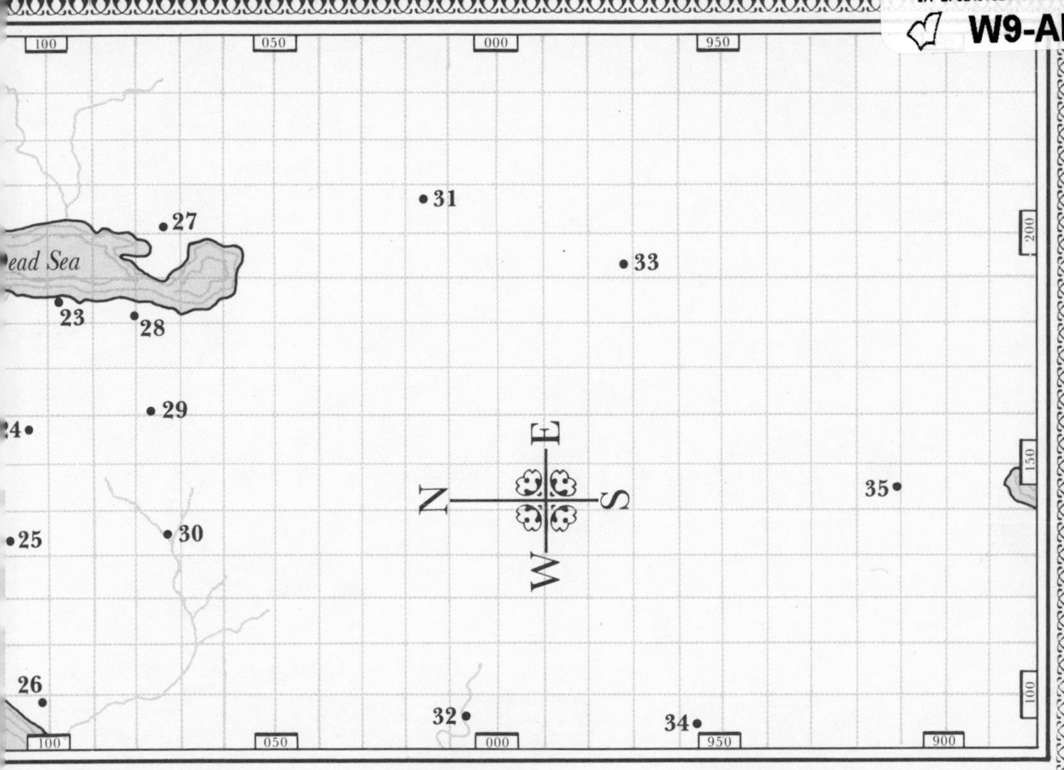

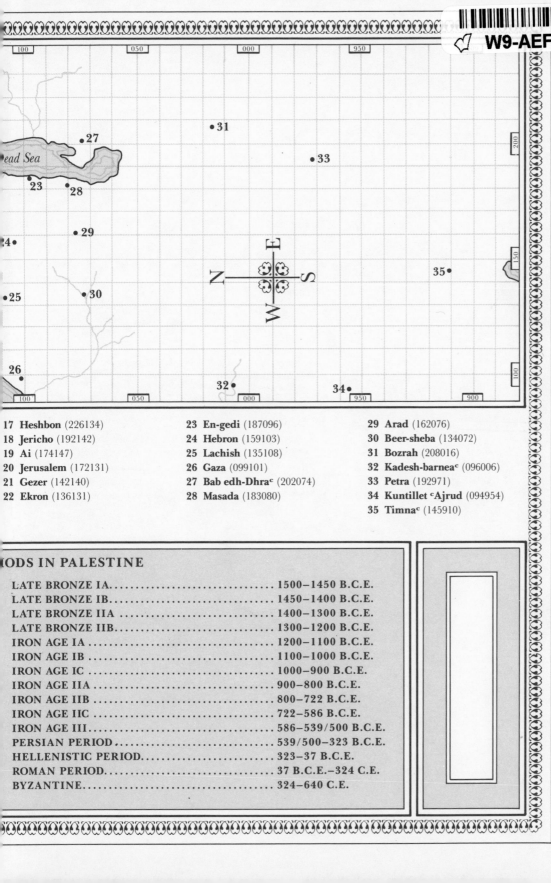

17 **Heshbon** (226134)
18 **Jericho** (192142)
19 **Ai** (174147)
20 **Jerusalem** (172131)
21 **Gezer** (142140)
22 **Ekron** (136131)
23 **En-gedi** (187096)
24 **Hebron** (159103)
25 **Lachish** (135108)
26 **Gaza** (099101)
27 **Bab edh-Dhra[c]** (202074)
28 **Masada** (183080)
29 **Arad** (162076)
30 **Beer-sheba** (134072)
31 **Bozrah** (208016)
32 **Kadesh-barnea[c]** (096006)
33 **Petra** (192971)
34 **Kuntillet [c]Ajrud** (094954)
35 **Timna[c]** (145910)

ODS IN PALESTINE

LATE BRONZE IA	1500–1450 B.C.E.
LATE BRONZE IB	1450–1400 B.C.E.
LATE BRONZE IIA	1400–1300 B.C.E.
LATE BRONZE IIB	1300–1200 B.C.E.
IRON AGE IA	1200–1100 B.C.E.
IRON AGE IB	1100–1000 B.C.E.
IRON AGE IC	1000–900 B.C.E.
IRON AGE IIA	900–800 B.C.E.
IRON AGE IIB	800–722 B.C.E.
IRON AGE IIC	722–586 B.C.E.
IRON AGE III	586–539/500 B.C.E.
PERSIAN PERIOD	539/500–323 B.C.E.
HELLENISTIC PERIOD	323–37 B.C.E.
ROMAN PERIOD	37 B.C.E.–324 C.E.
BYZANTINE	324–640 C.E.

THE ANCHOR BIBLE DICTIONARY

THE ANCHOR BIBLE DICTIONARY

VOLUME 1
A–C

David Noel Freedman
EDITOR-IN-CHIEF

ASSOCIATE EDITORS
Gary A. Herion • David F. Graf
John David Pleins

MANAGING EDITOR
Astrid B. Beck

DOUBLEDAY
NEW YORK • LONDON • TORONTO • SYDNEY • AUCKLAND

THE ANCHOR BIBLE DICTIONARY: VOLUME 1
PUBLISHED BY DOUBLEDAY
a division of Bantam Doubleday Dell Publishing Group, Inc.
666 Fifth Avenue, New York, New York 10103

THE ANCHOR BIBLE DICTIONARY, DOUBLEDAY,
and the portrayal of an anchor with the letters ABD
are trademarks of Doubleday,
a division of Bantam Doubleday Dell Publishing Group, Inc.

DESIGN BY Stanley S. Drate/Folio Graphics Company, Inc.

Library of Congress Cataloging-in-Publication Data
Anchor Bible dictionary / David Noel Freedman, editor-in-chief;
associate editors, Gary A. Herion, David F. Graf, John David Pleins;
managing editor, Astrid B. Beck.
—1st ed.
p. cm.
Includes bibliographical references.
1. Bible—Dictionaries. I. Freedman, David Noel, 1922– .
BS440.A54 1992
220.3—dc20 91-8385
CIP

Vol. 1 ISBN 0-385-19351-3
Vol. 2 ISBN 0-385-19360-2
Vol. 3 ISBN 0-385-19361-0
Vol. 4 ISBN 0-385-19362-9
Vol. 5 ISBN 0-385-19363-7
Vol. 6 ISBN 0-385-26190-X

Printed in the United States of America

10 9 8 7 6 5 4 3 2 1

FIRST EDITION

CONSULTANTS

HANS DIETER BETZ (Greco-Roman Religion)
Shailer Mathews Professor of NT Studies, University of Chicago

JAMES H. CHARLESWORTH (Apocrypha and Pseudepigrapha)
George L. Collord Professor of NT Language and Literature, Princeton Theological Seminary

FRANK MOORE CROSS (Old Testament)
Hancock Professor of Hebrew and Other Oriental Languages, Harvard University

WILLIAM G. DEVER (Archaeology)
Professor of Near Eastern Archaeology and Anthropology, University of Arizona

A. KIRK GRAYSON (Mesopotamia and Assyriology)
Professor, University of Toronto

PETER MACHINIST (Bible and Ancient Near East)
Professor of Near Eastern Languages and Civilizations, Harvard University

ABRAHAM J. MALHERBE (New Testament)
Buckingham Professor of New Testament Criticism and Interpretation, The Divinity School, Yale University

BIRGER A. PEARSON (Early Christianity)
Professor of Religious Studies, University of California at Santa Barbara

JACK M. SASSON (Bible and Ancient Near East)
Professor in Religious Studies, University of North Carolina

WILLIAM R. SCHOEDEL (Early Christian Literature)
University of Illinois at Urbana-Champaign

EDITORIAL STAFF

LIST OF CONTRIBUTORS

JAMES W. AAGESON
Assistant Professor, Concordia College, Moorhead, MN

PAUL J. ACHTEMEIER
Jackson Professor of Biblical Interpretation, Union Theological Seminary, Richmond, VA

PETER R. ACKROYD
Professor Emeritus, London University, London, England

ELAINE ALDER GOODFRIEND
Woodland Hills, CA

PAULINE ALBENDA
Brooklyn, NY

LARRY J. ALDERINK
Professor of Religion, Concordia College, Moorhead, MN

L. C. A. ALEXANDER
Firth College, University of Sheffield, Sheffield, England

PHILIP S. ALEXANDER
Senior Lecturer in Jewish Studies, University of Manchester, Manchester, England

JOSEPH M. ALEXANIAN
Professor of Biblical Studies, Trinity College, Deerfield, IL

JAMES P. ALLEN
Associate Curator, Metropolitan Museum of Art, New York, NY

LESLIE C. ALLEN
Professor of OT, Fuller Theological Seminary, Pasadena, CA

JOHN E. ALSUP
Professor of NT, Austin Presbyterian Theological Seminary, Austin, TX

ROBERT ALTER
Professor of Hebrew and Comparative Literature, University of California at Berkeley, Berkeley, CA

REV. DR. ROBERT ALTHANN
Pontifical Biblical Institute, Rome, Italy

FRANCIS I. ANDERSEN
Professor of OT, New College Berkeley, Berkeley, CA

CHARLES P. ANDERSON
Associate Professor of Religious Studies, University of British Columbia, Vancouver, Canada

GARY A. ANDERSON
Associate Professor of Biblical Studies, University of Virginia, Charlottesville, VA

REV. HUGH ANDERSON
Professor Emeritus, University of Edinburgh, Scotland

ROBERT T. ANDERSON
Professor, Michigan State University, East Lansing, MI

SHIMON APPLEBAUM
Professor M. M. Emeritus, Tel Aviv University, Tel Aviv, Israel

RAMI ARAV
University of Haifa, Haifa, Israel

YOËL L. ARBEITMAN
Senior Research Fellow, Institute of Semitic Studies, Princeton, NJ

BILL T. ARNOLD
Professor of OT and Biblical Languages, Wesley Biblical Seminary, Jackson, MS

CLINTON E. ARNOLD
Associate Professor of NT, Talbot School of Theology, La Mirada, CA

PATRICK M. ARNOLD, S.J.
Assistant Professor, University of San Diego, San Diego, CA

JOHN ASHTON
University of Oxford, Oxford, England

ELIZABETH ASMIS
Associate Professor, University of Chicago, Chicago, IL

JAN ASSMANN
Professor, Aegyptologisches Institut, Universität Heidelberg, Germany

MICHAEL C. ASTOUR
Professor of Historical Studies, Southern Illinois University, Edwardsville, IL

HAROLD W. ATTRIDGE
Professor, University of Notre Dame, Notre Dame, IN

LIST OF CONTRIBUTORS

GARY C. AUGUSTIN
Clinical Coordinator, Heartland Samaritan Counseling Center, St. Joseph, MO

DAVID E. AUNE
Professor of Religious Studies, Saint Xavier College, Chicago, IL

HECTOR AVALOS
Ph.D. Candidate, Harvard University, Cambridge, MA

ALAN J. AVERY-PECK
Director, Jewish Studies Program, Tulane University, New Orleans, LA

LARS E. AXELSSON
Kävlinge Församling, Kävlinge, Sweden

PROF. DR. T. BAARDA
Vrÿe Universiteit, Amsterdam, The Netherlands

ROGER S. BAGNALL
Professor of Classics and History and Dean of the Graduate School of Arts and Sciences, Columbia University, New York, NY

LLOYD R. BAILEY
Associate Professor, Duke Divinity School, Durham, NC

RANDALL C. BAILEY
Associate Professor of OT and Hebrew, Interdenominational Theological Center, Atlanta, GA

JOHN BAINES
Professor of Egyptology, University of Oxford, Oxford, England

WILLIAM BAIRD
Professor of NT, Brite Divinity School, Texas Christian University, Fort Worth, TX

DAVID W. BAKER
Professor of OT and Hebrew, Ashland Theological Seminary, Ashland, OH

DAVID L. BALCH
Associate Professor, Brite Divinity School, Texas Christian University, Fort Worth, TX

EDWARD B. BANNING
Assistant Professor, Dept. of Anthropology, University of Toronto, Toronto, Ontario, Canada

OFER BAR-YOSEF
Professor, Harvard University, Cambridge, MA

WILLIAM HAMILTON BARNES
Assistant Professor of Bible, Southeastern College of the Assemblies of God, Lakeland, FL

MICHAEL L. BARRÉ
Professor of Sacred Scripture, St. Patrick's Seminary, Menlo Park, CA

W. BOYD BARRICK
Dean, School of Arts and Sciences, Eastern Montana College, Billings, MT

S. SCOTT BARTCHY
Adjunct Associate Professor, Dept. of History, UCLA, Los Angeles, CA

JOHN R. BARTLETT
Associate Professor of Biblical Studies, Trinity College, Dublin, Ireland

JOHN BARTON
Reader in Biblical Studies, University of Oxford, Oxford, England

JOUETTE M. BASSLER
Associate Professor, Perkins School of Theology, Southern Methodist University, Dallas, TX

RICHARD BAUCKHAM
Reader in the History of Christian Thought, University of Manchester, Manchester, England

ALBERT I. BAUMGARTEN
Associate Professor, Bar-Ilan University, Ramat-Gan, Israel

GEORGE R. BEASLEY-MURRAY
Senior Professor of NT Interpretation, Southern Baptist Theological Seminary, Louisville, KY

ASTRID BILLES BECK
University of Michigan, Ann Arbor, MI

GARY BECKMAN
Associate Curator, Yale Babylonian Collection, New Haven, CT

PETER ROSS BEDFORD
Ph.D. Candidate, The Oriental Institute, University of Chicago, Chicago, IL

DEWEY M. BEEGLE
Professor Emeritus of OT, Wesley Theological Seminary, Washington, DC

MOSHE BEER
Professor, Bar-Ilan University, Ramat-Gan, Israel

A. F. L. BEESTON
Emeritus Professor of Arabic, St. John's College, Oxford, England

CHRISTOPHER T. BEGG
Professor, Catholic University, Washington, DC

ITZHAQ BEIT-ARIEH
Professor, Institute of Archaeology, Tel Aviv University, Tel Aviv, Israel

BARRY J. BEITZEL
Professor of OT and Semitic Languages, Trinity Evangelical Divinity School, Deerfield, IL

ALBERT A. BELL, JR.
Associate Professor of Classics and History, Hope College, Holland, MI

DAN BEN-AMOS
Professor, University of Pennsylvania, Philadelphia, PA

AMNON BEN-TOR
Professor, Institute of Archaeology, Hebrew University, Jerusalem, Israel

PAUL BENJAMIN
Principal and Professor of OT Studies, Theological College of Lanka, Pilimatalawa CP, Sri Lanka

CHANEY R. BERGDALL
Associate Professor of Bible and Religion, Huntington College, Huntington, IN

ADELE BERLIN
Professor of Hebrew, University of Maryland, College Park, MD

JOHN M. BERRIDGE
Professor, Dept. of Theology, St. Francis Xavier University, Antigonish, Nova Scotia, Canada

DONALD K. BERRY
Assistant Professor of Religion, Mobile College, Mobile, AL

JOHN WILSON BETLYON
Chaplain (Captain), United States Army, Fort Benning, GA

ARNOLD BETZ
Graduate Student, Vanderbilt University, Nashville, TN

HANS DIETER BETZ
Shailer Mathews Professor of NT Studies, University of Chicago, Chicago, IL

PROF. DR. JOHANNES BEUTLER
Phil.-Theol. Hochschule Sankt Georgen, Frankfurt am Main, Germany

BRYAN E. BEYER
Assistant Professor of Bible, Columbia Bible College and Seminary, Columbia, SC

M. ALFRED BICHSEL
Professor Emeritus of Church Music, Eastman School of Music–University of Rochester, Rochester, NY

ROBERT D. BIGGS
Professor of Assyriology, The Oriental Institute, University of Chicago, Chicago, IL

J. DANIEL BING
Associate Professor of History, University of Tennessee, Knoxville, TN

AVRAHAM BIRAN
Nelson Glueck School of Biblical Archaeology, Hebrew Union College–Jewish Institute of Religion, Jerusalem, Israel

PHYLLIS A. BIRD
Associate Professor of OT Interpretation, Garrett-Evangelical Theological Seminary, Evanston, IL

JAMES NEVILLE BIRDSALL
Professor Emeritus of NT Studies and Textual Criticism, University of Birmingham, Birmingham, England

ELIZABETH BLOCH-SMITH
New Haven, CT

LAWRENCE BOADT
Professor of Biblical Studies, Washington Theological Union, Silver Spring, MD

WALTER R. BODINE
Dallas, TX

PIERRE-MAURICE BOGAERT
Professeur ordinaire à la Faculté de Théologie, Université Catholique de Louvain, Louvain-la-Neuve, Belgium

REV. M.-É. BOISMARD
Professeur, École Biblique et Archéologique Française, Jerusalem, Israel

BARUCH M. BOKSER (deceased)
Professor of Talmud and Rabbinics, The Jewish Theological Seminary of America, New York, NY

ROBERT G. BOLING
Professor of OT, McCormick Theological Seminary, Chicago, IL

PIERRE BORDREUIL
Centre National de la Recherche Scientifique, Paris, France

MARCUS J. BORG
Professor of Religious Studies, Oregon State University, Corvallis, OR

PEDER BORGEN
Professor, University of Trondheim, Trondheim, Norway

M. EUGENE BORING
Professor, Texas Christian University, Fort Worth, TX

ODED BOROWSKI
Associate Professor and Chair, Emory University, Atlanta, GA

PROF. DR. FRANÇOIS BOVON
Faculté de théologie, Université, Geneva, Switzerland

CRAIG D. BOWMAN
Ph.D. Candidate, Princeton Theological Seminary, Princeton, NJ

MARY BOYCE
Professor Emerita, University of London, London, England

JOHN M. BRACKE
Dean for Academic Life and Assistant Professor of OT, Eden Theological Seminary, Webster Groves, MO

FREDERIC R. BRANDFON

JAMES A. BRASHLER
Dean of Ecumenical Institute, St. Mary's Seminary and University, Baltimore, MD

ELIOT BRAUN
Senior Excavating Archaeologist, Israel Antiquities Authority, Jerusalem, Israel

DAVID C. BRAUND
Exeter University, England

TERRY L. BRENSINGER
Associate Professor of Biblical Studies, Messiah College, Grantham, PA

MARC ZVI BRETTLER
Assistant Professor of Near Eastern and Judaic Studies, Brandeis University, Waltham, MA

PIERRE BRIANT
Professor, Université de Toulouse, Toulouse, France

SEBASTIAN PAUL BROCK
Reader in Aramaic and Syriac, Oriental Institute, University of Oxford, Oxford, England

HAROLD BRODSKY
Associate Professor, University of Maryland, College Park, MD

GEORGE J. BROOKE
Lecturer in Intertestamental Literature, University of Manchester, Manchester, England

ROGER BROOKS
Associate Professor, University of Notre Dame, Notre Dame, IN

MAGEN BROSHI
The Israel Museum, Jerusalem, Israel

RAYMOND E. BROWN
Auburn Distinguished Professor of Biblical Studies, Union Theological Seminary, New York, NY

S. KENT BROWN
Professor of Ancient Scripture, Brigham Young University, Provo, Utah

FREDERICK FYVIE BRUCE (deceased)
Professor Emeritus, University of Manchester, Manchester, England

WALTER BRUEGGEMANN
Professor of OT, Columbia Theological Seminary, Decatur, GA

JORUNN JACOBSEN BUCKLEY
Emory University, Atlanta, GA

MARIE-LOUISE BUHL
Former Keeper, Danish National Museum, Copenhagen, Denmark

DAVID BUNDY
Associate Professor of Christian Origins, Asbury Theological Seminary, Wilmore, KY

GARY T. BURKE
Windsor Locks, CT

RITA J. BURNS
Milwaukee, WI

FREDERIC W. BUSH
Associate Professor of OT, Fuller Theological Seminary, Pasadena, CA

BRENDAN BYRNE
Professor of NT, Jesuit Theological College, United Faculty of Theology, Parkville, Melbourne, Australia

JANE M. CAHILL
Archaeologist, City of David Archaeological Project, Hebrew University of Jerusalem, Jerusalem, Israel

JOSEPH A. CALLAWAY (deceased)
Former President of W. F. Albright Institute of Archaeological Research

RON CAMERON
Associate Professor of Religion, Wesleyan University, Middletown, CT

RICHARD I. CAPLICE
Professor of Assyriology, Pontifical Biblical Institute, Rome, Italy

MAURICE CARREZ
Professeur Emerite, Docteur de Paris et Strasbourg, Institut Protestant de Theologie Paris et Institut Catholique de Paris, Paris, France

ROBERT P. CARROLL
University of Glasgow, Glasgow, Scotland

SCOTT T. CARROLL
Assistant Professor of Ancient History, Gordon College and Gordon-Conwell Theological Seminary, Wenham, MA

KEVIN J. CATHCART
Professor, Dept. of Near Eastern Languages, University College Dublin, Dublin, Ireland

THOMAS SCOTT CAULLEY
Associate Professor of NT, Manhattan Christian College, Manhattan, KS

JACQUES CAUVIN
Directeur de Recherche, Centre National de la Recherche Scientifique, Institut de Préhistoire Orientale, Saint-Paul-le-Jeune, France

HENRI CAZELLES
Professor, Institut Catholique, École Pratique Hautes Études, Sorbonne, Paris, France

JAMES H. CHARLESWORTH
George L. Collord Professor of NT Language and Literature, Princeton Theological Seminary, Princeton, NJ

GLENN F. CHESNUT
Professor of History and Religious Studies, Indiana University at South Bend, South Bend, IN

RANDALL D. CHESNUTT
Associate Professor of Religion, Pepperdine University, Malibu, CA

REV. DR. BRUCE CHILTON
Bernard Iddings Bell Professor of Religion, Bard College, Annandale-on-Hudson, NY

DUANE L. CHRISTENSEN
Professor of OT Languages and Literature, American Baptist Seminary of the West and Graduate Theological Union, Berkeley, CA

MIGUEL CIVIL
The Oriental Institute, University of Chicago, Chicago, IL

JOHN J. CLABEAUX
Associate Professor of Ancient Languages and Theology, St. John's Seminary College, Boston, MA

G. W. CLARKE
Professor, Australian National University, Canberra, A.C.T., Australia

H. ELDON CLEM
Ph.D. Candidate, Hebrew Union College, Cincinnati, OH

RONALD E. CLEMENTS
Professor, King's College, University of London, London, England

RICHARD J. CLIFFORD, S.J.
Professor, Weston School of Theology, Cambridge, MA

DAVID J. A. CLINES
Professor of Biblical Studies, University of Sheffield, Sheffield, England

ANGELA E. CLOSE
Adjunct Professor, Southern Methodist University, Dallas, TX

GEORGE W. COATS
Professor of OT, Lexington Theological Seminary, Lexington, KY

GARETH LEE COCKERILL
Professor of NT and Biblical Theology, Wesley Biblical Seminary, Jackson, MS

MORDECHAI COGAN
Professor of Bible and Biblical History, Ben-Gurion University of the Negev, Beer-Sheva, Israel

SUSAN GUETTEL COLE
Associate Professor, University of Illinois at Chicago, Chicago, IL

JOHN J. COLLINS
Professor of Christianity and Judaism in Antiquity, University of Notre Dame, Notre Dame, IN

RAYMOND F. COLLINS
Professor-in-Ordinary of NT Studies, Catholic University of Leuven, Louvain, Belgium

JOHN G. COOK
Pastor, Reems Creek Presbyterian Parish, Weaverville, NC

JERROLD S. COOPER
Professor, Johns Hopkins University, Baltimore, MD

ROBERT B. COOTE
Professor, San Francisco Theological Seminary, San Anselmo, CA

FR. VIRGILIO C. CORBO, O.F.M.
Minzar Terra Santa–Capharnaum, Rosh Pinna, Israel

KATHLEEN E. CORLEY
Instructor of Religious Studies, Sioux Falls College, Sioux Falls, SD

CHARLES B. COUSAR
Professor of NT, Columbia Theological Seminary, Decatur, GA

ROBIN C. COVER
Assistant Professor, Dallas Theological Seminary, Dallas, TX

PETER W. COXON
Lecturer, University of St. Andrews, St. Andrews, Scotland

FRED B. CRADDOCK
Bandy Professor of Preaching and NT, Candler School of Theology, Emory University, Atlanta, GA

PETER C. CRAIGIE (deceased)
Associate Vice President, University of Calgary, Calgary, Alberta, Canada

JAMES L. CRENSHAW
Professor of OT, Duke University, Durham, NC

FRANK MOORE CROSS
Hancock Professor of Hebrew and other Oriental Languages, Harvard University, Cambridge, MA

JOHN DOMINIC CROSSAN
Professor of Religious Studies, DePaul University, Chicago, IL

J. H. CROUWEL
Professor of Aegean Archaeology, University of Amsterdam, Amsterdam, The Netherlands

KENNETH HUGH CUFFEY
Senior Pastor, Wyckoff Baptist Church, Wyckoff, NJ

R. ALAN CULPEPPER
James Buchanan Harrison Professor of NT, Southern Baptist Theological Seminary, Louisville, KY

EDWARD M. CURTIS
Associate Professor, Biola University, La Mirada, CA

EDWARD R. DALGLISH
Professor Emeritus, Baylor University, Waco, TX

M. DANDAMAYEV
Institute for Oriental Studies, Leningrad, U.S.S.R.

JON B. DANIELS
Assistant Professor of Religion, Defiance College, Defiance, OH

FREDERICK WILLIAM DANKER
Professor Emeritus of NT, Christ Seminary–Seminex/Lutheran School of Theology, Chicago, IL

SHIMON DAR
Land of Israel Studies, Bar-Ilan University, Ramat-Gan, Israel

G. I. DAVIES
Lecturer in Divinity and Fellow of Fitzwilliam College, University of Cambridge, Cambridge, England

MARGARET DAVIES
Lecturer, University of Bristol, Bristol, England

PHILIP R. DAVIES
Reader in Biblical Studies, University of Sheffield, Sheffield, England

JAMES R. DAVILA
Visiting Assistant Professor, Tulane University, New Orleans, LA

M. STEPHEN DAVIS
University Minister, Houston Baptist University, Houston, TX

JOHN DAY
Fellow and Tutor of Lady Margaret Hall and Lecturer in OT in the University of Oxford, Lady Margaret Hall, Oxford University, Oxford, England

MICHAL DAYAGI MENDELS
Curator, Biblical Archaeology, Israel Museum, Jerusalem, Israel

BERT DE VRIES
Director, American Center of Oriental Research, Amman, Jordan

J. ANDREW DEARMAN
Associate Professor of OT, Austin Presbyterian Theological Seminary, Austin, TX

RICHARD E. DEMARIS
Assistant Professor of Theology, Valparaiso University, Valparaiso, IN

STEPHEN G. DEMPSTER
Assistant Professor of Biblical Studies, Atlantic Baptist College, Moncton, New Brunswick, Canada

WILLIAM G. DEVER
Professor of Near Eastern Archaeology and Anthropology, University of Arizona, Tucson, AZ

LAMOINE DEVRIES
Adjunct Professor, Southwest Missouri State University, Springfield, MO

ALEXANDER A. DI LELLA, O.F.M.
Ordinary Professor, Catholic University of America, Washington, DC

ROBERT A. DI VITO
Adjunct Assistant Professor, Georgetown University, Washington, DC

MATTHEW W. DICKIE
Associate Professor, University of Illinois at Chicago, Chicago IL

RAYMOND B. DILLARD
Professor of OT Language and Literature, Westminster Theological Seminary, Philadelphia, PA

JOHN M. DILLON
Regius Professor of Greek, Trinity College, Dublin, Ireland

DEVORAH DIMANT
Professor, University of Haifa, Haifa, Israel

PAUL E. DION
Professor, University of Toronto, Toronto, Canada

GENEVIEVE DOLLFUS
Centre National de la Recherche Scientifique, Paris, France

JOHN R. DONAHUE, S.J.
Professor of NT, University of Notre Dame, Notre Dame, IN

KARL P. DONFRIED
Professor of Religion and Biblical Literature, Smith College, Northampton, MA

MARY ANN DONOVAN, S.C.
Associate Professor, Jesuit School of Theology, Berkeley, CA

RUDOLPH H. DORNEMANN
Curator of History, Milwaukee Public Museum, Milwaukee, WI

DAVID A. DORSEY
Professor of OT, Evangelical School of Theology, Myerstown, PA

MOSHE DOTHAN
Professor, University of Haifa, Haifa, Israel

TRUDE DOTHAN
E. L. Sukenik Professor of Archaeology, Institute of Archaeology, Hebrew University, Jerusalem, Israel

THOMAS B. DOZEMAN
Professor of OT, United Theological Seminary, Dayton, OH

JAN W. DRIJVERS
Dept. of History, Groningen State University, Groningen, The Netherlands

JOEL F. DRINKARD, JR.
Associate Professor of OT, Southern Baptist Theological Seminary, Louisville, KY

ARTHUR J. DROGE
Associate Professor of NT and Christian Origins, University of Chicago, Chicago, IL

PAUL BROOKS DUFF
Assistant Professor, College of St. Thomas, St. Paul, MN

RODNEY K. DUKE
Emory University, Atlanta, GA

DENNIS C. DULING
Professor, Canisius College, Buffalo, NY

DAVID L. DUNGAN
Professor, University of Tennessee, Knoxville, TN

JAMES D. G. DUNN
Professor of Divinity, University of Durham, Durham, England

ROBERT C. DUNSTON
Associate Professor, Cumberland College, Williamsburg, KY

JEAN-MARIE DURAND
École Pratique des Hautes Études, Sorbonne, Paris, France

ELMER H. DYCK
Assistant Professor of Biblical Studies, Regent College, Vancouver, British Columbia, Canada

ROBERT H. DYSON, JR.
Director, University Museum and Professor of Anthropology, University of Pennsylvania, Philadelphia, PA

KEITH L. EADES
Campus Ministry Associate for Rio Hondo College, Whittier Area Ecumenical Council, Whittier, CA

DIANA VIKANDER EDELMAN
Buffalo Grove, IL

GERSHON EDELSTEIN
Israel Antiquities Authority, Jerusalem, Israel

DOUGLAS R. EDWARDS
Assistant Professor, University of Puget Sound, Tacoma, WA

O. C. EDWARDS, JR.
Professor of Preaching, Seaburg-Western Theological Seminary, Evanston, IL

CARL S. EHRLICH
Ph.D. Candidate, Harvard University, Cambridge, MA

REV. DR. JOHN H. ELLIOTT
Professor of Theology and Religious Studies, University of San Francisco, San Francisco, CA

STEPHEN EMMEL
Yale University, New Haven, CT

JOHN C. ENDRES
Associate Professor of Scripture, Jesuit School of Theology at Berkeley, Berkeley, CA

ELDON JAY EPP
Harkness Professor of Biblical Literature, Case Western Reserve University, Cleveland, OH

MICHEL VAN ESBROECK
Professor, Univ. München, Bollandist, Ludwig-Maximilian Universität, Munich, Germany

TAMARA C. ESKENAZI
Associate Professor of Bible, Hebrew Union College–Jewish Institute of Religion, Los Angeles, CA

DOUGLAS ESSE
Assistant Professor, University of Chicago, Chicago, IL

CARL D. EVANS
Associate Professor of Religious Studies, University of South Carolina, Columbia, SC

CRAIG A. EVANS
Professor of Biblical Studies, Trinity Western University, Langley, British Columbia, Canada

JANET MEYER EVERTS
Assistant Professor, Hope College, Holland, MI

J. CHERYL EXUM
Associate Professor of Hebrew Bible, Boston College, Chestnut Hill, MA

RUTH FAGEN
Instructor, The Jewish Theological Seminary of America, New York, NY

JEFFREY A. FAGER
Assistant Professor of Religion and Philosophy, Kentucky Wesleyan College, Owensboro, KY

FREDERICK MARIO FALES
Verona, Italy

WANN MARBUD FANWAR
Adventist International Institute of Advanced Studies, Silang, Cavite, Philippines

VALERIE M. FARGO
Midland, MI

LOUIS H. FELDMAN
Professor, Yeshiva University, New York, NY

ARTHUR J. FERCH
Field Secretary, South Pacific Division of Seventh-Day Adventists, Sydney, N.S.W., Australia

EVERETT FERGUSON
Professor, Abilene Christian University, Abilene, TX

PAUL WAYNE FERRIS, JR.
Professor of Hebrew Bible and Semitics, Columbia Biblical Seminary, Columbia, SC

DANNA NOLAN FEWELL
Assistant Professor of OT, Perkins School of Theology, Southern Methodist University, Dallas, TX

ZBIGNIEW T. FIEMA
Dept. of Anthropology, University of Utah, Salt Lake City, UT

DAVID A. FIENSY
Pastor, Grape Grove Church of Christ, Jamestown, OH

ISRAEL FINKELSTEIN
Professor, Institute of Archaeology, Tel Aviv University, Tel Aviv, Israel

BENJAMIN FIORE
Professor, Canisius College, Buffalo, NY

EDWIN FIRMAGE
Graduate Student, University of California at Berkeley, Berkeley, CA

MOSHE FISCHER

THOMAS FISCHER
Dept. of History, Ruhr-University, Bochum, Germany

JOHN T. FITZGERALD
Associate Professor, University of Miami, Coral Gables, FL

JAMES W. FLANAGAN
Hallinan Professor, Case Western Reserve University, Cleveland, OH

PAUL V. M. FLESHER
Assistant Professor of the History and Literature of Religion, Northwestern University, Evanston, IL

DAVID FLUSSER
Professor, Hebrew University, Jerusalem, Israel

GERALD P. FOGARTY
Professor, University of Virginia, Charlottesville, VA

ELAINE R. FOLLIS
Jeanne and George Todd Professor of Religious Studies, Principia College, Elsah, IL

A. DEAN FORBES
Project Manager, Hewlett-Packard Laboratories, Palo Alto, CA

J. MASSYNGBAERDE FORD
Professor, University of Notre Dame, Notre Dame, IN

HAROLD O. FORSHEY
Professor, Miami University, Oxford, OH

ROBERT T. FORTNA
Professor of Religion, Vassar College, Poughkeepsie, NY

JARL FOSSUM
Associate Professor of NT Studies, University of Michigan, Ann Arbor, MI, and Adjunct Professor of Gnostic and Related Studies, C. G. Jung Institute, Zürich, Switzerland

BENJAMIN R. FOSTER
Professor of Near Eastern Languages, Yale University, New Haven, CT

JOHN L. FOSTER
Professor of English, Roosevelt University, Chicago, IL

MERVYN FOWLER
Chepstow, Gwent, England

MICHAEL V. FOX
Professor, University of Wisconsin, Madison, WI

STEVEN D. FRAADE
Mark Taper Professor of the History of Judaism, Yale University, New Haven, CT

JUDITH A. FRANKE
Director, Dickson Mounds Museum, Lewistown, IL

RAFAEL FRANKEL
Lecturer, Haifa University, Haifa, Israel

H. J. FRANKEN
Professor Emeritus, University of Leiden, Leiden, The Netherlands

PAUL NIMRAH FRANKLYN
Editor, Professional Books, Abingdon Press, Nashville, TN

ERNEST S. FRERICHS
Professor of Religious Studies and Judaic Studies, Brown University, Providence, RI

TERENCE E. FRETHEIM
Professor of OT, Luther Northwestern Theological Seminary, St. Paul, MN

MARK J. FRETZ
Assistant Professor of Religion, Bluffton College, Bluffton, OH

SEAN FREYNE
Professor, Trinity College, Dublin, Ireland

JÖRAN FRIBERG
Professor of Mathematics, Chalmers University of Technology, Gothenburg, Sweden

FRANK S. FRICK
Professor of Religious Studies, Albion College, Albion, MI

RICHARD ELLIOTT FRIEDMAN
Professor, University of California at San Diego, La Jolla, CA

BRUCE W. FRIER
Professor of Classics and Roman Law, University of Michigan, Ann Arbor, MI

DR. VOLKMAR FRITZ
Professor, Universität Giessen, Germany

VIRGIL R. L. FRY
Pastor, First Baptist Church, Mt. Pleasant, IA

TIKVA FRYMER-KENSKY
Reconstructionist Rabbinical College, Overbrook Hills, PA

WILLIAM J. FULCO, S.J.
Professor of Near Eastern Studies, Pontifical Biblical Institute, Jerusalem

RUSSELL FULLER
Wellesley College, Wellesley, MA

VICTOR PAUL FURNISH
University Distinguished Professor of NT, Perkins School of Theology, Southern Methodist University, Dallas, TX

HARRY Y. GAMBLE, JR.
Associate Professor of Religious Studies, University of Virginia, Charlottesville, VA

ANDREW N. GARRARD
Director, British Institute at Amman, Amman, Jordan

SUSAN R. GARRETT
Assistant Professor of NT, Yale Divinity School, New Haven, CT

W. WARD GASQUE
Provost and Professor of Biblical Studies, Eastern College, St. Davids, PA

BEVERLY ROBERTS GAVENTA
Professor of NT, Columbia Theological Seminary, Decatur, GA

MICHAEL GAWLIKOWSKI
Professor, Institute of Archaeology, Warsaw University, Warsaw, Poland

CONRAD GEMPF
Lecturer, The Centre for Undergraduate and Postgraduate Research, London Bible College, Northwood, Middlesex, England

LAWRENCE T. GERATY
Professor of Archaeology and President, Atlantic Union College, S. Lancaster, MA

C. H. J. DE GEUS
Associate Professor, Dept. of Near Eastern Languages, State University of Groningen, Groningen, The Netherlands

MORDECHAI GICHON
Professor, Tel Aviv University, Tel Aviv, Israel

FLORENCE MORGAN GILLMAN
Associate Professor, University of San Diego, San Diego, CA

JOHN L. GILLMAN
Lecturer, San Diego State University, San Diego, CA

SEYMOUR GITIN
Professor, Director of the W. F. Albright Institute of Archaeological Research, Jerusalem, Israel

PROF. DR. B. GLADIGOW
Seminar für Indologie und Vergleichende Religionswissenschaft, Universität Tübingen, Tübingen, Germany

DAVID A. GLATT
University of Pennsylvania, Philadelphia, PA

ALBERT E. GLOCK
Director, Institute of Archaeology, Birzeit University, Bir Zeit, West Bank

CAROL A. M. GLUCKER
Tel Aviv University, Tel Aviv, Israel

JAMES E. GOEHRING
Assistant Professor of Religion, Mary Washington College, Fredericksburg, VA

ROBERT GOLDENBERG
Associate Professor of Judaic Studies, State University of New York at Stony Brook, Stony Brook, NY

FRANCOLINO J. GONÇALVES
Professor, École Biblique et Archéologique Française, Jerusalem, Israel

HATICE GONNET
Chargé de Recherches, Centre National de la Recherche Scientifique, Paris, France

DAVID GOODBLATT
Professor, University of California at San Diego, La Jolla, CA

WILLIAM R. GOODMAN
Professor of Religious Studies, Lynchburg College, Lynchburg, VA

STEPHEN GORANSON
Instructor, North Carolina State University, Raleigh, NC

NAAHA GOREN-INBAR
Institute of Archaeology, Hebrew University, Jerusalem, Israel

PROF. DR. DR. MANFRED GÖRG
Institut für Biblische Exegese Katholisch-Theologische Fakultät der Universität München, Munich, Germany

NIGEL GORING-MORRIS
Institute of Archaeology, Hebrew University, Jerusalem, Israel

RONALD L. GORNY
Chicago, IL

MOSHE GOSHEN-GOTTSTEIN
Professor, Director, Hebrew University Bible Project, Jerusalem, Israel

NORMAN K. GOTTWALD
W. W. White Professor of Biblical Studies, New York Theological Seminary, New York, NY

M. H. GRACEY
William Hulme's Grammar School, Manchester, England

DAVID F. GRAF
Associate Professor of History, University of Miami, Coral Gables, FL

PROF. DR. FRITZ GRAF
Universität Basel, Basel, Switzerland

M. PATRICK GRAHAM
Cataloger, Pitts Theology Library, Emory University, Atlanta, GA

ROBERT M. GRANT
Professor Emeritus, University of Chicago, Chicago, IL

JOSEPH A. GRASSI
Professor, Santa Clara University, Santa Clara, CA

A. KIRK GRAYSON
Professor, University of Toronto, Toronto, Canada

JOEL B. GREEN
Academic Dean and Associate Professor of NT, New College for Advanced Christian Studies, Berkeley, CA

WILLIAM SCOTT GREEN
Professor of Religion, University of Rochester, Rochester, NY

RAPHAEL GREENBERG
Israel Antiquities Authority, Jerusalem, Israel

SAMUEL GREENGUS
Julian Morgenstern Professor of Bible and ANE Literature, Hebrew Union College–Jewish Institute of Religion, Cincinnati, OH

FREDERICK E. GREENSPAHN
Associate Professor of Judaic Studies, University of Denver, Denver, CO

LEONARD J. GREENSPOON
Professor of Religion, Clemson University, Clemson, SC

EDWARD L. GREENSTEIN
Professor of Bible, The Jewish Theological Seminary of America, New York, NY

ROWAN A. GREER
Professor of Anglican Studies, Yale Divinity School, New Haven, CT

HERBERT G. GRETHER
Fort Collins, CO

MIRIAM TAMARA GRIFFIN
Tutorial Fellow and University Lecturer, Somerville College, Oxford University, Oxford, England

DENNIS E. GROH
Professor of the History of Christianity, Garrett-Evangelical Theological Seminary, Evanston, IL

DOUGLAS M. GROPP
Assistant Professor of Semitics, Catholic University of America, Washington, DC

MICHAEL D. GUINAN, O.F.M.
Professor of OT and Semitic Languages, Franciscan School of Theology (Graduate Theological Union), Berkeley, CA

NORMAN R. GULLEY
Professor of Systematic Theology, Southern College of Seventh-Day Adventists, Collegedale, TN

DAVID M. GUNN
Professor of OT, Columbia Theological Seminary, Decatur, GA

ANN C. GUNTER
Assistant Curator, ANE Art, Arthur M. Sackler Gallery and Freer Gallery of Art, Smithsonian Institution, Washington, DC

CARRIE GUSTAVSON-GAUBE
Phoenix, AZ

KLAUS HAACKER
Professor, Kirchliche Hochschule Wuppertal, Wuppertal, Germany

ROBERT D. HAAK
Assistant Professor, Augustana College, Rock Island, IL

RACHEL HACHLILI
Professor, Dept. of Archaeology, University of Haifa, Haifa, Israel

JO ANN HACKETT
Professor, Harvard University, Cambridge, MA

ADNAN HADIDI
Associate Professor, University of Jordan, Amman, Jordan

DONALD A. HAGNER
Professor of NT, Fuller Theological Seminary, Pasadena, CA

JOHN F. HALL
Associate Professor of Classics and Ancient History, Brigham Young University, Provo, UT

ROBERT G. HALL
Assistant Professor of Religion, Hampden-Sydney College, Hampden-Sydney, VA

WILLIAM W. HALLO
W. M. Laffan Professor of Assyriology and Babylonian Literature, Yale University, New Haven, CT

BARUCH HALPERN
Professor, York University, Toronto, Ontario, Canada

JEFFRIES M. HAMILTON
Trenton, NJ

VICTOR P. HAMILTON
Professor of Religion, Asbury College, Wilmore, KY

DENNIS HAMM, S.J.
Associate Professor, Dept. of Theology, Creighton University, Omaha, NE

PAUL L. HAMMER
Professor of NT Interpretation, Colgate Rochester Divinity School, Bexley Hall, Crozer Theological Seminary, Rochester, NY

JIN HEE HAN
Assistant Professor of Biblical Studies, Alliance Theological Seminary, Nyack, NY

LOWELL K. HANDY
Lecturer, Loyola University of Chicago, Chicago, IL

THOMAS D. HANKS
Presbyterian Missionary, Metropolitan Community Church, Buenos Aires, Argentina

PAUL D. HANSON
Lamont Professor of Divinity, Harvard University, Cambridge, MA

MICHAEL E. HARDWICK
Director, School for the Diaconate, Episcopal Diocese of S. Ohio, Cincinnati, OH

DOUGLAS R. A. HARE
W. F. Orr Professor of NT, Pittsburgh Theological Seminary, Pittsburgh, PA

G. EDWIN HARMON
Director of Adult Day Programs, Babcock Center, Inc., Lexington, SC

DANIEL J. HARRINGTON
Professor of NT, Weston School of Theology, Cambridge, MA

J. GORDON HARRIS
Vice President for Academic Affairs and Professor of OT, North American Baptist Seminary, Sioux Falls, SD

RIVKAH HARRIS
Associate Professor of Liberal Arts, School of the Art Institute, Chicago, IL

STEPHEN HART
British Institute at Amman for Archaeology and History, Amman, Jordan

LARS HARTMAN
Professor, Uppsala University, Uppsala, Sweden

GERHARD F. HASEL
Professor of OT and Biblical Theology and Director of Ph.D./Th.D. Programs, Andrews University, Theological Seminary, Berrien Springs, MI

ALAN J. HAUSER
Professor, Appalachian State University, Boone, NC

RICHARD B. HAYS
Associate Professor of NT, Yale Divinity School, New Haven, CT

JOHN F. HEALEY
Lecturer in Semitic Studies, University of Manchester, Manchester, England

JOSEPH P. HEALEY
Associate Professor of Religious Studies, Hobart and William Smith Colleges, Geneva, NY

WARREN J. HEARD, JR.
Assistant Professor of NT, Trinity Evangelical Divinity School, Deerfield, IL

CHARLES W. HEDRICK
Professor, Southwest Missouri State University, Springfield, MO

GEORGE C. HEIDER
Vice President for Academic Affairs and Associate Professor of Theology, Concordia College, Seward, NE

RONALD E. HEINE
Director, Institut zur Erforschung des Urchristentums, Tübingen, Germany

RONALD S. HENDEL
Assistant Professor, Southern Methodist University, Dallas, TX

HOLLAND L. HENDRIX
Academic Dean, Union Theological Seminary, New York, NY

JOHN B. HENNESSEY
Head, Department of Archaeology, University of Sydney, Sydney, N.S.W., Australia

SHARON HERBERT
Professor of Classical Archaeology, University of Michigan, Ann Arbor, MI

GARY A. HERION
Assistant Professor of Biblical Studies, Hartwick College, Oneonta, NY

LARRY G. HERR
Professor of Religious Studies, Canadian Union College, College Heights, Alberta, Canada

PROF. DR. DR. SIEGFRIED HERRMANN
Evangelisch-Theologische Fakultät, Ruhr-Universität Bochum, Bochum, Germany

ZEʾEV HERZOG
Tel Aviv University, Tel Aviv, Israel

RICHARD S. HESS
Lecturer in Biblical Studies, Bible Training Institute, Glasgow, Scotland

THEODORE HIEBERT
Associate Professor of Hebrew Bible/OT, Harvard Divinity School, Harvard University, Cambridge, MA

RICHARD H. HIERS
Professor, University of Florida, Gainesville, FL

ANDREW E. HILL
Associate Professor of OT, Wheaton College, Wheaton, IL

DELBERT R. HILLERS
W. W. Spence Professor of Semitic Languages, Johns Hopkins University, Baltimore, MD

JULIAN V. HILLS
Assistant Professor of Theology, Marquette University, Milwaukee, WI

T. R. HOBBS
Professor of OT Interpretation, McMaster Divinity College, McMaster University, Hamilton, Ontario, Canada

RONALD F. HOCK
Associate Professor of Religion, University of Southern California, Los Angeles, CA

ROBERT HODGSON, JR.
Professor of Religious Studies, Southwest Missouri State University, Springfield, MO

DANIEL LEE HOFFMAN
Ph.D. Candidate, Miami University, Oxford, OH

JAMES K. HOFFMEIER
Associate Professor, Wheaton College, Wheaton, IL

ROBERT L. HOHLFELDER
Professor of History, University of Colorado, Boulder, CO

JOHN C. HOLBERT
Associate Professor of Homiletics, Perkins School of Theology, Dallas, TX

CARL R. HOLLADAY
Professor of NT, Candler School of Theology, Emory University, Atlanta, GA

JOHN S. HOLLADAY, JR.
Professor, University of Toronto, Toronto, Ontario, Canada

THOMAS A. HOLLAND
Publications Director, The Oriental Institute, University of Chicago, Chicago, IL

PAUL W. HOLLENBACH
Professor of Religious Studies, Iowa State University, Ames, IA

STEVEN W. HOLLOWAY
University of Chicago, Chicago, IL

SVEND HOLM-NIELSEN
Professor, University of Copenhagen, Denmark

PROF. DR. D. HOMÈS-FREDERICQ
Secrétaire-Trésorière, Comite Belge de Fouilles en Jordanie, A.S.B.L., Musées Royaux d'Art et d'Histoire, Ministère de l'Education Nationale et de la Culture, Brussels, Belgium

LESLIE J. HOPPE
Associate Professor, Catholic Theological Union, Chicago, IL

FRIEDRICH WILHELM HORN
Privatdozent, Vereinigte Theologische Seminare, Universität Göttingen, Göttingen, Germany

G. H. R. HORSLEY
Senior Lecturer in Hellenistic Greek, Division of Religious Studies, La Trobe University, Victoria, Australia

RICHARD A. HORSLEY
Chairman, Study of Religion Program, University of Massachusetts, Boston, MA

PIETER W. VAN DER HORST
Professor, Theological Faculty of the University of Utrecht, Utrecht, The Netherlands

EDWIN C. HOSTETTER
Ph.D. Candidate, Johns Hopkins University, Baltimore, MD

J. L. HOULDEN
Professor, King's College, London, England

PHILO H. J. HOUWINK TEN CATE
Archaeologisch-Historisch Instituut der Universiteit van Amsterdam, Amsterdam, The Netherlands

DAVID M. HOWARD, JR.
Assistant Professor of OT, Trinity Evangelical Divinity School, Deerfield, IL

GEORGE E. HOWARD
Professor of Religion, Head of the Dept. of Religion, University of Georgia, Athens, GA

JENS HØYRUP
Associate Professor, University of Roskilde, Roskilde, Denmark

PROF. DR. HANS HÜBNER
Theologische Fakultät, Georg-August-Universität, Göttingen, Germany

ULRICH HÜBNER
Wissenschaftlich-Theologische Seminar, Ruprecht-Karls-Universität Heidelberg, Heidelberg, Germany

JOHN R. HUDDLESTUN
Ph.D. Student, University of Michigan, Ann Arbor, MI

JOHN HUEHNERGARD
Professor of Semitic Philology, Harvard University, Cambridge, MA

HERBERT B. HUFFMON
Professor, Drew University, Madison, NJ

JOHN H. HULL, JR.
Torrance, CA

ANDERS HULTGÅRD
Dept. of the History of Religions, University of Bergen, Bergen, Norway

JEAN-BAPTISTE HUMBERT
Archaeologist, École Biblique Jérusalem, Jerusalem

MELVIN HUNT
Training Coordinator, East Bay International Studies Center, California State University at Hayward, Hayward, CA

L. D. HURST
Associate Professor of Religion, University of California at Davis, Davis, CA

LARRY W. HURTADO
Professor of Religion, University of Manitoba, Winnipeg, Manitoba, Canada

RODNEY R. HUTTON
Professor, Trinity Lutheran Seminary, Columbus, OH

ELIZABETH F. HUWILER
Lancaster Theological Seminary, Lancaster, PA

MOAWIYAH M. IBRAHIM
Professor, Institute of Archaeology and Anthropology, Yarmouk University, Irbid, Jordan

BRIAN P. IRWIN
Student of OT, Wycliffe College, University of Toronto, Toronto, Ontario, Canada

BENJAMIN ISAAC
Professor, Tel Aviv University, Ramat Aviv, Israel

EPHRAIM ISAAC
Professor, Institute of Semitic Studies, Princeton, NJ

WESLEY W. ISENBERG
Associate Professor of Theology, Concordia University, River Forest, IL

TOMOO ISHIDA
Professor, University of Tsukuba, Tsukuba-shi, Ibaraki-ken, Japan

HOWARD JACKSON
Pomona College, Claremont, CA

I. JACOB AND W. JACOB
Director and Associate, Rodef Shalom Biblical Botanical Garden, Pittsburgh, PA

WALDEMAR JANZEN
Professor of OT, Canadian Mennonite Bible College, Winnipeg, Manitoba, Canada

WERNER G. JEANROND
University of Dublin Trinity College, Dublin, Ireland

SHARON PACE JEANSONNE
Assistant Professor of Theology, Marquette University, Milwaukee, WI

CLAYTON N. JEFFORD
Assistant Professor of Scripture, St. Meinrad School of Theology, St. Meinrad, IN

ALAN W. JENKS
Associate Professor of Religious Studies, West Virginia University, Morgantown, WV

JOSEPH JENSEN
Associate Professor, Catholic University of America, Washington, DC

L. ANN JERVIS
Wycliffe College, Toronto School of Theology, University of Toronto, Toronto, Ontario, Canada

JANET H. JOHNSON
Professor of Egyptology, The Oriental Institute, University of Chicago, Chicago, IL

LUKE TIMOTHY JOHNSON
Professor, Indiana University, Bloomington, IN

SIEGFRIED S. JOHNSON
Graduate Student, University of Michigan, Ann Arbor, MI

BRIAN W. JONES
University of Queensland, Brisbane, Australia

DONALD L. JONES
Professor and Graduate Director, University of South Carolina, Columbia, SC

F. STANLEY JONES
Assistant Professor of NT and Ancient Christianity, California State University, Long Beach, CA

REV. DR. IVOR H. JONES
Wesley House, Cambridge, England

RICHARD N. JONES
Middle East Center, University of Utah, and Senior Technologist, Dept. of Immunology, Associated Regional and University Pathologists, Inc., Salt Lake City, UT

MARINUS DE JONGE
Professor of NT and Early Christian Literature, University of Leiden, Leiden, The Netherlands

KLAUS JUNACK
Chief-Custodian, Institute for NT Text Research, Münster, Germany

GERALD E. KADISH
Associate Professor of History and Near Eastern Studies, State University of New York at Binghamton, Binghamton, NY

ZEIDAN A. KAFAFI
Associate Professor, Institute of Archaeology and Anthropology, Yarmouk University, Irbid, Jordan

RICHARD KALMIN
Assistant Professor, The Jewish Theological Seminary, New York, NY

JOHN KAMPEN
Academic Dean/Professor of Bible, Payne Theological Seminary, Wilberforce, OH

HAYA RITTER KAPLAN
Museum of Antiquities of Tel Aviv/Jaffa, Tel Aviv, Israel

JACOB KAPLAN
Museum of Antiquities of Tel Aviv/Jaffa, Tel Aviv, Israel

ARYEH KASHER
Professor, Tel Aviv University, Tel Aviv, Israel

H. J. KATZENSTEIN
Associate Professor, Schocken Institute, Jerusalem, Israel

IVAN T. KAUFMAN
Professor of OT and Hebrew, Episcopal Divinity School, Cambridge, MA

STEPHEN A. KAUFMAN
Professor, Hebrew Union College, Cincinnati, OH

ROSALINDE ANNE KEARSLEY
Macquarie University, North Ryde, N.S.W., Australia

BRIAN E. KECK
Ph.D. Student, University of Michigan, Ann Arbor, MI

HOWARD CLARK KEE
Senior Research Fellow, University of Pennsylvania, Philadelphia, PA

PROF. DR. OTHMAR KEEL
Biblisches Institut der Universität, Freiburg, Switzerland

WERNER H. KELBER
Turner Professor of Religious Studies, Rice University, Houston, TX

GEORGE L. KELM
Professor of Archaeology, Southwestern Baptist Theological Seminary, Fort Worth, TX

CHARLES A. KENNEDY
Professor of Religion, Virginia Polytechnic Institute and State University, Blacksburg, VA

DAVID KENNEDY
Associate Professor, Dept. of Archaeology, Boston University, Boston, MA

JAMES KENNEDY
Lecturer, Baylor University, Waco, TX

LAWRENCE KEPPIE
Senior Curator, Hunterian Museum, University of Glasgow, Glasgow, Scotland

ISAAC M. KIKAWADA
Visiting Lecturer, University of California at Berkeley, Berkeley, CA

ALISTAIR KILLICK
Romsey, Hampshire, England

GERALDINE KING
London, England

KAREN L. KING
Associate Professor of Religious Studies, Occidental College, Los Angeles, CA

PHILIP J. KING
Professor, Boston College, Chestnut Hill, MA

K. A. KITCHEN
Professor of Egyptology, Oriental Studies, University of Liverpool, Liverpool, England

WILLIAM KLASSEN
Professor of Religion, University of Waterloo, Waterloo, Ontario, Canada

HANS-JOSEF KLAUCK
Universitätsprofessor and Chair of NT Studies, Universität Würzburg, Katholisch-Theologische Fakultät, Biblisches Institut, Würzburg, Germany

JACOB KLEIN
Professor of Assyriology and Bible, Bar-Ilan University, Ramat-Gan, Israel

RALPH W. KLEIN
Dean and Christ Seminary–Seminex Professor of OT, Lutheran School of Theology at Chicago, Chicago, IL

AMOS KLONER
Professor, Antiquities Authority and Bar-Ilan University, Jerusalem and Ramat-Gan, Israel

A. BERNARD KNAPP
Research Fellow in Archaeology, Cambridge University, Cambridge, England

ERNST AXEL KNAUF
Dr. theol. habil., Wissenschaftlich-Theologisches Seminar der Universität, Heidelberg, Germany

DOUGLAS A. KNIGHT
Professor of Hebrew Bible, Vanderbilt University, Nashville, TN

FREDERICK W. KNOBLOCH
Lecturer in Biblical Hebrew, University of Pennsylvania, Philadelphia, PA

YOSHITAKA KOBAYASHI
Chairman, OT Dept., Asia Adventist Theological Seminary, Silang, Cavite, Philippines

PROF. DR. DIETRICH-ALEX KOCH
Universität Münster, Münster, Germany

KLAUS KOCH
Professor for OT and History of Near Eastern Religions, Alttestamentliches Seminar, Universität Hamburg, Hamburg, Germany

MOSHE KOCHAVI
Professor of Archaeology, Tel Aviv University, Tel Aviv, Israel

JOHN KOENIG
Professor of NT, The General Theological Seminary, New York, NY

WADE R. KOTTER
Senior Lecturer, Dept. of Sociology and Anthropology, Towson State University, Towson, MD

DAVID KRAEMER
Associate Professor, Jewish Theological Seminary, New York, NY

ROBERT A. KRAFT
Professor of Religious Studies, University of Pennsylvania, Philadelphia, PA

CHARLES R. KRAHMALKOV
Professor of Ancient Near Eastern Languages and Literatures, University of Michigan, Ann Arbor, MI

EDGAR M. KRENTZ
Professor of NT, Lutheran School of Theology at Chicago, Chicago, IL

JOHN S. KSELMAN
Associate Professor of OT, Weston School of Theology, Cambridge, MA

JOANNE KUEMMERLIN-MCLEAN
Montana State University, Bozemann, MT

J. KENNETH KUNTZ
Professor of Religion, University of Iowa, Iowa City, IA

JOHN KUTSKO
Ph.D. Student, Harvard University, Cambridge, MA

ROBERT KYSAR
Adjunct Professor of NT, Lutheran Theological Seminary (Philadelphia) and Co-Pastor, Upper Dublin Lutheran Church, Ambler, PA

W. G. LAMBERT
Professor of Assyriology, University of Birmingham, Birmingham, England

PETER LAMPE
Professor of NT, Union Theological Seminary, Richmond, VA

H. DARRELL LANCE
Professor of OT Interpretation, Colgate Rochester Divinity School, Bexley Hall, Crozer Theological Seminary, Rochester, NY

HAYIM LAPIN
Ph.D. Student, Columbia University, New York, NY

NANCY L. LAPP
Lecturer, Pittsburgh Theological Seminary, Pittsburgh, PA

BERNARD C. LATEGAN
University of Stellenbosch, Stellenbosch, South Africa

DONALD LATEINER
Professor, Humanities-Classics, Ohio Wesleyan University, Delaware, OH

DALE F. LAUNDERVILLE, O.S.B.
Assistant Professor, St. John's University, Collegeville, MN

SOPHIE LAWS
Adjunct Fellow, Regent's College, London, England

ROBERT B. LAWTON, S.J.
Dean of the College, Georgetown University, Washington, DC

GARY LEASE
Professor, History of Consciousness, Associate Chancellor, University of California at Santa Cruz, Santa Cruz, CA

MONIQUE LECHEVALLIER
Chargée de recherche, Centre National de la Recherche Scientifique, Paris, France

JOHN H. LEITH
Pemberton Professor of Theology, Union Theological Seminary, Richmond, VA

ANDRÉ LEMAIRE
Directeur d'études, École Pratique des Hautes Études, Sorbonne, Paris, France

NIELS PETER LEMCHE
Professor, University of Copenhagen, Copenhagen, Denmark

WERNER E. LEMKE
Professor of OT Interpretation, Colgate Rochester Divinity School, Bexley Hall, Crozer Theological Seminary, Rochester, NY

C. J. LENZEN
Institute of Archaeology and Anthropology, Yarmouk University, Irbid, Jordan

RONALD J. LEPROHON
Associate Professor of Egyptology, University of Toronto, Toronto, Ontario, Canada

JON D. LEVENSON
A. A. List Professor of Jewish Studies, Harvard University, Cambridge, MA

BARUCH A. LEVINE
Professor of Hebrew and Judaic Studies, New York University, New York, NY

LEE I. LEVINE
Professor of Jewish History and Archaeology, Hebrew University and Seminary of Judaic Studies, Jerusalem, Israel

JOHN R. LEVISON
Assistant Professor of Biblical and Theological Studies, North Park College, Chicago, IL

JACK P. LEWIS
Professor of Bible, Retired, Harding Graduate School of Religion, Memphis, TN

THEODORE J. LEWIS
Assistant Professor, University of Georgia, Athens, GA

HAROLD A. LIEBOWITZ
Associate Professor, University of Texas at Austin, Austin, TX

DALE C. LIID
Instructor and N. California Representative, Center for the Study of Early Christianity, Jerusalem, Israel

BETTY JANE LILLIE, S.C.
Associate Professor of Biblical Studies, Athenaeum of Ohio, Mt. St. Mary's Seminary, Cincinnati, OH

JAMES LIMBURG
Professor, Luther Northwestern Theological Seminary, St. Paul, MN

MARY AIKEN LITTAUER
Syosset, NY

MARIO LIVERANI
Professor, University of Rome, Rome, Italy

PROF. DR. RÜDIGER LIWAK
Professor, Kirchliche Hochschule, Berlin, Germany

ALAN BRIAN LLOYD
Professor, University College of Swansea, Wales

HING CHOI LO
Associate Professor of OT, Hong Kong Baptist Theological Seminary, Hong Kong

FR. STANISLAO LOFFREDA, O.F.M.
Director and Dean, Studium Biblicum Franciscanum, Jerusalem, Israel

THOMAS R. W. LONGSTAFF
Professor of Religion, Colby College, Waterville, ME

JEFFREY K. LOTT
Ohio State University, Columbus, OH

J. P. LOUW
Professor, University of Pretoria, Pretoria, South Africa

KIRK E. LOWERY
Budapest, Hungary

MEIR LUBETSKI
Associate Professor, Baruch College, City University of New York, New York, NY

DIETER LÜHRMANN
Professor of NT, University of Marburg, Germany

LAMONTTE M. LUKER
Assistant Professor of OT, Lutheran Theological Southern Seminary, Columbia, SC

JACK R. LUNDBOM
Visiting Professor of OT, Uppsala University, Uppsala, Sweden

A. BOYD LUTER, JR.
Chair and Associate Professor of Bible Exposition, Talbot School of Theology, La Mirada, CA

BURTON MACDONALD
Professor, Dept. of Theology, St. Francis Xavier University, Antigonish, Nova Scotia, Canada

DENNIS RONALD MACDONALD
Professor of NT and Christian Origins, Iliff School of Theology, Denver, CO

M. C. A. MACDONALD
University of Oxford, Oxford, England

PETER MACHINIST
Professor, Dept. of Near Eastern Languages and Civilizations, Harvard University, Cambridge, MA

TEMBA L. JACKSON MAFICO
Professor, Interdenominational Theological Center, Atlanta, GA

BONNIE MAGNESS-GARDINER
Assistant Professor, Bryn Mawr College, Bryn Mawr, PA

RABBI DR. JONATHAN DAVID MAGONET
Leo Baeck College, London, England

WALTER ARTHUR MAIER III
Assistant Professor, Concordia Theological Seminary, Fort Wayne, IN

RUTH MAJERCIK
Lecturer, University of California at Santa Barbara, Santa Barbara, CA

F. MALBRAN-LABAT
Centre National de la Recherche Scientifique, Paris, France

DALE W. MANOR
Ph.D. Candidate, University of Arizona, Tucson, AZ

ZVI URI MAʿOZ
District Archaeologist–Golan, Israel Antiquities Authority, Kazrin, Israel

W. HAROLD MARE
Professor of NT, Covenant Theological Seminary, St. Louis, MO

JEAN-CLAUDE MARGUERON
École Pratique des Hautes Études, Sorbonne, Paris, France

CLAUDE F. MARIOTTINI
Associate Professor of OT, Northern Baptist Theological Seminary, Lombard, IL

BRUCE A. MARSHALL
Professor, University of New England, Armidale, N.S.W., Australia

I. HOWARD MARSHALL
Professor of NT Exegesis, University of Aberdeen, Aberdeen, Scotland

HUBERT M. MARTIN, JR.
Professor of Classics, University of Kentucky, Lexington, KY

RALPH P. MARTIN
Professor of Biblical Studies, University of Sheffield, Sheffield, England

THOMAS W. MARTIN
Adjunct Instructor, University of Nebraska at Omaha and Associate Pastor, First United Methodist Church, Fremont, NE

ROBERT MARTIN-ACHARD
Professeur honoraire aux Universités de Genève et de Neuchâtel, Switzerland

FRANK J. MATERA
Associate Professor, Catholic University of America, Washington, DC

KENNETH MATHEWS
Associate Professor of Divinity, Beeson Divinity School, Samford University, Birmingham, AL

KIKUO MATSUNAGA
Professor of NT Theology, Tokyo Union Theological Seminary, Tokyo, Japan

VICTOR H. MATTHEWS
Professor, Southwest Missouri State University, Springfield, MO

GERALD L. MATTINGLY
Professor of Biblical Studies, Johnson Bible College, Knoxville, TN

A. D. H. MAYES
Associate Professor, University of Dublin, Dublin, Ireland

AMIHAY MAZAR
Associate Professor, Hebrew University of Jerusalem, Jerusalem, Israel

J. CLINTON MCCANN, JR.
Assistant Professor of OT, Eden Theological Seminary, Webster Groves, MO

LEE MARTIN MCDONALD
Adjunct Professor of NT Studies, Fuller Theological Seminary Extension, Menlo Park, CA

REV. SUSAN MCGARRY
Ph.D. Student, University of Michigan, Ann Arbor, MI

MICHAEL DAVID MCGEHEE
Assistant Professor, College of St. Benedict, St. Joseph, MN

PATRICK E. MCGOVERN
Research Specialist, Museum Applied Science Center for Archaeology and Near East Section, University Museum, University of Pennsylvania, Philadelphia, PA

JOHN E. MCKENNA
Adjunct Professor of OT and Hebrew, Fuller Theological Seminary, Pasadena, CA

STEVEN L. MCKENZIE
Associate Professor, Rhodes College, Memphis, TN

DONALD K. MCKIM
Interim Pastor, Trinity Presbyterian Church, Berwyn, PA

BARBARA KELLEY MCLAUCHLIN
Associate Professor of Classics, San Francisco State University, San Francisco, CA

MARK D. MCLEAN
Associate Professor of Biblical Studies and Philosophy, Evangel College, Springfield, MO

GREGORY MCMAHON
Assistant Professor of Ancient History, University of New Hampshire, Durham, NH

PHILLIP E. MCMILLION
Associate Professor, Harding University Graduate School, Memphis, TN

JOHN MCRAY
Professor of NT and Archaeology, Wheaton College Graduate School, Wheaton, IL

KATHLEEN E. MCVEY
Associate Professor, Princeton Theological Seminary, Princeton, NJ

JOHN P. MEIER
Professor of NT, Catholic University of America, Washington, DC

SAMUEL A. MEIER
Assistant Professor of Hebrew, Ohio State University, Columbus, OH

EDMUND S. MELTZER
Associate Professor, Claremont Graduate School, Claremont, CA

DORON MENDELS
Associate Professor, Hebrew University of Jerusalem, Jerusalem, Israel

GEORGE E. MENDENHALL
Professor Emeritus, University of Michigan, Ann Arbor, MI, and Visiting Professor, Institute of Archaeology and Anthropology, Yarmouk University, Irbid, Jordan

REINHOLD MERKELBACH
Professor, University of Cologne, Germany

ZEʾEV MESHEL
Institute of Archaeology, Tel Aviv University, Tel Aviv, Israel

BEN FRANKLIN MEYER
Professor, McMaster University, Hamilton, Ontario, Canada

LESTER V. MEYER
Professor of Religion, Concordia College, Moorhead, MN

MARVIN W. MEYER
Associate Professor of Religion, Chapman College, Orange, CA

CAROL MEYERS
Professor, Duke University, Durham, NC

ERIC M. MEYERS
Professor of Religion, Duke University, Durham, NC

JOHN R. MILES
Book Editor, *Los Angeles Times,* Los Angeles, CA

JACOB MILGROM
Professor of Bible and Hebrew, University of California at Berkeley, Berkeley, CA

WILLIAM R. MILLAR
Professor of Religion, Linfield College, McMinnville, OR

ALAN RALPH MILLARD
Reader in Hebrew and Ancient Semitic Languages, University of Liverpool, Liverpool, England

J. MAXWELL MILLER
Professor of OT Studies, Emory University, Atlanta, GA

ROBERT D. MILLER II
Graduate Student, University of Michigan, Ann Arbor, MI

WATSON E. MILLS
Professor of NT Studies, Mercer University, Macon, GA

R. D. MILNS
Professor of Classics and Ancient History, University of Queensland, Brisbane, Australia

HANS-JÜRGEN VAN DER MINDE
Calden, Germany

PAUL S. MINEAR
Winkley Professor Emeritus of Biblical Theology, Yale University, New Haven, CT

FRANK T. MIOSI
Director, Ministry of Colleges and Universities, Toronto, Ontario, Canada

PAUL ALLAN MIRECKI
Assistant Professor, University of Kansas, Lawrence, KS

PIERRE DE MIROSCHEDJI
Chargé de Recherche, Centre National de la Recherche Scientifique, Jerusalem and Paris

MARGARET M. MITCHELL
Assistant Professor of Biblical Studies, McCormick Theological Seminary, Chicago, IL

STEPHEN MITCHELL
University College of Swansea, Wales, United Kingdom

PROF. DR. SIEGFRIED MITTMANN
Eberhard-Karls-Universität, Tübingen, Germany

CAREY A. MOORE
A. R. Strong Professor of Religion, Gettysburg College, Gettysburg, PA

REV. ROBERT MORGAN
University of Oxford, Oxford, England

MARTHA A. MORRISON
Adjunct Lecturer, Boston College, Chestnut Hill, MA, and Research Associate, University Museum, Philadelphia, PA

WILLIAM S. MORROW
Assistant Professor, Queen's Theological College, Kingston, Ontario, Canada

JAMES C. MOYER
Professor and Head of the Dept. of Religious Studies, Southwest Missouri State University, Springfield, MO

REV. DR. JOHN BERNARD MUDDIMAN
Official Fellow in NT Studies, Mansfield College, Oxford, England

JAMES R. MUELLER
Assistant Professor, University of Florida, Gainesville, FL

PROF. DR. MARTIN JAN MULDER
Rijksuniversiteit, Leiden, The Netherlands

E. THEODORE MULLEN, JR.
Associate Professor, Indiana University–Purdue University at Indianapolis, Indianapolis, IN

PROF. DR. WALTER W. MÜLLER
Philipps-Universität, Seminar für Semitistik, Marburg, Germany

ROBERT A. MULLINS
Lecturer in Biblical History, Institute of Holy Land Studies, Mt. Zion, Jerusalem, Israel

WILLIAM J. MURNANE
Associate Professor of History, Memphis State University, Memphis, TN

ROLAND E. MURPHY, O.CARM.
George Washington Ivey Emeritus Professor of Biblical Studies, Duke University, Durham, NC

JEROME MURPHY-O'CONNOR
Professor, École Biblique et Archéologique Française, Jerusalem, Israel

GERARD MUSSIES
Faculty of Theology, State University of Utrecht, The Netherlands

CHARLES D. MYERS, JR.
Assistant Professor of Religion, Gettysburg College, Gettysburg, PA

NADAV NA᾿AMAN
Professor, Dept. of Jewish History, Tel Aviv University, Ramat Aviv, Israel

JOSEPH NAVEH
Professor, Hebrew University, Jerusalem, Israel

AVRAHAM NEGEV
Professor, Hebrew University, Jerusalem, Israel

RICHARD D. NELSON
Professor of OT, Lutheran Theological Seminary, Gettysburg, PA

RUSSELL D. NELSON
Assistant Professor of Religious Studies, Concordia College, Edmonton, Alberta, Canada

EHUD NETZER
Senior Lecturer, Hebrew University, Jerusalem, Israel

KENNETH G. C. NEWPORT
Hong Kong Adventist College, Kowloon, Hong Kong

CAROL A. NEWSOM
Associate Professor of OT, Candler School of Theology, Emory University, Atlanta, GA

OLIVER NICHOLSON
Assistant Professor, Dept. of Classical and Near Eastern Studies, University of Minnesota, Twin Cities, Minneapolis, MN

GEORGE W. E. NICKELSBURG
Professor, University of Iowa, Iowa City, IA

EUGENE A. NIDA
Consultant, American Bible Society and United Bible Societies, Kennett Square, PA

KJELD NIELSEN
Lecturer, University of Copenhagen, Denmark

FREDERICK W. NORRIS
Professor of Christian Doctrine, Emmanuel School of Religion, Johnson City, TN

ROBERT NORTH, S.J.
Professor of Archaeology and OT Exegesis, Retired, Pontifical Biblical Institute, Rome, Italy

TAMAR NOY
Curator of Prehistoric Periods, The Israel Museum, Jerusalem, Israel

RICHARD W. NYSSE
Associate Professor of OT, Luther Northwestern Theological Seminary, St. Paul, MN

JULIA M. O'BRIEN
Assistant Professor, Meredith College, Raleigh, NC

J. RANDALL O'BRIEN
Senior Pastor, Calvary Baptist Church, Little Rock, AR

GERALD G. O'COLLINS
Professor, Gregorian University, Rome, Italy

GAIL R. O'DAY
Associate Professor of Biblical Preaching, Candler School of Theology, Emory University, Atlanta, GA

REV. J. C. O'NEILL
Professor, University of Edinburgh, Edinburgh, Scotland

ROBERT F. O'TOOLE, S.J.
Professor, Danforth Chair in Humanities, St. Louis University, St. Louis, MO

ROBERT A. ODEN, JR.
Headmaster, The Hotchkiss School, Lakeville, CT

J. P. OLESON
Professor, Dept. of Classics, University of Victoria, Victoria, British Columbia, Canada

GARY H. OLLER
Associate Professor of Classics, University of Akron, Akron, OH

DENNIS T. OLSON
Assistant Professor of OT, Princeton Theological Seminary, Princeton, NJ

MARK J. OLSON
Assistant Professor of Religion, Virginia Polytechnic Institute and State University, Blacksburg, VA

AHARON OPPENHEIMER
Professor, Tel Aviv University, Tel Aviv, Israel

ELIEZER D. OREN
Professor, Ben Gurion University, Beer-Sheva, Israel

HARRY M. ORLINSKY
Professor Emeritus of Bible, Hebrew Union College–Jewish Institute of Religion, New York, NY

CARROLL D. OSBURN
Walling Distinguished Professor of NT, Abilene Christian University, Abilene, TX

RICHARD E. OSTER, JR.
Professor of NT, Harding Graduate School of Religion, Memphis, TN

MAGNUS OTTOSSON
Professor, University of Uppsala, Uppsala, Sweden

ASHER OVADIAH
Professor, Tel Aviv University, Tel Aviv, Israel

J. ANDREW OVERMAN
Dept. of Religions and Classical Studies, University of Rochester, Rochester, NY

MITCHELL C. PACWA, S.J.
Assistant Professor, Loyola University of Chicago, Chicago, IL

RAPHAEL I. PANITZ
Consultant/Legislative Assistant, U.S. House of Representatives Committee on Science, Space, and Technology, Washington, DC

D. PARDEE
Professor, University of Chicago, Chicago, IL

REV. DR. D. C. PARKER
The Queen's College, Birmingham, England

S. THOMAS PARKER
Associate Professor, North Carolina State University, Raleigh, NC

PETER J. PARR
Senior Lecturer, Institute of Archaeology, University College London, London, England

DOUGLAS M. PARROTT
Professor, University of California at Riverside, Riverside, CA

H. VAN DYKE PARUNAK
Scientific Fellow, Industrial Technology Institute, Ann Arbor, MI

DALE PATRICK
Associate Professor of Bible, Drake University, Des Moines, IA

JERRY A. PATTENGALE
Assistant Professor, Azusa Pacific University, Azusa, CA

STEPHEN J. PATTERSON
Assistant Professor of NT, Eden Theological Seminary, St. Louis, MO

JON PAULIEN
Associate Professor of NT Interpretation, Andrews University, Berrien Springs, MI

MARY MARGARET PAZDAN
Associate Professor of Biblical Studies, Aquinas Institute of Theology, St. Louis, MO

BIRGER A. PEARSON
Professor of Religious Studies, University of California at Santa Barbara, Santa Barbara, CA

BRIAN PECKHAM
Associate Professor, Regis College, Toronto, Ontario

JOHN GRIFFITHS PEDLEY
Professor of Classical Archaeology and Greek, University of Michigan, Ann Arbor, MI

MALCOLM L. PEEL
Executive Director, The Greater Cedar Rapids Foundation, Cedar Rapids, IA

ROMANO PENNA
Professor of NT Exegesis, Pontificia Università Lateranense, Rome, Italy

HARRY LEE PERKINS
Teacher of Classics, Coordinator of Curriculum in Classical Languages, St. Catherine's School, Richmond, VA

LARRY PERKINS
Professor of Biblical Studies, Northwest Baptist Theological College and Seminary, Vancouver, British Columbia, Canada

PHEME PERKINS
Professor, Boston College, Chestnut Hill, MA

MELVIN K. H. PETERS
Associate Professor, Duke University, Durham, NC

DAVID L. PETERSEN
Professor of OT, Iliff School of Theology, Denver, CO

WILLIAM L. PETERSEN
Assistant Professor, Pennsylvania State University, University Park, PA

JOHN L. PETERSON
Dean, St. George's College, Jerusalem

GERALD J. PETTER
Grand Rapids, MI

STEPHEN J. PFANN
Director, Center for the Study of Early Christianity, Jerusalem, Israel

FR. MICHELE PICCIRILLO
Professor of Biblical History and Geography, Studium Biblicum Franciscanum, Jerusalem

STUART RICHARD PICKERING
Postdoctoral Fellow in History, Macquarie University, Sydney, N.S.W., Australia

ALBERT PIETERSMA
Professor, University of Toronto, Toronto, Ontario, Canada

STANLEY C. PIGUÈ
Lecturer, Averett College, Danville, VA

DANA M. PIKE
Lecturer, Rutgers University-Camden, Camden, NJ

STEPHEN PISANO, S.J.
Extraordinary Professor, Pontifical Biblical Institute, Rome, Italy

WAYNE T. PITARD
Assistant Professor, University of Illinois at Urbana-Champaign, Urbana, IL

FR. BARGIL PIXNER
Benedictine Dormition, Abbey, Benedictine Dormition Abbey, Jerusalem, Israel

ELIZABETH E. PLATT
Associate Professor of Biblical Studies, University of Dubuque Theological Seminary, Dubuque, IA

J. DAVID PLEINS
Assistant Professor, Santa Clara University, Santa Clara, CA

ECKHARD PLÜMACHER
Bibliothek der Kirchlichen Hochschule Berlin, Berlin, Germany

MARVIN H. POPE
Professor Emeritus, Semitic Languages and Literatures, Yale University, New Haven, CT

BEZALEL PORTEN
Professor, Hebrew University, Jerusalem, Israel

STANLEY E. PORTER
Associate Professor of Greek, Biola University, La Mirada, CA

GARY G. PORTON
Professor, University of Illinois at Urbana-Champaign, Urbana, IL

DAVID POTTER
Assistant Professor, University of Michigan, Ann Arbor, MI

MARVIN A. POWELL
Professor of Ancient History, Northern Illinois University, DeKalb, IL

GARY D. PRATICO
Associate Professor of OT, Gordon-Conwell Theological Seminary, S. Hamilton, MA

M. W. PRAUSNITZ
Dept. of Antiquities, State of Israel, Jerusalem, Israel

TERRENCE PRENDERGAST
Associate Professor, Regis College, University of Toronto, Toronto, Ontario, Canada

CAROLYN PRESSLER
Assistant Professor of OT Theology, United Theological Seminary of the Twin Cities, New Brighton, MN

JOHN F. PRIEST
Professor, Florida State University, Tallahassee, FL

JEAN-MARC PRIEUR
Professor, Faculté de théologie de Montpellier, France

WILLIAM H. PROPP
Professor, University of California at San Diego, La Jolla, CA

EMILE PUECH
Chercheur, Centre National de la Recherche Scientifique, Paris, and Professeur, École Biblique et Archéologique Française, Jerusalem

JAMES D. PURVIS
Professor of Religion, Boston University, Boston, MA

ALBERT DE PURY
Professor and Dean, Faculté de théologie, Université de Genève, Geneva, Switzerland

ELISHA QIMRON
Professor, Ben-Gurion University of the Negev, Beer-Sheva, Israel

MONSIGNOR JEROME D. QUINN (deceased)
The Saint Paul Seminary, Saint Paul, MN

PAUL R. RAABE
Assistant Professor of OT, Concordia Seminary, St. Louis, MO

TESSA RAJAK
Reader in Classics, University of Reading, Reading, England

GEORGE W. RAMSEY
Herrington Professor of Religion, Presbyterian College, Clinton, SC

C. NICHOLAS RAPHAEL
Professor of Geography, Eastern Michigan University, Ypsilanti, MI

URIEL RAPPAPORT
Professor, University of Haifa, Haifa, Israel

WALTER E. RAST
Professor of OT and Palestinian Archaeology, Valparaiso University, Valparaiso, IN

MITCHELL G. REDDISH
Associate Professor of Religion, Stetson University, DeLand, FL

PAUL L. REDDITT
Professor of OT, Georgetown College, Georgetown, KY

DONALD B. REDFORD
Professor, University of Toronto, Toronto, Ontario, Canada

STEPHEN A. REED
Dorot Project Researcher, Ancient Biblical Manuscript Center, Claremont, CA

DAVID G. REESE
Toccoa Falls College, Toccoa Falls, GA

MERLIN D. REHM
Professor of Religion, Concordia College, Bronxville, NY

HAROLD E. REMUS
Professor, Wilfrid Laurier University, Waterloo, Ontario, Canada

GARY A. RENDSBURG
Associate Professor, Cornell University, Ithaca, NY

JOHN REUMANN
Professor of NT and Greek, Lutheran Theological Seminary, Philadelphia, PA

E. J. REVELL
Professor, University of Toronto, Toronto, Ontario, Canada

HENNING GRAF REVENTLOW
Professor, Ruhr-Universität Bochum, Bochum, Germany

JEAN-PAUL REY-COQUAIS
Faculté des Sciences Humaines, Université de Bourgogne, Dijon, France

DAVID RHOADS
Professor of NT, Lutheran School of Theology, Chicago, IL

SUZANNE RICHARD
Assistant Professor, Drew University, Madison, NJ

KENT HAROLD RICHARDS
Professor of OT, Iliff School of Theology, Denver, CO

REV. JOHN RICHES
University of Glasgow, Glasgow, Scotland

STEPHEN D. RICKS
Associate Professor of Hebrew and Semitic Languages, Brigham Young University, Provo, UT

RAINER RIESNER
Universität Tübingen, Tübingen, Germany

RICHARD RIGSBY
Professor of OT, Talbot School of Theology, La Mirada, CA

HELMER RINGGREN
Professor Emeritus, University of Uppsala, Uppsala, Sweden

GREGORY ALLEN ROBBINS
Assistant Professor of Christian Origins, University of Denver, Denver, CO

VERNON K. ROBBINS
Professor of Religion, Emory University, Atlanta, GA

JOHN F. ROBERTSON
Associate Professor of History, Central Michigan University, Mt. Pleasant, MI

GESINE ROBINSON
Institute for Antiquity and Christianity, Claremont Graduate School, Claremont, CA

STEPHEN E. ROBINSON
Professor of Ancient Scripture, Brigham Young University, Provo, UT

THOMAS L. ROBINSON
Researcher, Consultant, Leonia, NJ

WILLIAM C. ROBINSON, JR.
Professor, Andover Newton Theological School, Newton, MA

FRANCESCA ROCHBERG-HALTON
Associate Professor, University of Notre Dame, Notre Dame, IN

JEFFREY S. ROGERS
Furman University, Greenville, SC

J. W. ROGERSON
Professor, University of Sheffield, Sheffield, England

ISRAEL ROLL
Professor, Dept. of Classics, Tel Aviv University, Tel Aviv, Israel

GARY O. ROLLEFSON
Professor of Anthropology, San Diego State University, San Diego, CA

C. GILBERT ROMERO
Visiting Professor, Seminario Mayor San Carlos, Trujillo, Peru

AVRAHAM RONEN
Professor, University of Haifa, Haifa, Israel

MARGARET ROOT
Associate Professor, University of Michigan, Ann Arbor, MI

MARTIN ROSE
Professor, University of Neuchâtel, Neuchâtel, Switzerland

STEVEN A. ROSEN
Senior Lecturer, Ben-Gurion University of the Negev–Archaeological Division, Beer-Sheva, Israel

JONATHAN ROSENBAUM
Greenberg Professor and Director, University of Hartford, West Hartford, CT

RENATE ROSENTHAL-HEGINBOTTOM
Seminar für Iranistik und Vorderasiatische Archäologie, Göttingen, Germany

RAY LEE ROTH
Professor, International Institute for Advanced Studies, Silang, Cavite, Philippines

CHRISTOPHER ROWLAND
Dean and University Lecturer, University of Cambridge, England

R. RUBINKIEWICZ
Professor, Catholic University of Lublin, Lublin, Poland

KAREN S. RUBINSON
New York, NY

PROF. DR. DR. KURT RUDOLPH
Philipps-Universität Marburg, Marburg, Germany

JOAN BRUEGGEMAN RUFE
University of Virginia, Charlottesville, VA

MICHAEL L. RUFFIN
Pastor, First Baptist Church, Adel, GA

JACQUES RYCKMANS
Professor Emeritus, Université Catholique de Louvain, Louvain-la-Neuve, Belgium

RONALD H. SACK
Professor of History, North Carolina State University, Raleigh, NC

KIYOSHI K. SACON
Professor and President, Tokyo Union Theological Seminary, Tokyo, Japan

KATHARINE DOOB SAKENFELD
Professor, Princeton Theological Seminary, Princeton, NJ

ANTHONY J. SALDARINI
Professor, Boston College, Chestnut Hill, MA

E. P. SANDERS
Arts and Sciences Professor of Religion, Duke University, Durham, NC

JAMES A. SANDERS
Professor of Biblical Studies, School of Theology at Claremont and the Claremont Graduate School, Claremont, CA

NAHUM M. SARNA
Professor Emeritus, Brandeis University, Waltham, MA

JACK M. SASSON
Professor in Religious Studies, University of North Carolina, Chapel Hill, NC

R. THOMAS SCHAUB
Professor, Indiana University of Pennsylvania, Indiana, PA

LINDA S. SCHEARING
Assistant Professor, Luther College, Decorah, IA

TAMAR SCHICK
Associate Registrar of Archaeology, Israel Museum, Jerusalem, Israel

LAWRENCE H. SCHIFFMAN
Professor of Hebrew and Judaic Studies, New York University, New York, NY

GOTTFRIED SCHILLE
Pfarrer Dr. habil., Kirchgemeinde Borsdorf, Borsdorf bei Leipzig, Germany

DONALD G. SCHLEY
Assistant Professor of Bible and Religion, College of Charleston, Charleston, SC

THOMAS SCHMELLER
Professor, Emory University, Atlanta, GA

FREDERICK W. SCHMIDT
Assistant Professor of NT Studies, Messiah College, Grantham, PA

JOHN J. SCHMITT
Associate Professor of OT, Marquette University, Milwaukee, WI

PHILIP C. SCHMITZ
Instructor, Dept. of History and Philosophy, Eastern Michigan University, Ypsilanti, MI

WILLIAM R. SCHOEDEL
University of Illinois at Urbana-Champaign, Urbana, IL

GENE M. SCHRAMM
Professor of Semitics and Professor of Linguistics, University of Michigan, Ann Arbor, MI

PROF. DR. KLAUS-DIETRICH SCHUNCK
Universität Rostock, Theologische Fakultät, Rostock, Germany

ELISABETH SCHÜSSLER FIORENZA
Stendahl Professor of Divinity, Harvard Divinity School, Cambridge, MA

DANIEL R. SCHWARTZ
Associate Professor, Hebrew University, Jerusalem, Israel

PROF. DR. R. EDUARD SCHWEIZER
Emeritus, University of Zurich, Zurich, Switzerland

JOHN J. SCULLION (deceased)
Professor of OT Exegesis, United Faculty of Theology, Melbourne, Victoria, Australia

J. A. SCURLOCK
Assistant Professor of History, Elmhurst College, Elmhurst, IL

DAVID R. SEELY
Assistant Professor, Brigham Young University, Provo, UT

JO ANN H. SEELY
Provo, UT

JOE D. SEGER
Professor of Religion and Anthropology, Director of the Cobb Institute of Archaeology, Mississippi State University, Mississippi State, MS

CHRISTOPHER R. SEITZ
Associate Professor of OT, Yale University Divinity School, New Haven, CT

PHILIP SELLEW
Associate Professor of Classical Studies, University of Minnesota, Minneapolis, MN

C. L. SEOW
Associate Professor of OT, Princeton Theological Seminary, Princeton, NJ

CLAUDIA J. SETZER
Columbia University and Union Theological Seminary, New York, NY

WILLIAM H. SHEA
Research Associate, Biblical Research Institute, Silver Spring, MD

RODNEY H. SHEARER
Pastor, Ono United Methodist Church, Ono, PA

A. R. R. SHEPPARD
London, England

GERALD T. SHEPPARD
Associate Professor of OT Literature and Exegesis, Emmanuel College of Victoria University and the Toronto School of Theology in the University of Toronto, Toronto, Ontario, Canada

ELIZABETH J. SHERMAN

GARY S. SHOGREN
Assistant Professor of NT, Biblical Theological Seminary, Hatfield, PA

PHILIP L. SHULER
Professor, McMurry University, Abilene, TX

REV. DR. R. J. H. SHUTT
Retired, Worcester College of Education, Worcester, England

STEVEN E. SIDEBOTHAM
Associate Professor, University of Delaware, Newark, DE

JOHN H. SIEBER
Professor of Religion, Luther College, Decorah, IA

DANIEL J. SIMUNDSON
Professor of OT, Luther Northwestern Theological Seminary, Saint Paul, MN

ITAMAR SINGER
Senior Lecturer, Tel Aviv University, Tel Aviv, Israel

JOEL C. SLAYTON
Professor of Religion, Central Baptist College, Conway, AR

DAVID CHANNING SMITH
Pastor, Fort Christmas Baptist Church, Christmas, FL

DENNIS E. SMITH
Associate Professor, Phillips Graduate Seminary, Enid, OK

MARK S. SMITH
Assistant Professor of Northwest Semitic Languages and Literatures, Yale University, New Haven, CT

ROBERT HOUSTON SMITH
Fox Professor of Religious Studies, College of Wooster, Wooster, OH

ROBERT WAYNE SMITH
Teaching Fellow, Miami University, Oxford, OH

DANIEL C. SNELL
Associate Professor of History, University of Oklahoma, Norman, OK

GRAYDON F. SNYDER
Academic Dean and Professor of NT, Chicago Theological Seminary, Chicago, IL

WILL SOLL
College of the Ozarks, Point Lookout, MO

RIFAT SONSINO
Rabbi, Temple Beth Shalom, Needham, MA

ANTHONY SPALINGER
Senior Lecturer, University of Auckland, Auckland, New Zealand

JOHN R. SPENCER
Associate Professor, John Carroll University, University Heights, OH

S. DAVID SPERLING
Professor of Bible, Hebrew Union College–Jewish Institute of Religion, New York, NY

FRANK ANTHONY SPINA
Professor of OT, Seattle Pacific University, Seattle, WA

RUSSELL P. SPITTLER
Professor of NT, Fuller Theological Seminary, Pasadena, CA

H. A. I. STADHOUDERS
Faculteit der Godgeleerdheid, Rijksuniversiteit Utrecht, Utrecht, The Netherlands

JOHN E. STAMBAUGH
Professor of Classics, Williams College, Williamstown, MA

IVAN STARR
Wayne State University, Detroit, MI

WILLIAM P. STEEGER
Professor and Director of Center for Christian Ministry, Ouachita Baptist University, Arkadelphia, AR

ZDRAVKO STEFANOVIC
Professor of OT, Asia Adventist Theological Seminary, Manila, Philippines

ROBERT H. STEIN
Professor of NT, Bethel Theological Seminary, St. Paul, MN

PIOTR STEINKELLER
Professor of Assyriology, Harvard University, Cambridge, MA

EPHRAIM STERN
B. M. Lauterman Professor of Biblical Archaeology, Institute of Archaeology, Hebrew University, Mount Scopus, Jerusalem, Israel

MATTHEW W. STOLPER
Professor of Assyriology, The Oriental Institute, University of Chicago, Chicago, IL

MICHAEL E. STONE
Professor, Hebrew University of Jerusalem, Israel

ROBERT F. STOOPS, JR.
Associate Professor, Dept. of Liberal Studies, Western Washington University, Bellingham, WA

STANLEY K. STOWERS
Associate Professor, Brown University, Providence, RI

JAMES F. STRANGE
Professor of Religious Studies, University of South Florida, Tampa, FL

PROF. DR. GEORG STRECKER
Fachbereich Theologie der Georg-August-Universität, Göttingen, Germany

WILLIAM D. STROKER
Drew University, Madison, NJ

DOUGLAS STUART
Chair, Division of Biblical Studies, Gordon-Conwell Theological Seminary, South Hamilton, MA

PAUL F. STUEHRENBERG
Monographs Librarian, Yale University Divinity Library, New Haven, CT

THEODORE STYLIANOPOULOS
Professor, Holy Cross Greek Orthodox School of Theology, Brookline, MA

DAVID E. SUITER
Regis College, Denver, CO

RICHARD D. SULLIVAN (deceased)
Adjunct Professor of History, Simon Fraser University, Vancouver, British Columbia, Canada

HENRY T. C. SUN
The Claremont Graduate School, Claremont, CA

M. SUSSMAN
Professor Emeritus of Bacteriology, Medical School, Newcastle Upon Tyne, England

STEVEN R. SWANSON
Instructor, Glendale Community College, Glendale, CA

JAMES L. SWAUGER
Curator Emeritus–Anthropology, Carnegie Museum of Natural History, Pittsburgh, PA

MARVIN A. SWEENEY
Associate Professor of Religious Studies, University of Miami, Coral Gables, FL

JAMES D. TABOR
Associate Professor, University of North Carolina, Charlotte, NC

CHARLES H. TALBERT
Wake Forest Professor of Religion, Wake Forest University, Winston-Salem, NC

DAVID TARLER
Archaeologist, The City of David Archaeological Project, Hebrew University of Jerusalem, Jerusalem, Israel

JEAN-MICHEL DE TARRAGON, O.P.
Professor of OT History and Ugaritic, École Biblique et Archéologique Française, Jerusalem, Israel

J. GLEN TAYLOR
Assistant Professor, Wycliffe College, University of Toronto, Toronto, Canada

MARION ANN TAYLOR
Assistant Professor, Wycliffe College, University of Toronto, Toronto, Canada

WALTER F. TAYLOR, JR.
Associate Professor of NT, Trinity Lutheran Seminary, Columbus, OH

PROF. DR. WINFRIED THIEL
Philipps-Universität, Marburg, Germany

JOHAN CARL THOM
Lecturer in Greek, University of Stellenbosch, Stellenbosch, South Africa

DANA ANDREW THOMASON
Assistant Counselor and Chaplain, Hendrix College, Conway, AR

DAVID L. THOMPSON
F. M. and Ada Thompson Professor of Biblical Studies, Asbury Theological Seminary, Wilmore, KY

REV. DR. HENRY O. THOMPSON
Professor of Bible and Ministry, Unification Theological Seminary, Barrytown, NY, and Adjunct Professor of Ethics, School of Nursing, University of Pennsylvania, Philadelphia, PA

THOMAS L. THOMPSON
Associate Professor, Marquette University, Milwaukee, WI

DONALD A. D. THORSEN
Associate Professor of Theology, Azusa Pacific University, Azusa, CA

DAVID L. TIEDE
President and Professor of NT, Luther Northwestern Seminary, St. Paul, MN

THOMAS H. TOBIN, S.J.
Associate Professor of Theology, Loyola University of Chicago, Chicago, IL

WESLEY IRWIN TOEWS
Assistant Professor, University of Manitoba, Winnipeg, Manitoba, Canada

LAWRENCE E. TOOMBS
Professor Emeritus, Wilfrid Laurier University, Waterloo, Ontario, Canada

KAREL VAN DER TOORN
Professor, Rijksuniversiteit Utrecht, The Netherlands

EMANUEL TOV
Professor, Dept. of Bible, Hebrew University, Jerusalem, Israel

JOHN T. TOWNSEND
Professor, The Episcopal Divinity School, Cambridge, MA

JOSEPH L. TRAFTON
Associate Professor of Religious Studies, Western Kentucky University, Bowling Green, KY

STEPHEN H. TRAVIS
Vice Principal, St. John's College, Nottingham, England

DIANE TREACY-COLE
Assistant Professor, University of Wisconsin at Oshkosh, Oshkosh, WI

JAY CURRY TREAT
Ph.D. Candidate, University of Pennsylvania, Philadelphia, PA

JULIO TREBOLLE
Professor, Universidad Complutense, Madrid, Spain

PHYLLIS TRIBLE
Baldwin Professor of Sacred Literature, Union Theological Seminary, New York, NY

JOSEPH W. TRIGG
Rector, St. Patrick's Episcopal Church, Falls Church, VA

JEFFREY A. TRUMBOWER
Doctoral Candidate, The Divinity School, University of Chicago, Chicago, IL

JONATHAN N. TUBB
The British Museum, Dept. of Western Asiatic Antiquities, London, England

C. M. TUCKETT
Senior Lecturer in NT Studies, Faculty of Theology, University of Manchester, Manchester, England

JOHN D. TURNER
Cotner Professor of Religious Studies and Professor of Classics and History, University of Nebraska at Lincoln, Lincoln, NE

A. DOUGLAS TUSHINGHAM
Emeritus Professor, Dept. of Near Eastern Studies, University of Toronto, and Chief Archaeologist (retired), Royal Ontario Museum, Toronto, Ontario, Canada

CHARLES L. TYER
Pastor, First Baptist Church, Belfast, ME

ROGER W. UITTI
Professor of OT, Lutheran Theological Seminary, Saskatoon, Saskatchewan, Canada

JEREMIAH UNTERMAN
Associate Professor and Director of Jewish Studies, Barry University, Miami Shores, FL

WILLIAM J. URBROCK
Professor of Religious Studies, University of Wisconsin at Oshkosh, Oshkosh, WI

DAVID USSISHKIN
Professor, Tel Aviv University, Tel Aviv, Israel

FRANÇOIS VALLAT
Directeur de Recherche, Centre National de la Recherche Scientifique, Paris, France

GUS W. VAN BEEK
Curator Old World Archaeology, Smithsonian Institution, Washington, DC

JOHN VAN ENGEN
Director, The Medieval Institute, University of Notre Dame, Notre Dame, IN

CHRISTIANA DE GROOT VAN HOUTEN
Assistant Professor, Calvin College, Grand Rapids, MI

JACK W. VANCIL
Associate Professor of OT, Harding Graduate School of Religion, Memphis, TN

JAMES C. VANDERKAM
Professor, North Carolina State University, Raleigh, NC

ALLEN D. VERHEY
Professor of Religion, Hope College, Holland, MI

BURTON L. VISOTZKY
Appleman Associate Professor of Midrash and Interreligious Studies, Jewish Theological Seminary of America, New York, NY

BENEDICT THOMAS VIVIANO, O.P.
Professor Ordinarius of NT, École Biblique et Archaeologique Française, Jerusalem, Israel

PAULINE A. VIVIANO
Associate Professor of Theology, Loyola University of Chicago, Chicago, IL

ERICH A. VON FANGE
Professor Emeritus, Concordia College, Ann Arbor, MI

PROF. DR. WILLEM S. VORSTER
University of South Africa, Republic of South Africa

KAREL J. H. VRIEZEN
Lecturer, Faculty of Theology, University of Utrecht, Utrecht, The Netherlands

WESLEY HIRAM WACHOB
Ph.D. Candidate, Emory University, Atlanta, GA

UTE WAGNER-LUX
Deutsches evangelisches Institut für Altertumswissenschaft des Heiligen Landes, Basel, Switzerland

ROBERT W. WALL
Professor of Biblical Studies, Seattle Pacific University, Seattle, WA

HOWARD N. WALLACE
United Theological College, North Parramatta, N.S.W., Australia

JEROME T. WALSH
Associate Professor, St. John's University, Jamaica, NY

STANLEY D. WALTERS
Professor of OT Languages and Literatures, Knox College, University of Toronto, Toronto, Ontario, Canada

BRUCE K. WALTKE
Professor of OT, Westminster Theological Seminary, Philadelphia, PA

WILLIAM A. WARD
Professor of Egyptology, Brown University, Providence, RI

DUANE F. WATSON
Assistant Professor of NT and Greek, Malone College, Canton, OH

JOANN FORD WATSON
Assistant Professor of Theology, Ashland Theological Seminary, Ashland, OH

ROBERT L. WEBB
University of Sheffield, Sheffield, England

PROF. DR. HANS WEDER
Universität Zürich, Zurich, Switzerland

HARRY WEEKS
Ph.D. Candidate, University of Michigan, Ann Arbor, MI

TOM F. WEI
Columbus, OH

MOSHE WEINFELD
Professor, Hebrew University, Jerusalem, Israel

JAMES M. WEINSTEIN
Lecturer in Classics, Cornell University, Ithaca, NY

RICHARD D. WEIS
Assistant Professor of OT, New Brunswick Theological Seminary, New Brunswick, NJ

HEROLD WEISS
Professor, Saint Mary's College, Notre Dame, IN

STEVEN WEITZMAN
Harvard University, Cambridge, MA

LAURENCE L. WELBORN
Assistant Professor of NT, McCormick Theological Seminary, Chicago, IL

COLIN M. WELLS
T. F. Murchison Distinguished Professor of Classical Studies, Trinity University, San Antonio, TX

FRED WENDORF
Henderson-Morrison Professor of Prehistory, Southern Methodist University, Dallas, TX

DAVID WENHAM
Tutor at Wycliffe Hall, Oxford, and member of University of Oxford Faculty of Theology, Oxford, England

EDWARD F. WENTE
Professor of Egyptology, The Oriental Institute, University of Chicago, Chicago, IL

RAYMOND WESTBROOK
Associate Professor, Johns Hopkins University, Baltimore, MD

FRANK E. WHEELER
Associate Professor of Biblical Studies, York College, York, NE

L. MICHAEL WHITE
Professor of Religion, Oberlin College, Oberlin, OH

RICHARD T. WHITE
New York, NY

SIDNIE ANN WHITE
Assistant Professor, Albright College, Reading, PA

JOHN WHITEHORNE
Reader in Classics and Ancient History, University of Queensland, Queensland, Australia

KEITH W. WHITELAM
Lecturer, University of Stirling, Stirling, Scotland

JOHN M. WIEBE
Adjunct Professor of Semitic Languages, Fuller Theological Seminary, Pasadena, CA

MAX WILCOX
Professor, Macquarie University, Sydney, N.S.W., Australia

MICHAEL J. WILKINS
Chair and Professor, Dept. of NT, Talbot School of Theology, La Mirada, CA

ERNEST WILL
Membre de l'Institut, Académie des Inscriptions et Belles Lettres, Paris, France

TOM WAYNE WILLETT
Unionville, IN

BRUCE B. WILLIAMS
Research Associate, The Oriental Institute, University of Chicago, Chicago, IL

DAVID SALTER WILLIAMS
Associate Professor, University of Georgia, Athens, GA

MICHAEL A. WILLIAMS
Associate Professor and Chairman, Comparative Religion Program, University of Washington, Seattle, WA

NORA A. WILLIAMS
Near Eastern Studies Dept., Johns Hopkins University, Baltimore, MD

RONALD J. WILLIAMS
Professor Emeritus, University of Toronto, Toronto, Ontario, Canada

H. G. M. WILLIAMSON
Reader in Hebrew and Aramaic, Faculty of Oriental Studies, University of Cambridge, Cambridge, England

BRUCE E. WILLOUGHBY
Managing Editor, The University of Michigan, Ann Arbor, MI

J. CHRISTIAN WILSON
Assistant Professor of Religion, Elon College, Elon College, NC

ROBERT R. WILSON
Professor of OT and Religious Studies, Yale University, New Haven, CT

STEPHEN G. WILSON
Professor of Religion, Carleton University, Ottawa, Ontario, Canada

DONALD H. WIMMER
Seton Hall University, South Orange, NJ

GERNOT L. WINDFUHR
Professor of Iranian Studies, University of Michigan, Ann Arbor, MI

JOHN D. WINELAND
Teaching Fellow, Miami University, Oxford, OH

DAVID WINSTON
Professor of Hellenistic and Judaic Studies, Graduate Theological Union, Berkeley, CA

ORVAL WINTERMUTE
Duke University, Durham, NC

MICHAEL O. WISE
Assistant Professor of Aramaic, University of Chicago, Chicago, IL

FREDERIK WISSE
Professor, McGill University, Montreal, Quebec, Canada

BEN WITHERINGTON, III
Associate Professor of Biblical and Wesleyan Studies, Ashland Theological Seminary, Ashland, OH

CHRISTIAN WOLFF
Dozent, Kirchliche Hochschule Berlin-Brandenburg, Berlin, Germany

BRYANT G. WOOD
Research Analyst, Associates for Biblical Research, Ephrata, PA

REV. DR. CHRISTOPHER J. H. WRIGHT
All Nations Christian College, Ware, Hertfordshire, England

DAVID P. WRIGHT
Salt Lake City, UT

HENRY T. WRIGHT
Professor of Anthropology and Curator of Archaeology, Museum of Anthropology, University of Michigan, Ann Arbor, MI

JOHN W. WRIGHT
Assistant Professor, St. Mary's College, Notre Dame, IN

REV. DR. N. T. WRIGHT
Oxford University, Oxford, England

EDWIN M. YAMAUCHI
Professor of History, Miami University, Oxford, OH

ADELA YARBRO COLLINS
Professor, University of Notre Dame, Notre Dame, IN

KHAIR N. YASSINE
Professor of ANE Archaeology, University of Jordan, Amman, Jordan

GALE A. YEE
Associate Professor, College of St. Thomas, St. Paul, MN

MARGUERITE YON
Directeur de Recherche, Centre National de la Recherche Scientifique, Lyon, France

T. CUYLER YOUNG, JR.
Director, Royal Ontario Museum, Toronto, Ontario, Canada

RONALD YOUNGBLOOD
Professor of OT and Hebrew, Bethel Theological Seminary West, San Diego, CA

RANDALL W. YOUNKER
Assistant Professor of OT and Biblical Archaeology, Andrews University, Berrien Springs, MI

TZVEE ZAHAVY
Professor, University of Minnesota, Minneapolis, MN

YAIR ZAKOVITCH
Associate Professor of Biblical Studies, Hebrew University of Jerusalem, Jerusalem, Israel

JURIS ZARINS
Professor, Southwest Missouri State University, Springfield, MO

ADAM ZERTAL
Dept. of Archaeology, Haifa University, Israel

REV. DR. GEORGE T. ZERVOS
Parish Priest, St. Nicholas Greek Orthodox Church, Wilmington, NC

PAUL E. ZIMANSKY
Associate Professor, Boston University, Boston, MA

MATTANYAH ZOHAR
Institute of Archaeology, Hebrew University of Jerusalem, Jerusalem, Israel

JEFFREY R. ZORN
University of California at Berkeley, Berkeley, CA

BRUCE ZUCKERMAN
Associate Professor, University of Southern California, Los Angeles, CA

ROCHUS ZUURMOND
University of Amsterdam, The Netherlands

PREFACE

In view of Gary Herion's comprehensive Introduction to the *Anchor Bible Dictionary,* very little needs to be added by way of preface, but a few words may be helpful. The project itself was initiated early in the 1980s by conversations between Robert Heller, then head of the Religion Department at Doubleday, and me. Because of the widespread acceptance and use of the Anchor Bible Critical Commentaries, we felt that a companion work, the *ABD,* was an appropriate undertaking. As a consequence, I prepared a master plan, which called for a set of fives: five volumes, five years, five hundred contributors, and five million words. As such, it would have matched generally earlier major works of the same kind: the justly regarded classic work of the turn of the century, *The Hastings' Dictionary of the Bible* (in five volumes, 1898–1904), and the well-known *Interpreter's Dictionary of the Bible* (also in five volumes, the first four appearing in 1962, with a fifth, supplemental volume in 1976). Now, at the end of the first major stage of this enterprise (the submission of the manuscript), the *ABD* has turned out to consist of six volumes, with nearly a thousand contributors, well over six million words, with the completed manuscript submitted to the publisher in just six years. That it was done within this period is a tribute to the last of the associate editors, Gary Herion, who delivered all six volumes in manuscript form from the beginning of June to the latter part of August, 1990. While a project of such magnitude is difficult to manage in its various aspects, the hardest part of all is to finish it and close it down. Getting started certainly was not easy, but once this huge vehicle was well under way, it threatened to become a runaway, moving faster and growing larger (like a snowball coursing down a mountainside) and sweeping everything in its path. It is difficult to imagine how dangerous a prospect this can be, of continuing and unlimited expansion, a never-ending process. It is not readily recognized that for each topic assigned there are many more that could be assigned, and between every two entries there could exist any number of others, all worthy of consideration. Even before the project has reached maximum speed and efficiency, and manuscripts are pouring in in large numbers, it is necessary to call a halt, turn off the power, and apply the brakes. The next most dramatic moment in the work comes with the decision to call a halt and the declaration that the dictionary is done. Of course it isn't (and never will be) "done" because the task of scholarship goes on, old entries need to be revised, and new entries need to be written; but when the deadline arrives, the work is finished. It takes a person of character and courage to make such a determination in the midst of the endless flow of words, but it is necessary. Not every assigned article is received within the time limits, and not every one that is received is finally acceptable. But at some point the declaration must be made, and the editors and the publisher must take what they have and go on to the second major stage: producing the work of a whole generation of scholars in book form.

Gary Herion proved to be the right person in the right place at the right time. He came on board after others had started the project and moved it along. But he finished it, and for that a special accolade is in order. He organized and coordinated the work force for this powerful push to the finish line, and he himself contributed a major effort in negotiating with authors, bringing in the manuscripts, reading and editing the latter. He set an example of conscientiousness and dedication that stirred the rest to emulation as well as embarrassment: he came earlier and stayed later as time wore on and the deadlines approached. He was the ideal coadjutor and chief of operations, and when the time came and the last whistle blew, he had successfully completed what others had started.

I wish to add a personal word of gratitude to all those who had a hand in this undertaking, and whose names are listed in Herion's Introduction. I want to mention in particular the administrative officers of the University of Michigan, who provided substantial material assistance for the *ABD,* in particular the several vice presidents for academic affairs who held the office during the life of the *ABD* project: Billy Frye, James Duderstadt, Charles Vest, and Gilbert Whitaker. Each VPAA in turn renewed the commitment and the support, the continuity being established and maintained by that most modest and self-effacing of associate vice presidents, Robert Holbrook, who has been a faithful backer of this project since its inception.

A final word of gratitude is owing to Astrid B. Beck, without whose constant and diligent oversight of the Project and the Program on Studies in Religion, neither would have succeeded or even survived. She maintained both at the highest levels of efficiency and equanimity during the most trying periods, when the entire building was being torn apart and rebuilt, and when the work force threatened to overwhelm the facilities, and the work load reached a crisis point. There is an unpayable debt owed by all of us.

DAVID NOEL FREEDMAN
EDITOR-IN-CHIEF
December 7, 1990
Ann Arbor, Michigan

INTRODUCTION

Every generation needs its own Dictionary of the Bible. Within its pages one can expect to find presented the essence of critical scholarship on subjects pertaining to the Bible, as those subjects are understood by students of that generation. Thus while such encyclopedic reference works provide a valuable service to their readers, in a larger sense they can never transcend the limits of their own historical contexts. In time they inevitably become outdated, and after a generation or so they can hope to achieve a sort of "second shelf life" as a valuable period piece, witness to where the field of biblical studies was at one point in its history.

It has been thirty years since the last major Bible dictionary appeared in America. The Biblical Theology movement was in its heyday, and a certain "consensus" on matters pertaining to the history and literature of both testaments had been established. When reviewing English-language Bible dictionaries of the time, one cannot help but notice the preponderance of word studies and of sweeping historical reconstructions that were characteristic of the field at midcentury. One critic at the time noted this and lamented that more attention was not being devoted to the critical issues of methods and assumptions. Baldly stated, it seems that scholarship at that time was more interested in presenting "the facts" than in considering critically how we know them to be "facts."

The emphasis in biblical studies has changed considerably since then. The mainstream American consensus that held in the 1950s and early '60s unravelled during the 1970s. Sweeping historical reconstructions became increasingly rare as OT and NT scholars alike began to engage in often fierce debates over methods and assumptions (e.g., about the role and value of archaeology, and about the "literary" nature of biblical historiography). And when syntheses were attempted, one would very often find scholars moving beyond the venerable limits of the canon itself: the vocation of "biblical scholar" increasingly required one to be competent in dealing with a wide range of later, extrabiblical texts attesting to the complex emergence of early Judaism and early Christianity (or, as many would now insist, "early Judaism*s* and early Christianit*ies*").

The *Anchor Bible Dictionary* is no less a product of its time. In some respects, the situation since the 1960s is now reversed: scholars now tend to be more preoccupied with considering how we know something to be a "fact" than in assembling those "facts" into a meaningful whole. Thus the overwhelming majority of major articles found in the following pages devotes a good deal of space to the basic epistemological question: "How do we know what we know about this topic?" One will be hard pressed to find in these pages any sort of sweeping historical synthesis that presumes a scholarly consensus. Scholarly consensus simply does not exist here at the end of the twentieth century.

Nevertheless in these six volumes there are still many new and refreshing insights one can discover about biblical texts, about histories and personalities referred to therein, about religious ideas and themes that find expression in its pages, about ancient Oriental and Hellenistic intellectual and cultural contexts that almost invariably lie just beneath the surface of the text (if not on the surface itself), and about the processes that helped to ensure the Bible's central place in nascent Judaism and Christianity. In short, the *ABD* provides the scholarly world and the general public with an up-to-date and comprehensive treatment of all biblical subjects and topics. Our goal has been to provide an eminently readable and yet authoritative reference source for all readers of the Bible. To achieve this, we have assembled an international host of scholars—including prominent archaeologists, Assyriologists, Egyptologists, classicists, philosophers, and ancient historians—who have been selected on the basis of their expertise and special contributions to biblical scholarship. They come with diverse professional and confessional backgrounds, reflecting the growing pluralism and interdisciplinary interests of the field.

A review of *ABD* entries should quickly convince the interested student of the Bible that the *ABD* is indeed an invaluable reference source and a powerful research tool. Yet the perceptive reader scanning these pages and comparing its entries with those of other Bible dictionaries will also discover that there is something to be learned here about the field of biblical studies itself. One may note, for example, the preponderance of new articles pertaining to the cultural history and social institutions that lie in the background of ancient Israel and early Christianity; this is so because these days there is a relatively large number of scholars with social science interests working in these areas. One will also note the large number of articles dealing with archaeological sites and excavations; this is so because the last twenty-five years have seen a veritable explosion of archaeological activity in the lands of the Bible. One will also note specific entries treating pseudepigraphic and apocryphal texts, Nag Hammadi tractates, and individual Dead Sea scrolls; this is so because the scope of scholarly interest has now extended beyond the conventional limits of the canon. One will note that the so-called "minor entries" on personal and place names usually go beyond the one- or two-sentence recapitulations often found in other Bible dictionaries; this is so because scholars today seem to have a keener interest in the often minute details associated with genealogies and toponyms, and they appreciate how a careful reexamination of these details can sometimes lead to fresh insights about the relationship between tradition and history. Conversely one will not find as many minor or midlevel entries dealing with biblical lexical items; this is so because we could not find many scholars interested in these subjects or able to push their presentations beyond those found in other Bible dictionaries. What this means is that in some areas related particularly to word studies the *ABD* simply does not replace such major English-language works as the *IDB* or the still-incomplete *TDOT*. This also reveals something about the agenda and the priorities of biblical scholarship in the 1970s and '80s.

One will also appreciate the extent to which biblical studies has become increasingly specialized and even fragmented during the past thirty years. This first became apparent to us during the assignment phase of the project, as more and more contributors expressed reservations about taking on assignments that did not lie within the immediate bounds of their particular "subject" or area of expertise. On the positive side, this means that most *ABD* entries devote greater attention to crucial matters of data and methodology, so that the reader usually gets an expert presentation of the basic issues associated with the study of this or that topic. However, as noted above, the drawback is a certain reluctance to place a given topic within a larger picture—to provide the sweeping and definitive synthesis that some readers desire and expect in a dictionary of the Bible. When presented, syntheses in *ABD* entries tend to be developed more cautiously than in earlier Bible dictionaries, and conclusions are frequently hedged with significant qualifications. That is simply the way responsible critical biblical scholarship tends to be practiced today. One ramification of this increased specialization is evident in our long list of contributors: those who would lament all this as "overspecialization" will no doubt delight in noting that in 1962 only 253 contributors were needed to write more than 7,500 entries for the *IDB,* while thirty years later almost four times as many were needed to write 6,200 entries for the *ABD.* This is an honest reflection of the nature of biblical scholarship here in the final decades of the second millennium.

If it really will be another generation before the next major English-language dictionary of the Bible is attempted, one senses that the *ABD* may in fact be one of the last of its kind. Somehow one suspects that the next major English-language Bible dictionary may not be something one "purchases" but something to which one "subscribes" (complete with annual updates and revisions); that—like money—its primary medium will not be ink-on-paper but electronic impulses (complete with three-dimensional, interactive, color graphics); that it will not be something you place on your shelf but that you load into your computer. Despite all the exciting possibilities this presents, it is also a bit discomforting. Perhaps more than anyone else, we who study the Bible should appreciate the power and the impact of the immutably printed word that, for better or worse, reflects an age and a perspective that cannot easily be erased or revised.

* * *

One of the happy duties associated with writing "introductions" is to acknowledge all those whose labors helped to bring these printed words before the reader. In the case of the *Anchor Bible Dictionary* this is a particularly happy assignment because of the camaraderie and friendships that developed over the years as dedicated people applied their respective talents to the common task. This is not to imply that the production of the *ABD* was without serious practical challenges. No one affiliated with its production was a professional "dictionary maker." Rules and procedures tended to be invented as the need arose. In short, we learned how to create a Bible dictionary primarily by creating a Bible dictionary.

Challenges such as this (especially when they are associated with omnipresent deadlines) either fray people's nerves and drive them apart or draw them closer together. Fortunately the latter was the case. Those bonds tended to be strengthened as together we faced hardships such as unpredictable power failures and periodic fire alarms, incessant jackhammers operating just outside the office door, day after day of dust, and (not surprisingly) chronic computer malfunctions. But in the long run what held the bonds intact was the sense that the work was meaningful. Everyone involved in the *ABD* project soon came to share David Noel Freedman's passionate commitment to the field of biblical studies, and his belief that the time was right for a new multivolume encyclopedic reference work on the Bible. Few other scholars can command the worldwide respect and admiration that are prerequisite to a major collaborative venture such as this. Fewer still possess the ability and skill needed to orchestrate effectively the many necessary resources and personalities. David Noel Freedman could. If indeed the *ABD* should reflect the epitome of biblical scholarship in the last half of this century, who can be surprised that he should be its chief editor?

At the beginning of the project, David F. Graf assisted Freedman as the first associate editor. One of Graf's initial tasks was to draw up a preliminary list of entries and to estimate projected lengths for each. Graf also expanded the enterprise from a purely textual project to a more comprehensive purview integrating the perspective of other related disciplines. In particular, there was an expansion of the archaeological entries for both the Ancient Near East and the

Classical world. David R. Seely, a graduate student in biblical studies at the University of Michigan at the time, helped Graf in this initial process of preparing lists of entries.

Perhaps Graf's most important task was to identify leading scholars who could write the major *ABD* entries. He assembled a staff of consultants from leading specialists in various biblical fields and related disciplines. These scholars were extremely helpful in recommending potential authors for specific dictionary assignments, not only in the first year of the project but also over the years that followed. In making contact with potential authors, Graf was a tireless and ubiquitous presence at professional conferences, not only in the United States but also throughout Europe and the Middle East, cornering scholars one-on-one and enlisting them for the project. Initially the challenges were formidable: many scholars needed to be convinced of the need for yet another multivolume Bible dictionary, while almost all needed to come to terms with the sacrifices they were being asked to make to ensure that this new dictionary would be available soon and at an affordable price. Graf's perseverance and success ensured not only that the very finest and most appropriate authorities would write the major entries for the *ABD;* it also seems to have helped characterize the emerging relationship between the project and its contributors, most of whom came to envision their association with the *ABD* not simply as another professional transaction but as a personal investment in the future of biblical studies.

In 1985 John David Pleins joined Graf and assisted in the administration and organization of the project, which by then had already expanded to involve almost twice as many contributors as had been involved in earlier major Bible dictionary projects. In 1986 he assumed the duties of associate editor while Graf, who had accepted a faculty position at the University of Miami, continued to serve in a consulting capacity, assisting in the assignment of the remaining major entries. Pleins concentrated on assigning the midlevel entries, reading the growing number of major entries that were beginning to arrive, and streamlining office procedures for managing the growing stable of authors and assignments.

During the summer of 1987 Pleins accepted a faculty position at Santa Clara University, and I was asked to serve as the third associate editor of the *ABD.* In the months before his departure, Pleins did a masterful job of orienting me about all the complexities of the project. Together we drafted a comprehensive style guide for authors, thereby facilitating the editorial process by ensuring that all contributions would now display a higher level of uniformity and standardization. In the months that followed, both Pleins and Graf continued to be a valuable and accessible resource to me. Many other projects would have been jeopardized by the number of staff transitions that affected the *ABD,* but Graf's and Pleins' continued cooperation and commitment to the project—and the good rapport that developed among the three of us—guaranteed significant continuity and made my task of completing the project much easier.

By early 1988 the *ABD* project had grown to include more than three times as many contributors as other dictionary projects, while the bulk of minor entries still remained unassigned. It became obvious that we would never be able to manage such a growing number of authors and assignments without a computerized data base. Robert Croninger of the Programs for Educational Opportunity in the University of Michigan's School of Education provided crucial advice and assistance as we initially began setting up this data base. Two graduate students at the University of Michigan, John Kutsko and Harry Weeks, played key roles in gathering data for these minor entry subjects and matching them with potential authors working in related areas of biblical studies. An emphasis in assigning minor entries was to recruit contributors from among the young scholars, women and men, who will be shaping the next generation of biblical studies. Mark Fretz, another graduate student, began researching and writing dozens of these entries to see how they might be improved beyond the usual one- or two-sentence recapitulations of the biblical text. His important work resulted in an *ABD* "Style Guide for Minor Entries," which gave contributors clear guidelines on how ideally to proceed. Although everyone realized that many minor entries simply cannot be expanded beyond one or two sentences, it was gratifying to observe that many of our contributors were able to provide far more informative "minor entries" than those typically found in other Bible dictionaries.

The basic task of editing manuscripts began as soon as the first entries arrived in 1985. Not surprisingly, the dual responsibilities of reading manuscripts and managing assignments proved more than any single editor could handle. Especially with the major entries, various consultants and other editors in specific areas (such as New Testament and Intertestamental literature) had opportunities initially to read and respond to many manuscripts: among these editors who deserve special thanks are Herbert Grether, James Mueller, Paul Mirecki, and William Ward. Also, beginning in the fall of 1988, various graduate students in biblical studies provided part-time assistance, editing the minor entries but also copy editing other manuscripts to ensure uniform use of abbreviations, bibliographic style, and other format conventions. In addition to Fretz, Kutsko, and Weeks, these included Arnold Betz, April DeConick, Marianna Giovino, John Huddlestun, Brian Keck, Glenn LaPoint, Tim LaVallee, Robert Miller, and Helen Richards.

In the last hectic year we added to the *ABD* staff a number of full-time assistants to help complete the editing of manuscripts. The first addition was Philip C. Schmitz, who joined the project full-time in the spring of 1989. In addition to editing a large number of manuscripts, Schmitz played a crucial role in supervising and coordinating the editorial activities of our various part-time graduate students and was a strong force in helping to guarantee that the bibliographies accompanying *ABD* articles met the most exacting standards of scholarly usefulness. In many respects Schmitz functioned as a fourth associate editor actively involved in every phase of the project providing extremely helpful advice and expertise on a wide range of matters.

Dale W. Manor, a doctoral candidate in archaeology at the University of Arizona, moved to Ann Arbor in the fall of 1989 to work full-time editing a large number of manuscripts dealing with archaeological and historical geographical matters. In implementing various editorial decisions for standardizing and improving the presentations of these subjects, Manor helped to set new standards that future dictionaries covering biblical places and archaeology must now strive to match.

In the spring of 1989 Leslie Barkley joined the project as Production Assistant, essentially serving as a full-time work coordinator. Within the first two months she learned how to direct the office routine and personnel better than I had done in the previous two years; as a consequence, our productivity and output increased significantly. She was extremely effective in identifying and anticipating problems and in establishing procedures for resolving them. In the year after we submitted manuscripts to the publisher, she remained on staff to help coordinate the final preparation of illustrations, prefatory material, corrigenda, and proofreading. She demonstrated a keen interest in the subject matter, an attention to detail, and a commitment to professional standards that would be the envy of many biblical scholars.

Between 1985 and 1990 the *ABD* project benefited from a rotating staff of part-time secretaries who handled the routine clerical duties associated with form letters, manuscripts, files, and phone calls. At various times this staff included Lisa Anderson, Kathleen Haviland, Amy Polack, Catherine Kiah, Lisa O'Donnell, Daniel Slager, Paul Slager, Debra Abbott, Shawn Herkimer,

Pamela Rejniak, Tina O'Donnell, and Sharon Manor. During the sometimes hectic times of transitions, Diane Feikema, Theresa Nehra, Lynette Lowey, and Jacqueline Phillips provided notable stability and continuity. Shereen Sauer of the University of Michigan Printing Services took an active interest in the *ABD* project, and consistently provided us with reliable and efficient photocopying assistance. In the final six months of the project, Dennis Moser provided invaluable assistance in the proofreading and in ensuring that the "mechanics" of the finished product indeed worked as intended.

The impression one may have from all of this is that the *ABD* office was always a crowded place buzzing with activity. That was not always the case. During the 1988–89 academic year—a critical phase in the life of the project—the *ABD* essentially had two staff persons: myself and my wife Carol. Although it is common for spouses to be mentioned in introductions, Carol's involvement in the project was uncommon. The year preceding the hiring of several full-time staff members was in many respects the most demanding (that was what justified the full staff), but Carol was there to handle the enormous onslaught of mail, the multitude of daily changes that needed to be made on the data base, the problems that seemed to be surfacing all around us, and all the minute details of managing work flow. She thereby freed me for the task of reading and editing the rapidly growing stack of manuscripts. While many people, thankfully, were on hand to share in the satisfactions of bringing this project to a close, I was very glad to have Carol with me during those months when the future of the project was most in doubt. (In addition, our third child, Daniel, was born in April of that year, and he became an intimate member of the "team.")

Not the least we need to give credit and express appreciation to the donors who made significant contributions to the dictionary through financial support. First and foremost among these is the University of Michigan through the office of the vice president for academic affairs, specifically through support from Robert S. Holbrook, who never wavered in his goodwill for this research project and who lobbied for us with the higher powers for continued funding. The University of Michigan supported us not only with funds, but also with space and equipment. We are indeed grateful. Drs. Charles C. and JoAnne Walton Dickinson were also very generous with their financial support. Their contributions made it possible for us to fund our first research assistant for the dictionary, Mark Fretz, and it came at a crucial time of necessary expansion for the project. They continued their support over time; we owe them a great vote of thanks. In addition, we received financial help from Joy Ungerleider-Mayerson through the Dorot Foundation early in the project, again at a crucial time when resources were slim. We heartily thank all our donors.

A word of appreciation is also due to the Religion Department of the Bantam, Doubleday, Dell Publishing Group. At various key moments in the life of this project, certain individuals were on hand to help move this project closer to publication. Theresa D'Orsogna provided helpful advice throughout most of the project, and James Bell was instrumental in helping us to coordinate our editorial work with that of the publisher. Michael Iannazzi was instrumental in steering the *ABD* through its final production stages.

One colleague stands out as deserving special notice. Dr. Astrid Beck, the Program Associate for the University of Michigan's Program on Studies in Religion, has been a constant source of support to all of us who worked on the project and a key to its success. Had she done nothing more than serve as chief financial officer for the project, meticulously ensuring that the costs of editing the *ABD* were covered, she would merit abundant accolades. But she has done considerably more. She was our principal liaison with the university community: in addition to managing the university's religious studies curriculum and maintaining her own teaching load, she provided for all the space, equipment, and personnel needs of the dictionary project. She was an untiring and effective advocate of the project and a particularly graceful and calming presence whenever we confronted the frustrations of bureaucratic "red tape." She always promised to resolve problems, and she always managed to do so. Astrid was also our principal liaison with the publisher; she taught all of us the ins and outs of dealing with a major publisher, and she especially sensitized me to publishing concerns of which I was completely ignorant. Furthermore she served the project directly as an author and as a translator; and whenever my own writing needed editing, I regularly turned to her. At every stage of the project—from its inception to its completion, in happy times and in sad ones—she has been a model of professionalism, a key adviser, and a good friend.

If it is true that one learns how to create a Bible dictionary simply by creating one, then it follows that the Bible dictionary in question will contain numerous mistakes and reflect occasional bad judgments. So it is with the *Anchor Bible Dictionary*. It also follows that the best time to start a major Bible dictionary project such as the *ABD* is immediately after one has completed a major Bible dictionary project such as the *ABD*—and then to make everything perfect and exactly right. That task, however, is perhaps best left to the next generation.

GARY A. HERION
ASSOCIATE EDITOR
December 6, 1990
Ann Arbor, Michigan

USING THE ANCHOR BIBLE DICTIONARY

Coverage

The *Anchor Bible Dictionary* strives to inform the educated reader of major developments and issues associated with the study of the Bible. It assumes that the reader has a general understanding of and interest in modern biblical scholarship. The *ABD* therefore is primarily a reference tool that will be a valued resource not only for professional scholars and graduate students, but also for clergy and laypersons interested in and familiar with critical biblical study.

The main element of any Bible dictionary is the biblical canon itself. Therefore in these pages readers will find surveys and summaries of issues related to every book of the Bible, including the Hebrew Bible, the Apocrypha, and the New Testament. However, there are also scores of additional entries covering the noncanonical texts: the so-called "Old Testament Pseudepigrapha," the Dead Sea Scrolls, the Nag Hammadi texts, early rabbinic writings, the Church Fathers, and the so-called "New Testament Apocrypha." Each such entry summarizes the contents and structure of the book, describes its literary character and relation to other ancient writings, its major theological ideas and motifs, and theories about the date, place, and identity of its author. In entries that deal with noncanonical texts, readers are also directed to the most useful English translations when such are available. In an effort to control the scope of the Dictionary, only texts that antedate the 4th century A.D. are treated (with a few important exceptions).

Because a concordance is a second element of a Bible dictionary, one will also find here entries on major words and on every name encountered in the Bible. The Revised Standard Version served as the base text in compiling this concordance of terms. However, because word studies have been very ably covered in earlier dictionary series, we have felt it appropriate to concentrate on other types of dictionary/encyclopedia entries; therefore the *ABD* has fewer lexicographic entries than earlier Bible dictionaries. Nevertheless all major theological *logoi* (from ANGELS to YOKEFELLOW) are represented by entries, as are all RSV words that represent transliterations of original Hebrew, Aramaic, or Greek words (e.g., EPHOD; MAMMON; RACA). All these articles treat the original biblical terms underlying the RSV word, attempting to define the word or topic, bringing in any significant insights or nuances provided by extrabiblical parallels, and surveying important scholarly statements on the term/topic.

Every proper name mentioned in the Bible is also reflected in entries, immediately followed by an indication whether the name belongs to a person, place, deity, or object. Whenever the same name belongs to both a person and a place, for example, the *ABD* will provide a separate entry for each; however, if more than one person or more than one place bear the same name, the separate individuals will generally be listed and treated within a single entry. All RSV variant and derivative forms of a name are also clearly indicated. The *ABD* has also attempted to establish new standards in the treatment of biblical place names; these new standards are designed to encourage and reward readers who seriously pursue the historical geographical aspect of biblical study (see "Archaeology and Historical Geography" below). There are also dozens of articles on important persons and places from antiquity who are not listed in any Bible concordance but who nevertheless bear on our understanding of the history and interpretation of the Bible (e.g., MERENPTAH; JOSEPHUS; UGARIT).

There are also hundreds of entries on various historical and archaeological subjects. Again, the *ABD* tends to focus on historical topics that antedate the 4th century A.D. The historical entries strive first to orient readers to the primary sources available for historical reconstruction and to the nature and limitations of those sources. Second, they provide a broad overview of the subject, directing readers to major cruxes of interpretation and to the variety of scholarly opinions expressed on such matters. The entries on archaeological subjects include especially current reports on the results of excavations. In addition, there are dozens of entries covering all important methodologies in biblical scholarship, all versions of the Bible, particular social and cultural institutions in the ancient world of the Bible, ancient religious sects and philosophical movements, major literary genres and motifs, etc. In selecting these topics, the editorial staff in conjunction with the Board of Consultants has made every effort to identify the current and major issues that have been focal points for scholarly study. In these entries, contributors have attempted first and foremost to address the fundamental epistemological question: How do we know what we know about the subject, especially if it is a phenomenon from antiquity? Individual presentations may be arranged in various different ways (topically, chronologically), but each always strives toward clarity and sense.

Headings and Structures of Entries

Each *ABD* entry consists of (1) a "heading," (2) a "body" or "text," and (3) a "bibliography" (although shorter entries may not include the latter).

Heading

ABD headings have deliberately been kept simple in an effort to get the reader into the body or text of the entry as quickly as possible. Unlike other Bible dictionaries, we have felt that Dictionary headings are not the proper place to accumulate technical data such as lists of textual variants or relevant Hebrew or Greek words with associated biblical citations; this information can more easily be presented in the body of the article or obtained from a good concordance or lexicon. We have also chosen not to list etymologies (or translations) of proper names in the headings, since these are usually conjectural at best and sometimes mislead readers into overstating the symbolic significance of biblical names. (However, because names often reveal something of religious or cultural significance, we have encouraged contributors to treat etymologies in the body of the entry.) We have also chosen not to provide pronunciation guides for names in the heading (or anywhere else) since there are (and can be) no uniform standards for these.

The heading of an *ABD* entry can have five component parts, which are used flexibly to accommodate the idiosyncracies of each individual entry. Although most entry headings have only two or three component parts, the five parts are typically formatted as follows:

ENTRY WORD (QUALIFYING TAG) [Heb/Gk *transliteration*]. Var. VARIANT FORMS. DERIVATIVE FORMS.

For example:

ZEBULUN (PERSON) [Heb *zĕbûlûn*]. Var. ZABULON. ZEBULUNITE.

(1) The entry word is the "title" of the article, set off in boldface type for easy recognition. All headings therefore contain an entry word, and many headings contain *only* an entry word (or phrase). Entry words are arranged in alphabetical order according to the spelling conventions of the RSV. Hyphens have been retained as they are presented in the RSV, and this affects the alphabetization scheme. For example, BAAL-ZEPHON appears before BAALAH; BETH-ZUR before BETHANY; EL-PARAN before ELA; and EN-TAPPUAH before ENAIM.

(2) The qualifying tag, set in caps within parentheses, is most frequently used to specify something about the entry word, usually whether it is the name of a person, place, deity, or other recurring category. All entries on biblical proper names will have a qualifying tag in the heading indicating whether the name, *in the context of the RSV presentation,* belongs to a person or a place. (The complex question of whether a particular biblical genealogy indeed lists a personal name or a toponym/ethnonym would then be addressed within the body of the entry.) If the entry word is an archaeological site, the qualifying tag can provide map coordinates for locating that site (see "Archaeological and Historical Geography" below). Qualifying tags are also used in entries dealing with particular Dead Sea Scroll manuscripts or Nag Hammadi codices, giving the reader the appropriate technical sigla accompanying it:

ADAM, APOCALYPSE OF (NHC V,*5*).
MELCHIZEDEK (NHC IX,*1*).
MELCHIZEDEK (11QMelch).
MIQSOT MAʿASEH HATORAH (4QMMT).

(3) The transliteration provides the original biblical form of the entry word, set in italics within brackets and preceded by an abbreviation indicating whether the form is Hebrew, Aramaic, Greek, or Latin. In proper names, usually only the primary form of the name is given; for example, names such as Abraham, Moses, and David occur in both the OT and NT, but only the Hebrew form is included in the heading since the OT is the base text in which the name first occurs. Noteworthy variants *in the original texts* (including Kethib-Qere readings and exceptional LXX forms) may be listed, separated either by commas or semicolons. For example:

ADNAH (PERSON) [Heb *ʿadnah; ʿadnâ*].
ABIGAIL (PERSON) [Heb *ʾăbîgayil; ʾăbîgal*].
BIRZAITH (PERSON) [Heb K *birzāwit;* Q *birzāyit*].
PROSTITUTION [Heb *zĕnût; zĕnûnîm; taznût*].

(4) Variant forms are listed in capitals and preceded by the abbreviation "Var." Usually these are spelling variants of an individual's name reflected in the RSV. For example, Azmaveth in Ezra 2:24 is reproduced as Beth-azmaveth in Neh 7:28 and as Bethasmoth in 1 Esdr 5:18; similarly, the NT form of Arpachshad is Arphaxad (Luke 3:36). However, variants also may

include secondary names borne by people (again, the RSV form is given). For example, Jacob also bore the name Israel, while Jehoahaz was also known as Ahaziah and Shallum. Multiple variants are separated by semicolons, and the end of the list of variants is signalled by a period. For example:

AI (PLACE) [Heb *hāʿay*]. Var. AIATH; AIJA.
JEHOADDIN (PERSON) [Heb *yĕhōʿaddîn*]. Var. JEHOADDAN.
PETER (PERSON) [Gk *Petros*]. Var. SIMON PETER; SIMON.

(5) The last component of the heading is a list of any RSV derivative forms. Derivatives are secondary forms derived usually from personal or place names (i.e., from other entry words). These are also capitalized, and if there is more than one derivative form, they are separated by semicolons. For example:

ABIEZER (PERSON) [Heb *ʾăbîʿezer*]. Var. IEZER. ABIEZRITE; IEZERITE.
EPHRAIM (PERSON) [Heb *ʾeprayim*]. EPHRAIMITES.

Body/Text

After the heading, most entries begin with a statement providing a general definition of the subject, often citing significant biblical passages referring to it. Some major entries have been prepared by combining several articles treating various aspects of the subject. For example, the entry on CHRISTIANITY contains eight articles treating the emergence of Christianity in various parts of the eastern Mediterranean world.

Outlines with corresponding section headers have been included for lengthier articles; midsize articles usually have just the section headers. These enable the reader either to trace the course of the presentation or quickly to identify where a particular aspect of the topic is treated. Whenever a proper name entry treats multiple persons or places bearing the same name, the treatment of each individual subject is introduced by a boldface Arabic numeral.

Bibliography

Most entries conclude with a bibliography, listing items alphabetically by author's last name, and then by year of publication. In some exceptional cases, bibliographies have been subdivided topically. The unique formatting of bibliographic items—each item on its own line with full information displayed instead of all items strung together in abbreviated form—has been designed to assist the serious student who wishes to move from the *ABD* entry into the library for more detailed research on the subject. Certain items that had not appeared in print before 1990 have been marked as "fc" (forthcoming).

Archaeology and Historical Geography

Dozens of *ABD* entry words are actually the names of archaeological sites where excavation work is shedding light on the material culture of Bible lands. The qualifying tags that usually follow these entry words are either a Map Reference (M.R.) number or a latitude-longitude number:

DEIR ʿALLA, TELL (M.R. 209178). A site in the E Jordan Valley, roughly halfway between the Lake of Tiberias and the Dead Sea, near the river Zerqa (biblical Jabbok).

AMARNA, TELL EL- (27°38′N; 30°52′E). The site of the premier city and residence of the Egyptian Pharaoh Amenhotep (Amenophis) IV (alias Akhenaten, ca. 1377–1360 B.C.); located on the east bank of the Nile ca. 180 miles S of modern Cairo.

Very often M.R. or latitude-longitude numbers are also given in the body of the entry itself in discussions that link biblical place names to actual sites. The six-digit M.R. number applies to a grid system frequently used by professional archaeologists to pinpoint sites located in and around Israel and Jordan. These numbers should be used in conjunction with the map conveniently printed on the inside front cover of each *ABD* volume. The first three digits specify the north-south axis while the final three digits specify the east-west axis. Therefore, when locating Deir ʿAlla on the inside cover map, the reader would first find line 209 in the right- or lefthand margin and would then follow that line across to the point where it intersects with line 178 (as indicated on the top or bottom margin of the map). The consistent application of this system within the *ABD* marks a clear break with other Bible dictionaries, which often locate archaeological sites (particularly in the central hill country of Palestine) with respect to modern towns and villages. However, since 1967 the demographics of this occupied territory have been constantly changing, rendering such *relative* locations obsolete. The map reference system employed in the *ABD* makes it possible now to provide *absolute* locations for sites, regardless of ongoing demographic and political upheavals in the Middle East.

The latitude-longitude system works similarly and should be used in conjunction with the map printed on the inside back cover of each *ABD* volume. For example, when locating Tell el-Amarna on that map, the reader would first find latitude 27°38′N in the right- or lefthand margin (keeping in mind that there are 60 minutes per degree), and then would follow that line across to the point where it intersects with the line representing longitude 30°52′E (as indicated on the top or bottom margins of the map).

Throughout the article the reader will encounter standardized references to various archaeological periods. For the reader's convenience, the chronological boundaries associated with each of these periods are listed in the inside front cover of each volume. However, our decision to provide standardized references should not be construed as indicating that scholars are in consensus either about this terminology or about the accompanying dates; in fact, in numerous *ABD* entries authors often have provided qualifying remarks about the period and date of specific archeological remains. It has been precisely the variety of competing chronologies and disagreement over these matters that has prompted us in the first place to insist upon a standard set of references. For example, some archeologists use the term "Middle Bronze I" to refer to the period 2350–2000 B.C., while others use it to refer to the period 2000–1800 B.C. Our intention in standardizing these references is simply to assist the reader by bringing uniformity to the Dictionary (inviting meaningful correlations between different sites presented in the Dictionary) and to do so with a scheme that will not soon be outdated.

Although we have standardized the dates pertaining to archaeological periods, we have not sought to impose uniformity to historical chronology especially as it pertains to regnal dates of ancient kings. As our entries on chronology attest, various dating systems are possible for Mesopotamia, Egypt, and the Israelite monarchy; we have therefore chosen simply to let each individual author utilize the dating scheme that most appeals to him or her. This inevitably results in some inconsistency and potential confusion between entries. For example, entry A may note that the famous "Israel" stela written early in the reign of Merenptah is dated to 1230 B.C., while entry B may note that Merenptah ruled 1223–1213 B.C. and entry C may give dates of 1213–1203 B.C. The reader must appreciate that there are various different ways by which historians calculate ancient regnal dates (although the reader may be confident that dates ultimately grounded in either the Neo-Assyrian or the Greco-Roman chronologies are correct and almost universally accepted).

We have also attempted to standardize the spelling of ancient (non-biblical) names with respect to the current conventions used by Egyptologists and Assyriologists. Pharaonic names are generally spelled according to the Egyptian form, with the familiar Greek form usually given in parenthesis.

Cross References

One asset of the *ABD* is the presence of cross-references that enable interested readers to pursue the continued discussion of a subject in another *ABD* entry. Cross-references are signalled by the entry word(s) being printed in CAPITAL LETTERS, sometimes reinforced by the preceding phrase "See" or "See also." These signals represent the editors' promise that some noteworthy elaboration on this subject will be found under the entry named. Because all biblical names also constitute entry words, the appearance of a proper name in any *ABD* article automatically constitutes an invitation to turn to that entry, regardless of whether or not the name is set in caps.

Abbreviations and Citations

For the convenience of the reader, an exhaustive list of abbreviations has been included at the front of each volume. In alphabetical order, the reader will find almost 2,000 abbreviations for all canonical and noncanonical writings, every leading journal and series pertaining to biblical and related studies (ancient history, archaeology, linguistics, etc.), as well as other technical matters. This list is not complete in providing abbreviations for ancient classical works; therefore, when readers encounter a citation for a lesser-known classical work not included in the abbreviation list, they should consult the lists published in *The Oxford Classical Dictionary,* Liddell and Scott's *A Greek-English Lexicon,* or *A Patristic Greek Lexicon* edited by G. W. H. Lampe.

To prevent bibliographies from becoming too cumbersome, we have chosen *not* to list in our bibliographies articles that have been published either in other Bible dictionaries, in well-known (and oft-cited) textbooks, or in commentaries that are part of a series. Instead, within the body of an entry we have incorporated abbreviated references to these various types of work, as well as volume and page numbers. For example:

> All these words appear in the LXX except possibly *dikaiokrisia* (*TDNT* 2: 24; Wilckens *Romans* EKKNT, 125–26).

> Other general surveys of Herod the Great may be found in *WHJP; HJP*^{2} 1: 287–329; PW 7/2: 1–158; and *CAH* 10: 316–36.

Abbreviations for all these items are found in the abbreviations list, where the reader could deduce, for example, that a scholar named Wilckens has written a commentary on the book of Romans as part of the Evangelisch-katholischer Kommentar zum Neuen Testament series. One would also learn, for example, that a general survey of Herod the Great can be found in the 2d edition (1973–87) of Emil Schürer's *The History of the Jewish People in the Age of Jesus Christ,* vol. 1, pp. 287–329, or that a discussion of the word *dikaiokrisia* can be found on p. 24 of vol. 2 of the *Theological Dictionary of the New Testament* (Grand Rapids, 1964–76). The point is that *ABD* bibliographies have been streamlined by moving references such as these into the body of the text.

While we have followed strict guidelines in standardizing citations to biblical and pseudepigraphic texts, some flexibility in citing chapter and verse in early rabbinic and classical texts has been necessary. As a rule, however, we have tried to move away from the use of Roman numerals in such citations. In citing Josephus we have tried to include, in addition to the book number, not only the chapter and paragraph numbers used in English translations, but also the verse number(s) associated with the original Greek text (the latter being signalled with § or §§):

> In this passage (*Ant* 18.3.3 §§63–64), Josephus notes that during the procuratorship of Pontius Pilate "there lived Jesus, a wise man, if indeed one ought to call him a man."

Hebrew and English versification often diverges, as does MT and LXX versification. In such instances, we have usually included first the Hebrew (MT) citation followed by an "em" dash and the English or LXX citation:

> Qoheleth's advice on religious observance is a good case in point (Eccl 4:17–5:19—Eng 5:1–20).

> This is also evident in the Greek translation of Josh 8:30–33 (—LXX 9:3–33).

When dealing with parallel verses, the tendency has been to use the equal sign (=) rather than parallel bars (//), even when there is not an exact verbatim correlation between pericopes. However, for simplicity we have often just noted the existence of parallels with the abbreviation "pars.":

> The account of 1 Esdr 2:1–15 (= Ezra 1:1–11) seems . . .

> As seen in Mark 1:7–8 (= Matt 3:11–12 = Luke 3:16), . . .

> All the Synoptic Gospels note that Jesus was questioned about this (Mark 12:18–27 and pars.).

We have chosen not to standarize B.C./A.D. and B.C.E./C.E. one way or the other, but instead to let individual authors use whichever system they are most comfortable with, although we have insisted on uniformity *within* each entry.

Notes and Bibliography

In lieu of footnotes, the *Anchor Bible Dictionary* follows a social-science system of citation and bibliography. The bibliography at the end of an article lists major sources relevant to the discussion. Within the body of the entry, references to bibliographic items are cited by author, date, and (where necessary) pages. Multiple references are separated by semicolons. For example:

> This observation has been made with less precision by Beckwith (1985: 97) on the basis of a cursory . . .

> Though the identity of the psalmists' "enemies" has not been determined with precision, they are seen to be such a great menace that they are better dead than alive (Westermann 1981: 188–94; Birkeland 1955; Keel 1969).

Illustrations

The editors of the *ABD* have made every effort to reserve space for line drawings, charts, and photographs illustrating important points made in the text of specific entries. However, the limitations of space and the desire to keep the six volumes listed at an affordable price have meant that we have had to sort through the many recommendations submitted by contributors to select primarily those illustrations that are essential to the comprehension of our articles. In other words, there are no gratuitous illustrations in this Dictionary, and consequently the *ABD* should not be considered a pictorial encyclopedia of the Bible.

The several hundred black-and-white illustrations contained in the *ABD* are identified by a code name consisting of the first three letters of the entry word with which it appears, followed by a two-digit number. References to *ABD* illustrations typically take the form: "See Fig. ART.07." The initial capital of "Fig." (for "Figure") is intended to distinguish an illustration published in the *ABD* from one that might be published elsewhere, in which the lowercase "fig." is used. For example:

> One example of a Canaanite temple is the Fosse Temple III at Lachish (see Mazar 1990: 254 and fig. 7.11). Its principle architectural features can be contrasted with the Iron Age *migdal* temple at Shechem. See Fig. TEM.08.

In this example, the first reference is to an illustration found in Mazar 1990, while the second reference is to an illustration found in the T-volume of the *ABD.*

THE EDITORS

LIST OF ABBREVIATIONS

1 Apoc. Jas.	*First Apocalypse of James* (NHC V,*3*)
1 Chr	1 Chronicles
1 Clem.	*1 Clement*
1 Cor	1 Corinthians
1 En.	*1 Enoch (Ethiopic Apocalypse)*
1 Esdr	1 Esdras
1 John	1 John
1 Kgdms	1 Samuel (LXX)
1 Kgs	1 Kings
1 Macc	1 Maccabees
1 Pet	1 Peter
1 Sam	1 Samuel
1 Thess	1 Thessalonians
1 Tim	1 Timothy
1Q, 2Q, 3Q, etc.	Numbered caves of Qumran, yielding written material; followed by abbreviation of biblical or apocryphal book
1QapGen	*Genesis Apocryphon* of Qumran Cave 1
1QH	*Hôdāyôt (Thanksgiving Hymns)* from Qumran Cave 1
1QIsa[a, b]	First or second copy of Isaiah from Qumran Cave 1
1QM	*Milḥāmāh (War Scroll)*
1QpHab	*Pesher on Habakkuk* from Qumran Cave 1
1QS	*Serek hayyaḥad (Rule of the Community, Manual of Discipline)*
1QSa	Appendix A *(Rule of the Congregation)* to 1QS
1QSb	Appendix B *(Blessings)* to 1QS
1st	first
2 Apoc. Jas.	*Second Apocalypse of James* (NHC V,*4*)
2 Bar.	*2 Baruch (Syriac Apocalypse)*
2 Chr	2 Chronicles
2 Clem.	*2 Clement*
2 Cor	2 Corinthians
2 En.	*2 Enoch (Slavonic Apocalypse)*
2 Esdr	2 Esdras
2 John	2 John
2 Kgdms	2 Samuel (LXX)
2 Kgs	2 Kings
2 Macc	2 Maccabees
2 Pet	2 Peter
2 Sam	2 Samuel
2 Thess	2 Thessalonians
2 Tim	2 Timothy
2d	second
3 Bar.	*3 Baruch (Greek Apocalypse)*
3 Cor.	*3 Corinthians*
3 En.	*3 Enoch (Hebrew Apocalypse)*
3 John	3 John
3 Kgdms	1 Kings (LXX)
3 Macc.	*3 Maccabees*
3d	third
3Q15	Copper Scroll from Qumran Cave 3
4 Bar.	*4 Baruch*
4 Ezra	*4 Ezra*
4 Kgdms	2 Kings (LXX)
4 Macc.	*4 Maccabees*
4QFlor	*Florilegium* (or *Eschatological Midrashim*) from Qumran Cave 4
4QMess ar	Aramaic "Messianic" text from Qumran Cave 4
4QPhyl	Phylacteries from Qumran Cave 4
4QPrNab	Prayer of Nabonidus from Qumran Cave 4
4QTestim	*Testimonia* text from Qumran Cave 4
4QTLevi	*Testament of Levi* from Qumran Cave 4
5 Apoc. Syr. Pss.	*Five Apocryphal Syriac Psalms*
5 Macc.	*5 Maccabees*
11QMelch	*Melchizedek* text from Qumran Cave 11
11QtgJob	*Targum of Job* from Qumran Cave 11
A	Codex Alexandrinus
ÄA	Ägyptologische Abhandlungen
AA	*Archäologischer Anzeiger,* Berlin
AAL	*Afroasiatic Linguistics,* Malibu, CA

AANLM	*Atti dell'Accademia Nazionale dei Lincei, Memorie, Classe di scienze morali, storiche e filologiche,* ser. 8
AANLR	*Atti dell'Accademia Nazionale dei Lincei, Rendiconti, Classe di scienze morali, storiche e filologiche,* ser. 8
AARAS	American Academy of Religion Academy Series
AARASR	American Academy of Religion Aids for the Study of Religion
AARCRS	American Academy of Religion Classics in Religious Studies
AARSR	American Academy of Religion Studies in Religion
AARTT	American Academy of Religion Texts and Translations
AASF	Annales Academiae Scientarum Fennicae, Helsinki
AASOR	Annual of the American Schools of Oriental Research
ÄAT	Ägypten und Altes Testament
AAWLM	*Abhandlungen der Akademie der Wissenschaften und der Literatur Mainz*
AB	Anchor Bible
ABAW	Abhandlungen der Bayerischen Akademie der Wissenschaften
AbB	Altbabylonische Briefe in Umschrift und Übersetzung, ed. F. R. Kraus. Leiden, 1964–
abbr.	abbreviated, abbreviation
ABD	*Anchor Bible Dictionary*
ABIUSJH	*Annual of Bar-Ilan University Studies in Judaica and the Humanities*
ABL	*Assyrian and Babylonian Letters,* 14 vols., ed. R. F. Harper. Chicago, 1892–1914
ABLA	M. Noth. 1971. *Aufsätze zur biblischen Landes- und Altertumskunde,* ed. H. W. Wolff. Neukirchen-Vluyn
ʿAbod. Zar.	*ʿAboda Zara*
ʾAbot	*ʾAbot*
ʾAbot R. Nat.	*ʾAbot de Rabbi Nathan*
Abr	Philo, *De Abrahamo*
ABR	*Australian Biblical Review*
ABRMW	H. Graf Reventlow. 1985. *The Authority of the Bible and the Rise of the Modern World.* Trans. J. Bowden. Philadelphia
AbrN	*Abr-Nahrain*
absol.	absolute
AcApos	*Acta Apostolorum Apocrypha.* 3 vols. Hildesheim, 1959
ACF	*Annuaire du Collège de France,* Paris
ACNT	Augsburg Commentary on the New Testament
AcOr	*Acta orientalia*
AcOrASH	*Acta orientalia Academiae Scientiarum Hungaricae*
ACR	*American Classical Review*
AcSum	*Acta Sumerologica*
act.	active
Acts	Acts (or Acts of the Apostles)
Acts Andr.	*Acts of Andrew*
Acts Andr. Mth.	*Acts of Andrew and Matthias*
Acts Andr. Paul	*Acts of Andrew and Paul*
Acts Barn.	*Acts of Barnabas*
Acts Jas.	*Acts of James the Great*
Acts John	*Acts of John*
Acts John Pro.	*Acts of John (by Prochorus)*
Acts Paul	*Acts of Paul*
Acts Pet.	*Acts of Peter*
Acts Pet. (Slav.)	*Slavonic Acts of Peter*
Acts Pet. 12 Apost.	*Acts of Peter and the Twelve Apostles* (NHC VI,*1*)
Acts Pet. Andr.	*Acts of Peter and Andrew*
Acts Pet. Paul	*Acts of Peter and Paul*
Acts Phil.	*Acts of Philip*
Acts Phil. (Syr.)	*Acts of Philip (Syriac)*
Acts Pil.	*Acts of Pilate*
Acts Thad.	*Acts of Thaddaeus*
Acts Thom.	*Acts of Thomas*
ActSS	*Acta Sanctorum*
ACW	Ancient Christian Writers
A.D.	*anno domini* (year)
ad loc.	*ad locum* (at the place)
ADAIK	Abhandlungen des deutschen archäologischen Instituts, Kairo
ADAJ	*Annual of the Department of Antiquities of Jordan*
Add Dan	Additions to Daniel
Add Esth	Additions to Esther
ADFU	Ausgrabungen der Deutschen Forschungsgemeinschaft in Uruk-Warka
adj.	adjective
ADOG	*Abhandlungen der Deutschen Orient-Gesellschaft,* Berlin
ADPV	Abhandlungen des Deutschen Palästina-Vereins
adv.	adverb
AE	*L'année épigraphique* [cited by year and no. of text]
AEB	*Annual Egyptological Bibliography*
Aeg	*Aegyptus: Revista italiana di egittologia e papirologia*
AEHE IV	*Annuaire de l'École pratique des Hautes Études,* IVᵉ section, Sc. hist. et philol., Paris
AEHE V	*Annuaire de l'École pratique des Hautes Études,* Vᵉ section, Sc. relig., Paris

AEHL — *Archaeological Excavations in the Holy Land,* ed. A. Negev. Englewood Cliffs, NJ, 1980
AEL — M. Lichtheim. 1971–80. *Ancient Egyptian Literature.* 3 vols. Berkeley
AER — *American Ecclesiastical Review*
AESH — B. Trigger, B. J. Kemp, D. O'Connor, and A. B. Lloyd. 1983. *Ancient Egypt: A Social History.* Cambridge
Aet — Philo, *De aeternitate mundi*
Aev — *Aevum: Rassegna di scienze storiche linguistiche e filologiche*
ÄF — Ägyptologische Forschungen
AFER — *African Ecclesiastical Review,* Eldoret, Kenya
AfL — *Archiv für Liturgiewissenschaft,* Regensburg
AFNW — *Arbeitsgemeinschaft für Forschung des Landes Nordrhein-Westfalen,* Cologne
AfO — *Archiv für Orientforschung,* Graz
AfrTJ — *Africa Theological Journal,* Arusha, Tanzania
AgAp — Josephus, *Against Apion (= Contra Apionem)*
ʾAg. Ber. — *ʾAggadat Berešit*
AGJU — Arbeiten zur Geschichte des antiken Judentums und des Urchristentums
Agr — Philo, *De agricultura*
AGSU — Arbeiten zur Geschichte des Spätjudentums und Urchristentums
AH — *An Aramaic Handbook,* ed. F. Rosenthal, 2 vols. Wiesbaden, 1967
Ah. — *Ahiqar*
AHAW — Abhandlungen der Heidelberger Akademie der Wissenschaften
AHG — B. Albrektson. 1967. *History and the Gods.* ConBOT 1. Lund
AHR — *American Historical Review*
AHW — *Akkadisches Handwörterbuch,* ed. W. von Soden. 3 vols. Wiesbaden, 1965–81
AI — Arad Inscription [cited according to Y. Aharoni. 1981. *Arad Inscriptions,* Jerusalem]
AION — *Annali dell'Istituto orientali di Napoli*
AIPHOS — *Annuaire de l'Institut de philologie et d'histoire orientales et slaves*
AIR — *Ancient Israelite Religion: Essays in Honor of Frank Moore Cross,* ed. P. D. Miller, P. D. Hanson, and S. D. McBride. Philadelphia, 1987
AIS — I. Finkelstein. 1988. *The Archaeology of the Israelite Settlement.* Jerusalem
AJA — *American Journal of Archaeology*
AJAS — *American Journal of Arabic Studies*
AJBA — *Australian Journal of Biblical Archaeology*
AJBI — Annual of the Japanese Biblical Institute, Tokyo
AJP — *American Journal of Philology*
AJSL — *American Journal of Semitic Languages and Literatures*
AJT — *American Journal of Theology*
Akk — Akkadian
AKM — *Abhandlungen zur Kunde des Morgenlandes (Leipzig)*
AL — *The Assyrian Laws,* ed. G. R. Driver and J. C. Miles. Oxford, 1935
ALBO — Analecta lovaniensia biblica et orientalia
ALGHJ — Arbeiten zur Literatur und Geschichte des hellenistischen Judentums
Allogenes — *Allogenes* (NHC XI,*3*)
Altertum — *Das Altertum,* Berlin
ALUOS — Annual of Leeds University Oriental Society
Am — *America,* New York
AmBenR — *American Benedictine Review*
AMI — Archäologische Mitteilungen aus Iran
Amos — Amos
AMT — R. C. Thompson. 1923. *Assyrian Medical Texts.* Oxford
AN — J. J. Stamm. 1939. *Die akkadische Namengebung.* MVÄG 44. Berlin
AnBib — Analecta Biblica
AnBoll — *Analecta Bollandiana*
AncIsr — R. de Vaux, 1961. *Ancient Israel: Its Life and Institutions.* Trans. J. McHugh. London. Repr. New York, 1965
ANE — Ancient Near East(ern)
ANEP — *Ancient Near East in Pictures Relating to the Old Testament,* 2d ed. with suppl., ed. J. B. Pritchard, Princeton, 1969
ANET — *Ancient Near Eastern Texts Relating to the Old Testament,* 3d ed. with suppl., ed. J. B. Pritchard, Princeton, 1969
ANF — The Ante-Nicene Fathers
Ang — *Angelicum,* Rome
ANHMW — *Annalen des Naturhistorische Museum in Wien*
Anim — Philo, *De animalibus*
Anon. Sam. — *Anonymous Samaritan Text*
AnOr — Analecta orientalia
ANQ — *Andover Newton Quarterly*
ANRW — *Aufstieg und Niedergang der römischen Welt,* ed. H. Temporini and W. Haase, Berlin, 1972–
AnSt — *Anatolian Studies*
Ant — Josephus, *Jewish Antiquities (= Antiquitates Judaicae)*
AntCl — *L'antiquité classique*

ANTF Arbeiten zur neutestamentlichen Textforschung

ANTJ Arbeiten zum Neuen Testament und Judentum

Anton *Antonianum*

Anuario *Anuario de Filología,* Barcelona

ANVAO Avhandlinger utgitt av det Norske Videnskaps-Akademi i Oslo

AO Der Alte Orient

AOAT Alter Orient und Altes Testament

AOATS Alter Orient und Altes Testament Sonderreihe

AÖAW *Anzeiger der Österreichischer Akademie der Wissenschaften,* Vienna

AOB[2] *Altorientalische Bilder zum Alten Testament,* 2d ed., ed. H. Gressman. Berlin and Leipzig, 1927

AOBib Altorientalische Bibliothek

AoF *Altorientalische Forschungen*

AOS American Oriental Series

AOSTS American Oriental Society Translation Series

AOT[2] *Altorientalische Texte zum Alten Testament,* 2d ed., ed. H. Gressman. Berlin and Leipzig, 1926

AP *L'année philologique*

Ap. Ezek. *Apocryphon of Ezekiel*

Ap. Jas. *Apocryphon of James* (NHC I,*2*)

Ap. John *Apocryphon of John* (NHC II,*1*; III,*1*; IV,*1*)

APAACS American Philological Association American Classical Studies

APAPM American Philological Association Philological Monographs

APAT *Die Apokryphen und Pseudepigraphen des Alten Testaments,* 2 vols., ed. E. Kautzch. Tübingen, 1900. Repr. 1975

APAW *Abhandlungen der Preussischen Akademie der Wissenschaft*

APEF *Annual of the Palestine Exploration Fund*

APNM H. B. Hoffman. 1965. *Amorite Personal Names in the Mari Texts.* Baltimore

Apoc. Ab. *Apocalypse of Abraham*

Apoc. Adam *Apocalypse of Adam* (NHC V,*5*)

Apoc. Dan. *Apocalypse of Daniel*

Apoc. Dosith. *Apocalypse of Dositheus*

Apoc. El. *Apocalypse of Elijah*

Apoc. Ezek. *Apocalypse of Ezekiel*

Apoc. Messos *Apocalypse of Messos*

Apoc. Mos. *Apocalypse of Moses*

Apoc. Paul *Apocalypse of Paul* (NHC V,*2*)

Apoc. Pet. *Apocalypse of Peter* (NHC VII,*3*)

Apoc. Sedr. *Apocalypse of Sedrach*

Apoc. Thom. *Apocalypse of Thomas*

Apoc. Vir. *Apocalypses of the Virgin*

Apoc. Zeph. *Apocalypse of Zephaniah*

Apoc. Zos. *Apocalypse of Zosimus*

Apocr. *Apocryphal, Apocrypha*

Apol Jud Philo, *Apologia pro Iudaeis*

Apos. Apostolic, Apostles

Apos. Con. *Apostolic Constitutions and Canons*

APOT *Apocrypha and Pseudepigrapha of the Old Testament,* 2 vols., ed. R. H. Charles. Oxford, 1913

Ar Arabic

AR Archaeological Reports

ʿArak. *ʿArakin*

Aram Aramaic

ArbT *Arbeitzen zur Theologie,* Stuttgart

Arch *Archaeology*

ArchEleph B. Porten. 1968. *Archives from Elephantine.* Berkeley

ArchPal W. F. Albright. 1960. *The Archaeology of Palestine.* 3d rev. ed. Harmondsworth. Repr. Gloucester, MA, 1971

ARE *Ancient Records of Egypt,* 5 vols., ed. J. H. Breasted. Chicago, 1906. Repr. New York, 1962

ARET Archivi reali di Ebla, Testi

ARG *Archiv für Reformationsgeschichte*

ARI W. F. Albright. 1968. *Archaeology and the Religion of Israel.* 5th ed. Baltimore

Aris. Ex. *Aristeas the Exegete*

Aristob. *Aristobulus*

ARM Archives royales de Mari

ARMT Archives royals de Mari: transcriptions et traductions

ARNA *Ancient Records from North Arabia,* ed. F. V. Winnett and W. L. Reed. Toronto, 1970

ArOr *Archiv orientální*

art. article

Art. *Artapanus*

ARW *Archiv für Religionswissenschaft*

AS Assyriological Studies

ASAE *Annales du Service des antiquités de l'Egypte*

ASAW *Abhandlungen der Sächsischen Akademie der Wissenschaften in Leipzig*

Asc. Jas. *Ascents of James*

Ascen. Is. *Ascension of Isaiah*

Asclepius *Asclepius 21–29* (NHC VI,*8*)

ASNU Acta seminarii neotestamentici upsaliensis

ASORDS American Schools of Oriental Research Dissertation Series

ASORMS — American Schools of Oriental Research Monograph Series
ASP — American Studies in Papyrology
ASS — *Acta sanctae sedis*
AsSeign — *Assemblées du Seigneur*
ASSR — *Archives des sciences sociales des religions*
Assum. Mos. — *Assumption of Moses*
Assum. Vir. — *Assumption of the Virgin*
Assur — *Assur,* Malibu, CA
ASTI — *Annual of the Swedish Theological Institute*
ASV — American Standard Version
ATAbh — Alttestamentliche Abhandlungen
ATANT — Abhandlungen zur Theologie des Alten und Neuen Testaments
ATAT — Arbeiten zu Text und Sprache im Alten Testament
ATD — Das Alte Testament Deutsch
ATDan — Acta theologica danica
ATG — *Archivo Teológico Granadino,* Granada
ATJ — *Ashland Theological Journal,* Ashland, OH
ATR — *Anglican Theological Review,* Evanston, IL
Aug — *Augustinianum,* Rome
AulaOr — *Aula Orientalis,* Barcelona
AuS — G. Dalman. 1928–42. *Arbeit und Sitte in Palästina.* 7 vols. BFCT 14, 17, 27, 29, 33, 36, 41. Gütersloh, 1928. Repr. Hildesheim, 1964
AusBR — *Australian Biblical Review*
AUSS — *Andrews University Seminary Studies,* Berrien Springs, MI
Auth. Teach. — *Authoritative Teaching* (NHC VI,*3*)
AUU — Acta universitatis upsaliensis
AV — Authorized Version
AW — *The Ancient World,* Chicago
AWEAT — Archiv für wissenschaftliche Erforschung des Alten Testaments
B — Codex Vaticanus
b. (Talm.) — Babylonian (Talmud) = "Babli"
B. Bat. — *Baba Batra*
B. Meṣ. — *Baba Meṣiʿa*
B. Qam. — *Baba Qamma*
BA — *Biblical Archaeologist*
Bab. — Babylonian
BAC — Biblioteca de autores cristianos
BAEO — Boletín de la asociación españala des orientalistas
BAfO — *Beihefte zur Archiv für Orientforschung,* Graz
BAGD — W. Bauer, W. F. Arndt, F. W. Gingrich, and F. W. Danker. 1979. *Greek-English Lexicon of the New Testament.* 2d ed. Chicago
BAIAS — *Bulletin of the Anglo-Israel Archaeological Society,* London
BANE — *The Bible in the Ancient Near East,* ed. G. E. Wright. Garden City, NY, 1961. Repr. Winona Lake, IN, 1979
Bar — Baruch
BAR — *Biblical Archaeologist Reader*
Bar. — *Baraita*
BARev — *Biblical Archaeology Review*
BARIS — British Archaeological Reports, International Series
Barn. — *Epistle of Barnabas*
BASOR — *Bulletin of the American Schools of Oriental Research*
BASORSup — BASOR Supplement
BASP — *Bulletin of the American Society of Papyrologists*
BASPSup — Bulletin of the American Society of Papyrologists Supplement
BAss — Beiträge zur Assyriologie und semitischen Sprachwissenschaft
BAT — Die Botschaft des Alten Testaments
BBB — Bonner biblische Beiträge
BBC — Broadman Bible Commentary
BBET — Beiträge zur biblischen Exegese und Theologie
BBLAK — *Beiträge zur biblischen Landes- und Altertumskunde,* Stuttgart
B.C. — before Christ
BC — Biblical Commentary, ed. C. F. Keil and F. Delitzsch. Edinburgh
B.C.E. — before the common (or Christian) era
BCH — *Bulletin du correspondance hellénique*
BCNHE — Bibliothèque copte de Nag Hammadi Section Études
BCNHT — Bibliothèque copte de Nag Hammadi Section Textes
BCPE — *Bulletin de Centre Protestant d'Études,* Geneva
BDB — F. Brown, S. R. Driver, and C. A. Briggs. 1907. *A Hebrew and English Lexicon of the Old Testament.* Oxford
BDF — F. Blass, A. Debrunner, and R. W. Funk. 1961. *A Greek Grammar of the New Testament and Other Early Christian Literature.* Chicago
BDR — F. Blass, A. Debrunner, and F. Rehkopf. 1984. *Grammatik des neutestamentlichen Griechisch.* 16th ed. Göttingen
BE — *Bulletin epigraphique,* ed. P. Gauthier. Paris
BE — Bibliothèque d'étude (Institut français d'Archéologie orientale)
BEFAR — Bibliothèque des Écoles françaises d'Athènes et de Rome
Bek. — *Bekorot*
Bel — Bel and the Dragon
Bened — *Benedictina,* Rome

BeO — *Bibbia e oriente,* Bornato
Ber. — *Berakot*
Berytus — *Berytus,* Beirut, Lebanon
BES — *Bulletin of the Egyptological Seminar,* Chico, CA
Beṣa — *Beṣa (= Yom Ṭob)*
Beth Mikra — *Beth Mikra,* Jerusalem
BETL — Bibliotheca ephemeridum theologicarum lovaniensium
BEvT — Beiträge zur evangelischen Theologie
BFCT — Beiträge zur Förderung christlicher Theologie
BGBE — Beiträge zur Geschichte der biblischen Exegese
BGU — *Berlin Griechische Urkunden*
BHG — *Bibliotheca Hagiographica Graeca.* Brussels, 1909
BHH — *Biblisch-Historisches Handwörterbuch,* ed. B. Reicke and L. Rost. Göttingen, 1962
BHI — J. Bright. 1981. *A History of Israel.* 3d ed. Philadelphia
BHK — *Biblia hebraica,* 3d ed., ed. R. Kittel
BHNTC — Black's/Harper's New Testament Commentaries
BHS — *Biblia hebraica stuttgartensia*
BHT — Beiträge zur historischen Theologie
BIATC — *Bulletin d'information de l'Académie de Théologie Catholique,* Warsaw
Bib — *Biblica,* Rome
BibAT — *Biblical Archeology Today: Proceedings of the International Congress on Biblical Archaeology, Jerusalem, April 1984.* Jerusalem, 1985
BibB — Biblische Beiträge
BibBh — *Biblebhashyam,* Kerala, India
bibliog. — bibliography
BibOr — Biblica et orientalia
BibS(F) — Biblische Studien (Freiburg, 1895–)
BibS(N) — Biblische Studien (Neukirchen, 1951–)
BIES — *Bulletin of the Israel Exploration Society (= Yediot)*
BIFAO — *Bulletin de l'institute français d'archéologie orientale,* Cairo
Bij — *Bijdragen: Tijdschrift voor Filosofie en Theologie,* Amsterdam
Bik. — *Bikkurim*
BiMes — Bibliotheca Mesopotamica
BIN — *Babylonian Inscriptions in the Collection of James B. Nies,* New Haven, 1917–54
BiOr — *Bibliotheca Orientalis,* Leiden
BIOSCS — *Bulletin of the International Organization for Septuagint and Cognate Studies*
BJPES — *Bulletin of the Jewish Palestine Exploration Society (= Yediot;* later *BIES)*
BJRL — *Bulletin of the John Rylands University Library of Manchester*
BJS — Brown Judaic Studies
BK — *Bibel und Kirche,* Stuttgart
BK — E. Bresciani and M. Kamil. 1966. Le lettere aramaiche di Hermopoli. *AANLM* 12/5: 357–428
bk. — book
Bk. Barn. — *Book of the Resurrection of Christ by Barnabas the Apostle*
Bk. Elch. — *Book of Elchasai*
Bk. Noah — *Book of Noah*
BKAT — Biblischer Kommentar: Altes Testament
BLE — *Bulletin de littérature ecclésiastique,* Toulouse
BLe — H. Bauer and P. Leander. 1918–22. *Historische Grammatik der hebräischen Sprache.* Halle, Repr. Hildesheim, 1962
BLit — *Bibel und Liturgie,* Klosterneuburg
BMAP — E. G. Kraeling. 1953. *The Brooklyn Museum Aramaic Papyri.* New Haven. Repr. 1969
BMMA — *Bulletin of the Metropolitan Museum of Art*
BMQ — *British Museum Quarterly*
BMS — *The Bible in Modern Scholarship,* ed. J. P. Hyatt. Nashville, 1965
BN — *Biblische Notizen,* Bamberg
Bo — Unpublished Boğazköy tablets (with catalog number)
BOSA — *Bulletin on Sumerian Agriculture,* Cambridge
B.P. — before (the) present (time)
BR — *Biblical Research,* Chicago
BRev — *Bible Review*
BRevuo — *Biblia Revuo,* Ravenna
BRL — K. Galling. 1937. *Biblisches Reallexikon.* Tübingen
BRM — *Babylonian Records in the Library of J. Pierpont Morgan,* ed. A. T. Clay, New York, 1912–23
BSac — *Bibliotheca Sacra*
BSAW — *Berichte über die Verhandlungen der Sächsischen Akademie der Wissenschaften zu Leipzig,* phil.-hist. Kl.
BSC — Bible Study Commentary
BSFE — *Bulletin de la Société française d'égyptologie*
BSOAS — *Bulletin of the School of Oriental and African Studies*
BTAVO — Beihefte zum Tübinger Atlas des Vorderen Orients
BTB — *Biblical Theology Bulletin*
BTF — *Bangalore Theological Forum,* Bangalore

BTNT	R. Bultmann. 1955. *Theology of the New Testament.* 2 vols. Trans. K. Grobel. New York and London
BToday	*Bible Today,* Collegeville, MN
BTrans	*Bible Translator,* Aberdeen
BTS	*Bible et terre sainte*
BTZ	*Berliner Theologische Zeitschrift*
BU	Biblische Untersuchungen
BuA	B. Meissner. 1920–25. *Babylonien und Assyrien.* 2 vols. Heidelberg
Burg	*Burgense,* Burgos, Spain
BurH	*Buried History,* Melbourne, Australia
BVC	*Bible et vie chrétienne*
BWANT	Beiträge zur Wissenschaft vom Alten und Neuen Testament
BWL	W. G. Lambert. 1960. *Babylonian Wisdom Literature.* Oxford
ByF	*Biblia y Fe,* Madrid, Spain
BZ	*Biblische Zeitschrift,* Paderborn
BZAW	Beihefte zur *ZAW*
BZNW	Beihefte zur *ZNW*
BZRGG	Beihefte zur *ZRGG*
BZVO	Berliner Beitrage zum Vorderen Orient
C	Codex Ephraemi
C&AH	*Catastrophism and Ancient History,* Los Angeles
ca.	*circa* (about, approximately)
CaByr	*Cahiers de Byrsa*
CAD	*The Assyrian Dictionary of the Oriental Institute of the University of Chicago*
CaE	*Cahiers Evangile,* Paris
CAH	*Cambridge Ancient History*
CahRB	Cahiers de la Revue biblique
CahThéol	Cahiers Théologiques
CaJ	*Cahiers de Josephologie,* Montreal
Cant	Song of Songs (or Canticles)
CaNum	*Cahiers de Numismatique,* Bologna
CAP	A. E. Cowley. 1923. *Aramaic Papyri of the Fifth Century B.C.* Oxford [cited by document number]
CAT	Commentaire de l'Ancient Testament
Cath	*Catholica,* Münster
Cav. Tr.	*Cave of Treasures*
CB	*Cultura biblica*
CBC	Cambridge Bible Commentary on the New English Bible
CBQ	*Catholic Biblical Quarterly,* Washington, DC
CBQMS	Catholic Biblical Quarterly Monograph Series
CBSC	Cambridge Bible for Schools and Colleges
CC	*Cross Currents,* West Nyack, NY
CCath	Corpus Catholicorum
CCER	*Cahiers du Cercle Ernest Renan,* Paris
CChr	Corpus Christianorum
CD	Cairo (Genizah), Damascus Document [= S. Schechter, *Documents of Jewish Sectaries,* vol. 1, *Fragments of a Zadokite Work,* Cambridge, 1910. Repr. New York, 1970]
CdÉ	*Chronique d'Égypte,* Brussels
C.E.	common (or Christian) era
Cerinthus	*Cerinthus*
cf.	*confer,* compare
CGTC	Cambridge Greek Testament Commentary
CGTSC	Cambridge Greek Testament for Schools and Colleges
CH	*Church History*
CH	Code of Hammurabi [cited according to G. R. Driver and J. C. Miles, eds. 1952–55. *The Babylonian Laws.* 2 vols. Oxford]
CHAL	*A Concise Hebrew and Aramaic Lexicon of the Old Testament,* ed. W. L. Holladay. Grand Rapids, 1971
chap(s).	chapter(s)
CHB	*The Cambridge History of the Bible,* 3 vols., ed. P. R. Ackroyd, G. W. M. Lampe, and S. L. Greenslade. Cambridge, 1963–70
CHD	Chicago Hittite Dictionary
Cher	Philo, *De cherubim*
CHI	*Cambridge History of Iran*
CHJ	*The Cambridge History of Judaism,* ed. W. D. Davies and L. Finkelstein. Cambridge, 1984–
CHR	*Catholic Historical Review*
CHSP	*Center for Hermeneutical Studies Protocol Series,* Berkeley, CA
CIG	*Corpus inscriptionum graecarum*
CII	*Corpus inscriptionum indicarum*
CIJ	*Corpvs inscriptionvm ivdaicarvm,* ed. J. B. Frey. Sussidi allo studio delle antichità cristiane, pub. per cura del Pontificio istituto di archeologia cristiana 1, 3. Vatican City, 1936–52
CIL	*Corpus inscriptionum latinarum*
CIS	*Corpus inscriptionum semiticarum*
CiuD	*Ciudad de Dios,* Madrid
CJ	*Concordia Journal,* St. Louis, MO
CJT	*Canadian Journal of Theology*
CL	*Communautés et Liturgies,* Ottignies, Belgium
CL	Code of Lipit-Ishtar [R. R. Steele. 1948. The Code of Lipit-Ishtar. *AJA* 52: 425–50]
Cl. Mal.	*Cleodemus Malchus*
CLA	*Canon Law Abstracts,* Melrose, Scotland
cm	centimeter(s)

CMHE	F. M. Cross. 1973. *Canaanite Myth and Hebrew Epic.* Cambridge, MA
CMIB	*Canadian Mediterranean Institute Bulletin,* Ottawa
CNFI	*Christian News From Israel,* Jerusalem, Israel
CNS	*Cristianesimo nella Storia,* Bologna, Italy
CNT	Commentaire du Nouveau Testament
CO	*Commentationes orientales,* Leiden
Col	Colossians
col(s).	column(s)
Coll	*Collationes,* Brugge, Belgium
Colloquium	*Colloquium,* Auckland/Sydney
ColT	*Collectanea Theologica,* Warsaw
comp.	compiled, compiler
ComViat	*Communio Viatorum,* Prague
ConBNT	Coniectanea biblica, New Testament
ConBOT	Coniectanea biblica, Old Testament
Concilium	Concilium
Conf	Philo, *De confusione linguarum*
Congr	Philo, *De congressu eruditionis gratia*
conj.	conjunction; conjugation
ConNT	*Coniectanea neotestamentica*
constr.	construction; construct
ContiRossini	K. Conti Rossini. 1931. *Chrestomathia Arabica meridionalis ephigraphica,* Rome
COut	Commentaar op het Oude Testament
CP	*Classical Philology*
CPJ	*Corpus papyrorum Judicarum,* ed. A. Tcherikover. 3 vols. Cambridge, MA, 1957–64
CQ	*Church Quarterly*
CQR	*Church Quarterly Review*
CR	*Clergy Review,* London
CRAIBL	*Comptes rendus de l'Académie des inscriptions et belles-lettres*
CRBR	*Critical Review of Books in Religion*
CRINT	Compendia rerum iudaicarum ad novum testamentum
CRRA	*Compte Rendu de . . . Recontre Assyriologique Internationale*
Crux	*Crux,* Vancouver, BC
CS	*Chicago Studies,* Mundelein, IL
CSCO	Corpus scriptorum christianorum orientalium
CSEL	Corpus scriptorum ecclesiasticorum latinorum
CSR	*Christian Scholars Review,* Houghton, NY
CT	*Cuneiform Texts from Babylonian Tablets . . . in the British Museum,* London, 1896–
CT	*The Egyptian Coffin Texts,* ed. A. de Buck and A. H. Gardiner. Chicago, 1935–47
CTA	A. Herdner. 1963. *Corpus des tablettes en cunéiformes alphabétiques découvertes à Ras Shamra-Ugarit de 1929 à 1939.* MRS 10. Paris
CTAED	S. Ahituv. 1984. *Canaanite Toponyms in Ancient Egyptian Documents.* Jerusalem
CTH	E. Laroche. 1971. *Catalogue des textes hittites.* Paris
CThM	Calwer Theologische Monographien
CTJ	*Calvin Theological Journal,* Grand Rapids, MI
CTM	*Concordia Theological Monthly*
CToday	*Christianity Today,* Carol Stream, IL
CTQ	*Concordia Theological Quarterly,* Fort Wayne, IN
CTSAP	*Catholic Theological Society of America Proceedings,* New York
CTSSR	College Theology Society Studies in Religion
CU	Code of Ur-Nammu [J. J. Finkelstein. 1960. The Laws of Ur-Nammu. *JCS* 14: 66–82; F. Yildiz. 1981. A Tablet of Codex Ur-Nammu from Sippar. *Or* 58: 87–97]
CurTM	*Currents in Theology and Mission,* Chicago
D	"Deuteronomic" source; or Codex Bezae
DACL	*Dictionnaire d'archéologie chrétienne et de liturgie*
DAGR	*Dictionnaire des antiquités grecques et romaines d'après les textes et les monuments,* ed. C. Daremberg and E. Saglio. 4 vols. Paris, 1877–1919
Dan	Daniel
DB	*Dictionnaire de la Bible,* 5 vols., ed. F. Vigouroux. Paris, 1895–1912
DBAT	*Dielheimer Blätter zum Alten Testament*
DBM	*Deltion Biblikon Meleton,* Athens
DBSup	*Dictionnaire de la Bible, Supplément,* ed. L. Pirot, A. Robert, H. Cazelles, and A. Feuillet. Paris, 1928–
DBTh	*Dictionary of Biblical Theology,* 2d ed., ed. X. Léon-Dufour. Trans. E. M. Stewart. New York, 1973
DC	*Doctor Communis,* Vatican City
DD	*Dor le Dor,* Jerusalem
DDSR	*Duke Divinity School Review*
Dec	Philo, *De decalogo*
Dem.	*Demetrius (the Chronographer)*
Dem.	*Demai*
Deo	Philo, *De Deo*
Der. Er. Rab.	*Derek Ereṣ Rabba*
Der. Er. Zuṭ.	*Derek Ereṣ Zuṭa*
Deut	Deuteronomy

DH	Deuteronomistic History/Historian
DHRP	Dissertationes ad historiam religionum pertinentes
Diakonia	*Diakonia,* Vienna
Dial. Sav.	*Dialogue of the Savior* (NHC III,*5*)
Dial. Trypho	Justin, *Dialogue with Trypho*
Did	*Didaskalia,* Portugal
Did.	*Didache*
Diogn.	*Epistle to Diognetes*
Direction	*Direction,* Fresno, CA
Disc. 8–9	*Discourse on the Eighth and Ninth* (NHC VI,*6*)
DISO	C.-F. Jean and J. Hoftijzer. 1965. *Dictionnaire des inscriptions sémitiques de l'ouest.* Leiden
diss.	dissertation
div.	division
Div	*Divinitas,* Vatican City
DivT	*Divus Thomas,* Piacenza, Italy
DJD	Discoveries in the Judean Desert
DL	*Doctrine and Life,* Dublin
DMOA	Documenta et Monumenta Orientis Antiqui
DN	divine name
DÖAW	*Denkschriften der Österreichischer Akademie der Wissenschaften,* Vienna
DOSA	J. Biella. 1982. *Dictionary of Old South Arabic: Sabaean Dialect.* HSS 25. Chico, CA
DOTT	*Documents from Old Testament Times,* ed. D. W. Thomas. Edinburgh, 1958. Repr. New York, 1961
DRev	*The Downside Review,* Bath
DS	Denzinger-Schönmetzer, *Enchiridion symbolorum*
DTC	*Dictionnaire de théologie catholique*
DTT	*Dansk Teologisk Tidsskrift,* Copenhagen
DunRev	*Dunwoodie Review*
E	east(ern); or "Elohist" source
EA	Tell el-Amarna tablets [cited from J. A. Knudtzon, O. Weber, and E. Ebeling, *Die El-Amarna Tafeln,* 2 vols., VAB 2, Leipzig, 1915; and A. F. Rainey, *El-Amarna Tablets 359–379: Supplement to J. A. Knudtzon, Die El-Amarna Tafeln,* 2d rev. ed., AOAT 8, Kevelaer and Neukirchen-Vluyn, 1970]
EAEHL	*Encyclopedia of Archaeological Excavations in the Holy Land,* 4 vols., ed. M. Avi-Yonah, 1975
EAJET	*East Africa Journal of Evangelical Theology,* Machakos, Kenya
EAJT	*East Asia Journal of Theology,* Singapore
EB	Early Bronze (Age); or Echter Bibel
EBib	Études bibliques
Ebr	Philo, *De ebrietate*
Ec	*The Ecumenist,* New York, NY
Eccl *or* Qoh	Ecclesiastes or Qoheleth
EcR	*The Ecumenical Review,* Geneva
Ecu	*Ecumenismo,* Ravenna, Italy
ed.	editor(s); edition; edited by
ED	Early Dynastic period
ʿEd.	*ʿEduyyot*
EDB	*Encyclopedic Dictionary of the Bible,* ed. and trans. L. F. Hartman. New York, 1963
e.g.	*exempli gratia* (for example)
Eg	Egyptian
ÉgT	*Église et Théologie,* Ottawa
EHAT	Exegetisches Handbuch zum Alten Testament
EHI	R. de Vaux. 1978. *The Early History of Israel.* Trans. D. Smith. Philadelphia
EHS	Einleitung in die Heilige Schrift
EI	*Eretz Israel*
EJ	*Encyclopedia Judaica,* 10 vols., ed. J. Klutzkin and I. Elbogen. Berlin, 1928–34
EKKNT	Evangelisch-katholischer Kommentar zum Neuen Testament
EKL	*Evangelisches Kirchenlexikon*
El. Mod.	*Eldad and Modad*
EM	*Ephemerides Mexicanae,* Mexico City
Emm	*Emmanuel,* New York
EncBib	*Encyclopaedia Biblica,* ed. T. K. Cheyne. London, 1800–1903. 2d ed. 1958
EncBibBarc	*Enciclopedia de la Biblia,* ed. A. Diez Macho and S. Bartina. Barcelona, 1963–65
EncBrit	*Encyclopaedia Britannica*
EnchBib	*Enchiridion biblicum*
EncJud	*Encyclopaedia Judaica* (1971)
EncMiqr	*Entsiqlopēdiā Miqrāʾīt-Encyclopaedia Biblica,* Jerusalem, 1950–
EncRel	*Encyclopedia of Religion,* 16 vols., ed. M. Eliade. New York, 1987
Eng	English
Entr	*Encounter,* Indianapolis, IN
Ep Jer	Epistle of Jeremiah
Ep. Alex.	*Epistle to the Alexandrians*
Ep. Apos.	*Epistle to the Apostles*
Ep. Barn.	*Epistle of Barnabas*
Ep. Chr. Abg.	*Epistle of Christ and Abgar*
Ep. Chr. Heav.	*Epistle of Christ from Heaven*
Ep. Lao.	*Epistle to the Laodiceans*
Ep. Lent.	*Epistle of Lentulus*
Ep. Paul Sen.	*Epistles of Paul and Seneca*

Ep. Pet. Phil.	*Letter of Peter to Philip* (NHC VIII,*2*)
Ep. Pol.	*Epistles of Polycarp*
Ep. Tit. (Apoc.)	*Apocryphal Epistle of Titus*
Eph	Ephesians
Eph.	see *Ign. Eph.*
EphC	*Ephemerides Carmelitica,* Rome
Ephem	M. Lidzbarski. 1900–15. *Ephemeris für semitische Epigraphik.* 3 vols. Giessen
EphLit	*Ephemerides Liturgicae,* Rome
EphMar	*Ephemerides Mariologicae,* Madrid
EPRO	Études préliminaires aux religions orientales dans l'Empire romain
ER	*Epworth Review,* London
ErbAuf	*Erbe und Auftrag*
ERE	*Encyclopaedia of Religion and Ethics,* 12 vols., ed. J. Hastings. Edinburgh and New York, 1908–22
ErFor	Erträge der Forschung
ErfThSt	Erfurter Theologische Studien
ErJb	*Eranos Jahrbuch*
ERT	*Evangelical Review of Theology,* Exeter
ʿErub.	*ʿErubin*
Escr Vedat	*Escritos del Vedat,* Torrente
esp.	especially
EspVie	*Esprit et Vie.,* Langres
EstBib	*Estudios Bíblicos,* Madrid
EstEcl	*Estudios Eclesiásticos,* Barcelona
EstFranc	*Estudios Franciscanos,* Barcelona
Esth	Esther
EstTeo	*Estudios Teológicos,* São Leopoldo, Brazil
ET	English translation
et al.	*et alii* (and others)
etc.	*et cetera* (and so forth)
Eth	Ethiopic
ETL	*Ephemerides Theologicae Lovanienses,* Louvain
ETOT	W. Eichrodt. 1961–67. *Theology of the Old Testament.* 2 vols. Trans. J. A. Baker. Philadelphia
ÉTR	*Études théologiques et Religieuses,* Montpellier, France
Études	*Études,* Paris
Eugnostos	*Eugnostos the Blessed* (NHC III,*3*; V,*1*)
EuntDoc	*Euntes Docete,* Rome
Eup.	*Eupolemus*
EV(V)	English version(s)
EvJ	*Evangelical Journal,* Myerstown, PA
EvK	Evangelische Kommentare
EvQ	*Evangelical Quarterly,* Derbyshire
EvT	*Evangelische Theologie,* Munich
EWNT	*Exegetisches Wörterbuch zum Neuen Testament,* ed. H. Balz and G. Schneider
Ex	*Explor,* Evanston, IL
ExB	Expositor's Bible
Exeg. Soul	*Exegesis on the Soul* (NHC II,*6*)
Exod	Exodus
ExpTim	*Expository Times,* Surrey
Ezek	Ezekiel
Ezek. Trag.	*Ezekiel the Tragedian*
Ezra	Ezra
f(f).	following page(s)
FAS	Freiburger Altorientalische Studien
FB	Forschuung zur Bibel
FBBS	Facet Books, Biblical Series
FC	Fathers of the Church
fc.	forthcoming (publication)
fem.	feminine; female
FFNT	Foundations and Facets: New Testament
FGLP	Forschungen zur Geschichte und Lehre des Protestantismus
FGrH	F. Jacoby. *Die Fragmente der griechischen Historiker.* 2d ed. 3 vols. in 10 pts. Leiden, 1957–64 [cited by fragment no.]
FH	*Fides et Historia,* Grand Rapids
fig(s).	figure(s)
FKT	*Forum Katholische Theologie,* Aschaffenburg
fl.	*floruit* (flourished)
Flacc	Philo, *In Flaccum*
FoiVie	*Foi et Vie,* Paris
Fond	*Fondamenti,* Bresica
Forum	*Forum,* Bonner, MT
FOTL	Forms of Old Testament Literature
FR	Freiburger Rundbrief
Fran	*Franciscanum,* Bogotá
Frg. Tg.	*Fragmentary Targum*
Frgs. Hist. Wrks.	*Fragments of Historical Works*
Frgs. Poet. Wrks.	*Fragments of Poetic Works*
FRLANT	Forschungen zur Religion und Literatur des Alten und Neuen Testaments
Frm.	*Fragments* (NHC XII,*3*)
FSAC	W. F. Albright. 1957. *From the Stone Age to Christianity.* 2d ed., repr. Garden City, NY
FTS	Freiburger Theologische Studien
FuF	*Forschungen und Fortschritte,* Berlin
Fuga	Philo, *De fuga et inventione*
Fund	*Fundamentum,* Riehen, Switzerland
Furrow	*Furrow,* Maynooth
FWSDFML	*Funk and Wagnall's Standard Dictionary of Folklore, Mythology and Legend*
FZPT	*Freiburger Zeitschrift für Philosophie und Theologie,* Fribourg
GAG	W. von Soden. 1969. *Grundriss der akkadischen Grammatik samt Ergänzungsheft.* AnOr 33/47. Rome

Gaium	Philo, *Legatio ad Gaium*
Gal	Galatians
GARI	A. K. Grayson. 1972. *Assyrian Royal Inscriptions.* RANE. Wiesbaden
GB	D. Baly. 1974. *The Geography of the Bible.* 2d ed. New York
GBS	Guides to Biblical Scholarship
GCS	Griechischen christlichen Schriftsteller
Gem.	*Gemara*
Gen	Genesis
GesB	W. Gesenius. *Hebräisches und aramäisches Handwörterbuch,* 17th ed., ed. F. Buhl. Berlin, 1921
GGR	M. P. Nilsson. *Geschichte der griechische Religion.* 2 vols. 2d ed. Munich, 1961
GHBW	R. R. Wilson. 1977. *Genealogy and History in the Biblical World.* YNER 7. New Haven
Gig	Philo, *De gigantibus*
Giṭ.	*Giṭṭin*
GJV	E. Schürer. 1901–9. *Geschichte des jüdisches Volkes im Zeitalter Jesu Christi.* Leipzig. Repr. Hildesheim, 1970
Gk	Greek
GK	*Gesenius' Hebräische Grammatik,* 28th ed., ed. by E. Kautzsch. Leipzig, 1909. Repr. Hildesheim, 1962
Gk. Apoc. Ezra	*Greek Apocalypse of Ezra*
GKB	G. Bergsträsser. 1918–29. *Hebräische Grammatik mit Benutzung der von E. Kautzsch bearbeiteten 28. Auflage von Wilhelm Gesenius' hebräischer Grammatik.* 2 vols. Leipzig. Repr. Hildesheim, 1962
GKC	*Gesenius' Hebrew Grammar,* 28th ed., ed. E. Kautzsch. Trans. A. E. Cowley. Oxford, 1910
GLECS	*Comptes Rendus du Groupe Linguistique d'Études Chamito-Sémitiques,* Paris
GM	*Göttinger Miszellen*
GN	geographical name
GNB	Good News Bible
GNC	Good News Commentary
GNS	Good News Studies
GNT	Grundrisse zum Neuen Testament
GO	Göttinger Orientforschungen
Gos. Barn.	*Gospel of Barnabas*
Gos. Bart.	*Gospel of Bartholomew*
Gos. Bas.	*Gospel of Basilides*
Gos. Bir. Mary	*Gospel of the Birth of Mary*
Gos. Eb.	*Gospel of the Ebionites*
Gos. Eg.	*Gospel of the Egyptians* (NHC III,*2*; IV,*2*)
Gos. Eve	*Gospel of Eve*
Gos. Gam.	*Gospel of Gamaliel*
Gos. Heb.	*Gospel of the Hebrews*
Gos. Inf.	*Infancy Gospels*
Gos. Inf. (Arab)	*Arabic Gospel of the Infancy*
Gos. Inf. (Arm)	*Armenian Gospel of the Infancy*
Gos. John (Apocr.)	*Apocryphal Gospel of John*
Gos. Marcion	*Gospel of Marcion*
Gos. Mary	*Gospel of Mary*
Gos. Naass.	*Gospel of the Naassenes*
Gos. Naz.	*Gospel of the Nazarenes*
Gos. Nic.	*Gospel of Nicodemus*
Gos. Pet.	*Gospel of Peter*
Gos. Phil.	*Gospel of Philip* (NHC II,*3*)
Gos. Thom.	*Gospel According to Thomas* (NHC II,*2*)
Gos. Trad. Mth.	*Gospel and Traditions of Matthias*
Gos. Truth	*Gospel of Truth* (NHC I,*3*; XII,*2*)
GOTR	*Greek Orthodox Theological Review,* Brookline, MA
GP	F. M. Abel. 1933. *Géographie de la Palestine,* 2 vols. Paris
GRBS	*Greek, Roman and Byzantine Studies,* Durham, NC
Great Pow.	*The Concept of Our Great Power* (NHC VI,*4*)
Greg	*Gregorianum,* Rome
GSAT	*Gesammelte Studien zum Alten Testament,* Munich
GTA	Göttinger theologische Arbeiten
GTJ	*Grace Theological Journal,* Winona Lake, IN
GTT	*Gereformeerd Theologisch Tijdschrift,* Netherlands
GTTOT	J. J. Simons. 1959. *The Geographical and Topographical Texts of the Old Testament.* Francisci Scholten memoriae dedicata 2. Leiden
GuL	*Geist und Leben,* Munich
GVG	C. Brockelmann. 1903–13. *Grundriss der vergleichenden Grammatik der semitischen Sprachen.* 2 vols. Berlin. Repr. 1961
ha.	hectares
Hab	Habakkuk
HAB	*Harper's Atlas of the Bible*
HÄB	Hildesheimer ägyptologische Beiträge
HAD	*Hebrew and Aramaic Dictionary of the OT,* ed. G. Fohrer. Trans W. Johnstone. Berlin, 1973
Hag	Haggai
Ḥag.	*Ḥagiga*
HAIJ	J. M. Miller and J. H. Hayes. 1986. *A History of Ancient Israel and Judah.* Philadelphia
Ḥal.	*Ḥalla*
HALAT	*Hebräisches und aramäisches Lexikon zum Alten Testament,* ed. W. Baumgartner et al.
HAR	*Hebrew Annual Review*

HAT	Handbuch zum Alten Testament
HAW	Handbuch der Altertumswissenschaft
HBC	*Harper's Bible Commentary*
HBD	*Harper's Bible Dictionary,* ed. P. J. Achtemeier. San Francisco, 1985
HBT	*Horizons in Biblical Theology,* Pittsburgh, PA
HDB	*Dictionary of the Bible,* 4 vols., ed. by J. Hastings et al. Edinburgh and New York, 1899–1904. Rev. by F. C. Grant and H. H. Rowley, 1963
HDR	Harvard Dissertations in Religion
HDS	Harvard Dissertation Series
Hdt.	Herodotus
Heb	Hebrew; Epistle to the Hebrews
Heb. Apoc. El.	*Hebrew Apocalypse of Elijah*
Hec. Ab	*Hecataeus of Abdera*
Hel. Syn. Pr.	*Hellenistic Synagogal Prayers*
Hen	*Henoch,* Torino, Italy
Heres	Philo, *Quis rerum divinarum heres*
Herm	*Hermathena,* Dublin, Ireland
Herm. Man.	*Hermas, Mandate*
Herm. Sim.	*Hermas, Similitude*
Herm. Vis.	*Hermas, Vision*
Hermeneia	Hermeneia: A Critical and Historical Commentary on the Bible
Ḥev	Naḥal Ḥever texts
HeyJ	*The Heythrop Journal,* London
HG	J. Friedrich. 1959. *Die hethitischen Gesetze.* DMOA 7. Leiden
HGB	Z. Kallai. 1986. *Historical Geography of the Bible.* Leiden
HHI	S. Herrmann. 1975. *A History of Israel in Old Testament Times.* 2d ed. Philadelphia
HibJ	*Hibbert Journal*
HIOTP	H. Jagersma. 1983. *A History of Israel in the Old Testament Period.* Trans. J. Bowden. Philadelphia
Hist. Eccl.	Eusebius, *Historia ecclesiastica (= Church History)*
Hist. Jos.	*History of Joseph*
Hist. Jos. Carp.	*History of Joseph the Carpenter*
Hist. Rech.	*History of the Rechabites*
Hit	Hittite
HJP[1]	E. Schürer. *The History of the Jewish People in the Time of Jesus Christ,* 5 vols., trans. J. Macpherson, S. Taylor, and P. Christie. Edinburgh, 1886–90
HJP[2]	E. Schürer. *The History of the Jewish People in the Age of Jesus Christ,* 3 vols., ed. and trans. G. Vermes et al. Edinburgh, 1973–87
HKAT	Handkommentar zum Alten Testament
HKL	R. Borger. 1967–75. *Handbuch der Keilschriftliteratur.* 3 vols. Berlin
HKNT	Handkommentar zum Neuen Testament
HL	Hittite Laws [*ANET,* 188–97]
HM	*Hamizrah Hehadash/Near East,* Jerusalem
HNT	Handbuch zum Neuen Testament
HNTC	Harper's NT Commentaries
HO	Handbuch der Orientalistik
Hokhma	*Hokhma,* La Sarraz, Switzerland
Hor	*Horizons,* Villanova, PA
Hor.	*Horayot*
Hos	Hosea
HPR	*Homiletic and Pastoral Review,* New York
HPT	M. Noth. 1981. *A History of Pentateuchal Traditions.* Trans. B. Anderson. Chico, CA
HR	*History of Religions,* Chicago
HS	*Hebrew Studies,* Madison, WI
HSAO	*Heidelberger Studien zum Alten Orient.* Wiesbaden, 1967
HSAT	*Die heilige Schrift des Alten Testaments,* 4th ed., ed. E. Kautzsch and A. Bertholet. Tübingen, 1922–23
HSCL	Harvard Studies in Comparative Literature
HSCP	*Harvard Studies in Classical Philology,* Cambridge, MA
HSM	Harvard Semitic Monographs
HSS	Harvard Semitic Studies
HTKNT	Herders theologischer Kommentar zum Neuen Testament
HTR	*Harvard Theological Review*
HTS	Harvard Theological Studies
HUCA	*Hebrew Union College Annual,* Cincinnati
Ḥul.	*Ḥullin*
Hymn Dance	*Hymn of the Dance*
Hyp. Arch.	*Hypostasis of the Archons* (NHC II,*4*)
Hypo	Philo, *Hypothetica*
Hypsiph.	*Hypsiphrone* (NHC XI,*4*)
IB	*Interpreter's Bible*
IBC	Interpretation: A Bible Commentary for Teaching and Preaching
ibid.	*ibidem* (in the same place)
IBS	*Irish Biblical Studies,* Belfast
ICC	International Critical Commentary
IDB	*Interpreter's Dictionary of the Bible,* ed. G. A. Buttrick. 4 vols. Nashville, 1962
IDBSup	*Interpreter's Dictionary of the Bible Supplementary Volume,* ed. K. Crim. Nashville, 1976
IEJ	*Israel Exploration Journal,* Jerusalem
IG	*Inscriptiones Graecae*
IGRR	*Inscriptiones Graecae ad res Romanas pertinentes,* ed. R. Cagnat, J. Toutain, et al. 3 vols. Paris, 1901–27. Repr. Rome, 1964

Ign. Eph.	*Ignatius, Letter to the Ephesians*
Ign. Magn.	*Ignatius, Letter to the Magnesians*
Ign. Phld.	*Ignatius, Letter to the Philadelphians*
Ign. Pol.	*Ignatius, Letter to the Polycarp*
Ign. Rom.	*Ignatius, Letter to the Romans*
Ign. Symrn.	*Ignatius, Letter to the Smyrnaeans*
Ign. Trall.	*Ignatius, Letter to the Trallians*
IGLS	Jalabert, L., and Mouterde, R. 1929–. *Inscriptions grecques et latines de la Syrie*. 6 vols. Paris
IGSK	Inschriften griechischer Städte aus Kleinasien
IJH	*Israelite and Judean History*, ed. J. Hayes and M. Miller. OTL. Philadelphia, 1977
IJT	*Indian Journal of Theology*, Calcutta
IKirZ	*Internationale Kirchliche Zeitschrift*, Bern
ILS	*Inscriptiones Latinae selectae*, ed. H. Dessau. 3 vols. in 5 pts. Berlin, 1892–1916. Repr.
Imm	*Immanuel*, Jerusalem
impf.	imperfect
impv.	imperative
inf.	infinitive
Inf. Gos. Thom.	*Infancy Gospel of Thomas*
INJ	*Israel Numismatic Journal*, Jerusalem
Int	*Interpretation*, Richmond, VA
Interp. Know.	*Interpretation of Knowledge* (NHC XI,*1*)
IOS	*Israel Oriental Studies*
IOTS	B. S. Childs. 1979. *Introduction to the Old Testament as Scripture*. Philadelphia
IPN	M. Noth. 1928. *Die israelitischen Personennamen*. BWANT 3/10. Stuttgart. Repr. Hildesheim, 1966
Iraq	*Iraq*
Irénikon	*Irénikon*
IRT	Issues in Religion and Theology
Isa	Isaiah
ISBE	*International Standard Bible Encyclopedia*, 2d ed., ed. G. W. Bromiley
ISEELA	*Instituto Superior de Estudios Eclesiasticos Libro Anual*, Mexico City
Istina	*Istina*, Paris
ITC	International Theological Commentary
ITQ	*Irish Theological Quarterly*, Maynooth
ITS	*Indian Theological Studies*, Bangalore
IvEph	*Die Inschriften von Ephesos*, ed. H. Wankel. 8 vols. IGSK 11–15
j. (Talm.)	Jerusalem (Talmud)
J	"Yahwist" source
JA	*Journal asiatique*
JAAR	*Journal of the American Academy of Religion*
JAC	*Jahrbuch für Antike und Christentum*
Jan. Jam.	*Jannes and Jambres*
JANES	*Journal of the Ancient Near Eastern Society of Columbia University*, New York
JAOS	*Journal of the American Oriental Society*, New Haven
JAOSSup	Journal of the American Oriental Society Supplement
JARCE	*Journal of the American Research Center in Egypt*, Boston
Jas	James
JAS	*Journal of Asian Studies*
JB	Jerusalem Bible
JBC	*The Jerome Biblical Commentary*, ed. R. E. Brown, J. A. Fitzmyer, and R. E. Murphy. 2 vols. in 1. Englewood Cliffs, NJ, 1968
JBL	*Journal of Biblical Literature*
JBR	*Journal of Bible and Religion*, Boston
JCS	*Journal of Cuneiform Studies*
JDAI	*Jahrbuch des deutschen archäologischen Instituts*
JDS	Judean Desert Studies
Jdt	Judith
JEA	*Journal of Egyptian Archaeology*, London
Jeev	*Jeevadhara*, Kottayam, Kerala, India
JEH	*Journal of Ecclesiastical History*, London
JEnc	*The Jewish Encyclopaedia*, 12 vols., ed. I. Singer et al. New York, 1901–6
JEOL	*Jaarbericht Vooraziatisch-Egyptisch Gezelschap "Ex Oriente Lux"*
Jer	Jeremiah
JES	*Journal of Ecumenical Studies*, Philadelphia
JESHO	*Journal of the Economic and Social History of the Orient*, Leiden
JETS	*Journal of the Evangelical Theological Society*
JFA	*Journal of Field Archaeology*
JFSR	*Journal of Feminist Studies in Religion*, Atlanta
JHNES	Johns Hopkins Near Eastern Studies
JHS	*Journal of Hellenic Studies*, London
JIBS	*Journal of Indian and Buddhist Studies*
JIPh	*Journal of Indian Philosophy*
JITC	*Journal of the Interdenominational Theological Center*, Atlanta
JJS	*Journal of Jewish Studies*, Oxford
JLA	*The Jewish Law Annual*, Leiden
JMES	*Journal of Middle Eastern Studies*
JMS	*Journal of Mithraic Studies*
JNES	*Journal of Near Eastern Studies*, Chicago
JNSL	*Journal of Northwest Semitic Languages*, Stellenbosch

Job	Job
Joel	Joel
John	John
Jonah	Jonah
Jos	Philo, *De Iosepho*
Jos. or Joseph.	Josephus
Jos. Asen.	*Joseph and Asenath*
Josh	Joshua
JPOS	*Journal of Palestine Oriental Society,* Jerusalem
JPSV	Jewish Publication Society Version
JPT	*Journal of Psychology and Theology,* La Mirada, CA
JQR	*Jewish Quarterly Review*
JQRMS	Jewish Quarterly Review Monograph Series
JR	*Journal of Religion,* Chicago
JRAI	*Journal of the Royal Anthropological Institute*
JRAS	*Journal of the Royal Asiatic Society*
JRE	*Journal of Religious Ethics*
JRelS	*Journal of Religious Studies,* Cleveland, OH
JRH	*Journal of Religious History*
JRS	*Journal of Roman Studies,* London
JRT	*Journal of Religious Thought,* Washington, DC
JSHRZ	Jüdische Schriften aus hellenistisch-römischer Zeit
JSJ	*Journal for the Study of Judaism,* Leiden
JSNT	*Journal for the Study of the New Testament,* Sheffield
JSNTSup	Journal for the Study of the New Testament Supplement Series
JSOT	*Journal for the Study of the Old Testament,* Sheffield
JSOTSup	Journal for the Study of the Old Testament Supplement Series
JSP	*Journal for the Study of the Pseudepigrapha*
JSPSup	Journal for the Study of the Pseudepigrapha Supplement
JSS	*Journal of Semitic Studies,* Manchester
JSSEA	*Journal of the Society for the Study of Egyptian Antiquities,* Mississauga, Ontario
JSSR	*Journal for the Scientific Study of Religion*
JTC	*Journal for Theology and the Church*
JTS	*Journal of Theological Studies,* Oxford
JTSoA	*Journal of Theology for Southern Africa,* Cape Town, South Africa
Jub.	*Jubilees*
Judaica	*Judaica: Beiträge zum Verständnis . . .*
Judaism	*Judaism,* New York
Jude	Jude
Judg	Judges
JW	Josephus, *The Jewish War (= Bellum Judaicum)*
JWH	*Journal of World History*
K	Kethib
K	Tablets in the Kouyunjik collection of the British Museum [cited by number]
KAI	*Kanaanäische und aramäische Inschriften,* 3 vols., ed. H. Donner and W. Röllig, Wiesbaden: Otto Harrassowitz, 1962
Kairos	*Kairos,* Salzburg
KAJ	*Keilschrifttexte aus Assur juristischen Inhalts,* ed. E. Ebeling. WVDOG 50. Leipzig, 1927
Kalla	*Kalla*
KAR	*Keilschrifttexte aus Assur religiösen Inhalts,* ed. E. Ebeling. WVDOG 28/34. Leipzig, 1919–23
KAT	Kommentar zum Alten Testament
KAV	*Keilschrifttexte aus Assur verschiedenen Inhalts,* ed. O. Schroeder. WVDOG 35. Leipzig, 1920
KB	*Keilschriftliche Bibliothek,* ed. E. Schrader. Berlin, 1889–1915
KB	L. Koehler and W. Baumgartner. 1953. *Lexicon in Veteris Testamenti libros.* Leiden; *Supplementum ad Lexicon in Veteris Testamenti libros.* Leiden, 1958
KBANT	Kommentare und Beiträge zum Alten und Neuen Testament
KBo	*Keilschrifttexte aus Boghazköi.* WVDOG 30/36/68–70/72– . Leipzig, 1916–23; Berlin, 1954–
KD	*Kerygma und Dogma,* Göttingen
KEHAT	*Kurzgefasstes exegetisches Handbuch zum Alten Testament,* ed. O. F. Fridelin, Leipzig, 1812–96
Kelim	*Kelim*
Ker.	*Keritot*
Ketub.	*Ketubot*
KG	H. Frankfort. 1948. *Kingship and the Gods.* Chicago. Repr. 1978
KHC	*Kurzer Handcommentar zum Alten Testament,* ed. K. Marti. Tübingen
Kil.	*Kilʾayim*
KJV	King James Version
KK	*Katorikku Kenkyu,* Tokyo, Japan
Klosterman	E. Klosterman. 1904. *Eusebius Das Onomastikon der Biblischen Ortsnamen.* Leipzig. Repr. 1966
KlPauly	*Der Kleine Pauly,* ed. K. Zeigler–W. Sontheimer, Stuttgart, 1964
KlSchr	*Kleine Schriften* (A. Alt, 1953–59, 1964 [3d ed.]; O. Eissfeldt, 1963–68; K. Ellinger, 1966)

KlT Kleine Texte
km kilometer(s)
KRI K. Kitchen. 1968– . *Ramesside Inscriptions, Historical and Biographical.* 7 vols. Oxford
KRI Y. Kaufmann. 1960. *The Religion of Israel.* Trans. M. Greenberg. New York
KTR *King's Theological Review,* London
KTU *Keilalphabetischen Texte aus Ugarit,* vol. 1, ed. M. Dietrich, O. Loretz, and J. Sanmartín. AOAT 24. Kevelaer and Neukirchen-Vluyn, 1976
KUB Staatliche Museen zu Berlin, Voderasiatische Abteilung (later Deutsche Orient-Gesellschaft) *Keilschrifturkunden aus Boghazköi,* 1921–
LÄ *Lexikon der Ägyptologie,* eds. W. Helck and E. Otto, Wiesbaden, 1972
L. A. B. *Liber Antiquitatum Biblicarum*
Lad. Jac. *Ladder of Jacob*
LAE *The Literature of Ancient Egypt,* ed. W. K. Simpson. New Haven, 1972
L. A. E. *Life of Adam and Eve*
Lam Lamentations
Lane E. W. Lane. 1863–93. *An Arabic-English Lexicon.* 8 vols. London. Repr. 1968
LAPO Littératures anciennes du Proche-Orient
LAR D. D. Luckenbill. 1926–27. *Ancient Records of Assyria and Babylonia.* Chicago
LÄS Leipziger ägyptologische Studien
LAS D. D. Luckenbill. 1924. *Annals of Sennacherib.* OIP 2. Chicago
LASBF *Liber Annuus Studii Biblici Franciscani,* Jerusalem
Lat Latin
Lat *Lateranum,* Vatican City
Laur *Laurentianum,* Rome
LavTP *Laval Théologique et Philosophique,* Quebec
LB Late Bronze (Age)
LB *Linguistica Biblica,* Bonn
LBAT *Late Babylonian Astronomical and Related Texts,* ed. T. G. Pinches and A. Sachs. Providence, RI, 1955
LBHG Y. Aharoni. 1979. *The Land of the Bible,* 3d ed., rev. and enl. by A. F. Rainey. Philadelphia, 1979
LBS Library of Biblical Studies
LCC Library of Christian Classics
LCL Loeb Classical Library
LD Lectio divina
LE Laws of Eshnunna [A. Goetze. 1956. *The Laws of Eshnunna.* AASOR 31. New Haven; *ANET,* 161–63]
Leg All I–III Philo, *Legum allegoriae* I–III
Leš *Lešonénu*
Let. Aris. *Letter of Aristeas*
Lev Leviticus
Levant *Levant,* London
LexLingAeth A. Dillmann. 1865. *Lexicon linguae aethiopicae.* Leipzig. Repr. New York, 1955; Osnabruck, 1970
LexSyr C. Brockelmann. 1928. *Lexicon Syriacum.* 2d ed. Halle. Repr.
LHA F. Zorrell. 1966. *Lexicon Hebraicum et Aramaicum Veteris Testamenti.* Rome
Life Josephus, *Life (= Vita)*
List *Listening: Journal of Religion and Culture,* River Forest, IL
lit. literally
Liv. Pro. *Lives of the Prophets*
LL *The Living Light,* Washington, DC
LLAVT *Lexicon Linguae aramaicae Veteris Testamenti documentis antiquis illustratum.* E. Vogt. 1971. Rome
loc. cit. *loco citato* (in the place cited)
Lost Tr. *The Lost Tribes*
LPGL G. W. H. Lampe. 1961–68. *A Patristic Greek Lexicon.* Oxford
LQ *Lutheran Quarterly*
LR *Lutherische Rundschau*
LS *Louvain Studies,* Louvain
LSJM H. G. Liddell and R. Scott. 1968. *A Greek-English Lexicon.* rev. ed., ed. H. S. Jones and R. McKenzie. Oxford
LSS Leipziger Semitistische Studien
LTJ *Lutheran Theological Journal,* Adelaide, S. Australia
LTK *Lexikon für Theologie und Kirche*
LTP *Laval Théologique et Philosophique*
LTQ *Lexington Theological Quarterly,* Lexington, KY
LUÅ Lunds universitets årsskrift
Luc Lucianic recension
Luke Luke
LumVie *Lumière et Vie,* Lyons, France
LumVit *Lumen Vitae,* Brussels
LW *Lutheran World*
LXX Septuagint
m meter(s)
MA Middle Assyrian
Maarav *Maarav,* Santa Monica, CA
Maᶜaś. *Maᶜaśerot*
Maᶜaś. Š. *Maᶜaśer Šeni*
MABL *The Moody Atlas of Bible Lands,* ed. B. J. Beitzel. Chicago, 1985
Magn. see *Ign. Magn.*
MaisDieu *Maison-Dieu,* Paris

Mak.	*Makkot*
Makš.	*Makširin (= Mašqin)*
Mal	Malachi
MAL	Middle Assyrian Laws
MAMA	*Monumenta Asiae Minoris Antiqua,* vol. 1, ed. W. M. Calder and J. M. R. Cormack. Publications of the American Society for Archaeological Research in Asia Minor. Manchester, 1928. Vol. 3, ed. J. Keil and A. Wilhelm, 1931. Vol. 4, ed. W. H. Buckler, W. M. Calder, W. K. C. Guthrie, 1933. Vol. 5, ed. C. W. M. Cox and A. Cameron, 1937. Vol. 6, ed. W. H. Buckler and W. M. Calder, 1939
Man	*Manuscripta,* St. Louis, MO
MANE	*Monographs on the Ancient Near East,* Malibu, CA
Mansrea	*Mansrea,* Madrid
MAOG	Mitteilungen der Altorientalischen Gesellschaft, Leipzig
Marianum	*Marianum,* Rome
Mark	Mark
Marsanes	*Marsanes* (NHC XI,*1*)
MarSt	*Marian Studies,* Dayton, OH
Mart. Bart.	*Martyrdom of Bartholomew*
Mart. Is.	*Martyrdom of Isaiah*
Mart. Mt.	*Martyrdom of Matthew*
Mart. Paul	*Martyrdom of Paul*
Mat. Pet.	*Martyrdom of Peter*
Mart. Pet. Paul	*Martyrdom of Peter and Paul*
Mart. Phil.	*Martyrdom of Philip*
Mart. Pol.	*Martyrdom of Polycarp*
Mas	Masada texts
MÄS	Münchner Ägyptologische Studien
masc.	masculine
Matt	Matthew
May	*Mayéutica,* Marcilla (Navarra), Spain
MB	Middle Bronze (Age)
MB	*Le Monde de la Bible*
MBA	Y. Aharoni and M. Avi-Yonah. 1977. *The Macmillan Bible Atlas.* Rev. ed. New York
MC	*Miscelánea Comillas,* Madrid
MCBW	R. K. Harrison. 1985. *Major Cities of the Biblical World.* New York, 1985
McCQ	*McCormick Quarterly*
MD	E. S. Drower and R. Macuch. 1963. *Mandaic Dictionary.* Oxford
MDAIK	Mitteilungen des deutschen archäologischen Instituts, Kairo
MDOG	Mitteilungen der deutschen Orient-Gesellschaft
MDP	Mémoires de la délégation en Perse
MedHab	Epigraphic Expedition, *Medinet Habu.* OIP 8 (1930), 9 (1932), Chicago
Meg.	*Megilla*
Meʿil.	*Meʿila*
Mek.	*Mekilta*
Melch.	*Melchizedek* (NHC IX,*1*)
Melkon	*Melkon*
MelT	*Melita Theologica,* Rabat, Malta
Mem. Apos.	*Memoria of Apostles*
Menaḥ.	*Menaḥot*
MEOL	*Medeelingen en Verhandelingen van het Vooraziatisch-Egyptisch Gezelschap "Ex Oriente Lux,"* Leiden
Mer	*Merleg,* Munich
MeyerK	H. A. W. Meyer, Kritisch-exegetischer Kommentar über das Neue Testament
MGWJ	*Monatsschrift für Geschichte und Wissenschaft des Judentums*
mi.	mile(s)
Mic	Micah
Mid.	*Middot*
Midr.	*Midraš;* cited with usual abbreviation for biblical book; but *Midr. Qoh.* = *Midraš Qohelet*
MIFAO	Mémoires publiés par les membres de l'Institut français d'archéologie orientale du Caire
Migr	Philo, *De migratione Abrahami*
MIO	*Mitteilungen des Instituts für Orientforschung,* Berlin
Miqw.	*Miqwaʾot*
Mird	Khirbet Mird texts
misc.	miscellaneous
MM	J. H. Moulton and G. Milligan. 1914–30. *The Vocabulary of the Greek Testament Illustrated from the Papyri and other Non-Literary Sources.* London. Repr. Grand Rapids, 1949
MNTC	Moffatt NT Commentary
ModChurch	*Modern Churchman,* Leominster, UK
Moʿed	*Moʿed*
Moʿed Qaṭ.	*Moʿed Qaṭan*
Month	*Month,* London
MPAIBL	*Mémoires présentés à l'Académie des inscriptions et belles-lettres*
MPAT	*A Manual of Palestinian Aramaic Texts,* ed. J. A. Fitzmyer and D. J. Harrington. BibOr 34. Rome, 1978
MRR	*The Magistrates of the Roman Republic,* ed. T. R. S. Broughton and M. L. Patterson. 2 vols. Philological Monographs 15. 1951–52. Suppl., 1960
MRS	Mission de Ras Shamra
ms (pl. mss)	manuscript(s)
MScRel	*Mélanges de science religieuse,* Lille
MSD	Materials for the Sumerian Dictionary
MSL	*Materialen zum sumerischen Lexikon,* Rome, 1937–

MSR *Mélanges de Science Religieuse,* Lille
MSU Mitteilungen des Septuaginta-Unternehmens
MT Masoretic Text
MTS Marburger Theologische Studien
MTZ *Münchner theologische Zeitschrift*
Mur Wadi Murabbaʿat texts
Mus *Le Muséon: Revue d'Études Orientales,* Paris
MUSJ *Mélanges de l'Université Saint-Joseph*
Mut Philo, *De mutatione nominum*
MVAG Mitteilungen der vorder-asiatisch-ägyptischen Gesellschaft
N north(ern)
n(n). note(s)
NA Neo-Assyrian
NAB New American Bible
Nah Nahum
NARCE *Newsletter of the American Research Center in Egypt*
NASB New American Standard Bible
Našim *Našim*
NAWG *Nachrichten der Akademie der Wissenschaften in Göttingen*
Nazir *Nazir*
NB Neo-Babylonian
N.B. *nota bene* (note well)
NBD *The New Bible Dictionary,* 2d ed., ed. J. D. Douglas and N. Hillyer. Leicester and Wheaton, IL
NCBC New Century Bible Commentary
NCCHS *New Catholic Commentary on Holy Scripture,* ed. R. D. Fuller et al.
NCE *New Catholic Encyclopedia,* ed. M. R. P. McGuire et al.
NCH M. Noth. 1986. *The Chronicler's History.* Trans. H. G. M. Williamson. JSOTSup 51. Sheffield [translates chaps. 14–25 of *ÜgS*]
NC1BC New Clarendon Bible Commentary
NDH M. Noth. 1981. *The Deuteronomistic History.* Trans. H. G. M. Williamson. JSOTSup 15. Sheffield [translates chaps. 1–13 of *ÜgS*]
NDIEC *New Documents Illustrating Early Christianity,* ed. G. H. K. Horsley. Macquarie University, 1976– [= 1981–]
NE northeast(ern)
NE M. Lidzbarski. 1898. *Handbuch der nordsemitischen Epigraphik.* 2 vols. Weimar
NEB New English Bible, Oxford, 1961–70
NEBib Neue Echter Bibel
Ned. *Nedarim*
NedTTs *Nederlands Theologisch Tijdschrift,* The Hague
Neg. *Negaʿim*
Neh Nehemiah
Neot *Neotestamentica,* Stellenbosch
NETR *The Near East School of Theology Theological Review,* Beirut
neut. neuter
Nez. *Neziqin*
NFT New Frontiers in Theology
NGTT *Nederduits Gereformeerde Teologiese Tydskrif,* Stellenbosch
NHC Nag Hammadi Codex
NHI M. Noth. 1960. *The History of Israel.* 2d ed. Trans. S. Godman, rev. P. R. Ackroyd. London
NHL *The Nag Hammadi Library in English,* 3d ed., ed. J. M. Robinson. San Francisco, 1978
NHS Nag Hammadi Studies
NHT S. R. Driver. 1913. *Notes on the Hebrew Text and the Topography of the Books of Samuel.* 2d ed. Oxford
NICNT New International Commentary on the New Testament
NICOT New International Commentary on the Old Testament
Nid. *Niddah*
NIDNTT *New International Dictionary of New Testament Theology,* 3 vols., ed. C. Brown. Grand Rapids, 1975–78
NIGTC New International Greek Testament Commentary
NIV New International Version
NJB New Jerusalem Bible
NJBC *New Jerome Bible Commentary*
NJPSV New Jewish Publication Society Version
NKJV New King James Version
NKZ *Neue kirchliche Zeitschrift*
no. number
Norea *The Thought of Norea* (NHC IX,*2*)
NorTT *Norsk Teologisk Tidsskrift,* Oslo, Norway
NovT *Novum Testamentum,* Leiden
NovTG[26] *Novum Testamentum Graece,* ed. E. Nestle and K. Aland. 26th ed. Stuttgart, 1979
NovTSup Novum Testamentum Supplements
NPNF Nicene and Post-Nicene Fathers
NRSV New Revised Standard Version
NRT *La nouvelle revue théologique*
n.s. new series
NSSEA *Newsletter of the Society for the Study of Egyptian Antiquities*
NT New Testament
NTA *New Testament Abstracts*

NTAbh	Neutestamentliche Abhandlungen
NTApocr	E. Henneke. *New Testament Apocrypha,* ed. W. Schneemelcher. Trans. R. McL. Wilson. 2 vols. Philadelphia, 1963–65
NTC	B. S. Childs. 1985. *The New Testament as Canon: An Introduction.* Philadelphia, 1985
NTCS	*Newsletter for Targumic and Cognate Studies,* Toronto
NTD	Das Neue Testament Deutsch
NTF	Neutestamentliche Forschungen
NTHIP	W. G. Kümmel. 1972. *The New Testament: The History of the Investigation of Its Problems.* Trans. S. M. Gilmour and H. C. Kee. Nashville
NTL	New Testament Library
NTM	New Testament Message
NTOA	Novum Testamentum et Orbis Antiquus
NTS	*New Testament Studies,* Cambridge, MA
NTT	*Nieuw theologisch Tijdschrift*
NTTS	New Testament Tools and Studies
Num	Numbers
Numen	*Numen: International Review for the History of Religions,* Leiden
NV	*Nova et Vetera,* Geneva
NW	northwest(ern)
NWDB	*The New Westminster Dictionary of the Bible,* ed. H. S. Gehman. Philadelphia, 1970
OA	Old Assyrian
OAkk	Old Akkadian
OB	Old Babylonian
Obad	Obadiah
OBO	Orbis biblicus et orientalis
ÖBS	Österreichische biblische Studien
OBT	Overtures to Biblical Theology
OC	*One in Christ,* London
OCA	Orientalia christiana analecta
OCD	*Oxford Classical Dictionary*
OCP	*Orientalia Christiana Periodica,* Rome
Odes Sol.	*Odes of Solomon*
OECT	*Oxford Editions of Cuneiform Texts,* ed. S. Langdon, 1923–
OED	*Oxford English Dictionary*
OG	Old Greek
OGIS	*Orientis graeci inscriptiones selectae,* ed. W. Dittenberger. 2 vols. Leipzig, 1903–5
Ohol.	*Oholot*
OIC	Oriental Institute Communications
OIP	Oriental Institute Publications
OL	Old Latin
OLA	Orientalia Lovaniensia Analecta
OLP	*Orientalia lovaniensia periodica*
OLZ	*Orientalistische Literaturzeitung,* Berlin
OMRO	*Oudheidkundige Medeelingen uit het Rijks-Museum van Oudheden te Leiden*
Onomast.	Eusebius, *Onomasticon*
Op	Philo, *De opificio mundi*
OP	*Occasional Papers on the Near East,* Malibu, CA
op. cit.	*opere citato* ([in] the work cited)
Or	*Orientalia*
ʿOr.	*ʿOrla*
OrAnt	*Oriens antiquus*
OrBibLov	Orientalia et biblica lovaniensia
OrChr	*Oriens christianus*
Orig. World	*On the Origin of the World* (NHC II,*5*; XIII,*2*)
OrSyr	*L'orient syrien*
o.s.	old series
OstStud	*Ostkirchliche Studien,* Würzburg
OT	Old Testament
OTA	*Old Testament Abstracts*
OTE	*Old Testament Essays,* Pretoria
OTG	Old Testament Guides
OTG	*The Old Testament in Greek according to the Text of Codex Vaticanus,* ed. A. E. Brooke, N. McLean, and H. St. J. Thackeray. Cambridge, 1906–40
ÖTK	Ökumenischer Taschenbuch-Kommentar
OTL	Old Testament Library
OTM	Old Testament Message
OTP	*Old Testament Pseudepigrapha,* 2 vols., ed. J. Charlesworth. Garden City, NY, 1983–87
OTS	*Oudtestamentische Studiën*
p	Pesher (commentary)
P	"Priestly" source
p(p).	page(s); past
PÄ	*Probleme der Ägyptologie,* Leiden
PAAJR	*Proceedings of the American Academy for Jewish Research,* Philadelphia
Pal.	*Palestinian*
Pal. Tgs.	*Palestinian Targums*
PalCl	*Palestra del Clero*
par(s).	paragraph(s); parallel(s)
Para	*Para*
Paraph. Shem	*Paraphrase of Shem* (NHC VII,*1*)
part.	participle
pass.	passive
passim	throughout
PBA	*Proceedings of the British Academy,* Oxford

PBS	University Museum, University of Pennsylvania, *Publications of the Babylonian Section,* Philadelphia
PCB	*Peake's Commentary on the Bible,* rev. ed., ed. M. Black and H. H. Rowley. New York, 1962
P.E.	Eusebius, *Praeparatio evangelica*
Peʾa	*Peʾa*
PEFA	Palestine Exploration Fund Annual
PEFQS	*Palestine Exploration Fund Quarterly Statement*
PEGLAMBS	*Proceedings of the Eastern Great Lakes and Midwest Biblical Societies*
PEGLBS	*Proceedings of the Eastern Great Lakes Biblical Society*
PEQ	*Palestine Exploration Quarterly,* London
perf.	perfect
Pers	Persian
Pesaḥ.	*Pesaḥim*
Pesiq. R.	*Pesiqta Rabbati*
Pesiq. Rab Kah.	*Pesiqta de Rab Kahana*
PG	J. Migne, *Patrologia graeca*
PGM	*Papyri graecae magicae,* 3 vols., ed. K. Preisendanz. Leipzig, 1928–41
Ph. E. Poet	*Philo the Epic Poet*
PhEW	*Philosophy East and West*
Phil	Philippians
Phil.-hist. Kl.	Philosophische-historische Klasse
Phld.	see *Ign. Phld.*
Phlm	Philemon
PHOE	G. von Rad. 1966. *The Problem of the Hexateuch and Other Essays.* Trans. E. Dicken. Edinburgh and New York
Phoen	Phoenician
PhönWest	*Phönizier im Westen,* ed. H. G. Neimeyer. Madrider Beiträge 8. Mainz, 1982
PhRev	*Philosophical Review*
PI	J. Pedersen. 1926–40. *Israel: Its Life and Culture.* 2 vols. Copenhagen
PIBA	*Proceedings of the Irish Biblical Association,* Dublin
PIOL	Publications de l'Institut orientaliste de Louvain
PIR	*Prosopographia imperii Romani saec. I.II.III,* 3 vols., ed. E. Klebs, H. Dessau, and P. von Rohden. Berlin, 1897–98
PIR[2]	*Prosopographia imperii Romani saec. I.II.III,* 2d ed., ed. E. Groag, A. Stein, and L. Petersen. 5 vols. Berlin and Leipzig, 1933–
Pirqe R. El.	*Pirqe Rabbi Eliezer*
P. J.	*Paraleipomena Jeremiou*
PJ	*Palästina-Jahrbuch*
PL	J. Migne, *Patrologia latina*
pl.	plural
pl(s).	plate(s)
Plant	Philo, *De plantatione*
Plato Rep.	*Plato: Republic 588B–589B* (NHC VI,*5*)
PMR	Charlesworth, J. H. 1976. *The Pseudepigrapha and Modern Research.* SCS 7. Missoula, MT
PN	personal name
PN A	Pottery Neolithic A
PN B	Pottery Neolithic B
PNPI	J. K. Stark. 1971. *Personal Names in Palmyrene Inscriptions.* Oxford
PNPPI	F. Benz. 1972. *Personal Names in the Phoenician and Punic Inscriptions.* Studia Pohl 8. Rome
PNTC	Pelican New Testament Commentaries
PO	Patrologia orientalis
Pol.	see *Ign. Pol.*
Post	Philo, *De posteritate Caini*
POTT	*Peoples of Old Testament Times,* ed. D. J. Wiseman. Oxford, 1973
POuT	De Prediking van het Oude Testament
PPN A	Pre-Pottery Neolithic A
PPN B	Pre-Pottery Neolithic B
Pr Azar	Prayer of Azariah
Pr. Jac.	*Prayer of Jacob*
Pr. Jos.	*Prayer of Joseph*
Pr Man	Prayer of Manasseh
Pr. Mos.	*Prayer of Moses*
Pr. Paul	*Prayer of the Apostle Paul* (NHC I,*1*)
Pr. Thanks.	*The Prayer of Thanksgiving* (NHC VI,7)
Praem	Philo, *De praemiis et poeniis*
Praep. Evang.	Eusebius, *Praeparatio evangelica*
Pre. Pet.	*Preaching of Peter*
Presbyterion	*Presbyterion,* St. Louis, MO
Prism	*Prism,* St. Paul, MN
Pro	*Proyección,* Granada, Spain
Prob	Philo, *Probus*
Procl	Proclamation Commentaries
Proof	*Prooftexts: A Journal of Jewish Literary History*
Prot. Jas.	*Protevangelium of James*
Prov	Proverbs
Provid I–II	Philo, *De providentia* I–II
PRS	*Perspectives in Religious Studies,* Macon, GA
PRU	*Le Palais Royal d'Ugarit,* ed. C. F. A. Schaeffer and J. Nougayrol. Paris
Ps(s)	Psalm(s)
Ps-Abd.	*Apostolic History of Pseudo-Abdias*
PSB	*Princeton Seminary Bulletin,* Princeton, NJ
PSBA	*Proceedings of the Society of Biblical Archaeology*
Ps-Clem.	*Pseudo-Clementines*

Ps-Eup.	*Pseudo-Eupolemus*
Ps-Hec.	*Pseudo-Hecataeus*
Ps-Mt.	*Gospel of Pseudo-Matthew*
Ps-Orph.	*Pseudo-Orpheus*
Ps-Philo	*Pseudo-Philo*
Ps-Phoc.	*Pseudo-Phocylides*
Pss. Sol.	*Psalms of Solomon*
PSt	*Process Studies,* Claremont, CA
PSTJ	*Perkins (School of Theology) Journal,* Dallas, TX
PT	*Perspectiva Teológica,* Venda Nova, Brazil
pt.	part
PThS	*Pretoria Theological Studies,* Leiden
PTMS	Pittsburgh Theological Monograph Series
PTU	F. Gröndahl. 1967. *Die Personennamen der Texte aus Ugarit.* Studia Pohl 1. Rome
Pun	Punic
PVTG	Pseudepigrapha Veteris Testamenti graece
PW	A. Pauly–G. Wissowa, *Real-Encyclopädie der classischen Altertumswissenschaft,* Stuttgart, 1839–; supplements, 1903–56, 11 vols.; 2d series, 1914–48
PWCJS	*Proceedings of the . . . World Congress of Jewish Studies*
PWSup	Supplement to PW
Pyr	K. Sethe. 1908–32. *Die altägyptischen Pyramidentexte.* 4 vols. Leipzig. Repr. Hildesheim, 1969
Q	Qere; "Q"-source; Qumran texts (e.g., 4QTestim)
Qad	*Qadmoniot,* Jerusalem
QD	Quaestiones disputatae
QDAP	*Quarterly of the Department of Antiquities in Palestine*
QHBT	*Qumran and the History of the Biblical Text,* ed. F. M. Cross and S. Talmon. Cambridge, MA, 1975
Qidd.	*Qiddušin*
Qinnim	*Qinnim*
QL	Qumran Literature
Qod.	*Qodašin*
Qoh or Eccl	Qoheleth or Ecclesiastes
Quaes Ex I–II	Philo, *Quaestiones et solutiones in Exodum* I–II
Quaes Gen I–IV	Philo, *Quaestiones et solutiones in Genesin* I–IV
Ques. Ezra	*Questions of Ezra*
Quod Det	Philo, *Quod deterius potiori insidiari soleat*
Quod Deus	Philo, *Quod deus immutabilis sit*
Quod Omn	Philo, *Quod omnis probus liber sit*
R	H. C. Rawlinson. 1861–1909. *The Cuneiform Inscriptions of Western Asia.* London
RA	*Revue d'Assyriologie et d'Archéologie orientale,* Paris
RAB	J. Rogerson. 1985. *Atlas of the Bible.* New York
Rab.	*Rabbah* (following abbreviation for biblical book: *Gen. Rab.* = *Genesis Rabbah*)
RAC	*Reallexikon für Antike und Christentum,* 10 vols., ed. T. Klauser, Stuttgart, 1950–78
RANE	Records of the Ancient Near East
RÄR	H. Bonnet. 1952. *Reallexikon der ägyptischen Religionsgeschichte.* Berlin
RArch	*Revue archéologique*
RasT	*Rassegna di Teologia,* Naples
RAT	*Revue Africaine de Théologie,* Kinshasa Limete, Zaire
RazFe	*Razón y Fe,* Madrid
RB	*Revue biblique,* Paris
RBén	*Revue bénédictine,* Maredsous
RBI	*Rivista biblica italiana,* Brescia
RBR	*Ricerche Bibliche e Religiose*
RCB	*Revista de Cultura Biblica,* São Paulo, Brazil
RCT	*Revista Catalana de Teología,* Barcelona, Spain
RDAC	*Report of the Department of Antiquities, Cyprus,* Nicosia
RdÉ	*Revue d'égyptologie*
RdM	*Die Religionen der Menschheit,* ed. C. M. Schröder, Stuttgart
RE	*Realencyklopädie für protestantische Theologie und Kirche,* 3d ed., ed. A. Hauck. Leipzig, 1897–1913
REA	*Revue des études anciennes*
REAug	*Revue des études augustiniennes,* Paris
REB	*Revista Eclesiástica Brasileira,* Brazil
RechBib	Recherches bibliques
RefRev	*Reformed Review,* Holland, MI
RefTR	*Reformed Theological Review,* Melbourne
REJ	*Revue des études juives,* Paris
RelArts	Religion and the Arts
RelLond	*Religion,* London, 1971–
RelNY	*Religion,* New York
RelS	*Religious Studies,* London
RelSoc	*Religion and Society*
RelSRev	*Religious Studies Review*
Renovatio	*Renovatio,* Bonn
repr.	reprint, reprinted
RES	*Revue des études sémitiques,* Paris
RES	*Répertoire d'épigraphie sémitique* [cited by number]

ResABib Die Reste der altlateinische Bibel
ResQ *Restoration Quarterly,* Abilene, TX
Rev Revelation
Rev. Ezra *Revelation of Ezra*
Rev. Steph. *Revelation of Stephen*
RevExp *Review and Expositor,* Louisville, KY
RevistB *Revista Bíblica,* Buenos Aires
RevistEspir *Revista de Espritualidad,* Madrid
RevQ *Revue de Qumran,* Paris
RevRef *La Revue Réformée,* Aix en Provence
RevRel *Review for Religious,* St. Louis, MO
RevScRel *Revue des sciences religieuses,* Strasbourg
RevSém *Revue sémitique*
RevThom *Revue thomiste,* Toulouse
RGG *Religion in Geschichte und Gegenwart*
RGTC *Répertoire géographique des textes cunéiformes,* 8 vols., ed. W. Röllig. BTAVO B7. Wiesbaden
RHA *Revue hittite et asianique*
RHE *Revue d'histoire ecclésiastique,* Louvain
RHLR *Revue d'histoire et de littérature religieuses,* Paris
RHPR *Revue d'histoire et de philosophie religieuses,* Strasbourg
RHR *Revue de l'histoire des religions,* Paris
RIC *The Roman Imperial Coinage,* ed. H. Mattingly et al. London, 1923–81
RIC^2 *The Roman Imperial Coinage,* 2d ed., ed. C. H. V. Sutherland and R. A. G. Carson. London, 1984–
RIDA *Revue internationale des droits de l'antiquité*
RIH J. de Rouge. 1877–78. *Inscriptions hiéroglyphiques copiées en Egypte.* 3 vols. Études égyptologiques 9–11. Paris
RivArCr *Rivista di archeologia cristiana,* Rome
RivB *Rivista biblica,* Bologna
RLA *Reallexikon der Assyriologie,* ed. G. Ebeling et al. Berlin, 1932–
RLT *Revista Latinoamericana de Teologia,* San Salvador
RNAB see *RAB*
RNT Regenesburger Neues Testament
RocTKan *Roczniki Teologiczno-Kanoniczne,* Lublin
Rom Romans
Rom. see *Ign. Rom.*
Roš Hš. *Roš Haššana*
ROTT G. von Rad. 1962–65. *Old Testament Theology.* 2 vols. Trans. D. M. G. Stalker. New York
RP *Revue de philologie*
RQ *Römische Quartalschrift für christliche Altertumskunde und Kirchengeschichte,* Vatican City
RR *Review of Religion*
RS *Ras Shamra*
RSLR *Rivista di storia letteratura religiosa,* Turin
RSO *Rivista degli studi orientali*
RSPT *Revue des sciences philosophiques et théolgiques,* Paris
RSR *Recherches de science religieuse,* Paris
RST *Religious Studies and Theology,* Edmonton, Alberta
RSV Revised Standard Version
RT *Recueil de travaux relatifs à la philologie et à l'archéologie égyptiennes et assyriennes*
RTAM *Recherches de Theologie Ancienne et Médiévale*
RTL *Revue théologique de Louvain*
RTP *Revue de théologie et de philosophie,* Lausanne
RUO *Revue de l'université d'Ottawa*
Ruth Ruth
RV Revised Version
RVV Religionsgeschichtliche Versuche und Vorarbeiten
Ry G. Ryckmans. 1927–59. Inscriptions sudarabes I–XVII. *Mus* 40–72 [cited by no. of text]
S south(ern)
S. ʿOlam Rab. *Seder ʿOlam Rabbah*
Šabb. *Šabbat*
SacDoc *Sacra Doctrina,* Bologna
SacEr *Sacris Erudiri: Jaarboek voor Godsdienstwetenschappen,* Brugge, Belgium
Sacr Philo, *De sacrificiis Abelis et Caini*
SAHG A. Falkenstein and W. von Soden. 1953. *Sumerische und akkadische Hymnen und Gebete.* Zurich
SAK *Studien zur Altägyptischen Kultur,* Hamburg
Sal *Salesianum,* Rome
Salman *Salmanticensis,* Salamanca
Sam. Pent. Samaritan Pentateuch
Sam. Tg. *Samaritan Targum*
SamOstr Samaria Ostracon/Ostraca
SANE *Sources From the Ancient Near East,* Malibu, CA
Sanh. *Sanhedrin*
SANT Studien zum Alten und Neuen Testament
SAOC Studies in Ancient Oriental Civilization
Sap *Sapienza,* Naples
SAQ Sammlung ausgewählter kirchen-und dogmengeschichtlicher Quellenschriften

SAT — *Die Schriften des Alten Testaments in Auswahl,* ed. and trans. H. Gunkel et al. Göttingen
SB — Sources bibliques
SBA — Studies in Biblical Archaeology
SBAW — Sitzungsberichten der (königlichen) bayerischen Akademie der Wissenschaften
SBB — Stuttgarter biblische Beiträge
SBibB — *Studies in Bibliography and Booklore,* Cincinnati, OH
SBJ — La sainte bible de Jérusalem
SBLABS — Society of Biblical Literature Archaeology and Biblical Studies
SBLAS — Society of Biblical Literature Aramaic Studies
SBLASP — Society of Biblical Literature Abstracts and Seminar Papers
SBLBAC — Society of Biblical Literature The Bible in American Culture
SBLBMI — Society of Biblical Literature The Bible and Its Modern Interpreters
SBLBSNA — Society of Biblical Literature Biblical Scholarship in North America
SBLDS — Society of Biblical Literature Dissertation Series
SBLMasS — Society of Biblical Literature Masoretic Studies
SBLMS — Society of Biblical Literature Monograph Series
SBLNTGF — Society of Biblical Literature: The New Testament in the Greek Fathers
SBLRBS — Society of Biblical Literature: Resources for Biblical Study
SBLSBS — Society of Biblical Literature: Sources for Biblical Study
SBLSCS — Society of Biblical Literature: Septuagint and Cognate Studies
SBLSP — *Society of Biblical Literature Seminar Papers*
SBLSS — Society of Biblical Literature: Semeia Studies
SBLTT — Society of Biblical Literature: Texts and Translations
SBLWAW — Society of Biblical Literature: Writings of the Ancient World
SBM — Stuttgarter biblische Monographien
SBS — Stuttgarter Bibelstudien
SBT — Studies in Biblical Theology
SC — Sources chrétiennes
SCCNH — *Studies on the Civilization and Culture of Nuzi and the Hurrians,* 2 vols., ed. D. I. Owen and M. A. Morrison. Winona Lake, IN, 1981–87
ScEccl — *Sciences ecclésiatiques*
ScEs — *Science et esprit,* Montreal
SCHNT — Studia ad corpus hellenisticum novi testamenti
Scr — *Scripture*
SCR — *Studies in Comparative Religion*
ScrB — *Scripture Bulletin*
ScrC — *Scripture in Church,* Dublin
ScrHier — *Scripta Hierosolymitana,* Jerusalem
Scrip — *Scriptorium,* Brussels
Scriptura — *Scriptura,* Stellenbosch
ScrT — *Scripta Theologica,* Barañain/Pamplona
SCS — Septuagint and Cognate Studies
ScuolC — *Scuola Cattolica,* Milan
SD — Studies and Documents
SDB — *Smith's Dictionary of the Bible,* ed. H. B. Hackett. Boston, 1880
SE — southeast(ern)
SE — *Studia Evangelica I, II, III* (= TU 73 [1959], 87 [1964], 88 [1964], etc.)
SEÅ — *Svensk Exegetisk Årsbok*
Search — *Search,* Dublin
Šeb. — *Šebiʿit*
Šebu. — *Šebuʿot*
sec. — section
Sec. Gos. Mk. — *Secret Gospel of Mark*
SecondCent — *Second Century,* Macon, GA
Sef — *Sefarad,* Madrid
SEG — *Supplementum Epigraphicum Graecum,* ed. J. J. E. Hondius. Leiden, 1923–
Sem — *Semitica,* Paris
Ṣem. — *Ṣemaḥot*
Semeia — *Semeia,* Chico, CA
SemiotBib — *Sémiotique et Bible,* Lyon
Semitics — *Semitics,* Pretoria
Sent. Sextus — *Sentences of Sextus* (NHC XII,*1*)
Šeqal. — *Šeqalim*
Seux — J. M. Seux. 1968. *Epithètes Royales Akkadiennes et Sumériennes.* Paris
SGL — A. Falkenstein. 1959. *Sumerische Götterlieder.* Heidelberg
SGV — *Sammlung gemeinverständlicher Vorträge und Schriften aus dem Gebiet der Theologie und Religionsgeschichte,* Tübingen
SHAW — Sitzungsberichte der Heidelberger Akademie der Wissenschaften
Shep. Herm. — *Shepherd of Hermas*
SHIB — R. M. Grant and D. Tracy. 1984. *A Short History of the Interpretation of the Bible.* 2d ed. Philadelphia
Shofar — *Shofar,* West Lafayette, IN
SHR — Studies in the History of Religions
SHT — Studies in Historical Theology

Sib. Or. — *Sibylline Oracles*
SICV — *Sylloge inscriptionum Christianorum veterum musei Vaticani,* ed. H. Zilliacus. Acta instituti Romani Finlandiae 1/1–2. Rome
SIDÅ — Scripta Instituti Donneriana Åboensis, Stockholm
SIDJC — *Service International de Documentation Judéo-chrétienne,* Rome
SIG[3] — *Sylloge Inscriptionum Graecarum,* ed. W. Dittenberger. 3d ed. Leipzig
SII — *Studies in Islam,* New Delhi
sing. — singular
Sipra — *Sipra*
Sipre — *Sipre*
Sir — Ecclesiasticus *or* Wisdom of Jesus Ben-Sira
SIRIS — *Sylloge inscriptionum religionis Isiacae et Serapicae,* ed. L. Vidman. RVV 28. Berlin, 1969
SJ — Studia Judaica
SJLA — Studies in Judaism in Late Antiquity
SJOT — *Scandinavian Journal of the Old Testament*
SJT — *Scottish Journal of Theology,* Edinburgh
SkrifK — *Skrif en Kerk,* Pretoria
SLAG — *Schriften der Luther-Agricola-Gesellschaft* (Finland)
SLJT — *Saint Luke's Journal of Theology,* Sewanee, TN
SMEA — *Studi Micenei ed Egeo-Anatolici*
SMS — *Syro-Mesopotamian Studies,* Malibu, CA
SMSR — *Studi e materiali di storia delle religioni*
Smyrn. — see *Ign. Smyrn.*
SNT — Studien zum Neuen Testament
SNTSMS — Society for New Testament Studies Monograph Series
SNTU — *Studien zum Neuen Testament und seiner Umwelt,* Linz
SNVAO — *Skrifter utgitt av det Norske Videnskaps-Akademi i Oslo*
SO — Symbolae osloenses
SÖAW — *Sitzungsberichte der Österreichen Akademie der Wissenschaften*
Sobr — Philo, *De sobrietate*
Somn I–II — Philo, *De somniis* I–II
SonB — Soncino Books of the Bible
Sop. — *Soperim*
Soph. Jes. Chr. — *Sophia of Jesus Christ* (NHC III,*4*)
Soṭa — *Soṭa*
SOTSBooklist — *Society for Old Testament Study Booklist*
SOTSMS — Society for Old Testament Study Monograph Series
Sou — *Soundings,* Nashville
SPap — *Studia papyrologica*
SPAW — Sitzungsberichte der preussischen Akademie der Wissenschaften
SPB — Studia postbiblica
Spec Leg I–IV — Philo, *De specialibus legibus* I–IV
SPhil — *Studia Philonica,* Chicago
SPIB — *Scripta Pontificii Instituti Biblici,* Rome
SpT — *Spirituality Today,* Dubuque, IA
SQAW — Schriften und Quellen der alten Welt
SR — *Studies in Religion/Sciences religieuses,* Waterloo, Ontario
SS — Studi semitici
SSAOI — *Sacra Scriptura Antiquitatibus Orientalibus Illustrata,* Rome
SSEA — Society for the Study of Egyptian Antiquities
SSN — *Studia Semitica Neerlandica,* Assen
SSS — Semitic Study Series
St — *Studium,* Madrid
ST — *Studia theologica*
STÅ — *Svendk teologisk årsskrift*
StadtrChr — P. Lampe. 1987. *Die stadtrömischen Christen in den ersten beiden Jahrhunderten.* WUNT 2/18. Tübingen
StANT — *Studien zum Alten und Neuen Testament,* Munich
StBT — *Studien zu den Boğazköy-Texten,* Wiesbaden
StDI — Studia et Documenta ad Iura Orientis Antiqui Pertinenti
STDJ — Studies on the Texts of the Desert of Judah
StEb — *Studi Eblaiti,* Rome
StEc — *Studi Ecumenici,* Verona, Italy
Steles Seth — *Three Steles of Seth* (NHC VII,*5*)
StFS — *Studia Francisci Scholten,* Leiden
STK — *Svensk teologisk kvartalskrift,* Lund
STL — Studia theologica Ludensia
StLtg — *Studia Liturgica,* Rotterdam
StMiss — *Studia Missionalia,* Rome
StOr — *Studia Orientalia,* Helsinki
StOvet — *Studium Ovetense,* Oviedo
StPat — *Studia Patavina,* Padua, Italy
StPatr — *Studia Patristica*
StPhilon — *Studia Philonica*
Str — *Stromata,* San Miguel, Argentina
Str-B — H. L. Strack and P. Billerbeck. 1922–61. *Kommentar zum NT aus Talmud und Midrasch.* 6 vols. Munich
STT — *The Sultantepe Tablets,* 2 vols., ed. O. R. Gurney, J. J. Finkelstein, and P. Hulin. Occasional Publications of the British School of Archaeology at Ankara 3, 7. London, 1957–64

StTh	*Studia Theologica*
StudBib	Studia biblica
StudBT	*Studia biblica et theologica,* Guilford, CT
Studium	*Studium,* Madrid
StudNeot	Studia neotestamentica, Studia
StudOr	Studia orientalia
StudPhoen	Studia Phoenicia [I–VIII]
STV	*Studia theologica varsaviensia*
Sukk.	*Sukka*
Sum	Sumerian
SUNT	Studien zur Umwelt des Neuen Testaments
suppl.	supplement
Sus	Susanna
SVF	*Stoicorum veterum fragmenta,* ed. J. von Arnim. 4 vols. Leipzig, 1903–24. Repr. Stuttgart, 1966; New York, 1986
SVTP	Studia in Veteris Testamenti pseudepigrapha
SVTQ	*St. Vladimir's Theological Quarterly,* Tuckahoe, NY
SW	southwest(ern)
SWBA	Social World of Biblical Antiquity
SwJT	*Southwestern Journal of Theology,* Fort Worth, TX
SWP	*Survey of Western Palestine:* *SWP* 1 = C. R. Conder and H. H. Kitchener. 1881. *Galilee.* London. *SWP* 2 = C. R. Conder and H. H. Kitchener. 1882. *Samaria.* London. *SWP* 3 = C. R. Conder and H. H. Kitchener. 1883. *Judaea.* London. *SWP* 4 = E. H. Palmer. 1881. *Arabic and English Name Lists.* London. *SWP* 5 = C. Wilson and C. Warren. 1881. *Special Papers.* London. *SWP* 6 = C. Warren and C. Warren, 1884. *Jerusalem.* London. *SWP* 7 = H. B. Tristram. 1884. *The Fauna and Flora of Palestine.* London.
SymBU	Symbolae biblicae upsalienses
Syr	Syriac
Syr	*Syria: Revue d'Art Oriental et d'Archéologie,* Paris
Syr. Men.	*Syriac Menander*
SZ	*Stimmen der Zeit,* Munich
T. 12 P.	*Testaments of the Twelve Patriarchs*
T. Ab.	*Testament of Abraham*
T. Adam	*Testament of Adam*
T. Ash.	*Testament of Asher*
T. Benj.	*Testament of Benjamin*
T. Dan.	*Testament of Daniel*
T. Gad	*Testament of Gad*
T. Hez.	*Testament of Hezekiah*
T. Isaac	*Testament of Isaac*
T. Iss.	*Testament of Issachar*
T. Jac.	*Testament of Jacob*
T. Job	*Testament of Job*
T. Jos.	*Testament of Joseph*
T. Jud.	*Testament of Judah*
T. Levi	*Testament of Levi*
T. Mos.	*Testament of Moses*
T. Naph.	*Testament of Naphtali*
T. Reu.	*Testament of Reuben*
T. Sim.	*Testament of Simeon*
T. Sol.	*Testament of Solomon*
Ṭ. Yom	*Ṭebul Yom*
T. Zeb.	*Testament of Zebulun*
TA	*Tel Aviv,* Tel Aviv
Taᶜan.	*Taᶜanit*
TAD	B. Porten and A. Yardeni. 1986. *Textbook of Aramaic Documents from Ancient Egypt.* Jerusalem *TAD* A = vol. 1, *Letters* *TAD* B = vol. 2, *Contracts* *TAD* C = vol. 3, *Literature and Lists* *TAD* D = vol. 4, *Fragments and Inscriptions*
TAik	*Teologinen Aikakauskirja,* Helsinki
Talm.	*Talmud*
TAM	*Tituli Asiae Minoris*
Tamid	*Tamid*
TAPA	*Transactions of the American Philological Association*
TAPhS	*Transactions of the American Philosophical Society,* Philadelphia
TBC	Torch Bible Commentary
TBei	*Theologische Beiträge,* Wuppertal
TBl	*Theologische Blätter*
TBT	*The Bible Today,* Collegeville, MN
TBü	Theologische Bücherei
TCGNT	B. M. Metzger. 1971. *A Textual Commentary on the Greek New Testament,* United Bible Societies
TCL	*Textes cunéiforms du Musée du Louvre,* Paris, 1910–
TCS	Texts from Cuneiform Sources: TCS 1 = E. Sollberger. 1966. *Business and Administrative Correspondence Under the Kings of Ur.* Locust Valley, NY. TCS 2 = R. Biggs. 1967. *ŠÀ.ZI.GA: Ancient Mesopotamian Potency Incantations.* TCS 3 = Å. Sjöberg, E. Bergmann, and G. Gragg. 1969. *The Collection of the Sumerian Temple Hymns.* TCS 4 = E. Leichty. 1970. *The Omen Series šumma izbu.* TCS 5 = A. K. Grayson. 1975. *Assyrian and Babylonian Chronicles.*

TD — *Theology Digest,* St. Louis, MO
TDNT — *Theological Dictionary of the New Testament,* 10 vols., ed. G. Kittel and G. Friedrich. Trans. G. W. Bromiley. Grand Rapids, 1964–76
TDOT — *Theological Dictionary of the Old Testament,* ed. G. J. Botterweck, H. Ringgren, and H. J. Fabry. Trans. J. T. Willis, G. W. Bromiley, and D. E. Green. Grand Rapids, 1974–
TE — *Theologica Evangelica,* Pretoria
Teach. Silv. — *Teachings of Silvanus* (NHC VII,*4*)
Tem. — *Temura*
Temenos — *Temenos: Studies in Comparative Religion,* Helsinki
Ter — *Teresianum,* Rome
Ter. — *Terumot*
Test — *Testimonianze,* Florence
Testim. Truth — *Testimony of Truth* (NHC IX,*3*)
TEV — Today's English Version
TextsS — Texts and Studies
TF — *Theologische Forschung*
Tg. Esth. I — *First Targum of Esther*
Tg. Esth. II — *Second Targum of Esther*
Tg. Isa. — *Targum of Isaiah*
Tg. Ket. — *Targum of the Writings*
Tg. Neb. — *Targum of the Prophets*
Tg. Neof. — *Targum Neofiti I*
Tg. Onq. — *Targum Onqelos*
Tg. Ps.-J. — *Targum Pseudo-Jonathan*
Tg. Yer. I — *Targum Yerušalmi I*
Tg. Yer. II — *Targum Yerušalmi II*
TGI — K. Galling. 1950. *Textbuch zur Geschichte Israels.* 2d ed. Tübingen
TGl — *Theologie und Glaube,* Paderborn
Thal. — *Thallus*
ThArb — *Theologische Arbeiten,* Berlin
THAT — *Theologisches Handwörterbuch zum Alten Testament,* 2 vols., ed. E. Jenni and C. Westermann. Munich, 1971–76
ThEd — *Theological Educator,* New Orleans
ThEH — *Theologische Existenz Heute,* Munich
Them — *Themelios,* Madison, WI
Theod. — *Theodotus*
Theology — *Theology,* London
THeth — Texte der Hethiter
ThH — *Théologie historique*
THKNT — Theologischer Handkommentar zum Neuen Testament
Thom. Cont. — *Book of Thomas the Contender* (NHC II,*7*)
Thomist — *Thomist,* Washington, D.C.
ThPh — *Theologie und Philosophie,* Freiburg
ThStud — Theologische Studien
Thund. — *The Thunder: Perfect Mind* (NHC VI,*2*)
ThV — *Theologische Versuche,* Berlin
ThViat — *Theologia Viatorum,* Berlin
TijdTheol — *Tijdschrift voor Theologie,* Nijmegen
Titus — Titus
TJ — *Trinity Journal,* Deerfield, IL
TJT — *Toronto Journal of Theology*
TLZ — *Theologische Literaturzeitung*
TNB — *The New Blackfriars,* Oxford
TNTC — Tyndale New Testament Commentary
Tob — Tobit
Ṭohar. — *Ṭoharot*
TOTC — Tyndale Old Testament Commentary
TP — *Theologie und Philosophie*
TPNAH — J. D. Fowler. 1988. *Theophoric Personal Names in Ancient Hebrew.* JSOTSup 49. Sheffield
TPQ — *Theologisch-Praktische Quartalschrift,* Austria
TQ — *Theologische Quartalschrift*
TR — P. Lucau. *Textes Religieux Égyptiens,* 1, Paris
Trad — *Tradition,* New York
Traditio — *Traditio,* New York
Trall. — see *Ign. Trall.*
TRE — *Theologische Realenzyklopädie*
Treat. Res. — *Treatise on Resurrection* (NHC I,*4*)
Treat. Seth — *Second Treatise of the Great Seth* (NHC VII,*2*)
Treat. Shem — *Treatise of Shem*
TRev — *Theologische Revue*
Tri. Trac. — *Tripartite Tractate* (NHC I,*5*)
Trim. Prot. — *Trimorphic Protennoia* (NHC XIII,*1*)
TRu — *Theologische Rundschau,* Tübingen
TS — *Theological Studies,* Washington, DC
TSK — *Theologische Studien und Kritiken*
TSSI — J. C. L. Gibson. 1971–82. *Textbook of Syrian Semitic Inscriptions.* 3 vols. Oxford
TT — *Teologisk Tidsskrift*
TTKi — *Tidsskrift for Teologie og Kirke,* Oslo, Norway
TTKY — *Türk Tarih Kurumu Kongresi Yayînlari.* Ankara
TToday — *Theology Today,* Princeton, NJ
TTS — Trierer Theologische Studien
TTZ — *Trierer theologische Zeitschrift*
TU — Texte und Untersuchungen
TUAT — Texte aus der Umwelt des Alten Testaments
TV — *Teología y Vida,* Santiago, Chile
TvT — *Tijdschrift voor Theologie,* Nijmegen, The Netherlands

TWAT	*Theologisches Wörterbuch zum Alten Testament,* ed. G. J. Botterweck, H. Ringgren, and H. J. Fabry. Stuttgart, 1970–
TWNT	*Theologisches Wörterbuch zum Neuen Testament,* 8 vols., ed. G. Kittel and G. Friedrich. Stuttgart, 1933–69
TynBul	*Tyndale Bulletin*
TZ	*Theologische Zeitschrift,* Basel, Switzerland
UBSGNT	*United Bible Societies Greek New Testament*
UCPNES	University of California Publications in Near Eastern Studies
UCPSP	University of California Publications in Semitic Philology
UET	Ur Excavations: Texts
UF	*Ugarit-Forschungen*
Ug	Ugaritic
UGAÄ	Untersuchungen zur Geschichte und Altertumskunde Aegyptens
ÜgS	M. Noth. 1967. *Überlieferungsgeschichtliche Studien.* 3d ed. Tübingen
UNT	Untersuchungen zum Neuen Testament
ʿUq.	*ʿUqṣin*
Urk. IV	*Urkunden des ägyptischen Altertums.* Abt. IV, *Urkunden der 18. Dynastie,* ed. K. Sethe and W. Helck. 22 fasc. Leipzig, 1903–58
US	*Una Sancta*
USQR	*Union Seminary Quarterly Review,* New York, NY
UT	C. H. Gordon. 1965. *Ugaritic Textbook.* AnOr 38. Rome; suppl. 1967
UUÅ	*Uppsala universitets Årsskrift*
v(v)	verse(s)
VAB	*Vorderasiatische Bibliothek,* Leipzig, 1907–16
Val. Exp.	*A Valentinian Exposition* (NHC XI,*2*)
VAT	Vorderasiatische Abteilung, Thontafelsammlung, Staatliche Musee zu Berlin
VC	*Vigiliae christianae*
VCaro	*Verbum caro*
VD	*Verbum domini*
VE	*Vox Evangilica*
VetChr	*Vetera Christianum,* Bari
VF	*Verkündigung und Forschung*
Vg	Vulgate
Vid	*Vidyajyoti,* Delhi
VigChrist	*Vigiliao Christianae*
VIO	Veröffentlichung der Institut für Orientforschung
Virt	Philo, *De virtutibus*
Vis. Ezra	*Vision of Ezra*
Vis. Is.	*Vision of Isaiah*
Vis. Paul	*Vision of Paul*
Vita	*Vita Adae et Evae*
Vita C	Eusebius, *Vita Constantini*
Vita Cont	Philo, *De vita contemplativa*
Vita Mos I–II	Philo, *De vita Mosis* I–II
VKGNT	*Vollständige Konkordanz zum griechischen Neuen Testament,* ed. K. Aland
VL	Vetus Latina
vol(s).	volume(s)
Vorsokr.	*Fragmente der Vorsokrater,* 4th ed., ed. H. Diels. Berlin, 1922
VR	*Vox Reformata,* Geelong, Victoria, Australia
VS	Vorderasiatische Schriftdenkmäler der königlichen Museen zu Berlin
VSpir	*Vie spirituelle,* Paris
VT	*Vetus Testamentum,* Leiden
VTSup	Vetus Testamentum Supplements
W	west(ern)
WA	["Weimar Ausgabe," =] *D. Martin Luthers Werke: Kritische Gesamtausgabe,* ed. J. K. F. Knaake et al. Weimar, 1883–
Way	*The Way,* London
WbÄS	A. Erman and H. Grapow. 1926–31. *Wörterbuch der ägyptischen Sprache.* 7 vols. Leipzig. Repr. 1963
WBC	World Bible Commentary
WBKL	Wiener Beitrage zur Kulturgeschichte und Linguistik
WbMyth	*Wörterbuch der Mythologie,* ed. H. W. Haussig, Stuttgart, 1961
WC	Westminster Commentaries, London
WD	*Wort und Dienst*
WDB	*Westminster Dictionary of the Bible*
Wehr	H. Wehr. 1976. *A Dictionary of Modern Written Arabic,* 3d ed., ed. J. M. Cowen. Ithaca
WF	Wege der Forschung
WGI	J. Wellhausen. 1878. *Geschichte Israels.* Berlin [see also *WPGI* and *WPHI*]
WHAB	*Westminster Historical Atlas of the Bible*
Whitaker	R. E. Whitaker. 1972. *A Concordance of the Ugaritic Literature.* Cambridge, MA
WHJP	*World History of the Jewish People*
Wis	Wisdom of Solomon
WLSGF	*The Word of the Lord Shall Go Forth: Essays in Honor of David Noel Freedman,* eds. C. L. Meyers and M. O'Connor. Winona Lake, IN, 1983
WMANT	Wissenschaftliche Monographien zum Alten und Neuen Testament
WO	*Die Welt des Orients*
WoAr	*World Archaeology*
Wor	*Worship,* Collegeville, MN
WordWorld	*Word and World,* St. Paul, MN
WPGI	J. Wellhausen. 1895. *Prolegomena zur Geschichte Israels.* 4th ed. Berlin

WPHI	J. Wellhausen. 1885. *Prolegomena to the History of Israel.* 2 vols. Trans. J. S. Black and A. Menzies. Edinburgh. Repr. Cleveland 1957; Gloucester, MA, 1973
WS	*World and Spirit,* Petersham, MA
WTJ	*Westminster Theological Journal,* Philadelphia, PA
WTM	J. Levy. 1924. *Wörterbuch über die Talmudim und Midraschim.* 5 vols. 2d ed., ed. L. Goldschmidt. Leipzig. Repr. 1963
WTS	E. Littmann and M. Höfner. 1962. *Wörterbuch der Tigre-Sprache.* Wiesbaden
WuD	*Wort und Dienst,* Bielefeld
WUNT	Wissenschaftliche Untersuchungen zum Neuen Testament
WUS	J. Aistleitner. 1974. *Wörterbuch der ugaritischen Sprache.* 4th ed., ed. O. Eissfeldt. BSAW 106/3. Berlin
WuW	*Wissenschaft und Weisheit,* Mönchengladbach
WVDOG	*Wissenschaftliche Veröffentlichungen der Deutschen Orient-Gesellschaft*
WW	*Word & World,* Fort Lee, NJ
WZ	*Wissenschaftliche Zeitschrift*
WZKM	*Wiener Zeitschrift für die Kunde des Morgenlandes*
WZKSO	*Wiener Zeitschrift für die Kunde Süd- und Ostasiens*
Yad.	*Yadayim*
Yal.	*Yalqut*
Yebam.	*Yebamot*
Yem. Tg.	*Yemenite Targum*
YES	Yale Egyptological Studies
YGC	W. F. Albright. 1969. *Yahweh and the Gods of Canaan.* Garden City, NY. Repr. Winona Lake, IN, 1990
YJS	*Yale Judaica Series,* New Haven
YNER	Yale Near Eastern Researches
Yoma	*Yoma (= Kippurim)*
YOS	Yale Oriental Series
y. (Talm.)	Jerusalem (Talmud) = "Yerushalmi"
ZA	*Zeitschrift für Assyriologie*
Zabim	*Zabim*
ZAH	*Zeitschrift für Althebräistic*
ZÄS	*Zeitschrift für Ägyptische Sprache und Altertumskunde*
ZAW	*Zeitschrift für die alttestamentliche Wissenschaft,* Berlin
ZB	Zürcher Bibelkommentare
ZDMG	*Zeitschrift der deutschen morgenländischen Gesellschaft*
ZDPV	*Zeitschrift des deutschen Palästina-Vereins*
Zebaḥ.	*Zebaḥim*
Zech	Zechariah
ZEE	*Zeitschrift für evangelische Ethik*
Zeph	Zephaniah
Zer.	*Zeraᶜim*
ZHT	*Zeitschrift für historische Theologie*
ZKG	*Zeitschrift für Kirchengeschichte*
ZKT	*Zeitschrift für katholische Theologie,* Innsbruck
ZMR	*Zeitschrift für Missionskunde und Religionswissenschaft*
ZNW	*Zeitschrift für die neutestamentliche Wissenschaft*
Zost.	*Zostrianos* (NHC VIII,*1*)
ZPE	*Zeitschrift für Papyrologie und Epigraphik*
ZPKT	*Zeitschrift für Philosophie und Katholische Theologie*
ZRGG	*Zeitschrift für Religions- und Geistesgeschichte,* Erlangen
ZST	*Zeitschrift für systematische Theologie*
ZTK	*Zeitschrift für Theologie und Kirche*
ZWT	*Zeitschrift für wissenschaftliche Theologie*
ZycMysl	*Zycie i Mysl*

AARON (PERSON) [Heb *ʾahărōn*]. AARONITES. The son of Amram and the brother of Moses and Miriam who was the eponymous ancestor of the priestly Aaronites and the paradigm for later priests. He dies at Mount Hur (Deut 32:50) and is succeeded by his son Eleazar (Num 20:22–29). Aaronites are the priests who claim descent from Levi through Aaron. They are often referred to as the "sons of Aaron" (Heb *bĕnê ʾahărōn*) (cf. Lev 3:8; 21:1; Num 10:8; Josh 21:4; 1 Chr 24:1; Neh 12:47) or as "belonging to Aaron" (Heb *lĕʾahărōn*) (cf. 1 Chr 12:28—Eng 12:27; 27:17). The meaning of the name "Aaron" is uncertain, although it is perhaps derived from Egyptian.

A. Introduction
B. Images of Aaron in the Biblical Literature
C. Aaron/Aaronite Relations with Others
D. The Priestly Functions of Aaron and the Aaronites
E. Summary

A. Introduction

The first task in understanding Aaron and the Aaronites is to examine the varied images of them in the biblical accounts. Sometimes there is a strong positive image of Aaron as the officially ordained priest of God. At other times, the picture is rather negative, portraying Aaron at odds with Moses and "mainline" religious practices. In examining these portrayals, it becomes clear that positive images appear in the later biblical materials and negative images are prominent in the earlier materials. It is also true that there is a significant body of biblical literature (the prophets—especially Ezekiel—and the Deuteronomistic History) in which priests are present but there is little or no reference to Aaron or his followers. Thus, in order to understand the images of Aaron and the Aaronites, one needs to be aware of the particular literature in which these references to Aaron are found, and the specific time frame in which that literature emerged.

A second set of concerns when discussing Aaron and the Aaronites focuses on their relationship to other people or priestly groups. In terms of individuals, the question is primarily Aaron's relationship with Moses. In terms of the Aaronites, the question is how they relate to the Levites and Zadokites, two other major priestly factions.

Finally, Aaron and his descendants are the preeminent models of what it means to be a priest. They are the ones who perform the most holy of rituals, who handle the holiest of sacred objects and who enter the holiest of places. In addition, they are the ones who oversee all priestly functions and groups, and monitor the activities of the priests at both the temple and the tabernacle.

B. Images of Aaron in the Biblical Literature

It is clear that there is some ambivalence in the biblical texts toward Aaron. On the one hand, he becomes involved with the construction of the GOLDEN CALF (Exodus 32) and joins Miriam in opposing Moses (Numbers 12). On the other hand, Aaron and his sons are singled out to serve God as priests (Exodus 28–29; Leviticus 8–9). Somewhere amid these two perspectives stands a remarkable silence on the Aaronites (e.g. 1–2 Kings, Ezekiel), in which they are neither good nor bad. There are other priests or priestly groups present, but Aaron and the Aaronites are not part of that presence.

This confusing portrayal has been the subject of speculation for some period. As early as Wellhausen *(WHPI)* and Kennett (1905), it was suggested that the positive portrayal of Aaron emerged only in the post-exilic period and that the negative or neutral portrayals dated from the pre-exilic period. Since those early discussions, Meek (1929), Welch (1939), North (1954) and Cody (1969, 1977) have offered slight variations on the same basic position—that the positive image of Aaron is a product of the post-exilic period.

Their arguments are based on an examination of the materials in which Aaron appears. There are 346 references to Aaron in the Hebrew Bible (several in the Apocrypha and Pseudepigrapha and 5 in the NT). A vast majority (296) appear in Exodus, Leviticus, and Numbers. The remainder are spread out in Deuteronomy (4), Joshua (6), Judges (1), 1 Samuel (2), Micah (1), Psalms (9), Ezra (1), Nehemiah (3), 1 Chronicles (16), and 2 Chronicles (7). The lack of appearances in Ezekiel, who is very concerned with priests, and the scarcity in Deuteronomy (4), where Moses plays a predominant role, are very curious. However, prior to drawing any conclusions, specific passages need to be investigated, and this investigation must be cognizant of the historical situation from which the passages emerge.

A safe place to begin such an examination is the work of the Chronicler, whose postexilic date is essentially undisputed. In 1–2 Chronicles one sees a prominent positive role for Aaron. He is the brother of Moses (1 Chr 5:29—Eng 6:3); he and his sons make sacrifices, offerings, and atonement in the most holy place in the temple (1 Chr 6:34—Eng 6:49); and Aaron and his sons are "set apart" to perform the most sacred of duties—to burn incense, to minister, and to bless (1 Chr 23:13; 24:19). Furthermore, in 2 Chr 26:16–21, it is explicitly indicated that only the sons of Aaron, and *not* King Uzziah, could burn incense to Yahweh.

There are many other positive portrayals of Aaron, but most are found in P (Priestly) material, a collection of material more problematical in terms of dating than the Chronicler's materials. The general consensus, albeit certainly not uniform, is that the present form of the P material reflects the understandings and perspectives of the early Second Temple period (i.e., postexilic period). Following that consensus yields a perspective on Aaron which is consistent with what emerged in the postexilic work of the Chronicler.

When one looks at the P material, one sees a very positive understanding of Aaron. A few examples from Exodus will support this point. Following the description of the ark and tabernacle (Exod 25:1–27:20), Aaron and his sons (the Aaronites) are to "tend" the tent of meeting (Exod 27:21), to serve Yahweh as priests (Exod 28:1), to wear priestly garments (Exod 28:3–43), including the Urim and Thummim (Exod 28:30), to be consecrated to Yahweh (Exod 29:1) and to be ordained (Exod 29:9, 35). To celebrate this ordination, a bull and two rams are to be sacrificed in Aaron's honor (Exod 29:10–37). Finally, Aaron and his sons shall be anointed and consecrated as priests of Yahweh with "holy oil" (Exod 30:30–31). This positive image of Aaron continues through most of Exodus (with the exception of Exodus 32, which will be discussed later), throughout all of Leviticus and most of Numbers.

In Leviticus, much time is spent describing specific offerings and the procedures for those offerings. Consistently, Aaron, or "Aaron's sons, the priests" are specified as the only people authorized to perform these rituals. In Lev 6:1–9:24—Eng 6:8–9:24, Aaron and his sons are instructed as to the law of the various offerings and their crucial role in these offerings. The ritual for anointing Aaron and his sons is spelled out in Lev 6:12–16—Eng 6:19–23. The actual ceremony for the ordination of Aaron and his sons is prescribed in Leviticus 8–9. The regulations for the actions of the Aaronites—"the priests, the sons of Aaron"—are spelled out in Leviticus 21. The concern is to maintain the holy status of the priests so that they do not become defiled by such actions as marrying a divorced woman (v 7), letting one's hair hang loose (v 10), or coming in contact with a dead body (v 11). In addition, no person with a blemish may "offer bread" to Yahweh (v 18).

In Numbers 1–4, Moses and Aaron conduct a census of the people in preparation for war. Three factors should be considered when examining the role of Aaron in this census. First, the Levites, another priestly group, are numbered separately from the rest of the people (Num 1:47; 3:16–37), and are to be given to Aaron to stand (Heb *ʿmd*) before and serve (Heb *šrt*) him (3:6). The second point is that the line of succession to Aaron is established. In Num 3:2–3 Aaron's sons are listed and identified as anointed priests "ordained to minister in the priest's office" (literally "whose hands are filled for the priesthood" [Heb *mlʾ yd lkhn*], "to fill the hand," is the common Hebrew expression used to indicate ordination). Since Nadab and Abihu, two of Aaron's sons, have died (Leviticus 10), Eleazar and Ithamar, Aaron's other sons, are the successors to Aaron. Finally, *only* Aaron and his sons are to be priests. All others who seek to come near the tent of meeting should be killed (Num 3:10).

This perspective on Aaron's exclusive role as priest is continued in Numbers 16. The account records the rebellion of Korah, Dathan, and Abiram against Moses and Aaron (Num 16:1–3) and contains the statement that only the descendants of Aaron can be priests (Num 17:5–Eng 16:40). This is curious since Korah, the son of Ishar, and Aaron, the son of Amram, are both seen as descendants of the priestly family of Levi (Exod 3:16–18; Num 3:17–19; 16:1). However, for the Priestly writer it is only Aaron's branch of the Levitical family which can claim the legitimate right to the priesthood at the temple and tabernacle. Other material in Numbers (except Numbers 12) conveys the same basic positive evaluation of Aaron. As with the Chronicler, the Priestly writer presents a positive image of Aaron.

In contrast to that perspective, one can find materials in which there is a negative, or at least neutral, image of Aaron. One example is in Deuteronomy. This material is examined first because it can be identified, with a comfortable degree of certainty, as having originated in a preexilic context. One example, in particular, is Deuteronomy 9, which contains part of Moses' presentation to the people. Of interest here is the telling of the story of Moses' descent from Mount Horeb after having received the two tablets of stone. Moses comes upon the people who have sinned and made a GOLDEN CALF (Deut 9:15–16). The story continues with a statement that Yahweh is so angry toward Aaron that he was about to destroy him. It appears that it is only Moses' intercessory prayer and his utter destruction of the Golden Calf which saves Aaron. It is certainly not a glowing recommendation of Aaron. Indeed, the only other appearance of Aaron in Deuteronomy is in 32:50, where Aaron is merely mentioned as a brother of Moses. Thus Deuteronomy neither presents a positive image of Aaron, nor contains a reference to Aaron as priest (unless one considers Aaron's role in the building of the Golden Calf as priestly—but even then it would not be seen as consistent with the mainline worship of Yahweh).

This negative perspective is not confined to this passage in Deuteronomy. In Exodus 32, although there is some discussion as to the integrity of the passage, Aaron is portrayed as the villain who receives the gold from the people (Exod 32:4a), makes the calf (Exod 32:4a, 35), declares, "These are your gods, O Israel, who brought you out of the land of Egypt!" (Exod 32:4b), and builds an altar before the calf (Exod 32:5). When Moses returns from the mountain, he indicates that Aaron has brought a great sin upon the people (Exod 32:21) and has allowed the people to "break loose" (Exod 32:25). While Aaron seeks to redirect Moses' anger (Exod 32:22–24), his culpability is clearly indicated.

A third example of this negative image of Aaron is found in Numbers 12. Here Aaron and his sister Miriam challenge Moses' authority (12:1) and claim that Yahweh speaks through them as well as through Moses (12:2). The response of Yahweh is clear; Moses is the specially chosen spokesperson, and no one should challenge him (12:5–8). As punishment, Yahweh makes Miriam leprous and subsequently heals her only after Aaron pleads with Moses to petition Yahweh on their behalf.

All three of these passages which convey either a negative or a nonpriestly image of Aaron are generally considered to be preexilic in date. The single reference to Aaron in the prophets (Mic 6:4), which is preexilic, merely refers to Aaron as having been sent to Egypt with Moses and Miriam. In addition, there are precious few references to Aaron in the pre-exilic and exilic work of the Deuteronomistic Historian, which is surprising, given the number of times priests or priestly factions are mentioned. It is only in Joshua, where cities are distributed to the Levites (Josh 21:4, 13, 19), that Aaron is referred to as a priest. Finally, Ezekiel, an exilic work which spends much time discussing the roles and functions of the priests and priestly groups, never refers to Aaron or the Aaronites.

The implication of this examination of the biblical passages which refer to Aaron is that the positive image of Aaron and the Aaronites, and of their role as priests, arises in the post-exilic period. This may be expected since it reflects, in general, the prominent position of priests in the postexilic period, and, in particular, the emergence of the role of the high priest. In contrast, in the pre-exilic period Aaron is mentioned only a few times, often in a neutral or negative way, and very rarely as a priest. Thus one must conclude that the prominence of Aaron and the Aaronites as priests is a post-exilic phenomenon.

C. Aaron/Aaronite Relations with Others

A second area of consideration is the relationship of Aaron to other individuals and of the Aaronites to other priestly groups. Aaron's relationship to Moses is of primary importance. In terms of the associations of the Aaronites, there are two other priestly factions which have a significant role in the Hebrew Bible—the Zadokites and the Levites. It is clear that there is struggle, conflict, and competition among these three groups over who is going to have control of the priesthood. As indicated in the previous section, one must remember that all of these relationships are fluid and that Aaron's priority is emphasized in the later biblical materials.

The close association of Moses and Aaron is a common theme in the Pentateuch (although not exclusively found there [Josh 24:5; 1 Sam 12:6; Ps 77:21—Eng 77:20, 99:6]), particularly in the later (Priestly) writings of the Pentateuch. The association begins with the claim that Aaron is Moses' brother (Exod 4:14; 6:20; 28:1; Num 26:59; 27:12–13; Deut 32:50; 1 Chr 5:29—Eng 6:3; 23:13). There are also over 65 instances where the phrase "Moses and Aaron" appears, almost like a word pair, and only a few instances where the phrase "Aaron and Moses" occurs (Exod 6:26; Num 3:1). What is striking about many of these instances is that the presence of "Aaron" is not crucial to the passage. It could easily be removed without a significant impact on the passage or its meaning (cf. Exod 7:8; 10:3; 16:6; Lev 9:23; 11:1; Num 4:1; 14:5; 33:1). So the evidence for a close association of Moses and Aaron is not absolutely certain, and it is primarily found in the later materials.

In the relationship between Moses and Aaron, it is clear that Moses has a more prominent role. Most often in the Torah, Yahweh speaks to Moses, who in turn speaks to Aaron (Exod 7:19; 16:32–34; Lev 17:1–2; Num 6:22–23; 8:1–2), or Yahweh speaks to Moses and Aaron at the same time (Exod 12:43; Lev 11:1; 14:33; Num 2:1; 19:1; 20:12). Only rarely does Yahweh speak directly to Aaron (Lev 10:8; Num 18:1). In addition, when one looks at the dynamics of the plague stories, there is a clear but subtle shift in the relationship between Moses and Aaron. At the beginning, Moses fumbles for words and pleads his incompetence until in anger Yahweh appoints Aaron to be Moses' spokesperson. Even then Aaron receives Yahweh's words through Moses (Exod 4:1–17; 7:19). Thus at the beginning of the plague stories Aaron has an important role. When both Moses and Aaron appear before Pharaoh (Exod 5:1, 7:10), it is Aaron's rod which becomes the serpent (7:10), swallows the rods of Pharaoh's magicians (7:12), is used to turn the Nile into blood (7:19), causes the plague of frogs (8:1—Eng 8:5), and brings about the plague of gnats (8:16–17). However, with Exodus 9, Aaron begins to fade from the scene, and it is Moses who brings the boils (9:10) and uses his own rod to bring hail and fire (9:23) and the locusts (10:12–13). One explanation of this shift is that the earlier plagues tend to be from the P writer and the later plagues tend to be from the older pentateuchal source, the J writer. Although there is considerable and justifiable discussion about the degree to which one can identify a particular passage or verse as J or P, the general perspective suggests that the older materials do not place an emphasis on Aaron whereas the newer materials do. Thus, like the prominence of Aaron as priest in the postexilic period, it seems that the association of Aaron with Moses also finds its greatest emphasis in the post-exilic materials.

Moses and Aaron also appear together when the people are "murmuring" during the Exodus. Usually this murmuring involves the rebellion of the people against the leadership. In Exodus 17 the people murmur against Moses (v 2). Aaron is not the target of the rebellion and his role in the incident is only that of holding up Moses' arms, along with Hur (v 12). In Numbers 12, the rebellion is again directed at Moses (v 1). However, this time it is Aaron and his sister Miriam who lead the rebellion against Moses. Finally, in Numbers 14 and 16, the rebellion is directed not just against Moses but also against Aaron (Num 14:2, 16:3). This confused situation becomes clear when one realizes that the early materials (Numbers 12, Exodus 17) either ignore Aaron or are negative toward him, whereas in the later materials (Numbers 14, 16) there is a positive picture of Aaron and a link with Moses.

When one turns to the priestly groups, it is apparent that the relations between the Zadokites and Aaronites change over time. During the monarchy, it is the Zadokites who play a prominent role in the priesthood and little is said about the Aaronites. One merely needs to look at the dearth of references to Aaron or Aaronites in Kings and Samuel (only 2 Samuel) in contrast to the 26 references to Zadok as the priest of the monarchy. At the end of David's reign, there is a conflict over the succession to the throne between Solomon and his followers and Adonijah and his followers (1 Kings 1–2). When Solomon is victorious in the struggle, he appoints Zadok as the priest of the Temple and expels Abiathar (1 Kgs 2:27), the associate of Adonijah. While there may be some debate over the actual association of Abiathar—whether he is Levite or Aaronite—it is clear that Zadok and his followers, the Zadokites, are the priests in good standing. That perspective continues in the late exilic work of Ezekiel; he never mentions the Aaronites. Rather, it is the Zadokites with the assistance of the Levites who are the priests (Ezek 40:46; 44:15; 48:11).

It is only in the post-exilic material of the Chronicler that any association between Aaron and Zadok appears, and the perspective is always that Zadok the priest is a descendant of Aaron (1 Chr 5:29–34—Eng 6:3–8; 6:35–38—Eng 6:50–53; Ezra 7:1–5), which preserves the priority of Aaron. In addition, the Chronicler seeks to clarify the relationship of Zadok and Abiathar, the two priests of David (2 Sam 8:17, cf. 1 Sam 22:20) who are rivals after his death. According to 1 Chr 24:3, Zadok is a descendant of Eleazar, the son of Aaron, and Abiathar is a descendant of Ithamar, also a son of Aaron. Thus, for the Chronicler, all priests are descendants of Aaron, which again stresses the post-exilic prominence of the Aaronites.

The relationship between the Aaronites and the Levites is much more confusing and more prone to be hostile than that between the Aaronites and the Zadokites. Nevertheless, this relationship also shows development and change. A prime example of the hostility emerges in Exodus 32. The complicity of Aaron in the Golden Calf apostasy has already been mentioned. At the end of that account, there is the punishment for those involved in the idolatry (Exod 32:25–29). Moses calls for those "on Yahweh's side" to join him in opposition to the people who "broke loose," and presumably that included Aaron. It is the Levites who respond to Moses' call and slay 3,000 people who participated in the apostasy. As a result of the Levites' actions, they are "ordained" to the service of Yahweh (Exod 32:29). The Hebrew text says "their hands are filled," which is a clear reference to their ordination as priests. It thus appears that the Levites' rise in status is directly related to their opposition to Aaron and his followers.

This same perspective is present when one examines 1 Kings 12. In this passage Jeroboam establishes two cultic centers in the Northern Kingdom at Dan and Bethel (vv 25–33), and makes two calves of gold for these centers (v 28). Jeroboam erects these calves and declares, "Behold your gods, O Israel, who brought you out of the land of Egypt," the same phrase as was used by Aaron in Exod 32:4. In addition, when Jeroboam selects priests for his temple he explicitly excludes Levites (1 Kgs 12:31). (According to 2 Chr 13:8–9, Jeroboam excludes both Levites and Aaronites, which reflects the later post-exilic perspective of the Chronicler in which Aaron is the only true priest and could not have participated in the apostasy of the Northern Kingdom.) A further piece of data which links these two golden calf incidents of Exodus 32 and 1 Kings 12 together is that the two eldest sons of Aaron and the sons of Jeroboam have virtually the same names: Nadab and Abihu for Aaron (Exod 6:23) and Nadab and Abijah for Jeroboam (1 Kgs 14:1, 20). Furthermore, all four of these sons die as a result of their idolatry (cf. Leviticus 10; 1 Kgs 14:1–14; 15:25–30). So based on these early materials, the improper cultic practices of Jeroboam are associated with those of Aaron, and the Levites either do not participate or actively oppose those idolatrous religious practices.

Numbers 16 is another passage in which there is opposition between Aaron and the Levites. However, in this instance, it is Aaron who is declared the righteous follower of God; and it is Korah, the descendant of Levi, who revolts against Moses and Aaron. Indeed, the followers of Aaron (Aaronites) are explicitly identified as the priests of Yahweh to the exclusion of Korah (Num 16:1–5—Eng 16:36–40).

This change in perspective on Aaron, where Aaron is now seen as the dominant priest, is reflective of the post-exilic materials of the Priestly writer and the Chronicler and again exemplifies the post-exilic relationship of Aaronites and Levites. It also shows that although all priestly factions traced their ancestry back to Levi, and Levi is considered ordained by God, the Levites' primary function is to serve the Aaronites.

When the census of the people is being taken by Aaron and Moses in Numbers, the Levites are explicitly set aside (Num 1:47) and not numbered at the beginning, since they have special tasks around the tabernacle. Later, however, the Levites are numbered and chosen by God to stand (Heb *ʾmd*) before Aaron and to "minister" (Heb *šrt*) to Aaron, since they are given to Aaron and his sons (Num 3:5–10; cf. 4:27). What is clear in this passage is that there is a distinction between the Aaronites as priests and the Levites, who, although also ordained, are secondary priests subordinate to Aaron.

Aaron is then to collect the Levites and consecrate them to service (Heb *ʿbd*) (Num 8:5–26; cf. 18:1–7). This perspective is continued in Chronicles, where there is a clear distinction between priests, understood to be Aaronites, and Levites (1 Chr 23:2; 24:31; 28:13, 21; and 2 Chr 7:6; 11:13; 13:9; 19:8; 23:4, 6). The Levites are to stand (Heb *ʾmd*) before the priests, the sons of Aaron (1 Chr 23:27–28), and guard (Heb *šmr*) the sons of Aaron (1 Chr 23:32; cf. 2 Chr 13:10; 35:14; Neh 12:47).

The priority of the Aaronites is illustrated in no better way than in the account in Num 17:16–28—Eng 17:1–13. According to the passage, each of the twelve tribes has a rod or staff, and each is to have the tribal ancestor's name placed on the rod. However, the rod representing Levi's tribe has Aaron's name written upon it. When all twelve rods are deposited in the tent of meeting to determine which of them will be chosen by God, it is the "rod of Aaron" which sprouts and bears "ripe almonds." This, of course, indicates Yahweh's selection of Aaron over all other (cf. *Ps-Philo* 17:1–4; 53:9). Finally, Aaron's rod, which is put before the "testimony" in the tent of meeting, is to become a sign that the people should not murmur against Yahweh (cf. Numbers 16).

In the following chapter (Numbers 18), where Aaron's priesthood and the role of the tribe of Levi are again discussed, the priority of Aaron and his sons as priests and the secondary status of the tribe of Levi are reiterated. The Levites are to minister to (Heb *šrt;* Num 18:2), to guard (Heb *šmr;* Num 18:3), and to serve (Heb *ʿbd;* Num 18:6) Aaron and his sons. This role of attending to Aaron and the Aaronites is given exclusively to the Levites (Num 18:4). However, the Levites are firmly cautioned *not* to approach the altar, lest they die (Num 18:3). This material in Numbers is late, again suggesting that the priority of Aaron and the Aaronites and the secondary status of the tribe of Levi (the Levites) emerges in the time of the Second Temple. In the material from the earlier periods, the Levites are often preferred, and it is the Aaronites whose activities are questionable and whose status is secondary to the Levites.

In general, it appears that Aaron's relationship with others has had the same mixed history as was seen in the review of Aaron in the biblical literature. In the monarchical period, Aaron and the Aaronites have a secondary, nonexistent, or negative status in relation to the other priestly groups. That perspective changes in the post-exilic period of the high priest, when Aaron and his sons (the Aaronites) become the high priests and establish their superiority over other groups. They do this by a genealogical link which traces their ancestry back to Moses and beyond to Levi, and by the accounts of Yahweh's selection of Aaron as the chosen priest, the paradigm—preferred over the other priestly factions (Levites and Zadokites). Indeed, the other priestly factions became servants to Aaron and the Aaronites.

D. The Priestly Functions of Aaron and the Aaronites

The role of Aaron as priest emerges in the activities and functions he and his descendants, the Aaronites, perform. Of course, one of their main functions is to preside at cultic ceremonies. However, there are other related activities in which they are involved.

There are numerous references in which Aaron (or his descendants) officiate at and participate in cultic rituals. In fact, the majority of the discussion in Leviticus is devoted to the priestly functions of Aaron and the Aaronites. They perform the "burnt offering" (Lev 1:3–17; 9:12–14), the "cereal offering" (Lev 2:1–16), and the "peace offering" (Lev 3:1–17; 9:18–21). Aaron is not explicitly mentioned when the "sin offering" (Lev 4:1–5:13) or "guilt offering" (Lev 5:14–26—Eng 5:14–6:7) are discussed. However, when the laws (Heb *tôrāt*) of the "sin offering" are presented (Lev 6:17–23—Eng 6:24–30; cf. 9:8, 16:6), it is the Aaronites who are addressed. For the "guilt offering" Aaron is again not specified, but it is always a priest who officiates (Lev 5:16, 5:25–26—Eng 6:6–7, 7:1–5), and Aaron is in charge when the offering of atonement is made (Leviticus 16). Thus the presumption that this anonymous priest should be understood as Aaron seems valid (cf. 1 Chr 6:34—Eng 6:49).

Another priestly function of the Aaronites is participation in ordination. Indeed, the Aaronites participate in their own ordination ceremony (Leviticus 8). It is run by Moses at Yahweh's command, but Aaron and his sons participate by laying their hands upon the bull of the "sin offering" (8:14), the ram of the "burnt offering" (8:18), and the ram of the "ordination" (8:22). Finally, they are to eat from the ordination offering (8:31–36).

An important passage which outlines Aaron's duties is Leviticus 10:8–11. This passage is unusual because it is one of the few places where Yahweh speaks directly to Aaron rather than through Moses. Here Aaron is told to do three things: avoid drinking when going into the tent of meeting; distinguish between the holy and the common and between the clean and the unclean; and teach the people Yahweh's statutes. One curiosity about the passage is how closely it echoes Ezekiel 44. In Ezekiel the reference is not to Aaron but to the priests who are the sons of Zadok and who also claim descent from Levi. Nevertheless, the functions of the priests are very similar: the sons of Zadok are told not to drink before going into the temple (Ezek 44:21); to distinguish between clean and unclean (Ezek 44:23b); to teach the people the difference between holy and common (Ezek 44:23a); to act as judge (Ezek 44:24a; cf. Exod 28:29–30); and to keep Yahweh's laws (Ezek 44:24b). Although the priestly faction in charge may have changed, the priestly functions relative to the central shrine remain essentially the same.

The distinction between clean and unclean is the focus of Leviticus 11–14. Moses and Aaron (Lev 11:1) are to speak to the people about this distinction, and people who are thought to be diseased are to be brought before Aaron and his sons for examination (Lev 13:1–2). It is Aaron who is to determine clean and unclean in relation to disease, and to deal with unclean houses and how to cleanse them (Lev 14:33–57). The same standards of purity apply to the Aaronites themselves. They are to be without blemish and pure in all ways (Leviticus 21). This is another means of distinguishing Aaron from others, and supports the contention that Aaron is chosen above the others to be priest (Ps 105:26, 106:16) and to have access to the holy things (1 Chr 23:13) in the temple (1 Chr 24:19) or in the tent of meeting (Exod 27:21, Num 17:1–5—Eng 16:36–40).

In Joshua 21, the Aaronites are to receive 48 Levitical cities from among the cities recently conquered by the twelve tribes (vv 4, 10, 13, 19). These cities, along with their pasture lands (but not, presumably, the agricultural lands [Num 35:1–8]), are to be set aside as land in which the priests can live and raise herds. This perspective is reiterated in 1 Chr 6:39–66—Eng 6:54–81, where there is a special reference to the sons of Aaron receiving cities of refuge (1 Chr 6:42–45—Eng 6:57–60). They are said to receive 13 cities, although only 11 are listed by name, in which a criminal may find refuge from pursuers. In the other major references to the cities of refuge (Num 35:9–15; Deut 19:1–10; Joshua 20), only 6 cities are set aside, and there is no mention of the cities being given to Aaron. The Aaronite control of these cities of refuge may well reflect the Chronicler's post-exilic perspective, in which there is a positive image of Aaron, and the Aaronites are in charge of the priesthood.

Finally, the Aaronites are given the Urim and Thummim (Exod 28:30, Lev 8:5–9). These "sacred lots" are used to determine the will of Yahweh (Num 27:21; 1 Sam 14:36–42, 27:6; cf. 1 Sam 10:20–24) and to indicate the juridical role of Aaron (Exod 28:29–30a; cf. Ezek 44:24). In Num 27:21, it is Eleazar, the son of Aaron, the next in the priestly line (cf. Num 20:22–29), who uses the Urim to inquire whether Joshua should succeed Moses. The Urim and Thummim are thus symbols of special access to God's will; and, according to parts of the biblical tradition, they belong in the hands of the Aaronites.

It is clear that Aaron and the Aaronites play a prominent role as priests. Their fulfillment of that role is emphasized in the Hebrew Bible, especially in the later materials. That perspective continues in the intertestamental literature (4 Macc 7:11; 3 *En.* 2:3; 48A:7), although there are surprisingly few references to Aaron in this material. In the New

Testament, the book of Hebrews speaks of Jesus being called by God, just like Aaron (Heb 5:4–5). However, to distinguish Jesus from the priests of his contemporary time, Jesus is said to be of the order of Melchizedek, not that of Aaron and the Levites (Heb 7:4–22). Thus the writer of Hebrews is claiming a priestly authority for Jesus which predates that of Aaron or Levi and comes through Melchizedek at the time of Abraham (Gen 14:17–24; Ps 110:4; Heb 7:1–3).

E. Summary

Aaron and the Aaronites play an important role in the religious structure of ancient Israel. The emphasis upon them and their functions clearly indicates their place as the preeminent priests. However, close examination of the biblical literature suggests that this prominent role was not present at the beginnings of Israel and was not won without a struggle. The earlier materials indicate a more significant role for the Levite and Zadokite priestly factions than for the Aaronites. It is only with the realignment and reorganization forced upon the Israelites by the trauma of the fall of Jerusalem in 586 B.C.E. that the Aaronites assume center stage. Then, in the writings of the postexilic period, the Aaronites are portrayed as the paradigm of priests, and the other priestly groups are relegated to secondary or servant status. (See also PRIESTS AND LEVITES.)

Bibliography

Aberbach, M., and Smolar, L. 1967. Aaron, Jeroboam, and the Golden Calves. *JBL* 86: 129–40.

Cody, A. 1969. *A History of Old Testament Priesthood.* AnBib 35. Rome.

———. 1977. Aaron: A Figure with Many Facets. *BToday* 88: 1089–94.

Gunneweg, A. H. J. 1965. *Leviten und Priester.* FRLANT 89. Göttingen.

Horbury, W. 1983. The Aaronic Priesthood in the Epistle to the Hebrews. *JSNT* 19: 43–71.

Judge, H. G. 1956. Aaron, Zadok and Abiathar. *JTS* n.s. 7: 70–74.

Kennett, R. H. 1905. Origin of the Aaronite Priesthood. *JTS* 6: 161–86.

Meek, T. J. 1929. Aaronites and Zadokites. *AJSL* 45: 149–66.

North, F. S. 1954. Aaron's Rise in Prestige. *ZAW* 66: 191–99.

Sabourin, L. 1973. *Priesthood: A Comparative Study.* SHR 25. Leiden.

Welch, A. C. 1939. *The Work of the Chronicler.* London.

JOHN R. SPENCER

AB [Heb *ʾāb*]. The fifth month of the Hebrew calendar, roughly corresponding to July and August. See CALENDAR.

ABADDON [Heb *ʾăbaddôn*]. Derived from Heb *ʾābad,* "became lost," "be ruined, destroyed," "perish," Abaddon has a variety of nuanced meanings.

A poetic synonym for the abode of the dead, meaning "Destruction," or "(the place of) destruction." Abaddon occurs in parallel and in conjunction with Sheol (Job 26:6 and Prov 15:11; 27:20). It is also found in conjunction with Death (Job 28:22) and in parallel with the grave (Ps 88:12—Eng 88:11). Although a place of mystery which is hidden from human eyes, Abaddon is clearly known by God (Job 26:6; Prov 15:11). It is twice personified: (1) along with Death, it speaks (Job 28:22); and (2) along with Sheol, it is insatiable (Prov 27:20). It is also remote: in Job 31:12, adultery becomes "a fire that consumes unto [as far as] Abaddon." See also DEAD, ABODE OF THE.

In Rev 9:11, the word "Abaddon" is personified as "the angel of the bottomless pit." It is also identified as the king of the demonic "locusts" described in Rev 9:3, 7–10, and is explained for Greek-speaking readers as Apollyon (Gk *apollyōn*), "destroyer."

The LXX usually translates Heb *ʾabaddon* as Gk *apōleia,* "destruction"; the Vg renders it as Latin *perditio,* "ruin, destruction" (whence Eng "perdition," which ordinarily means "hell"); in Syr (Peshitta), the cognate word means "destruction," and is sometimes used in the Psalms to render "the Pit," which is another OT synonym of Sheol.

In rabbinic literature, the word has come to mean the place of punishment reserved for the wicked. Current English versions render this word variously in the OT: "Abaddon," "Destruction/destruction," "the place of destruction," "Perdition/perdition," "the abyss," "the world of the dead." In the single NT occurrence, the word is consistently transliterated as "Abaddon."

HERBERT G. GRETHER

ABAGTHA (PERSON) [Heb *ʾăbagtāʾ*]. See MEHUMAN (PERSON).

ABANA (PLACE) [Heb *ʾăbānâ*]. One of two rivers of Damascus, which Naaman the Syrian considered to be superior to the Jordan (2 Kgs 5:12). The Awaj and the Barada are now the chief streams that flow through the city of Damascus, the former representing the Pharpar of the Hebrew text and the latter the Abana. The Barada (Abana) has as its source a large pool of great depth on a high plain rising 1149 feet (383 m) in the Anti-Lebanon Mountains, 23 miles (37 km) northwest of Damascus. Making a rapid descent down the mountains, the stream flows through a picturesque gorge, across a plain, through Damascus, and loses itself in the marshy lake Bahret el-Kibliyeh about 18 miles (29 km) east of the city.

RAY LEE ROTH

ABARIM (PLACE) [Heb *ʿăbārîm*]. A mountain range generally located east of the mouth of the Jordan river and northeast of the Dead Sea forming the northwestern rim of the Moabite tableland, thus separating the latter from the rift valley (Num 33:47–48). The highest peaks of this range rise about 600 feet above the Moabite plateau and overlook the Dead Sea some 4000 feet below their summits.

The mountains of Abarim, a southern extension of the Transjordan range, are located "in front of [the town of] Nebo" (Num 33:47). One of the peaks of this ridge is Mount Nebo (see also NEBO, MOUNT), which Moses ascended from the Plains of Moab (Num 27:12) and from which he viewed the land of Canaan prior to his death

(Deut 32:49). The Israelites camped in the mountains of Abarim after leaving Almon-diblathaim and before reaching the Plains of Moab, the final stage of the exodus from Egypt (Num 33:47–48).

In Jer 22:20 the RSV treats *ʿăbārîm* as a proper name, assuming it to be a region as are Lebanon to the north and Basham to the northeast. However, the KJV translates *ʿăbārîm* by "passages." Similarly, several ancient versions (LXX, Vg and Pesh) reflect in their translations of *ʿăbārîm* in Jer 22:20 the verbal root meaning "to cross over" or "to pass over." Abarim may originally have been an appellative (reflected in the Gk of the LXX translation of Num 27:12 *"to oros to en tō peran"* i.e. "[places] on the other side [of Judah])" before it became the proper name "Abarim." The NEB emends the RSV reading "valley of the travelers" in Ezek 39:11 to read "the valley of Abarim" (see also TRAVELERS, VALLEY OF).

While most maps confine the Abarim range to the highland north of the river Arnon, several scholars (*GP* 1:379; *GTTOT:* 261; van Zyl 1960: 51) infer from Jer 22:20 and the name of the encampment Iye-abarim, which by definition appears to be associated with the Abarim range, that the hills of Abarim also describe the mountains east of the southern end of the Dead Sea. Though the precise location of IYE-ABARIM is uncertain, scholars generally place it south of the Arnon gorge.

In antiquity Josephus (*Ant* 4. 8,§48), Jerome and Eusebius made reference to the Abarim hills (Lagarde 1966: 16,5; 89,8; 216,4). For references, see BEER (PLACE).

Arthur J. Ferch

ABBA. A form of the Aramaic word for "father" found in Gal 4:6; Rom 8:15; and Mark 14:36 alongside the Greek *ho patēr* as an address to God. The presence of *ho patēr* in every case (instead of the vocative *pater*) shows that the NT writers saw *abba* as a determinative form: *ʾabbāʾ*, "the father"; cf. Matt 11:16; Luke 10:21. Such forms are frequently used in Aramaic and Hebrew when a vocative is required: another example is *talitha* (Aram. *ṭalyĕtāʾ/ṭalyĕtāʾ*), rendered *to korasion* in Mark 5:41. Accordingly the explanation of *abba* as the determinative form of *ab* ("father") is almost certainly correct.

Alternatively the form has been explained as a rare vocative (in which case it could just as well be Hebrew as Aramaic) or as derived from children's baby talk (cf. "Papa," "Daddy"). If the last explanation were right, then the use of *abba* as an address to God in Mark 14:36 might be thought to imply a special, indeed a unique, intimacy. This view was held at one time by J. Jeremias, but he later came to regard it as "a piece of inadmissible naivety" (1967: 63). Wrong as it is, it deserves mention not only because of its extensive dissemination beyond the walls of academia but also because its influence can be detected even in the work of respected scholars such as J. G. D. Dunn (1975: 21–26; 1980: 22–23) and is explicit in the most recent writing of M. J. Borg (1987: 45). Apart from the intrinsic unlikelihood of the idea that Jesus ever addressed God as "Daddy," the suggestion is ruled out of court by one important fact: wherever *abba* is found with the meaning "father" or "my father" (in Mishnaic Hebrew or Targumic Aramaic), it is equally employed of the fathers of grown-up sons. One instance cited by G. Vermes (1983: 42) is Judah's threat to his unrecognized brother, Joseph, in the *Tg. Neof.* version of Gen 44:18: "I swear by the life of the head of *abba,* as you swear by the life of the head of Pharaoh your master. . . ." And as J. Barr (1988) emphasizes, inferences concerning the meaning of words must be based upon function, not upon origin or derivation.

There is no evidence in pre-Christian Palestinian Judaism that God was ever addressed as *abba* by an individual Jew in prayer. Jeremias (1967: 59) adduces two instances in the Babylonian Talmud (*b. Taʿan.* 23ab) from stories told of sages who lived in the 1st century B.C.; but Schelbert (1981: 398–405) has shown these attributions to be insecure, a point reemphasized by Fitzmyer (1985: 27) in the most comprehensive of all recent discussions of the subject. Though God is frequently alluded to as the father of his people in the OT and elsewhere, the earliest attestation of *abba* as a personal address to God is Gal 4:6. This should not be taken to imply that the sense of God as the father of the individual supplicant was not pre-Christian: there are a few passages that perhaps indicate it: Sir 23:1, 4; Wis 2:16; 14:3. This evidence, however, is neither abundant nor strong.

The question why the Aramaic *abba* was retained in the Spirit-inspired prayer of Greek-speaking communities cannot be answered with certainty. But even the single attribution of the term to Jesus (in the prayer in Gethsemane) lends plausibility to the suggestion that Christian usage was prompted by an authentic tradition of Jesus' own prayer. This is supported by Paul's association of the prayer of the community with the divine sonship of Christ "God has sent the spirit of his Son into our hearts, crying, 'Abba! Father!' " (Gal 4:6). The fact that Matthew and Luke have different renderings of Jesus' prayer to God in Gethsemane (*pater mou,* Matt 26:39; *pater,* Luke 22:42) may be explained in one of two ways: either the memory of Jesus' own prayer did not survive beyond the first written account; or else the use of *abba* in Christian prayer was no longer current in the Matthean and Lucan communities.

Finally, what are the christological implications of the use of the term by Jesus? Since the address was taken over by Christians in their own prayer, they cannot have seen it as evidence of an *exclusive* relationship between Jesus and God. Moreover, postbiblical usage (the only comparative material available) suggests that the nuance of *abba* as an address is closer to "Father" than the earlier Hebrew and Aramaic forms (*ʾābî* and *ʾăbî* respectively), which mean specifically "my father." These, like *abba,* can be used in speaking about one's father as well as in addressing him; but unlike *abba,* they are not used of another person's father. Besides, the Gospels portray Jesus as urging his disciples to regard God as a father and to address him as their father in prayer. Nevertheless, taken in conjunction with other gospel evidence (e.g. Matt 11:25–27 = Luke 10:21–22) for Jesus' own awareness of God as Father, the use of *abba* constitutes one especially strong argument for the view that the personal sense of the fatherhood of God was a typically Christian development of the Judaic tradition, and that this probably originated in a recollection of Jesus' teaching and of the example of his own prayer.

Bibliography

Barr, J. 1988. "Abba" Isn't "Daddy," *JTS* 39: 28–47.
Borg, M. J. 1987. *Jesus: A New Vision.* San Francisco.

Dalman, G. 1902. *The Words of Jesus.* Trans. D. M. Kay. Edinburgh.
Dunn, J. G. D. 1975. *Jesus and the Spirit.* London.
———. 1980. *Christology in the Making.* London.
Jeremias, J. 1967. *The Prayers of Jesus.* London.
Fitzmyer, J. A. 1988. *Abba* and Jesus' Relation to God. Pp. 15–38 in *À Cause de l'Évangile.* Lectio Divina 123. Paris.
Schelbert, G. 1981. Sprachgeschichtliches zu "Abba." Pp. 395–447 in *Mélanges Dominique Barthélémy,* ed. P. Casetti et al. Freiburg.
Vermes, G. 1983. *Jesus and the World of Judaism.* London.

JOHN ASHTON

ABDA (PERSON) [Heb *ʿabdāʾ*]. **1.** The father of Adoniram (1 Kgs 4:6), an official in charge of forced labor during King Solomon's reign (1 Kgs 5:27—Eng 5:14). Abda appears in a list of Solomon's high officials (1 Kgs 4:1–6).

2. The son of Shammua, and descendant of Jeduthun, one of 284 Levites listed among those who performed their duties in "the holy city" (Jerusalem) under Nehemiah (Neh 11:17; LXX variants of the name include *ōbēb* and *abdas*). As a descendant of Jeduthun, Abda was a member of a family set apart for musical service by King David (1 Chr 25:1–6). A parallel biblical list (1 Chr 9:14–16) mentions not Abda but Obadiah (also derived from the Heb root *ʿbd*), but the Neo-Babylonian Murašu Archive (dated ca. 429–428 B.C.E.) refers to an *Ab-da-ʾ* son of *Aplā* (Hilprecht 1898: 45.5; Zadok 1976: 17), demonstrating the contemporaneous use of this name in Babylon.

Bibliography

Hilprecht, H. V., ed. 1898. *The Babylonian Expedition of the University of Pennsylvania. Series A: Cuneiform Texts.* Vol. 9. Philadelphia.
Zadok, R. 1976. *The Jews in Babylonia in the Chaldean and Achaemenian Periods in the Light of the Babylonian Sources.* Tel Aviv.

MARK J. FRETZ

ABDEEL (PERSON) [Heb *ʿabdĕʾēl*]. The father of Shelemiah, an official of unspecified status under Jehoiakim, King of Judah (Jer 36:26—LXX 43:26). Together with Jerahmeel and Seraiah, Shelemiah was ordered by the king to seize Baruch the scribe and Jeremiah the prophet (cf. Jer 26:20–24—LXX 33:20–24, where Uriah the prophet was similarly seized, and then executed). The MT phrase including "Shelemiah the son of Abdeel" (Jer 36:26) is missing in the LXX, and was likely lost through homoioteleuton (note the similarities between Heb *ben-ʿabdĕʾēl* and the preceding *ben-ʿazrîʾēl*).

MARK J. FRETZ

ABDI (PERSON) [Heb *ʿabdî*]. **1.** A Levite of the clan of Merari, and father of Kishi and grandfather of Ethan (1 Chr 6:29—Eng 6:44). His name appears in an extended genealogy listing Levi's descendants (1 Chronicles 1–9). Abdi's son Kishi (Heb *qyšy*) is probably the Kushaiah (Heb *qwšyhw*) of 1 Chr 15:17. His grandson, Ethan, served as temple singer under King David and eventually supplanted Jeduthun as head of the third clan of temple singers (1 Chr 6:16–34—Eng 6:31–48; see Williamson 1979: 263).

2. The father of Kish, a Levite who helped cleanse the temple during the reign of King Hezekiah (2 Chr 29:12). See KISH. This Abdi is mentioned in a short list of Levites who cleansed the temple, rather than in an extended genealogy. However, the appearance of the name "Abdi" in lists from both the Davidic-Solomonic period (see above) and the Hezekiah period is noteworthy: both Abdi's were Levites of the clan of Merari, their sons had similar names (Kish/Kishi), and their descendants appear to have been involved in various aspects of temple service. On the one hand, this similarity may be historical: there may well have been two Levites named Abdi living three hundred years apart, the second of whom named his offspring Kish and thereby recalled the earlier "golden age" of David and Solomon. On the other hand, the similarity may be a purely literary creation, a technique whereby the Chronicler supported his portrayal of Hezekiah as a "second Solomon" (Williamson 1977: 119–25). A third view is that "Kish the son of Abdi" means "Kish the descendant of Abdi." According to this view, the legitimizing function of the Levitical genealogies (1 Chronicles 6) was utilized to indicate not a literal, biological father, but a real or fictive ancestor for this important Levite, who assisted in cleansing the temple in Hezekiah's time.

3. A descendant of Elam who returned from Babylonian exile. This Abdi was one of a number of returnees who married foreign women from "the people of the land" (Ezra 10:26 = 1 Esdr 9:27 [LXX *abdia* is a variant of *ōabdeios* in 9:27]). Under Ezra, he was subsequently forced by a covenant made with God to separate himself from his foreign wife and her children (Ezra 10:1–44 = 1 Esdr 8:88–9:36; see also Neh 13:23–31).

Bibliography

Williamson, H. G. M. 1977. *Israel in the Books of Chronicles.* Cambridge, MA.
———. 1979. The Origins of the Twenty-four Priestly Courses, A Study of 1 Chronicles xxiii–xxvii. Pp. 251–68 in *Studies in the Historical Books of the Old Testament,* ed. J. A. Emerton. VTSup 30. Leiden.

MARK J. FRETZ

ABDIEL (PERSON) [Heb *ʿabdîʾēl*]. The father of Ahi, a prominent member of the tribe of Gad (1 Chr 5:15) in the northern Transjordan during the reigns of King Jotham of Judah and Jeroboam II of Israel (mid-8th century B.C.E.). According to various LXX manuscripts, Abdiel is not the father of Ahi but instead the father of either *zaboucham,* or *achibouz,* or simply the brother (Heb *ʾḥy*) of Buz (Gk *bouz*). The name "Abdiel" occurs in an extended genealogy of Israel that also identifies tribal locations within Palestine (1 Chronicles 2–8).

MARK J. FRETZ

ABDON (PERSON) [Heb *ʿabdôn*]. Four individuals mentioned in the OT bear this name, which is formed on the root *ʿbd* with an abstract or diminutive ending, thus evoking the sense of "service" or, possibly, "servile."

1. Abdon son of Hillel was from the town of Pirathon in Ephraim (possibly at or near Farʿata, ca. 10 km southwest of Shechem). He is one of the tribal leaders who "judged Israel," for "eight years," in the premonarchy period (Judg 12:13–15). Information about him is sketchy. That he had "forty sons and thirty grandsons," an odd progression, "who rode on seventy donkeys" may indicate declining wealth and prominence of one extended family in the central hill country where the territory of Ephraim and Manasseh merged. Territorial claims were still so unsettled that the area where Abdon lived is also called "Amalekite hill country" (12:15).

2. Another Abdon is the first-mentioned (1 Chr 8:23) of eleven sons of Shashak in a second genealogy of Benjamin. In contrast to the genealogy in the preceding chapter (1 Chr 7:6–12), chapter 8 is organized to show distribution of Benjaminite families, at some time not specified, outside as well as within the "Deuteronomic" description of Benjamin's territory (Josh 18:11–28; Myers *1 Chronicles* AB, 53). Seemingly contradictory, or inconsistent, genealogies may coexist because they have different functions (Wilson 1977:203).

3. Another Abdon is the firstborn of Jeiel's 9 sons in a list of Saul's ancestors which is recorded twice (1 Chr 8:30 and 9:36).

4. Abdon son of Micah (2 Chr 34:20) is a member of the board of inquiry sent by King Josiah to the prophetess Huldah, for authentication of the rediscovered "book of the law." In the parallel account, however, the name is ACHBOR (2 Kgs 22:14).

Bibliography

Mullen, E. T. Jr. 1982. The "Minor Judges." *CBQ* 44: 185–201.

Wilson, R. R. 1977. *Genealogy and History in the Biblical World.* New Haven.

ROBERT G. BOLING

ABDON (PLACE) [Heb *ʿabdôn*]. Var. EBRON. Located in the tribe of Asher, Abdon is mentioned three times in the OT, once in the territorial allotment to Asher in Josh 19:28 (MT *ʿebrōn;* RSV Ebron) and twice in the Levitical City lists, Josh 21:30 and 1 Chr 6:59—Eng 6:74. The biblical site has been identified with Khirbet ʿAbda (M.R. 165272), a site located 6 km E of the coastal city, Tell ʾAchzib. (See Boling and Wright *Joshua* AB; Noth *Joshua* HAT; Peterson 1977: 29–39.)

Khirbet ʿAbda is situated in the coastal plain of Acco and on the important Wadi el-Qarn. Tell ʾAchzib is located at the W end of the wadi, and Khirbet ʿAbda is situated where the wadi emerges from the Galilean hills. The importance of this site should not be minimized since it appears to have dominated an important trade route from Phoenicia to the Galilee region. The remains lie on a fairly large natural hill, and so the tell itself is actually smaller than at first appears. The surrounding countryside is lush, with the coastal plain able to support much agricultural activity. There is an ample water supply at the site.

Since the mid-18th century many geographers have visited the site, identifying it with different degrees of probability. They include Guérin (1868: 2:67), Kitchener (1881: 170), Garstang (1931: 98), Saarisalo (1929: 39–40), a survey team from the Palestine Department of Antiquities, and most recently the Levitical City survey team. From the surface surveys conducted at Khirbet ʿAbda, there is indication of occupation in the LB Age, Iron I, Iron II, Roman, Byzantine, and Arabic periods.

Bibliography

Albright, W. F. 1921–23. Contributions to the Historical Geography of Palestine. AASOR 2–3.

Abel, F. M. 1938. *Géographie de la Palestine.* Vol. 2. Paris.

Conder, C. R., and Kitchener, H. H. 1881. *The Survey of Western Palestine.* Vol. 1. London.

Garstang, J. 1931. *Joshua, Judges.* London.

Guérin, M. V. 1868. *Description géographique, historique et archéologique de la Palestine.* Vol. 2. Paris.

Peterson, J. L. 1977. *A Topographical Surface Survey of the Levitical "Cities" of Joshua 21 and I Chronicles 6: Studies on the Levites in Israelite Life and Religion.* Diss. Seabury-Western Theological Seminary.

Saarisalo, A. 1929. Topographical Research in Galilee. *JPOS* 9: 37–40.

JOHN L. PETERSON

ABEDNEGO (PERSON) [Heb *ʿăbēd nĕgô*]. See SHADRACH, MESHACH, ABEDNEGO.

ABEL (PERSON) [Heb *hebel*]. Second son of Adam and Eve (Gen 4:2). Abel was a herdsman who gave as a sacrifice to the Lord the firstborn of his flock and their fat portions. Yahweh's acceptance of this sacrifice and the rejection of the gift of Abel's brother, Cain, set the latter at enmity with him, prompting Cain to murder Abel in a field (Gen 4:8). The subsequent birth of Seth to Adam and Eve is understood by Eve as a replacement for Abel (Gen 4:25). In the gospels, Jesus assigns the guilt of all righteous blood—from that of Abel to that of Zechariah—to the Pharisees of his generation (Matt 23:35; Luke 11:51). The writer of Hebrews notes that by faith Abel brought a more acceptable sacrifice than his brother, Cain (Heb 11:4). The next chapter of Hebrews argues for the superiority of the blood of Jesus to that of Abel (Heb 12:24). Three issues surround the figure of Abel in the Bible: the question as to why God looked with favor on the offering of Abel; the meaning of the phrase "the blood of Abel" as it is used in the NT; and the meaning of the name "Abel" and its usage in the story of Genesis.

The biblical text gives no explicit reason for God's preference for Abel's offering. This has given rise to speculation. Even the writer of Hebrews does little more than observe the offering as characteristic of faith. Explanations which focus on the difference in the type of offering of Cain and Abel (Gunkel *Genesis* HKAT, 37; Skinner *Genesis* ICC, 105) or on the difference in their disposition, like those which emphasize the inscrutable choice of God (von Rad *Genesis* OTL, 104; Westermann *Genesis 1–11* BKAT, 403–4), rely upon suppositions not explicit within the text. Nor is there any support for a rivalry between farmers and herdsmen (as disputed by Sarna 1970: 28). Note that *minḥāh,* "offering," can refer to a grain offering as well as to a meat offering. The text makes a distinction between Abel's offering of the "first" and Cain's offering of "some" (Cassuto 1961: 206–7; Sarna 1970: 29; Waltke 1986; Wenham *Genesis 1–15* WBC, 103–4). In offering the firstborn, Abel's act parallels that of Israelite sacrifices in which the firstborn represents both that which belongs to God as well as the entirety of the flock. By giving the firstborn and the best of the animal (i.e., the fat), Abel would be understood as having given everything to God.

Jesus' observation on the blood of Abel refers to the murder of Abel, which is interpreted as similar to that of a "prophet"; and to that of a martyr, apparently due to its association with the worship of God (Hill, *Matthew* NCBC, 315; Marshall, *Luke* NIGTC, 506; Légasse 1982; Fitzmyer, *Luke 20–24* AB, 946, 951).

The focus of Heb 11:4 is on the faith of Abel. He represents the first example of the righteous who are put to death for their faithfulness. In Heb 12:24 Abel's blood represents the murder of an innocent victim. It cries out for vengeance (Gen 4:10). The blood of Jesus could also represent the murder of an innocent victim. However, instead of a cry for vengeance, the blood of Jesus provides mercy before God (Le Déaut 1961:30–36; Moffatt, *Hebrews* ICC, 163–65, 218–19; Hughes 1977:453–57, 551–52).

Attempts to trace the meaning of the name "Abel" to the Akkadian *aplu,* "heir" (*IDB* 1: 4) or the Sumerian synonym, *ibila* (Landersdorfer 1916: 67–68), seem to be speculative. This is true despite the occurrence of these elements in Mesopotamian personal names. Nor is a relationship with the names Jabal and Jubal at the end of chapter 4 clear from the text (contra Skinner, *Genesis* ICC, 103). A simpler origin for the name can be found in the Hebrew root *hbl,* those meaning, "breath," reflects the more basic idea of that which is transitory (Cassuto 1961:202; von Rad, *Genesis* OTL, 104; Westermann, *Genesis 1–11* BKAT, 398; *TWAT* 2:337–38; Wenham, *Genesis 1–15* WBC, 102). In the narrative of Genesis 4, Abel represents a figure whose life is cut short before its full time is accomplished. Although one may argue that Abel's name was intended to signify the general condition of humanity as subject to death, it is better to see the name as an anticipation of Abel's premature death.

Bibliography

Cassuto, U. 1961. *A Commentary on the Book of Genesis.* Pt. 1, *From Adam to Noah.* Trans. I. Abrahams. Jerusalem.

Hughes, P. E. 1977. *A Commentary to the Epistle to the Hebrews.* Grand Rapids.

Landersdorfer, S. 1916. *Sumerisches Sprachgut im alten Testament.* Leipzig.

Légasse, S. 1982. L'oracle contre "cette génération" (Mt 23,34–36 par Lc 1,49–51) et la polémique judéo-chrétienne dans la source des logia. Pp. 237–256 in *Logia. Les Paroles de Jésus—The Sayings of Jesus,* ed. J. Delobel.

Le Déaut, R. 1961. Traditions targumiques dans le corpus Paluinien? (Hebr 11,4 et 12,24; Gal 4, 29–30; II Cor. 3, 16). *Bib* 42: 28–48.

Offord, J. 1916. Archaeological Notes on Jewish Antiquities. *PEFQS* 138–48.

Sarna, N. 1970. *Understanding Genesis.* Heritage of Biblical Israel 1. New York.

Waltke, B. K. 1986. Cain and His Offering. *WTJ* 48: 363–72.

RICHARD S. HESS

ABEL-BETH-MAACAH

ABEL-BETH-MAACAH (PLACE) [Heb *ʾābēl bêt-maʿăkâ*]. Var. ABEL OF BETH-MAACAH. A town in the N part of Israel conquered by Ben-hadad at the beginning of the 9th century B.C. (1 Kgs 15:20) and then by Tiglath-pileser III in 734 B.C. (2 Kgs 15:29). Its identification with *ʾbw3m* in the Execration texts (E47) (Alt 1941: 33) is doubtful, but it can be identified with *ibr* no. 92 in the list of Thutmoses III (*LBHG,* 150) and thus must have been one of the Canaanite centers in the country. Its role during the revolt of Sheba (2 Sam 20:14–18) may indicate both a certain independence during the reign of David and the continuation of the Canaanite population. According to the proverb in 2 Sam 20:18, Beth-Maacah must have been famous for its council. The city has been identified with Tell Abel el-Qamḥ (M.R. 204296), 7 km WNW of Dan.

Bibliography

Alt, A. 1941. Herren und Herrensitze Palästinas im Anfang des zweiten Jahrtansends v. Chr. *ZDPV* 64: 21–39.

VOLKMAR FRITZ

ABEL-KERAMIM

ABEL-KERAMIM (PLACE) [Heb *ʾābēl kĕrāmîm*]. A town on the border of the Ammonites (Judg 11:33), probably identical with *Abila* in Eusebius' *Onomast.* (32, 14–16 Klostermann). According to Eusebius, the distance from *Abila* to Philadelphia/Rabbath Ammon/Amman is 6 roman leagues. Based on this reference, suggestions for the location of Abel-Keramim form a circle around Amman: Nāʿūr (M.R. 228142; *GP* 2: 233f), Khirbet es-Suq (*KISchr* I: 159, n. 3), and Kōm Yājūz (M.R. 237160; Mittmann 1969: 75). These identifications were all ruled out by Redford (1982a; 1982b), who identified Abel-Keramim with the *krmm* of Thutmosis' III list of Asiatic toponyms (see *ANET,* 242). However, Redford's own identification of Abel-Keramim at Tell el-ʿUmeiri (M.R. 234142) is open to criticism, since excavations there did not corroborate the LB occupation assumed by Redford on the basis of his survey. See UMEIRI, TELL EL-. Knauf (1984) adduced evidence from the Islamic conquest narratives, and proposed identifying Abel-Keramim with Saḥāb. According to early Islamic tradition, in A.D. 634 a battle was fought between "Ābil, Zīzaʾ, and Qasṭal" (cf. Donner 1981: 113f). The plain N of Zīzaʾ, NE of Qasṭal, and S of the Ammonite hill country, now transversed by the Hijaz railway and the location of Amman's international airport, would indeed have formed a splendid battleground for cavalry. To the N, this plain is dominated by Saḥāb. Sahab was a walled city in the 15th century B.C., and extensively occupied during the Iron Age. See SAHAB. Its vicinity was densely occupied by hamlets and farmsteads in the Late Byzantine and Umayyad periods (Gustavson-Gaube and Ibrahim 1986).

Abel-Keramim can be translated "pasture of vineyards," or since *Karamīm/Karamen is previously attested as this place's name, "the pasture of the vineyard town." Place names containing the *abel* element have a high frequency in the OT and in the present toponymy of S Syria, Jordan, and Palestine. These names seem to have originated among the nonurban population of this area in the course of the LB and Early Iron Age transition. These names may indicate the sociopolitical change which took place in this period, i.e. the demise of the city-states and the formation of the Aramaean, Israelite, and Ammonite tribal states.

Bibliography

Donner, F. M. 1981. *The Early Islamic Conquests.* Princeton.

Gustavson-Gaube, C., and Ibrahim, M. 1986. Sahab Survey, 1984. *AFO* 33: 283–86.

Knauf, E. A. 1984. Abel Keramim. *ZDPV* 100: 119–121.

Mittmann, S. 1969. Aroer, Minnith und Abel Keramim (Jdc. 11, 33). *ZDPV* 85: 63–75.

Redford, D. 1982a. Contact between Egypt and Jordan in the New Kingdom: Some Comments on Sources. Pp. 115–19 in *Studies in the History and Archaeology of Jordan I,* ed. A. Hadidi. Amman.

———. 1982b. A Bronze Age Itinerary in Transjordan (Nos. 89–101 of Thutmose III's List of Asiatic Toponyms). *JSSEA* 12: 55–74.

Ernst Axel Knauf

ABEL-MEHOLAH (PLACE) [Heb. *ʾābēl mĕḥôlâ*]. A town located in the western Jordan ghor (Judg 7:22; 1 Kgs 4:12). It was the hometown of the prophet Elisha, son of Shaphat (1 Kgs 19:16), and probably also of Adriel ben Barzillai the Meholathite, the son-in-law of Saul, the first King of Israel (1 Sam 18:19; 2 Sam 21:8). The name of the settlement means "meadow of dancing." It is one of a group of compound names formed with *ʾābēl,* "meadow, well-watered land," as a descriptive first element. Other examples include Abel-maim, Abel-shittim, Abel-keramim, Abel-mizraim, and Abel-beth-maacah. While the present spelling and vocalization of the second element means "dancing," it is possible that before the medial *waw* was added as a vowel marker, the nonvocalized consonantal text *mḥlh* designated the Manassite clan of Mahlah (Num 26:33; 27:1; 36:11; Josh 17:3; 1 Chr 7:18), indicating that the meadow where the town was founded belonged to the Mahlah clan.

The location of the ancient settlement is disputed. 20th-century proposals have included two sites on the eastern side of the Jordan: Tell Maqlub (M.R. 214201) inland on the north bank of the Wadi el-Yabis (Glueck 1945–48: 215–23) and Tell el-Meqbereh/Tell Abu Kharaz, in the eastern ghor at the mouth of the Wadi el-Yabis (Alt 1928:44–46; Noth 1959: 52–60); and four sites in the western Jordan ghor; Ras Umm el-Harrube (M.R. 196175) in the hills above the north bank of the Wadi Faria (Burney 1914: 94–96); Tell Abu Sifri (S)/Khirbet Tell el-Hilu, which lies at the junction of Wadi el-Helwah and Wadi el-Malih north of the Wadi Faria (Albright 1925: 18; Alt 1928:45; *GP,* 234; Simons 1959: 294; *LOB,* 284, n. 222); Tell el-Hamme, which lies at the mouth of the Wadi Losm el-hamme, about 5.25 km north of Tell Abu Sifri (Hölscher 1910: 17–18); and Tell Abu Sus, which lies about 15 km south of Beth Sheʾan, at the southern edge of the Beth Sheʾan Valley (Naor 1947:90–93; Zobel 1966: 97–101; Mittmann 1970: 128; Rosel 1976: 15; Zori 1977: 38–9; *LOB* 313; *HGB,* 63). The town's location on the western side of the Jordan River is clearly indicated by the description of the fifth Solomonic district in 1 Kgs 4:12. The district included the lowland areas forming an arc around the Gilboa spur, from Taanach in the Esdraelon Plain, westward, through the Beth Sheʾan Valley, swinging south to include the western bank of the ghor to the southern boundary of Abel-Meholah, opposite Jokmeam.

A location in the western ghor is also indicated by the description of the flight of the Midianites from the Jezreel Valley in Judg 7:22–8:5. Attempting to return to their home in the east, which required the crossing of the Jordan (Judg 6:33), they are said to have moved southward from the Valley, to Beth-Shittah, as far as the riverbank of Abel-Meholah, near or opposite Tabbath. Gideon is to have sent mesengers to the inhabitants of the hill country of Ephraim to seize the waters as far as Beth-barah and also the Jordan against the retreating Midianites, to prevent them from fording the Jordan and escaping into Gilead or down the eastern ghor to the arabah region south of the Dead Sea. Their failure to act allowed the Midianites to cross the Jordan, forcing Gideon to cross in pursuit (Judg 8:1–5). Regardless of one's stance as to the historical reliability and date of the Gideon narrative (Payne 1983: 163–72), one can presume that the author of the story would have been familiar with the geography and the ancient road systems in the regions depicted in the story, which would not have changed significantly over time. The information provided requires a location for Abel-Meholah in the western ghor near the Jordan River, north of Beth-barah and near or opposite Tabbath, and north of the latitude of Succoth on the eastern bank of the Jordan, which was the first settlement Gideon reached after crossing the river. Eusebius places Abel-Meholah in the western ghor, identifying it with the Roman settlement known as Bethmaela ten Roman miles south of Scytholpolis (Beth Sheʾan). In light of the available information, Tell el-Meqbereh/Tell Abu Kharaz, Tell Maqlub, and Ras Umm el-Harrube can be eliminated from potential candidacy.

Archaelogical surveys at Tell Abu Sifri (S)/Khirbet Tell el-Hilu have indicated occupation during the EB I, MB I, IIB, LB, Iron I-II, Pers, Hell, Rom, Byz, Medieval, and Ottoman periods (Zertal 1986: 141; cf. Gophna and Porat 1972: 218; Mittmann 1970: 336), while similar surveys at Tell el-Hamme have uncovered evidence of occupation during EB I, MB I, IIB, LB, Iron I-II, Pers, Hell, Byz, Medieval, and Ottoman periods (Gophna and Porat 1972: 214; Mittmann 1970: 338; cf. Zori 1977: 37). Excavations were begun at Tell el-Hamme in 1988. A preliminary survey at Tell Abu Sus yielded diagnostic shards from EB I-II, Iron I, Byz, and Arabic periods (Zori 1977: 38–39).

Of the three proposed locations in the western ghor, Tell abu Sifri (S)/Khirbet Tell el-Hilu and Tell el-Hamme would both seem to be located too far inland from the Jordan to have been along the theoretical Midianite retreat path in Judg 7:22. While settlements often controlled outlying fields or territory beyond the settlement proper, the reference to Abel-Meholah's "riverbank" suggests that the town was located close to the Jordan. Tell Abu Sus seems to be the best candidate in light of the description in both Judg 7:22 and 1 Kgs 4:12. In order for the equation with Tell Abu Sus to be upheld, future survey work or excavations would need to confirm occupation during the Roman period, to corroborate Eusebius testimony, and probably also Iron II occupation, the period when the Gideon story may first have become part of the Deuteronomistic History.

Bibliography

Albright, W. F. 1925. Bronze Age Mounds of Northern Palestine and the Hauran. *BASOR* 19: 5–19.

Alt, A. 1928. Das Institut im Jahre 1927. Die Reise. *PJ* 24: 30–73.

Burney, C. F. 1914. The Topography of Gideon's Rout of the Midianites. *BZAW* 87–99.

Glueck, N. 1945–49. Explorations in Eastern Palestine, IV. *AASOR* 25–28.

Gophna, Y., and Porat, R. 1972. The Land of Ephraim and Manasseh. Pp. 196–243 in *Judaea Samaria and the Golan,* ed. M. Kochavi. Jerusalem.

Hölscher, G. 1910. Bemerkungen zur Topographie Pälastinas 2. *ZDPV* 33: 16–25.

Mittmann, S. 1970. *Beiträge zur Siedlungs- und Territorialgeschichte des nördlichen Ostjordanlandes.* Wiesbaden.

Naor, M. 1947. Jabesh-Gilead, Abel Meholah, and Zaretan. *BJPES* 13: 89–99 (in Hebrew).

Noth, M. 1959. Gilead und Gad. *ZDPV* 75: 14–73.

Payne, E. 1983. The Midianite Arc in Joshua and Judges. Pp. 163–172 in *Midian, Moab, and Edom,* ed. J. Sawyer and D. Clines. JSOTSup 24. Sheffield.

Rosel, H. 1975. Studien zur Topographie der Kriege in den Büchern Josua und Richter. *ZDPV* 92: 10–46.

Simons, J. 1959. *Geographical and Topographical Texts of the Old Testament.* Studia Francisci Scholten Memoriae Dicata 2. Leiden.

Zertal, A. 1986. The Israelite Settlement in the Hill-Country of Manasseh. Diss. Tel Aviv University (Hebrew).

Zobel, H. J. 1966. Abel-Mehola. *ZDPV* 82: 83–108.

Zori, N. 1977. *The Land of Issachar: Archaeological Survey.* Jerusalem.

DIANA V. EDELMAN

ABGAR, EPISTLE OF CHRIST TO. This correspondence consists of two letters, one from Abgar V Ukkama "the Black," toparch of Edessa to Jesus of Nazareth, and Jesus' reply. Both are pseudepigraphic. The earliest surviving versions of this apocryphal epistle, which appear in Eusebius' *Hist. Eccl.* 1.13.6–10 (ca. A.D. 303) may be summarized as follows: Addressing Jesus as "good Savior," Abgar professes admiration for his cures accomplished "without medicines or herbs" and asserts that he must be "God, and came down from heaven to do these things, or . . . a Son of God." He invites Jesus to come to Edessa, on the one hand, to heal him of an illness [*pathos*] and, on the other, to take refuge since "the Jews are mocking you and wish to ill-treat you." In response, Jesus praises the ruler for his belief "not having seen me" (cf. John 20:29). Yet he replies that he cannot come since he "must first complete here all for which I was sent, and after thus completing it be taken up to him who sent me" (cf. John 16:5; 17:4). He promises to send one of his disciples to cure Abgar and to "give life to you and all those with you."

Eusebius claimed to have translated the letters from Syriac documents in the archives of Edessa (*Hist. Eccl.* 1.13.5), and he concluded, again claiming to follow his Syriac source, with the story of the fulfillment after Pentecost of Jesus' promises to Abgar, when the apostle Thomas sent Thaddeus (= Syriac "Addai"), one of the seventy, to Edessa (*Hist. Eccl.* 1.13.11–22). The letters appear in their earliest Syriac versions at the beginning of the *Doctrine of Addai* ca. A.D. 400 (Howard 1981: 6–8 = *Doc.Add.*). Here Jesus' reply is spoken to Hanan, Abgar's messenger and archivist, who puts it into writing. The wording of the letters themselves in Syriac is almost identical to Eusebius' Greek version. Here, however, and in later references two new features appear: (1) Jesus' letter adds a blessing or promise of protection for the city of Edessa (*Doc.Add.* 8:19–20; cf. CChr Ser. Latina 175: 27–105) and (2) Hanan also paints a portrait of Jesus and brings it back to Abgar with the letter from Jesus (*Doc.Add.* 8:20–9:4; Evagrius *h.e.* 4.27). Apotropaic powers were subsequently ascribed to copies of the letter as well as to the painting, which came to be known as an *acheiropoietos* icon (Dobschütz 1899: 102–96; Segal 1970: 75; Runciman 1931: 245–51). Despite the fact that Jesus' letter to Abgar was included in the Gelasian decretals' list of apocrypha (A.D. 494), the story of King Abgar and Jesus retained its popularity into the medieval period (Segal 1970: 75). Early scholarly acceptance of the letters as genuine has given way to various degrees of skepticism. Following Gutschmid (1887), Burkitt (1904: 10–38) argued that the ruler in question was Abgar IX (d. ca. A.D. 216) rather than Abgar V (d. A.D. 50) since he is mentioned in the Bardaisanite *Book of the Laws of the Countries* (= *BLC, see* BARDAISAN OF EDESSA) as having forbidden emasculation in honor of Atargatis when he "came to the faith" (*BLC* 607). Burkitt held further that, although the letters were pseudepigraphic, together with the rest of the *Doctrine of Addai* they shed light on Jewish-Christian evangelization of Edessa, which began in the latter half of the 2d century. In 1934 Bauer denied any historical basis for the Abgar legend (Bauer 1971:2–12). Literary models for the legend have been seen in Josephus' account of the conversion of the Jewish rulers of Adiabene (Marquart 1903; Segal 1970: 67–69; cf. Murray 1975: 8–9) or in Manichaean literature (Drijvers 1980).

Bibliography

Bauer, W. 1963. The Abgar Legend. Pp. 437–44 in *New Testament Apocrypha,* by E. Hennecke, ed. W. Schneemelcher. Vol. 1. Philadelphia.

———. 1971. *Orthodoxy and Heresy in the Earliest Christianity.* Philadelphia.

Burkitt, F. C. 1904. *Early Eastern Christianity.* London.

Devos, P. 1967. Égérie à Édesse. S. Thomas L'Apôtre: Le Roi Abgar. *AnBoll* 85: 381–400.

Dodschütz, E. von 1899. *Christusbilder; Untersuchungen zur christlichen legende.* TU 18.1–2.

———. 1900. Der briefwechsel zwischen Abgar und Jesus. *ZWT* 43: 422–86.

Drijvers, H. J. W. 1980. Addai und Mani. Christentum und Manichäismus im dritten Jahrhundert in Syrien. OCA 221: 171–85.

Gutschmid, A. von 1887. *Untersuchungen über die Geschichte des königreiches Osroëne.* Mémoires de l'Académie impériale des Sciences de S. Pétersbourg. Sér. 7, 35.1.

Howard, G. 1981. *Labubna bar Sennak. The Teaching of Addai.* SBLTT 16. Ann Arbor. (= *Doc.Add.*)

Marquart, J. 1903. *Osteuropäische und Ostasiatische Streifzüge ethnologische und historisch-topographische Studien zur geschichte des 9. und 10. jahrhunderts (ca. 840–940).* Leipzig.

Phillips, G. 1876. *The doctrine of Addai the Apostle, Now First Edited in a Complete Form in the Original Syriac.* London.

Runciman, S. 1931. Some Remarks on the Image of Edessa. *Cambridge Historical Journal* 3: 238–52.
Segal, J. B. 1970. *Edessa 'The Blessed City.'* Oxford.
Tixeront, L.-J. 1888. *Les origines de l'église d'Édesse et la légende d'Abgar. Étude critique suivie de deux textes orientaux inédits.* Paris.

KATHLEEN E. MCVEY

ABI (PERSON) [Heb *ʾăbî*]. Var. ABIJAH. Wife of Ahaz, king of Judah, and mother of Hezekiah (2 Kgs 18:2 = 2 Chr 29:1). Abi's name appears in the regnal formula of her son, Hezekiah. She is the daughter of Zechariah, whose place of origin is unknown. In the Chronicler's parallel account she is called Abijah [Heb *ʾăbîyâ*]. See QUEEN.

LINDA S. SCHEARING

ABI-ALBON (PERSON) [Heb *ʾăbî-ʿalbôn*]. An Arbathite listed in a roster of King David's thirty chief warriors (2 Sam 23:31). His native town is probably Beth-arabah, possibly to be identified with *el-Gharabeh,* southeast of Jericho (cf. Jos 18:18, 22). The confusion associated with this name is signaled by the substitution of the name "Abiel" in the 1 Chr 11:32 parallel list. Several significant opinions about the name have been offered. Zadok (1979: 105) believes that Heb *ʾăbî-ʿalbôn* may be an altered form of an unattested *ʾabi-baʿlon,* and that the MT tendency to change pagan theophoric elements (such as *baʿlon*) to *ʾēl* accounts for the variant "Abiel" in 1 Chr 11:32. Mazar (1986: 94) holds that the original text read "Abibaal son of the Arbathite"; the replacement of the *baʿal* element with *ʾēl* rendered the Abiel associated with "the Arbathite" (preserved in 1 Chr 11:32), while the dropping of the *b* consonant in *bʿl* and fusion with the following word "son of" (Heb *bn*) rendered *ʾbyʿlbn* Abi-albon (2 Sam 23:31). McCarter (*2 Samuel* AB, 492) suggests that an even more complex textual history lies behind the MT reference to Abi-Albon. He believes that 2 Sam 23:31 originally read "Abial the Beth-arabathite" (Heb *ʾbyʿl bt hʿrbty*), but that the common prefix for town names, *bêt,* had been misread *bat,* "daughter of," and was "corrected" to *ben,* "son of." This "corrected" version is reflected in the LXX: *abiēl huios tou Arabōthitou,* "Abiel son of the Arabathite." Finally, a fusion of the name "Abial" with the word "son of" resulted in the name *ʾbyʿlbn,* vocalized Abi-Albon.

Bibliography

Mazar, B. 1986. *The Early Biblical Period, Historical Studies.* Ed. S. Aḥituv, and B. Levine. Jerusalem.
Zadok, R. 1979. *The Jews in Babylonia During the Chaldean and Achaemenian Periods, according to the Babylonian Sources.* Studies in the History of the Jewish People and the Land of Israel Monograph Series 3. Haifa.

MARK J. FRETZ

ABIASAPH (PERSON) [Heb *ʾăbîʾāsāp*]. One of three sons of Korah (Exod 6:24), who led an uprising against Moses and Aaron in the wilderness (Numbers 16). Abiasaph is listed as the head of a Korahite clan in a genealogy relating Aaron and Moses to the Levitical order (Exod 6:14–25; cf. Num 26:5–11).

MARK J. FRETZ

ABIATHAR (PERSON) [Heb *ʾebyātār*]. The son of Ahimelech and priest of David (1 Sam 22:20–23). Abiathar fled to David with an ephod after the massacre of the priests of Nob at the hands of Doeg the Edomite. Saul had ordered the slaughter after hearing that Ahimelech had harbored David, supplied him with bread and a sword, and also inquired of God on his behalf. The text is not consistent concerning the precise location of Abiathar's delivery of the ephod to David. Earlier David is reported to have been in the forest of Hereth in Judah (1 Sam 22:5), yet we are later informed that Abiathar had fled to David at Keilah (1 Sam 23:6). A common solution, based on the LXX, is to understand this verse as referring to Abiathar's earlier flight and that he later accompanied David to Keilah. There is some confusion concerning the relationship between Abiathar and Ahimelech. In 2 Sam 8:17 the MT reads "Ahimelech the son of Abiathar," which conflicts with 1 Sam 23:26 and 30:7, whereas the Syriac reads "Abiathar son of Ahimelek." The Hebrew of 1 Chr 18:16 points to a similar confusion, but reads "Abimelech son of Abiathar." The LXX, Syr, and Vg suggest "Ahimelech" in line with 2 Sam 8:17. The reference to Abiathar in Mark 2:26 is usually explained as a result of this confusion in 2 Sam 8:17. However, it is difficult to see how Mark could have made such an error when the reference was to the incident with David at Nob where he accepted the consecrated bread from Ahimelech. The parallel passages in Matt 12:1–8 and Luke 6:1–5 both omit any reference to Abiathar.

The episode represents an important transition in the narrative of Saul's decline and David's rise since Saul has become increasingly isolated, culminating in his complete estrangement from Yahweh. The murder of the priests of Nob and the transfer of the ephod to David by Abiathar symbolizes Yahweh's complete withdrawal from Saul and his continuing presence with David. Abiathar provides an important medium of communication between Yahweh and David by consulting the ephod on David's behalf (1 Sam 23:9–12). McCarter (*1 Samuel* AB, 366) understands the episode as depicting David as the protector and preserver of the priesthood of Nob, whereas Saul is depicted as its destroyer. Gunn (1980: 88) understands the episode in literary terms; Abiathar provides David with access to the ephod and thus access to the divine realm of foreknowledge.

Those who treat the narratives in historical terms also see the relationship between David and Abiathar as particularly significant. During the rebellion of Absalom, Abiathar is willing to accompany David in his flight from Jerusalem (2 Sam 15:24–36). He and Zadok are said to be responsible for the ark of the covenant of God. Zadok and Abiathar are told by David to return to Jerusalem (15:27–28). They later (17:15–22) inform David, through their sons, of Hushai's warning not to wait at the fords of the wilderness. Bright (*BHI,* 200–1) sees David's strategy here as a brilliant move to combine Abiathar, as the representative of tribal Israel, with Zadok, as the representative of the indigenous Jerusalemite priesthood. Abiathar's support for Adonijah and Zadok's support for Solomon in the struggle for succession to the throne of David is often understood in similar terms. The representatives of tribal Israel were ousted in a purge at the beginning of Solomon's reign with Abiathar being exiled to Anathoth. Solomon spared him only because of his service to David (1 Kgs 2:26). Zadok's appointment in his place (1 Kgs 2:35) is understood in terms of the victory of urban Canaanite religious specialists. However, in the subsequent list of Solomon's officers, Abiathar is still recorded as priest alongside Zadok (1 Kgs 4:4); presumably, this refers to the beginning of the reign. The exile of Abiathar is presented in the Deuteronomistic History as the fulfillment of the word of Yahweh against Eli (1 Sam 2:30–36). This forms part of the common prophecy-fulfillment scheme in Deuteronomistic History. The implicit assumption that Abiathar was a descendant of Eli presumably rests upon 1 Sam 14:3.

Bibliography

Gunn, D. 1980. *The Fate of King Saul.* Sheffield.

KEITH W. WHITELAM

ABIB [Heb *ʾābîb*]. The first month of the Canaanite calendar, roughly corresponding to March–April. See the CALENDARS articles.

ABIB, TEL. See TEL-ABIB (PLACE).

ABIDA (PERSON) [Heb *ʾăbîdāʿ*]. The son of Midian and grandson of Abraham's second wife, Keturah (Gen 25:4 = 1 Chr 1:33). The name "Abida" may be either a patronym or a toponym. Abida is used as a patronym both in the genealogy at the end of the Abraham narrative (Gen 25:1–4), and in the genealogy connecting Adam to Israel/Jacob (1 Chronicles 1). This patronym has traditionally been associated with the Arabian tribe of Ibadidi (*ANET,* 286; Glaser 1890: 259; Musil 1926: 292; Abel *GP,* 287); however, Ephʿal (1982: 89, 217) rejects this identification because it involves two radical a spelling change of the name "Ibadidi." Abida may also be a toponym associated with the modern town named *al-Badʿ* (or *al-Bedʿ;* a shortened form of Heb *ʾăbîdāʿ?*), located 25 km east of the Gulf of ʿAqaba and 120 km south of *al-ʿAqaba* in northwest Arabia, (Winnett 1970: 192; see also von Wissmann PWSup 12: 544 on *al-Badʿ* and *Mughayir Šuʿayb*).

Bibliography

Ephʿal, I. 1982. *The Ancient Arabs.* Jerusalem and Leiden.

Glaser, E. 1890. *Skizze der Geschichte und Geographie Arabiens* Vol. 2. Berlin.

Musil, A. 1926. The Northern Heǵâz. Vol. 1 of *American Geographical Society Oriental Explorations and Studies,* ed. J. K. Wright. New York.

Winnett, F. V. 1970. The Arabian Genealogies in the Book of Genesis. Pp. 171–96 in *Translating and Understanding the Old Testament,* ed. H. T. Frank and W. L. Reed. Nashville.

MARK J. FRETZ

ABIDAN (PERSON) [Heb *ʾăbîdān*]. The son of Gideoni and leader of the Benjaminites (Num 2:22; 10:24) who assisted Moses in taking a census of the Israelites in the wilderness of Sinai (Num 1:1–16). Abidan also contributed offerings on behalf of the Benjaminites on the ninth day of the tabernacle dedication (Num 7:60–65).

MARK J. FRETZ

ABIEL (PERSON) [Heb *ʾăbîʾēl*]. **1.** A Benjaminite, the father of Kish and Ner, and the grandfather of Saul and Abner (1 Sam 9:1; 14:51). The name probably means "my father is [the god] El." Abiel represents the fourth generation in the Saulide genealogy in 1 Sam 9:1. An identification of Abiel with Abijah, the son of Becher in the Chronicler's genealogy of Benjamin (1 Chr 7:8), has been suggested on the presumption that Becher can be equated with the Saulide ancestor Becorath, and that the final divine name elements have been interchanged (Malamat 1968: 171–72, n. 28).

Abiel's absence from the Saulide genealogy in 1 Chr 8:29–32 and 9:39–44 has been explained in different ways. One approach has been to argue that the name was dropped as the ancient records were adjusted to reflect altered rankings within Saul's extended family for possible succession to the Israelite throne (Flanagan 1981:59). A second approach has been to posit that the name is found in the Chronicles lists in the corrupted form Baʿal in 8:30 and 9:36 (Demsky 1971:17). In order for this view to be possible, it would also need to presume the principle espoused in the first approach to explain why Abiel becomes the son or brother of Kish in Chronicles instead of his father, as in Samuel. A third approach would be to suggest that Abiel has been deliberately removed from the genealogies in Chronicles and replaced by Ner as a means of secondarily linking the Saulide genealogy with the postexilic genealogy of Gibeon (1 Chr 9:35–38 = 1 Chr 8:29–32). The occurrence of a Ner in the late Gibeonite list (1 Chr 9:36) seems to have led to the truncation of the early Saulide genealogy and to the substitution of Ner, Saul's uncle, for Abiel, his grandfather. In this way the Ners would appear to be a single individual and the Saulide genealogy could be grafted onto the Gibeonite one (see NER).

2. The Arbathite, named in 1 Chr 11:32 as one of the "mighty men" of David's armies. In a list detailing the same group of individuals in 2 Sam 23:31 he appears as Abialbon, one of the military elite group known as the "Thirty." The variant LXX reading in 2 Sam 23:11, Abiel *son* of the Arbathite, may indicate that the original text of that verse read "Abiel/Abial son of the Arbathite," or "Abiʿal/Abibaʿal the Beth-Arabathite" (Mc Carter *2 Samuel* AB, 492; Mazar 1963: 316 n. 4). The name "Abial" would mean "my (divine) father is ʿAl (= the "High One"), while the name "Abibaal" would mean "my (divine) father is Baal (or 'the Lord')." The gentilic Arbathite indicates the person's town of origin, or clan association (see ARBATHITE).

Abiel's status within David's army is somewhat obscured by his twofold designation as a member of the "Mighty Men" and of "the Thirty." The correct vocalization and identity of the term usually translated "the Thirty," *šlyšm,* is disputed. One group understands it to designate the group of men who served as the third person of the chariot team (i.e., Haupt 1902). A second group suggests that it designated an institution not necessarily limited to thirty members that served either as the king's bodyguard (Elliger 1935: 68) or supreme command (Mazar 1963: 310). According to a third approach, the single form was a title meaning "of the third rank" that designated high-ranking officers (Mastin 1979: 153–54; Naʾaman 1988: 71, 75). Of the three possibilities, the last one requires the least number of textual emendations and provides the most cogent explanation for the required equation of the functions "military elite" *(gibbôrîm)* and "officers" *(šālîšîm)* that are assigned to the same list of individuals in the two texts in 2 Sam 23:8–39 and 1 Chr 11:10–47. The group of officers apparently was headed by the commander of the entire militia, Abishai, and he was followed in rank by "the Three," Josheb-bassebeth, Eleazer, and Shammah, who served as commanders of the three subunits of the professional army. The remaining individuals, including Abiel, then served as commanders over smaller divisions within the three subunits (Naʾaman 1988: 75). See also DAVID'S CHAMPIONS.

Bibliography

Demsky, A. 1971. The Genealogy of Gibeon (I Chronicles 9:35–44): Biblical and Epigraphic Considerations. *BASOR* 202: 16–23.

Elliger, K. 1935. Die dreissig Helden Davids. *PJ* 31: 29–75.

Flanagan, J. 1981. Chiefs in Israel. *JSOT* 20: 47–73.

Haupt, P. 1902. The Phrase *Rkbm ṣmdym* in 2 Kings ix.25. *JBL* 21: 74–78.

Malamat, A. 1968. King Lists of the Old Babylonian Period and Biblical Genealogies. *JAOS* 88: 163–73.

Mastin, B. A. 1971. Was the *šālîš* the Third Man in the Chariot? *VTSup* 30: 125–54.

Mazar, B. 1963. The Military Elite of King David. *VT* 13: 310–20.

Naʾaman, N. 1988. The List of David's Officers. *VT* 38: 71–79.

Diana V. Edelman

ABIEZER (PERSON) [Heb *ʾăbîʿezer*]. ABIEZRITE. Var. IEZER; IEZERITE. The name of two individuals in the Hebrew Bible. Although Abiezer may mean "father of help," or "my father is help," *ʾab* (father) is here a relational noun used as a theophoric (or divine name) element and the subject of a nominal clause: "Ab is help" (*IPN,* 33, 67–75, 154). The use of the relational nouns *ʾab* and *ʾaḥ* (brother) in a theophoric sense, according to Noth, derives from a period in early Semitic tribal history when the tribe maintained a familial identification with the tribal deity. This special relationship to the god of the tribe allowed that god to be designated "father" or "brother." Thus the name "Abiezer" would designate not a single god, universally identified as *ʾab,* but the deity of the respective tribe (cf. Abijah "Yahweh is father"). The NT use of the Aramaic *Abba* for the deity would therefore appear to have its antecedents in ancient Semitic tribal religion.

1. The name of one of the families of Manasseh (Josh 17:2), named for its male progenitor (1 Chr 7:18). This Abiezer was the "son" of Gilead, a descendant of Machir; the reference to Iezer (Heb *ʾiyʿezer*) among the "sons" of Gilead and to the family of the Iezerites in Numbers 26:30 probably applies to the same group. This family received its inheritance west of the Jordan, and the judge and deliverer Gideon belonged to it (Judg 6:11, 34; 8:2).

2. A Benjaminite warrior among David's champions, who was a native of Anathoth (2 Sam 23:27 = 1 Chr 11:28). The same village was home to Abiathar the priest, and his likely descendant, the prophet Jeremiah. This same Abiezer is listed as the officer over David's monthly levies of 24,000 in the ninth month (1 Chr 27:12). The historicity of this second list, however, and its concomitant figures, is doubtful. It is more likely that 1 Chronicles 27 reflects more of an idealized view of David's military organization than a real one. As one of David's champions (Heb *šālišîm;* RSV: The Thirty), Abiezer was more likely a member of an elite corps of fighters loyal only to the king, rather than an officer over his monthly levies. See DAVID'S CHAMPIONS.

D. G. Schley

ABIGAIL (PERSON) [Heb *ʾăbîgayil; ʾăbîgal*]. **1.** Wife, first of Nabal, then of David (1 Samuel 25). She appears as the second wife/mother mentioned in two lists of David's sons born in Hebron (2 Sam 3:2–5 and 1 Chr 3:1–3). The name of her son is problematic, being either Chileab (2 Sam 3:3), Daluiah (LXX—2 Kgdms 3:3), or Daniel (1 Chr 3:1). Abigail first appears in 1 Samuel 25 as the wife of Nabal the Calebite. She is portrayed as the "ideal wife"—both beautiful and intelligent—while her husband is presented as ill behaved and rude. When Nabal refuses to accommodate David's request for food, it is Abigail who, unknown to her husband, hastily amasses the food and delivers it to David. Her speech to David, a masterful example of tact and diplomacy (vv 24–31), succeeds in averting David's wrath at Nabal (vv 32–35). Upon hearing of his wife's generosity, Nabal's heart "died within him" (v 37) and ten days later he was dead. 1 Samuel 25 concludes with David's marriage to both Abigail of Carmel, and to Ahinoam of Jezreel.

Abigail's name appears five times in the OT outside of 1 Samuel 25. Three times it is linked with Ahinoam of Jezreel. Both Abigail and Ahinoam accompany David to Gath (1 Sam 27:3), where they are later captured by an invading group of Amalekites (1 Sam 30:5). After their rescue (1 Sam 30:18), they journey with David to Hebron (2 Sam 2:2) where they bear David children (2 Sam 3:3 = 1 Chr 3:1). Of the five times Abigail's name appears outside of 1 Samuel 25, all except one (1 Chr 3:1) carry with it the epithet "widow of Nabal."

Recent literary approaches to 1 Samuel 25 underscore Abigail's speech and character. J. D. Levenson (1978) argues 1 Samuel 25 is a "narrative analogy" presenting a "proleptic glimpse" of 2 Samuel 11. Unlike Bathsheba, Abigail is the "ideal woman" whose "rhetorical genius" prevents David from killing her husband (Levenson 1978: 11–28). D. Gunn (1980: 98–100), while sharing Levenson's appreciation for the speech's artistry, rejects (1980: 154, n. 13) his conclusion that the episode is a "moral allegory." Abigail's speech reveals her to be "shrewd" rather than good, while Nabal is "unwise" rather than evil. While both Levenson and Gunn analyze Abigail's speech, A. Berlin focuses on Abigail's characterization. Abigail is an exaggerated stereotype—the model wife. David's treatment of her (as well as of Michal, Abishag, and Bathsheba) represents an "indirect presentation" of David. Moreover, each "private" response to the women in his life corresponds to a phase of David's "public" life. Thus, David's "eager but gentlemanly response" to Abigail mirrors his "self assurance as a popular leader" (Berlin 1983: 30–33).

Behind the literary presentation of Abigail lies the sociopolitical realities of her marriage to David. Nabal was a wealthy and probably influential Calebite. David's marriage to Nabal's widow was useful in bringing David much needed support from the south. This support might have been instrumental in David's being crowned king at Hebron—an area associated with the figure of Caleb in the text (Levenson 1978: 24–28).

2. Sister of David (1 Chr 2:16) and Zeruiah (2 Sam 17:25, 1 Chr 2:16); mother of Amasa (2 Sam 17:25, 1 Chr 2:17). The name of Abigail's father is unclear. 1 Chr 2:13–16 identifies Jesse as the father of Abigail, while 2 Sam 17:25 says she was the "daughter of NAHASH." Most critics prefer the reading in 1 Chronicles 2, explaining the discrepancy by either: (1) understanding "Nahash" as the mother of Abigail rather than the father; (2) declaring the reading in 2 Sam 17:25 corrupt, an intrusion from v 27; or (3) positing an earlier husband (Nahash) of Jesse's wife, who fathered Abigail and Zeruiah.

The name of Abigail's husband is also problematic. The MT of 2 Sam 17:25 gives the name of Amasa's father as "ITHRA the Israelite," while 1 Chr 2:17 says it was "JETHER the Ishmaelite." The issue is further complicated by the variant reading in the LXX^{M} which identifies him as a "Jezreelite."

J. D. Levenson and B. Halpern (1980) argue that Ithra/Jethro was the real name of Abigail's husband ("Nabal") mentioned in 1 Samuel 25. They find it highly unlikely that the only two Abigails in the OT would be: (1) contemporaries, (2) sister-in-laws, and (3) married to men from the same geographical area (assuming Ithra/Jethro/Nabal to be from Jezreel and Jezreel to refer to the Judean town near Hebron). They therefore conclude there was only one Abigail—David's sister—who later became David's wife. Later tradition suppressed the memory of this incestuous union.

Bibliography

Berlin, A. 1983. *Poetics and Interpretation of Biblical Narrative.* Bible and Literature Series 9. Sheffield.

Fokkelman, J. P. 1986. *Narrative Art and Poetry in the Books of Samuel.* Vol. 2 of *The Crossing Fates (I Sam. 13–21 & II Sam. 1).*

Gunn, D. M. 1980. *The Fate of King Saul.* JSOTSup 14. Sheffield.

Levenson, J. D. 1978. I Samuel 25 as Literature and History. *CBQ* 40: 11–28.

Levenson, J. D., and Halpern, B. 1980. The Political Import of David's Marriages. *JBL* 99: 507–18.

LINDA S. SCHEARING

ABIHAIL (PERSON) [Heb *ʾăbîḥāyil*]. **1.** Father of Zuriel; descendant of Merari, Levi's youngest son (Num 3:35). Abihail's name appears in the epithet of his son found in the third and last division of the census list in Num 3:14–39. The census, ordered by Moses, involved the three Levitical branches of Gershon, Kohath, and Merari. Abihail's son was leader of the Merarite branch during their journey in the wilderness.

2. Wife of Abishur, of the House of Judah; mother of Ahban and Molid (1 Chr 2:29). Her name appears in a genealogy of Jerahmeel, the great-grandson of Judah and Tamar.

3. A Gadite (1 Chr 5:14). Abihail is mentioned in the Gadite genealogy found in 1 Chr 5:11–17.

4. Mother of Mahalath; wife of Jerimoth; and daughter of Eliab (2 Chr 11:18). Abihail's name occurs in a genealogical note concerning Rehoboam's wives. The reading of the verse, however, is problematic:

KJV: And Rehoboam took him Mahalath the daughter of Jerimoth the son of David to wife, *and Abihail* the daughter of Eliab the son of Jesse;

RSV: Rehoboam took as wife Mahalath the daughter of Jerimoth the son of David, *and of Abihail* . . .

Some translators (i.e. KJV) conclude v 18 mentions two wives (Mahalath and Abihail) while others (i.e. RSV) assume only one (Mahalath). Although the Hebrew of v 18 is unclear, the context is helpful in determining its meaning. Since the following verses (vv 19–20) refer to v 18 using only the feminine singular, it can be concluded that only one wife, Mahalath, is mentioned. Thus, the reading which understands Abihail as Mahalath's mother (RSV), is to be preferred.

Abihail's daughter, Mahalath, is one of eighteen wives credited to Rehoboam, king of Judah. The marriages of both mother and daughter are particularly interesting. Abihail's husband (Jerimoth) and father (Eliab) were both sons of David. Her daughter married David's grandson (Rehoboam). Thus both Abihail and Mahalath married their cousins. Their marriages reflect a period of intermarriage within the Davidic house not witnessed elsewhere in the text.

5. Father of Queen Esther; uncle of Mordecai (Esth 2:15; 9:29; cf. also 2:7). His name appears twice in the epithet of his daughter, the alleged wife of King Ahasuerus.

LINDA S. SCHEARING

ABIHU (PERSON) [Heb *ʾăbîhûʾ*]. One of four sons born to Aaron, the brother of Moses, by Elisheba (Exod 6:23). At Sinai, Abihu was singled out by God, along with Aaron and Nadab, as one of those leaders who would accompany Moses up the mountain (Exod 24:1, 9). He also performed priestly services for God as one of Aaron's sons (Exod 28:1; Num 3:2; 26:60; 1 Chr 5:29—Eng 6:3; 24:1). When Abihu and his brother Nadab offered "unholy fire" to the Lord, they were devoured by God's holy fire as punishment (Lev 10:1; Num 26:61; cf. Numbers 16). Although the sin committed by Abihu was not clearly defined (Lev 10:1–4; see Laughlin 1976 for various opinions), it served as a point of reference in identifying Abihu within the Bible (Num 3:4; 1 Chr 24:2). In Rabbinic literature the sins of Nadab and Abihu were multiplied and this incident (Lev 10:1–4) became the basis for teachings on cultic and ethical behavior in Judaism (see Shinan 1979).

Bibliography

Laughlin, J. C. H. 1976. The "Strange Fire" of Nadab and Abihu. *JBL* 95: 559–65.

Shinan, A. 1979. The Sins of Nadab and Abihu in Rabbinic Literature. *Tarbiz* 48: 201–14, II.

MARK J. FRETZ

ABIHUD (PERSON) [Heb *ʾăbîhûd*]. A grandson of Benjamin through Bela (1 Chr 8:3), the name "Abihud" is preserved in an extended genealogy of Israel that also identifies tribal locations within Palestine (1 Chronicles 2–8). According to the MT, the first three sons of Bela were "Addar, and Gera, and Abihud" (Heb *ʾaddār wĕgērāʾ waʾăbîhûd*); however, the text could easily be emended to read "Addar, and Gera, *that is,* the father of Ehud" (Heb *ʾaddār wĕgērāʾ waʾăbî ʾēhûd*). Baker (1980) argues that the two separate individuals named Gera listed as sons of Bela (1 Chr 8:3, 5) were distinguished by the waw explicative, which followed the first Gera, providing a detail about him being the father of Ehud. Thus, MT *waʾăbîhûd* is divided into *waʾăbî,* "that is, the father of," plus *ʾēhûd* "Ehud," the judge mentioned elsewhere in his own right as the son of Gera (Judg 3:15). Note also the EHUD who had a son named Gera (1 Chr 8:6–7). Kuhn (1923) observed that a misunderstanding of the phrase *ʾby hwdyh* produced the name *ʾăbîhûd* ("Abihud"), and the Gk *abioud* (Matt 1:13) was based on the LXX rendering of this synthetic name (see ABIUD).

Bibliography

Baker, D. W. 1980. Further Examples of the WAW EXPLICATIVUM. *VT* 30: 131–36.

Kuhn, G. 1923. Die Geschlechtsregister Jesu bei Lukas und Matthäus, nach ihrer Herkunft untersucht. *ZNW* 22: 206–28.

Meyer, E. 1986. *Die Entstehung des Judenthums.* Halle.

MARK J. FRETZ

ABIJAH (PERSON) [Heb *ʾăbîyâ*]. Var. ABIJAM; ABI. **1.** According to the MT, a man from the tribe of Benjamin (1 Chr 7:6, 8). He was the grandson of Benjamin, being the son of Becher who was Benjamin's son. But some scholars are suspicious of the text of 1 Chr 7:6a. Curtis and Madsen (*Chronicles* ICC, 145–49) present a detailed explanation in support of the contention that "Benjamin" in v 6 is a corruption of "Zebulun" and that 1 Chr 7:6–12 contains a Zebulunite genealogy. In that case Abijah would be from the tribe of Zebulun.

2. The second son of Samuel (1 Chr 6:13—Eng 6:28). When Samuel appointed him and his older brother, Joel, as judges over Israel (1 Sam 8:1), they were corrupted by bribery. This perversion of justice contributed to Israel's disillusionment with the office of judge, which in turn aroused among the people the desire for a king (1 Sam 8:5).

3. A chief among the descendants of either Eleazar or Ithamar, sons of Aaron (1 Chr 24:3–4, 10). When David assigned the priests to service in the temple according to divisions determined by lot, Abijah became the leader of the 8th (1 Chr 24:10) from among 24 divisions. In their service the members of his division (as of all divisions) were obligated to observe the procedures first instituted by Aaron (1 Chr 24:19). Zechariah, the father of John the Baptist, was serving in the temple with the division of Abijah (Luke 1:5) when he received the announcement that he would have a son.

4. According to the MT of 1 Chr 2:24, she was the wife of Hezron, the mother of Ashhur, and the grandmother of Tekoa. She was probably the daughter of Machir (1 Chr 2:21). But the MT is uncertain here, an uncertainty which the LXX confirms by giving a different reading for v 24a, though it follows the MT in identifying Abijah as the wife of Hezron. Noting the LXX's dissatisfaction with the MT, modern scholars have attempted to reconstruct the text, and in the process they have altered also the name "Abijah" and its immediate syntax. Curtis and Madsen (*Chronicles* ICC, 92) offer one reconstruction. In this reconstruction "Abijah" is corrected to "Abiu," or "Abihu," meaning "his father." The reconstructed passage then reads, "Caleb went in unto Ephrath, the wife of his father, and she bore . . ." In this reading, "Abijah" is no longer a proper name. Williamson (1979: 353–55) offers another reconstruction. He considers the phrase "and the wife of Hezron was Abijah" to be a gloss; this eliminates the word "Abijah," in any of its possible forms or meanings, from the original text. Both Curtis and Madsen and Williamson provide detailed accounts of their process of reconstruction. The RSV translates: "Caleb went in to Ephrathah, the wife of Hezron his father, and she bore . . ." This translation also eliminates "Abijah" as a proper name.

5. A son of Jeroboam, king of Israel (1 Kgs 14:1). During Jeroboam's reign he fell seriously ill, which prompted Jeroboam to seek from Ahijah the prophet a favorable word on the issue of the illness. But in his quest, Jeroboam proceeded in a manner which determined some of the details of a melancholy conclusion to Abijah's illness. Having conducted himself wickedly as king, Jeroboam had already gained the disfavor of Ahijah, who had designated him king (1 Kgs 11:28–30) in the name of Yahweh. Therefore he sent his wife in disguise to Shiloh to seek the word from the prophet. But the design failed. Through Yahweh's intervention, the prophet identified her when she arrived and spoke judgment on Abijah: he would die when she reentered Tirzah to return to her residence. The boy died in accordance with the prophet's word. After his death, the seal on his father's wickedness, Israel awarded him a dubious distinction: Israel mourned him and buried him with proper ceremony. By contrast, all other members of Jeroboam's family upon their death were unceremoniously eaten by either dogs, if they died in the city, or birds, if in the country (1 Kgs 14:1–18). Abijah was awarded this distinction because in him was found "something pleasing to the Lord" (1 Kgs 14:13); the text does not identify what in the child pleased the Lord. The LXX includes this account (3 Kgdms 12:24g–n) in another version and earlier in the narrative of Jeroboam's life, immediately after his return from a flight to Egypt and before his accession. It also preserves details about Abijah which are lacking in the MT. According to the LXX, Abijah was born in Egypt. His mother's name was Ano; she was an Egyptian and a sister-in-law of Susakim, king of Egypt. Accordingly, Abijah was Susakim's nephew. Debus (1967: 55–92) discusses in detail the differences between the versions of the narrative in the MT and the LXX.

6. See ABIJAH, KING OF JUDAH.

7. The mother of King Hezekiah (2 Chr 29:1 = 2 Kgs 18:2). She was the wife of King Ahaz and the daughter of Zechariah. In 2 Kings she is called "ABI" in the MT, and "Abou" in the LXX.

8. A priest during the governorship of Nehemiah (Neh 10:8—Eng 10:7). He endorsed, by the impress of his seal, a covenant which the people under Ezra's leadership made with Yahweh at the conclusion of the Feast of Tabernacles.

9. A priest, perhaps a Levitical priest, who returned from Babylon with Zerubbabel and Jeshua (Neh 12:1, 4). He was one of the chiefs of the priests in the days of Jeshua (Neh 12:7), and he was the father of Zichri upon whom his authority devolved (Neh 12:17) in the days of Jeshua's son, Joiakim (Neh 12:12).

Bibliography

Debus, J. 1967. *Studien zur Darstellung Jerobeams und der Geschichte des Nordreichs in der deuteronomistischen Geschichtsschreibung.* Göttingen.

Williamson, H. 1979. Sources and Redaction in the Chronicler's Genealogy of Judah. *JBL* 22: 351–59.

GERALD J. PETTER

ABIJAH, KING OF JUDAH.

Var. ABIJAM. The son of Rehoboam and king of Judah (1 Kgs 14:31), whose mother was Maacah, daughter of Abishalom (1 Kgs 15:2). The spelling of the same varies. In the MT of 1 Kings the name appears as Abijam (*ʾăbîyām);* some mss and the MT of Chronicles have Abijah (*ʾăbîyâ),* while the LXX has *Abiou.* It is also possible that the king's name was a theophoric compounded with the divine name "Yam," the Canaanite god of the sea, who is known from Ugaritic literature. Gray (*1-2 Kings*[3] OTL, 347, n. c) thinks that such a name of a king of Judah is inconceivable and that the divine element would have been a form of Yahweh. He argues that the LXX reading *Abiou* suggests a variant *Abiyo* in which the final *w* may have been corrupted to *m,* which it closely resembles in the photo-Hebraic script.

He is said to have reigned three years (ca. 913–911 B.C.E.), but it appears it may have been only two (1 Kgs 15:2; 2 Chr 13:2; cf. 1 Kgs 15:1, 9). LXX reads "6 years" for the length of his reign: this would suggest a confusion between *šš,* "6," and *šlš,* "3." Miller and Hayes (*HAIJ,* 240) speculate that, owing to the short length of his reign and the extended length of the reign of his successor, Abijah either died early and Asa was a minor when he became king, or the queen mother acted as regent during the early years of his son Asa.

The evidence concerning Abijah's mother is confusing and inconsistent. 1 Kgs 15:2 records that his mother's name was Maacah the daughter of Abishalom (*ʾăbîšālôm*) whereas 2 Chr 11:20 reads "Absalom" (*ʾabšālôm*). Gray (*1-2 Kings*[3] OTL, 347–78, n. g) accepts the reading "Absalom" and argues that Maacah may well have been the "granddaughter" of Absalom, David's son, particularly since the usual place of origin of the father of the queen mother has been omitted. A further difficulty is that at the accession of his son, Asa's mother is also said to be Maacah the daughter of Abishalom (1 Kgs 15:10 = 2 Chr 15:16). Gray (*1-2 Kings*[3] OTL, 348, n. f) believes that 1 Kgs 15:10 may indicate that Abijah and Asa were brothers rather than son (cf. *HAIJ,* 240). He offers the alternative explanation that since Abijah reigned for such a short time Maacah may have remained as "the principal lady," while the mother of Asa was omitted. However, the MT and Vg of 2 Chronicles 13 record the name of Abijah's mother as Micaiah, daughter of Uriel of Gibeah. The LXX and Syr follow 1 Kgs 15:2 in suggesting that the queen mother was Maacah.

Although Abijah was condemned in typical Deuteronomistic terms for apostasy, nevertheless the dynasty was established for David's sake. It is stated that despite his apostasy, Yahweh gave him a lamp in Jerusalem, set up a son after him, and established Jerusalem (1 Kgs 15:4). The establishment of Jerusalem is important in the theology of the Deuteronomistic History as the site of the central sanctuary. The treatment of the reign of Abijah admirably illustrates the theological bias and selectivity of the Deuteronomistic History. The negative presentation of his reign invites a direct comparison with that of Asa his son who is portrayed as a cultic reformer in line with Deuteronomistic principles, who even removed the Asherah of Abijah's wife Maacah (1 Kgs 15:13). The one political aspect of the reign which is mentioned briefly, without comment, is that Abijah and Jeroboam I ben Nebat were at war. The Deuteronomistic History provides little, if any, useful information for the historian.

The Chronicler presents a significantly different account, representing Abijah as righteous and divinely blessed (2 Chr 13). His 14 wives, 22 sons, and 16 daughters are presented as a sign of favor from Yahweh (2 Chr 13:21). Whereas the Deuteronomistic History merely notes that Abijah was involved in the continuing border warfare with the north (1 Kgs 15:7), the Chronicler preserves a tradition of a major military conflict near mount Zemaraim in the hill country of Ephraim (2 Chr 13:13–20). Abijah's moralizing speech to Jeroboam and Israel is in distinct contrast to his rejection in 1 Kgs 15:3 for apostasy. The speech is usually understood as representing the Chronicler's own ideology since it justifies the Davidic dynasty and the Jerusalem cult installed by David. It then acts as a rejection of the apostasy of the north with a strong claim that Yahweh is the god of Judah as demonstrated in the military victory. Williamson (1977: 114), however, rejects the common interpretation that this is a piece of anti-Samaritan polemic, arguing that, although the speech criticizes the northern kingdom, it carries within it an appeal for repentance. Following Abijah's speech of justification to Jeroboam, he wins an overwhelming victory capturing Bethel, Jeshanah, and Ephron with their villages (2 Chr 13:19). The historical reliability of this information is difficult to assess; Miller and Hayes (*HAIJ,* 247) think that at most it can only refer to a border skirmish. The exaggerated numbers (see Dillard *2 Chronicles* WBC, 106–7) are a further reason for questioning the veracity of this report. Williamson (1977: 114–17) has demonstrated the importance of 2 Chronicles 13 within the structure of the work of the Chronicler, who draws a sharp distinction between the faithfulness of Abijah and the apostasy of Ahaz in 2 Chronicles 28. Ahaz is utterly condemned in terms which echo Abijah's rejection of the north in his speech to Jeroboam.

Bibliography

Williamson, H. G. M. 1977. *Israel in the Books of Chronicles.* Cambridge.

KEITH W. WHITELAM

ABIJAM (PERSON) [Heb *ʾabîyām*]. See ABIJAH (PERSON).

ABILA OF THE DECAPOLIS (M.R. 231231). A city belonging to a league of cities called the Decapolis, originally having ten members.

A. Location and Identification

Abila of the Decapolis has been identified with Quailibah (M.R. 231231) in N Jordan. Eusebius (*Onomast.* 32.16) states that Abila was located twelve Roman miles E of Gadara. The name from this ancient site has continued to modern times—Schumacher (1889) found that local tradition attached the name Abil to the N tell. In the 1984 excavations a stone inscription with the name "Abila" written in Greek was found on the site. An inscription (A.D. 133–44) at Tayibeh near Palmyra speaks of "Well-heralded Abila of the Decapolis." Ptolemy (*Geog.* 5.14), lists this Abila separately from the Lysanias Abila (W of Damascus), and Hierokles (*Synekdemos* 720, 721) identifies it as part of Provincia Arabia. Abila probably became a Decapolis city sometime between Alexander's conquests and the zenith of Seleucid power (ca. 198 B.C.). Polybius (5.69–70) states that Antiochus III (ca. 218 B.C.) conquered Abila, Pella, and Gadara. The Decapolis as a region is mentioned in the Gospels (Matt 4:25, Mark 5:20; 7:31), but no specific cities are mentioned.

Abila consists of two tells, Abila (N) and Umm el ʾAmad (S) with a "saddle" joining the two. The site is bordered on the E by Wadi Quailibah, on the N by Wadi Abila, and on the S by Ain Quailibah and its wadi. Tombs and graves are cut into the soft limestone mainly along the wadi ledges on the E, S, and N.

B. Survey and Excavation

The major inquiry into the site began in 1978 when W. Harold Mare of Covenant Seminary visited Abila as part of an overview of several Decapolis cities. A cooperative effort ensued with Dr. Adnan Hadidi, Director of the Department of Antiquities of Jordan, and W. H. Mare as principal investigators to survey the area and excavate the site over several seasons beginning in 1980.

In 1980 a small survey team, using a time-controlled transect surface sherd collection technique in segments across the site, determined that there was occupation on the site at various times from the EB through the Umayyad periods. The heaviest concentration was in the Byzantine and Umayyad periods, diminishing in the Roman, Hellenistic, Iron Age II, and EB periods, with minimal evidence from the Chalcolithic, Neolithic, and Islamic periods. The subsequent excavations have confirmed the evidence of the 1980 survey project.

Ruins of a large rectangular building were found N of the stub of an E-W acropolis wall which stretches along the S crest of the tell. This building proved to be the remains of a 5th–6th-century triapsidal Byzantine basilica, with evidence at the central apse that it was built over an earlier Roman building (a temple?). The Umayyad rebuilding over the basilica and stockpiling of basilica architectural fragments for further use imply an Umayyad presence and possible construction of a mosque. Excavation N of the Byzantine basilica produced Byzantine and earlier materials—Byzantine loci and a water channel, remains of earlier Roman buildings, and reuse of still earlier Hellenistic walls. On the N slope was found a city wall preserved to a height of ca. 5 m; this proved to be at least of Roman-Byzantine origin. The S slope of the N tell had remains of a stairway and gate (?).

On the W side of the acropolis of Umm el ʾAmad were ruins of a residential section (areas D 5–7, 8–10) including a street, market, and a palaestra or residence with a two-column entrance. To the E of the residential section were the remains of a basilica (areas D 1–4, 11, 12), which Schumacher (1889) had suggested was a "temple," but which was another Byzantine basilica. Farther still to the E, was a theater nestled along the slopes of the "saddle." The theater overlooked the remains of a massive ruined building (a Roman bath?) and an ancient road which led eastward over a bridge crossing wadi Quailibah. A third Byzantine basilica was located on a ledge E of the theater. The three basilicas so far found at the site suggest a possible Byzantine bishopric headquarters at Abila.

Three underground aqueducts have been investigated. The Khureibah Aqueduct stretches 2.5 km, bringing water from the S to the Ain Qualibah area on the S of Umm el ʿAmad; this aqueduct was apparently dug during the Roman period. Two other aqueducts (ca. 1400 m long) direct water N from Ain Quailibah under the E edge of Umm el ʿAmad to the saddle area between the two tells. The upper aqueduct (one to two m higher on the ledge) seems to date from the Roman-Byzantine period, while the lower aqueduct was probably built in Hellenistic-Roman times or earlier (Persian or Iron Age).

The excavation of fourteen tombs (both loculus and arcosolium types) and nine simple graves along the E band of Wadi Quailibah (areas H and J) and the bank S of Ain Quailibah (area K) revealed important aspects of Early and Late Roman and Byzantine culture. Males and females and children (36 percent of the persons found had died before their 16th birthday) were buried with a variety of grave goods which imply a wide range of social stratification. Nine limestone anthropoid busts found in Tomb K 1 point to cult feasts or annual family reunions.

C. Summary

The research at Abila points to an Early Roman Abila of moderate size, with considerable expansion in the Late Roman and Byzantine periods. Evidence of the later Umayyad and earlier Hellenistic city is just emerging. The extent of later Islamic presence and earlier Hellenistic, Persian, Iron, and Bronze Age periods and still earlier habitations will be revealed through future excavation seasons.

Bibliography

Bowersock, G. W. 1971. A Report on Provincia Arabia. *JRS* 61: 219–42.

Brünnow, R. E., and Domazewski, A. 1904–9. *Die Provincia Arabia,* I–III. Strassburg.

Mare, W. H., et al. 1982. "The Decapolis Survey Project: Abila 1980," *ADAJ* 26: 37–65.

———. 1983. The Second Campaign at Abila of the Decapolis (1982). *Near East Archaeological Society Bulletin,* Pt. 1, 21: 5–55; Pt. 2, 22: 5–64.

———. 1985. The Third Campaign at Abila of the Decapolis (1984). *Near East Archaeological Society Bulletin,* Pt. 1, 24: 5–98; Pt. 2, 25: 5–70.

———. 1986. The Third Campaign at Abila of the Decapolis (1984). *Near East Archaeological Society Bulletin,* Pt. 3, 26: 5–70.

———. 1987. The Fourth Campaign at Abila of the Decapolis (1986). *Near East Archaeological Society Bulletin,* Pt. 1, 28: 35–76; Pt. 2, 29: 63–88.

McNichol, A.; Smith, R. H.; and Hennessy, B. 1982. *Pella in Jordan 1.* Canberra.

Schumacher, G. 1889. *Abila of the Decapolis.* London.

Smith, R. H. 1973. *Pella of the Decapolis.* Wooster, OH.

W. HAROLD MARE

ABILENE (PLACE) [Gk *Abilene*]. A tetrarchy named after its chief town, Abila, which is located on the bank of modern Barada (Abana) 18 miles NW of Damascus en route to Heliopolis (Baalbec). A Moslem legend places Abel's tomb near the ruins of an Abilenian temple, thereby preserving the ancient name. Luke 3:1 identifies Abilene as the tetrarchy of Lysanias (II) at the incipient stage of John the Baptist's ministry. Josephus is careful to associate Abila and Abilene with Lysanias, *he Lusaniou* (*JW* 2, 11.5; *Ant* 17, 6.10), an association found as late as the time of Ptolemy (ca. A.D. 170). Two Gk inscriptions from Abila support this association, and coincide with the chronology of Luke 3:1, i.e., between the years A.D. 14–29 (Yamauchi 1981: 99).

Abilene was originally part of the Ituraean kingdom of Ptolemy Menaeus (ca. 85–40 B.C.). In 36 B.C., M. Antonius executed Ptolemy's son, King Lysanias I, and divided Ituraea. Cleopatra received part of the kingdom, which in turn was transferred by her conqueror, Augustus, to Herod the Great in 20 B.C. (Bruce: 1971: 20, 248). Except for an Abila inscription identifying a second Lysanias (above), Abilene's history remains obscure until A.D. 37 when Gaius conferred the title "king" on his friend Herod Agrippa I, along with Abilene and additional territory. Procurators governed Abilene from the time of Agrippa I's death (A.D. 40) until Claudius conferred it upon Herod Agrippa II in A.D. 53. Upon the latter's death, Abilene became part of the province of Syria.

Bibliography

Bruce, F. F. 1971. *New Testament History.* New York.

Yamauchi, E. 1981. *The Stones and the Scriptures: An Introduction to Biblical Archaeology.* Grand Rapids.

JERRY A. PATTENGALE

ABIMAEL (PERSON) [Heb *ʾăbîmāʾēl*]. A son of Joktan and thus the name of an Arabian tribe (Gen 10:28; 1 Chr 1:22), which has not been identified nor localized in a satisfactory way. The name is either to be analyzed as *ʾăbî* + *mā* (as an emphasizing enclitic particle) + *ʾēl* "(my) father is truly God" or, less probably, as Old S Arabic *ʾbm* (in the absolute state) + *ʾl,* i.e., "Father is God," which may be compared to the apotropaic formula *ʾbm wdm* "Father is (the God) Waddum" (*CIS* IV, 475 and 476; etc.), or to the Akkadian name *abumilum* "Father is God."

Hommel (1893: 16) has already pointed out that Old Arabic has a name type that contains the enclitic *-m,* e.g., *ʾlmnbṭ* "God has truly brought to light," *ʾlmydʿ* "God truly knows," and *ʾbmʿṯtr* "Father is truly *ʿAṯtar.*" The last-mentioned name occurs as the name of a clan, *ʾhl/ʾbmʿṯtr,* in the early Sabaean inscription *RES* 2740,4 which was written not later than the 5th century B.C. and which had been found in the ruined ancient town of Haram in the Yemenite Jawf on the N side of the main wadi. The Sabaean boustrophedon text *CIS* IV, 516, in which the name *ʾlmnbṭ* is found (line 26), comes from the same place; and the fragmentary inscription *RES* 2847, in which the name *ʾlmydʿ* occurs, was discovered in the neighboring ancient site of Kamnā. From this epigraphic evidence, it can be concluded that proper names with the enclitic *-m* were only in use in the region of the town of Haram and are to be reckoned among the dialectal peculiarities which the inscriptions from this town show. With due reservation, it may therefore be supposed that the Hebrew form *ʾăbîmāʾēl* reflects a hitherto unattested Sabaean name **ʾbmʾl* which might have originated from the area of the ancient town of Haram.

The first who connected the biblical name *ʾăbîmāʾēl* with the Sabaean name *ʾbmʿṯtr* was Halévy (1885: 6–7); he thought, however, that both names contain the contracted form of the word for mother, *ʾm,* and are therefore to be interpreted respectively as "father of the mother of God" and "father of the mother of *ʿAṯtar.*" The explanation of *ʾăbîmāʾēl* as "father of *māʾēl*" must likewise be rejected, since at such an early time no names are attested which are compounded with the element *ʾabû* (or *ʾăbî*) "father of," which later on became common among the Arabs. Another rejected interpretation is the comparison of the last part of the name, proposed for the first time by Bochartus (1674: 144–45), with the people or region *mali* mentioned by the Greek author Theophrastus (*Hist. Pl.* 9.4); this is, however, only a variant of *mamali,* the designation of the W Arabian mining region.

Bibliography

Bochartus, S. 1674. *Geographia sacra. Pars prior Phaleg.* Francofurti ad Moenum.

Halévy, J. 1885. Recherches bibliques. 3. *REJ* 10: 1–9.

Hommel, F. 1893. *Süd-Arabische Chrestomathie.* Munich.

W. W. MÜLLER

ABIMELECH (PERSON) [Heb *ʾabîmelek*]. Two or three persons in the Hebrew Bible bear this name.

1. A king of Gerar mentioned in Genesis 20 and 26:1–33. He is tied to the patriarchal narratives with regard to their pastoral nomadic activities and the fear Abraham and Isaac display whenever entering the political domain of a powerful ruler. Each enter Gerar, between Kadesh and Shur, seeking pasturage and water. They obtain both through the use of the "Wife-Sister" deception in which the patriarch, to save his life, hides his true relationship with his wife (note the first use of this motif in Gen 12:10–20, where the Pharaoh is the dupe). Once the king has mistakenly taken the patriarch's wife, Yahweh's displeasure is aroused against him and his people. Subsequently, Abimelech returns the wife to her husband, and is forced (through embarrassment and fear) to grant to him, in the form of a parity treaty, grazing rights and the use of wells within his territory.

The fact that this preliminary episode is found in both the Abraham and Isaac narratives suggests a literary doublet. It is possible, however, that the name "Abimelech," like Pharaoh, is simply a throne name used by all kings of Gerar. Thus whenever the "Wife-Sister" deception is used, it is applied to a different ruler, but for the same reason, as a measure of self-defense by an immigrant against a powerful, indigenous ruler.

One additional problem in the Abimelech stories is found in Gen 26:1, where he is referred to as the "king of the Philistines." This is generally explained as an anachronism since the Philistines did not inhabit the area around Gerar until after the Sea Peoples' invasion of the Near East (*ca.* 1200 B.C.E.). Van Seters (1975: 52), however, takes this as evidence of the lack of historicity in the narrative, while Wiseman (1980: 150) points to the Gerarites as part of a settlement of Philistines prior to the mass invasions of the 13th century.

2. The name "Abimelech" also appears in the superscription of Psalm 34. The writer is either using the name as a generic title for all Philistine kings, or perhaps has confused Achish of Gath (1 Sam 21:10–15) with Ahimelech of 1 Sam 21:2.

Bibliography

Matthews, V. H. 1986. The Wells of Gerar. *BA* 49: 118–26.

Van Seters, J. 1975. *Abraham in History and Tradition.* New Haven.

Wiseman, D. J. 1980. Abraham Reassessed. Pp. 141–60 in *Essays on the Patriarchal Narratives,* ed. A. R. Millard and D. J. Wiseman. Winona Lake, IN.

VICTOR H. MATTHEWS

3. One of the sons of Jerubbaal who administered the central hill country (and by dint of conquest—Judg 8:1–17—Gilead) in the aftermath of their father's demise. The historian equates Jerubbaal with Gideon, and although the equation has often been questioned (e.g., Richter 1963: 157–67), the absence of any obvious reason for the historian to have inferred it (he could simply have introduced Abimelech as a filibuster) suggests that the equation was already traditional.

The name "Abimelech" means "the (divine) king is my father," and is of a type attested in Israel as well as its environs: cf. Ahimelech ("the king is my brother"; Old Palestinian variant Abimelech) in 1 Sam 21:2–9 (> Ps 34:1; 52:2); 22:10–16; 23:6; 26:6; 30:7; Abimilki, king of Tyre in the Amarna archive (EA 146–55); and the Philistine king Abimelech in Gen 20:2–18; 21:22–32; 26:1–26, where the name is evidently retrojected. It has no necessary monarchic overtones; but it is interesting that the earliest "king" in Israelite memory should have such a name, and it is possible that it is in fact a throne name.

Abimelech persuades the men of Shechem to prefer his personal kingship over the oligarchy of Gideon's sons. Killing his brothers, therefore, he enters into a covenant of kingship (9:5–21), characterized by a fable drawing on the normal topoi of Near Eastern royal apology, and sealed by the ordinary ceremony of blessings and curses (see Halpern 1978: 92–96). Abimelech resides in "*trmh*" (9:31; cf. Dossin 1957), probably identical with the "*ʾrmh*" of 9:41 (by interchange of *t* and ʾ), or Khirbet el-ʾUrma, about 7 km SE of Shechem (*WHJP* 1/3: 319 n. 56). Shechem's acceptance of his sovereignty makes him master of the central hills.

During Abimelech's reign, the Shechemites prey upon the trade routes leading through their territory (9:25), and sedition comes to the town (9:27–29). The name of the instigator, Gual (with Josephus) ben-Ebed, is probably invented—it means "despised, son of a slave." Abimelech's principal there is also named as in a folktale, Zabul ("prince," "magnate"). Zabul informs Abimelech that Gual plans to march from the temple of Baal/El Berit ("the lord/god of the covenant"), which was outside the town (9:46–49), in the aftermath of the feast of the vintage, and to lay siege to Shechem, the acropolis of which, at least, Zabul held (9:31–33). Abimelech therefore sets four ambushes in the field, and as Gual takes the field, his forces descend from all directions (those to the E are first confused with shadows, which, with 9:48, may have inspired the use of Burnam Wood in Macbeth). They worst Gual, who during the night is expelled from the town. The next day, therefore, Abimelech ambushes Gual and assaults and demolishes Shechem, and the "temple of El Berit" (9:30–49).

A similar action at Thebez (for an identification with Tirzah, see *WHJP* 1/3: 320 n. 61) ends in Abimelech's demise. Abimelech drives the defenders from the lower city to the citadel, and dies while attempting to burn the citadel. The manner of his death is proverbial—David cites it in 2 Sam 11:21: he is crushed by a grindstone a woman drops from atop the wall (9:50–54). The short flirtation with kingship ends just after it begins, and it is another century before monarchy is reintroduced in the hills.

The tradition concerning Abimelech is to be dated quite early (see Halpern 1978; Rösel 1983, both with bibliography), although different critics identify various pieces of the textual formulation as deriving from later retelling (see Soggin *Judges* OTL, 163–66). In any case, the archaeological record at Shechem dovetails nicely with the story: the site was apparently abandoned after a destruction in the mid-12th century B.C.E. (Wright 1967: 365–66; Campbell 1976: 41), its reoccupation in the 10th century B.C.E. coinciding with the return of a monarchic government (Shechem commands the interior trade routes of Ephraim and Manasseh, and is a natural seat of government for the region N of Jerusalem). The reference in 2 Sam 11:21 to Abimelech's death is generally understood to be a token of an early composition. And Abimelech campaigns for the kingship of Shechem with the slogan that he is their "flesh and blood" (9:2)—that is, he qualifies to be their king because he is their kin. This expression, which must be linked to the insistence on endogenous kingship in

Deut 17:14–16, appears elsewhere only in 10th century B.C.E. contexts, principally in connection with David (2 Sam 5:1–3; cf. 1 Chr 11:1–3; 12:23–41; and 2 Sam 19:11–13; note the transformation in J in Gen 2:23–24; 29:14, where Jacob ends by "serving" his kinsman). The slogan that repudiates the claim to kinship and kingship is "Who is Abimelech?" (9:28)—denouncing the claimant as a stranger. It, too, is used only in 10th century B.C.E. contexts, or in connection with 10th century figures (1 Sam 25:10; 2 Sam 20:1; 1 Kgs 12:16; see *BAR* 3: 170; Buccellati 1967: 100). Furthermore, it may be that the later historian misunderstood this tradition—which would be evidence that he inherited it: Abimelech becomes the son of Gideon's Shechemite concubine (Judg 8:31), i.e., a brother Shechemite, rather than a brother Israelite.

Finally, the memories of fighting at the city gate, differences between lower cities and citadels, dealing with citadels by burning them down, and socioethnic distinctions in Shechem all bear the mark of authenticity. The Shechemite depradations on the trade routes also probably reflect premonarchic reality (and cf. Judg 5:6). A 10th century B.C.E. date for the oldest version of the tale is the latest possible; the tradition itself probably extends at least into the 11th and perhaps into the 12th century B.C.E. It is possibly one of the oldest historical traditions Israel has preserved.

Bibliography

Buccellati, G. 1967. *Cities and Nations of Ancient Syria.* Studi Semitici 26. Rome.

Campbell, E. F. 1976. Two Amarna Notes: The Shechem City-State and Amarna Administrative Terminology. Pp. 39–54 in *Magnalia Dei: The Mighty Acts of God,* ed. F. M. Cross; P. D. Miller; and W. E. Lemke. Garden City, N.Y.

Halpern, B. 1978. The Rise of Abimelek ben-Jerubbaal. *HAR* 2: 79–100.

Richter, W. 1963. *Traditionsgeschichtliche Untersuchungen zum Richterbuch.* BBB 18. Bonn.

Rösel, H. N. 1983. Überlegungen zu Abimelech und Sichem im Jdc. ix. *VT* 33:500–3.

Wright, G. E. 1967. Shechem. Pp. 355–70 in *Archaeology and Old Testament Study,* ed. D. Winton Thomas. London.

BARUCH HALPERN

ABINADAB (PERSON) [Heb *ʾăbînādāb*]. The name of three individuals. It means "my father is noble."

1. The father of Eleazar, Uzzah, and possibly Ahio, if the latter is a proper name and not a reference to Eleazar "his brother" (1 Sam 7:1; Sam 6:3, 4; 1 Chr 13:7). The men of the Gibeonite enclave town of Kiriath-jearim are reported to have moved the ark from Beth-Shemesh to "the palace/temple of Abinadab on the hill" (1 Sam 6:19–7:1) at the request of the latter group. Abinadab's son Eleazar is said to have been consecrated as priest to have charge of the ark (1 Sam 7:1). The context suggests that the ambiguous Hebrew term *bêt,* which can mean simply "house," but also "palace" or "temple," here refers to a temple or place complex containing a temple. Since it is unlikely that the townspeople would have moved the ark to the home of a common citizen for safekeeping, and in light of the purported need to seek out someone who could minister to Yahweh appropriately (cf. Klein *1 Samuel* WBC, 60), without invoking divine wrath (1 Sam 6:19–20), it is likely that Abinadab was himself a well-known priest.

Abinadab need not have been a priest in Kiriath-Jearim; he could have been the high priest for the entire Gibeonite enclave, connected to the enclave's main sanctuary. Kiriath-jearim was one of four cities in the Benjaminite territory that formed a separate Hivite enclave. The main city of the enclave was Gibeon, and the remaining two were Chephirah and Beeroth. If the main goal of the author was to have the men of Beth-Shemesh turn the ark over to members of the neighboring Hivite enclave, it would have been natural to have them contact the closest Gibeonite city, Kiriath-jearim. It does not necessarily follow, however, that the men from the latter town are to be understood to have taken the ark home; it would have been more natural for them to have delivered it to the main Gibeonite sanctuary.

By having the men of Beth-Shemesh call out the nearest members of the Gibeonite enclave to remove the ark to their territory to deal with the wrathful Yahweh, who had just slain seventy of their men for looking into the ark, the biblical writer has indirectly implied that the Gibeonites would have known how to assuage the deity connected with the ark. The logical implication is that Yahweh was at home among the Gibeonites. An alternative understanding would see the choice of Kiriath-jearim to be based on the site's nodal point as the boundary between Judah, Benjamin, and Dan. Kiriath-jearim, Beth-Shemesh, and Ekron, the three reported stopping places of the ark on its return journey from Philistia, all occur in the Judahite boundary list in Josh 15:9b–11a, suggesting that the author of the narrative in 1 Sam 6:19–7:2 wanted to emphasize the ark's return within the boundaries of Judah, so linking it closely to the later tribe (Blenkinsopp 1969:147–48).

The "hill of Abinadab" is identified as KIRIATH-JEARIM in 1 Sam 7:2, compared to BAALE-JUDAH in 2 Sam 6:2. Both seem to be later glosses (Blenkinsopp 1969:156). The conflicting traditions are harmonized elsewhere in the Bible by equating the latter two names (Josh 15:9; 18:14; 1 Chr 13:6). Baale-Judah might itself be an artificial hybrid created by equating the town of Baalah (Josh 15:9; 1 Chr 13:6) with Kiriath-jearim (Blenkinsopp 1969:146; Mazar 1960:66). The site of "Abinadab's hill" is commonly linked with the place name "Gibeat-Kiriath (Jearim)" in the list of Benjaminite cities in Josh 18:28, although the final element in the name ("jearim") must be restored to the reading on the basis of purported haplography. It has been proposed that the Hill was the older Hivite-turned-Benjaminite town as opposed to the later Judahite settlement built on the adjoining hill (Aharoni 1959: 229), or simply a particular quarter of the city (McCarter *1 Samuel* AB, 137).

An alternative identification of "Abinadab's hill" can be made on the basis of historical consideration. The ark almost certainly played a central role within Saul's national cult, a fact that led David to move it to his new capital at Jerusalem. As the site of the ark prior to David's reign, it is plausible to conclude that "Abinadab's hill" is an oblique reference to the religious capital of Saul's state. Textual tradition (esp. 1 Kings 3–9 and 2 Chronicles 1–2) tends to indicate that the great *bāmâ* sanctuary of Gibeon served as Saul's religious capital (Schunk 1963: 131–38; Blenkinsopp 1974; Edelman 1990). It has been suggested that the actual sanctuary might have been located southwest of Gibeon proper on the height of Nebi Samwil (see bibliography cited in Blenkinsopp 1969: 151, n. 32; Edelman 1990). No Iron I remains have been detected from surface survey, however, so the latter proposal remains conjecture (Kallai 1972: 185–86).

2. The second son of Jesse and older brother of David (1 Sam 16:8, 1 Chr 2:13). He is reported to have been a soldier in Saul's army along with his brothers Eliab and Shamma. The three are said to have been among the Saulide forces at the battle against the Philistines in the Elah Valley, when Goliath was killed (1 Sam 17:13). David is depicted as having been sent by his father to deliver the three older brothers provisions while in camp during this confrontation, providing the biblical writer a motive for David's presence at the time of the battle and his eventual reported slaying of Goliath. Since a variant tradition in 2 Sam 21:19 reports that Elhanan son of Jaareoregim the Bethlehemite slew Goliath, the historical reliability of the narrative account in 1 Samuel 16 is doubtful (for bibliography, see Klein *1 Samuel* WBC, 268). Nevertheless, it is conceivable that Abinadab and his two brothers had been present at the battle where Goliath was killed, as members of Saul's professional military forces (1 Sam 14:52).

3. A son of Saul, probably the fourth-born son and sixth child born to Ahinoam, who died in battle alongside his father and two brothers, Jonathan and Malchishua, on Mt. Gilboa. He and his brother Eshbaal do not appear in the two-generation Saulide genealogy in 1 Sam 14:49, but both are named subsequently in the fourteen-generation genealogy in 1 Chr 8:33–39; 9:39–44. The logical conclusion is that they were both born after the first list was made. Abinadab must have been in his early twenties when he died, since he was eligible for military service, but apparently had not yet married or had any children. According to Num 26:2, 4, the military draft began at age twenty, although it is not certain whether this standard would have applied at the beginning of the monarchy. The age of marriage for ancient Israelite males, either for royalty or the common citizenry, is unknown.

4. For "son of Abinadab" (1 Kgs 4:11), see BEN-ABINADAB.

Bibliography

Aharoni, Y. 1959. The Province List of Judah. *VT* 9: 225–46.
Blenkinsopp, J. 1969. Kiriath-Jearim and the Ark. *JBL* 88: 143–56.
———. 1974. Did Saul Make Gibeon His Capital? *VT* 24: 1–7.
Edelman, D. 1990. *Saulide Israel.* Winona Lake, IN.
Kallai, Z. 1972. Benjamin and Mt. Ephraim. In *Judaea, Samaria and the Golan. Archaeological Survey 1967–1968,* ed. M. Kochavi. Jerusalem.
Mazar, B. 1960. The Cities of the Territory of Dan. *IEJ* 10: 65–77.
Schunk, K. D. 1963. *Benjamin.* Berlin.

DIANA V. EDELMAN

ABINOAM (PERSON) [Heb *ʾăbînōʿam*]. The father of Barak, the military leader summoned by Deborah the prophetess to lead the Israelites into battle against Sisera, commander of the Canaanite army (Judg 4:2, 6–7, 12). In the "Song of Deborah" (Judg 5:2–31), two out of the three occurrences of the name "Barak" (vv 1, 12) are identified by the patronym "Abinoam."

MARK J. FRETZ

ABIR. See NAMES OF GOD (OT).

ABIRAM (PERSON) [Heb *ʾăbîrām*]. **1.** Son of Eliab, a Reubenite, who with DATHAN, KORAH, and 250 leaders of Israel conspired against the exclusive leadership of Moses and Aaron in the wilderness (Num 16:1–40). The conspiracy ended when, in the aftermath of a ritual contest with Aaron, the earth "swallowed" the leaders and fire devoured the 250. The name is theophoric, meaning "the exalted one is (my) father" (same as Abram). In the LXX the name occurs as Abiron.

It is generally agreed that this narrative represents the later editing of two such independent conspiracy traditions. Owing to the interest of the postexilic priestly redactor, the dominant strand in the present text is that concerning the attempted encroachment of the Levite Korah upon Aaronide priestly rights. However, underlying the story of Abiram is a quite different conspiracy against Moses' political leadership attributable to the epic tradition (J). Here the concern is Moses' sole claim to be "prince" (*śar,* v 13) over the people. The reference to "putting out the eyes" of the conspirators (v 14) is not to be dismissed as a figure of speech (so Budd *Numbers* WBC, 187), but is to be understood as a typical punishment for political treason. Whereas the Korah tradition ended in conflagration (a case of the punishment matching the offense), the theme of the earth swallowing the conspirators is at home in the Dathan-Abiram tradition. This earlier form of the tradition lies behind both Deut 11:6 and Ps 106:17. If Ps 106:17 predates the present form of the story in Numbers, then the mention of fire in the psalm could account for the development of the "Korah" tradition. That the tradition in the psalm is early is suggested by the fact that it places the conspiracy prior to both the apostasy at Horeb and the aborted invasion of Canaan, clearly out of synchronization with the present form of the narrative. The story of Abiram is often understood as a reflection of the loss of prestige by the tribe of Reuben following the period of settlement.

2. The firstborn son of Hiel of Bethel, the man who rebuilt the city of Jericho in the days of Ahab (1 Kgs 16:34). The text suggests that Abiram was offered by his father as a sacrifice at the laying of the foundation in order to effect the successful completion of the building program, just as his brother SEGUB was offered at its conclusion. The offering of such "foundation sacrifices" reflects a custom attested by archaeological discovery in which infants placed in jars have been found buried within the gate complex of a city. Whether the children were sacrificed or died of natural causes, the deuteronomist regards this action as the working out of the curse on Jericho spoken by Joshua in Josh 6:26 (Gray *Kings* OTL, 334–35). He also links the episode to the evil deeds of Ahab, particularly Ahab's building projects. The rebuilding of

Jericho is thus placed within the context of the deuteronomistic judgment on "the sins of Jeroboam" (v 31).

Bibliography

Liver, J. 1961. Korah, Dathan and Abiram. Pp. 189–217 in *Studies in the Bible,* ed. C. Rabin. Jerusalem.

RODNEY R. HUTTON

ABISHAG (PERSON) [Heb *ʾăbîšag*]. A beautiful young woman from Shunem whose parents are unknown (1 Kgs 1:1–4). Her name, with the epithet "the Shunammite," occurs five times in the succession narrative in 1 Kgs 1–2 (1:3, 15; 2:17, 21, 22). Seeking a young maiden to attend the ailing king, David's servants locate Abishag "the Shunammite," who is "very beautiful." They bring her to David, but David "knows" her not (vv 3–4). Aside from a brief note about her ministering to David (1:15), nothing more is heard about Abishag until after David's death. Adonijah (Solomon's brother) asks Bathsheba to intercede with Solomon on his behalf. The purpose of this intercession is to secure Abishag as Adonijah's wife (2:16–18). Bathsheba does as Adonijah requests, but Solomon replies, "Ask for him the kingdom also . . ." (2:19–22) and has Adonijah put to death (2:24–25).

Attempts to reconstruct the historical Abishag focus on her relationship to David, the nature of her activities in David's court, and the political significance of Adonijah's request and Solomon's refusal.

Abishag's relationship to David is defined by her function in court. Commentators have alternatively suggested she was David's nurse (Montgomery *Kings* ICC, 72), his concubine (Gray *Kings* OTL, 77), or his queen (Mulder 1972: 43–54). The issue is whether Abishag's job was to cure or to test David. If Abishag's primary task was to cure him, then she is best likened to a nurse. Her actions constitute a kind of "contactual medicine" whereby the warmth of a beautiful young maiden was imbued—through contact—to an aging body. Both Josephus (*Ant* 7.14.3) and Galen (cited by Montgomery *Kings* ICC, 72) attest the practice. If, however, the issue was not David's health but his ability to rule, then Abishag's presence is better explained in terms of a test. The king's authority (and the nation's future) corresponded to his virility (Gray *Kings* OTL, 77). Abishag's presence "tests" the elderly David's sexual prowess. His failure to "know" Abishag (1:4) indicates his failure as king and precipitates the fight for succession which follows. If Abishag's function was to test David's virility, then it is possible she was admitted into David's harem either as concubine or wife.

After David's death, Adonijah's request for Abishag became the catalyst for his own death. What motivated this request and why did Solomon refuse? What was Abishag's political significance? Assuming Abishag was part of David's harem, Adonijah's request can be interpreted as an attempt to seize Solomon's throne. Since the appropriation of a king's harem appears to be tantamount to a bid for the throne itself (cf. 2 Sam 3:7ff.; 16:21ff.), the possession of Abishag as wife would be politically significant. One could argue, however, that Adonijah would have been a fool to make such an open bid. Instead, his request might have reflected nothing more ambitious than his desire for Abishag. Regardless of Adonijah's motives, however, Solomon chose to interpret his request as a direct threat (2:22). One can only speculate as to Solomon's reasons for this move. Either Solomon intentionally misunderstood Adonijah's motives; Adonijah did attempt to seize the throne; the whole accusation was a figment of Solomon's paranoid imagination (Gunn 1978: 137 n. 4); or Solomon realized Abishag—as witness to Bathsheba's conspiracy (cf. 1:15)—could be dangerous wed to his rival (Sanda, cited in Montgomery *Kings* ICC, 79).

Aside from historical considerations, the story and characterization of Abishag have been the object of recent literary analysis. David Gunn traces the political (David as King) and the personal (David as Man) themes found in the story of David and sees both converging in the story of Abishag. David's impotence as a man is echoed by his impotence as a ruler (Gunn 1978: 90–91). Adele Berlin accepts Gunn's observations, but focuses on the characterization of Abishag. For Berlin, Abishag is neither a fully developed character like other women in David's story (cf. Michal, Bathsheba), nor is she a stereotypical character (cf. Abigail). Rather, Abishag functions as an agent—a character about whom little is known that is not necessary for the plot. The reader knows Abishag only through the eyes of the narrator or the other characters in the story. Thus Abishag is the "younger woman" to Bathsheba, a token of kingship to Solomon, and a symbol of impotence to David (Berlin 1983: 23–33).

Bibliography

Berlin, A. 1983. *Poetics and Interpretation of Biblical Narrative.* Sheffield.

Gunn, D. M. 1978. *The Story of King David: Genre and Interpretation. JSOTSup* 6. Sheffield.

Mulder, M. J. 1972. Versuch zur Deutung von *sokenet* in 1 Kö. i.2, 4. *VT* 22: 43–54.

LINDA S. SCHEARING

ABISHAI (PERSON) [Heb *ʾăbîšay*]. One of the three sons of Zeruiah, David's sister (1 Chr 2:16; 2 Sam 17:25; see ZERUIAH). These men belonged to David's "inner circle" and presumably had served as his advisors and retainers since his early days as a fugitive from Saul (1 Sam 22:1).

The name Abishai is of obscure origin. It may be based on a theophoric element in a nominal clause, meaning something like "Father (Heb *ʾab-;* i.e., the god) is a gift (Heb *šay*)." It is also possible that the second particle is a shortened form of a longer three-radical root such as *šālôm,* in which case Abishai would be the equivalent of Absalom/Abisalom (see NAMES, HYPOCORISTIC). A third possibility is that Abishai is the Hebrew form of the Egyptian name *A/Ibša* (*AOT*[2], 51; cf. LXX *Abessa*) or the Akkadian name *Ibašši(-ilum).*

Abishai, who served as one of the chiefs of DAVID'S CHAMPIONS (Heb *šālišîm;* RSV: The Thirty; 2 Sam 23:8–39), is depicted as intensely combative toward the enemies of David, especially Saul (1 Sam 26:6–9) and Saul's kinsman Shimei (2 Sam 16:9–11). The narrator also implicates Abishai in the murder of Abner, the son of Ner (Saul's cousin and commander of the army) by his brother JOAB

(2 Sam 3:30). Still, no mention of Abishai's complicity in this act is made in the account of Abner's death (2 Sam 3:20–27), in David's curse upon the perpetrator (2 Sam 3:29), or in David's avenging of this deed (1 Kgs 2:5–6).

Abishai is also credited with having saved David's life during the Philistine wars when he struck down Ishbi-benob, one of the descendants of the Rephaim (1 Sam 21:16–17). Thus, he was a valiant warrior about whom heroic tales were told—the true mark of a great warrior in ancient society. (Examples from Greek legend are Achilles, Ajax, Diomedes, and Odysseus at Troy.) Indeed, David appears to have retired from active military service as a result of this incident, so that the sons of Zeruiah, Abishai and Joab, appear as the leaders of David's army in the campaigns from the time of the Ammonite wars (2 Samuel 10–11; 12:26–31) on. According to 2 Sam 23:18–19, Abishai was commander of the *šālišîm* (RSV: The Thirty), an elite corps of renowned warriors within David's private army. This position gave Abishai a command in the army second only to his brother, Joab, the commander-in-chief. Abishai served in this capacity during the Ammonite wars and in the revolt of Absalom (2 Sam 18:1–5). Prior to the revolt of Sheba ben Bichri, however, David had removed Joab from his command (probably for killing the rebel Absalom against the king's express orders), so that Abishai initially appeared as the commander of the Cherethites and Pelethites in that conflict (2 Sam 20:6–7). By the end of the campaign, Joab returned to his command after killing the tardy Amasa. Thus, not only was Abishai one of David's warrior elite, but he served as second-in-command of the army after Joab, probably because of his status as commander of the *šālišîm* (although this status is not mentioned in the summary lists of David's officials: 2 Sam 8:15–18; 20:23–25).

Because Abishai generally appears working closely with his brother Joab, his absence from the intrigue surrounding the selection of David's successor is remarkable (1 Kings 1–2). A logical explanation for this absence is that Abishai by this time was dead. Certainly, had he been alive, he would have lent his support to the cause of Adonijah, whom Joab had backed in place of Solomon. Indeed, David's warrior elite is depicted as supporting Solomon, and Joab's nemesis emerges in the figure of Benaiah ben Jehoiada, another of David's warrior elite who is variously described as commander of the foreign mercenaries (the Cherethites and Pelethites; 2 Sam 8:18; 20:23) or commander of the bodyguard (the *mišmaʿâ;* 2 Sam 23:23). Since Abishai had commanded the foreign mercenaries during the revolt of Sheba (2 Sam 20:7), it is likely that Benaiah was a latecomer to this position (Benaiah's most prominent role was as commander of the army under Solomon). It is perhaps not too bold to assume that Abishai had died prior to the attempt to crown Adonijah, necessitating the promotion of Benaiah. Abishai's departure from his accustomed command allowed for the entry of Benaiah into the drama surrounding Solomon's succession and guaranteed the victory of Solomon's party, and eventually, Joab's death.

Yet Abishai plays more than an historical role within the Davidic narratives: along with his brother, Joab, he is made a violent foil for the pious David. Thus the impetuous Abishai accompanies David into Saul's camp at night and urges David to let him kill the sleeping monarch (1 Sam 26:6–12). David righteously restrains the warrior, however, refusing to put his hand forth against the Lord's anointed. A further incident occurs in the murder of Abner. Although Abner's murder by men who are, after all, David's henchmen appears all too convenient to modern observers, the narrator seeks to exculpate David in the matter and lays the blame squarely on the heads of Joab and Abishai (2 Sam 3:30). Again David stands forth as the righteous man who refuses to shed the blood of the innocent and *who rejects stealth in killing,* while Joab and Abishai are portrayed as treacherous murderers (note the threat to kill Saul while he sleeps, and the slaying of Abner under the pretense of friendship). David says of Abner's death, "as one falls before the wicked you have fallen." Abishai appears as a foil a third time when David and his followers are abandoning Jerusalem in the face of Absalom and his rebel army (2 Sam 16:5–14). A man of the house of Saul, Shimei ben Gera, meets David and his retainers and curses them:

> Begone, begone you man of blood,
> you worthless fellow!
> The Lord has avenged upon you
> all the blood of the house of Saul,
> in whose place you have reigned.
> And the Lord has given the kingdom into the
> hand of your son Absalom.
> See! Your ruin is upon you—
> for you are a man of blood. (2 Sam 16:7–8)

Shimei's curse highlights a major *Tendenz* of the Davidic narratives: David's burden of guilt for his hand in the death of Saul and the extermination of Saul's line, and the writer's efforts to exonerate David in the matter. As in the camp of Saul, Abishai seeks David's permission to kill Shimei on the spot. David again refuses, rebuking Abishai and implying that Shimei has a right to curse him. Furthermore, David appeals to the Lord to look upon him in his affliction, and to repay him with good for this cursing. The impression thus created is that the sons of Zeruiah (who are addressed collectively here, though it is only Abishai who acts) are ruthless men of blood. Conversely, David righteously rejects even that claim upon his enemy's life and person which normally would have been granted him. Seen in this light, David emerges as the Wisdom tradition's paradigm of the righteous man who leaves vengeance in the hands of the Lord and does not put forth his hand in violence. Joab and Abishai are, conversely, the paradigmatic violent men—men of blood, ruthless and unrestrained in their wickedness. While Abishai fulfills this archetype in several instances, the final curse falls upon Joab, who is said to have avenged "in time of peace blood which had been shed in war," and to have put "the blood of war upon the girdle about his loins and upon the sandals on his feet" (1 Kgs 2:5, MT; *contra* RSV "*my* loins," "*my* feet"). It is precisely the juxtaposition of these two archetypes—the righteous man who will not put forth his hand to shed blood versus the wicked who is only too quick to draw his sword—that allows the author (or authors) of the Davidic narratives to place the blame for the blood shed under David (especially that of Saul's house) upon his nephews and loyal retainers, the sons of Zeruiah.

Thus two pictures of Abishai emerge from the Davidic narratives. As an historical figure, Abishai was probably one of David's staunchest supporters, a member of the king's own family who had probably been with him since his days as an exile from Saul in the Judean wilderness (1 Sam 22:1–2). As a literary figure, Abishai, along with his brother Joab, provides a violent foil for the self-renunciatory David, who will not lift his hand in to harm either his enemy, Saul, Saul's kinsmen, Abner and Shimei, or even his own rebellious son, Absalom.

D. G. Schley

ABISHALOM (PERSON) [Heb *ʾăbîšālôm*]. See ABSALOM (PERSON).

ABISHUA (PERSON) [Heb *ʾăbîšûaʿ*]. **1.** A high priest of the tribe of Levi and grandson of Eleazar (1 Chr 5:30–31—Eng 6:4–5; 6:35—Eng 6:50). In the post-exilic Jewish community, Ezra's authority was legitimized by proof of descent through the high priest Abishua (Ezra 7:5; 1 Esdr 8:2; 2 Esdr 1:2). Wilson (1977) notes that this is one of the functions of genealogical lists; sometimes these lists simply function to legitimize the positions of important individuals, rather than to transmit all the names of that person's ancestors and/or descendants.

2. A son of Bela the Benjaminite (1 Chr 8:4). This Abishua appears only in this extended genealogy of Israel (1 Chronicles 2–8), which also identifies tribal locations within Palestine.

Bibliography

Johnson, M. D. 1969. *The Purpose of Biblical Genealogies with Specific Reference to the Setting of the Genealogies of Jesus.* SNTSMS 8. Cambridge, MA.

Wilson, R. R. 1977. *Genealogy and History in the Biblical World.* YNER 7. New Haven.

Mark J. Fretz

ABISHUR (PERSON) [Heb *ʾăbîšûr*]. One of two sons of the Judahite Shammai, a descendant of Hezron (1 Chr 2:28–29). Abishur, his wife Abihail, and his two sons appear in an unparalleled list of Jerahmeel's descendants (1 Chr 2:25–33) contained within the Chronicler's larger genealogy of Israel (1 Chronicles 2–8).

Mark J. Fretz

ABITAL (PERSON) [Heb *ʾăbîṭāl*]. The mother of Shephatiah and a wife of King David (2 Sam 3:4 = 1 Chr 3:3). Abital's name occurs in two lists of sons born to David at Hebron. In one case (2 Sam 3:2–5), this list is inserted within the narrative concerning the strife between the houses of Saul and David; in the other case, its parallel (1 Chr 3:1–4) forms part of a larger genealogy of Israel (1 Chronicles 2–8).

Mark J. Fretz

ABITUB (PERSON) [Heb *ʾăbîṭûb*]. A son of Shaharaim the Benjaminite by Hushim, one of the two women whom Shaharaim subsequently sent away while he was living in Moab (1 Chr 8:8–11). The textually questionable MT refers to Hushim and Baara as "his (Shaharaim's) women" (Heb *nāšāyw*), but then calls Hodesh "his wife" (Heb *ʾištô*). Also, the children of the wife Hodesh are distinguished by the designation "heads of fathers' houses" (1 Chr 8:10), and are listed before the sons of the woman Hushim, who are simply named Abitub and Elpaal. Moreover, the text lists the descendants of Elpaal (1 Chr 8:12), but does not mention Abitub again, which may indicate Abitub's relative unimportance or else the author's disfavor of this son of Shaharaim.

Mark J. Fretz

ABIUD (PERSON) [Gk *Abioud*]. The son of Zerubbabel and father of Eliakim, according to Matthew's genealogy tying Joseph, the husband of Mary, to the royal house of David and Solomon (Matt 1:13). The name "Abiud," however, occurs neither in Luke's parallel genealogy of Joseph's ancestors (Luke 3:23–38), nor in the OT list of Solomon's descendants (1 Chr 3:10–24). This paradox has yielded no easy explanations. Kuhn (1923), for example, noted that the Chronicler lists a "HODAVIAH" (Heb *hôdawyāhû*) as a descendant of Zerubbabel (1 Chr 3:24), and that the Heb form *hôdîyâ* "HODIAH" is frequently confused with this term (1 Chr 4:19; Neh 10:10). He then suggests that Matthew's *abioud* represents Heb *ʾăbîhûd,* and that *ʾăbîhûd* resulted from a combination of *ʾby* and *hwdyh* in the (unattested) phrase *zrbbl ʾby hwdyh,* "Zerubbabel (was) the (fore)father of Hodiah," a phrase which perhaps telescopes the genealogy by conveniently leaping over all the names between Zerubbabel and Hodaviah/Hodiah. Kuhn believes that this "Hodiah" (Heb *hōdîyâ*) is rendered in Luke's parallel genealogy (3:26) as "JODA" (Gk *iōda*). Gundry (1982: 17) takes a less direct approach: he suggests that Matthew noted the name "Eliezer" in Luke's genealogy (3:29) and was reminded of the priestly lineage of Aaron (1 Chr 5:29—Eng 6:3), whose sons' names included a similarly spelled Eleazar and Abihu (MT *ʾăbîhûʾ*, but LXX *abioud*). Gundry proposes that Matthew mistakenly believed that LXX *abioud* represented Heb *ʾăbî yĕhûd(â)* ("My father is Judah"), and that he lifted the name from its priestly context and inserted it into the genealogy of Joseph to help underscore his Judaean royal lineage.

Bibliography

Gundry, R. H. 1982. *Matthew: A Commentary on His Literary and Theological Art.* Grand Rapids.

Kuhn, G. 1923. Die Geschlechtsregister Jesu bei Lukas und Matthäus, nach ihrer Herkunft untersucht. *ZNW* 22: 206–28.

Mark J. Fretz

ABNER (PERSON) [Heb *ʾabner*] Var. ABINER. The son of NER and cousin of Saul ben Kish. The name means "father is Ner" or "father is a lamp." The variant form "Abiner" means "my father is Ner"; "my father is a lamp." Abner served as commander of the first national Israelite army during the reigns of Saul and Eshbaal (1 Sam 14:50,

17:55; 2 Sam 2:8 etc.). The circumstances of his appointment are not related in the biblical texts, but it was common practice in ancient times to place blood relatives in positions of trust. The importance of Abner's position is indicated by his being seated beside King Saul at the observance of the New Moon festival (1 Sam 20:25). His status as commander seems to have prompted the Chronicler to report that he had dedicated war spoils for the maintenance of the temple, alongside Samuel, Saul, and Joab (1 Chr 26:27–28). Since the temple of Jerusalem did not exist during the time of any of those named, the tradition should probably be seen to derive from the Chronicler's pious imagination.

By having Saul request Abner to find out David's identity after the youth confronted Goliath (1 Sam 17:55–58), the biblical writer introduces irony into his narrative and at the same time, provides a basis from which to explore the motifs of loyalty and treachery. As Saul's loyal and trusted servant responsible for the kingdom's security, Abner is made responsible for the first formal introduction of David, the divinely chosen successor to Saul, the divinely rejected king. In addition, Saul's request to discover David's identity leads Abner to establish formal ties to the youth who will become his rival both within the Saulide military ranks, and within the political arena, for control of the Saulide throne.

The narrative tradition in 1 Samuel 26 portrays Abner in the additional role of the king's personal bodyguard. It reports that Abner slept next to the king in the camp during the pursuit of David, with the army surrounding the two, for protection. After David allegedly infiltrates the Saulide camp by night, stealing the king's spear and water jug, David chides Abner for not having kept a close enough watch over Saul in camp.

The historical reliability of Abner's depicted role as Saul's personal bodyguard in 1 Samuel 26 is doubtful. 1 Sam 22: 14 reports that David had served as the commander of Saul's personal bodyguard before his flight from the Saulide court. It appears that Saul had established a separate elite corps of professional soldiers who were not an official branch of the professional army but were loyal directly to him. David had a similar group, known as The Thirty (2 Sam 23:18). Abner apparently served as commander of the regular Israelite forces but was not involved directly with the royal bodyguard, which was under the command of another officer. It might be possible to presume that Saul was unable to find a suitable replacement the ranks of his bodyguard after David's flight and appointed Abner interim commander of both groups. It seems more likely, however, that the depiction of Abner in 1 Samuel 26 is to be understood as shaped by literary rather than historical concerns. Perhaps the author wanted to contrast David's superior service in protecting the king prior to his flight from court with that of Saul's most trusted servant, Abner. In this way he could illustrate the theme of David's blamelessness before Saul and Saul's unfounded suspicion and rejection of David.

In the wake of the disastrous battle at Mt. Gilboa that left Saul and his three eldest sons dead, Abner took Saul's remaining son ESHBAAL and crowned him as the new king of Israel at Mahanaim, the district capital of Saulide holdings in Gilead (2 Sam 2:8–9). Eshbaal was probably a youth under twenty at the time of his coronation. It can be presumed that Eshbaal's kingship would have been acclaimed by the surviving troops accompanying Abner, commander of the Saulide forces, to Mahanaim. (The army played a similar role, serving as a convenient quorum of assembled Israelite citizens, in the subsequent coronations of Omri [1 Kgs 16:16] and Joram [2 Kgs 11:4–12]). During Eshbaal's brief two-year reign, Abner continued to serve as commander of the national Israelite army.

Abner's first task as Eshbaal's commander-in-chief was to secure the town of Gibeon, which may have served as the Saulide capital (2 Kgdms 21: 1–9 LXX), against seizure by David (2 Sam 2:12–33). Engaging in representative combat with David's men, each side chose 12 men to fight and determine who would control the city. All 24 died, leading to a draw. In the wake of the fighting that ensued, Abner killed Asahel, the brother of JOAB, commander of David's forces (2 Sam 2:23). Both Asahel and Joab were David's nephews. Three hundred and sixty of Abner's men from Benjamin are reported slain in the ensuing melee, while only nineteen of David's men were killed (2 Sam 2:30–31). A desire to portray Judah as the stronger of the two, and as the unofficial victor, is evident.

According to 2 Sam 3:1, 6, during Eshbaal's 2-year reign, there was war between the house of Saul and the house of David, during which time Abner was making himself strong in the house of Saul. It seems that Abner decided to take advantage of Eshbaal's youth and inexperience in his effort to gain the Israelite throne. As the longtime commander of the Israelite forces, he would have had most of the army's support in his bid to replace Eshbaal. Abner made further attempt to usurp the throne by having sexual relations with Saul's concubine RIZPAH (2 Sam 3:7), for possession of the royal harem gave a person title to the throne (de Vaux 1965:115–19). David is later reported to have received Saul's wives when he became king over Israel (2 Sam 12:8). Likewise, Absalom asserted his claim to kingship in Jerusalem by erecting a tent on the palace roof and having sexual relations with the ten concubines whom David had left behind "to keep the house" when he fled to Gilead (2 Sam 15:16; 16:20–22). After his return, David put the ten concubines under guard in a separate house, where they were provided for but were left to live out their lives as if in widowhood (2 Sam 20:3).

The Bible reports that Eshbaal chastised Abner for his actions with Rizpah; in response, Abner vowed to set up the throne of David over both Israel and Judah, in fulfillment of the divine promise to David (2 Sam 3:9–10). To this end, Abner is said to have negotiated with David, with the consent and support of the elders of Israel and Benjamin, to make David king over Israel in place of Eshbaal (2 Sam 3:12–21). The course of historical events underlying the present narrative depiction may have been slightly different. Abner's negotiations with David may have taken place as part of a larger plan for a coup d'état, in which Abner sought David's help in accomplishing his coup in exchange for promised cooperation between the two neighboring states. The incident with Rizpah would have been an additional step in the planned coup. Alternatively, Abner may have offered to deliver Israel to David in exchange for a position as commander of the combined forces of Israel and Judah, thereby ousting Joab from his post as commander of the Judahite forces (Josephus *Ant* 7.1.5; Hertzberg *Samuel* OTL, 260; VanderKam 1980: 531; cf. Grønbaek 1971:234–42). The occurrence of some sort of collusion between David and Abner is indicated by David's later appointment of Abner's son Jaasiel to be the leader of Benjamin, after he succeeded Eshbaal to the throne of Israel (1 Chr 27:21).

During his negotiations with David, Abner was killed by Joab, David's commander, and Joab's brother Abishai, to avenge Abner's slaying of their brother Asahel at the battle at Gibeon. Upon learning that Abner had been conferring with David, Joab tried to convince David that Abner was acting as a spy on Eshbaal's behalf. Without David's knowledge, Joab sent messengers after Abner to have him return to Hebron, whereupon he slew Abner in the city gate while talking to him in private (2 Sam 3:22–30). In spite of the biblical apologetic, there is growing recognition that David was actively involved in Abner's murder, either directly in a murder plot with Joab; indirectly, through manipulation of Joab by allowing him to murder Abner as part of a standing blood feud; or independently in some unknown fashion covered up in the biblical account (i.e. Hertzberg *Samuel* OTL, 261; Lemche 1978: 16–17; VanderKam 1980: McCarter *2 Samuel* AB, 120–22; Cryer 1985: 392).

David cursed Joab and his father's house for the act of blood revenge, and had Abner buried in Hebron with a great display of public lamentation in order to convince both Judah and Israel that he had not plotted Abner's death (2 Sam 3:31–39). Ironically, Eshbaal's head would later be entombed with Abner's remains (2 Sam 4:12) after his similar assassination, probably at David's command. David's brief dirge over Abner (2 Sam 3:33–34), written with the chiastic structure abb′a′, may artfully maintain the ambiguity of his cause of death by carrying over the initial interrogative *he* to the fourth line, rendering the answer to the initial question with a further question (Freedman 1987:127; cf. McCarter *2 Samuel* AB, 111).

Bibliography

Cryer, F. H. 1985. David's Rise to Power and the Death of Abner. *VT* 35: 385–94.

Freedman, D. N. 1987. On the Death of Abiner. Pp. 125–27 in *Love and Death in the Ancient Near East,* ed. J. H. Marks and R. M. Good. Guilford, CT.

Grønbaek, J. H. 1971. *Die Geschichte vom Aufstieg Davids (1 Sam. 15–2. Sam. 5).* Copenhagen.

Lemche, N. P. 1978. David's Rise. *JSOT* 10: 2–25.

VanderKam, J. C. 1980. Davidic Complicity in the Deaths of Abner and Eshbaal. *JBL* 99: 521–39.

Vaux, R. de 1965. *Ancient Israel: Social Institutions.* Trans. John McHugh from French. New York.

DIANA V. EDELMAN

ABODE OF THE DEAD. See DEAD, ABODE OF THE.

ABOMINATION OF DESOLATION. A phrase occurring in the OT book of Daniel (11:31, 12:11, and perhaps 9:27), in 1 Maccabees 1:54, and in the teaching of Jesus as recorded in the synoptic gospels (Matt 24:15, Mark 13:14; see GOSPELS, LITTLE APOCALYPSE IN). The phrase refers in Daniel and 1 Maccabees to the desecration of the temple by the pagan emperor Antiochus Epiphanes in 167 B.C.E. and in the teaching of Jesus to some analagous disaster which he anticipates.

A. Daniel and 1 Maccabees

1. The Hebrew Phrase in Daniel. There are a number of textual and translational difficulties in the three Daniel texts. Dan 11:31 is most simply translated: "And they shall set up the abomination making desolate" *(wĕnātĕnû haš-šiqqûṣ mĕšōmēm).* Dan 12:11 speaks of "the time . . . for the setting up of an abomination being/making desolate" *(lātēt šiqqûṣ šōmēm).* Dan 9:27 reads literally: "and upon wing abominations making desolate" *(wĕ ʿal kĕnap šiqqûṣîm mĕšō-mēm),* which may mean: "upon the wing of abominations shall come one who makes desolate" (so RSV), or if the participle "making desolate" is construed with the noun "abominations" (even though in our texts the participle is singular and the noun plural), the text may mean: "On a wing . . . he will set up an abomination causing desolation" (so NIV). The meaning of the "wing" in 9:27 is in any case problematic, being variously explained by scholars, e.g. as referring to the "pinnacle" of the Jerusalem temple, to the "horns" of the altar in the temple, and/or to the "wings" of Baal portrayed as an eagle or winged sun. Other commentators have suggested emendation of the text, e.g. reading "and in its place" or "on their base" *(wĕ ʿal kannô/kannām).* (On these possibilities see Daniel commentaries and Goldstein *1 Maccabees* AB, 147.)

Despite the uncertainty of such details, the overall sense of the passages in Daniel is clear and the same in all three passages (cf. also 8:13). They refer to the coming to Jerusalem of a pagan invader, who will forcibly end the traditional worship of the temple, as epitomized by the daily burnt offering, and who will introduce pagan worship ("the abomination of desolation") until the time of the end.

2. Antiochus Epiphanes. Almost all commentators, including those who question the scholarly consensus that Daniel in its present form is to be dated in the second century B.C.E., see in the Danielic "abomination" a reference to the profanation of the temple by Antiochus IV ("Epiphanes") in 167 B.C.E. The phrase in 1 Macc 1:54 refers quite explicitly to this event: "On the fifteenth day of Chislev, in the one hundred and forty-fifth year, they erected a desolating sacrilege upon the altar of burnt offering." Antiochus was ruler of the Seleucid empire, of which Palestine was a part, and he responded to an act of defiance on the part of the Jews by attacking Jerusalem and by seeking to abolish the practice of the Jewish religion. His most horrifying action was the desecration of the temple and the introduction there of pagan worship (i.e. "the abomination of desolation"). His action met with courageous resistance, inspired and led by the family of Judas Maccabeus. Against all odds, the Jews defeated the Seleucid armies and regained a significant amount of control of their own affairs, including of the temple; this was cleansed of the "abomination" in 164 B.C.E., an event recalled ever after by the Jews in the feast of Hanukkah or Dedication (see MACCABEES, 1–2).

3. Further Observations. A number of further points about the Danielic "abomination" should be noted.

a. The unusual phrase "abomination of desolation" is commonly seen by scholars as a derogatory reference to the deity to whom Antiochus rededicated the Jerusalem temple. The new dedication was probably to Zeus Olympios (so 2 Macc 6:1), who may have been identified with, or at least given the Semitic name of, the Phoenician god *Baʿal šāmên* (= "Lord of heaven"). In order to avoid referring to the pagan deity directly, the author of Daniel parodies, substituting the term *šiqqûṣ* (i.e. abomination) for the name Baal (or Zeus) and the word *šōmēm* (i.e. desolating) for the consonantally similar *šāmêm* (i.e. of heaven). The term *šiqquṣ* is frequently used in the OT to designate something filthy or disgusting, and in particular idols; the substitution of this term for the name "Baal" can be compared to the use elsewhere in the OT of the word *bōšeth* ("shame") for Baal, as in the names in 2 Sam 4:1, 4, etc. (For a modification of this view, see Goldstein *1 Maccabees* AB, 143–52).

b. There is some doubt as to whether "of desolation" is the best translation for the relevant Hebrew word(s) in the Daniel texts. The Heb root *šmm* can have the sense of "being desolate," e.g., of deserted places; but it can also mean "to be appalled." The Greek versions of the OT opt for the first sense, using the verb *erēmoō;* but many modern scholars consider that the second meaning is more likely in Daniel, and that we should translate the whole phrase as "appalling sacrilege." It is possible, however, that the author of Daniel intended several connotations: the term may have been a parody of the name of the pagan god (see above), and may have suggested both the desolation brought to the temple (spiritual desolation at least), and the appalling nature of what had taken place; it is just possible that there is also an allusion to Antiochus' supposed madness, since the root *šmm* sometimes has this sense in postbiblical Hebrew (Rowley 1932: 265).

c. What form did the "abomination" set up by Antiochus take? A reading of 1 Maccabees (1:54,59) and of Josephus (*Ant* 12 §252) suggests that a pagan altar was erected on top of the altar of burnt offering in the temple. There is no explicit mention of an idol being erected, nor of one being destroyed when the temple was cleansed (1 Macc 4:43). However, the later Christian and Jewish tradition that a statue of Zeus was erected in the rededicated temple (perhaps also statues of Antiochus himself) may have some historical foundation. The phrase "abomination of desolation" could be a reference to such an unmentionable thing, or to some other stone structure(s) associated with pagan worship (Rowley 1953: 310–12; Goldstein *1 Maccabees* AB, 143–52). It has been suggested that Antiochus saw his rededication of the temple as the restoration of the original religion of the Jews rather than as the introduction of a new religion and deity; but whether this was his theory or whether he more simply saw himself as suppressing one undesirable and politically subversive religion and replacing it with something superior, the effect on the Jews was the same. (On Antiochus and his religious outlook, see Mørkholm 1966, and Goldstein *1 Maccabees* AB, 104–60).

d. The suggestion that the Babylonian creation myth with its account of Marduk slaying the chaos monster Tiamat has influenced the Danielic portrayal of the "abomination" is of interest (Heaton *Daniel* TBC, 92–96). However, while it is plausible to postulate connections between the Babylonian myth and the four sea beasts of Daniel 7 and then also with the "beast" of Revelation, it is not clear that the myth has contributed at all directly to the Danielic description of the abomination.

B. The Gospels and New Testament

The LXX translates the Danielic phrase "abomination of desolation" in 12:11 with the words *to bdelugma tēs erēmōseōs* (similar phraseology being used also in 9:26, 11:31; cf. *bdelugma erēmōseōs* in 1 Macc 1:54). Matthew and Mark use precisely this Greek phrase in their parallel accounts of Jesus' eschatological discourse (Matt 24:15; Mark 13:14). In speaking of the future, Jesus warns generally of sufferings to come, and then says particularly, "When you see the abomination of desolation standing where it ought not to be [so Mark; Matt "in the holy place"], then let those who are in Judea flee to the mountains . . ." The picture is of a disaster in Judea and of enormous and widespread suffering, to be ended only by the coming of the heavenly Son of Man. Luke's parallel passage does not have the phrase "abomination of desolation," but says, "When you see Jerusalem surrounded by armies, then know that its desolation has come near" (21:20).

The synoptic "abomination" has been variously interpreted (for a survey of views see, e.g., Ford 1979: 158–69). Many scholars have linked it to specific events in the 1st century, for example to the crisis that occurred in Palestine in 39–40 C.E., when the emperor Caligula ordered that his statue be placed in the Jerusalem temple (an order not eventually implemented, thanks to the emperor's death), or to the events leading up to the destruction of Jerusalem in 70 C.E. More particularly some have identified the "abomination" with the disgraceful and bloody wrangling of the Zealots during the Jewish war (Jos *JW* 4 §196–207, 377–94, etc.), or with the Roman standards advancing on Jerusalem.

Other scholars have declined to see such historical significance in the phrase, preferring instead to interpret the "abomination" as the coming of an eschatological antichrist figure, akin perhaps to the Pauline "man of lawlessness" and to the "beast" of Revelation. Others again have argued for a double reference to historical events in the 1st century and also to a future eschatological catastrophe.

To decide between such interpretations is a complicated task, entailing judgments about many related questions, e.g., about the history and authenticity of the traditions in question, about the respective dates of the synoptic Gospels, and about the nature of NT prophecy. And it may, of course, be that there are several interpretations of the "abomination" represented in the NT. However, a few further points may be noted.

1. The Origin of the Tradition. The Gospels ascribe the Christian "abomination" tradition to Jesus, but many scholars have questioned that attribution, arguing that the synoptic eschatological discourse contains a considerable amount of material that had its origin in the church (or even in Jewish tradition) rather than in Jesus' own teaching. They have argued on literary grounds for the composite nature of the eschatological discourse, and on theological and historical grounds for the tradition having its origin after Jesus' ministry, perhaps in the crisis situation provoked by Caligula in 39 C.E. This argument has been disputed by other scholars, who see the tradition as entirely congruous with other aspects of Jesus' teaching. (On the history of the discourse see commentaries, also Wenham 1984 for references.)

2. Background Considerations. In order to understand the NT use of the phrase "abomination of desolation," it is helpful, first, to be reminded of the historical and emotional importance of the Maccabean period and experience for the Jews of the 1st century C.E. It was natural for them to see parallels between their experience of Roman rule and the Maccabean experience of Seleucid rule and for them to regard the courageous stand of the Maccabees as an example and inspiration at times of tension or confrontation with Rome (even though there were differing views about what sort of resistance was called for). It was natural, too, for the Jews to be particularly sensitive to anything resembling the outrage perpetrated by Antiochus; thus, when Pilate ordered Roman legionary standards to be taken into Jerusalem, he was surprised by the massive outcry among the Jews (Jos *JW* 2 §175).

It is helpful, second, to recognize the importance of the book of Daniel within the Christian tradition of the NT period. It is not just the "abomination of desolation" that has a Danielic background, but also the tradition of the heavenly Son of Man, as now found in the Gospels; and it is possible that Jesus' kingdom teaching derives more from Daniel than anywhere else (Dan 2:44; 7:14, 27 etc.). It is hard to exaggerate the importance of Daniel for NT eschatology as a whole; Jesus' eschatological discourse in particular has been viewed as a midrash on Daniel (so Hartman 1966). The indebtedness of the NT to the book of Daniel is no doubt connected with the general interest of 1st-century Palestinian Jews in the Maccabean experience. That experience was seen as paradigmatic and prophetic.

Such an understanding is clear in Luke, who makes no reference to "the abomination," but who explicitly refers to "armies" surrounding Jerusalem, to the city's desolation, and then to the people being killed and taken captive, while the Gentiles trample the city. Luke's significant differences at this point from Matthew and Mark are often supposed to be a reflection of his post 70 C.E. standpoint; he has modified the Markan tradition in the light of his knowledge of the events and in order to distinguish clearly between the events of 70 C.E. and the eschatological coming of the Son of Man. Against this view it has been argued that Luke's changes betray no specific knowledge of the events of 70 C.E., and that they could be simple clarifications of the obscure Markan wording, or even independent early tradition.

Although it is less obvious what Mark and Matthew intend when they refer to the "abomination of desolation standing," it is quite likely that Luke has correctly conveyed their meaning. Mark intriguingly has a masculine participle "standing" *(hestēkota)* with the neuter noun "abomination" *(bdelugma)*, suggesting that he associated the awful event with an evil individual; he also refers to the abomination standing "where it ought not," whereas Matthew says more clearly "in the holy place." One possible explanation of Mark's obscurity is that he may have been writing at a sensitive time, when caution was appropriate; his gospel has often been dated to the period 66–70 C.E.. It is of interest to note that the Jewish writer Josephus sees Daniel's "abomination" as prophesying both the desolation of Antiochus and that perpetrated by the Romans (*Ant* 10 §276); the NT evangelists may have had the same understanding.

3. Concluding Observations on the Synoptic Phrase. If the Maccabean experience and the book of Daniel were so important in the 1st century C.E., then this is probably a clue that the NT "abomination" will have been understood by something analogous to the action of Antiochus, i.e., as an idolatrous attack on the people and temple of God by a powerful pagan force. The Gospels' own evidence supports the view that this was their understanding: Matthew specifically invites his readers to think back to Daniel (24:15), and it is possible that Mark's much debated "let the reader understand" is a similar invitation (13:14). All three evangelists include the injunction to those in Judea to "flee to the hills," a phrase reminiscent of 1 Macc 2:28 (cf. Matt 24:16; Mark 13:14; Luke 21:21). Luke has probable echoes of Daniel when he refers to the Gentiles treading down Jerusalem (Luke 21:24; cf. Dan 8:13).

Another clue to the evangelists' understanding of the abomination is the prediction of the destruction of the temple which in each Gospel precedes the eschatological discourse. Since the discourse, including the warning of the "abomination," is presented as explanatory of that prediction, there is a strong case for linking the setting up of the abomination with the predicted destruction of the temple (which is otherwise not mentioned in the discourse, unless the "coming of the Son of Man" is interpreted as a reference to that destruction). The picture, then, would appear to be of a major catastrophe, analogous to 167 B.C.E., but involving the profanation and destruction of the temple. The "desolation" in the synoptic phrase was probably understood literally.

4. Other Parts of the New Testament. Although the phrase "abomination of desolation" is not found in the NT outside the Gospels, the Danielic idea is probably reflected in the Pauline "man of lawlessness" in 2 Thessalonians 2, in the Johannine "Antichrist" of 1 John 2:18, 4:3, and in the "beast" of Revelation 13, 18. If we have in these different writings variations on a common eschatological theme and tradition, then 2 Thessalonians, if it is Pauline, is our earliest written contact with the tradition, showing it to be quite primitive. It may be that when Paul calls the lawless one "the man of perdition" or "of destruction," this is equivalent to the synoptic phrase "of desolation." But it is notable that both Paul and John, perhaps because they are writing in a Gentile context, describe the future evil in rather general religious terms without obvious political or military allusions (i.e., with no explicit reference to an attack on Jerusalem, though note Paul's reference to the man of lawlessness being in the "temple of God" and his remark about the Jews of Judea in 1 Thess 2:16), and also in terms of the appearance of an individual antichrist figure rather than in terms of an "abomination" being set up. It has been suggested that Paul was influenced in his thinking by Caligula's outrageous threat to the temple in

39–40 C.E., but his "man of lawlessness" is entirely explicable on the basis of the Danielic tradition. In Revelation the beast is clearly political in character, being the Roman empire, but the attack is now (after 70 C.E.?) not on the city of Jerusalem, but on the reconstituted people of God, i.e. the church.

Bibliography

Beasley-Murray, G. R. 1957. *A Commentary on Mark Thirteen.* London.

Bickerman, E. 1979. *The God of the Maccabees.* Leiden.

Dancy, J. C. 1954. *A Commentary on 1 Maccabees.* Oxford.

Ford, D. 1979. *The Abomination of Desolation in Biblical Eschatology.* Washington.

Gaston, L. 1970. *No Stone on Another.* Leiden.

Hartman, L. 1966. *Prophecy Interpreted.* Lund.

Mørkholm, O. 1966. *Antiochus IV of Syria.* Copenhagen.

Rowley, H. H. 1932. The Bilingual Problem of Daniel. *ZAW* 9:256–68.

———. 1953. Menelaus and the Abomination of Desolation. Pp. 303–15 in *Studia Orientalia Ioanni Pedersen.* Copenhagen.

Wenham, D. 1984. *The Rediscovery of Jesus' Eschatological Discourse.* Sheffield.

DAVID WENHAM

ABORTION IN ANTIQUITY. Abortion, natural and induced, is attested as a legal matter as early as the mid-2d millennium B.C. This article will consider abortion and related topics in the OT and the Ancient Near East, in ancient Judaism, the Greco-Roman world, and in early Christianity.

A. Abortion in ANE Law and the OT

With the exception of the Middle Assyrian Laws (ca. 1600 B.C.), the earliest Near Eastern law codes (including the legal materials in the OT) do not deal with the willful destruction of the fetus with the consent of the mother, but mention only natural miscarriages caused by a blow from another party. According to the injunctions outlined in the Middle Assyrian Laws, if a woman has had a miscarriage by her own act, when they have prosecuted her (and) convicted her, they shall impale her on stakes without burying her (Middle Assyrian Laws 53, in *ANET* 185). This code further directs that if the woman dies in the process of inducing the abortion, her body will still be impaled (as a kind of poetic justice) and will be denied burial.

Several of the law codes of the Ancient Near East, the Code of Hammurabi (ca. 1950 B.C.), the Lipit-ištar Laws, the Sumerian Laws (ca. 1800 B.C.), the Hittite Laws (ca. 1300 B.C.), as well as the Middle Assyrian Laws contain stipulations providing for compensation when a woman has been caused to miscarry because of a blow that she received from another person, thus providing at least indirect evidence concerning the status of the fetus in these societies. The Code of Hammurabi directs that if a seignior [a man of rank or authority] struck a(nother) seignior's daughter and caused her to miscarry, he shall pay ten shekels of silver for her fetus. If that woman has died, they shall put his daughter to death (Code of Hammurabi 209–10, *ANET,* 175). The Code of Hammurabi further provides for compensation for miscarriages caused to the daughter of a commoner and of a female slave. In each of these cases the penalty is commensurately smaller: the miscarriage of the fetus of a commoner's daughter is assessed at five shekels of silver, while her death must be compensated by a half mina of silver; causing the miscarriage of a female slave was fined at two shekels of silver, while the one causing her death was obliged to pay one third of a mina of silver (Code of Hammurabi 211–14). The Sumerian Laws (4.1–2, *ANET* 525), the Lipit-ištar Laws (iii.2′–5′, 7′–13′; Civil 1965: 5), and the Middle Assyrian Laws (21, 50–52, *ANET* 181, 184–85), contain provisions similar to those in the Code of Hammurabi, although the penalties in the Middle Assyrian Laws are somewhat more stringent: the man causing the miscarriage by his blow must compensate for her fetus with a life. Further, in both the Lipit-ištar and Middle Assyrian Laws, if the woman dies, the man himself will be put to death (Lipit-ištar iii.7′–8′, Civil 1965: 5; Middle Assyrian Laws 50, *ANET* 184). The Hittite Laws provide a further refinement: the fine assessed for a miscarriage caused in the tenth (lunar) month of pregnancy is twice the amount of the fine when the miscarriage occurred during the fifth month (Hittite Laws 1.17–18, *ANET* 190). The fine assessed for a miscarriage in the tenth (lunar) month of pregnancy suggests a distinction made in the status of the fetus and the loss that it implies for the father or family. Unlike the other law codes, in the Hittite Laws the assault on the woman and her possible death as a consequence are not considered.

The codes discussed above were not designed primarily to protect the unborn, although that was certainly one result of these injunctions, because the exposure or killing of abnormal, deformed, or otherwise unwanted children was both tolerated and practiced among them (Ebeling *RLA* 1:322). These laws and prohibitions were primarily sociopolitical in intent and protected the community from the potential loss of strength that a normal, healthy child could provide.

Exod 21:22–25 is frequently referred to in discussions of abortion. According to this passage, "When men strive together, and hurt a woman with child, so that there is a miscarriage, and yet no harm follows, the one who hurt her shall be fined, according as the woman's husband shall lay on him; and he shall pay as the judges determine. If any harm follows, then you shall give life for life, eye for eye, tooth for tooth, hand for hand, foot for foot, burn for burn, wound for wound, stripe for stripe" (RSV). These verses present numerous exegetical difficulties that have resulted in widely differing interpretations. According to one view, the "harm" (Heb *ʾāsôn*) in the Hebrew text refers to an injury done to the woman, since (according to this interpretation of the passage) the miscarriage is explicitly mentioned in contrast or juxtaposition to the "harm." Thus, the *ʾāsôn* done the woman, through either serious injury or death, is punished more severely than the miscarriage of the fetus, thereby indicating that the fetus was not viewed as fully human. Those holding to this view also note that this interpretation closely parallels evidence from other Near Eastern codes (Paul 1970: 71; Loewenstamm 1977: 356; Weinfeld 1977: 129; Sinclair 1978: 179–82; Sinclair 1980: 110). According to others, the first instance refers to a blow that results in a premature birth, but produces no further complications (*ʾāsôn)* to the child, while the second case refers to an instance in which the miscarriage results in the death of the fetus. Thus, according to this view, the fetus could be viewed as having a status similar or identical to that of human beings (Cottrell 1973: 8–9[604–15]; Jackson 1973: 273–304; Waltke 1976: 3–13; House 1978–79: 117–20). While these differing interpretations of Exod 22:21–25 influence the view of the status of the fetus in Hebrew law, they provide at best only indirect evidence for the case of induced abortions.

B. Abortion in the Hellenistic and Roman World

Greek philosophers offered opinions on abortion that diverged as widely as did their perspectives on the moment of ensoulment. Plato believed that the fetus is a living being (Plutarch *De placitis philosophorum* 5.15). Still, he recommended abortions for women who conceived after the age of forty (*Resp.* 5.9). Aristotle (*Pol.* 7.15.25[1335b]) allowed abortions only before "sense and life have begun" in the fetus, which he viewed as coming as forty days for males and ninety for females (*HA* 7.3; *GA* 4.1), and indicated by the movement of the fetus in the mother's womb. According to the Stoics, the fetus remains a part of the mother until it is born. Although no Greek Stoic whose writings are preserved takes a position on induced abortion, the Roman Stoic Musonius Rufus (whose views may have paralleled those of the earlier Greek Stoics) forbade induced abortions. However, it may also be here that the views of Aristotle and Musonius Rufus were more the result of a concern for the welfare of the state than for the fetus itself. The exposure of children was a practice tolerated, and in some instances even encouraged, by the same Greek philosophers and ethicists who took clear positions against abortion, probably for the same reasons, mentioned above, in the ancient Near Eastern societies: abortion was forbidden in order to protect the potential contribution to the society that the child would provide. However, once the child was born and found to be deformed in some way and, thus, a potential drain on the resources of the society, its death through exposure was allowed (Bennett 1923: 341–51; Eyben 1980–81: 12–19).

The paucity of Greek legislation on abortion makes it difficult to draw any definite conclusions concerning its legal status. According to a document falsely attributed to Galen, the lawmakers Lycurgus and Solon both enacted legislation prohibiting abortion and punishing its practice (Moòssides 1922: 64). While corroborating evidence is wanting, in the light of parallel laws in the ancient Near East, in particular the Middle Assyrian law punishing induced abortion, it is certainly not beyond the realm of possibility for induced abortion to have been forbidden in early Greek law as well. Indeed, according to the 1st-century Stoic philosopher, Aelius Theon, one of the orations by the Attic orator Lysias concerned "whether the fetus was human and whether abortions might be subject to penalty" (Dölger 1934: 10–12).

The Hippocratic oath forbids administering abortifacients (Nardi 1970: 59–60) except to expel a fetus that was already dead. On the other hand, there are reports of other methods recommended by Greek physicians in order to abort in the very earliest stages of pregnancy (Moòssides 1922: 68; Hèhnel 1936: 235; Crahay 1941: 14–15; Dickison 1973: 160). An inscription from Philadelphia in Asia Minor dating from about 100 B.C. includes prohibitions against the taking of drugs to prevent birth *(atokeion)* or to cause abortions *(phthoreion* [Nardi 1970: 193–94]). This differs from other *Kultsatzungen* of the Hellenistic period in that the use of birth control devices and abortifacients are not merely viewed as the source of cultic impurity, but as ethical and moral failings (Dölger 1934: 19–20; Weinfeld 1977: 132; but cf. Crahay 1941: 17).

While induced abortion is only occasionally mentioned in Rome during the period of the Republic, it seems to have been very common during the early centuries of the Empire. In reaction to this growing permissiveness, eminent writers of the period raised their voices in praise of those who avoided it and against those who practiced it. Borrowing a military metaphor, Ovid says that the woman who first aborted a fetus "deserved to die by her own weapons" (*Am.* 2.14.5–6). Seneca pays tribute to his own mother for never having "crushed the hope of children that were being nurtured in [her] body" (*Helv.* 16.3). Suetonius, Juvenal, and Pliny the Younger each report the tragic account of Julia, the niece of the emperor Domitian, whom he seduced and later compelled to undergo an abortion that resulted in her death (Suet. *Dom.* 22; Juv. 2.32–33; Pliny *Ep.* 4.11.16). Further, the exposure of unwanted infants, rare during the Republican period, appears also to have been commonplace under the Empire (Eyben 1980–81: 14).

C. Abortion in Ancient Judaism and in the NT

The LXX translators rendered Exod 21:22–23 in a manner that is markedly different from the received Hebrew text, apparently reflecting an awareness of the various strands of Greek philosophical thought on the status of the fetus: "If two men fight and they strike a woman who is pregnant, and her child comes out while not yet fully formed, he will be forced to pay a fine; whatever the woman's husband imposes, he will pay with a valuation. But if it is fully formed, he will give life for life, eye for eye, tooth for tooth, hand for hand, foot for foot, burning for burning, wound for wound, stripe for stripe." Whereas in the Hebrew text the term *ʾāsôn* may be understood as referring either to the fetus or to the woman, the LXX rendering of this phrase as "fully formed" makes explicit its reference to injuring the fetus, not the woman. Further, the use of the term "not fully formed" and "fully formed" is reminiscent of Aristotle's distinction between fetuses in which "sense and life have begun" and those that have not. The LXX translation implies a view about the status of the fetus that is basically Aristotelian and takes a middle position between the Stoic and Platonic views (Gorman 1982: 34–35; cf. Salvoni 1975: 27). It stipulates the death penalty in the event of the death of a fully developed fetus that was caused to miscarry when the woman was struck by another person.

Philo of Alexandria (25 B.C.–A.D. 41), in his treatise on

the Ten Commandments and other Jewish laws, *Special Laws* (*Spec Leg* III 108–9), discusses in the section on the commandment "Thou shalt not kill" the situation reflected in Exod 21:22–23. In this passage Philo says that if a man assaults a pregnant woman and strikes her in the belly, he will be required to pay a fine if the fetus is as yet unformed, as compensation both for the blow itself and for the fact that he has deprived "nature of bringing a human being into existence. However, if the fetus is formed, he will be put to death." Philo compares the formed fetus in the womb to "a statue lying in the sculptor's workshop needing nothing more than to be taken outside and released from confinement."

While retaining the LXX's distinction between the fetus that is "fully formed" and one that is not, Philo changes the specific situation that results in harm to the fetus from a fight between two men into one man's intentional assault on a pregnant woman. Most significant, however, is the moral tenor of his discussion. Unlike the text of Exodus, which is primarily concerned with nice legal distinctions, Philo emphasizes the moral wrongness of such an assault on the unborn. In Philo's view, one who injures a fetus that is not fully formed is guilty of an outrage against nature, while one who harms the formed fetus is guilty of the murder of a human being and is thus deserving of death (Gorman 1982: 35–36).

It is significant to note that the context in which Philo is speaking is part of an a fortiori argument against exposure. According to Philo, although Moses never includes exposure among prohibited practices, it is certainly implied, since Philo understands the law as prohibiting the destruction of life in utero. He is also challenging the justification of abortion by legal, medical, and philosophical authorities who, he declares, claim that "the child while still adhering to the womb below the belly is part of its future mother" (Philo *Spec Leg* III 117). Philo's perspective also differs significantly from those of the Hellenistic world and the ancient Near East in that he is not primarily concerned with the prerogatives of the father, or the needs of the state, but with the rights of the mother and unborn child.

The Jewish historian Flavius Josephus briefly discusses the injunction in Exod 21:22–25 (*Ant* 4§278). However, unlike Philo, Josephus follows the Hebrew text rather than the LXX in his rendering of this passage. Further, Josephus has recast the statute sufficiently that the ambiguity inherent in the Hebrew original concerning the object of the "harm" (Heb. *ʾāsôn*) is eliminated: in the view of Josephus, it is the woman, and not the fetus, who is intended. According to Josephus, whoever kicks a pregnant woman, thereby causing the fetus to miscarry, will be fined according to the judges' determination (which fine will be given to the aggrieved husband) "for having by the destruction of the fruit of her womb, diminished the population." He further indicates that if the woman dies from the blow she received, he will be put to death.

In his apology for Judaism, Josephus writes: "The Law orders all of the offspring to be brought up and forbids women either to abort or to do away with a fetus, but if she is convicted, she is viewed an infanticide because she destroys a soul and diminishes the race" (*AgAp* 2.202). It is somewhat difficult to reconcile Josephus' statement here with his view expressed in *Ant.* In the former, a clear distinction in penalty is made for the death of the fetus and the death of the woman. Here, however, Josephus explicitly states that the willful destruction of the fetus is equivalent to murder (although, strikingly, no penalty is stated). The contradictions in the two statements may, perhaps, be reconciled (if they are to be harmonized at all) in the following manner: although the willful destruction of a fetus is viewed in a manner not unlike murder, because Josephus regarded the woman and not the fetus as the primary target of the attack in the passage in Exodus 21, he may be treating the death of the fetus in a manner somewhat different from the death of the woman. In any case, it is significant that Josephus describes the fetus as having a soul, and clearly forbids a deliberate abortion of the fetus.

The rabbinic writings reflect an interest in the status of the fetus as well as a concern for the health and well-being of the mother. A passage in the *Mekilta* (*Nez.* 8) indicates that the blow to a woman that results in a miscarriage described in Exodus 22 is an act to be punished by a fine, but not by death, as it would be in the case of a capital crime. Similarly, according to the Mishnah (*Nid.* 5:3), only the killing of a child already born ("one day old") is an offense subject to the death penalty, whereas no mention is made of abortion as a capital offense. A fetus only becomes a person after it is born, when the "greater part of the head" (i.e., the forehead) emerges from the womb (Mishnah *Ohol.* 7:6; *Nid.* 3:5). If the mother's life is endangered by the pregnancy, then the obligatory principle of *piqqûaḥ-nepeš* ("safeguarding of life") is invoked, and the termination of the pregnancy is mandated. Thus, "if a woman is suffering hard labor, the child must be cut up while in her womb and brought out member by member, since the life of the mother takes precedence over that of the child" (*m. Ohol.* 7:6). On the other hand, this same passage indicates that if the greater part of its head has already emerged, then nothing is done to it since no preference may be given to one life over another. Subsequent Talmudic discussions reiterate these same principles (Sinclair 1980: 122–14, 119–22).

The early Christians opposed both abortion and infanticide. While there is no direct reference to either practice in the NT, the *pharmakoi* mentioned in Rev 21:8 and 22:15 may refer to those who obtained abortifacients (cf. 9:21; 18:23; Gal 5:20). However, other writings of the early period of Christianity, such as the *Didache* and the so-called *Epistle of Barnabas*, expressly condemn both abortion and infanticide. *Didache* 2:2, in writing about the "two ways," notes that there is a great difference between these two ways. In an exposition of the second great commandment ("Love thy neighbor as thyself") as part of the "Way of Life," the author makes a list of prohibitions modeled on the Ten Commandments, including: "Thou shalt not murder a child by abortion/destruction" *(ou phoneuseis teknon en phthora)*. The *Ep. Barn.* (19:5) contains the same prohibition immediately preceded by "thou shalt love thy neighbor more than thyself" (cf. *Apos. Con.* 7.3.2). According to *Did.* 5:2, among those who are on the "Way of Death" are "infanticides" and "those destroying the image of God" (cf. *Ep. Barn.* 20:2). Apparently, then, the fetus was viewed as being a neighbor with the same rights—

including the right to life—that the neighbor would have. Similarly, the early Christian apocalyptic literature reflects a moral abhorrence of willful abortion. The *Apocalypse of Peter,* roughly contemporary with the *Did.* and the *Ep. Barn.* and at one time included in the canon of scripture (in the *Muratorian Fragment* and by Clement of Alexandria), paints a graphic portrait of hell's population, which includes a scene in which women who have obtained abortions are in a gorge, up to their throats in excrement, while fire shoots forth from the infants who were aborted and strikes the women on the eyes. The *Apocalypse* continues by stating that the infants will be given to Temlakor, while the women who aborted them "will be tortured forever" (*Apoc. Pet.* [Ethiopic 8 = Akhmim Fragment 26]; cf. Clement of Alexandria *Ecl.* 41, 48–49 = *PG* 9.717–20; Quasten 1950: 144; Gorman 1982: 50–51).

From the 2d century on, opposition by Christian writers to induced abortion on ethical grounds continued, if not increased. The Christian apologist Athenagoras, in response to the charge that the Christians engaged in the ritual slaughter of children, asked what reason they might have to commit murder when they already assert that women who induce abortions are murderers and will have to give account of it to God. The same person, Athenagoras reasons, would not regard the fetus in the womb as a living thing and, therefore, an object of God's care and then kill it (*Presbeia* 35 = *PG* 6.969) For Clement of Alexandria (*Ecl.* 50.1–3 = *PG* 9.720–21; cf. Dölger 1934: 28–29), Tertullian (*An.* 27; cf. Emmel 1918: 33–44, 90–97), and Lactantius (*De opificio Dei* 17.7 = CSEL 27.56), ensoulment takes place at or immediately after conception. Thus, abortion at any stage of the pregnancy is viewed by them as unacceptable. The view in subsequent centuries is equally insistent on the moral right of the fetus to life. The councils of Elvira in A.D. 305 (Canons 63, 68 = *PL* 84:308–9; cf. Connery 1977: 46–49) and Ancyra in 314 (Canon 21; Cf. Nardi 1970: 496–501) contained canons against abortion. Similarly, the voices of Jerome (*Ep. 22 ad Eustochium* 13 = CSEL 54:160; *Ep. 121 ad Algasiam* 4 = CSEL 56:16), Ambrose (*Exameron* 5.18.58 = CSEL 32:184–85), and Augustine (*De nuptiis et concupiscentiis* 1.17 = CSEL 42:230) in the Latin West, and Basil of Caesarea (*Ep.* 188.2 = *PG* 32:671) and John Chrysostom (*Hom. in Rom.* 24 = *PG* 60:626–27) in the Greek East were raised against abortion and in defense of the life of the unborn (Nardi 1970: 483–582; Eyben 1980–81: 62–74; Gorman 1982: 53–73). See also *RAC* 1: 55–60; 2: 176–83.

D. Conclusion

In the ancient Near East, only the Middle Assyrian Laws provide explicit sanctions against those practicing the premeditated abortion of a fetus. The text in Exodus 22 gives only implicit evidence for the question of willful abortion. As a result, some scholars have attempted to elicit from other biblical texts an ethic that could be applied to the question of abortion (Waltke 1976: 3–13; Kline 1977: 193–201; Kurz 1986: 668–80). However, even where the evidence concerning the status of the fetus is somewhat ambiguous, there is no indication that premeditated abortion was tolerated in ancient Israel. On the other hand, the relatively permissive attitude in the ancient Near East toward the exposure of unwanted infants (for which there is no evidence available in ancient Israel) suggests that the prohibition of abortion, even where it existed, was designed more to protect the society from the loss of potentially productive members than from any particular concern with the rights of the fetus itself. A roughly analogous situation existed among the Greeks during the Hellenistic period: there was a general, though by no means uniform or monolithic, indisposition toward premeditated abortion, while the exposure of unwanted infants was widely tolerated. In Imperial Rome, the attitude toward abortion was more permissive than in the Hellenistic world, while exposure was also widely tolerated under the Empire. A significant development in attitude toward abortion can be seen in the writings of formative Judaism, particularly in Philo, as well as in early Christianity: not only is abortion prohibited—and exposure, too—but this prohibition rests upon an ethical concern for the fetus and the newly born. A further dimension to the discussion on abortion is added in the rabbinic writings, where the health and well-being of the expectant mother are taken into consideration.

Bibliography

Cottrell, J. W. 1973. Abortion and the Mosaic Law. *Christianity Today* 17: 602–5.

Civil, M. 1965. New Sumerian Law Fragments. Pp. 1–13 in *Studies in Honor of Benno Landsberger.* AS16. Chicago.

Crahay, R. 1941. Les Moralistes anciens et l'avortement. *L'antiquitè classique* 10: 9–23.

Dickison, S. K. 1973. Abortion in Antiquity. *Arethusa* 6: 159–66.

Dölger, F. 1934. Das Lebensrecht des ungeborenen Kindes und die Fruchtabtreibung in der Bewertung der heidnischen und christlichen Antike. *Antike und Christentum* 4: 1–61.

Emmel, K. 1918. *Das Fortleben der antiken Lehren von der Beseelung bei den Kirchenvätern.* Borna-Leipzig.

Eyben, E. 1980–81. Family Planning in Graeco-Roman Antiquity. *Ancient Society* 11: 5–81.

Feldman, D. 1968. *Birth Control in Jewish Law.* New York.

Gorman, M. J. 1982. *Abortion and the Early Church.* New York.

Hèhnel, R. 1936. Der künstliche Abortus im Altertum. *Archiv für Geschichte der Medizin* 29: 224–25.

House, H. W. 1978/79. Miscarriage or Premature Birth: Additional Thoughts on Exodus 21: 22–25. *WTJ* 41: 108–23.

Huser, R. J. 1942. *The Crime of Abortion in Canon Law.* Washington.

Ilberg, J. 1910. Zur gynäkologischen Ethik der Griechen. *ARW* 13: 1–19.

Jackson, B. S. 1977. The Problem of Exod. 21:22–25. *VT* 27: 352–60.

Kline, M. 1977. Les Talionis and the Human Fetus. *JETS* 20: 193–201.

Krenkel, W. A. 1971. Erotica I. Der Abortus in der Antike. *Wissenschaftliche Zeitschrift der Universität Rostock* 20: 443–52.

Kurz, W. S. 1986. Genesis and Abortion: An Exegetical Test of a Biblical Warrant in Ethics. *TS* 47: 668–80.

Moòssides, M. 1922. Contribution à la étude de l'avortement dans l'antiquité grecque. *Janus* 26: 59–85; 129–45.

Nardi, E. 1970. *Aborto procurato nel mondo grecoromano.* Milan.

Noonan, J. T., Jr. 1970. An Almost Absolute Value in History. Pp. 1–59 in *The Morality of Abortion,* ed. John T. Noonan, Jr. Cambridge, MA.

Paul, S. 1970. *Studies in the Book of the Covenant in the Light of Cuneiform and Biblical Law.* Leiden.

Quasten, J. 1950. *Patrology*. Vol. 1. Utrecht.
Rasmussen, J. A. 1979. Abortion: Historical and Biblical Perspectives. *Concordia Theological Quarterly* 43: 19–25.
Salvoni, F. 1975. Indagine veterotestamentaria, problemi dell'ominizzazione e indicazioni per i casi di aborto terapeutico ed eugenetico, la legge civile e l'etica del credente. *Ricerche Bibliche e Religiose* 10: 7–53.
Sinclair, D. 1980. The Legal Basis for the Prohibition of Abortion in Jewish Law. *Israel Law Review* 15: 109–30.
———. 1978. The Legal Basis for the Prohibition of Abortion in Jewish Law (in Comparison with Other Legal Systems). *Shenaton Hamishpat Haivri* 5: 177–207 (In Hebrew).
Waltke, B. K. 1976. Reflections from the Old Testament on Abortion. *JETS* 19: 3–13.
Weinfeld, M. 1977. The Genuine Jewish Attitude towards Abortion. *Zion* 42: 129–42 (in Hebrew).

STEPHEN D. RICKS

ABRAHAM (PERSON) [Heb *ʾabrāhām*]. Var. ABRAM. The biblical patriarch whose story is told in Genesis 12–25.

A. The Biblical Information

1. Outline of Abraham's Career. Abraham is portrayed as a member of a family associated with city life in Southern Babylonia, moving to Haran in Upper Mesopotamia *en route* to Canaan (Gen 11:31). In Haran, God called him to leave for the land which he would show him, so he and Lot, his nephew, went to Canaan. At Shechem in the center of the land, God made the promise that Abraham's descendants would own the land (Gen 12:1–9). Famine forced Abraham to seek food in Egypt, where the Pharaoh took Abraham's wife, Sarah, who Abraham had declared was his sister. Discovering the deception, the Pharaoh sent Abraham away with all the wealth he had acquired, and Sarah (Gen 12:10–12). In Canaan, Abraham and Lot separated in order to find adequate grazing, Lot settling in the luxuriant Jordan plain. God renewed the promise of Abraham's numberless descendants possessing the land (Genesis 13). Foreign invaders captured Lot, so Abraham with 318 men routed them and recovered Lot and the booty. This brought the blessing of Melchizedek, the priest-king of Salem to whom Abraham paid a tithe (Genesis 14). Following a reassuring vision, Abraham was promised that his childless condition would end and that his offspring would occupy the land, a promise solemnized with a sacrifice and a covenant (Genesis 15). Childless Sarah gave Abraham her maid Hagar to produce a son, then drove out the pregnant maid when she belittled her barren mistress. An angel sent Hagar home with a promise of a harsh life for her son, duly born and named Ishmael (Genesis 16). Thirteen years later God renewed his covenant with Abraham, changing his name from Abram, and Sarai's to Sarah, and imposing circumcision as a sign of membership for all in Abraham's household, born or bought. With this came the promise that Sarah, then ninety, would bear a son, Isaac, who would receive the covenant, Ishmael receiving a separate promise of many descendants (Genesis 17). Three visitors repeated the promise of a son (Gen 18:1–15). Lot meanwhile had settled in Sodom, which had become totally depraved and doomed. Abraham prayed that God would spare the city if ten righteous people could be found there, but they could not, so Sodom and its neighbor were destroyed, only Lot and his two daughters surviving (Gen 18:16–19:29). Abraham living in southern Canaan encountered the king of Gerar, who took Sarah on her husband's assertion that she was his sister. Warned by God, King Abimelech avoided adultery and made peace with Abraham (Genesis 20). Now Isaac was born and Hagar and Ishmael sent to wander in the desert, where divine provision protected them (Gen 21:1–20). The king of Gerar then made a treaty with Abraham to solve a water-rights quarrel at Beersheba (Gen 21:22–34). When Isaac was a boy, God called Abraham to offer him in sacrifice, only staying the father's hand at the last moment, and providing a substitute. A renewal of the covenant followed (Gen 22:1–19). At Sarah's death, Abraham bought a cave for her burial, with adjacent land, from a Hittite of Hebron (Genesis 23). To ensure the promise remained within his family, Abraham sent his servant back to his relatives in the Haran region to select Isaac's bride (Genesis 24). The succession settled, Abraham gave gifts to other sons, and when he died aged 175, Isaac and Ishmael buried him beside Sarah (Gen 25:1–11).

2. Abraham's Faith. Although it was Abraham's grandson Jacob who gave his name to Israel and fathered the Twelve Tribes, Abraham was regarded as the nation's progenitor (e.g., Exod 2:24; 4:5; 32:13; Isa 29:22; Ezek 33:24; Mic 7:20). Israel's claim to Canaan rested on the promises made to him, and the God worshipped by Israel was preeminently the God of Abraham (e.g., Exod 3:6, 15; 4:1; 1 Kgs 18:36; Ps 47:9). God's choice of Abraham was an act of divine sovereignty whose reason was never disclosed. The reason for Abraham's favor with God (cf. "my friend," Isa 41:8) is made clear in the famous verse, "Abraham believed God and he credited it to him as righteousness" (Gen 15:6; cf. Rom 4:1–3), and in other demonstrations of Abraham's trust (e.g., Gen 22:8). Convinced of God's call to live a seminomadic life (note Heb 11:9), Abraham never attempted to return to Haran or to Ur, and took care that his son should not marry a local girl and so gain the land by inheritance, presumably because the indigenous people were unacceptable to God (Gen 24:3; 15:16). Throughout his career he built altars and offered sacrifices, thereby displaying his devotion (Gen 12:7, 8; 13:4, 18), an attitude seen also in the tithe he gave to Melchizedek after his victory (Genesis 14). The places sacred to him were often marked by trees, a token of his intention to stay in the land (Gen 12:6; 13:18; 21:33). Abraham believed his God to be just, hence his concern for any righteous in Sodom (Gen 18:16ff.). Even so, he attempted to preempt God's actions by taking Hagar when Sarah was barren (Gen 16:1–4), and by pretending Sarah was not his wife. In the latter cases, God intervened to rescue him from the results of his own deliberate subterfuge because he had jeopardized the fulfilment of the promise (Gen 12:17f.; 20:3f.).

The God Abraham worshipped is usually referred to by the name *yhwh* (RSV LORD); twice Abraham "called on the name of the LORD" (Gen 12:8; 13:4), and his servant Eliezer spoke of the Lord, the God of Abraham (Gen 24:12, 27, 42, 48). The simple term "God" (*ʾĕlōhîm)* occurs in several passages, notably Gen 17:3ff; 19:29; 20 often; 21:2ff; 22. Additional divine names found in the Abraham narrative are: God Almighty (*ʾel šadday,* Gen 17:1), Eternal God (*yhwh ʾēl ʿôlām* Gen 21:33), God Most High (*ʾēl ʿelyôn* Gen 14:18–22), Sovereign Lord (*ʾădōnāy yhwh,* Gen 15:2, 8), and Lord God of heaven and earth (*yhwh ʾĕlōhê haššāmayim wĕhāʾāreṣ* Gen 24:3,7).

Abraham approached God without the intermediacy of priests (clearly in Genesis 22; elsewhere it could be argued that priests were present, acting as Abraham's agents but not mentioned). God spoke to Abraham by theophanic visions (Gen 12:7; 17:1; 18:1). In one case, the appearance was in human form, when the deity was accompanied by two angels (Gen 18; cf. v19). Perhaps God employed direct speech when no other means is specified (Gen 12:lf; 13:14; 15:1; 21:12; 22:1). Angels could intervene and give protection as extensions of God's person (Gen 22; 24:7, 40). Prayer was a natural activity (e.g., 20:17) in which Eliezer followed his master's example (Gen 24). Eliezer did not hesitate to speak of Abraham's faith and God's care for him which he had observed (Gen 24:27, 35). God commended Abraham to Abimelech as a prophet (Gen 20:7, *nābîʾ*). Abraham is portrayed as worshipping one God, albeit with different titles. Abraham's is a God who can be known and who explains his purposes, even if over a time span that stretches his devotee's patience.

3. Abraham's Life-style. Leaving Ur and Haran, Abraham exchanged an urban-based life for the seminomadic style of the pastoralist with no permanent home, living in tents (Gen 12:8, 9; 13:18; 18:1; cf. Heb 11:9), unlike his relations near Haran (Gen 24:10, 11). However, he stayed at some places for long periods (Mamre, Gen 13:18; 18:1; Beersheba, Gen 22:19; Philistia, Gen 21:3, 4), enjoyed good relations with settled communities (Gen 23:10, 18 mentions the city gate), had treaty alliances with some, and spoke on equal terms with kings and the Pharaoh (Gen 14:13; 20:2, 11–14; 21:22–24). He is represented as having owned only one piece of land, the cave of Machpelah (Genesis 23). Wealth flowed to him through his herds, and in gifts from others (Gen 12:16; 20:14, 16), so that he became rich, owning cattle, sheep, silver, gold, male and female slaves, camels and donkeys (Gen 24:35). He may have traded in other goods, for he knew the language of the marketplace (Genesis 23). His household was large enough to furnish 318 men to fight foreign kings (Genesis 14). He was concerned about having an heir, and so looked on Eliezer his servant before sons were born (Gen 15:2), and took care to provide for Isaac's half-brothers so that his patrimony should not diminish (Gen 24:36; 25:5, 6; cf. 17:18). While Sarah was his first wife, Abraham also married Keturah, and had children by her, by Hagar, and by concubines (Gen 25:1–6). His burial was in the cave with Sarah (Gen 25:9–10).

4. Abraham, Ancestor of the Chosen People. Belief in their ancestry reaching back to one man, Abraham, to whom God promised a land, was firmly fixed among Jews in the 1st century (e.g., John 8:33–58; cf. Philo), and is attested long before by the prophets of the latter days of the Judean Monarchy (Isa 41:8; 51:2; 63:16; Jer 33:26; Ezek 33:24; Mic 7:20). The historical books of the OT also contain references to Abraham (Josh 24:2, 3; 2 Kgs 13:23; 1 Chr 16:16–18; 2 Chr 20:7; 30:6; Neh 9:7, 8) as does Psalm 105. In the Pentateuch the promise is mentioned in each book after Genesis (Exod 2:24; 33:1, etc.; Lev 26:42; Num 32:11; Deut 1:8; etc.).

B. Abraham in Old Testament Study

1. Abraham as a Figure of Tradition. Building on meticulous literary analysis of the Pentateuch, Julius Wellhausen concluded ". . . we attain to no historical knowledge of the patriarchs, but only of the time when the stories about them arose in the Israelite people; this latter age is here unconsciously projected, in its inner and its outward features, into hoar antiquity, and is reflected there like a glorified mirage." And of Abraham he wrote, "Abraham alone is certainly not the name of a people like Isaac and Lot: he is somewhat difficult to interpret. That is not to say that in such a connection as this we may regard him as a historical person; he might with more likelihood be regarded as a free invention of unconscious art" (*WPHI,* 319f.). The literary sources of the early Monarchy, J and E, drawing on older traditions, preserved the Abraham stories. At the same time, Wellhausen treated the religious practices of Abraham as the most primitive in the evolution of Israelite religion. Hermann Gunkel, unlike Wellhausen, argued that investigating the documentary sources could allow penetration beyond their final form into the underlying traditions. Gunkel separated the narratives into story-units, often very short, which he alleged were the primary oral forms, duly collected into groups as sagas. These poems told the legends attached to different shrines in Canaan, or to individual heroes. Gradually combined around particular names, these stories were ultimately reduced to the prose sources which Wellhausen characterized. Gunkel believed the legends arose out of observations of life associated with surrounding traditions, obscuring any historical kernel: "Legend here has woven a poetic veil about the historical memories and hidden their outlines" (Gunkel 1901: 22). The question of Abraham's existence was unimportant, he asserted, for legends about him could not preserve a true picture of the vital element, his faith: "The religion of Abraham is in reality the religion of the narrators of the legends, ascribed by them to Abraham" (122).

The quest for the origins of these elements has continued ever since. Martin Noth tried to delineate the oral sources and their original settings, building on Gunkel's premises (Noth 1948), and Albrecht Alt investigated religious concepts of the expression "the gods of the fathers" in the light of Nabatean and other beliefs. He deduced that Genesis reflects an older stage of similar seminomadic life, the patriarchal figures being pegs on which the cult traditions hung (Alt 1966). The positions of Alt and Noth have influenced commentaries and studies on Abraham heavily during the past fifty years. At the same time, others have followed the literary sources in order to refine them and especially to discern their purposes and main motifs (e.g., von Rad *Genesis* OTL). For Abraham the consequence of these studies is the same, whether they view him as a dim shadow in Israel's prehistory, or as a purely literary creation: he is an example whose faith is to be emulated. The question of his actual existence is irrelevant; the stories about him illustrate how generations of Jews believed God had worked in a man's life, setting a pattern, and it is that belief, hallowed by the experience of many others, which is enshrined in them (see Ramsey 1981).

2. Abraham as a Figure of History. Several scholars have searched for positions which allow a measure of historical reality to Abraham. While accepting the literary sources as the channels of tradition, they have seen them as reflecting a common heritage which was handed down through different circles and so developed different emphases. This explains the nature of such apparently duplicate stories as Abraham's twice concealing Sarah's status (Gen 12:11–20; 20:2–18). W. F. Albright and E. A. Speiser were notable exponents of this position, constantly drawing on ancient Near Eastern sources, textual and material, to clarify the patriarch's ancient context. Albright claimed the Abraham stories fitted so well into the caravan society that he reconstructed for the 20th century B.C. "that there can be little doubt about their substantial historicity" (1973: 10). Textual and material sources included the cuneiform tablets from Mari and Nuzi and occupational evidence from Palestine. The Nuzi archives were thought to have yielded particularly striking analogies to family practices in the stories (see Speiser *Genesis* AB). These comparisons were widely accepted as signs of the antiquity of the narratives, and therefore as support for the contention that they reflected historical events. Even scholars who held firmly to the literary analyses took these parallels as illumination of the original settings of the traditions (e.g., *EHI*). In 1974 and 1975 T. L. Thompson and J. Van Seters published sharp and extensive attacks on the views Albright had fostered, Thompson urging a return to the position of Wellhausen, and van Seters arguing that the stories belonged to exilic times (Thompson 1974; Van Seters 1975). The impact of these studies was great. They showed clearly that there were faults of logic and interpretation in the use made of the Nuzi and other texts, and put serious doubt on the hypothesis of an Amorite "invasion" of Palestine about 2000 B.C. In several cases, they pointed to other parallels from the 1st millennium B.C. which seemed equally good, thus showing that comparisons could not establish an earlier date for the patriarchal stories. For many OT scholars the arguments of Thompson and Van Seters reinforced the primacy of the literary analysis of Genesis and its subsequent developments, allowing attention to be paid to the narratives as "stories" rather than to questions of historicity.

Inevitably, there have been reactions from a variety of scholars who wish to sustain the value of comparisons with texts from the 2d millennium B.C. These include an important study of the Nuzi material by M. J. Selman (1976) and investigations of the Mari texts in relation to nomadism by J. T. Luke (1965) and V. H. Matthews (1978). Equally important, however, are considerations of the methods appropriate for studying the Abraham narratives, and these will be discussed in the remainder of this article, with examples as appropriate.

C. Abraham—A Contextual Approach

When the literary criticism of the Old Testament was elaborated in the 19th century in conjunction with theories of the evolution of Israelite society and religion, the ancient Near East was hardly known. With increasing discoveries came the possibility of checking the strength of those hypotheses against the information ancient records and objects provide. Were Genesis a newly recovered ancient manuscript, it is doubtful that these hypotheses would be given priority in evaluating the text. A literary analysis is one approach to understanding the text, but it is an approach that should be followed beside others and deserves no preferential status.

The current analysis is unsatisfactory because it cannot be demonstrated to work for any other ancient composition. Changes can be traced between copies of ancient texts made at different periods only when both the earlier and the later manuscript are physically available (e.g., the Four Gospels and Tatian's *Diatessaron*). Moreover, the presuppositions of the usual literary analysis do not sustain themselves in the light of ancient scribal practices, for they require a very precise consistency on the part of redactors and copyists. Ancient scribes were not so hide-bound. Rather, the Abraham narratives should be judged in their contexts. They have two contexts. The first is the biblical one. Historically this sets Abraham long before Joseph and Moses, in current terms about 2000 B.C. (Bimson 1983: 86). Sociologically it places Abraham in the context of a seminomadic culture not controlled by the Mosaic laws, moving in a Canaan of city-states. Religiously it puts Abraham before the cultic laws of Moses, aware of God's uniqueness and righteousness, yet also of others who worshipped him, such as Melchizedek. To an ancient reader, there was no doubt that Abraham, who lived many years before the rise of the Israelite monarchy, was the ancestor of Israel, a position which carried with it the promise of the land of Canaan and of God's covenant blessing. That is the biblical context and it should not be disregarded (see Goldingay 1983). The detection of apparently duplicate or contradictory elements in the narratives, and of episodes hard to explain, is not sufficient reason for assuming the presence of variant or disparate traditions, nor are anachronisms necessarily a sign of composition long after the events described took place. These questions can only be considered when the narratives are set in their second context, the ancient Near Eastern world, at the period the biblical context indicates. Only if it proves impossible to fit them into that context should another be sought.

1. Abraham the Ancestor. Although Abraham's biography is unique among ancient texts, its role in recording his ancestral place is not. Other states emerging about 1000 B.C., like Israel, bore the names of eponymous ancestors (e.g., Aramean Bit Bahyan, Bit Agush). Some traced their royal lines back to the Late Bronze Age, and many of the states destroyed at the end of that period had dynasties reaching back over several centuries to founders early in the Middle Bronze Age (e.g., Ugarit). Assyria, which managed to survive the crisis at the start of the 1st millennium B.C., listed her kings back to that time, and even before, to the days when they lived in tents. In this context, the possibility of Israel preserving knowledge of her descent is real (cf. Wiseman 1983: 153–58). States or tribes named after ancestors are also attested in the 2d millennium B.C. (e.g., Kassite tribes, *RLA* 5: 464–73). Dynastic lineages are known because kings were involved. Other families preserved their lines, too, as lawsuits about properties reveal (in Egypt, Gaballa 1977; in Babylonia, King 1912: no. 3), but they had little cause to write comprehensive lists. Israel's descent from Abraham, the grandfather of her national eponym, is comparable inasmuch as he received the original promise of the land of Canaan. The ancient King Lists rarely incorporate anecdotal information (e.g., Sumerian King List, Assyrian King List; see *ANET,* 265, 564). However, ancient accounts of the deeds of heroes are not wholly dissimilar. Sargon of Akkad (ca. 2334–2279 B.C.), a king whose existence was denied when his story was first translated, is firmly placed in histories as the first Semitic emperor, well attested by copies of his own inscriptions made five centuries after his death, and by the records of his sons. Stories about Sargon were popular about 1700 B.C., and are included among the sources of information for his reign from which modern historians reconstruct his career. Other kings have left their own contemporary autobiographies (e.g., Idrimi of Alalakh, *ANET,* 557). All of these ancient texts convey factual information in the style and form considered appropriate by their authors. The analyses of their forms is part of their proper study. Finding a biography in an ancient Near Eastern document that combined concepts drawn from the family-tree form and from narratives about leaders, such as Genesis contains, preserved over centuries, would not lead scholars to assume the long processes of collecting, shaping, revising and editing normally alleged for the stories of Abraham.

2. Abraham's Career and Life-style. Journeys between Babylonia and the Levant were certainly made in the period 2100–1600 B.C. Kings of Ur had links with north Syrian cities and Byblos ca. 2050 B.C., and in Babylonia goods were traded with Turkey and Cyprus ca. 1700 B.C. A detailed itinerary survives for a military expedition from Larsa in southern Babylonia to Emar on the middle Euphrates, and others trace the route from Assyria to central Turkey. If Abraham was linked with the Amorites, as W. F. Albright argued, evidence that the Amorites moved from Upper Mesopotamia southward during the centuries around 2000 B.C. cannot invalidate the report of Abraham's journey in the opposite direction, as some have jejunely asserted (e.g., van Seters 1975: 23). Where the identifications are fixed and adequate explorations have been made, the towns Abraham visited—Ur, Haran, Shechem, Bethel, Salem (if Jerusalem), Hebron—appear to have been occupied about 2000 B.C. (Middle Bronze I; for a summary of archaeological material, see *IJH,* 70–148). Gerar remains unidentified, nor is there positive evidence for identifying the site now called Tel Beer-sheba with the Beer-sheba of Genesis (Millard 1983: 50). Genesis presents Abraham as a tent dweller, not living in an urban environment after he left Haran (cf. Heb 11:9).

Extensive archives from Mari, ca. 1800 B.C., illustrate the life of seminomadic tribesmen in relationship with that and other towns (see MARI LETTERS). General similarities as well as specific parallels (e.g., treaties between city rulers and tribes) can be seen with respect to Genesis. Some tribes were wealthy and their chieftains powerful men. When they trekked from one pasturage to another, their passage was marked and reported to the king of Mari. Town dwellers and steppe dwellers lived in dependence on each other.

In Canaan, Abraham had sheep and donkeys like the Mari tribes, and cattle as well. This difference does not disqualify the comparison (*pace* van Seters 1975: 16), for the Egyptian Sinuhe owned herds of cattle during his stay in the Levant about 1930 B.C. Like Abraham, Sinuhe spent some of his life in tents, and acquired wealth and high standing among the local people (*ANET*, 18–22; note that copies of this story were being made as early as 1800 B.C.). To strike camp and migrate for food was the practice of "Asiatics" within reach of Egypt, so much so that a wall or line of forts had to be built to control their influx (ca. 1980 B.C., see *ANET,* 446). The story of Sinuhe relates that the hero met several Egyptians in the Levant at this time (*ANET,* 18–22); the painting from a tomb at Beni Hasan depicts a party of 37 "Asiatics" (*ANEP,* 3), and excavations have revealed a Middle Bronze Age settlement in the Delta with a strong Palestinian presence (Bietak 1979). Military contingents brought together in coalitions traveled over great distances to face rebellious or threatening tribes, as in the affair of Genesis 14 (see below C5). In an era of petty kings, interstate rivalry was common and raids by hostile powers a threat to any settlement. To meet the persistent military threat, many cities throughout the Near East were strongly fortified during the Middle Bronze Age; fortification provided well-built gateways in which citizens could congregate (Gen 23:10, 18).

Disputes arose over grazing rights and water supplies. Abraham's pact at Gerar is typical, the agreement duly solemnized with an oath and offering of lambs. Abraham was a resident alien *(gēr)*, not a citizen (Gen 15:13; 23:4). Concern for the continuing family was normal. Marriage agreements of the time have clauses allowing for the provision of an heir by a slave girl should the wife prove barren (*ANET,* 543, no. 4; cf. Selman 1976:127–29). The line was also maintained through proper care of the dead, which involved regular ceremonies in Babylonia (see DEAD, CULT OF). Burial in the cave at Machpelah gave Abraham's family a focus which was valuable when they had no settled dwelling (cf., the expression in Gen 47:30). Comparisons made between Abraham's purchase of the cave reported in Genesis 23 and Hittite laws (Lehmann 1953) are now seen to be misleading (Hoffner 1969: 33–37). However, the report is not a transcript of a contract, and so cannot be tied in time to the "dialogue document" style fashionable in Babylonia from the 7th to 5th centuries B.C., as Van Seters and others have argued (Van Seters 1975: 98–100), and at least one Babylonian deed settling property rights survives in dialogue form from early in the 2 millennium B.C. (Kitchen 1977: 71 gives the reference).

3. Abraham's Names. Abram, "the father is exalted," is a name of common form, although no example of it is found in the West Semitic onomasticon of the early 2d millennium B.C. The replacement, Abraham, is given the meaning "father of a multitude" (Gen 17:5). That may be a popular etymology or a play on current forms of the name "Abram" in local dialects for the didactic purpose of the context, the inserted *h* having analogies in other West Semitic languages. The name "Aburahana" is found in the Egyptian Execration Texts of the 19th century B.C. (*m* and *n* readily interchange in Egyptian transcriptions of Semitic names [*EHI,* 197–98]). Genesis introduces the longer name as part of the covenant God made with Abram, so the new name confirmed God's control and marked a stage in the Patriarch's career (see Wiseman 1983: 158–60). No other person in the OT bears the names "Abram" or "Abraham" (or "Isaac" or "Jacob"); apparently they were names which held a special place in Hebrew tradition (like the names "David" and "Solomon").

4. Abraham's Faith. A monotheistic faith followed about 2000 B.C. is, so far as current sources reveal, unique, and therefore uncomfortable for the historian and accordingly reckoned unlikely and treated as a retrojection from much later times. The history of religions undermines that stance; the astonishing impact of Akhenaten's "heresy" and the explosion of Islam demonstrate the role a single man's vision may play, both imposing a monotheism upon a polytheistic society. Abraham's faith, quietly held and handed down in his family until its formulation under Moses, is equally credible.

Contextual research helps a little. Further study has traced the "gods of the fathers" concept far beyond Alt's Nabatean inscriptions to the early 2d millennium B.C., when the term referred to named deities, and the god El could be known as *Il-aba* "El is father" (Lambert 1981). Discussion of the various names and epithets for God in the Abraham narratives continues, revolving around the question whether they all refer to one deity or not (see Cross 1973; Wenham 1983). Some ancient texts which apply one or two of these epithets to separate gods (e.g., the pair *ʾl* "God" and *ʿlywn* "Most High," in an 8th-century Aramaic treaty, *ANET,* 659), may reflect later or different traditions; the religious patterns of the ancient Levant are so varied that it is dangerous to harmonize details from one time and place with those from another. The OT seems to equivocate over the antiquity of the divine name *yhwh.* Despite Exod 6:3, the Abraham narratives include the name often. Apart from the (unacceptable) documentary analysis, explanations range from retrojection of a (post-) Mosaic editor to explanations of Exod 6:3 allowing the name to be known to Abraham, but not its significance (see Wenham 1983:189–93). The latter opinion may find a partial analogy in the development of the Egyptian word *aten* from "sun disk" to the name of the supreme deity (Gardiner 1961: 216–18). However, the absence of the divine name as an indubitable element in any pre-Mosaic personal name should not be overlooked. Abraham naturally had a similar religious language to those around him, with animal sacrifices, altars, and gifts to his God after a victory. He found in Melchizedek another whose worship he could share, just as Moses found Jethro (Gen 14; Exod 2:15–22; 8), yet he never otherwise joined the cults of Canaan.

5. Objections to a 2d Millennium Context. a. Anachronisms. The texts about Sargon of Akkad are pertinent to the question of anachronisms in the Abraham stories. In those texts, Sargon is said to have campaigned to Turkey in aid of Mesopotamian merchants oppressed there. Documents from Kanesh in central Turkey attest to the activities of Assyrian merchants in the 19th century B.C., but not much earlier. Therefore the mention of Kanesh in texts about Sargon and his dynasty is considered anachronistic. At the same time, the incidents those texts report are treated as basically authentic and historically valuable (Grayson and Sollberger 1976: 108). The anachronism does not affect the sense of the narrative. In this light, the problem of the Philistines in Gen 21:32, 34 may be viewed as minimal. Naming a place after a people whose presence is only attested there six or seven centuries later than the setting of the story need not falsify it. A scribe may have replaced an outdated name, or people of the Philistine group may have resided in the area long before their name is found in other written sources. Certainly some pottery entered Palestine in the Middle Bronze Age from Cyprus, the region whence the Philistines came (Amiran 1969: 121–23). A similar position can be adopted with regard to the commonly cited objection of Abraham's camels. Although the camel did not come into general use in the Near East until after 1200 B.C., a few signs of its use earlier in the 2d millennium B.C. have been found (see CAMEL). It is as logical to treat the passages in Gen 12:16, 24 as valuable evidence for the presence of camels at that time as to view them as anachronistic. Contrariwise, the absence of horses from the Abraham narratives is to be noted, for horses could be a sign of wealth in the places where he lived (cf. 1 Kgs 4:26); horses are unmentioned in the list of Job's wealth (Job 1:3). Ancient Near Eastern sources show clearly that horses were known in the 3d millennium B.C., but only began to be widely used in the mid-2d millennium B.C., that is, after the period of Abraham's lifetime as envisaged here (Millard 1983: 43). Comparisons may be made also with information concerning iron working. A Hittite text tells how King Anitta (ca. 1725 B.C.) received an iron chair from his defeated foe. Recent research dates the tablet about 1600 B.C., yet iron only came into general use in the Near East when the Bronze Age ended and the Iron Age began, ca. 1200 B.C. Were the Anitta text preserved in a copy made a millennium after his time, its iron chair would be dismissed as a later writer's anachronism. It cannot be so treated; it is one important witness to iron working in the Middle Bronze Age (Millard 1988). Alleged anachronisms in the Abraham narratives are not compelling obstacles to setting them early in the 2d millennium B.C.

b. Absence of Evidence. Occasionally the absence of any trace of Abraham from extrabiblical sources is raised against belief in his existence soon after 2000 B.C. This is groundless. The proportion of surviving Babylonian and Egyptian documents to those once written is minute. If, for example, Abraham's treaty with Abimelech of Gerar (Genesis 21) was written, a papyrus manuscript would decay quickly in the ruined palace, or a clay tablet might remain, lie buried undamaged, awaiting the spade of an excavator who located Gerar (a problem!), happened upon the palace, and cleared the right room. If Abimelech's dynasty lasted several generations, old documents might have been discarded, the treaty with them. Egyptian state records are almost nonexistent owing to the perishability of papyrus, so no evidence for Abraham can be expected there.

Abraham's encounter with the kings of the east (Genesis 14) links the patriarch with international history, but regrettably, the kings of Elam, Shinar, Ellasar, and the nations have not been convincingly identified. R. de Vaux stated that "it is historically impossible for these five sites south of the Dead Sea to have at one time during the second millennium been the vassals of Elam, and that Elam never was at the head of a coalition uniting the four great near eastern powers of that period" (*EHI,* 219). Consequently, the account is explained as a literary invention of the exilic period (Astour 1966; Emerton 1971). At that date, its author would either be imagining a situation unlike any within his experience, or weaving a story around old traditions. If the former is true, he was surprisingly successful in constructing a scenario appropriate for the early 2d millennium B.C.; if the latter, then it is a matter of preference which components of the chapter are assumed to stem from earlier times. Yet the chapter may still be viewed as an account of events about 2000 B.C., as K. A. Kitchen has demonstrated (Kitchen 1977: 72 with references). A coalition of kings from Elam, Mesopotamia, and Turkey fits well into that time. To rule it "unhistorical" is to claim a far more detailed knowledge of the history of the age than anyone possesses. The span of the events is only fifteen years, and what is known shows how rapidly the political picture could change. Current inability to identify the royal names with recorded kings is frustrating; scribal error is an explanation of last resort; ignorance is the likelier reason, and as continuing discoveries make known more city-states and their rulers, clarification may emerge. (One may compare the amount of information derivable from the Ebla archives for the period about 2300 B.C. with the little available for the city's history over the next five hundred years.) Gen 14:13 terms Abram "the Hebrew." This epithet is appropriate in this context, where kings are defined by the states they ruled, for Abram had no state or fatherland. "Hebrew" denoted exactly that circumstance in the Middle Bronze Age (Buccellati 1977).

D. Duplicate Narratives

A major argument for the common literary analysis of the Abraham narratives, and for the merging of separate lines of tradition, is the presence of "duplicate" accounts of some events. Abraham and Isaac clashed with Abimelech of Gerar, and each represented his wife as his sister, an action Abraham had previously taken in Egypt (Gen 12:10–20; 20; 26). These three stories are interpreted as variations of one original in separate circles. That so strange a tale should have so secure a place in national memory demands a persuasive explanation, whatever weight is attached to it. In the ancient Near East, kings frequently gave their sisters or daughters in marriage to other rulers to cement alliances and demonstrate goodwill (examples abound throughout the 2d millennium B.C.). The actions of Abraham and Isaac may be better understood in this context, neither man having unmarried female relatives to hand. That they were afraid may reflect immediate pressures. For Isaac to repeat his father's procedure at Gerar is more intelligible as part of a well-established practice of renewing treaties with each generation than as a literary repetition (Hoffmeier fc.).

Abraham and Isaac both had trouble with the men of Gerar over water rights at Beer-sheba. Again, the narratives are counted as duplicates of a single tradition (Speiser *Genesis* AB, 202), and again two different episodes in the lives of a father and son living in the same area is as reasonable an explanation in the ancient context. One king might confront and defeat an enemy, the same king or his son having to repeat the action (e.g., Ramesses II and the Hittites, Kitchen 1982 *passim*). The naming of the wells at Beersheba, usually labeled contradictory, is also open to a straightforward interpretation in the light of Hebrew syntax which removes the conflict (*NBD,* 128).

E. Conclusion

To place Abraham at the beginning of the 2d millennium B.C. is, therefore, sustainable. While the extrabiblical information is not all limited to that era, for much of ancient life followed similar lines for centuries, and does not demand such a date, it certainly allows it, in accord with the biblical data. The advantage this brings is the possibility that Abraham was a real person whose life story, however handed down, has been preserved reliably. This is important for all who take biblical teaching about faith seriously. Faith is informed, not blind. God called Abraham with a promise and showed his faithfulness to him and his descendants. Abraham obeyed that call and experienced that faithfulness. Without Abraham, a major block in the foundations of both Judaism and Christianity is lost; a fictional Abraham might incorporate and illustrate communal beliefs, but could supply no rational evidence for faith because any other community could invent a totally different figure (and communal belief can be very wrong, as the fates of many "witches" recall). Inasmuch as the Bible claims uniqueness, and the absolute of divine revelation, the Abraham narratives deserve a positive, respectful approach; any other risks destroying any evidence they afford.

Bibliography

Albright, W. F. 1973. From the Patriarchs to Moses. 1. From Abraham to Joseph. *BA* 36: 5–33.

Alt, A. 1966. The Gods of the Fathers. Pp. 1–77 in *Essays on Old Testament History and Religion,* trans. R. A. Wilson. Oxford.

Amiran, R. B. K. 1969. *Ancient Pottery of the Holy Land.* New Brunswick, NJ.

Astour, M. C. 1966. Political and Cosmic Symbolism in Genesis 14 and its Babylonian Sources. Pp. 65–112 in *Biblical Motifs: Origin and Transformation,* ed. A. Altmann. Cambridge, MA.

Bietak, M. 1979. Avaris and Piramesse. *PBA* 65: 255–90.

Bimson, J. 1983. Archaeological Data and the Dating of the Patriarchs. Pp. 53–89 in Millard and Wiseman 1983.

Buccellati, G. 1977. *ʿApiru* and *Munnabtūtu:* The Stateless of the First Cosmopolitan Age. *JNES* 36: 145–47.

Clements, R. 1967. *Abraham and David.* SBT n.s. 5. London.

Cross, F. M. 1973. *Canaanite Myth and Hebrew Epic.* Cambridge, MA.

Emerton, J. A. 1971. Some False Clues in the Study of Genesis XIV. *VT* 21: 24–47.

Gaballa, G. A. 1977. *The Memphite Tomb-Chapel of Mose.* Warminster.

Gardiner, A. H. 1961. *Egypt of the Pharaohs.* Oxford.

Goldingay, J. 1983. The Patriarchs in Scripture and History. Pp. 1–34 in Millard and Wiseman 1983.

Grayson, A. K., and Sollberger, E. 1976. L'insurrection générale contre Narām-Suen. *RA* 70:103–28.

Gunkel, H. 1901. *The Legends of Genesis.* Trans. W. H. Carruth. Repr. 1964. New York.

Hoffmeier, J. fc. Once Again, the Wife-Sister Stories of Genesis 12, 20, and 26 and the Covenants of Abraham and Isaac at Beersheba. (Paper read at the SBL Annual Meeting, Boston, 1988.)

Hoffner, H. A. 1969. Some Contributions of Hittitology to Old Testament Study. *Tyndale Bulletin* 20: 27–55.

Irwin, D. 1978. *Mytharion.* AOAT 32. Neukirchen-Vluyn and Kevalaer.

King, L. W. 1912. *Babylonian Boundary Stones.* London.

Kitchen, K. A. 1966. Historical Method and Early Hebrew Tradition. *Tyn Bul* 17: 63–97.

———. 1977. *The Bible in Its World.* Downer's Grove, IL.

———. 1982. *Pharaoh Triumphant: The Life and Times of Ramesses II.* Warminster.

Lambert, W. G. 1981. Old Akkadian Ilaba = Ugaritic Ilib? *UF* 13: 299–301.

Lehmann, M. R. 1953. Abraham's Purchase of Machpelah and Hittite Law. *BASOR* 129: 15–18.

Luke, J. T. 1965. *Pastoralism and Politics in the Mari Period.* Ann Arbor.

Matthews, V. R. 1978. *Pastoral Nomadism in the Mari Kingdom.* ASORDS 3. Cambridge, MA.

Mendenhall, G. 1987. The Nature and Purpose of the Abraham Narratives. Pp. 337–56 in *AIR.*

Millard, A. R., and Wiseman, D. J., eds. 1983. *Essays on the Patriarchal Narratives.* 2d ed. Leicester.

Millard, A. R. 1983. Methods of Studying the Patriarchal Narratives as Ancient Texts. Pp. 35–51 in Millard and Wiseman, 1983.

———. 1988. King Og's Bed and Other Ancient Ironmongery. Pp. 481–92 in *Ascribe to the Lord,* ed. L. Eslinger. JSOTSup Sheffield.

Noth, M. 1948. *A History of the Pentateuchal Traditions.* Trans. B. W. Anderson. Englewood Cliffs, NJ. Repr.

Ramsey, G. W. 1981. *The Quest for the Historical Israel.* Atlanta.

Selman, M. J. 1976. The Social Environment of the Patriarchs. *Tyn Bul* 27: 114–36.

———. 1983. Comparative Customs and the Patriarchal Age. Pp. 91–139 in Millard and Wiseman 1983.

Thompson, T. L. 1974. *The Historicity of the Patriarchal Narratives.* Berlin.

Seters, J. van. 1975. *Abraham in History and Tradition.* New Haven.

Wenham, G. J. 1983. The Religion of the Patriarchs. Pp. 161–95 in Millard and Wiseman 1983.

Wiseman, D. J. 1983. Abraham Reassessed. Pp. 141–60 in Millard and Wiseman 1983.

A. R. Millard

ABRAHAM, APOCALYPSE OF. A midrash based on the text of Genesis 15 presented in the form of revelation. The title of the book is preserved only in manuscript S (Codex Silvester), where it runs as follows: "The Book of the Revelation of Abraham, son of Terah, son of Nahor, son of Serug, son of Arphaxad, son of Shem, son of Noah, son of Lamech, son of Methusaleh, son of Enoch, son of Jared."

A. Contents

The main subject of the book is the election of Abraham and the covenant between God and Abraham and his descendants. Chapters 1–8 tell about the call of Abraham out of the midst of idolaters. After a deep reflection on the various forms of their idolatry, Abraham wants to know the true God who created the universe. God then appears to him in the form of fire and commands him to leave the home of his father Terah and to sacrifice a heifer, a she-goat, a ram, a turtledove, and a pigeon (Genesis 15) on the high mountain. Chapters 9–32 describe Abraham's journey to the mount of Horeb, the offering of the sacrifice, and the visions imparted to him. Abraham sees, among other things, the seven sins of the world (24:3–25:2) and the destruction of the Temple in Jerusalem (27:1–12). God announces to him the punishment of the Gentiles and of the sinners belonging to the people of Israel (chap. 29). The vision of the "man going out from the left, the heathen side" (29:4) foretells the test of the people of God in the last days of this age. Before the age of justice, God will afflict "all earthly creation" with ten plagues (29:15, 30:2–8) and afterward send his Elect One, who will summon the people of God (31:1). Sinners will be punished and the righteous will triumph forever (chap. 32).

B. The Text

The *Apocalypse of Abraham (Apoc. Ab.)* is preserved only in Old Church Slavonic translation. According to common opinion, it was translated from Greek around A.D. 900 in Bulgaria, although translation from a Semitic original cannot be excluded (see below). The Old Church Slavonic copies of the text were very soon transferred, probably by monks, from Bulgaria to Russia and there diffused within some centuries in different transcripts. This fact explains why the present text of the book is influenced by the old Russian language. All nine extant manuscripts containing this pseudepigraphon are preserved in the museums and the libraries of the U.S.S.R. The oldest manuscript is the Codex Silvester (14th century), which is characterized by many omissions owing mostly to inadvertance of the copyists; the text itself is incomplete. The best text is preserved in manuscript B, which belongs to the Synodal Paleja Tolkovaja (Sin 211, Gosudarstvennyj Istoričeskij Muzej 869, fols. 76–90, Moscow) and dates to the 16th century (see Philonenko-Sayer and Philonenko 1981; Rubinkiewicz 1977; 1987).

C. The Integrity of the Text

Most critics distinguish two parts in the *Apocalypse of Abraham:* the haggadic section (chaps. 1–8) and the apocalyptic section (chaps. 9–32). The two sections were probably written by different authors. Later, the two documents were most likely joined together into a single work. It seems, however, that only chapter 7 did not belong to the original text of the pseudepigraphon, and maybe also chapter 23 (the description of the sin of Adam and Eve, which undoubtedly reflects Jewish sources; the chapter could have been introduced into the *Apocalypse of Abraham* from another pseudepigraphon). A special problem is presented by *Apoc. Ab.* 29:4–13. Generally one assumes that the Man "going out from the left, the heathen side" (29:4), worshipped by the great crowd of the heathen, and insulted by some of the people of Israel, represents the figure of Jesus. Therefore, some critics claim that this passage is a Christian interpolation (*ANRW* 2/19/1: 137–51) or that it could be a "Jewish view of Jesus as an apostle to the heathen" (*EncJud* 1: 125–27). However, an exact analysis of the vision in *Apoc. Ab.* 29:4–13 proves that it must be original, and that it "has little in common with a Christian view of Jesus but recalls the beast in Rev 13:1–4" (Hall 1988). The heathen man may be identified as the Roman emperor. Only "the phrase identifying the man who is worshiped as a child of Abraham (29:9b) must be understood as a gloss, probably by a Christian interpolator who found Christ in the author's 'antichrist' " (Hall 1988).

In addition to these three passages, we may note some glosses, perhaps because of the Bogomil editor (*ANRW* 2/19/1: 137–51; Rubinkiewicz 1987; contrary Philonenko-Sayar and Philonenko 1981). The very strange statement that Abraham's issue are "the people (associated) with Azazel" must be understood in the light of the gloss *"ljudii s Azazilomû sii sout"* (22:5), "this is the people with Azazel," found in one of the manuscripts in the correct form. In the other manuscripts it is slightly different and incorporated into the main phrase. This fact explains the strange association of Azazel with the people of God and is in the spirit of the medieval slavonic sect of the Bogomils.

D. Original Language

The original language of the *Apocalypse of Abraham* was undoubtedly Semitic, either Aramaic or Hebrew. Many Semitisms are found in the text which cannot be explained simply by the influence of Septuagintal style. For example, *Apoc. Ab.* uses the positive instead of the comparative, indicating a Semitic original. The awkward Slavonic construction "heavy of (a big stone)" (1:5) renders Semitic *kbd mn,* which should be interpreted "heavier than (a big stone)." Also, prepositions are sometimes used according to Hebrew rather than Slavonic syntax (e.g., 8:4; 12:10; see Rubinkiewicz 1980).

E. Date and Origin

The *Apocalypse of Abraham* was written after A.D. 70, as is evident from its reference to the destruction of the Temple. If one assumes that plagues 1, 3, 5, 7, 9, (*Apoc. Ab.* 30:4–8) refer to the events from A.D. 69 and 70, and that plagues 2, 4, 6, 8, 10 (*Apoc. Ab.* 30:4–8) refer to the eruption of Vesuvius in A.D. 79, then it may be surmised that the text was composed between A.D. 79–81. This opinion is reinforced by the symbolic interpretation of the haggadic material found in *Apoc. Ab.* 1–6 (the idols symbolize the hostile kingdoms and kings: Marumat = Rome, Barisat = Babylon, [Su]zuch = Persia, "five other gods" = Galba, Otho, Vitellius, Vespasian, and Titus), but this explanation must remain hypothetical (see Rubinkiewicz 1982).

The author of *Apoc. Ab.* belonged to the priestly environment. Some doctrinal affinities of the text with the Qumran writings—e.g., the opinion regarding the High Priest in the Temple, the liturgical milieu of the pseudepigraphon concentrated around the Feast of Tabernacles as the Feast of the renewal of the Covenant, and predeterminism contained in the text of this work—show at least some dependency on Essene doctrine. Despite these similarities, there is no convincing argument that the author of *Apoc. Ab.* was an Essene. The views expressed in the pseudepigraphon correspond equally well to the concepts represented by the priestly environment of Palestine in general, not just the Essene environment.

F. Theology

God is eternal (9:3) and He is the God who protects Abraham and his issue (9:4). He has created the universe, has elected Israel, has called her "my people" (22:5; 31:1), and will give her the victory over her enemies (31:1–2).

Angelology plays an important part in the pseudepigraphon. The most eminent person is the angel of God, Iaoel. His features resemble certain features of the Angel of God in Exod 23:20–23. His fundamental role is to protect and fortify Abraham (10:3). The chief of the fallen angels is Azazel (13:7). His power is on the earth (13:7–8; 14:6), but it is not unlimited; for example, Azazel has no power over the just (13:10).

The world is divided into two parts: (1) the land and the garden of Eden, and (2) the upper and lower waters. In the same way, mankind is divided into the people of God (Israel) and the Gentiles (21:3–7). However, there is no ontological dualism in *Apoc. Ab.* The world created by God is good (22:2). There is no other God except that one for whom Abraham searched and who is beloved (19:3). There is evil in the world, but it is not unavoidable. God has full control over the development of events and does not allow the body of the just man to fall under the control of Azazel (13:10). Azazel is wrong if he thinks that he may scoff at justice and disclose the secrets of heaven (14:4). He will be punished and banished to the desert, where he will remain forever (14:5).

The age of wickedness will consist of "twelve periods" (29:2). After this age comes the last judgment, preceded by the redemption of the righteous. First, however, ten plagues will affect all the world (29:15; 30:2–8). Then God will send his "Elect One" (31:1) and will gather the dispersed people of God. At this time, the Gentiles who oppressed Israel will be punished (31:2) and the apostates will be burned by the fire of Azazel's tongue (31:6). The Temple will be rebuilt and the cult restored (29:17–18). There is no explicit doctrine of the resurrection in the pseudepigraphon. However, this idea may be suggested by the symbol of the dew (19:4) and by the conviction expressed in 13:10 that the body of the just will not belong to Azazel. This may be connected with the exegesis of Ps 16:10, a Psalm utilized by Christians to prove the resurrection of Jesus (Acts 2:27).

G. The *Apocalypse of Abraham* and the Bible

The books of Genesis and Ezekiel play fundamental roles in *Apoc. Ab.* The author begins his work with an allusion to Gen 20:13, adduced in light of targumic exegesis, and closes with reference to Gen 15:13–16 (*Apoc. Ab.* 32:1–3). *Apoc. Ab.* 8:4 and 9:1–4 reflect the expression contained in Gen 12:1 and 15:1 seen in the light of Ps 22:2–3 and Deut 33:29. The author quotes Gen 15:9 (*Apoc. Ab.* 9:5) and employs the image of Gen 15:17a (*Apoc. Ab.* 15:1). The text of *Apoc. Ab.* 20:4 reminds one of Gen 18:27 and that of *Apoc. Ab.* 20:6 alludes to Gen 18:30. *Apoc. Ab.* 18–19 is based on Ezekiel 1, 10. Abraham sees four living creatures (*Apoc. Ab.* 18:3–12; cf. Ezek 3:12–13), the throne (*Apoc. Ab.* 18:3; cf. Ezek 1:26), and the Divine Chariot (*Apoc. Ab.* 18:12; cf. Ezekiel 1, 10).

There is no direct relation between the *Apocalypse of Abraham* and the NT. There are nonetheless many parallel expressions which show that the authors drew from the same tradition (for example, *Apoc. Ab.* 13:3–14 and Matt 4:1–11 par; *Apoc. Ab.* 9:5–8; 12:1–10 and Gal 4:21–31; *Apoc. Ab.* 18:11 and Rev 5:9; see Rubinkiewicz 1987).

H. The *Apocalypse of Abraham* and the Pseudepigrapha

The author of *Apoc. Ab.* follows the tradition of *1 Enoch* 1–36. The chief of the fallen angels is Azazel who rules over the stars and the main part of humanity. It is easy to find here the tradition of Gen 6:1–4 developed in *1 Enoch.* Azazel rebelled against God and, together with the other angels, united sexually with the daughters of men. He disclosed the secrets of heaven and caused great misfortune on earth. Therefore, he was expelled to the desert. Abraham, like Enoch, receives the power to tame Satan (*Apoc. Ab.* 14:3; 1 *En.* 14:3). The tradition of 1 *Enoch* 10 about Azazel underlying *Apoc. Ab.* 13–14 permits us to understand better the difficult text of Matt 22:11–14 (see Rubinkiewicz 1984).

The *Apocalypse of Abraham,* with its Palestinian origin, early date of composition, common tradition with *1 Enoch,* and connections with NT writings, finds a place for itself among the most significant works of the Jewish world in the 1st century A.D.

Bibliography

Charlesworth, J. H. 1976. *The Pseudepigrapha and Modern Research.* SCS 7. Missoula.

Denis, A.-M. 1970. *Introduction aux pseudepigraphes grecs d'Ancien Testament.* SVTP 1. Leiden.

Hall, R. G. 1988. The "Christian Interpolation" in the *Apocalypse of Abraham. JBL* 107: 107–10.

Lunt, H. 1985. On the Language of the Slavonic *Apocalypse of Abraham. Studia Hierosolymitana* 7: 55–62.

Philonenko-Sayar, B., and Philonenko, M. 1981. L'Apocalypse d'Abraham. *Sem* 31.

———. 1982. *Die Apocalypse Abrahams.* JSHRZ 5. Gütersloh.

Rubinkiewicz, R. 1977. L'Apocalypse d'Abraham en slave. 2 vols. Diss. Rome [typescript].

———. 1980. Les sémitismes dans l'Apocalypse d'Abraham. *Folia Orientalia* 21: 141–48.

———. 1982. Apokalipsa Abrahama 1–6: Propozycja interpretacji symbolicznej. *RocTKan* 29/1: 79–94.

———. 1984. *Die Eschatologie von Henoch 9–11 und das Neue Testament.* ÖBS 6. Klosterneuburg.

———. 1987. *L'Apocalypse d'Abraham en vieux slave.* Lublin.

Rubinstein, A. 1953. Hebraisms in the Slavonic "Apocalypse of Abraham." *JJS* 4: 108–15.

———. 1954. Hebraisms in the "Apocalypse of Abraham." *JJS* 5: 132–35.

———. 1957. A Problematic Passage in the Apocalypse of Abraham. *JJS.*

Ryszard Rubinkiewicz

ABRAHAM, TESTAMENT OF. Although titled a "testament" in many of the extant manuscripts, the Testament of Abraham exhibits few of the traits of that genre. Abraham is instructed to make a testament in preparation for his death, but he neither relates his own personal history in order to instruct his descendants, nor imparts ethical advice to those who have gathered at his bedside. The "Testament" of Abraham is more closely related to the apocalyptic dramas, the descriptions of otherworldly journeys, and the legends about the death of Moses, which circulated widely in the Hellenistic and Roman periods, than it is to the other testamentary literature. The "Testament" focuses on the inevitability of death, God's just and merciful judgment (in contrast to Abraham's quick condemnation of sinners), and the fate of souls after death. The figure of Abraham bears some resemblance to the biblical character in that he is presented as hospitable and righteous, but he is also seen in the story as disobedient (refusing to go with God's appointed messengers) and self-righteous (condemning nearly everyone that he sees during his heavenly journey).

The work survives in two distinct Greek recensions, a longer version (A) and a shorter version (B). The two recensions probably derive from a common source, but neither is directly dependent on the other. Whereas the long version is thought to preserve the more original contents and order, the short version often preserves earlier wording and simpler vocabulary (James 1892: 49; Nickelsburg 1976: 85–93).

The story contains two parallel and symmetrical divisions: In the first part, Michael is sent by God to retrieve Abraham's soul (chaps. 1–15); in the second part, Death is sent to complete the task (chaps. 16–20; Nickelsburg 1984: 61). In part one, Abraham receives the visitor Michael with great hospitality, but after he discovers why Michael has come, he refuses to die (A2–7; B = Abraham tries to postpone death). Michael continues to try to persuade Abraham to obey God's will, but Abraham instead strikes a bargain with Michael that would allow him to see all the inhabited world before he dies (A8–9; B = "all God's creation"). During the journey, Abraham is repulsed by the wickedness that he sees, and he immediately calls for the death of the sinners (A10). God orders the tour to stop before Abraham condemns everyone; he then instructs Michael to take Abraham to the place where Abel is carefully weighing the deeds of the dead so that Abraham can see God's compassionate judgment (A11–13). God's merciful treatment of the souls persuades Abraham to pray on behalf of those he had condemned during his journey (A14).

Although Michael has fulfilled his part of the bargain, Abraham still refuses to die. Michael then returns to heaven and God sends Death to reclaim Abraham's soul (A15–16). Death attempts to frighten Abraham by showing him all manner of gruesome deaths (A17), and then tries to persuade him that a swift death is something to be sought because such a death precludes any further punishment (A17–19). Abraham still is reluctant to die; finally he is tricked by Death, and dies. The story concludes with the angels taking Abraham's soul to heaven (A20).

Aside from the minor differences mentioned in the summary, the longer and shorter recensions differ in two major ways: (1) the shorter recension places the judgment scene before the tour of the world; and (2) the judgment scene in the shorter recension is much less fully developed.

The two recensions are preserved in approximately thirty Greek MSS ranging from the 13th to the 17th century (for a full list, cf. Schmidt 1986: 1–3; Denis 1970: 32–33). The noteworthy other languages are Coptic (which generally follows B, but some elements resemble A; cf. Sparks' introduction to Turner 1984: 393), Ethiopic (based on the Coptic; cf. *HJP*[2] 3/2: 765), Arabic (also based on the Coptic), Roumanian (cf. Turdeanu 1981: 201–18, 440), and Slavonic (follows B; cf. Turdeanu 1981: 201–18, 440).

Scholars such as Ginzberg and Kohler argued for a Hebrew original for the work, but the consensus today is that the longer version of the Testament was composed in Septuagintal, or Semitic, Greek (cf. *OTP* 1: 873; Delcor 1973: 32–34). This position is strengthened by the close vocabulary parallels between the long recension and other books such as the Wisdom of Solomon and 2,3,4 Maccabees, which were clearly composed in Greek. The shorter version can easily be retroverted to Hebrew, but as Sanders notes, the Hebrew that results is a classical biblical prose style, not the Hebrew of the Greco-Roman period as evidenced by the Dead Sea Scrolls and early rabbinic literature (*OTP* 1: 873). It is therefore likely, though still not settled, that the shorter recension was also composed in Greek (cf. Schmidt 1986).

There are no historical allusions in the Testament. Thus estimates of the date of composition have ranged from the 2d century B.C.E. up to the 6th century C.E. (for the final form of the long recension), although most scholars regard the 1st century B.C.E. or 1st century C.E. as the most likely (*OTP* 1: 874; Schmidt; Delcor: 73–77; Collins: 226; Denis 1970: 36).

An Egyptian provenience for the Testament has been widely accepted (*OTP* 1: 875; Collins: 226; Denis 1970: 36; Nickelsburg 1984: 63). Cited in its favor are the similarities in vocabulary between the Testament and other works thought to derive from Egyptian Jewry (3 Maccabees, Testament of Job, 3 Baruch), the balancing of deeds (weighing of souls; chaps. A11–13), the three levels of judgment (which may reflect the three levels of jurisdiction in Roman Egypt; cf. Sanders: 875; Delcor: 18), and the portrayal of the figure of death as a heavenly courtier and servant of God (Nickelsburg 1984: 63). Schmidt has argued for a Palestinian provenience (see also Janssen), but he bases his claim on the doubtful position that the shorter recension was composed in Hebrew.

Undoubtedly a Jewish work, the Testament (especially the longer recension) does contain a few Christian additions (most notably in the judgment scene; cf. *HJP*[2] 3/2: 763; Nickelsburg 1984: 63). Whether any identifiable group within Judaism is responsible for its composition is still debated. Kohler and Ginzberg suggested that the work derived from the Essenes, and that idea, in a slightly diluted form, has been picked up by Schmidt, who argues that the work originated from "a popular Essenism." Delcor (70–73) has suggested that the work may have been written by the Therapeutae, an Essenelike group, but Sanders has refuted this position convincingly, noting especially that Abraham is presented in the Testament as a city dweller whereas the Therapeutae were strictly nonurban dwellers (according to Philo), and that the Judaism presented in the Testament is a "lowest-common-denominator Judaism" which lacks any sectarian attributes (*OTP* 1: 876; but cf. *HJP*[2] 3/2: 762).

Bibliography

Delcor, M. 1973. *Le Testament d'Abraham.* SVTP 2. Leiden.

Denis, A. M. 1970. *Introduction aux pseudépigraphes grecs d'Ancien Testament.* SVTP 1. Leiden.

James, M. R. 1892. *The Testament of Abraham.* TextsS 2/2. Cambridge.

Janssen, E. 1975. Testament Abrahams. *JSHRZ* 3: 193–256.

Nickelsburg, G. W. E. 1976. *Studies on the Testament of Abraham.* SCS 6. Missoula, MT.

———. 1984. Stories of Biblical and Early Post-Biblical Times. Pp. 60–64 in *Jewish Writings of the Second Temple Period,* ed. M. E. Stone. CRINT 2.2. Philadelphia.

Schmidt, F. 1986. *Le Testament grec d'Abraham.* Texte und Studien zum Antiken Judentum 11. Tübingen.

Stone, M. E. 1972. *The Testament of Abraham.* SBLTT 2; Pseudepigrapha Series 2. Missoula, MT.

Turdeanu, E. 1981. Le Testament d'Abraham en slave et en roumain. Pp. 201–18, 440 in *Apocryphes slaves et roumains de l'Ancien Testament.* SVTP 5. Leiden.

Turner, N. 1984. The Testament of Abraham. Pp. 393–421 in *The Apocryphal Old Testament,* ed. H. F. D. Sparks. Oxford.

JAMES R. MUELLER

ABRAM (PERSON) [Heb *ʾabrām*]. See ABRAHAM (PERSON).

ABRON (PLACE) [Gk *abrōna*]. A wadi along which the Assyrian general Holofernes razed all the cities in his western campaign during the Persian period (Jud 2:24). However, the location of Abron is uncertain, and given the genre of the book of Judith, the historicity of this campaign and the "Assyrian" general is doubtful. The campaign is set in the territory of Cilicia (Jud 2:21–25), suggesting that Abron is located somewhere between the NW bend of the Euphrates and the Mediterranean Sea. The confusion is compounded by the textual variants (Codex Sinaiticus *chebrōn;* Vg *mambre* [2:14]), which suggest that some ancient translators may have located Abron in the Hebron/Mamre region of Palestine. Some scholars, following Movers (1835), explain Gk *abrōna* as a translator's misunderstanding of the Heb phrase *bʿbr hnhr* ("beyond the river"), designating "east of the Euphrates River," or "Mesopotamia" (cf. Josh 24:2, 14–15). However, from the Mesopotamian point of view, this phrase designated the region, or an administrative district, west of the northern bend of the Euphrates River (namely, Syria-Palestine; see Rainey 1969). In this phrase the Heb *ʿbr* was mistaken by the translator to be the actual name of the river. Others identify Abron with the Habur River (see HABOR), which joins the Euphrates 31 km NW of Dura (Soubigiou *Judith* Sainte Bible, 516).

Bibliography

Movers, F. C. 1835. Ueber die Ursprache der deuterocanonischen Bücher des alten Testaments. *ZPKT* 13: 31–48.

Rainey, A. F. 1969. The Strategy "Beyond the River." *AJBA* 1: 51–78.

MARK J. FRETZ

ABRONAH (PLACE) [Heb *ʿabrōnâ*]. An Israelite campsite on the exodus itinerary, located between the stations of Jotbathah and Ezion-geber, N of the Gulf of ʿAqaba (Num 33:34–35; see Deut 2:8; 10:6–7). The historical location of the site of Abronah remains uncertain, as do most of the sites on the wilderness itinerary (Num 33:1–49), and any proposed location of these sites presumes a theoretical travel route (Aharoni *LBHG,* 198). A modern site named both Ar *ʿAin ed-Defîyeh* or *Dāfiya,* and also *ʿEin Avrona* (Hebrew), located 15 km N of the Gulf of ʿAqaba, is one identification (Rothenberg, et al., 1961: 89; Baly 1963: 166; see also *RNAB,* 114), while Aharoni and Avi-Yonah (*MBA,* 174) allow for the tenuous possibility of Elat (modern *Umm Rashrash;* M.R. 145884), situated on the northern shore of the Gulf of ʿAqaba.

Bibliography

Baly, D. 1963. *Geographical Companion to the Bible.* London.

Rothenberg, Beno; Aharoni, Y.; and Hashimshoni, A. 1961. *God's Wilderness: Discoveries in Sinai.* London.

MARK J. FRETZ

ABSALOM (PERSON) [Heb *ʾabšālōm*]. Var. ABISHALOM.

1. Third son of David. His mother was a foreigner, MAACAH, daughter of Talmai, king of Geshur (2 Sam 3:3; 1 Chr 3:2). He was one of six sons born to David at Hebron by six different wives. He was at the center of a long-running series of troubles that David had with his sons: he killed his older brother AMNON and later rebelled against David himself.

Absalom first appears in the story of Amnon's rape of their sister Tamar (2 Samuel 13). After the rape was committed, Absalom hated Amnon (13:22) with the same hatred that the latter had shown for Tamar (13:15–19), and he bided his time for revenge.

After two years, Absalom was able to lure Amnon—who himself had lured his sister into a trap—as well as "all the king's sons" to festivities at Baal-hazor, near Ephraim, during the time of sheepshearing (13:23–29). There, Absalom had Amnon killed and the brothers fled. David first mourned the death of Amnon, and then he mourned the absence of Absalom, who had fled to his mother's household in Geshur, where he remained for three years (13:30–39). David appears here and throughout as a noble, yet somewhat passive and detached hero.

Absalom was finally brought back through the efforts of Joab, David's general and nephew (2 Samuel 14). In an episode reminiscent of Nathan's parable that entrapped David into acknowledging his sin, Joab recruited a wise woman from Tekoa to masquerade as a bereaved mother whose remaining son's life was threatened. When David's compassion led him to intercede, she pointed out to him that Absalom's lot was the same as her son's. Acknowledging her point, David restored Absalom from exile, but perhaps showed considerable insensitivity in not allowing him to come into his presence for 2 years (14:28). At this point we are told of Absalom's great beauty (just as his sister had been beautiful) and his full head of hair (14:25–27). A reconciliation with his father finally was brought about after some persistence on Absalom's part (14:29–33).

Immediately thereafter, Absalom began an active campaign of subversion against his father (15:1–12). Just as people had admired his great beauty (14:25), so they now admired what they saw as his great wisdom (15:3–6). He conspired to be made king at Hebron, his birthplace and—ironically—the place of his father's acclamation as king and early reign over Judah and all Israel. (The duration of this campaign is uncertain; it was likely 40 days or 4 years, and not the 40 years of the MT at 15:7; *see* Conroy 1978: 106–7, n. 40.)

In the narrative, Absalom temporarily fades into the background after 15:12; the story now focuses on David's flight to the Jordan River and his encounters with various opponents and supporters along the way (15:13–16:14). As the conspiracy gained supporters (15:12), David was persuaded to flee from Jerusalem, along with his household and warriors loyal to him (15:13–23). Among these loyal ones was Ittai, leader of six hundred men from Gath and one of three generals who led the climactic battle against Absalom (18:2). David directed the priests Abiathar and Zadok that the ark should not accompany him in his flight (15:24–29), a contrast with earlier attitudes toward the ark (1 Samuel 4). David also met Ziba and Shimei (16:1–14), foreshadowing later events unrelated to Absalom (19:17–31—Eng 19:16–30).

After David's departure, Absalom was able to enter Jerusalem without resistance (16:15). Ahithophel, David's respected counselor, had joined Absalom (15:12, 30–31), and he advised him to consolidate his position as king by taking his father's concubines, which Absalom did (16:20–23). He also counseled a selective strike that would kill only David (17:1–4). To counter Ahithophel's defection, David had enlisted one Hushai, the Archite, who then entered Absalom's court as a spy (15:32–37; 16:15–19). Hushai, acting in David's interests, advised a large-scale mobilization instead, and Absalom took his advice, prompting the rejected Ahithophel to commit suicide (17:5–14, 23). YHWH's hand was evident in this, since Ahithophel's advice had been good counsel (17:14)—the delay in mobilization allowed Hushai to send word to David about Absalom's plans via the two priests' sons Ahimaaz and Jonathan, setting the stage for the military confrontation (17:15–22).

The confrontation took place across the Jordan, in the dense Forest of Ephraim in Gilead. Absalom's forces were no match for David's seasoned followers, and many were lost to the sword or to the forest (18:1–8). The narrative slows to describe the death of Absalom and its announcement to David (18:9–32). Absalom's hair had gotten caught in a tree in the dense woods, and Joab killed him, aided by ten of his armor-bearers. The suspense builds as David awaits word of the battle, brought by two messengers. The moving climax is reached abruptly, in David's reaction to his son's death and his poignant lament (18:33).

Absalom had three sons, and a comely daughter whom he named after his sister (14:27). In light of 18:18, it appears that his sons died early in life. If he is the Abishalom of 2 Kgs 15:2, 10, then he had another daughter (or granddaughter), named for his mother, Maacah (contra the OG reading of 2 Sam 14:27b). She was the wife of Rehoboam, mother of Abijam, and (grand)mother of Asa (2 Kgs 15:2, 10, 13; cf. 2 Chr 11:20–22). The "Absalom's Monument" that he built to commemorate his own name due to his lack of heirs (2 Sam 18:18) is not the "Absalom's Tomb" that can be seen today on the eastern slope of the Kidron Valley. The latter dates to a much later period.

The story of Absalom has been seen as part of a large document known as the "Succession Narrative" (2 Samuel 9–20, 1 Kings 1–2; *see* Rost 1982, Whybray 1968), in which the primary concern is the struggle for succession to David's throne. However, this hypothesis fails to do justice to the appendix to 2 Samuel (chs. 21–24), and the evidence for the succession theme within the Absalom narrative itself (2 Samuel 13–18 [or 20]) is meager. Thus caution should be exercised here, to avoid subordinating too much to this one theme (Conroy 1978: 101–5; IOTS: 266–80).

2. The father of Mattathias, who was one of two who remained loyal to Jonathan Maccabeus when his army had been routed by the Syrians in 145 B.C.E. (1 Macc 11:70). This Absalom (GK *Apsalōmos*) also may have been the father of the Jonathan whom Simon Maccabeus sent on a mission to Joppe in 143 B.C.E. (1 Macc 13:11).

3. One of two envoys sent by the Jews to Lysias, Antiochus' deputy, to negotiate a peace after his defeat at Beth-Zur in 164 B.C.E. (GK *Abessalōm;* 2 Macc 11:17). The "House of Absalom" is mentioned in the Qumran commentary on Habakkuk, and it may have been an influential, pious family in the Maccabean period (Goldstein *2 Maccabees* AB, 410).

Bibliography

Conroy, C. 1978. *Absalom Absalom!* AnBib 81. Rome.

Rost, L. 1982. *The Succession to the Throne of David.* Historic Texts and Interpreters in Biblical Scholarship 1. Trans. M. D. Rutter and D. M. Gunn. Sheffield.

Whybray, R. N. 1968. *The Succession Narrative: A Study of II Sam. 9–20 and I Kings 1 and 2.* SBT, 2d Ser. 9. Naperville, IL.

David M. Howard, Jr.

ABU ET-TWEIN, KHIRBET

ABU ET-TWEIN, KHIRBET (M.R. 158119). An Iron Age fortress located on the summit of a remote ridge in the W slopes of the Hebron Hills, E of the Valley of Elah. The site was surveyed and excavated in 1974–75 by A. Mazar. The fortress is a square structure, ca. 30 × 30 m, with thin outer walls, yet the corners are built of large boulders. A gate chamber led from the E into a square inner courtyard, surrounded by a double row of rooms on all four sides. The rooms were constructed by placing a row of monolithic pillars between the outer wall of the fortress and the inner wall which surrounds the courtyard. Division walls created rooms of different sizes, some of which were perhaps for storage and stables (see Fig. ABU.01). The pottery found in the fortress is mainly of the Iron Age II, but there are also forms dated to the 6th and even the 5th centuries B.C., pointing to a continuous use of the fortress even after the destruction of Judah in 587 B.C.

A small village existed during the Iron Age II on a saddle at the foot of the hill on which the fortress was located. The village consisted of a number of houses scattered over a large area, with open spaces between them.

It appears that the fortress was constructed during the period of the Monarchy (perhaps during the 8th century B.C.) as a guard position and observation point in the remote region, which separated the extensive urban settlements in the Shephelah from those on the summit of the Judean Hills. Similar fortresses were discovered in surveys farther to the N and S in the same relative geographical proximity. It appears that these fortresses were used also as stations in a system of communication, serving as points to transmit fire signals from the Shephelah to Jerusalem in time of war (see Jer 6:1; Zeph 1:16; 3:18; Ps 74:3; and Lachish letter No. 4), while in times of peace they probably housed garrisons and perhaps officials of the Judean Monarchy.

Bibliography

Mazar, A. 1982. Iron Age Fortresses in the Judean Hills. *PEQ* 114: 87–109.

Amihay Mazar

ABU GHOSH

ABU GHOSH (M.R. 160134). A prepottery Neolithic B (PPNB) site located within the limits of the present-day village of the same name. It is in the Judean hills ca. 12 km

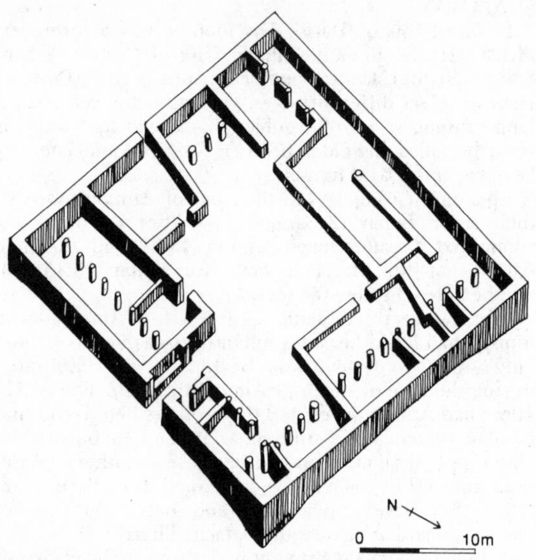

ABU.01. Isometric reconstruction of fortress at Abu et-Twein. *(Redrawn from Mazar 1982, fig. 12.)*

W of Jerusalem, 700 m above sea level. R. Neuville first explored the site in 1928 after flint artifacts and stone vessel fragments were found on the surface (Neuville 1929). In 1950, J. Perrott opened a trench (70 m^2) and recognized a 1 m thick archaeological layer (Perrott 1952). He recognized the similarities of the materials to the prepottery levels at Jericho, the only known stratified Neolithic site in Palestine at that time. New excavations were conducted at Abu Ghosh between 1967 and 1971, which opened an 800 m^2 area (Dollfus and Lechevallier 1969; Lechevallier 1978; Hesse 1978). As a result of the excavations, the following stratigraphic configuration was recognized: (a) a surface layer with terra rossa and coarse gravel, mixed with recent material (ca. 30 cm thick); (b) gray organic soil with angular stones and archaeological material *in situ* (ca. 0.50–1.10 m thick); and (c) sterile red clay (ca. 0.0–0.20 m thick) and bedrock.

Layer b yielded the remains of three levels of construction badly damaged by erosion and intrusive pits of later periods. In the relatively well-preserved intermediate level, the plans of large rectangular buildings were obtained. The walls, 0.60 to 1.10 m wide, were built with two rows of rough stones and rubble. The best preserved house measured 6.50 × 6 m. It had a white polished plaster floor with a band of red paint all along the walls. This house had been rebuilt once and the plaster floor showed evidence of two phases. Another house, also with remains of a plaster floor, had a row of three small compartments (0.80 × 1.00 m) along the S wall, which must have been used for storage. North of the buildings was an enclosure wall (18 m long), which seems to have marked the border of the settlement. Associated stone pavements, stone-lined pits, and hearths were located outside the buildings.

The remains of some thirty individuals, mostly represented by isolated bones, were recovered. In the undisturbed burials, the skeletons were in a flexed position (Arensburg, Smith, and Yakar 1978). Two adults, buried under the plastered floor of one house, were missing their skulls, but their mandibles were present. Five individuals had been buried in one location—the lower one, an adult, was undisturbed, while the remains of two adolescents and a child had been pushed aside to give place to the last burial of an adult.

The fauna included wild pig, cattle, gazelle, and deer, but the dominant species was goat (ca. 55 percent). From a study of the ages of the animals at death and the ratios of their sex, it appears that animal domestication was not fully developed (Ducos 1978).

The material culture is represented by the flint assemblage, polished stone artifacts, and bone tools. Fine brown, cream white, or reddish (most probably heat-treated) flint was used. The tools include small denticulated sickle blades (about 40 percent) and arrowheads of various types: tanged, winged and notched (Helwan and Jericho points), shouldered (Byblos) and foliated (Amuq) points, retouched by abrupt of flat pressure flaking. A few large amygdaloid axes with a polished edge, smaller axes with rectilinear sides, and small picks are present. Obsidian is represented by one arrowhead and a few bladelets. A good number of polished limestone bowls, basins, and flat dishes were present, as well as cupholes, grinding stones, and pestles (some in imported basalt). The bone tools were mainly awls, with some spatulas, and one needle. Other finds are scarce: a few animal figurines in unbaked clay, some beads in turquoise and green stone, a limestone pendant, and some worked cowrie shells.

From the data obtained through the geophysical survey and the excavations, the site seems to have covered an area of 2000–2500 m^2. The well-built stone houses and storage facilities suggest that this was a sedentary village. This is in agreement with the developing goat domestication and the reliance on harvesting and storing plants (cereals?) as inferred from the large number of sickle blades and grinding stones (no seeds were preserved). However, hunting was still an important source of food if one considers the wild species represented among the animal bones and the large number of arrowheads.

While no suitable samples were avilable for radiocarbon dating, the cultural features are consistent with the PPNB (7th millennium B.C.), most probably in its later phase. A later reoccupation of the site is indicated by the presence of small pressure-flaked arrowheads and a few large denticulated sickle elements.

Bibliography

Arensburg, B.; Smith, P.; and Yakar, R. 1978. The human remains from Abou Gosh. Pp. 95–105 in Lechevallier 1978.

Ducos, P. 1978. La faune d'Abou Gosh; proto-élevage de la chèvre au néolithique preé-céramique. Pp. 107–120 in Lechevallier 1978.

Dollfus, G., and Lechevallier, M. 1969. Les deux premières campagnes de fouilles à Abou Gosh (1967–1968). *Syr* 44: 279–87.

Hesse, A. 1978. Reconnaissance géophysique du site d'Abou Gosh. Pp. 83–90 in Lechevallier 1978.

Lechevallier, M. 1978. *Abou Gosh et Beisamoun.* Mémories et Travaux du Centre de Recherches préhistoriques français de Jérusalem, no. 2. Paris.

Neuville, R. 1929. Additions à la liste des stations préhistoriques de Palestine et Transjordanie. *JPOS* 9: 114–21.

Perrot, J. 1952. Le Néolithique d'Abou Gosh. *Syria* 29: 119–45.

MONIQUE LECHEVALLIER

ABU HAMID, TELL (M.R. 192204). A Neolithic/Chalcolithic site in the Jordan Valley, on the terrace left by the marls of the Pleistocene lake Lisan, at an altitude of 250 m below sea level. The site covers about 4.5 hectares, and is limited on its N and S by two deep wadis in which are perennial springs. Current annual precipitation is about 200 mm, allowing for some dry farming.

The site was discovered during the first season of the East Jordan Valley Survey in 1975 and has been dated to the Neolithic/Chalcolithic Period by Ibrahim, Sauer, and Yassin (1976: 51). The material collected during this survey was later discussed by Kafafi (1982). In the summer of 1985, G. Dollfus and Z. Kafafi revisited the site and initiated a joint Jordano-French expedition which conducted its first season of excavation in 1986.

In addition to a general survey of the site and a systematic collection of all the artifacts, various soundings at the site indicate that a maximum of 2.5 hectares were built up during one major phase of occupation, and the depth of deposits vary between 0.30 m to 1.20 m. The remainder of the site was apparently the scene of outdoor activities or enclosures for the herds.

Approximately 400 m² have been excavated, revealing two phases of construction. The basal level is characterized by planoconvex mudbrick walls defining rectangular rooms. No complete house has been excavated so far. The upper level is badly eroded, and consists of remains of walls and large numbers of pits (fire pits, storage pits, etc.) which disturb the earlier level. On the edge of the developed area, in what appears to be a storage area, one pit has produced a huge pithos—1.50 m high and 1 m in diameter.

The ceramic assemblage is homogeneous. Most of the vessels are handmade, while small conical bowls show traces of the use of a slow wheel. The surfaces are either rough or wet-smoothed, especially near the rim; slips and self-slips are frequent. The decoration consists of impressed designed, applied clay coils with nail impressions or lunates in relief; occasionally painted bands will also appear. Among the painted pottery, the designs are usually linear. Very few shards are covered with a dark red paint and burnished. Rare also are fragments with chevron designs. These categories of pottery show great similarities with those excavated at Tuleilat Ghassul, Tabaqat Fahil, Shuneh North, Neve Ur, and sites in the Golan and Hauran Heights ("Chalcolithic").

The flint industry consists of scrapers on tabular flints, end scrapers, micro end scrapers, sickle blades, adzes, axes, chisels, perforated disks of unknown function, borers, piercers, denticulated pieces, and notched pieces. The burins are rare and only three transverse-edge arrowheads have been collected so far. Ground stone tools, utensils, and vessels made out of basalt and limestone are abundant, as are also mace heads, some of which are made from hematite.

Preliminary analyses of faunal and botanical remains indicate that the subsistence strategy was mostly agropastoralism. Hunting does not seem to have played an important role: wild species represent a very low percentage of the faunal remains, and arrowheads are nearly absent.

While radiocarbon samples have not yet been analyzed, the architectural remains, the assemblage of the artifacts, and the subsistence activities suggest a date for the settlement in the first part of the 4th millennium B.C.

Bibliography

Dollfus, G., and Kafafi, Z. 1986. Abu Hamid, Jordanie. Premiers résultats. *Paléorient* 12/1: 91–100.

———. 1987. Preliminary results of the first season of the Joint Jordano-French Project at Abu Hamid. *ADAJ* 30: 353–80.

Ibrahim, M.; Sauer, J.; and Yassin, K. 1976. The East Jordan Valley Survey, 1975. *BASOR* 222:41–66.

Kafafi, Z. 1982. The Neolithic of Jordan (East Bank). Ph.D. Diss. Freie Universität. Berlin.

G. DOLLFUS
ZEIDAN A. KAFAFI

ABU THAWWAB, JEBEL (M.R. 230174). A late Neolithic-EB I site south of Wadi Zerka (Jabbok).

A. History of the Excavations/Explorations

During his intensive surveys and explorations of the East Bank of the Jordan, Glueck visited the area of Jebel Abu Thawwab and identified it as Abu Trab (Glueck 1939: 225). Near the top of the mountain, he recognized three caves and considered them the results of earlier mining. In 1975, Coughenour investigated the caves and suggested, "A furnace or smithing operation might well be located by test excavations" (1976: 74). The caves were revisited during the er-Rumman Survey in 1985.

Z. Kafafi and R. Gordon of the Institute of Archaeology and Anthropology at Yarmouk University visited the site in 1983 as a result of a note published by E. Gillet and C. Gillet (1983) in which they mentioned having collected Neolithic and EB pot sherds and flint tools. Several visits followed to gather surface sherds and flint tools, which were dated to the Late Neolithic (Yarmukian), EB I, Roman, and Byzantine periods. As a result of these preliminary investigations, the Institute of Archaeology and Anthropology of Yarmouk University sponsored two seasons of excavations in 1984 and 1985 (Kafafi 1985a; 1985b; 1986a; 1986b), and conducted a survey in the area around the site in 1985 (Gordon and Knauf 1986).

B. The Results of the Excavations

Two main occupational phases were identified—the earliest dates to the Late Neolithic 1, the second phase is assigned to the EB I. These two phases are separated by a mixed fill, consisting mostly of small-sized stones. Both phases yielded architectural remains. Those of the Late Neolithic consisted of rounded and rectangular houses in addition to storage pits (Kafafi 1985b). The EB I buildings were rectangular with benches. All were built of medium-sized boulders and the Neolithic floors were made of either mud or pebbles, while those of the EB were of plaster.

The Yarmukian pottery assemblage consisted of both fine and coarse wares, red painted slip, and decorations consisting of incised herringbone chevrons, and red paint with parallel incisions. The forms represented were cups, simple bowls, deep bowls, and simple hole-mouth and globular jars. The flint tools consisted primarily of arrowheads and sickle blades. In addition, points, knives, scrapers, burins, and spearheads were represented along with grinding and ground stones. The excavations also produced some bone tools, shells, and human and animal figurines.

The preliminary analysis of the botanical remains indicates that the following plants were predominant in the subsistence strategy: lentils, field pea, row barley, wheat, pistachio, and almond.

Although the samples for radiocarbon dating have not yet been analyzed, based on parallel, and stratigraphic, studies, the early phase of Abu Thawwab is consistent with the 6th millennium B.C. (Late Neolithic, "Yarmukian") and the late phase is consistent with the EB I.

Bibliography

Coughenour, R. A. 1976. Preliminary Report on the Exploration and Excavation of Mugharet el-Wardeh and Abu Thawab. *ADAJ* 21: 71–78.

Gillet, E., and Gillet, C. 1983. Jebel Abu Thawab, Jordan. *Levant* 15: 187–91.

Glueck, N. 1939. *Explorations in Eastern Palestine, III.* AASOR 18–19.

Gordon, R. L., and Knauf, E. A. 1986. Rumman-Survey. *AfO* 33: 282–83.

Kafafi, Z. A. 1985a. First Season of Excavations at Jebel Abu Thawwab (er-Rumman), 1984: Preliminary Report. *ADAJ* 30: 57–68.

———. 1985b. Late Neolithic Architecture from Jebel Abu Thawwab, Jordan. *Paléorient 11/1*: 125–27.

———. 1986a. Second Season of Excavations at jebel Abu Thawwab (er-Rumman), 1985: Preliminary Report. *ADAJ* 30: 57–68.

———. 1986b. Gabal Abu Tawwab. *AfO* 33: 156–68.

ZEIDAN A. KAFAFI

ABUBUS (PERSON) [Gk *Aboubos*]. The father of Ptolemy, son-in-law and murderer of the high priest Simon Maccabeus and governor over the plain of Jericho (1 Macc 16:11–12, 15). No other information concerning Abubus is available since his name occurs only in this narrative concerning the murder of Simon Maccabeus.

MARK J. FRETZ

ABYSS, THE [Gk *abyssos*]. "Bottomless," "unfathomed," or "unfathomable deep"; with the feminine article, it signifies "the deep" or "the underworld." The term occurs at least 34 times in the LXX, where in 30 instances it renders Heb. *tĕhôm* (or its plural); once for *mĕṣûlâ*, depths (Job 41:23—LXX 41:22—Eng 41:31); once for *ṣûlâ*, "depths" (Isa 44:27); and twice where the text is uncertain (Job 36:16; 41:24a—LXX 41:23a—Eng 41:32a).

In the OT, "the abyss" is not widely used in the English versions, although it is found in some of the more recent translations, rendering *tĕhôm* (NAB, 11 times; NEB, 7 times; NJB, 6 times; and AB, once). NAB uses the word 3 times for *ʾăbaddôn*, "destruction" (Job 31:12; Prov 15:11, 27:20). *JPS* uses it once for *maʿămaqqîm*, "depths" (Isa 51:10, where it is parallel with *tĕhôm*).

The more usual English renderings of the words behind the LXX *abyssos* in the OT are "the deep," "the depths," and "deep." These terms, along with "the abyss," are used in the following senses which reflect meanings of Heb *tĕhôm* and its synonyms: (1) the primordial ocean (e.g., Gen 1:2); (2) the (deep) sea (e.g., Jonah 2:6—Eng 2:5; Job 28:14, 38:16, 41:23—LXX 41:22—Eng 41:31); (3) the Red Sea (e.g., Ps 106:9—LXX 105:9; Isa 51:10, 63:13—with mythological overtones); (4) subterranean waters (e.g., Gen 7:11, 8:2; Prov 3:20; Ps 78:15—LXX 77:15); and (5) the depths of the earth, i.e., Sheol (Ps 71:20—LXX 70:20).

In intertestamental literature, "the abyss" carries a number of meanings: (1) the great deep under the earth, namely, that part of the universe set in opposition to the height of the heavens (Sir 1:3, 16:18, 24:5, 29, 42:18); (2) a poetic reference to the Red Sea where a personified wisdom delivered Israel (Wis 10:19); (3) the depths of the earth (*Jub.* 5:10); and (4) the abyss of fire, i.e., the place of torment for sinners and fallen angels (*1 En.* 10:13; 18:11).

In the NT, there are 9 occurrences of Gk *abyssos*, which, in the older English versions, are usually rendered by "the deep" (Luke 8:31, Rom 10:7) and "bottomless" or "the bottomless pit" (seven times in Revelation). Other English versions use "the abyss" or "the Abyss" with more or less frequency (RSV, twice; NASB, 7 times; JB, GNB, NIV, NJB, 8 times; NEB all 9 times). In 2 Pet. 2:4, NJB renders Gk *zophos*, "dark, gloomy (place)," as "the dark abyss" (i.e., hell).

There are two meanings for "the abyss" in the NT. First, it refers to (1) the place to which the forces of evil are consigned (e.g., the demons in Luke 8:31), and from which they come by way of a shaft (the demonic "locusts" of Rev 9:1–11; cf. ABADDON; Apollyon). From the abyss comes the beast (Rev 11:7), and into it is cast the dragon, i.e. Satan (Rev 20:1, 3). Second, in one passage "the abyss" is a synonym for Hades (Rom 10:7). See also DEAD, ABODE OF THE.

HERBERT G. GRETHER

ACACIA. See FLORA.

ACCAD (PLACE) [Heb *ʾakkad*]. One of the cities of Nimrod listed in the Table of Nations of the Yahwist (Gen 10:10). It is listed along with Babel and Erech (and possibly Calneh) in the land of Shinar. These cities are called the "*rēʾšît* of his kingdom." This Hebrew word can mean either "beginning" (cf. Isa 46:10) or "chief," "mainstay" (cf. Amos 6:1 and Jer 49:35). If the connotation "beginning" is correct, then it means that the cities formed the original nucleus of Nimrod's empire. But if the meaning is "mainstay," then Accad and the other cities are described as the most important ones of his kingdom (on the latter, see Speiser *Genesis* AB). Either interpretation is possible within the context.

Accad was known by the Sumerian name "Agade" (A-GA-DÈ^{ki}). This city was founded in the 24th century B.C.E. by Sargon I of Agade, and was the capital of his dynasty until it was destroyed during the fall of that dynasty in the 22d century B.C.E. It was never rebuilt. A Sumerian composition from the late 3d millennium B.C.E., known as *The Curse of Agade,* relates a legendary version of the demise of the city (for a translation and commentary, see Cooper 1983). Agade is mentioned occasionally in subsequent Mesopotamian literature, but its location has not yet been determined with any certainty. The name "Agade" continued to survive in the title "the land of Sumer and Akkad," referring to Babylonia, and in Akkadian (*akkadû*), the word for the Semitic language spoken by the people of Sargon. It is clear that Gen 10:10 refers to the city Agade, not the region of Babylonia, since it is listed along with other cities in Mesopotamia. It is interesting to note that the Yahwist must have had a source mentioning a city that had ceased to exist before the end of the 3d millennium B.C.E.

The reading of the LXX is *Archad.* There is no obvious reason for the change. It is possible that the *reš* was accidentally added in a Hebrew manuscript in reminiscence of the *reš* in the preceding word "Erech." In any case, this form of the name is clearly secondary and incorrect.

Bibliography
Cooper, J. S. 1983. *The Curse of Agade.* Baltimore.

JAMES R. DAVILA

ACCENTS, MASORETIC. See MASORETIC ACCENTS.

ACCO (PLACE) [Heb *ʿakkô*]. Var. PTOLEMAIS. One of the most prominent coastal cities in Canaan, mentioned only once in the OT in connection with the tribe of Asher's inability to drive out its inhabitants (Judg 1:31). On the basis of various Gk mss, it has been suggested that in Josh 19:30 Ummah (MT *ʿmh*) should be read Acco (*ʿkw*). The city was renamed Ptolemais during the Hellenistic-Roman periods, and it was there that the apostle Paul stayed for one day while en route from Tyre to Caesarea at the end of his third missionary journey (Acts 21:7).

Acco's importance may be attributed to its location at the juncture between the coastal road and the inland road leading through Galilee and Transjordan to Syria. OT Acco is identified with el-Fukhkhar (M.R. 158258) at modern Acre/Akko NE of the Naaman River and 700 m inland. The original size of the tell was ca. 200 dunams; however, its S side, apparently affected by its proximity to the river and by late destructions, has been almost totally destroyed. Here there are still remains of the swamps created near the outlet of the river. From the Persian period on, the settlement of Acco gradually moved off the tell and to the NW, along the Mediterranean.

A. History of the City

Acco is first mentioned in the Egyptian Middle Kingdom Execration Texts, where a Canaanite ruler of Acco named Tr'mw appears. Later, Acco is frequently mentioned in the Egyptian sources, which indicates that the population of the city was mainly Canaanite while the rulers were of Hurrian and Indoeuropean origins. These sources include the Karnak list of Thutmose III (*ANET,* 242), Amarna letters (13 times), and in a relief from the Karnak temple from the period of Rameses II, all of which testify to the city's importance. In the Ugaritic and Akkadian texts from Ugarit, Acco is among the few Canaanite cities mentioned. From the same period is a letter recently found in Aphek with the name of a high-ranked official, Adlaha of Acco.

In the 8th and the 7th centuries B.C., Acco appears to have been an important Phoenician city. According to Assyrian sources, the city (*Akku*) rebelled against Assyrian rule and was captured first by Sennacherib and finally by Ashurbanipal, who destroyed it and exiled its people. From the time of Cambyses on, Acco (Gk *akē*) was an important military and administrative center of the Persian empire.

In 332 B.C., Acco surrendered peacefully to Alexander the Great and remained autonomous. Throughout the wars of the Diadochi, it changed hands, but eventually, the city remained under Ptolemy II Philadelphus, who there established a *polis.* Acco-Ptolemais (as it was known) became a prominent trade center at that time, as indicated by the correspondence of Zenon. Following the Syrian wars, the city became a permanent part of the Seleucid empire and was renamed Antiochia-at-Ptolemais by Antiochus IV Epiphanes. Alexander Balas made Acco his second capital and royal fortress. During the Maccabean revolt, Acco was hostile to the Jewish cause; in fact, the city defeated Simon in 163 B.C., and it was there also that Jonathan was captured by Tryphon in 142 B.C. In 104 B.C., Alexander Jannaeus seized the city from him (later he had to surrender it to his mother, Cleopatra III). Acco was then captured by Tigranes of Armenia in 83 B.C.

The Roman phase in the history of Acco began with the arrival of Pompey and annexation of Judea to Rome in 63 B.C. Under Roman rule, Acco-Ptolemais became autonomous under the supervision of the Roman proconsul in Syria.

B. Excavations on the Tell

Prior to the systematic excavations in the 1970s, archaeological research of the city concentrated in uncovering tombs and in emergency digs occasioned by rubble-clearing work of new building projects in modern Acre. The tell itself, which had for hundreds of years been exposed to robbery and destruction and then to steady agricultural cultivation, had been subjected to several archaeological surveys, including that of Saarisalo (1929).

The systematic excavations of Tell el-Fukhkhar began in 1973 and thus far 10 seasons of excavations have been conducted in 8 areas on the tell. Also, 2 seasons were conducted in the lower (modern) city (Areas E and D), and short trial digs were also conducted there in Areas L, M, and N. Consequently, it is possible to obtain some sense of the history of Acco's settlement.

1. Late Chalcolithic—EB IA. Remains of the first stages of settlement were found in Area S on the S slope of the tell, opposite the fertile valley which extends along the N bank of the river and which may have served as an early anchorage. Foundations of stone-built walls, as well as several granary pits, were uncovered on the virgin soil. Sections of a few superimposed floors were cleared, and on the evidence of the pottery, the first settlement may date to the transitional period between the Late Chalcolithic and EB I. It appears to have ended abruptly after 2–3 generations; after its abandonment, there was most probably a gap in the settlement of Acco until the fortified MB I city was erected.

2. MB I. The earliest fortifications on the site were uncovered chiefly on the tell's N slope (Areas AB and B), and on the NW slope (Area F). It is still uncertain whether this fortification system encompassed the entire city or mainly its acropolis. Erected on the bedrock of the highest point of the hill, this fortification consisted in its base of a layer of hardened clay at least 2 m thick. Later a cyclopean wall of boulders ca. 3.5 m thick was erected on this rampart and a new layer of sloping rampart was attached to it. Over this, a brick wall with two bulging towers preserved up to 4 m high was constructed as a part of the fortification system. Attached to the N face of this enormous wall and traced for ca. 25 m was a stairway, consisting of 19 steps, which started from the top of the rampart. It seems that at least these first two stages of the fortification system belong to the MB I period. In the late stage, this rampart, including the stairway, was covered from the outside, and to its N the citadel ("Building A") was erected in the late MB I or early MB II period. The lowest level reached within the city to the S of the rampart (Area AB) and consisted of remains of stone walls, which supported and strengthened the inner slope of the rampart. On this slope, two burials in jars (one of a child and the other of an infant) accompanied by artifacts help to date it to the MB I period.

In Area F on the NW corner of the tell, a city gate ("Sea Gate") built into the rampart as part of the fortification system provided the best evidence for dating the earliest foundations of the city. The gate, preserved up to 3 m high, was approached by four steps and a rather narrow passage. It was composed of two interconnected units: a stone-built rectangular outer room and a square inner room built of bricks, with three pairs of gateway pilasters. The inner room, most probably a guardroom, had a second story, apparently leading to the towers on either side of the gate. The gate shows at least two phases of development within the MB I period, before it was filled in and went out of use. The quarter of the city ajoining the gate was partly excavated, and its architecture and the finds on all the floors, both in the gate itself and the gate quarter of the city, indicate its existence in at least three stages of the MB I period (ca. 2000–1800 B.C.).

3. MB II–III. The later stages of the fortification are characterized mainly by the citadel (Building A), a large brick building erected to the N of the rampart (Area AB). It probably served as a fortress from the end of the MB I until the end of the MB II period. In this two-story building was found an important stone-lined grave of a wealthy woman of high status. Skeletons of a woman and two children and a large number of burial gifts, including pottery vessels, jewelry, and scarabs, were discovered in the grave. On the inner face of the wall (constructed in the second stage of the fortification to support the rampart) were found scattered burials. Burials, either dug or built, continued in the MB III period, as for example, the burial found in a large square vaulted stone-built tomb in Area H. Beside local pottery, the artifacts also included fine pottery imported from N Syria or Anatolia, as well as scarabs, weapons, and jewelry. On the inner slope of the rampart, which was partly filled by now, a few structures, connecting walls, stone-built drainage installation, and granary pits were found. In the debris, many animal bones and a whole skeleton of a large donkey were found. This stratum was also found in the lowest level of Area C, where a handle of a large pithos bearing the impression of a Hyksos scarab was discovered.

Near the W end of the rampart (Area P), a section of a stone-built postern was excavated. It was about 2 m high outside and inside ca. 1.6 m. The floors consisted of flat stone slabs. It might have been used for both collecting water and communication from the city during seige or attack.

4. LB I–II. The citadel in Area AB continued during most of this period, though it was partly damaged possibly during Thutmose III's conquest. Into the additional layer of the rampart, LBI graves were installed. One of these was a very well-built stone grave; beside the skeleton were some rare types of bichrome ware and a large krater of the "chocolate-on-white" type. Some buildings were uncovered in Area A, among which was a public building made of mud bricks. The building was erected, according to the finds, at the end of the 15th or beginning of 14th century B.C. when Acco and its rulers are frequently mentioned in the El-Amarna tablets. A few burials with finds of the early LB period were found outside this building. Also uncovered was a well-preserved rectangular stone tomb with a low vault, a rare example in Canaan for this period. It was built into the NW slope of the rampart (Area H). Beside the pottery, the finds included scarabs, some of which were set in gold rings. In Area S, an outstanding find was an ivory cosmetic box in the form of a duck. Some damage inflicted on several buildings may be related to Seti I's campaign in the area.

Toward the end of this period, probably after Acco's destruction by Rameses II, the citadel fell into disuse and the place was partly converted into a workshop area. By then, there were almost no regular buildings, and instead, many silos and granaries were found in Area AB. Beside the local pottery, Cypriot and Mycenean sherds from the end of the LB II period were still found on the floors and in stone-lined pits and silos, testifying to a maritime trade relations between Acco, Cyprus, and the Aegean.

5. The LB–Early Iron Transition. The citadel disappeared at the end of the Bronze Age and the whole area was converted into an industrial quarter, associated with the making of pottery, the reworking of metals, and probably also the extraction of purple dye from murex shells. Layers of ash and workshop waste accumulated one on top of the other in the open spaces between craftsmen's installations and working floors. Among the finds in Area AB were crucibles, pieces of a clay tuyere, a stone jewelry mold, as well as remains of a furnace that was probably used for smelting copper and bronze for recasting. A large pottery oven with remains of a locally produced ware of Mycenean IIIc1 type was found. Such a pottery type was also found in a parallel stratum in Area F. Some whole local pottery vessels found in a pit, on top of the rampart (Area H) also belong to the transitional LB–Early Iron period. Typical to the local Canaanite culture are two small finds in Area K: one is a mold of a Canaanite goddess, probably an Asherah, and the other is a bronze male figurine with one hand raised, which probably represents the Canaanite god Reshef.

There are remains of poorly constructed houses mainly at the SW areas of the tell, as well as many granary pits. From Area H came a stone, mortar-shaped portable altar, bearing incised drawings of boats and boatmen; it was probably brought by newcomers to Acco. The presence of a large number of crushed murex shells (used also for the foundations of several floors) and a large piece of a jar covered with purple dye indicate the activity of the purple dye extracting. A scarab of Tausert found in Area AB, just below the workshop's floors, may help to date this stratum to the end of the 13th and beginning of the 12th century B.C.

This new material culture on the remains of the LB Canaanite city testify to a settlement of a non-Canaanite ethnic group, probably one of the "Sea Peoples" known to have invaded the country around that period. The evidence of the new material culture and specifically the pottery mentioned above provides grounds for assigning the finds to one of the "Sea Peoples," probably the Sherden, who are known mainly from Egyptian sources as having settled on the N coast of Canaan.

6. Iron Age I–II. The scarce architecture from the 11th and 10th centuries B.C. seems to indicate the decline of Acco, at the same time that to the N, Tyre was becoming a prominent city port in the region. The pottery includes vessels of the Phoenician "Achzib" type, as well as Cypriot "black-on-red" and "white painted" pottery, which seem to belong to the early stage of the Iron Age. A circular crucible found above the industrial area ascribed to the Sherden seems to indicate that the production of pottery continued in this place.

From the 9th century on, the city began to develop again, as inferred from the renewal of building activity, mainly for living quarters. The "bowl" of the city was by then filled in completely. The wall built in Area A to fill in and straighten the rampart formed a basis on which the city was leveled. In addition to the regular constructions on stone and brick, ashlar-built structures, probably public, appeared for the first time. A solid brick wall preserved to a height of 7 courses was found in one of the buildings which apparently continued to function in the early Assyrian period and was finally destroyed during the conquest of Sennacherib. Among the interesting finds was a hoard of little cubes of silver. In a later stratum a large building with a series of rooms still preserved to a height of 4 courses was destroyed by fire, indicating the destruction of the city probably during the period of Assurbanipal. The layers of ash contained fragments of various metals, testifying to the existence of a metal industry during this period. A stone construction, which might have been a part of a casemate wall, was traced in Area H. In Areas A and K, living quarters with a few industrial installations were uncovered. In Area A, there was evidence of a double destruction; the first may be assigned to the capture of the city by Sennacherib and the second should be related to Assurbanipal's conquest. In Area K, remains were found of what might be a fortification, but this is still unclear. In addition to local pottery, Phoenician and Cypriot types of wares were traced, as well as figurines dating from the 8th to the 6th centuries B.C. A tiny stone (perhaps used as an amulet) was found with a Phoenician inscription which reads *ʾšʾ* (Asha); also found was a stamped handle with an engraved horse and the inscription *ršp*.

7. The Persian Period. With the Persian conquest of Acco in the 6th century B.C., the city again became an important administrative, military, and economic center. In fact, the two well-defined Persian strata (5 and 4), starting with the last quarter of the 6th century (when Cambyses' expedition to Egypt took place) and ending with the city's conquest by Alexander the Great, provide evidence for an enormous expansion toward the bay. With the construction of a harbor, it became the major anchorage for military and mercantile traffic to and from Egypt. The results of the excavations show that although the city expanded beyond the tell itself, most of the population probably still lived on the tell during the period.

In Area K, where, as yet, only one stratum has been assigned to the Persian period, residential buildings with courts and ovens were excavated. The Persian level there is also represented by a series of deep pits, where a large amount of iron slag was found, testifying to the industrial character of this part of the city. A large cistern with a well-preserved plastered interior, which was probably built during this period, was linked with this industry. In Area A, remains of a three-room structure, built partly in the Phoenician style of stretchers and headers, was uncovered. It had probably been used for administrative and storage purposes. In a pit in its floor were found two Phoenician ostraca. One of them contained an order from the governor of Acco to the guild of metal craftsmen, to give a large number of metal vessels to the person "in charge of the temples." This provides evidence for the existence of Phoenician temples at Acco. Nearby, a well-constructed stone wall and some cultic artifacts were found, and these may have belonged to this temple. The finds, which include several zoomorphic and anthropomorphic male and female figurines, testify to the Phoenician character to this quarter.

A large quantity of imported Greek "black-on-red" figure pottery also turned up in the Persian strata, mainly on the W part of the tell. In Area F, among buildings constructed in the Phoenician style of headers and stretchers, a stone-lined pit, with a basalt base (*bothros*) was found, containing a large quantity of local, Cypriot, and Greek pottery. Among these was a rare Attic red-figured bell krater, portraying Heracles accompanied by satyrs and maenades, from the early 4th century B.C. The architecture and the finds indicate a prosperous city quarter, perhaps settled by Greek merchants.

8. The Hellenistic Period. The Hellenistic city on the tell was very well planned, and though the two strata from this period were subjected to robbery, destruction, and finally agricultural cultivation (at least from the Middle Ages on), one can still recognize the urban planning in most of the excavated areas of the tell. The town planning continued on the tell even after the main urban center of Acco had moved down to the maritime plain, to Ptolemais (see C below). A few structures, built in the Phoenician style of headers and stretchers, belong to the earliest stage of the era. The remains in Area K show well-planned buildings with open courtyards, where the artifacts, especially the pottery, were mainly Hellenistic. The pottery, including amphorae with stamped handles, mainly of the 2d century B.C., provide evidence for well-developed trade relations, mainly with the islands of the Mediterranean and the Aegean. Metal and stone ware, jewelry, as well as figurines of different types (e.g., of a woman with her hands over her head), were found.

Above the Hellenistic strata were several badly preserved remains of a settlement from the Roman and Byzantine periods. There was little evidence from the Crusader period (mainly from the S part of the tell), even though the Crusaders occupied the tell. A stone structure uncovered in Area B1, guarding the route to the Galilee, may be dated to the time of Saladin. In the Ottoman period the earlier building remains had already been covered with soil and blown sand, and the tell was used as a pasture.

C. Excavations in the "New City"

Several of the rescue excavations undertaken in the area between the tell and the Crusader Ottoman city of Acre confirmed the assumption that the new city of Acco developed to the W of the tell as early as the Persian period. In the lowest stratum (9), reached in Area D (ca. 600 m W of the tell), local and Greek ware was found from the 5th century B.C. To the next stratum (8) belonged a wall constructed of ashlar stones and rubble fill from the late 5th and early 4th centuries. The next two strata (7 and 6) provide evidence for a flourishing Hellenistic city with a specific architecture, an important tombstone of a Greek from Crete, and coins which provide a date for the strata. The following stratum (5) belongs to the Roman period. In the next stratum (4) remains of a well-paved street and a drainage system serve as evidence of the prosperity of this part of the city during the Byzantine period. The discovery of remains of a Crusader building (in stratum 2) raises the question whether the walls of the Crusader city should not have existed more to the E than is generally accepted. A remarkable find from this stratum is a very rare chalice bearing a fragmentary Latin inscription and a cross which might indicate a Crusader church on the site. The last occupation of this part of the city is represented by stone installations from the Ottoman period (stratum 1).

Other rescue operations were conducted to the SW of Area D, where remains of nine settlement strata were excavated (Area E). The lowest stratum yielded local and Greek pottery and some remains from the late 5th and early 4th centuries B.C. In the next stratum was found a segment of the foundations of a large round tower (ca. 20 m in diameter) built of ashlar stones. Attached to the tower were remains of walls which belonged to a fortification system of the early Hellenistic period. In one area, a large number of lead arrows and slingstones suggest that some of the structures served as an armory. The destroyed walls testify to the many battles for Acco during the "Syrian Wars" in the Hellenistic period. Along one of the walls, unused pots with lids dating to the 3d century B.C. were found still standing on a floor. This enigmatic find and a Tanit sign on a jar may point to a local cult. In the next stratum, some changes in the structures could be observed until the fortification fell into disuse, apparently during the time of Vespasian. In the later Roman and Byzantine periods, a podiumlike structure was erected on the site. During the Arab period, a large installation for lime production existed in the area.

The last among the significant excavations in the new city took place N of the areas described above (Area L). Part of a building was discovered, most likely a temenos, erected in a Hellenistic style. This building, which existed in only one stratum, yielded many pottery figurines and lamps from the 3d century B.C., and certainly was used for cultic purposes.

Bibliography

Ben-Arieh, S., and Edelstein, G. 1977. *Akko: Tombs Near the Persian Garden.* ᶜAtiqot, English Series 12. Jerusalem.

Dothan, M. 1974. A Sign of Tanit from Tel ᶜAkko. *IEJ* 24: 44–49.

———. 1976. Akko: Interim Excavation Report, First Season 1973/74. *BASOR* 224: 1–48.

———. 1985. A Phoenician Inscription from ᶜAkko. *IEJ* 35: 82–94.

Dothan, M., and Raban, A. 1980. The Sea Gate of Ancient Akko. *BA* 43/1: 35–39.

Galling, K. 1938. Die Syrisch-Palastinische Kuste nach der Beschreibung bei Pseudo-Skylax. *ZDPV.* 61: 66–96.

Goldman, Z. 1975. Accho. *EAEHL* 1: 14–23.

Kadman, L. 1961. *The Coins of Akko-Ptolemais.* Tel Aviv.

Rainey, A. F. 1971. Akko. *EncBib* 6: cols. 224–28.

Saarisalo, A. 1929. Topographical Researches in Galilee. *JPOS* 9: 27–40.

MOSHE DOTHAN

ACHAIA (PLACE) [Gk *Achaia*]. Var. ACHAEA. A Greek region which twice gave its name to all of Greece before its Achaean League (280–146 B.C.) fell to the Romans (Polyb. 2.41; Thuc. 1.111, 115). All relevant NT references involve Corinth, Achaia's capital (Acts 18:12, 27; I Cor 16:15; 2 Cor 1:1).

The Achaean people came from the east and pushed out the region's original inhabitants, the Ionians. The latter are credited with founding the twelve coastal cities which became the fulcrum of the Achaean League. Following the Dorian invasions (ca. 1250 B.C.) Achaia, thus named by Homer after Achilles' men and Agamemnon's followers, realized an alliance of powerful cities between Elis and Sicyon. It was a commander-in-chief of the Achaean League, Aratus of Sicyon, who spearheaded their constitution (251 B.C.). Achaia managed several successful colonies, e.g., Sybaris and Croton, and is perhaps part of Philistine ancestory (*AHL,* 214). Although Achaia aligned with Rome in 198 B.C., it lost its autonomy in 146 B.C., when, after years of disputes, the Romans razed Corinth. Julius Caesar turned Rome's attention again to Achaia in 46 B.C. and rebuilt its former isthmian city, which became the Roman capital of Achaia in 27 B.C. (Apul *Met.* 10.18). Achaia now included all of the southern half of the Greek peninsula (Paus. 8). In this same year the Romans made the northern part of (former) Achaia into Macedonia, with a southern border stretching from the Eubian gulf west-northwest to around Actium. This division prefaces the reference "Macedonia and Achaia" which generally implied all of Greece (Acts 19:21; Rom 15:26; I Thess 1:8). The Romans often just used "Achaia" to define the parameters of Greece, excluding Thessaly. The early Christians recognized Macedonia and Achaia as one of the thirteen major Roman provinces (*MCBW,* 218). By A.D. 65 the provinces of Thessaly and Epirus were clearly defined and constituted Achaia's northern border; Actium, and the coastal territory to its immediate south, became part of Epirus.

Paul's eighteen-month stay in Corinth is dated by an Achaean inscription at Delphi which chronicles the tenure of proconsul Gallio (*SIG* 3.108). By the time of Nero's accession, Christianity had a permanent hold in Achaia, already boasting at least twenty churches.

JERRY A. PATTENGALE

ACHAICUS (PERSON) [Gk *Achaikos*]. A Corinthian Christian who, along with Stephanas and Fortunatus, traveled from Corinth to be with Paul in Ephesus (1 Cor 16:17). The name "Achaicus," which means "one who is from Achaia," suggests that he was a slave or former slave from that region since slaves were often named after the province from which they came. Paul rejoiced at the arrival of these three messengers because, as Paul expressed it, they made up for the absence of the other Corinthians which Paul keenly felt (16:17). He remarks that their presence refreshed his spirit (16:18), apparently because they relieved some of his worries about the Corinthian community. In turn, Paul observed that their coming would also lift the Corinthians' spirits, probably because they would know their envoys had brought him much comfort. Finally, Paul urges the Corinthians to "recognize these people" (16:18). That Paul concludes with this appeal suggests that they were among "Paul's people" in the community (cf. 1:12).

It is possible that the three men had brought a letter to Paul, although one should not deduce that they were therefore among those Corinthians who delivered the communication referred to in 7:1, nor among "Chloe's people" (1:11), since those groups brought disturbing reports to Paul. After their visit with Paul, Achaicus and the others probably carried 1 Corinthians back with them to Corinth (see Fee *1 Corinthians* NICNT, 46–66).

The reference to the household of Stephanas immediately preceding the reference to Achaicus and Fortunatus in 16:17 could imply that the latter two were members of that household, either slaves or attached freedmen, and thus that they were numbered among Paul's first converts in Achaia and were themselves ministers to the community in Corinth (16:15). (Indeed a few mss in the Western tradition read "and Fortunatus and Achaicus" in 16:15, but their inclusion here is most likely an assimilation to v 17.)

JOHN GILLMAN

ACHAN (PERSON) [Heb *ʿakan*]. Var. ACHAR. Achan, the son of Carmi, son of Zabdi, son of Zerah, of the tribe of Judah, appears in the MT of Joshua 7 (the full form of his name is found in vv 1 and 18; shortened form in vv 19, 20, 24). In the Old Greek of Joshua and in the MT and Old Greek of 1 Chron 2:7, the name appears as Achar (in the preceding verse his grandfather's name is recorded as Zimri). This variation may be explained by graphic confusion between *resh* (*r*) and *nun* (*n*) at the end of the name in Hebrew. Or the two forms may represent a change from original "Achan" to "Achar" under the influence of the verbal root *ʿkr,* meaning to "trouble," which appears in Joshua 7:25 (so also in 6:18).

In defiance of a command from Joshua (6:17–19), Achan took of the booty from Jericho (specifically: "a beautiful mantle from Shinar, two hundred shekels of silver, and a bar of gold weighing fifty shekels") and hid the loot in his tent. He did not come forth on his own to confess. Rather, Joshua cast lots, beginning by tribes and working his way down to Achan himself. Confronted by this divine sleuthing, Achan finally confessed. His admission of guilt did not, however, save him from a drawn-out punishment of burning and stoning. Although the specific sin was Achan's, blame was shared widely. First by all Israel (see v 1), which suffered a defeat at Ai directly after Achan's theft. In some sense, Israel was to blame, if only indirectly. Achan's family was implicated more directly and suffered the same punishment as their leader.

Many scholars view Joshua 7:1–8:24 as a composite of two originally separate traditions—one dealing with Achan and the other with the battles for Ai. Some posit a primarily etiological basis for the Achan tale. They point to the statement, found in Joshua 7:26, that a mound of stones heaped upon Achan remained "to this day" in the Valley of Achor (a site usually identified by contemporary scholars with the modern el-Buqeʿah, a large plain SW of Jericho). Outside of Joshua 7, the Valley of Achor is found in Josh 15:7, Hos 2:15 ("I will make the Valley of Achor a door of hope"), and Isa 65:10 ("the Valley of Achor shall become a place for herds to lie down").

In the judgment of others, the story of Achan originated as intertribal polemic, with the tribe of Judah coming up on the losing side. Read in its present form, the story yields significant theological insight: all Israel must be totally obedient to Yahweh and his regulations for Divine Warfare if Israel is to be victorious. The sin of even a few is imputed to the entire community.

Although Achan/Achar is not mentioned in the Bible outside of the passages listed above, allusions to him have been detected at two points in the New Testament (see further Derrett 1986): in the story of Ananias and Sapphira (Acts 5:1–10) and in the Parable of the Pounds (Luke 19:11–27) or Talents (Matthew 24:14–30). Later Jewish traditions emphasize Achan's confession and the further trouble he averted thereby (so *Sanh.* 43b; also *ʾAbot R. Nat.* and *Num. Rab.*). Although his sin cost him his life in this world, his confession gained him a place in the world to come. See also *EncJud* 2:211; Boling and Wright *Joshua* AB; and Butler *Joshua* WBC.

Bibliography

Derrett, J. D. M. 1986. A Horrid Passage in Luke Explained (Lk 19:27). *ExpTim* 97: 136–38.

Drucker, R. 1982. *Yehoshua. The Book of Joshua.* ArtScroll Tanach Series. Brooklyn, NY.

LEONARD J. GREENSPOON

ACHBOR (PERSON) [Heb *ʿakbôr*]. **1.** Father of Baal-hanan, a king of the Edomites prior to Israel's monarchy (Gen 36:38–39; 1 Chr 1:49). Achbor's name occurs in parallel lists of Edomite kings, the dates and duration of whose reigns are uncertain (Gen 36:31–39 = 1 Chr 1:43–51).

2. The son of Micaiah, father of ELNATHAN, and a courtier of King Josiah (ca. 640–609 B.C.E.; 2 Kgs 22:12, 14; Jer 26:22; 36:12). After the book of the law was found and read to Josiah, Achbor was sent as part of a royal delegation to inquire of Huldah the prophetess concerning the words of this book (2 Kgs 22:11–20; see 2 Chr 34:19–28, where "Achbor son of Micaiah" is replaced by "Abdon the son of Micah" [v 20]). Elnathan the son of Achbor played an important role in the administration of King Jehoiakim (ca. 609–598 B.C.E.).

MARK J. FRETZ

ACHIM (PERSON) [Gk *Achim*]. The son of Zadok and father of Eliud in Matthew's genealogy of Joseph, the husband of Mary (Matt 1:14). Although Achim is absent in

Luke's parallel genealogy (3:23–38), his mention in Matt 1:14 may associate him with the lineage of the high priest Zadok (1 Chr 5:34–35—Eng 6:8–9; Gundry 1982: 18). Also, the name "Achim" may be a shortened form of the name of Zadok's son Ahimaaz (1 Chr 5:34–35—Eng 6:8–9; MT *ʾăḥîmāʿaṣ* = LXX *acheimaas*; for Gk *acheim*, cf. LXX 1 Chr 11:35; 24:16—Eng 24:17).

Bibliography

Gundry, R. H. 1982. *Matthew: A Commentary on His Literary and Theological Art.* Grand Rapids.

MARK J. FRETZ

ACHIOR (PERSON) [Gk *Achiōr*]. Achior the Ammonite appears only in Judith, in which he plays a prominent role as a gentile who embraces Judaism. He was among the leaders of Israel's neighbors whom Holofernes, general of Nebuchadnezzar, had summoned to inform him about the Israelite nation, who alone among the Western peoples dared to resist his army. In Jdt 5:5–21 Achior surveys Israel's biblical history from Chaldean origins to the post-exilic period. His rather deuteronomic claim that God would permit Holofernes to defeat them only if they had sinned nearly cost Achior his life (5:22). The general decided to postpone his execution and remarks ironically that the Ammonite would not see his face "until I take revenge on this race that came out of Egypt" (6:5). Achior was delivered to the Israelites of Bethulia, to whom he reported the conversation with Holofernes (6:10–21). Later Judith herself confirmed that what Achior had told the general was correct (11:9–10). Moreover, after Judith had beheaded Holofernes, Achior once more saw his face and was able to verify that the head she had brought to Bethulia was indeed the general's (14:5–10; Vg places these vv before 14:1). Achior then firmly believed in God and was circumcised, thus converting despite the command of Deut 23:3.

The name "Achior," which does not occur in the Hebrew Bible, has been explained in various ways (Steinmann 1953: 55–62; Moore *Judith* AB, 158, 162–63). One possibility is that it reproduces the Semitic name *ʾḥyʾwr* ("my brother is light"), which could be taken as a reference to the true insight which he brings in the book (Enslin 1972: 86). A second option, defended by H. Cazelles (1951: 125–37, 324–27), is to view it as a mistake for *ʾḥyqr*, the name of another gentile—the sage in the book of *Ahiqar* (in Tob 11:20 the Vg reads *Achior* where the LXX [v 19] has *Achikar*). Apart from the shared consonants at the beginning of the two names, there is little reason to think they have been confused. A third hypothesis is that the name is a corrupt form of *ʾḥyhwd* ("[my] brother is Judah"). In support of this option one should note that in Num 34:27 the name *ʾḥyhwd* appears in the LXX as *achiōr* (Cowley *APOT* 1: 252); and in the Syriac version of Judith *Achior* is spelled *ʾḥyhwd* (Steinmann 1953: 55). If this appealing suggestion is correct, then Achior's name, like that of Judith ("a Jewess"), would symbolize the role that he, a convert from a nation that was related to Israel (Gen 19:30–38), plays in the book.

Bibliography

Cazelles, H. 1951. Le personnage d'Achior dans le livre de Judith. *RSR* 39: 125–37, 324–27.
Enslin, M. S. 1972. *The Book of Judith.* Jewish Apocryphal Literature 7. Leiden.
Steinmann, J. 1953. *Lecture de Judith.* Paris.

JAMES C. VANDERKAM

ACHISH (PERSON) [Heb *ʾākîš*]. Philistine ruler of Gath, from whom David sought asylum when he fled from Saul. In 1 Sam 27:2 his father's name is given as Maoch (*māʿôk*), which closely resembles Maacah (*maʿăkâ*), father of King Achish of Gath according to 1 Kgs 2:39. There were probably two kings by this name: Achish I, son of Maoch, who was succeeded by Maacah, father of Achish II. In the title of Psalm 34, he is called Abimelech, a Semitic title perhaps adopted by Philistine rulers, rather than a personal name (cf. Gen 20:1–2; 21:34).

The name is not Semitic in form and has been related to Agchioses, a king in the neighborhood of Troy at the time of the Trojan War (Hom. *Il.* 2: 819). The name probably corresponds to that of *Ikausu* (ANET, 291), a Philistine king of Ekron in the days of Esarhaddon (681–669 B.C.) and Ashurbanipal (668–629 B.C.). Two names in a list of Keftui names from Egypt have been identified with Achish, particularly since the Philistines were reputed to have come from Caphtor (*Keftui*) in Amos 9:7 (Strange 1980). Corney (*IDB* 1: 27) has explained the name from Hurrian *akk sha(rur)*, "the king gives."

From a literary perspective, the figure of Achish is related to that of Goliath, another Philistine champion from Gath (1 Sam 17), in the narrative of David's rise to power (cf. Miscall 1986: 173–77). The story of David and Goliath concludes with the curious statement that "David took the head of the Philistine and brought it to Jerusalem" (1 Sam 17:54), foreshadowing David's rise to power in that city. When David slew Goliath, the women sang, "Saul has slain his thousands, and David his ten thousands" (1 Sam 18:7), a refrain which appears again on the lips of both the servants of Achish (1 Sam 21:11—Eng 21:10) and the Philistine commanders addressing Achish (1 Sam 29:5), forming a kind of frame around the story of David and Achish and connecting it to the earlier story of Goliath.

In his first encounter with Achish, David carried Goliath's sword with him, which he had received from the priest Ahimelech (1 Sam 21:9—Eng 21:8). Perhaps this explains his fear and feigned madness before Achish, king of Goliath's hometown (1 Sam 21:13–14—Eng 21:12–13). David's conduct on this occasion has been compared to that of other great men who feigned madness in difficult circumstances, such as Ulysses (Cic. *Off.* 3, 26), L. Junius Brutus (Dion Hal. 4, 68), the astronomer Meton (Ael. *VH* 13, 12), and the Arabian king Bacha (Schultens, *Anth. Vet. Hamasa*, p. 535). Subsequently, Achish accepted David and his men as mercenaries and gave David the city of Ziklag in exchange for his raids on southern tribes hostile to the Philistines (1 Sam 27:1–12). Because of the suspicion of some of his commanders, however, Achish excused David from participation in the fateful battle of Mount Gilboa in which Saul and his sons died.

There is an interesting play on the word "head" in the

concluding episodes of the story of David and Achish. The Philistine commanders suggested that David would be reconciled to his lord (Saul) "with the heads of the (Philistine) men here" (1 Sam 29:4). Earlier, Achish had appointed David to be "the keeper of my head forever" (i.e., his permanent body guard; 1 Sam 28:2). After the battle of Mount Gilboa, the Philistines "cut off (Saul's) head . . . and fastened his body to the wall of Beth-shan" (1 Sam 31:9–10). In the tradition of Jephthah of old, David became both "head and leader over them" (Jdg 11:11), as foreshadowed in the words of Achish and his Philistine cohorts.

Bibliography

Bertholet, A. 1896. *Die Stellung der Israelitu und der Juden zu den Freunden.*

Dothan, T. 1982. *The Philistines and Their Material Culture.* New Haven.

Mazar, B. 1964. The Philistines and the Rise of Israel and Tyre, *Israel Academy of Sciences and Humanities Proceedings,* 1: 1–22.

Miscall, P. D. 1986. *1 Samuel: A Literary Reading.* Bloomington, IN.

Strange, J. 1980. *Caphtor/keftui: A New Investigation.* Leiden.

DUANE L. CHRISTENSEN

ACHOR (PLACE) [Heb *ʿākōr*]. A valley (*ʿēmeq*) on Judah's northern border (Josh 15:7) identified with modern day *El Buqêʿah.* According to biblical tradition, Achan and his family were stoned and buried at the Valley of Achor after he violated the ban following the battle of Jericho. Achan's crime (Joshua 7) was the first Israelite act of disobedience after Israel crossed the Jordan; his death was the first divinely commanded punishment in the new land. Josh 7:25–27 (probably secondary) offers an etiological explanation of Achor's name. Joshua declares that Achan has troubled (Heb *ʿkr*) Israel and that God will trouble (*ʿkr*) him; the site of his execution is therefore called "trouble" (*ʿākôr*). The word play is further developed by LXX^{B}, Syriac, and 1 Chron 2:7, where Achan's name is rendered "Achar."

The Valley of Achor is included among the sites marking Judah's northern border (Josh 15:7), a list which moves uphill from the Jordan to Jerusalem. The reference to the Valley of Achor is omitted from the description of Benjamin's southern boundary (Josh 18:15–19), which otherwise parallels the list delineating Judah's northern border.

The negative character of both Achor's name and the Achan tradition allows Achor to function as a figure of eschatological change. According to Hos 2:17—Eng 2:15, the Valley of Trouble will be made a door of hope. Hosea's mention of Achor as a "doorway" may be a reference to an old road which F. M. Cross (*CMHE,* 110) has identified as an ancient route from the *Ḥajle* Ford through *El Buqêʿah* to Jerusalem. Isa 65:10 promises that the Valley of Sharon to the east and the Valley of Achor to the west will be given as rich pasture land to those who seek God.

Noth (1955: 42–55) has identified the Valley (*ʿēmeq*) of Achor with present day *El Buqêʿah* ("little valley"), a small plain (approximately five miles long and up to two miles wide) in the northern Judean wilderness, between Hyrcania and Qumran. *El Buqêʿah* is bounded on the north by the *Wâdī Dabr* system, and on the south by *Wâdī en-Nár* (the Kidron Valley). According to Noth, *El Buqêʿah* is the only site in the area around Jericho which could properly be called an *ʿēmeq* (that is, an arable, defensible depression, bordered by hills or mountains).

Noth's identification has achieved near consensus among biblical scholars. Wolff (1954: 76–81) has presented the strongest alternative proposal. He locates the Valley of Achor in *Wâdī en-Nuwēʿime,* a valley one-half mile wide by one mile long situated north of Jericho, a location which fits both the Benjaminite context of Joshua 7 and the northern prophet Hosea's reference to Achor. However, *Wâdī en-Nuwēʿime* is too far into Benjaminite territory (perhaps near the Ephramite border) to be cited as a marker for the Judean-Benjaminite boundary. That the Valley of Achor is included in the Judean but not the Benjaminite description of their joint border suggests that it belonged to Judah. Joshua 7 (long recognized as independent from the account of the conquest of Ai in Joshua 8) would then be a Judean story which had been carried to Gilgal and incorporated into its Benjaminite legends.

F. M. Cross and J. T. Milik's exploration of *El Buqêʿah* (1956: 5–17) uncovered three Iron Age II settlements (*Khirbet Abu Ṭabaq* [M.R. 188127], *Khirbet es Samrah* [M.R. 187125], and *Khirbet el Maqari* [M.R. 186123]) which they have identified with the desert cities Middin, Secacah, and Nibshan (Josh 15:61–62). The proposal has been well received; however, in the absence of evidence directly linking the desert cities to the Valley of Achor, or the Iron Age ruins to the desert cities, the identification must be considered tentative.

Bibliography

Cross, F. M., and Milik, J. T. 1956. Explorations in the Judaean Buqêʿah. *BASOR* 142: 5–17.

Noth, M. 1955. Das Deutsche Evangelische Institut für Altertumswissenschaft des Heiligen Landes Lehrkursus 1954. *ZDPV* 75.

Stager, L. E. 1974. El-Bouqêʿah. *RB* 81: 94–96.

———. 1976. Farming in the Judean Desert. *BASOR* 221: 145–58.

Wolff, H. W. 1954. Die Ebene Achor. *ZDPV* 70: 76–81.

CAROLYN J. PRESSLER

ACHSAH (PERSON) [Heb *ʿaksâ*]. The daughter of Caleb (1 Chr 2:49) and the wife of the Israelite judge Othniel (Josh 15:16–17 = Judg 1:12–13). For sacking the city Kiriath-sepher (Debir, see Josh 15:15 = Judg 1:11), Othniel received Achsah as a prize from Caleb. Subsequently, in addition to receiving territory in the Negeb, Achsah charmed Caleb into giving her the arable land known as the Upper and Lower Springs (Josh 15:13–19 = Judg 1:11–15; see Mosca 1984). Although the derivation of her name is uncertain, relating Achsah to those charming, seductive anklets that attracted attention in Isa 3:16–18 (Heb *hāʿakāsîm*) would certainly deepen our appreciation of the wordplays in these verses.

While in this story Achsah is Caleb's daughter and Othniel is "the son of Kenaz, the brother of Caleb" (Josh 15:17; cf. Judg 1:13; 3:9–11; 1 Chr 4:13), the genealogical relationship between Achsah and her spouse is not self-evident (see Webb 1987: 233, n. 25). Since the name "Caleb" occurs as the son of both Jephunneh (see e.g., Numbers 13–14; Joshua 14–15; Judges 1; 1 Chr 4:15) and

Hezron (1 Chronicles 2), but never occurs as the son of Kenaz (cf. 1 Chr. 4:15 where Caleb is the grandfather of Kenaz), therefore, contrary to the implication of Josh 15:17 = Judg 1:13, Achsah is not literally Othniel's niece. The relationship must be understood, rather, within the framework of how genealogies function in the Bible.

According to Wilson (1977: 183), genealogies can be used to delineate social and political ties between two groups and, in particular, to incorporate marginally affiliated clans in a central tribe. Since the genealogies of Caleb and Othniel are related in this way to the tribe of Judah (Yeivin 1971: 13–14), it can be inferred that Joshua uses the term "brother" to express that Caleb and Othniel belonged to a common group, which was assimilated into the tribe of Judah (Meyer 1906: 348–49; Johnson 1969: 6). Thus, the marriage of Achsah to Othniel would have functioned to strengthen the ties between the clans of Othniel and Caleb.

Bibliography

Johnson, M. D. 1969. *The Purpose of Biblical Genealogies with Specific Reference to the Setting of the Genealogies of Jesus.* SNTSMS 8. Cambridge, MA.

Meyer, E. 1906. *Die Israeliten und ihre Nachbarstämme.* Halle.

Mosca, P. 1984. Who Seduced Whom? A Note on Josh 15:18 // Judges 1:14. *CBQ* 46: 18–22.

Webb, B. G. 1987. *The Book of Judges: An Integrated Reading.* JSOTSup 46. Sheffield.

Wilson, R. R. 1977. *Genealogy and History in the Biblical World.* YNER 7. New Haven.

Yeivin, S. 1971. *The Israelite Conquest of Canaan.* Uitgaven van het Nederlands Historisch-Archaeologisch Instituut te Istanbul 27. Istanbul.

Mark J. Fretz

ACHSHAPH (PLACE) [Heb *ʾakšāp*]. An ancient Canaanite city-state. Its antiquity and importance are known from a few early records. The Egyptian Execration Texts (*ca.* 20th–18th century B.C.), lists Achshaph among 64 other place names. These were well-known city-states ruled by a king, so the fact that Achshaph was included in the list is indicative of its prominence. The Karnak List of Towns conquered by Thutmose III (15th century B.C.) refers to Achshaph as a city in the Plain of Jezreel and Acco, in the district of Gaza. The Tell el-Amarna Letters (*ca.* 14th century B.C.) state that the kings of Acco and Achshaph (spelled *ʾakšapa*) provided military assistance to the King of Jerusalem and Shuwardata (Gath). The Papyrus Anastasi 1 (13th century B.C.) indicates that a road from Megiddo reached the Plain of Acco close to Achshaph, although it spelled Achshaph with an *ʿayin* instead of an *ʾalep*.

Achshaph is mentioned in the Bible solely in the book of Joshua. It is one of the city-states that joined the coalition of the northern kings (Josh 11:1) to fight Joshua and the Israelites. Obviously, on being defeated, it became a part of Asher's territory (Josh 19:25).

The reference to Achshaph in the book of Joshua is significant for two reasons. First, the tradition behind the book preserved a memory that Achshaph was a royal city in the N plain during the ancient times. Second, by mentioning a renowned ancient city the Deuteronomistic theologian illustrated that when the Israelites were obedient to the Lord, the cities of the northern coalition, the powerful Achshaph included, were defeated and their land given to Israel.

The location of Achshaph remains uncertain. Some identify it with Tel Keisan, which is located 6 miles SE of Acco. Remains from the Bronze Age and early Iron Age were found there. See KEISAN, TELL. Another likely site is Khirbet el-Harbaj (M.R. 158240), which is situated at the S end of the plain of Acco.

Paul Benjamin

ACHZIB (PLACE) [Heb *ʾakzîb*]. Var. CHEZIB. **1.** A town allocated to the tribe of Judah (Josh 15:44). From the context of its placement among the other cities, it appears to have been in the Shephelah, probably at its juncture with the Judean hills. In Mic 1:14, it is mentioned among several towns on which the prophet presents various puns, playing upon the similarity of the sounds of the name of the town Achzib (Heb *ʾakzîb*) with "deceit" (Heb *ʾakzāb*). The town may be connected with the birth of Judah's son, Shelah, who was born to him by a Canaanite woman—the name of the city, CHEZIB (PLACE) (Heb *kēzîb*), is an apparent variation of Achzib.

While certain identification is not possible, Eusebius (*Onomast.* 172) identified the site with Chasbi, which is modern Tell el-Beida (M.R. 145116) near Adullam.

2. A tell on the Mediterranean coast (M.R. 159272) N of Acco. According to Josh 19:29, it was part of the territory of Asher, but they proved unsuccessful in expelling the Canaanites from the site (Judg 1:31).

Excavations directed by M. W. Prausnitz in 1963–64 revealed that at the end of the MB I, a trench had been dug in the *kurkar* E of the tell which had transformed the Achzib peninsula into a Mediterranean port and island city. The circumference was defended by earth walls, a glacis, and a fosse. Apparently sacked in the beginning of the LB (mid-16th century B.C.E.), Achzib was rebuilt, but was again laid waste at the end of the LB. From the Iron Age IB (11th century B.C.E.), the town expanded to its largest size during the 8th century (Iron Age II), when it was conquered by Sennacherib in 701 B.C.E. The rebuilt city, which is called Accipu in the Assyrian texts, flourished throughout the succeeding Persian period. The evidence from the storehouse excavations shows that it prospered until the beginning of the Roman period. Three squares excavated in the middle of the site attest to occupation by Byzantines, Crusaders, and Arabs.

Numerous excavations have been conducted in the various cemeteries (Central, Eastern, Southern, and Northern) beginning in 1941 and spanning over forty years. The first excavations were directed by I. Ben-Dor and the remaining operations since 1944 have been directed by M. Prausnitz. While all the cemeteries have produced Iron Age materials, only the Southern and Central cemeteries have produced burials from the MB I–II.

a. The Central Cemetery. Early Iron Age IB cist graves of the 12th–11th centuries B.C.E. have been excavated which contained one or two skeletons each. Characteristic grave goods were cylinder seals, bronze bowls, a bronze double axe, long-hafted lance heads, an ivory bowl with lion couchant, as well as numerous burnished bichrome pilgrim flasks and white-painted Cypriot bottles, all of which indicate a continuation of the LB Canaanite customs into the beginning of the Iron Age.

b. The Eastern Cemetery. At the end of the Iron Age IB, underground burial chambers with shafts were hewn into the rock. Inside each of the burial chambers were found the skeletons of 300 to 400 individuals. These were family tombs identical with contemporary Israelite funereal practices and architecture. The family vaults were apparently in continuous use for 250–300 years. The pottery inside the tombs consisted of a great number of red-burnished, and red-polished jugs with trefoil rims, as well as red-polished jugs with mushroom rims—all typical "Achzib" wares. Statistically the amount of early bichrome wares was minimal and pilgrim flasks were few and late. There was a range of proto Black-on-Red to Black-on-Red II/III wares dating from the end of the 11th to the 8th/7th centuries B.C.E. More than three fourths of all the pottery finds were jugs.

c. The Southern Cemetery. A different range of contemporary ceramics of the Iron Age II was predominate in this cemetery. Bichrome, Black-on-White, and Black-on-Pink pilgrim flasks represented the overwhelming majority of pottery in the early phase of the burials. Some chambers were built, some hewn into the rock. A shaft or dromos led to the entrance. Paradoxically the ceilings of the rock-cut chambers had been quarried to be covered again by a built upper structure—a *bamah* with altar, *maṣṣebah,* and a special ceramic repertoire of votives. These family vaults contained 250–300 bodies buried over a period of about 300 years. The early, middle, and final phases of these chambers are dated by the ceramics, scarabs, and cylinder and stamp seals.

The middle phase continued to use red-slipped flat pilgrim flasks reflecting the LB traditions. At this time (mid-9th century), however, white painted Cypriot wares disappear and were replaced by red-polished Achzib jugs with trefoil rims. There also appeared red-polished bowls and jugs with mushroom rims. This phase continued until the first third of the 7th century B.C.E. The final phase was highlighted by large storage jars used as ossuaries and receptacles for funeral gifts, which accompanied the deceased inside the family vault. To judge by seals and scarabs, the final phase ended in the beginning of the 6th century.

The Southern cemetery was also a burial ground for shaft burials of the 6th century. The absence of Attic wares strongly suggests that by midcentury, this sacred ground with its Canaanite and Sidonian traditions was no longer in use.

d. The Northern Cemetery. The areas excavated contained cremation urns and burials mainly of the Iron Age, Persian, and Hellenistic periods. Iron Age cremation urns had also been deposited in the sands of the peripheral regions of the Southern cemetery. Early cremation urns were large Sub-Mycenean kraters, White-Painted II–III geometric kraters, or Black-on-Red I–II wares belonging to the 10th–8th centuries B.C.E. Later cremation burials were made inside storage jars. Also significant was the custom of erecting a *maṣṣebah* immediately above the cremation urns or jars.

Cremation urns were also found clustered around the foundations of a large pavement covered by lime and chalk plaster which had been frequently resurfaced. There was an area surrounded by a wall in which was an altar—this is believed to have been a *bamah.* The absence of scarabs or other funerary gifts with the urns near the *bamah* leaves only typological and stratigraphic criteria for determining its date, apparently 8th century B.C.E. The types of kraters and storage jars used in this cemetery and the stelae have close parallels with those found in the lower levels of the Precinct of Tanit at Carthage. The preference for kraters as cremation urns in association with the contemporary Achzib red-slipped jugs clearly points to the continuation of Syro-Hittite traditions at Achzib.

Each of the cemeteries represents a separate cultural tradition—Late Canaanite-Sidonian, Israelite, and Syro-Hittite. Only after the 6th century B.C.E. did they become known as Phoenician.

Bibliography

Oren, E. D. 1975. The Pottery from the Achzib Defence System, Area D: 1963 and 1964 Seasons. *IEJ* 25: 211–25.

Prausnitz, M. W. 1963. Notes and News. Achzib. *IEJ* 13: 337–38.

———. 1965. Notes and News. Tel Achzib. *IEJ* 15: 256–58.

———. 1975. The Planning of the Middle Bronze Age Town at Achzib and its Defences. *IEJ* 25: 202–10.

M. W. PRAUSNITZ

ACRABA (PLACE) [Gk *Egrebēl*]. A town situated southeast of Dothan in the eastern hills of Samaria (Jdt 7:18). The Assyrian general Holofernes had the Edomites and Ammonites stationed in this area while his troops cut off the water supply to the Israelite town of Bethulia. However, the location of Acraba is uncertain, and given the genre of the book of Judith, the historicity of this campaign and the "Assyrian" general is doubtful. Most scholars (see Moore *Judith* AB, 173) identify Acraba with Acrabeta (modern *ʿAqraba*), located 40 km north-northeast of Jerusalem. Acraba may also be associated with the site AKRABATTENE (1 Macc 5:3), where Judas Maccabaeus defeated the Idumeans who were killing Jews in 164 B.C.E. (Goldstein *1 Maccabees* AB, 294).

MARK J. FRETZ

ACRE (PLACE). See ACCO (PLACE).

ACROSTIC. A device employed in poetry whereby the initial letters or signs of each line, read downward, constitute a name, a sentence, or an alphabetic pattern.

The earliest examples of *name/sentence acrostics* are Babylonian. Two can be dated to the reigns of Ashurbanipal and Nebuchadnezzar II respectively, since they mention those kings by name. The best-known Babylonian acrostic, the so-called *Babylonian Theodicy,* has been provisionally dated ca. 1000 B.C.E. (Lambert 1960: 67). The acrostic may spell out a name (e.g., "God Nabu") or a sentence (e.g., in the *Theodicy,* "I, Sag-gil-kinam-ubib, the incantation priest, am adorant of the god and the king"). Six of the seven extant Babylonian acrostic poems (surveyed in Soll 1988: 305–11) are stanzaic. In all but one of the stanzaic acrostics, each line within the strophe begins with the same sign that began the strophe. This repeating stanzaic pattern is the typical pattern for the Babylonian acrostics. In the Babylonian writing system, one sign could represent more than one sound. Most of the acrostics make use of this polyphony of sign values. Thus, the most important consideration was a conceptual or visual one: the use of the same sign. Two of the prayers incorporate not only an acrostic, but also a *telestic:* the terminal letters of each line, read downward, also form a phrase.

Name/sentence acrostics also occur in Greek literature. The Christian acrostic in the Sibylline Oracles 8.217–50 reads *iēsous chreistos theou huios sōtēr stauros,* which in turn utilizes the well-known Christian acrostic *ichthys.*

The Hebrew Bible contains a number of *alphabetic acrostics.* The earliest biblical acrostics are probably the damaged acrostic in Psalms 9–10 and the partial acrostic (through *kap*) in Nahum 1; both are usually dated to the period of the Judaean monarchy. Many of the remaining biblical acrostics are probably either exilic or postexilic. Psalm 37 and Lamentations 1, 2, and 4 are stanzaic acrostics (see LAMENTATIONS); repeating stanzaic acrostics may be found in Lamentations 3 (3-line strophes) and Psalm 119 (8-line strophes). In Psalms 111 and 112, each individual colon (half of a normal line) begins with a consecutive alphabetic character. Psalms 25 and 34 both omit a *waw* line and add a *pe* line after *taw.* This *pe* line thus becomes the last letter of the acrostic and combines with *ʾalep* and *lamed* (the first and middle letters of the acrostic) to form the consonants of the first letter of the alphabet, *ʾlp* (Skehan 1971: 74). The remaining biblical acrostics are Psalm 145 and Proverbs 31: 10–31. There are also three psalms from Qumran (see Sanders 1965) which are alphabetic acrostics: the Hebrew text of Sirach 51: 13–30 (11QPs^{a}Sirach, which also adds a *pe* line), the so-called Apostrophe to Zion (11QPs^{a}Zion) and the partial acrostic (through *pe*) 11QPs^{a}155 (also known [Syriac] Psalm III). For a more detailed discussion of alphabetic acrostics in the biblical period, see Marcus (1947), Holm-Nielsen (1960), and Soll (1990, chap. 1).

While acrostic poetry depends on knowledge of the art of writing and is therefore "scribal" in the sense that all ancient written literature is scribal, the acrostic should not be seen as exclusively, or even primarily, wisdom literature. Included among the biblical alphabetic acrostics are hymns (e.g., Psalm 145), prayers (e.g., Psalm 25), and wisdom poems (e.g., Prov 31:10–31). This same distribution of genres is found in Babylonian name/sentence acrostics as well.

While the biblical alphabetic acrostic is often considered to be a mnemonic device (e.g., Paul *IDBSup,* 600–1), this position is difficult to maintain in the light of parallel Babylonian acrostics, which no one supposes were written with a mnemonic end in view (for further discussion, see Soll 1988: 320–22). The use of the acrostic form is best understood by analogy with metrical or rhyme schemes as an aesthetic constraint. It provided ancient poets with stimulus, direction, and limit as they drew on their stock of divine epithets, lament motives, petitions, and other conventional features of religious poetry which could otherwise be piled on indefinitely.

In the case of a name/sentence acrostic, the acrostic identifies the poem's author, the purpose of the composition, the one to whom it is addressed, or some combination of these. Although the poet began with the acrostic text as a matrix for the work, habit causes the reader to begin reading horizontally rather than vertically. Thus the impression of the finished product is the reverse of the process of composition: the poem gives the appearance of generating the acrostic, as if revealing a secret about itself. All Babylonian name/sentence acrostics had some way of alerting the reader to the presence of the acrostic pattern.

The alphabetic framework is, by contrast, abstract; it does not say anything. Rather, it says everything, for the 22 letters of the alphabet can be used to make any combination of words. The alphabet is a ready metaphor for totality and completeness (Gottwald 1954: 23–32) and thus serves as an excellent frame for praising the qualities of God (Psalms 111 and 145), the just man (Psalm 112), or the capable woman (Prov 30:10–31). Even in poems not concerned with the enumeration of qualities, use of the alphabet evokes a sense of completeness without having to be comprehensive. The fact that the Semitic alphabet gave a much greater impression of organization than any of its adaptations to other languages and scripts (Driver 1976: 179–85) may also have led to its use as an ordering device for poetry.

The alphabetic framework was a fixed sequence that did not have to be justified, but was simply there, ready to be built on. The only variation in this order is the inversion of the *ʿayin-pe* sequence: *pe* precedes *ʿayin* in Lamentations 2, 3, and 4; Psalm 10; and the LXX of Proverbs 31:10–31. The *pe-ʿayin* inversion occurs in some epigraphic abecedaries as well (Cross 1980: 9–13), so variation on this point in the acrostics was not a question of poetic license, but of adherence to different ordering conventions.

The alphabetic sequence may have been understood as being complete numerically as well as linguistically, which would account for the 22-line poems in the Bible. This number of lines is clearly a deliberate choice in Lamentations 5, since the rest of the book consists of alphabetic acrostics. Psalms 33, 38, and 103 are also 22-line poems.

Bibliography

Cross, F. M. 1980. Newly Found Inscriptions in Old Canaanite and Early Phoenician Scripts. *BASOR* 238: 1–20.

Driver, G. R. 1976. *Semitic Writing.* London.

Freedman, D. N. 1972. Acrostics and Metrics in Hebrew Poetry. *HTR* 65: 367–92.

Gottwald, N. K. 1954. *Studies in the Book of Lamentations.* SBT 14. Chicago.

Holm-Nielsen, S. 1960. The Importance of Late Jewish Psalmody for the Understanding of the Old Testament Psalmodic Tradition. *ST* 14: 1–53.

Lambert, W. G. 1960. *Babylonian Wisdom Literature.* Oxford.

Marcus, R. 1947. Alphabetic Acrostics in the Hellenistic and Roman Periods. *JNES* 6: 109–15.

Sanders, J. A. 1965. *The Psalms Scroll of Qumran Cave 11.* DJD 4. Oxford.

Skehan, P. W. 1971. *Studies in Israelite Poetry and Wisdom.* CBQMS 1. Washington.

Soll, W. 1988. Babylonian and Biblical Acrostics. *Bib* 68: 305–23.
———. 1990. *Psalm 119: Matrix, Form and Setting.* CBQMS 24. Washington, DC.

WILL SOLL

ACTS OF ANDREW. See ANDREW, ACTS OF.

ACTS OF ANDREW AND MATTATHIAS. See ANDREW AND MATTATHIAS, ACTS OF.

ACTS OF JOHN (BY PROCHORUS). See JOHN, ACTS OF (BY PROCHORUS).

ACTS OF PAUL. See PAUL, ACTS OF.

ACTS OF PETER. See PETER, ACTS OF.

ACTS OF PETER AND PAUL. See PETER AND PAUL, ACTS OF.

ACTS OF PETER AND THE TWELVE. See PETER AND THE TWELVE, ACTS OF.

ACTS OF PHILIP. See PHILIP, ACTS OF.

ACTS OF PILATE. See PILATE, ACTS OF.

ACTS OF THE APOSTLES. See LUKE-ACTS, BOOK OF.

ACTS OF THEKLA. See THEKLA, ACTS OF.

ACTS OF THOMAS. See THOMAS, ACTS OF.

ACTS, BOOK OF. See LUKE-ACTS, BOOK OF.

ADADAH (PLACE) [Heb *ʿadʿādâ*]. A city situated in the Negeb region of Judah toward Edom (Josh 15:22). In the Bible this name occurs only as part of a list of Judah's territorial inheritance (Josh 15:20–63). According to most scholars (e.g., Boling and Wright *Joshua* AB, 379), the MT *wĕʿadʿādâ,* "and Adadah," should be emended to read Heb *wʿrʿrh,* "and Ararah" (cf. LXX variants *arouēl, arouēr,* as well as *adada*). Some scholars, therefore, identify Adadah with *ʿArʿarah* (modern *Khirbet Aroer*; see Alt 1934: 19; Keel and Küchler 1982: 337), a site located some 20 km southeast of Beer-sheba, to which David redistributed some of the spoils of the Amalekites (1 Sam 30:28; see McCarter *1 Samuel* AB, 436). Alternatively, Kallai (*KHG* 351) suggests that if no evidence of an Iron Age settlement is yielded from *ʿArʿarah,* then Tell ʾEsdar, located 2 km farther north-northeast should be considered. Aharoni (*LBHG,* 117) suggests that the name was originally Heb **Aroer-ʿArʿarah,* "ʿArʿarah the ruin" (Heb *ʿărôʿēr* indicates "a ruin" as does Arabic *khirbet*). Epigraphically, therefore, the name "Adadah" may have resulted from a transmutation in the name "ʿArʿarah" of the Heb letter *resh* to *daleth,* since these letters are difficult to distinguish in script.

Bibliography

Alt, A. 1934. Das Institut im Jahre 1933. *PJ* 30: 5–31.
Keel, O., and Küchler, M. 1982. *Orte und Landschaften der Bibel, Ein Handbuch und Studienreiseführer zum Heiligen Land.* Vol. 2. Göttingen and Zürich.

MARK J. FRETZ

ADAH (PERSON) [Heb *ʿādâ*]. The name "Adah" seems to have been common in the ancient Semitic world (compare Minaean *ʿdt* [?]; Thamudic *ʿdh/ʿdy*; Safaitic *ʿdʾ/ʿdy*; Aramaic *ʿdyh*; Neo-Punic *ʿdyt* [?]; Syrian *ʿaddā/ʿiddô*; Samaritan *ʿāda*; Nabataean *ʿdyw*; and Arabic *ʿaddijj*). It appears to be the shortened form of a personal name containing the element **ʿdw/y,* "to decorate, embellish" (Weippert 1971: 250; Stamm 1980: 130) (e.g., Heb *ʿadîʾēl, ʿadāyāh(û), ʾelʿādâ, ʿādîn(āʾ)* [?], and *ʿiddô(ʿ)* [?]; Sabaean/Safaitic/Ammonite [?] *ʿdʾl*; Libyanite *ʿdwn* [?]; Minaean/Safaitic *ʿdyn* [?]; and Gr *Kosadou* [gen. from *qsʿd*?]). Two women in the Hebrew Bible bear this name.

1. The first of Lamech's two wives, according to the genealogy in Gen 4:17–19. To her two sons, Jabal and Jubal, are attributed the life-style of the tentdweller and the herdsman, as well as the cultural achievement of musical performance.

2. The daughter of Elon the Hittite, and one of Esau's Canaanite wives (Gen 36:2). She was considered to be one of the Edomite tribal ancestresses alongside of Oholibamah and Basemath. Eliphaz, her only son and Esau's eldest, was born in Canaan (Gen 35:4, 10) and became the father of Teman, Omar, Zepho, Gatam, Kenaz, Amalek (and Korah?) (Gen 36:11–12), who are listed a few verses later as the "tribal chiefs" (*ʾallûpîm*) of Edom (vv 15–16). The three contradictory texts Gen 36:2–3, 26:34, and 28:9 are based on different traditions of P, hence the lack of harmony (Speiser *Genesis* AB, 279; Westermann *Genesis 1–11* BK, 684).

Bibliography

Moritz, B. 1926. Edomitische Genealogien I. *ZAW* 44: 81–93.
Stamm, J. J. 1980. *Beiträge zur hebräischen und altorientalischen Namenkunde.* OBO 30. Göttingen.
Weippert, M. 1971. *Edom. Studien und Materialien zur Geschichte der Edomiter auf Grund schriftlicher und archäologischer Quellen.* Diss. Tübingen.

ULRICH HÜBNER

ADAIAH (PERSON) [Heb *ʿădāyâ*; *ʿădāyāhû*]. **1.** A Levite of the clan of Gershom, son of Ethan, father of Zerah, and grandfather of Ethni (1 Chr 6:26–27—Eng 6:41–42). His name occurs in the middle of a genealogical list whose purpose was to substantiate the Levitical pedigree of Asaph, one of the temple singers appointed by King David (1 Chr 6:16–17, 33—Eng 6:31–32, 48). With some justification this Adaiah [*ʿădāyâ*] has been equated with Iddo [*ʿiddô*] in 1 Chr 6:6—Eng 6:21 (Schumacher *IDB* 1:42) but this identification is not absolutely certain. Although there are four names (Gershom, Jahath, Zimmah, Zerah) common to the two Gershomite Levitical lists involved (1 Chr 6:5–6—Eng 6:20–21; 1 Chr 6:24–28—Eng 6:39–43), the pertinent inner patterns Zimmah-Joah-*Iddo*-Jeatherai and then Zimmah-Ethan-*Adaiah*-Zerah-Ethni illustrate equally the configuration of differences. It is also worth noting that Chronicles traces Asaph's lineage through Adaiah to Levi's son "Gershom," not the more traditional "Gershon."

2. A Benjaminite, one of the sons of Shimei (1 Chr 8:21). His name is found in a list of Benjamin's descendants who are distinguished as heads of families living in Jerusalem (1 Chr 8:28). This Shimei [Heb *šimʿî*] is probably a textual corruption of the name SHEMA [Heb *šemaʿ*] mentioned ealier in 1 Chr 8:13. The complex 1 Chronicles 2–8 contains three epicenters: the lists of the tribe of Judah at the beginning, those of Levi in the middle, and those pertaining to the tribe of Benjamin at the end. This threefold arrangement reflected something of the territorial, social, and political realities of the postexilic period (see Weinberg 1981: 111–12).

3. The father of Maaseiah, who is seemingly listed as one of the "commanders of hundreds" [*śārê hammēʾôt*] that conspired with Jehoiada the priest to overthrow Queen Athaliah and install young Joash upon the Judean throne (2 Chr 23:1). According to 2 Kgs 11:4 these individuals were "the captains of the Carites and of the guards." By contrast, the Chronicler, true to his own ideology, apparently reports the plot as carried out exclusively by priestly and Levitical guards in order to avoid any hint of the desecration of the temple area by "foreign mercenaries" (Myers *2 Chronicles* AB, 131; Williamson *Chronicles* NCB, 315). On the connection of Levites with martial activities, see Spencer 1984: 270–71. Dillard, moreover, makes the intriguing observation that, whereas the first three occurrences of names (Azariah, Ishmael, Azariah) in 2 Chr 23:1 are introduced with the preposition *le,* the last two names (Maaseiah ben Adaiah, Elishaphat) are proceeded by the object marker *ʾet* before "the commanders of hundreds." While representative possibly of no more than a stylistic variation, this change in pattern may just as well indicate that for the Chronicler Maaseiah ben Adaiah was not intended to be included among the "commanders of hundreds." However, that the writer regarded the commanders as Levites seems to be implied in the activities envisioned in 1 Chr 23:6–7, 9 (see Dillard *2 Chronicles* WBC, 177 n.1c, 180–81).

4. The maternal grandfather of King Josiah (2 Kgs 22:1). It is characteristic of the Deuteronomistic history to introduce Judean kings through a fixed scribal formula. Included in this formula is the name of each king's mother. Jedidah, Josiah's mother, is cited as the daughter of Adaiah of Bozkath. BOZKATH (Josh 15:39) appears to be a SW Judean village in the vicinity of Lachish (Tell ed-Duweir) and Eglon (Tell el-Ḥesi).

5. A Judahite, the son of Joiarib, and father of Hazaiah (Neh 11:5). He is mentioned as an ancestor of Maaseiah, one of the Judean family heads resident in Jerusalem after the return from exile. The parallel text in 1 Chr 9:5 (RSV) makes no reference to Adaiah ben Joiarib but speaks rather of "the Shilonites: Asaiah [= Maaseiah?] the first-born, and his sons." However, the presence of Judah's two sons Perez (Neh 11:4; 1 Chr 9:4) and Zerah (1 Chr 9:6) in these two otherwise synoptic lists suggests that the MT behind the RSV's "the Shilonite/the Shilonites" [*haššîlōnî*/*haššîlōnî*] in Neh 9:5 and 1 Chr 9:5 might well be revocalized to read "the Shelanite/the Shelanites" [*haššēlānî*/*haššēlānî*] (see NEB), thus making this Adaiah actually a descendant of Judah through his third son Shelah (Gen 38:5; Num 26:20).

6. The son of Jeroham (1 Chr 9:12 = Neh 11:12) and one of the priests listed who returned from exile to live and work in Jerusalem. Adaiah and his brethren, heads of fathers' houses, are reported to have numbered 242 persons. A comparison of the two parallel verses cited reveals that Nehemiah 11 carries his ancestry back to the seventh generation, adding three additional names (Pelaliah, Amzi, Zechariah) to Adaiah's ancestry as given in 1 Chr 9:12.

7. A son of BANI (Ezra 10:29 = 1 Esdr 9:30) and **8.** a son of BINNUI (Ezra 10:39), two individuals who had married foreign women and who were induced to put them away along with their children, in the time of Ezra (Ezra 10:44 = 1 Esdr 9:36). The double occurrence of the name "Bani" in both Ezra 10:29 and 10:34 and the similar name "Binnui" in Ezra 10:39 have given rise to a number of textual emendations. Not all is settled even with respect to the name "Adaiah": thus LXX 1 Esdr 9:30 reads *iedaios* for Adaiah in Ezra 10:29; accordingly, the text-critical apparatus of BHS suggests that the name "Adaiah" here be amended to read either *yeʿadya* or *yedaʿya.* For the second Adaiah named in Ezra 10:39, there is no corresponding name parallel whatsoever in 1 Esdr 10:34. There, in fact, Binnui has become a one of Bani's sons!

Bibliography

Kellerman, U. 1966. Die Listen in Nehemiah 11 eine Dokumentation aus den letzten Jahren des Reiches Judas? *ZDPV* 82: 209–27.

Spencer, J. R. 1984. The Tasks of the Levites. *ZAW* 96: 267–71.

Weinberg, J. P. 1981. Das Wesen und die funktionelle Bestimmung der Listen in 1 Chr 1–9. *ZAW* 93: 91–114.

Roger W. Uitti

ADALIA (PERSON) [Heb *ʾădalyāʾ*]. One of the ten sons of Haman (Esth 9:8). The names of Haman's sons appear within Esth 9:1–19, a passage long thought to be the denouement of the Esther story, although recent research has shown it to be independent of both the main story (Esth 1–8) and the two appendices; one on the origin of Purim (Esth 9:20–32), the other the praise of Mordecai (Esth 10:1–3) (Clines 1984: 39–49, 158–62). This passage resolves the question of what happened after king Ahasuerus granted the Jews permission to defend themselves against the attacks of hostile neighbors incited by Haman (Esth 8:11–12). In this narrative context the killing of

Haman's male progeny is the reversal of his attempt to annihilate the Jews (Esth 3:9–15) (Berg 1979: 105ff.).

The authenticity of the names of Haman's sons is a matter of dispute. There are variant lists of the names in the LXX, the A-Text (= LXX L?) and other ancient versions (see the lists in Moore *Esther* AB, xlii–xliii; Haupt 1907–8: 175). It has been suggested from this that the spelling of certain names in MT may be corrupt, the Greek versions perhaps preserving a more accurate spelling (Moore *Esther* AB, xliv). Against this, the attestation in Iranian onomastica of a few of the names in MT Esther and the likelihood that many of them can be given sensible Iranian etymologies has renewed confidence in the superiority of the MT orthography (Millard 1977; Zadok 1986). While this also counters the claim that the names are the product of the writer's imagination, the use of probable real names proves nothing about the veracity of the story. Many of the names of Haman's sons are, however, otherwise unattested, perhaps reflecting our limited knowledge of Iranian onomastica. The current state of knowledge of Iranian dialects leaves the analysis of many of the names uncertain and the etymologies given are often conjectural. For the analysis of many of the names there is often no advancement on the classic studies of Oppert (1894: 35–41), Justi (1895), Scheftelowitz (1901), and Bartholomae (1904). Their work on Iranian names in Esther is summarized by Paton (1908: 66–71). The most recent comprehensive survey of Iranian names is Hinz (1975), supplemented by Zadok (1986) on names in Esther.

ʾădalyāʾ (LXX *barsa*) has a number of proposed Old Iranian etymologies for which see Paton (*Esther* ICC, 70f.) and Gehman (1924: 327), but none are convincing. *ʾădalyāʾ* may be related to the name *ʾdlyn* attested in a 6th century B.C.E. Aramaic text from Egypt (Bauer and Meissner 1936 line 16; *TAD,* 11–13), although this name also proves to be difficult to analyze (Grelot 1972: 500f.; Kornfeld 1978: 113 for Hurrian derivation). For an explanation of the LXX spelling, see Haupt (1907–8: 176).

Bibliography

Bartholomae, C. 1904. *Altiranisches Wörterbuch.* Strassburg.

Bauer, H., and Freedman, D. N. 1936. Ein aramäische Pachtvertrag aus dem 7. Jahre Darius' I. Pp. 414–24 in *Sitzungsberichte der Press. Akad. der Wiss., Philol.-hist. Kl.* Berlin: Adademie der Wissenschaften.

Berg, S. B. 1979. *The Book of Esther: Motifs, Themes and Structure.* SBLDS 44. Missoula, MT.

Clines, D. J. A. 1984. *The Esther Scroll.* JSOTSup 30. Sheffield.

Grelot, P. 1972. *Documents araméens d'Egypt.* LAPO Paris.

Haupt, P. 1907–8. Critical Notes on Esther. *AJSL* 24: 97–186. Repr., pp. 1–90 of *Studies in the Book of Esther,* ed C. A. Moore. New York, 1982.

Hinz, W. 1975. *Altiranisches Sprachgut der Nebenüberlieferungen.* Wiesbaden.

Kornfeld, W. 1978. *Onomastica Aramaica aus Ägypten.* Vienna.

Justi, F. 1895. *Iranisches Namenbuch.* Marburg. Repr. Hildescheim, 1963.

Millard, A. R. 1977. The Persian Names in the Book of Esther and the Reliability of the Hebrew Text. *JBL* 96: 481–88.

Oppert, J. 1894. Problèmes Bibliques. *Review des études juives* 28: 32–59.

Scheftelowitz, I. 1901. *Arisches in Alten Testament.* Vol. 1. Berlin.

Zadok, R. 1986. Notes on Esther. *ZAW* 98: 105–10.

PETER BEDFORD

ADAM (PERSON) [Heb *ʾādām*]. The Hebrew noun *ʾādām* generally denotes "human being," "humankind." The term is also used of the male individual in the Gen 2:4b–3:24 creation narrative.

A. Etymology and Use in the OT.

The etymology of the word is uncertain. *ʾādām* has often been associated with the root *ʾdm* "red." Evidence cited in support of this association is widespread. In Akkadian, *adamu* means "blood, red garment," and *adamatu* "black blood." In Aramaic, *ʾădām* and other cognate terms refer to "blood," while in biblical Hebrew *ʾādōm* means "red" (adj.), and the verb *ʾādōm* "to be red." The Ugaritic verb *ʾadm* appears in several places in connection with bodily cleansing and anointing, and is usually translated "to rouge or redden." It has been suggested that the use of *ʾādām* for "human" arises because of the reddish color of human skin.

The play on words in Gen 2:7 and 3:19 between *ʾādām* and *ʾădāmâ* "ground, earth," has not been overlooked in the search for an etymology of the former. The name *ʾādām* is given to the human creature believed to have come from the *ʾădāmâ.* Of course, word plays in themselves do not necessarily indicate the etymology of a word. They could simply be used by writers or editors for literary effect. However, in this case the suggested etymological connection ought not to be ruled out. The Akkadian *adamātu,* "dark red earth" (used as a dye), suggests that the Hebrew *ʾădāmâ* could also be derived from the root *ʾdm,* "to be red." *ʾādām* and *ʾădāmâ* could have been derived from the same root separately or the latter could have given rise to the former because of the similarity of skin tone to the color of the soil itself.

While we cannot draw any firm conclusions about the origins of biblical *ʾādām,* we should note that the word has cognates in other Northwest Semitic languages. *ʾdm* appears in both Ugaritic and Phoenician as "human being." In the former, the high god El is called *ʾab ʾadm,* "the father of humankind." The development of *ʾdm* for "humankind" would seem to have been confined to the Northwest Semitic domain since the Akkadian word for "human being" is *awīlum/amī(ē)lu.* Thus, any etymological connection between *ʾādām* and either *ʾdm* "to be red," or the root for "ground, earth," would appear to be a localized Northwest Semitic phenomenon. The cognates for the latter two words range across the whole Semitic family.

B. *ʾādām* in Genesis 1–11.

ʾādām is used widely throughout the OT for "humankind" or "human being." It also occurs as the proper name of the first of the forefathers of the human family in 1 Chr 1:1. This may also be the case in Job 31:33, Hos 6:7, and Deut 4:32. In Genesis 1–5 the situation is more complex.

The use of *ʾādām* in J is concentrated in the primeval history of Genesis 2–11. In Gen 2:4b–4:25, the term refers to a specific male being. Elsewhere in the primeval narrative, it refers to humankind in general, even in Gen 8:21, which recalls the curse of Gen 3:17–19. In the context of Genesis 2–11, the individuality of the figure ʾādām in Gen 2:4b–3:24 must be seen as representative. No doubt the sources of the stories dictated in part the shape of the J narrative. ʾādām usually appears with the definite article *hāʾādām* (exceptions being 2:5, 2:20, and 3:17, the last two of which many scholars have amended).

While the individuality of the ʾādām figure in Gen 2:4b–3:24 is evident throughout the story, the restriction of ʾādām to a male individual begins clearly only from 2:18. Thus the beginning of the story addresses the issue of human beings in general in the presence of Yahweh. The disobedience that follows is not to be blamed primarily on the woman in the garden, but is the responsibility of the whole human community, as the curses (3:14–19) reveal. In 4:1, 25, ʾādām is clearly used as the proper name of the father of Cain, Abel, and Seth. After these verses, J again employs the term in its broader context. We should note that the Septuagint and Vulgate begin to translate *hāʾādām* as a proper name in Genesis 2:19.

In Gen 1:26–28, P uses ʾādām collectively as male (*zākār*) and female (*nĕqēbâ*). A single couple is not indicated here. ʾādām in its composite whole as male and female is the image of God. In Gen 5:3–5, however, P clearly understands ʾādām as an individual, i.e., the father of Seth and other children. The writer even records Adam's age at death as 930 years. This transition in the P material cannot be properly understood apart from the intervening J narrative. Recent studies in the canonical shape of Genesis 1–11 (Childs *IOTS*, 148–50) have drawn attention to the interdependence of the J and P material and the theological import of their connection. Although Childs suggests that the J creation account plays a subsidiary role to that of P, he does point to the interconnection between creation (Genesis 1) and the history of humankind (Genesis 2). One should also note that, as the two chapters stand, they present a balanced picture of humanity. The creature made in the image of God, indeed invited into God's presence, is also the creature primarily responsible for the subsequent alienation and enmity within creation. The two sides of humanity presented in Ps 8:4–7 are seen in reverse order in Genesis 1–3.

The closeness and yet enmity between humans and creation is highlighted by the play on words between ʾādām either as "human being" or the first male individual, and ʾădāmâ "ground, earth." It is from ʾădāmâ that ʾādām is fashioned (Gen 2:7). The latter's task is to till the ground (2:6). When ʾādām disobeys Yahweh, the ʾădāmâ is cursed (3:17–19). This in turn causes hardship for ʾādām. The end of ʾādām is again to return to the ʾădāmâ (parallel to ʿāpār "dust"). This wordplay continues through the flood story and is highlighted in 4:11–12 and 5:29. The link between ʾādām and ʾădāmâ in terms of sin and curse is only alleviated in 8:21–22. The dependence of fertility on human behavior, which remains wicked (8:21; 9:18–27; 11:1–9), is broken.

While the wordplay between ʾādām and ʾădāmâ is unique to the biblical material, the notion that humans are in part formed from earth or clay was widespread in the ancient Near East. We find it in the Sumerian account of the creation of humans where Enki, in order to fashion servants for the gods, calls on Mammu to "mix the heart of the clay that is over the abyss" (see Kramer 1961: 72–73). Likewise in the story of Atrahasis, Ea assists Mami, "the mistress of all the gods," in fashioning humans by pinching off pieces of clay (Tablet I. 189–260; see Lambert and Millard 1969: 56–61; cf. *ANET*, 99–100).

C. ʾādām in Intertestamental Literature.

Little attention has been given to the ʾādām figure of Genesis 1–5 elsewhere in the OT. There are, however, possible allusions to ʾādām and the creation narrative in apocryphal literature (Sir 17:1; 49:16; Tob 8:6; Wis 2:23; 9:2; 10:1). Renewed interest in and speculation concerning ʾādām is found in pseudepigraphal, rabbinic, and gnostic texts. The Greek text *Apocalypse of Moses* is the most familiar of these. It tells of the life of Adam and Eve outside paradise, the death of Abel, the birth of Seth, Adam's illness, and the journey of Eve and Seth to paradise in search of the oil of the Tree of Life which would cure Adam. Adam dies and his soul is taken into the presence of God by the Cherubim. Through the prayers of the angels, Adam is pardoned and taken back into the third heaven. While a good portion of this material overlaps with its Latin counterpart, *The Life of Adam and Eve*, the exact nature of the relationship between these two texts is difficult to determine (see *OTP*, 249–95 for a translation and discussion of both texts). See ADAM AND EVE, LIFE OF.

Emphasis in the *Apocalypse of Moses* focuses on two matters: (1) the nature of sin and the present human condition and (2) the hope of resurrection. The sin of Adam and Eve is their deliberate disobedience of God's command (*Apoc. Mos.* 8:2; 10:2; 23:4, etc.). Eve is the one who initially succumbs to temptation and then dupes Adam into following her example (7:2–3; 9:2; 14:2; 21:1–6). Both lose the visible righteousness and glory of God which they had in the beginning (11:2; 20:1–2; 21:2). This sin brings hardship upon humanity. However, the image of God in which they were created is retained in their son Seth (10:13; 12:1), who is born according to the appointment of God (38:4).

While Adam's death is a result of sin, it eventually provides an avenue to hope in resurrection. In his mercy God promises to pardon Adam and to raise him up to enjoy the benefits of paradise once again (28:4; 37:1–6; 41:3). This comes to fruition after his death. His former glory is restored (39:1–3) and the power of Satan is overcome, turning grief to joy. Just as others participate in the consequences of Adam's sin, so there is hope that the "holy people," those who adhere to the covenant, will share in his resurrection (13:3–5; 41:3).

Speculation in various noncanonical works also focuses on the figure of Adam. Philo stresses Adam's perfection (*Op* 47:136–141), while various other works describe his honor and beauty above other living beings (e.g., Sir 49:16; *Pesiq. Rab Kah* 101). This beauty was lost with Adam's sin (*Gen. Rab.* 11:2; 12:6). A motif of rabbinic thought is the enormous size of Adam, whose body stretches across the cosmos (e.g., *Gen. Rab.* 8:1; 21:3; 24:2; *Pirqe R. El.* 11; *ʾAbot R. Nat.* B8, etc.). Other passages note Adam's great wisdom (*Gen. Rab.* 24:2; *Pesiq. R.* 115a).

D. Adam in the New Testament.

The most significant references to Adam in the NT are found in Rom 5:12–21 and 1 Cor 15:21–22, 45–49. Here Paul develops his Adam-Christ typology (on the debated origin of this typology, see discussion in Cranfield *Romans* ICC, 269–95; Kasemann *Romans* HNT, 139–58; and Beker 1980). In Rom 5:12–21 Paul emphasizes the analogy between Adam, the one through whom sin and condemnation to death come into the world, and Christ, the one through whom life is offered to all. While this analogy presents Adam and Christ as those who shape the destiny of the world, the contrast is not to be ignored. The reign of grace and righteousness which comes through the second Adam confronts the reign of sin and death introduced through the first Adam and overcomes it.

In 1 Cor 15:21–22, the emphasis of the typology focuses on Christ as the one through whom resurrection to life comes. This theme is carried through in vv 45–49. In resurrection, one has a spiritual body, like that of the heavenly Christ, in contrast to the physical body which all humanity has in common with the earthly Adam. Paul draws on Gen 2:7 (LXX) as support. Here Paul could well be using the type of exegesis Philo exhibits in his discussion of Genesis 1:27 and 2:7, wherein he contrasts the heavenly, archetypal person with the historic Adam, made from dust (*Legum Allegoriae,* i.31). However, Paul understands these figures not as types but as eschatological and historical figures respectively (1 Cor 15:47).

Elsewhere in the NT, reference is made to Adam as the first generation of humanity (Jude 14 and Luke 3:38). In the latter text, he is foremost in the genealogy that leads to Jesus. In 1 Tim 2:13–14, the Eden story is used to justify the denial of teaching roles and positions of authority to women at that time. The writer stresses the prior creation of Adam, as well as the fact that Eve was the one deceived by the serpent. Adam is seen as completely innocent, while the woman in the story is labeled the transgressor. Such a line of argument is in keeping with early Jewish exegetical interpretations of Genesis 3 (e.g. *Apoc. Mos.* 15–21; *Pirqe R. El.* 1, 13).

Bibliography

Beker, J. C. 1980. *Paul the Apostle: The Triumph of God in Life and Thought.* Philadelphia.

Kramer, S. N. 1961. *Sumerian Mythology.* Rev. ed. New York.

Lambert, W. G., and Millard, A. R. 1969. *Atrahasis: The Babylonian Story of the Flood.* Oxford.

Niditch, S. 1983. The Cosmic Adam: Man as Mediator in Rabbinic Literature. *JJS* 34: 137–46.

Sharp, J. L. 1973. Second Adam in the Apocalypse of Moses. *CBQ* 35: 35–46.

Wallace, H. N. 1985. *The Eden Narrative.* HSM 32. Atlanta.

Westermann, C. 1984. *Genesis 1–11.* Trans. J. Scullion. London.

HOWARD N. WALLACE

ADAM (PLACE) [Heb *ʾādām*]. A city located in the Transjordan N of the place where the Israelites crossed the Jordan into Palestine (Josh 3:14–17). According to the biblical account of the crossing, the waters of the Jordan "rose up in a heap" at Adam (Josh 3:16). A strategic city, Adam was situated near the fords of the Jordan (Judg 7:24), S of the mouth of the Jabbok River and N of the mouth of wadi *Farʿah.* At Adam, significant travel routes intersected (2 Sam 18:23; Hos 6:9), which made it easily accessible to Pharaoh Shishak individual (ca. 945–924 B.C.E.) of Egypt, who captured Adam while on a military campaign through Palestine (1 Kgs 14:25–28; 2 Chr 12:1–12; see Kitchen 1973: 438; Mazar 1986: 146). Most scholars have traditionally located this site at *Tell ed-Dāmiyeh* (modern *Damiya;* see Glueck 1951: 331; Boling and Wright *Joshua* AB, 169), where landslides have been known to dam up the Jordan (Aharoni *LBHG,* 34; Keel and Küchler 1982: 491; Noth *Josua* HAT, 37).

The translation of the MT of Josh 3:16 reads, "one heap arose a great distance from Adam, the city which is beside Zarethan," and the written text (Heb *bēʾādām*) differs from what is to be read (Heb *mēʾādām*). The LXX rendering differs quite radically from the MT: "forming a single heap over a very wide area, as far as the frontier of Kiryath-Jearim" (see Boling and Wright *Joshua* AB, 156). Whereas the MT identifies the location of the obstruction of the water in relation to Adam, the LXX expresses the expanse of the flooding in relation to Kiriath-Jearim. Thus, a single story about the extent of flooding is formulated from two different points of reference.

The city of Adam may also refer to a sacred location in biblical poetry (see Mazar 1985: 17–18). Several verses of poetry which contain the Heb word *ʾādām,* traditionally translated "man," could be clarified by translating it "(the city) Adam." Consequently, Ps 68:19–Eng 68:18 and Ps 78:60 could benefit from this proposal (Goitein 1947), as could Hos 6:7 (even though LXX *hōs anthrōpos,* "as man," supports the traditional rendering of "man"; see Andersen and Freedman *Hosea* AB, 439).

Bibliography

Glueck, N. 1951. *Explorations in Eastern Palestine, IV.* Pt. I: Text. AASOR 25–28. New Haven.

Goitein, S. D. 1947. The City of Adam in the Book of Psalms? *JPES* 13: 86–88.

Keel, O., and Küchler, M. 1982. *Orte und Landschaften der Bibel, Ein Handbuch und Studienreiseführer zum Heiligen Land.* Vol. 2. Göttingen and Zurich.

Kitchen, K. A. 1973. *The Third Intermediate Period in Egypt (1100–650 BC).* Warminster, England.

Mazar, B. 1985. Biblical Archaeology Today: The Historical Aspect. Pp. 16–20 in *BibAT.* Jerusalem.

———. 1986. *The Early Biblical Period, Historical Studies,* ed. S. Aḥituv and B. A. Levine. Jerusalem.

MARK J. FRETZ

ADAM AND EVE, LIFE OF. Among several related narrative elaborations of the biblical account of Adam and Eve, the most important are the Greek *Apocalypse of Moses* and the Latin *Vita Adae et Evae.* An Armenian recension was translated loosely from the *Apocalypse of Moses,* or possibly from the Syriac (Conybeare 1895: 216–35), at least by 1000 C.E., although more probably during the 5th or 6th centuries. A Slavonic recension, translated from the Greek between 950 and 1400 C.E., combines the *Apocalypse of Moses* and *Vita* 1–11. Other documents, while part of the Adam cycle of literature, have no direct literary relationship with the *Apocalypse of Moses* and *Vita Adae et Evae*: the *Cave of Treasures,* the *Combat of Adam and Eve* (Ethiopic), the *Testament of Adam,* and the *Apocalypse of Adam* from Nag Hammadi.

The *Apocalypse of Moses* and *Vita Adae et Evae,* though sharing much material, also contain unique traditions:

	Ap. Mos.	*Vita*
1. Adam and Eve search for food and repent by standing in the Jordan and Tigris rivers.	——	1–8
2. Satan, disguised as an angel, convinces Eve to curtail her penitence.	——	9–11
3. Satan explains his fall and consequent enmity toward Adam.	——	12–17
4. Eve escapes death and bears Cain by means of Adam's intercession.	——	18–22
5. Eve bears (Cain [*Ap. Mos.* 1:3]), Abel, Seth, *et al.*	1:1–5:1	23–24
6. Adam reveals to Seth his rapture to paradise to see God.	——	25–29
7. Adam, on his deathbed, sends Eve and Seth on an unsuccessful quest for the oil of mercy.	5:2–14:3	30–44
8. Eve exhorts her children to obey by recounting the temptation by Satan and expulsion from paradise.	15–30	——
9. Adam dies.	31–32	45
10. Adam is pardoned.	33–37	46
11. Adam is buried.	38:1–42:2	47–48
12. Eve commands her children to preserve her and Adam's life on tablets of stone and clay.	——	49:1–50:2
13. Eve dies and is buried.	42:3–43:4	50:3–51:3

The redactors of the *Apocalypse of Moses* and *Vita Adae et Evae* shape their mutual (e.g., *Apoc. Mos.* 5:2–14:3 and *Vita* 30–44) and unique (e.g., *Apoc. Mos.* 15–30) traditions in different ways, as a comparison of three major characteristics of both stories will demonstrate. First, Satan is prominent in *Apoc. Mos.* 15–30, where he is responsible for the deception of the serpent, Eve, and Adam, yet his role is even more prominent in *Vita Adae et Evae.* Satan deceives Eve a second time (chaps. 9–11), then explains thoroughly why he maliciously pursues Adam (chaps. 12–17). According to *Vita* 37–39, a "serpent" whom Seth recognizes as Satan, the "cursed enemy of truth, (and) chaotic destroyer," attacks him; in the parallel passage of *Apoc. Mos.* 10–12, only a rebellious "wild beast" attacks Seth.

Second, Eve is culpable for the first transgression in both accounts, but the redactor of *Vita Adae et Evae,* particularly in the unique material (chaps. 1–22), consciously denigrates Eve and exonerates Adam. Eve's unrealistic solution to hunger following explusion is to have Adam murder her, since she sinned, so that God may return him to paradise (chaps. 1–6); in contrast, Adam suggests sensibly that they repent. While the Jordan stops its flow and the entire animal world gathers around Adam when he repents, Eve succumbs again to Satan's deceit (chaps. 7–11). Subsequently, when she departs to die, Eve experiences birthpangs but receives no mercy, despite her desperate prayers, until Adam intercedes (chaps. 18–22).

Third, God's mercy, a significant theme in both stories, is interpreted differently. One message of *Vita Adae et Evae* is that penitence, properly performed, evokes God's mercy. The editor presents details of Adam's penitence in the Jordan (chaps. 6–8) and adds similar details to Seth's prayer at paradise (chap. 40; cf. *Apoc. Mos.* 13:1) to provide the readers with models of penitence. Because Adam repented properly, he was pardoned during his lifetime (chap. 46). In contrast, the main theme of the *Apocalypse of Moses* is that mercy is accessible only following death. Adam faces death, uncertain that God will be merciful (chaps. 31–32). He dies and, after a lengthy and suspenseful account of angelic intercession, is pardoned (chaps. 33–37). Finally, he receives the promise of resurrection twice (39:1–3; 41:2–3).

The preceding examples demonstrate that the *Apocalypse of Moses* and *Vita Adae et Evae* are similar, but significantly different from each other. The relationship between them is difficult to determine. Meyer (1895: 205–8) regarded the *Vita* as the older document. Fuchs (1900: 508–9) and Wells (*APOT* 2: 128–9) regarded the *Apocalypse of Moses* as earlier. It is equally possible that the two narratives were composed independently on the basis of traditions which they had in common (e.g., *Apoc. Mos.* 31–32 and *Vita* 45).

Many of the traditions underlying these texts were probably composed in Hebrew. However, the author of the *Apocalypse of Moses* was familiar with the LXX, and *Vita Adae et Evae* contains some Greek expressions (e.g., *plasma,* "creature," in 46:3), indicating that at least some of the original traditions may have been composed in Greek. There is little consensus, then, concerning the relationship of the Greek and Latin texts and the language of the traditions which preceded them other than that a diverse oral and literary history underlies these documents (Johnson *OTP* 2: 251).

Both sets of traditions are clearly Jewish, exhibiting parallels with many Jewish documents (notes in Johnson *OTP* 2: 258–95). Although *Apoc. Mos.* and *Vita* contain no historical allusions, several of these parallels indicate that the traditions embodied in both fit well into the 1st and early 2d centuries C.E. Josephus' *Ant* 1.2.3 contains a reference to tablets of stone and clay which is similar to *Vita* 49:1–50:2. The apostle Paul refers to Satan's being disguised as an angel of light (2 Cor 11:14 and *Vita* 9, *Ap. Mos.* 17) and to the location of paradise in the third heaven (2 Cor 12:2–3 and *Ap. Mos.* 37:5). The most important parallels which suggest a late 1st or early 2d century provenance are those between the *Apocalypse of Moses* and *4 Ezra* and *2 Baruch*: (1) the combination of allusions to Gen 1:26–27 and 2:7, the image of God and the work of God's hands, to appeal for divine mercy (*Apoc. Mos.* 33–37 and *4 Ezra* 8:44–45); (2) the loss of supramundane paradise (*Ap. Mos.* 27–29 and *2 Bar.* 4:3–7); and (3) emphasis upon the effects of the initial transgression on future generations, yet insistence upon individual responsibility as the prerequisite to eschatological glory (*Apoc. Mos.* 14, 28, 30 and *4 Ezra* 3:20–27; 4:26–32; 7:11–14; 7:116–31; *2 Bar.* 17:1–18:2; 23:4–5; 48:42–47; 54:13–19).

These parallels suggest that the traditions contained in these documents may belong to the 1st century C.E. The *terminus ad quem* for their composition is ca. 400 C.E., since several texts written shortly after that date, including the Armenian version, appear to depend upon them. No manuscripts date earlier than the 11th century for the *Apocalypse of Moses* and the 9th century for *Vita Adae et Evae*. See Johnson *OTP* 2: 249–95, and Wells *APOT* 2: 123–54 for text.

Bibliography

Bertrand, D. A. 1987. *La Vie grecque d'Adam et 'Eve.* Recherches Intertestamentaires 1. Paris.

Conybeare, F. C. 1895. On the Apocalypse of Moses. *JQR* 7: 216–35.

Fuchs, C. 1900. Das Leben Adams und Evas. Pp. 506–28 in *Die Apokryphen und Pseudepigraphen des Alten Testaments,* vol. 2, ed. E. Kautzsch. Tübingen.

Jagíc, V. 1893. Slavische Beiträge zu den biblischen Apokryphen. *Denkschriften der philosophisch-historische Klasse der kaiserlichen Akademie der Wissenschaften* 42: 1–104.

Kabisch, R. 1905. Die Entstehungszeit der Apokalypse Mose. *ZNW* 6: 109–34.

Levison, J. R. 1988. *Portraits of Adam in Early Judaism: From Sirach to 2 Baruch.* JSPSUP 1. Sheffield.

———. 1989. The Exoneration of Eve in the Apocalypse of Moses 15–30. *JSJ* 20: 135–50.

Meyer, W. 1878. Vita Adae et Evae. *Abhandlungen der philosophisch-philologischen Klasse der königlich bayerischen Akademie der Wissenschaften* 14/3: 187–250.

Nagel, M. 1972. La Vie grecque d'Adam et d'Eve. Diss. Strasbourg.

Nickelsburg, G. W. E. 1981. Some Related Traditions in the Apocalypse of Adam, the Books of Adam and Eve, and 1 Enoch. Pp. 515–39 in *The Rediscovery of Gnosticism,* vol. 2, ed. B. Layton. Studies in the History of Religions 41. Leiden.

Tischendorf, C. von. 1866. *Apocalypses Apocryphae.* Leipzig. Repr. Hildesheim, 1966.

JOHN R. LEVISON

ADAM, APOCALYPSE OF (NHC V,*5*). A Jewish-gnostic document found in the Nag Hammadi Library, a collection of papyrus manuscripts discovered in Upper Egypt in 1946. The *Apocalypse of Adam (Apoc. Adam)* purports to be a revelatory discourse that Adam delivered to his son Seth which was preserved for Seth's posterity. It is not to be identified with any previously known Adam text. Epiphanius (*Pan.* 26.8.1) mentions that the "gnostics" used "apocalypses of Adam," but little is known of them.

A. Setting.

Apoc. Adam is the fifth and final tractate in NHC V. *Apoc. Adam* is immediately preceded in NHC V by three other tractates bearing the title "apocalypse": an apocalypse of Paul and two apocalypses of James. The first tractate in NHC V is not an apocalypse but a highly fragmentary copy of *Eugnostos,* of which another copy is preserved in Codex III. The inclusion of four apocalypses in one book is unusual in the Nag Hammadi Library and does seem to be the result of a deliberate scribal collection.

B. Text.

The manuscript is preserved in the Coptic Museum in Old Cairo (codex inventory number 10548). The tops and bottoms of its 21 inscribed papyrus pages are all lacking text in varying degrees. Pages 69–70 are completely lacking all vestiges of first and last lines, while pages 67 (the verso, p. 68, is uninscribed), 71–72, and 77 are each lacking one to four lines at the bottom of the page.

As to its date and provenance, one cannot be certain. It was written in Greek sometime after the appearance of the Septuagint (250–200 B.C.E.), and then translated into Coptic (Sahidic dialect) sometime before the middle of the 4th century C.E., when the books of the Nag Hammadi Library were manufactured. It has been dated in its present form as early as the end of the 1st century C.E. Since its present form is thought to be the result of editorial redaction, the various component parts could perhaps be even earlier.

C. Character and Contents.

The narrative is cast as a revelatory discourse delivered by Adam to his son Seth "in the 700th year"; that is, just prior to Adam's death (cf. Gen 5:3–5 LXX). This feature suggests that the text is to be understood as the "last testament" of Adam, and to be associated with other testamentary literature in antiquity, such as the *Testaments of the Twelve Patriarchs.* The selection of Seth as the son to receive the revelation, and the identification of Seth's namesake as "that man who is the seed of the great generation" (NHC 65,6–9; cf. Gen 5:3), also associates the text with other Sethian literature in antiquity. It has been described as an original writing of the gnostic sect of the Sethians (Turner 1986).

Unlike other gnostic writings, Adam describes his original androgynous "creation" in highly positive language (NHC 64,6–12). His "fall" is portrayed as a lapse into ignorance that is brought about by separation into male and female entities (NHC 64,20–28; cf. Gen 2:21–23), rather than by an act of disobedience to God's command not to eat of the tree "of the knowledge of good and evil," as it is reported in the Jewish biblical tradition (Gen 2:15–17; 3:1–19). Three unnamed heavenly figures then appear to Adam and their revelation to him becomes the subject of Adam's last testament to Seth (NHC 67,14–21).

Adam describes to Seth the origin of a special race of men, and their struggle against God, The Almighty (Gk *pantocrator*), or Sakla, who is portrayed as the creator god of the Jewish biblical tradition. Three attempts are made by the Almighty to destroy this race of men who possess the knowledge of the "eternal God" (NHC 68,10–16), which Adam also possessed in his primordial state (NHC 64,6–14).

Two of these attempts to destroy this special race of "Sethians" (cf. NHC 65,6–9), that of flood (NHC 69,1–16—the Noah story) and fire (NHC 75,9–16—the Sodom/Gomorrah story) are well known in Jewish biblical tradition, but are here given new interpretations. For example, the biblical flood narrative is explained as the attempt of a wicked creator to destroy the pure race of men who possess special knowledge of the eternal God, rather than as the judgment of a righteous God upon the wickedness of humankind (cf. Gen. 6:1–7). A third threat is lost in lacunas (NHC 71,8–72,1), but may be assumed because of a clear account of a third deliverance (NHC 72,1–15).

At the conclusion of these three attempts of the Almighty to destroy the great race, Adam describes the descent of a heavenly figure, the Illuminator of Knowledge. The sudden appearance of this heavenly figure shakes the cosmos of the Almighty, disturbing his heavenly court, i.e., his powers and angels. The Illuminator comes to "redeem" the souls of the seed of Noah "from the day of death" and to leave for himself "fruit-bearing trees" (NHC 76,8–17). He performs "signs and wonders" (NHC 77,1–3). And as the man on whom "the holy spirit has come," he "suffers in his flesh," (NHC 77,16–18), yet the god of the powers and his hosts do not see the Illuminator or his glory (NHC 77,7–15).

Perplexed by these events, the "angels and all the generations of the powers" in confusion ask about the source of the disturbance (NHC 77,18–27). The narrative continues with thirteen erroneous explanations for the Illuminator's origin made by "kingdoms," followed by the correct explanation of the "kingless generation" (NHC 82,19–83,7). The narrative then reports an apocalyptic scene, reminiscent of Matthew 25, in which those who oppose the Illuminator fall under the condemnation of death, while those who receive his knowledge "live forever" (NHC 83,8–29). The document concludes with a description of competing baptismal traditions, and a statement that the "words of revelation" are not to be inscribed in a book but rather "on a high mountain, upon a rock of truth" (NHC 85,1–18).

The struggle between the Almighty and the special race of men who possess knowledge of the "eternal God" is cast in the form of a gnostic midrash on the biblical story in which elements of the story (NHC 67,22–69,10; 70,3–71,4; 72,15–17; 73,25–27) are followed by a gnostic interpretation (NHC 69,18–70,2; 71,8–72,15; 72,18–73,24; 73,27–76,7) that sets out a Sethian explanation for the events in the story. The author never quotes the biblical passages directly, however, but draws on material that has already been influenced by Jewish exegetical traditions.

The thirteen erroneous kingdom explanations (NHC 77,27–82,19) for the Illuminator's origin are cast in highly structured prose with a recurring refrain. For example:

> The twelfth kingdom says about him:
> "He came from two illuminators.
> He was nourished there.
> He received glory and power.
> And in this way he came to the water."
>
> The third kingdom says about him:
> "He came from a virgin womb.
> He was cast out of his city
> —he and his mother—and was
> taken to a desolate place.
> He was nourished there
> and received glory and power.
> And in this way he came to the water."

Each of the thirteen kingdoms offers an explanation for the Illuminator's origin followed by statements of nourishing (except numbers 5, 7, 10, and 13), receiving power and glory (except number 11), and the concluding refrain: "And in this way he came to the water."

It is generally agreed that the explanations of the Illuminator's origin constitute traditional material that was later incorporated into the present document (Hedrick 1980: 130–54). It has also been argued (Hedrick 1980) that the document breaks down into two sections that appear to be two separate sources harmonized by an ancient editor with appropriate redactional comments at the point of the literary seams. One source (NHC 64,1–65,23; 66,12–67,12; 67,22–76,7; 83,7–84,3; 85,19–22) stands near the border separating Jewish apocalypticism and gnosticism. The general character of its gnosticism and its extensive use of Jewish traditions suggest that this source reflects a type of emerging Jewish gnosticism. The second source (NHC 65,24–66,12; 67,12–67,21; 76,8–83,7) contains few overt references to Jewish traditions, but reflects a developed gnostic mythology. The two sources were brought together in a group that argued for a spiritualized understanding of baptism and an ascetic life-style. The polemic against baptism (NHC 84,4–85,18; 85,22–31) at the end of the tractate is not directed against Christian baptism but reflects competing views of baptism within rival gnostic communities. The theory that the text breaks down neatly into two sources has been criticized, but it seems clear that the text as it now appears has been subjected to redaction (Pearson 1986).

D. Significance.

The text documents the existence of a type of heterodox Jewish gnosticism. It is "Jewish" in its knowledge and use of Jewish traditions, but in its intention the document is radically anti-Jewish since it constitutes a thoroughgoing Sethian-gnostic transversion of usual Jewish traditions. There are some general parallels to the Christian tradition, but the document has no features that are necessarily Christian and it makes no use of New Testament texts. The redeemer-illuminator mythology in the document does not appear to have been derived from Christian groups or texts. Rather, the author draws instead (MacRae 1965) upon pre-Christian Jewish traditions of the persecution and subsequent exaltation of the righteous man as reflected, for example, in Wisdom 1–6 and Isaiah 52–53. *Apoc. Adam* reflects a type of non-Christian Jewish gnosticism prossessing a fully developed redeemer myth that did not pass through the Christian kerygma, but rather appears to be an independent parallel development.

Bibliography

Beltz, W. 1970. Die Adam-Apokalypse aus Codex V von Nag Hammadi. Dr. Theol. diss. Berlin.

Böhlig, A. 1968. Jüdisches und iranisches in der Adamapokalypse des Codex V von Nag Hammadi. Pp. 149–61 in *Mysterion und Wahrheit.* AGJU 6; Leiden.

Böhlig, A., and Labib, P., eds. 1963. *Koptisch-gnostische Apokalypsen aus Codex V von Nag Hammadi im koptischen Museum zu Alt-Kairo.* Halle-Wittenberg.

Hedrick, C. W. 1980. *The Apocalypse of Adam: A Literary and Source Analysis.* SBLDS 46. Chico, CA.

Hedrick, C. W., and Hodgson, R., Jr., eds. 1986. *Nag Hammadi, Gnosticism, and Early Christianity.* Peabody, MA.

Kasser, R. 1967. Bibliothèque gnostique V: Apocalypse d'Adam. *RTP*: 316–33.

Krause, M. 1972–74. The Apocalypse of Adam. Vol. 2, pp. 13–23 in *Gnosis: A Selection of Gnostic Texts,* ed. W. Foerster; trans. and ed. R. McL. Wilson. 2 vols. Oxford.

MacRae, G. 1965. The Coptic Gnostic Apocalypse of Adam. *HeyJ* 6: 27–35.

———. 1979. The Apocalypse of Adam. Pp. 151–95 in *Nag Hammadi Codices V, 2–5 and VI with Papyrus Berolinensis 8502, 1 and 4,* ed. D. M. Parrott. Leiden.

———. 1983. Apocalypse of Adam. *OTP* 1: 707–19.

Morard, F. 1985. *L'Apocalypse d'Adam (NH V,5): Texte établi et présenté.* BCNH, Section Textes 15. Quebec.

Pearson, B. 1986. The Problem of "Jewish Gnostic" Literature. Pp. 15–35 in Hedrick and Hodgson 1986.

Perkins, P. 1977. Apocalypse of Adam: The Genre and Function of a Gnostic Apocalypse. *CBQ* 39: 382–95.

———. 1972. Apocalyptic Schematization in the Apocalypse of Adam and the Gospel of the Egyptians. *SBLSP* 2: 591–95.

Robinson, J. M., ed. 1975. *The Facsimile Edition of the Nag Hammadi Codices: Codex V.* Leiden.

Rudolph, L. 1969. Gnosis und Gnostizismus, ein Forschungsbericht. *TRu* 34: 160–69.

Schottroff, L. 1969. Animae naturaliter salvandae: Zum Problem der himmlischen Herkunft des Gnostikers. Pp. 65–97 in *Christentum und Gnosis,* ed. W. Eltester. BZNW 37. Berlin.

Stroumsa, G. 1984. *Another Seed: Studies in Gnostic Mythology.* NHS 24. Leiden.

Troger, K.-W., ed. 1972. *Gnosis und Neues Testament.* Berlin.

Turner, J. 1986. Sethian Gnosticism: A Literary History. Pp. 55–86 in Hedrick and Hodgson 1986.

CHARLES W. HEDRICK

ADAM, THE TESTAMENT OF. Because of erroneous identification by 19th-century scholars, the *Testament of Adam* has only recently been classified as one of the pseudepigrapha of the OT. A composite document, the Testament is made up of three originally independent sections referred to as the Horarium, which is a catalog of the hours of the day and night, the Prophecy in which Adam foretells the future of the world, and the Hierarchy, which explains the names and functions of the different ranks of angels. In the Horarium (chaps. 1 and 2), father Adam is represented as revealing to his son Seth what parts of the created order, both natural and supernatural, render their praises to God at each hour of the day or night: demons at the first hour of the night, doves at the second, fish and fire at the third, etc.

In the second section, the Prophecy (chap. 3), Seth relates to the reader in Adam's own words what his father had prophesied just before his death concerning the future of the world. This is primarily an *ex eventu* prophecy of the coming of Jesus Christ and of the events of his life, death, and resurrection (as recorded in the NT), but the Prophecy also describes the Flood and the end of the world and answers questions about the Fall and related events. For example, we are informed that the forbidden fruit was really the fig, and that Cain actually killed Abel out of passion for Lebuda, one of their sisters. Seth also describes Adam's funeral in some detail. The most striking doctrinal feature of the Testament, the promised deification of Adam, is found in this section. Here Adam explains that it had been his wish and God's intention to make Adam a god, but that because of the Fall, the promised apotheosis had to be postponed until after the saving mission of Jesus Christ, at which time its occurrence was certain.

The third section of the Testament, the Hierarchy (chap. 4), lists the nine different kinds of angels and explains the role and function of each in the administration of the cosmos. For example, according to the Hierarchy the archons control the weather; the authorities take care of the sun, moon, and stars; and the powers keep the demons from destroying the whole of creation. The nine classes of angels are in ascending order: angels, archangels, archons, authorities, powers, dominions, thrones, seraphim, and cherubim.

Although versions of the Horarium and Prophecy sections of the Testament have been found in Greek, Arabic, Ethiopic, Old Georgian, and Armenian, Syriac has been demonstrated to be the original language of the document in all three of its sections. Evidence for this are the puns and wordplays in the text that work only in Syriac. Also, the manuscript evidence for the Syriac text is considerably older than that for any other version, the earliest being British Museum MS Add 14,624, which dates from the 9th century. Corruptions in the Greek version have proved to result from mistaking one Syriac word for another, therefore demonstrating that the Greek is dependent upon the Syriac. The Arabic, Old Georgian, and Armenian versions did not appear until after a Syriac version was well established and well attested, and must therefore be secondary to it. The Ethiopic version is dependent upon the Arabic.

It is likely that the first section of the Testament, the Horarium, is taken from Jewish traditions which circulated before the 3d century C.E., since it completely lacks the Christian elements which are so prominent in the Prophecy and Hierarchy and since it displays several affinities with the Wisdom literature of the OT. This Jewish material appears to have been joined together with the Prophecy by a Christian redactor in the 2d or 3d century to form the present *Testament of Adam.* The Prophecy itself, though heavily Christianized, preserves some Jewish traditions about Adam and Eve found in other Jewish literature but not in the OT, among them the idea that Adam left to his posterity an esoteric understanding of creation and a knowledge of the future history of the world. But in the present document, the substance of Adam's legacy has been turned by the redactor into a Christian proof text. Subsequently, perhaps between the 3d and 5th century, the Hierarchy was added to the Prophecy and Horarium, because its angelology complemented theirs, though the addition never really caught on, being found in only one Syriac MS.

Bibliography

Robinson, S. E. 1982. *The Testament of Adam: An Examination of Syriac and Greek Traditions.* Chico, CA.

———. 1983. The Testament of Adam. Pp. 989–95 in *OTP* 1.

STEPHEN E. ROBINSON

ADAMAH (PLACE) [Heb *ʾădāmâ*]. A fortified city within Naphtali's territorial boundaries, the exact location of which is unknown (Josh 19:36; LXX variants also reflect the uncertainty). Adamah is not to be identified with Adam in the Transjordon (Josh 3:16), nor with Adami-neqeb (Josh 19:33; see Boling and Wright *Joshua* AB, 459). Aharoni (*LBHG,* 429) suggests a location 7 km W of the Sea of Galilee associated with Shemesh-adam (modern *Qarn-ḥaṭṭin*). Rogerson (*RNAB,* 129) associates this same site with Madon (Josh 11:1; 12:19), and suggests that an unidentified location 7 km N of Capernaum may also be the location of biblical Adamah.

MARK J. FRETZ

ADAMI-NEKEB (PLACE) [Heb *ʾadāmî neqeb*]. After the conquest described in Joshua 6–12, the Transjordan tribes of Reuben, Gad, and half of Manasseh returned to the E bank of the Jordan River. The W bank proper was then divided among the remaining tribes. Several major tribal units were settled and Joshua cast lots (18:10) for the remaining seven. The sixth portion went to the tribe of Naphtali (Josh 19:32–39). The S border of Naphtali (and part of the N border of Issachar) ran from Heleph to the Jordan River where it comes out of the Sea of Galilee. Simons (*GTTOT* 194) says this is not a border but just a list of cities. Aharoni (*LBHG* 259) suggests the border ran just S of the line of Wadi Fajjas/Fegas. Kallai (*HGB* 235) considers it a border. RSV refers to the boundary while the Jerusalem Bible refers to the territory of Naphtali. One of the border sites, v 33, is Adami-nekeb.

Wright (*WHAB* 42) shows Adami-nekeb within the SW corner of Naphtali's territory, near its W boundary with Zebulun (which is Zebulun's E boundary). Verses 35–38 list Naphtali's fortified cities but these are not the boundary cities, except that v 36 includes Adamah. It is not impossible this is Adami-nekeb. However, Adamah is in sequence with Chinereth and Hazor, which suggests it is in the N (Naʿaman 1986: 134).

Adami-nekeb is described as a city or town between the Sea of Galilee and Mt. Tabor. Adam means "man" (BDB, 10) or "ground," and Nekeb means "pierce" (BDB, 666), and hence a "pass" that pierces the mountain. It has also been translated "red pass," since *ʾdm* means "red," perhaps a reference to the *terra rossa,* the "red soil" common to the land. Yet a third translation is "fortified hollow." The KJV translates it as two names, following the LXX which has two names, with various spelling. The Jerusalem Bible translates one name but spells it Adami-negeb. The Vulgate has "Adami which is Neceb." Aharoni (*LBHG,* 126–27) quotes the Jerusalem Talmud (Meg. 1, 77a) where Rabbi Yosi refers to Adami—Damin, the Nekeb—Saydatha. "Damin" is an Aramaic intermediate form between biblical Adami and Arabic Damiyeh.

The Palestine Exploration Survey maps locate Adamah at Khirbet Damiyeh, 7 m NW of the exit of the Jordan from the Sea of Galilee and Adami at Khirbet Adamah, 5–6 m S of the exit. However, Boling (*Joshua* AB, 458; *GTTOT* 196) et al. place Adami at Damiyeh. Gehman (*NWDS* 16) suggests that Adami of the narrow pass is called this to distinguish it from Adam of the ford, Josh 3:16. Khirbet Damiyeh is a Bronze Age and Iron Age site 5 m SW of Tiberias, on the W side of Sea of Galilee. It is above the Wadi Mu'allaqah, which flows into the Wadi Fegas (*HGB,* 235). The site called Darb el-Hawarnah was probably a fortress controlling the pass on the caravan route from Damascus by way of Hauran or Bashan, around the S end of Galilee to the plain of Acco. It was a major alternate route to the Via Maris (*LBHG,* 61).

The conquest lists of Thutmose III (1504–1450 B.C.) include a site, no. 57 at Karnak, called *nkbu* which may be Nekeb or Negeb (*GTTOT* 196; *GP* 398; *ANET* 242). However, Aharoni (*LBHG* 161, 183) identifies no. 57 as Tell Abu Hureireh, possibly biblical Gerar, while identifying no. 36, Adumim with Adami-nekeb, Kh. et-Tell, *above* Kh. ed-Damiyeh (he seems to identify the two tells, *LBHG* 429). While noting several authors who share this identification, S. Ahituve, identifies Thutmose's no. 36 with Tel Qarnei Hittin, the Horns of Hattin (quoted by Naʾaman 1986: 128 n.23). Aharoni identifies Adamim in Papyrus Anastasi I, an Egyptian letter of the scribe Hori, as Adami-nekeb (*ANET* 477). Kallai (*HGB* 235, n.287) explains the et-Tell and Damiyeh distinction by noting there are three ruins on Damiyeh. Kh. et-Tell is the highest of these at the top of the slope. Simons (*GTTOT* 196; *NWDB* 659) suggests that if Nekeb is a separate place, it may be Kh. el-Bassum (Bronze Age), SE of Kh. ed-Damiyeh, E of Kefr Sabt.

Some identify Nekeb by its Talmudic name with a ruin called Seiyadeh, but Kh. Sayadeh is a late ruin (Roman) with no ancient tell nearby. Aharoni thought it probable that "the Nekeb" is not an ancient name but an appellative to Adami. Kallai (*HGB* 235, n.287) acknowledges Roland de Vaux's discovery of a settlement *south* of the Wadi Muʾallaqah, opposite Damiyeh, with remains of the same Bronze and Iron Ages as Damiyeh. De Vaux assumed the double settlements reflect the double name but this has not been accepted by others. Van Beek (*IDB* 1: 45) cautions Adami-nekeb is not ʾUdm of the Keret Epic from Ugarit (*GP* 238), nor Amarna Letter no. 256, Udumu, a city in the land of Garu which was hostile to the Pharoah (*ANET* 486). These may be identified with Edom (Albright 1943: 14). It is of interest that all these names may be interpreted as "red" stone, object, thing, etc. The plural "Adummim" means "red stones," as in the red-streaked limestone cited earlier.

Bibliography

Albright, W. F. 1943. Two Little Understood Amarna Letters from the Middle Jordan Valley. *BASOR* 89: 7–17.

Beecher, W. J. 1976. Adami-nekeb. *ISBE* I: 54.

Kalland, E. S. 1975. Adami-nekeb. Vol. 1, pp. 58 in *The Zondervan Pictorial Encyclopedia of the Bible,* 5 vols., ed. M. C. Tenney and S. Barabas. Grand Rapids.

Naʾaman, N. 1986. *Borders and Districts in Biblical Historiography.* Jerusalem.

HENRY O. THOMPSON

ADAR [Heb *ʾădār*]. The twelfth month of the Hebrew calendar, roughly corresponding to February and March. See CALENDARS (HEBREW).

ADASA (PLACE) [Gk *Adasa*]. The town where Judas Maccabeus and his military band camped and subsequently defeated the Syrian general Nicanor and his troops (1 Macc 7:40–45). Josephus' account of this story locates Adasa 30 stades (ca. 4 km) from Beth-horon (*Ant* 12.10.5; see also his reference to the town Acedasa, in the province of Gophna, *JW* 1.1.6). Some scholars identify Adasa with modern *Khirbet ʿAdaseh,* a militarily strategic site located midway between Jerusalem and Beth-horon, ca. 8 km (60 stades) SE of Beth-horon, rather than the 30 stades recorded by Josephus (Abel *GP,* 238; Goldstein *1 Maccabees* AB, 341). Adasa has also been identified with the *ʾAdasa* northeast of Beth-horon in the province of Gophna, which was known to Eusebius (*HJP*[2] 1: 170).

MARK J. FRETZ

ADBEEL (PERSON) [Heb *ʾadbĕʾēl*]. The third of Ishmael's twelve sons (Gen 25:13 = 1 Chr 1:29). The LXX, however, transposing the letters *beta* and *delta,* spells the name *nabdeēl* (Gen 25:13) or *nabdaiēl* (1 Chr 1:29) in these parallel lists, and adds *ragouēl kai nabdeēl* "Ragouel (or Reuel) and Nabdeel" to the list of Dedan's sons in Gen 25:3. But the Lucianic version of 1 Chr 1:29 reads Gk *abdiēl,* and Josephus spells the name *abdeēlos* in his list of Ishmael's descendants (Ant 1.12.4). This rather consistent metathesis of the letters *beta* and *delta* in the Gk texts suggests that the difference in spelling is not simply a scribal error. Based on the LXX use of an initial *N,* Albright (1956: 13–14) suggests that *Nadab* is a hypocoristic doublet of Heb *ʾadbĕʾēl,* and identifies Nadab with the Arabic name *Idibaʾil.* Other scholars identify Adbeel with the Arabian tribal and personal name *Idibaʾilu,* which appears in the inscriptions of Tiglath-Pileser III (*ANET,* 283; Ephʿal 1982: 215–16; Montgomery 1934: 45; Musil 1926: 291). Tiglath-Pileser III (744–727 B.C.E.) first subjugated this northwest Arabian tribe, then appointed Idibiʾlu to the wardenship of the Egyptian border.

Bibliography

Albright, W. F. 1956. The Biblical Tribe of Massa' and Some Congeners. Vol. 1, pp. 1–14 in *Studi Orientalistici in Onore di Giorgio Levi della vida.* Rome.

Ephʿal, I. 1982. *The Ancient Arabs.* Jerusalem and Leiden.

Montgomery, J. A. 1934. *Arabia and the Bible.* Philadelphia.

Musil, A. 1926. *The Northern Ḥeğâz.* American Geographical Society Oriental Explorations and Studies 1. New York.

MARK J. FRETZ

ADDAN (PERSON) [Gk *Charaathalan, Charaathalar*]. A leader of the exiles, who returned to Palestine from Telmelah and Telharsha in Babylon (1 Esdr 5:36). The RSV form "Addan" is derived from the difficult LXX phrase, rendered by codex Vaticanus *hēgoumenos autōn charaathalan kai allar,* "their leaders (were) Charaathalan and Allar" (codex Alexandrinus spells the names *charaathalar* and *alar*). Bewer (1922: 30) argues that Gk *charaathalan* should be two words (*charaath* and *alan*), and that Gk *alan* resulted from a confusion in the transmission of Gk *adan,* since the triangular form of uppercase Gk *lambda* closely resembles the "tee pee" form of uppercase Gk *delta.* He bases this suggestion on the place name "Addan," attested in Ezra 2:59 and Neh 7:61. See ADDAN (PLACE). The occurrence of Addan as a personal name is unique to the list of returnees in 1 Esdras 5.

Bibliography

Bewer, J. A. 1922. *Der Text des Buches Ezra.* Göttingen.

MARK J. FRETZ

ADDAN (PLACE) [Heb *ʾaddān*]. Var. ADDON. A place in Babylon from which a group of Jews of undocumented ancestry returned to Palestine (Ezra 2:59 [LXX *ēdan*] = Neh 7:61 [Heb *ʾaddôn*; LXX *ērōn*]). The location of this site is unknown.

MARK J. FRETZ

ADDAR (PERSON) [Heb *ʾaddār*]. The first son of Bela and grandson of Benjamin (1 Chr 8:3). The name "Addar" appears only in this portion of an extended genealogy (1 Chronicles 7–8) listing Benjamin's descendants. Parallel genealogies list "Ard" as either a son of Bela (Num 26:40), or a son of Benjamin (Gen 46:21); however, the list of Benjamin's descendants in 1 Chronicles 7 has neither name. See ARD. Albright (1939: 179–80), noting the similarity of the Hebrew letters *dalet, kap,* and *reš* (cf. Josh 16:2, 5; 18:13), argues that the names "Addar" and "Ard" are actually corrupted forms of the (unattested) Hebrew clan name **erek* "Erech" (cf. the gentilic *ʾarkî* "Archite"). See ARCHITE.

Bibliography

Albright, W. F. 1939. Review of *GP.* Vol. 2. *JBL* 58: 177–87.

MARK J. FRETZ

ADDAR (PLACE) [Heb *ʾaddār*]. A border town in the southern Negeb region of Judah, near Hezron and Karka (Josh 15:3). The name "Addar" occurs as part of a lengthy list of Israelite tribal boundary sites (Joshua 15–17). The precise location of Addar is unknown. The name may be synonymous with Hazar-addar (cf. Num 34:4; see Noth 1935: 188), or possibly a parenthetical comment regarding the location of the border of Judah, e.g., "It went around Hezron (more specifically, it went up to Addar)" (see Boling and Wright *Joshua* AB, 365).

Bibliography

Noth, M. 1935. Studien zu den historisch-geographischen Dokumenten des Josuabuches. *ZDPV* 58: 185–255 = *ABLA* 1: 229–80.

MARK J. FRETZ

ADDAX. See ZOOLOGY.

ADDI (PERSON) [Gk *Addi*]. **1.** The patronym of a clan of Israelite laypersons who returned from Babylonian exile (1 Esdr 9:31). Members of the clan of Addi were listed (after the sons of Bani) with those who married foreign women from "the people of the land," and who, under Ezra, were subsequently forced by covenant to separate themselves from these foreign wives and their children (cf. Neh 13:23–31). The name "Addi" does not appear in Ezra's parallel list (Ezra 10:18–44), although there the name "ADNA" does appear right after the listing of the sons of Bani (Ezra 10:30).

2. The son of Cosam and father of Melchi in Luke's geneaology of Joseph, the husband of Mary (Luke 3:28). The name "Addi" is absent in Matthew's parallel genealogy (Matt 1:1–17). Kuhn (1923: 214) finds an analogue in the MT name *pĕdāyâ* (2 Kgs 23:36), which the LXX renders *edeil.* The LXX apparently presupposes Heb *ᶜdyl,* "ADIEL" (1 Chr 4:36; 9:12; 27:25), a variant of which combines Heb *ᶜdy* [Gk *addi*] and an alternate theophoric ending (Heb *yh*) resulting in "ADAIAH." Given the unpredictable occurrence of Gk *addi* as a variant in LXX manuscripts of four unrelated passages (Num 26:25—Eng 26:16, RSV "Iddo"; 1 Chr 6:21, RSV "Eri"; 2 Chr 28:12, RSV "Hadlai"; 1 Esdr 9:31, RSV "Addi"), and the tenuous nature of identifying a specific individual simply on the basis of a particular form of a name, the Addi in Luke 3:28 must remain anonymous.

Bibliography

Kuhn, G. 1923. Die Geschlechtsregister Jesu bei Lukas und Matthäus, nach ihrer Herkunft untersucht. *ZNW* 22: 206–28.

MARK J. FRETZ

ADDITIONS TO DANIEL. See DANIEL, ADDITIONS TO.

ADDITIONS TO ESTHER. See ESTHER, ADDITIONS TO.

ADDITIONS TO JEREMIAH. See JEREMIAH, ADDITIONS TO.

ADDON (PLACE) [Heb *ʾăddôn*]. See ADDAN (PLACE).

ADDUS (PERSON) [Gk *Addcus*]. The name of one of the 17 families descended from Solomon's servants that returned to Jerusalem from Babylon (1 Esdr 5:34). The name "Addus" occurs only in that portion of the list providing names not attested in parallel lists (Myers *1 & 2 Esdras* AB, 68). Those parallels instead list 10 families (Ezra 2:55–58 = Neh 7:57–60; LXX Neh 7:60 cites 11 families). Also, the summary in 1 Esdr 5:35 (and its LXX parallels in Ezra 2 and Nehemiah 7) numbers only 372 total "temple ministrants" and servants, while the MT parallels number 392 (Ezra 2:58; Neh 7:60).

MARK J. FRETZ

ADER, KHIRBET (M.R. 222068). A site in ancient Moab on the Transjordanian Plateau. It is located on the "King's Highway"—one of the major caravan routes in antiquity—some 7 km NE of the modern city of Kerak, Jordan. The ancient site comprises a large tell of about 10 acres and, separated by a small wadi, a much smaller mound. The modern village of Ader now occupies the site.

A. History of Exploration.

The site's best-known feature is its four *menhirs* (large upright monoliths), noted as early as 1806 by J. Seetzen and later by J. L. Burckhardt and A. Musil. W. F. Albright (1924; 1934) and N. Glueck (1933) investigated the architectural remains at the site and, by a study of the pottery, concluded that its main periods of occupation were the late EB, the Iron Age, and the Late Roman Period. In 1933, W. F. Albright and R. G. Head directed a two-week expedition, accounts of which were only published in preliminary fashion (Albright 1934; 1944). R. L. Cleveland (1960) later published the results of the original expedition.

B. The Early Iron Age Remains.

Khirbet Ader is most frequently referred to as one of a half-dozen or so excavated settlement sites found in the EB IV period, ca. 2400–2000 B.C. Given the growing evidence for a significant level of sedentism (small towns and villages) in Transjordan, it is now clear that this period was not the "nomadic interlude" as envisioned by K. Kenyon (Richard 1980). Both the 10-acre "city," as Albright describes it, and the small tell to the N were occupied in the EB IV; apparently only a portion of the main site was occupied during the Iron Age and Roman Period.

Almost 3 m of EB IV occupational debris attest to a permanently occupied agricultural settlement. Good arable land surrounds the site and nearby streams provide a permanent source of water. On the small tell, a trench measuring 10 m × 4 m revealed three occupational levels (A–C) with pottery that Albright compared with Tell Beit Mirsim strata I–J. Although the pottery appears mixed, clear stratification was present, consisting of the corner of a rectangular house in the latest level (A), a mudbrick wall, and much mudbrick debris and ash in level B, and an enigmatic level C that contained early pottery, particularly wavy ledge handles. A study of the pottery plates (Cleveland 1960) shows that the three phases exemplify the degenerate red-slipped and burnished pottery with rilled exterior that is characteristic of the end of the EB. On the basis of comparisons with other EB IV sites (Iktanu, Khirbet Iskander, ᶜAroᶜer, Bâb edh-Dhrâᶜ), one can date Ader to the early part of the EB IV period (i.e., EB IVA–B). Ader's two clear architectural phases compare well with these sites, where two to four phases have been identified. A typical EB IV shaft tomb was also excavated on the small mound.

Originally four *menhirs* were noted at the site, one of which rested upon a step in the portico of a temple. Near the temple lay a massive stone slab with two round depressions, obviously an altar for offerings. Unfortunately this building, which was to be excavated fully in 1933, had been almost totally destroyed in the interim since Albright's first visit. From Albright's description and a published, though hypothetical, plan (Cleveland 1960: fig. 8), the temple appeared to be of tripartite design with the center room slightly offset. If Albright's observations are correct, this temple would be the earliest example of a type known during the MB and LB from Syria-Palestine at such sites as Shechem, Ebla, Alalakh, and Hazor.

Although Albright originally referred to the structure as the "Moabite Temple," he later placed it in the Canaanite Period. Given the apparent sole discovery of EB IV sherds and occupation on the small tell, as well as the associated *menhir,* it is highly likely that the building belongs in the EB IV period. Large *menhirs* (some 4 meters high) like those at Ader are also known from other EB sites (e.g., Bâb edh-Dhrâᶜ, Khirbet Iskander, and Lejjun). In light of a recently excavated EB IV sanctuary at Bâb edh-Dhrâᶜ and the monumental EB IV architecture (fortifications and gateway) at Khirbet Iskander, it would not be impossible that such a temple could date to the EB IV. On the basis of excavations in Jordan over the past 15 years, it is becoming increasingly clear that the EB IV was a period of urban regression, and not a nomadic interlude. Moreover, the strong continuities now apparent between the EB III and the EB IV suggest that the collapse of the city-state system at the end of EB III and the subsequent adaptation to nonurban subsistence strategies (small towns, villages, and pastoralism) were a result of gradual internal processes, not nomadic invasions as earlier scholarship presupposed (Richard 1986).

C. Iron Age and Roman Remains.

On the main tell, excavation uncovered occupation of the Iron Age II and the Roman/Byzantine periods, although earlier EB IV occupation was noted. Only fragments of walls and associated Iron Age II pottery represent the Iron Age occupation on the mound. More substantial remains of the Roman/Byzantine period were found. The city wall was constructed in the Late Roman period (2d–3d centuries A.D.). Excavation showed that a tower on the N city wall, well built with a front wall of ashlars, dated to the Late Roman Period, but had been repaired in the Byzantine period. The domestic occupation uncovered within the city wall consisted of several walls comprising a fairly well-preserved room with a great deal of Roman (3d century) pottery. Below the floor of this room there was discovered a cist burial, in which some Nabatean sherds were also found. Interestingly, among the rubble within the room the excavators found a stone with a Hebrew inscription, thought to date from the Byzantine period.

Bibliography

Albright, W. F. 1924. The Archaeological Results of an Expedition to Moab and the Dead Sea. *BASOR* 14: 1–12.

———. 1934. Soundings at Ader, a Bronze Age City of Moab. *BASOR* 53: 13–18.

Albright, W. F.; Kelso, J. L.; and Palin, T. J. 1944. Early Bronze Pottery from Bâb ed-Drâᶜ in Moab. *BASOR* 95: 3–13.

Cleveland, R. L. 1960. *The Excavation of the Conway High Place (Petra) and Soundings at Khirbet Ader.* AASOR 34–35. Cambridge, MA.

Glueck, N. 1934. Explorations in Eastern Palestine. AASOR 14: 3, 45–47. Philadelphia.

Mallon, A. 1924. Voyage d'exploration au sud-est de la Mer Morte. *Bib* 5: 413–455.

Richard, S. 1980. Toward a Consensus of Opinion on the End of the Early Bronze Age in Palestine-Transjordan. *BASOR* 247: 4–37.

———. 1986. The Early Bronze Age: The Rise and Collapse of Urbanism. *BA* 50: 22–43.

SUZANNE RICHARD

ADIDA (PLACE) [Gk *Adida*]. Mentioned in 1 Macc 12:38 and 13:13 as a Judean town fortified and occupied by Simon, the second brother of Judah the Maccabee. Adida is probably the biblical Harim of Ezra 2:32 (Heb *ḥārim;* Gk *arōth*) and which occurs in Neh 7:37 as Hadid (Heb *ḥādid;* Gk *adid*). Ezra and Nehemiah list Harim/Hadid along with Lod and Ono in whose vicinity Adida lay. Josephus describes Adida as located on a hill overlooking the plains of Judea (*Ant* 13.6.5 §203). Abel (1926: 218, 511 and *GP* 2: 340) considers Josephus' description of a hill as an exaggeration but deems Adida to be the modern *ᵓel-Ḥaditheh* located 6 km NE of Lod (M.R. 145152).

Bibliography

Abel, F.–M. 1926. "Topographie des campagnes machabéennes," *RB* 35: 206–22 and 510–33.

MICHAEL E. HARDWICK

ADIEL (PERSON) [Heb *ᶜădîᵓēl*]. **1.** A Simeonite prince who, during Hezekiah's reign, was involved in Simeonite expansion to Gedor in search of pasture lands (1 Chr 4:36). His name appears in a list of Simeon's descendants (1 Chr 4:24–43) preserved within an extended genealogy of Israel (1 Chronicles 2–8).

2. The father of the priest Maasai, an exile who returned from Babylon to live in Jerusalem (1 Chr 9:12). In a parallel list of priests who lived in Jerusalem under Nehemiah (Neh 11:10–14), the name "Adiel" is replaced with Azarel (LXX variants include *esdriēl, ezriēl*). A possible connection between the names "Adiel" and "ADDI" must be rejected as being too tenuous.

3. The father of Azmaveth, the administrator in charge of the "treasuries" of King David, presumably in Jerusalem (1 Chr 27:25; see Rudolf *Chronikbücher* HAT, 180). This name occurs in a list of stewards of crown property (1 Chr 27:25–31).

MARK J. FRETZ

ADIN (PERSON) [Heb *ᶜādîn*]. The father of a clan of returnees who settled in the area of Jerusalem during the reign of the Persian ruler Artaxerexes (Ezra 2:15; 8:6; Neh 7:20; 1 Esdr 5:14 [where LXX renders the name variously as *adeiliou* and *adinou*]). While this leader's name occurs as a patronym in parallel lists of returnees (Ezra 2 = Nehemiah 7 = 1 Esdras 5), his descendants were variously numbered as 454 (Ezra 2:15 = 1 Esdr 5:14) or 655 (Neh 7:20; Codex Alexandrinus reads 654, as do variant readings of Ezra 2:15 and 1 Esdr 5:14; see Allrick 1954: 22). As a prince under Nehemiah, Adin set his seal to the covenant made with the Lord (Neh 10:17—Eng 10:16).

Bibliography

Allrik, H. L. 1954. The Lists of Zerubbabel (Nehemiah 7 and Ezra 2) and the Hebrew Numeral Notation. *BASOR* 136: 21–27.

MARK J. FRETZ

ADINA (PERSON) [Heb *ʿădînāʾ*]. The son of Shiza and leader of a band of Reubenites associated with King David's chief military men (1 Chr 11:42). This group of Reubenite warriors reinforced David's armies, perhaps during his wars in the Transjordan (Mazar 1986: 102). The Chronicler's expansion (1 Chr 11:41b–47) of the parallel lists of David's military elite (1 Chr 11:10–41a = 2 Sam 23:8–39) includes Adina and 15 other men from the Transjordan. There is general agreement that these verses were not part of the original list, and Williamson (*1 & 2 Chronicles* NCBC, 104) and others (Mazar 1986: 101–2; Rudolf *Chronikbücher* HAT, 101) have argued convincingly that the Chronicler or a later redactor did not fabricate these names.

Bibliography

Mazar, B. 1986. The Military Élite of King David. Pp. 83–103 in *The Early Biblical Period: Historical Studies,* ed. S. Aḥituv, and B. Levine. Jerusalem.

MARK J. FRETZ

ADITHAIM (PLACE) [Heb *ʿădîtayim*]. One of 14 towns grouped together in the Shephelah (foothills) of Judah (Josh 15:36). The name "Adithaim" occurs only here and the location is unknown. Abel (*GP* 2: 238; see also *RAB,* 148) suggests modern *el-Ḥadîtheh,* a site 4 km NNW of Yâlō, based on a comparison with Egyptian *kdtm* (no. 25 of the Shishak list); however, others dispute this and prefer to leave the location unspecified (Albright 1939; Noth *ABLA* 2: 78).

Bibliography

Albright, W. F. 1939. Review of *GP. JBL* 58: 177–87.

MARK J. FRETZ

ADLAI (PERSON) [Heb *ʿadlay*]. Father of Shaphat, the official in charge of King David's herds in the valleys (1 Chr 27:29). Adlai is unknown outside this list of stewards of crown property (1 Chr 27:25–31).

MARK J. FRETZ

ADMAH (PLACE) [Heb *ʾadmâ*]. One of the "cities of the plain" associated by biblical tradition with Sodom and Gomorrah (Gen 14:2, 8). Admah is mentioned (along with Sodom, Gomorrah, and Zeboiim) among the points marking the Canaanite's southern border (Gen 10:19). Shinab, King of Admah, was one of the five allies (along with the kings of Sodom, Gomorrah, Zeboiim, and Zoar) who were defeated by Chedorlaomer and his three confederates in the Battle of the Valley of Siddim (Gen 14:2, 8) (see also CHEDORLAOMER). While Admah is not specifically mentioned in the account of the destruction of Sodom and Gomorrah (Gen 19:24–28), the tradition that it was also destroyed as judgment for its sin is attested twice. Like Sodom and Gomorrah, Admah and Zeboiim function as proverbial symbols of divine judgment. The fate of all four cities is held out as a warning to Israel not to disobey the covenant (Deut 29:22—Eng 29:23). Hosea 11:8 also recalls the divine overthrow of Admah and Zeboiim (cf. Wis 10:6).

The historicity of Admah's association with Sodom and Gomorrah is uncertain. Several scholars cite the greater number of references to Sodom and Gomorrah as evidence that Admah and Zeboiim are secondary additions to a core tradition. Admah and Zeboiim are, however, consistently associated with Sodom and Gomorrah within the written biblical tradition.

The site of Admah is uncertain. Simons (1959: 222–29) and others locate the cities of the plain in the SE corner of the Jordan Valley, to the N of the Dead Sea. Albright (1924: 8), tentatively identifying Admah with Adamah (Josh 3:16), also suggests that Admah and Zeboiim were located in the Jordan Valley, although he situates Sodom and Gomorrah under the shallow S bay of the Dead Sea. The Early Bronze Age ruins of Bab edh-Draʿ, Numeira, Feifeh, Khanazir, and Es-Safi, on the SE edge of the Dead Sea, have been hailed as the cities of the plain (van Hattem, 1981: 87–92). However, the archaeological evidence is inconclusive. See also SODOM, ZEBOIIM.

Bibliography

Albright, W. F. 1924. The Expedition of Xenia Theological Seminary and the American Schools. *BASOR* 14: 1–12.

Harland, J. P. 1942. Sodom and Gomorrah. *BA* 5: 17–32.

Hattem, W. C. van 1981. Once Again: Sodom and Gomorrah. *BA* 44: 87–92.

Simons, J. 1959. *The Geographical and Topographical Texts of the Old Testament.* Leiden.

CAROLYN J. PRESSLER

ADMATHA (PERSON) [Heb *ʾadmātāʾ*]. One of seven wise princes who counseled King Ahasuerus concerning matters of the law and judgment (Esth 1:14; cf. Ezra 7:14). Since the historicity of the book of Esther is uncertain, the identification of the characters cannot be verified. The name "Admatha" is absent in the LXX, which seems to have suffered corruption in this verse since it lists only three names (Gk *arkesaios, sarsathaios,* and *malēsear*).

MARK J. FRETZ

ADMIN (PERSON) [Gk *Admin*]. The son of Arni and father of Aminadab (Luke 3:33) in Luke's genealogy of Joseph, the husband of Mary (Luke 3:23–38). Matthew's parallel genealogy (Matt 1:1–17), replaces Luke's name sequence of Hezron—Arni—Admin—Aminadab with the sequence Hezron—Aram—Aminadab. According to the LXX, this Aram is Aminadab's father in Ruth 4:19 (MT reads *rām;* LXX variants include *aram* and *arran*), and in 1 Chr 2:9–10 (MT reads *rām;* LXX lists *ram* and *aram*). Luke's passage (3:33) contains a number of variant spellings of the name (e.g., *admin, aram,* and *admi*), attesting to the problems encountered by the copyists in attempting to establish the identity of Admin (Brown 1979: 60).

Bibliography

Brown, R. E. 1979. *The Birth of the Messiah*. Garden City.

MARK J. FRETZ

ADNA (PERSON) [Heb *ʿadnāʾ*]. **1.** A descendant of Pahathmoab and one of a number of returning exiles who married foreign women (Ezra 10:30). Under Ezra, Adna was subsequently forced by covenant to separate himself from his foreign wife and her children (Ezra 10:1–44 = 1 Esdr 8:88–89:36; see also Neh 13:23–31). LXX variants include *aidaine, idane,* and *edne,* and the apparent parallel in 1 Esdr 9:31 lists *addi* (see ADDI).

2. Head of the priestly family of Harim in the days of the high priest Joiakim (Neh 12:15). Adna may have been a contemporary of Adna no. 1 above, since the name of his father, "HARIM," also appears in connection with the issue of foreign wives (see especially Ezra 10:21; Neh 3:11); his priestly lineage, however (Neh 12:12–21), sets this Adna apart from the descendent of Pahathmoab.

MARK J. FRETZ

ADNAH (PERSON) [Heb *ʿadnaḥ; ʿadnâ*]. **1.** One of seven military leaders from the tribe of Manasseh who defected from King Saul's troops to serve David (1 Chr 12:21—Eng 12:20) prior to the confrontation with the Philistines in which Saul died (1 Samuel 31). The wary Philistines did not permit David to enter into this battle (1 Samuel 29), and before David could return to Ziklag, Amalekites had raided the town; so Adnah (Heb *ʿadnaḥ*), and the others were in a position to assist David against these raiders (1 Chr 12:21; see also 1 Samuel 30).

2. One of King Jehoshaphat's chief military officials who commanded an army of 300,000 soldiers in Judah (2 Chr 17:14). In the Bible his name (Heb *ʿadnâ*) occurs in a large list of commanding officers who served Jehoshaphat (2 Chr 17:13b–19). This rare biblical name is inscribed on a stone bowl unearthed at Kuntillet-ʿAjrud. Based on archaeological and epigraphical evidence at ʿAjrud, and on Adnah's biblical connection with Jehoshaphat, Meshel (1978: 54) tentatively raises the possibility that the inscription and the Bible refer to the same person.

Bibliography

Meshel, Z. 1978. Kuntillet ʿAjrud, an Israelite Religious Center in Northern Sinai. *Expedition* 20: 50–54.

MARK J. FRETZ

ADONAI [Heb *ʾădōnāy*]. One of the various names of God in the Hebrew Bible. The term is derived from Heb *ʾādôn* ("lord"), which in the biblical text refers both to the deity and to human rulers. Adonai is a modified form of the plural of *ʾādôn:* it bears the first-person suffix "my" and has been vocalized in a slightly different manner than "my lords," receiving a lengthened final *a*. Although based on a plural, it is usually translated into English as "my lord" or simply "Lord."

Adonai appears in the MT both as a title in its own right and as a substitute for the personal name of God, Yahweh. In order to preserve the sanctity of the Name, the Masoretes placed the vowel letters of Adonai underneath the consonants of Yahweh. This common substitution technique, called *qere/kethib* ("read/written"), clues readers to pronounce the Name as Adonai. In cases in which Adonai already appears, the hybrid form is read "Elohim." The RSV renders the substitution form as "LORD" (with all letters capitalized) while Adonai itself is translated "Lord" (with only the first letter capitalized).

The failure to recognize this substitution technique led later translators of the Hebrew Bible to render the form as it appears. Vocalizing the consonants YHWH with the vowels of Adonai (e, o, a) produced the new form "Yehowah," or in English "Jehovah." According to Kaufmann Kohler (*JEnc* 1: 201), this misreading can be traced to a Christian translator working in 1520 C.E. (See also YAHWEH.)

JULIA M. O'BRIEN

ADONI-BEZEK (PERSON) [Heb *ʾădōnî bezeq*]. The name of a Canaanite king reportedly defeated by the tribe of Judah in battle near Bezek (Judg 1:4–7). Wright (1946: 105–14) argued that this king was identical with Adoni-Zedek of Jerusalem (who was defeated and killed by Joshua, [Joshua 10]). Since nothing is said of this king's ruling over Jerusalem, and both names are distinctive, there is no substantive textual reason indicating that Adoni-Zedek was corrupted to Adoni-Bezek. The difficulty with Adoni-Bezek is that while the name is constructed as if Bezek were a divine name (cf. Adoni-Zedek—"My Lord is *ZDQ*," or Adonijah—"My Lord is Yahweh"), Bezek is unattested as a divine name. It is possible that there was a deity, Bezek, whose name was related to the Hebrew word *bāzāq,* found once with the meaning of "lightning" (Ezek 1:14). Until the discovery of such a deity, however, this suggestion is no more than guesswork.

A better possibility is to derive Bezek from the Hebrew word *bezeq,* meaning "fragment," or "sherd." This term is found as the name of a (rocky?) place in Judg 1:4–7 and 1 Sam 11:8. The site in Judg 1:4–7 would seem to lie near Jerusalem; but that in 1 Sam 11:8 may be identified with modern *Ibziq,* northeast of Shechem on the road to Beth-Shean. Since Bezek was a city, Adoni-Bezek is best read as "Lord of Bezek" (with *ʾădōnî-* forming the construct of *ʾādôn,* as is frequently the case with masculine nouns in the construct state (*BLe,* 525, §65j). That Adoni-Bezek was the ruler of Bezek is implied in that the men of Judah "came upon Adoni-Bezek at Bezek" (Judg 1:4). Having captured this Canaanite king, the Israelites cut off his thumbs and big toes (Judg 1:6). Thereupon Adoni-Bezek said, "Seventy kings with their thumbs and big toes cut off used to pick the scraps from under my table; as I have done, so has God repaid me." That Adoni-Bezek was then carried back to Jerusalem, where he died, is probably a later gloss dating from the time when the Israelites controlled the city (See also ADONI-ZEDEK; BEZEK).

Bibliography

Wright, G. E. 1946. The Literary and Historical Problem of Joshua 10 and Judges 1. *JNES* 5: 105–14.

D. G. SCHLEY

ADONI-ZEDEK [Heb *ʾădōnî-ṣedeq*]. A Canaanite king of Jerusalem (Josh 10:1–3) whose name means either "My Lord is righteousness" (i.e., Heb *ṣedeq* = "righteousness"), or "My Lord is Zedek." The latter is more likely, since Adoni-Zedek is constructed as a noun clause with a theophoric element (or divine name). The Yahwistic equivalent of Adoni-Zedek is Adonijah—"My Lord is Yahweh." A Canaanite king of Salem (= Jerusalem; cf. Ps 76:2) bears a name with the same theophoric element: Melchi-Zedek (Gen 14:18; Ps 110:4)—"My King is Zedek." The theophoric element *ṣdq* also occurs in the syllabic writings from Ugarit in the names *Ili-Ṣaduq*—"My God is Ṣaduq"—and *Ḥammi-Ṣaduq*—"My Warmth (?) is Ṣaduq." *Adnṣdq* is also attested, providing a parallel to the biblical name Adoni-Zedek (*PTU,* 187). Although the term *sedeq* by itself never occurs in the Hebrew Bible as the name of a deity, the above evidence probably indicates the existence of an old Canaanite god, *Ṣedeq* (Ug *Ṣaduq*), who was at one time the patron deity in Jerusalem.

Further evidence indicates that this tradition continued into the Davidic monarchy. David's choice of a priest of unknown origin, Zadok (Heb *Ṣādôq,* Ug *Ṣaduq*), to serve alongside Abiathar, may have resulted from a desire (or need) to secure the loyalty of the Jebusite cult in Jerusalem. This was done by recognizing its priest-king (Zadok) as high priest in Israel. That the Davidic kings viewed themselves as heirs to the Jebusite royal tradition is suggested by the writer of Ecclesiastes, ostensibly Solomon, who boasts of acquiring wealth "more than all who had been before me in Jerusalem" (Qoh 2:7).

Adoni-Zedek is depicted in Joshua 10 as the leader of a coalition of five southern Canaanite cities—Jerusalem, Hebron, Jarmuth, Eglon, and Lachish—formed to punish the Gibeonites after they had made peace with Joshua. These kings came up against Gibeon and encamped by the city. Joshua, having made a forced march from Gilgal at night, surprised the Canaanite army and threw it into a panic. The Israelites smote them as they fled by way of the ascent of Beth-Horon (which runs west-southwest from Gibeon to the Shephelah). According to the biblical account, Yahweh also smote them with hailstones as they fled, and at Joshua's request, caused the sun to stand still while the Israelites finished the slaughter (Josh 10:11–13). The five kings escaped and hid themselves in the cave at Makkedah, whence Joshua took them and hanged them on five trees in the vicinity (Josh 10:16–27). It has been argued that this Adoni-Zedek is identical with Adoni-Bezek, the Canaanite king in Judges 1, but this proposition is doubtful. See also ADONI-BEZEK; ZADOK; MELCHIZEDEK (PERSON); GIBEON.

Bibliography

Baudissin, W. W. von. 1929. *Kyrios als Gottesname im Judentum.* Vol. 3. Giessen.

Johnson, A. 1967. *Sacral Kingship in Ancient Israel.* Cardiff.

Wright, G. E. 1946. The Literary and Historical Problem of Joshua 10 and Judges 1. *JNES* 5:105–14.

D. G. SCHLEY

ADONIJAH (PERSON) [Heb *ʾădōnîyāh(û)*]. A name given three OT characters which means "Yah(weh) is (my) Lord."

1. The fourth son of David by his wife Haggith in Hebron, while David was king of Judah (2 Sam 3:4; 1 Chr 3:1–2); and heir apparent to the throne at the time of Solomon's accession. Adonijah's personal ambition led to his own demise in a story that echoes that of the rebellion and death of his elder brother Absalom.

The story begins with a note on the feebleness of David in his old age. Since the elder half-brothers Amnon, Absalom, and presumably Chileab were dead (1 Kgs 2:22), it was assumed by Adonijah, and perhaps by the general populace, that he was next in line for the throne. Though David may have promised Bathsheba, his favorite queen, that her son Solomon would succeed him—a fact that finds some confirmation in the exclusion of Solomon from Adonijah's feast—that pledge does not appear to have been seriously considered. The subsequent nomination of Solomon came as a surprise to the followers of Adonijah, who himself later claimed in conversation with Bathsheba: "You know that the kingdom was mine, and that all Israel fully expected me to reign" (1 Kgs 2:15).

With the help of David's general Joab and the priest Abiathar, Adonijah prepared a sacrificial feast near the spring En-rogel, to which he invited "all his brothers, the king's sons (except for Solomon), and all the royal officials of Judah (except for Nathan, Zadok, and Benaiah)," hoping to become king before his aged father died (1 Kgs 1:9). His plans were thwarted by the prophet Nathan, the priest Zadok, and Benaiah, commander of the royal bodyguard, who allied themselves with Bathsheba to forestall his succession.

When Bathsheba informed David of the events at En-rogel and the threat to her own life if Adonijah became king (1 Kgs 1:21), Nathan opportunely appeared, confirming her words and making his own appeal on the basis of loyalty to old friends and counselors. Together Nathan and Bathsheba moved the aged David to decisive action; and he ordered that Solomon be conducted on the royal mule in a procession to the spring at Gihon to be anointed and proclaimed king by Zadok. The instructions were immediately carried out and the new king, Solomon, was joyfully acclaimed by the people.

When the resounding acclamations of Solomon's procession were interpreted by Jonathan, the son of Abiathar, to mean the ruin of Adonijah's hopes, his adherents fled and Adonijah himself took sanctuary in the Temple by laying hold of the horns of the altar. Adonijah was subsequently persuaded to leave his asylum only by Solomon's promise to spare his life (1 Kgs 1:40–53).

After David's death, Adonijah asked Bathsheba to intercede with Solomon to give him in marriage the beautiful Abishag, his father's concubine and nurse. Solomon interpreted this as a bid for the throne and ordered Adonijah's execution at the hands of Benaiah.

Close parallels between the stories of Absalom (2 Samuel 15–18) and Adonijah (1 Kings 1–2) have been noted (Fokkelman 1981: 345–410; Long 1984: 33–52; and Gunn 1987: 104–111). Both men are described as handsome and appealing figures, who were not adequately disciplined by their father. Adonijah enlisted the help of "chariots and horsemen and fifty men to run before him" (1 Kgs 1:5), as Absalom had done before him (2 Sam 15:1). Both sought the crown on their own without David's support; and both came to a violent end. Adonijah's request from Solomon that he be given Abishag as his wife is reminiscent of Absalom, who, after taking Jerusalem and in order to secure his political position, publicly took David's concubines as his own (2 Sam 16:20–23). Adonijah's desire to marry Abishag may have been motivated by his love for her; but that decision was his final undoing. Whatever his real motives or the political significance of his act may have been, in terms of the story, he was rebelling against the king.

The story of Adonijah's rebellion and fate in 1 Kings 1–2 may also be interpreted in relation to the law of the king in Deut 17:14–20, which forbade the monarch from relying solely on force of arms, alliances (through marriage), or wealth. Adonijah's violation of the prohibitions of the law of the king foreshadows the more flagrant violations of this same law on the part of Solomon. The king is to follow the law of Moses, which is in the hands of the Levites.

2. A Levite who, together with princes and priests, instructed the people in the law during a mission to the cities of Judah in the third year of Jehoshaphat (2 Chr 17:8).

3. A leading layman, one of the "chiefs of the people," who sealed the covenant of reform in the time of Ezra (Neh 10:17—Eng 10:16).

Bibliography

Fokkelman, J. P. 1981. *Narrative Art and Poetry in the Books of Samuel: King David.* vol. 1. Assen.

Gunn, D. M. 1978. *The Story of King David: Genre and Interpretation,* JSOTSup 6. Sheffield.

Langlamet, F. 1976. Pour ou Contre Salomon? *RB* 48: 321–79, 481–528.

Long, B. O. 1984. *1 Kings.* Grand Rapids.

Veijola, R. 1975. *Die Ewige Dynastie, David und die Entstehung seiner Dynastie nach der deuteronomistischen Darstellung.* Helsinki.

Zalewski, S. 1973. The Character of Adonijah. *Beth Mikra* 19: 229–55 (in Hebrew).

———. 1974. The Struggle between Adonijah and Solomon over the Kingdom. *Beth Mikra* 20: 490–510 (in Hebrew).

DUANE L. CHRISTENSEN

ADONIKAM (PERSON) [Heb *ʾădōnîqām*]. The father of a clan who, along with other lay families, returned from Babylon to Palestine (Ezra 2:13 = Neh 7:18 = 1 Esdr 5:14; also Ezra 8:13 = 1 Esdr 8:39). The precise number of returnees in Adonikam's clan is uncertain, owing to the occurrence of this name in multiple lists where the Hebrew-Aramaic numeral notation may have been miscounted (Allrik 1954). Adonikam may be identical with the ADONIJAH mentioned in a list of lay family heads (Neh 10:17—Eng 10:16), since both are listed in conjunction with otherwise similar persons (Myers *Ezra-Nehemiah* AB, 239: Williamson *Ezra, Nehemiah* WBC, 329).

Bibliography

Allrik, H. L. 1954. The Lists of Zerubbabel (Nehemiah 7 and Ezra 2) and the Hebrew Numeral Notation. *BASOR* 136: 21–27.

MARK J. FRETZ

ADONIRAM (PERSON) [Heb *ʾădōnîram*]. The son of Abda and an official in Solomon's court who was in charge of the forced labor used in many of the major building projects (1 Kgs 4:6; 9:15). This office was first mentioned late in David's reign and continued into the rule of Rehoboam (2 Sam 20:24; 1 Kgs 12:18). In the reign of David and Rehoboam, this office was held by Adoram. Some scholars take this to be a shortened form of the name "Adoniram." If this is the case, then one person held this office from late in David's reign until the crisis under Rehoboam—a period of some 40 years. The LXX supports this identification and uses the name "Adoniram" consistently in the passages referring to this official. Other scholars believe that it is possible, but not likely, that one person would have held this office for such a length of time.

Two factors suggest the importance of Adoniram's office: (1) the position is included in the small number of offices listed at the royal court, and (2) control of a force of 30,000 men certainly would have been given only to a most trusted individual (1 Kgs 5:28—Eng 5:14).

Forced labor was a part of many societies in the Ancient Near East. Israel's distaste for this practice is probably to be seen in the demand for lighter burdens under Rehoboam (1 Kgs 12:4). When Rehoboam refused to change his harsh policies, Adoniram, the overseer of the hated forced labor, was murdered by the angry Israelites (1 Kgs 12:18).

PHILLIP E. MCMILLION

ADOPTION. The creation of a kinship relationship between two individuals that is recognized as essentially equivalent to one stemming from natural descent. In the ancient Near East, such ties were typically between adoptive parent(s) and a son or daughter, but individuals were adopted into other roles as well. Frequently the parties were relatives before the adoption took place. Adoption differs from fosterage in that the latter is a temporary arrangement which is not legally binding. The foster child receives support but not the status of son or daughter.

A. Extrabiblical Sources.

Because biblical references to adoption are both limited in number and seldom unambiguous, they have been interpreted with the aid of extrabiblical sources, particularly cuneiform texts.

1. Cuneiform. Relevant documents date at least from the beginning of the 2d millennium B.C.E. to the Achaemenid period, the majority coming from Old Babylonian (OB) and Middle Babylonian (MB) times. Since our sources span both a wide geographical range and the better part of two millennia, details of adoption practice from a given time and place were not necessarily universal.

Law collections (often called law codes) and adoption contracts are our primary types of documentation. The latter are more abundant and also more reliable, since the function of the collections is debated and their treatment of adoption incomplete. Contracts have their limitations as well; they do not as a rule present the circumstances leading to the adoption, or the age of the parties. Stipulations regarding adoption differed from contract to contract and "code" to "code" so that one cannot expect to discover general laws which governed Mesopotamian (or biblical) practice.

Schorr (1913) and Kohler, Koschaker, and Ungnad (1909–23) have collected a number of OB adoption texts; see also texts and bibliography in Ellis 1975. Speiser (1930) and Cassin (1938) present MB Nuzi texts with discussion (see also dissertations cited in Eichler 1989: 116–17 nn. 51, 56). References to adoption in the law collections (see *ANET*) are Codex Hammurabi (CH) §§170–71, 185–93; Laws of Eshnunna §35; and Middle Assyrian Laws (MAL) §A 28; cf. doubtfully MAL §A 41, Lipit-Ištar §27.

Other types of documents occasionally mention adoption. We read of the adoption of a foundling in "The Legend of Sargon" (*ANET,* p. 119) and, with details of the adoption procedure, in the lexical series *ana ittišu* (Landsberger 1937: 44–47). In addition, there are records of litigation over custody or inheritance rights of adoptees.

The most common Akkadian way to say "adopt" is *ana mārūtim leqû* "take for son/daughtership." Individuals could also be adopted into other roles, such as that of brother (*aḫḫūti,* "brotherhood"), sister (*aḫātūti/atḫūti*), or even father (*abbūti*). In cases known especially from Nuzi, women adopted in order to be given in marriage would receive the "status of (adopted) daughter" (*mārtūtu*), daughter-in-law (*kall[at]ūtu*), daughter or daughter-in-law (*mārtūtu u kall[at]ūtu*), or sister (*aḫātūtu*); for literature see Eichler 1989; nn. 36, 56, 61.

Adoptions were usually effected by an agreement between two parties, the adopter and the parent or guardian of the adoptee, but occasionally adoptees would act on their own behalf. A written contract recording the adoption typically included a statement of the adoptive relationship, clauses regarding its dissolution, a record of the oath of the parties, the names of witnesses, and the date. Some sources hint at an adoption ceremony.

Adoption in the cuneiform *Kulturkreis* took many forms. An individual might be adopted as heir, or into apprenticeship. Slaves were manumitted by adoption (Schorr 1913: nos. 23–35), and illegitimate children legitimated. Females were often adopted with a view to giving them away in marriage. An adoptive sister relationship between co-wives could promote family unity. A man without male offspring might adopt his son-in-law to keep property within the family. Money, land, or services often played a role in the adoption arrangement. At Nuzi, in particular, land sales took the form of an adoption (Cassin 1938: 51–274). The buyer was adopted and given land as an "inheritance" in exchange for a "gift" of equivalent value. These "sale adoptions" have often been seen as circumventing a prohibition against alienating ancestral property (cf. Lev 25:23–28); for this and other interpretations see Maidman 1976: 92–123.

2. Egyptian. Far fewer texts are preserved from Egypt (see Allam 1972). The "Story of Sinuhe" may contain an example of the adoption of a son-in-law in Syro-Palestine (*ANET* pp. 19–20). The "Extraordinary Adoption" text (ca. 1100 B.C.E.; Thompson 1974: 229 n. 141) refers to the adoption of a wife as the daughter and heir of her childless husband. Following the latter's death, the wife freed and adopted three slaves (her husband's children by a concubine?). One of them, a woman, married the wife's brother, whom the wife then adopted as son and heir. In a text from ca. 656 B.C.E., the Nitocris Adoption Stela, Pharaoh Psammetichus had his daughter Nitocris adopted as successor to the celibate Divine Wife of Amon at Thebes.

3. Jewish. An Aramaic papyrus from the Jewish colony at Elephantine (*BMAP,* no. 8), dated to 416 B.C.E., refers to the manumission and adoption of a slave. Both adopter and adoptee bear Jewish names. Catacomb inscriptions attest to Jewish adoptions in the Roman period (Leon 1960: 232–33).

B. Adoption in the Bible.

1. Possible Cases. A list of proposed examples of adoption, arranged according to the identity of the adoptee, follows. In addition, Lev 18:9 may refer to an adopted daughter, but more probably to a case of remarriage.

a. Children of Surrogate Mother. Sarai, Rachel, and Leah each gave a female slave to her husband for the purpose of procreation (Gen 16:1–4; 30:1–13). Extrabiblical parallels are not decisive as to whether the primary wife in such a case adopted the surrogate's offspring (Thompson 1974: 254–59, 266–67). Two items in the biblical accounts may imply adoption by the wife: her regard of the children as her own (e.g., Gen 16:2; 30:3–13) and the possible allusion by Rachel to an adoption rite (Gen 30:3). The first point is generally conceded, but may be explained by the wife's ownership of the slave (Tigay *EncJud* 2:298). Moreover, the offspring are frequently called children of the slave. But (aside from source-critical considerations) it may be that, as in many societies, ties to the natural mother (or father, in the case of Ephraim and Manasseh) continued to be recognized. Regarding the second point, Rachel desired her slave to "give birth on my knees" (Gen 30:3), interpreted by Stade (1886) as referring ultimately to the practice of a woman giving birth onto her husband's knees. The husband's act, and by extension placing one's child on one's knees, was an acknowledgment of the child as a legitimate descendant (cf. Tigay *EncJud* 2: 299), while receiving or placing someone else's child on the knees signified adoption. Alternately, Rachel demonstrated her desire for children by assisting her slave in birth, or hoped to cure her own infertility (Tigay *EncJud* 2: 299).

b. Children of Foreign Wives. A proposal that the end of Ezra 10:44 refers to adoption has received new support from Akkadian and other parallels (Paul 1979–80: 183–85).

c. Foundling. After his abandonment, the infant Moses was discovered by Pharaoh's daughter "and he became her son" (*wayhî-lāh lĕbēn,* Exod 2:10). This verse and the fact that the adult Moses continued to live as an Egyptian

(2:11,19) speak against mere fosterage. Commentators are quick to point out that the account reflects at most an Egyptian custom, but the point loses some of its force if the story is seen not as primarily historical, but as the Hebrew version of the widespread "birth of the hero" myth (cf. *ANET,* p. 119). The payment of Moses' natural mother to nurse him (2:7–10) echoes identical arrangements in Mesopotamian adoption contracts (e.g., Schorr 1913: nos. 8, 83). Two NT passages apparently understand Moses as the adopted son of Pharaoh's daughter (Acts 7:21, Heb 11:24).

d. (Great-)Grandchildren. The adoption of grandchildren, well known in modern times, is also attested in an Ugaritic document (Mendelsohn 1959). Three biblical cases are relevant. Ephraim and Manasseh are adopted by their grandfather Jacob (Gen 48: 5–6), who tells Joseph: "Your two sons . . . are mine . . . as Reuben and Simeon are." The adoption serves an evident aetiological purpose: to explain the place of Ephraim and Manasseh, rather than their father Joseph, among the 12 tribes of Israel. Jacob's blessing in Gen 48:15–16, in which Joseph is omitted from the sequence of generations, also has been interpreted as implying adoption. The notice that Joseph removed his sons from Jacob's knees may hint at an adoption rite (Stade 1886: 144–45).

The sons of Machir "were born on Joseph's knees" (Gen 15:23). Even granting Stade's view, this may have been merely an acknowledgment of legitimate descent. On the other hand, a tradition of the adoption of the Machirites could have served two purposes: to explain their relative prominence (e.g., Judg 5:14), or to explain the incorporation of this originally foreign clan (1 Chr 7:14) into Israel. A number of scholars have deduced a direct relationship between Joseph and Machir on independent grounds.

A third possible case is that of Naomi and Obed. After Naomi's son Mahlon died childless, his widow Ruth had a child, Obed, by Mahlon's kinsman. According to the custom of levirate marriage, Obed would be considered as Mahlon's son and hence Naomi's grandson. At one point (Ruth 4:16–17), Naomi held Obed in her bosom *(bĕḥêqāh)* "and became his *ʾōmenet*" ("supporter," a vague term), whereupon the neighbors remarked "a son has been born to Naomi." The custom of an adoptive mother offering her breast to an adoptee is known among the Arabs and in other cultures, and an adoption account might have served to "Judaize" Obed (King David's ancestor), who would otherwise have had a Moabite mother. We do not know, however, that offering a breast to an adoptee was a Hebrew custom or that Naomi did so. The neighbors' words need not be taken literally. Adoption, it seems, would have deprived Ruth of someone to carry on Mahlon's name, and it is questionable if Naomi could unilaterally effect a change in Obed's status.

e. Illegitimate Son. Jephthah appears to have been legitimated and hence adopted, if legitimation in Israel was effected as in Mesopotamia (Schorr 1913: no. 12, Thompson 1974: 260; cf. CH §§170–71 [*ANET,* 173]). Although his mother was a prostitute, Jephthah was entitled to share his father's inheritance (Judg 11:1–2).

f. Nephew or Male Relative. The custom by which the offspring of a levirate marriage is ascribed to a childless deceased brother or male kinsman has been viewed as a postmortem adoption.

g. Orphan. Mordecai (Esth 2:7) supported his cousin Hadassah/Esther *(ōmēn ʾet-hădassâ)* and, after her parents' death, adopted her (*lĕqāḥāh . . . lĕbat*; similarly Akk *ana mār(t)ūtim leqû*). It is doubtful that an unmarried woman of Esther's age could live with Mordecai except for an adoptive relationship. Although both were Jewish, they were living under Persian rule (as were those in the Jewish text from Elephantine), so it is not certain that a Jewish practice is reflected.

h. Slave. Manumission of slaves by adoption is well known in the ancient Near East, and manumitted slaves occasionally are named heir (e.g., Schorr 1913: no. 35; Muhammad's adopted son Zaid ibn Ḥāritha). Abram's fear that his slave would be his heir (Gen 15:2–3) seems to imply the slave's (possibly future) adoption, since normally only a relative could inherit (see e.g., Num 27:8–11). Although in Hurrian law an unrelated *ewuru* "heir" could inherit by default, there is no hint of this in biblical law. On Genesis 15, see further Thompson 1974: 203–30.

Jarha (1 Chr 2:34–35) is a probable example of the manumission and adoption of a slave. According to the common Mesopotamian practice, the slave (and foreigner) Jarha would have been manumitted by adoption before being married to his master Sheshan's daughter. Jarha's children are listed as Sheshan's descendants.

i. Son-in-law. Jarha also serves as an example of an adopted son-in-law. Barzillai, who married and took his father-in-law's name (Ezra 2:61, Neh 7:63), is probably another. Many features of the Jacob and Laban narrative, and particularly parallels to two Nuzi adoption texts (*ANET,* pp. 219–20, nos. 2 and 3), have suggested it as another example. Other features, however, distinguish this case from standard Mesopotamian adoption arrangements, and similarities to herding contracts have been noted. See recently Eichler 1989: 114–16.

j. Wife. An adoption of a wife as daughter is known from Egypt, but the oft-repeated notion that in Hurrian practice a wife could be adopted as her husband's sister and that this explains the "wife-sister" motif in the Bible (Gen 12:13 and parallels) is now widely rejected as based upon the (mis)interpretation of a small number of texts (Eichler 1989: 112–13).

2. Metaphorical Use. The father-son relationship of Yahweh and Israel may have been conceived at times as an adoptive one (Jer 3:19; explicitly in Rom 9:4). The relationship between God and king is illustrated using what are evidently adoption formulae in Ps 2:7, 2 Sam 7:14 (Tigay *EncJud* 2: 300–1). See Paul 1979–80: 177–80, 184.

Adoption *(huiothesia)* appears as a metaphor five times in NT writings ascribed to Paul (Rom 8:14, 23; 9:4; Gal 4:5; Eph 1:5), where it serves to distinguish the believer's sonship from that of Jesus and to illustrate the Christian's change of status, both accomplished and prospective. The background of the metaphor has variously been seen as Roman, with its concept of strong paternal authority; Greek, as the term *huiothesia* implies; or Hebrew, as implied in Paul's use of the semitic term *abba* in describing the adoptive father.

3. Issues. Definitions of adoption have varied, leading to varying evaluations of the extent to which it was practiced in Israel. Attempts to adhere to the strict meaning of Latin *adoptio* have led some scholars to include as true adoption only those cases where a person under paternal authority *(patria potestas)* is transferred to the authority of a third (free) individual and appointed heir. Adoption, thus narrowly defined, has been said not to have existed in Israel. But in addition to running counter to the general usage by scholars of the ancient Near East, this definition ignores the concept of adoption reflected in our texts. Adoption into sonship *(ana mārūtim)*, for example, can occur when the adopter is a slave (Speiser 1930; no. 5) or a woman (Schorr 1913: no. 29); when the adoptee is a foundling (Landsberger 1937: 44–46), the adopter's illegitimate child (Schorr 1913: no. 12: cf. CH §§170–71) or a free individual (adrogation; Kohler, Koschaker, and Ungnad 1909–23: no. 1425); and in numerous cases where an inheritance is not mentioned.

Although adoption was practiced in ancient Israel, it is impossible to say to what extent this was true. Many of the biblical cases occur in the patriarchal narratives or on foreign soil, involve foreigners, or are uncertain. Moreover, adoption is not mentioned in biblical law. The nature of our sources is no doubt partly responsible for the seeming scarcity of biblical adoption. Biblical references are generally not explicit enough to allow confirmation (or denial) of proposed cases. The silence of biblical law collections may simply reflect their selective and incomplete nature; compare the haphazard notice adoption receives in the Mesopotamian collections. Since adoption was, it seems, of little theological interest (except as a metaphor), there was no particular reason to mention it; if we read of a barren woman, it is often only to set the stage for a miraculous birth.

The absence of adoption in postbiblical Jewish law, however, suggests that it was not prevalent in Israel, at least in later periods. Various explanations have been suggested (Boecker 1974): the importance of blood lineage to the Hebrews, the practice of polygyny, the custom of levirate marriage, and the belief that fertility or barrenness reflected God's will, which adoption would circumvent. No single explanation is completely satisfactory, and all address only the "demand" side of the equation, without explaining, for example, the place of orphaned or unwanted children in Israelite society.

For bibliography not listed below see especially Paul 1979–80: 175 n. 1.

Bibliography

Allam, S. 1972. De l'adoption en Egypte pharaonique. *OrAnt* 11: 277–95.

Boecker, H. J. 1974. Anmerkungen zur Adoption im Alten Testament. *ZAW* 86: 86–89.

Cassin, E.-M. 1938. L'Adoption à Nuzi. Paris.

Donner, H. 1969. Adoption oder Legitimation? Erwägungen zur Adoption im Alten Testament auf dem Hintergrund der altorientalischen Rechte. *OrAnt* 8: 87–119.

Eichler, B. L. 1989. Nuzi and the Bible: A Retrospective. Pp. 107–19 in *DUMU-E$_2$-DUB-BA-A: Studies in Honor of Åke W. Sjöberg*, ed. H. Behrens, D. Loding, and M. T. Roth. Philadelphia.

Ellis, M. de J. 1975. An Old Babylonian Adoption Contract from Tell Harmal. *JCS* 27: 130–51.

Kohler, J.; Koschaker, P.; and Ungnad, A. 1909–23. *Hammurabi's Gesetz.* Vols. 3–6. Leipzig.

Landsberger, B. 1937. *Die Serie* ana ittišu. MSL 1. Rome.

Leon, H. L. 1960. *The Jews of Ancient Rome.* Philadelphia.

Maidman, M. P. 1976. A Socio-economic Analysis of a Nuzi Family Archive. Ph.D. Diss. University of Pennsylvania.

Mendelsohn, I. 1959. A Ugaritic Parallel to the Adoption of Ephraim and Manasseh. *IEJ* 9: 180–83.

Paul, S. 1979–80. Adoption Formulae: A Study of Cuneiform and Biblical Legal Clauses. *Maarav* 2: 173–85.

Schoenberg, M. W. 1963. *Huiothesia:* The Word and the Institution. *Scr* 15: 115–23.

Schorr, M. 1913. *Urkunden des altbabylonischen Zivil- und Prozessrechts.* VAB 5. Leipzig.

Speiser, E. A. 1930. New Kirkuk Documents Relating to Family Laws. *AASOR* 10: 1–73.

Stade, B. 1886. Miscellen. 15. "Auf Jemandes Knieen gebären." *ZAW* 6: 143–56.

Thompson, T. L. 1974. *The Historicity of the Patriarchal Narratives.* BZAW 133. New York.

FREDERICK W. KNOBLOCH

ADORAIM (PLACE) [Heb *ʾadôrayim*]. Var. ADORA. A town in the central hill country of Judah, listed among the cities fortified by Rehoboam near the beginning of his reign (2 Chr 11:9). An examination of the list of cities fortified by Rehoboam (2 Chr 11: 5–12) shows that they form a logical and fairly consistent defensive line on the western, southern, and eastern frontiers of Rehoboam's domains, supplemented by additional fortresses at key road junctions (*LBHG,* 290–94). This strongly suggests that the author of Chronicles had access to some sort of official military document delineating the defenses of the Kingdom of Judah. During Hellenistic and Roman times, this fortress-town was known as Adora (GK *adōra*). According to 1 Macc 13:20–21, Simon Maccabeus stopped the advance of Trypho at Adora. Josephus records (*Ant* 13.9.1) that Adora was captured by John Hyrcanus following the death of Antiochus 7 in 129 B.C., and that it still remained in Hasmonean hands at the time of Janneaus (*Ant* 13.15.4). It must have fallen into Roman hands soon thereafter, for it was among the cities rebuilt in 59 B.C. by Gabinius, proconsul of Syria (*Ant* 14.5.3). In the form "Aduram," this town appears in the book of Jubilees (38:9–24) as the location of the burial of Esau following his battle with Jacob. The ancient name is clearly reflected in the modern town of Dura, located approximately 7 km W, and slightly S, of Hebron (M.R. 152101). There is little doubt that the ancient town is to be located here, or at least in the immediate vicinity.

WADE R. KOTTER

ADRAMMELECH (DEITY) [Heb *ʾadrammelek*]. In 2 Kgs 17:31 it is reported that the Babylonians who were resettled in Samaria "burned their children in the fire to Adrammelech and Anammelech, the gods of Sepharvaim." The place name "Sepharvaim" may refer to the Babylonian city of Sippar, but the identity of the Babylonian god Adrammelech is unknown.

A. KIRK GRAYSON

ADRAMMELECH (PERSON) [Heb *ʾadrammelek*]. According to 2 Kgs 19:37 (= Isa 37:38), one of the sons of the Assyrian king Sennacherib who, along with his brother Sharezer, assassinated their father. This Adrammelech may be identical with Arda-Mulishi, who is identified as a son of Sennacherib in Assyrian sources.

Bibliography

Parpola, S. 1980. The Murderer of Sennacherib. *Mesopotamia* 8: 171–182.

A. KIRK GRAYSON

ADRAMYTTIUM (PLACE) [Gk *Adramutteion*]. An ancient city of Mysia located along the NW coast of the Roman province of Asia (modern Turkey). A ship from this city, probably a small trading vessel, is mentioned in Acts 27:2. The ship was homeward bound when Paul, Luke, Aristarchus, and Julius the Centurion boarded it in order to journey from Caesaria to Rome via the Asian coast.

This city, located at the base of Mt. Ida, controlled a substantial port from its position at the head of the Gulf of Adramyttium (Hdt. 8: 42), which is across from the island of Lesbos. Today the harbor is filled with alluvial deposits and the site of the city is known as Karatash, while the original appellation is preserved in the name of the nearby town Edremit.

The founding of the city is problematic with three prevalent theories: it is the *Pedasus* of Homer; it was founded by Adramys, the brother of Croesus, in 3 B.C.; or it was one of many colonies established by merchants from the spice-rich area of S Arabia known as Hadhramaut (Harris 1925). The reading of the name with a rough breathing is indicated in the Vulgate rendering as *navem Hadrumetinam.* This may lend credence to Harris' theory.

The commercial importance of the city, indicated by the coins found at the site, peaked when Pergamum was the capital of the region but had faded by the NT period. Adramyttium, one of the chief cities of the province, was chosen to be the host of the provincial governor's law court, the assizes *(conventus)* of the NW district of the Roman province of Asia. It was the original place of the worship of Castor and Pollox and home of the orator Xenocles (the tutor of Cicero) (See Strabo 8: 1.66; Plutarch, Cicero 4). Adramyttium was noted for the production of a special ointment (Pliny N.H. 13: 2.5).

Bibliography

Harris, J. R. 1925. Adramyttium. *The Contemporary Review* 128: 194–202.

Leaf, W. 1923. *Strabo on the Troad.* Cambridge.

JOHN D. WINELAND

ADRIA, SEA OF (PLACE) [Greek *Adrias*]. An arm of the Mediterranean between Italy and the Balkan Peninsula joining the Ionian Sea in the southeast, commonly known as the Adriatic Sea. It is mentioned in the NT in relation to the apostle Paul's journey to Rome (Acts 27:27). Today, the name denotes the sea which extends from northwest to southeast, a length of nearly five hundred miles. The Italian shore is low, especially in the northeast basin around the delta of the Po, which is the largest river that flows into it. The east coast is rather rugged and fringed with islands. This allows for many good harbors on the Dalmatian coast as opposed to the relatively few found on the Italian side. The northeast winds, together with the prevalence of sudden squalls, makes navigation in winter difficult and dangerous.

The Sea was known in antiquity as Adrias, Adriatike Thalasa, Adriatikon Pelagos in Gk, and Adriaticum Mare, Adrianum Mare, or Mare Superum in Latin. According to Strabo (5.1), the name was derived from the old Etruscan city-colony ATRIA located north of the Po River. Justin (20, 1.9), however, suggests a Greek origin for the name. Originally, the name was applied to the upper (northwestern) part of the sea, but it became gradually extended southeastward some 6000 stadia (approx. 700 miles) as far as the Ionian Sea (Strabo 2,123), and even to the Sicilian Sea, including waters between Crete and Malta (Orosius 1, 2.90). Thus in antiquity it was understood that Malta lay at the western extremity of the Adriatic Sea (Procopius 1, 14), while Crete was surrounded by the same on the west (Strabo 3.17) and the same waters encompassed Sicily on the east (Strabo 3.4, 15). It seems that the name was first used interchangeably with the Ionian Sea, and gradually came to include it. "The Ionian Sea is part of what is now called the sea of Hadria," wrote Strabo (2, 5.20). According to Livy (5,33), Italy was surrounded by two seas, the Tuscan on the west and the Hadriatic on the east. The name therefore is more restricted today than it was in the past, when it not only included waters between Sicily and Crete, but might have been applied to the whole of the eastern Mediterranean with the exception of the Aegean Sea.

Therefore, it would be misleading to limit the reference from the Acts to what is today known as the Adriatic Sea. Because many of the Gk manuscripts call Malta *Melite* (with several variations in Greek and also Latin manuscripts), some have tried to see in the name an island other than Malta, namely modern Mljet in the Adriatic. Yet the most probable east-northeast direction of the wind called Northeaster (Gk *euroklydon* or *eurakylon,* Acts 27:14) would not support this suggestion. Scholars are still more inclined to understand the NT reference to *adrias* in a more general way, as opposed to the more restricted modern usage of the term.

To avoid a possible confusion in the use of different names some have suggested a strict distinction in the use of the terms the "Adrian Sea" and the "Adriatic Sea." Even though this may be done today, Ptolemy used the two names interchangeably (3. 4:Adria, and 3.17:Adriatic).

Acts 27:27 states that the vessel upon which Paul was going to Rome was "driven up and down" for fourteen days by high winds before its shipwreck on Malta. That the sea earned a tempestuous reputation in ancient times can be documented by records of such famous writers as Josephus (*Vita* 3) and Horace (Odes 1, 33).

Bibliography

Avi-Yonah, M., and Malamat, A., eds. *The World of the Bible.* New York.

Meinardus, Otto F. A. *St. Paul's Last Journey.* New Rochelle, NY.

ZDRAVKO STEFANOVIC

ADRIEL (PERSON) [Heb *ʿadrîʾēl*]. A Meholathite, the son of Barzillai, and son-in-law of King Saul through marriage to one of the two royal princesses. There is some confusion as to which daughter of Saul he married. According to 1 Sam 18:19, he married the elder daughter MERAB, who had been promised to David, while the MT and LXX Codex Vaticanus of 2 Sam 21:8 report that he married the younger daughter MICHAL (PERSON). In 2 Sam 21:8, other manuscripts (LXX^{LN} and 2 Heb mss) read Merab in agreement with 1 Sam 18:19 (instead of Michal). The Targum, in an attempt to resolve the conflicting readings, combines the names in the phrase *myrb drby't mykl,* lit. "Merab who is the [young] girl of Michal," which identifies Adriel's wife (Merab) while introducing a new element to the relationship between Michal and Merab. Most scholars favor Merab as the true spouse, although a minority favor Michal, in spite of the conflicting traditions, believing the MT testimony in 2 Sam 21:8 to be the more difficult reading and the tradition to be an older and more reliable source than 1 Sam 18:19 (i.e., Stoebe 1958: 229; Glück 1965; Lemche 1978: 7–8). The royal marriage produced at least five sons, who were later executed by the Gibeonites for Saul's bloodguilt (2 Sam 21:8).

As a Meholathite, Adriel was an inhabitant of the town of Abel-Meholah, probably located at Tell Abû Sûs, in the W ghor (see ABEL-MEHOLAH). His marriage to a Saulide princess may have sealed a treaty between his city-state and Saul's new Israelite state (Edelman 1990). Such diplomatic marriages were an established convention in the ancient Near East (Malamat 1963:8–10). Abel-Meholah did not become a corporate part of the Israelite state until David or Solomon's reign, as indicated by the city's inclusion in Solomon's fifth district (1 Kgs 4:12). His name means "El is my help," and seems to be Aramaic. Some manuscripts read *ʿzryʾl,* which has the same meaning, but substitutes the Hebrew word *ʿzr* for its Aramaic cognate *ʿdr* (Nestle 1897; McCarter *2 Samuel* AB, 439).

Bibliography

Edelman, D. 1990. *Saulide Israel: A Study in Secondary State Formation in Ancient Canaan.* Winona Lake.

Glück, J. J. 1965. Merab or Michal? *ZAW* 77: 72–81.

Lemche, N. P. 1978. David's Rise. *JSOT* 10: 2–25.

Malamat, A. 1963. Aspects of the Foreign Policies of David and Solomon. *JNES* 22: 1–17.

Nestle, E. 1897. Some Contributions to Hebrew Onomatology. *AJSL* 13: 169–76.

Stoebe, H. J. 1958. David und Michal—Überlegungen zur Jugendesgeschichte Davids. Pp. 224–43 in *Von Ugarit nach Qumran,* ed. W. F. Albright, W. Baumgartner, J. Lindblom, *et al. BZAW* 77. Berlin.

Diana V. Edelman
Mark J. Fretz

ADUEL (PERSON) [Gk *adouēl*]. The son of Gabael and great grandfather of Tobit, a descendant of the tribe of Naphtali (Tob 1:1). The name "Aduel" is a possible variant of ADIEL; the *yod* in Heb *ʿădîʾēl* (1 Chr 4:36; 9:12; 27:25), if replaced with *waw,* would result in the Heb consonants *ʿdwʾl,* logically transliterated as Gk *adouēl.* Nonetheless, the name "Aduel" only occurs in this genealogy of Tobit.

Mark J. Fretz

ADULLAM (PLACE) [Heb *ʿădūllām*]. ADULLAMITE. A city in the Shephelah region at approximately the midpoint of a line running from Bethlehem to Gath. It has been identified with modern Tell esh Sheikh Madhkur (Albright 1924:3–4; M.R. 150117).

In Gen 38:1, 12, and 20, in the story about Judah and Tamar, a character is identified as Hirah the Adullamite. He is called Judah's friend (38:12,20) and is entrusted with the deliverance of a pledge (38:20).

Adullam appears twice in Joshua. The king of Adullam is listed in Joshua 12 as one of the local kings whom the Israelites defeated on the west side of the Jordan (Josh 12:15). Adullam was allotted to the tribe of Judah (Josh 15:35).

Adullam occupies a prominent place in the story of David's rise to kingship. David fled from Saul to a cave near Adullam and there surrounded himself with a band of about 400 men (1 Sam 22:1). That this was a place of security for David's warriors is spelled out in 1 Chronicles 11, which refers to the place as "the rock." The syntax of the parallel passage in Samuel is confusing and probably the result of scribal error. Apparently there has been a substitution of the word for "harvest" or "harvesttime" (Heb *qāṣîr*; BDB, 894) for "the rock" or "the secure place" (Heb *haṣṣūr*; BDB, 849), the second of which is the term employed in Chronicles. Some versions of the LXX also have "the rock" instead of "harvesttime" at 1 Sam 23:13.

Chronicles lists Adullam as among the cities which Solomon's successor REHOBOAM fortified in anticipation of the invasion of Judah by the Pharaoh SHISHAK ca. 918 B.C.E. (2 Chr 11:7). Many commentators and historians accept the placing of this list in the reign of Rehoboam (see *BHI,* 233; Naʾaman 1986:6). Others, partly on the basis of archeological evidence at these sites, feel that the list belongs to the reign of another king, either JOSIAH (Fritz 1981) or HEZEKIAH (Naʾaman 1986).

MICAH, a contemporary of Hezekiah's, mourns over Adullam among the cities of the Shephalah (Mic 1:15), possibly in advance of Sennacherib's invasion (see 2 Kgs 18:13 = 2 Chr 32:1).

Adullam appears twice in postexilic contexts. It is named as one of the places where the people of Judah settled after the Exile (Neh 11:30). In the time of the Maccabean revolt, Adullam once again served as a refuge, this time for Judas Maccabeus and his army after they defeated GORGIAS, the governor of Idumea (2 Macc 12:38). Here the place is referred to with a variant Greek spelling, *odollam.*

Bibliography

Albright, W. F. 1924. Researches of the School in Western Judaea. *BASOR* 15: 2–11.

Fritz, V. 1981. The "List of Rehoboam's Fortresses" in 2 Chr 11:5–12: Document from the Time of Josiah. *EI* 15: 46–53.

Naʾaman, N. 1986. Hezekiah's Fortified Cities and the *LMLK* Stamps. *BASOR* 261: 5–21.

Jeffries M. Hamilton

ADULTERY [Heb *niʾupîm;* also *zĕnût, zĕnûnîm,* "whoredom," "harlotry"]. Sexual intercourse between a married or betrothed woman and any man other than her husband. The marital status of the woman's partner is inconsequential since only the married or betrothed woman is bound to fidelity. The infidelity of a married man is not punishable by law but is criticized (Mal 2:14–5; Prov 5:15–20). Biblical law shows similar leniency for sexual relations before a woman's betrothal (Exod 22:15–6; Deut 22:28–29; for possible exceptions [Lev 21:9, Deut 22:13–21], see below).

A. Adultery as a Crime and Sin
B. Adultery and the Betrothed Maiden
C. The Prosecution of Adultery
   1. The Death Penalty
   2. Divorce
   3. Public Stripping of Adulteress
   4. Mutilation
D. Means of Execution
E. Adultery in the ANE
F. Adultery in the Biblical Narrative
G. Adultery in the Prophetic Books
H. Adultery in Wisdom Literature

A. Adultery as a Crime and Sin.

Adultery was a capital crime according to Lev 20:10 and Deut 22:22. Both parties must die. The reasons for the gravity of this crime are never explicitly stated in the OT, yet the patrilineal nature of Israelite society strongly suggests that mistaken paternity would surely be dreaded. If an act of undetected adultery produced offspring, a likely result would be the bequeathal of the family inheritance to this illegitimate heir. This is emphasized by Ben Sira (23:22–23); for a similar thought, see Qoh 6:1–2. Philo remarks that the deceived husband would be like a "blind man knowing nothing of the covert intrigues of the past," yet "forced to cherish the children of his deadliest foe as his own flesh and blood" (*Dec* 24:126–29). Fustel de Coulanges (1956:97) writes ". . . by adultery the series of descendants was broken; the family, even though living men knew it not, became extinct and there was no more divine happiness for the ancestors." While these remarks concern ancient Greece in particular, it is probable that the same could be said regarding Israel. Dread of the extinction of the family line is evident in the Priestly Code, among other places, with its punishment of *karet* (Gen 17:14, Exod 30:33,38, Lev 17:4,9, 20:3,5–6, etc.) and childlessness (Lev 20:20–21). The term *karet,* according to traditional Jewish exegesis, refers to early death and childlessness or the death of one's progeny without issue (see Rashi, Ibn Ezra, and S. D. Luzzato on Gen 17:14). According to the LXX and traditional Jewish law, the issue from an adulterous union, like all prohibited unions, is the *mamzer* or "bastard" of Deut 23:3 (*m. Yebam.* 4:13; *m. Qidd,* 3:12), who is excluded from membership in the assembly of the Lord.

The economic aspect of the crime, i.e. as a simple violation of the husband's property, seems to have played a minor role compared with the social and religious dimensions of the crime. Adultery is the height of treachery (Jer 9:1; Mal 3:5; Ps 50:18) and adulterers are linked with murderers (Job 24:14–15). Adultery is an assault upon the sanctity of the nuclear family, which is divinely ordained (Gen 2:18,24; Prov 18:22). The prohibition of adultery, the 7th commandment of the Decalogue, along with the 5th—"Honor your father and mother . . ."—seek to protect this sacred institution. This may be the reason for the reversal of the 6th and 7th commandments and thus the juxtaposition of the 5th and 7th in the Nash Papyrus, some manuscripts of the LXX, and Philo (*Dec* 24:121).

Both parties to the illicit union are ritually defiled or rendered impure (*ṭmʾ*; Lev 18:20; Num 5:13; Ezek 18:6; 23:13,17; 33:26). The adulterer commits an "abomination" (*tôʿēbâ;* Ezek 22:11), while adultery is included in the Pentateuch's catalog of sexual crimes which defile the land of Israel, causing it to "spew out its inhabitants" (Lev 18:20,24–25). It is considered a "great sin" *(ḥăṭāʾâ gĕdōlâ)* by the biblical author (Gen 20:9) and a "sin against God" (Gen 20:6; 39:9; Ps 51:6).

This characterization of adultery as a "great sin" was not limited to Israel. It is found in texts from Ugarit (Moran 1956: 280–81) and Egypt (Rabinowitz 1956: 73; see *ANET,* 24, where adultery is labeled a "great crime"). In several Akkadian texts, *ḫaṭû,* cognate to Heb *ḥṭʾ,* "to sin," refers specifically to adultery (*CAD* 6:157); *ḫāṭītum* (fem. sing. part. of *ḫaṭû*) indicates an adulteress (*CAD* 6:153).

That the prohibition of adultery was included in the Decalogue, the only direct and unmediated address of YHWH to Israel (Exod 20:19; Deut 4:10; 5:20–21), indicates its grave nature. In accordance with the later conception of the Decalogue as the epitome of biblical law, Saadiah Gaon, followed by Abraham Ibn Ezra and Abarbanel, understood the 7th commandment as inclusive of all sexual acts prohibited in the Torah. While dealt with in the Decalogue and books of Leviticus (20:10) and Deuteronomy (22:22), adultery is neglected in the 4th major law collection of the Pentateuch, the so-called Covenant Code (Exodus 21–23).

B. Adultery and the Betrothed Maiden.

The betrothed maiden is one for whom a bride-price *(mōhar)* has been paid, but who still resides in her father's house awaiting consummation of the marriage (inferred from Exod 22:15–16; Deut 20:7 and comparative material, cf. Code of Hammurabi 130 [*ANET,* 171]; and the Laws of Eshnunna 26 [*ANET*, 162]). She is also subject to the Bible's harsh penalty for adultery. Deut 22:23–24 prescribes death for the betrothed woman who is found having sexual relations with a man "in the city" if their discovery is not prompted by her calls for help; her compliance is therefore assumed.

Deuteronomy's law concerning the slandered newlywed wife (22:13–21) may be another instance of the Bible's equation of betrothal and marriage. She is condemned to death for "whoring in her father's house" (v 21) but this, according to traditional Jewish exegesis, refers to her defloration subsequent to betrothal but before cohabition with her husband, when she still resided in her father's house. If, on the other hand, this law prescribes capital punishment for sexual relations which occurred before the woman's betrothal, Deuteronomy's harsh stand is unique both for the Bible and ancient Near Eastern law. Other laws prescribe a relatively light penalty for the ravisher of the unbetrothed virgin (Exod 22:15–16; Deut 22:28–29; also Code of Hammurabi 130 [*ANET,* 171] and Middle Assyrian Laws 55–56 [*ANET,* 185]). Finkelstein writes that while adultery was treated with the utmost gravity, the rape of an unmarried woman, by contrast, "seems to have been treated as a relatively mild offense, and except for the talionic element in Middle Assyrian Law 55 . . . was considered only an economic injury to the girl's father—or master, where the victim was a slave girl" (1966: 366–67).

According to Lev 19:20, the betrothed (*neherepet,* literally "assigned") slave girl and her lover are not executed because she "has not yet been freed," i.e. the regular penalty for adultery does not apply because she is still a slave and not because her "assignment"/betrothal is anything less than marriage (Milgrom 1977: 44–45): in the Bible, as in the ancient Near East in general, a slave girl is not a legal person and her sexual violation is treated as a transgression of her owner's property for which he would seek compensation, not prosecution (Finkelstein 1966: 360).

C. The Prosecution of Adultery

1. The Death Penalty. Determining the legal reality in ancient Israel for the prosecution and punishment of the adulteress and her partner is problematic. At the close of the law on adultery, the Deuteronomist commands his audience to "sweep away evil from Israel" (Deut 22:22), which suggests that members of the community have the right and obligation to initiate proceedings against known adulterers in their midst. The collective divine punishment envisioned by the legislators of Deuteronomy and the so-called Holiness Code (Leviticus 17–26) make it imperative that transgressors of the law be prosecuted irrespective of the wishes of the offended party (Lev 18:24–30; 26:14–41; Deut 28:15–68). M. Greenberg contends that the law codes' decree of capital punishment was carried out "in all events. There is no question of permitting the husband to mitigate or cancel the punishment. For adultery is not merely a wrong against the husband, it is a sin against God, an absolute wrong" (1960: 12).

Others maintain that in practice, however, the penalty for adultery in Israel was more flexible, and further, that the initiation of proceedings against the offenders was the exclusive right of the husband (Loewenstamm 1962: 55–59; Jackson 1973: 33–34; Yaron 1969: 188, n. 77; McKeating 1979: 62–65). According to this view, Israelite judicial practice would have resembled that of Mesopotamia. While Mesopotamian law codes allow for the death penalty, the injured husband retained the right of pardon (Code of Hammurabi 129 [*ANET,* 171]; Middle Assyrian Law 15 [*ANET,* 181]; Law of Eshnunna 28 [*ANET,* 162] on its face doesn't allow for mitigation, but see Yaron 1969: 188–90).

Greenberg thinks that the biblical law's demand for execution was uncompromising because of the Israelite view that adultery was a sin against God; thus man could not opt to forgo it. Yet ancient Mesopotamia seems to have held a similar view of adultery, i.e. as an offense to the deity (see above; Lambert *BWL,* 119, 131), but its law codes do indeed allow the husband to mitigate the punishment. Perhaps this same dichotomy existed de facto in Israel.

Prov 6:32–35 suggests that execution was the maximum penalty imposed and that the fate of the adulterers was at the husband's discretion. The enraged husband will "show no pity on his day of vengeance; he will not have regard for any ransom." The cuckold, according to Proverbs 6, will not accept ransom *(kōper)* because of his insatiable anger, not because of its prohibition. Num 35:31–32 specifically rules out ransom in the case of homicide but not adultery (in which case it may have been permissable). On the other hand, the compensation mentioned in Proverbs 6 may refer to an illegal payment of money to the husband to avert prosecution; *šoḥad,* the parallel of *kōper* in v 35 suggests this (cf. Exod 23:8; Isa 5:23). Further, the international flavor of the book of Proverbs and scholarship's imperfect understanding of the "foreign woman" pericopes (Proverbs 2 and 5–7; see below) advises against viewing Israelite jurisprudence in the light of Prov 6:32–35.

Job refers to marital infidelity as an *ʿăwōn pĕlîlîm* (31:11), which Speiser (1963: 304) translates as "an assessable transgression" in accordance with his view that all examples of the root *pll* in Hebrew share the underlying concept of "assess." This suggests that the adulterer could compensate the cuckolded husband, who would determine the amount of damages according to his own discretion. Yet this translation appears inaccurate given its context. Job also calls adultery *zimmâ,* a word used regularly for "indecent and disgusting sexual conduct" (Pope, *Job* AB, 203) and a "fire burning down to Abaddon" (31:12). "Assessable transgression," however, suggests the relative mildness of the offense, which can be compensated by payment rather than corporal or capital punishment. Until our understanding of the root *pll* in this verse and its counterparts (Job 31:28 and Deut 32:31) is more certain, the preferred translation remains "criminal iniquity" or "criminal offense," which better conveys the severity of the deed.

Several biblical texts suggest that other measures short of execution were utilized to punish the adulteress.

2. Divorce. The Pharisaic school of Shammai suggested that the legal, biblical term for divorce, *ʿerwat dābār* (Deut 24:1–4), literally "nakedness of a thing," referred to adultery as a ground for such action (*m. Git.* 9:10), but this has been convincingly rejected (Neufeld 1944: 178–89; Lieber, *EncJud* 6: 123–24). Both Jer 3:8 and Hos 2:4 suggest that the adulteress was divorced, but since the former text refers symbolically to the exile of the N kingdom, divorce (Heb *šlḥ,* literally "send off," "dismiss") provides the most appropriate metaphor. Hos 2:4 echoes the ancient Near Eastern formula for divorce, "You are not my wife" (Gordon 1936: 277–80, Yaron 1961: 46–47), although there is some doubt that divorce is intended here because "there would be no basis for all that follows" (Andersen and Freedman *Hosea* AB, 222).

3. Public Stripping of Adulteress. Stripping is mentioned in Hos 2:5, 12; Jer 13:22–26; Ezek 16:37, 39; and 23:26, 29. In all of these cases, the faithless wife who suffers this penalty is a symbol for apostate Israel (cf. Nah 3:5). Stripping, however, may have served as a prelude to execution rather than as an alternative to it (Ezek 16:37–41; Susanna 32). In *m. Soṭa* 1:5 the suspected adulteress is partially stripped before drinking the potion of "bitter waters" (Num 5:11–31).

4. Mutilation. Mutilation of the adulteress is mentioned

in Ezek 23:25, but this should not be viewed as an Israelite practice since the prophet himself states, "and they (Oholibah's former lovers) shall judge you according to their law" (v 24; cf. Middle Assyrian Law 15 [*ANET*, 181]).

It should be noted that the biblical texts alluding to divorce, public stripping, and mutilation contain prophetic metaphors and hence they are not dependable sources for actual Israelite legal practice. In Ezek 16:39 and 23:26, 29, personified Jerusalem is stripped by her lovers, not her husband. In Hos 2:5, Jer 13:26, and Akkadian sources, the offending wife is stripped by her husband or his family to symbolize the withdrawal of her maintenance (Gordon 1936: 277; Greenberg, *Ezekiel* AB, 287). Apparent in Ezekiel 16 and 23, then, is the intrusion of the tenor of the metaphor, Israel's pillaging by foreign armies.

Obviously the de facto procedure for the prosecution of adultery is uncertain. In the biblical law of murder, the prosecution and execution of the murderer is left in the hands of the wronged individual, the kinsman of the deceased or "redeemer of blood" (Num 35:19–21, Deut 19:6, 12), yet the Bible's legislation seeks to regulate this ancient practice and transfer some responsibility to the public domain with the appointment of the refuge cities and the participation of public officials to distinguish between the intentional and unwitting manslayer (Exod 21:13–14; Num 35:9–29; Deut 19:1–13). After all, if the redeemer shirks his responsibility or kills an unintentional manslayer (the intention of *dām nāqî*, "blood of the innocent" of Deut 19:10), all Israel would be subject to bloodguilt (Num 35:33–34; Deut 19:10). Similarly, the criminalization of adultery in Israel was an expected development. An act which transgressed Israel's covenent with YHWH, the basic principles of which are found in the Decalogue, endangered the entire community, and so it was only natural that the prosecution of adulterers be transformed from a right which individuals may forgo to a duty incumbent upon all members of the community.

D. Means of Execution.

The method of execution for the guilty pair is not stated explicitly in either Lev 20:10 or Deut 22:22. The unchastity of the betrothed virgin of Deut 22:24 is punished by stoning, as is the premature defloration of the newlywed bride in Deut 22:13–21. Ezek 16:40 and 23:47 list stoning and stabbing among the punishments for wayward Jerusalem, yet here the crime is compounded by idolatry and infanticide.

The LXX of Susanna, v 62, mentions flinging those who accused the heroine of adultery into a ravine (see Deut 19:16–19); this practice coincides with the rabbinic mode of "stoning"–casting the criminal into a rocky ravine rather than casting stones at the criminal (*m. Sanh.* 6:4). The Talmudic means of execution for adultery was strangulation; this according to the exegetical rule that anytime the death penalty was decreed but the means not specified in the biblical text, strangling was intended (Sipra, Qedoshim 10:8; *b. Talm. Sanh.* 52b; according to R. Josiah, this was because it was the most merciful).

Burning is mentioned in Genesis 38 as the penalty for Tamar, whose status was that of a married woman (because she was promised to her *levir* Shelah). While fornication for the lay Israelite is not penalized in the law codes (see above on Deut 22:13–21), a priest's daughter who "defiles herself through harlotry" is burned to death because of the extraordinary demand of holiness for the priesthood (Lev 21:9).

Both parties, when known, are executed (Lev 20:10; Deut 22: 21, 22). According to A. Phillips (1970: 110), the execution of the adulteress in addition to the adulterer is an innovation of the Deuteronomic reform, but this is based on his uncommon notion that the Decalogue was addressed only to male Israelites and therefore only they were penalized. In the Bible's decree of the death sentence in Lev 20:10b, a singular verb, *yûmat,* is found with the compound subject, "the adulterer and the adulteress," which suggests to some that the latter is an addition (Noth, *Leviticus* OTL, 150; Phillips 1970: 111). Yet this grammatical irregularity is common enough in Biblical Hebrew (GKC, 145o), while Fishbane attributes it to the fact that the penalty clause *môt yûmat* is a frozen technical term (1974: 25, n.2). The equal punishment of both parties is typical of Mesopotamian law (Code of Hammurabi 129 [*ANET*, 171]; Middle Assyrian Law 13 [*ANET*, 181]; Hittite Law 197–98 [*ANET*, 196]). This serves to preclude the possibility that two of the involved parties conspired against the third. The phrase *gam šĕnêham,* "one as well as the other," (Deut 22:22), echoes this demand for equal justice.

E. Adultery in the ANE.

Several features distinguish Israel's laws on adultery from those of her neighbors.

1. Hittite Law 197 (*ANET*, 196) and perhaps Middle Assyrian Law 15 (*ANET*, 181; see Driver and Miles 1975: 45–50) allow the cuckolded husband to execute the couple with impunity if he finds them *in flagranti delicto,* i.e., in the very act of adultery. The biblical laws of jurisprudence seem to forbid this (Deut 17:6–7, 19:15, Num 35:30).

2. The paramour's knowledge about or ignorance of the woman's marital status is taken into account. If he was not aware that she was married, he would be acquitted (Finkelstein 1966: 369–70; Middle Assyrian Laws 13–14 [*ANET*, 181]). Biblical laws make no such allowance. Gen 20:3 suggests that in YHWH's eyes, the guilt of adultery is absolute.

3. The Mesopotamian law codes are more comprehensive, dealing with other matters tangential to adultery. For example, all of the major law codes deal with the cohabitation of a married woman with a second man in the event of desertion by her husband or his prolonged captivity in a foreign land (Laws of Eshnunna 29–30 [*ANET*, 162]; Code of Hammurabi 134–36 [*ANET*, 171]; Middle Assyrian Law 36 [*ANET*, 183]). Only later Jewish law takes up this issue (for sources, see Schereschewsky, *EncJud* 2: 429–33). Akkadian laws also deal with the accusation of adultery by a third party (Middle Assyrian Law 17–18 [*ANET*, 181]; Code of Hammurabi 132 [*ANET*, 171]; the Bible deals only with accusation brought by the woman's husband [Num 5:11–31; Deut 22:13–21]); and pandering as incidental to adultery (Middle Assyrian Law 22–24 [*ANET*, 181–82]).

F. Adultery in Biblical Narrative.

The theme of adultery is found several times in the book of Genesis. Both Abraham and Isaac try to pass off their wives as their sisters, allowing them to be taken (or nearly taken) by foreigners (Genesis 12:10–20; 20; 26:1–11). Both patriarchs assume that the people of Gerar and Egypt took the "great sin" of adultery very seriously and would rather make widows out of Sarah and Rebecca than incur the guilt of adultery (David Kimchi). YHWH's punishment for adultery in all three chapters is collective (12:17; 20:7, 17; 26:10).

In Genesis 38, Judah sentences his daughter-in-law Tamar to be burned for apparent adultery, i.e., having sexual relations while waiting for her *levir* to come of age. In Genesis 39 is found another false accusation of adultery, here in the guise of the attempted rape of a married woman, which is treated alongside uncoerced adultery in the law codes (Deut 22:23–27; Law of Eshnunna 26; Code of Hammurabi 130; Hittite Law 197–98).

King David committed adultery with Bathsheba, daughter of Eliam and wife of Uriah the Hittite, one of his faithful warriors (2 Samuel 11; 23:39). David's guilt is compounded by his successful plot to have Uriah killed in battle. This was necessary to prevent the disclosure of the king's role in Bathsheba's pregnancy. His fear was prompted certainly by the expected popular censure of his deed (Prov 6:33) but perhaps also by the application of Israel's law even to the king himself (Deut 17:19; cf. 1 Kings 21, where the limitation of royal power in Israel is apparent).

G. Adultery in the Prophetic Books.

The prophets frequently indicted Israel for marital infidelity (Hos 4:2,13–14; Jer 5:7; 7:9; 13:27; Ezek 22:11; 33:26; Isa 57:3; Mal 3:5). Jeremiah specifically condemned the prophets of his day for this act of treachery (23:14; 29:23).

Adultery is used as a metaphor for apostasy in several prophetic books (Hosea 1–3, Jer 2:23–25; 3:1–13, Ezekiel 16; 23). This symbolism is apt because both represent the betrayal of exclusive fidelity. Raw material for the creation of this symbolism is found in the Pentateuch. Israel is commanded to revere only YHWH (Exod 20:3; 22:19; 34:14; etc.) and the formula used to express their covenant relationship is similar to the "solemn words" for marriage in ANE texts (Lev 26:12; Deut 26:17–18; 29:12; see Yaron 1961: 46–47; Muffs 1965). YHWH is "jealous" or "impassioned" *(qannāʾ)* where Israel is concerned (Exod 20:5; 34:14) and idolatry, specifically calf worship, becomes Israel's "great sin" (Exod 32:21; 2 Kgs 17:21). Israel's worship of other gods is called "whoring" (Exod 34:16; Deut 31:16). It has also been suggested that the promiscuous behavior supposedly typical of the Canaanite fertility cult lies at the background of this motif.

Hosea is the first prophet explicitly to analogize apostasy and adultery. Some suggest that this notion first came to him as the result of his wife Gomer's infidelity; YHWH's command to take a "wife of harlotry" (1:2), then, was written after the prophet's domestic adversities and conveys his understanding of these events as determined by God. Others discount the historicity of Hosea 1–2 because of the obscure and allegorical nature of these chapters, while in Hosea 3 the promiscuous woman is probably not the prophet's wife. Cohen argues that Hosea's perception may be an outgrowth of the Israelite religion itself—a sort of "midrash" based on the commonly held analogy in Israel of marriage and covenant—rather than the result of an experience unique to Hosea (1966: 9–11).

Jeremiah 3:1–5, uses the legal form of Deut 24:1–4 to illustrate the injurious effects of Israel's "whoring with many lovers." Verses 6–13 tell the tale of two sisters, "Rebel Israel" and "Faithless Judah," both of whom are married to YHWH. While the former is divorced for adultery (the exile of the northern kingdom), the latter repents only halfheartedly (a reference to Josiah's reform, 2 Kings 22–23), and then proceeds (v 13)—despite YHWH's pleas to repent—to "spread her legs to strangers under every leafy tree" (Rashi's paraphrase of the difficult *wattĕpazzĕrî ʾet-dĕrākayik*; others render the vague "you scattered your ways"). Several of Jeremiah's other references to adultery may also be references to idolatry (5:7; 7:9; 13:22).

Ezekiel devotes more verses to this motif than either of his two predecessors. Indeed, chap. 16, with 63 verses, is the longest in his book, yet its excessiveness is not limited to quantity. Jerusalem here is a murderous nymphomaniac who makes even Sodom (here her "sister") seem righteous. In chap. 23, Ezekiel in 49 verses reworks in a similarly extreme fashion the motif of Jer 3:6–12, YHWH's marriage to two sisters.

H. Adultery in Wisdom Literature.

The Book of Proverbs, chaps. 2 and 5–7, warns against consorting with the adulteress, labeled also "a woman of evil" (6:24), but most often a "foreign" or "strange" woman (2:16; 5:3,20; 6:24; 7:5). She is dressed like a harlot (7:10), although is not identified as one (6:26 contrasts the harlot to the adulteress). Only in Proverbs 5 is the correspondence between an adulteress and the "foreign woman" uncertain since only her intended victim is presented as married (vv 15–20). She lures foolish men to her home with crafty words (2:16; 5:3; 6:24; 7:14–20). Associating with her leads to "death" (2:18–19; 5:5; 7:26–27), which may be a reference to judicial execution, premature death at the hands of God, or perhaps spiritual demise. She has forgotten the "covenant of her God" (2:17), a reference either to the Decalogue, which prohibits adultery, or perhaps to her marriage vows.

Her characterization as "foreign" or "strange" is explained in several ways: (1) as a dissolute woman, she places herself outside the circle of proper relations or outside the norms of the community (Snijders 1954: 88–100); (2) *zār* here as in other places refers to a third party or one other than the members of a specific group, family, or tribe (Deut 25:5; 1 Kgs 3:18; Prov 5:10, 17); (3) she is indeed a foreigner. Egyptian wisdom warns against consorting with a "woman from abroad," traveling without her husband and waiting to ensnare the naive youth (*ANET,* 420). Bostrom argues that she is a non-Israelite devotee of a fertility goddess and that her sexual activity has a cultic function (1935: 103–55); or (4) she symbolizes either a Canaanite goddess and her cult, non-Israelite religion in general, or "the seductions of this world" (so Saadiah Gaon); most recently Fishbane (1974: 44) labeled Prov 6:20–35 an "inner biblical midrash on the Decalogue" in which the foreign woman symbolizes "the seduction of false wisdom" in direct contrast to divine wisdom in Proverbs 8 and 9.

Prov 30:20 underlines the nonchalance of the adulterous woman who euphemistically "eats, wipes her mouth," and then says, "I have done no wrong." According to Job, the adulterer wears a disguise to conceal his identity and, like the murderer and robber, waits for the cover of night to commit his crime (24:13–16). In his oath of piety, Job curses himself with his own wife's infidelity if "his heart was ravished by the wife of his neighbor and he lay in wait at his door" (31:9–12).

Bibliography

Bostrom, G. 1935. *Proverbia Studien: die Weisheit und das fremde Weib in Spr. 1–9.* LUÅ N.F. I, 30. Lund.

Cohen, G. 1966. The Song of Songs and the Jewish Religious Mentality. Pp. 1–21 in *The Samuel Friedland Lectures, 1960–66.* New York.

Driver, G. R., and Miles, J. C. 1975. *The Assyrian Laws.* Oxford.

Finkelstein, J. J. 1966. Sex Offenses in Sumerian Law. *JAOS* 86: 355–72.

Fishbane, M. 1974. Accusations of Adultery: A Study of Law and Scribal Practices in Num 5:11–31. *HUCA* 45: 25–45.

Fustel de Coulanges, Numa Denis. 1956. *The Ancient City.* Garden City, NY.

Gordon, C. 1936. Hosea 2:4–5 in the Light of New Semitic Inscriptions. *ZAW* 54: 277–80.

Greenberg, M. 1960. Some Postulates of Biblical Criminal Law. Pp. 5–28 in *Yehezkel Kaufmann Jubilee Volume,* ed. M. Haran. Jerusalem.

Jackson, B. 1973. Reflections of Biblical Criminal Law. *JJS* 24: 8–38.

Kornfeld, W. 1950. L'Adultere dans L'Orient Antique. *RB* 57: 92–109.

Loewenstamm, S. 1962. The Laws of Adultery and Murder in Biblical and Mesopotamian Law. *Beth Mikra* 13: 55–59 (in Hebrew).

———. 1964. The Laws of Adultery and Murder in the Bible. *Beth Mikra* 8–9: 77–78 (in Hebrew).

McKeating, H. 1979. Sanctions against Adultery. *JSOT* 11: 57–72.

Milgrom, J. 1976. *Cult and Conscience.* Leiden.

———. 1977. The Betrothed Slave Girl, Lev 19:20–22. *ZAW* 89: 43–50.

Moran, W. L. 1956. The Scandal of the "Great Sin" at Ugarit. *JNES* 18:280–81.

Muffs, Y. 1965. Studies in Biblical Law, IV: The Antiquity of P. *Lectures at the Jewish Theological Seminary of America.* New York (mimeographed).

Neufeld, E. 1944. *Ancient Hebrew Marriage Laws.* New York and London.

Phillips, A. 1970. *Ancient Israel's Criminal Law.* Oxford.

———. 1981. Another Look at Adultery. *JSOT* 20: 3–25.

Rabinowitz, J. J. 1956. The "Great Sin" in Ancient Egyptian Marriage Contracts. *JNES* 18:73.

Snijders, L. A. 1954. The Meaning of *zar* in the Old Testament. *OTS* 10: 1–154.

Speiser, E. 1963. The Root *pll* in Hebrew. *JBL* 82: 301–6.

Wenham, G. J. 1972. *Betulah:* "A Girl of Marriageable Age." *VT* 22: 326–48.

Yaron, R. 1961. *Introduction to the Law of the Aramaic Papyri.* Oxford.

———. 1969. *The Laws of Eshnunna.* Jerusalem.

Elaine Adler Goodfriend

ADUMMIM (PLACE) [Heb *ʾădummîm*]. After the conquest described in Joshua 6–12, Joshua divided the land by lot among the tribes of Israel. Joshua 15 describes the lot which fell to the tribe of Judah and gives a description of the boundaries of Judah. The N boundary (v 5) ran from the mouth of the Jordan River, where it empties into the Dead Sea, to Debir from the Valley of Achor and northward, turning toward Gilgal, which is opposite the ascent, *ma'aleh* of Adummim—which is on the S side of the valley (v 8). In Josh 18:11, we find a description of the lot falling to the tribe of Benjamin. The S boundary (v 15) goes from Kiriath-jearim to the Dead Sea and the mouth of the Jordan River (v 19). In 18:17 we read that the border goes from Enshemesh *(ʿên šemeš)* to Geliloth which is opposite the ascent of Adummim (LXX *Aithamin*).

The root means "red" (BDB, 10) and is in the plural form so one might translate it "double red" or "Big Red." It has also been translated "red places." Smith (1974:180–81) thinks the name is from the "curious red streaks" which appear from time to time on the stone. These in turn provided meaning for later names like the Red Khan (inn), Khan el-Ahmar (M.R. 181133), one of the sites of the Inn of the Good Samaritan (Luke 10:34). The Arabic name for a nearby hill and fortress NE or the Khan is Talʾat ed-Dumm, the ascent of blood, which probably also refers to the red marl rock formations, rather than the more pietistic derivation of the wounded traveler of the Good Samaritan story, or Jerome's reference that the pass was the way of the robbers.

The fortress was the Crusaders' Chastel or Citerne Rouge built by the Templars to protect the pilgrims going down to the Jordan River to the site of Jesus' baptism. The Crusaders also called the place la Tour Maledoin, perhaps following Eus. (*Onomast.* 260–340), who refers to the place as Maledomni, i.e., *maʾale-adum-mim,* the ascent of Adummim. It was already a fortress in an earlier day. Eus. refers to a castle. Jerome (342–420) lists Adummim as a stronghold midway between Jerusalem (2500 ft. above sea level) and Jericho (770 feet below sea level). It is ca. 6 m SW of Jericho. Josephus (*JW* 4.8.3 § 474) describes the Jericho-Jerusalem distance as 18 Roman mi. 150 stadioi. He claims the Tenth Legion (Fretensis) came this way for the seige of Jerusalem (5.2.3 §69–70). The road itself is the middle one of three ancient caravan or trade routes from the Jordan Valley to the hill country. It follows the Wadi Qelt up through this pass at Adummim to Jerusalem (the N one goes to Bethel and the S one to Mar Saba). From Adummim, Jericho can be seen in one direction and the Mt. of Olives at Jerusalem in the other.

The name "Adummim" appears in the lists of Thutmose III and Sheshonk I and again in Papyrus Anastasi I, the Egyptian letter of Hori (*ANET* 242, 475–79). The latter asks sarcastic questions of a would-be scribe named Amen-em-Opet. These refer to locations in Canaan such as Shechem, Hazor, Adummim, Beth-shan, the Jordan River, etc. (*ANET* 477). However, these references may be to a different Adummim. Aharoni (*LBHG,* 61) identifies this Adummim with Adami-Nekeb while S. Ahituve considers it Tel Qarnei Hittin, the Horns of Hittin (quoted by Naʾaman, 1986: 128 n.23).

Bibliography

Helmbold, A. K. 1975. Adummim. 1.66. *The Zondervan Pictorial Encyclopedia of the Bible,* 5 vols., ed. M. C. Tenney and S. Barabas. Grand Rapids.

Naʾaman, N. 1986. *Borders and Districts in Biblical Geographical Lists.* Jerusalem.
Smith, G. A. 1974. *The Historical Geography of the Holy Land,* 25th ed. London.

HENRY O. THOMPSON

ADVERSARY. See SATAN.

ADVOCATE [Gk *paraklētos*]. Originally *paraklētos* had a passive sense, "one who is called alongside [to someone's aid]," and so was rendered in Latin as *"advocatus."* In the NT it is used in an active sense (as is "advocate" in current English): "one who appears on another's behalf," "mediator," "intercessor," or "helper." In 1 John 2:1, Jesus Christ is referred to as our *paraklētos* who intercedes with (God) the Father on behalf of sinners. Some English versions paraphrase the word: "one to plead our cause" *(NEB),* "someone who pleads . . . on our behalf" (GNB), or "one who speaks in our defense" *(NIV).*

In the Gospel of John (14:16, 26; 15:26; 16:7), *paraklētos* is identified with the Holy Spirit and is variously translated as the "Comforter" *(KJV, ASV),* "Counselor" *(RSV, NIV),* "Advocate" *(JB, NEB),* and "Helper" *(GNB, NASB).* R. Brown (*John 13–21* AB, pp. 637, 649, 685, 703; note also appendix V), recognizing that no single English word covers all the meanings of *paraklētos,* employs a virtual transliteration, "Paraclete" (see also *NAB* and *NJB*).

HERBERT G. GRETHER

AENEAS (PERSON) [Gk *Aineas*]. A man at Lydda, bedridden with paralysis, whom Peter was instrumental in healing (Acts 9:32–35). This person is not otherwise attested, though the name itself is fairly common and is found in Greek classical writers and in Josephus (*Ant* 14.10.22).

HERBERT G. GRETHER

AENON (PLACE) [Gk *Ainon*]. John the Baptist baptized at this well-watered site along the Jordan River. According to Eus. (Onomast 40.1), this site is 6 miles S of Roman Scythopolis *(Beth-shean),* the capital of a Decapolis territory. John 3:23 identifies a nearby Salim (Salumias), a description in agreement with Eus. Aenon, perhaps from Ar *ʾain* spring, is appropriate for an area near Tell Sheikh Selim which has several springs. Wadi Farʿah qualifies Nablus, E of Shechem, as yet another possibility for Aenon (Albright 1954). Ironically, modern Salim, 3.5 miles E of Nablus, is also a contending site (Albright 1924). But the ancient location of Salim (Gen 14:18; Jer 48:5) was nearer to the aforementioned wadi Farʿah than the modern site bearing the same name.

A Madeba mosaic map (ca. 560 A.D.). from Jordan complicates a positive location of Aenon. The map, on a Madeba church floor, shows two Aenon sites. One of the two sites positions Aenon W of the Jordan and may be synonymous with modern Salim, mentioned above. The mapmaker identifies this vaguely placed site as "near Salim," and a row of bluish-green cubes. Atheria (ca. 385 A.D.) qualifies Aenon as in a garden with a pool or spring, perhaps represented by the colored cubes. The second map site is N of the Dead Sea, on the E side of the Jordan, yet S of the first map site. The second site, near a hill and a spring, may also be the hill of Elijah, i.e., where he ascended to heaven.

Bibliography

Albright, W. F. 1954. Recent Discoveries in Palestine and the Gospel of St. John. Pp. 153–55 in *The Background of the New Testament and its Eschatology,* ed. W. D. Davies and D. Daube. Cambridge.
———. 1924. Some Observations Favoring the Palestinian Origin of The Gospel of John. *HTR* 17:193–94.

JERRY A. PATTENGALE

AESORA (PLACE) [Gk *Aisōra*]. A site mentioned in the book of Judith, whose exact location is unknown (Jdt 4:4). It forms part of the list of towns N of Jerusalem called upon to defend the city from attack by HOLOFERNES. The Greek name may be a translation of the Hebrew Hazor (Heb *ḥāṣôr*) or Hebrew Jazer (Heb *yaʿzēr*; see HAZOR; JAZER). If it is a translation of biblical Hazor, there are five cities in the Hebrew Bible with this name (Josh 11:1; Josh 15:23; Josh 15:25; Neh 11:33; Jer 49:28). Of these five, the two likeliest candidates for identification are the Hazor in Josh 11:1, located 10 miles N of the Sea of Galilee (modern Tell el-Qedah), or the Hazor in Neh 11:33, a town located in Benjaminite territory (modern Kh. Hazzūr). The likelier identification is with biblical Jazer, a fortified city in Gilead (Num 21:32, 32:35), which was disputed among the Israelites, Ammonites, and Moabites. It has been identified by Avi-Yonah and Aharoni (*MBA,* 179, map 211) with Kh. es-Sar (M.R. 228150), located 7 miles SW of Philadelphia in Transjordan, and thus in the line called for by the book of Judith, between Samaria and Jerusalem. However, given the genre of the book of Judith, it is possible that the name is entirely fictitious.

SIDNIE ANN WHITE

ʿAFFULA, EL- (M.R. 177223). The remains of ancient ʿAffula are located within the modern town of that name, on the N slopes of the hill of Moreh in the heart of the Jezreel Valley. Little of the mound survives, but its occupation is known to extend from the mid-4th millennium through the Roman period, with Crusader and Ayyubid remains attested as well.

The name apparently derives from early Semitic *ʿōpel,* or "citadel." The site may be mentioned in the Egyptian Execration texts of the 19th century B.C., and again in the well-known list of Thutmose III in the 15th century B.C. In the Israelite period, ʿAffula would have been reckoned as one of the "daughters" of Megiddo (Josh 17:11). It may be identified with Arbela of Eusebius' *Onomasticon* (14.20) and with Afel of the medieval period.

ʿAffula was excavated by E. L. Sukenik in 1926 and 1931; again in 1937 by Sukenik and N. Avigad; and then in 1950–51 by I. Ben-Dor and M. Dothan. These excavations, however, were little more than scattered soundings and clearance of tombs, and no final reports have appeared.

Stratum X belongs to the Late Chalcolithic and EB I (mid-late 4th millennium B.C.). The remains were mostly hearth and pits/silos, with pottery of the gray-burnished "Esdraelon" type marking the latest occupation. Stratum IX, later in EB I, with band-slipped wares, had crude house foundations. After a gap, Stratum VIII represented a reoccupation in EB III; few building remains were found, but the characteristic KHIRBET KERAK WARE appears. Stratum VII belongs to EB IV (ca. 2400–2000 B.C.). Subrectangular dwellings with ovens were found, together with typical large storejars, with "folded envelope" ledge handles.

Strata VI–V belong to the MB, spanning perhaps the entire period ca. 2000–1500 B.C. A planned settlement revealed streets, courtyards, domestic dwellings, pits/silos, pottery kilns, and several dozen intermural tombs.

Late Bronze I was not attested, but Stratum IV belongs to LB II (ca. 1400–1200 B.C.). Little but tombs were found, some containing Mycenaean and Cypriot imported pottery.

Stratum IIIB-A was the only Iron Age settlement, belonging to Iron I, and following closely in the ceramic tradition of Stratum IV. Phase IVB contained some Philistine Bichrome ware; phase IIIA was apparently destroyed in the mid-11th century B.C., perhaps during the time of Saul. A few large courtyard houses marked the first phase, as well as granaries, a kiln, and a few tombs. Only a few Iron II remains were noted, including a few sherds of Samaria ware.

Stratum II dates to the Roman period (2d–4th centuries A.D.), and Stratum I to the Crusader and Ayyubid period (11th–13th centuries A.D.).

Bibliography

Dothan, M. 1955. The Excavations at ᶜAfula. *ᶜAtiqot* 1: 19–70 (in Hebrew).

———. 1975. ᶜAfula. *EAEHL* 1: 32–36.

Sukenik, E. L. 1936. Late Chalcolithic Pottery from ᶜAffuleh. *PEFQS*, 150–54.

———. 1948. Archaeological Investigations at ᶜAffula. *JPOS* 21: 1–79.

William G. Dever

AGABUS (PERSON) [Gk *Hagabos*].

A Christian prophet from Judea (Acts 11:27–30 and 21:10–14). In 11:27–30 Agabus goes with a group of other prophets from Jerusalem to Antioch and prophesies that there would be a famine "over all the world." Luke states that the prophecy was fulfilled during the reign of Emperor Claudius (41–54 C.E.). Although no worldwide famine occurred during the reign of Claudius, there are references to isolated famines throughout the Roman Empire during this time (Tac. *Ann.* 12.43; Seut. *Claud.* 18.2; Dio Cas. 60.11). According to Josephus (*Ant* 20.2.5 §49–53; 20.5.2 §100–1), there was a famine in Palestine during the procuratorship of Tiberius Alexander (46–48 C.E.), during which Queen Helena of Adiabene bought grain from Egypt and figs from Cyprus and distributed them in Jerusalem. Agabus's prophecy stirred the Christians in Antioch to send a collection by Paul and Barnabas to aid the Judean Christians (cf. Eus. *Hist. Eccl.* 2.3.4).

In 21:10–14 Agabus goes to Caesarea and delivers a prophecy accompanied by a vivid symbolic act in the fashion of the classical prophets (e.g. Isaiah 20; Jer 13:1–11; Ezekiel 4–5). He takes Paul's girdle and binds his own hands and feet and prophesies that the Jews would bind Paul and hand him over to the Romans if he proceeded to Jerusalem. His prophecy was not strictly fulfilled, for although the Jews did seize Paul, they did not hand him over to the Romans. Rather the Romans rescued Paul from the Jews and bound him in chains in order to protect him from the Jewish rabble (21:33). In any case, Luke clearly holds the Jews responsible for delivering Paul to the Romans (28:17).

Late tradition identifies Agabus as one of the Seventy and a martyr at Antioch.

Bibliography

Lake, K. 1933. The Famine in the Time of Claudius. Pp. 452–55 in *The Beginnings of Christianity*, vol. 5. Ed. F. J. Foakes Jackson and K. Lake. London.

Patsch, H. 1972. "Die Prophetie des Agabus." *TZ* 28: 228–32.

JoAnn Ford Watson

AGAG (PERSON) [Heb *ʾăgag*].

The name of two kings of the Amalekites (Num 24:7 and 1 Sam 15:8–9, 20, 32–33), and perhaps a traditional or common name of all their kings—like Pharaoh in Egypt and perhaps Abimelech (Achish) among the Philistines. Though the etymological meaning is not certain, it is usually taken from Akkadian *agāgum*, "to get angry, furious." The Greek name "Ogygos," which appears to be Semitic in origin, has been derived from *ʾāgag*, "to flame" (Astour 1964: 200).

1. The name of a (legendary?) king mentioned by Balaam in an archaic poetic context, "his king shall be higher than Agag" (Num 24:7). Its usage here appears to be a wordplay on the term *gag*, "roof," which is found in Ugaritic and South Canaanite (EA 287:37). The context suggests a mythological character, which is rendered by LXX as *Gōg*, a figure that later leads the evil forces that rise up to war against Yahweh in a climactic eschatological battle (Ezekiel 38–39). In Num 24:23 the term "Gog" (or more frequently "Og") is inserted by LXX in an obscure passage, which has been rendered (Albright *YGC* 14, n. 40):

> And he saw Gog and delivered an oracle about him, saying:
> The isles shall be gathered from the north,
>   And ships from the farthest sea;
> And they shall harass Aššur and harass ᶜEber,
>   But he (Gog) will perish forever.

2. The name of a king of the Amalekites whom Saul spared, contrary to a sacred ban imposed by Samuel in which the Amalekites were devoted to destruction because of their opposition to Israel at the time of the Exodus (1 Sam 15:2–3). Samuel's inference of perpetual war against the Amalekites seems to reflect the content of another fragment of archaic Hebrew poetry concerning Amalek

(Exod 17:16) which has been rendered (Christensen 1975: 48):

For the hand is on Yahweh's banner;
The battle belongs to Yahweh,
Against Amalek from generation to generation.

In the Holy War tradition of ancient Israel, Amalek apparently played the role of archenemy. It would appear that Agag was the name of the king of Amalek within a body of archaic poetry, the "Song of the Wars of Yahweh" (cf. Num 21:14).

W. R. Smith (1927: 491–92) has argued that Saul spared Agag in order that he might be sacrificed according to an ancient Arab pattern for victorious warriors on their return from a foray; and that Samuel actually accomplished this offering by slaying Agag "before Yahweh" in Gilgal. In the biblical story, Saul's disobedience at this point occasioned his final break with Samuel.

The term "Agag" appears also in the book of Esther as the gentilic name of Haman (ch. 3:1, 10; 8:3, 5; and 9:24). Haupt (1906: 8, 12–14, 42 [nn. 111, 112]) argued that the designation "Agagite" here, perhaps a Hebrew adaptation of the epithet Gagite (*Gōgaios,* "northern barbarian"), was used to indicate to a Hebrew what "Macedonian" would to a Greek; and that it meant "Amalekite" in the sense of a contemptible, hateful person, but not implying that Haman actually had any genealogical tie with Amalek. However, Jewish tradition makes much of the connection, arguing that Samuel's execution of Agag came one day too late. It was during that brief interval between Saul's sparing of Agag and his execution by Samuel that he became the progenitor of Haman (*Meg.* 13a, *Targ. Sheni*; to Esther 4:13). See also AGAGITE.

Bibliography

Astour, M. 1964. Greek Names in the Semitic World and Semitic Names in the Greek World. *JNES* 23: 193–201.

Christensen, D. L. 1975. *Transformations of the War Oracle in Old Testament Prophecy.* HDS 3. Missoula.

Haupt, P. 1906. *Purim.* Baltimore.

Smith, W. R. 1927. *Lectures on the Religion of the Semites.* 3d ed. New York.

Winckler, H. 1898. Gog. *Altorientalische Forschungen* 2. Leipzig.

DUANE L. CHRISTENSEN

AGAGITE (PERSON) [Heb *ʾăgāgî*]. A gentilic name identifying HAMAN, the enemy of the Jews in the book of Esther (Esth 3:1, 10; 8:3, 5; 9:24). By identifying Haman as an offspring of "Agag the descendant of Amalek" (Aram *ʾgg br ʿmlq*), the Targums elaborate on the MT, and Josephus supports this identification by referring to Haman as "the Amalekite" (*Ant* 11.6.5, 12). However, the LXX and its variant manuscripts prefer Gk *bougaion, gōgaion,* or *makedōn.* In the Latin witnesses, support is found for the MT (Vg. *Agag*), as well as for Gk *bougaion* (OL *bagogeum*).

Such diverse readings indicate that the ancient translators, like modern scholars, were attempting to interpret the term "Agagite." Of the modern scholars who support the MT reading, Paton (*Esther* ICC, 194) represents the position well. He suggests that the term "Agagite" literarily identified Haman as a descendant of Agag the king of the Amalekites, Israel's ancient and continual antagonists (Exod 18:8–16; Num 24:7; Deut 25:17–19; 1 Samuel 15). Based on this premise, other scholars point out that the term "Agagite" fits the typology of "the enemy" of the Jews, which may account for LXX variants like *bougaion, gōgaion,* and *makedōn,* since these were "the enemy" at different periods of time (Altheim and Stiehl 1963: 212; Ringgren and Weiser *Esther* ATD, 127; Moore *Esther* AB, 35; Stein 1982: 569). Other suggestions are that Agagite may be a nickname for Haman (Simons 1959: 485), possibly an official title like "Pharaoh" (Keil *Chronicles, Ezra, Nehemiah, Esther* BKAT, 632), or simply an Elamite name *A/Ag-ga-ga* (Zadok 1984).

Of those who emend the MT, Haupt (1908: 123) posits an original Heb **gʾgy,* "Gagean or northern barbarian," from Codex Vaticanus' *Gōgaios* (Esth 3:1; see LXX *gōg* in Num 24:7), and also based on the correspondence of spelling in Gk and Heb. He thus identifies Haman as a northern enemy of the Persians, rather than of the Jews. Lewy (1939: 134), viewing the LXX *bougaion* as a transmutation of the West-Iranian word *baga,* "god," proposes an original Heb **bwgy,* "Bougaite or worshipper of Baga," identifying Haman as a devotee of the god Mithra (Esth 3:1; Add Esth 12:6). He contends that a Babylonian story about the persecution of Marduk worshipers ("Mardukians") by their enemies, the "Bougaions" (worshipers of Mithra), was adapted to the Jewish experience by supplying the appellative "Agagite." In Homeric literature Gk *bougaion* means "braggart" (*Il.* 13.824; *Od.* 18.79), but this seemingly has no relation to the LXX use of the term. Finally, based on evidence also cited by Lewy (above), and on the assumption that Gk *bougaios* and *bagaios* are the same, Hoschander (1923: 23) emends Heb *hʾggy* to read *hbgy,* "the Bagoan." However, unlike Lewy, he views this not as the name of a deity, but as a Persian gentilic name.

On literary grounds, it can be seen that the term "Agagite" functions on more than one level. As the textual variants cited by most scholars suggest (see e.g. Paton *Esther* ICC, Moore *Esther* AB), the term "Agagite" harkens back to the story of Agag (1 Samuel 15), with which the Esther story has some parallels (McKane 1961: 260), especially since Mordecai, like Saul (1 Sam 9:1–2), was a "son of Kish, a Benjaminite" (Esth 2:5). Within the book of Esther, Haman's role as the sole enemy of the Jews is indicated by the term "Agagite" (3:10; cf. 8:1; 9:10; see Clines 1984: 14, 42). Definition of the term "Agagite" is provided by parallel occurrences of other appellatives with the name "Haman" (Jones 1978: 40): the most complete identification of Haman, "Haman, the Agagite, the son of Hammedatha, the enemy of (all) the Jews" (3:10; 9:24), can be abbreviated by omitting one or the other of the appellatives. Therefore, in Esth 3:1 and 8:5 Haman is identified simply as "the Agagite," whereas in 9:10 the only label applied to him is "the enemy of the Jews." Also, the identification "Haman, the enemy of the Jews" (8:1) is complemented by "Haman, the Agagite" (8:3). These variant identifications of Haman in parallel verses in Esther clearly make "Agagite" virtually synonymous with "the enemy of the Jews."

Bibliography

Altheim, F., and Stiehl, R. 1959–63. *Die aramäische Sprache unter den Achaimeniden,* Vol. 1/2. Frankfurt am Main.

Clines, D. J. A. 1984. *The Esther Scroll.* JSOTSup 30. Sheffield.

Haupt, P. 1908. Critical Notes on Esther. *AJSL* 24: 97–186.

Jones, B. W. 1978. The So-Called Appendix to the Book of Esther. *Semantics* 6: 36–43.

Hoschander, J. 1923. *The Book of Esther in the Light of History.* Philadelphia.

Lewy, J. 1939. The Feast of the 14th Day of Addar. *HUCA* 14:127–51.

McKane, W. 1961. A Note on Esther 9 and 1 Samuel 15. *JTS* 12: 260–61.

Simons, J. 1959. *The Geographical and Topographical Texts of the Old Testament.* Leiden.

Stein, E. 1982. Un Essai D'Adaptation de la Fête de Pourim dans L'Alexandrie Hellenistique. Pp. 567–76 in *Studies in the Book of Esther,* ed. C. A. Moore. New York.

Zadok, R. 1984. On the Historical Background of the Book of Esther. *BN* 24: 18–23.

MARK J. FRETZ

AGAPE MEAL [Gk *agapē*]. "Love feast," a specialized Christian use of the Greek word for love *(agapē)* to refer to a fellowship meal which was a principal occasion for charity to the poorer members of the church.

Agapē occurs with this meaning in the NT only in Jude 12 ("These are blemishes on your love feasts, as they boldly carouse together, looking after themselves") and as a variant reading in the parallel passage in 2 Pet 2:13. These passages reflect later problems associated with the agape—immoral conduct and selfish interest in the food more than genuine community love. Love *(agapē)* in early Christian usage was practical (1 John 3:17–18), so one use of the word came to be the meal served for benevolent purposes. The instructions of Jesus in Luke 14:12–14 were taken seriously in the early church. That *agapē* came to mean "love feast" is a testimony to the practical nature of early Christian love and to the prominence of a meal as a way of expressing love.

A. Greco-Roman Religious Meals

Greco-Roman society knew various types of religious meals. Especially important in the social life of the early Roman empire were the monthly banquets of the private associations. Whether based on nationality, a common occupation, or social concern, these clubs nearly always had a religious aspect (with a patron deity, a priest or priestess among the officials, and libations or other sacrifices as part of their gatherings) and provided burial services for their members. Whatever other functions these clubs served, the social fellowship of their regular meals together constituted an important feature. The members paid a monthly fee, but patrons often supplied the food or drink for the banquet. These convivial occasions had to be tightly regulated by statutes because of their rowdiness. Some of these regulations assess fines for disorderly conduct, prohibit a member taking another member to court to settle a dispute, and provide for functionaries to enforce proper conduct during the meetings (IG II^2 1368). Celsus, the 2d-century pagan critic of Christianity, compared the agape to meals in pagan secret associations (Origen, *C. Cels.* 1.1).

B. Jewish Religious Meals

Judaism also had its religious associations whose members ate together, especially on sabbaths and festivals. These gatherings were of a soberer and more disciplined character than Greco-Roman club meals. The Mishnah's report of rabbinic disputes about the order of activities reveals the following elements accompanying the meal: washing hands, lighting lamps, blessing and breaking of bread, and blessing a cup of wine (*m. Ber.* 8). These features appear in Christian accounts of the agape. The Qumran community had its group meals at which the priest blessed the bread and wine (1QS 6.3–6; 1QSa 2.17–22), and the Therapeutae in Egypt had a festal meal and vigil which included prayer, exposition of the scripture, hymns, and a meal of bread and water (Philo, *Vita Cont* 64–89). Jewish religious meals provided the immediate antecedent for the practice of Jesus and his disciples.

C. Jesus and His Disciples

Religious meals in the early church may have had their origin in Jesus' meals with his disciples. The NT places a particular emphasis on Jesus' eating and drinking with his disciples after the resurrection (Luke 24:30, 41–42; John 21:12–14; Acts 10:41). During the ministry of Jesus the feeding miracles occupied a prominent place (Mark 6:35–44; 8:1–9 pars.); Luke showed a special interest in Jesus' teachings associated with meals (Luke 14:1–24).

The Lord's Supper was instituted in the context of a Jewish religious meal (Mark 14:22–25 pars.), and it continued to be observed in a meal setting (1 Cor 11:20–34). The disturbances at Corinth which Paul sought to correct may have resulted from Greeks carrying over into a Christian setting the convivial practices of their own (religious) club life. The poorer members were humiliated, since those better off ate the food and drink they furnished instead of sharing it or ate the best portions provided from the common fund before the poorer (workers) could arrive (1 Cor 11:21–22).

D. Relation to Eucharist

When the eucharist was separated from the meal in time and location (as it may have been from the beginning in intention and purpose), the latter moved more decisively in the direction of fellowship and charity. Terminology, however, continued to be interchangeable. Ign., *Smyrn.* 8 appears to use *agapē* for the eucharist (*Smyrn.* 7; cf. *Ep. Apos.* 15, which uses agape for the remembrance of the Lord's death), and Hippolytus, *Ap. Trad.* 26 (in some of its versions) uses "Lord's supper" for the love feast. The lack of clear distinctions shows in the competing interpretations of *Did.* 9–10. Do the prayers refer to a eucharist, an agape, or to a eucharist in the context of an agape? Since the compiler called the prayers eucharistic, the absence of a memorial of the death and resurrection is hardly conclusive that an agape is described. Pliny the Younger at the beginning of the 2d century refers to two gatherings by Christians in Bithynia: one before dawn and another in the evening "to partake of food—but food of an ordinary and innocent kind" (*Ep.* 10.96). The latter meeting, he says, was suspended when he enforced the edict against unauthorized associations. The separate evening meeting and the willingness of Christians to give it up might suggest an agape rather than the eucharist. All later sources show a separation of the eucharist from the agape.

E. Purpose

The NT indicates the early disciples had meals for fellowship and/or benevolence. According to Acts 2:46, "Day by day . . . they partook of food with glad and generous hearts." The "daily distribution" to the widows in Acts 6:1–2 may have been of funds or of food. Such activities may have continued and later have been described by the word *agapē* or may have served as a precedent for the institution of the agape. A 2d-century apologist for Christianity declared that Christians "have their meals in common" (*Diogn.* 5).

F. Later Descriptions

The fullest descriptions of the love feast come from about the year 200. Tertullian gives this information:

> Our feast shows its motive by its name. It is called by the Greek word for love. Whatever is reckoned the cost, money spent in the name of piety is gain, since with that refreshment we benefit from the needy . . . We do not recline at the table before prayer to God is first tasted. We eat the amount that satisfies the hungry; we drink as much as is beneficial to the modest. We satisfy ourselves as those who remember that even during the night we must worship God; we converse as those who know that the Lord listens. After the washing of hands and lighting of lamps, each one who is able is called into the center to chant praise to God either from the holy scriptures or from his own talents. This is proof of how much is drunk. Prayer in like manner concludes the meal (*Apol.* 39.16–18).

The more detailed account by Hippolytus (*Ap. Trad.* 25–27) shows a concern with tight ecclesiastical control, for one of the clergy must preside. The benevolent purpose of the meal is highlighted and the recipients of the food were expected to pray for the host.

It was necessary that the love feasts be tightly regulated. Clement of Alexandria protested against the almost exclusive use of *agapē* for the social meal: "The meal occurs because of love, not love because of the meal" (*Paed.* 2.1.4–9). He attests that the meal had become the chief thing about Christianity for many, but he wanted to lift thoughts to a higher plane. Pagans misunderstood what they heard about the Christians' meal (Min. Fel. *Oct.* 9; 30–31), but their charges of immorality (Athenagoras, *Plea* 3) may have had some basis in fact in irregularities associated with the love feast (Tertullian, *Fasting* 17). Disorders in connection with love feasts led to efforts to suppress them in the 5th century. For further discussion see *DACL* 1: 775–848.

Art. Meal scenes are common in the Catacomb paintings. It is often difficult to know what is being depicted: a feeding miracle from the Gospels, the Last Supper, the eucharist, the heavenly banquet of the redeemed, a funerary meal in commemoration of the deceased, or an agape. The inscriptions "love" and "peace" suggest that some of the pictures depict an agape. These paintings may be a further confirmation of the central place which the common meal had in the religious experience of many ordinary Christians. The martyrs in the *Passion of Perpetua and Felicitas* 17 in their last meal on the day before their martyrdom, perhaps in anticipation of the heavenly banquet, partook of an agape "so far as they could."

Bibliography

Cole, R. L. 1916. *Love-Feasts: A History of the Christian Agape.* London.

Ferguson, E. 1987. *Early Christians Speak.* Abilene.

Hamman, A. 1970. Quelle est l'origine de l'agape? *Studia Patristica* 10: 351–54.

Hanssens, J. M. 1927–1928. L'Agape et l'Eucharistie. *Ephemerides liturgicae* 41: 525–48; 42: 545–71.

———. 1930. *Institutiones liturgicae de ritibus orientalibus.*, v. II. Rome.

Keating, J. F. 1906. *The Agape and the Eucharist in the Early Church.* London. Repr. 1969.

Reicke, B. 1951. *Diakonie, Festfreude, und Zelos in Verbindung mit der altchristlichen Agapenfeier.* Uppsala.

EVERETT FERGUSON

AGE In the OT usually in the sense of the age of a person or of people. In this sense it renders a number of terms or expressions in Hebrew. See OLD AGE. While this meaning also is found in the NT, much more often there it is used in the sense of one or both of the two ages (Gk *aiōn*) of the world, as conceived in late Jewish thought. This meaning is found in expressions such as "this age," "the present age," "the end of the age," and "that age," "the age to come."

HERBERT G. GRETHER

AGEE (PERSON) [Heb *ʾāgēʾ*]. The father of the Hararite Shammah, one of King David's three chief "mighty men" (2 Sam 23:11). The name Agee only occurs once within this roster of David's "mighty men" (2 Sam 23:8–17) and is conspicuously absent in the parallel passage 1 Chr 11:11–19; the Lucianic text of LXX reads *ēla,* to which Mazar (1986: 91) emends the MT. However, based on occurrences of the term "Hararite" in the Samuel list and its Chronicles parallel, Agee may be related to another of these "mighty men." Compare the MT of the following verses:

(1) 2 Sam 23:11a		*šammāʾ*	*ben-ʾāgēʾ*	*hărārî*
(2) 2 Sam 23:32b–33a	*yĕhônātān*	*šammâ*		*hahărārî*
(3) 1 Chr 11:34b	*yônātān*		*ben-šāgēh*	*hahărārî*

(1) "Shammah the son of Agee the Hararite" and (2) "Jonathan, Shammah the Hararite" become in Chronicles 11 (3) "Jonathan the son of Shagee the Hararite." It may be suggested that Heb *šāgēh* (1 Chr 11:34b) results from a combination of *šammāʾ* and *ʾāgēʾ* (2 Sam 23:11a), which reflects an association between Agee and Jonathan in 2 Samuel 23 (see Elliger 1935: 31). According to some scholars (McCarter *2 Samuel* AB, 493), the term "Hararite" (Heb *hrry;* see 2 Sam 23:11), together with its close variant

(*hhrry,* see 2 Sam 23:33 and 1 Chr 11:34–35) and other proximate forms in these lists (*hʾrry,* see 2 Sam 23:33; *hḥrdy,* see 2 Sam 23:25; *hhrwry,* see 1 Chr 11:27), is a gentilic associated with an unknown clan. Others hold that "Hararite" is the name of Agee's hometown, and identify it with "Araru" of the Amarna Letters (Elliger 1935: 56).

Bibliography

Elliger, K. 1935. Die dreissig Helden Davids. *PJ* 31: 29–75.

Mazar, B. 1986. *The Early Biblical Period, Historical Studies,* ed. S. Aḥituv and B. Levine. Jerusalem.

MARK J. FRETZ

AGIA (PERSON) [Gk *Augian*]. The daughter of Barzillai and wife of Jaddus, whose sons returned from exile and laid claim to the priestly office without proof of priestly ancestry (1 Esdr 5:38). The name Agia is absent in the parallel lists of Ezra 2:61 = Neh 7:63). Although the sons of Jaddus were excluded from priestly service, their ancestral lineage through Agia to Barzillai gave them venerable connection to Israel since the family of Barzillai had been especially favored by King David (2 Sam 17:27; 19:31–40; 1 Kgs 2:7).

MARK J. FRETZ

AGING. See OLD AGE.

AGORA (PLACE) [Gk *agora*]. A gathering place in the city or town that was used for business, social, and political purposes. The word derives from *ageirein,* meaning "to bring together." Paul and Silas were dragged to the *agora* at Philippi by irate citizens who were bringing a complaint there before the Roman authorities (Acts 16:19–21). Paul also debated with Epicurean and Stoic teachers in the *agora* in Athens (Acts 17:17). In view of such use of the space, some modern versions render the word as "public square" or "city square," rather than the traditional "market place" (RSV).

In the Gospels, the word is rendered "market place," and the contexts show that it referred to a place where more than buying and selling went on: An employer found workers (Matt 20:3), men liked to be greeted with respect (Matt 23:7 and parallel), and children played (Matt 11:16). But there is no evidence in the Gospels that the market places of Palestinian towns were used for political purposes.

HERBERT G. GRETHER

AGRAPHA. A word used to designate the noncanonical "sayings" of Jesus.

A. Toward a Definition

The term agrapha has been used since J. G. Koerner (1776) to refer primarily to "sayings attributed to Jesus which are not found in the four canonical Gospels." The choice of the designation agrapha, or unwritten sayings, was related to the idea that these materials were initially preserved orally and only later were incorporated into written documents, frequently as individual, isolated sayings. Sayings of Jesus such as those in Acts 20:35 and 1 Thess 4:15–17 have been referred to as agrapha, though they are within canonical writings. The vast majority of the agrapha are found outside the canonical writings. The term is currently used apart from the claim or attempt to demonstrate that the materials involved owe their existence to oral preservation of sayings or teachings of Jesus. The question of the origin of individual sayings is more an issue treated in investigating the materials than of defining the term.

Though the definition given above is the most widely used, one encounters others in the critical literature which warrant mention. Hennecke (1913: 17, 25) limited the designation agrapha to extracanonical, isolated sayings of Jesus. Quotations from known apocryphal writings were thus excluded. This distinction was related to the organization of his influential *New Testament Apocrypha* (1963), in which many of the sayings were treated elsewhere in the collection as parts of discussions of documents such as the apocryphal gospels. Mangenot (*DTC* 1: 625) restricted the designation to "authentic" or genuine sayings of Jesus not found in the four canonical Gospels. Resch (1906), in the second edition of his comprehensive collection of materials, used the term to refer to extracanonical scriptural fragments whether of the OT or NT.

In current usage the term agrapha is frequently a virtual synonym for, and may even be replaced by, "extracanonical sayings of Jesus." This latter designation is intended primarily to indicate location, not to suggest judgments concerning origin or theological or historical value. Most of the same range of materials is included, even those sayings attributed to Jesus in the canonical NT outside the Gospels, such as Acts 20:35. The major difference is that the term "extracanonical sayings of Jesus" usually includes more variant manuscript readings and citations from early Christian writings which parallel canonical sayings than was the case earlier with the designation agrapha. A major reason for this shift would seem to be the decreased emphasis on the search for "authentic" sayings and the increased emphasis on other types of studies of the formation and transmission of sayings of Jesus. More will be said in this regard when the value of the materials in the study of early Christianity is discussed below.

The sayings treated as agrapha are, in terms of their form, relatively analogous to those of the synoptic tradition. Most may be categorized using the form-critical designations initially developed by Rudolf Bultmann (1963) for the study of the synoptic tradition (parables, apophthegms, prophetic and apocalyptic sayings, wisdom sayings and proverbs, I-sayings, and community rules). Koester (1968) has used these categories in treating the sayings in the *Gospel of Thomas* and, more recently, Stroker (1988) has used them in categorizing the extracanonical sayings generally.

Since the term agrapha has been used primarily to refer to relatively short sayings essentially containing teachings, certain types of materials attributed to Jesus in early Christianity are usually excluded. (1) The infancy gospels contain some words attributed to Jesus, but these are usually comments on the miraculous deeds, or other events and encounters narrated, and are of a rather different nature from teachings. (2) Several documents are largely revelatory discourses of Jesus, usually in the form of dialogues between Jesus and one or more of his disciples. Lengthy dialogues, whether from the Nag Hammadi corpus or from analogous treatises in Codices Brucianus and Askewianus, and Papyrus Berolinensis 8502 are not treated as agrapha. The same is the case with most of the materials, also largely revelatory discourses, in the *Epistula Apostolorum, The Testament of the Lord,* and the Ethiopic *Apocalypse of Peter.* Shorter sayings from some of these documents are found in some collections of agrapha, however. (3) Sayings attributed to the preexistent Jesus are usually not included. (4) Quotations of biblical passages, whether from the OT or NT, are also not included when the understanding is present that Jesus was the one who spoke through the words of the biblical writers.

B. Sources

The sources in which agrapha or extracanonical sayings of Jesus are found are numerous and of wide variety. The following categorization is representative of those frequently found in the critical literature: (1) NT writings apart from the four Gospels; (2) variant readings or additions found in manuscripts of the Gospels; (3) quotations contained in the writings of the church fathers and other early Christian literature, such as the early liturgies and church orders; (4) manuscripts or fragments of manuscripts of noncanonical gospels and other noncanonical writings, usually designated NT apocrypha; (5) Manichaean and Mandaean writings; (6) ancient Jewish writings; and (7) Islamic writings.

Some documents from the Nag Hammadi corpus warrant special mention in this context, though they are a part of category 4 above. The importance of the *Gospel of Thomas* is unparalleled for the study of the extracanonical sayings. It consists of a collection of some 114 sayings, including parables, and is thus the largest single collection of sayings of Jesus outside the canonical tradition. Approximately one half of the sayings in Thomas have parallels within canonical materials, whereas the rest are without significant parallel. The relation of Thomas to the canonical gospels is debated, but an increasing number of scholars assess it as preserving a tradition of Jesus' sayings, literarily independent from the canonical tradition. Assessments of the agrapha since the initial publication of the *Gospel of Thomas* (Guillaumont 1959) have been significantly affected by this major new discovery. The sayings attributed to Jesus in the *Gospel of Philip* are easily distinguished from their context and are also to be included in collections and treatments of the agrapha.

Somewhat more complicated are the *Dialogue of the Savior,* the *Book of Thomas the Contender,* and the *Apocryphon of James.* These writings are currently in the literary form of revelation discourses. Recent studies indicate, however, that each may have made use of earlier collections of shorter sayings, many of which can be distinguished, at least tentatively, from their present literary context and reconstructed in an earlier form (Turner 1975; Koester 1979; Hedrick 1983; Cameron 1984; Emmell 1984). The analysis of these documents, and also of the revelation discourses mentioned earlier as usually not included among the agrapha, will likely yield an increasing number of shorter sayings, viewed as representing an earlier stage of tradition. These reconstructed, shorter sayings will likely become incorporated in future treatments of the agrapha or extracanonical sayings of Jesus.

C. Study of the Agrapha

The agrapha have been the subject of numerous and varied studies. Long before the major manuscript discoveries of the 19th and 20th centuries, scholars had called attention to these extracanonical sayings, had made collections of varying degrees of completeness, and had attempted to give some explanation of them and their place in the history of early Christianity. The best bibliography of the older literature was done by Pick (1908: 126–52). Resch (1906: 14–22) provides an assessment of much of the early works. Jeremias (1964: 4–13) has surveyed the materials since Resch.

The history of research is too extensive for inclusion here; nonetheless, a sketch of the major types of studies is necessary in order to understand current research and assessment of the importance of the agrapha.

An emphasis on collecting the materials understandably characterizes the first type of study. The earliest treatments of the agrapha were made by editors of the Apostolic Fathers and other early Christian writings, the first to my knowledge being that by Cotelier in 1672. He dealt with a number of important examples, citing parallel material, and was the first to indicate the wide distribution of extracanonical sayings of Jesus. Lists and short treatments of the agrapha are to be found from this time on. The first book which limited itself to the treatment of agrapha was by Dodd (1874).

An apex in collecting material was reached in 1889 with the publication of the first edition of Alfred Resch's work. Resch provided the most comprehensive collection of materials prior to the discovery of the Egerton Papyri and the Nag Hammadi Codices. The second edition of his work (1906) dealt with the newly discovered Oxyrhynchus Papyri. Resch's goal, more strongly stated in the first edition than in the second, was to restore an *Urevangelium* or original gospel, written in Hebrew, fragments of which could be reconstructed from some of the agrapha and other material he had collected. Despite the failure of his broader attempt, Resch's collection of materials has remained not only useful but also, until recently, the most comprehensive available.

Preuschen (1901) published a collection of isolated sayings as well as fragments of apocryphal NT writings. Still useful collections of the texts of much of the material in the original languages were made by Erich Klostermann (1911; 1929) which contain fragments of noncanonical gospels, the Oxyrhynchus sayings, and a collection of 88 additional agrapha. The most complete early collection of the materials in English translation was made by Pick (1908). His earlier work (1903) also contained a sizable listing of agrapha. A comprehensive collection of the materials, in original language with English translations and parallel materials, has recently been published (Stroker 1988).

The question of authenticity dominates the second type of study (i.e., whether the passages in question contain sayings to be viewed as spoken by the historical Jesus). Nestle (1896) treated 27 agrapha he considered to be authentic sayings of Jesus. Ropes (1896) provided a critical evaluation of Resch's work, not only of his general thesis, but also of the underlying treatment of the agrapha and related material. Ropes eliminated from the main focus of the discussion passages whose contexts did not claim they were sayings of Jesus and also quotations from canonical texts secondarily attributed to Jesus. The question of authenticity was asked with rigor and persistence. Only a few passages from the mass of material collected by Resch were considered by Ropes to have any real claim to authenticity. With the publication of Oxyrhynchus Papyri 1: 654, 655 (Grenfell and Hunt 1898; 1904) the question of authenticity was posed with renewed urgency and, with some notable exceptions, has dominated research on the agrapha until relatively recently.

Following Ropes no comprehensive treatment of the agrapha appeared until that of Joachim Jeremias (1958; 1964) whose work has been very influential. Jeremias treats in detail only a small number of sayings, but in the initial sections of his work has a survey of the larger body of material. In his introduction he speaks of the unfortunate overemphasis on the question of authenticity, while the meaning of the sayings has largely been neglected. Jeremias is, however, in essential continuity with the quest for authentic sayings, departing from this type of study only in giving an exposition of the agrapha selected as potentially authentic (21 initially, 18 in later editions) in terms of their religious significance, finding or constructing a situation in Jesus' life in which they could have been said and expounding the sayings on the basis of such a context.

Jeremias stands at the virtual end of an approach to the study of the agrapha for which the quest for authentic sayings of Jesus was the primary concern, a quest which has focused on an ever-diminishing number of passages and relegated the bulk of the materials to the periphery. Hofius (*TRE* 2: 103–10) eliminated half of Jeremias' 18 sayings and considers the question of authenticity properly to *begin* with the investigation of the remaining 9, for some of which he harbors doubts.

The question of authenticity will never fully be given up; it has the same validity as the quest for authentic sayings of Jesus within the canonical tradition. The value of the agrapha, however, lies primarily in other areas.

A third type of study focuses on the processes of the formation of the extracanonical sayings. Here the quest for authentic sayings of Jesus is not primary; rather, extracanonical sayings, including ones which parallel those within the canonical gospels, are studied for clues to understanding the ways in which Jesus' teachings were shaped and adapted in early Christianity. Walter Bauer (1909) is an early example of this type. As a methodological consideration, Bauer treats all sayings attributed to Jesus not found in the earliest reconstructable version of the NT as not originating from him or as modifications of earlier forms of Jesus' sayings. He then classifies the changes which can be observed by comparison with the canonical materials. Leon Wright (1952) is primarily concerned with materials which can be shown to have obvious contacts with the texts of the canonical Gospels. Differences between the agrapha and patristic quotations on the one hand, and the canonical versions on the other, are grouped in terms of types of motivations which the alterations seem to evidence. The categories chosen are ones generally recognized by textual critics. Wright concludes that by and large the agrapha are dependent upon the canonical, and thus not upon an independent, parallel tradition. Bultmann (1963) has made more use of extracanonical sayings than one is aware of at first reading. There is no separate study of the agrapha, but examples are used to show the continuation in the extracanonical and postcanonical materials of tendencies in the development of tradition which Bultmann holds he has discerned within the synoptic materials themselves.

Helmut Koester (1957b), while reviewing Jeremias' work, called for a rather different approach to the study of the agrapha. Koester asserts that the same type of treatment should be given the agrapha as given the canonical sayings of Jesus, since neither can be properly assessed primarily in terms of the question of authenticity. "This demand is to be placed on the study of the extracanonical sayings of the Lord. They receive their own proper value from their *Sitz im Leben* and are immune against the verdict of inauthenticity even if they have their *Sitz* not in the life of Jesus but in that of the community" (1957b: 222). Both groups of materials are to be regarded as units of early Christian tradition, to be understood as representing situations in the life and thought of the early Christian communities. Their place and use in the life, thought, and worship of the early church are the key to the value of the extracanonical sayings. Neither the distinction between canonical and noncanonical nor the question of authenticity should rob them of their significance.

Studies along the lines called for by Koester thus may be viewed as representing a fourth type: that is, treating the agrapha and extracanonical sayings that closely parallel the canonical as parts of a larger treatment of the tradition of Jesus' teachings in the works of a given writer or a given body of tradition. Examples of this type are Bellinzoni (1967) and Kline (1975).

D. The Value of the Agrapha

As already indicated, the value of the agrapha and other extracanonical traditions of Jesus' teachings cannot be limited to the search for those few sayings which might be viewed as authentic sayings of the historical Jesus. Rather, the importance of these materials lies in their role in broadening our understanding of the development and transmission of traditions of Jesus' teachings. The following three areas may be mentioned as especially important in this regard.

The canonical tradition and the sources immediately behind the canonical gospels were neither the only collections nor the sole bearers of the traditions of Jesus' teachings. Koester (1957a) has shown that many of the sayings in the Apostolic Fathers are independent of the synoptic gospels. Further, the sayings in the *Gospel of Thomas* are best viewed as stemming from a collection which is independent of, and perhaps earlier than, the canonical Gospels. Thus the question of the earliest stages of the tradition of Jesus' teachings cannot be investigated on the basis of the canonical Gospels alone. Extracanonical sources provide some sayings without parallel in the canonical Gospels which, on the basis of their form and content, are to be viewed as stemming from very early stages of the Jesus tradition. Further, extracanonical sayings sometimes preserve a less-developed version of a canonical saying and may give us thereby access to a stage of tradition earlier than that of the canonical Gospels.

Secondly, Jesus' sayings were transmitted and redacted independently of the canonical tradition as well as in dependence upon it. In both the extracanonical and the canonical traditions, sayings were shaped and redacted in large measure to meet the needs of the communities. The processes of redaction of individual sayings and groups of sayings are largely analogous in the canonical and extracanonical tradition. Thus the extracanonical sayings can help us achieve a more complete picture of the transmission and redaction of the sayings of Jesus and the relation of these processes to different groups within early Christianity.

Finally, the extracanonical tradition provides evidence that sayings from other sources have become attributed to Jesus. Our understanding of the extent to which sayings from other sources have become attributed to Jesus, a process discernible also in the canonical tradition, would necessitate study of the extracanonical materials.

Study of the agrapha or extracanonical sayings can thus broaden our understanding of the total picture of the early history of the Jesus tradition. In this context, the agrapha have considerable value, to the theologian as well as to the historian.

Bibliography

Bauer, W. 1909. *Das Leben Jesu im Zeitalter der neutestamentlichen Apokryphen.* Tübingen. Repr. 1967.

Bellinzoni, A. J. 1967. *The Sayings of Jesus in the Writings of Justin Martyr.* Leiden.

Bultmann, R. 1963. *History of the Synoptic Tradition.* Trans. John Marsh. New York.

Cameron, R. 1984. *Sayings Traditions in the Apocryphon of James.* HTS 34. Philadelphia.

Cotelier, J. B. 1672. *Patres Apostolici.* Paris.

Dodd, J. T. 1874. *Sayings Ascribed to our Lord by the Fathers and Other Primitive Writers.* Oxford.

Emmell, S. 1984. *Nag Hammadi Codex III, 5. The Dialogue of the Savior.* NHS 26. Leiden.

Grenfell, B. P., and Hunt, A. S. 1898. *The Oxyrhynchus Papyri.* Part 1. London.

———. 1904. *The Oxyrhynchus Papyri.* Part 4. London.

Guillaumont, A. et al. 1959. *The Gospel According to Thomas.* Leiden.

Hedrick, C. 1983. Kingdom Sayings and Parables of Jesus in the Apocryphon of James: Tradition and Redaction. *NTS* 29: 1–24.

Hennecke, E. 1913. Agrapha. Pp. 16–25 in *Realenzyklopädie für protestantische Theologie und Kirche* 23. 3d ed. Ed. A. Hauck. Leipzig.

Hennecke, E., and Schneemelcher, W. 1963. *New Testament Apocrypha.* Vol. 1: *Gospels and Related Writings.* Trans. R. McL. Wilson. Philadelphia.

Jeremias, J. 1958. *Unknown Sayings of Jesus.* London. Rev. ed. 1964.

Kline, L. L. 1975. *Sayings of Jesus in the Pseudo-Clementine Homilies.* Missoula, MT.

Klostermann, E. 1911. *Apocrypha 3: Agrapha, slavische Josephstücke, Oxyrhynchus-Fragmente.* 2d ed. *Kleine Texte für Vorlesungen und Übungen* 11. Ed. H. Lietzmann. Bonn.

———. 1929. *Apocrypha 2: Evangelien.* 3d ed. *Kleine Texte für Vorlesungen und Übungen* 8. Ed. H. Lietzmann. Bonn.

Koerner, J. G. 1776. *De sermonibus Christi agraphois.* Leipzig.

Koester, H. 1957a. *Synoptische Überlieferung bei den apostolischen Vätern.* TU 65. Berlin.

———. 1957b. Die ausserkanonischen Herrenworte als Produkte der christlichen Gemeinde. *ZNW* 48: 220–37.

———. 1968. One Jesus and Four Primitive Gospels. *HTR* 61: 203–47.

———. 1979. Dialogue und Spruchüberlieferung in den gnostischen Texte von Nag Hammadi. *EvT* 39: 532–56.

Nestle, E. 1896. *Novi Testamenti Graeci Supplementum.* Leipzig.

Pick, B. 1903. *The Extra-canonical Life of Christ.* New York.

———. 1908. *Paralipomena: Remains of Gospels and Sayings of Christ.* Chicago.

Preuschen, E. 1901. *Antilegomena: Die Reste der ausserkanonischen Evangelien und urchristlichen Überlieferung.* Giessen.

Resch, A. 1889. *Agrapha: Ausserkanonische Evangelienfragmente.* TU 5.4. Leipzig.

———. 1906. *Agrapha Ausserkanonische Schriftfragmente.* TU 15. 3–4. Leipzig.

Robinson, J. M. 1977. *The Nag Hammadi Library in English.* San Francisco.

Ropes, J. H. 1896. *Die Sprüche Jesu die in den kanonischen Evangelien nicht überliefert sind.* TU 14.2. Leipzig.

Stroker, W. D. 1988. *Extra-canonical Sayings of Jesus: Texts, Translations and Notes.* Atlanta.

Turner, J. 1975. *The Book of Thomas the Contender from Codex II of the Cairo Gnostic Library from Nag Hammadi,* CG II, 7. Missoula, MT.

Wright, L. 1952. *Alterations of the Words of Jesus as Quoted in the Literature of the Second Century.* Cambridge, MA.

WILLIAM D. STROKER

AGRICULTURE. Agriculture is the cultivation of the soil for food products or any other useful or valuable growth of the field or garden; also, by extension, it includes any industry practiced by a cultivator of the soil in connection with such cultivation, as fruit raising, animal husbandry, dairying, and gardening. The study of ancient agriculture relies on archaeological finds (installations, tools, organic remains), biblical and extrabiblical (including literary and economic) texts, and comparisons with traditional practices in preindustrial societies.

A. Background.

Agriculture was the economic backbone of biblical Israel, where it was practiced by city dwellers as well as villagers. Its influence was very strong on many facets of daily life, including religion, law, and social behavior. The biblical farmer was the heir to a long agricultural tradition which originated in the Near East some time before the Neolithic period (ca. 7000 B.C.E.) with the domestication of plants and animals (Butzer 1971; Flannery 1973). However, while the biblical farmer did not introduce any new species, he improved farming methods and techniques for utilizing the produce. Domestication of food plants and animals was an important factor in the establishment of permanent villages. The earliest domesticated plants were cereals (two-rowed barley, emmer wheat, and einkorn wheat; Renfrew 1973: 30–81) and legumes (lentils and peas; Zohary and Hopf 1973). Fruit trees were domesticated much later ca. 4000 B.C.E. and included olive, vine, date, pomegranate, and fig (Stager 1985b). Among the earliest domesticated animals were sheep and goats (Nissen 1988: 24–27) which continue to dominate animal husbandry up to the present. Documentary and archaeological evidence shows that the last animal to be domesticated was the camel during the transition period from the LB to the Early Iron Age. The appearance of the camel in the Bible as a household animal of the Midianites in the Gideon stories (Judg 6:5; 7:12; 8:26) agrees with archaeological finds, while any earlier mention (e.g., Genesis 24) is anachronistic. See also ZOOLOGY.

Canaan's agricultural richness was recognized already in early historical times as evidenced by Egyptian records from the Old, Middle, and New Kingdom. Her agricultural wealth made her a target for invading armies coming to loot (*ARE* 1: 143; 2: 187, 189, 191; *ANET* 19, 228).

The repertoire of plants cultivated by the biblical farmer included several types of cereals, legumes, vegetables and spices, and a variety of fruit trees, each of which was grown in the area most suitable for it. The country is divided into several regions, highlands and valleys, each dominated by different geomorphological and climatic conditions, which determine soil types and water availability, the most important factors in agriculture (Hopkins 1985: 55–133; see PALESTINE, CLIMATE OF). The short rainy season (mid-October to April; see RAIN), the fluctuation in precipitation, and the rocky and hilly nature of most of the terrain made agriculture hard to practice; yet by careful selection of the proper species it became the mainstay of the country's economy throughout history. Some solutions to these problems were provided by the development and wide use of terracing and run-off farming in the highlands and in the Negeb, and the improvement of water collection and storage in underground reservoirs. Some scholars suggest that these factors enabled the Israelites to settle the Galilean, Samarian, and Judean highlands and to overtake the land whether by force or slow encroachment (Aharoni 1956; Stager 1985a). Later, during the monarchical period, these methods allowed settlement in newly acquired lands and along trade routes, for defense and economical reasons (Evenari et al. 1971).

Land could be owned by individuals (Num 27:1–8; Deut 21:15–17, 1 Kgs 21:1–3), royalty (1 Chr 27:26–28), and the priesthood (Num 35:1–8), all of whom, according to Israelite ideology, served as safekeepers because the land ultimately belonged to YHWH.

B. Conditions.

Conditions for agriculture in the Near East, and especially in Israel, are not very favorable. Many hardships have been encountered by the farmer, and these include lack of sufficient amount of water and soil. The terrain in most cases is uneven and rocky, and very few natural water sources are available; thus, farming in biblical times depended heavily on rain (Deut 12:11) and on the ability of the farmer to clear and prepare land (Josh 17:17–18; Isa 5:2). In most cases, irrigation was out of the question. Since the rainy season is short (October to April) and droughts are common, agriculture was always considered dependent upon the grace of the supernatural, be it the Canaanite fertility and nature gods or YHWH. For the Israelite farmer, the dependence on YHWH meant the observance of the covenant, which was rewarded by "rain . . . in its season" (Deut 11:13–17). Other conditions which caused crop failure included diseases, locust attacks (Amos 7:1; Joel 1:4; 2:25), and other pests such as mice, worms, fruit bats, and weeds. Several of the plant diseases are mentioned either by name (smut, Heb *šiddāpôn;* rust, Heb *yērāqôn;* bunt, Heb *boʾšâ*) or by symptom (black rot in grapes, Heb *bĕʾūšîm,* Isa 5:2, 4; loss of olives to peacock eyespot, Deut 28:40; see Borowski 1987: 153–162).

On the other hand, the farmer could restore soil fertility and increase his yield by several methods which are not specifically mentioned in texts but can be surmised from written descriptions of certain practices or through analysis of the technology available to the farmer. Fallowing, using the Sabbatical Year (Exod 23:10–11) or another program, and organic fertilizing were probably used to a certain degree, the latter included the use of dung, compost, and ash. There is a very strong possibility that crop rotation, suggested by Isa 28:24–29 (see Borowski 1987: 148–151), was also used as a method for increasing crop yield and lowering plant diseases. One of the elements available to the biblical farmer for crop rotation and increased yield was "green manuring," the cultivation of legume plants to increase nitrogen presence and its availability to other plants (Borowski 1987: 148–149).

C. Agricultural Products. (See also FLORA.)

1. Field Crops. The biblical farmer did not introduce new plants to the variety already existing, however he chose those which suited his needs best. Field plants cultivated by the biblical farmer, as attested in the Bible and archaeological remains, included cereals (Heb *dāgān*), and legumes (Zohary 1982: 74–76, 82–84). Most common among the cereals were wheat (*Triticum durum* Desf. and *Triticum vulgare* [VIII.] Host.; Heb *ḥiṭṭutâ*), emmer (*T. dicoccum* [Schrank] Schuebl.; Heb *kussemet*), barley (*Hordeum;* Heb *śĕʿōrâ*), and millet (*Panicum miliaceum* and *Setaria italica;* Heb *dōḥan*). Legumes included lentil (*Lens culinaris* Medic.; Heb *ʿădāšîm*), broad bean (*Vicia faba;* Heb *pôl*), bitter vetch (*Vicia ervilia* Wild.), chick-pea (*Cicer arientum;* Heb *ḥāmîṣ*[?];), pea *(Pisum sativum),* and fenugreek *(Trigonela graecum).* In addition, the biblical farmer cultivated several spice plants such as black cumin (*Nigella sativa;* Heb *qeṣaḥ*), cumin (*Cuminum cyminum;* Heb *kammōn*), and coriander

(*Coriandrum sativum;* Heb *gad*). Other plants were flax (*Linum usitatissimum;* Heb *pištâ*) and sesame *(Sesamum indicum)*.

2. Vegetables. Vegetables (Heb *zērûʿîm; yārāq*) were part of the agricultural repertoire, although not as highly regarded as the other plants (Dan 1:11–16). They were grown in small plots or gardens and included cucumbers (*Cucumis sativus* or *C. chate;* Heb *qiššūʾîm*), watermelon or muskmelon (*Citrulus vulgaris* or *Cucumis melo;* Heb *ʾăbaṭṭîhîm*), leeks or other greens (Heb *ḥāṣîr*), onion (*Allium cepa;* Heb *bĕṣālîm*), and garlic (*Allium sativum;* Heb *šûmîm*).

3. Fruit Trees. Fruit trees were as important an element in biblical agriculture as field crops; however, they were not domesticated as early as cereals and legumes (Zohary and Spiegel-Roy 1975). The earliest remains of fruits in Canaan come mostly from the EB Age, although fig remains were found in Neolithic and Chalcolithic Jericho. The most popular fruit tree in biblical times was the grapevine (*Vitis vinifera;* Heb *gepen*), the fruit of which was used for making wine *(yayin)*, raisins *(ṣimmûqîm)*, and syrup *(mišrat ʿănābîm)*. Other common fruit trees were fig (*Ficus carica;* Heb *tĕʾēnâ*), pomegranate (*Punica granatum;* Heb *rimmôn*), date (*Phoenix dactylifera;* Heb *tāmār*) and sycamore (*Ficus sycomorus;* Heb *šiqmîm*). Less common were the *tappûăḥ* (possibly quince or apricot), and mulberry (Heb *bākāʾ*). One common tree not mentioned specifically in the Bible is the carob *(Ceratonia siliqua)*; however, there is no question that it was cultivated in biblical times.

The olive (*Olea europaea;* Heb *zayit*) was as important to the economy of ancient Israel as was the grapevine. Its fruit was made into oil (Heb *šemen*) to be used for cooking, lighting, ointments, and other religious and secular purposes. Like wine, oil was exported to other parts of the Near East and was one of the three main elements of the agricultural economy along with grain (Heb *dāgān*) and wine (Heb *tîrôš;* Hos 2:10—Eng 2:8; etc.).

Several nuts were also cultivated, including almond (*Prunus amygdalus* Stokes; Heb *šāqēd*), pistachio (*Pistacia atlantica* Desf.; Heb *boṭnîm*), and walnut (*Juglans regia;* Heb *ʾĕgôz*).

D. Field Work.

The agricultural seasons are well enumerated in the OT; however, the best source of information is the Gezer calendar, a 10th century B.C.E. inscription from the site of biblical Gezer, which reads:

> two months of ingathering [olives]/two months
> of sowing [cereals]/two months of late sowing [legumes and vegetables]
> a month of hoeing weeds [for hay]
> a month of harvesting barley
> a month of harvesting [wheat] and measuring [grain]
> two months of grape harvesting
> a month of ingathering summer fruit

A study of this inscription shows that sowing of cereals started after the Festival of Booths (Tabernacles) in the N Kingdom (end of October), harvesting barley commenced at the Passover festival (end of March), and the conclusion of wheat harvesting was celebrated with the festival of weeks/Pentecost (end of May; Borowski 1987: 31–44).

According to the Gezer calendar, sowing took place in the fall. Two months were devoted to sowing cereals and two more to late sowing and planting of legumes and vegetables. Since no sowing could have been done without plowing, either before or after, the farmer had to wait for the first autumn rains to soften the ground. Plowing was done with a wooden-frame plow to which a metal point (copper, bronze, and later iron) was attached, pulled by a team of animals, usually oxen. The same was done in large orchards and vineyards. In small plots, on slopes, and near the plants, a hand-held hoe was used. Sowing was performed either by broadcasting or by a seed drill attached to the plow.

Harvesting agricultural produce started in the spring, first with reaping barley, then wheat (see book of Ruth), followed by grapes and other fruit (see HARVESTS, HARVESTING). The Gezer calendar assigns seven months to the harvest. Harvesting cereals *(qāṣîr)* was followed very closely by threshing and winnowing to separate the grain. Grapes were immediately turned into wine or raisins and the same was done with other fruits. Storage of agricultural produce in its raw or finished state was done in specially constructed structures underground in pits and silos and above the ground in small rooms or large storehouses. The produce was stored in bulk or jars, depending on its nature and the nature of the storage facility.

Much of the technology used in processing agricultural produce is known from biblical descriptions, archaeological discoveries, and artistic representations from different parts of the Near East. Threshing was done either by stick for small quantities of certain types of plants (cumin) or by a threshing sledge or a wheel-thresher. Winnowing took place during times when the threshed material could be thrown in the air by a fork (*mizreh;* Isa 30:24) or a wooden shovel (*raḥat;* Isa 30:24) and be separated to its components (grain, straw, chaff) by the wind according to weight. Final cleaning was done with two different types of sieves, *kĕbārâ* (Amos 9:9) and *nāpâ* (Isa 30:28). The clean grain *(bār)* was stored in jars or in storage facilities such as grain pits *(ʾăsāmîm)* or storage houses *(miskĕnôt)*.

Wine had to be produced immediately after harvest (*zāmîr* or *bāṣîr*) because fresh grapes could not be stored. The grapes were treaded on a flat, hard surface, and the juice which ran into a reservoir hewn in the rock or built out of stones and clay was collected into large jars, which were put for fermentation in a cool storage place. Raisins and raisin cakes were also made at that time by drying fresh grapes. The same process was used for drying and making cakes of figs and dates. These and other fruits such as pomegranates were also used for wine making.

Oil, like wine, was one of the exported commodities produced in ancient Israel. During the Iron II period, oil production technology made great strides with the development of the beam press. Until then, oil production was a simple matter. The olives were beaten or cracked in a mortar and then placed in straw baskets directly under stone weights. The pressed oil flowed into a container from where it was scooped into jars and stored. Small quantities of oil were produced by placing the beaten olives in water and scooping the floating oil. The beam-press innovation enabled the exertion of a much greater pressure on the olives by tying weights to a beam used as a lever under which the baskets were placed. This method facilitated the production of larger quantities of oil in less time and less effort (Eitam 1979; Gitin 1985; Kelm and Mazar 1989: 47–49).

E. Influence on Culture.

Agriculture dominated not only the economy but the whole of Israelite daily life. The Bible is saturated with agricultural symbolism, similes, and metaphors in parables, proverbs, prophecies, admonitions, hymns, and other literary forms (Judg 8:2; 9:8–15; Isa 5:1–8; Ezek 17:6–10). Many laws related to agriculture were formulated, such as those protecting the family inheritance (Num 27:1–8), concerning the protection and support of the poor, taxation, etc. (Exod 23:11; Lev 23:22; Deut 24:21). Israelite laws also regulated many aspects of agriculture such as the age at which fruit trees could be harvested, types of plants and where they could be planted (the law of *kilʾayim,* Lev 19:19, Deut 22:9), and fallowing (sabbatical year). Religion and cult were strongly dominated by agricultural themes. The three main festivals associated with pilgrimages to Jerusalem all celebrate the beginning or ending of agricultural seasons. Passover (Heb *pesaḥ*) celebrates the beginning of cereal (barley) harvesting; Weeks (or Pentecost; Heb *šābūʿôt*) celebrates the end of the wheat harvest and with it the end of cereal harvesting; Booths (Heb *sukkôt*) marks the end of fruit ingathering and the beginning of the sowing season. Sacrifices and contributions to the Temple and its personnel were agricultural in nature (Num 18:8–32; Deut 18:1–9). Finally, and significantly, the rewards for observing the covenant with YHWH were spelled out in agricultural terms; ample rain in its appropriate season and resistance to plant diseases which led to abundance were the direct benefits of adherence to the covenant (Deut 28:22).

Bibliography

Aharoni, Y. 1956. A Survey of the Galilee: Israelite Settlements and Their Pottery. *EI* 4:56–64.

Borowski, O. 1987. *Agriculture in Iron Age Israel.* Winona Lake.

Butzer, K. W. 1971. Agricultural Origins in the Near East as a Geographical Problem. Pp. 209–35 in *Prehistoric Agriculture,* ed. S. Struever. Garden City.

Dimbleby, G. W. 1967. *Plants and Archaeology.* London.

Eitam, D. 1979. Olive Presses of the Israelite Period. *TA* 6: 146–55.

Evenari, M.; Shanan, L.; Tadmor, N.; and Itzhaki, Y. 1971. *The Negev: The Challenge of a Desert.* Cambridge.

Flannery, K. V. 1973. The Origin of Agriculture. *Annual Review of Anthropology* 2: 271–310.

Gitin, S. 1985. Dramatic Finds in Ekron. *ASOR Newsletter* 36(3): 2–3.

Hopkins, D. C. 1985. *The Highlands of Canaan.* Decatur, GA.

Kelm, G. L., and Mazar, A. 1989. Excavating in Samson's Country. *BARev* 15(1): 36–49.

Nissen, J. H. 1988. *The Early History of the Ancient Near East 9000–2000 B.C.* Trans. E. Lutzeier. Chicago.

Renfrew, J. M. 1973. *Palaeoethnobotany: The Prehistoric Food Plants of the Near East and Europe.* New York.

Stager, L. E. 1981. Highland Village Life in Palestine Some Three Thousand Years Ago. *The Oriental Institute News & Notes* 69: 1–3.

———. 1985a. The Archaeology of the Family in Ancient Israel. *BASOR* 260: 1–35.

———. 1985b. The Firstfruits of Civilization. Pp. 172–88 in *Palestine in the Bronze and Iron Ages,* ed. J. N. Tubb. London.

Zohary, D., and Hopf, M. 1973. Domestication of Pulses in the Old World. *Science* 182: 887–94.

Zohary, D., and Spiegel-Roy, P. 1975. Beginning of Fruit Growing in the Old World. *Science* 187: 319–27.

Zohary, M. 1982. *Plants of the Bible.* Cambridge.

Oded Borowski

AGRIPPA (PERSON) [Gk *Agrippas*]. The name held by two Herodian rulers in 1st century Palestine. Josephus' writings constitute our primary source of information for both, although both are also mentioned in the NT book of Acts: Agrippa I as the "Herod" who persecuted the early church in Jerusalem (12:1–23), and Agrippa II as the king who, years later, heard Paul's defense prior to Paul's journey to Rome (25:13–26:32).

1. Agrippa I was born in 10 B.C., son of Aristobulus and Bernice and thus, through Aristobulus, grandson of Herod. In early childhood he was sent with his mother to Rome. There he was brought up in the company of Claudius, who was his same age, and Drusus, son of Tiberius, who was slightly older. At the imperial court he made connections which were to prove vital to him in later life—not only with Claudius and Drusus, but also, through his mother, with Antonia, wife of the elder Drusus (Tiberius' brother), and with others besides, not least imperial freedmen (*Ant* 18.143, 191). It was largely in the pursuit of such connections that Agrippa borrowed and spent large sums of money. After the premature death of his companion Drusus in A.D. 23, Agrippa returned to Judea in a state of considerable poverty and, we are told, contemplating suicide.

By now Agrippa had married Cypros, daughter of Phasael. Her good offices won for Agrippa the help of his sister's husband, Antipas (*Ant* 18.145ff.). Antipas gave Agrippa an allowance and the post of *agoranomos* (market supervisor) at Tiberias, where he was to live. However, Agrippa soon found his position to be as ignominious as it was inadequate. We are told that Antipas taunted Agrippa over his dependence. Instead Agrippa looked to L. Pomponius Flaccus, Roman governor of Syria. He had become a friend of Flaccus during his time at Rome (*Ant* 18.149–50). At first Agrippa prospered in Flaccus' entourage. But he fell from favor when he took a bribe from the Damascenes to support their cause with Flaccus in a boundary dispute with the people of Sidon. Agrippa's brother and enemy, Aristobulus, had brought the bribe to Flaccus' attention (*Ant* 18.151–4).

Agrippa resolved to return to Italy but he lacked the funds to do so. He contracted a loan on disadvantageous terms with one Protos, a freedman of his mother whom she had left to Antonia. Agrippa sailed first for Alexandria, narrowly escaping the clutches of Herennius Capito, an imperial procurator who sought payment of Agrippa's outstanding debts to the imperial treasury (*Ant* 18.156–8). At Alexandria, Agrippa gained further funds through his wife, Cypros, who obtained a loan from Alexander the alabarch, who had already refused her husband (*Ant* 18.159–60).

Agrippa was received warmly by the emperor Tiberius on Capri, until a letter of complaint arrived from the outraged Capito. Tiberius now ordered that Agrippa be refused admission to him until his debt to the treasury had been paid. Antonia loaned Agrippa the necessary sum in memory of his mother and his upbringing with Claudius, her son. Tiberius now received him once more and placed him in the entourage of his grandson, Tiberius Gemellus. Meanwhile, Agrippa also sought the company of Antonia's grandson, Gaius, better-known by his nickname, "Caligula." A huge loan from a Samaritan freedman of Tiberius enabled Agrippa to pay his debt to Antonia and to spend lavishly as he pursued Gaius' favor (*Ant* 18.161–7). But Agrippa went so far in currying favor with Gaius that he found himself condemned by Tiberius on a charge of treason. Antonia's influence won him some privileges during his 6 months of imprisonment under the ever-present threat of execution (*Ant* 18.168–204).

Agrippa was only released upon Gaius' accession, after Tiberius' death, in A.D. 37. Gaius assigned him the northern domains of Philip the tetrarch and Lysanias with the title of king. Agrippa also received the symbols of the rank of praetor (*Ant* 18.228–37; Philo *In Flaccum* 40). Returning to Judaea in A.D. 38 he visited Alexandria where he eclipsed the Roman prefect of Egypt in his splendor (Philo *In Flaccum* 26–29). Upon the exile of Antipas in A.D. 39, Gaius gave Agrippa his tetrarchy (Galilee and Perea) in addition to Agrippa's other lands (*War* 2.183; *Ant* 18.255). At about this time Agrippa used his favor with Gaius and his diplomatic skills to block Gaius' plan of erecting a statue of his imperial self in the Temple at Jerusalem (Philo *Leg. ad Gaium* 261ff.).

At Rome again in A.D. 41, Agrippa is credited by Josephus with a major role in the tense negotiations which followed Gaius' assassination and which resulted in the accession of Claudius without full-blooded civil war. In reward, Claudius bestowed upon him the rest of the kingdom of Herod, his grandfather. Claudius formalized Agrippa's new position with a treaty ceremony in the Forum at Rome, held according to archaic custom, as Agrippa's coinage indicates (*Ant* 19.275 with *HJP*², 445 n. 19). Agrippa also received the symbols of the rank of consul. For his brother Herod, Agrippa won rule over Chalcis (Dio 60.8.2–3).

Agrippa soon returned to his newly enlarged kingdom where he ruled to the benefit of Jerusalem and other cities, notably Berytus in Syria (*Ant* 19.335ff.). Yet, despite his close relationship with Claudius, Agrippa was instructed to abandon his fortification of Jerusalem by the emperor through Marsus, governor of Syria. Such fortifications were considered to be a potential threat (*Ant* 19.326–7 with *HJP*², 448). On similar grounds Marsus broke up a gathering of kings which Agrippa had convened at Tiberias in A.D. 44 (*Ant* 19.338–42).

In general, Agrippa observed Jewish traditions scrupulously (*Ant* 19.331; though see *HJP*², 451 on his coinage). He persecuted the Christians James and Peter, executing the former and chaining the latter (Acts 12:1–5). He died in A.D. 44 after a short illness which suddenly afflicted him while he presided at a festival in the emperor's honor at Caesarea-Strato's Tower. At the festival, Agrippa dressed in a silver robe; the crowd, impressed with his radiance, acclaimed him a god. He did not reject the acclamation, and this act of vainglory was seen as the reason for his death (*Ant* 19.343–52; Acts 12:22–23).

Agrippa and Cypros had several children: Marcus Julius Agrippa (= Agrippa II); Drusus, who died before his father; Bernice; Mariamme; and Drusilla. Their names indicate a mixture of Jewish and family traditions with a concern for the Roman imperial family (Braund 1984: 111). Agrippa's own nomenclature, Julius Agrippa, indicates not only the Roman citizenship which he had inherited through Herod but also his family's links with the Roman Agrippa, a stalwart of Augustus' regime. Agrippa must have had a Roman forename, but this is not known: Marcus is usually assumed on the grounds that his son was Marcus, but it is also likely since the Roman Agrippa had also been Marcus. Like his son after him, Agrippa as king boasted the titles "Great King, Friend of Caesar, Pious and Friend of the Romans" (*HJP*², 452; cf. 475). The book of Acts is exceptional in according him the name "Herod."

2. Agrippa II—or, to give him his Roman name, Marcus Julius Agrippa—was born in A.D. 28 the son of Agrippa I and Cypros (*War* 2.220 with *Ant* 19.354). At the time of his father's death in 44 A.D., young Agrippa was in Rome, where he was being brought up at the court of the emperor Claudius. Claudius, we are told, wished immediately to appoint him as his father's successor on the throne: Josephus implies that Claudius' formal treaty with Agrippa I may have contained some mention of the succession (*Ant* 19.360–2). However, the emperor's advisers dissuaded him from this plan in the light of Agrippa's youth and the kingdom's importance. In his stead Claudius therefore appointed a Roman governor (*Ant* 19.363).

While at Claudius' court, Agrippa took the opportunity of representing Jewish causes (*Ant* 15.407; 20.10ff. and 135). Claudius gave him the kingdom left vacant by the death of Herod of Chalcis, husband of his sister Bernice, in about A.D. 50 (*Ant* 20.104; *War* 2.223, with *HJP*², Appendix 1). Josephus reckons the years of Agrippa's reign there from A.D. 49 (*JW* 2.284; cf. *Ant* 20.138). In 52 A.D. Agrippa was in Rome once more (*Ant* 20.134ff.). In A.D. 53, instead of Chalcis, he was given the former domains of Philip, Lysimachus, and Varus (*Ant* 20.138; with *HJP*², 472 n. 7). Nero added parts of Galilee and Peraea, most importantly Tiberias, Tarichea, and Julias (*Ant* 20.159; *War* 2.252). These additions may be linked with the new eras which appear on his coinage in 56 A.D. and 61 respectively. In Nero's honor he renamed Caesarea Philippi as Neronias (*Ant* 20.211).

Agrippa has been acccused of excessive slavishness towards the Romans (notably by Schürer [*HJP*², 474]); however, the accusation is not easily substantiated. His concern for Judaism is not in doubt; his discussions on Jewish legal matters with Rabbi Eliezer ben Hyrcanus tend to indicate as much (as Schürer [*HJP*², 475] allows). That Agrippa's sister's husbands underwent circumcision may or may not be a further indication (*pace HJP*², 475, who overemphasizes this). The book of Acts tends to suggest some interest in matters of religion, if a little detached, for he and his sister Bernice wished to see and hear Paul (25:22ff., especially 26:3). In particular, Agrippa's support of Jewish causes with Claudius ought not to be forgotten (above), nor the fact that he took costly steps to save the Temple from subsidence (*War* 5.36; *Ant* 15.391).

In A.D. 66 Agrippa was in Alexandria to congratulate Tiberius Julius Alexander, a man of Jewish origin who had become Roman prefect of Egypt. As the Jewish revolt developed in that year, Agrippa returned to Jerusalem to quell it. He failed to do so and became a target himself as the revolt flared up and split into factions (*War* 2.426). He was left little choice but to join with the Romans, which gave him the considerable military might and resources at his disposal (*War* 2.500–3; 523–5). Parts of his kingdom joined the revolt, notably Tiberias, Tarichea, and the fortress of Gamala, but Agrippa preferred to rule through delegates. He spent much of his time outside his kingdom at Berytus, a favorite city of the Herods, until the arrival of Vespasian in A.D. 67. Thereafter he kept close to Vespasian and his son Titus, who had also spent his youth at the court of Claudius (*HJP*², 477).

Upon Nero's death in A.D. 68, Agrippa left for Rome together with Titus in order to congratulate the new emperor, Galba. In the course of their journey news arrived that Galba had been assassinated and replaced. Agrippa continued to Rome, but Titus returned to his father. On July 1, A.D. 69, Vespasian was proclaimed emperor at Alexandria; war with the other claimant, Vitellius, followed, so Agrippa returned from Rome, staying with Titus, whom his father had left to deal with the Jewish revolt (Tacitus *Historiae* 2.1–2; 2.81; 5.1).

When Vespasian had established himself as emperor and the Jewish revolt had been crushed, Agrippa was rewarded for his loyalty with additional territory (details are lacking; see *HJP*², 478). In Rome in A.D. 75 Agrippa was awarded the symbols of praetorian rank. Thereafter he all but disappears from history. Josephus tells us that Agrippa corresponded with him on the subject of his book on the *Jewish War,* praising its accuracy and admitting that he owned a copy (*Life* 65; *AgAp* 1.9). Agrippa seems to have died in the reign of Vespasian's younger son, Domitian, about A.D. 93 (*HJP*², 480–83). His attitude toward the Romans, in part at least, is summed up in the speech which Josephus attributed to him. If Agrippa did not actually deliver this speech in trying to quell the revolt, he apparently later read and approved of it. The main point of the speech seems notably well-reasoned: namely, that the Romans were simply too strong to succumb to any uprising which Jewish revolutionaries could mount (*War* 2.345ff.).

Agrippa seems not to have married and not to have fathered any children. It was rumored that his relationship with his sister Bernice was incestuous: Josephus' denial of that rumor is as predictable and inconclusive as Juvenal's eager acceptance of it (*Ant* 20.145; Juv. 6.158).

Bibliography

Braund, D. C. 1984. *Rome and the Friendly King.* New York.

Schürer, E. 1973. *The History of the Jewish People in the Age of Jesus Christ (175 B.C.–A.D. 135).* Ed. G. Vermes and F. Millar. Edinburgh.

DAVID C. BRAUND

AGUE See SICKNESS AND DISEASE.

AGUR. (PERSON) [Heb *ʾāgûr*]. The son of Jakeh, and author of a collection of Proverbs beginning in Prov 30:1. It remains unclear whether the pericope ends with the conclusion of the chapter or at an earlier point (verse 14?). See McKane *Proverbs* OTL, 643 for discussion. Cohen (*Proverbs* SonB, 200) cited a midrash that identified Agur as Solomon, the one who "stored up" (*ʾagar)* wisdom and (*nqh*?) "spewed it out" (*hiqqi*—for Jakeh) by taking many wives. Another ancient view of the passage understood "Agur" allegorically, i.e., as a reference to Solomon and saw "Jakeh" as David. Apparently, the Vulgate translated *ʾāgûr* as a passive participle, hence, "the Assembler" (from *ʾāgûr* "to gather"), an appellative rather than a proper name. The LXX reads "fear (my words)" based on the Hebrew *gûr* or *tāgûr* (*BHS*:1315), from *gûr* ("to dread").

The collection displays no unique character that would aid in recovery of information on the obscure Agur. The translation of the proper names (Agur and Jakeh) provides a preferred solution for the difficult passage, but the solution itself is not beyond question. Some commentators (e.g., Ringgren *Sprüche* ATD; Scott *Proverbs* AB, 175) read *hammassaʾî* ("the Massaite") for the difficult *hammassāʾ* ("the oracle"). Keil and Delitzsch (1950: 266–67) translated Prov 30:1 as "The words of Agur the son of Jakeh, of the tribe (the country) of Massa," claiming that both Agur and LEMUEL were Arabs. The name Agur does occur in Sabean inscriptions, though it is not found elsewhere in the Hebrew Bible. The word *hamassāʾ* has been emended to *mašālô* ("his *mašal*") by a number of recent interpreters. The most popular approach has been to read *massāʾ* as the common noun meaning "burden" or "oracle." Toy's suggestion that the word be omitted as a gloss is the most extreme solution (*Proverbs* ICC, 518). He also suggested that Agur was either a sage who lived well after Solomon, or an older figure whose authority was used by a later writer.

Bibliography

Keil, C. F. and Delitzsch, F. 1950. *Biblical Commentary on the Proverbs of Solomon.* Vol. 2. Grand Rapids.

DONALD K. BERRY

AHAB (PERSON) [Heb *ʾaḥʾāb*]. The name of two persons in the Hebrew Bible.

1. Son and successor of Omri, who ruled N Israel during the second quarter of the 9th century B.C. The exact dates of his reign are disputed: 871–852 B.C. (Begrich 1929; Jepsen and Hanhart BZAW 88); 874–853 (Thiele 1965); 875–854 (Andersen 1969). The Deuteronomistic and prophetic traditions single him out as one of the worst kings of the N kingdom (1 Kgs 16:33; 2 Kgs 21:3, 13; Micah 6:16).

A. Sources

The sources for Ahab are 1 Kings 16:29–22:40, with the exception of chapter 19 (in which Ahab is mentioned only in verse 1, the introduction), chapter 20, and 22:1–38. These latter two references originally were not in the context of traditions about Ahab but instead of a later phase of the Omride dynasty or earlier phase of the Jehu dynasties, despite the occasional mention of Ahab's name (20:2, 13, 14; 22:20, see below). Given the tendentious nature of the remaining texts, however, caution is necessary when using them as historical sources. For example, the Elijah stories originate in prophetic circles of tradition which opposed the royal house of Omri (especially its religious policies), and which therefore depict Ahab as Elijah's antagonist. Also, the framework for the reign of Ahab (16:29–33; 22:39–40) is formed by the Deuteronomistic redactors of the book of Kings, who insert important traditional material here going back to the royal records of the N kingdom, but who utilize this material for their own negative assessment of Ahab.

These sparse historically relevant accounts of Ahab in the OT are supplemented by extrabiblical sources. Ahab is expressly mentioned in the so-called monolith inscription of the Assyrian king Shalmaneser III (see *ANET,* 277ff.). Likewise, the inscription of King Mesha of Moab refers in part to the reign of Ahab, without, however, mentioning him by name. The historical value of the excerpts from the historical work of Menander of Ephesus quoted by Josephus (*Ant* 8.13.2; cf. 8.13.1) is doubtful.

B. Ahab's Foreign Policy

Ahab was the exponent of a political program introduced by his father Omri, shaped mainly to counter the threat posed by the expanding power of the neighboring Aramean kingdom of Damascus (Unger 1957; Hallo 1960; Mazar 1962; Tadmor 1975; Lipiński 1978). Since the incursion of the Arameans into Galilee under Baasha (1 Kgs 15:16–22), the kingdom of Damascus remained a constant source of trouble which kept particularly the area E of the Jordan under pressure. However, we have no information about actual conflicts between Damascus and Israel in the time of Ahab. A massive Aramean invasion into the center of the Israelite territory, as reported in 1 Kings 20, is not likely to have occurred under Ahab. The story, originally transmitted anonymously, and referring to a later historical situation, was placed into the reign of Ahab by redactors, who inserted his name in various places (vv 2, 13, 14). The battle for Ramoth-Gilead, in which Ahab purportedly died (22:29–38), is also unhistorical. For a discussion of problems associated with the battles reported in 1 Kings 20 and 22, see ARAM (PLACE). Nevertheless, one may assume a constant state of tension between Aram-Damascus and Israel and possibly even border skirmishes.

These hostilities came to an end toward the end of Ahab's reign when a more dangerous enemy appeared on the scene and threatened both Syria and Palestine: the Assyrian king Shalmaneser III. Aram and Israel temporarily suspended their hostilities in order to oppose the Assyrians in a grand alliance of the Syro-Palestinian states ca. 853 B.C. The major part of Ahab's reign, however, seems to have been overshadowed by the Aramean threat. To meet this threat, Ahab conducted a deliberate policy of peace and alliances with the neighboring states, especially Judah and Phoenicia. The border skirmishes with Judah, which had erupted periodically since the division of the kingdom at the time of Rehoboam, were probably terminated by Omri, but certainly by Ahab. The new state of peace and alliance was sealed by a political marriage: ATHALIAH (more likely a sister [2 Kgs 8:26] than a daughter of Ahab [2 Kgs 8:18]) was given in marriage to the Judean crown prince Jehoram. In the following period the Judean kings appear as partners in alliance with the N Israelite monarchs of the Omride dynasty.

In similar fashion, the relationship with the Phoenicians was placed on a new footing. Ahab, probably already as crown prince, married the Phoenician princess Jezebel, daughter of "Ethbaal, King of the Sidonians" (1 Kgs 16:31) or "Ittobaal, king of Tyre and Sidon" (Josephus *Ant* 8.13.1). It is doubtful whether the area of Mt. Carmel—which from time to time was in the hands of the Phoenicians—was returned to Israel in connection with the new alliance (Alt, *RGG*[3] 1: 189). By the time of Ahab, however, it was firmly under Israelite control. Furthermore, the alliance with the Phoenicians probably was intended less to settle territorial disputes than to insure a condition of peace in the NW and to encourage trade with the Mediterranean coast.

Finally, even the border wars with the Philistines (1 Kgs 15:27; 16:15) ceased. During Ahab's reign and beyond, relations with the Philistine city states seem to have been peaceful (2 Kings 1). East of the Jordan Ahab initially maintained Israel's hegemony over Moab and secured the S frontier of the Israelite settlement of the wadi Heidan against the mounting pressure from the Moabites. He doesn't seem to have attempted to recapture the territory between the Heidan and the Arnon, which was occupied by the Moabites. Thus, Ahab achieved a truce on all borders, and in some areas even secured allies, in order to meet the Aramean threat in the N.

C. Ahab's Domestic Policies

Ahab's domestic policies likewise were aimed at consolidating power. In order to relieve and obviate internal tension he pursued a policy designed to strike a balance between the Israelite population and traditionally Canaanite segments of the population. The speculation that Ahab opened his new capital of Samaria to the Canaanite influence in particular while his secondary residence Jezreel was intended primarily for the Israelite component of the citizenry (Alt *KlSchr*[2] 3: 258–302) cannot be documented. Yet it has a certain ring of truth, because Jezreel maintained its role as royal residence only among the rulers from the House of Omri and apparently lost this function after the revolution of Jehu and the anti-Canaanite purge of Samaria (2 Kings 9–10).

Ahab's policy of balancing Israelite and Canaanite interests also had consequences in the religious sphere. The Canaanite cult of Baal attained equal status and even received special governmental support through the influence of Queen Jezebel and her court. In Samaria, Ahab erected a temple to Baal with a Baal altar and an image of Asherah (1 Kgs 16:32f.). The god Baal who was worshipped there was identical to the Phoenician god Melkart whom Jezebel knew from her homeland. Ahab himself, however, was hardly a Baal worshipper (contrary to 1 Kgs 16:31); the names of his sons Ahaziah and Jehoram contain the root of Yahweh's name, and these names were Ahab's way of demonstrating his attachment to the God of Israel. Nevertheless, his policies of religious compromise and coexistence earned him the opposition of circles more zealously loyal to Yahweh, especially the prophet Elijah, who viewed Ahab's policies as a challenge to the requirement of exclusive worship of Yahweh (cf. 1 Kgs 18:21). This violent opposition continued among the prophetic groups even after the death of Ahab and has led to the dim view of Ahab preserved in the biblical tradition. Subsequently this portrait was adopted and further intensified by the Deuteronomistic redactors of the book of Kings (1 Kgs 16:30–33).

D. Traditions about Ahab

1. The Drought and the Contest on Carmel. The reign of Ahab is linked to the tradition of a severe drought whose beginning and end was traced to the activity of Elijah the prophet (1 Kgs 17:1; 18:41–46). It seems, however, that at this point the two were not yet antagonists. It is debatable whether this drought is identical with the one which Menander of Ephesus alleges occurred under Ittobaal of Tyre in Phoenicia (Josephus *Ant* 8.13.2), or whether the link between them was established by Josephus himself. The implication that the drought was caused by Ahab's idolatry (1 Kgs 16:29–17:1) was a construction of the Deuteronomistic redaction: The original prophecy itself (17:1) contained no such attribution. It is possible (if not provable) that, like other originally basic information (e.g., a more detailed identification of the rank of Ahab and of the place of the prophecy), the original "cause" for the drought was deleted by the redactors in favor of their own explanation.

The tradition of the contest on Mt. Carmel was originally unrelated to Ahab. True, he is mentioned in the introduction (18:20), but he appears nowhere else in the entire narrative (18:21–40). The contest on Mt. Carmel was thus definitely not a "Haupt- und Staatsaktion" (Alt, *KlSchr*[4] 2: 147), but was likely a much more limited, local event in which the powers of state were unlikely to have participated. Nor does the first half of chapter 18 contain any historically reliable information on Ahab. The passage which describes how Ahab and his house minister, Obadiah, scour the whole country in search of feed for the royal mares (vv 3–6) most likely does not recount an historical incident, but is intended to demonstrate vividly the severity of the drought's burden on the land. The scene of the encounter between Ahab and Elijah (vv 16–20) serves primarily to link the theme of the drought to the tradition of the "divine judgment on Mt. Carmel."

2. Naboth's Vineyard. The story of Naboth's vineyard at Jezreel (1 Kings 21), on the other hand, is explicitly an Ahab tradition. In the present form of the chapter it is Jezebel, to be sure, who is the chief character of the episode. Yet it is Ahab who was most likely the original focus of the tradition. This is already evident in the fact that, at first, Elijah addresses only Ahab (vv 17–22), while the word of judgment over Jezebel appears as a later addition to the story (v 23). Furthermore, there exists a short parallel tradition to this story in 2 Kgs 9:25–26. Here, too, only Ahab is mentioned as the offender; Jezebel is not mentioned at all. Similarly, the story's motif of "intrigue"—Jezebel staging a fast day with Naboth presiding, bribing false witnesses to denounce him, and then putting him to death on trumped up charges—probably should be attributed to a secondary embellishment of the tradition. Originally it is probable that Ahab on his own initiative appropriated a piece of land belonging to Naboth of Jezreel (more likely a field outside the city [2 Kgs 9:25f] than a vineyard next to the royal palace [1 Kgs 21:1]) by falsely accusing Naboth (of high treason?) and executing him together with his sons (2 Kgs 9:26), who would retain a legal claim to the land.

This was probably an instance of conflict between the old Israelite property laws and the interests of the king. The former guaranteed the Israelite protection from sale or exchange of his inherited land, while the latter accommodated the expansion and consolidation of crown property. According to 1 Kgs 21:2, Ahab shared the belief common in the ancient Orient (as well as in Canaan) that property could be freely traded, bought, exchanged, or mortgaged (not unlike his father Omri, who purchased the hill of Samaria, 1 Kgs 16:24). He was thwarted, however, by Naboth's implicit appeal to the Israelite law of property (21:3) which prohibited the sale or exchange of inherited land except for its transferral as inheritance. The intent of this tradition was probably to show how Ahab employed the power of his royal office to eliminate Naboth and his sons unlawfully and to gain possession of their land. This instance of might before right was a perversion of the king's role, and indicates that in some ways the Israelite monarchy resembled ancient Oriental despotism. Consequently, Ahab received an announcement of impending judgment; in 1 Kgs 21:17ff. it is understood to have been conveyed by Elijah, but in 2 Kgs 9:25–26 it is mentioned only as the word of Yahweh without naming any prophet. According to the latter text the judgment was executed not against Ahab but his son Jehoram. See NABOTH.

3. Building Projects. The reign of Ahab brought Israel not only military strength and security, but also increase of commerce, economic prosperity, and material culture. As might be expected, Ahab's building activity is also emphasized by the Deuteronomistic frame (16:32f.; 22:39) which itself derives from the royal records. It is likely that he completed the construction of the new capital, Samaria, which his father Omri had founded. Mention has already been made of the construction of a Baal temple with altar and Asherah statue (16:32f.), which was intended primarily for Jezebel and her retinue, but also for a wider Canaanite population. The shrine was totally demolished during Jehu's rise to power (2 Kgs 10:25–27) and therefore it is no longer accessible to archaeological examination. According to 1 Kgs 22:39, Ahab also built an "ivory house": This designates the royal palace (or a part thereof), the walls of which were decorated with ivory carvings.

The excavations at SAMARIA illustrate this fact. The ivory plaques found there represent the most important collection of Palestinian miniature art of this era. At least a part of it belongs to Ahab's time (Dussaud 1925). The images manifest the strong influence of Egyptian style, but are probably of Phoenician origin. A fortified casemate wall (stratum 2) ascribed to the Ahab period demonstrates Ahab's efforts to enclose the city. The design of the palace is no longer exactly ascertainable because of numerous structural additions. Especially noteworthy, however, is the brilliant wall construction using ashlars in a nearly seamless headers-and-stretchers technique, which cannot be attributed to indigenous Israelite traditions of craftsmanship. It is more likely that Ahab, like Solomon before him, employed Phoenician specialists who contributed their technical expertise in the construction of the capital city.

Besides Samaria there are other cities in the land which Ahab completed or developed into fortifications (Pienaar 1981). The latter normally were sitated in strategically important locations. Hazor, Dan, and En Gev protected the land against the Aramean threat; Megiddo shielded the plain of Jezreel against incursions from the coastal plain, especially by the Philistines; while Jericho (1 Kgs 16:34) apparently served as protection against possible Moabite attacks, or as a base of operations in S Cis-Jordan. Of course, it is not possible in every case to determine precisely whether the strata in question belong to the time of Ahab or to other Omride kings; however, in view of the remark in 1 Kgs 22:39 it seems most likely that the bulk of these should properly be attributed to Ahab.

The most striking archaeological findings come from MEGIDDO and HAZOR, both of which were heavily garrisoned fortresses. In the W part of the Hazor settlement there was a large citadel with unusually thick walls and a monumental gate which was originally adorned with proto-aeolic columns (Stratum 8). The excavations in Megiddo between 1960 and 1970 have caused a considerable revision of the old stratigraphy (Yadin 1975). The famed "stables of Solomon" now have turned out to be buildings from the time of Ahab (Stratum 4a); their function, however, remains disputed. In view of the large contingent of war chariots at Ahab's disposal, their use as stables cannot be ruled out; however, their interpretation as storehouses, or even as garrisons, is currently favored. A similar columned building in Hazor from the same era (Stratum 8) is plainly a storehouse. The immense water systems in Megiddo and Hazor are particularly striking. They, too, may be dated to Ahab's time. They each consisted of a vertical shaft (of 35 m at Megiddo; 30 m at Hazor) leading, via a stairway, to a horizontal tunnel. At Hazor this tunnel of 25 m led to the groundwater table in a gentle descent. At Megiddo water from a spring protected externally by a wall was carried to the shaft over a distance of 63 m. Both structures were engineering masterpieces of their time, insuring unhindered access to water from inside the city in the event of a siege.

4. The Battle of Qarqar. Toward the end of Ahab's reign a newly emerging enemy upset the balance of power in Syria and Palestine: the kingdom of Assyria. In 853 B.C. the Assyrian king Shalmaneser III mounted his first campaign against Syria. This event is not mentioned in the OT, but is known from Assyrian sources, particularly from the so-called Monolith Inscription of Shalmaneser (*ANET,* 278f.). Observing the Assyrian expansion, the Syro-Palestinian states suspended their internecine hostilities and formed a protective alliance against the greater danger. At the head of this coalition apparently stood the Aramean king of Damascus, Hadadezer. Immediately following him, Irḫulēni, king of the Arameans of Hamath, and Ahab of Israel *(aḫabbū sirʾilāʾa)* are mentioned as most important allies. They were joined by lesser Syrian and Phoenician rulers as well as Arabian cameleers. With 2,000 war chariots, Ahab deployed the largest chariot force of all the allies. Shalmaneser had attacked the area of Hamath and had conquered and destroyed the town of Qarqar. It was here that the army of the allies challenged him. As may be expected from the style of the Assyrian royal inscriptions, the Assyrians won a brilliant victory; it was, however, more likely a failure, for Shalmaneser discontinued his advance and apparently gave up his plans of subjugating the enemy. In the years following he avoided marching into Syria and resuming the battle with the allies.

5. Ahab's Death. Ahab died shortly after the battle of Qarqar. According to 1 Kgs 22:29–38, he lost his life in a battle with the Arameans over the E Jordan city of Ramoth-Gilead. This implies that the Israelite-Aramean alliance disintegrated quickly. However, the formula in 22:40 ("he was laid to rest with his father," which is generally used for a nonviolent death) contradicts such an implication, reflecting correctly the actual historical facts. 1 Kgs 22:29–38 is not a tradition yielding reliable historical data; at best it may reflect residual memories of the wounding of Ahab's son Jehoram near Ramoth-Gilead (2 Kgs 8:28–29; 9:14ff.). Furthermore, a notice of fulfillment has been inserted (22:38; cf 21:19). Thus it seems likely that Ahab died a peaceful and natural death in Samaria.

E. Conclusion

The portrait of Ahab and his dynasty (the "House of Ahab") has been negatively distorted in the OT tradition primarily because of his religious policies which were seen as a danger to the traditional worship of God in circles loyal to Yahweh. His skillful foreign policies, which provided Israel with strength, security, and prosperity, which safeguarded peace and the balance of power, and which, finally, contributed to the (temporary) containment of Assyrian expansionism, may be inferred from the few sources that yield reliable historical data. However, his contributions in this regard were ignored in the decidedly theological perspective of the OT witnesses (Whitley 1952; Gooding 1964; Cohen 1975). The negative picture of Ahab in the OT is influenced (1) by the circles of opposing prophetic groups who transmitted the events of that time through their own biased perspective and (2) by the transitions accompanying the Jehu revolution, which put an end to the "House of Ahab". In the judgment of later Deuteronomistic circles, Ahab was the worst of all the kings of the N kingdom (1 Kgs 16:33). For them, his behavior yielded a negative criterion for the assessment of subsequent kings or groups and their fortunes (2 Kgs 21:3, 13; Micah 6:16).

2. The son of Kolaiah who, along with Zedekiah the son of Maaseiah, was condemned by Jeremiah for prophesying false things to the Judean exiles in Babylonia (Jer 29:21–23). The two were also accused of committing adultery. Although the LXX omits 29:16–20 (the Lucianic text preserves them in a different order), the context of the passage suggests that, like their contemporary Hananiah (Jeremiah 28), these two prophesied a quick end to the exile. Apparently their prophetic activity earned them the disfavor of Nebuchadnezzar, who had them executed (probably for sedition). Consequently, Jeremiah anticipated that their deaths would be cited in a popular curse: "May Yahweh make you like Zedekiah and Ahab, whom the king of Babylon roasted in the fire."

Bibliography

Andersen, K. T. 1969. Die Chronologie der Könige von Israel und Juda. *ST* 23: 69–114.

Begrich, J. 1929. *Die Chronologie der Könige von Israel und Juda.* BHT 3.

Cohen, M. A. 1975. In All Fairness to Ahab. *EI* 12: 87–94.

Dussaud, R. 1925. Samarie au temps d'Achab. *Syr* 6: 314–48.

Fohrer, G. 1978. Ahab. *TRE* 2: 123–25.

Gooding, D. W. 1964. Ahab According to the Septuagint. *ZAW* 76: 269–80.

Hallo, W. 1960. From Qarqar to Carchemish. *BA* 23: 34–61.

Ishida, T. 1975. "The House of Ahab." *IEJ* 25: 135–37.

Jepsen, A., ed. 1979. *Von Sinuhe bis Nebukadnezar.* 3d ed. Stuttgart.

Lipiński, E. 1978. Aramäer und Israel. *TRE* 3: 590–99.

Mazar, B. 1962. The Aramaean Empire and its Relations with Israel. *BA* 25: 98–120.

Miller, J. M. 1967. The Fall of the House of Ahab. *VT* 17: 307–24.

Parzen, H. 1940. The Prophets and the Omri Dynasty. *HTR* 33: 69–96.

Pienaar, D. N. 1981. The Role of Fortified Cities in the Northern Kingdom During the Reign of the Omride Dynasty. *JNSL* 9: 151–57.

Tadmor, H. 1975. Assyria and the West. Pp. 36–48 in *Unity and Diversity.* H. Goedicke and J. J. M. Roberts, eds. Baltimore.

Thiele, E. R. 1965. *The Mysterious Numbers of the Hebrew Kings.* Rev. ed. Grand Rapids, MI.

Timm, S. 1980. Die territoriale Ausdehnung des Staates Israel zur Zeit der Omriden. *ZDPV* 96: 20–40.

———. 1982. *Die Dynastie Omri.* FRLANT 124.

Unger, M. 1957. *Israel and the Aramaeans of Damascus.* Grand Rapids, MI.

Whitley, C. F. 1952. The Deuteronomic Presentation of the House of Omri. *VT* 2: 137–42.

Yadin, Y. 1975. *Hazor.* New York.

WINFRIED THIEL
Trans. Dietlinde M. Elliott

AHARAH (PERSON) [Heb *ʾaḥĕrah*]. The third son of Benjamin, following Bela and Ashbel in 1 Chr 8:1 (LXX variants include *aara, deira,* and *iaphaēl*). Since the name Aharah does not occur in parallel genealogies of Benjamin (Gen 46:21; Num 26:38; 1 Chr 7:6), it is difficult to identify him. These various genealogies differ in the names, number (from three to ten), and order of sons listed. The close variant name "Ahiram" is listed as the 3d son of Benjamin in Num 26:38 (like Aharah, this name occurs only once), suggesting that the list in 1 Chronicles 8 is dependent on Numbers 26.

MARK J. FRETZ

AHARHEL (PERSON) [Heb *ʾăḥarḥēl*]. The son of Harum and bearer of the family name (1 Chr 4:8). Located within a fragmented list of Judah's descendants (vv 1–23), the MT shows no connection between this verse and the surrounding context. The MT of v 8 (*wĕqôs hôlîd ʾet-ʿānûb wĕʾet-haṣṣobēbâ ûmišpĕḥōt ʾăḥarḥēl ben-hārûm,* "And Koz was father of Anub, and Zobebah, and the families of Aharhel the son of Harum") may be connected to v 7, if it is assumed that Heb *wĕqôṣ* has dropped out of the end of v 7 through haplography (Williamson *1, 2 Chronicles* NCBC, 59). This would make Koz the last named son of Ashhur and Helah, and thereby relate his offspring to Judah. Similarly, v 8 and v 9 are not interconnected, unless it is assumed that Jabez was also a son of Koz (Curtis and Madsen *Chronicles* ICC, 107).

Most scholars agree that the text of 1 Chr 4:5–9 is corrupt, and that v 8 stands apart from the preceding and succeeding verses. Therefore, genealogical connections between individuals in these verses are not easily established. If, as the MT suggests, Aharhel is indeed the son of Harum, it seems unlikely for him also to be a son of Koz (Rudolf *Chronikbücher* HAT, 30). If Harum is a gentilic variant of "Ram" (Heb *rûm*), with a prefixed definite article, then Aharhel is a descendant of Ram (Yeivin 1971: 199, n. 109). The LXX reading suggests a third possibility: The name Aharhel itself (*ʾăḥarḥēl*) is a textual corruption of the phrase *ʾăḥî rēkab,* "brother of Rechab" (*genneseis adelphou Rēchab huiou Iareim,* "the progeny of the brother of Rechab, the son of Iarim"). Since the names Aharhel and Harum do not occur elsewhere in the Bible, and the foregoing questions cannot be satisfactorily resolved, no clear identification of Aharhel is possible.

Bibliography

Yeivin, S. 1971. *The Israelite Conquest of Canaan.* Uitgaven van het Nederlands Historisch-Archaeologisch Instituut te Istanbul 27. Istanbul.

MARK J. FRETZ

AHASBAI (PERSON) [Heb *ʾăḥasbay*]. The father of Eliphelet (2 Sam 23:34), one of David's champions (the *šālišîm;* RSV: The Thirty). That Ahasbai was from Maacah may indicate that he was a Syrian (see MAACAH), making his son one of the many foreign nationals among David's retainers. The town of Abel, in Beth-Maacah (2 Sam 20:14) probably refers to the region of Maacah in southern Syria as well (cf. Aharoni *LBHG* 167). On the other hand, 1 Chr 2:48; 4:19 list Maacah as a family group in southern Judah, raising the possibility that Ahasbai was a Judean. The parallel list in Chronicles (1 Chr 11:35b–36a) reads Eliphal the son of Ur, followed by Hepher the Mecherathite, instead of Eliphelet, the son of Ahasbai of Maacah. In this case it seems probable that the scribe misread the Hebrew consonantal text *ʾḥsby* as *ʾwr ḥpr,* though in other instances it appears as if the Chronicler is working with a somewhat different text from that in 2 Sam 23:8–39 (see DAVID'S CHAMPIONS).

D. G. SCHLEY

AHASHTARITES [Heb *hāʾăḥaštārî*]. See HAAHASHTARI.

AHASUERUS (PERSON) [Heb *ʾăḥašwērôš;* Gk *asyēros*]. **1.** The Persian king who chose Esther to be his queen (Esth 1:1; 2:16–17; cf. also Ezra 4:6). See ESTHER. He is to be identified with the famous XERXES (485–465 B.C.), but was mistakenly identified in Jewish Midrash with Artaxerxes. Hoschander (1923) argued that Ahasuerus was to be identified with Artaxerxes II (403–359 B.C.). But extrabiblical evidence leaves little doubt that Ahasuerus was Xerxes, the son of Darius I. Shea (1976: 228) is able to list the spelling of both Xerxes and Artaxerxes in seven languages: Greek, Old Persian, Elamite, Aramaic, Hebrew, Akkadian, Egyptian (there is always a *t* in the spelling of the latter name).

Apart from Esther, this Ahasuerus is mentioned only in Ezra 4:6 in relation to an accusation which was lodged against the Jews in his reign. Morgenstern (1956, 1957, 1960, 1966) postulated a destruction of Jerusalem in 485 B.C. in the reign of Xerxes as the immediate background of Ezra and Nehemiah, but most scholars regard such a thesis as highly improbable.

Herodotus, in addition to depicting Xerxes' role in the invasion of Greece in 480 B.C., presents an unflattering portrait of the king as an impatient, hot-tempered monarch with a wandering eye for women. According to Herodotus (9.108–13), Xerxes (Gk *assouēros*) not only tried to have an affair with his brother's wife, but also did have an affair with her daughter.

According to Barucq (1961: 3), the role which Ahasuerus holds in Esther "conforms perfectly to Xerxes" as we know him from Herodotus. Moore (1975: 69) agrees: "Much of what the author of Esther says about King Xerxes corresponds fairly well with what the classical writers had to say about such things, for example, . . . his nasty and at times irrational temper (1:12; 7:7–8). . . ."

Ahasuerus is prominently portrayed on his throne in a fresco of the famous Dura Europos synagogue (Levit-Tawil 1983).

2. The father of Darius the Mede (Dan 9:1). See DARIUS THE MEDE.

3. The ruler who helped Nebuchadnezzar destroy the city of Nineveh (Tob 14:15). However, given the romantic and unhistorical nature of this apocryphal book, the identity of this character is in doubt. The author's chronological sequence seems to be so skewed (cf. Tob 1:4, which condenses events two centuries apart into one generation) that it is impossible to determine which ancient ruler he had in mind. He may have regarded this as the same Ahasuerus mentioned in Esth 1:1 and Ezra 4:6 (i.e., the Persian Xerxes; see 1. above), who came to the throne about 75 years after Nebuchadnezzar died. Other ancient sources confirm that Nineveh was actually destroyed in 612 B.C. by a coalition led by Nebuchadnezzar's father Nabopolassar and Cyaxares *(Uvaxšatra)* the Mede.

Bibliography

Barucq, A. 1961. Esther et la cour de Suse. *BTS* 39: 3–5.

Hoschander, J. 1923. *The Book of Esther in the Light of History.* Philadelphia.

Levit-Tawil, D. 1983. The Enthroned King Ahasuerus at Dura. *BASOR* 250: 57–78.

Littman, R. J. 1975. The Religious Policy of Xerxes and the *Book of Esther. JQR* 65: 145–55.

Millard, A. R. 1977. The Persian Names in Esther and the Reliability of the Hebrew Text. *JBL* 96: 481–88.

Moore, C. A. 1975. Archaeology and the Book of Esther. *BA* 38: 62–79.

Morgenstern, J. 1956. Jerusalem—485 B.C. *HUCA* 27: 101–79.

———. 1957. Idem. *HUCA* 28: 15–47.

———. 1960. Idem. *HUCA* 31: 1–29.

———. 1966. Further Light from the Book of Isaiah upon the Catastrophe of 485 B.C. *HUCA* 37: 1–28.

Olmstead, A. T. 1948. *History of the Persian Empire.* Chicago.

Shea, W. H. 1976. Esther and History. *AUSS* 14: 227–46.

Yamauchi, E. 1980. The Archaeological Background of Esther. *BSac* 137: 99–117.

EDWIN M. YAMAUCHI

AHAVA (PLACE) [Heb *ʾahăwāʾ*]. Var. THERAS. The river (and possibly also a town) mentioned in Ezra's memoirs as the place where Ezra first gathered the exiles and proclaimed a fast before departing to return to Palestine (Ezra 8:15, 21, 31). Although limited data is available, and all proposed identifications assume a particular route for Ezra's return, Ahava presumably was located within a radius of 200 km from Babylon (Zadok 1979: 117).

One obstacle to identification lies in the abundant textual variants found in the relevant verses. In v 15, the Ethiopic *ahua* reflects MT tradition, but LXX variants including *euei(m)* and *thousi* do not support the MT. In vv 21 and 31, the LXX reads variously *thoue, aoue, daouath.* The 1 Esdras 8 parallels read *theran* (41, 60—Eng 8:61), while a variant of v 41 reads *potamon* (river) as the proper name itself. Josephus mentions no name, but simply refers to the place as the "other side of the Euphrates" (*Ant* 11.5.2). It is difficult to decipher whether the various mss reflect different *vorlagen,* or whether the scribes were attempting to make an identification of the site.

Although the canal Ahava still has not been positively identified by scholars (Delitzsch 1881: 193), and may simply refer to a large, unsettled area outside Babylon, it may be associated with various settlement sites. According to Williamson (*1, 2 Chronicles* NCBC, 116), Ahava may have been one of Babylon's artificial canals or waterways constructed for defensive purposes, whose source was the Euphrates. Winckler (1901: 518) identifies Ahava with the ancient city of *Opis* (Babylonian *Upi*), which was probably located north of Sippar along the Tigris. Obermeyer (1929: 15) identifies Ahava with "Awa-na" (where "na" signifies a district), a village located ca. 53 km north of Baghdad near the Tigris. Based on LXX *aoue* and *euei,* Gutman (*EncMiqr* 1: 122) proposes *Itu* (modern *Hīt,* probably the same as *ʾIs*), a city located ca. 200 km northwest of Babylon on the Euphrates.

Bibliography

Delitzsch, F. 1881. *Wo lag das Paradies?* Leipzig.

Obermeyer, J. 1929. *Die Landschaften Babylonien im Zeitalter des Talmuds und des Gaonats.* Schriften der Gesellschaft zur Förderung der Wissenschaft des Judentums 30. Frankfurt am Main.

Winckler, H. 1901. *Altorientalische Forschungen.* Vol. 3. Leipzig.

Zadok, R. 1979. *The Jews in Babylonia During the Chaldean and*

Achaemenian Periods according to the Babylonian Sources. Studies in the History of the Jewish People and the Land of Israel Monograph Series 3. Haifa.

MARK J. FRETZ

AHAZ (PERSON) [Heb ʾāḥāz]. The name is a hypocoristicon: a shortened form of names such as Ahaziah and Jehoahaz, "the LORD holds." These names probably reflect confidence in God's imminent presence, as in Ps 73:23, "I am always with you, you hold (*ʾāḥaztā*) my right hand" (*IPN,* 179).

1. The great-great-grandson of Saul, mentioned only in post-exilic genealogies (1 Chr 8:35, 36, and 9:41, 42; Ahaz is absent in the Hebrew of 9:41, probably as a result of haplography). These verses appear in the two nearly identical genealogies of Saul's family in 1 Chr 8:33–40 and 1 Chr 9:39–44. This list is from the end of the First Temple period (Demsky 1971: 20), and was preserved by Benjaminite families that survived the Babylonian exile (Williamson 1979: 356). The existence and preservation of the Saulide genealogy probably reflects the continued prominence of Saul's family, and perhaps even their hope that they would return to power (Ackroyd, *Chronicles Ezra Nehemiah* CBC, 42; Flanagan 1982: 25). The genealogy of Benjamin in 1 Chronicles 8 corresponds to the genealogy of Judah in chaps. 2–4, forming a frame around the other tribes of Israel. Benjamin and Judah are given this prominent position by the Chronicler because of their past loyalty to David and the Temple (Williamson, *Chronicles* NCB, 46–47) and because they are the two main tribes that returned from the exile (Ezra 1:5). The repetition of the genealogy in chap. 9 serves as a bridge to the narrative of Saul's death in chap. 10 (Demsky 1971: 17).

Bibliography

Demsky, A. 1971. The Genealogy of Gibeon (1 Chronicles 9:35–44). *BASOR* 202: 16–23.

Flanagan, J. 1982. Genealogy and Dynasty in the Early Monarchy of Israel and Judah. Pp. 23–28 in *Proceedings of the Eighth World Congress of Jewish Studies. Division A: The Period of the Bible.* Jerusalem.

Williamson, H. G. M. 1979. Sources and Redaction in the Chronicler's Genealogy of Judah. *JBL* 98: 351–59.

MARC Z. BRETTLER

2. The son and successor of Jotham, who assumed the throne when he was 20 years old and reigned for 16 years, ca. 742–727 B.C.E. (2 Kgs 16:2). The fuller form of the name Jehoahaz is found in the Assyrian annals of Tiglath-pileser III as Yauhazi (*ANET,* 282–4). The chronological difficulties connected with this reign are notoriously difficult. The precise timing of Ahaz's accession is obscured by the conflicting references in 2 Kgs 16:2 and 2 Chr 28:1 when compared with the contradictory information about the death of Ahaz and the accession of Hezekiah (2 Kgs 16:19–20; 18:1). If Hezekiah succeeded Ahaz when he was 25 years old (2 Kgs 18:2), then Ahaz could only have been 11 years old when he became a father since he is said to have been 36 at the time of his death (2 Chr 28:2).

Various aspects of the reign of Ahaz are described in three separate accounts in 2 Kings 16, 2 Chronicles 28, and Isaiah 7, as well as in Assyrian annals and inscriptions (*ANET,* 282–84). These accounts give very different assessments of the reign of Ahaz, as well as a number of conflicting details which are difficult to reconcile. Historians have tried to reconstruct the Syro-Ephraimite war on the basis of the accounts of Ahaz's reign in Kings, Chronicles, and Isaiah. All note that the broad outline appears to be recognizable, while the actual details are much more contentious. See SYRO-EPHRAIMITE WAR. A good account of the various difficulties can be found in Bright (*BHI,* 276–77) or Miller and Hayes (*HAIJ,* 340–46). These accounts are dependent upon critical judgments about the date of the various narratives as well as assessments of the priority of various conflicting details in the different accounts. There is some dispute over the correct date of Ahaz's appeal to Tiglath-pileser for assistance in fending off the anti-Assyrian coalition formed by N Israel and Syria. Judah was deprived of the important economic and strategic port of Elath by the Arameans (according to the MT of 2 Kgs 16:6) or by the Edomites (as many commentators emend the text). According to the Chronicler, the Edomites joined the attack upon Judah (2 Chr 28:17–18), while the Philistines made incursions into the Shephelah and Negeb. However, it is clear that the Assyrians soon subdued the region and defeated the Syro-Ephraimite coalition (ca. 734–732 B.C.E.).

Furthermore, it is often concluded that the consequences of Ahaz's action was to reduce Judah to a vassal state of Assyria (*BHI,* 276–77). A particular area of debate (Cogan 1974; McKay 1973) has been whether or not Ahaz introduced the worship of Assyrian astral deities into the Jerusalem temple and so throughout Judah. Such a view is based on the description of Ahaz's voluntary introduction of the altar from Damascus into the Jerusalem temple after his visit to Tiglath-pileser (2 Kgs 16:10). This is then thought to be confirmed by the fact that Ahaz was forced to pay tribute, in the form of temple treasures, to his Assyrian overlord. However, this standard interpretation has been challenged, particularly by Cogan (1974) and McKay (1973). They question the fact that Tiglath-pileser ever imposed Assyrian religion upon vassals or that Ahaz was forced to modify indigenous cults (McKay 1973: 5–12). It has been pointed out that the Deuteronomistic condemnation of Ahaz was for the introduction of Palestinian indigenous cults rather than for those of Assyria (Cogan 1974: 72–88). Ahaz's sacrificial cult is described in 2 Chr 28:23 as being carried out in honor of the "gods of Damascus." This suggests that the Jerusalem cult was based on common Syro-Palestinian models, rather than necessarily subject to Assyrian imperial religion. Cogan and McKay deny that the type of altar described is found in Mesopotamia. Ahaz is also seen as reviving the cult of child sacrifice associated with Molech. The phrase "he made his son pass through the fire" is taken as a reference to child sacrifice rather than some ritual ordeal: RSV "he burned his son" (cf. Deut 18:10).

The differing biblical and scholarly assessments of Ahaz's reign highlight the tendentious nature of the biblical narratives. Ackroyd (1968) has highlighted the differing theological concerns in the three narratives and their difficulty as historical sources. He maintains that it is not possible to conflate the accounts in order to arrive at an historical picture. Thompson (1982) has produced the most detailed study of the theological shaping of these narratives. Ackroyd (1984) has recently argued that Ahaz's submission to Assyrian power enabled Judah to survive the catastrophe which overtook the northern kingdom in 722 B.C.E., whereas Hezekiah's rebellion against the Assyrians resulted in disaster. He concludes that the biblical assessments of Ahaz's reign from a purely theological point of view present the opposite of an historically accurate picture.

The account of Ahaz's reign in 2 Kings 16 forms an important part of the Deuteronomistic presentation of the climactic advance of the S kingdom to its ultimate fate at the hands of the Babylonians in 587 B.C.E. Ahaz's reign is highlighted by the Deuteronomists in a number of important ways. He is not only condemned with the standard assessment that "he did not do what was right in the eyes of the LORD . . . ," but his reign is introduced without mention of his mother, a very rare occurrence in regnal formulae paralleled only in the introduction to the reign of Jehoram (2 Kgs 8:16–17). Again, like Jehoram, Ahaz is also reviled further by being compared in his wickedness to the kings of Israel (2 Kgs 16:3; see 2 Kgs 8:18). The amount of space devoted to detailing Ahaz's religious and political deviations from the Deuteronomistic ideal highlights the significance of this chapter within the Deuteronomistic History. Ahaz is presented as adding significantly to this spiral of cultic decline by following the abominable practices of the nations driven out by Yahweh and sacrificing and burning incense on the high places, hills, and under every green tree. His cultic failings are couched in language that makes his crime in the eyes of the Deuteronomists unambiguous and unforgivable. The appeal to Tiglath-pileser against the Syro-Ephraimite coalition, his subsequent building of the altar on the Damascus model, the payment of tribute, and various alterations to the temple are introduced without explicit comment or condemnation. However, in the context of the severe condemnation in the opening verses of the chapter (2 Kgs 16:2–4), this has to be read as further evidence of the inherent corruption of Ahaz's reign. Most reigns of S kings who are judged as unworthy as Ahaz are dismissed in a few verses. The significance of this chapter is that it stands immediately before the important editorial section in 2 Kings 17 detailing the destruction of the N for its apostasy. The present context, therefore, highlights that the S kingdom is progressing at an ever increasing rate to a similar fate.

The Chronicler's presentation of the reign of Ahaz further highlights the different theological assumptions underlying these major complexes within the Hebrew Bible. It is generally recognized that the Chronicler reworks the material from Kings in line with his/her own tendentious design. The overall condemnation at the opening of the chapter remains very much the same. However the details of the account are often strikingly different while much of the material is unique to the Chronicler. The treatment of Judaean captives by the N kingdom (2 Chr 28:8–15) is an addition by the Chronicler. Ahaz's problems with Israel and Syria are not presented as due to a coalition but as separate matters. Whereas 2 Kings 16 and Isaiah 7 state that the coalition besieged Jerusalem but was unable to take it, the Chronicler details devastating defeats by Syria and Israel. Williamson (1977: 114–18) has pointed out the significance of the chapter within the Chronicler's work. The various additions and changes made by the Chronicler to the Kings account reverse the presentations of the S and N kingdoms in 2 Chronicles 13. He highlights very significant literary parallels between 2 Chronicles 28 and 2 Chronicles 13 which emphasize the tendentious way in which the material is presented. At the end of the reign of Ahaz both communities have been defeated and are in partial exile. It is made clear that Ahaz has reversed the religious policies of Abijah and that Judah has assumed the apostate role previously attributed to N Israel.

Isaiah 7 provides a different perspective on the Syro-Ephraimite coalition and Ahaz's role in the affair. Ahaz symbolizes a lack of faith and trust in Yahweh. The symbolic naming of the children, Shear-jashub and Immanuel, are signs of hope presented to the king confirming that the coalition will be divinely defeated, provided Judah remains faithful. The implicit threat is to the Davidic dynasty since the signs are given to "the house of David" (7:2). Clements (*Isaiah* NCBC, 84) also points out that the attempt by the coalition to place Ben Tabeel on the throne further symbolizes the threat since it is usually assumed that the reference is to an Aramaean of non-Davidic descent.

Bibliography

Ackroyd, P. R. 1968. Historians and Prophets. *SEÅ* 33: 18–54.

———. 1984. The Biblical Interpretation of the Reigns of Ahaz and Hezekiah. Pp. 247–59 in *In the Shelter of Elyon. Essays on Ancient Palestinian Life and Institutions in Honor of G. W. Ahlström,* ed. W. B. Barrick and J. R. Spencer. Sheffield.

Cogan, M. 1974. *Imperialism and Religion. Assyria, Judah and Israel in the Eighth and Seventh Centuries B.C.E.* Missoula.

McKay, J. W. 1973. *Religion in Judah under the Assyrians 732–609 B.C.* London.

Thompson, M. 1982. *Situation and Theology: Old Testament Interpretation of the Syro-Ephraimite War.* Sheffield.

Williamson, H. G. M. 1977. *Israel in the Books of Chronicles.* Cambridge.

Keith W. Whitelam

AHAZIAH (PERSON) [*ʾăḥazyāh(û)*]. The name of two kings in the OT. The name means "Yahweh has seized."

1. King of N Israel, the son and successor of Ahab, who reigned little more than one year. The calculations for his reign differ only slightly: 852–851 B.C.E. (Begrich and Jepsen), 853–852 (Thiele), 854–853 (Andersen).

The sources for Ahaziah of Israel are found in 1 Kgs 22:40, 50, 52–54; 2 Kgs 1:1–18; and 2 Chr 20:35, 37. The subsequent division of the book of Kings has split the account of Ahaziah's reign into two halves. Little is reported about the period of his reign. One can assume that it was too short a period of time to enable him to make changes in the policies he had inherited from his father Ahab, even if he had wanted to do so. He probably continued Ahab's policies, externally seeking peace and alliances and concentrating all his efforts on the prevention of a potential Syrian (and later an Assyrian) threat. Domestically, he probably continued to strive for a balance between the Israelite citizens and the traditionally Canaanite population by promoting equality of rights in social and religious affairs. This caused him (like his father Ahab before him) to be criticized by circles loyal to Yahweh, especially by the prophet Elijah. A concrete case of this is found in the narrative of 2 Kings 1. Because these few notices about Ahaziah derive from the prophetic tradition and the Deuteronomistic redactors, he is depicted negatively, as was his father Ahab.

2 Kgs 1:1, a noteworthy verse that seems rather abrupt, informs the reader that Moab rebelled against Israel after Ahab's death (i.e., during the reign of Ahaziah). This note appears in an almost identical formulation in 3:5, where it refers to the time of Jehoram, Ahaziah's successor. It introduces the narrative about the campaign of the kings of Israel, Judah, and Edom against King Mesha of Moab. This is most likely the original source of this information (3:5), but later Deuteronomistic redactors moved it to 2 Kgs 1:1, because it fit the chronological context better there ("after Ahab's death," which had just previously been reported). In this new context, however, this note served no purpose. Besides, the "defection of Moab" is difficult to imagine as a sudden event. In the last years of Ahab's reign the Moabites were probably already attempting to shake off their dependency, in order to exert more pressure on the areas of Israelite settlement in the N after Ahab's death (cf. *KAI* 2,174). The growing expansion of the Moabites under the rule of their king Mesha must have burdened the administrations of Ahaziah and Jehoram.

According to 1 Kgs 22:50 Ahaziah offered to let the Judean king Jehoshaphat participate in his naval enterprise in the Red Sea. It is certain that this notice depends on old reports. Jehoshaphat used his sovereignty over Edom in order to imitate the model of Solomon (1 Kgs 9:26–28; 10:11) and to resume his shipping trade headquartered at the Gulf of Aqabah. He had a fleet built at Ezion-geber (a location that has not yet been exactly determined near present-day Elath, perhaps Ğesīret Faraʿūn), which was supposed to travel to Ophir (probably in S Arabia) where it would acquire gold through trade (22:48–49). Ahaziah also wanted to be involved in this financially promising expedition. It is possible that he offered Jehoshaphat the chance to join the undertaking by introducing him to the arts of ship construction and nautical affairs, which the Israelites had learned in their dealings with the Phoenicians. Whatever the circumstances and the background for this may have been, Jehoshaphat rejected Ahaziah's offer. The expedition miscarried; soon after its departure the fleet, which had been constructed by Judeans inexperienced in shipbuilding, was dashed to pieces.

In 2 Chr 20:35–37, the sole passage in Chronicles that mentions Ahaziah, this event receives a theological interpretation. By changing the details of 1 Kgs 22:48–50, the naval project was depicted as an enterprise shared by both kings. The words of an otherwise unknown prophet announce and interpret this failure as God's punishment for Jehoshaphat's alliance with the impious Ahaziah.

The most extensive story about Ahaziah, found in 2 Kgs 1:2–17, is a tradition about Elijah. Ahaziah is mentioned by name only at the beginning (v 2), although it is almost certain that he was indeed Elijah's opponent in this conflict. The original story encompassed only vv 2–8, 17. It derives unquestionably from historical facts, but uses them only as a framework for a theological statement. This narrative reports that Ahaziah has had an accident, falling from his upper chamber—either through the wooden window lattice or through the enclosure surrounding the roof, injuring himself seriously. In this condition he sent messengers to Ekron to obtain an oracle concerning his fate. The name of the god to which he appealed in 2 Kgs 1:2 is Baal-zebub, "Lord of the Flies," which seems to be a distortion of the original name Baal-Zebul, "Prince Baal" (as attested in Ugaritic texts and even NT passages [Matt 10:25; Matt 12:24 = Mark 3:22 = Luke 11:15; Matt 12:27 = Luke 11:18f.; on the other hand, "Beelzebub" is attested in ms variants). This name refers to a salvation god of apparent supraregional importance. By sending messengers to this deity in Ekron rather than to Yahweh, Ahaziah behaved as if there were no god in Israel to impart information and to decide matters of life and death. For this reason Elijah announces to Ahaziah his death, which then comes to pass. Therefore, Ahaziah died as a result of falling from the upper chamber of his palace in Samaria. Since he had no son, his brother Jehoram followed him on the throne (2 Kgs 1:17–18, in a textually difficult formulation which arose from the combination of diverse textual components: the end of the original story about Elijah, a Deuteronomistic framework for Ahaziah, and a synchronistic dating).

In their introduction (1 Kgs 22:52–54) the Deuteronomistic redactors of the book of Kings assess Ahaziah negatively, presenting him as an adherent of Baal. That has a certain basis in the following story in which Ahaziah appeals to "Baal-zebub" of Ekron. As in the case of Ahab, it is questionable whether this evaluation is accurate in a strict sense. See also AHAB.

2. King of Judah, son of Jehoram and Athaliah, who ascended the throne as his father's successor at the age of 22 and reigned just barely one year, i.e., 845–44 (Begrich), 845 (Jepsen), 841 (Thiele) or 843–842 B.C.E. (Andersen).

Notices about Ahaziah of Judah are found in 2 Kgs 8:24–29; 9:16, 21–29; 10:13–14; and 2 Chr 22:1–2, 6–11. His name is mentioned also in 2 Kgs 11:1–2; 12:19; 13:1; 14:13; and 1 Chr 3:11. It is found in the distorted form "Azariah" in 2 Chr 22:6 (cf. 2 Kgs 8:29); he is called "Jehoahaz" in 2 Chr 21:17 (cf. 22:1) and 25:23 (cf. 2 Kgs 14:13), where the two elements that form the name are reversed. In all these cases the person's identity is guaranteed by the parallels.

The sources are diverse in nature. The Deuteronomistic framework for Ahaziah is found in 2 Kgs 8:25–27 and 9:28–29. It is possible that 8:28 derives from the notices of annals, and 8:29 corresponds nearly verbatim to the passage 9:15a, 16b. The large unit 9:1–10:17 was written to justify the demise of the Omride dominion and to legitimate the Jehu dynasty. In respect to Judah, it seems not to be tendentious.

According to 2 Kgs 8:28, Ahaziah, together with Jehoram of Israel, defended the E Jordanian boundary city Ramoth-Gilead (Tell er-Rāmīṯ) against the Syrians from Damascus who were led by their king Hazael. If this is true, Ahaziah had apparently little time to exert his power in Jerusalem and left the business of ruling principally to his mother Athaliah. In express contrast to 8:28, however,

9:14 knows nothing about Ahaziah's participation in the battles around Ramoth-Gilead. Like 9:16b, 8:29b knows only Ahaziah's visit to the wounded king Jehoram in Jezreel. Two possible solutions are imaginable. One can explain the conflict as a difference between S Judean (8:28) and N Israelite perspectives (8:29b = 9:16b; 9:14b, 15a), while a more radical solution anticipates the inauthenticity of the information in 8:28. The assumption of a small textual error at the beginning of 8:28 removes the subject Ahaziah from the sentence, producing the following reading: "And Joram, the son of Ahab, went into battle against Hazael, the king of Syria, in Ramoth-Gilead" (thus Würthwein *Kings* ATD 11/2, 324, following Ewald and Klostermann). Of course, this must be a very old textual corruption, since this wording is assumed in 2 Chr 22:5.

In any case, Ahaziah was present in Jezreel when Jehu arrived for the purpose of exterminating the Omride dynasty (8:28; 9:16b, 21, 23). Jehu killed Jehoram of Israel and also ordered the execution of Ahaziah of Judah, who fled S toward Beth-Haggan (En-Gannim) apparently hoping to fight his way back to Jerusalem. However, near Ibleam (Khirbet Belᶜame) he was seriously wounded by those who were pursuing him. He made it as far as Megiddo (Tell el-Mutesellim) where he died. His body was brought to Jerusalem and buried in the tombs of the kings (9:27–29). Concurrently, "forty-two brothers of Ahaziah," who likewise were staying in the N kingdom, presumably fell unexpectedly into the hands of Jehu, who had them executed (10:12–14). The authenticity of this bloody episode is not undisputed, although the number of Ahaziah's "brothers" seems unusually high. Either it is exaggerated, as often occurs in the OT, or the "brothers" should be understood in a nonliteral sense as members of the Davidic royal line, whose sovereign at that time was none other than King Ahaziah. The motives which led Jehu also to have the Judean king and his relatives killed are not entirely clear. Did he, by taking these measures, want only to prevent the dead king's (Jehoram's) cousin from taking blood revenge? Or did he also want to destroy the Omride dynasty along with its palpable allies? In any case, Jehu's sanguine deed ironically enabled the Omrides to come to power in Jerusalem (i.e., Queen Athaliah's assumption of the government [11:1–3]), something he could not have anticipated or desired.

The Deuteronomistic redactors judge Ahaziah's religious behavior negatively and equate it with the "way of the house of Ahab." The context attributes his behavior to the influence of his mother Athaliah (8:26–27). The Chronicler expressly states (2 Chr 22:3) that Ahaziah's mother encouraged his apostasy from God. Ahaziah is described in this context as a person who subjected himself both religiously and politically to the influence of the "house of Ahab" (22:4–5). Otherwise, Chronicles provides information that is not present in its Vorlage in the books of Kings. According to 2 Chr 21:17 and 22:1, Ahaziah was supposed to have been the youngest son of Jehoram, who came to the throne, because all of his older brothers had either been led away or killed by Philistines and Arabs who had invaded Judah. In this case, one may suggest that the Chronicler had access to a special source. However, the historicity of this information is subject to serious reconsideration. This especially applies to the Chronicler's depiction of the demise of Ahaziah (22:5–9), which in part consists of excerpts from 2 Kgs 8:28–10:14 (v 5 = 2 Kgs 8:28; v 6 = 2 Kgs 8:29), and in part of summaries reported in that text (v 7 = 2 Kgs 9:21; v 8 = 2 Kgs 10:12–14). However, Ahaziah's death is described quite differently by the Chronicler than by the Deuteronomistic redactors. According to 2 Chr 22:9, Ahaziah hid in Samaria, where he was discovered and killed by Jehu, and subsequently also buried there. This completely contradicts the information presented in 2 Kgs 9:27–28. Even if one should think that a special tradition was used in Chronicles, its presentation is much more improbable than that found in 2 Kgs 9:27–28.

Bibliography

Jepsen, A. 1962. Ahasja. *BHH* 1: 50.

Miller, J. M. 1967. The Fall of the House of Ahab. *VT* 17: 307–24.

Steck, O. H. 1967. Die Erzählung von Jahwes Einschreiten gegen die Orakelbefragung Ahasjas (2 Kön 1, 2–8. *17). *EvT* 27: 546–56.

WINFRIED THIEL
Trans. Phillip R. Callaway

AHBAN (PERSON) [Heb *ʾaḥbān*]. A son of Abishur and Abihail, of the tribe of Judah (1 Chr 2:29). The identity of Ahban is uncertain, a fact reflected by LXX variants (e.g., *achabar, ozabar,* and *adab*). The name itself occurs only in this extended genealogy of Israel identifying tribal locations within Palestine (1 Chronicles 2–8).

MARK J. FRETZ

AHER (PERSON) [Heb *ʾaḥēr*]. The father of Hushim according to the MT of 1 Chr 7:12; the name is attested only in this tribal genealogy. The MT of 1 Chr 7:12 reads *wěšuppim wěḥuppim běnê ᶜîr ḥūšim běnê ʾaḥēr,* lit. "And Shuppim and Huppim the sons of Ir, Hushim the sons of Aher." The difficult grammatical construction of a plural "sons" preceded by only one name (Hushim) is only one problem in this text; the other problem is the fact that although Dan is included in the list of Jacob's sons (1 Chr 2:2), there is no Danite lineage in the subsequent tribal genealogies (1 Chronicles 2–8). The occurrence of the word *ʾaḥēr* in this difficult text can be interpreted not only as a personal name, but also as an adjective; if the text is emended, one can reconstruct in its place either different personal names or a cardinal number.

Klostermann (*RE* 4: 94) emends 1 Chr 7:12 to read *bny dān ḥšm běnô ʾeḥād,* "Sons of Dan: Hushim his son, one." This solution is supported by Gen 46:23 and less so by Num 26:42, while the proposed reading *běnô,* is supported by the LXX reading *huios autou,* "his son." The emendation of MT *ʾaḥēr* to the cardinal number "one" (Heb *ʾeḥād*) is justified since the Heb letters *dalet* and *reš* are easily confused, and since the Chronicler tends to number the sons (cf. 1 Chr 7:1, 3, 6–7). Although Rudolf (*Chronikbücher* HAT, 68) concurs with Klostermann's conclusion, he presumes that a marginal note (Heb *lěpānîm lāᶜîr šēm ʾaḥēr,* "previously the city had another name") on Judg 18:29a (MT *wayyiqrěʾû šēm-hāᶜîr dān,* "and they call the name of the city Dan") became a gloss in Klostermann's proposed text of 1 Chr 7:12. According to Rudolf's explanation, ʾaḥēr is an adjective ("another") displaced through textual corruption. Along other lines Noth (*ÜgS* 1: 118) concludes that 1 Chr 7:12 should read ". . . and Shupham and Hupham. The sons of Dan: Suham. The sons of Asher [sic.]: . . ." Based on the assumption that the order of the tribes in Numbers 26 is the Chronicler's source, he completely revises the MT, and includes a postulated lacuna between vv 12 and 13. In order to place Dan and Asher in their proper order between Benjamin and Naphtali, according to Num 26:38–50 (cf. Gen 46:8–27), Aher (Heb *ʾaḥēr*) is either deleted, or emended to read Asher (Heb *ʾāšēr*). One other solution (Williamson 1973) is to emend the final word of 1 Chr 7:12 (MT *ʾaḥēr*) to read either *ʾard* (cf. Gen 46:21; Num 26:40 where Heb *ʾard* follows *ḥpm* in the order of names), or *ʾaddār* (cf. LXX of Num 26:40, *adar;* and 1 Chr 8:3 where a scribe may have mistaken the Heb letter *dalet* for *ḥet*). If, as Williamson proposes, 1 Chr 7:12 is a fragmentary verse that was added to vv 6–11, then the word Aher would have been produced by a scribal error. Thus, the absence of Dan is not a problem, because it did not occur in the fragment, which must be treated separately from the rest of the name list.

Bibliography

Williamson, H. G. M. 1973. A Note on 1 Chronicles 7:12. *VT* 23: 375–79.

MARK J. FRETZ

AHI (PERSON) [Heb *ʾăḥî*]. The son of Abdiel and chief of one of the Gadite clans in the "pasture lands of Sharon" during the overlapping reigns of Jotham of Judah and Jeroboam II of Israel (1 Chr 5:14–16). The name occurs in a textually corrupt genealogical list, and combined with the fact that it is a form of the Hebrew word for "brother," it has presented problems for translators and interpreters alike. The pattern "son of X, son of Y, son of Z, etc." in 1 Chr 5:14–15 is interrupted by Heb *ʾḥy*. One solution is to retain the MT and take *ʾḥy* as a personal name, possibly a shortened form of Ahijah (Rudolf *Chronikbücher* HAT, 46), without the expected "son of." Another option, reflected in various ancient versions, is to read *ʾḥy* as the construct form of the common noun ("brother of;" see LXX *adelphou* and Vg. *fratres*); however, an expected proper noun does not follow the construct "brother of" in these mss, therefore, the sense is no more clear with this translation. Another option is to emend the text, as do some other LXX mss (1 Chr 5:14) by transposing *ʾḥy* and the preceding name Buz (e.g. *zaboucham, achibouz*). Although Heb *ʾḥy* occurs 35 times in the MT, the RSV translates it "Ahi" only here. In a similar instance (1 Chr 7:34) the RSV prefers to emend the text (*ûbĕnê šāmer ʾăḥî wĕrāwhgâ*, lit. "The sons of Shemer: Ahi and Rohgah") to read "The son(s) of Shemer his brother: Rohgah . . ." (*ʾāḥîw rā[w]hgâ*). This emendation seems to be based on the parallel in v 35 (*ûben-hēlem ʾāḥîw*, "The son(s) of Helem his brother"). In 1 Chr 7:34 some LXX mss combine the two names (e.g., *achiouraoga, hēeigkairagous*), others render Ahi quite literally (*achi kai rooga*, "Achi and Rooga"); but in support of the RSV, other mss combine *ʾḥy* with the following *waw* (LXX *achiouia;* Armenian *achiu;* see also LXX v 35 *adelphou autou*). Since *ʾḥy* is a common element in NW Semitic names (*AI,* 93.6; *PNPI,* 263–64; *APNM,* 160–61), it is plausible to argue that Ahi is indeed a personal name in 1 Chr 5:15; however, because the text is corrupt, an emendation similar to that made by the RSV in 1 Chr 7:34 could just as easily solve the problem.

MARK J. FRETZ

AHIAH (PERSON) [Heb *ʾăḥîyāh*]. A clan leader who signed Nehemiah's pledge of reform (Neh 10:27—Eng 10:26). In this list of leaders (vv 2–28) Ahiah's is the only name preceded by the Heb conjunction *waw.* Meyer (1896: 142) suggests that this distinguishes *wʾḥyh;* thus, by emending it to *wʾḥyw,* he changes the text to read "Rehum, Hashabnah, Maaseiah, and his brother Hanan . . ." The LXX of Neh 10:27, however, renders the name as *ara,* suggesting the name Arah, a prominent family name mentioned in Ezra 2:5 (= Neh 7:10).

Bibliography

Meyer, E. 1896. *Die Entstehung des Judenthums.* Halle.

MARK J. FRETZ

AHIAM (PERSON) [Heb *ʾăḥîʾām*]. One of the Hararites listed in the parallel rosters of King David's warriors (2 Sam 23:33; 1 Chr 11:35). In the MT, these parallel lists spell the name of Ahiam's father as Sharar (2 Sam 23:33) or Sachar (1 Chr 11:35). Some variants of the LXX read *sacharō,* or *sachar ho*—lending support to Sachar as the original form. The designation "Hararite" possibly signifies either Ahiam's clan name (translated "the Urite" by McCarter *2 Samuel* AB, 493), or the name of his hometown, which Elliger (1935: 56) identifies with the town Araru of the Amarna letters.

Bibliography

Elliger, K. 1935. Die dreissig Helden Davids. *PJ* 31: 29–75.

MARK J. FRETZ

AHIAN (PERSON) [Heb *ʾaḥyān*]. The son of Shemida, and grandson of Manasseh (1 Chr 7:19) listed within the extended genealogy of Israel (1 Chronicles 2–8). Ahian is not mentioned elsewhere in connection with Shemida, who is allotted land in the Cisjordon (Num 26:32; Josh 17:2). According to ostraca discovered at Samaria (Reisner, Fisher, and Lyon 1924: 228–29), Shemida is either the name of a tribal unit involved in commerce, or a place name like Shechem which also appears in the ostraca. Although Ahian does not occur in the ostraca, since other names in the biblical genealogy which are or might very well be geographical names do appear there, Ahian may be the place name which came to be associated with a tribal unit located in the Manassite region of Samaria.

Bibliography

Reisner, G. A.; Fisher, C. S.; and Lyon, D. G. 1924. *Harvard Excavations at Samaria, 1908–1910.* Vol. 1. Cambridge, MA.

MARK J. FRETZ

AHIEZER (PERSON) [Heb *ʾăḥîʿezer*]. **1.** The son of Ammishaddai and leader of the tribe of Dan, who assisted Moses in taking a census of Israel (Num 1:12; 2:25). As tribal representative, Ahiezer contributed offerings on the 10th day of the tabernacle dedication (Num 7:66, 71) and commanded the Danites as a rear guard for Israel on the march from Sinai to Palestine (Num 10:25).

2. Chief of the Benjaminites who defected from King Saul to David at Ziklag (1 Chr 12:3). If the plural "sons" (Heb *bĕnê*) refers both to Joash and Ahiezer, as the RSV translates the MT, then Ahiezer would also be one of two sons of Shemaah the Gibeathite in this list of Benjaminite defectors. Of all the members of Saul's army who went over to serve David, some of the most noteworthy were these Benjaminites, since they were from Saul's own clan (see Rudolf *Chronikbücher* HAT, 105; Williamson 1981; Zeron 1974).

Bibliography

Williamson, H. G. M. 1981. 'We Are Yours, O David': The Setting and Purpose of 1 Chronicles 12:1–23. *OTS* 21: 164–76.
Zeron, A. 1974. Tag für Tag kam man zu David, um ihm zu helfen, 1 Chr 12, 1–22. *TZ* 30: 257–61.

MARK J. FRETZ

AHIHUD (PERSON) [Heb *ʾăḥîhûd; ʾăḥîḥud*]. Two individuals mentioned in the Hebrew Bible bear this name. In both its forms, this name has been translated "the brother (i.e., the god) is exalted" (*EncMiqr* 1: 215), with the kinship term *ʾaḥ* (brother) representing the theophoric element. Johnson (*IDB* 1: 67) offers the translations of "the (divine) brother is exalted" or "the (divine) brother is glorious." One suggestion (*Enemiqr* 1: 215; see esp. *IPN,* 146, 192) is that the name expresses the glory and majesty of the Lord that appear in nature and particularly in the heavens. However, the textual transmission of these vv has not been clear, as exemplified by the many LXX variants.

1. An Asherite, the son of Shelomi (Num 34:27), and one of those named (MT *ʾăḥîhûd*) in a list of tribal leaders. These leaders, *"neśî ʾîm,"* (Speiser: 1967), were appointed by Eleazar the Priest and Joshua the son of Nun to oversee the allotment of the land of Canaan W of the Jordan River to the 10 tribes of Israel. Based on the LXX variant (Gk *achiōr*) in this verse Ahihud has been identified with the name ACHIOR in the book of Judith (see Cowley 1913: 244).

2. A Benjaminite, his name (MT *ʾăḥîḥud*) appears in a genealogy which lists him as either the son of Heglam or the son of Gera (1 Chr 8:7). This genealogical ambiguity reflects the unclarity of the transmission of this and other vv in this passage. See ABIHUD.

Bibliography

Cowley, A. 1913. The Book of Judith. Vol. 1, pp. 242–67 in *APOT.* Oxford.
Speiser, E. A. 1967. Background and Function of the Biblical Nasiʾ. Pp. 113–122 in *Oriental and Biblical Studies,* ed. J. J. Finkelstein and M. Greenberg. Philadelphia.

RAPHAEL I. PANITZ

AHIJAH (PERSON) [Heb *ʾaḥîyāh*]. Nine persons in the Hebrew Bible/OT bear this name.

1. A priest, the son of Ahitub and great-grandson of Eli (1 Sam. 14:3). He was a priest in Shiloh and provided oracular guidance for Saul (1 Sam 14:18–19, 41–42). In 1 Sam 14:18, the MT indicates that Ahijah was in charge of the ark of God which was housed at Kiriath-jearim. The LXX reads instead "the ephod" which Ahijah is said to carry in 1 Sam 14:3. The ephod was an item of priestly apparel (Exod 28:1–43), which was also apparently used for oracular guidance. It is speculated that the garment contained a pouch to hold the Urim and Thummim. The fact that Saul requests oracular guidance is cited in support of the LXX reading against that of the MT. Since he was the son of Ahitub, it is assumed that he was also the brother of Ahimelech, the priest of Nob (1 Sam 22). Ahijah's connection to Saul is also important in literary terms, since the rejection of the house of Eli parallels the ultimate fate of Saul and his descendants.

2. A secretary within Solomon's bureaucracy (1 Kgs 4:3). Mettinger (1971: 24–30) believes that "Ahijah" disguises an Egyptian name similar to that of his brother "Elihoreph." The name of his father is Shisha, derived from the Egyptian *sš* "scribe." The phrase might be read as "sons of a scribe," i.e., members of a scribal guild. Mettinger has demonstrated that Solomon probably modelled his own bureaucracy on that of the Egyptians.

3. A prophet from Shiloh (1 Kgs 11:9) who supported Jeroboam's abortive coup against Solomon. He plays a crucial role in the Deuteronomistic History's portrayal of the split between the S and N kingdoms during the reign of Rehoboam. Ahijah meets Jeroboam, Solomon's overseer over compulsory labor, outside Jerusalem and through symbolic action and prophetic utterance provides the theological justification for the division of the kingdom after Solomon's death. The rending of Ahijah's cloak into 12 pieces and the giving of 10 to Jeroboam is reminiscent of Samuel's rejection of Saul in 1 Samuel 15. However, the LXX differs in a number of details from the MT, including the claim that this action was carried out by Shemaiah and not Ahijah. It is made clear that, although the socioeconomic reasons for the division stem from the oppression of the Davidic monarchy brought to a head by the policies of Rehoboam (1 Kings 12), the theological justification offered is the apostasy of Solomon. Ahijah promises Jeroboam a "sure house" (1 Kgs 11:38), echoing the dynastic promise to David in 2 Samuel 7. The final break brought about by the heavy tax burden levied by Rehoboam is presented in typical Deuteronomistic terms as the fulfillment of the prophecy of Ahijah (1 Kgs 12:15).

Later Jeroboam sends his disguised wife to Ahijah in old age in order to enquire if his son Abijah will survive his childhood illness (1 Kgs 14:1–18). The prophecy delivered by Ahijah is the fulcrum for the Deuteronomistic rejection of all N kings. Jeroboam is rejected for his apostasy, particularly the setting up of the rival N shrines of Bethel and Dan. The dynastic promise, which was couched in conditional terms in 1 Kgs 11:38–39, is withdrawn. The death of the child is again presented as confirmation of the prophecy of Ahijah. It is further fulfilled with the slaughter of the house of Jeroboam by Baasha (1 Kgs 15:29).

The prophecies of Ahijah are presented in Deuteronomistic terms and play a central role in the overall design of the Deuteronomistic History. Ahijah represents the ideal Deuteronomistic prophet whose words are fulfilled. Despite this clear Deuteronomic shaping, the narratives are thought to be multilayered. Many commentators accept that these narratives preserve authentic historical information about the nature of Israelite prophecy and sociopolitical disputes at the time of the division of the kingdom. Cohen (1965; 1971) believes that Ahijah represents a Shilonite priestly faction who supported Jeroboam's struggle with Rehoboam. This faction is thought to represent the pre-monarchic religious specialists, identified with Abiathar, who had become increasingly marginalized by the centralizing policies of Solomon. Jeroboam's establishment of royal shrines at Dan and Bethel also failed to restore the fortunes of the Shilonite priesthood. The view that Ahijah championed the restoration of the shrine at Shiloh was challenged by Noth (1966: 132–144) who argued that he was in favor of the political break with the S but not with a break with the Jerusalem cult. Wilson (1980: 184–87) has followed this general analysis in his discussion of Ahijah as a typical peripheral prophet from Ephraim. He represents the views of a group outside of and opposed to the royal establishment. His support group is presumably drawn from Ephraimites and probably from the old Shilonite priesthood ousted by Solomon. Ahijah challenged the royal establishment in an attempt to redress the balance in this struggle for power. Similarly, his rejection of Jeroboam is to be understood in factional terms of a center-periphery struggle for power.

The Chronicler refers to "the prophecy of Ahijah" as one of the sources for the reign of Solomon (2 Chr 9:29). There is no agreement over whether or not this refers to the material preserved in 1 Kings 11 and 14 or is a collection of material which did not find its way into the canon of the Hebrew Bible.

4. The father of Baasha, king of Israel, and member of the tribe of Issachar (1 Kgs 15:27, 33; 21:22; 2 Kgs 9:9). The LXX reads "who was of Beth Belaan" for "Issachar." Gray (*1–2 Kings*[3] OTL, 357, n.b) suspects that Beth indicated a place name in Issachar, yet only Bethshemesh appears in the tribal list in Josh 19:17–23. Belaan is not mentioned elsewhere as part of Issachar. The house of Baasha ben Ahijah becomes as reviled as that of Jeroboam I ben Nebat, who was the symbol of royal apostasy in the Deuteronomistic History (1 Kgs 21:22; 2 Kgs 9:9).

5. One of the sons of Ehud, a Benjaminite, carried into captivity (1 Chr 8:7). Ahijah may be a variant of Ahoah in v 4, as suggested by LXX^{B} and the Syriac. The MT is difficult. 1 Chr 8:6 reports that the sons of Ehud were the heads of clans in Geba who were exiled to Manahath. However, Braun (*1 Chronicles* WBC, pp. 120–1) understands the phrase *wayyaqlûm* as "who were moved," i.e., emigrated, rather than as "they were carried into exile." Geba is mentioned in the list of Levitical cities (Josh 21:17; 1 Chr 6:60) and was fortified by Asa (1 Kgs 15:22; 2 Chr 16:6). The location of Manahath is disputed, but often identified with Malah near Jerusalem (*LBHG,* 381). The list of Ehud's sons in 1 Chr 8:7 begins with a conjunction suggesting that a name or phrase is missing. Furthermore, the names of two of the sons, Naaman and Gera, appear as sons of Bela (1 Chr 8:4–5). The various lists of Benjamin's and Bela's sons and their descendants show considerable variation (Genesis 46; Numbers 26; 1 Chronicles 7 and 8) and numerous textual difficulties, as evidenced in 1 Chr 8:6–7.

6. One of David's mighty men, a Pelonite (1 Chr 11:36). The MT of the corresponding list of David's mighty men in 2 Sam 23:8–39 provides an entirely different reading: "Eliam son of Ahithophel the Gilonite" (2 Sam 23:34). The two lists not only show considerable variations but are placed in different positions in relation to the reign of David. The Chronicler places the list at the very beginning of his reign, whereas in 2 Samuel it is found as an appendix to the reign of David. The list in Chronicles functions as a legitimation of David through the support of these warriors and all Israel (1 Chr 11:10).

7. One of the sons of Jerahmeel, a member of the tribe of Judah (1 Chr 2:25). Some mss of the LXX suggest that this is not a proper name but read "his brothers," while the Syriac reads "your brothers." Williamson (1979) has noted that the list of Jerahmeel's descendants (1 Chr 2:25–33, 33–41) forms the center of a chiasm within the genealogy of Judah. Interestingly the first part of Jerahmeel's genealogy (1 Chr 2:25–33) is segmented, while the latter half (1 Chr 2:33–41) is linear.

8. A Levite in charge of the temple treasury (1 Chr 26:20). There is some doubt whether a personal name is contained here or a more general phrase that introduces the Levitical families in charge of the temple treasuries. The LXX reads "Levites, their brothers," while NIV and Braun (1 Chronicles WBC, 248) translate the phrase as "their fellow Levites."

9. Ahiah, one of the chiefs of the people, who set his seal on the covenant of Nehemiah (Neh 10:27—Eng 10:26). It is puzzling that this is the only name in the list of signatories to be preceded by the conjunction "and," *waʾăḥîyāh.* The originality of the list of signatories placed at the beginning of the document has been disputed (see Williamson, *Ezra, Nehemiah* WBC, 325–31 for a discussion of the various proposals).

Bibliography

Cohen, M. A. 1965. The Rebellions during the Reign of David: An Inquiry into Social Dynamics in Ancient Israel. Pp. 91–112 in *Studies in Jewish Bibliography, History and Literature in Honor of I. Edward Kiev,* ed. C. Berlin. New York.

———. 1971. The Role of the Shilonite Priesthood in the United Monarchy of Ancient Israel. *HUCA* 36: 59–98.

Mettinger, T. N. D. 1971. *Solomonic State Officials. A Study of the Civil Government Officials of the Israelite Monarchy.* Lund.

Noth, M. 1966. *The Laws of the Pentateuch and Other Studies.* Edinburgh.

Williamson, H. G. M. 1979. Sources and Redaction in the Chronicler's Genealogy of Judah. *JBL* 98: 351–59.

Wilson, R. 1980. *Prophecy and Society in Ancient Israel.* Philadelphia.

KEITH W. WHITELAM

AHIKAM (PERSON) [Heb *ʾăḥîqām*]. The son of Shaphan, and member of a very prominent Jerusalem family who held government office under Josiah (ca. 640–609 B.C.E.) and Jehoiakim (ca. 609–598 B.C.E.).

Ahikam's father, Shaphan, was royal secretary during the reign of Josiah (2 Kgs 22:3–20). Ahikam's brothers, Elasah (Jer 29:3) and Gemariah (Jer 36:10–12, 25), and Gemariah's son Micaiah (Jer 36:11–13), were also court officials. Although Ahikam's title is not given in the Hebrew Bible, it is evident that he was high-ranking. The office of *ăšer ʿal habbayit* ("who is over the house;" see, e.g., 1 Kgs 16:9; 18:3; 2 Kgs 18:18) was probably held by Ahikam's son Gedaliah. Most scholars now believe that a contemporary seal inscribed "to Gedaliah, who is over the house" belonged to this Gedaliah, son of Ahikam. It is possible that this office was hereditary and had earlier been held by Ahikam himself (cf. Katzenstein 1960: 153–54; Lohfink 1978: 338).

During the reign of Josiah, Ahikam (along with his father Shaphan) was appointed to a delegation sent to consult the prophetess Huldah on the occasion of the finding of the lawbook (2 Kgs 22:12–13; 2 Chr 34:20–21). Following Jeremiah's fiery "temple sermon" at the beginning of Jehoiakim's reign, Ahikam is reported to have saved the prophet from execution at the hands of the people (Jer 26:24; this note is preceded in Jer 26:20–23 by an account of how the prophet Uriah, who had delivered a similar message, had been executed). This incident not only attests the influence wielded by Ahikam, but also indicates that he, like other members of the family of Shaphan, was kindly disposed toward Jeremiah. Furthermore, Ahikam and his family were undoubtedly sympathetic to the pro-Babylonian position supported by Jeremiah. Ahikam's son, Gedaliah, was appointed ruler of Judah by Nebuchadnezzar after the fall of Jerusalem in 587–586 B.C.E. (2 Kgs 25:22; Jer 40:7).

While it is possible that Ahikam was deported in 597 B.C.E. (passages such as Jer 38:1–6 reveal that a new group of court officials surrounded Zedekiah), the fact that Ahikam's name fails to appear in Jer 36:9–26 suggests that he may have died some time before the reading of Jeremiah's scroll in Jehoiakim's 5th year.

Bibliography

Hooke, S. H. 1935. A Scarab and Sealing from Tell Duweir. *PEQ* 67: 195–97.

Katzenstein, H. J. 1960. The Royal Steward *(Asher ʿal ha-Bayith)*. *IEJ* 10: 149–54.

Lohfink, N. 1978. Die Gattung der "Historischen Kurzgeschichte" in den letzten Jahren von Juda und in der Zeit des Babylonischen Exils. *ZAW* 90: 319–47.

JOHN M. BERRIDGE

AHIKAR/AHIQAR (PERSON). Ahiqar has long been familiar as an Assyrian sage who was the hero of a book that was read and preserved by Jews of antiquity. There is no doubt that the many versions of the work that bears his name are nonhistorical in character, but recent discoveries have made it quite likely that there once was an Assyrian scholar by this name who served in the time of Esarhaddon (680–669 B.C.E.). The name is spelled *ʾḥyqr* in the Aramaic papyrus from Elephantine. It means "my brother is precious/valuable."

A. Ahiqar in the Book of Ahiqar

The earliest extant form of the book is the fragmentary Aramaic text copied on a late-5th-century papyrus from Elephantine (Naveh 1970: 35). See also AHIQAR, BOOK OF. The text (text: Cowley 1923; translation: Lindenberger *OTP* 2: 479–507) describes him as "a wise and skillful scribe" (i.1: *spr ḥkym wmhyr*) who was "[ke]eper of the seal of Sennacherib" (i.3: *ṣb*]*yt ʿzqth zyśnḥʾryb*). He was also "father of all Assyria, on whose counsel King Sennacherib and [all] the Assyrian Army [used to rely]" (iv.55: *ʾbwh zy ʾtwr klh zy ʿl ʿṭth snḥʾryb mlkʾ wḥyl ʾtwr* [*klʾ hww*]). He continued to hold high office into the time of Sennacherib's successor Esarhaddon (i.4–5), who calls him "O wise [s]cribe, counselor of all Assyria" (i.12: *s*]*prʾ ḥkymʾ yʿṭ ʾtwr klh*). By this time, however, Ahiqar had reached an advanced age. As he had no son, he adopted his nephew Nadin and taught him his wisdom so that he could become his replacement. The nephew proved to be a scoundrel who plotted against his uncle and convinced Esarhaddon that he should be executed. (According to later, more complete versions of the story Nadin forged correspondence from Ahiqar which showed that he was scheming to seize the kingdom with foreign assistance.) A royal officer named Nabushumishkun was commissioned to kill Ahiqar, but the clever sage reminded him that under reversed circumstances he had saved the officer's life. A eunuch was executed instead of Ahiqar, and the Nabushumishkun hid the fallen wise man in his house. The preserved portion of the Aramaic narrative ends at this point in the story. The fuller versions (e.g., the Syriac, Armenian, and Arabic) continue the tale by relating that Esarhaddon soon needed Ahiqar's remarkable savoir faire because the Egyptian king, who had heard of the sage's "death," challenged the Assyrian monarch to send him someone who could construct a palace between heaven and earth. If he could, he would receive Egypt's revenue for 3 years; if he could not, Egypt would receive a similar amount from Assyria. Just when Esarhaddon feared that the challenge would prove disastrously costly, the officer told him that Ahiqar was alive. He was swiftly retrieved from his hiding place and dispatched to Egypt where he handled all difficulties with astonishing flair. He returned with great wealth to Assyria where he promptly settled accounts with Nadin. After Ahiqar had beat him severely and lectured him at length, Nadin died.

B. Ahiqar in the Book of Tobit

Although the Ahiqar papyrus was found at the Jewish military colony at Elephantine, nothing in the text suggests Jewish authorship of the work or even Jewish influence on it. Indeed, the presence of divine names such as El (vii.107; x,154,156,161 [?]; xii. 173 [?]), Šamaš (vi.92, 93; vii.108; ix.138; xi.171) and Šamayn (? vii.95) betray a polytheistic origin for the book. In the deuterocanonical book of Tobit, however, Ahiqar has been transformed from an Assyrian to an Israelite of the tribe of Naphtali who is a relative of Tobit. Tobit, which may date from the 3d century B.C.E. (Doran 1986: 299), manifests a number of important similarities with the book of *Ahiqar* (Greenfield 1981: 329–36). Both are set in Assyria at the time of the kings who ruled around the time of the destruction of Samaria (Tobit mentions Shalmaneser, Sennacherib, and

Esarhaddon [1:15–22]) and both are sapiential novels in which wise instructions are conveyed by an elderly character to his son at two similar locations. The book of Tobit mentions Ahiqar in four passages. In 1:21–22 Tobit reports that Esarhaddon "appointed Ahikar *[Achicharon],* son of my brother Anael to supervise all the finances of his kingdom; he had control of the entire administration. Then Ahikar interceded on my behalf and I came back to Nineveh. For he had been chief cupbearer, keeper of the privy seal, comptroller, and treasurer when Sennacherib was king of Assyria; and Esarhaddon renewed the appointments. Ahikar was my nephew and so one of my kinsmen" (NEB). The picture presented here resembles that in the book of *Ahiqar* except that the sage is now an Israelite. Later Tobit, after he became blind, notes that Ahikar cared for him for two years (2:10). Further evidence that the author of Tobit knew the Ahiqar story comes from 11:18 (v 19 in Greek) in which he mentions Ahiqar and Nadab (= Nadin), who are both identified as Tobit's cousins (so Sinaiticus *[hoi exadelphoi]*) or, in Vaticanus and Alexandrinus, Nadab is called Ahikar's nephew *(ho exadelphos autou)*. Finally, 14:10 alludes to another part of the Ahiqar narrative: "My son, think what Nadab did to Ahikar who brought him up: he forced him to hide in a living grave. Ahikar survived to see God requite the dishonour done to him; he came out into the light of day, but Nadab passed into eternal darkness for his attempt to kill Ahikar. Because I [?] gave alms, Ahikar escaped from the fatal trap Nadab set for him, and Nadab fell into the trap himself and was destroyed" (NEB). The end of this passage reflects the words of the final proverb in Ahiqar (Syriac 8:41; Greenfield 1981: 333–34).

C. Other References

Several ancient writers mention a character whose name closely resembles that of Ahiqar; they may be referring to the hero of the book (Harris, Lewis, Conybeare *APOT* 2: 715–17; Küchler 1979: 344–46; Lindenberger *OTP* 2: 491). The Christian writer Clement of Alexandria (ca. 150–215) claimed that the Greek author Democritus (ca. 460–370 B.C.E.) plagiarized from a stele of Ahiqar (*tēn Akikarou stēlēn* [*Str.* 1.69, 4]). In this connection, the Persian Muslim philosopher Shahrastani (1071–1153), in a collection of sayings from Democritus, cites three sayings which agree very closely with proverbs from the versions of Ahiqar. Strabo (ca. 63 B.C.E.–23 C.E.), in his *Geography* 16,2,39, gives from Poseidonius (135–51 B.C.E.) the names of famous seers; among them he names *Achaikaros* as being among the people from the Bosporus. It has been suggested that *Bosporus* is an error for *Borsippa,* so that the Mesopotamian savant could be intended (Harris, Lewis, Conybeare *APOT* 2: 716). This must be regarded, however, as quite uncertain. Diogenes Laertius (3d century C.E.) provides a list of the works by Theophrastus (372–287 B.C.E.), among which is one named *Akicharosa.* If all of these intend the Ahiqar known from the story and proverbs, they show that his fame, especially as a dispenser of wise words, was early and spread over a wider area than the Semitic world. The same could be concluded from the fact that the Greek *Life of Aesop* borrows heavily from the story and proverbs of Ahiqar in chaps. 23–32. It has also been suggested that Ahiqar's name should be restored on the 3d-century C.E. Roman mosaic of Monnus in Trier. In it there are 9 octagonal sections in each of which are pictured a Muse with a symbol of the art with which she is connected and an expert in that art or founder of it. In the section for Polymnia, the Muse often associated with dance and mime, is a figure only part of whose name is preserved. The letters *-icar* could well be part of Acicarus or Ahiqar (Lindenberger *OTP* 2: 492), though combining him with Polymnia is surprising (Küchler 1979: 352–55).

D. Ahiqar as a Figure of History

There have been several attempts to relate aspects of the Ahiqar story to history. W. von Soden (1936: 1–13) argued that Adad-šum-uṣur, one of Esarhaddon's advisors, was the historical point of origin for the Ahiqar legends. This official wrote many letters and exercised considerable influence in the court. As Ahiqar did, he requested from the king that his son Arad-Gula be given an important position. The son eventually did gain a post. Moreover, there is evidence that Adad-šum-uṣur fell from grace, though it is not known whether he was restored to his former status. But, as von Soden noted, no high official in the time of Sennacherib and Esarhaddon bore the name Ahiqar. In his opinion, a change of names took place during the transmission of the story so that Adad-šum-uṣur became Ahiqar. E. Reiner (1961: 7–8) has observed that the theme which provides the framework of the Ahiqar story—the "disgrace and rehabilitation of a minister"—was known in Babylonia and that it was fused with the other major theme—the "ungrateful nephew." A recent discovery at the site of ancient Uruk has cast some interesting new light on the Ahiqar tradition. German excavations there in 1959–60 unearthed in a room next to the *reš*-sanctuary a tablet (W 20030, 7) which provides a list of Assyrian kings from before and after the flood (van Dijk 1962: 44–52). An official called an *ummānu*—a term for both a learned man and high official (Reiner 1961: 9)—is named for each of the kings. For the time of King Esarhaddon (11. 19–20) it mentions that a man named ^{1}a-ba-^{d}NINNU-da-ri (= aba-enlil-dari) was the *ummānu* and notes that the Ahlamu (= the Arameans) called him ^{1}a-ḫu-'u-qa-a-ri. This is the name Ahuqar or Ahiqar. Consequently, there is now documentary evidence that Esarhaddon, who is the king with the primary royal role in the book of *Ahiqar,* had a chief advisor whose Aramaic name was the one found in the Aramaic version of the book. The list in which his name appears was copied in the year 147 of the Seleucid Era (= 165 B.C.E.), when Antiochus (IV) was king (11.23–24). It has also been noted that the only case of an Assyrian proverb that parallels one in *Ahiqar* (the Syriac version) is quoted in one of Esarhaddon's letters (Greenfield 1981: 335 n. 20), and that the name Nabushumishkun is the same as that of Merodach-Baladan's son who was taken captive by Sennacherib (Greenfield 1981: 335 n. 21).

It is clear from the reference to Ahiqar in the Uruk list that some sort of historical kernel lies behind the story. There was a wise man, possibly an author (Lindenberger 1983: 22), named Ahiqar in the court of Esarhaddon. Nevertheless, it is just as evident that the book which now bears his name has assumed folkloristic traits (Niditch and Doran 1977: 182–85) and can hardly be termed a historical document.

Bibliography

Cowley, A. 1923. *Aramaic Papyri of the Fifth Century B.C.* Oxford. Repr. Osnabrück, 1967.

Dijk, J. van. 1962. Die Inschriftenfunde. Pp. 39–62 in *XVIII. vorläufiger Bericht über die von dem Deutschen Archäologischen Institut und der Deutschen Orient-Gesellschaft aus Mitteln der Deutschen Forschungsgemeinschaft unternommenen Ausgrabungen in Uruk-Warka,* ed. H. J. Lenzen. Berlin.

Doran, R. 1986. Narrative Literature. Pp. 287–310 in *Early Judaism and Its Modern Interpreters,* ed. R. A. Kraft and G. W. E. Nickelsburg. The Bible and Its Modern Interpreters 2. Philadelphia and Atlanta.

Greenfield, J. C. 1981. Aḥiqar in the Book of Tobit. Pp. 329–36 in *De la Torah au Messie,* ed. J. Doré, P. Grelot, and M. Carrez. Paris.

Küchler, M. 1979. Frühjüdische Weisheit in den Achikar-Traditionen? Pp. 319–413 in *Frühjüdische Weisheitstraditionen.* OBO 26. Göttingen.

Lindenberger, J. M. 1983. *The Proverbs of Ahiqar.* JHNES. Baltimore.

Naveh, J. 1970. *The Development of the Aramaic Script.* Proceedings of the Israel Academy of Sciences and Humanities 5/1. Jerusalem.

Niditch, S., and Doran, R. 1977. The Success Story of the Wise Courtier. *JBL* 96: 179–93.

Reiner, E. 1961. The Etiological Myth of the "Seven Sages." *Or* 30: 1–11.

Soden, W. von. 1936. Die Unterweltsvision eines assyrischen Kronprinzen. *ZA* 43: 1–31.

JAMES C. VANDERKAM

AHILUD (PERSON) [Heb *ʾăḥîlûd*]. **1.** The father of Jehoshaphat, the "recorder" in the royal administrations of David and Solomon (2 Sam 8:16; 20:24; 1 Kgs 4:3; 1 Chr 18:15). In the parallel lists of officials (2 Sam 8:16–18 = 1 Chr 18:15–17), the Gk provides numerous variants of the name Ahilud, tending to substitute more familiar names from nearby verses. For example, LXX *acheia* may be associated with *ʾăḥîyāh* (Ahijah), mentioned along with Ahilud in the list of Solomonic officials (1 Kgs 4:3); LXX *achimelech* (Ahimelech) is listed on verse after Ahilud (2 Sam 8:17) as one of the priests; while LXX *abimelech* (Abimelech) appears in the parallel of 1 Chr 18:16; Lucian's *acheinaab* may reflect Heb *ʾăḥînādāb* (Ahinadab), which occurs in the list of Solomonic officials (1 Kgs 4:12). Callaway's (1983) recent find of a jar handle with the name Ahilud on it makes it likely that by the end of the 11th cent. it was a common name.

The title held by Ahilud's son Jehoshaphat (Heb *mzkyr*) is usually translated "recorder," "herald." The extensive discussion of this term (see McCarter *2 Samuel* AB, 254 for citations) leads one to conclude that JEHOSHAPHAT was some type of spokesperson for the royal court. Accordingly, it can be presumed that Ahilud's family had a favored position during the United Monarchy.

2. The father of Baana, prefect over the fifth of King Solomon's 12 administrative districts that included at least Taanach, Megiddo, and Beth-shean (1 Kgs 4:12; see *HG,* 61–64). Baana no doubt was favored because of the high status of his father's family within Israel. Presumably this Ahilud is the same as the father of Jehoshaphat (see above); the political situation would have favored the appointment of two brothers from a seemingly loyal family, the one (Jehoshaphat) as trusted "recorder," the other (Baana) as district prefect (see Mettinger 1971: 121).

Bibliography

Callaway, J. A. 1983. A Visit with Ahilud. *BARev* 9/5: 42–53.

Mettinger, T. N. D. 1971. *Solomonic State Officials.* ConBOT 5. Lund.

MARK J. FRETZ

AHIMAAZ (PERSON) [Heb *ʾăḥîmaʿaṣ*]. The meaning of the name Ahimaaz is uncertain. Ar *maʿiḍa* "be angry" may be related, and thus BDB (p. 591) interprets the name as "my brother is wrath" (cf. the Safaitic personal name *ʾmʿd;* Ryckmans 1934: 131a). See, however, *IPN,* 235: 97. Three different men in the OT bear this name.

1. The father of Saul's wife Ahinoam. Both father and daughter appear only in 1 Sam 14:50.

2. Son of the priest Zadok; Ahimaaz was one of the supporters of David who stayed in Jerusalem or its environs after the king was forced to flee the city in the coup d'etat by his son Absalom (2 Sam 15:27). Ahimaaz and a companion, Jonathan the son of the priest Abiathar, were stationed at En-Rogel, a short walk from Jerusalem. From there they relayed information about Absalom's activities to the exiled king. In one celebrated incident (2 Sam 17:15–23), Ahimaaz and Jonathan, on their way to David with vital information about an impending attack by Absalom, were forced to hide in a well in Bahurim while agents of Absalom searched for them.

Although the son of a priest of the highest rank, Ahimaaz served David as a messenger (at least during the king's exile), evidently having an athletic bent; hence David's choice of him to bring word from En-Rogel. On one occasion Ahimaaz outran another messenger (2 Sam 18:23) and was identified from afar by a watchman on the basis of his gait (v 27), a detail which shows that he regularly brought messages to the king. He is nowhere said to perform a priestly role; rather it was Zadok's son Azariah (1 Kgs 4:12) who served as priest in Solomon's temple. (It is possible, however, that Azariah was Zadok's grandson, Ahimaaz's son; cf. 1 Chr 5:34–6—Eng 6:8–10; the gloss at 5:36 is evidently placed with the wrong Azariah.)

The events related in 2 Sam 18:19–33 are informative with regard to Ahimaaz's character. Upon Absalom's death and the defeat of his army in the Forest of Ephraim, Ahimaaz volunteered to take word to David in Mahanaim. But Joab, the commander of David's forces, feared the king's reaction to news of his son's death, and sent an unnamed Cushite messenger instead. Ahimaaz, however, refused to be dissuaded, in spite of Joab's protest (v 22) that he would not be rewarded for his efforts. After asking for a third time, and less politely (v 23; the polite particle *nāʾ* is dropped and a simple future ("I will run") is used in place of the previous cohortative), he obtained Joab's leave. Although setting out later than the Cushite, Ahimaaz passed him by taking the apparently faster "Way of the Plain" (see Budde *Samuel* KHC, 287). Upon reaching David, he related only the defeat of Absalom's army; it devolved upon the hapless Cushite to tell David that his son was dead.

Some commentators have argued that Ahimaaz had good intentions, but became confused (Klaus) or evasive (Hertzberg *1 and 2 Samuel* OTL) under David's questioning, or that he acted in good faith throughout, having not heard of Absalom's death (McCarter *2 Samuel* AB). The latter is a difficult position to maintain; it was Absalom's death that brought an end to the fighting between the armies of David and Absalom (2 Sam 18:16), and as even Ahimaaz hints (v 29), it caused a great tumult. Even if Ahimaaz somehow had not previously heard the news—which was surely on everyone's lips—Joab mentions Absalom's death to him in v 20. McCarter (*2 Samuel* AB, 408) suggests that these are the narrator's words, not Joab's, but it nevertheless appears from Ahimaaz's conversation with Joab (particularly Ahimaaz's words in vv 22–3) that he understands Joab's reason for not sending him to David. Moreover, Ahimaaz's claim of ignorance about Absalom's welfare (that he heard a commotion but left before learning what it was about) is patently false, since it is without foundation in the preceding narrative, and since the Cushite, who left earlier, knew of Absalom's death. Ahimaaz, who was high-born and on close terms with David's general Joab (the latter calls him "my son" and tries to protect him from David's displeasure; Ahimaaz, for his part, is not afraid to argue with Joab), can hardly have been ignorant of Absalom's execution at the hands of Joab and his ten armor-bearers (18:14–5). Lastly, if Ahimaaz were to be seen as acting in good faith, the narrative would lose much of its rich irony and literary raison d'être.

It appears, on the contrary, that Ahimaaz possessed the same sort of craftiness that made Jacob an entertaining figure. The nameless Cushite, doubtless running along with dreams of a handsome reward from David, acts as a foil for Ahimaaz. (The notice of the latter's quicker route rules out the interpretation that the Cushite was passed because he ran slowly, reluctant through fear of David's response; on the contrary, as is seen in his words to David [vv 31–32], he believed that he carried good news.) The reader knows what the Cushite does not: that David will be devastated by the "good news," and that Ahimaaz is in hot pursuit. On the other hand, the reader is led to see Ahimaaz as an overeager naïf who carries news which is both bad and (since the Cushite left first) no longer new. But Ahimaaz takes this no-win situation and turns it to his advantage, first by taking a shortcut and reaching David first, and second by appropriating the good news for himself, leaving the Cushite with the bad. In a final twist, however, Ahimaaz's actions come to nought as David senses that he has not been told everything, and bids Ahimaaz to stand by until the second messenger arrives.

David's statement that Ahimaaz "is a good man, and comes with good tidings" (v 27), is not to be taken at face value, but as an ironic touch. It is not Ahimaaz's goodness, but rather his opportunism, which makes him a bearer of good news. Similar irony is apparent when Jonathan (Ahimaaz's companion in 2 Sam 15:27, 36 and 17:17–21) comes bearing news for Adonijah (1 Kgs 1:42); the latter exclaims "Come in, for you are a worthy man and bring good news," but Jonathan replies (v 43), "No, for our lord King David has made Solomon king . . ."

3. A son-in-law of King Solomon and prefect over the district of Naphtali, charged with supplying provisions for the palace in the 8th month of every year (1 Kgs 4:15, cf. 4:7). Ahimaaz married Solomon's daughter Basmath. His name (found only in 1 Kgs 4:15) is lacking a patronym. Possibly "Ahimaaz" is in fact the surviving part of a patronym, since 5 of the preceding 7 names listed in 1 Kgs 4:8–14 are in patronymic form (i.e., early damage to the text may have destroyed the personal names of these individuals). Possibly identical to Ahimaaz 2.

Maaz, a shortened form of Ahimaaz or of a similar name, appears in 1 Chr 2:37. The related name Abimaaz was found on a seal impression from Jerusalem which reads *lṣpn ʾlbmʿṣ* "belonging to *ṣpn* (the son of) Abimaaz" (Avigad 1970: 131 and pl. 30:c). A seal impression which, though missing one letter, appears to contain the same inscription was found at Azekah (Bliss 1900: 14–15, and 18 Cut 2/2).

Bibliography

Avigad, N. 1970. Excavations in the Jewish Quarter of the Old City of Jerusalem, 1970 (Second Preliminary Report). *IEJ* 20: 129–40.

Bliss, F. J. 1900. Fourth Report on the Excavations at Tell Zakarîya. *PEFQS:* 7–16.

Klaus, N. 1983. David's Bad News—A Literary Analysis. *Beth Mikra* 95: 358–67 (in Hebrew).

Ryckmans, G. 1934. *Les noms propres sud-semitiques.* Vol. 1. Louvain.

FREDERICK W. KNOBLOCH

AHIMAN (PERSON) [Heb *ʾăḥîman*]. Name of two people in the OT.

1. One of the "giant" descendants of ANAK (Num 13:22; Josh 15:14; Judg 1:10). Although it is possible that Ahiman could be the son of Anak (Josh 15:13), it seems unlikely since Anak is related to the legendary Nephilim (Num 13:33; see also Gen 6:4) which seems to put Anak himself back in the mists of history. Ahiman, along with Sheshai and Talmai, was probably a leader of the Anakim in the Hebron area (Num 13:22; Judg 1:10). The spies who were sent out by Moses to investigate Canaan were the first to encounter Ahiman (Num 13:22). The Anakim, whose unusual height and strength made them appear invincible (Num 13:33), were cited by 10 of the spies as the prime reason for their belief that Israel could not conquer Canaan. The biblical writers apparently felt it necessary to ensure that the eventual destruction of the Anakim was recorded in detail to indicate the power of God to triumph over even his most fearsome enemies. Although the text is unclear as to who conquered the Anakim (Joshua in Josh 11:21; Caleb in Josh 15:14; and Judah in Judg 1:10), both Joshua and Caleb, the spies who were confident that Israel could conquer Canaan, are associated with the conquest of Ahiman and the other Anakim. This desire to provide specific instances in which faithful individuals triumphed against incredible odds is probably responsible for the names of Ahiman, Sheshai, and Talmai being recorded throughout Israel's dealings with the Anakim rather than merely listing the Anakim as one of the nations conquered by Israel.

2. A Levite who was one of the gatekeepers in the temple after the return from exile in Babylon (1 Chr 9:17). According to 1 Chr 9:17, Ahiman is 1 of 4 gatekeepers, but Neh 11:19 excludes Ahiman and Shallum and lists only Akkub and Talmon. Curtis and Madsen (*Chronicles* ICC, 174) and Braun (*1 Chronicles* WBC, 136) suggest that since Ahiman is the last gatekeeper mentioned in the list in 1 Chr 9:17, the text should read *ʾăḥêhem* "their brothers" as does Neh 11:19 (rather than the proper name Ahiman). 1 Chr 9:24–26 emphasizes the fact that there were 4 gatekeepers, 1 for each side of the temple. The Chronicler may well have added the name Shallum to the list in Neh 11:19 and changed "their brothers" in Neh 11:19 into the proper name Ahiman to produce the required 4 gatekeepers. At this time, however, it is impossible to decide definitely on the historicity of Ahiman. Neh 11:19 may well list only the 2 significant gatekeepers while 1 Chr 9:17 lists all 4 of the gatekeepers.

ROBERT C. DUNSTON

AHIMELECH (PERSON) [Heb *ʾăḥîmelek*]. **1.** The son of Ahitub, and father of Abiathar (1 Sam 21:2–10—Eng 21:1–9; 22:9–20; 23:6; 30:7). Ahimelech is sometimes identified with Ahijah (1 Sam 14:3, 18), but it is more likely that Ahijah is his brother (McCarter, *1 Samuel* AB, 239). If true, this would make Ahimelech the great-grandson of Eli.

Ahimelech was in charge of the priests at Nob located N of Jerusalem and close to Gibeah where Saul lived. Therefore, he was part of the religious establishment of Saul's kingdom. On one occasion David came to Ahimelech seeking food and a weapon. David pretended he was on a mission for Saul though he was really taking flight from Saul. Even though he was suspicious of David, Ahimelech gave him sacred bread and the sword of Goliath. Like Michal and Jonathan before him, Ahimelech was another of Saul's supporters who helped to preserve David's life. Unlike the others, he did not knowingly help David escape from Saul. However, Doeg the Edomite witnessed Ahimelech's act and later told Saul. Saul accused Ahimelech of treason, refused to accept his denial, and told his servants to kill Ahimelech and the other priests. When his own servants refused, Saul returned to Doeg. Doeg, who apparently had no reverence for Israelite priests, killed Ahimelech and 84 other priests, and wiped out the town of Nob. Only Abiathar, son of Ahimelech, escaped and fled to David. This fulfilled the prophecy of 1 Sam 2:31ff. about punishment on the house of Eli. It also shows that Saul was without further benefit of priestly counsel while David protected and preserved Abiathar. Later, Abiathar came to share priestly duties with Zadok.

2. A Hittite (Heb *ḥittî*) companion of David who remained silent when asked by David to accompany him into Saul's camp (1 Sam 26:6). The names of persons called "Hittites" in the OT are almost all good Semitic names, e.g., Ephron and Zohar, Gen 23:8; Judith, Gen 26:32; Adah, Gen 36:2, etc. Ahimelech likewise is a good Semitic name, meaning "my brother is king." Therefore, it is most likely that Ahimelech is part of a group of Canaanites and not a Hittite from Anatolia.

3. Son of Abiathar and grandson of Ahimelech in 1. above, according to 1 Chr 24:3, 6, 31. This Ahimelech worked with Zadok to organize the priests into 24 ancestral classes. His identity can be supported by the common practice (1 Chr 5:30–41) of naming the grandson after his grandfather (*CMHE,* 212–214). Others (e.g., Braun, *1 Chronicles* WBC, 238) argue against a separate identity for this Ahimelech for two reasons. First, Ahimelech is Abiathar's *father* elsewhere (1 Sam 22:20; 23:6; 30:7). Abiathar was active with Zadok (2 Sam 20:25) during David's reign and was replaced by Zadok (1 Kg 2:35) in Solomon's reign. Those verses that read "Ahimelech, son of Abiathar" could be either a scribal error, or the writer's judgment on Abiathar for supporting Adonijah instead of Solomon for the kingship. Second, the later Ahimelech is descended from Ithamar (1 Chr 24:3) while the earlier Ahimelech is descended (with Zadok) from Eleazar. This makes the later Ahimelech's lineage subordinate to Zadok. "Ahimelech, son of Abiathar" in 2 Sam 8:17 is usually taken as a scribal error and should be "Abiathar son of Ahimelech" (McCarter, *2 Samuel* AB, 253). The same approach is suggested for the parallel passage 1 Chr 18:16 (Abimelech is a scribal error there for Ahimelech).

JAMES C. MOYER

AHIMOTH (PERSON) [Heb *ʾăḥîmôt*]. The son of Elkanah, brother of Amasai, and father of another Elkanah, all Levites descended from Kohath (1 Chr 6:10—Eng 6:25). In a subsequent genealogy, this line of descent differs by naming Mahath as the son of Amasai and father of Elkanah (1 Chr 6:20–21—Eng 6:35–36; cf. 2 Chr 29:12). Rudolf (*Chronikbücher* HAT, 54) suggests that the name Ahimoth resulted from the conflation of an original MAHATH (Heb *maḥat*) with a later marginal gloss "his brother" (Heb *ʾāḥîw*); thus *ʾāḥîw* plus *maḥat* became *ʾăḥîmôt*. Further speculation on his identity is difficult, because the name Ahimoth is unattested outside this genealogy of Levites (1 Chr 6:1–15—Eng 6:16–30).

MARK J. FRETZ

AHINADAB (PERSON) [Heb *ʾăḥînādāb*]. The son of Iddo and prefect over the seventh of King Solomon's twelve administrative districts named after the town Mahanaim (1 Kgs 4:14). As prefect, Ahinadab was in charge of supplying the royal court (family, servants, officials) one month per year. The district comprised the southern half of the Transjordan and included tribal territory from Gad (*HGB*, 65, 262–73; Jones *1 and 2 Kings. Vol. 1.* NCBC, 143) and possibly also from Manasseh and Reuben (Mettinger 1971: 118). The appointment of Ahinadab as prefect indicates that his family enjoyed high social standing at the time of Solomon.

Bibliography

Mettinger, T. N. D. 1971. *Solomonic State Officials.* ConBOT 5. Lund.

MARK J. FRETZ

AHINOAM (PERSON) [Heb *ʾăḥînōʿam*]. **1.** The daughter of Ahimaaz (1 Sam 14:50), who became the wife of SAUL BEN KISH, and the first queen of the Israelite state. The name means, "my brother is joy." The Bible does not record her hometown. It appears that she bore Saul seven children: five sons and two daughters. According to the list of offspring in 1 Sam 14:47–48, which seems to derive from the early years of Saul's reign, Merab was the first-born; then Jonathan, the eldest male; Ishvi; Malchishua; and Michal, the younger daughter. Abinadab and Eshbaal, who are not named in the first list, but who are included in the Saulide genealogies in 1 Chr 8:33–40 and 1 Chr 9:39–44, appear to have been the last two born, with Eshbaal the youngest. Ishvi is not mentioned in the later genealogies, and probably died as a youth (see ISHVI).

2. A woman from the town of Jezreel, who became one of David's early wives (1 Sam 25:43; 27:3; 30:5; 2 Sam 2:2; 3:2; 1 Chr 3:1). While he was in flight from Saul, David is reported to have married her along with Abigail, the widow of Nabal (1 Sam 25:43), and the two women were to have accompanied him to Gath and resided there during his early mercenary service (1 Sam 27:3). Both Ahinoam and Abigail are reported to have been among those taken captive from Ziklag by the Amalekites while David was joining the Philistine troop muster at Aphek to do battle against Saul (1 Sam 30:5). The authenticity of the Amalekite incident is questionable; it serves on a literary level to contrast David's actions against the Amalekites with Saul's failure to eradicate them at Yahweh's command in 1 Samuel 15 (i.e. Gunn 1980: 110), illustrating once more his legitimate role as divinely anointed heir-elect to the throne on the eve of Saul's death. His defeat of the Amalekites emphasized his ability to serve as God's earthly vice-regent and military commander, while providing him with a convenient alibi for his whereabouts as Saul died on the battlefield at Gilboa (Edelman 1990). She bore David his first child, Amnon, after David had terminated his service to Achish of Gath and had moved from the Philistine town of Ziklag to Hebron (2 Sam 2:2; 3:2; 1 Chr 3:1).

It has been proposed that the two Ahinoams were the same individual on the basis of Nathan's comment to David that Yahweh had given him "his master's wives" in 2 Sam 12:8 (Levenson 1978: 27). Such a presumption would require David to have run off with the queen mother while Saul was still on the throne, which seems unlikely. In view of the possession of the royal harem as a claim to royal legitimacy (see ABNER), Nathan's comment can be related to David's eventual possession of Saul's wives after he ascended the throne in the wake of Eshbaal's death. Nathan refers to David's possession of more than a single wife of Saul's in v 23, which precludes the application of the phrase to Ahinoam alone. it is likely that the Jezreel that was Ahinoam's home was the town in S Judah, rather than the town in the Jezreel Valley. In his bid to build a rival state to Saul's in the hills of Judah, it would have been expedient for David to have wed the daughter of an important member of the community of Jezreel in the vicinity of Carmel (Josh 15:55, 56; Kh. Tewana ?), an area with established viticulture that could offer David a possible economic base for his political growth (see DAVID).

Bibliography

Edelman, D. 1990. *Saulide Israel: A Study in Secondary State Formation in Ancient Canaan.* Winona Lake, IN.

Gunn, D. 1980. *The Fate of King Saul.* JSOTSup 14. Sheffield.

Levenson, J. 1978. 1 Samuel 25 as Literature and History. *CBQ* 40: 11–28.

Diana V. Edelman

AHIO (PERSON) [Heb *ʾaḥyô*]. According to the Hebrew text, 3 different people were named Ahio. However, since the consonantal spelling of Ahio *(ʾḥyw)* is identical with the word "his brother" or "his brothers," it is uncertain if all these Ahios should be read with the MT as personal nouns. The form of the name is unique; it is the only name in the Hebrew Bible to end with *-yô.* This might suggest that *ʾḥyw* should never be read as a personal name. However, extrabiblical epigraphic evidence of various types suggests that the suffix *-yô* was used in preexilic Israel: it is found in names in the Samaria ostraca (e.g., Gadio *[gdyw]; KAI* 185), on seals (e.g., Abio [*ʾbyw*]; Hestrin and Dayagi-Mendels 1978: 36) and on the Kuntillet Ajrud inscriptions (e.g., Shemaio [*šmʿyw*]; Meshel 1978). Furthermore, the name Ahio itself is attested to in a preexilic seal, "Belonging to Ahio son of Saul" (*lʾḥyw bn šʾl;* Avigad 1975) and on a bronze bowl probably of Palestinian origin found in Nimrud (Barnett 1967: 4–6). The Ahio son of Saul seal is especially tantalizing given the connection of the name Ahio to the tribe of Benjamin and specifically to the family of Saul. In later sources, the name Ahio is used of at least 3 individuals in the Elephantine papyri. Thus, Ahio certainly existed as a personal name in Israel and the relative merit of the reading Ahio or "his brother(s)" must be decided on a case by case basis.

The recent epigraphic evidence suggests that the *-yô* element is theophoric (Zevit 1980: 12), and the name is a variant of Ahijah and should be understood as "my (divine) brother is YHWH." The suggestion that it is a profane name, "my little brother" (Noth *IPN,* 22) is unlikely given the newer evidence of *-yô* as a theophoric element.

Ahio refers to the following 3 individuals:

1. Son of Abinadab, who along with his brother Uzzah, drove the cart that transported the ark (2 Sam 6:3–4 = 1 Chr 13:7). Uzzah plays a major role in that narrative; when the cattle leading the cart stop, he steadies the ark, is killed by God, and David names the site Perez-Uzzah (2 Sam 6:6–8). Since Ahio played such an insignificant role in that narrative, there is no obvious reason why his name should have been remembered. Indeed, several ancient translations to 1 Chr 13:7 read the common noun "his brother(s)" rather than the proper noun, Ahio. These factors have suggested that Ahio in Samuel be emended to "his brother" or "his brothers." This is possible, though not compelling. The more radical solution of Budde (1934: 48–49), that Ahio has replaced an earlier "and his brother Zadok" *(wʾḥyw ṣdq)* involves too many conjectures concerning the text and the origins of the Zadokite priesthood.

2. A Benjaminite mentioned only in 1 Chr 8:14. His exact relation to others in the genealogy is unclear; some have seen him as the son of Beriah, mentioned in the previous verse (e.g., NEB), while others have suggested that he is descended from Elpa'al, mentioned in verses 12 and 18 (e.g., RSV). The abruptness of this genealogy and its use of parenthetic geographical statements make it unusually difficult to know how the people mentioned in it are related, and several scholars have rearranged it (Hogg 1899; Rudolph *Chronikbücher* HAT, 78). Furthermore, many have followed the Lucianic family of the LXX, and have emended Ahio to *ʾăḥêhem,* "their brothers" (so BHS). However, there is no contextual or syntactic reason to expect *ʾăḥêhem,* "their brothers" to appear in the genealogy at this point. Therefore, the vocalized Hebrew text Ahio, as a personal name, should probably be retained. In this case, it is noteworthy that another Benjaminite Ahio is mentioned in 1 Chr 8:31 = 9:37 (although that text too is beset with textual problems). Either the same individual is referred to, and he is placed in varying positions in different genealogies because of the respective author's differing conceptions about Ahio's importance, or Ahio might have been a traditional name among the Benjaminites. (See ALEMETH.)

3. A Benjaminite of the clan of Gibeon, brother of Kish (1 Chr 8:31 = 9:37). On the repetition of this genealogy in chap. 8 and 9, see AHAZ #1. It is unclear if this Ahio is related to Saul; this depends on whether the Kish of 1 Chr 8:30 is to be identified with the Kish of v 33 (Demsky 1971: 16–20) and whether we assume (with Curtis and Madsen *Chronicles* ICC, 164) that the Chronicler has intentionally substituted Gibeon for Gibeah, Saul's birthplace. The Septuagint translates "and his brother," reading *wĕʾāḥîw,* but this is probably a misreading of the consonantal *wʾḥyw* by the translator; there is no contextual or syntactic reason for "and his brother" to appear in this type of genealogy. As noted above, the relationship between this Ahio and the Ahio of the Benjaminite genealogy in 8:14 is uncertain.

Bibliography

Avigad, N. 1975. New Names on Hebrew Seals. *EI* 12: 66–71 (in Hebrew).

Barnett, R. 1967. Layard's Nimrud Bronzes and Their Inscriptions. *EI* 8: 1*–7*.

Budde, K. 1934. Die Herkunft Ṣadoḳ's. *ZAW* 52: 42–50.

Demsky, A. 1971. The Genealogy of Gibeon (1 Chronicles 9:35–44): Biblical and Epigraphic Considerations. *BASOR* 202: 16–23.

Hestrin, R., and Dayagi-Mendels, M. 1978. *Seals from the First Temple Period.* Jerusalem (in Hebrew).

Hogg, H. 1899. The Genealogy of Benjamin: A Criticism of 1 Chronicles VIII. *JQR* 11: 102–14.

Meshel, Z. 1978. *Kuntillet Ajrud.* Jerusalem (in Hebrew).

Zevit, Z. 1980. MATRES LECTIONIS *in Ancient Hebrew Epigraphs.* ASORMS 2. Cambridge, MA.

MARC Z. BRETTLER

AHIQAR, BOOK OF. The book of *Ahiqar* is a rare example of a polytheistic work which was used and adapted by some Jewish groups. Like Tobit, it is a sapiential novel, i.e., it combines a dramatic story with wise instruction. It is the most ancient of the extrabiblical works preserved and read by Jewish people.

A. The Story

According to the most fully preserved versions of the plot, Ahiqar was a wise scribe and counsellor of the Assyrian kings Sennacherib and Esarhaddon (their order is reversed in the later versions). See AHIKAR/AHIQAR. As he lacked a son, the sage adopted his nephew Nadin whom he trained to be his successor by instructing him with wise words. Nadin did succeed the aging Ahiqar, but far from exhibiting appropriate gratitude to his uncle, Nadin framed him by forging treasonous letters in Ahiqar's name. When Esarhaddon was informed of Ahiqar's alleged crime, he sentenced him to death. It happened that Nabushumishkun, the officer commissioned to execute Ahiqar, had been saved by him at an earlier time when their roles were reversed and Ahiqar had been ordered to kill him. The officer agreed to spare Ahiqar and to kill a eunuch in his place. Once it became known abroad that Ahiqar was dead, the Egyptian king issued a challenge to the Assyrian monarch: If he sent him someone who could construct a palace between heaven and earth, Esarhaddon would receive the revenue for 3 years from Egypt. If no such expert could be found, then the Assyrian king would have to pay the Egyptian sovereign a similar sum. Esarhaddon bemoaned the loss of Ahiqar and was overjoyed to discover that his earlier order had been countermanded. Once he had recovered from his confinement, Ahiqar went to Egypt and handled all problems with stunning wit and wisdom. He returned to Assyria with the Egyptian revenue and took his revenge on Nadin. He severely punished him and scathingly criticized him for what he had done; the battered Nadin then swelled up and died.

B. Versions

The earliest extant version of Ahiqar is the fragmentary Aramaic text which was found at Elephantine. The papyrus dates from the late 5th century B.C.E. and contains parts of the narrative in 5 columns (through the "execution" of Ahiqar) and sayings on the remaining 9. Later, many other versions of the book appeared. Some small, very fragmentary parts of what may have been a 1st-century C.E. Demotic translation of Ahiqar have been identified (Küchler 1979: 333–37; Lindenberger 1983: 310–12), but their nature remains unclear. The two fragments with narrative sections do not agree in all details with known versions of the story, and the one fragment with sapiential teachings offers no correspondence with the other texts. Ahiqar was, in all likelihood, translated into Greek, but no copy of this version has been found. The Gk *Life of Aesop* (chaps. 23–32) does, however, contain sections which parallel the book, with Aesop assuming the role of Ahiqar and the Babylonian king Lykeros that of the ruler whom he serves. The hypothetical Greek Ahiqar eventually served as the base for translations into Rumanian and Slavonic, with the latter becoming the *Vorlage* of Russian and Serbian editions. The Syriac translation, which exists in more than one recension, is the oldest and most valuable of the complete versions. From it Armenian and Arabic (and Karshuni) renderings were made, with the Armenian becoming the base for Georgian and Old Turkish translations. Some of the proverbs of Ahiqar are included in the Ethiopic *Book of the Wise Philosophers* which was translated from Arabic (Lindenberger 1983: 4–7). In some instances Ahiqar has been included as an appendix to *A Thousand and One Nights.*

C. Date and Origin

Even before the Elephantine papyrus was found, it was known that Ahiqar was pre-Christian in date because elements of its story, some of its principal characters, and aspects of its instruction are mentioned in Tobit (1:21–22 [Ahikar is called Tobit's nephew; see also 4QTobaram[a]];

2:10; 11:18–19; 14:10 [see 4QTobaram[d]; his name in some mss at 14:15 is a mistake, perhaps for Cyaxares]). The discoveries in Egypt simply confirmed the antiquity of the work. The script of the Elephantine papyrus can be classified as ". . . formal or semi-formal of the end of the fifth century" (Naveh 1970: 35; Cowley 1923: 204). The story must, therefore, have been written at some time after the beginning of Esarhaddon's reign (680 B.C.E.) and before the copy of it from Elephantine was made. This battered text, which does not appear to be the autograph (Lindenberger 1983: 19), contains parts of both the narrative and the sayings, but the point (or points) where there was a change (or changes) from one to the other has not survived. This raises the problem whether the book as it stands is a unity (and thus probably composed at one time) or is a later combination of narrative and sayings which were originally separate and from different dates. As far back as the story can be traced, they are combined, but the proverbs or sayings appear to be written in an older form of Aramaic—in a Western dialect—than the official Aramaic of the narrative (Greenfield 1978: 97; Lindenberger 1983: 19, 279–304). If this is true, it may mean that different authors composed them and that it would then be possible to date the proverbs at an earlier time than the *terminus a quo* implied by the narrative; but the conclusion is not inevitable, in as much as traditional material such as the proverbs would naturally be in a more archaic or poetic diction than the narrative. Moreover, even in the Aramaic there are references to the narrative in the sayings. Finally, as noted by Küchler (1979: 330), the first words of the Aramaic papyrus (*ʾlh m*]*ly ʾḥyqr* [these are the words of Ahiqar]) imply that sayings are involved.

It was once thought that Hebrew might have been the original language of the book, but scholarly views changed with the discovery of the Aramaic text. The Assyrian setting of the tale suggested to some that the author wrote in Akkadian (so Cowley 1923: 205–08; Grelot 1972: 429) from which the Aramaic was translated (Cowley posited a Persian intermediary translation). Nevertheless, while this view continues to find defenders, it now seems more likely that both narrative and sayings were composed in Aramaic (Lindenberger 1983: 16–17, who notes an Aramaic word play in saying 41 [*ḥṭ* (arrow) and *ḥṭʾ* (sin)]).

D. Structure

As indicated above, it has been claimed that the sayings originated separately from the narrative so that the present combination of the two is due to a later editorial operation. All extant texts, however, contain both, but questions remain about the shape of the book because of uncertainties regarding the exact location of the sayings. It is obvious that major differences separate the Aramaic sayings and those of the later versions, and that for the sapiential material the latter also show variation relative to one another. But a more significant structural problem has to do with the original location of the proverbs, once they were joined to the narrative (if they were ever separate). In the Aramaic text, the columns numbered i–v contain narrative and vi–xiv offer sayings. None of the fragmentary narrative lines indicates a transition to the proverbs. This may entail that in the Aramaic version the sayings came at the end of the narrative (Cowley 1923: 210; Lindenberger *OTP* 2: 480). Grelot (1972: 432–51) attempts to integrate the two by arranging the columns in the order i, vi–xiv, ii–v, but the state of the text makes any conclusion quite uncertain. The major later versions—Syriac, Armenian, and Arabic—present two sets of sayings: the first (chap. 2) contains Ahiqar's instruction of Nadin and the second (chap. 8) his harsh words for him near the conclusion. The parallel sections in the *Life of Aesop* are distinctive in that the one section of sayings which Aesop delivers to his adoptive son Ennus is found before Aesop leaves for Egypt and just before Ennus' death. As nothing definite can be deduced from the Aramaic text and the Aesop material is a special case, it is reasonable to suppose that the arrangement as given in the Syriac, Armenian, and Arabic versions is the original one. See also *ANET* 427–30; *APOT* 2: 715–84; *Proverbs* OTL.

Bibliography

Cowley, A. 1923. *Aramaic Papyri of the Fifth Century B.C.* Oxford. Repr. Osnabrück, 1967.

Greenfield, J. C. 1978. The Dialects of Early Aramaic. JNES 37: 93–99.

Grelot, P. 1972. Histoire et sagesse de'Aḥîqar l'assyrien. Pp. 427–52 in *Documents araméens d'Egypte.* LAPO. Paris.

Küchler, M. 1979. Frühjüdische Weisheit in den Achikar-Traditionen? Pp. 319–413 in *Frühjüdische Weisheitstraditionen.* OBO 26. Göttingen.

Lindenberger, J. M. 1983. *The Aramaic Proverbs of Ahiqar.* JHNES. Baltimore.

Naveh, J. 1970. *The Development of the Aramaic Script.* Proceedings of the Israel Academy of Sciences and Humanities 5/1. Jerusalem.

JAMES C. VANDERKAM

AHIRA (PERSON) [Heb *ʾăḥîraʿ*]. The son of Enan and leader of the tribe of Naphtali, who assisted Moses in taking a census of Israel (Num 1:15; 2:29). As tribal leader, Ahira contributed offerings on the 12th day of the tabernacle dedication (Num 7:78, 83), and took charge of the military troop of Naphtali throughout Israel's march from Sinai to Palestine (Num 10:27).

MARK J. FRETZ

AHIRAM (PERSON) [Heb *ʾaḥîrām*]. AHIRAMITES. The third of 5 sons of Benjamin and head of the Ahiramites, according to one Benjaminite genealogy (Num 26:38). While this is the only occurrence of the name, scholars have suggested that corrupt forms of "Ahiram" may exist in several other Benjaminite genealogies. One such case is Genesis 46:21, which lists 10 sons of Benjamin, including "Ehi, Rosh, Muppim, Huppim." It is widely agreed (e.g., Speiser *Genesis* AB, 343) that these 4 names are a mechanical corruption of "Ahiram, Shephupham, Huppim." This correction would bring these names to agree with the 3d, 4th, and 5th sons of Numbers 26:38–9. A metathesis of the final *mem* of "Ahiram" and the initial *šin* of "Shephupham" would have created a name with the consonants *ʾalep-ḥet-reš-šin,* which could then have been broken into 2 names, "Ehi, Rosh." The resulting names, "Ehi, Rosh, and Muppim" do not occur in any other Benjaminite genealogy. Another possible occurrence of the name "Ahiram" is in the name "Aharah" who is listed in 1 Chr 8:1 as the 3d son of Benjamin. Schumacher (IDB 1:70) suggests that yet another corrupt form of "Ahiram" exists in the name "Aher" in 1 Chr 7:12. While this may seem superficially to be the case, most scholars follow the suggestion of Klostermann (*RE* 4) that the name should be read *ʾeḥād,* "one." There are other possibilities for the name "Aher" (which is nowhere else attested), including that of reading "Addar" (="Ard"), a name found in several Benjaminite genealogies (Williamson *1 Chronicles* NCBC, 78).

SIEGFRIED S. JOHNSON

AHISAMACH (PERSON) [Heb *ʾăḥîsāmāk*]. A Danite and father of tabernacle craftsman OHOLIAB (Exod 31:6, 35:34, 38:23). Ahisamach is a rather typical W Semitic verbal sentence name (*IPN* 66–70). In such names kinship elements such as *ʾāb* "father" and *ʾāḥ* "brother" are "generally theophoric, the deity being identified as a protective relative." (*IDB* Sup, 620) The name, then, means "My [divine] brother supports/has supported." A similar name with the same verb, *Semachiah* "Yahweh supports/has supported" (1 Chr 26:7) is clearly theophoric. See also *TDOT* 1:7, 193.

STEPHEN A. REED

AHISHAHAR (PERSON) [Heb *ʾăḥîšaḥar*]. A son of Bilhan (1 Chr 7:10), grandson of Jediael, appearing in a curious Benjaminite genealogy in 1 Chr 7:6–12a. The name means "brother of the dawn." This is the only appearance of the name in the MT (LXX *Achisaar*), and it does not appear in the Apocrypha or the deuterocanonical literature. Scholarship has been divided concerning the authenticity of this genealogy because of its place in the text, the more complete Benjaminite genealogy which follows in 1 Chr 8:1–40, the lack of reference to Zebulun and Dan within 1 Chronicles 1–9, the naming of only 3 sons of Benjamin (Bela, Becher, and Jediael), and the singular appearance of Jediael in the genealogy. Curtis and Madsen (*Chronicles* ICC, 147) and Brunet (1953: 485f.) opt for the possibility of the genealogy being that of Zebulun. However, this approach suggests corruption of the text without sufficient manuscript support. Coggins (*Chronicles* CBC, 49), Braun (*1 Chronicles* WBC, 108), and Williamson (*Chronicles* NCBC, 78) suggest that this genealogy has replaced the tradition of Gen 46:21 at this point and reflects a postexilic military census list complete with inflated numbers of fighting men (see also Meyers *1 Chronicles* AB, lii). Since Ahishahar and the other sons of Bilhan are called *rāʾšē hāʾābôt,* or heads of families, political and social organization may be reflected somewhat, as well as military organization. In early Israel, and probably continuing even as late as postexilic times, the *bēt ʾāb* was the basic and most important socioeconomic unit. Harmon (1983: 150) has indicated that the head man of a *bēt ʾāb* may have functioned along the lines of the bigmen of anthropological terminology. Orme (1981: 139) states that bigmen are successful, involved in community affairs, associated with feasts, and involved in arbitration in local disputes.

Bibliography

Brunet, A.-M. 1953. Le Chroniste et ses Sources. *RB* 60: 481–508.

Harmon, G. E. 1983. *Floor Area and Population Determination: A Method for Estimating Village Population in the Central Hill Country during the Period of the Judges (Iron Age I).* Diss.

Orme, Bryony. 1981. *Anthropology for Archaeologists.* Ithaca.

G. EDWIN HARMON

AHISHAR (PERSON) [Heb *ʾăḥîšār*]. One of Solomon's high officials (*śārîm),* who was in charge of the palace (1 Kgs 4:6). His duties as royal chamberlain, or majordomo (*ʿal-habbāyit,* "over the house"), were centered on the administration of the royal household. Near Eastern parallels to this office suggest that he regularly received instructions from the king, controlled important communications and access to the palace, and oversaw other officials (*AncIsr* 1: 128–31; cf. Isa 22:22). In Israel the office may not yet have gained the importance which it held in other lands, as is suggested both by the occurrence of Ahishar's name toward the end of the list (1 Kgs 4:2–6), and by the fact, unusual for this list, that the name of his father is not mentioned. J. Gray (*Kings* OTL, 133) speculates that the lack of a patronymic may indicate the inferior nature of the office, or that Ahishar was of foreign, or humble, origin.

Even the form of the name is uncertain. As it stands, the name might mean "my brother has sung" (*ISBE* 1: 81). The Gk has *Achei* (G[B]) or *Achiēl* (G[L]). Montgomery (*Kings* ICC, 119) suggested that in the Gk text *Achei ēn,* the *ēn* may have been an error for *ēl,* pointing to a Heb *ʾḥyʾl,* with *šr* as a remainder of the patronym. Another possibility would be to vocalize *ʾaḥyāšār* ("my brother is righteous," *IPN* 189).

KENNETH H. CUFFEY

AHITHOPHEL (PERSON) [Heb *ʾăḥîtōpel*]. A famed wise man and royal counselor of David who figured prominently in Absalom's revolt against his father.

The name itself is composed of the theophoric element *ʾăḥî-* followed by the obscure *tōpel,* otherwise unknown except as a place name in the lower Transjordan (Deut 1:1), which is to be identified with modern *Ṭafîla.* Noth suggests that the 2d particle be identified with the later Heb word *ṭpl* = *tpl,* meaning "to add to" (*IPN* 236).

Ahithophel's role in Absalom's revolt earned him a permanent place in the later Syriac vocabulary, where his name became an adjective—*ʾaḥitōpēlājā*—meaning "traitor." This same wise man was also the father of Eliam, one of David's champions (the *šālišîm;* RSV: The Thirty), who may be identified with Ammiel (*IPN* 15, n.2), the father of Bath-shua (= Bath-sheba, 1 Chr 3:5; see below).

As a wise man, Ahithophel was reputed to be "like the oracle of God" (2 Sam 16:23). Thus it was a fortunate turn of events for Absalom when Ahithophel threw in his hand with the rebels. It was on Ahithophel's advice that Absalom violated David's concubines "in the sight of all Israel" (2 Sam 16:21–23), as prophesied by Nathan (2 Sam 12:11), in order to demonstrate Absalom's complete break from his father. (In the ancient Near East, the usurpation of the royal authority of one's father also meant the usurpation of his male virility, hence the great symbolic power of Absalom's act.) Ahithophel further advised Absalom to let him take a body of 12,000 men and strike David and his men immediately, while they were still weak and dispirited from the coup. Absalom was at first pleased with this suggestion, but Hushai the Archite, one of David's counselors (who was secretly working to undo Ahithophel's sound advice), opposed the plan. Hushai argued instead that Absalom should wait until all Israel had gathered to him. Then, when Absalom and the Israelites met David and his professional soldiers in the field, they would overrun David and his men by sheer force of numbers. When Absalom chose to follow the advice of Hushai, Ahithophel, certain of the impending disaster, went home and set his affairs in order, and hanged himself.

Ahithophel's participation in Absalom's revolt is indicative of the deep dissatisfaction with David's rule, even within the inner circle at court. While many may have joined the rebels in order to anoint a king who took a more direct interest in the affairs of the people than David (2 Sam 15:1–6), Ahithophel's reasons may have been private. That is, he may have been motivated by David's treacherous murder of Bath-sheba's husband, Uriah. If Ammiel, father of Bath-shua (1 Chr 3:5; Bath-shua, as the mother of Solomon, is to be read Bath-sheba) is the same person as Eliam, son of Ahithophel (2 Sam 23:34)—and this is not certain: the names are related, but in the same way that Joab [= Yahweh is father] is related to Abijah [= father is Yahweh], so that they are not identical—Bath-sheba would have been the granddaughter of Ahithophel. Ahithophel would then have had a very real and personal stake in the rebels' cause, namely revenge. One should wonder, however, at the absence of Ammiel (Eliam?) from among the conspirators. Bath-sheba's father would certainly not have been ignorant of what his own father had known of his daughter's marriage. In the end, Ahithophel's relationship to Bath-sheba must remain uncertain, as must his reasons for joining Absalom's revolt.

Bibliography

Bailey, R. C. 1989. *David in Love and War: the Pursuit of Power in 1 Samuel 10–12*. JSOTSup 75. Sheffield.

D. G. SCHLEY

AHITUB (PERSON) [Heb *ʾăḥîṭûb*]. **1.** A Levitical priest, the father of Ahijah and Ahimelech, and grandfather of Abiathar (1 Sam 14:3; 22:9, 11–12, 20). Ahijah was priest to Saul in Shiloh (1 Sam 14:3) and served the same king at Gibeah in his warfare with the Philistines (1 Sam 14:18–19, 36). Ahimelech the priest (contra the gloss in Mark 2:26) gave David holy bread and Goliath's sword at Nob (1 Sam 21:7, 10—Eng 21:6, 9) and perished when Doeg the Edomite massacred the priesthood there (1 Sam 22:18). Ahimelech's son Abiathar escaped to serve David as his chaplain during his "outlaw" period (1 Sam 22:20; 23:6; 30:7) and remained an important priest during David's early kingship (2 Sam 15:35; 20:25; 1 Chr 27:34?). Moreover, it is difficult to reconcile the claim that Ahimelech was Abiathar's son (2 Sam 8:17 = 1 Chr 18:16; also 1 Chr 24:6) unless there was an Ahimelech II. We are told that Abiathar's son/Ahitub's great-grandson, Jonathan, stayed behind in Jerusalem as one of David's spies after David's flight from Absalom (2 Sam 15:27, 36). Ahitub's brother's name was Ichabod, and both men are termed sons of Phinehas and grandsons of Eli, the high priest at Shiloh in the days of young Samuel (1 Sam 1:3; 4:21; 14:3). While one tradition traces Ahitub's ancestry through Eli back to Eleazar, Aaron's third son (2 Esdr 1:1–3), another tradition links this Ahitub through his son Ahimelech and grandfather Eli with Ithamar, the fourth son of Aaron (1 Chr 24:3; Josephus, *Ant* 5.11.5).

2. A Levitical priest, the son of Amariah (I?), father of Zadok (I?), and grandfather of Ahimaaz (2 Sam 8:17 = 1 Chr 18:16; 1 Chr 5:33–34—Eng 6:7–8; 6:37–38—Eng 6:52–53). Zadok (I?), with Abiathar, was a priest to David (2 Sam 15:35; 2 Sam 8:17; 20:25; 1 Chr 18:16). When Abiathar supported Adonijah as David's successor instead of Solomon, Solomon appointed Zadok (I?) as his high priest in place of Abiathar (1 Kgs 2:35). Ahimaaz, son of Zadok (I?) and grandson of Ahitub (I?), together with Jonathan ben Abiathar, likewise kept David informed of developments in Jerusalem following Absalom's conspiracy (2 Sam 15:27, 36).

3. A Levitical priest, the son of Amariah (II?), and the father of Zadok (II?), and grandfather of Shallum (1 Chr 5:37–38—Eng 6:11–12). This Ahitub (II?) appears to be the same person listed in Neh 11:11 and 1 Chr 9:11 as the father of Meraioth and grandfather of Zadok (II?) and great-grandfather of Meshullam (= Shallum above?).

It may well be that 3. and 2. (and even 1.) above are actually all one and the same person (Curtis and Madsen *Chronicles* ICC, 128–29). Beside the Ahitub of Eli's lineage, the name Ahitub appears in 7 biblical genealogical lists: Neh 11:11; 1 Chr 9:11; Ezra 7:1–5; 1 Chr 5:27–41—Eng 6:1–15; 1 Chr 6:35–38—Eng 6:50–53; 1 Esdr 8:1–2; and 2 Esdr 1:1–3. Yet in only one of these lists, namely 1 Chr 5:27–41—Eng 6:1–15, does the name Ahitub appear more than once. The fact that the pattern Amariah-Ahitub-Zadok occurs twice only in this one particular list readily suggests either a copyist's error or some deliberate scribal intention. This list is a long one, covering 26 generations in all, from Levi to Jehozadak, the high priest who went into exile (1 Chr 5:4—Eng 6:15). The 2d list in the same chapter (1 Chr 6:35–38—Eng 6:50–53) limits itself to repeat only the 12 names from the first half of its chapter counterpart, the high priests from Aaron through Ahimaaz. On the other hand, Neh 11:11 and 1 Chr 9:11 represent lists of only 6 names each, but names more suggestive of the lower half of the same long list in 1 Chr 5:27–41—Eng 6:1–15. Neh 11:11 reads the names Ahitub-Meraioth-Zadok-Meshullam-Hilkiah-Seraiah; 1 Chr 9:11 reiterates the same first 5 names but changes the last name to Azariah. If Neh 11:11 and 1 Chr 9:11 should exhibit an early form of the list, Ezra 7:1–5 reflects another stage in its development as it solves the previous last name mixup through conflation (Azariah-Amariah-Ahitub-Zadok-Shallum-Hilkiah-Azariah-Seraiah-Ezra) and expands the upper end of the list to include the high priests from Aaron down through Meraioth. The long list in 1 Chr 5:27–41—Eng 6:1–15 goes further, repeating the upper and lower pattern of names from Neh 11:11; 1 Chr 9:11; and Ezra 7:1–5. What turns up basically new in this long list are the hitherto unparalleled names Amariah-Ahitub-Zadok-Ahimaaz-Azariah-Johanan, filling the gap between Meraioth and Azariah of the former lists. Significantly the first 3 names of this addition of 6 names contribute to the double pattern of Amariah-Ahitub-Zadok already noted above. The remaining 2 somewhat-later lists from 1 and 2 Esdras then go on to presuppose the final stage reflected in the long list as the 12 names of 1 Esdr 8:1–2 draw from both the top and the bottom of the long list. 2 Esdr 1:1–3 parallels Ezra 7:1–5 closely, but between Amariah and Ahitub it includes 3 names completely new to all the previous lists: the names Eli-Phinehas-Ahijah. This suggests that the Ahitub intended in this last list is Ahijah, person 1. above, and, this, in a list which purports to link Ezra the priest to the line of Eleazar, not Ithamar.

If the double names Zadok and Ahitub in the long list are in fact a literary fiction created to supply a lineage to an otherwise unknown Zadok, the name of Ahitub known from the house of Eli (the house which Zadok displaced) could have been singled out by the biblical writer as a convenient and appropriate priestly ancestor (Rehm, *IDBSup*, 976–77). On the other hand, were it granted that the long list, though unique, is reliable, and that there were in fact historically more than one Ahitub and one Zadok in the priesthood descendent from Eleazar, the threefold delineation above might stand.

Interestingly, Katzenstein (1962), in his study of the high priests from Solomon to Jehozadak, thinks there may have been as many as 22 high priests in office during this time span. This would add 9 names to the 13 currently on record in 1 Chr 5:34–41—Eng 6:8–15 for this span in the long list. Besides the one Ahitub expected in this part of the list, he postulates 3 Zadok's, 4 Azariah's, and 2 Amariah's. Katzenstein follows closely the sequence of high priests given by Josephus (*Ant* 9.1.1; 9.7.1; 9.10.4; 10.8.5–6) and believes that the extra names in Josephus were omitted by the biblical writers because they knew these priests to be non-Zadokites (see Katzenstein 1962: 382–84).

4. The son of Elijah and the father of Raphaim and the distant ancestor of Judith, the heroine of the apocryphal book of the same name (Jdt 8:1). As Judith's supposed ancestry is traced back 16 generations to Israel or Jacob, the author sought to impress upon his readers the rich Jewish heritage of the God-fearing widow of Bethulia who single-handedly captivated and decapitated the fearsome invader Holofernes.

Bibliography

Johnson, M. D. 1969. Genealogies in Ezra-Nehemiah and Chronicles. Pp. 37–76 in *The Purpose of Biblical Genealogies.* Cambridge.

Katzenstein, H. J. 1962. Some Remarks on the Lists of the Chief Priests of the Temple of Solomon. *JBL* 81: 377–84.

ROGER W. UITTI

AHLAB (PLACE) [Heb *ʾaḥlāb*]. A town within the tribal boundaries of Asher whose non-Israelite inhabitants were driven out during the Heb conquest of Palestine (Judg 1:31). Although in Josh 19:24–31 the list of towns located on Asher's territorial boundary does not mention Ahlab, LXX^B of Josh 19:29 reads *apo leb* "from Leb," which may reflect a Heb *vorlage* of **mlb*. However, the LXX reading *aalaph* in Judg 1:31 supports a derivation from Heb *ʾḥlb* rather than *ḥlb*.

Discussion focuses on a metathesis within the name of the letters *lamed* and *bet*. Whereas Judg 1:31 reads "Ahlab, and Achzib, and Helbah," Josh 19:29 concludes with "Mehebel to Achzib." Boling and Wright (*Joshua* AB, 453) argue that Heb *mʾḥlb* "from Ahlab" was the original reading in Josh 19:29, and identify Ahlab with Mehebel. Other scholars identify the two towns, but view Ahlab as an equivalent or variant of Mehebel (Meyer 1906: 540; Fisher 1975: 286). More specifically, Abel (*GP*2: 67), followed by Aharoni (*LBHG*, 235), concludes that the doublet of Ahlab and Helbah in Judg 1:31 expresses a metathesis of Mehebel. In contrast, Kallai (*HGB*, 222) suggests that Ahlab has no parallel in Josh 19:29, whereas Helbah matches a proposed reconstruction Heb **mḥlb* (MT *mḥbl*). This might be supported by the Assyrian inscription of Sennacherib (*ANET*, 287), which lists towns in the area of Sidon, and mentions the town of Maḫalliba. Since the time of Delitzsch (1881: 284), scholars have associated Ahlab with this Maḫalliba, identifying Ahlab with modern *Khirbet el-Maḥalib* located ca. 6 km northeast of Tyre (Boling and Wright *Joshua* AB, 455). See also MAHALAB.

Bibliography

Delitzsch, F. 1881. *Wo Lag Das Paradies?*. Liepzig.

Fisher, L. R. 1975. *Ras Shamra Parallels: The Texts from Ugarit and the Hebrew Bible Vol. 2.* AnOr 50. Rome.

Meyer, E. 1906. *Die Israeliten und Ihre Nachbarstämme.* Halle.

MARK J. FRETZ

AHLAI (PERSON) [Heb *ʾaḥlāy*]. **1.** Although listed as a son of Sheshan (1 Chr 2:31), Ahlai probably was a daughter (in view of v 34) given in marriage to Sheshan's Egyptian slave, Jarha (v 35). However, some scholars understand vv 34–41 as representing a different genealogical source and feel no need to harmonize this passage with v 31, thus concluding that Ahlai was a son. The expression "son(s) of" may be used in the sense of "descendant" or "offspring." Since the MT of 1 Chr 2:31 uses the plural "the sons of," the single daughter (or son) Ahlai, may possibly be understood here as the progenitor of a clan or family bearing her/his name. Because of Sheshan's failure to produce sons, Ahlai probably was the founder of a branch of the important family of Jerahmeel, the first-born of Hezron, grandson of Judah. The Jerahmeelites' association with the Kenites (1 Sam 27:10; 30:29), the similarity of several of their names with the Edomite genealogy in 1 Chronicles 1, and the correspondence of some personal names with place names, allows some scholars to identify them with foreign elements in Israel (Gen 15:19) and the shift of Edomites from southern Judah northward following the destruction of Jerusalem (Braun, *1 Chronicles* WBC, 45 and Myers, *1 Chronicles* AB, 15).

2. The mother (or possibly father) of Zabad, who was one of the mighty men of the armies of David (1 Chr 11:41b). Zabad is listed as a descendant of Sheshan's daughter in 1 Chr 2:36, supporting the conclusion that Ahlai was his mother and identical with #1 above. 1 Chr 11:41b–47 appears to be a continuation of the comparable list in Samuel (2 Sam 23:24–39) and contains names not found there.

Bibliography

Williamson, H. G. M. 1979. Sources and Redaction in the Chronicler's Genealogy of Judah. *JBL* 98: 351–59.
Wilson, R. R. 1977. *Genealogy and History in the Biblical World.* New Haven.

W. P. STEEGER

AHLAMU. See ARAMEANS.

AHOAH (PERSON) [Heb *ʾaḥôaḥ*]. 6th son of Bela and grandson of Benjamin, according to one Benjaminite genealogy (1 Chr 8:4). Many scholars have proposed that "Ahoah" is a mistake for AHIJAH (e.g. Williamson *1 and 2 Chronicles* NCBC, 84), due to the evident dittography in v 7, "Naaman, Ahijah, and Gera." The Hebrew script of the two names *ʾaḥôaḥ* and *ʾahîyāh* are nearly identical. This proposal is supported by the Gk (LXX), Syr, and Aramaic versions. The Gk reads *achia* for the name in both v 4 and v 7.

SIEGFRIED S. JOHNSON

AHOHI (PERSON) [Heb *ʾăḥôḥî*]. Var. AHOAH. AHOHITE. Although seen by some as a corruption of Ahijah (Heb *ʾăḥîyāh* vs. *ʾăḥôḥî*), Ahohi is a gentilic noun designating membership in the clan of Ahoah (Heb *ʾăḥôaḥ*), which was counted among the descendants of Benjamin (1 Chr 8:4). That David usurped the Israelite throne from the Benjaminite king Saul did not prevent a number of Benjaminites, including some from the clan of Ahoah, from fighting in David's service. These included Eleazar the son of Dodo (2 Sam 23:9–10; 1 Chr 11:12), the second of "the three," one of David's most renowned warriors. Although the RSV lists Eleazar as "the son of Dodo, the son of Ahohi," the correct reading is probably "Eleazar, the son of Dodo, son of an Ahohite." Either reading would reflect the same Hebrew phraseology; it simply makes more sense to read Ahohi in its plain sense as a gentilic noun, rather than construing it as a proper name.

In the Chronicler's list of David's heroes, the deeds of Eleazar, the son of Dodo, and Shammah, the son of Agee the Hararite, have been combined into a single account (1 Chr 11:12–14; probably when the copyist skipped from the Hebrew *neʾespû-šām* [2 Sam 23:9b] to *wattĕhî-šām* [2 Sam 23:11]). Besides Eleazar, 2 Sam 23:28 recalls one Zalmon, the Ahohite, whose name parallels that of Ilai (Heb *ʿîlay*, emend to *ṣîlay*?) the Ahohite in 1 Chr 11:29. See ILAI; ZALMON.

Finally, the mention of Dodai the Ahohite in the list of monthly levies (1 Chr 27:4) may refer to the father of Eleazar the son of Dodo. Thus, at least two or three Benjaminites from the clan of Ahoah fought in David's select corps of heroic warriors, a fact which may testify both to David's popularity among Saul's picked men (cf. 1 Sam 18:6–8), and to the antiquity of David's own corps of champions (Heb *šālišîm*).

Bibliography

Elliger, K. 1935. Die dreissig Helden Davids. *PJ* 31: 29–75 (esp. 44–45).

D. G. SCHLEY

AHRIMAN. See ZOROASTER, ZOROASTRIANISM.

AHUMAI (PERSON) [Heb *ʾăḥûmay*]. A member of the tribe of Judah and the son of Jahath (1 Chr 4:1–2). However, he may have been a Calebite, since Shobal, the grandfather of Ahumai, is identified as a descendant of Caleb in 1 Chr 2:50, 52. The genealogy found in 1 Chr 4:1–7 was originally a Calebite list, which has been incorporated into the overall genealogical list of Judah (1 Chr 2:3–4:23). The motivation for this incorporation may have been the Chronicler's interest in "all Israel" as a whole and the tribe of Judah in particular. (For further discussion, see Curtis and Madsen *Chronicles* ICC; Braun *1 Chronicles* WBC; Williamson *1 and 2 Chronicles* NCBC.)

H. C. LO

AHURA MAZDA (DEITY). The name of the supreme god worshipped in the Zoroastrian religion. Ahura means "Lord" and Mazda means "Wisdom". The name was originally an appellation of an ancient Iranian divinity, conceived of as the spirit or force of wisdom. His earthly prototype was presumably the high priest who counseled and guided the tribe. Zoroaster, in founding the religion, exalted him as the one eternal Being, wholly wise and good, and very powerful, but not yet omnipotent, that is, his power is presently limited by that of the Evil Spirit, likewise self-existent (see ZORASTER, ZOROASTRIANISM), whom at the end of time he will destroy. For this purpose Ahura Mazda created by his thought lesser divinities and this world (*Y[asna]* 31.11). This creative act was accomplished with the aid of the Holy Spirit (*Y.*44.7, 51.7, cf. 31.3), who is one with him, and yet distinct. The lesser divinities are of the same essence and will as their Creator, and to venerate any one of them is to venerate Ahura Mazda. Zoroastrianism is also known to its adherents as "the Mazda-worshipping religion," which emphasizes its essential monotheism.

Zoroaster invoked Ahura Mazda in all his hymns (the *Gathas*), and the whole *Avesta* was regarded by the orthodox as revealed by him to his prophet. This view is still upheld by some, on the grounds that, though of multiple authorship, it all derives essentially from Zoroaster's teachings, and so is informed by Ahura Mazda's omniscience. All devotional acts begin with veneration of Ahura Mazda, and the 5 obligatory daily prayers in Avestan are prefaced by the affirmation in Persian: "Ohrmazd is Lord." The Sassanian king Vahram V answered Christian accusations of polytheism by declaring that "he acknowledged only one God. The rest were but as courtiers of the King" (Hoffmann 1880: 42).

Zoroaster believed that he saw and spoke with Ahura Mazda repeatedly. He declared himself "eager to behold and take counsel" with him (*Y.*33.6), and when rejected as his prophet turned to him for aid. "Take heed of it, Lord, granting the support which friend should give to friend" (*Y*.46.2). He saw him anthropomorphically ("the tongue of Thy mouth" *Y*.31.3, cf. *Y*.28.11; "the hand with which Thou holdest . . ." *Y*.43.4); but also with awe, as clad with the sky as garment (*Y*.30.5), the One who "established the course of the sun and stars . . . upheld the earth from below, and the heavens from falling" (*Y*.44.3, 4).

The earliest recorded reference to Ahura Mazda, as *as-sa-ra ma-za-aš,* is in an Assyrian cuneiform text of probably the 8th century B.C. This was presumably the Old Iranian divinity, since Zoroastrianism had probably then only just reached western Iran. Ahura Mazda was named many times by Darius the Great (522–486 B.C.) in his inscriptions; and Western scholars used to think that he was represented on Achaemenian monuments by a crowned male figure in a winged circle. This is now interpreted rather as a symbol of the Royal Fortune. Zoroastrianism remained, it seems, aniconic until the late 5th century B.C., after which cult statues were created of Ahura Mazda and other divinities. None of these survives, because of the successful iconoclasm of the Sassanians (224–652 A.D.). Rock sculptures show him as a kingly figure, standing or on horseback, and once holding the *barsom,* the priestly bundle of rods (Pope 1938: 154A, 156, 160A; Christensen 1936: 90–1, 226–7, 255). No representations of him are now made, but in living Zoroastrianism, as in the religion's earliest days, his worship is conducted in the presence of ever-burning fire, regarded as a symbol of truth and enlightenment.

Bibliography

For the *Avesta, Gathas, Yasna* and Old Persian inscriptions see under ZOROASTER, ZOROASTRIANISM.

Benveniste, E. 1970. Le terme iranien *mazdayasna. BSOAS* 33: 5–9.

Boyce, M. 1975. *The Early Period.* Vol. 1 of *A History of Zoroastrianism.* Ed. B. Spuler. Handbuch der Orientalistik. Leiden.

———. 1982. *Under the Achaemenians.* Vol. 2 of *A History of Zoroastrianism.*

———. 1984. Ahura Mazdā. *Encyclopaedia Iranica* 1:685–87. London.

Christensen, A. 1936. *L'Iran sous les Sassanides.* Copenhagen. Repr. 1944.

Duchesne-Guillemin, J. 1953. *Ormazd et Ahriman. L'aventure dualiste dans l' antiquité.* Paris.

Hoffman, G. 1880. *Auszüge aus syrischen Akten persischer Märtyrer.* Abhandlungen für die Kunde des Morgenlandes 7/3. Leipzig. Repr. Nendeln, Liechtenstein, 1966.

Humbach, H. 1957. Ahura Mazdā und die Daēvas. *Wiener Zeitschrift für die Kunde Süd- und Ostasiens* 1: 81–94.

Konow, S. 1937. Medhā and Mazdā. Pp. 217–22 in *Jhā Commemoration Volume. Essays on Oriental Subjects.* Poona, India.

Kuiper, F. B. J. 1957. Avestan Mazdā. *Indo-Iranian Journal* 1: 86–95.

———. 1976. Ahura Mazdā 'Lord Wisdom'. *Indo-Iranian Journal* 18: 25–42.

Lommel. H. 1930. *Die Religion Zarathustras nach dem Awesta dargestellt.* Tübingen. Repr. 1971.

Pope, A. U. 1938. *A Survey of Persian Art.* Vol. 1. Oxford. Repr. Wiesbaden, 1977.

Robert, L. 1975. Une nouvelle inscription grecque de Sardes. *CRAIBL,* 306–31.

Thieme, P. 1970. Die vedischen Āditya und die zarathustrischen Amaša Spanta. Pp. 397–412, in *Zarathustra,* ed. B. Schlerath. Wege der Forschung 169. Darmstadt.

MARY BOYCE

AHUZZAM (PERSON) [Heb *ʾăḥuzzām*]. A member of the tribe of Judah and son of Asshur (1 Chr 4:5–6). According to the problematic MT text of 1 Chr 2:24, Ashhur was the posthumous son of Hezron. On the other hand, the LXX text indicates that Ashhur was the son of Caleb who, after the death of Hezron, married Ephrathah, Hezron's wife. Thus Ahuzzam may have been a Calebite. The incorporation of the Calebite descendants into the Judahite genealogy may reflect a later period when the tribe of Caleb was absorbed into the tribe of Judah.

H. C. LO

AHUZZATH (PERSON) [Heb *ʾăḥûzat*]. Accompanied Abimelech, king of Gerar, and Phicol to make a covenant with Isaac (Gen 26:26—only occurrence of the name in OT). Ahuzzath is referred to as Abimelech's "friend" (*mērēʿēhû*). This was an official title devoid of emotional connotation; it denoted a counselor to the king on various administrative matters (Donner 1961; Van Selms 1957). A priest named Zabud, for example, is called a "friend of the king" in a list of court officials (*śārîm;* 1 Kgs 4:2–6; cf. Hushai, 2 Sam 15:37; 16:16–17). Abimelech and Phicol also appear in Genesis 21 when they make a covenant with Abraham. The long time span between this covenant and the one with Isaac makes it unlikely that the same parties were involved in both instances. Thus, scholars have suggested that either "Abimelech" and "Phicol" were recurring titles or family names (Kidner 1967: 154), or that only one covenant was actually made but it was differently reported in variant traditions (Speiser *Genesis* AB, 203).

Bibliography

Donner, H. 1961. "Der 'Freund des Königs,' " *ZAW* 73: 269–77.

Kidner, D. 1967. *Genesis.* Downers Grove, IL.

Van Selms, A. 1957. The Origin of the Title "The King's Friend." *JNES* 16: 118–23.

DAVID SALTER WILLIAMS

AHZAI (PERSON) [Heb *ʾaḥza(y)*]. Father of Azarel and grandfather of Amashsai who is cited as a leader of one of the important priestly families in Jerusalem at the time of the rebuilding of the walls of Jerusalem by Nehemiah (Neh 11:13). Meshillemoth and Immer are reported as his father and grandfather. In the comparable list of 1 Chr 9:12 this person seems to be known by the name of Jahzerah (Heb *yaḥzērâ;* LXX[B] *iediou*). There Meshullam, Meshillemith, and Immer are named as his ancestors.

ROGER W. UITTI

AI (PLACE) [Heb *hāʿay*]. Var. AIATH; AIJA? The name (meaning "the ruin") of a place mentioned in connection with Abram's early migration into the land of Canaan (Genesis 12–13), and with Joshua's subsequent conquest of that land (Joshua 7–8). It is usually identified with Et-Tell

(M.R. 174147), a 27.5 acre site E of modern Beitin (biblical Bethel).

A. Biblical References
B. Location and Description
C. History of Excavations
   1. The Garstang Soundings (1928)
   2. The Rothschild Expedition (1933–35)
   3. The Joint Archaeological Expedition (1964–76)
D. Settlement Phases
   1. The Pre-Urban Village
   2. The Urban A Walled City
   3. The Urban B Remodeled City
   4. The Urban C Reconstructed City
   5. The Iron Age I Village
E. The Problem of the Conquest of Ai

A. Biblical References

Genesis 12:8 reports that Abram "removed to the mountain on the east of Bethel, and pitched his tent, with Bethel on the west and Ai on the east." Bethel and Ai seem to be landmarks locating the mountain on which Abram built his altar to the Lord, as is the case also in Gen 13:3–4. The conquest of Ai, related in Josh 7:2–5 and 8:1–29, is related from the perspective of the site as a landmark: "So Joshua burned Ai, and made it forever a heap of ruins, as it is to this day" (8:28). Topographical descriptions in the accounts indicate that it is the same landmark referred to in Gen 12:8. Ai is mentioned again in Josh 10:1–2 and 12:9, first in relation to Gibeon (el-Jib), and second, to Bethel. The statement in 10:2 that Gibeon "was greater than Ai" does not appear in the Septuagint, and is probably an expansion of the tradition similar to that found in Joshua 7–8 in the MT. In 12:9, Ai is located "beside Bethel," similar to the location in 7:2.

The name "Aiath," which seems to be a variation of Ai, appears in Isa 10:28 in association with Rimmon (possibly modern Rammun, E of et-Tell), Michmash (Muchmas), Geba, Ramah (er-Ram), and Gibeah (Tell el-Ful). Whether the reference is to Et-Tell is not clear, although Aiath would be in the same vicinity. Neh 11:31 lists an "Aija" among the villages of Benjamin in the postexilic period, among the same villages named in Isa 10:28f., and since "Bethel and Ai" are named in the list in Neh 7:32, Ai and Aija seem to be understood as two different places. However, it should be noted that the reference to "Aija" does not appear in the Septuagint. The biblical evidence thus favors identification of Ai with the landmark site known as et-Tell, E of Beitin and atop the watershed plateau overlooking Jericho 9 miles eastward in the Jordan Valley.

B. Location and Description

In his *Onomasticon,* Eusebius wrote that Bethel was located 12 Roman miles N of Jerusalem on the right side of the road leading to Neapolis (modern Nablus), and that Ai was located at a minor ruin E of Bethel. Whether he referred to the site of et-Tell is not certain, because there are other small ruins in the vicinity. It is possible that only the acropolis area of et-Tell was regarded as Ai, because John Garstang in 1928 made the same identification, overlooking the other three-fourths of the ancient tell that stretched down the slope eastward (see Callaway 1972: 14–18).

Et-Tell and another site in the SE edge of modern Deir Dibwan, Khirbet Haiyan (M.R. 175145), were suggested by E. Robinson in 1838 as possible locations of biblical Ai. The position of et-Tell recommended itself to Robinson, but he did not discern the presence of ancient walls and buildings because they were covered with heaps of unworked stones. Thus he favored the small ruin just S of Deir Dibwan whose name he did not record. It was later identified as Khirbet Haiyan by C. R. Conder in the Palestine Exploration Fund Survey (Saunders 1881: 95–96).

Captain Charles Wilson did a reconnaissance survey from Nablus to Jerusalem in 1866, and gave particular attention to Bethel and Ai. He noted the modern village of Beitin, 9 miles S of Shiloh, which he identified with biblical Bethel. On a hill adjoining the village, and E of it, was a fortified Christian church, and E of it the hilltop ruins locally known as "Et-Tel, 'the heap'." Its location corresponded to the description in Gen 12:8 and Joshua 7–8, so Wilson identified et-Tell with biblical Ai on the evidence of the biblical references and the topography of the area.

In a surface survey of the region E of Bethel in 1924, W. F. Albright became convinced that et-Tell was indeed the ruin of an ancient city, and that no other proposed site could possibly date to the time of the Israelite settlement in Canaan. Khirbet Haiyan had no surface pottery that could be attributed to the LB Age, or to Iron Age I. The tradition that Joshua "burnt Ai and made it a heap (tell) forever" (Josh 8:28) seemed to support his position. Albright's identification of et-Tell with Ai was therefore based upon biblical traditions and the topography of the region and was supported by the evidence of an ancient city of the Canaanites which lay under the heaps of stones. His location of the site of Ai has not been seriously challenged in the last half-century (*EAEHL* 1: 36).

C. History of Excavations

1. The Garstang Soundings (1928). The first excavations at Ai (et-Tell) were conducted by John Garstang in September, 1928. 8 trenches were opened, 5 against the outer face of the S city wall, and 3 inside the city in the acropolis area. The results of his work were never published although a summary report of 3 typed pages and a sketch plan was submitted to the Department of Antiquities. He did claim in a later book that LB pottery dating to ca. 1400 B.C. was found, and was left "in the collection of the American School," now the Albright Institute in Jerusalem. This pottery has not been located for a 2d opinion of its dating. The supposed discovery of a 1400 B.C. city at Ai supported Garstang's dating of the fall of Jericho at the same time, and confirmed the traditional date for the Exodus and Conquest generally accepted at the time (Callaway 1980: 1–4).

2. The Rothschild Expedition (1933–35). Judith Marquet-Krause directed the second excavation at Ai, with the support of Baron Edmond de Rothschild of Paris. Inspired by the prospect of "resurrecting" the ancient biblical city of Ai from the dust of its ruins, she embarked upon a series of annual campaigns in 1933 which were abruptly terminated by her death in 1936 as she prepared for the 4th year of work.

The Rothschild excavations were confined to the upper part of et-Tell, between contours 835 and 850 on the site plan (see fig. AIP.01). This was the area sketched by Garstang in 1928 as the entire site. During 2 months of work in the 1st campaign, the so-called palace was unearthed, a part of the Iron Age I village was discovered and tombs in the necropolis NE of the tell were excavated. A long and productive six-month campaign in 1934 continued excavations of the Iron Age village, uncovered the lower-city fortifications near contour 835, and discovered the "sanctuary" in the citadel area of the acropolis (see D.4. below). A final campaign in 1935 focused on completing excavation of the Iron Age village, which was found to be constructed on top of EB remains with no intervening occupation evidence. The lower city was also extended inside the city walls, and the "Postern Gate" inside an elliptical tower was found. All of the lower-city remains belonged in the EB Age. This limited the Iron Age village to the acropolis area (Callaway 1972: 18–22; 1980: 4–7). See fig. AIP.01.

3. The Joint Archaeological Expedition (1964–76). Beginning in 1964, J. Callaway directed 9 seasons of work at Ai and other sites in the region until 1976. 8 sites were opened at et-Tell in areas adjacent to the Rothschild excavations and in new areas along the lower E city walls as follows: site A, the sanctuary and citadel fortifications; site B, the Iron Age village; site C, the lower city near contour 835; site D, the temple-palace complex on the acropolis; site G, the lower-city residential area; site H, the east city-wall fortifications; site J, the wadi gate fortifications; and site K, the corner gate and reservoir (see fig. AIP.01). All of the city below contour 845 on the site plan was found to be EB, dating before ca. 2400 B.C., with Iron Age agricultural terraces indicating it was placed in cultivation by the founders of the Iron Age village ca. 1200 B.C.

Three sites in the vicinity of et-Tell were excavated to complete an archaeological profile of the region. Khirbet Haiyan, located on the regional plan and a candidate for the location of biblical Ai, was excavated as site E in 1964 and 1969. It was found to be a Byzantine settlement founded on scattered remains of the First Temple period, or 1st century A.D. Khirbet Khudriya, E of et-Tell, was excavated as site F in 1966 and 1968, and was also a Byzantine settlement or possibly a monastery. Tombs in the valley adjacent to the settlement yielded pottery, ossuaries, and objects from as early as the 1st century B.C.

Salvage excavations were conducted in 1969, 1970, 1972, and 1974 at Khirbet Raddana (M.R. 169146), in the N edge of modern Bireh, with sites designated R, S, and T. Hewn pillars of two Iron Age I houses, contemporary with those at site B at et-Tell, were uncovered during the construction of a new road on the site, and the Joint Expedition was invited to excavate them. It was thought that the evidence of these houses would supplement that of the houses at et-Tell. They were found to be part of a small unfortified village settled about 1200 B.C., and abandoned about 1050 B.C., the same as the village at Ai (et-Tell) (Callaway 1972: 22–26; 1980: 7–18).

D. Settlement Phases

The following settlement phases have been identified:

STRATUM	PHASE	DESCRIPTION	PERIOD	CHRONOLOGY
Pre-Urban	I–II	Unfortified Village	EB IB	3200–3100 B.C.
Urban A	III	Walled City of 27.5 Acres	EB IC	3100–2950 B.C.
Urban B	IV–V	Remodeled Buildings and Fortifications	EB II	2950–2775 B.C.
Urban C	VI–VIII	Reconstructed City and Fortifications	EB III	2775–2400 B.C.
Intermediate	IX	Site Abandoned	——	2400–1200 B.C.
Iron Age	X–XI	Unfortified Village above Contour 845	Iron Age I	1200–1050 B.C.
Byzantine-Islamic	XII	Site Terraced and Cultivated	——	5th Century to Present

1. The Pre-Urban Village. Remains of an unfortified village, reaching from site C at contour 835 to the acropolis area, were found underneath the first-city wall system. The village was at least 200 m in length, making it larger than the Iron Age village built centuries later. Artifacts from this phase reflect a population made up of overflow from other sites, such as Jericho 9 miles away in the Jordan Valley, together with an increment of newcomers to the region. The new elements in the village culture at Ai eventually dominated in later periods that carried over from Chalcolithic by the indigenous population. There seem to have been movements of population from N Syria and Anatolia as early as EB IA that introduced pottery forms such as carinate platters, holemouth jars with inward rolled rims, and painted decorations of line-group designs.

2. The Urban A Walled City. A well-planned walled city enclosing about 27.5 acres was constructed at the beginning of EB IC, or ca. 3100 B.C. Its fortifications were laid out on natural contours of the hilltop site, and they fixed the limits of the city in its succeeding phases until final destruction about 2400 B.C. There is debate among scholars whether the EB IC walled city grew out of the previous unwalled village, or was imposed upon the village by newcomers (see Schaub 1982: 67–75). My view is that newcomers who brought with them experience in city-building imposed the Urban A plan upon the local villagers. Fortifications at sites A and C were built over large areas of village houses, and the entire site was carefully divided into spatial components seemingly too sophisticated to have emerged from the village culture.

Components of the city that can be located on the site plan are: (1) the acropolis complex at site D; (2) the citadel and later sanctuary at site A; (3) a market and residential area at site C, houses at site G, and 4 city-gate complexes at sites A, K, J, and L. Urban life in the city revolved around the temple-palace compound on the acropolis. Enclosed by its own walls (2-m-wide) inside the city, the temple and palace lay side by side with the temple on the E, and the palace structures (that continued in use until EB III) enclosing both ends and the back side of the temple (see D on fig. AIP.01).

Of the 4 city gates in the Urban A phase, 3 were 1 m wide and constructed straight through the fortification

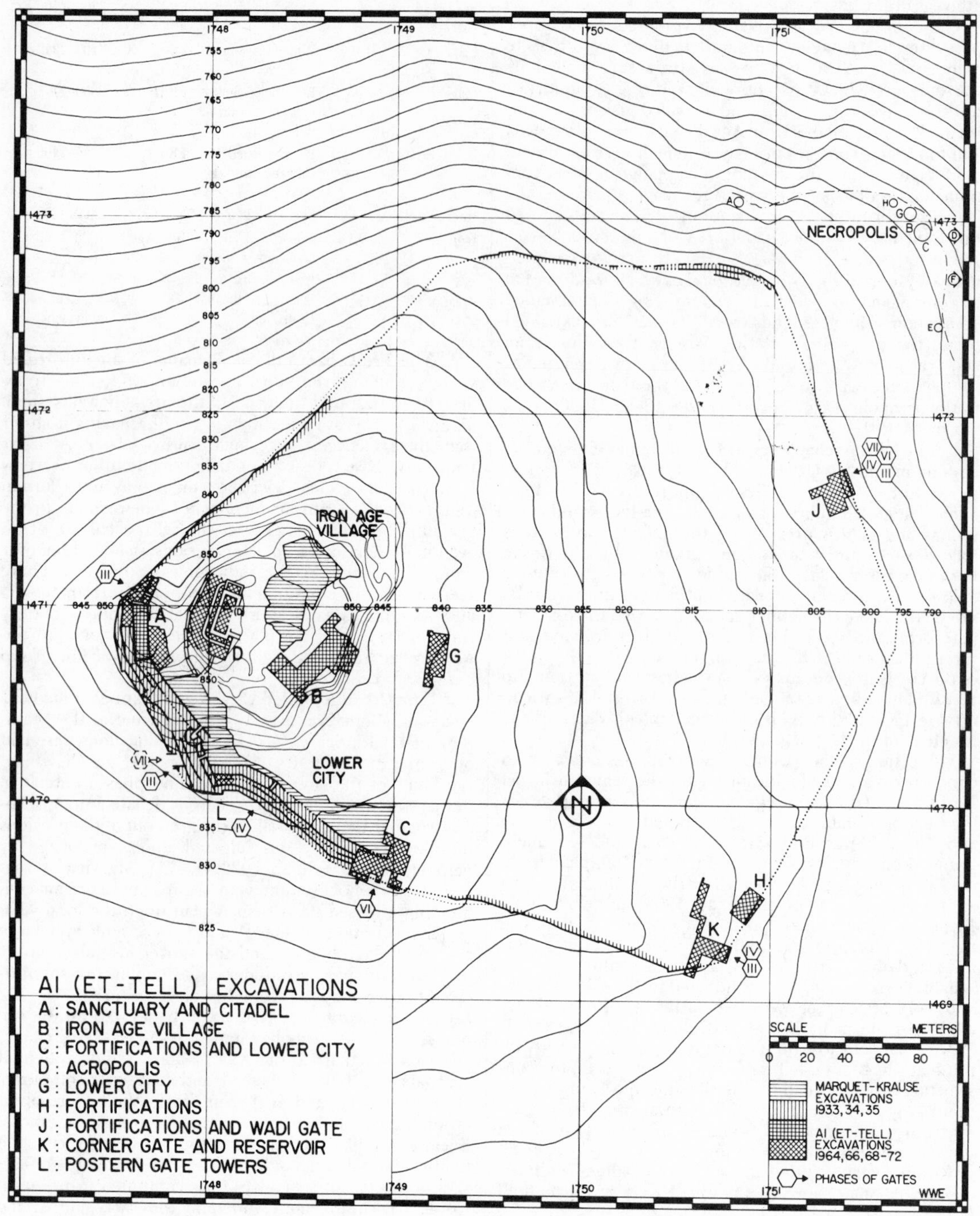

AI.P.01. Site plan of excavations at Ai. *(Courtesy of J. A. Callaway.)*

walls. These were the citadel (site A), postern (site L), and corner (site K) gates. Walls at the postern gate were preserved more than 2 m high, and there was evidence that the narrow passageway was covered, making it a kind of tunnel through the wall. Only 1 side of the wadi gate (site J) was uncovered, and since the excavated area was more than 1 m wide, this gate must have been wider than the others.

The Urban A city was inhabited by a substantial element of indigenous people whose pottery culture is rooted in the Chalcolithic period, indicating that the village population of EB IB was largely absorbed by those whom I regard as newcomers in EB IC. Radical changes in lifestyle from village to urban life, with the imaginative spatial planning of the new city, indicates that new leadership was imposed from the outside. Antecedents of this culture are traced to coastal and N Syria, as well as to S Anatolia.

3. The Urban B Remodeled City. Violent destruction abruptly terminated the Urban A phase at Ai ca. 2950 B.C. The citadel at site A was burned, leaving scorched stones as mute testimony of the event. A blanket of ashes covered the acropolis building floors of polished plaster. New leadership seems to have been imposed upon the population, and the city was rebuilt and extensively modified.

The culture of the new regime contrasts with that of the preceding one. Fortifications were widened and strengthened. The citadel gate was closed by an addition of about 0.75 m to the width of the original wall, and the postern gate was closed and discontinued. The lower-city gate in site C was constructed in this phase, presumably because the location was more easily fortified than the postern gate site. The temple-palace at site D was rebuilt, and the palace area was constricted to about half its original size by construction of a wall (2 m wide) with curved corners in the middle of the previous space. These modifications suggest ad hoc building and remodeling inferior to that of the original city.

Analysis of pottery and artifacts suggests that the transition to Urban B was brought about by local conflict rather than by outsiders. A movement from N to S can be traced in the pottery forms of the Urban B phase, suggesting that ultimate outside influences came from the N through settlements in N Canaan.

A massive destruction by fire over all of the excavated areas brought the Urban B city to an end shortly before the beginning of the 3d Dyn. in Egypt. At sites A and C, collapsed roof beams were covered over by stones from walls and clay which covered the beams; they smoldered with enough intensity to dissolve the stones into calcined masses, cementing pieces of pottery into lumps and baking sun-dried bricks into a pottery-like consistency. At site D, the temple-palace compound, walls either collapsed or tilted precariously, suggesting that an earthquake struck the city. In the N wall of the temple, a rift in bedrock sliced through the main room and through the wall, leaving stones tilted into the break. When the city was rebuilt in the Urban C phase, the tilted curved corner wall of the temple-palace was buttressed and preserved in the reconstruction.

4. The Urban C Reconstructed City. That the Urban B city lay in ruins for some time is evident in erosion channels in some houses that were built over in the Urban C phase. At Site A, the fortifications were rebuilt first, then houses were constructed against the inner face of the walls. Some 20 to 40 years must have elapsed, therefore, between the destruction of the Urban B phase and the completion of the Urban C city.

Egyptian involvement in the rebuilding is evident at the temple-palace area on the acropolis and at site K in the SE corner of the fortifications. Pier bases in the temple were shaped with copper saws, probably like those known in Egypt from the 1st Dyn., and the temple wall (2 m wide) was built of hammer-dressed stones shaped like bricks and laid in mud mortar like bricks. The interior of the wall was plastered, with the plaster continuing on the floor and up to the piers resting on the rectangular-shaped bases. Alabaster and stone vessels imported from Egypt were among the temple furnishings (see Callaway 1972: 248).

At site K, a carefully engineered open-water reservoir was constructed inside the corner of the city wall. A closely laid stone-paved floor was set in a backing of red clay, and a dam of red clay (2.5 m high) faced with stones formed the perimeter on three sides. The floor sloped from W to E toward the city wall. Estimates of the capacity of the reservoir (25 m wide) range from 1,800 to 2,000 cubic m. This would be enough to supplement rainfall and other sources for a population of 2,000 inhabitants (see *EAEHL* 1: 45).

An interruption in the Urban C city seems to have occurred about 2550 B.C., evidenced by broken down and rebuilt city walls, and major changes in the temple area. It seems that the fortifications inside the city around the temple were again strengthened, completely eliminating the former palace area back of the temple. The temple was made into a royal residence, and a modest sanctuary was constructed against the Citadel at site A in what had been a residence. This is the "Sanctuary" discovered by Marquet-Krause in 1934, which was actually a sanctuary only during the last half of the Urban C phase. Khirbet Kerak pottery and objects on the altar of the new sanctuary and in adjacent rooms imply a new influence from the N of Canaan during this phase (Callaway 1978: 52–55).

Another violent destruction overtook the city about 2400 B.C., during the 5th Dyn. of Egypt. No definite identity of the aggressor is known, but a scene in the tomb of Inti at Dishashi depicts the capture of a Canaanite town, and a mutilated inscription names two cities, neither of which can be identified. If Ai was taken from control of Egypt about 2550 B.C., it would be among the cities in Canaan listed for recapture in any campaign to regain control of the region. In any case, the city was completely destroyed and abandoned, and was not reoccupied until Iron Age settlers came upon the ruins of the site 1,200 years later, ca. 1200 B.C.

5. The Iron Age I Village. Waves of settlers from the N, S, E, and W made their way into the highlands of Canaan about 1200 B.C., in an unprecedented series of disruptions around the E Mediterranean combined with the decline of major powers that had controlled the area. Those who settled the small village of Ai seem to have come from the W, being part of a larger migration of refugees fleeing from the recent and more war-like newcomers to the coastal region. By the time of this migration, the original name of the ancient city had been lost in a litterbox of history, and it was simply The Ruin, a popular designation of the mound as a landmark.

The new villagers were able to wrest a living from their arid environment by the introduction of two new technologies. First, they dug cisterns in the soft limestone underneath and beside their houses to capture rainwater. Second, they terraced hillside slopes on contours and planted them in various crops. At Ai, the village was located on the acropolis above contour 845, and the remainder of the ancient ruin was terraced and placed in cultivation. The only fortifications were those left standing from the EB city, which were broken down in places and covered over by heaps of stones. Estimates of the population range from 150 to 300 persons.

That the new settlers had experience in hill-country farming is evident in their subsistence strategy and the village layout and houses. Houses were characterized by piers, either of stacked stones or hewn monoliths, that supported the roofs and divided space in the "greatrooms." Some houses had a 3d room across the back of the main area. Streets at Ai were paved with cobblestones set in red clay which led to the thresholds of the closely spaced houses. A high dividing wall separated two compounds of houses in site B, suggesting that several extended families made up the population of the village.

An interruption in the life of the village occurred about 1125 B.C., and there seems to have been an increase in the population. Numerous silo granaries were built in open areas around houses and even in the streets. The ruins of the EB temple were occupied with a crude stone wall separating the spacious interior into 2 living areas. Silos were built in the corners of the ancient structure. The introduction of silo granaries in the new phase represents a difference in storage methods from the earlier phase, when large storejars were used for grain and other foods and occasional silos were cut into the bedrock floors of houses. The latter phase of occupation lacks the orderliness in both houses and streets of the original phase (see Callaway 1985: 37–43).

E. The Problem of the Conquest of Ai

Reconciliation of the archaeological evidence with the biblical account of the capture of Ai is difficult, because the evidence does not agree with the prevailing views of the event. The older view of a 1400 B.C. conquest based upon 1 Kings 6:1 (held by Garstang) is not supported because there was no occupation of the site at that time. Albright's view of a conquest about 1250–1230 B.C. is also unsupported, which he himself recognized. He ascribed the conquest related in Josh 8:1–29 to nearby Bethel which was destroyed at the time, instead of to Ai, and conjectured that later tradition confused the accounts and attributed the destruction to Ai. This view is weakened by the LXX omission of reference to men of Bethel participating in the defense of Ai in Josh 8:17. A fragmentary text of Josh 8:3–18 from Qumran Cave 4 is also a shortened version similar to that of the LXX, although the reference in Josh 8:17 is one of the missing fragments. It is quite probable, however, that the mention of Bethel is a Masoretic expansion and is, therefore, secondary. Martin Noth held that the Ai account in Joshua 8 is legendary and etiological in nature, and is therefore unhistorical. Marquet-Krause and de Vaux, and, more recently, Yigael Yadin and A. Malamat, view the account as primarily etiological.

We are left with the options of discounting the historicity of the Ai account or of placing the conquest in a chronological context later than LB. The latter is here proposed, and it is suggested that the interruption of the Iron Age village about 1125 B.C. would be an appropriate time (Callaway *IDB* Sup., 16). However, there is increasing evidence from excavations and surveys of the hill country from the Negeb to Esdraelon that a military conquest as described in Joshua 1–11 is without archaeological support, and that the settlement depicted in the book of Judges matches the evidence more accurately. The hundreds of villages, among which was that at Ai, founded on hilltops and supported by an agricultural subsistence, were occupied by people who fled from conflicts and violence to the safety of the hills. Indeed, the original settlers at Ai seem to have come to the highlands by way of the lowlands to the W and N instead of from the E (as depicted in popular "conquest" and "sedentarization" reconstructions). The people at Ai would thus be part of the large population of villagers in the highlands that emerged as the Israel we know in the book of Judges.

Bibliography

Callaway, J. A. 1972. *The Early Bronze Age Sanctuary at Ai (et-Tell)*. London.

———. 1978. New Perspectives on Early Bronze III in Canaan. Pp. 46–58 in *Archaeology in the Levant*. Eds. R. Moorey and P. Parr. Warminster.

———. 1980. *The Early Bronze Age Citadel and Lower City at Ai (et-Tell)*. Cambridge, MA.

———. 1985. A New Perspective on the Hill Country Settlement of Canaan in Iron Age I. Pp. 31–49 in *Palestine in the Bronze and Iron Ages*, ed. J. N. Tubb. London.

Saunders, T. 1881. *An Introduction to the Survey of Western Palestine*. London.

Schaub, R. T. 1982. The Origins of the Early Bronze Age Walled Town Culture of Jordan. Pp. 67–75 in *Studies in the History and Archaeology of Jordan*, ed. A. Hadidi. Amman.

JOSEPH A. CALLAWAY

AIAH (PERSON) [Heb *ʾayyâ*]. The name means "hawk" or "falcon" (Lev 11:14; Deut 14:13; Job 28:7), and Hicks (*IDB* 1: 73) suggests it was a nickname. According to Westermann (*Genesis 12–36* BK, 567), the presence of animal names in genealogies (e.g., Genesis 36) suggests that the list developed in an early period.

1. First of the two sons of Zibeon, the son of Seir, a Horite living in Edom (Gen 36:24; 1 Chr 1:40). His brother Anah was probably the father of Oholibamah, one of Esau's wives (Gen 36:2, 18). This assumes that the Anah in Gen 36:2 is the *son* of Zibeon (reading Heb *ben* with the LXX, Syriac, and Sam Pent, rather than the MT *bat* "daughter") and therefore the brother of Aiah (Gen 36:24). Aiah's name occurs in a brief Horite lineage placed among Edomite genealogical lists in Genesis 36 and 1 Chr 1:36–42. His father was the head of a Horite clan (Gen 36:20–21) and his brother was noted for discovering "hot springs" of water in the desert (Gen 36:24). These facts are the biblical witnesses to the close relation between the

Edomites and the Horites (see Bartlett 1969). The latter probably comprised the pre-Edomite population of Edom, which later became assimilated to the Edomites (Deut 2:12).

2. The father of Rizpah, a concubine of Saul (2 Sam 3:7). The name occurs four times in 2 Samuel and is exclusively used as a patronym, "Rizpah, the daughter of Aiah" (2 Sam 3:7; 21:8, 10, 11). Aiah's importance stems from the fact that his daughter was a member of the first Israelite king's harem. After Saul's death she became the concubine of his successor and son Ishbosheth, and was at the center of royal intrigue, when Abner (the military commander) was accused of sleeping with her (2 Sam 3:7). Such an act constituted an attempt to seize the leadership from Ishbosheth (cf. 2 Sam 16:21–22; 1 Kgs 2:13–25). Aiah's daughter also bore two sons for Saul: Armoni and Mephibosheth. Both were killed to appease Yahweh for a previous treacherous act of Saul against the Gibeonites (2 Sam 21:1–14).

Bibliography

Bartlett, J. R. 1969. The Land of Seir and the Brotherhood of Edom. *JTS* 20: 1–20.

STEPHEN G. DEMPSTER

AIATH (PLACE) [Heb *ʿayyāt*]. See AI (PLACE).

AIJALON (PLACE) [Heb *ʾayyālôn*]. Located in the tribe of Dan, Aijalon was an important city in the history of ancient Israel. The first reference to the city is in EA 273, where Aijalon and Gaza are mentioned as "falling away to the Habiru." However, Dussaud (1927: 230) has suggested that Aijalon was known to the Egyptians even earlier in the Middle Kingdom period.

Judg 1:35 reports that the Danites had initially failed in their attempt to take Aijalon from the Amorites. When it eventually fell to the Israelites it was assigned to the tribe of Dan on or near the border with Ephraim (Josh 19:42). Aijalon is mentioned in a poetic fragment, in parallelism with Gibeon, as a place where the moon and sun respectively halted at the command of Joshua (Josh 10:12). Saul and Jonathan defeated the Philistines at Aijalon after the battle of Michmash (1 Sam 14:31). Jonathan was responsible for the initial success, but Saul and the rest of the army shared in the subsequent battle. If it is correct to identify Elon as Aijalon, the next mention of Aijalon is in 1 Kgs 4:9. The RSV notes that Elon-beth-hanan belongs to the second administrative district of Solomon; the consonantal MT *(ʾylwn),* however, raises the possibility that Aijalon is the intended reference. When the monarchy was divided, Aijalon was included in the tribe of Benjamin. In 2 Chr 11:10 Aijalon, built by Rehoboam as a defensive city, belonged to Judah and/or Benjamin, while in 2 Chr 28:18 the city belonged to Judah. In the Levitical city (Albright 1945; Peterson 1977: 340–51) lists Aijalon is the third Danite city in Joshua (21:24), while in the 1 Chronicles list there is no mention of the tribe of Dan and instead Aijalon is a continuation of the Ephraim allotment (6:54—Eng 6:69).

Aijalon was located at the W end of the Valley of Aijalon on the major trunk road which led into the hill county, past Gibeon, and ultimately reached Jerusalem. The importance of Aijalon in the biblical record depended on its strategic location. The Valley of Aijalon is the most important of all the natural trade routes through the Shephelah. There is no reference to Aijalon during or after the exile, although the Aijalon Valley continued to be an important trade route. According to Josephus (*JW* 2.513–16) Cestius Gallus, governor of Syria, took the Aijalon Valley route in his campaign against Jerusalem in A.D. 66. Eusebius mentions Aijalon in his *Onomasticon* (18:13–14). (See also Epiph. *Adv. Haeres* 2.702.)

There are two sites that have been identified with biblical Aijalon, Yalo and Tell Qoqa. Since Robinson (1841: 63–65) all major geographers have identified Yalo (M.R. 152138) with Aijalon. It was Albright (1924: 10) who first observed that Tell Qoqa had many EB shards on it, making it the "older Aijalon," while Yalo has many of the later periods.

Yalo is located three kilometers E of Imwas, twenty kilometers WNW of Jerusalem, and ten kilometers ESE of Gezer. From the summit of the mound, one has a perfect view of the Aijalon Valley as it wraps itself around the N, NW, and NE sides of the tell and then disappears to the NE into the surrounding hills.

Tell Qoqa is situated immediately to the SE of Yalo, separated by a little valley. While Albright argued that Tell Qoqa was the older city, there is evidence that both sites were occupied during the same periods and that the boundary separating EB Qoqa and fortified Yalo is not as distinct as had been argued earlier.

From the surface surveys conducted at Tell Qoqa, pottery has been found from the Early Bronze Age, Middle Bronze Age II, Late Bronze Age, Iron I, and Iron II periods. At Yalo there is indication of Middle Bronze Age II, Late Bronze Age, Iron I, Iron II, Persian, Hellenistic, Roman-Byzantine, and Middle Ages and Ottoman occupation.

Bibliography

Albright, W. F. 1924. Research of the School in Western Judaea. *BASOR* 15: 2–11.

———. 1945. The List of Levitic Cities. Pp. 49–73 in *Louis Ginzberg Jubilee Volume.* New York.

Clermont-Ganneau, C. 1896. *Archaeological Researches in Palestine During the Years 1873–1874.* Trans. John Macfarlane. London.

Conder, C. R., and Kitchener, H. H. 1881. *Survey of Western Palestine.* Vol. 3. London.

Dussaud, R. 1927. Nouveaux Renseignements sur la Palestine et la Syrie Vers 2000 Avant Notre Ére. *Syria* 8: 216–33.

Guérin, H. V. 1868–69. *Description géographique, historique et archéologique de la Palestine, Judée.* 3 Vols. 1. Paris.

Peterson J. L. 1977. *A Topographical Surface Survey of the Levitical "Cities" of Joshua 21 and I Chronicles 6: Studies on the Levites in Israelite Life and Religion.* Diss. Seabury-Western Theological Seminary.

Robinson, E. 1841. *Biblical Researches in Palestine.* Vol. 3. Boston.

Smith, G. A. 1899. *The Historical Geography of the Holy Land.* 6th ed. New York.

JOHN L. PETERSON

AIN (PLACE) [Heb *ʿayīn*]. Var. ASHAN. **1.** A town marking the idealized E border of the "promised land," located in the vicinity of the Sea of Galilee (Num 34:11). The location of the place is unknown. The text indicates that Ain is located W of Riblah; if this is the same Riblah mentioned in 2 Kgs 23:33, then Ain would be near Kadesh on the Orontes River in modern Syria near the NE border of Lebanon. On the other hand, since the Vulgate here refers to Riblah in connection with "the spring (Heb *ᶜên*) of Daphne," it is possible that Ain is actually identical to Kh. Dufna (M.R. 209292), 24 miles N of the Sea of Galilee (and 1.5 miles W of Tel Dan). It is also possible to identify Ain with Kh. Ayun (M.R. 212236), 2.5 miles E of the S tip of the Sea of Galilee.

2. A Levitical city mentioned three times in the OT, first in Josh 15:32, where it is assigned to the tribe of Judah and is a part of the administrative district of Hormah; second in the Levitical city list in Josh 21:16, where it is the seventh city in the Judah/Simeon list; and third in 1 Chr 4:32, where Ain is given to the descendants of Judah and Simeon.

The city of Ain presents problems, regarding even its name. In Josh 21:16 the city is called Ain *(ᶜayin)*, while in the parallel Levitical city list in 1 Chr 6:44 (—Eng 6:59) it is called Ashan *(ᶜāšān)*. Albright (1945: 61) has suggested that Ashan should also be read in Joshua 21 as in the Chronicler. He argued that between the 2d century B.C. and the 3d century A.D. the Hebrew "Ain" replaced the correct "Ashan." Consistently the Greek texts have *Asan*.

There is a lack of clear understanding regarding the identification of the biblical Ain. It was Robinson (1841: 625) who first suggested the identification of Kh. Anim el-Ghuwein (M.R. 156084). Kh. Anim is an unimpressive small mound in the center of a small, shallow, circular valley. The surrounding hills are low. Immediately to the W of the tell is Wadi Sha'b el Jabu, which leads into Nahal Anim. The site is located not too far from the ancient highway from Hebron to Arad that passed through Juttah and es-Samu.

There have been no archaeological excavations conducted at Kh. Anim, although there have been archaeological surveys. The Archaeological Survey of Israel visited the site and there identified Iron II, Hellenistic, Roman-Byzantine, and Medieval pottery. The levitical city survey team also found Iron II, Roman-Byzantine, and Arab shards at the site.

However, the identification of Ain with Kh. Anim was challenged by Wilson (1847: 354) following the text of the Chronicler, and it was Musil (1907: 66) and others who identified Ain with Ashan. Kh. Asan is 3.2 km N of Beersheba, near Nahl Asan. There are good reasons to identify biblical Ain/Ashan with Kh. Asan simply on linguistic grounds, but there are also geographical considerations. Although the site remains archaeologically unknown, it is clearly in the tribe of Simeon and on a major trade route leading N into the Shephelah.

Bibliography

Albright, W. F. 1945. The List of Levitic Cities. Pp. 49–73 in *Louis Ginzberg Jubilee Volume on the Occasion of His Seventieth Birthday.* New York.

Cross, F. M., Jr., and Wright, G. E. 1956. The Boundary and Province Lists of the Kingdom of Judah. *JBL* 75: 202–26.

Mazar, B. 1957. The Cities of the Priests and the Levites. VTSup 7: 193–205.

Musil, A. 1907. *Arabic Petraea.* Vol. 2. Vienna.

Peterson, J. L. 1977. *A Topographical Surface of the Levitical "Cities" of Joshua 21 and I Chronicles 6: Studies on the Levites in Israelite Life and Religion.* Unpubl. diss. Seabury-Western Theological Seminary.

Robinson, E. 1841. *Biblical Researches in Palestine.* Vol. 2. Boston.

Wilson, J. 1847. *The Lands of the Biblical Visited and Described.* Vol. 1. Edinburgh.

JOHN L. PETERSON

ᶜAIN GHAZAL. A Neolithic village located on the Zarqa (Jabbok) River at the NE edge of the modern city of Amman. Although badly disturbed by highway, commercial, and civic construction until 1981, four seasons of "rescue archaeology" in the years 1982–85 have produced a relatively complete picture of the site's history.

Three major occupational phases occurred at ᶜAin Ghazal: the Pre-Pottery Neolithic B (PPNB; ca. 7250–6200 B.C.), the PPNC period (ca. 6200–5800 B.C.), and the Yarmukian phase (ca. 5400–5000 B.C.) of the early ceramic Neolithic. Early in its development, ᶜAin Ghazal was already a thriving village of some 10–12 acres, supported by goat herding and such agricultural products as peas, lentils, wheat, barley, and chick-peas. Hunting of wild game (especially gazelle and cattle) and the collection of wild plants (especially figs, almonds, and pistachios) still provided about half of the dietary needs. Long-range contacts are evidenced by Anatolian obsidian, S Jordan minerals, asphalt from the Dead Sea, and shells from the Mediterranean and Red Seas. As early as 7100 B.C. ᶜAin Ghazal was also an important Levantine religious center, with plaster human statuary reflecting a sophisticated system of public ritual and ceremony. Smaller clay human and animal figurines indicated more personal, family-oriented concerns on health, fertility, and magic/luck in hunting. Housing consisted of spacious and sturdy rectangular stone dwellings with well-made plaster floors, many decorated on the interior walls and floors with geometric and linear designs.

By 6500 B.C. the village had doubled in size, reflecting the excellent environmental resources to sustain population growth, and by the end of the 7th millennium it extended over more than 30 acres, more than three times the size of contemporary Jericho, making ᶜAin Ghazal one of the largest population centers of the Near East.

Shortly after 6200 B.C., a sudden alteration in the character of the archaeological material at ᶜAin Ghazal indicates that a significant cultural change had occurred despite the evidence of occupational continuity. Conspicuously different architecture, stone tools, economic foci, and human burial practices emerged that have no counterparts in other areas of the Levant, suggesting that the Jordanian highlands underwent a locally inspired cultural adaptation, possibly associated with an increased emphasis on exploiting desert regions to the E.

It is not known yet how long this peculiarly Jordanian Neolithic development lasted, but ᶜAin Ghazal was eventually abandoned sometime in the early 6th millennium. Several centuries later a new social group appeared at the site, radically different in cultural terms because of the production of well-made pottery, though the construction of flimsy and impermanent pit dwellings continued. Preliminary analysis suggests these new Yarmukian people were no longer full-time farmers but relied instead on nomadic pastoralism centering on herds of goats, sheep(?), cattle, and perhaps pigs, aided by domestic dogs.

A multiyear campaign of excavations will resume at ᶜAin Ghazal, and it is anticipated that significantly greater resolution will emerge concerning the daily lives of the people of this important site.

Bibliography

Banning, E., and Byrd, B. 1984. The Architecture of PPNB ᶜAin Ghazal, Jordan. *BASOR* 255: 15–20.

Rollefson, G. 1983a. The 1982 Season at Ain Ghazal: Preliminary Report. *ADAJ* 27: 1–15.

———. 1983b. Ritual and Ceremony at Neolithic Ain Ghazal (Jordan). *Paleorient* 9/2: 29–38.

———. 1983c. 8,000 Year Old Statues from PPNB ᶜAin Ghazal. *ASOR Newsletter* 35/2: 1–3.

———. 1984a. ᶜAin Ghazal: An Early Neolithic Community in Highland Jordan, Near Amman. *BASOR* 255: 3–14.

———. 1984b. Early Neolithic Statuary from Ain Ghazal (Jordan). *MDOG* 116: 185–192.

———. 1985. The 1983 Season at the Early Neolithic Site of ᶜAin Ghazal. *National Geographic Research* 1/1: 44–62.

Rollefson, G., and Simmons, A. H. 1984. The 1983 Season at ᶜAin Ghazal: Preliminary Report. *ADAJ* 28: 13–30.

———. 1985a. The Early Neolithic Village of ᶜAin Ghazal, Jordan: Preliminary Report on the 1983 Season. *BASORSup* 23: 35–52.

———. 1985b. Excavation at ᶜAin Ghazal 1984: Preliminary Report. *ADAJ* 29: 11–30.

———. 1986. The 1985 Season at ᶜAin Ghazal: Preliminary Report. *ADAJ* 30: 41–56.

GARY O. ROLLEFSON

ᶜAJJUL, TELL EL- (M.R. 093097). A large site (ca. 28 acres) of the MB to LB located ca. 7 km SW of Gaza. According to Albright (1938: 337), the name means "Mound of the Little Calf." The tell is situated ca. 1.5 km inland from the Mediterranean coast on the N bank of Nahal Besor (Wadi Ghazzeh). The coastline S of Gaza is composed of steep slopes and low cliffs except where the Nahal Besor empties into the sea. Here the estuary meanders through low, rolling sand dunes that once provided convenient access from the sea to Tell el-ᶜAjjul and the coastal road. It was along the Nahal Besor, a natural frontier between Egypt and Canaan, that the Hyksos built several fortifications including Tell el-ᶜAjjul. These control points were all protected with a typical "Hyksos" rampart and fosse of the MB period.

A. Identification

Excavations at Tell el-ᶜAjjul have produced no inscriptional evidence to suggest its name in antiquity. F. Petrie assumed the site to be ancient Gaza, but the consensus of modern scholarship suggests that Tell el-ᶜAjjul is Eusebius' "Beth-Aglaim" (*Onomast.* 48:19), 8 Roman miles (11.6 kms or 7.3 miles) from Gaza. While the direction from Gaza is unclear in Eusebius and the Madeba Map places a "Bethagidea" SE of Gaza, Jerome locates it on the coast by referring to it as "Bethagla maritima." The objection that Eusebius' Beth-Aglaim was 8 Roman miles from Gaza rather than the 6 of Tell el-ᶜAjjul is not major. First, the ancient road probably did not go straight to Gaza but skirted the sand dunes by connecting with the "kurkar" ridge S of Gaza, making the road longer. Secondly, the Nahal Besor is the only convenient access from the coast to Tell el-ᶜAjjul and the coastal road for several kms.

B. Archaeological Evidence

J. Starkey first took note of Tell el-ᶜAjjul and persuaded F. Petrie to excavate there. Petrie began excavations in 1930 and continued until 1934 for a total of four seasons. A fifth season of excavating at Tell el-ᶜAjjul was carried on by E. H. Mackay and M. Murray in 1938. Petrie quickly published four well-illustrated volumes of the results of his excavations (Petrie 1931–34), but his methods were somewhat lacking and any early material from Tell el-ᶜAjjul should be used with caution. Since it is difficult to identify Tell el-ᶜAjjul in ancient sources as a particular historical site during the MB, we must rely on the archaeological remains to recreate the history of this city and ancient texts to provide the context in which this city flourished. Several eras of the settlement are represented by the terms City I, City II, and City III. There is evidence of a settlement before these three cities and of continued occupation by a military garrison after City III began its decline into the Iron Age.

1. Early Settlements. The first signs of occupation at Tell el-ᶜAjjul may have been found by James Starkey on the S bank of the Nahal Besor opposite Tell el-ᶜAjjul. He dated his finds to the EB. On the N side of the estuary, Petrie uncovered a cemetery W of the tell in which he found a profusion of copper weapons after which he named the area the "Copper Age Cemetery." He erroneously attributed this cemetery and a small find of vases and shards to the Chalcolithic Age (before 3150 B.C.E.). The cemetery is actually of the EB IV (as early as 2200 B.C.E. or as late as 2000 B.C.E.). The settlement at Tell el-ᶜAjjul began to urbanize during the Egyptian 12th Dynasty of the MB I (Rainey 1972: 369–408). The evidence for this community were found in artifacts from the S quarter of the mound (Kempinski 1974: 147) and the contents of the "courtyard cemetery" in the N quarter that date from the late 12th to the early 13th Dyn.

2. City III and Palace I. The middle of the 18th century B.C.E. saw internal and domestic problems in Egypt. With Egypt's weakened central authority, Tell el-ᶜAjjul's fortunes apparently improved. They built some of the most notable fortifications and public buildings in Canaan. In constructing the fosse around the fortification, they excavated blocks of sandstone, which were used for the foundation of the palace. The fosse measured some 6 m deep and 15–18 m across. From the bottom of the fosse to the top of the fortification was probably over 45 m. One entry faced the sea, and another was in the center of the NE wall toward Gaza. Inside the secured perimeter was built the largest palace (Palace I) of this age ever found in Palestine. It measured ca. 50 by 39 m. The walls of the palace were 2 m thick (suggesting a possible second story), and it had rooms on three sides around a courtyard. Palace

I was destroyed with the coming of the 15th Dyn. or the "Hyksos" period (1668 B.C.E.).

3. City II and Palace II. The remains of City II and Palace II reflect a period of great prosperity during the MB III "Hyksos" period. This came about as a result of Tell el-ᶜAjjul's strategic position at the W end of the trade routes that came from the E via Elath and the Negeb. Three particular finds of this period reveal some of Tell el-ᶜAjjul's commercial and political activity. First, stylized Cypriot pottery inspired local potters to make what has become known as "Bichrome Ware." It is characterized by geometric ("Union Jack") patterns, fish, and birds. It became so popular along the coast that it has become a diagnostic indicator of this period. Secondly, the tomb of a Hyksos nobleman was uncovered and with him were found his chariot and horses. Since chariots were a new military innovation of the period and were financed and controlled by affluent nobility, it appears that Tell el-ᶜAjjul was ruled by such feudal lords. Confirming the presence of an affluent nobility was the third discovery of a hoard of gold jewelry of superb craftsmanship.

4. City I and Palaces (Fortresses) III–V. With the defeat of the Hyksos by Ahmose I and the establishment of the 19th Dyn. (1567–1320 B.C.E.), Egypt gained control of trade from the E. This reduced the economic prospects of Tell el-ᶜAjjul, and City I began its decline with a major part of the population moving to Gaza (the site of the new administrative center of the 19th Dyn. in Canaan). The debate continues concerning the date of Palace (Fortress) V and the continuing occupation at Tell el-ᶜAjjul. Some contend (Kempinski 1974: 148) that the fortresses continued at Tell el-ᶜAjjul until the middle 12th century B.C.E., after which it was abandoned near the end of the 12th century B.C.E. with the influx of Philistines into S Palestine. Others (Albright 1938: 358), relying on evidence of the cemetery near the fortress, have dated the fortress to the latter part of Iron Age I (1000–900 B.C.E.) and have proposed occupation on the site until that time.

Bibliography

Albright, W. F. 1938. The Chronology of a South Palestinian City, Tell el-ᶜAjjul. *AJSL* 55: 337–359.

Kempinski, A. 1974. Tell el-ᶜAjjul—Beth-Aglayim or Sharuhen? *IEJ* 24: 145–152.

Negbi, O. 1970. *The Hoards of Goldwork from Tell el-ᶜAjjul.* Studies in Mediterranean Archaeology 25. Goteborg.

Petrie, W. M. F. et al. 1931–34. *Ancient Gaza I–IV.* London.

Rainey, A. F. 1972. The World of Sinuhe. *IOS* 2: 369–408.

Stewart, J. R. 1974. *Tell el-ᶜAjjul. The Middle Bronze Age Remains.* Studies in Mediterranean Archaeology 38. Goteborg.

Tufnell, O. 1976. El-ᶜAjjul, Tell (Beth ᶜEglayim). *EAEHL* 1: 52–61.

DALE C. LIID

AKAN (PERSON) [Heb *ᶜaqān*]. Var. JAAKAN. A clan name mentioned in the genealogy of Seir the Horite in Gen 36:27. Akan is listed as one of the three sons of Ezer, and he is thus a grandson of Seir. The name in this form only appears in Genesis 36, but it is equivalent to the name JAAKAN found in the matching genealogical clan list in 1 Chr 1:42. These clans, not to be equated with the Hurrians, are part of the original "inhabitants of the land" mentioned in Gen 36:20, who lived in the area of Edom (perhaps as cave dwellers) prior to the coming of the Esau clans.

VICTOR H. MATTHEWS

AKELDAMA (PLACE) [Gk *Akeldamach*]. An uninhabited area outside Jerusalem where Judas Iscariot committed suicide and was buried (Acts 1:19). The name "Akeldama" is derived from the Aramaic expression *ḥăqēl dĕmaʾ* ("field of blood"), which came to be attached to the location through its connection with Judas Iscariot (on the form, see BDF §39.3). Klostermann (*apud* Lake 1965: 13) suggests that the translation of the Aramaic in the Acts account was generated by later Christians eager to promote their perspective and that the phrase originally referred to "field of sleep" and was a euphemism for a cemetery. Klostermann's position is rejected by Kirsopp Lake, who questions the etymological argument that substitutes the word for "blood" with the word for "sleep." Lake also suggests that there is no usage of the term "field of sleep" meaning cemetery in associated ancient literature (Lake 1965: 13). The transliteration provided in Acts 1 is superior. Acts 1:18 identifies Judas as purchasing this property with the blood money acquired from the priests for betraying Jesus. Judas' purchase of the land, however, was effected only after his suicide, by the proxy of the priests (Matt 27:3). The plot they purchased with the blood money was reportedly the potter's field in which Judas had committed suicide (Matt 27:5). The potter's field was subsequently set aside as a cemetery for foreigners.

The place known as the potter's field could have been either the possession of a specific potter or a place that acquired that name through its association with potters. The significance of the previous ownership of the land arises in that the purchase of the potter's field is reported by Matt 27:10 to be a fulfillment of a prophecy of Jeremiah. This citation, however, appears to be a combination of Zech 11:12–13; Jer 18:2–12, Jer 19:1–13, and Jer 32:6–9.

The description of Akeldama as the potter's field has contributed to locating the site. The OT frequently associates the S side of Jerusalem with potters. The area beyond the Potsherd Gate (Jer 19:2) in the Hinnom Valley was the location of Jeremiah's demonstration of the smashing of a newly purchased clay jar to proclaim the coming events of the Babylonian expansion. The Potsherd Gate is equated with the Dung Gate (Neh 2:13) in the Tg. Yer. It is maintained by many that it attained its name because it overlooked a pottery dump. In Jeremiah's message he implies that the name of the location would change from Topeth or Valley of Ben Hinnom to the "valley of slaughter" following the Babylonian advance (Jer 19:6). This final description is close to the later Aramaic name.

The Hinnom Valley S of Jerusalem is argued to be the location of Akeldama. This valley was desecrated in the eyes of pious Jews from the time of Kings Ahaz and Manasseh, who promoted Molech worship there (2 Kgs 23:10). In the 1st century A.D. the valley was used as a refuse dump for the city of Jerusalem (see Mark 9:47). These aspects would have contributed to the non-occupation of the site. The priests would have been able to purchase the land there at a relatively low price, and foreigners not concerned with Jewish religion would have had no problems with being buried in that location.

In the 4th century Jerome affirmed a S location of Akeldama in opposition to Eus., who held that it was N of Jerusalem. The traditional site is located on a level space on the S side of the Hinnom Valley, just before it joins the Kidron Valley. A ruined structure 24 m by 17 m is located on the site today. This structure was used as a communal burial place for centuries. Today a Greek monastery stands near the site and carries the name. This site cannot be conclusively shown to be the actual site of Akeldama.

Bibliography

Lake, K. 1965. *The Beginnings of Christianity. Pt. I: The Acts of the Apostles.* Vol. 4, ed. F. J. Foakes Jackson and K. Lake. Grand Rapids.

ROBERT W. SMITH

AKHENATEN. Second son of Amenhotep (Amenophis) III of the 18th Dynasty by his great king's-wife Tiye, and king of Egypt for nearly 17 years (Wenig 1972), 1377–1361 (Redford 1984: 57) or 1350–1334 (Wente and Van Siclen 1976: 218).

Born probably in Memphis while his father yet resided in the northern capital, Akhenaten is not pictured on any known monument prior to his accession and would not have been in line for the throne had his older brother Thutmose not died prematurely (Gauthier 1912: 335f.). When the royal family took up residence in Thebes for the first jubilee (Redford 1984: 51–52f.) Akhenaten accompanied them. There he appears as "king's-son" in dockets from his father's reign (Hayes 1951: 172, fig. 27[KK]), and there he came to the throne as Amenhotep IV when Amenophis III died, there being no substantial evidence for any coregency (Redford 1967: 88ff.; Von Beckerath 1984: 11f.; contra Aldred 1988).

For the first few months of his reign he continued work on monuments left unfinished at his father's death: the gate of the 2d Pylon (Lauffray 1980: 87ff.), and the decoration of a monumental portal on the south of Karnak (Redford 1983: 368). On the latter the falcon-headed Re-Harakhty is the only god who appears as the recipient of Akhenaten's worship, a harbinger of things to come. To his name is added an epithet that had enjoyed some currency in solar theology: "He who rejoices in the horizon in his name 'Light which is in the Disc' " (Gunn 1923; Fecht 1967; Munro 1981; Redford 1976: 54, n. 123). That the predilection for one god constituted something more than mere henotheism is strongly suggested in an early "speech from the throne" in which Akhenaten introduces his god to the court. Therein he describes his celestial deity in terms of uniqueness, transcendence, and permanence that were to become common throughout the reign, while at the same time accusing the gods of having "ceased one after the other" (Redford 1981).

Throughout the reign frequent mention is made of the king's "teaching," which may be merely the largely poetic description of the wonders of the sun-spawned universe seen through the eyes of a sensitive aesthete. The Hymn to the Sun-disc (Auffret 1981; Bernhardt 1969; *AEL,* 96–107; von Nordheim 1979), echoes of which seem later to be heard in Psalm 104, describe the solar deity as the creator and sustainer of the universe, the guarantor of life and the eternal hypostasis of pharaonic monarchy in the heavens. In the latter capacity the deity is granted the double cartouche, hailed in royal terms, and conceived in art as the mirror image in the heavens of king Akhenaten upon earth. Pursuant to his iconoclastic urges, Akhenaten rid the cult of images of deity as well as mythology, and even the decorative arts and the script were purified of anthropomorphic and theriomorphic elements (Redford 1984: 173ff.). The great Hope of all Egyptians, the multifarious world of the Beyond, the Underworld over which Osiris and his congeners presided, was done away with; and although outward forms, such as shawabtis, mortuary texts, and sun hymns were retained, they were expurgated of all allusions to the Underworld (Assmann 1972; Redford 1980; Redford 1984: 169ff.).

Akhenaten honored his god by inaugurating a new icon, a new art style, and by championing a temple design influenced by Heliopolis. The new icon was derived from the earlier Re-Harakhty figure by the simple expedient of suppressing the figure, retaining the disc, and appending a multitude of sticklike arms. Introduced in anticipation of the jubilee to be celebrated in the 2d and 3d year, the "Sun-disc" (as Akhenaten referred to his deity) was termed "the Great, living Disc which is in jubilee, Lord of heaven and earth," and suffered its lengthy name to be confined within two cartouches. The new art-style, an "expressionistic" treatment of natural forms based on an accentuation of the salient features of the king's personal appearance and showing a predilection for feminine softness, was introduced at the same time as the brainchild of Akhenaten himself, who issued the appropriate directives to his master artists (Aldred 1968 and 1973; Pillet 1961; Schäfer 1931).

The "Heliopolitan" type of temple consisted of a simple series of open courts (in contrast to the closed processional temples), oriented eastward and centering upon an altar. At Thebes, the erstwhile residence, four major temples were constructed, the largest of which (the *Gm[t]-p³-itn*) was the venue of the great jubilee (Redford 1973, 1975, 1977; Smith and Redford, 1977). Additional structures were the *Rwd-mnw,* the *Tni-mnw,* and the "Mansion of the *bnbn,*" given over to the queen and centered upon the sole obelisk of Thutmose IV, E of the Amun temple. Another *Gm-itn* was erected at Kawa in Nubia (Breasted 1902; Porter and Moss 1952: 180ff.), Memphis (Löhr 1975) and Heliopolis (Habachi 1971; Löhr 1974) were both provided with temples to the Sun-disc, and offering lists allude to cult installations throughout the Delta (Saad 1971). After year 5 two vast temples were included in the new city "Horizon of the Disc" (Amarna), one the "House of the Sun-disc" incorporating another *Gm-p³-itn* and a *Ḥwt-bnbn,* and a "Mansion of the Sun-disc," possibly a royal mortuary temple (Petrie 1894; Gunn and Pendelbury, 1923–51; Samson 1972; reliefs: Roeder 1969; Hanke 1978).

The royal family is already in evidence at the outset of the reign. Nefertiti, the Great Royal Wife, of unknown parentage but undoubtedly of Egyptian birth (Seele 1955: 170), appears in the jubilee with her first daughter, Meretaten. Before the 5th year two additional daughters had been born in rapid succession, Meketaten and Ankhesenpaaten; and at Amarna three more girls appeared before year 9, but these apparently died in infancy (Smith and Redford 1977: 83ff.). Sons are conspicuous by their absence, but one Amarna text refers to the "bodily son of the king, Tut-ankhu-aten" (Roeder 1969, pl. 106). Nefertiti herself seems to lose influence and drop out of sight toward the close of the reign, but may have survived her husband (Redford 1975: 11f.). Of the other wives the best known is Kiya, who appears briefly at Amarna (Fairman 1961: 29; Harris 1974; Hanke 1978). That Nefertiti appears at the close of the reign under the guise of a *male* coregent, Smenkhkare, has been mooted but remains highly controversial (Harris 1973; 1974; 1977; Samson 1981; 1982; Tawfik 1981).

The decision to abandon the old capital, Thebes, was taken perhaps as early as year 4, when the high priest of Amun is found working in the quarries (Redford 1963). Shortly after followed the wholesale destruction of Amun's name and iconography throughout the land. By year 6 construction at the new site of Amarna, the "horizon" which the Sun-disc had chosen (Aldred, 1976), was far enough advanced for the court to take up residence. Akhetaten was the god's site, and owed nothing to Thebes or Memphis: it was planned from the outset for the services of the new god (Smith 1981, 314ff.; Samson 1972; O'Connor fc.). The old administrative families were ignored, and a roster of "new men" replaced them. Chief among these were the chamberlain Tutu, the general Maya, the high priest Meryre; of the "old guard," Ay, the general and emanuensis, and Parennefer, the butler, found places in the new order (Hari 1976). Though Akhenaten might contemplate travel abroad, the new city was to be the permanent residence of court and government.

The army remained prominent throughout the reign (Schulman 1964), but Akhenaten's aversion to accompanying his troops in the field and his self-confessed refusal to "deal harshly" in foreign affairs lent his administration an irresolute character (cf. EA 162.40–1; Helck 1971, 168ff.; Kitchen 1962; Redford 1984, 185ff.; Several 1972). A campaign was mounted in Nubia (Helck 1980; Schulman 1982), and some sort of punitive action in Asia may have been contemplated before his death. But in the north, action seems to have been largely restricted to exiling recalcitrant natives (Edzard 1970) and removing dissidents and suspects to Egypt for interrogation (EA 162.67–77). Neutralized in the war between Khatte and Mitanni, Akhenaten watched inactive as the Hittites swiftly destroyed Mitanni and subverted her erstwhile dependencies in North Syria (Astour 1981). An incipient revolt in Nukhashshe looked to Egypt for help, but this did not materialize, and the rebels were crushed (Redford 1984: 197ff.). Before the end of the reign, the border state of Kadesh had defected to the Hittites, to be followed upon the return of Asiru, its king, from detention in Egypt, by Amurru (Freydank 1960; Klengel 1965).

Akhenaten passed away probably less than 6 months into his 17th year of rule, perhaps in the early summer. He was probably buried in his tomb in the royal wadi at Amarna (Martin 1974), but because of pillaging, virtually nothing remains of the interment. The extent to which any of the grave goods in tomb 55 of the Valley of the Kings represents his mortuary paraphernalia is a moot point (Schnabel 1976; Reeves 1981). Branded a rebel by later generations, and omitted from the king lists (Gardiner 1938), Akhenaten lived on in a folklore only partly preserved for us (Krauss 1976; Redford 1985, chap. 8).

Bibliography

Aldred, C. 1968. *Akenaten Pharaoh of Egypt.* London.

———. 1973. *Akhenaten and Nefertity.* New York.

———. 1976. The Horizon of the Aten. *JEA* 62.

———. 1988. *Akhenaten Pharaoh of Egypt.* Rev. ed. London.

Assmann, J. 1972. Die "Häresie" des Echnaton: Aspekte der Amarna-Religion. *Saeculum* 23: 109–26.

Astour, M. 1981. Ugarit and the Great Powers. Pp. 3ff. in *Ugarit in Retrospect,* ed. G. D. Young. Winona Lake, Ind.

Auffret, P. 1981. *Hymnes d'Égypte et d'Israël.* OBO 34. Freiburg and Göttingen.

Beckerath, J. von. 1984. Eine Bemerkung zu der vermuteten Koregenz Amenophis' III und IV. *GM* 83: 11ff.

Bernhardt, K.-H. 1969. Amenophis IV and Psalm 104. *MIO* 15: 193ff.

Breasted, J. H. 1902. A City of Akhenaten in Nubia. *ZÄS* 40: 106ff.

Edzard, D. O. 1970. Die Tontafeln von Kamid el-Loz. Pp. 55ff. in *Kamid el-Loz-Kumidi.* Bonn.

Fairman, H. W. 1961. Once again the So-called Coffin of Akhenaten. *JEA* 47: 25ff.

Fecht, G. 1967. Zur Frühform der Amarna-Theologie. *ZÄS* 94: 25ff.

Freydank, H. 1960. Eine hethitische Fassung des Vertrages zwischen dem Hethiterkönig Suppiluliuma und Aziru von Amurru. *MIO* 7: 356ff.

Gardiner, H. 1938. A Later Allusion to Akhenaten. *JEA* 24: 124ff.

Gauthier, H. 1912. *Le livre des rois d'Égypte.* Vol. 2. Cairo.

Gunn, B. 1923. Notes on the Aten and His Names. *JEA* 9: 168ff.

Gunn, B., and Pendelbury, J. D. S. 1923–51. *The City of Akhenaten.* 3 vols. Oxford.

Habachi, L. 1971. Akhenaten in Heliopolis. *Beiträge zur ägyptischen Bauforschung und Altertumskunde* 12: 35ff.

Hanke, R. 1978. *Amarna-Reliefs aus Hermopolis.* Hildesheim.

Hari, R. 1976. *Repertoire onomastique amarnien.* Geneva.

Harris, J. R. 1973. Nefertiti Rediviva. *AcOr* 35: 5ff.

———. 1974. Kiya. *CdÉ* 49: 25ff.

———. 1977. Akhenaten or Nefertiti. *AcOr* 38: 5ff.

Hayes, W. C. 1951. Inscriptions from the Palace of Amenhotep III. *JNES* 10: 35–40; 82–104; 156–82; 231–42.

Helck, H. W. 1971. *Die Beziehungen Ägyptens zur Vorderasiens im 3. und 2. Jahrtausend v. Chr.* 2d ed. ÄA 8. Wiesbaden.

———. 1980. Eine Feldzug unter Amenophis IV gegen Nubien. *SAK* 8: 117ff.

Kitchen, K. A. 1962. *Suppiluliuma and the Amarna Pharaohs.* Liverpool.

Klengel, H. 1965. Einige Bemerkungen zur Syrienpolitik des Amenophis IV/Echnaton. *Altertum* 11: 131ff.

Krauss, R. 1976. *Das Ende der Amarnazeit.* Hildesheim.

Lauffray, J. 1980. Les *"talatat"* du IXe pylone de Karnak et le *Tenymenou. Karnak* 6: 67ff.

Löhr, B. 1974. Ahanjati in Heliopolis. *GM* 11: 33ff.

———. 1975. Ahanjati in Memphis. *SAK* 2: 139ff.

Martin, G. T. 1974. *The Royal Tomb at El-Amarna.* Vol. 1. London.

Munro, P. 1981. Frühform oder Deckname des Jati (Aton) in Heliopolis? *MDAIK* 37: 359ff.

Nordheim, E. von. 1979. Der grosse Hymnus des Echnaton und Psalm 104. *SAK* 7: 227ff.

O'Connor, D. fc. Tell el-Amarna: Microcosm of the Universe.
Petrie, W. M. F. 1894. *Tell el-Amarna.* London.
Pillet, M. 1961. L'art d'Akhenaton. Pp. 81ff. in *Melanges Mariette.* Cairo.
Porter, B., and Moss, R. 1952. *Topographical Bibliography of Ancient Egyptian Hieroglyphic Texts, Reliefs and Paintings.* Vol. 7. Oxford.
Redford, D. B. 1963. The Identity of the High Priest of Amun at the beginning of Akhenaten's Reign. *JAOS* 83: 240–41.
———. 1967. *History and Chronology of the Eighteenth Dynasty of Egypt: Seven Studies.* Near and Middle East Series 3. Toronto.
———. 1973. Studies on Akhenaten at Thebes, I. *JARCE* 10: 77ff.
———. 1975. Studies on Akhenaten at Thebes, II. *JARCE* 12: 9ff.
———. 1976. The Sun-disc in Akhenaten's Program, Its Worship and Antecedents, I. *JARCE* 13: 47ff.
———. 1977. Preliminary Report on the First Season of excavations in East Karnak, 1975–1976. *JARCE* 14: 9ff.
———. 1980. The Sun-disc in Akhenaten's Program, Its Worship and Antecedents, II. 17: 21ff.
———. 1981. A Royal Speech from the Blocks of the 10th Pylon. *BES* 3: 87ff.
———. 1983. A Head-smiting Scene from the 10th Pylon. *Fontes atque Pontes* 362ff.
———. 1984. *Akhenaten, the Heretic King.* Princeton.
———. 1985. *Pharaonic King-Lists, Annals and Day-Books.* SSEA Publication 4. Mississauga, Ontario.
Reeves, C. N. 1981. A Reappraisal of Tomb 55 in the Valley of the Kings. *JEA* 67: 48ff.
Roeder, G. 1969. *Amarna-Reliefs aus Hermopolis.* Hildesheim.
Saad, R. 1971. A Unique Offering List of Amenophis IV Recently Found at Karnak. *JEA* 57: 70ff.
Samson, J. 1972. *Amarna, City of Akhenaten and Nefertity.* London.
———. 1981. Akhenaten's Coregent Ankhkheprure-Nefernefruaten. *GM* 53: 51ff.
———. 1982. Akhenaten's Coregent and Successor. *GM* 57: 57ff.
Schäfer, H. 1931. *Amarna in Religion und Kunst.* Leipzig.
Schnabel, D. 1976. Die Rätsel des Grabes no. 55 im "Tal der Könige." *Altertum* 22: 226ff.
Schulman, A. R. 1964. Some Observations on the Military Background of the Amarna Period. *JARCE* 3: 51ff.
———. 1982. The Nubian War of Akhenaten. Pp. 299ff. in *Colloques internationaux de CNRS* no 595. Paris.
Seele, K. C. 1955. King Ay and the Close of the Amarna Age. *JNES* 14: 168–80.
Several, M. W. 1972. Reconsidering the Egyptian Empire in Palestine during the Amarna Period. *PEQ* 104: 123ff.
Smith, W. S. 1981. *The Art and Architecture of Ancient Egypt.* Harmondsworth.
Smith, R. W., and Redford, D. B. 1977. *The Akhenaten Temple Project.* Vol. 1, *The Initial Discoveries.* Warminster.
Tawfik, S. 1981. Aton Studies. *MDAIK* 37: 469ff.
Wenig, S. 1972. Amenophis IV. *LÄ* 1: 210ff.
Wente, E., and Siclen, C. van. 1976. A Chronology of the New Kingdom. Pp. 217–61 in *Studies in Honor of George R. Hughes,* ed. J. H. Johnson and E. F. Wente. SAOC 39. Chicago.

DONALD B. REDFORD

AKHETATEN (PLACE). See AMARNA, TELL EL-.

AKIBA, RABBI. Leading rabbinic teacher of the first third of the 2d century C.E. (d. 135). Akiba's influence on the early development of the rabbinic tradition was very great; the vast majority of the authorities cited in the Mishnah were Akiba's disciples and successors, and indeed the major texts of the early rabbinic canon are said to have been the work of these disciples (see *Sanh.* 86a). Reflecting this influence, the image of Akiba presented in rabbinic texts is that of the ideal devotee of Torah; as one might expect with any such idealized portrait, traditional narratives concerning him are so colored with legend and reverential exaggeration that biographical conclusions cannot easily be drawn from them.

The picture of Akiba as ideal Torah scholar emerges from several well-known stories. He is described as having been born to poverty (*Ber.* 27b) and has having been in his early years a bitter enemy of the emerging learned elite (*Pesaḥ.* 49b), but is said then to have devoted years of study to the Torah and finally to have become the greatest Torah master of his day. His role in historical memory as Sage par excellence is reflected as well in a number of stories putting Akiba at the center of rabbinic-Patriarchal politics of the late 1st and early 2d centuries (*Ber.* 27b–28a, *j. (Talm.) Ber.* 4:1 7cd; *Roš. Haš.* 2:9), while the end of Akiba's life too was remembered as exemplary: he joyously died a martyr's death during Hadrian's persecution of Judaism because he could not abandon the public teaching of Torah (*Sanh.* 12a, *Ber.* 61b).

Akiba's influence on the developing tradition was primarily of two sorts. He is identified as the individual chiefly responsible for the systematic arrangement of Oral Torah according to subject matter (*j [Talm.] Šeqal.* 5:1 48c, *t. Zabim.* 1:5, *ʾAbot R. Nat.* 18), and he is credited with having devised an elaborate hermeneutic of Scripture which allowed him to find meaning in every letter and every diacritical mark of the text (*Menaḥ.* 29b). The inference from the perfection of Scripture that every detail of the text has meaning was opposed by Akiba's great contemporary Ishmael b. Elisha, who insisted to the contrary that "Scripture speaks the sort of language that people use" (*Ber.* 31b), but Akiba's hermeneutic is reflected in much subsequent *midrash* (the *Mekhilta* of R. Simeon b. Yohai, *Sifra,* and *Sifre Zuta* on Numbers, along with numerous Talmudic passages), and according to Jerome (*ad* Isa 7:14) it stimulated the production of a new Greek translation of the Bible as well. The aggadic image (*Menaḥ.* 29b) of Moses visiting Akiba's academy and finding himself unable to understand the interpretations of the Torah propounded there offers later rabbis' acknowledgment that Akiba's hermeneutic was strikingly original but only tenuously linked to the apparently intended meaning of the text; interpretation letter by letter allowed for great freedom, but also led to disregard for context and plausibility in both aggadic and halakhic contexts (*Ḥag.* 14a, *Sanh.* 38b, 51a, 67b).

Akiba's willingness to discover unexpected and far-reaching implications in Scripture is reflected as well in his apparent interest in the more recondite aspects of early rabbinic religion, such as *merkabah* ("chariot") mysticism and the other secret teachings that came to be known as *Pardes* (the "garden"). Even in such realms, however, Akiba remained the model for later generations to emulate; of the four who "entered the garden," only he "entered in peace and came out in peace" (see *t. Ḥag.* 2:2, *j. (Talm.) Ḥag.* 2:1 77b, *b. (Talm.) Ḥag.* 14b).

On the basis of one Talmudic tradition (*j (Talm.) Taʿan.* 4:7 68d), much recent historiography has described Akiba as an enthusiastic supporter of Bar Kokhba's rebellion against Rome, but the most recent investigations (Schaefer) have cast doubt on this conception. (See also *EncJud* 2: 488–92; *JEnc* 1: 304–10.)

Bibliography

Finkelstein, L. 1936. *Akiba: Scholar, Saint and Martyr.* New York.

Heschel, A. J. 1962–5. *Torah min ha-Shamayim ba-Aspaklaria shel ha-Dorot.* 2 vols. Theology of Ancient Judaism. London and New York.

Schaefer, P. 1980. Rabbi Aqiva and Bar Kokhba. Vol. 2, pp. 113–30 in *Approaches to Ancient Judaism,* ed. W. S. Green. Chico.

ROBERT GOLDENBERG

AKITU. The Sum Á-KI-TI, and its Akk cognate *akī tu(m),* may refer either to the *akītu* festival proper or to a temple in which this festival was celebrated. The origin and etymology of this noun is unknown. On account of the Akk plural form *akiā ti,* some scholars consider Sum Á-KI-TI to be a Sem loanword, borrowed from Old Akk (cf. *AHW:* 29). The Sum term for "New Year" is ZAG-MU(-K), lit. "the (end) limit of the year," borrowed into Akk as *zagmukku/zammukku.* Both the Sum and Akk terms may refer either to New Year's Day or to the New Year festival proper.

A. The *akītu* and the New Year Festivals in Sumerian Religion (ca. 2500–1800 B.C.E.)

The *akītu* and the New Year (ZAG-MU-K) seem to have been two distinct festivals in Sumerian religion.

1. The Sumerian *akītu* Festival. The earliest references to the *akītu* festival are implied in Pre-Sargonic economic texts from Ur and Adab, dated to the "Month of Á-KI-TI," i.e., the sixth month and first month of the local calendars, respectively. The *akītu* festival in Ur, during the Ur III period (ca. 2100–2000 B.C.E.) and the Isin-Larsa period (ca. 2000–1760 B.C.E.), took place twice a year: in the sixth (or seventh) month, i.e., in the beginning of the barley sowing season; and in the first (or twelfth) month, i.e., when the barley harvest began. This duality arose as a result of a shift in the beginning of the calendar year from the seventh month (i.e. the autumn) to the first month (i.e. the spring), which resulted in two *akītu* festivals: the "*akītu* of the sowing (season)" and the "*akītu* of the harvest (season)." The same duality can also be observed in the Bible, where both the first month (Nisan) and the seventh month (Tishre) are referred to as the turning points of the year (cf. Exod 12:2; 23:16). The *akītu* in Nippur, on the other hand, took place in the fourth and twelfth months, in Lagash and Umma, perhaps once a year, in the eighth month. The exact day of the month on which the festival was celebrated is not known. The *akītu* was celebrated in a special temple in the open country, situated near a canal. It was usually dedicated to the city god, and therefore offerings were presented there to his statue or emblem. A major and joyful event of the festival was the procession, in the course of which the god's statue and his entourage were carried from his temple to the *akītu* temple and back, partly by chariot and partly by boat. The responsibility for the festival fell on the king. As to its religious significance, it is assumed that the *akītu* festival marked the beginning of the agricultural year, or semiannual season. In the course of his visit to the *akītu* temple, the city god was believed to have blessed the fields, in anticipation of the renewal of agricultural work (Falkenstein 1959: 166).

2. The New Year Festival in the Neo-Sumerian Period (ca. 2100–1800 B.C.E.). The inscriptions of Gudea (ca. 2100 B.C.E.) and some cultic-literary texts from the OB period indicate that in the Neo-Sumerian period. New Year's Day was considered as an important festival, on which special cultic rites (Sum PILLUDA) were performed, under the aegis, and probably with the personal participation, of the king. The most important cultic event in the Sumerian New Year festival was the Sacred Marriage rite *(hieros gamos).* In Lagash and elsewhere, this rite was probably conceived as having taken place on the divine level, i.e., between the city god and his wife. The Ur III kings, however, seem to have introduced a new feature into the cult, borrowed from the Uruk tradition: sacred union between the deified king in the role of the fertility god Dumuzi, and a priestess representing Inanna, the goddess of love (cf. van Dijk 1954: 83–8; J. Klein 1981: 124–66). The kings of Isin also celebrated the sacred marriage rite on New Year's Day in their capital with a priestess, who represented Inanna, identified with the city goddess Ninisinna. The celebrations in Isin involved a great variety of cultic personnel, including transvestites (Römer 1965: 128–49; Reisman 1973: 185–92). The sacred union between the god and the goddess, or their earthly representatives, was believed to fertilize nature and society alike for the coming year, and thus ensure plenty and abundance for the land (Jacobsen 1975: 68–71). Another important feature of the New Year festival in Sumer was the ceremony of the "Determining of Fates." The sacred marriage itself usually culminated in a blessing (lit. "fate-decreeing") for abundance and fertility, which the goddess bestowed upon the king and the land. The Lagash sources also indicate that on New Year's Day, major religious and political decisions were taken, probably by oracular guidance, including the appointment of rulers and state and temple officials. On this day, criminals and immoral persons were excluded from the communal meal in the temple, and the rights of the orphans and widows were enforced (Heimpel 1981: 66–8; 88).

B. The *akītu* (New Year) Festival in the 1st Millennium B.C.E.

1. In Babylon. In Babylon, unlike in other Mesopotamian cities, from early times the *akītu* was celebrated only once a year, in the month of Nisan, and thus it gradually merged and became identified with the New Year festival *(zagmukku).* In the 2d millennium B.C.E., with the rise of Babylon to supremacy, the *akītu*/New Year of Nisan, which was dedicated to Marduk, became the most important festival in Mesopotamia, including the city of Assur. In 1st millennium Babylon, the New Year festival was celebrated in a great pomp and rejoicing, during the first eleven days of Nisan. The climactic event of this festival was the divine procession to the *akītu* temple and the celebration of the *akītu* ritual there. The participation of the king in the *akītu*/New Year festival was obligatory, and his duties included, *inter alia,* a declaration of innocence before Marduk on the fifth of Nisan, and "seizing the hand of Bēl" (i.e., Marduk) and accompanying him to the *akītu* temple. The ritual of the Babylonian New Year festival is described in detail in a text from the Seleucid period (i.e. the 3d century B.C.E.), containing instructions to the high priest *(šešgallu),* as to the cultic activities to be performed in the temple, from the second to the fifth of Nisan (Thureau-Dangin 1921: 127–54; *ANET,* 331–34). During these days, prayers and incantations are recited to Marduk, beseeching him to calm his anger and bless the king and the people for the coming year. On the fourth day, the great Babylonian mythic poem *enūma eliš,* describing Marduk's victory over Tiamat (the primeval sea) and the creation of the world by him, is recited before the god. On the fifth day, after the temple has been thoroughly purified, the king is led before Marduk. The high priest takes away from him his royal insignia, strikes him on his cheeks, pulls his ears, and makes him bow down to the ground. At this point, the king has to utter a declaration of innocence, in which he asserts that he did not neglect the worship of the god, nor did he harm the sacred city of Babylon or its protected people. Thereupon, the high priest utters a favorable oracle, assuring the king that Marduk listened to his prayer and will bless his kingship and destroy his enemies. After the high priest returns to the king his royal insignia, he again strikes his cheek, and if "his tears flow—Bēl is appeased; if his tears do not flow—Bēl is angry; an enemy will rise and bring about his downfall" (*ANET,* 334, 429–52). The description of the *akītu* ritual in the above text has been lost. Nevertheless, some of its highlights can be culled from the inscriptions of NA and NB kings. On the fifth day of Nisan, the statues of Nabû and other deities arrived at Babylon. The festive procession to the *akītu* temple took place most probably on the ninth of Nisan (Berger 1970: 156). The king "seizes" the hand of Marduk and conducts him to the *akītu* temple outside the city. There, on the tenth of Nisan, a cultic drama, symbolizing Marduk's primordial victory over Tiamat and the forces of chaos, was enacted in some way (Lambert 1968: 104–12; 1963: 25: 189–90). The purpose and meaning of this ritual is not clear. Some see in it society's identification with the powers of nature, when the seasons change and natural life renews itself (Frankfort 1948: 314); others assume that the *akītu,* originally an agricultural festival, became a national festival, commemorating the establishment of the Babylonian empire or its reunification, in the guise of a primordial cosmic battle (Jacobsen 1975: 76). It is interesting to note that the association of the New Year with the creation of the world survived in the rabbinic interpretation of the Jewish New Year festival. Since New Year's Day was considered to be the time of decreeing the fates for the coming year, the ritual of Fate Decreeing was performed during the festival twice: once on the fifth (or sixth) of Nisan, in the sanctuary of Nabû in Babylon, called the "Dais of Fates" (Akk *parak šīmāti*), and a second time in Marduk's temple, upon his return from the *akītu* temple. The New Year festival ended on the eleventh day, and on the twelfth day Nabû and all the gods returned to their cities. According to an earlier hypothesis (Zimmern 1918: 2–20; Pallis 1926: 221–43), the New Year festival's cultic drama included another episode, in which Marduk, prior to his battle with Tiamat, was put to death, taken down to the netherworld, and resurrected, in imitation of the cult of the dying god Dumuzi—Tammuz. However, the NA cultic commentary, on which this hypothesis is based, turned out to be nothing but an anti-Babylonian or pro-Babylonian propaganda. The purpose of this text was either to justify Sennacherib's destruction of Babylon and capture of Marduk's statue, in terms of a divine trial (von Soden 1955:51: 130–166), or to explain Marduk's exile and his return to his city, in terms of death, descent to the netherworld, and resurrection (Frymer-Kensky 1983: 131–44). In any case, this vestigial and late addition to the New Year's Day ritual has nothing to do with the motif of the dying fertility god.

2. In Assur and Other Cities. In early times, most probably, the Babylonian god Marduk played the central role in the New Year celebrations in Assur. Only after Sennacherib destroyed Babylon, capturing Marduk's statue (in 684 B.C.E.) and elevating Assur to the rank of Marduk, did Assur become the central figure in the celebrations. Sennacherib reports in his inscriptions that he rebuilt the old *akītu* temple in honor of his god Assur, and renewed the *akītu* festival there. From his description of the representations engraved on the bronze gates of this temple we learn that, in Assur, just like in Babylon, a cultic drama, symbolizing Assur's victory over Tiamat, was enacted in the *akītu* temple (*LAS,* 135–43). However, contrary to an erroneous hypothesis, Sennacherib did *not* embody the god Assur in this cultic drama (cf. *LAS,* 142:15 + 1; *Enc Miqr* 7: 310; *CAD* K, 289a). Other Mesopotamian cities, in the 1st millennium, beside Babylon and Assur, preserved ancient local traditions and did not normally celebrate the *akītu* festival on New Year's day (cf. Falkenstein 1959: 159; 177, note 52). Thus, in Uruk two *akītu* festivals were celebrated: one in Nisan and one in Tishre. The *akītu* of Nineveh was probably celebrated on the 16th of Ṭebēt (i.e., the sixth month), whereas that of Arbela (Milkiya), sometime in the month of Ab (i.e., the fifth month).

Bibliography

Berger, P.-R. 1970. Das Neujahrsfest nach Königsinschriften des ausgehenden babylonischen Reiches. Pp. 155–59 in *Actes de la XVIIe Rencontre Assyriologique Internationale.*

van Dijk, J. J. A. 1954. Le fête du nouvel an dans un texte de Šulgi. *BiOr* 11: 83–88.

van Driel, G. 1969. *The Cult of Assur.* Assen.

Falkenstein, A. 1959. *akitu*-Fest und *akitu*-Festhaus. Pp. 147–93 in *J. Friedrich Festschrift,* ed. R. van Kienle et al.

Frankfort, H. 1948. *Kingship and the Gods.* Chicago.

Frymer-Kensky, T. 1983. The Tribulations of Marduk: The So-called "Marduk Ordeal Text." *JAOS* 103: 131–41.

Grayson, A. K. 1970. Chronicles and the Akitu Festival. Pp. 160–70 in *Actes de la XVII[e] Recontre Assyriologique Internationale.*

Heimpel, W. 1981. The Nanshe Hymn. *JCS* 33: 65–139.

Jacobsen, Th. 1975. Religious Drama in Ancient Mesopotamia. Pp. 65–77 in *Unity and Diversity,* ed. H. Goedicke and J.J.M. Roberts. Baltimore.

Klein, J. 1981. *Three Šulgi Hymns: Sumerian Royal Hymns Glorifying King Šulgi of Ur.* Ramat-Gan.

Köcher, F. 1952. Ein mittel assyrisches Ritualfragment zum Neujahrfest. *ZA* 16: 192–202.

Lambert, W. G. 1954–55. An Address of Marduk to Demons. *AfO* 17: 315.

———. 1963. The Great Battle of the Mesopotamian Religious Year: The Conflict in the Akitu House. *Iraq* 25: 189–190.
———. 1968. Myth and Ritual as Conceived by the Babylonians. *JSS* 13: 104–12.
Landsberger, B. 1915. *Der kultische Kalender der babylonier und assyrer I.* LSS 6/1–2. Leipzig.
Nakata, I. 1968. Problems of the Babylonian Akitu Festival. *JANES* 1: 41–49.
Pallis, S. A. 1926. *The Babylonian Akitu Festival.* Copenhagen.
Postgate, J. N. 1974. The *bīt-akī ti* in Assyrian Nabu Temples. *Sumer* 30: 51–74.
Reisman, D. 1973. Iddin-Dagan's Sacred Marriage Hymn. *JCS* 25: 185–202.
Römer, W. H. Ph. 1965. *Sumerische 'Königshymnen' der Isin-Zeit.* Leiden.
Schmidt, J. 1973. Babylon. *AfO* 24: 164–66.
von Soden, W. 1955. Gibt es ein Zeugnis dafür, dass die Babylonier an Wiederaufstehung Marduks geglaubt haben? *ZA* 51: 130–66.
———. 1957. Ein neues Bruchstück des assyrischen Kommentar zum Marduk-Ordeal. *ZA* 52: 224–34.
Thureau-Dangin, F. 1921. *Rituels accadiens.* Paris.
Zimmern, H. 1906. *Zum babylonischen Neujahrsfest.* Leipzig.
———. 1918. *Zum babylonischen Neujahrsfest, zweiter Beitrag.* Leipzig.

JACOB KLEIN

AKKADIAN LANGUAGE. *See* LANGUAGES (AKKADIAN).

AKKO (PLACE). See ACCO (PLACE).

AKKUB (PERSON) [Heb *ʿaqqûb*]. **1.** Head of a family of temple gatekeepers in the postexilic period who are listed as returnees from Babylonian exile under the leadership of Zerubbabel and others (Ezra 2:42 = Neh 7:45 = 1 Esd 5:28). While this list appears in Ezra 2 immediately after the return of Sheshbazzar, there are several indicators that it is not a list of that group who first responded to Cyrus' edict. Not least of these is the absence of the name "Sheshbazzar," which raises the question of the relationship between SHESHBAZZAR and ZERUBBABEL. Myers (*1 Chronicles* AB, 15–16, 146) surveys various views about the origin and purpose of this list. Recent scholarship tends to follow Rudolph (*Ezra und Nehemia* HAT, 17) in understanding it as a composite list of groups who returned from exile in the early years of the Persian period (Clines 1984: 44; Williamson *Ezra, Nehemiah* WBC, 31–32). It is uncertain whether Ezra 2 is copied from Nehemiah 7, or Nehemiah 7 is copied from Ezra 2, or both are copied from some other original document (Fensham 1982: 49; Clines 1984: 44–45). The list is also found in 1 Esdras 5 as those who returned with Zerubbabel during the reign of Darius.

The family of Akkub continued as gatekeepers throughout the postexilic period (1 Chr 9:17; Neh 11:19; 12:25), the individual names in these verses being properly understood as names of families.

2. Head of a family of NETHINIM (temple servants) who also are listed as returnees from Babylonian exile under the leadership of Zerubbabel and others (Ezra 2:45 = 1 Esdr 5:30). The names Akkub and Hagab are lacking in the parallel list at Neh 7:48. Either the Ezra list has made repetition of Akkub from v 42 and Hagabah from earlier in v 45 (Batten *Ezra, Nehemiah* ICC, 90) or the scribe copying the list for Nehemiah 7 skipped from Hagabah to Hagab (Williamson *Ezra, Nehemiah* WBC, 26). The nature of the scribal error is related to the larger issue of the literary relationship between the lists.

3. One of the men who assisted Ezra in the public reading of the law by explaining the reading to the people (Neh 8:7–8). That Akkub and his fellows are properly identified as Levites (1 Esdr 9:48 and Vg as opposed to MT) is supported by Neh 8:9 and the references to the teaching role of the Levites in 2 Chr 17:7–9; 35:3. Understanding what these men did hinges on the meaning of v 8, especially the word *mĕpōrāš* (RSV "clearly"). Traditionally this has been understood as referring to the Levites' translation from Hebrew to Aramaic. However, it may refer to their explaining the meaning and implication of the old law in a new setting. Some have understood the term as referring to the activity of the men standing with Ezra (v 4), meaning that they read clearly or divided the reading into paragraphs, pausing to allow the Levites to give their explanation. (Ackroyd *Chronicles, Ezra, Nehemiah* TBC 295–96; Kidner 1979: 106; Williamson *Ezra, Nehemiah* WBC, 277–79, 290.)

4. A post-exilic member of the royal family of David descended from King Jehoiachin (1 Chr 3:24). According to the MT, Akkub is the eighth generation from Jehoiachin. However, in v 22 "the sons of Shemaiah" may be a dittograph, because the list of five sons of Shemaiah is followed by the numeral six. If the phrase is deleted, v 22 then lists the six sons of Shecaniah, yielding only seven generations from Jehoiachin to Akkub. At v 21 the RSV follows LXX, Vg, and Syr in reading "his son" *(bnw)* instead of "the sons of" *(bny)* before the last four names in the verse. Such a reading adds four generations, yielding eleven or twelve generations from Jehoiachin to Akkub. This uncertainty about the number of generations involved affects attempts to date the list and, as a consequence, the generation of Akkub. (See Ackroyd *Chronicles* TBC, 34 and Williamson 1982: 58.)

Bibliography

Clines, D. J. 1984. *Ezra, Nehemiah, Esther.* Grand Rapids.
Fensham, F. C. 1982. *The Books of Ezra and Nehemiah.* Grand Rapids.
Galling, K. 1951. The Gōlā-List According to Ezra 2 and Nehemiah 7. *JBL* 70: 149–58.
———. 1964. Die Liste der aus dem Exil Heimgekehrten. Pp. 89–108 in *Studien zur Geschichte Israels im persischen Zeitalter.* Tübingen.
Kidner, D. 1979. *Ezra and Nehemiah.* Grand Rapids.
Williamson, H. G. M. 1982. *1 and 2 Chronicles.* Grand Rapids.

CHANEY R. BERGDALL

AKRABATTENE (PLACE) [Gk *Akrabattēnē*]. The district where Judas Maccabeus defeated the "sons of Esau," i.e., the Idumeans or Edomites (1 Macc 5:3). The Hellenistic form of the name may be associated with Akrabbim, an important ascent from the Arabah to the northern Negev at the southern border of Judean territory. Josephus (*JW*

2.12.4; 4.9.9) mentions a toparchy near Shechem (Nablus) with the same name, but it is not clear whether this is identical with the area where Judas fought. Regardless, the Akrabattene of Josephus should be connected with the "Akrabattine" of the Onomasticon of Eusebius (cf. Klostermann 1904: 14,10; 86,25; 108,20; 156,30; 160,14).

Bibliography

Klostermann, E. 1904. *Eusebius. Das Onomastikon der biblischen Ortsnamen.* Leipzig.

Schunck, K.-D. 1980. I. Makkabäerbuch. *JSHRZ* I, 287–373.

M. GÖRG

AKRABBIM (PLACE) [Heb *ʿaqrabbîm*]. The name, meaning "scorpions," is part of the compound geographical name *maʿăleh ʿaqrabbîm* ("ascent of scorpions"). According to Num 34:4; Josh 15:3; Judg 1:36, Akrabbim was an outermost point on the S borderline of the Judean territory SW of the Dead Sea. The name may be equated with hieroglyphic *ʿqrbt* mentioned in the topographical lists of the mortuary temple of Amenhotep III at Thebes (Edel: list "B_N li.11"), which in turn seems to be identical with a name preserved as *mqrpt* in the great Palestine List of Thutmose III (No. 94). The latter is probably a misreading of a form *ʿqrpt* supposedly existing in an earlier version of the list (Görg 1974a; but see Redford 1982). The ascent of Akrabbim should be connected with one of the passes between the Arabah and the Wadi Fiqre and Kurnub. It is usually identified with Naqb eṣ-Ṣfar (Abel 1933; Noth *Joshua* HAT; but cf. Aharoni *LBHG*). There were three way stations from the bottom to the top, known today as Rugm Ṣfar, Khirbet Ṣfar, and Qaṣr Ṣfar, all of which were "Nabataean in origin, Roman in repair, and Byzantine in reconstruction" (Glueck 1959: 207). The ascent may have been a station point on the ancient expedition routes of Egyptian kings to the different copper mines near the Arabah and to Transjordanian places as early as the 18th dyn. (Haider 1987). In Roman and Byzantine times the pass served as a convenient and important way from the Mediterranean Sea to Edom, Moab, and Elat (Harel 1959; 1967). Named after the ascent, the adjacent area seems to be the AKRABATTENE where Judas Maccabeus defeated the Idumeans (1 Macc 5:3).

Bibliography

Abel, F.-M. 1933. *Géographie de la Palestine, I.* Paris.

Edel, E. 1966. *Die Ortsnamenlisten aus dem Totentempel Amenophis III.* Bonn.

Glueck, N. 1959. *Rivers in the Desert.* New York.

Görg, M. 1974a. Zum "Skorpionenpass" (Num. XXXIV 4; Jos. XV 3). *VT* 24: 508–9.

———. 1974b. *Untersuchungen zu hieroglyphischen Wiedergabe palästinischer Ortsnamen.* Bonner Orientalistische Studien, n.s. 29. Bonn.

Haider, P. 1987. Zum Moab-Feldzug Ramses' II. *SAK* 14: 107–23.

Harel, N. 1959. The Roman Road at the Ma aleh Aqrabim (the "Ascent of the Scorpions"). *IEJ* 9: 175–79.

———. 1967. Israelite and Roman Roads in the Judaean Desert. *IEJ* 17: 18–26.

Keel, O., and Küchler, M. 1982. *Orte und Landschaften der Bibel. II.* Zürich.

Redford, D. 1982. A Bronze Age Itinerary in Transjordan. *JSSEA* 12: 55–74.

M. GÖRG

AL ʾUBAID (30°59′N; 46°03′E). A small tell (350 m long and 7–8 m high) in S Mesopotamia, 6 km W of Ur, excavated by H. R. Hall in the spring of 1919 and by L. Woolley in 1923 and 1924. It is famous for having been the site of a 3d millennium B.C. Sumerian temple and for having furnished the first proof of painted ceramics characteristic of the long Neolithic period in Iraq. Consequently, the name of the site has been used to designate the Neolithic culture of Iraq.

A. The Temple and Its Artifacts

The sanctuary belonged to the series of temples built on terraces; it stands inside an oval enclosure characteristic of the Early Dynastic period (first half of the 3d millennium). Some inscriptions on bricks prove that it was still in use during the era of the third Dynasty of Ur (21st century) and that it was dedicated to Ninhursag, goddess of the mountain. Nothing has been found of the temple itself, but a study has been made of the platform that supported it (33 by 26 m), its stairway leading to the SE side and a second one leading to the NW side, and its subsequent phases of reconstruction. It was surrounded by an oval enclosure which was possibly double (85 by 65 m) and which delimited the sacred area. A magnificent collection of artwork was found where it had been deliberately stuffed into the masonry during the reconstruction of the building. Among these works were representations of bulls, birds, bronze lion heads, copper columns nailed onto wooden beams (or with mosaic incrustations encased in bitumen and pressed against the trunks of palm trees), heads of nails from the architectural decorations, and the famous relief of the Imdugud, with its lion-headed eagle binding two stags. Also discovered were several statues (some complete, others in fragments) among which is the one of Kurlil; a golden jewel belonging to Aannipadda, King of Ur and one of the most ancient kings of history; the foundation inscription of the temple dedicated to Ninhursag by this king; fragments of inscribed vases; and a very famous frieze of the dairy in stone and shell on a base of bitumen. This series of artwork represents the most beautiful collection found on one site in Mesopotamia; it is all the more remarkable given the small area and limited period of occupation of this site. This collection alone would have ensured the reputation of Al-ʾUbaid.

B. The Neolithic Culture

In his excavations, Woolley also found potsherds of painted ceramics with black motifs generally in geometric shapes on a background of greenish hue (the color of the paste) which could be dated back to a prehistoric era. Further research carried out on neighboring sites such as Eridu and later throughout Mesopotamia produced findings that indicated a particularly important phase of the historical development. It is now known that this "Ubaid culture" represents the last great stage in the evolution of

Near-Eastern Neolithic societies before the intensified urbanization toward the end of the 4th millennium. This culture acquired its main characteristics during the 6th millennium and disappeared toward 3700 B.C. after having influenced in varying degrees and in various ways the entire region between the E Mediterranean and Iran, the Anatolian plateau, and the end of the Arabian peninsula.

It is from the birth of this culture that the emergence of a distinctive "Mesopotamia" is dated. Before then, the alluvial valleys in the desert areas were not subject to the agricultural techniques of the first Neolithic or pre-Neolithic societies; the colonization of this area along the Tigris and Euphrates rivers was not undertaken until the 7th millennium, and it was a fairly slow process beginning in the S regions. It is in the S—at Eridu (Ubaid 1), then at Hajji Muhammad (Ubaid 2)—that one can see the first evidence of this new culture, characterized by its ceramics, the use of curved nails and clay sickles, as well as by architecture which progressed rapidly towards a certain monumentality (thanks to the application of new techniques such as molded bricks or the use of pilasters in reinforcing the building without increasing the amount of masonry).

From Ubaid 2, this culture began to appear beyond its Mesopotamian cradle; indeed, it spread rapidly toward the N and NW along the great rivers; it is in the regions of Mandali (Hamrin basin) as well as in Assyria (Tepe Gawra) that its first developments have best been analyzed. But this culture also dominated the entire area of the Khuzistan, where it was to contribute to the elaboration of the Susiane; finally it progressed S toward the Persian Gulf also, where its presence can be seen on many sites on the coast of Saudi Arabia. The full expansion and the greatest extension of Ubaid culture took place between 4500 and 3700 B.C. corresponding to the Ubaid 3 and 4 phases; its two centers—one in S Mesopotamia, the other in Assyria and the Hamrin—express two aspects of this culture which continue to progress in the Gulf, on the Iranian plateau, and particularly toward the countries of the Mediterranean Levant and Anatolia. Yet, the further one goes from the Mesopotamian bases, the more the unique features of Ubaid are diminished in favor of local and regional tendencies and influences.

The society associated with this Ubaid culture became increasingly complex during its two-millennia span. There was hardly anything in common between most of the 6th millennium villages and the great centers of the mid-4th millennium. These changes are seen first of all in the technical capabilities evident in the production of most of the material goods and in the economic foundations of the social structure. Originally in the marshes of S Mesopotamia, the basic occupations of life were fishing and hunting in the swamps and the neighboring deserts. But the originality of the inhabitants who settled in that region lay in their ability to apply irrigation techniques in non-marshy areas in order to develop the crops, techniques similar to those used previously during the Samarra era. This included a remarkable new step, drainage, without which it would have been impossible to cultivate the land for very long because of the high salt concentration. Irrigation and drainage also entailed a change in the group's habits and life-style; the traditional and more individualistic methods of economic subsistence would not facilitate the new strategy for exploiting the land. Without reinforcing community practices, irrigation would have been impossible. Other discoveries characterize this period, in particular one dealing with the uses of fire. Ceramics became more widespread but were still done by hand; also, metal began to appear, still on a very small scale, and primarily in the form of jewelry. Nevertheless, this indicates a growing mastery of metallurgy which would eventually take firmer hold some centuries later with the beginnings of the Bronze Age.

This better technical ability both in agriculture and in the production of material objects (pottery and metal) had important consequences on the evolution of society. If the villages showed no sign of social differentiation at the beginning of the 6th millennium, the same cannot be said during the 4th: Tepe Gawra (levels 12 and 11) in particular clearly shows the juxtaposition of simple buildings accommodating common people with larger homes which belonged to the dominant group (who undoubtedly held the power); certain other buildings seem to have been considered as specialized shops.

But why this emergence of S Mesopotamia beginning with Ubaid 2? Why was it accompanied by such a vigorous geographical diffusion of its cultural traits? Finally, why was it succeeded by a new supremacy in that region at the time of Uruk (3300–3100 B.C.), during the 3d millennium? The answers are still uncertain, but it could be that "necessity was the mother of invention": the tension created by the absence of basic raw materials (such as wood) and the need to acquire these prompted a search for other ways to meet the basic human needs. Natural waterways would have become the most favored means of transportation in order to ensure such supplies, and consequently those routes became the avenues along which the cultural characteristics of Ubaid would have spread to the surrounding countries. Therefore the transmission of ceramics is merely a material reflection of a much more vigorous exchange which resulted in a sort of standardization of Near-Eastern civilization. This uniformity began with the elaborate forms in S Mesopotamia, particularly in the region of Ubaid, where it was first recognized by modern scholars.

Bibliography

Hall, H. R., and Woolley, L. 1927. *Ur Excavations, I. Al'Ubaid.* London.

Huot, J. -L., et al. 1987. *Préhistoire de la Mesopotamie: La Mesopotamie préhistorique et l'exploration recente du djebel Hamrin.* Paris.

Lloyd, S. 1984. *The Archaeology of Mesopotamia.* Rev. ed. London.

Oates, J. 1973. The Background and Development of Early Farming Communities in Mesopotamia and the Zagros. *Proceedings of the Prehistoric Society* 39: 147–81.

JEAN-CLAUDE MARGUERON
Trans. Paul Sager

AL-ʿULA. See DEDAN.

ALALAKH. A Bronze Age city identified with Tell ʿAṭšan (or Atchana; 36°15′N; 36°23′E). See also AMUQ PLAIN.

A. The Site and Its Yield

The Bronze Age city of Alalakh was uncovered by the British mission headed by Sir Leonard Woolley, in the years 1937–1939 and 1946–1949, at the large mound called Tell ᶜAṭšan (Turk Açana). It is situated in the S part of the Plain of Antioch, some 400 m E of the Orontes and less than 3 km SE of the bridge where the road from Antakya to Aleppo crosses the river. The excavations disclosed seventeen levels of occupation, with remains of private and public buildings (palaces, temples, and fortifications), artifacts, and works of art, but most important, a rich epigraphic corpus represented by over five hundred cuneiform tablets (principally from the Levels VII and IV) and a long historical inscription engraved on a royal statue at the time of Level IV. The excavator's report (Woolley 1955; cf. 1953) was later corrected and modified in several points dealing with chronology and historical reconstruction (i.e., by Mellink 1957; Albright 1957; Astour 1972; Gates 1976, 1981, 1987). The inscription on the statue of King Idrimi was first published by S. Smith (1949) and subsequently studied and published anew by several other scholars (an English translation, *ANET*, 557–58; a collated hand copy, transliteration, and translation by Dietrich and Loretz 1981, with a commentary by Klengel 1981). A catalog of tablets numbered from one through 453a and comprising 466 items, many of them presented in copies and/or transliterations, with a general introduction, was published by Wiseman (1953, supplemented by his 1954, 1958, 1959a, and 1959b). A number of items in Wiseman's publications were collated and published in full (in transliteration) by Dietrich and Loretz 1969a, 1969b, and 1970, with an additional forty-three tablets (all from Level IV), which brings the total number of known tablets to 509; but several of them remain unpublished, and there may still be some tablets unaccounted for in the Museum of Antakya. The seal impressions on the Alalakh tablets have been collected and commented upon by Collon (1975).

B. History of Alalakh

The earliest occupational strata of Tell ᶜAṭšan were found to lie below the present level of groundwater. The potsherds extracted from the liquid mud at the bottom of a special caisson pit included a small number of specimens attributable to the Amuq I and J phases of the ceramic sequence of other excavated mounds of the area and datable, respectively, to ca. 2400–2250 and 2250–2000 B.C. This proves that the site was already inhabited in the period of the EBLA archives. Alalakh appears indeed in the Ebla texts under the name *A-la-la-ḫu*^{ki}, more often spelled ᵓA_{x} (NI)-*la-la-ḫu*^{ki}, as a dependency of Ebla and apparently not having a vassal king of its own. Later, in the records of the Third Dynasty of Ur (2063–1955 B.C., low chronology), a state *Mu-ki-iš*^{ki} or *Mu*-⌜x⌝-*gi*$_4$-*iš*^{ki} is mentioned (along with Ebla and two other cities formerly subject to Ebla) among the vassals of the kings of Ur. Late Bronze Age sources from Alalakh, Ugarit, and Hatti make certain that Mukiš was the name of the Plain of Antioch and adjacent hill areas with Alalakh as its capital. The construction of the first palace in Level XIII of Alalakh (the sequential position of which seems to coincide with the period of Ur III) also testifies to Alalakh's achievement of autonomous statehood. In the 18th century B.C. Alalakh came under the sway of the new, powerful kingdom of Yamḫad with its capital at Ḫalab (Aleppo). It must have been one of the unnamed cities of the Cedar and Boxwood Mountains and the seacoast raided by King Yaḫdun-Lim of Mari ca. 1740 B.C. (an event marked perhaps by the end of Level X at Alalakh). No inscriptional material has been found in Levels XVII–VIII.

Written documentation on the history of Alalakh (and, to an extent, of Yamḫad) first appears in Level VII, which should be dated ca. 1650–1570 B.C. According to the tablets AT 1 and 456, King Abbān I of Yamḫad gave Alalakh to his younger brother Yarim-Lim in appreciation of his loyalty to him during a civil war and as compensation for the loss of his former fief, Irridi, east of the Euphrates. Yarim-Lim's installation as the appanage king of Alalakh was marked by the erection of a new great palace, a total rebuilding of the temple of Ištar, and the construction of a citadel. The palace archives yielded at least 175 Akkadian-written tablets, including legal contracts, judicial acts, deeds of purchase or exchange of towns, deliveries of food staples, loans, ration lists, etc. The texts bear witness to Alalakh's commercial relations with Emar and Carchemish on the Euphrates; with Ebla and other cities of Yamḫad; with Ugarit on the seacoast and Alashiya (Cyprus); with Tunip, Qatna, and Amurru in central Syria; and even with remote Babylonia. They also testify to a growing presence of a Hurrian-speaking element in northern Syria.

The period of Level VII encompassed the reigns of Yarim-Lim and his son Ammitaqum and ended in the destruction of Alalakh by the Hittite king Hattušiliš I. This event marked the beginning of a long series of Hittite campaigns aiming at the conquest of Yamḫad, which caused great destruction in northern Syria and culminated in the sack of Aleppo by Muršiliš I, ca. 1531 B.C. As for Alalakh, it was quickly rebuilt and regained a certain prosperity (Level VI) but no longer had a king of its own. Northern Syria became an object of contention among the Hittites, the Hurrian kingdom of Mitanni in northern Mesopotamia, and the 18th Dynasty of Egypt. An independent kingdom was briefly restored at Aleppo, ca. 1525 B.C., by Ilim-ilimma I, an offspring of the old dynasty of Yamḫad. The new king was, however, soon overthrown, probably at the instigation of Mitanni. A younger son of Ilim-ilimma, Idrimi, fled to Ammia in northern Phoenicia, where he was able to build ships and recruit troops and, after seven years of exile, to land in force on the coast of his homeland. He made Alalakh his capital and recovered his father's domain but was forced, after seven more years of hostilities, to enter into a vassalage treaty with Parattarna I, king of Mitanni, and to help him against the Hittites. Out of the Hittite booty he built a palace at Alalakh, part of which was uncovered in Level V. Idrimi reigned for thirty years (until ca. 1480 B.C.) and was succeeded by his son Adad-nirari, as stated in Idrimi's pseudo-autobiographical inscription.

No records survived from Level V (reigns of Idrimi and Adad-nirari) except for three of Idrimi's tablets that had been transferred to the archives of the Level IV palace. But it is known from the annals of Thutmose III and other Egyptian records of his time that, during that Pharaoh's war with Mitanni, he conquered northern Syria up to the Euphrates (in 1472 B.C.) and received tribute from Alalakh (in 1467 B.C.). In 1463 B.C., however, the Mitannians recovered all of northern Syria. The throne of Alalakh passed now to Idrimi's other son, Niqmepa, a loyal vassal of Mitanni. He built a new palace, different from the previous one in its architecture and orientation. The palace was expanded by Niqmepa's son Ilim-ilimma II, but was burned and destroyed, probably by the Hittite king Tudhaliyaš I in ca. 1430 B.C. The period of the existence of Niqmepa's palace forms Level IV of Alalakh. The ruins of the palace revealed an archive of about three hundred tablets which include interstate treaties, testimonies of Alalakh's relations with its Mitannian overlords, legal documents, census lists by settlements and socio-legal classes, ration lists, inventories, and other records. The tablets display a very significant increase of Hurrian influence in onomastica and vocabulary, which no doubt reflects the political influence of Mitanni. The inscribed statue of Idrimi dates from the time of Level IV.

Very little epigraphic material comes from Level III. Alalakh and most of the rest of northern Syria remained under the overlordship of Mitanni. When the Hittite king Šuppiluliumas I invaded Syria in 1366 B.C., the king of Mukiš-Alalakh, Itur-Addu, and his allies of Niya and Nuḫašše resisted him but finally lost. The fall of Alalakh to Šuppiluliumaš marks the transition to Level II. The victorious Hittite king gave much of Alalakh's territory to the pro-Hittite kingdom of Ugarit and to the newly established kingdom of Carchemiš and created from the rest of it another Hittite appanage under the name "Kingdom of Halab." After that, Alalakh was ruled by Hittite princes. Hittite presence is evidenced from a couple of Hittite tablets, several Hittite stamps, and a stele with a Hittite hieroglyphic inscription. Along with the Hittite capital, Hattušaš, and most cities of western Syria, Alalakh was utterly destroyed by the invasion of the Sea Peoples soon after 1200 B.C., and was never rebuilt.

C. Importance of the Alalakh Finds

Alalakh has no direct bearing on the Bible because of the geographical and chronological distance between them. Indirectly, however, it is of interest to biblical studies by the light it sheds on the Syro-Palestinian and Near Eastern context of biblical *realia*. The relevant points are here succinctly summarized.

1. The inscriptional and stratigraphical material from Alalakh, with its direct and indirect synchronisms with Mari, Assyria, Babylonia, the Hittite kingdom, and Egypt, was of paramount importance for the revision of ancient Near Eastern chronology of the second millennium B.C.

2. The texts from Level VII disclosed the political structure of the Great Kingdom of Yamḫad, the largest West Semitic state of the Middle Bronze Age. Of particular interest is the vassalage treaty between King Abbān of Yamḫad and his brother Yarim-Lim of Alalakh.

3. The texts of Level IV present a vivid picture of a medium-sized Syrian state of the Late Bronze Age, at the time of Mitannian hegemony. They show us a stratified society of several legally determined classes, from the highest *(mariannu)* to the lowest *(ḫubšu),* and give us a clearer notion of their respective obligations and privileges than do other sources. The term *ḫubšu* has been often equated with Heb *ḥopšî* "freeman," but most likely incorrectly.

4. The ubiquitous ḪABIRU are mentioned in several texts of Level IV (and probably in a date formula of Level VII) as a specific group of the population. Far from being described as a heterogenous and despised assemblage of refugees, fugitives, and outlaws without civil rights (as claimed by a widely accepted theory), they appear as bearers of arms in census lists, one of them is registered as a priest of the goddess Išḫara, and we hear of a Ḫapiru "house" (in this case, as often in Akk and Heb phraseology, meaning a tribal unit) consisting of 1,436 men, eighty of whom owned chariots, which would put them on the same military level as the *mariannu* class.

5. The treaties between Idrimi and Pilliya (AT 3) and between Niqmepa and Ir-[d]IM, of Tunip (AT 2) (both translated by Reiner in *ANET*, 531–32) are among the earliest of their kind in the Near East and of considerable juridical and diplomatic interest.

6. The texts of Level VII and especially of Level IV, though none of them is written in Hurrian, contain so many Hurrian personal names and Hurrian loan words that they have made an important contribution to our knowledge of the Hurrian language (see Draffkorn 1955).

7. The biographical inscription of Idrimi, written in the first person but actually composed some years after his death, is an early and in many ways unique specimen of Syro-Palestinian narrative literature, unique in its time but anticipating, in a way, such biblical biographical stories as those of Joseph and David (see Wiseman 1955 for this and other parallels).

8. Finally, the succession of palaces and temples at Alalakh forms a chapter in the history of Syro-Palestinian secular and sacral architecture, including those of Israel and Judah.

Bibliography

Albright, W. F. 1957. Further Observations on the Chronology of Alalaḫ. *BASOR* 146: 26–34.

Astour, M. C. 1969. The Partition of the Confederacy of Mukiš-Nuḫašše-Nii by Šuppiluliuma. *Or* n.s. 38: 381–414, Pl. 51.

———. 1972. Ḫattušiliš, Ḫalab, and Ḫanigalbat. *JNES* 31: 102–9.

———. 1989. *Hittite History and Absolute Chronology of the Bronze Age.* Partille, Sweden.

Collon, D. 1975. *The Seal Impressions from Tell Atchana/Alalakh.* AOAT 27. Kevelaer and Neukirchen-Vluyn.

Dietrich, M., and Loretz, O. 1969a. Die soziale Struktur von Alalaḫ und Ugarit (II). *WO* 5: 57–93.

———. 1969b. Die soziale Struktur von Alalaḫ und Ugarit (V). *UF* 1: 37–64.

———. 1970. Die soziale Struktur von Alalaḫ und Ugarit (IV). *ZA* 60: 88–123.

———. 1981. Die Inschrift der Statue des Königs Idrimi von Alalaḫ. *UF* 13: 201–69.

Draffkorn, A. 1955. *Hurrians and Hurrian at Alalaḫ.* Diss. Pennsylvania.

Gates, M. -H. C. 1976. *Alalakh-Tell Atchana, Levels VI and V.* Diss. Yale.

———. 1981. Alalakh Levels VI and V. *SMS* 4: 11–50.

———. 1987. Alalakh and Chronology Again. Pp. 60–86 in *High, Middle, or Low?*, ed. P. Åström. Gothenburg.

Klengel, H. 1965. *Geschichte Syriens im 2.* Jahrtausend v.u.Z. Vol. 1. Berlin.
———. 1981. Historischer Kommentar zur Inschrift des Idrimi von Alalaḫ. *UF* 13: 269–78.
Mellink, M. 1957. Review of *Alalakh* by L. Woolley. *AJA* 61: 395–400.
Smith, S. 1940. *Alalakh and Chronology.* London.
———. 1949. *The Statue of Idri-mi.* London.
Wiseman, D. J. 1953. *The Alalakh Tablets.* London.
———. 1954. Supplementary Copies of Alalakh Tablets. *JCS* 8: 1–30.
———. 1958. Abban and Alalaḫ. *JCS* 12: 124–29.
———. 1959a. Ration Lists from Alalakh VII. *JCS* 13: 19–33.
———. 1959b. Ration Lists from Alalakh IV. *JCS* 13: 50–59.
———. 1967. Alalakh. Pp. 117–35 in *Archaeology and Old Testament Study,* ed. D. Winton Thomas. Oxford.
Woolley, L. 1953. *A Forgotten Kingdom.* Baltimore.
———. 1955. *Alalakh: An Account of the Excavations at Tell Atchana in the Hatay, 1937–1949.* Oxford.

Michael C. Astour

ALCIMUS (PERSON) [Gk *Alkimos*]. Name of a high priest who held office in Jerusalem in the years 161–159 B.C.E. (1 Maccabees 7; 9; 2 Maccabees 14). He is condemned by the author of 1 Maccabees as the leader of the "lawless and irreligious" Jews (1 Macc 7:5). The name "Alcimus" is Greek, and it probably stands for the Hebrew *"Yakim,"* which may be equivalent to *"Eliakim"* (cf. 1 Chr 24:12 in the LXX).

Alcimus was probably appointed to office by Antiochus V and Lysias to succeed Menelaus. When Demetrius I took over the Seleucid throne, Alcimus approached him and was reconfirmed by him in his office. About two years later he passed away, and the high priesthood remained vacant for several years.

The ancient sources are inimical towards Alcimus. According to 2 Maccabees he "defiled himself" in the time of the persecutions (14:3), while 1 Maccabees inculpates him in the treacherous murder of sixty Hasidim (7:12–16); and his death is explained as a punishment for his tearing down a wall in the temple (9:54–56). This information should be treated skeptically, since both authors had their reasons to criticize Alcimus, who was an opponent of Judas and a contender for the high priesthood, which was taken by the Hasmoneans shortly afterward (152 B.C.E.).

It is impossible to place Alcimus exactly within the various groups within Jewish society at that time. The fact that he replaced Menelaus and was negotiating with the Hasidim would show him to be lesser a Hellenizer than 1 and 2 Maccabees would like us to believe. Nevertheless the breach between him and the Hasidim, and the legend concerning him and the sage Yosi son of Yoezer (*Gen. Rab.* 65:26 and parallels) point to a certain division between him and the Hasidim which might have been on religious grounds, as well as with Judas and his followers on political grounds. The additional meager information from Josephus is that he was not of the Oniad house (*Ant* 12. 387), but we do know that he was a priest (*Ant* 20. 235). According to *Genesis Rabbah* (65. 26) Alcimus was the nephew of Rabbi Josi ben Yoezer, who himself was of priestly family. There his name is Yakim Iṣ Zerorot. Alcimus' position within Jewish society of that time is hard to define. Scholars propose various suggestions, from mild hellenizer to pietist leader. However, the most we can assume is to envision Alcimus as politically pro-Seleucid, culturally a non-hellenizer and socially opposed to the Hasmoneans.

Uriel Rappaport

ALEMA (PLACE) [Gk *Alema*]. Usually understood as one of six cities in Gilead where Jews were being held captive by the Gentile inhabitants of the cities after the rededication of the Temple (1 Macc 5:26). News of their plight was delivered by Nabateans to Judas Maccabeus, who was already three days' journey across the Jordan, coming to the defense of Jews who had fled Gentile persecution to the city of Dathema. After Judas rescued the Jews in Dathema, he turned to attack a city whose name is listed as Alema in several MSS, and liberated Jews in Chaspo, Maked, Bosor, Carnaim, "and the other cities of Gilead" (5:36, 44). Thus, 1 Macc 5:35–44 seems to describe the defeat of five of the six cities mentioned by the Nabateans. The site of Alema is unknown, but is often identified with Alma, located eight and one-half miles SE of Bosor (Abel *GP,* 241; Baly *GB,* 216). Some scholars (e.g. Abel *GP,* 34) suggest it might also be the city of Helam mentioned in 2 Sam 10:16.

This reading of 1 Macc 5:26, 35 is by no means certain, however. Goldstein (*1 Maccabees* AB, 301) notes a change in prepositions from *"eis"* (at) to *"en"* (in) before the word "Alema," suggesting that "Alema" was the name of the district in which Bosor was located and that Jews were under siege in only five cities: Bozrah, Bosor in Alema, Chaspho, Maked, and Carnaim. Also, the mention of "Alema" in 5:35 is by no means certain. Various MSS of 1 Maccabees read "Mella," "Mala," "Mapha," or "Maapha." Goldstein cogently argues (*1 Maccabees* AB, 302) that a scribe would hardly alter a text in which one of the places mentioned in 5:26 reappeared, but might well supply a name from 5:26 not specifically listed in 5:35 as being defeated. Hence, he concluded that the place name in 5:35 was irretrievably lost.

Bibliography

Tedesche, S., and Zeitlin, S. 1950. *The First Book of Maccabees.* New York.

Paul L. Redditt

ALEMETH (PERSON) [Heb *ʿālemet*]. The name of two men in the book of 1 Chronicles.

1. Son of Becher and grandson of Benjamin according to 1 Chr 7:8. The genealogy of Benjamin in that chapter is at variance with the Benjamin genealogies in the Torah (Gen 46:21; Num 26:38–41) and elsewhere in 1 Chronicles (8:1–40); this, combined with other factors, has led some scholars to assume that 1 Chr 7:8–12 originally described another tribe, and was incorrectly attributed to Benjamin (*Chronicles* ICC, 147–149). However, it is not unusual for variant genealogical traditions to exist for a single tribe, since each variant might have served a different function, might date from a different period, or might reflect a different understanding of the power relationships within the tribe (Johnson 1969 and Wilson 1977). Thus, the received text is probably correct, and 1 Chr 7:8–12 should be understood as a Benjaminite genealogy (*Chronicles* NCBC, 77–78). Some evidence suggests that this genealogy in its final form might date to the postexilic period (*1 Chronicles* AB, 53). According to 1 Chr 6:45(— Eng 6:60), Alemeth was a levitical city in Benjamin (See ALEMETH [PLACE]). Anathoth, also a city in Benjamin, is mentioned alongside Alemeth. Thus, the creator of this section of the genealogy was defining a relationship between various Benjaminite cities by positing an ancient kinship relationship between ancestors with the city names. This practice is typical of genealogical thinking (Wilson 1977), and is found elsewhere in biblical genealogies (Demsky 1982). The connection of the personal name "Alemeth" to a specifically Benjaminite city suggests that the attribution of the genealogy to Benjamin in 1 Chr 7:6 is correct. The connection to Benjamin is further fostered by the overlap of the names Jeremoth/Jerimoth and Elioenai/Elienai in both chapter 7 (vv 7 and 8) and in the Benjamin genealogy in chapter 8 (vv 14 and 20). The minimal extent of overlap between these two genealogies and the placement of Alemeth at radically different periods of the tribe's history is not surprising; it is not unusual for very different relationships between ancestors or clans to be posited by different genealogies of the same tribe.

2. A descendant of Saul, son of either Jehoaddah (1 Chr 8:36) or Jarah (1 Chr 9:42). If we accept the reading of 9:42 and connect Jarah *(yᶜrh)* with the city Kiriath-jearim *(qryt yᶜrym),* then this verse which mentions Alemeth, Azmaveth, and Moza, all city names in Benjamin, is using genealogical language to describe the dispersion of the Benjaminite clans (Demsky 1971: 19). On the doubling of the Benjamin genealogy in 1 Chronicles 8 and 9, see AHAZ.

Bibliography

Demsky, A. 1971. The Genealogy of Gibeon (1 Chr 9:35–44): Biblical and Epigraphic Considerations. *BASOR* 202: 16–23.

———. 1982. The Genealogy of Menasseh and the Placement of the Inheritance of Milcah Daughter of Zelophehad. *EI* 16:70–75. (In Hebrew).

Johnson, M. 1969. *The Purpose of the Biblical Genealogies.* Cambridge.

Wilson, R. R. 1977. *Genealogy and History in the Biblical World.* New Haven.

MARC Z. BRETTLER

ʾALEP. The first letter of the Hebrew alphabet.

ALEXANDER THE GREAT (PERSON). Alexander III of Macedon, "the Great," was born in July 356 B.C., the son of Philip II and the Epirote princess Olympias. His childhood years coincided with the expansion of Macedonian power both S into the Greek peninsula and E through the Balkans. Greek authors of the time described Philip II as a man of extreme ambition, a trait which Alexander himself was to display in great measure throughout his life. His mother, to whom Alexander had a much closer attachment than to his father, was also ambitious, both for herself and for her son, and may be largely responsible for his belief that he had a special relationship with the gods. For about three years (ca. 342–340) Aristotle acted as Alexander's tutor. It is impossible to say how far he influenced the thinking of his royal pupil, though Alexander's love for Homer's *Iliad* may be due in part to Aristotle.

Alexander acted as regent for his father in 340, and in 338 commanded the left wing of the Macedonian army, facing the Theban Sacred Band at the battle of Chaeronea, at which the combined forces of Thebes and Athens were crushed and Macedonia became the arbiter of the destiny of the Greek states. After the battle, Alexander escorted the bones of the Athenian dead to Athens—the only occasion on which he visited that city.

In 337, Philip divorced Olympias and married the much younger Cleopatra, daughter of a Macedonian noble. The marriage caused great dissension in the royal family, with Alexander both indignant for his mother's sake and concerned about his own prospects of succession. Hence when Philip was assassinated in the following year, there was some suspicion that Olympias and Alexander were behind the assassination. Nevertheless, Alexander succeeded with little difficulty, thanks to the support of senior generals such as Antipater and Parmenion, though there did occur the usual liquidation of potential rivals and enemies. In Greece, he was swiftly recognized as *hēgēmōn* (Leader) of the Greek League of Corinth established by his father in the previous year and as commander-in-chief of the forces for the impending invasion of the Persian Empire. The following year, 335, was spent in securing the N frontier of Macedonia against barbarian uprisings and in suppressing a rebellion in Greece led by Thebes. The ruthless destruction and enslavement of Thebes was an act of terror to deter similar revolts during the king's absence in Asia.

The campaign against Persia was the major legacy of Philip to Alexander. It was to be a joint campaign of Macedonians and the Greeks of the League of Corinth under the command of Philip, the Macedonian king. The publicly proclaimed reasons for the attack were to liberate the Greek cities of Asia Minor from Persian control and to punish the Persians for the burning of Greek temples 150 years earlier under Xerxes. Other factors motivating Philip will have been the prospect of plunder and the acquisition of territory. A Macedonian army had been operating in NW Asia Minor since 336. We do not know how far, if at all, Philip's intentions went beyond those publicly proclaimed; and this is true also for Alexander, when he crossed into Asia in the spring of 334. The army which he led amounted to about 40,000 men and 160 ships. The kernel of the army was about 15,000 Macedonians, superbly trained and organized by Philip. The League of Corinth supplied 7,000 troops and the fleet, in whose loyalty Alexander appeared to have little confidence.

The first two years of the war (334–333) saw the majority of the coast of Asia Minor and the major centers in the interior fall into Macedonian hands. The Persian armies were twice defeated in pitched battles: at the river Granicus, soon after the crossing, and at Issus in November 333. At Issus the Persian king Darius himself led his army; his flight from the battlefield left his family hostage to Alexander. Soon after the Granicus victory, the Greek cities of Asia Minor who joined Alexander were given their freedom and democratic governments. But at the same time, his lack of confidence in his Greek fleet and the strength of the Persian fleet caused him to disband his fleet and adopt the strategy of conquering the Persian fleet from the land. This meant gaining control of all bases used by the Persians and also opened up the real danger of a Persian naval counterattack on Greece and Macedonia. Indeed, the Persians made such good use of their naval opportunities in the Aegean that Alexander was obliged to form a new navy in 333 and the danger was not finally averted until mid-332. To gain control of the home bases of the Persian fleet, Alexander was committed to the conquest of the seaboard as far south as Egypt—far beyond the limits of Asia Minor. His expanding ambitions can be further seen in his reply to the offer of peace made by Darius after Issus, in which Alexander rejects peace and claims now to be "Lord of Asia," that is, the Persian empire, only a small part of which he had hitherto conquered.

The greater part of 332 was taken up with the seven-month siege of Tyre, which supplied the main contingent to the Persian fleet. During the siege, a second peace offer, in which Darius offered to cede the whole W part of his empire as far as the river Euphrates, was rejected. The capture and enslavement of Tyre, preceded by the final breakup of the Persian fleet, was reminiscent of the brutality of the capture of Thebes. Then moving S and capturing Gaza after a two-month siege, Alexander entered the Persian satrapy of Egypt unopposed. Here, as well as honoring the local gods, he was crowned Pharaoh, thus becoming the son of Amun-Re. This divine sonship may have been one of the factors which impelled him to visit the famous oracle of Ammon in the desert at Siwah. Ammon (Amun) had long been equated by Greeks with Zeus, and sonship of Ammon could well be understood as meaning the sonship of Zeus. Certainly Alexander visited the oracle because Perseus and Heracles, to both of whom he traced his ancestry, had consulted it; and emulation of his divine ancestors increasingly played an important part in Alexander's actions. What questions he put and what answers he received are beyond our knowledge, but it is possible that any belief he may have had in his own superhuman nature was strengthened by the visit. It was probably before the visit that he laid the foundations of what was rapidly to become the greatest city in the Mediterranean world (see ALEXANDRIA).

In spring 331, Alexander left Egypt to strike into the heart of the Persian empire for the decisive engagement with Darius, who had been gathering a new army for almost two years. The battle that took place at Gaugamela on October 1st sealed the fate of Darius and his empire, though Darius once again escaped from the battlefield. One source tells us that after the battle Alexander was proclaimed King of Asia, presumably by his Macedonians.

Instead of pursuing Darius E, Alexander turned S to seize the major cities of the Persian empire, especially Babylon, Susa, and Persepolis. At Babylon, he appointed a former Persian enemy as satrap (governor)—the first of a series of such appointments in the central and E satrapies. This practice may have been calculated to win over the Iranian governing class, but it was bound to be controversial with the Macedonians. The climax of his lengthy stay at Persepolis was the deliberate burning of the royal palace, perhaps intended as a symbol of the overthrow of Achaemenid Persia.

In late spring 330, Alexander set out in pursuit of Darius, who had been trying to raise a new army in Media. Significantly, the Greek troops of the League of Corinth were now discharged and sent home, a sign that the original purpose of the expedition was now completed. The hapless Darius was betrayed by his lieutenants and murdered. His alleged dying request to Alexander to avenge his murder enabled the Macedonian to portray himself as the legitimate successor and avenger of Darius and the assassins as regicides and rebels. When the leading regicide, Bessus, was captured, he was punished and executed in the traditional Persian way of dealing with rebels—another sign of Alexander's growing assumption of the style of the Great King. Soon after Darius' death, in Hyrcania, Alexander began to wear the dress of the defeated Medes and Persians, though perhaps at first only in his dealings with the Iranians.

The next two-and-a-half years, until early 327, were occupied with the reduction of the satrapies of the E and NE of the Persian empire, especially Bactria and Sogdiana. The fighting encountered in this area was perhaps the most difficult and constant yet encountered by the Macedonians, since for the first time they were facing what might be called "nationalist" resistance against the foreign conqueror, whatever claims to legitimacy he might make. Indeed, Alexander's marriage to the Sogdian princess Rhoxane (late 328) was probably more a political gesture than the love match described by ancient sources; it was certainly not popular with the Macedonians, who regarded it as degrading for their king to marry a foreign captive. The founding in this area of a large number of "cities," populated mainly by Macedonian veterans and Greek mercenaries, is a testimony to its warlike and rebellious nature. For the cities were intended primarily as garrisons; economic and "cultural" motives were purely secondary.

During these years in the E satrapies, there occurred three incidents which indicate a growing undercurrent of hostility and resentment among the Macedonian nobility toward Alexander, especially in connection with his orientalizing practices. The first, in late 330, was the alleged conspiracy of Philotas, the commander of the elite Companion cavalry. The execution of Philotas and subsequent murder of his father, Parmenion, removed a powerful family group inherited by Alexander from Philip. The murder by Alexander of Clitus, another of the older Macedonians, during a drunken quarrel at Bactra in 328 was caused by Clitus' outspoken criticism of Alexander's growing "orientalism." An attempt, perhaps in early 327, by Alexander to extend to Macedonians and Greeks the Persian practice of *proskynēsis*, or abasement before the king, foundered on the opposition led by Alexander's own court historian, the Greek Callisthenes, nephew of Aristotle. It is possible that Alexander's reason for trying to introduce this ceremony went beyond a desire to have a uniform court ceremonial. To Greeks and Macedonians, prostration implied the worship of a god, and Alexander, the descendent of Heracles and son of Zeus-Ammon, may have been paving the way for the announcement of his own divinity. Soon after this a conspiracy to murder the king, formed by the Royal Pages, was discovered. Their leader, when arrested, gave Alexander's increasing orientalism and un-Macedonian behavior as the impulse for their attempt. The Pageboys were executed, as was their tutor, Callisthenes, whom Alexander believed to be behind the plot. The killing of Callisthenes probably exercised a deep influence on the attitude towards Alexander of the Peripatetic school of philosophy, founded by Aristotle, Callisthenes' uncle.

In the spring of 327, the army crossed the Hindu Kusch to begin the invasion and conquest of what the Greeks called India (roughly modern Pakistan). The Indian campaign, which lasted for over two years, had been planned by Alexander for at least three years. India had once been a part of the Achaemenid empire; Heracles and Dionysus were believed to have been there; and contemporary geography conceived of India as being much smaller than it really was and as terminating eastward in the encircling ocean. The desire to reclaim his rightful inheritance, to equal and even surpass the exploits of his ancestor and of Dionysus, and to reach the bounds of Asia and the world were powerful motives for Alexander's invasion. After securing the voluntary submission of the ruler of Taxila, Alexander defeated the neighboring king, Porus, in a battle on the river Hydaspes (modern Jhelum) in June 326. Porus was reinstated in his kingdom, but as Alexander's vassal. By now the Macedonians were probably aware that the end of India was not near; it stretched eastward interminably, with endless marching and fighting in prospect. It is not therefore surprising that at the river Hyphasis (modern Beas), the soldiers refused to go further, forcing Alexander to abandon his ambitions in this direction. The army did not, however, simply retrace its route westward, for Alexander put into operation another long-matured plan—to voyage down the river Indus to the sea and then to attempt a land march and sea voyage along the coast to the Persian Gulf and back to the center of the empire. The joint naval and military descent of the Indus involved much savage and brutal fighting, with the Brahmins leading the native resistance and Alexander pursuing a policy of wholesale slaughter. The king himself was nearly killed in the assault on one town, and the severity of his wound may have contributed to his early death. Despite the awful slaughter, the conquest of India was largely ephemeral and a failure.

Arriving at the Indus delta in the summer of 325, Alexander set about preparations for the joint naval and military expedition westward. The fleet was commanded by the king's old friend Nearchus; Alexander himself led the army, less a large detachment that had already been sent westward by an easier route. The army was to leave first and was ostensibly to reconnoitre possible harbors and leave supplies for the fleet. Its march led it through the Gedrosian desert (Makran), whose inhospitable nature Alexander must have known; but he was eager to succeed in bringing an army through a region where Cyrus the Great and the legendary Semiramis had failed. Heat and lack of food and water turned the march into an unparalleled disaster, in which as many as 90,000 persons may have died. It was a grave blow to Alexander's pride and reputation. The fleet, too, suffered great privations, but eventually, about December 325, it joined up with the remnants of the army in Carmania. The voyage had, at any rate, shown that it was possible to sail from the Indus to the Euphrates.

On his return to the center of the empire early in 324, Alexander found a state of turmoil and confusion. His prolonged absence in India had led many to believe that he would never return. Consequently many satraps had engaged in oppression and mismanagement and were behaving as independent dynasts. Many of the oppressive satraps were Iranians, but prominent Macedonians were also found guilty. Alexander's friend and treasurer, Harpalus, had grossly abused his position and fled westward to Greece before Alexander's arrival, taking with him a large amount of money and many mercenary soldiers. Harpalus' money was to play an important part in the Athenian-led revolt against Macedonia which broke out upon Alexander's death. The task of punishing the guilty and reestablishing the king's authority lasted for several months into 324.

The year 324 was eventful in other ways. Despite opposition amongst the Macedonian nobility and the apparent failure of his Iranian satraps, Alexander pressed on with his orientalizing policy. At Susa, a mass wedding celebration was held at which eighty of the king's close friends and companions married noble Iranian brides. The ordinary Macedonian soldiers too had their unions with native women solemnly legitimized. About 30,000 Persian youths, trained in Macedonian weaponry and significantly called by Alexander his "successors," reached Susa and were incorporated in the army. This last event especially vexed the Macedonian soldiers, whose resentment of Alexander's orientalizing practices had been steadily growing over the years. Soon after, at Opis, Alexander's demobilizing of 10,000 veteran Macedonians provoked them to mutiny. They believed that their king no longer held them in high regard and was trying to get rid of them and replace them with orientals. The mutiny was broken by Alexander's clever use of psychological tactics, and the men agreed to their discharge. Before their departure Alexander, in a grand symbolic gesture, held a huge banquet for 9,000 Macedonians and Persians, with the Macedonians holding the places of honor. At the banquet Alexander pronounced his famous prayer for "concord and partnership of the empire for Macedonians and Persians." Scholarly opinion is divided as to whether this was a genuinely programmatic utterance or merely an empty gesture at the end of a dangerous incident. Certainly the basic problem still remained: if Alexander was to continue as Lord of Asia, what was his relationship to be with the Macedonians, who had won Asia for him and on whom he was still greatly dependent?

A little before this, Alexander had issued a decree to all the Greek cities to receive back their political exiles. His motives for this are puzzling: he may have wished to ensure for himself partisans in the Greek cities which were hostile to Macedonian domination, or it may have been intended as a beneficent gesture which would solve a long festering and disruptive pattern among the Greeks. But the decree, a clear breach of the covenant of the League of Corinth, was a major factor in the decision of Athens and other cities to try to shake off the Macedonian yoke. Some scholars believe that this decree was accompanied by a request from Alexander to the Greeks to worship him as a god. A god, it is suggested, could properly interfere in the internal affairs of the League of Corinth, though its Macedonian leader could not. Such an argument is almost certainly mistaken. Yet it is certain that Greek cities in 324 debated and in some instances agreed to Alexander's deification, and it is highly likely that the impulse came from Alexander himself. Why Alexander wished to be worshiped by the Greeks must remain a matter for speculation. It is improbable that he wanted to establish a theocratic empire. There is no evidence that Persians and other Iranians received such a request, and he must have been fully conscious of the hostility of his Macedonians to such an idea. But there were precedents among the Greeks for the worship of a living ruler; indeed, it is almost certain that cults of Alexander himself had already been established by the Greek cities of Asia Minor at the time of their liberation. It is almost certain too that Philip himself had, at the end of his life, both believed in his own divinity and been the object of cult worship in some Greek cities. Alexander, the son of Zeus-Ammon and the descendant of the god Heracles, had surpassed all mortals, as well as Heracles and the god Dionysus, in the magnitude of his achievements. He may well have considered that the appropriate recognition of his greatness was to be worshiped as a living god and that the Greeks were the appropriate people to accord him this honor. His deification created a powerful precedent for his successors (see below) who, in Ptolemaic Egypt and Seleucid Syria, established cults of themselves and their relatives. The worship of Roman emperors may be seen as the continuation and extension of the well-established tradition of ruler-cult among the Greeks.

But if he was given divine status by the Greeks, he did not live long to enjoy it. The death of his closest friend and virtual deputy, Hephaestion, in late 324 was a devastating blow to the king. In the late spring of 323, he was in Babylon preparing the enormous naval and military forces needed for his projected conquest of the Arabian peninsula. The motives for the expedition, which was associated with plans to colonize the Persian Gulf, were commercial and personal. Arabia was famed for its spices; but Alexander, hearing that the Arabs worshiped only two gods, was eager to be added to that number. The preparations were well advanced when the king was struck by an illness and died on 10 June 323. Some believed that he was poisoned, but it is more likely that his death was the result of disease, perhaps malaria, exacerbated by constant heavy drinking and a constitution weakened by wounds and years of hardship. His body, after lying in state in Babylon, was to have been transported to Aegeae in Macedonia, there to be buried with the other kings of Macedonia. But Ptolemy, after gaining the satrapy of Egypt in the division of the empire among the leading generals, seized the body and took it to Egypt, where it lay for centuries in the king's own city, Alexandria.

The nature of our ancient evidence, with its tendency to heroize Alexander, makes it difficult to give an accurate assessment of the king and his achievements. Some traits in his personality seem certain: he was passionate in his nature and capable of great excesses in his emotions; he could be extravagantly generous to his friends and to those who voluntarily submitted themselves to him, but ruthless and brutal in suppressing opposition, real or imagined. He was a hard drinker and capable of great violence when drunk. His admiration for Greek culture, especially the poetry of Homer, cannot be doubted. He was deeply conscious of his heroic and divine ancestors, Achilles and Heracles, and eager to emulate and surpass them, particularly Heracles. Those who speak of his "heroic" nature refer mainly to his insatiable and consuming desire for glory, which was to be gained by conquest and doing what nobody before him had done, and his constant desire to do something new was complemented by a mind that was always eager to see something new. From his early years, perhaps under the influence of his mother, he had regarded himself as set apart from the rest of humanity; and it is no cause for surprise that in his later years he should have become convinced of his own divinity.

As a general he owed much to the army and officers he inherited from Philip. He was a great tactician and cavalry commander, but his ability as a grand strategist is open to question. The siege of Tyre shows not necessarily his siegecraft, but his single-minded determination. That he was a great and inspiring leader of men is obvious from the fact that his Macedonians followed him as far as India before refusing to go further, despite the years away from home and the appalling hardships frequently encountered. Even the meeting at Opis was partly motivated by the men's jealousy for Alexander's affections, and their grief at his death was deep, though significantly they later insisted that Philip Arrhidaeus, the feebleminded but Macedonian-born half-brother of Alexander, should succeed Alexander in joint kingship with Alexander IV, the infant son of the oriental Rhoxane. They loved his person while rejecting his policies.

There are many deficiencies in Alexander as a ruler. His lust for overseas glory and conquest meant that his native Macedonia was deprived of its king for virtually the whole of his reign, though the demands made on Macedonian manpower for these conquests may have permanently weakened the homeland. His failure to reconcile the Greek city-states to Macedonian rule resulted in the widespread revolt which broke out on the news of his death. In Asia itself he made only minor changes to the Achaemenid system of government, perhaps because he regarded it as generally satisfactory, perhaps because he did not have the time, but perhaps because he was not interested in the art of government. Certainly the turmoil in which he found the empire on his return from India demonstrated the need for a period of firm and benevolent government. Yet Alexander's main concern in these last years seems to have been with plans for ever more conquest on an enormous scale. The claim of one ancient writer that "under Alexander's kingship it was not possible for the ruled to be the victims of injustice at the hands of their rulers" cannot be taken as universally valid. It is highly improbable that, as has been claimed, Alexander was a believer in universal "Brotherhood of Man" or that he wished to blend together, "as in a loving-cup," all the many different peoples of his empire. He was certainly aware of the problem facing him as a foreign conqueror ruling over a proud people with an imperial heritage. If he was to remain Lord of Asia, he must win the adherence of the traditional governing class and try to reconcile these people and the Macedonians to each other, at least as long as he needed the Macedonians. He may have intended Macedonians and Iranians to become the joint ruling class of the empire, but there are signs that his inclinations were increasingly toward the ways of the East rather than the more austere and independent ways of Macedonia. Had he lived longer, the hardest task before Alexander would have been that of defining his relationship with his Macedonians.

The effects of Alexander's reign and conquests were far reaching. From the wars which broke out among his generals after his death there eventually emerged the great successor kingdoms of the East, each under its Macedonian dynastic family; the most important are Ptolemaic Egypt and Seleucid Syria. These are the states in which Hellenic civilization became modified into what is now called Hellenistic civilization. The Near East was opened up to Greek and Macedonian settlement and exploitation. Great cosmopolitan cities, each with its Greco-Macedonian upper class, grew up in the successor kingdoms, the most famous of which was Alexander's own Alexandria in Egypt, with its royally founded and endowed library and museum. Greek, in its modified *koine* form, became the language of the educated classes throughout the Near East. As early as the third century the OT was translated into Greek at Alexandria and Greek was the language of the NT (see SEPTUAGINT). The Greeks who migrated to these new cities took with them their culture as well as their language and thus brought about the spread of Hellenism. Nor was the process one-sided; Asian art, literature, and, above all, religion exerted increasing influence on the Greeks. For Greek religion offered little, either in the present or the future, to the ordinary person. But the mysteries of Isis and Osiris, Sarapis, Mithras, and eventually Christianity, which promised a life of bliss hereafter, were eagerly embraced by Greeks and Macedonians both in Asia and in the old country. During the second century Rome rapidly became the dominant power in the eastern Mediterranean, and it was this Hellenistic Greek civilization that overcame the fierce victors. Greek ideas, science, and literature were absorbed by the Romans and modified by their own native traditions and ways. The resulting Greco-Roman culture was in its turn transported by the Romans to their western provinces and so formed the basis of the civilization not only of the Latin countries, but of all western Europe.

Bibliography

Work on Alexander up to 1972:

Seibert, J. 1972. *Alexander der Grosse.* Erträge der Forschung 10. Darmstadt.

Special studies of Alexander:

Fox, R. L. 1973. *Alexander the Great.* London.

Hammond, N. G. L. 1981. *Alexander the Great: King, Commander and Statesman.* London.

Levi, M. A. 1981. *Alessandro Magno.* Milan.

Schachermeyr, F. 1973. *Alexander der Grosse.* Vienna.

Will, W. 1986. *Alexander der Grosse.* Stuttgart.

Influence of Alexander and his career:

Walbank, F. W. 1981. *The Hellenistic World.* Glasgow.

Welles, C. B. 1970. *Alexander and the Hellenistic World.* Toronto.

Wilcken, U. 1967. *Alexander the Great.* Trans. G. C. Richards and ed. E. N. Borza. New York.

R. D. Milns

ALEXANDER (PERSON) [Heb *Alexandros*]. **1.** Alexander Balas, also known as Alexander Epiphanes, was a pretender and eventual ruler of the Seleucid kingdom between 158 and 145 B.C.E. (1 Macc 10:1, 15–21, 47–67, 88–89; 11:1–17). The author of 1 Macc 10:1 calls him "Alexander Epiphanes, son of Antiochus (IV)," while other ancient authors call him "Alexander Balas." He claimed to be the son of Antiochus IV and therefore the rightful heir of the Seleucid throne. However, among the ancient sources only 1 Maccabees, Josephus, and Strabo believe his claim; the rest deny it. The name "Balas" may have been his original family name (Just. *Epit.* xxxv.1.6) or it may have been a form of Baal, a Syrian divine name equivalent to Alexander's divine name "Epiphanes."

When Demetrius I overthrew the weak Antiochus V and his prime minister Lysias, he incurred Rome's displeasure. Roman mistrust, plus Demetrius' foreign policies, disaffected him from the kings of Asia Minor and Egypt. Therefore, these kings and the Romans were willing to support a pretender to the throne.

In 158 B.C.E. Alexander Balas claimed to be the son of Antiochus IV; he even resembled his claimed brother, Antiochus V. The next year, Attalus II, king of Pergamum and enemy of Demetrius, sent Alexander to Cilicia, on the border of the Seleucid Kingdom, to establish Alexander's claim and threaten Demetrius. In the summer of 153, Alexander received the support of the Roman Senate for his claims to the Seleucid throne with the help of Laodice, the daughter of Antiochus IV, and Heracleides of Miletus, another enemy of Demetrius. While Demetrius developed a drinking problem, Alexander and Heracleides developed support and an army. In 152 Alexander took control of Ptolmais, with the help of a populace disgusted with Demetrius.

Demetrius sought the help of the Jews against Alexander by offering Jonathan, the brother of Judas Maccabees (1 Macc 9:28–31), the right to raise an army and rebuild the walls of Jerusalem. Alexander made Jonathan a counteroffer that included the high priesthood, royal honors, and military benefits. Despite Demetrius' further offer of lower taxes, freedom of religion, and political rights, Jonathan sided with Alexander (1 Macc 10:7–47; 11:28–37).

The ancient sources do not describe clearly the war between Alexander and Demetrius. Yet they do agree that in the summer of 150 Alexander secured the throne after Demetrius died in battle when he fell from his horse into a swamp. At that point the 23-year-old Alexander declared himself king. Ptolemy VI (Philometer) came to Ptolemais, where he gave his daughter, Cleopatra, in marriage to Alexander. Jonathan rode in state from Jerusalem to Ptolemais where Alexander honored him with a royal purple robe, the privilege of "Friend of First Rank," and the military and administrative governorship of Judah and three sections of Samaria (1 Macc 10:51–66).

Unfortunately, Alexander was lazy, inept, and licentious. Domination by his mistresses and friends alienated him from the populace. His friend Ammonius used the position of prime minister to eliminate his personal enemies. While Alexander lived at Ptolmais, his friends, Hierax and Diodotus (Tryphon), oppressively ruled Antioch.

After four years of growing discontent, Demetrius II, son of the dead king, sailed from his refuge at Knidos, Crete, with a mercenary army to Cilicia. Alexander moved from Ptolmais to Antioch to halt Demetrius' advance. The governor of Palestine, Appollonius, rebelled against Alexander, but Jonathan stopped the revolt. In 145, Ptolemy came to Alexander's aid with a land army and a navy. However, Ptolemy switched his allegiance from Alexander to Demetrius, claiming there was an attempt on his life by Alexander's friend Ammonius. When Alexander would not hand over Ammonius for punishment, Ptolemy assumed that Alexander had conspired against him. The sources do not agree on the story. Diodorus (32.9) claims that Ptolemy invented the story in order to justify his change of allegiance (1 Macc 11:8–12).

Alexander left Antioch and went to the area around Cilicia, presumably to fight Demetrius. Hierax and Tryphon also switched allegiance and turned the people of Antioch against Alexander. Ammonius tried to escape the city dressed as a woman but was found out and killed. Ptolemy VI then marched into Antioch and crowned himself the king of Asia. Then he offered his daughter, Cleopatra, to Demetrius II, along with a promise of support. Demetrius accepted both offers and came to Antioch, where Ptolemy crowned him as king of Asia and therefore as vassal to Egypt.

At this point Alexander returned from Cilicia to Antioch, where his army fought the armies of Demetrius and Ptolemy on the plains next to the Oinoparas River. When Alexander's army lost, he fled to Abai in Arabia, probably in the Syrian desert. He took refuge with a sheik variously named by the ancient sources as Diocles or Iamblichos (Diodorus), Zabdiel (1 Macc 11:17), or Eimalkouai (1 Macc 11:39). Alexander had left his infant son in the safekeeping of this sheik a year earlier. Assassins decapitated Alexander at Abai, though sources do not agree on their identity. Diodorus says that it was two of Alexander's friends, Heliades and Cassius (32.9c–10.1), while 1 Macc 11:17 says it was Zabdiel the Arab. Perhaps Zabdiel was the Arabic name of either Heliades or Cassius (Goldstein *1 Maccabees* AB, 428). Alexander's assassins brought his head to Ptolemy, just before Ptolemy died of battle wounds. Thus, Demetrius II Nicator replaced Alexander Balas.

Bibliography

Bevan, E. R. 1902. Vol. 1 of *The House of Seleucus*. New York.

Volkmann, H. 1925. Demetrius I und Alexander I von Syrien. *Klio* 19: 373–412.

MITCHELL C. PACWA

2. Son of Simon of Cyrene and brother of Rufus (Mark 15:21). In view of the large Jewish community in Cyrene and the probability that Simon had come to Jerusalem for the pilgrimage feast of Passover, we may assume Alexander and his family were Greek-speaking Jews (cf. Acts 2:10; 6:9; 11:20; 13:1). This judgment may receive further support from an ossuary discovered in the Kidron Valley in 1941, on which were found Greek and Hebrew inscriptions identifying the box as having been prepared for "Alexander, son of Simon" and, perhaps, "Alexander the Cyrenian." This latter reading is debated, though additional evidence in the tomb suggests that its owners were a family from the Diaspora Jewish community of Cyrenaica. Presumably, Alexander and his brother are mentioned by Mark because they were known to Mark's intended audience. This is suggested, first, by the fact that Simon is introduced curiously, not with reference to his father, as we might expect (cf. Mark 1:19; 2:14; 3:17, 18; 10:46), but to his sons. Second is the problem of the retention of the names by Mark; their omission by Matthew and Luke—most likely dependent on Mark—suggests that these two names had an additional significance beyond mere received tradition. This significance is obviously known only to Mark, but not important to Luke or Matthew. Indeed, elsewhere Mark is sparing enough with his use of proper names. Third, although mention of Simon in Mark allows a minor character to exemplify the humble role of a disciple, an important Markan motif, no such theological role can be assigned to the casual naming of Simon's sons. Some scholars find additional evidence of the connection of Alexander and Rufus with Mark's intended audience in the reference to Rufus, "chosen in the Lord," in Rom 16:13, but this begs many questions related to the location of Mark's church, the authorship of Romans 16, and the possibility of multiple persons bearing this name.

3. A relative of the high priest Annas (Acts 4:6). In this passage, Alexander appears to exert considerable influence in the affairs of the temple as a member of the high priest's family, which is contrasted with the uneducated apostles (Acts 4:13). Apart from this reference, nothing is known of this Alexander.

4. A Jew of Ephesus (Acts 19:33). In the course of Paul's evangelistic mission at Ephesus, the silversmith Demetrius incited a riot among the smiths of the city, who feared damage to their industry as a result of the iconoclasm of Paul's converts (Acts 19:23–41). During the confusion of the ensuing rally for Artemis in the theater, the Jews put forward Alexander as their spokesperson. Presumably, they expected him to disassociate the Jews from the followers of the Way. Recognizing Alexander was a Jew, thus no friend to Artemis, however, the mob refused him the opportunity to speak. Some have suggested that Alexander was himself a smith and was thus well suited to speak in this instance, and that this same Alexander reappears as an enemy of Paul in 2 Tim 4:14 (see #6 below); this is highly speculative.

5. False teacher at Ephesus (1 Tim 1:20). Alexander, together with Hymenaeus, is identified as having repudiated the faith (i.e., the gospel) and a good conscience, then as a result, as having been excommunicated from the church. If Alexander's teaching was consistent with the false teaching with which 1 Timothy is concerned, it was speculative, argumentative, given to asceticism, dualistic (with an attendant dim view of the material world), and possessive of an over-realized eschatology (cf. 1 Tim 1:3–7; 3:1–13; 4:3; 6:3–10). In spite of the reference to *gnosis* (knowledge) in 1 Tim 6:20–21, it is doubtful that we can claim Alexander as an early teacher of Gnosticism per se. It is easier to find here a less-developed attempt to syncretize the Christian faith with Jewish and Hellenistic philosophy. In any case, as a result of his activity, Alexander has been "handed over to Satan," an apparent reference to his being set outside the fellowship of the Christian community. Some, however, influenced by the parallel expression in 1 Cor 5:1–5, see here a more focused reference to Satan's role in physical punishment. The goal of this disciplinary action was restorative—i.e., that Alexander be taught not to blaspheme. Some have tried to identify this Alexander with that mentioned as Paul's foe in 2 Tim 4:14 (see #6 below). In this regard, it is noteworthy that both references, 1 Tim 1:20 and 2 Tim 4:14, refer to his being judged. Proponents of this view assume that, by the time of the writing of 2 Timothy, either Alexander has not yet been excommunicated or, even after having left Ephesus, he continues to pose a threat to Christian leaders like Timothy.

6. Metalworker at Ephesus (2 Tim 4:14). According to 2 Tim 4:14–15, Alexander had done great harm to Paul and had strongly opposed his message. It has been argued that this great harm should be identified with Alexander's role as a witness for the prosecution in Paul's trial in Rome. Others, noting that Timothy was warned to beware of Alexander in Asia Minor, have argued that he was instrumental in Paul's arrest. There is no firm evidence to identify this Alexander with either of the two men of the same name in Acts 19:33 and 1 Tim 1:20 (see #4–5 above). The name itself was common in the Hellenistic and Roman periods. (See Fee *Timothy, Titus* GNC).

Bibliography

Avigad, N. 1962. A Depository of Inscribed Ossuaries in the Kidron Valley. *IEJ* 12: 1–12.

Dibelius, M., and Conzelmann, H. 1972. The Pastoral Epistles. Hermeneia. Philadelphia.

Hengel, M. 1985. *Studies in the Gospel of Mark.* London.

Lee, G. M. 1975. Mark 15:21, "The Father of Alexander and Rufus." *NovT* 17: 303.

JOEL B. GREEN

ALEXANDRA SALOME (PERSON) [Gk *Alexandra Salome*]. Var. SALINA. Wife of the Hasmonean kings Aristobulus I and Alexander Jannaeus; mother of the high priest John Hyrcanus II and of the pretender to the throne Aristobulus II; and ruler of Judaea 78–69 B.C.E. (*Ant* 13.11.2; 13.12.1; 13.15.5; 13.16.1–6). Alexandra's first husband, Aristobulus I, had seized power from his mother, imprisoned her and his brothers, and let her starve in prison. As Aristobulus lay dying, Alexandra engineered the death of his brother and successor Antigonus in order to avoid her mother-in-law's fate. When Alexandra succeeded Aristobulus, she freed his brothers from prison and married the youngest, Alexander Jannaeus. Expecting him to be weak, she hoped to influence him to favor the Pharisee party. However, his monarchical claims and his aggressive foreign policy alienated the Pharisees, leading to an unsuccessful rebellion (90–85 B.C.E.) that cost 50,000 lives.

In 78 B.C.E., upon Alexander's death, Alexandra completed the conquest of Ragaba and triumphantly returned to Jerusalem as the queen. She made peace with the Pharisees and appointed as high priest her elder, weaker son, John Hyrcanus, a supporter of the Pharisees. The Pharisees executed anyone who helped Alexander Jannaeus persecute them, including Diogenes, the leader of the Sadducees. Her younger son, Aristobulus, a Sadducee supporter, complained to Alexandra. She acceded to his demand for control of some Judaean forts, unfortunately setting the stage for civil war after her death.

In foreign policy, Alexandra remained neutral in wars of Roman expansion and in Seleucid and Ptolmaic disputes. She fostered Judaean security by enlarging her army and by taking hostages from neighboring territories. The only military expedition during her reign was a futile attempt by her son, Aristobulus, to prevent the conquest of Damascus. Later, when Tigranes, king of Armenia, attacked Phoenicia, Alexandra avoided conflict by paying him large tribute. Otherwise, her reign was exceptionally prosperous.

In 69 B.C.E., when Alexandra fell ill, Aristobulus revolted by capturing twenty-two Judaean cities. Though reluctant to believe that he was rebelling, Alexandra eventually took his wife and children hostage. She underestimated Aristobulus' power when she advised Hyrcanus and the Pharisees not to worry. After her death, Aristobulus and Hyrcanus fought a civil war that led to Roman intervention and domination.

Bibliography

Klausner, J. 1972. Queen Salome Alexandra. Pp. 242–54 in *The Hellenistic Age,* Vol. 6 of *WHJP,* ed. A. Schalit. New Brunswick, NJ.

MITCHELL C. PACWA

ALEXANDRIA (PLACE) [Gk *Alexandreia*]. This article will focus mainly on the archeological evidence for the Jewish community in Alexandria up to 117 C.E. and for Christianity before Constantine.

A. History

Alexandria was founded by Alexander the Great in 331 B.C.E. on a site already partially occupied by a native Egyptian village, Rhakotis (31° N; 30° E). (The name "Rakote" was retained as a designation for Alexandria in Coptic usage.) Cleomenes of Naukratis was its first governor, and Deinokrates of Rhodes was its first architect. Upon the death of Alexander in 323 B.C.E. Egypt came under the rule of Ptolemy, a Macedonian general and companion of Alexander. Under Ptolemy I ("Soter") the city became the capital of Egypt, though as a Greek city it was often distinguished from Egypt proper. The city prospered under the Ptolemies and quickly became the cultural and educational center of the Hellenistic world.

1. The Jewish Community. Jewish immigration into Egypt from Palestine had begun as early as the 6th century B.C.E., and Jews flowed into the new city in large numbers almost from the beginning, many as prisoners of war. (Josephus reports that Alexander himself settled Jews in the city, *JW* 2.487; cf. *AgAp* 2.35.) The earliest archeological evidence for the Jewish community of Alexandria consists of tombs in the E necropolis of Ibrahimiya dating to the time of Ptolemy II, or perhaps as early as Ptolemy I (323–285 B.C.E.).

The Jews were organized as a *politeuma* ("Community"; cf. *Let. Aris.* 310), and were encouraged by the Ptolemies and later by the Roman emperors to live according to their ancestral customs. By the 1st century C.E. the Jewish population in Alexandria numbered in the hundreds of thousands. Philo claims that in his time there were at least a million Jews in Egypt (*Flacc* 43), and a large proportion of these must have lived in Alexandria.

With the coming of Roman rule in 30 B.C.E., the economic situation of the Jews in Egypt began to change. With the imposition of the *laographia* ("poll-tax") in 24/23 B.C.E., applicable to native Egyptians and other non-Greek groups, the concern for civic rights among many of the Jews became acute, and relations with the Greek population became strained. A pogrom against the Jews in 38 C.E. prompted a group of Jews, led by Philo, to appeal to the emperor, an appeal that was unsuccessful. The assassination of Caligula in 41 and the favorable attitude adopted by Claudius brought a temporary lull in the strife. Matters came to a head again in 66 when, with great loss of life, a riot was put down by Philo's apostate nephew, Tiberius Alexander, Prefect of Egypt (*JW* 2.487–98). A revolt of the Jews under Trajan in 115 brought massive destruction, and by the time it was put down in 117 the Jewish community had been virtually annihilated (Eus. *Hist. Eccl.* 4.2). One monument destroyed by the Jews during that revolt was the Nemeseion, built by Julius Caesar for the head of Pompey (Appian *BCiv.* 2.380), a structure some scholars have identified with the famous "Alabaster Tomb" now located in the Latin cemetery (cf. Fraser 1972,2: 108).

Jews did not become a significant presence in the city thereafter until the 4th century C.E. From that time a good deal of tension existed between them and the Christians, culminating in the destruction of the Jewish community under Archbishop Cyril in 415.

2. The Christian Community. The origins of Christianity in Alexandria are obscure, but it is safe to assume that the earliest Christians were Jews from Palestine. During the 2d century C.E. Christianity became a significant presence in the city, although archeological evidence for Christianity before the 4th century is very scanty.

After the Jewish revolt of 115–17 Hadrian sponsored considerable rebuilding in the city, but from the time of Caracella on (211–217) a number of disasters ensued: the city was sacked by Caracella in 215, by Aurelian in 273, and by Diocletian in 295. Further destruction, aimed at uprooting paganism, occurred under Christian rule. The most significant was the destruction of the Serapeum under Theodosius I in 391, led by Archbishop Theophilus. Further devastations occurred with the invasion of the Persians in 617 and its aftermath.

After the Arab conquest of Alexandria in 641, the city entered a period of many centuries of decline, eclipsed by the new capital at Fustat (Old Cairo) and by the maritime city of Rashid (Rosetta) on the mouth of the W branch of the Nile. By the time Napoleon and his forces arrived in Alexandria in 1798 it had been reduced to a small village of a few thousand inhabitants. The modern development of Alexandria as a city began under Muhammad Ali (1805–1848).

B. Topography

Alexandria was built on a ridge of land lying between the Mediterranean Sea to the NW and Lake Mareotis to the S. The dominant feature of the area is the bay formed by a promontory called in ancient times "Lochias" (modern Silsileh), protected by the island of Pharos lying offshore. Our knowledge of the topography of ancient Alexandria is based almost exclusively on the detailed description provided in Book 17 of the *Geography* written by Strabo, who was resident in the city ca. 24–20 B.C.E. (For extensive discussion of Strabo's account and the correlative evidence, see Fraser 1972,1: 7–37; 2: 12–111 [notes].) Unfortunately, many of the details of his account cannot be corroborated archeologically, since in the last century intense building activity has taken place in those areas which could have yielded important archeological information had scientific excavations been carried out in time. In addition, Alexandria lies on land which has subsided some four meters since antiquity. Hence the contours of the shoreline have changed; some built-up areas of the ancient city now lie submerged beneath the sea, and early occupation levels in some parts of the city are now below the water table.

Strabo gives the dimensions of the city as 30 stades in length (E–W) and 7 or 8 stades in width (N–S). He mentions the wide streets intersecting the city, the two broadest of which cut one another into sections at right angles (17.1.8). The long one, Via Canopica, ran from the Necropolis in the W to the Canopic Gate in the E (1.10), and is now thought to correspond generally with the modern Sharia el-Hurriya.

Up to a third of the entire city was occupied by an area called "the Palaces" *(ta basileia),* resplendent with beautiful buildings such as the Museum (presumably including the Library, which, however, Strabo does not mention) and the *Sēma,* containing the burial places of Alexander and the Ptolemies (1.8). The sites of these structures are unknown, but the "Palaces" neighborhood extended from Cape Lochias W and S. In the Roman period that area was called "Brucheion" (Bruchium) and was largely abandoned during the reign of Aurelian. Strabo distinguishes that larger area from the "inner royal palaces" (*ta endoterō basileia,* 1.9) concentrated on and near Lochias.

Strabo next describes the city as one would encounter it if sailing into the Great Harbor (the E harbor, now silted up and used only for small craft). To the right lay the island of Pharos, with its famous lighthouse. (That island is the traditional site of the translation of the LXX; cf. *Let. Aris.* 301; Philo *Vita Mos* II.35–36.) To the left were the reefs and promontory of Lochias, with its royal palace and private royal harbor. Opposite that small harbor was Antirrhodos, an island with a royal palace and another harbor. Rising in the background was the Theater, and the Poseidium, an elbow of land on which was a temple of Poseidon. Mark Antony had extended a mole from there out into the harbor, at the end of which he built a palace called the "Timonium" (1.9). No certainly identifiable remains of the Theater have turned up, but it is thought to have been situated near the modern Government Hospital. Remains of the Poseidium and Timonium were visible in the 19th century, and underwater excavations could probably even now turn up some evidence of value. See fig. ALE.01.

Strabo continues his discussion by referring to structures further W: the Caesarium, the Emporium and warehouses, and ship buildings extending as far as the Heptastadion. The Heptastadion ("seven stades" long) was a mole connecting the mainland with Pharos; it served to divide the Great (E) Harbor from the Eunostos (W) Harbor (1.9). No trace of the Heptastadion remains; it has been silted over, with the result that Pharos is no longer an island. The site of the Caesarium, or Sebasteion (cf. Philo *Gaium* 151) is known, and the obelisks standing at its entrance remained until the 19th century, when they were removed respectively to London ("Cleopatra's Needle") and New York. The Caesarium was turned into a church in the 4th century and became the Patriarchal Cathedral until its destruction in 912.

Strabo next describes the W part of the city. The Eunostos Harbor, today the main harbor of Alexandria, had within it an artificial harbor called "Kibotos," which was connected to Lake Mareotis by a canal. The Kibotos was the main commercial harbor for boat traffic from the Nile River inland. A "Necropolis" is mentioned as lying outside of the city to the W. The only building specifically mentioned for this part of the city is the Serapeum (1.10). Strabo saw the Ptolemaic Serapeum, but it was greatly extended in the Roman period and then destroyed by Christian zeal in 391. It is the only temple in Alexandria that has been excavated (see Adriani 1966: 90–100; plates 28–31, for summary and full bibliography). Its ruins lie in what was the native Egyptian neighborhood Rhakotis. One of its prominent landmarks is the so-called "Pompey's Pillar" (set up in honor of Diocletian).

Strabo next turns his attention to the central part of the city, mentioning the beautiful Gymnasium with its porticoes and groves, situated on the main E–W street (Via Canopica), and the Paneium, a sanctuary of Pan lying on a hill (1.10). No certain archeological corroboration is available for these structures (cf. Adriani 1966: 222, 233). Proximity of the Gymnasium to the Great Synagogue (see below) is suggested by Philo's account of the troubles in 38 C.E. (*Gaium* 132–35; cf. Pearson 1986: 148, n. 85). Outside the Canopic Gate to the E lay the Hippodrome (cf. *3*

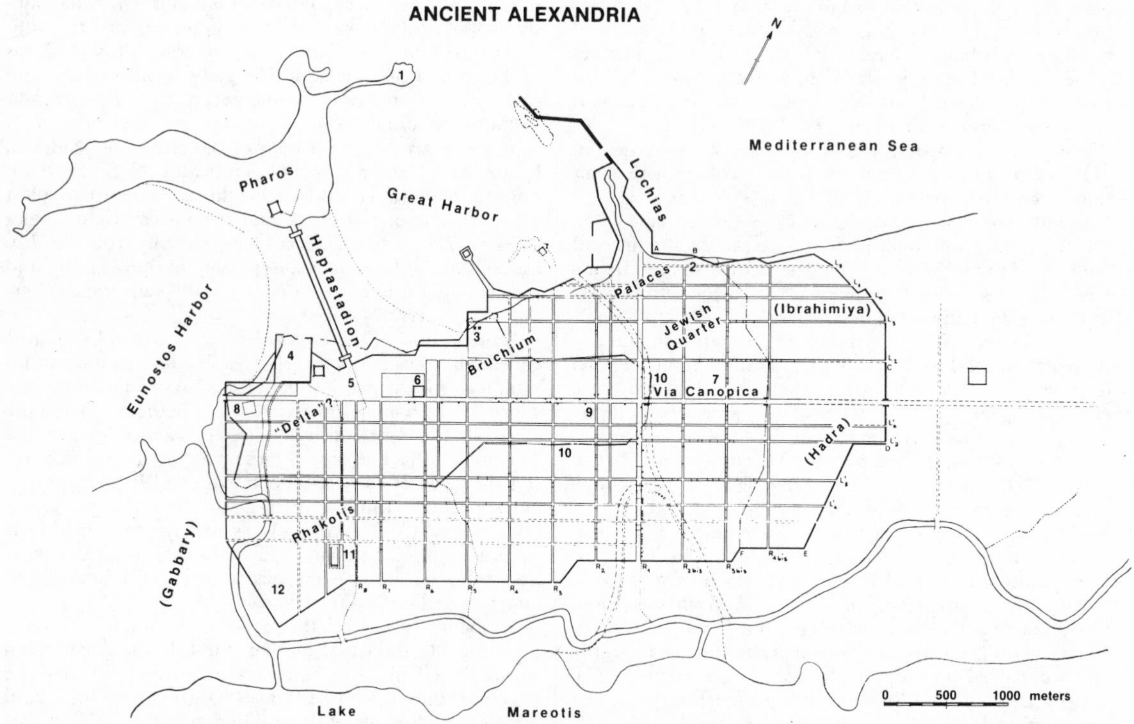

ALE.01. Map of ancient Alexandria. *1,* Pharos lighthouse; *2,* Martyrium of St. Mark; *3,* Caesarium; *4,* "Kibotos" harbor; *5,* western Agora; *6,* Bendideion (Mendideion); *7,* "Alabaster tomb"; *8,* St. Theonas Church; *9,* Gymnasium; *10,* Arab wall; *11,* Serapeum; and *12,* Wescher catacomb. This map (cf. Pearson 1986: 157–59) is adapted from Adriani 1966: 269, tavola A. It is a reconstruction based on the "Carte del'antique Alexandrie et de ses fauborgs" in Mahmoud-Bey 1872. The street grid is Mahmoud-Bey's reconstruction of the street system of Alexandria in the early Roman period. The sites indicated in parenthesis (Gabbary, Ibrahimiya, and Hadra) are sections of the modern city; in antiquity the main W and E necropoleis were located in these areas. *(Courtesy of B. Pearson.)*

Maccabees 4–6), and then, 30 stades from Alexandria, Nicopolis (1.10), a new community founded by Augustus Caesar.

Strabo does not provide any details concerning the city wall, nor does he mention the necropoleis that lay to the E of the city. The first systematic attempt to locate the ancient walls and the street grid on the basis of archeological probes was that of the astronomer Mahmoud-Bey, whose map showing the walls and the streets has been the basis for subsequent topographical research (Mahmoud-Bey 1872). Unfortunately, his results are not reliable, though his street grid, representing the Roman (not Ptolemaic) streets, is widely used (cf. Fig. ALE.01). Especially problematic is his location of the E wall, which would accordingly have enclosed the Ptolemaic necropoleis of Shatby, Ibrahimiya, and Hadra. These necropoleis, as dictated by custom, must necessarily have lain *outside* the original wall of the city. The 9th century Arab wall, of which some traces remain, enclosed a much smaller area of the city.

Strabo does not say anything concerning the location of the Jewish neighborhoods, or those of other ethnic groups, nor does he mention the division of the city into quarters named for the first five letters of the Greek alphabet (cf. *Ps.-Callisthenes* 1.32). However, in his lost historical work *(Historica Hypomnemata)* he states that a "great part" of the city of Alexandria had been alloted to the Jews (quoted in Josephus *Ant* 14.117; cf. Stern 1976: 277–82). Philo reports that two of the "letters" were predominantly Jewish, though Jews lived elsewhere in the city as well (*Flacc* 55). In his *Jewish War* Josephus describes the 66 C.E. Roman attack on the Jews concentrated in "Delta" (*JW* 2.495). The "Delta" quarter has often been identified with the Jewish neighborhood he mentions elsewhere as the city's finest residential quarter, adjacent to the palaces, by the sea "without a harbor" (*AgAp* 2.33–36), an area easily identifiable as the section to the E of Lochias (modern Silsileh) near Shatby Beach. But, since a papyrus dated to 13 B.C.E. locates the Kibotos harbor "in Delta" (*BGU* 1151, lines 40–41), "Delta" must have been in the W part of the city. It would therefore have been one of the *two* predominantly Jewish quarters mentioned by Philo (Adriani 1966: 239; Pearson 1986: 147).

The neighborhood E of Lochias was probably Alexandria's oldest and most important Jewish section. Here was probably located the greatest of Alexandria's many synagogues (see Philo *Gaium* 132–135; cf. *Flacc* 41), a double-colonnade basilica described in rabbinic sources as "the glory of Israel" (*t. Sukk.* 4.6; *j. Sukk.* 5.1; *b. Sukk.* 51b), and destroyed by Trajan during the revolt of 115–117. No archeological evidence for Jewish habitation in this area has been found, although synagogue inscriptions have been found in Hadra to the E, and in Gabbary, W of the ancient city. Jewish tombs were found in the E and W necropoleis in the early part of this century, but no trace of them remains today (see C below).

Topographical references in the legendary *Acts of Mark*, narrating the story of the founding of Christianity in Alexandria, correlate well with the two "Jewish" areas mentioned, "Delta" in the NW part of the city, and the main residential area in the NE, thus also reinforcing the supposition that the earliest Christians in Alexandria were Jews (cf. Pearson 1986: 151–54; see D below). For the early 3d century, a good case has been made for locating the "catechetical school" and the center of ecclesiastical Christianity in general in the main Greek area of the city, Bruchium (Andresen 1979: 428–52). By the 2d century, if not earlier, Christians would have been found among the Egyptians residing in Rhakotis. It may have been among these Christians that the apocryphal *Gospel of the Egyptians* first circulated (Pearson 1986: 150).

C. Jewish Papyri and Inscriptions

No papyri have survived the humid climate of Alexandria, but numerous papyri attesting to Jewish life in Alexandria have been found elsewhere in Egypt, and have been published in *CPJ* (Tcherikover et al. 1957–64; see index, vol. 3: 197–98).

The Jewish inscriptions from Egypt comprise nos. 1424–1539 of *CII* (Frey 1952), conveniently republished in *CPJ* 3: 138–66. Sixteen of these are from Alexandria (1424–39).

Nos. 1424–31 are tomb inscriptions from the early Ptolemaic necropolis of Ibrahimiya. The first three, presumably the oldest, are in Aramaic, the others in Greek. (On this Jewish necropolis see esp. Breccia 1907; cf. Goodenough 1953: 62–63, figs. 863–64.) No. 1434, very fragmentary, is possibly a dedication by Jews to the royal house, found in the necropolis of Kom al-Shuqafa. Nos. 1435–38 are votive inscriptions, 1439 an inscription of ownership *(Ioulianou)* on a plaster amphora, with menorah.

The most important of the inscriptions are nos. 1432 and 1433, both fragmentary synagogue inscriptions, neither found *in situ*. No. 1432, found in Gabbary (the W necropolis area in antiquity) records the building of the synagogue *(proseuchē)* by Alypos and its dedication to "the great God who listens to prayer" "on behalf of the queen and the king" (Cleopatra VII and Antony), 37 B.C.E. No. 1433, found in Hadra (part of the E complex of necropoleis in antiquity), was dedicated to "God Most High" *(theō hypsistō)*, and probably dates from the 2d century B.C.E.

Of the other synagogue inscriptions found in Egypt, no. 1440 from Schedia (modern Kafr el-Dawar), not far from Alexandria, records the dedication of a *proseuche* built by "the Jews" in honor of "King Ptolemy (III Euergetes) and Queen Berenice his sister and wife and their children." This inscription, and one from Crocodilopolis with the same kind of dedication (1532A), are the oldest synagogue inscriptions in existence, dating from between 246–221 B.C.E.

Two other inscriptions from Egypt, provenience unknown, may be from Alexandria: no. 1446, a votive inscription, and 1447, a dedicatory inscription on a statue base.

Two inscriptions not included in the corpus are worth mentioning here. The first is a tombstone of uncertain provenience now in the Greco-Roman Museum in Alexandria, inscribed (in Greek) *Iouda* over a "solar" menorah, with shofar and palm-branch (cf. Goodenough 1953: 63, fig. 896). The other one is a partial Hebrew inscription *(brkm)* on a piece of an amphora dated to the 1st or 2d century C.E. and probably imported from Palestine. It was uncovered in the Polish excavations at Kom el-Dikka in downtown Alexandria (Fiema 1985).

D. Christian Evidence

1. Churches. The evidence for the existence of church buildings in Alexandria before the 4th century is very scanty. Church buildings certainly existed in Egypt before the 4th century, for Eusebius reports on the massive destruction of churches during the Diocletianic persecutions (*Hist. Eccl.* 8.2), and there is documentary evidence for church buildings in Egypt (with the use of the term "ekklesia" for such buildings) as early as the 3d century (Judge and Pickering 1977: 59–61, 69). Church buildings would have existed in Alexandria as well.

Epiphanius, writing in the late 4th century, lists the Alexandrian churches known to him (*Haer.* 69.2): (1) "Caesarea" (built on the site of the Caesareum under Archbishop Athanasius in 368); (2) "Of Dionysius" (location unknown, attested from the time of Athanasius but presumably connected in some way with Bishop Dionysius [246–64], replaced because of its inadequate size by the church of St. Athanasius [see (7) below]); (3) "Of Theonas" (see below); (4) "Of Pierius" (location unknown, presumably named for the 3d century Alexandrian presbyter mentioned by Eusebius [*Hist. Eccl.* 7.32.26–30]); (5) "Of Persaea" (unidentified); (6) "Of Dizya" (unidentified); (7) "Of Mendidion" (a church built by Athanasius near the temple called either "Bendidion" [for the god Bendis] or "Mendidion" [for the Egyptian god Mendes], and eventually converted into the Mosque of the Souq al-Attarin after the Arab conquest); (8) "Of Annianus" (location unknown, but possibly connected in local legend with the traditional successor of St. Mark, Annianus [68–83, but see below]); and (9) "Of Baukalis" (the memorial to St. Mark attested from the 4th century and located in an area then called *Boukolou,* earlier part of the ancient Jewish quarter E of Lochias.)

Epiphanius' list ends with the phrase "and others." One prominent church left unmentioned by Epiphanius should have been known to him: the church of St. Michael (or the church of Alexander), which Bishop Alexander (313–26) created from a temple previously dedicated to Saturn. This church was situated near the Paneum, E of the Caesarea church. Perhaps Epiphanius' reference to a church "of Annianus" (no. 8 above) is mistaken and should have read "of Alexander" instead.

For our purposes, the most important of these churches mentioned by Epiphanius are the "Baukalis" church (#9 above) and the church of St. Theonas (no. 3 above). The former is reputed to have been founded in the time of St. Mark as the first church in Alexandria (*Acts of Mark* 5). In the early 4th century it was a parish church served by the presbyter (and later heretic) Arius. No trace of it remains. The church of St. Theonas, named for the Alexandrian bishop (282–300), is the earliest church building for which we have adequate documentation. It was rededicated by Bishop Alexander to the Virgin Mary, and was eventually turned into the "Mosque of a Thousand Pillars." It was severely damaged by the French in 1798, and its remains were obliterated in 1829. (On the churches of Alexandria *see* esp. Leclercq *DACL* 1: 1107–25.)

2. Cemeteries. The earliest reference to Christian cemeteries in Alexandria is found in a letter of Bishop Dionysius (246–264) quoted by Eusebius (*Hist. Eccl.* 7.11.10; cf. 7.13.1). A cemetery located in the W suburbs is mentioned in the *Passio* of St. Peter I (Bishop of Alexandria, 300–311); it had been constructed by him and served as his own burial place (Viteau 1897: 83).

Christian tombs have been found in both the E and W necropoleis, but almost all have been obliterated during this century, many of them without adequate documentation. Most of them seem to have dated from the period after the Peace of the Church (313). (*See* esp. Leclercq, *DACL* 1:1125–54; Adriani 1966: 122–23, 183–86; plates 41, 102–104; Krause 1966: 105–107). By far the most important are the Wescher Catacomb discovered in 1858 in the Karmuz district, not far from Pompey's Pillar, and the famous catacomb complex of Kom al-Shuqafa. The latter was discovered in 1900 and is still a tourist attraction (Adriani 1966: 172–180; plates 96–101). The Wescher Catacomb (Leclercq, *DACL* 1: 1125–45; Adriani 1966: 184–86; plates 103–104) was an elaborate tomb complex with rich decoration. Two staircases led down to an open chamber with an apse in the W wall. To the E was a gallery of 32 loculi on two levels, and to the N a chamber with three arcosolia. The main chamber contained a baptistry, and was evidently also used for *refrigeria* (memorial meals) and other Christian services. The paintings and frescoes representing Christ, saints, and prophets are now thought to have dated from the end of the 4th to the 7th centuries (Krause 1966: 107). Of this important Christian monument nothing remains.

3. Papyri and Inscriptions. No papyri have been found in Alexandria itself, and very little papyrus documentation exists for Alexandrian Christianity prior to Constantine. One very important piece of evidence does exist, however, a papyrus from the Fayyum in the Amherst collection (P. Amh. I [1900] 3a; see Judge and Pickering 1977: 48, 54–55; Snyder 1985: 152–53). This papyrus, dating from 264–282, is a fragmentary letter from a Roman Christian to Christian brethren in Arsinoe (presumably a church). In it the Alexandrian church, under the leadership of "Maximus the Papa" (Bishop 264–282), is understood to be performing banking functions as a financial intermediary for Christians. Other Alexandrians named in the letter include Theonas, presumably then serving as a financial secretary to Maximus, who eventually succeeded Maximus as Bishop (282–300).

A corpus of Christian Greek inscriptions from Egypt was published early in this century but is now unfortunately out of date (Lefebvre 1907). Of the inscriptions published in this corpus, nos. 1–56 are from Alexandria. A few of these, all tomb inscriptions, are dated by Lefebvre to the period before Constantine. Nos. 21 and 22 are from Gabbary (W necropolis), and no. 47 is from Hadra (E necropolis). No. 33 is a group of inscriptions from the Wescher Catacomb; Lefebvre's dating (3d or 4th century) is probably too early. Nos. 34 and 35 are inscriptions from the "Tomb of Rufinus" in Karmuz (cf. Leclercq *DACL* 1: 1149–50) and are dated to the Antonine period (2d century). No. 54, from Mafrouza, is dated to 148. Nos. 34, 35, and 54 may not be Christian; they have only the formula *eupsychei,* "farewell," a formula widely used both by pagans and Christians.

To conclude, it must be acknowledged that the documentary evidence provides a very incomplete picture of the social life of Christians in Alexandria before the time of Constantine.

Bibliography

Adriani, A. 1934. Saggio di una pianta archeologica di Alessandria. *Annuario del Museo Greco-Romano* 1: 55–96 + map.

———. 1966. *Repertorio d'arte dell' Egitto greco-romano.* Series C, Volumes 1 (Testo) and 2 (Tavole). Palermo.

Andresen, C. 1979. "Siegreiche Kirche" in Aufstieg des Christentums: Untersuchungen zu Eusebius von Caesarea und Dionysios von Alexandrien. *ANRW* 2.23.1: 387–495.

Botti, G. 1898. *Plan de la ville d'Alexandrie à l'époque ptolémaïque.* Alexandria.

Breccia, E. 1907. La Necropoli de l'Ibrahimieh. *Bulletin de la Société Archéologique d'Alexandrie* 9: 35–86.

———. 1922. *Alexandrea ad Aegyptum.* Bergamo, Italy.

Calderini, A. 1935. *Dizionario dei nomi geografici e topografici dell' Egitto greco-romano.* Vol. 1, fasc. 1. Milan.

Fiema, Z. 1985. A Hebrew Inscription from Kom el-Dikka, Alexandria, Egypt. *JARCE* 22: 117–18.

Fraser, P. M. 1972. *Ptolemaic Alexandria.* 3 vols. Oxford.

Frey, J.-B. 1952. *Corpus Inscriptionum Iudaicarum.* Vol. 2. Vatican.

Goodenough, E. R. 1953. *Jewish Symbols in the Greco-Roman Period.* Vols. 2 (text) and 3 (illustrations). New York.

Judge, E. A., and Pickering, S. R. 1977. Papyrus Documentation of Church and Community in Egypt to the Mid-Fourth Century. *JAC* 20: 47–71.

Krause, M. 1966. Alexandria. Vol. 1, cols. 99–111 in *Reallexikon zur Byzantinischen Kunst,* ed. K. Wessel. Stuttgart.

Lefebvre, M. G. 1907. *Recueil des inscriptions grecques-chrétiennes d'Egypte.* Cairo.

Mahmoud-Bey. 1872. *Mémoire sur l'antique Alexandrie.* Copenhagen.

Neroutsos-Bey. 1888. *L'Ancienne Alexandrie.* Paris.

Pagenstecher, R. 1919. *Nekropolis: Untersuchungen über Gestalt und Entwicklung der Alexandrinischen Grabanlagen und ihrer Malereien.* Leipzig.

Pearson, B. A. 1986. Earliest Christianity in Egypt. Pp. 132–59 in *The Roots of Egyptian Christianity,* ed. B. A. Pearson and J. E. Goehring. Studies in Antiquity and Christianity 1. Philadelphia.

Rodziewicz, M. 1984. *Les habitations romaines tardives d'Alexandrie à la lumière des fouilles polonaises à Kôm el-Dikka.* Vol. 3 of *Alexandrie.* Warsaw.

Snyder, G. F. 1985. *Ante Pacem: Archaeological Evidence of Church Life Before Constantine.* Macon, GA.

Stern, M. 1976. *From Herodotus to Plutarch.* Vol. 1 in *Greek and Latin Authors on Jews and Judaism.* Jerusalem.

Tcherikover, V., et al. 1957–64. *Corpus Papyrorum Judaicarum.* 3 vols. Cambridge, MA.

Viteau, J. 1897. *Passions des Saints Ecaterine et Pierre d'Alexandrie.* Paris.

BIRGER A. PEARSON

ALEXANDRINUS. See CODEX ALEXANDRINUS.

ALGEBRA. See MATHEMATICS, ALGEBRA, AND GEOMETRY.

ᶜALI, TELL (M.R. 202234). A Neolithic/Chalcolithic site on the W bank of the Jordan River, one mile S of the Sea of Galilee, on a terrace 10–15 m above an important junction, E–W from the Yarmuk Valley (Sha'ar Hagolan) to the Mediterranean coast, and N–S from the Huleh (Beisamoun) to Munhata and Jericho. The site was blessed with copious springs and drainage into the Jordan (Prausnitz 1959).

Four seasons of excavations (1955–1957, 1959) undertaken by the Israel Department of Antiquities (Prausnitz 1970) revealed four superimposed strata beginning with IV$^{a\text{-}b}$ to I $^{(a)\text{-}b\text{-}c}$, ranging chronologically from Pre-Pottery Neolithic B (PPNB) and Pottery Neolithic (PN), to the Early Chalcolithic.

The architecture of stratum IV consisted of straight walls with rounded corners and round huts (?), whose pebble floors which had been sunk into the earth were characteristic of stratum IV^{a,b}. In stratum III a straight wall with a thin plaster floor was unearthed. Beneath the floor a crouched, decapitated skeleton was discovered. Stratum II revealed a large, irregular, built enclosure 13.60 × 8.80 m with what appears to be a row of two or three rooms, 2.50 × 3.50 m, placed inside the outer walls to face an inner court which is paved with pebbles. The buildings of the uppermost stratum, I$^{(a)\text{-}b\text{-}c}$, were rectangular houses 6 to 10 m long and about 4 m wide, set in clusters around a central area and adjacent to large tracts of arable land on the terrace (Vita-Finzi and Higgs 1970).

Flint and stone industries of stratum IV contain a number of microlithic blades and a crescent. According to recent terminology (Crowfoot-Payne 1983), stratum IV would thus belong to an incipient PPNB of the middle of the 7th millennium B.C. The double-ended (including naviform) cores typical of the PPNB, long blades, and "reaping knives" are common from strata IV to II. Pressure-flaked long blades and daggers come from stratum I^{c}. Among the arrowheads found at the site were the Jericho point, with marked, notched tang and wings (represented from IV to I^{c}); the Byblos point, without wings (stratum III); and the Amuq point, leaf-shaped with a tang and the oval point (strata II–I^{b}). The latter two types of points are pressure-flaked and fluted.

Pottery vessels were first discovered in stratum II, although an animal figurine was found in IV (PPNB). Thick-walled, handmade, chaff-tempered clay hole-mouth jars with lug handles were the earliest local ceramics. Probably imported were bowls decorated by painted and burnished red bands around the rim and reserved unpainted areas, decorated by cuts and slabs, as well as incised straight and wavy lines. This pottery has exact parallels in the "Coastal Neolithic" at Hazorea (Anati 1973), at Ras Shamra V$^{A\text{-}B}$ (de Contenson 1977), which places Tell ᶜAli II to the middle/last quarter of the 6th millennium B.C. A third type of pottery had been decorated by glossy bands of creamy paint in dark to medium red. The paint had been allowed to trickle down the body in stripes. Stratum I$^{b\text{-}c}$ produced fine monochrome burnished pottery in various shades of black to gray and dark brown to red. This pottery belongs to the dark-faced burnished ware, which at Hazorea is an upper part of the "Coastal Neolithic," at Munhata 2^{A} is called "wadi Rabah phase" (Perrot 1968), and is also known in the Amuq C-D. The upper stratum (I^{a}) at Tell ᶜAli brought to light thumb-impressed and painted ware, which is well known all over N Palestine and dated to the Early Chalcolithic, the turn of the last quarter of the 5th millennium B.C.

At Tell ᶜAli, from the PPNB to the Early Chalcolithic an archaeological, stratigraphic sequence was traced for the first time. Later work at Munhata and Hazorea proved the sequence for the whole of N Palestine. Links were established along the coast of the N Levant with Byblos and Ras Shamra and inland Ramad and Amuq (Mellaart *CAH*³ 1/1: 264–9).

Bibliography

Anati, E., et al. 1973. *Hazorea I.* Brescia, Italy.

Cauvin, J. 1968. *Fouilles de Byblos IV.* Paris.

Contenson, H. de. 1977. Le Neolithique de Ras Shamra V d'après les campagnes 1972–76 dans le Sondage SH. *Syria* 54: 1–23.

Crowfoot-Payne, J. 1983. The Flint Industries of Jericho. *Excavations at Jericho V,* ed. K. M. Kenyon and T. A. Holland. Oxford.

Perrot, J. 1968. Prehistoire Palestinienne, *DBSup,* col. 416.

Prausnitz, M. W. 1959. The First Agricultural Settlements in Galilee. *IEJ* 9: 166–74.

———. 1970. *From Hunter to Farmer and Trader.* Bonn.

Vita-Finzi, C. and Higgs, E. S. 1970. Prehistoric Economy in the Mount Carmel area of Palestine. Site Catchment Analysis. *Proceedings of the Prehistoric Society* 36: 28–37.

M. W. Prausnitz

ALIA AIRPORT (PLACE). A cemetery of the 2d–3d century A.D. discovered at the present Queen ᶜAlia International Airport S of Amman, Jordan. In 1978, a number of tombs and an inscription were noticed during the construction of the maintenance hangar area. After further investigation, it was clear that the site consisted of a large cemetery below a series of hills on which some ruined structures were found. The tombs were covered by relatively level soil 1.5–2.0 m thick. The inscription, which is Thamudic, was one of the key finds for the interpretation of the site.

M. Ibrahim directed a rescue excavation of the cemetery. All soil from within the graves was sifted, and five burials were lifted entirely. These remains were then examined by B. Frohlich at the Smithsonian Institution. Apparently these were remains of an Arab tribe which lived just outside the border of the Roman Empire between the arable plateau and the arid land. The site lay some 6 km beyond permanent settlements and cultivation and was in an area of pastoral grazing. Although a few shards indicate activity during the early Islamic period, the cemetery belongs entirely to the Roman Imperial period. It occupies an area of 65 m square. Most of the families were buried in individual graves forming rows.

Among the burial goods, leather was quite prevalent. In addition to leather footwear and possibly folded clothing, large sheets of leather were buried. They were thin (0.2 cm.) and were originally quite supple. It seems most likely that these large sheets of leather were made to cover the backs of horses or camels. Square saddles are shown in numerous representations in the art of Palmyra and S Syria of the 3d century A.D. Other artifacts show a close relationship between this community and the Roman settlers. Women and children were adorned with jewelry, including earrings, necklaces, finger rings, bracelets, and anklets—mostly of bronze. A few of the women were provided with gold earrings and additional toilet articles. Four seals were found in the graves. One was a scarab seal set in a pendant in a bronze band with a loop behind it. It shows a monkey and a griffin facing each other above a crocodile and winged uraei. Another seal is of a dark green stone and may have originated in Saudi Arabia. It is believed to have been held as an heirloom for at least 700 years before being deposited in the grave. Some 225 beads were found, some of precious stone such as carnelian, amethyst, agate, and coral. Fifteen rings of hollow gold beads were also found. Cosmetic items include spatulae and cosmetic spoons, kohl tubes, hairpins, a wooden comb, and a glass rod. The epigraphic evidence, burial practices, leather finds, and the location of the cemetery all support the attribution of these graves to the Arab population rather than to the Roman army.

Bibliography

Ibrihim, M. M., and Gordon, R. L. 1987. *A Cemetery at Queen Alia International Airport.* Wiesbaden.

Moawiyah M. Ibrahim

ALIAH (PERSON) [Heb *ᶜalyâ*]. See ALVAH (PERSON).

ᶜALLA, DEIR. See DEIR ᶜALLA.

ALLAMMELECH (PLACE) [Heb *ʾalammelek*]. A town located in the inheritance of the tribe of Asher (Josh 19:26). The OT form can be translated as "oak of the king." However, the LXX has preserved variants, such as *alimelech,* which have led some scholars to suggest that the original Semitic form of the name was *ʾltmlk.* Scholars (*LBHG,* 160) have used this hypothesis to equate Allammelech with town Number 45 (Eg *rtmrk*) in the conquest list of Thutmose III at Karnak. If this supposition is correct, the history of Allammelech can be extended into the Late Bronze Age.

Scholars have concluded that Allammelech was located in the southern part of the territory, in the Plain of Acco, from the position of Allammelech in the list of border towns. The Plain of Acco was densely settled in the Iron Age (*HGB,* 429), and several tells have been suggested as the location of Allammelech. The site most frequently mentioned (*GP,* 66) is Tell en-Nahal (M.R. 157245), which provides a general indication of the probable location of Allammelech, although the evidence in support of any identification is slight.

Melvin Hunt

ALLOGENES (NHC XI,*3*). A Gnostic apocalypse, written in the form of an epistle, relating the secret revelations and extra-bodily visions of Allogenes to his son, Messos. The name and title "Allogenes" literally means "the stranger" or "the foreigner." It is, however, a pseudonym and tells us nothing about the historical identity of the author.

Allogenes clearly belongs to a tradition, reported by Epiphanius, which designates Seth as "Allogenes" and attributes various books to him (*Pan.* 39.1.5; 40.2.1–2; and 40.7.1–5). The text also shows close affinity with a group of other texts discovered near Nag Hammadi which are usually designated as "Sethian" (Schenke 1974; Turner 1986). *Allogenes* shares with these texts the following characteristics: self-designation of gnostics as "seed" (56,30); Allogenes-Seth as the Gnostic savior; the divine triad, Father-Mother-Son (the Invisible Spirit, Barbelo and Autogenes); and the salvific role of the "illuminators." There is a particularly close affinity with *The Three Steles of Seth, Marsanes,* and *Zostrianos;* all three of these texts depend heavily upon technical philosophical terminology. *Allogenes,* however, contains no specifically Jewish or Christian language of any kind, but does draw heavily upon technical philosophical terminology.

It is highly probable that Plotinus knew a Greek version of *Allogenes.* Porphyry writes that Plotinus was acquainted with revelations by Allogenes and Messos, among others, and attacked them in lectures and in his treatise *Against the Gnostics* (*Plot.* 16). Although Plotinus' work cannot be read solely as an attack on *Allogenes, Allogenes* does contain the type of philosophical language and conceptuality Plotinus may have felt deserved refutation. It draws heavily upon philosophical terms and concepts current in Middle Platonism, especially with regard to the philosophical speculation on the rise of the soul and the divine hierarchy. The divine hierarchy of Plotinus, for example, is quite close to that of Allogenes. Compare:

Plotinus
One
Mind
Soul 1. directed toward intelligible realities
 2. mediator
 3. directed toward things of this world

Allogenes
One — Invisible Spirit
Mind — Barbelo
Logos (Son) — 1. Kalyptos (the intelligible *logos*)
 2. Protophanes (mind actualized)
 3. Autogenes (savior, acts in particulars for their correction)

The author of *Allogenes* combines in a unique and coherent manner traditional Sethian materials (its basic mythological pattern, magical prayers, and the ritual of ascent) with contemporary philosophical speculation on the rise of the soul and the divine hierarchy. He does not reduce Sethian mythology to a philosophical system, nor does he allow either mythology or philosophical conceptuality to control the flow of logic in the text. But there is a clear shift away from a more typically Gnostic view of salvation as escape from this evil world toward a view of salvation as the experience of self-recognition and direct apprehension of God.

The narrative progression in *Allogenes* is found in the account of the character Allogenes' reaction to his experiences. This account provides the reader with a clear description of the progression of the soul toward salvation. Allogenes moves from fear, ignorance, and disturbance of soul to knowledge, stability, praise, silence, and finally joy. The main point of the text is to convey an understanding of the nature and process of salvation. Salvation itself is understood as knowledge of God and Self, achieved first through auditory, and then through visionary, revelation. The emphasis in the content of the auditory revelations is on epistemology and ontology, that is to say, on coming to knowledge of true Being. The visionary revelation describes the direct apprehension of Self and God in the extra-bodily ascent of the soul. *Allogenes* is most probably closely connected with the Sethian rite of ascension in that it provides mythological-philosophical reflection upon the necessity for an ascension, the content of the ascent (insofar as that can be communicated), and its ultimate significance (Schenke 1981: 601–2).

Discovered in 1945 near Nag Hammadi in Egypt, the text survives in only one manuscript dating to the first half of the 4th century. Though originally written in Greek, it survives only in Coptic translation (Sahidic).

The underlying Greek text may be dated to the first quarter of the 3d century since it is highly probable that a version was known to Plotinus. It should not be dated earlier since the philosophical treatment of epistemology and ontology reflects philosophical conceptuality current in the late 2d and early 3d centuries.

Although translation into Coptic cannot decisively lead to the conclusion that the original was composed in Egypt, nonetheless the particular combinations of mythological elements and philosophical speculation make Alexandria a distinct possibility.

Bibliography

King, K. L. fc. *Allogenes: Text, Translation, and Notes.* California Classical Library 1. Sonoma, CA.

Robinson, J. M. 1977. The Three Steles of Seth and the Gnostics of Plotinus. Pp. 132–42 in *Proceedings of the International Colloquium on Gnosticism, Stockholm, August 20–25, 1973.* Kungl. Vitterhets Historie och Antikvitets Akademiens, Handlingar, Filologisk-filosofiska serien 17. Stockholm and Leiden.

Schenke, H.-M. 1974. Das Sethianische System nach Nag-Hammadi-Handschriften. Pp. 165–74 in *Studia Coptica,* ed. P. Nagel. Berlin.

———. 1981. The Phenomenon and Significance of Gnostic Sethianism. Vol. 2, pp. 588–616 in *The Rediscovery of Gnosticism,* ed. B. Layton. SHR 41. Leiden.

Turner, J. 1980. The Gnostic Threefold Path to Enlightenment. *NovT* 22: 324–51.

———. 1986. Sethian Gnosticism: A Literary History. Pp. 55–86 in *Nag Hammadi, Gnosticism, And Early Christianity,* ed. C. W. Hedrick and R. Hodgson, Jr. Peabody, MA.

Turner, J. fc. Allogenes. In *Nag Hammadi Codex XI,* ed. C. Hedrick. The Coptic Gnostic Library. Leiden.

Williams, M. A. 1981. Stability as a Soteriological Theme in Gnosticism. Vol. 2, pp. 819–29 in *The Rediscovery of Gnosticism,* ed. B. Layton. Leiden.

———. 1985. *The Immovable Race: A Gnostic Designation and the Theme of Stability in Late Antiquity.* NHS 29. Leiden.

Karen L. King

ALLON (PERSON) [Heb *ʾallōn*]. Descendant of Simeon. The only reference to him occurs in 1 Chr 4:37, where he is recorded as the grandfather of Ziza. The list of individuals in 1 Chr 4:34–37 were "princes in their families" (1 Chr 4:38). This certainly means that Meshobab, Jamlech, Joshah, Joel, Jehu, Elioenai, Jaakobah, Jeshohaiah, Asaiah, Adiel, Jesimiel, Benaiah, and Ziza were all princes of the tribe of Simeon in the days of the Judean King Hezekiah (late 8th century). While most scholars seem to assume that Allon is also a prince, the text is not at all clear that the antecedent of "these" (Heb *ʾēlleh*) also includes their ancestors when named. Allon is not mentioned in the Syr Peshitta version, since it omits entirely the list of Simeonite princes. In their place the Syr reads, "And they had a great name. And their dwellings were beautiful and quietness and peace was around them." This is an indication that there were variant traditions of this passage extant in ancient times (for discussion and bibliography see Williamson *Chronicles* NCBC). However, since the Peshitta is left with no antecedent for its reference in 4:38—"And these are the names of the princes who were there"—it is more likely that the Peshitta text represents an omission, rather than the original situation (although some scholars disagree). The word "*ʾallôn*" refers to some kind of vigorous tree, possibly an oak, and is probably derived from the root "*ʾwl*" meaning "be in front, strong" (KB, 19).

H. Eldon Clem

ALLON-BACUTH (PLACE) [Heb *ʾallôn-bākût*]. A place in the vicinity of Bethel where Deborah, Rebekah's nurse, was buried (Gen 35:8). The name literally means "oak of weeping." In Judg 4:5 there is a reference to a "palm tree of Deborah" located between Ramah and Bethel in the hill country of Ephraim, but the context explicitly mentions a different type of tree and implies an association with a different Deborah (the prophetess/judge, not the nurse of Rebekah).

Gary A. Herion

ALMIGHTY [Heb *šadday, ʾel šadday;* Gk *pantokrator*]. General name given to the patriarchal family god and later identified with Yahweh. "Almighty" translates the Hebrew *Shaddai* of the pre-Mosaic tradition (Gen 17:1; Cross *CMHE*, 13–75) and is identified with Yahweh in the Mosaic tradition (Exod 3:13–17; 6:2–3). See GOD, NAMES OF.

Albright (1935: 192–193) has shown that the name derives from northern Mesopotamian roots and came to Canaan with the ancestors of the Israelites as a patriarchal family god. Wright (1962: 51) sees the relationship of the clan to its deity as probable background for the later covenant relationship between God and Israel (Exod 6:4). Anderson (1986: 44) indicates points of similarity between Shaddai and the Canaanite god El, but notes that theological differences in the nature of Israel's God and the covenant relationship called for essentially different response in worship and morality. DeVaux (*AncIsr*, 294) points to enhanced qualities of Yahweh worship at cult sites formerly used for El worship.

The Greek of the Apocrypha and New Testament renders the Hebrew "Shaddai" by *pantokrator,* a compound of *pan* (all) and *krátos* (power, might). In the Intertestamental Period the living tradition is reflected in the prayer of Jonathan (2 Macc 1:24–29) recalling both divine attributes and covenant relationship. During events of Jewish history from 180 to 161 B.C.E. the people of Israel under the leadership of the Maccabees invoked God's almighty power in military confrontations (2 Macc 7:35; 8:11); and to strengthen their conviction of divine fidelity to their eternal covenant with the Lord (2 Macc 1:25; 3:22; 5:20; 6:26; 7:38). In the New Testament ten instances of *pantokrátor* are predominantly in Revelation, with only one in 2 Cor 6:18. Thus the descriptive designation "Almighty" in connection with the name of the Lord God is consistent in biblical usage.

Bibliography

Albright, W. F. 1935. The Names of Shaddai and Abram. *JBL* 54: 180–193.

Anderson, B. W. 1986. *Understanding the Old Testament.* Englewood Cliffs, NJ.

Wright, G. E. 1962. *Biblical Archaeology.* Philadelphia.

Betty Jane Lillie

ALMODAD (PERSON) [Heb *ʾalmôdād*]. Firstborn son of Joktan and hence the name of a South Arabian tribe (Gen 10:26; 1 Chr 1:20), which, however, has neither been identified nor localized in a satisfactory way. Retaining the Masoretic vocalization, the first syllable could be conceived as Arabic *ʾāl,* "family, clan," the name of a specific clan could then be seen in the following part of the name, probably *ʾāl mawdad.* There are attestations of such a name in Old South Arabic; in Sabaean *mwddm* occurs as a proper name (*CIS* IV, 94,5), and in Qatabanian *mwddn* is to be found as a clan name (*RES* 3902, No. 98,2). The Hebrew form *-môdād* could very well be derived from an Old South Arabic *mwdd-n, mawdad-ān,* and in this case it cannot be excluded that the region where the tribe of *ʾalmôdād* lived has to be localized somewhere in the area of the ancient kingdom of Qatabān, the center of which was the capital Timnaʿ in the Wadi Bayḥān in present-day South Yemen. Qatabān is mentioned for the first time in the Old Sabaean text *RES* 3945; the earliest Qatabanian inscriptions, however, do not go back to the time in which the biblical table of nations originated.

Glaser (1890: 425) was inclined to recognize in *ʾalmôdād* the Minaean clan of Gabʾān, members of which are called "friends" of the king during the time concerned in the inscriptions (*ʾhl gbʾn mwddt* . . . "clan of Gabʾān, friends of . . . ;" *RES* 2771,2; *RES* 2774,1; etc.). The interpretation of the first syllable of *ʾalmôdād* as the Arabic article *al-,* according to which the meaning of the name would be "the friend," is hardly acceptable and was already rejected by Gesenius-Kautzsch (GK, 118).

In case one gives preference to the vocalization of the LXX, *elmōdad,* the first syllable of the name could be conceived as the name of "God," Heb *ʾēl.* Reading the name in this way, *ʾelmôdād* could be interpreted as "God is loved" or "God is a friend"; cf. also Old Sabaean *mwd,* "friend," and the Heb proper name Medad, LXX *mōdad* (Num 11:26), the Aramaic *mwdd* inscribed on a clay-tablet from Niniveh (*CIS* 11, 43, R6), in cuneiform writing *mudadu,* Akkadian *mudādum,* all of which mean "friend, beloved." Hommel (*HAW* 3.1.1: 554–5), however, regarded the *m* in *ʾlmwdd* as an emphasizing enclitic particle, and wanted to read the name *ʾelī-mā-wadd,* "(my) God is truly Wadd," Wadd being an ancient Sabaean deity and the main god of the Minaeans.

Certainly erroneous is the connection, first proposed by Bochartus (1674: 112–13), of *ʾalmôdād* with the *alumaiōtai* in Ptolemaeus (*Geog.* 6.7.24), an otherwise unattested tribe at the NE coast of the Arabian peninsula.

Bibliography

Bochartus, S. 1674. *Geographia sacra. Pars prior Phaleg.* Francofurti ad Moenum.

Glaser, E. 1890. *Skizze der Geschichte und Geographie Arabiens.* Berlin.

W. W. Müller

ALMON (PLACE) [Heb *ʿalmôn*]. Var. ALEMETH. A city given to the descendents of Aaron the priest (Josh 21:18). BDB (p. 761) derived it from *ʿlam,* "conceal, hidden;" others suggest it means "sign" or "road mark." Albright thought the meaning of the name was obscure. It is spelled *Gamala* in LXX, *Almon* in LXX Codex Alexandrinus, *Amala* in LXX Codex Vaticanus, *Elmon* in LXX Lucian, and *Alemeth (Allemeth)* in 1 Chr 6:45 (—Eng 6: 45; *Galemeth* in LXX; *Alamoth* in LXX Lucian). Almon and Alemeth both come from the same root. Josh 21:1ff describes the allotment of 48 cities and their pasture lands (not cultivated lands) to the Levites according to the commandment of Moses in Num 35:1–8, since they did not get territorial allotments as such. Boling (*Joshua* AB, 492–494) dates the list to the mid-8th century on archaeological grounds: surface collection of potshards and other data show most of the sites were occupied then, with ʿAlmon occupied in the 9th and 8th centuries. Myers, on the other hand, dates them to the reign of David on historical grounds—when the country was still divided among tribes and before Solomon separated it into administrative districts (*1 Chronicles* AB, 48).

Almon is one of 13 cities given to the priests (the sons of Aaron) and one of 4 cities in the tribal territory of Benjamin. The four in Josh 21:17–18 include Gibeon (el-Jib), Geba (Jaba'), Anathoth (Anata), and Almon, while 1 Chr 6:60 leaves out Gibeon (Geba is at times a short form of Gibeon and Gibeah [Tell el-Ful]), all NE of Jerusalem. ʿAlmon is ca. 5 mi. from Jerusalem. Neither ʿAlmon nor Anathoth is in the list of Benjaminite cities in Josh 18:21–28. ʿAlmon is identified with Kh. ʿAlmit (M.R. 176136), a tell between Geba and Anathoth, 1 mi. NE of Anata, on the road to Ain Farah which runs into the Wadi Qelt to Jericho. Albright (1924) suggested the modern ending shows the pointing is wrong in Chronicles and in turn, "the relation between *ʿAlmon* and *ʿAlmit* is dialectical, and is precisely like that between *tahton* and *tahfit,* the *ît* being the archaic feminine of the *nisbeh* in *î* . . ." Avi-Yonah (*EJ* 1: 666) notes that "Almon" is erroneously identified with Ailamon (Aijalon) on the Madeba map (6th century A.D.) based on a reference in Eus. (*Onomast.* 18: 14). In the Crusader period, Amieth (Alemeth) is mentioned along with Aneth (Anathoth) and Farafonte (Ayn Fara).

Bibliography

Albright, W. F. 1924. Alameth and Azmaveth. AASOR 4: 156–57.

Henry O. Thompson

ALMON-DIBLATHAIM (PLACE) [Heb *ʿalmōn diblātayim*]. One of Israel's wilderness wandering encampments located within the territory of Moab between Dibon-gad and the mountains of Abarim (Num 33:46, 47). It has been equated by some with Beth-diblathaim (mentioned in Jer 48:22 and in the Moabite stone, line 30), a site which has been tentatively identified with *Deleilat esh-Sherqiyeh* (M.R. 228116), a small town about halfway between Dibon and Medeba. Others have thought that Almon was a daughter settlement of Diblathaim, that is Beth-diblathaim, and have located the former at nearby *ʿAin ed Dib.* All of the suggestions are speculative at present.

Randall W. Younker

ALMOND. See FLORA.

ALOES. See PERFUMES AND SPICES; FLORA.

ALPHA. The first letter of the Greek alphabet.

ALPHA AND OMEGA. The first and last letters of the Greek alphabet. The phrase "the Alpha and the Omega" is used three times in the book of Revelation, twice as a self-designation of God (1:8; 21:6) and once as a self-designation of Christ (22:13). The meaning of "alpha and omega" is evident from the descriptive phrases used in conjunction with it. Rev 1:8 further describes God as the one "who is and who was and who is to come, the Almighty," whereas in 21:6 "the Alpha and the Omega" is supplemented by the phrase "the beginning and the end." Christ identifies himself as "the Alpha and the Omega, the first and the last, the beginning and the end" (22:13). The juxtaposition of the terms "alpha" and "omega" unites creation and eschatology. The God who brought the world into existence is the same one who will bring the world to completion. As the Alpha, God is the creator of all things; everything has its beginning in God (Rev 4:11). To refer to God as the Omega is to affirm that all of creation finds its purpose and meaning in God, for God will bring the universe to its final consummation. What God commenced "in the beginning" (Gen 1:1), God will direct to its conclusion.

Furthermore, all of history is under the control of God, not just its beginning and ending. In later rabbinic writings the first and last letters of the alphabet were used to denote something in its entirety. Abraham was said to have kept the law from *ʾalep* to *taw* (the first and last letters of the Hebrew alphabet), meaning that he obeyed the entire law. In a similar way, to describe God as the Alpha and the Omega is not a restriction of God to only the beginning and the end but is a declaration of the totality of God's power and control. God is "the Almighty," and as such all "salvation and glory and power belong to our God" (Rev

19:1). Nothing is outside the purview of God. The claim that God is the one "who is and who was and who is to come" is a restatement of the same idea.

The author of Revelation, because of his exalted Christology, can apply the same phrases to Christ that he used for God. He too is the first and the last, the beginning and the end, the Alpha and the Omega. Elsewhere in the NT, Christ's role in creation is explicitly stated (John 1:3; Col 1:16). The idea of Christ as the Omega or the end is particularly appropriate in Revelation which depicts Christ as the means through which God's purposes are accomplished, not only as the slain lamb (5:9), but also as the victorious rider on the white horse (19:11–21).

The source for the author of Revelation's description of God as the first and the last was likely the Hebrew Bible, specifically Isa 41:4; 44:6; and 48:12, passages which emphasize the uniqueness of God. Although the symbolic use of the first and last letters of the alphabet is not found there, this practice can be documented in Hellenistic writings, in Josephus, and in rabbinic literature.

Bibliography

Farrer, A. 1949. *A Rebirth of Images.* Westminster.

Kittel, G. 1964. Alpha, Omega. *TDNT* 1: 1–3.

MITCHELL G. REDDISH

ALPHAEUS (PERSON) [Gk *halphaios*]. **1.** Father of Levi the tax-collector (Mark 2:14; Luke 5:27 [D]; *Gos. Pet.* 14:60).

2. Father of James the apostle, as distinguished from the apostle James the son of Zebedee (Matt 10:3; Mark 3:18; Luke 6:15; Acts 1:13).

Although nothing more is known for certain about either Alphaeus, it has been suggested that the two are actually the same person. Assuming that Levi is to be identified with Matthew the apostle, then another pair of brothers in addition to Peter, Andrew, James, and John would be among the twelve, i.e., James and Matthew. The manner in which Alphaeus is used in the lists of the apostles, however, strongly suggests two different individuals are intended. Alphaeus is used to distinguish this James from the son of Zebedee. Furthermore, since two sets of brothers among the twelve are identified (Matt 10:3), if there were a third set, they surely would also have been identified as such.

Several textual witnesses for Mark 2:14 read "James the son of Alphaeus" rather than "Levi the son of Alphaeus," thus eliminating one difficulty, but suggesting that another tax-collector, named James, was a follower of Jesus. The textual variation is likely an attempt to harmonize Mark 2:14 with Mark 3:18 and Matt 10:3 = Luke 6:15. But it creates another difficulty when compared to its parallel, Luke 5:27, which reads "a tax-collector named Levi." The variant reading is unlikely original.

The second Alphaeus is sometimes identified with Clopas (John 19:25) or Cleopas (Luke 24:18). The identification with Clopas is based on the assumption that only three women at the cross are mentioned in John 19:25 (and not four) as in the parallel verses (Matt 27:56; Mark 15:40). Thus, Mary the sister of Jesus' mother is said to be the wife of Clopas, and is supposedly listed second in Matt 27:56 and Mark 15:40 as Mary the mother of James and Joseph (Joses in Mark). Consequently, James is the son of Alphaeus (Clopas) and Mary, thus making him a cousin of Jesus. This conclusion would suggest that five cousins of Jesus were among the twelve apostles. While such possibilities are interesting they are more speculative than provable.

Identifying Alphaeus with Clopas/Cleopas is based on the claim that they are variations of a common Aramaic original (e.g., Edersheim 1899,2: 603). Since the form of the original has not been established, such an argument offers little support for identifying Alphaeus with Clopas. Cleopas is an abbreviated form of the Greek name Cleopatros and should not be identified with Clopas. See also CLOPAS, CLEOPAS, JAMES (PERSON), LEVI, MARY (PERSON), MATTHEW.

Bibliography

Edersheim, A. 1899. *The Life and Times of Jesus the Messiah.* 2 vols. 8th ed. New York.

FRANK E. WHEELER

ALTAR [Heb *mizbēaḥ;* Gk *thusiastērion, bōmos*]. Altars occur in a wide range of religions, both geographically and chronologically, often related to the concept of tables, hearths, thrones, or burial mounds. In the ancient world, any surface on which offerings were made or placed for a deity could be considered an altar. Altars could be portable or stationary, simple or elaborate (*EncRel* 1: 222–27).

A. Altars in the Hebrew Bible

While scholars speak of altars in connection with a variety of phenomena, the primary term for altar in the Hebrew Bible is *mizbēaḥ* (400x) which is derived from the root *zbḥ,* "to slaughter." Altars are distinguished from other cultic structures such as temples and high places. Although all temples had associated altars, it appears that not all altars were part of a temple complex. Altars were constructed at places which were considered to have a sacred character, points where contact between the human and the divine could occur. For a discussion of Heb *bāmâ,* see HIGH PLACE.

1. Construction. Throughout the period of the monarchy, it was the king who was held accountable for the construction and maintenance of altars and related structures (Ahlström 1982: 1–9). It is uncertain if altars were built by private persons. Although a variety of nonroyal figures from the Hebrew Bible are credited with the construction of altars (e.g., Noah, Abraham, Moses, etc.), it may be that these figures were given "royal" prerogatives in the tradition because of their status. While there are other clear cases of nonroyal figures constructing altars (e.g., Balaam in Numbers 23), these figures are acting on the authority of a royal patron.

It appears that "natural" rock altars were used for rituals in some cases (Judg 13:15–20), although the term *mizbēaḥ* is not always used in the description of this type of situation (1 Sam 6:14–15; 14:33–34). The terminology associated with altars in the Hebrew Bible indicates that altars were normally thought of as being constructed in some sense. The most common verbs used for the establishment of altars are "to build" *(bnh)* and "to make" *(ʿśh)*. In some cases these are used interchangeably (cf. Gen 35:1–7) although *bnh* is not used with altars constructed with metal. Other terms associated with the construction of altars are "to establish" *(qûm)*, "to set up" *(nṣb)*, "to put/place" *(śîm)*, "to arrange/set in order" *(ʿrk)*, and "to found" *(kûn)*. The terms used to describe the repair of altars include "to heal" *(rpʾ)*, "to make new" *(ḥdš)*, and "to purify" *(ṭhr)*.

Within the Hebrew Bible are several accounts of religious "reforms" which include the decommissioning or destruction of altars. A variety of terms are used for this activity. Since these same terms are often used for the demolition of buildings and other man-made structures, it indicates that altars also were normally constructed. The most common verb for destruction is "to tear down" *(ntṣ)*, occurring often in the Deuteronomic material. Other terms include "to cause to depart/decommission" *(śîr)*, "to throw down" *(hrs)*, "to tear apart" *(qrʿ)*, "to smash" *(šbr)*, "to be waste" *(ḥrb)*, "to be desolate" *(šmm)*, and "to break" *(ʿrp)*.

Although very often single altars are assumed in the Hebrew Bible, it is clear that multiple altars were known. This is indicated by the occurrence of the plural *(mizbĕḥôt)* and from the fact that it was necessary to distinguish certain altars (e.g., the altar of burnt offering). The story of Balaam's construction of seven altars (Numbers 23), while not necessarily reflecting historical reality, also indicates knowledge of the use of multiple altars.

One feature of the design of Israelite altars was the presence of "horns" *(qĕrānôt)*. As can be seen in numerous examples of smaller incense altars and from the larger altar found at Beer-sheba (see below), these "horns" were projections from the corners. The precise significance of the horns is not known. One theory is that the original function of the horns was to aid in binding a victim to the altar. This may be given some support in Ps 118:27. Also, owing to the special sanctity of the altar, a person accused of a murder could "grasp" the horns of the altar to receive a measure of protection (but cf. Exod 21:14; 1 Kgs 2:28–34; Milgrom 1980). Jer 17:1 seems to indicate that the horns could be engraved, but the text is possibly corrupt. The cutting off of the horns is used as a symbol of the destruction in Amos 3:14. Horned altars are not unique to Israel. They are found in Canaanite contexts (Stendebach 1976: 190–92), in excavations at temples in Cyprus (cf. Karageorghis 1981; Ionas 1985), and other locations throughout the ancient Near East (cf. Yavis 1949: 165–66).

Altars associated with the tabernacle were considered portable, being equipped with rings through which poles could be inserted for transport. While portable altars are known from nomadic contexts, there is no evidence that the altars constructed during the period of the Israelite or Judahite monarchies were normally moved. The historical evaluation of the portable altars of the tabernacle is dependent on the larger historical questions surrounding the tabernacle itself.

2. Materials. The Hebrew Bible mentions a variety of materials used for the construction of altars. It would appear that the ideology concerning the materials of the altar changed over time and/or from place to place. In the introductory material to the Covenant Code (Exod 20:24–25), an initial command is given that an "altar of earth" *(mizbēaḥ ʾădāmâ)* be constructed. The precise meaning of this unique term is uncertain. Robertson (1948) thinks it means simply an altar of "natural" materials. Galling (IDB 1: 97) states that it refers to an altar constructed as a "low cube of clods of clay." The existence of mudbrick altars in this region would make it more likely that some type of earthen brick is intended (cf. Isa 65:3).

In Exodus 20, however, the possibility of construction of a stone altar is admitted. As might be expected in Israel, stone is the assumed building material for altars. In Exod 20:25, Josh 8:31, and Deut 27:5–7, where altars of stone *(mizbēaḥ ʾăbānîm)* are specified, it is commanded that these stones be unworked by iron. This command may reflect the idea that the unworked stone contained something of the "natural" presence of the deity which would be dissipated through the working with iron (Galling IDB 1: 97). Most scholars believe that Exod 20:25 is the earliest of the three passages, reflecting an attempt at cultic reform prior to the Deuteronomist. This prescription was not universally followed since altars constructed of hewn stone were constructed in Judah (cf. Beer-sheba below). It would appear that altars which included horns could not be either of "earth" or "unworked stone" (cf. Wiener 1927: 2–3).

Exod 20:26 gives an impression of the size of an altar by commanding that the altar not be mounted by means of steps in order that the "nakedness" of the priest not be exposed. This command implies that steps were part of the normal construction of the altar. Altars with steps are known from early times in Canaan (cf. Megiddo below), but steps are not conspicuous in the description of altars from the period of the Israelite and Judahite monarchies (cf. Beer-sheba below however). It would appear that the problem of exposure was solved differently in Exod 28:42–43, which commands the wearing of "pants" by Aaron and the officiating priests (cf. Lev 6:3—Eng 6:10).

Several types of altars constructed with metal are also prominent. Two different bronze altars are mentioned as being located in the forecourt of the tabernacle/temple. (Note the mention of bronze altars also in Phoenician *KAI* I:2 #10.4 and Punic *KAI* I:14 #66.1.) The altar associated with the tabernacle (Exod 27:1–8; 38:1–7) is described as constructed of acacia wood (5 by 5 by 3 cubits) and overlaid *(ṣph)* with bronze. While it is clear that the description of this altar does not derive from a "nomadic" past, the source of the description is unclear. Some scholars believe that the description of the tabernacle derives from the Davidic period but is based on a premonarchic model (Cross 1984). Others date it to Solomonic (Haran 1978: 189–204) or even later periods. The altar in the forecourt at which the regular sacrifices were conducted was called the "altar of burnt offering" *(āh mizbēaḥ hāʿôllāh)* in the Priestly source and in Chronicles (but cf. Gadegaard 1978).

The Chronicler believed that Solomon also constructed a bronze altar (20 by 20 by 10 cubits) in the forecourt of his temple (2 Chr 4:1). It should be noted, however, that the construction of this altar is omitted from the parallel description in 1 Kings 7 although the presence of a bronze altar is assumed in 1 Kgs 8:64, 2 Kgs 16:14–15, and Ezek 9:2. Some scholars believe that the notice of construction has been displaced from its original location in 1 Kings to Chronicles. It is possible that this altar should be differentiated from an altar of stone (note the use of *bnh*) built by Solomon mentioned in 1 Kgs 9:25. This stone altar may also be implied in the wording of 2 Kgs 16:14. (Additional support for the existence of two altars can be found in Gadegaard 1978: 40–41 although his interpretation of "high place" may be questioned.) This stone altar constructed by Solomon may be the one which is replaced (2 Kgs 16:10–16) with a "great altar" *(hammizbēaḥ haggādôl)* modeled after an altar seen by Ahaz in Damascus. At that time the bronze altar was moved and reserved for inquiries by the king himself. The regular sacrifices of the nation and king were conducted on the new "great altar."

Another noteworthy altar is that described in some detail in Ezek 43:13–17. At the center of the reconstructed land, Ezekiel envisions a three-tiered altar mounted by steps (12 by 12 cubits on the top tier and 16 by 16 cubits on the lowest tier). This idea may be based on a Babylonian model (Albright 1920: 139–41) or even on Ahaz's "great altar" (*IDB* 1: 98; Haran 1978: 194).

The normal placement of sacrificial altars in the Hebrew Bible was in the courtyard in front of the temple, although altars on the roof were also known (cf. 2 Kgs 23:12, Judg 6:26). (Note may also be made of the Ugaritic text *UT* Krt:73–80, which speaks of the hero offering sacrifices on a wall // tower // roof.)

There is no evidence of the use of sacrificial altars in the interior of the tabernacle or temple. In fact, sacrificial rituals are specifically excluded from the temple itself in Exod 30:9. The normal activities associated with a sacrificial altar are also indicated in Josh 22:28–29 where the trans-Jordanian tribes claim that their "altar" is in fact a "memorial" (see below). They claim their "memorial" is not intended for the normal activities of "burnt offering, cereal offering, or for sacrifice" (v 29). Even types of offerings which might be associated with a "presentation" altar are burned (Exod 29:25). Vessels and offerings were placed "before" *(lipnê)* the altar, not upon it (cf. Deut 26:4; Zech 14:20). It is also possible that images of gods were placed near the altar (cf. 1 Sam 6:15; Ezek 6:13).

Within the interior of the tabernacle/temple were "altars" connected to the use of incense. Exod 30:1–10 and 37:25 describe an "altar" of acacia wood overlaid with gold (1 by 1 by 2 cubits) within the tabernacle. Most scholars think that this "altar" was not part of the original description since its presence is not noted in Exodus 25 or 26:33–37 as expected. This altar is paralleled by the description of an altar of cedar overlaid with gold constructed by Solomon (1 Kgs 6:20, 22). For further discussion of these altars, see INCENSE ALTARS where the "altar of incense" *(mizbēaḥ haqqĕṭōret)* and "incense altars" *(ḥammānîm)* are treated. Ezekiel also mentions an "altar of wood" (*hammizbēaḥ ʿēṣ*; Ezek 41:22) found within the temple, but goes on to describe this rather as a "table" *(haššulhān)*.

3. Activities Associated with Altars. The most common activities associated with altars in the Hebrew Bible are the burning of sacrifices upon the altar. Some passages (e.g., Gen 22:9–10) might indicate that the offering was actually slain upon the altar (cf. Gadegaard 1978: 35–36). The usual practice reflected in the text, however, is the slaying of the victim beside *(ʿl)* or in front of *(lipnê)* the altar in order that blood could be collected for other ritual purposes.

Several verbs are used to describe the actions of cultic personnel in connection with the altar. The most common terms refer to the offering of sacrifices, "to cause a sacrifice to ascend" *(ʿlh)* and "to burn offerings" *(qṭr)*. In addition to the obvious role of the altar in the burning of offerings to the god, the altar (especially the foundation [*yĕsôd*] and the horns) was the recipient of blood from the sacrificial victims. A wide range of terms is used to describe the application of blood to the altar, including (prominently) "to toss, throw" *(zrq)*. While blood and oil were applied to the altar, the altar did not function as a libation table as found in earlier Canaanite practice (cf. Megiddo below).

The significance of the preposition *(ʿl)* used with these verbs is unclear. In some instances it seems to indicate that the action takes places "upon," i.e., on top of, the altar (e.g., 1 Kgs 9:25). In other cases, it denotes proximity (e.g., 2 Chr 1:6). The clear picture seems to be that wood was placed on the top of the altar. The sacrifice was then placed upon the wood. The precise function of a bronze grating mentioned in connection with the tabernacle altar (cf. Exod 27:4) is not known. As discussed earlier, the altar is assumed to be large enough and high enough to need steps. The verb "to descend" is used when Aaron leaves the altar in Lev 9:22. (Note might be taken of the similar Ugaritic use of *mdbḥt* with the verb *yrd,* "to go down," in *UT* 1.20.)

Although the tabernacle altar is described as hollow *(nĕbūb),* in no case are actions described which indicate that the sacrifice was burned within the altar. It may be that the altar was filled with earth in order to dissipate the heat generated in the burning of sacrifices. Several examples of altars constructed with a fill of ash or earth/rubble are noted by Yavis (1949: 62–63, 84, 97, 100, 111, 115, 129, 154, 169, 175–76, 178–80, 204, 207–13). This method of construction might answer the principal objection to the use of these altars as burnt-offering altars made by Gadegaard (1978). This method was suggested earlier by the rabbis but rejected by Robertson (1948: 17–18).

In several cases it appears that the normal usage of *mizbēaḥ* has been extended. The only apparent reference to a "presentation altar" is in Ezek 41:22 where an "altar of wood" (2 by 2 by 3 cubits) is described as "a table which is before Yahweh." It also seems that the altar located within the tabernacle/temple was used only for the burning of incense, not other sacrifices (see above). It is more likely that the understanding of the term "altar" has expanded to include these cases rather than an otherwise unknown ancient use of the term having been preserved.

The term *mizbēaḥ* is also used for another type of construction which serves primarily as a "memorial" within the Hebrew Bible. Several "altars" are given names, often in connection with some unusual event (cf. Gen 33:20; 35:7; Exod 17:15; Josh 22:10–34; and Judg 6:24). In none of these cases are sacrifices actually offered upon these "altars." Whether these constructions were memorials which the author calls "altars" or whether they were altars which later authors attempted to legitimize by assigning an acceptable function is not clear (cf. Snaith 1978; Van Seters 1980: 232). A similar case of a rock being designated as a named "memorial" is found in 1 Sam 7:12, but without the term *mizbēaḥ* being used.

Altars did have other functions. Altars were built to mark the territory associated with the deity (cf. 1 Kgs 18:17–40; 2 Kgs 5:17) although altars in foreign territories were also known (e.g., Elephantine, cf. Wiener 1927: 8–9). As noted above, within Israel the altar also served as a place of asylum.

There are differences among the various "authors" of the Hebrew Bible in their portrayal of altars. The Yahwist assumes Levitical distinctions for the altars even in the pre-Mosaic period. The Priestly author does not allow Levitical distinctions before Sinai. He assumes the existence of only one altar since Sinai but in some senses has reduced its sanctity compared to earlier ideas (e.g., it no longer provides asylum; Milgrom 1980). The Deuteronomist (Deut 12:15–24) loosens the connection between the altar and the slaughter of animals prescribed in earlier writings (Lev 17:1–7).

B. Archaeological Evidence

A survey of the literature would seem to indicate that the archaeological evidence for altars is quite extensive. In fact, from an archaeological perspective, there is little agreement on the type of installation to which the term "altar" is applied. It is used for everything from large platforms to somewhat smaller installations with evidence of burning in courtyards of temples to numerous types of flat surfaces with "cup marks" found in a wide variety of contexts (cf. Kittel 1908: 98–146). These later examples are extremely difficult to evaluate archaeologically since they often occur outside of obvious cultic contexts and are impossible to date with any confidence. It may even be questioned whether their function is cultic rather than practical. It is clear that cultic activities took place within the context of wine and olive pressing and threshing floors (cf. Ahlström 1982: 25 n 89). It is doubtful, however, that these installations should be termed "altars" on the basis of the usage of the term in the literature of the Hebrew Bible.

An example of these difficulties can be seen with an "altar" found at Ṣarᶜa west of Jerusalem. There is found a large, stepped stone block (2.16 by 2.16 by 1.3m) on which is a series of channels and cup marks (Kittel 1908: 104–8; *IDB* 1: 100). Many scholars have related this installation to the offering of Manoah reported in Judges 13. It must be noted, however, that the date of this installation is unknown, and also that the term "altar" is only indirectly applied to the rock upon which the offerings were made in the Judges account. Whether there is, in fact, any connection between these two pieces of evidence is unknown.

1. Early Altars in Canaan. There existed in Canaan a long tradition of altar construction prior to the Israelite period. Already in the Chalcolithic period there is evidence that altars were in use. In a broadroom sanctuary at Ein Gedi, directly opposite the entry, a horseshoe-shaped altar composed of large stones was found. Bones and broken clay figurines were found within the ashes of the altar (Ussishkin 1971: 29).

The tradition of broadroom temples with raised platforms opposite the entry may be carried on into the Early Bronze Age (cf. Megiddo XIX Temple 4050 and Megiddo XV Temples 5192 and 4040, although no evidence of sacrifice is present). One of the most impressive altars discovered in Canaan was unearthed at the site of Megiddo (Structure 4017). Located in an area surrounded by temples, this large, nearly circular stone altar (8m diameter) stands 1.4m high and was mounted by a flight of steps. The altar and surrounding enclosure was in existence through at least four phases during EB III–IV. The surrounding area was littered with bone and pottery fragments and the top had indications of burning (Loud 1948: 61–64, 70–84). (Concerning the Early Bronze Age "temples" and associated altars claimed for Ai [et-Tell], cf. Ottosson 1980: 128–30 n.2.)

Structures similar to the circular altar at Megiddo have also been found at a temple dated to MB II B–C at Nahariyah. A three-phase circular stone structure (14m diameter) with two steps was found in the courtyard of the temple. Among the stones of this structure was organic material which may have been the remains of offerings. About 4m distance from the circular structure the excavators discovered a small stone installation they described as an altar. However, they give no evidence of its use. Finds from the courtyard include ash, bones, figurines, and pottery associated with cultic activity. Ottosson's conclusion that the circular structure may have functioned as an altar is more likely than the smaller installation indicated by the excavators (Ottosson 1980: 99–101; Dothan 1974: 14–25). Cf. also the circular structures dated to MB IIB–LB I at Tell Kittan (Eisenberg 1977: 77–81).

A later level (VIII) at Megiddo also reveals evidence of a small (1.10 by 1.10 by .55m), lime-plastered mudbrick "altar" or "table" in court 5020. Although no evidence connects this building to cultic activity, its similarities to the Acropolis Temple at Lachish might be noted. If this connection is valid, the strong Egyptian influence at Lachish would make identification as a "table" or "presentation altar" more likely since blood sacrifice was apparently not part of the Egyptian ritual at that time. No direct evidence of burning or sacrifice is mentioned on or near the structure (Loud 1948: 113–14).

Galling has related this structure to others found at Tell ᶜAjjul and Shechem (*IDB* 1: 99). It would seem, however, that these latter examples are altars in courtyards in front of the temple while the example from Megiddo is differently located within an internal court. The altar from Shechem may have been founded in the courtyard of the *migdal*-type Temple Ib and was prominent in its position directly in front of the entrance of Temple 2. It is constructed of mudbrick and stone (2.2 by 1.65 by .35m?).

Late Bronze Age Hazor also has an example in Area H of a centrally located altar in front of a temple which was used through several levels. In the forecourt of the temple of Stratum 2 (LB I) containing ash and bone remains, a large (3.5 by 2 by .3m?) altar (2534) and nearby a smaller one (2554) were found. In the course of time the courtyard was enclosed (but remained unroofed?). It seems likely that the installation (2218) in a similar position in front of the later Temple IA (LB III) is the remains of an altar carrying on the same tradition.

In the main room (2113) of this same temple, several "libation" and "offering" tables were found. Other finds also imply that liquid offerings were important in this sanctuary (cf. Ottosson 1980: 32). This is also evident in the placement of a "libation altar" in the passageway just outside the forecourt of the Stratum IB temple. Also during Stratum I in Area F, a large stone block (2.4 by .85

by 1.2m) with two depressions was found. Although there were finds of pottery and bones around this "altar," it differs from the other "altars" in that there is no clearly related temple. If this was an altar, it is not evident what type of offerings were associated with it. The prominence of libation installations in Area H might indicate that this "altar" also functioned as a libation table (cf. Yadin 1972: 100–1 and fig. 25). A similar large stone was found at the MB II–LB "High Place" at Gezer in front of the monoliths. Its function is also unknown.

A recent study of the mudbrick "altars" from the Beth Shan IX has found little support for their designation as altars (Ottosson 1980: 63–66). The "altar" associated with the Fosse Temple at Lachish may better be termed a dais since this building was clearly roofed and the installation would not have functioned for burning sacrifices.

2. Altars from the Israelite Period. A series of Philistine temples from Iron Age I have been excavated at Tel Qasile. In the courtyard (111) of the Stratum X temple, a low (1.3 by 1.5 by .1m) stone foundation for an altar was discovered. The floor of the courtyard contained sherds, animal bones, and ash. A less well preserved altar (108) may be found in the following Stratum IX courtyard (Mazar 1980: 40–41, 51).

Also dated to the early Iron Age is an installation located on Mt. Ebal near ancient Shechem (Zertal 1985, 1988). This installation has been connected to the altar described in Josh 8:30–35 by the excavator. Others have claimed that the ruins are a house/watchtower (Kempinski 1986). The main structure is approximately 9 by 7m and is preserved to a height of 3.27m. It contains a fill of pottery, ash, and bones. According to the excavator, the structure is approached by ramps, one of which is 1.2m wide. The structure is surrounded by an inner courtyard which contains numerous "installations" with ash, animal bones, or clay vessels. The entire area is surrounded by an enclosure wall (250 by 52m). The "altar" complex was preceded by a circular stone structure (2m diameter) also filled with ash and bones.

Within the Judahite fortress at Tel Arad, a shrine was discovered including an altar which continued in use over several periods. It is reported by the excavator that near a square stone altar in an open area of the lowest level were pits with burned bones. During the following periods, the sanctuary was constructed with a square earth and fieldstone altar (5 cubits^2) centrally located in the courtyard. A large flint slab was found on top of this altar. In later strata the altar was rebuilt in the same location, but an addition of a wall to the north of the courtyard meant that it was no longer centrally located. According to the excavator, the altar was not in use in the final temple complex, a fact which is attributed to the "reforms" of Hezekiah (Aharoni 1968: 2–32). Problems with the stratigraphy and reporting of the evidence from Arad make these historical conclusions difficult to verify. It is likely that the altar(s) of this shrine should be dated to the 7th century B.C.E. (cf. Ussishkin 1988: 142–57).

Similar controversy surrounds the discovery of a large (1.57m high) horned altar at Tel Beer-sheba. This altar, made up of a number of dressed stones, was found reused in the walls of a storehouse from Stratum II just east of the gate. The excavators believe it was part of a now destroyed sanctuary of an earlier level (Aharoni 1974: 2–6). Yadin has argued that it belongs to a sanctuary of Stratum II (reconstructed in Building 430 to the west of the gate). He believes that the steps of this room originally led to the top of the altar (Yadin 1976: 5–14). Since there is no evidence of burning on the stones of the altar, its actual function is unclear. Because its form is similar to that of numerous smaller incense altars, it may be that it was used for incense rather than burnt offerings.

Generally, the conclusions from the archaeological evidence confirm those reached from textual evidence. Altars for burnt offerings stood in the forecourt of the temple. Only incense altars were found within the interior. (cf. Ottosson 1980: 117, 119 n.14). Altars were constructed primarily of stone, although mudbrick and stone-and-earth constructions were also known. As would be expected, no altars constructed with precious metals have survived.

C. Altars in the NT

The LXX and NT generally distinguish between legitimate *(thusiastērion)* and illegitimate *(bōmos)* altars. The latter term is the common word for altar in classical Greek. For study of the archaeological evidence for Greek altars, cf. Yavis (1949).

The term *bōmos* is found only once in the NT in Paul's speech in Athens (Acts 17:23). The basis for his speech is the observation of an altar dedicated to "The Unknown God." There is evidence both from archaeology and from ancient authors to indicate that this type of altar may have been known in Athens. This evidence includes an inscribed altar from 2d century C. E. Pergamum probably reading "to unknown gods" (*IDBSup,* 19).

A number of references in the NT refer back to altars *(thusiastērion)* within the accounts of the Hebrew Bible (cf. Matt 23:35, Luke 11:51, Rom 11:3, Jas 2:21). Another group (Matt 23:18–20, 1 Cor 9:13, etc.) refer to the contemporary altar in the temple of Herod. This altar is described by Josephus (*JW* 5.5.225) as large (50 by 50 by 15 cubits) with a ramp approach. These measurements are somewhat larger than indicated in the Mishnah (30 by 30 by 5 cubits; *Mid.* 3:1).

The reference in Luke 1:11 speaks of Zechariah's service at the altar of incense within the temple. A group of passages in Revelation also imply the existence of a golden horned altar (probably for incense) within the heavenly temple (cf. Rev 9:13).

The only direct reference to a Christian altar is in the metaphor found in Heb 13:10, and its significance is disputed. Some think that the reference is to the cross, others to the communion table, etc. (cf. *IDBSup,* 19–20; *TDNT* 3: 183). For a survey of the ideology of later Christian altars, cf. *EncRel* 1: 225–26.

Bibliography

Aharoni, Y. 1968. Arad: Its Inscriptions and Temple. *BA* 31: 2–32.

———. 1974. The Horned Altar of Beer-sheba. *BA* 37: 2–6.

Ahlström, G. W. 1982. *Royal Administration and National Religion in Ancient Palestine.* Studies in the History of the Ancient Near East 1. Leiden.

Albright, W. F. 1920. The Babylonian Temple-Tower and the Altar of Burnt-Offering. *JBL* 39: 137–42.

Cross, F. M. 1984. The Priestly Tabernacle in the Light of Recent Research. Pp. 91–105 in *The Temple in Antiquity,* ed. Truman G. Madsen. Religious Studies Monograph Series 9. Provo, UT.

Dothan, M. 1974. The Excavations at Nahariyah. *IEJ* 6: 14–25.

Eisenberg, E. 1977. The Temples at Tell Kittan. *BA* 40: 77–81.

Gadegaard, N. H. 1978. On the So-Called Burnt Offering Altar in the Old Testament. *PEQ* 110: 35–45.

Galling, K. 1925. *Der Altar in den Kulturen des alten Orients.* Berlin.

Haran, M. 1978. *Temples and Temple-Service in Ancient Israel.* Oxford.

Ionas, I. 1985. The Altar at Myrtou-*Pigadhes*: A Re-examination of Its Reconstruction. *RDAC* 1985: 137–42.

Karageorghis, V. 1981. The Sacred Area of Kition. Pp. 82–90 in *Temples and High Places in Biblical Times,* ed. Avraham Biran. Jerusalem.

Kempinski, A. 1986. Joshua's Altar—An Iron Age I Watchtower. *BARev* 12,1: 42, 44–49.

Kittel, R. 1908. *Studien zur Hebräischen Archäologie und Religionsgeschichte.* Beiträge zur Wissenschaft vom Alten Testament 1. Leipzig.

Loud, G. 1948. *Megiddo II Seasons of 1935–39: Text.* OIP 62. Chicago.

Mazar, A. 1980. *Excavations at Tell Qasile Part One The Philistine Sanctuary: Architecture and Cult Objects.* Qedem 12. Jerusalem.

Milgrom, J. 1980. Sancta Contagion and Altar/City Asylum. Pp. 278–310 in *Congress Volume,* ed. J. A. Emerton. VTSup 32, Leiden.

Ottosson, M. 1980. *Temples and Cult Places in Palestine.* Boreas 12. Uppsala.

Robertson, E. 1948. The Altar of Earth (Exodus XX, 24–26). *JJS* 1: 12–21.

Snaith, H. H. 1978. The Altar at Gilgal: Joshua XXII 23–29. *VT* 28: 330–35.

Stendebach, F. J. 1976. Altarformen im kanaanäisch-israelitischen Raum. *BZ* n.s. 20: 180–96.

Ussishkin, D. 1971. The "Ghassulian" Temple in Ein Gedi and the Origin of the Hoard from Nahal Mishmar. *BA* 34: 23–39.

———. 1988. The Date of the Judaean Shrine at Arad. *IEJ* 38: 142–57.

Van Seters, J. 1980. The Religion of the Patriarchs in Genesis. *Bib* 61: 220–33.

Wiener, H. M. 1927. *The Altars of the Old Testament.* Beigabe zur orientalistischen Literatur-Zeitung. Leipzig.

Yadin, Y. 1972. *Hazor.* The Schweich Lectures of the British Academy 1970. London.

———. 1976. Beer-sheba: The High Place Destroyed by King Josiah. *BASOR* 222: 5–17.

Yavis, C. G. 1949. *Greek Altars.* Saint Louis University Studies Monograph Series: Humanities No. 1. St. Louis.

Zertal, A. 1985. Has Joshua's Altar Been Found on Mt. Ebal? *BARev* 11,1: 26–43.

———. 1988. A Cultic Center with a Burnt-Offering Altar from Early Iron Age I Period at Mt. Ebal. Pp. 137–47 in *Wünschet Jerusalem Frieden: Collected Communications to the XIIth Congress of the International Organization for the Study of the Old Testament, Jerusalem 1986,* ed. M. Augustin and K. D. Schunck. Frankfurt.

ROBERT D. HAAK

ALTAR OF WITNESS. See WITNESS, ALTAR OF (PLACE).

ALTARS, INCENSE. See INCENSE ALTARS.

ALUSH (PLACE) [Heb *ʾālûš*]. A place in the desert where the Israelites camped after leaving Egypt (Num 33:13). It is listed between Dophkah and Rephidim, and is located somewhere in the area between the Wilderness of Sin and that of Sinai. It may possibly be identified with Wadi el-'Eshsh (cf. *Numbers* WBC, 355). The Sam. Pent. reads "Alish."

GARY A. HERION

ALVAH (PERSON) [Heb *ʿalwâ*]. Var. ALIAH. One of the tribal chiefs of Edom/Esau, according to the list of the chiefs in Gen 36:40–43 (= 1 Chr 1:51b–54). The two variant forms of this name (*ʿalwâ* in Gen 36:40; *ʿalyâ* in 1 Chr 1:51 [but note Qere *ʿlwh*!]), along with the two variant forms of the name of the first son of Shobal (Alvan/Alyan; Heb *ʿalwān*/*ʿalyān*; Gen 36:23 = 1 Chr 1:40), all refer to the same Seiritic-Horitic clan belonging to the tribe of Shobal. See ALVAN (PERSON). The derivation of the name from Hurrian (Feiler 1939; Ginsberg and Maisler 1934) cannot be verified. Rather, it seems to be derived from a Semitic root: **ʿlw* (Arabic) or **ʿly* (NW Semitic), meaning "to be high/lofty/elevated" (cf. Arabic *ʿlwʾn*; Sabaean, Liḥyanite, Safaitic *ʿlyn*). Alvah/Alvan probably represents the Edomite form of the name (while Aliah/Alian conveys the "Hebraized" form), formed according to **Paʿl* with "Bildungs suffixe" *-ā* and *-an* (Weippert 1971: 244, 260).

Bibliography

Feiler, W. 1939. Hurritische Namen im Alten Testament. *ZA* 45: 216–29.

Ginsberg, H. L., and Maisler (Mazar), B. 1934. Semitised Hurrians in Syria and Palestine. *JPOS* 14: 243–67.

Kornfeld, W. 1985. Die Edomiterlisten (Gn 36; 1 C 1) im Lichte des altarabischen Namensmateriales. *AOAT* 215: 231–36.

Moritz, B. 1926. Edomitische Genealogien I. *ZAW* 44: 81–93.

Weippert, M. 1971. *Edom. Studien und Materialien zur Geschichte der Edomiter auf Grund schriftlicher und archäologischer Quellen.* Diss. Tübingen.

ULRICH HÜBNER

ALVAN (PERSON) [Heb *ʿalwān*] Var. ALIAN. A clan name mentioned in the genealogy of Seir the Horite in Gen 36:23. These clans, not to be confused with Hurrian groups in Mesopotamia, are mentioned as the original "inhabitants of the land" of Edom (perhaps as cave dwellers). Alvan is listed as one of the five sons of Shobal and he is thus the grandson of Seir. The name in this form only appears in Genesis 36, but an alternate form, Alian, does appear in the matching genealogical clan list in 1 Chr 1:40. This variant may be due to the confusion between *waw* and *yod.* (But see discussion in ALVAH.) See Deut 2:12–22 for mention of the dispossession of the Horite clans in the region of Seir (Edom) by the encroaching "sons of Esau." This conquest is paired in the text with the conquest by the Israelite tribes of Canaan.

VICTOR H. MATTHEWS

AM HAʾAREZ. A Hebrew term (sing. *ʿăm hāʾārĕṣ;* pl. *ʿămmê hāʾāreṣ, ʿămmê hāʾărāṣôt*) literally meaning "people of the land." The term occurs 73 times in the OT (51 times in sing. forms and 22 times in pl. forms). The LXX translates the term *tò laòs tēs gēs,* though in Lev 20:2 and Dan 9:6 it is translated *to ethnos to epi tēs gēs* and in Lev 20:4 *hoi autochthones tēs gēs.*

Because of its frequency the term has generated a variety of opinions as to its exact meaning. The term *ʿăm* is contrasted with the term *gôy* (Rost 1934: 147). The latter is taken to refer to people in general, while *ʿăm* is thought to refer to the specific population of a territory. There is also a general consensus that *ʾărĕṣ* is interchangeable with certain other terms, e.g., *ʿăm yĕhûdāh* (2 Kgs 14:21). *ʿăm* likewise is said to be coterminal with the term *ʾănšê,* as in *ʾănšê yĕhûdāh* (2 Sam 2:4) (Würthwein 1936: 15).

The debate over the term centers around its use as a *terminus technicus.* The most extreme point of view on its technical sense is represented in the classic work of Mayer Sulzberger (1909). Sulzberger argues that in ancient Israel there existed a national assembly (Edah) composed of two houses (Nesiim and Zekenim). The Nesiim was the smaller of the two chambers (12 members) and the Zekenim the larger (70 members). The Zekenim were elected representatives from the 11 tribes exclusive of Levi (Sulzberger 1909: 8–13). Sulzberger notes that the Edah was dissolved upon the death of Joshua. He then attempts to identify an entity which carried on those functions between the death of Joshua and the clear emergence of a political body in the Gerusia of the Hellenistic period. In his view, the *ʿăm hāʾārĕs* was this entity, and he cites a number of passages to support this (Gen 23:7, 12, 13; Lev 4:27; 20:2, 4). Chiefly, however, it is in the events surrounding the downfall of Athaliah and the critical role that the *ʿăm hāʾārĕs* played in that episode (2 Kings 11, esp. vv 14, 18–20) that Sulzberger sees the clear evidence of the political function of the group.

Sulzberger's views, however, were generally considered to be too extreme, too tendentious, and too heavily dependent on textual interpretations that failed to take into account the complex nature of the use of the term and the contexts in which it occurred.

The prevalent position on the term was elaborated by Ernst Würthwein (1936). He argues that the term indicates the cadre of fully enfranchised male citizens (1936: 18). This group represents a sort of power elite, the band of those who form the solid core of the nation. Würthwein argues that this group not only formed a distinct social group but that they represented, in effect, a powerful class whose economic, social, and military power combined to make them a critical faction in the functioning of the state (1936: 15–18).

He traces the development of this group from the earliest period of the monarchy, identifying the *ʿăm hāʾārĕṣ* with the *ʾănšê yĕhûdāh* of 2 Sam 2:4. The power of the group was most prevalent in the early period of the Davidic-Solomonic monarchy when the interests of the various "tribal" groups had to be carefully manipulated to achieve consensus on the monarchy and on the specific choice of kings. This sense of independence from the monarch was stronger certainly in N Israel than in S Judah, where the symbiosis of royal and group interests had been largely accomplished through the political skills exercised by David in his acquisition of power. In Judah the interests of the monarch had become, in effect, the interests of the people. But at the earliest stages there were still vestiges of this independent power. The power was certainly based in tradition, but the real power of the group rested on its military capacity as a militia.

In response to this old ideology of a militia, both David and Solomon were able to develop significant independent military power by gathering a personal bodyguard and armed force whose loyalty was to the king and not to the nation as a whole (Würthwein 1936: 20).

But despite this older sense of a body of freeholders, the most significant development of the concept of the *ʿăm hāʾārĕṣ* came after the breakup of the two kingdoms, and specifically in Judah in the period between Athaliah (842–837 B.C.E.) and the Exile (589 B.C.E.). During this period, according to Würthwein, we can clearly see the term being used to designate a specific, identifiable class. The cases cited are first the role of the *ʿăm hāʾārĕṣ* in the overthrow of Athaliah and the selection of Joash (2 Kings 11; 2 Chronicles 23). In that instance the *ʿăm hāʾārĕṣ* are associated with other clearly designated groups (priests, palace officials, military leaders) in the revolution and enthronement of the new king. There is also a note in 1 Kgs 11:18 which associates the *ʿăm hāʾārĕṣ* with the military group who destroyed the temple of Ba'al (though this reference is omitted in 2 Chronicles 23). A second case is 2 Kgs 21:25 (= 2 Chr 33:25), where the "people of the land" slay the assassins of Amon (642–640 B.C.E.) and participate in the election and enthronement of Josiah (640–609 B.C.E.). A third instance is 2 Kgs 23:30 (= 2 Chr 26:1), which associates the "people of the land" with the enthronement of Jehoahaz.

More evidence of a class of "people of the land" is found in 2 Kgs 23:35, where the "people of the land" are taxed to raise tribute for Pharaoh Neco. There is a regular association of the *ʿăm hāʾārĕṣ* with recognized social classes in other areas as well. In Jer 1:15; 34:19; 37:2; 44:21, they are associated with princes and priests, eunuchs, servants of the king, and the king himself, all of which would seem to indicate some sense of a distinct group at this period.

While acknowledging the work that Würthwein has done, Nicholson examines the term outside the Kings-Chronicles-Jerusalem complex (i.e., royal establishment) and argues that in these other instances (Gen 23:7, 12, 13; 42:6; Exod 5:5; Leviticus 20) the term is ambiguous at best and in many ways nearly generic (1965: 60–62). He further considers the main texts from Kings, and in each of these he raises doubts about the specific uses of the term. Stretching further into Ezekiel (12:19; 33:2; 39:13; 45:22; 46:3, 9), he makes the case for a contextually based interpretation of the term.

Nicholson's arguments parallel in some sense the position taken by de Vaux (*AncIsr,* 70–72). De Vaux sees the term as simply designating the "body of free men, enjoying civic rights in a given territory" (p. 70). He considers the term's use in three periods. First, in the preexilic period, it is associated with specific groups: the king or the prince, the king and his servants, priests and chiefs, the chiefs, the priests, and the prophets, and with no others. But he argues that it designates simply the "whole body of citizens" (p. 71). De Vaux is at pains to show that in 2 Kgs 11:20, where a distinction apparently is made between "the people of the land" and the inhabitants of Jerusalem, the distinction is not based on "class" differences but simply on residency (those inside and outside the city). Second, at the time of the return from Exile, the term at first has this old meaning, but in Ezra and Nehemiah it begins to change. Finally, in the rabbinic literature, it becomes a pejorative term.

Halpern (1981) considers the evidence and argues that the term *ʿam* is the consanguineous unit, the corporation of Israel, and the people *(ʿăm-)* of the land are the people who have the land in common (1981: 196–98). He argues against any connection between the people of the land and military units, and generally supports a contextual interpretation.

There is no question that the term changes meaning dramatically after the exile. De Vaux and others show that in Haggai (2:4) and Ezekiel (7:27; 12:19; 22:19; 22:29; 33:2; 39:13; 45:16; 45:22; 46:3; 46:9) the term retains its preexilic sense. This may also be the case in Dan 9:6. But in Ezra and Nehemiah the term begins to take on a different meaning. On the one hand, Ezra 2:2 and Neh 7:7 seem to designate the men/people of Israel and the men/people of the land much as in the preexilic period. But, on the other hand, Ezra 4:4 contrasts the "people of the land" and the "people of Judah" in a way that indicates a conflict of interests.

Most significantly, the term is used in the plural in the postexilic period; it is used either to indicate the group which opposed the restoration of the temple state or to refer to the heterogeneous population which the returnees found in the land. This population is characteristically viewed with disdain (Ezra 9:1, 2; 10:2, 11; Neh 10:20–31).

In a recent study of this late development in the use of the term, Gunneweg has proposed that the term *gôlâ* takes on a revised and enriched meaning. The *běnê hāggôlâ* are the true congregation in contradistinction to all the inhabitants of the land, the *ʿămmê hāʾărāṣôt.* Thus the terms intend a theological meaning for what were once sociological groups. Gunneweg designates this a "semantic revolution" (1983: 437–40). The rabbinic use then picks up on this late development and the term eventually comes to have a pejorative meaning. It refers to the ignorant, the impious, the nonobservant, etc.

From this general review it is clear that there is little evidence to support extreme interpretations of the term. But there is sufficient evidence in various periods to indicate that within a carefully defined context the term may have specific senses. Our growing knowledge of the social construction of early Israel may help clarify the specific contextual situations that justify one or another use of the term.

Bibliography

Gunneweg, A. H. J. 1983. ʿAM HAʾAREṢ—A Semantic Revolution. *ZAW* 95: 437–40.

Halpern, B. 1981. *The Constitution of the Monarchy in Israel.* HSM 25. Chico.

Nicholson, E. W. 1965. The Meaning of the Expression ʿam haʾarez in the Old Testament. *JSS* 10: 59–66.

Oppenheimer, A. 1977. *The ʿAM HA-ARETZ.* Trans. I. H. Levine. ALGHJ. Leiden.

Rost, L. 1934. Die Bezeichnungen für Land und Volk im Alten Testament. Pp. 125–48 in *Festschrift Otto Pröcksch,* ed. Albrecht Alt et al. Leipzig.

Sulzberger, M. 1909. *The AM HA-ARETZ: The Ancient Hebrew Parliament.* Philadelphia.

Würthwein, E. 1936. *Der ʿamm haʾaretz im Alten Testament.* BWANT 17. Stuttgart.

Zeitlin, S. 1933. The AM HAAREZ: A Study in the Social and Economic Life of the Jews before and after the Destruction of the Second Temple. *JQR* 23: 45–61.

JOSEPH P. HEALEY

AMAD (PLACE) [Heb *ʿamʿād*]. A town in the inheritance of Asher (Josh 19:26). From the position of Amad in the list of border cities, its general location should be sought in the S portion of the tribal territory. Evidence is not sufficient to determine an identification with any site.

MELVIN HUNT

AMAL (PERSON) [Heb *ʿāmāl*]. A descendant of Asher, whose name appears in an abbreviated genealogy in 1 Chr 7:30–40, which lists the "men of Asher" who were "heads of fathers' houses, approved, mighty warriors, chief of the princes." One third of the names given in Asher's genealogy are found nowhere else in Scripture; such is the case with the name Amal. Little is known of him, except that his name means "heavy labor," "vexation," or "trouble," that his father's name is Helem, and that Zophah, Imna, and Shelesh are listed as his brothers.

J. RANDALL O'BRIEN

AMALEK (PERSON) [Heb *ʿămālēq*]. AMALEKITE. One of the six sons of Eliphaz and a grandson of Esau, whose mother was Timna, Eliphaz's concubine (Gen 36:11, 12; cf. 1 Chr 1:36). Amalek was one of the "chiefs of Eliphaz in the land of Edom" (Gen 36:15,16). In the biblical tradition, the terms "Amalek," "Amalekite," and "Amalekites" are used to designate the descendants of Eliphaz who, like Esau, are linked with the land of Edom. The Amalekites were a nomadic or seminomadic people, descendants of Esau and one of Israel's traditional enemies. They are not mentioned by name in any extra-biblical source, so the OT provides the only written evidence on this relatively obscure people.

A. Origin

Gen 14:7 says that Chedorlaomer and the coalition of eastern kings "subdued all the country of the Amalekites" at a place called Enmishpat, i.e., Kadesh (Khirbet el-Qudeirat in N Sinai?). Various explanations have been given for the apparent contradiction this verse seems to raise: how a "country of the Amalekites" could be attached to an episode that antedated Esau, Eliphaz, and Amalek. Some scholars regard this reference as a blatant anachronism, while others say it is simply an editorial insertion. an updating of the text by a later editor who knew that the Amalekites occupied the region mentioned in Gen 14:7

during his lifetime or sometime before. It would have been perfectly normal to link Kadesh with the Amalekites through much of Israel's history. Still others suggest that the descendants of Esau intermarried with related but earlier nomadic groups, became dominant, and the designation was used retroactively.

In one of his oracles, Balaam referred to Amalek as "the first of the nations" (Num 24:20). This verse, too, has been the focus of a wide range of interpretation, but it is possible that the diviner was alluding to Amalek's status as one of the most ancient peoples. By whichever argument one explains the problem with Gen 14:7, it should be noted that the use of the term "Amalekites" in a patriarchal narrative is not completely incongruous with Amalek's genealogy in Gen 36:9–12.

B. Territory

As reported in Gen 36:16, Amalek was associated initially with Edom. The highly mobile—nomadic or seminomadic—lifestyle of the Amalekites, as described in all biblical passages that mention their name, should prepare the reader to understand Edom as a homeland from which later generations ranged far and wide. Throughout their entire history, as far as it is known, Amalekite social and economic institutions were shaped by two major factors. First, most of the Amalekites seem to have occupied the less desirable fringe areas adjacent to land capable of supporting more sedentary populations. Their seasonal migrations or raiding expeditions did take them as far north as the hill country of Ephraim (Judg 12:15) and as far west as the Philistine territory around Ziklag (1 Sam 30:1–2). Most episodes involving the Amalekites take place along the transitional zone of S Canaan or Judah, where desert and sown come together.

Second, the Amalekites were scattered across a vast territory. Num 13:29 notes that "the Amalekites dwell in the land of the Negeb," but this verse does not reflect the whole picture; it simply isolates this people from other peoples who lived in the same proximity at a point in time. The full scope of the Amalekites' wanderings, at least in the time of Saul, is described in 1 Sam 15:7: "And Saul defeated the Amalekites, from Havilah as far as Shur, which is east of Egypt." Thus, Amalekite tribes inhabited the wilderness between W Sinai and the Arabah of Arabia, depending on the meaning of Havilah in this verse. In fact, the Amalekite way of life is better understood when it is observed that the Ishmaelites ranged over a similarly defined territory (Gen 25:18). Though some scholars regard these statements as "geographical hyperbole," it can be reasonably assumed that the various Amalekite tribes indeed needed such a large area in which to live given its limited sources of water and food. It should be remembered that for at least part of their history the Amalekites used camels for transportation in times of war and peace (cf. Judg 6:5; 7:12).

C. History

Because of Amalek's occupation on the border of Palestine, in Sinai and the Negeb, these tribes were in conflict with the Hebrews from the time of their wilderness wanderings until the early monarchy. Indeed, every encounter between Amalek and Israel recorded in the OT is marked by hostility. It is likely that the other sedentary peoples near ancient Israel (e.g., Egypt, Edom, Moab) had similar problems with the Amalekites, but information on these other lands is unavailable.

The hostilities between Amalek and Israel began during the Hebrew sojourn in the Sinai. Exod 17:8–13 describes this first encounter, an apparently unprovoked attack upon Israel at Rephidim. It is possible that the Amalekites feared the Israelite incursion into the region of Kadesh (cf. Gen 14:7, where this place is linked with Amalek). Perhaps the Amalekites thought the Hebrews represented competition for water or would interfere with their trade routes. At any rate, Deut 25:17–18 says that the Amalekite attacks were merciless; this harassment led to great enmity between Israel and Amalek. The Amalekites were defeated (Exod 17:13), and they were placed under a permanent ban (17:14–16; Deut 25:17–19). Memory of Amalek's opposition to Israel was still alive in the days of Samuel and Saul (1 Sam 15:2–3).

With the defeat of the Amalekites, Israel controlled Kadesh-barnea (cf. Num 10:11–21:3). When the Hebrew spies returned to Kadesh (13:26), they reported that the Amalekites, among other peoples, blocked Israel's ambition to enter and occupy Canaan (13:29). According to Num 14:25, the Lord warned Israel to avoid contact with Amalek and take a more circuitous route to the promised land. This warning was not heeded, the Hebrews attempted to enter the hill country of southern Canaan, and they were repelled by the Amalekites and Canaanites (14:44–45; Deut 1:44). The Israelites were pursued all the way to Hormah (Tel Masos?), a settlement that was probably in Amalekite hands during other periods. One of the most interesting references to the Amalekites from the period of the Israelite wilderness wanderings is found in Num 24:20, where Balaam makes what could be interpreted as the only positive statement about this people in the whole Bible. Also important is the fact that Balaam "looked on Amalek," presumably from "the top of Peor, that overlooks the desert" (23:28), perhaps localizing the Amalekites to the S Jordan Valley.

Several significant references to Amalek come from the book of Judges, which deals with the Israelites after they had assumed a more sedentary existence within what they regarded as their own territory. According to Judg 3:12–14, Eglon, the king of Moab, allied himself with or hired as mercenaries the Ammonites and Amalekites to attack Israel. This Transjordanian confederacy defeated the Hebrews and captured "the city of palms," almost certainly the environs of Jericho. While this passage seems to locate an Amalekite center in Transjordan, Judg 12:15 mentions the existence of a similar enclave in the territory of Ephraim at Pirathon, which the text identifies as "the hill country of the Amalekites." Once again, this reference highlights the wide geographical range of Amalek.

In a similar raid from across the Jordan, the Amalekites are named as one of the peoples who invaded the regions west of the Jordan, including "the neighborhood of Gaza" (Judg 6:3–5) and the valley of Jezreel (6:33). Both of these episodes link Amalek with the Midianites and the people of the East (Qedemites), and both raids were made with the use of camels (6:5; 7:12). Although Judges says that Gideon defeated these nomadic invaders, they continued to threaten the security of Israel's settled communities on other occasions.

The most detailed and most decisive encounters between Amalek and Israel are found in the Samuel narratives on Saul. Soon after he became king of Israel, this great warrior resumed the traditional warfare with the Amalekites (1 Sam 15:2–3). From the town of Telaim, whose exact location is unknown, Saul moved against the Amalekite frontier to the south of Judah and attacked "the city of Amalek" (15:4–5). This is the first recorded instance in which Israel invaded Amalekite territory, actually striking what must have been the tribal center at that time. While it is not necessary to take the word "city" literally in this instance, since it is likely that "the city of Amalek" was more of a fortified camp, some scholars (e.g., Herzog 1983: 43, 47) have identified this ancient place with Tel Masos (M.R. 146069), located 7 miles east-southeast of Beer-sheba (cf. Edelman 1986: 82). Others locate the Amalekite center in N Sinai, somewhere in the vicinity of Kadesh-barnea.

In 1 Sam 15:6 intriguing reference is made to the presence of the Kenites among Amalek. Because his war was with the traditional foe of Israel, the Amalekites, Saul allowed the Kenites to depart. Saul's military victory is noted in 15:7, but his failure to execute the ban against Amalek constituted a spiritual failure. Saul's retaliation was not complete, since he took booty and a prisoner, Agag, the king of Amalek, who was later killed by Samuel (cf. 15:8–9, 20, 32–33). Agag was a traditional name or title for Amalekite kings (cf. Num 24:7), who were undoubtedly tribal chiefs like the "kings" of Midian and other nomadic groups (cf. Num 31:8, etc.). Most important is the fact that the name (or title) Agag is the only known Amalekite proper name. See AGAG; AGAGITE.

After David was given Ziklag by Achish, the Philistine, he continued the Hebrew offensive on Amalek's territory (1 Sam 27:8–9). While David's small army was away, the Amalekites carried out a retaliatory raid against David's Negeb base, burning Ziklag and taking prisoners (30:1–2). With the help of an Egyptian who had been a slave of the Amalekites, David located their camp beyond the Besor (Wadi Ghazzeh), defeated them in a pitched battle, and recovered all spoil (30:11–20). In fact, David looted the Amalekite encampment while 400 of their young men fled on camels (30:17, 20).

According to 2 Sam 1:1–10, David learned that Saul had been killed by an Amalekite, probably a mercenary in the Philistine army (cf. 1 Sam 31:1–6; 2 Sam 4:9–10). Most important are the statements that summarize David's military activities and name the Amalekites among those subdued (2 Sam 8:12; 1 Chr 18:11). David's victories seem to have brought an end to the threat that the Amalekites posed to the communities of Israel, for these enemies are no longer named as serious opponents after the days of Saul and David (cf. Ps 83:5–11 for a list of Israel's enemies in an unknown context, including Amalek in v 7).

Eph^cal (1982: 63) observes that the names Hagarites, Ishmaelites, Midianites, and Amalekites are not mentioned in biblical accounts that narrate events after the mid-10th century B.C. (with the exception of 1 Chr 4:43). Instead, the collective term Arab(s) appears, along with a number of other names (e.g., Buz, Dedan, Qedar, Sheba). Not surprising is the fact that the vague designation, "people of the East," occurs in passages on both sides of the mid-10th century. So the specific name, Amalekites, seems to disappear from the historical memory of the biblical writers, but the people themselves merged with other groups, took on new names, or were identified by the generic term Arab.

As noted above, the only reference to Amalekites after David's era is found in 1 Chr 4:43. This verse observes that only a "remnant of the Amalekites" was left in the time of Hezekiah (late 8th century B.C.), and this group was defeated by the Simeonites in Mt. Seir. Landes (*IDB* 1: 102) suggests that Amalekite history ended where it had begun, in Edom. Eph^cal (1982: 66, 80) says that Seir could refer to both sides of the Arabah in this instance. If so, this verse provides the only datum on the Negeb's inhabitants in the 9th–8th centuries B.C.

D. Archaeological Remains

Landes (*IDB* 1:102) and other scholars state that archaeological research has thrown no light on the Amalekites. Though some progress has been made in associating specific groups of nomads with archaeological evidence (cf. Parr 1982; Sawyer and Clines 1983; Rosen 1988), no recovered data are attributed to Amalek with any degree of certainty. Intensive surveys make it possible to say that the Negeb had very little occupation in the Late Bronze Age and that its resettlement began in the early Iron Age, especially in the 11th–early 10th centuries B.C. As Rothenberg (1967: 92–97) suggested, some of the small fortified settlements in the Negeb highlands can be linked to the Amalekites. Certain scholars (e.g., Herzog 1983: 43, 47) have identified Tel Masos with the place called "the city of Amalek" in 1 Sam 15:5. Of course, more data must be recovered before such conjectures can be verified.

Bibliography

Edelman, D. 1986. Saul's Battle Against Amaleq (1 Sam 15). *JSOT* 35: 71–84.

Eph^cal, I. 1982. *The Ancient Arabs: Nomads on the Borders of the Fertile Crescent 9th–5th Centuries B.C.* Leiden.

Herzog, Z. 1983. Enclosed Settlements in the Negeb and the Wilderness of Beer-sheba. *BASOR* 250: 41–49.

Irvine, A. K. 1973. The Arabs and Ethiopians. Pp. 287–311 in *Peoples of Old Testament Times*, ed. D. J. Wiseman. Oxford.

Parr, P. 1982. Contacts between North West Arabia and Jordan in the Late Bronze and Iron Ages. Vol. 1, pp. 127–33 in *Studies in the History and Archaeology of Jordan*, ed. A. Hadidi. Amman.

Rosen, S. A. 1988. Finding Evidence of Ancient Nomads. *BARev* 14/5: 46–53, 58–59.

Rothenberg, B. 1967. *Negeb, Archaeology in the Negeb and the Aravah.* Ramat Gan. (In Hebrew.)

Sawyer, J. F. A., and Clines, J. A. 1983. *Midian, Moab and Edom: The History and Archaeology of Late Bronze and Iron Age Jordan and North-West Arabia.* Sheffield.

GERALD L. MATTINGLY

AMAM (PLACE) [Heb *ʾămām*]. A town in the Negeb district of the tribal inheritance of Judah (Josh 15:26). Although its site has not been definitively located, it lay in the area E and S of Beer-sheba (Josh 15:21; Cross and

Wright 1956: 212). Abel (*GP* 2: 242) proposed placing Amam on the Wadi eṣ-Ṣîni on the basis of the variant *sēn* in LXX^B. Recently Naʾaman (1980: 146) has advocated locating Amam at the site of Beʾer Nevatim (Bir el-Hamam) on the Nahal Beʾer-Sheva (Wadi Meshash). Amam may be mentioned in the longer form of its name as Beth-amam ("House of Amam") in one of the ostraca from Beer-sheba (Aharoni 1973: 71–72).

Bibliography

Aharoni, Y. 1973. The Hebrew Inscriptions. Pp. 71–78 in *Beer-Sheba I*, ed. Y. Aharoni. Tel-Aviv.

Cross, F. M., and Wright, G. E. 1956. The Boundary and Province Lists of the Kingdom of Judah. *JBL* 75: 202–26.

Naʾaman, N. 1980. The Inheritance of the Sons of Simeon. *ZDPV* 96: 136–52.

CARL S. EHRLICH

AMANA (PLACE) [Heb *ʾămānâ*]. A mountain cited along with Lebanon, Senir, and Hermon (Cant 4:8). Probably one of the mountains near the source of the Amana River comprising the Anti-Lebanon range. Solomon bids the Shulammite maiden (Cant 6:13) to leave these beautiful mountain peaks of her northern country land.

RAY LEE ROTH

AMANUENSIS. This term, taken from Latin ("of the hand"), denotes one who writes what another dictates, or copies what another has written, and thus means a secretary or scribe. A person performing this function is designated in the Hebrew Bible as a *sōpēr,* and in the Greek NT as a *grammateus.* In both cases, however, it is necessary to distinguish between the scribe as a person skilled in writing who works as a secretary, and the scribe as a member of a professional class devoted to the study and interpretation of the Torah of Moses. Most of the biblical references to scribes have the latter meaning in view and occur in post-exilic biblical literature. This article, however, will treat only the former sense, i.e., a secretary skilled in the art of writing or copying manuscripts.

Allusions to *sōpēr* as "secretary" are frequent in the Hebrew Bible. The scribe was a traditional and necessary functionary of the royal court; specific mention is made of the secretaries of David (2 Sam 20:25, 2 Kgs 12:10), Hezekiah (2 Kgs 18:18, 37; 19:2), Josiah (2 Kgs 22:3–12, 2 Chr 34:15–20), Joash (2 Chr 24:11), and Jehoiakim (Jer 36:12, 20). The activities of royal secretaries included, among other things, record-keeping and the drafting of royal letters and decrees; in some cases, the secretary also served as a counselor in matters of state, since the scribe, by reason of training and experience, was not only skilled in writing but was also often "a man of understanding" (cf. 1 Chr 27:32). Military commanders regularly relied on secretaries to maintain rolls and records, and to draft orders and communiqués (2 Kgs 25:19, 2 Chr 26:11, Jer 52:25). Even a prophet could employ an amanuensis if circumstances warranted. The signal instance of this is Jeremiah's reliance on Baruch to transcribe the prophet's oracles from dictation and read them in the temple precincts, a place where Jeremiah himself had been forbidden to appear (Jer 36).

The Greek term *grammateus* occurs only once in the NT in its normal sense of "clerk" or "secretary" (Acts 19:35), yet here the term designates not a "secretary," in the simple sense, but a high civic official whose duties included the drafting of decrees of the citizenry, administering civic funds, and transacting affairs of the city. (The frequent translation "town clerk" is not quite apposite.) Still, the activity of secretaries is elsewhere intimated in the NT, especially in the letters of Paul. It was apparently Paul's custom to dictate his letters to a secretary. The "oral style" of the letters is only one indication of this. In Rom 16:22, one Tertius expressly designates himself as the transcriber of the letter. Paul's practice in other letters of adding greetings (1 Cor 16:21, 2 Thess 3:17, Col 4:18), an asseveration (Phlm 19), and a summary statement (Gal 6:11–18) in his own handwriting implies that the letters themselves were written at the hands of amanuenses who transcribed at Paul's dictation. Indeed, 2 Thess 3:17 claims that Paul's appended greeting, written in his own hand, was a "sign" or "mark" employed in each of his letters. This practice suggests that these letters were normally in the handwriting of a secretary. A similar use of an amanuensis is also indicated by 1 Pet 5:12. In dictating his letters to a secretary, Paul was following a well-established practice in antiquity. Many papyrus letters preserved from the period were written in the hand of a secretary, with the final greeting or other closing matter written in the hand of the sender. In addition, classical literature often attests the use of a secretary. Cicero, a prolific letter writer, often dictated letters to his secretary, Tiro, and frequently alluded to this practice. Plutarch mentions it for Caesar (*Vit. Caes.* 17.3), Pliny the Younger mentions it for his uncle (*Ep.* 3.5, 9.36), and Quintilian objects to its widespread use (*Inst.* 10,3,19) (Bahr, 1966, concisely surveys the evidence).

The use of amanuenses by Paul has occasioned the development of various "secretary hypotheses," each of which seeks to explain why some letters attributed to Paul (e.g., Ephesians, Colossians, 1–2 Timothy, Titus) differ significantly in vocabulary, style, and conceptuality from the undoubtedly authentic letters. It is claimed that Paul did not dictate all his letters verbatim but sometimes provided only an outline or rough notes, leaving the actual composition to an amanuensis. While such theories might help to explain rather wide variations in vocabulary and style among letters attributed to Paul, they do not satisfactorily account for conceptual and situational differences. Nevertheless, Paul's use of amanuenses, together with the fact that he often names others as co-senders with himself (1 Cor 1:1; 2 Cor 1:1; Phil 1:1; Col 1:1; 1 Thess 1:1; 2 Thess 1:1; Phlm 1), suggests that the problem of the authorship of some Pauline letters may be even more complex than is usually assumed.

Bibliography

Bahr, G. J. 1966. Paul and Letter Writing in the First Century. *CBQ* 28: 465–77.

———. 1968. The Subscriptions in the Pauline Letters. *JBL* 87: 27–41.

Longenecker, R. N. 1974. Ancient Amanuenses and the Pauline

Epistles. Pp. 281–97 in *New Dimensions in New Testament Study,* ed. R. N. Longenecker and M. C. Tenny. Grand Rapids.
Robinson, E. T. 1917. Composition and Dictation in the New Testament Books. *JTS* 18: 288–301.
Roller, O. 1933. *Das Formular der paulinischen Briefe.* Stuttgart.

HARRY Y. GAMBLE

AMARIAH (PERSON) [Heb *ʾămaryâ; ʾămaryāhû*]. **1.** A Levitical high priest, the son of Meraioth and father of Ahitub and grandfather of Zadok (I) (1 Chr 5:33–34—Eng 6:7–8; 1 Chr 6:37–38—Eng 6:52–53). The name occurs in the most extensive and perhaps most recent of all the preexilic priestly genealogies in the OT (1 Chr 5:29–41—Eng 6:3–15) and also in a comparable abbreviated high priestly list from the same chapter (1 Chr 6:35–38—Eng 6:50–53). Unlike the longer list which traces the high priesthood from Aaron through Eleazar down to the Exile, this second comparable list traces the high priestly lineage from Aaron on through Eleazar only as far as Ahimaaz, the son of Zadok (I) (Williamson *Chronicles* NCB, 74).

2. A Levite of the Kohathite clan, the second of four sons of Hebron (1 Chr 23:19; 24:23). He is presented as a contemporary of David. His name is found in a supplemental list of Levites (1 Chr 24:20–31) which presupposes a still earlier Levitical list (1 Chr 23:6–23).

3. A Levitical high priest, the son of Azariah and father of Ahitub (II?) and grandfather of Zadok (II?) (1 Chr 5:37–38—Eng 6:11–12; Ezra 7:2–3). Within the long high priestly list of 1 Chr 5:29–41—Eng 6:3–15 the threefold pattern of Amariah-Ahitub-Zadok occurs twice (1 Chr 5:33–34, 37–38—Eng 6:7–8, 11–12). The reliability of this list is undermined by the fact that in no other high priestly list of the OT does one find such repetition with respect to these names. Also, the names of known high priests for the period from the narratives of Kings and Chronicles do not always correlate with their supposed high priestly correspondents in this long list. (For the suggestion that the Chronicler's list included only those high priests who were known to have been Zakokites, see Katzenstein 1962: 382–84.) Still, the period between the Exodus and the Exile, from Aaron through Ezra, requires more names than the 14 (1 Esdr 8:1–2), 17 (Ezra 7:1–5), or even 20 (2 Esdr 1:1–3) given in the other lists. The 23 names (from Aaron to Jehozadak) given in the long list of 1 Chr 5:29–41—Eng 6:3–15 are more salutory, even if they, too, seem to fall short (since 23 generations × 25 years per generation yields only 575 years for a period estimated to be closer to 700 years long). Accordingly, were the long list to be regarded as somewhat authentic, there would be no need to equate this Amariah with 1. above. Moreover, all three lists which cite Amariah as an ancestor of Ezra the priest (Ezra 7:1–5; 1 Esdr 8:1–2; 2 Esdr 1:1–3) list Zadok as the father of Shallum, and two of the three lists name Azariah as Amariah's father (Ezra 7:3; 2 Esdr 1:2), suggesting also that the Amariah intended here is Amariah II, not I. 1 Esdras 8 complicates the issue, though, in that while it knows Zadok as Shallum's father it cites Uzzi as Amariah's immediate predecessor, prompting linkage in this case with the upper half of the longer priestly list. Neh 11:11 and 1 Chr 9:11, on the other hand, appear to focus on the bottom end of the same long list, with Ahitub named as the father of Meraioth and Zadok (II?), but there is no mention of Amariah whatsoever. In 2 Esdr 1:1–3, Amariah's son, grandson, great-grandson, and great-great-grandson are purported to have been Eli, Phinehas, Ahitub, and Zadok (II?) respectively. The names Eli, Phinehas, and Ahitub, however, are not paralleled at this point in Ezra 7:3 (= 1 Esdr 8:2) or in any other high priestly list and are therefore most suspect.

4. A high priest in King Jehoshaphat's time (873–849 B.C.), placed in charge over all ecclesiastical and religious matters (2 Chr 19:11). His father is not named. He may be the same as 3. above (Schumacher *IDB* 1: 102–3).

5. A Levite, one of six persons appointed by King Hezekiah (787/86–715 B.C.) to assist in the distribution of the portions of the free-will offerings in the cities of the priests (2 Chr 31:15).

6. The son of Hezekiah and father of Gedaliah (Zeph 1:1). He is cited as a progenitor of the prophet Zephaniah ben Cushi, active during the reign of King Josiah (640–609 B.C.). In view of the unusual length of the opening prophetic genealogy, the ancestor intended may well be King Hezekiah (KJV Hizkiah) of Judah.

7. A Levitical priest (Neh 12:2). His name occurs on a list of priests and Levites who returned from Babylon with Zerubbabel and Jeshua (Neh 12:1, 7). His descendant, Jehohanan, represented one of the priestly courses active during the high priesthood of Joiakim, Jeshua's successor (Neh 12:13).

8. A priest, a contemporary of Nehemiah (Neh 10:4, 9—Eng 10:3, 8). He is listed as one of the persons who set their seal to the covenant document reconstituting the postexilic community.

9. A Judahite, the son of Shephatiah, descendant of Perez (Neh 11:4). He is cited as an ancestor of the Judahite Athaiah [*ʿătāyâ*] ben Uzziah, one of the 10 percent of the people in the days of Nehemiah who volunteered to live in Jerusalem rather than with the majority in the country towns of Judah. In the otherwise parallel verse, 1 Chr 9:4, there is no mention of any Athaiah; instead Uthai [*ʿûtay*] ben Ammihud, descended from Perez, is named. The nearest 1 Chr 9:4 comes to Amariah [*ʾămaryâ*] is in the name "Imri" [*ʾimrî*] (Myers *Ezra-Nehemiah* AB, 185–86).

10. One of the sons of Binnui (RSV), and a contemporary of Ezra (Ezra 10:42). His name appears on a list of those who had married foreign women and who were induced by Ezra to send such wives away along with their children (Ezra 10:44 = 1 Esdr 9:36). The RSV has adopted the suggested reading of *BHS,* namely, "and of the sons of Binnui" (Ezra 10:38) [= *ûmibbĕnê binnûy* for MT's "and Bani and Binnui" = *ûbānî ûbinnûy* = KJV]; NEB supports the RSV with "of the family of Binnui." Cf. LXX "the sons of Banui = *hoi huioi banoui.* In the interest of consistency, the RSV's synoptic parallel (1 Esdr 9:34) has adopted the reading "Amariah" [= Gk *amaria*] for the present Greek text's "Zambris" [LXX *zambris; zambrei*], even though the father of this person is said to be "Ezora" [LXX *ezōra*].

Bibliography

Katzenstein, A. J. 1962. Some Remarks on the Lists of the Chief Priests of the Temple of Solomon. *JBL* 81: 377–84.

ROGER W. UITTI

AMARNA LETTERS.

An important corpus of cuneiform documents found at Tell el-Amarna in Egypt.

A. Discovery and Publication

In the late autumn of 1887 a woman of the bedouin tribe of Beni ᶜAmrān discovered a number of tablets in the ruins near the village of Hajji Qandil. The place where the tablets were found is located on the eastern bank of the Nile, ca. 300 km south of Cairo and was called by scholars el-Amarna, after the name of the bedouin tribe. The site of el-Amarna was known to be the seat of Akhetaten ("the Horizon of Aten"), the residence of the Egyptian king Akhenaten, and the tablets unearthed there were part of the royal archive of the Pharaoh.

The local bedouin excavated the site and sold the tablets to a local dealer. The tablets were then sent to Upper Egypt and sold to the representatives of European museums. The Berlin museum got the majority (201 tablets), the British Museum (82 tablets), and the local museum of Cairo (51 tablets) also obtained large collections, and other museums and private persons bought numerous tablets (*PWCJS* 9: 11–14). Overall, 336 tablets are known today from this illegal dig. A certain part of the tablets was totally destroyed at that time, though it is impossible to verify their number (Knudtzon, Weber, and Ebeling 1915: 1–15; Sayce 1917).

A few years after the discovery, in 1891–92, a systematic excavation was conducted at the site by Sir Flinders Petrie (1894). He dug where the tablets were found (House No. 19) and its neighborhood and discovered 21 additional tablet fragments. In later years, three other archaeological expeditions worked at the site of el-Amarna (in 1911–14, 1921–23, 1926–37) and a further 23 tablet fragments were discovered. The overall number of tablets published is now 380 (Moran 1987; *PWCJS* 9: 3–16).

Publication of the Amarna tablets began soon after their discovery (Winckler and Abel 1889–90; Bezold and Budge 1892; Winckler 1896). A decisive step was made by J. A. Knudtzon, who systematically collated all tablets discovered until 1907 and published a comprehensive text edition (EA Nos. 1–358), accompanied by extensive historical commentary by O. Weber and detailed indexes by E. Ebeling (Knudtzon, Weber, and Ebeling 1915). At the same time, Schroeder (1915) published a new facsimile of the largest collection of Amarna tablets, that of the Berlin museum.

Twenty-two additional tablets were uncovered and published in various publications between 1915 and 1970 and were collected and edited in one volume by A. F. Rainey (1970). A final tablet was published by Walker (1979). Recently, W. L. Moran (1987) has published a new edition of all the letters, in which were included many new readings, extensive philological discussions, and detailed indexes. Moran's edition considerably advances the understanding of the corpus and marks a new stage in the research of the archive.

B. The Archive and Its Chronology

The tablets were discovered in the "office-house of the letters of Pharaoh," which was the place where the cuneiform staff of the foreign department must have been located. Of the corpus of 380 tablets, only 32 were not letters. These tablets served for the study of the art of cuneiform writing and reading. Among them were lexical texts (EA 351–54, 373), a list of gods (EA 374), syllabaries (EA 348, 350, 379), and literary texts (EA 340–41, 356–59, 375) (*PWCJS* 9: 27–33). These texts are closely related to well-known lexical and literary ancient Near Eastern tablets. Among the literary compositions one may note the Myth of Adapa, the Myth of Nergal and Ereshkigal, and the text entitled "The King of the Battle." Notable also is an Egyptian-Akkadian dictionary (EA 368), in which the Egyptian words are written syllabically by cuneiform signs.

The corpus of letters can be divided into two distinct groups: a small group of 44 letters that were exchanged between Egypt and other great powers and a much larger group of over 300 tablets that were exchanged between Egypt and vassal kingdoms in Canaan and northern Syria.

Numerous tablets written by the pharaohs either to "great kings" (EA 1, 5, 14, 31) or to vassal rulers (EA 99, 162–63, 190, 367, 369–70) were discovered among the Amarna tablets and may be regarded as letters that—for unknown reasons—were not dispatched abroad (i.e., they are not copies of the original letters) (Moran 1987: 19–20).

The city of Akhetaten (el-Amarna) was founded on virgin soil by Amenhotep IV (Akhenaten) (ca. 1350–1334) in his 4th year and became his residency in his 7th year. It served as the capital city until his death and was abandoned by the royal court in the 3d year of Tutankhamen (ca. 1334–1325) (Hornung 1964: 79–94; Redford 1967: 156–62). However, the earlier tablets discovered in the archive were written in the last decade of Amenhotep III, Akhenaten's father. It is thus clear that many letters were brought from the previous capital (Thebes) to the new capital when the royal court moved there. These must have been those that were necessary for future correspondence. One may further assume that certain letters were taken from Akhetaten at the time of its abandonment. The number of letters transferred in both cases is unknown nor do we know how many tablets were destroyed when the archive was discovered and before the value of the tablets was recognized (Campbell 1964: 32–35). What was left at el-Amarna is a unique collection which is different in its assemblage from all other ancient Near Eastern archives (Riedel 1939; Campbell 1964: 35–36; Naʾaman 1981a: 173–74).

The archive covers less than thirty years (from ca. the 30th year of Amenhotep III to Tutankhamen's 3d year). The exact time span depends on whether or not there was a coregency between Amenhotep III and Akhenaten, a problem still debated by scholars (e.g., Kitchen 1962; Campbell 1964; Redford 1967; Kühne 1973; Krauss 1978).

C. Script and Language

The Amarna letters were written in cuneiform signs on clay tablets. The cuneiform script was already known in northern Syria in the 2d half of the 3d millennium B.C. (at Ebla). The Canaanite cuneiform tradition is rooted in the north Mesopotamian and north Syrian traditions of the OB period (18th–17th centuries B.C.) (Anbar and Naʾaman 1986–87). Almost all the letters in the Amarna archive are written in Akkadian, i.e., an East Semitic language. Thus, letters exchanged between the Egyptian pharaohs and their vassals in Canaan were written in a language that was foreign to both. Akkadian (i.e., Babylonian) had acquired in the 14th century B.C. the status of an international language *(lingua franca)*, by which kings reigning all over the Near East were able to communicate.

The art of reading and writing cuneiform was known only to a relatively small group of experts who studied this craft for a period of many years. The diffusion of the Amarna letters all over Canaan and the many local variants show that expert scribes were situated in all of the important kingdoms. Since all diplomatic correspondence was in their hands, they attained a high social position and had certain influence on the direction of foreign affairs. A number of letters (EA 286:61–64; 287:64–70; 286:62–66; 289:47–51; 316:16–20) illustrate how important it was at that time to find ways to flatter and patronize the Egyptian royal scribes.

A small number of letters to "great kings" were written in their local language, i.e., Assyrian (EA 15), Hurrian (EA 24), and Hittite (EA 31–32), while the rest were written in Akkadian, although the dialect of these letters is sometimes regarded as "peripheral." That is because the language of these letters has retained certain archaic features, such as sign forms, logograms, vocabulary, and grammar, which were considered "classical" in earlier periods but have already disappeared from the cuneiform tradition of Mesopotamia and have been preserved only in the western periphery (Moran 1987: 22–24).

Two cuneiform traditions may be detected in the Canaanite and north Syrian letters. The one is Hurro-Akkadian, which is typical of tablets emanating from the north, that is, Hurrian-speaking kingdoms that were governed and influenced by Mitanni (Wilhelm 1970; Izreʿel 1985; Moran 1987: 24–27). The other tradition is widespread in all areas of Canaan and was strongly influenced by the current West Semitic language. The grammar of these documents was so deeply transformed by the local language and dialects that the letters may be regarded as being "West Semitized" (Rainey 1975: 395). The Canaanite Amarna letters (with the exception of the letters from Jerusalem and Tyre: see Moran 1975a; Grave 1980: 216–18; 1982: 178–79) may be regarded as eastern in their vocabulary and as western in their grammar (Moran 1987: 27). It goes without saying that they constitute a very important source for the study of the dialects current in Canaan in the 14th century B.C. (Moran 1950; 1960; 1965; Rainey 1971; 1973; 1975; 1978; Izreʿel 1978).

D. The International Correspondence

The relations between Egypt and the other great powers of the ancient Near East occupy a central place in the correspondence. The latter powers were Babylon (EA 1–14), Assyria (EA 15–16), Mitanni (EA 17, 19–30), Arzawa (EA 31–32), Alashia (EA 33–40), and Hatti (EA 41–44). Their kings called each other by proper names (Alashia is an exception) and expressed their equal political status by the addressing formula (e.g., "Say to PN, king of GN . . . thus says PN_2, king of GN_2 . . ."), by the denomination "brother" (i.e., a king of equal rank), and by employing the same words for greeting. Moreover, only they were entitled to be called "great king," that is a king who was a suzerain of vassal states and was equal in his political status to the other great powers (Moran 1987: 62).

The "great kings" exchanged messengers who traveled between the capital cities and transmitted letters, verbal messages, and gifts from one court to another. These gifts had symbolic as well as economic value (Liverani 1972; Zaccagnini 1973). Bringing a gift was an inseparable element of the international correspondence; but gifts were also supposed to be of equal value and there are many complaints in the letters about the inferior quality and the poor value of received gifts. Egypt was the source of gold for all other countries and there are many requests in the letters for Egyptian gold (Edzard 1960). The correlation between good relations and expensive gifts is illustrated by the words of a Babylonian king who described a reaction to a previous rich shipment of gold by the words (EA 11 rev. 21–23): "The gold [is abundant. Among] the kings there are brotherhood, friendliness, peace and [good] relations. [He is] rich with precious stones, rich with silver, rich with [gold]."

Exchanging gifts was sometimes regarded as a kind of indirect commerce, but there were also direct commercial relations, both by land and at sea, between the great powers, and as a rule every king was responsible for the safety of the foreign merchants who stayed in the territories under his authority. Thus, when his merchants were robbed and murdered at Ḫannathon, the king of Babylon wrote to the king of Egypt (EA 8:25–33): "Canaan is your land and its kings are your servants. It was in your land that I have been robbed. Investigate them and repay the money that they took. Execute the men who slew my servants and avenge their blood. But if you do not slay these men, they will do it again and attack either one of my caravans or even your messengers and relations will be cut off between us."

Diplomatic marriage between a "great king" and the daughter of another is well attested in the letters (Pintore 1978). It was always the Pharaoh, however, who married foreign princesses and brought them to his harem. Egyptian kings refused to marry their daughters to other kings and to send them abroad (EA 4:6–7): "From old, the daughter of an Egyptian king has not been given in marriage to anyone") (Pintore 1978: 78–79; Schulman 1979). Thus, Amenhotep III, who enjoyed a long reign of 38 years, married two Babylonian princesses, two Mitannian princesses, and one from Arzawa (Schulman 1979: 183–84). Marriages between kings were negotiated by the two courts and the marriage gifts were an important (though delicate) element within the negotiation. Indeed, the richest lists of gifts known from the Amarna archive were recorded on such occasions (EA 14, 22). The foreign princesses did not attain the position of "great wife of the king" (i.e., queen) in the Egyptian harem but remained wives of second rank (Schulman 1979: 183).

The Amarna archive is our earliest witness for the international character of the Late Bronze Age. These relations were first established in the 15th century and lasted (though with considerable changes) until the end of the 13th century, encompassing all major civilizations of western Asia. The great powers divided among themselves the entire civilized world, each dominating its vassals, and established a set of strict rules for international correspondence (Kestemont 1974).

Impressive as it is, one should not be dazzled by the polite tone and the external gestures that find expression in the international correspondence. Much more important than all these were the *realpolitik* and the actual struggle for power and for dominion, and indeed, these struggles dominated international relations in the late stages of the Amarna period.

Since the 15th century B.C., the kingdom of Mitanni had been a strong power whose vassal's border in Syria reached the northern boundary of the land of Canaan. In the course of the Amarna period, Šuppiluliumas, the Hittite king, conducted several campaigns against Mitanni and conquered the former Mitannian vassal kingdoms in northern Syria, thus reviving the Hittite's old claims over these areas. Aššur-uballiṭ, king of Assyria, took advantage of the situation and attacked the crumbling kingdom of Mitanni in order to expand the Assyrian territories. At the same time he tried to be recognized as a "great king" by the other western Asiatic great powers and to establish with them diplomatic relations (EA 15–16) (Artzi 1978).

The immediate result of the Hittite expansion to northern Syria was the deterioration of Hittite-Egyptian relations. Both kingdoms claimed domination over Amurru and Kadesh (Qidshu) and the armed struggle between the two powers is mentioned in the latest letters of the archive and would last for several decades (Kitchen 1962; Helck 1971: 168–214; Krauss 1978; Murnane 1985).

E. The Vassal Letters

The majority of the letters in the archive were sent by the vassals in Canaan and in northern Syria. The latter's tablets were probably sent at a relatively late stage when Mitanni, their overlord, was defeated by the Hittites and they addressed Egypt for help (Redford 1967: 216–25; Naʾaman 1975: 15–17, 210–14, 229–30). There are also seven letters (EA 99, 162–63, 190, 367, 369–70) that were addressed by the Pharaoh to his vassals in Canaan (see above). One may easily compare the ways in which one side addressed the other.

The humiliated tone of the vassal letters as against the commanding words of the letters of the pharaohs is the most conspicuous formal trait of the correspondence. In spite of regional variations, the vassal letters closely resemble each other in their words. "Speak to the king, my lord . . . ; thus says PN, your servant . . ." is typical of the addresses to letters in which the lord-vassal relations are deliberately emphasized. The Pharaoh is only called by the title "king" (with the exception of the two northern letters from Qatna, EA 53:1 and 55:1). Greeting formulas are quite rare, the main exception being the letters of Byblos (e.g., "Rib-Addi speaks to his lord, king of all countries, the great king, king of the battle. May the Lady of Byblos give strength to the king, my lord."). In place of greetings in the introductions to most of the letters one finds expressions of humiliation emphasizing the inferior status of the vassal as against his lord. To illustrate the introduction of a vassal letter we shall translate a typical south Canaanite letter (EA 328:1–16):

> To the king, my lord, my god, my Sun, the Sun from heaven; thus says Yabni-ilu, the ruler of Lachish, your servant, the dust under your feet, the groom of your horses. At the feet of the king, my lord, my god, my Sun, the Sun from heaven, I have fallen seven and seven times, on the belly and on the back.

The king, on the other hand, addressed his vassals by short words: "To PN, ruler of GN, speak! Thus [says] the king." There is no greeting and the tenor of the letters is a combination of commands and threats.

However, the commanding tone of the royal letters and the humiliated expressions of the vassals should not obscure the historical reality. When examining the letters, it becomes clear that the vassals enjoyed much more freedom than one may deduce from the formal analysis of the letters and often they operated on their own behalf, contrary to the obvious Egyptian interests in the land of Canaan.

The major events occurring within the land of Canaan during the Amarna period were the foundation of the strong kingdom of Amurru in the north and the expansion of Labʾayu of Shechem and his sons in central Palestine. The first episode is directly linked with the armed struggle between Mitanni and Hatti over the domination of Syria. The rulers of Amurru took advantage of the situation and greatly expanded their territory along the coast and the middle Orontes Valley. During the last stages of the archive, ʿAziru of Amurru was still an Egyptian vassal, but soon afterward he had signed a vassal treaty with the Hittites, thus transgressing his oath to the Pharaoh and joining his enemies (Klengel 1969: 178–208, 245–99; Altman 1973).

The offensive of Labʾayu of Shechem and his sons was motivated by the desire to expand their territory and become the strongest and most influential power in the country and by their hatred of the newly established Egyptian centers of government, in particular that of Beth-shean (Campbell 1965; Naʾaman 1975: 27–46; Spalinger 1983: 96). They formed a powerful coalition that included Gezer in the south and Gath-Carmel in the north. A countercoalition, headed by the kings of Megiddo and Acco and supported by the Egyptian authorities, was formed in reaction and succeeded in bringing the Shechemite offensive to an end.

When examining the Amarna letters it is clear that the ambitions of local rulers, the power of the nonurban elements in local affairs, and the readiness of Egypt to interfere and operate in local disputes were the principal factors that influenced internal affairs in Canaan. Egypt was strong enough to quell all rebellions and to bring to an end all inner struggles, save possibly for the northernmost area, where its vassals bordered on another imperial power.

The Amarna archive is our main (and sometimes only) source for the study of many aspects of Canaan in the Late Bronze Age prior to the Israelite settlement in the land. Some of these aspects will be examined in the following paragraphs (Helck 1971: 246–55, 474–91; *CAH*[3] 2/2: 98–116; Frandsen 1979; Naʾaman 1982: 195–241; Groll 1983).

F. Egyptian Government in Canaan

Soon after the conquest of Canaan by Thutmose III (1482 or 1457), the Egyptians tried to organize it as a province. The main source of information for the measures undertaken at that time are the Amarna tablets, written ca. 100 years after the foundation of the Egyptian province in Asia.

The Egyptians left the array of Canaanite kingdoms which they conquered and established a network of six garrison cities to administer and rule the land. Four were situated along the coast: Gaza and Joppa in the south and Ullasa and Ṣumur in the north. Two other centers of government were established on the main crossroads: Beth-shean in northern Palestine and Kumidi in the south of the Beqaʿ Valley of Lebanon (Helck 1971: 251–52; Naʾaman 1981a: 177–78). The garrison cities also controlled considerable surrounding farmlands. For example, the fields west of the city of Beth-shean were annexed by Thutmose III and administered by the Egyptians (Naʾaman 1981b). The cities themselves served as centers for the Egyptian personnel in Canaan and for the garrison troops stationed in the land. They were also the gathering places for the tributes and gifts of the vassals. The latter were required to guard the cities and the special installations therein and to cultivate and harvest their territories.

The number of Egyptian troops stationed in Canaan was relatively small. They included only the garrison troops *(ṣābē maṣṣarti)* installed either in the garrison cities or in certain strategic or vulnerable city-states (e.g., Jerusalem, Megiddo, Acco, Byblos). These troops are mentioned many times in the vassal letters; their number vary from less than fifty soldiers to three hundred (Pintore 1972; 101–6). The regular troops (*ṣābē piṭāti,* "archers") were stationed in Egypt and embarked on campaigns when the situation demanded their presence. On such occasions they were accompanied by chariot troops and usually returned to Egypt after completing their mission (Pintore 1972; 1973).

The territory in Asia under Egyptian rule was apparently divided into subunits; their number, however, is debated among scholars. According to the common view, it was separated into three districts: Palestine with its seat at Gaza, the coast of Lebanon with its center at Sumur, and south Syria with its seat at Kumidi (Helck 1971: 248–52; *LBHG,* 146–53; De Vaux 1968: 25–28). According to another view, it was divided into two subunits: Palestine plus the Phoenician coast and south Syria (including the Bashan and the kingdom of Hazor). This twofold division was the outcome of the historical situation of the Middle Bronze Age (Naʾaman 1975: 166–72, 227; 1981a: 183–84). The assumption that the garrison city of Beth-shean was the seat of another (fourth) district (Hachmann 1982a: 44–47) is not very likely.

At the head of the Egyptian hierarchy in Canaan were the governors, possibly one in each province. Their Egyptian title was "messenger of the king to every foreign land" (Edel 1953: 55–63; Singer 1983: 18–21). Other officials were of various Egyptian ranks and titles, but the Canaanite scribes usually employed one and the same title, *rābiṣu* ("commissary"), to denote all ranks and titles of Egyptian functionaries serving in Canaan. It is impossible therefore to be precise concerning the Egyptian titles (unless they can be identified with well-known Egyptian officials) and exact analysis of the Amarna correspondence might only reveal the relative status of the various functionaries mentioned therein. The situation is even more complicated since some of the officials arrived on special missions from Egypt and were not part of the bureaucratic apparatus in the land.

A set of prohibitions was imposed upon the vassals and the Egyptian officers were responsible for their fulfillment. Examination of the letters reveals that the Egyptian apparatus was often rather flexible in what was permissible or prohibited to the vassal, not to mention those cases in which two Egyptian commissioners supported different sides of a conflict.

The vassals were obliged to pay tribute and send gifts, though only a small part of these were recorded in the letters. They served in the Egyptian garrison cities, cultivated their territories, and secured the caravan routes traversing their kingdoms. They provided armed forces for Egyptian campaigns and served as a supply network for armies that moved in Canaan and along the coast. It is evident that the Canaanite city-states were an important support for the Egyptian government abroad, enabling her to control, with the help of only a few officials and a relatively small number of troops, its Asiatic province. The various military, strategic, and economic advantages that Egypt gained in the Amarna period from the occupation of Canaan was bought for a relatively low price (see Naʾaman 1981a). It was only at a later time that conditions changed, obliging Egypt to alter its policy and to intensify its involvement in the land (Weinstein 1981: 17–23; Naʾaman 1982: 241–51; Singer 1988).

G. The Network of Canaanite City-States

The land of Canaan was divided into a network of kingdoms of various sizes and strengths. Since only the rulers of these political units were allowed to correspond with the Pharaoh, the Amarna letters are our main source for composing the list of city-states. The gaps of information may be filled by the Egyptian topographical lists and particularly by the Egyptian royal inscriptions. The relative strength of the kingdoms may be deduced from analysis of these sources.

The three most important kingdoms in Palestine in the 14th century B.C. were Gezer in the northern Shephelah, Shechem in the central hill country, and Hazor in the north. Other important city-states in the south were Ashkelon, Lachish, and Gath(?) (Tell es-Ṣāfi); Jerusalem (and Debir, according to archaeological excavations) dominated the southern part of the hill country, Gath-padalla was the strongest kingdom in the Sharon region, while Rehob, Megiddo, Shimʿon, Acco, and Akhshaph were the most important kingdoms in the northern plains. Shechem and Hazor may be regarded as the only territorial kingdoms, the others may be characterized as city-states (Naʾaman 1988).

The coast of Lebanon was divided among several kingdoms of equal strength (Tyre, Sidon, Byblos), and Amurru in the north emerged as an important territorial kingdom in the course of the Amarna period (see above). Damascus was the most influential kingdom in south Syria; its ruler enjoyed an outstanding high status and prestige and functioned as the main supporter of the Egyptian governor of Kumidi (Hachmann 1970; 1982b). Many other kingdoms were located in the area of the Beqaʿ of Lebanon (e.g., Ḫashabu, Tushulti, Ḫasi, Ṭubiḫu, Enishazi), in the Bashan (Ashtaroth, Buṣruna, Ḫalunnu) and east of Mount Lebanon (Ruḫizzi, Lapana). Their relative strength in the Amarna period cannot be established, owing to the paucity of documentary evidence (Klengel 1970: 4–29, 56–70, 96–112; Hachmann 1970: 84–88; Ahituv 1984).

North of the land of Canaan was the strong kingdom of Kadesh (Qidshu), which dominated the land of Takhshi. It was a vassal of Mitanni, but when that kingdom fell, it tried to expand its territory and conquer parts of the land of ʿAmqi (the Beqaʿ of Lebanon), thus attacking the vassals of Egypt situated there (EA 140, 170, 174–76, 363) (Klengel 1969: 139–71; Krauss 1978: 63–70).

The network of Canaanite units was composed of kingdoms of higher and lesser rank. The chain of events was determined primarily by the former while the latter cooperated with them, either willingly or not. The strong kingdoms were able to dictate the policy of the lesser kingdoms and even to intervene in their inner affairs.

At the head of each kingdom stood the local ruler. In his relations with the Pharaoh he was regarded as a city ruler *(ḫazannu)*, like any other Egyptian mayor *(ḥʾty-ʿ)*. The title was intended to emphasize the fact that he occupied his position with the approval of the Egyptian overlord. However, only in exceptional cases did the Pharaoh actually intervene in matters of succession, enforcing his own candidate (always of the local dynasty) as city ruler. In internal relations within Canaan and in contacts with his subjects, the local ruler was considered a king who ascended the throne through the dynastic principle and, in turn, left his throne to his heir after him (see EA 8:25, 30:1, 70:20, 88:46, 92:32–34, 109:46, 139:14–15, 140:10–12, 147:67, 148:40–41, 197:14–15, 41–42, 227:3, 256:7–8, 306:24).

Not enough details of the internal structure of the kingdoms are reported in the letters since they mainly reflect foreign affairs, that is, relations with Egypt and with neighboring kingdoms. We do know that the capital city was the focus of each unit, and usually it was either its sole or its principal urban center. The king's palace was the center of government for the kingdom and the bureaucratic apparatus operated either in the palace or in its vicinity. Around the capital city were tracts of agricultural fields cultivated by its inhabitants and in the peripheral areas were numerous villages and hamlets with their own fields and pasture land.

The actual power of the king in his city and territory varied from place to place and from period to period. It was dependent upon external factors and upon the power of the civil instititions. Several episodes are described in the letters in which a king was deposed and removed from his town (i.e., Rib-Addi of Byblos and Yashdata of Taanach) or even killed (Aduna of Irqata, Zimredda of Lachish, and the rulers of Ammiya and Ardata). The power in certain cases (i.e., Byblos, Taanach, Irqata, Ammiya, and also Tunip) was in the hands of the citizenry, although such an oligarchical rule in a city-state was only temporary and apparently did not last long. The only exception is that of Arwada, a small island near the coast of Lebanon, in which the power was (as far as we know) permanently in the hands of the council of elders.

H. The Nonurban Elements (ʿApiru and Sutu)

During the 16th century B.C. the urban culture of Canaan suffered a heavy blow. Many fortified cities were destroyed and some were deserted for a long period of time. It has been estimated that the total occupied area in Palestine decreased in the Late Bronze Age I to a third of that of the Middle Bronze Age II and that the number of settlements was only ca. 30–40 percent (Gonen 1981: 63–69) of what it had been. The destruction was particularly severe in the hill country, the lower Jordan Valley, and the Negeb. The decline of urban life brought about an immediate increase of the pastoral and brigand elements and resulted in the growing insecurity of the land.

It is against this background that the frequent mention of the ʿApiru (and the Sutu as well) in the Amarna letters should be evaluated. In the ancient Near Eastern documentation, ʿApiru is a designation for people who were uprooted from their original political and social frameworks and forced to adapt to a new environment and way of life. The ʿApiru are known from many western Asiatic societies in the 2d millennium B.C. Their different traits and social behavior in each area were the outcome of this adaptation to new circumstances. The Amarna tablets are the largest single group of documents in which the term ʿApiru is mentioned. According to the letters, they were scattered all over Canaan and had an important effect on events which took place in the land (Bottéro 1954; Greenberg 1955; Loretz 1984).

However, the Amarna letters show a unique development in the meaning of the appellation ʿApiru. On many occasions, the term became a derogatory designation for rebels against Egyptian authority (Mendenhall 1973; Naʾaman 1986a: 275–78). In the letters of Byblos, for example, the term ʿApiru was frequently applied to ʿAbdi-Ashirta of Amurru and his son ʿAziru. Also the expression "to become ʿApiru," which is repeated in many letters from all areas of Canaan, implies desertion from the Pharaoh and his supporters, the city-states' rulers, and defection to the side of his opponents, who were thus regarded as outlaws (Liverani 1979). The extension of the term ʿApiru in order to denigrate these elements that opposed the authors of the letters is the result of the political nature of the Amarna correspondence, in which every ruler tried to justify his deeds before the Pharaoh and to slander his opponents. This must be taken into consideration when trying to determine the role of the authentic bands, brigands, and mercenaries in the Amarna period.

Even after the elimination of those letters which, directly or indirectly, refer in general terms to city-states' rulers and their supporters, it is evident that the nonurban elements played an important role in Canaan in the 14th century B.C. They appear in letters either as bands or as individuals who were recruited and served as mercenaries in the army. As bands, they operated on their own behalf or took advantage of the conflicts between rulers and cooperated with one side or another (e.g., the conflicts between Amurru and Byblos or between Shechem and its neighbors). Alongside the ʿApiru appear also the Sutu (EA 195:24–29; 246 r. 6–7; 318:10–14), which was the Akkadian appellation for the pastoral nomadic elements.

As an illustration of the historical role of the ʿApiru one may present a group of letters from south Canaan, in all of which city-states' rulers bitterly complained of distress and serious difficulties in their kingdoms, and indeed, soon afterward they all disappeared from the historical arena and were replaced by others (Naʾaman 1975: 145–53; 1979: 676–82). The reason for the short period of unrest and rebellion, of which the ʿApiru are accused, was probably the temporary strengthening of the nonurban elements in these areas. In another case, a band of ʿApiru stayed in the city of Tushulti under the patronage of its ruler, raided the neighboring cities, and set them on fire, until they were attacked by Tushulti's neighboring rulers and forced to leave their shelter in the city (EA 185–86).

The existence of large groups of nomads and refugees may well explain the power of kingdoms situated in the hill country (e.g., Shechem, Hazor, and Amurru). Located near the nomadic enclaves, they were able either to hire soldiers from their members or to cooperate with their leaders (e.g., EA 71:20–22; 87:21–24; 148:41–43; 195:24–32; 246:5–10; 254:31–37).

I. The Amarna Letters and the Bible

Numerous details that appear in biblical descriptions of pre-Israelite Canaan fit nicely into the picture constructed from the Amarna tablets. These are the division of the land into many entities, each ruled by a king; the description of certain entities as being composed of a major city and its surrounding villages (compare EA 74:19–24; 228:13–17, 238:4–8 to Josh 15:45–47; 17:11, 16: Judg 1:27); the coalition of kingdoms as a means to gain power (compare EA 366 to Joshua 10–11); and the chariots (though anachronistically described as built of iron) as the main basis of Canaanite military power.

However, other details do not fit nicely into the picture described by the Amarna letters. Many sites that appear as Canaanite in biblical descriptions are not mentioned in the Amarna archive and, according to archaeological excavations, were either small villages or entirely uninhabited in the Late Bronze Age (e.g., Jericho, Ai, Jarmuth, Hebron, Beer-sheba, Arad). Most prominent is the city of Hebron, which, according to biblical tradition, was an important center in the time of the Patriarchs and in the conquest period, whereas the city is not mentioned in any source of the Late Bronze Age and the site of ancient Hebron (Tell er-Rumeideh) was uninhabited in this period. Also, the king of Jerusalem appears at the head of a coalition of kingdoms located in the hill country and the Shephelah (Joshua 10). The territory and the political standing of the king of Jerusalem, according to the Amarna tablets, seem to have been relatively modest and one would hardly assume that its king was able to head a coalition in which remote cities like Lachish and Eglon took part (Naʾaman 1975: 104–15; 1986b: 470–72).

There is no indication in the Amarna tablets of a diversity of ethnic groups in the land of Canaan; the inhabitants of the land were all considered to be Canaanites (De Vaux 1968). The biblical tradition, however, mentions groups of variegated ethnic origin in different parts of the land (e.g., Philistines, Hivvites, Hittites, Jebusites, Girgashites, Perizzites), which hardly fits the perceived reality of the Amarna period. It rather reflects the Iron Age, when biblical descriptions of the land and its inhabitants were first recorded (Mendenhall 1973: 142–63; Mazar 1981).

The description of the city of Shechem in the days of Abimelech (Judges 9) is closely related to that of the Canaanite cities in the Amarna tablets. The institution of the lords *(baʿalê)* of Shechem is the same as the *bēlē āli* of the Amarna letters (EA 102:22; 138:49). The role of Zebul as a magistrate *(śar hāʿiyr)* who administered the city for the ruler (Abimelech) is parallel to that of the *ḫazannu* ("mayor") in ancient Near Eastern societies. However, the general situation drastically changed: Shechem was subjugated by the tribe of Manasseh and the tribal leader, Abimelech, resided within his clan and had nominated a mayor as his representative in the city. The city council tried to regain power by hiring a band of ʿApiru under the leadership of Gaal, just as Canaanite rulers in the Amarna period would do to attain the same goal, or as the lords *(baʿalê)* of Keilah did when they hired David and his band to protect the city against the Philistine raids (1 Sam 21:1–13). Abimelech's immediate attack on the city of Shechem and the expulsion of the band of Gaal (Judg 9:34–41) finds an exact parallel in the above cited case of the ruler of Tushulti, who, under pressure by his neighboring rulers, was forced to drive the band of ʿApiru out of his city (EA 185–86).

The description of "the justice *(mišpāṭ)* of the king" in 1 Sam 8:10–18 has sometimes been compared with Canaanite and north Syrian societies of the Late Bronze Age (Mendelsohn 1956). However, the distorted outlines of the institution of kingship in Samuel's antimonarchical polemical speech hardly fit any ancient Near Eastern kingship either in the 2d or the 1st millennium B.C. Isolated kings may well have treated their subjects in such an arbitrary and vicious manner, but despotism of the kind portrayed in the speech was not typical of well-established kingdoms, including the Canaanite city-states of the 2d millennium B.C. It has been alternatively suggested that the "king's justice" was originally a disguised polemical composition written against the despotic institution of kingship established in Israel by King Solomon (Crüsemann 1978: 66–73), but the discourse was probably composed at a much later time, either in the 7th or the 6th century, when the failure of the Israelite kingdom to provide security for its subjects became historical reality.

Overall, the image of Canaanite civilization as reflected in the Bible is far from accurate. Only certain outlines are precise, whereas other details reflect the reality of the time in which they were written, that is, the 1st millennium B.C. The history of the land of Canaan and its civilization must be studied from external sources and particularly from the Amarna letters. The authenticity of biblical data should always be examined against this background.

Bibliography

Ahituv, S. 1984. *Canaanite Toponyms in Ancient Egyptian Documents.* Jerusalem.

Albright, W. F. 1937. The Egyptian Correspondence of Abimilki, Prince of Tyre. *JEA* 23:190–203.

———. 1943. Two Little Understood Amarna Letters from the Middle Jordan Valley. *BASOR* 89: 7–17.

Alt, A. 1924. Neues über Palästina aus dem Archiv Amenophis' IV. *PJ* 20: 22–41. Repr. vol. 3, pp. 158–75 in *Kleine Schriften zur Geschichte des Volkes Israel,* Munich, 1959.

———. 1925. Die Landnahme der Israeliten in Palästina. *Reformationsprogramm der Universität Leipzig:* 1–35. Repr. vol. 1, pp. 89–125 in *Kleine Schriften zur Geschichte des Volkes Israel.* Munich, 1953.

———. 1950. Das Stützpunktsystem der Pharaonen an der phönikischen Küste und im syrischen Binnenland. *ZDPV* 68: 97–133. Repr. vol. 3, pp. 107–40 in *Kleine Schriften zur Geschichte des Volkes Israel,* Munich, 1959.

Altman, A. 1973. *The Kingdom of Amurru and "The Land of Amurru" 1500–1200 B.C.* Vol. 1–2. Diss. Ramat Gan: Bar-Ilan University (Hebrew).

Anbar, W., and Naʾaman, N. 1986–87. An Account Tablet of Sheep from Ancient Hebron. *TA* 13–14: 3–12.

Artzi, P. 1963. The "Glosses" in the Amarna Tablets (and in Ugarit), in *Bar-Ilan. Annual of Bar-Ilan University* 1: 24–57 (Hebrew).

———. 1978. The Rise of the Middle-Assyrian Kingdom according to El-Amarna Letters 15 and 16. Pp. 25–41 in *Bar-Ilan Studies in History.* Ramat Gan.

Bezold, C., and Budge, E. A. W. 1892. *The Tell el-Amarna Tablets in the British Museum.* London.

Bottéro, J. 1954. *Le Problème des Ḫabiru à la 4ᵉ Rencontre Assyriologique Internationale.* Cahiers de la sociéte asiatique XII. Paris.

Campbell, E. F. 1964. *The Chronology of the Amarna Letters with Special Reference to the Hypothetical Coregency of Amenophis III and Akhenaten.* Baltimore.

———. 1965. Shechem in the Amarna Archive. Pp. 191–207 in *Shechem: The Biography of a Biblical City.* G. E. Wright. London.

———. 1976. Two Amarna Notes: The Shechem City-State and Amarna Administrative Terminology. Pp. 39–54 in *Magnalia Dei. The Mighty Acts of God. Essays on the Bible and Archaeology in Memory of G. Ernest Wright,* ed. F. M. Cross, W. E. Lemke, and P. D. Miller. Garden City, NY.

Crüsemann, F. 1978. *Der Widerstand gegen das Königtum. Die antiköniglichen Texte des Alten Testamentes und der Kampf um den frühen israelitischen Staat.* WMANT 49. Neukirchen-Vluyn.

De Vaux, R. de. 1968. Le Pays de Canaan. Pp. 23–30 in *Essays in Memory of E. A. Speiser,* ed. W. W. Hallo. AOS 53, New Haven.

Edel, E. 1953. Weitere Briefe aus der Heiratskorrespondenz Ramses' II.: KUB III 37 + KB_0 I 17 und KUB III 57. Pp. 29–63 in *Geschichte und Altes Testame, Festschrift für Albrecht Alt.* Tübingen.

Edzard, D. O. 1960. Die Beziehungen Babyloniens und Ägyptens in der Mittelbabylonischen Zeit und das Gold. *JESHO* 3: 38–55.

———. 1985. Amarna und die Archive seiner Korrespondenten zwischen Ugarit und Gaza. Pp. 248–59 in *Biblical Archaeology Today: Proceedings of the International Congress on Biblical Archaeology Jerusalem, April 1984,* ed. J. Amitai. Jerusalem.

Frandsen, J. F. 1979. Egyptian Imperialism. Pp. 167–90 in *Power and Propaganda. A Symposium on Ancient Empires,* ed. M. T. Larsen. Mesopotamia 7. Copenhagen.

Gonen, R. 1981. Urban Canaan in the Late Bronze Age. *BASOR* 253: 61–73.

Gordon, C. H. 1947. The New Amarna Tablets. *Or* 16: 1–21.

Grave, C. 1980. On the Use of an Egyptian Idiom in an Amarna Letter from Tyre and in a Hymn to the Aten. *OrAnt* 19: 205–18.

———. 1982. Northwest Semitic *ṣapānu* in a Break-up of an Egyptian Stereotype Phrase in EA 147. *Or* 51: 161–83.

Greenberg, M. 1955. *The Ḫab/piru.* AOS 39. New Haven.

Groll, S. I. 1983. The Egyptian Administrative System in Syria and Palestine in the 18th Dynasty. Pp. 234–42 in *Fontes Atque Pontes. Eine Festgabe für Hellmut Brunner.* Ägyptens und Altes Testament 5. Wiesbaden.

Hachmann, R. 1970. Kāmid el-Lōz—Kumidi. Pp. 63–94 in *Kamid el-Loz—Kumidi. Schriftdokumente aus Kamid el-Loz,* ed. D. O. Edzard, R. Hachmann, P. Maiberger, and G. Mansfeld. Saarbrücker Beiträge zur Altertumskunde 7. Bonn.

———. 1982a. Die ägyptische Verwaltung in Syrien während der Amarnazeit. *ZDPV* 98: 17–49.

———. 1982b. Arahattu—Biriawaza—Puhuru. Pp. 137–61 in *Kamid el-Loz 1971–74,* ed. R. Hachmann. Saarbrücker Beiträge zur Altertumskunde 32. Bonn.

Heintz, J.-G. 1982. *Index documentaire d'El-Amarna. Liste/Codage des textes: Index des ouvrages de référence.* Wiesbaden.

Helck, W. 1971. *Die Beziehungen Ägyptens zu Vorderasien im 3. und 2. Jahrtausend v. Chr.* 2d rev. ed. Wiesbaden.

Hess, R. S. 1985. Personal Names from Amarna: Alternative Readings and Interpretations. *UF* 17: 157–67.

———. 1986. Divine Names in Amarna Texts. *UF* 18: 149–68.

Hornung, E. 1964. *Untersuchungen zur Chronologie und Geschichte des Neuen Reiches.* Wiesbaden.

Izreʿel, S. 1978. The Gezer Letters of the el-Amarna Archive—Linguistic Analysis. *IOS* 8: 13–90.

———. 1985. *The Akkadian Dialect of the Scribes of Amurru in the 14th–13th Centuries B.C.* Diss. Tel Aviv University (in Hebrew).

Kestemont, G. 1974. *Diplomatique et droit internationale en Asie Occidentale (1600–1200 av. J.C.).* Louvain-La-Neuve.

Kitchen, K. A. 1962. *Suppiluliuma and the Amarna Pharaohs.* Liverpool.

Klengel, H. 1969. *Geschichte Syriens im 2. Jahrtausend, v.u. Z.* Vol. 2 of *Mittel-und Südsyrien.* Berlin.

———. 1970. *Geschichte Syriens im 2. Jahrtausend v.u.Z.* Vol. 3 of *Historische Geographie und Allgemeine Darstellung.* Berlin.

Knudtzon, J. A.; Weber, O.; and Ebeling, E. 1915. *Die el-Amarna Tafeln mit Einleitung und Erlauterungen.* Vol. 1–2. VAB 2. Leipzig.

Krauss, R. 1978. *Das Ende der Amarnazeit. Beiträge zur Geschichte und Chronologie des Neuen Reiches.* Hildesheimer Ägyptologische Beiträge 7. Hildesheim.

Kühne, C. 1973. *Die Chronologie der internationalen Korrespondenz von El-Amarna. AOAT* 17: Kevelaer and Neukirchen-Vluyn.

Liverani, M. 1972. Elementi "irrazionali" nel commercio amarniaco. *OrAnt* 11: 297–317. Trans. "Irrational" Elements in the Amarna Trade. Pp. 21–33 in *Three Amarna Essays,* M. Liverani. MANE 1/5. Malibu, CA, 1979.

———. 1979. Farsi Ḫabiru. *Vicino Oriente* 2: 65–77.

———. 1983. Political Lexicon and Political Ideologies in the Amarna Letters. *Berytus* 31: 41–56.

Loretz, O. 1984. *Ḫabiru-Hebräer: Eine sozio-linguistische Studie über die Herkunft des Gentiliziums ʿibrî vom Appelativum ḫabiru.* BZAW 160. Berlin and New York.

Lorton, D. 1974. *The Juridical Terminology of International Relations in Egyptian Texts through Dyn. XVIII.* Baltimore.
Mazar, B. 1981. The Early Israelite Settlement in the Hill Country. *BASOR* 241: 75–85.
Mendelsohn, I. 1956. Samuel's Denunciation of Kingship in Light of Akkadian Documents from Ugarit. *BASOR* 143: 17–22.
Mendenhall, G. E. 1973. *The Tenth Generation. The Origins of the Biblical Tradition.* Baltimore and London.
Mohammad, W. A.-K. 1959. The Administration of Syro-Palestine during the New Kingdom. *ASAE* 56: 105–37.
Moran, W. L. 1950. *A Syntactical Study of the Dialect of Byblos as Reflected in the Amarna Tablets.* Diss. Johns Hopkins University.
———. 1960. Early Canaanite *yaqtula. Or* 29: 1–19.
———. 1965. The Hebrew Language in Its Northwest Semitic Background. Pp. 59–84 in *The Bible and the Ancient Near East,* ed. G. E. Wright. Garden City, NY.
———. 1973. The Dual Personal Pronouns in Western Peripheral Akkadian. *BASOR* 211: 50–53.
———. 1975a. The Syrian Scribe of the Jerusalem Amarna Letters. Pp. 146–66 in *Unity and Diversity. Essays in the History, Literature and Religion of the Ancient Near East,* ed. H. Goedicke and J. J. M. Roberts. Baltimore and London.
———. 1975b. Amarna Glosses. *RA* 69: 147–58.
———. 1984. Additions to the Amarna Lexicon. *Or* 53: 297–302.
———. 1987. *Les Lettres d'El-Amarna.* Littératures Anciennes du Proche-Orient 13. Paris.
Murnane, W. J. 1985. *The Road to Kadesh. A Historical Interpretation of the Battle Reliefs of King Sety I at Karnak.* Studies in Ancient Oriental Civilization 42. Chicago.
Naʾaman, N. 1975. *The Political Disposition and Historical Development of Eretz-Israel According to the Amarna Letters.* Diss. Tel Aviv University (Hebrew).
———. 1979. The Origin and Historical Background of Several Amarna Letters. *UF* 11: 673–84.
———. 1981a. Economic Aspects of the Egyptian Occupation of Canaan. *IEJ* 31: 172–85.
———. 1981b. Royal Estates in the Jezreel Valley in the Late Bronze Age and Under the Israelite Monarchy. *EI* 15: 140–44 (Hebrew).
———. 1982. Eretz Israel in the Canaanite Period: The Middle Bronze Age and the Late Bronze Age (ca. 2000–1200 B.C.E.). Vol. 1, pp. 129–256 in *The History of Eretz Israel,* ed. I. Ephʿal. Jerusalem (Hebrew).
———. 1986a. Ḫabiru and Hebrews: The Transfer of a Social Term to the Literary Sphere. *JNES* 45: 271–88.
———. 1986b. The Canaanite City-States in the Late Bronze Age and the Inheritances of the Israelite Tribes. *Tarbiz* 55: 463–88 (Hebrew).
———. 1988. Historical-Geographical Aspects of the Amarna Tablets. Pp. 17–26 in *Proceedings of the Ninth World Congress of Jewish Studies. Panel Sessions Bible and Ancient Near East.* Jerusalem.
Petrie, W. M. F. 1894. *Tell el-Amarna.* London.
Pintore, E. 1972. Transiti di truppe e schemi epistolari nella Siria Egiziana dell'età di el-Amarna. *OrAnt* 11: 101–31.
———. 1973. La prassi della marcia armata nella Siria Egiziana dell'età di el-Amarna. *OrAnt* 12: 299–318.
———. 1978. *Il matrimonio interdinastico nel Vicino Oriente durante i secoli XV–XIII.* Orientis Antiqui Collectio 14. Rome.
Rainey, A. F. 1970. *El-Amarna Tablets 359–379. Supplement to J. A. Knudtzon, Die EL-Amarna Tafeln. AOAT* 8. 2d rev. ed. 1978. Kevelaer and Neukirchen-Vluyn.
———. 1971. Verbal Forms with Infix -t- in the West Semitic el-Amarna Letters. *IOS* 1: 86–102.
———. 1973. Reflections on the Suffix Conjugation in West Semitized Amarna Tablets. *UF* 5: 235–62.
———. 1975. Morphology and the Prefix-Tenses of West Semitized el-Amarna Tablets. *UF* 7: 395–432.
———. 1978. The Barth-Ginsberg Law in the Amarna Tablets. *EI* 14: 8–13.
Redford, D. B. 1967. *History and Chronology of the Eighteenth Dynasty of Egypt. Seven Studies.* Toronto.
Riedel, W. 1939. Das Archiv Amenophis IV. *OLZ* 42: 145–48.
Sayce, A. H. 1917. The Discovery of the Tel el-Amarna Tablets. *AJSL* 33: 89–90.
Schroeder, O. 1915. *Die Tontafeln von el-Amarna in akkadischer Sprache.* Vol. 1–2. VS XI–XII. Leipzig.
Schulman, A. R. 1979. Diplomatic Marriage in the Egyptian New Kingdom. *JNES* 38: 177–93.
Several, M. W. 1972. Reconsidering the Egyptian Empire in Palestine during the Amarna Period. *PEQ* 104: 123–33.
Singer, I. 1983. Takuḫlinu and Ḫaya: Two Governors in the Ugarit Letter from Tel Aphek. *TA* 10: 3–25.
———. 1988. Merneptah's Campaign to Canaan and the Egyptian Occupation of the Southern Coastal Plain of Palestine in the Ramesside Period. *BASOR* 269: 1–10.
Spalinger, A. 1983. The Historical Implications of the Year 9 Campaign of Amenophis II. *JARCE* 13: 89–101.
Walker, C. B. F. 1979. Another Fragment from el-Amarna (EA 380). *JCS* 31: 249.
Weinstein, J. M. 1981. The Egyptian Empire in Palestine: A Reassessment. *BASOR* 241: 1–28.
Wilhelm, G. 1970. *Untersuchungen zum Hurro-Akkadischen von Nuzi.* AOAT 9. Kevelaer and Neukirchen-Vluyn.
Winckler, H. 1896. *The Tell-el-Amarna Letters.* Trans. J. Metcalf. New York.
Winckler, H., and Abel, L. 1889–90. *Der Thontafelfund von el-Amarna.* Vol. 1–3. Berlin.
Zaccagnini, C. 1973. *Lo scambio dei doni del Vicino Oriente durante i secoli XV–XIII.* Rome.

NADAV NAʾAMAN

AMARNA, TELL EL- (27°38′ N; 30°52′ E). The site of the premier city and residence of the Egyptian Pharaoh Amenophis (Amenhotep) IV (alias Akhenaten ca. 1377–1360 B.C.); located on the east bank of the Nile in the 15th nome (township) of Upper Egypt, ca. 180 miles S of modern Cairo. The Pharaoh named his new city Akhetaten (Eg *3ḫt-itn* "the horizon of the Sun-disc").

Although the area had been frequented in earlier periods by mining expeditions to neighboring Hatnub, the decision to found a city must have been taken no later than Akhenaten's 4th year. By year 6, the king's family was in residence, and the greater city and environs (on both banks) delimited by a series of boundary stelae.

Chosen perhaps because the eastern cliffs resembled the hieroglyphic sign *3ḫt* "horizon," the city became the center of worship of the king's sole god, the Sun-disc. Two major temples to the god occupied its central area, the "Mansion of the Sun-disc" (Eg *ḥwt-ıtn*), and the *Gm-ʾitn* ("The Sun-disc is found") with ancilliary shrines in the N and S suburbs.

The settlement constituted a "planned" city, arranged

along a broad N–S avenue, connecting the king's residence on the N with the central city and the "Viewing Place of the Disc" on the S. The city housed a formal palace, administrative blocks and granaries, residences for the immediate members of the royal family, and well-planned villas for the state officers and courtiers. The necropolis on the E was divided into a N and S cemetery, flanking the E wadi wherein the royal tomb was located.

In the 3d year of Tutankhamen (ca. 357 B.C.), after approximately 16 years of residence, the royal family left the city for Memphis, and the court and general populace soon thereafter moved out. Under Horemheb (ca. 1347–1318 B.C.) the temples and public buildings were systematically demolished, and the masonry shipped to other sites (especially Hermopolis) for reuse. There is some evidence of very limited building activity under the Ramessides.

The site is also famous for the discovery in 1888–89 of the cache of tablets known as the "Tell el-Amarna Letters"—the "dead files" of international state correspondence from the reigns of Amenophis III, Akhenaten, and Tutankhamen. See also AMARNA LETTERS; AKHENATEN.

Bibliography

Aldred, C. 1968. *Akhenaten, King of Egypt.* London.

———. 1973. *Akhenaten and Nefertiti.* London and New York.

Kemp, B. J. 1986. Tell el-Amarna. *LÄ* 6: 309–19.

Peet, T. E.; Frankfort, H.; Pendlebury, J. D. S.; and Fairman, H. W. 1923–51. *The City of Akhenaten.* 4 vols. London.

Pendlebury, J. D. S. 1935. *Tell el-Amarna.* London.

Petrie, W. M. F. 1894. *Tell el-Amarna.* London.

Redford, D. B. 1984. *Akhenaten, the Heretic King.* Princeton.

Samson, J. 1972. *Amarna: City of Akhenaten and Nefertiti.* London.

DONALD B. REDFORD

AMASA (PERSON) [Heb *ʿămāśāʾ*]. **1.** Kinsman of David (2 Sam 19:14—Eng 19:13) whom Absalom appointed to replace Joab as commander of the army during his rebellion against David (2 Sam 17:25), a post Amasa retained after David's return to power, only to be murdered by Joab in the early stages of the suppression of Sheba's rebellion. According to 2 Sam 17:25, his father was Ithra, the Israelite, (according to 1 Chr 2:17, Jether the Ishmaelite) and his mother Abigail the daughter of Nahash. However, this latter name may be a textual corruption from 2 Sam 17:27, because Abigail is also identified as the sister of Joab's mother Zeruiah. According to 1 Chr 1:16–17, both these women were sisters of David and presumably daughters of Jesse. It has been alternately suggested that Abigail was David's half-sister and not Jesse's daughter. The wording of 2 Sam 17:25 suggests that there was something unusual or irregular about Abigail's marital relationship with Ithra.

Although it remains a matter of dispute whether the tribe of Judah joined the northern tribes in rebellion against David or remained neutral, Amasa's support of Absalom indicates that high-ranking Judahites were active in opposing David. Although the professional troops of David commanded by Joab defeated the national militia led by Amasa, David's position was still tenuous enough to require special overtures to Judah for a quick return to the throne. The appointment of Amasa was one factor in David's successful appeal to his fellow Judahites (2 Sam 19:12–15—Eng 19:11–14). David's tilt to Judah seems to have precipitated Sheba's subsequent rebellion.

Amasa failed to carry out David's orders to muster the militia of Judah in three days to meet the Sheba crisis (2 Sam 20:4–5). Perhaps he simply did not have enough time, or perhaps he felt it would be personally inexpedient to attack Israel with the militia of Judah. David's professional troops set out alone, among them Joab (vv 6–7). Amasa encountered them at Gibeon and was treacherously stabbed by Joab, who immediately took back effective control of the army (vv 8–11). The details of this murder are obscure but imply premeditation and trickery. The sight of Amasa's body was not permitted to hinder the army's progress (vv 12–13). Amasa's murder would later help justify the liquidation of Joab upon Solomon's accession (1 Kgs 2:5, 32). From a literary standpoint, the biblical author seems to treat David's offer to Amasa as one of several errors in personal and political judgment (for other examples, see 2 Sam 13:21; 18:5; 19:2–4—Eng 19:1–3; 19:42–44—Eng 41–43; 1 Kgs 1:6).

Amasa has sometimes been identified with Amasai (Heb *ʿămāśay*), the chief of the "Thirty" (1 Chr 12:19—Eng 12:18), who pledged loyalty and peace to David when Saul was hunting for him (See DAVID'S CHAMPIONS). There is no solid evidence either for or against this proposal.

2. Son of Hadlai, one of four chiefs of Emphraim who supported the prophet Oded in opposing a proposal to take captives from Judah into Samaria, cared for them instead, and returned them south (2 Chr 28:12–15). Luke's parable of the Good Samaritan reflects this narrative (compare v 15 with Luke 10:34).

RICHARD D. NELSON

AMASAI (PERSON) [Heb *ʿămāśay*]. A name found throughout Chronicles in the Hebrew Bible.

1. A Levite from the clan of Kohath, a descendant of Elkanah and relative of Ahimoth (1 Chr 6:10—Eng 6:25). He is also mentioned as the father of Mahath and as a Levitical musician in the genealogy of Heman (1 Chr 6:20—Eng 6:35). Both contexts appear concerned to trace the lineage of Samuel the prophet, to whom the Chronicler assigns Levitical ancestry (1 Chr 6:13, 18—Eng 6:28, 33; cf. 1 Sam 1:1); this reflects the Chronicler's pervasive interest in the prophetic function of the Levitical musicians (1 Chr 25:1–8; 2 Chr 20:14; 29:25; 34:30; 35:15). Since Mahath is mentioned in 1 Chr 6:20—Eng 6:35; (cf. 2 Chr 29:12), some correct Ahimoth to *ʾăḥîw maḥat,* "his brother Mahath" (cf. *BHS*).

2. One of the priests appointed by David to blow the trumpets before the ark during its transfer from the house of Obed-edom to Jerusalem (1 Chr 15:24).

3. The father of Mahath, a Kohathite at the time of Hezekiah (2 Chr 29:12). Since #1 and #3 both involve an Amasai, father of Mahath, some have equated these figures, though they were presumably separated by centuries. More probably the recurrence of the names reflects the practice of papponymy (naming sons for grandfathers) or some other naming convention.

4. Chief of the "Thirty," a group of David's military

elite (1 Chr 12:19—Eng 12:18). The only other person known to have held this title, according to the MT, was Jashobeam (1 Chr 11:11, though he is chief of the "Three" in some LXX mss). This Amasai is occasionally equated with either (1) Abishai the brother of Joab, chief of the "Three" (2 Sam 23:18, MT; but "Thirty" in two Hebrew mss and Syr), or (2) Amasa, another prominent military figure (2 Sam 17:25; 20:4–13). Assessing this Amasai is complicated by debate regarding the identification of the "Three" and the "Thirty" (see DAVID'S CHAMPIONS). The Chronicler in this context is concerned to show growing support for David among those formerly loyal to Saul (1 Chr 12:1–8, 17—Eng 12:1–7, 16).

Bibliography

Mazar, B. 1963. The Military Elite of King David. VT 13: 310–20.

Naʾaman, N. 1988. The List of David's Officers. VT 38: 71–79.

Williamson, H. G. M. 1981. "We Are Yours, O David." *OTS* 21: 164–76.

RAYMOND B. DILLARD

AMASHSAI (PERSON) [Heb *ʿămašsa(y)*]. Var. MAASAI. A Levitical priest, the son of Azarel and grandson of Ahzai (Neh 11:13). His name calls to mind one of the important priestly families listed as resident and active in Jerusalem at the time of Nehemiah, ca. 444 B.C. In the parallel verse in 1 Chr 9:12 his name occurs as Maasai [Heb *maʿśa(y)* or *maʿăśa(y)*] ben Adiel ben Jahzerah. The textual apparatus of *BHS* itself posits his name as more originally either AMASAI [Heb *ʿămāśa(y)*] or Amasai [Heb *ʿămāsa(y)*]. Such a name is common elsewhere in Chronicles: 1 Chr 6:10—Eng 6:25; 6:20—Eng 6:35; 12:19—Eng 12:18; 15:24; 2 Chr 29:12. Both 1 Chronicles and Nehemiah trace his lineage back to Immer, a Levitical priest descended from Aaron through his son Eleazar (1 Chr 24:14). Amashsai and his brethren are said to have numbered 128 men.

ROGER W. UITTI

AMASIAH (PERSON) [Heb *ʿămasyâ*]. Amasiah (meaning "Yahweh carried or supported"), son of Zichri, was from the tribe of Judah and a lieutenant of Adnah, commander of Jehoshaphat's standing army (2 Chr 17:16). He stands out in this list of military commanders for his piety and altruistic motives for service. His volunteering for Yahweh's service is perhaps in contrast to the other commanders who possibly, along with the rest of the army, were conscripts (*AncIsr* 1: 231). He is said to have commanded 200,000 men. Meyers (*2 Chronicles* AB, 78, 98) suggested that these numbers are best explained by translating the Heb *ʾelep* as "(military) unit" of unknown strength rather than "thousand." Amasiah would have then commanded 200 "units."

KIRK E. LOWERY

AMAW (PLACE) [Heb *ʿammô*]. According to the RSV, the land "near the River" in which was located Pethor, the city from which Balaam traveled to curse the Israelites (Num 22:5). The KJV and the AV follow the MT and LXX, which read "the land of the sons of his people *(ʿammo)*" while the Syriac, Vulgate, and Samaritan versions have "the land of the Ammonites *(bene-ʿammon)*." Gray (*Numbers*, ICC, 325) suggested that MT lost the final nun and thus changed Ammon to *ʿammo*. "The River" has been taken to mean the Euphrates River. Pethor has been identified with Pitru, near Carchemish, 400 miles and 20 days' journey by camel to the N of Moab and hence a minimum of 80 days for the two round trips described in 22:7–36. Ammon, on the other hand, is easily a donkey's journey from Moab. While the Ammonites did not live by the Jordan River, it is not impossible that here "the River" is the Jordan.

Excavations in 1967 at Tell Deir ʿAlla (biblical Succoth?) in the Jordan Valley discovered a series of texts written in ink on plaster. They record the vision and interpretation of Balaam the son of Beor. While the texts date from centuries later, their contents could be from an earlier time, but in any case they reveal a Jordan Valley tradition about a diviner named Balaam. The story recorded in Numbers 22–24 may refer to the same prophet or a different one. But the Deir ʿAlla texts strengthen the translation which has Balaam coming from the Ammonite area.

Amaw, however, still has support. Deut 23:4 records Balaam as coming from Pethor in Mesopotamia. Albright (1950: 15–16 n. 13; 20) translated ʿAmau on a statue of King Idrimi excavated in 1939 by Sir Leonard Woolley at Atchana, ancient Alalakh, in Syria, near Antioch on the Orontes. The statue is dated ca. 1450 B.C. by Albright and 1375 B.C. by Woolley and Sidney Smith. The translation in *ANET* spells it Amaʾe (p. 557). Idrimi lived in the city of Emar and later ruled Halab (Aleppo), Mukishkhi, Niʾ, and Amaʾe (or Amaw). Pitru in Amaw was actually not on the Euphrates itself but on the Sajur River, a few miles from its juncture with the Euphrates. The Sajur is a tributary from the W. It is a sizable stream whose lower stretch flows between two ranges of low chalk hills. Amaw or Amau is in the valley of the Sajur, between Aleppo and the Euphrates. Pethor or Pitru is mentioned by Shalmaneser III (860–825 B.C.). Pethor as *Pe-d-rui* appears in the lists of Thutmose III (1504–1450 B.C.) who conquered Amaw. The country is also mentioned in the tomb of Qen-Amun, an Egyptian officer of Amenhotep II (1450–1425 B.C.), the son of Thutmose III. Egyptian *ʿmw* means Asiatic or Syrian. This may influence the interpretation of these Egyptian references. Similarly, some find a reference to Amaw in Exod 15:14 where RSV has "the peoples" in parallel with Philistia, Edom, Moab, and Canaan; i.e., Amaw may be listed here as another land like these others.

Bibliography

Albright, W. F. 1950. Some Important Recent Discoveries: Alphabetic Origins at the Idrimi Statue. *BASOR* 118: 11–20.

Barabas, S. 1975. Amaw. I: 126. *The Zondervan Pictorial Encyclopedia of the Bible,* 5 vols., ed. M. C. Tenney and S. Barabas. Grand Rapids.

Goetze, A. 1957. The Syrian Town of Emar. *BASOR* 147: 22–27.

Thompson, H. O. 1986. Balaam in the Bible and at Deir ʿAlla. *BA* 49: 218–19.

HENRY O. THOMPSON

AMAZIAH (PERSON) [Heb *ʾămaṣyāhû*]. The name held by four persons in the Hebrew Bible. The name means "Yahu is strong" (*TPNAH* 75: 163).

1. The 9th ruler of the southern kingdom of Judah (ca. 800–783 B.C.), the son of Joash, king of Judah (ca. 837–800 B.C.).

The accounts of Amaziah's reign in Kings and Chronicles (2 Kings 14 = 2 Chronicles 25) are in substantial agreement, with the exception of material in Chronicles which explains Amaziah's disastrous motivation for his war with Israel and his subsequent fall (see 2 Chr 25:5–10). Scholars are in disagreement concerning the historical reliability of this material, which is unique to Chronicles.

2 Kings 14 gives Amaziah's age as twenty-five when he was made king following the assassination of his father. The length of his reign is given as 29 years with the additional synchronism in 2 Kgs 14:17 that he lived fifteen years beyond the death of Jehoahaz, king of Israel, i.e. to ca. 769 B.C. The unusual length of the reign of his son and successor Azariah (Uzziah), 52 years, has led to the suggestion that he had his son rule with him as coregent, a practice known also in Israel (Gray *Kings* OTL, 65–68; Barnes, fc., 197 n. l, m).

His father, Joash, was murdered by two of his retainers (2 Kgs 12:20–21). As soon as Amaziah's rule was secure, he had these men, who were still in royal service, executed (2 Kgs 14:5 = 2 Chr 25:3–4). The sources do not explain what Amaziah had to do in order to consolidate his power.

The first major recorded event of his reign which our sources report is his war against Edom. He is said to have slain 10,000 in the otherwise unknown Valley of Salt (Heb *gayĕʾ hamelaḥ*), the location of which is uncertain. The Arabah just S of the Dead Sea has been proposed (*LBHG*, 313), as has the *Wadi Milh* E of Beer-sheba (Gray *Kings* OTL, 605).

Amaziah then took Sela and renamed it Joktheel. The identification of Sela with the later site of Petra was first given in LXX and later accepted by Eusebius (*Onomast.* 36.13; 142.7; 144.7). This identification has been accepted by many scholars (Avi-Yonah *EAEHL*, 943) although contested by Haram (1968: 201–12). Aharoni has proposed *es-Sela* (*LBHG*, 37).

In addition to the 10,000 slain in the Valley of Salt, 2 Chr 25:37 adds that Amaziah slew an additional 10,000 by throwing them from the cliffs above the valley. This detail is repeated by Josephus (*Ant* 9 §191).

Following his successful clash with Edom, nothing more is recorded of any Judean expansion to the S or E. The consolidation of Judean control of the S end of the King's Highway as far as Elath had to wait until the reign of Amaziah's son and successor Azariah (2 Kgs 14:22).

For reasons which are unclear, Amaziah challenged Jehoash, king of Israel, to battle. They met at Beth-shemesh in Judah, E of Jerusalem, where the Judean army was routed and Amaziah taken prisoner. He was taken to Jerusalem, where Jehoash broke down a portion of the N wall and plundered both the palace and the temple. Jehoash returned to the N, taking with him hostages to ensure Amaziah's good behavior.

While the origin of this dispute is not given in the account in 2 Kings 25, 2 Chronicles 14 adds that mercenaries from Israel hired by Amaziah for his war with Edom, but then released prior to the battle, vented their anger at being denied the chance for plunder by plundering some Judean villages on their way home. Amaziah, angered by this, then declared war on Israel. Another possibility is that the conflict began as a border dispute, or that it began over control of the W terminus of the trade routes leading to the Gulf of Aqaba. A combination of the latter two possibilities seems likely (Gray *Kings* OTL, 608).

Amaziah, like his father, fell victim to an assassination plot. Our sources record that, although he fled from Jerusalem to Lachish in order to escape, he was handed over to the conspirators and killed. His body was brought up to Jerusalem on a horse, an act of disrespect, where he was buried with his ancestors in the city of David.

2. The priest at the N, royal sanctuary of Bethel during the reign of Jeroboam II (ca. 786–746 B.C.). He attempted to expel the prophet Amos from the temple there, forbidding him to prophesy in the N kingdom and reporting his pessimistic oracles, which were weakening the land, to the king (Amos 7:10–17).

3. The son of Hilkiah and father of Hashabiah, a descendant of Merari son of Levi. 1 Chr 6:31–47 is a text which is concerned with presenting the legitimacy of the office and descent of the Levitical singers. The appointment of temple singers is here traced back to the reign of David after he brought the ark to Jerusalem.

4. Father of Joshah, and a descendant of Simeon mentioned in 1 Chr 4:34.

Bibliography

Barnes, W. fc. *Studies in the Chronology of the Divided Monarchy of Israel.* HSM. Atlanta.

Haran, M. 1968. Observations on the Historical Background of Amos 1.2–2.6 *IEJ* 18: 201–12.

RUSSELL FULLER

AMEN [Heb *ʾāmēn*]. Within the Hebrew Bible, "Amen" typically appears at the close of commands, blessings, curses, doxologies, and prayers. Fundamentally, it is used to confirm what has been said before, by way of response (Num 5:22; Deut 27:15–26; 1 Kgs 1:36; Jer 11:5; 28:6; 1 Chr 16:36; Neh 5:13; 8:6). That it acquired the status of a formal response at an early period is shown clearly by Jer 28:6, where the prophet appears to confirm that Hananiah has said, by a conventional usage of "Amen," and then proceeds to contradict it. The majority of usages already cited appear in public, often liturgical contexts, so that the responsive usage in Psalms comes as no surprise (Pss 41:13; 72:19; 89:52; 106:48). The last usage is—together with 1 Chr 16:36; Neh 5:13; 8:6—especially instructive, as "the people" are explicitly instructed to say "Amen" (and "Hallelujah," rendered "Praise the Lord" in the RSV). In function and formal usage, "Amen" serves to confirm what has gone before, usually—but not exclusively—in public, liturgical contexts of divine praise. The usage of 1 Kgs 1:36 (cf. also Isa 65:16) establishes the idiomatic, nonliturgical origins of the usage.

The translation of the word has proved problematic, although its function is straightforward. The verbal *ʾmn* is associated with several meanings in its various forms, from "support," "be faithful" *(Qal)* through "sure," "established" *(Nipʿal)*, to "stand firm," "believe" *(Hipʿil)*. A meaning such as "truly," "surely," or "so be it," seems clear, although none of those renderings entirely captures the nuance of the Hebrew. Within the manuscripts of the LXX, there is a notable variety of renderings of Heb *ʾāmēn*. Predominantly, "so be it" *(genoito)* is the preferred rendering (Num 5:22; Deut 27:15–26; Jer 11:5). But "truly" *(alēthôs)* is also possible (Jer 35:6 LXX), and there are several occasions (1 Chr 16:36; Neh 5:13; 8:6 [the latter two being 2 Esdr 15:13 and 18:6 in the LXX]) when Heb *ʾāmēn* is simply transliterated as *amēn.* 1 Esdr 9:47 and Tob 8:8 demonstrate that the transliteration had gained some currency in the Greek-speaking circles for which the Septuagint was intended; the latter passage also shows the propriety of "Amen" within private prayer. Just as the development of a generic affirmation into a public, often liturgical, response is attested in the Hebrew Bible, the LXX reveals a tendency for the word to be used in other religious contexts. Notably, there is even support among some manuscripts of the LXX to close books with a solemn "Amen" (Tobit, *3* and *4 Maccabees*).

Generally speaking, the use of "Amen" within the NT is predictable, once the evidence of the Hebrew Bible and the LXX is taken into account. Pauline habits in this regard are representative, as he uses "Amen" to round off blessings and doxologies (Rom 1:25; 9:5; 11:36; 15:33; Gal 1:5; Phil 4:20). He also uses it to confirm his own prayers by way of closing his letters, although some of the usages (in 1 and 2 Corinthians and Romans) are probably scribal additions. But in both the range of its usage and the variety of its manuscripts, the Pauline corpus stands within the precedents of the LXX, although Pauline usage is both more frequent and more consistent than is the LXX. Paul also gives some hint of the reason for this greater frequency and consistency when he refers to "Amen" as a liturgical response of the church in Corinth (1 Cor 14:16; cf. 2 Cor 1:20).

Pauline usage is also consistent with that of the deutero-Pauline corpus, as well as of the Pastorals (Eph 3:21; 1 Tim 1:17; 6:16; 2 Tim 4:18; Heb 13:21). The ubiquity of "Amen" was by no means limited to the Pauline circle, as much the same usage can be encountered in 1 Pet 4:11; 5:11; Jude 25, and such passages could be augmented by means of reference to variant readings. Revelation might particularly be noted, however, as evidencing a liturgical, responsorial usage in early Christian worship (1:6, 7; 5:14; 7:12; 19:4; 22:20); indeed, Jesus Christ can here be known as "the Amen," because his witness is sure (3:14). Such a development is innovative, but in line with the liturgical and christological tendency of the document.

Curiously, the only oddity of usage within the NT (as judged in comparison with the Hebrew Bible and the LXX) is attributed to Jesus himself. Instead of a responsive, liturgical usage, Jesus presents "Amen" as introductory and asseverative, in the form "Amen, I say to you . . ." (Matt 5:18 plus 73x in the gospels). The agreement among the gospels in respect of this diction becomes all the more striking when certain deviations in Luke and John are explained. Luke's relative infrequency is mitigated by his use of "truly" *(alēthôs)* and "in truth" *(epʾ alētheias)* as a virtual equivalent of *ʾāmēn* (4:25; 9:27; 12:44; 21:3). The LXX is commonly appealed to by way of precedent for Luke's procedure, and "truly" clearly conveys the sense of "Amen," but the translation is syntactically sensitive. The introductory position of *ʾāmēn* makes the natural equivalent in Greek *(genoito)* impracticable, with the result that Lukan style is at this point scarcely Septuagintal. The Johannine doubling *Amēn amēn* (John 1:51, etc.) is normally said to be liturgical, and in this instance the usage of the Hebrew Bible and the LXX does appear to be antecedent.

The mystery remains: why should an unusual, introductory, and asseverative usage be ascribed to Jesus, when the normal usage of "Amen," even within the NT, is responsive? A straightforward answer to that question was provided by Joachim Jeremias, who argued that Jesus himself employed well-known language in a radically fresh way, in order to assert in advance the authority of his pronouncements. As is frequently the case in his work, Jeremias proceeds by comparing dominical diction with rabbinic conventions (Jeremias 1971: 35–36) and concludes that deviations of the former from the latter are hallmarks of Jesus' own message.

Such an approach remains widely represented and particularly serves the interests of those who argue that Christianity in some sense transcends Judaism. In this particular case, Jeremias' argument has encountered two obstacles. First, it has been suggested that there is some precedent, prior to Jesus, for introductory "Amen" (Strugnell 1974). Indeed, some of the uses within the Hebrew Bible may be so described (1 Kgs 1:36; Jer 28:6) and may be among the best examples of the usage with its basic meaning. Even in such cases, however, although the usage is introductory within dialogue, it is in fact responsive to a previously established statement. It is the proleptically asseverative function of Jesus' use of "Amen" which makes it appear unusual. To that extent, Jeremias' argument may be justified, although it also must be refined somewhat. The second challenge of Jeremias' position is far more radical. K. Berger has attacked the consensus that "Amen" is essentially a locution of Hebrew-speaking Judaism. He urges the view that, on the turf of Hellenistic Judaism, Hebrew "Amen" was used with the introductory function of *ē mēn* in Greek. This usage, he argues, was taken up within Christian communities to mark the faithful transmission of tradition (Berger 1970: 72, 93, 147, 151, 159–63).

The evidential basis of Berger's case is slender. Chiefly, he relies upon the introduction, "Amen, I say to you," in the *T. Ab.* 8:7 (Berger 1970: 15). What is crucial for Berger is that the introduction precedes a quotation of Gen 22:17, which commences with *ē mēn* in the LXX. Such evidence falls far short of constituting an analogy to the ubiquity of asseverative "Amen" in the gospels, but it does at least establish that the idiom is meaningful within the context of Hellenistic Judaism. In any case, as Berger admits (1972: 47–50), the usage in the *T. Ab.* is certainly not to be seen as an antecedent of dominical usage in the gospels. Neither the date nor the tradition history of the document admits of such a conclusion (Sanders *APOT* 1: 871–81). But Berger successfully explodes any confidence that introductory "Amen" must be seen as an instance of Semitism, and he raises the possibility that the idiom is at home within Hellenistic, Greek-speaking Judaism.

A mediating point of view has been articulated by B. D. Chilton, on the basis of the Old Syriac gospels and Targumic diction (Chilton 1978). The Syriac versions are of interest, in view of the relatively close relationship between that language and the Aramaic of 1st-century Palestine. Curiously, the Old Syriac gospels simply read ʾ*myn* where *amēn* appears in the Greek, but there are occasions when the term is omitted. That would tend to support Berger's contention, in that it makes "Amen" appear more natural in Greek than in Syriac. On the other hand, the Syriac versions also suggest that another introductory asseveration analogous to *amēn* in the Greek gospels survived from Aramaic. The locution in question is "in truth" (Syr *bqwštʾ*), an unusual usage in the Syriac gospels but a common expression in Aramaic. It appears, for example, at Gen 3:1; 17:19; 18:13; 20:12; 42:21 in *Targum Onqelos,* corresponding to a variety of introductions in the Hebrew and Greek texts; similarly, it occurs at *T. Isa.* 37:18; 45:14, 15. *T. Isa.* 37:18 is of special interest, because ʾ*mnm* (which is closely related to "Amen") is the corresponding term in Hebrew, while "in truth" *(epʾ alētheias)* appears in Greek (cf. also Gen 18:13; 20:12 LXX). The clear possibility emerges that "Amen" in the gospels represents "in truth" in the Aramaic tradition of Jesus' words, as Luke's presentation at 4:25; 9:27; 12:44; 21:3 would also suggest.

Introductory and asseverative "Amen" in the gospels may therefore represent dominical usage, but not in the direct manner Jeremias suggested. The Aramaic assurance, "in truth," was transformed within Hellenistic circles steeped in the language of Judaism and became "Amen." That added weight to the authority and liturgical impact of Jesus' sayings, and conveyed the theological conviction that the one who spoke was sufficiently credible as to be called "the Amen" (Rev 3:14).

Bibliography

Berger, K. 1970. *Die Amen-Worte Jesu.* BZNW 39. Göttingen.

———. 1972. Zur Geschichte der Einleitungsformel "Amen ich sage euch." *ZNW* 63: 45–75.

Chilton, B. D. 1978. "Amen": An Approach through Syriac Gospels. *ZNW* 69: 203–11. Repr. pp. 15–23 in *Targumic Approaches to the Gospels.* Studies in Judaism. Lanham, MD, 1986.

Hasler, V. 1969. *Amen: Redaktionsgeschichtliche Untersuchungenen zur Einführungsformel der Herrenworte "Wahrlich ich sage euch."* Zurich.

Jeremias, J. 1971. *New Testament Theology.* Vol. 1, *The Proclamation of Jesus.* New York.

Strugnell, J. 1974. "Amen, I Say Unto You" in the Sayings of Jesus and in Early Christian Literature. *HTR* 67:177–82.

Bruce Chilton

AMERICAN SCHOOLS OF ORIENTAL RESEARCH, HISTORY OF THE.

A. Beginnings: 1900–18

During the 19th century only a handful of Americans were engaged in archaeological research centering on the ancient Near East; most notable among them was Edward Robinson, explorer-biblical scholar, whose travels in the Holy Land signaled a new era in the topographical study of that part of the world. It was only at the turn of the century that Americans became involved in a concerted way; the year 1900 marked the establishment in Jerusalem of the American School for Oriental Study and Research, shortened later to the American Schools of Oriental Research; it is even better known today by the acronym ASOR.

Sponsored by three similar professional organizations—the American Oriental Society, the Archaeological Institute of America, and the Society of Biblical Literature—ASOR came into being; but the individual most responsible for the establishment of ASOR was J. Henry Thayer, professor of NT at Harvard. As president of the Society of Biblical Literature, he advocated strongly that such action be taken and worked tirelessly to make it happen.

According to ASOR's original constitution, "The main object of said School shall be to enable properly qualified persons to prosecute Biblical, linguistic, archaeological, historical, and other kindred studies and researches under more favorable conditions than can be secured at a distance from the Holy Land."

In the summer of 1900, Charles C. Torrey of Yale went to Jerusalem to set up ASOR's first overseas institute; he also served as its director during that academic year. ASOR's original quarters in Jerusalem consisted of only one large room in the Grand New Hotel (today, the New Imperial Hotel), in the vicinity of the Jaffa Gate. Torrey's first objective, shared by all his successors, was to build a research library for the School.

From 1900 to the beginning of World War I the School was managed by annual directors, who were scholars in one or another aspect of Near Eastern studies, including the Bible. However, they had no firsthand contact with the Near East. Thus, they spent most of their time familiarizing themselves with the land and visiting historical sites, and consequently had little opportunity to develop a coherent academic program for the School. Nonetheless their presence during those early years marked an important beginning for the School.

When David G. Lyon of Harvard was director of the School in 1906, he secured permission from the Ottoman government to excavate the site of ancient Samaria, situated near the modern village of Sebastiyeh. This Harvard-sponsored project was the first American dig conducted in Palestine. George A. Reisner, prominent Egyptologist, played a leading role in this undertaking; at the same time he set the standards for archaeological method and recording in Palestine, thereby influencing all future archaeologists.

James A. Montgomery of the University of Pennsylvania, director of the School immediately before the outbreak of World War I, was forced to leave Jerusalem after only three months. The activities of the School in Jerusalem were at a standstill for the remainder of the war. Montgomery continued to exercise great influence on the affairs of the School from Philadelphia, eventually being elected ASOR's first president (1921–34).

B. Between the Wars: 1919–45

The School in Jerusalem reopened in 1919. That same year saw the appearance of the *Bulletin of the American Schools of Oriental Research (BASOR),* today a leading journal in the field of Near Eastern archaeology, edited successively by Montgomery, William F. Albright, Delbert R. Hillers, David N. Freedman, William G. Dever, and Walter E. Rast. In 1921 when the American Schools of Oriental

Research was legally incorporated, "Schools" was deliberately pluralized to make room for other institutes that might eventually be established in the Near East.

The most prominent name associated with the Jerusalem School in the 1920s, as well as with ASOR for the next five decades, was William F. Albright, who was director of the School from 1920 to 1929, again from 1933 to 1936. When he completed his directorship in Jerusalem, Albright returned to America and became the W. W. Spence Professor of Semitic Languages at Johns Hopkins University.

Under Albright the Jerusalem School became an important research center, as well as a base for archaeological excavations. The field trips conducted by Albright have become legendary; during such trips the participants collected artifacts of all kinds, including pottery, and did limited surveys of selected sites. Albright brought to bear on these trips his extraordinary knowledge of philology, geography, pottery, and several other specialties, to the great benefit of his traveling companions.

Albright also conducted excavations, beginning at Tell el-Ful (Gibeah) in 1922. Between 1926 and 1932 Albright excavated at Tell Beit Mirsim, 12 miles SW of Hebron. Classifying the stylistic changes in potsherds at Tell Beit Mirsim, Albright constructed a ceramic typology, which he correlated with the stratigraphy of the tell. Through a combination of stratigraphy and typology, the two basic techniques of the archaeologist, Albright established the pottery chronology for Palestine. In 1927 and 1934 he directed the excavations at Bethel, one of the cities most frequently mentioned in the Bible.

Because many ASOR members had great professional interest in ancient Mesopotamia, Baghdad was chosen as the site of ASOR's second overseas institute. George A. Barton of the University of Pennsylvania was its first director, and Albert T. Clay of Yale the resident professor. Formally inaugurated in 1923, this School was the first American research institute in Baghdad. Because it lacked its own building, the American consulate provided office space for the Baghdad School. By 1925 the Jerusalem School was housed in permanent quarters, but the Baghdad School has never had its own residence.

Initially the Baghdad School conducted archaeological surveys, in addition to detailed study of all the excavated sites. Excavations were also undertaken by Americans at such well-known sites as Yorghan Tepe (Nuzi), Khorsabad, Tepe Gawra, and Tarkhalan.

Meanwhile the Jerusalem School continued to sponsor excavations at such sites as Tell en-Nasbeh (Mizpah), Gerasa (Jerash), Beth-zur, and Beth-shemesh.

The next long-term director of the School in Jerusalem, after Albright, was Nelson Glueck, who served in the 1930s and '40s, a period marked by serious political disturbances. While director of the Jerusalem School, Glueck inaugurated the *Newsletter,* an informal account of current projects; it has become an integral part of ASOR's publications program.

Glueck was a scholar-explorer in the tradition of Edward Robinson. Having learned excavation method and pottery chronology from Albright at Tell Beit Mirsim, he was well prepared for the monumental explorations he undertook in Transjordan and the Negeb; in all, he surveyed more than 1500 sites. Many of his conclusions have withstood the test of time, even though more sophisticated methods have been developed meanwhile.

Second only to Albright among the leading ASOR figures was G. Ernest Wright of Harvard. Although he was more prominent in ASOR after World War II, already in 1938 he launched the *Biblical Archaeologist (BA),* ASOR's popular quarterly. Never content to be an ivory-tower scholar, Wright was eager to communicate to the interested nonspecialist the results of scientific research. It is a special tribute to Wright that in 1987 the *Biblical Archaeologist* celebrated its golden jubilee. Subsequent editors, including Edward F. Campbell, H. Darrell Lance, David N. Freedman, and Eric M. Meyers, have maintained the high standards set by Wright.

C. A Decade of Development: 1945–55

In this postwar era archaeology continued to develop as a scientific discipline. Individual excavations were overshadowed, however, by the accidental discovery of the Dead Sea Scrolls, the most exciting event in the history of biblical archaeology. ASOR played its role in the identification and ongoing decipherment of these texts through the scholarly efforts of John C. Trever, Millar Burrows, William H. Brownlee, Frank M. Cross, and a host of other epigraphists, archaeologists, and biblical specialists.

After the inevitable disruptions caused by World War II in both Syria-Palestine and Iraq, the Baghdad School undertook a new phase of excavations at Nippur, which continued for 25 years. Albrecht Goetze of Yale directed the Baghdad School after the war and was responsible for founding in 1947 the *Journal of Cuneiform Studies (JCS),* a scholarly review of the literature, languages, and cultures of ancient Mesopotamia. The Baghdad School also participated in several surface surveys in Iraq, notably those under the supervision of Robert McC. Adams of the University of Chicago.

D. An Era of Expansion: 1956–67

The most significant American undertaking of this period was the Shechem excavations in central Palestine, under the direction of G. Ernest Wright, who combined stratigraphic digging and daily ceramic analysis with a detailed recording system. Shechem was the training ground for prospective American archaeologists; almost every later excavation, including Gezer, Hesi, Shema, Lahav, and Idalion (in Cyprus), reflected the influence of the Shechem expedition.

Another prominent ASOR figure was James B. Pritchard, associated with the University Museum of the University of Pennsylvania. In this era he excavated three important sites: el-Jib (Gibeon), Tell es-Saidiyeh (Zarethan), and Sarafand (Zarephath). Joseph A. Callaway of the Southern Baptist Theological Seminary excavated at et-Tell (biblical Ai) between 1964 and 1972. Apart from its merit as an exemplary field project, this dig demonstrated that archaeology and the biblical text are sometimes in conflict. The lack of artifactual evidence from the Late Bronze Age (1550–1200 B.C.) at this site makes it difficult to reconcile the traditional date of the "conquest" of Canaan, as recounted in the book of Joshua, with the archaeological record.

One of the most promising American archaeologists of this period was Paul Lapp, another long-term director of the Jerusalem School, whose career was cut short by a drowning accident in 1970. Before the tragedy he had already excavated at seven sites, including Araq el-Emir, Taanach, and Bab edh-Dhra. He has been accurately described as "the outstanding Palestinian archaeologist of his generation."

In 1964, G. Ernest Wright led a small expedition to Gezer in Israel but soon turned the project over to his students, William G. Dever and H. Darrell Lance. Applying what they had learned at Shechem, and at the same time introducing some new techniques, the Gezer staff fielded a quality dig. Hundreds of American volunteers were initiated into archaeology at the Gezer field school; several of them have become directors of their own excavations.

E. The Modern Period: 1967–85

In the aftermath of the 1967 Arab-Israeli War, ASOR established an institute in Amman to provide for American archaeology in Jordan. The newly erected international boundaries along the Jordan River prevented the Jerusalem School from filling that role, as it had done in the past. In response to the political reality, the institutes in Jerusalem and Amman were separately incorporated; the Jerusalem School was renamed appropriately the W. F. Albright Institute of Archaeological Research (AIAR), while the Amman School was named the American Center of Oriental Research (ACOR). Among the fine directors of ACOR, James A. Sauer deserves to be singled out; more than any other, he shaped the destiny of this center. As a result, ACOR has become a leading research center in Jordan. Sauer also led surveys, advised the Department of Antiquities, and lectured regularly in the University of Jordan.

ACOR has sponsored several excavations in Jordan; among the more significant are the ongoing dig at Bab edh-Dhra directed by Walter E. Rast and R. Thomas Schaub, as well as the long-term project at Tell Hesban, under the direction of Siegfried H. Horn, and later Lawrence T. Geraty of Andrews University, with Roger S. Boraas as chief archaeologist. In conjunction with the excavation of this latter site, a regional survey was conducted. Incorporating new techniques, this project was a model of interdisciplinary research and environmental studies.

Beginning in 1971, William G. Dever became the fourth long-term director of the Albright Institute. Building on the achievements of his predecessors, he expanded the archaeological facilities and the academic program of AIAR. His long-term successor, Albert E. Glock, continued these programs, and the current director, Seymour Gitin, has further developed them.

In addition to sponsoring traditional excavations relating to the Bronze and Iron Ages, both AIAR and ACOR are expanding the temporal horizons by digging sites that fit in both early (e.g., prehistory) and late (e.g., early Judaism, the beginnings of Christianity, and Islam) on the archaeological time scale.

ASOR has also expanded its traditional geographical boundaries. Prevented by civil war from digging in Lebanon, ASOR pursued the Phoenicians at two of their principal colonies—Cyprus and Carthage. To facilitate excavation, ASOR established a temporary institute at Carthage and a permanent one in Nicosia, called the Cyprus American Archaeological Research Institute (CAARI). Anita Walker of the University of Connecticut was its first director, followed by Ian Todd of Brandeis, and Stuart Swiny.

Because the land of Syria and its cultural heritage are central to ASOR's interests, Damascus would be an ideal place to establish a research institute. Few countries in the Near East can match the archives at Mari, Ugarit, and Ebla, all in Syria. Efforts to have a center in Syria have thus far not been successful, but ASOR maintains a cordial relationship with Syrian archaeologists and has also conducted limited excavations and surveys in Syria.

After World War II archaeological field method, including the techniques of retrieval and recording, improved considerably; by 1970 the method became far more sophisticated. The most obvious development is in the composition of the dig staff; today, both natural and social scientists are present in the field alongside the archaeologists. In the past the primary concern was with events such as warfare and conquest, which constitute political history. Today's objective is to recover every aspect of the ancient people's daily life, including their social organization, economic structure, population expansion, and trade patterns. Natural and social scientists, especially anthropologists, are rendering invaluable assistance to archaeologists as they pursue this holistic approach.

To guarantee that ASOR-sponsored projects meet the standards set by the new technology, the Committee on Archaeological Policy was instituted to oversee all field work. As first chairman of this committee, Edward F. Campbell, with the able assistance of Michael D. Coogan, played a substantial role in raising the standards of ASOR's digs. As Campbell's successor, William G. Dever has continued to insist upon professionalism in all aspects of ASOR's archaeological projects.

On the occasion of ASOR's 85th birthday in 1985, its members rejoiced in the accomplishments of the organization; at the same time they were vitally aware of how much remains to be done. The achievements are the result of innumerable scholars, many of them anonymous (as in this article), working together. Only cooperative effort of this kind will insure the success of ASOR in the years ahead.

Bibliography

King, P. J. 1983. *American Archaeology in the Mideast.* Philadelphia.

Wright, G. E. 1970. The Phenomenon of American Archaeology in the Near East. Pp. 3–40 in *Near Eastern Archaeology in the Twentieth Century,* ed. J. A. Sanders. Garden City, NY.

PHILIP J. KING

AMERICAN VERSIONS. See VERSIONS, ENGLISH (AMERICAN VERSIONS).

AMI (PERSON) [Heb *ʾāmî*]. A variant form of "Amon" in Ezra 2:57, it is therefore also the RSV rendering of the Gk *Allōn* in 1 Esdr 5:34. For both, see AMON (PERSON).

AMITTAI (PERSON) [Heb *ʾămittay*]. According to 2 Kgs 14:25 and Jonah 1:1, the father of the prophet Jonah. Noth (*IPN,* 162) suggested that the name is a shortened form of a nominal sentence using the Hebrew word for "truth" or "faithfulness" (*ʾemet*). Thus it means literally "my truth" or "my faithfulness," but that presumably stands for "God is my truth" or "God is my faithfulness."

RICHARD D. WEIS

AMMAH (PLACE) [Heb *ʾammâ*]. A hill E of Gibeon that lies "before Giah on the way of the wilderness of Gibeon" (2 Sam 2:24) that descends to the Jordan Valley. On the evening of the battle at Gibeon between the men of Israel and the servants of David, Joab (David's captain) and his brother Abishai came to this hill at sunset while pursuing Abner (Israel's captain). Abner and his men were fleeing toward the Jordan River and the city of Mahanaim. While the location of Ammah has not been conclusively identified, scholars have speculated about its location. This speculation is based on both linguistic analysis and practical geographic considerations. The Hebrew word *ʾammâ* may come from the Akk *ammatu,* cubit or foundation (Borée 1930: 35). In Rabbinic Hebrew, however, *ʾammâ* can mean a canal for water or a sewer (*m. Šabb.* 3:4; *Kil.* 3:2). Though the LXX transliterates the name of the hill as *Amman,* both Aquila and Theodotian translate the Hebrew word *ʾammâ* as *hydragōgos* (a water lead or channel). The Vulgate likewise provides *aqua ductus* as a translation. Since Giah (Heb *gîaḥ*) may indicate a spring (from the verb *gîaḥ*, to burst forth), one could conclude that the hill, Ammah, was a hill with a water channel related to the water source, Giah. The LXX, however, transliterates *gîaḥ* as the proper name *Gai,* a transliteration of the Hebrew word *gayʾ* (valley). Aquila and Theodotian translate it as *pharaggos* (chasm, ravine, or gully), and the Vulgate translates it as *vallis* (valley). This has led investigators to conclude that Giah is a valley and that Ammah stands at its side (*EncMiqr* 2: 419). Press (1951: 158) identified this valley as Sahel Geba, which is E of Gibeon and lies S of Wadi Suweinit, which separates Geba (modern Jebaʿ, M.R. 175140) from Michmash (modern Mukhmas, M.R. 176142). See also GEBA. Along the side of the valley there is a cave called Heb *maʿārat ʾl gāyâ.* According to Press, the earlier name of the valley continues in the name of this cave. It is true that Sahel Geba lies along a possible route that Abner may have taken to reach the Jordan Valley, but in order to accept it as an accurate identification one must assume that the common word for valley, *gayʾ*, was replaced, in the text, by the rare form *gîaḥ*. Scholars have, therefore, not agreed upon a place identification for Ammah. It is accepted that Ammah lies somewhere E of Gibeon on what the text calls "the way to the wilderness of Gibeon." Aharoni (*LBHG,* 60) identified "the way to the wilderness of Gibeon" as a branch of the "way of the wilderness" that ran more or less along the traditional boundaries between Benjamin and the House of Joseph (Josh 16:1–2; 18:12–13).

Bibliography

Borée, W. 1930. *Die alten Ortsnamen Pälestinas.* Leipzig.

Press, I. 1951. *A Topographical-Historical Encyclopaedia of Palestine.* Vol. 1. Jerusalem (in Hebrew).

SUSAN E. MCGARRY

AMMAN (M.R. 238151). The capital city of the modern Hashemite kingdom of Jordan, situated in the Transjordan tableland E of the Jordan Rift Valley. Archaeological explorations in the environs of the city have revealed evidence of its character in biblical times. In OT times the city was known as "Rabbah of the Ammonites," while through the Hellenistic-Roman period it was known by the name "Philadelphia." Modern Amman thus overlies the classical Philadelphia, which in turn overlies OT Rabbah of the Ammonites. Indeed, the springs that still provide water to Amman have made this place a site of habitation since Paleolithic times.

A. Description

During the last few decades, the city has grown out of all proportion, and an important part of downtown Amman has been built on the major ruins of the Roman city in an area less than 2 sq. km. Its well-preserved buildings and striking features of its Roman town plan show the various aspects of Roman art and engineering.

The old city consists of an upper and a lower section. See Fig. AMM.01. The former is built on a prominent hill and constitutes the acropolis (now the Citadel) of the city. This hill is a strategic natural L-shaped oblong plateau overlooking the forum area in the lower section to the S. It consists of two rectangles of unequal dimensions. Steep wadis surround the acropolis on all sides except on the N, where the acropolis was separated from the rest of the hill by an artificial depression. The acropolis area itself rises from E to W in three terraces. From very early times this hill had been a fortress of great importance. The lower city is associated with the wadi bed below and to the S of the acropolis; the *Seil Amman* divides this lower area into two long narrow strips of land. In Roman times, streets, public buildings, and a forum were built along this wadi bed.

B. The Ammonite Period

The Iron Age, or Ammonite period, is well represented throughout the city of Amman. These remains attest the Ammonite capital city of Rabbah, where David sent Uriah the Hittite, husband of Bathsheba, to die in battle (2 Sam 11:14–21). On the Citadel, building remains and artifacts were located on the upper and lower terraces. An early 9th-century Ammonite inscription in Aramaic was discovered outside the walls of the Citadel and is believed to have been a royal record of a magnificent building scheme which was undertaken at Rabbath Ammon (i.e., Amman). It is one of the most important stone inscriptions yet found in the area from a linguistic and paleographic view. Some scholars see in it a closer relationship between Ammonite and Hebrew than between Moabite and Hebrew prose in the 9th century B.C. (*BASOR* 193: 2f.; *BASOR* 198: 38f.). Another Ammonite inscription was found on a small bronze bottle discovered at Tell Siran near Amman. The inscription speaks of vineyards, gardens, and cisterns which belong to the time of two Amminadabs, kings of the Ammonites in the 7th century B.C. (*ADAJ* 18: 5; *BASOR* 212: 14; *Berytus* 22: 115f.; *BA* 37: 13f.).

Many Iron Age tombs discovered in the vicinity of Amman contained a good range of pottery objects, anthropoid coffins, figurines, various seals, jewelry, and mirrors

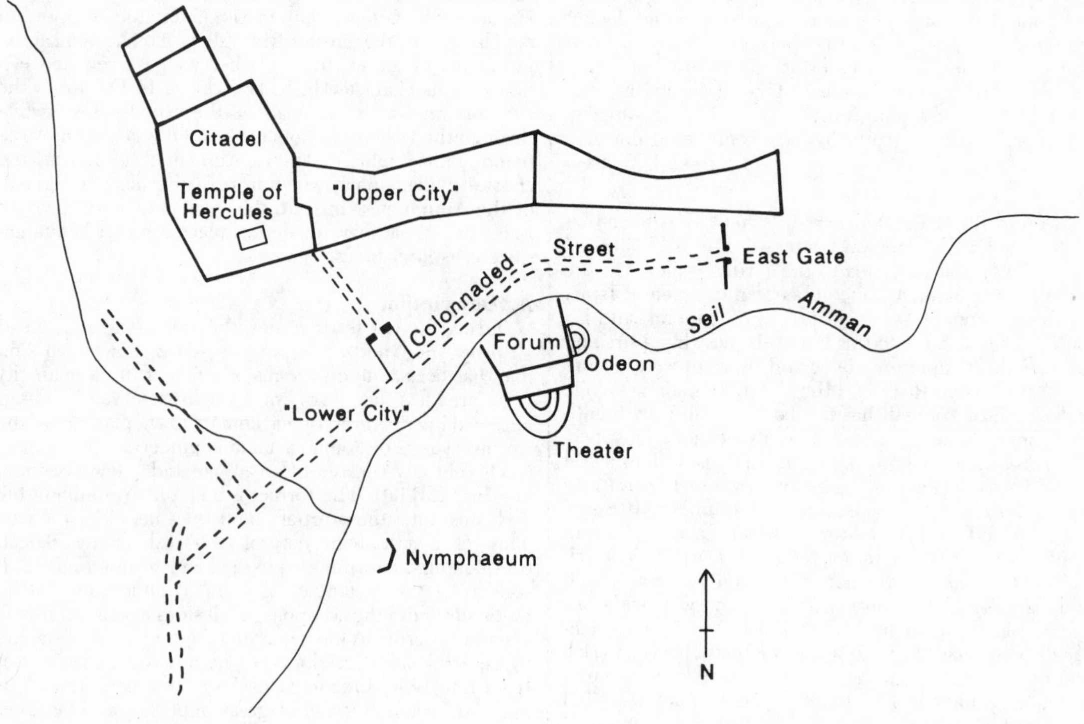

AMM.01. Town plan of Philadelphia (modern Amman)—Roman period.

(*QDAP* 11: 81; *ADAJ* 11: 41f.; *ADAJ* 20: 57f.; *ADAJ* 16: 91f.; *AUSS* 9: 179f.). Ammonite pottery, as all Iron Age pottery of E Jordan, shows a highly developed industry. Much of this pottery is covered with red or brown slip, highly polished, and often decorated with bands of dark brown paint and sometimes with bands of white paint between them (*AJA* 36: 295f.; *QDAP* 11: 67f.; *QDAP* 13: 92f.; *QDAP* 14: 44f.; *APEF* 48f.). In plastic art, the Ammonites show an advanced stage in this field. Historically important are a group of clay figurines which represent a horse-and-rider type and a small statue in limestone bearing the inscription in Aramaic, "Yarahᶜazar, chief of the horse," which indicate the existence of Ammonite cavalry apparently modeled on Assyrian cavalry (*QDAP* 11: 67f.; *ADAJ* 1: 34f.).

C. The Classical Period

In the Hellenistic period the city was renamed Philadelphia to honor Ptolemy II Philadelphos, the Hellenistic ruler of Egypt (285–247 B.C.). In 218 B.C. it was captured by Antiochus III the Great, the Hellenistic ruler of Syria. For about a century before the Roman conquest of the Near East, Amman belonged to the Nabataeans. When Pompey conquered Syria and Palestine (ca. 63 B.C.), Philadelphia became the southernmost member of the Decapolis. In 106 A.D., it became a city in the Roman province of Arabia. Situated on the magnificent Via Nova Traiana which joined Bosra with the Red Sea, Philadelphia enjoyed a long period of prosperity during the 2d century A.D.

1. The Acropolis. On the acropolis close to the S wall was built a temple dedicated to Hercules. See Fig. AMM.02. Only part of its podium and the column bases of the *pronaos* remain *in situ.* Apparently the temple was *prostyle tetrastyle* with one column on either side of the portico. The antae, which were made of half columns, terminate in rectangular pilasters set at the angles of the cella wall. The podium on which the temple was erected is a rectangle 8m × 19m. A fragmentary inscription discovered in the debris around the temple indicates that it was built during the reign of Marcus Aurelius (169–80 A.D.). Partial excavation near the temple shows that it was built on the site of a sacred rock which, as shown by pottery finds, has quite a long history, beginning in the EB Age (ca. 3000 B.C.).

Recognizing its strategic value for the region of Amman, the Romans rebuilt the ancient fortress on the acropolis and surrounded it with massive walls which rank among the finest of ancient fortifications. These walls consist of lower courses which incline inward in steps of heavy, well-jointed, rusticated stonework with drafted edges overlaid by a wall of smooth square stones of excellent quality.

2. The Lower City. Along the N bank of the *Seil Amman* ran the colonnaded street and on the E end was a monumental gateway. Another monumental gateway apparently

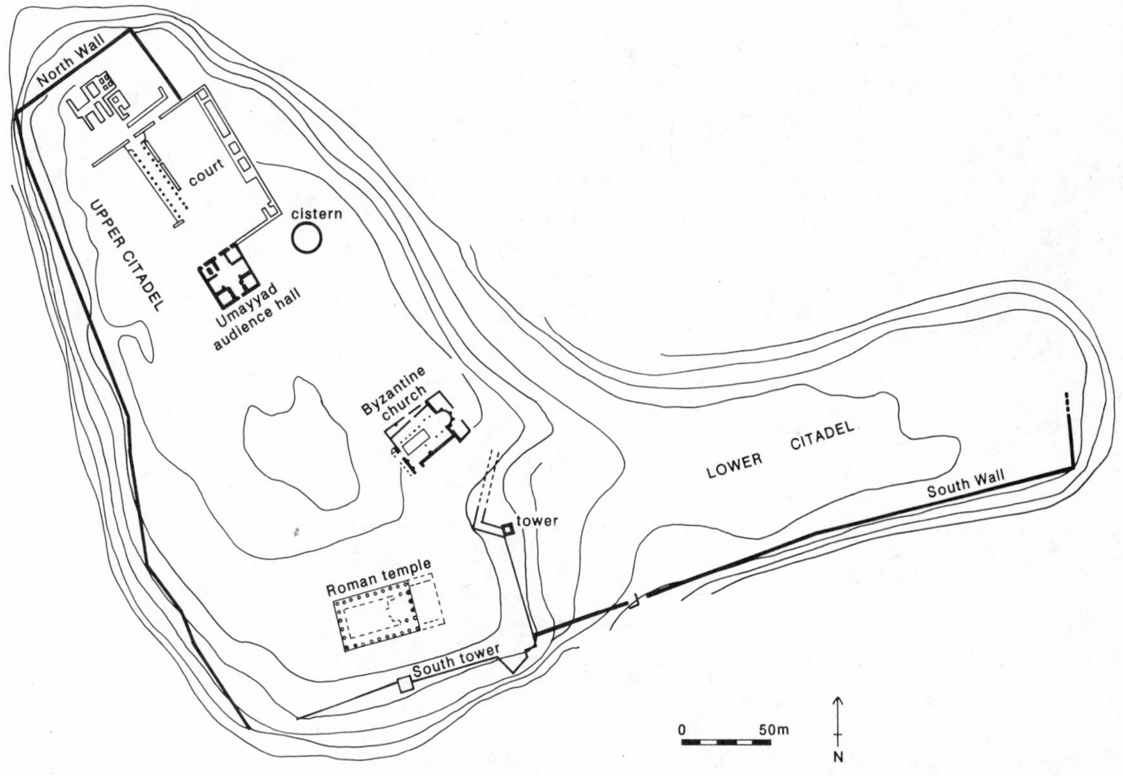

AMM.02. Area plan of acropolis at Philadelphia. *(Redrawn from* ADAJ *22: 21, fig. 1.)*

led up to the temple on the hill. South of the *Seil* were situated the forum, the theater, the odeon, and the nymphaeum. See Fig. AMM.01.

The forum is bordered by porticos on three sides and closed on the N by the bend in the *Seil* and the colonnaded street beyond. The forum and porticos constitute an irregular ensemble in the form of a trapezoid rather than a rectangle. Including the colonnades, the forum measures 100m on the S side, 48m on the W, and 50m on the E side. See Fig. AMM. 03. The total area of the forum is approximately 7620 sq. m. Thus, the forum at Amman ranks among the largest of Roman imperial fora.

The theater is located against a natural recess at the foot of a rocky hill to the S of the forum. The *cavea* was apparently at least partially hollowed from the hillside and the artificial portions were built upon masses of stonework and barrel vaults. The theater is semicircular in plan with three horizontal divisions of seats. The external diameter of the auditorium is 85m and its internal diameter is 40m. The height of the theater from the ground in front to the top of the back wall is about 25m. Numismatic evidence indicates that the theater was built in the middle of the 2d century A.D.

The odeon is semicircular in plan with a stage building that is connected with an outer wall by a barrel-vaulted passage with a corner tower at each end. The *cavea* is oriented to the W and is built up entirely from ground level of well-dressed blocks of limestone sometimes bossed and drafted especially in the interior sections. The external diameter of the *cavea* is 38m and its internal diameter is 22m. Stratigraphic as well as stylistic evidence indicates that the odeon was built in the first quarter of the 2d century A.D.

The nymphaeum, which lies farther SW, is very close to the point where a small branch of the *Seil Amman* flowing from N to S empties into the main stream. Unfortunately, it is presently impossible to determine the actual extent and complexity of the building, since today the area is jammed with modern structures which have sadly encroached upon the ancient remains. The dimensions and architectural elements of the existing S wall indicate that the building was truly monumental. This wall is built in the form of a half octagon with three large apsidal recessions, each flanked by small niches. The center apse measures 8.5m in width and each of the side apses is 5.5m wide. The width of each of the small niches is 1.25m. The

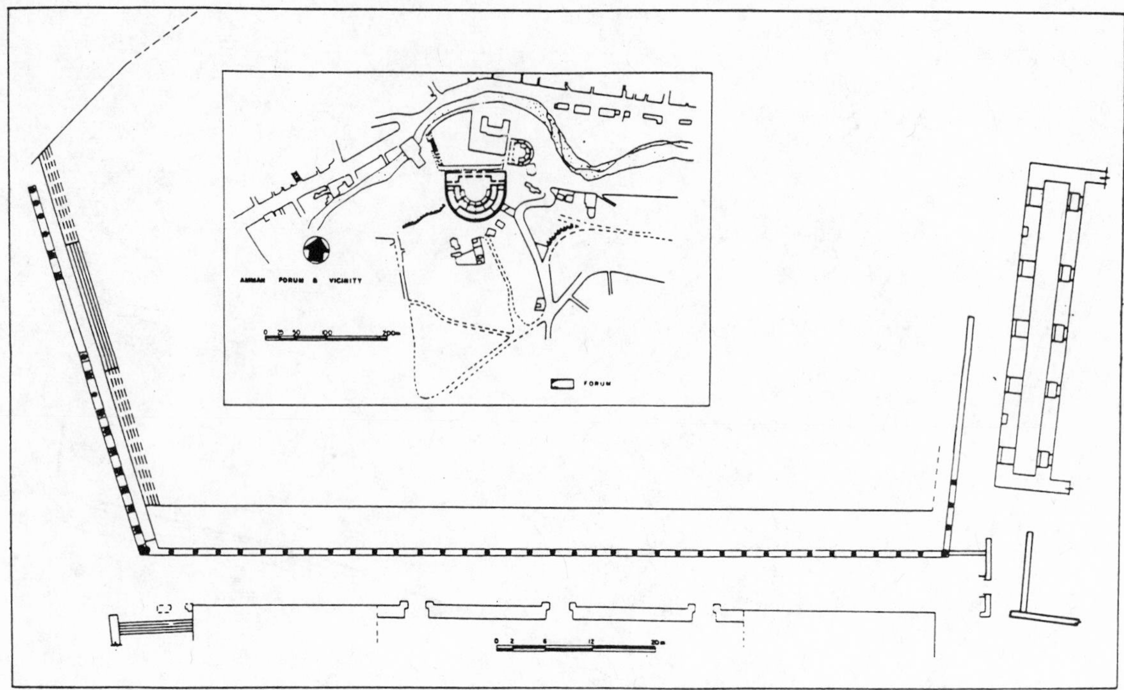

AMM.03. Area plan of Roman Forum, Theater, and Odeon at Philadelphia. *(Courtesy of A. Hadidi.)*

order of the colonnade which originally ran parallel to the four sides of the wall was Corinthian. The nymphaeum was built in the 2d century A.D.

Bibliography

Brunnow, R. E., and Domaszewski, A. V. 1905. *Provincia Arabia,* vol. 2. Strassburg.

Butler, H. C. 1921. *Syria, Div. II, Sec. A.* Leiden.

Conder, C. R. 1889. *The Survey of Eastern Palestine.* London.

Hadidi, A. 1974. The Excavation of the Roman Forum at Amman (Philadelphia) 1964–67. *ADAJ* 19: 71–91.

Harding, G. L. 1956. *The Antiquities of Jordan.* London.

ADNAN HADIDI

AMMIDIANS [Gk *Ammidioi*]. A family returning from exile in Babylon with Zerubbabel (1 Esdr 5:20). Although 1 Esdras is often assumed to have been compiled from Ezra and Nehemiah, this family does not appear among their lists of returning exiles. Omissions like this also raise questions about 1 Esdras being used as a source by Ezra or Nehemiah. Furthermore, problems associated with dating events and persons described in 1 Esdras have cast doubt on the historicity of the text. Heltzer (1977: 64–65) has argued that the name of this family's progenitor was Heb *ʿmdyh.* (See also Myers *1–2 Esdras* AB.)

Bibliography

Heltzer, M. 1977. Ein epigraphischer Blick auf das 3. Esrabuch. *Bib* 58: 62–72.

MICHAEL DAVID MCGEHEE

AMMIEL (PERSON) [Heb *ʿammîʾēl*]. Var. ELIAM. The name Ammiel is a compound of the Hebrew words *ʿam* ("people, relatives") and *ʾel* ("God"), thus signifying "My kinsman (relative?) is God." The name was given to four different OT individuals.

1. A son of GEMALLI, Ammiel represented the tribe of Dan among the twelve men Moses sent to spy out the land of Canaan (Num 13:12). Though not the head of the tribe of Dan (cf. 7:66), he was one of its leading members (13:2, 3) and was no doubt selected because of his suitability for the mission to be carried out.

2. The father of MACHIR, who hid MEPHIBOSHETH, the son of Jonathan, from David in his house at Lodebar (2 Sam 9:4, 5), located east of the Jordan River somewhere near Mahanaim. The people in this exposed region, in constant peril of raids from the E and the N, appear to have been supportive of strong central governments which could provide protection and, therefore, were opposed to insurrections such as those of David and later Absalom. Thus Ammiel and his family were strong supporters of Saul and his son Ishbosheth, who set up his throne at Mahanaim. Machir became loyal to David after

Ishbosheth's death, possibly because of his kindness toward Mephibosheth, and is listed as one of the three individuals who brought provisions to David in exile at Mahanaim during Absalom's rebellion (17:27). The fact that Ammiel is mentioned in 2 Samuel 17 is a clue that Machir's considerable wealth may have been inherited. Mauchline (*Samuel* NCBC, 243), infers that the family belonged to the tribe of Manasseh.

3. The father of BATHSHUA (a phonetic variation of BATHSHEBA), one of David's wives, and thus the grandfather of Solomon (1 Chr 3:5). In a parallel text, 2 Sam 11:3, the two parts of his name are transposed into Eliam, which means "My God is a kinsman." McCarter (*2 Samuel* AB, 285) proposes that the mention of a married woman's father implies that Ammiel/Eliam (see ELIAM) was an important man. It is an unlikely possibility that the father of Bathshua and the father of Machir were the same person, which could explain Machir's change of heart toward David. If that is true, and Hertzberg (*Samuel* OTL, 309–10) is also correct that Ammiel/Eliam was the son of Ahithophel mentioned in 2 Sam 23:34, it would help explain some of the intrigues in David's court. For further discussion, see Smith *Samuel* ICC.

4. The sixth son of OBED-EDOM, a Levite, one of the doorkeepers who took care of the S gate of the temple complex and who also were in charge of the storehouse (1 Chr 26:5, 15). This appointment was made toward the end of David's lifetime (1 Chr 23:1).

JON PAULIEN

AMMIHUD (PERSON) [Heb *ʿammîhûd*; *ʿammîḥûr*]. Five individuals mentioned in the Hebrew Bible bear this name. Ammihud is a theophoric name, comprised of the kinship term *ʿam* (kinsman) representing the divine, and the root *hwd,* "glory, exaltation," and may be translated as "The divine is exalted" (*EncMiqr* 6: 287). An alternate translation is "My kinsman is splendor" (*IDB* 1: 107). The name is similar in form and meaning to the names Abihud and Ahihud. Note that, in the Targum to 2 Sam 13:37, Ammihud appears instead of the MT Ammihur, and the LXX of Num 34:28 translates the entire gentilic *benamioud* (Heb *ben-ʿammîhûd*).

1. The father of Elishama, who was one of the leaders (Heb *nĕśîʾîm*) of the tribe of Ephraim during the journey through the Sinai wilderness (Num 1:10; 2:18; 7:48, 53; 10:22). According to 1 Chr 7:26, Ammihud was the great-grandfather of Joshua.

2. The father of Samuel, who was one of the leaders of the tribe of Simeon at the time of the allotment of the land of Canaan to the Israelites (Num 34:20).

3. The father of Pedahel, who was one of the leaders of the tribe of Naphtali at the time of the distribution of the land of Canaan to the Israelites (Num 34:28).

4. In 2 Sam 13:37, the MT is written *ʿammîḥûr,* but read *ʿammîhûd.* This person was the father of Talmai, the king of Gesher, uncle of Absalom. The latter had fled to Talmai after murdering Amnon, the half-brother of Absalom, and resided with him for three years.

5. The son of Omri, from the clan of Perez, who was the son of Judah and the father of Uthai. This Uthai was the head of the clan listed among the first postexilic settlers of Jerusalem (1 Chr 9:4).

RAPHAEL I. PANITZ

AMMINADAB (PERSON) [Heb *ʿammînādāb*]. The name of four individuals in the Hebrew Bible.

1. A Judean, a descendant of Perez and ancestor of David through Boaz (1 Chr 2:10; Ruth 4:19–20). He was the father of Nahshon, a prominent figure in the tribe of Judah (Num 1:7; 2:3; 7:12, 17; 10:14), and Elisheba, the wife of Aaron (Exod 6:23). He is also mentioned in the genealogy of Jesus (Matt 1:4; Luke 3:33; Gk *Aminadab*).

2. A son of Kohath and father of Korah (1 Chr 6:7—Eng 6:22). Amminadab is not found in other lists of the sons of Kohath; in these other texts Izhar is found instead of Amminadab, and Korah is the son of Izhar (Exod 6:18, 21; cf. 1 Chr 5:28, 6:3—Eng 6:2, 18; Num 3:19). LXX^{A,L} have Izhar in 1 Chr 6:7—Eng 6:22, though this reading more probably developed as a correction. Williamson (*1 and 2 Chronicles* NCBC, 71) and Rudolph (*Chronikbücher* HAT, 54) both provide detailed and somewhat ingenious explanations of how this difficulty may have arisen. Within the context of 1 Chr 6:7–18—Eng 6:22–33 the Chronicler appears to be concerned with the lineage of Samuel the prophet (1 Chr 6:13, 18—Eng 6:28, 33), to whom he assigns Levitical ancestry (1 Sam 1:1). This reflects the Chronicler's pervasive interest in the prophetic function of the Levitical musicians (1 Chr 25:1–8; 2 Chr 20:14; 29:25; 34:30; 35:15).

3. A descendant of Kohath, leader of a family in the clan of Uzziel, who takes part in the transfer of the ark from the House of Obed-edom to Jerusalem (1 Chr 15:10–11).

4. The father of Esther according to the LXX of Esth 2:15; 9:29. MT identifies her father as Abihail.

RAYMOND B. DILLARD

AMMISHADDAI (PERSON) [Heb *ʿammîšaddāy*]. The father of Ahiezer, who was a captain of Dan during the wilderness journey (Num 1:12; 2:25; 7:66, 71; 10:25). The name occurs only as a patronym of Ahiezer. Rather than the late, artificial "people of the Almighty," his name means "my kinsman is Shaddai," the theophoric element (Heb *šaddāy*) being common in the ancient Near East (see Fowler 1988: 53–54, 251).

Bibliography

Fowler, J. D. 1988. *Thophoric Personal Names in Ancient Hebrew.* JSOT Sup 49. Sheffield.

JOEL C. SLAYTON

AMMIZABAD (PERSON) [Heb *ʿammîzābād*]. The son of Benaiah son of Jehoiada, commander of David's corps of champions.

The name itself is constructed from the theophoric element *ʿammî,* literally "the father's brother," or "uncle," and the verb, *zābād,* "to give (as a gift)." Here *ʿammî* is a familial particle used to refer to the family, clan, or tribal deity (cf. *IPN* 15, n.2; 47, 66–79, esp. 77).

Ammizabad is recorded in the Chronicles as having commanded Benaiah's division of the monthly levies of 24,000 troops (1 Chr 27:6), possibly while Benaiah was commander of David's champions, although this list is of dubious historical value (see DAVID'S CHAMPIONS; see also BENAIAH). The Heb has "his [Benaiah's] division was Ammizabad his son."

D. G. SCHLEY

AMMON (PERSON) [Heb *ᶜammôn*]. AMMONITE. The son of Abraham's nephew Lot, who was the product of an incestuous union between Lot and one of his daughters (Gen 19:36–38). As such, Ammon serves as the eponymous ancestor of the Ammonites, a Transjordanian people whose kingdom the Israelites encountered in their exodus march to the Promised Land (Num 21: 24–35; Deut 2:16–37). Later David waged war against the Ammonites (2 Samuel 11–12).

The history of Ammon is known from written sources only from the 8th century B.C., when it is mentioned in the Neo-Assyrian annals. The historical value of the biblical references to the Ammonite kingdom is hard to evaluate because of the partly legendary character of the sources relating to the Exodus and the relatively late date of the final redaction of the unit. Most recent research tends, in fact, to lower the date of the biblical redaction to almost the same period as the Neo-Assyrian annals. Therefore, nothing is scientifically certain about Ammon and the Ammonites before the 8th century. The Ammonites are not mentioned in Egyptian historical writings.

Happily, archaeology provides abundant proof of the existence of the Ammonites before the 8th century. The site of the capital, Rabbath-Ammon, was occupied from the EB Age, and became a powerful city-state in the MB II period (18th century B.C.). It is known that a decrease in population marks the LB Age (16th–13th centuries). Some traces testify to a new occupation in the Early Iron Age (but it is unlikely that Iron Age Rabbath-Ammon had a rampart before the 10th century). The region around Rabbath-Ammon also shows signs of occupation in the Early Iron Age; the transition from LB to Early Iron Age passed peacefully there. Archaeology can no longer cite as evidence the monuments popularly called the "Ammonite towers" in dating the occupation. These watchtowers of the region were used in successive periods from the 8th century B.C. and their foundation is spread over different periods.

A. The Biblical Traditions

The historical origin of the Ammonites is not specified in the OT; they were already present in Transjordan when the Hebrews arrived. A popular tradition derives the name from the incest of Lot (Gen 19:36–38); the Ammonites would thus be "Arameans" in the OT sense. It is possible that in another biblical tradition the Ammonites are considered "Amorites," as are their immediate neighbors, the Moabites (seen as a brother in Gen 19:36). But the OT designation "Amorites" does not have the precision frequently given it by modern historians. Nothing proves that the Ammonites were the fruit of an invasion, Aramean or Amorite, or that they must have settled down (Pitard 1987: 87). The archaeology of the capital city shows a continuous, if irregular, occupation. We still do not know precisely who the Bronze Age Ammonites were. Most probably, they were simply the native people of the country.

1. The Accounts of the Conquest. There is no biblical reference to the conquest of an Ammonite kingdom. Moses and his forces go around the region of Amman. According to the schema of Num 21:24–35, the Hebrews subdue the Amorite kingdom of Heshbon, then the town of Jazer, and finally, after a detour, that of Edrei in Bashan. In Deut 2:19 and 37, there is recounted an explicit order of God not to attack Ammon. The territories around Ammon are therefore divided between the tribes of Reuben, Gad, and the half-tribe of Manasseh. Gad is the closest to Ammon, with Jazer as its nearest neighboring city. This territory is the nucleus of Gilead, a geographic name which will have greater territorial expansion over the ages. It will extend N as far as the Yarmuk, country of Machir-Manasseh (cf. Num 32:39). However, it should be noted that Num 32:34–38 implies that Gad had a territory so vast as to encompass Reuben and approach Moab. These Hebrew neighbors of Ammon fought with one another and with Moab. They weakened with time (as Gad absorbed Reuben, and then it was absorbed by the Arameans of Damascus).

From the biblical schema of the conquest it is difficult to ascertain what historical factors can account for the fact that the "Amorite" kingdom of Sihon was fought and conquered (Num 21:21–31) while the kingdom of Ammon was not. Furthermore, there is no formal mention of the "kingdom" of Ammon in the accounts of the conquest. It is possible that, at the period in which these accounts are set, Ammon was only a mediocre political entity. But Ammon had been urbanized centuries before the time proposed for the arrival of the Hebrews. It certainly had a local "kingdom." More probably, the silence concerning Ammon reflects the period when these accounts were written, and a later political situation of the Aramean period, when no one could possibly imagine the Hebrews conquering such a powerful kingdom.

2. The Period of the Judges. Ammon is mentioned in connection with Israel's conflicts in the period of the Judges. The first incident is minor, connected with the struggle between the Benjaminites and Moab. In Judg 3:13, it is mentioned that the Moabite king, Eglon, was allied with the Ammonites; but these latter play no part in the rest of the account. Judg 11:4, 12–33 refers to Gileadite resistance (led by Jephthah) against the Ammonites. Here for the first time there is reference to an unnamed "king" of the Ammonites. But the account of Jephthah vv 15–26 is untrustworthy: Ammon and Moab are confused, and the Moabite god, Chemosh, is attributed to the Ammonites.

3. The Period of Saul and David. The Ammonite king, Nahash, besieged Jabesh of Gilead, which was rescued by Saul in 1 Sam 11:1–11. Nahash was succeeded by his son Hanun, a contemporary of David. The conquest of the Ammonite capital, Rabbath-Ammon, by David (2 Samuel 10–12) marks the true entry of the Ammonites into history. At the time of the revolt of Absalom, "Shobi, son of

Nahash, from Rabbah of the Ammonites" came to bring material aid to David, although he did not offer military assistance (2 Sam 17:27). This Shobi, if he really was the son of the king Nahash, would then be the brother of Hanun. He may have been enthroned by David in place of Hanun after the conquest of Rabbath-Ammon.

The OT has nothing more to say about the Ammonites during the time of David. Probably their history was independent of that of the Hebrews after the death of Solomon. The only significant point of contact is the mention of family links between Hebrews and Ammonites. Solomon had Ammonites among his foreign wives (1 Kgs 11:1). Naamah, mother of King Rehoboam, was an Ammonite.

4. The Preexilic Period. In the 9th century, during the reign of Jehoshaphat, Ammon, Moab, and Edom united in order to attack Judah; they were unsuccessful, probably because of dissension among the allies (2 Chr 20:1, 10, 22–23). A similar coalition took place during the reign of Jehoiakim, at the end of the 7th and beginning of the 6th centuries (2 Kgs 24:2). Before this, however, Uzziah of Judah and his son Jotham received tribute from Ammon in the 8th century (2 Chr 26:8; 27:5). Just before the fall of Jerusalem, there was an attempt to form an alliance between Judah and her neighbors, including the Ammonites (Jer 27:3). But this alliance was preceded by an attack by the "Chaldeans, Arameans, Moabites, and Ammonites" against Judah about 601 B.C. (2 Kgs 24:2). Ezek 21:25, 33 suggests that Nebuchadnezzar attacked Ammon.

5. Exilic and Postexilic Periods. After the destruction of Jerusalem, the assassin of Gedaliah took refuge with the Ammonites (Jer 41:10, 15). In the time of Nehemiah the Ammonites opposed the rebuilding of Jerusalem (Neh 4:1–2). The Ammonites are cited as adversaries one last time in the Maccabean wars (1 Macc 5:6–7).

6. The Prophetic Literature. Special mention must be made of the references to Ammon in the prophetic oracles. These are often outside the context of precise biblical chronology and belong to a stereotyped literary genre, where Ammon is found as the traditional enemy of Israel, generally associated with Moab and Edom. This is the case in Amos 1:13–15; Isa 11:14; Jer 9:25; 25:21; 49:1–6; Ezek 25:1–5; Dan 11:41; and Zeph 2:8–9. Other texts, which are not oracles, make the same association, e.g., Jer 27:3.

Apart from this prophetic literature, allusions to Ammon are found in Ps 83:7–9; Ezra 9:1; Neh 13:23; Jdt 5:2; 7:17–18. These are clearly late, and the precise historical context is difficult to determine.

B. The Extrabiblical Evidence

The evidence of biblical historiography must be compared with the extrabiblical historical evidence. The earliest document is Neo-Assyrian and dates from the time of Tiglath-pileser III. The author states that toward 733 B.C. the king Shanib (or Shanip) of Bit-Ammon paid tribute (*ANET,* 282a). The campaign of Tiglath-pileser probably had serious consequences, destabilizing the whole region (Oded 1970: 177) and leaving a relative vacuum which enabled incursions by desert nomads.

A letter from Nimrud mentions the tribute of the "sons of Ammon" under an Assyrian king who reigned between Tiglath-Pileser and Sargon II (Saggs 1955: 135, text XVI, line 35). The king Shanib was the grandfather of a certain Yarih-Ezer (who was probably not king), who is quoted in the inscription of a statue discovered at Amman in 1949. In 701 B.C. Sennacherib mentions a king of Ammon, Pudu-Ilu, or Buduili (*ANET,* 287b) who was still reigning at the time of Esarhaddon, about 677 (Borger 1956: 60, line 62). Assurbanipal mentions Pudu-Ilu's successor Amminadab, who about 667 paid tribute to the Assyrians (*ANET,* 294a). The names of these three kings are confirmed by local epigraphic documents, in particular the seals of their ministers (Bordreuil 1986: 134, 137). Among these documents may be noted the Tell Siran bottle (Zayadine and Thompson 1973: 135), which ennumerates "Amminadab, king of the Ammonites, son of Hiṣṣal-El, king of the Ammonites, son of Amminadab, king of the Ammonites." Thus we discover that Amminadab I was succeeded by Hiṣṣal-El, who in turn was succeeded by Amminadab II, taking us down to about 600–590 B.C. Toward 587, the king Baalis (Jer 40:14) is attested by a seal of Tell Umeiri, which names him "Baal-Yasha" (Herr 1985: 170). This is the last Ammonite king whose name has been preserved. Josephus (*Ant* 10.181–82) states that Nebuchadnezzar defeated the Ammonites and the Moabites in 582–581 B.C. This marked the end of the Ammonites as a political force.

The Ammonite Kings

King	Reference
Nahash (ca. 1030–1000)	1 Sam 11:1–12; 12:12; 2 Sam 10:2
Hanun son of Nahash	2 Sam 10:1–4; 1 Chr 19:2–6
Shobi son of Nahash	2 Sam 17:27
Shanib (ca. 733)	*ANET*, 282 (Tiglath-pileser III)
Zakur son of Shanib	Ammonite Statue J.1656
Yarih-Ezer (?)	Ammonite Statue J.1656
Pudu-Ilu/Buduili (ca. 701–677)	Borger 1956: 60 (Sennacherib and Esarhaddon)
ʿAmminadab I (ca. 667)	*ANET,* 294 (Assurbanipal)
Hiṣṣal-El, son of Amminiadab	Tell Siran bottle
ʿAmminadab II, son of Hiṣṣal-El	Tell Siran bottle
Baʿalis/Baal-Yasha (ca. 587)	Jer 40:14; bulla of Tell ʿUmeiri

Under the Persian Empire, Ammon was a district of the fifth satrapy, "Beyond-the-River," under the authority of a *peḥa* or Governor. In Neh 2:9–10, Tobiah, "the Ammonite servant" (*ʿbd*), appears at the side of Sanballat the Horonite of Samaria and Geshem the Arab (Neh 2:19) to oppose the rebuilding of the walls and temple of Jerusalem. He was therefore a functionary of the king, as suggested by Neh 2:19.

In the Hellenistic period, the capital of the Ammonites kept the name of Rabbatamana, as attested by Polybius *Histories* V.71, who mentions it in connection with the siege of Antiochus III in 218 B.C. The Seleucid king conquered the city by gaining control of the water-supply system of the acropolis (the cistern and access tunnel to the N). Under Ptolemy Philadelphus II, about 250 B.C., the name of the city was changed to Philadelphia, in honor of the king's sister-wife Arsinoe Philadelphia. Nevertheless the Zenon papyrus, PSI 616, mentions Rabbatamana, and the papyrus PCZ 59009, which dates from April to May 259 B.C., is signed at Birtha of Ammanitis. In fact, in this document the cleruchies of Tobias appear.

In the Hasmonean period, the Bible suggests that Judas Maccabeus subdued the region W of Amman (i.e., the city of Jazer and its dependent towns) in 163 B.C., after defeating a certain Timothy, chief of the Ammonites (1 Macc. 5:6–7). This W section was called Peraea. There is very little information concerning its late history up to the Roman conquest.

Bibliography

Abou Assaf, A. 1980. Untersuchungen zur ammonitischen Rundbildkunst. *UF* 12: 7–102.

Albright, W. F. 1953. Notes on Ammonite History. Pp. 131–36 in *Miscellanea Biblica B. Ubach.* Scripta et Documenta I. Montserrat.

Avigad, N. 1970. Ammonite and Moabite Seals. Pp. 284–95 in *Near Eastern Archaeology in the Twentieth Century,* ed. J. A. Sanders. New York.

Bartlett, J. R. 1978. Ammon und Israel. *TRE* 2: 455–63.

Block, D. I. 1984. *Bny ʿmwn:* The Sons of Ammon. *AUSS* 22: 197–212.

Boling, R. G. 1988. *The Early Biblical Community in Transjordan.* SWBA 6. Sheffield.

Bordreuil, P. 1986. Sceaux transjordaniens inscrits. Pp. 128–41 in *La Voie Royale. 9 000 ans d'art au royaume de Jordanie.* Paris.

Borger, R. 1956. *Die Inschriften Asarhaddons Konigs von Assyrien. AfO* 9. Graz.

Dornemann, R. H. 1983. *The Archaeology of the Transjordan in the Bronze and Iron Ages.* Milwaukee, WI.

Herr, L. G. 1985. The Servant of Baalis. *BA* 48: 169–72.

Landes, G. M. 1961. The Material Civilization of the Ammonites. *BA* 24: 65–88.

Lemaire, A. 1987. Ammon, Moab, Edom: l'époque du Fer en Jordanie. Pp. 47–74 (53–59) in *Rencontres de l'École du Louvre. La Jordanie de l'âge de la pierre à l'époque byzantine.* Paris.

Oded, B. 1970. Observations on Methods of Assyrian Rule in Transjordania. *JNES* 29: 177–86.

Pitard, W. T. 1987. *Ancient Damascus.* Winona Lake, IN.

Puech É. 1985. L'inscription de la statue d'Amman et la paléographie ammonite. *RB* 92: 5–24.

Saggs, H. F. W. 1955. The Nimrud Letters, 1952, II. *Iraq* 17: 126–54.

Sauer, J. A. 1985. Ammon, Moab and Edom. Pp. 206–14 in *Biblical Archaeology Today.* Jerusalem.

———. 1986. Transjordan in the Bronze and Iron Ages: a Critique of Glueck's Synthesis. *BASOR* 263: 1–26.

Younker, R. W. 1985. Israel, Judah and Ammon and the Motifs on the Baalis Seal from Tell el ʿUmeiri. *BA* 48: 173–80.

Zadok, R. 1977. Historical and Onomastic Notes, *WO* 9: 35–56.

Zayadine, F. 1973. Recent Excavations on the Citadel of Amman. *ADAJ* 18: 17–35.

———. 1974. Note sur l'inscription de la statue d'Amman, J.1656 *Syria* 51: 129–36.

———. 1987. Recent Excavations on the Citadel of Amman. *ADAJ* 31: 299–311.

Zayadine, F., and Thompson, H. O. 1973. The Ammonite Inscription from Tell Siran. *Berytus* 22: 115–40.

JEAN-MICHEL DE TARRAGON
Trans. Gerard J. Norton

AMMON (PLACE) [Heb *ʿammôn*]. See RABBAH (AMMON).

AMMONITE LANGUAGE. See LANGUAGES (INTRODUCTORY SURVEY).

AMNON (PERSON) [Heb *ʾamnōn*]. **1.** Firstborn son of David. His mother was Ahinoam of Jezreel (2 Sam 3:2; 2 Chr 3:1), whom David had taken as a wife at the same time as Abigail (1 Sam 25:42–43). He was one of six sons born to David at Hebron by six different wives.

Amnon otherwise is known only for an episode recounted in 2 Samuel 13, where he raped his half-sister Tamar. He is lovesick over his beautiful sister and is encouraged by a cousin, Jonadab, to gain access to her via a trick (2 Sam 13:1–5). When he does so, he first attempts to persuade her to lie with him, but she refuses to do so without their father's sanction (vv 6–13). He then forcibly rapes her and disgustedly casts her away (vv 14–19). Their brother Absalom hears of this and plots revenge, which is not accomplished for two years, when Amnon is killed, ironically, by a ruse on Absalom's part (vv 20–29).

The story is a masterpiece of drama, suspense, and irony. It is the first of several stories of David's troubles with his children following his own sin in 2 Sam 11–12, and it echoes that story (Fokkelmann 1981: 124–25; Gunn 1978: 98–100). Both David and Amnon, for example, see and desire a beautiful woman and conspire to get her. David attempts to cover his sin by a murder; Amnon ironically, David's son, is himself murdered.

Within the Amnon story the literary and dramatic climax is reached with the actual rape, in v 14 (Ridout 1974: 80–84; Fokkelmann 1981: 99–114). The climax is approached with a drawn-out, suspense-building account of the scene and the dialogue in Amnon's bedroom (vv 8–13). The shift from love (or lust) to hate and disgust after the rape is sudden, forceful, and dramatic (vv 15–17; cf. 22). Amnon's death is related in a matter-of-fact way (v 29), highlighting the emerging status of Absalom.

2. A son of Shimon, in the genealogy of descendants of Judah (2 Chr 4:20). Nothing further is known of father or son.

Bibliography

Conroy, C. 1978. *Absalom Absalom!* AnBib 81. Rome.

Fokkelmann, J. P. 1981. *King David (II Sam. 9–20 & I Kings 1–2).* Vol. 1 of *Narrative Art and Poetry in the Books of Samuel.* Assen, The Netherlands.

Gunn, D. M. 1978. *The Story of King David. JSOTSup* 6. Sheffield.

Long, B. O. 1981. Wounded Beginnings: David and Two Sons. Pp. 26–34 in *Images of Man and God,* ed. B. O. Long. Sheffield.

Ridout, G. 1974. The Rape of Tamar. Pp. 75–84 in *Rhetorical Criticism,* ed. J. J. Jackson and M. Kessler. Pittsburgh.

DAVID M. HOWARD, JR.

AMOK (PERSON) [Heb *ʿāmôq*]. A priest mentioned in the list of Israelites who returned from exile to Jerusalem in the days of Zerubbabel (Neh 12:7). His name, along with some 14 others, is lacking in the major LXX manuscripts, but this probably represents a secondary scribal omission. Later in the same chapter (v 20), Amok is again part of a list in the MT, this time cited as the father of Eber, the head of a priestly family. Once again, many manuscripts of the LXX omit his name (as well as many of the other names of priestly households). As Myers (*Ezra-Nehemiah* AB, lxvi) has pointed out, such omissions in the Greek characterize quite a number of the lists of Nehemiah (especially in Codex Vaticanus); the majority of these omissions cannot simply be explained as mechanical errors such as homoioteleuton or homoioarkton.

Although the Heb *ʿāmôq* appears only twice in the MT as a proper name (both instances having already been noted), the essentially identical term *ʿāmōq* appears some 17 times as an adjective meaning "deep" or "unfathomable." R. A. Bowman (*IB* 3: 785) is probably correct in translating the priestly name Amok as metaphorical, "inscrutable" or "wise" (cf. also the Akkadian parallels which he cites). Very possibly the full priestly name was Amokiah ("Yah[weh] is wise/inscrutable") or Amokel ("El [God] is wise/inscrutable"), or the like.

Recently, Williamson (*Ezra, Nehemiah* WBC, 355–66) has argued persuasively for the relative primacy of the list of priestly families found in Neh 12:12–21, arguing that from this list a later editor has transcribed vv 1–7. As Williamson points out, it is less likely that someone invented the names of the added generation in vv 12–21, names which are not paralleled elsewhere, than that the names of the family heads were merely transferred from this list to the list found in vv 1–7. He further notes that the names found in vv 19–21 (as well as the analogous vv 6a–7a), namely Joiarib, Jedaiah, Sallai (Sallu), Amok, Hilkiah, and Jedaiah, probably represent a later expansion of the original list, attributable to the same or a later editor. Both the inclusion of the conjunction "and" in the MT before both lists (and used nowhere else in either list), as well as the observation that precisely these same six names are lacking from the list of priests in Neh 10:3–9 (—Eng 10:2–8), lend strong support to his proposed reconstruction. Thus, the original list underlying both lists of priests in Nehemiah 12 (as well as the one in Nehemiah 10) appears to have been considerably shorter; and more to the point, it probably did not include the name Amok at all (see also the comments of Bowman [*IB* 3: 784], and the references cited there). Presumably such an addition was made to align the lists with the actual priestly hierarchy in later times.

WILLIAM H. BARNES

AMON (DEITY) [Heb *ʾāmôn*]. An Egyptian deity who was recognized as the "king of the gods" by the time of the New Kingdom. He was connected with the city of Thebes, an association remembered by some of the later biblical writers. In Egyptian his name means "hidden" or "invisible one" (Eg *Imn*). His name is found twice in the OT: in Nah 3:8, where the Egyptian city of Thebes is called *nō ʾāmôn,* and in Jer 46:25, where Jeremiah declares that Yahweh will punish Amon of Thebes (Heb *ʾāmôn minnôʾ*) through Nebuchadrezzar, king of Babylon.

In Egypt, Amon is often associated with the wind and air and even the "breath of life." He is usually portrayed in human shape with a crown of two tall upright plumes, although some representations also incorporate elements of his sacred animal, the ram, and his sacred bird, the goose. Herodotus tells an amusing story which was meant to explain Amon's association with the ram as well as why Egyptians refused to sacrifice the ram except once a year (Hdt 2.42; Armour 1986: 140). Amon, together with the vulture goddess Mut and the god Khons, formed the Theban triad of father, mother, and son. Amon is also identified with Min, the fertility god of Coptos and Akhmim. In these instances he bears the name Amon-Min and, like Min, he is represented in ithyphallic form.

Amon is first mentioned in the Unas Pyramid Texts (§446) as a primeval deity belonging to the Ogdoad of Hermopolis ("the City of the Eight Primeval Gods") where he is accompanied by his female counterpart, Amaunet. He was worshiped at Thebes in the 11th Dynasty, but it was with the emergence of the powerful 12th Dynasty that he became prominent (cf. the personal name of the founder of the 12th Dynasty, Amenemhat, "Amon is Supreme").

Amon became state god of Egypt with the emergence of the 18th Dynasty and the foundation of the New Kingdom. Prior to this, the Hyksos (Dynasties 15 and 16) had established Avaris in the Delta as their capital and had elevated the importance of the god Seth. After Ahmose, founder of the 18th Dynasty, expelled the Hyksos he once again chose Thebes to be the capital city. As the empire expanded in the New Kingdom under such mighty pharaohs as Thuītmose III, so did the power of Amon, who was seen as being responsible for all of the military successes. Amon was especially credited with victories over foreigners, including the driving out of the Hyksos and the subsequent military excursions into Asia Minor. Having thus subjugated all of the foreign deities, he became "king of the gods." At the same time, the priesthood of Amon greatly increased their power and wealth, the wide influence of Amon's priesthood being reflected in the numerous and elaborate temples and shrines devoted to Amon which spread throughout Egypt, especially on the banks of the Nile.

As Amon rose to preeminence among the gods, he also took on characteristics of Re, the sun god. Amon, "the king of the gods," and Re, the creative power in the sun, were seen as one and the same and henceforth referred to as the supreme god, Amon-Re. Amon had gone from a local deity to a national war god and then to an omnipotent deity who absorbed the elaborate creation mythology surrounding Re. A new cosmogony was developed centering around the creative power of Amon and the city of Thebes as the place where creation had originated. Frankfort (*KG,* 160) has stressed that the fusion of Amon with Re was not a "trick of priestly syncretism intended to add glamour to the god of the capital of Thebes. In reality," Frankfort suggests, "it was a truly creative thought which realized the potentialities of a combination of the concept of the creator-sun with that of Amon, the 'breath of life,' 'the hidden one,' who, as one of the Eight of Hermopolis, was part of the uncreated chaos." Be that as it may, the priests of Amon were nevertheless the direct beneficiaries of their god's new elevated status.

The supremacy of Amon was interrupted for a brief period of time. Amenophis IV, better known as the heretic pharaoh Akhenaten (ca. 1377–1360 B.C.E.), broke with the cult of Amon and favored a solar monotheism which worshiped Aten, the Sun-disc. Akhenaten went to great lengths to extirpate the Amon cult, including expunging the god's name from monuments, destroying sacred images of Amon, and purging any mention of Amon in ritual or mythology. Yet Akhenaten's efforts ultimately proved unsuccessful. Shortly after his death, his religious beliefs in Aten as well as his capital Akhetaten were abandoned. The cult of Amon, which was never totally relinquished, started to resurge even in Akhenaten's last year and grew even stronger during the reign of Smenkhkare. Amon worship was fully restored by Tutankhamen with Thebes serving again as the capital. A famous text from Ramses III of the 20th Dynasty known as the Harris papyrus gives an inventory list of the great wealth of Amon's temples which included "5000 divine statues, 86,486 servants, 421,362 head of cattle, 433 gardens and orchards, 691,334 acres of land, 83 ships, 46 workshops, 65 cities and towns" as well as vast amounts of gold, silver, and incense (see *ANET,* 260–62).

Nahum 3:8 uses the sacking of Thebes (Heb *nōʾ ʾāmôn*) in 663 B.C.E. by the Assyrians as a warning of divine judgment against the equally powerful city of Nineveh.

Bibliography

Armour, R. A. 1986. *Gods and Myths of Ancient Egypt.* Cairo.

Assmann, J. 1983. *Re und Amun. Die Krise des polytheistischen Weltbildes im Ägypten der 18.-20. Dynastie.* Göttingen.

Nelson, H. H. 1942. The Identity of Amon-Re of United-With-Eternity. *JNES* 1: 127–55.

Otto, E. 1968. *Ancient Egyptian Art. The Cults of Osiris and Amon.* New York.

Sethe, K. 1929. *Amun und die acht Urgötter von Hermopolis.* APAW 4. Berlin.

Wainwright, G. A. 1934. Some Aspects of Amūn. *JEA* 20: 139–53.

———. 1963. The Origin of Amum. *JEA* 49: 21–23.

Watterson, B. 1984. *The Gods of Ancient Egypt.* New York.

THEODORE J. LEWIS

AMON (PERSON) [Heb *ʾāmôn*]. Var. AMI. **1.** The son of Manasseh, who ruled over Judah for two years, ca. 642-640 B.C.E. (2 Kgs 21:19–26 = 2 Chr 33:21–25). Amon came to the throne at the age of twenty-two, being one of Manasseh's youngest sons. His reign was cut short by an assassination plot carried out during a palace revolt by his courtiers. These conspirators were in turn killed by the "People of the Land" (Heb *ʿam hāʾāreṣ*), who then put Amon's eight-year-old son Josiah on the throne.

The silence of the biblical text with regard to the motive for the assassination has intrigued scholars, who have attempted to conjecture as to the underlying political and religious causes behind the coup d'état. Malamat (1953: 26–29) has argued that Amon was assassinated by those who objected to his pro-Assyrian policy. Such a hypothesis would fit well with what we know of the general uprising against Assurbanipal in 640 B.C.E. Perhaps owing to Egyptian incitement, the conspirators felt it was time to throw off the Assyrian yoke. Yet this view has recently been challenged by Cogan and Tadmor on chronological grounds (*2 Kings* AB, 275–76).

Other scholars have suggested that the conspirators were religiously motivated. Both accounts by the Deuteronomist and the Chronicler state that Amon practiced the abominable ways of his father Manasseh. Thus it has been conjectured that Amon was assassinated by those who favored the religious reforms of Hezekiah. Nielsen (1967: 103–6), for example, notes the struggle going on between the Jerusalem priesthood and those who favored Manasseh's religious policies.

Finally, it has also been suggested (Cogan and Tadmor *2 Kings* AB, 276) that perhaps Manasseh's older sons who were passed over for the throne may have been behind the assassination of their younger brother.

It is, of course, impossible to decide the extent to which Amon's assassination was politically or religiously motivated based on the data at hand. Our theological historians (the Deuteronomistic account followed by the Chronicler) are more interested in articulating the damning report that Amon "did what was displeasing to Yahweh just as Manasseh his father had done" with idolatry being singled out for special mention (2 Kgs 21:20–22 = 2 Chr 33:22). Some scholars have suggested that this may argue against the historicity of the Chronicler's description of Manasseh's repentance. In order to be consistent with his earlier description of Manasseh's repentance, the Chronicler departs from the Deuteronomistic account by pointing out that "Amon did not humble himself before Yahweh as had his father Manasseh" (2 Chr 33:23).

2. A governor (Heb *śar hāʿîr;* cf. Avigad 1976: 178–82) of Samaria during the days of Ahab (1 Kgs 22:26 = 2 Chr 19:25). Some scholars would rewrite his name *ʾmr* (cf. LXX's *sem(m)ēr/em(m)ēr*) instead of MT's *ʾmn* (cf. Stade 1885: 173–75). In this narrative Ahab charged Amon and Joash, "the son of the King," with keeping the prophet Micaiah under arrest and feeding him bread and water until Ahab returned "safely" from the fatal battle at Ramoth-gilead.

3. In a census list, Nehemiah 7:59 mentions the "children of Amon" as among those who returned from the exile under Zerubbabel and Jeshua's leadership. They are listed among the "children of Solomon's servants." In the parallel list in Ezra 2:57 they are called "children of Ami [Heb *ʾāmî*]."

Bibliography

Avigad, N. 1976. The Governor of the City. *IEJ* 26: 178–82.

Malamat, A. 1953. The Historical Background of the Assassination of Amon, King of Judah. *IEJ* 3: 26–29.

Nielsen, E. 1967. *Political Conditions and Cultural Developments in Israel and Judah During the Reign of Manasseh.* Vol. 1, pp. 103–6 in *Proceedings of the Fourth World Congress of Jewish Studies.* Jerusalem.

Stade, B. 1885. Der Name der Stadt Samarien und seine Herkunft. *ZAW* 5: 165–75.

THEODORE J. LEWIS

AMORA, AMORAIM. The traditional title for the Jewish rabbinic authorities ("rabbis") living from about 200 C.E. to around 500 C.E. (the "Amoraic period" of rabbinic Judaism). The term (Heb *ʾămôrʾa* [sing.], *ʾamôrʾaîm* [pl.]) comes from the root (*ʾmr*) which means "to speak" or "to interpret." The name stems from their activities in interpreting the Mishnah.

The location and importance of the rabbis changed during this period. Palestine comprised the Amoraim's first center, but after approximately 400 C.E., they disappeared from history. The Amoraim in Babylonia were initially subordinate to the Palestinians, but after 400 they constituted the only rabbinic movement. As archaeological and literary evidence makes clear, however, in neither area did the Amoraim control the religious activities of the Jewish people early on. It was not until about 500 C.E. that the Babylonian Amoraim gained authority among the populace.

Each group of rabbis bears responsibility for a legal compilation called a TALMUD. The two Talmuds show similarities in form and goal. Each text is organized as a "commentary" on the Mishnah. The Amoraim thus reinterpret the Mishnah's focus on the temple cult as a way of life based on the synagogue and school—with emphasis on prayer, study, and right actions. This transformation also appears in Leviticus Rabbah—a "commentary" to Leviticus—which changes Leviticus' focus on temple worship to an interest in morality and prayer. Thus, the Amoraim played the pivotal role in transforming Judaism from a religion of sanctification through the temple cult to a religion of salvation through sanctification by ethical behavior, prayer, and study.

There is a second, rare, usage of the term *amora* found in the Talmuds. It is a technical term designating someone who interprets for teachers. In a school, the teacher would briefly make a point, usually in a low voice; the Amora would then repeat the point in a louder voice and in a simpler manner so that all could hear and understand.

Bibliography

Mielziner, M., and Guttmann, A. 1968. *Introduction to the Talmud. With a New Bibliography, 1925–1967.* 4th ed. New York.

Neusner, J. 1972. *There We Sat Down.* Nashville.

———. 1985. *The Oral Torah.* San Francisco.

PAUL V. M. FLESHER

AMORITES [Heb *ʾemōrî*]. In biblical tradition, the designation of one of the seven to ten nations (Josh 7:10; Gen 15:19–21) that inhabited Canaan before the formation of the Israelite federation.

A. The Name

The term *amurru* first occurs in Old Akkadian sources as the general designation of "the West," referring to the W wind, and to the geographical area lying to the (N) W of Mesopotamia. The most frequent usage of the term refers to the population of that W region as an ethnic designation. Its semantic equivalent, Sumerian MAR.TU was used already in the mid-3d millennium B.C. even at Ebla in an ethnic or cultural sense, designating the population of the "West" that was recognized to be foreign to the population of Mesopotamia proper by culture as well as by language. It was also the name of a deity the characteristics of which are obscure. The meaning of the Sumerian term and how it came to designate the Amorites is unknown.

B. The Language

Amorite was a very important factor in the history of the Semitic languages, but information about it derives almost exclusively from personal names that can be identified as Amorite by grammatical and other contrasts to the standard onomastics of Akkadian. Nevertheless, considerable information concerning the language has been obtained from these names (Huffmon 1965). Some 6000 Amorite and other non-Akkadian personal names have been identified (Gelb 1980), and in addition some Amorite words appear in cuneiform sources, especially the archives of Mari.

Though early investigations of the language induced some scholars to term it "East-Canaanite" (Bauer 1926), it is clear that Amorite was an independent branch of Northwest Semitic, though it is far from clear to what extent it contrasted to the languages of the inland Syrian region to its W, and to the languages of the coastal region of Palestine and Lebanon (Mendenhall 1985; fc.c). Its West Semitic affiliation is guaranteed by the verbal system with prefixed and suffixed tenses, and preformatives with *ya-* instead of the East Semitic *i-*, as well as by a predominantly West Semitic lexical inventory (but see below).

C. The People and Culture

It has been a conventional scholarly opinion for decades that the Amorites were a nomadic population of the Syro-Arabian steppeland (Kupper 1957), who infiltrated into N Syria, gradually became sedentary, and then civilized enough to form states and empires. This view was based ultimately upon old 19th-century romantic ideas about the nomadic origins of all Semitic populations (Kupper 1957: xiv), and probably more immediately on the Sumerian satire on the Amorites preserved in Sumerian literature of the OB period. In this famous satire the Amorites are described as not burying their dead, eating uncooked meat, not living in houses—in short, as uncivilized nomadic barbarians (Cooper 1983). Though the description is patently untrue, or perhaps only technically apposite, the scholarly world seems to have taken this urban Sumero-Akkadian scurrilous description of Amorite culture at face value because it fitted in with preconceived theories about successive waves of nomads from the Arabian desert as the origin of the Semitic-speaking populations.

In sharp contrast to traditional ideas, a much more productive and realistic approach to the problem of Amorite culture is based upon a recognition of the fact that this population complex had its homeland in the region from the Euphrates River to the upper Khabur and Balikh river valleys S of the Anatolian mountains (Luke 1965). The many hundreds of small unfortified village *tells* in this region (Mallowan 1947: 10–11; Meijer 1986), many of which were occupied already in the Chalcolithic period, identify the culture as basically a village farming culture from time immemorial, but characterized also by a constant contact with urban cultures that were themselves powerfully influenced by the Sumero-Akkadian urban civilization of Mesopotamia. This region also was traversed by the main trade routes between Mesopotamia, Syria, and Anatolia. It is entirely possible that in early 3d-millennium sources the entire region from the Euphrates to the Mediterranean Sea may have been included in what the Sumerians called MAR.TU (Haldar 1970), and that the term may already have been applied therefore to non-Semitic-speaking persons as well.

The N part of this region was characterized by adequate rainfall for agriculture and intensive utilization of arable land. The archaeological record of the dense population of this region inevitably meant that an increasing portion of the population was dependent upon large-scale animal husbandry as their economic base. This was in turn greatly facilitated by the enormous range of steppeland to the S, extending all the way from W Mesopotamia to the Arabian desert, and to the SW to the fringe area of E Syria through the oasis of Palmyra. This large-scale sheepherding in turn implied a symbiotic relationship with urban societies that utilized the wool for the production of, and international trade in, textiles that is already attested in the texts from Ebla (Matthiae 1980). The seasonal movements of village shepherds, especially those residing along the Euphrates Valley, with their flocks between these steppe regions to the S and what is termed the "Upper Country" in the Mari texts, probably led to a contrast designated by the Amorites themselves as the group called *Banu-Yamina* "Southerners," i.e., residents of the Euphrates Valley region who engaged in irrigation agriculture as well as pastoralism, and the *Banu-Simʾal* "Northerners," of the rainfall agriculture region. This seasonal movement also has usually been confused by modern scholars with relatively recent nomadic cultural adaptations.

The economic base of the old Amorite society was thus a diversified one combining the high productivity of agricultural villages with the equally high productivity of animal husbandry. The bureaucratic archives of Mari in the 18th century B.C. give abundant evidence of this. The tax receipts of the palace indicate that persons with Amorite names made contributions of *agricultural* produce equally with such contributions made by persons who had Akkadian names. It is interesting, however, that tax payments of *animals* were made by persons who bore Amorite names only (Kerestes 1982). The evidence strongly suggests that, at least in the irrigation-based villages around Mari, the population engaged in agriculture was much more likely to become "Akkadianized" than were the shepherds. It is probable that the irrigation canals maintained by the king of Mari created a dependency and tendency toward assimilation to the Akkadian urban culture on the part of village farmers that was not characteristic of her much more independent shepherds.

Already at the dawn of history urban societies within the Amorite geographical region had been powerfully influenced by the urban cultures to the east (Matthiae 1980), but not until the Mari texts of the Old Babylonian period do we have some concrete evidence for the potential and actual friction between the urban society and the village/pastoral productive complex upon which it was dependent. The famous warning to the king of Mari not to ride upon a horse but upon a donkey because he was the king "not only of the Akkadians, but also of the Khana" illustrates the contrast. Much more important, however, is the evidence for the nearly constant conflict between successive kings of Mari and a coalition of tribes called "Benjaminites." The conflict ultimately stemmed from the fact that two generations earlier a king of Mari had, through military conquest, extended his control over city/village complexes to the W, absorbing their territory and populations into his imperial domain (see Kupper 1957: 47–81, who completely misunderstood the historical situation).

The tribal organization of the Benjaminites as well as other social entities referred to in the Mari texts had nothing to do with nomadism; rather, such organization is a constant in village society, especially when solidarity among villages is necessary to counterbalance the increasing domination of a central government. See also BEDOUIN AND BEDOUIN STATES. Unfortunately, little is known of the internal social organization of Amorite populations: they had officials known as *rabi amurrim* ("chief of Amurru") and *ʾabi amurrim* ("father of Amurru") and Amorite towns and villages had officials appointed by the king. These village heads were called *sugagum* in Amorite but *šāpirum* in Akkadian, and had to pay large sums to the royal treasury for their appointment (*CAD s.v. sugagum*). Furthermore, some regions had kings (*šarrum*) such as those defeated by the grandfather of Zimri-Lim. Their territory became part of the Mari empire, and their cities (Abattum, Tuttul, and Terqa, as well as no doubt others) became seats of provincial governors.

D. Amorite History Reconstructed

Contrary to present accepted opinion, it is probable that the sedentary Amorite culture of NE Syria had a continuity from the Chalcolithic or even Neolithic period on to the end of the MB Age. Though earlier Assyriologists identified this region of high population density with the land of Subartu and a non-Semitic-speaking folk, all the evidence we have indicates persons of the region have perfectly good Amorite names. It is not until the end of the MB Age that there is evidence for a massive shift of population in the entire N Syrian region, with the establishment of the empire of Mitanni and its predominantly Hurrian and Indo-European population.

In the absence of usable written documents prior to the EB Age, there is no way of proving or disproving this thesis. What does appear to be certain is that the growth of population in this region resulted in increasing emigration to the E, and there is now no reason to believe that what was happening in the W was any different. By the end of the 3d millennium B.C. Amorites were already settled in fairly large numbers in the cities of Mesopotamia (Bucellati 1966). Before the end of the 3d Dynasty of Ur, the king had erected a long wall that was intended to stop the Amorite infiltration and incursions into his territory. According to ancient traditions, a coalition of Amorites and Elamites destroyed Ur (ca. 1960 B.C.), and within a century virtually all of the old cities of Mesopotamia were ruled by kings who bore Amorite names.

It is certain that a similar process was taking place in the W regions along the Mediterranean coastal plain (Mendenhall 1985), though the evidence is very meager compared with that available for Mesopotamia and provides little, if any, basis for a chronology of the process. Ugarit had an Amorite dynasty in control of the city by about 1900 B.C. that continued in power until the city was destroyed at the end of the LB period. Similarly, Byblos had kings with Amorite names by about 1800 B.C., and it is perhaps no coincidence that the first (known) Amorite king of Byblos, Shemu-Abu, had the same name as that of the founder of the 1st Dynasty of Babylon, Sumu-Abum. Whether or not the destruction or collapse of the city-states of Palestine and Lebanon at the end of the EB III period (about 2300 B.C.) had anything to do with Amorite infiltration is at present an unanswerable question. It would seem improbable, to judge from what is known of Mesopotamian history. Furthermore, the earliest evidence for Amorite political control of coastal city-states comes half a millennium after the EB III destructions, and therefore makes most implausible the theory that Amorite incursions were responsible.

The turbulent times that attended the transition from the MB to the LB Age (16th century B.C.) seem also to have seen the disintegration of the old Amorite culture in the N Syrian homeland. There can be little doubt that this was brought about by incursions of Anatolian populations from the N. It is possible that the process was already beginning in the earlier phases of the MB period, and may help account for the Amorite migrations to the E and W. By the end of the 16th century the whole of N Syria was under the domination of the Hurrian empire of Mitanni; by the beginning of the 14th century many of the city-states of Syria, the coastal region, and Palestine (as far S as the Hebron area) were ruled by kings who bore Hurrian or Indo-European names. Alalakh in N Syria shows a significant population shift from very predominantly Semitic names to equally predominant Hurrian names between the 18th and 15th centuries. Ugarit on the coast had a population less than 40 percent Semitic, and in most of N Syria and the coastal region dynastic names shifted from Semitic, to Hurrian, and then to Luwian. By the Iron Age N Syria was known as *mat ḫatti*, "land of the Hittites."

During the LB Age, the Amorites had evidently become thoroughly assimilated into local populations both in the E and the W, as well as in the NE Syrian homeland, so that after that is no longer possible to identify a specific Amorite cultural/linguistic population group.

E. "Amorite" as a Political Designation

It was noted above that in native Amorite society there were already kings and other titles that designated political functions or offices. Following the diaspora of Amorites in the 20th to 19th centuries, there was evidently a multitude of political titles that made use of the term Amurru or the Sumerian MAR.TU. The term "father of the land of Amurru" was used at Larsa by an Elamite king, and subsequently by other kings including Hammurapi. The title became "king of the Amorites" by Hammurapi's 35th year and was a standard appellative of kings from then on, obviously devoid of any ethnic connotations. It was even included in standard lexicographical texts: LUGAL MAR.TU = *šar-ru a-mur-ri-i* (Kupper 1957: 174–77).

In the LB Age there was established a kingdom of Amurru in the upper Orontes Valley region of Syria. It is attested already in the Alalakh texts of the 15th century, and its history is well recorded in the Hittite and Amarna archives until its destruction at the beginning of the Iron Age. Abdu-Ashirta, a vassal of the Egyptians, established a dynasty in that kingdom that can be traced for six generations. His successor, Aziru, became a vassal of the Hittites as Egyptian power in the N began to wane, and we even have the text of the suzerainty treaty between him and the Hittites.

The next and last occurrence of the royal title "king of the Amorites" occurs in the biblical references to Sihon, who associated with Heshbon in Transjordan, and who was defeated in the earliest recorded battle of the newly established Israelite federation (Numbers 21). There can be little doubt of the historicity of the event, even though the present narratives are of course garbled by the overlay of later tradition and interpretations. His royal title must have derived from, and represented a continuation of, the political traditions of the old N Syrian principality of Amurru. Together with a number of other puzzling traditions (notably the Balaam narratives), this title strongly indicates a considerable influx of population into Transjordan and Palestine at the time when destructions in N Syria were leaving much of that region virtually depopulated. At the same time (i.e., the transition from LB to Early Iron Ages) the population of Transjordan saw a very sharp rise in density, and the only reasonable source for this rapid growth was the region to the N. Even the name Sihon (as well as Og of Bashan, who is also identified as an "Amorite" king) has no reasonable Semitic etymology. As was true also in Mesopotamia, the term "Amorite" no longer had any ethnic or linguistic significance and had simply become part of the traditional titulary of kings with N Syrian cultural connections. The conclusion is inescapable that Sihon and others were the remnants of N political entities that attempted to reestablish their old political regimes in another region—exactly as the neo-Hittite state of Carchemish successfully did for a time, after the destruction of the Hittite state and empire ca. 1200 B.C.

That Sihon and Og were not the only illustrations of such a process is indicated by the fact that the Amorites are also included in all of the various "Tables of Nations" scattered through the Pentateuch and Joshua. These lists designate political regimes and not merely "ethnic" groups. This is evident both from the fact that they are labeled *gôyîm* (which is probably best defined as "a politically organized military gang") and from the fact that some of them, such as the Jebusites of Jersualem, can definitely be identified with specific city-states. It has been established that the regime of Jerusalem already in the Amarna period derived from N Syria (Moran 1975). Its Amorite derivation is indicated not only by its name, *Yebus* (which is Amorite *Yabusum*), but also by the bitter condemnation of the prophet Ezekiel (16:2–3), who accurately described its origin as a hybrid of Amorite and "Hittite" (i.e., N Syrian) forebears. Even the language of standard biblical prose, that of Jerusalem, betrays its Syro-Hittite heritage in its use of the verb *hyh,* "to become," that is attested elsewhere only in Amorite and at Zenjirli (and of course in the much later attested Aramaic), instead of the otherwise standard Phoenician-Arabic verb *kwn* that stems from the EB Old Coastal Dialect of Palestine.

F. The Amorite Cultural and Religious Legacy

To the E, the disappearance of the Old Akkadian language and its replacement by Old Babylonian and Old Assyrian is most probably the result of Amorite influence in Mesopotamian speech and eventually writing. A similar but not identical process took place in the W. The Old Coastal Semitic of the Byblos Syllabic texts was replaced by a complex of local dialects that have long been termed "Canaanite," but all of which exhibit a blend of the older dialect with very strong influence from Amorite that can be traced especially in proper names and vocabulary (Mendenhall 1985: chap. 10; fc.b). In contrast to the E, where the older Old Akkadian disappeared entirely, the basic structure of the older language, the Old Coastal Semitic, survived in various fringe areas from the Biqaᶜ of Lebanon to the Sinai peninsula, and eventually became literate in the inscriptions of Old North Arabic and Old South Arabic.

Historically more important, however, is increasing evidence suggesting that venerable cultural and religious traits all over the ANE have Amorite origins. Long ago it was noted that the myth of cosmic conflict was probably Amorite in origin, and was adapted in the E in the Babylonian creation epic, and in the W in the Ugaritic myth of the conflict of Baᶜal and Yamm. Accompanying the mythical motifs, the Amorite deities Dagan, Hadad, and ᶜAnat became established in the W superimposed upon earlier deities of ᵓAthirat and Yamm, ᵓIl, ᵓIlat (Baᶜalat), and a Baᶜal, whose proper name is unknown, but who is later identified with the Amorite storm god Hadad. The details of the process remain to be worked out, but the syncretistic process itself can hardly be questioned (Vine 1965).

Furthermore, it is now possible to trace, at least in theory, the reasons for the extremely close parallels between biblical and Old Babylonian literary works. It is virtually certain that such motifs as the flood story were mediated to the Palestinian region through N Syrian (Hurrian) versions of an old Amorite narrative. However, much more impressive is the earliest biblical law code of Exodus 21–23: its striking similarities to the Code of Hammurapi and other Mesopotamian law codes reflect their common derivation from Amorite traditions and customary law.

Probably the single most important Amorite contribution to the biblical tradition was the Abraham narrative in Genesis, which was in all probability a specifically Palestinian epic tradition (for the archaeological correlations, see Dever *IJH,* 70–120). In spite of the fact that it has been thoroughly reworked to fit the political concerns of a *much* later period (Mendenhall *AIR,* 337–56), the basic structure of the narrative fits entirely the nature of the historical process of Amorite migrations attested in the Bronze Age sources: from infiltration to political control legitimized through a divine gift of the land (though the latter stage is, of course, presented in the biblical narrative as realized only with King David).

Finally, it should be noted that some of the most important concepts in the theological vocabulary of the Hebrew Bible are either demonstrably or probably of Amorite origin. Foremost is the concept of divine deliverance that became the concept of "salvation" expressed in various forms of the root *yšᶜ*. At least sixteen gods and divine epithets appear as subjects of the verb "to save" in the Amorite personal names. Other key theological terms that are probably Amorite are *ṣdq,* "righteous"; *nqm,* "vindication"; *yšr,* "upright" (there was probably a native Coastal Dialect cognate, but with a semantic contrast); *špṭ,* "to judge"; *ḥsd,* "faithful," and perhaps *zkr,* "remember" (Mendenhall fc.b).

In summary, from the MB Age on there was no region of the Levant that had not been influenced by the Amorite language and culture in various ways and various degrees. Their cultural and linguistic influence was a lasting one that is gradually coming to light, especially in the areas of religion and law. Past generations of scholars credited the Babylonians with these cultural achievements; however, it now appears that the Babylonians themselves were merely the recipients, in part the product, and to some degree the vectors of the ancient Amorite village heritage, until they succumbed to the perpetual temptation of urban imperialism. It is equally clear that the Amorite populations were themselves drastically modified by the various cultures into which they became integrated in the later phases of the Bronze Age, so that eventually they ceased to exist as a distinct cultural group.

Bibliography

Bauer, T. 1926. *Die Ostkanaanäer.* Leipzig.

Bucellati, G. 1966. *The Amorites of the Ur III Period.* Vol. 1. Naples.

Cooper, J. 1983. *The Curse of Agade.* Baltimore.

Gelb, I. 1980. *Computer-Aided Analysis of Amorite.* AS 21. Chicago.

Haldar, A. 1970. *Who Were the Amorites?* Leiden.

Huffmon, H. 1965. *Amorite Personal Names in the Mari Texts.* Baltimore.

Kerestes, T. 1982. *Indices to Economic Texts from the Palace of Zimri-Lim (ca. 1782–1759 B.C.)* Diss. Michigan.

Kupper, J. 1957. *Les Nomades en Mesopotamie au temps des rois de Mari.* Paris.

Luke, T. 1965. *Pastoralism and Politics in the Mari Period: A Re-Examination of the Character and Political Significance of the Major West Semitic Tribal Groups on the Middle Euphrates.* Diss. Michigan.

Mallowan, M. 1947. Excavations at Brak and Chagar Bazar. *Iraq* 9: 10–11.

Matthiae, P. 1980. *Ebla: An Empire Rediscovered.* London.

Meijer, D. 1986. *A Survey in Northeastern Syria.* Leiden.

Mendenhall, G. 1985. *The Syllabic Inscriptions from Byblos.* Beirut.

———. fc.a. Jerusalem 1000–63 B.C. *History of Jerusalem.*

———. fc.b. Toward a Method for the Historical Lexicography of Semitic Languages. Abdel-Massih Memorial Volume.

———. fc.c. The Amorite Migrations. *Mari at Fifty.*

Moran, W. 1975. The Syrian Scribe of the Jerusalem Amarna Letters. Pp. 146–66 in *Unity and Diversity,* ed. H. Goedicke and J. Roberts. Baltimore.

Vine, K. 1965. *The Establishment of Baal at Ugarit.* Diss. Michigan.

George E. Mendenhall

AMOS (PERSON) [Heb *ᶜāmôs*]. **1.** See AMOS, BOOK OF.

2. The son of Manasseh and father of Josiah, according to Matthew's genealogy tying Joseph, the husband of Mary, to the House of David and Solomon (Matt 1:10). Amos is unknown as an ancestor of Jesus in any other biblical documents, except Luke's genealogy (see below), but there is a significant textual variant with Amon, Gk *amōn* (see ASAPH). The external evidence for Amos is strong (Sinaiticus B, C, [D^{Luke}], St. Gall, Tiflis, Leningrad, f^{1}, 33, $it^{c, d Luke, ff1, g1, k, q}$ $cop^{sa, bo, fay}$, arm, eth, geo), with Alexandrian and some Caesarean witnesses, as well as Eastern versions, in comparison with the weaker external evidence for Amon (K, L, W, Leningrad, f^{13}, *Byz Lect*^{m}, it^{a}, Vg, $syr^{c, s, p, h, pal}$). The UBS committee "was impressed by the weight of the external evidence" (*TCGNT* 2) for Amos, though it recognized opposing positions (cf. Borland 1982: 501–3). If Amos is adopted—as it is by only a few standard versions, including RSV and NAB (contra AV, NEB, NASB, NIV, JB)—the genealogy appears to be in error, possibly with insertion of the OT prophet Amos (Luz *Matthew 1–7* EKK, 90 n.14) for the more historically correct Amon, found in the king-list of 1 Chr 3:13–14 and in 2 Kgs 21:18. Gundry (1982: 16) believes Matthew may have chosen or coined the spelling "Amos" for a secondary allusion to the prophet, as he did with Asaph (RSV Asa) (1:7–8), but this is dubious (cf. Brown 1977: 60–61). Amon probably should be read instead, on the basis of the OT evidence, although, unlike the MT, the LXX on which Matthew may well depend illustrates a diversity of readings, including Amos and Amon.

3. The father of Mattathias and son of Nahum, according to Luke's genealogy tying Joseph, the "supposed father" of Jesus, to descent from Adam (Luke 3:25). It falls within a list of seventeen otherwise unknown antecedents of Jesus (Fitzmyer *Luke 1–9* AB, 500), except for Matthew's genealogy (which appears in adapted form in Luke 3:23–31 in the codex Bezae) (see above). Whereas Amos may, according to Marshall (*Luke* NIGTC, 163), represent the king Amon (2 Kgs 21:18), Amoz the father of Isaiah (2 Kgs 19:2), or the prophet, the name here probably is not to be equated with any OT person bearing a similar name (cf. Hervey 1853: 136–37), even in light of Luke's theme of Jesus as prophet (see Johnson 1969: 240–52). Kuhn (1923: 211) must stretch the evidence to see a relation between Amos and Simeon (3:30) as a result of corrupt writing and placement.

Bibliography

Borland. J. A. 1982. Re-Examining NT Textual-Critical Principles and Practices used to Negate Inerrancy. *JETS* 25: 499–506.

Brown, R. E. 1977. *The Birth of the Messiah: A Commentary on the Infancy Narratives in Matthew and Luke.* Garden City, NY.

Gundry, R. H. 1982. *Matthew: A Commentary on His Literary and Theological Art.* Grand Rapids.

Hervey, A. 1853. *The Genealogies of Our Lord and Saviour Jesus Christ, As Contained in the Gospels of St. Matthew and St. Luke.* Cambridge.

Johnson, M. D. 1969. *The Purpose of the Biblical Genealogies, with Special Reference to the Setting of the Genealogies of Jesus.* SNTSMS 8. Cambridge.

Kuhn, G. 1923. Die Geschlechtsregister Jesu bei Lukas und Matthäus, nach ihrer Herkunft untersucht. *ZNW* 22: 206–28.

STANLEY E. PORTER

AMOS, BOOK OF. Amos (Heb *ᶜāmôs*) was an 8th-century Hebrew prophet who was born in the S kingdom of Judah but whose ministry was directed mainly to the N kingdom of Israel. Prophesying probably shortly after 760 B.C.E., Amos is reckoned as the earliest of the so-called writing prophets. The book bearing his name contains both oracles by him and some biographical information about him. It is the sixth book in the prophetic section of the Hebrew Bible and the third book of the "minor Prophets" (in the LXX it is the second book, before Joel).

A. Biography
B. Historical Setting
C. Theological Ideas and Motifs
D. Structure and Content
E. Literary and Rhetorical Features
F. Text and Canon

A. Biography

Our knowledge of Amos the man is restricted to the information provided in the book of Amos. He was from Tekoa (Amos 1:1), a small garrisoned fortress ca. 10 miles S of Jerusalem and slightly W of the wilderness of Judah, a barren and rocky wasteland that falls toward the Dead Sea. He was variously described as a *nōqēd,* "shepherd" (1:1), a *bôqēr,* "cattleman" (7:14), and a *bôlēs,* "gouger [of sycamore figs]" (7:14). Undoubtedly, then, he came from an agricultural background, but the exact natures of his duties are in doubt. Early scholarship assumed that Amos was a poor manual laborer, a shepherd and goatherd who, possibly in the off season, worked as a dresser of the sycamore trees that grew in the lowlands in the Jericho Valley. The latter work involved cutting the fruit while it was still on the tree so that it would ripen at the proper time. It was generally assumed that the figs were eaten by the poor, including Amos, who may also have cut figs in exchange for grazing rights.

These early interpretations arose not so much from an understanding of the words used to describe Amos' profession—*nōqēd* occurs in only one other place in the OT, and both *bôqēr* and *bôlēs* are *hapax legomena*—as from the thrust of Amos' message. Scholars assumed that, since Amos was a champion of the poor and a critic of the wealthy, he must have had a modest upbringing. For a number of reasons this conclusion must be rejected.

The one other OT occurrence of *nōqēd* is in a reference to Mesha, king of Moab (2 Kgs 3:4). Mesha was obviously the "owner of herds," a breeder on a large scale, not a poor shepherd. *nōqēd* also occurs at Ugarit in the colophon of a text that indicates a possible cultic significance to the term (*CTA* 6.6 = *UT* 62.55): *rb khnm*/*rb nqdm,* "Chief of Priests/Chief of (Temple)-herdsmen" (*ANET,* 141b). Both these references suggest that Amos was either a shepherd who owned his sheep or an official who tended the royal or temple herds.

The Ugaritic text creates the intriguing possibility that Amos worked as an official in the service of Uzziah (2 Chr

26:10) or the Jerusalem temple. This cannot be ruled out. However, it appears that the term *nōqēd* is not in and of itself a cultic or royal term but one that derives those connotations from the surrounding text (cf. *CTA* 71.71 = *UT* 113.71). Thus, we would argue that Amos was not a royal or cultic figure but one of the *ʿăm-hāʾārēṣ*, the well-to-do class of citizens who owned cattle, sheep, and goats. The *ʿăm-hāʾārēṣ* maintained tribal authority and Yahwistic orthodoxy, two characteristics of Amos' message (see Soggin 1987: 10–11).

This interpretation of Amos' vocation clears up the problem of understanding *nōqēd* and *bôqēr* together. *nōqēd* has generally been interpreted as a herder or breeder of small animals (sheep and goats), while *bôqēr* has been reserved for one who breeds large animals (cattle) (cf. the Kilamuwa inscription from Zinjirli [*KAI* 24:12]). It has been argued that the terms are incongruous, that poor farmers did not have the resources to breed and tend both small and large domestic animals. This led to emendations of the text: since *nun* and *bet* are often confused in writing, as are *dalet* and *reš,* scholars sometimes emended the MT to read *bôqēr* for *nōqēd* or *nōqēd* for *bôqēr,* thereby eliminating the problem. Others suggested that the reference to "flock" in Amos 7:15 influences the reading of *bôqēr* (from large animals to small) (7:14). Neither proposal is necessary, however, when we accept that Amos was rich enough to own sheep, goats, and cattle.

Finally, although the poor did eat sycamore figs, the fruit was mostly used for cattle fodder. Thus, the description of Amos as a *bôlēs* may refer to his ownership of sycamore orchards as a feed crop rather than to the specific act of cutting the figs.

The information regarding Amos is scarce, so that which does exist is worked and reworked, interpreted and reinterpreted in an attempt to enhance our understanding of the prophet. Since we have no first-person account of Amos' call to prophesy—as we do, for example, with Jeremiah—intense attention has been paid to the biographical record of Amos' confrontation with Amaziah, the high priest of Bethel (7:10–17), for it is there that Amos proclaimed to Amaziah that Yahweh "took him from following the flock" and called him to "go and prophesy to my people Israel" (7:15). Amos also states: *lōʾ nābîʾ ʾānōkî, wĕlōʾ ben-nābîʾ ʾānōkî* "Not a prophet I, nor the son of a prophet I" (7:14).

Much has been written about this statement, and scholars uniformly agree only on one point: the term *ben-nābîʾ*, "son of a prophet," refers to a member of a prophetic guild (1 Kgs 20:35; 2 Kgs 2:3; 4:1, 38). As the monarchy developed, those who anointed kings and supposedly had a direct line to Yahweh established guilds to perpetuate their profession by recruiting and training future prophets. The guilds were undoubtedly supported from the royal treasury: in troubled times the royal family would need favorable predictions to secure the support of the populace, who would have looked to the prophets as messengers of Yahweh. By Amos' time there were probably few, if any, independent prophets. Part of the importance of Amos and his oracles lies in the fact that he was the first prominent independent prophet of the monarchy. His message is not that of the prophetic guilds; anyone can prophesy who hears Yahweh (Amos 3:8).

In Hebrew Amos 7:14 is a nominal verbless clause. In such instances, the tense of the implied verb "to be" is understood from context. Here, it can be either present tense (from the influence of v 13b) or past tense (from the influence of v 15). The reading "I *am* not a prophet nor the son of a prophet" would suggest that Amos had separated himself from the prophets of the palace, whom he considered corrupt and unable to speak for Yahweh. "Amos is bent on *contradicting* Amaziah's assumption that he is a professional prophet, not somehow *reinforcing* it" (Auld 1986: 26), as a reading in the past tense might suggest. Auld (pp. 26–27) also suggests that the present tense is to be read unless context dictates otherwise; that the three nominal clauses in v 14 (*lōʾ nābîʾ ʾānōkî / wĕlōʾ ben-nābîʾ ʾānōkî / kî bôqēr ʾānōkî ûbôlēs*) suggest a continuing present; and that the *lōʾ*, "not," is an emphatic negative, not the *lʾ* affirmative as in Ugaritic. He concludes that Amos was reinforcing his independence of the corrupt prophetic unions that announced only what their employer, the king, allowed.

The reading "I *was* not a prophet" would suggest that Amos was emphasizing that he was not a prophet at the time of his calling, that he had no prophetic training, and that he did not turn to prophecy for economic or other ulterior motives. Scholars (see, e.g., Mays, *Amos* OTL, 137–39) who argue for a past tense note that Amos referred to prophets (2:11; 3:7), spoke in oracles and sayings like other prophets, and interceded like other prophets (7:2, 5). Amaziah called what Amos was doing "prophesying" (*tinnābēʾ*, 7:12, 16), and Amos said that he was called and sent to "prophesy" (*hinnābēʾ*, 7:15). Soggin (1987: 8) notes that "throughout the book the verb *nbʾ* and the noun *nābîʾ* (the verb six times, the noun four times) never have negative connotations." Amos also received visions like other prophets (7:1–9; 8:1–9:6) and was called a *ḥōzeh,* "seer" (7:12), a synonym for *nābîʾ* and a term usually appearing in the titles of prophetic books and the Chronicler's work—the term *rōʾeh,* "public seer," is not used and may be yet another way that Amos denied his connection to the paid religious profession. Based on this evidence, one could argue that Amos did not consider all prophets to be corrupt and thus was not denying that he was a prophet, although he might be denying that he was the son of a prophet.

It is possible to propose a new solution to the problem of tense in this passage. It may be that Amos 7:14b–15—that is, Amos' response to Amaziah—is part of the dialogue between Amos and Yahweh at the time of Amos' call. We have, in compressed form, Amos' excuse for not wanting to obey Yahweh and Yahweh's response. Just as Jeremiah (Jer 1:4–10, esp. vv 6–7) responded, "I do not know how to speak, for I am only a youth," so Amos responded, "I am not a prophet nor the son of a prophet, but just a cattleman and fig cutter." Yahweh's response to Jeremiah was, "Go to whom I send you; speak what I command," and Yahweh's response to Amos was, "Go, prophesy." Thus, the tense of the verbless clause is present, which satisfies the linguistic arguments, but it references a past situation, which allows for a better interpretation of Amos as a prophet. And in reiterating his call, or part of it, Amos responded to Amaziah's concerns. Zevit (1975) notes that Amaziah assumed that Amos earned his living as a prophet, usually spoke in Judah, and was on his own in Bethel (Amos 7:12). Amos countered that he did not earn a living as a prophet, had a divine mission to Israel, and was not on his own but was called by Yahweh (7:14–15). Amos supplied all of this information to Amaziah through a recollection of his call.

The sayings and oracles of Amos convince us that he was cognizant of the history of Judah, Israel, and their neighbors (1:3–2:16). He knew about the cultic and political centers of Israel and Judah and their practices (Jerusalem—2:5, 6:1; Samaria—3:9, 4:1, 6:1; Bethel—3:14, 4:4, 5:5–6, 7:13; Gilgal—4:4, 5:5, Beer-sheba—5:5, 8:14; Dan—8:14). Amos was also aware of the social hierarchy and power structures that existed. The variety of his literary structures and his heightened rhetoric convince us that he was a gifted orator (see E below). All these factors lend credence to the view that Amos was a very gifted, highly educated individual, not a poor shepherd. It is romantic but highly unreasonable to think that the lofty motifs and grand oration of the book of Amos came from an uneducated manual laborer. It has also been suggested that the bold and brash statements of Amos (4:1, 5:5, 6:12, etc.) show that Amos is young. Yet the problems depicted by Amos would lead even older men and women to decry the situation with boldness and sarcasm.

In summary, Amos was an economically independent landed aristocrat who, believing that he had been called by Yahweh, became a prophet to the N kingdom of Israel. After the events of 7:10–17, it is assumed that Amos returned to his ranch in Judah. There is a pseudepigraphic legend that Amos was tortured by Amaziah and then was killed by Amaziah's son (see *OTP,* 391), and another that he was killed by King Uzziah (Ginzberg 1937–66: vol. 4: 262; vol. 6: 357 [*Shalshelet ha-Kabbalah 97*]). We have no evidence that there is any truth to either story.

B. Historical Setting

Amos' ministry is dated to the reigns of Jeroboam II (786–746 B.C.E.), king of Israel, and Uzziah (783–742 B.C.E.), king of Judah, "two years before the earthquake" (1:1). The earthquake, remembered centuries later (Zech 14:4–5), was severe, and evidence of its occurrence appears in the remains of Stratum VI at Hazor (King 1988: 21, 38), which can be dated to the mid-8th century. Josephus (*Ant* 9.222–27) connects the earthquake with an act of impiety on Uzziah's part around 760 B.C.E. (see 2 Kgs 15:5; 2 Chr 26:16–20).

If we date the earthquake to around 760 B.C.E., this coincides with Jeroboam's reconquest of Transjordan (Amos 6:14; see 2 Kgs 14:23–29), which also occurred around 760 B.C.E., and with Uzziah's impiety and subsequent leprosy. Jotham, Uzziah's son, reigned as regent from 750 to 742 B.C.E., and then, after his father's death, as king from 742 to 735 B.C.E. (2 Kgs 15:6; 2 Chr 26:21). If Amos' ministry had fallen in the regency of Jotham (750 B.C.E. onward), then presumably Jotham would have been mentioned in the superscription to the book. Thus, we can date Amos shortly before 750 B.C.E., or around 760 B.C.E.

The extraordinary length of the reigns of Jeroboam and Uzziah gives some clue to the historical situation during the early to mid-8th century B.C.E. First, this was a period of peace and expansion for Israel and Judah. The wars that threatened the two kingdoms during the reigns of the predecessors of Jeroboam and Uzziah were over. Assyria to the NE and Egypt to the S were both on the decline and were no threat to the smaller nations of Syria-Palestine. Israel and Judah took the opportunity to expand their borders to those of the old and revered Davidic-Solomonic empire.

The most important annexation for Israel was Gilead and the Transjordanian cities of Lo-debar and Karnaim (6:13–14). The King's Highway, the major trade route from the Tigris-Euphrates river valley to the Gulf of Aqaba and Egypt, ran through Gilead and the Transjordan. Thus, Gilead had been continually contested by Israel and Aram (Syria). With the Assyrian destruction of Damascus, the capital of Aram, Aram went into a decline around 801 B.C.E., which allowed Israel to assume control. Jeroboam, the greatest king of the Jehu dynasty, annexed the area of Gilead and occupied the Transjordan and Judah. Israel thus controlled the major trade route in the area and thereby reaped great wealth.

This was therefore a period of great prosperity for Israel. The stability of the region allowed for the safe conduct of caravans down the King's Highway, which was in Israelite hands. Trading with Egypt and Arabia in the S and Byblos and Syria in the N greatly increased the wealth of Israel and Judah. Amos describes this wealth, which is also evidenced in the archaeological remains of the time. Samaria, located 42 miles N of Jerusalem on a hill about 300 feet above the valley, was established by Omri (876–869 B.C.E.) as the third capital of Israel after Shechem and Tirzah, and excavations there and elsewhere have confirmed the wealth of the rulers and leaders of Israel. Over 500 ivory fragments from the 9th and 8th centuries have been found at Samaria (cf. Amos 3:15). Finds from other cities include over 300 ivories from Megiddo, a bed of ivory from Salamis in Cyprus (6:4), and two palaces facing in opposite directions, from Zinjirli, possibly evidence of the winter and summer houses in Amos 3:15 (also 6:11; cf. 1 Kgs 21:1, 18; Jer 36:22; *KAI* 216.17–20). Houses of hewn stone, or ashlar masonry (Amos 5:11), are found at Samaria. (See King 1988 for descriptions of the archaeological excavations and their findings.)

Auld (1986: 13) argues that, by the time of Amos, Israel was not prosperous but in decline: "The disparity between rich and poor which Amos found so objectionable may have been the result, not of recent prosperity acquired by some under Jeroboam's long reign, but of a longer established decline which bore most heavily on the poor." Hayes (1988) agrees with this interpretation of the historical situation. Yet the archaeological evidence argues for prosperity, not depression, during the mid-8th century. Further evidence comes from Tirzah, the capital of Israel before it was moved to Samaria. Excavations at that city have revealed that in the 10th century B.C.E. houses were of uniform size throughout the city, but by the 8th century one section of the city contained large houses, evidence of prosperity, while the other section contained the small houses of the poor. Megiddo was also a prosperous city during Jeroboam's reign (King 1988: 39). And Amos' description of the elaborate *marzēaḥ* banquets held by the rich (6:4–7) and his reference to the rich women of Israel as the "cows of Bashan" (4:1), fattened on their wealth and security, do not suggest a long-established decline. Thus, we can assume that Israel's domination of Gilead and the King's Highway led to a prosperity that enveloped the royal family and prominent members of society but did not trickle down to the poor. It is this uneven distribution of wealth in the 8th century that set the atmosphere for the social crimes that Amos so violently abhorred.

C. Theological Ideas and Motifs

The Israelites were a religious people. Pilgrimages to Bethel, Gilgal, and Beer-sheba, the sacred precincts of Israel, were commonplace (4:4; 5:5). Freewill and thanksgiving offerings and tithes were performed regularly (4:4), and there were many religious assemblies and festivals (5:21–23). By all criteria, then, the Israelites assumed that they were performing the cultic and ritual requirements necessary to appease Yahweh. Furthermore, they considered their wealth and security as evidence that Yahweh was pleased. They assumed that their steadfast devotion to cultic ritual exempted them from the requirements of righteousness and social justice and from the consequences of wrongdoing. Through sacrifice they could guarantee divine favor and their own survival. The peace and prosperity the nation enjoyed must have, to many Israelites, validated their lives, values, and assumptions as the chosen people of God.

Yet the people had turned the official view around and were reasoning in reverse: their prosperity proved that they were righteous. The distinction, while a fine one, is nevertheless important: the obligation of the covenant was to pursue righteousness and justice; prosperity would follow as a by-product of God's pleasure. The pursuit of wealth rather than righteousness was an unacceptable short cut, and wholly abhorrent to Yahweh, according to the prophet. "Amos' severe judgment is a repudiation, not of the cult itself, but of the cult as it was practiced in the eighth century B.C.E. . . . One's conduct in the marketplace must always conform to one's attitude in the holy place" (King 1988: 89).

And Israel's did not. Amos decried the social injustice, the oppression of the poor, and the lack of any moral or ethical values on the part of the rich and powerful. According to Amos, the spokesman of Yahweh, Israel was a violent, oppressive, and exploitative society. The poor had to sell themselves into slavery to pay off trivial debts (2:6; 8:6). The rich falsified weights and measures (8:5) and traded dishonestly (8:6). Even the courts, the last bastion of hope for the poor, were corrupt. Judges were bribed to cheat the poor out of what little they had (2:7; 5:10, 12). In fact, Israel was no longer capable of acting with justice (3:10; cf. 5:7, 24; 6:12). Truth and honesty were now hated (5:10).

Huffmon (1983: 111–12) is correct in suggesting that, when these social crimes are placed in historical context, four ideological points in Amos' message can be discerned: (1) the socioeconomic lifestyle of the Israelites is opposed to traditional values; (2) socioeconomic reorganization without compassion is not acceptable; (3) the resulting oppression of the poor cannot be tolerated; and (4) participation in the cultus gives a false sense of confidence.

Israel had profaned the true tradition upon which the nation was founded, the Book of the Covenant. The ancient prohibitions against sexual abuse (Exod 21:7–9), debt slavery (22:24), charging interest to the poor (22:25), the misappropriation of collateral (22:26–27), the corruption of the legal process (23:6–8), and fraudulent weights and measures (Deut 25:13–16) were ignored (Amos 2:7; 2:6; 5:11; 2:8; 5:10, 12; and 8:5, respectively) in the greedy race for more wealth. Partial corroboration of these practices comes from the Meṣad Ḥashavyahu ostracon (ca. 625 B.C.E.), whereon a reaper complains that his garment (*beged*) had been impounded and asks the military governor to intervene and retrieve it (King 1988: 24–25).

In the wake of these social crimes, Amos cried: "Let justice (*mišpāṭ*) roll down like waters, and righteousness (*ṣĕdāqāh*) like an overflowing stream" (5:24). In the ancient Near East deities were uniformly considered the source of water. Amos noted that it is justice and righteousness, not cultic ritual alone, that bring forth the divine salvific waters.

Given the peace and prosperity that existed, Amos undoubtedly knew that he had an uphill battle to convince the nation of the truth of his message. He thus took every opportunity to show that his message was Yahweh's message. In his confrontation with Amaziah (7:10–17) Amos denied any relationship to the prophetic unions and claimed that his ministry and message were the direct result of a call from Yahweh (see A above). Were it not for Yahweh's call, he would be tending to his agricultural business. Amos also emphasized the importance of his message through exaggerated and sarcastic rhetoric (see E below). But more importantly, Amos switched the meaning of common, traditional religious ideas, such as the election of Israel, "the day of Yahweh," and salvation history.

Israel viewed themselves as the elect of God, chosen by Yahweh to be His people, His nation; and they considered that election as an occasion of privilege and prosperity. Yet, for Amos, the people had turned the doctrine of election upside down. Election meant, first and foremost, special responsibility and obligation, which Israel could discharge only through the proper treatment of their fellow human beings. Amos measured the moral health of Israel and found the country fatally ill. Amid the peace, prosperity, and religious enthusiasm there was no fundamental loyalty to God, social justice, and ethical standards. Amos declared that Yahweh had thus rejected Israel's corrupt cult (5:21–24), which had produced a false sense of security and encouraged moral depravity. Amos cried out: "You only have I known of all the families of the earth. Therefore, I will punish you for all your iniquities" (Amos 3:2).

The concept of election included not only the assurance that Yahweh would preserve them as a people, but also the anticipation that the "day of Yahweh" would come, a day of salvation when all Israel's enemies would be destroyed and Israel would stand before the world as a testimony to God's power and authority. With the expansion of the kingdom and with the peace that existed, many Israelites must have thought that "the day" had come and that Jeroboam was the "messiah." Amos, however, reversed the popular interpretation of the "day of Yahweh." It became a day of destruction, not salvation; of darkness, not light; of punishment, not prosperity (4:12; 5:18–20; 8:9–10).

So salvation history became judgment history. In a beautiful parody of the salvation story of Israel's deliverance from Egypt and entrance into the land of Canaan (Pss 105; 136:10–22), Amos turned the plagues of Egypt upon Israel (4:6–13). Unlike the Egyptians, however, Israel did not respond. The God of the conquest was now the God of destruction (2:9–16); the God of the Exodus was now the God of all nations, and the specialness of His relationship with Israel was now destruction, not election. Just as He will destroy the nations surrounding Israel and Judah, so will He destroy Israel and Judah.

With no evidence of a remorseful Israel, Amos had no choice but to become, and thus to forever be known as, a prophet of doom, whose images are those of war (3:11; 6:14; 7:17), defeat (5:3), deportation (4:2–3; 6:7; 7:11, 17), and death (5:2–3, 16; 6:9; 7:11, 17; 8:3; 9:10). He predicted the destruction of Israel (3:12, 15; 5:2, 17; 7:9, 11; 9:8), the razing of the capital Samaria (6:8), the captivity of the Israelites by the Assyrians (5:27; 6:7; 7:11), and the destruction of Damascus, Philistia, Tyre, Edom, Ammon, Moab, and Judah (1:3–2:5). All of this began to take place in 734 B.C.E. when Tiglath-pileser III (745–727 B.C.E.), king of Assyria, mounted his first campaign to the W, conquering the coastal areas of Palestine. Hazor, Megiddo, Galilee, and Gilead were captured in 733 B.C.E., and Damascus and Syria in 732 B.C.E. By 727 B.C.E. the small nations of Syria and Palestine, including Israel and Judah, were vassals of Assyria. In 722 B.C.E., after a brief revolt, Samaria was razed, the leaders of Israel were exiled, and Israel became a province of Assyria.

The question has always existed in Amos studies: Did Amos hold out any hope of redemption and renewal? "Many of Amos's words are very bleak: their surface meaning can be read no other way. But is their intent simply at worst to jeer at those on their way to deserved perdition, or at best to annotate their record and arraign them before capital sentence is carried out? Or is the purpose of Amos's sharp criticism to shock his people into self-understanding *and a commitment to amelioration?* He refuses to commit his God to a positive response, but he does leave the door open" (Auld 1986: 65). Auld and others assume that every prophet brought a message of both doom and hope, that every prophet presented a futuristic picture of hope no matter what the crimes and the punishment. It could be argued, however, that Amos' original message did not contain even a shred of hope for Israel. (For a discussion of the oracle of hope and restoration in 9:11–15, as well as the doxologies, see F below.)

According to the prophet, the Israelites were beyond redemption (3:10; 5:10) and ready for the punishment that Amos must have sensed was on the horizon. Why would he have projected hope if he knew it was a matter of time before Assyria turned its attention to the west? It is important to note that, unlike other prophets who held out great promise for a remnant that would survive, Amos assumed that there would be no remnant (4:2b; 6:10), or at least that that remnant was in jeopardy. One could also argue that, even if Amos had wanted to present some hope, to do so to such a self-righteous audience enjoying peace and prosperity would have softened the message and led them to turn a deaf ear.

D. Structure and Content

Scholars have divided the book of Amos in a number of ways. Koch and others (1976), for instance, divide the book into four parts (chaps. 1–2, chaps. 3–4, 5:1–9:6, and 9:7–15). Van der Wal and Talstra (1984), criticizing Koch's four-part structure, divide the book into two parts (chaps. 1–6 and 7–9). They argue that the superscription implies that two books, one of "words" and one of "visions," were joined together. Most recently, Limburg (1987) has proposed a sevenfold division of the book, each division further subdivided into seven parts. He would propose a three-part structure. Chaps. 1–2 are clearly a unit. Whether chaps. 3–6 should be subdivided into any smaller units is debatable, but it seems clear that this section should be separated from the visions at the end of the book (chaps. 7–9), the third section.

1. Chapters 1–2. The book of Amos begins with a classical prophetic superscription (1:1, cf. Hos 1:1; Isa 1:1; Jer 1:1). It contains chronological and geographical information on the prophet's ministry and identifies his profession; it also provides a description of the contents of the book—"the words of Amos . . . which he saw." The patronym of the prophet, another feature of the standard superscription, is here missing. The awkwardness of the two dependent clauses has led Mays (*Amos* OTL), Soggin (1987), and others to suggest that the original superscription was as follows: "The words of Amos of Tekoa which he saw concerning Israel two years before the earthquake." The rest they consider the work of a Deuteronomic redactor during Josiah's reform or the Exile. Whether or not this is true, it is important to note that the original superscription is a late addition to the book and not original with Amos. This is not unusual and in fact is the case with all of the prophetic superscriptions of the OT.

After a detached oracle (1:2), there is a series of indictments and sentences against various nations who were adjacent to and had contact with Israel throughout its history (1:3–2:5). (1) *Damascus,* the capital of the Aramaean kingdom to the NE of Israel, was accused of ruthless warfare (1:3–5). It had "threshed Gilead with iron threshing sledges," perhaps a reference to King Hazael's conquest of Gilead (2 Kgs 10:32–33). (2) Yahweh indicted the *Philistines,* Israel's rival for possession of the land of Canaan, because of their exile of a people to Edom (1:6–8). This was possibly a reference to the practice of trading captured prisoners to Edom as slaves to be used in the copper mines located there. (3) *Tyre,* the ancient trading center along the Mediterranean, was convicted of the same practice as the Philistines, as well as for broken agreements (1:9–10). (4) *Edom,* which lay SE of Judah, was the target of the fourth oracle (1:11–12). With the exception of Judah, Edom was the most closely associated with Israel: the nation descended from Esau, Jacob's brother (Genesis 36). Edom had "pursued his brother [Israel] with a sword," a reference to the hostility between the two brothers that was symbolic of the animosity between the two nations throughout their existence. (5) *Ammon* was the next nation to be indicted by Yahweh (1:13–15). The nation, which lay E of the Jordan bordering the Israelite territory of Gilead, was accused of a brutal aggression against Israel, one that included "ripping open" pregnant women. (6) *Moab,* which lay E of the Dead Sea and whose S border joined Edom's N limits, was accused of desecrating the dead, defiling the bones of the king of Edom (2:1–3). (7) *Judah,* the sister kingdom of Israel, was convicted of "rejecting the law of

Yahweh" (2:4–5). Except for the latter oracle against Judah, all of the others refer to crimes against humans. This, and the use of Deuteronomic language (*tôrāh* and *šāmar*), has led some scholars to regard the oracle against Judah as a secondary addition, but its exclusion would destroy the formal structure of the whole, as we shall see.

The condemnation and judgment upon each nation began, "For three transgressions . . . and for four . . . ," a poetic technique that provided a formal structure to the whole (this technique of X, X + 1 was common in the wisdom literature of the ancient Near East; see Prov 6:16; 30:15; *Ahiqar* vi.92 [*ANET,* 428b]; *UT* 51.iii.17–18 [*ANET,* 132b]). Thus, there are seven indictments against seven nations, that is, the sum of three plus four. And certainly not lost on the audience was the fact that, when Israel conquered Canaan, it displaced seven nations whom Yahweh condemned and removed from the land because of their inhumanity to humans. Seven nations are now again subject to removal. Yet the climax comes with the addition of one more nation, *Israel* itself—the seventh plus one, the last, separate from the others. Israel, charged with social injustice, had proven to be no better than the Amorites, whom they displaced when they entered the land of Canaan (2:6–11). Just as Israel's seven neighbors were to be punished for various breaches of international law and morality—a sentence that Israel would have applauded—so Israel was to be punished for its lack of justice and compassion to fellow human beings.

When Amos finished his oracle on Judah, the seventh, the audience must have thought he was finished. How shocking it must have been to hear him continue, and to condemn them. "Amos [here was] original in asserting that social injustices and transgressions of the moral code in Israelite society (perhaps equated with 'the law') have the same moral status as transgressions of the much more 'self-evident' laws of international conduct and of the practice of war" (Barton 1980: 49). And, as we have noted, Amos was unique in turning the doctrine of election upside down with his belief that "Israel was not indemnified against punishment but was all the more accountable in view of her election" (Barton 1980: 49).

2. Chapters 3–6. This section contains oracles against Israel and predictions of its destruction, and the vast majority of scholars consider this section of the book to contain the actual words of Amos. This section begins with Amos' new interpretation of what election means to Israel: "You only have I known of all the families of the earth; therefore I will punish you for all your iniquities" (3:2). This sets the tone and provides the main theme for this section.

Amos then fortifies his position as a prophet, and his message as one that comes from Yahweh, with a series of rhetorical questions (3:3–8). Here Amos uses exaggeration to point out the obvious. The questions, all demanding a "No" answer, lead the audience to anticipate the confirmation of Amos as a prophet, who is speaking only because Yahweh has spoken to him.

After confirming his role as the messenger of God, Amos delivers a series of oracles against Samaria and Bethel. The arrangement is an A, B, A′, B′ pattern: first those who dwell in Samaria are condemned (3:9–12), then those at the sanctuary of Bethel (3:13–15), then the women of Samaria (4:1–3), and then those at the sanctuaries of Bethel and Gilgal (4:4–5). Amos addresses both the political and cultic centers in his denunciation of Israel's corrupt social practices.

As we noted above (C), 4:6–13 contains a parody of the salvation history of Israel. This parody is arranged in a 2 + 2 + 1 pattern (see Gese 1981), with a doxology (v 13) at the end. As we will see, this is the same pattern that appears with the visions (7:1–9; 8:1–3; 9:6) (see Gese 1981: 75–78). There are two pairs of visions, plus a fifth, with a doxology (9:5–6) at the end of the section.

Amos' references to Israel's past would have been familiar to all Israelites. Yet Amos reinterpreted their significance. Just as Yahweh plagued Egypt in order to exact the deliverance of His people, so Yahweh plagued His people Israel to exact their return to Him. Just as He destroyed Sodom and Gomorrah, so He destroyed part of Israel. These calamities were brought upon the nation by God to effect its repentance and return to righteousness. But each attempt at reconciliation ended in failure: " 'Yet you did not return to me,' says Yahweh." When they did not respond, Amos taunted, "Prepare to meet your God, O Israel!" (4:12). A meeting that Israel could only have imagined as a pleasant experience now becomes an occasion for the wrath of God to rain down upon those who are present.

Lest Israel think that Amos is happy about the destruction to come, a lamentation over the fallen house of Israel immediately follows (5:1–2). In the classic *qinah* meter of a lament, Amos communicates Yahweh's sorrow over the near complete devastation of Israel—only 10 percent of the population will survive.

The lament in 5:1–2 begins a lengthy section that utilizes a chiastic pattern (A, B, B′, A′) to organize the material. Scholars have argued until recently tht 5:1–17 contains fragments of various sayings given by Amos at different times. That now appears not to be the case. De Waard (1977) demonstrated that 5:1–17 was a palistrophe with the following sections: A—elegy (vv 1–3); B—"seek and live" (4–6); C—complaint (7); D—doxology (8–9); C′—complaint (10–13); B′—"seek good, not evil" (14–15); and A′—mourning (16–17). Lust (1981), expanding on De Waard's structure, considers the entire section from 4:1 to 6:7 to be a chiasm. Again, the doxology at 5:8–9 is the turning point for the structure.

A note about the doxologies is in order. There are three doxologies in the book of Amos (4:13; 5:8–9; and 9:5–6), each significantly placed as an integral part of its respective literary pattern. They underscore Yahweh's power throughout history, emphasizing the point that, if He chooses, He can do *against* Israel what He has previously done *for* Israel. Although most scholars consider the doxologies late editions to the book of Amos (see F below), the fact that they are inherent in the literary structures suggests either that they are original or that both they and the structure are late. The former seems preferable, and it is best to regard the structures and the sayings as original.

A series of woes appears from 5:18 to 6:14. Subjects include "the day of Yahweh" (5:18–20), the cult (5:21–27), the military security of the nation (6:1–3), the *marzēaḥ* feast (6:4–7), and the destruction to come (6:8–14). Amos' description of the *marzēaḥ* feast is particularly intriguing.

The feast, attested from the 14th century B.C.E. to Roman times, had either a religious or a funerary significance. It lasted for several days, during which time meat and wine were served to banqueters who were prostrate on couches. There was much eating, anointing with oil, and music (*nebel* is a lyre, not "harp" as RSV [see King 1988: 154]). Amos seems to address the practice of the feast both to show the injustice of such luxurious feasting while the poor are in such misery and to suggest that, if the feast is a funerary feast, then the participants should mourn for the poor and for the destruction that is soon to take place.

3. Chapters 7–9. This unit contains five visions which are broken by a biographical narrative (7:10–17, see A above) and a series of condemnations against Israel (8:4–14). Through these five visions Amos demonstrated the meaning of "prophet" as "seer." He saw events or objects, whether in visions or in everyday life, which he interpreted or which were interpreted for him with respect to the religious situation in Israel. The visions are grouped in pairs in which the imagery is different but the message and its meaning are the same. Within each pair the imagery intensifies, becoming more cataclysmic.

The first pair of visions was a locust plague destroying crops before they were harvested (7:1–3) and a cosmic fire that devoured both the land and the great deep (7:4–6). Although the visions were different, the message was the same: destruction had been decreed against Yahweh's people. When the prophet interceded with Yahweh on behalf of the threatened people, Yahweh agreed and spared the people, or at least postponed the punishment. In both visions, the Lord repented, saying, "It shall not be."

The second pair of visions likewise differed in content and imagery, but the message communicated by them was the same: Yahweh will no longer relent or forgive; the time for mercy is past, and destructive judgment is now certain. The prophet no longer intercedes. In the third vision, Amos saw Yahweh standing beside a wall, with a plumb line in His hand (7:7–9). Much as a mason or a carpenter plumbs a wall to determine if it is straight, so Yahweh plumbed His people, measuring them against His standard of justice and righteousness. Israel failed the test, and this time Yahweh would not spare them. God declared that the land would be made desolate, that Israel would be laid waste, and that He would "rise against the house of Jeroboam with the sword." The fourth vision contains a play on words. Amos saw a basket of summer fruit (*qayiṣ*), and Yahweh interpreted it for him as the end (*qēṣ*) of His people (8:1–3). As in the third vision, so here, Yahweh will not spare those who would make a mockery of His moral teachings. As one gathers in the summer fruit, so Yahweh will gather His people for destruction.

Sandwiched between the third and fourth visions is a narrative about the prophet and his dramatic confrontation with Amaziah, the high priest at the Bethel sanctuary (7:10–17). The words of Amos were unpopular with the religious and political leaders of Israel and posed a threat to Amaziah's authority and control over the cult. Whether Amos threatened Jeroboam—which would have been treason—or whether Amaziah distorted Amos' words for his own gain is difficult to determine and has been the subject of much scholarly debate, but the text shows that Amaziah went to King Jeroboam and reported that Amos had threatened the king's life (vv 10–11). With this report, Amaziah undoubtedly received royal permission to escort Amos across the border. Amaziah thus ordered Amos to go back to Judah, to prophesy in his own land, and never to prophesy at Bethel again (vv 12–13). Amos recounted his call from Yahweh to be a prophet to Israel and indicated that it was his duty to prophesy and preach against Israel (vv 14–16). He then gave Amaziah a personal message concerning his destiny: Amaziah was to be carried away to be executed in an alien country after witnessing his wife's prostitution and his family's death (v 17).

The reason that this narrative is sandwiched between the third and fourth visions is to explain why Yahweh's decision to destroy Israel is irreversible. The behavior of the high priest—in rejecting the message of Amos with its divine warning and in going further by effectively denying the prophet's right and necessity to speak—closes off the last chance Israel has to hear the truth and repent. Thus, Yahweh cannot rescue and spare Israel now that the opportunity for repentance is gone for good.

After an interlude of oracles, including one likening the "day of the Lord" to a solar eclipse (8:9–10), two of which Amos could have witnessed (784 and 763 B.C.E.), the fifth vision points beyond the destruction of the nation and the exile of the people to the obliteration of the leadership, the final act in the drama of judgment. Yahweh stood beside the altar of the temple and ordered its destruction and the elimination of all the people (9:1–6). Not only will Yahweh destroy the land and its inhabitants, but He will raze the sacred precinct where He was worshiped and kill all those who maintained His cult. No one will escape the wrath of Yahweh, no matter where they may hide. Yahweh, the God of hosts, the creator and sustainer of the world, will perform His judgment upon Israel.

The visions are followed by two oracles that close the book. The first (9:7–10) is a prophecy of terrible destruction on the nation Israel. The imagery is vivid: no one shall escape the evil destruction, not even those who think they can hide in foreign countries, for Yahweh will scoop up and shake the nations through His sieve, and not one Israelite shall fall through. All Israel shall be caught in the coming destruction.

This vivid oracle of destruction is followed by a vision of the last days when the land and its fruitfulness will be restored and renewed and a new age of reconciliation and restoration will begin. The vision describes the restoration of the Davidic kingdom, prosperity, and security (9:11–15). Scholarly consensus is that this last promise of renewal is a 6th-century exilic addition. Eighth-century prophetic oracles were often revised and reapplied to the similar 6th-century experience of Judah (e.g., Micah), and consequently 8th-century materials were often interlaced with those of the sixth. That appears to be the case here. First, v14b contradicts 5:11b. Second, there is a discordant tension between the severe oracle of destruction in the preceding verses (7–10) and the glorious hope of renewal here. Third, as we have noticed above, nowhere else in Amos is his judgment and condemnation of Israel mitigated. Fourth, the phrase "unsteady booth of David" most likely refers to the imminent destruction of Judah in 587/6 B.C.E., over a century and a half later than Amos. The phrase "restore the fortunes" is clearly later terminology (see Isa

63:9; Micah 7:14). Fifth, the "remnant of Edom" probably refers to those left after Edom's destruction by the Babylonians, also in the 6th century (Ezek 25:12–14). For these reasons, it seems likely that 9:11–15 is a late addition to Amos (see F below for a discussion of other late additions).

E. Literary and Rhetorical Features

The language is rich and the literary features abundant in the book of Amos. In addition to the literary structures (chiasm, alternation) pointed out in the previous section, Amos uses a number of other features to formulate his message. The use of divine appellatives, the alternation between first and third person, and between second and third person with reference to addressees, and the creation of sound patterns all aid in knitting together the larger structure of 4:1–6:7 (Tromp 1984). Amos is fond of progressive numerical formulas, using them to structure at least three sections of the book: the X+1 pattern of 1:3–2:14 and the 2+2+1 quinary patterns of 4:6–13 and chaps. 7–9.

Amos employs a variety of types of literature. The messenger formula typical of diplomatic correspondence in the ancient Near East (2 Kgs 19:10–19) is used abundantly by prophets, including Amos. The introductory formula "thus Yahweh has said/says" and its variations ("Yahweh has sworn," "an oracle of Yahweh") is used approximately twenty times throughout the book. Amos presents visions, as we have noticed, testimony ("Hear this word," 3:1; 4:1; 5:1), woes ("Woe to," 5:18; 6:1; 6:4), proverbs (3:3–6), wisdom (5:13), laments (in 3/2 *qinah* meter, 5:1–2), and doxologies (4:13; 5:8–9; 9:5–6). Judgments in the form of reproaches and oracles of doom of course appear throughout the book.

Amos' use of rhetorical features include exaggeration (2:6–8; 3:9–11; 4:1–3; 5:21; 6:12–13), word play (5:5b; 8:1–2), antithesis (2:13; 5:4–5, 24), verbless sentences (5:18; 6:1–3, 6, 8, 14), taunts (4:4–5), riddles (6:12), comparisons (2:9; 5:2, 7, 19), and metaphors (1:3; 2:13; 3:12; 9:9).

F. Text and Canon

The book of Amos for the most part contains the words of Amos, the 8th-century prophet. There are, however, sections that everyone agrees are not written by Amos: the superscription (1:1) and the biographical account of the prophet's confrontation with Amaziah (7:10–17). It is generally assumed that the disciples of Amos supplied these sections when they preserved Amos' words in writing, either during or shortly after his ministry. His disciples also may have organized Amos' oracles into the present patterns that we have. For instance, the oracles to the foreign nations in 1:3–2:5 may have been separate oracles that were brought together by those who followed Amos.

The general consensus is that the social matters are the true words of Amos. Although Koch and others (1976; 1982/3) argue that the doxologies (4:13; 5:8–9; 9:5–6) are late, de Waard (1977) and Tromp (1984) have shown that they are an integral part of the structure present in their respective sections (see the discussion in D above). To consider them late, then, is to consider the structuring of these sections a late editorial function. Since the doxologies reaffirm the power of Yahweh to act as the prophet has said he would and do not go against the grain of any sections that are considered original with Amos, it seems best to attribute the doxologies to Amos and/or his disciples.

Lust (1981) has suggested that 5:4–6 and 5:14–15 are part of the Deuteronomic redaction since they mimic Deut 12:5 and 30:15, respectively. But which work influenced the other? It is possible that the "seek X, not Y" phrase and its variations such as "seek X and live" were common examples of the rhetoric of the monarchy. Amos could easily have been the first to record them. Amos 1:2 is sometimes rejected as late on the basis of its similarity with Joel 3:16 and Jer 25:30–31, but again, Joel and Jeremiah could have been copying Amos.

Some scholars also reject the originality of the oracles against the nations of Tyre (1:9–10), Edom (1:11–12), and Judah (2:4–5; see D above). It has been argued that the oracle against Tyre should be dated post-604 B.C.E. to the time of Nebuchadnezzar II (cf. Ezek 26:1–28:19). Ezekiel's proclamation against Edom (25:12–14) has led some to regard Amos' oracle against that nation as similarly emanating from the exilic period. As we have noted, the Deuteronomic language in the oracle against Judah suggests a 7th- or 6th-century date (see Barton 1980: 24). Yet all of the smaller nations of Syria-Palestine were alternately strong independent states and then vassal provinces numerous times from the 8th century until the conquest of the Near East by Cyrus the Persian. There were ample occasions to condemn each of the above, and the prophecies of Ezekiel almost two centuries later should not deter us from assuming that the prophets of Yahweh also had problems with these nations in the 8th century. Furthermore, an elimination of these oracles from the set destroys the entire structure of chaps. 1–2 and eliminates the movement toward the ultimate climax of the series, the oracle against Israel. As noted above, there can be little doubt that 9:11–15 is a later addition to the book.

Scholars disagree on what other sections can be attributed to Amos or his disciples and on the development of the text of the book. Hammershaimb (1970), for instance, considers the entire book to be the genuine sayings of Amos that were put together by his disciples. Gordis (1971) and, more recently, Limburg (1987) assume that the book is substantially the unified work of Amos. Hayes (1988) believes that the book is the result of later redactors pulling together short snippets of the genuine speeches of Amos. Mays (*Amos* OTL) considers 1:3–6:14 to be from Amos, with the rest the result of redactions that reached down into the exilic period. Rudolf (*Joel, Amos, Obadjah, Jona* KAT) reduces the material original to Amos to 1:3–2:16. He assumes that Amos' disciples developed the rest of the book, except for 9:11–15, which Rudolf argues is late.

Wolff (*Joel and Amos* Hermeneia) believes that chaps. 3–6 are from Amos and that the rest has been developed in six layers: (1) chaps. 1 and 2 and (2) the five-part series of oracles and visions from Amos himself (cf. Gese 1981); (3) the Amos school (disciples); (4) the Bethel interpretation during the period of the Josianic reform (3:14b; 5:5b; 9:1–4); (5) the Deuteronomic redaction; and (6) the postexilic salvation eschatology. Coote (1981), adapting Wolff's work, assigns the book to a three-stage process of growth: (1) "the words of Amos"; (2) "Justice and the Scribe," the message reactualized in the 7th century; and (3) "Exile and Beyond." More than likely there were three stages in the development of the book of Amos: (1) the original words of Amos, including the sayings (1:3–6:14; 8:4–14; 9:7–10) and the first-person narratives ("visions," 7:1–9; 8:1–3; 9:1–6); (2) the work of the disciples, including the superscription (1:1) and the third-person narrative (7:10–17); and (3) a later editing that appended the oracle of hope to the end of the book (9:11–15).

The book of Amos, in its present form except for 9:11–15, was undoubtedly part of the first edition of the Hebrew Bible. That edition, compiled between 560 and 540 B.C.E. by the Jewish community in exile, included the Primary History (Genesis–2 Kings) and the prophetic corpus associated with that history (1 Isaiah, Jeremiah, Ezekiel, and the first 9 books of the minor prophets). The last date recorded in this material is 561 B.C.E., the 37th year of the exile of Jehoiachin and the 1st year of the reign of Awil-Marduk, king of Babylon. This may refer to the actual date and place of publication. Amos 9:11–15 was probably added to the book after Jewish hopes were aroused by the decree of Cyrus in 538 B.C.E. By the dedication of the second temple in 515 B.C.E., the book of Amos was in its present form.

As far as the text is concerned, "in the main the ancient versions of Amos attest the same text of the book as the familiar Hebrew" (Auld 1986: 57). The LXX lacks "the oracle of Yahweh, God of Hosts" in 6:8 and 6:14, and some Gk versions lack 3:10, but otherwise the LXX and the other versions represent a text similar to the MT; there are no important variations. Furthermore, the MT is in good condition. The text is difficult in places (2:7; 3:12; 5:6, 26; 7:2; and 8:1) where some scholars recommend emending the MT, but in general problems with interpretation of the text arise from our lack of understanding, not the corruption of the text itself.

Bibliography

For a comprehensive, annotated bibliography on Amos, see van der Wal 1986. This article was completed before Andersen and Freedman 1989 was available.

Ackroyd, P. R. 1977. A Judgment Narrative between Kings and Chronicles? An Approach to Amos 7:9–17. Pp. 71–87 in *Canon and Authority*, ed. G. W. Coats and B. O. Long. Philadelphia.

Andersen, F. I., and Freedman, D. N. 1989. *Amos*. AB Garden City, NY.

Auld, A. G. 1986. *Amos*. OT Guides. Sheffield.

Barstad, H. M. 1984. *The Religious Polemics of Amos*. VTSup 34. Leiden.

Barton, J. 1980. *Amos's Oracles against the Nations: A Study of Amos 1:3–2:5*. SOTSMS 6. Cambridge.

Berridge, J. M. 1976. Die Intention der Botschaft des Amos, exegetische Überlegungen zu Amos. 5. *TZ* 32: 321–40.

Cazelles, H. 1977. L'Arrière-Plan Historique d'Amos 1, 9–10. Pp. 71–76 in *Proceedings of the Sixth World Congress of Jewish Studies*. Vol. 1. Jerusalem.

Coote, R. B. 1981. *Amos among the Prophets*. Philadelphia.

Eichrodt, W. 1977. Die Vollmacht des Amos. Pp. 124–31 in *Beiträge zur alttestamentlichen Theologie: Festschrift für Walther Zimmerli zum 70 Geburtstag*, ed. H. Donner; R. Hanhart; and R. Smend. Göttingen.

Gese, H. 1979. Das Problem von Amos 9,7. Pp. 33–38 in *Textgemäss: Festschrift E. Würthwein*, ed. A. H. J. Gunneweg and O. Kaiser. Göttingen.

———. 1981. Komposition bei Amos. Pp. 74–95 in *Congress Volume*, VTSup 32. Leiden.

Ginzberg, L. 1937–66. *The Legends of the Jews*. 7 vols. Trans. H. Szold. Philadelphia.

Gitay, Y. 1980. A Study of Amos's Art of Speech: A Rhetorical Analysis of Amos 3:1–15. *CBQ* 42: 293–309.

Gordis, R. 1971. The Composition and Structure of Amos. Pp. 217–29 in *Poets, Prophets and Sages: Essays in Biblical Interpretation*, ed. R. Gordis. Bloomington and London.

Hammershaimb, E. 1970. *The Book of Amos*. Oxford.

Hayes, J. H. 1988. *Amos: His Times and His Preaching*. Nashville.

Howard, G. 1970. Some Notes on the Septuagint of Amos. VT 20: 108–12.

———. 1982. Revisions toward the Hebrew in the Septuagint Text of Amos. *EI* 16: 125*–33*.

Huffmon, H. B. 1983. The Social Role of Amos' Message. Pp. 109–16 in *The Quest for the Kingdom of God: Studies in Honor of George E. Mendenhall*, ed. H. B. Huffmon, F. A. Spina, and A. R. W. Green. Winona Lake, IN.

King, P. J. 1988. *Amos, Hosea, Micah—An Archaeological Commentary*. Philadelphia.

Knierim, R. P. 1977. "I will not cause it to return" in Amos 1 and 2. Pp. 163–75 in *Canon and Authority*, ed. G. W. Coats and B. O. Long. Philadelphia.

Koch, K. 1982/3. *The Prophets*. 2 vols. London.

Koch, K. et al. 1976. *Amos: Untersucht mit den Methoden einer strukturalen Formgeschichte*. 3 vols. *AOAT* 30. Neukirchen-Vluyn.

Limburg, J. 1987. Sevenfold Structures in the Book of Amos. *JBL* 106: 217–22.

Lindström, F. 1983. *God and the Origin of Evil*. ConBOT 21. Lund.

Lust, J. 1981. Remarks on the Redaction of Amos V, 4–6, 14–15. *OTS* 21: 129–54.

Martin-Achard, R. 1984. *God's People in Crisis*. International Theological Commentary. Grand Rapids.

Morgenstern, J. 1936–61. Amos Studies I, II, III, IV. *HUCA* 11: 19–140; 12–13: 1–53; 15: 59–304; 32: 295–350.

Mulder, M. J. 1984. Ein Vorschlag zur Übersetzung von Amos III 6b. VT 34:106–8.

Polley, M. 1989. *Amos and the Davidic Empire*. Oxford.

Segert, S. 1984. A Controlling Device for Copying Stereotype Passages? (Amos i 3–ii 8, vi 1–6). VT 34: 481–82.

Smalley, W. A. 1979. Recursion Patterns and the Sectioning of Amos. *BTrans* 30: 118–27.

Soggin, J. A. 1987. *The Prophet Amos*. Trans. John Bowden. London.

Story, C. I. K. 1980. Amos—Prophet of Praise. VT 30: 67–80.

Tromp, N. J. 1984. Amos V 1–17: Towards a Stylistic and Rhetorical Analysis. *OTS* 23: 65–85.

Waard, J. de. 1977. The Chiastic Structure of Amos V, 1–17. VT 27: 170–77.

———. 1978. Translation Techniques used by the Greek Translators of Amos. *Bib* 59: 339–50.

Wal, A. van der. 1983. The Structure of Amos. *JSOT* 26: 107–13.

———. 1986. *Amos: A Classified Bibliography*. 3d ed. Amsterdam.

Wal, A. van der, and Talstra, E. 1984. *Amos*. Amsterdam.

Weippert, H. 1985. Amos. Pp. 1–29 in *Beiträge zur prophetischen Bildsprache*, ed. H. Weippert et al. OBO 64. Freiburg.

Wolff, H. W. 1973. *Amos the Prophet*. Philadelphia.

Woude, A. S. van der. 1982. Three Classical Prophets: Amos, Hosea and Micah. Pp. 32–57 in *Israel's Prophetic Tradition,* ed. R. Coggins; A. Phillips; and M. Knibb. Cambridge.

Zevit, Z. 1975. A Misunderstanding at Bethel, Amos 7:12–17. VT 25: 783–90.

Zobel, H. J. 1985. Prophet in Israel und in Judah. Das prophetische Verständnis des Hosea und Amos. *ZTK* 82: 281–99.

BRUCE E. WILLOUGHBY

AMOZ (PERSON) [Heb *ʾāmôṣ*]. The father of the prophet Isaiah (Isa 1:1). Other than his name, the Hebrew Bible gives us no information about Amoz. Furthermore, this name is the only direct information we have about Isaiah's origins. See ISAIAH. The name occurs thirteen times in the Hebrew Bible and is always part of the phrase "Isaiah the son of Amoz" (Isa 1:1; 2:1; 13:1; 20:2; 37:2, 21 [=2 Kgs 19:2, 20; cf. 2 Chr 32:20]; 38:1 [=2 Kgs 20:1]; 2 Chr 26:22; 32:32). According to Jewish tradition, Amoz was the brother of King Amaziah, the father of King Uzziah (*Meg.* 10b; *Soṭa* 10b). Hence, Isaiah would have been in the line of David. While there are a number of other indications that Isaiah possessed a close connection to the court, it is impossible to confirm this late tradition. The name Amoz is the short form of the name Amaziah, Heb *ʾămaṣyāhû* ("YHWH is strong"). This type of name is at home in the world of cult poetry in which one recognizes that YHWH is the source of strength for his adherents. In addition to Amaziah, the names of the other Judean kings of the 8th century B.C.E. are formed in a similar manner: Uzziah ("YHWH is my strength"), Jotham ("YHWH is upright"), Ahaz (short form of Joahaz="YHWH has seized"), Hezekiah ("YHWH is my strength") (Wildberger *Isaiah 1–12* BKAT, 5; *IPN,* 190). The name *ʾāmôṣ* also appears on a seal of unknown provenance. Although Anderson (1960: 57–58) has argued that this seal belonged to a professional scribe who was none other than the father of Isaiah, it is highly unlikely that this seal ever belonged to the biblical Amoz (Kaiser *Isaiah 1–12* OTL, 2; Wildberger *Isaiah 1–12* BKAT, 5).

Bibliography

Anderson, R. T. 1960. Was Isaiah a Scribe? *JBL* 79: 57–58.

JOHN H. HULL, JR.

AMPHICTYONY. That premonarchic Israel had a structure analogous to that of the classical amphictyony is a theory which enjoyed wide acceptance over half a century. The success of the theory resulted from its explanatory power: it not only provided a credible and illuminating account of an early obscure period, but it also supplied a context within which to locate the formative stages of the Pentateuch and the origins of distinctively Israelite institutions and traditions which could not be explained within the frame of reference of Israel as a monarchic state. Recent criticism of the theory, while not necessarily leading to its absolute rejection, has at least made such comprehensive use of the analogy inappropriate.

A. The Classical Amphictyony

"Amphictyony," probably originally the proper name of a tribe rather than a compound expression meaning "to dwell around," was the term applied by Demosthenes in the 4th century B.C.E. to a sacred league which, from the beginning of the 6th century B.C.E., had its center at the shrine of Apollo at Delphi. It is to this league that the term originally belongs, and only by analogy is it later applied to other leagues. Thus, Strabo (9.2.33) refers to the amphictyony at Onchestos, and also (8.6.14) to the 7-member amphictyony at Calauria, both centered on sanctuaries of Poseidon. The Delphi league, the institution about which most information exists (though deriving from a relatively late date in its history) and the league to which the term "amphictyony" properly applied, is, therefore, the model against which the appropriateness of any analogous use of the term is to be tested.

The Delphi amphictyony was a sacred league of 12 peoples; their number remained constant, though political events sometimes led to changes in the identity of the members. It was originally based on the sanctuary of Demeter at Thermopylae, but later came to take the sanctuary of Apollo at Delphi also under its protection. The chief functions of the league related to the sanctuary, which the amphictyonic members undertook to maintain and defend. This task was organized by the *hieromnemones,* the chosen delegates of the amphictyonic members (perhaps together with the *pylagoroi,* apparently either the original delegates of the league when it was based on Pylae, or delegates charged with particular functions). The *hieromnemones* met regularly in assembly at the sanctuary for festivals, to administer the finances of the amphictyony, and to keep the sanctuary and its access roads in good repair. Although the cultic focus is essential—a characteristic reflected also in the manifest lack of political unity among the members, between whom internecine warfare was not unknown—the purpose of the amphictyony was not wholly cultic. The members undertook not to destroy any of the towns of the league and not to cut off their water supplies, within the framework of attempting to preserve a state of political equilibrium between the members. Thus, it was not simply for the purpose of maintaining a sanctuary that the amphictyony came into existence, but rather in order to give cultic expression to an agreed state of mutual relations which had already been achieved.

B. The Theory of an Israelite Amphictyony

Amphictyonic structures have been proposed for the Philistines (by Rahtjen) and the Sumerians (by Hallo), but it is with reference to Israel that the analogy has been most extensively developed outside the classical world. The term "amphictyony" had already been long introduced into the

Israelite context (by, for example, Alt 1929: 438–39; see further Bächli 1977: 17–20) when Noth published his highly influential study *Das System der zwölf Stämme Israels* in 1930. Here the analogy was convincingly expounded in full detail. Further studies by Noth of the pentateuchal laws, the history of the pentateuchal traditions, and the "judge of Israel," culminating in his *The History of Israel,* elaborated his primary study and developed its consequences for associated areas of OT study. Through the use of this analogy, Noth was able to give institutional form to a premonarchic Israel which he, under the strong influence of Weber, conceived of as a religious entity, the covenant people of Yahweh.

Noth (1930: 3–39) based his study on the OT tribal lists. These lists describe Israel, in common with other non-Israelite peoples, as a community of twelve tribes, descended from the twelve sons of Jacob. The lists may be, as in Genesis 29–30, of the sons of Jacob, or, as in Numbers 26, of the tribes of Israel; but the number twelve is consistently maintained. Even when there is variation in the constituent elements of the lists the total number remains fixed. The main discrepancy between the lists and the one which divides them into two basic categories is that some lists include the tribe of Levi while others do not: Genesis 49 is taken as the basic form of the former group, and Numbers 26 of the latter. The sons of Jacob appear in Genesis 49 in the following order: Reuben, Simeon, Levi, Judah, Zebulun, Issachar, Dan, Gad, Asher, Naphtali, Joseph, and Benjamin. The birth story of Genesis 29–30 shows that the first six are sons of Jacob by his wife Leah, the next four by the handmaids Bilhah and Zilpah, and the last two by his second wife Rachel. The tribes of Israel are listed in Numbers 26 in the following order: Reuben, Simeon, Gad, Judah, Issachar, Zebulun, Manasseh, Ephraim, Benjamin, Dan, Asher, and Naphtali.

The chief variation between these lists, the presence or absence of Levi, is important in that it allows a chronological ordering of the lists, for the type which includes Levi is probably older than that which does not. The reason is that it is easier to explain how Levi should have been secondarily omitted from the list than to explain its secondary inclusion. Levi's inclusion in Genesis 49 among the other brothers presupposes that, as in Genesis 34, it is a "secular" tribe. Otherwise, however, and historically, Levi is known only as a priestly tribe separate from its fellow tribes and having no land possession; it is this later status of Levi which is reflected in its omission from the list of Numbers 26. Both lists, in terms of their absolute date, must reflect conditions of the premonarchic period. The later of them, Numbers 26, supports this conclusion since it assigns to the tribes families which may be identified as city-states of the mountain territories of Palestine (Shechem, Tirzah, and Hepher), but none which may be identified as city-states of the plains. These presupposed conditions would antedate Israelite expansion into the plains, especially in the time of David.

Other variations between the lists, following on the omission of Levi, include the substitution of Manasseh and Ephraim for the single Joseph, and the transfer of the tribe of Gad from a position near the end of the Genesis 49 list to a new position among the Leah group of tribes formerly occupied by Levi. Both changes are significant, the one reflecting a concern to maintain the total of twelve, and the other intending to preserve a total of six for those tribes reckoned as descended from the sons of Leah. It is this concern for consistency which suggests that there is a historical reality behind the lists in the actual life and constitution of Israel in the period of the judges from which these lists derive.

It is at this point that Noth (1930: 39–60) introduced the analogy of the classical amphictyony through which the reality of premonarchic Israelite life might be clarified. The number twelve of the tribes of Israel is an institutional necessity to be understood within the framework of a tribal federation analogous to the later Greek amphictyony at Delphi. In both cases the number is related to the months of the year and the need to maintain the central sanctuary on a rota basis. As in Greece, so in Israel, that number remained constant while the constituent elements of the total were open to variation. In the Israelite context the concern for the number six of the Leah group of tribes should be given a similar explanation. This group represents an older amphictyonic organization of six tribes, only secondarily extended to twelve (Noth 1930: 75–80). Historically, this presupposes that the Leah tribes were the older inhabitants of the land; their organization was extended to a membership of twelve through the inclusion of the handmaid tribes (Dan, Gad, Asher, Naphtali) on the occasion of the entry into the land of the Rachel tribes (Joseph and Benjamin) under the leadership of Joshua. This older six-tribe Leah amphictyony was superseded by the twelve-tribe amphictyony, but alongside the latter there coexisted a six-tribe amphictyony comprising the southern tribes living on the mountains of Judah: Judah, Caleb, Othniel, Cain, Jerahmeel, and Simeon. Thus, Judah and Simeon effectively belonged to two amphictyonies: the larger one was centered on Shechem, to which Joshua summoned the tribes at the conclusion of the entry of the Rachel tribes (Joshua 24), and the smaller one was centered on Hebron and formed the base of David's later elevation to kingship. These were the cult centers which the tribes undertook to maintain; it was here that they, in their representatives, the *nĕśîʾîm* (a list of whom appears in Num 1:5–15), met to conduct the business of the amphictyony and to participate in the common worship of their amphictyonic God, Yahweh. Shechem, the first center of the twelve-tribe amphictyony, was where the ark was kept; following the movements of the ark, it may then be conjectured that the amphictyonic central sanctuary was subsequently to be found at Bethel, Gilgal, and, finally, Shiloh (*NHI,* 94–95). Through its common cult the amphictyony expressed its essential character as a sacral union. Joshua 24, which records the foundation of the twelve-tribe amphictyony, also reflects the form by which these tribes worshiped Yahweh: it was a covenant form, in which the tribes regularly affirmed their acceptance of the conditions of the covenant proclaimed to them as the law of Yahweh. The amphictyony was, therefore, the institution through which the people of Yahweh came into existence.

Noth's reconstruction was highly influential for a number of reasons. As Sasson (1981: 8–9) has noted, it reflected contemporary German historiographic interest, rooted in recent German history, in the rise of the nation-state, and thus integrated Israel's early history directly and meaningfully into more general historical experience. Moreover, it supplied a framework of historical explanation which was credible for Israelite traditions and institutions of the premonarchic period and beyond. Thus, in general terms, it provided a theory of the nature of an Israel distinct from the monarchic state and presupposed by the monarchic state and also indeed by pentateuchal tradition in general: the monarchy was an institution founded on an already existing Israel; the pentateuchal tradition has its focus on an Israel of the type of the amphictyony rather than the monarchy. It is to such an Israel that the laws of the Pentateuch are addressed, rather than to a monarchic state (Noth 1966: 20–36), and it is within such an Israel that the "minor judges" (Judg 10:1–5; 12:7–15) should be understood to have functioned (Noth 1950: 404–17). The war between the tribe of Benjamin and the rest of the tribes of Israel (Judges 19–21) was an amphictyonic war with a direct parallel in the Greek context (Noth 1930: 100–6). The traditions behind Deuteronomy and the covenant faith which was found to be reflected in both psalms and prophets could all be seen as rooted in amphictyonic Israel of the premonarchic period (Nicholson 1967: 37–57). Thus, the explanatory power of the amphictyony model together with its conformity to contemporary historiographic interests and values ensured the more or less general acceptance of the theory in OT scholarship.

C. Reception of the Theory

The theory of an Israelite amphictyony received its definitive formulation in the work of Noth; it is, therefore, to Noth's presentation that criticism has, especially in the last two decades, been directed. The historical and geographical distance which separates premonarchic Israel from the classical amphictyony, together with the lack of any Hebrew term which might be a possible counterpart to the Greek "amphictyony," have been considered by, for example, Fohrer (1966: 801–16) general points of weakness in the analogy (though, it should be emphasized, issues such as influence or dependence of one culture on another do not arise in the context of an analogy); but it is in three major areas that the appropriateness of the analogy has been substantively questioned.

1. The Tribal Lists. Noth's fundamental dependence on the OT tribal lists is problematic for at least two reasons. In the first place, the essential characteristic of the amphictyony was its central sanctuary; but the primary evidence for the presence of an analogous institution in Israel is the consistency of the number twelve of the Israelite tribes. In the classical context, however, associations with varying numbers of members could be termed amphictyonies, the number of members being a secondary or even irrelevant matter. Even when the number twelve is found in the Greek context it is doubtful that it is to be related to the amphictyonic duties of the members. These duties were probably not discharged by the members on a regular monthly rota, but rather by the council of the amphictyonic representatives gathered at the central sanctuary. The number twelve, as De Vaux (EHI: 702–3; see also Mayes 1974: 117 n.57) has recognized, expresses totality (as in 1 Kgs 7:44; 10:20; 19:19) and need not be related to practical concerns. Its presence or absence in any context is, therefore, generally irrelevant to the issue of the existence of an amphictyonic institution.

Secondly, Noth's treatment of the relationship and dating of the tribal lists is generally questionable. The argument that there is a chronological relationship between them begs the question of their purpose, for it is apparent that the very different types of list which are being compared (genealogical, tribal, territorial) need have no direct relationship: thus, Genesis 49 could be older or later than Numbers 26. That any of them belong to the premonarchic period is also doubtful. The order of tribes which Numbers 26 offers can be adequately explained only in the late context of the priestly writing (Hoftijzer 1959: 241–63; Mayes 1974: 16–34), which, in a series of lists (Num 1:20–43; 2:3–31; 26), is describing the layout of the Israelite camp in four companies, each company consisting of three tribes: the effect of the priestly ordering is that Judah, the favored tribe, is the leading tribe of its company encamped on the eastward side. The priestly background of this list effectively removes it from consideration for an institutional structure of Israel in the premonarchic period. The list of the type of Genesis 49 is no more closely related to that time. That the entity Joseph, which appears there, is the original entity which later split into Ephraim and Manasseh (and Ephraim appears in the early Judges 5), is in fact unlikely. The earliest and original use appears to have been "House of Joseph" and this expression came into existence in the monarchic period as a collective designation for a northern group, parallel to the designation "House of Judah." "Joseph" is, in other words, a secondary formation which presupposes the existence of Ephraim and Manasseh and also the stabilization of very complex tribal movements and relationships which were still in progress throughout the whole of the premonarchic period and beyond. In the case of neither Numbers 26 nor Genesis 49 can a premonarchic background credibly be claimed, and thus the view that these lists are to be explained within the framework of an Israelite amphictyony must come under serious question.

2. The Central Sanctuary. The amphictyonic central sanctuary was, by definition, integral to that organization. In the Israelite context, however, the information on such a sanctuary is sparse, and this aspect of the theory in fact played a secondary role in Noth's presentation. It was only on the basis of having already, through consideration of the tribal lists, established the existence of an Israelite amphictyony, that Noth then addressed the question of its central sanctuary. Here, in a concrete expression of their common allegiance to Yahweh, the tribes of Israel were supposed regularly to have celebrated a covenant festival. The focal point of the Israelite amphictyony was its sacred ark, and, as reflected in its movements through the period of the judges, the central sanctuary was established first of all at Shechem, and then subsequently at Bethel, Gilgal, and Shiloh, the last-mentioned being the sanctuary of the ark at the end of the premonarchic period.

The criteria proposed to determine whether or not a particular sanctuary was an amphictyonic central sanctuary are largely circumstantial. This in itself is not a decisive weakness, but it must be of some significance that the laws of the OT, and in particular the book of the covenant (Exod 20:23–23:33), which has been identified as amphictyonic law, make no reference to obligations laid on the Israelite tribes to maintain and protect a central sanctuary (and in fact the Book of the Covenant surely envisages a number of local sanctuaries); nor does this law identify the Israelite *nĕśîʾîm* as tribal representatives gathered at such a sanctuary (Exod 22:27—Eng 28). In the absence of such direct evidence two specific criteria (the presence of the ark and the celebration of the covenant festival), together with one general criterion (acknowledgment as supreme by all the tribes of Israel), are taken to determine the existence of a central sanctuary (Irwin 1965: 161–84).

It must be said, however, that even granted the sufficiency of these criteria they provide no certain evidence of the central status of any premonarchic Israelite sanctuary (Mayes 1974: 34–55). The celebration of a covenant festival at any sanctuary in pre-Deuteronomic times is increasingly a matter of doubt; the ark was certainly to be found at Gilgal and Shiloh (and perhaps also at Bethel, Judg 20:27), though its connection with Shechem (Josh 8:30–35) is attested only in what is certainly a Deuteronomistic passage. These may not, however, be considered particularly pressing issues, derived as they are from OT rather than classical contexts. Yet on the question of the general acknowledgment of a sanctuary as central by all the members of amphictyonic Israel, the result is no clearer. The summoning of all the tribes to Shechem (Joshua 24) is related only in a post-Deuteronomistic story of highly dubious historical value (Mayes 1983: 49–51). Gilgal and Shiloh were sanctuaries of clearly quite distinct Yahwistic traditions, the first of which formed the eventual background for Saul's kingship while the second provided the theological basis for David's kingship. These cannot be treated in any respect as central sanctuaries of a unified Israelite cult. The evidence relating to Bethel is also unclear: the story of the rape and murder of the Levite's concubine in Judges 19–21, which Noth treated as an authentic amphictyonic tradition, forms the context for the statement that "the people of Israel arose and went up to Bethel, and enquired of God" (Judg 20:18), but Shiloh is also mentioned here as the sanctuary of a yearly feast of Yahweh (21:16–21), while in the same story (20:1) it is at Mizpah that "the congregation assembled as one man to the Lord." Although it is certainly conceivable that secondary expansion of the story has overlaid an original reference to just one sanctuary, it is also more than probable that any critical procedure undertaken to recover that older story will also remove its "all-Israel" (and so its "amphictyonic") frame of reference. It appears, therefore, that with regard to this, the fundamental aspect of the amphictyonic organization, there is no unequivocal support for an analogous structure in premonarchic Israel.

3. The Function of the Amphictyony. It is possible that the classical amphictyony could still be claimed as an analogy of some heuristic value for premonarchic Israel even in the face of the weaknesses already noted. This would require, however, a form of theory rather different than that originally proposed by Noth and elaborated by himself and others later. As Gottwald (1979: 376–86) has noted, in the classical context the amphictyony was a cultic organization; it did not provide the framework within which a social and political entity was founded, but rather presupposed those historical, social, and political developments which led to the existence of a people; it was by a people, already united in military and other leagues, that an amphictyonic structure was adopted for the purpose of maintaining the balance of political and social power which had already been achieved.

Within the Israelite context, however, the amphictyony has been made to serve a much more comprehensive function. It is here not only a cultic organization, but also social, political, ethnic, and perhaps also military. Even if (with Smend 1970) the practice of holy war is to be seen as an activity of a military league quite independent of the amphictyonic institution, the latter still has a range of functions which sets it apart from the classical organization. It is within the amphictyony that Israelite political, social, and ethnic consciousness is held to have been formed. Not only did her tribal representatives meet at the central sanctuary, but here also her judges functioned, while it was within that framework that there gradually evolved the normative account of Israelite ethnic origins which eventually found its deposit in the Pentateuch. Moreover, this Israelite amphictyony is held to have been so integral to Israelite identity that it survived the introduction of the monarchy and lived on alongside the monarchic institution as that essential Israel addressed by prophecy and law. The analogy cannot possibly bear the weight of theory with which it is here elaborated.

It is clear that Noth was by no means unaware of this problem, for he himself pointed to the artificial and schematic character of the tribal lists as well as the inconsistency between the particular tribes which they include on the one hand, and the historical role (or lack of it) of these same tribes, on the other. He argued (1930: 40–41), however, that this artificiality did not in itself invalidate the historical reality of the institution, for the latter is an administrative organization created from already existing raw material: just as Solomon, for the maintenance of his royal court, established twelve districts in his kingdom, districts which did not reflect any natural divisions of Israelite tribal territories, so also the amphictyony was an artificial but nevertheless historical institution erected on given social and political realities. The implication of this argument was, as Noth (1930: 55–56) acknowledged, that it was not in fact through the amphictyony that the tribes of Israel first came together. Rather, through the accidents of history, such as common invasion of a new land and common opposition to outside forces, the unity of Israel was first established, a unity which the amphictyony was then designed to preserve. In the elaboration of the theory of an Israelite amphictyony, this significant aspect of its background and context has been generally overlooked.

D. Alternative Models for Premonarchic Israel

In recent study of the premonarchic period attention has shifted away from the issue of an Israelite amphictyony both toward other possible analogies for understanding the totality "Israel" and toward the study of the basic social units of which any possible Israelite federation was composed. In the latter context the significance of the family and clan, over against the tribe, as the basic social and economic units has been stressed, especially by Gottwald (1979: 239–92); and as a framework within which they may have been comprehended, the possibility of using the segmentary lineage system, known among African tribes, has been explored, by Crüsemann (1978: 201–8) and Frick (1985: 51–69). Either as an alternative or as a supplement to the analogy of the segmentary society, Israel has also been described as an association of chiefdoms (Flanagan 1981: 47–73; Frick 1985: 71–97; Rogerson 1986: 17–26), the chiefdom analogy being particularly appropriate for the rule of Saul, though perhaps also suitable for the earlier premonarchic period.

None of these more recent developments is in fact incompatible with the theory of an amphictyony in premonarchic Israel, at least insofar as the functions of the latter are restricted to what is suggested by the classical model. Thus, while it must be admitted that, for the present, the evidence in favor of such an organization in Israel is not convincing, the possibility is still open that, within an Israel organized as a segmentary society or an association of chiefdoms, amphictyonic relationships existed between larger or smaller groups of tribes or other social units already united on other grounds. It might be through such relationships that the complex and still uncertain history of the development of Yahwism within Israel will be better understood; but it is unlikely that the analogy will become reestablished as a form by which the nature of the totality of Israel, at any period, is to be expressed. See also Noth, *HPT.*

Bibliography

Alt, A. 1929. Israel, politische Geschichte. Cols. 437–42 in *RGG* 3. Tübingen.

Anderson, G. W. 1970. Israel: Amphictyony; ᶜAM; ḲĀHĀL; ᶜĒḎÂH. Pp. 135–51 in *Translating and Understanding the Old Testament,* ed. H. T. Frank and W. L. Reed. Nashville.

Bächli, O. 1977. *Amphiktyonie im Alten Testament.* Basel.

Chambers, H. E. 1983. Ancient Amphictyonies, sic et non. Pp. 39–59 in *Scripture in Context II,* ed. W. W. Hallo; J. C. Moyer; and L. G. Perdue. Winona Lake, IN.

Crüsemann, F. 1978. *Der Widerstand gegen das Königtum.* WMANT 49. Neukirchen-Vluyn.

Flanagan, J. W. 1981. Chiefs in Israel. *JSOT* 20: 47–73.

Fohrer, G. 1966. Altes Testament—"Amphiktyonie" und "Bund." *TLZ* 91: 801–16, 893–904 = Pp. 84–119 in *Studien zur alttestamentlichen Theologie und Geschichte 1949–1966. BZAW* 115. 1969. Berlin.

Frick, F. S. 1985. *The Formation of the State in Ancient Israel.* The Social World of Biblical Antiquity Series 4. Sheffield.

Geus, C. H. J. de. 1976. *The Tribes of Israel.* Assen.

Gottwald, N. K. 1979. *The Tribes of Yahweh.* Maryknoll, NY.

Hallo, W. W. 1960. A Sumerian Amphictyony. *JCS* 14: 88–96.

Hoftijzer, J. 1959. Enige opmerkingen rond het israëlitische 12-stammensysteem. *Nederlands Theologisch Tidsskrift* 14: 241–63.

Irwin, W. H. 1965. Le sanctuaire central israélite avant l'établissement de la monarchie. *RB* 72: 161–84.

Lemche, N. P. 1977. The Greek "Amphictyony"—Could It Be a Prototype for the Israelite Society in the Period of the Judges? *JSOT* 4: 48–59.

———. 1985. *Early Israel.* VTSup 37. Leiden.

Mayes, A. D. H. 1973. Israel in the Pre-Monarchy Period. VT 23: 151–70.

———. 1974. *Israel in the Period of the Judges.* SBT, 2d. Series 29. Naperville, IL.

———. 1977. The Period of the Judges and the Rise of the Monarchy. Pp. 285–331 in *IJH.*

———. 1983. *The Story of Israel between Settlement and Exile.* London.

———. 1985. *Judges.* Sheffield.

Nicholson, E. W. 1967. *Deuteronomy and Tradition.* Oxford.

Noth, M. 1930. *Das System der zwölf Stämme Israels. BWANT* 4,1. Stuttgart.

———. 1950. Das Amt des "Richters Israels." Pp. 404–17 in *Festschrift für Alfred Bertholet,* ed. W. Baumgartner et al. Tübingen. pp. 71–85 in *Gesammelte Studien* 2. TBü 39. 1969. München.

———. 1966. The Laws in the Pentateuch: Their Assumptions and Meaning. Pp. 1–107 in *The Laws in the Pentateuch and Other Essays.* Trans. D. R. Ap-Thomas. Edinburgh.

Orlinsky, H. M. 1962. The Tribal System of Israel and Related Groups in the Period of the Judges. Pp. 375–87 in *Studies and Essays in Honor of A. A. Neuman,* ed. M. Ben-Horin; B. D. Weinryb; and S. Zeitlin. Philadelphia.

Ploeg, J. van der. 1950. Les Chefs du peuple d'Israël et leurs titres. *RB* 57: 40–61.

Rad, G. von. 1951. *Der heilige Krieg im alten Israel.* ATANT 20. Zürich.

Rahtjen, B. D. 1965. Philistine and Hebrew Amphictyonies. *JNES* 24: 100–4.

Rogerson, J. W. 1986. Was Early Israel a Segmentary Society? *JSOT* 36: 17–26.

Sasson, J. 1981. On Choosing Models for Recreating Israelite Premonarchic History. *JSOT* 21: 3–24.

Smend, R. 1970. *Yahweh War and Tribal Confederation.* Nashville.

———. 1971. Zur Frage der altisraelitischen Amphiktyonie. *EvT* 31: 623–30.

Speiser, E. A. 1963. Background and Function of the Biblical Nāśī. *CBQ* 25: 111–17 = Pp. 113–23 in *Oriental and Biblical Studies,* ed. J. J. Finkelstein and M. Greenberg. 1967. Philadelphia.

Thiel, W. 1980. *Die soziale Entwicklung Israels in vorstaatlicher Zeit.* Neukirchen-Vluyn.

Weber, M. 1952. *Ancient Judaism.* Trans. H. H. Gerth and D. Martindale. New York.

Weippert, H. 1973. Das geographische System der Stämme Israels. VT 23: 76–89.

Zobel, H. J. 1965. *Stammesspruch und Geschichte. BZAW* 95. Berlin.

A. D. H. Mayes

AMPHIPOLIS (PLACE) [Gk *Amphipolis*]. An ancient city of Macedonia located on a terraced hill on the E bank of the Strymon River just S of Lake Cercinitis and about 4 km N of the estuary of the river and the harbor city of Eion. On his second missionary journey, Paul with Silas passed through this city while traveling on the Via Egnatia from Philippi (approximately 50 km to the E) to Thessalonica (Acts 17:1). The city was set on a hill surrounded by the river on three sides and protected by a wall on the E side. This geographical situation of Amphipolis and its prominent position provides the rationale for its name, which means "around the city" (Thuc. 4.102).

The Thracian founders of the city originally called it *Ennea Hodoi* or "Nine Ways," which indicates its early importance as a commercial and military center. Athenian attempts to colonize the city failed in 497, 476, and 465 B.C. but succeeded in 436 B.C. under the leadership of Hagnon. Amphipolis came under Spartan control in 424

B.C. when Brasidas conquered the city. The efforts of Thucydides, general over Thrace, only succeeded in saving the harbor city of Eion. Despite the efforts of the Athenians to regain control of Amphipolis it remained a free city until Philip the Great of Macedonia conquered it in 357 B.C. After the Romans conquered the region at the Battle of Pydna in 168 B.C. they divided Macedonia into four districts, designating Amphipolis as a free city and the chief city of the first district (Livy 45.17–18, 29–30).

The city, which lies in a fertile river valley, was noted for its wine, oil, and wood. Silver and gold were mined in the adjacent hills and fine woolen textiles were manufactured in this region. During the Roman period the city commanded a strategic position along the Via Egnatia, the bridge across the Strymon River.

Excavations at the city have revealed several tombs from the classical and Hellenistic periods. Four early Byzantine basilicas have been uncovered and they house beautiful mosaic floors. Several coins and inscriptions have been discovered at the city.

Bibliography

Stikas, E. 1985. Les Fouilles d'Amphipolis paléochrétienne en Macedoine Orientale. *Byzantine Studies* 12: 351–85.

Voutiras, E. 1986. Victa Macedonia: remarques sur une dédicace d'Amphipolis. *BCH* 110/1: 347–55.

JOHN D. WINELAND

AMPLIATUS (PERSON) [Gk *ampliatos*]. A Roman Christian who received greetings from Paul in Rom 16:8 as "my beloved in the Lord." Since he was known personally by Paul, who had not yet been in Rome, Ampliatus must have lived in the E of the Roman Empire for a while before he came to Rome. His name, a typical slave name, shows that he probably was a slave or freedman (see the epigraphical material in Lampe *StadtrChr,* 144, 152–53). A connection to Flavia Domitilla and the Ampliatus-Cubiculum in the Roman catacomb "Domitilla" (Cranfield *Romans* ICC, 790) does not exist (Lampe *StadtrChr,* 20–21).

PETER LAMPE

AMRAM (PERSON) [Heb *ʿamrām*]. Var. AMBRAM (LXX). The name of two men in the OT.

1. A second-generation Levite, the son of Kohath, and the father of Moses, Aaron, and Miriam (1 Chr 5:24–29—Eng. 6:2–3). Amram is a biblical figure without a narrative; he appears only in late genealogical lists. The earliest attestation of Amram appears in Exod 6:18. Amram's presence in the genealogy of Exod 6:14–25 most likely resulted from the priestly writer's unification of three or four authentic genealogical sources (Möhlenbrink 1934: 187–90). Once Amram entered the pentateuchal tradition, the priestly writer utilized the name in order to establish a distinct levitical family with specific roles for the conquest of the land (Num 3:19, 27). The appearance of Amram follows a similar pattern in Chronicles. The Chronicler, probably drawing upon the levitical lists in Exodus 6 and Numbers 2–3, included Amram as an individual (1 Chr 5:29—Eng 6:3) and as the name for a levitical family (e.g., 1 Chr 26:23).

2. A son of Bani who lived in the Persian province of Judah during the mission of Ezra (Ezra 10:34). Amram was one of many Judeans who had married non-Judean wives. He consented to divorce his wife during the reforms of Ezra under the threat of complete ostracism from the Jerusalem temple-state.

Bibliography

Möhlenbrink, K. 1934. Die levitischen Überlieferungen des Alten Testaments. *ZAW* 52: 184–231.

JOHN W. WRIGHT

AMRAPHEL (PERSON) [Heb *ʾamrāpel*]. King of Shinar (Gen 14:1, 9), one of the allies of Chedorlaomer. Shinar is an alternate name of Babylonia in the OT and in some Egyptian and cuneiform records of the 2d millennium (1QapGen 21:23 and the Targums render it by *bbl* "Babel"). Amraphel was identified with Hammurapi by Schrader (*SPAW* 1887: 600–5), who assumed that the biblical form of the name arose from a miswritten Hebrew rendering of a variant of the cuneiform name. This identification, once widely accepted, was later virtually abandoned, mainly because Hammurapi was never active in the W.

If one proceeds from the premise that the four eastern kings of Genesis 14 were modeled on the four kings of the "Chedorlaomer texts" (see CHEDORLAOMER), one must look among them for the one who is attested as a king of Babylonia. This is ^{m}*I-bil-*^{d}*Tu-tu* (Spartoli 158 + 962: rev. 27) who, according to his characteristic there (rev. 24–29) and in Spartoli III,2: 3–9 (where the name is broken off), clearly corresponds to Marduk-apal-iddina II (Merodach-baladan), chief of the Chaldean tribe of Bīt-Yakin in the Sea Land, who twice seized the throne of Babylon from Assyria (722–710 and 703 B.C.). He was viewed as an alien usurper by the Babylonian priesthood and patriciate and especially hated because of his removal of divine statues from Babylon and other cultic centers of Babylonia when he twice retreated to the Sea Land. In extant versions of the Chedorlaomer text, the form *I-bil-Tu-tu* represents a pseudonym or cryptogram of the common ideographic spelling of the name Marduk-apal-iddina, which was AMAR.UTU.IBILA.SUM^{na}. The IBILA element was simply moved to the initial position and rendered phonetically as *i-bil,* while the AMAR.UTU (Akk "Marduk") element was replaced by another common name for that god, Tutu. The author of Genesis 14, however, seems to have had at his disposal a version in which the correct ideographic spelling was preserved: he simply read the first element (AMAR.UTU) phonetically as *ʾamar,* and gave the second element (IBILA) its regular Akkadian value *apal* (commonly pronounced *pal* in composite names). The result would hence have been **ʾamarpal* (cf. LXX *amarphal;* Astour 1966: 94–99).

Bibliography

Astour, M. C. 1966. Political and Cosmic Symbolism in Genesis 14 and in Its Babylonian Sources. Pp. 65–112 in *Biblical Motifs: Origins and Transformations,* ed. A. Altman. Cambridge, MA.

Brinkman, J. A. 1964. Merodach-Baladan II. Pp. 6–53 in *Studies Presented to A. Leo Oppenheim.* Chicago.
Dhorme, P. (later E.) 1908. Hammurabi-Amraphel. *RB* 17: 205–26.

MICHAEL C. ASTOUR

AMULET. See MAGIC (ANE).

AMUQ PLAIN. A small plain in S Turkey located on the curve of the Orontes, a river which runs S–N to this point, where it then flows S–W to empty into the Mediterranean. It forms a meeting point, or crossroads, of the following: the Ghab Valley through which the Orontes flows; the N road which runs along the E border of the Amanus; and the road which goes E to Aleppo and to the Euphrates. Thanks to this last section of the Orontes River, this area is directly linked to the coastal region. This situation explains why, in spite of its marshy and unhealthy conditions, this plain has been inhabited by man almost continuously since the Neolithic period.

Two different expeditions have helped to uncover the history of the region. The first was under the auspices of the Oriental Institute of Chicago. It excavated the sites of Chatal Hüyük, Tell Jdeide, and Tell Tayinat between 1933 and 1937 under the direction of C. W. McEwan and R. J. Braidwood. Information gathered pertained mainly to the Neolithic period as well as the 3d and 1st millennia. The second expedition was led by Sir Leonard Woolley to Tell Atchana; its first stage was from 1937 to 1939, and its second stage from 1946 to 1949. It very satisfactorily completed the sequence thanks to the discovery of Alalakh, a city that existed in the 2d millennium.

Occupation of the region seems to have begun in the 6th millennium. The Neolithic era was then well under way: agriculture and the rearing of livestock were the basic activities, and ceramics had already been introduced. Through an in-depth study of ceramics and of its association with the various categories of lithic materials found at Chatal Hüyük and especially at Tell Jdeide, R. J. Braidwood and his team divided the period which extends from 6000 to 2000 B.C. into ten clearly defined phases which they designated from A to J. These letters mark high points of the evolution of N Syria and the progressive transformation of lifestyles during the Neolithic period and the growth of the villages (phases A–E from 6000 to 3500 B.C.), the chalcolithic period, and the still very gradual introduction of the use of metal (phase F, 3500–3000), and finally the Bronze Age which, in the 3d millennium (phases G–J), saw the progressive spread of tools and metal armaments, the building of the first cities, and the birth of writing. During almost the whole of this long period, N Syria appears to have been culturally dependent on Mesopotamia, and it seems that its development was largely the result of the exceptional dynamism of the civilization of the Region of the Two Rivers. Nevertheless, as Ebla reveals, the power of the Syrian economy grew rapidly in the 3d millennium, allowing real originality to soar to great heights. Evidence of this is a group of little bronze statues found at Tell Jdeide which is perhaps one of the most ancient expressions of a type of statue for which the Syrians became particularly renowned throughout ancient times.

Nevertheless, it is the rise of the city of Alalakh about 2000 B.C. that prompts the observation that this region was involved in the profound changes that affected Syria. Indeed, this city looks like a small regional capital within the kingdom of Aleppo, or the kingdom of Yamhad, and at the same time it reflects the life of N Syria during the 2d millennium. The excavations brought to light the existence of seventeen levels (not all of which correspond to a real historical phase). Woolley dated their development between 3200 and 1200 B.C. In reality, the beginnings of the city certainly do not go back further than 2000, and the first important period seems to have been a level 7, which must be dated to the 18th century. The site is famous for having yielded clay tablets which illustrate various areas of public and private life. The architectural documentation consists of a sanctuary, the center of political power, the city gate, and some houses.

One can follow the transformations of the temple throughout the millennium thanks to the seven phases which have been discovered and which show that the basic plan was always respected, even if some modifications gave each one its own particular appearance. The different levels were very simply organized: starting with a large room which was approximately a square with a porch on its SE side overlooking a small courtyard, these levels do not, in most cases, have characteristic furnishings for worship, since these were certainly to be found at a higher level; thus it is generally thought that the temple was shaped like a tower and belonged to a typical Levantine series of which the most famous examples have been found at Ugarit. The palace on level 7, or the palace of Yarim-Lim, a contemporary of Hammurapi of Babylon (18th century), which unfortunately is incomplete, extended immediately E from the temple. Evidently it had a floor where royal apartments were probably located, and large reception rooms, while the servants' quarters were located on the ground floor. The quality of the construction in dressed stone for the door jambs and certain sections of the walls and an armature of wooden beams filled with unbaked bricks on the upper levels clearly show that this building belonged to the E Mediterranean world. This is also confirmed by the presence of mural paintings in which one can recognize strong Minoan features.

The palace on level 4 or the palace of Niqmepas (late 15th to early 14th centuries) followed a totally different concept, for there one finds many elements belonging to the architectural style called *Hilani.* This style, which was highly favored at the beginning of the 1st millennium, emphasizes the existence of a southern influence undoubtedly linked to the development of the prestigious Hittite empire. Elements of the fortification system and the gigantic gate give some idea of the protection of the city, and the house designs, which were unfortunately all too often reduced to just the foundations, depict certain aspects of daily life.

Evidence of the artistic life of the city has come to light thanks to the discovery of statues and fragments of statues, among which one can mention the superb head in diorite found on the floor of the temple at level 7. Woolley thought the head represented the king Yarim-Lim who was described in various written texts, but he had not the slightest proof for that identification. The quality of this portrait, unique in Alalakh, is so remarkable that it seems highly improbable that it came from a local workshop. On the other hand, the statue of King Idrimi is dated about 1400 B.C.—it portrays him in a sitting position on a slightly raised throne that has been poorly separated from the original block of white magnesite. This statue shows unskilled workmanship: its poorly traced features and complete lack of artistic quality indicate that it could very well have been made in a local workshop that was little prepared for such a great endeavor. Concerning the inscription, the text engraved on the statue also holds some surprises which seem to indicate a lack of experience more easily attributable to the stonecutter than to the scribe.

The hundreds of cuneiform tablets discovered mainly on levels 7 and 4 show that people had a perfect grasp of writing in the city of Alalakh in the 18th century. This fact should not be surprising, for even if the city did not play a regional political role, its position on the busy commercial route implied habitual use of this technique. Thanks to these tablets, valuable information has been gathered on the Syrian situation pertaining to the 18th as well as to the 14th centuries; they have even contributed to calling into question the chronology accepted until the Second World War regarding the 1st Babylonian Dynasty.

Alalakh is important to us for providing information on a small city in N Syria, and also for partially filling in the gaps left by the absence of findings in Aleppo, the true capital of the kingdom of Yamhad in the Middle Bronze Age.

During the 1st millennium, the Orontes River maintained its importance. The port of El-Mina and the city of Antioch clearly show this. But one must take particular note here of the site of Tell Tayinat, which was excavated by the team from the Oriental Institute of Chicago. This site revealed levels of the Iron Age where many of the famous *Hilani*-style buildings were discovered.

Secondly, and perhaps more importantly, there are remains of a temple in elongated shape, exactly like a megaron which appears to be characteristic of N Syria and which provided the model of the famous temple of Solomon in Jerusalem.

Bibliography

Braidwood, R. J., and Braidwood, L. S. 1960. *Excavations in the Plain of Antioch, I. The Earliest Assemblages, Phase A–J.* Chicago.

Smith, S., and Sewell, J. 1940. *Alalakh and Chronology.* London.

Woolley, L. 1953. *A Forgotten Kingdom.* Baltimore.

———. 1955. *Alalakh, An Account of the Excavations at Tell Atchana.* Oxford.

JEAN-CLAUDE MARGUERON
Trans. Paul Sager

AMZI (PERSON) [Heb *ʾamṣî*]. **1.** A Levite, the son of Bani, the father of Hilkiah, and the grandfather of Amaziah (1 Chr 6:30–31—Eng 6:45–46). His name occurs in a list of twelve descendants of Merari, Levi's son, which legitimizes Ethan ben Kishi as one of three levitical singers appointed by King David. The Ethanites were to stand at the left side (1 Chr 6:29—Eng 6:44) of Heman, the more prominent levitical musician.

2. A levitical priest, the son of Zechariah and the father of Pelatiah (Neh 11:12). He is cited as a progenitor of Adaiah, one of the priests living in Jerusalem at the time of Nehemiah. Unfortunately, Amzi is not mentioned in the abbreviated list of Adaiah's ancestors in 1 Chr 9:12.

ROGER W. UITTI

ANAB (PLACE) [Heb *ʿănāb*]. A city in the southernmost part of the hill country of Judah (Josh 15:48–50). It is about three miles west of Debir (Dahariyeh). The Egyptian texts of the 19th Dynasty refer to it as *Qrt ʿnb,* hence its original name is likely to have been *Kiriat-ʿanab.* Its modern Arab name is *Khirbet ʿUnnâb eṣ-Ṣeghîreh,* but is called Tel Rekhesh in modern Hebrew. The remains of an Iron Age city have been found at the site.

The book of Joshua mentions it as one of the cities inhabited by the Anakim (Josh 11:21). When Joshua launched his attack, the Anakim, though mighty, could not stand before him. Joshua and his armies took Anab and it was allotted to the tribe of Judah (Josh 15:20, 50).

PAUL BENJAMIN

ANAEL (PERSON) [Gk *Anaēl*]. The brother of Tobit (Tob 1:21). Tobit claimed that Anael was the father of Ahikar, whom Esarhaddon (Assyrian ruler from 681 to 669 B.C.) appointed accountant and chief administrator over his whole empire. See AHIKAR. No name better demonstrates the fictional nature of the book of Tobit and its characters than Anael, through whom the well-known figure of Ahikar was made not only Jewish but a relative of Tobit; indeed, one who interceded with Esarhaddon to have Tobit pardoned for past "crimes" against the state (e.g., burying the bodies of faithful Jews left exposed) and allowed to return to Nineveh from hiding.

PAUL L. REDDITT

ANAFA, TEL (M.R. 210286). A Hellenistic and Roman site in the Huleh Basin.

A. Identification and Location

Tel Anafa is situated in the upper Galilee at the base of the Golan Heights. The site lies near the crossroads of the N–S trade route through the Jordan and Massyas valleys with the E–W road from Damascus to Tyre which in the Late Hellenistic and Roman eras constituted one of the major outlets of the immensely profitable trans-desert trade route to the W. The tel is small, about 160 m long and 110 m wide, and rises some 10 m above the surrounding Huleh Basin. Although excavations have shown that the mound was occupied almost continuously from the EB Age through the 1st century C.E., the best-preserved and most impressive remains belong to the Late Hellenistic era when the occupants appear to have profited greatly from their location near the trade routes. At that time the tel served as the acropolis of a larger town, the walls of which were revealed in the fish-pond construction of the early 1970s but which are now covered by the surrounding cotton fields. After ten years of excavation there is still no evidence for the ancient name of the town in Hellenistic times; the presence of several other Hellenistic settlements nearby in the Huleh Basin make it impossible to identify the tel confidently with any particular Hellenistic settlement mentioned in texts or inscriptions.

B. Excavations

Ten seasons of field work have been carried out in two series of excavations at Tel Anafa. The first series, under the directorship of S. Weinberg, was in the field for five seasons between 1968 and 1973. The second series fielded five summer campaigns between 1978 and 1986, under the codirectorship of S. Weinberg and S. Herbert.

In the ten seasons of excavations approximately 1000 m^2 of the tel were dug to depths of as much as 6 m, although the average depth of penetration was ca. 2.5 m. The earliest habitation levels reached in the deeper probes belong to the MB period, but pottery found in terrace fills and other secondary deposits bears witness to the occupation of the site in the latter part of the EB Age. Nowhere on the tel was sterile soil or bedrock reached. When, in the early years of the excavation, it became clear that there were over 3 m of Hellenistic accumulation, well stratified into several major architectural phases, the decision was taken to concentrate on the Hellenistic remains, opening large areas to clarify the extent and plan of the Hellenistic buildings.

C. Hellenistic and Roman Era Buildings

The N half of the tel is dominated by the substantial remains of a large Hellenistic building (the LHSB) ca. 38 m square. The walls of this building are a mixture of cut limestone ashlar blocks and basalt fieldstones and are preserved in a few instances to a height of over 2 m. The mixed ashlar/rubble construction technique is characteristic of Phoenician settlements from the Iron Age through Hellenistic eras. The use in some of the walls of the Greek dry masonry elements, such as swallowtail clamps and rectangular dowels sealed with lead, points to a mixed Greco-Phoenician tradition. Also indicative of Greek building tradition was the decorative stucco which faced many of the walls. The painted and gilded stucco imitated drafted blocks, egg-and-dart moldings, and Ionic and Corinthian column capitals. The plan of the building can be restored as suites of rooms on four sides opening onto a central courtyard measuring 9 × 12 m. There is a major paved entrance to the NW. A bath complex along the E side of the court bears witness to the luxurious standard of living of the inhabitants. The bath complex consists of three rooms, the southernmost the working area for heating the water, the middle and northern rooms for bathing and dressing. The bathing room contains a large plaster basin for the heated water and a decorated mosaic floor. The mosaic measures 3.5 × 2.3 m. It is the earliest decorated mosiac pavement yet found in Syro-Palestine. The mosaic is made up of black diorite and white marble tesserae between 1 and 1.5 cm square. The design includes a black border around the edges of the mosaic; the interior is divided into three panels of unequal size by black bands running N to S. The westernmost panel contains a clear checkerboard design, the other two panels are decorated with non-representational curvilinear motifs in the manner of Hellenistic irregular mosaics. Excavation under the mosaic and plaster basin revealed a primitive hypocaust system of mudbrick pillars separated by heating channels which ran underground from a stone firing pit in the S room. Such elaborate bathing suites are not common in Greek houses or palaces in the Hellenistic era and the presence of such a complex in the LHSB at Tel Anafa is another indication of the mixed cultural background of the Hellenistic inhabitants of the tel.

The evidence of the numerous coins and stamped amphora handles found at Tel Anafa points to a date late in the third quarter or early in the fourth quarter of the 2d century B.C.E. for the original construction of the LHSB. A coin of Alexander Zebina (128–125 B.C.E.) found in the construction fill of the S room of the bath is the latest find under any of the original floors of the building. Also present under these floors were small amounts of Eastern Sigillata A wares. A massive leveling and terracing operation took place with the construction of the LHSB, obliterating earlier architectural remains. In only a few spots are earlier Hellenistic structures preserved. These take the form of boulder walls with pebble floors and are tentatively dated to the 3d century B.C.E. and are associated with the coins of Ptolemy II and III found on the site. Hellenistic black slipped wares and "Parthian" green glazed pottery were found in the Early Hellenistic fills.

In the first quarter of the 1st century B.C.E. the LSHB underwent substantial alterations in which it was divided into a number of separate units. First a large building with thick rubble walls was built over its NE corner. Shortly thereafter the North Building was built up against the W wall of the Northeast Building. At the time of the construction of the North Building, the paved entrance at the NW was blocked and the W rooms of the LHSB were realigned; in addition, the floor levels of the W rooms and central court were raised ca. 0.5 m and paved with basalt. The bath remained in use throughout the remodeling. Coins of independent Tyre and Sidon, and Rhodian stamped amphora handles of period VI (108–80 B.C.E.) date the alterations to the first quarter of the 1st century B.C.E.

Although the area as remodeled in the 1st century B.C.E. is less grandiose in plan, both the architecture and the finds show that this was still a period of prosperity and Greek influence. Both the North and Northeast buildings are relatively large and spacious structures; the North Building is decorated with painted stucco, albeit simpler than on the LHSB; imported luxury products such as the Late Hellenistic redwares and molded glass bowls are still abundant at these levels; stamped amphora handles of period VI (108–80 B.C.E.) are common; Hellenized coins of 1st century B.C.E. independent Sidon are the largest single issue present at the site. There are no signs that this period of prosperity was brought to an end by military conquest or violence of any sort. Although there are some signs of fire in the houses on the S slope there is no general layer of conflagration on the site. The archaeological record instead shows a picture of abandonment and gradual decay of the Hellenistic buildings. The evidence of the coins and the stamped amphora handles suggests strongly that this abandonment took place early in the second quarter of the 1st century B.C.E. Of 319 coins found at Tel Anafa, only one must be dated between 75 B.C.E. and the early years of the 1st-century C.E.; none of the 122 stamped amphora handles found in the excavations need be dated after 80 B.C.E.

The site was resettled early in the 1st century C.E., probably under the impetus of Herod Philip, whose coins appear in and under the walls of this phase. The buildings of this period are much smaller and simpler than their Hellenistic predecessors, the most common plan being long and narrow 2-room structures built of undecorated rubble. The walls of this phase are sometimes founded directly on the preceding Hellenistic structures and often use blocks robbed from these earlier walls. In addition to the Herod Philip coins, Early Roman lamps with molded discus and sigillata wares in Early Roman shapes date this occupation phase to the 1st century C.E. By the end of the 1st or early 2d century C.E. the site is again abandoned and never reoccupied in any major way.

D. Summary and History

The results of ten seasons of excavation show the site of Tel Anafa to have been occupied almost continuously from the EB Age through the 1st century C.E. The large and deeply founded buildings of the Late Hellenistic era have disturbed and largely obscured the remains of the earlier habitations, but give us a vivid picture of a rich Hellenized settlement of Late Seleucid times. The evidence of the coins and stamped amphora handles together with the architectural remains of the Hellenistic levels indicates that there was a minor Ptolemaic settlement on the site in the 3d century B.C.E. This was succeeded in the second half of the 2d century B.C.E. by a prosperous Seleucid settlement which took an active part in the trade of the Late Seleucid Empire and flourished through the first quarter of the 1st century B.C.E. The chaotic conditions surrounding the disintegration of the Seleucid Empire probably led to the site's abandonment sometime shortly after 75 B.C.E. The tel was reoccupied in the early years of the 1st century C.E. as part of the reorganization of the Galilee under Herod Philip, whose capital was at nearby Caesarea Philippi (modern Banias). It was again abandoned toward the end of the century and not reoccupied in antiquity.

Bibliography

Herbert, S. 1978. New Campaign at Tel Anafa, 1978. *Muse* 12: 21–29.
———. 1979. Tel Anafa 1978: Preliminary Report. *BASOR* 234: 67–81.
———. 1979. Tel Anafa 1979. *Muse* 13: 16–21.
———. 1980. Tel Anafa 1980. *Muse* 14: 24–30.
———. 1981. Tel Anafa. The 1981 Season. *Muse* 14: 23–29.
Weinberg, G. D. 1970. Hellenistic Glass from Tel Anafa in Upper Galilee. *Journal of Glass Studies* 12: 17–27.
Weinberg, S. S. 1969. Tel Anafa—A Problem-Oriented Excavation. *Muse* 3: 16–23.
———. 1970. Tel Anafa: The Second Season. *Muse* 4: 15–24.
———. 1970. Excavations at Tel Anafa. *Qad* 3: 135–38 (in Hebrew).
———. 1970. *Tel Anafa: The Hellenistic Town.* Jerusalem.
———. 1971. Tel Anafa: The Third Season. *Muse* 5: 8–16.
———. 1971. Tel Anafa: The Hellenistic Town. *IEJ* 21: 86–109.
———. 1972. Tel Anafa—1972: The Fourth Season. *Muse* 6: 8–18.
———. 1974. Excavations at Tel Anafa, 1973. *Muse* 8: 14–28.

S. C. HERBERT

ANAH (PERSON) [Heb *ʿănâ*]. One of the sons of Zibeon, and the father of Esau's wife Oholibamah (Gen 36:2, 14, 18, 25; 1 Chr 1:40). MT Gen 36:2, 14 *bat* ("daughter") is to be corrected to *ben* ("son") according to Gen 36:24; 1 Chr 1:38, 40. According to the tribal system of the Edomites, Anah was considered to be a Seiritic-Horitic clan of the tribe of Zibeon (Weippert 1971: 439–51).

Anah is also identified as the one "who found the 'water' [MT hapax legomenon *hayyēmim*] in the wilderness as he pastured the asses of Zibeon his father" (Gen 36:24), and this passage has been the subject of some debate (cf. Yellin 1933; Glaser 1933). Beeston (1974) translated Heb *yēmim* according to the LXX as "lakes"; Anah fell victim to a mirage—says Beeston—and acquired a nickname: "the one who found lakes in the desert." Driver (1975) derived Heb *yēmim* from a supposed Heb **ym* "[a kind of] fish, living in lakes and marshes" (cf. Syr *ymmʾ*, Ar *yamm*). Speiser (*Genesis* AB, 279–80) and Grill (1967) suppose a metathesis of *y* and *m* in *hayyēmim,* and reads *hammayim* "water" (cf. Vg *aquas calidas*).

The interpretation of the name Anah is uncertain. Earlier it was frequently derived from Arabic *ʿāna* ("wild donkey"). The derivations from Hurrian (Feiler 1939; Ginsberg and Maisler 1934) are open to doubt. Anah is most likely the shortened form of a name constructed with **ʿny* "to answer" (Weippert 1971: 245).

Bibliography

Beeston, A. F. L. 1974. What Did Anah See? VT 24: 109–10.
Driver, G. R. 1975. Gen XXXVI 24: Mules or Fishes. VT 25: 109–10.
Feiler, W. 1939. Hurritische Namen im Alten Testament. *ZA* 45: 216–29.
Ginsberg, H. L., and Maisler (Mazar), B. 1934. Semitised Ḫurrians in Syria and Palestine. *JPOS* 14: 243–67.
Glaser, O. 1933. Der wasserspendende Esel (Gen XXXVI 24). *ZS* 9: 134–36.
Grill, S. 1967. Ischodadh von Merw und die hajjemin Gn 36,24. *BZ* 11: 116–17.
Horwitz, W. J. 1973. Were There Twelve Horite Tribes?, *CBQ* 35: 69–71.
Kornfeld, W. 1985. Die Edomiterlisten (Gn 36; 1C1) im Lichte des altarabischen Namensmaterials. Pp. 231–36 in AOAT 215.
Moritz, B. 1926. Edomitische Genealogien I. *ZAW* 44: 81–93.
Weippert, M. 1971. *Edom. Studien und Materialien zur Geschichte der Edomiter auf Grund schriftlicher und archäologischer Quellen.* Diss., Tübingen.
Yellin, D. 1933. Recherches bibliques: 1. hayyemin (Genèse 36,24). *ZS* 9: 134–36.

ULRICH HÜBNER

ANAHARATH (PLACE) [Heb *ʾănāḥărāt*]. The sixth place listed in the description of the territory of Issachar (Josh 19:19). The name also appears in the topographical list of Thutmose III (no. 52: *i-n-h-r-t;* Simons 1937: 117). Amenhotep II captured Anaharath in his second campaign to Asia. The list of booty included 17 *maryanu,* six children of princes, 68 "Asiatics," and seven chariots of silver and gold. Anaharath was the northernmost place mentioned, and from there Amenhotep II apparently returned to Megiddo (*ANET,* 247; Edel 1953: 134–35, 157; Aharoni 1960: 181–83).

The biblical references and the position of the town in Thutmose's list show that Anaharath was located in the hill country of Issachar. It was suggested that the ancient name had survived in that of the village Nᵓaurah (de Saulcy 1877: 22–23; Albright 1926: 229). Another identification put forward was that of Tell el-ᶜAjjul (M.R. 093097), a site overlooking the main N–S route, the so-called "Via maris" (*EncMiqr* 1: 451). Aharoni (1967) has shown, however, that the only true tel in the region with suitable LB finds is Tell el-Mukharkhash (Tel Rekes; M.R. 194228), 7 km SE of Mt. Tabor. Recent surveys (Zori 1977: 116–20; Gal 1980: 33–40) and excavations (Gal 1981) have confirmed this identification.

Bibliography

Aharoni, Y. 1960. Some Geographical Remarks Concerning the Campaigns of Amenhotep II. *JNES* 19: 177–83.

———. 1967. Anaharath. *JNES* 26: 212–15.

Albright, W. F. 1926. The Topography of the Tribe of Issachar. *ZAW* 3: 225–36.

Edel, E. 1953. Die Stelen Amenophis II aus Karnak und Memphis mit dem Bericht über der asiatischer Feldzuge des Königs. *ZDPV* 69: 97–176.

Gal, Z. 1980. *Ramat Issachar.* Tel Aviv (in Hebrew).

———. 1981. Tell Rekhesh and Tel Karnei Hittin. *EI* 15: 213–21 (in Hebrew).

Saulcy, F. de. 1877. *Dictionnaire topographique abrégé de la Terre Sainte,* Paris.

Simons, J. J. 1937. *Handbook for the Study of Egyptian Topographical Lists Relating to Western Africa.* Leiden.

Zori, N. 1977. *The Land of Issachar: Archaeological Survey.* Jerusalem (in Hebrew).

Rafael Frankel

ANAIAH (PERSON) [Heb *ᶜanāyāh*]. One of the men standing at Ezra's right hand when Ezra stood before the Water Gate and read from the Book of the Law of Moses (Neh 8:4). He is also listed as one of the brethren who set their seal to the covenant (Neh 10:23—Eng 10:22). The name Anaiah means "The Lord has answered one's prayer." This form is found frequently in hymns of thanksgiving (Pss 69:14, 17, 18; 143:1, 7).

Gary C. Augustin

ANAK (PERSON) [Heb *ᶜănāq*]. ANAKIM. A people who occupied Canaan before the arrival of Israel and traced their ancestry back to Anak. Apparently, *anaq* was originally a common noun whose meaning was "neck" or "necklace," and gradually Anakim became the name of a tribe, with the possible meaning "long necked" (= giant).

Anak was the son of Arba (Josh 15:13; 21:11), the founder of Kiriath-arba (i.e., Hebron; Josh 21:11). Though his son's name gave rise to the gentilic, Arba was regarded as "the greatest man among the Anakim" (Josh 14:15).

All of the biblical references agree that the descendants of Anak were tall, of gigantic size (Deut 2:10, 21; 9:2). When the Hebrew spies returned from their mission in Canaan, they warned Israel about the Amalekites, Hittites, Jebusites, Amorites, and Canaanites (cf. Num 13:29), but the spies were especially concerned about the Anakim. In Num 13:28 it is recorded that the spies made general comments about the strong people who lived in the land, in large and fortified towns, but then they added, "and besides, we saw the descendants of Anak there" (cf. Deut 1:28). Num 13:33 connects the Anakim with the infamous Nephilim: "the sons of Anak, who come from the Nephilim" (cf. Gen 6:4). Deut 2:10, 20–21, and 9:2 identify the Anakim with the Emim, Zamzummim, and Rephaim. So it is not surprising that the hearts of the grasshopper-sized Hebrew spies melted at the sight of these giants, and this report had the same result on the Israelites who heard it. But Moses predicted that the Lord would give the Israelites victory over the Anakim, "a people great and tall" (Deut 9:2–3).

While most biblical references locate the Anakim in S Canaan, more specifically in the environs of Hebron (Num 13:22; Josh 14:12–15), there is a single passage that says the Anakim originally inhabited a much wider territory. This passage, Josh 11:21–22, reports that Anakim used to occupy the hill country of Judah (at Hebron, Debir, and Anab specifically) *and* the hill country of Israel. More importantly, it reports that this dreaded enemy was virtually wiped out by Joshua (with Caleb being responsible for the expulsion of the Anakim from Hebron; cf. Josh 14:12–15; 15:13–14; Judg 1:10), with the only survivors remaining in the Philistine cities of Gaza, Gath, and Ashdod. Incidentally, the RSV rendering of Jer 47:5 follows this tradition and places the Anakim in a Philistine context as well. It is most probable that Goliath of Gath and the other giants of 2 Sam 21:16–22 (cf. 1 Chr 20:4–8) were regarded as descendants of the Anakim remnant in Philistia.

In the Egyptian Execration Texts (*ANET,* 328–29), there are references to several princes with Semitic names who are identified as rulers of *Iy-ᶜanaq.* Many scholars regard this as a tribal name related to the Anakim, but this connection is not certain (cf. Albright 1928). Apart from these texts, which date to the 19–18th centuries B.C., there are no other extrabiblical references that shed light on the Anakim.

Bibliography

Albright, W. F. 1928. The Egyptian Empire in Asia in the Twenty-first Century B.C. *JPES* 8: 223–56.

Gerald L. Mattingly

ANAMIM [Heb *ᶜănāmîm*]. The third "offspring" of Egypt (Gen 10:13). On the basis of the plural suffix marker, *-îm,* this figure seems to be the name of an ethnic group, the identification of which remains uncertain. Albright (1920–21: 191–92) attempted to find this name in a Neo-Assyrian text (KAV no. 92 line 41), occurring beside the place name of Caphtor. He equated the latter with Crete and the former *(a-na-mi)* with Cyrene. Later studies of this text have read this name as *a-na-kù,* eliminating the possibility of a reference to the Anamim (Albright 1925: 236–37; Weidner 1952–53: 22).

A second suggestion (Skinner *Genesis* ICC, 212) is to emend the text, following LXX *ʾenemetiem,* and to read *knmtym,* identifying the place with Egyptian *knmt* in the Libyan desert. A third option, following targum Pseudo-Jonathan and some of the fragmentary targums, is to interpret Anamim as referring to *mrywtʾy,* a place identified as W of Alexandria (Cassuto et al. *EncBib* 6: 309). While the other "offspring" of Egypt appear to reflect place names or people who lived in or near Egypt, there remains uncertainty as to the identification of a number of them (cf. LUD and NAPHTUHIM), including Anamim. The order of the names appear to be according to the number of consonants in the root, beginning with two (Lud) and proceeding to four (Naphtuhim and all the names of v 14), thus the order is probably not intended to follow a geographical sequence (Wenham *Genesis 1–15* WBC, 224).

Bibliography

Albright, W. F. 1920–21. A Colony of Cretan Mercenaries on the Coast of the Negeb. *JPOS* 1: 187–94.

———. 1925. A Babylonian Geographical Treatise on Sargon of Akkad's Empire. *JAOS* 45: 193–245.

Weidner, E. 1952–53. Das Reich Sargons von Akkad. *AfO* 16: 1–24.

RICHARD S. HESS

ANAMMELECH (DEITY) [Heb *ʿănammelek*]. A god or goddess to whom, along with Adrammelech, the former inhabitants of Sepharvaim offered child sacrifice (2 Kgs 17:31). Sargon II had settled the Sepharvites in Samaria after deporting much of the local populace.

The interpretation of this otherwise unknown god-name depends in some part on the understanding of the name Adrammelech. Some who follow Albright (*ARI,* 163) in assuming that *ʿadra(m)-* conceals an incorrectly written form of Hadad would find in *ʿana(m)-* the name of the goddess Anat. Thus NAB translates "King Hadad and his consort Anath," and Gese (Gese et al. 1970: 110), "Hadad König, ʿAnat des Königs." The very existence of such a god as Hadad-milki or the like has been called into question, however (see Kaufman 1978). An alternate interpretation (Albright *ARI,* 163; Cogan and Tadmor *2 Kings* AB, 212) suggests a reflex of the name of the Sumerian sky god Anu in Anammelech. In fact, neither of these explanations is completely satisfactory.

The reference to child sacrifice with this divinity might indicate that the *-melek* element of the name does not have to do with the word for king, but with the much-discussed word (from a root *y/hlk?*) for sacrifice which also appears in the name Molech or Moloch (see Gibson *TSSI* 3: 74–75; and, specifically with the name Anammelech, Green 1975: 179–87).

Kaufman (1978: 102–3) argues from both literary and linguistic considerations that Sepharvaim was a city in Phoenicia, not in Syria, Babylonia, or even Elam as many assume.

Bibliography

Gese, H.; Höfner, M.; and Rudolph, K. 1970. *Die Religionen Altsyriens, Altarabiens und der Mandäer.* Vol. 10/2 of *Die Religionen der Menschheit,* ed. C. M. Schröder. Stuttgart.

Green, A. R. W. 1975. *The Role of Human Sacrifice in the Ancient Near East.* Missoula, MT.

Kaufman, S. A. 1978. The Enigmatic Adad-Milki. *JNES* 37: 101–9.

WILLIAM J. FULCO

ANAN (PERSON) [Heb *ʿānān*]. A signatory to the code of Nehemiah and a lay leader of the people (Neh 10:26). The name comes from the Heb root *ʿnn* = "appear." Along with Anani, who is mentioned in 1 Chr 3:24, the name may be an abbreviated form of the name Ananiah, who is a lay leader mentioned in Neh 3:23 (Brockington *Ezra, Nehemiah, Esther* NCBC, 142).

FREDERICK W. SCHMIDT

ANANI (PERSON) [Heb *ʿănānî*]. The last recorded descendant of Jehoiachin, the last king of the S kingdom of Judah. In 1 Chr 3:24 he is listed as the seventh and final son of Elioenai. He *may* be mentioned in a letter written in Aramaic from the Jewish mercenaries settled on the island of Elephantine in Egypt to Bogoas, the Persian governor of Judah ca. 413 B.C.E. The letter is a petition for permission to rebuild their temple dedicated to "Yahu the God of Heaven" (*ANET,* 491–92). If the reconstruction by Cross (1975) of the Judean restoration is correct and the Anani mentioned in the Elephantine letter is indeed the same as the Anani of 1 Chr 3:24, then he would have been the contemporary of the Jerusalem High Priests Johanan II and Jaddua II. For a contrasting view of the period, see Widengren (1977: 489–538). The name may mean "(Yahweh) has revealed himself" (*ISBE* 1: 120).

Bibliography

Cross, F. M. 1975. A Reconstruction of the Judean Restoration. *Int* 29: 187–203.

Widengren, G. 1977. The Persian Period. Pp. 489–538 in *IJH.*

RUSSELL FULLER

ANANIAH (PERSON) [Heb *ʿănanyāh*]. Father of Maaseiah, whose son, Azariah, was involved in the repair and reconstruction of Jerusalem's walls under the direction of Nehemiah (Neh 3:23). He is identified by some scholars with Anan, who is mentioned in Neh 10:26, and with Anani, who is mentioned in 1 Chr 3:24, both of which may be abbreviated forms of Ananiah (Brockington *Ezra, Nehemiah, Esther* NCBC, 142). The name is comprised of two elements: the Heb root *ʿnn,* "appear," and the theophoric name *yah* = "Yaweh." The normal translation for the name is "Yahweh has appeared" (Fowler 1988: 103).

Bibliography

Fowler, J. D. 1988. *Theophoric Personal Names in Ancient Hebrew.* *JSOTSup* 49. Sheffield.

FREDERICK W. SCHMIDT

ANANIAH (PLACE) (Heb *ʿănanyāh*). One of the villages in the territory of Benjamin where the children of Benjamin lived after the return from exile in Babylon (Neh 11:32). Though the verse that lists Ananiah among the Benjaminite towns is missing from the LXX, it appears as Gk *Anania* in the Codex Sinaiticus and the recension Luciani. Some scholars identify Ananiah as modern Bêt Hannîna (Press 1955: 742–73) 4 km NNW of Jerusalem. Others (Albright 1923: 9) would dispute this identification because the three towns listed in this verse, Anathoth, Nob, and Ananiah, move from N to S geographically. Beth Hannina is NW of them all while Ananiah should be found S of the others and E of Jerusalem. There are two villages here, Bahurim (Râs el-Tumein, M.R. 174133) and Bethany (el-ʿAzarîyeh, M.R. 174131). Albright (1923: 9) identified Ananiah with Bethany. Citing parallel examples from the Bible, he argued that Beth ʿAnaniah (after the founder Ananiah) and ʿAnnaiah were interchangeable and the slight difference between Beth ʿAnaniah and Beth ʿAniah is due to syllabic haplology. Early claims that Bethany lay not in Benjamin but in Judah (Press 1955: 43) were answered first by the explanation that the old borders of Judah may have been altered in the days of Nehemiah (Kallai 1960: 86). Later identifications of several places whose names appear in the boundary descriptions between Judah and Benjamin (Josh 15: 7; 18: 16–17) affirm the possibility that the border passed just S of Bethany (*EncMiqr* 6: 311). En-shemesh, for instance, has been identified with ʿAin Ḥoḍ (M.R. 175131) and En-rogel with Bir Alyub (M.R. 172130). Thus Bethany lies near the S border of Benjamin and could be this Persian-period village. During the excavations of the old city W of the present town of Bethany, a number of objects from the Persian period were found (Saller 1957: 374), giving additional support to the theory that this is the site of the postexilic village of Ananiah. See also BETHANY.

Bibliography

Albright, W. F. 1923. Bethany in the Old Testament. *BASOR* 9: 8–10.

———. 1924. Bethany in the Old Testament. AHSOR 4: 158–60.

Kallai, Z. 1960. *The Northern Boundaries of Judah from the Settlement of the Tribes until the Beginning of the Hasmonaean Period.* Jerusalem (in Hebrew).

Press, I. 1955. *A Topographical-Historical Encyclopaedia of Palestine.* Vol. 4. Jerusalem (in Hebrew).

Saller, S. J. 1957. *Excavations at Bethany 1949–1953.* Jerusalem.

SUSAN E. MCGARRY

ANANIAS (PERSON) [Gk *Hananias*]. Probably a transcription of the not uncommon Hebrew name *ḥănanĕyāh,* "God is merciful," with a Greek ending. Here we are concerned with five individuals who bore this name.

1. The angel Raphael claims that he is Tobit's kinsman Azariah, the son of the great and noble Hananiah, i.e., "God helps, son of God is merciful" (Tob 5:13). Given the edifying nature of the book of Tobit, there is probably a play on the meaning of the names (Zimmermann 1958: 75).

2. An Ananias is named in the genealogy of Judith (8:1). Since this book likewise is an edifying story, any serious treatment of the genealogy is wasted effort (Enslin 1972: 110). Rather, the genealogy stresses the purity of the heroine's descent from Israel, and some of its fictitious names may have been borrowed from Numbers (1:6, 8; 26:8, 57) and from Nehemiah (12:12–21; Craven 1983: 84–85).

3. Ananias, a Christian of Jerusalem, appears in a story of a rule miracle of punishment (very similar to divine judgment) paralleled by that of his wife, SAPPHIRA (Acts 5:1–11). Luke portrays women as men to suggest equality (O'Toole 1984: 118–26).

Although they were free to do as they wished with their property, both before and after the sale, Ananias and Sapphira agreed to deceive the apostles and the community about the price of a field, and so Ananias places only a part of the proceeds at Peter's feet. But Peter asks Ananias, "Why has Satan filled your heart to lie to the Holy Spirit?" and further describes his crime as lying to God, not to human beings. The victory of the Spirit and God, represented by Peter and the community, over Satan in Ananias and Sapphira is complete. When reproved by Peter, Ananias says nothing. Rather he falls down and dies, and others wrap him up, carry him out, and bury him. The resultant effect is that great fear comes on all who hear of the event.

What originally happened cannot now be deciphered. The names, Ananias and Sapphira, and the analogous story in 1 Cor 5:1–8 show the possibility of a historical kernel for Acts 5:1–11 (Lüdemann 1987: 71). Luke surely contrasts Ananias (Sapphira) and Barnabas of the preceding pericope (Acts 4:36–37); also the parallels to Judas, the condemnation of Simon (Acts 8:20–23), and the blinding of Elymas (Acts 13:6–11) come to the fore.

4. In Damascus, a Jewish Christian, Ananias (Acts 9:10–7; 22:12–6), who is a devout observer of the law and well spoken of by all the Jews, has a vision of Christ, who sends him to lay hands on Paul and cure his blindness, to baptize him so that he may wash away his sins and be filled with the Holy Spirit. Ananias protests because of Paul's reputation and the harm he has done to the Christians. In the meantime, Paul has received a vision about Ananias' coming. When Ananias arrives, he performs his assignment and likewise tells Paul that God appointed him to know his will and to see the Just One whose witness he must be and for whom he will suffer.

This portrayal of Ananias is largely due to Luke. Ananias is not mentioned in the conversation story of Paul in Acts 26, and what is said in Acts 22 would not be completely intelligible, if one had not already read chap. 9. Moreover, the particular vision genre is found in the NT only in Luke (Acts 9:4–6, 10–16; 10:3–6; 22:7–10; 26:14–18; Lohfink 1965: 53–60). Lüdemann (1987: 119–20) argues that it is hardly possible to make a well-grounded historical judgment about the person of Ananias and his part in the conversion/call of Saul, but there remains the problem of the name which Luke surely would not have otherwise introduced (cf. Acts 5:1–11; 23:1–5; 24:1). Stählin (*Acts* NTD, 136) concludes that Ananias was from Palestine, which may well be an indication of an independent, probably chronologically prior to the persecution of the Christian Hellenists, spread of the gospel and community beyond Palestine. To be sure, Acts 22:14–16 are more Jewish in tone. Ananias' protest represents a traditional motif which stresses either the significance and unprecedented nature of the command (cf. Exod 3:11; Jer 1:6; Luke 1:18–20) and/or the remarkable nature of the conversion (Roloff *Acts* NTD, 106, 323). According to Hengel (1979: 84), Ananias was probably an important intermediary between the Christians and Damascus and Paul.

5. Ananias, the son of Nedebaeus, was high priest under Claudius and Nero ca. 47–58 C.E. Paul appears before him claiming innocence (Acts 23:1–10), and Ananias orders one of the attendants to strike him on the mouth (cf. John 18:22–23). Paul retorts with the prophetical (Haenchen *Acts* Meyerk, 637) statement, "God shall strike you, you whitewashed wall," and points out that such an action is contrary to the law according to which Paul is supposedly being judged. When informed that he is speaking against the high priest, Paul apologizes with a scriptural citation (Exod 22:28). Later (Acts 24:1), Ananias leads the Jewish accusers of Paul before Felix.

Lüdemann (1987: 252–53, 258) sees Paul's presentation before the high priest whom he insulted and the names of Ananias and the lawyer Tertullus in Acts 24:1 as historical, because there was no good reason for creating such a tradition. The presence of Ananias in Acts 24:1 reveals for Luke the weight that the Jewish officials attached to Paul's case. Finally, it is hard to see how Paul could have been ignorant of Ananias' office. Did he not know who gave the command to strike him or was Paul being ironical: one would not expect a high priest to transgress the law (Munck *Acts* AB, 223)?

Josephus provides further information. Ananias was assigned the high priestly office by Herod, king of Chalcis (*Ant* 20 §103). After an outbreak of violence between the Jews and Samaritans, the governor of Syria, Quadratus, sent Ananias and others off in chains to Caesar (*JW* 2 §243; *Ant* 20 §131), but they were rescued through the influence of Agrippa II. Ananias may have enjoyed something of a reputation among the people; he certainly used his wealth to bribe individuals and to pay court to the procurator, Albinus, and the high priest who succeeded him. Through the capture of his son and other household members, the Sicarii forced Ananias to convince Albinus to release many of their followers. On the other hand, Ananias' slaves went to the threshing floors and took by force the tithes of the priests. They beat those who refused to yield. As a result, some poor priests died from starvation (*Ant* 20 §205–13). During the Jewish War, Ananias was seen as a friend of the Romans and his house was burned. Although he managed to flee to the palace of Herod the Great, he and his brother, Ezechias, were later caught and killed by Zealots (*JW* 2 §426, 429, 441–42).

Bibliography

Craven, T. 1983. *Artistry and Faith in the Book of Judith.* SBLDS 70. Chico, CA.

Enslin, M. S. 1972. *The Book of Judith.* Jewish Apocryphal Literature 7. Philadelphia.

Hengel, M. 1979. *Acts and the History of Earliest Christianity.* Trans. J. Bowden. Philadelphia.

Lohfink, G. 1965. *Paulus vor Damaskus: Arbeitsweisen der neueren Bibelwissenschaft dargestellt an den Texten Apg 9, 1–19; 22, 3–21; 26, 9–18.* SBS 4. Stuttgart.

Lüdemann, G. 1987. *Das frühe Christentum nach den Traditionen der Apostelgeschichte: Ein Kommentar.* Göttingen.

O'Toole, R. F. 1984. *The Unity of Luke's Theology: An Analysis of Luke-Acts.* GNS 9. Wilmington, DE.

Zimmermann, F. 1958. *The Book of Tobit.* Jewish Apocryphal Literature. New York.

ROBERT F. O'TOOLE

ANANIEL (PERSON) [Gk *Ananiēl*]. The grandfather of Tobit (Tob 1:1). In Codex Sinaiticus the name Ananiel appears also in 1:8, which reads in part: "as Deborah, the wife of Ananiel my father, commanded." This verse designates Ananiel as the father, rather than the grandfather, of Tobit. It contradicts Alexandrinus and Vaticanus, as well as Tob 1:1 in Sinaiticus itself, in all three of which Ananiel is listed as Tobit's grandfather. Zimmermann (1958: 49) suggests that the problem is due to the error of a copyist, whose eye strayed to the name Anna in v 9, causing him to insert the similar name Ananiel in v 8. Without the name Ananiel, the phrase in Sinaiticus would read identically with the phrase in Alexandrinus and Vaticanus.

The Hebrew form of the name *(ḥănîʾēl)* is a compound of the noun *ḥănînâ* (favor) and the noun *ʾel* (God), meaning "favor of God" or "God is merciful." The name appears twice in the OT, designating a prince of the tribe of Manasseh (Num 34:23) and a chief of the tribe of Asher (1 Chr 7:39).

Bibliography

Zimmermann, F. 1958. *The Book of Tobit.* New York.

PAUL L. REDDITT

ANASIB (PERSON) [Gk *Anasib*]. Ancestor of a priestly family who returned from exile in Babylon with Zerubbabel (1 Esdr 5:24). Although 1 Esdras is often assumed to have been compiled from Ezra and Nehemiah, this family does not appear among their lists of returning exiles (cf. Ezra 2:36; Neh 7:39). Omissions such as this also raise questions about 1 Esdras being used as a source by Ezra or Nehemiah. Moreover, problems associated with dating events and persons described in 1 Esdras have cast doubt on the historicity of the text. Identification of Anasib is further complicated by numerous textual variants. The most significant of these variants listed in Hanhart (1974) are: Lat *Eliasib* in the Vg, Gk *sanabeis* in Codex Vaticanus, and Gk *sanaseib* or *sanasēb* in various minuscules.

Bibliography

Hanhart, R. 1974. *Esdrae liber I.* Vol. 8/1 in *Septuaginta: Vetus Testamentum Graecum.* Göttingen.

MICHAEL DAVID MCGEHEE

ANATH (DEITY) [Heb *ʿănāt*]. An ANE goddess.

A. Anath According to Nonbiblical Sources

Anath apparently was worshiped by the Amorites already in the 3rd millennium B.C. Her cult is attested in records from the Amorite kingdom at Mari during the reign of Zimri-lim (ca. 1780–1758 B.C.). The goddess was closely associated with the city Ḫanat (about 75 miles SE of Mari), which may have been a cult center of Anath.

Literature from Ugarit is the most important source for an understanding of the goddess. In a passage in the Baal Epic, Anath is depicted as a fierce, invincible warrior, slaughtering people, tying their heads and hands to her person, wading knee deep in the blood and gore of those she has slain, reveling in fighting and destruction. Sated with battling, Anath calmly wipes her victims' blood from her house and washes herself. Later in the epic Anath is Baal's ally in his quest for El's permission to build a palace. She presents Baal's petition before El in a most disrespectful manner, threatening him with physical violence. Because El does not give the desired response, Baal and Anath next persuade Asherah to intercede on Baal's behalf. When El finally issues his permission, Anath is the one who announces the good news to Baal. After his palace is built, Baal comes under the power of Mot ("Death"). Anath finds Baal, buries him, and, in mourning for him, makes incisions on her body, besides sacrificing many animals. Her heart yearning for Baal "like the heart of a cow for her calf, like the heart of a ewe for her lamb," Anath seizes Mot and destroys him. With this victory of Anath, Baal revives and returns to his throne.

In the story of Aqhat, Anath desires a bow and arrows, made by the craftsman of the gods, which are possessed by Aqhat. She offers the hero gold and even immortality. Refusing Anath's proposal, Aqhat not only accuses the goddess of lying, but also insults her by implying that she is unable to use the bow. Furious, Anath appears before El, addressing him in the same disrespectful way she does when presenting Baal's petition before El in the Baal Epic. After El acquiesces to her plan for revenge, Anath plots with her servant Yatpan, who evidently takes on the form of a bird. Hovering above Aqhat in the midst of a flock of birds, Anath releases Yatpan, who swoops down and fatally strikes Aqhat. Anath weeps for Aqhat; further, she fails to acquire his bow, which somehow falls into the water and is broken.

The dominant characterization of Anath presented by the extant Ugaritic texts is that of a warlike, bloodthirsty, violent goddess. Insolent, impetuous, relentless, she is the outstanding goddess of these texts (as compared to Asherah and Ashtoreth), due not to her position or rank, but to the force of her personality. Anath, having an intense love for Baal, is usually paired with him as his consort and ally (one exception being the story of Aqhat). See also BAAL (DEITY). In fact, victories over certain enemies which are ascribed to Baal in some Ugaritic passages are attributed to Anath in others. This may be a case of variants, or it may be due to the fact that both Baal and Anath fighting as a pair achieved these triumphs; perhaps the battles of one deity had become blended together with those of the other in the people's minds. There are allusions to the beauty and fertility of Anath, but no preserved text clearly depicts her as giving birth to offspring. However, Anath can be viewed as a fertility goddess in this sense: she is Baal's partner, zealous for his cause, aiding him, and by her defeat of Mot, enabling Baal to come back to life. Moreover, in the Kirta Epic, Kirta is promised that his firstborn son will be suckled by Anath. Finally, Anath is portrayed a number of times as a winged goddess.

Epithets of Anath seen in the Ugaritic literature include "Mistress of Royalty," "Mistress of Dominion," "Mistress of the Highest Heavens," "Lady," and "Maiden." She is referred to as the sister of Baal, probably not in the literal sense, but because of their close companionship. Her title "Virgin" is not to be understood literally, since texts picture her as having intercourse with Baal. Among proposals of scholars are that "Virgin" indicates Anath's perpetual youth, beauty, and nubility; her never bringing forth offspring; her ability to restore her own virginity; her cultic chastity; or her inaccessibility (as an unconquerable martial divinity). Another title of the goddess, Ug *ybmt lʾimm,* remains enigmatic. Both words have received various translations: the first, for example, "Sister-in-Law," "Progenitress," "Nubile Widow"; the second, "People(s)," "Nations," "Rulers," "Mighty One."

Anath was also worshipped in Egypt, particularly during the 19th Dynasty. Rameses II seems to have had a special preference for the goddess. Statues have been found depicting the pharaoh with Anath. A few preserved steles with identifying inscriptions portray Anath being petitioned. One, dating to the reign of Rameses III, was found outside Egypt: it belonged to an Egyptian official in Beth-shan. In a short offering prayer the dedicator asks for "life, welfare and health." The Egyptian representations show Anath clothed, wearing a crown, sitting or standing (Beth-shan), and either armed or unarmed. On the Beth-shan stele she holds a scepter and sign of life. In the magical texts Anath repulses angry demons in battle. The Egyptians closely associated Anath with Ashtoreth (an association evidenced in Ugaritic passages). Both are mentioned in a magical text (13th century B.C.) as the "great goddesses who conceive but cannot bring forth." See ASHTORETH.

There is less evidence concerning Anath from the 1st millennium B.C. Personal names with "Anath" (or some variant) as a theophoric element appear in upper Mesopotamia, and as far W as Carthage and Hadrumetum. Inscriptions mentioning the goddess come primarily from Cyprus. One of these, from Lapethos, is a 4th-century Phoenician-Greek bilingual, which identifies Anath (named in the Phoenician section) with Athena (named in the Greek section). Anath is called the "refuge of the living." In the lore of Sakkuniathon, Anath is probably to be identified with "Athena."

Texts from the 5th-century Jewish colony at Elephantine indicate the worship of Yahweh, but also of Anath-bethel and Anath-yahu. Basically two proposals for understanding these names have been presented by scholars. The first is that the names demonstrate the worship of Anath at Elephantine; she was regarded as Yahweh's consort. The second, more likely to be correct, is that "Anath" in these names is a hypostatized aspect or quality of Yahweh: it is an Aramaic noun meaning "Providence," "Sign," or "Time." Thus, "Anath-bethel" is "Providence/Sign of the House of God," "Anath-yahu" is "Providence/Sign of Yahweh."

It is probable that at least the memory of Anath continued as late as the 3rd century A.D. Evidence from Palmyra (specifically, theophorous names) points to this conclusion.

Also, in the opinion of most scholars, Anath is one of the goddesses included in the composite deity Atargatis, the Syrian goddess whose worship eventually spread throughout the entire Mediterranean world.

B. Anath in the OT

There are only indirect and very limited traces of the cult of Anath in the OT. Of the three great Canaanite goddesses (Asherah, Anath, Ashtoreth), Anath is the least attested. Three place names—Anathoth (e.g., Josh 21:18; Jer 1:1), Beth-anath (Josh 19:38; Judg 1:33), and Beth-anoth (Josh 15:59)—have usually been explained as involving the name of the goddess. Since "Anathoth" may be a shortened form of "Beth-anathoth," it is conceivable that the three had the same general meaning, "House of Anath." The names would then indicate that at one time Anath was worshiped in these locations.

Shamgar, a mighty fighter in Judges (3:31; 5:6), is designated *ben ʿănāt,* "the son of Anath." The name "Shamgar" is non-Israelite (best seen as Hurrian in origin). Scholarly opinion varies as to understanding "the son of Anath." For example, this designation is seen as indicating Shamgar's community; Shamgar was from Beth-anath (*IDB* 4: 306). Another interpretation, seeing in the designation mention of the war divinity Anath, is that it is a military title or epithet (Craigie 1972: 239–40). However, Cross (1980: 7) thinks that *ben ʿănāt* may be a simple personal name. After comparing inscriptions on two arrowheads dating to the late 12th and late 11th centuries B.C., he suggests that the designation be understood as "the (son of) Son of Anath." Ben Anath ("Son of Anath") was Shamgar's father, who was named after the goddess. Extrabiblical onomastic data indicate that personal names often consisted of "Son of" plus the name of a deity. Since Ben Anath was named after the warrior goddess Anath it is quite possible that he came from a military family.

Bibliography

Craigie, P. C. 1972. A Reconsideration of Shamgar ben Anath (Judg 3:31 and 5:6). *JBL* 91: 239–40.

Cross, F. M. 1980. Newly Found Inscriptions in Old Canaanite and Early Phoenician Scripts. *BASOR* 238: 1–20.

Eaton, A. W. 1964. *The Goddess Anat: The History of Her Cult, Her Mythology and Her Iconography.* Diss. Yale University.

Kapelrud, A. S. 1969. *The Violent Goddess: Anat in the Ras Shamra Texts.* Oslo.

Stadelmann, R. 1967. *Syrisch-Palästinenische Gottheiten in Ägypten.* Probleme der Ägyptologie 5. Leiden.

WALTER A. MAIER III

ANATH (PERSON) [Heb *ʿănāt*]. Ostensibly the father of Shamgar, a judge of Israel (Judg 3:31), his identity and even reality have been questioned. Albright (*ARI,* 111) first suggested that the phrase *ben-ʿănāt* actually should be read *bêt-ʿănāt* ("house or temple of Anath"), a city in Galilee. Shamgar then becomes a (the chief?) citizen of that town which Israel was unable to conquer (Judg 1:33). Others identified the city as Anathoth, the birthplace of the prophet Jeremiah (Gray 1957: 127–29). Craigie (1972: 239) interprets *ben-ʿănāt* as a military name or title. Anath was the Ugaritic goddess not only of fertility but of war as well, appearing in Egyptian and Mari texts in a martial role. Further, the name *bn.ʿnt* appears in two lists of personal names from Ugarit (*PRU* 2/43: 12; 61: 6). In this case, the translation of the phrase might very well be "mercenary." If Anath was an actual person, it is unlikely that he was an Israelite or a convert to Yahweh, for we would not expect him to hold the name of a competing deity during a period when Israel is contending with the Canaanites for the land.

Bibliography

Albright, W. F. 1925. The Evolution of the West-Semitic Divinity ʿAn-ʿAnat-ʿAtta. *AJSL* 41: 73–101.

Craigie, P. C. 1972. A Reconsideration of Shamgar ben Anath (Judg 3:31 and 5:6). *JBL* 91: 239–40.

———. 1978. Deborah and Anat: A Study of Poetic Imagery (Judges 5). *ZAW* 90: 374–81.

Fensham, F. C. 1961. Shamgar ben Anat. *JNES* 20: 197–98.

Gray, J. 1957. *The Legacy of Canaan: The Ras Shamra Texts and Their Relevance to the Old Testament.* VTSup 5. Leiden.

KIRK E. LOWERY

ANATHOTH (PLACE) [Heb *ʿănātôt*]. A priestly city in the tribal territory of Benjamin, first mentioned in the Bible as the home of Abiezer and Jehu, two of David's bodyguards (2 Sam 23:27; 1 Chr 11:28; 12:3; 27:12). This important town is not mentioned in any of the early narratives dealing with events such as the conquest or the allotment of cities to the tribes.

Abiathar, the last chief priest of Eli's family, was exiled to his estate in Anathoth because he had supported Solomon's rival, Adonijah. Solomon said that Abiathar deserved death, but because he had carried the ark of the Lord before David, Solomon instead deposed him from the priesthood and exiled him to Anathoth (1 Kgs 2:26). Anathoth is mentioned by Isaiah (10:30) as one of the places on the Assyrian route, but the city was spared destruction.

The prophet Jeremiah was born in Anathoth (Jer 1:1). It was here that he began to prophesy and here that the people of Anathoth rebuked him because he had accused them of breaking the covenant and had prophesied that evil would come upon them. Later, Jeremiah purchased the field of Hanamel in Anathoth as a symbol of God's promise that life someday would return to normal (32:7–9). Jeremiah's last reference to Anathoth appears in a letter from the exiles in Babylon to the religious authorities in Jerusalem (29:27). After the Exile, 128 men of Anathoth returned with Zerubbabel to their town (Ezra 2:23; Neh 7:27) and Anathoth was resettled by the Benjaminites (Neh 11:32).

The debate over Anathoth's location is whether it lies on the high mound (Ras el-Kharrubeh) immediately S of the village of Anata or in the valley next to Anata (M.R. 175135). Anata is situated on a broad ridge composed of three hills connected by saddles. To the S of Anata is a low plateau, and then the N slope of Ras el-Kharrubeh.

Ras el-Kharrubeh is a hill 4.5 km NE of Jerusalem. A low valley and several small hills lie between Ras el-Kharrubeh and the ridge which the Mount of Olives occupies. Wadi Farah with its steep, rocky sides is the nearest water supply to Ras el-Kharrubeh. Neither Ras el-Kharrubeh nor Anata lies on a major highway, but they are within 3 km of the main road from Jerusalem to Shechem and near the junction of the "Way of Beth Horons."

The early historians who identified biblical Anathoth all associated the site with Anata. Josephus (*Ant* 10 §114) identified Anathoth as the home of Jeremiah "which is twenty stades distant from Jerusalem." Eusebius (*Onomast.* 26.27–29) placed Anathoth 3 miles N of Jerusalem in the tribe of Benjamin.

Many pilgrims—including Burchard of Mt. Zion, Marino Santo, John Poloner, and Brother Felix—visited biblical Anathoth during the time of the Crusades. Following the Crusades, the site is not mentioned again until the last century, when E. Robinson also identified ancient Anathoth with Anata. The French geographer M. V. Guérin (1869: 76–79) was the first person to record a visit to Ras el-Kharrubeh.

The most important archaeological work at Anata and Ras el-Kharrubeh was done over fifty years ago by E. P. Blair and A. Bergman (Biran). This work was initiated because Alt had earlier suggested that OT Anathoth was initially at Ras el-Kharrubeh but was moved to Anata after the exile. Blair was given the responsibility of conducting soundings at Anata. As he walked the surface, he was convinced there was not enough debris to indicate that an ancient settlement had occupied this site. His five probes supported that observation, yielding only Arabic, Byzantine, Hellenistic, and Roman deposits (Blair 1936). Because there were no pre-Hellenistic remains, Blair concluded that Alt's views were correct.

Biran's survey at Ras el-Kharrubeh identified pottery from Iron I to Byzantine (Bergman 1936). Out of two probes a few sherds were found from the end of Iron I, some from Iron II, and a few more from the Persian-Hellenistic and Roman periods. Biran concluded that the site was occupied from about the 9th century to Byzantine times. The settlement reached its peak in Iron II (between 800 and 600 B.C.), although it continued to exist in Persian-Hellenistic times, finally coming to an end in the Byzantine period. As a result of the work done by Blair and Biran, the identification of Ras el-Kharrubeh with Anathoth is universally accepted among Israeli, European, and American archaeologists.

There was no subsequent archaeological work at either Anata or Ras el-Kharrubeh until the Levitical City survey team visited the two sites in 1971. At Anata, all the sherds found were Arab and Byzantine (as Blair had observed), with the exception of one possible Iron II sherd. At Ras el-Kharrubeh there was an abundance of pottery dating from Iron II as well as Hellenistic, Roman, and Byzantine periods. The earliest sherd from Iron II was from the 9th century, and the 8th century had the most impressive amount.

The Levitical City survey work at Ras-Kharrubeh and Anata supports the original claims of Alt (Peterson 1977: 409–26). At these two sites we have another example of an Iron Age/Persian city shifting locations during the Hellenistic and Roman periods. During the Iron Age the biblical city of Anathoth was located at Ras el-Kharrubeh, but during the Hellenistic-Roman periods it was relocated down the valley to the village that today bears its name.

Bibliography

Albright, W. F. 1936. Archaeological Notes. *BASOR* 61: 23–25; 62: 25–26; 63: 23.

Bergman (Biran), A. 1936. Sounding at the Supposed Site of OT Anathoth. *BASOR* 62: 22–25; 63: 22–23.

Blair, E. P. 1936. Soundings at Anata (Roman Anathoth). *BASOR* 62: 18–21.

Guérin, M. V. 1869. *Description géographique, historique et archéologique de la Palestine.* Vol. 3. Paris.

Peterson, J. L. 1977. *A Topographical Surface Survey of the Levitical "Cities" of Joshua 21 and I Chronicles 6.* Evanston, IL.

JOHN L. PETERSON

ANATOLIA. The Asian portion of the modern republic of Turkey. The area shows a great deal of topographic variation; some of the main features include a central plateau, a mountainous region in the east, and a fertile plain in the southern region around Adana. See Fig. ANA.01. Because it was one of the crossroads of the ancient Mediterranean world, it has a rich and diverse history, including numerous historical and cultural contacts with Syro-Palestine and its people. This entry will survey the prehistory and history of Anatolia, and will summarize some of the broad features of Anatolian mythology, especially that preserved by the Hittites. See also the entry on HITTITES.

PREHISTORY OF ANATOLIA

The prehistoric period in Anatolia runs from the Lower Paleolithic (ca. 400,000 B.P.) to the end of the EB III period (ca. 2000 B.C.). The beginning of the historic era is marked by the emergence of the Hittites.

A. Paleolithic

Finds from the Paleolithic period are relatively few. Although they occur in both open-air and cave sites, the data are uneven owing to a lack of concerted systematic surveys. The Karain cave near Antalya currently offers the best continuous chronological sequence for prehistoric Anatolia (Mellaart 1975: 93), showing evidence of occupation from the Lower (ca. 400,000 B.P.) to the Upper Paleolithic periods (ca. 30,000–13,000 B.C.). Of special interest is the final undisturbed Upper Paleolithic level (II) which yielded the remains of both *Homo neanderthalensis* and *sapiens* (Esin and Benedict 1963: 340). A final Neolithic phase from Karain can be roughly correllated with the Cilician Neolithic periods (cf. Mellink 1965: 105–6). New excavation is currently being carried on by Turkish and American excavators at Yarimburgaz cave, near Istanbul, where the earliest evidence of human habitation in Turkey is being uncovered Stone tools and fossilized faunal remains unearthed in the cave date to at least 700,000 B.C. Other late-Paleolithic-period sites have been found at Macun Çay near Ankara and Tekköy on the Black Sea coast (Esin and Benedict 1963). Sites such as these indicate that early food-gathering and -collecting communities existed somewhat N of the regions traditionally associated with Anatolia's earliest human habitation.

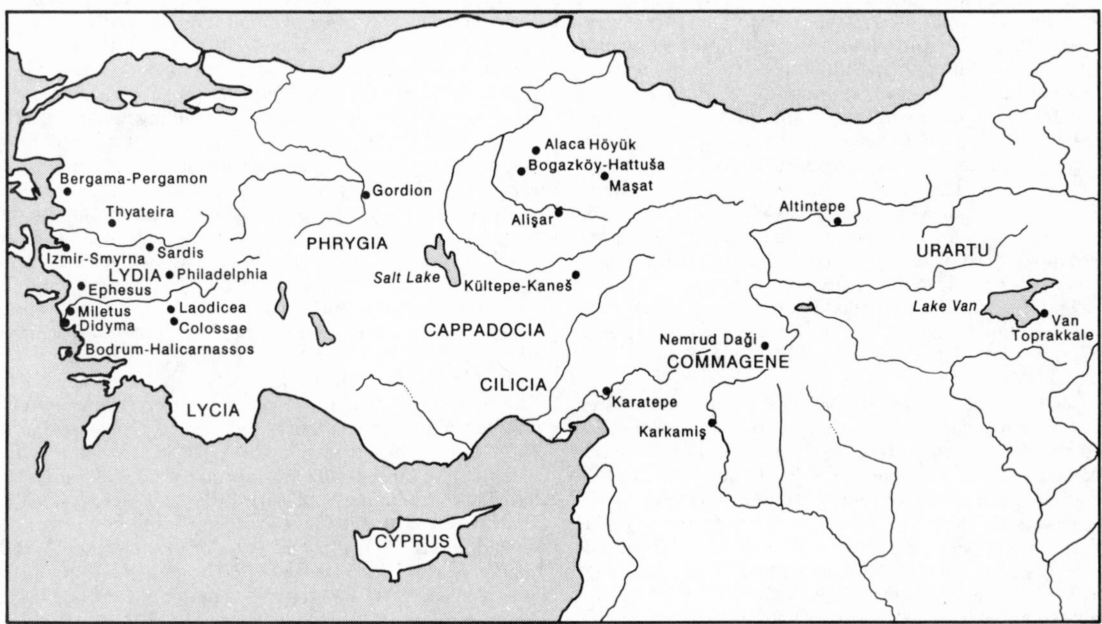

ANA.01. Map of Anatolia.

B. Epipaleolithic

The Epipaleolithic period (ca. 13,000 B.C. to 8,500 B.C.) was a time of intense experimentation. While true agriculture was still unknown, the subsistence pattern of the previous era was gradually supplemented by what has been termed "incipient agriculture." Preadaptive technologies associated with this strategy allowed for a greater exploitation of available food resources. The chipped-stone industry underwent a marked development which is especially apparent in the microlithic tools. Sites attributed to this period are concentrated in a series of caves located on the lower elevations of the once heavily forested Taurus range, overlooking both the Lycian plain and the Mediterranean (Mellaart 1975: 34–35, 92–94). Two such sites are Belbaşı (ca. 13,000 B.C.) and Bildibi (ca. 9,000 B.C.), both of which display hunter-gatherer economies. While Bildibi C showed some evidence of experimentation with grains, the environment proved unsuitable for the adaptation of agriculture and the region was bypassed in succeeding periods in favor of arable lands farther north.

C. Neolithic

The earliest evidence of settled life in Anatolia dates to the Neolithic age (Mellaart 1975; Todd 1980). At the outset of the period (8500–5500 B.C.), man was already experimenting with the plants and animals living around him, and soon began to realize the possibility of manipulating the environment for his own benefit (Reed 1977; Wright 1971). The "incipient agriculture" of the preceding period gave way to a primitive form of true agriculture and the development of village-farming sites across the "fertile crescent." The SE stretch of Anatolia formed the N arc of this crescent and sites such as Çayönü served as bases from which agriculture expanded into W Anatolia.

The Anatolian Neolithic is commonly divided into two phases, the aceramic and the ceramic (Mellaart 1975; but cf. Todd 1980). During the aceramic phase (8500–6500 B.C.) settled communities first appear in conjunction with domesticated plants and animals. The results of archaeological exploration suggest that regional differences already existed during the earliest phase of the Neolithic. Data are uneven, however, as the pertinent sites are few and scattered. The ceramic phase (6500–5500 B.C.), as its name suggests, is characterized by the first appearance of pottery. The economies of both Neolithic phases were similar. Dry-farming communities predominated and were located in areas with arable lands. Such sites were also near local sources of water and scattered examples of irrigation are known. Animal husbandry was introduced early but became more prevalent during the later stages of the Neolithic. Faunal remains show that wild game was also heavily exploited, especially in the period's early phase. Some communities supplemented this base economy by using local resources (i.e., obsidian) as a means of trade. At present, most of the information concerning the Neolithic derives from sites located in the S reaches of the peninsula. Recent salvage excavations along the Euphrates, however, have provided important new information at sites such as Hayar Höyük, Gritille, and Cafer Höyük.

Çayönü is currently the earliest settled site known in Anatolia. Evidence suggests that it was occupied as early as 8000 B.C. and provides fascinating information about the shift from a hunting and gathering to a village-farming economy (cf. Braidwood et al. 1981). The site covered about 30,000 m^2 and housed several hundred people. Hand-worked obsidian and flint tools were found in abundance at Çayönü, as were grinding stones and other materials for food processing. Bone and antler tools also appeared, as did small beads, pendants, and figurines. Copper artifacts were more abundant than expected for such an early date. True pottery was completely absent from the site, but white plaster vessels *(vaisselles blanches)* occur in the upper levels. While botanical remains suggest the appearance of domesticated grains by 7000 B.C., evidence of domesticated animals does not appear, with the exception of the dog (ca. 7000 B.C.), until somewhat later. This situation is not unlike that of other transitional Anatolian Neolithic sites such as Aşikli Höyük, Suberde, and Hacilar (V).

Çatal Höyük (East) is the best known of the Neolithic sites in Anatolia and best represents the developments which were taking place during the later part of the period (Mellaart 1967). The site was well planned and carefully constructed, made up of contiguous mudbrick houses with entryways through the roof. The walls and floors were plastered and burnished as in contemporary Jericho. Pottery was found in all thirteen excavated levels, though aceramic levels undoubtedly lie farther below. While the pottery appears to be strictly utilitarian in nature, other arts and crafts attest to a nonutilitarian aspect in the culture. Although no altars were found, the discovery of shrines with bucrania, wall paintings, plaster reliefs, and cult figurines suggests a strong religious orientation. Taken together, these materials provide evidence for a sophistication not previously suspected in central Anatolia.

The chipped-stone industry of Çatal Höyük is particularly significant. The people who inhabited Çatal Höyük made almost exclusive use of obsidian from nearby volcanic flows for their tools and weapons. The fact that local Anatolian obsidian was found at Jericho, among other places in the Levant, suggests that the inhabitants of Çatal Höyük were involved in some form of long-distance trade (Renfrew, Dixon, and Cann 1966). While one need not understand the term "trade" in an exaggerated sense, some sort of exchange must be hypothesized in order to account for the movement of Konya obsidian so far abroad. The occurrence of Mediterranean shells, metal ores, and pigments not found locally also point to the existence of such trade. The economy of Çatal Höyük, however, continued to be based on agriculture, and irrigation appears at Çatal Höyük around 6000 B.C. The diet of Çatal Höyük remains one of the most varied yet discovered in the Neolithic. Although no definite proof was found of domesticated animals, animal husbandry probably played a significant role in the town's economy. Weapons, wall paintings portraying hunt scenes, and the bones of wild animals, however, indicate that hunting was still important. Çatal Höyük comes to an end around 5400 B.C., although after a short interval a new settlement is founded across the river. This later settlement belongs to the Early Chalcolithic period.

D. The Chalcolithic Period

The three phases of the succeeding Chalcolithic period last from about 5500 to 3000 B.C. and seem to have gradually developed out of the Neolithic period with no clear signs of cultural upheaval. The Early Chalcolithic period (5500–4500 B.C.) is best known from sites localized S of the Kizil Irmak. This initial phase is sometimes called the "late Neolithic" because its economy shows little change from the preceding Neolithic, remaining agriculturally based. Faunal studies are incomplete, but animal husbandry probably existed at Hacilar, much as at contemporary sites such as Erbaba and Can Hasan where sheep, goats, cattle, and perhaps pigs were kept. Botanical remains indicate that foodstuffs were much like those at Çatal Höyük with einkorn, emmer, as well as 2- and 6-rowed barley being mainstays along with peas, lentils, chick-peas, acorns, and hackberries. The distinguishing characteristic of the period is the development of painted pottery, the earliest examples of which apparently come from Mersin. The principal Anatolian site of the Early Chalcolithic is Hacilar, where the red-on-creme pottery attained a high degree of development (Mellaart 1975: 111). The examples from levels V–II are considered the hallmark of the period. Two distinct phases of fine clay figurines are found at Hacilar, the first (levels IX–VI) which displays the statuary at its unrivaled best, and the second (levels V–II) which lacks much of the creativity and charisma of the earlier examples. Nonetheless, the statuary, as a whole, is unmatched by anything else of its time. Early levels were unfortified, but security is enhanced in period II, with the addition of an outer defense wall formed by employing a line of contiguous structures on the perimeter of the site as a defensive measure. The site was destroyed and abandoned about 4800 B.C., leaving no apparent links to succeeding cultures.

Subsequent phases of the Chalcolithic are not well documented, especially in central Anatolia. The Middle Chalcolithic period (4500–3500 B.C.) is most evident along the Euphrates River where Late Ubaid cultural remains indicate a Mesopotamian intervention. This interlude represents the beginning of a persistent pattern of Mesopotamian riverine expansion which continues through the Middle Bronze Age (Marfoe 1987). Ubaid pottery at sites along the land route to the Ergani-Maden copper mines near Diyarbakir seems to confirm the motivation behind this expansion, and Ubaid pottery from Fraktin suggests that Mesopotamian influence may have also extended into central Anatolia at this time. The Late Chalcolithic (3500–3000 B.C.) is imprecisely understood in both western and central Anatolia (Yakar 1985, cf. chart 107). In the east, the Uruk culture succeeded the Ubaid and, like its predecessor, followed the main river routes north. Uruk expansion into Anatolia is documented in a series of enclaves which included sites such as Tepe Gawra, Tell Brak, Tarsus, Carchemish, Habuba Kabira, Kurban Höyük, and Norşuntepe before its sudden collapse around 3000 B.C. (Algaze 1987).

The legacy of early Anatolian prehistory is one of innovation, growth, and preparation. Important changes occurred inside Anatolia related to the development of greater food production and sedentism. The Early Bronze Age (3000–2000 B.C.) ushered man into a new age. Rapid developments in metallurgy, a greater accumulation of wealth and property, larger cities, and increased social organization all occur. Trade and military ventures bring

Anatolia increasingly into contact with the outside world. In spite of its "internationalism," however, small villages with an agriculturally based economy remain the backbone of the country. The Early Bronze Age of Anatolia is conveniently divided into three periods.

E. The EB I Period

The initial phase of the Early Bronze in Anatolia (3000–2800 B.C.) displays a proto-urban village character marked by the first appearance of distinct, though parochial, cultural regions. EB I is represented in the NW by the pre-Troy I cultures of the Troad and related island sites off the coast such as Poliochni (on Lemnos), Thermi (on Lesbos), and Emporio (on Chios). The exact placement of the pre-Troy I sequence is not completely understood, but on the basis of comparative ceramics it appears to antedate Troy I with Kumtepe Ic coming near the end of EB I (Yakar 1985; Mellink 1986). The small and later fortified town of Troy I can only begin then near the end of the EB I period (ca. 2800 B.C.; cf. Yakar 1985: 116). It should be noted, however, that attempts to interpret the evidence from Troy have led to serious disagreement over Anatolian chronology which stems, in part, from differences in the chronological systems currently in use. While some scholars would put more reliance on European and Aegean sequences established on the basis of comprehensive radiocarbon dates (Easton 1976), others feel that it is more productive to link Troy to the Aegean only after it is securely tied to central Anatolia and, through historical synchronisms, to the better-established Near Eastern chronologies (cf. Yakar 1985: 111).

The EB I is not easily demarcated in central Anatolia. It may be part of a cultural complex that is not totally indigenous to the region, perhaps including parts of Thrace, the Troad, and the Pontic regions. Evidence is found in the ceramics of Alişar, Kültepe, and Alaca Höyük, but details are unclear because of a lack of clear ties to more secure chronologies. EB I levels are dated primarily on the basis of affinities in the material culture to the preceding Chalcolithic period and the lack of foreign imports prevalent in the succeeding EB II (cf. Mellink 1965: 110–13). Because its upper chronological limit is sometimes thought to overlap with the Chalcolithic, the complex is often referred to as "Late Chalcolithic." Other north-central sites tied to this horizon include Büyük Güllücek, Horoztepe, and Maşat Höyük. The EB I is also represented at Bağbaşı in Elmalı plain, and Beycesultan (XX–XL) near Denizli.

Eastern Anatolia became the theater of the Early Trans-Caucasian movement (ETC) about this same time (Kelly-Buccelati 1974). Also known as the Khirbet Kerak, Kura-Araxes, or Karaz culture (in reference to other areas where it has been isolated), the ETC movement is defined by the distinctive red-black polished ware with fluted and grooved decoration found in its wake. The movement begins in the Araxes Valley situated between the Black and Caspian seas during the 4th millennium, and then spreads E into Iran. It has been suggested that the impetus of this movement originated, as it so often does in Anatolia's history, in the desire to obtain raw materials in the form of native copper and copper ores (Kelly-Buccelati 1974: 353). The first elements of the ETC arrive in eastern Anatolia around 2800 B.C.

F. EB II

The EB II sequence (ca. 2800–2400 B.C.) is composed of roughly contemporary cultures whose contemporaneity is based on clear synchronisms in the following period. Among these are middle and late Troy I (including Troy IIa) in the NW, the "Copper Age" cultures of central Anatolia, and the Cilician EB II. Urbanism is on the rise and imposing walls begin to appear at regional centers like Troy, Alaca Höyük, Kültepe, Norşuntepe, and Arslantepe. Fortified cities such as these suggest aggressive kingdoms vying for power. The number of metal weapons such as battle-axes, swords, and spears found at these sites provide further evidence of militarism and the need for defense. The reason behind this urban growth and apparent aggressiveness is debated. Much of it, especially in the eastern and central regions, may be a response to the Mesopotamian movement into the region in search of raw materials. As Anatolian metals such as copper, lead, gold, silver, and electrum were among the most highly coveted of these resources, those who controlled the access to them must have reaped startling wealth, not to mention jealous competitors.

In the northwest, Troy I survives until about 2600 B.C. and is followed by a hiatus in occupation before the EB II concludes with the complete rebuilding of the Troy IIa citadel around 2500 B.C. (cf. Mellink 1986: 149, pl. 16; Yakar 1985), an event which is approximately contemporary with the last phase of the Early Dynastic III period in Mesopotamia (cf. Yakar 1976: 56). Inland, its influence is felt as far away as Beycesultan (XIX–XVII).

The EB II of central Anatolia is represented by "Copper Age" levels at Alişar Höyük, Acemhöyük, and Kültepe. The development of small settlements into large fortified cities suggests an increasingly urban orientation. Alaca Höyük is of particular importance for this period. Among the discoveries at Alaca are the royal tombs (Yakar 1985: 185). These rectangular shaft tombs must have been the final resting places for several generations of the city's royal house. The men were buried with weapons and the women with domestic articles and jewelry. Also among the contents of these tombs are the enigmatic "standards" and the metal remains of furniture. The numerous metal remains found in the tombs reveal the same advanced technological skills as found at Troy.

The origins of the Alaca culture are disputed. Unfortunately, the royal tombs cannot be stratigraphically dated, but on the basis of "Copper Age" pottery found in the tomb, they were tentatively placed at the end of the EB II or early in the EB IIIa, though some tombs seem to date a little later (cf. Yakar 1985: 176, 177–79, 185). While some have tried to link the Alaca culture to the Kurgan cultures of the north, and the Black Sea coast site of Maikop in particular (Yakar 1985: 185), there is no clearly definable means of tracing its origins.

Meanwhile, eastern Anatolia continued to bear the brunt of the Early Trans-Caucasian movement which reached the area of the Keban dam and Malatya around 2800 B.C., later finding its way to the Amuq around 2600 B.C. ETC influence is also felt at this same time in central

Anatolian "Copper Age" sites such as Kültepe and Alaca Höyük (Kelly-Buccelati 1974: 301–33). Farther south, the seizure and occupation of the town of Purušḫanda (perhaps located at Acemhöyük) by Sargon I (ca. 2400 B.C.) renewed the Mesopotamian presence in the region and suggests that this part of Anatolia was well known to Mesopotamians as early as the 24th century B.C.

G. EB III Period

The last phase of the Early Bronze Age (ca. 2400–2000 B.C.) witnessed major developments taking place throughout Anatolia. The upper limit of subphase EB IIIA is determined by the inauguration of the Cilicio-Troadic connection and the introduction of wheel-made pottery to Troy IIb. These events provide clear chronological synchronisms between Troy IIb–g and the Cilician EB IIIA. In the case of Tarsus, the evidence is strong enough to postulate an intrusive settlement of West Anatolians (Mellink 1986: 149–51). This intrusion may have been brought about by seafaring warriors and merchants who followed the coast, much like the "Sea Peoples" of the later 13th–early 12th centuries.

The EB IIIA in central Anatolia is characterized by a continuity that goes back to the EB II (Yakar 1985: 183). The region, however, was not isolated from the larger events of the period. Depatas and one-handled cups found at such sites as Alişar, Kültepe, and Acemhöyük indicate that the region was intimate with the affairs of the EB IIIA (Özgüç 1986; Mellink 1986). The similarity of jewelry from Troy, Alaca, and Eskiyapar provides another indication of strong relations between Troy and her central Anatolian counterparts (Mellink 1986: 142).

In the E, a middle phase of the ETC movement begins about 2400 B.C., but its energy is apparently spent by 2100 B.C. In fact, a pattern of cultural fragmentation has already developed in the E in which numerous local cultures flourish during the last part of the 3d millennium. This patchwork of small polities is characterized by large walled towns and many local ceramic traditions which actually begin in the middle of the 3d millennium and continue into the 2d (Marfoe 1987: 34).

The EB IIIA period came to an end around 2300 B.C. when Troy II was overrun and the Cilicio-Troadic connections were severed by a force of uncertain origin (cf. Mellink 1986: 151). The EB IIIB is marked by the erection of Troy III–V, which were roughly contemporary with the later central Anatolian EB III. Along the coastal areas of W and SW Anatolia the Minoans became the dominant seafarers, supplanting the native West Anatolians, while the inland areas of W and S Anatolia are thought to have provided the backdrop for the movement of the Indo-European-speaking peoples into Anatolia (cf. Yakar 1976).

The areas N of the Kizil Irmak do not seem to have been affected by the aggressive action which brought an end to Troy II (above) and many of the principalities to the S (Yakar 1985: 183). Important EB III settlements maintained themselves at Alaca Höyük, Maşat, Kültepe, Acemhöyük, Karahöyük-Konya, and Alişar Höyük. It may be that in the cities of this area, especially those farther N, are to be found the "indigenous" Hattians who preceded the Hittites and bequeathed to them so many of their cultural trappings.

Although it was not uncommon for these EB III settlements to be overthrown from time to time, occupation is quickly resumed with no signs of cultural collapse. Signs point to internal or internecine conflict rather than external force, a point which is confirmed in the cultural continuity seen between the EB III and succeeding MB/LB cultures, as well as the expanding foreign contacts. Kültepe-Kaneš, in anticipation of its role as the nexus of the Old Assyrian trade network in the Middle Bronze Age, shows signs of increasing prosperity from its foreign trade (Özgüç 1986). Other towns also grow, either in response to similar economic catalysts or as places of refuge from the internecine struggles convulsing the region. Near the end of the period the Mesopotamian link is again apparent in the form of traders from Ur (III) and Assyria who successively followed the long-established trade routes to central Anatolia. As a result of such external influences, the cultural horizon of central Anatolia was considerably broadened in advance of the political shift which was to turn the focus of the ancient world to Anatolia for much of the 2d millennium. When the EB III came to an end around 2000 B.C., the stage was already set for the emergence of the Hittites.

Bibliography

Algaze, G. 1987. *Mesopotamian Expansion and its Consequences.* Diss. Chicago.

Blegan, C. W. 1963. *Troy and the Trojans.* London.

Braidwood, R. J.; Cambel, H.; and Schirmer, W. 1981. Beginnings of Village-Farming Communities in Southeastern Turkey: Çayönü Tepesi, 1978 and 1979. *Journal of Field Archaeology* 8: 249–58.

Easton, D. F. 1976. Towards a Chronology for the Anatolian Early Bronze Age. *AnSt* 26: 145–67.

Esin, U., and Benedict, P. 1963. Recent Developments in the Prehistory of Anatolia. *Current Anthropology* 4: 339–46.

Kelly-Buccelati, M. 1974. *The Early Transcaucasian Culture.* Diss. Chicago.

Marfoe, L. 1987. Cedar Forest to Silver Mountain: Social Change and the Development of Long-Distance Trade. Pp. 25–35 in *Early Near Eastern Societies, in Center and Periphery in the Ancient World,* ed. M. Rowlands; M. Larsen; and K. Kristiansen. Cambridge.

Mellaart, J. 1967. *Çatal Höyük: A Neolithic Town in Anatolia.* London.

———. 1975. *The Neolithic of the Near East.* London.

Mellink, M. 1965. The Chronology of Anatolia. Pp. 101–31 in *Chronologies in Old World Archaeology.* Chicago.

———. 1986. The Early Bronze Age in West Anatolia. Pp. 139–52 in *The End of the Bronze Age in the Aegean,* ed. G. Cadogan. Leiden.

Özgüç, T. 1986. New Observations on the Relationship of Kültepe with Southeast Anatolia and North Syria during the Third Millennium B.C. Pp. 31–47 in *Ancient Anatolia: Aspects of Change and Cultural Development.* Madison.

Reed, C., ed. 1977. *Origins of Agriculture.* Paris.

Renfrew, C.; Dixon, J. E.; and Cann, J. R. 1966. Obsidian and Early Cultural Contact in the Near East. *Proceedings of the Prehistoric Society* 22: 30–72.

Todd, I. 1980. *The Prehistory of Central Anatolia I: The Neolithic Period.* Studies in Mediterranean Archaeology. Göteborg.

Wright, G. A. 1969. *Obsidian Analyses and Prehistoric Near Eastern Trade 7500 to 3500.* Anthropological Papers 37. Ann Arbor.

———. 1971. Origins of Food Production in Southwestern Asia: A Survey of Ideas. *Current Anthropology* 12: 447–76.

Yakar, J. 1976. Anatolia and the "Great Movement" of Indo-Europeans, ca. 2300 B.C.E.—Another Look. *Tel Aviv* 3: 151–57.

———. 1985. *The Later Prehistory of Anatolia.* BAR International Series 268, 2 vols. London.

RONALD L. GORNY

HISTORY OF ANCIENT ANATOLIA

Both archaeological and textual source material is abundant for ancient Anatolia. Many sites have been excavated and have yielded a wealth of evidence about architecture, city planning, pottery, metallurgy, and material culture in general for all periods of Anatolian history. Textual remains from a number of sites have provided philologists and historians with material for the history of early Asia Minor. The many different languages, scripts, and writing media reflect the diversity of the area's history. The cuneiform system of writing is represented by clay tablets written in at least two dialects of Akkadian, Hittite, and Urartian, as well as Urartian monumental inscriptions in stone. From the Hittite kingdom and many Neo-Hittite cities, steles and monuments written in the Luwian hieroglyphic script are extant. Phrygians and Lydians left inscriptions in their own languages and distinctive scripts based on Phoenician or Greek alphabets. There is a wealth of inscriptional material in Greek and Latin from the later periods, as well as information in some Greek and Roman writers.

A. Old Assyrian Merchants

History begins in Anatolia with the tablets of the Old Assyrian merchants. These merchants, based in Aššur, came into Anatolia near the beginning of the 2d millennium B.C. and established trading colonies (Old Assyrian *kārum*) to facilitate regular trade between Aššur and Anatolia. The most important of these colonies was at the city of Kaneš, modern Kültepe. In the upper levels of the *kārum* were discovered a number of tablets, primarily economic documents, written in cuneiform in the Old Assyrian script and dialect. Formal trade agreements were drawn up with local Anatolian rulers, who offered the merchants protection but also exacted taxes on their commerce. Indo-European names occur in some of the documents, indicating that the Hittites were already present in Anatolia in this period, although not as a recognizable political entity. Also found in the *kārum* district were a number of cylinder seals, a distinctively Mesopotamian type of seal which was rolled across a wet clay bulla or tablet as a signature. The seals show Mesopotamian and Syrian as well as native Anatolian motifs.

On the site of the city itself a palace has been identified. Tablets in Old Assyrian were also found in this building; the local ruler apparently employed scribes from the *kārum.* One of the most interesting is a letter from another Anatolian ruler to the king of Kaneš. In another building was found a dagger or spearhead inscribed "the palace of Anitta the king." Opinion is divided as to whether this indicates that Anitta was king at Kaneš or that he sacked the city and the dagger was lost there.

The advent of the Assyrian traders begins the historical period in Anatolia; those merchants brought with them among other things the concept of writing and the use of cylinder seals. Later Hittite texts refer to a city called Neša (Kaneš) as their city of origin, which accords well with the evidence of the Hittite names in the Kaneš tablets. Thus the Hittites were exposed to the cultural influence of the foreign merchants from Aššur, some elements of which are discernible in the Hittite cultural tradition.

B. Hittites

The main textual source for Hittite history is the large corpus of cuneiform texts discovered at the Hittite capital of Ḫattuša, modern Boğazköy, in central Turkey. Most of the texts are in Hittite, the earliest attested Indo-European language. Archaeological evidence for the Hittites is extensive; major sites include Boğazköy, Maşat, Alaca Höyük, and Alişar.

The first recorded king of the Hittites was Anitta, very probably the same king whose dagger was found at Kültepe. The one major text attributable to him lists the cities which he conquered. One of these was Ḫattuša, which was resettled and made the capital by the Hittites under Ḫattusilis I ca. 1650 B.C. Perhaps the most important document for this king's reign in his "Political Testament," in which he addresses the assembled nobles on the subject of his adoption of a new heir after the treachery of his own son. His adopted successor, Muršili I, expanded Ḫattusilis' empire and even made a raid deep into Mesopotamia, conquering Babylon and ending the OB dynasty of Hammurapi ca. 1595. However, Muršili on his return was murdered in the first of a long series of dynastic disputes. The Old Hittite period ends with the king Telepinu, who promulgated an edict defining rules for dynastic succession designed to end the intrigues which had crippled the kingdom since Muršili's assassination.

After a Middle Hittite period of somewhat meager documentation, the New Hittite period begins with the reign of Šuppiluliumas I, who embarked on an ambitious program of empire building. Later kings maintained and increased the conquered lands, administering an empire extending in all directions from Ḫattuša. Important texts in this period include the annals of Muršili II, in which are detailed year by year the campaigns of the king, a treaty between Ḫattusilis III and Rameses II which is famous because it is extent in copies both from Ḫattuša and from Egypt, and the "Apology" of Ḫattusilis III, an early piece of political justification in which the king defends his usurpation of the throne from his nephew. The reign of Ḫattusilis' successor, Tudḫaliya IV, is characterized by his religious reforms. Shortly after that king's reign the capital was captured and burned and the empire collapsed. Scholars have yet to penetrate the mystery of who it was that so dramatically brought to an end one of the great empires of the Near East. See also HITTITES.

C. Neo-Hittite States

Although the collapse of the capital at Ḫattuša signaled the end of the Hittite empire, many of the cities throughout the empire retained their Hittite character for centuries after the imperial structure had vanished. The culture of these Neo-Hittite cities shows a mixture of Hittite and Aramean elements. An important source for their political history are the annals of the kings of Assyria, who eventually incorporated all of these cities one at a time into their empire. The archaeological record from this period includes excellent architectural remains and wonderful examples of sculpture, both relief and in the round. There are also a number of inscriptions in hieroglyphic Luwian, although there is no corpus of nonmonumental documentation analogous to the Hittite archives at Ḫattuša.

Karkamiş, on the modern Syria-Turkey border, was a provincial capital during the Hittite empire and became one of the most important Neo-Hittite cities. Much of the 1st-millennium city has been excavated, revealing the truly magnificent series of orthostats (stone slabs, carved in low relief, used to decorate the walls of public buildings). Many of these orthostats may now be seen in the Ankara museum. The art of Karkamiş influenced all of the surrounding states and was probably transmitted to the Greeks by the Phrygians.

One of the most spectacular of all the Neo-Hittite sites is Karatepe. Here the orthostats have been preserved *in situ,* giving the modern visitor an idea of the layout of the city and its decoration. The reliefs and the long bilingual inscription of King Azitawanda in hieroglyphic Luwian and Phoenician illustrates the blending of Hittite and Phoenician elements at Karatepe.

The history of the Neo-Hittite period is one of many small city-states, heirs at least in part to Hittite culture, which maintained themselves as independent principalities but were never able to reunite the area as the Hittite empire had done. This made them susceptible to attack, and their history as independent states ended as each individual city was incorporated into the expanding Assyrian empire in the first half of the 1st millennium B.C. Thereafter their distinctive Hittite-Aramean character was lost and they were absorbed culturally as well as politically into the Assyrian empire. The period immediately after the Neo-Hittite states is thus for southern Anatolia one of Assyrian domination.

D. Urartians

The extremely mountainous E region of Anatolia was called by the Assyrians of the late 2d and 1st millennia Urartu or Uruatri. A number of Urartian sites have been discovered. These include Van, Toprakkale, Altıntepe, and Çavuştepe in Turkey and Karmir-Blur and Erin-Berd in the Soviet Union. Urartian cities follow the general pattern of utilizing the region's steep-sided hills as natural fortification, supplemented with defensive walls. The cities normally have huge cisterns cut in the rock and an extensive system of storage jars, for withstanding the sieges of the Assyrians mentioned below.

Archeology has also brought to light a number of monumental rock inscriptions of the Urartians, written in Assyrian cuneiform but in the Urartian language, which shows some affinities to Hurrian. Approximately 25 tablets have been found in addition to the rock inscriptions. Still, much of our understanding of Urartian political history comes from the Assyrian sources.

The Urartian homeland is well protected by mountains and rather inaccessible from Assyria, its main enemy. The Assyrians could only campaign in Urartu for a few weeks out of the year, because the passes through which they had to go were only open for a short time. This dictated the Urartian strategy for defending their homeland, which was simply to withdraw within their walled fortress towns and utilize their stored provisions to wait out the Assyrian siege. The development of Urartian political organization from a tribal system to a unified monarchy may be traced in the Assyrian sources over a period of several centuries. By the 9th century B.C., Urartu was the object of regular campaigns by the Assyrians. In the first half of the 8th century, Urartian power was at its zenith as they pushed west to the Mediterranean, coming into contact with the Neo-Hittite states. The Urartians managed to hold some of their conquered lands until Tiglath-pileser III reasserted Assyrian control and pushed the Urartians back into their mountainous homeland. Thereafter the history of Urartu is primarily one of defense against periodic campaigns of the Assyrians. Urartu as an independent kingdom in the written sources disappeared with its conquest by the Medes in the later 7th century B.C. The Urartians are best known to us today through their excellent metalwork and ivory carving, their jewelry, and their armor.

E. Phrygians and Lydians

The Phrygians were contemporaries of the Urartians who lived in central Anatolia around the Halys River, the modern Kızıl Irmak. Primary written sources for their history are Greek legends, such as the Midas story, and Assyrian historical documents. The Phrygians had their own alphabetic writing system based on the Phoenician alphabet, but the corpus of Phrygian is very small and is limited mostly to monumental inscriptions. Their main site is the capital at Gordion. Outside the ancient city are several huge burial tumuli. The largest of these is referred to as that of Midas, but there is no evidence for this identification. Another site is a rock-cut building façade at Midas city in W Anatolia which includes an inscription.

The Phrygians may appear in written sources as early as the 11th century B.C., in the reign of the Assyrian king Tiglath-pileser I. Sargon II (8th century) records a military confrontation with the Phrygian king Mita (the Greek Midas) in Cilicia in S Anatolia. Soon after this clash with Assyria the Cimmerians ca. 690 B.C. swept into Anatolia and took Gordion, with Midas, according to tradition, committing suicide at the loss of his kingdom. After the Cimmerian invasion, Gordion was rebuilt, but although the architecture and material culture closely resemble that of the earlier city, the rebuilding was done by the Lydians, not Phrygians. The Phrygians worshiped the goddess Kubaba/Cybele, who in later periods became an important mother-goddess in Anatolia.

The Lydians, as noted above, added the Phrygian region to their own when Gordion was destroyed by the Cimmerians. The Cimmerians also attacked the Lydian capital of Sardis in W Anatolia, but King Alyattes managed to repel them. Written sources for the Lydians are meager, including a few texts in Lydian and mention of them in Homer and Herodotus. From Herodotus, we learn that Alyattes pushed his kingdom to the Mediterranean, destroying Smyrna (modern Izmir) at the beginning of the 6th century B.C. Excavation at Sardis has brought to light much of the material culture of the Lydians. They were in close contact with the Greeks throughout their history, and much of their art shows affinities with that of the Greeks of the Archaic period. Croesus, the last Lydian king, ca. 561–547 B.C., consulted the oracle at Delphi and attacked the Persians on the strength of the oracle's reply. The result of his attempt to expand his kingdom at the expense of the Persians, however, was that the Persians took Sardis and ended the Lydian kingdom.

F. Ionian City-States

The W coast of Anatolia of the 1st millennium is referred to as Ionia because of the many Ionian Greek city-states founded there during the migrations at the end of the Bronze Age. Important sites include Ephesus, Priene, Miletus, and Didyma. Greek literary sources supplement the extensive archaeological record.

Throughout the 7th century B.C. several Lydian kings in succession attacked various Ionian cities in their expansion to the west. Alyattes, mentioned above, laid siege to the important port city of Miletus for 12 years and succeeded in taking Smyrna. His successor Croesus is recorded as giving gifts to Ionian temples, especially the temple of Artemis at Ephesus, but he attacked that city as well. A number of the mainland Ionian cities were paying tribute to Lydia up until the fall of that kingdom to the Persians. The island cities were free of this burden as the Lydians had no fleet. The Ionian city-states are well known for their intellectual life; the pre-Socratic philosophers Thales, Anaximander, and Anaximenes all came from Ionian Anatolia.

G. Persian Period

Greek and Persian literary sources furnish the main evidence for the Persian occupation of Anatolia, as the Persians left little distinctive archaeological evidence. The Medes, a group associated with the Persians, are recorded in Anatolia early in the 6th century B.C., fighting with Lydia. In 546 the last Lydian king, Croesus, attacked the first Achaemenid (Persian) king, Cyrus. When Cyrus took the Lydian capital of Sardis the remainder of Anatolia rapidly followed. For the next two centuries the Persians ruled Anatolia from several different satrapies, or provincial administrative centers. One of the best-known satraps was Mausolus of Halicarnassos, whose funerary monument was the Mausoleum, one of the 7 wonders of the world.

The Ionian city-states, taken by the Persians in the wake of their conquest of Sardis, revolted in 499 B.C., winning only a temporary freedom. After quelling the revolt, the Persians attempted to placate the Ionian cities in order to secure their flank before launching their invasion of the Greek mainland. The failure of Xerxes' Greek invasion weakened Persian control of the Greek cities in Anatolia as well, although it was not until Alexander the Great's campaigns through Anatolia in the middle of the 4th century B.C. that the Persians were expelled. The Persians ruled Asia Minor politically, but had little influence culturally, the various pre-Persian cultures of Anatolia remaining essentially the same.

H. Hellenistic Period

This is the period between Alexander's expulsion of the Persians and the coming of the Romans. Sources for this period include the various Greek historical sources on Alexander and his successors as well as archaeological evidence from many sites. Some parts of Anatolia were incorporated into the empire of Alexander and his successors, while other areas managed to escape conquest or reasserted their independence, forming small kingdoms. The north central region was never conquered by Alexander and remained independent until the Roman period.

An important kingdom of this period was that of Pergamon (modern Bergama), located on the W coast. The foundation of the kingdom dates to Philetaeros, 283–263 B.C. The remains of the city on its acropolis are still very impressive. Attalus I (241–197 B.C.) built the magnificent altar of Zeus, now on exhibit in Berlin, to commemorate a victory over the Gauls of central Anatolia. Pergamon's close cultural contact with mainland Greece is indicated by Attalus II's endowing of a stoa at Athes. The last Pergamene king, Attalus III, bequeathed the kingdom to Rome at his death in 133 B.C.

One of the best known of the independent Hellenistic kingdoms of Anatolia is that of Commagene, situated in SE Anatolia. It is justly famous for the funerary monument of its king, Antiochus I Epiphanes, deep in the mountains at Nemrud Dağı. The site contains a huge burial tumulus with pavilions facing both the rising and setting sun with colossal stone statues of Hellenistic gods, in which group Antiochus included himself. There are also other monuments and inscriptions in the area. The culture of Commagene as preserved shows a unique mixture of Greek and Iranian elements. The kingdom remained independent until A.D. 72, when it was incorporated into the province of Syria by Vespasian.

I. Roman Period

Rome began expanding into Anatolia in the 2d century B.C. and eventually took all of the region, splitting it into several provinces, the largest of which were Asia, Galatia, and Cappadocia. Besides the acquisition of Pergamon and Commagene mentioned above, a landmark in the Roman takeover was the final conquest by Pompey ca. 67 B.C. of the district of Pontus on the Black Sea after three wars with its last ruler, Mithridates VI. Abundant Roman sites in Anatolia have yielded archaeological evidence and many inscriptions in Greek and Latin. A number of Roman writers mention Asia Minor as well. Important sites include Ephesus (modern Selcuk), Hierapolis (modern Pamukkale), and Aphrodisias. The seven churches of Revelation are all located in Anatolia; some of them are at cities with extensive Roman remains; at others almost nothing is left today. For the archaeology of the seven churches, see the comprehensive study of Edwin Yamauchi cited in the bibliography.

Unlike the Persian rulers of Anatolia, who left little in the archaeological record, the Romans built cities in Anatolia which are distinctively Roman, with the normal elements of Roman cities such as baths, a forum, theater, and stadium. The culture was a mixture of Greek and Roman elements with an additional Anatolian admixture. Artemis of Ephesus was a syncretized deity distinctive to this Anatolian Greco-Roman city, and Cybele, attested (as Kubaba) from the Hittite and Phrygian periods, was worshiped throughout Roman Anatolia as a mother goddess. The last major influence on the culture was the advent of the new religion of Christianity, which revolutionized the beliefs of its formerly pagan converts and eventually led to the founding by Constantine of a new capital of the now Christian empire just across the Bosporus from the Anatolia where Christianity experienced much of its early growth.

Bibliography

Alkim, U. Bahadır. 1968. *Anatolia I.* Archeologia Mundi. Geneva.

Calder, W. M., and Bean, G. E. 1958. *A Classical Map of Asia Minor.* London.

Gurney, O. R. 1981. *The Hittites.* 2d rev. ed. New York.

Lloyd, S. H. 1967. *Early Highland Peoples of Anatolia.* London.

Metzger, H. 1969. *Anatolia II.* Trans. J. Hogarth. Archeologia Mundi. Geneva.

Yamauchi, E. M. 1980. *The Archaeology of New Testament Cities in Western Asia Minor.* Grand Rapids, MI.

Zimansky, P. E. 1985. *Ecology and Empire: The Structure of the Urartian State.* SAOC 41. Chicago.

GREGORY MCMAHON

ANATOLIAN MYTHOLOGY

Although many different peoples lived in Anatolia in ancient times, we know little about any Anatolian mythology outside of that preserved by the Hittites. A few myths for later Anatolian peoples are found in Greek and Latin sources. The cuneiform texts found in the Hittite archives at their capital of Ḫattuša, modern Boğazköy, include a number of mythological tales. Most of these mythological texts are in the Hittite language, but there are also some in Hattic, Hurrian, and Akkadian. As is the case with any archive of clay tablets, portions of the texts are often missing where the tablet has been broken or abraded away.

The mythology preserved in the Hittite archives reflects two main borrowed traditions: that of the Hattians (pre-Hittite inhabitants of Anatolia), and that of the Hurrians, a people of N Mesopotamia who exerted great cultural influence on the Hittites in their later history, transmitting elements both of their own and Mesopotamian culture to their northern neighbors. The Hattian myths are not independent literary creations; rather, each forms an integral part of a ritual and had a magical potency as it was recited at the performing of the ritual. These Hattian myths, reflecting a native Anatolian tradition, date from the Old Hittite period, when the influence of the Hattians was strongest on the developing Hittite culture. The foreign mythology borrowed from the Hurrians, and to a lesser extent the Mesopotamians and Canaanites, dates from the New Hittite or Empire period. A more complete treatment of Hittite mythology is available in the article, on which some of the following depends, by Güterbock (1961) (see also Goetze *ANET*[3], 120–28).

A. Old Hittite Mythology

Although the Hattian myths are preserved mostly in Hittite copies, their origins in the Hattian tradition may be seen in the Hattian names for all of the major deities and their location in the Hattian homeland in north central Anatolia. The motif running through most of the Old Hittite myths is that of a crisis in the Hittite lands caused by the disappearance or incapacitation of a deity. This requires the gods to convene and work out a solution to restore the missing god, a solution which often involves the assistance of a mortal. When the god once again assumes his proper place, the land is restored to full vigor and produces its bounty for the people.

The myth of the "Moon That Fell from Heaven" exists in a bilingual Hattic-Hittite copy. Its fragmentary condition renders its unclear story even more difficult to understand. All that we can understand from this myth is that the moon (i.e., the moon god) falls down from heaven and various deities then send messengers after it in an attempt to retrieve it and restore it to its proper place in the heavens. The accompanying ritual is designed to propitiate the storm god and is to be performed "when the storm god thunders." It is not clear how the myth's plot is related to the accompanying ritual.

The myth of the "Disappearing Deity" is actually a series of myths with more or less the same plot and different deities cast in the lead role. Although the extant copies of these myths are in Hittite, their locale and primary characters again indicate a Hattian origin. The main theme involves the disappearance of one deity in a fit of anger, the quest to find and bring him back, and his restoration to the company of the gods.

The best-known example of this myth is the one in which the god Telepinu disappears. When in anger he deserts the populated areas and goes out into the hinterland, the resultant cessation of fertility and growth threatens the people with famine. When the gods assemble, they realize that Telepinu is absent and, afraid of dying of hunger themselves (because the people cannot make sacrifices), send out a bee to find Telepinu. The bee finds the sulking god and stings him awake. Telepinu, further enraged, causes more havoc in the land, at which point Kamrušepa, the goddess of healing and magic, is commissioned to bring him back. There follows a description of the ritual designed to appease the god, who eventually returns, restoring fertility to the land.

In other versions of the myth other gods, e.g., the sun god, Inara, disappear, and the methods used to find the absentee god vary somewhat. It is usually not specified what has caused the god to become so angry that he deserts his people. In the story of the disappearance of the storm god, the sin of his father is given as the reason for the god's leaving. It is interesting that the gods themselves must resort to magic to restore the missing deity to their company. The dependence of the gods on the offerings of man is reflected in the concern they feel for their own well-being when man's food supply is threatened. These Old Hittite disappearing deity myths should not be confused with the "dying god" myths of other ancient cultures. They exhibit marked differences from such myths; for example, the god does not die but only disappears. Unlike dying god myths, the disappearing deity myths are not related to any seasonal pattern.

Another myth from the Hattian tradition is that of Illuyanka. Unlike the other Old Hittite myths, which are integrated into a ritual procedure performed only as needed, the Illuyanka myth was recited as part of the state cult, at the yearly *purulli* festival. The word *illuyanka* is the Hittite noun "serpent, snake." There are two different versions of the story. In one the serpent defeats the storm god in battle, whereupon the storm god seeks assistance from the other gods to regain supremacy. To aid him the goddess Inara prepares a feast which includes an abundance of alcoholic refreshment and secures the assistance of a mortal, Ḫupašiya, who promises to help in return for Inara's love. Inara then invites the serpent to the feast, at the end of which he is too inebriated or too swollen to go back down into his hole. When Ḫupašiya has tied him up and rendered him harmless the storm god comes and kills him, thus restoring his supremacy. In the rather tragic conclusion, Ḫupašiya goes to live with Inara but finds that he misses his wife and children. After looking out the window and seeing his family, he is killed by Inara when he expresses his desire to rejoin them.

In the other version of the myth the serpent takes the eyes and heart of the storm god when he defeats him in battle. The storm god then marries a mortal woman and has a son, whom he gives to the serpent's daughter in marriage. Instructed by his father the storm god, the son, upon entering his new bride's house, asks for his father's heart and eyes from the serpent, which he then takes to his father. When the storm god has thus restored his body to full capacity, he is able to destroy the serpent and his family. Again the plot contains an element of tragedy, as the storm god's son, now a member of the serpent's family, tells his father to kill him along with his new father-in-law, the serpent. This second version must be understood in light of the *antiyant-* form of marriage, in which a man enters his bride's house and, in lieu of bringing a bride price, receives a gift from his new father-in-law for leaving his own family and becoming part of his bride's family. The storm god's heart and eyes are the marriage gift which the son requests, but as an *antiyant-* husband he has joined his life to that of his new family and must share their fate.

Other Old Hittite myths include that of "Telepinu and the Daughter of the Sea God," in which the sea god becomes angry, but instead of leaving the land, he carries off another god, the sun god. His anger is understandable, because he has given the sun god to Telepinu as a marriage gift in an *antiyant-* marriage, but Telepinu has not remained in his house as an *antiyant-* husband should, but has returned to the house of his father the storm god.

In a ritual for the erection of a new palace some mythological passages are included in the magical proceedings which give a rare glimpse into Hittite conceptions of the netherworld. Goddesses spinning the thread of life are depicted, and the ritual includes a prayer to them to give long life to the owner of the new palace. The story elements, as part of a magical procedure, were considered to have magical potency in securing the desired result.

B. New Hittite Mythology

The mythology of the New Hittite or Empire period reflects the strong influence of the Hurrians on the culture of the Hittite kingdom in its later period. As most of the myths are not preserved in Hurrian-language copies, we are fortunate to have these myths preserved in their Hittite versions. We do not know how closely these versions followed the Hurrian originals. The main characters, all Hurrian or Mesopotamian deities, and the settings of the myths in the Hurrian homeland indicate the Hurrian origin of the material.

There is a cycle of Hurrian myths describing the struggle among the gods for supremacy in heaven, with different generations battling against each other to establish themselves as king. One of this cycle is the myth often referred to as "Kingship in Heaven." The plot involves Anu (the Mesopotamian sky god) deposing his lord Alalu, a lesser-known Mesopotamian god. Kumarbi, a Hurrian deity identified as the "father of the gods," serves Anu, but in his turn seeks to depose him. Kumarbi, as he chases Anu, swallows his "manhood" and eventually gives birth to the storm god (Hurrian Tešub), who as the issue of Anu's "manhood" is considered the son of Anu, not of Kumarbi. Ea, the Mesopotamian god of wisdom, becomes involved in the dynastic dispute, but the end of the text is missing. Although we do not have the resolution of the story we may infer from Tešub's position in the Hittite pantheon that he became king of the gods.

Another myth in this cycle of cosmic battles, the "Song of Ullikummi," tells more of the battle between Kumarbi and Tešub. Kumarbi, in plotting to regain his throne from the usurper Tešub, sleeps with a rock, the issue of which is the giant Ullikummi. He is placed on the shoulder of Ubelluri, the giant who supports the earth and seas on his shoulders. With so solid a foundation, the stone monster grows rapidly and in 15 days has reached the heavens. The first to notice him is the sun god, who reports the matter to Tešub. Tešub, Tašmišu, and Ištar, the Mesopotamian goddess of love, go out to observe the monster. When Ullikummi proves immune to Ištar's blandishments, Tešub is forced to battle the monster. Tešub is defeated, and Kummiya, his city, is threatened by the monster. Tešub's brother Tašmišu recommends getting help from Ea, the god of wisdom, who suggests weakening Ullikummi by cutting his bond with Ubelluri with the cleaver which was used at creation to separate the heavens from the earth. Again the ending of the tablet is broken away; we leave the story with the renewal of battle between Tešub and Ullikummi, the latter boasting of his prowess. The final result, however, must have been a victory for Tešub, again inferred from his position at the head of the Hittite pantheon. The cycle of succeeding generations of gods overthrowing their forebears and usurping the throne of heaven is thus broken with Tešub, who manages to take the throne from Kumarbi, but also successfully defends it from the next generation as represented by Ullikummi. The motif of generations of gods ruling successively in the heavens is seen in the Babylonian creation epic, *Enuma Eliš,* and was probably borrowed by the Hurrians. In turn the close parallels in these Hurrian-Hittite myths to Hesiod's *Theogony* may indicate influence from the Hittites on Greek cosmology.

The myth of the "Kingship of KAL" presents a similar story of the struggle for supremacy in heaven. Again Tešub's position is threatened, and he in fact loses the throne when Ea appoints KAL king of heaven. The god KAL becomes arrogant in his rule of heaven, causing Ea to regret his action. Ironically, Ea seeks help from Tešub's old rival Kumarbi in reinstating Tešub on the throne of heaven. The gods decide on action against KAL when his rebelliousness becomes contagious and the people stop providing food and drink offerings for them. Once again the tablet is broken before the end of the story, but it seems that Tešub was restored to the kingship and KAL was punished. In this story, as in that of Ullikummi, Ea is involved in dynastic disputes and seems to have some authority over who rules in heaven.

The myth of "Silver" is another Hurrian myth in which the protagonist, called Silver with no divine determinative, is upset because the gods do not recognize him. He pulls the sun and moon down to earth; when they worship him and ask for mercy he has pity on them. In another episode he hits an orphan with a stick, who responds by reminding Silver that he too was once an orphan. Silver is moved to tears by this and goes to his mother's house, apparently for comfort. In the next episode, probably related to the preceding one, Silver forces his mother to tell him who his father is. He learns that his father is Kumarbi and his brother is the storm god, Hurrian Tešub. Thus in this myth Kumarbi, not Anu, is the father of Tešub. In Urkiš, Kumarbi's home, Silver looks for his father but does not find him. Eventually the storm god (Tešub) goes to see Silver because he is agitating the land, at which point the text is lost.

The story shows some interesting points. Although Silver is obviously very powerful if he can pull down the sun and moon, he does not occur elsewhere among the gods of the Hittites. His name is written without the divine determinative almost invariably used for names of gods. Silver's classification as an orphan offers an interesting insight into Hittite-Hurrian society. Although his mother is still alive, Silver is considered an orphan because he has no father, or at least he does not know his father and thus has no lineage. When he is told who his father is, he can recognize his ancestry and is therefore no longer an orphan. There is no character quite like Silver in other ancient Near Eastern mythology, and because he does not occur elsewhere in the Hittite corpus he remains a somewhat mysterious figure.

In the myth of the sun god, the cow, and the fisherman, the divine and mortal come into direct contact. The sun god observes the cow from the heavens and, overcome with desire, approaches and talks with her in the guise of a young man. In a very broken passage of the tablet he apparently sleeps with her, after which the counting of months signals a pregnancy, followed by the birth of a child. When the child is born the cow complains that her offspring looks human and not like a calf. What follows has been interpreted in two different ways. Friedrich in his early edition (1949) described the scene in which the cow opens her mouth like a lion and goes to her child as the cow's attempt to kill her child, which did not resemble the calf that she was expecting. More recently Hoffner (1981: 192–93), has suggested that the cow opened her mouth wide to lick the child as she cared for it. However we interpret the passage, the child lives, the sun god delights in his child, and he sends animals to protect it. Eventually a fisherman finds the child and somehow realizes that it is the sun god's child. When he brings it home his barren wife simulates birth pains for the benefit of the neighbors and then brings forth the baby as her own. The cow's attitude toward the child is not completely clear, but the fisherman and his wife consider it a blessing from the sun god.

The myth of Appu contains a strongly drawn moral lesson, beginning with a statement about the vindication of just men and retribution for evil men. Appu is a man of great wealth but no offspring. The reason becomes clear: he has never "taken hold" of his wife. When he tells the sun god of his childlessness, that deity suggests that he drink himself into a state of intoxication and then sleep with his wife. The result is two sons for Appu; the first he names Idalu, "evil one," and the second Ḫandanza, "just one."

After Appu dies, Idalu forces a division of the father's property, taking the good cow and giving Ḫandanza the bad one. The sun god intervenes, however, and makes the poorer cow prosper, which inspires Idalu to covet the beast which he maliciously assigned to his brother. The issue eventually goes to the gods to be resolved, with the sun god and then Ištar of Nineveh rendering judgment.

The myth, through the use of characters with allegorical names, makes it easy to understand the moral of the story. Ḫandanza the just one, despite the machinations of Idalu the evil one, prospers because of his righteousness. The sun god as the god of justice (an association going back to Mesopotamian antecedents) makes Ḫandanza's inferior cow surpass Idalu's good cow. The myth offers interesting insights into Hittite ideals of moral rectitude and justice being worked out in the earthly sphere through divine intervention.

Another Hurrian myth preserved in a Hittite version is that of Kešši. Kešši is a hunter who after his marriage to a beautiful woman neglects all of his former activities, the most notable of these being sacrifices of bread and wine to the gods, and hunting. His retirement from hunting angers his mother, to whom he had been in the habit of bringing part of the fruits of his hunting expeditions. He responds to his mother's resentment at the cessation of these gifts by going back out to the field to hunt. Unfortunately the gods in their anger at the loss of Kešši's sacrifices have hidden all the game. After wandering for three months, loath to return to the city empty-handed, Kešši eventually falls ill and has a series of dreams. Most of these dreams are lost in the broken portion of the tablet. The fourth dream involves a boulder which falls from the sky and crushes some servants. In the sixth dream, Kešši dreams that he has a collar on his neck and a woman's anklet on his foot. When he does return home, his mother interprets the dreams for him, but the interpretations, like most of the dreams, are broken away in the tablet. This particular myth is unusual in that it exists in a Hittite version, a Hurrian version, and an Akkadian version from the Amarna scribal school.

There are two other Hurrian myths which exist only in fragmentary Hittite versions. In one the protagonist is Gurparanzaḫ, a name derived from the Hurrian name for the Tigris River. We may infer that the myth was borrowed from Mesopotamia by the Hurrians from the fact that the action of the story takes place not in the Hurrian homeland but in central Mesopotamia. Here again the Hurrians have transmitted a Mesopotamian theme to the Hittites. Another fragmentary Hurrian myth is that of the devouring serpent Ḫedammu who succumbs to Ištar's attractions.

A "Hittite" myth which has a Canaanite instead of Hurrian background, judging from the names of the divine characters, is that of Elkuniršа. This name is a Hittite rendering of the Canaanite *ʾēl qônê ʾereṣ*, "El creator of the earth." In this myth Ašertu (Canaanite Ašerah), wife of Elkunirša, propositions Elkunirša's son, the Canaanite storm god Baal, who goes and tells his father about it. The significance of this appears to be Ašertu's questioning of her husband's virility and a consequent appeal to a younger generation's vitality. Elkunirša tells Baal to go ahead and sleep with Ašertu and humiliate her. When he does this she is angered and works her way back into Elkunirša's favor so that she can revenge herself on Baal, to which her husband eventually agrees. The goddess called Ištar in the text, representing the Canaanite Astarte or ʿAnat, overhears Ašertu's plans for revenge and warns her brother Baal so that he can protect himself. In the Hurrian myths Tešub the storm god was Ištar's brother, and we see the same sibling relationship in this Canaanite myth.

Güterbock (1961: 155) has identified a Syrian origin for another myth, that of Mt. Pišaiša. The text is fragmentary; we may discern that Mt. Pišaiša rapes Ištar and then asks for clemency when she exacts revenge.

In addition to the foreign Hurrian and Syrian myths preserved in Hittite versions from Boğazköy, the Mesopotamian Gilgamesh epic is also extant in copies from the Hittite capital. Güterbock (1961: 154) has pointed out that the Hurrian version of this epic from Boğazköy is evidence for the role of the Hurrians in transmitting this element of Mesopotamian culture to the Hittites. Hittite and Akkadian versions for Gilgamesh exist as well.

The two main streams of Hittite mythology reflect the two primary influences on their culture. In the early period the gods and the myths that define their relationships were adopted from their Anatolian predecessors, the Hattians. They thus preserve an older prehistoric mythological tradition. As the Hittite state matured it came increasingly into contact with the Hurrians to the S, who both served as transmitters of Mesopotamian cultural elements and also passed on their own characteristic culture. Although some of the characters are Mesopotamian, the myths preserved by the Hittites are distinctively Hurrian and provide a rare glimpse into the Hurrian world. The Hittites thus play their most important role as preservers rather than originators of Anatolian mythology.

C. Later Mythology

Mythological material concerning later Anatolian peoples is preserved in some Greek and Latin authors. With the political and cultural integration of Anatolia into the Greek and Roman world, it becomes increasingly difficult to define what is distinctively "Anatolian" mythology. Without wishing to impose a distinction between classical and Anatolian mythology which the ancients did not recognize, we may note several myths which appear to be based on Phrygian or Lydian originals. Further references to mythological passages in classical writers may be found in *The Oxford Classical Dictionary* sub Attis, Cycnus, Heracles, Laomedon, and Midas.

Several Phrygian myths revolve around the character of Midas. There is a historically documented Midas, a Phrygian king of the 8th century B.C. who appears in Assyrian sources. Uncertainty about the relation of this king to the Midas of legend is reflected in the separation of the two entries for Midas in the *OCD.* In one of the Midas stories the king, reflecting the classical tradition that satyrs are privy to valuable wisdom which they will divulge if forced to do so, plots the capture of a satyr who regularly visits his garden. By mixing wine with the water of the garden's well or spring where the satyr normally drinks, the king gets him too intoxicated to escape. Midas then questions his captive; various ancient authors differ on what wisdom the satyr imparted to the Phrygian king.

Another story about Midas told both in Hyg., *Fab.* 191.1 and Ov. *Met.* 11.146–93 describes the musical contest between Pan and Apollo. When Midas rejects the decision for Apollo by the judge, Mt. Timolus, Apollo punishes the king's preference for the pipes of Pan by giving him donkey ears. Although Midas hides those ears beneath a cap, he cannot keep the secret from his barber. The barber, unable to contain the secret but bound not to reveal it to anyone, goes and whispers it in a hole in the ground, which he then covers up. The reeds which grow up on the spot are privy to the secret and whisper it as the wind blows them.

The most famous of the Midas stories (Ov. *Met.* 11. 84–145) is that of the Midas touch. In gratitude for the king's returning Silenus to him, Dionysius offers Midas whatever he wishes. The king requests that whatever he touches be turned to gold. After the first flush of excitement, as he sits down to a meal, he discovers that food and drink are also susceptible to his golden touch. Dionysius, answering Midas' prayer to be rid of the accursed gift, instructs him to wash it away in the headwaters of the Pactolus River. Thus this etiological myth explains why the Pactolus is such a rich gold-bearing stream. In one variation to the story Midas turns his daughter to gold before ridding himself of the "gift"; in another he dies of starvation because he cannot cleanse himself of the golden touch.

Another Anatolian myth of the Phrygian-Lydian milieu is that of Attis and Agdistis. Pausanias 7.17.9–12 relates two versions of the story, of which the first is probably Lydian. In this story Attis, born a eunuch of a Phrygian father, moves to Lydia where he officiates at Lydian rites for the mother goddess (Cybele). Zeus becomes angry at Attis' increased favor with the mother goddess and attacks the Lydians by sending a boar to ravage their crops. Among those killed by the boar is Cybele's favorite, Attis. Probably dependent on this version is the tale told by Hdt. 1.34–45, of Atys, son of the Lydian king Croesus, who was killed by a spear during a boar hunt.

In the second version, probably Phrygian, the demon Agdistis, who was the product of seed dropped on the ground by Zeus while asleep, is hermaphroditic. In their fear of Agdistis the gods castrate the demon. An almond tree grows up from the cut-off member, the fruit of which fertilizes a daughter of the Sangarius River, who bears Attis. Exposed at birth, the young Attis is nurtured by a billy goat, and when he reaches maturity, Agdistis falls in love with him. Attis meanwhile has been betrothed, but during the wedding ceremony Agdistis appears, causing Attis to go mad and castrate himself, as does his prospective father-in-law. Agdistis repents of the deed, and although the story does not state that Attis died, this is implicit in Agdistis' petition to Zeus to grant Attis' body immunity from decomposition. Ov. *Fast.* 4.221–44 tells a different version in which Cybele drives Attis mad in vengeance for his forsaking her for the nymph Sagaritis (whose name looks like the name of the river Sangarius, whose daughter bore Attis in the Phrygian version of Pausanias). In the insanity induced by Cybele, Attis castrates himself, which for Ovid explains why the devotees of Cybele and Attis castrate themselves while evoking the writhings of Attis in his madness. The similarity of these two versions and the later role of Attis as the consort of Cybele in the great Cybele cult indicates that we should see in Agdistis some form of Cybele. Note, however, that both Agdistis and Cybele appear in the myth as told by Arnobius (*Adv. Nat.* 5.5–7).

Bibliography

Beckman, G. 1982. The Anatolian Myth of Illuyanka. *JANES* 14: 11–25.

Friedrich, J. 1949. Churritische Märchen und Sagen in hethitischer Sprache. *ZA* 49: 213–55.

Güterbock, H. G. 1961. Hittite Mythology. Pp. 139–79 in *Mythologies in the Ancient World,* ed. S. N. Kramer. Garden City, NY.

Hoffner, H. A. 1965. The Elkunirsa Myth Reconsidered. *RHA* 76: 5–16.

———. 1981. The Hurrian Story of the Sungod, the Cow and the Fisherman. Pp. 189–94 in *Studies on the Civilization and Culture of Nuzi and the Hurrians.* Winona Lake, IN.

———. fc. The Song of Silver. In *Festschrift Heinrich Otten.*

Siegelová, Jana. 1971. *Appu-Märchen und Ḫedammu-Mythus.* Studien zu den Boğazköy-Texten 14. Wiesbaden.

GREGORY MCMAHON

ANATOLIAN LANGUAGES.

See LANGUAGES (INTRODUCTORY SURVEY)

ANCESTOR WORSHIP.

Ancestor worship and cults of the dead reflect acts directed toward the deceased, functioning either to placate the dead or to secure favors from them. See DEAD, CULT OF THE. The study of ancestor worship in the Bible was popular at the end of the 19th century among both anthropologists and biblical scholars who felt that death rites held the key to Israelite religion (see Spronk 1986: 3–83 for history of research). There has also been a resurgence of interest in ancestor worship and related death rituals in recent scholarship (Heider 1985; Spronk 1986; Lewis 1989), which has attempted to set the biblical data within its ANE context. The Yahwism which became normative in ancient Israel was resolute in its condemnation of ancestor worship. Yet ancient Israel shared a solidarity with the other cultures of the ANE and it should not be surprising to find cults of the dead in some forms of popular religion.

A. Ancestor Worship in the ANE

In the ancient Near East the dead were perceived to be able to bestow blessings on those who provided them with the proper cult. Conversely, the dead might occasionally act malevolently if they were not accorded the proper services. Magical literature from Mesopotamia mentions the restless ghost who returns to haunt the living.

1. In Egypt. The cult of the dead in ancient Egypt is well known, owing to the fascination surrounding the pyramids, mummification, and the Book of the Dead. The Egyptian preoccupation with death has been described by many scholars (e.g., Gardiner 1935: 5–45; Frankfort 1948: 88–123). It is not the fear of the dead which takes center stage in ancient Egypt but rather the provision for the deceased. A great deal of resources were devoted to making sure that the dead, including royalty, nobility, and to a lesser degree commoners, would have everything they needed to exist comfortably in the hereafter. The tomb of Tutankhamen is our best example of how the pharaoh was provided with elaborate furnishings for his next life. The dead were also greatly dependent on others to continue to provide them with the essential offerings long after the initial interment (cf. the contractual agreements mentioned in Gardiner 1935: 27, 43–44).

2. In Mesopotamia. A concise example of ancestor worship in Mesopotamia is found in the following plea from a *kispu* text: "Come (O dead ancestors), eat this, drink this and bless Ammiṣaduqa, son of Ammiditana, the king of Babylon" (Finkelstein 1966: 96–97). In the Mesopotamian cult of the dead a "caretaker" (*pāqidu*) was responsible for the care of the ghost (*eṭemmu*) of his deceased ancestor. This care included essential services such as making funerary offerings (*kispa kasāpu*), pouring water (*mê naqû*), and invoking the name (*šuma zakāru*) (Bayliss 1973: 116). Newly published texts from the Kuyunjik collection have given us new insights into the intricate art of necromancy in ancient Mesopotamia (Finkel 1983–84: 1–17).

3. At Ugarit. Our understanding of Canaanite ancestor worship has been greatly enhanced by the publication of the Ugaritic texts. One text (*KTU* 1.161) describes a liturgy of a mortuary ritual directed toward the deceased royal ancestors, some of whom are called *rapiʾūma* (see REPHAIM). The deceased are invoked to assist in bestowing blessings upon the reigning king. Other texts (*KTU* 1.6.6.45–49; 1.113) refer to the deceased as "gods" (*ilu*). This was an attempt to describe the preternatural character of the deceased who were not "deified" in the sense that they became like one of the high gods of the Ugaritic pantheon. After all, even though King Keret is the god El's son, he still must die like a mortal.

Some scholars (e.g., Pope 1981: 176) have also argued that the *marzeaḥ* at Ugarit and elsewhere was "a feast for and with departed ancestors corresponding to the Mesopotamian *kispu*" (see Lewis 1989: 80–94 and BANQUETING HALL/HOUSE).

The importance of ancestor worship at Ugarit is also underscored by the frequent occurrences of *ilib,* the "divine ancestor," which occurs characteristically at the head of pantheon lists as well as various other genres such as epic texts and sacrificial and offering lists (Lewis 1989: 56–59).

All evidence points to a vibrant cult of ancestor worship at Ugarit as in Mesopotamia and Egypt. This is further confirmed by the archaeological excavations at Ras Shamra which have documented the use of pipes leading from ground level down into the tomb. These pipes (cf. Akk *arūtu*) were used to provide the deceased with water, which was one of the essential services (Schaeffer 1939: 50; cf. *mê naqû* above). Libations were also offered to the dead through openings in the top of corbel vaults (Schaeffer 1938: fig. 42).

B. Ancestor Worship in Ancient Israel

In the past, scholars were all too eager to emphasize the "uniqueness" of Israelite religion over against her pagan neighbors (see Miller 1985: 201–12). Thus, scholars of such stature as de Vaux (*AncIsr,* 60), Wright (*Deuteronomy IB,* 487) and Kaufmann (*KRI,* 312–16) asserted quite dogmatically that ancestor worship was nowhere to be found in the Bible. More recently scholars have started to appreciate the cultural solidarity which ancient Israel shared with her neighbors (e.g., *CMHE*). As it developed, Yahwism borrowed many Canaanite motifs while rejecting others. In its earliest periods it is difficult to distinguish between Israelite and Canaanite religion. As Yahwism progresses, we may talk of a "normative Yahwism" as reflected in the prophetic and Deuteronomistic literature. This Yahwism which became normative condemned ancestor worship. Yet a strong case can be made for the existence of ancestor worship in some forms of "popular religion" (for discussion of terminology, see Lewis 1989: 1–2). What emerges from various biblical texts is the picture of an ongoing battle throughout ancient Israel's history between adherents of what becomes normative Yahwism and those who practiced death rituals.

1. Deuteronomistic Literature. Deuteronomistic legal material contains clear restrictions against consulting one's dead ancestors (Deut 18:10–11), giving offerings to the dead (Deut 26:14) and engaging in self-laceration rituals (Deut 14:1) which were typical of Canaanite death cult practice. It can safely be inferred from these laws that cults of the dead existed and flourished in ancient Israel to the extent that they were considered a threat to what becomes normative Yahwism.

Deuteronomistic narrative material also preserves vestiges of death cult practices. The *locus classicus* for any examination of necromancy in the Hebrew Bible is Saul's encounter with the necromancer at Endor in 1 Samuel 28. Despite Deuteronomistic editing, the efficacy of the practice of necromancy is left intact. The dead Samuel who is conjured from the netherworld in this narrative is called an *ʾĕlōhîm* "god," or better yet, a "preternatural being" as elsewhere in the ancient Near East. Other passages which may contain vestiges of death cult practices are 2 Sam 12:15–24; 18:18; 2 Kgs 9:34–37; 13:20–21 (see Lewis 1989: 99–127).

2. Prophetic Literature. The prophets also encountered the practice of consulting one's deceased ancestors within some segments of Israelite society. Isaiah of Jerusalem and the person(s) responsible for collecting the oracles against the nations used necromantic imagery with pejorative overtones (Isa 8:19; 29:4; 19:3). Halpern (1986: 118–19) also places Isaiah 28 in the context of the ancestral cult.

Jer 16:5–8 speaks against those who go to the funeral banquet house (Heb *marzēah;* see BANQUETING HALL/HOUSE) and those who lacerate themselves for the dead. Ezek 43:7–9 refers to an abominable practice done by kings upon their death. It seems that they had engaged in the practice of placing either their corpses or their royal mortuary steles in close proximity to the temple precinct, resulting in its defilement. Isa 57:6 and 65:4 (cf. 45:18–19) also contain a good deal of death cult imagery, including libations and offerings given to the dead ancestors and all-night vigils in tombs (Lewis 1989: 143–60; 1987: 267–84).

In summary, the prophetic literature supports the picture we get from the Deuteronomistic literature. Necromancy and other death cult practices involving ancestor worship seem to have been so common in certain segments of ancient Israelite society that the prophets could freely pick up on this imagery in their critiques.

3. The Holiness Code and Other Priestly Material. The HOLINESS CODE contains prohibitions against conjuring and consulting one's dead ancestors (Lev 19:26–32; 20:6, 27) which were being practiced in certain "nonorthodox" segments of Israelite society. Other priestly material seems almost preoccupied with the defiling nature of the corpse, the bones, and the grave. It has been suggested that this too is a reflection of an attempt to combat a cult of the dead (Meyers 1983: 102, 104).

4. Psalms. Spronk (1986: 249, 334–37) has argued that the "holy ones who are in the earth" in Ps 16:3 is a reference to deified ancestors. Ps 106:28 also makes mention of "sacrifices to dead ancestors" *(zibḥê mētîm)* in its description of the Baal Peor incident (cf. Num 25:1–5).

5. Wisdom Literature. The attitude of the wisdom tradition toward ancestor worship is represented in Job 14:21 and Qoh 9:4–6, 10. These passages provide a remarkable contrast to 1 Samuel 28 (see above). In the latter, the dead are represented as having knowledge about the affairs of the living and necromancy is portrayed as an efficacious practice. The wisdom tradition, as represented by these two passages, gives no credence to necromancy. The deceased are not knowledgeable about the affairs of the living. Ancestor worship would prove fruitless because the dead do not have the ability to grant favors to the living.

6. Archaeological Data. We can never be too cautious when it comes to drawing inferences from physical remains. Albright (1957: 242–58) hypothesized that the "high places" *(bāmôt)* were funerary in character, yet the archaeological and textual material with which he supported his thesis has not borne up under closer scrutiny (Barrick 1975: 565–95). Ribar (1973: 45–71) has identified several tomb installations which, he believes, suggest that offerings were made to deceased ancestors on a repeated basis and hence qualify as denoting a cult of the dead. What is of particular interest in this regard is the practice of cutting apertures into the ceilings of tombs through which offerings for the dead were introduced. Storage jars were often placed directly over the heads of corpses. Cooley (1983: 47–58) has recently published more of the material from Dothan, one of the most important sites relating to ancestor worship and secondary burials. In short, the archaeological evidence corroborates the hints we glean from the textual material, namely, that cults of the dead existed in ancient Israel despite the best efforts to eradicate their existence.

C. Conclusions

Ancient Israelites shared a cultural solidarity with their neighbors with regard to their attitude toward ancestor worship. The texts mentioned above (apart from the Wisdom Literature) support the notion that there was an ongoing battle by the Yahwism which emerges as normative against the practice of necromancy and other death rituals such as self-laceration and presenting offerings to one's deceased ancestors. This Yahwism condemned ancestor worship as blatant acts of disobedience against Yahweh, whose sovereignty was challenged when one looked elsewhere to control human destiny.

In priestly phraseology, when one dies he is "gathered to his kin" *(neʾĕsap ʾel ʿammāyw)*. In Deuteronomistic terminology one "sleeps with one's fathers" *(šākab ʿim ʾăbôtāyw)* (Alfrink 1943: 106–18; 1948: 118–31). Such usage regarding joining one's ancestors in the underworld is closely tied to clan solidarity (cf. *qabūṣī didāni,* "the 'gathered ones' of the Didanu tribe" [*//rapiʾī arṣi*] in *KTU* 1.161.3, 10). This solidarity was strengthened and promoted by ancestor worship, which was practiced despite efforts to the contrary.

Bibliography

Albright, W. F. 1957. The High Place in Ancient Palestine. VTSup 4: 242–58.

Alfrink, B. 1943. L'Expression *šākab ʿim ʾăbôtāyw. OTS* 2: 106–18.

———. 1948. L'Expression *neʾĕsap ʾel ʿammāyw. OTS* 5: 118–31.

Barrick, W. B. 1975. The Funerary Character of "High-Places" in Ancient Palestine: A Reassessment. VT 25: 565–95.

Bayliss, M. 1973. The Cult of Dead Kin in Assyria and Babylonia. *Iraq* 35: 115–25.

Bordreuil, P., and Pardee, D. 1982. Le Rituel funéraire ougaritique RS 34.126. *Syr.* 59: 121–28.

Brichto, H. C. 1973. Kin, Cult, Land and Afterlife—A Biblical Complex. *HUCA* 44: 1–54.

Burns, J. B. 1978. Necromancy and the Spirits of the Dead in the Old Testament. *Transactions of the Glasgow University Oriental Society* 26: 1–14.

Chapman, R.; Kinnes, I.; and Randsborg, K. 1981. *The Archaeology of Death.* Cambridge.

Cooley, R. E. 1983. Gathered to His People: A Study of a Dothan Family Tomb. Pp. 47–58 in *The Living and Active Word of God,* ed. M. Inch and R. Youngblood. Winona Lake, IN.

Finkel, I. J. 1983–84. Necromancy in Ancient Mesopotamia. *AfO* 29–30: 1–17.

Finkelstein, J. J. 1966. The Genealogy of the Hammurapi Dynasty. *JCS* 20: 95–118.

Frankfort, H. 1948. *Ancient Egyptian Religion.* New York.

Gardiner, A. H. 1935. *The Attitude of the Ancient Egyptians to Death and the Dead.* Cambridge.

Halpern, B. 1986. "The Excremental Vision": The Doomed Priests of Doom in Isaiah 28. *HAR* 10: 109–21.

Heider, G. C. 1985. *The Cult of Molek: A Reassessment.* JSOTSup 43. Sheffield.

Huntington, R., and Metcalf, P. 1979. *Celebrations of Death: The Anthropology of Mortuary Ritual.* Cambridge.

Levine, B. A., and Tarragon, J. M. de. 1984. Dead Kings and Rephaim: The Patrons of the Ugaritic Dynasty. *JAOS* 104: 649–59.

Lewis, T. J. 1987. Dealth Cult Imagery in Isaiah 57. *HAR* 11: 267–84.

———. 1989. *Cults of the Dead in Ancient Israel and Ugarit.* HSM 39. Atlanta.

Meyers, E. M. 1983. Secondary Burial in Palestine. *BAR* 4: 94–114.

Miller, P. D. 1985. Israelite Religion. Pp. 201–37 in *The Hebrew Bible and Its Modern Interpreters,* ed. D. A. Knight and G. M. Tucker. Chico, CA.

Pitard, W. T. 1978. The Ugaritic Funerary Text RS 34.126. *BASOR* 232: 65–75.

Pope, M. H. 1981. The Cult of the Dead at Ugarit. Pp. 159–79 in *Ugarit in Retrospect,* ed. G. D. Young. Winona Lake, IN.

Ribar, J. W. 1973. *Death Cult Practices in Ancient Palestine.* Diss. University of Michigan.

Schaeffer, C. F. A. 1938. Les Fouilles de Ras Shamra-Ugarit, neuvième campagne (printemps 1937): Rapport sommaire. *Syr.* 19: 193–255.

———. 1939. *The Cuneiform Texts of Ras Shamra Ugarit.* London.

Spronk, K. 1986. *Beatific Afterlife in Ancient Israel and in the Ancient Near East.* AOAT 219. Neukirchen-Vluyn.

Tromp, N. 1969. *Primitive Conceptions of Death and the Nether World in the Old Testament.* BibOr 21. Rome.

THEODORE J. LEWIS

ANCIENT VERSIONS. See VERSIONS, ANCIENT.

ANDREW (PERSON) [Gk *Andreas*]. The NT shows little interest in Andrew. His name occurs only twelve times, four of these merely in lists of apostles (Mark 3:18; Matt 10:2; Luke 6:14; Acts 1:13). According to Mark, Jesus called Andrew and his brother Peter to leave their nets to "become fishers of men" (1:16–18); at their home in Capernaum Jesus healed Peter's mother-in-law (1:29–31); and Andrew—along with Peter, James, and John—heard Jesus predict the destruction of the temple (13:3). Matthew adds nothing to Mark's picture of Andrew, and in fact omits the name in his redacting of Mark 1:29–31 and 13:3 (cf. Matt. 8:14 and 24:3). Outside of lists of apostles, the author of Luke/Acts omits reference to Andrew altogether.

Andrew fares somewhat better in the fourth gospel. He is the first of the apostles called by Jesus (1:35–40). He brings his brother Simon Peter to Jesus (1:41–42), and he informs Jesus concerning the lad with the expandable lunch (6:8–9) and about Greeks who wanted to see him (12:22). None of these narratives appears in the Synoptic Gospels, and some of the information in them in fact contradicts the Synoptics. According to John, Andrew's home was not Capernaum but Bethsaida (1:49), and he was called not from fishing but from the retinue of John the Baptist (1:35–40).

Andrew also appears in the *Gospel of the Ebionites* (Epiph. *Haer.* 30.13), the *Gospel of Peter* (14[60]), *Epistula apostolorum* (2), *Pistis Sophia* (e.g., 96 and 136), but none of these apocrypha develops the portrait of the apostle beyond that already in the NT. Andrew is little more than Peter's shadow and Jesus' occasional interlocutor. The *Muratorian Fragment* adds only that Christ told Andrew that John would write his gospel.

This near silence stands in stark contrast to the late 2d century *Acts of Andrew,* one of the five major apocryphal Acts of Apostles. Although the book no longer survives in its entirety, it must have been expansive. Gregory of Tours (6th century) epitomized the *Acts of Andrew* in order to rescue it from rejection by many "because of its excessive verbosity." According to Gregory, the *Acts of Andrew* narrated Andrew's departure from Jerusalem to missionize Achaea, but he soon left Achaea to rescue Matthias from cannibals. After doing so he returned to Achaea by northern Anatolia, Thrace, and Macedonia, converting pagans, exorcising demons, healing the sick, raising the dead, and breaking up families with his preaching of mandatory celibacy. When he arrived in Patras, Achaea, he converted Maximilla, the wife of the proconsul Aegeates; she thereafter forswore sex with her husband. Aegeates crucified the apostle next to the sea (see ANDREW, ACTS OF).

This explosion of interest in the apostle issues not from a latent Andrean tradition that simply had found no earlier expression but from the author's decision to write a Christian *Odyssey,* for which Andrew was well qualified. He once was a fisherman, he had brought Greeks to Jesus, and his very name resonated with the Greek word for courage (*andreia*). Like Odysseus, Andrew sails from Achaea to rescue Matthias from Myrmidons. Myrmidons appear in Homer as allies to Achilles, but a contrived etymology later generated a myth that Zeus once transformed ants (Gk *myrmēkes*) into humans, who retained their former, formic traits. Andrew returns to Achaea through a series of dangerous adventures and in the end dies at the edge of the sea, tied to his cross like Odysseus at the mast. The apostle thus returns to his heavenly home beyond the flux, temptations, and dangers of this world. Patras, the place of his execution, was the closest major Achaean city to Ithaca, Odysseus' island home. In addition, the *Acts of Andrew* contained a visit to the netherworld, danger at sea, and Christianized counterparts to Penelope and Telemachus, Odysseus' wife and son. The proconsul who ordered Andrew's crucifixion is Aegeates ("one from Aegae"), a figure inspired by Odysseus' nemesis, Poseidon, whose Homeric home was Aegae.

Even after the composition of the *Acts of Andrew,* the apostle remained relatively obscure for nearly six centuries. Because of its popularity among Manicheans, the *Acts of Andrew* itself was poorly transmitted except for the Myrmidon story, which soon circulated independently as the *Acts of Andrew and Matthias in the City of the Cannibals.* In 357, Constantius II deposited the apostle's putative remains in the Church of the Holy Apostles in Constantinople, along with those of Luke and Timothy. By the 6th century, Patras and Sinope boasted of having been evangelized by Andrew, but there is little evidence that Christians elsewhere gave the apostle special attention.

Sometime in the 8th century, however, Andrew was pressed into service to legitimate Byzantine claims to apostolicity. For centuries, the church in Rome had claimed Peter as its founder. On the other hand, Byzantium, largely the product of Constantine's relocation of the imperial capital to the E, could claim no founding apostle. This was not so problematic when Rome and Byzantium were on good terms, but when the two great ecclesiastical centers parted ways, Byzantium was in desperate need of apostolic pedigree. Andrew was perfectly suited for the purpose. According to the gospel of John, he was the first of the apostles to come to Jesus, and later he brought his brother Peter, Rome's favorite, to the Lord. The *Acts of Andrew* and traditions derived from it had placed Andrew's ministry in the region of the Black Sea, and if one can trust the epitome of Gregory of Tours, the Acts in fact sent the apostle to Byzantium. Furthermore, from the time of Constantius II, Andrew's relics reposed in Constantinople's Church of the Holy Apostles.

Such long-standing associations between Andrew and the city generated a legend that when Andrew, the *Protokletos* (First-Called), visited Byzantium he appointed as bishop Stachys (cf. Rom 16:9), who inaugurated an unbroken line of bishops. In the 9th century, soon after the origin of this legend, several versions of his passion appeared along with three different Byzantine "Lives" of Andrew. A monk named Epiphanius, the author of one of these "Lives," claimed that virtually every tribe on the shores of the Black Sea appealed to Andrew as the founder of its church: the Scythians, the Sogdians, the Gorsini, the Iberi, the Sousi, the Phousti, the Alani. Andrew also allegedly visited Amisus, Trapezunta, Iberia, Phrygia, Ephesus, Bithynia, Laodicea, Mysia, Odyssopolis, Chalcedon, Heraclea, Amastra, Zalichus, Neocaesarea, Sebastopolis Magna, Zecchia, and Sinope. His reputation in the East now was secure. He remains the patron of Russian Orthodoxy by dint of a legend that he preached as far north as Kiev.

Andrew also became popular in the West. In 1204, crusaders stole Andrew's relics from Constantinople and took them to Amalfi, Italy. According to ancient Celtic tradition, St. Regulus (4th century) took the apostle's arm to St. Andrews, Scotland, where the archdiocese still celebrates the event each May 9. The Anglo-Saxon epic *Andreas,* a poetic recasting of the *Acts of Andrew and Matthias,* shows the importance of the apostle in the British Isles at an early date.

In iconography, Andrew often appears with unkempt hair and a long beard, attended by a ship, a fish, or a net. His most distinctive signature is his X-shaped cross, a feature not attested prior to the 7th century. Andrew's feast day is November 30.

Bibliography

Dvornik, F. 1958. *The Idea of Apostolicity in Byzantium and the Legend of the Apostle Andrew.* Dumbarton Oaks Studies 4. Cambridge, MA.

Flamion, J. 1911. *Les Acts apocryphes de l'apôtre André.* Recueil de travaux d'histoire et de philologie 33. Louvain.

Mykytiuk, B. G. 1979. *Die ukrainischen Andreas-bräuche und ver-*

wandtes Brauchtum. Veröffentlichungen des Osteuropa-Instituts München, Reihe Geschichte 47. Wiesbaden.

Peterson, P. M. 1958. *Andrew, Brother of Simon Peter, His History and His Legends.* NovTSup 1. Leiden.

DENNIS R. MACDONALD

ANDREW AND MATTHIAS, ACTS OF. An early Christian apocryphal tale featuring two of the disciples of Jesus. The *Acts of Andrew and Matthias* begins with the apostles casting lots to see where they will preach. Andrew goes to Achaea and Matthias to the city of the cannibals, which the Latin and Anglo-Saxon witnesses (along with one Greek manuscript) name Myrmidonia. Myrmidonia is home to Myrmidons, Achilles' allies in Homer. After Homer there arose a myth that Myrmidons once were ants (Gk *myrmēkes*), who retained some formic traits even after becoming human. Some authors emphasized the positive qualities of ants, e.g., thrift, industry, organization, while others emphasized their imperialism, might, and ferocity. Even the Greek versions of the *Acts of Andrew and Matthias* that lack the word "Myrmidonia" witness to the cannibals' ancestry from ants. In the middle of the city they had built a large furnace (Gk *klibanos*) for roasting their victims. (Such furnaces were mud structures reminiscent of anthills.) When Matthias arrives, they drug him and incarcerate him for thirty days of fattening. Andrew leaves Achaea to rescue Matthias and floods the cannibals as one might flood ants. They repent, and Andrew stops the flood but plunges the worst of the cannibals into an abyss in the middle of the city, like so many ants down an ant hole. In the abyss they see places of eternal bliss and torment, but Andrew promises to return to raise them up again.

Insofar as Andrew never returns to raise the Myrmidons, the *Acts of Andrew and Matthias* obviously is incomplete. Originally it seems to have continued in the late 2d-century *Acts of Andrew.* The best surviving witness to the *Acts of Andrew,* a 6th-century epitome by Gregory of Tours, begins by narrating Andrew's rescue of Matthias from Myrmidonia. Three Byzantine "Lives" of Andrew likewise attest to this story near the beginning of Andrew's career. The *Acts of Thomas* and the *Acts of Philip,* both of which borrowed extensively from the *Acts of Andrew,* likewise knew of the Myrmidon story. On the other hand, chaps. 11–15 of the *Acts of Andrew and Matthias* could not have been written prior to the 4th century. Here Andrew narrates how Jesus refuted Jewish high priests by making a sphinx in a pagan temple summon Abraham from his tomb to witness to Jesus' divinity. These chapters also seem to anticipate the transformation of pagan temples into churches, a practice not common until the 5th century. Not only do these chapters come from a later period, they are foreign to the content and narrative flow of the rest of the *Acts of Andrew and Matthias* and are poorly attested in textual and in external witnesses.

One therefore should assume that the frame-story of the *Acts of Andrew and Matthias* first appeared at the beginning of the 2d-century *Acts of Andrew,* just as it does in the epitome by Gregory of Tours. In the 5th century, someone detached the story from the rest of the *Acts of Andrew* and inserted chaps. 11–15 in order to support the controversial Christian reappropriation of pagan temples. Later, the Greek manuscript tradition dropped all references to Myrmidonia because of its associations with pagan mythology. The story was popular in the Middle Ages: it exists in Syriac, Coptic, Armenian, Old Slavonic, Latin, and Anglo-Saxon as well as in Greek. It received its most famous expression in the Anglo-Saxon heroic epic, *Andreas,* but it also inspired episodes in the *Acts of Thomas, Acts of Philip, Acts of Mark, Acts of Peter and Andrew, Acts of Andrew and Philemon,* and the *Martyrdom of Matthew.*

Bibliography

The Greek text of the *Acts of Andrew and Matthias* appears in *Acta apostolorum apocrypha,* ed. R. A. Lipsius and M. Bonnet, 2/1.65–116. The most important Latin version is in Blatt, F. 1930. *Die lateinischen Bearbeitungen der Acta Andreae et Matthiae apud Anthropohagos.* BZNW 12, 32–95. Geissen.

An English translation of the Greek versions appears in *Ante-Nicene Fathers* 8: 517–34.

Baumler, E. B. 1985. Andrew in the City of the Cannibals: A Comparative Study of the Latin, Greek, and Old English Texts. Diss. Kansas.

Brooks, K. R. 1961. *Andreas and the Fates of the Apostles.* Oxford.

Flamion, J. 1911. *Les Actes apocryphes de l'apôtre André. Les Actes d'André et de Mathias, de Pierre et d'André et les textes apparentés.* Recueil de travaux d'histoire et de philologie 33. Louvain.

Löfstedt, B. 1975. Zu de lateinischen Bearbeitungen der Acta Andreae et Matthiae apud Anthropophagos. *Habis* 6: 167–76.

MacDonald, D. R. 1986. *The Acts of Andrew and Matthias* and *The Acts of Andrew,* and Response to Jean-Marc Prieur. *Semeia* 38: 9–26, 35–39.

Reinach, S. 1904. Les Apôtres chez les anthropophages. *RHLR* 9: 305–20.

DENNIS R. MACDONALD

ANDREW, ACTS OF. The *Acts of Andrew* is an important account of Andrew's travels, beginning in Pontus and ending in Patras, Achaea, where the apostle is martyred. Andrew goes from city to city, performing miracles, preaching the word of salvation, and converting the crowds.

He travels by way of Amasia, Sinope, Nicea, Nicodemia, Byzantium, Thrace, Perinthus, Philippi, and Thessalonica. On arriving in Patras, he converts the city (including the proconsul Lesbios) and performs many miracles. Then he visits several Achaean cities: Corinth, Megara, and perhaps Sparta. He then is warned by a vision about returning to Patras. Upon his return to this city, he heals and converts Maximilla, the wife of Aegeates, the new proconsul. He performs many healings and then converts Stratocles, Aegeates' brother. After her conversion Maximilla becomes celibate, which provokes the furor of Aegeates such that he arrests Andrew. The converts reconvene in the prison to hear the apostle's preaching. It is here that the martyrdom of Andrew begins. Because Maximilla refuses to return to conjugal life, Aegeates, out of revenge, crucifies the apostle. He dies after having preached from his cross to the assembled inhabitants of Patras for three days.

The *Acts of Andrew* is an original and homogeneous work insofar as it was composed from start to finish by the same author, who had no need to introduce or to compile preexisting literary materials. The apostle's speeches, which are important in this work, are rich in content and betray signs of educated style and composition. They transmit the basic features of the author's theology.

A. Transmission of the Text

The *Acts of Andrew* was written in Greek, but unfortunately has not come down to us in its original form. There are, however, five types of documentation that allow partial reconstruction.

1. The *Liber de miraculis* (Gregory of Tours) (Bonnet 1884: 821–46). The Gallic bishop, Gregory of Tours (6th century) held in his hands the complete text of *Acts Andr.*, most likely in Latin translation. His Latin summary of this book preserves the basic features of the narrative framework, and for this reason it is priceless: it is the only document that now permits one to recognize the general layout of the work and of the collective accounts of Andrew's travels. A comparison with the sources that represent some of the primitive content of the *Acts Andr.* (especially Coptic papyrus *Utrecht 1, Laudatio,* and JS) show that Gregory (1) omitted the speeches, (2) often modified the structure of the text, and (3) twisted the meaning of the work to make it more acceptable to Catholic conscience. After chap. 36, he very briefly summarized the account of the martyrdom by referring to a Latin *Passio* which already existed (surely *Passio sancti Andreae Apostoli* known by the title *Conversante et docente*; Bonnet 1894: 374–78).

2. Coptic papyrus *Utrecht 1* (Quispel 1956: 129–48). This papyrus contains the translation of an excerpt from *Acts Andr.* corresponding to chap. 18 of *Liber de miraculis,* an episode located in Philippi. It was not transmitted together with other sections of *Acts Andr.*, for it ends with the title "The Act of Andrew." The excerpt occupies pp. 1–15 in the manuscript, but the first eight pages as well as pages 11 and 12 are lost.

3. The *Armenian Passio* (Tcherakian 1904: 146–67; Leloir 1986: 228–57). This translation dates to the 6th century and is a complete version of the end of *Acts Andr.* comprising the martyrdom of Andrew in Patras and part of the speech spoken in prison just prior to the martyrdom. It preserves some of the sections of the text omitted by all of the Greek witnesses. The translator sometimes bends the text to make it more "orthodox" and more biblical.

4. Five Gk recensions of the end of the *Acts Andr.* The end of *Acts Andr.* is preserved in five Gk recensions. The problem here is that the documents reproduce the primitive text of *Acts Andr.,* but they do not cover the same portions of the text, and they do not always preserve the same elements.

a. The *Passio of Andrew* preserved in two manuscripts: Sinai *gr. 526* (fol. 121v–132) and Jerusalem, *Saint Sabas* 103 (fol. 155–168v) (Detorakis 1981–82: 325–52). This *Passio,* designated by JS, is the longest. It begins well before the *Armenian Passio,* narrating what Andrew did and said in Patras before his martyrdom. It begins with an account of the healing of a servant of Stratocles, Aegeates' brother, and continues to the end of *Acts Andr.* A comparison with the *Armenian Passio* and other Gk witnesses shows that it has not preserved all the elements of the text. The scribe who initiated this version was particularly fond of abbreviating the speeches.

b. The excerpt of *Acts Andr.* preserved in Vatican *gr. 808* (fol. 507–12) (Bonnet 1898: 38–45). This fragment of *Acts Andr.* is mutilated at the beginning and end. It takes place in the narrative sequence of JS, ending just prior to the beginning of the martyrdom. It reproduces faithfully the portion of the *Acts* that it covers.

c. The *Passio of Andrew* preserved in Ann Arbor 36 (fol. 60v–66v). This unedited *Passio* covers the narrative of Andrew's martyrdom. It begins immediately after the mutilated ending of the Vatican *gr. 808.* Like JS, it has not preserved all the elements of the primitive text. The speeches in particular fell victim to abbreviation, but these lacunae are not the same as those in JS, demonstrating that Ann Arbor 36 did not derive from JS, but that they are two text types derived from a common ancestor: the *Acts of Andrew.*

d. The *Passio of Andrew* attested to by Paris, *B.N. 770* (fol. 43v–46), and by Jerusalem, *Saint Sabas 30* (fol. 154v–156v), known as *Martyrium alterum A* (Bonnet 1898: 58–64). Like Ann Arbor 36, this recension covers all of the martyrdom, but with some deletions, much more numerous and significant than in the recensions treated above.

e. The *Passio of Andrew* contained in Paris, *B.N. 1539* (fol. 304–305v), known as *Martyrium alterum B* (Bonnet 1898: 58–64). Like the two *Passio* below, this version preserves the whole of the martyrdom, but with even more numerous deletions.

5. Some excerpts of *Acts Andr.* are preserved in Gk revisions. There exist Lives or *Passio* of Andrew, dependent on *Acts Andr.,* which preserve some Gk extractions from the apocryphon:

a. A Gk version of the *Letter of the Presbyters and Deacons of Achaea* (Bonnet 1898: 1–37). This letter, originally written in Latin, was translated into two major Gk versions. One of them, which begins with *haper tois ophthalmois hēmōn,* also included in chaps. 10–15 some important excerpts from the primitive *Acts Andr.* These excerpts, found at the end of the martyrdom, without exception can be identified in the other Gk witnesses.

b. Two versions that derive from the same recension of the *Acts Andr.* These are *Martyrium prius* (8th century) (Bonnet 1898: 46–57) and a work of Nicetas the Paphlagonian known as *Laudatio* (9th–10th century) (Bonnet 1894: 311–52). They report the conversion of Patras and of the proconsul Lesbios (*Martyrium prius* 3–8; *Laudatio* 34–37) and Andrew's speech to the cross (*Martyrium prius* 14; *Laudatio* 46). *Laudatio,* however, also contains the account of the healing of Stratocles' servant (chap. 43), which conforms to the beginning of JS. It also contains some lines (chap. 48, p. 348, ll. 8–22) identifiable in Gk witnesses to the martyrdom. It presents also an account of a healing at Patras (chap. 41) that correlates with chap. 33 of *Liber de miraculis.*

From these five Gk recensions of the ending of *Acts Andr.* and from the excerpts preserved by the three Gk revisions identified above, it is possible to reconstruct a single text. The reconstruction does not try to reproduce the exact text of *Acts Andr.*; a comparison with the *Armenian Passio* demonstrates that some passages remain lost in all of the Gk witnesses. Rather, the reconstruction seeks to establish the original text as much as possible, and thus enlarges considerably a basis from which to study the theology of this apocryphon.

One should add to these five types of witness a second Sahidic Coptic fragment (4th century) of two badly preserved folios (Barns 1960: 70–76). It contains a conversation between Jesus and Andrew in which the apostle presents a short balance sheet for his apostolic activity. Barns proposes to attach it to an apocryphal gospel or better to *Acts Andr.* The hypothesis concerning the appropriateness of this fragment for *Acts Andr.* appears reasonable enough, although one cannot demonstrate it with certainty.

B. The Author's Theological Perspective

The author of *Acts Andr.,* even though he tells a story of Andrew's travels and martyrdom, has little interest in writing a biography. His intent, rather, is to transmit a message of salvation. The *Acts of Andrew* is propagandistic, meant for anyone who wished to hear and receive that message.

This salvation consists of liberation by means of self-realization, a realization that the soul (or "new man"), which is of divine origin, is captive in the body—a prey to the vicissitudes inherent in this condition, deceived and dominated by demonic forces. As soon as a person becomes aware of this fact, he or she is liberated from constraints bound to the corporeal and demonstrates this by adhering to sexual abstinence, dietary frugality, and rejection of worldly honors. The believer lives spiritually with those who have experienced the same liberation and who are of the same nature. He or she awaits death as the definitive liberation from all corporeal bounds, when he or she will return to God, will meditate on Him, and be united with Him insofar as they share the same nature.

The apostle (see Prieur 1981: 121–39) is the one who bears this revelation of salvation. His words which resonate in the "new man" are like a mirror in which one recognizes one's true nature.

The incarnate Christ, the dead and risen one, the preacher of God's reign, plays no role in this process of salvation. The *Acts of Andrew* makes virtually no distinction between the Father and the Son. It is one and the same divinity who is in turn named God, Father, Jesus, Christ. The Holy Spirit is absent. The *Acts of Andrew* contains no reflections on the origin of the world or of evil: everything focuses on human salvation.

C. Origin of *Acts Andr.*

1. Gnosticism. The *Acts of Andrew* displays certain obvious affinities to Gnosticism. Lipsius considered it a gnostic writing, like the other apocryphal Acts (1883: I, 543–622). Flamion combatted this idea by arguing that the author of *Acts Andr.* moved within the context of the Great Church (1911: 145–77). Quispel returned to the alleged gnostic character of *Acts Andr.,* but claimed more precisely that one could have professed the ideas contained in it without leaving the Catholic Church (1956: 129–48). Hornschuh, though recognizing the gnostic traits in *Acts Andr.,* did not believe it was possible to label it gnostic (1964: 270–97).

The affinities between *Acts Andr.* and Gnosticism obtain especially to dualism. They also concern salvation. But dualism does not determine what the human essence is in terms of natural inherent properties. In the context of the message of salvation, one must make a decision to align oneself on the side of the light or on the side of darkness. However, *Acts Andr.* offers no explanation for the fall of the soul. It appeals neither to the notion of the Pleroma nor to that of the Aeons. It offers no gnostic cosmogony. Properly speaking, *Acts Andr.* is therefore not a gnostic text; rather it shares a gnosticizing mentality current at the time.

2. Platonism. Several features relate *Acts Andr.* to Platonism: the discovery of the interior human essence presented as a spiritual childbirth; Andrew presented as a master of maieutics, whose death resembles that of Socrates; the spiritual mirror: the liberation and flight of the soul; and God presented as the good and the beautiful.

Flamion (1911) thought that *Acts Andr.* was Neoplatonic, but that would place it in the 3d century, which is too late. Hornschuh, however, saw affinities between *Acts Andr.* and Middle Platonism on the one hand and with the thought of Tatian on the other.

3. Stoicism. The *Acts of Andrew* also exhibits some stoic characteristics, especially in matters of morality. Andrew exhorts his listeners not to be carried away by their passions but to unify their behavior with their interior disposition. He is unflinching in the face of death, not because he was insensitive to sorrow, but by virtue of his spiritual elevation.

4. Reflections of the Mentality of the Age. It would seem impossible to relate *Acts Andr.* to a particular philosophical or religious milieu. We already have seen several different currents of thought to which one might compare the *Acts,* though without being able to identify it with any of them precisely. It is better to try to see in these various currents witnesses to an age. It is a spiritual atmosphere, influenced by Platonism and Neopythagorism, which blossomed in the 2d and 3d centuries.

5. Time and Place of Origin. The *Manichean Psalter,* which contains some allusions to the content of *Acts Andr.* (Allberry 1938: 142, 143, 192), establishes the 3d century as the *terminus ad quem* for the redaction of the apocryphon, but the *Acts* had to have originated earlier, between 150 and 200, closer to 150 than to 200. The distinctive christology of the text, its silence concerning the historical and biblical Jesus, and its distance from later institutional organization and ecclesiastical rites militate for an early dating. Moreover, its serene tone and unawareness of any polemic against some of its ideas as heterodox, particularly in the area of the christology, show that it derived from a period when the christology of the Great Church had not yet taken firm shape. One might repeat here the line of argumentation employed by Junod and Kaestli for locating the *Acts of John* in the same period (1983: 695). Moreover, *Acts John* displays several affinities with *Acts Andr.,* such as the literary genre, structure, and theological orientations.

Concerning the place of origin, there is nothing that can settle the matter in favor of one region over another. The text could have been drawn up as easily in Greece or in Asia Minor, in Syria or in Egypt. Alexandria in particular commends itself for the spiritual and intellectual milieu where a text like *Acts Andr.* might first have seen the light of day.

Bibliography

Allberry, C. R. C. 1938. *A Manichean Psalm-Book* 2. Stuttgart.

Barns, J. 1960. A Coptic Apocryphal Fragment in the Bodleian Library. *JTS* N.S. 11: 70–76.

Bonnet, M. 1884. Edition of the *Liber de miraculis beati Andreae apostoli* of Gregory of Tours. *Monumenta Germaniae historica. Scriptores rerum Merovingicarum* I. Hannover: 821–46.

———. 1894. *Supplementum codicis apocryphi* II. *AnBoll* 13. Edition of the *Laudatio: Acta Andreae apostoli cum laudatione contexte:* 311–52. Edition of *Conversante et docente: Passio sancti Andreae apostoli:* 374–78.

———. 1898. *Acta apostolorum apocrypha.* Leipzig. Repr. Darmstadt 1959.

Detorakis, T. 1981–82. An unpublished "Martyrdom" of St. Andrew the Apostle. Pp. 325–52 in *Acts of the Second International Congress of Peloponnesian Studies* 1, ed. T. A. Gritsopoulos; D. V. Vayakalos; and C. L. Kotsonis. Athens.

Dvornik, F. 1958. *The Idea of Apostolicity in Byzantium and the Legend of the Apostle Andrew. Dumbarton Oaks Studies* 4. Cambridge, MA.

Flamion, J. 1911. *Les Actes apocryphes de l'apôtre André. Les Actes d'André et de Matthias, de Pierre et d'André et les textes apparentés.* Louvain.

Hornschuh, M. 1964. Andreasakten. Pp. 270–297. Vol. 2 in *Neutestamentliche Apokryphen. Apostolisches, Apokalypsen, und Verwandtes,* ed. E. Hennecke and W. Schneemelcher. Tübingen.

Junod, E., and Kaestli, J.-D. 1983. *Acts Iohannis.* CChr Series Apocryphorum 1–2. Turnhout.

Leloir, L. 1986. *Ecrits apocryphes sur les apôtres.* CChr Series Apocryphorum 3. Turnhout.

Lipsius, R. A. 1883. *Die Apokryphen Apostelgeschichten und Apostelegenden* 1. Braunschweig. Repr. Amsterdam 1976. 543–622.

Prieur, J.-M. 1981. La Figure de l'apôtre dans les Actes apocryphes d'André. Pp. 121–39 in *Les Actes apocryphes des apôtres. Christianisme et monde païen,* ed. F. Boven. Geneva.

———. 1989. *Acta Andreae.* CChr Series Apocryphorum 5–6. Turnhout.

Quispel, G. 1956. An Unknown Fragment of the Acts of Andrew. *VC* 10: 129–48.

Tcherakian, C. 1904. *Anakanon Girkh Arakhelakankh.* Venezia.

JEAN-MARC PRIEUR

ANDREW, FRAGMENTARY STORY. See ANDREW, ACTS OF.

ANDRONICUS (PERSON) [Gk *Andronikos*]. **1.** A deputy of Antiochus IV Epiphanes (2 Macc 4:31, 32, 34, 38). According to the account in 2 Macc 4:30–38, when a revolt broke out in Tarsus and Mallus, Antiochus left Andronicus, a Friend of the King (v 38), in charge as his deputy. Menelaus used this opportunity to bribe Andronicus with gold vessels stolen from the temple in Jerusalem. After Onias exposed this episode publicly, he fled to the temple of Daphne at Antioch for sanctuary. On the advice of Menelaus, Andronicus brought Onias out of the temple by deceit and murdered him. Learning of this murder upon his return, Antiochus stripped Andronicus of his rank, publicly humiliated him, and put him to death at the very spot of Onias' death. Classical sources (Diodorus Siculus 30.7.2–3 and John of Antioch) state that the reason for Andronicus' death was his murder of Antiochus, son of Seleucus IV, on behalf of Antiochus IV. A number of solutions for the differing accounts of Andronicus' death have been proposed: (1) the date of Andronicus' death was the same year as Onias' (170/169 B.C.) and may have suggested to the writer of 2 Maccabees a cause-and-effect relationship; (2) the author of 2 Maccabees may have fabricated the story for his own theological reasons (Hengel 1974: 2: 183 n. 132; 185 n. 142); Antiochus IV may have used this incident as a pretext for silencing Andronicus before he could implicate Antiochus IV in the murder of the younger Antiochus (Goldstein *2 Maccabees* AB, 238–39).

2. Official of Antiochus IV Epiphanes (2 Macc 5:23). Andronicus was placed over the temple on Mt. Gerizim after Antiochus IV invaded Judea and Samaria. If Andronicus' position was the same as Philip's in v 22, then he was commander of a garrison stationed on Mt. Gerizim. Goldstein (*2 Maccabees* AB, 261) further proposes that Andronicus may have been the predecessor of Apollonius, a military commander (1 Macc 3:10) or governor of Samaria (*Ant* 12.5.5 §261).

Bibliography

Hengel, M. 1974. *Judaism and Hellenism.* 2 vols. Trans. John Bowden. Philadelphia.

RUSSELL D. NELSON

3. A Christian apostle in the time of Paul, born a Jew. Both Andronicus and Junia, who were apostles prior to Paul (Rom 16:7; cf. 1 Cor 15:7–8), belonged to the limited number (but exceeding "twelve") of early Christian apostles who had seen the resurrected Christ (cf. 1 Cor 15:5–9; 9:1, 5–6; Gal 1:17). Because of their Greek names they may have belonged to the Greek-speaking Jewish-Christian group in Jerusalem (Acts 6; Cranfield *Romans* ICC, 190), and later to the early missionaries based in Antioch who initiated the mission to the gentiles (11:20) and whom Paul joined (13:1; 11:19–26; Gal 1:21; cf. Lüdemann 1987: 144 for the historicity of the Acts traditions). In any case, Andronicus and Junia at some point worked with Paul in the missionary effort to the gentiles, because all three of them went to prison together (Rom 16:7; Lampe *StadtrChr,* 58, 148–49). As Rom 15:24, 16–20, 30–32 presume, they also consented to Paul's program of a worldwide mission to the gentiles.

Andronicus and Junia, who possibly was his wife and had accompanied him as an active missionary (Rom 16:7; cf. 1 Cor 9:5), moved to Rome before Paul did. Paul greets both of them in Rom 16:7 and calls them "outstanding among the apostles" (not "in the eyes of the apostles"). This compliment served at the same time as a recommendation for Paul himself, who no doubt was trying to establish himself in Rome: being highly controversial in the east because of his law-free gentile mission, Paul could point out that these outstanding Jewish-Christian apostles were close to him.

Bibliography

Lüdemann, G. 1987. *Das Frühe Christentum nach den Traditionen der Apostelgeschichte.* Göttingen.

Ollrog, W. H. 1979. *Paulus und seine Mitarbeiter.* WMANT 50. Neukirchen.
Roloff, J. 1965. *Apostolat-Verkündigung-Kirche.* Gütersloh.

PETER LAMPE

ANEM (PLACE) [Heb *ʿānēm*]. A town in the inheritance of Issachar assigned to the Gershomite clan of the Levites as a levitical city (1 Chr 6:58—Eng 6:73). Another list of levitical cities is preserved in Joshua 21, where in v 29 Anem is replaced by En-gannim.

Most researchers have concluded that the two OT lists of levitical cities were derived from a single original. As a result, a number of attempts have been made to equate Anem and En-gannim. Albright argued (1926: 231), using evidence from the LXX, that both Anem and En-gannim obscured an original Heb form of *ʿnʿnm,* which he located at Olam (M.R. 197230). While a number of scholars have accepted Albright's identification, Kallai (*HGB,* 425) has noted that Albright's argument requires a series of scribal errors to be correct, and has rejected it.

Kallai has suggested that the consonantal *ʿnm* is either an abbreviation or merely a shortened form of the toponym En-gannim, *ʿngnm.* If this theory is correct, Anem/En-gannim should be located at Jenin (M.R. 178207). See also EN-GANNIM (PLACE).

It remains a possibility that Anem is a distinct location, unrelated to En-gannim. Abel (*GP,* 244) has suggested Khirbet Anim (M.R. 202231) as a likely location for an independent Anem.

Bibliography

Albright, W. F. 1926. The Topography of the Tribe of Issachar. *ZAW* 44: 225–36.

MELVIN HUNT

ANER (PERSON) [Heb *ʿānēr*]. A brother of Mamre and of Eshkol (Gen 14:13), all three of whom are described as Abram's allies (Gen 13:24). The latter verse belongs to the passage vv 17, 21–24 about the contest in generosity between the king of Sodom and Abram, which contradicts v 10 (that the kings of Sodom and Gomorrah had perished in asphalt pits) and vv 14–15 (that Abram routed the army of the four eastern kings with just his own 318 house-born men), and is obviously an interpolation. From there, the names of Aner and Eshkol were added by an editor to v 13 along with the ethnic "Amorite" for Mamre. Elsewhere in the OT, Eshcol and Mamre are names of places near Hebron and not persons; it is therefore probable that Aner was originally also a toponym in the same area. (*ʿnr* in the list of levitical cities in the territory of Manasseh, 1 Chr 6:55, is a miscopy of *tʿnk* "Taanach" in Josh 21:25.) The divergent forms of the name in LXX, Samuel, and QL raise a doubt about the correctness of its writing in the MT, but its original form and etymology cannot be reconstructed.

MICHAEL C. ASTOUR

ANER (PLACE) [Heb *ʿānēr*]. A town of the tribe of Manasseh assigned as a levitical city to the Kohathites of the tribe of Levi (1 Chr 6:55—Eng 6:70). In a second list of levitical cities (Josh 21:25), Aner is replaced by Taanach. Most scholars have concluded that both OT lists reflect a single original, so attempts have been made to equate the two toponyms.

The generally accepted solution has been the proposal that Aner was derived from Taanach (Heb *taʿnak*) because of two simple scribal errors. The initial *taw* of Taanach was lost to the preceding word, while the final *kap* was changed to a *reš* (the form of both letters being similar in antiquity). If this hypothesis is correct (*HGB,* 470), then Aner should be equated with Taanach (M.R. 171214).

If Aner is an independent town, unconnected with Taanach, then its location is not known.

MELVIN HUNT

ANGELS. In modern usage the term "angels" refers to heavenly beings whose function it is to serve God and to execute God's will.

OLD TESTAMENT

A. General Matters
   1. Terminology
   2. Historical Development
B. Preexilic Concepts
   1. The Divine Council
   2. The Heavenly Army
   3. Agents and Messengers
C. Exilic and Early Postexilic Developments
   1. Ezekiel
   2. Zechariah
   3. The *Śāṭān*
   4. Other
D. Second Temple Period
   1. Functions and Appearance of Angels
   2. The Heavenly Court/Temple
   3. The Angelic Hierarchy
   4. War in Heaven
   5. Angelic Dualism
   6. Communion with the Angels

A. General Matters

1. Terminology. Although no single term corresponding precisely to the English word "angels" occurs in the Hebrew Bible, there is a rich vocabulary for such beings. Some of the expressions either denote their divine status (e.g., *běnê (hā) ĕlōhîm,* lit., "sons of God" [such grammatical constructions identify generic categories (divine beings), not genealogical relationships], Gen 6:2, 4; Job 1:6; 2:1; 38:7; *běnê ʾēlîm,* "sons of gods, divine beings," Ps 29:1; 89:7—Eng 89:6; *ʾĕlōhîm,* "gods," Ps 82:1) or denote their special sanctity (*qĕdōšîm,* "holy ones," Ps 89:6, 8—Eng 89:5, 7). Other terms refer to their functions (*měšārětîm,* "ministers," Ps 103:21; *śār,* "commander," Josh 5:14; *ṣěbāʾôt,* "hosts, army," Ps 89:9—Eng 89:8; 103:21). The most common of these functional terms if *malʾāk,* "messenger, envoy." It is from the translation of *malʾāk* in the LXX (Gk *aggelos*) that the English word "angel" derives. As terms denoting functions, both *aggelos* and *malʾāk* can refer equally to human or angelic beings. Consequently, there are occasionally passages in which it remains disputed whether the reference is to a heavenly being or a human one (see Judg 2:1; Mal 3:1). It was only with the Vulgate that a systematic distinction was made between angelic emissaries (Lat *angelus*) and human ones (Lat *nuntius*). Nevertheless, there are indications that already in the LXX *aggelos* was beginning to take on the quasi-technical meaning of heavenly being. In several instances *aggelos* is used for terms such as *bĕnê (hā) ʾĕlōhîm* (Gen 6:2; Deut 32:8; Job 1:6; 2:1; 38:7), *ʾĕlōhîm* (Ps 8:6; 97:7; 138:1), and *śār* (Dan 10:21; 12:1), and in one case *malʾāk* is translated as *theos* (Qoh 5:55—Eng 5:6). There is even one instance in the Hebrew Bible (Judg 13:6) in which a character implies a distinction between a "man of God" (*ʾîš ʾĕlōhîm*) and a "messenger/angel of Yahweh" (*malʾāk yhwh*).

Extrabiblical literature from the late Second Temple period (3d century B.C.E.–1st century C.E.) reflects many additional terms for angels. These include "watchers" (Aram *ʿîrîn*, Dan 4:10, 14, 20; *Jub.* 4:15, 22; *1 En.* 1:5); "spirits" (Heb *rûḥôt*, 1QH 1:11; 1QM 12:9; *Jub.* 15:31; *1 En.* 15:4; cf. 1 Kgs 22:21); "glorious ones" (Heb *nikbĕdîm*, 1QH 10:8; *2 En.* 21:1, 3; "thrones" (Gk *thronoi*, *T. Levi* 3:8; *2 En.* 20:1); "authorities" (Gk *exousiai*, *1 En.* 61:10; *T. Levi* 3:8); "powers" (Gk *dynameis*, *2 En.* 20:1); and many other descriptive and functional terms.

2. Historical Development. Any survey of the concept of angels has to take account of the growth and development of the idea over the centuries, the different literary genres in which references occur, and the different social contexts from which the ideas emerge. Although references to angels occur in the oldest strata of the OT (in pentateuchal narratives and in early poetry), there is a clear increase in speculation about the heavenly world in prophetic writings from the exilic and early postexilic periods. It is in the late Second Temple period, however, that the most developed speculations occur. Why there should have been such a development in lore about heavenly beings is not fully understood. Increasing contact with Babylonian and Persian religious traditions may be one element (Russell 1964: 257–62), though most of the features of the developed angelology have clear antecedents in preexilic Israelite tradition. Perhaps much of the speculation on the heavenly world was not really new but represents old Israelite popular religion which only finds its way into literary sources in the postexilic writings (Collins 1977: 101–4). Be that as it may, the increase in discourse about angels in the later sources indicates that those authors found the speculation on the heavenly world a useful way to explore serious religious and theological issues—the weakness of Israel in a world of empires, the difficulty of understanding cosmos and history, the existence of evil, the failure of human religious institutions, the hope and experience of transformation, and so on.

B. Preexilic Concepts

1. The Divine Council. In Israel, as in the ANE in general, the underlying conception of the heavenly world was that of a royal court. Yahweh was envisioned as a king, and at his service were divine beings who served as counselors, political subordinates, warriors, and general agents. These divine beings were often referred to as a collective group (Gen 28:12; 33:1–2; Pss 29:1; 89:6–9) and were understood to constitute a council ("the council of El," *ʿădat ʾēl*, Ps 82:1; "the conclave of Yahweh/Eloah," *sôd yhwh*, Jer 23:18; *sôd ʾĕlôah*, Job 15:8), "the conclave/assembly of the holy ones" (*sôd/qāhāl qĕdōšîm*, Ps 89:6, 9). Similar expressions occur in ANE sources (Phoen: *mpḥrt ʾil gbl qdšm*; Ug: *pẖr ʾilm, pẖr bn ʾilm, dr ʾil*, etc.; Akk: *puḫur ilāni*; see Mullen 1980). The most extensive description of the council and its tasks in the OT is found in 1 Kgs 22:19–22. There, the prophet Micaiah ben Imlah sees the enthroned Yahweh with "all the host of heaven standing about him on his right and on his left." When Yahweh poses a question to the council, there is general discussion ("and one said one thing and another said another"), until a specific proposal emerges ("then a spirit came forth and stood before Yahweh and said . . ."). Prophets might stand in the council of Yahweh to receive a word (Jer 23:18, 22; Isaiah 6). The council was also a place of accusation and judgment (Psalm 82). Perhaps because of their privileged place in the divine council, angels were considered to be paragons of knowledge and discernment (2 Sam 14:17, 29; 19:28).

According to Deut 32:8 (LXX and 4QDeut), when God organized the political structure of the world, each of the nations was assigned to one of the angels/minor deities, with Israel reserved for Yahweh's own possession. Psalm 82 assumes a similar setup but describes the revocation of the arrangement. In that text God brings accusation before the divine council concerning the failure of these minor deities to ensure justice, for which they are to be ousted and killed. See DIVINE ASSEMBLY.

2. The Heavenly Army. In Deut 33:2, Yahweh is said to be accompanied by ten thousand holy ones as he advances from the southland (cf. the reference in Ps 68:18 to the many thousands of chariots with Yahweh at Sinai). These are undoubtedly the angelic armies that are referred to in the common divine title Yahweh of Hosts. In one of the rare instances in which an individual angelic being with a clearly defined office is mentioned, Joshua encounters a mysterious figure with a drawn sword who identifies himself as "the commander of the army of Yahweh" (*śār ṣābaʾ yhwh*, Josh 5:14). When the prophet Elisha was besieged, he was given protection by "horses and chariotry of fire," invisible to all whose eyes were not opened by Yahweh (2 Kgs 6:17).

3. Agents and Messengers. a. Role and Significance. In addition to the various roles that the angelic beings play as a group, there are many texts which describe the actions of a single angelic figure. Almost always in these instances the term *malʾāk* ("messenger") or *malʾāk yhwh/(hā) ʾĕlōhîm* ("messenger of Yahweh/God") is used. The term "messenger" should not be construed too narrowly, however, for these divine beings carry out a variety of tasks. They do announce births (of Ishmael, Gen 16:11–12; Isaac, Gen 18:9–15; Samson, Judg 13:3–5), give reassurances (to Jacob, Gen 31:11–13), commission persons to tasks (Moses, Exod 3:2; Gideon, Judg 6:11–24), and communicate God's word to prophets (Elijah, 2 Kgs 1:3, 15; a man of God, 1 Kgs 13:18; cf. 1 Kgs 22:19–22; Isaiah 6; Jer 23:18, 23). But the angel may also intervene at crucial moments to change or guide a person's actions (Hagar, Gen 16:9; Abraham, Gen 22:11–12; Balaam, Num 22:31–35; the people of Israel, Judg 2:1–5) and may communicate divine promises or reveal the future in the course of such intervention. In addition angels may be the agents of protection for individuals or for Israel as a whole (Gen 24:7, 40; 48:16; Exod 14:19–20; 23:20, 23; 32:34; Num 20:16; 1 Kgs 19:5–8; 2 Kgs 19:35 = Isa 37:36; Pss 34:8—Eng 34:7; 91:11). But they may also be Yahweh's agents for punishment (Genesis 19; Num 22:33; 2 Samuel 24 = 1 Chronicles 21; Pss 35:5–6; 78:49).

In contrast to later writings, these texts exhibit almost no interest in the heavenly messengers themselves. They are not individuated in any way. They do not have personal names or definite offices (though see Josh 5:14). It is generally argued that the term *malʾāk yhwh* should not be translated "*the* messenger of Yahweh," as though referring to a particular divine being, but simply "*a* messenger of Yahweh" (Hirth 1975: 25–31). Either translation is grammatically possible. The messengers are not described (see Judg 13:6 for a partial exception) and are often not even recognized. When human beings do realize the identity of the one who speaks with them, the reaction varies. In some narratives no reaction at all is described (e.g., Genesis 19), while in others the reaction is reverence (Josh 5:14–15) or fear (Judg 13:21). In short, these texts show no speculative interest in the divine messenger whatever. The messenger is of significance solely for the sake of the message (Westermann 1985: 244).

b. Relationship to Yahweh. Many of these narratives about the *malʾāk yhwh* pose a long-standing problem of interpretation: what is the relationship between the messenger/angel of Yahweh and Yahweh? In many of the narratives the *malʾāk* initially appears to be a distinct figure. But at some point in the account it appears as though Yahweh were personally present instead of the *malʾāk yhwh.* In Gen 16:7, for example, when Hagar has run away from Sarai's cruel treatment, the text says that "a *malʾāk yhwh* found her by a well in the wilderness." The two converse and the narrator again identifies the one who speaks with Hagar as a "*malʾāk yhwh*" in vv 9, 10, and 11. But the words which the *malʾāk yhwh* speaks in v 10 ("I will multiply your descendants . . .") appear rather to be the first-person speech of Yahweh himself. In the following verse, however, the *malʾāk yhwh* again speaks of Yahweh in the third person. Yet v 13 begins, "Hagar called the name of Yahweh who spoke with her, 'You are a God of seeing.' . . ." The end of the verse is textually corrupt but is probably to be translated "I have indeed seen God after He saw me." The apparent interchangeability of the *malʾāk yhwh* and Yahweh cannot be resolved by assuming a clumsy merging of two traditional stories. The same ambiguity occurs in many narratives (e.g., Gen 21:15–21; 22:11–12; 31:11–13; Exod 3:2–6; Judg 6:11–24). Numerous suggestions have been put forward to account for this peculiar feature (e.g., that the *malʾāk yhwh* is a sort of hypostasis of the deity; that a functional identity exists between messenger and sender; that the phrase *malʾāk yhwh* is a late, pious interpolation; that the alternation between Yahweh and *malʾāk yhwh* has to do with point of view; etc. See the review in Hirth 1975: 13–23). But the explanation that seems most likely is that the interchange between Yahweh and *malʾāk yhwh* in various texts is the expression of a tension or paradox: Yahweh's authority and presence in these encounters is to be affirmed, but yet it is not possible for human beings to have an unmediated encounter with God (cf. *TWAT* 4: 901; Hirth 1975: 83–84). Hagar is correct—she has seen God. But the narrator is also correct that the one who appeared to her was a *malʾāk yhwh.* The unresolved ambiguity in the narrative allows the reader to experience the paradox. It would be misleading, however, to suggest that this perspective was a dogmatic belief of ancient Israelite religion. There are other narratives in which God appears and converses with human beings, with no reference to a *malʾāk yhwh* (e.g., Genesis 15), and yet others in which the *malʾāk yhwh* is consistently distinguished from Yahweh (e.g., 1 Kings 19). Religious beliefs and forms of expression were probably no more uniform in ancient Israel than in any other age.

The quality of ambiguity which attaches to the *malʾāk yhwh* allows it to be used to stress either God's presence or distance, as in the various traditions that a *malʾāk* accompanied the Israelites on the exodus from Egypt (Exod 14:9; 20:20–23; 32:34; Num 20:16). In Exod 14:9 the *malʾāk* is associated with the pillar of cloud and, like it, functions as a manifestation of the presence of Yahweh with the people. There is a degree of theological speculation in Exod 23:20–23 in the subtle way in which the presence of Yahweh is understood to be manifest. Yahweh speaks of sending the *malʾāk* before the people to protect and guide them and warns the people to obey the *malʾāk,* "because my name is in him." Deuteronomistic theology uses the same concept of the name of God to describe the way in which Yahweh is present in the Jerusalem temple (1 Kgs 8:16, 29; 9:3; cf. Jer 7:12). By contrast, Exod 33:2–3 uses the image of the *malʾāk* to describe Yahweh's absence. The passage follows the account of the apostasy with the golden calf. "I will send a *malʾāk* before you . . . for I will not go up in your midst, because you are such an obstinate people that I might consume you on the way."

c. Relations between Angels and Humans. Although speculation about the angelic world or the relation between divine and human beings does not seem to have attracted much attention in preexilic writings, there is one brief text which raises such questions, Gen 6:1–4. There the interbreeding between divine beings (*bĕnê hā ʾĕlōhîm*) and human women is described. Although the passage is obscure in many respects, the offspring of the union become the ancient warriors of reknown (LXX, *gigantes,* "giants"). Although not presented as a rebellion in heaven or as a "fall" of divine beings, the results of the mating are troubling to Yahweh, who decrees a limit to the human life span as a consequence. It has recently been argued that this passage preserves an old alternate introduction to the flood story, in which the flood was sent to eliminate these half-human/half-divine beings who threatened the order of creation (Hendel 1987: 13–26). Whatever role the tradition may have played in ancient Israel, it became the source of intense speculative development in later centuries.

C. Exilic and Early Postexilic Developments

It is probably not accidental that the 6th century saw a considerable increase in speculation about the heavenly world and its angelic inhabitants, especially in the prophetic literature. The problem of the destruction and the reconstitution of Judah's national institutions required a mode of thinking that could encompass the disaster in some coherent and meaningful structure and provide confidence in the possibility of reconstruction.

1. Ezekiel. Ezekiel's vision of the coming destruction of Jerusalem (Ezekiel 8–11) begins with the appearance of an angelic being who is described in terms derived from the account of the glory of Yahweh (*kābôd yhwh*) in 1:27. The destruction of Jerusalem is carried out at Yahweh's command by other angelic figures described only as six armed men (9:2). An angelic scribe ("a man clothed in linen who had a writing case at his side," 9:3) marks those who are to be spared. Ezekiel's vision of the angelic destroyers provides a graphic reassurance that the destruction, terrible as it is, remains under the direct control of the God of Israel and does not simply represent the triumph of the Babylonians (cf. *2 Baruch* 6–8, written after the destruction of the Second Temple by the Romans). Corresponding to Ezekiel's vision of the destruction of Jerusalem is his vision of the temple as it is to be rebuilt (Ezekiel 40–48). Ezekiel is guided through the structure by an angel ("a man whose appearance was like that of bronze," 40:3) who measures the various structures for Ezekiel and explains the purposes of some of them (e.g., 42:13–14).

The cherubim or living creatures (*kĕrûbîm; ḥayyôt*) described in Ezekiel 1 and 10 are not, properly speaking, angels. The description in Ezekiel and the graphic depictions of similar figures from the ANE indicate that they were winged creatures combining human and animal features. Indeed, they may be described as the animals of the heavenly world. Unlike the "messengers" or the "sons of God," cherubim have only limited functions. They serve as watchdog-like guardians (Gen 3:24; Ezek 28:14), as winged mounts (2 Sam 22:1; Ps 18:11—Eng 18:10), and as bearers of the throne chariot (Pss 80:1; 99:1; Isa 37:16; Ezekiel 1; 10). Perhaps because of their protective role, they were frequently used as decorative motifs in temples and on cultic furnishings (Exod 25:18–20; 26:31; 1 Sam 4:4; 1 Kgs 6:23–36). Similarly, the seraphim of Isaiah 6 are not angels but winged serpentine figures associated with the iconography of the Yahwistic cult (Isa 14:29; 30:6; cf. Num 21:6–9; 2 Kgs 18:4). Isaiah has partially assimilated them to the role of members of the divine council. Later tradition interpreted both seraphim and cherubim as classes of angels.

2. Zechariah. Faced with serious issues of social restructuring and institutional restoration, Zechariah, one of the early postexilic prophets, articulated his message largely in terms of angelic visions. According to Petersen (*Haggai and Zechariah 1–8* OTL, 115–16), "rather than proposing, as had Haggai, that the temple needed to be rebuilt, or that Zerubbabel was to be anointed as king, Zechariah experienced Yahweh's angelic agents and discerned how the new religious and social order was to be initiated. What Zechariah reports in these visions is initial restoration within the cosmic order. . . . Yahweh's steeds and angelic host are busy with the work of creating a new social and religious structure that will affect the entire world, not just Judah." Zechariah's message is made particularly authoritative through his claim that he is not only announcing what should be done on earth but what is already being done in heaven and will soon become evident on earth.

Zechariah concretizes the ancient notion of the army of Yahweh by describing the horses, riders, and chariots which roam the earth, returning to report to the angel of Yahweh and to present themselves before Yahweh (Zech 1:7–17; 6:1–8). The chariots are identified with the four winds (Zech 6:5; cf. Ps 104:4). It appears that in Zechariah's visions the figure identified as the *malʾāk yhwh* has become a distinct and powerful figure in the heavenly world. He has several functions in the visions: guide and interpreter for Zechariah (Zechariah 1–6 *passim*); intercessor for Israel, who receives words of consolation that he commands Zechariah to proclaim (1:12–17; cf. Isa 40:1–9); presider and judge in the divine council (Zechariah 3); and commander of the angelic patrols (Zech 1:11; 6:7).

3. The *Śāṭān*. The angelic figure of the *śāṭān* in Zech 3:1–2 is not to be understood as the cosmic enemy of God of later angelology. The word is a common noun ("opponent, accuser") and is related to the verb *śāṭan,* "to accuse." Both noun and verb can be used of human beings as well as of angelic ones (Num 22:22; 1 Sam 29:4; Zech 3:1; Ps 109:4). Here one should translate, "He showed me Joshua the high priest standing before the *malʾāk yhwh,* and the accuser was standing at his right hand to accuse him." The accuser is simply a member of the divine council who has brought to judgment a high priest who is cultically impure. The picture is very close to that of Job 1–2. "At the time when the sons of God came to present themselves before Yahweh, the *śāṭān* also came among them" (1:6; see also 2:1). There, too, the *śāṭān* raises questions about a person whom he suspects of self-interested piety. The only other contemporary text which mentions this figure is 1 Chr 21:1. A comparison with the parallel text, 2 Sam 24:1, shows that "the anger of Yahweh" in 2 Samuel has been concretized by the Chronicler as the action of a member of the divine council. While the *śāṭān* is not depicted as an enemy of God in any of these texts, the fact that in Zechariah and Job his view is repudiated by God and *malʾāk yhwh* indicates the beginning of the development of the *śāṭān* as a sinister figure (see Petersen (*Hagai and Zechariah 1–8* OTL, 189–90). The notion of an angel who has particular responsibility for an individual, guiding and interceding on behalf of that person, is developed in Job 33:23–26 (cf. 5:1; 16:19). A close parallel to this conception is the "personal god" of Mesopotamian religion (Jacobsen 1976: 147–64).

4. Other. In general, 1–2 Chronicles tends to be somewhat more vivid in its description of angelic figures than parallel texts in Samuel-Kings (compare 2 Sam 24:16–17 with 1 Chr 21:15–30). The idea of heavenly beings as a chorus of praise, reflected already in Psalm 29, is associated with God's act of creation in Job 38:7 (see also *11QPs*[a] *Creat* 26:13; Neh 9:6). In Ps. 148:2 the angelic chorus (*malʾākîm//ṣĕbāʾôt*) is the first in a chain of praise embracing all creation (cf. Ps 103:20–22).

D. Second Temple Period

It is in the late Second Temple period that speculation about the heavenly world and its inhabitants becomes fully developed. There are some new developments in angelology, the most significant being the dualistic notion of evil angels opposed to God, but most of the beliefs about angels are essentially expansions and concretizings of older notions. Numerous references to angels can be found in many genres of literature produced in different social settings, suggesting that a general body of lore concerning angels was common to the popular religion of the era. But the concentration of extensive angelological speculation in certain genres of literature (esp. apocalypses) and in the literature of certain communities (e.g., Qumran) reminds one that the religious and intellectual significance of angelology differed among various Jewish groups.

1. Functions and Appearance of Angels. The general function of the angel as the agent of God's will is widely attested. Retellings of OT narratives (especially *Jubilees* and *Pseudo-Philo*) tend to introduce angels where they did not occur in the OT, oftentimes as performing some act which the OT attributes directly to God (e.g., *Jub.* 38:10; 10:22–23; 14:20; 19:3; 32:21; 41:24; 48:2; *Ps-Philo* 11:5; 15:5; 19:12, 16; 61:5). In the book of Tobit the belief in a protecting angel (cf. Gen 24:7) is dramatized with all the ironic and humorous potential of the situation richly realized (*HBD,* 791–803). Angels help and protect the pious and bring their prayers before God (Dan 3:25, 28; *1 En.* 100:5; *1QM* 13:10; *T. Jud.* 3:10; *T. Dan.* 6:5; *T. Naph.* 8:4; *T. Jos.* 6:7; *T. Benj.* 6:1; *Ps-Philo* 38:3; 59:4; *3 Macc.* 6:18–19; *Vita* 21). Angels also decree and execute punishment in accordance with God's will (Dan 4:13–26; *T. Naph.* 8:6; *1 Enoch* 56). An angelic scribe keeps records which are opened at the time of judgment (Dan 7:10; *1 En.* 89:61–77; 90:14–20; *2 En.* 19:5; *Ap. Zeph.* 3; 7).

The angel as teacher and mediator of revelation is a well-attested motif, even in nonapocalyptic texts (*Joseph and Asenath* 14–15; *Jub.* 1:27–29; 10:10–14 [cf. *1 Enoch* 8]; *T. Reu.* 5:3; *T. Levi* 9:6; *T. Iss.* 2:1; *T. Jos.* 6:6). In apocalyptic writings, the angelic revealer, heavenly guide, and interpreter of mysteries and visions becomes a standard feature (e.g., Daniel 7–12; *1 Enoch* 17–36; *Apocalypse of Abraham* 10–18; *4 Ezra* 3–14). The appearance of the angel often evokes an acute emotional reaction from the person who sees it (Dan 10:7–9; *2 En.* 1:3–8; *Ap. Ab.* 11:2–6).

Certain angels are identified by personal names, the most frequently named being Michael, Gabriel, Raphael, and Uriel (Dan 9:21; 10:13; Tob 12:15; *1 En.* 9:1; 21:10; *4 Ezra* 4:1; *Sib. Or.* 2:215; *1QM* 9:15–16). For various lists of other angels, see *1 En.* 8; 20; 82:13–20. Frequently, the angel's appearance is described in terms of light, fire, shining metals, or precious stones, a tradition based on Ezekiel's description of the glory of God (Dan 10:5–6; 2 Macc 3:25–26; *Jos. As.* 14:9; *2 En.* 1:3–5; *Ap. Ab.* 11:1–3; *Ap. Zeph.* 6:11–15). Their garments are white linen or white with golden sashes (Dan 10:5; 12:6; 2 Macc 3:26; 11:8; *T. Levi* 8:2; but see *Ap. Ab.* 11:2). Angels are assumed to be spiritual creatures whose physical manifestations and apparent eating and drinking are shams (Tob 12:19; *Ap. Ab.* 13:4; *T. Ab.* 4:9–10; Philo, *Quest. Gen.* 4:9; Jos. *Ant.* 1.11.2 §197). There was even speculation on special angelic food and its qualities (*Jos. As.* 16:12–16; Wis 16:20; *Vita* 4:2; cf. Ps 78:23–25). Although angels are spirits and may be called "gods" (*ʾēlîm, ʾĕlōhîm*), they are created beings (*Jub.* 2:2). There is some evidence that certain Jewish groups believed the angels to have assisted God in the creation of the world (Fossum 1985: 192–213). Rabbinic Judaism found the notion theologically dangerous and vigorously rebutted it (Segal 1977). In *Jubilees,* even though angels are created on the first day, they have no role in the creation of the world except to praise the work of God (*Jub.* 2:3; cf. *11QPs*[a] *Creat* 26:13; Job 38:7).

2. The Heavenly Court/Temple. The old notion of the divine council continued to be central for the image of the angelic world. In QL in particular the language of council (*ʿēdāh*), assembly (*qāhāl*), and conclave (*sôd*) is prominent (esp. in *Hodayot; ŠirŠabb*). Graphic depictions of the heavenly court are frequent in apocalypses, though the emphases differ from those of OT sources. The splendor and magnitude of the scene are stressed, but the deliberative role of the council is all but eliminated (Dan 7:9–10; *1 En.* 14:19–23; 40:1–7; *2 Enoch* 20; *4 Ezra* 8:21–22). Rather, it is a place of judgment (Dan 7:10–14; *1 En.* 60:2–6), of revelatory pronouncements (Dan 7:13–14; *1 Enoch* 15–16), and of praise (*1 En.* 61:9–13; *2 En.* 20:4–21:1; *Ap. Ab.* 10:9; 18:11–14; *Ps.-Philo* 18:6). According to some sources, the praise is sung in a special angelic dialect (*T. Job* 48–50; cf. *Ap. Zeph.* 8:4).

Not only royal court but also temple imagery informs the picture of the heavenly world (*1 Enoch* 14). Consequently, the angels may be described as priests who serve in the heavenly temple (*Jub.* 30:18; 31:14; *T. Levi* 3:5–6; *1QSb* 4:24–26; *ŠirŠabb, passim*). In *Jubilees* the angels of the presence and the angels of holiness observe the Sabbath and the Feast of Weeks and are said to have been created circumcised (*Jub.* 2:17–18; 6:18; 15:27). Later rabbinic tradition rejected the notion that the Torah is observed by the angels (see Schäfer 1975: 111–59, 229).

3. The Angelic Hierarchy. The angels are organized in a hierarchical manner. There may be a single superior angel and/or a small group of archangels (usually four or seven), sometimes designated as the angel(s) of the presence (Tob 12:15; *T. Levi* 8:2; *Jub.* 1:27, 29; 2:1–2, 18; 15:27; *1 En.* 9:1; 20:1–7; 40:1–10; 71:9–13; 90:21; *1QM* 9:15–16; *1QSb* 4:25; *1QH* 6:13; cf. Isa 63:9). Where a single angel heads the hierarchy, he is sometimes identified as Michael, the angel who has particular responsibility for the people of Israel (Dan 12:1; *Vita* 13–15). The figure known as the Angel of Truth (*1QS* 3:24) or the Prince of Light (*CD* 5:18; *1QS* 3:20; *1QM* 13:10) in Qumran literature is in all probability to be identified with Michael (compare *1QM* 13:10 with 17:6–8), as is Melchizedek in *11QMelch.* Many sources also identify various groups and classes of angels (*Jub.* 2:2, the angels of the presence and the angels of holiness; *ŠirŠabb*[d] [4Q403 1 i 1–29] and *ŠirŠabb*[f] [4Q405 13 4–7], seven chief and deputy princes; *1 En.* 61:10, cherubim, seraphim, ophanim, angels of power, angels of the principalities; *2 Enoch* 20, ten classes of angels in the seventh heaven; *T. Levi* 3:5–8, archangels, messengers, thrones, authorities; etc.). In some texts the classes of angels are assigned to different heavens (e.g., *T. Levi* 3; *2 Enoch* 3–20). There also developed the notion that all the physical processes of the cosmos (e.g., the movement of sun, moon, and stars; the phenomena of fire, wind, rain; the growth of plants and animals; etc.) are all under the control of particular angels or groups of angels (*Jub.* 2:2; *1 En.* 60:16–22; 82:9–20; *2 Enoch* 19; *1QH* 1:10–11).

For apocalyptic literature, the detailed speculation about the heavenly world, its angelic beings, and their functions is not mere window dressing for the historical and eschatological message which the seer often receives. Rather, such knowledge in itself serves the purpose of theodicy, inasmuch as it provides insight into a system of order and purposive power.

4. War in Heaven. The angels are also closely related to the historical process and its outcome. Just as there are angels over the natural workings of the cosmos, so there are angelic leaders of the nations. Their actions are sometimes directed by God, but on occasion they exceed their orders (*1 En.* 89:59–64) or act to oppose the angels God has assigned to help Israel (Dan 10:13, 20; 12:1). The notion that Israel was aided in times of crisis by angelic warriors was widely shared (2 Macc 3:25–26; 11:8; 15:22–23; cf. Jos. *JW* 6.5.3 §298), but received a distinctive development in apocalyptic and related literature. While older Israelite tradition had described the conflict between Yahweh and the kings of nations opposed to Israel, apocalypses imagine a two-tiered, mirror-image conflict. The conflict on earth between Israel and its enemies is the counterpart of the conflict in heaven between angelic armies. Victory will mean the establishment of the kingdom of Michael among the angels and of Israel among the nations (*1QM* 17:6–8; *As. Mos.* 10:1–10; cf. Dan 7:13–14, 26–27). Although references to angelic armies are very frequent in the apocalypses, the most detailed account of the eschatological battle and the role of the angels is to be found in the Qumran War Scroll (*1QM*).

5. Angelic Dualism. The development of the old notions of the angels of the nations and of God's angelic army is probably one source of the dualistic thinking characteristic of much of the angelology of this period. The influence of Iranian religion is also usually assumed, though it is difficult to demonstrate in detail. In some texts the opposition between an angelic ruler of the forces of light and an angelic ruler of the forces of darkness is made explicit (*4Q^c^Amram*; *1QS* 3:13–4:14). Various names attach to the leader of the evil angels: Melchiresha (*4Q^c^Amram*^b^ 2 3′; *4QṬeharot*^d^ [*4Q280*] 2 2); Belial (*1QM* 1:1; 13:11; *1QS* 2:4–5; *CD* 5:17–19); Beliar (*Jub.* 1:20; *T. Reu.* 2:2; *T. Jud.* 25:3); Mastema (*Jub.* 10:8; *1QM* 13:11); Satan (*1QH* fr. 4, line 6; *Vita* 9–16). In retellings of biblical narrative he is depicted as the enemy of Israel's ancestors (*CD* 5:17–19; *Jub.* 17:15–18; 48:2, 9, 17).

The speculative reinterpretation of Gen 6:1–4 was another important aspect of dualistic theology. In the Enoch literature the angels who mate with women corrupt the earth and its inhabitants, prompting the intercession of the archangels. Although the immediate consequences of the breach are resolved, the mating produces a race of evil spirits subject to Mastema (*1 Enoch* 6–16; *Jub.* 10:1–14; cf. *Genesis Apocryphon* 2). Only in the eschatological victory and final judgment would the rebellious angels, the evil spirits, and their human allies be completely destroyed (*1 En.* 90:17–27; *As. Mos.* 10:1–10; *T. Sim.* 6:3–6).

6. Communion with the Angels. While the angelic armies figure prominently in eschatological visions of salvation, access to the heavenly world and the company of angels during one's lifetime or at death was also desired as a form of deliverance. Enoch's sojourn with the angels was a special case (*Jub.* 4:21–26; *2 En.* 1:8–10). But the tradition that Enoch and other seers were clothed with heavenly garments and became like the angels may describe a kind of transformation which was sought by apocalyptic communities (*2 Enoch* 22; *Ap. Zeph.* 8:3; cf. *1QS* 4:6–8). According to some sources, the righteous dead will dwell with the angels (*1 En.* 39:4–8; cf. Rev 6:9–11). The literature of the Qumran community, however, speaks of enjoying present communion with the angels as part of the blessedness of membership in the community of the new covenant (*1QS* 11:7–8; *1QSa* 3:3–11; *1QH* 3:21–22; 6:12–13; 11:10–14).

Bibliography

Bietenhard, H. 1951. *Die himmlische Welt im Urchristentum und Spätjudentum.* WUNT 2. Tübingen.

Collins, J. J. 1977. *The Apocalyptic Vision of the Book of Daniel.* HSM 16. Missoula, MT.

Fossum, J. E. 1985. *The Name of God and the Angel of the Lord.* WUNT 36. Tübingen.

Hendel, R. S. 1987. Of Demigods and the Deluge: Toward an Interpretation of Genesis 6:1–4. *JBL* 106: 13–26.

Hirth, V. 1975. *Gottes Boten im Alten Testament.* Theologische Arbeiten 32. Berlin.

Jacobsen, T. 1976. *The Treasures of Darkness.* New Haven.

Mullen, E. T. 1980. *The Assembly of the Gods: The Divine Council in Canaanite and Early Hebrew Literature.* HSM 24. Chico, CA.

Rowland, C. 1982. *The Open Heaven.* New York.

Russell, D. S. 1964. *The Method and Message of Jewish Apocalyptic.* OTL. Philadelphia.

Schäfer, P. 1975. *Rivalität zwischen Engeln und Menschen.* Studia Judaica 8. Berlin.

Segal, A. 1977. *Two Powers in Heaven.* SJLA 25. Leiden.

Westermann, C. 1985. *Genesis 12–36.* Trans. J. J. Scullion S.J. Minneapolis.

Carol A. Newsom

NEW TESTAMENT

The NT conception of angels (Gk *aggeloi*) is derived from that of the OT and Judaism and does not make any important modifications or innovations of its own (see above). The NT does not provide a systematic discussion of angels. Rather, angels are incidental characters in the story of redemption. Consequently references to them are concentrated in the accounts of Jesus' birth and resurrection in the Synoptic Gospels, the account of the founding of the Church in Acts, and the account of the final consummation in Revelation.

A. Their Nature

Angels are supernatural heavenly beings created by God (Col 1:16). They are described as spirits (Heb 1:7, 14) and as holy (Mark 8:38; Luke 9:26; Acts 10:22; Rev 14:10). They are presented as robed in white garments (Matt 28:3 = Mark 16:5; John 20:12; Acts 1:10; Rev 19:14) and radiating great light (Matt 28:3; Luke 24:4; Acts 10:30; Rev 10:1; 15:6; 18:1). By their very nature they also radiate the glory of God (Luke 2:9; 9:26; Acts 12:7; 2 Pet 2:10; Jude 8; cf. Acts 6:15) and praise him (Luke 2:13–14; Rev 5:8–14; 7:11–12; 19:1–8).

In form they are akin to humankind and are often referred to as men (Mark 16:5; Luke 24:4; Acts 12:15; Heb 13:2), but are different enough to evoke fear in (Matt 28:1–8; Mark 16:5–8; Luke 1:11–12; 2:9–10; 24:5; Acts 10:4) and worship from (Rev 19:10; 22:8–9) human beings. Angels are asexual (Matt 22:30 par.) and transcend time (Luke 20:34–36). Their knowledge is more comprehensive than humankind, but not unlimited (Matt 24:36 = Mark 13:32; Eph 3:10; 1 Pet 1:12). Their strength is also a notable feature (2 Thess 1:7; 2 Pet 2:11; Rev 5:2; 10:1; 18:21). They possess their own languages (1 Cor 13:1) and are intently concerned with the salvation of humankind (Luke 15:10; Eph 3:10; 1 Tim 5:21; Pet 1:12; cf. 1 Cor 4:9), offering the prayers of the saints on the golden altar (Rev 5:8; 8:3–4), observing worship (1 Cor 11:10), and ministering to the Christian (Heb 1:14).

There are myriads and legions of angels (Matt 26:53; Luke 2:13; Heb 12:22; Jude 14; Rev 5:11; 9:16), but only two are named, the archangels Gabriel (Luke 1:19) and Michael (Jude 9; Rev 12:7). Gabriel is a messenger and Michael a warrior. An archangel is referred to in 1 Thess 4:16 and possibly others in 1 Tim 5:21. In Revelation there appear to be vestiges of the Jewish notion of four or seven archangels in the references to seven spirits (1:4; 3:1; 4:5; 5:6) or angels (8:2) before the throne, four living creatures waiting on the throne (4:6; 5:6), and four angels who preside over the four corners of the earth (7:1). The latter indicates a job differentiation among angels as well, for there are angels over the elements, including water (Rev 16:5; cf. John 5:4 var), fire (Rev 14:18; cf. Heb 1:7), and wind (Rev 7:1; cf. Heb 1:7). The elemental spirits (*stoicheia tou kosmou*) of Gal 4:3 and Col 2:8, 20 may be a reference to demonic angels ruling the world. See ELEMENT, ELEMENTAL SPIRIT.

The category of archangels is indicative of a hierarchy among angels, a hierarchy which is also found among evil angels with Satan as their head (Matt 25:41). Unlike other Jewish works, in the NT these hierarchies remain unelaborated, but are implied in the designation "principalities and powers" (Rom 8:38; 1 Cor 15:24; Eph 1:21; 2:2; 3:10; 6:12; Col 1:16; 2:10, 15; 1 Pet 3:22).

Angels have free will, and those in heaven chose to obey (Matt 6:10) while others chose to rebel (Jude 6; 2 Pet 2:4). The latter are led by Satan (Matt 25:41; Rev 12:7–9) and he seeks to imitate the angels of light (2 Cor 11:14). In the final conflagration, Michael and his angelic host will fight and defeat Satan and his angelic hosts (Rev 12:7–9). Their fate is to be cast into the lake of fire (Matt 25:41).

In the early christological debates, the superiority of Christ over the angels was stressed (Eph 1:21; Col 2:15; Heb 1–2; 1 Pet 3:22) and worship of angels strictly prohibited (Col 2:18; Rev 19:10; 22:8–9). In fact, angels are said to worship Christ (Heb 1:6). Evil angels are to be judged by the saints (1 Cor. 6:3).

B. Their Function

Angels also serve as guardians of individuals and churches. The angels of children in Matt 18:10 are apparently guardian angels. The seven angels of the seven churches in Revelation 2–3 have been identified by some as guardian angels. Belief in a guardian angel underlies Acts 12:15 where Peter is mistaken for his angel. In a guardian capacity, an angel releases the apostles (Acts 5:19–20) and Peter (Acts 12:6–11) from prison.

In part functioning as guardians and in their role as servants which they share with humankind (Rev 19:10; 22:8–9), angels minister to Jesus while he was accomplishing his mission. During the temptation, Satan points to the extremes to which the angels will go to keep Jesus from harm (Matt 4:6 = Luke 4:10–11), and angels come and minister to Jesus after the temptation (Matt 4:11; Mark 1:13). They also minister to Jesus in Gethsemane once he has accepted his fate (Luke 22:43 var). Twelve legions of angels are readied for Jesus' defense at his arrest (Matt 26:53), and angels roll the stone from the entrance of the tomb at the resurrection (Matt 28:2). In short, Jesus spoke of them as "ascending and descending upon him" (John 1:51).

A major function of angels is as messengers and instructors. The thought of angels speaking to someone was not foreign to the audience of the NT (John 12:29). As well as by a direct presence, angels often deliver their message in a dream (Matt 1:20–21; 2:13, 19–20, 22) or a vision (Acts 10:3–6; Rev 1:10).

Moses received the Law from an angel (Acts 7:38, 53; Gal 3:19; Heb 2:2). Angels were witnesses to the incarnation (1 Tim 3:16). Paul assumes that angels can preach a gospel (Gal 1:8) and the Pharisees assume that an angel could have spoken with Paul (Acts 23:9). Angels are harbingers of the births of John the Baptist (Luke 1:11–20) and Jesus (Luke 1:26–38). They advise Joseph about the nature of Mary's child (Matt 1:20–21). They proclaim the birth of Jesus to the shepherds (Luke 2:8–14). They warn Joseph to flee to Egypt with Mary and Jesus (Matt 2:13) as well as when to return (Matt 2:20). They give instructions to the women at the tomb (Matt 28:5–7 = Mark 16:6–7 = Luke 24:4–7). Two angels speak to the disciples at Christ's ascension (Acts 1:10). An angel speaks to Moses in the burning bush (Acts 7:30, 35, 38), advises Philip where to travel (Acts 8:26) and Cornelius to send for Peter (Acts 10:3–6, 22, 30–32; 11:13–14), and reassures Paul that he would stand before Caesar (Acts 27:23–24). As typical of apocalyptic writings, an angel escorts John through his visions (e.g., Rev 17:7).

Angels are integrally involved in judgment, both ongoing and at the final consummation. In an ongoing capacity, angels killed Herod because he accepted the worship of the crowd (Acts 12:20–23). In the final consummation an archangel announces Christ's descent at the parousia (1 Thess 4:16) and other angels announce phases of the final judgment (Rev 10:1–7; 14:6–7), begin its initial processes (Rev 5:1–2; 14:14–16), and are active in it (Rev 8–9; 15–16; 20:1–3). They will accompany Christ at his parousia (Matt 16:27; 25:31; Mark 8:38 = Luke 9:26; 2 Thess 1:7; Jude 14–15), will gather the elect (Matt 24:31 = Mark 13:27), and will separate the evildoers for destruction in the fire (Matt 13:39–42, 49–50; 25:31–46; Jude 14–15). Possibly as a council, they will witness Christ's denial of those who denied him (Mark 8:38 = Luke 9:26; 12:8–9; Rev 3:5; cf. Rev 14:10). The role of angels is often portrayed in military fashion (Rev 19:14, 19), as warriors at Christ's bidding (Matt 26:53).

Bibliography

Benoit, P. 1983. Pauline Angelology and Demonology. Reflexions on the Designations of the Heavenly Powers and on the Origin of Angelic Evil According to Paul. *Religious Studies Bulletin.* 3/1: 1–18.

Bishop, E. F. F. 1964. Angelology in Judaism, Islam, and Christianity. *ATR* 46: 142–54.

Schlier, H. 1968. *The Relevance of the New Testament.* Pp. 172–92. Trans. W. J. O'Hara. New York.

DUANE F. WATSON

ANGELS OF THE SEVEN CHURCHES (Gk *aggeloi tōn hepta ekklēsiōn*). This expression is found only in Rev 1:20 in the preparatory vision of the risen Lord (1:9–20). Here the angels of the seven churches are equated with the seven stars in the Lord's right hand (cf. 1:16). The identity of the seven angels is uncertain, with both human and superhuman identifications being possible (see Hemer 1986: 32–34; McNamara 1966: 192–98).

A. Human Identifications

It has been proposed that the angels are messengers from the seven churches sent to John and/or the messengers from John entrusted to deliver the letters. Although virtually always being a reference to a heavenly messenger, *aggelos* is used occasionally in both the OT (Mal 2:7; 3:1) and the NT (Matt 11:10; Luke 7:24; 9:52; Jas 2:25) to refer to a human messenger. The leaders of the church, perhaps their bishops, is also a possible identification. However, elsewhere in the NT *aggelos* is never used to designate a church leader.

Against both of these identifications is the fact that the content of the letters of chaps. 2–3 pertain to the churches themselves, not to a third party, whoever the angels may be. Against any identification of the angels with any human being is the fact that all of the other 66 occurrences of *aggelos* in Revelation and virtually all other known occurrences refer to supernatural beings. Also, the use of angels to represent human beings or churches is virtually unknown in apocalyptic literature.

However, it should be noted that *Tg. Ps.-J.* on Exod 39:37; 40:4 identifies the seven lamps of the lampstand of the tabernacle as the seven stars or planets, and the latter in turn as "the just that shine unto eternity in their righteousness." This equation supports a human identification for angels and corresponds to the symbolism of Revelation in which the lampstands represent churches.

B. Superhuman Identifications

The seven angels have been identified as the guardian angels of the seven churches. Nations (Deut 32:8 LXX; Dan 10:13, 20; 12:1; Sir 17:17) and individuals (*Jub.* 35:17; Matt 18:10; Acts 12:15) are portrayed as having guardian angels. However, this identification is not satisfactory because of the difficulty of the resulting scenario in which Christ directs John to write a letter to the churches, but John in turn addresses it to their guardian angels instead (1:11).

Widely accepted is the position that the angels are personifications of the prevailing spirit of the churches, the spiritual counterpart of the earthly reality. This would make the angels akin to the Persian *fravashis,* heavenly counterparts of earthly individuals and communities. The difficulty that the letters are addressed to the angels but pertain to the churches is thus eliminated, for both can be addressed simultaneously. However, although the stars and the lampstands are distinguished in Revelation as angels and churches respectively, in this solution they are now virtually equated. Ultimately no identification has as yet been totally satisfactory.

Bibliography

Hemer, C. J. 1986. *The Letters to the Seven Churches of Asia in Their Local Setting.* JSNTSup 11. Sheffield.

McNamara, M. 1966. *The New Testament and the Palestinian Targum to the Pentateuch.* AnBib 27. Rome.

DUANE F. WATSON

ANGER. See VIRTUE/VICE LISTS; WRATH OF GOD.

ANGLE, THE (PLACE) [Heb *hammiqṣōaʿ*]. "Place of corner-structure," "corner buttress": corner of a building (Exod 26:24; 36:29); corner of a court (Ezek 46:21); corner post of the altar (Ezek 41:22). Particularly, an important and well-known part of the defense structure of Jerusalem, built by Uzziah king of Judah when he fortified the city by constructing towers at the Corner Gate, at the Valley Gate, and at the angle (2 Chr 26:9). Destroyed in the conquest of Jerusalem by Nebuchadnezzar, this section (Neh 3:19–20, 24–25) and other sections of the wall were repaired by Nehemiah, ca. 430 B.C. Being mentioned in the vicinity of the Water Gate (3:26), the wall of Ophel (3:27), and the East Gate (v 29), "the Angle" seems to have been located along the E wall of Jerusalem, somewhere near the Water Gate (which may have led to the Gihon Spring) and the earlier house (palace) of David (Mare 1987: 123–26).

Bibliography

Mare, W. H. 1987. *The Archaeology of the Jerusalem Area.* Grand Rapids.

W. HAROLD MARE

ANIAM (PERSON) [Heb *ʾănîʿām*]. The fourth son of Shemida (1 Chr 7:19) in the genealogy of Manasseh (7:14–19). His name occurs only once in the Bible and may have meant "people's lament" (*ʾānâ* + *ʿam*) or "I am kinsman" (*ʾănî* + *ʿam*). Noth (*IPN,* 237) suggested that the name is a scribal mistake for Noah, one of the five daughters of Zelophehad (Num 26:33).

1 Chr 7:19 is a genealogical fragment whose relationship to the rest of the Manassite genealogy (7:14–18) is unclear. The verse records the names of Shemida and his four sons, but it does not link them to the Manassites who were listed earlier. Consequently, a number of proposals have been made to integrate the verse more effectively into the rest of the Manassite genealogy. Curtis and Madsen (*Chronicles* ICC, 152) have proposed, for example, that Shemida was the fourth son of Hammolecheth (v 18); this would make Aniam her grandson. Others, however, have argued that Gilead was the father of Shemida, just as Num 26:30–32 indicates (cf. Josh 17:1–3). In this case, Aniam would have been Gilead's grandson. Rudolph (*Chronikbücher* HAT, 69–71) is the most persuasive of those who

favor this position, and his presentation involves a comprehensive emendation of the Manassite genealogy in 1 Chronicles 7 on the basis of Num 26:28–34.

M. PATRICK GRAHAM

ANIM (PLACE) [Heb *ʿānîm*]. A town situated in the SW hill country of Judah (Josh 15:50), within the same district as Debir. The only OT reference to this settlement, whose name means "springs," occurs in the list of towns within the tribal allotment of Judah (Josh 15:21–62). The theory that this list is derived from an administrative roster compiled under the Judean monarchy (Alt 1925) has been widely accepted, although controversy continues over the precise makeup of the districts, the proper context of the town lists of Benjamin and Dan, and the period of the monarchy to which the original roster belongs (Boling and Wright *Joshua* AB, 64–72). Anim may be the same place as Hawini of the Amarna Letters (Boling and Wright *Joshua* AB, 388). Eusebius (*Onomast.* 26.9) associates Anim with the Christian town of Anaia, situated nine Roman miles S of Hebron. Anim is most probably to be identified with Khirbet Ghuwein et-Tahta (Aharoni *LBHG* 300; M.R. 156084), located approximately 20 km S of Hebron and 4 km S of es-Samu (ancient Eshtemoh?). Khirbet Ghuwein et-Foqa, just to the northeast, may be the location of Christian Anaia (Gold *IDB* 1: 300).

Bibliography

Alt, A. 1925. Judas Gaue unter Josia. *PJ* 21: 100–16.

WADE R. KOTTER

ANIMAL. See ZOOLOGY.

ANKLETS [Heb *ʿăkāsîm*]. The word *ʿekes,* found only in the plural in the Hebrew Bible, indicates a piece of jewelry worn around the ankle, as are bracelets worn encircling the wrist. The only biblical text mentioning anklets is Isa 3:18, in which the decadent garb of self-indulgent Israelites is listed in considerable quantity. Twenty-one items are presented, and anklets head the list. Perhaps their position at the top of the list, where they are followed by "headbands," is meant to indicate that the items that follow are those that adorn the entire body, from foot to head.

Anklets were usually made of metal, although some glass examples have been found. Of the metal ones, bronze examples are most common, but the existence of gold, silver, and iron specimens can be established either through the discovery of actual examples or through analogy with the more commonly found bracelets or rings. All of these circular metal items of adornment were made by bending straight wires or bands into a rounded shape. Sometimes the ends were left open; on some examples they have been welded or twisted together. Metal anklets were usually undecorated except for the occasional clubbing or flattening of the free ends in unclosed examples.

Although bracelets, armlets, necklaces, and rings were apparently worn by both men and women, it is difficult to determine whether the same can be said for anklets. In graphic art from the ancient Semitic world, depictions of human figures tend to be those of upper-class individuals, clad in ceremonial garb. This means that long cloaks or outer garments cover the lower legs and obscure the areas in which anklets would be worn. However, certain renderings of deities, especially those depicted nude or seminude, are instructive. Although such figures are often very simple and stylized, the use of jewelry as adornment stands out in the absence of items of clothing. A comparison of female and male Canaanite gods rendered in metal (see Negbi 1976) shows a number of examples of female figures with anklets but only one or two possible males so adorned.

The graphic information is valuable in showing the way the anklets were worn. Several examples of single anklets, that is, one on each ankle, can be seen. But in the preponderance of instances, anklets were worn in sets of three and four, and probably also in sets of five and maybe even six (Seibert 1974: pls. 41, 54, 56, 59, 63). The fact that anklets were worn in groups informs the meaning of Isa 3:16, in which the prophet mocks the haughty daughters of Zion, who strut about wantonly, "tinkling with their feet." The verb in this passage is derived from the word for anklet and indicates the jingling noise produced by the movement of the feet of a person wearing anklets.

Bibliography

Negbi, O. 1976. *Canaanite Gods in Metal.* Tel Aviv.
Seibert, I. 1974. *Woman in Ancient Near East.* Leipzig.

CAROL MEYERS

ANNA (PERSON) [Gk *Hanna; Anna*]. **1.** The wife of Tobit and mother of Tobias. Anna serves three roles in the story of Tobit. First, she is the object of piety for Tobit and Tobias. Tobit marries Anna, who is a member of his paternal clan, and thereby provides a good example for Tobias and other Jews in the Diaspora (1:9). Tobit instructs Tobias to honor his mother after Tobit's death and to bury her in Tobit's grave (4:3–4), which Tobias does (14:10).

Second, she is the ideal wife. When Tobit no longer hides from Sennacherib, he returns to Anna and Tobias (1:20). Later, when Tobit is blinded by the sparrow droppings, Anna takes up "women's work," which the Vg explains as weaving cloth (2:11 LXX—2:19 Vg). Thus she exemplifies the ideal wife of Prov 31:10–31. She values Tobias more than any riches he can bring back from his dangerous journey (5:18–23), and she watches the road for his return (11:5–6, 9).

Her third role is to be a foil to Tobit's piety. When her employers give her a kid as a bonus, Tobit accuses her of theft. Her retort in LXX questions the value of his piety if it makes him such a blind know-it-all (2:14). In Vg, which explicitly compares Tobit to Job (2:15 Vg), Anna says his piety is vain (2:22 Vg), making her more like Job's wife. Whereas Tobit trusts that God's angel will take care of Tobias (10:1–3), Anna rejects his belief and despairs of Tobias' life with fasting and lament (10:4–7). Yet it is Anna who watches for Tobias daily (11:5–6, 9) and who sees him first, so even her despair was not without hope.

Bibliography

Pfeiffer, R. 1949. *History of NT Times, With Introduction to the Apocrypha.* Westport, CT.

MITCHELL C. PACWA

2. An elderly and especially devout Jewish widow portrayed in Luke 2:36–38 who should not be confused with the Anna of Tobit, a deuterocanonical book. Strikingly, Anna is the only woman in NT called a prophetess (using the Greek noun form of the word). Thus, she is to be understood in the light of such OT figures as Deborah and Huldah. Comparisons should also be made with the intertestamental figure of Judith who, like Anna, was devout, lived to about the same age (105), and did not remarry after her husband died (Judith 16:23). The Lukan material raises the question of whether or not there was some sort of Jewish order of widows who had specific functions in the temple, for example, to pray (Witherington 1988: 140–41). This might explain her apparently constant presence in the temple. It should also be noted that, according to Luke's portrait of Anna, she, unlike Simeon, goes forth to proclaim the good news about the Messiah (Plummer *Luke* ICC, 71). This foreshadows one of the roles assumed by female believers in Luke's 2-vol. work (cf. Priscilla in Acts 18). It is also possible that Luke intends for the reader to see parallels between Luke 1–2 and Acts 1–2, in which case Anna anticipates what will happen when the spirit is poured out on all flesh, and both sons and daughters prophesy (Stahlin *TDNT* 9: 451). There may also be some truth in the suggestion that Anna is portrayed by Luke as one of the *ʾanawim*, i.e., the pious Jewish poor (Brown 1977: 446). Luke does seem to have a special interest in such people, and in view of his theme of reversal of fortunes (cf. Luke 4:17–19), he seems to promote women like Anna as examples of how the gospel affects human lives. Anna may also be seen as a model of faith in action, one who responds positively and properly to the coming of the Messiah.

Bibliography

Brown, R. 1977. *The Birth of the Messiah.* Garden City, NY.
Witherington, B. 1988. *Women in the Earliest Churches.* Cambridge.

BEN WITHERINGTON III

ANNAN (PERSON) [Gk *Annan*]. See HARIM.

ANNAS (PERSON) [Gk *Hannas*]. High priest in Jerusalem between ca. A.D. 6, when he was appointed by Quirinius, and A.D. 15, when he was removed by Valerius Gratus (*Ant* 18.2.1, 2 §§ 26–35; Luke 3:2). Annas' later prominence, long after his deposition, and the success of his family in high priestly office, make it seem unlikely that he was deposed as a result of official displeasure; he served the accommodation with Rome very well (Smallwood 1976: 155–56, 159). Although, as we shall see, there are references in the gospels to his being high priest during the capital proceedings against Jesus, that claim is incorrect: Caiaphas was high priest at the time, and—in chronological terms—he was the most successful high priest of the period (see CAIAPHAS). But the influence of Annas survived his personal high priesthood. Five of his sons—Eleazar, Jonathan, Theophilus, Matthias, and the younger Annas—all held that office (*Ant* 20.9.1 §198; Enelow *JEnc* 1: 610), and the claim is made in John 18:13 that Caiaphas was actually his son-in-law.

The continuing influence of Annas makes certain misstatements in the NT explicable. The odd reference to the joint high priesthood of Annas and Caiaphas, in Luke 3:2, and the unqualified reference to him alone as high priest in Acts 4:6, are perhaps the most obvious instances. But the latter case might give us pause, before we dismiss it as a simple error. The scene in Acts 4 represents an inquisition of Peter and John by the Sanhedrin in Jerusalem, following their healing of a lame man at the Beautiful Gate of the temple (Acts 3:1–26). The mention of Annas occurs within a description of the assemblage of the council (4:5f), which is specifically said to include, not only priests, but "rulers, and elders, and scribes" (v 5). After referring to Annas as high priest, v 6 mentions "Caiaphas, and John, and Alexander, and as many as were from high priestly stock." It seems quite clear that Acts refers to Annas' position of leadership within a vital faction of the Sanhedrin, to his driving force behind the inquisition. The primary opposition to Jesus is priestly (cf. vv 1–3), and Annas appears to be leading the opposition. The usage of the term "high priest" is therefore loose (and technically incorrect), but scarcely incomprehensible.

The family of Annas appears in consistent, sometimes deadly, opposition to Jesus' movement during its early years. Aside from Annas' personal involvement in the condemnation of Jesus, to which we shall turn below, we see in Acts 4 a formality of opposition, which hardens Jesus' movement in its tendency toward a formal break with Judaism. Peter boldly proclaims, "Let it be known to you, and all Israel, that by the name of Messiah Jesus of Nazareth—whom you crucified, but whom God raised from the dead—this man stands before you whole" (4:10); that amounts to a stinging, personal statement of judgment against Annas, Caiaphas, and anyone else who had anything to do with Jesus' execution. The presentation of Acts therefore uses Annas as emblematic of the distinction between the rulers who crucified Jesus and those Jews who decided to follow him (cf. v 4 and see GAMALIEL). The "John" mentioned in v 6 may be Annas' son, a future high priest (cf. the full spelling, "Jonathan," in representatives of the so-called Western text; Lake and Cadbury 1933: 42; and Jeremias 1969: 197 n. 161). In ca. A.D. 62, Annas' son and namesake took the opportunity of a hiatus in Roman rule to arrange the death of James, the brother of Jesus (*Ant* 20.9.1 §§ 197–203; Smallwood 1976: 279–80). That the very name "Annas" should have become something of an inverted icon within the NT, a symbol of hierarchical opposition to Christianity, is therefore quite understandable.

It is nonetheless surprising to find the uniquely Johannine scene of the session at Annas' house (18:12–24). Annas is insistently called "high priest" (vv 15, 16, 19, 22) despite the fact that Caiaphas is as well (cf., above all, the confusion caused by the usage in v 24); indeed, Jesus is struck for answering Annas as high priest sharply (v 22). Annas' very residence is said to be high priestly (v 15), and Jesus is brought there by a contingent of Roman and Jewish forces (v 12). Moreover, the Johannnine scene poses the gravamen against Jesus in terms quite different from the Synoptics': Annas is concerned about Jesus' disciples and teaching, while Caiaphas' focus in the Synoptics is the temple and christology. It seems obvious that Annas features in John, at least to some extent, as typological of Jewish enmity toward Jesus and his movement.

Behind the text of John, however, there may be an important trace of historical reminiscence. The issue which mortally opposed Caiaphas to Jesus had been Jesus' inflammatory action of occupying the temple. The immediate occasion of Jesus' act was his opposition to the placement of vendors of sacrificial animals in the precincts of the temple. Given that such an arrangement was unusual, and could have caused opposition, the question arises, why would Caiaphas have permitted it? It has become conventional, among Christian scholars of the NT, to claim that references in rabbinica to "the sons of Ḫanan," merchants of such animals, should be identified with Annas' family (cf. Jeremias 1969: 20, 49; Edwards *ISBE* 1: 128).

A full acceptance of the suggested identification would provide a picture in which Annas opposed Jesus for economic, not simply theological, reasons. A certain amount of evidence might be said indirectly to support it. The family of Ḫanan is decried for its conniving practices in Talmud (*Pesaḥ.* 57a), and problems of extortionate pricing by merchants of sacrificial animals are addressed in Mishnah (*Ker.* 1.7). But to make of Annas a 1st-century equivalent to Shylock on the basis of such evidence is more to indulge the rhetorical reference to Annas in the NT than to describe it. The fact is that Ḫanan is a common name in rabbinica; indeed, the name is used to refer to a real or fictitious scoundrel on some occasions (cf. *B.Qam.* 37a, 115a). To ascribe the sitting of the merchants, the resulting occupation of the temple by Jesus, and the complicated proceedings against him all to Annas' venal motives, and simply because he bore a common name which was also associated with vendors, appears tendentious in the extreme. The very prominence of Annas and his family during the period, and his possible relationship to Caiaphas, suggest that the sitting of the merchants (and their subsequent removal) occurred with his approval. But to speculate on his character—and especially to suggest that his motivation was economic—is to proceed far beyond the evidence and to desert exegesis in favor of a long-discredited, apologetic stance.

Bibliography

Jeremias, J. 1969. *Jerusalem in the Time of Jesus.* Trans. F. H. and C. H. Cave. London.

Lake, K., and Cadbury, H. J. 1933. Vol. 4 of *The Beginnings of Christianity.* London.

Smallwood, E. M. 1976. *The Jews under Roman Rule.* SJLA 20. Leiden.

BRUCE CHILTON

ANNIAS (PERSON) [Gk *Annias*]. Ancestor of a family who returned from Babylon with Zerubbabel (1 Esdr 5:16). Although 1 Esdras is often assumed to have been compiled from Ezra and Nehemiah, this family does not appear among their lists of returning exiles (cf. Ezra 2:17; Neh 7:23). Omissions such as this also raise questions about 1 Esdras being used as a source by Ezra or Nehemiah. Furthermore, problems associated with dating events and persons described in 1 Esdras have cast doubt on the historicity of the text.

MICHAEL DAVID MCGEHEE

ANNIUTH (PERSON) [Gk *Anniouth*]. See BANI.

ANNUNUS (PERSON) [Gk *Announos*]. One of the priests or Levites recruited upon Ezra's request to return with him to Jerusalem and serve in the temple (1 Esdr 8:47—Eng 8:48; not included in the parallel list in Ezra 8:19).

There is a discrepancy between Ezra 8 and 1 Esdras 8. Ezra 8 says that Ezra assembled only Levites missing from the first group to return to Jerusalem (8: 17–19). Ezra takes measures to secure the "ministers" (*mšrtym*), apparently for menial work. In 1 Esdras, both priests and Levites are absent, and Ezra sends for priests (*tous hierateusontas*; 1 Esdr 8:45—Eng 8:46).

The list of the priests and the temple servants in 1 Esdr 8:47–49—Eng vv 46–48 seems to be excerpted from a complete list. In Codex Alexandrinus, Annunus is identified as the brother of Jeshaiah, another priest in the same list. Codex Vaticanus omits the first half of 1 Esdr 8:47—Eng v 48, where both Annunus and Jeshaiah (his brother) are mentioned.

The absence of the name in Ezra 8:19 leads C. T. Fritsch (*IDB* 1: 138) to suspect that a corruption of *wĕʾittô*, "and with him," in Ezra 8:19 gave rise to the name Annunus.

JIN HEE HAN

ANOINTED, THE. See CHRIST; MESSIAH.

ANT. See ZOOLOGY.

ANTELOPE. See ZOOLOGY.

ANTHOTHIJAH (PERSON) [Heb *ʿantōtîyāh*]. One of the sons of Shashak, according to the longer genealogy of Benjamin given by the Chronicler (1 Chr 8:24).

SIEGFRIED S. JOHNSON

ANTHROPOLOGY AND THE OT. As an academic discipline, anthropology is organized differently in different countries. In North America the subject is often called cultural anthropology. It is interested in the comparative study of societies and cultures, seeking to formulate general theories about how culture changes in response to such things as alterations in the environment, population increase and control, and the introduction of new technologies. In Britain it is usually called social anthropology, focusing on the study of single societies. The aim is not to produce general theories of culture, but to show how in each given case a society's beliefs, kinship system, exercise of power, etc., form a coherent set of symbols which reflect and constitute that society's understanding of the world.

A. The Interface with OT Study

The way in which anthropology is organized in different parts of the world has affected the way in which it has been used in OT studies. Thus, recent attempts in North America to reconstruct the origin of the Israelite tribes and the emergence of the Israelite state have depended on general theories of culture change. In Britain attention has been focused upon OT sacrifice and ritual as part of a set of coherent symbols. The continent of Europe has been more influenced by the British than by the North American approach; indeed, the French sociologist E. Durkheim exerted considerable influence upon the development of British social anthropology in the present century.

Twenty years ago there was broad agreement in OT study on a number of issues that overlapped with anthropology. With regard to Israel's origins, it was believed that the Israelites were seminomads who had entered Canaan either forcefully or peacefully, and had then settled down (sedentarized). The intellectual life of the ancient Israelites was thought in many ways to resemble that of "primitives": they could not distinguish easily between the individual and the group, and the personality of one person could merge into that of another so that, for example, a messenger was simply an extension of the personality of whoever had given him the message. It was held that in matters of worship the Israelites used sacred drama which differed little from magical beliefs, and that, by enacting the humiliation of the king and his restoration, the Israelites sought to influence the agricultural cycle for the coming year. It was also believed that the Israelites had little idea of scientific causation and therefore readily regarded as miraculous what modern observers would explain in natural terms.

In the past twenty years the picture has changed considerably. The view that the Israelites were sedentarizing seminomads has been strongly challenged by an alternative theory: that they were peasants who had rebelled against their Canaanite overlords and had established an alternative, egalitarian society. The previous view of the intellectual life of the Israelites has been shown to rest upon ideas about primitives that hardly apply to the Israelites, who, culturally, were far more advanced.

In Britain the impetus for a new evaluation came from anthropologists themselves. E. R. Leach applied to the opening chapters of Genesis the interpretation of myths then being pioneered by the French sociologist C. Lévi-Strauss, and he followed this up with a paper entitled "The Legitimacy of Solomon" (1969). However, Leach believed that OT narratives had no historical value whatsoever, and that they were texts which sought to resolve the paradox that Israel was a separate people yet in full contact with other peoples. At the same time, by inviting refutation, Leach's articles forced British OT scholars to become familiar with the type of anthropology to which Leach was indebted. Probably the most influential work at this time was that of anthropologist Mary Douglas, which was both an attack on the idea of "primitive mentality" and an attempt to show that the animals listed in Leviticus 11 were prohibited because they were anomalies with respect to the classification of the world implied in Genesis 1 (see below).

In North America the impetus came not from anthropologists but from OT scholars, arising from their strengths in archaeology and in the study of the ANE in general. The mention of nomads in the Mari correspondence, of *šasu* and *sutu* nomads in Egyptian and Akkadian texts respectively, not to mention the *ḫabiru* of the Amarna and other texts, made it necessary to turn to anthropology to try to discover the precise nature of these groups. G. E. Mendenhall was the first scholar to question the seminomad "sedentarization" hypothesis on the basis of studies derived from anthropology (1962), although his contribution was overlooked until it was restated in his *Tenth Generation* (1973). Since then, especially in North America, there has been an explosion of interest in anthropology among OT scholars, although most of the attention has focused on Israel's origins and the nature of Israelite prophecy.

B. Israel's Self-awareness

As noted above, Mary Douglas' essay "The Abominations of Leviticus" (1966: 41–58) argued that certain creatures are prohibited in the OT because they are anomalous. According to Genesis 1, the world is divided into heavens, earth, and seas; and the creatures appropriate to these areas are, respectively, those with wings and two legs, those with two legs who walk or four legs who go on all fours, and those with fins. Other creatures, such as those with wings and four legs, or land creatures with no legs at all, do not fit the classification and are therefore prohibited. Although Douglas' explanation can be faulted at a number of points, her intention was to see these prohibitions as something essentially logical, given the Israelite world view. The prohibitions were part of a complex set of social mechanisms that ordered the world and marked off the sacred from the secular.

This sort of approach was taken further by Douglas Davies (1977) and applied to Israelite sacrifice. The complicated ritual for the rehabilitation of the "leper" in Leviticus 14 shows how the Israelites divided the world into sectors with strong barriers, that needed powerful social rituals to enable them to be crossed. The restored leper, for example, after shaving off all his hair, washing all his clothes, and bathing, had to spend seven days in a sort of social limbo, inside the camp but outside his own tent. On the eighth day he again shaved, washed his clothes, and bathed, so that the final offerings for his full restoration to society could be made. In the Day of Atonement ceremony, there are very powerful rituals used to counterbalance the social effects of individual and corporate wrongdoing during the previous year. The entire sanctuary is cleansed by means of blood sprinkling, and a goat over whom all the sins of the people have been confessed is led across boundaries, from the sanctuary through the camp and out into the wilderness, symbolizing and effecting the removal of what is socially disruptive from the ordered relationships of the camp.

It becomes clear that, if Israelite self-awareness begins to be approached in this sort of manner, a quite different picture emerges from that of the "primitive" living in a mystical sort of communion with nature and fellow Israelites. Reality for the Israelite, in fact, was carefully ordered and structured; therefore, the task of future research should be directed toward elucidating this order more thoroughly. There remains, however, a different problem. When was Israelite self-awareness ordered in this manner? Was this self-awareness held by all the people, or just some of them? Leach was able to avoid this problem by supposing that OT narratives were devoid of historical (diachronic) value, resembling the (synchronic) data collected by a field anthropologist. Douglas Davies qualified his study by saying that views he described were those of the Israelite leaders after the Exile. It is obvious from the OT itself, however, that diverse self-conceptions existed in Israel: the common people and their rulers often refused to accept the prophetic interpretation of Israel's religion, and many Israelites found the fertility religion of Canaan more attractive than the ethical monotheism of the prophets. Thus, for all its value, study of the mental life of the Israelites in terms of a single coherent system of symbols cannot deal with the diverse religious conflicts recorded in the OT.

C. Israelite Prophecy

Recent work on Israelite prophecy from an anthropological perspective has been able to make a start on this matter of religious conflict. Whereas older scholarship dealing with prophecy was interested in the mental states of the prophets (esp. the role of "ecstasy"), the anthropological approach has sought to identify the part played by society in the processes by which people become prophets and act out their prophetic roles. Petersen (1981) divides Israelite prophecy into two main types: peripheral possession prophecy and central morality prophecy. The former is common among groups who are at the margins of society, their leaders have support groups, and their god is sometimes amoral. Central morality prophets are active in times of national difficulty, often lack support groups, and affirm the standard morality of the state. This typology certainly makes sense of some OT material. The prophetic groups led by Elijah and Elisha resemble peripheral possession prophets, while Isaiah and Jeremiah resemble central morality prophets. Undoubtedly there is more to the matter than this, but the anthropological approach immediately sets up a typology unavailable to approaches simply asking questions that ignore social dimensions. Long (1981) has investigated the matter of conflict between prophets and regards such conflict as common, if not normal. In the case of such prophetic conflict, Wilson (1980) suggests that the outcome is often determined by the relative strengths of the prophets' support groups. This is an area where much remains to be done.

D. Israel's Origins and Early Social Organization

Work on Israel's origins has engendered keen debate and posed fundamental questions of method. Mendenhall (1962; 1973) and Norman Gottwald (1979), whose somewhat similar but different accounts of Israel's origins in terms of a peasants' revolt have challenged the seminomad immigration theory, are dependent upon a type of American cultural anthropology which assigns an important role to factors such as technological innovation and population growth and response in the development of societies. This is one reason why both have eschewed the idea of Israel's origins in terms of the immigration implied in the book of Joshua in favor of an explanation in terms of developments within Canaanite society itself. On the other hand, Niels Peter Lemche (1985), in what is the most comprehensive discussion in this area so far, has insisted that OT scholars must be as widely read as possible in the anthropological literature, and must be aware of the differing schools in anthropology and their assumptions. He maintains that the aim of such reading must be to circumscribe the use of common sense by indicating how societies actually function and what manifestations are likely and unlikely.

Lemche shows that nomadism is a very complex phenomenon encompassing peoples without leaders as well as peoples with princely families that traditionally offer leadership. Nomads may well be related to settled peoples in nearby villages. Some may become day laborers out of necessity and be forced to settle down. Others may settle down because they become rich, investing their surplus in land. There is no particular type of land especially suited to nomadism, and sedentarization is not something particularly desired by nomads. Settling down involves losing freedom to move around, and it may bring the likelihood of having to pay taxes. Nomadism is a multi-resource phenomenon which adapts to the prevailing political circumstances.

Lemche rejects the idea that farmers and cities are often in conflict, a view central to Gottwald's work. He cites examples of farmers living in close harmony with cities. Indeed, cities may be best defined as geographical collections of disparate units. On segmentary and egalitarian societies, Lemche shows that segmentary societies are not necessarily egalitarian, and that societies that have an egalitarian ideology do not necessarily have egalitarian praxis. He rejects on anthropological grounds the views of Mendenhall and Gottwald, and although he does not himself subscribe to an immigration type view of Israelite origins, he indicates that it cannot be ruled out on anthropological grounds.

Lemche also devotes a section to an analysis of early Israelite social structure. In the late 1970s a consensus seems to have emerged according to which Israelite society consisted of three major elements: family, clan, and tribe, indicated by the Hebrew terms *bêt ʾab, mišpaḥâ* and *šebeṭ*. Tribes were geographical associations of groups. Lemche convincingly challenges this consensus and establishes an alternative. He argues that the term *bêt ʾab* designates both the family and the lineage, the difference between the two being that a family is a residential group while the lineage is a descent group that links families. He also argues that *mišpaḥâ* overlaps with *bêt ʾab* in designating a lineage, and that it probably also designates a maximal lineage, that is, a reckoning of descent from a family to a founder of a tribe or major group. Lemche notes that *mišpaḥâ* is much less frequent in the OT than *bêt ʾab,* and that no leader comes from a *mišpaḥâ*. On the evidence available to us from the book of Judges, Israelite tribes were not segmentary egalitarian societies. They were territorial groups with potential for united action under single leaders. Even the so-called "minor judges" of Judges 10:1–5 and 12:8–15 seem to have been wealthy and powerful individuals, with large families. In the case of three of them, it is noteworthy that a tribal area is called a land (Heb *ʾereṣ*; cf. Judg 10:4; 12:11, 15).

On the matter of the origin of the tribes, anthropology does not give much assistance. It seems likely that Gottwald's view cannot be established on anthropological grounds, namely, that Israelite tribes were not "true" tribes, but were secondary formations in response to the oppressive policy of Canaanite cities. Although some of the tribal names, e.g., Judah and Ephraim, may be geographical designations taken over by groups living in those areas, this is not true for all tribal names, some of which are clearly personal names. Some sort of nomadic origin cannot be ruled out in these cases, although it is difficult to say when and under what circumstances these groups became sedentary. Another difficult question is that of the origin of the twelve-tribe system. Granted the now widespread rejection of Noth's theory that Israel was a twelve-tribe amphictyony in the period of the judges, it may be necessary to look for the origin of the twelve-tribe system in the united monarchy of David and Solomon, intended to be a legitimation of the rule of Judah over a group of tribes that had not previously been united, unless they had united under Saul in the face of the Philistine threat. It is clear from texts such as Genesis 49 and Deuteronomy 32 that tribal fortunes varied and that some tribes, for example Simeon, were absorbed into other tribes. It is usually held that these adjustments must have taken place before the monarchy; but this assumes that we know more about Israelite tribes than we actually do. If tribal adjustments involved shifts in inner loyalties that posed no threat to the state and its administration, then adjustments could have taken place during the monarchy, and may have been reflected in texts such as Genesis 49 and Deuteronomy 33.

In fact, the way in which anthropology is used in connection with Israel's origins will depend on the view that individual scholars take of the date and manner of composition of the Pentateuch and the Deuteronomic History. If the trend toward dating the "Yahwist" source to the postexilic period becomes anything like a consensus, this will have important consequences for the use of anthropology in determining Israel's origins. In short, anthropology can indicate what is likely and what is not likely in the structure and function of societies, but it cannot be a substitute for historical critical study of the OT text.

E. Emics and Etics in OT Study

A fundamental difference between Mendenhall and Gottwald concerns the place of Israel's religious ideology in the formation of the Israelite people. For Mendenhall, the revolt that brought Israel into being was inspired by the ideology of the God who had redeemed a group of slaves from Egypt and had made a covenant with them. For Gottwald, religious ideology was the *product* of economic and social circumstances, not the cause; therefore, Israel's religious ideology resulted from the formation of an egalitarian society in the period 1250–1050 B.C. In taking this view, Gottwald has put the issue of "emics" and "etics" on the agenda of OT study.

One of the main sources for this part of Gottwald's approach is the American anthropologist Marvin Harris, who has provided a persuasive presentation of what is known as cultural materialism (1979). Following Marx, Harris maintains that the mode of production in the material life of a society determines the general character of its social, political, and spiritual processes. If society is divided into infrastructure, structure, and superstructure (with the first term designating mode of production, population size, patterns of work, etc.; the second term designating kinship systems and political life, etc.; and the third term designating myths, symbols, magic, and religion), then changes in the infrastructure will affect the structure and superstructure, but not vice versa. (For example, if an animal is hunted to near extinction, it will be necessary for a society to hunt a different animal. This may entail changes in social organization and may also result in myths that explain why the near extinct animal is "taboo.") Harris' approach is etic, that is, he wishes anthropology to make quasi-scientific generalizations about societies that can be verified or falsified. Emic explanations, on the other hand, which Harris eschews, are explanations of societies in terms of what their members think about themselves. As such, emic explanations are not open to verification or falsification.

The difference between etic and emic explanations is well illustrated by Harris' disagreement with Mary Douglas about why pigs are unclean animals in the OT. Douglas' explanation is emic, that is, in terms of the world view of the OT itself. Pigs do not fit the classification system in which four-legged animals must chew the cud and part the hoof. Harris' explanation is etic, that is, in terms of a general theory of culture. According to him, the pig is prohibited because its natural habitat—forests and the edge of swamps—was not readily available in Israel and in other parts of the NE, whereas it was available, for example, in Europe (where there was no such prohibition). Harris therefore makes a good case for etic explanations and attacks the sort of British social anthropology described above (see B). While taking Harris' point, however, it is difficult to see how Israelite sacrifice could be explained in purely etic terms. There are parts of human life, such as uncertainty, illness, and death, that are essentially questions of human existence, and which demand answers that belong to the realm of religion and symbolism.

Gottwald identifies himself as a cultural materialist (1979: sec. 50–51) and at the end of his book he makes a plea for a biblical sociology. This would investigate the infrastructure of ancient Israel at every stage of its development, with a view toward establishing how changes in the infrastructure led to changes in social organization and religious belief. There is also a hermeneutical dimension to this. Biblical sociology would investigate the fortunes of what Gottwald holds to be the pristine manifestation of Yahwism, namely, the establishment of a liberated egalitarian society, which was eventually eclipsed when power was centralized under the monarchy. The OT approached in this way becomes a challenge to establish today a liberated egalitarian society appropriate to our world.

Etic studies are already beginning to become a feature of OT scholarship, especially with the investigation of Iron Age agriculture in Israel. In the matter of the formation of the Israelite state, it is recognized that environmental factors played a part which, compounded with the Philistine threat, brought about the need for a new type of social organization (see Frick 1985). Yet etic approaches must be combined with the fact, attested in the anthropological literature, that individuals such as Saul and David played a part in facing crises, and can substantially affect their outcome.

Serious anthropological study of the OT is only just beginning; but, compared with the situation twenty years ago, OT scholars now have available to them resources that should enable considerable progress to be made.

Bibliography

Davies, D. 1977. An Interpretation of Sacrifice in Leviticus. *ZAW* 89: 388–98.

Douglas, M. 1966. *Purity and Danger.* London.

———. 1975. *Implicit Meanings, Essays in Anthropology.* London.

Flanagan, J. 1981. Chiefs in Israel. *JSOT* 20: 47–73.

Frick, F. S. 1977. *The City in Ancient Israel.* SBLDS. Missoula.

———. 1985. *The Formation of the State in Ancient Israel.* Sheffield.

Geus, C. H. J. de. 1976. *The Tribes of Israel. An Investigation into Some of the Presuppositions of Martin Noth's Amphictyony Hypothesis.* Assen.

Gottwald, N. K. 1979. *The Tribes of Yahweh. A Sociology of the Religion of Liberated Israel 1250–1050 BCE.* Maryknoll, NY.

Harris, M. 1976. History and Significance of the Emic/Etic Distinction. *Annual Review of Anthropology* 5: 329–50.

———. 1979. *Cultural Materialism. The Struggle for a Science of Culture.* New York.

Lang, B. 1980. *Wie wird man Prophet in Israel? Aufsätze zum Alten Testament.* Düsseldorf.

Lang, B., ed. 1985. *Anthropological Approaches to the Old Testament.* London.

Leach, E. R. 1969. *Genesis as Myth and Other Essays.* London.

———. 1976. *Culture and Communication.* Cambridge.

Lemche, N. P. 1985. *Early Israel. Anthropological and Historical Studies on the Israelite Society before the Monarchy.* VTSup 37. Leiden.

Long, B. O. 1981. Social Dimensions of Prophetic Conflict. *Semeia* 21: 31–53.

Mendenhall, G. E. 1962. The Hebrew Conquest of Palestine. *BA* 25: 66–87.

———. 1973. *The Tenth Generation.* Baltimore.

Petersen, D. L. 1981. *The Roles of Israel's Prophets.* JSOTSup 17. Sheffield.

Rogerson, J. W. 1978. *Anthropology and the Old Testament.* Oxford.

———. 1977. The Old Testament View of Nature: Some Preliminary Questions. *OTS* 20.

———. 1980. Sacrifice in the Old Testament. Pp. 45–59 in *Sacrifice,* ed. M. F. C. Bourdillion and M. Fortes. London.

———. 1986. Was Israel a Segmentary Society? *JSOT* 36: 17–26.

Wilson, R. R. 1980. *Prophecy and Society in Ancient Israel.* Philadelphia.

J. W. ROGERSON

ANTHROPOMORPHISM. See YAHWIST ("J") SOURCE.

ANTILEBANON (PLACE) [Gk *Antilibanos*]. Geographical region NE of Galilee situated between Lebanon and Damascus, the major feature of which is a range of mountains running SW to NE (Jdt 1:7). The region of Antilebanon is separated from Lebanon by the Al-Biqa^{c} Valley (known as Coele-Syria in antiquity), the N extension of the Rift Valley. Mt. Hermon (2750 m), known as Sirion to the Sidonians and Senir to the Amorites (Deut 3:9), dominates the S part of the Antilebanon region and the range of mountains which also has this designation.

The Antilebanon region receives mention in the biblical tradition only in Jdt 1:7 within a list of regional names which includes Cilicia, Lebanon, and Damascus. The Vulgate translation, which generally is shorter than the Greek text, omits any reference to it. In the story of Judith the "Assyrian" king, Nebuchadnezzar, seeks assistance from the W part of his empire in a war against King Arphaxad. Antilebanon, part of Nebuchadnezzar's empire, refuses along with many other W regions to send him assistance. Because of this challenge to his authority Nebuchadnezzar initiates a military campaign to enforce his rule, and this sets the scene for the story of Judith's heroic feat.

Although Antilebanon is not mentioned by name in the OT, presumably reference is made to this region or portions of it under other names such as Lebanon and Mt. Hermon.

L. J. PERKINS

ANTI-MARCIONITE (GOSPEL) PROLOGUES. Short prefixes to the gospels of Mark, Luke, and John (if one existed for Matthew, it has been lost) which at one time were widely believed to have an anti-Marcion bias. The anti-Marcionite Prologues were found together for the first time in the 8th century Latin ms T (Toletanus) and later in the mss FNS. They were designated "anti-Marcionite Prologues" by Donatien de Bruyne (1928), who argued that these prefixes formed a single literary unit, were anti-Marcion in sentiment, and were written in the last half of the 2d century (ca. 160–180). He also claimed that Irenaeus, ca. 180 C.E., was acquainted with them and that the *Monarchian Prologues,* ca. 4th century, depended on their Latin translations. It is generally agreed, as De Bruyne claimed, that all of these prologues were originally written in Greek even though the only surviving Greek ms is of the Lukan prologue (*Athens 91* or =*A*). The Mark and John prologues are only found in Latin.

Although many leading scholars after De Bruyne (e.g., Julicher, Lietzmann, and especially Harnack) agreed with his conclusions, more recently scholars have moved away from those views, contending that, with the exception of the prologue to John, the prologues are neither anti-Marcion in sentiment nor is there a common literary thread which links them together. Further, some scholars argue that they may have originated sometime after the mid-4th century and perhaps followed the *Monarchian Prologues,* though others continue to believe that the Markan and Lukan prologues stem from a time before Irenaeus. The evidence is inconclusive. What is more certain is that the Lukan prologue circulated at first independently of other prologues as is obvious from its inclusion of other writings (the Apocalypse and the gospel of John), its manifestly different style, and its considerably longer length than the prologues to Mark and John.

The prologue to John continues to be the most disputed of the prologues because of its claims that John the apostle dictated his gospel to Papias and that he (John) both opposed and condemned Marcion. Most scholars today agree that this prologue is both anachronistic and historically false. It appears that its author based some of his comments on a faulty reading of Tertullian's *Adv. Marc.* 4.5,3. The current lack of confidence in the prologue to John, however, does not carry over to those of Mark and Luke, whose importance for critical studies should be examined separately.

The prologues support the widespread traditions of the Church regarding the authorship of the canonical gospels and they also suggest the importance of these gospels in the life and worship of the Christian churches at least by the end of the 4th century. Their value for canonical questions is, however, limited because of the difficulty of dating them with precision.

Bibliography

Bruce, F. F. 1988. *The Canon of Scripture.* Downers Grove, IL.

Bruyne, D. de. 1928. Les Plus Anciens Prologues latin des évangiles. *RB* 40: 193–214.

Grant, R. M. 1941. The Oldest Gospel Prologues. *ATR* 23: 231–45.

Gutwenger, E. 1946. The Anti-Marcionite Prologues. *TS* 7: 393–409.

Haenchen, E. 1971. *The Acts of the Apostles.* Philadelphia.

Harnack, A., von. 1928. Die ältesten Evangelien-Prologe und die Bildung des Neuen Testaments. SBAW 24: 322–41.

Heard, R. G. 1955. The Old Gospel Prologues. *JTS* 6: 1–16.

Howard, W. F. 1935/36. The Anti-Marcionite Prologues to the Gospels. *ExpTim* 47: 534–38.

Quasten, J. 1953. *Patrology.* Vol. 2. Utrecht.

Regul, J. 1969. *Die Antimarcion. Evangelienprologe.* Freiburg.

LEE MARTIN MCDONALD

ANTINOMIANISM. The conviction that believers are freed from the demands of God's law by depending upon God's grace for their salvation (thus *anti* "against" + *nomos* "law"). Although the word "antinomian" is not found in Scripture, Scripture's own history tells of the struggle to maintain balance between law and grace—between an appreciation of God's merciful and unconditional response toward God's people on the one hand, and their obliged and obedient response to God's law on the other. Believers, who emphasize the unconditional promises that God makes when covenanting with His people, but then downplay what God expects of His people, tend toward an antinomistic faith; the opposite emphasis leads to legalistic faith.

The OT does not speak of an antinomistic threat to Israel's covenant with God. It does, however, speak of two different covenant traditions, sometimes placing them in tension (Hillers 1969; Brueggemann 1979): the Davidic tradition which emphasizes God's unconditional commitment to Israel, and the Mosaic which emphasizes Israel's obligations to its God. When Israel understood itself primarily in Davidic terms, as God's prophets were inclined to point out, it was inclined to depreciate God's Torah both as gospel and as demand.

Earliest Christianity's antinomistic struggles are clearly envisioned by the NT (Wall 1987). Paul battled legalistic religion by emphasizing the importance of what God does through Christ to fulfill the promise of salvation. According to Paul's "theo-logic," moral righteousness is the *anticipated* outcome of God's justification of those who depend upon Christ's death and resurrection rather than works in keeping with the Law (Torah). Such faith places the redeemed community "in Christ"—a place where God's spirit can now lead God's people to ethical fruit (Gal 5:16–25), and where the "righteousness of God" has now released them from the obligation to obey Torah as a condition of covenant blessings (Rom 7:1–8:17; cf. 2 Cor 5:21). This moral calculus, which clearly subordinates ethical concerns to theological convictions, led some of his converts to lawlessness (1 Corinthians) and his opponents to accuse him of a disregard for ethical conduct (Rom 3:1–8).

In response, Paul clarified that God's grace brings liberty from sin and not liberty to sin (Rom 6:1–11). However, the antinomian trajectory, first sounded within some gnostic communions of the 1st and 2d centuries (e.g., Valentinians) with continuing echoes in some charismatic communions today, finds most of its biblical warrants from Paul (and to a lesser extent from John, who always refers to *nomos* in a pejorative way). Thus, one must look to the non-Pauline corpus for Scripture's own built-in corrective. The writer of Hebrews reminds the reader that salvation itself is jeopardized if the demand of the gospel is forsaken (5:11–6:8). James speaks of the eschatological banishment (2:12–13) of the "worthless religion" (1:26) which confesses right faith but fails to obey God's law of mercy (2:14–26); eschatological Israel is justified by works, not by *sola fide* (2:24). 2 Peter condemns a Pauline group for promising moral freedom (2:19) when virtue is what saves (1:5–11). Finally, 1 John was no doubt written against gnosticizing Christian teachers who claimed to have a sinless nature (1:10) and so lived without sin (1:8). According to 1 John, to act upon their moral claims would yield a life of "lawlessness"—an indifference to Christ's death (2:1–2) and to sin, and thus to God's law of love (3:4–15).

While the synoptic evangelists depict Jesus as a Torah-observant Jew (Moo 1984), Luke's emphasis is on the risen Jesus, who viewed the Law primarily as God's *promise,* not His demand (Wilson 1983)—an antinomistic disposition. Matthew's emphasis, on the other hand, is on a scribal Jesus who viewed obedience to his rigorist interpretation of Torah as necessary for salvation (5:17–20). Further, the evangelist's use of the word group *anomia/anomos* polemicizes against antinomians in his own church (Barth 1963).

Thus, these self-correcting, canonical "conversations" call the Church from the margins of the gospel to its center, where both God's grace and God's demand are found.

Bibliography

Barth, G. 1963. Matthew's Understanding of the Law. Pp. 58–164 in *Tradition and Interpretation in Matthew.* Philadelphia.

Brueggemann, W. 1979. Trajectories in OT Literature and the Sociology of Ancient Israel. *JBL* 98: 161–85.

Hillers, D. 1969. *Covenant: The History of a Biblical Idea.* Baltimore.

Moo, D. 1984. Jesus and the Authority of the Mosaic Law. *JSNT* 20: 3–49.

Wall, R. 1987. Law and Gospel, Church and Canon. *WTJ* 22: 38–70.
Wilson, S. 1983. *Luke and the Law.* Cambridge.

ROBERT W. WALL

ANTIOCH (PLACE) [Gk *Antiocheia*]. A number of cities built by various Seleucid kings bore the name "Antioch." The two that had the most important impact on the peoples of the Bible were the Antioch in Pisidia (south central Turkey) and the Antioch on the Orontes River in Turkey near the modern border with Syria.

ANTIOCH OF PISIDIA

Pisidian Antioch was a city in south central Turkey founded in the 3d century B.C. by one of the Seleucid kings, probably Antiochus I or Antiochus II, and initially occupied by settlers from Magnesia on the Maeander in Ionia. The city has been identified with ruins just east of the modern town of Yalvaç (38°17′N; 31°11′E). Around the middle of the 2d century B.C. a fine Ionic temple was built at the extramural sanctuary of Mên Askaênos, an Anatolian deity and the most important god of the city (Mitchell and Waelkens fc., chaps. 2–3). Little else is known of Antioch's history in the Hellenistic period, but it became prominent in 25 B.C. when the Roman emperor Augustus annexed the central Anatolian province of Galatia, to which it belonged, and refounded the city as a Roman colony populated by veterans from the Roman legions V and VII (Levick 1967: 29–41). It swiftly became an important and successful commmunity. Between 15 B.C. and A.D. 35 three members of the imperial household—Drusus, brother of the future emperor Tiberius; C. Domitius Ahenobarbus, the father of the emperor Nero; and L. Cornelius Sulla Felix, son-in-law of Germanicus—as well as two Augustan generals, P. Sulpicius Quirinius and M. Servilius, held honorary magistracies in the colony. At the same time the city center was adorned with a magnificent series of buildings connected with the imperial cult: a Roman-style podium temple set in front of a semicircular portico at the head of a large colonnaded square, a colonnaded street named after the emperor Tiberius, a triple arched gateway, which was completed in A.D. 50, and a staircase linking the street with the imperial sanctuary (Robinson 1926; Mitchell and Waelkens fc., chap. 4). Also during this period members of Antioch's leading families began to hold important positions in the Roman military and administrative hierarchy, and the elite of the colony were among the first easterners to enter the Senate at Rome (Levick 1967: 103–20; Halfmann 1979). The colony continued to prosper through the 2d and 3d centuries and under Diocletian became the metropolis of the newly constituted province of Pisidia. An early 4th-century governor, Valerius Diogenes, was responsible for an important building program and was also active in the persecution of Christians (*MAMA* 1 no. 170; Calder 1920), but by the end of the century Antioch had an orthodox bishop in correspondence with St. Basil, and had witnessed the construction of several major churches (Mitchell and Waelkens fc., chap. 2 and appendix 1; Kitzinger 1974).

The time of Antioch's greatest prosperity came during the 1st century after its refoundation by Augustus, and it is against this background that the most famous episode in its Christian history, St. Paul's mission, should be viewed. Paul visited Antioch three times (Acts 13:13–52; 16:1–6; 18:23—on the last two occasions Antioch is not named but a visit may be presumed). On his first missionary journey Antioch was his first stopping point in Asia Minor, and the first place where he proselytized among both gentiles and Jews (Acts 13:42–49). This visit, perhaps in A.D. 47, occurred precisely as the great building program for the city center was nearing completion. The choice of Antioch reveals much about the character and strategy of Paul's mission. He had come from Perga in Pamphylia, on Turkey's south coast, where he had not stopped to preach, and before that from Paphos on Cyprus, where he had won over, at least temporarily, his most distinguished convert, the governor Sergius Paulus (Acts 13:5–12). We now know that Sergius Paullus (as his name should be written) himself came from Pisidian Antioch: members of his family received honors there and intermarried with another prominent local family, the Caristanii. They also acquired large estates in central Anatolia (Halfmann 1979; Mitchell, *ANRW* 2/72: 1073–4; Mitchell 1981). It is overwhelmingly likely that Paul, who had almost certainly adopted the Latin name in place of the Hebrew Saul in recognition of the meeting with Sergius Paullus (Dessau 1910), was directed to Antioch by his recent convert. There were other reasons why Antioch should have been an attractive destination. The clear purpose of Paul's journeys was to visit major cities in the eastern parts of the Roman Empire: colonies such as Alexandria Troas, Philippi, and Corinth; or leading provincial cities like Thessalonica, Beroea, Athens, and Ephesus. The ultimate goal, demonstrated not only by events but by the early Epistle to the Romans, was Rome itself. Although in the event most of Paul's known converts came from lower-class backgrounds (Meeks 1982), he clearly had ambitions to win over the leaders of society in the cities. Pisidian Antioch was a natural target for his activities. It not only contained a large population of Roman citizens, but was even divided, following Roman practice, into wards (*vici*) which were named after prominent landmarks or institutions of the city of Rome itself (Levick 1967: 76–78). The splendid buildings associated with the imperial cult were on a scale that could hardly be paralleled in the Greek part of the empire and emphatically underlined these associations. Antioch would have appeared to Paul as a model of the capital itself.

Paul's first addresses in Antioch and nearby Iconium were in the synagogues, which may have had their origins in the Hellenistic period when the Seleucid Antiochus III is known to have settled Babylonian Jews in Phrygia (Josephus *Ant* 12 § 147). He reminded them of the tradition to which they belonged and identified Jesus as the savior descended from David whose coming had been prophesied to the Jews. The address contains one of Paul's most explicit descriptions of the crucifixion and resurrection as proof of the fulfillment of those prophecies. According to Acts, the mission attracted so much attention that on the Sabbath following the first address almost the whole city, Jew and gentile alike, turned out to hear Paul, causing the leaders of the Jewish community to turn against him. They looked for support from leading persons in the city and from highborn women who were "god-fearers" (*sebomenai*). This expression distinguishes the group from the *Ioudaioi,* Jews in the full sense, and it is illuminated by other passages in Acts which separate Jewish sympathizers from Jews, and by inscriptions from Asia Minor which make clear that these divisions were characteristic of most of the communities of the Diaspora (Millar and Vermes 1986: 150–77). Since the leading women of Antioch were certainly members of the Roman colonial families settled by Augustus, it is clear that, as in contemporary Rome, Judaism was winning converts among the aristocracy of the period.

Some twenty years after Paul's visit to Antioch, the Phrygian city of Acmonia, which also had a prominent Roman community, had a synagogue built with funds provided by a highborn woman of Galatian descent, Iulia Severa. She had close associations with the locally established Roman family of the Turronii, one of whom was the leading member of the synagogue, another a high priest of the Roman imperial cult (*MAMA* 6 nos. 264–65). This cultural milieu is strikingly similar to that implied by the account in Acts of Paul's experience in Antioch.

In the longer term the mission failed. Apart from the information that can be extracted from the apocryphal 2d-century *Acts of Paul and Thecla,* relating the martyrdom of one of Paul's notable converts, there is virtually no trace of Christianity in Pisidian Antioch before the peace of the Church in the 4th century A.D.

Bibliography

Calder, W. M. 1920. Two Episcopal Epitaphs from Laodicea Combusta. *JRS* 10: 42–59.

Dessau, H. 1910. Der Name des Apostels Paulus. *Hermes* 44: 347–68.

Halfmann, H. 1979. *Die Senatoren aus dem östlichen Teil des Imperium Romanum bis zum Ende des 2. Jh. n. Chr.* Göttingen.

Kitzinger, E. 1974. A Fourth Century Mosaic Floor in Pisidian Antioch. Pp. 385–95 in *Mélanges Mansel.* Ankara.

Levick, B. M. 1967. *Roman Colonies in Southern Asia Minor.* Oxford.

Meeks, W. A. 1982. *The First Urban Christians.* New Haven.

Millar, F., and Vermes, G. eds. 1986. *The History of the Jewish People in the Age of Jesus Christ.* Vol. 3/1. Edinburgh.

Mitchell, S. 1981. Review of Halfmann 1979. *JRS 71:* 191–93.

Mitchell, S., and Waelkens, M. fc. *Pisidian Antioch. The Site and Its Monuments.*

Robinson, D. M. 1926. Roman Sculptures from Colonia Caesarea (Pisidian Antioch). *Art Bulletin* 9.1: 5–69.

STEPHEN MITCHELL

ANTIOCH OF SYRIA

Antioch of Syria was built on the Orontes River (36°14′N; 36°07′E; now in modern Turkey) about 300 B.C.E. by Seleucus I. It continued to grow in size and influence during the Hellenistic period. Legends and some archaeological remains suggest that pioneering Greeks had settled in the area before the city was founded. Its lush river valley and the plain to the north—which included a lake—normally provided ample supplies of grain, olives, grapes, and fish. From springs to the south in Daphne, the favored summer home of the wealthy, fresh water reached the city via two aqueducts. Antioch flourished, despite its vulnerable military position between the mountains north of it and the broad valley around it. Seleucia Pieria, its port, lay less than a day's walk from Antioch. The two cities were connected by the Orontes, which usually carried cargo from the port to the metropolis. A break in the Lebanese mountains fostered trade with the East. Chinese porcelain was discovered in the excavations and a silk industry still exists in the village of Samandaği, not far from the site of Seleucia. Antioch also became an important military center after it was incorporated into the Roman Empire in 64 B.C.E. and served as a staging area for wars between Rome and its eastern adversaries.

When Seleucia Ctesiphon was destroyed in 165 C.E., Syrian Antioch ranked as the third largest city of the Roman world next to Rome and Alexandria. Ancient and modern estimates of its size vary. Ancient sources range from 600,000 (Pliny *HN* 6.122 for Seleucia Ctesiphon's population) to 200,000 (Chrysostom *Pan. Ign.* 4). Modern historians suggest about 100,000 in the 1st century C.E., but if the metropolitan region as well as slaves are included, the number well may exceed this conservative estimate.

The site is still breathtaking. On a clear day one can see from Mt. Casius southwest of Antioch all the way to Cyprus. Temperatures are moderate and rainfall is usually sufficient. But frequent earthquakes and the shifting trade routes led to rapid decline after the Arab invasions. Modern Antakya is a bustling small city that occupies much of the ancient site. Ruins of the walls, the hippodrome, a large structure that might be the foundation of Diocletian's palace, masonry works to control flooding, and portions of the aqueducts can still be seen. The most important artifacts, however, are the magnificent mosaics found during the 1932–39 excavations (Princeton University and the Sorbonne). Most of them are displayed in the Antakya museum (others at Princeton and the Louvre). They form perhaps the best single collection in the world.

Seleucus I built Antioch on the SE side of the Orontes, setting up the streets in a normal grid pattern, except for the main one. This thoroughfare, complete with temples and shops, baths and beggars, ran NNE from the S gate to a central point within the city and then NE to the E gate. It was finished in the Roman period when Herod the Great paved it with marble, and Tiberius later built the colonnades. Thus, in the 1st century C.E. Antioch was a beautiful, important center of commerce, culture, and political power.

A. Judaism

No specific piece of literature about Jews in Antioch was written in the city or addressed to the Jewish community there. But a number of sources important for the history of the city, including not only the Talmud and Josephus, but also the *Chronographia* of Malalas, contain information about Antiochene Jewry.

The earliest settlers of Seleucus' city—aside from the native Syrians and perhaps Greek pioneers—were his own soldiers, which included Cretans, Cypriots, and Jews. Josephus claims that the Jews were granted rites as a *politeuma,* a "political state," by Seleucus, but corroborating evidence for such early status is lacking (*AgAp* 2 §39, *Ant* 12 § 119, *JW* 7 § 43). The situation of the Jewish community in Antioch during the reign of Antiochus Epiphanes (175–163 B.C.E.) was apparently quite difficult. Epiphanes' successors returned brass votive offerings, previously sent by Antiochene Jews to Jerusalem and confiscated there, but large-scale repression of Jews at Antioch is unknown. 2 Macc 4:33–38 speaks of a former Jewish high priest, Onias II, who lived in greater Antioch, most likely at Daphne. He came to the metropolis after Jason had assumed the high priesthood. When Antiochus Epiphanes marched away from Antioch, he left a man named Andronicus in charge. Onias discovered that a certain Menelaus had stolen vessels of gold from the Jerusalem temple and sold them. Overwhelmed with anger, Onias made the deed public but, fearing for his life, he fled to a place of refuge in Daphne, possibly the temple of Apollo. Antiochus' deputy Andronicus agreed to give him protection but then killed him when he left the sanctuary. Andronicus' reason was simple: he had in his possession some of the golden pieces Menelaus stole.

Even though its size warranted respect, the Jewish community often did not fare well with the general populace of Antioch. A rebellion under Demetrius II (145–139 B.C.E.) was put down not only by the ruler's Cypriot mercenaries, but also by troops he requested from Jonathan of Israel. Thus Jewish soldiers were among those who ravaged the city and killed a number of its Jewish citizens. Alexander Jannaeus of Israel later refused to recruit Syrian troops for his army, perhaps because of their hatred for Jews (Josephus *Ant* 13 §137; 1 Macc 11:45–47).

After the coming of the Romans, Jews at Antioch showed their continued importance, a power that both exalted their position and made them objects of envy. Between 30 and 20 B.C.E. Herod the Great used his enormous wealth to demonstrate his allegiance to Rome by paving the main street of Antioch with marble (Josephus *JW* 1 §425; *Ant* 16 §148). In 9–6 B.C.E. a Jewish emir, a "military commander," from Babylon named Zamaris was allowed to take up residence in greater Antioch. Because he brought 100 relatives and 500 mounted bowmen, he was settled north of the walled city in the plain. That decision implies that some Jews were already living there, perhaps as farmers (Josephus *Ant* 17 §23–27).

When Caligula decided to have a statue of himself as Zeus made and set up within the Jerusalem temple, he ordered the governor of Syria, Petronius, to carry out his will. The statue was constructed at Sidon. Either there or at Ptolemais Jews offered their first protests. But a strange account of an Antiochene circus riot between Blues and Greens during the governorship of Petronius (39–41 C.E.), may be related to Caligula's plan. Petronius supported the Greens and so did the Jews. The Blues were angered by the games, became violent, eventually burned at least one synagogue, and killed a number of Jews. Perhaps the Jewish community wanted to influence Petronius quietly through the available city institutions by supporting his party. Whatever their intention, they became the target of the riot (Malalas 244.15–245.1).

In the sixties, Antiochus, the son of a Jewish leader, rushed into a crowded theater and shouted that the Jews were plotting to burn the city. He led the angered crowd in making various Jews sacrifice to pagan gods or die, and was given command of troops who forced his people to break the Sabbath by working as they did on other days. A few years later, when fire broke out in the business and administrative center of the city and Antiochus repeated his charges, only the intervention of C. Pompeius Collega, the governor of Syria, prevented a pogrom (Josephus *JW* 7 §46–62).

The Roman general and future emperor Titus received much political attention with his triumphal entry into Antioch after the fall of Jerusalem in 70 C.E. A mass of Antiochene citizens pleaded with him to destroy their Jewish community, but he refused to annihilate the Jews, to expel them, or to withdraw their rights as a *politeuma.* Yet to please the citizens he took some of the booty from Jerusalem, bronze cherubim from the temple, and placed them at the Daphne Gate. At a higher place on the gate itself he put up statuary that probably depicted Aeternitas and thus reminded everyone of Rome's victory in Jerusalem. Since most of Antioch's Jews lived in the southern quarter around the Daphne Gate, they were continually humiliated by these strong symbols of their defeat (Josephus *JW* 7 §96–111; *Ant* 12 §121–124; Malalas 281.4–5).

Both the influence and the financial position of Jews within the city waned even into the early part of the second century. When Rabbis Akiba, Eliezar, and Jehoshua came to collect support for Jewish scholars, the assembled funds were meager, nothing like the gold sent to Jerusalem in the earlier periods (*j. Hor.* 3, 48a). But by the end of the century, there is some evidence that the Jewish community was recovering. The Jew Asabinos was an owner of important property and a member of the city Senate (Malalas 290.14–20).

B. Christianity

No biblical literature explicitly claims that it was composed in Antioch; neither is any Scripture specifically addressed to Christianity in the city. Many NT scholars suppose that Matthew was written in Antioch. Meier, following Streeter (1924), has argued that Matthew originated in the city but, like Streeter, he offers only conjectural argument (Brown and Meier 1983). The claims rest on Streeter's contention that no gospel could have gained wide acceptance had it not come from a major center. Matthew was used by Syrian writers such as Ignatius of Antioch, but no point in the text of the gospel demands that it was written in Antioch. Kingsbury (1977) claims on the basis of internal evidence that Matthew must have come from a wealthy urban church, and thus from Antioch, the great Syrian center. History does not require that wealth, culture, and influence exist only in great urban centers. But, given those strictures, Antioch is the best candidate for the place where Matthew was composed.

Shepherd (1956) argued that the letter of James was written in Syria, but he did not claim it came from Antioch. Following patristic citations, Fitzmyer supports Antioch as the city in which Luke wrote his gospel (Fitzmyer *Luke 1–9* AB). No clear detail in the gospel or Acts demands that they were composed in Antioch. Harnack (1908) proposed a written Antiochene source for the book of Acts. Jeremias (1966) and Bultmann (1967) basically agreed, but

Dupont (1960) and Haenchen (1968) have disputed that suggestion.

The only firsthand report of events in Antiochene Christianity comes from Paul (Gal 2:11–14). The conflict between Peter and Paul focused on gentile and Jewish Christians eating together, perhaps celebrating agape feasts. They ignored either the strict laws about food or those concerning table fellowship, rules important to both conservative Judaism and conservative Jewish Christianity. According to Paul's account, Peter agreed to these meals and participated in them until men "sent by James" from Jerusalem challenged his position. Although Gal 2:11–14 provides the basis of this report, the entire letter forms Paul's defense of Christian freedom against the demands of Judaizers.

Peter's position deserves closer attention. Paul claims that "the rest of the Jews [i.e., Jewish Christians] and Barnabas" accepted Peter's decision. This acceptance evidently was based on the concern Jewish Christians had for their counterparts in Palestine. With Judaism still well established in that region, there would be difficulty recruiting new members were the initiates called upon to break the established customs. Peter's reversal may have been affected by his concern for evangelism in Palestine and unity in the whole Church.

If that description of the conflict between Peter and Paul is correct, then perhaps the following relationship between Galatians 1–2 and Acts 15 makes sense. The conference in Jerusalem debated the validity of gentile mission and probably occurred before Paul's confrontation with Peter. It decided that missions to Jews and to gentiles were appropriate. But the leaders did not foresee that areas of overwhelming gentile populations might lead to congregations including both Jewish and gentile Christians. In that atmosphere, all the food laws and the rules for table fellowship would come under pressure.

The relationship between Galatians and Acts 15 remains confused. The reported letter from the Jerusalem conference indicates that Jewish Christians compromised but did not sacrifice what was in their view necessary for Jewish mission and Christian unity. If Paul accepted such a decision, which is itself uncertain, he did not allow it to dictate his sense of growing gentile mission or his understanding of practice within Jewish-gentile congregations.

The background for this interpretation is provided by Acts 11:19–20. Haenchen (1968) and others find these comments to be editorial transitions of questionable historical value. But if a group of Jewish Christians fled the persecution in Jerusalem and preached in Antioch *only* to Jews, then an audience ready to hear Peter's position and that of James' representatives was in place. Paul was prepared to do almost anything consistent with the gospel to win followers to Christ (Philippians and Romans), but some Jewish Christians in Antioch originally were willing only to continue the tradition they knew. For them, Jesus was the Messiah of Jews. Yet others rejected such restrictions; they preached also to Greeks. The stage was set for conflicts not debated at the Jerusalem council.

Perhaps the early problems in Jerusalem concerning Jewish and Hellenistic widows had demanded discussions about the nature of the community in the midst of such cultural variations (Acts 6). Judaism had partially solved the problems by organizing itself into various synagogues; at least, we know that in Jerusalem there were synagogues of Cypriots and Hellenists. The earliest Christians, however, found such separations difficult. They apparently appointed functionaries to deal with the problems, one of whom, Nicolaus, had come from Antioch. But the details are slight, and the accounts questioned by many careful scholars.

Acts 11:26 indicates that the term "Christians" was first used in Antioch. No evidence suggests that it arose elsewhere. Tacitus, Suetonius, Pliny, and other non-Christians found some form of the word to be descriptive. Among the so-called Apostolic Fathers it occurs only in Ignatius' letters, and appears again in Theophilus' apology. The verb form in Acts 11:26 does not specify whether the Antiochene Christians gave themselves that name or it was given to them by outsiders. Malalas (252.8–13) reports that Evodius, the bishop who followed Peter, created the term, but his account primarily indicates that later Christians found it important to claim they chose the name for themselves. Bikerman (1949) has argued persuasively for the name being the Christians' choice, yet Downey (1961), who brilliantly connected the incident with the circus conflict during the reign of Caligula, saw the term as a Roman creation. If this word arose in a time when Jews were suffering a pogrom, the Christians' need to distinguish themselves from Jews and the authorities' need to identify them as non-Jews well may have coincided.

The reference to a large famine under Claudius (Acts 11:27–30) forms the context of yet another story about Antiochene Christianity. Some historians take the reference seriously as an attempt by Luke to tie his account to important events. Within the NT, the visit of Paul and Barnabas to Jerusalem with relief creates problems of chronology. Textual variants for Acts 12:25 demonstrate the difficulties early Christians had with this sequence. In various manuscripts Paul and Barnabas return "to Jerusalem," "from Jerusalem," or "to Antioch." Paul specifically claims in Gal 1:18 and 2:1 that he did not go to Jerusalem until 14 years after his conversion. That amount of time does not appear to elapse between Acts 11:29–30 and 14:25–15:35. Although it is plausible that Antiochene Christians aided Jerusalem Christians during a famine, the chronology is indecipherable.

In Acts 13:1 the mention of prophets and teachers as leaders suggests the earliest organizational pattern for the Christian community in Antioch. It is they who send Paul and Barnabas on a mission to the wider world. Those named are of interest. Symeon and Manaen bear Semitic names while Symeon's name *Niger* is ambiguous. Although it might refer to his skin coloring, in ancient literature it can also refer to temperament or some important event in the bearer's life.

Manaen, the *suntrophos* of Herod the Tetrarch, most probably was a man of position, who worked within the inner circle of Herod Antipas' court. The word *suntrophos* could mean only that he was the child of a wet nurse or a household servant, one who was a companion of the king during his youth. But it is unlikely that Luke would have emphasized that connection. Herod the Great had paved the central street of Antioch and doubtless had an embassy in the city to oversee the project. Perhaps his son also placed prominent people in the metropolis.

Lucius of Cyrene indicates another interesting relationship. The North African city of Cyrene had a large Jewish colony. Perhaps Lucius came directly from that city. He might have heard the gospel there or he might have become a Christian as a result of evangelization of a synagogue like that of the Cyrenes in Jerusalem or some other city. We cannot tell. At best we know that Lucius considered Cyrene to be his home and that he was a Christian leader in Antioch. His Latin praenomen, Lucius, perhaps like that of Paul, suggests important Roman connections.

Acts does not speak of the confrontation between Paul and Peter at Antioch. But if Barnabas remained convinced of Peter's position as Paul describes it in Gal 2:13, his disagreement with Paul about John Mark in Acts 15:36–41 may have involved another issue. Barnabas and John Mark might represent a team that intended to preach more to Jews than to gentiles, or at least a twosome that was willing to leave the decisions of the Jerusalem council intact, and thus avoid the problems Antiochene Christianity presented for Jerusalem Christians.

Such an explanation strengthens the interpretation that Antioch developed into a center of Jewish Christianity led by people who did not agree with Paul's position. Some have found Acts 18:22–23 to imply that Paul returned, argued his case once more, and was again rejected. Yet that well may be a misinterpretation. According to Acts 15:40, when Paul and Silas left Antioch on the so-called second missionary journey, the church at Antioch supported their mission.

In Gal 2:13 Paul did not say that gentile Christians in Antioch had disagreed with his views. Furthermore Paul praises Barnabas in 1 Cor 9:6. The event described in that passage occurred after the disagreement in Antioch. Perhaps Paul and Barnabas were eventually reconciled. At least no one should claim that Pauline Christianity definitely lost its place in Antioch during the apostle's lifetime.

Ignatius, who flourished in Trajan's reign, turned certain Pauline positions upside down; others he kept fundamentally intact. He argued for monepiscopacy and his own personal authority, but fought both docetic and Judaizing treatments of christology. During the last half of the 2d century, various gnostics taught in the metropolis. Menander, Saturninus, Cerdon, Tatian, and Axionicus have all been associated with Antioch (Just. *Apol.* 1.26; Iren. *Haer.* 1.22; Eus. *Hist. Eccl.* 4.10–5.2; Epiph. *Anac.* 46.1; Tert. *Adv. Valent.* 4.3).

The Jewish Christian character of Antiochene Christianity is apparent. About 180 C.E. Theophilus, the bishop of Antioch, wrote a Christian apology so marked by Hellenistic Jewish arguments that it might almost pass for Jewish literature. And Eusebius (*Hist. Eccl.* 3.22, 36) employed lists of bishops for the metropolis that begin with Peter and fail to mention Paul. Even the later history of Antiochene Christianity often indicates the strength of gentile appeal, rooted in an appreciation for and appropriation of Jewish tradition and hermeneutic.

The metropolis served as a crucible in which more than one understanding of Christianity took shape. There Christianity became a world religion. It supported a mission to gentiles, insisted upon close connections to Judaism, and formed a Jewish-gentile Christian community.

C. Other Religions

In the process of founding Antioch, Seleucus I apparently offered sacrifices to Zeus Kasios in Seleucia Pieria, to Zeus Keraunios in Iopolis, and to Zeus Battiaios on the site (Malalas 198.23–201.3). The importance of Zeus is indicated by the various names under which he was represented in the city: Epikarpios, Nemean, Nikephoros, Philios, Soter, as well as the Olympian Zeus (Lib. *Ep.* 11.51; Just. *Epit.* 39.2.5–6; Julian *Mis.* 346B–D; Malalas 275.10; 283.4–9 [Jeffreys et al. 1986]). Only the Tyche of Antioch has a similar significance in the fragmentary remains from the metropolis. Her statue was created early and dominated Antiochene life (Malalas 201.1–2; 276.6–9). Statuettes and coins depict her presence. Apollo was worshipped at Daphne in a marvelous temple that burned in the 4th century C.E. (Lib. *Ep.* 11.94–99; Sozom. *Hist. Eccl.* 5.19). A beautiful statue of Artemis graced the city from Hellenistic times (Lib. *Ep.* 11.59–65).

The metropolis had an Isis cult; lamps, statuary, inscriptions, and mosaics, as well as the ruins of a temple, evidence its presence. The Romans built temples to their pantheon and set up statues to honor their former rulers. By the time of Augustus, deified emperors were well represented in the city. In 7/6 B.C. he appears on coins issued in Antioch as the high priest of his own cult. About 117 C.E., Hadrian built a small but lovely shrine to the deified Trajan and constructed a temple to the nymphs that included a statue of himself represented as Zeus (*Suda* s.v. Iobianos).

Julian (*Mis.* 346B–D), Libanius (*Ep.* 11.16–27), Livy (41.20.9), and Malalas (29.15–16; 30.2–3; 235.6–7; 246.10–19; 263.11–17; 283.4–9; 302.6–9; 307.5–20) also speak of temples or shrines built to honor Aphrodite, Ares, Asclepius, Athena, Calliope, Demeter, Dionysus, Hecate, Herakles, Hermes, Io, Jupiter Capitolinus, Kronos, Minos, the Muses, and Nemesis as well as statuary honoring many other gods. Most of these worship centers were active during the Roman period.

The famous Antiochene Olympic games always involved Greek and Roman gods. A Syrian Maiuma festival was incorporated into the celebrations for Dionysus and Aphrodite (Malalas 284.21–285.11). Mosaics and the visit of Apollonius of Tyana indicate the influence of magic within the city in the 1st century C.E. (Philostr. *VA* 6.38). Euphrates of Tyre, a popular Stoic preacher, may also have been in the metropolis during that period (Pliny *Ep.* 1.10).

Many of these religions had declined by the 4th century C.E., as Libanius and Julian indicate, but they continued to be influential. In the 6th century two Antiochenes were prosecuted in Constantinople for pagan practices (Michael the Syrian 2:271). Thus Syrian Antioch was a center of many Greco-Roman religions well beyond the period of interest to biblical students.

Bibliography

Bikerman, E. 1949. The Name of Christians. *HTR* 42: 109–24.
Brown, R., and Meier, J. 1983. *Antioch and Rome.* New York.
Bultmann, R. 1967. *Exegetica.* Tübingen.
Downey, G. 1961. *A History of Antioch in Syria.* Princeton.

Dupont, J. 1960. *Les Sources du livre des Actes.* Paris.
Elderkin, G. W.; Stillwell, R.; Waagé, F.; Waagé, D.; and Lassus, J. 1934–72. *Antioch-on-the-Orontes.* Princeton.
Haenchen, E. 1968. *Die Apostelgeschichte.* Göttingen.
Hann, R. 1987. Antioch: Charisma and Conflict in the First Century. *JRH* 14: 341–60.
Harnack, A. 1908. *Die Apostelgeschichte.* Leipzig.
Jalabert, L., and Mouterde, R. 1950–53. *Inscriptions grecques et latines de la Syrie.* Paris.
Jeffreys, E.; Jeffreys, M.; Scott, R.; et al. 1986. *The Chronicle of John Malalas: A Translation.* Byzantina Australiensia 4. Melbourne.
Jeremias, J. 1966. *Abba.* Göttingen.
Kingsbury, J. 1977. *Matthew.* Proclamation Commentary. Philadelphia.
Kraeling, C. 1932. The Jewish Community at Antioch. *JBL* 51: 130–60.
Liebeschutz, J. 1972. *Antioch: City and Imperial Administration in the Later Roman Empire.* Oxford.
Meeks, W., and Wilken, R. 1978. *Jews and Christians in Antioch in the First Four Centuries of the Common Era.* Missoula, MT.
Shepherd, M. 1956. The Epistle of James and the Gospel of Matthew. *JBL* 75: 40–51.
Streeter, B. 1924. *The Four Gospels.* New York.
Wallace-Hadrill, D. 1982. *Christian Antioch: A Study of Early Christian Thought in the East.* Cambridge.

FREDERICK W. NORRIS

ANTIOCHIANS [Gk *Antiocheis*]. Hellenized Jews living in Jerusalem enrolled as privileged citizens of Antioch (2 Macc 4:9, 19; see 1 Macc 1:13–14). "Antiochians" is the rendering of 2 Macc 4:9, 19 in the NAB. The term is variously rendered in other versions: "citizens of Antioch" or "Antiochian citizens" (RSV, GNB), "Antiochenes" (NEB), and "Antiochists" (JB, NJB). When Jason bought the high priesthood from Antiochus IV, his deal included the Hellenization of Jewish citizens through institution of the gymnasium, citizenship training, and enrollment as Antiochian citizens.

These Hellenized Jews did not form a united party in Jerusalem. In 175 some supported Jason, an Oniad, while by 172 another group supported Menelaus, a Tobiad whom Antiochus appointed high priest in Jason's place for a bribe (2 Macc 4:23–50). In 169, Jason and his supporters tried to retake Jerusalem upon hearing the false rumor that Antiochus IV had died in Egypt. Jason took the city, forcing the supporters of Menelaus to flee to the citadel for their lives. However, Antiochus' return forced Jason to flee. This power play among the Antiochian Jews incited Antiochus' violence against Jerusalem and his despoiling of the temple treasury, with Menelaus' help (2 Macc 5:1–16). In 167, Antiochus built a fortress and a mercenary garrison in Jerusalem to protect the Antiochians (2 Macc 5:22–26; 1 Macc 1:29–33). The Antiochian citizens became irrelevant after the success of the Maccabean revolt.

Three theories try to explain the nature of the Antiochian citizenship. First, Antiochus gave privileges to cities of his empire by making them into "Antiochs" and their citizens into "Antiochians" (Bevan 1966; Tcherikover 1959). Second, the Antiochians were a group of Hellenized citizens who gathered around the gymnasium as a surrogate for a true polis until a polis could be established (Bickermann 1979). Third, Antiochus, formerly a hostage in Rome, tried to imitate Roman extension of citizenship to people in cities of his empire in order to insure their loyalty (Goldstein *Maccabees* AB).

Bibliography

Bevan, E. R. 1966. *House of Seleucus.* Vol. 2. New York.
Bickermann, E. 1979. *The God of the Maccabees.* Leiden.
Tcherikover, V. 1959. *Hellenistic Civilization and the Jews.* Philadelphia.

MITCHELL C. PACWA

ANTIOCHIS (PERSON) [Gk *Antiochis*]. Concubine of Antiochus Epiphanes IV (2 Macc 4:30). Antiochus IV's official queen was Laodice, who may have been his sister. According to oriental custom, Antiochus IV assigned the maintenance of Tarsus and Mallus, two Cilician towns, to Antiochis' care. The Seleucid kings ruled by right of conquest and had sovereign authority over their conquered domain to dispose of their lands as they wished. The revenues of the two cities were assigned to Antiochis for her maintenance, and she was probably given authority to intervene in official affairs of state, perhaps affronting the Cicilians' pride. The citizens of the two cities revolted in A.D. 170, demanding the immediate attention of Antiochus IV.

The coins of Tarsus indicate that Antiochus conferred the privileges of an Antiochene city upon Tarsus. An inscription from A.D. 166 indicates that Tarsus continued to enjoy the privileges of Antiochene citizenship after the revolt against Antiochis. Nothing is known of Antiochis or this rebellion apart from the reference in 2 Maccabees.

SCOTT T. CARROLL

ANTIOCHUS (PERSON). A Macedonian name (*"opposer"*) borne by the father of Seleucus I, founder of the Seleucid dynasty of Syria, hence favored by the following kings of the dynasty.

1. Antiochus I Soter (*"savior"*) (281–261 B.C.). Born 324 B.C., the son of Seleucus I and the Bactrian princess Apama, he was coregent before becoming king after his father was assassinated in 281 B.C. Having consolidated control over Syria, Antiochus renounced the Macedonian ambitions of Seleucus (a treaty made with Antigonus Gonatas, 278 B.C.) and concentrated upon expanding Seleucid power into Asia Minor. This brought him into conflict in 280/279 B.C. with Ptolemy II of Egypt, and later with the Gauls (Galatians), who had crossed the Hellespont in 278/277 B.C. after devastating Greece and Macedonia. The exact outcome of the First Syrian War (274–271 B.C.) with Ptolemy II is unclear, except that Coele-Syria continued under Egyptian control. It was Antiochus' victory over the Gauls in the so-called elephant battle of 275 (or 270) B.C. which gained him his title Soter, but he was defeated at Sardis in 262 B.C. by the Galatian mercenaries of Eumenes of Pergamum (paid for by Ptolemy). Like his father, Antiochus keenly promoted Hellenism through colonization, founding many cities particularly in Iran, and it was he who established the Seleucid ruler cult.

2. Antiochus II Theos (*"god"*) (261–246 B.C.). Coregent (from 268 B.C.) before succeeding his father, Antiochus I. His control of Asia Minor was soon challenged by Ptolemy II (Second Syrian War, 260–253[?] B.C.). Antiochus seems to have emerged the overall victor, but by offering a huge dowry Ptolemy prevailed upon him to make a dynastic marriage with his daughter Berenice. His repudiated wife, Laodice (Antiochus' half-sister), set up a rival court at Ephesus, which Antiochus had recently liberated (259/258 B.C.) from the tyrant Timarchus (it was this action which gained Antiochus his title Theos). Strife between the two queens was to culminate after Antiochus' death (246 B.C.) in the murder of Berenice and her son by Antiochus, and the Third Syrian (or Laodicean) War (246–241 B.C.) between Ptolemy III, Berenice's brother, and Seleucus II, Antiochus' son by Laodice. The events of his reign are alluded to in Dan 11:6–9.

3. Antiochus III the Great (223–187 B.C.). Born 241 B.C., the younger son of Seleucus II Callinicus, he succeeded his brother Seleucus III Soter in 223 B.C. In the Fourth Syrian War against Egypt (221–217 B.C., but interrupted in 220 B.C. by the revolt of Molon in Media) he reached Ptolemais in Phoenicia in winter 218/217 B.C. before being defeated by Ptolemy IV Philopator at Raphia in Gaza on 22 June 217 B.C. (Polybius 5.51–87). Ptolemy thus regained control of Coele-Syria and Antiochus turned his attention eastward against Parthia, Armenia, and Bactria; it was his conquests there (212–205 B.C.) which gained him the title of the Great. On the accession of the young Ptolemy V Epiphanes (204 B.C.), he formed a secret alliance with Philip of Macedon to conquer and partition Egypt (Livy 31.14), and the Fifth Syrian War (202–200[?] B.C.) saw him extend Seleucid domination to the Sinai. An invasion of his kingdom from Pergamum, engineered by the Romans, who were becoming alarmed by Antiochus' energy and ambition, allowed the Egyptian general Scopas to recover the lost ground temporarily but Antiochus finally defeated the Egyptians at the Battle of Panium (200 B.C.). He thus gained control of all of Palestine. Military governors and a system of tax farming were introduced throughout Judea but the high temple of Jerusalem was guaranteed inviolate and granted subsidies (Josephus, *Ant* 12.3.3–4 §§129–53). Under the peace settlement of 195 B.C., Antiochus gave Ptolemy his daughter Cleopatra I with the revenues of Coele-Syria and Palestine as dowry but kept control of those areas himself. He now turned toward Asia Minor, settling 2000 Jewish families from Mesopotamia in Lydia and Phrygia as part of his pacification effort. His invasion of Thrace (194 B.C.) finally wore out Roman patience and a lengthy war ensued, which ended in his defeat at Magnesia in 190 B.C. The treaty of Apamea (188 B.C.) compelled him to send twenty hostages, including his son Antiochus IV, to Rome and to yield any claim to Asia Minor W of the Taurus. Warlike to the last, Antiochus was killed in 187 B.C., plundering the temple of Baal in Susa. The major events of his reign are alluded to in Dan 11:10–19.

4. Antiochus IV Epiphanes (*"manifest" [as a god]*) (175–164 B.C.). Younger son of Antiochus III, he returned from Rome when his brother Seleucus IV Philopator sent his own son Demetrius as hostage in his stead, and usurped the throne after Seleucus was assassinated. His unpredictable character—at one time generous to a fault, at another fiercely tyrannical—is described by Polybius, who gave him the nickname Epimanes (*"utterly mad"*) (26.1a.1), and by Diodorus (29.32) and Livy (41.20). It was his instability, verging upon insanity, which was to lead to the excessively harsh treatment meted out to the Jews by this otherwise energetic and capable ruler.

Antiochus' ambition was to use the common culture of Hellenism to unify the diversity of the Seleucid empire. Accordingly, he was easily won over by promise of payment from Jason, leader of the pro-Greek faction in Jerusalem, to make him high priest in place of his brother Onias III, and willingly allowed him to Hellenize the city by establishing a gymnasium and an ephebic class and by inscribing its citizens as Antiochenes (i.e., Jason may have wished to reorganize Jerusalem as a Greek polis called Antioch, although the exact interpretation is disputed).

This state of affairs, described in 2 Macc 4:7–22, lasted from ca. 174 B.C. to ca. 171 B.C. until Menelaus, another pro-Hellenist whose conduct was to be even more offensive to the orthodox, supplanted Jason by offering Antiochus even more for the high priesthood. Jason, however, reasserted his claim, apparently believing Antiochus had died while on his second campaign against Egypt (170/169 B.C.). He seized Jerusalem and besieged Menelaus in the citadel (2 Macc 5:5). Antiochus construed this as rebellion and, returning with his army to Syria in late 169 B.C., he savagely attacked the city, butchering its inhabitants and looting the high temple (2 Macc 5:11–23; Josephus, *Ant* 12.5.3 §§246–47).

Worse followed. Invading Egypt again the next year, Antiochus was met outside Alexandria by a Roman delegation led by C. Popilius Laenas and given an ultimatum to desist at once from all hostilities against Egypt or her territories. With his stick Popilius drew a circle in the sand around Antiochus, who had asked for time for consultation, and insisted that he decide before stepping out of it (Polybius 29.27; a famous incident retold by many other sources). Antiochus had no choice but to withdraw his forces. According to Dan 11:30, it was outrage at this affront that decided Antiochus to enforce his Hellenization policy upon the Jews, even to the extent of completely exterminating them and their religion.

In 167 B.C., Apollonius, his chief tax collector, was dispatched with 22,000 men and attacked Jerusalem on the Sabbath. Most of the male population was killed and the women and children enslaved; those few who could left the city. The city walls were demolished and the old city of David refortified (the Akra) and furnished with a military garrison (1 Macc 1:29–36; 2 Macc 5:24–26). There followed the prohibition of all Jewish rites and the rededication of the high temple to Olympian Zeus. A monthly check was made, and anyone found with a copy of the Book of the Law or a child who had been circumcised was put to death (1 Macc 1:54–64; *Ant* 12.5.4–5 §§248–64). In December 167 B.C. (on 25 Kislev) the first pagan sacrifice was performed on the altar to Zeus which had been erected over the altar of burnt offering in the temple: this is *"the abomination of desolation"* alluded to in Dan 11:31 and 12:11 (cf. 1 Macc 1:54; Mark 13:14 in a Gk version).

Antiochus' decree, promoted vigorously throughout all his domains (2 Macc 6:8–9), was met at first only with passive resistance from the Jews, although of the most heroic kind (2 Macc 6:10–7:42; further elborated in *4 Maccabees*). Open defiance, however, soon followed, first at Modein, a village NW of Jerusalem, where the priest Mattathias refused to obey the local Syrian commissioner and sacrifice to the heathen gods. He killed the commissioner, overturned the altar, and fled with his sons to the hills (1 Macc 2:1–28; *Ant* 12.6.1–2 §§265–72). They were joined by others but many were massacred in a Syrian attack when they refused to defend themselves on a Sabbath (1 Macc 2:32–38; *Ant* 12.6.2 §§272–78). Mattathias persuaded the survivors that the right of self-defense had to take precedence and he was now joined by many of the Hasidim. His guerrilla bands traveled Judea, defying the prohibitions and harassing the Syrians (1 Macc 2:42–48).

When Mattathias died (166/165 B.C.), the leadership was taken over by one of his five sons, Judas Maccabeus, advised by his brother Simon. As the Jewish forces grew more confident, Judas continued his father's successes. These culminated in the rout of one Syrian force under Apollonius, whom Judas himself killed, and then another larger army under Seron, the local commander-in-chief (1 Macc 3:10–24; *Ant* 12.7.1 §§287–92).

News of the widespread revolt in Judea reached Antiochus when he was about to embark on a campaign in the E (165 B.C.). Lysias, left as vice-regent and guardian of Antiochus V, was ordered to depopulate the country. His generals Ptolemy, Nicanor, and Gorgias arrived in Judea with a large force, so confident that they had with them slave traders ready to purchase the Jewish prisoners (1 Macc 3:38–41; 2 Macc 8:8–11; *Ant* 12.7.3 §§298–99). That confidence, though, was misplaced. The Jewish forces under Judas, now organized into a regular army, evaded a large search party under Gorgias and fell upon the main force in camp at Emmaus, completely routing it. Finding their camp ablaze when they returned and the Jews ready to offer battle, Gorgias and his troops fled the country (1 Macc 4:1–25; 2 Macc 8:12–36; *Ant* 12.7.4 §§305–12).

The campaign was resumed (probably in fall or winter 165/164 B.C.) by Lysias himself with a larger army (1 Macc 4:28–35; *Ant* 12.7.5 §§313–15; although the historicity of this campaign is disputed). Judas met him near Beth-zur and once again won the day. The subsequent peace negotiations, which resulted in an amnesty for the Jews and an end to their active persecution, are probably reflected in the letters quoted in 2 Macc 11:16–21, 27–33, and 34–38.

Judas was now established in control of all Judea, except for the Akra (occupied by Syrian troops until their final expulsion by Simon in 142/141 B.C.), and could attend to purifying and restoring the temple. The new altar of burnt offering was dedicated in December 164, three years to the day (25 Kislev) after it had first been profaned (1 Macc 4:52–59; *Megillath Taanith* [ed. Lichtenstein] §23).

Antiochus meanwhile, after quelling the revolt of Artaxias of Armenia (165 B.C.), had invaded Elymais (Elam), where he was foiled in an attempt to sack the temple of Artemis (Aphrodite in some accounts). He withdrew to Tabae in Persia and died there in late 164 B.C. of consumption (according to Appian, *Syr.* 66), although several lurid accounts of his death through divine retribution are given by 1 Macc 6:1–17 (cf. *Ant* 12.9.1 §§354–59) and 2 Macc 1:13–17 and 9:1–29.

5. Antiochus V Eupator (*"born of a noble father"*) (164–162 B.C.), second son of Antiochus IV. Left under the guardianship of Epiphanes' foster brother Philip, he was only nine years old when he became king in 164 B.C. and was seized by the army commander Lysias, who made himself guardian and regent. After the Maccabean recovery of the high temple (December 164 B.C.; the letter in 2 Macc 11:22–26, purporting to be from Antiochus to Lysias, which guarantees Jewish religious rights, may come here rather than be part of the settlement of 162 B.C.), Judas laid siege to the Syrian garrison in the citadel (163/162 B.C.). Antiochus and Lysias responded by invading Judea and besieging Beth-zur (1 Macc 6:18–31). After defeating Judas' army at Beth-zachariah (1 Macc 6:32–46; misrepresented as a Jewish victory by 2 Macc 13:15–17), they took Beth-zur and put Mt. Zion under siege. But news that Philip was advancing on Antioch compelled them to lift the siege and grant lenient terms. The Jewish fortifications were destroyed and the Jews again made subject to Syria but they had kept their religious freedom intact. Antiochus and Lysias soon defeated Philip but shortly afterward they were betrayed to a new pretender, Demetrius I Soter (162–150 B.C.) and were murdered (1 Macc 7:1–4; 2 Macc 14:1–2; *Ant* 12.10.1 §§389–90).

6. Antiochus VI Epiphanes Dionysus (*"the manifest Dionysus"*) (145–142 B.C.), son of Alexander Balas and Cleopatra Thea. He was still a child when Alexander's general Diodotus Tryphon promoted him as a claimant to the Seleucid throne, then occupied by Demetrius II Nicator (145–140/139 B.C.). Jonathan, who had initially helped Demetrius quell a revolt in Antioch by sending 3000 armed men (1 Macc 11:38–53), took their side when Demetrius broke his promise to withdraw from the fortresses of Judea. After Antiochus was set up as king, Jonathan and Simon were made his generals (1 Macc 11:54–59) but their subsequent successes alarmed Tryphon. He captured Jonathan by trickery and eventually killed him in 143/142 B.C. (1 Macc 12:39–53; 13:23–4) before having Antiochus murdered (by corrupt surgeons, according to some sources) and assuming the throne himself (1 Macc 13:31–32; *Ant* 13.7.1 §§218–20).

7. Antiochus VII Sidetes (*"man of Side"*) (138–129 B.C.), so called because his youth was spent at Side in Pamphylia. Younger brother of Demetrius II Nicator, he successfully contested the throne after the latter's capture by the Parthians, defeating the usurper Tryphon (*Ant* 13.7.1–2 §§221–24; Strabo 14.5.2 §668). To ensure Jewish support, he granted Simon the right to mint coinage as well as confirming all earlier privileges (1 Macc 15:1–9), but after his success he reneged and demanded the surrender of Joppa, Gazara, and the citadel of Jerusalem and the arrears of their tribute (1 Macc 15:26–36). Refusal led to war and the rout of his general Cendebeus by Simon's sons (1 Macc 15:38–41; 16:1–10; *Ant* 13.7.3 §§225–27). Later Antiochus himself invaded Judea and besieged John Hyrcanus in Jerusalem (135/134 B.C.). After a lengthy siege the city was surrendered on terms and its walls demolished (*Ant* 13.8.2–3 §§236–48; the exact dates of the siege remain uncertain). Antiochus was killed in 129 B.C. while campaigning against the Parthians, leaving the way clear for Hyrcanus to continue the expansionist policies of Jonathan and Simon.

8. Antiochus VIII Grypus (*"hook-nosed"*) (125–96 B.C.). Born 141 B.C., the second son of Demetrius II Nicator and Cleopatra Thea. He reigned jointly with her from 125 to 121 B.C. In 114/113 B.C. he was deposed by his half-brother Antiochus IX Cyzicenus but returned in 111 B.C. and regained most of Syria, Cyzicenus retaining only Coele-Syria (Porphyry, Eusebius *Chron.* I. col. 260). The continuing conflict between them meant that Judea under John Hyrcanus was once more completely independent of Syria (*Ant* 13.10.1 §§273–74).

9. Antiochus X Eusebes (*"pious"*) (95–83 B.C.). Son of Antiochus IX Cyzicenus, he spent most of his reign in dynastic struggles with the five sons of Antiochus Grypus (Seleucus VI, deposed in 95 B.C.; Antiochus XI Philadelphus, defeated and killed after a brief time in power [94 B.C.]; Philip I Philadelphus [94–83 B.C.]; Demetrius III Philopator [95–88, B.C.]; and Antiochus XII Dionysus [87–84 B.C.], killed in battle against the Nabateans). These years, described in detail by Josephus (*Ant* 13.13.4 §§365–71; 14.3–15.1 §§384–91), represent the death throes of the Seleucid dynasty. In 83 B.C., Tigranes, king of Armenia, seized Syria and ruled it for fourteen years via a viceroy until his own defeat by the Romans (69 B.C.).

10. Antiochus XIII Asiaticus (69–64 B.C.), son of Antiochus X Eusebes. Set up as a client king by Lucullus after the defeat of Tigranes, Antiochus was challenged and deposed by Philip II, grandson of Antiochus Grypus, in 65/64 B.C. The Seleucids' rule over Syria was finally ended by Pompey in 64 B.C. and Syria was made a Roman province (63 B.C.).

11. Unrelated to the Seleucid dynasty is Antiochus, father of the Numenius who was one of the envoys sent by Jonathan Maccabeus in 144/143 B.C. to negotiate friendly relations with Sparta and to renew the treaty made by Judas Maccabeus with the Romans (1 Macc 12:16; 14:22; *Ant* 13.5.8 §§163–70).

Bibliography

Bevan, E. R. 1902. *The House of Seleucus.* 2 vols. London.
Bickermann, E. 1937. *Der Gott der Makkabäer.* Berlin.
Bouché-Leclerq, A. 1913–14. *Histoire des Séleucides (232–64 avant J.-C.).* 2 vols. Paris.
Mørkholm, O. 1966. *Antiochus IV of Syria.* Classica et Mediavalia Diss. 8. Copenhagen.
Russell, D. S. 1967. *The Jews from Alexander to Herod.* Oxford.
Schmitt, H. H. 1964. *Untersuchungen zur Geschichte Antiochus des Grossen und seiner Zeit.* Historia Einzelschriften 6. Wiesbaden.
Tcherikover, V. 1959. *Hellenistic Civilization and the Jews.* Philadelphia.

JOHN WHITEHORNE

ANTIPAS (PERSON) [Gk *Antipas*].

An abbreviated form of the name *Antipatros* (Antipater).

1. A martyr of the Church in Pergamum, described as Christ's faithful witness (Rev 2:13); the same description is given to Christ himself (Rev 1:5). Legend among later hagiographers (e.g., Simon Metaphrastes and the Bollandists) has it that Antipas was slowly roasted to death in a brass bull during the reign of Domitian (Mounce, *Revelation* NICNT, 97).

2. Father of Antipater (see no. 3, below). According to Josephus, King Alexander and his wife made Antipas "general of all Idumea" (*Ant* 14.1.3).

3. Father of Herod the Great, also known as Antipater. Josephus described him as an Idumean who was procurator of Judea (*Ant* 14.1.3). See HEROD THE GREAT.

4. Son of Herod the Great and Malthrace who was appointed tetrarch of Galilee and Peraea (Hoehner 1980; *HJP*[2] 1: 340–53). In the NT he is always referred to as Herod and is mentioned in the gospels as the king who had John the Baptist arrested and executed (Matt 14:3–12 = Mark 6:17–29; *Ant* 18.5.2) and subsequently interrogated Jesus during his trial in Jerusalem (Luke 23:6–12). See also HEROD ANTIPAS; HERODIAS.

Bibliography

Hoehner, H. W. 1980. *Herod Antipas. A Contemporary of Jesus Christ.* Grand Rapids.

FRANK E. WHEELER

ANTIPATER (PERSON) [Gk *Antipatros*].

Son of Jason (1 Macc 12:16; 14:22). He is mentioned twice as an envoy sent by Jonathan with Numenius, son of Antiochus, to Rome and Sparta. Their purpose was to seek the renewal of friendship and alliance with Rome and Sparta (1 Macc 12:1–23). The successful completion of their mission to Sparta is recorded in a letter from Sparta (1 Macc 14:20–23) which mentions the honorable reception of the envoys. If, as scholars suggest, 1 Macc 15:15–24 is dislocated in the present text and should be relocated after 14:24, then the Roman response would be seen in the letter from the consul Lucius. In this case Antipater would still be in the company of Numenius (1 Macc 15:15), who would have been directed back to Rome after Jonathan's death on behalf of Simon (Goldstein *1 Maccabees* AB, 492–500). Antipater was chosen as envoy because of his father Jason, son of Eleazar, who undertook a similar mission under Judas Maccabeus (1 Macc 8:17–32).

RUSSELL D. NELSON

ANTIPATRIS (PLACE) [Gk *antipatris*].

The city to which Paul was taken on his way from Jerusalem to Caesarea (Acts 23:31). Also, at Matt 13:54 Codex Sinaiticus originally had Jesus "coming to Antipatris," but the *anti-* was subsequently crossed out so that it read (correctly) "home country" (Gk *patris*). Antipatris has been identified with Tell Ras el-ʿAin (M.R. 143168) on the source of the Yarkon River 26 miles S of Caesarea. One of the five biblical towns named "Aphek/Aphekah" occupied this site in pre-Hellenistic times. See APHEK, no. 4. Extensive archaeological excavations (see bibliography) and the abundance of written documents mentioning this city make it possible to reconstruct the long history of the site.

A. Bronze Age

The earliest occupation at Ras el-ʿAin dates to the Chalcolithic period (4th millennium B.C.), but the first walled city was erected there only in the EB Age (ca. 3200 B.C.). The site was therefore one of the earliest walled cities in Palestine, comprising more than 30 acres at the time. Fine earthenware bowls produced in this EB city were appreciated by many of the inhabitants of the cities in the central hill country and Negeb. This town was probably the central city of the Sharon plain during most of the 3d millennium B.C.

After the collapse of the EB civilization the site was deserted for a time (2300–2000 B.C.), but a new town was built there at the advent of the MB Age (2000–1550 B.C.). The archaeological finds and the historical sources demonstrate that during the MB Age this city—Aphek—was once again the most prominent city of the Sharon plain. In the Egyptian Execration Texts of the 19th–18th centuries B.C. it was listed as the town of "Apiqum," ruled by "Yanakilu," a prince with an Amorite name. Its importance at that time is probably reflected in the appelation "Aphek of the Sharon" in the LXX (Josh 12:18). Six archaeological stages have been distinguished at MB Aphek: (1) resettlement of the site; (2) building of the city walls and of Palace I; (3) building of Palace II and restoration of the city walls; (4) Palace II abandoned; (5) building of Palace III; and (6) restoration of Palace III. There was violent destruction of the site by the mid-16th century B.C.

Under the Egyptian empire (LB Age), the city of Aphek was reduced to a strategic stronghold on the Via Maris. It appears among the cities on the coastal road in Thutmose III's topographical lists and as a town in the S Sharon in the annals of Amenhotep II (*ANET,* 246). Palaces IV and V (of the 15th–14th centuries B.C.) were built on the acropolis on a smaller scale but with the same orientation as the MB palaces. Palace VI of the 13th century, however, was just a small fortified residency built for the Egyptian governor who now ruled Aphek in place of a local prince. This reverse in government probably occurred when Rameses II took measures to strengthen his military bases in Canaan before marching into battle against the Hittite forces in Syria. Two similar lime-coated winepresses were found near this Palace VI residency, containing Canaanite wine jars of the same type as those from the residency's storerooms. Egyptian pottery bowls and other Egyptian artifacts were found in the debris, fallen from the residency's upper story.

The Palace VI residency appears to have been attacked, conquered, and put to fire during the last third of the 13th century. Egyptian artifacts and various inscriptions were found in the debris of its upper floor; however, two cuneiform tablets warrant special mention. One is a trilingual lexicon (the first and only of its kind) that has, in addition to Akkadian and Sumerian, Canaanite written in its third column. The other is a letter sent from the governor of Ugarit to the Egyptian high commissioner of Canaan. Written in Akkadian, it deals with the transactions of wheat between Canaan and Ugarit, taking place in the harbor cities of Jaffa and Acco. The letter has been dated to ca. 1230 B.C. on prosopographic grounds (see Owen et al. 1987), and this must have also been the date of the final destruction of Canaanite Aphek. In the OT, Aphek is mentioned for the first time in the roster of Canaanite cities conquered by Joshua (Josh 12:18).

B. Iron Age

Aphek was resettled during the 12th century B.C. by a people of unknown origin. The architecture of their houses is paralleled only at Tell Abu Huwam in Haifa Bay. Fishing was essential in their subsistence economy. Typical Philistine artifacts, including several female deity figurines ("Ashdodah"), attest to the presence of the Philistines at Aphek during the 11th century B.C. A clay tablet from this level, bearing an undeciphered inscription, may be a clue to the yet unknown Philistine script. This Aphek is mentioned several times in the Bible as a Philistine base. It was there that the Philistines had gathered their armies before the Battle of Ebenezer (1 Sam 4:1) and from there David was sent back to Ziklag when the Philistines summoned their armies before the Battle of Gilboa (1 Samuel 29). ʾIzbet Sartah, an early Israelite settlement located 2 miles E of Aphek, has been suggested as the possible site of Ebenezer.

Israelite Aphek was rebuilt during the period of the united monarchy, but was devastated by an enemy around 900 B.C. and never totally recovered. Because of its strategic location the site was mentioned in several documents of the time. The OT states that Hazael took from the hands of Jehoahaz king of Israel the seacoast as far as Aphek (2 Kgs 13:22b). Esarhaddon, king of Assyria, mentioned "Apiqu, which is on the border of Samaria," as a station on his march toward Egypt. In an Aramaic letter of about 600 B.C., written to the pharaoh probably by the king of Ekron, Aphek is mentioned as the place at which the marauding Babylonians were last intercepted.

C. Hellenistic and Roman

The town prospered again in the Hellenistic period under the name of Pegai, and it was renamed "Antipatris" by Herod the Great, in honor of his father Antipater (*Ant* 16.5.2; *JW* 1.21.9). Its importance during the Roman period was mainly as a crossroad town, halfway between Jerusalem and Caesarea. Paul stayed there overnight on his two-day journey from Jerusalem to Caesarea (Acts 23:31). The town was destroyed by Vespasian during the Jewish War (*JW* 4.8.1), was rebuilt again on a larger scale, and was totally decimated by the earthquake of A.D. 363, never to be restored.

Archaeological rescue excavations were carried out at Ras al-ʿAin (or Tel Aphek) by the Palestine Department of Antiquities and by the Israel Department of Antiquities. Major excavations were carried out at the site by Tel Aviv University Institute of Archaeology from 1972 to 1985.

Bibliography

Albright, W. F. 1923. The Site of Aphek in the Sharon. *JPOS* 3: 50–53.

Eitan, A. 1967. A Sarcophagus and an Ornamental Arch from the Mausoleum at Rosh Haʿayin. *EI* 8: 114–18 (in Hebrew).

———. 1969. Excavations at the Foot of Tel Rosh Haʿayin. *ʿAtiqot* 5: 49–68 (in Hebrew).

Iliffe, J. H. 1936. Pottery from Ras el-ʿAin. *QDAP* 5: 113–26.

Kochavi, M. 1981. The History and Archaeology of Aphek-Antipatris, a Biblical City in the Sharon Plain. *BA* 44: 75–86.

———. 1989. *Aphek-Antipatris. Excavating Five Thousand Years of History.* Tel Aviv (in Hebrew).

Kochavi, M., and Beck, P. 1976. *Aphek-Antipatris 1972–1973: Preliminary Report.* Tel Aviv.

Kochavi, M., et al. 1978. *Aphek-Antipatris 1974–1977: The Inscriptions.* Tel Aviv.

———. 1979. Aphek-Antipatris, Tel Poleg, Tel Zeror and Tel

Borga. Four Fortified Sites of the Middle Bronze Age IIA in the Sharon Plain. *ZDPV* 95: 121–65.
Ory, J. 1936. Excavations at Ras el ʿAin. *QDAP* 5: 111–12.
———. 1937. Excavations at Ras el ʿAin II. *QDAP* 6: 99–120.
Owen, D. I., et al. 1987. *Aphek-Antipatris 1978–1985: The Letter from Ugarit. Philological, Historical and Archaeological Considerations.* Tel Aviv.

MOSHE KOCHAVI

ANTIPHRASIS. Saying the opposite of what is meant, as for example when Job's wife urges Job to "bless" (*brk;* i.e., curse) God and die (Job 2:9). See BIBLE, EUPHEMISM AND DYSPHEMISM IN THE.

ANTONIA, TOWER OF (PLACE) [Gk *to anastēma tēs Antonias*; Lat *turris Antonia*]. Primary military fortification of Jerusalem adjoining Herod's temple under both Herodian and Roman rule and called the Antonian Fortress (*JW* 5.5.8 §240).

Specific reference to the fortress does not occur in the NT, but rather in the pages of historians, particularly Josephus. The latter describes the structure in meticulous detail, providing information that it was located where the N and W angles of the temple conjoined, built upon a rock 50 cubits high and from there rising an additional 40 cubits. At each corner of its rectangular walls the fortress was surmounted by turrets that reached the height of 50 cubits in all but its SE corner. There, in a commanding position, a great turret of 70 cubits overlooked the temple and its courtyards. Inside, the fortress was furnished as lavishly as a palace with baths, courtyards, and quarters for a large number of troops (*JW* 5.5.8 §§238–45). Clearly the fortress was strategically located to accomplish Herod's purpose of dominating the temple through a garrison which could readily allay any disturbance that might arise in the temple precincts (*JW* 1.21.1 §401).

The fortress was not actually a new construction by Herod, but rather a major renovation and expansion of an existing fortification known as the Baris [Heb *bira* fortress]. According to Josephus (*Ant* 15.11.4 §403), this structure dated from the time of Hyrcanus I (135–105 B.C.) and occupied the site of an even earlier fortification, the Tower of the Hundred in Nehemiah's wall (Neh. 3:1). The Baris was much used and "formed a safe and convenient residence for the Hasmonean princes at the times when they were obliged to perform high priestly duties in the temple" (Paton 1977: 131). The exact ground on which the Antonian tower was constructed has yet to be determined. The fortress itself was destroyed during Titus' siege of Jerusalem in 70 A.D. when it was invested and later razed by the V and XII Roman legions (*JW* 5.11.4 §467; 6.2.1 §93). The site of the tower, along with the whole temple area, comprised the location of one of two fora in Hadrian's Aelia Capitolina, built over the ruins of Jerusalem a century after its destruction. Foundation stones often attributed to Herod's fortress complex seem rather to belong to Hadrian's forum, and archaeological efforts to locate the fortress precisely remain inconclusive (Benoit 1976: 87–89; Benoit 1952: 545–50; Peters 1985: 76).

Herod named his fortress in honor of his friend, the Roman triumvir Marcus Antonius (Tac. *Hist.* 5.11; *JW* 1.21.1 §401; *Ant* 15.11.4 §409). It was to Mark Antony that Herod owed his rule over Judea. When the Hasmonean Antigonus, with the aid of Parthian intervention, wrested back control from Herod's father, the Roman procurator Antipater, Herod fled to Rome and, with Antony's support and a compliment of 11 legions under the command of Antony's lieutenant Sosius, reasserted his authority in Judea. At Antony's urging, the Roman Senate created Herod king of Judea (Tac. *Hist.* 5.9; App. *BCiv.* 5.75; Dio Cass. 49.22; *JW* 1.14.3 §280–18.3 §357; *Ant* 14.14.3 §377–16.4 §491; Huzar 1978: 160–66). The strategic position of the Antonian fortress on a height commanding both city and temple did not escape the notice of the Romans, who after Herod also garrisoned the tower (Tac. *Hist.* 5.11–12; Peters 1985: 75–76). Whether the tower served as the *praetorium,* or administrative headquarters of the Roman procurator, is questionable. Herod's palace was more likely used in this capacity and as residence of the governor (Benoit 1952: 531–45).

Bibliography

Benoit, P. 1952. Pretoire, Lithostroton et Gabbatha. *RB* 59: 531–50.
———. 1976. The Archaeological Reconstruction of the Antonia Fortress. Pp. 87–89 in *Jerusalem Revealed,* ed. Y. Yadin. New Haven.
Huzar, E. G. 1978. *Mark Antony.* Minneapolis.
Paton, L. B. 1908. *Jerusalem in Bible Times.* Repr. 1977. New York.
Peters, F. E. 1985. *Jerusalem.* Princeton.

JOHN F. HALL

ANTONY, MARK. See MARK ANTONY.

ANUB (PERSON) [Heb *ʿānûb*]. A son of Koz recorded in a preexilic list from the genealogy of Judah (1 Chr 4:8). The name has been identified with ANAB in Josh 11:21 and 15:50. Grammatically, Anub is a passive participle ostensibly from the root *ʿnb,* the nominal form of which means "grape." The meaning of the name itself is not clear and has been variously defined as "bound, tied" or "modest."

JAMES M. KENNEDY

APAME (PERSON) [Gk *Apamē*]. A concubine of Darius I (521–486 B.C.) who wielded much power over her king, according to 1 Esdr 4:29–32. The apocryphal author informs us that it was not one of Darius' wives, i.e., Atossa, Artystone, Parmys, and the daughter of Otanes, but Apame, daughter of Bartacus the Illustrious (or Thaumastos Bartacus), who "dominated" the king. Apame's historical significance is preserved solely through an illustration of women's power given at "The Banquet of Darius" (1 Esdr 3:1–4:63). Darius probably captured Apame during his conquest of the Greeks (Herodotus 3–6).

Concubines were commonplace at the Persian court. Darius' father, Artaxerxes, had 360 concubines, seeing one per day. Persian soldiers had permission to take concubines on military excursions. However, Apame's actions—teasing and mocking the king—are inconsistent with the contemporary mores and gender roles. Even the queens survived under the mercy of the king (Esth 1:15–20; and the role of Darius' queen Atossa in Aeschylus' *Pers.*). The context of the Apame story obviously stands in stark contrast to the biblical account (Ezra 1–8). Three major differences between the accounts are (1) the king under whom Zerubbabel returned—Cyrus (Ezra 2:2) or Darius (1 Esdr 4:13); (2) the nature of Zerubbabel's authority—God of Israel and King Cyrus (Ezra 4:3) or King Darius (1 Esdr 4:47–58); and (3) Zerubbabel's reason for involvement—heritage and the law of Moses (Ezra 3:2) or cleverness and application of the Apame story (1 Esdr 3:1–4:63).

Numerous cognates of Apame and references to Persian concubines are known: wives of Seleucus I Nicator, Magas, and Prusias were all named Apama. And at least six ancient sites were named Apamea.

JERRY A. PATTENGALE

APELLES (PERSON) [Gk *Apellēs*]. A Roman Christian who received greetings from Paul in Rom 16:10. Paul called him "approved in Christ." Within the literary sources and in more than 37,000 Roman inscriptions, Apelles' name occurs only twenty-seven times (Lampe *StadtrChr,* 138–42, 149, 153). Since the name was not common there, it probably indicates that Apelles had immigrated to Rome from the east of the Roman Empire.

Sinaiticus and some minuscules read *apellēs* instead of *apollōs* in Acts 18:24 and 19:1. These writers probably identified the Christian Alexandrian scholar of Acts 18:24–28 with the Roman Christian of Rom 16:10, and suggested that the latter was "approved" because "through grace he greatly helped [the Christians in Greece] . . . showing by the scriptures that the Christ was Jesus" (Acts 18:27–28). Indeed, in the 2d century C.E. a (gnostic-Marcionite) scholar named Apelles had studied in Alexandria and afterward taught in Rome (see Lampe *StadtrChr,* 350–51). With this in mind and by confusing the 1st and 2d centuries, Sinaiticus may have merged the two NT persons. All other important manuscripts correctly read *apollōs* in Acts 18–19 (cf. also 19:1 with 1 Cor 1:12; 3:4–15).

PETER LAMPE

APHAIREMA (PLACE) [Gk *Aphairema*]. Samarian district that became part of Judea during the early Hasmonean era (1 Macc 11:34). The unprincipled Demetrius II Nicator ("the conqueror"; 145–141 B.C.) promised Aphairema ("separation") to Judea's high priest/governor in exchange for loyalty (1 Macc 11:34). The Seleucid king also promised the Samaritan districts of Lydda (Lod) and Ramathaim (Arimathea). But Judea did not realize the actual confirmation of these transfers until the reign of Antiochus VI—who was still preoccupied with the Seleucid-Ptolemaic power struggle. Aphairema consisted of the SE region of Samaria, which was predominantly mountainous (Ezra 2:33; Neh. 7:37). Later, as the NE region of Judea, Herod the Great (d. 4 B.C.) renamed Aphairema as the Thamniticam toparchy, after its new capital Thamna—W of the town Ahairema. During Rome's municipal territory system, the town Ahairema (*et Taiyibe,* Eusebius' Ephraim, *On.* 24.3) was in the Aelia Capitolina territory and just S of the Neapolis boundary. The Romans most likely routed the Jerusalem–Gophna road through Aphairema during the Bar Kokhba revolt (Avi-Yonah 1976: 185).

Bibliography

Avi-Yonah, M. 1976. *The Holy Land.* Grand Rapids, MI.

JERRY A. PATTENGALE

APHEK (PLACE) [Heb *ʾăpēq; ʾăpēqâ; ʾăpîq*]. Var. APHIK; APHEKAH. The place name Aphek appears eight times in the MT as *ʾăpēq* or *ʾăpēqâ* (Josh 12:18; 13:4; 19:30; 1 Sam 4:1; 29:1; 1 Kgs 20:26, 30; 2 Kgs 13:17). A ninth reference to *ʾăpēqâ* (Josh 15:53) is translated "Aphekah" in the RSV (see APHEKAH; and no. 5 below). The form *ʾapîq* (RSV "Aphik") occurs in Judg 1:31. The Lucianic version of the LXX provides a final scriptural reference to Aphek in a verse appearing after 2 Kgs 13:22 (see no. 4 below).

To the earliest scholars it was already clear that these referred to several places. Eusebius, for example, already distinguished four places of this name (Klosterman 1904: 22, line 21; 26, line 15; 30, line 16; 34, line 11). However, the exact number and their geographical locations remain a matter of controversy. The name also appears in other ancient written sources. Some of these references—such as those appearing in the topographical list of Thutmose III, in the description of the military campaign of Amenhotep II, and the reference to "the tower of Aphek" by Josephus (*JW* 11.19.1)—can each be related to one of the biblical Apheks (see no. 4 below). Other references, such as that in the Execration Texts (Posener 1940: 69, E9), lack additional geographical information and are therefore difficult to relate to one specific Aphek.

Albright's (1922) suggestion that there were five biblical Apheks is accepted here. Albright also suggested, however, that the name Aphek is connected with the Assyrian *apēqu*—"be strong, firm, solid"—and means a fortress. Other scholars relate the name to the Hebrew *ʾapîq*—valley bed/river torrent (Alt 1925: 52–53, 53 n.1). Since some of the sites proposed for these various Apheks are situated alongside rivers or near springs of water, the latter explanation seems preferable.

1. Aphek of Asher. A town in the tribal territory of Asher listed in the group of cities at the end of the description of the territory of Asher (Josh 19:29–30) and again (as Aphik) in the list of cities that the tribe of Asher did not inherit (Judg 1:31). These two lists were almost certainly derived from a common source. Some have identified this Aphek with Tel Kurdana (M.R. 160250) at the sources of the Na'aman River 9 km SE of Acco (Alt 1928: 58–59; Mazar 1939), and consequently the kibbutz founded nearby has been named Aphek. Alternatively, others (Saarisalo 1929: 32, no. 1) have associated it with Tel Kabri (M.R. 164268), a large site of 32 hectares, 4 km E of Nahariya. There are four large springs in its vicinity, the richest in the center of the site. The name Tel Kabri is a modern one, the site encompassing the ruins of the villages et-Tell, en-Nahr, and the N area, Dhahrat et-Tell. The site is presently being excavated (Kempinski and Miron 1987; Kempinski 1987; 1988). The cities not inherited by Asher were more probably in the northerly parts of the coastal plain, and therefore the identification with Tel Kabri is preferable. Both Tel Kurdana and Tel Kabri contain considerable MB remains, allowing for the identification of the Aphek of the Execration Texts at either site.

2. Aphek of Aram. A town in or near the territory of Aram (Syria) from which Ben-hadad, king of Damascus, departed for battle against Ahab, and to which he retreated after being defeated (1 Kgs 20:26–30). The reference to the God of Israel being a God of the mountains (1 Kgs 20:23, 28) implies that the battle took place in the plain. Elisha's prophecy (2 Kgs 13:17) presumably refers to the same Aphek. Thus, Aphek is to be sought in Aramean territory but near or in the plain and on the route to Israel.

Eusebius (Klosterman 1904: 22, lines 19–22) refers to "a large village called Apheka of the town Hippos" in the Golan area; however, there he located the Aphek (Heb *ʾăpēqâ*) of Josh 13:4 (see no. 3 below), not the one mentioned in 1–2 Kings. The Apheka of Eusebius is to be identified with modern Fiq (M.R. 216242), 4 km E of Qalat al Hisn (Hippos-Suseita). Early finds have not been reported from this site, and Aharoni (*LBHG,* 304, n.60) suggested placing the biblical Aphek instead at Kh. el'Asheq (ʿEin Gev) on the shore of Lake Kinnereth (M.R. 210243). Recently, however, D. Ben Ami has discovered a tell by the name of Tel Soreq (M.R. 215242) in the valley to the NW of Fiq and suggested that it is the biblical Aphek. In excavations carried out at this site Iron Age fortifications of the 8th and 9th centuries have been uncovered, as have finds from the EB IV, MB II, and LB II periods (Beck and Kochavi 1987–88). The site is very small, however, so that identification with Aphek remains in doubt.

3. Aphek in Lebanon. A town defining a portion of the border of "the land that yet remains (to be possessed)," mentioned alongside references to Sidonian and Amorite territories (Josh 13:4). Eusebius, who understood "the borders of the Amorites" to refer to Transjordan (Exodus 21; Numbers 21, 32, etc.), located this Aphek in the Golan (Klosterman 1904: 22, lines 19–22). However, although the text is corrupt and attempts at complete restoration remain conjectural, vv 4–6 almost certainly demarcate a region the N border of which is the border of the land of Canaan (Num 34:7–9), while its S border constitutes the N limit of the tribal territories as described in Joshua (Aharoni *LBHG,* 215–17; Naʾaman 1986: 39–73). Noth (1938: 48–49) understood Aphek to mark the S border of "the land that remains" and suggested that it was probably the Aphek of Asher (see no. 1 above) or even that in Sharon (see no. 4 below). The other portions of the description are from S to N, however, and the identification of Aphek with Afqa (M.R. 231382) on the sources of Nahr Ibrahim in Lebanon NE of Beirut seems likely (Dussaud 1927:14). This reinforces the identification of Lebo Hamat ("the entrance to Hamath," Num 34:8) with Lebwe to the E of Afqa (Elliger 1936: 44), thus placing Aphek on the N border of Canaan.

4. Aphek in Sharon. A town in the Sharon plain area whose king was listed as being defeated by the Israelites at the time of Joshua (Josh 12:18). The text is problematic, however. The MT reads, "the king of Aphek, one; the king of Lasharon, one," while the LXX seems to presuppose "the king of Aphek of Sharon, one." Its relative proximity to Philistine territory is confirmed by 1 Sam 4:1 and 29:1, as well as by the Lucianic version of the LXX, in which the note that "Hazael took from [Jehoahaz'] hands all Philistia from the Western Sea to Aphek" appears after 2 Kgs 13:22 (=4 Kgdms 13:22). This Aphek on the coastal plain is referred to in a number of other ancient sources, most notably Thutmose III's topographical list (No. 66) (Simons 1937: 117), Amenhotep II's second Asiatic campaign (Edel 1953; *ANET,* 246), Esarhaddon's campaign to Egypt (*ANET,* 292), an Aramaic papyrus mentioning the king of Babylon at Aphek (Porten 1981: 36), and the tower of Aphek in or near Antipatris (*JW* 2.19.1).

Early scholars did not identify a town by the name Aphek in the Sharon; without exception they followed Eusebius in placing the Aphek of 1 Sam 29:1 in the Jezreel Valley (Klosterman 1904: 30, line 16). The current identification of this Aphek with the tell of Ras el-ʿAin (M.R. 143168) at the sources of the Yarkon River was the result of the work of a series of scholars over a period of several decades. Wellhausen (1889: 254) was the first to show that the Philistines mustered their forces at Aphek *before* going up to Jezreel, demonstrating that the events took place in the following order: (1) 1 Sam 28:1–2; (2) 1 Samuel 29; and (3) 1 Sam 28:3–25. He also suggested that at the Battle of Ebenezer (1 Sam 4:1) the Philistines mustered their forces at this same Aphek, and that the later battles against Aram (see no. 2 above) were fought at the same Aphek somewhere in the N Sharon. Smith (1895), however, was the first to utilize Egyptian documents to show that Aphek was in the S Sharon. Guthe (1911) showed that Josephus' reference to the tower of Aphek connected Aphek to Antipatris, which was already known to be on Tel Ras el-ʿAin. Alt was the first to suggest that Aphek was actually on the tell, but it was Albright (1923a; 1923b) who published his views first, Alt only publishing his later (Alt 1925: 50–53). See also ANTIPATRIS.

5. Aphekah in Judah. One of the nine towns listed in the sixth district of Judah, the capital of which is presumed to have been Hebron; the RSV renders the name as APHEKAH (Josh 15:33). Alt (1932: 16–17) identified this town with Kh. el Hadab (M.R. 155098) 7 km SW of Hebron, while Abel (*GP,* 2: 247) identified it with Kh. Kan'an (M.R. 157102) 3 km SW of Hebron. Kochavi's recent survey, however, confirms the identification of this Aphekah with Kh. el Hadab, a site 4.5 acres in size with remains of fortifications and large quantities of Iron Age sherds. Below the site are two large springs, ʿEin el Dibleh and ʿEin Fawar (Kochavi 1972: Site 176, 22, 29, 62, 68).

Bibliography

Albright, W. F. 1922. Notes and Comments. One Aphek or Four? *JPOS* 2: 184–89.

———. 1923a. The Site of Aphek in Sharon. *JPOS* 3: 50–53.

———. 1923b. Some Archaeological and Topographical Results of a Trip through Palestine. *BASOR* 2: 3–14.

Alt, D. A. 1925. Das Institut im Jahre 1924. *PJ* 21: 5–58.

———. 1928. Das Institut im Jahre 1927. *PJ* 24: 1–73.

———. 1932. Das Institut im Jahre 1931. *PJ* 28: 5–46.

Beck, P., and Kochavi, M. 1987–88. The Land of Geshur. *Excavations and Surveys in Israel* 6: 75–78.

Dussaud, R. 1927. *Topogaphie historique de la Syrie Antique et Médiévale.* Paris.

Edel, E. 1953. Die Stelen Amenophis II aus Karnak und Memphis mit dem Bericht über der Asiatischen Feldzuge des Konigs. *ZDPV* 69: 97–176.

Elliger, K. 1936. Die Nordgrenze des Reiches Davids. *PJ* 32: 34–73.

Guthe, H. 1911. Beitrage zur Ortskunde Palästinas: Aphek Apheka. *Mitteilungen und Nachrichten des Deutschen Palästina-vereins* 17: 33–44.

Kempinski, A. 1987. *Excavations at Kabri Preliminary Report of 1986 Season.* Tel Aviv.

———. 1988. *Excavations at Kabri Preliminary Report of 1987 Season.* Tel Aviv.

Kempinski, A., and Miron, E. 1987. Kabri 1986–1987. *IEJ* 37: 176–77.

Klosterman, E. 1904. *Eusebius: Das Onomastikon der biblischen Ortsnamen.* Leipzig (Repr. 1966).

Kochavi, M. 1972. *Judaea, Samaria and the Golan Archaeological Survey 1967–1968.* Jerusalem (in Hebrew).

Mazar, B. 1939. Aphek in the Territory of Asher. *Bulletin of the Jewish Palestine Exploration Society* 6: 151–56 (in Hebrew).

Naʾaman, N. 1986. *Borders and Districts in Biblical Historiography.* Jerusalem.

Noth, M. 1938. *Das Buch Josua.* Tübingen.

Porten, B. 1981. The Identity of King Adon. *BA* 44: 36–52.

Posener, G. 1940. *Princes et pays d'Asie et de Nubie.* Bruxelles.

Saarisalo, A. 1927. *The Boundary between Issachar and Naphtali.* Helsinki.

———. 1929. Topographical researches in Galilee. *JPOS* 9: 27–40.

Simons, J. J. 1937. *Handbook for the Study of Egyptian Topographical Lists Relating to Western Asia.* Leiden.

Smith, G. A. 1895. On Aphek in Sharon. *Palestine Exploration Fund Quarterly Statement* 28: 252–53.

Wellhausen, J. 1889. *Composition des Hexateuchs und de historischen Bucher des Alten Testaments.* Berlin.

RAFAEL FRANKEL

APHEKAH (PLACE) [Heb *ʾăpēqâ*]. A town situated in the central hill country of Judah (Josh 15:53), within the same district as Hebron. The only OT reference to this settlement, whose name perhaps means "enclosure" or "fortress" (from the root *ʾpq,* "hold," "be strong"), occurs in the list of towns within the tribal allotment of Judah (Josh 15:21–62). The theory that this list is derived from an administrative roster compiled under the Judean monarchy (Alt 1925) has been widely accepted, although controversy continues over the precise makeup of the districts, the proper context of the town lists of Benjamin and Dan, and the period of the monarchy to which the original roster belongs (Boling and Wright *Joshua* AB, 64–72). The location of Aphekah is not well known, although it most probably lay SW of Hebron. Suggested identifications include Khirbet Kana'an (*GP,* 247; M.R. 157102), Khirbet el-Hadab (Alt 1925; M.R. 155098), and Khirbet Marajim (Boling and Wright *Joshua* AB, 389; M.R. 152099). Only the latter identification is supported by evidence of occupation during the Iron Age (Kochavi 1974: 3 n.2).

Bibliography

Alt, A. 1925. Judas Gaue unter Josia. *PJ* 21: 100–16.

Kochavi, M. 1974. Khirbet Rabûd = Debir. *TA* 1: 2–33.

WADE R. KOTTER

APHERRA (PERSON) [Gk *Apherra*]. A servant of Solomon whose descendants returned from exile in Babylon with Zerubbabel (1 Esdr 5:34). Although 1 Esdras is often assumed to have been compiled from Ezra and Nehemiah, this family does not appear among their lists of returning exiles (cf. Ezra 2:57; Neh 7:59). Omissions such as this also raise questions about 1 Esdras being used as a source by Ezra or Nehemiah. Furthermore, problems associated with dating events and persons described in 1 Esdras have cast doubt on the historicity of the text. Heltzer (1977: 66) suggests that Apherra is a Gk rendering of the Heb *ʾprḥ.*

Bibliography

Heltzer, M. 1977. Ein epigraphischer Blick auf das 3. Esrabuch. *Bib* 58: 62–72.

MICHAEL DAVID MCGEHEE

APHIAH (PERSON) [Heb *ʾăpîaḥ*]. The ancestor of Saul ben Kish, the first King of Israel (1 Sam 9:1). The name may mean "sooty" (McCarter *1 Samuel* AB, 168) or, alternatively, "large foreheaded" (*IPN,* 227). LXX^{A} offers the variant form Aphech, which presumes a final *qop* instead of a final *ḥet.*

The genealogy for Saul in 1 Sam 9:1 probably represents a use of the motif of the seven-generation pedigree as a literary device to emphasize Saul's destiny to greatness from birth (Sasson 1978: 185). Apparently only six generations of names from Saul's family were known, forcing the author to include an unnamed "Yimnite man" as Aphiah's father and the founding generation to enable him to employ the literary device. The MT and LXX^{B} both describe Aphiah as "the son of a Yim(i)nite man." The LXX offers a variant reading, "a Yim(i)nite man," which would appear to indicate Aphiah's own clan affiliation instead of that of his father, and which loses the seventh generation from the genealogy. Since the opening phrase in the verse describes Kish as a Benjaminite, there is no need to repeat the Benjaminite affiliation of the founding ancestor, and the Hebrew text does not read "*Ben*jaminite" for Aphiah's father, but merely "Yiminite."

It appears that the founder of the Saulide family is not to be associated with the tribe of Benjamin, which is the common presumption (i.e., Hertzberg *1 and 2 Samuel* OTL, 75; McCarter *1 Samuel* AB, 164, 167), but rather with the neighboring Asherite clan of Yimnah (1 Chr 7:35), probably located in southeastern Mt. Ephraim in the vicinity of Bethel (Edelman 1988: 44–58). The same clan is found subsequently in the story in v 4 as the third territory within Mt. Ephraim that Saul traversed in search of his father's lost asses. The author of the story appears to have deliberately introduced word play between *Ben*jaminite (*bnymyny*) and Yimnite (*ym(y)ny*) and to have used it to foreshadow Saul's kingship over the portion of Mt. Ephraim that was toured in quest of the asses, the symbol of royalty par excellence in Israel and other Semitic ANE societies.

He was implying that Saul had a legitimate claim to dominion in the area because of his ancestral roots in Yimnah. Later editors apparently misunderstood the original author's intention and presumed that "Yimnite" was a shortened or defective reference to "Benjaminite," leading one to introduce the medial *yod* into both occurrences of the name in 1 Samuel. A similar misunderstanding probably produced "Yiminite" from an original reading "Yimnite" in 2 Sam 20:1 and Esth 2:5. The Syr and Targum readings reflect the same presumption that the phrase designates Benjamin.

It is possible to suggest that the MT and LXX[B] text preserves a conflated reading of the two variants "Yim(i)nite man" and "Benjaminite" (i.e., Hertzberg *1 and 2 Samuel* OTL, 75; McCarter *1 Samuel* AB, 168). However, four factors indicate that the MT and LXX[B] reading is correct as it stands: the genealogical context of the list, which would favor the retention of the term "son" to express the filial relationship between Aphiah and the following person; the existence of the seven-generation motif as a documented ancient literary device; the introductory identification of Kish as a Benjaminite that would render a subsequent mention of Benjamin superfluous; and the identification of Aphiah's father as a Yim(i)nite rather than a *Ben*jaminite. The LXX[L] would appear to reflect a loss or dropping of the word "son" by a scribe who did not understand the force of the phrase.

Aphiah's absence from the Saulide genealogy in 1 Chr 8:33–40 and 1 Chr 9:39–44 is probably due to the Chronicler's artificial grafting of the Saulide family tree onto the postexilic genealogy of the clans inhabiting Gibeon, which resulted in the deletion of the names of four known Saulide ancestors (for details and alternate suggestions, see NER and ABIEL).

Bibliography

Edelman, D. 1988. Saul's Journey through Mt. Ephraim and Samuel's Ramah (1 Sam 9:4–5; 10:2–5). *ZDPV* 104: 44–58.

Sasson, J. M. 1978. A Genealogical "Convention" in Biblical Chronology? *ZAW* 90: 171–85.

Diana V. Edelman

APHID. See ZOOLOGY.

ʿAPIRU. See HABIRU, HAPIRU.

APIS (DEITY). The sacred bull-god of Egypt, whose sudden departure is ridiculed by the prophet Jeremiah as a signal of the catastrophe that is about to befall Egypt (Jer 46:13–15). The biblical passage is problematic. The MT suggests that v 15 is a bicolon: *maddûaʿ nisḥap ʾabbîreykā / lōʾ ʿāmad kî yhwh hădāpô* ("Why was your majesty [?] swept away? / It could not stand because Yahweh expelled it")—although some Heb mss read a singular *ʾbyrk,* "your bull." The LXX translates the verb *nisḥap* ("it was swept away") as *ephygen ho Apis* ("Apis has run away"), suggesting a Heb *Vorlage* of **nās ḥap* ("Apis has fled")—*ḥap* being the Heb form for the name of this bull-god (cf. Eg *ḥpw*). Thus, v 15 would be rendered as a tricolon that makes explicit reference to this well-known Egyptian deity: "Why has Apis fled? / Your bull not stand? / Surely Yahweh has expelled him!"

Festivals associated with Apis began very early in Egyptian history and are recorded on 1st Dynasty inscriptions as well as on the Palermo stone (recto iii:12; see also Ael. *NA* 11.10). Although he was a fertility deity associated with procreation as well as agricultural bounty, Apis also enjoyed celestial associations. During the New Kingdom period he came into close association with Ptah, the principal deity of Memphis, and was invoked as the "manifestation" and "hypostasis" of Ptah (Sandman 1946: 196–98). While this might suggest that Apis was simply the visible form of Ptah (Hornung 1982: 136), the two were nevertheless distinct deities and were never confused.

When an Apis bull died, his successor was diligently sought throughout Egypt and could be identified by coloration and distinctive markings: black coat with a white triangle on the forehead, a white vulture on its back, and a "scarab" beneath its tongue (Herodotus 3.28). The temple to which he was immediately taken stood S of the Ptah temple in Memphis, and comprised *inter alia* a colonnaded court where the bull could be viewed (Herodotus 2.153; Stabo 17.807) as well as an embalming chamber. Classical sources which mention the ritual drowning of an aged bull (Griffiths 1970: 511) are not confirmed by native Egyptian texts, and during the 1st millennium B.C. the average life span of a bull was 16–19 years (Kitchen 1982: 62).

The obsequies attendant upon the death of an Apis entailed lavish expense and involved the entire kingdom. Until the Ramesside age the bulls were buried above ground in the Saqqara necropolis; but during the reign of Rameses II a special hypogeum with galleries and chambers was carved out in the same area (Lauer 1976: 11ff., 217ff.). An adjacent gallery was devoted to the burials of the "Mothers of Apis." At each interment, numerous commemorative steles were deposited by the priests and workmen who had officiated at the ceremony, and these memorials (especially those dating from the 8th century B.C. through Ptolemaic times) often contain important genealogical and chronological information (Malinine et al. 1968).

During the late period, as Memphis became a key political center where accreditation had to be secured by those who aspired to rule Egypt (see MEMPHIS), the worship of Apis took on the form of a national cult. In this connection, Jeremiah's ridicule of the fleeing Apis (44:15) can be seen as a metaphorical reference to the dissolution of the Egyptian kingdom. Libyan, Kushite, Saite, and Ptolemaic kings all carefully honored the bull cult (Crawford 1980; Redford 1986: 276ff.); and Apis, when identified with Osiris, became a major ingredient of the Greco-Roman deity "Serapis" (Stambaugh 1972). Roman emperors, while generally acting against the interests of its priests, were nevertheless careful not to offend Apis (Redford 1986: 301f.), and the cult survived probably until the late 4th century A.D.

Bibliography

Crawford, D. J. 1980. Ptolemy, Ptah and Apis in Hellenistic Memphis. Pp. 1–42 in *Studies on Ptolemaic Memphis.* Louvain.

Griffiths, J. G. 1970. *Plutarch's De Iside et Osiride.* Cardiff.

Hornung, E. 1982. *Conceptions of God in Ancient Egypt.* Ithaca.
Kitchen, K. A. 1982. Further Thoughts on Egyptian Chronology in the Third Intermediate Period. *RdÉ* 34: 59–69.
Lauer, J. P. 1976. *Saqqara, the Royal Cemetery of Memphis.* London.
Malinine, M., et al. 1968. *Catalogues des steles du Serapeum de Memphis.* Vol. 1. Paris.
Redford, D. B. 1986. *Pharaonic King-lists, Annals and Daybooks.* Toronto.
Sandman, M. 1946. *The God Ptah.* Lund.
Stambaugh, J. 1972. *Serapis under the Early Ptolemies.* Leiden.

DONALD B. REDFORD

APOCALYPSE, LITTLE. See GOSPELS, LITTLE APOCALYPSES IN THE.

APOCALYPSES AND APOCALYPTICISM.

This entry consists of five separate articles. The first two discuss the genre of "apocalypse" and provide an introductory overview to the subject. The third covers "apocalyptic" literature in Mesopotamia and the question of its connection to biblical apocalyptic writings. The fourth and fifth articles respectively provide more in-depth discussions of early Jewish and early Christian "apocalyptic" writings.

THE GENRE

A. Definition

In recent attempts to add precision to the terminology used in discussing the phenomenon loosely called apocalyptic, "apocalypse" has come to designate a literary genre in contrast to the related concepts "apocalyptic eschatology" and "apocalypticism" (see also the heading "Early Jewish Apocalypticism" later in this article). This triad and the specific definitions given to each of its members are of considerable heuristic value in the scholarly attempt to clarify a complex ancient phenomenon (Koch 1972: 23–28; Hanson *IDBSup,* 27–28). Heuristic devices must not be regarded as more than they are, however, namely, tools useful to the extent that they shed light on the ancient materials themselves. In using such tools, one does well to remember that the ancient apocalyptic writers did not distinguish rigidly between genre, perspective, and ideology, and from this it follows that such categories should be used only with great sensitivity to the integrity and complexity of the compositions themselves.

In using the term "apocalypse" to designate a genre, we are utilizing a derivative of the Greek noun *apokalypsis* ("revelation, disclosure"). The first attested use of the term to refer to a literary work is in the opening line of the book of Revelation, "The *apokalypsis* of Jesus Christ." This bears both historical and formal significance: historical inasmuch as the book of Revelation has exercised considerable influence on the Western understanding of the genre; formal inasmuch as the book exhibits nearly all of the principal characteristics of this genre (pseudonymity being one notable exception).

The first two verses of the book of Revelation contain *in nuce* the narrative structure of the genre: a *revelation* is given by God through an otherworldly *mediator* to a *human seer* disclosing *future events.* V 3 contains an added feature commonly found (or implied) in apocalypses, namely, an *admonition.* Beyond these three verses the book of Revelation as a whole casts further light on this genre. It offers descriptions of the seer's response to awesome revelatory experiences that resemble those recurring in other apocalypses. True to the structural complexity of many apocalypses, the book of Revelation embraces a series of vision accounts, interspersed with smaller genres like the epistle, the doxology, the victory song, and the blessing. And while the emphasis is on the visionary experience of the seer as the mode of revelation, in chap. 4 the seer, following a heavenly summons to "come up hither," finds himself in the heavenly throne room, thus providing an example of the "heavenly journey" found, often in vastly elaborated form, in other apocalypses.

A group headed by J. J. Collins expanded on earlier studies of the genre apocalypse by analyzing all of the texts classifiable as apocalypses from the period 250 B.C.E. to 250 C.E. and concluded with this definition: " 'Apocalypse' is a genre of revelatory literature with a narrative framework, in which a revelation is mediated by an otherworldly being to a human recipient, disclosing a transcendent reality which is both temporal, insofar as it envisages eschatological salvation, and spatial, insofar as it involves another, supernatural world" (Collins 1979: 9). The distinction between a temporal and a spatial axis in the mode of revelation found in this definition reflects the fact that, while the eschatological perspective stemming from prophecy is of central importance in early Jewish and Christian apocalypses, descriptions of otherworldly journeys, lists of natural phenomena, and diverse kinds of cosmic and celestial speculations also are found in some of those apocalypses. When consideration is given to the perennial tension between temporal and spatial definitions of salvation (e.g., mythic versus epic views of reality in antiquity and historical versus existential views today), the juxtaposition of temporal and spatial axes within ancient apocalypses seems conceptually fitting.

B. Antecedents

While fully developed apocalypses first appear in the 3d and 2d centuries B.C.E., two biblical books from the 6th century B.C.E. adumbrate many of the formal features of the genre and can be viewed as important sources. In the opening verse of the book of Ezekiel the prophet reports that "the heavens were opened and I saw visions of God." In its present form the book of Ezekiel is constructed around five visions, revealing both future judgment and future salvation. In a series of eight visions in Zechariah 1–6 the prophet views supernatural phenomena which are then explained by an interpreting angel as bearing on future events. It seems plausible to assume that later visionaries considered themselves to stand in the tradition of such worthy predecessors.

C. Important Apocalypses

Smaller units embedded in the gospels and epistles of the NT aside, chaps. 7–12 of the book of Daniel share with the book of Revelation the distinction of alone representing the genre of the apocalypse in the Bible. Like the book of Revelation, Daniel 7–12 contains a series of visions (7, 8, and 10–12). In all three cases the seer receives the vision through an angelic mediator and the content has bearing on future judgment and salvation.

1 Enoch, which is actually an anthology of apocalyptic writings ascribed to the antediluvian figure Enoch and arising over a period of at least two centuries, is preserved in an Ethiopic translation of a Greek version (partially preserved) of Aramaic originals (fragments discovered among the Dead Sea Scrolls). The earliest of the Enochic apocalypses originated at least a half century before Daniel 7–12. Notable among these earliest materials are chaps. 6–11, which trace the rise of evil in the world to the rebellion in heaven alluded to in Gen. 6:1–4, and chaps. 17–36, which describe the heavenly journeys of Enoch. Clearly datable to the period of the Maccabean revolt is the allegorical history of the world in chaps. 89–90 referred to as the "Animal Apocalypse," and the "Apocalypse of Weeks" in *1 En.* 93 and 91:12–17. These apocalypses from *1 Enoch* illustrate the eclectic nature of the genre as it took shape in the Hellenistic period, for we find eschatological visions in continuity with earlier prophecy combined with sapiential and speculative materials reflecting other influences. Nevertheless, the dominant emphasis of these apocalypses and those discussed below is harmonious with the themes of earlier Israelite religion, for they reveal a time/place beyond the fallen present in which God's sovereignty will be restored and the righteous will be vindicated.

4 Ezra and *2 Baruch.* These two works are closely tied together by common themes and a shared setting in the aftermath of the Roman destruction of Jerusalem and the temple. In *4 Ezra* three dialogues between seer and an angel are followed by three visions which, in an allegorical fashion recalling Daniel and the Maccabean period apocalypses of *1 Enoch,* desribe the movement of history through the ages down to the concluding divine denouement. *2 Baruch* similarly combines dialogue and visions into a tapestry of apocalypses and other genres subservient to the eschatological theme of the fulfillment of human history in final judgment and salvation.

D. Setting and Function

Though the degree to which the above-mentioned apocalypses preserve traces of their historical setting varies, it is evident in general terms that they all reflect a situation of crisis and aim at offering assurance of salvation to those alienated from the power structures of this world and suffering for their religious convictions. Daniel envisions the imminent destruction of Antiochus IV and the conferral of the kingdom on the "saints of the Most High." In *4 Ezra* the angel explains that the vision of the transformation of the woman from mourning and weeping to glory signifies the transformation that is about to happen to Zion. In the book of Revelation, visions of the downfall of the beast and the victory of the lamb gave assurance of the final vindication of those suffering under Roman persecution. Though more difficult to integrate into the theme of assurance in time of crisis, even those sections revealing the mysteries of the heavens and the secrets of the vast cosmos contribute to the effort to establish a basis for hope transcending the ever changing experiences of this world. The setting and function that can be glimpsed behind the Jewish and Christian apocalypses thus indicate that, while those communities and movements that we can characterize under the rubric of "apocalypticism" expressed themselves in genres ranging all the way from the testament to the song of victory, the genre of the apocalypse is more intimately related to the phenomenon of apocalyptic than any other literary form.

Bibliography

Collins, J. J., ed. 1979. *Apocalypse: The Morphology of a Genre. Semeia* 14. Missoula, MT.

Hanson, P. 1987. *Old Testament Apocalyptic.* Philadelphia.

Hellholm, D., ed. 1983. *Apocalypticism in the Mediterranean World and the Near East.* Tübingen.

Koch, K. 1972. *The Rediscovery of Apocalyptic.* SBT 2/22. Naperville, IL.

PAUL D. HANSON

INTRODUCTORY OVERVIEW

The word "apocalyptic," though properly an adjective, in common parlance has come to designate the phenomenon of the disclosure of heavenly secrets in visionary form to a seer for the benefit of a religious community experiencing suffering or perceiving itself victimized by some form of deprivation. The book of Daniel is the foremost literary example of this phenomenon in the world of Jewish antiquity, though Jewish apocalyptic writings range far beyond the Bible and betray connections with related phenomena in other cultures.

The problem with the proper usage is that it leaves unclear what qualities determine whether a given experience or written account fits the category apocalyptic: whether literary characteristics, a particular world view or pattern of ideas, or a certain type of social setting. This unclarity has led scholars to prefer a triad of definitions, differentiating between "apocalypse" as a literary genre, "apocalyptic eschatology" as a religious perspective, and "apocalypticism" as a community or movement enbodying an apocalyptic perspective as its ideology (Koch 1972; P. Hanson *IBDSup,* pp. 28–34; Collins 1984).

A. Apocalypse

Though the phenomenon designated "Jewish apocalyptic" comes to expression in more than one genre, the specific genre "apocalypse" occupied a privileged position. First used explicitly as the designation of a writing in antiquity in Rev. 1:1, the structure of the apocalypse reflects more closely than any other genre the essential characteristics of the apocalyptic phenomenon, and its history is more closely intertwined with the history of Jewish apocalyptic than is the history of any other genre.

B. Apocalyptic Eschatology

The ideas and concepts that come to expression in apocalyptic writings range broadly from ancient mythic motifs to biblical themes to speculation reflecting a Hellenistic milieu. Nevertheless, as the genre "apocalypse" enjoys pride of place on the literary plane, a world view we can designate "apocalyptic eschatology" more frequently than any other perspective provides the conceptual framework within which the diverse materials encompassed by the apocalyptic writings are interpreted.

Eschatology, as the study of "end-time" events, developed earlier in biblical prophecy. The perspective of apocalyptic eschatology can best be understood as an outgrowth from prophetic eschatology. Common to both is the belief that, in accordance with divine plan, the adverse conditions of the present world would end in judgment of the wicked and vindication of the righteous, thereby ushering in a new era of prosperity and peace. In an early postexilic prophetic oracle, Yahweh announces:

> For the former troubles will be forgotten,
> They will be hidden from my eyes;
> For now I create new heavens
> and a new earth (Isa 65:16b–17a).

Prophetic eschatology and apocalyptic eschatology are best viewed as two sides of a continuum. The development from the one to the other is not ineluctably chronological, however, but is intertwined with changes in social and political conditions. Periods and conditions permitting members of the protagonist community to sense that human effort would be repaid by improved fortune tended to foster prophetic eschatology, that is, the view that God's new order would unfold within the realities of this world. Periods of extreme suffering, whether at the hands of opponents within the community or those of foreign adversaries, tended to cast doubts on the effectiveness of human reform and thus to abet apocalyptic eschatology, with its more rigidly dualistic view of divine deliverance, entailing destruction of this world and resurrection of the faithful to a blessed heavenly existence.

C. Apocalypticism

The social and political setting within which most of the Jewish apocalyptic writings arose is a matter of scholarly conjecture. A noteworthy exception is the corpus of sectarian writings found at Qumran. Though actual examples of the genre of the apocalypse at Qumran are rare and fragmentary in form, the sectarian writings are permeated with the perspective designated above as "apocalyptic eschatology." Within the community at Qumran, the perspective of apocalyptic eschatology had been elevated to the status of an ideology, functioning to inform its interpretation of Scripture, to provide the basis for its understanding of Jewish and gentile adversaries, and to supply a historiographic point of view from which to develop a detailed scenario of final conflict and divine vindication of the elect.

Apocalypses and other writings sharing the perspective of apocalyptic eschatology originating outside of the Qumran community were copied and studied within that community (e.g., the writings within the Ethiopic corpus designated *1 Enoch,* minus the parables, and *Jubilees*). Though these writings differ at important points from the Qumran writings, shared views on calendar, angelology, demonology, cosmology, and eschatology suggest that different communities embodying the perspective of apocalyptic eschatology maintained contact with one another, possibly with the consciousness of being united under the umbrella of a wider Essene movement.

Hopefully future archaeological findings coupled with intensified study of existing written and archaeological material will shed further light on Jewish apocalypticism. In such scholarship the temptation to try to homogenize all apocalyptic writings into one broad movement must be eshewed. *4 Ezra* and *2 Baruch,* bearing affinities as they do with Pharisaic teachings, illustrate that not all apocalyses come from the Essenes. Apocalyptic themes in later rabbinic writings indicate that an apocalyptic motif in a literary composition does not constitute proof of origin in an apocalyptic movement (Block 1952). Apocalypticism, as a designation for a movement that has adopted the perspective of apocalyptic eschatology as its ideology, must accordingly be used with great caution and only in cases where sufficient evidence accumulates to point to a community that has constructed its identity upon the world view of apocalyptic eschatology.

D. Sources of Jewish Apocalyptic

What were the influences that fostered the development of Jewish apocalyptic? Scholars were once confident that the source could be traced to a form of Persian dualism with which Judaism came into contact in the Second Temple period. Support for this view has evaporated as the result of studies indicating that the Persian sources upon which the hypothesis rested were written over a half millennium after the period of alleged influence.

Gerhard von Rad, reviving an idea advanced in the 19th century, argued that the Wisdom tradition was the source of Jewish apocalyptic (Von Rad 1972). This he did by identifying the heart of apocalyptic not in eschatology but in a deterministic interpretation of history. Von Rad's hypothesis has found few followers and many critics, largely due to the fact that apocalyptic eschatology—while not excluding other patterns of thought—frequently provides the conceptual framework into which other materials are integrated and on the basis of which they are interpreted (Von der Osten-Sachen 1969).

The source that continues to emerge from the debate concerning origins with the highest degree of credibility is biblical prophecy. Here the key lies within a group of writings that can either be designated "late prophecy" or "early apocalyptic" (e.g., Isaiah 24–27; Isaiah 56–66; Zechariah 9–14), insofar as they occupy a transitional position between the more historically oriented perspective of classical prophecy and the more transcendent view of salvation characteristic of the apocalyptic writings. Challenges to the prophetic source theory, however, have also made a contribution: they have indicated that Jewish apocalyptic becomes increasingly complex over the course of the centuries and especially as it enters the Hellenistic era, at which point it draws freely upon rather refined sciences such as learned speculation on celestial and terrestrial phenomena and sapiential reflection betraying stronger connections with Mesopotamian mantic traditions than with Egyptian or Israelite wisdom (Collins 1977; Stone 1976).

E. Theological Meaning

As the writer of the book of Daniel drew upon the words of the prophet Jeremiah to explain his troubled times, and as the teachers of Qumran expounded on the books of Habakkuk and Nahum to reveal the eschatological significance of current events, so too Herbert Armstrong and Hal Lindsay command the attention of millions with their biblically based predictions of apocalyptic denouement. Diligent historical-critical study, combined with hermeneutical theory that pays attention to the multivalence of symbols and the complexities involved in the transfer of meaning from ancient settings to a world far removed in time, can restrain reckless readings of Jewish apocalyptic writings that abet international tension and can serve instead as a guide to a more accurate understanding of these mysterious compositions and to a more fitting appreciation of the abiding significance of the messages addressed by ancient apocalyptic seers to those engulfed by suffering and overwhelmed by dread (Hanson 1987).

Bibliography

Block, J. 1952. *On the Apocalyptic in Judaism.* JQRMS 2. Philadelphia.

Collins, J. J. 1977. Cosmos and Salvation: Jewish Wisdom and Apocalyptic in the Hellenistic Age. *HR* 17: 121–42.

———. 1984. *The Prophetic Imagination in Ancient Judaism.* New York.

Hanson, P. D. 1975. *The Dawn of Apocalyptic.* Philadelphia.

———. 1987. *Old Testament Apocalyptic.* Philadelphia.

Koch, K. 1972. *The Rediscovery of Apocalyptic.* SBT 2/22. Naperville, IL.

Osten-Sachen, P. von der. 1969. *Die Apokalyptik in ihrem Verhältnis zu Prophetie und Weisheit.* ThEH 157. Munich.

Rad, G. von. 1972. *Wisdom in Israel.* Nashville.

Stone, M. E. 1976. Lists of Revealed Things in the Apocalyptic Literature. Pp. 414–52 in *Magnalia Dei: The Mighty Acts of God,* ed. F. M. Cross et al. Garden City, NY.

Paul D. Hanson

AKKADIAN "APOCALYPTIC" LITERATURE

Research in Akkadian literature over the last decade or so has led to the suggestion that the origins of apocalyptic literature may be found there. The particular type of Akkadian literature in question is the so-called "Akkadian prophecies." This article will first describe briefly the Akkadian prophecies and their purpose, then go on to discuss the question of whether or not these are eschatological in nature and what possible relationship they may have to Jewish apocalyptic literature.

Akkadian prophecies are actually pseudoprophecies, for they consist in the main of predictions after the event (*vaticinia ex eventu*). The predictions are presented as a chronological sequence of reigns and are often introduced by some such phrase as "a prince will arise." It is a feature of Akkadian prophecies that the rules are never mentioned by name but it is often possible to identify them since various details such as the length of their reigns are often given. The reigns themselves are described as "good" or "bad" and the vocabulary and literary style of these prophecies generally is that of Akkadian omen literature.

Akkadian prophecies are a purely literary phenomenon and there is no evidence for any oral background. This is in contrast to Akkadian oracles which, as the name implies, were oral pronouncements to the king by ecstatics and are not relevant to our discussion of apocalyptic literature. The number of Akkadian prophecies so far recovered is quite small; in fact only five main compositions are as yet known. Of these five only two are directly relevant to the present topic: the *Dynastic Prophecy* and the *Uruk Prophecy.*

Scholars generally agree that the writer of an Akkadian prophecy wished to justify or advocate an idea, institution, or development in his own time by means of a long preamble in which he pretends to have predicted other ideas, events, and institutions of previous times. He then concludes this series of pseudopredictions with a prophecy that the particular idea or institution which he wished to justify or advocate would be established by the gods. Now the peculiarity of the two prophecies just mentioned, the *Dynastic Prophecy* and the *Uruk Prophecy,* is that each seems to conclude with a real prophecy; that is, something that the writer himself only wished would come about but had not actually done so in his lifetime. Thus the *Dynastic Prophecy* seems (the text is unfortunately badly broken) to conclude with a prediction that the Seleucid Empire in Babylonia will fall. In other words, it is the product of anti-Macedonian feeling in Babylonia. The conclusion of the *Uruk Prophecy* is even more significant. After prophesying various good and bad reigns for the city of Uruk, the writer ends with a prediction that a king will arise in Uruk and rule the four quarters: that is, the world. The last two sentences read, "His reign will be established forever. The kings of Uruk will exercise dominion like the gods." There is no doubt that this is a real prediction since in fact such an event never happened. There is more significance, however, than that to these sentences; they are clearly eschatological in nature.

The evidence for eschatology in the Akkadian prophecies immediately provides a major link with apocalyptic literature. The idea that world history will end in a millennium, when all wrongs will be righted and all just people rewarded, is a major feature of Jewish apocalyptic literature, such as the book of Daniel and, by extension, the Christian book of Revelation, and of the apocalyptic tradition which developed in medieval times. We cannot give any specific date to the *Uruk Prophecy* in Mesopotamia but it is well established that the genre called Akkadian prophecy was present before 1000 B.C. It cannot yet be shown that the earlier Akkadian prophecies had eschatological ideas in them; indeed this has been debated in scholarly circles. Nevertheless, the presence of eschatology in the later prophecies seems to fit well in the context of this genre and probably is an indigenous development. Thus there is good reason to suggest, even though it cannot be proven, that apocalyptic literature has its origin in the Mesopotamian literary genre called Akkadian prophecies.

Bibliography

Biggs, R. 1967. More Babylonian Prophecies. *Iraq* 29: 117–32.

———. 1987. Babylonian Prophecies, Astrology, and a New Source for "Prophecy Text B." Pp. 1–14 in *Language, Literature and History,* ed. F. Rochberg-Halton. AOS 67. New Haven.

Grayson, A. K. 1975. *Babylonian Historical Literary Texts.* Toronto Semitic Texts and Studies 3. Toronto.

Grayson, A. K., and Lambert, W. G. 1964. Akkadian Prophecies. *JCS* 18: 12–16.

Hallo, W. 1966. Akkadian Apocalypses. *IEJ* 16: 231–42.

Hunger, H., and Kaufman, S. 1975. A New Akkadian Prophecy Text. *JAOS* 95: 371–75.

A. Kirk Grayson

EARLY JEWISH APOCALYPTICISM

The term "apocalypticism" is derived from the Greek word *apokalypsis,* "revelation," which is used to designate the book of Revelation in the NT (Rev 1:1). The term is variously used to refer to a social movement or movements, a system of thought, or, more vaguely, a spiritual movement. The starting point, however, for any use of "apocalyptic," "apocalypticism," and related terms is a distinctive body of literature from ancient Judaism and early Christianity.

A. Literary Genre

Historically this corpus has been recognized because of its resemblance to the canonical Apocalypse of John, or book of Revelation. "Apocalypse" was a well-known genre label in Christian antiquity, beginning from the end of the 1st century C.E., when it appears as the introductory designation in Rev 1:1 (Smith 1983: 18–19). Thereafter apocalypses are attributed to both NT (Peter, Paul) and OT figures (e.g., the gnostic *Apocalypse of Adam,* the Cologne Mani Codex speaks of apocalypses of Adam, Sethel, Enosh, Shem, and Enoch). Prior to the late 1st century C.E. the title is not used. (Its occurrence in the manuscripts of *2* and *3 Baruch* may be secondary.) It is possible, nonetheless, to identify a corpus of Jewish writings from this earlier period which fit a common definition (Collins 1979: 21–59). This definition is first of all formal: *an apocalypse is a genre of revelatory literature with a narrative framework, in which a revelation is mediated by an otherworldly being to a human recipient.* It also recognizes a common core of content: an apocalypse *envisages eschatological salvation and involves a supernatural world.* Finally, there is, on a rather general level, a common function: an apocalypse is *intended to interpret present, earthly circumstances in light of the supernatural world and of the future, and to influence both the understanding and the behavior of the audience by means of divine authority* (Yarbro Collins 1986: 7). This definition fits all the Jewish writings which are generally classified as apocalypses: Daniel, *1 Enoch, 2 Enoch, 2 Baruch, 3 Baruch, 4 Ezra, Apoc. Abraham,* and a few works of mixed genre (*Jubilees, T. Abraham*). Note also *T. Levi* 2–5 which is part of a larger work, and *Apoc. Zephaniah,* which is problematic because of its fragmentary character. It also fits an extensive corpus of Christian writings, beginning with Revelation, *Hermas,* and *Apoc. Peter.* Examples can also be found, with some distinctive variations, in Gnosticism (*Apoc. Adam, 2 Apoc. James*), among the later Jewish mystical texts (e.g., *3 Enoch*), and also in Greek, Latin, and Persian literature (see the various essays in Collins 1979).

The definition of apocalypse given above fits an extensive body of literature, which was produced over several hundred years. It is not suggested that the genre remained static or was consistently uniform. In fact, the definition serves only to delimit the corpus, and allows for considerable variation and development within it. To begin with, it is possible to distinguish two broad types of apocalypses: the historical type (e.g., Daniel) in which revelation is most often conveyed in symbolic visions and presents an overview of history culminating in a crisis, and the otherworldly journeys (of which the earliest example is found in the *Book of the Watchers, 1 Enoch* 1–36), which are more mystical in orientation. It is also possible to distinguish various historical clusters of apocalypses which have their own distinctive emphases and concerns—e.g., within the Jewish corpus one might distinguish the early Enoch literature, the apocalypses of the Diaspora, or those composed after the fall of Jerusalem, *4 Ezra* and *2 Baruch* (see Collins 1984). Moreover, there is always some overlap between the apocalypses and other genres, e.g., the historical reviews which are characteristic of the historical apocalypses are also typical of the *Sibylline Oracles* and of the testamentary literature. While the apocalypses constitute a distinct genre, they cannot be understood in isolation from the various types of related literature.

B. From Apocalypse to Apocalypticism

We have seen that the genre apocalypse is characterized in part by core elements of content, specifically a lively belief in the supernatural world and the expectation of eschatological salvation.

Belief in a supernatural world is, of course, characteristic of religion in general. Against the background of the Hebrew Bible, however, the apocalyptic literature shows a heightened interest both in otherworldly regions and in supernatural beings. So Enoch describes the abodes of the dead and the places of judgment, and ascribes the origin of evil to the sin of the Watchers, or fallen angels. This aspect of apocalypticism has often been overlooked because of a preoccupation with eschatology, but it has been repeatedly emphasized in recent years (e.g., Gruenwald 1980; Rowland 1982). It is an important feature of all the apocalypses, not only of the heavenly journeys.

Eschatology, too, was characteristic of much of the prophetic tradition. In the apocalyptic literature, however, it takes on a new character. The distinctive novelty here was the belief in the judgment of the dead. An apocalypse like Daniel might still proclaim an eschatological kingdom of Israel, but it also promised that the faithful would rise in glory, and thereby offered a perspective on life which was very different from that of the Hebrew prophets.

Taken together, these core elements of content constitute *a world view,* which was new and distinctive in Judaism when it first emerged in the Hellenistic period, although it subsequently came to be widely accepted. The belief in a judgment beyond death and in the influence of angels and demons on human life created a framework for human decisions and actions. *This world view or "symbolic universe" which is extrapolated from the apocalypses is what we call "apocalypticism."* It can also be expressed in other literary forms. The *Discourse on the Two Spirits* and the *War Scroll* from Qumran are not presented as revelations mediated by an angel, but they are generally and rightly recognized as apocalyptic in the broader sense that they exhibit the apocalyptic world view. Apocalypticism, then, is a broader phenomenon than the literary genre. From the historical point of view, the world view is prior to the production of apocalypses (i.e., people who believe in angels and demons and in an eschatological judgment are likely to write apocalypses, although they may also express themselves in other genres). From the viewpoint of the modern scholar, however, the literary genre is prior (i.e., the world view is recognized by analogy with the apocalypses).

In his influential article in *IDBSup*, Paul Hanson defined apocalypticism not only as a "symbolic universe" but as "the symbolic universe in which an apocalyptic movement codifies its identity and interpretation of reality" (*IDBSup*, 30). One of the strengths of Hanson's article lay in his realization that one cannot speak simply of *the* apocalyptic movement: there is no demonstrable historical link between the people who produced the early Enoch literature and those who wrote *4 Ezra* and *2 Baruch*, or the other distinct clusters of apocalyptic texts. He was also right in recognizing that apocalypticism *can* serve as the "symbolic universe" of a movement. Nonetheless, there is no automatic connection between apocalypticism and social movements. In many cases we know very little of the social matrix in which apocalyptic literature was produced. A work like *4 Ezra* may have been the product of a relatively isolated individual, who was not part of a movement in any meaningful sense of the word. We should beware of inferring social movements too readily from literary evidence.

C. Israelite Background

Jewish apocalypticism first emerges clearly in the Hellenistic age, but it is in many respects a development of old strands in the religion of Israel (see Collins 1987: 548–50). There is obvious continuity between the apocalyptic expectation of a final judgment and the prophetic "day of the Lord." The idea of a cosmic day of judgment is widely attested in the prophets and the psalms (e.g., Pss 96, 98; Isa 2:4). The apocalyptic interest in the heavenly world is a development of older ideas of the heavenly council (e.g., Ps 82:1) which can be traced back to Canaan and Mesopotamia in the 2d millennium (Mullen 1980). The degree of continuity between the apocalyptic world view and the older religion of Israel is hard to assess, because the mythological elements in Israelite religion are not well represented in the Hebrew Bible. We read in Isa 24:21–23 that "on that day the Lord will punish the host of heaven, in heaven, and the kings of the earth, on the earth. . . . They will be shut up in a prison, and after many days they will be punished." This passage evidently presupposes a fuller narrative than is now extant. In *1 Enoch* 18, Enoch is shown the prison of the host of heaven. We cannot infer that all the transcendent world toured by Enoch was presupposed in Isaiah 24, but we must recognize that the apocalyptic writers had at their disposal a much fuller mythology than is now extant in the Hebrew Bible. Light has been shed on some apocalyptic passages, notably Daniel 7, by the Ugaritic myths, which were written down over a millennium earlier (Collins 1977: 96–103). Because of the high degree of selectivity in the editing of the Hebrew Bible, the lines by which this material was transmitted down to the Hellenistic age are no longer in evidence.

Paul Hanson claims to find the perspective of apocalyptic eschatology already in the late 6th century B.C.E., especially in the oracles of Isaiah 56–66 (Hanson 1975). On Hanson's reconstruction, the authors of these oracles belonged to a disenfranchised group, which was excluded from power in the restored Jerusalem temple. As they despaired of rectifying this situation by human means, they called on their God to "rend the heavens and come down" (Isa 64:1) and envisaged "a new heaven and a new earth" (Isa 65:17). Hanson traces a movement which persisted from the time of the Exile to the end of the 5th century and is attested in Zechariah 9–14, Isaiah 24–27, Malachi, and possibly Joel. Perhaps the most radical vision is found in Isaiah 24–27, where we are told that God "will swallow up death forever" (Isa 25:8).

This bold reconstruction of a social movement is quite hypothetical, but its historical plausibility does not concern us here. For our purposes, the essential point is that the world view of these postexilic writings is significantly different from what we will later find in *1 Enoch* and Daniel. The crucial difference can be seen in the nature of the eschatology. In Isaiah 65 the new creation is one where "the child shall die a hundred years old, and the sinner a hundred years old shall be accursed," but they will die nonetheless. There is no question of personal immortality. Even Isaiah 24–27, which speaks of the destruction of death and says that God's dead shall live (Isa 26:19), most probably only envisages the resurrection of the Israelite people, in the manner of Ezekiel 37. There is still no suggestion that a human being can pass over to the world of the angels or become a companion to the host of heaven. Consequently these oracles retain the this-worldly emphasis traditional in biblical prophecy. In view of this, the oracles of Isaiah 56–66 and other postexilic prophecies are best regarded as examples of late prophecy, even though some of their themes are later taken up in a new context in the apocalypses. This is also true of the visions of Zechariah 1–6, which are closer formally to the apocalyptic visions than any material in the Hebrew Bible before the book of Daniel, and which are more obviously supportive of the cultic institutions than Isaiah 56–66. There again, the goal envisaged is the restoration of Israel so that everyone would invite his neighbor under his vine and under his fig tree (Zech 3:10).

D. Foreign Influences

The development of apocalypticism in the Hellenistic period cannot be understood exclusively against the background of older Israelite religion. Judaism was exposed to a wide range of influences in the postexilic era and there were some analogous developments in other traditions at this time. The earliest Jewish apocalypses are those attributed to Enoch and Daniel, both of whom have strong links with Mesopotamia. The figure of Enoch seems to be modeled to a great degree on legendary Mesopotamian sages, especially Enmeduranki, founder of the guild of *barus* or Babylonian diviners (VanderKam 1984: 38–45). One of the earliest of the writings attributed to him is primarily concerned with the movements of the stars, a topic which enjoyed much greater prominence in Babylonian tradition than in Israel. The book of Daniel is set in the Babylonian Exile, and Daniel is portrayed as a professional sage, skilled in the interpretation of dreams like his Chaldean colleagues. There is, then, reason to suspect that the earliest stages of Jewish apocalypticism developed in the eastern Diaspora, though conclusive evidence is lacking.

It is not surprising, then, that some scholars have sought

the background of Jewish apocalypticism in Mesopotamian traditions (Lambert 1978; VanderKam 1984; Kvanvig 1987). There is no evidence that the Babylonians ever developed an apocalyptic tradition, but some aspects of Babylonian thought may have had an influence on the development in Judaism. Many scholars have observed the affinities between apocalyptic revelation and the "mantic wisdom" of the Chaldeans (Müller 1972). Both involve the interpretation of mysterious signs and symbols and both carry overtones of determinism. The omen collections, which are the primary literature of Babylonian divination, are very different from the Jewish apocalypses. There are, however, two Mesopotamian genres which are significant for the background of Jewish apocalypticism. One is the dream vision, whose influence is undeniable in the case of Daniel, but is also in evidence in the Enochic *Book of Dreams* (*1 Enoch* 83–90). The most interesting example is the 7th-century Assyrian *Vision of the Netherworld,* in which a prince, in his dream, is taken before the king of the netherworld, issued a warning, and allowed to return to life. The attempt to demonstrate direct influence of this composition on the apocalypses of Enoch and Daniel has not been convincing (Kvanvig 1987), but it is potentially important for the development of the subgenre of otherworldly journeys. Unfortunately we have as yet few examples of such visions of the netherworld (see also the death dream of Enkidu in the Epic of Gilgamesh). The second Mesopotamian genre which is relevant here is more closely related to the historical apocalypses and has only come to light in recent years. This is the genre of Akkadian prophecy, defined as "a prose composition consisting in the main of a number of 'predictions' of past events. It then concludes either with a 'prediction' of phenomena in the writer's day or with a genuine attempt to forecast future events" (Grayson 1975: 6). In at least some cases they are pseudonymous (Marduk, Shulgi; the attribution of other oracles is uncertain because of fragmentary preservation). Examples range in date from the 12th century to the Seleucid era. Such *vaticinia ex eventu* figure prominently in the historical apocalypses (e.g., Dan 8:23–25, Daniel 11. See Lambert 1978). These Babylonian prophecies do not end with the transcendent, cosmic eschatology which characterizes apocalypticism, and are not properly called "apocalyptic," but they provide one of the building blocks for one type of apocalypse.

Unlike the Babylonians, the Persians had a well-developed apocalyptic tradition, which has often been assumed to be the source of Jewish apocalypticism (e.g., Bousset 1966: 478–83). In recent years scholars have become reticent about positing Persian influence, because of the notorious difficulties of dating. Most of the relevant Persian material is extant in Pahlavi works, which are as late as the 9th century C.E. The traditions involved are certainly much older than this but are difficult to date with any confidence. One of the primary texts in dispute is the *Bahman Yasht,* or *Zand-i Vohuman Yasn,* a full-blown apocalypse of the historical type, which includes a vision of a tree with four metal branches symbolizing kingdoms (cf. the statue in Daniel 2). This composition has been widely thought to be based on a lost Zand of the Avesta, which was widely influential in the Hellenistic age (Eddy 1961: 17–20; Widengren 1983: 105–27). Recently, however, the existence of this Avestan Zand has been questioned, and the possibility of Jewish influence on Persian apocalypticism has been raised (Gignoux 1987: 355). Another major witness to pre-Christian Persian apocalypticism is the *Oracle of Hystaspes,* which is not extant and must be reconstructed from the writings of Lactantius. This work has sometimes been regarded as a Jewish pseudepigraph (so Flusser 1982) and, while most scholars accept it as Persian, the uncertainty of provenance is symptomatic of the problems of Persian apocalypticism.

Despite the problems, the possible influence of Persian apocalypticism of Judaism cannot be discounted. A brief (and problematic) account of Persian religion attributed to Theopompus (about 300 B.C.E.) attests a belief in an ongoing dualistic struggle between light and darkness, the activity of angelic and demonic beings, and the division of history into periods (Plut. *De Is. et Os.* 47). Belief in resurrection is undisputedly old in Persian religion (Widengren 1983: 81), as is the motif of the heavenly journey (Gignoux 1987: 364). Persian influence on the dualism of the Dead Sea Scrolls is widely admitted. The full relationship between Persian and Jewish apocalypticism, and the degree of influence of the one on the other, remains one of the major unresolved problems in the study of apocalypticism.

Many of the features of apocalypticism which are paralleled in Babylonian and Persian material are also paralleled more widely in the Hellenistic world. There was a long-standing tradition of political prophecy in Egypt, which was adapted in the Hellenistic period in the *Potter's Oracle* (Griffiths 1983: 283–93). The *Sibylline Oracles,* adapted in Judaism and Christianity, were in origin a Greek genre. The motif of the otherworldly journey was widespread in the Hellenistic-Roman world, as were various forms of belief in immortality. The currency of these ideas in the general environment may have stimulated their acceptance in Judaism. This is not to detract from the thoroughly Jewish character of apocalypticism as it developed in *1 Enoch* and Daniel, but to recognize that Hellenistic Judaism was a product of its age and should be studied in its cultural context.

E. Earliest Jewish Movements

The earliest Jewish apocalyptic movement is that associated with the figure of Enoch. In this case we have a cluster of apocalypses (the *Book of the Watchers,* the *Astronomical Book,* the *Book of Dreams,* the *Apocalypse of Weeks,* all now gathered in *1 Enoch*) which are in demonstrable continuity with one another. All are ascribed pseudonymously to the antediluvian figure of Enoch. The Aramaic fragments from Qumran require a 3d-century date for the earliest stages of this movement (Milik 1976; Stone 1980: 27–35). The earliest documents of this corpus (the *Astronomical Book* and the *Book of the Watchers*) are largely concerned with cosmological lore. In both cases, however, the order of the cosmos has been disrupted: in the *Astronomical Book* by "many heads of the stars" who go astray (*1 Enoch* 80) and in the *Book of the Watchers* by the fallen angels. It is disputed whether the *Book of the Watchers* is a reflection on the problem of evil in general (Sacchi 1982) or a more specific reaction to the cultural changes of the Hellenistic age (Nickelsburg 1977). Neither of these early apocalypses shows the expectation of imminent divine intervention which is often taken to be constitutive of apocalypticism (cf. Daniel and Revelation), but they do affirm an ultimate divine judgment. The Mesopotamian parallels to the figure of Enoch and the interest in the astral world in the *Astronomical Book* suggest that the earliest stages of this tradition were formed in the eastern Diaspora, although the evidence is not conclusive (VanderKam 1984). The Enoch tradition undergoes some development in the *Apocalypse of Weeks* and the *Book of Dreams*. These documents were produced closer to the time of the Maccabean revolt and were certainly written in Palestine. Both apocalypses contain lengthy reviews of history in the guise of prophecy and culminate with divine intervention and a final judgment. Both also give clear indications of the formation of a distinct group, called "small lambs" in *1 Enoch* 90:6 and "the chosen righteous from the eternal plant of righteousness" in *1 Enoch* 93:10. We know nothing of the organization of this group. They endorsed the military action of Judas Maccabee and the use of the sword against sinners (91:11), and claimed to have a sevenfold teaching (93:10) of which the writings attributed to Enoch are presumably representative. It is possible that they are identical with the Hasidim who are mentioned as supporters of Judas Maccabee in 2 Macc 14:6 (cf. 1 Macc 2:42; 7:12–13) but the Hasidim are not otherwise known to have had the range of cosmological interests attested in the books of *Enoch*.

A contemporary but distinct apocalyptic movement is attested in the book of Daniel. In Daniel 11–12 we read of wise teachers (*maskilim*) who instruct the many in a time of persecution and some of whom are martyred. Unlike the militant "lambs" of Enoch, these people appear to be quietists, who look to their heavenly patron Michael for victory. Some of their traditions are related to those of the Enoch literature (compare the visions of the divine throne in Daniel 7 and *1 Enoch* 14) but the two groups cannot be simply identified.

The book of Daniel has its own tradition history, which is reflected in the tales in Daniel 1–6. Here again there is reason to suspect that the early stages of the tradition were formed in the eastern Diaspora, although the apocalyptic visions of chaps. 7–12 were certainly composed in Palestine.

F. Qumran

The Qumran community presents a special set of problems for the study of Jewish apocalypticism. The Qumran library included multiple copies of the apocalypses of Daniel and Enoch. It also included some fragmentary works which are possibly apocalypses (4Qᶜ Amram, *The New Jerusalem*) and some eschatological revelations related to Daniel, which contain the four-kingdom motif (4QPsDan ar, and an unpublished vision of four talking trees, Garcia-Martínez 1987: 206–7). On the other hand, none of the major works of the sect is in the form of an apocalypse, and it is not clear that any apocalypse was composed at Qumran (Stegemann 1983: 495–530). Nonetheless, Qumran has often been described as an apocalyptic community, and with justification (Collins 1990). The *Community Rule* (1QS), the most authoritative description of the community we have, contains a treatise on the two spirits, which is thoroughly apocalyptic in its world view: human life is ruled by the warring spirits of light and darkness, but in the end God will intervene and reward the children of light with life without end (1QS 3–4). The *Damascus Document* (CD), which legislates for a wider community, alludes to this cosmic dualism (CD 5:18) although it does not expound it in the manner of 1QS, and it anticipates the destruction of the wicked by the hand of the angels of destruction (CD 2:6). The *War Scroll* (1QM) provides the rule for the eschatological war of the sons of light against the sons of darkness, in which the heavenly host mingles with the human combatants, and Michael is finally exalted over Belial. The sectarians believed they were living in the age of wrath, the last age, when the final battle was imminent (CD 1:5; 1QH 3:28). Other documents reflect the community's interest in the heavenly world. The *Hōdāyôt* express the belief that the members of the community were already in fellowship with the angelic council (1QH 3:19–22), and the *Songs of the Sabbath Sacrifice* describe the divine praises uttered by the various classes of angels. The fact that the community did not produce apocalypses may be due to the belief that the Teacher of Righteousness had become the medium of revelation for the community (1QpHab 7:4–5).

There is no doubt that the Qumran community was influenced by the world view expounded in the apocalypses of Daniel and Enoch. The precise relation of the community to those apocalyptic movements is unclear, however. CD 1 describes the emergence of "a plant root" in the "age of wrath." Many scholars have noted the similarity to the "chosen righteous from the eternal plant of righteousness" in the *Apocalypse of Weeks* (*1 Enoch* 93:10) and assumed that the Enoch movement was simply the early stage of the Essene sect, before the arrival of the Teacher of Righteousness or the settlement at Qumran, or that both texts refer to the formation of the Hasidim, who are then taken to be the percursors of the Essenes (see Nickelsburg 1983: 641–54). The Qumran sect shared with the Enoch group the 364-day calendar, and we know that a dispute over the calendar was an important factor in the formation of the sect. Nonetheless it is too simple to identify either the early Essenes or their precursors with the Enoch movement. We have seen reason to believe that the book of Daniel was the product of a different group than the Enoch literature. Yet it was no less influential at Qumran. Moreover, the halachic (legal and ritual) concerns which are so important at Qumran are not reflected at all in either *1 Enoch* or Daniel. We must resist the temptation to conflate all apocalyptic groups of the early 2d century into one movement. The Dead Sea sect was certainly influenced by the apocalypses, but it is best considered as a distinct movement.

The Qumran community provides the only instance in which we have substantial evidence about the social organization of an apocalyptic movement. In many respects it runs counter to the stereotypical ideas of such movements. It is rigidly hierarchical, legalistic, and preoccupied with questions of purity. We should not infer that all apocalyptic movements were organized in this way. The character of the Qumran community was shaped to a great degree by the priestly traditions of its members. An apocalyptic world view does not in itself imply a particular form of social organization.

G. Other Jewish Apocalyptic Movements

We are very poorly informed about Jewish apocalyptic movements apart from the Dead Sea sect, but it is salutary to remember that even the Qumran community was unknown half a century ago. The *Similitudes of Enoch* speak of "the community of the righteous" (*1 Enoch* 38:1) but tells us nothing about how that community was organized. We know of various movements in the 1st century C.E. which may have had an apocalyptic character. The preaching of John the Baptist evidently concerned "the wrath to come" but our information about his world view is very sketchy. Josephus writes of "deceivers and impostors, who under the pretense of divine inspiration fostering revolutionary changes, persuaded the multitude to act like madmen" (*JW* 2.13.4 § 258–60). Again, we do not know enough about these people to say whether their world view can properly be described as apocalyptic. At the end of the 1st century, *4 Ezra* and *2 Baruch* witness to a debate going on in some circles about the justice of God, which was conducted within an apocalyptic world view. Whether this debate implies any significant social movement, however, is an open question. In the Diaspora, the *Sibylline Oracles* attest a tradition which extended over more than 200 years. That tradition, in its earlier phase (Book 3), was closer to the this-worldly eschatology of the prophets than to apocalypticism but it developed strongly apocalyptic features in later books (especially Books 1–2 and 4, see SIBYLLINE ORACLES).

H. Function of Apocalypticism

It is apparent from this brief sketch that our knowledge of the social settings of Jewish apocalypticism is quite limited. This limitation cannot be overcome by adopting ideal models from cultural anthropology and deducing social settings from them, but only by the discovery of new information about the actual historical circumstances of ancient Judaism. It should be apparent, however, that those settings are diverse.

It has been generally assumed that apocalypticism arises from the experience of alienation, or in times of crisis (e.g., Hanson 1987: 75). This assumption is defensible if we grant that alienation, and crises, may be of many kinds. Apocalypticism can provide support in the face of persecution (Daniel), reassurance in the face of culture shock (the *Book of the Watchers*) or social powerlessness (the *Similitudes of Enoch*), reorientation in the face of national trauma (*2 Baruch, 3 Baruch*), consolation for the fate of humanity (*4 Ezra*). What is constant is not the kind of problem addressed but the manner in which it is addressed. In each case the apocalyptic revelation diverts the attention from the distressful present to the heavenly world and the eschatological future. This diversion should not be seen as a flight from reality. Rather it is a way of coping with reality by providing a meaningful framework within which human beings can make decisions and take action (compare the *maskilim* in Dan 11: 32–34).

Finally we should note that, just as apocalypticism cannot be identified with a single social movement, so it cannot be identified with a single strand of theology. To be sure, it involves some consistent assumptions about the way the world works, e.g., the inevitability of a final judgment. Within the framework provided by these assumptions, however, there is room for diversity of theological traditions. There is a great difference between the priestly legalism of Qumran and the sapiential traditions which inform *4 Ezra* and *2 Baruch,* which are closer to the mindset of the rabbinical schools. It could also be adapted to a radical departure from traditional Judaism in the rise of Christianity.

Bibliography

Bousset, W. 1966. *Die Religion des Judentums im Späthellenistischen Zeitalter.* Ed. H. Gressmann. 4th ed. Tübingen.

Collins, J. J. 1977. *The Apocalyptic Vision of the Book of Daniel.* HSM 16. Missoula.

———. 1979. *Apocalypse. The Morphology of a Genre. Semeia* 14. Missoula.

———. 1984. *The Apocalyptic Imagination.* New York.

———. 1987. The Place of Apocalypticism in the Religion of Israel. Pp. 539–58 in *AIR*.

———. 1990. Was the Dead Sea Sect an Apocalyptic Movement? In *Archaeology and History in the Dead Sea Scrolls,* ed. L. H. Schiffman. Sheffield.

Eddy, S. K. 1961. *The King Is Dead.* Lincoln, NE.

Flusser, D. 1982. John of Patmos and Hystapses. Pp. 12–75 in *Irano Judaica,* ed. S. Shaked. Jerusalem.

Garcia-Martínez, F. 1987. Les Traditions apocalyptiques à Qumran. Pp. 201–35 in *Apocalypses et voyages dans l'Au-Delà,* ed. C. Kappler. Paris.

Gignoux, P. 1987. Apocalypses et voyages extra-terrestres dans l'Iran Mazdéen. Pp. 351–74 in *Apocalypses et voyages dans l'Au-Delà,* ed. C. Kappler. Paris.

Grayson, A. K. 1975. *Babylonian Historical-Literary Texts.* Toronto.

Griffiths, J. G. 1983. Apocalyptic in the Hellenistic Era. Pp. 273–94 in Hellholm, 1983.

Gruenwald, I. 1980. *Apocalyptic and Merkavah Mysticism.* Leiden.

Hanson, P.D. 1975. *The Dawn of Apocalyptic.* Philadelphia.

———. 1987. *Old Testament Apocalyptic.* Nashville.

Hellholm, D., ed. 1983. *Apocalypticism in the Mediterranean World and the Near East.* Tübingen.

Koch, K. 1972. *The Rediscovery of Apocalyptic.* Naperville.

Kvanvig, H. 1987. *Roots of Apocalyptic.* Neukirchen-Vluyn.

Lambert, W. G. 1978. *The Background of Jewish Apocalyptic.* London.

Milik, J. T. 1976. *The Books of Enoch.* Oxford.

Mullen, E. T., Jr. 1980. *The Assembly of the Gods.* HSM 24. Chico.

Müller, H.-P. 1972. *Mantische Weisheit und Apokalyptik.* VTSup 22. Leiden.

Nickelsburg, G. W. 1977. Apocalyptic and Myth in 1 Enoch 6–11. *JBL* 96: 386–405.

———. 1983. Social Aspects of Palestinian Jewish Apocalypticism. Pp. 639–52 in Hellholm, 1983.

Rowland, C. 1982. *The Open Heaven. A Study of Apocalyptic in Judaism and Christianity.* New York.

Sacchi, P. 1982. Ordine cosmico e prospettiva ultraterrena nel postesilio. Il Problema del male e l'origine dell apocalittica. *RivB* 30: 11–33.

Smith, M. 1983. On the History of Apokalypto and Apokalypsis. Pp. 9–20 in Hellholm, 1983.

Stegemann, H. 1983. Die Bedeutung der Qumranfunde für die Erforschung der Apokalyptik. Pp. 495–530 in Hellholm, 1983.

Stone, M. E. 1980. *Scriptures, Sects and Visions.* Philadelphia.

———. 1984. Apocalyptic Literature. Pp. 383–441 in *Jewish Writings of the Second Temple Period,* ed. M. E. Stone. Philadelphia.

VanderKam, J. 1984. *Enoch and the Growth of an Apocalyptic Tradition.* CBQMS 16. Washington, D.C.

Widengren, G. 1983. Leitende Ideen und Quellen der iranischen Apokalyptik. Pp. 77–162 in Hellholm, 1983.

Yarbro Collins, A., ed. 1986. *Early Christian Apocalypticism. Semeia* 36. Chico.

JOHN J. COLLINS

EARLY CHRISTIAN

A. The Milieu of Jesus

As is now generally accepted, Judaism in the time of Jesus was diverse (Nickelsburg and Stone 1983: 1). Although Jesus lived between the two main periods during which most of the Palestinian Jewish apocalypses were composed (the 3d–2d centuries B.C.E. and the late 1st century C.E.), there is evidence that the apocalyptic world view was widespread in Palestine during his time and that this world view was frequently linked to political issues. As was noted above, the community at Qumran had copies of Daniel and apocalypses attributed to Enoch. Even if they did not compose apocalypses themselves, their major works expressed an apocalyptic world view. Their expectations of the future included an eschatological battle in which foreign rulers (the Romans in the later documents) and their Jewish collaborators would be defeated. There is no evidence that Jesus had direct contact with the community at Qumran. Nevertheless, the fact that Philo and Josephus wrote descriptions of their way of life and beliefs shows that these were not unknown, even outside Palestine, assuming that the members of the community were ESSENES; (for the texts from Philo and Josephus in English translation, see Dupont-Sommer 1973: 21–36). The fact that at least some of the manuscripts of the *War Scroll* are in Herodian script shows that this document was very important from about 30 B.C.E. to about 70 C.E. (Cross 1961: 118, 120 n.20).

The *Assumption* or *Testament of Moses* is not an apocalypse but is closely related to the genre. This work was composed in the 2d century B.C.E. but was updated after the death of Herod in 4 B.C.E. (Collins 1979: 45). This work is especially important for the context of Jesus' teaching because it refers to God's kingdom in an apocalyptic context (*Testament of Moses* 10). That context includes vengeance on the enemies of Israel (vv 2, 7, 10). In the revised form of the work, the enemies were understood to be the Romans (Yarbro Collins 1976: 186).

It is likely that the occasion for the revision of the *Testament of Moses* was the unrest that followed the death of Herod the Great in 4 B.C.E. (Jos. *Ant* 17.9.1 § 206–17.12.2 § 338). This unrest included the activities of three messianic pretenders, Judas the Galilean, Simon, and Athronges (9.5 § 271–9.8 § 285). The *Testament of Moses,* however, has greater affinity with the earlier nonviolent protest of Judas and Matthias, the interpreters of the law, than with the activist royal pretenders (Yarbro Collins 1976: 186; see Horsley and Hanson 1985: 110–17).

When Archelaus was deposed and exiled, Judea, Samaria, and Idumea were annexed to the Roman province of Syria. Unrest broke out again in 6 C.E. when Quirinius, Octavian's legate, took a census of the property of the Jews. Judas the Galilean led the revolt (Jos. *Ant* 18.1.1 § 1–18.2.1 § 26; see Fitzmyer *Luke 1–9* AB, 393, 401–2). Besides this violent uprising, two further incidents of nonviolent resistance occurred. The first, in 26 C.E., involved opposition to Pilate's bringing Roman standards into Jerusalem, because of the images of the emperor (presumably Tiberius) on them (Jos. *Ant* 18.3.1 § 55–59; *JW* 2.9.2 § 169–2.9.3 § 174). The other centered on Gaius' command, in about 40 C.E., that his legate to Syria, Petronius, erect his statue in the temple (*Ant* 18.8.2 § 261–18.8.9 § 309; *JW* 2.10.1 § 184–2.10.5 § 203).

At some point during the reign of Tiberius, and probably during the time of Pontius Pilate was prefect of Judea, John the Baptist preached a message and performed a baptism of repentance (in addition to the gospels of the NT, see Jos. *Ant* 18.5.2 § 116–19). Josephus' account of John's message is very uneschatological, whereas the accounts of the gospels are thoroughly eschatological. The lack of eschatology in Josephus' picture is probably due to his well-known bias in that regard. It is likely that John announced the "wrath to come" (see the saying from Q, the Synoptic Sayings Source, preserved in Matt 3:7–10 = Luke 3:7–9). This "wrath to come" was probably an element of the apocalyptic eschatology shared by John and the fourth book of the *Sibylline Oracles* (see especially lines 152–74).

Besides the evidence for the prevalence of apocalyptic eschatology during the time of Jesus, it is probable that at least one apocalypse was written around that time in Palestine. The *Similitudes of Enoch,* preserved in *1 Enoch* 37–71, was apparently not part of the collection of Enoch books at Qumran. This lack allowed J. T. Milik to argue that the *Similitudes* is a Christian work of the 3d century (1976: 89–98). His argument has not won support, however, and most specialists date the work between the reign of Herod the Great and the destruction of the temple in 70 C.E. (Yarbro Collins 1987: 404–5). Since the latest historical allusions relate to the Parthian invasion of Palestine in 40 B.C.E. and Herod's treatment in the warm springs of Callirrhoe, the usual methods of dating lead to a date around the turn of the era (Collins: 1979: 39; cf. 1984: 143).

The apocalyptic texts mentioned in this section, especially Daniel, had an influence on the people living in Jesus' time and no doubt on Jesus himself. The political unrest following Herod's death was still vivid for those who had experienced it, and they probably spoke of it now and then to their children. The tensions that gave rise to that unrest were not far beneath the surface and, at least in some circles, were linked to apocalyptic eschatology.

B. Jesus

During most of the 19th century, Jesus was viewed primarily as a teacher and social reformer (Schweitzer 1968). In 1892, Johannes Weiss published a study that led to the rediscovery of the apocalyptic aspect of the teaching of Jesus. Much of the work of biblical scholars and theologians in the first half of the 20th century centered on the task of assimilating this discovery and its consequences. A certain shift occurred in 1960 when Ernst Käsemann declared that, although Jesus made the apocalyptically determined message of John his point of departure, his own preaching was not fundamentally apocalyptic but proclaimed God as near at hand. Käsemann was "convinced that no one who took this step can have been prepared to wait for the coming Son of Man, the restoration of the Twelve Tribes in the Messianic kingdom and the dawning of the Parousia . . ." (1969: 101). The positions of Philip Vielhauer (1965: 87–91) and Norman Perrin (1967: 154–206) are similar.

In recent work on the historical Jesus, his life and teaching have been placed in the context of Jewish restoration eschatology (Sanders 1985). Events of Jesus' life that make this reconstruction credible are his baptism by John; his choosing twelve disciples to have a special role, presumably a role symbolic of the renewal of the twelve tribes of Israel; his carrying out a prophetic symbolic action in the temple that probably foretold its destruction and renewal; and his execution by the Romans for sedition. Jesus' proclamation of the kingdom of God and the miracles attributed to him can and ought to be interpreted in the context suggested by the major features of his life, namely Jewish restoration eschatology.

If Jesus' teaching about the eschatological restoration included the activity of the heavenly "son of man" foretold in Daniel 7, it would be appropriate to speak of his teaching as apocalyptic. Scholars are divided on this issue. Some argue that the Son of Man sayings were composed by Jesus' followers after the appearances to them of Jesus as the risen Lord (e.g., Vielhauer 1965; Perrin 1974: 10–93). Others argue that Jesus spoke of a heavenly Son of Man but did not identify himself with that figure (e.g., Bultmann 1968: 112, 122, 128, 151–52; Yarbro Collins 1987). Others argue that Jesus not only spoke of a Son of Man but identified himself with that heavenly being (e.g., Caragounis 1986: 174–75).

An argument in favor of Jesus' having an apocalyptic orientation is that the movement with which he associated himself (that of John the Baptist) seems to have been apocalyptic and the movement that commenced among his followers very shortly after his death, the earliest Christian community in Jerusalem, also seems to have been apocalyptic (Perrin and Duling 1982: 71–79; Käsemann 1969: 102). It is more credible historically that Jesus' life and teaching stood in continuity with these movements rather than in discontinuity.

C. The Synoptic Tradition

The synoptic tradition is a diverse body of oral and written materials centering on the life and teaching of Jesus that circulated in Christian circles in the first two centuries C.E. It is known primarily from the Synoptic Gospels, Mark, Matthew, and Luke, but also from several early apocryphal gospels (Koester 1980: 112). As indicated above, there is a widespread consensus that the earliest Christian community was an apocalyptic community (see also *BTNT* 1: 37–42; Allison 1985; Sanders 1985: 91–95).

1. The Sayings Source. According to the explanation of synoptic relationships called the Two Source Theory, the authors of Matthew and Luke used two written sources, the gospel of Mark and the Synoptic Sayings source, often referred to as "Q" (from the German *Quelle,* meaning "source"). The latter does not survive independently but must be reconstructed by synoptic comparison. The soundest method of reconstruction is to include material found in Matthew and Luke but not in Mark, or in all three but in two forms in either Matthew or Luke (a Markan form and a Q form). Such a reconstruction suggests that Q contained a variety of smaller literary forms, including brief narratives, such as the story of Satan's testing Jesus, wisdom sayings, pronouncement stories, and prophetic and apocalyptic sayings. It is likely that Q concluded with an apocalyptic or eschatological discourse (Kümmel 1975: 66, Perrin and Duling 1982: 102).

As reconstructed from Matthew and Luke, the Sayings Source is heavily influenced by apocalyptic eschatology. Most often its apocalyptic hope is expressed in sayings about the return of Jesus from heaven as the Son of Man, e.g., Luke 12:40 = Matt 24:44. His coming was expected to be like lightning or the primordial flood (Luke 17:24 = Matt 24:27; Luke 17:26 = Matt 24:37). The social setting of this apocalyptic material was an environment of persecution by "this generation," leaders in Jerusalem, and Pharisaic leaders (Perrin and Duling 1982: 103–7).

Recently, John Kloppenborg has argued that the apocalyptic form of Q is secondary and that, in its original form, the Sayings Source was a nonapocalyptic wisdom document, belonging to the genre "instruction" (Kloppenborg 1987a). Kloppenborg has certainly advanced the discussion of the genre of Q, but his argument regarding an early nonapocalyptic form is problematic because of its differentiation of source and redaction along "pure" formal lines (Yarbro Collins, forthcoming a and b). Kloppenborg has also argued that the Sayings Source, even in its latest recoverable form, is not apocalyptic because "it does not fully share the situation of anomie which impels apocalypticism towards its vision of a transformed future" (1987b). This argument is not compelling because it uses a single hypothetical characteristic of apocalypticism to determine whether a work is apocalyptic or not.

2. Mark. With Mark the gospel tradition reaches its apocalyptic peak. Its genre has been seen as parabolic (Kelber 1983: 117–29). Joel Marcus has pointed out the apocalyptic character of the parables in Mark (1986: 62–65, 229–33). According to Norman Perrin, the gospel of Mark presents "an apocalyptic drama" in three acts, involving the work of John the Baptist, the work of Jesus, and finally the mission of the disciples into the world (Perrin and Duling 1982: 238). Although in some ways the gospel of Mark resembles ancient biographies (Aune 1987: 46; Talbert 1988), its genre is better described as historiography in the apocalyptic mode (Yarbro Collins 1990: 148).

Mark begins with the words, "The beginning of the good news of Jesus the Messiah." The "good news" (gospel) here refers to the entire work and teaching of Jesus. Mark's account of this good news begins with a prophecy attributed to Isaiah (1:2–3) and the indication that this prophecy was fulfilled in the activity of John the Baptist (1:4). John himself then prophesies the coming of one mightier than he (1:7–8). This prophecy is fulfilled in the narrated arrival of Jesus to be baptized (1:9–11). Jesus later prophesies his own death and resurrection (8:31; 9:31; 10:32–34). The reader is led to understand the narration of the fulfillment of this prophecy as an apocalyptic-eschatological event in light of the two major discourses of Jesus, both of which are apocalyptic in character (chaps. 4 and 13; see Marcus 1986; Brandenburger 1984; Allison 1985: 26–39). The ending of Mark is open-ended (Kelber 1983: 129). It does not signify closure at the point of the failure of the male disciples of Jesus to stand by him at the cross or of the female disciples to announce the resurrection. Rather, it demands that the readers bring to mind the unnarrated portion of the story (Magness 1986: 114–17). The rest of the story includes the apocalyptic-eschatological events of the proclamation of the good news to all nations (13:10) and the revelation of the Son of Man (13:24–27).

3. Matthew and Luke. Besides preserving the apocalyptic material of Mark and adding that of Q, the gospel of Matthew has modified, in an apocalyptic direction, certain passages taken from Mark. For example, Matthew's parable chapter has become even more apocalyptic than Mark's with the addition of the parable of the weeds and its interpretation (13:24–30, 36–43). To Mark's account of the transfiguration, Matthew has added elements typical of apocalyptic visions (17: 2, 6–7). To the apocalyptic discourse, Matthew has added phrases like "the close of the age" (24:3), "the sign (of the Son of Man)" (v 30), and the reference to a loud trumpet call that will accompany the sending out of the angels to gather the elect (v 31). Likewise, the death and resurrection of Jesus are accompanied by apocalyptic signs not mentioned by Mark (27:51b–53; 28:2–4). The emphasis in Matthew is more on the aspect of fulfillment than on expectation of the conclusion of the apocalyptic scenario. This impression is given primarily by the theme of the presence of the risen Lord with the community (18:20; 28:20).

It is now generally agreed that Conzelmann overstated the degree to which the author of Luke-Acts departed from the world view of apocalyptic eschatology (see, e.g., Fitzmyer, *Luke* AB, 18–23, commenting on Conzelmann 1960 et al.). Nevertheless, a shift is evident from the expectation of an imminent revelation of the Son of Man to the concerns of the daily life as a Christian. This shift is evident in the use of apocalyptic traditions in ethical exhortation (Tannehill 1986: 243, 246–51).

D. Paul

It is widely agreed that Paul's world view was apocalyptic (Käsemann 1980; Beker 1980). Paul viewed the resurrection of Jesus as the beginning of the apocalyptic event of the general resurrection (1 Cor 15:12–20; cf. Dan 12:2–3). In his earliest letter, the focus is on the imminent return of the risen Lord and the union of Christians in fellowship with him, both the few Christians who have died and the majority expected to survive (1 Thess 4:13–18; cf. 1 Cor 15:51–52). In his later letters, Paul accepts the possibility that he will die before the return of Christ (Phil 1:19–26; cf. 2 Cor 5:1–10). Since the literary genre apocalypse and related texts expressing apocalyptic eschatology are not always characterized by imminent expectation, this shift in Paul's thought may not be used to argue that his later letters are not apocalyptic. The understanding of history expressed in Rom 8:18–25, for example, is apocalyptic. The primordial past is portrayed indirectly as a lost age of glory and freedom from decay (note the allusion to Gen 3:17 in v 20). The sufferings of the present time are the eschatological woes that precede the new age of glory and freedom that will begin with the general resurrection, the "redemption of our bodies" (v 23; cf. 1 Cor 15:20–28).

Besides the temporal apocalyptic dimension, Paul reflects interest in the spatial dimension of apocalyptic revelation (Segal 1986). His conversion or call is described as "a revelation of Jesus Christ" (Gal 1:12). In 2 Cor 12:1, he speaks of "visions and revelations of the Lord." By way of example, he speaks of a man who was caught up to the third heaven, to paradise, where he received secret revelations (vv 2–4). His remark that "a thorn was given me in the flesh" to keep him from being too elated by the abundance of revelations (v 7) implies that the "man" taken up to the third heaven was Paul himself. In 1 Corinthians 2, Paul speaks of "a secret and hidden wisdom of God, which God decreed before the ages for our glorification" (v 7). This combination of heavenly and eschatological revelation in Paul is comparable to what we find in the book of Daniel.

E. The Book of Revelation

The book of Revelation is the only apocalypse in the NT, and even it is a mixed genre, since the account of the revelation received by John is embedded in an epistolary framework (1:4–6; 22:21). Like the book of Daniel, Revelation brings heavenly mysteries to bear on a social crisis. In this case, the crisis is the tension between Roman ideology and Christian messianism (Yarbro Collins 1984; cf. Schüssler Fiorenza 1985). For a discussion of this work, see the article on REVELATION, BOOK OF.

F. The Apostolic Literature

Among the works conventionally called the "apostolic fathers" by modern scholars is one apocalypse, the *Shepherd of Hermas*. Internal evidence suggests that this work was composed by a Jewish Christian freedman in Rome. It was written, perhaps in stages, between about 90 and 150 C.E. (Osiek forthcoming in *NTApocr* 3). The work consists of three parts: visions, mandates, and similitudes. At least the part containing the visions is an apocalypse (Hellholm 1980), but it is appropriate to speak of the entire work as an apocalypse (Osiek 1986).

Heavenly revelation plays a major role in the work. In Visions I–II, a heavenly figure, an elderly lady, allows Hermas to copy the content of a heavenly book so that he can communicate it to the faithful. The mandates or commandments and the similitudes or parables, that constitute the bulk of the work, are presented as the revelation given to Hermas by a heavenly being in the dress of a shepherd (Visions V.1–5). The work also has a strong eschatological interest. The term *thlipsis* is used both for persecution and for the impending eschatological crisis (Vis II.ii.7–8, iii.4; III.vi.5; IV.i.1, ii.5, iii.6; cf. Sim

VIII.iii.6–7). Apparently the apocalyptic eschatology of this work included the transformation of the faithful to an angelic state after death (Vis II.ii.7).

Although the *Didache* is a church order in terms of genre, it expresses apocalyptic eschatology. This is especially apparent in the concluding chapter (16), a short apocalyptic discourse. This discourse is related to Mark 13 and parallels, especially to Matthew 24. *Didache* 16, however, does not follow that text closely, but seems to be largely independent, perhaps drawing on oral tradition. It shares with Matthew 24 the notion of a "sign" linked to the appearance of the Lord (Son of Man) on the clouds and the motif of a trumpet call. Its distinctive elements, relative to the synoptic apocalyptic discourse, are the fiery trial and the deceiver of the world. The latter is presented in terms reminiscent of the lawless one in 2 Thessalonians 2 (cf. Holland 1988).

G. The Gnostic Apocalypses

There is an emerging consensus that the religious philosophy called "Gnosis" (or Gnosticism, especially in its more developed forms) originated in the diverse matrix of Judaism in the late Hellenistic period (Rudolph 1983: 277). Thus, Gnosticism should no longer be described as a Christian heresy. In spite of the essential independence of Gnosticism from Christianity, the two movements came into contact early, perhaps already in Paul's time (Rudolph 1983: 300–2) and a gnostic form of Christianity emerged in the 2d century (Layton 1987: 20–21).

The literature produced by Christian gnostics included a number of apocalypses (Fallon 1979: 124). An early and classic example is the *Apocryphon* or *Secret Book of John* (Fallon 1979: 130–31; Layton 1987: 23–51). This work was composed in Greek (although it survives only in Coptic), probably in the 2d century C.E. The narrative framework involves Jesus' appearance after his resurrection to John the son of Zebedee on the Mount of Olives. In a dialogue between the two, the Savior reveals the nature of God as the source of all being, the structure of the divine world *(pleroma)* before creation, the story of creation (Genesis 1–4 retold from a gnostic perspective), and the secrets of salvation. John is commissioned to relate these mysteries to those who are like him in spirit. In the concluding narrative framework he communicates the revelation to his fellow disciples.

Several gnostic apocalypses include a heavenly journey (Fallon 1979: 136–39). One of these is the *Apocalypse of Paul* (preserved in Coptic and not to be confused with the Christian aprocyphal *Apocalypse of Paul* preserved primarily in Latin). The narrative framework involves an appearance of the Holy Spirit as a little child to Paul on a mountain near Jerusalem. The Spirit then takes Paul on a journey through the ten heavens (the longer, later version of *2 Enoch* also has a journey through ten heavens). In the seventh heaven is an "old man," probably the God of the Jewish Bible, who tries to prevent Paul from going beyond that heaven. Paul, however, with the help of the Spirit and a special sign, is able to ascend further. In the tenth heaven Paul meets his fellow spirits. The descent of Paul is not narrated and there is no concluding narrative framework.

H. The Christian Apocrypha

The *Apocalypse of Peter* (preserved in Greek fragments and in Ethiopic) is one of the oldest Christian apocryphal apocalypses. It was probably composed around 135 C.E., since the activity of the Jewish messianic claimant, Bar Kokhba is indirectly portrayed as the eschatological crisis. Like many of the gnostic apocalypses, its narrative setting seems to be after the resurrection of Jesus (Yarbro Collins 1979: 72–73). Jesus is the mediator of heavenly revelation, in this case, of the signs and events of the end and visions of the places of reward and punishment (Himmelfarb 1983: 8–11). Other Christian apocryphal apocalypses in which revelation is mediated through epiphanies, visions, and auditions include *Jacob's Ladder*, the *Book of Elchasai*, the *Apocalypse of St. John the Theologian* (modeled on the canonical book of Revelation), the *Questions of Bartholomew*, the *Book of the Resurrection of Jesus Christ by Bartholomew the Apostle*, and parts of other works (Yarbro Collins 1979).

The oldest Christian apocryphal apocalypse of the heavenly journey type is the *Ascension of Isaiah*. This work is probably a composite made up of two originally independent works, a Martyrdom of Isaiah and a Vision or Ascent of Isaiah. The latter is the apocalypse and is contained in chaps. 6–11 (Yarbro Collins 1979: 84). Isaiah's journey is through the seven heavens and involves revelation of the different kinds of angels inhabiting each. The climax is a "prophecy" of the descent of "the Beloved" (Christ) through the seven heavens, his mission on earth, and his ascent back into the seventh heaven. In the present time it is the wicked angel Sammael and the angels of the firmament who determine events on earth. The strife on earth reflects the strife among the angels. Other Christian apocryphal apocalypses of the journey type include the Latin *Apocalypse of Paul*, the Greek *Apocalypse of Ezra*, the Ethiopic *Apocalypse of the Virgin Mary*, the *Story of Zosimus*, the Greek *Apocalypse of the Holy Mother of God*, a Coptic *Apocalypse of James* unrelated to the two discovered at Nag Hammadi, a Coptic work entitled *The Mysteries of St. John the Apostle and Holy Virgin*, the Greek *Apocalypse of Sedrach*, and parts of other works (Yarbro Collins 1979). Many of these works are concerned with punishments (Himmelfarb 1983) and rewards after death. They are important for many reasons, one of which is that they formed the raw material for Dante's *Divine Comedy*. On apocalypticism in the Middle Ages, see McGinn (1979).

Bibliography

Allison, D. C. 1985. *The End of the Ages Has Come.* Philadelphia.

Aune, D. E. 1987. *The New Testament in Its Literary Environment.* Philadelphia.

Beker, J. C. 1980. *Paul the Apostle: The Triumph of God in Life and Thought.* Philadelphia.

Brandenburger, E. 1984. *Markus 13 und die Apokalyptik.* Göttingen.

Bultmann, R. 1968. *The History of the Synoptic Tradition.* New York.

Caragounis, C. C. 1986. *The Son of Man: Vision and Interpretation.* Tübingen.

Collins, J. J. 1979. The Jewish Apocalypses. *Semeia* 14: 21–59.

———. 1984. *The Apocalyptic Imagination.* New York.

Conzelmann, H. 1960. *The Theology of St. Luke.* New York.

Cross, F. M. 1961. *The Ancient Library of Qumran and Modern Biblical Studies.* Rev. ed. Garden City, NY.

Dupont-Sommer, A. 1973. *The Essene Writings from Qumran.* Gloucester, MA.
Fallon, F. T. 1979. The Gnostic Apocalypses. *Semeia* 14: 123–58.
Hellholm, D. 1980. *Das Visionenbuch des Hermas als Apocalypse.* Vol. 1. Lund.
Himmelfarb, M. 1983. *Tours of Hell: An Apocalyptic Form in Jewish and Christian Literature.* Philadelphia.
Holland, G. S. 1988. *The Tradition That You Received from Us: 2 Thessalonians in the Pauline Tradition.* Tübingen.
Horsley, R. A., and Hanson, J. S. 1985. *Bandits, Prophets and Messiahs.* Minneapolis.
Käsemann, E. 1969. The Beginnings of Christian Theology. *New Testament Questions of Today.* Philadelphia.
———. 1980. *Commentary on Romans.* Grand Rapids.
Kelber, W. H. 1983. *The Oral and the Written Gospel.* Philadelphia.
Kloppenberg, J. S. 1987a. *The Formation of Q.* Philadelphia.
———. 1987b. Symbolic Eschatology and the Apocalypticism of Q. *HTR* 80: 287–306.
Koester, H. 1980. Apocryphal and Canonical Gospels. *HTR* 73: 105–30.
Kümmel, W. G. 1975. *Introduction to the New Testament.* Rev. ed. Nashville.
Layton, B. 1987. *The Gnostic Scriptures.* Garden City, NY.
Mack, B. L. 1988. *A Myth of Innocence: Mark and Christian Origins.* Philadelphia.
Magness, J. L. 1986. *Sense and Absence: Structure and Suspension in the Ending of Mark's Gospel.* Atlanta.
Marcus, J. 1986. *The Mystery of the Kingdom of God.* Atlanta.
McGinn, B. 1979. *Visions of the End: Apocalyptic Traditions in the Middle Ages.* New York.
Milik, J. T. 1976. *The Books of Enoch.* Oxford.
Nickelsburg, G. W. E., and Stone, M. E. 1983. *Faith and Piety in Early Judaism.* Philadelphia.
Osiek, C. 1986. The Genre and Function of the Shepherd of Hermas. *Semeia* 36: 113–21.
Perkins, P. 1980. *The Gnostic Dialogue: The Early Church and the Crisis of Gnosticism.* New York.
Perrin, N. 1967. *Rediscovering the Teaching of Jesus.* New York.
———. 1974. *A Modern Pilgrimage in New Testament Christology.* Philadelphia.
Perrin, N., and Duling, D. C. 1982. *The New Testament: An Introduction.* 2d ed. New York.
Rudolph, K. 1983. *Gnosis: The Nature and History of Gnosticism.* San Francisco.
Sanders, E. P. 1985. *Jesus and Judaism.* Philadelphia.
Schüssler Fiorenza, E. 1985. *The Book of Revelation.* Philadelphia.
Schweitzer, A. 1968. *The Quest of the Historical Jesus.* New York.
Segal, A. F. 1986. Paul and Ecstasy. Pp. 555–80 in *SBLSP.* Atlanta.
Talbert, C. H. 1988. Once Again: Gospel Genre. *Semeia* 43: 53–73.
Tannehill, R. C. 1986. *The Narrative Unity of Luke-Acts.* Vol. 1. Philadelphia.
Vielhauer, P. 1965. *Gottesreich und Menschensohn in der Verkündigung Jesu.* Aufsätze zum Neuen Testament. Munich.
Weiss, J. 1971. *Jesus' Proclamation of the Kingdom of God.* Philadelphia.
Yarbro Collins, A. 1976. Composition and Redaction in the Testament of Moses 10. *HTR* 69: 179–86.
———. 1979. The Early Christian Apocalypses. *Semeia* 14: 61–121.
———. 1984. *Crisis and Catharsis: The Power of the Apocalypse.* Philadelphia.
———. 1987. The Origin of the Designation of Jesus as Son of Man. *HTR* 80: 391–407.
———. 1990. Narrative, History and Gospel: A General Response. *Semeia* 43: 145–53.
———. fc.a. The Son of Man Sayings in the Sayings Source. *To Touch the Text.* New York.
———. fc.b. Review of Kloppenborg 1987a. *JBL.*

ADELA YARBRO COLLINS

APOCRYPHA.

APOCRYPHA. The Greek noun *apokrypha* means "hidden." It is used to denote writings on the fringes of the canon of the OT and NT. See also the CANON articles.

OLD TESTAMENT APOCRYPHA

The term "Old Testament Apocrypha" signifies numerous Jewish religious writings that date from approximately 300 B.C.E. to 70 C.E.

Today "apocrypha" does not refer to "hidden" secrets, as in Dan 12:9–10 and *4 Ezra* 14:44–48. According to a wide consensus, and to the definition of PSEUDEPIGRAPHA as an open literary category, the OT Apocrypha should be defined as a closed and focused collection. This ancient literary collection, therefore, contains 13 works found in the old Greek codices of the OT—namely Codex Vaticanus, Codex Sinaiticus, and Codex Alexandrinus—but not in the *Biblia Hebraica* or OT.

All were written in a Semitic language and in Palestine, except for the Wisdom of Solomon and 2 Maccabees, which were composed in Greek, probably in Alexandria. All are preserved in Greek, in one or more of the Greek uncials already mentioned, and sometimes also in other languages.

Many Jews by the 2d century B.C.E. contended that prophecy lasted only from Moses to Ezra (see Josephus, *AgAp* 1; *4 Ezra* 14; *B. Bat.* 14b–15c). The Apocrypha were composed long after Ezra and were thus attributed to biblical heroes, like Jeremiah, Baruch, and Solomon, who antedated Ezra, were internal expansions to Esther or Daniel, or were "histories" of the successes or excesses of the Maccabees.

These Jewish documents were considered authoritative and inspired by many early Jews. They were not used, however, by Alexandrian Jews to fill out the canon in contrast to a Palestinian canon. While different Jewish groups, especially the Essenes and the Samaritans, had expanded or contracted collections of sacred writings, there were not two Jewish canons in prerabbinic Judaism. Philo of Alexandria did not use the Apocrypha as authoritative scripture. He quoted especially the Torah. Today Jews do not consider the Apocrypha canonical; their canon is the *Biblia Hebraica,* which is completed by the Mishna, Tosephta, and the two Talmuds.

The early Greek codices of the Bible are Christian collections; they contain not only the OT but also the NT, the Apocrypha, sometimes one or more of the Pseudepigrapha, and even additional Christian compositions. Hence, the inclusion of the Apocrypha into a canon may well be a Christian innovation.

In the 4th century C.E. Jerome was dissatisfied with the Old Latin version of the OT. He translated the canonical books from Hebrew into Latin, and produced the Vulgate, which is still authoritative in Roman Catholicism. Since he worked from the Hebrew and not the Greek version of the OT, he limited his Vulgate to the Hebrew canon. He considered the additional documents in the Greek canon of scripture to be "apocryphal." Later the Western church added to the Vulgate the Apocrypha, probably using the Old Latin version. In reaction to the Protestant Reformation and Luther's relegation of the Apocrypha, the Roman Catholic Church, on April 8, 1546, at the Council of Trent, declared the Apocrypha to be part of the Christian canon. Hence, today Roman Catholics contend these works are "Deuterocanonical" and inspired.

In the 16th century, Luther and the early Protestants rejected as canonical the additional books in the canon. They were antipathetic to apocalyptic thought, and had a distorted view of 2 Maccabees, because 12:43–45 had been used to support the Roman Catholic idea of purgatory, and of Tobit and other works in the Apocrypha, because they had been used to prove the doctrine of works righteousness. Luther placed the apocryphal works at the end of his translation of the OT and labeled them "Apocrypha." Protestants today do not consider the Apocrypha canonical, even though some books, especially Ben Sira, are often considered authoritative and even inspired.

The *Epistle of Jeremiah* was written well before 100 B.C.E. Confirmation of this date is now evident, because a Greek fragment was found in Qumran Cave VII that dates from circa 100 B.C.E. The original was composed sometime around 300 B.C.E. Containing only 72 or 73 verses, the work, influenced by Jeremiah 10:1–16, is an exhortation not to fear or worship idols.

Tobit was probably composed around 180 B.C.E. It is a romantic story instructing, among other values, that God does indeed help those faithful to his laws. The *dramatis personae* are Tobit, a righteous exile in Nineveh; Anna, his wife; Tobias, his son; Sarah, a bride who loses seven bridegrooms in succession; Asmodeus, a demon who successively slays Sarah's bridegrooms on their wedding nights; and Raphael, the angel who defeats the demon.

Judith, composed around 150 B.C.E., is a story about how the heroine Judith defeats and beheads Holofernes, the Assyrian general, and delivers her nation. The author intended to exhort Jews to reject evil, especially when it is represented by an invading enemy, and to be obedient to Torah. One of the most startling features of *Judith* is that the author had Judith pray to God to help her to lie.

3 Ezra (also named 1 Esdras and even III Esdras), was written sometime between 150 and 100 B.C.E. It is a conserted attempt to rewrite 2 Chr 35:1–36:23, Ezra, and Nehemiah 7:38–8:12. 3 Ezra 3:1–5:6 is independent of the OT. Tendencies in the book are the elevation of Ezra as "high priest," the celebration of the Temple, and the preoccupation with Zerubabel.

Additions to Esther are six expansions to Esther in its Greek form: Mordecai's dream, Artaxerxes' letter which orders the Jews to be exterminated, prayers by Mordecai and Esther, Esther's successful audience before King Artaxerxes, the king's second letter which praises the Jews, and the interpretation of Mordecai's dream. The date for these additions is clearly pre-70 C.E., but they may have been added to Esther in different years from 167 to 114 B.C.E., or sometime in the 1st century B.C.E. The authors of these additions added color to the story, provided an apology for Judaism, and—most importantly—supplied God's name, the theological words, and ideas conspicuously absent in Esther. For example, salvation now comes not as a result of Esther's courage but because of her piety.

The Prayer of Azariah and the Song of the Three Young Men, Susanna, and *Bel and the Dragon* are three documents added to Daniel and date between 165 and ca. 100 B.C.E. *The Prayer of Azariah* turns the reader's attention to the Jews facing martyrdom and away from the wicked king. It stresses that there is only one God and that he is just.

Susanna is an attractive tale about a desirable and virtuous woman who is charged by two elders because she refuses to have sex with them. She is rescued by Daniel, who cross-examines them and reveals that they are lying.

Bel and the Dragon preserves two stories. One describes how Daniel proves that the priests, not the idol Bel, eat the food presented to it. The other tells how Daniel destroys an idol but is saved by Habakkuk, who is aided by angels.

1 Baruch dates from the 1st or 2d centuries B.C.E., and is composite. It opens with an acknowledgment that Jerusalem was destroyed because of Israel's sins and with a plea for God's forgiveness. It then moves through a poetic celebration of wisdom, to a description of how the lament from Jerusalem was heard.

Ben Sira (Sirach or Ecclesiasticus) was probably composed around 180 B.C.E. by a conservative teacher in Jerusalem. It is an apology for Judaism and a critique of Greek culture. Typical themes are the reverence for the Temple, the Torah, and the belief in one God who is just and merciful. A Heb mss of *Ben Sira* was found at Masada.

The *Wisdom of Solomon,* perhaps written in the 1st century B.C.E., is a blend of Jewish wisdom traditions with Greek and Egyptian ideas. Wisdom is clearly personified.

1 Maccabees, composed near the end of the 2d century B.C.E., celebrates the military exploits of the Maccabees up to the rule of John Hyrcanus. The author is pro-Hasmonean, but does not articulate the importance or value of martyrdom. This document is a major source for studying the history of 2d-century Palestine.

2 Maccabees, written in the latter part of the 2d century or the early decades of the 1st century B.C.E., is an epitome of the lost five-volume history by Jason of Cyrene. Much more theologically oriented than 1 Maccabees, 2 Maccabees stresses the resurrection of the body, the efficaciousness of martyrdom, and the revelatory dimension of miracles. It is anti-Hasmonean. Two letters introduce the Epitome. The first is probably authentic, was composed around 124 B.C.E. in a Semitic language, and is an appeal to celebrate Hanukkah. The second letter is probably inauthentic, dates between 103 and 60 B.C.E., and may have been composed in Greek.

Formerly *4 Ezra* (also called II Esdras and even the Apocalypse of Ezra) and the *Prayer of Manasseh* were considered a part of the OT Apocrypha. However, they are not found in the oldest Greek codices of the LXX, are pseudepigraphical, are not found in many collections of the Apocrypha, and are now frequently and rightly considered among the books in the OT Pseudepigrapha.

For additional information, consult the entries on each of the documents mentioned above. For texts, see *APOT* and *APAT.* See also JSHRZ and *HJP*^{2} 3/2.

Bibliography

Anderson, G. W. 1970. Canonical and Non-Canonical. In *CHB* 1:113–59.

Collins, J. J. 1981. *Daniel, 1–2 Maccabees.* OTM 16. Wilmington, DE.

Goodspeed, E. J. 1939. *The Story of the Apocrypha.* Chicago.

Metzger, B. M. 1957. *An Introduction to the Apocrypha.* New York.

Nickelsburg, G. W. E. 1981. *Jewish Literature Between the Bible and the Mishnah.* Philadelphia.

Oesterley, W. O. E. 1935. *An Introduction to the Books of the Apocrypha.* New York.

Pfeiffer, R. H. 1949. *History of NT Times with an Introduction to the Apocrypha.* New York.

Stone, M. E., ed. 1984. *Jewish Writings of the Second Temple Period.* CRINT 2.2. Assen and Philadelphia.

JAMES H. CHARLESWORTH

NEW TESTAMENT APOCRYPHA

Although there are problems with the definition (see below), the term "New Testament Apocrypha" has generally come to refer to various early Christian writings that are not included in the canonical NT.

A. The Problem of Definition

In general, the term "New Testament Apocrypha" has come to refer to that corpus of early Christian literature that shares with the writings of the NT proper—with respect either to form and content, or to similar claims to apostolic derivation—a common self-consciousness in laying claim to the authority that derives from the age of Christian origins. Like the books of the NT, the apocryphal NT writings derive from various early Christian communities and from various time periods. But unlike the books that have come down to us as the "canonical NT," the apocryphal writings generally did not achieve the level of widespread ecclesiastical use that would have prompted their inclusion in most of the early Christian canonical lists.

When one attempts to go beyond a definition of this general sort, one inevitably encounters difficulty. For example, if one follows the natural inclination to develop a definition of "apocrypha" based upon the use of its cognate Greek and Latin terms by early Christian authorities, the inconsistency with which the word is applied to various works inevitably poses a problem. The dilemma is illustrated by the disparate uses of the term in the latter part of the 2d century and the beginning of the 3d. On one hand, Clement of Alexandria can use "apocryphal" in quite a literal sense to refer to certain "secret" books said to be in the possession of followers of the heretic Prodicus (*Strom.* 1.15.69.9). The books in question, incidentally, have little to do with the NT at all but are of Persian origin, and thus fall outside of what most scholars today would choose to treat as NT Apocrypha. On the other hand, Tertullian seems to use the term without regard for its literal meaning "secret." For him it has become simply a term of disparagement, since he uses it in tandem with the adjective *falsa* to indicate his low opinion of the *Shepherd of Hermas* (*De pud.* 10.6). And again, it is instructive to note that the term is applied to a book which few today would treat under the rubric of NT Apocrypha, assigning it instead to that special (though similarly ill-defined) category of early Christian literature known as the "Apostolic Fathers." Finally, one finds the term employed by Irenaeus to refer to certain writings of the Marcosians, who have as their intent, as he puts it, the "perversion" of scripture (*Adv. haer.*, 1.20 [xiii], 1), as though the books in question were simply heretical adaptations of writings Irenaeus regards as having scriptural authority. Though the Secret Gospel of Mark provides at least one example where this was in fact the case (Koester 1980a), Irenaeus' use of the term here would not apply to most of the books modern students would consider to fall within the category "NT Apocrypha."

Scholars have not shown any greater degree of unanimity in defining just what is meant by the term "NT Apocrypha." The use of "apocrypha" generally to denote early Christian works not found in the canonical NT occurs already in the title of Michael Neander's 16th century collection of apocryphal NT writings: *Apocrypha: hoc est, narrationes de Christo, Maria, Joseph, cognatione et familia Christi, extra Biblia.* It is doubtful that this usage bears any direct relationship to ancient uses of the word "apocrypha," but derives instead analogically from the Protestant reformers' use of "Apocrypha" to refer to those OT writings accepted as canonical by the Council of Trent, but rejected by Luther as "not held equal to the sacred scriptures," and thus relegated to an appendix in his landmark German translation of the Bible.

But in this century, prominent scholars have pressed for a definition of NT Apocrypha which goes beyond the simple meaning "extrabiblical," or "noncanonical." In his learned volume on the *Apocryphal New Testament,* M. R. James used the term "apocryphal" primarily in its common, or popular, sense of connoting "false or spurious" (p. xiv), thus implying that the chief characteristic separating this material from the NT proper is the fact that it, unlike the canonical writings, does not derive from the apostolic hands to which it lays claim. However, today, when most critical NT scholarship entertains similar doubts about roughly two thirds of the canonical NT itself, such a definition clearly will not suffice. Wilhelm Schneemelcher also sought a definition in history, calling apocryphal those books which "from the point of view of Form Criticism further develop and mould the kinds of style created and received in the New Testament . . . , which are distinguished by the fact not merely that they did not come into the New Testament but also that they were intended to take the place of the four Gospels of the canon (this holds good for the earlier texts) or to stand as enlargement of them side by side with them." (*NTApocr* 1:27–28). But as Koester (1980a) has pointed out, this sort of stratifying approach, which regards the corpus of canonical writings as necessarily early, and all of the apocryphal literature as part of a late, secondary effort to continue that which the NT had already started, is not supported by the MSS evidence, and may reflect more our own canonical predispositions than the literary histories of the books themselves. At the very least, such a definition could only be applied with great difficulty to a work such as the *Gospel of Thomas,* which is certainly not modeled upon any NT writing (and possibly predates many of them), a problem Schneemelcher himself could already foresee (*NTApocr* 1:60–64).

B. The Range of NT Apocryphal Literature

Most recent collections have chosen to organize and present the corpus of NT apocryphal literature in terms of the four genres represented in the NT itself: gospels, acts, letters, and apocalypses. This, of course, presupposes the sort of definition proffered by Schneemelcher, in which apocryphal works are regarded primarily as secondary attempts to supplant various NT writings. If one can no longer accept this view of apocryphal literature, it serves no useful purpose to retain these categories, especially since the parameters suggested by them, if taken seriously, would exclude from consideration many important early Christian apocryphal works. Schneemelcher himself was already testing the limits of these parameters by including in his collection such works as the *Books of Jeu* or *Thomas the Contender* under the rubric of "gospels." These two works are but a few droplets of the great flood of new material that has recently come onto the field owing largely to the discovery in 1945 of a hoard of Coptic gnostic texts at Nag Hammadi in upper Egypt. As the publication and study of these new documents proceeds, the range of types and genres of literature to be considered under the heading of NT Apocrypha will have to be expanded greatly. It clearly will no longer suffice to organize all of NT apocryphal literature into the four traditional categories represented in the canonical NT. The categories of material indicated in the following list of apocryphal works is suggestive of the great variety of NT apocryphal literature written and used by early Christians (see also related entries in the ABD).

New Testament Apocrypha

1. Gospels and Related Forms
   a. *Narrative Gospels*
      - *The Gospel of the Ebionites*
      - *The Gospel of the Hebrews*
      - *The Gospel of the Nazoreans*
      - *The Gospel of Nicodemus (The Acts of Pilate)*
      - *The Gospel of Peter*
      - *The Infancy Gospel of Thomas*
      - P. Egerton 2 (a fragment of an unknown narrative gospel)
      - P. Oxy. 840 (a fragment of an unknown narrative gospel)
      - *The Protevangelium of James*

   b. *Revelation Dialogues and Discourses*
      - *The (First) Apocalypse of James* (NHC V)
      - *The (Second) Apocalypse of James* (NHC V)
      - *The Apocryphon of James* (NHC I) (a revelation discourse cast in an epistolary framework)
      - *The Apocryphon of John* (NHC II, III, IV, and BG 8502)
      - *The Book of Thomas the Contender* (NHC II)
      - *The Dialogue of the Savior* (NHC III)
      - The *Epistula Apostolorum* (a revelation discourse cast in an epistolary framework)
      - *The Gospel of the Egyptians* (distinct from the Coptic Gospel of the Egyptians—cf. below under Treatises)
      - *The Gospel of Mary* (BG 8502)
      - *The Gospel of Philip* (NHC II)
      - *The Letter of Peter to Philip* (NHC VIII) (a revelation discourse cast in an epistolary framework)
      - *Pistis Sophia*
      - *The Questions of Mary*
      - *The Questions of Bartholomew*
      - *The Second Treatise of the Great Seth* (NHC VII)
      - *The Sophia of Jesus Christ* (NHC III and BG 8502)
      - The Two *Books of Jeu*
      - Bodlian Copt. MS d54 (a fragmentary dialogue between Jesus and John)

   c. *Sayings Gospels and Collections*
      - *The Gospel of Thomas* (NHC II)
      - The Synoptic Sayings Source (Q)
      - *The Teachings of Silvanus* (NHC VII)

2. Treatises
   - *On the Origin of the World* (NHC II)
   - *The (Coptic) Gospel of the Egyptians* (NHC III and IV)
   - *The Gospel of Truth* (NHC I and XII)
   - *The Hypostasis of the Archons* (NHC II)
   - *The Treatise on Resurrection* (NHC I) (a treatise cast in epistolary form)
   - *The Tripartite Tractate* (NHC I)

3. Apocalypses
   - *The (Coptic) Apocalypse of Elijah*
   - *The (Arabic) Apocalypse of Peter*
   - *The (Coptic) Apocalypse of Peter* (NHC VII)
   - *The (Greek/Ethiopic) Apocalypse of Peter*
   - *The (Coptic) Apocalypse of Paul* (NHC V)
   - *The (Latin) Apocalypse of Paul*
   - *The Apocalypse of Sophonias*
   - *The Apocalypse of Thomas*
   - *The Ascension of Isaiah* (chap. 6–11)
   - *The Christian Sibyllines*
   - *The Concept of Our Great Power* (NHC VI)
   - *The Book of Elchasai*
   - *V* and *VI Ezra*
   - *Melchizidek* (NHC IX)
   - *The Mysteries of St. John the Apostle and the Holy Virgin*

4. Acts
   - *The Acts of Andrew*
   - *The Acts of Andrew and Matthias*
   - *The Acts of John*
   - *The Acts of Paul (and Thecla)*
   - *The (Coptic) Act of Peter* (BG 8502)
   - *The (Greek) Acts of Peter*
   - *The Acts of Peter and the Twelve* (NHC VI)
   - *The Acts of Philip*
   - *The Acts of Thomas*
   - *The Kerygmata Petrou*

5. Letters
   - *The Abgar Legend*
   - *The Correspondence between Paul and Seneca*

- *The Epistle of Pseudo-Titus*
- *Paul's Letter to the Laodiceans*

6. Liturgical Materials
   a. *Homilies*
      - *The Interpretation of Knowledge* (NHC XI)
      - *The Kerygma of Peter*
      - *The Testimony of Truth* (NHC IX)
      - *A Valentinian Exposition* (NHC XI)
   b. *Psalms*
      - *The Odes of Solomon*
   c. *Prayers*
      - *On the Annointing* (NHC XI)
      - *On Baptism A* (NHC XI)
      - *On Baptism B* (NHC XI)
      - *On the Eucharist A* (NHC XI)
      - *On the Eucharist B* (NHC XI)
      - *A Prayer of the Apostle Paul* (NHC I)

Though this list is relatively inclusive, it is not exhaustive of all the works that might come under consideration as NT Apocrypha. For example, in the early editions of his *Neutestamentliche Apokryphen,* Edgar Hennecke included the *Didache,* the letters of Clement of Rome, and other works normally associated with the corpus "Apostolic Fathers," which some today would still insist on including in any complete listing of the NT Apocrypha. There is also the question of how far to extend the chronological limits of the designation NT Apocrypha. For example, should one consider the later apocryphal acts, such as the *Acts of Xanthippe and Polexena* or the *Martyrdom of Peter,* as also belonging to this corpus? The current trend seems to be toward inclusivity rather than limitation, since such a designation as NT Apocrypha, as abstract as it may be, does tend to be suggestive of a "canon" of texts worthy of scholarly attention. Over the last two decades, a group of Swiss scholars forming *l'Association pour l'étude de la litterature apocryphe chrétienne* has been attempting to rectify the years of scholarly neglect under which many such later apocryphal works have suffered by publishing new critical editions and French translations of (eventually) all the Christian apocrypha (including OT Apocrypha) in the Series Apocryphorum of Corpus Christianorum.

C. The Value of NT Apocrypha

It has been customary to speak of the NT Apocrypha in terms of their value in bearing witness to the history of early Christianity only as it developed in the 2d and 3d centuries or later. More recent investigations of particular apocryphal works, however, have called into question this scholarly convention by dating certain books, or the traditions of which they have made use, to the 1st century. For example, Helmut Koester and James M. Robinson have argued for a view of Christianity in the 1st century that takes account of the traditions and tradition-historical tendencies at work in the *Gospel of Thomas,* which many today have come to view as a 1st-century Christian text (Robinson and Koester 1971: 71–113, 114–57, 158–204). In a separate article Koester (1980b) has suggested that in addition to the *Gospel of Thomas,* the *Dialogue of the Savior* may also bear witness to the development of the early Christian sayings tradition in the 1st century. Following upon an earlier suggestion of Koester (1980a: 126–30), John Dominic Crossan has argued in a recent monograph (1988) that the *Gospel of Peter* can be used to reconstruct a version of the passion narrative that predates both the synoptic version and that of John. Finally, Charles Hedrick (1988) has edited a collection of essays by various scholars exploring the value of apocryphal gospel traditions for addressing the question of the historical Jesus. All of these efforts reflect a current trend, especially among American scholars, to reexamine old historical assumptions about apocryphal literature in general, and to view apocryphal literature as the product, not of various attempts to rewrite or supplement the canonical texts, but of the great diversity of belief and practice that existed in early Christianity almost from its inception.

D. Sources

English translations or summaries of most of the works listed above may be found in M. R. James, *The Apocryphal New Testament,* or Edgar Hennecke and Wilhelm Schneemelcher, *New Testament Apocrypha (NTApocr),* an English translation of the 4th edition (1959) of their German collection, *Neutestamentliche Apocryphen.* The latter has recently appeared in a new German edition (1987), and a new edition of James' collection is currently being prepared by J. Keith Elliott. A new four-volume collection of apocryphal texts sponsored by Polebridge Press is also currently in production. For the Nag Hammadi texts, and those found in BG 8502, English translations are to be found in James M. Robinson, General Editor, *The Nag Hammadi Library.*

Critical editions of most of these texts are also available. Greek texts of many of the apocryphal gospels are to be found in Tischendorf, *Evangelia apocrypha,* published originally in 1853, and reissued in 1966. The standard text for the apocryphal acts is that of Lipsius and Bonnet, *Acta apostolorum apocrypha* (1959), also an update of an earlier volume assembled by Tischendorf (1851). Members of *l'Association pour l'étude de la litterature apocryphe chrétienne* have begun issuing new editions of the apocryphal acts in the Series Apocryphorum of Corpus Christianorum, including Eric Junod and Jean-Daniel Kaesteli, *Acta Iohannis* (1983), and Louis Leloir, *Acta Apostolorum Armenaica* (1986). Critical editions of the Nag Hammadi texts have appeared in the series Nag Hammadi Studies, including *Codex I* (H. W. Attridge, ed.), *Codices III,2 and IV,2: The Gospel of the Egyptians* (A. Bohlig, F. Wisse, P. Labib, eds.), *Codex III,5: The Dialogue of the Savior* (S. Emmel, ed.), *Codices V,2–5 and VI with P. Berol. 8502, 1 and 4* (D. M. Parrott, ed.), *Codices IX and X* (B. A. Pearson, ed.). Critical editions of all of the Nag Hammadi Codices are currently in production or imminently forthcoming in this series. Carl Schmidt's text of the *Pistis Sophia* has been published in the same series (Nag Hammadi Studies 9, R. McL. Wilson, ed.), as well as his text of the *Books of Jeu* from the Bruce Codex (Nag Hammadi Studies 13, R. McL. Wilson, ed.). The entire text of BG 8502 was published originally by Walter Till in 1955, and reissued in a revised edition by Hans-Martin Schenke in 1972. The Syriac text of the *Odes of Solomon* is published with an English translation by James H. Charlesworth in the SBLTT series. The texts pertinent to the reconstruction of the Synoptic Sayings Source (Q) have been published by John Kloppenborg. A new fragment of P. Egerton 2 has just been published by Michael Gronewald, and should thus be added to the fragment originally published by Bell and Skeat. For critical texts of other NT apocryphal works and fragments, one should consult the appropriate sections of Hennecke-Schneemelcher, *NTApocr.*

Bibliography

Attridge, H. W. 1985. *Nag Hammadi Codex I (The Jung Codex).* NHS 22–23. Leiden.

Bell, H. I., and Skeat, T. C. 1935. *Fragments of an Unknown Gospel and Other Early Christian Papyri.* London.

Bohlig. A., and Wisse, F., with P. Labib. 1975. *Nag Hammadi Codices III,2 and IV,2: The Gospel of the Egyptians.* NHS 4. Leiden.

Charlesworth, J. H. 1977. *The Odes of Solomon.* SBLTT 13, Pseudepigrapha Series 7. Chico, CA.

Crossan, J. D. 1988. *The Cross That Spoke. The Origins of the Passion Narrative.* San Francisco.

Emmel, S. 1984. *Nag Hammadi Codex III,5: The Dialogue of the Savior.* NHS 26. Leiden.

Gronewald, M. 1987. Unbekanntes Evangelium oder Evangelienharmonie (Fragment aus dem "Evangelium Egerton"). Pp. 136–45 in *Kölner Papyri* (P. Köln Series) Band 6, Sonderreihe Papyrologica Colonensia, Vol. 7. Cologne.

Hedrick, C., ed. 1988. *The Historical Jesus and the Rejected Gospels.* Atlanta.

James, M. R. 1924. *The Apocryphal New Testament.* Oxford.

Junod, E., and Kaesteli, J.-D. 1983. *Acta Iohannis.* CChr Series apocryphorum 1 and 2. Turnhout.

Kloppenborg, J. 1987. *Q Parallels: Synopsis, Critical Notes, and Concordance.* Sonoma, CA.

Koester, H. 1980a. Apocryphal and Canonical Gospels. *HTR* 73: 105–30.

———. 1980b. Gnostic Writings as Witnesses for the Development of the Sayings Tradition. Pp. 238–56 in *The Rediscovery of Gnosticism,* Vol. I; ed. B. Layton. SHR 16. Leiden.

———. 1983. History and Development of Mark's Gospel (From Mark to *Secret Mark* and "Canonical" Mark). Pp. 35–57 in *Colloquy on New Testament Studies,* ed. Bruce Corely. Macon GA.

Leloir, L. 1986. *Acta apostolorum armenaica.* CChr Series apocryphorum 3. Turnhout.

Lipsius, R., and Bonnet, M. 1959. *Acta apostolorum apocrypha.* Hildesheim.

Parrott, D. M. 1979. *Nag Hammadi Codices V,2–5 and VI with Papyrus Berolinensis 8502.1 and 4.* NHS 11. Leiden.

Pearson, B. A. 1981. *Nag Hammadi Codices IX and X.* NHS 15. Leiden.

Robinson, J. M., ed. 1988. *The Nag Hammadi Library.* 3d rev. ed. San Francisco.

Robinson, J. M. and Koester, H. 1971. *Trajectories Through Early Christianity.* Philadelphia.

Scholer, D. M. 1971. *Nag Hammadi Bibliography.* NHS 1. Leiden.

Till, W., and Schenke, H.-M. 1972. *Die gnostischen Schriften des koptischen Papyrus Berolinensis 8502.* TU 60^2. Berlin.

Tischendorf, C. von. 1851. *Acta apostolorum apocrypha.* Lipsiae.

———. 1853. *Evangelia apocrypha.* Lipsiae. [Reprint 1966: Hildesheim].

Wilson, R. McL., ed. 1978a. *The Books of Jeu and the Untitled Text in the Bruce Codex.* Text ed. by C. Schmidt; trans. and notes by V. MacDermot. NHS 13. Leiden.

———. 1978b. *Pistis Sophia.* Text ed. by C. Schmidt; trans. and notes by V. MacDermot. NHS 9. Leiden.

STEPHEN J. PATTERSON

APOLLO (DEITY). After Zeus, the most important deity in the Greek pantheon, and the most Greek of all the gods. His cult was prominent throughout the Mediterranean world. As a vegetation deity, he guards against plagues of mice, grasshoppers, and plant diseases, and as a god of herds, he offers protection, especially against wolves. Very early he has a reputation for healing powers, but in time his son Asclepius takes over this function. Warding off evil usually implies power to effect its opposite, and as the god of purity, Apollo sends in retribution destructive plagues or sickness. Hence purification and expiation rites were a strong feature in his cult.

In the Greco-Roman world, prophetic powers were associated especially with Apollo, whose principal oracle was located at Delphi. Strabo (9.3.12) reports that Apollo slew the Python, a serpent or dragon that guarded this oracle. The Greek term *pythōn* came to be used in reference to the Python's spirit of divination that inspired the deity's medium at the shrine in Delphi (Plut. *De def. or.* 414e). Acts 16:16 uses the term in apposition to *pneuma* (spirit) in a description of a woman similarly possessed.

That Paul sets high value on prophecy is apparent from 1 Cor 14:1–5. Since women were used as oracular media for Apollo at some oracles in Greece, it is not surprising that prophecy is associated also with female members of the Corinthian church (1 Corinthians 11). But Apollo is a deity of order, and Paul, for whatever other reasons, relates to this cultural feature with his insistence that female prophets wear appropriate head covering (vv 11–16).

The Greek instinct for moderation found in Apollo the balance to Dionysos, who was especially associated with ecstatic worship and had found an early welcome at Delphi. Since Apollo sponsors reasoned discourse, his priest at Delphi interpreted the Pythia's responses. A related concern for harmony is evident in Paul's instruction concerning prophecy and the interpreter's role in connection with ecstatic speech ("tongues" 1 Cor 14:22–25). He also teaches that the "spirits of prophets are subject to prophets, for God does not encourage disorder *(akatastasia)* but harmony *(eirēne)*" (vv 32–33). Paul's declaration that he would rather speak five intelligible words than tens of thousands in ecstatic utterance (v 19) would be well understood in Hellas.

The broad range of talent exhibited at Corinth (1 Cor 14:26) parallels the beneficent civilizing influence that was traditionally associated with Apollo. At the same time it attests the depth of Paul's awareness of basic Hellenic values (Rom 1:14; 1 Cor 9:19–23), the cultivation of which contributed to a pervasive symmetry that was so highly prized among Greeks and expressed in maxims that were inscribed at Delphi: *gnōthi sauton* (know yourself), *mēden agan* (nothing too much). These maxims attest the reputation that Delphi had for a civilizing influence.

Apollo's oracle at Delphi became world-renowned for the counsel it gave in ordering the lives of those who sought advice on commercial ventures, political issues, and a variety of personal problems, but in St. Paul's time its influence had declined. Yet Apollo's reputation for moral earnestness was so well established that if Christianity was to prevail in Greece, it was imperative that spirit-filled leaders in Christian communities be able to assist people in need of counsel. Paul met the need by including in his Corinthian correspondence a number of answers to perplexing problems. Of special interest is the fact that his letters to Corinth contain the highest concentration of his own claim to be spirit-inspired.

Numerous stories illustrate that Apollo's advice was not to be taken lightly, for sacrilegiousness paid an especially dreadful fee (Parke and Wormell 1956:1. 378–92). In like manner, Christian rites are to be approached with due reverence and concern for their moral implications (1 Cor 5). As at Delphi, trivializing of rites can be disastrous. Unworthy participation in the Eucharist accounts for an unusual incidence of sickness and death (11:30).

In one most vital respect there was an unbridgeable gulf between Apollo and Jesus Christ. Apollo in all his purity remains at a distance from humanity. No devotee of his would ever have said, "I live in Apollo and Apollo lives in me." Apollo had no defense against Paul's oracle in Gal 2:20 and one in 2 Cor 13:4: "Jesus was crucified in weakness, but lives by the power of God. For we are weak in him, but in dealing with you we shall live with him by the power of God."

Bibliography

Aune, D. E. 1983. *Prophecy in Early Christianity and the Ancient Mediterranean World.* Grand Rapids (pp. 23–79).

Farnell, L. 1907. *The Cults of the Greek City States.* Vol. 4. Oxford (pp. 98–355).

Latte, K. 1956. *Römische Religionsgeschichte.* HAW 5.4. Munich (pp. 221–25, 303–4).

Otto, W. F. 1983. *The Homeric Gods.* Trans. M. Hadas. New York.

Parke, H. W., and Wormell, D. E. H. 1956. *The Delphic Oracle,* 2 vols. Oxford.

Wilamowitz-Moellendorf, U. von. 1932. *Der Glaube der Hellenen,* vol. 2. Berlin (pp. 26–42).

FREDERICK W. DANKER

APOLLONIA (M.R. 131178). A Persian to Byzantine site located on a sandstone cliff on the shore of the S Sharon Plain, 17 km N of Jaffa, and 34 km S of Caesarea. The site in Arabic is called ʾArsuf. The shoreline includes a small natural haven, still used by local fishermen.

A. Research and Excavations

The site was first identified with Apollonia by Reland (1714: 570). Its main remains aboveground, which include the Early Arabic city wall and the Crusader castle, have been described by Guérin (1875: 375–82) and by Conder (1882: 137–40). Rescue excavations were conducted in 1950 (Ben-Dor and Kahane 1951: 41–43), and in 1962 and 1976 (Israel Dept. Ant. 1962: 11; 1976: 63; see Ovadiah and Birnbaum 1989). Excavations on a larger scale were undertaken in 1977 in the commercial quarter in the city's center (areas A–D), and in 1980–81 on both sides of the S city wall (area E), as well as in the *donjon* of the Crusader castle (area F_1; Roll and Ayalon 1989: 23–117). Since 1982, excavations have been carried out by I. Roll in the W of the city (area H) and in the castle's chapel (area F_2).

B. Early Remains

Scattered surface finds of Neolithic flint tools and some sherds from EB I indicate sporadic occupation of the site in those early periods. A few sherds from Iron Age IIA (9th century B.C.) found at the bottom of area H, and an Ushebti statuette of the 26th Dyn. (late 7th–early 6th centuries B.C.) from the surface (Giveon 1970: 347–8), indicate occasional occupation also in OT times. Therefore, there are no grounds for identifying the site with the biblical "town of Resheph" supposedly mentioned in 1 Chr 7:25 (Clermont-Ganneau 1896b: 259–60; see Kallai 1986: 155 n. 121), nor with one of the cities named in the campaign lists of Tiglath-pileser III (Forrer 1920: 61; see Tadmor 1985: 180–82).

C. The Persian Period

Architectural remains from two consecutive phases, uncovered in area H on the virgin soil, indicate that the earliest permanent settlement on the site belongs to that period. Infant burials in jars found in the NE and a large rubbish pit uncovered in area D show that this settlement was confined to the cliff's W edge. The finds include: (1) local pottery—mainly storage jars typical to the inland; (2) imported pottery—mainly Black Glazed Ware from Greece; (3) a great number of *Murex brandaris* shells, from which royal purple has been extracted; (4) a lot of twenty coins—all, except one, minted in Sidon; (5) an ostracon that mentions Eshmun, the chief god of Sidon. Clermont-Ganneau (1876: 374–75) was the first to point out that the Arabic toponym *ʾArsūf* derives from the name of the Phoenician god Resheph; hence it has been suggested that the original name of the site was *(A)rsôp* (Albright 1931–32: 167 n. 20) or rather *(A)ršōf* (Yzreel 1989). That makes one more link with the kingdom of Sidon, which was also known as "the Land of the Reshephs" (*KAI* 15; see Fulco 1976: 47). This data indicates that the earliest settlement at Apollonia was Sidonian, that it served as a trading center which had commercial ties with inland Palestine on one hand and with the Greek world on the other, and that it possessed a purple dye industry. The beginnings seem to date to the early 5th century B.C., when the Sidonian king Eshmunazar II was rewarded by the Persians with "Dor and Jaffa [and] the rich corn lands in the Plain of Sharon," as attested in the inscription on his sarcophagus (*KAI* 14.1.19), in return for the employ of his fleet against the Greeks (Kelly 1987: 39–56).

D. The Hellenistic Period

This period is represented mainly by assemblages of pottery uncovered in areas D and H and in two more spots along the cliff's W end, which indicate that the inhabited area was more or less the same as previously. The pottery includes local types, as well as imported wares from the main Hellenistic centers of the E Mediterranean. Large numbers of unbroken *Murex brandaris* shells have been found, and some *Murex trunculus* shells with their back knocked off; these seem to indicate that not only Royal purple (*ʾargāmān*) was produced in Hellenistic times, but also the much appreciated Hyacinthine purple *(tĕkēlet)* (Ziderman 1987: 15–33; see, however, McGovern et al. 1988: 81–90). Josephus, who provides the earliest historical records on the site, mentions Apollonia as a town that belonged to the Jews under Alexander Jannaeus (*Ant* 13.15.4 §395), then as a city restored by Gabinius (*JW* 1.8.4 §166). The name "Apollonia" derives from that of the Greek god Apollo, who was identified with the Phoenician god Resheph already in the early 4th century B.C. (*KAI* 39, 41; see Clermont-Ganneau 1876: 374–75; 1896b: 260; Fulco 1976: 50–52). Hence, there is no reason to think that the town was founded by Seleucus I (Hölscher 1903: 60), or by Apollonius, the Seleucid general under Demetrius II (Conder 1882: 137; Tcherikover 1970: 93).

E. The Roman Period

To the Roman period belongs an architectural complex with underground storage rooms, from the 2d (phase I) and early 3d (phase II) centuries A.D., uncovered in area E close to the main descent to the haven. The pottery includes large numbers of rough local storage jars, as well as finer pieces of Eastern Sigillata ware and African Red Slip ware. The latter indicate commercial ties with the main centers of pottery making along the Syro-Phoenician coast and in N Africa. Finds from the surface include: the sculpture of an eagle with a monogram of Emperor Julian and two inscribed stelae (Clermont-Ganneau 1882: 96, 134; Vincent 1909: 445–46), an ostracon with a love formula and a ring with a wish for good health (*SEG* 1957: 846; 1964: 466), all in Greek. That reflects a typical Greco-Roman city of the Mediterranean Orient and Apollonia is indeed recorded as such, between Caesarea and Jaffa (Shürer 1979: 114–15), by Pliny (*HN* 5.13.69), by Ptolemy (*Geog.* 5.15.2), and on the *Tabula Peutingeriana.* Apollonia is not mentioned in the Rabbinic literature nor in the NT. However, one may consider the possibility that the men sent by the centurion Cornelius from Caesarea to Jaffa to bring Peter (Acts 10:1–9) did spend the night at Apollonia, which is at the distance of one day's travel from Caesarea.

F. The Byzantine Period

This is the period when the city reached its largest expansion, up to 130 acres according to the pottery spread over the surface. It included a commercial area in the center, a large church in the SE, an industrial area in the N where oil, wine, and glass have been produced, and an anchorage along the shore. More manufacturing installations were found in the S and in the W. Byzantine Apollonia emerged as a main commercial, industrial, and maritime center, which served not only the whole of S Sharon, but also much of W Samaria. Various finds indicate that the city's prosperity was due mainly to its growing and lucrative Samaritan community (Sussman 1983: 71–96). There are no grounds for thinking that the name of the city was changed to Sozousa and to Aphthoria—a theory suggested by Clermont-Ganneau (1896a: 337–39; 1897: 18–20) and widely accepted ever since. Stephanus of Byzantium (ed. Meineke 1849: 106, 596) mentions both, Apollonia (no. 13, "near Jaffa") and Sozousa ("in Phoenicia"), as two different cities. Aphthoria is described by Petrus the Iberian (ed. Raabe 1895: 112) as a village located only 12 miles S of Caesarea.

Bibliography

Albright, W. F. 1931–32. The Syro-Mesopotamian God Šulmân-Ešmûn and Related Figures. *AfO* 7: 164–69.

Ben-Dor, I., and Kahane, I. 1951. Rishpon (Apollonia). *Bulletin of the Department of Antiquities of the State of Israel* 3: 41–43 (in Hebrew).

Clermont-Ganneau, Ch. 1876. Horus et Saint Georges d'après un bas-relief inédit du Louvre. *RA* 32: 196–204; 372–99.

———. 1882. *Rapports sur une mission en Palestine et en Phénicie entreprise en 1881.* Paris.

———. 1896a. *Archaeological Researches in Palestine during the Years 1873–1874,* 2. London.

———. 1896b. Notes on the April "Quarterly Statement." *PEFQS* 2: 259–61.

———. 1897. Aphthoria–Apollonia?. Pp. 18–20 in *Études d'archéologie orientale,* 2. Paris.

Conder, C. W., and Kitchener, H. H. 1882. *The Survey of Western Palestine,* 2. *Samaria.* London.

Forrer, E. 1920. *Die Provinzeinteilung des assyrischen Reiches.* Leipzig.

Fulco, W. J. 1976. *The Canaanite God Rešep.* New Haven.

Giveon, R. 1970. Three "Shawabti" Statuettes of the 26th Dynasty from Israel. Pp. 342–48 in *Sepher Shemuel Yeivin,* ed. S. Abramski et al. Jerusalem (in Hebrew).

Guérin, V. 1875. *Description géographique, historique et archéologique de la Palestine. Samarie,* 2. Paris.

Hölscher, G. 1903. *Palästina in der persischen und hellenistischen Zeit.* Berlin.

Israel Dept. Ant. 1962. Mosaic Floor in Apollonia. *Hadashot Arkheologiyot* 3: 11 (in Hebrew).

———. 1976. Apollonia. *Hadashot Arkheologiyot* 59–60: 63 (in Hebrew).

Kallai, Z. 1986. *Historical Geography of the Bible.* Jerusalem/Leiden.

Kelly, T. 1987. Herodotus and the Chronology of the Kings of Sidon. *BASOR* 268: 39–56.

McGovern, P. E., et al. 1988. Has Authentic *Tĕkēlet* Been Identified? *BASOR* 269: 81–90.

Meineke, A., ed. 1849. *Stephani Byzantii Ethnicorum quae supersunt.* Berlin.

Ovadiah, A., and Birnbaum, R. 1989. Greek Inscription from the Early Byzantine Church Discovered at Apollonia. Pp. 279–88 in Roll and Ayalon, eds. 1989.

Raabe, R., ed. 1895. *Petrus der Iberer.* Leipzig.

Reland, H. 1714. *Palaestina ex monumentis veteribus illustrata.* Trajecti Batavorum: Broedelet.

Roll, I., and Ayalon, E. 1987. The Market Street at Apollonia—Arsuf. *BASOR* 267: 61–76.

Roll, I., and Ayalon, E., eds. 1989. *Apollonia and Southern Sharon.* Tel Aviv (in Hebrew, with English summaries).

Schürer, E. 1979. *The History of the Jewish People in the Age of Jesus Christ (175 B.C.–A.D. 135),* 2. Rev. and ed. G. Vermes; F. Millar; and M. Black. Edinburgh.

Sussman, V. 1983. *The Samaritan Oil Lamp from Apollonia-Arsuf. TA* 10: 71–96.

Tadmor, H. 1985. Rashpuna—A Case of Epigraphic Error. *EI* 18: 180–82 (in Hebrew, with English summary on p. 71*).

Tcherikover, V. 1970. *Hellenistic Civilization and the Jews.* New York.

Vincent, H. 1909. Glanures archéologiques. *RB* 6: 445–46.

Yzreel, S. 1989. ʾArsūf is Arshof. Pp. 245–58 in Roll and Ayalon, *Sharon.*

Ziderman, I. 1987. First Identification of Authentic Tĕkēlet. *BASOR* 265: 25–33.

ISRAEL ROLL

APOLLONIUS (PERSON) [Gk *Apollōnios*]. The name of five men mentioned in their several capacities in 1 and 2 Maccabees.

1. The Son of Thraseas or (with a slight emendation) a son or native of Tarsus (2 Macc 3:5), and governor of Colesyria under Seleucus IV Philopater (the brother of Antiochus Epiphanes). Polybius (31.13.2–3) tells of a man named Apollonius who was removed from office after the murder of Seleucus by his minister Heliodorus in 175 B.C. (cf. Hengel 1974: 2.11, 272) and retired to Miletus. Polybius' Apollonius could be the son of Thraseas, but certainty is impossible. During the reign of Seleucus IV (187–175 B.C.), a Benjaminite (or a man from the clan of Bilgah) named Simon opposed the high priest Onias III, and turned to Apollonius for help. To entice Apollonius to act, Simon told him about money deposited at the Temple. Apollonius, in turn, informed Seleucus, who dispatched Heliodorus to Jerusalem to investigate (2 Macc 3:4–8). When Heliodorus attempted to confiscate Temple funds, he was struck by a heavenly apparition and nearly died (3:22–25). (In the account of this same event in *4 Macc.* 4:1–14, Apollonius himself, rather than Heliodorus, attempted the confiscation with similar results.)

The identity of the next-mentioned Apollonius (2 Macc 4:4) is debated, because the text is obscure. If one accepts the reading *Apollònion Menestheōs* (Apollonius, son of Menestheos), he is the same person who appears in 4:21. Goldstein argues (*2 Maccabees* AB, 222) that he is different from the Apollonius in 3:5 or 5:24. Bartlett (*Maccabees* CBC, 236) also accepts the reading, but identifies him with the native of Tarsus (as opposed to the son of Thraseas) in 3:5. The defective text, however, gives reason for suspecting the name *Menestheōs,* which could have been supplied from 4:21. On the whole, in fact, it appears that the Apollonius of 4:4 was the same as Apollonius, the son of Thraseas/Tarsus (3:5, 7) since both passages describe an Apollonius who (1) was governor of Colesyria and Phoenicia during the life of Seleucus and (2) supported Simon against Onias III. The author mentions the death of Seleucus in 4:7, so if the son of Thraseas was the same as the Apollonius mentioned by Polybius, he left office for Miletus.

2. The Son of Menestheus, sent by Antiochus IV Epiphanes (ruled 175–163 B.C.) to Egypt for the coronation of Philometer ca. 172 B.C. (2 Macc 4:21). Scholars often assume that this Apollonius was also the unnamed collector of tribute sent by Antiochus IV with 22,000 soldiers to Jerusalem in 167 B.C. (1 Macc 1:29–30). The same event is retold in 2 Macc 5:24–26, in which the official, Apollonius, was called a "captain of the Mysians," who were mercenaries from Mysia in NW Asia Minor (Goldstein *1 Maccabees* AB, 211). As mentioned above, it is possible that this Apollonius was the same as the native of Tarsus or even the governor of Samaria (see below; cf. Dickson *HDB* 1: 123–24). Also, one cannot exclude the possibility that the son of Menestheus and the captain of the Mysians are different people. On the whole, however, it seems best to see 2 Macc 4:21, 5:24–26 and 1 Macc 1:29–30 as referring to the same person, the son of Menestheus, who seemed not to have been a governor but to have been a trusted emissary of Antiochus.

3. The Governor of Samaria, killed in battle by Judas Maccabeus (who captured and used the sword of Apollonius the rest of his life [1 Macc 3:12]). This Apollonius appears suddenly in 1 Macc 3:10, with no introduction and no further designation. Josephus, however, identifies him as the governor of Samaria (*Ant.* 12.7.1 §287). Goldstein accepts that identification and argues that his army would have included surrounding gentiles (Arabs, Idumeans) and Greeks from Samaria itself, but no Samarians (*1 Maccabees* AB, 245–46).

4. The Son of Gennaeus, one of five regional rulers under Antiochus V Eupater (ruled 164–162) who persecuted Jews (2 Macc 12:2).

5. The Governor of Colesyria and Phoenicia under Alexander Balas (see Joseph. *Ant* 13.4.3 §88, who calls him Apollonius Daus) and Demetrius II Nicator. He is sometimes considered to be the son of Apollonius, son of Thraseas/Tarsus. Polybius mentions (31.19.6 and 21.2) an Apollonius who was the foster brother and confidant of Demetrius I Soter, and who helped him escape from Rome, where he was held hostage. Demetrius landed in Tripolis and ousted Antiochus V Eupater (1 Macc 7:1; 2 Macc 14:1). If the Apollonius in Polybius is the same as the Apollonius in 1 Macc 10:69, his close relationship to Demetrius II Nicator (ruled 145–139 and 129–125) would be explained on the basis of his previous relationship to the father Demetrius I. At any rate, in 147 B.C. Demetrius II sailed to Cilicia from Crete with a large mercenary army, intending to unseat Alexander Balas. As governor of Colesyria he named Apollonius, who apparently already held that position under Alexander Balas (Jos. *Ant* 13.4.3 §88), if not Demetrius I. Apollonius gathered a large army and besieged Jamnia. Meanwhile, he threatened Jonathan, the high priest, in Jerusalem, who attacked Joppa with an army of ten thousand men. Apollonius appeared to retreat from Joppa toward Azotus, taking 3,000 cavalry with him, but leaving 1,000 in hiding to surround Jonathan when he followed. The ambush failed; Jonathan attacked, and at the height of the battle Simon and his forces joined Jonathan. The Seleucids were routed, Azotus and the Temple of Dagan burned (1 Macc 10:67–85).

Bibliography

Dancy, J. C. 1954. *A Commentary on I Maccabees.* Oxford.

Hengel, M. 1974. *Judaism and Hellenism.* Trans. J. Bowden. Philadelphia.

Hutchison, J. Apollonius. *ISBE* 1: 188.

Tedesche, S., and Zeitlin, S. 1950. *The First Book of Maccabees.* New York.

———. 1956. *The Second Book of Maccabees.* New York.

PAUL L. REDDITT

APOLLOPHANES (PERSON) [Gk *Apollophanēs*]. A Syrian whom the army of Judah the Maccabee slew at the fortress of Gazara (2 Macc 10:37). The Maccabean forces had pursued Timotheus, the defeated commander of an invading Syrian army, to the fortress at Gazara, in the low hills of W Judaea. Jason of Cyrene, the author of 2 Maccabees, should have written Jazer, a town in Moab where this action probably took place (see 1 Macc 5:6–8; and *Ant* 12.8.1). The Maccabean soldiers killed Timotheus and his brother, Chaireas, the only other inhabitants of the town mentioned by name along with Apollophanes. Nothing is known about Apollophanes' position in the city. (See Goldstein *2 Maccabees* AB.)

MITCHELL C. PACWA

APOLLOS (PERSON) [Gk *Apollōs*]. A charismatic young convert in the early Christian community, described as "a man of learning, powerful in the scriptures" (Acts 18:24, NEB) who eventually had some impact on the churches of Achaia, notably Corinth (Acts 18:27; cf. 1 Cor 1:12; 3:4–6; etc.). As a native of Alexandria, Apollos (or Apollonios, according to Codex D) grew up in the leading center of Hellenistic and Platonic thinking E of Greece. We can only speculate about his intellectual links there, and a number of scholars have suggested he had direct acquaintance with Philo or the Therapeutae. He is presented in Acts as an eloquent speaker with more than a little skill at debating, although it is possible (if not probable) that Luke has exaggerated Apollos' abilities; regardless, there is no doubt that in general his credentials, at least within the context of the synagogue, were impressive.

The note that he was "instructed in his own country (Codex D) in the word of the Lord" (Acts 18:25), if genuine (as claimed by Foakes-Jackson, *Acts* MNTC), does not prove that Christianity had reached Alexandria by A.D. 50. The phrase "word of the Lord" probably refers to the LXX, not the Christian gospel. The possibility that he had contact with John the Baptist is also tenuous, even though according to Luke "he knew only the baptism of John" (Acts 18:25). It is most likely that this knowledge came either from contact with some of John's disciples or from a fragmentary report of the events in Palestine between A.D. 25–30. Apollos is also said to have "taught accurately the things concerning Jesus" (Acts 18:25), which for Luke apparently meant an accurate acquaintance with the facts of Jesus' life (cf. the "orderly account" of Luke 1:3), probably including the account of the resurrection. Yet it seems not to have included any knowledge about what took place immediately after Jesus' ascension; i.e., the coming of the Holy Spirit. Thus, the note in Acts 18:25 that Apollos was *zeōn tō pneumati* ("fervent in spirit," RSV) cannot refer to the Holy Spirit, since this would be inconsistent with his subsequent experience with Aquila and Priscilla (v 26) and with Paul's subsequent experience preaching in Apollos' wake (Acts 19:1–7).

Apollos' fervor appears to have impelled him to become an itinerant Jewish preacher, whose travels eventually brought him to Ephesus. There he began "to speak boldly in the synagogue" (Acts 18:26), an activity made possible by the customary invitation to visitors to make any comments they wished. At that time, Priscilla and Aquila—already introduced in Acts 18:2 as residents of Corinth who had earlier been victims of Claudius' general expulsion of all Jews from Rome (A.D. 49)—were present in the synagogue at Ephesus. They appear to have found his message deficient, and "they took him and expounded to him the way of God more accurately" (18:26). This would appear to have been more than just a casual exchange, and may have involved taking Apollos to their home for an indefinite stay. The "way" they expounded was probably stamped with Paul's distinctive influence, since the couple appear to have been Paul's friends and colleagues from their earlier days together in Corinth.

From Ephesus, Apollos wished to take his freshly supplemented message to Achaia (i.e., Greece), and he received the enthusiastic support of the Ephesian Christians in this endeavor (18:27). According to Codex D, Apollos' trip was urged by some Corinthian Christians currently living at Ephesus (Aquila and Priscilla might possibly fit into such a category). At Corinth, Apollos "greatly helped those who through grace had believed" (18:27), apparently a reference to catechetical instruction of new converts, and he "powerfully confuted the Jews in public, showing by the scriptures that the Christ was Jesus" (18:28). It is not clear what kind of scriptural exegesis is intended by this phrase, although it may be safe to infer that it was stamped by Paul's own christological exegesis of the OT (cf., e.g., Rom 10:6ff.; 1 Cor 10:1ff.; Gal 4:22ff.). That it was "allegorical" in the tradition of Philo's exegesis is purely a guess drawn from Apollos' Alexandrian background.

The church at Corinth apparently lionized Apollos to the point of making him the object of partisan loyalty, a point that is readily apparent in Paul's first epistle to that church (1 Cor 1:12). In that letter, Paul met the challenge not by directly confronting Apollos, but by attacking the Corinthian tendency toward factiousness (1 Cor 4:6). Indeed, Paul lists Apollos as among those who were with him at Ephesus when he composed 1 Corinthians (15:12). Some in the Corinthian church apparently wanted Apollos to return to minister to them, but Apollos refused, presumably out of concern for (and disapproval of) their factiousness. The only other NT reference to Apollos occurs in Titus 3:13, where Titus is asked "to speed Zenas the lawyer and Apollos on their way." The apparent meaning of these words is that the two had been commissioned by Paul to take the letter to Titus, but that they should not tarry long at Crete after delivering it.

The figure of Apollos has become symbolic of both eloquence and knowledge of scripture. Certainly the picture of him that emerges from the NT is of one who was a firm supporter of Paul, and of one who was, despite his natural abilities, in no way interested in competing with or subverting Paul's influence and authority. He seems to have preferred taking the subsidiary role of helping to strengthen churches which had already been established.

Luther suggested that Apollos was the author of the Epistle to the Hebrews, a suggestion which has received renewed popularity in recent years because of the implied connection with Alexandrian exegesis (cf. Heb 11:8–16 with Philo *Abr*) and to the suggestion that there is a complex interplay between Hebrews and Paul's Corinthian correspondence (Montefiore *Hebrews* BHNTC). But since we have no sample of writing from Apollos with which to compare Hebrews, the suggestion appears to be extremely tenuous (Hurst 1985).

Bibliography

Hurst, L. 1985. Apollos, Hebrews and Corinth. *SJT* 38: 505–13.

L. D. HURST

APOLLYON [Gk *Apollyōn*]. The Greek name, meaning "Destroyer," given in Rev 9:11 for "the angel of the bottomless pit" (in Hebrew called ABADDON), also identified as the king of the demonic "locusts" described in Rev 9:3–10. These "locusts" rise out of the bottomless pit (see ABYSS) and for five months torture "those of mankind who have not the seal of God upon their foreheads."

In one manuscript (syr ph), instead of Apollyon the text reads "Apollo," the Greek god of death and pestilence as well as of the sun, music, poetry, crops and herds, and medicine. Apollyon is no doubt the correct reading. But the name Apollo (Gk *Apollōn*) was often linked in ancient Greek writings with the verb *apollymi* or *apollyō*, "destroy" (cf. Aesch. *Ag.* 1080–82). From this time of Grotius, "Apollyon" has often been taken here to be a play on the name Apollo (*TDNT* 1: 397). The locust was an emblem of this god, who poisoned his victims, and the name "Apollyon" may be used allusively in Revelation to attack the pagan god (Ford *Revelation* AB, 152) and so indirectly the Roman emperor Domitian, who liked to be regarded as Apollo incarnate (Caird *Revelation* BHNTC, 120). See also DEAD, ABODE OF THE.

HERBERT G. GRETHER

APOLOGETICS, NT. Apologetics in the NT comprises a study of the "art of persuasion" employed by the early Christians. Such persuasion evolved in a context of Jewish and Hellenistic thought and laid a foundation for the 2d century apologists.

A. Introduction

Much of early Christian literature, including the NT, was written to promote and defend the Christian movement. As the early Christians attempted to appeal to the inhabitants of the Greco-Roman world at large, use was made of the strategies and methods of Hellenistic religious propaganda. The appropriation of such apologetic-propagandistic forms was essential if Christianity was to succeed in the face of competition from other religions (Fiorenza 1976: 1–25; cf. Georgi 1971: 124–31).

The study of early Christian apologetics typically begins with the writings of the Greek apologists of the 2d century: Quadratus and Aristides, but especially Justin, Tatian, Athenagoras, Melito, and Theophilus. It would be incorrect, however, to presume that these were the *first* Christian apologists. As early as the 1st century, Christians were compelled to defend their religious convictions against a variety of opponents, both within and without, and their apologetic arguments can be discerned in the NT itself. Indeed, many of these arguments were subsequently picked up and developed by the apologists of the 2d century (Droge 1988).

Apologetics as the "art of persuasion" is a function of rhetoric, specifically the rhetoric of the law courts (Betz 1976: 100). An "apology" *(apologia)* is, *sensu strictu*, a speech of defense in reply to a speech of the prosecution. The earliest Christian preaching is reported to have occurred in a context of this sort (Acts 2:14–35; cf. 22:1; 24:10; 25:8, 16; 26:1, 24; Phil 1:7, 16; 2 Tim 4:16). According to Luke, Jesus himself predicted that his disciples would be required to make an apology *(apologeomai)* before the legal authorities of their day (Luke 12:11). More generally, the author of 1 Peter exhorts his readers to "be prepared to make a defense *(apologia)* to anyone who calls you to account for the hope that is within you" (3:15). Yet, examples of apologetic arguments can also be found in the NT where the terms *apologia/apologeomai* are not explicitly used. For convenience these may be arranged into four broad categories: defense against (1) Judaism, (2) paganism, (3) the Roman Empire, and (4) other forms of Christianity. The impression should not be left, however, that these categories are mutually exclusive. In some instances, apologetic arguments have two or more opponents in view at one time.

B. Judaism

Apologetics in the NT takes as its starting point the crucifixion of Jesus, because the idea that the messiah was to suffer and die completely contradicted Jewish expectation. The historically undeniable fact of the crucifixion therefore required a defense of Jesus' messianic status against the Jewish objection that "a hanged man is accursed by God" (Deut 21:23; cf. Gal 3:13–14). The Christian response came most often in the form of an appeal to the Jewish scriptures themselves, for it was believed that these ancient oracles had predicted that the messiah would suffer, die, and be raised from the dead: "Was it not necessary that the Christ should suffer these things and enter into his glory? And beginning with Moses and all the prophets, he [sc. Jesus] interpreted to them in all the scriptures the things concerning himself" (Luke 24:26–27; cf. Acts 3:18–25; 8:30–35; 26:22–23; 1 Cor 15:3–8). The OT passages which figure prominently in this "passion apologetic" include Isaiah 42–44; 49–51; 52–53; 61; Psalms 22; 31; 34; 41; 42–43; 69; 109; 118; and Zechariah 9–14. The argument from prophecy (in reality an act of historical imperialism) became the hallmark of Christian apologetic toward Judaism, not only in the NT but also in Christian apologetics of the 2d century (e.g., the *Preaching of Peter;* Aristo's *Dialogue of Jason and Papiscus;* and Justin's *Dialogue with Trypho*). However, it was not without its appeal to Greeks (cf. Acts 10:43; Justin, *1 Apol* 33.5; 34.1–11; 48.1–6).

Matthew carries this hermeneutical principle one step further, for he is concerned to demonstrate that not only Jesus' passion but his entire life and teaching were in agreement with the Jewish scriptures. For example, he expands upon sayings of Jesus by adding quotations from the OT (9:13; 12:5–8, 40; 21:16), and he repeatedly emphasizes that the events of Jesus' life fulfilled divine prophecy: "This took place to fulfill *(hina plērothē)* what the Lord had spoken by the prophet . . ." (1:22; 2:15, 17, 23; 4:14–16; 8:17; 12:17–21; 13:14–15, 35; 21:4–5). Matthew also enters into controversy with Judaism in the Sermon on the Mount by criticizing popular Jewish piety (6:2, 5, 16; 7:5) and presenting Jesus as the legislator of a righteousness superior to that of the scribes and Pharisees (5:20).

Mark takes a somewhat different approach. In addition

to the argument from prophecy, he places the necessity for Jesus' suffering and death on the lips of Jesus himself in the form of "passion predictions" (8:31; 9:30–31; 10:32–34, 45). Like the other evangelists, Mark is also anxious to respond to Jewish accusations that Jesus was demon-possessed (3:19b–30 par.), that he did not fast (2:18–22 par.), keep the sabbath (2:23–3:6 par.), or observe laws of ritual purity (7:1–23 par.), and that he associated with sinners (2:15–17 par.) and claimed authority to forgive sins (2:1–12 par.).

Obviously, the resurrection itself was used by Christians as an important argument for the messianic status of Jesus, predictions of it being found, for example, in Psalms 16; 110; and Jonah 1. Apparently, however, allegations were made that the disciples of Jesus had stolen his body and thus faked the resurrection. The apologetic story of the setting of the guard at the tomb of Jesus is clearly an attempt to refute this accusation (Matt 27:62–66; 28:4, 11–15; cf. Craig 1984: 273–81).

The argument from prophecy gave rise to another problem. If Jesus had indeed been the promised messiah, why did the Jews for the most part reject him? The answer comes again in the form of OT citations about the failure of Israel to recognize the messiah (Ps 118:22; Isa 6:9–10; 8:14; 28:16; 29:10). Paradoxically, the unbelief of the Jews becomes a *proof* for Jesus having been the messiah! In the gospels, Jesus repeatedly draws attention to the failure of the Jews to believe in him, just as their ancestors had refused to believe the prophets (Matt 13:10–15 par.; 21:33–45 par.; cf. Acts 4:11; 28:26–27; 1 Pet 2:7–8). Paul expresses a similar view in Rom 9:30–33 and 11:7–10. The author of the Fourth Gospel also shares this perspective (12:37–41), but he carries it to a sinister extreme by demonizing the Jews (8:43–47). The problem of Jewish unbelief is one of the themes of Stephen's speech in Acts (7:51–53), but the speech goes considerably beyond this to argue that Christianity has superseded Judaism as a world religion. In particular, Stephen is sharply critical of the Jewish law and temple cult (Acts 6:11, 13), as Jesus himself seems to have been (Mark 7:18–19; 14:58; John 2:19).

In Gal 3:1–29 Paul engages in a critique of Judaism and presents a theoretical justification for his rejection of the Jewish law. A striking feature of Paul's argument is that the *lateness* of the law proves its lack of validity (Grant 1952: 223–24). On the other hand, God's covenant with Abraham (who is a type of the pagan convert) has both chronological and theological priority. According to Paul, the law of Moses represents a decline from an originally superior state of affairs. Indeed, the law brings with it a "curse" (Gal 3:10, 19–25; cf. Betz, *Galatians* Hermeneia, 144–46). A similar view was expressed before Paul's time by the influential polymath Posidonius of Apamea in his studies of primitive religion (Grant 1952: 224). His account of the origin of Judaism (preserved by Strabo 16.2.35–39; Nock 1959: 8, however, posits a Jewish source for Strabo) describes how the pure religion which Moses established in Jerusalem was later corrupted by "superstitious and tyrannical men" who instituted dietary regulations, ritual observances, and circumcision. Something like this informs Paul's rejection of the law in Galatians. He radicalizes it, however, by placing the point of decline earlier: the corruption of Moses' successors has become the corruption of Moses *himself,* or of the (fallen?) angels who gave him the law (Gal 3:19; cf. Grant 1952: 224). Paul takes a similar position with respect to Judaism in Rom 2:1–4:25, though his tone is far more conciliatory.

The appeal to the Jewish scriptures also had a positive apologetic value. In addition to vindicating the "crucified messiah," the appeal had the effect of providing Christianity with a past history, indeed, an ancient and venerable one. In the Greco-Roman period, it was axiomatic that nothing could be both new *and* true (cf. Celsus, according to Origen, *Cels* 4.14). The attempt to anchor Christianity backward in the ancient writings of Moses and the prophets gave the impression at least that Christianity had antiquity on its side. Thus, Christianity becomes the "true Israel," and Christians the true descendants of Abraham (Gal 3:7, 9, 14, 29; 6:16; Rom 9:6–8). It was the task of the apologists of the 2d century to draw out the implications of this (see especially Justin, *1 Apol* 23.1; 31.8; 44.8–10; Tatian, *Orat* 31.1; Theophilus, *Autol* 3.16–30; Tertullian, *Apol* 19.1).

C. Paganism

If the idea of a crucified messiah was scandalous to Jews, it also offended Greek sensibilities (Celsus, according to Origen, *Cels* 1:54: "Celsus . . . reproaches the savior for his passion, saying that he was not helped by his father, nor was he able to help himself"; cf. 1.66, 69; 2.16, 36, 55, 63, 67–70). In the NT almost no attempt is made to alleviate the offense of the cross. Paul, for example, admits that the doctrine of "Christ crucified" *(Christos estauromenos)* is foolishness, at least according to recognized standards of wisdom; but he insists nevertheless that through the crucified (and resurrected) Christ, God has accomplished what human wisdom and philosophy could not: the redemption of mankind from the demonic powers of the cosmos (1 Cor 1:18–2:16; cf. 2 Cor 13:4; Gal 6:14). It is really only the author of the Fourth Gospel who, in gnosticizing fashion, reinterprets the crucifixion and thereby reduces its importance as a vicarious sacrifice.

One way the NT attempts to establish the divinity of Jesus is through the miracles he is said to have performed. The gospels of Mark and John, for example, portray Jesus as a wandering miracle worker who demonstrated his divine power by his deeds (Mark 4:35–5:43; 7:24–8:9; John 2:1–11; 4:46–5:9; 6:1–14; 9:1–7; 11:1–44). There is, however, an inherent weakness in the "argument from miracle," because opponents of Christianity could use the miracles as evidence that Jesus was a *magician,* not the son of God (so Celsus, according to Origen, *Cels* 1.68; 2.48–53). The 2d-century apologists are acutely aware of this. There is relatively little appeal in Justin to the miracles as evidence of Jesus' divinity. Justin recognizes that miracles only carry conviction to those who are actual eyewitnesses, and evoke no wonder in those who are dependent on secondhand testimony (*Dial. Trypho* 69.6).

In its attitude toward Greek religion the NT adopts a tradition going back to Hellenistic Judaism (Wisdom of Solomon 13–15). This tradition finds its clearest expression in Rom 1:18–32, where Paul criticizes pagan religion (Castellino 1963: 255–63). According to him, the history of Greek religion is one of degradation and corruption spurred on by men who have suppressed the truth. It therefore stands under divine wrath (1:18). This was not always the case, however, for originally mankind had a better, albeit approximate, conception of deity. These initial religious beliefs arose from man's intellectual contemplation of God's invisible nature insofar as it could be discerned in the creation (1:20; cf. Wis 13:1, 5; Philo, *Praem* 43). Paul characterizes this primordial religion simply as the knowledge of God (1:21). At some point, however, a process of corruption began. Instead of rendering proper worship to God, men "directed their thoughts to worthless things" and began to worship the images of men and animals (1:21–23; cf. Wis 13:10, 13–14; 14:17; 15:18). Thus, "they exchanged the truth for a lie and worshipped the creation instead of the creator" (1:25). The corruption of religion consequently brought about the perversion of morality, for having abandoned a proper understanding of God, men fell prey to their passions and engaged in unnatural sexual practices and assorted crimes (1:26–28). Indeed, according to Paul, it is the invention of idolatry which is the origin and cause of all the vices which destroy society (1:29–31; cf. Wis 14:12, 17). In this way the curse of God's wrath accomplishes its purpose. Paul's concern here is to demonstrate on the basis of a *theologia naturalis* that the Greeks are "without excuse" (*anapologētoi,* 1:20; 2:1), for there is a sufficient knowledge of God available to all men to ensure their responsibility (Ferguson 1962: 193).

Elsewhere Paul exhorts Christians to "shun the worship of idols," for whoever participates in pagan religious ceremonies is in reality worshipping *demons,* not God (1 Cor 10:14, 20–21; cf. 1 Thess 1:9–10; 2 Cor 6:15–16; 1 John 5:21; Rev 9:20). The belief that the traditional gods of Greek religion and myth were actually demons derives from Jewish tradition (*1 En.* 19:1; 99:7; *Jub.* 1:11; 22:17), but it is also found in the Academic critique of popular religion (Plut. *De def. or.* 417 CE; *De Is. et Os.* 360F; 361B; cf. Decharme 1904: 220–32, 454–64). The apologists of the 2d century employ both traditions to support their criticism of Greco-Roman religion (Justin, *1 Apol* 5.2–6.1; *2 Apol* 5.2–5; Athenagoras, *leg.* 24.3–27.2). The fact that many Christians refused to participate in pagan worship led directly to the charge that they were "atheists."

There are two passages in Acts in which Luke brings Christianity into direct confrontation with paganism (Acts 14:8–18; 17:16–34; cf. Grant 1986: 25–26, 49–51). In the first episode, Paul and Barnabas visit the Roman colony at Lystra, where Paul heals a man who had been crippled from birth. The Lystrans are so awed by the miracle that they suppose "the gods have come down . . . in the likeness of men" (14:11). Indeed, Barnabas and Paul are called Zeus and Hermes, and sacrifices are prepared for them. Paul, however, delivers a brief speech to dissuade the Lystrans (14:15–17). This is the first instance in Acts where Paul preaches to pagans without any link to the synagogue or Judaism (Haenchen *The Acts of the Apostles* MeyerK, 431). Paul urges the Lystrans to turn from "vain idols" (*ta mataia;* cf. LXX Jer 2:5) to a living God who created the world (14:15, citing Exod 20:11; cf. 1 Thess 1:9–10). Although in past generations God has allowed the pagans *(ta ethnē)* "to walk in their own ways" (Acts 17:30), he can still be perceived in the natural order of the cosmos: "For he did good and gave you from heaven rains and fruitful seasons, satisfying your hearts with food and gladness" (14:16–17; cf. Rom 1:20). It is interesting that in this non-Jewish context Paul's preaching is based on a kind of natural theology instead of the argument from prophecy. The fact that the name of Jesus is never used (not even in the miracle) is striking.

The apologetic theme of Paul's speech at Lystra is more fully developed in his speech at Athens (Acts 17:16–34). Once again Paul condemns idolatry, but this time the debate is with Epicurean and Stoic philosophers as well as with the officials of the Areopagus (on the historical problems, see Haenchen *Acts* MeyerK, 527–29). Furthermore, Paul's preaching at Athens contains an explicit reference to "Jesus and the resurrection." The Epicureans dismiss Paul as a "babbler" *(spermologos),* while the Stoics regard him as a "preacher of foreign divinities" (*kataggeleus xenōn daimoniōn*), presumably Jesus and his consort "Anastasis" (17:18). The educated reader of Acts could scarcely overlook the similarity to the charge against Socrates (*kaina daimonia eispherōn,* Xenophon, *Mem* 1.1.1; cf. Haenchen, *Acts* MeyerK, 527). Consequently Paul is brought before the court of the Areopagus in order to determine what his "new teaching" is (17:20). Paul begins his defense by calling the Athenians "very religious" (*deisidaimonesteroi,* 17:22; cf. 25:19), for while wandering through the city he discovered an altar dedicated "To an unknown god" (*agnostō theō,* 17:23). Paul concludes from this that the Athenians, or pagans generally, stand in a positive and negative relation to the one, true God: they worship him (along with many other gods!), yet they do not know him (Haenchen, *Acts* MeyerK, 521). Hence, Paul proclaims him. Alluding to Isa 42:5, he argues that the creator and lord of the cosmos does not live in man-made temples, nor is he in need of sacrifices from men. On the contrary, he is the one who "gives to all men life and breath and everything" (17:24–25; cf. 14:17). It is man's obligation therefore to seek God, for "he is not far from each one of us" (17:27). As proof of this, Paul quotes a line from the Stoic Aratus' poem *Phainomena* (5), a widely read and valued text: "For we are indeed his [according to Aratus, Zeus'] offspring" (17:28; cf. Cadbury 1955: 46–49). Paul goes on to point out that since we are God's offspring, we should not imagine that the deity is like an idol (17:29). The Hellenistic-Jewish philosopher Aristobulus (2d century B.C.) had cited this passage from Aratus to make a similar point (according to Eus. *Praep. Evang.* 13.12.3–7). Paul's polemic is directed not so much at the religion of the philosophers as it is aimed at Greek popular religion (Haenchen, *Acts* Meyer K, 525). At this point the speech takes a different turn. In the past, God has overlooked "the times of ignorance" (i.e., he had not punished the Greeks as they deserved; cf. 14:16; *contra* Rom 1:18–32); but now a decisive change has occurred: all men must repent because God is going to judge the world by "a man" (Jesus, though he is not named). The proof of this is that God has raised Jesus from the dead (17:30–31). With this, God ceases to be *unknown* (Haenchen, *Acts* MeyerK, 525). Once again the proclamation of the resurrection is incomprehensible to Paul's hearers: the Epicureans openly mock it, while the Stoics postpone a decision. "Some," however, are converted (17:32–34).

Both the Areopagus speech and Paul's address at Lystra

anticipate some of the main lines of 2d-century Christian apologetics (Geffcken 1907: xxxii–xxxiii).

D. Roman Empire

Examples of political apologetic abound in the NT, especially in the Lukan writings. It is Luke alone, for example, who connects the birth of Jesus with the census decree of Augustus (2:1–7; similarly, 3:1–2), implying thereby that Christianity rightfully belongs to the general course of world history (cf. Acts 26:26, "for this was not done in a corner"). The 2d-century apologist Melito of Sardis delights in pointing out that the birth of Christ coincided with the establishment of the Roman Empire by Augustus (according to Eusebius, *Hist. Eccl.* 4.26.7–8). Like the other evangelists, Luke is concerned to prove that Jesus was devoid of revolutionary intentions. In response to the provocative question about the payment of taxes to the emperor, Jesus insists that they should be paid (20:20–26 par.). Paul makes much the same point in Rom 13:1–7, as does the author of 1 Pet 2:13–17. In the Fourth Gospel an attempt is made to clear Jesus of the charge of being a political revolutionary by having him refuse to become king by popular acclamation (6:15; cf. 18:36). Luke is also anxious to demonstrate that Jesus was innocent of the charge of sedition. According to Luke, Pilate does not condemn Jesus (23:25; *contra* Mark 15:15; Matt 27:26); instead he pronounces him innocent on three occasions (23:4, 14, 22; cf. John 18:38; 19:4, 6). Furthermore, Luke exonerates the Romans of all culpability in the execution of Jesus: the Jewish authorities are the ones who willfully conspire to have Jesus condemned as a political revolutionary (20:20; 23:2, 5, 18–19, 23; cf. Matt 27:24–25). This in turn prepares the way for the defense of Christianity against the charge of sedition in Acts (Légasse 1981: 249–55). Once again it is the Jews who make the accusation: "They are all acting against the decrees of Caesar, saying that there is another king, Jesus" (Acts 17:7; cf. 24:5). Paul's response is typical: "Neither against the law of the Jews, nor against the temple, nor against Caesar have I offended at all" (25:8). Throughout Acts, Luke introduces an impressive array of Roman officials who display benevolence toward Christian missionaries (especially Paul) and who repeatedly attest that the charges brought against them have no factual basis (Acts 13:7, 12; 16:37–39; 18:12–16; 19:35–40; 23:26–30; 25:24–27; 26:30–32). Indeed, Paul is permitted to carry on his missionary work "openly and unhindered" even while being detained under military surveillance in Rome (28:30–31). Luke's political apologetic is intended to emphasize that there is nothing seditious about Christianity; on the contrary, Christians are law-abiding subjects of the Roman Empire. The apologists of the 2d century make the same claim (Justin *1 Apol* 17.1–3; Tertullian, *Apol* 21–24; 30–4; 32.1–3; 39.2).

An altogether negative evaluation of the Roman Empire is found in the Apocalypse of John, the result perhaps of active persecution of Christians by the state. The Pauline and Lukan view of the Empire as, on the whole, just and beneficent is here replaced by one which sees the Empire as energized by demonic forces bent on destroying the churches of God. This hostility is expressed through two principal agents: the "beasts" of Revelation 13. The first of these, the beast from the sea, is the Roman Empire itself (13:1–10); the second, the beast from the earth (or the false prophet), is the imperial cult (13:11–18). In the face of this onslaught, the apocalyptic writer advocates martyrdom, not violent resistance, for he is convinced that God and Christ will eventually triumph over the forces of evil in a great cosmic battle. The importance of Revelation should not be underestimated even though it is scarcely at the center of the NT.

E. Other Forms of Christianity

In the 1st century, Christianity lacked a uniform church structure and theology. Instead Christian communities tended to be shaped theologically and organizationally by their respective founders. Relations among these groups often ranged from close cooperation to competition and outright hostility. Nowhere is this clearer than in the Galatian churches established by Paul. His letter to these churches presents the first systematic apology for Christianity, not to outsiders but to Christians themselves (Betz 1976: 99–114). In Galatians, Paul defends what he calls "the truth of the gospel" (2:5, 14), that is, *his* gospel, "the gospel of the uncircumcision" (2:7; cf. 1:6–7; 5:6; 6:15).

Sometime after Paul's departure from Galatia, Jewish-Christian missionaries arrived from Jerusalem and attempted to persuade the Galatians that they were obligated to observe the law of Moses and receive circumcision if they hoped to achieve salvation (2:15–21; 3:2–5; 4:21; 5:2–12; 6:12–17). Paul's defense takes the form of an "apologetic letter" (Betz, *Galatians* Hermeneia, 14–15, 24, 28, 30). He begins by placing his opponents in historical perspective, identifying as their predecessors the dissenting faction at the Jerusalem council: the "false brethren" (2:4–5), the "men from James" (2:12), and the "circumcision faction" (2:12), as well as the Cephas group at Antioch (2:11–14). Furthermore, Paul contends that his "law-free" gospel was officially recognized by the "pillar apostles" of the Jerusalem church (2:1–10). Next, Paul appeals to scripture to prove that his gospel to the Gentiles represents the fulfillment of God's covenant with Abraham (3:1–29). Since Paul's opponents had success in winning the Galatians over to their side (i.e., to a form of Christian Judaism), Paul is compelled to define and defend his theology over against Judaism (see above, section B). Finally, in the allegory of Hagar and Sarah (4:21–31), Paul argues that only those who rely on faith and not the law are the true children of Abraham.

In its polemic against the doctrine of justification by faith, the letter of James provides evidence for the theology and continued existence of Paul's Jewish-Christian opponents (Jas 2:14–26; cf. Luedemann 1983: 194–205).

Galatians was not the only letter in which Paul had to defend himself against rival missionaries. In the letter fragment preserved in Phil 3:2–4:3 we learn that, like the opponents in Galatia, the adversaries encountered in Philippi also advocated a form of Christianity which included observance of the Jewish law and circumcision. Paul angrily refers to these opponents as "dogs" (3:2), turning on them the common term of abuse used by Jews of pagans (cf. Mark 7:27). In hyperbolic fashion Paul redefines circumcision as a form of ritual mutilation (3:2; cf. Gal 5:12) and argues that righteousness cannot be obtained through the law but only through faith in Christ (3:9; cf. Gal 2:16).

Paul also encountered Jewish-Christian missionaries in Corinth who boasted that they were "Hebrews, Israelites, and descendants of Abraham" as well as "servants of Christ" (2 Cor 11:22–23; cf. Georgi 1964: 31–82, 219–46). These "super-apostles" (11:5; 12:11) arrived in Corinth carrying letters of recommendation (3:1, from Jerusalem?) and claiming that they had performed miracles (12:11–12) and received mystical experiences (12:1–9). Since, however, they do not mention the law or circumcision, they appear not to have been the same opponents Paul encountered in Galatia and Philippi. These missionaries criticized Paul, saying that "his letters are weighty and strong, but his bodily presence is weak, and his speech of no account" (10:10–12). Furthermore, they argued that Paul's refusal to accept money from the Corinthians was either because he had no apostolic authority (12:11–18; cf. 11:7–9) or because he planned to steal from the collection (12:17). Paul first responded to these opponents in the letter fragment of 2 Cor 2:14–6:13 and 7:2–4. This letter appears to have been unsuccessful, however, for after a personal visit to Corinth, Paul was again compelled to defend himself in a letter partially preserved in 2 Corinthians 10–13, the so-called "letter of tears" mentioned in 2:4. This letter is a defense (cf. *apologeomai* in 12:19) of Paul's apostleship and ministry and displays a considerable amount of literary and rhetorical sophistication (Betz 1972: 13–42). Although Paul asks the Corinthians not to evaluate him by his opponents' criteria (10:1–18), he finally does so himself in the "fool's speech" of 11:16–12:13. Paul contends that he fully measures up to his opponents in terms of pedigree and spirituality (11:22–23; 12:1–16). Paradoxically, however, he insists that his superiority consists of the dangers, insults, and misfortunes that have plagued his career as an apostle: "If I must boast, I will boast of the things that show my weakness" (11:23–33; cf. 12:7–10, the "thorn in the flesh"). In this way, Paul makes clear that the Corinthians should not judge him in comparison with his opponents. Instead they must examine themselves to see whether they are holding the faith and whether Christ is present among them (13:5). If this is the case, then Paul has stood the test (Koester 1982: 2.130).

A completely different situation is presupposed by Paul's first letter to the Corinthians. Here Paul is not contending with *outside* rivals (but note the references to Apollos, 1:12; 3:4–6, 22; 4:6; 16:12). His polemic is addressed instead to the Corinthians themselves. In fact, the problems with which Paul deals seem to have resulted from a misunderstanding of what he himself had preached. Since he does not accuse the Corinthians of believing a "different gospel," 1 Corinthians is not an apologetic letter like Galatians or 2 Corinthians 10–13 (Koester 1982: 2.121).

In Colossians, Paul (or a Paulinist) is once again arguing with Jewish-Christian opponents who advocate circumcision (2:11) and the observance of dietary regulations and festivals like new moon and sabbath (2:16, 21). This is reminiscent of the situation in Galatians and Philippians, but in Colossians there is a gnostic dimension to the opponents' theology (*philosophia,* 2:8; cf. Koester 1982: 2.264–65). The opponents regard Christ as the head of a hierarchy of cosmic powers (1:16; 2:10). Union with Christ therefore could only be achieved through the mediation of angelic powers, probably in the context of a mystery-like initiation (2:18). In responding to this form of Christianity, the author of Colossians admits that Christ is the chief of the cosmic powers (1:15–20; 2:10; cf. Eph 1:21–22); but he maintains that through Christ's death these cosmic powers have been conquered and disarmed (2:15). At the same time the author contends that the Jewish law has also been canceled through Christ's death (2:14).

The precise identity of the opponents attacked by the author of the Pastoral Letters is difficult to determine. There are references which seem to fit both Jewish-Christians (1 Tim 1:7; 4:3; Titus 1:10, 14) and "gnostics" (1 Tim 6:20; 2 Tim 2:18), as well as false teachers generally (1 Tim 6:5, 10; 2 Tim 3:6–7; Titus 1:11). Only rarely, however, does the author enter into theological debate with his opponents (1 Tim 4:1–5). Instead, he prefers name-calling (Karris 1973: 549–64). The Pastorals seem therefore to have been designed as a manual or handbook to enable church leaders to identify and reject "heretical" brands of Christianity (Koester 1982: 2.304).

The author of the document known as 2 Peter warns his readers about those who distort the scriptures, including Paul's writings (3:16), with "cleverly designed myths" (1:16; cf. 2:1–22). In particular, these opponents reject the doctrine of Christ's parousia: "Where is the promise of his coming? For ever since the fathers fell asleep, all things have continued as they were from the beginning of creation" (3:4). The author of 2 Peter does not defend the traditional understanding of the parousia, but presents a general eschatological view of the dissolution of the cosmos, similar to the Stoic doctrine of "conflagration," *ekpyrōsis* (3:5–13; cf. Käsemann 1964: 169–95), with criticisms by Neyrey 1980: 407–31).

The author of 1 John argues against a "gnostic" interpretation of the Gospel of John. He identifies his opponents as those who deny that Jesus "came in the flesh" (4:2) and who refuse to identify the heavenly Christ with the earthly Jesus (2:22). In response, the author of 1 John insists on their identity (5:6–8) and maintains that such a view is in full accord with the intentions of the gospel (1:1–4). The author of 3 John is critical of a certain Diotrephes, who "does not acknowledge my authority" (9–10). The problem, however, seems to be more one of ecclesiastical politics than of theological controversy.

F. Conclusion

On the basis of this general survey of apologetics in the NT, the following conclusions may be drawn: (1) The appeal to the Jewish scriptures lies at the heart of the apologetic enterprise, both with respect to Judaism and the wider Greco-Roman world. It is on this basis that Jesus' messianic status is said to be proven and that Christianity's claim to be a world religion is established. In some instances even intramural controversies are resolved by an appeal to the OT. (2) The NT response to Greek religion is decidedly negative. Greek religion is rejected as idolatrous and the gods of the Greeks are exposed as demons who have deceived and enslaved mankind. Here the NT adopts the perspective of Hellenistic Judaism and, indeed, of Greek philosophy itself. Nevertheless, on the basis of an appeal to natural theology, pagans are held accountable, for there is sufficient knowledge of God available to them to ensure their responsibility. (3) With one exception, the NT uniformly views the Roman Empire as just and beneficent. Likewise, Christians are portrayed as loyal, law-abiding subjects of the Empire. (4) Many of the apologetic arguments found in the NT anticipate the main outlines of 2d-century apologetics. (See Bardy *RAC* 1: 533–43; Kamlah *RGG*³ 1: 477–500.)

Bibliography

Betz, H. D. 1972. *Der Apostel Paulus und die sokratische Tradition: Eine exegetische Untersuchung zu seiner "Apologie" 2 Korinther 10–13.* BHT 45. Tübingen.

———. 1976. In Defense of the Spirit: Paul's Letter to the Galatians as a Document of Early Christian Apologetics. Pp. 99–114 in *Aspects of Religious Propaganda in Judaism and Early Christianity,* ed. E. S. Fiorenza. Notre Dame.

Bruce, F. F. 1959. *The Defense of the Gospel.* Grand Rapids.

Cadbury, H. J. 1955. *The Book of Acts in History.* New York.

Castellino, G. 1963. Il paganesimo di Romani 1, Sapienza 13–14 e la storia delle religioni. Vol. 2, pp. 255–63 in *Studiorum Paulinorum Congressus Internationalis Catholicus 1961.* Rome.

Craig, W. 1984. The Guard at the Tomb (Mt 27:62–66; 28:4, 11–15). *NTS* 30: 273–81.

Decharme, P. 1904. *La critique des traditions religieuses chez les grecs des origines au temp de Plutarque.* Paris.

Dibelius, M. 1951. Paul on the Areopagus. *Studies in the Acts of the Apostles.* New York.

Dodd, C. H. 1953. *According to the Scriptures.* New York.

Droge, A. J. 1988. *Homer or Moses? Early Christian Interpretations of the History of Culture.* Hermeneutische Untersuchungen zur Theologie 26. Tübingen.

Ferguson, E. 1962. Apologetics in the New Testament. *ResQ* 6: 189–96.

Fiorenza, E. S. 1976. Miracles, Mission, and Apologetics: An Introduction. Pp. 1–25 in *Aspects of Religious Propaganda in Judaism and Early Christianity,* ed. E. S. Fiorenza. Notre Dame.

Gaertner, B. 1955. *The Areopagus Speech and Natural Revelation.* ASNU 21. Lund.

Geffcken, J. 1907. *Zwei griechische Apologeten.* Leipzig and Berlin.

Georgi, D. 1964. *Die Gegner des Paulus im 2 Korintherbrief: Studien zur religiösen Propaganda in der Spätantike.* WMANT II. Neukirchen-Vluyn.

———. 1971. Forms of Religious Propaganda. Pp. 124–31 in *Jesus and His Time,* ed. H. J. Schultz. Philadelphia.

Goodspeed, E. J., ed. 1914. *Die ältesten Apologeten.* Göttingen.

Grant, R. M. 1952. Hellenistic Elements in Galatians. *ATR* 34: 223–26.

———. 1986. *Gods and the One God.* Philadelphia.

Heffern, A. D. 1922. *Apology and Polemic in the New Testament.* New York.

Jervell, J. S. 1968. Paulus—Der Lehrer Israels: Zu den apologetischen Paulusreden in der Apostelgeschichte. *NovT* 10: 164–90.

Käsemann, E. 1964. An Apologia for Primitive Christian Eschatology. *Essays on New Testament Themes.* London.

Karris, R. J. 1973. Background and Significance of the Polemic of the Pastoral Epistles. *JBL* 92: 549–64.

Koester, H. 1982. *Introduction to the New Testament.* 2 vols. Philadelphia.

Légasse, S. 1981. L'apologetique à l'égard de Rome dans le procès de Paul (Actes 21, 27–26, 32). *RSR* 69: 249–55.

Lindars, B. 1961. *New Testament Apologetic: The Doctrinal Significance of the Old Testament Quotations.* Philadelphia.

Luedemann, G. 1983. *Paulus, der Heidenapostel: Vol. 2: Antipaulinisums im frühen Christentum.* FRLANT 130. Goettingen.

Malherbe, A. J. 1985/6. "Not in a Corner": Early Christian Apologetic in Acts 26:26. *SecondCent* 5: 193–210.

Nestle, W. 1952. Zur altchristliche Apologetik im Neuen Testament. *ZRGG* 4: 115–23.

Neyrey, J. 1980. The Form and Background of the Polemic in 2 Peter. *JBL* 99: 407–31.

Nock, A. D. 1959. Posidonius. *JRS* 49: 1–15.

Paulsen, H. 1977. Das Kerygma Petri und die urchristliche Apologetik. *ZKG* 88: 1–37.

Reagan, J. N. 1923. *The Preaching of Peter: The Beginning of Christian Apologetic.* Chicago.

Scott, E. F. 1907. *The Apologetic of the New Testament.* London.

Wernle, P. 1900. Altchristliche Apologetik im Neuen Testament: Ein Beitrag zur Evangelienfrage. *ZNW* 1: 42–65.

Williams, A. L. 1935. *Adversus Judaeos: A Bird's-Eye View of Christian Apologiae until the Renaissance.* Cambridge.

A. J. Droge

APOPHTHEGM. New Testament interpreters have used five different terms to refer to brief narratives that culminate in a saying of Jesus: (1) apophthegm; (2) paradigm; (3) pronouncement story; (4) chreia; and (5) anecdote. R. Bultmann, who used the term apophthegm, defined the form as "sayings of Jesus set in a brief context" (1963: 11). M. Dibelius, who used the term "paradigm," defined the form as an example narrative, "a record of a particular situation in a form which is as far as possible free of tendency and therefore of individuality and color" (1934: 37). He added that "many a Paradigm reaches its point in, and at the same time concludes with, a word of Jesus" (1934: 56). V. Taylor, using the term "pronouncement story," defined the form as stories that "quickly reach their climax in a saying of Jesus which was of interest to the first Christians because it bore directly upon questions of faith and practice" (1949: 23). R. Tannehill, using at one time the term "apophthegm" (*ANRW* 2/25/2: 1792–1829) and at another time "pronouncement story" (1981a, 1981b), expanded the definition to: a brief narrative in which the climactic (and often final) element is a pronouncement which is presented as a particular person's response to something said or observed on a particular occasion of the past. There are two main parts of a pronouncement story: the pronouncement and its setting, i.e., the response and the situation provoking the response. The movement from the one to the other is the main development in these brief stories (Tannehill 1981a: 1; cf. *ANRW* 2/25/2: 1792–93).

In recent years, as rhetorical analysis of the New Testament has come under the influence of the study of ancient rhetoric, a growing number of interpreters have started to use the term "chreia" for these units. According to our earliest extant definition, a chreia is a concise statement or action attributed with aptness to some specified character or to something analogous to a character (Butts 1987: 187; cf. Hock and O'Neil 1986: 83). This definition calls attention to action as well as speech, but even more important is the rhetorical framework in which the definition occurs.

Ancient rhetoricians manipulated the chreia by adding comments at the beginning and end, by expanding situations, questions and answers, and by elaborating the chreia into an argumentative sequence of units or into an essay. This means that a concise statement or action attributed to a specific person was a primary means for exploring, transmitting, and clarifying information about life in the world. The form, therefore, was not closed and unchangeable, but open and fluid. Since most of the features of the chreia discussed by the rhetoricians appear in the NT (see Robbins 1988a), interpreters have begun to analyze brief, medium, and longer units as instances of abbreviated, expanded, and elaborated chreiai (Mack 1988; Mack and Robbins 1988).

With the use of the term "chreia," interpreters have broadened the understanding of the relation of early Christian stories to stories in Hellenistic and Roman literature and society. Many more instances of chreiai exist in contemporary Greek and Roman literature than in contemporary Jewish literature. In the context of this observation, K. Berger, B. Mack, and V. K. Robbins have used the more general term "anecdote" as well as chreia, pronouncement story, and apophthegm to refer to the units (Berger *ANRW* 2/25/2: 1034–1432; 1984; Mack 1987; Robbins 1988b). This terminology reflects an awareness of fluidity within the form and of widespread existence of the form in Hellenistic and Roman culture.

No matter which of the five terms interpreters have used, all of them consider eleven well-known stories to represent the form: Eating with Tax Collectors and Sinners (Mark 2:15–17); the Question about Fasting (Mark 2:18–22); Plucking Grain on the Sabbath (Mark 2:23–28); True Relatives of Jesus (Mark 3:31–34); Blessing the Children (Mark 10:13–16); The Rich Young Man (Mark 10:17–22); The Sons of Zebedee (Mark 10:35–40); Paying Taxes to Caesar (Mark 12:13–17); On the Resurrection (Mark 12:18–27); The Anointing at Bethany (Mark 14:3–9); and Healing of the Man with Dropsy (Luke 14:1–6).

Dibelius, using the term "paradigm," discussed seven stories beyond this common group. One of them, Prophet without Honor (Mark 6:1–6), has been included by most interpreters except Taylor, who called it a "story about Jesus" rather than a "pronouncement story" (1949: 75). Cleansing the Temple (Mark 11:15-17) often is not included since the saying of Jesus derives from scripture. A third story, the Inhospitable Samaritans (Luke 9:51–55), often is not included since most early manuscripts do not contain the response, "and he [Jesus] said, 'You do not know what manner of spirit you are of; for the Son of Man came not to destroy men's lives but to save them.' " Dibelius also included four healing stories in addition to Luke 14:1–6: The Demoniac in the Synagogue (Mark 1:23–28); The Paralytic (Mark 2:1–12); The Man with the Withered Hand (Mark 3:1–6); and Blind Bartimaeus (Mark 10:46–52). Many interpreters today include the first three, because of the decisive speech and action of Jesus, but only a few include the healing of blind Bartimaeus.

Bultmann discussed forty-seven stories in the section on apophthegms in the Synoptic Gospels. During the 1980s this list expanded dramatically. In 1984, Berger presented a list of sixty-seven units (1984: 80–82) and Tannehill discussed approximately eighty-five units (*ANRW* 2/25/2: 1792–1829). In addition to the eleven units universally accepted and Prophet without Honor (Mark 6:1–6), Berger and Tannehill discussed twenty-two units Bultmann had discussed in his investigation of apophthegms: Beelzebul Controversy (Mark 3:22[23]–30); Defilement (Mark 7:1–15); Dispute about Greatness (Mark 9:33–37); Strange Exorcist (Mark 9:38–40); Who Can Be Saved? (Mark 10:23[26]–27); Already Left Family (Mark 10:28–31); Question of Authority (Mark 11:27–33); Greatest Commandment (Mark 12:28–34); Widow's Penny (Mark 12:41–44); Temple Destruction (Mark 13:1–2); Following (Matt 8:19–22; Luke 9:57–62); Baptist's Question (Matt 11:2–6; Luke 7:18–23); Praise of Children (Matt 21:14–16); Shekel in Fish's Mouth (Matt 17:24–27); Mary and Martha (Luke 10:38[40]–42); Woman Blesses Jesus' Mother (Luke 11:27–28); Parable of Rich Fool (Luke 12:13–21); Repentance or Destruction (Luke 13:1–5[9]); Prophet Perish in Jerusalem (Luke 13:31–33); Kingdom of God in You (Luke 17:20–21); Zaccheus (Luke 19:1–10); and Disciples Praise Mighty Works (Luke 19:37–40). In addition, Berger and Tannehill included ten units not included by Bultmann among apophthegms: Sign Request (Mark 8:11–12); Question about David's Son (Mark 12:35–37); Temptation of Jesus (Matt 4:1–11; Luke 4:1–13); Forgiveness (Matt 18:21–35); Inquiries to the Baptist (Luke 3:10–15); Return of the Seventy (Luke 10:17–20); Continuation of the Greatest Commandment (Luke 10:29–37); Narrow Door (Luke 13:22–30); Lovers of Money (Luke 16:14–15[31]); and Faith and Worthy Servant (Luke 17:5–6[10]). Beyond this, Tannehill (1981b) includes approximately thirty-five Synoptic Gospel units that Berger (1984) does not include. In turn, Berger introduces ten units from the Gospel of John and two from Acts: Why Do You Baptize? (John 1:24–27); Temple Cleansing (John 13:22); Question to John about Jesus (John 3:25–36); Jesus' Food (John 4:31–34); Work of God Is to Believe (John 6:28–29); Request for Sign (John 6:30–34); Refusal to Go to Jerusalem Openly (John 7:1–9); Adulterous Woman (John 8:1–11); Going to Jerusalem Again? (John 11:8–10); Mary Anoints Jesus (John 12:1–8); What Should We Do? (Acts 2:37–39); What Should I Do? (Acts 16:30–31).

When the lists of Berger and Tannehill are combined, approximately one hundred units in the Gospels and Acts now are being discussed as apophthegms or pronouncement stories. Along with this expansion of the list has come significantly new systems for classifying the units. A classification system among the forms began with Bultmann, who distinguished biographical apophthegms from controversy and didactic apophthegms. Tannehill grouped the synoptic units under five categories: (1) correction stories; (2) commendation stories; (3) quest stories; (4) objection stories; and (5) inquiry stories (1981a; 1981b; *ANRW* 2/25/2: 1792–1829). Berger and Robbins have introduced the categories of deliberative, judicial, and epideictic rhetoric in their classifications of stories (Berger 1984: 91–92; Robbins 1984). In addition, Robbins has grouped more than 1700 stories from antiquity according to the life cycle of a person and the major groups of people with whom the person interacts during the adult stage (1988b). The life-cycle categories are: (1) conception and birth; (2) childhood through beginning of adult career; (3) adult career; (4) old age; and (5) death. During the adult stage, the main character interacts with eight different kinds of people or groups: (1) associate or friend (individual); (2) associates or friends (group); (3) family; (4) feminine person(s); (5) general person or audience; (6) leader or representative (of a group or type); (7) specified group; (8) young person(s). This classification shows that these brief stories, each attributed to a specific person, are natural constituents in a biography of a person's life (cf. Berger 1984: 82).

Bibliography

Berger, K. 1984. *Formgeschichte des Neuen Testaments.* Heidelberg.

Bultmann, R. 1963. *The History of the Synoptic Tradition.* New York.

Butts, J. R. 1987. *The "Progymnasmata" of Theon: A New Text with Translation and Commentary.* Diss. Claremont.

Dibelius, M. 1934. *From Tradition to Gospel.* New York.

Hock, R. F., and O'Neil, E. N. 1986. *The Chreia in Ancient Rhetoric.* Volume 1, *The Progymnasmata.* Atlanta.

Mack, B. L. 1987. Anecdotes and Arguments: The Chreia in Antiquity and Early Christianity. *Occasional Papers of the Institute for Antiquity and Christianity* 10: 1–48.

———. 1988. *A Myth of Innocence: Mark and Christian Origins.* Philadelphia.

Mack, B. L., and Robbins, V. K. 1988. *Patterns of Persuasion in the Gospels.* Sonoma, CA.

Robbins, V. K. 1984. A Rhetorical Typology for Classifying and Analyzing Pronouncement Stories. *SBLSP* 23: 93–122.

———. 1988a. The Chreia and the New Testament. Pp. 1–24 in *Greco-Roman Literature and the New Testament: Selected Forms and Genres,* ed. David E. Aune. SBLSBS 21. Atlanta.

———. 1988b. *Ancient Quotes and Anecdotes.* Sonoma, CA.

Tannehill, R. C. 1981a. Introduction: The Pronouncement Story and Its Types. *Semeia* 21: 1–13.

———. 1981b. Varieties of Synoptic Pronouncement Stories. *Semeia* 21: 101–19.

Taylor, V. 1949. *The Formation of the Gospel Tradition.* London.

VERNON K. ROBBINS

APOSTASY. See PUNISHMENTS AND CRIMES.

APOSTLE. An apostle in the NT is an envoy, an ambassador, or a missionary. In the NT the term "apostle" is applied to one who carries the message of the gospel.

A. Definition and Origin

The early Christian title of apostle, although well attested in the NT and other early Christian sources, presents a number of still unresolved problems. The noun "apostle" *(apostolos)* is originally an adjective derived from the verb *apostellō* ("send"), found in the NT with a considerable range of meanings. The basic concept is that of the sending of messengers or envoys; an apostle can also be called *angelos* ("messenger," e.g., Luke 7:24; 9:52) or *kērux* ("herald," e.g., 1 Tim 2:7, 2 Tim 1:11; cf. Mark 1:45; 2 Cor 5:20). Apostles can be human or divine, sent by human or divine authorities.

The original adjective *apostolos* is attested only infrequently in Greek literature, referring to an envoy or a bearer of a message in a general sense (e.g., Herodotus 1.21; Plato, *Ep.* 7.346a). This technical meaning conforms to the Aramaic *selîaḥ* (Ezra 7:14; Dan 5:24; cf. 2 Chr 17:7–9; for references and bibliography, see Spicq, 1982). In the Hellenistic era, the concept of the divine envoy was applied by Epictetus to the ideal cynic (*Diss.* 3.22.3; 4.8.31), but the term *apostolos* does not occur. Christianity, therefore, appears to have picked a secular term and made it into a specific office and title.

In addition to evidencing a bewildering range of applications of the title of apostle, the NT and the early patristic literature also attempt to define it. Since scholarship is still divided on many of the questions, the following definitions must be seen as part of the argument and not as final answers.

The basic definition given by Origen (*Jo.* 32.17, ed. Preuschen 1903: 453, line 17) is simple: "Everyone who is sent by someone is an apostle of the one who sent him." The concept involves legal and administrative aspects and is basic to all types of representatives, envoys, and ambassadors. In the area of Christian religion, the term "apostle" can refer to a messenger, human or divine, sent by God or Christ to reveal messages or to reveal *the* message of the gospel. Origen's definition, although later, is grounded in the NT itself; e.g., John 13:16: "Truly, truly I say to you, a servant is not greater than his master; nor is he who is sent greater than the one who sent him" (cf. also Matt 10:40–42; Gal 4:14). More specific is the definition given in Acts 1:21–22, according to which an apostle must be "one of the men who have accompanied us during all the time that the Lord Jesus went in and out among us, beginning from the baptism of John until the day when he was taken up from us. . . ." Paul mentions (2 Cor 12:12; cf. Rom 15:19; Acts 5:12) the practice of the apostle legitimating himself by "the signs of the apostle" (*ta sēmeia tou apostolou*): i.e., "by signs and miracles and wondrous deeds." In the Petrine traditions, the task of the apostle is seen as transmitting the words of the prophets and of Jesus to the church (2 Pet 3:2; cf. the prophetic function of the apostles in Jude 17). Paul did not conform to any of these definitions, a fact that explains his position as an outsider and the difficulties he had obtaining recognition.

B. Apostles as Missionaries

Chronologically, in the earliest use of the term in the NT, *apostolos* is an administrative designation for envoys, delegates, and representatives. Their title and function are given in 2 Cor 8:23 (cf. Phil 2:25) as "envoys of the churches" *(apostoloi ekklēsiōn)*, that is, envoys appointed and sent out by the churches to represent them (see Betz *2 Corinthians 8 and 9* Hermeneia, 73, 81, 86). In other places, the term "apostle" is understood in a more religious sense as a missionary and preacher of the gospel. Acts 1:21–26 and 13:1–3, passages describing the appointment of different types of "apostles," show that such appointments did not exclude divine intervention and authorization. The tasks of these apostles could vary but they seem to be centered in the proclamation of the gospel and the founding and administering of new churches (see 1 Cor 9:5, 12:28; Eph 2:20; 3:5; 4:11; Rev 18:20; *Did.* 11:3–6). Rom 16:3–16 includes a long list of greetings, among them the two apostles Andronicus and Junias (Rom 16:7). Perhaps the name "Junias" was corrected by scribes to replace Junia, a female name; such a correction would indicate that a woman (here possibly a married couple like Prisca and Aquila in 16:3, and Philologus and Julia in 16:15, although none of them is called apostle) could serve as a missionary apostle (see BAGD: 380, s.v. *Iounias*; Schüssler-Fiorenza 1983: 160–204).

C. Jesus' Disciples as Apostles

A different concept of apostle is presupposed when the title is attributed to former disciples *(mathētai)* of Jesus who had been witnesses of his resurrection (Matt 10:2, 28:16–20; Mark 16:14–18; Luke 24:47–49; John 20:19–23; cf. 1 Cor 9:1). There are, however, complications. The decisive passage, 1 Cor 15:3–7, cites a composite formula combining different terminological usages (see Conzelmann *1 Corinthians* Hermeneia, 251–60): v 5 names Cephas, Peter and the Twelve, v 7 includes James, the brother of Jesus (not called apostle in Gal 1:19; 1 Cor 9:5; see Betz *Galatians* Hermeneia, 78), and "all the apostles" without clarifying how they are related to the "500 brothers" (v 6) not called apostles. At a later stage, the gospel writers, especially Luke, identify the disciples of Jesus during his life on earth with the apostles and the Twelve, creating the concept of the Twelve Apostles (see Matt 10:1–2; Mark 3:14 with variant readings; Luke 6:13; Acts 1:23–26; Klein 1961). Originally, either in the earliest church or in Jesus' lifetime, the Twelve *(hoi dōdeka)* were a separate institution (see 1 Cor 15:5; Acts 6:2) representing the twelve tribes of Israel (Matt 19:28; see Sanders 1985: 98–106). While their number was fixed, the names in the lists of the apostles vary to some extent (see Mark 3:16–19; Matt 10:2–4; Luke 6:14–16; Acts 1:13, 23, 26; for later lists, see *NTApocr,* 35–79; cf. also Mark 14:10, 43 and parallels; John 6:71, 12:4, 20:24; Acts 6:2). Luke's concept of the Twelve Apostles in effect limits the number to the disciples of the historical Jesus and denies the title of apostle to Paul (except Acts 14:4, 14, where Barnabas and Paul, owing to a pre-Lukan source, are called apostles). For Luke, the Twelve Apostles are the leaders of the Jerusalem church (see especially Acts 4:35–37; 5:2, 27–32; 6:6; 8:1, 14, 18; 9:27; 11:1; 15:1–6, 22–23; 16:4 [the last time apostles are mentioned in Acts]). Consequently, Luke does not call the missionaries apostles.

D. Paul as Apostle of the Gentiles

The origins of Paul's concept of apostleship are still shrouded in mystery. In early Christianity the term was controversial, as can be seen from the NT. Paul's letters reveal some developments. In accordance with an earlier stage of the tradition, Barnabas and Paul served as missionary "apostles" (cf. Rom 16:7; Acts 13:2–4; 14:4, 14; 1 Thess 2:1–7). Paul's bold attempt to rank himself alongside Cephas and the Twelve (1 Cor 15:3–10), however, met resistance, especially in the churches not founded by Paul, causing fierce debates about what constitutes apostleship. These debates reflect the fact that Paul's own interpretation of the title and office rested on rather different theological presuppositions by which he gave apostleship a completely new interpretation. This can have occurred only at a somewhat later time, not at the beginning of Paul's ministry. At the conference in Jerusalem (Gal 2:8; see Betz *Galatians,* 98–99; Lüdemann 1984: 76–77; 1980–83, 2: 62–63), and even in the prescript of the early letter of 1 Thessalonians (cf. also Phil 1:1; 2:25; Phlm 1), he did not call himself apostle (cf. its ambiguous usage in 1 Thess 2:7). The title appears as Paul's self-description in an epistolary prescript first in Gal 1:1, perhaps as a result of the conflict in Antioch (2:11–14), and then becomes standard (1 Cor: 2:7; 2 Cor 1:1; Rom 1:1; then Col 1:1; Eph 1:1; 1 Tim 1:1; 2 Tim 1:1, 11; Tit 1:1; differently 2 Thess 1:1).

Paul's reinterpretation of the concept questioned fundamental assumptions held by the church before Paul. He rejected the idea that having known the historical Jesus personally was a valid criterion (2 Cor 5:16). Indeed, the gospels point out that those who knew Jesus best during his life on earth—his disciples and his family—came to understand his message only after the resurrection. On the other hand, if witnessing the resurrection was the criterion, Paul qualified as an apostle, since he too had a vision of the risen Lord (Gal 1:16; 1 Cor 9:1–5; 15:1–10). If founding churches was the criterion, Paul had worked more in this task than everyone else (1 Cor 15:10). Looking back at his mission, he calls himself the "apostle of the Gentiles" (Rom 11:13; cf. 1:5–7, 13–15). When Christ appeared to him and called him to preach the gospel to the Gentiles (Gal 1:15–16), Paul took this call to mean that he was given a unique role in salvation history. In Rom 1:1; 1 Cor 1:1, Paul claims to be a "called apostle" *(klētos apostolos),* analogous to the former disciples of Jesus (cf. Mark 1:16–20 and parallels; 6:7; Matt 10:1, etc.). Not appointed by human authorities (Gal 1:1, 12) but by the risen Christ himself, he came to regard himself as the personal representative *(mimētēs)* of Christ on earth (1 Thess 1:6; 11:1; Phil 3:17; see Betz 1967). This fact implied that Paul's entire physical and spiritual existence was to be understood as an epiphany of the crucified and resurrected redeemer (Gal 6:14, 17; 2 Cor 2:14–5:21; 6:4–10; 12:7–10; 13:3–4; Phil 3:10). His missionary campaigns were to be regarded as a decisive phase prior to the *parousia,* in which the gospel had to be preached "from Jerusalem in a wide curve as far as Illyricum" (Rom 15:19) and indeed as far as Spain (Rom 15:24). This mission, when completed, would be regarded as the "offering of the gentiles" in which he officiated as the chief "celebrant" (Rom 15:16). In the Last Judgment, Paul expected to present his gentile churches unblemished and pure to Christ (1 Thess 2:10–12; 5:23; 1 Cor 1:8; 2 Cor 1:14; 11:2; Phil 2:15; furthermore Col 1:22; Eph 5:27).

Paul's concept of apostleship, while not conforming to the common criteria as exemplified by Luke-Acts, effectively changed these criteria, a process reflected in the NT. In this reinterpretation, other influences came into play. Widengren (1950; for bibliography, see Betz *Galatians,* 75) pointed to notions in Syriac Gnosticism that may have contributed to Paul's concept of apostleship. Betz (1972) showed that Paul was influenced by the Socratic tradition in which Socrates was seen as a messenger sent by the deity. Whatever influences there may have been, however, Paul, through his debates and struggles, and through his own suffering and death (cf. Col 1:24), defined the concept of apostleship in a radically new way that also determined its understanding and application in the post-NT era.

E. False Apostles

Paul's claim to apostleship reflects a more general confusion about the question of who was truly an apostle. Was James, "the brother of the Lord," an apostle (see Gal 1:19; 1 Cor 9:5; see Betz *Galatians,* 78)? The evidence is ambiguous. Contrary to Acts 14:4, 14, Paul himself evidently avoided attributing the title to Barnabas (cf. Gal 2:1–10, 13; 1 Cor 9:6). Paul sometimes mentions other missionary apostles whom he apparently considers to be inferior in status when compared to himself (see B, above). When he ridicules his opponents as "false apostles" (*pseudapostoloi,* 2 Cor 11:13) or "superapostles" (*hyperlian apostoloi,* 2 Cor 11:5; 12:11), he unfortunately does not reveal their names. That these opponents had even less respectful titles for him is suggested by the term "miscarriage" (*ektrōma,* 1 Cor 15:8). The struggle over the definition and criteria of true and false apostleship (see also Rev 2:2), in analogy to that over true and false prophecy, raged well into later church history as part of the battles against heresy (see *NTApocr,* 35–74; furthermore HERESY AND ORTHODOXY IN THE NT).

F. Christ as Apostle

Peculiar is the fact that only Heb 3:1 calls Christ an apostle: "Jesus, the apostle and high priest of our confession" (see Braun *An die Hebräer* HNT, 71–74, 78). This, however, appears to be a late application of the term which may have older roots (cf. Matt 15:24; Luke 4:18, 43). The Fourth Gospel still contains what seem to be traces of an older usage. We find here not only the definitive statement of 13:16 (cited above, A) but also, through the terminology of sending *(apostellō),* the description of Christ's entire mission. Jesus Christ, the Logos and Son of God, was sent by God into this world (3:16–17, 34; 5:36–38; 6:29, 57; 7:29; 10:36; 11:42; 17:3, 8, 18, 21, 23, 25; 20:21; cf. 1 John 4:9, 10, 14). In turn, Jesus sends out his disciples (4:38; 17:18; 20:21). They are called the Twelve, not apostles (6:67, 70–71; 20:24). It seems that the Fourth Gospel, without offering reasons, studiously avoids the title of apostle, while presuming the concept and terminology of sending. Perhaps the matter is related to the general similarity between Johannine christology and Pauline apostleship, a similarity which may reflect the still unexplained relationship between Johannine and Pauline Christianity.

Bibliography

Agnew, F. 1976. On the Origin of the Term Apostolos. *CBQ* 38: 49–53.

———. 1986. The Origin of the NT Apostle-Concept: A Review of Research. *JBL* 105: 75–96.

Barrett, C. K. 1970. *Pseudapostoloi* (2 Cor. 11:13). Pp. 377–96 in *Mélanges bibliques en hommage au R. P. Béda Rigaux.* Gembloux. Repr. pp. 87–107 in *Essays on Paul.* Philadelphia, 1982.

Betz, H. D. 1967. *Nachfolge und Nachahmung Jesu Christi im Neuen Testament.* BHT 37. Tübingen.

———. 1972. *Der Apostel Paulus und die sokratische Tradition.* BHT 45. Tübingen.

Brooten, B. 1982. *Women Leaders in the Ancient Synagogue.* BJS 36. Chico, CA.

Bühner, J.-A. 1977. *Der Gesandte und sein Weg im 4. Evangelium.* WUNT 2.2. Tübingen.

Hock, R. F. 1980. *The Social Context of Paul's Ministry.* Philadelphia.

Krik, J. A. 1974/75. Apostleship since Rengstorf. *NTS* 21:249–64.

Klein, G. 1961. *Die Zwölf Apostel.* FRLANT 77. Göttingen.

Lüdemann, G. 1980–83. *Paulus der Heidenapostel.* 2 vols. FRLANT 123, 130. Göttingen.

———. 1984. *Paul, Apostle to the Gentiles.* Trans. F. S. Jones. Philadelphia.

Munck, J. 1959 (1954). *Paul and the Salvation of Mankind.* Trans. F. Clarke. London.

Sanders, E. P. 1985. *Jesus and Judaism.* London and Philadelphia.

Schmithals, W. 1969. *The Office of the Apostle.* Trans. J. E. Steele. Nashville.

Schnackenburg, R. 1970. Apostles before and during Paul's Time. Pp. 287–303 in *Apostolic History and the Gospel.* ed. W. W. Gasque and R. P. Martin. Grand Rapids.

Schoeps, H. J. 1959. *Paul.* Trans. H. Knight. Philadelphia.

Schüssler Fiorenza, E. 1983. *In Memory of Her.* New York.

Spicq, C. 1982. *Notes de lexicographie néo-testamentaire, Supplément.* Pp. 54–63 in OBO 22/3. Freiburg. Éditions universitaires; Göttingen.

Widengren, G. 1950. *The Ascension of the Apostle and the Heavenly Book.* Uppsala.

Hans Dieter Betz

APOSTLES, EPISTLE OF. The *Epistle of the Apostles* (or *Epistula Apostolorum*) is an early apocryphal Christian work of unknown authorship. Originally written in Greek, the *Ep. Apos.* survives only in Ethiopic (complete text), Coptic (approx. two thirds), and Latin (fragments). The title has been inferred from the opening sentence, "What Jesus Christ revealed to his disciples as a letter . . ." (1.1; Duensing 1963: 191); but this translation of Ethiopic *maṣḥaf* ("book," "writing") has been questioned (Vanovermeire 1962: 112; Hills 1989: 2). The date and place of writing are disputed. Schmidt (1919) argued for 170–180 C.E. and Asia Minor; more recently Hornschuh (1965) has made a strong case for Egyptian provenance and a date ca. 120 C.E.; late 2d-century Syria has also been suggested (De Zwaan 1933).

What is clear is the *Ep. Apos.*'s genre. Chaps. 1–12 and 51 frame the body of the work (chaps. 13–50), which is a post-Easter dialogue between Jesus and the apostles. The former speaks as the risen Revealer, the latter as united witnesses to the Revealer's words and deeds (see esp. 29.5). The speeches' stereotyped introductions (e.g., "He [± answered and] said to us"; "We said to him") and rhetorical expressions (e.g., "Until what day do you ask?" [22.2]; "What you wish, say to me, and I will tell you without grudging" [24.5]) are conventional in contemporary literary dialogues (e.g., in *Shep. Herm.* and the Nag Hammadi tractates *Ap. Jas.* [NHC I,*2*], *Thom. Cont.* [NHC II,*7*], and *Dial. Sav.* [NHC III,*5*]).

The principal topics of the dialogue are the Lord's heavenly descent and incarnation (chaps. 13–14); the remembrance of his death and his second coming (15–18);

resurrection and judgment (19–29; 38–39); the mission of Paul (31–33); the signs of the end (34–37, adapted from an apocalypse; cf. the 5th-century *Testament of the Lord* 1–11, where the same apocalypse has been used); the commission of the disciples to preach, teach, and baptize (40–42); and orthodoxy and discipline (43–50). These diverse topics are unified by the author's concern to define the community in terms of keeping the Lord's commandments, to summarize the "faith" of the apostles (see esp. 5.21–22), and to offer a "revelation" that has present and ethical, as well as future and heavenly, content.

Of special interest is the use of gospel traditions, both in the dialogue (chaps. 13–50) and in its preface (1–12). For example, in *Ep. Apos.* 4–5 a list of miracles is expanded to include dialogue; this list is in turn appended to the hymnic or poetic chap. 3. Chaps. 3–5 thus constitute a christological aretalogy, whose function is to affirm the authority of the apostles and the traditions they reveal. In chaps. 41–42 a dominical saying prohibiting titles (cf. Matt 23:8–9) is reformulated to suit the author's situation. In *Ep. Apos.* 43–45 the parable of the Wise and Foolish Maidens, familiar from Matt 25:1–13, is narrated and explained through dialogue. In each of these sections some knowledge of the NT Gospels is probable. But there are no certain quotations from any NT writing, and the author appears to write without any awareness of a "canon" of NT scriptures. Indeed, among the proof texts quoted in the *Ep. Apos.* are several sayings not found in extant Jewish and Christian literature (see esp. 11.8).

Most commentators have seen as the work's primary purpose an orthodox defense against gnostic Christianity, since the author warns against "Simon and Cerinthus" in chaps. 1 and 7; these two are commonly identified as first among heretics by other 2d- and 3d-century writers. But this judgment must be treated with caution. First, the position of the "opponents" is never spelled out, nor is it explicitly contradicted. Second, the *Ep. Apos.* itself falls short of later 2d-century definitions of orthodoxy (e.g., in Irenaeus). Third, the author appears as much concerned with catechism and church order as with theological debate; the condemnation of heresy is standard in later church orders (e.g., Hippolytus *Apostolic Tradition* [ca. 215 C.E.] and the several church orders deriving from it; cf. also the *Catechetical Lectures* of Cyril of Jerusalem [d. 386 C.E.]).

More conspicuous is the author's emphasis on the disciples, as successors to the risen Lord and as "founders" of the Church (see esp. *Ep. Apos.* 33.2). The importance of baptism is stressed (e.g., in 5.21, where the best mss read "great Christians," an Ethiopic idiom for "the baptized"; 27.2; 42.3, 7), as is the eucharist (or "agape," in chap. 15) and the idea of a universal mission (e.g., in 30.1). This suggests that the *Ep. Apos.* is witness to the flowering of an ecclesiastical self-consciousness in an environment of competing Christian groups, but before the emergence of the "Great [or Catholic] Church."

Bibliography

Bardy, G. 1921. Review of *Gespräche Jesu mit seinen Jüngern nach der Auferstehung,* by C. Schmidt. *RB* 30: 110–34.

De Zwaan, J. 1933. Date and Origin of the Epistle of the Eleven Apostles. Pp. 344–55 in *Amicitiae Corolla: A Volume of Essays Presented to James Rendel Harris, D.Litt. on the Occasion of His Eightieth Birthday,* ed. H. G. Wood. London.

Duensing, H. 1925. *Epistula Apostolorum: nach dem äthiopischen und koptischen Texte.* KlT 152. Bonn.

———. 1963. Epistula Apostolorum. Trans. R. E. Taylor. Pp. 189–227 in *New Testament Apocrypha,* vol. 1: *Gospels and Related Writings,* ed. E. Hennecke, rev. W. Schneemelcher, trans. ed. R. McL. Wilson. Philadelphia.

Guerrier, L., and Grébaut, S. 1913. "Le testament en Galilée de Notre-Seigneur Jésus-Christ." *PO* 9: 141–236.

Hills, J. 1986. The *Epistula Apostolorum* and the Genre "Apocalypse." SBLASP 25: 581–95.

———. 1989. *Tradition and Composition in the Epistula Apostolorum.* HDR 26. Philadelphia.

Hornschuh, M. 1965. *Studien zur Epistula Apostolorum.* Patrîstische Texte und Studien 5. Berlin.

Lake, K. 1920. The Epistola Apostolorum. *HTR* 14: 15–29.

Lietzmann, H. 1921. Review of *Gespräche Jesu mit seinen Jüngern nach der Auferstehung,* by C. Schmidt. *ZNW* 20: 173–76.

Schmidt, C. 1919. *Gespräche Jesu mit seinen Jüngern nach der Auferstehung.* TU 43. Leipzig.

Vanovermeire, P. 1962. Livre que Jésus-Christ a révélé a ses disciples. Diss. Institut catholique de Paris.

JULIAN V. HILLS

APOSTOLIC CONSTITUTIONS AND CANONS.

APOSTOLIC CONSTITUTIONS AND CANONS. An early church manual of liturgical and ecclesiastical regulations that usually is dated to the end of the 4th century (ca. C.E. 380) and is ascribed to the region of Syria. The text is divided into 8 books, each of which incorporates several more ancient writings. Ancient Syriac texts, and subsequently Ethiopic and Arabic translations, indicate a knowledge of only the first 6 books, which suggests that these books formed the original core of the work to which Books 7–8 were added later. The complete corpus of materials has been preserved in Greek, Latin, and Coptic editions.

With the addition of occasional editorial alterations, Books 1–6 are formulated around the *Didascalia Apostolorum* (3d century). Book 7 utilizes much of the *Didache* (2d century) and the *Kadusha* prayer of early Jewish liturgy. The *Apostolic Tradition of Hippolytus* serves as a foundation for the 85 legislative canons that appear in Book 8, where a familiarity with the *Clementine Liturgy* also is evident.

The author of *Apos. Con.* has not been identified with certainty. The complete form of the title *(Constitutions of the Holy Apostles)* suggests that the 1st-century apostles have authored these materials, but this undoubtedly is a pseudepigraphical feature. So, too, the attestation within the text that these instructions originally were transmitted through the agency of "Clement" (6.18.11; presumably Clement I of Rome) should be rejected. It is much more likely that a later compiler, perhaps the Pseudo-Ignatius, who is responsible for the "longer recension" of the epistles of Ignatius, should be considered as the appropriate compiler of the text. The consistency in style and editorial technique further support the argument that a single editor is responsible for the final form of the text.

The contents of *Apos. Con.,* which include numerous moral exhortations and the outline of specific religious obligations, have been carefully arranged to meet the needs of early Christian believers. Throughout the text there is a strict dependence upon the authority of the OT and the NT, in addition to a rigid, legalistic interpretation of both. Book 1 is directed toward the circumstances of the laity, who are encouraged to follow a strictly ethical code of daily existence. Book 2 focuses upon the qualifications and obligations of the clerical orders. The offices of deacon and widow are addressed in Book 3, as are instructions for the correct observation of baptism ritual. Specific issues with regard to charity are discussed in Book 4. The fate and situation of those who are persecuted and martyred for the Christian faith are summarized in Book 5, followed by a review of heresies and schisms in Book 6. The "Two Ways" motif of early Jewish-Christian literature serves as the background of Book 7, where numerous ancient exhortations and liturgical traditions have been preserved. Book 8 concludes the text with a review of spiritual gifts and numerous points of worship and ecclesiastical order for the clergy.

Several special features characterize the corpus. The text recognizes a well-developed series of ecclesiastical offices, which includes the positions of bishop, presbyter, deacon, widow, sub-deacon, door keeper, and others. The role of the bishop in this structure is exalted greatly. At the conclusion of *Apos. Con.*, a list of canonized texts is offered which omits Revelation, but which includes *3 Maccabees, 1* and *2 Clement,* and *Apos. Con.* itself. While the text incorporates a significant number of prayers that reveal distinctly Jewish origins (see Books 7–8; Goodenough 1935: 306–58), it bears a distinct antipathy toward Jewish customs as they were practiced among early Christians.

The authenticity of *Apos. Con.* ultimately was rejected by the Council of Trullo in 692, an act which served to diminish its influence within later ecclesiastical tradition. The entire corpus of the Canons was accepted as genuine by John of Constantinople, however, and subsequently it gained authority throughout the Eastern Church, where it still is used today.

Bibliography

Altaner, B. 1960. *Patrology.* Trans. H. C. Graef. Freiburg im Breisgau.

Donaldson, J. 1951. Constitutions of the Holy Apostles. *ANF* 387–505.

Goodenough, E. R. 1935. *By Light, Light: The Mystic Gospel of Hellenistic Judaism.* New Haven.

Quasten, J. 1948. *The Ante-Nicene Literature after Irenaeus.* Vol. 2 in *Patrology.* Utrecht and Antwerp.

Turner, C. H. 1914. Notes on the Apostolic Constitutions: The Compiler an Arian. *JTS* 16:54–61.

———. 1915. Notes on the Apostolic Constitutions. The Apostolic Canons. *JTS* 16: 523–38.

———. 1930. Notes on the Apostolic Constitutions. The Text of the Eighth Book. *JTS* 31: 128–41.

Clayton N. Jefford

APOSTOLIC COUNCIL. See JERUSALEM, COUNCIL OF.

APOSTOLIC FATHERS. A collection of early Christian writings traditionally regarded as having been set down by people directly or indirectly associated with the apostles. A complete modern edition will include the following (the order varies considerably): *1 Clement, 2 Clement, Ignatius, Polycarp, Didache, Barnabas, Papias, Hermas, Martyrdom of Polycarp, Diognetus,* and *Quadratus* (cf. Bihlmeyer, Fischer). Separate discussions of each of these writings is provided in this dictionary. The purpose of the present article is to discuss the history of the collection as a whole and to indicate the bearing that the study of the Apostolic Fathers (AF) has on the study of the NT and early Christianity.

A line of distinguished editions of the AF leads back to a work published by the French scholar, J.-B. Cotelier, in Paris in 1672. The attention given to this body of material in the 17th century was prompted as much by the concern of humanism to return to the authentic sources of Western civilization as by the theological polemics of the reformation and counterreformation. The use of the expression "Apostolical Fathers" can be traced back at least as far as William Wake, who in 1693 published a translation of *1 Clement, Polycarp, Ignatius, Martyrdom of Ignatius, Martyrdom of Polycarp, Barnabas, Hermas,* and *2 Clement* (de Jonge). The subtitle of the work spoke of these writings as "being together with the Holy Scriptures of the NT, a complete collection of the most primitive antiquity for about CL years after Christ." And in the introduction to the third edition (1719), we are told that these works were "truly written by those whose names they bear, and that those writers lived so near the apostolical times, that it cannot be doubted, but that they do indeed represent to us the doctrine, government, and discipline of the church, as they received it from the apostles; the apostles from Christ, and that blessed Spirit, who directed them both in what they taught, and in what they ordain'd." Wake (now Archbishop of Canterbury) also noted that all this "is so exactly agreeable to the present doctrine, government, and discipline of the church of England by law establish'd; that no one who allows of the one can reasonably make any exceptions against the other." The expression "Apostolic Fathers" was also soon employed by the Lutheran theologian and scholar Thomas Ittig in his edition of 1699 (with reference only to materials associated with the names of Clement, Ignatius, and Polycarp) and by the Reformed (Armenian) biblical scholar and theologian Joh. Clericus (Jean Le Clerc) in his reedition of Cotelier in 1698 (with reference to materials associated with the names of Barnabas, Hermas, Clement, Ignatius, and Polycarp).

The previous work of two other English scholars—Patrick Young and James Ussher—is important in accounting for the emergence of the special attention given to the AF in this period. As early as 1633, Young in his capacity as Royal Librarian published *1 Clement* from Codex Alexandrinus, the celebrated 5th-century biblical manuscript presented in 1628 to Charles I by Cyril Lucar, patriarch of Constantinople. Young refers to the author as being "of almost the same time as the apostles, the disciple of Paul, and the successor of Peter," and to the writing as "this divine and clearly apostolic epistle." He also expresses the wish that the English king may be granted in his own realm the peace and harmony urged by Clement on the dissenters in Corinth long ago.

Even more important from the point of view of the impetus given to the scholarly investigation of the AF and the early church was the brilliant discovery by Archbishop Ussher of the shorter form of the letters of Ignatius (1644), which is generally accepted as genuine today. The discovery also had the effect of upholding the episcopal system as a feature of the earliest period. This was one reason that not long afterward the Reformed theologian and scholar, Jean Daillé, published an important study of Dionysius the Areopagite and the (shorter form of the) letters of Ignatius (1666) in which he attempted to prove the inauthenticity of both bodies of writings (Harrison 1936: 135). Posterity has accepted his judgment about the Areopagite but not (for the most part) about Ignatius. John Pearson, bishop of Chester, wrote an especially influential book defending the authenticity of the shorter form of the letters of Ignatius (1672). In the long run, however, Daillé's general insistence that the fathers of the church possess no special theological authority and must be approached historically was prophetic of the spirit that was to dominate the study of the early church in Western Christianity.

Additions to the roster of AF were subsequently made by Andreas Gallandi (a forerunner of Migne), who included also the letter to Diognetus, the fragments of Papias, and the fragment of Quadratus (1765). And finally, the startling discovery of the Didache by Bryennios (published in 1883) led to the inclusion of that document also among the AF.

The Bryennios manuscript (an A.D. 1056 codex of the Greek patriarchate in Jerusalem, formerly in the library of the Hospice of the Church of the Holy Sepulchre in Constantinople) represents a convenient point from which to look back to the role of the AF before modern times. The first writing in the codex is a brief "Synopsis (Survey) of the Old and New Testament" attributed (wrongly) to John Chrysostom. This is followed by *Barnabas, 1 Clement, 2 Clement,* the *Didache,* and the long recension of the letters of Ignatius (Harnack 1893: 11–12). The manuscript suggests an interest in the AF comparable in some ways to that of the later and more critical age already discussed. This is all the more surprising since the collection was put together at a time when (from the end of the 7th century on) little had been heard of the AF (other than Ignatius), and people's conception of the early period had been shaped primarily by forgeries long associated with the names not only of Ignatius but also of Clement of Rome, Dionysius the Areopagite, and Justin Martyr (Grant 1962: 428–29).

More real knowledge of the AF was available to the contestants in the Christological debates of the 5th and 6th centuries. Here interest in the AF centered primarily on Ignatius, who was appealed to by all sides. What stands out in this connection is that ultimately the short (and presumably authentic) recension of the letters of Ignatius proved most congenial to the monophysite cause (Grant 1962: 426–27). Much less significant use was made of *Polycarp, 1 Clement, 2 Clement,* and *Hermas* in this period; and appeals to *Papias* were even more isolated (Grant 1967: 24–32). Moreover, authentic early materials had to compete with the whole range of pseudepigraphical writings already noted.

Clearer conceptions of who and what the AF represented can be found in the 2d, 3d, and 4th centuries. Irenaeus, Clement of Alexandria, Origen, and Eusebius shed particularly important light on their reception (Grant 1962: 421–26). In these writers most of the AF were provided with rather direct links to the apostolic age; but forgeries were only beginning to cloud the horizon, and in some quarters problems of authenticity were discussed. Thus Eusebius set *Hermas, Barnabas,* and the *Didache* among the "spurious" items that make up the second component of the writings "not universally accepted" as scriptural (antilegomena); he noted that *1 Clement* was still read in many churches; he observed that *2 Clement* was not used by the ancients; he declared the romances written in the names of Clement of Rome forgeries; he suggested (in line with Alexandrian tradition) that *Hermas* was useful for elementary instruction; and he expressed his doubts about the intelligence of *Papias.* A wide range of concerns affecting theology, spirituality, ethics, and church order were involved in the appeal to these writings in this period. Although they rarely dominate any discussion, their importance should not be underrated. It may be noted (for example) that Irenaeus' millennialism owed a good deal to what he knew of *Papias;* that striking passages such as the lines from *Hermas* on the oneness of God who contains all but is himself contained by nothing, or the verses from *Ignatius* on the hidden entrance of Christ into the world, set the tone in a variety of contexts; and that the reworking of the material of the *Didache* in later church orders (the *Didascalia* and the *Apostolic Constitutions*) attests to its prestige.

It follows from what has been said that attention to the AF in the early church often took the form of a consideration of their possible canonicity (Ruwet 1942; 1948; 1952; Andry 1951; Grant 1964: 13–33; Kümmel 1966: 344–51). For the presumed association of their authors with the apostles gave them credentials as strong as some of the writings ultimately accepted into the NT. The most important points are these (though some are matters of dispute): Irenaeus came close to treating *1 Clement* and *Hermas* as scripture (but seems not actually to have done so). Tertullian dealt with *Hermas* as scripture in his pre-Montanist period. Clement of Alexandria regarded *1 Clement, Hermas, Barnabas,* and the *Didache* as inspired writings. Origen dealt with *Hermas, Barnabas,* and the *Didache* similarly, but at the same time seems not to have regarded them as canonical. Eusebius, as we have seen, is less receptive to these three books and regards them as spurious. Finally, Athanasius (in his famous festal letter on the topic) clearly sets the *Didache* and *Hermas* outside of the canon, but does so in such a way as still to reflect the high evaluation of these writings in the Alexandrian tradition. It should also be noted that Codex Sinaiticus (4th century) included *Barnabas* and *Hermas;* that Codex Alexandrinus (5th century) contained *1 Clement* and *2 Clement;* and that a catalog found in Codex Claromantanus (6th century) lists among the books of the NT (in addition to two other unusual works) *Barnabas* and *Hermas* (though all four items are set off by a dash).

Clearly the criterion that obtained most widely in thinking about the AF and drawing them together as a group in ancient and modern times was their presumed connection with the apostles or at least their presumed antiquity relative to (most) other noncanonical writings of the early church. In other respects they are very diverse indeed, and the difficulties inherent in defining the collection have grown rather than lessened over time (Jouassard 1957). As regards form, most of the AF in the modern collections are letters. But whereas *1 Clement, Ignatius,* and *Polycarp* are true letters, *Barnabas* (a theological tract), the *Martyrdom of Polycarp* (a martyrology), and *Diognetus* (an apology) are letters only in an external sense. The other writings of the AF represent a homily *(2 Clement),* a church order *(Didache),* and a kind of apocalypse *(Hermas).* Papias' discussion of the words and deeds of Jesus is known to us only in a series of fragments, and we have but one tiny quotation from the apologist Quadratus.

The status of the authors of these writings is also diverse: Ignatius, Polycarp, and (probably) Clement had some kind of official standing in their churches; the author of the *Martyrdom of Polycarp* recedes behind the authority of the church for which he writes; the individual who wrote to Diognetus is unknown; *Barnabas, 2 Clement* and the *Didache* are pseudonymous; *Hermas* was written by a man who sets himself apart from the clergy.

Moreover, rather different forms of the early Christian experience are represented by these writings. Aspects of the literary and theological world of Paul are reflected in some of the letters. But whereas *Polycarp* breathes the spirit of the Pastorals, and *1 Clement*'s Christianity is almost equally unadventuresome, Ignatius infuses his Paulinism with qualities reminiscent of John and other mystical (perhaps even quasignostic) strands of thought. Yet both Clement with his idea of succession and Ignatius with his emphasis on monepiscopacy set the stage for the further development of a catholic conception of ministerial authority. And this in turn may well be connected with the greater openness of *1 Clement* and *Ignatius* to elements derived from the popular culture of the Greco-Roman world. Indeed, the remarkable fact about most of the other Apostolic Fathers is the extent to which they remain indebted to various forms of Judaism. Thus the *Didache* not only looks like an extension of the concerns of Matthew's gospel, but also falls back on Jewish and Jewish-Christian materials in the realm of ethics and ritual that are not derived from the NT. *Barnabas* is reminiscent especially of Hebrews, but is even more clearly indebted to Jewish lore and at the same time more negatively disposed to Judaism as a historical and social fact. *2 Clement* represents (in the words of Hans Windisch) "a Synoptic-Gospels Christianity reformulated and domesticated in the light of late Judaism" (cf. Bihlmeyer 1956: xxix). And *Papias'* millennialism shows that themes from fully developed forms of apocalyptic thought were still alive in some circles. Similarly, *Hermas* registers the impact of a wide range of Jewish theological, angeological, and ethical ideas within the framework of an apocalyptic outlook (though elements from popular Greco-Roman culture also play an interesting role in his thought). Different again is the *Martyrdom of Polycarp,* which represents a complex weaving together of Jewish, Christian, and more popular elements that gave rise to the church's version of the holy man. And finally, the apologetic strategies of *Diognetus* (and *Quadratus*) belong to another whole order of theological and literary activity.

Modern views about the authenticity, dating, and historical setting of the AF have robbed even the criterion of antiquity of much of its significance. Most of the AF are, to be sure, relatively early. But no significant link between any of them and the apostles now seems particularly likely. Indeed, the *Didache, Barnabas,* and *2 Clement* all seem to be pseudonymous. And the reason for including *Diognetus* in the collection is undercut by the recognition that its last two chapters, which include the ambiguous reference to the author as "a disciple of apostles" (11.1), do not belong to the writing. A glance at the articles on the separate writings will also show that there is much dispute about the dating of most of these books and that at least some of them probably fall outside the period in question. Conversely, there are other early Christian works, both canonical and noncanonical, that seem to fall into this period. Above all, we are much more acutely aware today of the striking differences between the forms of Christianity reflected in the AF whatever their date may be. The conclusion seems inescapable that as a collection they represent nothing very definite in either theological or historical terms. NT scholarship, then, is moving even more consciously (in spite of the many difficulties involved) toward an integration of the AF with the later materials of the NT and with early noncanonical literature not included in the AF (cf. Koester 1982, 2: 147–347).

The very diversity of the AF has meant, however, that studies that have focused on this collection as a whole (usually with the exception of the apologetic materials) have worked with a sample of early Christian literature sufficiently broad to guarantee interesting results. Of particular importance here for NT scholarship have been the efforts to read the AF for the light they can shed on the reception of the various books of the NT. The report of the committee of the Oxford Society on this problem (1905) is still fundamental. But commentaries on the biblical books and studies of the individual writings of the AF have introduced many refinements. Nothing like an adequate summary of these discussions is possible here (for a survey of the findings, see Kümmel 1966: 337–40). It may be noted, however, that especially interesting investigations have been undertaken regarding the use of the Synoptic Gospels and of synoptic tradition in the AF. The debate is dominated by two books: Massaux (1950) and Koester (1957). The full range of possibilities are taken into account in these works: quotation of (or allusion to) one or the other of the Synoptic Gospels, reliance on some kind of harmonization of the written Gospels, knowledge of oral tradition, independent access to tradition peculiar to one of the Gospels, and so forth. In general, it may be said that Massaux (who worked with the whole range of Christian literature to the time of Irenaeus) emphasized the importance of Matthew to the church from the earliest times and the reliance by the majority of authors on Matthew in a written form. Koester, on the other hand, emphasized the extent to which the AF were indebted to oral tradition. Many of Koester's conclusions have been questioned by Grant (1964: 35–86), and the whole issue has been thoroughly reviewed by Köhler (1987), who finds himself closer to the position of Massaux than of Koester.

It is clear, however, that the work of Koester has contributed to a considerably more flexible notion of the possibilities in the reception of the Synoptic Gospels and of synoptic tradition in the early church.

Other studies devoted to the AF as a whole also retain their value in characterizing the Christianity of the period. Thus Torrance's classic treatment of grace in the AF (1948) is still useful even though he measured them too exclusively against Paul, took a Barthian approach to Paul too much for granted in so doing, and failed to note the elements in the AF that represent to some extent functional equivalents of the category of grace. Klevinghaus' demonstration of the eclipse of the significance of Israel as a historical reality in the AF (1948) remains generally convincing. More recently, Eijk's careful analysis of the doctrine of the resurrection in the AF (1974) is distinguished by special sensitivity to the differences between the individual writings. Other more or less useful studies on the AF as a whole are to be found on such topics as the connection between ethics and dogma (Hörmann 1952), the terminology for evil spirits (Gokey 1961), views of material re-creation (O'Hagan 1968), and moral teachings (Liébaert 1970). Naturally attention to the AF (sometimes as a distinct group) will also be found in histories of Christian thought, the ministry, the liturgy, spirituality, and so forth. Although peculiarities of one kind or the other are associated with each of the AF, it is perhaps Ignatius who strikes commentators most as rising above expectations in literary and theological terms.

It should be noted in conclusion that the basic tools for the study of the NT—Bauer's lexicon, Kittel's theological wordbook, and the grammar of Blass and Debrunner—give significant attention also to the AF. An excellent concordance to these writings was published by Heinrich Kraft in 1963.

Bibliography

Andry, C. F. 1951. Barnabae Epist. Ver. DCCCL. *JBL* 70: 233-38.

Bihlmeyer, K. 1956. *Didache, Barnabas, Klemens I und II, Ignatius, Polykarp, Papias, Quadratus, Diognetbrief.* Vol. 1 of Die Apostolischen Väter, ed. Wilhelm Schneemelcher. 2d ed. Tübingen.

Bryennios, P. 1883. *Didachē tōn dōdeka apostolōn ek tou hierosolymitikou cheirographou nyn prōton ekdidomenē meta prolegomenōn kai sēmeiōseōn.* Constantinople.

Clericus (Le Clerc), J. 1698. *SS. Patrum qui temporibus apostolicis floruerunt, Barnabae, Clementis, Hermae, Ignatii, Polycarpi opera edita et inedita, vera et supposititia, una cum Clementis, Ignatii, Polycarpi actis atque martyriis.* 2 vols. Antwerp.

Cotelerius (Cotelier), J. B. 1672. *SS. Patrum qui temporibus apostolicis floruerunt, Barnabae, Clementis, Hermae, Ignatii, Polycarpi opera edita et inedita, vera et supposititia, una cum Clementis, Ignatii, Polycarpi actis atque martyriis.* 2 vols. Paris.

Dallaeus (Daillé), I. (J.) 1666. *De scriptis quae sub Dionysii Areopagitae et Ignatii Antiocheni nominibus circumferuntur.* Geneva.

Eijk, T. H. C. van. 1974. *La résurrection des morts chez les pères apostoliques. ThH* 25. Paris.

Fischer, J. A. 1956. *Die Apostolischen Väter.* Munich.

Gallandi, A. 1765–81. *Bibliotheca veterum patrum antiquorumque scriptorum ecclesiasticorum graeco-latina.* 14 vols. Venice.

Gokey, F. X. 1961. *The Terminology for the Devil and Evil Spirits in the Apostolic Fathers.* The Catholic University of America Patristic Studies 93. Washington.

Grant, R. M. 1962. The Apostolic Fathers' First Thousand Years. *CH* 31: 421–29.

———. 1964. *The Apostolic Fathers.* Vol. 1. New York.

———. 1967. The Use of the Early Fathers from Irenaeus to John of Damascus. Pp. 20–34 in *After the New Testament,* ed. Robert M. Grant. Philadelphia.

Harnack, A. 1893. *Lehre der zwölf Apostel.* TU 2/1. Leipzig.

Harrison, P. N. 1936. *Polycarp's Two Epistles to the Philippians.* Cambridge.

Hörmann, K. 1952. *Leben in Christus, Zusammenhänge zwischen Dogma und Sitte bei den apostolischen Vätern.* Vienna.

Ittig, T. 1699. *Bibliotheca patrum apostolicorum graeco-latina: I. Clementis Romani prior et posterior ad Corinthios epistola, II. S. Ignatii epistolae septem genuinae quibus eiusdem interpolatae et spuriae epistolae necnon acta Ignatiani martyrii accedunt, III. S. Polycarpi epistola ad Philippenses cui praeter fragmenta Polycarpi ecclesiae Smyrnensis de Polycarpi matyrio epistola integra adjungitur.* Leipzig.

Jonge, H. J. de. 1978. On the Origin of the Term "Apostolic Fathers." *JTS* n.s. 29: 503–5.

Jouassard, G. 1957. Le groupement des Pères dits apostoliques. *MSR* 14: 129–34.

Klevinghaus, J. 1948. *Die theologische Stellung der apostolischen Väter zur alttestamentlichen Offenbarung.* BFCT 44/1. Gütersloh.

Köhler, W.-D. 1987. *Die Rezeption des Matthäusevangeliums in der Zeit vor Irenäus.* WUNT 2/24. Tübingen.

Koester, H. 1957. *Synoptische Überlieferung bei den Apostolischen Vätern.* TU 65. Berlin.

———. 1982. *Introduction to the New Testament.* 2 vols. Philadelphia.

Kraft, H. 1963. *Clavis patrum apostolicorum.* Munich.

Kümmel, W. G. 1966. *Introduction to the New Testament.* Nashville.

Liébaert, J. 1970. *Les enseignements moraux des Pères Apostoliques.* Recherches et synthèses, section de morale 4. Gembloux.

Massaux, É. 1950. *Influence de l'évangile de saint Matthieu sur la littérature chrétienne avant Saint Irénée.* Universitas catholica Lovanensis 2/42. Louvain. Repr. 1986.

O'Hagan, A. P. 1968. *Material Re-Creation in the Apostolic Fathers.* TU 100. Berlin.

Oxford Society. 1905. *The New Testament in the Apostolic Fathers.* Oxford.

Pearson, J. 1672. *Vindiciae epistolarum S. Ignatii.* Cambridge: John Hayes. Repr. 1852.

Ruwet, J. 1942. Les Antilegomena dans les oeuvres d'Origène. *Bib* 23: 18–42.

———. 1948. Clément d'Alexandrie: Canon d'écritures et apocryphes. *Bib* 29: 240–68.

———. 1952. Le canon Alexandrin des écritures: Saint Athanase. *Bib* 33: 1–29.

Torrance, T. F. 1948. *The Doctrine of Grace in the Apostolic Fathers.* Edinburgh.

Ussher, J. 1644. *Polycarpi et Ignatii epistolae.* Oxford.

Wake, W. 1693. *The Genuine Epistles of the Apostolical Fathers, S. Barnabas, S. Clement, S. Ignatius, S. Polycarp, The Shepherd of Hermas, and the Martyrdoms of St. Ignatius and St. Polycarp.* London. Repr. 1719.

Young (Junius), P. 1633. *Clementis ad Corinthios epistola prior.* Oxford.

WILLIAM R. SCHOEDEL

APPAIM (PERSON) [Heb *ʾappayim*]. One of the two sons of Nadab (1 Chr 2:30). Since his brother died childless, Appaim's descendants are an important part of the family of Jerahmeel, the firstborn son of Hezron, grandson of

Judah. The MT uses the plural "The sons of" in recording Appaim's issue (1 Chr 2:31); however, the single son, Ishi, may be understood here as the progenitor of a clan or family bearing his name. Appaim is a dual form meaning "nostrils" but may also mean "nose," "anger," or "temper" and is derived from the verb meaning "to be angry."

W. P. STEEGER

APPEAL TO CAESAR. Under the Empire, all holders of Roman citizenship possessed among their citizen rights the *ius appellationis ad Caesarem,* or right of appeal to Caesar. According to the great 3d-century jurist, Ulpian, the right of appeal was guaranteed to all Roman citizens, whether residents of Italy or the provinces under the provisions of a *lex Iulia de vi publica,* ennacted at the beginning of the Empire by Augustus, who thereby instructed Roman magistrates and officials that citizens should not only have the right of appeal from local judicial authority to Rome, but should also not be inflicted with death, scourging, prolonged imprisonment, or torture without full due process of law, including the right of *appellatio* (*Dig.* 48.6.7). There is some question as to when Augustus' law came to be extended to the provinces (Millar 1977: 508–9; Jones 1960: 54–55), but "late in the reign of Augustus there is a clear instance, in the second edict of Augustus from Cyrene, . . . that by that date the *lex Iulia* was being applied to actions in the provinces" (Sherwin-White 1963: 60). This process, along with other aspects of the emperor's judicial role, seems to have been regularized under successive emperors (Millar 1977: 509–14) so that by the early 3d century Severus Alexander was quick to warn provincial officials of any obstruction or abuse against those who made appeals. (*Dig.* 49.1.25 = *P.Oxy.* 2104).

The right of *appellatio* in the Empire replaced an earlier basic citizen right of the Roman Republic, the *ius provocationis ad populum,* or right of calling *(provocare)* on the entire body of citizens in assembly to overturn the judicial decisions of magistrates. Extended to all Roman citizens by the terms of a *lex Valeria* of 300 B.C., the exercise of *provocatio* was guaranteed in all capital cases, and could be exercised as well in other criminal cases, but apparently not in civil cases (*OCD* 892–93). Before 300 B.C. *provocatio* may have been utilized, but without assurance of receiving hearing before the *populus* assembled in the *Comitia Tributa,* or Tribal Assembly. The tribune of the plebs *(tribunus plebis)* was the presiding officer of this assembly and may have referred appeals to the body as a function of his *ius auxilii,* the right of rendering aid to any citizen whom he judged the victim of unjust magisterial authority *(coercitio).* The tribune could take action himself, or through the assembly, to overturn magisterial decisions either upon appeal or on his own initiative (Kunkel 1966: 54, 72; *OCD* 892–93). It is likely that the *appellatio ad Caesarem* derived directly from this tribunician *ius auxilii.* Cassius Dio (51.19.6–7) reports that in 30 B.C. Octavian Caesar was granted the tribunician authority of *ius auxilii* for life. The remaining powers of the tribune *(tribunicia potestas)* were granted to Octavian after his accession as Augustus, and it was from this tribunician power that Augustus and all subsequent emperors exercised judicial authority as the special protector of the Roman citizen body, a role which under the Republic had belonged to the plebeian tribune (Millar 1977: 509; Jones 1960: 54; Crook 1967: 70–71).

The exercise of *appellatio* was common among provincial Christians with Roman citizen status who had been accused of wrongdoing. The most familiar instance of appeal to Caesar is, of course, that of Paul. When about to be subjected to scourging under the direction of Felix, Procurator of Judaea (*OCD* 434), Paul "lays claim to the protection afforded by his Roman citizenship" (Millar 1977: 511), under the provisions of the *lex Iulia,* demanding that as a Roman he not be beaten uncondemned of any crime and protected from the same at the hands of the Jews (Acts 22:25–30; 23:27). It was when Paul was about to be tried before the tribunal of Porcius Festus, the successor of Felix as Judean procurator, that he proclaimed his appeal to Caesar (Acts 24:27–25:22). There is some difficulty, however, in understanding the precise nature of Paul's *appellatio,* since "it has the character of a rejection of one court in favor of another one rather than of an appeal from a verdict" (Millar 1977: 511). It has been suggested that the *lex Iulia* entailed not only appeal to the emperor after verdicts were rendered, but also the right to challenge the jurisdiction of a particular court by requesting a change of venue to Rome, a process that may more properly be referred to as *provocatio* than *appellatio* (Sherwin-White 1963: 115–16). Apparently provincial governors were not strictly bound to refer criminal cases to Rome. The well-known correspondence between Pliny and Trajan concerning the procedure for trying Christians with Roman citizenship indicates some confusion in the matter of jurisdiction (Pliny, *Ep.* 10.96.4). Certainly there is ample attestation of governors both trying and executing citizens in the provinces, suggesting that as a matter of practicality jurisdiction was retained by local magisterial authority unless there was by the defendant formal recourse to *provocatio* or to *appellatio* (Sherwin-White 1963: 58–63).

Bibliography

Crook, J. 1967. *The Law and Life of Rome 90 B.C.–A.D. 212.* Ithaca, NY.

Jones, A. H. M. 1960. *Studies in Roman Government and Law.* Oxford.

Kunkel, W. 1966. *An Introduction to Roman Legal and Constitutional History.* Oxford.

Millar, F. 1977. *The Emperor in the Roman World.* Ithaca, NY.

Sherwin-White, A.N. 1963. *Roman Society and Roman Law in the New Testament.* Oxford.

JOHN F. HALL

APPHIA (PERSON) [Gk *ʾApphia*]. A Christian greeted in the salutation of the letter to Philemon (Phlm 2). While some have proposed that this woman's name was spelled incorrectly in the aspirated form "Apphia" in Philemon, rather than the more familiar unaspirated Roman name "Appia," copious documentation exists for the aspirated form from Phrygian inscriptions, where the name appears to be of native origin (Lightfoot 1879: 306–8). A Phrygian provenance for Apphia's name also accords with the widely held opinion that Philemon was addressed to Christians living in Phrygia, most probably in the small town of Colossae.

Why Apphia, along with PHILEMON and ARCHIPPUS, was singled out for special greetings in Philemon 1–2 has occasioned much speculation. A common assumption has been that she was Philemon's wife (or daughter) and Archippus was their son (or her brother). This is related to the supposition, based on the phrase "your house" (Philemon 2), that all three lived in the same household. However, the possessive in this instance is singular in the Greek, leaving open the possibility that the house referred to was the domicile of Archippus, although many commentators nevertheless read the "you" as referring back to Philemon. The latter tend to see Apphia as having a leadership role in the house church owing to the presence of that group in the home where she and her husband (or her father) lived. That may be a correct analysis, but it remains possible that, if the house was rather that of Archippus, then Apphia's mention by Paul, with her obvious importance among the Colossian Christians, must rest on different grounds.

In this connection, it is noteworthy that Paul addresses Apphia as "sister" in the same context in which he calls Timothy "brother," Philemon "beloved fellow-worker," and Archippus "fellow-soldier." While the RSV prefaces each of these appellatives with "our," the Greek refers to Timothy as "the brother" *(ho adelphos)* and Apphia as "the sister" *(tē adelphē)*. Paul thus appears to distinguish between titles with which he uses the definite article and those with the possessive pronoun (cf. Phil 2:25 where the Gk identifies Epaphroditus as "*the* brother and *my* fellow worker and fellow soldier").

It has been argued that in using the definite article rather than the possessive pronoun, Paul focuses on the social positions of brother and sister, not on the individual's relationship with him. Further, whenever Paul uses the definite article with "brother(s)" or "sister(s)," the general sense conveyed is that one is a believer. This leads N. Petersen, for example, to conclude that "the brother or sister is thus an egalitarian identification applicable to all members of the church, whereas the use of the possessive pronoun has . . . a hierarchical connotation because it links those of whom it is used to Paul's *position" e.g. as his* fellow-worker or *his* fellow-soldier (1985: 172; his italics in quote).

These observations suggest that in Paul's greeting of Apphia, her role as a believer and community member was foremost in his mind. Thus, he probably did not single her out because of her relationship to Philemon or Archippus, nor to himself, but because she was an outstanding, faithful member and leader of the Colossian community whom he happened to know.

Bibliography

Lightfoot, J. B. 1879. *St. Paul's Epistles to the Colossians and to Philemon.* London. Repr. 1978, Grand Rapids.

Petersen, N. 1985. *Rediscovering Paul.* Philadelphia.

FLORENCE MORGAN GILLMAN

APPHUS (PERSON) [Gk *Apphous*]. Nickname of Mattathias' youngest son Jonathan (1 Macc 2:5), the successor of Judas Maccabeus. Two Hebrew roots may be conjectured for the nickname: *hpṣ*, "to seek, search," or *ḥpṣ*, "to desire." The second one may best suit a child's nickname—"desired, favorite." For the nicknames of Mattathias' sons, see GADDI. See also JONATHAN.

URIEL RAPPAPORT

APPIAN WAY (PLACE). Roman road connecting Rome, Capua on the Bay of Naples, and Brundisium on the Adriatic. It was constructed under the Roman censor Appius Claudius Caecus in 312 B.C.

Until the harbor of Ostia was developed by the emperors Claudius and Trajan, Puteoli, on the Bay of Naples, served as the major seaport for Rome. From the 2d century B.C. until the 1st century A.D., the normal route in approaching Rome by sea was to sail to Puteoli, as Paul did (Acts 28:13–15). The traveler then used the suburban roadways to reach Capua, from which the journey to Rome, 132 Roman miles, normally took five or six days. Landmarks of the journey were the rich fields of Campania, the shore of the Gulf of Gaeta, the plain of Fundi, and the seaside bluff at Tarracina. Here the wetlands of the Pomptine Marshes permitted a canal to be built, 19 Roman miles long. Canal boats allowed the traveler to continue the journey during the night somewhat more comfortably than on the road: the poet Horace (*Sat.* 1.5) includes an account of this boat in his colorful, detailed description of a trip on the Appian Way from Rome to Brundisium. At Forum Appii, the canal ended and the road continued in a straight line past Tres Tabernae and the hill towns of Lanuvium and Aricia to the Porta Capena in Rome, located at the end of the Circus Maximus.

The roadway, 14 Roman feet wide, was covered with gravel, and flanked by wide pedestrian walkways of pounded earth. Travelers used horses, carriages, or their feet, and could stay overnight at inns or the villas of acquaintances. All along the road were tombs, houses, shrines, and commemorative monuments. Towns and villages like Forum Appii and Tres Tabernae ("Three Taverns") offered lodging, stables, and food. Under Domitian (A.D. 95) a shortcut, the Via Domitiana, bypassed Capua and went directly along the coastline from Sinuessa to the harbor at Puteoli—its construction is the subject of Statius, *Silv.* 4.3: 40–55.

Bibliography

Chevallier, R. 1976. *Roman Roads.* Trans. N. H. Field. Berkeley and Los Angeles.

Quilici, L. 1976. *La Via Appia da Roma a Bovillae.* Rome.

JOHN E. STAMBAUGH

APPIUS, FORUM OF. See FORUM OF APPIUS.

APPLE. See FLORA, BIBLICAL.

APRON. Translates a word in Gen 3:7 that is rendered "girdle" in other passages in which it is used and represents an item of clothing. The Hebrew word has its root in a verb, *hgr*, which has a primary meaning of "gird." Thus it refers to a garment that is wrapped around the body.

Its basic usage in the Bible is to indicate an undergarment of some sort, that is, a garment that covers the upper part of the lower body. For men, at least, such a garment would have been one that covered the genital organs. Apparently, in ancient Semitic custom, young children ran about with a loose shirt or cloak. As they reached sexual maturity, they began to wear an "apron" or loincloth. This custom seems to underlie a passage in 2 Kgs 3:21, which describes a comprehensive military muster involving all who were able to bear arms, from youngest to oldest. The youngest in this instance were those who had begun to wear the apron or girdle; wearing that item of clothing represented adulthood with respect to military service. In this sense, it might also be linked with military garb, since a warrior would be stripped down to this minimal garment when going into battle.

The appearance of "apron" in the Eden story in Genesis also points to its meaning as a fundamental item of clothing, one that would cover the sexual organs of females as well as males. The woman and man in the garden, after eating of the forbidden fruit, gain human cognition. This involves realization that they are naked, a condition to which they respond with the human characteristic of making clothing—aprons of fig leaves—for themselves.

Although the apron is a basic item of clothing, listed along with "sandals" in 1 Kgs 2:5 to represent the garb of a man, David, upon whom innocent blood had been spilled in peace time, it evidently also came to mean a decorative piece of clothing, such as a belt or sash. Such accessory items could be extravagantly made, either of costly fabrics or perhaps even studded with precious gems. The prophet Isaiah contrasts the ostentatious apparel of wealthy women with what they will wear in the day of God's judgment. Among the radical changes in their garb will be the use of a rope in place of a "girdle" (Isa 3:24). Similarly, the value of the apron or girdle appears in 2 Sam 18:11, where Joab says he would have given a lot—"ten pieces of silver and a girdle"—if only the man who brought him news of Absalom's hanging had cut the body down from the tree.

Carol Meyers

AQIBA (PERSON). See AKIBA, RABBI.

AQUILA (PERSON) [Gk *Akylas*]. Aquila, an important Christian missionary in the mid-1st century C.E., is mentioned in 1 Cor 16:19, Rom 16:3–5, Acts 18:2–3 (historically reliable traditions; Lüdemann 1987: 206, 209–10); 18:18, 26; and 2 Tim 4:19.

A. Pontus and the First Stay in Rome

Aquila was probably freeborn; the epigraphical material indicates that ordinarily the name "Aquila" was not a slave name (see Lampe *StadtrChr,* 142, 151–52). A Jew from Pontus (Acts 18:2), Aquila was among the first Christians in Rome who still belonged to the synagogues of the city. Together with his wife, Prisca, and others, he propagated Christianity in at least one of the Roman synagogues. This Christian proclamation led to tumultuous controversies among the Roman Jews, so that the administration of the emperor Claudius expelled the main quarrelers, including Aquila and Prisca, from the city in 49 C.E. (Acts 18:2, Suet. *Claud.* 25.4: *"Iudaeos impulsore Chresto* [sic] *assidue tumultuantes Roma expulit," Oros.* 7.6.15–16, cf. Cass. Dio 60.6.6–7). Alternative interpretations would be that the commotion was caused not by Christians but by a Roman Jew, Chrestus (e.g., Solin *ANRW* 2/29/2: 659, 690), and that Aquila was not converted before he arrived at Corinth (e.g., Lüdemann 1987: 209). This is not probable for several reasons (for detailed discussion see Lampe *StadtrChr,* 4–7): (1) The Roman inscriptions never show the name "Chrestus" as a Jewish name; (2) it would have been a strange coincidence if, as a Jew in Rome, Aquila had been involved in a commotion caused by a certain Jew "Chrestus" and later, as a Christian, had worked as a missionary of "Christus;" (3) since Lat *Christus*/Gk *christos* was unusual for pagan ears and *Chrestus* a common pagan name (see Lampe *StadtrChr,* 6), both could easily be confused by pagan writers like Suetonius. The Christians were indeed often called *Chrestianoi* by pagan people (see Tac. *Ann.* 15.44; Tert. *Apol.* 3; *Ad Nat.* 1.3; Lactant. *Div. Inst.* 4.7). (4) Aquila was already a Christian before Paul settled in Corinth: Paul lived in Aquila's dwelling in Corinth (Acts 18:3), but his first christening in the city was Stephanas, not Aquila. In addition, Paul baptized no one else in Corinth except Crispus, Gaius, and Stephanas' household (1 Cor 1:14–16; 16:15). If Aquila had been christened by somebody other than Paul in Corinth, e.g., by Silas or Timotheus, Luke would have liked to report such success (cf. e.g., Acts 18:8). (5) It is not likely that the unbaptized Jew Aquila housed the Christian missionary Paul in Corinth and even gave him a job to support him (Acts 18:2–3), especially if the Jew Aquila had acted on the Jewish side of the controversies in Rome, fighting Christian preaching about Christ. Finally, (6) Gk *Ioudaios* in Acts 18:2 can be easily understood as Jewish-Christian (see Acts 16:1,20; 21:39; 22:3,12; cf. 9:10; Gal 2:13).

B. Corinth Profession and Social Status

From Rome the couple moved on to Corinth, where Paul first met and lodged with them and worked in Aquila's workshop (Acts 18:2–3). Their craft was tent making (Acts 18:3). Contrary to the traditional view that both were leather workers selling primarily to the military, they more likely sewed linen tents for private customers for use as tents on the beach, sunshades in the atrium, or market stalls (see Lampe 1987; leather tents for the military were sewn mainly by imperial slaves and freedmen or by the soldiers themselves, many of whom were craftsmen, as attested in Vegetius *de re militari* 2.11 and inscriptions at Hadrian's Wall).

Aquila has often been described as a wealthy man who owned one or more houses and ran a rather large business which employed several workers (e.g., Hengel 1973: 46; Lüdemann 1987: 209; Ollrog 1979: 26–27; Wilckens *Romans* EKKNT, 134) but evidence points in a different direction (Lampe *StadtrChr,* 158–64). Like most independent craftsmen, Aquila belonged to the poor strata of society; only a few craftsmen—mostly producers of luxury articles such as goldsmiths and jewelers—were wealthier. Paul "was in want" while he made his living by working in Aquila's shop (2 Cor 11:9). He himself considered his choice of work as a tentmaker as humiliating (2 Cor 11:7;

cf. 1 Cor 4:11–13; 1 Thess 2:9). In Corinth, he did not preach in Aquila's dwelling, although he lodged there. Also, Aquila's dwelling in Ephesus did not seem to have enough space for Paul's audience, although a subgroup of the Ephesian Christians met there as a house church (Acts 18:7, 2; 19:9; on these as historically reliable traditions, see Lüdemann 1987: 209–11, 222). Aquila's ability to travel (Lüdemann 1987: 209) is not an indication of considerable financial means (Lampe, *StadtrChr,* 162–64).

C. Ephesus

After more than one and a half years (Acts 18:11, 2; cf. Lüdemann 1987: 207), Aquila and Prisca moved from Corinth to Ephesus, where they were again active as missionary co-workers of Paul and formed a church in their home (1 Cor 16:19; cf. 2 Tim 4:19; Acts 18:18). The couple "risked their necks" for Paul's life (Rom 16:4) probably during their stay in Ephesus, where Paul was exposed to serious dangers (1 Cor 15:32; 2 Cor 1:8–9). The historicity of the Ephesian episode about Apollos told in Acts 18:26 is very doubtful (Lüdemann 1987: 215–16); *parrēsiazesthai* is a Lukan word, and there is a tension between v 25 and v 26: Apollos already taught "accurately" about Jesus (v 25) before he was instructed "more accurately" by Prisca and Aquila (v 26). Luke, the advocate of the apostle Paul, suggests in v 26 that Prisca and Aquila turned Apollos into a staunch supporter of Pauline Christianity. The pre-Lukan tradition (cf. vv 24–25), however, only knew that Apollos once worked in Ephesus at the same time Paul, Prisca, and Aquila did (cf. also 1 Cor 16:12, 19), and that Apollos was a Christian pneumatic (cf. also the Apollos party in Corinth [1 Cor 1:12] in the context of the Corinthian pneumatics and enthusiasts, e.g., 1 Corinthians 12–14). As such, Apollos was more likely a competitor of Paul (1 Cor 1:12; cf. 3:10b, 12–15) on whom the apostle could not impose his plans while he stayed in Ephesus (1 Cor 16:12). We do not know whether Prisca and Aquila at least housed Apollos in Ephesus (Acts 18:26; Weiser 1985: 508).

D. Second Stay in Rome.

Around 55–56 C.E. (after Claudius' death in 54 C.E. and between the writing of 1 Corinthians and Romans), the couple returned to Rome (majority opinion now holds that Rom 16:3–5 is part of the original letter to the Romans, Lampe *StadtrChr,* 124–35). This last move may have been strategically motivated: Aquila and Prisca were possibly sent as Paul's vanguard to Rome, where he wanted to get a firm footing with his gospel before continuing to Spain. In Rome, Aquila and Prisca again hosted a house church (Cranfield *Romans* ICC, 786). They were the first to receive greeting from Paul in Romans 16, where Paul praised them. Their prominence as Paul's co-workers was remembered by the later church: 2 Timothy used their names for the epistle's fictitious historical frame, at the beginning of a list of greeting (4:19). Church tradition of the 6th century claimed that the house church of Aquila and Prisca was the basis of the later Roman "title" church, "Prisca" on the Aventine. There is no proof for this connection (Lampe *StadtrChr,* 11).

Bibliography

Gielen, M. 1986. Zur Interpretation der paulinischen Formel *hē kat' oikon ekklēsia. ZNW* 77: 109–25.

Hengel, M. 1973. *Eigentum und reichtum in der frühen Kirche.* Stuttgart.

Hock, R. F. 1980. *The Social Context of Paul's Ministry.* Philadelphia.

Lampe, P. 1987. Paulus—Zeltmacher. *BZ* 31: 211–21.

Lüdemann, G. 1987. *Das frühe Christentum nach den Traditionen der Apostelgeschichte.* Göttingen.

Ollrog, W.-H. 1979. *Paulus und seine Mitarbeiter.* WMANT 50. Neukirchen.

Weiser, A. 1980. Akylas Priska Priskilla. Vol. 1, cols. 134–35 in *EWNT.*

———. 1985. *Die Apostelgeschichte II.* ÖTK. Gütersloh.

PETER LAMPE

AQUILA'S VERSION. Aquila was a Jewish translator active in the first quarter of the 2d century C.E. His Greek version of the OT was preserved by Origen in the third column of his Hexapla (compiled during the second quarter of the 3d century). According to tradition, Aquila, born a pagan, converted to Christianity and thence to Judaism. He studied with a number of rabbis, of whom Akiba was one. His version of the biblical text is marked by extreme literalism, in which he sought to reproduce closely not only the meaning, but also the form of his Hebrew *Vorlage.* In so doing, he does not seem to have been influenced by the exegetical emphases of Akiba or of any other particular rabbinic tradition (cf. Barthélemy 1963). Although it has been suggested that Aquila and Onqelos (to whom a Targum on the Pentateuch is attributed) are one and the same, the evidence for such an identification is not convincing.

As argued persuasively by Barthélemy (1963), Aquila should be seen as the culmination of at least a century's worth of translational activity within the Jewish community. Most of his techniques find their antecedents in an earlier recension designated by Barthélemy as *kaige* (see THEODOTION). In fact, it is likely that Aquila's version was a revision of this *kaige* Greek text and that he had no independent knowledge of the Old Greek (or original Greek translation) for most books of the OT. It is difficult to imagine that a reader with no knowledge of Hebrew could have easily followed Aquila's text, so completely did he shape his Greek into the Semitic mold. It would, however, be useful as a textbook and as a source for quotations on the Jewish side of the continuing polemics with Christians.

Because of its many literalistic tendencies and its frequent recourse to stereotyped or etymological renderings for Hebrew words and phrases, Aquila's version is also valuable for modern textual critics and exegetes. Up until the beginning of this century, his work was known mainly through brief citations in rabbinic and patristic sources and from textual notes in the margins or body of a few manuscripts. (It is also suggested that the "Septuagint" text of Qoheleth was produced by Aquila.) Today we have, in addition, some continuous text (for details, see Jellicoe 1968). Although for some this material simply confirms a negative assessment of Aquila's efforts, a fairer assessment of it serves to remind contemporary scholars that his approach was not nearly so heavy-handed and mechanistic as it is often portrayed. Moreover, the literalism Aquila exemplified was undoubtedly compatible with the exegetical concerns of his own day, and for this he was praised even by Christians like Origen and Jerome.

Bibliography

Barr, J. 1979. *The Typology of Literalism in Ancient Biblical Translations.* MSU 15. Göttingen.

Barthélemy, D. 1963. *Les Devanciers d'Aquila.* VTSup 10. Leiden.

Grabbe, L. 1982. Aquila's Translation and Rabbinic Exegesis. *JJS* 33: 527–36.

Jellicoe, S. 1968. *The Septuagint and Modern Study.* Oxford.

Reider, J. 1966. *An Index to Aquila.* Completed and rev. N. Turner. VTSup 12. Leiden.

Swete, H. B. 1914. *An Introduction to the Old Testament in Greek.* Rev. R. R. Ottley. Cambridge.

LEONARD J. GREENSPOON

AR (PLACE) [Heb *ʿār*]. A Moabite toponym used as the name of a town, a region, or both. As the name of a town, Ar could refer to a particular site (i.e., the proper name of a town), or it could be used as a general term for "city." (Moabite *ʿār* is the equivalent of Hebrew *ʿîr,* "city.") Because of the diverse usage of the term, the exact location of Ar cannot be determined with certainty on the basis of the OT, though the historical and geographical data in the Bible provide tantalizing clues for this task.

In the biblical tradition, the designation Ar is found almost exclusively in Numbers and Deuteronomy, in passages dealing with the Israelites' passage through and around Moabite territory. Most of these verses bear directly upon the subject of Moab's northern border at the time of the Hebrew migration, with all data supporting the view that Ar—as the name of a town or a region—was located near this northern boundary, the Arnon. In Num 21:14–15, the "seat of Ar" (i.e., "dwelling of Ar") is mentioned in connection with "the valleys of the Arnon," "the slope of the valleys," and "the border of Moab." Deut 2:18 refers to Ar's proximity to "the boundary of Moab" and, like the forementioned text, probably refers to the name of a prominent town on or near the Arnon (cf. Num 21:28, though some read "as far as" or "cities of" in place of the proper noun "Ar" in this verse). It is possible that "the city of Moab" *(ʿîr moab),* mentioned in Num 22:36, and "the city that is in the valley" (Deut 2:36; Josh 13:9, 16; 2 Sam 24:5) allude to Ar, but this is quite uncertain.

In contrast to the passages that use the designation Ar with reference to a city, specifically or generally, are verses that seem to use Ar as the name of a region, as a synonym for Moab (Deut 2:9, 29). The appearance of Ar in Isa 15:1 may be still another way in which this term was used in the OT. In this verse, the only occurrence of Ar in a poetic text, the prophet refers to a successful campaign against the Moabites. Ar and Kir are named in parallel lines, and it is difficult, if not impossible, to decide which of the following interpretations is correct: (1) Ar and Kir were the two principal towns of Moab (perhaps capitals in different periods), south of the Arnon, and Isaiah narrates the spread of news about the attack from city to city; (2) these terms refer to the towns of Moab in general (*ʿār* = Moabite for "city" and *qir* = Heb for "wall" or "walled city"); or (3) Ar and Kir are identical, with the poetic parallelism requiring two different designations for the same place (cf. Schottroff 1966: 179–81; Weippert 1979: 17–18).

Among the sites that have been identified as Ar of Moab are Kerak (probably ancient Kir/Kir-hareseth), Rabbah (ancient Areopolis/Rabbath Moab), Khirbet el-Miṣnaʿ (M.R. 223767), Khirbet el-Medeineh (M.R. 330768), and Khirbet el-Bālūʿ (M.R. 244855). Although it is impossible, at present, to state with certainty that any of these sites was ancient Ar, it is fair to say that the available geographical, historical, and archaeological evidence seem to favor Khirbet el-Bālūʿ (Miller 1989).

Bibliography

Miller, J. M. 1989. The Israelite Journey through (around) Moab and Moabite Toponymy. *JBL* 108: 577–95.

Schottroff, W. 1966. Horonaim, Nimrim, Luhith und der Westrand des "Landes Ataroth." *ZDPV* 82: 163–208.

Weippert, M. 1979. The Israelite "Conquest" and the Evidence from Transjordan. Pp. 15–34 in *Symposia Celebrating the Seventy-fifth Anniversary of the Founding of the American Schools of Oriental Research,* ed. Frank Moore Cross. Cambridge, MA.

GERALD L. MATTINGLY

ARA (PERSON) [Heb *ʾărāʾ*]. One of the descendants of Asher listed in the select genealogy in 1 Chr 7:30–40. Ara, whose name, perhaps, means "lion," is described as one of the "heads of fathers' houses, approved, mighty warriors, chief of the princes," in Asher's genealogy. Perhaps since Asher was a lesser tribe, originating from the Jacob-Zilpah union (cf. Gen 46:17–18), little emphasis is placed on his lineage. One third of the names listed in this genealogy in 1 Chronicles 7 are found only here in Scripture. Indeed, the name "Ara" appears nowhere else.

J. RANDALL O'BRIEN

ARAB (PLACE) [Heb *ʾărāb*]. A town situated in the central hill country of Judah (Josh 15:52), within the same district as Hebron. This settlement, whose name perhaps means "hiding place" (from Heb *ʾrb* "to lie in ambush"), is listed among the towns within the tribal allotment of Judah (Josh 15:21–62; see also BETH-DAGON). Arab may also have been the home of PAARAI the Arbite (Heb *haʾarbî*), one of David's champions (2 Sam 23:35). The ancient name is clearly reflected at modern Khirbet er-Rabiyeh (*LBHG* 372; M.R. 153093), which lies approximately 13 km SW of Hebron. Although the location is quite acceptable, it is not yet known whether Khirbet er-Rabiyeh was occupied during OT times.

Bibliography

Alt, A. 1925. Judas Gaue unter Josia. *PJ* 21: 100–16.

WADE R. KOTTER

ARABAH (PLACE) [Heb *ʿărābâ*]. A biblical term variously used referring to all or portions of the Great Rift valley in Palestine, running from the Sea of Chinnereth (Galilee) in the N, through the Jordan Valley to the Dead

Sea, and from there to the Gulf of Aqaba in the S. Along with the coastal plains, the Shephelah, the Negev, and the mountains, it is one of the principal geographical regions in Palestine (Josh 11:16). This region is a depression in the earth, for the most part below sea level, which provided a natural barrier and a border between Israel and her neighbors Ammon, Moab, and Edom to the E.

A. Description

Arabah refers to the section in Palestine of the Syrian-East African Rift—the Great Rift—which runs from Turkey to Mozambique. It can be divided into three distinct areas: the Jordan Valley, extending from the Sea of Chinnereth, including both sides of the Jordan river, to the Dead Sea; the region of the Dead Sea itself, including the desert wasteland on either side; and the modern Wadi el-ʿArabah, which designates the region running from the southern end of the Dead Sea, slightly W and S to the Gulf of Aqaba. While the biblical term was used in reference to the whole or parts of this entire area, in modern usage the designation "Arabah" refers specifically to the wilderness area in the S portion, the Wadi el-ʿArabah, from the S end of the Dead Sea to the Gulf of Aqaba.

The Jordan Valley extends from the S end of the Sea of Chinnereth to the Dead Sea and is divided between the Galilee-Beth-sheʾan Basin in the N and the Ghôr in the S by a narrowing referred to as the "Jordan waist." The Jordan winds its way from the Sea of Chinnereth 65 mi (105 km) before entering the Dead Sea (all statistics from Orni and Efrat 1980), and the valley ranges in width from 15 mi to 4 mi and dropping from about 700 ft (213 m) below sea level at the Sea of Chinnereth to 1300 ft (396 m) below sea level at the Dead Sea. See also JORDAN RIVER. The N half of the valley is well watered and relatively fertile while the S portion is drier and less cultivated. In the lower Ghôr is found the site of the ford of Adam (Josh 3:16) and farther S a rugged territory called in the Bible the "jungle of the Jordan" (Jer 12:5; 49:19; 50:44; Zech 11:3), a wilderness area known for its lions. From the E the Jordan River is joined by the rivers Yarmuq, ʿArab, Taiyebeh, Ziqlab, Yabis (perhaps biblical "brook Cherith" 1 Kgs 17:3), Jabbok, and Fariʿa. On the E bank of the southernmost portion of the Jordan River is the area called the well-watered "plains of Moab" (*ʿarĕbôt-môʾab),* the site of biblical Abel-shittim (Num 33:49; Josh 2:1, 3:1; Mic 6:5), while the W bank is the area of the "plains of Jericho" (*ʿarĕbôt-yĕrʾiḥô).*

The Dead Sea, sometimes referred to as the "Sea of the Arabah" *(yām hāʿărābâ),* extends 50 mi (80 km) S from the mouth of the Jordan, and at its widest point is 11 mi (18 km) wide. The level of the water has fluctuated throughout history but presently is about 1300 ft (396 m) below sea level. The Rift Valley extends beneath the level of the water another 1300 ft (396 m) to 2625 ft (800 m) below sea level, making it the deepest continental depression in the world. The sea is surrounded by a narrow shore on either side at the foot of the mountains—the highlands of Judah to the W and the plateau of Moab on the E. Besides the Jordan River, the Dead Sea is fed by the rivers Zerqa, Maʿin, Arnon, and Kerak from the E, while on the W are found the springs of ʿAin Feshka (near Qumran), En-gedi, and En Bokek. In biblical times the cities of Sodom and Gomorrah were located along with the cities of the plain somewhere in the S part of this region which, according to the Bible, was consideraly more fertile than it is today (Gen 13:10). Today this whole region is largely desolate, the S portion containing a salt plain and mountain, Har Sdom.

The southernmost section of the Arabah or Great Rift in Palestine extends from the S end of the Dead Sea 103 mi (165 km) to the S and slightly W to the Gulf of Aqaba. It varies in width from 20 mi (32 km) in the central sections to only 3 mi (5 km) in the S section near Elat. It rises abruptly in altitude going S from about 1300 ft (396 m) below sea level at the Dead Sea to 690 ft (210 m) in only a couple of miles and then ascends gradually to sea level at Elat in the area of ancient Ezion-geber. This area is covered with alluvial sand and gravel, and because of the lack of precipitation, the vegetation consists of sagebrush, camel thorns, and acacia. This area was of particular significance throughout history because it contained the only deposits of iron and copper in ancient Israel (Deut 8:9) which have been mined and smelted since Chalcolithic times. This area and the copper industry have been documented by Glueck (1970: 59–103) and Rothenberg (1962; 1972). See TIMNA. In addition, the port of Ezion-geber and/or Elat was the gateway for trade with Egypt, Africa, and Arabia and hence was the beginning of important trade routes that led N connecting with Gaza and the Via Maris to the W and through Edom, to the King's Highway in the E.

The route leading from the Gulf of Aqaba to Syria through the Great Rift is called by some the Rift Valley Road. It diverged into two roads from the Gulf of Aqaba to Syria interrupted by the cliffs of the Dead Sea and a basalt dam N of the Sea of Chinnereth. The W branch ran from Elat through Oboth to En-gedi and the E branch from Elat to Punon and the Wadi Kerak. From the Dead Sea N, both roads continued to Galilee but continuing from there to the N there was only one road (Baly, *GB,* 98).

B. Terminology and Occurrences

In the past some have argued the root of the word "Arabah" (Heb *ʿ-r-b)* originally meant "arid" or "sterile" (*BDB,* 787). In recent times this view has been seen as tenuous. The term "arabah" does often occur in contexts suggesting a general reference to "desert" or "wilderness" without a specific geographical point of reference. In most of these cases the term occurs without the definite article. It is possible the word developed the general sense of "wilderness" or "desert" simply from the fact that much of the area within the Arabah, especially in the S section of the Arabah, is in fact arid and desolate. This general usage is primarily found in poetry, especially in the prophets, and RSV usually translates "desert." See, for example, "Sharon is like a desert" (Isa 33:9); "a wolf from the desert" (Jer 5:6). The word is rendered as "plain" in "the whole land shall be turned into a plain" (Zech 14:10). Often the term "arabah" occurs in conjunction with other words meaning "wilderness" or "dry land." It is found as a parallel term to *midbār,* RSV "wilderness," in several passages: "waters shall break forth in the wilderness *(bammidbār)* and streams in the desert *(bāʿărābâ)*" (Isa 35:6). See also Isa 33:9; 40:3; 41:19; 51:3; Jer 17:6; Job 24:5. In addition, it is found in conjunction with other terms meaning "wilderness" or "dry land": "the wilderness *(midbār)* and dry land *(ṣiyyâ)* shall be glad, the desert *(ʿărābâ)* shall rejoice and blossom like a crocus" (Isa 35:1). See also Jer 2:6; 50:12; 51:43, where it occurs with *ṣiyyâ* and *midbār* and with "salt land" *(mlḥh)* in Job 39:6. Even where such a general sense is intended, it is possible that some of these contexts are a reference to the Arabah proper.

When "arabah" occurs with the definite article *(hāʿărābâ),* it is rendered by RSV as "Arabah," and in most cases designates a specific geographical place or area within the Rift Valley. Josh 11:16 lists this region as one of the major geographical areas in the Promised Land: "Joshua took all the land, the hill country, and all the Negeb, and all the land of Goshen, and the lowland, and the Arabah and the hill country of Israel" (Josh 11:16). There is a reference to the Arabah as the region on both banks of the Jordan Valley crossed by Abner on his way from Gibeon to Mahanaim (2 Sam 2:29). Several references are made to the Arabah as the E bank of the Jordan Valley from the Sea of Chinnereth to the Dead Sea (Deut 3:17; 4:49; Josh 12:1, 3), and there are references to the W bank of the Jordan Valley where Gilgal is located (Deut 11:30) and where the men of Ai went out to meet Israel in battle (Josh 8:14). The "plains of Jericho," where the fleeing King Zedekiah was apprehended by the Babylonians (2 Kgs 25:4; Jer 39:4; 52:7), are also referred to as the Arabah. The region to the W of the Dead Sea is referred to in 1 Sam 23:24: "David and his men in the wilderness of Maon, in the Arabah to the south of Jeshimon." Ezek 47:8 ("the water flows towards the eastern region and goes down into the Arabah") refers to the region of the Dead Sea and perhaps by extension to the whole of the S Arabah. The only explicit reference to the S portion of the Arabah, present-day Wadi el-ʿArabah, is found in Deut 2:8, where the children of Israel moved S from Kadesh "from the Arabah road from Elat and Ezion-geber."

The term "arabah" is occasionally used as a designation of a road or route, and Heb *derek hāʿărābâ* is variously translated: "Arabah road" (Deut 2:8), the road in the vicinity of Elat and Ezion-geber; "way of the Arabah" (2 Sam 4:7), the route from Mahanaim to Hebron; and "direction of the Arabah" designating a route from Jerusalem to the area of Jericho (2 Kgs 25:4; Jer 39:4; 52:7). The plural form *(ʿărābôt)* occurs in two expressions where it is translated as "plains": *ʿarĕbôt-môʾāb* "plains of Moab" (Num 22:1; 26:3, 63; 31:12; 33:48–50; 35:1; 36:13; Deut 34:1, 8) and *ʿarĕbôt-yĕrʾiḥô* "plains of Jericho" (Josh 4:13; 5:10; 2 Kgs 25:5; Jer 39:5; 52:8).

Several times the Dead Sea is referred to as the "Sea of the Arabah" *(yām hāʿărābâ),* often qualified as the Salt Sea. This term is found referring to the Dead Sea as a landmark delineating the boundaries of the tribes of Israel across the Jordan (Deut 3:17; 4:49; Josh 12:3), as well as in the description of the Jordan "flowing down toward the sea of the Arabah, the Salt Sea" (Josh 3:16). It is also found as the border of the N kingdom when Jeroboam II "restored the border of Israel from the entrance of Hamath as far as the Sea of the Arabah" (2 Kgs 14:25). In Amos 6:14 there is mention of the "brook of the Arabah" *(naḥal hāʿârābâ)* also in the context of the borders of Israel "from the entrance of Hamath to the Brook of the Arabah" in a passage that suggests Amos might be parodying Jeroboam's achievement mentioned in 2 Kgs 14:25. It is not certain if Amos intends a specific brook of water in the region such as the Wadi Qelt or the brook Zered (called in Isa 15:7 *naḥal hāʿârābîm* "brook of the willows") as the S border. Some have suggested that Amos may intend the Wadi el-ʿArabah, and Arabic term, referring to the whole area from the Dead Sea to the Gulf of Aqaba.

In addition there is a reference to the "plains of the wilderness" (*ʿrbwt hmdbr;* Qere in 2 Sam 15:28 and 17:16), which in its context suggests that part of the Arabah on the borders of the Judean wilderness, probably the Jordan Valley N of the Dead Sea. RSV, however, follows the Kethib reading "fords of the wilderness" *(ʿabĕrôt hāmmidbār),* referring to the crossing point of the Jordan in this area.

C. History

While not specifically mentioned, the area of the Arabah played a significant part in the patriarchal narratives. When there was conflict between the servants of Abraham and Lot over the shortage of pastureland, they divided the land between them. Lot chose the Jordan Valley because it was well watered, and he settled in the area around Sodom (Gen 13:2–13). The wealth and prosperity of the cities of the plain attracted the kings from the E, who sacked the cities of Sodom and Gomorrah and were pursued and caught by Abraham (Genesis 14). Later the cities of Sodom and Gomorrah were totally destroyed by "brimstone and fire from the Lord out of heaven" (Gen 19:24).

In the 14th–12th centuries B.C. mines in the S Arabah were heavily worked by the Egyptians, but later in Iron Age I–II production was left again to the local tribes of Midianites and Kenites. As prophesied by Moses, it was the site where iron and copper could be found in the Promised Land (Deut 8:9).

The children of Israel passed through the Arabah on their journey from Kadesh-barnea to Ezion-geber (Deut 2:8) before turning N and E to avoid the borders of Edom and Moab. The Amorites under Sihon had seized the Moabite portion of the Arabah, which was in turn captured and populated by the Israelites (Num 21:21–30; Deut 2:24–37). This area was the scene of the apostasy at Abel-shittim (Numbers 25). The plains of Moab *(ʿarĕbôt-môʾāb)* on the E bank of the Jordan N of the Dead Sea was the site of the Israelite camp that witnessed the final acts and received the final words of Moses (Numbers 32–36; Deut 1:1, 7). It is the area where the Israelites camped before they crossed to Jericho (Num 22:1; 3:48–50; 35:1; 36:13); where the census of Israel was taken before the entry into the Promised Land (Num 26:3, 63); where the booty was taken after the defeat of the Midianites (Num 31:12); the place from whence Moses ascended to Mt. Nebo in order to view the Promised Land (Deut 34:1, 8); and a landmark in the designation of the inheritance allotted to the tribes on the other side of the Jordan (Deut 3:17; 4:49; Josh 12:1, 3). Israel witnessed the miraculous parting of the Jordan (Josh 3:14–17) and crossed the Jordan under the direction of Joshua to the "plains of Jericho" *(ʿarĕbôt-*

yĕr'iḥô), camping at Gilgal, which became the headquarters for the first phase of the Conquest. On the plains of Jericho, Israel prepared for the capture of Jericho (Josh 4:13), here is where they renewed the covenant through circumcision, celebrated Passover, and where the manna stopped (Josh 5:1–10).

The N portion of the Arabah is the scene of the incident of Abner fleeing after his defeat at Gibeon (2 Sam 2:29), and the area which the assassins of Ishbosheth crossed from Mahanaim to bring the head of their king to David at Hebron (2 Sam 4:7). Throughout the history of Israel the S Arabah was a strategic area, both because of the copper industry as well as the seaport. It is recorded that Solomon "built a fleet of ships at Ezion-geber" (1 Kgs 9:26–28; 10:11; 2 Chr 8:17–18; 9:10–11), which pursued trade with Arabia and Africa. After Solomon's death, the area reverted to the Edomites, only to be reconquered by Jehoshaphat of Judah, who also built a fleet of ships (1 Kgs 22:48; 2 Chr 20:36). The dispute with Edom continued as Elath was recaptured by Amaziah (2 Kgs 14:22) or Uzziah (2 Chr 26:2), finally falling to the Edomites (2 Kgs 16:6). When Zedekiah fled Jerusalem toward the wilderness, he was captured by the Babylonians in the plains of Jericho in the Arabah, near Jericho (2 Kgs 25:5; Jer 39:5; 52:8).

The S section of the biblical Arabah was inhabited by the Nabateans in the 3d century B.C., and the Romans reopened copper mining in this area in the 1st–3d centuries A.D.

Bibliography

Glueck, N. 1970. *The Other Side of the Jordan.* Cambridge, MA.
Orni, E. and Efrat, E. 1980. *Geography of Israel.* 4th ed. Jerusalem.
Rothenberg, B. 1962. Ancient Copper Industries in the Western Arabah. *PEQ* 1962: 5–71.
———. 1972. *Timna.* London.

David R. Seely

ARABAH, BROOK OF THE (PLACE) [Heb *naḥal hāʿărābâ*]. A place mentioned in Amos's pronouncement of doom against Israel (Amos 6:14). Together with the "entrance of Hamath," the Brook of the Arabah is used to delineate the geographical extent of Yahweh's punishment: since the former (Heb *lĕbōʾ ḥămat*) seems to designate the N border of the promised land (Num 34:7–9; Josh 13:5; Ezek 47:15–16), the latter presumably designates the S border. However, elsewhere the S border is characteristically referred to as the "Brook of Egypt" (Josh 15:4; Ezek 47:19) or as "the Shihor, which is east of Egypt" (Josh 13:3). On the one hand, it is possible that the Brook of the Arabah is one of these, and therefore provides a coastal referent for the S boundary of Yahweh's punishment. The Brook of Egypt is usually identified with Wadi el-ʿArish, which drains the central Sinai N into the Mediterranean, while Shihor (Eg *š hor*) may be the easternmost branch of the Nile delta (*IDB* 4: 328; *ISBE* 1:549). On the other hand, it is possible that the Brook of the Arabah provides an inland referent for the S boundary. It may be equivalent to the Brook of Zered SE of the Dead Sea, a suggestion supported by the fact that the word "Arabah" is usually used to designate the Dead Sea basin and the area directly S of it to Aqaba. See also ARABAH; EGYPT, BROOK OF; SHIHOR.

Gary A. Herion

ARABAH, SEA OF. See SALT SEA.

ARABIA (PLACE) [Heb *ʿărab*]. ARABIAN. The OT has no true geographical place name "Arabia," the collective noun *ʿărāb* ("Arabs") being used to designate the region; the geographical term "Arabia" appears only in Greek texts. Arabs are also sometimes referred to in the OT as *bĕnê qedem* "people [literally "sons"] of the East" (*e.g.,* Judg 6:3, 1 Kgs 4:30) and their region as *ʾereṣ qedem,* "land of the East," or simply *qedem,* "East" (so Gen 25:6, Isa 2:6).

A. History and Geography

The origin of the Arabs is debated; the conventional view is that they originated in the central or S part of the Arabian peninsula (e.g., Montgomery 1934, Hitti 1970). The inclusion of the S part of the peninsula in the designation "Arabia" is not, however, attested until Roman times, nor do people identified as "Arabs" appear in ancient texts as inhabitants of the S region until the same period (Ephʿal 1982:8); prior to that time the S region was known by the names of the various kingdoms that inhabited it, such as Saba, Qataban, and Hadhramaut. Considerable evidence favors the theory that the Arabs first appeared on the N, W, and E edges of the Syrian desert, with an extension into the Negev, the Sinai peninsula, and the N part of the Hejaz (the NW coast and mountain range of the Arabian peninsula).

Egyptian texts as early as the 3d millennium B.C. refer to inhabitants of the S Levant as "sand-dwellers," a term that originally must have alluded to nomads, although even at that early date it also applied to sedentary Levantine peoples. The homeland of these Asiatics was sometimes designated, as in the Egyptian story of Sinuhe which originated in the 20th century B.C., by the Semitic word *qedem.* Archaeological investigations have shown that nomads were much in evidence in Syro-Palestinian life during the period 2200–1900 B.C., following the collapse of the EB cultures, but partially withdrew to the S and E desert regions during the subsequent centuries of ascendancy of the Canaanite city-states. The tendency of nomads to press into Palestine and W Transjordan as the Canaanite culture began to disintegrate during the latter part of the 1st millennium B.C. was impeded by the establishment of Edom, Moab, Israel, and other fledgling kingdoms. During much of the 1st millennium B.C. Arabs moved about on the fringes of the settled regions, not only providing the sedentary peoples with sheep, goats, camels, asses, and animal by-products such as skins and wool, but also serving as itinerant merchants trading in spices, dates, embroidery, incense, iron, copper, gold, precious stones, pearls, and other commodities, some of which originated in distant places (see Gen 2:11, 1 Kgs 10:2, Ezek 27:21–22).

Arabs were also active in the extreme S part of Palestine and Transjordan during the OT period. Nomadic groups, often called by tribal names rather than the generic term

"Arab," had long moved about in the W part of the Negeb between Judah and the "Brook of Egypt" (Wadi el-ʿArish, the traditional border between Palestine and Egypt) and in the rugged terrain E toward Edom and Midian. The Midianites, who were related to, if not identical with, the biblical Ishmaelites, were of Arab stock, and engaged in caravaneering. The biblical story of Joseph describes a Midianite caravan on its way from Gilead in the Transjordanian highlands to Egypt, passing through the vicinity of Dothan in N Palestine (Gen 37:25–28). The traders carried with them stock items of resin, balm, and myrrh, and also trafficked in slaves. Some Arab tribes probably made their living, as they did at later times in history, by preying upon such caravans, or by raiding villages or the encampments of other Arabs.

The earliest known appearance of the word "Arab" in extrabiblical texts is in an Assyrian record from the time of Shalmaneser III which states that an Arab leader named Gindibuʾ, who probably had his home on the SW edge of the Syrian desert, went with troops and 1000 camels to participate in a military coalition against the Assyrians that culminated in the battle of Qarqar in 853 B.C. Arabs appear frequently in the records of a number of later Assyrian monarchs, from Tiglath-pileser III through Ashurbanipal (745–627 B.C.), sometimes as allies and sometimes as the vanquished. Tiglath-pileser's annals identify various Arab tribes or leaders that were nominally integrated into the Assyrian empire. Under Sargon II, some Arabs were resettled in Palestine and elsewhere, either voluntarily or otherwise (see Ephʿal 1982: 105–8). Arabs also appear sporadically in the records of the subsequent Neo-Babylonian and Persian empires. None of the Near Eastern empires could, however, effectively control these nomads or their territories permanently; at most they could make incursions into the inhospitable desert regions, and usually had to content themselves with striking bargains with the Bedouin leaders to achieve their main goal, that of keeping commercial routes open. See BEDOUIN AND BEDOUIN STATES.

During the Greco-Roman period, the Arabs became much better known than previously. Geographers began to make rudimentary distinctions among the regions inhabited by Arabs, referring to the North Arabian region as "Arabia Deserta" and the SW coast of the Arabian peninsula as "Arabia Felix." Damascus was generally regarded as standing at the NW corner of Arabia Deserta (cf. Jdt 2:25). A third region, Arabia Petraea, emerged in Edom as one group of Arabs, the Nabataeans, rose to prominence during the 3d–1st centuries B.C. Transforming tribal leadership into kingship and their nomadic way of life into a sedentary existence, the Nabataeans gradually increased their cultural sphere N and W during this time, becoming prosperous through trade. They vigorously and creatively adapted Hellenistic-Roman culture to their indigenous traditions, particularly in their capital city of Petra. By the early 1st century A.D., at its zenith, the kingdom of Nabatea dominated a large part of Transjordan and the Negev (see Glueck 1959 and 1970, Bowersock 1983, and Negev 1986). See also NABATEANS.

The Romans, who had actively entered the governance of the Levant with Pompey's conquest of Syria and Palestine in 64–63 B.C., maintained the Nabataeans as a client state within the larger geographical region they called "Arabia" (comprising portions of Transjordan, S Syria, the Negev, and the NW Arabian peninsula) for well over a century, but in A.D. 106 annexed a large part of the Nabatean kingdom as a Roman province. Subsequently, attempting to prevent the still populous non-Nabatean Arab groups situated farther to the E and S from encroaching upon the boundaries of the empire, the Romans established a series of military posts in Transjordan (see Bowersock 1983 and Parker 1986), but these only partially achieved their purpose and after several centuries were abandoned; ultimately the Romans proved to have little more success than previous empires in controlling the Arabs. During the 4th–6th centuries A.D. the Arabs had considerable contact with the Byzantine world, but it was only when Islam emerged in the 7th century A.D. that they moved to the forefront of Near Eastern history.

B. In the OT and Intertestamental Literature

Ephʿal (1982: 60–63) points out that in the earlier historical texts in the OT bedouin peoples are referred to by various tribal names (chiefly Amalekites, Midianites, and Ishmaelites) or simply as people of the East; in later passages they still sometimes appear as people of the East, but are also designated by the generic term "Arab" or by names representing kingdoms, oasis cities, or other previously unknown groups. Ephʿal suggests that the change of terminology occurred in the mid-10th century B.C., at the end of the reign of King David. While such may have been the case, the biblical evidence for the change in terminology is scanty and somewhat questionable prior to the 7th century B.C. The first mention of Arabs in the records of the Hebrew monarchy appears in 1 Kgs 10:15 (=2 Chr 9:14), where the somewhat uncertain Hebrew text can be read as stating that Solomon received gold from "all the kings of the Arabs [or Arabia]." Inasmuch as Solomon is reported to have fostered commerce via the Red Sea, the passage may attest to gifts proffered by rulers of the kingdoms of the SW Arabian peninsula; the LXX, however, does not mention Arabs or Arabia but states that Solomon received tribute from "all the kings of the coast"—by which is perhaps meant the N Hejaz, where Tema, Dedan, and other caravan centers were located. Similarly the account of the visit of the Queen of Sheba to Solomon's court (1 Kgs 10:1–13) may have concerned the ruler of a N branch of the Sabaeans, located in the Hejaz and conducting operations both S along the Red Sea and N into the Negev. A case can, however, be made for the traditional interpretation of the story, which identifies Sheba with the Sabaean kingdom of the SW Arabian peninsula (see Ephʿal 1982: 63–64, 88–89, 227–29). Vv 11–12 of the account, which mention wood and precious stones that Solomon is said to have brought from Ophir, concern trade with more distant places than the Hejaz, but this information is an addition to the story.

Arabs are referred to several times in the Chronicler's history of the Northern and Southern Kingdoms. 2 Chr 17:11 states that Arabs gave large gifts of sheep and goats to Jehoshaphat, king of Judah (873–849 B.C.), who had attempted to reactivate Solomonic trade routes through the Red Sea (1 Kgs 22:47–49). 2 Chr 21:16 (cf. 22:1) alludes to a brief but destructive invasion carried out against Judah by the Philistines and "the Arabs who are near the Ethiopians" during the reign of Jehoram (859–853 B.C.). The Chronicler also mentions several times an Arab tribe known as the Meunites (2 Chr 20:1, 26:7; Ezra 2:50 = Neh 7:52), who are also attested in Assyrian records. That same work speaks of the Philistines, the Meunites, and "the Arabs that dwelt in Gurbaal" (26:7; cf. 14:12–14) as groups attacked by King Uzziah of Judah (783–750 B.C.); such a war, if historical, probably was waged out of concern not to acquire more territory but to control lucrative trade routes through the S end of the Levant. Precisely how historical these various states are is difficult to determine, since Chronicles is a relatively late postexilic work, and references in it to Arabs may reflect, in part, contemporaneous circumstances (cf. Eph^cal 1982: 65–71). The corresponding narratives in 2 Kings do not mention Arabs, and the LXX versions of the passages in 2 Chronicles often differ slightly from the Hebrew text, either omitting reference to Arabs or apparently attempting some clarification (e.g., "the Arabs and those who bordered on the Ethiopians" in 2 Chr 21:16 and "those that dwelt on the rock" in 2 Chron 26:7, the latter perhaps alluding to the Edomite stronghold at Petra or its vicinity).

In the prophetic tradition of the late 8th–early 6th centuries B.C. North Arabia continues sometimes to be alluded to as the East (e.g., Isa 11:14, Jer 49:28), and older tribal terminology occasionally appears, but the newer names of Arab groups such as Dedan, Tema, and Kedar (Qedar) are also frequent. The latter, all located in the NW corner of the Arabian peninsula, are often linked in prophetic poetry. Isa 21:11–17, which includes an oracle "concerning Arabia," uses all three names; the fact, however, that this oracle is lacking in the LXX raises some doubt as to its date. Jer 25:23–24 (LXX 32:23–24) refers to Dedan, Tema, Buz, and the Arabs who "cut the corners of their hair [i.e., have a distinctive tonsure]; all the kings of Arabia and all the kings of the mixed tribes that dwell in the desert." Montgomery (1934: 29–30) has pointed out that this may be the earliest unquestionable OT reference to "Arabs" dating from the latter part of the 7th or the early 6th century B.C. Ezekiel's list of nations that traded with the city of Tyre names not only Dedan and Kedar but also Sheba and Ramah as well, and gives important details regarding their commerce (Ezek. 27:20–22).

Some of the wisdom literature of the OT and the intertestamental period indicates that Arabia had a reputation for fostering men of wisdom, an idea that is also found occasionally in prophetic literature (e.g., Obad 8, Jer 49:7). The conventional presupposition about Arab wisdom is found in 1 Kgs 4:29–31, where Solomon's wisdom is said to have surpassed even that of the "people of the East." Epigrams and other wise sayings were sometimes believed to have an Arab origin (1 Sam 24:13 and perhaps Prov 30:1, 31:1). The postexilic wisdom book of Job refers to its protagonist as the greatest of the people of the East (Job 1:3), and makes allusions to persons and places in North Arabia, such as the Sabaeans (Job 1:15), the oasis of Tema (Job 6:19), and the land of Uz (Job 1:3; see also Lam 4:21, where Edom and Uz were paired); it has been thought by some scholars that the book had its origins in that region (but compare Montgomery 1934: 172–73).

The scanty references to the Arabs in the postexilic historical accounts in the OT, which should probably include at least some of the passages in Chronicles, show that the Arabs continued to be a force in the Levant during the 5th–3d centuries B.C. During the rebuilding of the walls of Jerusalem around 445 B.C. Nehemiah's efforts on behalf of the Jews were opposed by a coalition of several groups, the leaders of which were Sanballat the Horonite, Tobiah the Ammonite, and Geshem the Arab (Neh. 2:19; cf. 4:1—Eng 4:7, 6:1). The question of the identification of this personage is discussed in Eph^cal (1982: 197, 210–14), who suggests that Geshem probably ruled a group of Arabs that lived in the desert to the south of Judah. Extrabiblical sources attest to a king of Kedar named Gashmu, who was contemporary with the biblical Geshem, if not identical with him.

Jewish concern with Arabs in the 2d–1st centuries B.C. and the early 1st century A.D. tended to focus on the bedouin of Transjordan and the Negev; those in other regions are rarely mentioned. Zabdiel the Arab, who figures briefly in 1 Macc 11:16, and the Arabs called Zabadeans, who appear in 1 Macc 12:31, may have inhabited a part of the Negev. The word "Arab" sometimes was used with its old connotation of "nomad" (e.g., 2 Macc 12:10–12, where it is asserted that 5000 Arabs with 500 horsemen attacked Judas Maccabeus and were defeated, after which they "departed to their tents"); other references, however, show that the term could be used as a virtual equivalent of "Nabatean" (1 Macc 5:25, 39, 9:35, and 2 Macc 5:8).

C. In the NT

"Arabians" (i.e., inhabitants of Arabia, not necessarily entirely synonymous with "Arabs") are mentioned only once, as such, in the NT, as one of many kinds of foreigners living in Jerusalem who participated in the outpouring of the Holy Spirit at Pentecost (Acts 2:11). Paul mentions Arabia in his brief allusion to his conversion and subsequent departure "into Arabia," followed by his return to Damascus (Gal 1:17). This Arabian sojourn, of unspecified duration, took place somewhere on the edge of the Syrian desert or in Transjordan. Paul's famous escape from Damascus (2 Cor 11:32–33) took place under the kingship of Aretas IV, during a period of domination of the city by the Nabataeans.

D. In Biblical Theology and Imagery

Arab influence on the Bible was most intensively examined during a half-century period, from around 1885 to 1935. Julius Wellhausen wrote the first extensive modern treatise on the subject with his *Reste arabischen Heidentums*, published in 1887. His pioneering work was followed by others, among which were W. Robertson Smith's *The Religion of the Semites* (1894), G. Jacob's *Altarabische Parallelen zum Alten Testament* (1897), M.-J. Lagrange's *Études sur les religions sémitiques* (1905), D. S. Margoliouth's *The Relations between Arabs and Israelites prior to the Rise of Islam* (1924), Albrecht Alt's *Der Gott der Väter* (1929), and James Montgomery's comprehensive (and still highly useful) *Arabia and the Bible* in 1934. The historical and ethnographic work that was done decades ago has shown that the impact of Arabia and the Arab culture on the Bible was far greater than the occurrences of the words "Arabs" and "Arabia" in the Bible might suggest, a fact that is being reinforced by more recent research. The Arabs constituted a significant factor in the formation of the Israelite thought, not simply as an environmental presence but as a wellspring of influential cultural and religious concepts, only a few aspects of which can be touched upon here.

The OT recognition of the closeness of Arab and Hebrew cultures is reflected in the lineages incorporated in Genesis. Although lacking in ethnographic sophistication, these priestly genealogical constructions acknowledge nomadic groups as near relatives of the Hebrews. Unfortunately the dating of information in the lists is very uncertain and interpretation is replete with difficulties (see Ephᶜal 1982: 231–40). Some Arab tribes, including ones found in the Hejaz, are said to be descended from Abraham's son Ishmael by his less-favored wife, Hagar (Gen 25:12–18), while others, which were geographically closer to Palestine, such as Midian, are alleged to be Abraham's sons by his wife Keturah (Gen 25:1–6). The Joktanite tribes, whose separation from the Hebrews is ascribed to an era before Abraham (Gen 10:26–29), include some of the peoples of South Arabia who may have had ancient non-Arab origins. The descent of "those who dwell in tents and have herds" (Gen 4:20) from Jubal represents yet another genealogical tradition incorporated into Genesis, as does the lineage of the Edomites from Esau (Genesis 36).

Although the OT distinguishes between Hebrews and Arabs, numerous passages indicate that there was widespread recognition of the concept that Israel's physical and spiritual origins lay in the desert. The story of Cain and Abel in the JE epic tradition suggests a divine preference for Abel the shepherd rather than Cain the agriculturist (Gen 4:2–5; but see ABEL). Many aspects of patriarchal traditions are clarified by Arab concepts and practices, such as the welcome which Abraham gives to his angelic visitors (Gen 18:1–8) and the practice of a leader's returning to his tribe to obtain a wife for his son (Genesis 24). Arab customs that illuminate early biblical traditions are discussed in detail by Montgomery (1934) and others. (Since, however, Arab customs persisted throughout the biblical period, these affinities cannot be used as evidence for the historicity or antiquity of any particular sources or passages.) More normative yet for Hebrew theology is the account of the Hebrew exodus from Egypt, which has a subtle, multifaceted relationship to Bedouin culture, tracing Israel's fundamental encounter with God and his law to an experience in the wilderness of Sinai at a time when the Israelites were living in a manner much like that of the Arabs. The tradition has overtones of the rejection of both agricultural and urbanized life in favor of the more rigorous but purer life of the nomad. Furthermore, Moses is said to have gained knowledge about Yahweh, the Hebrew God, from his father-in-law, Jethro, a Midianite Arab.

By virtue of this communal memory of desert origins, biblical writers cherished the concept of the wilderness as the home to which Israel must return, if only figuratively, for spiritual sustenance. When the Northern Kingdom seceded from the Davidic monarchy, the poetic cry was "every man to his tents, O Israel" (2 Sam 20:1). The traditions about Elijah, and to a lesser extent Elisha, emphasize the prophets' orientation toward the wilderness. The theme appears in later prophets, among them Jer (2:2) and Hos (2:14). Arabia continued to exert a powerful influence in the thought of earliest Christianity. The Gospels emphasize the wilderness tradition when presenting Jesus as the successor to John the Baptist, an Elijah-like figure whose life and message echo the sternness and spiritual integrity of the Hebrew experience of the exodus (Mark 1:4–9 and par). When on the verge of his public ministry, Jesus goes into the wilderness, where he contemplates, and rejects, the temptations of materialism and urban culture (Mark 1:14–13 and par). The concept again reappears in the apostle Paul's withdrawal to Arabia following his conversion (Gal 1:17).

Bibliography

Bowersock, G. W. 1983. *Roman Arabia.* Cambridge, MA.

Ephᶜal, I. 1982. *The Ancient Arabs: Nomads on the Borders of the Fertile Crescent, 9th–5th Centuries B.C.* Jerusalem.

Glueck, N. 1959. *Rivers in the Desert.* New York.

———. 1965. *Deities and Dolphins.* New York.

Hitti, P. K. 1970. *History of the Arabs, from the Earliest Times to the Present.* New York.

Irvine, A. K. 1973. The Arabs and Ethiopians. Pp. 287–311 in *POTT.*

Margoliouth, D. S. 1924. *The Relations between Arabs and Israelites, prior to the Rise of Islam.* London.

Montgomery, J. A. 1934. *Arabia and the Bible.* Philadelphia.

Negev, A. 1986. *Nabatean Archaeology Today.* New York.

Parker, S. T. 1986. *Romans and Saracens: A History of the Arabian Frontier.* Durham, NC.

Sawyer, J. F. A., and Clines, D. J. A. 1983. *Midian, Moab and Edom: The History of Archaeology of Late Bronze and Iron Age Jordan and Northwest Arabia.* Sheffield.

ROBERT HOUSTON SMITH

ARABIA, LANGUAGES OF (SOUTH). See LANGUAGES (INTRODUCTORY SURVEY) and (PRE-ISLAMIC SOUTH ARABIA).

ARABIA, PREHISTORY OF. Some 80 years have elapsed between Hogarth's seminal work, *The Penetration of Arabia* (1904), and the first synthesis of recent archaeological work on the peninsula by Tosi (1986). While much of the Near East and particularly the "Holy Land" had been increasingly scrutinized by archaeologists since Hogarth's work, investigation into the Arabian past lagged behind. The Danish expeditions to the Arab Gulf countries beginning in the 1950s were the first to open up the potential not only for archaeology but for biblical readers as well.

Defining "Arabia" remains a complex and difficult task. Workable definitions depend on historical perspective, geomorphology (including flora/fauna, climatology), and the definition of archaeological assemblages and political considerations. If we were to strictly apply the concept of "Arabian peninsula" as defined by the Persian Gulf and Red Sea, following the 30° lat. we would place the upper boundary of Arabia just north of the Nafud desert at Jauf. However, much of the desert/steppe north of the Nafud has historically been defined as *Arabia Deserta,* so perhaps a better criterion for defining the northern limit of Arabia would be the 250 mm isohyet. This rainfall line divides the

Fertile Crescent from the steppe/desert. Using this criterion, we can briefly suggest 10 major divisions: (1) the North Arabian Desert, encompassing southern Syria, western Iraq, eastern Jordan, and northern Saudi Arabia extending to the Nafud desert, (2) the Nafud Desert and the eastern arm—the Dahna, (3) Eastern Arabia, stretching from Kuwait to the United Arab Emirates, (4) Oman including Dhofar, (5) the Najd, covering the center of the Arabian peninsula, bounded on the north and south by the Nafud and the Rub al-Khali and on the east by Eastern Arabia respectively, (6) the Hejaz, located along the northern Red Sea and including Midian, (7) the Asir/Yemen, defining the western highlands of the peninsula, (8) the Tihama, which is the Red Sea coast along the southern portion of the peninsula, (9) the Rub al-Khali sand desert, and (10) the Hadhramaut, stretching along the Arabian Sea.

The question of "prehistory" involves chronological considerations. Strictly speaking, our discussion ends when formal writing systems are developed in the peninsula. These are generally regarded as offshoots of the Proto-Sinaitic alphabet system (Gelb 1963: 122–27; Albright 1969; Millard 1986: 392–95) and do not antedate the early 1st millennium B.C. Thus, properly speaking, the prehistory of the Arabian peninsula begins with the appearance of hominids in the early Pleistocene and ends with the advent of early Iron Age oases' states ca. 1000 B.C. However, "history" as an expression of written records impinges on the Arabian experience almost from the beginning of writing. Thus, Dilmun (Eastern Arabia) seems to occur in Uruk period IV texts ca. 3000 B.C. (Nissen 1985: 229–30, 1986; Englund 1983) and continues to be mentioned along with later Magan (Oman) well through the 1st millennium B.C. (Potts 1978, 1983, fc.a, fc.b). Amorites (MAR.TU) as early pastoral nomads inhabiting the North Arabian desert are known from both the Ebla and Mesopotamian texts (ca. 2500 B.C.) (Archi 1985; *POTT,* 103). Equally early may be the Tihama of the southern Red Sea mentioned as part of Punt in the 5th Egyptian Dynasty (ca. 2400 B.C.) (*CAH* 1/2/14: 183). Finally, Midian occurs in Middle Kingdom Egyptian Execration Texts datable to ca. 1800 B.C. (Posener 1940: 88–90; *CAH* 1/2/21: 554–55).

Biblical references to the Arabian peninsula begin at a very early date and can be divided into two groups: (1) semihistorical attributions datable to a pre-Israel state period (Joseph account, Gen 37:25–28; Moses and the Exodus, Exod 2:15ff.; Gideon and the Midianites, Judg 6:11ff.) and (2) historical descriptions of Iron Age Arabia contemporary to the OT state of Israel (e.g. "Kings of Arabia" in 1 Kgs 10:15; Ophir and Tarshish in 1 Kgs 10:11ff.; Dumah in Gen 25:14, Josh 15:52; Dedan in Gen 10:7, Jer 25:23; Teima in Gen 25:15, Job 6:19; Qedar in 1 Chr 1:29, Ps 120:5 and "Arabs" in Neh 4:7, 6:1ff.). The latter also clearly help define the *terminus* for our brief introduction to Arabian prehistory and the former can be perhaps integrated in brief summaries of the relevant regions of Arabian prehistory.

Keeping in mind the strictures concerning the nature of the peninsula, we can summarize its prehistory in roughly four major blocks: (1) the Paleolithic, (2) the Neolithic, (3) the Chalcolithic/Early Bronze Age, and (4) the 2d millennium B.C. (Middle–Late Bronze Ages). The Paleolithic at this point has little relevance for Biblical studies although the evidence to date suggests that the Pliocene–Pleistocene epochs had a profound impact on the human and natural landscape of both Arabia and the Levant (Sayari and Zotl eds. 1978; Jado and Zotl eds. 1984; McClure 1984). North and West Arabia, in many respects, mirror the archaeological record generated along the Levantine coast and Syria. Already by the Oldowan period (ca. 1.5 million B.P.), sites have been recorded both in the Dead Sea rift valley (Ubeidiyah), the Negev and the Orontes River Valley, as well as the North Arabian desert in the vicinity of Jauf (Parr et al. 1978: 34; Whalen personal com.). The Acheulean is well represented in the Arabian peninsula, particularly by the sites of the Mindel-Riss interglacial (ca. 300,000 B.P.) (Zarins et al. 1980: 12–15; Zarins et al. 1981: 14–16; Whalen et al. 1981: 46–47). Work in the central Najd at such sites as Dawadmi (Whalen et al. 1983: 9–21; Whalen et al. 1984: 9–24) and at embayments along the southern Red Sea (Zarins et al. 1982: 35–36) has been particularly illuminating in reconstructing the distant human past. The Mousterian Middle Paleolithic (ca. 50,000 B.P.) can be found at virtually every Paleolithic site (see the above Acheulean references). In this regard, the evidence again parallels finds from the Levantine coast. The Upper and Epi-Paleolithic periods (40,000–10,000 B.P.) are seemingly absent from the peninsula, except along the northern fringes in the Northern Arabian desert (Copeland and Hours 1971; Garrard et al. 1986; Fujimoto 1978). In sum, the Paleolithic of the peninsula can be found along the northern and western portions of the peninsula swinging south along an arc through the Najd into the Hadhramaut. The entire Eastern Province and Oman seems devoid of this extremely long period in human development. By 10,000 B.P., most of the peninsula may have been abandoned as well. In addition, with the advent of the Holocene, the established climatological patterns of the previous epochs also disappeared, creating new hydrological, climatological, and landform expressions (Whitney 1983; Potts 1985: 677–80).

The Neolithic period saw the beginning of the "Agricultural Revolution" along the "Fertile Crescent" (Mellaart 1975; Bar-Yosef 1980; Moore 1982) and the re-establishment of people throughout the peninsula. The Neolithic experience in Arabia expressed itself in three different ways. First, the idea of pastoral nomadism began in the Northern Arabian desert (Zarins fc.a). This began around 6000 B.C. in conjunction with animal domestication in the Fertile Crescent (Zarins 1989a). Its earliest archaeological manifestation consisted of rock art, structural remains (habitation sites, kites, tumuli, pillars) and material culture (Tosi 1986: 473–74). Initial dependence was on both sheep/goats and cattle. By 5000 B.C. the phenomenon was widespread throughout the Northern Arabian Desert, the Najd, the Asir, and the Hejaz/Midian (Zarins 1979; Zarins et al. 1980: 17–20; Zarins et al. 1981: 19–23; Zarins et al. 1982: 30–32). Second, slightly after 5500 B.C. Eastern Arabia and Oman experienced the direct effects of Mesopotamian and Iranian contacts, and sedentary village life became characteristic of the region. The Ubaid Tradition of southern Mesopotamia has been found in Kuwait, Saudi Arabia, Bahrain, Qatar, and the U.A.E. (Masry 1974; Potts 1978; fc.b; 1985: 681–82; Oates 1978; 1986; Tosi 1986:

468). Subsequent developments in the region demonstrated a well-knit international network tying together the eastern part of the Arabian peninsula with the Indian subcontinent, Mesopotamia, and eastern Africa (Tosi 1986: 476). The Neolithic of Highland Yemen and the Asir took the form of a hybrid (DiMario fc.; Fedele 1985; fc.a; fc.b; Zarins et al. 1981: 21). Sedentary influences from Eastern Arabia via the Hadhramaut were integrated into a local culture influenced by the pastoral nomadism of the Najd and the Rub al-Khali "Neolithic" (Edens 1982, fc.). The third manifestation of the Neolithic period may have begun much earlier, but our recoverable record only begins with 7000 B.C. Here we are dealing with the shell middens of the Tihama, Oman, and the southern Arabian Ocean littoral. A series of site successions demonstrate close ties with East Africa, Eastern Arabia, Irtan, and India (Biagi et al. 1984; Zarins and Zahrani 1985; Zarins and Badr 1986; Tosi 1985: 363–69; 1986: 472; personal com.).

The subsequent period, 4000–2000 B.C., we have labeled Chalcolithic/EB, following the Levantine terminology. The trends established for the previous period in the peninsula continued to develop. People continued to herd goats/sheep and cattle. Donkeys and horses were introduced, which increased the population's mobility and range. Pastoral nomadism in its early form reached a climax but began a precipitous decline by 2000 B.C. (Zarins fc.a). Sites from the period are widespread in Northern Arabia, the Najd, Hejaz, and Asir/Yemen. The sedentary settlements of the Eastern Province continued to expand with such sites as the Qalat on Bahrain (Bibby 1969; Hoejlund 1986) and Hili 8 (Cleuziou 1981; 1982; 1986) providing long-term sequences. Tumuli fields in the U.A.E./Oman (Frifelt 1975; Vogt 1985; DeCardi 1978), Bahrain (Ibrahim 1982; Mughal 1983), Qatar (Tixier et al. 1980), and Eastern Saudi Arabia (Zarins ed. 1984; Adams et al. 1977; Potts et al. 1978) also provided additional data for reconstructing past cultural manifestations (Larsen 1983; Potts 1985: 683–94; Tosi 1986: 469). The latest work in Yemen has also provided data on the stage prior to the development of South Arabic civilization (De Maigret 1981, 1982, 1983, 1984). Midden coastal sites along the Red Sea and the Indian Ocean continued to enjoy relative prosperity. (See relevant citations in Neolithic section.)

The last period under review here, 2000–1000 B.C. (MB–LB), represents enigmatic developments on all fronts in Arabia. For pastoral nomadism, the emphasis on herding sheep/goats, cattle, and equids began to change radically during this period and camel domestication became preeminent (Bulliet 1975; Zarins 1989b). Concomitantly, structural remains became more ephemeral as greater mobility was demanded. Climatic and ecological change may have been tied to altered monsoonal rain patterns. Historical development during this period saw the change from Amorites to Shosu/Arameans and later Arabs. Site remains which definitely can be attributed to this period are so far rare (Zarins et al. 1981: 28–31 and pl. 11). The settled sites of the period along Eastern Arabia also became rare (Edens 1986; Bibby 1969) and the oasis concept which began to unite with the incipient rise of the South Arabian states can be attributed to this period (Parr and Gazdar 1980). The Midianite entity (Sawyer and Clines eds. 1983; Mendenhall 1984) also arose at this time in the Hejaz/Midian, and sites when adequately surveyed (Ingraham et al. 1981: 71–75) and excavated (Rothenberg 1972) may go a long way in shedding light on the related biblical accounts of Joseph, Moses, and Gideon. The key to our understanding of the Midianites and their biblical associations may lie in the future excavations at Qurayya. Midden sites on the Red Sea coast and the Arabian Sea have also been located and show promise in linking the Red Sea with Egyptian expansion during the Middle and New Kingdoms (Zarins fc.b.).

Bibliography

Adams, R. Mc.; Parr, P. J.; Ibrahim, M.; and Mughannum, A. S. 1977. Saudi Arabian Archaeological Reconnaissance—1976, Preliminary Report on the First Phase of the Comprehensive Archaeological Survey Program. *Atlal* 1: 21–40.

Albright, W. F. 1969. *The Proto-Sinaitic Inscriptions and Their Decipherment.* Cambridge, MA.

Archi, A. 1985. Mardu in the Ebla Texts. *Or* n.s. 54: 7–13.

Bar-Yosef, O. 1980. Prehistory of the Levant. *Annual Review of Anthropology* 9: 101–33.

Biagi, P.; Torke, W.; Tosi, M.; and Uerpmann, H.-P. 1984. Qurum, a Case Study of Coastal Archaeology in Northern Oman. *World Archaeology* 16: 43–61.

Bibby, G. 1969. *Looking for Dilmun.* Baltimore.

Bulliet, R. 1975. *The Camel and the Wheel.* Cambridge, MA.

Cleuziou, S. 1981. Oman Peninsula in the Early Second Millennium B.C. Pp. 279–93 in *South Asian Archaeology 1979,* ed. H. Hartel. Berlin.

———. 1982. Hili and the Beginning of Oasis Life in Eastern Arabia. *Proc. Sem. Arabian Stud.* 12: 15–22.

———. 1986. The Chronology of Protohistoric Oman, as Seen from Hili. In *Oman Studies,* ed. P. M. Costa, M. Tosi. Orientalia Romana 7. Rome.

Copeland, L., and Hours, F. 1971. A Microlithic Flint Site in the Wadi Rum, Jordan and a Review of the Epi-Paleolithic of Northern Arabia. *Proc. Sem. Arabian Stud.* 3: 7–23.

DeCardi, B. ed. 1978. *Qatar Archaeological Report Excavations 1973.* Oxford.

DeMaigret, A. 1981. Two Prehistoric Cultures and a New Sabaean Site in the Eastern Highlands of North Yemen. *Raydan* 4: 191–204.

———. 1982. Ricerche Archeologiche Italiane Nella Repubblica Araba Yemenita Notizia di una Seconda Ricognizione (1981). *OrAnt* 21: 237–53.

———. 1983. Activities of the Italian Archaeological Mission in the Yemen Arab Republic (1983 Campaign). *East and West* 33: 340–45.

———. 1984. A Bronze Age for Southern Arabia. *East and West* 34: 75–125.

DiMario, F. fc. The Western ar-Rub' al-Khali "Neolithic": New Data from the Ramlat Sabᶜatayn (Yemen Arab Republic). *Annali di Istituto Universitario Orientale (Napoli).*

Edens, C. 1982. Towards a Definition of the Rub al Khali "Neolithic." *Atlal* 6: 109–24.

———. 1986. Bahrain and the Arabian Gulf during the Second Millennium B.C.: Urban Crisis and Colonialism. Pp. 195–216 in *Bahrain through the Ages, the Archaeology,* ed. S. H. al Khalifa and M. Rice. London.

———. fc. The Rub al Khali "Neolithic" Revisited: The View from Nadqan. In *Essays in Arabian Archaeology in Memory of M. Golding,* ed. D. Potts.

Englund, R. 1983. Dilmun in the Archaic Uruk Corpus. Pp. 35–37 in *Dilmun, New Studies in the Archaeology and Early History of Bahrain,* ed. D. Potts. Berlin.

Fedele, F. G. 1985. Research on Neolithic and Holocene Paleoecology in the Yemeni Highlands. *East and West* 35: 369–73.

———. fc.a. IsMEO Activities: The Neolithic. *East and West* 36.

———. fc.b. North Yemen: The Neolithic. In *Aus dem Reich von Saba, 3000 Jahre Kunst und Kultur des Glucklichen Arabien,* ed. W. Daum. Munich.

Frifelt, K. 1975. On Prehistoric Settlements and Chronology of the Oman Peninsula. *East and West* 25: 329–424.

Fujimoto, T. 1978. The Assemblages of Site 50. Pp. 99–106 in *Paleolithic Site of the Douara Cave and Paleogeography of Palmyra Basin in Syria,* ed. K. Hanihara and Y. Sakaguchi. Tokyo.

Garrard, A. N.; Byrd, B.; and Betts, A. 1986. Prehistoric Environment and Settlement in the Azraq Basin: An Interim Report on the 1984 Excavation Season. *Levant* 18: 5–24.

Gelb, I. J. 1963. *A Study of Writing.* Chicago.

Hoejlund, F. 1986. The Chronology of City II and III at Qalʾat al-Bahrain. Pp. 217–24 in *Bahrain through the Ages, the Archaeology,* ed. S. H. al Khalifa and M. Rice. London.

Hogarth, D. G. 1904. *The Penetration of Arabia: A Record of the Development of Western Knowledge Concerning the Arabian Peninsula.* London.

Ibrahim, M. 1982. *Excavations of the Arab Expedition at Sar el-Jisr, Bahrain, State of Bahrain.* Manama.

Ingraham, M.; Johnson, T.; Rihani, B.; and Shatla, I. 1981. Preliminary Report on a Reconnaissance Survey of the Northwestern Province. *Atlal* 5: 59–84.

Jado, A. R., and Zotl, J. G., eds. 1984. *Quaternary Period in Saudi Arabia,* vol. 2. Vienna.

Larsen, C. 1983. *Life and Land Use on the Bahrain Islands: The Geoarchaeology of an Ancient Society.* Chicago.

Masry, A. 1974. *Prehistory in Northeastern Arabia: The Problem of Interregional Interaction.* Miami.

McClure, H. 1984. Late Quaternary Paleoenvironments of the Rub al Khali. Diss. London.

Mellaart, J. 1975. *The Neolithic of the Near East.* London.

Mendenhall, G. E. 1984. Qurayya and the Midianites. Pp. 137–45 in *Pre-Islamica Arabia,* vol. 2. Ed. A. al Rahman al Ansary. Riyadh.

Millard, A. R. 1986. The Infancy of the Alphabet. *World Archaeology* 17: 390–98.

Moore, A. M. T. 1982. A Four Stage Sequence for the Levantine Neolithic, ca. 8500–3750 B.C. *BASOR* 246: 1–34.

Mughal, R. 1983. *The Dilmun Complex at Sar. The 1980–82 Excavations in Bahrain.* Manama.

Nissen, H. 1985. Ortsnamen in den archaischen Texten aus Uruk. *Or n.s.* 54: 226–33.

———. 1986. The Occurrence of Dilmun in the Oldest Texts of Mesopotamia. Pp. 335–39 in *Bahrain through the Ages, the Archaeology,* ed. S. H. al Khalifa and M. Rice. London.

Oates, J. 1978. Ubaid Mesopotamia and Its Relation to Gulf Countries. Pp. 39–52 in *Qatar Archaeological Report Excavations 1973,* ed. B. deCardi. Oxford.

———. 1986. The Gulf in Prehistory. Pp. 79–86 in *Bahrain through the Ages, the Archaeology,* ed. S. H. al Khalifa and M. Rice. London.

Parr, P. J., et. al. 1978. Comprehensive Archaeological Survey Program: b. Preliminary Report on the Second Phase of the Northern Province Survey, 1397/1977. *Atlal* 2: 29–50.

Parr, P. J., and Gazdar, M. 1980. A Report on the Soundings at Zubaidah (al-Amara) in the al-Qasim Region: 1979. *Atlal* 4: 107–17.

Posener, G. 1940. *Princes et Pays d'Asie et du Nubie.* Brussels.

Potts, D. T. 1978. Towards an Integrated History of Culture Change in the Arabian Gulf Area: Notes on Dilmun, Makkan and the Economy of Ancient Sumer. *Journal of Oman Studies* 4: 29–51.

———. 1983. *Dilmun, New Studies in the Archaeology and Early History of Bahrain.* Berlin.

———. 1985. Reflections on the History and Archaeology of Bahrain. *JAOS* 105: 675–710.

———. fc.a. Southern Iran and Arabia in the Third Millennium B.C.: A New Perspective on the Problem of Magan." *OrAnt.*

———. fc.b. The Chronology of the Archaeological Assemblages from the Head of the Arabian Gulf to the Arabian Sea. In *Chronologies in Old World Archaeology,* ed. R. Ehrich. Chicago.

Potts, D. T.; al-Mughannum, A.; Frye, J.; and Sanders, D. 1978. Comprehensive Archaeological Survey Program: a. Preliminary Report on the Second Phase of the Northern Province. *Atlal* 2: 7–28.

Rothenberg, B. 1972. *Timna.* London.

Sawyer, J. F. A., and Clines, D. J. A. eds. 1983. *Midian, Moab, and Edom.* Sheffield.

Sayari, S., and Zotl, J. G. eds. 1978. *Quaternary Period in Saudi Arabia,* vol. 1. Vienna.

Tixier, J. ed. 1980. *Mission archéologique française à Qatar.* Paris.

Tosi, M. 1985. Tihamah Coastal Archaeology Survey. *East and West* 35: 363–69.

———. 1986. The Emerging Picture of Prehistoric Arabia. *The Annual Review of Anthropology* 15: 461–90.

Vogt, B. 1985. The Umm-an-Nar Tomb A at Hili North: A Preliminary Report on Three Seasons of Excavations, 1982–84. *Archaeology U.A.E.* 4: 20–38.

Whalen, N.; Killick, A.; James, N.; Morsi, G.; and Kamal, M. 1981. Saudi Arabian Archaeological Reconnaissance 1980: b. Preliminary Report on the Western Province Survey. *Atlal* 5: 43–58.

Whalen, N.; Sindi, H.; Wahidah, G.; and Ali, J. 1983. Excavation of Acheulean Sites Near Saffaqah in al-Dawadami (1402/1982). *Atlal* 7: 9–21.

Whalen, N.; Siraj-Ali, J.; and Davis, W. 1984. Excavation of Acheulean Sites near Saffaqah, Saudi Arabia 1403 AH 1983. *Atlal* 8: 9–24.

Whitney, J. W. 1983. *Erosional History and Surficial Geology of Western Saudi Arabia.* Technical Record USGS-TR-04-1. Jeddah.

Zarins, J. 1979. Rajajil, A Unique Arabian Site in the Fourth Millennium B.C. *Atlal* 3: 73–78.

———. 1989a. Jebel Bishri and the Amorite Homeland: The PPNB Phase. In *To the Euphrates and Beyond: Archaeological Studies in Honour of Maurits N. Van Loon,* ed. O. Haex; H. Curvers; and P. Akkermans. Rotterdam.

———. 1989b. Pastoralism in Southwest Asia: The Second Millennium B.C. In *The Walking Larder,* ed. J. Clutton-Brock. London.

———. fc.a. Archaeological and Chronological Problems within the Greater Southwest Asian Arid Zone: 8500–1850 B.C. In *Chronologies in Old World Archaeology,* ed. R. Ehrich. Chicago.

———. fc.b. Ancient Egypt and the Red Sea Trade: The Case for Obsidian in the Predynastic and Archaic Periods. In *H. Kantor Festschrift,* ed. B. Williams; T. Logan; and A. Leonard. Chicago.

———; Whalen, N.; Ibrahim, M.; Morad, A.; and Khan, M. 1980. Comprehensive Archaeological Survey Program: Preliminary

Report on the Central and Southwestern Provinces Survey. *Atlal* 4: 9–36.
———; Murad, A.; and al-Yish, K. 1981. Comprehensive Archaeological Survey Program: a. The Second Preliminary Report on the Southwestern Province. *Atlal* 5: 9–42.
———; Rihbini, A.; and Kamal, M. 1982. Comprehensive Survey of the Central Nejd—The Riyadh Environs. *Atlal* 6: 25–38.
———; Mughannum, A.; and Kamal, M. 1984. Excavations at Dhahran South—The Tumuli Field (208–91), 1403 AH/1983. A Preliminary Report. *Atlal* 8: 25–54.
———, and Zahrani, A. 1985. Recent Archaeological Investigations in the Southern Tihama Plain, (including Athar, 217–108 and Sihi, 217–107), 1404/1984. *Atlal* 9.
———, and Badr, H. 1986. Archaeological Investigations in the Southern Tihama Plain II (including Sihi, 217–107 and Sharja, 217–172), 1405/1985. *Atlal* 10.

JURIS ZARINS

ARABIA, RELIGION OF (SOUTH). See SOUTH ARABIA, RELIGION OF.

ARABIC LANGUAGE. See LANGUAGES (INTRODUCTORY SURVEY).

ARAD (PERSON) [Heb *ᶜarād*]. One of the six sons of Beriah, according to the longer genealogy of Benjamin given by the Chronicler (1 Chr 8:15). The Greek (LXX) reads *ōrēr* and *ōdēd* instead of *ᶜarād* and *ᶜāder,* evidencing confusion between the Hebrew letters *reš* and *dalet.*

SIEGFRIED S. JOHNSON

ARAD (PLACE) [Heb *ᶜărād*]. A town in the S Negeb of Judah, mentioned four times in the Bible, mainly in connection with the Canaanite king of Arad who defeated the Israelites when they first attempted a S entrance into Canaan (Num 21:1; 33:40). Later, the king of Arad is listed among the conquered kings of Canaan (Josh 12:14). The area was subsequently allotted to the Kenites who were descendants of Hobab, Moses' father-in-law (Judg 1:16). A fifth reference to Arad may be found in Josh 15:21, where the MT *ᶜeder* may reflect a transposition of the *reš* and *dalet* (LXX^B reads *Ara*).

A. Identification and History of Excavations
B. Results of Excavations
  1. Early Bronze Age
  2. Iron Age (Strata XII–VI)
  3. Later Periods (Strata V–II)
C. Controversies

A. Identification and History of Excavations

The site of Arad ("Greater Arad"?) can be identified by a perfect preservation of the name in the Arabic form of Tell ᶜArâd. The site (M.R. 162076) stands on a prominent mound in the NE section of the Beer Shevaᶜ Valley, exactly where Eusebius (*Onomast.* 14.1–3) located it—4 miles from Malaatha (Tell Milḥ) and 20 miles from Hebron. The identification of the site with ancient Arad is further strengthened by the discovery of inscriptions from the site which also preserve the name (see Herzog et al. 1987: 22 [photograph]).

R. Amiran and Y. Aharoni began excavations at Arad in 1962, and because of the unique nature of each of the areas of investigation, it proved advantageous to separate the projects into two distinctive efforts. Amiran's work concentrated on the huge EB town on the lower tell. Her work has provided valuable information about 4th–3d millennium B.C. town planning, trade connections, cultic paraphernalia, and ceramic collections. Aharoni directed five seasons (1962–67) on the upper tell, mainly on the Iron Age fortress. In 1976, Z. Herzog directed an additional season which focused specifically on the E gates of the fortress and was done in conjunction with reconstruction work being carried out by J. Campbell.

After his survey of the Beer Shevaᶜ basin in the late 1950s, Aharoni sought to implement a regional excavation study which began with his project at Arad. Following the work at Arad, seven seasons of study focused on BEER-SHEBA, while other expeditions studied Tell el-Milḥ (Tel Malhata) and Kh. el-Meshâsh (Tel Masos). See MALHATA, TEL, and MESHASH, KHIRBET El-. Other projects have since worked at sites such as Kh. Gharrah and Kh. Ghazzah. See IRA, TEL and UZA, HORVAT respectively. In this comprehensive effort, Aharoni had sought to apply A. Alt's (1925) territorial history model to field exploration. The goal has been to coordinate and compare the material and epigraphic remains from the field research with information obtained from biblical and other historical sources in order to arrive at a more comprehensive understanding of the political history of the E Negeb.

Among other innovative techniques, the Arad expedition initiated the practice of carefully dipping all sherds in water to expose any evidence of ink-written inscriptions. Fortunately, the dry climate helped to preserve many inscriptions that became visible in the dipping process. This has allowed over 100 Iron Age Hebrew inscriptions to be identified, as well as several dozen additional inscriptions written in Aramaic from the late Persian period. A few others were found written in Greek and Arabic.

A significant consequence of this large inscriptional repertoire is that the alphabet has now been paleographically documented through several Iron Age strata. See ARAD OSTRACA. The later strata particularly have yielded a sufficiently large corpus to provide a fairly broad base for analyzing the Hebrew script and orthography. The stratum VI archive pertaining to Eliashib (see B.2.f below) attests to the daily operation of an administrative supply center which served the needs of local patrols and probably catered in part to the trade caravans passing through the area. The language of these inscriptions is standard late biblical Hebrew exhibiting linguistic and syntactical parallels with the Bible. The few historical details that are referred to are tantalizing, but are seldom explicit enough for adequate reconstruction (see Yadin 1976; however cf. Aharoni 1981: 104 n. 2 [remark by A. Rainey]).

B. Results of Excavations

1. Early Bronze Age. The lower city, which is fortified with a stone wall and projecting towers, encloses ca. 22 acres (90 dunams) and has four strata of settlement from the EB (evidence of an earlier Chalcolithic occupation, stratum V, was also discovered). Stratum IV was an unfortified village of the late EB I. The EB II strata (III and II) were the principal fortified urban phases. For a site plan, see Fig. CIT.02. With its blocks of private residences, its cultic and public buildings, and an efficient water collection and storage system (especially important since no wadis, springs, or wells exist in the immediate vicinity), the EB town had many of the basic features of a typical urban center. The semicircular towers of the city wall correspond to the stylized Egyptian representation of a Canaanite city (cf. the Narmer palette; *ANEP,* fig. 297). EB Arad apparently had fairly extensive trade connections with Egypt, as inferred from the presence of Egyptian ceramic pieces in every stratum (as well as other small finds), and inferred especially from the discovery of a *serekh* of Narmer of Egypt (Amiran 1974). Stratum I was a squatters' village in the late EB II, resting on the ruins of the earlier strata. The site was essentially deserted by the beginning of EB III. For further discussion of the EB city, see Amiran 1965, 1970, 1972; Amiran et al. 1978; Amiran, Goethert, and Ilan 1987; and Dever 1982.

2. Iron Age (Strata XII–VI). The excavators of the upper tell of Arad have identified seven strata spanning the Iron Age. Their hope was to use the data gathered from the excavation—the stratigraphic profile of Arad, the extensive ceramic collection (which spans the Iron Age), and the relatively large number of epigraphic finds (mostly ostraca from the upper strata)—in conjunction with information found in historical sources, and to synthesize these into a comprehensive political history of the region.

Almost from the beginning, the excavations at Arad have generated controversy (e.g., Yadin 1965), much of which centers around fundamental stratigraphic questions and their implications for chronological reconstruction. Consequently there are competing and often irreconcilable syntheses about the "history" attested by the ruins. The presentation here generally follows the major summary of the excavation team, but strives to point out along the way some of the questions and issues that have been raised by others (see especially C below).

a. The Unfortified Site (Stratum XII). The first Iron Age establishment was an unwalled village with evidence of a low wall at some points along the perimeter, and with remains of dwellings found on the W side. In the center of the settlement was a courtyard in which stood a circular brick-filled platform (ca. 6 m diameter) and a smaller rectangular stone platform (an altar?), which may indicate some priestly connections (see Fig. ARA.01). This suggestion is corroborated by the reference in Judg 1:16 which mentions that "descendants of the Kenite, Moses' father-in-law" (LXX reads: "sons of Hobab the Kenite") settled near this area (Herzog et al. 1984: 2–6). The E Negeb was later referred to as "the Negeb of the Kenites" (1 Sam 27:10).

b. The 10th Century (Stratum XI). A square fortress (ca. 50 by 50 m) was built on the ruins of Stratum XII. Its fortifications used the common casemate construction, consisting of two parallel walls divided into chambers by cross walls. Large rooms lined the E wall, and the gate, which faced E, stood in the NE corner.

A temple (or shrine) stood in the NW quadrant of the

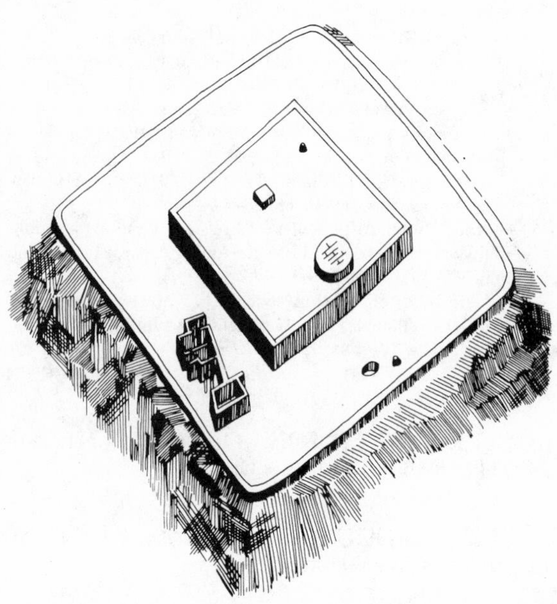

ARA.01. Isometric view of village at Arad—Stratum XII. *(Redrawn from Herzog et al. 1984: fig. 4.)*

fortress. This entire religious complex was aligned along an E-W axis, and consisted of an outer courtyard on the E end, and a sanctuary with a raised cubicle (ca. 1.2 by 1.2 m) in its back wall on the W end. In the W cubicle (i.e., the Holy of Holies) were found flint stelae still bearing traces of red pigment. Two small stone incense altars (made without horns), which probably originated in this stratum, were found lying on the second of three steps which led into the W cubicle (these altars still bore on their upper surfaces traces of burnt material which has been analyzed as animal fat; Aharoni 1967: 247 n. 29). In the courtyard apparently stood a sacrificial altar of which only the foundation stones remain (these became the foundation and step of the altar in the later strata; see below).

The details of the building plans of the cultic installation at Arad and the description of the Temple are remarkably similar—only the "Holy Place" is significantly different. While the Tabernacle and the Temple are both described as having a long room as the "Holy Place" (cf. Exod 26:15–25; 1 Kgs 6:2), the building at Arad instead has a broad room (its opening in one of the long walls).

The rear wall of the temple was built solidly against the inner casemate wall of stratum XI; this has contributed to the conclusion that the shrine was contemporary with the fortification wall (Aharoni 1971: 36). However, from the reports published thus far, it is unclear whether the back wall of the shrine (i.e., the Holy of Holies) was actually bonded into the casemate wall or simply abutted it (see further, C below). However, the temple seems to have remained in use through the next three strata (X–VIII). Its association with Yahweh is inferred from the discovery of letter 18, which mentions the "House of YHWH" (Heb *bêt YHWH*; Aharoni 1981: 35–38).

Stratum XI was destroyed by fire (Herzog et al. 1984: 8). It is possible that this destruction can be correlated with Shishak's 925 B.C. campaign into Israel (1 Kgs 14:25–26; 2 Chr 12:2–9) when he conquered, among other sites, two fortresses in S Israel which he recorded on the Karnak inscription (nos. 107–112): *ḥgrm ʿrd rbt ʿrd n-bt Yrḥm* (i.e., "the citadels of Greater Arad and Arad of the house of Jeruḥam"; *LBHG,* 215–16). Thus, stratum XI was a royal outpost probably founded during the United Monarchy, and its pottery may be a standard example of 10th-century Israelite wares (Herzog et al. 1984: 8–9); however, some have suggested that the fortress may have been founded in the 9th century instead (e.g., Mazar and Netzer 1986: 89–90; Mazar 1990: 439).

c. 9th Century (Stratum X). In the next stratum, the fortress wall was significantly modified (see Fig. ARA.02). The surviving casemate rooms were filled with stone and earth to form a solid wall, but a new wall was constructed on the W side. The renovation involved constructing a "sawtooth" semibuttressing pattern on the outside of the fortification walls; the purpose of this semibuttressing pattern is unclear. The NE corner, where the original gate had been, became the site of a storehouse, and the gate was relocated to the center of the E wall.

Because of the sanctity of the temple's site, the area was thoroughly cleaned and the temple repaired, with a northward extension added to the Holy Place. Aharoni (1971: 39–40) argues that the reconstructed shrine adopted a new "royal cubit" standard of measurement equivalent to 52.5 cm whereas the earlier standard for the cubit had been 45 cm.

In contrast to the expansion of the temple buildings, part of the area of the courtyard was lost with the addition

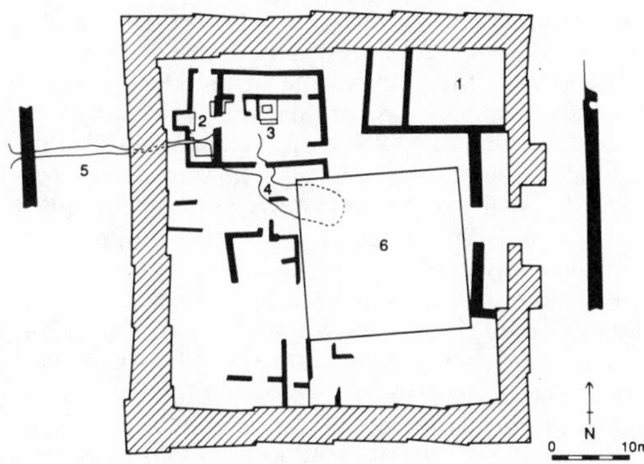

ARA.02. Plan of the fortress at Arad—Stratum X. *1,* storehouse; *2,* temple; *3,* temple courtyard with altar; *4,* underground cisterns; *5,* water channel; *6,* area of later Hellenistic tower. *(Redrawn from Herzog et al. 1984: fig. 10.)*

of a N side chamber. A water channel to the cisterns below the temple passed through a tunnel under the solid W exterior wall. These underground cisterns may have been used during the earlier stratum, and may have been natural caves predating the construction of the fort (although the contemporaneity of this water system with stratum X has been questioned; see C below).

The sacrificial altar in the courtyard was rebuilt using as its foundation the altar remains from stratum XI. Part of the old altar became the step for the new one. The new altar measured 5 by 5 cubits and 3 cubits high—according to the description of the tabernacle altar (Exod 27:1). It was constructed of unworked field stones with a clay and mud core. The top of the altar was a slab of flint surrounded by a plaster channel to drain fluids. Since the four corners of the altar were broken off, it remains unclear whether this altar originally had horns like that at Beer-sheba.

Two small bowls (nos. 102 and 103), each inscribed with (the same) two signs, were discovered on the step of the altar. Some controversy has surrounded how the signs (esp. the "three-pronged" second sign) are to be read, as well as the implications these readings have for the dating of stratum X. The excavation team reads the signs as the two Hebrew letters *qop-kap* (abbreviation for *qōdeš kôhănîm,* "sacred to the priests"), insisting that the script—particularly the round-bottomed *kap* on bowl 103—is archaic, suggesting that the bowls may have been preserved from an even earlier period (Herzog et al. 1984: 32). Cross (1979), however, contends that the letters are Phoenician *qop-šin* (abbreviation for *qdš,* "sacred"), and that the round-bottomed *"kap"* on bowl 103 is actually a "perfectly normal" three-pronged *šin* paleographically dating to the late 7th–early 6th century B.C. (p. 75). He also notes that the *"kap"* on bowl 102 has a variant trident form also found in late 7th–early 6th century Phoenician *šins,* and that the *qop* on both bowls has the shape of "a type which flourished in the 7th century" (p. 76). In response, the Arad team focused on Cross' trident-shaped *"šin"* (bowl 102) and argued that it is actually a vertical stroke that "can only belong to a [Hebrew] *kap*" (Herzog et al. 1984: 32). There seems to be no easy resolution to this *kap-šin* dispute, and a great deal obviously hinges on the handwriting standards of the ancient inscriber as well as on contemporary judgments about whether the vertical stroke on bowl 102 is an extension of the right-hand "prong" (suggesting a *kap*) or an extension of the middle "prong" (suggesting a *šin*). If it is the former, the balance is tipped toward a 9th-century date for stratum X; if it is the latter, the balance is tipped toward a 7th-century date. Furthermore, the ceramic typology of these two bowls has been attributed by some to a date "considerably later" than the 9th century (cf. Dever 1970: 173–74 and n. 76). The excavators point out, however, that the bowls were sealed *below* floor levels of strata VIII, VII, and VI, and on one of these later floors was found smashed 7th-century pottery (Herzog et al. 1984: 12). Since the earliest attributed stratum beneath which the bowls were sealed was VIII, one wonders if the bowls then should be associated with stratum IX instead of X. Indeed, the excavators have expressed varied opinions of the stratigraphic provenance of these bowls. Aharoni's report in 1964 states that the bowls were found "on a step in front of an earlier (stratum IX [sic!]) altar structure" (Aharoni and Amiran 1964: 282), but he later revised his conclusion and attributed them to stratum X (Aharoni 1968: 20). If the first assignment is valid, then the bowls would have to be associated with stratum VIII remains *at the earliest!*

Stratum X may have been constructed either by Asa (ca. 910–870 B.C.; 2 Chr 14:4–6; 1 Kgs 15:23), or Jehoshaphat (870–848 B.C.; 2 Chr 17:1–2, 12–13; 21:3), the two strongest kings of Judah in the 9th century. Their purpose was probably to control the route to Elath (1 Kgs 22:47–48; 2 Chr 17:10–12). As noted above, the date of the destruction of the stratum is even less certain. It may have been destroyed during the reign of Jehoram (848–841 B.C.), either when Edom revolted against Judah (2 Chr 21:8, 10) or when the Philistines and Arabs invaded Judah and sacked the palace (2 Chr 21:16–17). An alternative date could be during the reign of Joash, when Hazael invaded Judah (ca. 815 B.C.; 2 Kgs 12:18–19 [—Eng 12:17–18]; 2 Chr 24:23–24), but it is unclear if Hazael's invasion affected the S districts of Judah. Because of its similarity with the ceramic repertoire of strata IX and VIII, Y. Aharoni dated the end of stratum X to ca. 800 B.C. (see statement in Herzog et al. 1984: 12). M. Aharoni (1985) attributes the destruction to the first quarter of the 8th century, which essentially agrees with Mazar and Netzer's (1986: 89–90) and Ussishkin's (1988) 8th-century assignment of the stratum (see C below).

d. The 8th Century (Strata IX–VIII). With only minor modifications, the plan of the fortress in stratum IX remained essentially unchanged from that of stratum X. The area adjacent to and inside the S wall served as living quarters, and included seven dwelling units. The reorganized temple compound accommodated the addition of a new compartment to the E, its entrance was moved to the SE corner, and a stone-lined pit was dug next to the altar.

The stratum IX renovation probably occurred during the reign of Uzziah (ca. 767 B.C.; 2 Kgs 14:22; 2 Chr 26:2, 7–8), when he regained control over the Negeb and the caravan routes which passed from Arabia to the Mediterranean coast. It was probably destroyed during the Syro-Ephraimite war against Ahaz (734 B.C.) when the Philistines and Edomites to the W and S also conspired against Judah (2 Kgs 16:6; 2 Chr 28:17–18).

Stratum VIII represents the newly rebuilt fortress. The outer wall was reused, but the temple underwent radical changes. The main hall and the "Holy of Holies" remained essentially unchanged. However, the excavators report that a 1 m deep fill in the courtyard "completely covered" the sacrificial altar at this time (Herzog et al. 1984: 19). Presumably it was at this time that the two inscribed bowls (mentioned above) were buried at the foot of the abandoned altar (see above).

Not only was the level of the courtyard raised at this time, but also its area was diminished by the construction of a multiroom structure in the NE corner. In one of its rooms was found inscription 49 (notations written on the outside of a deep bowl), which refers to the "Sons of Korah" and the "Sons of Bezal[el]." Another room, S of the Holy of Holies, yielded inscriptions 50–52, which contain typical Levitical names. This suggests that the staff of the Arad temple either included guilds of cultic personnel similar to those in Jerusalem, or that these cultic officials were present (late 8th century B.C.) to supervise Hezekiah's reforms (which included the elimination of places of sacrifice outside of Jerusalem; cf. 2 Kgs 18:4; 2 Chr 31:1).

Two features of stratum VIII seem to imply an association with Hezekiah: the abandonment of the altar, and the ceramic repertoire (which is identical to that of Lachish stratum III). Hezekiah attempted to unite the remaining N tribes with Judah (2 Chr 30:6), and to make Jerusalem the exclusive site for worship around 715 B.C. To facilitate his plan, he eliminated the local shrines and destroyed their altars (2 Kgs 18:22; Isa 36:7; 2 Chr 31:1; 32:12). The fortification of Arad stratum VIII, however, probably was part of Hezekiah's futile defensive measures against the military threat of Assyria (2 Chr 32:27–29; also 2 Kgs 18:8). The destruction of this stratum likely occurred when Sennacherib invaded Judah in 701 B.C.

e. Late 7th Century (Stratum VII). At this time the temple itself was abandoned, and the incense altars were buried at the entrance to the Holy of Holies when the ruins of the temple were covered over. The solid wall of stratum VIII had been badly damaged on its S side, and the initial strategy to secure the fortress involved building a new wall 2 m inside the older line; an outer wall was then built on the foundations of the older one, making a casemate system. Apparently the other three walls were rebuilt as solid walls (cf. Herzog et al. 1984: 22). One of the S rooms yielded three seals which had belonged to "Eliashib son of Oshiahu," along with several ostraca listing commodities in Egyptian hieratic symbols (Israelite scribes had earlier adopted hieratic symbols for numbers, measures, and commodities).

It is unclear when this construction occurred—Manasseh probably could not have refortified Arad until after the death of Esarhaddon, king of Assyria (648 B.C.), and after he was freed from personal exile (2 Chr 33:11–17). Perhaps Manasseh (who died ca. 642 B.C.) or his grandson, Josiah (reigned 641–609 B.C.), built Arad stratum VII. Josiah began his reforms in his 12th year (ca. 629 B.C.), shortly after Assurbanipal had stepped down from the throne of Assyria. Stratum VII was probably destroyed during one of Nebuchadnezzar's campaigns into Judah (597 B.C.; cf. 2 Kgs 24:2; Jer 13:18–19).

f. Early 6th Century (Stratum VI). Very shortly after the destruction of Arad VII, a new casemate wall was constructed over the ruins of the former solid wall. This new defensive system was fortified with projecting towers on the W corners and along the W wall, while another small tower stood along the S wall. The foundation trench of the inner wall of the casemate system penetrated into the old sanctuary buried below. The gate, a simple passage through the casemate system with no defensive towers flanking it, was moved from the E to the N side.

The interior of the fortress appears to have been a large open area. The date of this stratum is inferred from the late Iron Age pottery found *in situ* on the floors which were laid against the walls of the stratum VI buildings. The excavators contend that the comb-tooth patterns on some of the stones in this stratum (which some would attribute to the Hellenistic period; see C below) were already in secondary use and therefore originated even earlier than stratum VI (Herzog et al. 1984: 26–27).

The occupants of the site, however, appear still to have been Judeans, as inferred from the archive of ostraca found in a room on the S side. Most of these were addressed to Eliashib (see above), indicating that he had returned as a commander (or at least as custodian of supplies). The paleographic similarity with the Lachish Letters (i.e., Lachish II) imply a date at the end of the Judean monarchy. Stratum VI may have been built after Zedekiah was called to Babylon (ca. 594 B.C.) to explain his participation in earlier anti-Babylonian activities (Jer 51:59; cf. 27:2–28:17). The site probably was destroyed by the Edomites during Nebuchadnezzar's campaign against Judah in 587 B.C. (Obad 10–14; Ps 137:7). Strengthening this historical reconstruction was the discovery of inscription 24 (found in the ruins outside the fort), which ordered Eliashib to dispatch reinforcements to the nearby town of Ramoth-negeb, "lest the Edomite should come there."

3. Later Periods (Strata V–II). In the Persian period, the Arabian king of Kedar, who had helped Cambyses invade Egypt, controlled the caravan routes. He also controlled Gaza and the N Sinai coast as far as Ienysos (el-Arish?; Hdt. 3.4–5). Thus, Arad was within his area of control. Somewhat typical of the Persian period in Palestine, no architectural remains were preserved in Arad V—only ash pits, in which were discovered 85 Aramaic ostraca dating from the mid-4th century B.C. The inscriptional data indicate that Arad served as a supply station along the caravan routes; the pits were used to store goods for the animals and personnel.

During the Hellenistic period (stratum IV), a massive rectangular tower (ca. 20 by 20 m) was built in the SE corner of the mound (see Fig. ARA.02). It was founded on bedrock, which meant that in removing the earlier remains, the builders disrupted the stratigraphy of the site in that quadrant. A courtyard, in which were various rooms, joined the N and W sides of the tower. The Hellenistic installation reused portions of the earlier stratum VI fortification walls as portions of the enclosure walls for this tower complex. It is unknown who built the tower, but it is possible that John Hyrcanus, who recaptured control of Idumea (including the Negeb) in 125 B.C. (*Ant* 5.1.22 §82; cf. 13.9.1 §257–58; *JW* 1.2.6 §63), may have built it as part of his defensive line.

Probably in the latter part of the 1st century B.C., and as a means of protecting the S frontier of his kingdom, Herod authorized construction of a small rectangular fort (ca. 31 by 37 m) on the SW corner of the Arad mound. The few small finds (including two Greek ostraca) date to the 1st century A.D. When the Romans conquered the Nabateans in A.D. 106, the frontier advanced farther S, rendering the forts in the Negeb generally obsolete. After an occupational gap of some 500 years, a caravanserai was built on the ruins of the earlier remains.

C. Controversies

While there are many questions regarding the interpretation of Arad (too many to detail in this article), the most recent work which brings much of the material together is by D. Ussishkin (1988). Among other problems, he questions the contemporaneity of the water channel and cistern with the shrine in stratum X (see Fig. ARA.02), and furthermore he insists that the shrine did not even exist earlier in stratum XI of the fortress. This conclusion is partially based upon the fact that the shrine lacks any evidence of fire destruction. Since the excavators attributed the destruction of stratum XI to fire during the campaign of Shishak (Aharoni 1968: 6; Herzog et al. 1984: 8), it seems peculiar that, if the shrine had existed in that stratum, no scars of such a conflagration would be present, even after a thorough cleaning. Furthermore, Ussishkin points out that an insufficient amount of stratum XI ceramic evidence was discovered with the shrine (which one might attribute to the cleaning operation) to necessitate the shrine's attribution to that stratum. The main argument then for its stratum XI attribution seems to be the fact that the rear wall of the Holy of Holies was built up against the inner casemate wall of stratum XI (but see B.2.b above).

Along with other archaeologists (e.g., Zimhoni 1985: 85–86; Mazar and Netzer 1986), Ussishkin furthermore argues that the ceramic repertoire of strata X–VIII shows such a significant degree of homogeneity that all of these strata might be compressed into the 8th century (cf. the implication of M. Aharoni 1985). He then places the founding of the shrine not in stratum XI of the fortress (10th century), but in stratum VII (i.e., either the late 8th or early 7th century; this stratigraphic reassignment of the shrine would then agree with Cross' [1979] paleographic analysis of the inscribed bowls found near the altar [although see Herzog et al. 1984: 12]).

Ussishkin, with others (e.g., Yadin 1965; Nylander 1967), challenges the overall stratigraphic assignments by suggesting that the stratum VI casemate wall should not be dated to the early 6th century B.C. but was actually contemporaneous with the stratum IV Hellenistic tower. Therefore he dates the wall to the Hellenistic/Roman period, basing this conclusion largely on the presence of characteristic tooth-combed Hellenistic style ashlars in the casemate wall, and on the stratigraphic relationship of that casemate wall to the Hellenistic tower (however, see B.2.f above).

Obviously much uncertainy exists, and the implications of these problems on the intended historical/archaeological construct (e.g., Arad's association with Asa, Jehoshaphat, Hezekiah, etc.) are great and may demand significant revision.

The chronological reassignments by Ussishkin and others of the strata at Arad, however, have difficulties when studied in conjunction with the paleographic analyses of the ostraca, which have been used to further our understanding of paleographic evolution. See ARAD OSTRACA. According to the excavators, the ostraca were found in various strata and in various areas, and given the arguments of Ussishkin and others, severe disruptions ensue if the ostraca are chronologically reassigned. At least four options exist to explain these tensions: (1) the paleographic analysis by Aharoni and company is essentially correct, and assuming the excavators attributed the ostraca to the correct strata, Ussishkin's arguments will need to be revised significantly or rejected; (2) if Ussishkin and others have provided workable stratigraphic interpretations, then the ostraca may have been mistakenly assigned to the wrong strata (cf. Zimhoni 1985: 84–85; Ussishkin 1988: 153); (3) if Ussishkin and others have provided correct analysis of the stratigraphy of the shrine, and if the ostraca are then reassigned correspondingly, the contribution that these ostraca make in comparative paleographic study will need to be reevaluated; or (4) a proper understanding of the materials has not been determined.

It remains unclear whether any of these matters can ever be resolved. Most of the site has already been excavated, providing limited opportunities for excavators to go back to the site to reinvestigate particular aspects of the stratigraphy. Hopefully, the final excavation reports will clarify these issues.

Bibliography

Aharoni, M. 1985. On "The Israelite Fortress at Arad." *BASOR* 258: 73.

Aharoni, Y. 1967. Excavations at Tel Arad: Preliminary Report on the Second Season, 1963. *IEJ* 17/4: 233–49.

———. 1968. Arad: Its Inscriptions and Temple. *BA* 31: 20–32.

———. 1971. The Israelite Sanctuary at Arad. Pp. 28–44 in *New Directions in Biblical Archaeology,* ed. D. N. Freedman and J. C. Greenfield. Garden City, NY.

———. 1981. *Arad Inscriptions.* Jerusalem.

Aharoni, Y., and Amiran, R. 1964. Notes and News: Tel Arad. *IEJ* 14: 280–83.

———. 1975. Arad. Pp. 74–89 in *EAEHL.*

Alt, A. 1925. *Die Landnahme der Israeliten in Palästina. Territorialgeschichtliche Studien.* Leipzig.

Amiran, R. 1965. A Preliminary Note on the Synchronisms between the Early Bronze Strata of Arad and the First Dynasty. *BASOR* 179: 30–33.

———. 1970. The Beginnings of Urbanization in Canaan. Pp. 83–96 in *Near Eastern Archaeology in the Twentieth Century,* ed. J. A. Sanders. New York.

———. 1972. A Cult Stele from Arad. *IEJ* 22: 86–88.

———. 1974. An Egyptian Jar Fragment with the Name of Narmer from Arad. *IEJ* 24: 4–12.

Amiran, R., et al. 1978. *Early Arad.* Jerusalem.

Amiran, R.; Goethert, R.; and Ilan, O. 1987. The Well at Arad. *BARev* 13/2: 40–44.

Cross, F. M. 1979. Two Offering Dishes with Phoenician Inscriptions from the Sanctuary of ʿArad. *BASOR* 235: 75–78.

Dever, W. G. 1970. Iron Age Epigraphic Material from the Area of Khirbet El-Kôm. *HUCA* 40–41: 139–204.

———. 1982. Review of *Early Arad. IEJ* 32: 170–75.

Herzog, Z.; Aharoni, M.; Rainey, A. F.; and Moshkovitz, S. 1984. The Israelite Fortress at Arad. *BASOR* 254: 1–34.

———. 1987. Arad: An Ancient Israelite Fortress with a Temple to Yahweh. *BARev* 13/2: 16–35.

Mazar, A. 1990. *Archaeology and the Land of the Bible.* Anchor Bible Reference Library. New York.

Mazar, A., and Netzer, E. 1986. On the Israelite Fortress at Arad. *BASOR* 263: 87–91.

Nylander, C. 1967. A Note on the Stonecutting and Masonry of Tel Arad. *IEJ* 17: 56–59.

Ussishkin, D. 1988. The Date of the Judaean Shrine at Arad. *IEJ* 38: 142–57.

Yadin, Y. 1965. A Note on the Stratigraphy of Arad. *IEJ* 15: 180.

———. 1976. The Historical Significance of Inscription 88 from Arad: A Suggestion. *IEJ* 26/1: 9–14.

Zimhoni, O. 1985. The Iron Age Pottery of Tel ʿEton and Its Relation to the Lachish, Tell Beit Mirsim and Arad Assemblages. *TA* 12: 63–90.

Dale W. Manor
Gary A. Herion

ARAD OSTRACA. Eighty-eight Hebrew, eighty-five Aramaic, five Arabic, and two Greek ostraca were discovered during excavations at Tell Arad, in the eastern Negeb, from 1962–1967 (with the exception of Hebrew ostracon 88, found in 1974). Three more Hebrew ostraca were found in 1976. As indicated by paleography and archaeological context, the Hebrew ostraca come from the 10th–6th centuries, the Aramaic from the 5th–4th centuries, the Greek from the 1st–2d centuries C.E., and the Arabic from the 7th–9th centuries C.E. Many of these texts, however, are fragmentary. Among the Hebrew ostraca, for example, only 15 are whole, and 7 of these include only 1 name. Twenty preserve only single letters. Most of the Aramaic ostraca are poorly preserved, with only a few entirely legible. The 5 Arabic sherds are also fragmentary, and the 2 Greek inscriptions are too incomplete to understand.

The Hebrew ostraca have attracted the most attention. They come from strata XI through VI, that is from the 10th to the 6th century B.C.E. The original excavators are certain about the dates of the earliest and latest Hebrew strata, on the basis of archaeological, historical, and paleographic considerations. They feel fairly confident about their dating of the intermediate strata. However, on controversies surrounding the stratigraphic dates, see ARAD (PLACE). Among preexilic Hebrew inscriptions, only the Lachish ostraca are comparable in number and significance. That so fragmentary a collection is considered so significant testifies, though, more to the relative paucity of inscriptional material from ancient Israel than to its intrinsic importance. In most disciplines such material would hardly win a nod, much less a covert glance.

A. Orthography and Syntax

The Hebrew ostraca from Arad tell us a number of things. In general they confirm our understanding of the orthography and syntax of preexilic Hebrew. The principles of Hebrew orthography developed by Cross and Freedman (1952) hold, except that the existence of internal *matres lectionis,* only suspected previously, has now been proven (*yod* for medial *î* is regular at Arad, and *waw* for medial *û* is almost universal). Other medial long vowels are consistently unmarked. As for final vowels, Aharoni (1975; 1981), who published the first complete edition of the Arad material, believed that final *-ā* on *qtl* 2d masculine singular forms is represented by the *mater lectionis h* in *wktbth* (7.6) and *ydʿth* (40.9). While possible, this explanation is not the most probable one. Given the clues of the Masoretic text (the short form of the *qtl* 2nd masculine singular preserved in the orthography, apparently reflecting the popular speech we would also expect in the nonliterary Arad texts) and the evidence of other inscriptions, it is better to take the *h* in these cases as a *mater* for the 3rd masculine singular pronominal suffix *ō*.

The ostraca add to the evidence for a Judahite dialect which, before the exile, generally did not contract diphthongs. The consistent use of the theophoric element *yahū* (as opposed to *yaw* or *yô*) in personal names at Arad may be further evidence for such a dialect (approximately 30 of roughly 85 different personal names are formed with this element). In short, the Arad ostraca expand rather than alter our knowledge of Hebrew orthography. The same is true with regard to syntax. One small point should be noted in passing. In 3.2–3 and 16.4 Aharoni read *waw* with perfect forms as conjunctive. P. Miller has observed that "while there appear to be such forms in late preexilic prose of the Bible, one should not assume too easily that the *waw* with perfect is conjunctive. Both . . . may be cases of perfect consecutives" (1985: 504). These perfects are simply examples of a use of the perfect long known from Old Testament prose (see Gesenius-Kautzsch-Cowley, 106 i; Joüon, *Grammaire de l'hébrew biblique* 112f.). If one wants to give them a name, the linguistic category "performatives" should be used (the word itself accomplishes something: e.g. "I decree/order/command") and they should be designated "performative perfects." Here and elsewhere the ostraca merely follow what had already been known about preexilic prose.

B. Content

Aharoni summarized the content of these inscriptions as "epistles to commanders of Arad with military and administrative information; instructions for the supply of wine and bread to military units and other people; instructions for the sending of consignments of oil and food to various fortresses; taxes from various places; lists of people, some with the addition of numbers; lists of the apportionment of wheat and other commodities; inventory lists of the storehouses, one of them in hieratic; registration of dates; offerings and donations to the sanctuary; and various other partial lists" (1981: 141). Given the fragmentary character of these inscriptions, one suspects that far too much has been deduced from such a limited base of evidence.

Unquestionably, a certain "Eliashib" is either addressed or referred to in many of the inscriptions. It is not clear what his position was, nor is the extent of his authority evident. A number of the ostraca contain intriguing references. Ostracon 24 (found outside the fortress on the W slope and dated on basis of orthography), for example, indicates fear of an Edomite advance against Ramat-negeb. Both Aharoni (1981: 149) and Lindsay (1976: 25) have tried to sketch the historical circumstances surrounding this reference; but paleography does not yet enable us to date inscriptions as precisely as their reconstructions demand, nor is our knowledge of this time period very full. Aharoni likewise tries to elaborate the Edomite background to Ostracon 40, but here the reconstruction is even more tenuous than with 24 since the inscription is so poorly preserved.

Aharoni concludes his discussion of the historical information gathered from these ostraca by stating: "We could not have expected a more surprising confirmation to our historical hypotheses than the epistle of Jehoahaz (Inscription 88), in which he announces his crowning, insists on energetic military preparations, and mentions the king of Egypt. This is full confirmation of the destruction of Stratum VIII in the year 609 B.C.E., and an additional proof of the high position of Eliashib, who received his instructions directly from the king" (1981: 150). The text which bears such weight simply reads as follows:

(1) *ʾny mlkty bk[l]* . . .	(1) I have come to reign in all . . .
(2) *ʾmṣzrʿw* . . .	(2) Take strength and . . .
(3) *mlk mṣryn l* . . .	(3) King of Egypt to . . .

It is impossible here to catalog all that has been derived from these texts, but historical statements based on the Arad ostraca should always be compared against the actual inscriptions themselves.

Bibliography

Aharoni, Y., with the cooperation of Naveh, J. 1975. *Arad Inscriptions.* Jerusalem (in Hebrew).

———. 1981. *Arad Inscriptions,* ed. and rev. A. F. Rainey. Jerusalem.

Cross, F. M., and Freedman, D. N. 1952. *Early Hebrew Orthography.* American Oriental Series 36. New Haven, CT.

Lindsay, J. 1976. The Babylonian Kings and Edom, 605–550 B.C. *PEQ* 108: 23–39.

Miller, P. 1985. Review of Arad Inscriptions, by Y. Aharoni. *CBQ* 47: 503–5.

Pardee, D. 1982. *Handbook of Ancient Hebrew Letters.* Chico, CA.

Parunak, H. 1978. The Orthography of the Arad Ostraca. *BASOR* 230: 25–31.

ROBERT B. LAWTON

ARADUS (PLACE) [Gk *Arados*]. An island and a city 3 km off the Phoenician (modern Lebanese) coast, 3 miles N of Beirut (1 Macc 15:23). Strabo (16.2.13–17) records that the inhabitants were descendants of exiles from Sidon, which would agree with the biblical references to the corresponding Hebrew eponym ARVAD (Gen 10:18; 1 Chr 1:16). Aradus was prominent enough to receive a letter from Lucius, consul of the Romans, in 139 B.C. (1 Macc 15:23). Being a well-protected island producing warriors and seamen famous in their service to Tyre (Ezek 27:8, 11), Aradus was always commercially productive and remained independent until the time of Nebuchadnezzar, ca. 627 B.C. Although its commercial productivity declined somewhat, the prominence of Aradus rose again under the rule of the Persians and Seleucids (Rostovtzeff 1967: 846; Seyrig 1950: 17–20; Elai, 1987). Specifically through an alliance with Seleucus Callinicus of the Seleucids, Aradians exerted their influence extensively on the mainland. In general, Strabo describes the Aradians as a prudent and industrious people with respect to their maritime affairs. Along with their good fortunes (for example, Seleucus Callinicus' granting of the right of *asylia*) they prospered.

Bibliography

Elayi, J. 1987. *Recherches sur les cités phéniciennes à l'époque perse.* AIONSup 51. Naples.

Jones, A. H. M. 1937. Pp. 235–36 in *The Cities of the Eastern Roman Provinces.* Oxford.

Rostovtzeff, M. 1967. *The Social and Economic History of the Hellenistic World.* Vol. 2. Oxford.

Seyrig, H. 1950. *Notes of Syrian Coins.* New York.

TOM F. WEI

ARAH (PERSON) [Heb *ʾārāḥ*]. **1.** Head of a family of Babylonian exiles who are listed as returnees under the leadership of Zerubbabel and others (Ezra 2:5 = Neh 7:10 = 1 Esdr 5:10). Later in the postexilic period Tobiah, the adversary of Nehemiah, married a woman from the family of Arah (Neh 6:18). For further discussion and bibliography, see AKKUB.

2. A son of Ulla listed in the preexilic genealogy of the tribe of Asher (1 Chr 7:39). Because Ulla is not mentioned earlier in the list, some emend the name to coincide with a previous one; but Braun (1986: 118–19) argues against such emendation.

Bibliography

Braun, R. 1986. *1 Chronicles.* Waco, TX.

CHANEY R. BERGDALL

ARAM (PERSON) [Heb *ʾărām*]. **1.** The fifth son of Shem in the genealogical list of Genesis 10, which is known as the Table of Nations (Gen 10:22). Aram is the eponymous ancestor of the ARAMEANS, an important West Semitic people. The section of the Table of Nations in which Aram appears is usually attributed to the Priestly source of the Pentateuch. P has placed Aram in the same generation as the eponymous ancestors of Elam and Assyria (Ashur), two generations earlier than the eponymous ancestor of the Hebrews (Eber—Gen 10:24). The position of Aram as a son of Shem reflects the importance of the Aramean tribes during the 1st millennium B.C.E. Four sons of Aram are listed in v 23. These apparently represent certain Aramean tribal groups, although little is known concerning any of the four. These sons are listed as brothers of Aram in the genealogical list of Chronicles (1:17), but this is probably due to a haplography of the phrase "The sons of Aram" from the text of Chronicles.

2. Son of Kemuel, grandson of Abraham's brother, Nahor (Gen 22:21). The genealogy of Nahor (22: 20–24) reflects a different (and probably earlier) tradition about the ancestry of the Arameans from the one found in Genesis 10 (see above). The twelve sons of Nahor, including Aram's father, Kemuel, appear to be eponymous ancestors of various Aramean tribes. Aram himself (here perhaps to be understood as the ancestor of the state of Aram-Damascus) is placed in the same generation as Jacob/Israel. This genealogical tradition stresses the idea of the close relationship between Israel and the Arameans, which pervades the book of Genesis (cf. Deut 26:5).

3. A son of Shemer in the genealogy of Asher in 1 Chr 7:34.

4. The Greek rendering of the name RAM in the genealogy of Jesus, Matt 1:3. The KJV has "Aram" here, while modern translations tend to replace it with "Ram" [cf. 1 Chr 2:9–10]. The name "Aram" also appears in the genealogy of Jesus in Luke 3:33 in the KJV. Later translations substitute the name ARNI, following the text of the most ancient manuscripts, where "Aram" was found in the Textus Receptus.

Bibliography

Malamat, A. 1967. Aspects of Tribal Societies in Mari and Israel. p. 129–38 in *XVe rencontre assyriologique internationale: La civilisation de Mari.* Liège.

———. 1973. The Aramaeans. Pp. 134–55 in *POTT.*

Mazar, B. 1962. The Aramaean Empire and Its Relations with Israel. *BA* 25: 98–120.

Noth, M. 1951. Beiträge zur Geschichte des Ostjordanlandes III. *ZDPV* 68: 19–36.

WAYNE T. PITARD

ARAM (PLACE) [Heb *ʾărām*]. The name of an important Aramean nation, located in southern Syria, which flourished between the 11th and 8th centuries B.C.E. Its capital was Damascus, currently the capital of the modern state of Syria. In many English translations, the name "Aram," when referring to this state, is translated (inaccurately) as Syria.

A. The Name

The use of the name "Aram" as a political or ethnic designation is not restricted, however, to this particular state. It occurs many times in compound names of states largely populated by Arameans, who were one of the most important ethnic groups in the Near East during the late 2d and the 1st millennia B.C.E. Thus there are references to Aram-Beth-Rehob, Aram-Damascus, Aram-Maacah, Aram-Naharaim, Aram-Zobah, and Paddan-Aram. In a few cases the name "Aram" alone is used to designate Aram-Naharaim (Num 23:7; Judg 3:10; Hosea 12:13) or Aram-Zobah (2 Sam 10 = 1 Chr 19; see ARAM-NAHARAIM; ZOBAH; DAMASCUS; PADDAN-ARAM; etc.). In some other occurrences, "Aram" is used more generally to refer to the Aramean kingdoms or people as a whole (1 Kgs 10:29 = 2 Chr 1:17; Judg 10:6; Amos 9:7). From 6th-century sources which deal with the destruction of Jerusalem (2 Kgs 24:2 and Jer 35:11), the name refers to Aramean tribes that lived in Mesopotamia, and from which Nebuchadnezzar had assembled his army.

But by far the most common usage of the term "Aram" in the Bible is as the name of the state centered around Damascus. This is the virtually exclusive use of the name in the books of Kings, Chronicles, and Isaiah, where the majority of the attestations occur.

B. History of Aram

Our knowledge of the history of Aram-Damascus is unfortunately limited. No written documents directly from the kingdom itself have been discovered to date, so that the only sources of information available are writings from neighboring states (mainly Israelite [i.e., biblical] and Assyrian texts). These, quite naturally, do not give a full picture of Aram, since they deal only with their own state's relations with that kingdom. Because of this, our knowledge centers upon Aram's role in the realm of international politics, while details of its internal life and culture remain obscure.

1. Early Relations with Israel. The kingdom of Aram-Damascus makes its first appearance in historical documents in 2 Sam 8:5–6. During a decisive conflict between Israel and Zobah, the two major powers of Syria-Palestine during the late 11th and early 10th centuries B.C.E., the army of Aram-Damascus is reported to have taken to the field in support of Zobah and its king Hadadezer (Aramaic, Hadad-ʿid̲r). David, the king of Israel, defeated the army and took control of Damascus, placing garrison troops there. Aram-Damascus thus became part of the empire of David, apparently as an occupied territory rather than as a vassal state.

Nothing else is known about Aram until the time of Solomon (mid-10th century). 1 Kgs 11:23–24 states that during Solomon's reign, a certain Rezon, son of Eliada, who had been a servant of the king of Zobah whom David had defeated, gathered together a group of malcontents, seized Damascus, and there proclaimed himself king. Rezon went on to remove Damascus from Israelite control. There is no indication that Israel was able to significantly oppose this action, and 11:25 suggests that Damascus remained outside Israel's control for a substantial part of Solomon's reign.

With the division of Solomon's kingdom into two smaller states ca. 932, and the resultant collapse of Israelite hegemony in the region, a period ensued when there was no dominant political power in Syria-Palestine. But by the beginning of the 9th century, Aram, with its capital at Damascus, had become a significant influence in the region. Little is known about Aram between the time of Rezon (about the middle of the 10th century) and the reign of Bir-Hadad I (biblical Ben-Hadad), who is mentioned in 1 Kgs 15:16–22 (= 2 Chr 16:1–6) in connection with a boundary war between Baasha of Israel and Asa of Judah (early 9th century). However, Bir-Hadad's patronymic in 15:18, "Ben-Hadad, the son of Tab-Rimmon, the son of Hezion," apparently furnishes the names of Bir-Hadad's two predecessors on the throne. There is also a reference in v 19 to a treaty that had been made between Bir-Hadad's father and Asa's father, although the details of this treaty are not known. But it is clear that Aram had become a state of comparable stature to Israel and Judah during the decades following the death of Solomon.

When Bir-Hadad I became involved in this boundary dispute between Israel and Judah, he sided with Judah (after a substantial bribe was sent to him by Asa) and attacked Israel from the north while Baasha's forces were concentrated in the south against Judah. He attacked and destroyed a number of major towns in Israel's territory to the north of the Sea of Galilee (1 Kgs 15:20). Baasha was forced to withdraw his army from the border with Judah and come to terms with Bir-Hadad, although no information is given concerning what these terms were.

2. Mid-9th Century B.C.E. a. Hadad-ʿid̲r and Assyria. By the fifth decade of the 9th century B.C.E., Aram had become one of the most powerful states in Syria-Palestine, if not actually the most powerful. This coincided with the first Assyrian attempts to extend their domination into central and southern Syria. In 853, Shalmaneser III of Assyria marched into the territory of the kingdom of Hamath, where his forces were met by a coalition of Syro-Palestinian states near the town of Qarqar. The coalition is described in an inscription of Shalmaneser III (known as the Monolith Inscription; *ANET,* 278–79) as having been made up of twelve states. The leader of the coalition is named as Adad-idri of Aram (Aramaic Hadad-ʿid̲r, the namesake of the king of Zobah defeated by David; see above), and he is said to have brought with him 1200 chariots, 1200 horsemen, and 20,000 footsoldiers. This is the largest contingent of horsemen and footsoldiers and the second largest group of chariots contributed by a member of the coalition. He was joined by two other major powers in the region, Irḫulena of Hamath and Ahab of Israel, who contributed the majority of the rest of the army (the other nine members of the coalition were more modestly represented). The coalition appears to have been successful at stopping Shalmaneser's advance. Although Shalmaneser claims to have won, it is clear from the inscription that he was obliged to return immediately to his homeland, without making further moves against any members of the coalition. Nor did he return to Syria for another four years.

The leadership of this coalition continued to rest in Hadad-ʿid̲r's hands for several years. Shalmaneser returned to Syria in his tenth, eleventh, and fourteenth years (849, 848, and 845 respectively), each time battling with the coalition, always headed by Hadad-ʿid̲r. At no time was Shalmaneser able to decisively defeat the coalition. Hadad-ʿid̲r's continued leadership role in this alliance indicates the prestige which Aram enjoyed in relation to the other states of central and southern Syria and Palestine during these years.

b. "Ben-Hadad" and Ahab. There has been considerable scholarly discussion concerning the relationship between Hadad-ʿid̲r of the Assyrian inscriptions and the king of Aram called Ben-Hadad in 1 Kings 20 and 22. These two chapters describe three battles between Israel and Aram, which are said to have taken place during the final five years of the reign of Ahab of Israel. If these chapters are reliable, then the king called Ben-Hadad in 1 Kings 20 (or "Ben-Hadad II," according to many scholars) should probably be identified with Hadad-ʿid̲r of the Assyrian inscriptions.

However, there are a number of elements in these two chapters which have led several scholars (including Jepsen 1941–45: 154–59; Miller 1966; and Pitard 1987: 115–25) to propose that the accounts of the war between Israel and Aram here do not belong originally to the period of Ahab, but rather to the time of Joash (or Joahaz, according to Miller 1966: 442–43) some fifty years later. A number of arguments have been put forward to substantiate this proposal. For example, literary analysis indicates that the accounts of the two battles in 1 Kings 20 did not originally provide the name of the king of Israel. Furthermore, the description of Israel's political situation in this chapter is seriously at odds with what is known of the reigns of both Omri and Ahab from other biblical passages (cf. 1 Kgs 16:27; 22:39), as well as extrabiblical texts. For example, Shalmaneser's Monolith Inscription reports that Ahab furnished 2000 chariots (the largest contingent of chariots from any member of the coalition) and 10,000 footsoldiers to the battle of Qarqar. Also, the Stela of Mesha, the king of Moab (*ANET,* 320–21), describes the domination of Moab by Omri and Ahab. Finally, archaeological evidence demonstrates that Israel was economically prosperous and able to support significant civilian and military building projects during this time. All of these suggest quite clearly that Ahab and Omri were very powerful kings (see AHAB), in contrast to the king of Israel in 1 Kings 20, who is portrayed as a weak vassal of Ben-Hadad of Aram (cf. 1 Kgs 20:1–9, esp. v 9) and his father, who is also described as having been dominated by Aram (20:34).

While such a portrayal does not fit well with the times of Omri and Ahab (i.e. ca. 886–853), it does match excellently with the reigns of Joahaz and Joash (ca. 814–782), when Israel was dominated by Hazael and his son Bir-Hadad (Heb Ben-Hadad; see 2 Kgs 13:22–25). It was during the reign of this Bir-Hadad that Joash was able to rebel successfully against Aram and defeat Bir-Hadad's army in a decisive battle near Aphek (2 Kgs 13:17). It should be noted that the decisive battle in 1 Kings 20 is also fought at Aphek. With regard to the account of Ahab's death in battle against Aram at Ramoth-Gilead (1 Kgs 22:1–36), scholars have suggested that this account has developed from the story of the wounding of Ahab's son, Joram, in battle at Ramoth-Gilead during the time of Hazael (2 Kgs 9:14–15; see Miller 1966: 444–46). Thus, it appears unlikely that there was a major war between Aram and Israel during the reign of Ahab. The stories in 1 Kings 20 rather illuminate events that took place some fifty to sixty years after the death of Ahab. The king of Aram called Ben-Hadad in these stories, as well as in the stories of Elisha and the Aramaeans in 2 Kings 5–7 (insofar as they may be regarded as historical), should be identified with Bir-Hadad, the son of Hazael (often referred to as "Ben-Hadad III" by many scholars; see B.3.b below). The only exception to this is the story in 2 Kgs 8:7–15.

Major changes occurred in Aram between 845 and 842, although the exact details are not known. 2 Kgs 8:7–15 gives an account of how a usurper named Hazael assassinated the king of Aram and seized the throne. The name of the king of Aram in this passage is Ben-Hadad. It is possible that the incorporation of the Ben-Hadad stories into the account of the period of Ahab has led to the use of his name in this story as well, and that the correct name of the king assassinated by Hazael was actually Hadad-ʿid̲r. But it is also possible that Hadad-ʿid̲r died sometime between 845 and 842 and was succeeded by a Bir-Hadad, who in turn was assassinated by Hazael. Unfortunately there is not enough evidence to determine the actual course of events.

3. The Aramean Empire. a. The Reign of Hazael. After Hazael seized the throne, ca. 842, the anti-Assyrian coalition that had been headed by Hadad-ʿid̲r collapsed and war broke out between Aram and Israel. A battle took place between Hazael's troops and the army of Joram of Israel near Ramoth-Gilead, a border town in the northern part of Israel's Transjordanian territory (2 Kgs 8:28–29; 9:14–15a). During this battle, Joram was wounded and was forced to retire from the area. It was at Ramoth-Gilead during this period of tension that Jehu began the revolution that would result in the assassination of Joram and Jehu's seizure of power in Israel (ca. 842/41, 2 Kgs 9). Relations between the two states did not improve after Jehu's rebellion, but Hazael had to turn his attention elsewhere in 841, when Shalmaneser III returned to Syria. With the coalition in shambles, most of the Syro-Palestinian states, including Hamath and Israel, submitted to the Assyrian king. But Hazael did not. Aram's army was defeated by Shalmaneser near Mt. Senir (the Mt. Hermon area), and the Assyrian army temporarily beseiged Damascus. But the city was not captured, and Shalmaneser marched on to the coast, where he received the submission of several kings, including Jehu of Israel (*ANET,* 280).

Hazael had to fight the Assyrians alone two more times (apparently Shalmaneser's 21st and 22d years, 838 and 837) as well. We know virtually nothing of the circumstances of these campaigns. But afterward, Shalmaneser's attention turned to lands in the north, and thirty years would elapse before the Assyrians would again march into southern Syria.

Once the pressure from the Assyrians subsided, Hazael returned to his policy against Israel. Jehu's bloody purge of supporters of the overthrown Omride dynasty had weakened Israel to the point that Hazael was able to annex Israel's Transjordanian territories (2 Kgs 10:32–33). By the reign of Jehu's son, Joahaz, Israel was virtually, if not actually, a vassal to Aram-Damascus. According to the Lucianic mss of the LXX (following 2 Kgs 13:22), Hazael also invaded and conquered Philistia. He then turned eastward and attacked Judah. Jehoash, the king of Judah, sent Hazael an extensive tribute, thereby presumably becoming a vassal, and Hazael then withdrew from Jerusalem (2 Kgs 12:17–18).

Thus during the reign of Hazael, Aram developed into a significant empire which covered much, if not all, of southern Syria and Palestine. Some scholars have proposed that Hazael also dominated northern Syria (Mazar 1962: 114; Jepsen 1941–45: 168), but none of the evidence adduced for this proposal is compelling. As far as can be determined from current evidence, Hazael's empire extended only as far north as Hamath's southern boundary. But even if he did not control northern Syria, Hazael had made Aram into one of the most significant states in the Levant. Hazael's reign, while beginning so poorly, appears to have become the period of Aram's greatest strength.

b. Bir-Hadad and the Collapse of the Empire. Hazael was succeeded, probably ca. 800 B.C.E., by his son Bir-Hadad (traditionally known in most scholarship as Ben-Hadad III, since Hadad-ʿid̲r was normally identified with the Ben-Hadad of 1 Kings 20 and thus designated Bir-Hadad II). Bir-Hadad is known from the Bible (2 Kgs 13:3–7, 22–25; and probably, 1 Kings 20; 2 Kgs 6:24–7:20), from a stone inscription of Zakkur (formerly vocalized as "Zakir"), king of Hamath and Luash (*ANET,* 655–56), and from Assyrian inscriptions of Adad-nirari III. All of these sources of information indicate that Bir-Hadad was unable to hold on to the political power established by his father. The Assyrian king Adad-nirari III besieged Damascus, probably in 796 B.C.E., and received a substantial tribute from the king of Aram, who is called Marʾi in the Assyrian inscriptions. Marʾi, which in Aramaic means "my lord," is almost certainly a title of Bir-Hadad. The inscription of Zakkur describes an attack on his capital city in Luash by a coalition of kings that was led by Bir-Hadad. In this campaign, Bir-Hadad was unsuccessful, being forced to lift the siege around the city before a surrender. He also suffered serious losses to Israel, which regained its independence at this time (see particularly 2 Kgs 13:22–25). As suggested above (B.2.b), it is probable that the accounts of two battles between Israel and Aram in 1 Kings

20 should be attributed to the time of Bir-Hadad, the son of Hazael, and Joash of Israel. We do not know in which chronological order all of these political reverses took place, but it is clear that by the end of Bir-Hadad's reign, Aram had lost much of its political power.

It is not known how long Bir-Hadad ruled, but it does appear that Aram's fortunes continued to decline during the first half of the 8th century. Only a few facts are known from this period, but they reveal the situation fairly well. In 773, the Assyrians, under Shalmaneser IV, once again attacked Aram, and a recently discovered (but as yet unpublished) stela describes the tribute given to Shalmaneser by the king of Aram, named Hadianu. During the same period, Israel experienced its last major revival under Jeroboam II (ca. 782–748). 2 Kgs 14:25, 28 suggest that Jeroboam was able to dominate Aram during his reign.

4. Raḏyan's Coalition and the End of Aram. Aram's last period of political influence and independence began about the middle of the 8th century with the reign of Aram's last king, called Rezin in the Bible (Aram, Raḏyān). Raḏyan was on the throne by 738, when his name appears on a list of vassals who brought tribute to Tiglath-Pileser III of Assyria that year. During the years 737–735, Tiglath-Pileser was involved in a series of campaigns to the north and east of Assyria. Raḏyan at this time formed a new coalition of Syro-Palestinian states (including Tyre and Israel) which rebelled against Assyria.

The coalition included Tyre and Israel, and apparently in an attempt to force Judah to join the coalition, Raḏyan and Pekah of Israel attacked Judah and besieged Jerusalem (see 2 Kgs 15:37; 16:5–9). Their plan was to replace the young king Ahaz of Judah with an anti-Assyrian puppet ruler, named Tabeel in Isa 7:6. Ahaz, against the advice of Isaiah (cf. Isaiah 7), sent a large gift to Tiglath-Pileser, asking for help against Aram and Israel. Tiglath-Pileser marched into Syria in 734, apparently capturing Tyre and the Philistine coast that year. Over the next two years, Tiglath-Pileser turned his attention directly toward Aram and Israel. During the campaign of 732, Aram was finally and fully defeated by the Assyrians. Accounts of the fall of Aram are found both in 2 Kgs 16:9 and in the inscriptions of Tiglath-Pileser. The Assyrian king claims to have destroyed 591 towns in the sixteen districts of Aram during the course of the campaign. In the end, Damascus was captured, and Raḏyan was killed. The Assyrians annexed the land of Aram into the empire, and the land was divided up into provinces. This was the end of the independent state of Aram. (For more details of the coalition formed by Raḏyan, see SYRO-EPHRAIMITE WAR; see also *POTT* pp. 134–55.)

Bibliography

Dupont-Sommer, A. 1949. *Les Araméens.* Paris.

Jepsen, A. 1941–45. Israel und Damaskus. *AfO* 14: 153–72.

Mazar, B. 1962. The Aramean Empire and Its Relations with Israel. *BA* 25: 98–120.

Miller, J. M. 1964. *The Omride Dynasty in the Light of Recent Literary and Archaeological Research.* Diss. Emory University.

———. 1966. The Elisha Cycle and the Accounts of the Omride Wars. *JBL* 85: 441–54.

Pitard, W. T. 1987. *Ancient Damascus.* Winona Lake, IN.

Unger, M. 1957. *Israel and the Aramaeans of Damascus.* Grand Rapids.

WAYNE T. PITARD

ARAM-MAACAH (PLACE) [Heb *ʾăram maʿăkâ*]. See MAACAH (PLACE).

ARAM-NAHARAIM (PLACE) [Heb *ʾăram nahărayim*]. Geographical name of an area in upper Mesopotamia, located around the great bend of the Euphrates River in N Syria. The name occurs five times in the Bible, and is often translated "Mesopotamia" in English versions, following the LXX rendering. It appears as the name of the ancestral home of Abraham's family in Gen 24:10 (the same area seems to be designated Paddan-Aram in the Priestly Pentateuchal source). It is also named as the homeland of Balaam, the son of Beor (Deut 23:5), and the country of Cushan-Rishathaim, the first of the oppressors of Israel in the book of Judges (Judg 3:8). David is said to have fought with troops from this area, during his war with Ammon and its Aramaean allies (1 Chr 19:6, cf. Ps 60, superscription [v 2 in Hebrew]). There are also two, possibly three, cases in which this area is simply designated by the term "Aram" (Judg 3:10; Hosea 12:13; and Num 23:7[?]). Various commentaries discuss the problems of the homelands of both Balaam and Cushan-Rishathaim.

A number of extrabiblical sources make reference to this land during the last half of the 2d millennium B.C.E. Several Egyptian pharaohs of the New Kingdom had dealings with or attempted to conquer this area, which they called Naharin(a). Attestations of this name are found in texts from the time of Thutmosis I (late 16th century) to the reign of Rameses III (early 12th century). The region is also known from the Amarna Letters (14th century) in the forms *na-aḫ-rí-ma* and *na-rí-ma.* Only in the Bible does the name occur prefixed with "Aram." In those instances where the term appears in connection with the patriarchs (and probably the other attestations as well), it is being used anachronistically, since the area probably was not under Aramaean control prior to the 1st millennium. From the 1st millennium B.C.E., there are no extrabiblical references to this area either as Naharaim or Aram-Naharaim.

Precise boundaries of the land of Naharaim cannot be determined from the preserved texts, but the towns said to be located in the land include Harran, Nahor, Pethor, and Tunip. These indicate that the designation covered areas on both the west and east sides of the Euphrates, as well as the Balikh River valley and perhaps part of the Habur River triangle (Finkelstein 1962: 84–86). See also ARAM (PLACE); MESOPOTAMIA; and *POTT* pp. 134–55.

Bibliography

Finkelstein, J. J. 1962. Mesopotamia. *JNES* 21: 73–92.

O'Callaghan, R. T. 1948. *Aram Naharaim.* AnOr 26. Rome.

WAYNE T. PITARD

ARAMAIC LANGUAGE.
See LANGUAGES (ARAMAIC).

ARAMAIC LETTERS.
See LETTERS (ARAMAIC).

ARAMAIC "MESSIANIC" TEXT (4QMess ar).

The siglum "4QMess ar" refers to ten little fragments in Aramaic found in cave 4 at Qumran. The fragments are written on soft leather, and the maximum dimensions of the whole are 20 × 38 cm. The script dates between 30 B.C. and A.D. 20. Their first editor, Jean Starcky (1964), labeled them an "Aramaic messianic text"; indeed he believed that they constituted an astrological text about the Messiah, since the child described in the fragments is said to be the Elect of God (*baḥîr ʾelaha*). The main assertions about the child are that "in his youth he will become like a man who does not know anything, until the time when he shall become skilled in the three books. Then he will become wise and will be endowed with discretion. . . . His calculations [will succeed] because he is the Elect of God" (Fitzmyer 1974: 142–43). In the second column, which is badly fragmented, it is stated that "waters will cease" and a Holy One and Watcher (more correctly, a Wakeful, Vigilant, Watchful, or Alert One) is mentioned.

Shortly after its first publication and the publication of the related horoscope (Allegro 1964), Fitzmyer published a radically different interpretation: the text is not a horoscope (because there are no stars or signs of the Zodiac) and is not messianic (because "Elect of God" is not always a messianic title), but is part of the physical description of the forefather Noah (1974). J. C. Greenfield (1973: xx–xxi) preferred an identification with Melchizedek, but the Noachic identification has prevailed in later studies. P. Grelot (1975) then proceeded to identify the three books mentioned in the fragments with the three books of Enoch mentioned in Jubilees 4:16–26. These three books are probably found in 1 Enoch: the Astronomical Book, the Book of Dreams, and the Book of the Wakeful. (Other books were subsequently added to these three in 1 Enoch.) In *Jub.* 7:38, Noah is said to receive the complete tradition of Enoch, his great-grandfather. The Noachic identification rests on the link between the three books mentioned in our text and Enoch the ancestor of Noah, on the phrase "waters will cease" (taken as a reference to the Deluge), on the mention of Holy One and Wakeful both here and in col. 2 of 1QapGen which deals with the birth of Noah, and on the fascination with the birth of Noah in intertestamental literature (*1 Enoch* 106–8; *Jubilees* 4–10) and in as yet unpublished Qumran fragments from caves 4 and 11.

The thorough study by Florentino García-Martínez (1981) concludes that our fragments form part of a lost book of Noah mentioned in *Jub.* 10:13 and 21:10 and in patristic references. These suggest that the book of Noah was among other things an herbalary or medical guide to healing plants that also provided halachic prescriptions for food and blood. Parts of this lost book may have been incorporated in *1 Enoch* and *Jubilees.*

4QMess ar provides a parallel to Simeon's declaration on the destiny of the child Jesus in Luke 2:34–35. The term "elect" is used 24 times in the NT, 20 times in the plural referring to the predestined saints, and 4 times in the singular with reference to the messiah (Luke 23:35; John 1:34 variant reading; 1 Pet 2:4, 6). Thus by the time of the NT, the term "elect of God" in the singular as found in our text had taken on a messianic significance in certain circles. In the OT the term "my Chosen One" or "my Elect" is used of David (Ps 89:4), the Servant of Yahweh (Isa 42:1), and Moses (Ps 106:23). Our text helps to fill out the intertestamental picture.

Bibliography

Allegro, J. M. 1964. An Astrological Cryptic Document from Qumran. *JSS* 9: 291–94.

Fitzmyer, J. A. 1974. The Aramaic "Elect of God" Text from Qumran Cave 4. Pp. 127–160 in *Essays on the Semitic Background of the New Testament.* Missoula.

García-Martínez, F. 1981. 4 Q Mes. Aram. y el Libro de Noe. Pp. 195–232 in *Escritos de Biblia y Oriente: Miscelánea conmemorativa del 25° anniversario del Instituto Español Bíblico y Arqueológico (Casa de Santiago) de Jerusalén,* ed. R. Aguirre and F. García Lopez. Bibliotheca Salmanticensis 38. Salamanca and Jerusalem.

———. 1987. Estudios Qumranicos 1975–1985: Panorama Critico (I). *EstBib* 45: 125–206.

Greenfield, J. C. 1973. Prolegomenon in Odeberg, *3 Enoch.* New York.

Grelot, P. 1975. Hénoch et ses écritures. *RB* 82: 481–500.

Starcky, J. 1964. Un texte messianique araméen de la grotte 4 de Qumran. Pp. 51–56 in *Mémorial du cinquantenaire de l'École des langues orientales anciennes de l'Institut Catholique de Paris.* Paris.

B. T. VIVIANO

ARAMAIC SCRIPT.

About 1100 B.C. the Aramaeans adopted the alphabetic script which was employed at that time by the Canaanites and Phoenicians. They wrote in this same script until the mid-8th century B.C. Moreover, at the beginning they may even have written in the Phoenician language as well, because by the end of the 9th century B.C. the stele of Kilamu, king of Yadi (Samʾal, where an Aramaic dialect was spoken), was inscribed in the Phoenician language. However, two later texts from Samʾal, the so-called Hadad inscription and the Panammu inscription, were written in the local Aramaic (Samʾalian) dialect. Only at the end of the 8th century B.C., Bar-Rekub, king of Samʾal, wrote his stele in the Aramaic language, which does not differ from that of Bar-Hadad king of Damascus, Zakkur king of Hamath, and the Old Aramaic inscription from Sefire.

In the scripts of all the inscriptions mentioned above and of other Aramaic monumental inscriptions, no clear Aramaic features are discernible; except for the two-bar *ḥet* in the inscription of Bar-Rekub, the scripts are generally Phoenician in character. The first distinctively Aramaic features appear in the mid-8th century B.C. cursive scripts, e.g., on the inscribed bricks from Hammat, where there is a one-bar *ḥet* (see also the inscribed lion weights from Nineveh, from the last quarter of the 8th century B.C.).

In 1979, reports of the discovery of the life-size statue of a man with a bilingual Assyrian-Aramaic inscription from Tell Fekheriye, near Gozan, aroused some doubts concerning the formerly held theory of the early development of the Aramaic script and its branching off from the Phoenician ca. 750 B.C. (which was described above). It is almost generally accepted that this statue with its inscription was erected in the 9th century B.C. However, the script of the Aramaic version of the inscription does not resemble the scripts of the contemporary Aramaic and Phoenician (or Moabite) inscriptions, but rather the 11th-century B.C. Proto-Canaanite script. If the Aramaic version on the Fekheriye statue was indeed written in the 9th century B.C., and not—as the paleographic criterion would indicate—in the 11th century B.C., then we may assume that this is a deliberate archaization, i.e., a successful imitation of a set of letters which was used 200 years earlier. Otherwise we should have to conclude that people speaking Aramaic in the region of Gozan managed to preserve for two centuries an archaic script which was not influenced by the development that took place elsewhere.

The impact of the Phoenician script on people who wrote in Aramaic was so strong that they took over the set of 22 letters employed by the Phoenicians without adding to it a single character, even though the phonetic system of the Aramaic language was much richer than that of the Phoenician. In Aramaic there were e.g., *ḏ* and *z*; but they wrote in the Phoenician way only *z* (*zy, znh, zhb*); there were *ṯ* and *š*, but both consonants were represented only by *š* (*šlš, šql*). Only in the 5th-century B.C. Aramaic inscriptions and documents we find "gold" written *dhb* and "to weigh" written as *tql*. Even in the Tell Fekheriye inscription, only 22 letters were used; the only exception there is that *ṯ* was expressed by *s* and not by the usual *š*.

At the beginning of the 1st millennium B.C. the Aramaic script and language were employed only—or mainly—by the inhabitants of the Aramean kingdoms, but from the 8th century B.C., after the Assyrians conquered these states and realized that the Aramaic script was much more convenient than their cuneiform writing, they granted the Aramaic language and script a special status. Aramaic became an official means of communication in the western provinces of the Assyrian empire. Very soon it turned into an international language in diplomacy and trade. Not only did the ministers of Hezekiah ask Rab-shakeh to speak to them in Aramaic "for we understand it" (2 Kgs 18:26), but 100 years later, at the end of the 7th century B.C. Adon the king of a certain Philistine (or Phoenician) city wrote to Pharaoh king of Egypt an Aramaic letter in which he asked for military aid against the advancing Babylonian troops that had already conquered Aphek (*KAI* 266). The diffusion of the Aramaic language and script increased in the Babylonian and Persian kingdoms.

After 732 B.C., the year of the Assyrian conquest of Damascus (the southernmost Aramaic city-state), the Aramaic script ceased to be a national script, and people of various national or ethnic origins began writing in it. Therefore the Aramaic script, not being restricted by the conservativeness which characterizes national writing traditions, was used for purely practical purposes. This phenomenon enabled the evolution of a cursive script which did not preserve the older letter forms, and any unnecessary strokes were dropped from the letters. As early as the end of the 7th century B.C., the Aramaic script looked like shorthand in comparison with the Phoenician and, particularly, with the Hebrew script.

Aramaic script was widely used in all the provinces of the Assyrian, Babylonian, and Persian empires. In a vast area extending from Asia Minor and Afghanistan to Egypt and North Arabia, the type of Aramaic script encountered was uniform, and no regional variations evolved even in the remotest provinces. The standards were fixed by the royal scribes, who wrote in a conservative formal cursive style. Everybody who learned to write was taught to follow the standard calligraphy of the formal cursive script but practically only the scribes adhered to the scribal rules. Other educated persons allowed themselves to write faster and thus to introduce innovations in the forms of the letters. This kind of writing—i.e., the free cursive style—caused the changes which eventually led to the development of the script. Those who learned reading and writing and had only a limited use for this knowledge tried imitating the formal style, but wrote clumsily in the vulgar cursive style. Besides the cursive style (with its three sub-styles: formal, free, and vulgar) the Aramaic script also had a lapidary style, which was practiced mainly for engraving on hard material, but even on stone the cursive (mainly the formal cursive) style very often prevailed.

The scripts of the 9th- and 8th-century Aramaic monumental inscriptions, which resemble those of the contemporary Phoenician ones, can be defined as lapidary. The influence of the Aramaic cursive can be seen only in the late 8th-century lapidary writing (e.g., the two-bar *ḥet* in the Bar-Rekub inscription). However, soon the Aramaic cursive became dominant, and even on stelae and seals cursive letters were engraved. The lapidary style, of course, was known everywhere, its most famous representatives from the Persian period being the inscriptions from Asia Minor, Tema in North Arabia as well as the "Yehud" and "Mozah" jar stamps stemming from various Judaean sites. With the fall of the Persian empire, the lapidary Aramaic style fell into disuse. However, its cursive counterpart survived, and its descendants exist even today.

The Aramaic inscriptions and manuscripts from the 8th to the 3rd century B.C. were written in the uniform Aramaic script. The number of these texts is quite large, including graffiti, dedicatory inscriptions, stelae, burial inscriptions, boundary inscriptions, seals, coin legends, clay tablets, ostraca (among them dozens from Elephantine, Arad, and Beer-Sheba), and manuscripts written on parchment and papyrus. The majority of the papyri belong to the 5th century B.C. and stem from the Jewish military colony in Elephantine in Upper Egypt, but papyri have also been found in Hermopolis, Saqqarah, and Edfu in Egypt (the Edfu papyri are generally from the 3d century B.C.), as well as in Wadi Daliyeh, E of Samaria in Palestine (from the 4th century B.C.).

The ca. 100 papyri from Elephantine include name lists, private and official letters, legal documents, and three literary texts—an Aramaic version of the Behistun inscription, the Proverbs of Ahiqar, and a fragmentary narrative text of Bar-Punesh (*CAP* 71). The Elephantine papyri and ostraca are very important for the study of the Aramaic script in the 5th century B.C.: the legal documents bear exact dates and mention the names of the scribes who were either professionals, writing in a semiformal hand, or chance scribes, writing in a free cursive hand. In addition to the possibility of examining the handwriting of the various Elephantine scribes at fixed dates, the autograph signatures display the writing of the witnesses with various degrees of penmanship. Thus in these signatures the vulgar cursive style, the writing of the unskilled writer, is also represented.

There is a clear distinction between the writing of the professional scribes from Elephantine and that of the scribes of Arsham, the Persian governor in Egypt. The latter wrote in a very formal cursive hand, whereas the former wrote in the less conservative, semiformal style, more influenced by the free cursive. However, the professional scribes of the Elephantine documents and those of the Arsham letters wrote in shaded scripts, i.e., they distinguished between the horizontal thick strokes and the thinner vertical strokes, while the chance scribes and the writers of the private letters wrote more carelessly without shading and generally in more developed handwritings. Thus in the Elephantine documents the three substyles of the cursive (free, formal, and vulgar) can be seen. This indicates that in the 5th century B.C. a large number of the inhabitants of Elephantine knew how to read and write, a fact which is evidence of a literate society, not only there but most probably in various areas in the Persian period and presumably even earlier (the Hebrew epigraphic material from the 7th-century B.C. Judah provides similar evidence).

Whereas in the Hebrew and Phoenician scripts the rightward diagonal downstrokes were shaded, in the Aramaic script the horizontal bars were thickened. This phenomenon can be followed from the 8th-century B.C. ink-written texts onward. This kind of shading is characteristic of all the scripts which evolved from the uniform Aramaic script. The modern descendants, like Jewish (square Hebrew), Arabic, and Syriac, follow this tradition. It is difficult to explain why the Aramaic script deviated from the system of shading that was employed by the Phoenicians, but possibly the reason may be found in the method of writing used by the Aramaic scribes in the Assyrian and Babylonian empires. It seems likely that most of these scribes, who were probably not of Aramaean origin, were bilingual and thus were used to writing in the cuneiform script with a stylus on soft clay. Actually there are dozens of clay tablets written in the cuneiform writing that bear Aramaic endorsements, and there are other clay tablets bearing only Aramaic texts. The way of holding the stylus for writing the cuneiform wedge-shaped marks has not been studied thoroughly, but perhaps the scribes who wrote in Aramaic were influenced by the cuneiform scribes, and this may account for the horizontal shading in the Aramaic script and its descendants.

It seems likely that the eastern neighbors of the Israelites, i.e., the Ammonites, Moabites, and Edomites, who spoke in dialects akin to Hebrew, learned the alphabet only in the 9th century B.C. Mesha, king of Moab, wrote his stele in the Moabite language but employed the Hebrew script, as it was used at that time by the inhabitants of Israel and Judah. Although no contemporary Edomite inscription is known at present, there is enough evidence to suppose that in the 9th century B.C. the Edomites also wrote in the Hebrew script. The Ammonites, however, adopted the Aramaic script from their northern neighbors Aram-Damascus (for an example of this, see the Amman Citadel Inscription). See EPIGRAPHY, TRANSJORDANIAN.

After the fall of Damascus in 732 B.C. and with the beginning of the Assyrian control of the King's Highway in Ammon, Moab, and Edom, the political and cultural influence of Israel and Judah on Moab and Edom came to an end. Because Aramaic was the official script in the western provinces of the Assyrian empire, Aramaic elements began to intrude into the scripts of Moab and Edom. Thus, while in the 7th-century B.C. inscriptions of the Moabites and Edomites there are Hebrew, Aramaic, and some peculiar local letter forms, in the 6th century B.C. the Aramaic forms prevail, and eventually the Hebrew elements disappear altogether. In the late 6th and 5th centuries no letter forms specifically Ammonite, Moabite, or Edomite are discernible, and the inscriptions were written solely in the Aramaic script, even those written in the Canaanite dialects.

After the conquest of Alexander the Great and the fall of the Persian empire, Greek replaced Aramaic as the official language and script of the government. However, Aramaic was already so deeply implanted that it continued to be spoken and written by all the nations who had formerly been under the Persian rule. The uniform Aramaic script continued to exist almost for 100 years; only in the middle of the 3rd century B.C. the various descendants began to crystalize.

Among the Eastern offshoots of the Aramaic script the following branches are discernible:

1. *The Syriac-Palmyrene branch.* As the Syriac and Palmyrene scripts have many common characteristics, the conclusion that they had a common ancestor is almost inevitable. It seems likely that both the Syriac and the Palmyrene scripts developed from the Aramaic chancellery script which was used in the 3d and 2d centuries B.C. in the Seleucid royal court in addition to the official script. In time, Syriac became the language and script of the Christian community whose center was in Edessa, but it was also adopted by the Palestinian Christians. The Palmyrene script was used mainly by the inhabitants of Palmyra and by Palmyrene emigrants all over the Roman empire; it was also accepted in Babylonia (where magic bowls were inscribed in it), as well as by the Manichaeans, who wrote sectarian texts in an Iranian dialect.

2. *The North Mesopotamian branch* is primarily known from the inscriptions discovered in Hatra, an oasis between the Tigris and the Euphrates, where a small kingdom flourished under Parthian suzerainty. This script was also accepted in Assur and Dura-Europus and even extended to Armenia and Georgia. The Armenians and Georgians did not speak Aramaic but wrote in this script, probably using the Aramaic words as ideograms.

3. *The South Mesopotamian branch* is best known from the script which was used from antiquity until modern times by the Mandaeans, a gnostic sect in Khuzistan and in the neighboring regions in Iran and Iraq. The earliest Mandaic texts probably stem from the 4th century, but the largest number come from the 6th century A.D. The Mandaic script developed from the Aramaic offshoot which

was used in Elymais, where another petty kingdom under Parthian suzerainty existed.

4. *The Iranian branch.* The Parthians, the Persians, and the Sogdians wrote in scripts that evolved from the uniform Aramaic script during the Achaemenid period. They generally used Aramaic ideograms, but in time the phonetic writing prevailed.

In the West, two scripts developed from the uniform Aramaic script:

5. *The Jewish script* is the ancestor of the medieval and modern (square) Hebrew script. F. M. Cross distinguished in its early evolutions three phases: Archaic or Proto-Jewish (ca. 250–150 B.C.), Hasmonaean (ca. 150–30 B.C.), and Herodian (ca. 30 B.C.–A.D. 70). This classification is mainly based on the variety of manuscripts found in Qumran, known as the Dead Sea Scrolls (Cross 1961: 174). The Jews, preferring this script, neglected their old Hebrew script, which was the national script of the inhabitants of Israel and Judah in the First Temple period. However, the original Palaeo-Hebrew script continued to be used in the Second Temple period by narrow circles. Its connotation was mainly nationalistic (coins) or religious (Pentateuch scrolls and the Tetragrammaton in texts written in the Jewish script), but it was also occasionally used in daily life.

Not only was the Palaeo-Hebrew script abandoned by the Jews (and preserved only by the Samaritans), but also the Jewish cursive (see the papyri from Wadi Murabbaʿat and Nahal Hever) ceased to exist after the defeat of Bar-Kokhba in 135 A.D.

6. *The Nabatean script* is well known from the monumental inscriptions which have survived in Nabatean cities, and from the graffiti found in the Sinai. Some Nabatean deeds were found in Nahal Hever which have been dated to the beginning of the 2d century A.D. The (formal and free) cursive style employed in these deeds clearly shows that the Nabatean script is the ancestor of the (classical) Arabic script.

Bibliography

Cross, F. M. 1961. The Development of the Jewish Scripts. Pp. 170–264 in *BANE*.

Naveh, J. 1970. *The Development of the Aramaic Script.* Jerusalem.

———. 1982. *Early History of the Alphabet.* Leiden.

JOSEPH NAVEH

ARAMEAN CONCUBINE. See ASRIEL; MACHIR; MANASSEH (PERSON).

ARAMEANS. Assyrian and biblical texts reveal the presence of people called Arameans living in most parts of Syria from the end of the 2d millennium B.C.

A. History of the Arameans

1. 11th to 9th Centuries B.C. a. Assyrian Sources. Tiglath-pileser I (ca. 1114–1076) campaigned from Assyria westward against an enemy named *ahlamē armāya* early in his reign, crossing the Euphrates in doing so. A badly broken Assyrian Chronicle may imply that Arameans pressed into Assyria itself later in his reign (TCS 5: 189). His son Aššur-bel-kala (ca. 1073–1056) followed his father's steps, but his inscriptions are less extensive and less explicit; they simply refer to *māt arime,* "the land of Aram." Both kings relate where they encountered these people: along the Euphrates from the Babylonian frontier at Rapiqu to Carchemish, in Mount Bishri, Tadmor (Palmyra) in Amurru, as far as the foot of the Lebanon mountains. Aššur-bel-kala met them in the mountains to the north, around the sources of the river Habur, an area where his father had fought the Mushki (often identified with the Phrygians). However, this was not the Arameans' most easterly penetration. They moved near to the heart of Assyria, settled E of the Tigris, and brought about a "dark age" from about 1050 to 930. When Assyrian royal reports resume under Aššur-dan II (ca. 934–912), the king relates his conquest of areas near the capital city of Aššur, and of Arameans who were evidently also not too distant. Adad-nirari II (ca. 911–891) continued his father's expansive policies, conquering Aramean sheikhs living in the Zagros foothills, an Aramean tribe called Teman near Nisibin, and reestablished Assyrian control over upper Mesopotamia as far W as the Habur River. Here the Assyrians faced the Aramean state of Bit-Bahyan, ruled by Abi-Salam at Guzan (biblical Gozan, now Tell Halaf), and took tribute. Campaign reports by Aššurnasirpal II and Shalmaneser III (ca. 883–859 and 858–824) disclose the presence of other Aramean states as far W as the river Euphrates, the major ones being Bit-Adini, Bit-Bahyan, Bit-Khalupe, and Bit-Zaman. References in various Assyrian inscriptions mention Aramean tribes taking control of these areas at the end of the 11th century, and the Assyrian kings plainly felt they had a right to rule there as their forebears had done in the 13th century. Other Aramean groups settled along the lower course of the Euphrates and farther E, all the way into Babylonia.

These Assyrian kings subjected the rulers they conquered, but allowed them, or chosen replacements, to continue to rule, requiring only loyalty and regular tribute. This was the case, it seems, at Guzan, where local princes ruled their people with the title "king" (*mlk*), but in their own Assyrian text they were called "governor" (*šaknu;* Abou-Assaf, Bordreuil and Millard 1982). Refusal of some to remain submissive or joining alliances with still independent states brought Assyrian troops back in punitive campaigns which occasionally led to the installation of Assyrian governors and officials in place of the local rulers. The career of Akhuni of Bit-Adini exemplifies the process. Having submitted to Assyria in 876 B.C., he was hostile to the next Assyrian king, Shalmaneser III, who eventually disposed of him and made his major town, Til-Barsip, an Assyrian stronghold (855 B.C.).

Under the leadership of Adad-idri (Hadadezer) of Damascus, an alliance of kings opposed the Assyrians. Among them were Urhilina of Hamath (whose name is neo-Hittite) and Ahab of Israel. The battle of Qarqar in 853 was followed by Assyrian attacks in 849, 848, and 845 until the coalition broke down. Two Assyrian campaigns against Damascus (841, 838) brought home booty, including a bead from a temple in a city of Hazael, king of Damascus (*ANET,* 281), but Damascus itself was not taken. Shalmaneser fought in Cilicia as well, defeating the Aramean king of Samʾal, Khayan, in 858. Khayan, together with Arame of Aguš (Arpad), paid tribute to him in 853 B.C.

The years of unrest and relative weakness of Assyria which followed allowed some of the Syrian states to strengthen themselves. A revolt in Gozan (Tell Halaf), suppressed in 808 B.C., was perhaps the outburst of nationalism by King Kapara, whose sculptures the German excavators found (see C, below). However, since he and his father, Khayan, remain unattested in other texts, the date cannot be set, and some would place him almost a century earlier (Abou-Assaf, Bordreuil, and Millard 1982: 100–1; Sader 1987: 30–44).

b. Hebrew Sources. In the SW, Aramean expansion met another recently established people, Israel. Apart from the obscure Cushan-rishathaim of Aram-naharaim who oppressed Israel early in the settlement period (Judg 3:8–10), the first Aramean groups encountered by Israel are the states of Zobah and Beth-Rehob in the days of Saul and David (1 Sam 14:47; 2 Sam 8:3, 5; 10:6–19; 13:37–39). These lay in the Lebanon Valley with Zobah extending to the N. The king of Zobah whom David fought was Hadadezer of Beth-rehob, his name being the same as that of the 9th-century king of Damascus who faced Shalmaneser III (in Assyrian texts Hadad-idri). Hadadezer had made himself overlord of all Syria, and David's final conquest of him "when he went to restore his control along the Euphrates River," and of the forces that came to his aid, gave Israel suzerainty over the whole of that territory at one blow (2 Sam 8:3–8, an event which apparently followed the campaigns in Transjordan, 2 Sam 10–12). A later Assyrian report of Aram capturing Pethor and Mutkinu on the Euphrates at about 1000 may refer to Hadadezer's rule (*LAR* 1.603). Hadadezer's intervention in Transjordan is the first sign of a long-continuing Syrian interest in that area (2 Samuel 10). Hadadezer did not rule in Damascus, but during Solomon's reign one Rezin set himself up as king there. At the end of the 10th century, Asa of Judah (ca. 911–870) hired "Ben-Hadad son of Tabrimmon, the son of Hezion, king of Aram, who was ruling in Damascus" against Israel, asking him to break his pact with Baasha of Israel and institute treaty relations such as had existed between their fathers (1 Kgs 15:18, 19). Some scholars suggest the ancestor Hezion was identical with Rezin, the names being linguistically equivalent (see *POTT,* n.23). The description "king of Aram, who was ruling in Damascus" may imply that the title "king of Aram" was not yet as tightly bound to that city as it became in Israelite perspective (cf. 1 Kgs 20:1). That the Ben-Hadad of Asa's time was the same as the Ben-Hadad of Ahab's is disputed (see BEN-HADAD). The name is possibly a dynastic one, and the Ben-Hadad who fought Ahab (1 Kings 20) and whom Hazael murdered (2 Kgs 8:7–15) could be a successor, the Adad-idri of the Qarqar alliance (see a. above). There is no support for W. F. Albright's contention that the Melqart Stele (*ANET,* 501; *ANEP,* 499), found near Aleppo, was erected by Ben-Hadad, son of Tab-rimmon (Pitard 1987: 138–44; note that the reading proposed there is as speculative as all others because the surface of the stone is too abraded to permit any certain reading of line 2). Ben-Hadad enjoyed both success and failure in his attempts to dominate Israel (1 Kings 20, 22). Some coercion may have brought Ahab of Israel to his side at Qarqar (853), the battle which resulted in Ahab's death and also demonstrated that there was no deep bond between the two kings (ca. 852; 1 Kings 22), despite occasional trade agreements (1 Kgs 20:34). Hazael, whose accession is set about 843 by Assyrian texts, continued to harass Israel (2 Kgs 8–12; 13:3, 7). During its period of power, Damascus absorbed the kingdoms of Zobah, Geshur, and Maacah, and overran Israelite territory in the NE (1 Chr 2:23; Mazar 1986: 121–22).

c. Aramean Sources. No Aramean chronicles or annals survive. From the 9th century B.C. there are a very few royal inscriptions and no other Aramaic texts. Of primary importance is the statue of a ruler from Tell Fekheriyeh (ancient Sikan, next to Tell Halaf, ancient Gozan), which reveals that the local king and his father doubled as Assyrian prefects for the region about 870–825 (Abou-Assaf, Bordreuil, and Millard 1982; a later date is canvassed by H. Sader [1987: 26, 27], but on the less than compelling grounds of artistic style). A king of Aram named Bar-Hadad dedicated a stele to Melqart (of Tyre), but the location of his realm is uncertain (see above). From the same date are two ivory plaques inscribed "for our lord Hazael" which had been taken as booty to Assyrian palaces at Arslan-Tash (ancient Hadatu) and Nimrud (ancient Kalhu); neither yield much information.

From these varied sources the following very incomplete outline of the Arameans in the 9th century emerges. Independent tribal states had grown up around various old urban centers where Arameans had overcome the local populace and replaced or dominated them. However, some towns of the earlier dynasties, survivors from the Hittite Empire, continued to maintain themselves.

2. 8th Century B.C. Combining sources gives a more coherent picture (for greater detail, see *CAH* 3/1:372–441). About the year 800 B.C. Hazael apparently still ruled a powerful Damascus, giving way ca. 797–796 to his son Ben-Hadad III, who was still able to dominate Israel. In the north of Syria, Arpad, overcome by Shalmaneser III, was now resurgent under Atar-šumki, son of Adramu. He led a group of eight princes who suffered renewed Assyrian attacks in 805 and 804, then submitted to Adad-nirari III without losing independence. All the Aramean regions to the east were now under Assyrian control, their governors in some cases still being local dignitaries (e.g., Bur-Sagale of Gozan, Millard 1972: Oded 1979), although there were rebellions from time to time (Gozan in 759–758). Adad-nirari III and his three sons who succeeded him were either content to, or not able to do more than, hold formal suzerainty over the states of west Syria, not interfering unless they acted against Assyrian interests. The apparent weakness of Assyria between 800 and 745 is partially belied by the campaigns against Aramean states on several separate occasions, and by Assyria's role in determining the boundary between two of them.

The kingdom of Hamath (modern Ḥama) separated Arpad from Damascus. In the 10th century, Hamath and Damascus had been hostile toward each other (2 Sam 8:9), but in the 9th century they joined forces against Shalmaneser III. At that time the rulers of Hamath bore "neo-Hittite" names (cf. "the kings of the Hittites" 2 Kgs 7:6), but early in the 8th century one with a West Semitic name, Zakkur, seized the throne. A usurper, perhaps from Ana on the mid-Euphrates (Millard fc.), he incurred the enmity of his neighbors. Ben-Hadad (Bar-Hadad) of Damascus led a coalition against him including kings of Arpad, Que, the Amq, Gurgum, Samʾal, and Melid (*ANET,* 655). They besieged Zakkur in Hazrak, north of Hamath, capital of the Lu'ash region, but divine intervention saved Zakkur, whose stele commemorates it. This event is plausibly associated with an Assyrian campaign "against Mansuate" in 796. Mansuate was evidently NW of Damascus, and part of its territory, so the same campaign is identified with the one in which Adad-nirari III took heavy tribute from "Mariʾ" king of Damascus (Mariʾ, Aramaic for "my lord," being a title of the king). The death of Hazael may have given the Assyrians the opportunity they needed to reassert control over S Syria and to support a pro-Assyrian king in Hamath. The Assyrian king then drew the border between Arpad and Hamath. All Syria's main states were subject to him. No Assyrian armies invaded for twenty years afterward, according to the available records.

Ben-Hadad III began his rule continuing Hazael's domination of Israel, but "the Lord provided a deliverer" (2 Kgs 13:3–5). This unidentified deliverer may be seen as the Assyrian king Adad-nirari III or his commander-in-chief, Šami-ilu, in the expedition of 796 (Millard 1973: 162). Whoever the deliverer was, Damascus became weaker, so that Jehoash of Israel defeated Ben-Hadad three times, recovering territory lost to Hazael (2 Kgs 13:25). The next king of Israel, Jeroboam II (ca. 793–753) created a realm that encompassed Damascus, reaching the border of the Hamathite kingdom, if not claiming authority over it (2 Kgs 14:25, 28). Jeroboam's ascendancy may have followed Assyrian campaigns against Damascus in 773 and Hazrak in 772. With his death that power was lost because an isolated Assyrian document mentions that Khayan ruled Damascus about 773. Whether this was the personal name of Ben-hadad III or a successor is unknown. Sometime after 750, Rezin occupied the throne of Damascus. Tiglath-pileser II names him among his tributaries from 738 B.C. onward. With Tyre and Israel, Rezin tried to force Judah to join a league against Assyria, but Ahaz secured his position by submitting to Tiglath-pileser (2 Kgs 15:5–9). Damascus fell and Rezin was executed in Assyrian campaigns of 733 and 732 and the region became an Assyrian province.

In the north, Matiʿ-ʾel followed his father Atar-šumki on the throne of Arpad. In 754 Aššur-nirari V of Assyria imposed a vassal treaty on him (*ANET,* 532–33). Matiʿ-ʾel also entered another pact with a suzerain called Bar-gaʾyah, king of a country whose name is written *ktk,* whose identity is a riddle still awaiting a convincing solution (for an impressive attempt see Lemaire and Durand 1984). The Aramaic stelae presenting the terms of the treaty, although incomplete, are the longest specimens of Old Aramaic. This agreement may have been the cause of Ashur-nirari V's attack or, if Arpad joined with Bar-gaʾyah afterward, the cause of further Assyrian campaigns against Arpad in 743–740.

Accidental preservation of a series of stone monuments at Zinjirli (ancient Samʾal) reveals the history of this small state between ca. 800 and 725. King Panammu, son of QRL (reading unknown), perhaps a son of Kilamuwa, boasts of his prosperity on a statue erected to honor the god Hadad. Family quarrels led to the death of Bar-Ṣur, probably a son of Panammu, and seventy royal sons (cf. 2 Kgs 10:1–11). Eventually the Assyrian Tiglath-pileser II set Panammu II, son of Bar-Ṣur, on the throne. His son, Bar-Rakkab, inscribed a statue in memory of his father, who died fighting with the Assyrians at Damascus, ca. 732. Bar-Rakkab's own inscriptions record his loyalty to Tiglath-pileser III, who died in 727. Sometime thereafter Samʾal was annexed by the Assyrians and Esarhaddon erected a stele there (see CAH 3/1:372–441; Sader 1987: 153–84; *TSSI* 2: 60–93).

Sargon II of Assyria crushed a revolt in Hamath led by Yau-biʾdi (720) and with that blow extinguished any flickering hopes of Aramean nationalism. All the former Aramean territories had already become provinces of the Assyrian empire. Arameans continued to live in them, but their identity was diluted by the Assyrian deportations (Oded 1979). The tribes in Babylonia maintained a quasi-independent status, joining Chaldeans and Elamites in anti-Assyrian uprisings, but their identity, too, became blurred during the Neo-Babylonian empire.

3. Later Times. The adjective "Aramean" continued in use as a description of individuals after all the Aramean states had disappeared. Sennacherib's counselor Ahiqar was so titled in the 5th-century B.C. papyrus copy of his story, and Jews living in Egypt were sometimes called Arameans at Elephantine at the same time (*CAP,* 15–16; Kraeling 1969: 47). The term probably came to denote one whose native language was Aramaic, and it was through their language and script that the Arameans left their mark on world history, and in the New Testament.

B. Prehistory of the Arameans

The scribes of Tiglath-pileser I qualified the Arameans as *ahlamu* (see as above). None of the various explanations proposed for *ahlamu* have proved satisfactory, and it may be a proper name (see Moscati 1959). After the texts of Tiglath-pileser I and Aššur-bel-kala, the word almost disappears from cuneiform records, except in one aspect of scribal tradition. Babylonian academics included some foreign words in the lexical texts they compiled, and among them are a few plant names which are labeled "Ahlamite," and in certain Persian and Seleucid period texts Ahlamite clearly means Aramaic or Aramean (Brinkman 1968: n. 1799). Thus this name was well rooted in Babylonian. Persons described as Ahlamite appear sporadically in documents of the latter half of the 2d millennium B.C., and as far back as the reign of Ammiṣaduqa of Babylon (ca. 1646–1626 B.C.) a tribe of Ahlamites was living near Sippar (*RGTC* 5:5; *RGTC* 3:5; van Lerberghe 1982). Although the relationship of Ahlamu to Arameans is unclear, the Assyrians saw it as very close, so a scribe of the 9th century might have termed "Aramean" the people whom his predecessor in the 13th century B.C. would have termed "Ahlamite." The situation can be understood if the Ahlamites were the section or group of the Arameans whom the Babylonians first encountered. (A similar situation led Europeans to give the name "Chinese" to all the Han peoples because the rulers of the Ch'in state controlled the regions to the west; see Bishop: 1938.)

Besides the cuneiform references to Ahlamu before 1100 B.C., various occurrences of Aram have been cited as evidence that this name was current in earlier periods to denote the Aramean people (Dupont-Sommer 1953). Further investigation has shown that none of these can be definitely linked with Aram, and all are personal or place names, never gentilics (Kupper 1957: 112–14). Exceptions to this verdict are two examples of Aram in Egyptian texts. A list of place names from the reign of Amenophis III (ca. 1390–1352) mentions "the one of Aram" (Eg *p3-jrm*), and a report from an officer on the eastern frontier of the Delta about 1210 tells of a colleague arriving from a town "in the district of Aram" (Edel 1966: 28; *ANET*, 258–59). When only the second text was available, scholars emended Aram to Amor, but the discovery of the earlier text makes that unlikely). At Ugarit a king gave away land including "fields of Arami" which might, in the light of the Egyptian evidence, be the same name. These are the earliest occurrences of Aram which could be identified with the Arameans and their territory, outside the Old Testament text.

The Patriarchal Narratives of Genesis claim the presence of Arameans in upper Mesopotamia early in the 2d millennium B.C. (for the date, see ABRAHAM). It was to Aram-naharaim that Abraham's servant went to find a wife for Isaac, and her relatives are titled "Arameans" (Gen 24:10; 25:20, cf. 28:5; 31:20, 24). Commentators usually call these references anachronistic, assuming that they are additions to old stories, or that they came naturally to writers of the late Monarchy, the exilic, or postexilic periods, who were rewriting traditional tales, or inventing the stories. If that were the case, their portrayal of a specific region "Aram" in upper Mesopotamia at a time when all independent states had been absorbed into provinces of the Assyrian, Babylonian, or Persian empires reflects knowledge of either an older position, or an ethnic or geographic rather than political terminology, otherwise unknown to us. After the mainly hostile relations between the national states of Israel, Judah, and the Arameans of Damascus during the Monarchy, it would be startling to find Israel asserting her ancestors were Arameans without any qualification, so claiming kinship with a different people, and jeopardizing their national distinctiveness. If, on the other hand, the Genesis and related references to Aram are accepted as coming from the early 2d millennium B.C. with the narratives in which they stand, they tell of Aramean people living in upper Mesopotamia at least 6 centuries before other sources mention such a people there. Before discounting this as incredible, it is necessary to ask if it is possible. Studies of ANE cultures show that it is. Documentation is sporadic even for major centers like Nineveh and Babylon; knowledge of upper Mesopotamia depends largely upon what was recorded in other places (e.g., Mari, Aššur, Nineveh, Hattušas), only a few texts have been found in that area itself. One town, Sikan, is known to have existed in the 9th century because both Assyrian texts and the inscription of a local king attest it (Abou-Assaf, Bordreuil, and Millard 1982), but it is also mentioned in a text written at the end of the 3d millennium B.C. (Salvini 1982: 18; *RGTC* 2: 164). Unless the town was known by the slightly different name *Waššukanni* in the 2d millennium B.C., there is a large gap in its history, and from the 1st millennium sources alone it might have been considered a place first built by the Arameans. (For other examples of words and types of objects "hibernating" in this way, see Millard 1984 and 1986). That the Pentateuch preserves very ancient information about the Arameans in a comparable way should not, therefore, be totally rejected; to do so is to risk deforming the evidence.

Of course, the Patriarchal Narratives reached their present form long after the events they describe; Laban the Aramean probably did not speak what is now recognized as Aramaic, any more than Abraham spoke biblical Hebrew. A picture of the Arameans originating as a tribe in Upper Mesopotamia about 2000, remaining there for several centuries, gradually growing, until increased numbers, drought, famine, and other agents forced them to spread E and W seems plausible. The eruption of the Aramean tribes into upper Mesopotamia and their expansion into Babylonia is comparable with the spread of the Amorites along the same routes a millennium earlier. Kinship of Arameans and Amorites is possible, but the attempt by M. Noth (1961) to prove the Arameans originated from the Amorites was disproved by D. O. Edzard (1964). Certainly there are a few similarities, such as names beginning with *ya* or ending with *-an,* and although when the only distinctive Aramean feature, the language, can be analyzed—and none survives from before ca. 850 B.C.—it has some markedly different characteristics (see the ARAMAIC articles), no more can be said at present than that both stem from a common NW Semitic ancestor. The declaration of Deut 26:5, "My father was a wandering Aramean," which asserts a shift to a higher status, reflects the same traditions, and can be understood well in the light of 2d millennium B.C. society (Millard 1980).

The prehistory of the Arameans remains to be elucidated through future discoveries of texts from the region which seems to have been their home, the "land between the two rivers," sometimes specified as "Aram between the rivers" (Aram-naharaim). It is noteworthy that the earliest occurrences of the name "Naharaim," outside the Bible, are in Egyptian texts which present it in the form *nhrn* with a shift of final *m* to *n,* a feature later found in Aramaic (*NBD,* 67). The construction Aram plus qualifier recurs in the expressions Aram-Beth-Rehob, Aram-Damascus, Aram-Maacah, and Aram-Zobah in the OT, and is reminiscent of the reverse forms such as Sippar-Amnanum and Sippar-Yahrurum of the OB period (Kupper 1957: 51–52; 75–76). The former define the segment of the tribe by its settlement, the latter define the segment of the settlement by the resident tribe. For a people to be called after the region they inhabited early in their history is a normal occurrence. Aram, therefore, may have been a region in upper Mesopotamia from which the Arameans took their name.

Relationships between the people and the men named Aram in Genesis are not clear. Aram, son of Shem, Asshur, and Elam (Gen 10:22, 23) appear to be intended as national ancestors of their respective nations. The Aram son of Kemuel, son of Nahor, and Chesed son of Nahor (Gen 22:21) may be coincidental rather than ancestors of the Arameans and Chaldeans.

C. Aramean Society

The Mesopotamian cuneiform texts provide valuable information about the Arameans. There were numerous tribes or clans; the names of over forty are listed for Babylonia. The meager evidence about them shows they retained some measure of identity until the rise of the Neo-Babylonian state late in the 7th century B.C. and that they were scattered in many small villages rather than occupying large towns (Brinkman 1984: 12–15). When the Arameans set up recognizable states in N Mesopotamia and Syria, these were mostly distinguished by tribal names. Some were descriptive, like Teman, "southerner," others perhaps derived from eponymous ancestors, such as Bit-Aguš, for which an ancestor named Guš or Aguš seems to be attested. The tribes clustered around tribal centers which sometimes gave their names to the kingdoms that developed, such as Damascus. Each tribe was ruled by its own chieftains or sheikhs, whom Assyrian texts perhaps entitled *našiku* (Heb *nāsîk* Josh 13:21). Adad-nirari II of Assyria faced three different rulers of the Teman tribe (*GARI* 2: 424–30), and there were a number governing the Laqê tribes on the mid-Euphrates at the same time. According to 1 Kgs 20:1–34, when Ben-Hadad II of Damascus failed to capture Samaria with thirty-two kings in his alliance, he replaced them with governors.

During the 9th century B.C. most of the Aramean states developed into monarchies, their kings vying with one another for power and greater realms. There was probably never an Aramean empire (contra Mazar 1986), rather an ever-changing pattern of alliances dominated by the strongest king of the moment, which was often the king of Damascus (as Bar-Hadad II at the Battle of Qarqar, Bar-Hadad III against Zakkur of Hamath).

The Arameans were seminomadic pastoralists, based in villages set in the countryside near good sources of water. Some of the populace remained in the villages throughout the year, while others took the flocks to find pasture. In this they followed the style attested for the Amorites a millennium before, for Laban and his family (Genesis 29–30), and for others since. The term *kaprum*, "village," known in the Mari tablets, continued as a designation for Aramean settlements (Aram *kĕpar*). The Aramean lifestyle affected the Assyrian language, which took over their terms for steppe and hill country (*mudabiru*, cf. Heb *midbar*, and *gabᶜani*, cf. Heb *gibᶜâ*).

Assyrian lists of booty taken from Aramean towns include grain, cattle, and sheep, and about 700 B.C. the area around Harran was occupied by small farmers raising livestock, grain, and vines, according to the "Harran Census" (Fales 1973). Unfortunately, lacking Aramaic documents, legal deeds, and any literature, it is impossible to describe their social customs in any detail.

D. Aramean Culture and Religion

The Aramean states were centered around existing cities and absorbed the remnants of LB populations. Although many cities in the W suffered in the upheavals of the 12th century, knowledge and skills survived. Aramean tribesmen assimilated much of the material culture of their predecessors and the continuing traditions of the Hittites. Of prime importance was the adoption of the Phoenician alphabet for writing the Aramaic dialects even though the phonemes did not correspond exactly. This script spread with the Arameans all over the Near East and, with the Persians, into India. The simplicity of the alphabet enabled it to supplant cuneiform, a process already beginning in Mesopotamia under the Assyrians (Millard 1983).

1. Art of the Arameans. Palaces of Aramean kings unearthed at Tell Halaf and Zinjirli display the plan identified by scholars as the *bīt hīlani* which Assyrian kings admired and copied as a "Hittite" (i.e. western) style. A wide portico led to a long reception or throne room with a latrine and stairwell at one end and sometimes smaller rooms behind. The stairs probably rose to an upper story containing a major room above the portico lit by a series of recessed windows.

These and other important buildings were adorned with sculptures. Usually they were carved in low relief on slabs up to three feet high. Doorways were guarded by lions, bulls, or mythical beasts, and at Tell Halaf the pillars of the portico were divine or human figures carved in basalt. (Other palaces may have had carved wooden pillars which do not survive.) These carvings follow Hittite styles and were presumably made by artists trained in a few central schools. It is almost impossible to distinguish sculptures made for neo-Hittite rulers at Malatya (ancient Melid), Carchemish, or Hamath from those made for Aramean kings at Zinjirli or Tell Halaf (*CAH* 3: Plates, 65–91). Assyrian influences do appear in some cases, however, as in the Tell Fekheriye statue of Hadda-yishᶜi, king of Gozan (Abou-Assaf, Bordreuil, and Millard 1982). The Melqart Stele of an unidentified Bar-Hadad and a slab carved with a sphinx found in Damascus have Phoenician models (see *ANEP*, 494). Thus no truly Aramean sculptural style can be identified.

Aramean seals are equally without distinguishing features. Both stamp and cylinder seals carry common Phoenician, Assyrian, Babylonian, or Persian motifs; only the correlation of script and name forms allow them to be identified as Aramean (Bordreuil 1986: 75–107 shows good examples).

Carved ivory panels decorating wooden furniture found at Assyrian and Syrian sites (Nimrud, Tell Halaf, Tell Taᶜyinat, Hamath) share a somewhat heavy style which is comparable with the neo-Hittite stone carving and may indicate a school of craftsmen at home in N Syria, perhaps at Hamath. In contrast, plaques of finer, more elegant appearance, with evident Egyptian models, may stem from a workshop in Damascus (Winter 1976; 1981). Both styles are local adaptations of motifs current elsewhere.

No specifically Aramean metalwork or jewelry can be isolated, although some bronze bowls found at Nimrud show similar artistic forms to the S Syrian ivories and have been claimed as "Aramean Art" (Barnett 1967). In pottery the red burnish known in early Iron Age Palestine is widespread among Aramean settlements, but its origin is not yet known.

2. Aramean Religion. Scattered Aramean inscriptions, rare references in the OT and cuneiform texts, later recollections, and the evidence of personal names are the only sources for knowledge of Aramean religion during the time of the native kingdoms. More extensive information from the Persian and Hellenistic eras (notably from the Elephantine papyri and the Palmyrene inscriptions) may echo earlier phases, but only very careful investigation can separate the concepts of different periods.

Each city had its own pantheon and patron deity, sometimes tied to the ruling family (as Rakkab-el at Zinjirli). However, Hadad or Hadda was the most prominent deity and patron of the kings of Damascus who called themselves Bar-Hadad, "Son of Hadad." He had a temple in Damascus—probably where the Umayyad Mosque stands—where he was also known as Ramman, "the Thunderer" (Greenfield 1987). Whether he or El, the supreme god, was known as Beᶜel-šamem ("lord of heaven") is unclear. Beᶜel-šamem was the one who gave victory to Zakkur of Hamath, advising him through prophets and oracles, yet Zakkur erected his stele of thanksgiving to El-wer, his patron, a form of the god Hadad. In the N the moon god was prominent, Harran being his ancient seat. He was known either by his West Semitic name Šahr, or by the Aramaic form of the Babylonian moon god Sin, Siʾ. Other gods named include Šemeš, the sun; Rešep, god of plague; Baᶜalat; ᶜAtar (earlier Athtar); and ᶜAtta (earlier ᶜAnat). All of these divinities were indigenous; the Arameans only adopted them and made certain culture-specific changes. Others were adopted from Assyrian and Babylonian: Nabu, Našuh (Nusku), (N)Inurta, and Nergal. In the Sefire treaty the divinities invoked include several pairs, El and ᶜElyon, Heaven and Earth, Day and Night. These pairs which are apparently sometimes hypostatizations, but not necessarily in male and female oppositions (*ANET,* 659). Personal names often reveal the traditional or popular attitudes to the gods (see Fowler 1988).

Temples and shrines certainly existed, but so far, excavations reveal little concerning them. The small temple beside the palace at Tell Taᶜyinat, although built in a neo-Hittite town, may indicate that the simple plan of entry, main hall, and shrine, inherited from the 2d millennium, was normal. There is no doubt that hilltops and springs must have been sites for pilgrimage and worship. Prayers and vows, festivals with communal meals, and celebrations of the dead are known from various Aramaic texts.

Bibliography

Abou-Assaf, A.; Bordreuil, P.; and Millard, A. R. 1982. *La Statue de Tell Fekherye et son inscription bilingue assyro-araméenne.* Paris.

Barnett, R. D. 1967. Layard's Nimrud Bronzes and their Inscriptions. *EI* 8: 1–7.

Bishop, C. W. 1938. An Ancient Chinese Capital. *Antiquity* 12: 68–78.

Bordreuil, P. 1986. *Catalogue des sceaux ouest-sémitiques inscrits.* Paris.

Brinkman, J. A. 1968. *A Political History of Post-Kassite Babylonia, 1158–722 B.C.* 43. Rome.

———. 1984. *Prelude to Empire. Babylonian Society and Politics 747–626 B.C.* Philadelphia.

Dupont-Sommer, A. 1953. Les débuts de l'histoire araméenne. VT Sup. 1: 40–49.

Edel, E. 1966. *Die Ortsnamenlisten aus dem Toten Tempel Amenophis III.* Bonn.

Edzard, D. O. 1964. Mari und Aramäer? *ZA* 56 n.22: 142–49.

Fales, F. M. 1973. *Censimenti e Catasti di Epoca Neo-Assira.* Rome.

Fowler, J. D. 1988. *Theophoric Personal Names in Ancient Hebrew. A Comparative Study.* JSOT Supp. Series 49. Sheffield.

Garbini, G. 1959. Il problema dell'Arte Aramaica. *Revist a degli Studi Orientali* 34: 141–47.

Greenfield, J. C. 1987. Aspects of Aramean Religion. Pp. 67–78 in *Ancient Israelite Religion: Essays in Honor of Frank Moore Cross,* ed. P. D. Miller, Jr., P. D. Hanson, and S. D. McBride. Philadelphia.

Kraeling, E. G. 1969. *The Brooklyn Museum Aramaic Papyri.* New Haven.

Kupper, J.-R. 1957. *Les nomades en Mésopotamie au temps des rois de Mari.* Paris.

Lemaire, A., and Durand, J.-M. 1984. *Les inscriptions araméennes de Sefireé et l'Assyrie de Shamshi-ilu.* Geneva and Paris.

Lerberghe, K. van. 1982. New Data from the Archive Found in the House of Ur-Utu at Tell ed-Dēr. Pp. 380–83 in *Vorträge gehalten auf der 28 Rencontre Internationale in Wien 6.–10. Juli 1981.* AfO Beiheft 19, ed. H. Hirsch. Horn, Austria.

Mazar, B. 1961. Geshur and Maacah. *JBL* 80: 16–28. Repr. Pp. 113–25 in *The Early Biblical Period, Historical Studies,* B. Mazar. Jerusalem. 1986.

———. 1962. The Aramean Empire and Its Relations with Israel. *BA* 25: 97–120. Repr. Pp. 151–72 in *Early Biblical Period.*

Millard, A. R. 1972. ⸢*ša ekalli - šgl -* ᵈ*sagale. UF* 4: 161.

———. 1973. Adad-nirari III, Aram and Arpad. *PEQ* 105: 161–64.

———. 1980. A Wandering Aramean. *JNES* 39: 153–55.

———. 1983. Assyrians and Aramaeans. *Iraq* 45: 101–8.

———. fc. The Home of Zakkur. *Semitica* 38.

Moscati, S. 1959. The Aramaean Ahlamu. *JSS* 4: 303–7.

Noth, M. 1961. *Die Ursprünge des alten Israel im Licht neuer Quellen.* Arbeitsgemeinschaft für Forschung des Landes Nordrhein-Westfalen, Geisteswissenschaften 94. Cologne.

Oded, B. 1979. *Mass Deportations and Deportees in the Neo-Assyrian Empire.* Wiesbaden.

Pitard, W. T. 1987. *Ancient Damascus. A Historical Study of the Syrian City-State from Earliest Times until Its Fall to the Assyrians in 732 B.C.E.* Winona Lake, IN.

Sader, H. 1987. *Les états araméens de Syrie depuis leur fondation jusqu'à leur transformation en provinces assyriennes.* Beiruter Texte und Studien 36. Beirut and Wiesbaden.

Salvini, M., and Pecorella, P. E. 1982. *Tell Barri—Kahat* 1. Rome.

Winter, I. J. 1976. Phoenician and North Syrian Ivory Carving in Historical Context: Questions of Style and Distribution. *Iraq* 38: 1–22.

———. 1981. Is There a Syrian Style of Ivory Carving in the Early First Millennium B.C.? *Iraq* 43: 101–30.

Zadok, R. 1985. Some Problems in Early Aramean History. Pp. 81–85 in *XXII Deutscher Orientalistentag vom 21. bis 25. Marz 1983 in Tübingen,* ed. W. Röllig. *ZDMGSup* 6. Wiesbaden.

A. R. MILLARD

ARAN (PERSON) [Heb ʾ*arān*]. A clan name associated with tribal groups living in the region of Edom and mentioned in the genealogy of Seir the Horite. These peoples, not to be confused with Hurrians, inhabited that area prior to the coming of the Esau clans, a more aggressive people who subsequently dispossessed them (Deut 2:12–22). Their designation as "cave dwellers" may be a reflection of their true condition, or it may be a disparaging remark by their conquerors. Aran is listed as the second of the two sons of Dishan, and he is thus the grandson of Seir. The name appears in this form in both Gen 36:28 and in the matching genealogical clan list in 1 Chr 1:42. Aran may be a variant of the name OREN, a man (clan name) mentioned in the genealogy of the tribe of Judah in 1 Chr 2:25 as the son of Jerameel.

VICTOR H. MATTHEWS

ARARAT (PLACE) [Heb *ʾărārāṭ*]. A country located in eastern Asia Minor which flourished from the 9th to the 6th centuries B.C.E. Its center was near Lake Van and its boundaries (uncertain at times and places) extended into modern Iran, Iraq, Russia, and Turkey. A conservative estimate of its area is roughly that of the state of Kansas (ca. 82,000 sq. mi.) and the maximum estimate is about 200,000 sq. mi. It was within the "mountains of Ararat" that, according to the biblical account (Gen 8:4), Noah's ark came to rest. A specific peak is not mentioned, and the modern designation "Mt. Ararat" does not occur in Scripture. (See ARK, NOAH'S.)

Jeremiah uses the term to designate a large geographical area when he speaks of "kingdoms" being summoned by the deity: Ararat, Minni, and Ashkenaz (51:27). Similarly, the author of 2 Kgs refers to assassins fleeing to "the land of Ararat" (19:37; cf. Isa 37:38). Assyrian records often refer to the same area as a country called Urartu.

A. The History of Ararat/Urartu

The term, of Assyrian origin, seems to be geographically descriptive ("mountainous country"?) rather than ethnic, and first occurs in the records of King Shalmaneser I (early 13th century, B.C.E.). He used it to refer to a collection of eight political entities situated southeast of Lake Van, against whom he mounted a successful military campaign. His son (Tukulti-Ninurta) refers to the same area as "the lands of Nairi" and mentions forty-three local rulers whom he defeated there. For a while, the terms "Urartu" and "Nairi" are used concurrently, but finally the more comprehensive geographical term (Urartu) predominates. Natives of the area, however, prefer the designation "the land of Biainili," and only one known inscription refers to it as "Urartu."

By the late 9th century, a unified Urartian state emerged under the rule of King Sarduri I, whose dynasty was to continue for the next two centuries. Mutual defense against Assyrian incursion may have contributed to the process of unification (Zimansky 1985: chap. 4). Since the country was situated at the junction of major mountain ranges (Pontic, Zagros, and Caucasus), multiple access was available to the potential invader through valleys. At the same time, the partitions of the area, created by high ridges, insulated it from sustained foreign control.

Expansion, especially to the SW in order to control trade routes and to gain access to the Mediterranean, brought resistance from Assyria, beginning with Sarduri's predecessor, Aramu. Shalmaneser III was forced to campaign against him, and then depicted his activities on the huge bronze gates of the city Imgur-Enlil (modern Balawat), SE of Nineveh. This outstanding example of Assyrian art shows, in successive registers, not only the victorious activities of Shalmaneser's army, but also the nature of Urartian dress, weapons, and valuables which were seized.

At the zenith of their country's power, Urartian monarchs pursued a vigorous program of building which included towns, temples, massive citadels, and irrigation projects (including an aqueduct fifty mi. in length). Financial support came from the natural resources of the area (metals, salt, agricultural products, and horses). Objects of Urartian origin have been found as far afield as Greece and Italy. Manpower for the construction projects was provided by thousands of prisoners who had been captured through the conquest of surrounding territory.

The native hieroglyphic script was inadequate for the needs of a rising bureaucracy and of international diplomacy, and Assyrian cuneiform script was adopted for such purposes. Similar borrowing is evident in Urartian literary style, in the design of military equipment, and in the arts.

An Assyrian revival, under the energetic Tiglath-pileser III (744–727 B.C.E.), included the recovery of territory that had been lost to the Urartians in Syria. Sarduri II lost a major battle (743) but was not pursued into the homeland. In 735, however, the Assyrian king laid seige to the Urartian capitol, Tushpa, on Lake Van. The fortress proved impregnable, but the devastation of the surrounding territory weakened Urartian power and led to the loss of surrounding vassal states. Only with difficulty did the next ruler, Rusa I, succeed in restoring the state, even as the Assyrians were preoccupied with internal problems.

Another Assyrian resurgence began with Sargon II (721–705 B.C.E.), who, in 714, regained territory all along the S and W border of Urartu and even invaded the SE part of the homeland. He reports that he laid waste pastures, agricultural land, and irrigation projects, as well as capturing the sacred city of Musasir and carrying off the statue of the national deity, Haldi. He lists plunder in the amount of a ton of gold, 10 tons of silver, 109 tons of bronze, and more than 300,000 other items (Piotrovsky 1969: 112). Sargon also depicted aspects of his campaign, in massive relief, on the walls of his palace at Dur-Šarrukin (Khorsabad). King Rusa of Urartu, overcome with remorse, committed suicide. Nonetheless, the Urartian state remained intact, even if severely chastened. Restoration began immediately under King Argišti II and his son Rusa II. This included (usually) friendly relations with a massive influx of nomadic tribes from across the Caucasus Range, initially the Cimmerians [Heb *gōmer*] and then the Scythians, much to the consternation of the Assyrians. (Eventually, the Cimmerians skirted Urartu to the NW and settled in central Asia Minor.)

The building of new towns and massive fortifications characterized Urartian royal activity during much of the 7th century, and in this they were so successful that the Assyrians (with troubles of their own) did not desire to renew hostilities.

The end of the Urartian state came swiftly, and from an unexpected source. The Medes, residents of what is now NW Iran, had joined with the Babylonians in bringing the

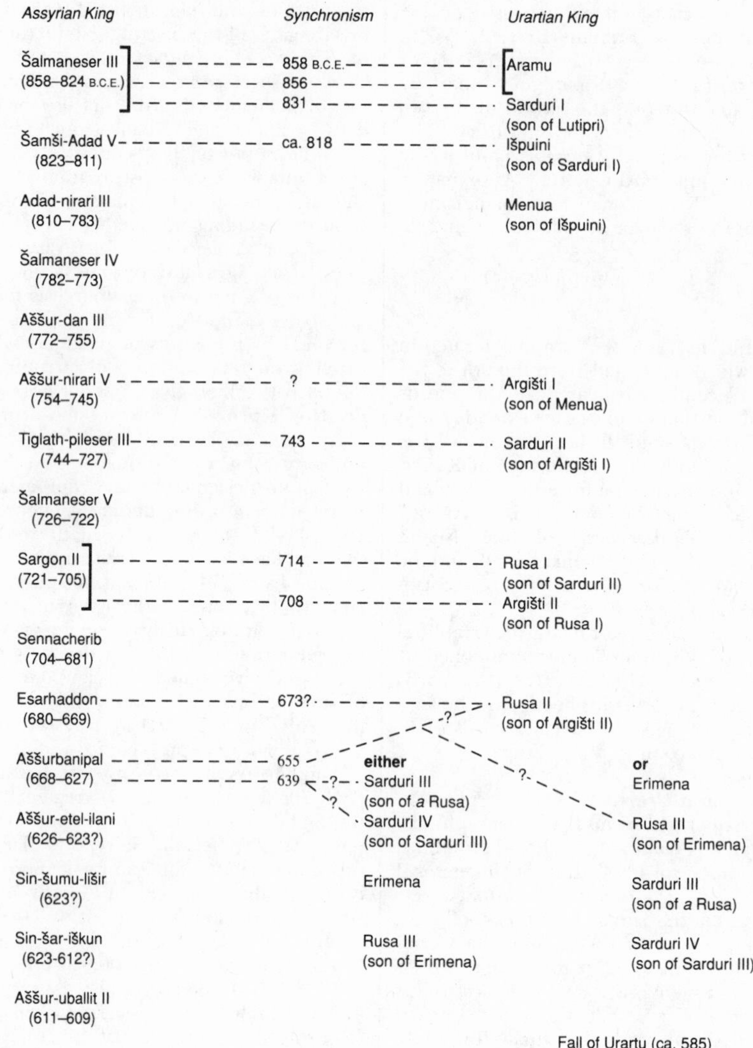

RULERS OF URARTU
Assyrian King
Synchronism
Urartian King
Šalmaneser III
(858–824 B.C.E.)
858 B.C.E.
856
831
Aramu
Sarduri I
(son of Lutipri)
Šamši-Adad V
(823–811)
ca. 818
Išpuini
(son of Sarduri I)
Adad-nirari III
(810–783)
Menua
(son of Išpuini)
Šalmaneser IV
(782–773)
Aššur-dan III
(772–755)
Aššur-nirari V
(754–745)
?
Argišti I
(son of Menua)
Tiglath-pileser III
(744–727)
743
Sarduri II
(son of Argišti I)
Šalmaneser V
(726–722)
Sargon II
(721–705)
714
708
Rusa I
(son of Sarduri II)
Argišti II
(son of Rusa I)
Sennacherib
(704–681)
Esarhaddon
(680–669)
673?
Rusa II
(son of Argišti II)
Aššurbanipal
(668–627)
655
639
either
Sarduri III
(son of a Rusa)
Sarduri IV
(son of Sarduri III)
or
Erimena
Rusa III
(son of Erimena)
Aššur-etel-ilani
(626–623?)
Sin-šumu-lišir
(623?)
Erimena
Sarduri III
(son of a Rusa)
Sin-šar-iškun
(623-612?)
Rusa III
(son of Erimena)
Sarduri IV
(son of Sarduri III)
Aššur-uballit II
(611–609)
Fall of Urartu (ca. 585)

ARA.03. Rulers of Uratu and Assyria—885–585 B.C.E. The sequence of Urartian kings becomes unclear after Rusa II. The length of individual reigns cannot be precisely determined. *(Adapted from the chronological chart in Zimansky 1985: 99.).*

Assyrian Empire to an end. They destroyed the old capital at Ashur in 614 B.C.E. and the new capital at Nineveh in 612. (It is slightly later, in 594, when Jeremiah attests to the existence of the Urartian state, as cited above.) The Medes, assisted by Scythians, then mounted a massive campaign about 585 B.C.E., sweeping over the Urartians and Cimmerians, on their way to battle the king of Lydia, in W Asia Minor. Shortly thereafter, the area was incorporated into the empire of the Persians.

A population element from the SW (mentioned as early as the 7th century by King Sarduri II as "Arme") moved into the former boundaries of Urartu, mingling with the local population. Thus Darius the Persian, reporting his conquest of the area (ca. 520 B.C.E.), refers to it as "Armenia," a designation that endures to the present day. However, the older designation (Urartu/"Ararat") was retained for one of the NE subdivisions. Thus, St. Jerome (4th century, C.E.) can remark that "Ararat is a region in Armenia on the Araxis [River]." This shift in terminology has produced a modern confusion about the location of the biblical "mountains of Ararat" (Gen 8:4) and the landing place of Noah's ark.

B. "Mount Ararat" and Noah's Ark

Within the Araratic subdivision of Armenia (39°42′N; 44°18′E) is a spectacular and isolated mountain, nearly

17,000 feet in elevation, which the Armenian population called Masis. It is now known by the Turks as Büyük ("mount") Ağri Dağ. Around the 11th–12th centuries (C.E.), the tradition developed that it was the landing place of Noah's vessel, and thus modern "ark searchers" have come to call it "Mount Ararat." Claims have been made, without foundation, that remnants of the biblical craft are still to be found there. (See NOAH AND THE ARK.)

Since the ancient kingdom of "Ararat" was much more extensive than the Armenian subdivision, early Jews, Christians, and Muslims sought the ark's landing place on the southern border where the mountains first arise from the Mesopotamian plain. The area of choice was called Qardu(n), and hence the Aramaic and Syriac versions of the Bible render Gen 8:4 as "the mountains of Qardu." Greek and Latin writers refer to the area as that of the Karduchi-people or as Gordyaea (the consonants *g, k,* and *q* easily interchange in these languages). In Turkish, the specific peak is known as Cudi Dağ, and atop its peak Nestorian Christians had erected several monasteries, including one at the summit known as the Cloister of the Ark. Later, the Muslim conquerors erected a mosque at the site and claimed to have removed enough wood of the ark to construct another mosque at the base of the mountain. To them, the mountain was known as Jabal ("mount") Judi, a designation in the Quran for the landing place (11:44). Even in recent times, persons of various faiths gathered annually atop this peak to commemorate Noah's first sacrifice after leaving the Ark (Bell 1911: 38).

Bibliography

Bell, G. L. 1911. *Amurath to Amurath.* New York.

Piotrovsky, B. B. 1969. *The Ancient Civilization of Urartu.* New York.

Zimansky, P. E. 1985. *Ecology and Empire: The Structure of the Urartian State.* SAOC 41. Chicago.

LLOYD R. BAILEY

ARATUS (PERSON). A Stoic poet of Soli in Cilicia (315–240 B.C.E.). A portion of the opening invocation to Zeus from his astronomical poem *Phaenomena* is quoted in the speech of Paul at the Areopagus (Acts 17:28): "For we are indeed his [God's] offspring." *Phaenomena,* Aratus' only completely extant poem, was widely known and liked in the Roman world; it was translated into Latin by Cicero, Caesar Germanicus, and Avienus. The latter two of these translations survive, along with fragments of Cicero's.

HERBERT G. GRETHER

ARAUNAH (PERSON) [Heb *ʾărawnâ*] Var. ORNAN. A Jebusite (non-Israelite native of Jerusalem) who sold David a threshing floor on which the king erected an altar (2 Sam 24:16–25 = 1 Chr 21:15–27). This story established the sanctity of what would become the site of Solomon's temple (1 Chr 22:1, 2 Chr 3:1) by asserting that it was the place where the angel of pestilence had stopped to spare Jerusalem and that David's sacrifice there had averted the epidemic (2 Sam 24:16, 25). The narrative also served to legitimate the temple's location on Jebusite soil by emphasizing that David had purchased the threshing floor in proper legal form and that he had done so at the command of God's prophet, Gad. If historical information can be derived from this sanctuary legend, a possibility denied by Fuss (1962: 164), it may reflect David's tolerant assimilation of the Jebusite elements within his new capital and respect for their property rights outside the walls of the city. It might also indicate that David made some sort of provision for the temple his son would build.

Both Araunah and his threshing floor have been the focus of intense scholarly interest. His puzzling name occurs in several different variants: as Awarnah and Aranyah as well as Araunah in the MT tradition of 2 Samuel 24, as Ornan in Chronicles, and as Orna in the LXX and 4QSam[a]. The name has been explained as the Hittite word for "aristocrat" and more believably as the Hurrian term for "lord." Such suggestions indicate that Araunah was a title rather than a personal name. This observation, coupled with the apparent designation of Araunah as "king" in the MT of 2 Sam 24:23, have led to the opinion, at least as old as Luther, that Araunah was the last Jebusite king of Jerusalem. One scholar has even identified him with Uriah the Hittite (Wyatt 1985: 41–49). It has also been suggested that his "threshing floor" was already a Jebusite holy place and that David took it over for the worship of Yahweh. According to this hypothesis, elements of a pre-Israelite sanctuary legend featuring Araunah as the cult founder can be traced within the present narrative (Ruprecht 1976: 5–17). The disturbed state of the text of 2 Samuel 24 makes it difficult to assess these theories.

The version of this story in 1 Chronicles describes Araunah (Ornan) as a further witness to the angel's appearance along with four of his sons.

Bibliography

Fuss, W. 1962. II Samuel 24. *ZAW* 74: 145–64.

Rupprecht, K. 1976. *Der Tempel von Jerusalem: Gründung Salomos oder jebusitisches Erbe?* BZAW 144. Berlin.

Wyatt, N. 1985. "Araunah the Jebusite" and the Throne of David. *ST* 39: 39–53.

RICHARD D. NELSON

ARBA (PERSON) [Heb *ʾarbaʿ*]. Presented alternately as the greatest of the Anakim (Josh 14:15) and as the father of Anak (Josh 15:13; 21:11). It is unlikely, however, that Arba, which means four, is a personal name. The LXX treats Arba as the name of the principal city of the Anakim and not as the name of its most renowned citizen. Various suggestions for the meaning of Kiriath-arba, the ancient name of the city of Hebron, have been proposed: "city of four clans," "city of four districts," "city of four famous persons." (See Soggin *Joshua* OTL; Miller and Tucker *Joshua* CBC; Noth *Joshua* HAT.)

PAULINE A. VIVIANO

ARBATHITE [Heb *ʿarbātî*]. A gentilic noun, possibly derived from the place name "Arabah" (Heb *ʿărābâh*) (2 Sam 23:31 and 1 Chr 11:32). This place name may be associated with the Arabah (Heb *ʿărābâh*), that is, the Rift (or Jordan) Valley. Applied to one Abi-albon/Abiel in the list of DAVID'S CHAMPIONS, the term "Arbathite" would designate this warrior as an inhabitant of the Arabah. Another, perhaps better, possibility is that Arbathite refers to an inhabitant of Beth-Arabah (M.R. 197139) (Heb *bêt-ʿărābāh*), a village on the border of Judah with Benjamin (cf. Josh 15:6, 61; 18:22; also, LXX Josh 18:18: *Baitharaba*).

D. G. Schley

ARBATTA (PLACE) [Gk *Arbatta*]. Arbatta's only historical mention is in connection with the successful attacks by Simon Maccabaeus against the heathens (1 Macc 5:23). This passage reveals only three certain identifications: Arbatta was N of Jerusalem, S of Ptolemais, and contained a Jewish constituency—perhaps a strong minority. Simon Maccabaeus, the Hasmonaean leader, assisted the "Jews of Galilee and Arbetta" in their S journey to Judea. Suggestions for Arbatta's location include: El-Bateiha, the plain N of the Sea of Galilee, the Arabah, and the toparchy of Akrabattis. The latter is an erroneous association (1 Macc 5:3) and the first two are within the boundaries of Hasmonaean Galilee—an inconsistency with the text. "From Arbatta" may likely be a scribal mistranslation of "from Narbatta." Narbatta, a Jewish enclave in Hasmonaean Caesarea, fits the context of the apocryphal account. The district was inland and on the logical route of Simon, i.e. from Ptolemais, around Mt. Carmel, through the W edge of Galilee, proceeding along the coastal route and then ascending to Jerusalem (Goldstein *1 Maccabees* AB, 300, 533).

Jerry A. Pattengale

ARBELA (PLACE) [Gk *Arbela*]. A city in Galilee captured from Judah in 160 B.C. Demetrius I Soter (Seleucid ruler 162–150 B.C.) sent Bacchides and Alcimus to Judah to battle Judas, eventuating in his death (1 Macc 9:22). The Syrian army departed from Antioch (Josephus, *Ant.* 12.11.1 §421) and came to Arbela in Galilee. 1 Macc 9:2, however, says they traveled "by the road which leads to Gilgal." Goldstein (*1 Maccabees* AB, 372) follows Josephus and reads "*galgala*" as "Galilee," instead of "Gilgal." This reading is appropriate since Greek scribes wrote "*galgala*" for "Galilee" at Josh 22:10 and "Gilgal" for "Galilee" at Josh 12:23 (Goldstein *1 Maccabees* AB, 372).

Arbela (M.R. 195246), probably the same place as Beth-Arbel in Hos 10:14, has long been identified with the unexcavated ruins at the modern village of Irbid, which sits on the SE side of the Wadi Hamam, with a row of caves on the opposite face of the ravine (Grove *SDB*, 148). Josephus says that Bacchides besieged and captured Jews who had fled (presumably from Arbela) into nearby caves (*Ant.* 12.11.1 §421). The full designation of the place of battle in 1 Macc 9:2 is "Messaloth in Arbella." The Heb word *mĕsillôṯ* refers to a raised way, often a highway (but never a city street) or stairs. It is assumed that the "*Messaloth*" of 9:2 was the name for the caves in the vicinity of Arbela. Josephus mentions the caves again as the hideout of robbers (*Ant.* 14.15.4 §415; 14.15.5 §422–28), who were extracted from the caves with hooks when Herod had his men lowered over the face of the cliffs. Josephus also reports that he fortified Arbela (*Life* 37 §188) and held a conference of Jews at the village (*Life* 60 §34).

Bibliography

Tedesche, S., and Zeitlin, S. 1950. *The First Book of Maccabees.* New York.

Paul L. Redditt

ARBITE [Heb *ʾarbî*]. A gentilic noun designating Paarai, one of David's champions (2 Sam 23:35). Arbite is probably derived from the place *ʾărāb,* in the hill country of Judah (Josh 15:52).

D. G. Schley

ARCHAEOLOGY, SYRO-PALESTINIAN AND BIBLICAL. Syro-Palestinian, as well as "biblical" archaeology, have been periodically surveyed by several specialists, including W. F. Albright (1938, 1951, 1969), G. E. Wright (1947, 1958, 1969a, 1969b), P. W. Lapp (1969), A. E. Glock (1985, 1986), W. G. Dever (1974, 1976, 1981, 1985, 1988, fc.b.), Toombs (1987), and P. R. S. Moorey (1981). The present essay will attempt to update the discussion by describing the current "state of the art" with special reference to: (1) the development of this branch of archaeology as a discipline; (2) the elaboration of its theoretical position since ca. 1970; and (3) the distinctive approach of the American "school." Since the purpose of this article is general orientation, the reader will more easily find the *results* of recent archaeology under other entries on specific sites, periods, and topics. Nor will we treat in much detail recent advances in archaeological field *method* (which in most discussions has meant simply excavation technique), since that has been adequately done elsewhere, and indeed a consensus has now been reached on what constitutes good field archaeology (see Dever and Lance 1978; Dever 1980b, 1985; Lance 1981; but cf. Harris 1979, Chapman fc. for still newer techniques).

A few words of explanation may be in order regarding what could seem a narrow and overly speculative approach.

1. The overriding emphasis here on theoretical trends is deliberate and programmatic. Even though it has infrequently been attempted, it is only by placing Syro-Palestinian and biblical archaeology in their changing conceptual framework that we can really appreciate what is happening today. Archaeology is not merely an antiquarian pursuit, the discovery of fascinating relics; it is an intellectual inquiry, one that seeks to penetrate and illumine human experience in the past. Thus *theory*—by which we mean not "speculation," but the basic way in which the discipline of archaeology sees itself—is clearly fundamental.

2. No apology is made, either, for emphasizing the American intellectual horizon. This is not to assert that American contributions have been pivotal (although they have), but simply to acknowledge that this article is primarily directed to an audience that is largely American. Furthermore, there really is no such thing as Syro-Palestinian or "biblical" archaeology per se. Each of the various "schools" that obviously exist, whether American, European, or Middle Eastern, is the product of a distinctive cultural and social environment, in some ways unique, each constantly changing. We shall therefore seek to explain *why* archaeology has taken the particular form that it

has in recent developments in America, as well as predict where the discipline may be headed. (Hereafter we shall use the term "Syro-Palestinian archaeology" for the overall discipline, relating it, of course, to biblical studies where pertinent.)

A. The Maturation of the "New Archaeology"

The first trend we wish to highlight has, according to some scholars, virtually revolutionized our field. In the past decade or so, several treatments have analyzed the somewhat belated impact of the "New Archaeology" of the 1960s in Americanist circles on our branch of archaeology (see most explicitly Dever 1976, 1981, 1985, 1988; Glock 1985; Toombs 1987). Since trends in that direction are by now well established (indeed they are dominant), it will be sufficient to summarize them here. Beginning on American digs of the late 1960s, various of the following theoretical and methodological tenets, mostly pioneered by New World archaeologists in America, had come to influence research design, fieldwork, and (to a lesser degree) analysis and publication of material. Let us look at them in turn, assessing in each case how far we have come.

1. A Multidisciplinary Approach. This grew out of the attempt to retrieve more than simply architectural and ceramic phases, which had been the conventional foci. We began to pay attention to floral and faunal remains, traces of past subsistence systems, evidence for environmental change, and indeed *all* data on material culture that by chance had been preserved in the archaeological record. That meant that alongside traditional stratigraphers and ceramic experts (and of course, biblical historians), expedition dig staffs included colleagues from many branches of both the social and the natural sciences. Typically one might find geographers, geomorphologists, climatologists, paleobotanists and paleozoologists, physical and cultural anthropologists, historians of technology, computer programmers, and still other specialists in fields formerly thought quite remote from archaeology.

The first multidisciplinary approaches at Gezer and elsewhere were, of course, purely pragmatic, rather than representing any far-reaching theoretical reformulation. The new look remained tentative and frankly experimental for many years, and demonstrably superior results are still not available in fully digested and integrated final reports. Nevertheless, the impact of the multidisciplinary approach is probably stronger than that of any other aspect of the "new archaeology," and the commitment to it greater. This is seen particularly in vastly more sophisticated research design. The proposals from Syro-Palestinian (and NE) archaeologists that come up for review in committees of the American Schools of Oriental Research, the National Endowment for the Humanities, or the National Geographic Society are now routinely multidisciplinary (and, of course, would not be funded otherwise). The best of these proposals measure up to the theoretical standards of modern archaeology anywhere. This is all the more impressive, since only 15 years ago our branch of archaeology was often dismissed by other archaeologists as hopelessly parochial, naïve, and amateurish. (One recalls Sir Mortimer Wheeler's famous comment: "Palestine, that perennial example of bad field archaeology.") It is a sign of our coming of age that we are finally able to compete successfully for both approval and financial support, even from secular circles. It is probably the adoption of a multidisciplinary approach, more than any other single change, that has helped to bring Syro-Palestinian archaeology into the mainstream.

The new field methods that the multidisciplinary approach brought into vogue were often essentially simple, but their results were revolutionary. They included principally fine-sieving, froth flotation, and palynology (the analysis of pollen grains) for the identification of plant and animal remains, and thus of ancient climate, subsistence, diet, and the like (for other tools, see A.3). Among American multidisciplinary projects of high caliber in the 1970s–1980s, we might single out, in Israel, the Central Negev Highlands Project of W. G. Dever and R. Cohen; the Shema-Meiron-Nabratein project of E. M. Meyers, C. Meyers, and J. F. Strange; the Lahav excavations of J. D. Seger; the Shiqmim excavations of T. E. Levy; and the joint project of S. Gitin (with T. Dothan) at Tel Miqne. In Jordan, we would note the Bâb edh-Dhrâᶜ excavation of R. T. Schaub and W. E. Rast; the Madeba Plains project of L. T. Geraty and others; the ᶜAin Ghazzal excavations of G. Rollefson; the Khirbet Iskander excavations of S. Richard and R. Boraas; and the Tell el-Hayyāt excavations of S. Falconer and B. Magness-Gardiner.

2. An Ecological Orientation. The employment of multidisciplinary staffs inevitably broadened the scope of Syro-Palestinian archaeology. At first, this was largely to accommodate the diverse theoretical interests of staff specialists, but gradually larger questions were asked of the archaeological enterprise itself. Many of these, and especially those that appeared most amenable to archaeological investigation, centered around the fundamental question of the site's (and therefore, the culture's) relation to the environment. Previously, individual archaeological sites had been excavated as phenomena in themselves, with little regard for their relationship either to each other or to their settings. (Some Palestinian sites might as well have been in Nebraska, the way they were dug and published.) Most excavators seemed to assume that intersite and environmental relationships were self-evident, others that they were unworthy of consideration. But the failure was probably due more to Syro-Palestinian archaeology's traditional *historical* (i.e., biblical) orientation, so that explanations of cultural change had been sought in ideological, rather than in material factors. Soon, however, borrowing the "new archaeology's" dominantly anthropological and *ecological* orientation brought about the recognition that any culture's distinctive form may be largely (although, of course, not exclusively) due to economic factors, and these in turn are heavily conditioned by the natural environment. In the newer view, culture is an adaptation to such factors as geographical situation, climate, proximity to natural resources and trade routes, and the availability of raw materials. Thus, while rightly eschewing either historical or economic determinism, Syro-Palestinian archaeologists in the 1970s began to study sites in their larger setting, both cultural/historical and natural.

The major research strategies that evolved entailed more surveys and excavations carried out on a regional scale; the comparative study of changing settlement types and patterns of distribution, often using tools developed by economic geographers (such as rank-size hierarchies, Central Place Theory, or other forms of locational analysis); attempts to reconstruct ancient climate and subsistence systems, including technological adaptation; and the first serious demographic projections yet done in our field. All of these questions were not pursued with equal urgency on all projects or for all periods. But the general orientation has proven so pervasive and so salutary that one can scarcely imagine the field before its introduction. The environmental data now being accumulated, when fully processed and published, will open up vistas undreamed of a generation ago and will allow the first comprehensive grasp of many periods and problems. All of the excavation projects mentioned above in Israel and Jordan, as well as surface surveys too numerous to mention, would be examples of the newer ecological orientation in fieldwork. In interpretation, a series of articles by both Israeli and American archaeologists has dealt with demographic issues in periods from the Early Bronze Age through the Roman period.

3. Systems Theory. Closely related to both the multidisciplinary and ecological approaches is the employment of some of the basic principles and categories of several disciplines commonly grouped under the rubric of General Systems Theory. The fundamental postulate is that the "organized state" consists of a number of adaptive subsystems, the whole being greater than the sum of its parts. These subsystems are all organically interrelated in a delicate but dynamic and constantly changing equilibrium, so that a change in any part of the system will have an effect on the rest of the system. Depending upon the balance of inputs and outputs of information and energy, as well as the action of "feedback loops" and "deviation amplifying" or "reducing" mechanisms, systems may succeed in maintaining "homeostasis," evolve to higher levels of integration, or collapse altogether (cf. orientation in Dever 1989).

While originally applied to the investigation of biological phenomena, systems theory has increasingly been adapted to many aspects of humanistic studies, including economics, data management, social planning, and the like. A recent citations analysis (Schiffer 1978) has shown systems theory now to be the dominant theoretical approach in Americanist archaeology. As applied to archaeology, the systemic paradigm might operate on the following assumptions: (1) culture is a uniquely human adaptive response to the natural environment; (2) culture is specific to particular conditions in time and space, collective, patterned, cumulative, transmittable; (3) culture is thus "systemic," i.e., it is the total adaptive system, comprising the interaction of a number of subsystems, such as settlement location in relation to natural habitat, technology, economic strategies, kinship and social structure, political organization—as well as ideology (including art, philosophy, and religion). Obviously, the operations of all these subsystems do not leave equal traces in the archaeological record (thus the difficulty of reconstructing philosophy and religion in the absence of texts). Yet insofar as material remains are not mere chance, but reflect patterned human thought and action, the archaeological record contains the "material correlates of behavior." Therefore archaeologists should seek to discern the nature, effect, and interaction of *all* the various subsystems that may leave identifiable physical remains. Fortunately, the multidisciplinary and ecological approaches noted above provide us with the necessary tools to exploit the archaeological record better. In summary, if the evolution of culture (not to mention the elucidation of the cultural process) is a major goal of archaeology, and not merely the writing of a narrow sort of "political history," then archaeologists *must* be systemic in their approach.

Thus far the theory and rationale may appear to be impeccable. The implementation, however, is another matter, and one that may confront seemingly insurmountable barriers. Among the difficulties are the incomplete nature of the archaeological record as preserved in a typical Middle Eastern mound; the daunting prospect of inferring cultural patterns from "mute" artifacts; and the sheer intractability of human social systems, past or present. Nevertheless, the systemic approach has sufficient practical and heuristic advantages that it is likely here to stay. If nothing else, paying attention to the subsystems noted above is a more efficient approach, in that it allows us to organize our research better, according to more convenient categories; to collect more varied data; and to undertake analysis more systematically, so as to answer specific questions regarding society and economy. At the present stage of research, we have been most successful in recovering settlement patterns and subsistence systems for ancient Palestine, with growing potential for demographic studies. The reconstruction of social organization is still in the beginning stages, although some useful evidence is now at hand. Ideology and religion have been neglected and are admittedly the most formidable subsystems to fathom, especially for the preliterate periods. But even here progress is being made, especially in illuminating the popular cult. (On the latter, see C.3 below.) One barrier is that the *enormous* quantity of data now being generated by the multidisciplinary and systemic approaches simply cannot be managed, much less published, with existing systems. Computerization of archaeology will obviously be necessary, both in basic recording of information and in multivariate statistical analysis, yet predictions made some years ago as to a "computer revolution" in our branch of archaeology (as Dever 1976) have not yet materialized.

The remaining trends that characterized American "new archaeology" in the 1960s and 1970s were: (4) *the use of "ethnoarchaeology,"* or analogies drawn from still-surviving primitive cultures in order to explicate archaeological remains from the remote past; (5) *dependence upon evolutionary models,* drawn from parallels in biological evolution, to explain cultural change, with emphasis, however, on a multilinear trajectory, on the distinctive nature of human behavior, and on human evolution; (6) *insisting on exploiting archaeology's full potential for explaining human behavior,* as well as elucidating the (presumably) universal character of the cultural process, as discerned through comparative and cross-cultural analyses; and (7) *the preference, in some circles, for an "explicitly scientific," or "nomothetic" approach,* which attempts to apply the methods of the natural sciences (especially as seen in the philosopher of science, Carl Hempel), with the major goal presumed to be the formulation and testing of universal "laws" of the cultural process.

These latter four trends, while exerting some influence upon Syro-Palestinian archaeology, have not been nearly as determinative as the first three. Ethnoarchaeology, for instance, despite its obvious potential and its common sense application on a small scale from the very beginning, has had little sustained attraction. This may be partly explained by the lack of anthropological and ethnographic training on the part of practitioners in our field, partly by a colonialist (and later a local nationalist) disdain for "native customs" that appeared too primitive to shed light on ancient high civilizations. Or again, "evolution" in any form was anathema to most archaeologists in our field, given their frequent biblical background (although the bias was more a matter of instinct, or even ignorance, than of conscious rejection).

The behavioralist-processualist and nomothetic schools were simply too esoteric to win many followers. Many might have objected (had they paid any attention at all) that the realm of human nature, unlike the biological realm, does not easily conform to any "laws," certainly not to those subject to verification by predictability. There is also the problem of whether culture, i.e., in the sense of a universal phenomenon, can be adequately described, much less "explained." Above all, there is room for doubt as to whether the archaeological record preserves enough evidence, even when fully exploited, to enlighten us sufficiently on the past cultural process, much less the present. For many, the basic question would have been whether archaeology can aspire to true "scientific method." (The question should have been *which* scientific method; see C.2 below.) Meanwhile, the current discussion in archaeology has been deflected somewhat away from the behavioralist and nomothetic schools by the trenchant critique of Ian Hodder (1986) and his call for a "post-processualist" approach that may be more closely aligned again with historical archaeology. Even more radical is the recent Neo-Marxist work of Shanks and Tilley (1987), arguing for a "post-modern," socially aware archaeology—a view so revolutionary that reviewers have described the impact of the work as "the loss of innocence." Thus the "new archaeology" of the 1970s–1980s is becoming *passé* before we have even caught up with it.

Underlying much of the skepticism in our own field, one suspects, was the assumption (albeit unspoken, or even unconscious) that ancient Palestine, especially Israel in the biblical period, was unique—somehow "superhistorical," not governed by the normal principles of cultural evolution. In its cruder form, this is simply religious fundamentalism, a rejection of "secular" history. But even in more sophisticated versions, it cannot escape the charge of special pleading. In any case, the real (and quite plausible) reasons for misgivings regarding these latter aspects of the "new archaeology" were ignored in favor of particularist or "historical" explanations, in an apparently unquestioned belief that the latter were sufficient.

Each of the above tenets of New World archaeology had varying influence in our field. Furthermore, they were often borrowed rather naïvely, with little appreciation for the difficulty of applying them to the mounds of the ANE, with their long history and exceedingly complex stratification. Nevertheless, there is little doubt that it was precisely the major trends of American "new archaeology" in the 1960s that provided the theoretical framework, such as it was, for Syro-Palestinian archaeology as it developed in the 1970s, and even more in the 1980s (see further Dever 1981, 1985; Glock 1985). It would be gratifying to think that the "revolution" was born of inner intellectual ferment, as our disciple matured, but that was not the case (see C.2 below).

B. Toward an Independent Discipline?

The several trends that we have just discussed suggested to some that by the early 1970s American Syro-Palestinian archaeology was moving out from under the domination of biblical studies that had characterized the Albright-Wright era, toward status as an independent discipline. It was clear that the domination of the classic "biblical archaeology" movement was threatened not only by external developments, in the form of the challenge of the "new archaeology," but also by internal weaknesses, both historical and theological. In particular, the goal of utilizing archaeology to provide historical validation for such episodes in the biblical tradition as the patriarchal and conquest eras was not met. As D. N. Freedman—one of Albright's most prominent disciples, and an eloquent advocate of "biblical archaeology"—recently admitted with admirable candor (1985: 6):

> Albright's great plan and expectation to set the Bible firmly on the foundation of archaeology buttressed by verifiable data seems to have foundered or at least floundered. After all the digging, done and being done and yet to be done, how much has been accomplished? The fierce debates and arguments about the relevance of archaeology to the Bible and vice versa indicate that many issues remain unresolved. Can anyone say anything with confidence about the patriarchs or the patriarchal age? The fact that skeptical voices now dominate the scene indicates that Albrightian synthesis has become unglued and we are further from a solution than we ever were. Archaeology has not proved decisive or even greatly helpful in answering the questions most often asked and has failed to prove the historicity of Biblical persons and events, especially in the early periods.

1. The Collapse of the "Biblical Archaeology" Movement. In retrospect, it is clear that the "archaeological revolution" envisioned by Albright and his followers simply never materialized. After a generation or so, mainstream American biblical scholarship moved away from reactionary and positivist positions such as Albright's, more in the direction of Continental scholarship—particularly of the German school, which had remained suspicious of American-style "biblical archaeology" all along. It could be argued that in America, "biblical archaeology's" demise in the 1960s coincided with the much-discussed "death of biblical theology." In any event, there were soon calls for "biblical archaeology's" replacement by a more specialized, professional secular discipline termed "Syro-Palestinian archaeology" (reviving Albright's 1938 alternate term; on the above, see Dever 1974 and many subsequent treatments, especially 1980a, 1985). There was heated opposition at first, much of it the result of semantic confusion or emotional overreaction from biblical scholars and threatened amateurs (cf. Dever 1982; Lance 1982; Glock 1986). Nearly all archaeologists, however, especially the younger generation, but also including most former "biblical archaeologists," embraced the "new archaeology" (above) with enthusiasm. The relatively easy transition may seem surprising, but it was probably due to the fact that little intellectual or theoretical revolution was involved; the "new archaeology" was exhilarating simply because it promised freer inquiry and more exciting results (cf. Wright 1974). American Syro-Palestinian archaeology, always pragmatic, remained so, and in this lay much of its stability in a period of crisis and change.

It is beyond dispute that in the struggle of the "two archaeologies" (the term of Glock 1985) in the 1970s and 1980s, Syro-Palestinian has triumphed. The new look is evident everywhere: in typical proposals and in nearly all projects in the Middle East; in papers in the leading journals and at the national professional meetings; and particularly in the several graduate programs (see C.2), where the cutting edge of research is visible. There may be a good deal of nostalgia for the older style of "biblical archaeology" (along with legitimate concerns for preserving the biblical connection), but virtually no one in America *does* such archaeology anymore, not even fundamentalists. (In Europe and the Middle East, few ever did, so these developments may be construed largely as a chapter in *American* intellectual and religious history; cf. Dever 1985; fc.a.). What has happened can perhaps best be summarized by noting that in the past decade or so Syro-Palestinian archaeology has "come of age," although still conscious of its parentage. Emerging to dominate the field, it may be characterized as: (1) specialized, (2) professional, and (3) secular.

2. Syro-Palestinian Archaeology as a Putative Discipline. Thus the debate about "biblical archaeology" now seems over, in both biblical and archaeological circles. But can that be taken as evidence that Syro-Palestinian archaeology has become an "independent, autonomous *discipline*," as some had advocated and others now simply assume? In order to answer that question, we may suggest the following criteria by which disciplines may normally be distinguished. A field of inquiry may be said to constitute a "discipline" when it possesses: (1) a class of distinct phenomena to be investigated, and data that are pertinent to the task; (2) a coherent body of appropriate theory, from which specific methods and standards are derived; (3) a group of practitioners who have the minimum professional and academic positions needed to survive; (4) educational and training programs sufficient to replace personnel; (5) the necessary financial resources to underwrite basic, continuing research; (6) professional organizations that foster a sense of corporate identity, facilitate collaborative projects, guarantee standards, and promote the discipline's interests; (7) adequate organs for dissemination and publication of results; (8) self-conscious, well-worked-out relationships with other allied disciplines; and (9) adequate public support to enable the discipline to compete in the marketplace of ideas and institutions.

Without going into documentary detail, it may be asserted that Syro-Palestinian archaeology at its present stage of progress *does* meet all these criteria, at least in modest measure. In fact, some of these tests were met long ago, even by "biblical archaeology," and others have now been met by the earnest and deliberate efforts of the current generation to create a discipline. Thus Syro-Palestinian archaeology exists as at least a fledgling professional and academic discipline—one, however, which remains pathetically small (despite a large popular following) and one whose future is by no means secure (see C.2 below). Meanwhile, "biblical archaeology" also survives, although not as an academic discipline per se (which it never actually became). In our view, the latter is better conceived as an interdisciplinary pursuit, popular or serious, i.e., a *dialogue between* several disciplines (including, of course, Syro-Palestinian archaeology; Dever 1974, 1976, 1980a, 1981, 1985; and C.3 below). The debate over the "disciplinary" question, however, is not fully resolved. A few scholars think that Syro-Palestinian archaeology should remain a branch of biblical studies (Wright 1969a), or even specifically of "biblical archaeology" (Cross 1973). Others hold that both types of archaeology have attained or can attain full disciplinary status (Lance 1982; Toombs 1982; Glock 1986).

3. Possibilities for a Dialogue between Disciplines. The fundamental question, often overlooked in the recent debate, is not whether Syro-Palestinian archaeology is, or should be, a separate discipline (it is in any case); or whether it can still be related to its parent-disciplines, ANE and biblical studies (it must be, however that relationship is construed). Such questions reveal a serious misunderstanding of archaeology today, and they only perpetuate sterile controversies. The misconceptions may take several forms. The most naïve is that the rationale and purpose of "biblical archaeology" (and, by extrapolation, Syro-Palestinian archaeology) is simply to elucidate the Bible, or the lands of the Bible. Scarcely more enlightened, however, is the contention of some scholars that archaeology is only the "handmaiden of history"; that archaeologists, by mastering the tools of their trade, become "mere technicians," isolated from humanistic studies; or that "professionalism" is to be decried in a discipline (that is, in other than one's own). It is worth noting that these supposedly serious objections to archaeology as a discipline come almost exclusively from biblical historians, Northwest Semitic/Hebrew epigraphers, Assyriologists, and other students of *texts,* who although highly specialized themselves, value archaeology mainly for producing literary remains (thus Cross 1973; but cf. Dever 1982, Lance 1982). These scholars seem oblivious to the equally valid historical data to be derived solely from the analysis of *material culture remains.* That is where archaeology today can make a valuable, indeed unique, contribution to humanistic studies.

Virtually all these and other objections to archaeology as a discipline may be removed simply by recalling what the original thrust of the "new archaeology" in the early 1970s was. It was not to make Syro-Palestinian archaeology "autonomous" in the sense of isolating it from other disciplines, but only to free it from its exclusive dependence upon ANE and biblical studies, so that it could develop according to its own inner dynamics, as a branch of general archaeology. From the beginning, the stress was upon the *inter*disciplinary character of all archaeology today, and thus upon the need for *dialogue* with many disciplines (see Dever 1974 and all subsequent treatments). The partners in this dialogue would still include, of course, the parent disciplines of ANE and biblical studies; but they would also include many of the other social sciences, especially anthropology, and increasingly the natural sciences. The intent was not to narrow the discipline, but to broaden it; not to cut off dialogue with biblical studies, but to promote it, this time on a new and sounder basis, with archaeology now an equal partner. Unfortunately, as we shall see, while the "declaration of independence," as well as the fresh perspective and degree of specialization that distance allowed, took place in archaeology in the past decade or so, the renewed dialogue has scarcely begun.

It may be pertinent at this point to look at the way other disciplines develop, that is, how they reshape themselves and form new alignments with allied disciplines. Here Thomas J. Kuhn's classic work *The Structure of Scientific Revolution* (rev. ed., Chicago, 1970) is most instructive. Kuhn's point of reference is, of course, the natural sciences, but his arguments are quite plausible when applied to the social sciences as well. Kuhn shows that periodic "revolutions" typically take place in a discipline not as a result of the overturning of the basic *theoretical* orientation owing either to external or internal changes, but rather as the result of largely pragmatic considerations. After a period of "normal science," during which the majority of younger practitioners happen upon a better way of doing science, there subsequently ensues a struggle between competing paradigms, in the course of which the established view is challenged but never entirely displaced. When a new majority consensus is reached, however, a new phase of "normal science" may be said to have been achieved—after which, in due time, the process will repeat itself.

On Kuhn's analogy, we may argue that the period from ca. 1970–1985 witnessed a true "revolution" in "biblical" and Syro-Palestinian archaeology. There was not then, nor has there been since, an integrated plan of action, much less the laying of a comprehensive intellectual groundwork (i.e., theory). Nor is there yet much published evidence to justify the claims often made for superior results. Finally, the "new archaeology" has not discovered for the first time the "right" way of doing archaeology, or the final truth about any archaeological interpretations. What *has* happened is precisely Kuhn's "paradigm shift," followed by a generational struggle. Elsewhere it has been argued (Dever 1988) that this development constitutes Syro-Palestinian archaeology's "fourth revolution," following the stratigraphic revolution of the 1950s–1960s. If so, then we are now entering a period of "normal science" when we can expect less controversy and more productivity as new data are generated by new research procedures. Furthermore, since theoretical formulations usually *follow* revolutions, it is also a time for reflection and critical assessment, such as we are attempting here.

We may now return to the unresolved issue above, concerning the relationship of the "post-revolutionary" discipline of archaeology to other disciplines. The issue was often posed in this manner: Is Syro-Palestinian archaeology still to remain a branch of ANE and biblical *history,* or of *anthropology* (Cross 1973)? This, however, is a false dichotomy. Archaeology today is not a "branch" of any discipline; it is a discipline itself (above), not "ancillary" to any (i.e. subservient; cf. Lat. *ancillarius,* "relating to maidservants"). As for choosing between the two supposed alternative target disciplines, it is true that Syro-Palestinian archaeology has recently moved somewhat closer to the discipline of anthropology. This is regarded by many as salutary, since it has often been observed than on the academic scene "American archaeology is anthropology, or it is nothing." Nevertheless, archaeology today is, as we have noted, *inter*disciplinary in character, and it should draw its strength and vitality from that fact. As for the best "home" for the discipline, this has more to do with matters of academic convenience than with intellectual issues. One of Syro-Palestinian archaeology's most impressive and beneficial recent achievements is that today the discipline could be readily housed in a Near or Middle Eastern, religious studies, history, classics, or anthropology department; and certainly in one of the few archaeology departments in North America. The latter development—the establishment of nonareal, all-embracing departments of archaeology, independent of anthropology, Near Eastern, or classical departments—is perhaps the clearest indication that archaeology *is* a viable academic discipline today (see Wiseman 1980). Syro-Palestinian archaeology still draws upon ANE and biblical studies for much of its areal content, i.e., its subject matter. But increasingly it looks to the natural sciences for its analytical procedures, and to anthropology and the other social sciences for its theoretical orientation. Rather than seeking to confine archaeology within such labels as "history," "anthropology," or "science," we should celebrate its multifaceted variety (cf. also Schiffer 1988). Archaeology (like anthropology) benefits from and contributes to many other disciplines. (For the question of whether archaeology possesses a unique epistemology or methodology of its own, see C.2 below.)

C. The Shape of the Future

To use an analogy we have already implied, Syro-Palestinian archaeology is a child of venerable parents, recently "come of age." But does the young adult have a future? We may suppose so. In attempting to answer that question fully, however, we need to catalog several desiderata, all of which must be achieved in some measure if our discipline is to survive and prosper in America. Let us look first at external circumstances, i.e., the situation in the Middle East.

1. Fieldwork Abroad. It is obvious that American Syro-

Palestinian archaeology—as a serious scholarly enterprise, devoted to original research and to innovative teaching—is dependent upon fieldwork possibilities in the Middle East. It is equally obvious that there are, however, many conditions that threaten our future, conditions over which we often have no control.

While American archaeologists (along with Europeans) pioneered nearly all the formative developments in archaeology in the Middle East over the past century, today they are restricted, and even excluded, in many countries. Thus there is little current American fieldwork in Turkey, Syria, Iraq, or Egypt; none in Lebanon, Saudi Arabia, the Gulf States, or Iran. Only Israel, Jordan, and Cyprus actively facilitate American excavation and research. Even in the latter three countries, however, the American role is inevitably diminishing as the national schools come to dominate the scene. These national schools enjoy formidable advantages: continual access to and choice of all the sites; the freedom to work out priorities on a national scale; logistical support of national institutions such as government departments, universities and museums, and various research facilities; a vast, largely unpublished database to which they have constant and expert recourse; hundreds of secure professional positions; and an increasingly enlightened public that at its best generates a large-scale, national consciousness of and identification with the archaeology of the region (especially in Israel) that not even "biblical archaeology" in its heyday could match. (On the Israeli school, see further Dever 1973, 1980b; Ussishkin 1982; Bar-Yosef and Mazar 1982; Stern 1987; A. Mazar 1988; and further on the Israeli and other national schools, see also Dever 1985.)

As the national schools mature rapidly, continually adopting the best of foreign methods to add to their own, they seem to lack only adequate funds and workforce. Much of the slack has been taken up, of course, by foreign and "joint projects." In Israel, for instance, most of the budget on many so-called "joint projects" is American, and nearly all the laborers are American student volunteers. But such arrangements will probably be counterproductive for us in the long run. They may provide many amateurs with the adventure of archaeology, but they are unlikely to train or help to place the necessary number of professionals needed to sustain American archaeology as an independent school. In this post-Colonial era the reduced role of foreign excavators is probably appropriate, but nevertheless it could bode ill for the future of our discipline. Some fear that we may end up spectators at a game we invented! More serious is the possibility that we shall eventually lose the capability of doing original (i.e., field) research, without which archaeology has neither control of the basic data nor the critical stance necessary for sustained scholarship. Furthermore, at the risk of sounding chauvinistic, we must insist that there are unique and legitimate *American* interests in the archaeology of the Middle East. Our intellectual and spiritual roots are there, too, and it is not unreasonable to suppose that American scholarship can serve our own interests best.

It is not primarily the growing competition with the national schools that is worrisome, however. After all, we should applaud the progress of archaeology anywhere and relish the competition. Of much greater concern are several conditions created by the fact that the Middle East is a developing area. The first is the rapid modernization and escalation of the economy throughout the area. This not only destroys thousands of archaeological sites before they are even mapped, but also makes the costs of doing both salvage and excavation work almost astronomical. The local schools can barely manage to keep up; but if archaeology has become an expensive necessity for them, it may soon be an impossible luxury for us. The second is the rising tide of nationalism and extremism in the area, often coupled with religious fanaticism, as well as violently anti-American sentiments. This obviously creates political instability, which may render local archaeology tenuous but threatens foreign archaeology with extinction. One disturbing side development of nationalism that affects archaeology, even where it is still able to plan and carry out long-term projects, is the unfortunate creation of an atmosphere where archaeology can easily be perverted to foster ethnic rivalry, or simply to serve the ends of national policy. (This trend, albeit minor, may already be perceived in a heightened interest in "pan-Islamic" archaeology in the Arab world; or in increased focus on ancient Israelite settlements in modern Israeli-occupied territories such as the West Bank, or "Judea" and "Samaria," as they are now being called.) Still more ominous is the outright opposition of some extreme elements to archaeology per se. Both the Muslim Brotherhood in several Arab countries and the ultra-Orthodox in Israel have harassed archaeologists in the field, vandalized monuments, and lobbied to outlaw excavations. If local archaeologists incur such wrath by offending traditional and religious sensitivities, we can easily imagine that foreign archaeologists may be placed in an absolutely impossible situation. Of course, one hopes that saner, more civil heads will prevail, but it is not easy to be sanguine about the Middle East today. Whatever transpires in the near future, it appears that archaeology in the Middle East will become more politicized, not less so.

The picture is not, however, entirely bleak for American archaeology in the Middle East. For one thing, we are obviously still needed and welcomed in several countries. Israel, Jordan, and Cyprus all encourage and support an astonishing number and variety of international projects, as well as many foreign archaeological institutes. The American Schools of Oriental Research, for instance, maintains flourishing and indeed expanding archaeological institutes in all three countries, as well as coordinating more than forty current American field projects. In these countries we may also take comfort in the existence of fully competent and enlightened Departments of Antiquities that are vigorously opposing all the threatening developments that we have noted above. But we must ask: what should the *American* role be in the future?

There remain a number of things that we can and should do, even if the initiative has now passed from us to the indigenous national schools. First, American archaeologists must vigilantly maintain our oft-asserted position of strict political neutrality—even at the risk of disappointing our beleaguered local friends on both side, who might welcome a warmer personal identification or emotional commitment. We must remain "disinterested scholars" in the best sense. The recent emergence of a more secular school of American archaeology should help us to avoid certain sentimental or pious motivations that have always been dangerous in archaeology, now more so. (Certainly, the typical Protestant theological mentality of many earlier archaeologists is hardly an asset in Israel today, nor is the Bible in any form in the Arab countries; cf. Dever fc.a.)

Second, the keyword should not be "competition," but "cooperation." Rather than duplicating the efforts of the national schools, we should be developing complementary projects—especially those that focus on neglected or little-known sites, periods, or problems. This will probably mean fewer large, long-term excavations of major tells, and more work with experimental methods, regional surveys, small one-period sites, and in general more of the specific "problem-solving" archaeology that is now in vogue. Not only are the expenses and logistics of such projects more manageable for foreign excavators, but the returns on the investment may be vastly superior in terms of readily published results, pertinent to the ongoing archaeological discussion. A final strategy may be to attempt fewer unilateral projects and to participate more in the cooperative or "joint" projects now being seen in Israel and Jordan. These projects pose many organizational difficulties, of course, and they sometimes offer limited opportunities for the development of the American partners, but they may be attractive, even necessary, in the future. Whatever happens, American Syro-Palestinian archaeology must remain in the field, but in the future it will need to concentrate a relatively greater proportion of its resources on *scholarship.* This will entail theoretical reformulations; creative synthesis and integration of the data; publication of past and continuing fieldwork; and above all, increasing attention to promoting the health of the discipline in America, both in terms of academic and popular support (see C.2 below).

2. The Discipline at Home. The internal factors that affect the future of American Syro-Palestinian archaeology may seem less intractable, but they are, if anything, even more formidable. Let us look initially at the practical, then the theoretical aspects (on the following, see further Dever 1982, 1985).

a. Some Practical Considerations. First and foremost, it is obvious that we must guarantee the survival of the field, which has managed rather remarkably in the past two decades or so to establish itself as a fledgling discipline. That is, *in addition* to winning over and maintaining the considerable popular support that "biblical archaeology" has always enjoyed in America, Syro-Palestinian archaeology must successfully make the final transition to professional and academic status. If it cannot do so, the entire enterprise may collapse, because archaeology has now become too complex, sophisticated, and expensive to survive solely on an amateur basis. Such support is vital (after all, "amateurs" are the truest "lovers" of all), but full-time specialists in fieldwork, research, and teaching are also essential. (Where would American archaeology be if its only clientele consisted of fascinated lay people, collectors, and a few pot hunters, i.e., it if could not support excavations, museums, and university departments of anthropology?)

Providing jobs will require retaining many essentially part-time positions in small church-related schools, in college departments of religion, or in seminaries. But it also means creating new positions, whether in university departments of Near Eastern studies, anthropology, or elsewhere, in order to supplement the few that we already have. Already relatively small but thriving graduate programs specializing in Syro-Palestinian archaeology (sic) exist at Toronto, Chicago, Harvard, Pennsylvania, Duke, and the University of Arizona. (Only the chair at Harvard is endowed, however.) At least forty Ph.D. students, of very high caliber and with considerable field experience, are in training in these programs, but it remains to be seen how (or whether) they can be placed. Clearly, the future of the discipline depends largely upon the fortunes of this upcoming generation, who embody all the ideals of the "revolution" we have sketched above, but whose careers are in jeopardy.

In addition to employment, it is clear that we also need funds for fieldwork and publications, our basic forms of research. To its credit, the "newer archaeology" has recently won substantial grants from secular sources such as the National Endowment for the Humanities, as well as several other public and private foundations. It is absolutely essential to retain and increase such funding as archaeology becomes less directly related to religious and theological concerns, and at the same time enormously more expensive.

Related to funding, but also to other basic problems, is the necessity for publishing prompt preliminary field reports: full-scale, integrative final reports; synthetic overviews of various periods and problems; and especially interpretive treatments relating recent discoveries to biblical studies, ANE studies, general archaeology and anthropology, and other disciplines. Here we have been so negligent and undisciplined that specialists in other fields can scarcely be faulted for not keeping up with progress in our branch of archaeology or making use of the data that we regard as crucial (unpublished "data" cannot be said to be "given," or made public, in any significant sense; see further below). The complexity and expense of modern archaeology have, of course, made publication immeasurably more difficult (cf. Dever 1982, 1985), but more urgent than ever, especially if Syro-Palestinian archaeology aspires to be a truly scholarly discipline.

A final desideratum may be fundamental to all our needs, the strengthening of learned societies and professional organizations. In our case, this is primarily the American Schools of Oriental Research (ASOR), which since 1900 has effectively served the interests of both lay people and academicians in the fields of ANE languages, history, and archaeology, as well as many aspects of biblical studies (King 1983). ASOR's in-country institutes and many field projects in the Middle East have already been mentioned. Here we should emphasize that ASOR, despite its traditional character and the formidable obstacles to the full development of archaeology, has been able not only to accommodate the thrust of the newer archaeology but to facilitate it. Indeed, ASOR today has become the principal institutional spokesman for the emerging discipline of Syro-Palestinian archaeology, while still retaining its venerable biblical connection (a considerable achievement). It sponsors the majority of American field projects in the Middle East, and its annual meetings and many publications serve as the main forum for presenting the results. Furthermore, ASOR's overseas institutes have long been not only significant research centers but also stepping stones in the careers of young archaeologists who were long-time directors (Albright, Glueck, Lapp, and others). Yet ASOR has not been as successful in another area that has now become crucial, i.e., the education of the American public and the promotion of archaeology on a broader scale. ASOR has only recently begun to reach beyond biblical circles for its audience, or to lobby effectively for federal support of Syro-Palestinian archaeology (although the short-term progress is impressive). And ASOR has yet even to face the challenge of creating new professional and academic positions, which in America can probably be done only with widespread public sympathy and support. We need *urgently* to "mainstream" Syro-Palestinian archaeology and "biblical archaeology" if we are to survive in the melée of ideas and institutions in a democratic society. Our motto should be: "Out of the cloister, into the academy, and even the marketplace."

b. Theoretical Considerations. Here again we would argue that theory, while it is not necessarily prior in the sense of initially provoking changes in a discipline, is nevertheless of primary importance in sustaining ferment and growth once begun. Biblical and Syro-Palestinian archaeology, however, have always been deficient in awareness of the importance of theory and method, being practically inclined instead. Thus there is virtually no bibliography on theory and method in our field before the 1970s, and little critical discussion even now—in surprising contrast to the voluminous and lively literature in Americanist archaeology (see Schiffer 1978, esp. 1988). This lack may be explained by the rather parochial and backward nature of our discipline until recently, as well as the fact that the impetus for change has been largely derived from other branches of archaeology. The characteristic pragmatism is best seen in the fact that when "method" finally began to be treated in the literature, the discussion was largely confined to field technique, i.e., "how to dig." Thus various stratigraphic and recording methods were hotly debated in the 1970s (see Wright 1969b; Dever 1973, 1980b; Lance 1981; cf. Chapman 1986). Yet we would argue that the fundamental *intellectual* issues in archaeology, i.e., theory, have never been seriously addressed by our branch. (But see programmatic essays by Dever 1981, 1985, fc.a; Strange 1982; Glock 1985, 1986; and even as early as Wright 1974; cf. Chapman fc. for a reactionary critique, from a British perspective.)

It was apparently overlooked that method *is* theory—in the sense that the questions selected for investigation inevitably shape the manner of inquiry. Thus our indictment is not that "biblical archaeology" lacked a theoretical framework, but rather that its assumptions were: (1) drawn from issues in biblical history and theology, not archaeology; and (2) rarely made explicit, much less critically evaluated. As an example, the desire to comment upon the "historicity of the Patriarchs" may be a fruitful inquiry in *biblical* scholarship, but it hardly constitutes appropriate archaeological theory, much less a research strategy (as was assumed by a former generation). Ironically, some of the same "biblical archaeologists" who became deeply involved in developing theological hermeneutics, such as G. E. Wright, never sought to formulate an *archaeological* hermeneutic. Albright came closest, in some of his mature synthetic treatments (like *FSAC*), and especially in several candid essays late in life on various philosophies of history (sic, *not* archaeology) and their impact on his thinking (see Dever 1981; contra Chapman fc.).

We are not suggesting that interpretive issues were avoided. On the contrary, the interpretation of nearly every discovery of "biblical" and Syro-Palestinian archaeology has been endlessly discussed, in lively and often polemical disputes that have come to characterize these disciplines in the minds of many. That most controversies were never resolved, however, is due largely to the fact that the discipline never developed a truly archaeological epistemology, that is, there existed no consensus on basic interpretive method. Even as "historical" archaeology, this approach was deficient. Evidence was gathered selectively, conclusions were drawn and debated, and interpretations advanced—all on the basis of an appeal to "history" (usually some school of biblical history). But what history *was,* and how a modern historiography was possible using archaeological data, were questions scarcely raised. Rarely was it specified what was meant by "history" (except as *Heilsgeschichte,* or "salvation history"), and "archaeology" was seldom given even minimal definition. (A definition of "culture" was rarer still.)

By epistemology we mean, of course, theory and method at their most fundamental level—a theory of knowledge—without which the word "discipline" is a tragic misnomer for a field of inquiry. A properly archaeological epistemology would confront such "obvious" questions as these, among others. What is the nature of the site-formation process, both natural and cultural (i.e., what is a tell?)? How does context affect the interpretation of an archaeological find (i.e., what is a locus?)? What constitutes an archaeological datum? What is the role of analogy in archaeological reasoning? Is there a uniquely archaeological logic? How may we extrapolate behavior from artifacts? What determines culture and culture change? The list could be expanded, but the point is clear: until we have wrestled long and earnestly with such basic questions of knowledge, archaeology is likely to remain little more than treasure hunting—a collection of chance finds, miscellaneous objects, and random "facts," without reference to an intellectual framework in which they might become meaningful. (For virtually the only explicit pleas for theory, see Dever 1981, 1985; Strange 1982; Glock 1985.)

Epistemology, however, operates at a level even *more* fundamental than the interpretive: it effectively determines the quality of the data we gather. In most research, but particularly in archaeology, what we "discover" is usually not by chance but is rather the direct outcome of what we think we know, what more we are trying to find out, and how we propose to go about the inquiry. To put it another way, there are few "facts" in archaeology. There are *artifacts* which can *become* "data," but only when they are properly excavated in context, interpreted in relation to a pertinent question, and published (i.e., "given") in full. The notion that the archaeologist is an "objective" scientist, who approaches a site with a mind that is a tabula rasa, is incredibly naïve—and dangerous. We see in the dirt only what we are sensitized to see; and unfortunately, we unwittingly destroy the rest of the evidence in getting it out of the ground. Field archaeology is, after all, an unrepeatable experiment. For example, an earlier generation routinely discarded animal bones, because (as it would have been said) "we already know what people ate in antiquity." Thus unique opportunities to study subsistence were irrevocably lost, since the necessary data were not collected. The present generation, therefore, which would like to ask new questions of the data, often cannot even formulate an adequate hypothesis until it gathers a better set of data. Archaeology can progress as a branch of learning, humanistic or scientific, only by such rigorous, systematic, cumulative theory building and theory testing. That is what we mean by epistemology.

The point may be driven home by an example or two. An earlier article on the Middle Bronze Age in Palestine, by the eminent Israeli historian and archaeologist Benyamin Mazar (1968), is now regarded, and rightly so, as a classic. It was a brilliant synthesis of what was known at the time, given the orientation of nearly all Syro-Palestinian archaeologists to what we have termed above "political history." The major data surveyed, in masterly fashion, bear upon the stratigraphy of the sites, fortifications, epigraphic remains, international relations in the Levant, and ethnic movements. The focus is on the great ideas, individuals, and institutions of the time, i.e., *public* events, or "political history." As a historical survey, much of this is still valid, and indeed a fundamental starting point for further research. But in this article there is virtually no reference to concerns that we would consider essential today: settlement patterns, technology, social and economic history, and demography. Even aesthetics and religion are neglected. Such terms as "culture" never appear. The treatment of the Middle Bronze Age in the illustrious CAH[3] by Kenyon (1973) is not much different in emphasis.

Now Mazar and Kenyon may be forgiven for not addressing these issues in the 1960s, because the data were not then available. But the data were unavailable *because* archaeologists and historians had been asking the wrong questions, or more accurately, questions that were simply inadequate in terms of stimulating explicit research designs that could focus on the *whole* range of data that were potentially available. The almost exclusive orientation of most Syro-Palestinian archaeologists toward "political history" was, of course, never explicitly stated, but it can be extrapolated from the typical methods employed and the results obtained. The twin foci were: (1) stratigraphy, or learning how to dig correctly, so as to separate major architectural phases; and (2) ceramic chronology, fixing absolute dates for the strata, mostly of destruction layers, in order to correlate them with biblical and other texts that described major episodes in political history. Field projects concentrated on large tells, especially ones that could be identified with biblical sites; and there the objective was mostly the clearance of fortifications, i.e., major architectural remains that could be expected to produce datable pottery and objects. Exposures were often narrow, with a preference for deep sondages that sampled all strata.

It needs to be stressed again that the chief goals of this kind of archaeology, although rarely acknowledged, were: (1) an outline of the political history of the major sites; and (2) a correctly dated local ceramic sequence. On sites being dug, there was relatively little exposure of domestic areas, i.e., of private dwellings, of storage and industrial installations, or of terraces, courtyards, and other open areas. There was virtually no interest in off-tell features (except for cemeteries) that might have revealed the use of water, land, and other natural resources. Smaller satellite villages, encampments, and the rural hinterland remained totally unknown, since there was little interest in environmental setting, and almost no regional survey work was undertaken.

It is true that the earlier generation of Syro-Palestinian and "biblical archaeologists" (the "third revolution," ca. 1930–1960) did hone the tools of comparative stratigraphy and ceramic chronology to a fine edge, perhaps unmatched anywhere else in the Middle East. But even here, the limited objectives are clear in retrospect. Stratigraphy in the Wheeler-Kenyon (or better, "baulk/debris-layer"; cf. Dever 1973) method focused somewhat mechanically on observing and recording soil layers empirically, so as to separate "loci" cleanly. But there was inadequate awareness of what we would now call "site formation processes," or the cultural and natural activities that *formed* these depositional features in the first place, and thus were capable of explaining their function in a larger context (Schiffer 1987). Or again, the common pottery of Palestine was exhaustively analyzed and catalogued (mostly on the basis of shape and decoration) so as to chart its typological development, which resulted in a relatively precise ceramic chronology. But with very few exceptions, pottery was not studied with a view to what it might contribute to our knowledge of the history of technology, to aesthetics, or to international relations and trade, i.e., to *culture* and *cultural change.* Above all, it is the models of cultural change themselves that were deficient. Most were reductionist and diffusionist. The term "culture" usually meant little more than a ceramic assemblage; and a new "pottery culture" meant a "new people," probably a new ideology. Major ethnic movements and foreign invasions (i.e., "historical" events) were invoked to explain nearly every transition in ancient Palestine. There was little emphasis on indigenous socioeconomic factors, technological innovation, or the overall evolution of local culture in any sense. In all these characteristic emphases of the former generation we see clearly the paradigm at work: the objective was "political history," *not* socioeconomic, technological, or true cultural history (in contrast to the typical *Kulturgeschichte,* for which the earlier approach is now faulted).

Syro-Palestinian archaeology will progress not so much by further mastery of stratigraphy and ceramic chronology, or by perfecting field technique (although progress in these areas was and is a necessary goal), but rather by becoming more sophisticated in its epistemology. That will necessitate our beginning to see "theory" not negatively, as we have done ("speculation" or "unsubstantiated claims"), but rather positively, as simply a body of heuristic principles that are capable of governing and advancing archaeological research (Schiffer 1988). Such theory should be comprehensive, systematic, clearly focused, and as empirically verifiable as possible. That is really what we mean by speaking, as we do so often today, of "research design."

An alternate model to "political history" in the future might be derived from the *annales* school of social and economic history, which utilizes massive archival documentation to look behind ideology, beyond the great episodic public events, to the daily life and environment of countless individuals, over vast sweeps of time. Thus Fernand Braudel's well-known *The Mediterranean and the Mediterranean World in the Age of Phillip II* (1970) sets forth a three-tier system. The upper level is a "history of events," a history that moves rapidly but is superficial. Beneath that, a second level comprises the "history of social groupings and their interactions," which moves much more slowly. Deeper still is an "undercurrent" of smaller groups and individuals in the setting of the natural environment, in which all the higher levels of history are rooted, whose movement unfolds gradually and can only be measured in millennia, *la longue durée.* Another instructive work of this school is E. Le Roy Ladurie's *The Peasants of Languedoc* (1974).

Archaeology does not, of course, possess the extensive written documentation that can be sifted through by historians of the *annales* school, nor can it perhaps ever write really fine-grained individual history. But archaeology today is ecological and focuses on setting; it turns up masses of obscure artifactual data that reflect the daily life of ordinary individuals; and it is unique among all disciplines in its sensitivity to cultural change over very long periods of time. Thus there is good reason to believe that Syro-Palestinian archaeology has scarcely begun to fulfill its potential for writing social and economic history on a much broader scale than formerly thought possible. (See further Dever 1988 on the "fourth revolution.") The tools are at hand, because the very multidisciplinary, ecological, and systemic approaches noted above already point promisingly in the right direction.

Insofar as we may succeed in broadening the scope of Syro-Palestinian archaeology's focus, we may achieve yet another goal that many find desirable today, that of integrating the discipline into the general field of archaeology and anthropology. (At the same time, we may still conceive our discipline as "historical archaeology," provided that the history writing is not one-dimensional.) That this goal has not been achieved, or even seriously attempted, is painfully obvious. Ancient Palestine has several attractions: a pivotal geopolitical situation in the Fertile Crescent, the great cradle of civilization; a long history of archaeological investigation that is more intensive relative to land area than that of any other country in the Middle East, with a rapidly growing database; and enormous popular appeal as the Land of the Bible. Yet anthropologists and social historians seeking cross-cultural comparisons typically ignore Palestine as a case study, especially in contrast to Egypt and Mesopotamia, and even poorly known Syria. Why is this?

Part of the neglect may be due simply to a secularist, antibiblical bias among many anthropologists (who, after all, can be parochial too). Some of it may also be due to suspicions, unfortunately well founded, about the quality of our data, much of it indeed poorly excavated in the past, as well as to others' ignorance of better work done recently. But it must be admitted that the isolation of Syro-Palestinian archaeology is largely our own fault. Until recently we had conceived the field as a branch of biblical studies, remaining aloof from the ongoing history of American archaeology and anthropology as an intellectual and disciplinary enterprise (see the illuminating history of American archaeology in Willey and Sabloff 1980). Indeed, we had prided ourselves on our "amateur" status and had often resisted professionalization. This meant that most archaeologists in our field were simply not asking the same questions as archaeologists generally. They did not read or publish in mainstream journals; they did not participate in professional societies or annual meetings of other archaeological and anthropological organizations; above all, they did not teach in or share programs with university departments of anthropology, where most of New World and European archaeology, as well as Near Eastern prehistorical archaeology, was being done.

Among recent and current issues in world archaeology would be the following, for example: (1) the rise and collapse of complex society; (2) the balance of idealist and materialist paradigms in the reconstruction of cultural change; (3) the social history of archaeology/anthropology; (4) space-time systematics, artifact variability, cultural patterning, and the material correlates of behavior; (5) site-formation processes and the nature of the archaeological record; and (6) archaeological identification of ethnicity. In addition, the several theoretical thrusts of the "new archaeology" noted above all reflect a number of specific questions about settlement types, subsistence, social structure, population growth, and the like. A dispassionate survey of the way Syro-Palestinian archaeology is taught, or a comparative citations analysis of the literature in our field and in the field of archaeology in general, would reveal that we have contributed very little to the discussion of these key issues, and we have only begun even to be aware of them. (If American Syro-Palestinian archaeology lags behind, the national schools in the Middle East, with the exception of Levantine prehistory, are even further behind—although their isolation is perhaps more understandable.) Younger specialists may be committed to the task of "mainstreaming" Syro-Palestinian archaeology, but it will likely take a generation for the new orientation to produce tangible results. (The best measure may be to keep up with journals like *American Antiquity*; or especially the ongoing volumes edited by M. B. Schiffer, *Advances in Archaeological Theory and Method,* London, 1978 and following.) Not until then will the "revolution" be complete.

3. Toward a New "Biblical Archaeology" as "Dialogue." The developments we have sketched above, as well as those predicted for the future, may be regarded as legitimate, even inevitable. But they nonetheless raise a prospect that many may find rather daunting: the possibility that the newer, "secular" Syro-Palestinian archaeology may no longer offer much to the elucidation of the Bible. In conclusion, we shall try to show that precisely the opposite is true, that indeed a *new style* of "biblical archaeology" is emerging. It emphasizes the possibility of a renewed and more fruitful dialogue *between* the two disciplines, now that they are attaining maturity (much as had been [perhaps overly-optimistically] predicted in Dever 1974 and several subsequent works, especially 1981, 1985).

There are, of course, formidable obstacles in the way of such a dialogue. Many observers believe that the two disciplines continue to move farther apart, and there is indeed some evidence of that. But we do not consider that primarily the fault of archaeologists, because we have supposedly become, as some critics put it, "overspecialized," "narrowly professional," "technicians rather than humanistic scholars." The simple fact is that, on the one hand, the practitioners of "biblical archaeology" failed to carry out their program of validating biblical history and faith through archaeology, and then gave up. On the other hand, biblical scholarship has increasingly moved away from its original historical-critical concerns to increasingly *literary* concerns, or to structural linguistics and the "metahistorical" understanding of language, finally to canonical criticism and the like. In all such cases, archaeology's attempt to recover the original context and events of the biblical texts—"the history behind the history"—tends to be regarded as simply irrelevant. History has become merely hermeneutics. Yet we would contend, exactly as Albright and Wright did (especially 1969, 1969a), that without the corrective of archaeology, its provision of "external" data, its unique ability to penetrate *behind* the tradition in the literature, to a more objective "secular" history, biblical studies is in constant danger of degenerating into subjective speculation, carrying neither historical nor theological conviction. (For the necessity of holding the two disciplines together, see, in addition to Dever as cited above, Albright 1969; Wright 1969a; Lapp 1969; Lance 1982; Sauer 1982; Meyers 1984; Glock 1986.) Whether the biblical texts are truly "historical" or merely possess an essential "historicality," it really *does* matter what actually happened in the past, not just how the religious community came to interpret the supposed events for its own needs in its own time and circumstance.

The time is now ripe for a renewed dialogue between the "new archaeology" and contemporary biblical studies. Such a dialogue is timely precisely because both disciplines have now moved away from the positivist Albrightian synthesis toward what appears to be an emerging consensus, though still largely inarticulate and even unself-conscious. Ironically, the new "secular" archaeology is better equipped to contribute to the coming dialogue than the old archaeology was, because it is more competent professionally, more open and flexible in its presuppositions, and at the same time less mired in tendentious theological views that have little to do with proper archaeological investigation. We may be coming, at last, to the point of Morton Smith's remarks over twenty years ago in his presidential address before the Society of Biblical Literature: "For a correct history of the Israelites we must have the archaeological facts determined quite objectively and independently by competent archaeologists, and the Biblical texts likewise by competent philologians, and then we can begin to compare them" (1969: 34).

But what can *archaeology* contribute specifically to the dialogue? Or to use a phrase turned by two of "biblical archaeology's" most eminent exponents, in their final treatments (Wright 1971; de Vaux 1970), "What is it that archaeology can and cannot do?" Implied, of course, is the fundamental question of the relation of artifacts to texts, of material culture to culture, of archaeology to history—all of which will have to be rethought in this post-Albrightian, "post-positivist" era.

a. Textual Remains and Their Contribution. While the task of literary interpretation is best left to specialists, the archaeologist is entitled to remind us that texts, too, are limited as a source of history, because of the fundamental problem of interpretation, both ancient and modern. Thus the Hebrew Bible must be regarded by the historian as a largely late, composite document; highly selective and incomplete in the materials it includes; basically establishment-oriented and therefore "elitist" in outlook. The Bible is theocratic history, sometimes blatantly propagandistic, not history but *Heilsgeschichte.* (The Bible usually does not pretend to be otherwise; it is we who are often naïve, not the biblical writers.) It is obvious that in the Hebrew Bible there is little or no "objective history" to be found, perhaps for the premonarchical period little material that is even useful to the historian. Nor is the problem confined to the Hebrew Bible Old Testament (although virtually all "biblical archaeology" concerned itself with that part of the Bible; but cf. Strange 1982). Archaeology can no more aid directly in the task of "rediscovering the historical Jesus" than it can in recovering the "patriarchal" or "conquest" eras at ancient Israel. As historians we are limited ultimately by the fact that the Bible asks not so much "What happened?" as "What did it *mean?*" Systematic theology goes further, of course, to ask "What *does* it mean?" To put it in another fashion, archaeology may aid in small but significant ways in getting at the "history behind the history," i.e., in the task of writing a history of Israel, or even a history of the religion of Israel, but scarcely at all in the task of formulating an Old Testament theology.

Furthermore, in considering the problem of interpretation, the common notion that "texts are eloquent but artifacts are mute" must be laid to rest. How effectively *either* class of data mediates past realities to us is dependent upon how skillfully and sensitively the data are interpreted. A text, biblical or otherwise, simply by virtue of exhibiting written signs, rather than other symbolic expressions of human thought and behavior, may be no more "objective" in the witness it bears than any other object, no more comprehensive than an archaeological sample, no more transparent in significance than an artifact. With both types of evidence, we must try to "decode" the meaning (or various meanings) in another time and place and circumstance (that will always remain elusive), then try to translate this for our own situation.

The analogy between the role of interpretation in understanding texts and artifacts may be carried even further. The Bible itself, at least in human terms, is an artifact from the past, one that reflects the lives and thoughts of those who shaped it. Yet there is one unique feature. The Bible as we have it is clearly both what it *was* in its original context and usage, plus what it has *become* over the centuries as Scripture, constantly reinterpreted by Synagogue and Church. For the secular historian (sic), the primary difference between the Bible as a literary *corpus* and other texts that have been brought to light by archaeology is simply that the former was never discarded or lost, but rather was continually preserved and revised by a still-living community. Thus the Bible, in *archaeological* terms, is what we may call a "curated artifact." The problems of interpretation are similar—but just as difficult.

b. Artifactual Remains and Their Contribution. Most

of the data from ancient Palestine that happen to be preserved are artifactual, not textual (the Bible being, as we have observed, a notable exception). Such data are often poorly preserved and in any case constitute an atypical representation of what must once have been present in the archaeological record. The context necessary to supply meaning may be missing, or misunderstood owing to faulty excavation. From these tantalizing physical remains—bits and pieces of the past—what can we learn, if anything, of history and culture that will *complement* and supplement the study of texts?

We have attempted above to show how much *more* illuminating the "new archaeology" can be than the old. To summarize briefly here, first, archaeology may contribute a knowledge of the larger context in which the Bible emerged, both physical and cultural, without which it cannot be fully understood. Archaeology alone is capable of bringing to life again the ANE setting, the neighboring lands and people and cultures. This provides the background against which the Bible can be portrayed so as to give it a credibility—an immediate, vivid, flesh-and-blood reality—that it cannot possibly have when read solely as Scripture, or as a long-lost literature isolated from its origins.

Second, archaeology, while it may not be able to give an ultimate explanation of events, historical or theological, can provide at least what we may call the "ecology of change." At any given period it can document the local conditions in Palestine that may have given rise to a situation that made changes possible, as well as putting these changes into the context of the natural environment and long settlement history of Palestine. Thus archaeology need not ignore, much less contradict, the historical and primarily religious affirmations of the ancient biblical writers. But it can, and should, supplement these partial explanations with an understanding of *other* factors that we moderns find helpful in assessing change—environmental, cultural, technological, socioeconomic, and other. Concerning these powerful agents of change, the Bible tells us next to nothing. This parallel and complementary "natural history," or "secular history," of ancient Palestine is recoverable only through archaeology (including, of course, additional extrabiblical texts that may be brought to light), and indeed only beginning now with the new tools at our disposal. Thus the book of Joshua and the works of the Deuteronomistic historians (Joshua-Kings) portray the emergence of Israel in Canaan as the result of a sudden, unified military conquest of the Twelve-Tribe League under the leadership of Joshua—a miraculous gift of Yahweh. Archaeological evidence, however, shows beyond doubt that most Late Bronze Age Canaanite sites in Palestine were not destroyed ca. 1200 B.C., and that nearly all the identifiable early Israelite settlements were established peacefully on virgin soil (Finkelstein *AIS*). Therefore, from the point of the secular historian, the ascendancy of Israel was part of a gradual, exceedingly complex process of socioeconomic change on the Late Bronze–Iron I horizon, not a "miracle" at all. See also ISRAEL, HISTORY OF (ARCHAEOLOGY AND THE ISRAELITE "CONQUEST") and SETTLEMENT OF CANAAN.

Finally, archaeology can look at the "other side of the coin," that is, at popular culture, at folk religion, possibly even at individual history in some cases (such as the *annales* school attempts). For instance, normative Israelite religion as reflected in the Hebrew Bible was supposedly Yahwistic. Archaeology, however, reveals that folk religion was highly syncretistic, that the popular cults of ancient Israel were strongly influenced by the Canaanite fertility religions.

D. Conclusion

In this essay we have tried to look briefly at Syro-Palestinian and "biblical" archaeology—at their history, their changing relationships, and especially their future prospects. The latter perspective is necessary, but risky, for archaeology by definition is full of surprises. Archaeology is also one of the fastest-moving of all the social science disciplines today, both in theoretical reformulations and in the astonishing type and array of new data that it is turning up. The "archaeological revolution" predicted by Albright is not over, as many seem to believe, but scarcely begun (even if it is not happening in the way he expected). And among Syro-Palestinian archaeology's many future accomplishments will certainly be the writing of a more comprehensive and satisfying history of ancient Palestine in both the Old and New Testament periods.

What archaeology cannot do, however, even at its best, is to "prove" the Bible in any sense—either by demonstrating that the events claimed by the biblical writers as central to the "salvation history" actually happened, much less by validating the theological inferences that are drawn from these events, whether ancient or modern. The notion that historical proofs can confirm, or even enhance, religious *faith* is a contradiction in terms.

Bibliography

Albright, W. F. 1938. The Present State of Syro-Palestinian Archaeology. Pp. 1–46 in *The Haverford Symposium on Archaeology and the Bible*, ed. E. Grant. New Haven.

———. 1951. The Old Testament and the Archaeology of Palestine. Pp. 1–26 in *The Old Testament and Modern Study*, ed. H. R. Rowley. Oxford.

———. 1969. The Impact of Archaeology on Biblical Research—1966. Pp. 1–14 in *New Directions in Biblical Archaeology*, ed. D. N. Freedman and J. C. Greenfield. Garden City, NY.

Bar-Yosef, O., and Mazar, A. 1982. Israeli Archaeology. *World Archaeology* 13: 310–25.

Chapman, R. 1986. Excavation Techniques and Recording Systems: A Theoretical Study. *PEQ* 118: 5–20.

———. fc. Ideas and Approaches in the Archaeology of the Levant: Petrie to the Present. *BASOR*.

Cross, F. M. 1973. W. F. Albright's View of Biblical Archaeology and Its Methodology. *BA* 36: 2–5.

Dever, W. G. 1973. *Archaeology and Biblical Studies: Retrospects and Prospects*. Evanston.

———. 1974. Two Approaches to Archaeological Method—The Architectural and the Stratigraphic. *EI* 11: *1–*8.

———. 1976. Archaeology. Pp. 44–52 in *IDBSup*.

———. 1980a. Biblical Theology and Biblical Archaeology: An Appreciation of G. Ernest Wright. *HTR* 73: 1–15.

———. 1980b. Archaeological Method in Israel: A Continuing Revolution. *BA* 43: 40–48.

———. 1981. The Impact of the "New Archaeology" on Syro-Palestinian Archaeology. *BASOR* 242: 14–29.

———. 1982. Retrospects and Prospects in Biblical and Syro-Palestinian Archaeology. *BA* 45: 103–7.
———. 1985. Syro-Palestinian and Biblical Archaeology. Pp. 31–74 in *The Hebrew Bible and Its Modern Interpreters,* ed. D. A. Knight and G. M. Tucker. Philadelphia.
———. 1988. Impact of the New Archaeology. Pp. 337–52 in *Benchmarks in Time and Culture,* ed. J. F. Drinkard, G. L. Mattingly, and J. M. Miller. Atlanta.
———. 1989. Yigael Yadin: Prototypical Israeli "Biblical Archaeologist." Pp. 44–51 in *EI* 20.
———. fc.a. AASOR. Baltimore.
———. fc.b. The Collapse of the Urban Early Bronze Age in Palestine: Toward a Systemic Analysis. In *L'urbanization de la Palestine ã l'âge du Bronze,* ed. P. de Miroschedji.
Dever, W. G., and Lance, H. D., eds. 1978. *A Manual for Field Archaeologists.* New York.
Freedman, D. N. 1985. The Relationship of Archaeology to the Bible. *BARev* 11/1:6.
Glock, A. E. 1985. Tradition and Change in Two Archaeologies. *American Antiquity* 50: 464–77.
———. 1986. Biblical Archaeology, An Emerging Discipline? Pp. 85–101 in *The Archaeology of Jordan and Other Essays Presented to Siegfried H. Horn,* ed. L. T. Geraty and L. G. Herr. Berrien Springs, MI.
Harris, E. C. 1979. *Principles of Archaeological Stratigraphy.* London.
Hodder, I. 1986. *Reading the Past.* Cambridge.
King, P. J. 1983. *American Archaeology in the Mideast.* Philadelphia.
Lance, H. D. 1981. *The Old Testament and the Archaeologist.* Philadelphia.
———. 1982. American Biblical Archaeology in Perspective. *BA* 45: 97–101.
Lapp, P. W. 1969. *Biblical Archaeology and History.* Cleveland.
Mazar, A. 1988. *Benchmarks in Time and Culture. Essays in Honor of Joseph A. Callaway,* ed. J. F. Drinkard, G. L. Mattingly, and J. M. Miller. Atlanta.
Mazar, B. 1968. The Middle Bronze Age in Palestine. *IEJ* 18: 65–97.
Meyers, E. M. 1984. The Bible and Archaeology. *BA* 47: 36–40.
Moorey, P. R. S. 1981. *Excavation in Palestine.* Grand Rapids.
Sauer, J. A. 1982. Syro-Palestinian Archaeology, History, and Biblical Studies. *BA* 45: 201–9.
Schiffer, M. B. 1978. Taking the Pulse of Method and Theory in American Archaeology. *American Antiquity* 43: 153–58.
———. 1987. *Formation Processes of the Archaeological Record.* Albuquerque.
———. 1988. The Structure of Archaeological Theory. *American Antiquity* 53: 461–85.
Shanks, M., and Tilley, C. 1987. *Social Theory and Archaeology.* Cambridge.
Smith, M. S. 1969. The Present State of Old Testament Studies. *JBL* 88: 19–35.
Stern, E. 1987. The Bible and Israeli Archaeology. Pp. 31–40 in *Archaeology and Biblical Interpretation,* ed. L. G. Perdue, L. E. Toombs, and G. L. Johnson. Atlanta.
Strange, J. F. 1982. New Developments in Greco-Roman Archaeology in Palestine. *BA* 45: 85–88.
Toombs, L. E. 1982. The Development of Palestinian Archaeology as a Discipline. *BA* 45: 89–91.
———. 1987. A Perspective on the New Archaeology. Pp. 41–52 in *Archaeology and Biblical Interpretation,* ed. L. G. Perdue, L. E. Toombs, and G. L. Johnson. Atlanta.
Ussishkin, D. 1982. Where Is Israeli Archaeology Going? *BA* 45: 93–95.
Vaux, R. de. 1970. On Right and Wrong Uses of Archaeology. Pp. 64–80 in *Near Eastern Archaeology in the Twentieth Century,* ed. J. A. Sanders. Garden City, NY.
Willey, G. R., and Sabloff, J. A. 1980. *A History of American Archaeology.* Rev. ed. San Francisco.
Wiseman, J. 1980. Archaeology in the Future. *AJA* 84: 279–85.
Wright, G. E. 1947. The Present State of Biblical Archaeology. Pp. 74–97 in *The Study of the Bible Today and Tomorrow,* ed. H. R. Willoughby. Chicago.
———. 1958. Archaeology and Old Testament Studies. *JBL* 77: 39–51.
———. 1969a. Biblical Archaeology Today. Pp. 149–65 in *New Directions in Biblical Archaeology,* ed. D. N. Freedman and J. C. Greenfield. Garden City, NY.
———. 1969b. Archaeological Method in Palestine. *EI* 9: *3–*4.
———. 1971. What Archaeology Can and Cannot Do. *BA* 34: 70–76.
———. 1974. The "New Archaeology." *BA* 38: 104–15.

WILLIAM G. DEVER

ARCHELAUS (PERSON) [Gk *Archelaos*]. The eldest son and successor of Herod the Great (cf. Matt 2:22), who ruled over Judea and Samaria from 4 B.C. until A.D. 6. Most of what we know about Archelaus comes from the Jewish historian Josephus. He reports that Archelaus and his brother Antipas, Herod's two sons by Malthace, a Samaritan, were raised in Rome.

In Judea, Antipater accused Archelaus (who was in Rome) not only of denouncing Herod for the murder of his half-brothers Aristobulus and Alexander, but also of claiming that Antipater would soon be another of Herod's victims (Jos. *Ant* 17.80), accusations which caused Herod to hate Archelaus (Jos. *Ant* 17.146). But shortly before his own death, Herod discovered that he had been duped by the scheming Antipater, and drafted the final version of his will naming Archelaus as principal heir to his kingdom (Jos. *Ant* 17.188–89).

Archelaus arranged Herod's funeral, and, we are told, he refrained punctiliously from accepting the royal title "king" until it had been confirmed by Augustus (Jos. *Ant* 17.202). He promised to rule more mildly than Herod, and was immediately showered with demands for the reduction and abolition of taxes, the release of prisoners, retribution against Herod's favorites, and replacement of the high priest appointed by Herod. Although Archelaus took a conciliatory stance, serious unrest developed, especially under the influence of those who supported the memory of Judas and Matthias, traditionalist Jews who had opposed Herod (Jos. *Ant* 17.149–67). This unrest reached such a point that Archelaus ordered his cavalry to put a stop to it; they killed some 3000 Jews in the Temple precinct during Passover (Jos. *Ant* 17.218).

Archelaus sailed for Rome to press his case with Augustus, taking with him Nicolas of Damascus, who had been Herod's great orator, and Herod's sister, Salome (who intended, we are told, to undermine Archelaus by drawing Augustus' attention to the disorder and carnage associated with Archelaus' brief rule). At the same time, Antipas also made his way to Rome to lay claim to Herod's throne. We are told that in Rome he gained the support of Herod's relatives, all of whom hated Archelaus. Meanwhile, Sabinus, imperial procurator of Syria, wrote to Augustus leveling accusations against Archelaus, who had thwarted his attempts to seize Herod's wealth (cf. Jos. *Ant* 17.221).

During Archelaus' absence in Rome, unrest had grown to large-scale rebellion. Varus, Roman governor of Syria, restored order. He also gave permission for a Jewish delegation to sail for Rome to request annexation and direct Roman rule over Judea (Jos. *Ant* 17.299–314). Augustus finally decided upon a compromise: Archelaus was awarded a large part of his father's kingdom (Judea proper, Samaria, and Idumaea, together with the cities of Strato's Tower-Caesarea, Sebaste, Joppa, and Jerusalem). From these territories Archelaus received an annual income of 600 talents. But Archelaus was not made "king" of these territories; instead, he was given the title of "ethnarch," probably to reconcile the Jewish delegation which had requested the abolition of the monarchy (Braund 1984: 142). However, Augustus is also said to have promised Archelaus that he would be awarded the royal title if and when he had proved himself a capable ruler (Jos. *Ant* 17.317). The coins of Archelaus (which bear no image) indicate that he was known as "Herod, ethnarch" (*HJP*[2] 354 n.4). Josephus, however, calls him "king," which, although technically inaccurate, might also constitute "oblique evidence on the scope of the office of ethnarch" (Sullivan *ANRW* 2/8: 309).

Archelaus remained in office until A.D. 6, and few details of his brief rule are known. He founded a town, which he named Archelais; he rebuilt the royal palace at Jericho in lavish style; and near Jericho he irrigated a plain and planted it with palm trees. Josephus indicates that he was not a popular ruler: he reports that leading Jews and Samaritans "finding his savagery and tyranny intolerable" brought accusations against him before Augustus (Jos. *Ant* 17.342); and that Archelaus, "remembering past differences, behaved savagely not only towards the Jews but also towards the Samaritans" (*JW* 2.111). Augustus summoned Archelaus through a man (also called Archelaus) who was responsible for the ethnarch's affairs at Rome; the manner of summons was a calculated insult. After a brief hearing, Augustus confiscated Archelaus' property and exiled him to Vienne in Gaul. Archelaus probably lived out his days in Vienne, although his tomb was later pointed out to those who visited Bethlehem (Jos. *Ant* 17.342–44; *HJP*[2] 356 n.13).

Many of Archelaus' troubles were inherited from Herod, although he himself had offended Jewish tradition in a number of ways. First, he had deposed the high priest Joazar (because he had supported Jewish malcontents) and he had appointed Eleazar, Joazar's brother, to take his place (cf. Jos. *Ant* 18.93 on priestly vestments). Second, he had married Glaphyra, daughter of Archelaus I of Cappadocia, a union which offended Jewish tradition because Glaphyra had already borne a son to Archelaus' brother, Alexander, her first husband. In fact, Archelaus was Glaphyra's third husband, since she had married King Juba II of Mauretania after Alexander's death (Jos. *Ant* 17.339; Sullivan *ANRW* 2/8: 296–394).

Bibliography

Braund, D. C. 1984. *Rome and the Friendly King*. New York.

DAVID C. BRAUND

ARCHER.
See MILITARY ORGANIZATION IN MESOPOTAMIA.

ARCHIPPUS

ARCHIPPUS (PERSON) [Gk *Archippos*]. A Christian greeted in the salutation of the letter to Philemon, identified as a "fellow soldier" of Paul (Philemon 2), and as one urged to fulfill the "ministry" (*diakonia*) he had received in the Lord (Col 4:17). Since Archippus is mentioned immediately after PHILEMON and APPHIA in Philemon 2, he is usually taken to have been a member of Philemon's household, perhaps a close relative of Philemon and Apphia, such as a son or a brother.

The evidence, however, may also be read plausibly to identify Archippus as the head of the household and, as such, the owner of the slave Onesimus (Knox *Philemon IB*, 49–51). It has been argued, first, based on the grammatical rule that a pronoun agrees with its nearest antecedent, that the singular pronoun "you" in the phrase "the church in your (Gk *sou*) house" (Philemon 2) could refer to Archippus. Second, the "ministry" that Archippus is asked to fulfill in Col 4:17, not further specified in that context, could be a reference to the veiled request in Philemon 13–14 to free Onesimus. Finally, Philemon 1 presupposes that Paul's "beloved fellow worker," Philemon, is to read the letter to the house church. If Philemon were the slaveowner, nothing would stop him from destroying the letter and punishing Onesimus. But if Archippus is the household head, then Paul would be effectively applying pressure on him to free Onesimus by having the letter read in his own house church and a decision thus made in the context of his Christian community (Cope 1985: 47). Nevertheless, against this identification of Archippus is the fact that the letter is addressed first of all to Philemon; for this reason he is usually taken to be its primary addressee and the owner of Onesimus.

The greeting in Philemon 2 also identifies Archippus as Paul's "fellow soldier" (Gk *sustratiōtēs*), i.e., his "fellow worker" (cf. Philippians 2:25, which indicates the two epithets are synonymous). The circumstances under which Paul came to know Archippus, however, are unknown. The military metaphor may indicate that Archippus, like Paul or perhaps at some time along with him, experienced conflict in his service of the church, probably in a position of leadership.

In Col 4:17, Archippus, who by implication is not presumed to be in Colossae, is said to have received a "ministry" in the Lord, although the nature of his role is not further specified. J. B. Lightfoot (1879: 244) has argued that the solemnity of the warning to fulfill that ministry "points to a continuous service, rather than an immediate service." Just prior to this warning in Col 4:16 is a reference to the neighboring church of Laodicea, which suggests that Archippus served that church, perhaps as its leader. But had he been neglectful or timid or somehow in need of an admonition to do his work? Or was his service of such difficulty that it required the courage of a soldier? Given Paul's respectful salutation to this Christian in the opening words of Philemon, the latter is more likely.

Bibliography

Cope, L. 1985. On Rethinking the Philemon-Colossians Connection. *BR* 30: 35–50.

Lightfoot, J. B. 1879. *Saint Paul's Epistles to the Colossians and to Philemon.* London. Repr. Grand Rapids, MI, 1978.

John Gillman

ARCHITE [Heb *ʾarkî*]. A gentilic formation referring to a clan located SW of Bethel which became a part of Benjamin (Josh 16:2). Five of the six occurrences of the word refer to Hushai, the most celebrated member of the clan, famous for his distinguished service as David's counselor (2 Sam 15:32; 16:16; 17:5, 14; 1 Chr 27:33). The term in Joshua 16:2 has to do with the marking of the S boundary of the tribe of Joseph at "ATAROTH, the territory of the Archites." This has caused confusion because of another Ataroth mentioned in v 7 as being on Ephraim's N border. The S Ataroth marks the border of the Archite clan and is called "Ataroth-addar" in Joshua 16:5 and 18:13, which may mean "Greater Ataroth" (Boling and Wright *Joshua* AB, 397–9).

Siegfried S. Johnson

ARCHITECTURE. See ART AND ARCHITECTURE articles.

ARCHIVES OF MURASHU. See MURASHU, ARCHIVE OF.

ARCHONS, HYPOSTASIS OF. See HYPOSTASIS OF THE ARCHONS (NHC II,*4*).

ARD (PERSON) [Heb *ʾārd*]. Var. ADDAR. ARDITES. One of Benjamin's ten sons, according to the Benjaminite genealogy of Gen 46:21, and head of the Ardites (Num 26:40). The variant form of the name, i.e., "Addar," is easily explained as a transposition of the Hebrew consonants *reš* and *dalet.* The LXX of Num 26:30 reads *adar.* Several variants for the name as it appears in 1 Chr 8:3 exist in the Gk, where the MT also transposes the consonants to read *ʾaddār.* Ard's relationship to Benjamin also varies. In Gen 46:21 he is numbered among ten sons of Benjamin, whereas in Num 26:40 and 1 Chr 8:3 he is a son of Bela and, thus, a grandson of Benjamin. Gen 46:21 also considers two other sons of Bela (Naaman and Gera) to be sons of Benjamin. This variance in family relationship raises the question of how to interpret the expression "sons of," whether it refers to direct family relationships or to clan affiliation (Williamson *1 and 2 Chronicles* NCBC, 83). Williamson finds the name "Ard" in yet another Benjaminite genealogy (1 Chr 7:12). He suggests that the name "Aher" in that verse is a slip for "Addar" or "Ard" (*1 and 2 Chronicles* NCBC, 78). However, most scholars still follow the suggestion of Klostermann in reading the word *ʾeḥād,* "one," an emendation supposing yet another confusion of *reš* and *dalet* (*RE* 4:94).

Siegfried S. Johnson

ARDAT (PLACE) [Lat *Ardath*]. The name of the field to which Ezra was directed (2 Esdr 9:26), by whose bounty he was nourished, and upon whose slopes he received a vision. As with most of 2 Esdras, there is no surviving Gk form of this place name. The Syriac form is *ʾrpd* and the Aramaic *ʾrbd* (perhaps meaning a grain measure). The Latin versions also vary: Ardat (Codex Sangermanesis), Ardad (Codex Ambianesis), Ardas (Codex Complutensis), and Ardaf (Codex Mazarinaeus). Jacob Meyers suggests that Ardat is the name of a small locality near Babylon (*1–2 Esdras* AB, 270). Supporting this suggestion, Abel offered the ruins of Orthosia (Ard) on the site of Ullaza, which is not far from Sumer as a possibility (*GP* 1: 4). He identified this site as the Egyptian *ʾrt,* which occurs in the description of the fifth campaign of Thutmose III as a destroyed city (*ANET,* 239). Another possibility mentioned by both Meyers and Abel is the village of Ardat mentioned a number of times in the Amarna letters near Tripoli or Byblos. There has been no conclusive site identification.

Susan E. McGarry

ARDON (PERSON) [Heb *ʾardôn*]. One of the sons of Caleb (1 Chr 2:18). In the LXX, the name *Orna,* which is otherwise unknown, appears in the place of Ardon. Thus it is not certain whether Orna is a variant of Ardon or whether it refers to a different person.

H. C. Lo

AREINI, TELL EL- (M.R. 129113). Tell esh-Sheikh Aḥmed el-ʿAreini (Arabic "Mound of Sheikh Aḥmed al-ʿAreini") is a mound of some 70 acres (exact limits undefined) on the N outskirts of the modern development town of Gat, just at the junction of the Coastal Plain and the Shephelah, on the S bank of the Wâdi Lachish. It was initially renamed "Tel Gath" by the Israel Geographic Names Committee, following the early identification with "Gath of the Philistines" proposed by Albright, Alt, and others, but the failure of more recent excavations to produce any pertinent Iron I material has resulted in the site's being renamed "Tel ʿErani." Alternate identifications might be Eglon or Mamshat (S. Yeivin), or possibly Libnah (Condor, B. Mazar). Limited soundings were carried out by S. Yeivin in 1956–1961, but only scant preliminary notices of the extensive material have been published (Yeivin, *EAEHL* 1:89–97 and references there; and cf. Weinstein 1984).

The lower city, comprising the bulk of the site, has a lower terrace (area D) and a higher terrace, the former of which has produced the greatest variety and quantity of Egyptian Predynastic and Early Dynastic material of any site in Palestine. The stratification of area D was poorly observed, however, and is much debated, so only a tentative outline of its phases can be given. Strata XII–VII are equivalent to the Egyptian Gerzean/Predynastic period (ca. 3500–3200 B.C.); stratum VI corresponds to the Late Predynastic and may have had a city wall (ca. 3200–3100); stratum V, in which Narmer's *serekh* was found, corresponds to the 1st Dynasty (ca. 3100–2800); strata IV–II correspond to the late 1st into 2d Dynasty (ca. 2800–2650); and stratum I has no clear Egyptian material (ca. 2650–?).

The major question regarding area D concerns Yeivin's sometime claim (never clearly articulated) that stratum VI ends in a major destruction, which should be attributed to Pharoah Narmer of the 1st Dynasty, whose *serekh* (signature) was found on a stratum V sherd (cf. Weinstein 1984 for the evidence and an opposing view). In any case, the succeeding city, which contains the bulk of the Egyptian material, was one of the sites in Palestine most closely connected with Early Dynastic Egypt, whether by trade contacts or otherwise. After the beginning of Dynasty III and the Old Kingdom period (at the latest), the lower city was abandoned, and it lay unoccupied throughout the remainder of the Early Bronze, Middle Bronze, Late Bronze, and Iron I Ages.

The Iron II and later upper city (principally areas A/G) of the NE corner rises some 45–55 ft. above the lower city, but it is only about 15 acres in extent. There were few impressive remains. The phases would appear to be roughly dated as follows:

Stratum	Century (B.C.)
IX	8th
VIII	late 8th
VII	8th/7th
VI	early 7th
V	mid-late 7th
IV	early 6th
III–II	Persian
I	Hellenistic

Byzantine and modern Arab burials lie on and around the mound. On the highest point is the *wêli* (tomb) of the sheikh after whom the mound is named; and nearby are the ruins of the abandoned modern village of ʿIraq el-Manshiyeh.

Bibliography

Weinstein, J. M. 1984. The Significance of Tell Areini for Egyptian-Palestinian Relations at the Beginning of the Bronze Age. *BASOR* 256: 61–69.

Yeivin, S. 1961. *First Preliminary Report on the Excavations of Tel "Gat" (Tell Sheyk ʿAhmed el ʿAreyny) Seasons 1956–1958.* Jerusalem.

William G. Dever

ARELI

ARELI (PERSON) [Heb *ʾarʾēlî*]. ARELITE. A son of Gad, grandson of Zilpah and Jacob, and ancestral head of the Arelites. His name is entered last among the seven sons of Gad mentioned in the list of the descendants of Israel that went to Egypt (Gen 46:16; *Jub.* 44:20 places him second to last). In the census reported in Numbers 26, he is again the last mentioned of the seven descendants of Gad whose names were adopted as clan names (Num 26:17—LXX 26:26). The LXX readings in Gen 46:16 (*ariēlis*) and Num 26:26 (*ariēl*—MT 26:17) suggest the Hebrew spelling *ʾarîʾel,* but the Samaritan Pentateuch reads *ʾrwly,* and the Syriac reads "Adil."

Richard W. Nysse

AREOPAGUS

AREOPAGUS (PLACE) [Gk *ho Areios pagos*]. The Areopagus, or Mars' Hill, was one of the more prominent topographical features of ancient Athens. It reaches a height of 377 ft. and appears to have received its name from an association with Ares, the Greek god of war, though some moderns have derived the name from *Arai* ("Curses"), interpreted as a term designating the Furies, whose cave was located on the NE slope of the hill. It was on the Areopagus that St. Paul stood in A.D. 51 when he delivered his sermon on the unknown god (Acts 17:19–22; Gärtner 1955: 45–65). The Acropolis, some 140 ft. higher, stands a short distance to the SE; and the agora, where Paul talked with passersby and disputed with Stoic and Epicurean philosophers before being taken to the Areopagus (Acts 17:16–18), spreads out below it almost directly to the north. On his ascent from the agora, Paul probably would have rounded the precipitous NE brow of the hill, the Cave of the Furies above him and to his right, and would have climbed toward the summit from the extreme SE by the stairway cut into the rock that is still in use today. (For a map, see ATHENS.) As they had since classical times, the slopes of the Areopagus constituted a residential area when Paul was in Athens.

Paul's conversion of Dionysius the Areopagite (Acts 17:34), whose surname signifies that he was a member of the Council of the Areopagus, gave the hill Christian associations that have persisted into modern times. Dionysius himself became the patron saint of Athens as well as, by tradition, her first bishop and a Christian martyr. The ruins of the Church of St. Dionysius, constructed in the 16th century, are presently visible on the high terrace just below the NE brow of the Areopagus (Travlos and Frantz 1965). At the E end of the church are the remains of the well, supposedly near the home of the Areopagite, where according to local tradition St. Paul was hidden from his persecutors.

A. The Council of the Areopagus

The ancient references to the Council, or Boule, of the Areopagus are usually imprecise, and its history can for the most part be written only in general terms. Named after the hill where it met, and descended from a Homeric-style council of elders that advised the king (see, e.g., *Iliad* 2.53 ff., 10.194 ff.), the council was long composed exclusively of aristocrats, and in the transition from monarchy to aristocracy it gradually assumed many previously regal powers and functions. In the first half of the 7th century B.C., still at the height of its authority, the Council of the Areopagus was the main governing body of Athens, with far-reaching and undefined religious, judicial, censorial, and political power, including a general control over the annual selection of the nine archons, the city's chief magistrates who "went up to the Areopagus" after their term of office, where they then sat for life.

The story of the slow and comparatively gentle democ-

ARE.01. View of the areopagus, looking W from the Acropolis at Athens. *(Courtesy of April D. De Conick.)*

ratization of Athens—which was over 150 years in the making and began imperceptibly about 620 B.C. when Draco codified the laws, thereby defining, and so limiting, the powers of the magistrates and the Council—is also the story of the gradual demise of the Council's authority. Solon confirmed that authority when he rewrote the laws in 594 B.C., but simultaneously laid the foundation for its deterioration, by allowing appeal from the judicial decisions of magistrates to his new people's court, and by opening the archonships, which would provide all future Areopagites, to men of wealth who were not aristocrats. It appeared to emerge without further damage from the constitutional reforms of Cleisthenes at the end of the 6th century B.C., but here again his institution of a council attached to the popular assembly could not but reduce the influence of the Council of the Areopagus and encourage the assumption of its functions by the new body.

A substantial loss of Areopagitic prestige was indirectly assured in 487 B.C. by the expansion of the role of sortition in the selection of archons. But the renewal of the Council's prestige and authority that resulted from its patriotic conduct during Xerxes' invasion (480–479 B.C.) was not undergirded by any constitutional change that would give it permanency. The *coup de grace* was seemingly delivered in 462 B.C. by Ephialtes, who made the only direct attack on the Council's integrity that is recorded and, with perhaps some assistance from Pericles, persuaded the assembly to transfer to itself, its own council, and the popular courts the bulk of the Areopagites' responsibilities. The largely honorific body that remained nevertheless continued to survive, though it took on an increasingly popular appearance itself during the years after 460 B.C., with first the reduction and then the effectual removal of property qualifications for appointment to the nine archonships that constituted the single source of Areopagites.

The reason for this survival is not far to seek. The Council of the Areopagus was a body hallowed by its antique origins, and as such it exercised certain functions so deeply rooted in religious tradition as to be virtually sacrosanct. It was never deprived of these, preeminently the jurisdiction in specific types of homicide cases. In the mythological version of its origins presented in Aeschylus' *Eumenides* (11.397–753), Athena herself founds the Council as a homicide court for the initial purpose of trying Orestes for the murder of his mother Clytemnestra; and Pausanias (I.28.5–6), writing a century after Paul's visit to Athens, indicates that when the Council convened on its hill to judge homicide cases, the accused still stood on the Rock of Insolence and the accuser on the Rock of No-Mercy (Frazer 1913: 362–66). It was this residue of sacred responsibility that preserved the Council in the wake of Ephialtes' assault, and which served as the basis for its eventual resurgence into an important political institution.

We find signs of its revival in the late 5th and the 4th century B.C., when it assumed special public duties in times of crisis, for example after the Athenian defeats by the Spartans at Aegospotami (405 B.C.) and by Philip of Macedon at Chaeronea (338 B.C.). The process of resurgence continued into the Roman period, with the result that by the middle of the 1st century B.C. the Council had reverted to its early status and become the chief governing body of Athens, its membership no doubt again limited to men of wealth and oligarchic sentiment with whom the Romans preferred to deal. Yet there were differences: Roman dignitaries were now sometimes numbered among the Areopagites, and gone forever was the old freedom of judgment and action. It was a Council of the Areopagus so reconstituted that directed the public life of Athens when Paul was there, and would apparently continue to do so until the end of classical antiquity.

B. Paul at the Areopagus

The Acts 17 references to the Areopagus have generated a considerable outpouring of scholarly ink over the past 250 years. The interpretive problem hinges on the exact meaning of "the Areopagus" (*ho Areios pagos*), and the solutions essayed may be divided into two basic groups. One view, supported by a tradition prevalent among the Church Fathers, holds that the term in question is an abbreviated designation for "the Council of the Areopagus," and that Paul was subjected to a formal judicial process, regardless of whether this was a trial or some sort of hearing, and regardless of whether the Council was meeting on the hill that gave it its name or at the Stoa Basileios in the agora (where its sessions had commonly been held since the 4th century B.C.). The other view, which seems preferable, regards *ho Areios pagos* as simply a reference to Mars' Hill, and contends that Acts provides no evidence of judicial proceedings, only an indication that Paul preached on the Hill in response to the request of those with whom he had conversed in the agora.

Bibliography

Bonner, R. J., and Smith, G. 1930–38. *The Administration of Justice from Homer to Aristotle.* 2 vols. Chicago.

Frazer, J. G. 1913. *Pausanias's Description of Greece.* Vol. 2. London.

Gärtner, B. 1955. *The Areopagus Speech and Natural Revelation.* Uppsala.

Hignett, C. 1952. *A History of the Athenian Constitution.* Oxford.

Travlos, J., and Frantz, A. 1965. The Church of St. Dionysios the Areopagite and the Palace of the Archbishop of Athens in the 16th Century. *Hesperia* 34: 157–202.

HUBERT M. MARTIN, JR.

ARETALOGY.

The recitation of the *aretai* (Gk "virtues," "mighty deeds") of a god, hero, or charismatic figure.

A. The Greco-Roman World

The term "aretalogy" includes a variety of forms of a common practice of hellenistic religion and politics. Many laudatory inscriptions, carefully phrased encomiums, and eulogistic biographies are still extant. Scholars have investigated the popular appeal and propagandistic value of a wide variety of such "aretalogical" accounts and have demonstrated that the differences among these texts and recitations of praise are at least as interesting as their commonality.

The term "aretalogy" was used rarely in antiquity and possessed no specific literary or oral form (see Sir 36:13 [14] and Strab. *Geographus* 17.1.17). On the other hand, Isis inscriptions from Delos speak of an "aretalogist" who was a dream interpreter, perhaps recounting the miraculous cures which Isis performed in dreams (see *IG* 11.4.1263). In turn, those who recited fabulous wonders were scorned by Roman authors as entertaining liars (Juv. *Egyptian Satire,* 15: Suet. *Aug.* 74). Modern scholars of the history of religions have thus identified "aretalogy" with the recitations of the "aretalogists," paying particular attention to its value as a mode of religious proclamation or propaganda. The chief example remained the appeal which Oriental and Egyptian traditions made to a broader public on the basis of the recitations of the mighty deeds and virtues of a god or cult figure.

Such cultic recitation took on a distinctive form in the "self-praises of Isis." Several inscriptions display a well-wrought form in which Isis declares "I am . . . ," announcing herself as the ruler of heaven and earth, mistress of fate and weather, legislator of helpful human ordinances, dispenser of wealth and source of wisdom. Such catalogs of her "virtues" could also be recited by others in third-person declarations, "She who . . ." These lists of glorious attributes and mighty acts may also be compared with the inscriptions of the healings which were placarded at Epidaurus in praise of Asclepius. Those lists for the healing cult were another form of "aretalogy" in the religious marketplace of the Greco-Roman world.

Laudatory biographies and letters of recommendation of charismatic prophets, healers, and itinerant philosophers have also been identified as "aretalogical" by modern scholars. Such cycles of stories and claims produced a peculiar literature which the satirists such as Lucian of Samosata could mock. In the effort to promote a particular figure as inspired or divine or as a "divine man" (Gk *theios anēr*), authors adopted various catalogs of virtues or mighty acts (*aretai*). Philosophers, rulers, and wonder workers could all be credited with divine or semidivine status although the specific criteria for such deifications were distinct. The praise of the wisdom of Socrates or the self-sufficiency of Diogenes may even be formally similar to the glorification of Alexander's courage or the recitation of the miraculous power of Asclepius' cures.

All of these distinct "aretalogical" traditions provide a window on the religious marketplace of the Greco-Roman world. Egyptian cults were striving for recognition and support for adherents in the west, exporting Isis to Rome along with the grain of the Nile and seeking recognition and support for Egypt's spiritual heritage and institutions were as legitimate as any in the dominant culture.

Popular philosophers competed for converts and healing shrines for adherents. The virtues of the philosophers could be catalogued in direct praise of their oral example or as cynic displays of disdain for conventional standards. Miraculous cures and mighty acts of shamans and rulers were listed as documentation of divine authority or agency. At the end of the 2d century C.E., Philostratus' *Life of Apollonius of Tyana* presented a synthesized portrait of the wonder-working Pythagorean philosopher. Earlier sources telling of Apollonius' marvelous acts of magic and supernatural power may still be identified within Philostratus' "life" of the philosopher, but Philostratus had produced a new example of a more complex "aretalogical" literature.

B. Jewish Wisdom and Mission

Many forms of contemporary Jewish tradition clearly participated in this Greco-Roman religious marketplace, and a variety of texts may be called "aretalogical" in close comparison with the traditions discussed above. The cleanest parallels can be drawn with Hellenistic Jewish texts of Egyptian provenance, but the competition among religious and philosophical traditions for adherents and converts is much more extensive.

The praise of Wisdom in both Proverbs 8 and Wis 9:18–10:21 recalls conventions of the praises of Isis. Whether Wisdom recites her own praises or is praised in third-person declaration, her "aretalogy" rivals that of Isis both in form and in the mythic creative and saving roles which she plays. Like Isis, Wisdom has become the consort of God whom the king desires as his bride (Wis 8:2–9). Still, her tasks are explicitly identified with Jewish scriptural traditions, and no accommodation is offered to those outside of "a holy people and blameless race" (Wis 10:15). Thus the audience for this "aretalogy" does not appear to be a broad public in the Greco-Roman world. Wisdom was being praised for the benefit of Jews who were intimidated by the power of Isis and the Egyptian royal theology which she represented.

The glorification of Moses by Artapanus was another kind of aretalogy, imitating the novelistic glorification of Egyptian and other nationalistic heroes. The biblical Moses is still central, but this worker of plagues and liberator of Israel is also praised as the founder of the nomes of Egypt, the inventor of ships, and a godlike Hermes who gives the Egyptians their sacred letters and interprets them. The folklore of national heroes is not as theologically particular as wisdom traditions nor so discriminating of moral virtue as the lives of the philosophers. But Artapanus' glorious portrait of Moses placed him in the proud company of such rulers and champions as Semiramis the Babylonian and Sesostris the Egyptian. Once again, the audience for such extravagant stories of Moses was probably only Egyptian Jews who were eager to be assured of the importance of their heritage within the dominant culture.

Philo's *Life of Moses* raised the aretalogy of Moses to a new level of the glorification of the "sage" and "divine man" who is at once the ideal king, lawgiver, high priest, and prophet (I.334; II.2–7, 187, 292). Whether written for Hellenistic Jews or non-Jews, Philo's account adapted the biblical account freely, dressing Moses in the philosopher's cloak and the robe of the statesman. Even the biblical miracles were heavily rationalized, ignored or turned into verifications of Moses' possession of the virtue of piety (*Vita Mos* II. 284). The recitation of miracles was not primary in this aretalogy. The hellenistic ideal of kingship is much more the controlling standard.

Josephus also indulged in effusive praise of Moses as the "most excellent general, the wisest adviser and the most conscientious of all guardians." Next to him such lawgivers as Lycurgus, Solon, and Zaleucus were only born yesterday (*AgAp* 2.154–58). Josephus was explicitly responding to the charges of others that Moses was an evil leper who organized the outcast Jews with the advice to attack the Egyptian population, showing goodwill to no one (*AgAp* 1.237–50, 304–8, 2.121–22). Writing in a time when the Roman order had driven the Jews into fighting for their right to live, Josephus' aretalogy is transparent in its defense of Moses' virtue, wisdom, and power.

C. New Testament Aretalogies and Mission

Early Christian proclamations of Jesus quickly adopted and adapted many forms of praise and testified to Jesus as Messiah, Savior, Son of God, Lord, and Son of Man. All such recitations of Jesus' words, works, life, death, and resurrection could be broadly called aretalogical. After all, the Christian mission also had to make its way in the Greco-Roman religious marketplace. But more specific comparisons have proved helpful in a few areas.

The "superlative apostles" of 2 Corinthians (12:11–12) may reflect a kind of Jewish Christian missionizing in which a particular kind of inspired exegesis, signs, wonders and mighty works were standard credentials. Perhaps Paul is contending with a kind of "divine man" tradition in which these star performers have their letters of recommendation and their loyal adherents. Then Paul's "foolish" recitation of his weakness and suffering is a counter-aretalogy, intended to discredit the self-praises of these "false apostles."

If the probability of pre-Gospel collections of miracle stories is high, then were these sources a kind of aretalogy? John probably used a Signs Source, and Mark may have drawn upon a cycle of miracle stories but subsumed them in a cross-resurrection narrative structure. Perhaps the Gospel genre is a kind of critique of the aretalogical traditions of the Greco-Roman religious marketplace.

On the other hand, perhaps the Gospels themselves should be viewed as aretalogies too. Luke-Acts in particular appears to appropriate the miracle traditions and glorify the Lord and the apostles without any sharp caution about the misuse of the Jesus traditions (apart from the clear perversion by Simon Magus and the Sons of Sceva in Acts 8 and 19). Some interpreters also regard the Fourth Gospel as using the Signs quite uncritically in a straightforward effort to glorify Jesus as the Son of God "striding over the earth."

The discussion is important since it requires the interpreter of the New Testament to view the mission of the early church within the competitive religious context of the 1st century. Paul and the evangelists have been described by some scholars as confounding the aretalogies of contemporary religious propaganda with the kerygma of Christ crucified. Other interpreters have argued that even the Gospels and Paul's recitations of his "foolishness" are distinctive aretalogies but not formally unique. Since the term is not technically specific, the discussion of "aretalogies" will continue to provide fruitful occasions for the comparison and contrast of the Gospels and early Christian proclamation with a wide range of religious and political recitations of praise of saviors, lords, cult figures, and gods.

Bibliography

Festugiere, A. J. 1949. A propos des aretalogies d'Isis. *HTR* 42: 209–34.

Fortna, R. T. 1975. Christology in the Fourth Gospel: Redaction-Critical Perspectives. *NTS* 21: 489–504.

Georgi, D. 1964. *Die Gegner des paulus im 2. Korintherbrief.* WMANT 11. Neukirchen-Vluyn.

Kee, H. C. 1973. Aretalogy and Gospel. *JBL* 92: 402–22.

Kloppenburg, J. S. 1982. Isis and Sophia in the Book of Wisdom. *HTR* 75: 57–84.

Loester, H. 1968. One Jesus and Four Gospels. *HTR* 61: 230–36.

Petzke, G. 1970. *Die Traditionen über Apollonius von Tyana und das Neue Testament.* SCHNT 1. Leiden.

Reitzensten, R. 1906. *Hellenistische Wundererzählungen.* Darmstadt.

Smith, J. Z. 1975. Good News Is No News: Aretalogy and Gospel. Pp. 21–38 in Part One of *Christianity, Judaism and Other Greco-Roman Cults,* ed. J. Neusner. Leiden.

Smith, M. 1971. Prolegomena to a Discussion of Aretalogies, Divine Men, the Gospels and Jesus. *JBL* 90: 174–99.

Tiede, D. L. 1972. *The Charismatic Figure as Miracle Worker.* SBLDS 1. Missoula.

DAVID L. TIEDE

ARETAS. Dynastic name of at least four kings of the royal house of Nabatea located at Petra. The earliest Nabatean Aramaic inscription from Elusa on the Petra-Gaza road in the Negev mentions an "Aretas, King of the Nabateans." Proposals for a date of the inscription vary from the beginning to the end of the 2d century B.C. (see Wenning 1987: 141). The Aramaic spelling of the name, *ḥrtt,* occurs rarely and is of disputed etymology, but it does appear as a personal name occasionally in Safaitic (Harding 1971: 282). It has been associated with the common Arabic name of *ḥarita,* "ploughman" (al-Khraysheh 1986: 93) and it is interesting that the name "*ḥāriṯat,* king of Hagar" appears in Aramaic on coins of the mid-2d century B.C. found at Susa (Robin 1974: 110). Hagar has been connected with the *Agraioi* of Greek sources, a people who controlled the E sector of the caravan route leading from Babylon through Dumat al-Jandal (Jauf) to Petra and the Mediterranean port at Gaza (Eratosthenes apud Strabo 16.4.2). The proposal that the original homeland of the Nabateans was located in this same region of the Persian

Gulf (Milik 1982) offers some support to these connections and may help explain other features of Nabatean culture, e.g., the use of Aramaic and the name of "Hagiru" for the queens and princesses of the Nabatean royal house (as known from coins; see Meshorer 1975: 79).

1. *Aretas I (ca. 170–160 B.C. fl.).* The first known dynast of the Nabateans is a contemporary of the early Hasmonean rulers. In 168, the Jewish high priest Jason sought refuge with an "Aretas, tyrant of the Arabs," before whom he was tried and/or imprisoned (2 Macc 5:8; cf. Goldstein *2 Maccabees* AB, 256). This Aretas is most likely the same king of the Nabateans referred to in the Elusa inscription as "tyrant," a word frequently used as a synonym for "king." The Nabateans under his rule appear to have been friends with the Maccabean rulers Judas (1 Macc 5:24–28; cf. Jos *Ant* 12.8.3 §335) and Jonathan (15.22). A perplexing reference to Arab nomads who skirmished with Judas (2 Macc 12:10–12) probably refers to Arabs existing outside the Nabatean circle (Bowersock 1983: 19–20), perhaps the Itureans (Kasher 1988: 30; see also ITURAEA).

2. *Aretas II (ca. 100 B.C. fl.).* Under his reign, the Nabateans first came into conflict with the Hasmonean kingdom. In 100 B.C., Alexander Jannaeus beseiged the important commercial port of Gaza. Aretas had pledged to protect the town, but he failed to send military assistance in time to defend it from the attack by the Hasmonean ruler (Jos. *Ant* 13.13.3 §358–64). Justinus' Latin epitome of Pompeius Trogus' *Historiae Philippicae* (39.5.5–6) mentions an Arab king named Herotimus who led campaigns into Syria and Egypt. Herotimus probably is to be identified with Aretas II. These conflicts have been interpreted as a struggle for control of the lucrative trade routes of Palestine during the decline of the Hellenistic powers of Syria and Egypt. This Aretas is also alluded to in the oldest Nabatean inscription known from Petra, where he appears as the father of Obodas I, his successor as king of the Nabateans (ca. 93–85 B.C.). This has led to the suggestion that he is the "founder of the Nabatean dynasty" (*HJP*[2] 1: 577), but this ignores the evidence for the earlier monarchs (Starcky *DBSup* 7: 905). Some archaic Nabatean coins known from Gaza and Petra have also been associated with his reign (Meshorer 1975: 10–11), the earliest issues by any of the Nabatean kings.

3. *Aretas III (ca. 85–62 B.C.).* The early years of his reign represent a period of Nabatean expansion. As a young prince, he founded the settlement of Aurara (modern Hymayma) between Petra and Aqaba, evidently to promote the trade along this important route that connected the Nabatean capital with the Red Sea (Uranius' *Arabicus* apud F. Jacoby *FGrH* 675 F1b; Eadie 1984). In 85, after the death of the Seleucid ruler Antiochus XII, Aretas acquired Coele-Syria and Damascus as part of his realm (Jos. *Ant* 13.5.2 §392). In coins struck at Damascus between 84–72 B.C., Aretas is entitled in the Greek legend the "Philhellene" (Meshorer 1975: 12–16), indicating the adoption of the Hellenistic tradition of the region. In 82, he launched a campaign into Judea where he defeated Alexander Jannaeus in a battle at Adida. After the setback, however, the Hasmonean ruler led a counterattack that saw the loss of Nabatean territories in Moab and Gilead (*Ant* 13.5.3–4 §393–97). In 72–71 B.C., the invasion of Tigranes of Armenia into Syria also forced Aretas to withdraw from Damascus (13.16.4 §419). After the death of Alexander Jannaeus in 76 B.C., his widow, Queen Alexandra, assumed ule until her death in 67 B.C. Afterward, a dynastic quarrel broke out between her sons, Hyrcanus and Aristobulus. The Idumean ruler Antipater, who supported Hyrcanus, had established friendly relations with the Nabateans, as a result of his marriage to a prominent Nabatean woman named Cypros, the mother of Herod the Great (*Ant* 14.7.3 §121; *JW* 1.181). As a result, he advised Hyrcanus to flee for refuge to "Aretas of Arabia" and enlist his support. Forming an alliance with the Nabatean ruler, Antipas and Hyrcanus then led a campaign against the opposition party of Aristobulus at Jerusalem. In response, the Roman general Pompey sent his envoy Scaurus to help defend Aristobulus. Under threat of being declared an enemy of Rome, Aretas withdrew from Jerusalem, but 6000 of his forces were slain by Aristobulus at Papyron, near Jericho, during their retreat (*Ant* 14.1.1–2.3 §1–33). Afterward, Scaurus beseiged Petra, but withdrew after the king paid him 3000 talents (*Ant* 14.5.1 §80–81; *JW* 1.124–30). During his aedileship in 58 B.C., Scaurus issued coins at Rome depicting a long-haired Aretas kneeling beside his camel in submission to himself (Crawford 1974: 446, no. 422). Henceforth, Nabatea came under Roman sway as a client kingdom.

4. *Aretas IV (9–8 B.C.–A.D. 40–41).* The zenith of Nabatean political and economic fortunes took place during the almost half-century of his lengthy reign. After the death of Obodas III in 9 B.C., Syllaeus, "the brother of the king" and chief administrator of the kingdom, assumed control of the state and even issued coinage depicting him as the monarch (Meshorer 1975: 36–40). Augustus recognized him as the official ruler, but an Aeneas assumed control of the throne at Petra under the name of Aretas (IV) and sent an embassy to Rome to plead his case and condemn Syllaeus. Although not a direct descendant of Obodas III, Aeneas appears to have been from a collateral line of the royal house, related to Malichus I (58–30 B.C.). However, the Roman emperor dismissed Aretas' claims, sending his envoys and their gifts back to Nabatea, as he had failed to request the emperor's permission before assuming rule. In spite of his initial rejection of Aretas' petition, Augustus found other complaints about Syllaeus more persuasive. These were issued by Herod the Great through his agent Nicolaus of Damascus. As a result, Syllaeus was condemned and later executed by Augustus, who reluctantly recognized Aretas as the legitimate ruler of Nabatea (Jos. *Ant* 16.9.1–4 §271–99 and 10.8–9 §335–55).

The lengthy reign of Aretas is the best documented of any Nabatean monarch. The coinage issued in his reign is immense, representing an estimated 80 percent of all Nabatean coinage. It has been found at scattered sites throughout the Levant (including Cyrus, Dura-Europos, and Susa) and even in Europe (Aventicum, Switzerland). It is also important for the portraiture of the monarch, who is depicted with a mustache after A.D. 18. A gap in the issues and inscriptions of his reign between 4–1 B.C. and a cryptic comment by Strabo (16.4.21) has led to the suggestion that the Nabatean kingdom had been annexed briefly, then transformed again to the status of a client state (Bowersock 1983: 54–55). The motive may be associated with Herod's death in 4 B.C., when Aretas provided auxiliaries to assist the Syrian legate Varus in quelling political unrest in Judea (*Ant* 17.10.9 §287; *JW* 2.68). Their disobedience of the Roman commander's orders during the affair prompted their dismissal and perhaps Roman intervention in Nabatea (*Ant* 17.10.10 §296). Nevertheless, other chronological gaps in the coinage and inscriptions of Aretas' reign exist, rendering this interpretation inconclusive. Moreover, the standard epithet "lover of his people" (*raḥem ʿanmeh*) that appears on Aretas' coinage has been interpreted as an implicit rejection of such titles as *philoromaios* and *philokaisar* used by other Roman client kings and a protest against any suggestion of servility (*HJP*² 1: 582). The epithet appears on his coins and inscriptions from the beginning to the end of his reign.

Under Aretas, the formative stage of Nabatean material culture took place. Their distinctive art, architecture, pottery, and peculiar Aramaic script all developed their classical style during his reign. Many of the monumental structures at Petra have been assigned to his time, such as the construction of the theater and Qaṣr al-Bint; the famous Khazneh at the terminus of the Siq has also been proposed as the great king's final resting place. The development of the Negev cities at the time—Oboda, Mampsis, Nessana, Elusa, and Sobata—further reflects the economic prosperity of the period. In addition, Madāʾin ṣaliḥ (ancient Hegra) appears to have been founded early in his reign, serving as an important emporium for the caravan trade in aromatics from South Arabia. Nabatean merchants in A.D. 3–6 even erected a sanctuary at the port of Puteoli in Italy (CIS II 158). The administrative and military organization of Aretas' realm reflect these foreign contacts; his officers bear titles adopted from the Hellenistic and Roman overlords: strategoi, hipparchoi, chiliarchoi, and even a centurion appear in inscriptions during his reign. In many respects, the cultural achievements of Aretas IV represent a fitting parallel to those of his contemporary in Judea, Herod the Great.

Aretas had at least two wives during his lengthy reign: Huldu (from 9 B.C.–A.D. 16) and Shuqailat (from A.D. 18). They are not designated his "sisters" (*ʾḥt*) on coins during his reign, in contrast to the wives of his royal successors Malichus II (A.D. 40–70) and Rabbel II (A.D. 71–106), but inscriptions indicate that both Huldu (CIS II 158) and Shuqailat (CIS II 354; Khairy 1981) were entitled his "sister." The "title" has been taken literally, but it many only represent an important rank in the hierarchy of the royal court of Nabatea (Meshorer 1975: 61). Syllaeus was also called the "brother of the king [i.e., Obodas II]," although he was the son of Teimu, not Obodas II. The members of the royal family of Aretas IV late in his reign are listed in a recent inscription found at Wadi Musa (Khairy 1981). It names four sons (Malichus II, Obodas, Rabbel, and Phasael) and four daughters (Shaʿdat, Shaqilat II, Gamilat, and Hageru); the latter princess was also the mother of a child named Aretas, the grandson of Aretas IV. Intermarriages between the royal families of the various monarchies were common in the East and existed in the relations of the Petraean royal house with the Herodian dynasty: one of Aretas' daughters—perhaps Shaʿudat (Starcky *DBSup* 7: 914)—was married to the tetrarch Herod Antipas before he divorced her to marry Herodias, the wife of his half-brother Herod Philip. John the Baptist condemned the action and was imprisoned and finally executed by Antipas around A.D. 29 (Matt 14:3–12 and par.). Aretas' anger found revenge only later, in A.D. 36, when he attacked and defeated the army of Antipas. Tiberius sent Vitellius the governor of Syria to punish Aretas for his action, but the Roman emperor's death in A.D. 36–37 canceled the expedition (*Ant* 18.5.1–3 §109–25).

The only specific biblical reference to Aretas IV appears in Paul's letter of 2 Corinthians in which he refers to his escape in a basket lowered from a window in the city wall that was guarded by the "governor [*ethnarch*] under king Aretas" (11:32–33). The circumstances remain obscure, but the Jewish and Nabatean Arab community appear to have acted in concert against Paul (cf. Acts 9:24). The ethnarch of Aretas has been taken to be a royal official charged with oversight of the Nabatean commercial colony established at Damascus (*DBSup* 7: 915; Rey-Coquais 1978: 50; Knauf 1983), rather than an indication the city constituted part of the Nabatean realm. A parallel has been found in an official with the title of "ethnarch" who was responsible for the Jewish community at Alexandria (Jos. *Ant* 14.17). But others feel that Paul's description of the incident seems to place the Syrian city clearly under Nabatean control, however briefly (Bowersock 1983: 68). Since the episode appears to have occurred in the reign of the emperor Caligula (A.D. 37–41), it has been associated with his general policy of extending the territories of the client kings in the East (Jewett 1979: 30–33, 99). No coinage from Damascus appears to have been struck during his reign or that of Claudius. Paul's prior contacts with Nabatea (Gal 1:17) may also account for the animosity of Aretas' official in Damascus, but the sources are silent about his Arabian sojourn. The odd inclusion of the incident in his list of hardships (see Fitzgerald 1988: 18–19) has been explained as an inversion of Roman military imagery, emphasizing the apostle's humiliation in retreating over a wall, in contrast to the distinguished award (*corona muralis*) given to the first courageous Roman soldier to scale the wall of the enemy (Judge 1968: 47; cf. Furnish *2 Corinthians* AB, 542). As such, it illustrates again the "weakness" of Paul.

Bibliography

Bowersock, G. W. 1983. *Roman Arabia.* Cambridge, MA.

Crawford, M. 1974. *Roman Republican Coinage,* Vol. 1. Cambridge.

Eadie, J. W. 1984. Humayma 1983: The Regional Survey. *ADAJ* 28: 211–24.

Fitzgerald, J. T. 1988. *Cracks in an Earthen Vessel: An Examination of the Catalogues of Hardships in the Corinthian Correspondence.* SBLDS 99. Atlanta.

Harding, G. L. 1971. *An Index and Concordance of Pre-Islamic Arabian Names and Inscriptions.* Near and Middle East Series 8. Toronto.

Jewett, R. 1979. *A Chronology of Paul's Life.* Philadelphia.

Judge, E. A. 1968. Paul's Boasting in Relation to Contemporary Professional Practice. *ABR* 16: 37–50.

Kasher, A. 1988. *Jews, Idumaeans, and Ancient Arabs.* Texte und Studien zum Antiken Judentum 18. Tübingen.

Khairy, N. 1981. A New Dedicatory Nabataean Inscription from Wadi Musa. *PEQ* 113: 19–26.

Knauf, E. A. 1983. Zum *Ethnarchen* des *Aretas* 2 Kor 11, 32. *ZAW* 74: 145–47.

Kraysheh, F. Al-. 1986. *Die Personennamen in den nabatäischen Inschriften des Corpus Inscriptionum Semiticarum.* Diss. Marburg.

Meshorer, Y. 1975. *Nabataean Coins.* Monographs of the Institute of Archaeology 3. Jerusalem.

Milik, J. T. 1982. Origines des Nabatéens. Pp. 261–65 in *Studies in the History and Archaeology of Jordan,* I. Ed. A. Hadidi. Amman.

Rey-Coquais, J.-P. 1978. Syrie romaine, de Pompée à Dioclétien. *JRS* 68: 44–73.

Robin, C. 1974. Monnaies provenant de l'Arabie du Nord Est. *Sem* 24: 83–125.

Wenning, R. 1987. *Die Nabatäer—Denkmäler und Geschichte.* Göttingen.

DAVID F. GRAF

ARGOB (PLACE) [Heb *ʾargōb*]. A district E of the Jordan valley of uncertain location. The name Argob occurs three times in the chapter of Deuteronomy recounting the capture of the Amorite kingdom of BASHAN that was ruled by OG (Deut 3:4, 13, 14) and once in the account of Solomon's administrative districts (1 Kgs 4:14). The name consistently appears in the construction *ḥebel ʾargōb,* and its proper interpretation presents several problems. The Hebrew noun *ḥebel* can denote a measured tract or area (note LXX *schoinismos* [1 Kgs 4:13]), and thus would seem to imply a clearly delineated section of Bashan. The etymology of the name "Argob" suggests a possible identification of the area, though difficulties remain. The toponym *ʾargōb* is probably related to the rare noun *regeb* "clod (of earth)" (found only in Job 21:33; 38:38), perhaps referring to a tract of arable land. The name is replaced in *Tg. Yer.* with the word *tarkona,* which may be a transliteration of Gk *trachōn,* a substantive meaning "rugged, stony region" and also the name of the large basalt formation about 20 mi. S of Damascus (called in Arabic *el-Leja* "the Refuge"; see TRACHONITIS). The location of this formation well E of the Jordan stands in the way of its identification with Argob, because Deut 3:14 implies that the region of Argob extended W "as far as the border of the Geshurites and Maacathites"; that border is generally placed at the Nahr er-Raqqad, the westernmost N-S tributary of the river Yarmuk.

Other locations have been proposed for Argob, though none can claim consensus. The region known as Batanea to the W and S of Trachonitis is one possibility (*GB,* 215). Its rich soil has been farmed by the Druze in more recent times. Simons (*GTTOT,* 8–9, 13) extends the region of Argob W to Nahr er-Raqqad and N to Mt. Hermon (although *GTTOT* Map V twice shows Argob lying along the Wadi al-Harir [also called Hreir or Ehrer], considerably E of Raqqad). Mazar (1961: 24) located Argob along the banks of the Wadi el-ʾAllan (another Yarmuk tributary situated between Raqqad and Harir). Avi-Yonah (*EncJud* 1) placed Argob between the wadis Raqqad and ʾAllan.

Bergman (1936: 239) suggested Jebel Druz as the location of Argob, though he doubted that the Israelite conquest included territory N of the Yarmuk. Ottosson (1969: 111–12) places Argob in N Gilead, *south* of the Yarmuk and S of Bashan (although he appears to extend Bashan S of the Yarmuk).

The location and extent of the region of Argob is further complicated by the biblical statement (Deut 3:13) that it is conterminous with the kingdom of Og and apparently also with the region called HAVVOTH-JAIR (Deut 3:14). The latter cities are said to be in Bashan (Josh 13:30) but also in Gilead (Num 32:40–41; Judg 10:4). The sixth Solomonic administrative district comprised Havvoth-jair in Gilead and the region of Argob in Bashan (1 Kgs 4:13), clearly distinguishing the locations of the two regions.

Another biblical reference to Argob (2 Kgs 15:25) is textually problematic. The phrase *ʾet-ʾargōb wĕʾet-hāʾaryê* may be misplaced from v 29, a list of places captured by the Assyrian king Tiglath-pileser. The second member of the pair may be a corrupt reading of *yāʾîr* from the place name Havvoth-jair. If this reasoning is correct, then Argob is distinguished from Havvoth-jair in this instance as well.

Bibliography

Bergman, A. 1936. The Israelite Tribe of Half-Manasseh. *JPOS* 16: 224–54.

Mazar, B. 1961. Geshur and Maacah. *JBL* 80: 16–28.

Ottosson, M. 1969. *Gilead: Tradition and History.* Lund.

HENRY O. THOMPSON

ARGOB AND ARIEH (PERSONS) [Heb *ʾargōb* and *ʾaryēh*]. Possibly two coconspirators with Pekah or victims along with the king, Pekahiah, of Pekah's conspiracy (2 Kgs 15:25), but more likely place names. The MT includes these two names in a grammatically difficult sentence, but they are omitted in many English translations (RSV, NAB, NEB). Various solutions to the problems posed by these two names have been suggested. Klostermann emends the text to read "with his four hundred warriors" suggesting that Pekah was able to eradicate the entire royal guard. Geller proposes that the text should be translated "near eagle and lion" indicating the place where Pekahiah was murdered. Geller argues that as Sennacherib was murdered between statues of protective deities set up at the gates of the royal palace, so Pekahiah was murdered between guardian statues of his palace. Most modern translators accept Stade's solution that Argob and Arieh are place names and should be omitted. It is possible that a scribe's eyes wandered from the Gilead of v 29 to the Gilead of v 25, where he then inserted place names that should actually be in v 29. Argob is the name of a district of Bashan (Deut 3:4, 13, 14; 1 Kgs 4:13). Arieh, similar in spelling to Havvoth-jair which is elsewhere associated with Argob (Deut 3:14), refers to a group of settlements in the area. (See Gray *Kings* OTL; Jones Vol. 2 of *Kings* NCBC.)

Bibliography

Geller, M. J. 1976. A New Translation for 2 Kings XV 25. *VT* 26/3: 374–77.

Klostermann, A. 1887. *Die Bücher Samuelis und der Könige.* Kurgefasster Kommentar zu den heiligen Schriften Alten und Neuen Testament, A/3. Nordlingen.

Stade, B. 1886. Anmerkungen zu 2 Kö, 15–21. *ZAW* 6: 156–89.

PAULINE A. VIVIANO

ARIANISM. See ARIUS, ARIANISM.

ARIARATHES (PERSON) [Gk *Ariarathēs*]. Ariarathes V Eusebes Philopater, king of Cappadocia (ca. 163–130 B.C.), [1 Macc 15:22]. He appears in a list of recipients of the letter sent by the consul Lucius endorsing the leadership of Simon, the High Priest. The letter stresses the renewal of friendship and alliance between Rome and Judea, forbids war against Judea by Roman allies, and allows for the extradition of prisoners. The placement of Ariarathes V after Attalus II reflects accurately both their submission to Rome and the strong ties between the two men. Attalus II married Ariarathes' sister, Stratonice. He also came to Ariarathes' aid when the latter's half-brother, Orophernes, had seized the throne of Cappadocia. Later they together attacked the city of Priene in an attempt to regain funds stolen by Orophernes, but they withdrew after Rome ordered them to cease. Ariarathes V died during the battle of Leucae while fighting with the Romans against Aristonicus, who attempted to seize the throne of Pergamum after the death of Attalus III.

Bibliography

Hansen, E. V. 1971. *The Attalids of Pergamon.* 2d ed. Ithaca, NY.
Magie, D. 1950. *Roman Rule in Asia Minor.* 2 vols. Princeton.

RUSSELL D. NELSON

ARIDAI (PERSON) [Heb *ʾarīday, ʾărîday*]. One of the ten sons of Haman (Esth 9:9). On problems surrounding this list of names, see ADALIA. Aridai (LXX *arsaion*) possibly renders the otherwise unattested Old Iranian name **Arya-dāyah-* "the Iranian tending for", or **Arya-da-hyu-* "of Iranian land, country."

Bibliography

Zadok, R. 1986. Notes on Esther. *ZAW* 98: 105–10.

PETER BEDFORD

ARIDATHA (PERSON) [Heb *ʾărîdātāʾ*]. One of the ten sons of Haman (Esth 9:8). On problems surrounding this list of names, see ADALIA. Aridatha (LXX *sarbaka* cannot be harmonized with Aridatha and must represent another name) possibly renders the otherwise unattested Old Iranian name **Arya-dāta*—"brought forth from the Aryan."

Bibliography

Hinz, W. 1975. *Altiranisches Sprachgut der Nebenüberlieferungen.* Wiesbaden.
Scheftelowitz, I. 1901. *Arisches im Alten Testament.* Vol. I. Berlin.

PETER BEDFORD

ARIEH. See ARGOB AND ARIEH.

ARIEL (PERSON) [Heb *ʾărîʾēl*]. Var. IDUEL. Even though the Hebrew terms that stand behind the transliteration "ariel" occur rarely in the Bible, "ariel" seems to carry a wide range of meanings: (1) a poetic name for Jerusalem (Isa 29:1–2, 7); (2) a common noun for "heroes" or "champions" (2 Sam 23:20; 1 Chr 11:22; cf. Isa 33:7); (3) a common noun for "altar hearth" (Ezek 43:15–16; cf. Mesha Inscription, line 12); and (4) a personal name, a proper noun (Ezra 8:16). This rapid overview actually reduces a complicated discussion to its simplest form, and the balance of this entry pursues the use of this word as a personal name. At the outset it should be recognized that there is much dispute over the etymology of "ariel" (lion of God?) and how the word was used in the ways listed above (Segert 1961: 241; *KAI* 2: 175; Andersen 1966: 90; *TSSI* 1: 80).

In Ezra 8:16, the personal name "Ariel" occurs in a list of "leading men" who helped Ezra solve a problem. In the parallel text in 1 Esdr 8:43, he is called Iduel (Gk Idouēlos). During the reign of Artaxerxes, Ezra received permission to lead a party of exiled Judeans from Babylonia back to Jerusalem. When he had gathered this group of men at "the river that runs to Ahava," whose exact location is unknown, Ezra took note of the fact that there were no "sons of Levi" among the large number. (A similar scarcity of Levites is noted in Ezra 2:40.) Accordingly, he summoned some of the leading men of the day, including Ariel, and apprised them of the situation. They were dispatched to a place called Casiphia, also unidentified, to speak to a leader named Iddo; he and his "brethren" were the temple servants (Hebrew *nĕtînîm*) at Casiphia. Apparently, the appeal of men like Ariel was successful, since "ministers for the house of God" were found to accompany Ezra and his party of émigrés (Ezra 8:15–20).

An intriguing use of the word "ariel" occurs in 2 Sam 23:20 (paralleled in 1 Chr 11:22). These verses mention the valor of Benaiah, the son of Jehoiada, one of David's mighty men. To illustrate his courage, the last part of the sentence reports that Benaiah "smote *two ariels of Moab*" (RSV), while the KJV renders this line "he slew *two lionlike men of Moab.*" A marginal note in the RSV informs the reader that the meaning of the term "ariel" is not known, and the KJV translators informed their readers that "ariel(s)" should be translated literally "lions of God." The KJV has chosen to follow the MT and translate "two ariels" into English as "two lionlike men" (i.e., "heroes" or "champions," which is probably a correct rendering). Likewise, the RSV follows the MT's wording, "two ariels," but leaves ariels untranslated. On the other hand, the LXX reconstructs the phrase to say *"The two sons of Ariel of Moab,"* thereby making Ariel a proper noun, the name of a Moabite father whose sons were slain by Banaiah. This use of "ariel" as a Moabite name can be compared with one of the proposed translations of a phrase in line 12 of the Mesha Inscription, *ʾrʾl dwdh* "Arel its commander" or "Arel its chief." Though the use of *ʾrʾl* as a man's name still finds support in scholarly circles, most seem to prefer "altar hearth" in this expression, as in Ezek 43:15–16 (Kaiser *Isaiah* OTL, 266–67).

Bibliography

Andersen, F. I. 1966. Moabite Syntax. *Or n.s.* 35: 81–120.
Segert, S. 1961. Die Sprache Der Moabitischen Königsinschrift. *ArOr* 29: 197–267.

GERALD L. MATTINGLY

ARIEL (PLACE) [Heb *ʾarîʾēl*]. When used to refer to a place, Ariel is a descriptive term applied to the city of Jerusalem: "Ho Ariel, Ariel, the city where David encamped"; "Yet I will distress Ariel . . ."; "And the multitudes of all the nations that fight against Ariel . . ." (Isa 29:1, 2, 7). The suggestion that the term is a compound of *ʾari* and *ʾel* to mean "lion[ness] of God" is inferred by some from references to Judah (whose capital was Jerusalem) as "a lion's whelp" (Gen 49:9) and to the leader of Judah, Jesus Christ, "the Lion of the tribe of Judah, the Root of David" (Rev 5:5). References in 2 Sam 23:20 to one of David's men as a valiant man who killed men of Moab and a lion, and in Isa 33:7 (where some postulate *ʾerʾellam* to be derived from *ʾariʾel*; cf. *BDB,* 72) to the brave men of Judah during Sennacherib's onslaught are cited in support of this view. It is noted that in 2 Sam 23:20 the LXX reads, "the two sons of Ariel of Moab," while the MT has "the two ariel(s) of Moab." In Ezek 43:15 there is a curious MT reading, *harʾēl,* "mountain of God," in the context of a description of the altar; some versions here have *ʾariʾēl* ("lioness of God") and *ʾariʾêl* ("altar hearth, hearth of God"; the *Qere* has *ʾariʾêl*). This latter interpretation, "altar hearth, hearth of God," is supported by some scholars because it fits the meaning of Ezek 43:15 where an altar for Jerusalem is described, an altar with four "horns," or projections, one at each of the four corners, and they see a parallel in the *ʾarʾel* (?) *dwd* which the Moabite Stone (line 12) says Mesha king of Moab dragged before the god Chemosh (*ANET,* 320). On this view the concept of altar hearth comes for *ʾarah,* "burn," similar to the Arabic *ʾira tun,* feminine "hearth." If this is the root, the *lamed* at the end of the word *ʾariʾel* is considered a formative. Thus, Isa 29:1, 2, 7 speaks of Jerusalem in solemn terms as the city on which God will bring his wrath, and Jerusalem will be like a burning altar hearth.

W. HAROLD MARE

ARIMATHEA (PLACE) [Gk *Arimathaia*]. Var. ARIMATHAEA; HARMATHAIM; RAMATHEM; RAMATHA; RAMAH; RAMA; ER-RAM. Each of the Gospels mentions this town only once, and always in association with JOSEPH OF ARIMATHEA—who placed Christ's body in his own tomb (Matt 27:57; Mark 15:43; Luke 23:50; John 19:38). This Jewish town (Luke 23:50) was in the Shephelah hills area, approximately 20 mi. E of modern Jaffa, and it most likely is identical with either modern Ramathain (Jos. *Ant* 13.4.9) or Rathamein—Samaritan toparchies. In 145 B.C., the Syrian king Demetrius II Nicator delivered three Samaritan toparchies, including Arimathea, to the Jewish leader Jonathan (1 Macc 11:34).

Both Eusebius and Jerome identify Arimathea with the birthplace of Samuel, i.e., Ramah or Ramathaim-zophim, "the two Ramahs" or "twin heights" within Ephraim (1 Sam 1:19). The *Onomasticon* identifies it with this site (Aramathem-Sophim) near Thamna and Lydda (Euseb. *Onomast.* 144.28; 1 Sam 1:1). In the 4th century Jerome reported that the Holy Paula visited this location. Strong traditions from the Middle Ages buttress this claim, celebrating this town as the prophet's original home. And even a monastery of Joseph of Arimathea was erected there. Conflicting traditions urge Arimathea's location at modern Rentis, 15 mi. E of Jaffa. Other suggestions for Arimathea include er-Ram and el-Birah-Ramallah, 5 and 8 mi. N of Jerusalem, respectively. The mosaic Madeba Map also warrants attention, listing Armathem and Arimathe.

All of the above suggestions coincide with the Heb *hārāmāta,* Ramathaim (1 Sam 1:1). The directive *he-*, "toward Rama," geographically accommodates the above selections. *Hārāmāta* becomes *Armathaim* in the LXX.

JERRY A. PATTENGALE

ARIMATHEA, JOSEPH OF. See JOSEPH OF ARIMATHEA.

ARIOCH (PERSON) [Heb *ʾaryôk*]. **1.** King of Ellasar and one of the allies of Chedorlaomer (Gen 14:1, 9). The identities of both Arioch and his kingdom have been controversial since ancient times (see ELLASAR on its identifications in ancient versions). After the decipherment of cuneiform and the emergence of the first fragmentary data on Babylonian history, E. Schrader (1883: 135) identified Ellasar with Larsa in S Babylonia, and Arioch, with one of its kings, (W)arad-Sin, via the hypothetical variant spelling of his name as ^{m}*Èri-*^{d}*A-ku* (both signifying "servant of the Moon-god"). A little later, the same scholar identified Amraphel with Hammurapi. When it was ascertained that the reign of Warad-Sin was not contemporaneous with that of Hammurapi, Dhorme (1908: 209; 1931: 262) replaced Warad-Sin as the prototype of Arioch with his brother and successor Rim-Sin. But the onomastic side of the equation was so convoluted and contrary to Akkadian phonetics and writing that Dhorme himself later abandoned it. Böhl (1930: 23) identified Ellasar with Telassar and explained *ʾaryôk* as Iranian **aryaka* "the Aryan." When the Mari texts disclosed the existence of a "son" (i.e., a vassal) of King Zimri-Lim named *Ar-ri-wu-uk,* Böhl (1945: 66; 1946: 17) transferred to him the identification with Arioch, though—as stated by Noth (1951)—without substantiation. Moreover, Dossin (1934: 118–19) pointed out that a kingdom listed in Genesis 14 along with Elam, Babylonia, and Hatti (see TIDAL), must have also been a major power. He explained Ellasar as a transcription of one of the cuneiform writings of *Aššur.* Böhl (1953: 46) and Dhorme (1956: 42) reached the same conclusion independently. (On Lipiński's connection of the name "Arioch" with that of a satrap of Armenia Minor in the 3d century B.C., written *Ariukēs* in Greek and *hry*[*w*]*kʾ* in Aramaic, see ELLASAR.)

It has been noted since the publication of the "Chedorlaomer texts" (see CHEDORLAOMER) that the patronymic of one of their four royal characters, written ^{m}ÌR-É-*ku-a* and ^{m}ÌR-^{d}É-*a-ku,* resembles the name "Arioch." The name of the king himself is written ideographically. After the initial efforts of transliterating it by various scholars, Astour (1966: 83) ascertained that its actual writing is ^{m}BÀD.MAḪ-^{d}MAŠ, to be read ^{m}*Tukulti-*^{d}*Ninurta.* The "Chedorlaomer texts" recount how the king in question plundered and flooded Babylon, killed its people, sat on the throne of Babylon as its lord, carried away its gods among the booty, and was murdered by his own son. This fits the Assyrian and Babylonian evidence about Tukulti-Ninurta I, king of Assyria (1243–1207 B.C.). His pseudo-patronymic in the "Chedorlaomer texts," preceded by the unusual relative-determinative pronoun *šá*, is actually a descriptive epithet (with a play of homophones, often used in these texts): "(he) who sacked *É-ku-a*," the central cella of the temple Esagila in Babylon, from which the historical Tukulti-Ninurta I carried away to Assur the revered statue of Babylon's patron god Marduk. The other occurrence of the pseudo-patronymic in these texts reverses the final two signs as *É-a-ku*. It is apparently the latter form that underlies Arioch in Genesis 14, where he is correctly ascribed the kingship of Assur, albeit in the cryptic transcription "Ellasar."

2. The captain of Nebuchadnezzar's guard (Dan 2:14, 15, 24, 25).

3. King of the Elymeans (Elamites), Jdt 1:6. The name of the latter two characters has evidently been borrowed from Genesis 14.

Bibliography

Astour, M. C. 1966. Political and Cosmic Symbolism in Genesis 14 and in its Babylonian Sources. Pp. 65–112 in *Biblical Motifs: Origins and Transformations*, ed. A. Altmann. Philip W. Lown Institute of Advanced Judaic Studies 3. Cambridge, MA.

Böhl, F. M. Th. de Liagre. 1930. *Das Zeitalter Abrahams*. Der Alte Orient 29/1. Leipzig.

———. 1945. Brieven uit het archief van Mari (Tell Hariri). *BiOr* 2: 63–67.

———. 1946. *King Hammurabi of Babylon in the Setting of His Time (about 1700 B.C.)*. Amsterdam.

———. 1953. *Opera Minora, Studies en Bijdragen op Assyriologisch en Oudtestamentisch Terrein*. Groningen.

Dhorme, E. 1908. Hammurabi-Amraphel. *RB* 17: 205–26.

———. 1931. Abraham dans le cadre de l'histoire, part IV. *RB* 40: 503–18; repr. as pp. 256–72 in *Recueil Édouard Dhorme*, Paris. 1951.

———. 1956. *La Bible: L'Ancien Testament*, vol. I. Bibliothèque de la Pléiade 139. Paris.

Dossin, G. 1934. Le site de Reḥobot-Ir et de Resen. *Mus*: 107–21.

Noth, M. 1951. Arioch-Arriwuk. *VT* 1: 136–40.

Schrader, E. 1883. *Die Keilinschriften und das Alte Testament*. 2d ed. Giessen.

Michael C. Astour

ARISAI (PERSON) [Heb *ʾarîsay*]. One of the ten sons of Haman (Esth 9:9). On problems surrounding this list of names, see ADALIA. Arisai (LXX *rouphaion*) perhaps renders the otherwise unattested Old Iranian name **Arya-sāya*—"Iranian protector/defender." For an explanation of the Greek name as a corruption of MT, see Haupt (1982: 70).

Bibliography

Haupt, P. 1982. Critical Notes on Esther. Pp. 1–90 of *Studies in the Book of Esther*, ed. C. A. Moore. New York.

Hinz, W. 1975. *Altiranisches Sprachgut der Nebenüberlieferungen*. Wiesbaden.

Peter Bedford

ARISTARCHUS (PERSON) [Gk *Aristarchos*]. A Jewish Christian from Thessalonica in Macedonia, one of Paul's travel companions (Acts 19:29), fellow workers (Col 4:11; Phlm 24), and fellow prisoners (Col 4:10). Present with Paul when Colossians and Philemon were written, Aristarchus sends his greetings to the recipients of both letters. The identification of Aristarchus in Col 4:10 as Paul's "fellow prisoner" (Gk *sunaichmalōtos*, lit. "prisoner of war") is probably to be taken in the strict sense referring to a time and place when Aristarchus was imprisoned with Paul (Ephesus, Caesarea, or Rome). However, it is not known when or where Aristarchus was actually imprisoned. For this reason the term has sometimes been interpreted in a metaphorical sense, meaning that Aristarchus, like Paul, was held "captive" by Christ.

Col 4:11 also names Aristarchus, Mark, and Jesus, called Justus, as the only "men of the circumcision" among Paul's "fellow workers for the kingdom of God" who were with him during his imprisonment. The presence of these Jewish Christian missionaries is comforting to Paul (Col 4:11). This would be particularly the case in light of the earlier crisis at Antioch (Gal 2:11–21), and its aftereffects (cf. Gal; Phil 3) when Paul was opposed by many Jewish Christian missionaries (see Ollrog 1979: 45–46).

In Acts, Aristarchus is identified as a Macedonian in 19:29, as being from Thessalonica in 20:4, and as both in 27:2. In the first text, he is linked with GAIUS, another Macedonian. These two travel companions of Paul were present with him at the riot led by the silversmiths in Ephesus. In that confusion, Aristarchus and Gaius were seized and dragged into the immense Ephesian theater, probably to be questioned about Paul's activities. Apparently they were freed shortly after the town clerk had diffused the fracas. Since Acts refers to Aristarchus twice within "we-passages" (20:4; 27:2), it has been speculated that Aristarchus knew Luke and that the notably vivid scene of the riot in 19:29, not a "we-passage," may nonetheless be attributed to an eyewitness account that Aristarchus provided for Luke (Bruce 1977: 289).

When the rioting ceased, Paul, presumably with Aristarchus and Gaius, departed for Macedonia and then for Greece. Later, Aristarchus, Secundus (also a Thessalonian), and others accompanied Paul on his return from Greece (Corinth) to Macedonia; from there they went ahead of him to Troas (20:5). A few years later, Aristarchus also traveled with Paul from Caesarea to Rome (27:2), where he may have shared in his imprisonment, possibly voluntarily (cf. Col 4:10). In Rome, Aristarchus may have come into contact with Epaphras, another fellow prisoner of Paul (Phlm 23).

One other possible reference to Aristarchus occurs in 2 Cor 8:18–19, where Paul, commending Titus to the Corinthians, mentions sending also "the brother who is famous among all the churches for his preaching of the gospel," a person who "has been appointed by the churches to travel with us." The strongest literary evidence for identifying Aristarchus as this brother is the parallel use of the term "travel companion" (*sunekdēmos*) found in the NT only here in 2 Cor 8:19 and in Acts 19:29 where Aristarchus is so described (Redlich 1913: 217–18). An identification of this unnamed brother with Aristarchus, however, remains hypothetical.

Bibliography

Bruce, F. F. 1977. *Paul: Apostle of the Heart Set Free.* Grand Rapids.

Ollrog, W.-H. 1979. *Paulus und seine Mitarbeiter.* WMANT 50. Neukirchen-Vluyn.

Redlich, E. B. 1913. *S. Paul and His Companions.* London.

JOHN GILLMAN

ARISTEAS THE EXEGETE. A Jewish author who flourished prior to the mid-1st century B.C.E. whose work *On the Jews* treated, at the very least, the biblical figure Job. To what extent he treated other matters is not known. He is generally designated "exegete" or "historian" because of his interest in the biblical text, especially its historical and genealogical features. This designation also serves to distinguish him from the author of the Letter of Aristeas to Philocrates, which relates the story of the translation of the Hebrew Bible into Greek (see ARISTEAS, LETTER OF).

The primary testimony for Aristeas is Eusebius *Praep. Evang.* 9.25.1–4, a section of some thirty lines taken from the pagan author Alexander Polyhistor, who, instead of giving a direct quotation, merely summarizes Aristeas' account of Job.

There is also a possible allusion to Aristeas in *Let. Aris.* 6, which mentions a previous communication in which the author "related the facts about the Jewish race." This may be a reference to another work, however, or it may even be a literary fiction. It has also been suggested that the author of the *Letter of Aristeas* borrowed his name from Aristeas the Exegete. Given the ambiguity of the evidence, these two pieces of testimony are perhaps best left unrelated. *Let. Aris.* 6 does become an important consideration, however, in the question of dating.

Similar to other noncanonical traditions (e.g. *T. Job* 1:1; 2:1–2; 3:1), Aristeas identifies Job with Jobab, one of the Edomite kings mentioned in Gen 36:31–39. In fact, Job is said to be the son of Esau and Bassara. Since the biblical account identifies Jobab as the great-grandson of Esau (Gen 36:33), the text of Eusebius may be corrupt at this point. In any case, Aristeas places Job within the lineage of Esau in the patriarchal period, as is the case in other traditions (*Ps-Philo* 8:8; *Tg. Ps.-J.* on Gen 36:11). He also locates Job in the land of Ausitis (LXX Job 1:1; MT "Uz"), which he further identifies as being near Idumaea and Arabia.

The overall portrait that emerges in Aristeas' account of the biblical story is Job the Patient; the image of Job the Questioner is completely absent (Doran, *OTP* 2: 855).

In spite of the brevity of Polyhistor's summary, it is clear that Aristeas is dependent on the LXX. This is seen in the proper names he employs, such as Jobab (Gen 36:33–34), Bassara (Gen 36:33), Ausitis (Job 1:1), Zophar, king of the Minnaites (Job 2:11), as well as in the close correspondence between his description of Job's possessions and that in LXX Job 1:3, the similarity of language used to describe his afflictions, and his designation of the three friends as "kings" (LXX Job 2:11; the titles are absent in MT).

One of the chief critical problems is how Aristeas relates to the LXX epilogue to Job (*Add. Job* 42:17b–e). The similarity of material suggests either that one depended on the other, or that both drew on a common tradition.

Since Aristeas was preserved by Alexander Polyhistor (ca. 105–30 B.C.E.), it is certain that he flourished prior to the mid-1st century B.C.E. Since he used a Greek translation of Genesis and Job, he appears to have flourished after the mid-3d century B.C.E., when these Hebrew texts began to become available in Greek. If there is a definitive connection between *Let. Aris.* 6 and Aristeas the Exegete's work, it must antedate the *Letter of Aristeas,* which may be as early as the 3d century B.C.E. But as noted earlier, this connection is very tenuous. Accordingly, scholars have generally dated him from the 2d century to the mid-1st century B.C.E.

Because of his apparently exclusive dependence on the LXX, scholars have tended to locate him in a Greek-speaking setting such as Egypt. Given the brevity of the fragment, however, the provenance must remain an open question.

Bibliography

Holladay, C. R. 1983. Aristeas. Pp. 261–75 in *Fragments from Hellenistic Jewish Authors.* Vol. 1. SBLTT 20. Pseudepigrapha Series 10. Chico, CA.

Schürer, E. 1986. Pp. 525–26 in *HJP* 3/1.

Walter, N. 1975. Aristeas. Pp. 293–96 in *Jüdische Schriften aus hellenistisch-römischer Zeit* 3/2, ed. W. G. Kümmel. Gütersloh.

CARL R. HOLLADAY

ARISTEAS, LETTER OF. The Letter of Aristeas addressed by Aristeas to a certain Philocrates describes the translation of the Pentateuch into Greek. As such, it is one of the principal sources of information about the origins of the SEPTUAGINT (LXX).

A. Summary

The contents of the Letter (*Let. Aris.*) can be summarized as follows: Aristeas relates how Ptolemy II King of Egypt (285–247 B.C.) requested Demetrius his librarian to make a complete worldwide collection of books for his library at Alexandria (vv 1–8). He soon collected over 200,000 books and told the king that his target was 500,000. There were also the laws of the Jews which needed translation and to be put into the library. So the king ordered a letter to be sent to the Jewish high priest about this matter (vv 9–11). Aristeas took this opportunity of raising with the king the question of the Jewish prisoners, about 100,000 in number, held in Egypt. Their release was successfully negotiated, and the king also paid compensation, 20 drachmas per prisoner, and decreed accordingly (vv 12–27). After this the king required Demetrius to report to him on the Jewish Scriptures. His report quoted in full emphasized the need for a version of them in the library, and suggested asking the high priest at Jerusalem to send 72 delegates, 6 from each of the 12 tribes (vv 28–32). The king agreed, and wrote accordingly, sending gifts and news of the release of the prisoners (vv 33–34). His letter and Eleazar's reply are given in full (vv 35–51); also a description of the gifts (vv 51–82).

A description of the temple at Jerusalem follows (vv 83–

104). This "digression" (v 112) ends with a description of the countryside (vv 112–20). Eleazar dispatched the envoys, and there is a lengthy apology for the Jewish Law, especially its monotheism, in contrast with the polytheism of its neighbors and their worship of sacred animals and idols (vv 121–71). When the embassy arrived in Alexandria, a royal banquet lasting 7 days was held in welcome, during which the king questioned the guests in turn about their religion, the nature and its relevance to the exercise of royalty. Each question is answered (vv 173–294). The banquet ends and Aristeas apologizes to Philocrates for the length of this account, but insists on its accuracy (vv 295–300).

After the banquet, the work of translation soon began. Drafts were made, compared, and a final Greek version was completed in just 72 days, whereupon it was read to the Jewish community and approved (vv 301–11). Demetrius was ordered to guard the books carefully, and finally gifts were exchanged and the translators returned home (vv 312–21).

B. Authorship and Date

Aristeas wrote the *Let. Aris.* to his brother Philocrates. He was one of the envoys but no further details are given about him. We can conjecture that he was a Jew living in Alexandria (Pelletier 1962: 56). His familiarity with Jewish worship and way of life is apparent, but his interests were not limited within that area.

In one passage (v 16) he seems to associate himself with those who also call God the Creator "Zeus," i.e., Greeks or Hellenists, but this somewhat inconclusive statement is outweighed by his special knowledge of Jerusalem and the temple worship (vv 83–118). This would indicate that Aristeas was probably a Jew. It is tempting to conclude from the setting of *Let. Aris.* that its author likewise came from Alexandria, but this is conjectural.

The reference to the Egyptian King Ptolemy Philadelphus (285–247 B.C.) and the use by Josephus (A.D. 37–?110) of *Let. Aris.* as a source (*Jewish Antiquities* 12.2.118) provide broad indications of the date. Within these limits the suggested dates, as summarized by Jellicoe (1968: 48–50) fall into three groups: early, ca. 150–100 B.C., and 1st century B.C. It is less probably a contemporary document—and therefore early—because the Pentateuch seems to be assumed by the author to be a well-established version, the origin of which he describes.

C. Translation

The consideration of the translation involves identifying the original which was translated, together with the method and procedure adopted in the undertaking. In respect of the first, *Let. Aris.* (v 30) states "the books of the law of the Jews, with some others, are wanting [i.e., not in the Library at Alexandria], for these works are written [Gk *legomena* lit. "spoken"] in Hebrew letters and language, but they have been transcribed [Gk *sesēmantai*] somewhat carelessly and not as they should be." It is not clear whether *Let. Aris.* is referring to Hebrew copies of the Law, or to existing Greek versions in the Library at Alexandria: in both cases they are criticized as somewhat inadequate. Moreover the crucial words (v 30) are ambiguous, as Pelletier (1962: 118–20) clearly indicated. There is difficulty too with *sesēmantai,* which is variously thought to have meant "written," "interpreted," and "rendered" (Shutt *OTP* 2: 25–29). If the view is taken that earlier Greek versions of the Law were consulted by the Seventy, it is possible to try and identify them. Jellicoe (1968: 50) thinks that *Let. Aris.* was written to defend a rival Greek version emanating from Leontopolis.

The amount of space given to the actual work of translation is short (vv 301–11). In addition to the difficulty mentioned above, *Let. Aris.* (v 302 and Pelletier [1962: 230 n. 2]), says simply that the translators "harmonized" their drafts, by comparing and agreeing on a final version. There must have been some guidelines for such harmonization. The ease and speed with which agreement was reached raise further suspicions, and all these considerations confirm the view that *Let. Aris.* in its account of the actual work of translation is inadequate and unreliable.

D. Purpose

The foregoing raises the difficult question of the purpose of *Let. Aris.* Clearly part of its purpose was to describe the translation of the Jewish Law into Greek. But equally clearly, that explanation is insufficient to account for the brevity of that passage, which is covered by vv 301–11 out of vv 322. The preceding sections are longer and more detailed, as the Summary indicates. There is a lengthy description of Palestine and Jerusalem, and at the banquet each one of the Seventy is questioned and gives his answer. If then, as seems likely, the actual translation is not the only focus of *Let. Aris.* can we identify the wider purpose? The content of the questions and answers at the banquet may provide a clue. They are concerned with Judaism and the Law, and the desire to present an apology for both in an environment which does not pay much attention to such things, and knows little or nothing about Palestine. *Let. Aris.* seeks to redress that balance, and this wider purpose would be more understandable if, as seems likely, the work emanated from Alexandria and even from the Jewish community which was established there.

In the Christian era the LXX version was highly esteemed (Swete 1902: 29), and the Hebrew version was neglected until Origen (ca. A.D. 185–254) revived interest in the Hebrew by comparing it with the Greek version. Similarities and differences were established in the texts, and the Greek version was defended against the Hebrew. *Let. Aris.* was used in that defense, and was considered to be verbally inspired (Pelletier 1962: 81–86). In spite of its limitations, it cannot be ignored in the study of the Septuagint.

Bibliography

Jellicoe, S. 1968. *The Septuagint and Modern Study.* Cambridge.

Nestle, E. 1902. Septuagint. *HDB* 4: 438–39.

Orlinsky, H. M. 1975. The Septuagint as Holy Writ and the Philosophy of the Translators. *HUCA* 46: 89–114.

Pelletier, A. 1962. *Lettre D'Aristee a Philocrate.* SC 89. Paris.

Schutt, R. J. H. 1977. Notes on the Letter of Aristeas. *BIOSCS* 10: 22–30.

Swete, H. B., ed. 1902. *An Introduction to the Old Testament in Greek.* Cambridge.

Thackeray, H. St. J. 1902. The Letter of Aristeas. Pp. 499–574 in *An Introduction to the Old Testament in Greek,* ed. H. B. Swete. Cambridge.

R. JAMES H. SHUTT

ARISTIDES (PERSON). According to Eusebius, both Quadratus and Aristides presented Christian apologies to the Emperor Hadrian at Athens, probably in 124 C.E. Aristides was unknown to scholars for many years, though his work survived in at least two 4th-century papyri (*POxy.* 15: 1778). The Mechitarists of Venice published an Armenian fragment in 1878, and in 1889 J. R. Harris discovered the whole apology in a 7th-century Syriac manuscript at St. Catherine's on Sinai. J. A. Robinson immediately found that the Greek apology had been used for a lengthy section of the Greek novel *Barlaam and Josaphat,* ascribed to John of Damascus. The text can be reconstructed from the last two witnesses and confirmed by the fragmentary papyri.

Arguments have continued about the recipient's identity, for the Syriac version is addressed by "Marcianus Aristides the Athenian philosopher" to Antoninus Pius, while the Armenian agrees with Eusebius that he addressed Hadrian. Conceivably the original version is reflected in the Greek text, which was later revised and expanded for his successor Antoninus. In any event the apology is quite early, antedating the more ambitious work of Justin.

The arrangement is simple: The work begins with a semiphilosophical description of God and then shows how the gods of various nations fall short. These are the Chaldaeans, who worship the elements/planets; the Greeks, who worship human beings, vulnerable and erratic; and the Egyptians, who worship animals. The Jews are better than any of these people but worship angels and observe the ritual law. Christians are best, for they trace their genealogy back to Jesus the Christ and practice pure love and benevolence. The Syriac version emphasizes their dislike of homosexuality, perhaps more appropriately mentioned to Antoninus than to Hadrian. Christians are slandered by the Greeks but they are just and holy.

Presumably Aristides belongs to the sequence of important Christians at Athens in the 1st and 2d centuries, beginning with Paul's address there and the historical Dionysius the Areopagite, and continuing through Aristides and perhaps Quadratus to the Athenian correspondents of Dionysius of Corinth and to another philosopher-apologist, Athenagoras.

The 4th-century papyri show that Aristides was still read even though later Greek Christians fail to mention Aristides or quote from the apology. Its simplicity must have seemed unfortunate in a period of increasing literary sophistication, when even Diognetus was forgotten. Later Christians liked to see quotations from Scripture, but Aristides supplied none.

Bibliography

Geffcken, J. 1907. *Zwei griechische Apologeten.* Berlin.

Harris, J. R., and Robinson, J. A. 1893. *The Apology of Aristides.* TextsS 1/1. Cambridge.

Milne, H. J. M. 1924. A New Fragment of the Apology of Aristides. *JTS* 25: 73–77.

Unnik, W. C. van. 1961. Die Gotteslehre bei Aristides und in gnostischen Schriften. *TZ* 17: 166–74.

ROBERT M. GRANT

ARISTOBULUS (PERSON) [Gk *Aristoboulos*]. Several significant people in ancient and sacred history. It is a common Greek name meaning "best counselor." See also ARISTOBULUS (OT PSEUDEPIGRAPHA).

1. Greek historian who accompanied Alexander the Great on his campaigns. At 85 years of age he wrote a work on Alexander which was highly regarded in the ancient world for its trustworthiness. Only fragments of the work are extant.

2. Jewish priest referred to in 2 Macc 1:10, who lived in Egypt during the reign of Ptolemy VII. In a letter written by Judas Maccabaeus in 165 B.C.E., Aristobulus is addressed as a representative of the Egyptian Jews and teacher or counselor of Ptolemy VII.

3. Eldest of five sons of John Hyrcanus, who was named Jehuda or Judas but is better known by his Greek name "Aristobulus." In 110 B.C.E., with his brother Antigonus, he laid siege to Samaria (Josephus *Ant* 13.10.2–3; and *War* 1.2.7). When Hyrcanus died in 107 B.C.E., he decreed that his widow should succeed him and that Aristobulus should serve as high priest (Josephus *Ant* 13.11.1). Aristobulus usurped the reign in 104 B.C.E. and may have been the first Hasmonean to arrogate to himself the title of "king" (Josephus *Ant* 13.11.1; compare, however, Strabo). He also apparently allowed himself to be called "Philhellene" because of the favor he showed to the Greeks (Josephus *Ant* 13.11.3; and *War* 1.3). Aristobulus subdued the Ituraeans and compelled them to convert to Judaism. To secure his power, he imprisoned and starved to death his mother and three of his brothers. Aristobulus' favorite brother, Antigonus, later came under false accusations made by a number of jealous enemies including Aristobulus' wife, Salome Alexandra. Antigonus was also murdered but Aristobulus himself died within the same year (104 B.C.E.) with a conscience stricken with self-remorse (Josephus *Ant* 13.11.1–3; and *War* 1.3.1–6).

4. Younger son of Alexander Jannaeus by Alexandra (Josephus *Ant* 13.16.1; and *War* 1.5.1). During Alexandra's 9-year reign, he opposed the Pharisees, whose influence his mother had sought. When Alexandra died in 70 B.C.E., she was succeeded by her eldest son, Hyrcanus, whom Aristobulus engaged in war, forcing Hyrcanus to resign his crown and high priesthood (Josephus *Ant* 13.16; 14.1.2; *War* 1.5; 6.1). Hyrcanus was given refuge by Aretas, King of Arabia Petraea. In 65 B.C.E., Aretas invaded Judea, defeated Aristobulus' forces, and laid seige to Jerusalem (Josephus *Ant* 14.1.3–4; and idem., *War* 1.6.2). In this connection, Josephus refers to a certain Onias, whom he describes as "a righteous man and dear to God," and whose prayers for rain in a time of drought were miraculously answered. The followers of Hyrcanus tried unsuccessfully to force Onias to place a curse on Aristobulus. Instead Onias prayed that neither side would succeed, and as a result, the infuriated mob stoned him to death (Josephus *Ant* 14.2.1). Some scholars associate Onias with the Teacher of Righteousness mentioned in the Dead Sea Scrolls and either Hyrcanus II or Aristobulus II as the

Wicked Priest. In 65 B.C.E., Rome interceded in the Judean affairs, initially supporting Aristobulus, but the following year Pompey decided to support Hyrcanus II, and Aristobulus and his two daughters were taken to Rome. In 56 Aristobulus escaped from Rome and appeared in Palestine, again claiming the throne. He was severely wounded in battle, captured, and sent as a prisoner to Rome with his son Antigonus. In 49 Julius Caesar freed Aristobulus, and supplied him with two legions in an attempt to recover Judea and weaken Pompey's political position. Quintus Metellus Scipio, Governor of Syria, had Aristobulus poisoned on his way to Palestine.

5. The grandson of number four, the son of Alexander and the brother of Herod the Great's wife, Mariamne. His mother, Alexandra, attempted to obtain the high priesthood for her son by persuading Cleopatra to influence Antony. Consequently Herod deposed Ananelus and bestowed the office to Aristobulus. Alexandra renewed complaints against Herod to Cleopatra and, under increasing suspicion, attempted to escape with her son to the protection of the Egyptian court. In 35 B.C.E., Herod had Aristobulus drowned at Jericho (Josephus *Ant* 15.2.3; and *War* 1.22.2).

6. One of the sons of Herod the Great by Mariamne, who was sent with his brother Alexander to Rome, where they were educated in the house of Pollio (Josephus *Ant* 15.10.1). Upon their return to Judea, their brother Antipater excited the suspicions of Herod against them, which were exasperated by the indignation the brothers showed at the murder of their mother. Aristobulus and Alexander were accused by Herod before Augustus at Aquilea in 11 B.C.E. but were temporarily reconciled with their father through the mediation of the Roman Emperor. In 6 B.C.E. the brothers were again charged with plotting against Herod but were reconciled through the efforts of Archelaus, King of Cappadocia, the father-in-law of Alexander. After being accused for a third time in 6 B.C.E., Augustus permitted Herod to arraign the two before a council which convened at Berytus. The brothers were condemned and strangled soon after at Sebaste (Josephus *Ant* 16.1–4; 8; 10; 11; and *War* 1.23–27; see also Strabo 16.756).

7. Son of Aristobulus, discussed above in number 6, and Berenice, surnamed "the younger" (Josephus *Ant* 21.2), the grandson of Herod the Great. He was educated in Rome with his two brothers together with the future Emperor Claudius (Josephus *Ant* 18.5.4; 6.1; and 20.1.2). Aristobulus lived at enmity with his brother Agrippa I. He accused Agrippa I of taking a bribe from the Damascenes, ultimately placing Agrippa at variance with Flaccus, the Roman Proconsul of Syria (Josephus *Ant* 18.6.3). Aristobulus joined the protest in Jerusalem against Caligula when the emperor attempted to erect statues in the Temple (Josephus *Ant* 18.8; *War* 2.10; and Tacitus *Hist* 5.9). Aristobulus was married to Jotapa, a princess from Emessa, by whom he had a daughter with the same name (Josephus *Ant* 18.5.4; and *War* 2.11.6). Aristobulus survived his brother Agrippa I, who died in 44 C.E. (Josephus *Ant* 20.1.2.; and *War* 2.11.6).

8. Son of Herod, King of Chalcis, great-grandson of Herod the Great, and grandson of Aristobulus. Aristobulus obtained his father's kingdom of Chalcis from the Romans sometime after 52 C.E. when it was taken from his cousin Agrippa II (Josephus *War* 7.7.11). Nero made Aristobulus King of Armenia Minor in 55 C.E. and added to his dominions a portion of Greater Armenia (Josephus *Ant* 20.8.4; and Tacitus *Ann* 13.7; 14.25). In 73 C.E., Aristobulus joined forces with Cassenius Paetus, the Roman Consul of Syria, to fight against Antiochus, King of Commagene. Aristobulus was married to the daughter of Herodias, Salome, by whom he had three sons (Josephus *Ant* 18.5.4).

9. A Roman named by Paul in Rom 16:10. According to tradition, Aristobulus was the brother of Barnabas, one of the 70 disciples, ordained a bishop, and was eventually a missionary to Britain.

SCOTT T. CARROLL

ARISTOBULUS (OT PSEUDEPIGRAPHA).

Jewish philosopher-exegete who flourished in Alexandria in the 2d century B.C.E. He wrote a work in Greek, possibly multivolumed and entitled *Explanations of the Book of Moses*, of which only several short fragments survive. The exegetically focused exposition employed a form of allegorical interpretation and had an explicit philosophical orientation. In both respects, Aristobulus anticipates Philo of Alexandria, although there are important qualitative differences in their approach and outlook. Common to both, however, is a concerted effort to address issues of biblical interpretation in light of current Greek philosophical positions and modes of interpretation, and in doing so, show that the best of Hellenistic thought and culture had already been embodied in the Mosaic law.

Five fragments from Aristobulus' work have survived. The first fragment, preserved in Eusebius *Hist. Eccl.* 7.32.16–18, is from an earlier treatise on the Passover by Anatolius, bishop of Laodicea (d. ca. 282 C.E.). Here Aristobulus asserts that the feast of Passover occurs during simultaneous solar and lunar equinoxes, thus when the sun and moon are at polar opposites in their orbiting positions.

The remaining four fragments, which are preserved in Eusebius' *Praeparatio Evangelica,* are direct quotations. Portions of these fragments are quoted earlier in Clement of Alexandria *Strom.* 6.3.32.5–33.1 and 6.3.32.3–4 (Frg. 2); 1.22.150.1–3 and 1.22.148.1 (Frg. 3); 5.14.99.3 and 5.14.101.4 (Frg. 4); 6.16.137.4–138.4; 6.16.141.7b–142.1; 6.16.138.4b; 6.16.142.4b–144.3; and 5.14.107.1–4 [+108.1] (Frg. 5). Portions of Frg. 4 are also contained in Clement *Protr.* 7.73.2.

Frg. 2 (*Praep. Evang.* 8.9.38–10.17) defends the biblical use of anthropomorphisms, based on interpretation "according to the laws of nature" (*phusikos*), as opposed to a "mythical and human way of thinking about God" used by those "devoted to the letter alone." Using a primitive, relatively undeveloped form of allegorical interpretation, Aristobulus explains biblical references to God's hand (power), standing (universal supremacy), and descent (the manifestation of God's universal majesty).

Frg. 3 (*Praep. Evang.* 13.12.1–2) asserts that Plato and Pythagoras borrowed much of their teaching from an early Greek translation of the Mosaic law. This fragment represents an explicit, well-developed example of the tradition, which circulated in a variety of forms, that Greek philosophy is traceable to Hebrew origins.

Frg. 4 (*Praep. Evang.* 13.12.3–8) explains the anthropomorphic expression "God spoke" and further expands the argument for Greek dependence on Moses by providing a lengthy quotation attributed to Orpheus which contains faint echoes of the biblical text. It also contains a quotation from the *Phaenomena* of Aratus (ca. 315–240 B.C.E.), altered to show that this Greek author was actually speaking unwittingly of the God of the Jews.

Frg. 5 (*Praep. Evang.* 13.12.9–16), which focuses on the sabbath, provides an allegorical interpretation of certain biblical statements, e.g., God rested on the seventh day. Through the use of number speculation drawn from various philosophical traditions, Aristobulus also interprets the sabbath as expressing the primal significance of the number seven as the ordering principle of the universe. He further posits Greek dependence on the Mosaic law by citing references attributed to Hesiod, Homer, and the mythical figure Linus attesting the special significance of the seventh day.

There is strong evidence for dating Aristobulus during the reign of Ptolemy VI Philometor (181–145 B.C.E.). "Ptolemy the King" to whom the work is dedicated and addressed is identified by Clement (*Strom.* 1.22.150.1) and derivatively by Eusebius (*Praep. Evang.* 9.6.6) as Philometor. This fits with Aristobulus' own reference to Ptolemy II Philadelphus (283–247 B.C.E.) as the addressee's "ancestor" (*Praep. Evang.* 13.12.2). Roughly the same period is envisioned when Clement (*Strom.* 5.14.97.7) and Eusebius (*Praep. Evang.* 8.9.38) identify him as the Aristobulus of 2 Macc 1:10, the leading addressee of the letter sent by Judas Maccabeus and the Judean Jews to the Jewish community in Egypt. This latter piece of evidence is controversial, however, since it may have influenced Clement (and therefore Eusebius) in their historical reconstruction (Walter 1964: 13–16).

Conflicting, but less compelling, evidence for an earlier date during the reign of Philadelphus occurs in Anatolius, who identifies Aristobulus as one of the 70 who translated the Hebrew Bible into Greek (Eusebius *Hist. Eccl.* 7.32.16; similarly, one textual tradition of Clement *Strom.* 5.14.97.7).

Aristobulus is clearly Jewish since he speaks of "our Law" (*Praep. Evang.* 8.10.1, 8; 13.12.8; also cf. 13.12.1, 13) and calls Solomon "one of our ancestors" (13.12.11) and Moses "our lawgiver" (8.10.3). What is clear from his writings is made explicit in the tradition: he is a self-styled philosopher. Clement (*Strom.* 1.15.72.4) and Eusebius (*Praep. Evang.* 9.6.6; 13.11.3–12.1 [title]) identify him as a Peripatetic, familiar "with Aristotelian philosophy" (*Praep. Evang.* 8.9.38). The term, however, should not be taken as a technical description of a particular philosophical school since it had a wider connotation during the Hellenistic period. Aristobulus' philosophical position is more appropriately described as eclectic, showing traces of Pythagorean, Platonic, Aristotelian, and Stoic influence. 2 Macc 1:10, while problematic, suggests that he was of a priestly family and served as "teacher of Ptolemy the king." The latter may mean that, in keeping with the tradition of the sage who instructs the king, he tutored the young Philometor and addressed a didactic work to him commending Jewish wisdom as the true philosophy (Hengel 1973, 1: 164). But whether he exercised such influence in the Ptolemaic court at that time is disputed (Collins, *OTP* 2: 833).

His role as exegete is reflected in Anatolius' characterization of his work as "exegetical books on the law of Moses" (Eusebius *Hist. Eccl.* 7.32.16) and also echoed by Eusebius' own description (*Praep. Evang.* 7.13.7) of his work as "interpretation of the sacred laws."

An Alexandrian provenance is suggested by the close association, both within the fragments themselves and in the later tradition, of Aristobulus with Ptolemaic Egypt. This is reinforced even more if 2 Macc 1:10 is reliable testimony to Aristobulus, since it specifically includes him with the "Jews in Egypt." Besides these numerous explicit connections, the philosophical tenor of the exposition, the allegorical mode of interpretation, and the broad familiarity with a wide range of classical Greek texts and philosophical positions fit well an Alexandrian setting. It has even been suggested that he was a member of the Alexandrian Museum (*HJP*[2] 3/1: 579).

Earlier scholars seriously doubted the authenticity of the fragments, arguing that the presence of forged quotations within them and signs of dependence on Philo of Alexandria require them to be dated in the Christian era. More recent scholarship, especially Walter (1964: 35–123), has defended their genuineness by noting, for example, that the style of language and relatively undeveloped form of allegorical interpretation fit the Hellenistic period.

Bibliography

Denis, A. M. 1970. Pp. 217–28 in *Fragmenta pseudepigraphorum quae supersunt Graeca una cum historicorum et auctorum Judaeorum hellenistarum fragmentis.* Leiden.

Fraser, P. M. 1972. *Ptolemaic Alexandria.* 3 vols. (1: 694–96; 2: 103–20). Oxford.

Hengel, M. 1973. *Judaism and Hellenism.* 2 vols. (1: 163–69; 2: 105–10). Trans. J. Bowden. Philadelphia.

Walter, N. 1964. *Der Thoraausleger Aristobulos.* TU 86. Berlin.

———. 1975. Aristobulos. Pp. 261–79 in *Jüdische Schriften aus hellenistisch-römischer Zeit* 3/2, ed. W. G. Kümmel. Gütersloh.

CARL R. HOLLADAY

ARIUS, ARIANISM.

Arius (256–336 C.E.), a presbyter of the Baucalis region of Alexandria (Boulerand 1964: 175), began a controversy ca. 318 (Schneemelcher 1954: 394) with Bishop Alexander of Alexandria over the nature of Christ's relation to the Father (Gregg and Groh 1977: 263). This controversy led ultimately to Arius' condemnation by the Council of Nicaea (325 C.E.), to the exclusion of his ideas from orthodoxy in the Creed and Anathemas of Nicaea, and to the movement known as Arianism.

Nothing is known about Arius' biography other than a probable birth in Libya sometime in the 3d century and an ordination to the office of deacon by Peter of Alexandria and to the office of presbyter by Achillas (Williams 1987: 29–32, 40). Reports of Arius' death in 336 may be reliable, though the circumstances were embellishments of his enemies (Williams 1987: 80–81). Current scholars are divided on the extent of Arius' personal impact on the movement, between those who see Arius as an essentially isolated figure and those who see him as an influential member of the circle of early Arians (Groh 1986).

Orthodox opposition to the emergence of a new wave of Arian theologians in the 350s, called in the scholarly literature Neo-Arians, led to the formation of the classic doctrine of the Trinity associated with the so-called Creed of the Council of Constantinople (381), which Christians recite today as the "Nicene" Creed (Kelly 1972: 296).

Kopecek has shown that the thought and liturgical emphases of these Neo-Arians should not be confused with those of Arius, especially, and the other early Arians (1979: 20–21, 25; Kannengiesser 1982b: 54–57; Gregg 1985: 174–75; Gregg and Groh 1981: ix, 8 and n. 38).

It is the *early* Arians (ca. 318–ca. 341 C.E.) who are most important in regard to biblical exegesis within the "Antiochene" tradition of Lucian (Bardy 1936). In addition to Arius, especially important are Asterius the Sophist (d. ca. 341; also called the "Sacrificer" because of his lapse in a persecution) and Eusebius of Nicomedia (d. ca. 342), bishop successively of Berytus, Nicomedia, and Constantinople. Although Eusebius' literary legacy amounts to only a single letter (Opitz 1935b: 15–17), his prominence as the acknowledged leader of the Arian movement after Nicaea and his favor with the imperial court were probably due to the fact that he was a patrician and a relative of the future emperor Julian (361–363 C.E.) (Barnes 1981: 70 and n. 79).

A. Sources

The sources collected and edited by Optiz (1935a–b) need to be supplemented for Arius by quotations and commentary in the writings of Bishop Athanasius of Alexandria (328–73 C.E.) and by the sources collected by Bardy (1936: 221–95; 1930: 266). Recently, an original text of Athanasius' *Ar.*, one of the most important sources for Arianism, has been established as contained in the first two extant *Ar.* (Kannengiesser 1983 and *tableau récapitulatif*). Kannengiesser rules out Athanasian authorship for *Ar.* 3 (1983: 310–68, 409), but his thesis that *Ar.* 3 was composed by Apollinaris of Laodicea (1982a: 994–95) or his school (1983: 414–16) is problematic. *Ar.* 3 should be considered to be most probably an anti-Arian writing by Athanasius from an as yet unspecified redaction or treatise.

A major debate is also under way (Kannengiesser 1982b: 12–17; Williams, Hall, Kannengiesser in Gregg 1985: 1–78; Stead 1978) over the best text and the exact original wording of Arius' *Thalia* in the three systematic citations of it reported by Athanasius (*Ar.* 1.5–6; *ep. Aeg. Lib.*12; *syn.* 15); and attempts to uncover the metric scheme (Stead 1978: 40–52) have not succeeded in guiding us to a normative text of Arius' systematic thinking (Kannengiesser, Gregg 1985: 61). Doctrinal disagreements among the versions seem, however, overdrawn; and an attempt to attribute a Neo-Arian redaction to *syn.* 15, thus lowering its value as a source for Arius' own thought, has been advanced and disproved in the same volume (in Kannengiesser 1982b: 54–57). Firm judgments about Athanasius' general trustworthiness as a reporter of opponents' opinions must await a better understanding of his methods (Stead 1976: 129–35) and a sifting of the mass of recent scholarly literature on Athanasius (Kannengiesser 1985).

The fragments of Asterius' *Syntagma* (Bardy 1936: 341–57) have recently been discriminated according to their two preserving sources by Wiles, who has shown that their content does not necessarily conflict with each other (Gregg 1985: 120). Asterius' *Homilies on the Psalms* (Richard 1956) Wiles has also shown to reflect differing, but not necessarily conflicting, emphases than the fragments (Gregg 1985: 135). To the homilies adjudged Asterian by Richard (1956), Wiles has further authenticated homilies 1, 10, 14, 24.4–15 (Gregg 1985: 140–44).

B. Christological Emphases

Scholarship of the last hundred years had tended to stress uncompromising monotheism, either Jewish or philosophical (Ricken 1969; Boulerand 1972: 101–74), as the central Arian motivation in subordinating Christ to God. More recent scholars (as chronicled in Norderval 1985) have ruled out such concerns and focused attention on the centrality of the Arians' distinctive Christology (Lorenz 1979: 223–24; Gregg and Groh 1981: 1–42, 77–129). Against the insistence of their orthodox opponents that Christ was the eternal essence, Word, Wisdom of the Father, Arians stressed Christ's creaturely dependence on God's will, emphasizing the Son's limited knowledge of the Father (Gregg and Groh 1977: 266). For Arius and Asterius, these affirmations of Christ's creaturehood safeguarded a true incarnation, in which the redeemer could suffer and save (Gregg and Groh 1981: 4; considerably extended, qualified, and refined by Wiles and Hanson in Gregg 1985: 135–37, 181–83). Thus our earliest (ca. 324 C.E.) systematic orthodox source against the Arians (Alex. Al. *Ep. Alex.*, Optiz 1935b: 25) criticizes them for emphasizing all the Gospel and Epistle passages, including Phil 2:5–11, which mention Christ's passion and humiliation and for ignoring all those texts which, to the orthodox, stress Christ's common nature or essence with the Father.

Thus, in opposition to the orthodox, Arians accented the creaturely commonality of Christ with those he was to redeem and, hence, Christ's importance as representative creature and model (Gregg and Groh 1981). In other contexts they emphasized the special role that Christ played in the work of creation and salvation (Casey 1935: 10; Tetz 1952–53), as Wiles has recently suggested on the basis of the Asterian homilies (in Gregg 1985: 135). Thus they seem to have made a slightly different (but not necessarily contradictory) aim or appeal depending on the context: on the one hand, Christ is special, and even sole agent by which creation and salvation are accomplished; on the other hand, Christ is the model of the perfect (= perfected) creature.

This double aim or appeal informs their use of the Christological title "only-begotten" *(monogenes)* (John 1:14; 3:16; 1 John 4:9). It can mean the only creature brought into being directly by God, or *firstborn* (that is, first in a series), or even *identical image;* but the term always carried with it notions of "first Son" or "favored Son," rather than "absolutely unique Son of God," as in orthodox texts (Gregg and Groh 1984: 315–16; expanded on and corrected in Gregg and Groh 1978: 276–78).

C. Uses of Scripture

In their use of Scripture, the Arians excelled as rhetors and tended toward literal and typological exegesis. In dogmatic contexts, they used the Scriptures to provide terminological distinctions and definitions (Gregg and Groh 1981: 7–8, 21, 89–90, 166–68). In homiletical contexts, they, often rhetorically, pursued the moral meaning and application of texts and exhortation of the hearers (Casey 1935: 10), as Wiles has observed (in Gregg 1985: 124–25).

Traces of the allegorizing of scriptural texts as practiced by the Alexandrian school are absent in Arian exegesis. This absence makes claims that the Arian crisis was a conflict of Alexandrian hermeneutics (Kannengiesser 1982b: 1–4) problematic, though Wiles (Gregg 1985: 125) has shown that Asterius stressed the titles of the Psalms in his homilies, as did Origen and some of his disciples.

The long-term importance of Arius and his circle for scriptural exegesis and interpretation seems to reside in their forcing Alexandrian orthodoxy to develop clearly its hermeneutic of Scripture (*Ar.* 3.26; Alex. Al. *Ep. Alex.* 35, Opitz 1935b: 25); and if Athanasius' later account of the discussions at Nicaea is to be believed (*decr.* 19–20, Opitz 1935a: 17), Arian exegetical strategy can be credited with forcing the insertion of a nonscriptural term "of the same essence" *(homoousios)* into a key article of the Creed for the first time in Christian history.

Bibliography

Bardy, G. 1930. Fragments attribués à Arius. *RHE* 26: 253–68.

———. 1936. *Recherches sur Saint Lucien d'Antioch et son école.* Études de théologie historique. Paris.

Barnes, T. D. 1981. *Constantine and Eusebius.* Cambridge, MA.

Boulerand, E. 1964. Les debuts d'Arius. *BLE* 65: 175–203.

———. 1972. *L'Heresie d'Arius et la "foi" de Nicée.* Paris.

Casey, R. P. 1935. An Early Homily Ascribed to Athanasius of Alexandria. *JTS* 36: 1–10.

Gregg, R. C., ed. 1985. *Arianism. Historical and Theological Reassessments. Papers from the Ninth International Conference on Patristic Studies September 5–10, 1983, Oxford, England.* Philadelphia Patristic Monograph Series 11. Philadelphia.

Gregg, R. C., and Groh, D. E. 1977. The Centrality of Soteriology in Early Arianism. *ATR* 59: 260–78. A later revised and augmented version of Gregg and Groh 1984 [1975].

———. 1981. *Early Arianism—A View of Salvation.* Philadelphia.

———. 1984. The Centrality of Soteriology in Early Arianism. *Studia Patristica* 15: 305–16. TU 128. Berlin.

Groh, D. E. 1986. Review Article: New Directions in Arian Research. *ATR* 68: 347–55.

Kannengiesser, C. 1982a. Athanasius of Alexandria *Three Orations against the Arians:* A Reappraisal. Pp. 981–95 in *Studia Patristica* 17, ed. E. A. Livingstone. Oxford.

———. 1982b. *Holy Scripture and Hellenistic Hermeneutics in Alexandrian Christology: The Arian Crisis.* Protocol of the Colloquy of the Center for Hermeneutical Studies in Hellenistic and Modern Culture 41. Berkeley.

———. 1983. *Athanase d'Alexandrie évêque et écrivain.* Théologie historique 40. Paris.

———. 1985. The Athanasian Decade 1974–84: A Bibliographical Report. *TS* 46: 524–41.

Kelly, J. N. D. 1972. *Early Christian Creeds.* 3d ed. New York.

Kopecek, T. A. 1979. *A History of Neo-Arianism.* 2 vols. Patristic Monograph Series 8. Philadelphia.

Lorenz, R. 1979. *Arius judaizans? Untersuchungen zur dogmengeschichtlichen Einordnung des Arius.* Forschungen zur Kirchen— und Dogmengeschichte 31. Göttingen.

Norderval, Ø. 1985. Arius Redivivus? Tendenser innenfor Ariusforskningen. *NorTT* 86: 79–90.

Opitz, H.-G. 1935a. *Athanasius: Werke.* Vol. 2. Berlin.

———. 1935b. *Athanasius: Werke.* Vol. 3, *Urkunden zur Geschichte des arianischen Streites 318–328.* Berlin.

Richard, M., ed. 1956. *Asterii Sophistae commentariorum in Psalmos quae supersunt accedunt aliquot homiliae anonymae.* Oslo.

Ricken, F. 1969. Nikaia als Krisis des altchristlichen Platonismus. *TP* 44: 321–41.

Schneemelcher, W. 1954. Zur Chronologie des arianischen Streits. *TZ* 79: 394–99.

Stead, G. C. 1976. Rhetorical Method in Athanasius. *VC* 30: 121–37.

———. 1978. The *Thalia* of Arius and the Testimony of Athanasius. *JTS* 39: 20–52.

Tetz, M. 1952–53. Eine arianische Homilie unter dem Namen des Athanasius von Alexandrien. *ZKG* 64: 299–307.

Williams, R. 1987. *Arius, Heresy and Tradition.* London.

DENNIS E. GROH

ARK OF THE COVENANT. A sacred object that represented the presence of God in ancient Israelite religion.

A. Designations

There are two Hebrew words translated as "ark" (Lat. *arca* "box, chest") in the English: (1) *ʾărôn,* ancient Israel's most sacred cultic object which was probably originally a box of some sort, and (2) *tēbāh,* the boat which Noah built. In addition to the sacred ark, *ʾărôn* also refers to a collection box in the temple (2 Kgs 12:10, 11—Eng 12:9, 10; 2 Chr 24:8, 10, 11) and the sarcophagus of Joseph (Gen 50:26). References to the ark appear in different formulations 195 times. Only 53 examples (a little over a quarter of the total number) refer to the ark without any qualification, and very few of these occur without an antecedent referent with a fuller name for the ark. It appears, therefore, that the qualifications are important for one's understanding of the significance of the ark in the various traditions (Maier 1965: 82–83).

1. Ark of God/YHWH. The ark is most often (82 times) associated with some divine name: "ark of God," "ark of YHWH," "ark of the God of Israel," "ark of the lord of all the earth," or the like. Most of these occur in the Deuteronomistic History; the rest are in Chronicles. In the Ark Narrative of 1 Samuel 4–6, we learn that the ark was associated with the divine name "YHWH of Hosts who sits enthroned upon the cherubim" (1 Sam 4:4; cf. 2 Sam 6:2; 1 Chr 13:6). This is usually regarded as the fullest and most ancient liturgical name of the ark. Some scholars have argued for the priority of the "ark of God" designations (von Rad, *PHOE,* 115–16), suggesting that it was only at Shiloh that the name of the ark was changed from "ark of God" to the more specific "ark of YHWH." But this is extremely difficult to demonstrate, as is the claim that the two sets of names represent two different strata in the ark stories. Indeed, the occasional juxtaposition of the two divine names (e.g., Deut 10:8; 31:9; Josh 3:3; 1 Kgs 2:26) and sometimes the translation of the names in the versions (e.g., LXX 1 Sam 4:3, 22; 5:2) suggest that the designations "ark of God" an "ark of YHWH" are probably to be treated for the most part as interchangeable names. The variations are usually stylistic rather than ideological. An exception is the name "ark of the god of Israel," all 7 occurrences of which are put in the mouth of the Philistines in connection with the ark's sojourn in Philistine territory (1 Sam 5:7, 8 [3x], 10, 11; 6:3). In the same literary context, the ark is most often called the "ark of YHWH" by the narrator (1 Sam 5:3, 4; 6:1, 2, 11, 15, 18, 19; 7:1). If any significance is to be attached to the specific designations in the narrative about the ark's sojourn, it is surely that the ark represents the power of Israel's God, the "hand" of YHWH (see D.1 below).

2. Ark of the Covenant. This designation appears 40 times, 30 times with various forms of the divine name. Thus, one finds "ark of the covenant of YHWH," "ark of the covenant of God," "ark of the covenant of the lord of all the earth," and so forth. In all cases, the term "covenant" appears to define the ark. The association of the ark with the covenant is typical of the Deuteronomists; it is their special designation of the ark. The statistic that stands out in this category, however, is not so much the places where the name does occur, but where it does not. It does not occur at all in the P work (Seow 1985: 186–87). Instead of "ark of the covenant," P uses a substitute name for the ark, even though the covenant is a key theological concept for P.

3. Ark of the "Testimony." This designation occurs, with one possible exception (Josh 4:16, which is generally taken to be a Priestly gloss), only in the Priestly material in the Tetrateuch. It is P's distinctive term for the ark; no one else uses it. The word that is usually translated as "testimony" *(ʿēdût)* is actually a synonym for "covenant" (Seow 1985: 192–93). We know this from cognates in Egyptian, Akkadian, and Old Aramaic. In Hebrew poetry *ʿēdût* is found in parallelism with *bĕrît,* the normal word for covenant in the Hebrew Bible (e.g., Ps 25:10; 132:12). In certain contexts, the Priestly writer uses *ʿēdût* where another writer would have used *bĕrît.* Thus, whereas Deuteronomy calls the tablets given at Sinai "tablets of the *bĕrît*" (Deut 9:9, 15), P calls them "tablets of the *ʿēdût*" (Exod 27:8; 31:18). It follows, then, that "ark of the *ʿēdût*" is P's equivalent of the Deuteronomistic "ark of the *bĕrît.*" Since P knows the word *bĕrît,* the difference between the designations of the Deuteronomist(s) and P should be explored (see D.3 below).

4. Allusions to the Ark. Outside the Pentateuch and the historical writings, the ark is mentioned by name only once in the Psalter (Ps 132:8) and once in the Prophets (Jer 3:16). This has led some to conclude that the ark was no longer in existence throughout most of the monarchical period (Haran 1963: 46–58). It should be noted, however, that in poetic texts and cultic contexts the ark, which represented the real presence of the deity, may be known simply by the divine name or some theological term. In similar manner, divine images of Mesopotamia were not always called statues, they were regularly referred to as "gods." Alternatively, the name of the god or goddess may be mentioned where the image of the deity is meant. Thus, the reference to YHWH dwelling in a tent (2 Sam 7:6) is clearly to be equated with the ark being in the tent (2 Sam 7:2). So, too, the expression "before YHWH" or "before God" may frequently be synonymous with "before the ark" (e.g., Lev 16:1–2; 2 Sam 6:4–5, 14, 16, 17, 21; 1 Sam 10:25; 2 Kgs 16:14; 1 Kgs 8:59, 62–65; 9:25; Josh 6:8; 1 Chr 1:6; 13:10 [cf. 2 Sam 6:7]; Judg 20:26–27). Related to this, the mention of YHWH's presence *(pānîm)* may also be an allusion to the ark (e.g., Num 10:35; Ps 105:4).

It is probable that Ps 47:6 [—Eng 47:5] refers to a procession of the ark, even though the ark is not mentioned by name (cf. the vocabulary of 2 Sam 6:15). The opening verse of Psalm 68 is similar to the incipit of the ancient Song of the Ark in Num 10:35 and is, perhaps, part of a liturgical text used in connection with the procession of the ark in the early monarchy. In Ps 78:61, there is an allusion to the ark's capture by the Philistines (1 Sam 4:10–11), but the ark is not mentioned by name. Rather, the ark is called simply "his might" and "his glory." This verse echoes the designation "the ark of your might" in Ps 132:8. Some scholars argue, therefore, that the exhortation to "seek YHWH and his strength" (Ps 105:4) contains an allusion to the ark. Indeed, this very portion of the Psalm is cited by the Chronicler (1 Chr 16:11) as part of a liturgy used with the procession of the ark, albeit he places the procession in the time of Solomon's inauguration of the temple. In the same liturgy, the Chronicler quotes from Psalm 96, which states that YHWH's "might and glory" (the same pair of words as in Ps 78:61) are in the temple (Ps 96:6; cf. 1 Chr 16:27). It should be noted that "glory" *(kābôd)* denotes the ark in 1 Sam 4:21–22, where the capture of the ark is lamented as the departure of glory from Israel.

It is commonly acknowledged that Psalm 24 contains an "entrance liturgy" used during the procession of the ark. The psalm celebrates YHWH's cultic return as mighty warrior and glorious king (Cross, *CMHE,* 91–99). This return of YHWH was, no doubt, represented by the procession of the ark. The psalm was perhaps sung antiphonally, with those who led the procession and the "gatekeepers of the ark" (cf. 1 Chr 15:23–24) singing different portions of the liturgical text. Just outside the gates of the city, or the doors of the temple, the celebrants heralded the arrival of the ark:

> Lift up your heads, O Gates;
> Be lifted up, O Ancient Doors
> That the King of Glory may come in!
> Who is this "King of Glory?"
> YHWH strong and mighty,
> YHWH the mighty warrior.
>
> Lift up your heads, O Gates;
> Lift up, O Ancient Doors
> That the King of Glory may enter.
> Who is the "king of Glory"?
> YHWH of Hosts, He is the King of Glory!
> (Ps 24:7–10)

B. Parallels

In order to shed light on the antiquity of the ark and its function, scholars this century have tried to relate the ark to various cult objects in the ANE. Accordingly, the ark has been compared with the Egyptian procession barques on which statues of the gods were placed (Gressman 1926), the sarcophagus of Osiris or the Tammuz chest of the Babylonians (Hartmann 1917–18: 209–14), the step shrine of Petra which was known also among the Hittites (Reimpell 1916: 326–331), and ceramic miniature temples at Megiddo (May 1935–36), among others. Two parallels merit attention here.

1. Tent Shrine. Early in its history, the ark was closely associated with divine presence. In fact, it was so closely associated with the presence of YHWH that it was thought to be an extension of YHWH's personality. YHWH was thought to be present whenever the ark was present. The ark led the people in their wanderings "to search for them a resting place" (Num 10:33). Whenever the ark proceeded, YHWH would be addressed directly:

> Arise, O YHWH,
> Let your enemies be scattered
> Let your foes flee from your presence.
> (Num 10:35)

By the same token, the homeward march of the ark was initiated by the call to YHWH to return (Num 10:36). The martial language in these fragments of an ancient liturgy recalls the use of the ark as a war palladium (Num 14:44; 1 Sam 4:2–9). The ark was the place where the leaders of the tribes of Israel sought oracles for holy war (Judg 20:26–27; 2 Sam 5:19, 23).

Such portrayals of the ark in relatively early sources has prompted comparison of the ark with the *qubbāh,* a pre-Islamic tent shrine of the Arab bedouin (Morgenstern 1945; Cross 1961). The *qubbāh* (cf. Num 25:8) was carried from place to place by the nomads; it led the tribes in their search for water and campsites, was used for divination, and functioned as a war palladium. It was made of red leather (cf. Exod 26:14) and contained two sacred stones (betyls). A bas-relief from a temple of Bel at Palmyra (ca. 1st century B.C.E.) shows a camel in procession, carrying a tent whose red color is still faintly visible. Several Palmyrene texts indeed mention the *qubbāh* (Zobel *TDOT* 1: 367). Variations of this cult object survived in the *ʿuṭfāh* (also called *markab*) and *maḥmal* of later Muslim bedouin. Some of these receptacles carried the Quran.

According to Diodorus Siculus, the Carthaginians also had a "holy tent" *(hiera skēnē)* which they carried with them to battle (Diod. 20.65). An altar was located near this tent shrine. Philo Byblius, quoting Sanchuniathon's "Phoenician history" (ca. 7th century), speaks of an ox-drawn shrine among the Phoenicians (*Praep. Evang.* 10.12; cf. 1 Sam 6:7, 11; 2 Sam 6:3).

There is a strong tradition in the Bible linking the ark with a tent. Referring to the capture of the ark by the Philistines (1 Sam 4:1–7:2), one text speaks of YHWH's forsaking "the tabernacle of Shiloh, the tent where he dwelled" (Ps 78:60–61; cf. 1 Sam 2:22), although the sanctuary at Shiloh is called *hêkāl* (temple/palace) in 1 Sam 1:9; 3:3. (A common view is that there was, in fact, no temple at Shiloh and that the allusions to a temple are anachronistic retrojections from the later Jerusalem temple (Cross, *CMHE,* 73; Haran 1962: 14–24). But it has been pointed out that both notions of the divine abode were already associated with the Canaanite high god, El [Seow 1989: 33–41].) In this connection, it is possible to argue that the tent shrine housing the ark was somehow *in* the temple (cf. the priestly gloss in Josh 18:1 about the establishing of the tent of meeting at Shiloh). According to one source, it was David who built a tent in which the ark was enshrined (2 Sam 6:17; 1 Chr 15:1, 3). Nathan's oracle is explicit that YHWH (i.e., the ark) had not remained *(yāšab)* in a temple but had been moving about "in a tent *and* in a tabernacle" (2 Sam 7:6). According to 1 Kgs 8:4 (cf. 2 Chr 5:5), Solomon brought the ark in procession with the "tent of meeting" and other cultic appurtenances—as if the tent which sheltered the ark was brought into the sanctuary along with the ark.

There is no text more emphatic about the ark being enshrined in a portable tent than P, although the precise relationship of the "tent" and "tabernacle" in P is difficult to sort out. In P, the ark is hidden by the *pārōket* veil which was "over the ark"—even as the *kappōret* was "over the ark" (Exod 30:6; 40:3)—and covering it (Exod 40:3; 21; cf. Num 4:5 and *b. Sukk.* 7b; *b. Soṭa* 37a). The verb "cover" in this context is the same as the verb for the cherubim's overshadowing of the ark. It is interesting, therefore, to note that Josephus describes the wings of the cherubim covering the ark "as under a tent or dome" (*Ant* 7.103–104). Josephus also reports that the ark and tent were both brought into the temple together (*Ant* 8.101). Jewish traditions suggest that the tent and the ark were removed from the temple during the destruction of Jerusalem (2 Macc 2:4–8; cf. *b. Yoma* 53b). Finally, the tradition of the tent shrine housing the ark is known in Heb 9:4 where the ark is said to be located "behind the second curtain," *in a tent.*

2. Throne Footstool. The ark at the Shiloh sanctuary is associated with the divine name "YHWH of Hosts who sits enthroned upon the cherubim" (1 Sam 4:4). This divine epithet combines the notions of YHWH as warrior and king. Moreover, the sanctuary is called a *hêkāl,* "temple" or "palace" (1 Sam 1:9; 3:3). The royal background of the cult at Shiloh has prompted some to argue that the origin of the ark is to be located not in the desert, but in the urban centers of Canaan. The nomads of the desert, it is presumed, would not have used the analogy of kingship prior to the establishment of the monarchy. This is fallacious, however. The idea of YHWH's kingship is presumed in several archaic, premonarchical poems (see Exod 15:18; Num 23:21; Deut 33:5). Moreover, the idea of a tent dwelling for God does not rule out the concept of YHWH's kingship. The chief god of the Canaanite pantheon, El, is regularly depicted in iconography and in the Ugaritic texts as a divine king. Yet El's domicile is explicitly stated to be a tent (*CTA* 4.4.20–26; *ANET,* 133).

In the Solomonic temple, the ark is placed in the innermost sanctum *(dĕbîr),* beneath the outspread wings of the cherubim (1 Kgs 8:6–7). Another passage says the cherubim were each 10 cubits high with the span of their outstretched wings 10 cubits wide (1 Kgs 6:23–28). The two cherubim together appear to have formed some sort of a throne for the invisible God (Mettinger 1982: 19–24). Cherubim thrones are well attested in Syria-Palestine. A beautiful ivory plaque has been excavated from the LB level Megiddo showing a king on a throne seat supported by winged sphinxes, with a procession of people paying homage to him. From the same site and period comes a tiny ivory model of an empty throne, again with winged creatures. The bas-relief from the sarcophagus of Ahiram, king of Byblos (ca. 10th century B.C.E.) likewise depicts a human or divine king sitting on a cherubim throne. A Punic stela from Sousse (Hadrumetum) and a scarab from Sardinia both show the god El as king on a throne.

Scholars from early in this century have proposed that the ark was such a throne and that the cherubim were carved on the side of the ark. But this is problematic. According to the dimensions of the cherubim and the account of the emplacement of the ark, it appears that the ark was not the cherubim-throne. Rather, the ark was probably regarded as the footstool of the invisibly enthroned deity. As such, it is closely associated with the notion of YHWH's enthronement, but it is not the throne *per se.* It should be noted that footstools regularly came with the throne in the ANE. The cherubim thrones of the sarcophagus of Ahiram and the ivory plaque of Megiddo both show boxlike footstools at the base of the throne. The god El, the enthroned deity par excellence among the West Semitic deities, also has a stool (*hdm,* as in Hebrew) on which he places his feet (*CTA* 4.4.29–30; *ANET;* 133).

It has been argued that when a treaty was sealed in the ANE, the treaty document was sometimes placed in a container which served as the footstool of a deity (de Vaux 1967). Thus, for example, a copy of the treaty between Rameses II (an Egyptian) and Ḫattusilis III (a Hittite) was placed at the feet of the images of Re and Teshub respectively. It is interesting in this connection to note that footstools from the Hittite kingdom were frequently boxlike. Tutankhamen's footstool was also boxlike, as was Ahiram's. Footstools from Urartu were made of wood (ebony or acacia), and were sometimes ornately decorated and gold-plated.

The ark is called the footstool explicitly in 1 Chr 28:2 in the words of David: "I had it in my heart to build a house of rest for the ark of the covenant of YHWH, for the footstool of our God." In Psalm 99, YHWH is said to be enthroned on the cherubim as a mighty king, and people are summoned to worship "at his footstool" (Ps 99:5). In a psalm that concerns the procession of the ark, a similar exhortation is issued: "Let us enter his dwelling, let us worship at his footstool" (Ps 132:7).

C. History

1. Premonarchical Period. The precise provenance of the ark is obscure. The biblical traditions point to an early premonarchical origin, and there is nothing to preclude that possibility. The ark is associated with Moses not only in the late sources, but also in the earliest texts. The Song of the Ark (Num 10:35–36) is placed in the context of the wilderness wandering under the leadership of Moses. A defeat of the Israelites in this same period is attributed to the lack of divine support: "neither the covenant-ark of YHWH nor Moses departed from the camp" (Num 14:44).

The ark was from the start a cultic and political symbol; its presence signified the presence of YHWH. According to the book of Joshua, the ark led the people in a conquest ritual (Josh 3:1–5:1; 6:1–25). The text is not written as a historical narrative about the conquest. Rather the interest appears to be in the ritual legitimation of Joshua and Israel.

When the ark entered the Jordan, the waters were held back and stood in a heap (cf. Psalm 114). Its crossing, therefore, was equated with the crossing of YHWH: "Lo! The ark of the Covenant, the Lord of all the earth is crossing over before you in the Jordan!" (Josh 3:11). The political significance of the ritual is never in doubt: that Israel might know that YHWH was with Joshua (Josh 3:7), and that all the nations might know that YHWH was with Israel (Josh 4:10, 24; 5:1).

Upon crossing the Jordan, a sanctuary was established at Gilgal (Josh 4:19). Sometime after the establishing of the Gilgal sanctuary, the ark was moved. The mention in Judg 2:1 that "the angel of YHWH" went up from Gilgal to Bochim is generally taken to be an allusion to the transfer of the ark. The site of Bochim is not known, but it is probably in the vicinity of Bethel (cf. LXX here assumes Hebrew "to Bochim and to Bethel"). The verb used of the angel's going to Bochim is commonly used in conjunction with processions (see Ps 47:6—Eng 47:5; 2 Sam 6:1, 15; 1 Kgs 8:1; etc.) At all events, the ark ended up in Bethel where an oracle was sought by the leaders of the tribal confederacy, in preparation for holy war against the tribe of Benjamin (Judg 20:18, 26–27). Both Gilgal and Bethel were situated within the territory of Ephraim, as was Shiloh, where the ark was located prior to its transfer to Jerusalem. All evidence suggests that the ark was originally the emblem of the northern (Ephraimite) confederacy, and Gilgal, Bethel, and Shiloh each served as its central sanctuary at some time. This shifting of sanctuaries is recalled in Nathan's oracle: "I (YHWH) have been moving about in a tent and a tabernacle" (2 Sam 7:6). According to a Priestly gloss, it was at Shiloh that "tent of meeting" was established (Josh 18:1).

At Shiloh the ark was kept in the sanctuary, where an annual festival was celebrated (Judg 21:19; 1 Sam 1:3, 21; 2:19). In the time of Samuel the ark was in the custody of Eli and his family, who traced their roots to Moses himself. It was at Shiloh that the ark was first called by the name of "YHWH of Hosts who sits enthroned upon the cherubim."

The ark continued to be used as a war palladium. According to the Ark Narrative of 1 Samuel 4–6, the ark was brought into battle with the Philistines near Shiloh. It was a desperate measure to avert defeat. However, the ark was captured by the Philistines, and when the news of its capture was reported to Eli, he fell backward, broke his neck, and died. The loss of the ark was mourned as the departure of YHWH's glory. According to the narrator, the ark was in Philistine possession for 7 months. Finally it was returned because it was causing the Philistines much trouble: a bubonic plague broke out in the Philistine cities.

2. Early Monarchical Period. The ark was moved from Philistine territory to Kiriath-jearim, where it remained in the custody of Abinadab the son of Eleazar for 20 years (1 Sam 6:21–7:2). It fell into oblivion during the days of Saul. The Chronicler says that it was neglected (1 Chr 13:3) and Ps 132:6 assumes that it was lost. Saul may be vindicated by 1 Sam 14:18, but "ark" in that text is usually taken to be a mistake for "ephod" (as some Gk mss suggest). So it may be true, after all, that Saul was not interested in the ark.

Given its obvious importance for the unity of the N confederacy, it is surprising that the ark did not play a more prominent role in the politics of Saul. In the light of the league's punitive war against the Benjaminites (Judg 19–21)—a war that was waged after an oracle was sought before the ark at Bethel (Judg 20:8, 26–27)—it is possible that Saul, a Benjaminite, may have been at odds with the leadership at Shiloh, the new center of the league (cf. Josh 22:12). Saul's break with Samuel and the priests of Nob may be evidence of this conflict.

In any case, the ark remained in Kiriath-jearim until David "found" it there "in the Highland of Jaar" (Ps 132:6). The political significance of David's action is commonly recognized. In contrast to Saul, David sought to ally himself with the Shilonite confederacy. The ark that was transferred to Jerusalem bore the very name of "YHWH of Hosts who sits enthroned upon the cherubim" (2 Sam 6:2; 1 Chr 13:6). That was precisely the name of the ark at Shiloh (1 Sam 4:4). David brought the ark in cultic procession into "the City of David" and set it in its place, in the tent. In his time, the ark continued to function as a war palladium from time to time (cf. 2 Sam 11:11; 1 Sam 15:24–29).

By all accounts, David did not build a temple to house the ark. Rather, it fell upon Solomon to do so. Upon the completion of the temple, Solomon brought the ark in procession into the innermost sanctum (1 Kgs 8:1–12). Although 1 Kings 8 is composite, with considerable exilic material embedded therein, it is still possible to discern a historical kernel. The gist of the account of the transmission of the ark is certainly pre-Deuteronomistic, as is a poetic fragment possibly from the Book of Jashar but now put in the mouth of Solomon:

> YHWH [LXX adds: "has established the sun in the heavens"]
> He said he would dwell in a storm cloud.
> I have indeed built for you a royal house
> the dais of your throne forever (vv 12–13).

Although the temple was completed in the month of Bul (1 Kgs 6:38), the procession was not held until the month of Ethanim, almost a year later (1 Kgs 8:1–2). The inauguration was deferred probably to coincide with the autumn New Year, a season for the celebration of divine kingship. That was a time for inauguration and renewal of temples in the ANE. The procession also coincided with the Feast of Sukkoth (1 Kgs 8:2, 65; cf. Josephus, *Ant* 8.100), which is called "the yearly feast of YHWH at Shiloh" (Judg 21:19; cf. 1 Sam 1:3, 21; 2:19).

Beyond the processions under David and Solomon, it is difficult to speak with certainty about cultic processions of the ark in the monarchical period. The ark is said to have had poles enabling it to be carried in cultic processions. In Solomon's temple, the poles were so long that their ends were seen "from the holy place before the inner sanctuary" (1 Kgs 8:7). Psalm 132 alludes to David's transfer of the ark and may, in an earlier version, have been used in conjunction with that procession or with the one under the auspices of Solomon. Psalms 24, 47, and 68 should probably be dated to the early monarchy, and may have been used in ritual processions of the ark (Fretheim 1967).

3. Disappearance. It is not certain precisely when and how the ark was lost; the Bible is silent on this matter. Some have conjectured that it was destroyed or removed in the monarchical period as a result of Shishak's raid in the 10th century (1 Kgs 14:25–28), or when Jehoash king of Israel plundered the temple in the wake of Judah's defeat (2 Kgs 14:8–14), or during Manasseh's syncretistic renovation of the temple (2 Kgs 21:4–6). The problem is compounded by the fact that the ark is not listed among the spoils from the temple that Nebuchadrezzar took to Babylon when Jerusalem was sacked (2 Kgs 25:13–17; Jer 52:17–23). This does not, of course, preclude a different date for the capture of the ark (say, 597 B.C.E.) or a different fate for it (i.e., destruction).

Several traditions place the disappearance of the ark to a date around the end of the 7th century and the beginning of the 6th. According to the Chronicler, along with his other reforms, Josiah ordered that the "holy ark" be placed in the temple because "you need not carry it upon your shoulders" (2 Chr 35:3). This text is problematic; its veracity is difficult to authenticate. The Chronicler believed that the ark was still in existence in the time of Josiah, but it was in transition—as it had been at one time. Perhaps he was making the point that Josiah reinstated the ark which had been removed from the adytum (possibly in the time of Manasseh) and had been in temporary shelters. In any case, Jeremiah spoke—*vaticinium ex eventu?*—against overconfidence in "the ark of the covenant." The ark's presence in the temple gave people a false sense of security about YHWH's permanent presence in their midst. Jeremiah declared that people would no longer say "the ark of the covenant of YHWH" (Jer 3:16). They would no longer remember the ark, visit it, or make it again.

According to some Jewish traditions, the Babylonians removed the vessels of gold, silver, and bronze, but Jeremiah removed the ark and the sacred tablets and hid them from the Babylonians. This tradition may be traced at least to the historian Eupolemus (see Eusebius, *Praep. Evang.* 9.39). A similar account is related by Alexander Polyhistor of Miletus in the 1st century B.C.E., but he was probably dependent on Eupolemus for this story. In a variant of this account, Jeremiah hid the tent, the ark, and the altar of incense in a cave on the mountain from which Moses saw the Promised Land (2 Macc 2:4–8). Another source has it that Josiah hid the ark under a rock "in its place" (*b. Yoma* 53b–54a; *m. Šeqal.* 6:1–2). According to a legend, an angel descended from heaven during the destruction of Jerusalem and removed the sacred vessels from the temple (*2 Bar.* 6:7). These accounts are obviously ways of coping with the unthinkable destruction of the ark of divine presence at the hands of Gentile invaders. More credible is the lament over the desecration of the temple and plundering of the ark during the destruction of the First Temple (2 Esdr 10:20–23). In any case, all traditions point to the exilic period for the disappearance of the ark.

It appears that the ark was not rebuilt for the Second Temple. Jeremiah declared that it was not to be made again (Jer 3:16). There is no mention of the ark anywhere in Ezekiel's blueprint for the new temple (Ezekiel 40–48). In the spot where the ark would have stood, there was, instead, a "stone of foundation" three fingers high (see *m. Yoma* 5:2). Otherwise, the adytum appears to have been empty. Josephus reports that such was the case (*JW* 5.5), and the Roman historian Tacitus concurs with this report (*Hist.* V.9). According to Josephus, when Pompey forced his way into the temple in 64 B.C.E., the Romans saw the sacred objects, which Josephus then enumerates without mentioning the ark (*Ant* 14.71–72; *JW* 1.152–53).

D. Theology

1. The Ark Narrative. The narrative in 1 Samuel 4–6 recounts the capture of the ark by the Philistines. Scholars have demonstrated that the ark functions here as Israel's equivalent of the divine statue in Mesopotamia (Delcor 1964; Miller and Roberts 1977). The ark represents the presence of YHWH.

In their battle against the Philistines, the elders of Israel called for the ark to be brought. The narrator reports that even the Philistines recognized the theological significance of the ark. They cried, "Woe to us! Who can deliver us from the *hand* (Heb "hand" = "power") of these gods?" (1 Sam 4:8). This was the significance of the ark in the narrative: it manifested the power of YHWH (see Miller and Roberts 1977). Indeed, in this ark story as elsewhere, the ark's presence demonstrated the power of YHWH. Likewise the purpose of the procession of the ark in Joshua is stated thus: "that all the peoples of the earth may know that the *hand* of YHWH is mighty" (Josh 4:24).

In desperation, the Israelites brought the ark. The presence of the ark was supposed to assure victory against the enemies. But the ark was captured instead, and the Israelites fled (1 Sam 4:10, 17). Things were not supposed to happen that way with the ark. When the ark, representing the presence of God, came into battle, the enemies were supposed to flee (Num 10:35; Pss 68:2—Eng 68:1; 114:3, 5). In the Ugaritic myth, when the divine warrior Baal-Hadad gave forth his voice, the enemies fled to the forests (*CTA* 4.7.29–37; *ANET,* 135). But in the Ark Narrative of 1 Samuel, it is YHWH's army that flees, and the enemies capture the ark.

For the narrator, the ark's capture provided an opportunity to argue again for YHWH's power. The ark was deposited in the temple of the Philistine god, Dagon, in Ashdod. The next day, "Dagon had fallen face to the ground before the ark of YHWH" (1 Sam 5:3). The wording recalls Joshua's gesture of penitence: "he fell face to the ground before the ark of YHWH" (Josh 7:6). The Philistines raised the statue of Dagon again. But the next day, "Dagon had fallen face to the ground before the ark of YHWH" (1 Sam 5:4). This time, Dagon's head and both his hands are cut off. Thus the hand of YHWH was demonstrated against the god of the Philistines; the hands of Dagon were cut off. According to the narrator, the hand of YHWH was heavy upon the people of Ashdod (1 Sam 5:6) and they were smitten with tumors. The people of Ashdod concluded: "The ark of the god of Israel must not remain with us, for his hand is heavy upon us and upon Dagon our god" (1 Sam 5:7).

The ark was sent to Gath and the hand of YHWH was against that city (1 Sam 5:9). When the ark came to Ekron, the people there concluded that it was brought there to slay them. Again, "the hand of God was heavy" in Ekron because the ark was there (1 Sam 5:11). Indeed, the presence of the ark in Philistine territory showed that the hand of YHWH was against them (2 Sam 5:3). And so the ark was returned "to its place" in Israel.

2. Transfer of the Ark. The ark that David transferred to Jerusalem is called the ark of "YHWH of Hosts who sits enthroned upon the cherubim" (2 Sam 6:2). The epithet brings to mind the image of YHWH as victorious warrior. Indeed, it appears that the procession appropriately follows YHWH's triumph over the Philistines at Baal-perazim. Having received an oracle from YHWH (we presume before the ark, cf. Judg 20:8, 27), David defeated the Philistines. Thereupon, he likened the victory to the divine warrior's cosmogonic defeat of chaotic waters: "YHWH has broken my enemies like the breaking of Waters" (2 Sam 5:20; cf. 6:8). After a second oracle and victory of the divine warrior, David brought the ark from Baale-judah (= Kiriath-jearim) to Jerusalem. The ark was marched into the city with cultic dancing, dramatizing the victorious return of the Warrior (Seow 1989). Finally the ark was placed in the newly won place. With this dramatic procession, many of Judah's theological traditions may be associated. Some of the traditions may even have grown from that significant event—traditions concerning YHWH's eternal choice of both David and Zion and traditions about Zion's inviolability in the face of enemy encroachments. Certainly many of these themes may be located in Psalm 132, some form of which may have been used in connection with David's procession of the ark.

3. The Ark in Deuteronomy. In contradistinction to earlier tendencies, Deuteronomy appears to downplay the importance of the ark. Accordingly, the ark does not appear anywhere in Deuteronomy in connection with the enthronement of YHWH. It is neither a war palladium, nor is it associated with the presence of God. The ark does not have that mysterious power that strikes people dead (1 Sam 6:19; 2 Sam 6:6–8; Lev 16:1). Rather, the ark in Deuteronomy is, as von Rad says, a demythologized ark (*PHOE,* 103–24). It is viewed merely as a receptacle for the tablets of the covenant (Fretheim 1968). It appears always to be mentioned incidentally. The narrator's interest in every case is on the covenant and the tablets that represent the covenant. So when the second set of tablets were commissioned at Sinai, the ark was also ordered—as if for the sake of the tablets alone. The author wastes no time in specifying the nature of the ark: it is a wooden *ʾărôn,* "box" (Deut 10:1), an ark of acacia wood (Deut 10:3). After YHWH had written on the tablets, they were placed in the ark (Deut 10:5). Likewise, when the "book of the Law" was completed, Moses commanded the Levites to put it by the side of the ark of the covenant "that it be there as a witness against you" (Deut 31:26). The Deuteronomic ark has no significance by itself; it is merely a receptacle in which and beside which the covenant documents are placed. Nothing is mentioned in D about the cherubim, or anything else that may suggest the throne. Nothing is said about the acacia wood being gold-plated. The ark in Deuteronomy seems to be, simply, an *ʾărôn,* "box, chest."

4. The Ark in P. By far the most detailed and meticulous description of the ark is found in P. Exod 25:10–22 purports to be part of a heavenly blueprint which Moses received for the construction of the tabernacle and its appurtenances. The ark was then constructed by a certain Bezalel (Exod 37:1–15). According to the plan from on high, the ark was to be a chest of acacia wood, 2.5 cubits long, and 1.5 cubits wide and high (i.e., 4 feet 2 inches by 30 inches by 30 inches). The wood was to be overlaid with gold on every side, with a molding of gold "upon it" all around—probably upon all four sides of the ark. In addition, there were four "feet" on each of which the builder was to then add a golden ring to hold two carrying poles. These poles were also to be made of acacia wood and plated with gold. The poles were always to be left in the rings, ready to be carried. The tablets (called "the stones of *ʿēdût* or, simply, *ʿēdût* in P) were to be deposited in the ark. On top of the ark there was to be a *kappōret* (covering) made of pure gold. It was to be as long and wide as the ark, but nothing is said of its thickness. This was for P a covering for the ark as well as a symbol of the propitiation of sins epitomized by the ritual before the ark on *yom kippūr,* "the day of atonement" (Lev 16:2ff.). Two cherubim were to be crafted "from the *kappōret*" (i.e., all of one piece), one cherub at each end of the *kappōret.* The cherubim were to face one another and have outstretched wings overshadowing the *kappōret.*

There is no chance in the description of P for the ark to be mistaken for a throne, or the footstool of a throne. It is emphatically a box in which the tablets were kept. To that extent, P's description is like that in Deuteronomy. The cherubim are not part of a throne. They are small ornate handiwork on the covering of the ark, unlike the huge cherubim described in 1 Kgs 6:23–28; 8:6–7 which are separated from the ark. Moreover, in contrast to the creatures on cherubim thrones, P has the cherubim facing each other: "their faces one to another, toward the *kappōret* were their faces" (Exod 25:20). Their outspread wings cover the ark. Thus, P leaves no room for the interpretation of the ark as a throne or the footstool of a throne. The ark was a *rendezvous* where God would meet the people, but it was not the locus of a throning presence. Such is the nature of divine presence, according to P: it is not confined to one place; rather, it is manifested from time to time as the deity wills (Lev 16:2). According to P, in the time of Moses YHWH chose to speak from between the cherubim on the *kappōret* of the ark (Num 7:89). That was a chosen place; it was theologically significant. While P admits that the ark may be one meeting point for God and the congregation, he takes pain to dissociate God from the ark (Seow 1985). The ark is associated with some form of the divine name 112 times in the Bible; but it never once occurs with the divine name in P. It appears that P was reacting to a misconception of divine immanence. Confidence in YHWH's presence had apparently become overly dependent on the ark's presence, so that the disappearance of the ark was causing an undue crisis of faith. For P the ark was not in any way to be associated with God's kingship; it was also not the indispensable mark of God's presence.

Related to the issue of God's abiding presence is the question of the covenant's validity. Whereas the ark is called "the ark of the covenant" (*ʾărôn habbĕrît*), "the ark of YHWH's covenant" (*ʾărôn bĕrît yhwh*), or the like in 40 cases throughout the Bible, the ark is not associated with the *bĕrît* in the Priestly work. Instead of *bĕrît,* P uses the synonym *ʿēdût* (incorrectly translated as "testimony" in many English translations) and speaks of the "ark of the *ʿēdût*" (Exod 25:22; 26:33, 34; 30:6; etc.). But P knows the word *bĕrît.* The *bĕrît* for P is eternal and never to be destroyed (Gen 9:8–17; 17:1–27). The eternal validity of that covenant is indicated by signs, like the rainbow, that cannot ever be eradicated or removed. The *ʿēdût* is never used of the covenant per se, only for the covenant tablets. Hence the instruction: "you shall put the *ʿēdût* into the ark" (Exod 25:16, 21). In this way, then, P was able to speak of the eternal validity of God's covenant with Israel, even in the face of the disappearance of the ark. The tablets may be shattered, but the covenant is eternal.

5. The Ark in Chronicles. Many of the Chronicler's references to the ark are parallel to and essentially derived from the accounts embedded in the Deuteronomistic History concerning the transmission of the ark under the aegis of David and Solomon. There are distinctive elements in Chronicles, however. It is reiterated time and again that the sacred ark was to be handled only by the priests and Levites (1 Chr 15:2, 12; 16:4), "gatekeepers of the ark" (1 Chr 16:23–24) and certain ministers of music (1 Chr 6:31–32; 16:37). By all accounts, the ark came into prominence under the patronage of David. The Chronicler states that the ark was indeed neglected in the days of Saul, and it was David who restored it to its rightful place (1 Chr 13:3–4). The contrast here between the negligent Saul and the pious David reminds one of the propagandistic claims in the royal inscriptions of Mesopotamia that portray the legitimate king as the "restorer of the forgotten cult" (Seow 1989). This view is certainly consonant with the ritual behind Psalm 132, which the Chronicler quotes (2 Chr 6:41). Faithful David swore that he would not rest until the rightful place of YHWH be restored and the ark was "rediscovered" (Ps 132:1–5). The procession of the ark by Solomon receives considerably more attention than in 1 Kings 8, but no significance may be discerned in most of the Chronicler's embellishments.

E. NT References

The Greek word *kibōtos* (the equivalent for Heb *ʾărôn*) occurs 6 times in the NT. Only 2 of these (Heb 9:3–5; Rev 11:19) refer to the cult object; the rest concern Noah's ark.

The account of the ark in Hebrews 9 purports to be a description of the ark under the "first covenant" which is superceded by the new covenant. The description is in substantial agreement with the account of P, although the name of the cult object here is "the ark of the covenant," which never occurs in P. The ark was enshrined in a tent behind the second curtain, together with the golden altar. It was gold-plated, and the cherubim were perched atop the covering (Propitiatory), overshadowing it (vv 3–5). The Gk word *hilastērion* used here to translate the Heb *kappōret* is found also in Rom 3:25, but it is impossible to know if the author here was thinking of the *kappōret* or the expiatory function of it. The writer of Hebrews lists the ark's content: a golden jar of manna, Aaron's rod that blossomed, and the tablets of the covenant. The jar of manna and rod of Aaron are both mentioned in P, but there the items are placed "before the *ʿēdût*" (Exod 16:32–34; Num 17:8–10)—that is, before the ark (cf. Exod 27:21; 30:36; Lev 16:13; 24:3).

In Rev 11:19 the ark is called "(God's) ark of the covenant" *(hē kibōtos tēs diathēkēs autou),* which represents a Greek adaptation of the Deuteronomistic name. In the vision of the eschatological temple, the disciple sees the ark in God's temple in heaven, with all the signs that in the Hebrew Bible normally accompany the theophany of the storm god, the divine warrior. So the ark is once again associated with the presence of God.

Bibliography

Ahlström, A. 1984. The Travels of the Ark: A Religio-Political Composition. *JNES* 43: 141–49.

Arnold, W. R. 1917. *Ephod and Ark.* HTS 3. Cambridge, MA.

Blenkinsopp, J. 1969. Kiriath-jearim and the Ark. *JBL* 88: 143–56.

Campbell, A. F. 1975. *The Ark Narrative (1 Sam 4–6; 2 Sam 6).* SBLDS 16. Missoula.

———. 1979. Yahweh and the Ark. *JBL* 98: 31–43.

Clements, R. E. 1965. *God and Temple.* Oxford.

Coats, G. W. 1985. The Ark of the Covenant in Joshua: A Probe into the History of Tradition. *HAR* 9: 137–57.

Cross, F. M. 1961. The Priestly Tabernacle. Pp. 201–28 in *BAR* 1.

———. 1981. The Priestly Tabernacle in the Light of Recent Research. Pp. 70–90 in *Temples and High Places in Biblical Times,* ed. A. Biran. Jerusalem.

Davis, G. H. 1967. The Ark of the Covenant. *ASTI* 5: 30–47.

Delcor, M. 1964. Yahweh et Dagon ou le Jahwisme face à la religion des Philistins, d'après 1 Sam. V. *VT* 14: 136–54.

Dibelius, M. 1906. *Die Lade Jahves.* FRLANT 98. Göttingen.

Dus, J. 1961. Der Brauch der Ladewanderung im alten Testament. *TZ* 17: 1–16.

———. 1963a. Die Erzählung über den Velust der Lade 1 Sam. IV. *VT* 13: 333–37.

———. 1963b. Noch zum Brauch der "Ladewanderung." *VT* 13: 126–32.

Eissfeldt, O. 1940–41. Lade und Stierbild. *ZAW* 58: 190–215.

Fretheim, T. E. 1967. *The Cultic Use of the Ark in the Monarchial Period.* Ph.D. Diss. Princeton.

———. 1968. The Ark in Deuteronomy. *CBQ* 30: 1–14.

Fritz, V. 1977. *Tempel und Zelt.* Neukirchen-Vluyn.

Gressmann, H. 1926. *Die Lade allerheiligste des salomonische Temples.* New York and Berlin.

Gutman, J. 1971. The History of the Ark. *ZAW* 87: 22–30.

Haran, M. 1959. The Ark and the Cherubim. *IEJ* 9: 30–38, 89–94.

———. 1962. Shiloh and Jerusalem: The Origin of the Priestly Tradition in the Pentateuch. *JBL* 81: 14–24.

———. 1963. The Disappearance of the Ark. *IEJ* 13: 46–58.

———. 1975. The Bas-Reliefs of the Sarcophagus of Ahiram King of Byblos in the Light of Archaeological and Literary Parallels from the Ancient Near East. *IEJ* 8: 15–25.

Hartmann, R. 1917–18. Zelt und Lade. *ZAW* 37: 209–44.

Hillers, D. R. 1968. Ritual Procession of the Ark and Psalm 132. *CBQ* 30: 48–55.

Maier, J. 1965. *Das israelitische Heiligtum* BZAW 93. Berlin.

Mettinger, T. N. D. 1982. *The Dethronement of Sabaoth.* ConBOT 18. Lund: Gleerup.

Miller, P. D., Jr., and Roberts, J. J. M. 1977. *The Hand of the Lord.* JHNES 9. Baltimore.

Morgenstern, J. 1945. *The Ark, the Ephod and the Tent of Meeting.* Cincinnati.

Porter, J. R. 1954. The Interpretation of 2 Samuel VI and Psalm CXXXII. *JTS* 5: 161–73.

Rad, G. von. 1966. The Tent and the Ark. Pp. 103–124 in *The Problems of the Hexateuch and Other Essays.* New York.

Reimpell, W. 1916. Der Ursprung der Lade Jahwes. *OLZ* 19: 326–31.

Roberts, J. J. M. 1971. The Hand of Yahweh. *VT* 21: 244–51.

Schicklberger, F. 1973. *Die Ladeerzählungen des ersten Samuel-Buches.* FB 7. Würzburg.

Schmidt, H. 1923. Kerubenthron und Lade. Pp. 120–44 in *Eucharistion* I. Göttingen.

Schmitt, R. 1972. *Zelt und Lade als Thema alttestamentlicher Wissenschaft.* Gütersloh.

Seow, C. L. 1985. The Designation of the Ark in Priestly Theology. *HAR* 8: 185–98.

———. 1989. *Myth, Drama, and the Politics of David's Dance.* HSM. Atlanta.

Timm, H. 1966. Die Ladeerzählung (1 Sam 4–6; 2 Sam 6) und das Kerygma des deuteronomistischen Geschichtswerks. *EvT* 29: 509–26.

Tur-Sinai, N. H. 1951. The Ark of God at Beit Shemesh (1 Sam. VI) and Peres 'Uzza (2 Sam. VI; 1 Chron. XIII). *VT* 1: 275–86.

Woudstra, M. H. 1965. *The Ark of the Covenant from Conquest to Kingship.* Philadelphia.

Vaux, R. de. 1967. Les cherubins et l'arche d'alliance, les sphinx gardiens et les trones divins dans l'ancien orient. *Bible et Orient.* Paris.

C. L. Seow

ARK, NOAH'S. See the NOAH AND THE ARK articles.

ARKITE (PERSON) [Heb *ʿarqî*]. One of the offspring of Canaan (Gen 10:17). The *-î* suffix suggests that this is a gentilic, reflecting the inhabitants of the coastal Phoenician town of Irqata. The name of this town appears in Egyptian *(ʿ3qty/ʿ3qtm),* Hittite *(ir-qà-ta),* and Akkadian sources, including the 2d millenium B.C. Amarna letters (*ir-qat, ir-qàt, ir-qa-ta, ir-qà-ta;* cf. Hess 1984: 495) and 1st millenium B.C. Neo-Assyrian texts (*ar-qa-a, ir-qa-na-ta-a-a;* cf. Parpola 1970: 31, 176; for the second spelling as a mistake, cf.

Tadmor 1961: 245 n. 49). The name of this town also appears in later Classical sources (Honigmann *RLA* 1: 153–54; Hawkins *RLA* 5:165–66). Irqata has been identified with Roman Caesarea of Liban, modern Tell Arqa (M.R. 250436), 12 mi. NE of Tripoli, where excavations have revealed occupation throughout the Bronze and Iron ages (Dussaud 1927: 80–91; Thalman 1978; Wenham *Gen 1–15* WB, 226). Just as Gen 10:16–18 associates the Arkites with Heth, the Amorites, Arvad, the Zemarites, and Hamath; so also does a Hittite prayer mention Irqata in association with Amurru, and the Neo-Assyrian sources associate Arqa/Irqa(na)ta with Arwada, Ṣimirra, and Ḫamat.

Bibliography

Dussaud, R. 1927. *Topographie historique de la Syrie antique et médiévale.* Paris.

Hess, R. S. 1984. *Amarna Proper Names.* Diss. Hebrew Union College.

Parpola, S. 1970. *Neo-Assyrian Toponyms.* AOAT 6. Kevelaer.

Tadmor, H. 1961. Azriyau of Yaudi. *ScrHier* 8: 232–71.

Thalman, J.-P. 1978. Tell-Arqa (Liban Nord) Campagnes I–III (1972–1974) Chantier I. Rapport préliminaire. *Syr* 55: 1–151.

RICHARD S. HESS

ARMAGEDDON (PLACE) [Gk *Armagedōn*]. The location of the final battle of earth's history as described in the book of Revelation. The word appears only once in the Bible and is Hebrew in origin (Rev 16:16). (See REVELATION, BOOK OF.) The most natural understanding of the Greek found in most manuscripts is "mountain (from the Hebrew *har*) of MEGIDDO." While the Greek spelling differs considerably from the Hebrew word "Megiddo," it is identical to the Septuagint transliteration in Josh 12:21 (ms A *mageddōn*), Judg 1:27 (ms A), and 2 Chr 35:22. Another transliteration of Megiddo in the LXX parallels the manuscript variant *mageddōn* (4 Kgdms 9:27—Eng 2 Kgs 9:27). Thus Nestle (*HDB* 2: 305) considered an allusion to Megiddo the most probable explanation of the term "Armageddon." It is interesting, however, that the only place in the OT where the Hebrew adds a final "n" to Megiddo, Zech 12:11, the LXX does not transliterate, instead it translates "Valley of Megiddo" as "(the pomegranate grove) cut down in the plain" *(ekkoptomenou)*.

The region of Megiddo was an ancient battleground. There the armies of Israel under DEBORAH and BARAK defeated SISERA and his Canaanite army (Judg 5:19 and context). Later, it was the scene of the fatal struggle between JOSIAH and Pharaoh NECO (2 Kgs 23:29, 30; 2 Chr 35:22). This was such a memorable event in Israel's history that the mourning for Josiah was recalled a hundred years later (Zech 12:11). Thus, if the writer of Revelation was alluding to this ancient battleground, its significance for ancient Israel made it an appropriate background to his description of the final battle between the forces of good and evil.

Bousset (*Revelation* MeyerK, 399), however, pointed out that the phrase "Mountain of Megiddo" is problematic. While the OT knows of a city of Megiddo (Josh 17:11; Judg 1:27; 1 Kgs 4:12; 9:15; 2 Kgs 9:27; 23:29, 30), a king of Megiddo (Josh 12:21), a valley of Megiddo (2 Chr 35:22; Zech 12:11), and waters of Megiddo (Judg 5:19), it knows of no "Mountain of Megiddo." A number of solutions to this problem have been offered over the centuries and continue to be offered.

Early Church Fathers, such as Hippolytus and Jerome, sought to locate Armageddon in Palestine, offering suggestions such as the Valley of Jehoshaphat (cf. Joel 3:2, 12) or Mount Tabor (cf. Judg 4:6, 12). The first proposal to gain wide currency was advanced by the earliest commentators on the book of Revelation, Oecumenius (early 6th cent.—see Hoskier 1928: 179–80) and Andreas of Caesarea (ca. 600 A.D.—see Schmid 1955: 1/175). Perhaps taking their cue from the LXX translators of Zech 12:11, who apparently understood *mĕgiddôn* to be derived from the Hebrew root *gdd* which means "to cut" or "to gash," they argued that the kings of the earth are gathered in Rev 16 to the "Mountain of Slaughter" to be exterminated. Supported by LaRondelle (1985: 23, 1989: 71–73), this view has never been refuted, yet does not attract wide support among scholars.

F. Junius (1599) associated Armageddon with "the mountain places of Megiddo." In marginal notes to the *Geneva Bible* he suggested that the battle of Armageddon is God's reversal of the reproach His people suffered with the defeat of Josiah. Several 19th-century scholars (see Bousset *Revelation* MeyerK, 399) sought to overcome the absence of a "mountain of Megiddo" in the OT by linking the battles at Megiddo with Ezekiel's description of Gog being defeated on the "mountains of Israel" (see Ezekiel 38 and 39, a passage alluded to in Rev 20:8–10).

Lohmeyer (*Revelation* HNT, 133–34) added a new twist to the "mountain of Megiddo" interpretation by associating Armageddon with Mount Carmel, an allusion to Elijah's confuting of the prophets of Baal. He appealed for support to *Ginza,* a much-later Mandean work, where demonic powers gather on Mount Carmel to plan their final assault on the forces of God. Shea (1980: 160–62) carries the argument a step further by seeing a multitude of allusions throughout Revelation to Elijah's experience on Mount Carmel, with dragon, beast, and false prophet being the latter-day counterparts of Ahab, Jezebel, and the prophets of Baal. As in the original instance, the issue is settled in Revelation by fire and by sword (Rev 19:20, 21).

While the first two explanations are based on how the translators of the LXX understood the Hebrew Bible, a number of attempts at emendation have also come into play. Many 19th-century scholars (see Nestle *HDB* 2:304–5 and Bousset *Revelation* MeyerK) noted that the difference between *har* and *ar* in Greek is a simple breathing mark, and such markings are generally omitted in the earliest manuscripts. Thus *ar-magedon* could be the equivalent of the Hebrew "city of Megiddo" *(ʿîr-mĕgiddô),* an allusion to the fortress city which guarded ancient Israel's most critical mountain pass.

Other scholars, beginning with an unsigned article in *ZAW* (1887: 170–71), gave attention to emendations of *magedōn.* In unpointed Hebrew *mĕgiddô* is identical in form to *migdô* which means "fruitful" or "his fruitfulness," "his choicest gifts." Thus, Bowman (*IDB* 1: 227) feels that Armageddon means "his fruitful mountain," a reference to eschatological Jerusalem (Joel 4:16–18—Eng 3:16–18, cf. Zechariah 14). This would associate the final battle scene with Jerusalem, as is also the case in Rev 14:14–20 and 20:7–10. Charles (*Revelation* ICC, 2: 50) combines both emendations; Armageddon means "fruitful city," which recalls John's title for the heavenly city in 20:9 (Gk *tēn polin tēn ēgapēmenēn,* "the beloved city").

One of the most popular emendations of *magedōn* was proposed by Hommel (1890). He suggested that the Greek *gamma* in *magedōn* is a transliteration, not of the Hebrew *gimel* but of the Hebrew *ᶜayin.* Thus *har-magedōn* would be a corruption of the Hebrew *har-môᶜēd,* or "mountain of assembly." Torrey (1938: 244–48) argues that Armageddon is a reference to Isa 14:13 where the "mountain of assembly" is the heavenly court in which God's throne is located. In Isaiah 14 the King of Babylon is called the "Day Star," a term applied to Christ in Revelation. Thus, *har-môᶜēd* recalls Hebrew mythology, where Mount Zion is the earthly counterpart of the heavenly throne room (Ps 48:3—Eng 48:2). Armageddon, then, is Babylon's final attempt to usurp the throne of God in its attack on end-time Jerusalem.

Gunkel (1895: 263–66) understood Armageddon to be a name with mythic origins, probably based on *1 Enoch* 6 where the evil angels gather on Mount Hermon to prepare for their assault on the daughters of men. Bousset follows Gunkel in suggesting that behind this reference lies an ancient myth, preserved in Mandean works, which described the assault on the holy mountain of the gods by an army of demons that is gathered by evil spirits, then destroyed by the gods of light.

The abundance of solutions and the great creativity with which they have been developed suggests that it is unwise to be dogmatic about the etymology of Armageddon. Nevertheless, current scholarship generally settles on a link with Megiddo or *har-môᶜēd* as the best explanation of *harmagedōn.*

The major difficulty with the *har-môᶜēd* interpretation is the great linguistic distance between *môᶜēd* and *magedōn.* While it is true that *gamma* is the only Greek letter that could correspond to the Hebrew *ᶜayin,* there is no external evidence that *môᶜēd* was ever transliterated as *magedōn* or even *mogēd,* whereas LXX evidence exists for transliterations of *mĕgiddô* and *mĕgiddôn.* Furthermore, the strength of Torrey's argument is largely diluted if one doesn't accept his theory that the Apocalypse is the translation of a Hebrew original.

It is probably safest, then, to avoid emendation and to either follow the Church Fathers or Lohmeyer and Shea, or to consider the problem unresolved. Many arguments have been raised against the "Mountain of Megiddo" interpretations, particularly by Jeremias (1932) and Torrey (1938): (1) there is no Mount Megiddo in pre-NT literature; (2) the earliest exegetes never interpreted it in this way; (3) the mythical world mountain was never associated with Megiddo in apocalyptic; (4) in Hebrew eschatology the final struggle is fought around Jerusalem (Zechariah 12 and 14; Joel 4—Eng 3; cf. Revelation 14; 20:7–10). These are, however, basically arguments from silence. They do not preclude the possibility that the author of Revelation saw elements of the ideological battle on Mount Carmel as decisive in the final battle between good and evil.

In fact, as Shea (1980: 158–60) points out, Megiddo is often used to speak of something else in the geographical area. The phrase "waters of Megiddo" (Jdg 5:19) is a reference to the Kishon River. And while Megiddo was not a mountain, it wasn't a valley either—it was located on an elevation overlooking the Plain of Jezreel or Esdraelon. Since the city was located at the foot of the Carmel range, "mountain of Megiddo" could easily be a reference to Mount Carmel (1 Kgs 18:19, 20; 2 Kgs 2:25; 4:25). It was on Mount Carmel that fire was called down from heaven to prove that Yahweh was the true God (cf. Rev 13:13, 14). It was there that the false prophets were defeated (cf. Rev 16:13–16). If John was alluding to Elijah's experience on Mount Carmel, he understood the battle of Armageddon to be a spiritual conflict over worship (cf. Rev 13:4, 8, 12, 15; 14:7, 9, 11; cf. 16:15; 17:14) in which all would be brought to a fateful decision with permanent results.

As part of the sixth bowl plague (16:12–16), the battle of Armageddon comes at a pivotal point in the book of Revelation. It parallels the sixth trumpet plague (9:13–21), where military imagery is combined with descriptions of demonic beings. The gathering effected by the three unclean spirits (16:13) is the demonic counterpart to the gathering call of the three angels of Rev 14:6–11. The reference to the demonic trinity connects this passage also with chaps. 13 and 19, where the same characters are at work. And finally, the battle is described in other but parallel terms in 17:12–17. The sixth bowl plague is not the battle of Armageddon itself; it is the gathering of forces for the battle. The battle itself accomplishes the fall of Babylon, which is outlined in the seventh bowl plague (16:17–21), in 17:16 and in chap. 18. For further discussion see *ISBE* 1:294–95, *EncBib* 1:310–11, *TDNT* 1:468, and *EWNT,* 366–67.

Bibliography

Anonymous. 1887. Die hebräische Grundlage der Apokalypse. *ZAW* 7: 167–76.

Gunkel, H. 1895. *Schöpfung und Chaos.* Göttingen.

Hommel, F. 1890. Inschriftliche Glossen und Exkurse zur Genesis und zu den Propheten. *NKZ* 1: 407–8.

Hoskier, H. C., ed. 1928. *The Complete Commentary of Oecumenius on the Apocalypse.* Ann Arbor.

Jeremias, J. 1932. Har Magedon (Apc 16:16). *ZNW* 31: 73–77.

Junius, F. 1599. Annotations on Revelation. *The Geneva Bible.* London.

LaRondelle, H. K. 1985. The Biblical Concept of Armageddon. *JETS* 28: 21–31.

———. 1989. The Etymology of Har-Magedon (Rev 16:16). *AUSS* 27: 69–73.

Rissi, M. 1966. *Time and History: A Study on the Revelation.* Richmond.

Schmid, J. 1955. *Studien zur Geschichte des Griechischen Apokalypse-Textes.* Munich.

Shea, W. H. 1980. The Location and Significance of Armageddon in Rev 16:16. *AUSS* 18: 157–62.

Swete, H. B. 1907. *The Apocalypse of St. John.* Repr. 1951. Grand Rapids.

Torrey, C. C. 1938. Armageddon. *HTR* 31: 237–48.

Violet, B. 1932. Har Magedon. *ZNW* 31: 204–5.

Yarbro Collins, A. 1979. *The Apocalypse.* Wilmington, DE.

Jon Paulien

ARMENIA (PLACE). A country constituting a series of plateaus joining Asia Minor to Iran. Great variation in altitude, terrain, climate, and plant life lead to strong regional disparities. Some mountains rear up to 17,000 feet, as does Ararat; they and their flanks impede travel. The prevailing E-W direction of the mountain ranges especially hampers N-S movement. The Euphrates River rises in Armenia, leading S; two other large rivers flow to the Caspian Sea.

The *Armenioi* were known to Greeks from at least the 6th century B.C. Armenia is listed on the Behistun inscription of Darius, and received Persian governors. The Orontids, a line of Persian descent, ruled there from about 400 B.C., and assumed the title of "King" after Alexander's day. Upon the defeat of the Seleucid Antiochus the Great by Romans and their allies in 190/189 B.C., the Armenian descendants of Artaxias formed a royal house which lasted until the time of Christ. A branch of the Armenian royal family also ruled in Commagene.

Armenia's greatest impact on the world of the Bible occurred in the reign of the Artaxiad King Tigranes. He had grown to maturity as a hostage at the Parthian court, but was released about 95 B.C. in return for "seventy valleys in Armenia" (Strabo 11.14.15.532). Tigranes married the daughter of Mithradates Eupator of Pontus and set out to aid that monarch in his long contest with Rome. He jointly raided Cappadocia, and conquered adjacent Sophene, thus extending Armenia's territory to a point across the Euphrates from Cappadocia. Tigranes eventually took to carrying off Cappadocians to populate his new fortress, Tigranocerta, near the upper Tigris.

Tigranes linked himself to Parthia, sending a daughter for marriage to Mithradates II. He also proved willing to contend with Parthians for territory. The Armenian holdings rapidly expanded, as Tigranes recovered the seventy valleys and seized territories which were nominally Parthian. He overcame Atropatene, Gordyene, Osrhoene, Adiabene, most of Mesopotamia, and Greater Media. In Eastern fashion, he left kings in place, often married to his own daughters. Thus on his coinage appeared the proud title "King of Kings" after Mithradates II died in 88/87 B.C.

The Parthian monarchs Orodes I and Sinatruces could not prevent the rapid expansion of Armenia at this time. Nor could the last Seleucids. Tigranes crossed the Euphrates about 87 B.C., assuming the hegemony of Commagene and Syria (Justin 40.1).

Tigranes took Antioch, effectively terminating the Seleucid Empire after more than two centuries. As a "successor" *(diadochus)* to the Seleucids, he continued their coinage and dynastic era. For fourteen or more years he ruled in Antioch, calmly adding to his territories and moving toward Judea. It escaped domination through timely negotiation and gifts, first by Alexander Janneus and then by his widow, Alexandra Salome (Sullivan 1970, chap. 5, §11 with n. 8–10 and chap. 3, §9.iii).

In 69 B.C., Tigranes had to face a challenge at home, necessitating withdrawal from Syria. Near Tigranocerta, he fought the Roman Lucullus but lost. For the rest of his reign (down to ca. 55 B.C.), he remained in control of his ancestral kingdom, but no longer of Syria. The last Seleucids sought to resume rule there, but Pompey pointed out that Tigranes had conquered them and Rome had conquered Tigranes.

In 67 B.C., Tigranes again took the field in Cappadocia, but an invasion of Armenia by his renegade son, supported by Phraates III of Parthia, drew him home. Tigranes gradually withdrew his support for Mithradates Eupator, thus dooming him to eventual Roman conquest.

The reputation of Tigranes for inflicting discomfort on his neighbors masks his service to Armenia. During a long reign (95–55 B.C.), he brought it safely through the Seleucid collapse, the rise and fall of Eupator in Pontus, the advent of Rome in the East, and threats from Parthia. His family continued to rule there for over half a century more.

King Artavasdes II (55–34 B.C.), son of Tigranes, continued his father's policy of marriage ties with Parthia. Nevertheless, he offered to support Crassus in 53 B.C. during an invasion of Parthian territory; Crassus declined and met disaster at Carrhae.

Armenia could not be counted a Roman ally in the aftermath. Cicero in 51 B.C. camped near Cybistra "so that Artavasdes, the Armenian King, whatever his policy might be, would know that an army of the Roman people was not far from his territory." He heard that "the Armenian King was about to make an attack on Cappadocia" (Cic. *Fam.* 15.2.2; 15.3.1). Perhaps as a consequence of Carrhae, Artavasdes assumed his father's title, "King of Kings," on his coinage.

Increased Roman activity against Parthia involved Artavasdes when Mark Antony proceeded against Parthia in 36 B.C. Among his allies stood "the greatest of all, Artavasdes of Armenia" with a large force. Antony allowed him to guide the expedition, and found himself detouring by way of Media Atropatene, where Artavasdes had scores to settle. When Artavasdes abruptly withdrew, Antony had to face winter and a Parthian army; he extricated only a portion of his men.

Antony seized Artavasdes in 34 and deported him to Egypt, where he died probably by Cleopatra's hand in 30 B.C. This proved a blunder, bringing no gain to Rome despite Antony's claim of an Armenian conquest. Armenians denied Antony access to their treasuries, one of his motives. The affair left a legacy of bitterness still discernible fifty years later (Tac. *Ann.* 2.3.2).

Artaxias II, son of Artavasdes, succeeded without interval, supported by the nobility. With Parthian assistance, he maintained himself (34–20 B.C.) and even carried out a massacre of Roman residents in the kingdom. He appears to have fallen to a family conspiracy (Dio 49.39 f.; Joseph. *Ant* 15.104f.; Tac. *Ann.* 2.3).

The death of Artaxias in 20 B.C. opened a century of intensified maneuvering to gain control of Armenia. A series of Artaxiad descendants of Tigranes the Great carried out brief reigns with Roman recognition. After their eclipse about A.D. 1, two kings of Atropatene also ruled Armenia briefly, but the Parthian Vonones I replaced them about A.D. 7. From A.D. 18 to 34, a successful Roman nominee, Zeno-Artaxias, proceeded from the dynasty of Pontus to the Armenian throne. Two Judaeans, descended from Archelaus of Cappadocia, tried to rule Armenia with the blessings of Rome. The first of these, Tigranes V, died in A.D. 36; the second, Tigranes VI, ruled Armenia in A.D. 60–62. Two Roman nominees from Asiatic Iberia also tried Armenia. Interspersed with these were rulers drawn from the Parthian royal house. (See *ANRW* 2/8: 300, 938; and Sullivan 1970, Chaps. 2 and 5.)

The "Armenian Question" in Roman-Parthian relations persisted. Long Roman supply lines precluded an effective military policy in Armenia. For instance, Corbulo's forces in A.D. 62 had to carry provisions by camel, and at times suffered real privation (Tac. *Ann.* 13.39; 14.24; 15.12). Romans also had difficulty delivering sufficient troops and had to rely on allies in Commagene and elsewhere. Armenians, both commoners and nobility, exhibited hostility to Rome (Tac. *Ann.* 15.27).

A compromise in A.D. 66 allowed Nero to invest the Arsacid Tiridates as king of Armenia at a ceremony in Rome (Dio 63.1–7). This arrangement held for half a century with Arsacids ruling Armenia and recognized by Rome.

Trajan tried to convert Armenia into a province in 114, but by 116/7 the Parthians again furnished a king for it. A long series of Arsacid kings appeared there in the 2d and early 3d centuries. Sometimes they bore Arsacid names reflecting in addition a grant of Roman citizenship, such as Aurelius Pacorus, "Great King of Armenia," known from an inscription in Rome (*OGIS* 382; see too *ANRW* 2/8, Parthian stemma after p. 938 and Magie 1950; 1528f. n. 2).

Armenia suffered occasionally from other invasions, as when the Alans raided it sometime before A.D. 137 (Dio 69.15). Parthians attacked it early in the reign of Marcus Aurelius, but in A.D. 163 the counterinvasion by Lucius Verus resulted in a Roman appointee as king, Sohaemus, whose name suggests descent from the royal house of Emesa, from which another Sohaemus had been chosen by Nero to rule nearby Sophene (Tac. *Ann.* 13.7). An invasion by the troops of Caracalla failed in ca. A.D. 215.

The Sassanid Persian overthrow of the Arsacids about A.D. 227 led to a change in Armenia as well, with greater receptivity to a Roman alliance, since the Arsacid dynasty sought to rule on in Armenia. Between 251 and 253, King Shapur invaded Armenia (Magie 1950: 1568 n. 29). In A.D. 297, Romans obtained by negotiation with Persia important satrapies along the Tigris in the vicinity of Armenia, but eventually returned several of these (Jones 1971: 224).

From late in the 3d century until well into the 4th, a locally acceptable king ruled Armenia with Roman support, and a peace between Rome and the Iranians led to a much-needed period of peace. A portion of Armenia itself was obtained by Rome in A.D. 387.

In early Byzantine times, further satrapies were detached, and the territory termed "Inner Armenia." The administration continued to be through local rulers. The legal system remained the "old law" of Armenia.

In Armenia, little essentially changed from the time of Tigranes to that of Justinian 600 years later. In those centuries, Armenia maintained its integrity and preserved the traditions which produced a long line of native kings in the middle ages, despite continued pressure from the outside. Eventually, emperors of Armenian extraction ascended the Byzantine throne.

The claim has been made that Armenia became the first state to recognize Christianity officially, early in the 4th century. This religion slowly replaced the variegated pantheon of syncretistic Iranian divinities previously worshiped there, and it became a vigorous institution, like Armenia itself.

Bibliography

Burney, C., and Lang, D. M. 1971. *The Peoples of the Hills: Ancient Ararat and Caucasus.* London.

Der Nersessian, S. 1969. *The Armenians.* London.

Jones, A. H. M. 1971. *The Cities of the Eastern Roman Provinces.* 2d ed. Oxford.

Lehmann-Haupt, C. F. 1910–31. *Armenien einst und jetzt.* 2 vols. Berlin.

Magie, D. 1950. *Roman Rule in Asia Minor.* 2 vols. Princeton.

Manandian, H. 1963. *Tigrane II et Rome.* Lisbon.

Sullivan, R. D. 1989. *Near Eastern Royalty and Rome, 100–30 B.C.* Toronto.

———. 1970. *Some Dynastic Answers to the Armenian Question.* Diss. California.

Toumanoff, C. 1966. Armenia and Georgia. *Cambridge Medieval History* 4: chap. xiv.

———. 1976. *Manuel de généalogie et de chronologie pour l'histoire de la Caucasie chrétienne (Arménie—Géorgie—Albanie).* Rome.

———. 1963. *Studies in Christian Caucasian History.* Washington.

Tournebise, H. F. 1910. *Histoire politique et religieux de l'Arménie.* Vol. 1. Paris.

RICHARD D. SULLIVAN

ARMENIAN VERSONS. See VERSIONS, ANCIENT (ARMENIAN).

ARMLET. See JEWELRY.

ARMONI (PERSON) [Heb *ʾarmōnî*]. A son of Saul, probably the eldest son borne by Saul's concubine Rizpah, the daughter of Aiath (2 Sam 21:8). The name means "my citadel." Armoni was publicly executed (Polzin 1969) during a religious barley harvest festival along with 6 other Saulides in the early years of David's accession to the Israelite throne after Eshbaal's murder (2 Sam 21: 1–14). The present report provides two explanations for the execution: (1) bloodguilt on Saul and his house for Saul's killing of the Gibeonites (v 1) (Prado 1954: 51), and (2) Saul's breaking of a treaty that was established between Israel and the Gibeonites by Joshua, by seeking to slay the Gibeonites "in his zeal for Israel and Judah" (v 2; Malamat 1955). Both reasons are presented as having led to a 3-year famine during David's reign.

After oracular consultation to determine the cause of the famine, David is said to have called the remaining Gibeonites to him to determine how expiation could be made for Saul's action. They are said to have demanded that 7 Saulides be turned over to them so that they could execute them at GIBEON on the mountain of Yahweh, following the LXX reading *(bgbʿwn bhr yhwh)*. The MT locates the place of execution "at Gibeah/the hill of Saul, the chosen one of Yahweh" *(bgbʿt šʾwl bḥyr yhwh)*. The MT reading reflects a substitution of Gibeah of Saul for Gibeon, and the further attempt to disguise the reference to Gibeon as the mountain of Yahweh by changing "mountain" into the passive participle "chosen one," substituting ḥet for *he*. The existence of a famous *bāmâ* sanctuary at Gibeon with Yahwistic connections (1 Kgs 3:5; 2 Chr 1:3–13 with much fictional embellishment) favors the LXX reading as genuine. In addition, while the adjective "chosen" is used to describe Saul's legitimate choice by Yahweh to be king in 1 Sam 10:24, it is similarly used in connection with David's relationship to Yahweh and appointment of king-elect after Saul's rejection by Yahweh in 2 Sam 6:21. The expression is by no means unique to Saul or distinguishes him from David in the context. It is hard to understand why the author would want to stress Saul's legitimate royal associations in connection with the site of execution, unless perhaps he wanted to highlight Saul's fall from grace by reminding the reader that the family of the former chosen one was now being punished by the new chosen one. The MT phrasing is awkward, reflects the anti-Gibeonite bias that permeates the Deuteronomistic writings (Kearney 1973), and may have arisen from a pious scribe who was influenced by this bias and altered the original wording to harmonize with 1 Sam 10:24 and 11:4 (for another explanation, see McCarter *2 Samuel* AB, 438).

The bodies of the 7 were left exposed until rain fell, from mid-April until October or November, and their bones were subsequently buried together with the exhumed remains of Saul and Jonathan in the family tomb in Benjaminite Zela. It has been suggested that the execution was done as part of a fertility rite, in which the bodies of the dead would have been dismembered and scattered in the fields to bring fertility to the land (i.e. Cazelles 1955: 167–69; Kapelrud 1955:120).

Bibliography

Cazelles, H. 1955. David's Monarchy and the Gibeonite Claim. *PEQ* 87: 165–75.

Kapelrud, A. S. 1955. King and Fertility. A Discussion of II Sam 21:1–14, Pp. 113–22 in *Interpretations ad Vetus Testamentum Pertinentes Sigmundo Mowinckel Septuagenario Missae,* ed. N.A. Dahl and A. S. Kapelrud. Oslo.

Kearney, P. 1973. The Role of the Gibeonites in the Deuteronomistic History. *CBQ* 35: 1–19.

Malamat, A. 1955. Doctrines of Causality in Hittite and Biblical Historiography: A Parallel. *VT* 5: 1–12.

Polzin, R. 1969. 'HWQY' and Covenantal Institutions in Early Israel. *HTR* 62: 227–40.

Prado, J. 1954. El extermino de la familia de Saul (2 Sam 21, 1–14). *Sefarad* 14: 43–57.

DIANA V. EDELMAN

ARMORY. See WEAPONS AND IMPLEMENTS OF WARFARE.

ARMY (MESOPOTAMIA). See MILITARY ORGANIZATION IN MESOPOTAMIA.

ARMY, HERODIAN. See HERODIAN ARMY.

ARMY, ROMAN. See ROMAN ARMY.

ARNA (PERSON) [Lat *Arna*]. An ancestor of Ezra, the father of Meraioth and the son of Uzzi according to the genealogy of Ezra in 2 Esdr 1:1–3. Slightly different pedigrees of Ezra are found in Ezra 7:1–5 and 1 Esdr 8:1–2 (cf. 1 Chr 5:27–40—Eng 6:1–14). Though the name Arna does not appear in the Ezra text, the order of the names suggests that Arna is in parallel to Zerahiah in Ezra 7:4 (see also 1 Chr 5:32—Eng 6:6). The genealogy in 1 Esdr 8:1–2 leaves out Arna (Zerahiah) along with the two generations after him.

JIN HEE HAN

ARNAN (PERSON) [Heb *ʾarnān*]. The fourth son of Hananiah the son of ZERUBBABEL and brother of Obadiah and Rephaiah, in 1 Chr 3:21, the genealogy which records the postexilic descent of the line of David. The RSV follows the Gk and Vg. The Heb, however, makes Arnan the son of Obadiah and father of Rephaiah.

RUSSELL FULLER

ARNI (PERSON) [Gk *Arni*]. An ancestor of Jesus, according to a textually confused part of the Lukan genealogy (3:33a). The reading of this name is adopted by the *UBSGNT* as part of a series of 3 names which are "the least satisfactory form of the text, a reading that was current in the Alexandrian church at an early period" (Metzger 1971: 136). It is also in the text of Nestle–Aland *Nov TG.* The name is not found, however, in many ancient Gk manuscripts of the NT, nor is it contained in the OT genealogies of 1 Chronicles 2 or Ruth 4.

Bibliography

Metzger, B. M. 1971. *A Textual Commentary on the Greek New Testament.* New York.

HERBERT G. GRETHER

ARNON (PLACE) [Heb *ʾarnôn*]. A perennial stream whose tributaries drain much of the Moabite plateau on both sides of the Arnon gorge (modern Wadi Mojib). The Arnon's source is near Lejjun, ca. 10 miles NE of Kerak. From its meager beginning, the stream flows NNW for ca. 15 miles, and then it courses an equal distance to the W, finally emptying into the Dead Sea. The Arnon's mouth is just north of the halfway point on the Dead Sea's eastern shore, at Ras el-Ghor; its perennial flow makes the Arnon the most important river on the sea's E side. The outflow of the Arnon itself is greatly increased by the water of Wadi Heidan, which merges (from the N) with the Arnon 2 miles from the latter's mouth (cf. Mattingly 1983).

The Arnon is named in the Bible 25 times, but it is most famous because its small, rapidly descending stream has created, through the millennia, a huge canyon along its E–W route. The section of Wadi Mojib whose N rim is less than 2 miles south of Dhiban is almost 3 miles across, from rim to rim. Its depth varies from 1,300 feet to 2,300 feet. Naturally, the wadi's length and depth made N–S travel in this area difficult—and certainly more time-consuming. Such streams, which cut across Transjordan's tableland, partially explain why the King's Highway was situated so far to the E. Because it bypassed the W edge of the escarpment and the deep gorges that run E–W, the so-called Desert Highway became an important N–S thoroughfare. A major confluence of the Arnon is located ca. 2 miles E of where the modern highway (perhaps following the route of the ancient King's Highway) crosses the riverbed. This point is just south of Aroer, a site which the Bible frequently identifies as sitting on the edge of the Arnon. The biblical designation "valleys of the Arnon" (Num 21:14) is quite appropriate for the convergence of canyons at this spot.

All of Transjordan is subdivided into 5 smaller regions by 4 wadi systems that run from E to W, draining the water from the plateau into the Jordan Rift: from the N these are (1) Yarmuk, (2) Jabbok, (3) Arnon, and (4) Zered. The Arnon itself divided Moab into 2 parts. While the S boundary of Moabite territory was fixed by the Zered (modern Wadi el-Hesa), Moab's N border fluctuated. In times of strength, the Moabites controlled the land between the Zered and the vicinity of Heshbon ca. 22 miles N of the Arnon. After he reclaimed northern Moab from the Israelites, King Mesha repaired the highway that crossed the Arnon at Aroer (Mesha Inscription, line 26), an event illustrating the unification of both parts of Moab. When Moabite power waned, their domain was reduced to the undisputed heartland of Moab, the territory between the Zered and the Arnon. Thus, the Arnon served as a natural boundary when political and military factors assigned it that purpose, but it was not enough of a barrier to create cultural differences on its two sides.

As noted above, the Arnon sometimes served as a boundary between the Moabites, Amorites (Num 21:13, 24, 26; and 22:36), and the Israelites (Deut 2:24, 36; 3:8, 16; Josh 13:16; 2 Kgs 10:33; cf. 2 Sam 24:5). References to the Arnon in the oracles of Isaiah (16:2) and Jeremiah (48:20) allude to its status as an important point in the N–S route through Moab.

Bibliography

Mattingly, G. L. 1983. The Natural Environment of Central Moab. *ADAJ* 27: 597–605.

Gerald L. Mattingly

ARODI (PERSON) [Heb *ʾarôdî*]. Var. AROD. ARODITES. The 6th of 7 sons of Gad named in the genealogy relating Joseph to Jacob (Gen 46:16). In a parallel genealogy which identifies the clans that constituted the 40,500 Gadites in the wilderness census (Num 26:17—LXX 26:26), the personal name is Arod (Heb *ʾarôd*) and the clan name is Arodites (Heb *ʾarôdî*). Several factors favor the long spelling: (1) the names of 5 of Gad's sons have the *î* ending, in both lists (Gen 46:16 = Num 26:15–17—LXX 26:24–27); (2) the LXX, Syr, and Samaritan Pentateuch texts read the *î* ending in Num 26:17; (3) in this sequence of names with the same ending, the *î* could easily have dropped out. Regardless of the original spelling, there is no doubt that the two genealogies list the same person.

Joel C. Slayton

AROER (PLACE) [Heb *ʿărōʿēr*]. AROERITE. Since it is likely that the name means "crest of a mountain" or "juniper," such frequent use of this place-name is not unusual.

1. The overwhelming number of references to a place named Aroer are made in connection with the so-called "Aroer on the Arnon." This settlement, more properly viewed as a fortress throughout most of its history, was situated on the N rim of Wadi el-Mujib, the biblical River Arnon. In fact, many of the biblical verses that mention this particular Aroer refer specifically to its location on the edge of the spectacular canyon that the Mujib has formed (e.g., Deut 2:36; 4:48; Josh 12:2; 13:16). Aroer's strategic location made it a natural checkpoint on a territorial border, as in the day of the Amorite kingdom of Sihon (Deut 4:48; Josh 12:2; cf. Judg 11:22) and during the Hebrew conquest and settlement in Transjordan (Deut 2:36; Josh 13:9). In both of these cases, the Arnon and, consequently, the fortress of Aroer marked the frontier with Moabite territory, to the S of the Arnon.

According to Num 32:34, Aroer was refortified by the Israelite tribe of Gad, though it was originally assigned to the Reubenites (Josh 13:16). At the time of David's census, Aroer was a logical starting point for the numbering of Hebrews who lived E of the Jordan. Aroer's strategic significance on the rim of the Arnon is highlighted again in the 2d half of the 9th century B.C., when Aroer is named as the S limit of the Syrian king Hazael's control of Transjordan (2 Kings 10:33). Very important is the reference to Aroer in line 26 of the Mesha Inscription (ca. 830 B.C.), where the Moabite king Mesha was credited with refortifying the site after his victory over Israel. Aroer was under Moabite control when it is mentioned for the last time in the Bible, in Jer 48:19.

Ancient Aroer is linked with certainty to the site of a small Arab village—and its imposing tell—named ʿAraʿir, which is located ca. 3 miles SE of Dhiban (biblical Dibon) and 2½ miles E of the so-called King's Highway (M.R. 228097). Excavations were conducted in 3 seasons of fieldwork, from 1964 to 1966, by a Spanish team which was under the direction of Emilio Olávarri (*EAEHL* 1: 98–100). ʿAraʿir yielded pottery and other artifacts that dated from ca. 2250 B.C. until the 3d century A.D., though the site was not occupied continuously over this long period. There was, for example, an occupational gap during the Middle Bronze Age, but evidence from the Late Bronze Age and Iron Age was recovered. The most important excavated structure is a fortress that measures ca. 50 yards on each side and was built of large blocks of stone laid in header-stretcher style. Olávarri attributes the construction of this fortress to Mesha.

2. Located in Transjordan and mentioned in Josh 13:25 and Judg 11:33. According to the former, this Aroer was "E of ["opposite" or "before"] Rabbah" (M.R. 238151) (modern Amman) and formed part of the boundary between the Israelite tribe of Gad's territory and Ammonite country. This description has been used to place this Aroer in the vicinity of es-Sweiwina, which is located south of Amman, but no excavations have been made that allow scholars to identify the location of this second Transjordanian Aroer with any certainty.

3. Place located E of the Jordan Rift has become known because of its appearance in the Heb text—and in the King James Version—in Isa 17:2a ["the cities of Aroer are deserted"]. If this reading is followed, it would seem to indicate that there was another Aroer in the neighborhood of Damascus. While this is possible, many translations, including the RSV, omit any reference to an Aroer by following the LXX and rendering 17:2a as "her cities will be deserted for ever."

4. Place located in the Bible to the W of the Jordan (1 Sam. 30:28). In this verse, the Hebrew historian says that David distributed loot to the elders of Aroer, after he recovered his wives from the Amalekites who had raided Ziklag. It is assumed that this was the home of Hotham the Aroerite, father of two of David's "mighty men" (1 Chron 11:44). Since the time of Edward Robinson's 1838 travels through Palestine, this Aroer has been linked with the Negev site of ʿArʿarah, which is located ca. 12 miles SE of BEER-SHEBA (M.R. 148062).

ʿArʿarah was excavated between 1975 and 1981 by A. Biran and R. Cohen. They concluded that this 5-acre site was first settled in the 7th century B.C. and was occupied, intermittently, until ca. A.D. 70. Though it is possible that further excavations might uncover remains from the 11th or 10th centuries B.C., it does not appear that ʿArʿarah was occupied in the time of David. Biran has suggested that Davidic Aroer can be identified with Tel Esdar, which is located ca. 1½ miles N of ʿArʿarah, and that the name Aroer was transferred to the latter site when it was founded in the 7th century B.C. Excavations at Tel Esdar did recover remains from the 11th–10th centuries B.C., but there is no other assurance that Biran's suggestion is correct.

The name Adadah (Josh 15:22) may be a corruption of ʿArʿara, another form for Aroer; the LXX reads Aruel for this place-name. It has also been identified with Khirbet ʿArʿarah, though this, too, is uncertain.

Bibliography

Biran, A. 1983. And David Sent Spoils to the Elders in Aroer. *BARev* 9: 28–37.

GERALD L. MATTINGLY

AROM (PERSON) [Gk *Arom*]. Ancestor of a family returned from exile in Babylon with Zerubbabel (1 Esdr 5:16). Although 1 Esdras is often assumed to have been compiled from Ezra and Nehemiah, this family does not appear among their lists of returning exiles (cf. Ezra 2:17; Neh 7:23). Omissions such as this also raise questions about 1 Esdras being used as a source by Ezra or Nehemiah. Furthermore, problems associated with dating events and persons described in 1 Esdras have cast doubt on the historicity of the text. Fritsch (*IDB* 1: 231) indicates that Arom may be a variant of HASHUM found in Ezra 2:19 and Neh 7:22. Although this is possible, the location of Hashum differs in the sequence of names found in Ezra 2 and Nehemiah 7, and Hashum (Gk *Asom*) itself occurs in 1 Esdr 9:33.

MICHAEL DAVID MCGEHEE

AROMATIC CANE. See PERFUMES AND SPICES.

ARPACHSHAD (PERSON) [Heb *ʾarpakšad*]. **1.** A son of Shem and the father of Shelah in the MT (Gen 10:22, 24). In the LXX and in the NT (Luke 3:36; cf. also Jubilees 8:1), Cainan is inserted in the genealogy between Arpachshad and Shelah. In the MT, the lifespan of Arpachshad is given as 438 years, with thirty-five as the age at which he fathered Shelah. Analyses of the personal name have included: the 1st part of the name as the geographic name *Arrapḫa*, probably situated at modern Kirkuk; and the 2d part of the name as *kaśdîm*, the gentilic, Chaldeans. This analysis of the first name would seemingly locate the name in the geographic context of Arpachshad's brothers (Gen 10:22) and assign it a Hurrian etymology (Albright 1924: 388–89; Cazelles *POTT* 22). Cf. also the suggestion of Gordon (*IDB* 1: 231) to identify the 1st 3 letters with the putative Hurrian element *arip*. This understanding of the 2d element might explain the absence of Babylon in the Table of Nations (Simons 1959: 9–10). However, these interpretations fail to explain the entire name. The *pataḥ-šĕwā* pattern, repeated 3 times, may suggest an artificiality in the pronunciation, reflecting an early loss of the original understanding of the six-consonant, non-Semitic(?) name. Two problems arise related to the mention of Arpachshad in Gen 11:10. First, the verse describes Shem as begetting Arpachshad 2 years after the flood when he was 100 years old. If Noah fathered Shem at 500 (Gen 5:32) and the Flood occurred in his 600th year (Gen 7:6, 11), then a discrepancy of 2 years appears. A temporal interpretation of the waw-consecutives in Gen 5:32 (Cryer 1985: 247–248), combined with Shem's position as 2d born (Cassuto *Genesis,* pp. 260–61), allows for a period of 2 years. Then Shem would have been born in Noah's 502d year and Arpachshad in Noah's 602d year (Cryer 1985: 247–48). A second problem arises when it is observed that the genealogies designate the eldest son of the new generation by listing him first or alone. This occurs in Gen 11:10–11 with Arpachshad. However, in Gen 10:22 Arpachshad appears 3d among the offspring of Shem. Unlike Genesis 11, which relates Abram's ancestry to Shem, Genesis 10 describes the geographical distribution of peoples in the known world. The "brothers" of Arpachshad are all gentilic or geographic names, and the order of the names in the text has nothing to do with order of birth.

2. The leader of the Medes who was defeated by Nebuchadrezzar (Jdt 1: 1). This figure is otherwise unknown in ancient sources. Attempts to identify Arpachshad with a Scythian king and to argue for an Iranian etymology are speculative (Brandenstein 1954: 60, 62).

Bibliography

Albright, W. F. 1924. Contributions to Biblical Archaeology and Philology. *JBL* 43: 363–93.

Brandenstein, W. 1954. Bemerkungen zur Völkertafel in der Genesis. Pp. 57–83 in *Sprachgeschichte und Wortbedeutung. Festschrift Albert Debrunner.* Berlin.

Cheyne, T. K. 1897. Arpachshad. *ZAW* 17: 190.

Cryer, F. H. 1985. The Interrelationships of Gen 5:32; 11:10–11 and the Chronology of the Flood (Gen 6–9). *Bib* 66: 241–61.

Simons, J. 1959. *The Geographical and Topographical Texts of the Old Testament.* Leiden.

RICHARD S. HESS

ARPAD (PLACE) [Heb *ʾarpād*]. City in N Syria identified with modern Tell Rifaat (36° 28′ N; 37° 06′ E). Biblical references (2 Kgs 18:34 = Isa 36:19; 2 Kgs 19:13 = Isa 37:13; Isa 10:9; and Jer 49:23) to its conquest by Assyria reflect Arpad's importance in the 9th and 8th centuries B.C.E. when it served as capital of the land of Bit-Agusi. A series of archaeological excavations at Arpad in the 1950s and 1960s by M. V. Seton-Williams and of the surrounding region in the 1970s by J. Matthers (1981) have uncovered architectural, ceramic, osteological, and other types of remains which span from the Chalcolithic in the 5th millennium B.C.E. to the Islamic era.

The main sources for the history of Arpad in the 9th and 8th centuries B.C.E. are Assyrian historical texts. The records of Adad-nirari III (810–783) mark the first known reference to the place as Arpad, but more common names include Yakhan and Bit-Agusi. Despite intermittent independence, Arpad paid tribute to Assurnasirpal (885–860), and suffered significant attacks from Shalmaneser III in 849 and Adad-nirari III in 805. Perhaps describing events in 796, Zakkur of Hamath reports in his Aram inscription (*KAI*, #202) that he was delivered, possibly with the help of Adad-nirari III, from an attacking coalition headed by Bargush (= Atar-shumki?) of Arpad. Matiʾ-ilu of Arpad concluded a treaty with Ashur-nirari V (754–746) in 754, and later, as recorded in the Sefire inscriptions (*KAI*, #222), another with a still obscure Bar-gaʾyah of *ktk*. Matiʾ-ilu's apparent revolt led to the conquest and reduction of Arpad to an Assyrian province by Tiglath-pileser III in 740. After 740 Arpad never regained its former power, although it did participate in an uprising suppressed by Sargon in 720.

Precise reconstruction of the royal line of Arpad in the 9th and 8th centuries B.C.E. remains a difficult problem. W. Pitard's (1988) recent identification of a certain Attarhamek in the much discussed Melqart Stele may suggest the existence of previously unrecognized kings of Arpad. However, the numerous uncertainties associated with the stele, ascribed to the kingdom of Damascus by many scholars, leaves the following relative chronology as the most certain: Agusi (1st half of 9th century); Arame (ca. 858–ca. 834); Atar-shumki (ca. 805–ca. 796?); and Matiʾ-ilu (ca. 754?–740).

Bibliography

Matthers, J., ed. 1981. *The River Qoueiq, Northern Syria and its Catchment: Studies Arising from the Tell Rifa at Survey 1977–79.* Oxford.

Pitard, W. 1988. The Identity of the Bir-Hadad of the Melqart Stela. *BASOR* 272: 3–21.

HECTOR AVALOS

ARPHAXAD (PERSON) [Gk *Arphaxad*]. **1.** Ruler over the Medes (Jdt 1:1). He rebuilt the wall of Ecbatana, and was defeated by Nebuchadnezzar in the mountains of Rages.

However, according to our historical sources, no Persian or Median king by the name of Arphaxad ever existed. Therefore, the character is usually considered fictitious, although Ball suggests that the name may be a corruption of "Arbaces," the name of the first Median king. The name is probably taken from the book of Genesis, where it is given as Arpachshad (Heb *ʾarpakšad*). He is the 3d son of Shem, born after the flood, who became the grandfather of Eber, the ancestor of Abraham. The name Arpachshad may be geographic in origin, indicating an area of Mesopotamia.

2. Ancestor of Jesus (Luke 3:36). See ARPACHSHAD.

Bibliography

Ball, C. J. 1888. *Judith.* Apocrypha of the Speaker's Commentary, ed. Henry Wace, I. London.

SIDNIE ANN WHITE

ARRAY, BATTLE. See WEAPONS AND IMPLEMENTS OF WAR.

ARSACES (PERSON) [Gk *Arsakēs*]. Name or title of Parthian kings, including the one who captured Demetrius II (1 Macc 14:2–3). The name may have been simply a title used by Parthian kings who claimed descent from Artaxerxes II, whose name was Arsaces before he took the Persian throne.

Appian (*Syrian Wars* 67) identifies the Arsaces who captured Demetrius II with Phraates (176–171 B.C.E.). However, his dates are 30 years too early. It must have been his younger brother, Mithradates I (171–138).

This Arsaces influenced Jewish history in 165, when Antiochus IV marched E, perhaps because of Parthian threats. On his return to Syria after a defeat by Mithradates I, Antiochus died at Gabae. Mithradates was then able to conquer Media and Mesopotamia.

Jewish history mentions him explicitly because in 142 Demetrius II mustered an international army to invade Mesopotamia. The purpose was to secure Mesopotamia for the Seleucids and to raise a force strong enough to defeat Trypho, a pretender to the Seleucid throne. After some initial successes, Arsaces Mithradates defeated Demetrius' army and captured Demetrius (1 Macc 14:2–3). Mithradates treated Demetrius very well and even gave the prisoner his own daughter, Rhodogune, in marriage. Mithradates died in 138. Demetrius remained a Parthian prisoner until 130, when Arsaces Phraates II set him free during an unsuccessful invasion by Demetrius' brother, Antiochus VII.

Bibliography

Bevan, E. R. 1966. Vol. 2 of *The House of Seleucus.* New York.

Debevoise, N. C. 1938. *A Political History of Parthia.* Chicago.

MITCHELL C. PACWA

ART AND ARCHITECTURE. Seven articles are included under this general heading. The first two, respectively, provide broad historical surveys of ANE art and of ANE architecture, excluding Egypt. The third article focuses more closely upon the art and architecture specifically of Mesopotamia, while the fourth provides an overview specifically of Egyptian art and architecture. The fifth article treats Persian art of the Achaemenid period, while the final two cover, respectively, early Jewish art and architecture and early Christian art.

ANCIENT NEAR EASTERN ART

Ancient Near Eastern art customarily includes the sculpture, pottery, painting, and glyptic produced in W Asia from their earliest appearances until the fall of the Achaemenid Persian Empire in 331 B.C. At the end of that period, the systematic introduction of Greek forms and styles in architecture and the visual arts throughout western and central Asia created new fusions of indigenous and Eastern Mediterranean forms in addition to Near Eastern traditions. In the mid-7th century of our era, the Islamic conquest of W Asia brought about significant changes in the forms and institutions of Near Eastern art and architecture. Yet established trends in a variety of media continued to flourish, and a neat division between pre-Islamic and Islamic Near Eastern art is difficult to establish (Ettinghausen 1962; Grabar 1973).

A. Scope

Unlike "Egyptian" or "Greek" art, the term "ancient Near Eastern art" does not embrace a coherent body of works of art linked by an obvious unity of style, purpose, or means of expression. Moreover, it includes works made by artisans of a variety of ethnic identities. No histories of art survive from the ANE; typological, aesthetic, and historical categories and trends have been established only in modern times. Because the modern distinction between art and craft is difficult to apply to the ANE, scholars generally admit a wide range of objects to the realm of art.

Although often treated as a geographical and cultural entity, the ANE encompassed a long history and a diverse set of physical environments. In artistic developments, as in other forms of cultural expression, such as languages, component regions in large measure followed independent avenues. It is customary to subdivide the Near East into several principal geographical regions—Mesopotamia, Iran, the Levant, and Anatolia—and to trace developments in art and architecture accordingly. Those divisions are generally agreed to correspond in significant ways to regionally characteristic and long-lived patterns of artistic and architectural expression, although it is also true that at most periods in antiquity each region was open to outside influence through movements of works of art, of patrons and artisans, and of conquerors and prophets. Because Mesopotamia alone provides a continuous sequence of excavated building remains and works of art accompanied by written records beginning about 3200 B.C., it continues to serve as a framework for ANE art as a whole. Yet all regions of the Near East displayed independent artistic traditions, and Mesopotamia, at various periods in its history, was in turn the recipient of forms, styles, and techniques of manufacture that had originated elsewhere.

That diversity of environment and culture helped to shape regional differences in the development of materials, technologies, and traditions employed for works of art or architecture. In Mesopotamia, in the major river valleys of the Tigris and Euphrates, natural resources for materials used in building or in fashioning works of art were limited primarily to plentiful quantities of clay and reeds. Gypsum and alabaster, stones suitable for building or for carving sculptures, existed in N Mesopotamia. Sources of ores, including gold, silver, copper, and iron, as well as certain varieties of stone, were available in the mountainous regions of Anatolia and W Iran. Works of art also employed prized materials imported to the Near East by sea or by land, often from considerable distances. The hard stone diorite, for example, used in Mesopotamia at certain periods for large-scale sculptures, was probably imported from islands in the Persian Gulf or from coastal ports along the shores of the Indian Ocean (Heimpel 1987). Lapis lazuli, a semiprecious stone favored for jewelry and also used together with other materials for decorative inlays, was very likely transported to the Near East via overland routes from present-day Afghanistan (Herrmann 1968). Ivory, another luxury material employed for furniture, inlays, and cosmetic items, came from elephant and hippopotamus hunted in Egypt and W Asia (Lucas 1962: 32–33; Barnett 1982: 3–15).

The periods under consideration also witnessed the development of critical technologies that shaped artistic energies as well as economies and societies. The domestication of animals and cultivation of plants, and the development of metallurgy in copper, gold, silver, and iron, took place in the ANE. Those technologies created materials for works of art as well as ways of fashioning or decorating them. Metal tools for carving stone, the use of plants or mineral pigments for coloring dyes or paint, and wool for textiles, in turn allowed new opportunities for artistic expression (Moorey 1985; Lucas 1962; Singer, Holmyard, and Hall 1954). Pyrotechnologies that made possible the production of good-quality ceramic objects fired at high temperatures, together with the materials faience (the common term for glazed sintered quartz) and glass, were all invented in the ANE (Moorey 1985). The invention of writing, a dramatic step in communications technology, took place in Mesopotamia about 3200 B.C. Among its many profound effects on Near Eastern history and society was the development of means of communication among artisans and architects (Cooper 1988; Kilmer 1990; Michalowski 1990).

A history of art depends on determining the sequence of forms and styles, as well as the relationships between works of art produced in different areas of a region. Works of ANE art are located within a relative chronological framework based on stratigraphic sequences discovered during excavations. In relative chronologies, works of art can be assigned a place in a series established through stratigraphic evidence. Many of them can also be dated in years, that is, in relation to our time, through such scientific means as radiocarbon dating of organic materials, or thermoluminescence of fired clay (Brothwell and Higgs 1970: 35–108). After the invention of writing in Mesopotamia, about 3200 B.C., written sources can be added to the evidence of archaeological context to assist in dating a monument. Inscriptions preserved on works of art, or names of individuals known from written documents, often make it possible to link a building or work of art with a dynasty or ruler known from cuneiform sources, which can in turn be dated via Mesopotamian, N Syrian, and Egyptian absolute chronologies (*CAH* 1/2: 173–93, 193–239).

Historians of ANE art investigate the forms, styles, subjects, and function of examples of painting, sculpture, and glyptic, seeking to compile a descriptive history of those categories of material and their sequence of development. They also investigate the social, political, and cultural contexts of works of art, their makers, patrons, and owners. When available, written sources—literary texts, correspondence, administrative records, annals, or inscriptions—are used to help reconstruct those contexts. Works of ANE art are usually classified and studied with close attention to the social and political circumstances in which they were made and used. Such evidence serves not only to help establish a probable date and place of manufacture for an object, but also contributes significantly toward understanding the circumstances of its creation, function, and meaning. Through study of their forms, subjects, and development, works of art and architecture can furnish information about the rituals, aesthetic sensibilities, or cultural traditions that engendered them. In turn, therefore, they help to supplement information available in ancient texts by providing an independent, rich, and complex set of sources documenting aspects of religion, politics, economics, and society. Works of art play a significant role in reconstructing the broader cultural history of the ANE.

A history of ANE art has been compiled principally by studying remains of buildings and artifacts recovered from excavations carried out during the 19th and 20th centuries. In addition, many objects purportedly of ANE origin have entered museums or private collections via the art market; for such material, authenticity or provenance must be established through technical criteria or by visual comparisons with works of known date and place of manufacture. Finally, ANE texts often describe or mention works of art or techniques of manufacture poorly represented in the archaeological record, thereby helping to reconstruct a more accurate and complete picture of the scope, purpose, and historical significance of artistic production in the ANE.

B. Western Discovery of ANE Art

Prior to archaeological confirmation of their civilizations, many ANE peoples and places were already known through the Bible and through classical accounts, those texts that had long formed the core of the Western tradition. European knowledge was based on biblical sources preserving names of ancient Mesopotamian cities, and on descriptions by classical authors, including Herodotus, Xenophon, Arrian, and Strabo, mentioning cities and monuments of Asia Minor, Babylonia, and Persia.

The historical interest of the Near East as the "Holy Land," in addition to its commercial and political importance, first prompted Western curiosity about its past. Many ancient monuments, in particular those dating to late antiquity, remained visible; consequently, they were the first sets of ruins that attracted the attention of European merchants or diplomats. Architectural remains and rock reliefs of Achaemenid and Sassanian Persia, for example, were described in Western travelers' accounts of the 16th and 17th centuries. The 18th and 19th centuries brought additional opportunities for Europeans to visit the ancient monuments of Mesopotamia; sites identified included the visible ruins of ancient cities named in biblical accounts, such as Babylon and Nineveh. European travelers to the Near East initiated modern awareness of its antiquities, and published illustrated narratives of their journeys that disseminated information to a wide and fascinated public.

As British and European interest in Near Eastern antiquities grew, travelers with sketchbooks were often succeeded by explorers with pick and shovel. Systematic, large-scale investigation of ruins began during the 1840s at sites in N Mesopotamia identified as Assyrian cities mentioned in the Bible. In 1843, Paul Emile Botta, then French consul at Mosul, uncovered the palace and sculptures of the Neo-Assyrian king Sargon at the site of Khorsabad. In 1845, the Englishman Austen Henry Layard (1817–1894) began digging at the site of Nimrud in N Mesopotamia, uncovering monumental architecture and sculpture, clay tablets and stones inscribed in the cuneiform script, and other finds (Lloyd 1980; Silberman 1982). The initial focus on places named in the Bible granted the monuments—and the cultures that had produced them—a status as part of the Western tradition, and imperial rivalries fed the demand for antiquities at home. As a result of British, French, and later German efforts, vast quantities of objects were transported to national museums in London, Paris, and Berlin. The presence of those monuments, in turn, helped to inspire scholarly attempts to integrate ANE monuments into the histories of other ancient arts, especially those of Egypt, Greece, and Rome (Bohrer 1989).

The decipherment of cuneiform, achieved during the 1840s and 1850s, served to open a new vista on the whole of Mesopotamian civilization as well as to enhance interest in Mesopotamian antiquities. Study of the texts revealed that Babylonia, as well as Assyria, had been home to important civilizations, and the later 19th century saw the investigation of S Mesopotamia and the discovery of civilizations predating the Neo-Assyrian Empire. European and American campaigns devoted to the recovery of early Mesopotamian monuments began in the late 19th century, at the Sumerian cities of Nippur and Telloh. A new, earlier era of Mesopotamian civilization was revealed through German excavations at Warka, ancient Uruk (biblical Erech), which began in 1912 and continued after the World Wars. In the 1920s and 1930s, then commencing again after World War II, archaeological investigations grew significantly in number and began to explore systematically the regions beyond the Tigris and Euphrates valleys. Excavation of increasingly earlier occupation became a priority of field research (Lloyd 1980). Those investigations revealed that the beginnings of art in the ANE were to be found at least as early as the Neolithic era.

Classical, and later biblical, references also supplied the initial impetus for European exploration of ruins in Anatolia. Travelers in search of monuments described by classical authors also came upon ruins which were, by the mid-19th century, recognized as those of earlier, pre-Greek cultures. Monuments with "hieroglyphic" inscriptions found in parts of present-day SE Turkey and N Syria were identified as the work of the Hittites, a people known from references in the Bible and in Egyptian and Assyrian records. In 1906, a German team began excavations at the modern site of Boğazköy, in north central Turkey, identified as ancient Hattusha, the capital of the Hittite Empire (Bittel 1970: 3–23). Since the 1930s, archaeological investigations carried out over a wide region of Turkey have also revealed extensive evidence for developed artistic styles and iconographies dating as early as the 7th millennium B.C.

Ruins dating to the Seleucid, Parthian, and Sassanian eras, many of them comparatively well preserved, early on attracted the attention of Western travelers. Scholarly interest in the art or architecture of those eras generally came later, however, and was directed principally toward sites in Syria and Mesopotamia (including Aššur, Dura Europus, Seleucia-on-Tigris, and Hatra). Excavation and analysis of the material was initially undertaken primarily as a branch of Hellenistic, Roman, or Islamic studies, and has only in recent decades been systematically investigated as an independent field of ANE art (Colledge 1977; Downey 1988; Herrmann 1977; see also EARLY CHRISTIAN ART, EARLY JEWISH ART AND ARCHITECTURE, below).

C. The Production of Art in the ANE

Only an incomplete account of ANE art can be reconstructed from available archaeological and textual sources. The initial concentration on S Mesopotamia in excavations and research of the 19th and early 20th centuries has shifted since the 1930s in favor of a more balanced interest in the art produced in all regions of the ANE. Yet not all regions played an equally significant role in the history of art, and there were in any given period centers of artistic production that exercised influence beyond their political boundaries. The creation and development of forms and styles in architecture, sculpture, seals, vessels, and jewelry are known in their main outlines from Mesopotamia, Anatolia, and the Levant. A comparably extensive series of sites with stratified occupation sequences and well-dated monuments is at present lacking for Iran.

Historians of ANE art must also contend with the uneven recovery and preservation of relevant categories of evidence. Organic materials, such as woven textiles, and fragile media, such as wall painting, are preserved only under exceptional circumstances; the scope of their production and their place in the history of ANE art is therefore extremely difficult to judge. Metalwork, a principal medium of ANE art, survives in only a small proportion to its original abundance. Ancient written sources, such as texts describing the manufacture or commercial exchange of those materials, or inscriptions preserved on statue bases, help to indicate the kinds and quantities of works of art once produced in the ANE.

For the vast eras of prehistory, the circumstances of artistic production can only be surmised. The shift from food-collecting to food-producing economies, or the "Neolithic revolution," is generally considered to have made possible the support of full-time artisans. Already in Neolithic times, there was a long-distance exchange of valued materials, such as obsidian, for tools and other artifacts (Cann, Dixon, and Renfrew 1970). Craftsmen may have specialized not only in the full-time manufacture of objects for utilitarian or ornamental use, but also in the design and shaping of specific raw materials.

Although no detailed records describing the organization of artistic production survive from historical periods, references preserved in the cuneiform literature of several cultures can be used to reconstruct aspects of the social and economic circumstances in which works of art were made. Philologists and historians have retrieved from administrative records, correspondence and inscriptions information on the artisan, his social role, and the conditions of his employment. In most cases, artisans were organized in palace or temple workshops, where they held lifetime positions. In those institutions, specialized personnel were given temporary or long-term assignments, either within the capital or in peripheral locations administered by the palace or temple. Most abundant among the documents concerning craftsmen employed by such institutions are the MB Age archives from the palace at Mari. At Mari, the category "artisan" (Akk *mār ummênim*) included physicians, scribes, barbers, cooks, and masons, all of whom were part of the palace bureaucracy (Zaccagnini 1983: 247–49; Sasson 1990).

Artisans were also employed by assignment from one court to another, usually at a foreign ruler's express request. Thus, specialized craftsmen—including physicians and diviners as well as sculptors—were sent to and from Egypt, Babylonia, and Hatti during the LB Age. During the 1st millennium B.C., it seems that there was a higher number of slaves among those engaged in specialized crafts during this period. At the same time, there are examples of groups of artisans in Neo-Babylonian Eanna who bargained with their employers over aspects of their professional responsibilities and working conditions (Zaccagnini 1983: 250–64).

Since archaeological investigations in the Near East have devoted most time and effort to the exposure of palace and temple complexes, including the archives of those institutions, we are best informed on the production of art for political and religious purposes. In a number of cultures, art helped to define the relationship between the ruler and society, both human and divine. To that end, works of art were often used to create and circulate an image of a ruler that conformed to social expectations, or that sought to introduce a new order or set of relationships. In addition, kings were directly involved with rituals in the construction of temples and palaces, and sometimes also participated in the design and decoration of buildings or works of art (Root 1979: 16–23).

Artistic interaction between different regions of the ANE came about through a variety of mechanisms, involving the movement of artisans as well as works of art. Trade, diplomacy, imperial expansion, and voluntary or forced population movements were among those mechanisms. Key sculptural monuments displayed in Mesopotamian sanctuaries were moved to the site of Susa, in SW Iran, through a series of raids on Mesopotamian cities by kings of Elam in the 12th century B.C. (*CAH* 2/2: 486). Cult images, endowed with powers of healing, were transported over long distances, usually in response to the express wish of an individual ruler (*CAH* 2/1: 346).

Relatively little is known of the production of art for private, nonroyal settings, at least before the Roman era. Personal possessions recovered from tombs, for example, help to determine the kinds of objects individuals of nonroyal status would have owned and treasured. The abundant category of cylinder seals and their impressions, many inscribed with the names of their owners, furnishes an exceptional opportunity to investigate works of art belonging to individuals of different social levels, the personal selection of subjects or styles, and the function, meaning, and reuse of those works of art (Gibson and Biggs 1977; Collon 1987).

D. Artistic Developments before 4000 B.C.

With the development of agriculture and animal husbandry in the Near East around 9000 B.C., permanently inhabited settlements provided a new and hospitable environment for artistic energies. Sources for reconstructing the beginnings of art are sculptures, vessels, or ornaments, made of clay or stone, found in settlements or graves over a wide region of W Asia (Mellink and Filip 1974; Mellaart 1975). Works of art seem to have been created for purposes of cult and magic, as far as we can reliably reconstruct their meanings and function. At Neolithic Çatal Hüyük, in south central Turkey, wall paintings and plastered relief sculptures document an elaborate cultic iconography involving bulls, felines, and human female figures. Plastered human skulls from Neolithic Jericho suggest that art functioned in a cult of ancestors. Common to Neolithic sites over a wide area of the Near East are figurines made of clay or stone in the shape of humans, most often females, or of animals.

Less practical ambitions must also have fed the urge to fashion clay, stone, or perishable materials into an image or pattern, or to decorate a surface. The medium of pottery developed early in the Near East, initially for the manufacture of simple containers; the earliest known examples, from the sites of Mureybit in N Syria, and Ganj Dareh Tepe, in W Iran, date to about 8000 B.C. By the 5th millennium B.C., potters at a number of sites in the Near East were producing ceramic vessels of high technical quality, and had adopted the medium as an important vehicle of artistic expression. A material that permits unlimited variations and ways of shaping, clay can also be transformed through firing; in addition, it provides a wealth of opportunities for decoration through incision, relief ornament, and the addition of a colored slip or paint. Excavations in northern and central Mesopotamia have yielded the painted pottery styles known as Samarra and Halaf. In Anatolia, a painted pottery style best known from the site of Hacilar also appeared during the late 6th millennium B.C. (Mellink and Filip 1974).

Architectural remains dating to this period are usually made of perishable or readily weathered building materials, including sun-dried mudbrick or reeds. Most buildings seem to have been ordinary dwellings, with adjacent space used for keeping animals. Several Neolithic sites have also yielded examples of substantial stone architecture, or of functionally specialized structures, such as fortifications or storerooms. A series of temples unearthed at sites of the Ubaid culture in Mesopotamia, dating to the 5th millennium B.C., bears witness to the standardization of ritual in the form of building plan, interior furnishings, and exterior decoration (see ANCIENT NEAR EASTERN ARCHITECTURE below).

E. Arts of the Early Urban Communities (to ca. 2350 B.C.)

With the invention of writing in Mesopotamia around 3200 B.C., new sources became available for understanding the purpose and meaning of architecture and works of art. In addition, writing appeared increasingly on works of art, in association with images. This close link between art and writing in Mesopotamia, forged early, continued throughout its history (Cooper 1988). Another key artistic development of the period was the invention of the cylinder seal in Mesopotamia. Engraved with patterned or figured designs, the seals were rolled across wet clay tablets or lumps of clay used to seal vessels, consignments of goods, and door latches of storerooms (Collon 1987). Seals and seal impressions have been recovered from every period of Mesopotamian history, furnishing the largest and richest source for tracing the variety and development of artistic styles and iconography. The appearance of this characteristic object elsewhere in the Near East also documents Mesopotamian commercial or cultural influence (Collon 1987; Gibson and Biggs 1977).

The art and architecture of the early urban settlements has been most thoroughly investigated at the site of Uruk, in S Mesopotamia (see also ANCIENT NEAR EASTERN ARCHITECTURE; MESOPOTAMIAN ART AND ARCHITECTURE below). The construction of monumental temple complexes built of molded, sun-dried mudbrick, following a standard plan and decoration, continued the developments in religious architecture of the Ubaid period. Along with standardized, monumental constructions for religious practices came the use of statuary in temple complexes. Preserved examples display a wide range of forms and styles, including life-sized, composite sculptures made of stone and other materials. Uruk has also yielded the first appearance of the *stele*, a block of stone carved in low relief on one or both sides, which remained a characteristic form of commemorative art throughout Mesopotamian history.

The first fully literate period in Mesopotamia, known as the Early Dynastic period (ca. 3000–2350 B.C.), allows us to chart developments in art and architecture in the city-states of Sumer. Excavations at several sites offer a stratification of building remains and also of associated finds, such as sculptures and cylinder seals. Temple complexes continued as the principal form of monumental architecture in the city-states of Early Dynastic Sumer. Along with inherited notions of building design and decoration, votive statuary placed in temples suggests a continuity of religious rituals and their artistic expression. Small sculptures in the form of stylized human worshippers were made of stone or metal; stone plaques carved in relief depicted worshippers in ceremonies, such as banqueting or the construction of temples.

The Early Dynastic period coincided with the rapid development of metallurgy in gold, silver, and copper alloy. Throughout the Near East, metal became the preeminent prestige material for vessels, weapons, jewelry, and other portable objects. Testifying to the technical and aesthetic achievements of early metalsmiths as well as to an elite taste in works of art are the remarkable objects recovered from the Royal Cemetery at the site of Ur. Grave goods included weapons, jewelry, vessels, and musical instruments, made of a wide variety of materials (shell, mother-of-pearl, lapis lazuli, wood, gold, silver, copper), often in combination with each other (Moorey 1982: 51–103). These objects, many carefully placed in royal graves, attest to a demand at the highest social levels for these imported precious materials, skillfully worked by local artisans. Secular energies in Early Dynastic Sumer were also manifested in works of art depicting military victories of the ruler, which became more frequent toward the end of the period (e.g., the stele of Eannatum: Orthmann 1975: pls. 90–91).

Independent artistic traditions in ceramics and metalwork flourished in central Anatolia during the 3d millennium B.C. At the site of Alaca Hüyük, in north central Turkey, a cemetery of shaft graves contained rich treasures made of copper alloy, gold, and silver, including vessels, jewelry, and sculptures in the form of human figures or of animals. These sculptures often combine different metals on a single object, producing a distinctive surface pattern or emphasizing parts of figures with gold or silver (Bittel 1976: 30–50). The decoration of pottery with black or copper-red slipped, polished surfaces also reflects the influence of metalwork. The "treasures" from the citadel at Troy, dating from the end of the 3d millennium, attest to another sophisticated metalworking center in NW Anatolia.

F. The First Empires (ca. 2350–1200 B.C.)

The rise of the Akkadian dynasty ca. 2350 B.C. brought an end to the political organization of Sumer in independent city-states. With the new concept of world empire, works of art could also serve to transmit imperial messages; this purpose of art would be increasingly exploited throughout antiquity. Although the capital of the dynasty, Agade, has not been discovered, art produced during the period of Akkadian domination has been recovered from several sites in Mesopotamia and N Syria. In addition, examples of Akkadian royal sculpture have come to light at the site of Susa, in SW Iran, where they were taken during raids by Elamite kings in the 12th century B.C. and rediscovered in the 20th century by a French team of excavators. One of the masterpieces recovered from Susa was the stele of Naram-Sin (Orthmann 1975: pl. 104).

After the Akkadian domination of Mesopotamia was brought to an end around 2200 B.C., a revival of Sumerian art and architecture ensued in the old city-states of S Mesopotamia. Traditional forms of religious architecture and of commemorative art were promoted energetically by the rulers of the Third Dynasty of Ur (ca. 2112–2000 B.C.). A series of statues of Gudea, ruler of Lagash (reigned ca. 2130 B.C.) also illustrates the intentional revival of Sumerian artistic traditions. The statues, many of them carved from blocks of diorite, depict the ruler in the traditional roles of pious worshipper and builder of temples (Orthmann 1975: pls. 53–57). Babylonia was also a powerful center under the First Dynasty of Babylon (ca. 2000–1600 B.C.), but almost nothing is known of its monumental art. The stele of Hammurabi, recovered from Susa, continues the tradition of earlier Mesopotamian stelae (Orthmann 1975: pl. 181). More eloquent testimony to the artistic achievements of this period are the palace, wall paintings, and sculptures preserved and excavated at the site of Mari, on the Euphrates River in N Syria (Parrot 1974). Mari, founded in Early Dynastic times, now rose to a new prominence as the capital of a kingdom ruled by a powerful local dynasty. Its MB Age remains and archives help to supplement the almost complete lack of material from Hammurabi's Babylon.

During the first half of the 2d millennium B.C., monumental art and architecture of individual style and consequence were developing on the Anatolian plateau under the auspices of the Hittites, an Indo-European-speaking people who probably moved into the area of present-day central Turkey around 2000 B.C. The official art of the Hittite Empire, preserved in rock reliefs, architectural sculptures, and seals, frequently depicted the king engaged in worship or religious ceremonies (Bittel 1976: 166–219). Hittite architecture has been most extensively revealed at the site of Boğazköy, ancient Hattusha, capital of the Old Hittite Kingdom and Empire (ca. 1650–1200 B.C.). Cuneiform archives recovered from several complexes at the site have permitted identification of some of the structures. The Hittite royal palace was a complex of adjacent, individual structures connected by large open courtyards. Built of massive stone foundations with mudbrick and timber superstructures, the palace buildings included large halls filled with wooden columns. Excavations at the capital have also furnished extensive evidence for Hittite temples, which followed a precise plan of axial entrance, central courtyard, and rear room containing the cult image (Bittel 1976: 105–35; Orthmann 1975: 399–419).

In the late 2d millennium B.C., a lively artistic exchange linked the Near East with Egypt and the Aegean world. Correspondence preserved at the city of Tell el-Amarna in Egypt, dating from ca. 1380–1362 B.C., bears eloquent witness to that internationalism, cultivated by the most powerful rulers of the Near East. The kings of Mitanni, of Kassite Babylonia, of Ugarit in Phoenicia, and of the Hittites, as well as the rulers of the 18th Dynasty in Egypt, exchanged artisans as well as works of art (Smith 1965).

G. The Neo-Assyrian and Achaemenid Persian Empires (ca. 1200–330 B.C.)

A series of destructions on the coasts of the Aegean and the E Mediterranean, dated to ca. 1200 B.C., brought an end to a number of important cities. Following those destructions, Mesopotamia regained political ascendance in W Asia under the Assyrians. Dramatic testimony to Assyrian military and imperial ambitions are the remains of their capitals, located in the "Assyrian triangle" of N Mesopotamia. The interior walls of the palaces at Nimrud, Khorsabad, and Nineveh were decorated with carved, painted reliefs depicting detailed narratives of military campaigns and ritual scenes. Fragmentary wall paintings survive from the palace of Sargon at Khorsabad, and from the governor's palace at Til Barsip in N Syria.

Important centers of ivory-carving flourished in N Syria and Phoenicia in the early 1st millennium B.C., in part under Assyrian royal patronage. Assyria was also involved in artistic exchanges with its neighbors in Phrygia, Urartu, and W Iran. The 9th through 7th centuries B.C. also saw the export of Near Eastern metalwork, ivories, and textiles to the Aegean world and to Etruria, stimulating the local production of "Orientalizing" styles.

The end of Assyrian rule in 612 B.C. was followed by the rise of the Achaemenid Persian dynasty to the status of world empire in W Asia. Under the leadership of Cyrus (reigned ca. 560–539 B.C.) and his successors, the Achaemenid Persians came to rule over western and central Asia, parts of SE Europe, and Egypt. With the shift of Near Eastern power to the dynasty's homeland in Iran, Iranian traditions played an increasingly central role in the creation of art and architecture for royal and elite patrons. Achaemenid Persian art also drew on the traditions of Assyria, Egypt, and Anatolia (see PERSIAN ART below). The monumental art and architecture of Achaemenid Persia are best known from the site of Persepolis, located in SW Iran. Built on an artificial platform with limited access, buildings consisted of individual rectangular structures, made of locally quarried limestone, with frequent use of stone columned interiors. On the exterior walls of several of the buildings, sculptures in low relief depicted processions of Medes and Persians, processions of tribute bearers from throughout the empire, and scenes of the Persian king enthroned or engaged in ritual combat (Root 1979). Achaemenid Persian imperial art was also created and circulated throughout the empire in the form of seals, coins, and official gifts, often vessels, made of precious metal. Other centers of artistic production in the empire have been investigated primarily in Anatolia, where art flourished under the patronage of local dynasts; artisans trained in Greek, Persian, and Anatolian traditions were employed to design and execute seals, coins, palaces, sanctuaries, and tombs (*CAH* 4: 211–33).

H. Hellenism and Near Eastern Traditions (ca. 330 B.C.–A.D. 250)

The Asian conquests of Alexander the Great in the 330s B.C. brought the Achaemenid Persian Empire to an end. The Seleucids, the successors of Alexander's general Seleucus, ruled over Mesopotamia and Syria from ca. 312–130 B.C. Under the Seleucids, cities with substantial Greek populations were founded over a wide region of western and central Asia. These foundations introduced into the Near Eastern repertoire on a large and systematic scale Hellenistic forms and styles in architecture, sculpture, metalwork, and painting (Colledge 1987).

In 246 B.C., the Parthians, an Iranian-speaking tribe originally from NE Iran, defeated the Seleucid armies and established rule over Mesopotamia and Iran. Their official art is known only from coins and from a few rock reliefs; but in the areas under their control flourished developments in art and architecture that drew on a vast range of traditions extending from the E Mediterranean to Han China. Art produced in the Parthian empire has been most extensively studied at sanctuary complexes in Syria, Iraq, Iran, and the Soviet Union, revealing a great variety in concurrent styles and techniques employed for architecture and sculpture (Colledge 1977; Downey 1988). Among the architectural forms developed in this era was the *iwan*, a barrel-vaulted three-sided hall, that became a principal element in Sasanian Persian and Islamic architecture.

I. Arts of Late Antiquity (ca. A.D. 250–650)

Following their victory over the Parthians in A.D. 246, the Sasanian Persian dynasty revived Iranian traditions in art and architecture while maintaining artistic exchanges with the Roman, and later Byzantine, empires. In addition, the Sasanian Persians pursued commercial and cultural relations with central Asia and China.

Monuments of the Sasanian era have been most extensively preserved and investigated in Mesopotamia and W Iran (*CHI* 3: 1055–1112). Architectural remains, mainly of palaces, have been investigated at Kish, Bishapur, Sarvistan, and Qasr-i Shirin; they demonstrate a continuity of Hellenistic and Roman forms and styles along with Near Eastern developments, including the *iwan*. A characteristic form of royal Sasanian art was the commemorative rock relief, carved on the natural cliff face, in the dynasty's homeland of SW Iran; most depict the investiture of the king or the king engaged in a ritual hunt. The royal hunt was also a principal theme of the decorated silver plates that were manufactured during the Sasanian era (Harper and Meyers 1981). Sasanian glass was exported over a wide area of western, central, and East Asia; patterned silks became highly prized in W Asia and Europe. The legacy of Sasanian Persian art and architecture included the transmission of ANE traditions to the West via the art of the Roman and Byzantine empires.

Bibliography

Amiet, P. 1980. *Art of the Ancient Near East.* New York.

Barnett, R. D. 1982. *Ancient Ivories in the Middle East and Adjacent Countries.* Qedem 14. Jerusalem.

Bittel, K. 1970. *Hattusha, The Capital of the Hittites.* New York.

———. 1976. *Die Hethiter.* Munich.

Bohrer, F. N. 1989. Assyria as Art: A Perspective on the Early Reception of Ancient Near Eastern Artifacts. *Culture and History* 4: 7–33.

Brothwell, D., and Higgs, E., eds. 1970. *Science in Archaeology. A Survey of Progress and Research.* Rev. ed. New York.

Cann, J. R.; Dixon, J. E.; and Renfrew, Colin. 1970. Obsidian Analysis and the Obsidian Trade. Pp. 578–91 in *Science in Archaeology. A Survey of Progress and Research,* ed. D. Brothwell, and E. Higgs. Rev. ed. New York.

Colledge, M. 1977. *Parthian Art.* Ithaca, N.Y.

———. 1987. Greek and Non-Greek Interaction in the Art and Architecture of the Hellenistic East. Pp. 134–62 in *Hellenism and the East,* ed. A. Kuhrt, and S. Sherwin-White. Berkeley.

Collon, D. 1987. *First Impressions. Cylinder Seals in the Ancient Near East.* Chicago.

Cooper, J. S. 1988. Writing in *Encyclopedia of Communications.*

Downey, S. B. 1988. *Mesopotamian Religious Architecture: Alexander through the Parthians.* Princeton.

Ettinghausen, R. 1962. *Arab Painting.* Geneva.

Frankfort, H. 1970. *The Art and Architecture of the Ancient Orient.* Rev. ed. Harmondsworth.

Gibson, M., and Biggs, R. D., eds. 1977. *Seals and Sealing in the Ancient Near East.* BiMes 6. Malibu.

Grabar, O. 1973. *The Formation of Islamic Art.* New Haven.

Groenewegen-Frankfort, H. A. 1951. *Arrest and Movement. An Essay on Space and Time in the Representational Art of the Ancient Near East.* London.

Harper, P. O., and Meyers, P. 1981. *Silver Vessels of the Sasanian Era. Vol. I: Royal Imagery.* New York.

Heimpel, W. 1987. Das Unter Meer. *ZA* 77: 21–91.

Herrmann, G. 1987. Lapis Lazuli: The Early Phases of Its Trade. *Iraq* 30: 21–57.

———. 1977. *The Iranian Revival.* Oxford.

Kilmer, A. D. 1990. Akkadian Names for Designs and Geometric Shapes. In *Investigating Artistic Environments in the Ancient Near East,* ed. Ann C. Gunter, Washington, D.C.

Lloyd, S. 1980. *Foundations in the Dust.* London.

Lucas, A. 1962. *Ancient Egyptian Materials and Industries.* 4th ed. London.

Mellaart, J. 1975. *The Neolithic of the Near East.* London.

Mellink, M. J., and Filip, J., eds. 1974. *Frühe Stufen der Kunst.* Propylaen Kunstgeschichte 13. Berlin.

Michalowski, P. 1990. Early Mesopotamian Communicative Systems: Art, Literature, and Writing. In *Investigating Artistic Environments in the Ancient Near East,* ed. Ann C. Gunter. Washington, D.C.

Moorey, P. R. S. 1982. *Ur "of the Chaldees."* Ithaca, N.Y.

———. 1985. *Materials and Manufacture in Ancient Mesopotamia: The Evidence of Archaeology and Art. Metals and Metalwork, Glazed Materials and Glass.* BAR International Series 237. Oxford.

Nissen, H. J. 1987. *The Early History of the Ancient Near East, 9000–2000 B.C.* Chicago.

Orthmann, W., ed. 1975. *Der alte Orient.* Propylaen Kunstgeschichte 14. Berlin.

Parrot, A. 1974. *Mari, capitale fabuleuse.* Paris.

Porada, E. 1965. *The Art of Ancient Iran.* New York.

Root, M. C. 1979. *The King and Kingship in Achaemenid Art.* Acta Iranica 9. Leiden.

Sasson, J. 1990. Artisans . . . Artists: Documentary Perspectives from Mari. In *Investigating Artistic Environments in the Ancient Near East,* ed. Ann C. Gunter, Washington, D.C.

Silberman, N. A. 1982. *Digging for God and Country.* New York.

Singer, C.; Holmyard, E. J.; and Hall, A. R., eds. 1954. *A History of Technology, Vol. I, From Early Times to the Fall of the Ancient Empires.* New York.

Smith, W. S. 1965. *Interconnections in the Ancient Near East.* New Haven.

Zaccagnini, C. 1983. Patterns of Mobility among Ancient Near Eastern Craftsmen. *JNES* 42: 245–64.

Ann C. Gunter

ANCIENT NEAR EASTERN ARCHITECTURE

If architecture is defined as building conditioned by aesthetic considerations, the Near East may reasonably claim the longest architectural history of any region on earth. Yet it is by no means easy to isolate and delineate a single dominant tradition in the area—comparable, for example, to Egyptian, Roman, or Gothic architecture—since the rubric "ancient Near East" covers many millennia and much cultural diversity in which recognizable, enduring monuments that would foster adherence to a uniform canon are lacking. Any general treatment of the subject, therefore, inevitably involves a rather artificial process of grouping and selection. The distinction between Mesopotamia, Anatolia, and the Levant employed here is no exception. Each of these subregions was subject to the others' influences and boundaries between them were never static, while, on the other hand, there is often evidence of independent local development within each area. Nevertheless, there are certain unities that prevail over the entire Near East and the convention of devoting a chapter to the ANE in general surveys of the history of architecture is not entirely without justification.

A. General Comments

One unifying feature of crucial significance is the prevailing use of mud brick as the primary building material. In many cases, particularly in S Mesopotamia, this is virtually all that remains for the archaeological study of architecture since such supplemental materials as stone, timber, and even baked bricks were valued and consequently removed from ruined buildings for reuse. Elsewhere in the Near East substantial stone foundations often remain as evidence of ground plans, but even under these circumstances, most of the above-ground walls of buildings were made of unbaked mud brick.

A consequence of reliance on this water-soluble building material is that ANE architecture did not last long. Under the best of circumstances, with annual replasterings and continuous maintenance, a mud-brick building has a life expectancy of less than a century. An abandoned edifice loses its architectural definition in a few years. Even the most monumental and massive structures in the area, city walls and the solid ziggurats of Mesopotamia, had to be shored up periodically in antiquity and survive today only as eroded and barely recognizable shadows of their former grandeur. The study of ANE architecture, therefore, is largely the study of building plans, not existing structures; and elevations must be reconstructed on basis of limited secondary sources such as pictorial representations and literary descriptions.

Mud brick has also done much to shape the character of Near Eastern archaeology; structures composed of it tend to be relatively massive, and their rapid decay leads to the buildup of cultural debris in artificial hills, or tells. It is not surprising that archaeological research has tended to focus on these, since they are obvious repositories of cultural information in stratified contexts. The excavation of tells is a labor-intensive process which has been conducted with varying degrees of skill over the last century. Every tell is made up of mud brick in various states of decay, and it is not always easy to judge what is or is not in a relevant position for architectural reconstruction. No economical system of preserving original mud brick exists, and since buildings are superimposed excavation implies destruction. Usually nothing remains at the end but notes, photographs, and plans, and there is often much uncertainty if not skepticism about specific aspects of any given building. The broad horizontal exposures that were typical of early 20th-century archaeology in the Near East involved hundreds of workmen moving tons of earth and are no longer economically feasible. Modern excavators have tended to select smaller sites, and specific edifices, rather than attempting to expose neighborhoods or entire city plans. All of these factors lend an unusual measure of uncertainty to our understanding of the history of architecture in the Near East.

B. Preurban Developments

The earliest buildings appear in the Levant before the introduction of agriculture and the domestication of animals. What remains of the earliest open-air structures are circular pits, 2 to 7 m in diameter, sunk to a depth of roughly 0.5 m. Field stones were often used for flooring and a portion of the above-ground walls. Although the superstructural detail of these is unknown, occasional traces of postmolds suggest that they were made of perishable materials. The earliest example, found associated with Kebaran lithics at ʿEn Gev in the Golan, is isolated, but groups of such structures dating to the range of 10,000 to 8000 B.C. were found at such sites as Muryebat on the Euphrates and ʿAin Mallaha near Lake Huleh. This appears to be the only type of edifice constructed by human beings at that time (Wright 1985, 1: 24).

This architectural uniformity, however, disintegrates quite early in the Neolithic and never returns. Perhaps the most celebrated example of early Neolithic sophistication is Jericho, where around 8000 B.C. there is ample evidence of collective, organized building activity in the form of a substantial wall along the perimeter of the site and an abutting stone tower 8 m high containing a staircase. Although the original interpretation of these as defensive structures has been challenged as anachronistic (Bar-Yosef 1986: 157–62), there can be no doubt that they represent landmarks of architectural sophistication.

Elsewhere there is equally dramatic evidence of early experimentation with building forms and materials. The range of functional differentiation in architecture can be illustrated merely by looking at three sites: 7th-millennium aceramic Çayönü in S Turkey, Beidha in Jordan, and 6th-millennium Umm Dabaghiyah in Iraq's N Jezira. At Çayönü the variety of building styles varies over time, beginning with simple pit houses followed by those with grill plans, broad pavements, cell plans, and finally large rooms. Most interesting are the broad pavement plans which have, as the name implies, pavements of flagstones or, in one case, pink terrazzo with white stripes. These buildings frequently have freestanding stones preserved within them and have therefore been interpreted as having some religious function. On the other hand, each cell of the cell-plan structures held different goods—an indication that these buildings were used for manufacturing or storage. At Beidha a similar pattern can be seen. After a developmental sequence from round to rectilinear structures was completed, three contemporary building types have been found. There, too, special purpose structures with stone pavements and standing stones have been interpreted as serving a religious purpose. Single-room, freestanding houses constructed of handmade mud bricks with a heavy, sometimes painted, plaster floor were clearly residential, and plans of this type remained popular in the Levant until the 3d millennium (Wright 1985, 1: 284). Associated with these at Beidha were "passageway houses," which may be conceived as a single long room divided into six alcoves by internal buttresses (see Fig. ART. 01). From the objects found in each bay, these have been interpreted as manufacturing areas by the excavator. At the slightly later site of Umm Dabaghiyah and at other sites with Hassunan pottery, residential structures consisting of two or three rooms are clustered around a series of very long buildings consisting of as many as 50 small rooms. The excavator has argued that these were used for centralized storage.

These examples present a picture of Neolithic architectural diversity which is repeated at many other sites in the Near East. One may also speak of a broad trend, with many exceptions, of round house forms being supplanted

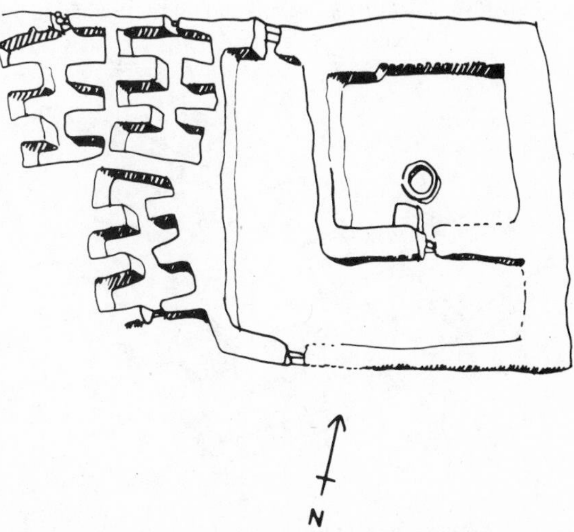

ART.01. Isometric reconstruction of Neolithic Passageway Houses at Beida, Jordan—Level 2. *(Redrawn from* PEQ *[1966]: 12, fig. 2.)*

by rectilinear ones, semisubterranean structures replaced by those laid out on the surface, and *tauf* superseded first by handmade mud brick and then by molded mud brick.

Some sites, of which the most dramatic is 6th-millennium Çatal Hüyük, located in Turkey's Konya Plain, exhibit architectural traditions all their own. Although only a portion of its settled area has been excavated, the exposures suffice to reveal a densely settled neighborhood of adjoining houses built of rectangular, mold-made mud bricks (see Fig. ART. 02). There appears to be a standard house plan, consisting of one square "living" room with sleeping platforms and a cooking area, and two subsidiary rooms, an air shaft and, sometimes a shared courtyard. Houses at Çatal Hüyük shared common walls, stepping up the mound to provide light, and access was by ladders through the roof. Çatal Hüyük's uniqueness lies in the many houses which were distinguished by elaborate painted and molded decorative elements, associated with especially rich grave goods accompanying the dead who were, as at many Neolithic sites, buried beneath the floors. These features have led the excavator to single such houses out as "shrines," but since one house in three is apparently so favored the socioreligious implications are perhaps less straightforward than this term would suggest.

C. Mesopotamia

1. General Remarks. It is customary to subdivide discussions of the Mesopotamian archaeological record between Assyria in the N and Babylonia, or Sumer and Akkad, in the S. There are, in fact, major differences in the architectural traditions of the two areas, but for historical periods the primacy of the S, particularly with regard to public buildings, is indisputable. The most obvious factor discriminating the two regions is the relative poverty of the S in terms of building materials; the only local resources available to the creators of the first urban civilization were mud, straw, reeds, date palms, and water. There was no stone of any kind in the immediate vicinity and wood suitable for roof beams and doors also had to be

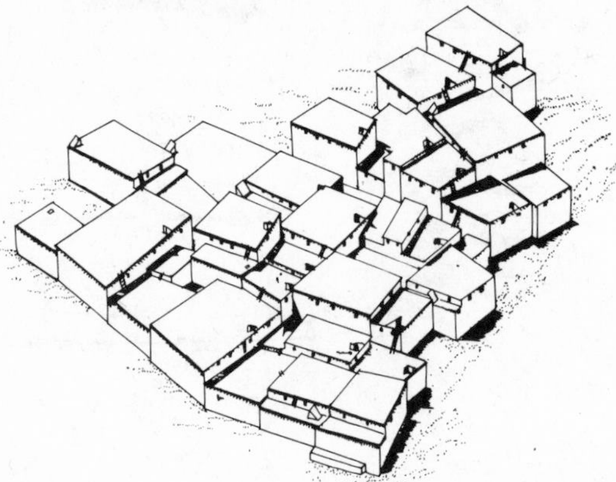

ART.02. Schematic reconstruction of houses at Çatal Hüyük—Level VI. (*Redrawn from J. Mellaart,* Çatal Hüyük: A Neolithic Town in Anatolia *[New York, 1967], 62, fig. 12.)*

imported. Nor was there a readily available supply of fuel for firing bricks, so the favored building material, at least insofar as it appears in the archaeological record, was unfired mud brick. In most cases this was either laid directly on the ground or put in recessed foundation trenches; there was no tradition of using stone foundations as damp courses in S Mesopotamia as there was in other parts of the ANE, although in some cases baked bricks served this purpose. Reed matting was used both in roofs and on floors, where traces of it were frequently preserved. There was doubtless also much building in reeds alone, with bundles tied together and bent into arches over which mats were thrown to form a kind of vault. Such structures, attested on cylinder seal designs and still seen in modern villages in marsh areas, are more or less archaeologically invisible. They may actually have been a fairly common house type that is underrepresented in an archaeological record based primarily on the investigation of tells. In Assyria both stone and timber were more readily available from the foothills of the nearby Taurus and Zagros flanks, but mud brick was the basic building material there as well.

2. Domestic Architecture and Town Plans. For most of the post-Neolithic Mesopotamian sequence, the basic house consists of mud-brick walls delineating rectilinear rooms around an internal courtyard. In the early periods some other plans are to be found, especially in the N. These include round houses, a distinctive T-shaped plan at the Samarran site of Tell es-Sawwan, and the ʿUbaid tripartite house with a long central room and a row of subordinate rooms on each of the long sides. It has been argued that the latter was the origin of what was to be a basic temple form (Roaf 1984).

The ideal Mesopotamian courtyard house, as seen in house plans drawn on clay tablets and in rare examples found archaeologically, consisted of a central court with rooms arranged on all four sides. Functional distinctions between entrance chambers, kitchens, bathrooms, storage and living rooms can often be made. In reality this ideal plan was usually distorted by the location of surrounding structures, the needs of the particular family, and the need to accommodate various nonresidential functions. Such distortion was facilitated by the malleability of mud brick—in which doorways can be opened and closed at will—and by the tradition of using party walls that characterizes Mesopotamian cities. Thus houses with rooms on only two or three sides of a court, those with multiple courts, and those with trapezoidal or even triangular rooms and courts are common, and over time the transformation of one type of organization into another is very common.

Despite nearly a century of excavation, evidence for the actual layout of cities in Mesopotamia is disappointingly meager, although this is an area in which recent research is making significant contributions. Significant residential districts have been uncovered at 3d-millennium Tell Taya, Abu Salabikh, and Khafajah, and at the 2d-millennium sites of Ur, Sippar, and Nippur. Nearly all show the pattern of narrow winding streets with houses tightly clustered together which is typical of the organic growth of residential districts in the absence of centralized planning. Within these areas, small chapels and possible shops have been identified, but by and large the areas are overwhelmingly domestic in nature (see Fig. ART. 03).

All such areas so far uncovered have exhibited an intermingling of large and small houses. This suggests that such neighborhoods were not segregated by wealth and class, an impression which is confirmed by the available cuneiform documentation. Thus the older idea that each Mesopotamian city was divided into specialized quarters is unsupported by current research. It is suggested instead that the city itself grew around several different focal points, where an initial larger building would be surrounded by the houses of its clients, kinsmen, or dependents. One of the clearest examples of this is seen at Khafajah, where the Temple Oval has a walled residential quarter occupied by temple dependents built up against it.

There were, of course, parts of the city marked off for the major institutions, and in most cities the ziggurat was part of a complex of temples and related structures that were physically separated from the residential areas by their own enclosures. Sacred buildings, however, were not confined to a single part of the city, and each Mesopotamian city-state was served by a number of temples.

3. Sacred Architecture. The term "temple" has two different, but not mutually exclusive nuances: (1) a residence of the god or his cult, and (2) a place of worship. It is clear that Mesopotamian temples also had important economic functions, since their role in storage, rationing, trade, and landholding is well established by texts. In both Assyria and Babylonia the core element of sacred architecture was an elongated room, the cella, in which the image of the god was placed in a niche or on a raised podium at one end. The configuration of rooms around this room, and the place from which one gained access to this key room varied, and the emphasis once given in scholarly writings to the cultic significance of bent-axis as opposed to straight-axis approaches to the altar has been blurred by recent discoveries.

Two sites provide the basic paradigms for the development of sacred architecture through the 5th and 4th millennia: Eridu in the S and Tepe Gawra in the N. Excavations at the former have revealed a sequence of superimposed cultic structures beneath a later ziggurat, the earliest of which is little more than a single square room with internal buttresses. Over time later shrines were built over older ones, the cella became increasingly elongated, subsidiary rooms were added, and the whole was increasingly embellished until in the late ʿUbaid period (early 4th millennium) the temple stood on a platform, had a clearly developed tripartite form with smaller rooms flanking the cella, was oriented with its corners to the cardinal points of the compass, and was decorated with a niched brick facade. All of these features are characteristic of sacred architecture in the succeeding period of urban development.

At Tepe Gawra there is more variety in temple plans. Round structures are present in the earliest levels and a seventeen-room circular building approximately 19 m in diameter reiterates the form found in the early Uruk period (level 11A). In between, there are some tripartite temples which bear a resemblance to the later ʿUbaid temples of Eridu, and in the later Uruk period a new temple form with a direct axis through a porch to a long cella is found.

It is in the Uruk and Jemdet Nasr periods that the increase in scale and complexity of sacred architecture so typical of S Mesopotamian cities is first found. The largest exposures from this period are found at Uruk, where the 50 × 80 m dimensions of Temple D, in the Eanna district, make it some four times the size of the latest ʿUbaid temple at Eridu, yet still recognizable as a building of the same form. The celebrated "White Temple," the last of a series in the area of the Anu ziggurat, may be taken to exemplify the practice of raising some temples onto platforms in a process that is felt to culminate in the emergence of the ziggurat in the 3d millennium (Lenzen 1941). In addition to the increase in building size, this period saw, more than any other, experimentation with the embellishment of temples. Colored baked clay and occasionally stone cones were driven into the plaster of the walls to make patterns of diamonds and chevrons, and at one site, Tell Uqair, the complex painted designs that decorated the interior were recovered.

Temples formed administrative centers of the emerging Mesopotamian cities and one of their primary functions was storage. The earliest complex recording devices that have yet been discovered—clay bullae, cylinder seal impressions, and archaic cuneiform tablets—are all associated with these buildings.

In the 3d millennium the temple type established earlier persisted, accompanied by increasing elaborative embellishments, especially of the associated courtyard and outbuildings. Perhaps the best example of long-term development from the late 4th through the first half of the 3d millennium is seen in the Sin Temple at Khafajah (Delougaz and Lloyd 1942). One dramatic new development, which proved to be short-lived, was a temple precinct surrounded by an oval enclosure wall. Temple ovals were some of the largest religious structures in their day, and examples have been found at Khafajah, ʿUbaid, al-Hibba, and Bahrain. The oval at Khafajah, the best known example, is a double enclosure that separates a temple platform off from the rest of the community, and contains a residence, generally felt to be that of the head priest of the temple, between the inner and outer oval. Although this specific form is confined to the Early Dynastic period, the idea of separating off the sacred area continued, and may be seen with particular clarity in the sacred precinct around the ziggurat at Ur in the Ur III period.

The emergence of the ziggurat, that most memorable of Mesopotamian sacred architectural forms, is probably to be related to the elevated temple platforms that can be seen in this period. The early history of ziggurats, however, is obscured by later rebuilding (Lenzen 1941). Most of the major ones that survive today date to the massive building projects of the Third Dynasty of Ur, when economic conditions apparently made it possible to fire prodigious numbers of bricks to be used as outer sheeting. The best preserved of these in S Iraq is at Ur (see Fig. ART. 04), where the lower stages and arrangement of approaching staircases were still clearly visible before reconstruction. Nowhere is the uppermost stage or summit temple preserved, and Herodotus' description of seven stages has perhaps been overused in reconstructing earlier ziggurats.

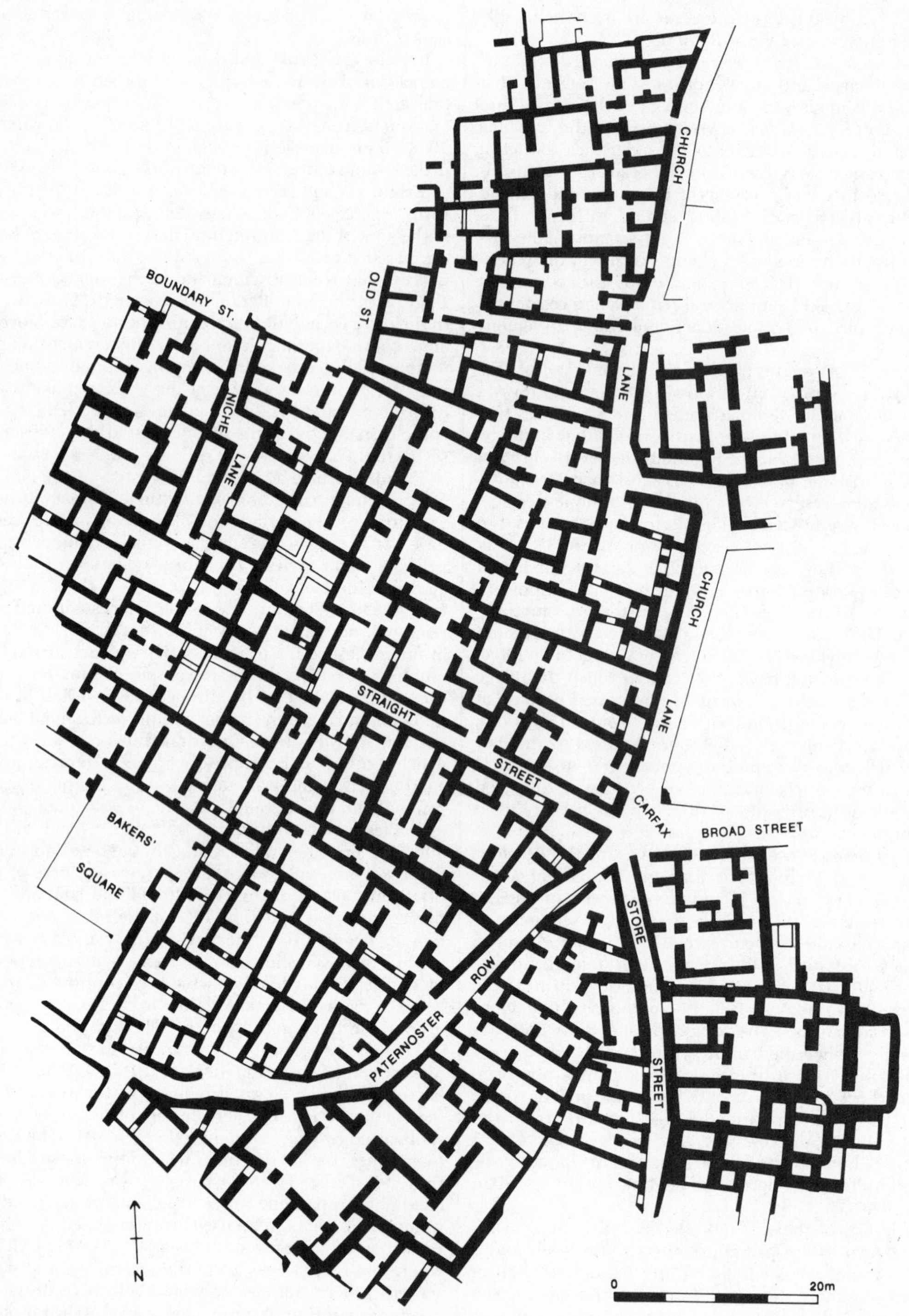

ART.03. Plan of residential area at Ur—Isin-Larsa/Old Babylonian Period. *(Redrawn from L. Woolley and M. Mallowan,* The Old Babylonian Period. *Ur Excavations 7 [Philadelphia and London: British Museum and University Museum, 1976], pl. 124.)*

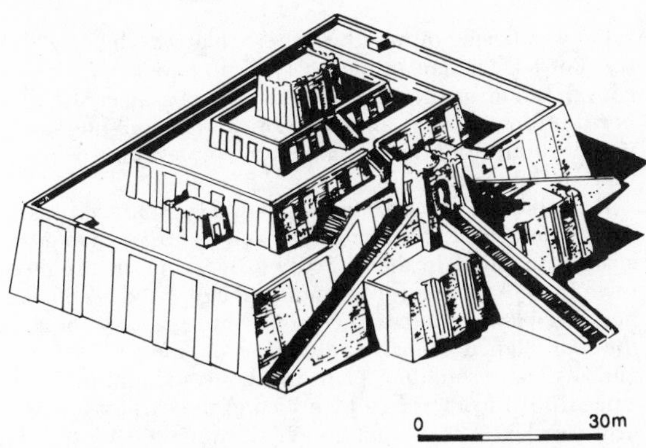

ART.04. Reconstruction of Ur-Nammu's ziggurat at Ur. *(Redrawn from P. R. S. Moorey,* Ur of the Chaldees *[Ithaca, NY: Cornell University Press, 1982], 148.)*

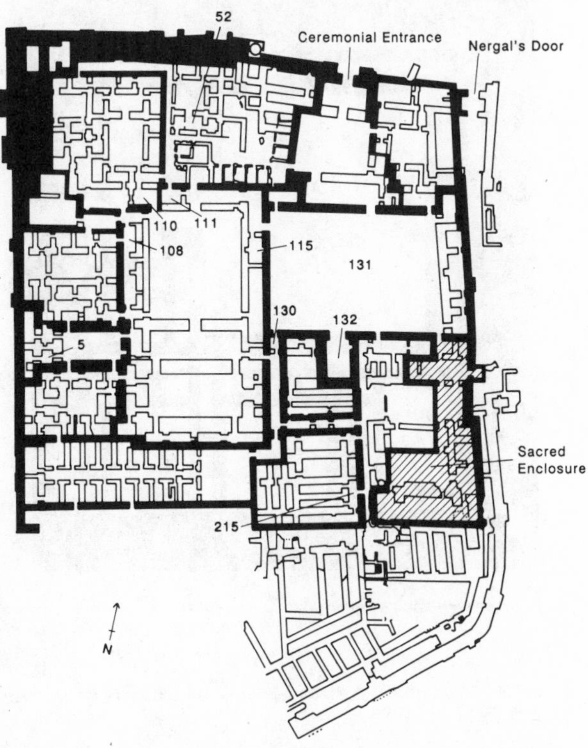

ART.05. Plan of palace of Zimri-Lim at Mari—OB Period. Texts were found in rooms 5, 52, 108, 110, 111, 115, and 215. *(Redrawn from J. Margueron,* Recherches sur les palais mésopotamiens de l'age du bronze. *Vol. 2. Bibliotéque Archéologique et Historique 107 [Paris: Paul Geuthner, 1982], fig. 147.)*

4. Secular Structures. a. Palaces. Buildings defined as palaces appear later in the Mesopotamian sequence than temples. There is a rather enigmatic building at the site of Jemdet Nasr itself, but the best preserved early palace is the "A palace" at Kish, dating to the second quarter of the 3d millennium. This is an elaborate residence, with separate areas grouped around different courtyards and connected to each other by narrow passageways. The whole is separated off from the community at large by a wall, through which there was only one point of access. The conglomerate character of palaces is best illustrated by the Old Babylonian palace at Mari which was destroyed in the 18th century B.C. (see Fig. ART. 05). Here the function of various areas—reception, residential, storage, manufacturing, recording, etc.—can tentatively be identified on the basis of textual and artifactual evidence. Palaces such as these, in which there were subunits grouped around different courtyards within the larger compound, were almost certainly the norm in Mesopotamia.

A thoroughly regular planned administrative structure can be seen in the rectangular palace at Tell Brak, in NE Syria (see Fig. ART. 06), which was built of mud bricks, some of which were stamped with the inscription of the Akkadian king Naram-Sin. This building, of which only the foundations survive, is undoubtedly the artifact of an imperial administration in an outlying region of the Akkadian Empire. No similar buildings are found in the more central territories of that empire but similarly planned structures with more specialized functions dating to the following Ur III period have been excavated near the ziggurat at Ur. One other building that has been called a palace, the Northern Palace at Tell Asmar, is also atypical in plan. But this structure, with its complex drainage system, has more recently been interpreted as a manufacturing center, probably used for tanning leather or fulling cloth (Delougaz, Hill, and Lloyd 1967: 196–98). It would appear that special-purpose buildings, many of which may indeed have been under royal aegis, had a variety of plans and should not be included under the rubric of "palace" because they lacked the residential function that is crucial in the definition of Mesopotamian palaces.

Assyrian palaces show the same general principle as Babylonian palaces—being organized into suites of rooms surrounding courts—but they have a much more standardized form. In essence there are two major courtyards, one which is the center of public functions and the other which belongs to the ruler's private residence. A group of rooms constituted the interface between these, among which was the long, narrow throne room, with side entrances and a dais at one end where the king held court (Turner 1972).

b. Fortifications and Defenses. Although some early sites, such as Tell es-Sawwan and Chogha Mami, had walls or other means of delimiting the perimeter of the community, the first really massive city walls date to the beginning of the 3d millennium B.C. While at places like Uruk it is relatively easy to trace the perimeter of the 3d-millennium city walls, the state of preservation of the mud brick is nowhere good enough to offer information on the technique of construction, or the details of their gateways.

The best-preserved walls and gateways that we have from the area come from the 1st millennium, particularly from Assyrian sites. At the late-8th-century Assyrian capital of Khorsabad the walls bore stone crenelation of a type that also appears to have been standard in Urartu. Each gateway was flanked by two towers, and attached sculptures, in this case winged bulls *(lamassu),* stood on either side of

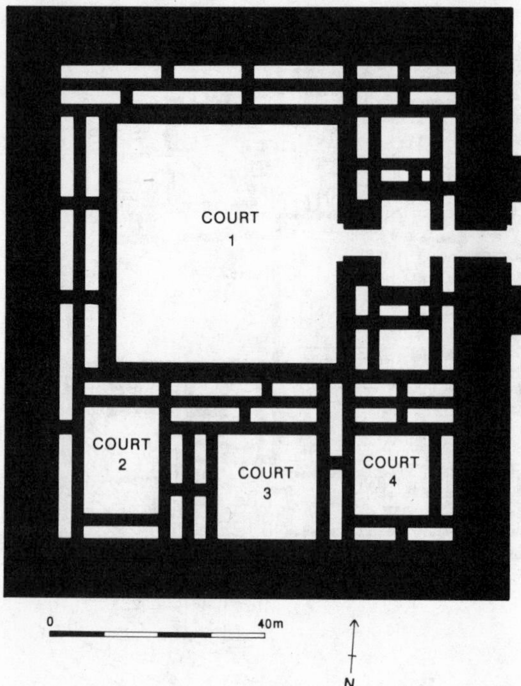

ART.06. Plan of palace of Naram-Sin at Tell Brak—Old Akkadian Period. *(Redrawn from* Iraq *9 [1947]: pl. LX.)*

each entrance. Assyrian reliefs also provide some information on what fortifications of the time must have looked like.

D. Anatolia

1. General Remarks. The architectural traditions of Anatolia are distinctly different from those of Mesopotamia despite cultural contact that manifests itself in religion, literary tradition, and other forms of art. Urbanism was not as pervasive in Bronze Age Asia Minor as in Mesopotamia, although there were interludes during which settlement mounds of 20 or more hectares were not uncommon, such as in the MB Age when Assyrian merchants brought literacy to the Anatolian Plateau for the first time. However, the creators of Anatolia's greatest civilization, the Hittites, lavished their efforts on one particular site, the imperial capital at Hattusha (modern Boğazköy), at the expense of other cities and even this, as recent excavations have shown, was more a city of temples than a dense concentration of inhabitants.

Anatolia is geographically quite diverse and relatively rich in natural resources and building materials by Near Eastern standards. Parts of it were heavily forested and suitable building stone was readily available in all areas. Although it is difficult to generalize about so extensive an area, which includes coastal regions, mountains, deserts, and a central plateau, precipitation is generally abundant and the extreme differences in temperatures between the hot, dry summers and the cold, damp, winters led to more rapid weathering of mud brick here than was the case S of the Taurus. Tectonic instability is felt to have been a major consideration in the development of a characteristic timber-reinforced stone and mud-brick wall building technique. Stone foundations are more or less the rule for walls in this area.

2. Domestic Architecture. Anatolia's character as a bridge between Europe and Asia and a mosaic of regionalism is manifest in the diversity of its domestic architecture. In W Anatolia, for example, an elongated rectilinear building plan with an antechamber and primary room at the rear aligned along a single axis is the most noteworthy and distinctive building plan of the 3d millennium. This "megaron" form was first identified in the earliest levels of Troy (see Fig. ART. 07), but is well documented at other W Anatolian sites such as Beycesultan, and appears also on the S coast of Asia Minor.

Another fundamentally Anatolian house type is more characteristic of, but by no means limited to, the Central Plateau and the period of Hittite domination in the 2d millennium. Its basic component is a unit of two rectangular rooms side by side, both of which face onto a courtyard that is delineated by a wall. There was generally a second story over the two rooms which was reached by a staircase from the court that led up to a balcony. Ground floors were apparently used for business activities and the second floor served for the basic living and sleeping areas. Complexes of these basic units, closely packed together and often with some modifications, can be seen at such sites as Kültepe and Boğazköy (Naumann 1971: 368–376).

Diversity rather than conformity to clearly defined types is most characteristic of Anatolian domestic architecture, however. Most houses seem to have reached their final configuration through agglutination of groups of rectangular or trapezoidal rooms. Although the use of interior courtyards is not unknown in Anatolia—in fact they are essential components in temples and palaces—they are

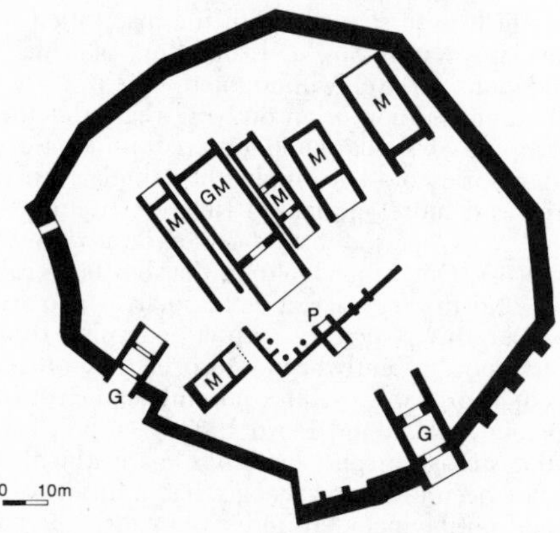

ART.07. Plan of citadel with Megara at Troy—Level IIc. *GM,* the great *megaron* (hall of state); *M, megara; G,* gates; *P,* propylon. *(Redrawn from C. W. Blegen,* Troy and the Trojans. *Ancient People and Places 32 [London: Thames and Hudson, 1963], 65, fig. 15.)*

rare in domestic architecture. Courtyards are more apt to lie beside or in front of freestanding houses, and in some cases there are rooms on two sides of a court. The idea of a house which enclosed open space with rooms on three or four sides, so fundamental in Mesopotamia, seems to have been foreign to the lands north of the Taurus (Naumann 1971: 381).

3. Sacred Architecture. The number of Hittite temples known has been dramatically increased through recent excavations on the upper city at Boğazköy. Until a decade ago the number stood at five, but it now exceeds thirty. While these vary somewhat in plan, they are all composed of the same basic elements: a gate; a staircase, probably to the roof rather than a second story; a large, nearly square courtyard; a porch opening on the courtyard and through which one had to pass to reach, albeit indirectly, the cella; one or more cellae in which there was a podium for the cult image; and a suite of rooms that could only be reached through the cella (Naumann 1971: 451–58). The largest of these temples and the only one extant in the lower city, the "Great Temple" at the foot of Büyükkale is surrounded by a massive complex of narrow storerooms, within several of which were found the temple archives (see Fig. ART. 08). Many of the features of these temples are also seen in the imperial buildings that limited access to the nearby open-air rock sanctuary of Yazilikaya. Unlike Hittite sculptural style and hieroglyphic writing which survived in modified form south of the Taurus in the Iron Age, the Hittite temple plan disappears with the collapse of the empire.

One other noteworthy Anatolian form is the Urartian *susi,* or tower temple. It had a regular ground plan with thick walls in the form of a square enclosing a single square room. The corners were strongly reinforced and the doorway was emphasized by niching that recalls similarly recessed cult sites that the Urartians carved on rock faces and used as places of worship. These give some idea of the towerlike dimensions of the *susi* and invalidate earlier attempts to reconstruct a much lower elevation for these buildings based on an Assyrian relief.

4. Secular Structures. a. Palaces. There is no definable "Anatolian" style of palace plan; virtually every building so identified is unique, and it is not always possible to be entirely confident in assigning functions to buildings, particularly in those cases where documentary evidence is lacking. For example, the group of *megara* that forms the core of the Troy II citadel is distinguished from ordinary houses by monumentality, but is this due to cultic or secular significance? Major buildings composed of suites of rectilinear rooms built around courtyards in an additive process at such sites as Beycesultan, Acemhüyük, and Kültepe are more confidently deemed to have served as residences of rulers and administrative centers. One would expect to find the grandest Anatolian palace on Büyükkale, the royal acropolis of the Hittite capital (see Fig. ART. 09), and what appears there is a unique complex of individual structures grouped around an ascending series of four courtyards rather than a single edifice (Bittel 1970: 63–90). The general arrangement of these was dictated by the topography of the eminence on which they were built, which was a natural fortress further isolated from the rest of the site by a fortification wall through which there were three gates. Like the courtyards of the temples, those of the palace complex were bordered by open pillared halls. Of the residential and administrative buildings coming off of these, one particularly noteworthy structure has foundations that appear to have supported a grid of 25 pillars to roof a 25 × 25 m audience hall. If this reconstruction is correct, it provides a clear antecedent for the pillared audience halls of Urartu and Achaemenid Persia.

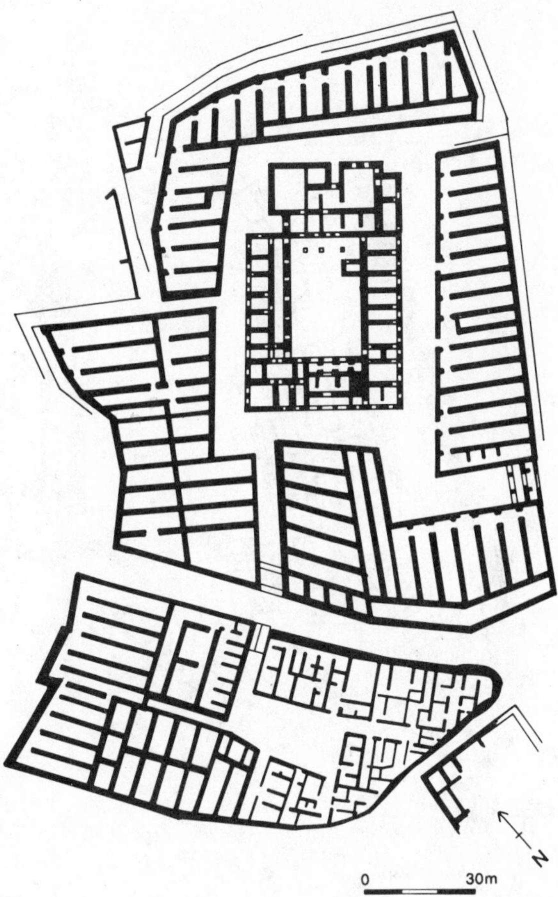

ART.08. Plan of Great Temple at Boğazköy—Lower City Level 2. *(Redrawn from K. Bittel,* Hattusha *[New York: Oxford University Press, 1970], 56, fig. 13.)*

That the palace/administrative architecture of Büyükkale is typical of the Hittite Empire is demonstrated by other sites on the Plateau. At Massat Hüyük the organizing feature is a again large courtyard bordered by pillars. At Alaca Hüyük a monumental gateway decorated with sculpted orthostats gives access to a small square out of which another, smaller gateway opens into a long, narrow court with porticoes on either side and a group of public buildings. Hittite texts make it clear that there were many such palaces in the Empire.

b. Fortifications and Defenses. Walled and fortified sites were characteristic of Anatolia from the Chalcolithic period on, to judge by the evidence of such sites at Hacilar

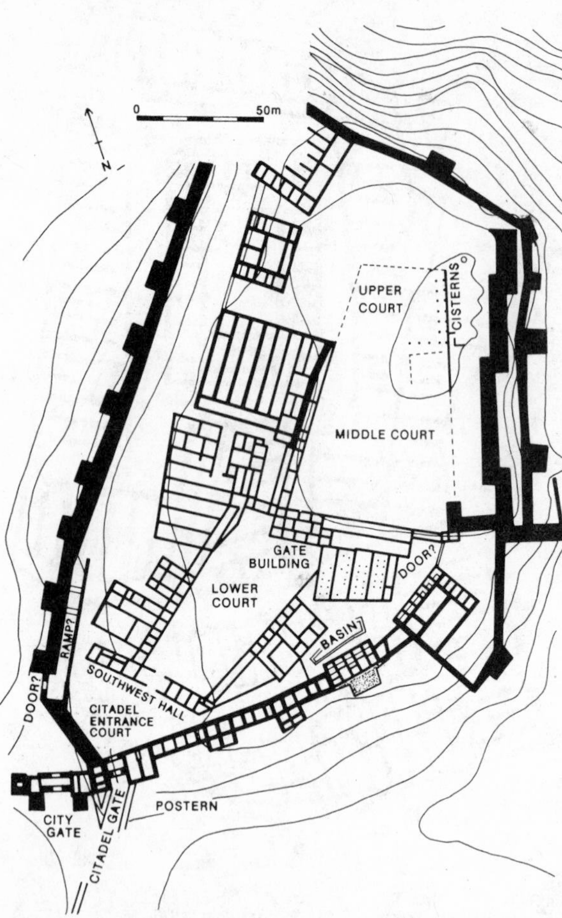

ART.09. Area plan of Royal Citadel (Büyükkale) at Boğazköy. *(Redrawn from K. Bittel,* Hattusha *[New York: Oxford University Press, 1970], 75, fig. 19.)*

and Mersin. Even at such modest villages as EB Age Demircihüyük there were clear arrangements made for defense, in this case a circular arrangement of houses facing inward with a stone and mud-brick wall forming the outer perimeter.

The 2d millennium saw the emergence of much stronger fortifications. Those of Troy VI, in which a substantial wall of drafted stones is buttressed and battered, are particularly noteworthy. The most elaborate fortifications, however, are to be seen at Hattusha, particularly in the great wall of the upper city. This enclosure is composed of a massive rampart, on top of which a casemate wall was constructed of cyclopean masonry. It was marked at regular intervals by towers and a smaller defensive wall ran in front of it to provide additional protection. The arched gateways, each flanked by relief sculpture, had two internal buttresses and towers on either side. Beneath the sphinx gate, the southernmost of the city, there was a 70-m-long underground passageway of cyclopean stonework to provide a more clandestine means of leaving the city.

The art of fortress building in Anatolia attained its highest level in the kingdom of Urartu, which from the 9th through the 7th centuries B.C. dominated the territory of what is now E Turkey, NW Iran, and the Armenian Soviet Republic. Urartian architecture is almost exclusively fortress architecture, and although some settlement areas have been excavated, these are almost all areas of elite housing associated with major citadels. Zernaki Tepe, a site at the NE end of Lake Van where there is evidence of a planned settlement of rectilinear houses laid out on a grid plan, remains something of an anomaly in the area. Although frequently cited as an example of Urartian building, it has produced little evidence of actual occupation and thus cannot be dated to the Urartian period with any confidence.

The favored sites for fortress construction in Urartu were on rock spurs overlooking plains in which intensive irrigation was practiced. Foundations for fortress walls were grounded on bedrock, with stone steps carved in the living rock to secure a solid footing. There is evidence that the Hittites pioneered this technique at Büyükkale and the hilltop structure at Gavurkale, but the Urartians used it much more regularly and extensively. The stone course of walls could be up to two meters high, but generally was more on the order of one meter, above which the walls were built in large, standardized mud brick. These walls stepped up and down sharply graded inclines and often rose to several stories in height, to judge by their thickness (in some cases five or six meters) and from contemporary drawings of fortresses on Urartian bronze belts, as well as a bronze model of a fortress facade found in excavations at Toprakkale.

5. Mortuary Architecture. Burial customs in Anatolia hardly merit treatment in a discussion of architecture before the Iron Age, although the imperial Hittite shrine of Yazilikaya should be mentioned in this context. In the 1st millennium, massive burial mounds are found associated with the three major kingdoms that dominated inland Asia Minor prior to its inclusion in the Persian Empire: Lydia, Phrygia, and Urartu. In the latter case these mounds appear to be an early form of elite burial that was later replaced by large burial chambers carved out of solid rock, the best preserved examples of which have been found in the cliff on which the citadel rock of Van is constructed. The Lydian and Phrygian mounds are much more numerous and prominent, and in each case they are grouped around the capital of the kingdom. None of the Lydian tombs has been found intact, although an ashlar burial chamber has been found in one of them, the "Tomb of Gyges." The tombs at Gordion, on the other hand, have been excavated with spectacular results. The largest of these, the so-called Midas tomb, contained a royal burial rich in grave-goods such as bronze cauldrons, numerous fibulae, and wooden furniture. The tomb itself was comprised of a conical mound of earth heaped up over a burial chamber that consisted of a log cabin protected by an additional outer log wall. In later burials, such as those at Midas City to the W, the Phrygians also carved out burial chambers with decorated facades in living rock.

E. Syria and Palestine

1. General Remarks. Although subject to the influence of Egypt, Anatolia, and Mesopotamia, the Levant developed a cultural tradition of its own, with distinctive architectural forms that are not paralleled in any of the surrounding areas. It is precisely these that have been of particular interest to biblical scholarship.

The climate of the Levant is more moderate than Anatolia, with its temperature extremes, or Mesopotamia, with its aridity. Building materials are more abundant than in Mesopotamia, but less so than in Anatolia. The basic material used for walls was again mud brick—usually, but not invariably, with stone socles. The Amanus and Lebanon ranges were celebrated for their timber in antiquity, but this resource does not seem to have been a major factor in the architectural record of the Levant.

2. Domestic Architecture. There appears to have been a certain amount of continuity in domestic architecture in the transition to urban life, at least insofar as the individual, broad-roomed house remained the most common form. See also CITIES (LEVANT). This form loses its predominance at the end of the EB Age, and in the second major urban period, the MB Age, private houses tend to be of a more elaborate, multiroomed type. There appears to be a great deal of diversity in the region, however, with numerous examples of both Mesopotamian courtyard houses and houses, perhaps of Egyptian inspiration, in which crosswalls divide the building into sections that are then subdivided into square rooms. A residential district at MB Halawa, on the Euphrates, displays nearly a score of houses of similar plan coming off of narrow streets and alleys laid out in a not quite perpendicular grid. In each case the single entrance from the street enters a courtyard, off of which there are two or three rooms. At Tell el-Ajjul, near Gaza, one sees neighborhoods in which much less planning is in evidence and wealthy houses are scattered among those that appear to be considerably smaller and more impoverished.

In the early part of the Iron Age, a distinctive building known as the "four room" house emerged, and because of the temporal coincidence, has been termed the "Israelite" house. See also HOUSE, ISRAELITE. The basic elements are a rectangular ground plan entered on one of the short sides, the division of the front part of the building into three sections by walls or columns running parallel to the long walls, and a broad room at the back of the building. This type of building is an autonomous development in the S Levant with antecedents in the Bronze Age. The designation "Israelite" is accurate only insofar as many Israelites lived in them—the same form is also found in Philistine settlements.

3. Sacred Architecture. The most famous building of the ANE, Solomon's temple in Jerusalem, is known only through literary testimony (1 Kings 5–6; 2 Chronicles 2–3; Ezekiel 41). It is described as a long building with two columns at its entrance, a vestibule *(ʾûlām)*, a cella *(hêkāl)* in the rear of which was another division, the *dĕbîr*—the holiest part of the sanctuary. Around three sides of the building was a three-story annex *(yāṣûaʿ)* containing storerooms. Busink's (1970) admirable and thorough study of both the philological evidence and archaeological comparanda for the reconstruction of this building has, however, failed to produce a consensus on many of its key features. See also TEMPLE, JERUSALEM.

One of the reasons for this uncertainty is that there are so many paradigms of sacred architecture in the Levant to chose from. Here, as elsewhere, temples originally seem to have developed out of domestic architecture, not surprisingly since they were conceived as residences for deities. In the Chalcolithic, for example, there is a celebrated example at Ein Gedi, where the basic form of the main structure is simply a large broad-roomed house with a platform against its rear wall. That this was a very special building, however, is made clear from its dominant position in a precinct that is walled off from the rest of the site and can be entered only through a monumental gateway. Even in the 3d millennium, however, there are other temple forms in existence, such as the twin porch temples of Megiddo and the Acropolis temple of Ai, with its annex and row of columns running along the long axis of the central room. In the 2d millennium, even more diversity is evident in the major urban sites. Ugarit has two major temples, the ground plans of both showing two more or less square adjoining units, the smaller being the entranceway and the latter the cella. At Shechem, Kamid el-Loz, and Megiddo one sees tower temples, where heavy reinforcement on either side of the entrance to the single-room cella must have created an impressive entranceway. There are square temples, such as the one excavated at the Amman Airport; temples based on the four-room house plan, e.g., at Tell el Far'ah; and the Fosse Temples of Lachish, in which the main room is distinguished by four columns in a square arrangement. In LB Hazor at least three different temple types appear to have been functioning at the same time.

One particular type of N Syrian temple form does show a coherent strain of stylistic evolution for over a millennium, beginning in the MB Age. The earliest known example is at Ebla, but it also appears at Alalakh, Hama, and, most spectacularly, ʿAin Dara. It is essentially a long, freestanding building of tripartite form, which has its entrance through an open porch, often between two columns, on one of the short sides. There is an intervening court, and then a main chamber, at the rear of which is a raised area. In some cases, a raised ambulatory runs along one, two, or three of the sides of the building.

Despite the diversity of Levantine sacred buildings, however, one would not be likely to confuse any of them with Anatolian or Mesopotamian temples, and one may hazard a few generalizations about their character. By and large, Syro-Palestinian temples are smaller than others in the Near East and they are more apt to be freestanding buildings with a direct-axis approach to the altar. They are more apt to be designed to create an impression from the outside, rather than emphasize interior space and obstruct their appearance confused by annexed rooms and storehouses.

4. Secular Structures. a. Palaces. The most clearly defined early palaces in the Levant are found in Syria—at Ebla, Alalakh, and Ugarit. The S Levant, where textual evidence is meager and palaces are normally defined as residential structures distinguished by larger-than-normal size, has nothing to match those sites in the 3d and 2d millennia. Palace G at Ebla, in which the royal archives were discovered, is only partially preserved around two sides of a large, unroofed courtyard (see Fig. ART. 10). At the N end of this there is a podium and, in the corner nearby, a staircase and guard chamber. On the E a ceremonial staircase of a quite different order ascends from the courtyard and not far from it, an unprepossessing annex of thin mud-brick walls projected from the same facade. Around its interior were the shelves on which the tablets of the archive were stored. Behind the massive walls that ringed the courtyard were other administrative rooms of the palace. Unfortunately, it is difficult to make much sense of this partial plan. The excavators have argued that it was not an internal courtyard, but rather an external one, but if so, it is unique. A second major palace at Ebla, dating to the MB Age and as yet incompletely published, included an almost "industrial" workshop where rows of grinding stones indicate that production was highly organized. A group of princely tombs were hollowed out beneath the floors of this palace, in keeping with a general Near Eastern tradition of royal burials in palaces, best known in Mesopotamia.

The palace at Ugarit is also a major monument of Levantine royal architecture, and displays many of the same characteristics that we have noted in palaces elsewhere: it is a composite structure of more than 90 rooms built around a multiplicity of courtyards, put together in a way suggestive of frequent additions, modifications, and expansions made to the original edifice. Unlike the palace at Mari, there was more than one entrance to this complex, but only the one on the W side had any monumentality and, to judge by tablet finds in the vicinity, it was through this that the public and administrative business of the palace passed.

A characteristic N Syrian architectural form that also has a relationship to palaces is the so-called *bīt hilani*, although the archaeological referent of this Assyrian term is not securely established. The edifice generally associated with this term in archaeological parlance is a broad room with an opening to a portico which was often flanked by subordinate rooms. The best preserved examples are found in 1st-millennium sites S of the Taurus, such as Zincirli, Carchemish, and Tell Halaf, although the 15th-century palace at Alalakh also contains this element and it has been argued that the *bīt hilani* was originally an Hittite innovation.

b. Fortifications, Gateways, and Defenses. As in other parts of the Near East, the first consistent tradition of city wall building belongs to the early part of the 3d millennium. At EB II Arad there is a stone wall built at ground level, punctuated with semicircular tower bastions (see Fig. CIT. 02). The Ebla texts speak of various city gates so it would appear that site was also walled, presumably around the edge of the natural mesa on which the site is built, where in fact the walls of the MB city have been excavated

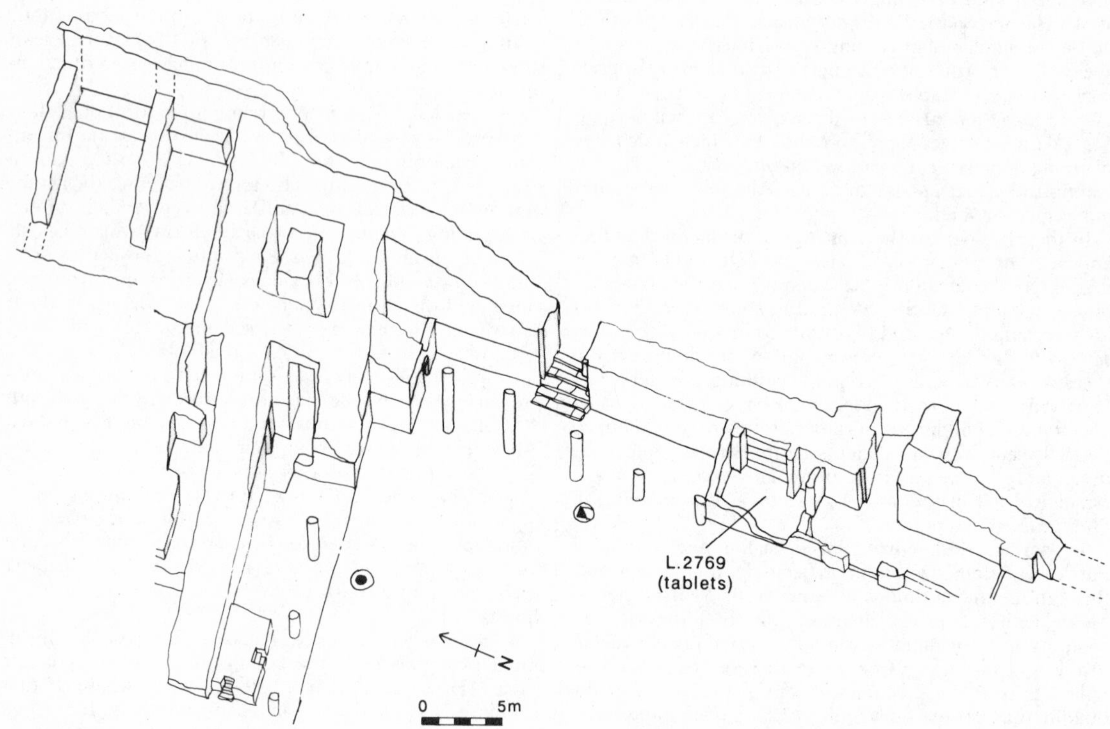

ART.10. Isometric plan of Palace G at Ebla (Tell Mardikh)—Level IIB1. Tablets and remains of shelving were found in the room L.2769 to the right. *(Redrawn from H. Weiss [ed.],* Ebla to Damascus *[Washington, DC: Smithsonian, 1985], 136, fig. 36.)*

and one major gateway dating to that period has been uncovered which is in a good state of preservation.

In the early 2d millennium, changes in the technology of warfare demanded much more solid fortification walls than had been customary in the previous era. Earthen ramparts were used to raise the level of the wall's foundation and presumably make it more difficult for a battering ram or siege engine to approach. Middle Bronze fortifications were stout enough that they continued to be used at many sites until the end of the Bronze Age, centuries after their original construction.

The last major innovation in wall construction was the introduction of casemate walls in the Iron Age. Although casemate walls were not as strong as solid constructions, they presented an impression of mass and solidity that was perhaps as important as real strength in an age in which royal propaganda appears to have been an international passion.

Gateways show an evolution toward increasing complexity from the 3d through the 1st millennium B.C. Initially consisting of simply reinforced towers or buttresses on either side of the entrance, they developed a multichambered form at the beginning of the 2d millennium. This gatehouse form persisted into the Iron Age, although it was further elaborated into the "Solomonic Gate" with four, rather than three, portals. The Levantine tradition of the S did not include sculptural decoration of these gateways, although the early example from MB Ebla does make use of ashlar masonry. In northern Syria, the Hittite tradition of reliefs on orthostats was maintained in Iron Age principalities.

c. Other Public Buildings. It is probable that much of the administrative activity of sites of the ancient Levant was in fact conducted in ordinary residential buildings which give no architectural manifestations of this additional function, except perhaps size. One distinctive form of a planned public building is quite conspicuous at most major sites in the S during the Iron Age, however, and has parallels in Urartian sites of the same era. The essence of the ground plan is a large rectangular building with two parallel rows of columns flanking its long axis. The floors between the columns and the walls were paved, but the central corridor was not. Sometimes groups of these structures were placed next to each other, sharing long walls. The function of these buildings has long been a matter of controversy; when first discovered at Megiddo they were identified as royal stables and many still hold to this view, but it has also been argued that they are storehouses, or possibly even markets (Herr 1988). See also STABLE, STABLES.

F. The Legacy of ANE Architecture

It would be hard to make a case for any strong persistence of ANE architectural traditions in the modern world. Mud brick, whose characteristics so conditioned ancient monumental building in the area, is not much favored today, except in rural vernacular architecture. While many of the architectural forms have continued directly up to the present, particularly at the level of domestic architecture (e.g., the courtyard house) on the more monumental level one must look only for indirect influences. Long after the megaron form was first attested in Anatolia it became a hallmark of Mycenaean architecture and its plan is mimicked within the peristyle of the Greek temple. Some Hittite influence is seen in Urartu, and Urartu's influence, such as it was, is apparent in the architecture of Achaemenid Persia. But generally, monumental building traditions of the ANE died out as they were modified and transformed during the Persian, Hellenistic, and Parthian eras, the periods in which Mesopotamian civilization itself faded and eventually died.

Bibliography

Aurenche, O. 1981. *La maison orientale: l'architecture du Proche Orient ancien des origines au milieu du IVe millénaire.* Bibliothéque Archéologique et Historique 109. 3 vols. Paris.

Bar-Yosef, O. 1986. The Walls of Jericho: An Alternative Interpretation. *Current Anthropology* 27: 157–62.

Bittel, K. 1970. *Hattusha: The Capital of the Hittites.* New York.

Braemer, F. 1982. *L'architecture domestique du Levant à l'âge du Fer.* Éditions Recherche sur les civilizations 8. Paris.

Busink, T. 1970. *Der Tempel von Jerusalem I.* Leiden.

Crawford, H. 1977. *The Architecture of Iraq in the Third Millennium B.C.* Mesopotamia 5. Copenhagen.

Delougaz, P. 1940. *The Temple Oval at Khafajah.* OIP 53. Chicago.

Delougaz, P., and Lloyd, S. 1942. *Pre-Sargonid Temples in the Diyala Region.* OIP 58. Chicago.

Delougaz, P.; Hill, H.; and Lloyd, S. 1967. *Private Houses and Graves in the Diyala Region.* OIP 88. Chicago.

Frankfort, H. 1970. *The Art and Architecture of the Ancient Orient.* Harmondsworth.

Herr, L. 1988. Tripartite Pillared Buildings, and the Market Place in Iron Age Palestine. *BASOR* 272: 47–67.

Kubba, S. A. A. 1987. *Mesopotamian Architecture and Town Planning from the Mesolithic to the End of the Proto-historic Period c. 10,000–3,500 B.C.* 2 vols. BAR International Series 367. Oxford.

Leick, G. 1988. *A Dictionary of Ancient Near Eastern Architecture.* London.

Lenzen, H. 1941. *Die Entwicklung der Zikkurat von ihren Anfängen bis zur Zeit der III Dynastie von Ur.* Leipzig.

———. 1955. Mesopotamische Tempelanlagen von der Frühzeit zum zweiten Jahrtausend. *Zeitschrift für Assyriologie* 17: 1–36.

Margueron, J. 1982. *Recherches sur les palais Mésopotamiens de l'age du bronze.* Bibliothéque Archéologique et Historique 107. 2 vols. Paris.

Naumann, R. 1971. *Architectur Kleinasiens von ihren Anfängen bis zum Ende der hethitischen Zeit.* 2d ed. Tübingen.

Roaf, M. 1984. Ubaid Houses and Temples. *Sumer* 43: 80–90.

Shiloh, Y. 1987. The Casemate Wall, the Four Room House, and Early Planning in the Israelite City. *BASOR* 268: 3–15.

Stager, L. 1985. The Archaeology of the Family in Ancient Israel. *BASOR* 260: 1–35.

Turner, G. 1972. The State Apartments of Late Assyrian Palaces. *Iraq* 32: 177–213.

Wright, G. 1985. *Ancient Building in South Syria and Palestine.* 2 vols. Handbuch der Orientalistik 1/2/B/3. Leiden.

PAUL ZIMANSKY

MESOPOTAMIAN ART AND ARCHITECTURE

The art and architecture of ancient Mesopotamia (now Iraq) have their foundations in the fertile area between the Tigris and Euphrates rivers, Mesopotamian art began in the late 4th millennium B.C., during the Uruk and Jemdet

Nasr periods; developed in the 3d millennium under the Sumerians and Akkadians; and flourished in the 2d and 1st millennia under the Babylonians, Mitannians, Kassites, and Assyrians. A well-defined architecture, although in the beginning very simple, evolved into elaborately planned temple sanctuaries and secular edifices. Artistic creativeness was expressed in a long tradition of sculpture and relief carving. Wall paintings were utilized during the historical periods, and their subjects range from figural compositions to ornamental bands of animal, floral, and patterned motifs. The chief vehicle of pictorial art is the cylinder seal, whose entire surface was covered with carvings (known as glyptic), so that when it is impressed in a soft clay, the design in reverse appears in relief and can be endlessly reproduced by rolling.

A. Protohistoric and Early Dynastic Periods (ca. 3500–2334 B.C.)

1. Architecture. The earliest monumental buildings consist of temples and sanctuaries. Temples were constructed on an elongated, rectangular plan. The nucleus of the layout is a T-shaped room. On each of the two sides of the long room were smaller ones, and on one short side was the cult room, flanked on each side by a smaller room. The entrance to the temple was on one of the long sides, termed the bent-axis approach. The outside walls of the building were decorated with niches in three steps. The cycle of collapse and rebuilding, of many centuries, brought about the raised site of the temple, above the level of its surroundings (Moortgat 1969: 1–2).

A characteristic feature of the buildings was the use of sun-dried mud brick, reed, and wood. Structures were occasionally strengthened with limestone facing. Another method was the use of baked nail-shaped clay cones set into a clay bed. The cones were generally painted in red, blue, black, or white, which resulted in mosaic designs resembling textile patterns. In the Eanna sanctuary at Uruk was a large cone-mosaic court that included a pillared terrace covered with mosaic (see Fig. ART. 11). A small temple in the same sanctuary had the walls of the open court entirely decorated with mosaic (Frankfort 1970: 24–25; Moortgat 1969: 3; Strommenger 1964: 378–82).

After 3000 B.C., a fundamental change in religious architecture occurred. The sacred structure, containing a gate room with stairs, one or more shrines, workrooms, and living quarters, was conceived as a unity. All the rooms were grouped around a central courtyard, and a protective wall surrounded the sanctuary. Sanctuaries of the type with the central courtyard, known as the House Plan temple, have been excavated in the Diyala region, at Khafaje, Tell Agrab, and Tell Asmar. Closely associated with temples was the ziggurat. It was a tower of one or more receding stages, more or less square, and at the top was a shrine. A ramp or flight of stairs led to the upper levels. Evidence for ziggurats in the Early Dynastic period occur at Kish, Nippur, Ur, and Uruk. The palacelike complex at Kish was an imposing residential and administrative center. The main building forms an oblong rectangle and a flight of stairs led to the monumental entrance, flanked by towers. The central area is a large square courtyard, with many rooms arranged along the four sides. The walls were white-plastered and fragments of inlaid friezes, showing walking sheep, men and women performing daily activities, and processions of chained prisoners, were found near the monumental entrance (Crawford 1977: 24; Moortgat 1969: 20–25; Strommenger 1964: 398).

2. Sculpture and Relief. Sculptured figures in the round in Mesopotamia before 3000 B.C. consist of idol-like figurines molded from clay. Male and female statuettes of later date are carved from alabaster and gypsum and molded. The statuettes are fixed onto bases and show distinctive anatomical and facial features. Statuettes of males are bearded, with or without long hair, or beardless and bald, and their wrap-around skirts with tufts reach below the knees (see Fig. ART. 12). Those of females show a variety of hairstyles and headdresses, and their long garments cover one or both shoulders. All the figures are posed frontally, their bare feet kept slightly apart, and their hands clasped at the waist. Many statuettes are worshipper types, both standing and seated, each placed in the temple as a substitute for the worshipper himself. Statuettes are sometimes embellished with inlay eyes of shell and black limestone, and hair and beard blackened with bitumen (Frankfort 1970: 45–59; Moortgat 1969: 33–35, 37–41; Strommenger 1964: 394).

Reliefs were employed to decorate cult vessels formed as bowls, libation jars, and tall cylinder-shaped containers. On the stone objects the reliefs vary from flat to high, to the extent of parts being in the round. Their subjects include domestic animals (ox and sheep), beasts of prey (lion and eagle), and mythical scenes. Two alabaster vessels, both from Uruk, have the outside surfaces decorated with extensive friezes. One object, shaped like a trough, shows a herd of sheep around a reed hut. The other object, a tall container, has rows of friezes on which a long parade of figures offering sacrifices, a herd of sheep, and produce of the fields are depicted. The stele, an upright stone block with narrow sides and rounded top, was decorated in relief with pictorial scenes and in later times had carved inscriptions. A basalt fragment of the Protohistoric period depicts two episodes of a king fighting a lion. The historical stele is exemplified by the limestone slab belonging to Eannatum (ca. 2600 B.C.), a ruler of Lagash, ancient Girsu. All four sides are covered with narrative scenes commemorating a military victory, and a detailed inscription fills the

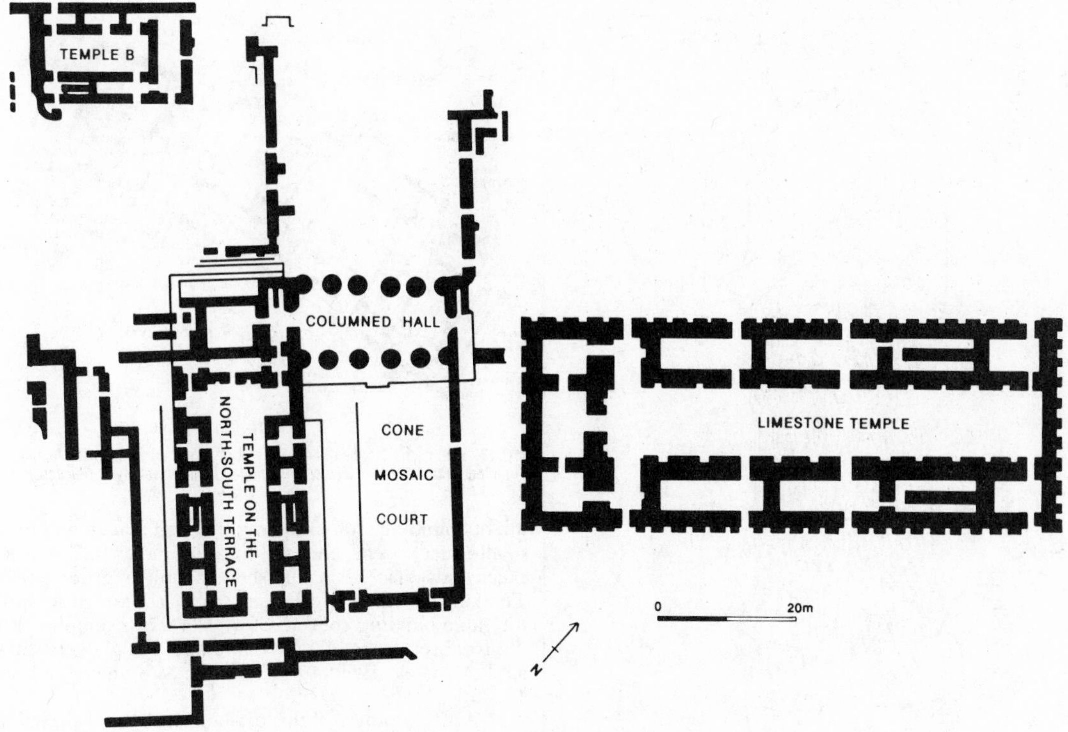

ART.11. Plan of Eanna Temple at Uruk—Level V/IV. *(Redrawn from Strommenger and Hirmer 1964: 379, fig. 4.)*

open spaces between the pictures. Votive plaques of stone with a perforated center, square in shape, have relief decorations divided into several registers. Themes include the ritual banquet, ritual scenes with gods seated on thrones, wrestling, and animal battles. Stone maces decorated with relief also served as votive objects (Frankfort 1970: 24–31, 67–73; Moortgat 1969: 41–44; Strommenger 1964: 396).

3. Decorative Art and Seal Design. Decorative art objects of the Early Dynastic period were made from precious metal, wood, and stone. A fine example is the engraved silver vessel from Tello. Two pictorial friezes encircle the vessel: cattle lying down, and lion-headed eagles (Imduguds) hovering above grasping lions and goats. A large relief of sheet copper from Tell ʿUbaid, almost a sculpture in the round, again depicts the lion-headed bird Imdugud, this time grasping a stag in each claw. The panel was nailed over a wooden core and set up on the facade of a temple. Exquisite examples of the goldsmiths' work were discovered in the Royal Cemetery at Ur (ca. 2650 B.C.). Objects include fluted beakers, bowls and cops, a helmet of beaten gold in the shape of a hairstyle with added perforated ears, a dagger whose blade and sheath are of gold, and its hilt of lapis lazuli studded with golden nails. There are also statues of a ram by a flowering shrub, the famous "Standard of Ur" with narrative scenes on both sides, lyres and chests, all of which are adorned with red stone, blue lapis lazuli, gold leaf, and white shell inlay over a wooden core (Frankfort 1970: 60–66, 71–75; Moortgat 1969: 41–42; Strommenger 1964: 397–99).

Early cylinder seals are cut from limestone, darker stones, lapis lazuli, rock crystal, and talc (steatite). Designs on seals and sealings (impressions on clay) depict recurrent themes: rows of animals, a bearded man in a variety of roles, boating scenes, activities connected with the production of manufactured goods, and patterns based on the rosette, circle, lozenge, and chevron. Contest scenes have elaborate compositions and among the contestants are a lion, bull, human-headed bull, and naked human figure. In banquet scenes participants drink from a large vessel through drinking tubes, or from cups. Frequently, musicians and servants accompany the banquet (Collon 1987: 14–31; Frankfort 1970: 35–37, 77–82). See also SEALS, MESOPOTAMIAN.

B. Dynasty of Akkad and the Neo-Sumerian Period (ca. 2334–2000 B.C.)

1. Architecture. A new development in temple building was the arrangement on one axis of a succession of courts and rooms leading to the main chamber, which contained the niche for the image of the deity. Examples of this method of building are the Ningal temple and the Enki

ART.12. Drawing of an alabaster statuette of a man from the Nintu Temple at Khafaje.

temple, both at Ur. The Gimilsin (Shu-Sin) Temple at Tell Asmar, ancient Eshnunna, is a square building with a similar ground plan (see Fig. ART. 13). The outside is decorated with flat buttresses, but the entrance is emphasized by two towers ornamented with stepped recesses. The best preserved ziggurat is that of the moon god Nanna at Ur. The four corners are oriented to the four points of the compass, and the casing of baked bricks is arranged in niches and flat buttresses. A central and two side staircases lead to the first level, where a gatehouse was built. The central stair continued to the highest platform, on which the actual temple was built. The temple tower of Innin (Inanna) at Uruk was simpler, and the outside walls were provided with flat buttresses. The ziggurat is constructed of brickwork, and layers of reed matting and reed straw are built into the structure at regular intervals. In addition, horizontal channels in which are thick reed ropes probably served to anchor the outside walls against the pressure of the weight of the bricks from inside (Frankfort 1970: 104–9; Moortgat 1969: 45, 56–59; Strommenger 1964: 406–9).

The palace became of greater importance than it had been in Early Dynastic times. The so-called Akkadian Palace at Tell Asmar is an enlarged dwelling house. The palace at Tell Brak discloses a new formal concept. It was a mighty building, 100 m square, that had a main and three small court systems enclosed by a perimeter wall. The so-called old palace at Ashur shows a similar ground plan. The kings of the Third Dynasty of Ur continued to apply the same building concept of a palace, as exemplified by the royal residence of Ur-Nammu and Shulgi (2112–2047 B.C.) (Moortgat 1969: 45–47, 59–60; Strommenger 1964: 402–3).

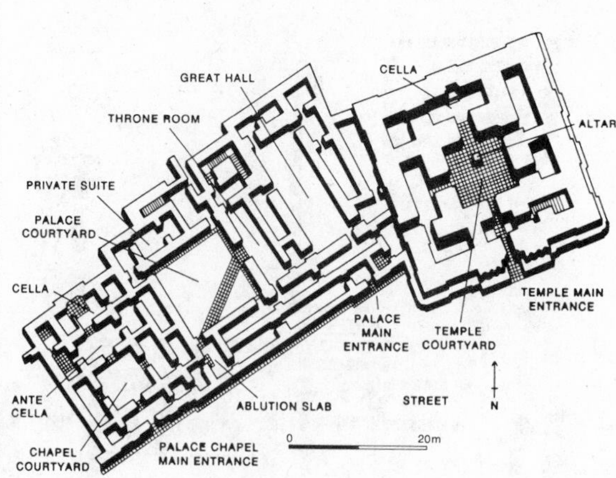

ART.13. Plan of the Temple of Shu-Sin and Governor's Palace at Tell Asmar—Ur III period. *(Courtesy of The Oriental Institute of The University of Chicago.)*

2. Art. Sculptures of this period, which show a relationship to the previous ED, have plastic form and gain in calm monumentality. Modeling is more detailed, limbs have more organic proportion than before, and individual differences are prominent. Considerable life-size diorite statues seem to have been made of several rulers; unfortunately, no excavated statue is preserved entire. There are torsos of life-size statues of the Akkadian ruler Manishtusu (2269–2255 B.C.); numerous statues of Gudea (ca. 2200 B.C.), a local ruler of Lagash; and fragmentary statues and statuettes of other kings and women. Portrait heads are often strikingly naturalistic (see Fig. ART. 14), and features are symmetrically placed and reflect a canon of proportion (Frankfort 1970: 84–86, 93–97; Moortgat 1969: 48–51, 62–65).

A fragment of a victory stele of Sargon of Akkad (2334–2279 B.C.) contains the portrait of the king, accompanied by a servant with a sunshade. Fragments of other stelae bearing reliefs depict battle scenes arranged in registers. The celebrated stele of Naram-Sin (2254–2218 B.C.) was erected in Sippar. The scene on the stone monument is a dynamic composition in which the Akkadian king, considerably larger than his companions, places his left foot on the bodies of two fallen enemies (see Fig. ART. 15). Votive stelae and stone plaques from Tello generally show scenes related to religious ceremonies. The great stele of Ur-Nammu has as its subject matter the cult functions of the ruler as temple builder and builder of canals (Frankfort 1970: 86–87, 102; Moortgat 1969: 47–49, 51–52, 65–68; Strommenger 1964: 404–6).

Akkadian cylinder seals are cut in deeper relief, the compositions are better balanced, and the style acquires a

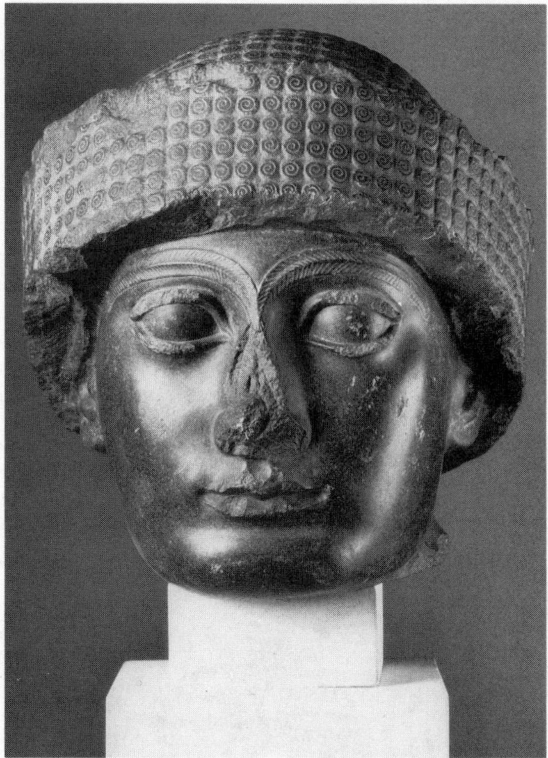

ART.14. Polished diorite head—Gudean Period (2290–2255 B.C.). *(Courtesy of the Musée du Louvre, Paris [copyright Réunion des Musées Nationaux].)*

new dynamism. Contest scenes were generally reduced to two pairs of equally matched opponents. In Akkadian times the banquet scene was often replaced by presentation scenes before a deity. The sun god was the most popular, and other popular deities were the water god, vegetation gods and goddesses, and a snake god. Seals of the post-Akkad period depict birds, boats, or two figures on either side of a tree. Presentation scenes become more standardized and there are few variations: a worshipper is led by a goddess before a seated deity, and an inscription is almost always added (Collon 1987: 32–39; Frankfort 1970: 89–91).

C. Dynasties of Isin/Larsa, Babylon, Mitanni, and Kassite (ca. 2000–1150 B.C.)

1. Architecture. Religious sanctuaries excavated so far, both large and small, disclose distinctive ground plans, and architectural decorations are occasionally added. Foundation walls of the main sanctuary at Ashur, dated to the reign of Shamshi-Adad I (1813–1781 B.C.), show that the building was composed of a central courtyard complex and several forecourts laid out at different levels. The Ishtar-Kititum building at Ishchali, ancient Neribtum (ca. 1800 B.C.), was a vast complex joining three temples in a large rectangle. The actual Kititum temple follows the one-axis arrangement of courts and rooms. The small Mitanni temple at Tell Brak (ca. 1600 B.C.), nearly square

ART.15. Victory stele of Naram-Sin, king of Akkad, from Susa. *(Courtesy of the Musée du Louvre, Paris [copyright Réunion des Musées Nationaux].)*

in plan, has the facade decorated with inset panels of three engaged half-columns. The entrance leads into a wide chamber, with a shallow niche almost opposite the door. The niche is flanked by half-columns, and from it a stepped dais projects into the chamber. The great Karana temple at Tell al-Rimah was entirely symmetrical in plan and attached to a rectangular ziggurat on one side (ca. 1600–1350 B.C.). The building was constructed with an elaborate architectural decoration of multiformed half-columns and pilasters surrounding the courtyard and the facade of one large chamber. Associated with the door of this chamber are stone orthostats with reliefs of divine figures and hybrid creatures. A modest temple of the Kassite king Karaindash (1445–1427 B.C.) was built at Uruk and dedicated to the goddess Inanna. The building is rectangular and freestanding, its entrance is situated on the main axis, and at the corners are bastions. Entirely new, the outer wall has recesses made out of molded bricks, in which male and female deities who stand and hold vases with water streams flowing from them are depicted. The molded reliefs form the oldest examples of Kassite architectural sculptures (Frankfort 1970: 107–9, 127–29; Moortgat 1969: 76–78, 93–98, 106–8, 116–18; Oates 1967: 78–80, 88–90; 1987: 181–87; Strommenger 1964: 416–17, 423–24, 434–35).

2. Sculpture and Painting. The few examples of stone sculpture in the round that survive are fragmentary, and the finest one is the expressive head of a king (ca. 1750 B.C.). Stone vases in the form of animals retain a precise, decorative style. Among the known small bronze statuettes of the Old Babylonian period are two from Ishchali. One is of a god stepping with the left foot on a couchant lamb, and the other is of a goddess seated on a simple stool. Both deities have four faces (Frankfort 1970: 110–19; Moortgat 1969: 88–89; Strommenger 1964: 420, 422).

Stone reliefs are represented by a number of fragments, which show military battles and the representation of a king beside an inscription. At the top of the stele on which Hammurabi's legal code is inscribed (ca. 1760 B.C.), the king stands alone before the throne of the sun god. The scene is worked in rounded relief. An important type of monument of the Kassite period is the so-called *kudurru* (or "boundary stone"), which recorded a grant of land and was shaped like a stele. Its subject matter consists mainly of symbolic emblems of deities (see Fig. ART. 16). The character of the divine symbols is an iconographic picture-language, with the symbols arranged in friezes, one above the other, from the astral gods to the chthonic powers. Reliefs on the front sides of two stone pedestals, supports for divine emblems, are fine examples of Middle Assyrian art (ca. 1240 B.C.). One work illustrates the king as worshipper, once standing and again kneeling, and the other illustrates the king standing between two hero figures who grasp tall wheel-topped standards. Small terra-cotta plaques, showing reliefs pressed from molds, were especially popular in the Old Babylonian period. A majority of the plaques represent deities, and other subjects include mythical scenes, scenes of family life, and individual figures of musicians, craftsmen, and animals (Frankfort 1970: 119–23, 129–30, 131–35; Moortgat 1969: 85–86, 100–3; Oates 1979: 99–101).

Evidence for wall paintings is rare. Impressive wall paintings found at Mari include the so-called Investiture of Zimri-Lim (ca. 1780 B.C.). Those from the palace at Nuzi (ca. 1400–1350 B.C.) are preserved only in small fragments. The designs consist of horizontal and vertical bands and metopes decorated with palmette trees, human and bulls' heads, and geometric patterns. The paintings are in red, pink, white, black, and gray on plaster. A Kassite palace built at Aqar Quf, ancient Dur Kurigalzu, was decorated with wall paintings showing geometric themes, floral patterns, and processions of men in white garments, dark hair, and red faces and arms against the gray walls. A few fragments of wall paintings from the MA palace at Kar-Tukulti-Ninurta (ca. 1240 B.C.) had pictorial motifs placed in metopelike panels and framed by ornamental bands (Frankfort 1970: 132, 135–37; Moortgat 1969: 99–100, 118–19; Oates 1979: 62–63; Strommenger 1964: 421).

ART.16. *Kudurru,* land grant boundary stone in white limestone, dating from the reign of Nebuchadnezzar I, ca. 1125–1104 B.C.E. *(Reproduced by Courtesy of the Trustees of the British Museum.)*

3. Seal Design. The business archives (inscribed clay tablets) of the merchants of Ashur (ca. 1920–1800 B.C.), who had a trading colony just outside Kültepe in Anatolia, were sealed with cylinder seals of Assyrian and foreign manufacture. The seals of Ashur are based on previous styles, but the execution is often crude. Figures are flat and linear, or elongated. Isin/Larsa seals are often made from heametite, a hard iron oxide. Presentation scenes continue from earlier periods, but filling motifs are now added in the spaces surrounding the figures. The worshipper stands with his hands clasped and almost invariably faces the seated deified king. Scenes of later date depict only standing figures, which consist of the king with a mace, a suppliant goddess, or the warrior goddess. About 1600 B.C. sintered quartz, also known as faience, frit, or paste, appeared as a new material for seals. It was easy to cut, could be fired or glazed, and was mass-produced. Subjects include horned animals, stylized human figures, decorative bands of net patterns, and linked chevron trees, center-dot circles, stars, and guilloches. Kassite seals were made of hard stones, such as chalcedony, and the designs reflect their dependence on Mesopotamian traditions. Most of the seals have prominent inscriptions, leaving little space for the designs. Seals of the MA period (ca. 1350–1150 B.C.) reflect a new, vital, and original style. Popular themes are winged griffin-demons holding up their prey by the legs, an animal striding toward a tree, and fights between animals (Collon 1987: 41–47, 58–59, 65–69; Frankfort 1970: 140–42).

D. Late Assyrian Period (ca. 1150–612 B.C.)

1. Architecture. Major evidence for Assyrian architecture comes from four cities: Ashur, Kalhu (Nimrud), Dur-Sharrukin (Khorsabad), and Nineveh. The main plan of the Assyrian temple is a long room, with or without an anteroom, that leads to a small cult room on a low platform, reached by a flight of stairs. The double temple at Ashur was dedicated to the gods Anu and Adad (ca. 1120 B.C.). The temple proper consists of two long chambers with deep cult niches and side rooms between two massive stepped towers. In front is a rectangular courtyard surrounded by a suite of rooms. The temple precinct with ziggurat at Khorsabad, ancient Dur-Sharrukin, contained five shrines of the Assyrian plan arranged around open courts enclosed by small rooms (late 8th century B.C.). Each shrine was dedicated to a different deity. More elaborate is the temple of Nabu at the same site. It is placed on a terrace and is divided into a forecourt and central court; the temple itself lies behind the latter and is enclosed by long corridors on three sides. Ezida, an enormous religious structure at Nimrud, ancient Kalhu, contained within it the temple of Nabu. There were over 35 rooms, in addition to four large courts and a number of long corridors. Ezida was organized like a fortress: there was a defensive wall and the only access to the building was up a ramp that led through a gate with heavy buttresses on either side. It remained in use from the 9th through 7th centuries (Mallowan 1975: 231–38; Oates 1968: 115–120; Strommenger 1964: 444–47).

The Assyrian palace, together with temples and administrative buildings, was situated within the fortified acropolis of the city. The NW Palace at Nimrud was built in the reign of Ashurnasirpal II (883–859 B.C.). It includes the forecourt (the *bābānu*) and the primary apartments, reception halls, domestic quarters, and an administrative wing (the *bītānu*). The largest room in the whole layout is the throne room, the true center of the whole palace. The plan radiates about a great open court; all the groupings of the chambers and smaller courts are neatly balanced and articulated. Other palaces excavated at Nimrud are the so-called Center Palace of Shalmaneser III (858–824 B.C.), the Central Palace of Tiglath-pileser III (745–727 B.C.), the SW Palace of Esarhaddon (680–669 B.C.), and the remains of a palace of Ashur-etel-ilani (after 626 B.C.). The palace of Sargon II (721–705 B.C.) at his newly founded city of Dur-Sharrukin stands on its own terrace and extends outside the city wall and at the same time forms its strongest bastion (see Fig. ART. 17). The great throne room has three entrances that face onto a vast open court. The two palaces of Sennacherib (704–681 B.C.) and Ashurbanipal (668–627 B.C.) are situated on the hill of Nineveh. Sennacherib described his royal residence as the "palace without a rival," and it was built in accordance with a new ground-plan design. The palace has at least three main entrances, of which two are provided with huge triple portals. The room arrangements grouped around the courts are completely different in shape and function; moreover, the room complexes are accessible from several sides. The North Palace of Ashurbanipal was only partially excavated. Within the complex is a large, long rectangular room that can be reached from a great hall through a triple portal. In particular a series of connecting long corridors or ramps lead up from a columned entrance to the main palace area (Frankfort 1970: 143–51; Mallowan 1975: 93–97, 164–65, 200–5; Moortgat 1969: 126–29, 151–53; Strommenger 1964: 437–88, 450–51).

Fort Shalmaneser at Nimrud, the so-called *ekal-masharti,* was an independent military installation. Its exclusive character is indicated by the line of the outer wall, reinforced externally by towers set at regular intervals. The fort proper with its 200-odd rooms and four separate quadrants had residential quarters for officers, barracks, stables, workshops, magazines, and the residency for the king and his court. Fort Shalmaneser was built in the reign of Shalmaneser III and continued in use till 612 B.C. Palace F at Dur-Sharrukin copied the *ekal-masharti* in Nimrud. It was the royal arsenal, the military center of Sargon II (Mallowan 1975: 369–83; Moortgat 1969: 137–39).

2. Sculpture and Decorated Monument. A rare bronze statuette dedicated to an Assyrian king, probably Ashur-dan I (1178–1133 B.C.), is of a slender figure dressed in a tunic, with a small shoulder shawl. Missing are the head, arms, and feet. Another unusual work is the torso of a statue of a nude woman, modeled in stone and inscribed with the name of Ashur-bel-kala (1073–1056 B.C.). There are several large stone statues of 9th-century-B.C. Assyrian kings. The royal figures are posed frontally and dressed in long wraparound shawl garments. Statues of deities, each distinguished by a horned cap and holding a box in both hands or else a vase from which streams of water flow, were placed in temple precincts (Frankfort 1970: 152; Mallowan 1975: 88–89; Moortgat 1969: 121–22; Strommenger 1964: 440–41, 443).

Reliefs with historical subjects appear on pillarlike stone monuments described as obelisks. The Broken Obelisk shows within a recessed panel bound captives before the Assyrian king, and above the scene are divine symbols (ca. 1070 B.C.). The White Obelisk has relief friezes in eight registers that extend around all four sides. The pictorial themes include warlike expeditions, ritual activities, and the hunt of wild animals. The monument is dated to the reign of Ashurnasirpal I (1049–1031 B.C.) or Ashurnasirpal II. The Black Obelisk of Shalmaneser III has five registers of panel reliefs on each of the four sides. The scenes show local rulers paying homage to the Assyrian king, while attendants from different regions bring tribute. On royal stelae, the Assyrian king is always portrayed with shoulder-length hair and long beard; he is dressed in the prescribed royal costume and carries the weapons of kingship. In the space above and in front of the ruler's

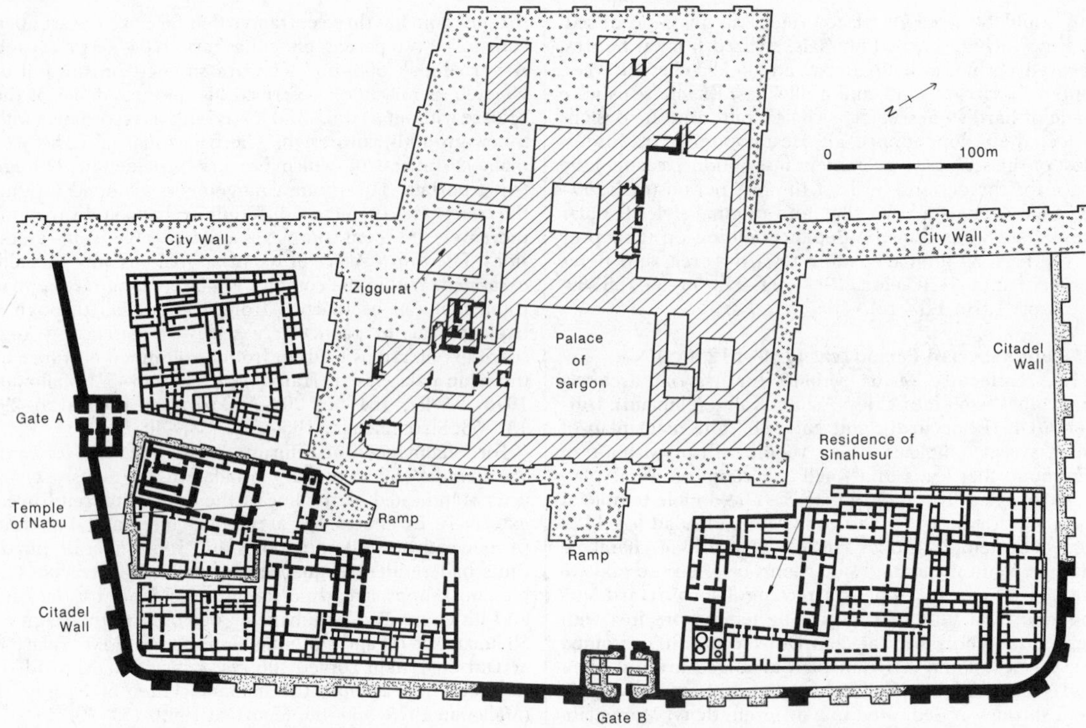

ART.17. Plan of citadel with palace of Sargon II at Khorsabad (Dur-Sharrukin). *(Courtesy of The Oriental Institute of The University of Chicago.)*

head are symbols of important deities whose awesome splendors are conferred upon the king, pictorially. The royal stelae were set up in temples, at city gates, and in captured foreign cities. Rock reliefs of Assyrian kings were carved at the sides of mountains located in different parts of the Near East, and many are extant (Barnett 1975: pl. 2; Mallowan 1975: 62–63; Moortgat 1969: 122–23; Strommenger 1964: 208).

3. Wall Relief and Ivory Work. The integration of architecture and pictorial art occurred early in the 9th century B.C., when wall reliefs replaced painting in the Assyrian palace. The unity of art and architecture was maintained throughout the following two centuries. Important portals throughout the palace area were lined with huge winged human-headed bull *(lamassu)* and winged human-headed lion *(šedu)* sculptures, whose duty it was to prevent evil spirits from entering. Stone slabs framing the doors were carved with winged and wingless human-headed and bird-headed genies and their images engendered a divine, protective atmosphere. Whole rooms within the palace had the lower part of their walls covered with limestone blocks, several meters high. Narrative scenes carved in relief on the stone blocks are essentially historical and deal with the Assyrian king's great deeds in war and hunting (see Fig. ART. 18). The events are expressed in monumental manner. Pictorial compositions, which became a determining factor in the development of style, are arranged in various ways. The episodic scene centers around a single activity; the narrative frieze shows a sequence of related events in one or more registers; the mural-type scene abandons the use of registers and, instead, dominates the entire surface of the stone block; and processions of large-scale human figures consist of soldiers, Assyrian officials, priests and musicians, and foreigners advancing to the Assyrian king and his personal attendants (Barnett 1975; Frankfort 1970: 157–60, 168–71, 174–94; Strommenger 1964: 441, 443, 448, 451).

Ivory carving as an art form was established in the Near East by the start of the 1st millennium B.C. Ivories in Assyrian style generally consist of flat plaques carved with incised designs of subjects and persons familiar from the palace wall reliefs. Other plaques show highly skilled carving in flat, low-relief style. Many decorated ivories were overlays for furniture and smaller objects. Purely Assyrian-style ivories became rare in the 8th century, in consequence of overhunting and extermination of herds of elephants which roamed parts of Syria (Mallowan 1978: 12–25; Herrmann and Mallowan 1974).

E. Neo-Babylonian Dynasty (625–539 B.C.)

Babylon's principal palace was the Southern Palace, built in the reign of Nebuchadnezzer II (604–562 B.C.). It contains five great courtyard complexes in parallel arrangement, resembling the multiplicity of the ordinary dwelling house. The decoration of the facade of the vast throne room facing the outer court was made of multicolored glazed bricks. Richly decorated glazed bricks were also used for the massive walls of the so-called Processional

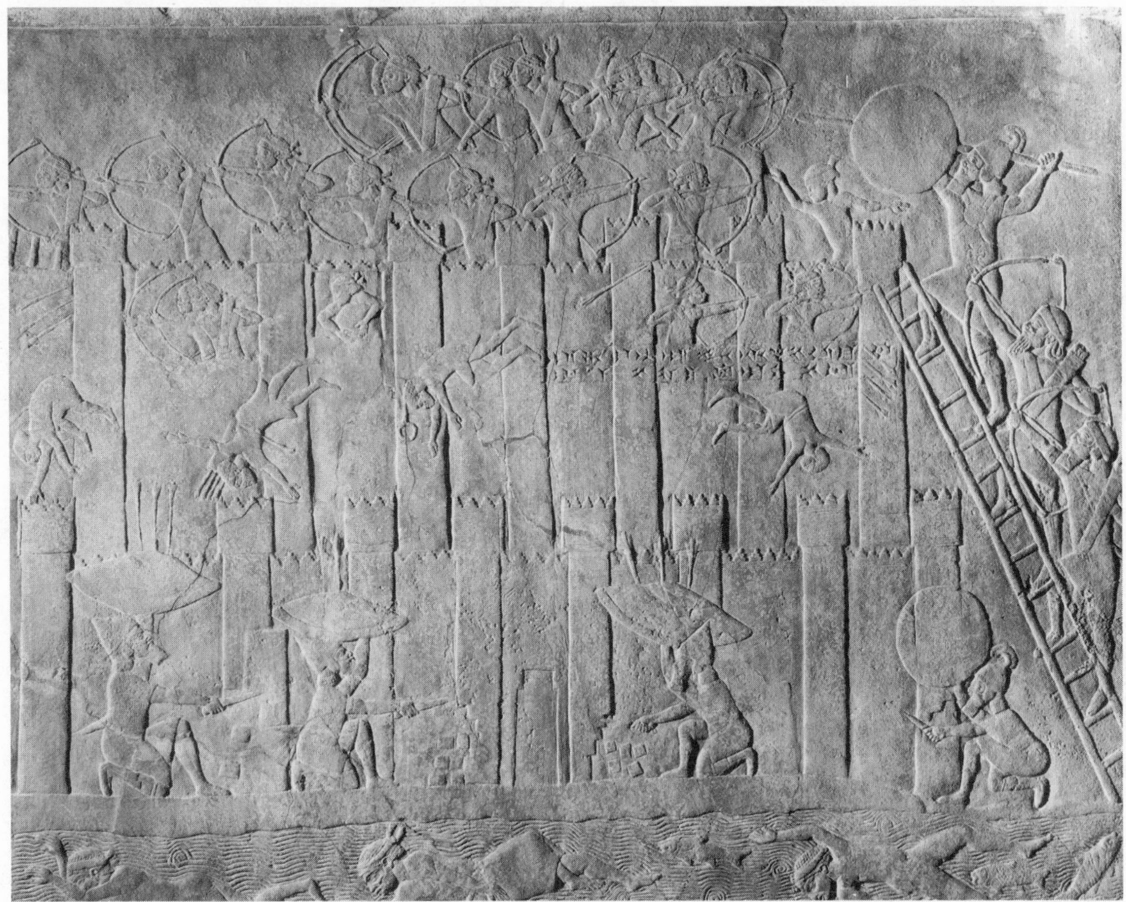

ART.18. Alabaster war relief in N Palace at Nineveh. Ashurbanipal and his troops storming the Elamite city of Ḫamanu. *(Reproduced by Courtesy of the Trustees of the British Museum.)*

Way and Ishtar Gate. Enamel brick technique in Babylon had two variants: a completely flat, painted and glazed surface or a glazed relief composed of molded bricks. The subject matter consists of slender trees with volute capitals, friezes of palmettes, and lions, bulls, and serpent-dragons *(mušhuš)*. Babylon's most important temple was Esagila, the dwelling place of the god Marduk. The Marduk sanctuary is a complex of buildings around open courts, the temple, and the ziggurat, all of which are enclosed by a rectangular perimeter wall. Remains of impressive NB temples have been found at excavated cities, including Sippar, Ur, Borsippa, and Kish (Frankfort 1970: 203–5; Moortgat 1969: 158–62; Oates, 1979: 144–46).

Art objects of the Neo-Babylonian period are sparse. The upper part of a stele of Nabonidus (555–539 B.C.) illustrates the royal figure standing below three divine symbols. Seals of Babylon, both in iconography and style, were probably influenced by Assyrian glyptic. One class of NB seals depicts a priest before the symbols of various deities (Collon 1987: 80–83).

F. Summary and Trend

Throughout the millennia, the art and architecture of Mesopotamia were linked by a unified tradition which stemmed from a comprehensive religious, political, social, and economic outlook that was homogeneous. The essential character of works of art may be defined as a striving for harmony, symmetry, and lucid description. Moreover, specific structures and works of art display a striving for monumentality, magnificence, and dynamic description, such as the ziggurat, Assyrian palace, and stele of Naram-Sin. The complexity and outward variations between artworks reflect the different levels of technical skill and feeling for style prevailing at any one time.

Systematic studies on Mesopotamian art have progressed in several important ways. One method of study focuses upon stylistic development and art-historical interpretation (Schlossman 1979; 1981–82; Reade 1979a, b; 1980a, b). Another method examines works of art within the context of administrative, historical, or social settings (Gibson and Biggs 1977; Winter 1976). Both approaches have contributed to the understanding of Mesopotamian art. Finally, recent archaeological exploration has uncovered additional ancient edifices, and those discoveries have enlarged the understanding of Mesopotamian architecture (Weiss 1985: 6–19).

Bibliography

Barnett, R. D., and Lorenzi, A. 1975. *Assyrian Sculpture in the British Museum.* Toronto.

Collon, D. 1987. *First Impressions. Cylinder Seals in the Ancient Near East.* Chicago and London.

Crawford, H. E. W. 1977. *The Architecture of Iraq in the Third Millennium B.C.* Mesopotamia 5. Copenhagen.

Frankfort, H. 1970. *The Art and Architecture of the Ancient Orient.* 4th rev. ed. London.

Gibson, M., and Biggs, R. D., eds. 1977. *Seals and Sealing in the Ancient Near East.* BibMes 6. Malibu.

Herrmann, G., and Mallowan, M. 1974. *Furniture from SW.7 Fort Shalmaneser. Commentary, Catalogue and Plates.* Ivories from Nimrud (1949–1963) Fascicle 3. London.

Mallowan, M. E. L. 1975. *Nimrud and Its Remains.* Vols. 1, 2, 2d ed. London.

———. 1978. *The Nimrud Ivories.* London.

Moortgat A. 1969. *The Art of Mesopotamia. The Classical Art of the Near East.* Trans. Judith Filson. London and New York.

Oates, D. 1967. The Excavations at Tell al Rimah, 1966. *Iraq* 29: 70–96.

———. 1968. The Excavations at Tell al Rimah, 1967. *Iraq* 30: 115–38.

———. 1987. Excavations at Tell Brak 1985–86. *Iraq* 49: 175–91.

Oates, J. 1979. *Babylon.* London.

Reade, J. E. 1979a. Assyrian Architectural Decoration: Techniques and Subject-Matter. *Baghdader Mitteilungen* 10: 17–49.

———. 1979b. Narrative Composition in Assyrian Sculpture. *Baghdader Mitteilungen* 10: 52–110.

———. 1980a. Space, Scale, and Significance in Assyrian Art. *Baghdader Mitteilungen* 11: 71–74.

———. 1980b. Architectural Context of Assyrian Sculpture. *Baghdader Mitteilungen* 11: 75–87.

Schlossman, B. L. 1979. Portraiture in Mesopotamia in the Late Third and Early Second Millennium B.C. Part 1. *AfO* 26: 56–77.

———. 1981/1982. Portraiture in Mesopotamia in the Late Third and Early Second Millennium B.C. Part 2. *AfO* 28: 143–70.

Strommenger, E., and Hirmer, M. 1964. *5000 Years of the Art of Mesopotamia.* Trans. C. Haglud. New York.

Weiss, H. 1985. Tell Leilan on the Habur Plains of Syria. *BA* 48: 6–32.

Winter, I. J. 1976. Phoenician and North Syrian Ivory Carving in Historical Context: Questions of Style and Distribution. *Iraq* 38: 1–22.

PAULINE ALBENDA

EGYPTIAN ART AND ARCHITECTURE

Egyptian architectural monuments and the other works of art which they contained constitute the largest visible legacy from pre-Classical times in the Near East. Their traditions continued into the early centuries A.D., and were very influential in much of the ancient world. Architecture and representational art formed an integrated system, whose basic organization was created around the beginning of the dynastic period (Baines 1989a). The majority of works of all periods down to Roman times fit within this system, which forms the most important presentation of ideology. Writing also partakes of the system: much preserved writing is on permanent monuments incorporated within architectural and artistic contexts, and has its full meaning within those contexts. Art was central to Egyptian high culture; in times of prosperity, a high proportion of resources was used to create works of art (see in general Aldred 1980).

Representational art in particular must be understood in terms of iconographic as well as representational conventions (see C.3 below). Both these types of convention affected compositions in ways that are sufficiently alien from those of Western art to need explicit study. Iconography related to a system of decorum which governed what was depicted and how it was shown in most contexts, and had extensions outside the artistic sphere (Baines 1985a: 277–305).

A. The Status of Art
B. Architecture
  1. Introductory: Domestic and Other Structures
  2. Materials and Forms
C. Representational Art
  1. Introduction
  2. Sculpture in the Round
  3. Relief and Painting
D. Minor Arts
E. Change; Legacy to the Near East

A. The Status of Art

It is often wrongly claimed that Egyptian art is not "art": that there was no Egyptian word for art, the concept of artistic creativity was lacking, and all works had a function (e.g., Wolf 1957: 66–68; Junge fc.). The linguistic argument is based on the fact that the Egyptian word *hmt* means "craftsmanship" rather than Western "art," but it is invalid, because Egyptian lacks words for many comparable abstractions, such as religion or politics, yet this does not show that Egypt lacked those phenomena. The absence of these words demonstrates something about Egyptian classification, but not about art (see Müller fc.). The other components of the argument implicitly use an over-narrow Westernizing conception of art—that it must be the expression of an individual personality and is essentially functionless. They cannot be sustained in the face of the demonstrable high status of some artists (e.g., Krauss 1983), the meaningful variation and stylistic development of works of art, and the resources and prestige vested in their production. Artists worked in teams, as is normal in most artistic traditions and necessary for manipulating intractable materials and creating very large works. This does not imply any devaluation of the resulting product or of those who were responsible for its design and execution. What can hardly be attributed to Egypt is the ideologically and behaviorally loaded Western conception of the "artist" (see also Drenkhahn 1976: 62–72).

Another debate has been about the interpretation of artistic production as having a "re-creative" purpose. Rituals that might be depicted on temple walls would substitute for their real performance, while statues of the deceased and the decoration of his tomb would enable him to survive the loss of his mummy and the cessation of his mortuary cult. The unquestionable "realism" of Egyptian representational forms would be explained along the same lines, as being required so that what was shown should come to life in the correct form (e.g., Iversen 1975: 5–7). This interpretation is not based on texts, but rather seeks to explain the choice of subject matter in temple and tomb decoration and some particular features of the record, such as the mutilation of signs representing human and animal figures in the Pyramid Texts inscribed in the mortuary chambers of late 5th and 6th Dynasty pyramids (Lacau 1914). Although some aspects of decoration have "performative" elements (Derchain 1989), this approach is generally implausible. In these areas, Egyptian art partakes of the character of central symbolic statements, and comparable phenomena could be found in many cultures.

B. Architecture

1. Introductory: Domestic and Other Structures. Architecture is both the principal artistic form and the context for other works of art (Jéquier 1920–24; Badawy 1954–68; de Cenival 1964; Smith 1981). The ultimate context of architecture is the Egyptian natural and social environment. Any general influence of the natural environment on architectural forms is, however, uncertain, except insofar as the dry, hot climate allowed the use of flat forms and encouraged measures to circulate air. An important environmental element is orientation. One or two temples have an astronomical orientation (Krauss 1985: 49), but the main astronomically oriented structures are mortuary, in particular the pyramids, whose sides face the cardinal points. Most temples are oriented to the Nile. Those on the west bank are entered from their "east" side and have an axis facing "west"; the reverse applies to those on the east bank. These orientations are variable according to the local direction of the river, so that, for example, the temple of Dendara faces north; the orientation of many other buildings was dependent on their connections with different structures on the same site.

The social environment is more significant than the natural. The highly centripetal Egyptian state was organized around the king, the capital or residence of the king, and, in earlier periods, the king's mortuary monument. In the New Kingdom and later, the royal city had a cosmic significance and formed a stage on which the king's actions and the life of the whole settlement assumed "historical" meaning. Rather similar meaning should be attributed to the royal palace, whose design shows many analogies with temples (O'Connor fc.a; fc.). At the other end of the scale of society and of architectural grandeur, everyday dwellings could have had architectural significance, as in many societies, but such a meaning can hardly be recovered. Most preserved nonelite housing is proletarian in organization and acquires architectural value chiefly through its context in large planned settlements. Elite manorial houses, as depicted especially in New Kingdom tombs, were set in large garden compounds, and had an urban counterpart in the elite "villas" of el-Amarna. These structures had both prestige and religious aspects, but have hardly been investigated for their architectural meaning (collection of material on domestic architecture: Roik 1988). Rural housing of the nonelite, which could have preserved more general cultural significance, is almost wholly unknown.

The majority of preserved architecture is stone built and funerary, consisting of freestanding or rock-cut tombs sited on the edge of the Nile Valley between Cairo and Aswan. These include royal tombs, varying in size from modest structures to the Great Pyramid. Preserved temple complexes belong principally to the New Kingdom and Greco-Roman period. There are also rock-cut temples in the desert escarpment in Egypt and Lower Nubia.

2. Materials and Forms. The principal constructional materials were stone and brick, but reed and matting were widespread for temporary structures, while some prestige building, for example of baldachins for royal and divine thrones, was in wood.

a. Brick. Mud brick, which survives less well than stone, was used for religious and secular structures from temples to houses (Spencer 1979). The earliest preserved brick dates to the Naqada II period, before the unification of the country. At first, the material was used for prestige purposes, becoming widespread only later. Nongeometric use of mud, as in wattle-and-daub, was probably always the standard technique for rural houses.

Mud brick was used with skill and imagination. Rich effects were created in elaborately paneled facades to the enclosures and outside walls of palaces and tombs. The characteristic "palace facade" form of these was perhaps originally royal, and remained a royal symbol, but it was used by others as well, especially in mortuary contexts. Its design is comparable with Mesopotamian motifs, but may not have been derived from them.

Brick enclosures were often on a colossal scale, especially in the Late Period; some walls are as much as 15 m thick. A characteristic feature of enclosure walls is the alternation of level sections of brickwork with undulating or concave and convex ones (e.g., Barguet 1962: 29–40). The purpose of this practice has been argued by different authors to be symbolic of the primeval waters, or to be structural (see Spencer 1979: 114–16, favoring the symbolic interpretation).

In brick buildings with interior spaces, the Egyptians mastered difficult structural elements such as wide unsupported vaults and domes. One reason for developing these techniques, which are more commonly found in burnt-brick traditions, is the scarcity of structural timber in Egypt. These forms contributed to the impressive appearance of utilitarian buildings, such as groups of magazines within temple complexes (see Fig. ART. 20; Vandersleyen 1975: pl. VII). But the design of large dwelling and ceremonial areas, such as palaces, which have to be studied principally from ground plans, appears superficially less orderly, and is not well understood.

b. Stone: Forms and Symbolism. Most of the main preserved monuments are built of limestone or sandstone (with parts in granite and other hard stones). Their struc-

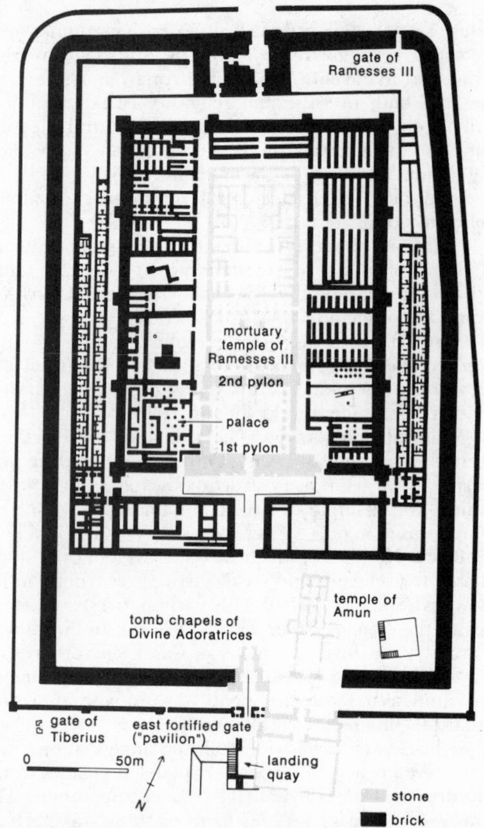

ART.20. Plan of temple complex of Ramesses III at Medinet Habu, W Thebes. (*Redrawn from J. Baines and J. Málek,* Atlas of Ancient Egypt *[London: Phaidon Press, 1980], 98.)*

tural forms are simpler than those of mud brick, but their symbolism is more elaborate. The earliest large-scale buildings, in the 3d Dynasty step pyramid complex of Djoser at Saqqara, look to plant models, from reeds and flowers to tree trunks, for the forms of columns and of decorative motifs. The complex is a successor of mortuary enclosures of the first two dynasties, in which similar structures may have been built in mud brick (O'Connor fc.b.), but brick hardly influenced the stone forms.

Stone structures are either largely solid, like the pyramids, or are based on load-bearing walls, columns, and pillars (Clarke and Engelbach 1930). Roofs are flat, and the distance spanned by roof beams is restricted to the maximum length for an unsupported architrave, about 3 m for limestone and 7 m for sandstone (used from the New Kingdom on). Forms are generally rectilinear, but are relieved by the characteristic batter of external surfaces (perhaps derived from brickwork or building in mud), by column styles, and by decorative features. Only a few buildings are geometric, the best known being the Valley Temple of Chephren at Giza (e.g., Lange and Hirmer 1968: pls. 32–33) and the cenotaph of Sety I at Abydos (Frankfort 1930); both are constructed mainly of granite. Large internal spaces are interrupted by the columns which carry the roof, and include the typical hypostyle halls of temples. In contrast with the generally axial design of temples, these halls have strong transverse accents.

Arches were not used in stone until the Late Period, and the only vaulting was corbelling, which was carved in New Kingdom temples to produce curved ceilings for sanctuaries and occurs in the rock-cut burial chambers of New Kingdom royal tombs (e.g., Vandersleyen 1975: pl. 93).

Most columns have capitals, and abaci are common (*LÄ* 5: 343–48). Their forms are generally derived from aquatic plants, especially papyrus, but including lotus, date palms, and, in late times, elaborate composites. The date palm, which is also a common model, should be considered aquatic, because palms frequently have their bases in marshy ground. Fluted and polygonal columns are known. Two characteristic features of wall design are the torus moulding, a cylindrical treatment of edges and corners applied to the most varied structures and features, and the cavetto cornice, a form which flares forward above a vertical or battered surface. Detailed examples of these suggest plant models in the lashing of edges of panels and the gathering of heads of plants at their tops. Two vital decorative motifs are the uraeus, or protective rearing cobra, which often occurs as a frieze, and the sun disk, which is found typically in the cavetto cornice above doorways.

Wall surfaces of stone structures were decorated with painted reliefs. By the 4th Dynasty some royal mortuary temples had a rich repertory of scenes, whose subjects included the worship of the gods, the provisioning of the temple by its estates, and "historical" events primarily showing the king's dominance of the world and maintenance of order. The relief area of a wall was set off by a dado of horizontal moulding lines at the bottom, and at the top the hieroglyph for sky or a *kheker* frieze, which seems to derive from tassels at the edge of a fabric.

Temples in particular exploited the potential of light and darkness (see Fig. ART. 21). They were theoretically oriented to face sunrise or sunset, and their outer areas were relatively light, but light struck directly into the interior only down the axis, when the inner doors were opened. Small window openings were cut in roofs, in the upper parts of walls, and at the juncture of wall and roof. Side rooms were completely dark. The decoration, whose primary purpose was its enacting of the symbolic world depicted in the reliefs, rather than creating something to be seen, could be seen only when illuminated by lamps. As in many other traditions, the completed work of art was hardly intended to be viewed.

In addition to their decoration, temples contained ritual equipment and many large and small statues. They were surrounded by service buildings and enclosed within mud-brick enclosure walls. Priests alone could enter temples and the gods, whose dwellings they were, left them only at festivals. Despite this seclusion, temples had a central significance as symbolic, sanctified representations of the perfect world at creation (Barguet 1962: 336–40; Baines 1976; Finnestad 1985). This meaning can be read in linear fashion off the plan of a complex, from the enclosure wall through the various areas and rooms into the sanctuary, or vertically, in the decoration of single walls. The slightly raised floor level of the sanctuary marked the original

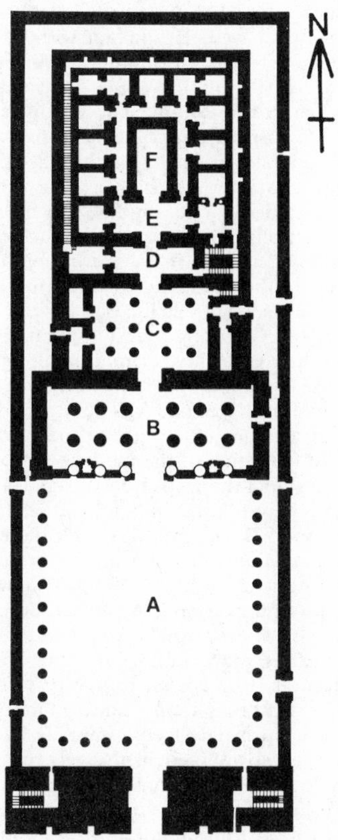

ART.21. The temple of Horus at Edfu. One approached the sanctuary *(F)* by passing through the outer courtyard *(A)*, the first and second hypostyle halls (*B* and *C*), the offering hall *(D)*, and the vestibule *(E)*. The architecture is such that the natural sunlight gradually diminishes as one moves deeper into the temple complex.

mound of creation, while the individual scenes and the wall surface as a whole represented the sanctified cosmos, terminating in the sky at the top. The entrance pylon of a temple (e.g., Vandersleyen 1975: pls. 91, 103), which consisted of a pair of high walls with battered faces flanking a central doorway, was its largest single element and was decorated with semi-apotropaic scenes of the king slaughtering his enemies. The wall decoration within the temples added to its meaning. Their reliefs show the king (in Graeco-Roman times the Ptolemy or Roman Emperor) offering to the gods and receiving benefits from them, and are organized into registers with sequences of scenes that summarize the stages of rituals or obey more abstract schemas. The world of the reliefs is almost exclusively divine and royal; its relation to humanity is indirect.

The forms of tombs are more various than those of temples and their meaning less well understood. There was almost always a distinction in location and form between royal and nonroyal tombs.

Royal tombs developed from the unmarked brick-lined pits of the first two dynasties at Abydos, through the pyramid complexes of the Old and Middle Kingdoms (Edwards 1985–86), to the rock-cut tombs of the New Kingdom in the Valley of the Kings (Hornung 1988) with their accompanying mortuary temples at the Nile Valley edge, and small Late Period structures in temple enclosures (Stadelmann 1971). Early royal tombs point to a cosmic destiny of the king in the next life. The pyramids have a stellar orientation, but may also be related to solar beliefs, while perhaps further symbolizing the first created matter. Their meaning seems closely related to that of the obelisk, which was both a cult object in its own right and a decorative element placed in pairs outside tombs and later temples. New Kingdom royal tombs are decorated with compositions concerned with the nightly passage of the sun god through the underworld, and their design too may symbolize the underworld.

Early nonroyal tombs, which are termed mastabas, have the form of stylized mounds with battered sides (in stone constructions from the 4th Dynasty on); the symbolism of this form is uncertain. The deceased was buried in a chamber at the bottom of a shaft cut within the mastaba structure. The mortuary cult centered on a niche, normally at the south end of the tomb, whose form derived from a section of mud-brick paneling. This niche became the Old Kingdom "false door," through which the deceased's spirit received offerings, while the area before it was extended to form a chapel, and much of the originally solid mastaba superstructure was gradually taken up by additional decorated rooms.

Rock-cut nonroyal tombs were constructed in all periods from the late 4th Dynasty on. Their decoration and focus on the false door were similar to mastabas, and their burials were also at the bottoms of shafts. Often rock-cut tomb complexes consist of a forecourt and paneled facade in front of the internal rooms. The standard form of a New Kingdom Theban tomb comprised a transverse room, parts of which might have "secular" decoration, with a longitudinal room behind leading to an offering place at the back. In the 18th Dynasty these tombs began to have religious scenes among the decoration, and by the 20th Dynasty almost all secular decoration had disappeared. In the artisans' tombs at Deir el-Medina, the decorated chambers were often underground and had vaulted ceilings, assimilating them to the forms of sarcophagi and burial chambers; these rooms had exclusively mortuary decoration.

From the mid–New Kingdom on, new forms of free-standing tombs modeled on temple designs developed in the Memphite area. These were influential into very late times, producing such masterpieces as the 4th–3rd-century-B.C. tomb of Petosiris at Tuna el-Gebel (Lefebvre 1923–24). By that date, however, few of the elite built major tombs, and this type is relatively poorly known. Examples at such sites as Saqqara have been more thoroughly destroyed than earlier tombs.

C. Representational Art

1. Introduction. The images that filled architectural spaces and decorated their surfaces were all designed on the same basic principles. Egyptian art therefore has a stylistic unity which has been recognized since antiquity. The application of its principles is best seen in the canon of proportions (e.g., Robins 1986), which provided a convenient and accurate means of depicting objects, especially the human form, on squared grids (see Fig. ART. 22), while facilitating the organization of artists in teams. The rendering of nature, which underlay the canon of proportions and has analogies in sculpture in the round, is very different from that of Western art. Its most important characteristics are its reliance on outlines and nonincorporation of foreshortening and related optical phenomena. Within its conventions, it strove toward what may be termed realism, that is, proportional accuracy and approximation to visual schemata, rather than toward extremes of stylization. For Westerners, there has often seemed to be a contradiction between its nonuse of perspective and its realism, and this problem has been alternately overlooked and commented on at length. Since perspective and foreshortening are characteristic of few artistic traditions, the methods so clearly exemplified in Egyptian art should be considered universal (Baines 1985b) and perspective a special case, rather than the other way around. Although the Westerner's difficulty with finding a way to approach Egyptian representation results largely from its realism, there is nothing inherently contradictory in the presence of realism in a nonperspective tradition.

As in many cultures, almost all works were planned to be painted, or were naturally colored (cf. Reutersward 1958). With few exceptions, coloring was polychrome. The basic coloring system consisted of black, white, red, yellow, green, blue, with gray both as a hue and as a neutral; brown and pink were later added to the repertory. Colors could appear in more than one shade. The color classification visible on the monuments is more complex than that known from the Egyptian language, but both fit the universal "color encoding sequence" of Berlin and Kay (Baines 1985c). Painting was the last stage of work on sculpture and relief; because many works were not finished, people will have been familiar with the appearance of unpainted works (see also Smith 1949: 105–29; 244–72).

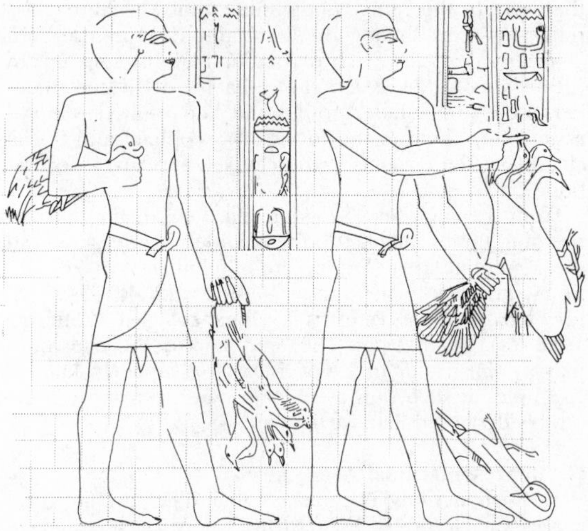

ART.22. Two figures with original grid on tomb of Wekhkotep at Meir—12th Dynasty. *(Redrawn from A. M. Blackman,* The Rock Tombs of Meir, *Vol. 2. Archaeological Survey of Egypt 23 [London: Egyptian Exploration Society, 1915], pl. XI.)*

2. Sculpture in the Round. The products of Egyptian techniques are easily appreciated in statuary (e.g., Russmann fc., Vandersleyen 1975: pls. 115–236). Apart from a geometrical character which is basic to the system and was probably valued for its dignity, the human figure is depicted realistically. Great mastery was achieved in stoneworking, in rendering the masses of the human form and of detail, and in the modeling of faces and of the upper part of the body (see Fig. ART. 23).

Except for the Old Kingdom, most statues come from temples and show gods, kings, and human beings more or less in repose, standing with the left foot forward, or seated or squatting (see Fig. ART. 24), singly or in small groups. They are idealized, with a concept of beauty not very different from that of the modern West. Transient or dynamic poses and the depiction of aged and careworn features are relatively rare, but are characteristic of many of the finest works. Iconographic details indicate the identity of many gods and of the king, but in addition most statues are inscribed with the owners' names and titles; statue and inscription complement each other so that the statue is the last "hieroglyph" of the text (which does not mean that text is more important than statue; Fischer 1974). Sculptures from colossi 15 m high to figurines of a few centimeters are remarkably uniform in style, but small works can be surprisingly free, especially in wood (which is greatly underrepresented in the record). This applies particularly to decorative figures like unguent jars in the form of offering bearers carrying pots (see Fig. ART. 25).

Art-historical work has tended to focus on the faces of statues and on problems of dating. The question of whether the Egyptians made "portraits" is much debated. While the features of some individuals, especially of royalty, are evidently depicted in statuary, the term "portrait" is so culturally loaded as to make its application to alien traditions problematic; meaningful answers to these questions depend on clarifying what is being asked. It is clear that the features chiefly at issue are those of kings (e.g., Tefnin 1979; Müller 1988), and that during the periods when distinctive royal faces were carved many other people were depicted with faces similar to those of kings. The only time when faces have a very clear iconographic significance was the later 12th Dynasty, when Senwosret III and Amenemhat III were depicted with suffering countenances probably signifying the role of the "suffering king." For other periods, especially the Late Period (Bothmer 1969; Brooklyn Museum 1988), marks of age were typical of nonroyal sculpture. Statues additionally derived acquired much of their meaning from iconography. People commissioned many statues of themselves with differing iconography that included the physique, which was youthfully slender in most cases, and prosperously obese for older, wiser figures.

The two principal contexts for sculpture were tomb and temple. There is little evidence for statues in other public places, except where large areas of a city were linked by avenues, principally of sphinxes (best known in Thebes). In addition to stone and wood, statues were made in

ART.23. Statue of Senwosret III in attitude of prayer. *(Courtesy of Hirmer Fotoarchiv, Munich.)*

ART.24. Scribe statue of Amenhotep, son of Hapu—Reign of Amenhotep III. *(Courtesy of Hirmer Fotoarchiv, Munich.)*

ART.25. Boxwood statue of servant girl. *(Durham University Oriental Museum.)*

copper or bronze and precious metals, and sometimes in composites of different substances. Very little bronze sculpture is known from before the Late Period, but casting was mastered impressively, if only for royal statues (Wildung 1984: 209, fig. 184; Old Kingdom molded statue Lange and Hirmer 1968: pl. 80). Temple reliefs depicting cult statues show a far wider range of types than is physically preserved (e.g., Davies 1953: pls. 1–5), most of them being made of wood, metal, or a mixture of the two.

Sculpture of different periods varies greatly in style and character. The time of the widest range of contemporary variation was the Late Period, when statues were the principal monuments of most members of the elite (Bothmer 1969; one group of royal sculpture: Russmann 1974).

3. Relief and Painting. Egyptian principles of representation have more distinctive consequences in relief and painting (Schäfer 1986). Despite fundamental differences of type, these two media share a linear mode of representation, and reliefs could be carved on the basis of existing paintings (e.g., Baines 1989b); preparatory drawings for both were essentially the same. Low raised relief was normal indoors and sunk relief, in which the stone of the background between the figures was not removed, outdoors; sunk relief shows up better in sunlight.

Compositions are organized as groupings conveying information visually, not as visual or perceptual images (see Fig. ART. 26). The picture surface is an area to be filled, not three-dimensional space or a specific location, and there is no fixed point from which compositions are to be viewed. Figures are related to one another by their actions and gestures or by overlapping, while relative size indicates relative importance, not distance. The chief organizing element in compositions is the register, a sequence of figures or separate scenes on a single baseline. A set of registers fills a wall surface, while principal figures or scenes may be the height of several registers and bracket them together. Designs are arranged to fill a surface evenly and arrange it meaningfully, rather as in the layout of an illustrated book. The register compositions of temples (see Fig. ART. 27), especially of the Late and Greco-Roman Periods, are more rigid than those of nonroyal tombs, and exhibit complex ordering principles that unify entire walls (Winter 1968: Part 1). The composition of scenes is so highly conventionalized that it is often meaningless to ask what locations or furnishings are shown in the scenes. The most prominent exceptions to, or extensions of, the normal principles of composition are in the royal battle reliefs of the New Kingdom (e.g., Gaballa 1976; Epigraphic Survey 1986).

The human figure exemplifies representational principles most fully. The body is treated as a set of aspects unified by its outline (the composition of male and female figures differs slightly). For figures standing at rest, a profile head encloses a single, mostly enlarged eye, and the shoulders are shown at full width, while a front profile joins the forward armpit to the waist. The hips and legs are again in profile; the feet are mostly separate. This construction retains proportional accuracy and allows figures to interact naturally on the picture surface, as well as being in harmony with Egyptian ideals of physical beauty. Because full faces are not shown, it does not address itself to the viewer or suggest the third dimension strongly. Similar compositional principles govern the representation of most objects. Any conventional form is necessarily a choice among many possibilities; once forms were devised, they mostly varied only in detail.

Private tombs of the Old-Middle Kingdoms contain a wide range of scenes of "daily life," such as agriculture, fishing, marsh pursuits (see Fig. ART. 28), and craftsmen; religious elements are largely confined to burial scenes and texts (Vandier 1964–78; Harpur 1987). The absence of scenes of gods and kings is probably determined by decorum. The purpose of the decoration is little understood and is hardly stated in the accompanying texts. Essential aspects seem to be commemoration of a successful life and praise of the deceased (Assmann 1983), and the preparation of offerings for the mortuary cult. The deceased "observes" the agricultural activities around him and only participates actively in hunting in the marshes, which probably symbolizes in part passage into the next world (Groenewegen-Frankfort 1951: 28–62). In the New Kingdom, scenes of the king rewarding the tomb owner were added to the repertory. Almost all scenes have identifying and descriptive text captions. Most Old Kingdom tombs at Giza and Saqqara are decorated in relief, while New Kingdom Theban tombs have more paintings, whose flexible medium encourages freer and livelier effects (see Fig. ART. 29; Davies and Gardiner 1936; Mekhitarian 1954); relief, however, was used in some of the finest Theban tombs (e.g., Lange and Hirmer 1968: pls. 166–77). Late Period reliefs divide into Theban (e.g., Kuhlmann and Schenkel 1983) and Lower Egyptian types (Leahy 1988). Both regions are significant for their artistic innovations, for their inclusion of new subject matter, such as the major underworld compositions characteristic of New Kingdom royal tombs, and for their complex mix of innovation and eclectic use of models from earlier periods.

D. Minor Arts

In prosperous periods, especially the mid–New Kingdom, vast numbers of decorative everyday and funerary objects were made (e.g., Hayes 1959; Boston 1982; Hildesheim 1987). These followed the same representational principles as relief and painting, and, because of the diagrammatic character of representation, depictions of items such as boxes and preserved pieces can correspond closely to each other.

The "minor art" which consumed most resources may have been jewelry (see Fig. ART. 30; Aldred 1971; Wilkinson 1971), for which gold, silver, and precious stones were used in great quantities. Egypt was the major producer of gold in the ANE, and the Eastern Desert abounded in semiprecious stones, but some materials, such as lapis lazuli, were imported from great distances at corresponding cost. Both royal and nonroyal jewelry are known, apart from its probably extensive use in the cult of the gods and deposition in burials, while body ornaments were worn by men and women in many contexts. Some jewelry, for example from the tomb of Tutankhamen, is of great symbolic and iconographic complexity.

Egyptian furniture, which is the chief preserved corpus from the ancient world (Fischer 1986: 169–240), is remarkably elegant and sophisticated, and several other genres, such as cosmetic equipment, were as highly developed.

ART.26. Schema of relief composition from the tomb of Ptahhetep at Saqqara—end of the 5th Dynasty. *(Reprinted from N. de G. Davies,* The Chapel of Ptahhetep and the Hieroglyphs. *Part I of* The Mastaba of Ptahhetep and Akhethetep at Saqqareh. *Archaeological Survey of Egypt 8 [London: Egypt Exploration Fund, 1900], pl. XXI.)*

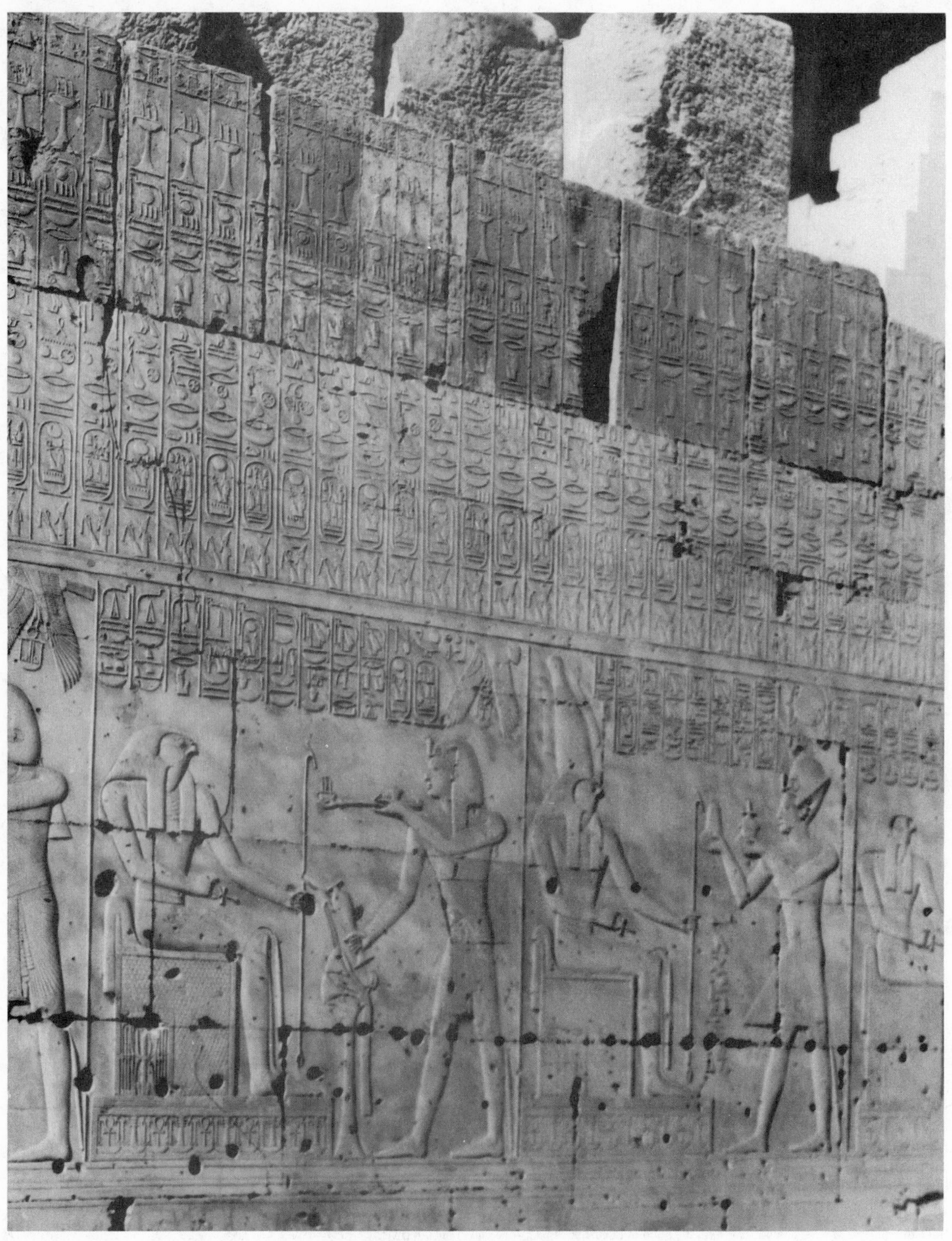

ART.27. Hall of Sokar in temple of Sety I at Abydos. *(Courtesy of Hirmer Fotoarchiv, Munich.)*

ART.28. Marsh scene in the tomb of Mereruka at Saqqara—early 6th Dynasty. *(Courtesy of Hirmer Fotoarchiv, Munich.)*

Art was thus not confined to temples and tombs, but pervaded elite life as a whole. Nonetheless, the principal preserved record is from tombs, and includes very important categories of material, such as coffins and sarcophagi. Despite the constraints of decorum, there was stylistic and formal uniformity across the genres of minor art, from temple and tomb to objects of household use.

Some categories of objects were generally devoid of artistic significance. Most pottery is plain and utilitarian, and painted wares are known only from one or two short periods (Bourriau 1981; Hope 1981, 1987). The reason for this is probably in part that the focus of elite interest in vessels was on stone—worked with astonishing virtuosity in the Early Dynastic Period (el-Khouli 1978)—and metal. Metal vases were widespread, but few are preserved (see Insley Green 1987).

E. Change; Legacy to the Near East

Egyptian art may seem static and rigid, but within its representational system it evolved very greatly. Development tended to be uniform in direction within major periods, mostly moving toward greater complexity and richness, but artists often sought inspiration in works of much earlier times than their own (cf. Baines 1988: 133–40). This tension between continuity with the immediate past and innovation with a backward glance is known from many long-lasting traditions. The fruitful development of native Egyptian art continued at least until the Roman conquest. The only time of truly radical departures was the attempted religious "revolution" of Akhenaten, during which both the style and the subject matter of reliefs and statuary were transformed, while representational conventions also changed significantly; most of these innovations were soon rejected. The motivation for Akhenaten's artistic changes may have been principally a desire for a radical break with what went before. The king will have commissioned the artists who produced the new style, among whom Bak is known by name and from his mortuary monument, but the phrases with which Bak describes his dependence on the king for teaching turn out to be conventional, so that they may not support the hypothesis of a special role for Akhenaten (Krauss 1986).

Egyptian artistic forms were very influential in the ANE. From the Old Kingdom or earlier, Egypt had close relations with Byblos, from which it imported timber in particular, and to which it exported both works of art and raw materials. Poorly provenanced finds of this period have appeared in Anatolia and the Aegean (e.g., Smith 1965: figs. 10–11). By the early 2d millennium B.C., objects and motifs like scarabs and the winged solar disk, as well as

ART.29. Painting of field with equids—mid-18th Dynasty. *(Reproduced by Courtesy of the Trustees of the British Museum.)*

ART.30. Pectoral of Princess Sit-Ḥat-Ḥor-Yunet—12th Dynasty. *(The Metropolitan Museum of Art, Purchase, Rogers Fund and Henry Walters Gift, 1916. [16.1.3].)*

more general Egyptian iconography, spread to Syria (Teissier 1989). During the late 2d and early 1st millennium, Egypt exercised a dominant cultural influence in parts of Syria-Palestine, while particular categories of objects, such as ivories, acquired an "Egyptian" style and were disseminated as far afield as Mesopotamia (e.g., Herrmann 1986: 18–19; Kitchen 1986).

In the case of ivories, the medium for transmission of this influence may have been the material itself, for which Egypt was the principal source, but the influence may be earlier than the date of the objects discovered. In other cases, it is more difficult to assess what objects carried artistic styles abroad, because the most easily transported materials, such as wood or Egyptian faience (e.g., Tait 1963), are seldom well preserved archaeologically, while jewelry, which is known, for example, from Byblos (Vandersleyen 1975: pl. 396b), will have tended to be recycled, and has largely vanished. Here, the inventories of gifts in the Amarna letters (Moran 1987: e.g., nos. 13–14, 22, 25), which describe objects by weight of materials used and largely ignore their manufacture, have similar implications. In addition, fragile objects, particularly ones used in everyday contexts, are poorly known from Egypt. Such gaps in the material will tend to suggest that Egyptian exports and influence in the Near East were less significant than they may in fact have been.

Bibliography

Aldred, C. 1971. *Jewels of the Pharaohs: Egyptian Jewellery of the Dynastic Period.* London.

———. 1980. *Egyptian Art in the Days of the Pharaohs, 3100–320 BC.* London.

Assmann, J. 1983. Schrift, Tod und Identität: Das Grab als Vorschule der Literatur im alten Ägypten. Pp. 64–93 in *Schrift und Gedächtnis: Archäologie der literarischen Kommunikation* 1. Munich.

Badawy, A. 1954–68. *A History of Egyptian Architecture.* 3 vols. vol. 1: Giza. Vols. 2–3: Berkeley.

Baines, J. 1976. Temple Symbolism. *Royal Anthropological Institute News* 15: 10–15.

———. 1985a. *Fecundity Figures: Egyptian Personification and the Iconology of a Genre.* Warminster.

———. 1985b. Theories and Universals of Representation: Heinrich Schäfer and Egyptian Art. *Art History* 8: 1–25.

———. 1985c. Color Terminology and Color Classification: Ancient Egyptian Color Terminology and Polychromy. *American Anthropologist* 87: 282–97.

———. 1988. Ancient Egyptian Concepts and Uses of the Past: 3rd to 2nd Millennium B.C. evidence. Pp. 131–49 in *Who Needs the Past? Indigenous Values and Archaeology,* ed. R. Layton. London.

———. 1989a. Communication and Display: The Integration of Early Egyptian Art and Writing. *Antiquity* 63: 471–80.

———. 1989b. Techniques of Decoration in the Hall of Barques in the Temple of Sethos I at Abydos. *JEA* 75: 13–36.

Barguet, P. 1962. *Le temple d'Amon-Re à Karnak.* Institut français d'Archéologie orientale, Recherches d'Archéologie, de Philologie, et d'Histoire 21. Cairo.

Boston, Museum of Fine Arts. 1982. *Egypt's Golden Age: The Art of Living in the New Kingdom 1558–1085 B.C.* Exhibition catalog. Boston.

Bothmer, B. V. 1969. *Egyptian Sculpture of the Late Period, 700 B.C. to A.D. 100.* Exhibition catalog, the Brooklyn Museum. Corrected reprint. New York.

Bourriau, J. 1981. *Umm el-Gaᶜab: Pottery from the Nile Valley before the Arab Conquest.* Exhibition catalog, Fitzwilliam Museum. Cambridge.

Brooklyn Museum. 1988. *Cleopatra's Egypt: Age of the Ptolemies.* Exhibition catalog. Brooklyn.

Clarke, S., and Engelbach, R. 1930. *Ancient Egyptian Masonry: The Building Craft.* London.

Davies, A. M. (Nina), and Gardiner, A. H. 1936. *Ancient Egyptian Paintings.* 3 vols. Chicago.

Davies, N. de G. 1953. *The Temple of Hibis in el Khargeh Oasis* 3: *The Decoration.* The Metropolitan Museum of Art, Egyptian Expedition Publications 17. New York.

de Cenival, J.-L. 1964. *Living Architecture: Egyptian.* London.

Derchain, P. 1989. A propos de performativité: pensers anciens et articles récents. *Göttinger Miszellen* 110: 13–18.

Drenkhahn, R. 1976. *Die Handwerker und Ihre Tätigkeiten im alten Ägypten.* Ägyptologische Abhandlungen 31. Wiesbaden.

Eaton-Krauss, M., and Graefe, E., eds. 1989. *Studien zur ägyptischen Kunstgeschichte.* Hildesheimer Ägyptologische Beiträge 20. Hildesheim.

Edwards, I. E. S. 1985–86. *The Pyramids of Egypt.* Rev. ed. Harmondsworth.

el-Khouli, Ali Abdel-Rahman Hassanein. 1978. *Egyptian Stone Vessels, Predynastic Period to Dynasty III: Typology and Analysis.* 3 vols. Mainz am Rhein.

Epigraphic Survey. 1986. *The Battle Reliefs of King Sety I.* Reliefs and Inscriptions at Karnak 4. OIP 107. Chicago.

Finnestad, R. B. 1985. *Image of the World and Symbol of the Creator: On the Cosmological and Iconological Values of the Temple of Edfu.* Studies in Oriental Religions 10. Wiesbaden.

Fischer, H. G. 1974. Redundant Determinatives in the Old Kingdom. *Metropolitan Museum Journal* 8: 7–25.

———. 1986. *L'écriture et l'art de l'Égypte ancienne: quatre leçons sur la paléographie et l'épigraphie pharaoniques.* Collège de France, Essais et Conférences. Paris.

Frankfort, H., et al. 1930. *The Cenotaph of Seti I at Abydos.* 2 vols. Egypt Exploration Society, Memoir 39. London.

Gaballa, G. A. 1976. *Narrative in Egyptian Art.* Deutsches Archäologisches Institut, Abteilung Kairo. Mainz am Rhein.

Groenewegen-Frankfort, H. A. 1951. *Arrest and Movement: An Essay on Space and Time in the Representational Art of the Ancient Near East.* London.

Harpur, Y. 1987. *Decoration in Egyptian Tombs of the Old Kingdom: Studies in Orientation and Scene Content.* London.

Hayes, W. C. 1959. *The Scepter of Egypt.* Cambridge, MA.

Herrmann, G. 1986. *Ivories from Room SW 37 Fort Shalmaneser.* 2 vols. Ivories from Nimrud (1949–1963) 4. London.

Hildesheim. 1987. *Ägyptens Aufstieg zur Weltmacht.* Exhibition catalog, Roemer- und Pelizaeus-Museum, Hildesheim. Mainz am Rhein.

Hope, C. 1981. The Blue-Painted Pottery of the Eighteenth Dynasty. Diss. University of London.

———. 1987. *Egyptian Pottery.* Shire Egyptology. Princes Risborough, England.

Hornung, E. 1988. *Tal der Könige: Die Ruhestätte der Pharaonen.* 4th ed. Zurich.

Insley Green, C. 1987. *The Temple Furniture from the Sacred Animal Necropolis at North Saqqara, 1964–1976.* Egypt Exploration Society, Excavation Memoir 53. London.

Iversen, E. 1975. *Canon and Proportions in Egyptian Art.* 2d ed. Warminster.

Jéquier, G. 1920–24. *L'architecture et la décoration dans l'ancienne Égypte.* 3 vols. Paris.

Junge, F. fc. Versuch zu einer Ästhetik der ägyptischen Kunst. In Eaton-Krauss and Graefe.

Kitchen, K. A. 1986. Egyptianizing Features in the Nimrud Ivories. Pp. 37–42 in Herrmann 1986.

Krauss, R. 1983. Der Bildhauer Thutmose in Amarna. *Jahrbuch Preussischer Kulturbesitz* 20: 119–32.

———. 1985. *Sothis- und Monddaten: Studien zur astronomischen und technischen Chronologie Altägyptens.* Hildesheimer Ägyptologische Beiträge 20. Hildesheim.

———. 1986. Der Oberbildhauer Bak und sein Denkstein in Berlin. *Jahrbuch der Berliner Museen* 28: 5–46.

Kuhlmann. K. P., and Schenkel, W. 1983. *Das Grab des Ibi, Obergutsverwalters der Gottesgemahlin des Amun (Thebanisches Grab Nr. 36)* 1: *Beschreibung der unterirdischen Kult- und Bestattungsanlage.* Deutsches Archäologisches Institut, Abteilung Kairo, Archäologische Veröffentlichung 15. Mainz am Rhein.

Lacau, P. 1914. Suppressions et modifications de signes dans les textes funéraires. *ZÄS* 51: 1–64.

Lange, K., and Hirmer, M. 1968. *Egypt: Architecture, Sculpture, Painting.* 4th ed. London.

Leahy, L. M. 1988. Private Tomb Reliefs of the Late Period from Lower Egypt. Diss. Oxford.

Lefebvre, G. 1923–24. *Le tombeau de Petosiris.* Service des Antiquités de l'Égypte. Cairo.

Mekhitarian, A. 1954. *Egyptian Painting.* Geneva.

Moran, W. L., *et al.* 1987. *Les lettres d'el-Amarna: Correspondance diplomatique du pharaon.* Littératures Anciennes du Proche-Orient. Paris.

Müller, M. 1988. *Die Kunst Amenophis' III. und Echnatons.* Basel.

———. fc. Die ägyptische Kunst aus kunsthistorischer Sicht. In Eaton-Krauss and Graefe.

O'Connor, D. fc. *City and Cosmos in Ancient Egypt.*

———. fc.a. Palace and City in New Kingdom Egypt. *Sociétés Urbaines en Égypte et au Soudan: Cahiers de Recherches de l'Institut de Papyrologie et d'Égyptologie de Lille.*

———. fc.b. Preliminary Report on the Excavations of the Pennsylvania-Yale Expedition to Abydos. *Journal of the American Research Center in Egypt* 26.

Reuterswärd, P. 1958. *Studien zur Polychromie der Plastik* 1: *Ägypten.* Acta Universitatis Stockholmiensis: Stockholm Studies in History of Art 3: 1. Stockholm.

Robins, G. 1986. *Egyptian Painting and Relief.* Shire Egyptology. Princes Risborough.

Roik, E. 1988. *Das altägyptische Wohnhaus und seine Darstellung im Flachbild.* 2 vols. Europäische Hochsculschriften 28: Archäologie 15. Frankfurt.

Russmann, E. R. 1974. *The Representation of the King in the XXVth Dynasty.* Monographies Reine Élisabeth 3. Brussels.

———. fc. *The Ancient Sculpture of Egypt in the Cairo and Luxor Museums.* Austin.

Schäfer, H. 1986. *Principles of Egyptian Art,* ed. E. Brunner-Traut. Trans. and ed. J. Baines. Rev. repr. Oxford.

Smith, W. S. 1949. *A History of Egyptian Sculpture and Painting in the Old Kingdom.* 2d ed. London.

———. 1965. *Interconnections in the Ancient Near East.* New Haven.

———. 1981. *The Art and Architecture of Ancient Egypt.* 3d ed. Harmondsworth.

Spencer, A. J. 1979. *Brick Architecture in Ancient Egypt.* Warminster.

Stadelmann, R. 1971. Das Grab im Tempelhof: Der Typus des Königsgrabs in der Spätzeit. *Mitteilungen des Deutschen Archäologischen Instituts, Abteilung Kairo* 27: 111–23.

Tait, G. A. D. 1963. The Egyptian Relief Chalice. *JEA* 49: 93–139.

Tefnin, R. 1979. *La statuaire d'Hatshepsout: Portrait royal et politique sous la 18e dynastie.* Monumenta Aegyptiaca 4. Brussels.

Teissier, B. 1989. diss. Oxford.

Vandersleyen, C. 1975. *Das alte Ägypten.* Propyläen-Kunstgeschichte 15. Berlin.

Vandier, J. 1958. *Manuel d'archéologie égyptienne* 3: *La statuaire.* 2 vols. Paris.

———. 1964–78. *Manuel d'archéologie égyptienne* 4–6. 3 vols. in 5. Paris.

Wildung, D. 1984. *Sesostris und Amenemhet: Ägypten im Mittleren Reich.* Freiburg and Munich.

Wilkinson, A. 1971. *Ancient Egyptian Jewellery.* London.

Winter, E. 1968. *Untersuchungen zu den ägyptischen Tempelinschriften der griechisch-römischen Zeit.* Österreichische Akademie der Wissenschaften, phil.-hist. Klasse, Denkschriften 98. Vienna.

Wolf, W. 1957. *Die Kunst Ägyptens: Gestalt und Geschichte.* Stuttgart.

John Baines

PERSIAN ART

This article will focus on the art of the Achaemenid Persian empire (ca. 538–330 B.C.), but will also include some comments about Persian architecture. The art of this period not only reflects the complexity and diversity of the empire itself; it also ideologically reinforces the notion of a world now under control.

A. Historical Background

The Persians, like the Medes, were of the Indo-European linguistic family. They had gradually migrated from an aboriginal eastern homeland to the Zagros mountains of W Iran by the close of the second millennium B.C. By the 9th century B.C., these Persian and Median tribes had established themselves securely along the E fringe of the Assyrian empire. The heads of the Persian tribes were vassals of the Medes during the critical period when the Assyrian empire was overthrown by a Median and Babylonian alliance (612 B.C.). The Persian Cyrus II (reg ca. 550–538 B.C.) was a prince of the Achaemenid clan. When he overthrew the yoke of Median domination, he fell heir to the large territories acquired by the Medes from the earlier Assyrian realm.

It was once thought that the Medes and Persians were nomadic groups without traditions of monumental architecture and sculpture up until the time of Cyrus the Great. More recent discussion (Root 1979: 28–42) has attempted to place these peoples firmly in a context of settled patterns of assimilation within the Mesopotamian/Iranian cultural sphere. We learn from Assyrian annals that Medes and Persians lived in fortified citadels as early as the 9th century B.C. Archaeological investigations in the W Zagros area have now verified these Assyrian records by retrieving sites in Median territory which show the architectural sophistication of these citadels and, in some cases, their closeness to representations of W Iranian settlements on Assyrian historical reliefs (Young 1969; Young and Levine 1974; Stronach 1969; Gunter 1982). Even in its preempire phase, then, the Achaemenid dynasty enjoyed access to the ancient traditions of Mesopotamia and Elam. In art, these traditions form a critical backdrop to the imperial program created by the early Achaemenid kings. Again from Assyrian royal annals we know that Cyrus I, grandfather of Cyrus the Great, sent one of his sons to the court of King Assurbanipal (mid-7th century) in a diplomatic maneuver. This demonstrates the integration of the dynasty already in its preimperial period within the political networks of the time. It also shows that these Persians were actively exposed to the visual grandeur of Assyrian palatial contexts. At the end of the same century, paylists record Persians working alongside Egyptians, Ionians, Lydians, Medes, and Elamites at the court of Nebuchadnezzar II of Babylon. This demonstrates the integration of the Persians within the systems of artistic *production* as well as consumption in Mesopotamia before the formation of their empire. Persian interaction with the indigenous Elamites in SW Iran was also an important factor in their ultimate imperial artistic formulations. The Achaemenid dynasts took over the ancient Elamite title King of Anshan; they used Elamite as an administrative language; and it is becoming increasingly clear that they also drew extensively upon Elamite artistic models in the creation of their own imperial style.

Under Cyrus II the Achaemenids pushed all the way to Lydia, conquering the mighty Croesus in 547 B.C. Babylon fell to Cyrus in 539 B.C. The empire reached its greatest extent under Darius I (reg 521–486 B.C.)—stretching from India into N Greece and across Egypt. The Achaemenids maintained power until 330 B.C., when Alexander finally succeeded in crippling the Persian regime after prolonged campaigning.

Achaemenid art must be understood against the historical background of the ANE cultures which preceded it. It must also be understood with reference to the factors of cultural idiosyncracy which the Persians brought with them into the Mesopotamian/Iranian sphere. And finally, it must be understood in terms of the diversity of regionalisms reflected in the vastness of the imperial domain.

B. An Overview of the Evidence

Achaemenid art is preserved in a full range of media: official architecture in stone and brick, architectural sculpture in stone and molded brick, freestanding sculpture in stone and metal, rock relief, wall painting, seals (preserved as actual artifacts and as impressions on documents), imperial and provincial (satrapal) coins, jewelry, horse trappings and weaponry, vessels of stone, glass, and metal, ornamental ivory and wood carving, and textiles. Only tantalizing vestiges of wall paintings, textiles, glassware, metalwork, ivory and wood carving have been preserved—owing to their ephemeral nature and to the tendency for metal to be melted down for reuse. The major sites from which evidence has come for the study of Achaemenid art are the capitals of Pasargadae (Stronach 1978), Persepolis/Naqsh-i Rustam (Schmidt 1953–70; Tilia 1972–78), and Susa (Perrot 1981; Perrot et al. 1971; 1972; 1974)—all in SW Iran—and the rock relief and inscription at Behistun in NW Iran (Root 1979: 58–61, 182–226). Retrieved Achaemenid remains from Babylon are significant but not extensive (Haerinck 1973; Seidl 1976). Ecbatana, the Median capital in NW Iran which was occupied later by the Achaemenids as a summer residence, lies under modern Hamadan and has not been systematically explored (Muscarella 1980: 31–35). To date, no satrapal governor's palace has been excavated, although the site of the important palace at Daskyleion in Anatolia has been identified and surveyed, with an impressive corpus of small finds awaiting full publication (Balkan 1959).

Significant random finds from outlying sectors of the Achaemenid sphere provide glimpses of art and society under the Persian kings which add to the picture encapsulated most completely at Persepolis. Nevertheless, it remains unfortunate that at present very little is yet known archaeologically about the eastern periphery of the empire. New perspectives on the history of the Achaemenids in this region should encourage further archaeological investigation (Briant 1984).

One of the difficulties in dealing with aspects of Achaemenid art relates to the types of textual sources available for interpretive assistance. The official imperial texts which have come down to us are informative on a certain level (Kent 1953); but some tend to be neglected by art historians and others tend to be misinterpreted (Root 1979: 7–11; 1988; fc.). A good example of the latter phenomenon is the so-called Susa Foundation Charter of Darius the Great. This text enumerates specific tasks performed by specific subject peoples in the construction and decoration of the palace at Susa. Its function as a propaganda text meant metaphorically to characterize imperial domain has usually been overlooked in favor of a interpretation which takes literally the allocation of tasks along strict ethnic lines. The absence of Persians in the listing has been used to show that Persian artisans must have had no role in the building of Achaemenid Susa. It seems clear, on the contrary, that the absence of Persians in the list reflects the idea that the text is a way of describing Persian political power over other peoples.

None of the imperial texts preserves an explicit narrative account of court ceremonies, such as might help to fathom some of the iconographical intricacies of official representations. Similarly, there are no extant travelogues written by Persians of the Achaemenid period giving descriptions of cities or monuments. Administrative documents, letters, and graffiti provide valuable but oblique views of certain aspects of artistic production (Roaf 1980; Root 1979).

The texts most often culled for information on Persian art and society are the Greek sources such as Herodotus' *Histories* (5th century B.C.) and Xenophon's *Anabasis* (4th century B.C.). The classical texts are rich; but they are problematic because of the externality of their perspectives on the Persian empire—an externality which is compounded by the naturally Greek-oriented focus of most of the scholars who comment upon them. Important recent discussions, however, are attempting to redress the balance (Sancisi-Weerdenburg, ed., 1988; Sancisi-Weerdenburg and Kuhrt, eds., 1988; Kuhrt and Sancisi-Weerdenburg, eds., 1988).

The OT contains little *explicit* information on Achaemenid art, although it may well be that careful analysis can reveal more suggestive material than was once thought (see below).

C. Achaemenid Monumental Art

Pasargadae was founded by Cyrus II after his victory over Croesus of Lydia in 547 B.C. It features a fortified citadel (originally intended to accommodate administrative and ceremonial structures). In the plain below, palaces, a garden pavilion, a gatehouse, a tower (probably for the safekeeping of ritual paraphernalia) and the house-type tomb of Cyrus have been excavated and studied. Remains of the stone water courses for a formal garden provide our first documented example of the Persian "paradeisos" (see Fig. ART. 31). This predilection for reception palaces with deep shady porticoes overlooking gracious symmetrical gardens is echoed throughout the subsequent history of Persian architecture. A striking reminiscence of the paradise ambiance of Pasargadae is the 17th-century-A.D. palace of Chehel Sutun at Isfahan, where the features of architecture and environmental tableau are still well enough preserved explicitly to evoke the original aesthetic and conceptual principles common to both the medieval and the ancient sites.

At Pasargadae, as at Persepolis somewhat later, the palace architecture uses stone for the skeletal structure: for foundations, stairs, columns, and door and window frames. Mud brick originally fleshed out these elements. The stoneworking at Pasargadae displays significant characteristics of Lydian and Ionian technique and aesthetic (Nylander 1970). The masonry of the citadel platform clearly reflects a desire to emulate Hellenic forms of drafted ashlar blocks, for instance. And the technical details of joining and tooling suggest the important part played here by masons from the west brought to work at the Persian court in the wake of the fall of Sardis.

The buildings at Pasargadae also incorporate elements of ANE tradition. With great doorways and columns of stone, the Pasargadae Gatehouse was designed to impress the visitor with allusions to the triumphs and aspirations of the king. Assyrianizing attached sculptures of guardian bulls protruded from the main portals, while the jambs of the side doors were decorated in low relief with the image of a winged figure wearing the royal robe of Elam and an elaborate Egyptian war crown. See Fig. ART. 31. An accompanying inscription declared, "I am Cyrus, an Achaemenian." The inscription may well have been meant to

ART.31. Doorjamb relief from the gatehouse at Pasargadae. *(Courtesy of M. C. Root.)*

suggest that the representation showed the king himself in an allegorical mode of imperial aspiration. In this context, the wings acquire interest as an echo of the benevolent guardian figures of Assyrian palace reliefs. They may have been intended to allude to the protective, nurturing properties of these magical creatures—creatures who in manifold variants figured prominently in the symbol-laden architectural decoration of Israelite palaces as well (e.g., 1 Kgs 6:23–37). The wings possibly also relate more specifically to a prophetic dream recorded by Herodotus (I. 209). Here, Cyrus is supposed to have envisioned Darius with wings overshadowing the entirety of the Achaemenid empire encompassing both Europe and Asia. Thus the winged figure of Pasargadae may symbolize at once the perpetuation of venerable Near Eastern traditions of guardian creatures and also a more assertive allegorical concept of world dominion.

Indeed, the concept of harmonious world order is the central theme of the entire program of Achaemenid Persian imperial art. This art is not historical in the annalistic sense. Rather, it is historical in a cosmic sense. Ideas about political events and relationships are distilled for presentation in elaborate metaphorical statements. Quasi-realistic depiction of the events themselves (such as are featured in Assyrian palace reliefs) have no place in the extant repertory of official Achaemenid art.

The monument of Darius I at Behistun emphasizes this aspect of Achaemenid art. See Fig. ART. 32. Often characterized as the sole example of Achaemenid historical art, this rock relief is in essence highly abstract in its depiction of history. The inscription gives details of a series of battles against rebels fought by various of Darius' generals in far-flung regions of the empire over the course of more than one year. But the accompanying relief offers an ideological précis of this narrative. Here, Darius stands with one foot upon the squirming prostrate figure of the pretender Gaumata. Behind the king, two of his generals and weapon bearers symbolize the full host of loyal men who backed the newly declared monarch. Stretching out before Darius is a row of bound captives—the rebels who in the historical narrative were described as having been dispatched separately in diverse encounters. Hovering above the entire scene, facing Darius, appears the figure of Ahuramazda in the winged disc.

The god Ahuramazda is repeatedly invoked in the imperial texts as the agent of imperial success with whom the king appears to enjoy a symbiotic relationship. The rendering as a half-length human figure emerging from a winged disc hearkens back to Neo-Assyrian representations of the god Assur. Because the image of Ahuramazda is never actually labeled in Achaemenid art, it has generated much controversy among scholars. Some have rejected the traditional interpretation in favor of variant nuances of the idea that the figure in the winged disc represents the "Xvarnah"—the essence of glory—of the king himself as this concept is articulated in later (post-Achaemenid period) Zoroastrian texts (Shahbazi 1974; 1980; Calmeyer 1979; Jacobs 1987). Others have urged retention of the traditional interpretation as the one which suits the conceptualizations apparent from texts of the Achaemenid period itself (Root 1979: 162–81; Lecoq 1984). The figure of Ahuramazda (as this article will persist in characterizing it) plays a role in many representational contexts of Achaemenid art. The very fact that the divine figure resembles the royal figure in dress and attitude correlates neatly with the complete marriage of goals between god and king as portrayed in the texts.

The controversy over the identity of the figure within the winged disc is particularly significant in the context of biblical studies because it forces us into the vexing issue of the religion practiced at the Achaemenid court (Herrenschmidt 1980). Although Ahuramazda is the primary deity invoked in the official texts, allusions do exist in the documentary evidence to the veneration of other gods as well, e.g., Behistun (Kent 1953: 132). Similarly, some evidence exists for *representations* of gods other than Ahuramazda in Achaemenid art (characterized with reference to seals in Moorey 1979). If the Achaemenids were Zoroastrians, their Zoroastrianism was of a variety not fully clarified through non-Achaemenid texts. Certainly, for instance, it

ART.32. Rock relief and inscription of Darius I at Behistun—519 B.C.E. *(Photograph by G. Cameron, courtesy of Kelsey Museum of Archaeology—University of Michigan)*

was not strictly monotheistic, and the rendering of divine images was not prohibited.

Official Achaemenid policy emphasized the pragmatism of condoning regional spiritual behavior as well as regional political and economic structure. In keeping with this policy, the Achaemenid king might display himself as Pharaoh, Son of Ra, in Egypt (Posener 1936; Root 1979: 61–72); he might rebuild the temple at Jerusalem; and he might patronize an artistic establishment in the Persian heartland which drank deeply of ancient Mesopotamian/ Iranian cult practices. It is difficult to assess the extent to which the ecumenicalism of official policy reflects active cult belief as opposed to purely formal embrace of the imagery and protocols of other cultures (Kuhrt 1987). The monumental art of the dynasty in the heartland suggests conscious reinforcement of links with the critical ancient traditions of the empire. This is seen first at Pasargadae (where we have already noted the winged figure of the Gatehouse). In the partially preserved door-jamb reliefs of Palace S, creatures of the Assyro-Babylonian cult world (a bull-man, a fish-garbed priest, an eagle-footed, human-legged creature) proceed out of the courtly chamber along with a presumably sacrificial bovine (Stronach 1978: 68–77).

At Persepolis, founded by Darius II in ca. 515 B.C., the program of architectural reliefs is more elaborate and more subtle in its evocations of ecumenical hegemony. The carved facade of Darius' rock-cut tomb at nearby Naqsh-i Rustam (copied by all subsequent Achaemenid kings) shows the king before a blazing fire altar with Ahuramazda and an emblem of the sun and moon in the field above. See Fig. ART. 33. The king and his altar stand atop a great carved platform which is raised off the ground by personifications of the lands of the empire. Darius' platform recalls the throne of Solomon (2 Chr 6:12) upon which Solomon stood in appearance before the assembly of Israel. Interestingly, the Achaemenid representation is the only preserved illustration of a royal appearance atop a dais of such dimensions from the entire ANE, excluding Egypt.

The lifting of the platform by peoples of the empire is frankly metaphorical. As the tomb inscription states: "If now thou shalt think that, 'How many are the countries which King Darius held?' look at the sculptures [of those] who bear the throne, then thou shalt know, then it shall become known to thee: the spear of a Persian man has gone forth far . . ." (Kent 1953: 138).

The supporting figures on the Achaemenid relief lift up

ART.33. Facade of the tomb of Darius I at Naqsh-i Rustam (near Persepolis). *(Courtesy of The Oriental Institute of The University of Chicago.)*

their king by assuming the ancient Atlas pose—frontal torso, with arms raised above the head and burden resting effortlessly on outspread fingertips. Within the iconographical traditions of the ANE, from Egypt to Iran, this pose had consistent and significant cosmic implications relating to the joyous elevation of celestial bodies (Root 1979: 131–61, for full discussion of this image). Under the patronage of Darius, a conflation of political and cosmic associations was achieved in imperial art. A provocative parallelism occurs here with the poetic metaphor of Psalm 22—where Yahweh is characterized as enthroned on the praises of Israel (v 4—Eng v 3).

Another important representational type depicting the Achaemenid king in monumental art is preserved on the stairway facades of the great Apadana at Persepolis (Root 1979: 227–84; 1985 passim). See Fig. ART. 34. Here, in its original state, both the N and the E stairway were decorated with the same relief program. At the center an over-life-size representation of the king enthroned under a baldachino acts as a visual and conceptual fulcrum for a vast expanse of figural imagery. An official bows before the king, serving to announce the imminence of a procession of gift bearers from the subject lands. Ranged in three registers of relief facing the central royal tableau appear depictions of delegates of non-Persian peoples of the empire. A Persian usher takes the leader of each delegation by the hand. This motif places the scene squarely within the ancient Mesopotamian tradition of presentation scenes in which a petitioner is brought forward by the hand or the wrist into the presence of a deity or a deified king. The specific sculptural formula used for the execution of the Apadana image of hand-holding is a conscious reminiscence of a traditional Egyptian patterning of interlaced hands. In the Egyptian context, the image and its precisely articulated rendering was used from the Old Kingdom through the Late Period in depictions of the deceased being brought forward into the presence of Osiris for the last judgment.

The Apadana reliefs thus offer another example of a conflation of political and spiritual message. The Achaemenid king has assumed the role of a quasi-divinity before whom a regiment of pious, gift-bearing petitioners will be led by the hand. In this case, the petitioners are the members of the imperial world created by the Persian

ART.34. Relief of Syrian tribute bearers on N stair of the Apadana at Persepolis. *(Courtesy of The Oriental Institute of The University of Chicago.)*

king. This world has been characterized in the official artistic program of the dynasty as a harmoniously ordered enterprise. The force of the Persian king is played out in terms evocative of a kind of spiritual power which is more compelling than mere military might described in annalistic detail.

The question naturally arises as to whether or not the reliefs of the Persian kings show him as a deified ruler who was actually worshiped at the court. At this point in our understanding of the issue it seems best to acknowledge the suggestiveness of the artistic program without insisting upon any specificity of underlying cult activity. We have absolutely no Persian textual reinforcement of Achaemenid date for the worship of the king as a god. The nature of Achaemenid kingship is certainly revealed in part through careful analysis of the imperial art (Root 1979). It becomes clear that the Persians established a concept or ideal of kingship which stressed the notion of peaceful coexistence centered around the charismatic persona of the Great King, King of Kings. But many questions remain (Kuhrt 1984; 1987). Hopefully the time will soon be ripe for an informed reappraisal of several brilliant, if problematic, commentaries on the impact of Achaemenid concepts of kingship upon the imperial cults of later periods—from Alexander to the Hellenistic and Roman rulers and the dynasts of Sasanian Persia (e.g., Taylor 1927; 1931; L'Orange 1953).

D. Achaemenid Seals

Numerically, the single most frequently depicted image in Achaemenid art—both monumental and small-scale—is the image of the hero mastering beasts. See Fig. ART. 35. This motif, in many variants, accounts for roughly two thirds of all extant Achaemenid representations in the medium of seal carving (Garrison 1988; Greenfield 1962). Research currently underway (Root and Garrison fc.a. and fc.b.) will soon provide the material basis for reassessing the relationships in meaning between the many privately owned seals bearing the hero image and the examples of the image employed in official contexts of imperial relief sculpture and imperial administrative seals.

The variant of hero motif which portrays the human protagonist controlling two symmetrically placed beasts may ultimately prove particularly interesting in this re-

ART.35. Royal name seal of Darius I. Seal impressed on the Persepolis Fortification Tablets. *(Courtesy of M. C. Root.)*

gard. Like most imagery in Achaemenid art, this one has a very ancient pedigree. Under the patronage of the early Achaemenid kings, its significance may, however, have achieved a subtle tuning—just as other venerable images were adapted to a new imperial environment. The tomb inscription of Darius the Great emphasizes the supreme moral importance of the blameless life: e.g., "By the favor of Ahuramazda, I am of such a sort that I am a friend to the right, I am not a friend to the wrong" (Kent 1953: 140). On Achaemenid seals, the image of the master of beasts—quietly and without weaponry controlling the forces of animal violence in an emblem of balanced accomplishment—suggests the possibility of a specific meaning. In Daniel 6 (which is set in Achaemenid times although not written in Achaemenid times), Daniel is delivered from the lions by the force of his blamelessness, as one who has done no wrong. Post-Achaemenid seal imagery in Iran develops the antique master-of-beasts image into an illustration specifically meant to allude to the Daniel story (Lerner 1977: 22–30). It seems plausible that under the Achaemenids, the popularity of this image on private seals already reflected a conceptual reworking of the ancient visual formula. In the Achaemenid context, the reworking took place, of course, before the writing of Daniel. Thus, its significance to Daniel is of a different order. The Achaemenid motif would have been popularized specifically to display an emblem of officially sanctioned virtue: the owner as a blameless person whose rectitude and right-minded attitude toward the king was symbolized by his portrayal as pacifier of wild beasts. In this case, the story in the book of Daniel would carry historical weight as the reflection on some level of a metaphorically expressed ethos actually current at the time when the story was intended to be set. An interesting issue—too complex for full discussion here—involves the fact that the hero on these seals often seems to wear a Persian royal crown. Without pursuing all the ramifications of this feature, one relevant possibility emerges in the context of biblical studies. The easiest solution to the issue of identifying the crowned figure would name it an image of the king himself. In this case, it would be the king depicted on innumerable private seals as the Blameless One, rather than a generalized personage meant to epitomize the *owner* of any particular seal. On the other hand, further insights may possibly be gleaned from Esth 6:6 and 8:15. Here, Mordecai is decked out in the robes and crown of the king for a public appearance in order to demonstrate the royal favor bestowed upon him. The private seals of the Achaemenid period showing crowned masters of beasts may thus relate to an actual Persian tradition of bestowing honor—a tradition reflected also in the later textual allusions in Esther.

E. Conclusion

The last 20 years have witnessed great scholarly advancement of our knowledge about Achaemenid Persian art in the dynastic heartland of SW Iran. The impact of this art upon the cultures under imperial control is, however, largely an undeveloped topic. One overview of the material evidence provides an indispensible step in the right direction (Moorey 1980). Specifically regarding the impact of Persian rule in Israel, major efforts now enable us to begin an evaluation of the penetration of Achaemenid art (Stern 1973). Analytical studies are moving in the direction of seeing far greater Persian artistic impact in the provincial regions than was once thought. And some scholars are making significant advances in correlating occurrences of strong artistic influence from Persia with specific historical events and political climates within the 200-year span of the empire (e.g., Mørkholm and Zahle 1972).

As we are told in the book of Esther, decrees of the Persian king were sent out far and wide, translated into the languages of specific localities. We learn the same from Darius' own words at Behistun. The discovery that an Aramaic version of the Behistun text from Elephantine in Egypt incorporates segments drawn from Darius' *tomb* text as well enhances our appreciation of the availability of material originally created in the heartland (Greenfield and Porten 1982). Now we know that the Behistun relief of Darius was copied for Babylon along with the text (Seidl 1976).

Official Persian art was designed for widespread dissemination and message conveyance, just as the official decrees were. From the imperial coinage emblazoned with imagery of the king-as-archer (Carradice 1987; Root 1989) to the grandiose metaphorical displays on the architectural facades of Persepolis, the overarching message is one of a world under control. The pervasive image of kingship stresses dynastic identity rather than personal idiosyncracy. The pervasive image of imperial domain and social hierarchy stresses cooperative—even joyous—service and the virtues of blamelessness.

Bibliography

Amiet, P. 1974. L'art achéménide. *Acta Iranica* 1: 163–70.

Balkan, K. 1959. Inscribed Bullae from Daskyleion-Ergill. *Anatolia* 4: 123–28.

Briant, P. 1984, *L'asie centrale et les royaumes proche-orientaux du premier millénaire.* Paris.

Calmeyer, P. 1979. Fortuna-Tyche-Khvarnah. *Jahrbuch des deutschen archäologischen Instituts* 94: 347–65.

Carradice, I. 1987. The "Regal" Coinage of the Persian Empire. Pp. 73–95 in *Coinage and Administration in the Athenian and Persian Empires,* ed. I. Carradice. BARIS 343. Oxford.

Garrison, M. B. 1988. *Seal Workshops and Artists in Persepolis.* Diss., Univ. of Michigan.

Greenfield, J. 1962. Studies in Aramaic Lexicography I. *JAOS* 82: 290–99.
Greenfield, J., and Porten, B. 1982. *The Bisitun Inscription of Darius the Great—Aramaic Version.* London.
Gunter, A. 1982. Representations of Urartian and Western Iranian Fortress Architecture in the Assyrian Reliefs. *Iran* 20: 103–12.
Haerinck, E. 1973. Le palais achéménide de Babylon. *Iranica Antiqua* 10: 103–32.
Herrenschmidt, C. 1980. La religion des achéménides. *Studia Iranica* 9: 325–39.
Jacobs, B. 1987. Das Chvarnah—zum Stand der Forschung. *MDOG* 119: 215–48.
Kent, R. G. 1953. *Old Persian Grammar, Texts, Lexicon.* 2d ed. New Haven.
Kuhrt, A. 1984. The Achaemenid Concept of Kingship. *Iran* 22: 156–60.
———. 1987. Review of *Reichsidee und Reichsorganisation im Perserreich* by P. Frei and K. Koch. *BiOr* 44 no. 1/2: 280–304.
Kuhrt, A., and Sancisi-Weerdenburg, H., eds. 1988. *Achaemenid History III.* Leiden.
Lecoq, P. 1984. Un problème de religion achéménide: Ahura Mazda ou xvarnah? *Acta Iranica* 23: 301–26.
Lerner, J. A. 1977. *Christian Seals of the Sasanian Period.* Leiden.
L'Orange, H. P. 1953. *Studies in the Iconography of Cosmic Kingship in the Ancient World.* Oslo.
Moorey, P. R. S. 1979. Aspects of Worship and Ritual on Achaemenid Seals. Pp. 218–24 in *VII. International Congress on Iranian Art and Archaeology.* Berlin.
———. 1980. *Cemeteries of the First Millennium B.C. at Deve Hüyük.* Oxford.
Mørkholm, O., and Zahle, J. 1972. The Coinage of Kuprlli. *Acta Archaeologica* 43: 57–113.
Muscarella, O. W. 1980. Excavated and Unexcavated Achaemenian Art. Pp. 23–42 in *Ancient Persia—The Art of an Empire,* ed. D. Schmandt-Besserat. Malibu, CA.
Nylander, C. 1970. *Ionians in Pasargadae.* Uppsala.
Perrot, J. 1981. L'architecture militaire et palatiale des Achéménides à Suse. Pp. 79–94 in *150 Jahre deutsches archäologisches Institut 1829–1979.* Mainz.
Perrot, J., et al. 1971. Recherches à Suse et en Susiane: Chaour. *Syria* 48: 36–51.
———. 1972. Une statue de Darius découverte à Suse. *Journal Asiatique* 250: 235–66.
———. 1974. Recherches dans le secteur de tepe de l'Apadana. *Cahiers de la délégation archéologique française en Iran* 4. Paris.
Posener, G. 1936. *La première domination perse en Égypte.* Cairo.
Roaf, M. 1980. Texts about the Sculptures and Sculptors of Persepolis. *Iran* 18: 65–74.
Root, M. C. 1979. *The King and Kingship in Achaemenid Art.* Leiden.
———. 1985. The Parthenon Frieze and the Apadana Reliefs at Persepolis. *AJA* 89: 103–20.
———. 1988. Evidence from Persepolis for the Dating of Persian and Archaic Greek coinage. *Numismatic Chronicle* 148: 1–12.
———. 1989. The Persian Archer at Persepolis. *Revue des études anciennes* 91.
———. fc. *Persia and the Parthenon: Essays on the Art of Emulation.*
Root, M. C., and Garrison, M. B. fc.a. Royal Name Seals of the Persian Empire. *Archäologische Mitteilungen aus Iran.*
———. fc.b. *The Seal Impressions on the Persepolis Fortification Tablets: A Catalogue Raisonné.* Oriental Institute Publications.
Sancisi-Weerdenburg, H., ed. 1988. *Achaemenid History I.* Leiden.
Sancisi-Weerdenburg, H., and Kuhrt, A., eds. 1988. *Achaemenid History II.* Leiden.
Schmidt, E. F. 1953–70. *Persepolis I-III.* OIP 68–70. Chicago.
Seidl, U. 1976. Ein Relief Dareios' I. in Babylon. *Archäologische Mitteilungen aus Iran* n.F. 9: 125–30.
Shahbazi, A. S. 1974. An Achaemenid Symbol I: A Farewell to "Fravahr" and "Ahuramazda." *Archäologische Mitteilungen aus Iran* n.F. 7: 135–44.
———. 1980. An Achaemenid Symbol II: Farnah (God Given) Fortune "Symbolized." *Archäologische Mitteilungen aus Iran* n.F. 13: 119–47.
Stern, E. 1973. *Material Culture of the Land of the Bible in the Persian Period 538–332 B.C.* Warminster.
Stronach, D. 1969. Excavations at Tepe Nush-i Jan 1967. *Iran* 7: 1–20.
———. 1978. *Pasargadae.* Oxford.
Taylor, L. R. 1927. The "Proskynesis" and the Hellenistic Ruler Cult. *JHS* 47: 53–62.
Tilia, A. B. 1972–78. *Studies and Restorations at Persepolis and Other Sites in Fars.* 2 vols. Rome.
Young, T. C., Jr. 1969. *Excavations at Godin Tepe.* Toronto.
Young, T. C., Jr., and Levine, L. D. 1974. *Excavations of the Godin Project.* Toronto.

MARGARET COOL ROOT

EARLY JEWISH ART AND ARCHITECTURE

This article will focus on two distinctive periods when Jewish art and architecture flourished: late in the Second Temple period (Hellenistic and Early Roman), and in the period of late antiquity immediately following (Late Roman and Byzantine). Differences between these two periods are significant, and are primarily political and social. In the former period, when the Jews enjoyed varying degrees of political autonomy, the art reflects not only the influence of the larger Greco-Roman culture but also the attempt to withstand those influences through the development of strictly aniconic features. In contrast to the national spirit of Second Temple period art, that of late antiquity is more an expression of communal and local life, and is replete with concrete visual images that are both figurative and symbolic.

A. Late Second Temple Period

During the Second Temple period, when there was a Jewish state in Palestine and a central Temple in Jerusalem, the ruling classes, though Hellenized, retained parts of their Jewish faith and laws. The art and architecture of the period show connections with the neighboring Greco-Roman culture. However, at the same time it reflects an attempt to withstand those influences by evolving strictly aniconic features. It is characterized by highly skilled indigenous stonework, by the predominant oriental elements of endless patterns, by the elements of *horror vacui,* by plasticity of carving, and by symmetrical stylization.

1. Architecture. The architecture of the late Second Temple period is reflected in Hasmonean remains found in sites and in structures that were later reconstructed or completely renovated in connection with subsequent Herodian architectural projects. These buildings and renovations left an enduring mark upon the art and architecture of the period.

a. Hasmonean. Hasmonean architecture mostly survives in remains of fortifications, desert fortresses, in funerary art, water systems, and the recently excavated Hasmonean palace at Jericho. The Hasmonean palaces especially exhibit clear architectural features. The characteristic features of the Hasmonean palaces include a central court surrounded by rooms. A hall with two columns *in antis* in the southern part of the court led to the triclinium, and probably served as a reception hall. This basic plan characterizes all the palaces at Masada, as well as the twin palaces at Jericho probably built at the same time, and was inspired by Hellenistic architecture.

b. Herodian. Comprehensive and monumental building projects were undertaken during Herod's reign (37–4 B.C.E.). The two sources of data relating to the Herodian construction projects are literary and archaeological. The major literary sources are the works of Josephus, particularly *Ant.* 15–17 and *JW* 1–2 and 5. Extensive archaeological excavations undertaken recently add information which both complements and contradicts the literary sources.

Josephus mentions 33 building projects, 20 of which were within the borders of Herod's kingdom while 13 were in other countries. This list of Herodian architectural projects includes references to the construction, reconstruction, and extension of towns, fortifications, palaces, and fortresses, as well as references to the Temple in Jerusalem, the largest single structure (the Royal Stoa), the largest palace (the 50-acre palace at Herodium), and one of the largest harbors ever constructed in antiquity (at Caesarea). Many of these monumental structures have survived and have been excavated in the last decades. See HEROD'S BUILDING PROGRAM; HERODIUM (M.R. 173119); CAESAREA (PLACE); etc. Most of these structures were built during Herod's reign, but renovations and reconstructions were undertaken during the 1st century C.E. until the destruction of the Second Temple in 70 C.E.

Herod built three new towns: Antipatris, Caesarea with its magnificent harbor, and Sebaste (Samaria) with its temple of Augustus. In the newly established towns Herod built temples, palaces, theaters, stadia, fortifications, and harbors. Within the Jewish Kingdom Herod carried out several projects. He built extensively in Jerusalem, particularly its Temple, a palace, town fortifications, and towers, as well as many public buildings and institutions. In the Judean desert he constructed or renovated several splendid palace-fortresses: Masada, Herodium, Alexandrion (Sartaba), Cypros, Machaerus, and the winter palaces at Jericho. The Herodian building projects included public structures and private buildings, as well as other structures such as palace-fortresses which incorporated monumental as well as utilitarian, functional sections. The palace-fortresses in particular combined luxurious, leisurely living with the need for security.

(1) Jerusalem Temple. Herod's temple in Jerusalem is the largest known temple in antiquity. One of the architectural wonders of the ancient world, and a unique structure, it must have made a magnificent impression on visitors. The Temple was the focal point for the Jewish nation, the center for worship, and the place where political, economic, and spiritual affairs of world Jewry could be discussed and determined. It was also the destination for pilgrims during the festivals, and therefore needed to accommodate thousands of people who gathered there to celebrate. One of the major reasons behind the enormity of the Herodian Temple building project was to meet this need.

The archaeological excavations carried out during the course of a decade (1968–78) have resulted in important data being disclosed concerning the areas of the Temple Mount gates and the areas outside the west, south, and east retaining walls. Streets, squares, and monumental passageways have been uncovered. See also TEMPLE, JERUSALEM.

(2) Palaces. King Herod's reign is remarkable, in the architectural sphere, for the many monumental edifices either renovated or newly built in both towns and fortresses. Herod concerned himself especially with the building of palaces which could be used both for administrative as well as for recreational purposes.

The typical architectural features of these palaces followed the common plans of the Roman *domus* and *villa* ("townhouse" and "country-house" respectively). A Herodian palace was usually an elaborate building with several wings. The main wing contained the triclinium (a peristyle court with rows of columns and double columns in its corners), an inner garden, a bathhouse, and dwelling rooms. The extended palace complex usually also included recreational facilities, including pools for swimming and sailing boats, and elaborate gardens, such as the sunken garden at Jericho (palace III). Water installations, such as aqueducts and channels, brought water to the pools and gardens, as well as to the residential wings.

(3) Fortresses. Seven fortresses known to have been built in the Judean desert (Masada, Herodium, Cypros, Hyrcania, Alexandrium, Machaerus, and Dok) constitute an important component of Herodian architecture. The fortresses were located in the desert, within view of each other. They were isolated and autonomous. Built on mountaintops, they were each strongly fortified, and had extensive systems for the entrapment and storage of water. They functioned primarily as military bases for defense, but also as places of refuge for political and spiritual reasons. In times of violent confrontation and upheaval, they acted as shelters. The fortresses also served as administrative centers for important routes, and for agricultural and royal farm areas and palaces; they were also used for guarding the borders. They even served as burial places both for the Hasmoneans and for Herod. Elaborate palaces were constructed on their premises. Masada was the most spacious of all and had several palaces on its summit, which served as leisure resorts. The fortresses sometimes extended into the lower areas of their mountains; Herodium had buildings and installations built below the mount.

2. Art. Second Temple period Jewish art is a purely decorative art characterized by a mixture of native traditions and Hellenistic-Roman features. Hellenistic-Roman culture greatly influenced the upper classes (of all the Near Eastern countries), as is attested to by the predominance of Hellenistic-Roman architecture and by the use of the Greek language and its institutions which affected many aspects of everyday life. Politically, the country was first under Hellenistic and later Roman rule. However, resistance to the intrusive culture was strong, in part because of the force and vitality of the Jewish religion which continued to influence the community's activities. Traditional aspects of Judaism so conceptually dominated its decorative art that neither figurative nor symbolic representation were depicted.

The various ornamental devices and the repertoire of motifs were part of the general stream of Roman art, especially its provincial and eastern tributaries. Decoration in Herodian architecture attests to the influence of Roman art. Hellenistic tradition, moreover, survived into the later Herodian period. A locally developed style is encountered mainly in funerary art, on tomb facades, on ossuaries, and on sarcophagi (see BURIALS, JEWISH). The style of Jewish art followed the basic oriental elements: (a) the "endless" and "all-over" patterns, (b) symmetrical stylization; (c) deep carving resulting in contrasts between parts, intensifying the play of light and shadow; and the so-called (d) *horror vacui*—the ornament filling of all available space.

Decoration of buildings, palaces, houses, and bathhouses of the Second Temple period mainly focused on the use of wall paintings, stucco-plaster moldings, and ornamental floor pavements. The decorative elements, motifs, and designs are characterized by a total lack of animate motifs or symbolic emblems. This stems from the reluctance of all Jews, including the ruling families such as that of Herod and his dynasty, to decorate any building or tomb with religious or iconic symbols. The biblical prohibition of "no graven image" (Exod 20:4; Deut 4:16; 27:15) was carefully kept.

Jewish art in the late Second Temple period exhibits several characteristic features. First, stonework, carving, and use of relief characterize Jewish Second Temple–period art and continue later in Jewish synagogal art. Stonework was one of the most prevalent crafts of Jewish art that flourished in Herodian times. It utilized the locally available stone, and created a new type of ornament. The designs were sketched in by compass and ruler and carved out by chisel in a deeply incised and stylized manner. Stonework is found in the architecture of buildings and tombs and in funerary art. Stone craft is also used for objects of daily life, such as ornamented stone tables and domestic vessels. Second, the repertoire of ornamental aniconic motifs reflects a rigid choice of floral, geometric, and architectural patterns, some of which were adopted from Hellenistic art. Third, Jewish art also displays many oriental elements, including the simple local art encountered mainly in Jewish burials as well as that seen in the palaces and tombs. The difference lies usually in the quality of execution and in the attention paid to decorative details.

Thus, there evolved a local Jewish art, strictly aniconic, using neither figures nor symbols. In their struggle against paganism and idolatry, the Jews refrained from using animate motifs and representational art. Only with the decline of paganism during the 3d century did the attitude of Jewish art change, resulting in the use of figurative motifs (see B. 2 below).

3. Synagogues. Several public structures of the Second Temple period which have been discovered in the last decades are considered to be synagogues. These include structures found at Masada, Herodium, Gamla, and Migdal, a recently uncovered structure at Capernaum (under the later synagogue), and another synagogue—now lost—reported at Chorazin.

The excavated structures are assumed by scholars to be synagogues because of the circumstantial evidence of similarity to each other in architectural plan and, therefore, in function, even though no actual proof has been uncovered. All the structures were built as oblong halls, and the halls were divided by rows of columns into a central nave and surrounding aisles. See Fig. ART. 36. Stepped benches were erected along all four walls of the hall facing the center. The structures also share a similar date for their construction in the 1st century C.E. (although Gamla may have been erected as early as the end of the 1st century B.C.E.).

Upon the evidence of the structures themselves, it should be noted that they differ from later synagogues in plan, function, and decoration. First, from the architectural point of view, no new conceptions in construction

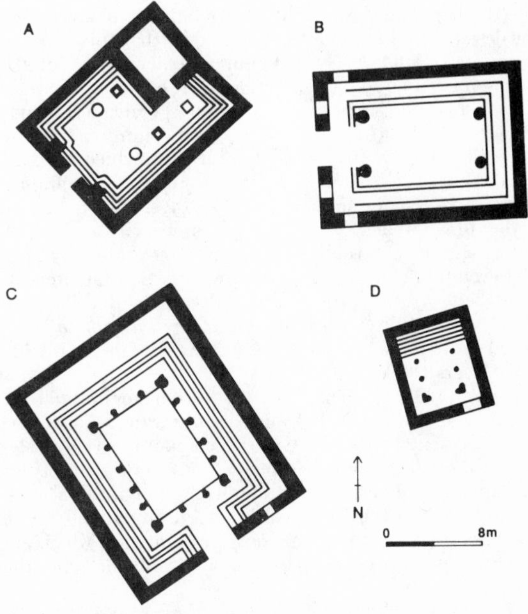

ART.36. Plans of synagogues—Second Temple Period. *A*, Masada; *B*, Herodium; *C*, Gamla; *D*, Migdal building (possibly synagogue). *(Redrawn from Hachlili 1987: 85, fig. 1.)*

have been discerned, but the impression is rather one of local extemporization. Second, these structures existed only for a short time in the 1st century C.E., and were never built again, except for Capernaum. Only in the case of the 1st-century building found under a later synagogue at Capernaum can one assume that it is a synagogue, due to its location. Third, these assembly halls lack the most important feature of the later synagogue: the Torah shrine. Finally, during the 1st century the Temple in Jerusalem was still the center for worship and ritual for the entire Jewish community in Judea and the Diaspora; it was *there* that one could participate most fully in the ceremonies, in the teaching of the Law conducted in the Temple courtyards, and in the resolution of administrative questions. These local centers of worship probably existed as community assembly halls, where services would be conducted probably only on Sabbaths and feast days. The assembly structures at the fortresses of Masada, Herodium, and Gamla probably served as local assembly halls during the years of the revolt against Rome, a time during which it was extremely difficult for their respective congregations to travel to Jerusalem to participate in Temple worship. At the same time as these structures were serving as small community centers, worship was presumably also being conducted in them, although no convincing proof of this has been found. With the destruction of the Jerusalem Temple in 70 C.E., local structures began to flourish which necessarily became sites of local worship and community centers. In these halls Torah reading came to be emphasized, and thus the distinctive feature of the later synagogues, the Torah shrine, begins to emerge.

B. Late Antiquity

1. Synagogue Architecture. An important innovation of Jewish art in Late Antiquity (3d–7th cents. C.E.) is associated with the construction and decoration of the synagogue. The synagogue building functioned as an assembly hall for the local congregation as well as a spiritual, religious, and social center. Its use as a community assembly hall determined its architectural plan, which took the form of a large hall divided only by supporting columns, with benches along the walls. But the diverse architectural styles uncovered indicate that no universal or uniform synagogue plan existed. Opinions vary considerably as to the evolution of synagogue architecture. Several attempts have been made to categorize and explain the different types and the divergence in style of the synagogues scattered throughout many regions (see Avi-Yonah 1981: 272–73; Meyers 1980: 97–108).

Generally the internal plan of the synagogue building consists of two rows of stone columns which divide the main hall lengthwise into a central nave and two side aisles (as in the late Second Temple period). The majority of synagogue plans are oblong and all have longitudinal axes. In addition, synagogues within Israel itself exhibit several other common features, the most prominent of which are the facades and its portals, the Torah shrine, and the gallery.

The major architectural feature they shared was the Torah shrine. From its inception following the destruction of the Jerusalem Temple, the Torah shrine became a permanent fixture in the synagogue building. Always built on the wall facing Jerusalem, the Torah shrine housed the Ark of the scrolls and structurally took the form of either an aedicula, a niche, or an apse. See Fig. ART. 37. The preponderance of *aediculae* found in excavated Galilean and Golan synagogues indicates that the aedicula was the characteristic structure for containing the Ark in these regions. In the case of synagogues which possessed two flanking aediculae, it seems that they had separate functions. One aedicula served to house the Ark of the Scrolls, while the other possibly held the menorah. Synagogues with *niches* have been found scattered throughout Palestine. There may have been local as well as traditional influences at work, because two of the niched synagogues are located at Tiberias while three are in Judea within close proximity of each other (Susiya, Eshtemoa, and Rimmon). The *apse* is a dominant architectural feature in the synagogue from the 6th century on, functioning as the container for the Ark and, possibly, the menoroth. The orientation of the apse is toward Jerusalem. Typological differences in the Torah shrines should be attributed either to local preferences, popular vogues, or historical development. Chronologically, the aedicula is the earliest type of Torah shrine (already in existence by the 2d century) and the most popular type in Galilean and Golan synagogues.

Construction of new synagogues in the 6th century shows a significant change in synagogue architecture by the addition of the apse as Torah shrine enclosure. Several renovated synagogues had their aedicula or niche replaced by an apse already in the 5th century (Ḥammath-Gader and Maʿoz Ḥayim). In the 6th century the apse was an integrally planned structure. The aedicula, on the other hand, even though built to be used as a permanent structure, was an appendage built onto the original internal wall only after the synagogue building had been constructed.

The most striking feature of synagogue architecture is the fundamental uniformity of design among synagogue structures. Differences occur, however, when certain structural features have to be adapted to liturgical requirements: to the changes, for example, in form of the Torah shrine (aedicula, niche, and apse) or to the development of the monumental facade in Galilean and Golan synagogues. Generally, the Jews tended to use a spacious hall to serve the congregation for reading the Torah and for prayer, but added the specific features of Torah shrine, benches, and gallery to suit their particular needs. Nevertheless, a definite originality of design can be distinguished in the characteristic triple facade of the building, and in the ornamentation infused with Jewish motifs and symbols (see below).

Scholarly opinion differs concerning the origin of the synagogue building plan and its sources of inspiration, such as the Hellenistic basilica, pagan triclinium, or other public structures. It appears most likely that synagogue structures were a synthesis and accumulation of a variety of plans and architectural features which were themselves influenced by traditional customs as well as by contemporary vogues, together with the Jewish congregation's social and religious needs. The rich ornamentation of the fa-

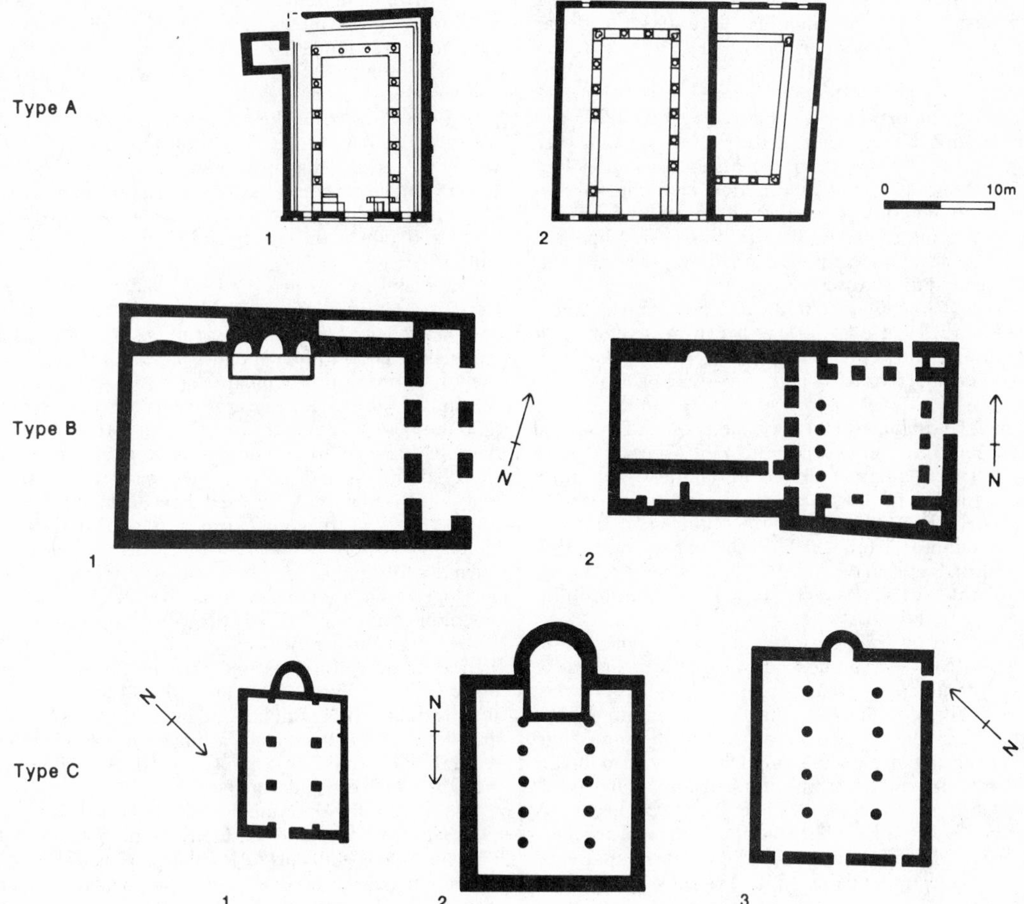

ART.37. Plans of synagogue types. *Type A,* aedicula: *1,* Chorazin; *2,* Capernaum. *Type B,* niche; *1,* Eshtemoa; *2,* Susiya. *Type C,* apse: *1,* Jericho; *2,* Maʿoz Ḥayim; *3,* Maon. *(Redrawn from Hachlili 1987: 144, fig. 1; 146, fig. 3; 147, fig. 4.)*

cade, walls, floors, and other areas of the synagogue was influenced by contemporary architectural styles in secular and religious buildings in both Israel and Syria. A combination of all these elements resulted in a house of worship functionally planned and lavishly decorated by the Jewish congregation. Utilizing previously constituted tenets within their own tradition, the Jews also adapted various elements of architecture and art from their neighbors. In this way, they succeeded in creating aesthetic and monumental structures.

Synagogues were not built according to a stereotyped plan, nor were they designed according to fixed custom or law. Synagogue building plans can be classified in two distinct categories: (1) those where the longitudinal stone structure is columnated, has benches, and is characterized by a richly decorated stone facade (distinctive of the Galilean and Golan synagogues); and (2) those where the broadhouse or "basilical" type of building is characterized by an axial court and narthex in front of the prayer hall, which obviates the need for a decorated facade. Buildings of this latter type were usually constructed of concrete, and constitute most synagogues found in Palestine.

Furthermore, several features encountered in most of the excavated and surveyed synagogues direct attention to an originality and individuality in their plans. These features include the Torah shrine, the triple portal, and the gallery, as well as various methods of ornamentation of the facade, interior, and floors. The highly ornamented facade exterior, characteristic of the Galilean and Golan synagogues, is an additional original synagogue structural feature.

Differences in plans among contemporary synagogues are usually due to regional and local traditions and local priorities as well as fashion. Changes in synagogue designs probably came about as a result of changes in theological concepts. Whereas Galilean synagogues indicate a preference for entrances and Torah shrines both on the same, Jerusalem-oriented wall, in other localities the Torah shrine is on the Jerusalem-oriented wall with the entrance on another.

2. Art. In contrast to Second Temple–period art which was aniconic and devoid of any figurative designs, a major change occurred at the end of the 2d century and even more so during the 3d century when representational art began to flourish. It was at this time that the barriers within which Judaism protected itself against foreign influences were being shattered. During this period the Jews acquired some of the customs and decorative elements from surrounding cultures; despite the traditional prohibition of such art contained in the Second Commandment (Exod 20:4–5; Deut 5:8–9), Jews began to develop their own figurative and representational art, using pagan motifs, figures, and animals, both for synogogal and for funerary art.

Symbolic and figurative art became possible for several reasons. First, the attitude of the rabbis became more tolerant. Such changes, reflected in Talmudic literature, were the result of political, economic, and social circumstances (Urbach 1959). Second, the influence of the surrounding cultures, from which certain pagan and mythological motifs were taken, became much stronger. Third, Jewish literature, legends, and Midrashim began to influence artistic traditions.

Judaism had no tradition of figurative art, and consequently the Jews were influenced by Hellenistic figurative art, using contemporary pattern books as well as creating their own. The Jewish attitude that developed with respect to art was basically to regard it as decorative—something to add beauty and ornamentation to buildings. Even mythological scenes found their way into Jewish buildings (such as the House of Leontis) as did many other pagan motifs (e.g., funerary art of Beth Shearim and synagogal architectural decoration and pavements). Jews of this period were unafraid of idolatry, and indeed felt that they were allowed to depict religious subjects. Judaism seems to have been indifferent to pictures and did not ascribe to them any sanctity. Therefore, for example, there was no reason to prevent the depiction of representations on pavements which were trodden upon; furthermore, walking upon pavements with such depictions insured that no sanctity or sacred quality would be attached to the scenes. Such a depiction was not considered to be a "graven image" such as those prohibited by the law. This might have been the reason why even pagan elements such as the zodiac were used. Judaism instead attached much more importance to the written word; this may be inferred from the iconoclastic destruction of the Naʿaran synagogue pavement, in which the letters, however, were preserved, or from the synagogues at Rehov and En Gedi, where floors paved with long inscriptions were left untouched.

a. Jewish Symbols. Specific Jewish symbols, such as the menorah, the Ark, and the ritual objects are attested in both synagogal and funerary art. These symbols express profound and significant values distinctly associated with Judaism, and thus were used frequently throughout Late Antiquity by Jews not only within Israel but also in the Diaspora, where they held a prominent place in the repertoire of Jewish art. These chosen religious symbols were derived from the Temple rites and ceremonies, which is why only a few symbols were actually used and why the repertoire is so limited.

Many other symbols and images were taken from the contemporary Hellenistic-Roman world; forms were borrowed but divested of their original meaning. Even if the form of the pagan motif was appropriated it would be wrong to assume that its symbolic value was also transferred. On the contrary, a symbol has a certain value which is applicable only within its context; it loses that significance and value when transplanted into another cultural context.

The real threat to Judaism's survival from this time on was from Christianity, which developed out of Judaism and had religious and cultural affinities with it. This challenge to Judaism's independence was even stronger from the 4th century on, when Christianity became the official religion of the Roman Empire. It was this time especially that the Jews needed to assert their own identity and therefore turned to certain symbolic expressions. They chose specific symbols which the Jewish communities as well as individuals felt expressed their distinctive faith, and could represent religious ideas with which they could identify.

An interesting example of the way in which a sign developed into a symbol may be seen in the case of the menorah. The menorah was probably a professional sign of the priests during the Second Temple period, signifying their duty and office, as well the sacred Temple vessel, along with the Table. Only after the destruction of the Temple did the menorah image change from a limited and specific official emblem into a more universal symbol of general but profound connotation, thus becoming the principal symbol of Judaism itself.

The major Jewish symbols were objects such as the menorah, the Ark, the ritual utensils, and the conch shell. The motifs and emblems in Jewish art borrowed from the pagan world were used without their original meaning, and for their decorative effect only, or were given a different significance in Jewish art (such as the zodiac, which now served as a calendar, and lions, which now signified the guarding of the Jewish symbols such as the menorah and the Ark). Jews carefully selected motifs and iconography of a symbolic character and depicted them in their synagogal and funerary art.

Due to extensive synagogue excavations as well as historical research, knowledge and evidence are now much more extensive than before. It seems reasonable to infer that an Ark of the Scrolls (in the shape of a wooden chest) stood inside the architectural structure of the Torah shrine in the synagogue building. Representations of the Ark in Jewish art confirm that in the synagogues of Late Antiquity a wooden Ark of the Scrolls stood inside the Torah shrine, regardless of its form (aedicula, niche, or apse). Nevertheless the Ark was also part of the symbolic repertoire of Jewish art: it represented much deeper connotations, being an integral part of the focal point of Jewish worship, the Torah. It also symbolized the place of prayer and of the Scriptures and their study in the destroyed Temple. Renditions of the Ark are encountered on tomb walls and doors, and on lamps found outside a synagogue context. On mosaic floors the Torah shrine is commonly depicted

ART.38. Synagogue floor mosaics depicting the ark of the scrolls, menorahs, and ritual objects. **Top**, panel from Hammath Tiberias; **bottom**, panel from Beth Alpha. *(Courtesy of R. Hachlili.)*

with two menoroth flanking it; this probably represents the actual positioning of the Torah shrine and menoroth in their prominent place on display in the synagogue building (see Fig. ART.38).

Depictions of a menorah flanked by ritual objects, or of the more elaborate Torah Shrine flanked by menoroth and ritual objects, came to symbolize participation in the annual pilgrimages, the Feast of the Tabernacles (the most important annual festival), and, by association, the Temple and its eventual rebuilding.

b. Figurative Art. The repertoire of Jewish figurative art included themes such as biblical stories, mythological designs, and motifs of animals and human figures which also occur in Jewish poetry. The significance of these symbolic and iconographic themes lies in its contrast with the contemporaneous aniconic Christian art; these artistic themes thus became a means of emphasizing the difference between the Jewish and Christian arts.

(1) Biblical Scenes. Biblical themes on synagogue mosaics were selected from a relatively small number of familiar biblical stories: the Sacrifice of Isaac, Noah's Ark, Daniel in the Lions' Den, the Twelve Tribes, and King David. Noteworthy is the recurrence of biblical scenes in more than one synagogue mosaic pavement within Palestine and on mosaics and frescoes in the Diaspora: *The Offering of Isaac* at Beth ʾAlpha (see Fig. ART. 39) and Dura Europos; *Noah's Ark* at Gerassa and Misis-Mopsuestia in Cilicia; *Daniel in the Lions' Den* at Naʿaran and Susiya; and *David* (= Orpheus) at Gaza and Dura Europos, and

ART.39. Beth ʾAlpha synagogue mosaic depicting the sacrifice of Isaac. *(Redrawn from Hachlili 1987: 289, fig. 31.)*

with Goliath's weapons at Marous. They were depicted in simple narratives, although some of the scenes as a whole may have had symbolic meanings. The scenes had in common the illustration of the theme of salvation and were associated with prayers offered in time of drought. The choice of themes was derived from the religiocultural climate of the period and meant to be a reminder of and reference to traditional historical events; there was no intention of using these themes for symbolic or didactic purposes, as suggested by some scholars (Goodenough 1953, 1: 253 ff.). However, the style, form, and artistic depiction on each of these floors is completely different, and each scene may be traced back to a distinct influence or source. The biblical scenes found so far do not seem to have a common denominator as regards style or origins. However, some similarity does exist in the arrangement of connecting panels and subject matter found both at Beth ʾAlpha and Naʿaran, suggesting a common source of social affinities.

(2) The Zodiac Panel. Four of the ancient synagogues discovered so far in Israel, ranging in date from the 4th to 6th centuries, contain mosaics showing the zodiac cycle: Ḥammath Tiberias, Beth ʾAlpha, Ḥuseifa, Naʿaran. A fifth synagogue, that of Susiya near Hebron, at one time also contained a zodiac mosaic floor, but it was later changed into a geometric pattern. The mosaic at the ʿEn Gedi synagogue yielded an inscription which includes the names of the zodiac signs followed by the names of the corresponding Jewish months.

It is highly characteristic of Jewish art that a pagan subject (in this case the zodiac) should be adapted to express a Jewish idea (such as an annual calendar). In the Roman world zodiac signs are of solely cosmic and astronomical significance, whereas in Christian, as in Roman, art, the calendar is represented by the labors of the months. Jewish art preferred an abstract and symbolic zodiac, rather than the naturalistic representation of human activity depicted on the Christian examples, in order to assure the people of the religious nature of the calendar. The fact that the zodiac was used frequently makes it clear that the Jewish community was not interested merely in a strictly decorative design for its floors. The fundamentally pagan zodiac cycle came to serve the Jewish community as a popular, symbolic calendar, and was employed as a significant framework for the annual synagogue rituals.

c. Artistic Motifs. Popular and common motifs in Jewish art indicate a persistent preference for particular themes in Jewish ornamentation. Sources for the motifs used in Jewish art include (1) tradition and the continuation of popular motifs deriving from Jewish art of the Second Temple period; (2) selected decorative patterns and motifs taken from contemporary (Greco-Roman, Syrian, and Nabatean) art, but now devoid of their symbolic context and significance; (3) chosen motifs from pattern books; and (4) motifs of symbols significant for Judaism. A motif consists either of a combination of several antithetic or heraldic elements such as lions flanking a menorah or Nikae flanking a wreath, or of a single image or object such as a rosette. The motifs include: flora and plant ornaments, geometric motifs, fauna and animal motifs, human figures, mythological motifs, and genre motifs.

Definite tendencies are revealed in the persistent selection of heraldic and antithetic symmetrical designs, such as lions, eagles, bulls, Nikae, peacocks, birds, horned animals, dolphins, and rosettes, which are depicted on sarcophagi, synagogue lintels, friezes, and mosaic floors. A common source for the motifs in Jewish art, most probably a pattern book, is indicated by the stylization of pose and posture as well as the patterning when representing animals, plants, and other ornaments; it is less likely that such motifs were copied directly from nature.

C. Conclusions

The strictly aniconic and nonsymbolic art characterizing the Second Temple period was the outcome of Judaism's struggle against paganism and idolatry. By the rigid observance of the prohibition against animate images, the Jews retained their own identity and distinctiveness.

This quality of the art of the Second Temple period completely disappeared during the period of Late Antiquity. In Late Antiquity, art and architecture were influenced by political and social changes in Palestine, most particularly by the destruction of the Jerusalem Temple and the removal of the center of Jewish life to Galilee. The prevailing architectural structure was now the synagogue, which replaced the Temple as the center of Jewish religious, national, and social life. In addition, the decline of paganism and the rise and expansion of Christianity caused a change in the Jewish attitude toward its own art; it now expressed its ornamentation and decorative architecture by figurative and symbolic means. With the destruction of the Temple, the need for a concrete visual image became strongly felt. Thus, only during this period do the Temple implements take on a symbolic significance in synagogal and funerary art.

Jewish art is an example of an art lacking figurative tradition, and having a weakly developed visual sense and an environment with strong external cultural influences. It is based on the ability and skill with which the artists related to the needs and requirements of their patrons, whose prerequisites were based mainly on decorative demands. A limited selection of symbols and subjects were chosen by the Jewish community and by its donors, who made their choice from available pattern books. Certain original aspects of ancient Jewish art which continually occur could be explained as being the result of the specific needs of the Jewish community, of its traditions, and of artists' innovations.

Jewish art was essentially a decorative art with both ornamental and iconographic functions. It was an art which consisted of an indigenous local tradition, with at the same time appropriations from the surrounding Greco-Roman and Christian cultures; it possessed an oriental style, and was characterized by the use of specific symbols, motifs, and iconography. However, despite those elements borrowed from neighboring cultures, Jewish art retained within it the fundamental beliefs, customs, and traditions of the Jewish people.

Bibliography

Avigad, N. 1981. The Galilean Synagogue and Its Predecessors. Pp. 42–44 in Levine 1981.

Avi-Yonah, M. 1961. *Oriental Art in Roman Palestine.* Rome.

———. 1981. Ancient Synagogues. Pp. 271–81 in *Art in Ancient Palestine.* Jerusalem.

Goodenough, E. 1953. *Jewish Symbols in the Greco-Roman Period.* Vol. I. New York.

Gutmann, J., ed. 1975. *The Synagogue: Studies in Origins, Archaeology and Architecture.* New York.

———. 1981. *Ancient Synagogues: The State of Research.* Ann Arbor, MI.

Hachlili, R. 1976. The Niche and the Ark in Ancient Synagogues. *BASOR* 223: 43–53.

———. 1977. The Zodiac in Ancient Jewish Art: Representation and Significance. *BASOR* 228: 61–77.

———. 1987. *Ancient Jewish Art and Archaeology in the Land of Israel.* Leiden.

Hachlili, R., and Merhav, R. 1985. The Menorah in the First and Second Temple Times in the Light of the Sources and Archaeology. *EI* 18: 256–67 (in Hebrew).

Levine, L. I., ed. 1981. *Ancient Synagogues Revealed.* Jerusalem.

Meyers, E. M. 1980. Ancient Synagogues in Galilee: Their Religious and Cultural Setting: *BA* 43: 97–108.

Naveh, J. 1978. *On Stone and Mosaic: The Aramaic and Hebrew Inscriptions from Ancient Synagogues.* Jerusalem (in Hebrew).

Netzer, E. 1975. The Hasmonean and Herodian Winter Palaces at Jericho. *IEJ* 25: 89–100.

———. 1981a. *Greater Herodium.* Qedem 13. Jerusalem.

———. 1981b. Herod's Building Projects: State Necessity or Personal Need? A Symposium. *The Jerusalem Cathedra* 1: 48–80.

Sukenik, E. L. 1934. *Ancient Synagogues in Palestine and Greece.* London.

Urbach, E. 1959. The Rabbinical Laws of Idolatry in the 2d and 3d Centuries in the Light of Archaeological and Historical Facts. *IEJ* 9: 149–65, 229–45.

RACHEL HACHLILI

EARLY CHRISTIAN ART

While some elements of early Christian art have always been available for observation, our present knowledge depends on the advent of archaeology as a scientific discipline. Early Christian archaeology has been closely, though not exclusively, attached to the excavation of the catacombs in Rome. It was there that Giuseppe Marchi (1795–1860) projected a series of studies which would encompass inscriptions, architecture, pictures, and sculptures. The expedition of this gigantic task fell on the able shoulders of Giovanni B. de Rossi (1822–94), then secretary of the Vatican Library. From his efforts sprung a school of collecting, organizing, and interpreting—a school which produced many journals and dictionaries (e.g., *DACL* and the more recent *Enciclopedia cattolica*). The school at Rome tended to interpret early Christian art in light of concerns found in contemporaneous patristic literature, or in terms of later dogmatic considerations.

There were detractors from this position, but not until about 1930 did another school of interpretation arise. Scholars like Hans Lietzmann, Franz Joseph Dölger, Theodor Klauser, and Erich Dinkler formed a group that interpreted early Christian art in light of the culture of the Mediterranean world. This more contextual approach has inspired a prodigious number of studies and is best represented by the *RAC* and the serial *JAC*.

A. Stages

The first art of the Christians bore little resemblance to Jewish art as we know it. Though we can note similarities in style and in relationship to the Hellenistic environment, there is little correspondence in content. The art of the floor of the synagogue at Beth ʾAlpha, for example, or the front wall of the synagogue of Dura-Europos reflects either the influence of non-Jewish artisans (such as the use of the zodiac) or an interest in illustrating Jewish practices and episodes from the Hebrew Bible. See EARLY JEWISH ART AND ARCHITECTURE, above. Similar concerns do not appear in the earliest Christian art.

For the first 150 years of the church there was no type of Christian pictorial art. As the Christian faith interacted with Hellenistic culture it slowly developed, independent of Judaism, its own symbol system and eventually pictorial art itself. If there were a Christian art it now lies indistinguishable from contemporary Greco-Roman materials. The first art consisted of symbols derived primarily from the Hellenistic social matrix. About the turn of the 2d century Clement approved certain of these key Christian symbols:

> Let our seals be the dove, or the fish, or a ship sailing before a fair wind, or the lyre for music, which seal Polycrates used, or a ship's anchor, which Seleucus carved on his device, and if there be a fisherman, he will recall an apostle and children drawn from the water. (*paed.* 3,11)

All of the symbols mentioned by Clement can be found at the earliest stages of Christian art. Near the end of the 2d century, about 180 C.E., pictorial representations began to appear which could be identified as Christian. The themes of these representations derived from Hellenistic culture, often utilizing the earliest symbols, though the context often reflected a biblical story or a liturgical practice. Christian pictures appeared simultaneously as plastic carvings on sarcophagi and as frescoes in catacombs and house churches. Though most of the early Christian pictorial representations were utilized in Christian contexts, they obviously addressed those formed by the contemporary Hellenistic culture. Eventually, as the culture became more Christian, and as Christianity was recognized as a legitimate faith expression, Christian art took on more of an illustrative and pedagogical role. For the sake of epochal clarity we speak of that change as the accession of Constantine in 313 C.E., though the time of the Roman Bishop Damasus (366–84) better represents the beginning of Christian orthodoxy. Any discussion of early Christian art would note the changes which might occur through these historical stages.

B. Sources

In order to distinguish stages in early Christian art it becomes necessary to determine what elements preceded the Constantinian era. For such a determination accuracy in dating is preferable to completeness. A narrow list of sources for 3d-century *frescoes* includes the baptistry at Dura-Europos, the sacrament chapels at St. Callixtus (Rome), the double chamber of the Lucina Area in St. Callixtus, the Flavian Gallery in the Domitilla catacomb (Rome), the Capella Greca in the Priscilla catacomb (Rome), and the hypogea in the catacomb of St. Gennaro (Naples).

There are also numerous early *plastic scenes on sarcophagi:* one found in the Kaisar Friedrich Museum, Berlin; the Sta. Maria Antiqua sarcophagus, Rome (see Fig. ART. 40); Museo Pio cristiano 119, the Vatican; Ny Carlsberg 832, Copenhagen; the Jonah Sarcophagus in the British Museum, London; the Sarcophagus of Hertofile in the Thermal Museum, Rome; Museo Pio cristiano 236, Julia Juliane, the Vatican; the Noah sarcophagus in the Rheinisches Landesmuseum, Trier; the Jonah-Sarkophag, Prinz-Paul-Museum-Garten, Belgrade; le Mas d'Aire Sarcophagus in l'eglise Sainte Quitterie du Mas, Aire-sur-l'Adour, France (see Fig. ART. 41); the Albana sarcophagus, Quirinius-Kappelle, Friedhof St. Matthias, Trier. In addition to these complete sarcophagi, there are a number of fragments in Rome and elsewhere throughout the ancient Roman Empire. Some pieces, found in the provinces, though 4th-century pieces actually parallel Roman Christianity of the 3d century (e.g., the remarkable collection found in the Musée d'Art Chretien in Arles, France).

There are no known certain *sculptures* which predate Constantine. The remarkable Jonah statues (Jonah Swallowed, Jonah Cast Up, Jonah at Rest, and Jonah as an Orante) as well as the Good Shepherd, now lodged in the Cleveland Museum of Art, appear early in many respects

ART.40. Sarcophagus in Sta. Maria Antiqua (Rome). Likely the oldest example of early Christian plastic art. *(Courtesy of G. F. Snyder.)*

but cannot be accurately dated. The *mosaics* of Mausoleum M in the Vatican necropolis are the only certain 3d-century Christian mosaics, though one can hardly ignore the floor on the N hall of the cathedral at Aquileia. Yet, little can be learned from its animal scenes. The S floor at Aquileia, with its Jonah and Good Shepherd, could be considered borderline 3d century.

C. Major Symbols

As in any culture the first Christian symbols not only identify the developing faith, but serve as an artistic resolution for what otherwise are significant conflicts or tensions for the community. Symbols are to be read in terms of such temporal conflicts rather than necessarily as dogmatic theological signs. This is especially evident in several of the earliest nautical symbols which reflect a conflict with the environment.

1. The Anchor. As a simple symbol the anchor appeared frequently on catacomb *tituli* (marble grave markers) of the 3d century. See Fig. ART. 42. By the 4th century it had almost totally disappeared. The anchor had no significant prior use as a religious symbol. Since any significance in Hellenistic culture was lacking, it has been suggested that the anchor represents a hidden cross, a disguise no longer needed when Christianity went public. However, in 3d-century popular Christianity there were few, if any, symbols of efficacious suffering and dying. As a popular symbol the cross was not hidden; it simply was not utilized. As a Christian metaphor the anchor occurs only once in the NT (Heb 6:19, as a symbol of hope). Since early Christian symbols or scenes seldom reflect any biblical meaning, there is no reason to assign the sense of hope to the anchor. Along with the other nautical symbols mentioned by Clement, the anchor reflects Christian conflict with the environment (implied by water). In the faith community the believer finds security.

2. The Boat. Like the anchor, the boat expresses security in an alien environment; but unlike the anchor it had a prior history. In some ancient religions the boat bore the dead to the other world, while in the Bible boats normally protected from threatening waters—e.g., the ark (Gen 6:19); Jonah's boat (Jonah 1:4); and the stilling of the storm (Mark 6:45–52). While the boats of early Christianity are not yet the salvific Church of the 4th century (Cyprian, *de catholicae ecclesiae unitate,* 6), they do offer deliverance to a threatened people.

3. The Fish. Though one of the most frequently used symbols of the early church, nevertheless the fish defies accurate analysis. Like the other nautical symbols the fish signifies secure life in conflictive situations. It is found with another nautical symbol, the anchor. One famous stela, that of Licinia (Museo Nazionale, Rome) contains a fish on

ART.41. Mas d'Aire Sarcophagus. Located in L'eglise Sainte Quitterie du Mass, Aire-sur-l'Adour, France. *(Courtesy of G. F. Snyder.)*

ART.42. Incomplete catacomb *titulus* at Rome showing tree, dove, and anchor. *(Courtesy of G. F. Snyder.)*

each side of an anchor. An inscription reads "fish of the living" (Gk *ichthus zōntōn*).

Some suppose this inscription, and the fish itself, refers to the use of Gk *ichthus* ("fish") as an acrostic meaning "Jesus Christ, God's Son, Savior." While no other symbols bear such a dogmatic meaning, and many uses of the fish symbol cannot refer to the Jesus acrostic, still the identification of the fish with Jesus cannot be denied. Tertullian wrote: "But we little fish, according to our *ichthun* Jesus Christ, are born in the water, nor were we saved in any other manner than by remaining in the water" (*De Bapt.* 1).

While Tertullian knew the social context of the fish (the newly baptized Christian remains in the water), he also knew the acrostic reference of "fish" to Jesus.

Apart from the acrostic, Jesus can be identified with the fish of the agape meal. Every known representation of the agape meal prior to Constantine shows fish, bread, and wine. While the meal may be based on the NT eucharistic passage of the Feeding of the Five Thousand (Mark 6:30–44), other inscriptional material identifies the fish meal with "the Fish from the Fountain, the very great, the pure, which the holy virgin seized" (Epitaph of Abercius). Fourth-century literary material can speak of the eucharist as the Christ feeding the people with 5 loaves and 2 fishes, and Christ is himself that bread and that fish (Paulinus of Nola, *epist.* 13, 11).

The fish symbol then refers both to the social implication of entering the faith community (baptism into a community of security) and a major means of maintaining membership in that community (the fish of the eucharist and/or agape). By the end of the 2d century this powerful symbol had also started to take on the dogmatic nature of the famous acrostic.

4. The Bread. Like the fish, the symbol of bread refers primarily to liturgical practices. It always appears in meal scenes with fish and wine (note the well-known combination symbol from the crypt of Lucina in S. Callixtus, Rome). Normally the artist portrayed bread as a small round object, often placed in a basket. In the eucharistic meal scenes there are 5 or 7 such baskets (see Mark 6:30–44 and 8:1–10). Such loaves or baskets of bread can be found in the symbol systems of many religions (Goodenough 1953–68; 5: 62–95). For most unofficial religions of the Mediterranean area, bread symbolized the fellowship of a religious meal or fellowship with the extended family and community through meals for the dead.

5. The Vase. While the vase does not appear as a eucharistic calix (or chalice) until the peace of Constantine, it does appear fairly often as a symbol in early Christian art. It cannot be the container from which the eucharist/agape wine was drunk, which was a small glass beaker. The vase occurs often with a dove, the primary symbol of peace for early Christians. Given that meaning and its frequency in both Christian and non-Christian burial areas, we can suppose it represents the unity of the extended family or faith community. As such it symbolically held the wine for the nearly universal meal for the dead. After Constantine its meaning and function shifted to the newly formed orthodox eucharist, where it was now portrayed as a calix.

6. The Vine and Grapes. The artistically ubiquitous vine brought a rich history of meaning. In Judaism and early Christianity it signified the source of life, especially the life of the faith community (Isa 5:1–7; John 15:1–11), and was prominent in Hellenistic religions (e.g., the cult of Dionysus'. The most prominent use of the vine in early Christianity occurs in Mausoleum M in the necropolis of St. Peter's. A green vine surrounds a gold sky with Christ Helios driving across it. See Fig. ART. 47.

Grapes sometimes occur with the vine, though more often with a dove. The dove signifies the peace of the faith community, achieved by eating the grapes (drinking the wine) of the community meal. As with the fish and bread, eventually the grape was identified with Christ, a grape (wine as blood) which suffered for us (Clem. *paed.* 2,2). The grape survived the peace of Constantine because it took on the Christological, cultic meaning.

7. The Lamb. In most instances the lamb of early Christianity appears in bucolic scenes, either with the Good Shepherd or an Orpheus-like figure. See Fig. ART. 40. While it would be tempting to identify the lamb with such biblical images as the innocent ewe lamb of Nathan's parable (2 Sam 12:1–6), it is more probable that pastoral scenes reflect the hospitality of the early church. Like the sheep of John 10:1–8, the lamb symbolizes the religious actor enjoying the presence of (and community associated with) the Good Shepherd. That sense of community can be found as late as in the apse of S. Apollinare in Classe, Ravenna, though there restricted to the community of the apostles.

After the peace of Constantine the lamb became a major symbol of the crucified Christ (Gallia Placida, Ravenna). The celebrative Passover lamb, as Jesus (1 Cor 5:7 and John 1:29), has become the sacrificial *agnus dei* (Rev 5:6).

8. The Dove. This symbol has a rich and extensive history. In other cultures it can refer to fertility, sexuality, love, and religious sentiments. In early Christianity the dove, as a symbol, appears often with the olive branch, a symbol of peace (see Figs. ART. 42 and ART. 43), and frequently with the inscription *IN PACE* (see Table 1, from Bruun 1963).

Table 1

	WITHOUT *IN PACE*	WITH *IN PACE*
Dove alone	45	37
Dove with olive branch or tree	21	30
Dove with Christogram	17	24
Dove with other symbols	16	15

Prior to Constantine (and the Christogram) the dove must have signified that peace and satisfaction deriving from faith and participation in the faith community. The dove and its counterpart, the Orante (see below), occurred often in biblical scenes of conflict. After the peace of Constantine, when social conflict had lessened, the dove referred more to peace of the soul, while the Orante eventually disappeared altogether.

9. The Olive Branch. The olive branch occurs primarily with the dove, though sometimes alone. In biblical scenes it is found almost always in Noah and the Ark, sometimes in Jonah, and sometimes in The Three Young Men in the Fiery Furnace. Its consistent placement makes fairly certain its symbolic identification with *pax*—the peace of the community in the face of conflict, as well as the peace of the *refrigerium* (meal with extended family and special religious dead).

10. The Orante. One of the two human symbols consists of a woman with upraised hands. See Figs. ART. 40, 43, 44. Her head is nearly always covered with a veil and a tunic of the 3d century *(orans tunicata et velata).* She exists as a separate figure, but, more important, through the 4th

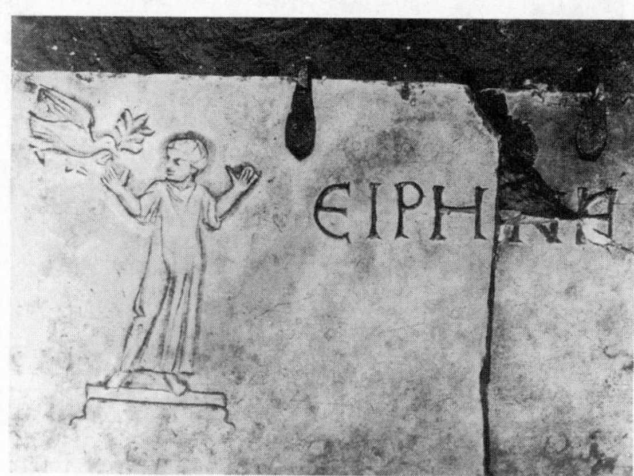

ART.43. Catacomb *titulus* for Eirene with dove, olive branch, and Orante (Rome). *(Courtesy of G. F. Snyder.)*

century is the main figure of nearly every biblical scene, both fresco and sculpture. She is Noah in the Ark, Jonah in the Boat, Jonah Spewed Out of the Sea Monster (Fig. ART. 41, right side of lid), Daniel Between the Lions (Fig. ART. 41, left of center), Susannah with the Elders (Fig. ART. 44), The Three Young Men in the Fiery Furnace, and sometimes Lazarus. She is the most important symbol in early Christian art.

The Orante has a long history in the Greco-Roman social matrix. Since there seems to be no major significance assigned to the biblical contexts in which the Orante is placed, it must be assumed the Orante has kept its traditional meaning, now transferred to a Christian pictorial backdrop. From examples of the Orante in public art (coins) and sepulchral art, it seems to have been associated mainly with familial piety. Given the biblical contexts used by the artists, the scenes must indicate a community (familial) victory in the midst of various conflicts (deliverance). Once the conflicts diminished during the reign of Constantine, the Orante essentially disappeared from Christian art.

11. The Good Shepherd. The second human figure is a male shepherd pictured with a member of the sheep family, normally a ram, on his shoulders. See Fig. ART. 40. The symbol, a *criophorus,* has an ancient history dating as far back as 1000 B.C.E. in Near Eastern circles. A number of meanings for the symbol have been suggested. The use of the Good Shepherd in baptistries (Dura-Europos, Naples?) as well as catacombs and meeting places indicates that the shepherd bore the religious actor into the faith community (or family of the dead). For that reason the Good Shepherd has been identified as *humanitas,* in contrast to the Orante as *pietas.* One might think of it as ecclesial hospitality. After Constantine, the Good Shepherd became the most popular symbol for Christ himself.

D. Pictorial Representations

Given the sources for early Christian art as noted, we can make a comparative analysis of subjects. Despite the limited number of pre-Constantinian sources, nevertheless a numerical count of artistic subjects is possible (see Table 2). Such a count reveals some remarkable data. The Jonah story completely dominates the subject matter of early Christian art (60 percent of all subjects represented belong to it); of subjects derived from the OT, 72 percent are specifically from Jonah. The story of Jonah stresses deliverance (often Jonah appears as the Orante), and most other subjects drawn from the OT also stress deliverance: Noah in the Ark, the Sacrifice of Isaac (Isaac also as an Orante, though see Fig. ART. 41, left lid of sarcophagus), Moses Striking the Rock, Jonah Cast into the Sea, Jonah and the Ketos (or Sea Monster), Jonah at Rest (see Fig. ART. 40, left), Three Young Men in the Fiery Furnace, Daniel in the Lion's Den (see Fig. ART. 41, left of center), Susannah and the Elders (see Fig. ART. 44), and David and Goliath. Of all early Christian pictorial interpretations, 74 percent deal with deliverance and, even more striking, 94% of all subjects from the OT involve the deliverance motif. While the biblical narrative appears to have no place in this material, perhaps the crisis represented does: threat of water (social environment), threat of religious persecution, threat of starvation, threat of death, threat of oppression by the state, and the threat of legal prejudice. After the time of Constantine all of these scenes disappeared except Noah and the Ark (which remained now as a symbol of the church) and Moses Striking the Rock (shifted to Peter Striking the Rock).

ART.44. Scene of Susanna (Orante to the left) being rescued by Daniel. From Capella Greca in the Priscilla catacomb (Rome). *(Courtesy of G. F. Snyder.)*

Adam and Eve is the only biblical scene of any consequence which does not convey deliverance. See Fig. ART. 45. For most of later Christian history the scene portrays the fall of the first man and woman, but in these earliest scenes there is no sign of sin. Instead, the scene represents the same bucolic paradise of Jonah at Rest or the Good Shepherd.

The Jonah cycle requires special consideration. There are three Jonah stories: (1) Jonah, often as an Orante, standing on a troubled boat; (2) Jonah, often as an Orante, coughed up from inside a sea monster; and finally (3) Jonah lying under a vine. See Fig. ART. 40 left. In the latter scene the iconography of Jonah matches precisely the iconography of Endymion (a mythical companion of the moon goddess Selene), who is also pictured reclining in paradisiacal repose (Endymion was a favorite figure on Roman sarcophagi). The three scenes, not always seriatim, represent chapters of the book of Jonah. Yet each stands on its own. Jonah in the boat and with the sea monster are both nautical scenes in which the Orante Jonah finds deliverance. According to the Jonah narrative there is no reason for Jonah to "be delivered" while in the boat. The last scene simply combines the pastoral scene of the Good Shepherd with the well-known iconography of Endymion.

Scenes from the NT center on Jesus rather than the Orante. Though deliverance often occurs, the artists focus on the deliverer, Jesus. Normally they portrayed Jesus as a young, curly-haired, beardless, wonder-worker. The figure reminds one of contemporary Hercules iconography. Of 31 NT scenes, 12 show Jesus healing (e.g., the paralytic; see Fig. ART. 41 lid, left of center) or raising from the dead (e.g., Lazarus; see Fig. ART. 41, left). In these Jesus often has his hand outstretched toward the healed, although sometimes he points with a wand.

Despite the emphasis on healing, the baptism of Jesus

Table 2

Biblical Representation	Fresco	Mosaic	II Sarc	Roman Frag	Other	Total
1. Giving Life to Eve					1	1
2. Adam and Eve	1		2		1	4
3. Noah in the Ark	3		3	2		8
4. Sacrifice of Isaac	2		1	2		5
5. Harassment of Moses			1			1
6. Moses Striking the Rock	4		1			5
7. Moses and the Bush				1		1
8. Ascension of Elijah				1		1
9. Jonah Cast into the Sea	4	1	8	23	2	38
10. Jonah and the Ketos	1		8	17	2	28
11. Jonah at Rest	5		7	25	5	42
12. Tobit and Fish			1			1
13. Three Young Men in the Fiery Furnace	1			3		4
14. Daniel in the Lion's Den	2		2		2	6
15. Susannah and the Elders	3			1		4
16. David and Goliath	1					1
17. Wisemen	1					1
18. Baptism of Jesus	3		1	2		6
19. Jesus Teaching			1	1		2
20. Healing of the Paralytic	2		1			3
21. Healing of the Demon Possessed			1			1
22. Healing of the Lame				1		1
23. Healing of the Crippled				1		1
24. Multiplication of the Loaves and Fishes			1	1		2
25. Woman at the Well	2					2
26. Resurrection of Lazarus	2		2	1		5
27. Walking on the Water	1					1
28. Women at the Tomb	1					1
29. Fisherman		1	2			3
30. Woman with Flow of Blood			1			1
31. Christ Helios		1				1

ART.45. Early 4th century sarcophagus cover with Adam and Eve. Musée d'Art Chrétien, Arles, France. *(Courtesy of G. F. Snyder.)*

ART.46. Fresco from Capella Greca in the Priscilla catacomb (Rome). The scene depicts the wisemen approaching Mary. *(Courtesy of G. F. Snyder.)*

appears more often than any other scene. Jesus appears as an older child being baptized by a bearded adult (typical iconography representation of a river God), while a dove hovers overhead. See Fig. ART. 40, right. While we may have an illustration of the baptism of Jesus with the descent of the Spirit, more likely the scene reflects the baptismal practice of the 3d-century church: an adolescent is baptized into the peace (dove) of the faith community. If this reflects baptism, then the Multiplication of the Loaves and Fishes signifies the agape meal (also a rather frequent scene) with its inevitable fish and baskets of bread. The Multiplication scene might refer to deliverance for the hungry, but more likely it associates the meals of the early church with the popular feeding of the five thousand (recounted 4 times in the Synoptics). The meal could be the eucharist, the Love Feast *(agape)*, or the meal with the dead *(refrigerium)*.

Most of the NT scenes relate iconographically to the Hellenistic social matrix. The scene of the wise men portrays representatives of foreign powers giving a crown of gold *(aurum coronarium)* to the emperor. See Fig. ART. 46.

In the birth scene, Mary and Jesus are represented iconographically similar to Isis and the child Horus.

On Roman sarcophagi or in mausoleums the deceased (male) often was portrayed reading to a younger person. Transferred to Christian sarcophagi (see Fig. ART. 40) the scene has been taken by some as the *traditio legis,* the passing of the law the next generation (Jesus to Peter). If the teaching figure is indeed Jesus, the iconography fits better with that of wandering philosophers. In addition to the wonder-worker Jesus there was in the earliest art a *Christus philosophicus* who taught the faith community (sarcophagus of Velletri). Only after the peace of Constantine did that shift to Jesus teaching only the apostles (based on scenes of the emperor with the officers of the empire; see the arch of Constantine and then eventually the Jesus of the Byzantine apses, the *maiestas domini.*

A beautiful mosaic of Christ Helios was discovered in mausoleum M of the necropolis under St. Peter's. See Fig. ART. 47. The scene shows a Christ figure, with sun rays streaming from his head, crossing a golden sky in a biga. Earlier some Jewish artists had portrayed the ascension of Elijah as a contrast to the intensely popular Sol Invictus (synagogue of Dura-Europos). Christians followed the example. While the carving on the wooden doors of 5th-century S. Sabina shows the same scene, the artist of Mausoleum M took an extra step: Christ, in the iconography of Elijah, became the sun god himself.

E. Conclusion

One critical scene (the crucifixion of Jesus) and its accompanying symbol (the cross) did not occur in early Christian art. Probably the first scene of Jesus suffering occurs on the Vatican's Passion sarcophagus, carved ca. mid-4th century. About the same time one artist transformed the Constantinian *chi-rho* to a cross, the *crux immissa.* This may be the first clear use of the cross as a symbol, if we discount as a prank the so-called Palatine cross, a donkey on a cross. See Fig. ART. 48.

In the social matrix from which Christianity arose, the major concerns were deliverance, security, kinship, and healing. The symbol of suffering and criminal death did not appeal to an oppressed people. After the peace of Constantine the passion narrative and the cross could symbolize the redemptive use of power. Thus, attempts to find hidden crosses in anchors, ship masts, palm trees, and cryptic language miss this important point.

ART.47. Mosaic of Christ Helios in mausoleum M under St. Peter's at Rome. *(Courtesy of G. F. Snyder.)*

ART.48. Graffito found on the Palatine in Rome. The drawing may be a caricature of the crucifixion. *(Drawing adapted by J. Wine.)*

Bibliography

Bovini, G. 1968. *Gli studi di archeologia cristiana.* Bologna.

Bruun, P. 1963. Symboles, signes et monogrammes. *Acta instituti Romani Finlandiae* 1/2: 73–166.

Dassmann, E. 1973. *Sündenvergebung durch Taufe, Busse und Martyrerfürbitte in den Zeugnissen frühchristlicher Frömmigkeit und Kunst.* Münster.

Deichmann, F. W.; Bovini, G.; and Brandenburg, H. 1967. *Repertorium der christlich-antiken Sarkophage.* Vol. 1. Wiesbaden.

Goodenough, E. R. 1953–68. *Jewish Symbols in the Greco-Roman Period.* Vols. 1–13. New York.

Grabar, A. 1967. *The Beginnings of Christian Art.* London.

Milburn, R. 1988. *Early Christian Art and Architecture.* Berkeley.

Nestori, A. 1975. *Repertorio topografico delle pitture delle catacombe Romane.* Rome.

Snyder, G. F. 1985. *Ante Pacem.* Macon, GA.

Testa, E. 1962. *Il simbolismo dei guideo-cristiani.* Pubblicazioni dello Studium Biblicum Franciscanum 14. Jerusalem.

GRAYDON F. SNYDER

ARTAPANUS. A Jewish author who flourished in Egypt prior to the mid-1st century B.C.E. and wrote a historical romance entitled *On the Jews* (perhaps *Judaica*). Three short fragments of the work survive, treating respectively Abraham, Joseph, and Moses, primarily as they relate to Egypt. The fragments display a remarkable level of syncretism, reflected by the manner and extent to which popular religious and cultural traditions from Egypt and the Graeco-Roman world are interwoven into the biblical story.

No verbatim excerpts from Artapanus' work survive. Instead, portions were summarized by the pagan author Alexander Polyhistor, who flourished in Rome in the mid-1st century B.C.E., and these summaries were later quoted directly in Eusebius *Praep. Evang.* 9.18, 23, 27. Prior to the time of Eusebius (ca. 260–340 C.E.), a brief portion of the third fragment concerning Moses was quoted by Clement of Alexandria (ca. 150–215 C.E.) in *Strom.* 1.23.154.2–3.

The first fragment (*Praep. Evang.* 9.18.1), consisting of only a few lines, describes Abraham's migration to Egypt and his subsequent return to Syria twenty years later, noting especially his role in providing astrological instruction to Pharaoh.

A somewhat longer second fragment (*Praep. Evang.* 9.23.1–4) depicts the circumstances of Joseph's coming to Egypt and his subsequent rise to power. The biblical account is embellished considerably as Joseph is made responsible for impressive land reforms and the discovery of measures, both of which earned him high esteem among the Egyptians. Also mentioned is his marriage to the Egyptian Asenath, daughter of a priest of Heliopolis.

A considerably longer third fragment (*Praep. Evang.* 9.27.1–37) focuses on Moses, covering the period from his birth until the arrival of the Israelites in the wilderness. It follows the storyline of Exodus but includes many nonbiblical features which give the story a distinctively Egyptian cast. Like Abraham and Joseph, Artapanus' Moses emerges as a cultural benefactor of the Egyptians, but his list of achievements exceeds that of his biblical predecessors. Besides being a brilliant military strategist who protects Egypt from the Ethiopians (also reported in Josephus *Ant* 2.10.1–2 §§ 238–53), he embodies the Hellenistic ideal of scientific discovery as the inventor of ships, military weapons, and other implements useful to Egyptian life. Perhaps most important, he emerges as the originator of philosophy. His role as renowned sage is underscored in the claim that he became the teacher of Orpheus and came to be identified with the god Hermes. Artapanus also credits him with the efficient organization and administration of the state, as well as the founding and organizing of Egyptian religious cults, a role in which the Egyptians came to revere him as divine. Another nonbiblical feature is an encounter between Moses and Pharaoh in which Pharaoh died for blaspheming the name of God but was miraculously restored to life by Moses. Artapanus also modifies the biblical account of the plagues and omits reference to the Passover. He also reports local traditions explaining how the Israelites crossed the Red Sea.

What is known about the author is derived largely from the surviving fragments themselves. Other than the above mentioned passages, he is referred to nowhere else. His unusual name seems to be of Persian origin, and this may suggest a mixed descent. Though earlier scholarship found it difficult to conceive of a Jewish author capable of such a high level of syncretism (and for this reason viewed him either as non-Jewish or as an apostate Jew), recent scholarship is much more certain of his Jewish identity, primarily because of the subject matter of the fragments. His main concern is to relate sympathetically the biblical story, which he knows from the LXX. He not only portrays Abraham, Joseph, and Moses in heroic terms, enhancing their stature as worthy religious leaders and cultural benefactors of Egypt, but also appears to be responding to negative criticisms. Thus he both promotes and defends the biblical story. His ardent zeal for his own religious tradition typifies the popular romance literature during the Hellenistic period: concern to establish legitimacy for one's own cultural tradition *vis-à-vis* other national traditions by presenting an attractive, interesting account of the heroes of that tradition based on one's own sacred books.

As to his date, it is only known for certain that he preceded Alexander Polyhistor (ca. 105–30 B.C.E.), who summarized his work (see Freudenthal 1875: 143–74, 215–18). His use of the LXX would place him after the mid-3d century B.C.E., when a Greek translation of the Hebrew Bible probably began to become available. If he is responding to anti-Jewish accounts of the Exodus, such as those of Manetho (ca. 280 B.C.E.), as seems likely, this would also establish an earlier reference point for dating. Within this 200-year range, 250–50 B.C.E., other dates have been suggested based on specific evidence. References in the fragments to the worship of Isis and allusions to mystery religions have been correlated with efforts by Ptolemy IV Philopator (221–205 B.C.E.) to promote the worship of Dionysus among Jews in Egypt (cf. *3 Macc.* 2:29–30). The reference to the conscription of Egyptian farmers (Frg. 3.7) may also point to the time of Philopator, who initiated the practice prior to the battle of Raphia (217 B.C.E.). If the mention of a Jewish temple built in Heliopolis (Frg. 2.4) is a reference to the temple at Leontopolis (established by Onias IV ca. 167–164 B.C.E.), this would suggest a time during the reign of Ptolemy VI Philometor (180–145 B.C.E.). Another clue to dating may be provided by Artapanus' mention of elephantiasis as the cause of the Egyptian king's death (Frg. 3.20). Although Plutarch (*Mor.* 731A) reports that the disease was first identified in the 1st century B.C.E., it appears to have been known and described in Egypt by Bolus of Mendes as early as the 3d century B.C.E. The strong apologetic tone of the fragments would suggest a period from the end of the 3d century to the middle of the 2d century B.C.E. The level of confidence they reflect would point to a period of relative stability reminiscent of the reign of Ptolemy VI Philometor.

As for the provenance, the thorough Egyptian cast of the fragments and the explicit preoccupation with Egyptian names and places makes an Egyptian setting almost certain. Whether the setting was specifically Alexandrian is not as certain, primarily because Artapanus reflects awareness of a broader range of native Egyptian traditions, and in certain respects differs conspicuously both in outlook and literary sophistication from other Jewish literature generally associated with Alexandria.

The Artapanus fragments are generally grouped with Hellenistic Jewish historical writings, but they are "history" only in the minimal sense that they rehearse the biblical story. Their nationalistic flavor, their conspicuous tendency to glorify ancestral heroes, and the incorporation of a wide range of popular traditions suggests that Artapanus' work belonged to the genre of popular, historical-romance literature.

While the Artapanus fragments provide some useful information relating to Egypt and Egyptian Judaism, their value does not depend on whether what they report is historically accurate, but rather on what they reveal about the historical situation out of which they arose and to which they attest. Specifically, Artapanus becomes a valuable resource for understanding the historical reality of Greek-speaking Judaism in an Egyptian setting perhaps as early as mid-3d century B.C.E. Scholars have always been intrigued by the extent of syncretism reflected in the fragments, even though their assessment of Artapanus' motives and ultimate loyalties have differed widely. Because of his portraits of Joseph and Moses in particular, he has figured prominently in the "divine man" debate. Scholars continue to debate what it meant for a Jewish author during the Hellenistic period to elevate Moses to near-divine status and offer such a positive description of Egyptian religion. All such assessments, however, must reckon with the question of genre in determining appropriate criteria for judging Artapanus' literary achievement. The widely acknowledged apologetic dimension in the Artapanus fragments makes them a valuable resource for understanding the social dynamics of Jewish responses to anti-Jewish polemics in the Hellenistic period. To the extent that the fragments reflect Artapanus' attempt to clarify misconceptions about Judaism and thereby gain cultural respectability, his work belongs within the tradition of "competitive historiography" that became well developed in the Hellenistic age (Collins, *OTP* 2:891–92). Yet, however outwardly directed his work might have been, it doubtless functioned to reinforce the faith and confidence of his fellow Jews.

Bibliography

Freudenthal, J. 1875. *Alexander Polyhistor und die von him erhaltenen Reste judäischer und samaritanischer Geschichtswerke.* Hellenistische Studien, 1–2. Breslau.

Holladay, C. R. 1983. "Artapanus." Pp. 189–243 in *Fragments from Hellenistic Jewish Authors,* Volume 1. SBLTT 20. Pseudepigrapha Series 10. Chico, CA.

Schürer, E. 1986. *HJP*² 3/1: 521–25.

Walter, N. 1976. Artapanos. Pp. 121–36 in *Jüdische Schriften aus hellenistisch-römischer Zeit* 1/2, ed. W. G. Kümmel. Gütersloh.

CARL R. HOLLADAY

ARTAXERXES (PERSON) [Aram *ʾartaḥšaśtaʾ;* Gk *Artaxérxēs*]. Persian king in whose reign the missions of Ezra (Ezra 7:1) and Nehemiah (Neh 2:1) took place. There were three Persian kings having this name, yet the biblical text neither specifies nor distinguishes among them: Artaxerxes I (Longimanus) son and successor of Xerxes I, ruled 465–425 B.C.E.; Artaxerxes II (Mnemon) son and successor of Darius II, ruled 404–358 B.C.E.; and Artaxerxes III (Ochus) son and successor of Artaxerxes II, ruled 359–338 B.C.E. The name may also have been assumed by Arses who ruled 338–336 B.C.E., and Bessos, who claimed the throne soon after Alexander's conquest (Cook 1983).

The name Artaxerxes appears in the books of Ezra and Nehemiah in five distinct contexts:

1. Ezra 4:7 relates that a letter was sent to Artaxerxes by BISHLAM, MIDREDETH, AND TABEEL. Nothing of the contents of this correspondence is told.

2. Ezra 4:8–23, in Aramaic, reports correspondence from REHUM and SHIMSHAI to Artaxerxes; included is a copy of a letter from Persian officials notifying Artaxerxes that repatriated Jews are rebuilding Jerusalem—the wall and its foundations are specifically mentioned (Ezra 4:12–13). Also included with this report is a rescript from Artaxerxes ordering a halt to all such building in Jerusalem "until a decree is made by me" (Ezra 4:21). Olmstead (1948:313) suggested that the complaint to Artaxerxes in Ezra 4:8–23 is a result of a nationalist faction who tried to gain independence after Ezra's mission but before Nehemiah's. Others have seen the complaint of Ezra 4:8–23 as a result of Nehemiah's work on the wall. See Rowley (1955:554–57) for a discussion of these and other positions.

3. Ezra 6:14, still part of the Aramaic source, is a summary statement attributing the completion of the Temple to the Persian rulers CYRUS, DARIUS, and Artaxerxes. The anachronistic character of the mention of Artaxerxes in the context of the building of the Temple has been a point of much discussion on the composition of the Aramaic section and of the books of Ezra and Nehemiah as a whole.

4. The mission of Ezra in the reign of Artaxerxes is introduced at Ezra 7:8; included is a rescript in Aramaic from Artaxerxes authorizing Ezra's religious and judicial duties, and instructing the treasurers of the satrapy Beyond the River to provide support to Ezra. Ezra began his mission in the "seventh year of the king" (Ezra 7:8); along with Ezra a contingency of people were allowed to emigrate to Judea "in the seventh year of Artaxerxes the king" (Ezra 7:7). If Artaxerxes I is the intended king then the mission occurred in 458 B.C.E. Herrmann (*HHI,* 309) argues that this is the view of the final editor. However, some scholars, most recently Miller and Hayes (1986), argue that Ezra's mission occurred under the authority of Artaxerxes II, that is, in 398 B.C.E. Bright *(BHI)* and Noth *(NHI),* by emending or rejecting the dates in the text, have argued that Ezra's mission occurred late in the reign of Artaxerxes I.

5. Neh 2:1 states that "in the twentieth year of King Artaxerxes" Nehemiah made his request directly to Artaxerxes to return to Jerusalem to rebuild it. Neh 5:14 identifies the inclusive dates of Nehemiah's mission in the reign of Artaxerxes "from the 20th year to the 32d year of Artaxerxes the king, 12 years." See also Neh 13:6. If Artaxerxes I is the intended ruler the 20th year would be 444 B.C.E. and the 32d year would be 427 B.C.E. Nehemiah made a return visit to Judea sometime after Artaxerxes's 32d year and remained in Judea for an unspecified time (Neh 13:6). Texts from Elephantine (*CAP* no. 30) and the Samaria Papyri (Cross 1975) have provided external evidence for identifying SANBALLAT, Nehemiah's rival, as the governor of Samaria in the reign of Artaxerxes I. Most

scholars are now agreed that Nehemiah's mission occurred in the reign of Artaxerxes I.

Artaxerxes's name is rendered with 2 spellings in the MT: (1) *ʾartaḥšaśtěʾ* in Ezra 4:8, 11, 23 and 6:14 (but note the variant *ʾartaḥšaśtāʾ* in Ezra 4:7); and (2) *ʾartaḥšastěʾ* beginning in Ezra 7:1. The 2d spelling is used to the end of Ezra and throughout the text of Nehemiah. Torrey (1910:38) suggested that the change from the Hebrew *śin* to *samek* is indicative of Artaxerxes I and Artaxerxes II respectively: the enemy of the Jews in Ezra 4 is Artaxerxes I, while the friend of the Jews in Ezra 7 and Nehemiah 2 is Artaxerxes II. Aramaic texts from Elephantine (*BMAP,* 132) spell Artaxerxes's name with the *samek.* Kraeling's papyrus 12, an Aramaic text dated to the reign of Artaxerxes II, uses the same spelling as those texts dated to Artaxerxes I (*BMAP,* 270). Other variants are involved as well which make Torrey's correlation difficult since variants occur even when the same ruler is intended (see *BMAP,* 142). Despite the difficulty of arguing that a practice in Egypt is the same as that of the redactor of Ezra and Nehemiah, Torrey's suggestion has not met with widespread acceptance.

Bibliography

Cook, J. M. 1983. *The Persian Empire.* New York.

Cross, F. M. 1975. A Reconstruction of the Judean Restoration. *JBL* 94:4–18.

Miller, J. M., and Hayes, J. H. 1986. *A History of Ancient Israel and Judah.* Philadelphia.

Olmstead, A. T. 1948. *History of the Persian Empire.* Chicago.

Rowley, H. H. 1955. Nehemiah's Mission and Its Background. *BJRL* 37:528–61.

Torrey, C. C. 1910. *Ezra Studies.* Chicago.

DAVID E. SUITER

ARTEMAS (PERSON) [Gk *ʾArtemas*]. A companion of Paul in the later years of Paul's career (Tit 3:12). It is never mentioned, however, where Artemas and Paul met. The letter to Titus portrays Paul as planning to send either Artemas or Tychicus to Crete, presumably to take Titus' place temporarily as the leader of the church there. Thus freed, Titus would be able to meet Paul at Nicopolis where he had decided to spend the winter. Of the several cities named Nicopolis, most commentators judge the reference in Tit 3:12 to be Nicopolis in Epirus on the W coast of Greece. Since there is a tradition preserved in 2 Tim 3:10 that Titus went to Dalmatia, to the north of Nicopolis, it is probable that he visited Paul along the way in Nicopolis and that Artemas (or Tychicus), if Paul followed through with his plan, spent time in Crete serving the church while Titus was away.

Bibliography

Dibelius, M., and Conzelmann, H. 1972. *The Pastoral Epistles.* Hermeneia. Trans. P. Buttolph and A. Yarbro. Philadelphia.

FLORENCE MORGAN GILLMAN

ARTEMIS (DEITY). Probably the most popular of the Hellenic deities, Artemis was worshiped wherever the Greeks settled and by the Romans as Diana after she was identified with the Italian goddess of that name. Her occasional identification with the Greek moon-goddess Selene had begun by the 5th century B.C., but she did not popularly become the moon until the advent of astrology religion in the Hellenistic age. Daughter of Zeus by the Titaness Leto and twin sister of Apollo, Artemis was born either on the island of Delos, where the Horn Altar, constructed of the horns of goats sacrificed to her, became famous as one of the wonders of the ancient world, or on the nearby island Ortygia. She consistently appears among the twelve Olympians, as in the Parthenon frieze, and is prominent in Greek literature, art, and public festivals from the Homeric period on. Her name, however, is etymologically obscure and her personality multifaceted and enigmatic.

Her typical form in literature and art (see, e.g., *Od.* 6.99–109, *Hymn. Hom. Ven.* 16–20, Eur. *Hipp.;* Callim. *Dian.* 1–182) is that of the Lady of the Wilds (Agrotera), a virgin huntress, pure and inviolable *(hagne),* who ranges the woodlands and mountains amid a retinue of sportive, dancing nymphs. Youthful, lithe, and dispassionately beautiful, she is often accompanied by a deer, and the bow is her constant attribute. She could be deadly and remorseless toward those who threaten her chastity or offend her, as when she turned Actaeon into a stag and let his own hounds tear him apart because he came upon her at her bath in a mountain stream, or when she sent the Calydonian boar to ravage the lands of Oeneus who had ignored her at sacrifice, or when she slew the daughters of Niobe with her arrows—as did Apollo her sons—to avenge Niobe's disparagement of Leto. Her role in the destruction of the giant Tityus, who attempted to rape Leto, and of the giants Otus and Ephialtes, who assaulted respectively her chastity and Hera's, seems, at least to a modern, more justifiable.

Before Artemis became one of the great gods, she may have been merely a wood nymph herself; for in the Peloponnesus she bore such epithets as Limnatis (Lady of the Lake), Lygodesma (Willow-Bound), and Cedreatis (Cedarn). She may at some point in her development have exhibited theriomorphic qualities: The visual arts sometimes represent her as winged, and in her cult at Brauron, in Attica, girls in her service pretended to be bears (cf. the varying accounts of her attendant nymph Callisto, who was seduced by Zeus and then turned into a bear).

Artemis the virgin huntress paradoxically contained within her personality obvious characteristics of a mother goddess, probably acquired in Asia Minor and from the Creton goddesses Britomartis and Dictynna, with whom she was sometimes identified. She zealously protects the suckling young of all wild animals, nuturing at their birth the very creatures she will later slaughter in the hunt; see, e.g., Aesch. *Ag.* 134–143, where she is incensed with Zeus' two eagles for devouring a pregnant hare. Fertility characteristics are strikingly apparent in her cult at Ephesus in Asia Minor: The Artemis whom the Ephesian mobs proclaim as "Great" at Acts 19:23–40 is a multi-mammary grotesque. In her capacity as mother goddess, Artemis was even the protectress of human children and was often identified with Eileithyia, the goddess-proper of human childbirth.

The darker aspect of Artemis' personality is perhaps

summed up and symbolized in her frequent identification with Hecate, a goddess of witchcraft and the moon who roves the night and was worshiped at the traditionally haunted-crossroad. It is an aspect alluded to in *Il.* 21.479–88, where Hera reviles Artemis for being a "lion to women" with a Zeus-given right to kill them at her pleasure, presumably at childbirth; and it is present in the myths of Actaeon, Niobe, and the Calydonian boar. Nowhere does this aspect come to the fore more starkly than: (1) at *Ag.* 104–247, when Artemis demands, and receives, the sacrifice of Agamemnon's virgin daughter Iphigenia, as simultaneously an atonement for the eagles' slaughter of the pregnant hare and a propiatory act to procure the release of the wind-bound Greek fleet from Aulis for the expedition against Troy; and (2) in Eur. *IT* when Iphigenia, saved from sacrifice at Aulis by the miraculous substitution of a hind and transported by Artemis to the land of the Taurians on the farthest shores of the Black Sea (according to the variant legend here followed), presides as priestess of Artemis over the sacrifice of all foreigners who wander to that land. There was probably a symbolic reminiscence of human sacrifice in the cultic rites of Artemis Tauropolus in Attica (a man's throat is scratched to the point of bleeding with a sword), whither according to the *IT* (see especially 1446–1461) Orestes and Iphigenia brought the goddess' cult statue after they escaped from Taurica. The shedding of human blood was also an important component in the rites of Artemis Ortheia at Sparta; during these events, which became a tourist attraction in Roman times, youths were whipped until they bled. Similarly, human sacrifice may lie behind the holocausts of fruit and live animals in honor of Artemis Laphria at Patrae. The substitution of a hind for the sacrificial victim (see Eur. *IA* 1532–1618 for an account of this miracle) bears comparison with that of the ram for Isaac in Genesis 22.

We may, at least to a point, account for the confusing multiplicity and ambivalence in Artemis' personality by regarding her as a humanized representation of untamed nature, which appears benign and life-giving at one time or place and cruel and destructive at another. And we may risk going somewhat further by regarding her as simultaneously a representation of what the Greek male, in the collective psyche of a male-dominated society, both admired and feared in the female. But Artemis is perhaps the most difficult of the Hellenic deities to comprehend and will undoubtedly always elude full explanation.

Bibliography

Burkert, W. 1972. *Homo Necans.* Berlin and New York.

———. 1985. *Greek Religion.* Trans. J. Raffan. Cambridge, MA.

Farnell, L. R. 1896. *The Cults of the Greek States.* Vol. 2. Oxford.

Graves, R. 1960. *The Greek Myths.* 2 vols. New York.

Guthrie, W. K. C. 1954. *The Greeks and Their Gods.* Boston.

Nilsson, M. P. 1961a. *Greek Folk Religion.* New York.

———. 1961b. *Geschichte der griechischen Religion.* Vol. 2, 2d ed. Munich.

———. 1967. *Geschichte der griechischen Religion.* Vol. 1, 3d. ed. Munich.

Otto, W. F. 1954. *The Homeric Gods.* New York.

Rose, H. J. 1958. *A Handbook of Greek Mythology.* London and New York.

Wilamowitz-Moellendorff, U. von. 1955. *Der Glaube der Hellenen.* 2 vols. Tübingen.

HUBERT M. MARTIN, JR.

ARTHROPODS. See ZOOLOGY.

ARUBBOTH (PLACE) [Heb *ʾărubbôt*].

A city mentioned only once in the Bible as the seat of Ben Hesed, governor of Solomon's 3d district (1 Kgs 4:10). The difficulty in identifying the city is a result of this singular reference, containing no specific geographic indicators. Its identification therefore requires a proper overview of the nature and character of this Solomonic district list (1 Kgs 4:7–19).

A. Location of Solomon's Third District

Two primary approaches have been suggested for understanding the geographic principles of the district divisions. According to the first (Alt, *KlSchr* 2: 76–89; Aharoni 1976), the districts were of 2 different types, the first being identical to the Israelite tribal territories, and the second including former Canaanite areas in the coastal plain and large valleys (the latter being defined by a listing of cities). The 3d district is defined as follows: "Ben Hesed in Arubboth, to him belonged Socoh and all the land of Hepher." According to this first approach, the fact that this district included a list of cities means that this district was formerly "Canaanite," located in the N Sharon between the Yarkon and Wadi ez-Zerqah rivers. (Consequently, in this approach the first district [the hill country of Ephraim] would have stretched far N of the tribe's original inheritance to include, during the period of the district division, the tribal territory of Manasseh as well.) Thus, Mazar (1935) suggested locating Hepher at Tel Iphshar (M.R. 141197), and Arubboth at Tel el-Assawir (M.R. 151210), near the W opening of the ʿIron pass leading to Megiddo.

Albright (1925) in particular offered another approach, pointing out the methodological problem of identifying Arubboth and Hepher in the coastal plain. The daughters of Zelophehad (the granddaughters of Hepher, Josh 17:1–4), appear in the Samaria Ostraca as territorial units in the NE part of the Manasseh hill country. Tirzah, for example, who belongs to Hepher's family, is located well inland, about 10 km NE of Shechem. Therefore, it seems more likely that the 'Land of Hepher' should be located in the hill country *within* the nuclear tribal allotment rather than in the formerly Canaanite area in the coastal plain (annexed to the monarchy only in the time of David). A coastal plain locale for the 3d district is also challenged by the archaeological data: Tel Iphshar is too small to have been a Canaanite city-state like Hepher (Josh 12:17), and Tel Assawir contained no sherds of the 10th century B.C.E. The site therefore could not have been a district capital during this period.

B. Other Possible References to Arubboth

Certain assistance for the identification of Arubboth is found in the fact that the city (and the district) of that name probably existed throughout the Iron Age, the Persian, Hellenistic and Early Roman Periods as well. According to Grintz (1957: 31), the tradition in Taanit Scroll, describing Jewish fortified cities in the Samaria region in either the Persian or the Hellenistic period, is linked with the Jewish settlement in the Dothan Valley, as told in the book of Judith. Others relate it to the settlement of the area by Jews after its conquest by John Hyrcanus in 106 B.C.E. It is possible that the name of the area in the Taanit Scroll, *Nabrachta,* is connected to one of the offshoots of the geographic name Arubboth (see below).

The area is mentioned in 1 Macc 5: 21–23: Simon the Hasmonean, after his victory over the Gentiles at Acre, brought to Jerusalem the Jews of Galilee and "Arbattoi," which seems to be a Jewish district located between the W Galilee and Jerusalem. The syntax of the name indicates a possible connection to Arubboth, since only the suffix differs from the original, without change in the basic consonants of the name.

The Byzantine historian Georghios Kedrenos cites a list of the Herodian toparchies (divided among Herod's sons), where the toparchy of Narbatton is mentioned along with Galilee and Perea. All 3 came under the jurisdiction of Herod Antipas. This list suggests that during the Herodian period there existed in N Samaria a Jewish district named Narbatton. Since both Galilee and Perea were Jewish districts, we may assume that this division was based upon the necessity of separating the Jewish toparchies from those of the Gentiles. It is worth noting, however, that this Byzantine source is controversial.

Finally, the area is mentioned twice by Josephus, along with a definition of its geographic location. First, in his description of the events close to the outbreak of the Jewish Revolt in May, A.D. 66, Josephus reports that a clash broke out between Greeks and Jews around the Great Synagogue of Caesarea; after the emperor Nero ruled in favor of the Greeks, the Jews took their Torah scrolls and went to one of their inheritances called Narbata, located 20 stadia from Caesarea (*JW* 2: 291). The second reference is connected with the report about Cestius Gallus' punitive campaign against Jerusalem in October A.D. 66; Josephus reports that Gallus sent forces of cavalry from Caesarea to Narbata, who "destroyed the district and set the villages aflame" (*JW* 2: 509).

The name of the area is not mentioned again. An analysis of the sources suggests a linguistic connection in the series Arubboth–Nabrachta–Arbatta–Narbata, based on the preservation of the ancient nucleus *r-b-t,* whose meaning is uncertain. The changes over a millennium are probably connected with the influx of Aram prefixes and suffixes into spoken Hebrew. Such include the prefix *n-* and the geographic suffix *-a* (as in Suseita and Gamla). Kampffmeyer (1892) showed that changes in suffix and prefix do not alter the nucleus of the name, and therefore we have in these sources evidence for the continuity of the district and the city in the same area (N Samaria, not the N Sharon valley). As for the distance of 20 stadia (12 km) from Caesarea to Narbata (*JW* 2: 291), Avi-Yonah (1962: 12, 127) showed that most of Josephus' distance indicators relate to distances between the district capital and the toparchy's border. We may, therefore, suggest that the border between the boundary of Caesarea and the toparchy of Narbata was the point where the Coastal Plain meets the Samaria hills, at a distance of 12 km from Caesarea.

C. Khirbet el-Hamam

1. Location and Description. During the course of a detailed archaeological survey on behalf of Tel Aviv and Haifa Universities, a previously unknown tell—Kh. el-Hamam—was discovered in 1978. This site seems to fit well the identification of Arubboth-Narbata. The site (M.R. 163201) rises S of the riverbed of Wadi Jiz, in a rugged and stony hill area, between the Dothan valley and the Coastal Plain.

The city stretches across two hilltops. The N hilltop is approx. 70 dunams in size; it is fortified naturally by means of steep slopes at the W, N, and E; at the S it is connected to the lower slope by means of a gradual and convenient downgrade. Its upper acropolis, about 25 dunams, was surrounded by a double city wall. The S hilltop is the larger one, and contains remnants of structures and caves with no indication of fortification.

A sophisticated Roman siege system surrounding the city was discovered and explored, including a circumvallation, three camps, and a siege ramp. The circumvallation is 1,516 m long and 2.2 m thick, encompassing the city from the W, N, and E. Alongside it were discovered Camp B (excavated) and Camps C–D (unexcavated). The supposed location of Camp A was the S hilltop.

2. Excavations. The siege system and the city itself were excavated during 1980–1984 (Zertal 1984). Camp B of the siege system lies on the el-Birkeh hill, approx. 600 m E of the city. It is a square structure (22 × 22 m) with opposite gates at the N and S. Rooms and floors were unearthed inside, upon which were found cooking pots and other vessels dated to the 1st century A.D., very similar to the material of Masada. In addition, a coin of Herod Archelaus (4 B.C.E.–A.D. 6) was found. The excavated part of the circumvallation was found to be identical in structure and dimensions to the E circumvallation and the walls of Camp A at Masada. Some towers were discovered along the circumvallation. Camp C at Kh. el-Hamam is a small structure (10 × 10 m), and camp D which lies on a slope next to the paved road that led to the city from the important Caesarea-Ginae road, is similar to Camp B. The siege system at Kh. el-Hamam is one of 4 extant, complete Roman systems connected with the Jewish Revolt (A.D. 66–70) and the Bar-Kokhba Revolt (A.D. 132–135): Masada, Bethar, Machaerus, and Narbata (Kh. el-Hamam). The latter is the only one found N of Jerusalem.

Three areas within the city itself were excavated: (1) the central section and the siege ramp; (2) the S wall; and (3) a group of houses in the upper W part of the city. In the central section a continuity of pottery groups was discovered, ranging from the 10th century B.C.E. until the 2d century A.D., confirming the conclusions of the survey. The city wall of the Iron Age dates to the 10th century B.C.E. and should possibly be identified as the Solomonic city wall of Arubboth. It is approx. 3 m thick, and was founded upon a low stone cliff. This wall continued to be in use during Iron II (the Israelite kingdom), and possibly also through the Persian period into Hasmonean times (2d century B.C.E.), when the city was refortified by an additional and new wall. At this stage, the Iron Age city wall became a supporting wall which encircled the city and lay outside the new wall. The entrance to this new wall was from the protected N side. The width of the Hasmonean wall is approx. 2 m, and it was the wall used to protect the city during the Jewish Revolt in A.D. 66. Two blocks of structures were excavated in the upper W area, dating to the Hellenistic-Herodian periods. Beneath it, fragmented Iron Age structures were exposed.

Beneath and outside the line of the walls, a sophisticated water system was explored and partially excavated. This includes 3 hewn cisterns in the form of subterranean chambers, plastered with a special plaster identical to that of the water system at Masada. Each of the chambers contained 600–1,000 cubic m of water, and were filled by means of a hewn opening. An aqueduct, whose entire route is as yet unknown, was connected to the cisterns.

The small finds include nearly 100 coins, dating from Ptolemy II (beginning of the 3d century B.C.E.), through the beginning of the 2d century A.D. In addition, carved stone vessels were unearthed, typical of Jewish settlements during the Second Temple period.

From a historical point of view, the results of the excavation support the identification of the city as Narbata, which was the only city in Samaria to take part in the Jewish Revolt. According to Josephus, it was also the only Jewish region in this area, otherwise populated by veterans of the Hellenistic and Roman armies (Sebaste) and by Samaritans. A few arrowheads, catapult stones, and a partial level of destruction at Kh. el-Hamam indicate that the battle over the city did not last long. We may assume that the city surrendered not long after the siege system was built. It is unclear why there is no mention of the siege of Narbata by Josephus. Despite that, there are actually no alternate identifications for the site, and it fits the location of Arubboth-Narbata in 3 major criteria: (1) the archaeological and historical periods of occupation, (2) the geographical context and location, and (3) the preservation of the name. The latter is still preserved in the vicinity in the form of Arrabeh (M.R. 169201), a village some 6 km to the SE, at the S fringe of the Dothan Valley. Apparently, the name shifted there after the destruction or abandonment of the city Narbata.

D. The History of Arubboth-Narbata

The results of the excavation indicate that the city was founded at the middle of the 10th century B.C.E., but there may have been a small village there founded a few decades earlier. Along with the foundation of the city the N hilltop was fortified, evidently creating an administrative center and seat of the regional governor. This foundation coincides with the intentions of the authorities, who preferred founding new sites, free of previous tribal traditions. Wright (1967) and Mazar (1975: 131) showed that Makaz (probably the capital of the 2d district) and Arubboth belong in this category.

The existence of the city, which was supported by the Arubboth district, continued during the period of the N Israelite kingdom. It is probable that the Jewish district of the Persian period in the Dothan valley, mentioned in the book of Judith, was connected somehow with the Arubboth district. Upon the Hasmonean conquest of Samaria by John Hyrcanus, the city underwent great development. A new city wall was built, thus creating a kind of fortified acropolis. During this period, or a bit later, the city of Arbatta grew and many new homes were built on the slopes of both the N and S hilltops. During the 1st century A.D. the name was changed to Narbata, and the city maintained some connection with the Jews of Caesarea.

Upon the outbreak of the Jewish Revolt, some of the Caesarean Jews moved to Narbata, taking with them their Torah scrolls. In this account, Josephus is possibly referring to persons belonging to the Zealot party in Caesarea, who thus declared an open revolt against the Romans (Zertal 1982). The place was finally abandoned at the beginning of the 2d century A.D.

From a geographic-historic viewpoint, it seems that the 3d Solomonic district coincided with the boundaries of Manasseh in the hill country (Josh 16:5–9; 17:7–13). This conclusion, which supports in broad lines Albright's approach (see A above), is also based upon the recent identification of Hepher (Josh 12:17) with Tel Muhaffar, a large fortified site situated at the N boundary of the Dothan valley. The identification of Hepher and Arubboth within the bounds of the Manasseh hill country conforms with the biblical data, the evidence of the Samaria Ostraca, and the Second Temple traditions.

Bibliography

Aharoni, Y. 1976. The Solomonic Districts. *TA* 3: 5–15.

Albright, W. F. 1925. The Administrative Division of Israel and Judah. *JPOS* 5: 17–54.

Avi-Yonah, M. 1962. *Historical Geography of Palestine.* Jerusalem (in Hebrew).

Grintz, Y. M. 1957. *Sefer Yehudith* (The Book of Judith). Jerusalem (in Hebrew).

Kampffmeyer, G. 1892. Alte Namen in Heutige Palastina und Syrien I: Namen des Alten Testaments. *ZDPV* 15: 1–33; 65–118.

Mazar, B. 1935. Die westlich Linie des Meerweges. *ZDPV* 58: 79–84.

———. 1975. *Cities and Districts in Eretz-Israel.* Jerusalem (in Hebrew).

Wright, G. E. 1967. The Provinces of Solomon. *EI* 8: 58*–69*.

Zertal, A. 1982. The Siege of Narbata and the Start of the Great Revolt. *Zmanim* 2 (10): 32–46 (in Hebrew).

———. 1984. *Arubboth, Hepher and the Third Solomonic District.* Tel Aviv (in Hebrew).

ADAM ZERTAL

ARUMAH (PLACE) [Heb *ʾărûmâ]. A town in Ephraim mentioned once or twice in the story of Abimelech son of Gideon (Judges 9). According to Judg 9:41, Abimelech resided briefly at Arumah. The text of Judg 9:31 is problematic. MT reads "he (scil. Zebul) sent messengers to Abimelech *bĕtormāh";* the last word consists of the Heb preposition *bĕ-* "in, at, by means of," and an otherwise unattested noun *tormâ,* whose root is possibly *rmh* "to deceive" (thus LXX[B] *en kryphē,* "in secret" [cf. LXX[A] *meta dōrōn* "with gifts," reading *trmh* as *tĕrūmâ* "offering, gift"]; KJV "privily"; ASV "craftily"; Boling *Judges* AB, 179 "by a ruse"). The consonants *btrmh* of MT should perhaps be read **bêt* [ʾă]*rūmâ* "Beth Arumah," thus creating a second mention of the site (*GTTOT,* 297).

Arumah is generally located at Khirbet el-ᶜOrmah (M.R. 180172) 5 miles SE of Shechem (*LBHG*, 242). It is not to be identified with RUMAH further N (*LBHG*, 329–31).

HENRY O. THOMPSON

ARVAD (PERSON) [Heb *ʾarwād*]. ARVADITES. One of the "offspring" of Canaan (Gen 10:18), who supplied rowers and guards for Tyre (Ezek 27:8, 11). Arvad is named in the list of places to which the Roman consul sent his proclamation of alliance with Simon (1 Macc 15: 23, if the textual rearrangement of Goldstein *Maccabees* AB, pp. 492–500 is followed). The Genesis reference has the gentilic suffix -*î*.

The city of Arvad, modern Ruad (M.R. 229473), is the most nothern of the Phoenician cities, located on an island adjacent to the coast. It is mentioned in an Egyptian text (*ʾá-r-du;* cf. Helck 1962: 310). In the Amarna letters it seems to have allied with Amurru against Byblos and Tyre (*ar-wa-da;* cf. Klengel 1969: 206; Katzenstein 1973: 42; Hess 1984: 436). It appears frequently in Assyrian and Babylonian texts on into the 1st millennium B.C., having to do with Syria (Unger *RLA* 1: 160–61).

Of some interest for comparison with the military aspect of the Arvadites mentioned in Ezekiel 27 is the mention of 200 soldiers from Arvad who fought with the opponents of Shalmaneser III at the battle of Qarqar in 853 B.C. (cf. Katzenstein 1973: 156). For the Assyrian kings, Arvad was the city "in the midst of the sea" (*qabal tamtim;* cf. Wiseman 1951: 24). There is a possible portrayal of Arvad as the island receiving wood in a Khorsabad relief (Parrot 1961 plate 48; Katzenstein 1973: 243). In this context, the Ezekiel passage associating renowned rowers with Arvad becomes meaningful (Ezek 27:8). Apparently it was sufficiently independent of the Seleucids in the mid-2d century B.C. to receive a proclamation from Rome.

Bibliography

Helck, W. 1962. *Untersuchungen Ägyptens zu Vorderasien im 3, und 2, Jahrtausend v. Chr.* AA 5. Wiesbaden.

Hess, R. S. 1984. *Amarna Proper Names.* Diss. Hebrew Union College.

Katzenstein, H. J. 1973. *The History of Tyre. From the Beginning of the Second Millennium B.C.E. until the Fall of the Neo-Babylonian Empire in 538 B.C.E.* Jerusalem.

Klengel, H. 1969. *Geschichte Syriens im 2. Jahrtausend v.u.z. Teil 2. Mittel-und Südsyrien.* Deutsche Akademie der Wissenschaften zu Berlin Institut für Orientforschung Veröffentlichung 70. Berlin.

Parrot, A. 1961. *Nineveh and Babylon.* Trans. S. Gilbert and J. Emmons. London.

Wiseman, D. J. 1951. Two Historical Inscriptions from Nimrud. *Iraq* 13: 21–26.

RICHARD S. HESS

ARZA (PERSON) [Heb *ʾarṣāʾ*]. Chamberlain of Elah, king of Israel, at Tirzah (1 Kgs 16:9). Though it was at the house of Arza that an intoxicated Elah was assassinated by Zimri, it is not known if Azra was a part of the conspiracy against the king. As chamberlain, literally "over the house," Arza may have been responsible for the royal property at Tirzah as well as the king's domestic affairs. The name, Arza, may be derived from the root, *rṣh*, (to be pleased, acceptable). Noth suggests an Arabic derivation from *ʾaraḍatun* "wood fretter" (IPN, 230). (See Gray *Kings* OTL; Noth *Könige* BKAT; Würthwein *Könige: 1 Könige 1–16* ATD; De Vries *1 Kings* WBC.)

PAULINE A. VIVIANO

ARZARETH (PLACE) [Lat *Arzareth; Arsareth*]. A land to which the 10 tribes of Israel were deported; to reach this region required a journey of a year and a half from the Euphrates river (2 Esdr 13:45). No place by this name is attested. To understand this reference, one must appreciate that the original Heb or Aram of 2 Esdras is no longer extant, and that all we have are Lat (and other) translations. Thus, some have suggested that the name preserves a corruption of Heb *ʾ*ereṣ ʾarat,* "land of Ar(ar)at" (i.e., N Armenia). However, it is more likely that the Lat here contains and conceals the Heb *ʾereṣ ʾăḥeret,* "another land" (cf. also 2 Esdr 13:40). This phrase appears in Deut 29:27 (—Eng 29:28), an exilic addition attributing to Moses the prediction about the scattering and deportation of the sinful Israelites. It is noteworthy that the early rabbis applied this phrase in their discussions about the dispersion of the Ten Tribes (*m. Sanh.* 10:3). Therefore, it is likely that the Semitic original of 2 Esdras did the same, and that the Lat translator has corrupted the original and transformed it erroneously into a proper name "Arzareth" (see Wright 1871).

Bibliography

Wright, W. A. 1871. Note on the "Azareth" of 4 Esdr XIII.45. *Journal of Philology* 3: 113–14.

GARY A. HERION

ASA (PERSON) [Heb *ʾāsāʾ*]. Son and successor of Abijam/Abijah and the 3d king of Judah after the division of the united monarchy. According to the synchronisms provided in 1 Kings, Asa's rule began while Israel's first king, Jeroboam, was still in power (15:9); it spanned the reigns of Nadab, Baasha, Elah, Zimri, and Omri; and it ended in the early years of Ahab's rule (16:29). He ruled for 41 years (1 Kgs 15:10; 2 Chr 16:13), which Albright (1945) dated to 913–873 B.C.E.

A. Sources

The primary account of Asa's reign is given by the Deuteronomistic historian in 1 Kgs 15:9–24. The author indicates that he has drawn his information from the annals of the kings of Judah (1 Kgs 15:23), but his ideological perspective is clearly stamped on the account.

The Chronicler presents a somewhat longer account in 2 Chr 13:23b–16:14 (—Eng 14:1b–16:14), parts of which parallel the account in 1 Kings but the rest includes added material of debated historical worth. It is clear that the Chronicler has used the Kings account as a principal source, even as he reshaped and added to it in order to present his own perspective on Asa's reign. Whether the Chronicler has used sources beyond 1 Kings to present his account of Asa is uncertain, but it is possible that he has. For example, the Chronicler's detailed information about

Asa's army (2 Chr 14:7) and related notes elsewhere in his work (cf. 17:14–19; 25:5 and 26:11–15) may preserve "authentic material relating to the conscript army" (Williamson *Chronicles* NCBC, 20, 261–2). Welten, however, contends that these passages are pure fabrications, reflecting the organization of Hellenistic armies in the time of the Chronicler (1973: 79–114). Whether the Chronicler's added information is based on additional sources or not, it must be used with caution in reconstructing the events of Asa's reign.

Two major aspects of Asa's reign are covered by both the Deuteronomistic historian and the Chronicler: (1) a religious reform and (2) a successful response to Baasha's invasion of Judah.

B. Asa's Reform

The account in 1 Kings indicates that the reform included the following actions by Asa, who (a) expelled the male cult prostitutes from the land; (b) removed all the images which his predecessors had made; (c) deposed his mother (grandmother?) Maacah from her position as queen mother *(gĕbîrâ)* because she had made an abominable image *(mipleṣet)* for Asherah; (d) destroyed this image by cutting it down and burning it; and (e) brought votive offerings into the temple. The Deuteronomistic historian praises Asa for doing "that which was right in the sight of Yahweh, like David his father" (15:11) and claims that, although the "high places" *(bāmôt)* were not abolished, the king was completely loyal to Yahweh all his life (15:14).

The Chronicler adds that Asa abolished the foreign altars and incense altars, and also claims (2 Chr 15:9–12) that Asa, in the 3d month of the 15th year of his reign, assembled all of Judah, Benjamin, and those who had come to live with them from Ephraim, Manasseh, and Simeon, to enter into a covenant to seek guidance from Yahweh. Those who refused to seek Yahweh, whether old or young, male or female, were put to death (2 Chr 15:13). Whether such a covenant ceremony took place is debated, but Williamson has suggested that the Chronicler's account of these matters is based on a special source and presents a plausible rendering of what took place (*Chronicles* NCBC, 269–71).

Asa's removal of Maacah from the position of queen mother is mentioned in 1 Kgs 15:13 and 2 Chr 15:16. Because her association with the goddess Asherah would have brought her into conflict with Asa's reform, Ahlström has concluded the queen mother's position was essentially cultic in nature (1963: 57–85). Other possibilities for understanding the queen mother's role have been reviewed recently by Andreasen (1983).

C. Asa's Response to Baasha's Invasion

1 Kgs 15:16 indicates that border conflicts between Judah and Israel continued throughout the reigns of Asa and Baasha, but the Deuteronomistic historian focuses on a decisive phase of the struggle. According to this account, Baasha marched into Judah as far as Ramah, which he fortified to cut off access to Jerusalem. Asa responded by sending an appeal, sweetened with a good portion of Judah's treasure, to Ben-hadad, the king of Aram, in Damascus. At that time Aram and Israel were allies, but Asa's request was for Ben-hadad to break off the alliance with Israel. Ben-hadad did so, and sent his forces into N Israelite territory, forcing Baasha to abandon Ramah. Asa then issued a proclamation to all Judah, with no exemptions, and they dismantled Baasha's fortifications at Ramah and used the stones and timbers to fortify Geba and Mizpah (vv 17–22).

The Chronicler's account places these events in the 36th year of Asa's reign (2 Chr 16:1; this conflicts, however, with 1 Kgs 16:6 and 8 which indicate that Baasha had died some 10 years earlier). On the theory that the Chronicler's chronology is based on a source which referred to the 36th year of the division of the monarchy, not of Asa's reign, Baasha's invasion and the related events would have taken place in the 16th year of Asa's reign (Williamson *Chronicles* NCBC, 256–7). It is possible, however, that the Chronicler's chronology serves theological rather than historical purposes (Rudolph 1952; Dillard 1980).

D. The Chronicler's Other Additions

The Chronicler has also added to his narrative about Asa an account of the invasion of Zerah the "Cushite" (14:7–13) and speeches to Asa by Azariah ben Oded (15:2–7) and the seer Hanani (16:7–10).

The speeches of Azariah and Hanani are taken by most scholars to be creations of the Chronicler. Azariah's speech is inserted between Asa's victory over Zerah and the account of Asa's religious reform. The Chronicler uses it to depict Asa's reform as inspired by Yahweh. Hanani's speech, on the other hand, condemns Asa for relying on Ben-hadad in the affair with Baasha, rather than on Yahweh as he did in the victory over Zerah. Von Rad has maintained that these and other speeches in 1 and 2 Chr reflect standard Levitical homiletic practice which the Chronicler has employed for his own theological purposes (*PHOE,* 267–80).

Many scholars believe that the account of Asa's victory over Zerah, though written in the Chronicler's style, is based on an event which the Chronicler knew from one of his sources. There is debate, however, over the identity of the invading forces. One view is that Zerah "the Cushite" was an Ethiopian general dispatched to Judah by Osorkon I in his latter years (Kitchen 1973: 309); another view is that the invading forces were a mercenary group stationed at Gerar from the time of Sheshonk's campaign against Judah (*BHI,* 234–35); still another view is that "Cush" in this context refers to an ethnic Bedouin group in the vicinity of Judah which menacingly invaded Asa's territory (Hidal 1976–77: 100–1). In the absence of more evidence, all of these theories remain mere speculation.

The Chronicler also credits Asa with the fortification of cities in Judah (2 Chr 14:6–7). Without entirely ruling out building activity in Asa's reign (cf. 1 Kgs. 15:23), Williamson notes the Chronicler's thematic emphasis in these verses, i.e., the author seeks to establish a connection between Asa's building activity and the peace that Yahweh had supposedly given him as a result of his reform (*Chronicles* NCBC, 260; cf. Welten 1973: 15–19).

E. Asa's Death

Asa developed a disease "in his feet" near the end of his life (1 Kgs 15:23); the Chronicler says this happened in the 39th year of his reign (2 Chr 16:12). The nature of this disease has been much discussed. Gout, dropsie, or gangrene have been most frequently suggested. The possibility cannot be excluded, however, that "feet" in this instance, as elsewhere in the Hebrew Bible, is a euphemism for genitals (Williamson *Chronicles* NCBC, 276–7; *HAIJ,* 241). Asa was buried in Jerusalem and succeeded by his son Jehoshaphat.

Bibliography

Ahlström, G. W. 1963. *Aspects of Syncretism in Israelite Religion.* Horae Soederblomianae 5. Lund.

Albright, W. F. 1945. The Chronology of the Divided Monarchy of Israel. *BASOR* 100: 16–22.

Andreasen, N.-E. A. 1983. The Role of the Queen Mother in Israelite Society. *CBQ* 45: 179–94.

Dillard, R. 1980. The Reign of Asa (2 Chronicles 14–16): An Example of the Chronicler's Theological Method. *JETS* 23: 207–18.

Hidal, S. 1976/77. The Land of Cush in the Old Testament. *SEÅ* 41–42: 97–106.

Kitchen, K. A. 1973. *The Third Intermediate Period in Egypt (1100–650 B.C.).* Warminster.

Rudolph, W. 1952. Der Aufbau der Asa-Geschichte. *VT* 2: 367–71.

Welten, P. 1973. *Geschichte und Geschichtsdarstellung in den Chronikbüchern.* WMANT 42. Neukirchen-Vluyn.

CARL D. EVANS

ASAHEL (PERSON) [Heb *ʿăśâʾēl;* Gk *Asael*]. The name of 4 or 5 men in the OT. The name Asahel is formed as a sentence using the verb *ʿaśâ* "to make," "to do" with the divine name El. Asahel means "El has done" or "El has made."

1. Asahel was one of the 3 sons of Zeruiah, David's nephews and retainers (see ZERUIAH, SONS OF). As with other figures of tradition, Asahel was remembered by a brief descriptive verse: he was "fleet as the gazelle" (cf. Goliath of Gath, "the shaft of whose spear was like a weaver's beam," 2 Sam 21:19; 1 Chr 20:5). While his brothers served throughout David's reign, Asahel was killed by Abner, the son of Ner, during the war between David and Ish-bosheth, the successor to King Saul (2 Sam 2:18–32); he was buried in the tomb of his father in Bethlehem. Joab, his brother, treacherously slew Abner in revenge for Asahel's death (2 Sam 3:22–30), an act which brought bloodguilt onto David's house, and in expiation for which David had his son and successor Solomon kill Joab (1 Kgs 2:5–6).

The inclusion of Asahel in the lists of David's heroic warriors (2 Sam 23:24; 1 Chr 11:26) suggests that these lists go back to the beginning of David's reign. That this same Asahel is listed as an officer over David's monthly levies (1 Chr 27:7), by which time he should have been dead, however, calls into question the historicity of that list (see DAVID'S CHAMPIONS), unless his name was placed upon this division posthumously to honor him (*IDB* 1:244).

Naʾaman's argument (1988: 77–79) that the story of Asahel's death at the hands of Abner was fabricated upon the strength of his mention in these lists is merely meant to support his own view that David's champions were really his high officer corps. 1 Chronicles 27 is the only text where a significant number of David's heroic warriors are presented as officers. Naʾaman's thesis requires him to discredit the account of Asahel's death during David's reign in Hebron, since it is highly unlikely that David had actually had a highly organized standing army based on successive monthly levies of 24,000 men each, 288,000 in all, *before* he became king of Israel. (Even the inflated figures of 1 Samuel 11 give Judah only 30,000 men; but cf. *IDB* 1:244.) The story of Asahel's death then, while likely embellished (storytelling and the writing of history were not mutually exclusive categories in the ancient Near East), is probably based on solid historical traditions.

2. One of six Levites sent in the 3d year of Jehoshaphat into the villages of Judah with the priests Elishama and Jehoram to teach the book of the law (2 Chr 17:7–8).

3. A Levite who assisted in the collection of tithes and devoted offerings in the temple during Hezekiah's attempted centralization of worship (2 Chr 31:11–13; cf. Hayes and Irvine 1987: 48–49).

4. The name of the (otherwise unknown) father of one Jonathan, an exile at the time of Ezra. Along with Jahzeiah, the son of Tikvah, this Jonathan opposed Ezra the scribe in his efforts to get the exiles to put away their foreign wives and children (Ezra 10:1–15, esp. v 15).

Although there is some ambiguity about this verse (cf. Vg and NJPSV, which put Jonathan and Jahzeiah in charge of Ezra's commission), Williamson (*Ezra, Nehemiah* AB, 156–57) has convincingly argued for the RSV rendering. 1 Esdras 9:14, however, clearly agrees with the Vg and NJPSV Ezra.

5. One of the "sons of Ezora" who dismissed his foreign wife following Ezra's action (1 Esd 9:34). The RSV name is AZAEL, as in Ezra 10:41, but it is rendered "Asahel" in AB, and Meyers equates it with the name in Ezra 10:15 (Meyers *Esdras* AB, 89). It is *azaelos* in the LXX. The name is also found as *aazaēlos, azēlos* at Murabbaʿat (Meyers *Esdras* AB, 93; DJD 2.227; *Les Grottes de Murabbaʿat,* DJD 2/94:12). If this person is the same as Asahel (4) above, then it is understandable that Jonathan would oppose an action which would result in the expulsion of his mother.

Bibliography

Hayes, J. H., and Irvine, S. A. 1987. *Isaiah: The Eighth-Century Prophet.* Nashville.

Naʾaman, N. 1988. The List of David's Officers. *VT* 38:71–79.

D. G. SCHLEY

ASAIAH (PERSON) [Heb *ʿăśāyāh*]. The name of 4 individuals in the Hebrew Bible.

1. A Levite from the Merari clan, one of the leaders appointed by David to move the ark from the house of Obed-edom to Jerusalem (1 Chr 6:15—Eng 6:30; 15:6, 11). Many regard 15:4–10 as a later insertion into Chronicles; however, Talmon (*IDBSup,* 322) and Williamson (*1 and 2 Chronicles* NCBC, 89, 121–22) argue that the repetition of the names in 15:11 is a literary device marking an insertion of source material by the original author.

2. One of the royal officials under Josiah, sent as part of a delegation to consult with the prophetess Huldah regarding the discovery of a book of the law in the temple (2 Kgs 22:12, 14; 2 Chr 34:20).

3. One of the leaders of the tribe of Simeon (1 Chr 4:36), among those who fought near Gedor (= Gerar?) and against the Meunites (1 Chr 4:38–43).

4. One of the descendants of Judah's son Shelah who returned to Jerusalem after the Babylonian captivity (1 Chr 9:5). Since the Chronicler gives the total number of those from the tribe of Judah who returned (1 Chr 9:6b), and since he lists descendants of Judah through Perez (1 Chr 9:4) and through Zerah (1 Chr 9:6a), MT Shilonites should be revocalized to Shelanites, the descendants of Judah's son Shelah (cf. Num 26:20; Neh 11:4–6).

RAYMOND B. DILLARD

ASAIAS (PERSON) [Gk *Asaias*]. A descendant of Annan and one of the returned exiles who was required by Ezra to divorce his foreign wife (1 Esdr 9:32). In the parallel text of Ezra 10:31, the name ISSHIJAH appears in the position Asaias holds in 1 Esdr 9:32.

JEFFREY A. FAGER

ASAPH (PERSON) [Heb *ʾāsāp*]. ASAPHITE. Three individuals in the OT bear the name Asaph (see also 4. below). In addition, this name occurs in the inscription *lʾsp* on a seal from Megiddo which has been variously dated to the 8th or 7th century B.C.E. (Diringer 1934: 168–69).

1. Son of Berechiah, eponymous ancestor of "the Asaphites" (RSV: "sons of Asaph"), and one of the great families or guilds of musicians and singers in the Jerusalem temple (1 Chr 6:39; 25:1, 2; 2 Chr 5:12). The headings of 12 psalms (50,73–83) include the designation *lĕʾāsāp,* most likely an indication that they were a part of an Asaphic collection or were performed according to the style or tradition of the guild bearing Asaph's name (note also the Asaphic attribution of the psalm anthology in 1 Chr 16:7–36). The theory that the Asaphic tradition was of N Israelite origins (Buss 1963) is intriguing but highly speculative, given that the rationale for attribution in the headings of the psalms remains uncertain.

At the time of the return from the exile, "temple singers" (1 Esdr 5:27; 1:15) in general could be referred to simply as "Asaphites" (Ezra 2:41 [= Neh 7:44; 1 Esdr 5:27]). The prominence of this guild is also apparent in the designation of the Asaphite Uzzi the son of Bani as "the overseer of the Levites" *(pāqîd halĕwiyyim)* over the work of the house of God (Neh 11:22). The subsequent reference to Persian support (Neh 11:23; see Rudolph *Esra Nehemia* HAT, 187) and the contrast of Uzzi's area of responsibility with that of Pethahiah the son of Meshezabel in the succeeding verse ("all matters concerning the people," Neh 11:24) support the suggestion that this guild at some point oversaw the Jerusalem cultus under Persian sponsorship (for a differing view see Clines *Ezra, Nehemiah, Esther* NCBC, 219). This scenario would accord well with the prominence given to the ancestor Asaph in 1 Chr 16:1–6, 37–42, where he is designated "the chief" *(hārōʾš)* of the Levites minstering before the ark in Jerusalem, while the priest Zadok and the singers Heman and Jeduthun were appointed by David to serve at Gibeon. Postexilic development in the guilds of singers (Gese 1974, Williamson *Chronicles* NCBC, 120–22; opposed by Clines *Ezra, Nehemiah, Esther* NCBC, 55–56) resulted in the replacement of the Asaphites by the guild of Heman as the preeminent group (cf. esp. 1 Chr 25:5).

Of Asaph himself, little can be said with confidence. According to the Chronicler, Asaph was a descendant of Gershom the son of Levi and one of three Levitical singers whom David placed in charge of the service of song in the house of YHWH (1 Chr 6:16–33—Eng 6:31–48; 15:16–19). Nevertheless, both the Levitical and Davidic connections are so characteristic of the Chronicler's attempts to legitimate the cultus of his own day (Williamson *Chronicles* NCBC, 73, 122) that they must remain suspect. Mowinckel speculated that if Asaph was a historical figure at all, he "probably belonged to the temple personnel after the reconstruction under Zerubbabel, or perhaps in late preexilic times" (1962: 2: 96; contrast, however, Clines [*Ezra, Nehemiah, Esther* NCBC, 56] Asaph "was not improbably a contemporary of David"). That Asaph is designated "the seer" (*haḥōzeh,* 2 Chr 29:30; see also Heman in 1 Chr 25:5, Jeduthun in 2 Chr 35:15, and "who should prophesy" [Qere: *hannibbĕʾîm*] in 1 Chr 25:1) is probably an indication that the musical guilds of the Chronicler's day fulfilled the function of cultic prophesy (see Johnson 1962: 69–74).

2. Father (or possibly "ancestor") of Joah the recorder under Hezekiah (2 Kgs 18:18,37 = Isa 36:3, 22). Nothing more is known of this individual.

3. "Keeper of the forest" under the Persian king Artaxerxes (Neh 2:8). Nehemiah requested authorization from Artaxerxes to procure timber from the forest under Asaph's jurisdiction for rebuilding Jerusalem's wall and temple. This Asaph may have been a Jew who, as Nehemiah did, rose to a position of some administrative prominence under Persian rule. It is also possible, however, that the name is an assimilation into Hebrew of a Phoenician or Persian name (Clines *Ezra, Nehemiah, Esther* NCBC, 143). The location of the forest is unknown.

4. "From the sons of Asaph" in 1 Chr 26:1 should be read "son of Ebiasaph" with LXX^{B} and with 1 Chr 9:19. Asaph of the Levitical genealogies (see item 1 above) belonged to the family of Gershom; it was Ebiasaph who was of the lineage of Kohath (Exod 6:25; 1 Chr 6:8,22—Eng 6:23,37).

Bibliography

Buss, M. J. 1963. The Psalms of Asaph and Korah. *JBL* 82: 382–91.

Diringer, D. 1934. *Le Iscrizioni Antico-Ebraiche Palestinesi.* Firenze.

Gese, H. 1974. Zur Geschichte der Kultsaenger am Zweiten Tempel. Pp. 147–58 in *Vom Sinai zum Zion. Altestamentliche Beitraege zur biblischen Theologie.* BEvT 64. Munich.

Johnson, A. R. 1962. *The Cultic Prophet in Ancient Israel.* 2d ed. Cardiff.

Mowinckel, S. 1962. *The Psalms in Israel's Worship.* 2 vol. Nashville.

J. S. ROGERS

ASARAMEL (PLACE) [Gk *Asaramel*]. According to 1 Macc 14:27–28, "on the eighteenth day of Elul, in the one hundred and seventy-second year, which is the third year of Simon the great high priest, in Asaramel in the great assembly of the priests and the people and the rulers of the nation and the elders of the country, the following was proclaimed to us." Asaramel (*en asaramel* in Codex Alexandrinus, VL, and Vg; *en saramel* in all other witnesses) appears to be the location where a proclamation was made recognizing the contribution of the Hasmoneans in the defense of Judaism and the Jewish people. One cannot escape the conclusion that the Gk text treats Asaramel (or Saramel) as a place, and yet no such location is known to have existed. Asaramel has been generally treated by translators as a corruption of the original Heb occurring during translation into Gk or during the transmission of the Gk text. Goldstein (*1 Maccabees* AB, 501) notes that although there is mss evidence that the point of origin could be included in a decree, our text places the reference "in Asaramel" after the date and not after the reference to the assembly (14: 28) according to the form of extant witnesses. One possibility is that *en asaramel* is a corruption of the Heb *ḥāṣēr* ʿ*am* ʾ*ēl*, "the court of God's people." This means that Simon was the great high priest in the Temple. Such an interpretation raises the question of why the term would have been transliterated rather than translated. The Syr translator of 1 Macc translated the Gk as *rb*ʾ *b*ʾ*sryl* (or *db*ʾ*sryl*), "prince of Israel." Syr uses *rb*ʾ to translate the Heb *śar* (cf. Sir 10:24). If the Syr is correct, the original Heb behind Asaramel was *śar* ʿ*am* ʾ*ēl*, "the Prince of God's People." We are therefore dealing with a title rather than a location. This possibility is supported by 1 Macc 13:42 and 15:1 which accord Simon a political title as well as the priestly. Thus 1 Macc 14:27 declares Simon to be both a great high priest and prince. Zeitlin (1950: 227) proposed that the preposition *en* which preceded *asaramel* could have been added later to make sense out of what was thought to have been a place name, and Goldstein (1976 *1 Maccabees* AB, 502) suggested that an original *waw* ("and") was changed into a *bet* ("in") owing to an error in phonetic spelling or hearing or perhaps a garbled Gk text. It is also possible that a later scribe, thinking Asaramel to be a place name, altered the "and" to an "in" in order for the text to make sense.

Bibliography

Zeitlin, S. 1950. *The First Book of Maccabees.* Trans. and ed. S. Tedesche and S. Zeitlin. NY.

MICHAEL E. HARDWICK

ASAREL (PERSON) [Heb ʾ*ăśarʾēl*]. One of the 4 sons of Jahallelel in the genealogy of Judah (1 Chr 4:16). In the LXX, the name appears as *Iserael,* which Curtis (*Chr* ICC, 110) believes to be an altered form of "Israel." Among the brothers of Asarel, Ziph is actually the name of a town in southern Judah (*LBHG,* 256, 291) so there is a possibility that Asarel may also be an eponym. (For further discussion, see Myers *1 Chr* AB; Williamson *Chr* NCBC.)

H. C. LO

ASCENSION OF CHRIST. The doctrine of the ascension includes the ascent, the session at God's right hand, and the judgment. It has been interpreted through the Person of Christ, through the work of Christ, and through both (Walker 1968: 80–81). There is "no incident in the life of Jesus at one and the same time so beset with difficulties and so essential as the Ascension" (Barclay 1961: 315). It may well be the most neglected doctrine of the church (Jansen 1959: 17), even though it is considered one of the most important themes of the NT, and the heavenly intercession and PAROUSIA are inexplicable apart from it (Donne 1977: 567) and the doctrine of God makes no sense without it (Haroutunian 1956: 280).

A. OT Roots of the Ascension

The coronation psalms (24, 47, 68, 110, 118) prefigure the ascension, exaltation, and session (Toon 1984: 21–29). In the LXX ascent language is used in Psalms 24(25):3, 47(48):5 and 68(69):18, and the phrase "sit at my right hand" of Ps 110(111):1 prefigures Christ's exaltation and is the most quoted OT text in the NT. Enoch (Gen 5:24, Heb 11:5) and Elijah's (2 Kgs 2:1–18) ascensions give other historical examples. The word *anelēmphthē,* used of Elijah's translation in the LXX of 2 Kgs (4 Kgdms) 2:11, is used of Christ's ascension in Mark 16:19 and 1 Tim 3:16.

B. NT Witness

The ascension is considered the essential link between the Jesus of history and the Christ of faith (Donne 1983: 25). For the NT, the description of the ascension is secondary to its theological meaning (Robinson *IDB* 1: 246). Nearly all NT writers testify to the ascension, although the Epistles (Rom 8:34, Ephes 1:20–21, 4:8–11, Heb 6:20) assume rather than describe it (Holwerda *ISBE* 1: 311). The Gospels focus on the physical aspects, whereas Paul, the theologian, emphasizes Christ's spiritual body (Simpson 1968: 419–20). The Johannine pericopes do not mention the ascension, but imply it on several occasions (John 8:14, 21; 13:3, 33, 36; 14:4, 5, 28; 16:5, 10, 17, 28). They portray Christ in the descent-ascent motif of his journey from and to his Father.

Gk terms describing or referring to Christ's ascension include *analēmpseōs* "received up," "assumption" (Luke 9:51); *diestē ap*ʾ *autōn* "withdrew from them" (Luke 24:51); *hypagō* "I go" (John 7:33; 8:14; 13:3, 33, 36); *metabę ek tou kosmou* "remove out of the world" (John 13:1); *poreuomai* "going away" (John 14:2; cf. *apelthō,* John 16:7); *aphiēmi ton kosmon* "I leave the world" (John 16:28); *kai poreuomai pros ton patera* "and go to the Father" (just as in the incarnation he came from the Father, *egō para thou Theou exēlthon* [John 16:27]; cf. *pros se erchomai* "I come to you" [John 17:11, 13]); *analēmphtheis ap*ʾ *humōn eis ton ouranon* "taken up from you into heaven" (Acts 1:11); *anabas eis hyphos,* "ascended on high" (Eph 4:8); *hyperypsōsen* "highly exalted" (Phil 2:9); *anelēmphthē en doxę* "was taken up in glory" (1 Tim 3:16); *poreutheis eis ouranon* "gone into heaven" (1 Pet 3:22); and *hērpasthē* "was snatched up" (Rev 12:5). In Luke 24:51, Acts 1:11, 22 and 1 Tim 3:16 the verbs are all passive, whereas in John 3:13, 6:62, Eph 4:10 and Heb 4:14 they are all active—indicating that Christ is drawn from the world by God and also goes of his own volition (cf. Metzger 1968: 80).

C. History of the Doctrine

"Belief in the ascension was universal in the early church, both in East and West" (Swete 1910: 1), but its critics are found through the centuries. By the 4th century the ascension was celebrated in the liturgy, although even after Augustine (354–430 C.E.) its doctrinal development continued (Bray 1988: 47).

The only direct reference to the ascension in the Apostolic Fathers is the phrase *anebē eis ouranous* "He ascended into heaven" (*Ep. Barn.* 15.9), showing already the confessional formulation of the doctrine. This is also evident in Justin Martyr (*1 Apol.* 21.1; 31.7; 42.4; 46.5; 50.12; 54.7; *Dial.* 34.2; 39.4; 63.1; 85.1; 108.2; 132.1). Melito of Sardis refers to the ascension in his paschal homily (*Pass.* 104.788). The doctrine is assumed by Irenaeus (*Haer.* 1.10.1; 3.4.2) and Origen (*Princ. praef.* 4) and adverted to by Tertullian (*Adv. Prax.* 2; *Praescr.* 13; *Virg. vel.* 1). Its formulation in the Apostles' Creed—*ascendit in caelis sedit ad dextram Patris* ("he ascended into heaven, seated at the right hand of the Father")—became normative for the theology of the western churches.

The scholastic interpretation of the ascension in medieval theology is exemplified in the *Summa Theologiae* of Thomas of Aquinas. It was fitting that Christ's unchanging life after his resurrection take place in heaven, the "place of incorruptibility," rather than on earth, a place subject to change and corruption (*Summa* 3 q. 57a 1).

With the Reformation, early Protestant orthodoxy appropriated the doctrine of the ascension particularly in the context of disputes concerning the Real Presence of Christ in the Eucharist.

In the 16th century, Melancthon was the first to attempt to harmonize the ascension with science, and Calvin produced a Copernican revolution through his ascension studies. Whereas previously scholars focused on Christ present with his Body—the Church—making it impossible (they thought) to be bodily present at God's throne, Calvin reversed this by stressing the bodily presence of Christ in heaven alone (*Institutes* [1559] 4.17.12, 26). Whereas, too, emphasis had been on the person of Christ, Calvin considered the work of Christ—Godwards and manwards, breaking new ground in his *triplex munus* (threefold office) of the ascended Christ as prophet, king, and priest. Calvin upheld the bodily ascension of Christ to God's throne, with no bodily presence in church or sacrament (*Institutes* [1559] 4.17.12). He supported a localized humanity of the ascended Jesus in contrast to Luther's ubiquitous omnipresence of his humanity (WA [1527] 23.133).

Friedrich Schleiermacher (1768–1834) rejected the ascension as having any part in the doctrine of Christ's person (*Christian Faith* [1830] 2.99). The century was preoccupied with history rather than with the session at God's throne, with individualism rather than with the corporate humanity in Christ, with his prophetic ministry on earth rather than also with his priestly ministry in heaven. Most of the 19th-century "lives of Jesus" omitted the ascension, ending with the resurrection, and systematic theologians (Hodge, Shedd) barely mentioned it. By contrast, Milligan's book broke new ground by presenting the ascension's authenticity.

Cosmological questions, biblical criticism and secularization reduced interest in the ascension in the 20th century (Toon 1984: 141). Harnack's article "Das Apostolische Glaubensbekenntniss" ("The Apostles' Creed") (1892) had questioned the biblical data because of its cosmology. Today the 16th-century Eucharistic controversy is deemed by some irrelevant, because Christ is viewed as above space and time (Harvey 1966: 28). Karl Barth (1960: 453–54) opposed visualizing the ascension "as a literal event, like going up in a balloon." Rather it was an entrance into a dimension of the created world "provisionally inaccessible" to the disciples. T. F. Torrance presented (1976) the reality of the ascension within a post-Copernican cosmology, and many concur that the ascension is not destroyed by an outdated cosmology.

Bibliography

Argyle, A. W. 1955. The Ascension. *ExpTim* 66: 240–42.

Barclay, W. 1961. *The Mind of Jesus.* New York.

Barth, K. 1960. *Church Dogmatics* 3/2. Edinburgh.

Berger, K. 1976. *Die Auferstehung des Propheten und die Erhöhung des Menschensohns.* SUNT 13. Göttingen.

Bray, G. L. 1988. Ascension and Heavenly Session of Christ. Pp. 46–47 in *New Dictionary of Theology,* ed. S. B. Ferguson, D. F. Wright, and J. I. Packer. Downers Grove, IL.

Conzleman, H. 1961. *The Theology of St. Luke.* New York.

Cullman, O. 1963. *The Christology of the New Testament.* Philadelphia.

Davies, J. D. 1955. The Prefigurement of the Ascension in the Third Gospel. *JTS* 6: 229–33.

Donne, B. K. 1977. The Significance of the Ascension of Jesus Christ in the NT. *SJT* 30: 558–68.

———. 1983. *Christ Ascended.* Exeter.

Fitzmyer, J. A. 1984. The Ascension and Pentecost. *TS* 45: 409–40.

Haroutunian, J. 1956. The Doctrine of the Ascension. *Int* 10: 270–81.

Harvey, V. A. 1964. *A Handbook of Theological Terms.* New York.

Jansen, J. F. 1959. The Ascension, the Church and Theology. *TToday* 16: 17–29.

Kerr, H. T. 1986. The Presence of the Absence. *TToday* 43: 1–5.

Lohfink, G. 1971. *Die Himmelfahrt Jesu.* SANT 26. Munich.

Metzger, B. M. 1968. *Historical and Literary Studies, Pagan, Jewish and Christian.* Grand Rapids.

Milligan, W. 1908. *The Ascension and Heavenly Priesthood of Our Lord.* London.

Moule, C. F. D. 1957. Expository Problems: The Ascension—Acts 1:9. *ExpTim* 68: 205–9.

———. 1958–59. The Interpretation of the Ascension in Luke and Acts. *NTS* 5: 30–32.

Parsons, M. C. 1988. The Text of Acts 1:2 Reconsidered. *CBQ* 50: 58–71.

Plooij, P. 1929. The Ascension in the 'Western' Textual Tradition. Amsterdam.

Simpson, W. J. 1968. *The Resurrection and the Christian Faith.* Grand Rapids.

Steinmetz, D. C. 1983. Scripture and the Lord's Supper in Christian Theology. *Int* 37: 253–65.

Stempvoort, P. A. van. 1958. The Interpretation of the Ascension in Luke-Acts. *NTS* 8: 30–42.

Swete, A. B. 1910. *The Ascended Christ.* London.

Thompson, C. 1964. *Received Up into Glory.* New York.

Toon, P. J. 1984. *The Ascension of Our Lord.* Nashville.

Torrance, T. F. 1976. *Space, Time, and Resurrection.* Grand Rapids.

Trudinger, P. 1968. *Arpagmos* and the Christological Significance of the Session. *ExpTim* 79: 279.
Walker, W. G. 1968. The Doctrine of the Ascension of Christ in Reformed Theology. Ph.D. diss. Vanderbilt.
Wilder, A. N. 1943. Variant Traditions of the Resurrection of Act. *JBL* 62: 307–18.

NORMAN R. GULLEY

ASCENT OF HERES (PLACE). See HERES, ASCENT OF (PLACE).

ASCENT TO HEAVEN. See HEAVEN, ASCENT TO.

ASCLEPIUS (NHC VI,*8*). The title assigned to the 8th tractate in codex VI of the collection of 4th-century Nag Hammadi Coptic manuscripts. The text, which extends from line 15 of p. 65 to line 43 of p. 78 of codex VI, has suffered considerable damage to the first half-dozen lines or so of each page beginning with p. 67. The Coptic dialect of NHC VI is Sahidic, with some Akhmimic and Subakhmimic variants.

The document lacks a title in the manuscript. The title *Asclepius* derives from the fact that this tractate represents a Coptic translation of a portion (sections 21–29) of the Hermetic dialogue which is so entitled in its Lat translation (the only version preserving the complete dialogue). The title *Asclepius* derives from the name of one of the interlocutors of the dialogue, the Greek and Roman demigod Asclepios/Aesculapius. The Greek original underlying both the Coptic and the Lat versions was entitled *The Perfect Discourse,* fragments of which are preserved in citations made by later authors. The earliest of these authors, the church father Lactantius, proves that *The Perfect Discourse* existed at the beginning of the 4th century C.E.; its composition may therefore be plausibly assigned to the 3d century. In those passages where the Gk original can be compared with both the Lat and the Coptic, the Coptic is markedly and consistently closer to the Gk than is the Lat, confirming that it more faithfully translates *The Perfect Discourse* than does the paraphrastic Lat *Asclepius.*

It is uncertain why the parameters of the Coptic excerpt are such as they are. It is possible that the Coptic text represents one or more of what may have been originally smaller, independent units of Hermetic literature that were eventually redacted into a larger Gk tract summarizing all Hermetic doctrine, hence a "perfect" discourse. This may also help to explain why the prayer that concludes the Latin *Asclepius* (sec. 41) appears in Coptic as a separate, *preceding* tractate in NHC VI (see THANKSGIVING, PRAYER OF). It is equally possible, however, that the current parameters of the Coptic *Asclepius* are simply due to the whims either of the Coptic translator or, more likely, of the copyist. In a note which immediately precedes the excerpt (65.8–14) and which he may have intended in part as an introduction to it, the translator/copyist informs the reader that many Hermetic discourses are in his hands and that he hesitates to copy them all.

As defined by the parameters of the Coptic excerpt, at any rate, *Asclepius* preserves the typically Hermetic form of a dialogue between mystagogue (in this case Hermes Trismegistos) and initiate (here Asclepios), covering a wide range of topics. Beginning with an exposition of the mystery of sexual intercourse (65.15–34), Hermes expounds on the distinction between the many who have no knowledge of God's mysteries and the few who do (65.34–66.25). For the latter, this *gnosis* is a healing of their passions, while the passions of the former are incurable. Although mortal and subject to passions because of their material bodies, humanity has been granted such knowledge from God, making man immortal and akin to God (66.26–68.19). This kinship with God enables man, like God himself, to create gods, if only in human likeness (68.20–69.27). Such gods are truly living gods, not merely the statues by which they are portrayed, as disbelievers think. There will come a day, however, when Egypt's worship of the gods will be scorned by blasphemous foreigners who will prohibit their worship, persecute the faithful, and fill the land with tombs. Egypt, the temple of the world, will be deserted by the gods and desecrated by the crimes of these men (69.27–73.22). But the Creator, who desires the Good, will destroy this perverted society as he has before, with water and fire, finally restoring the world and the faithful (73.23–at least 75.36). The excerpt closes by describing death and depicting the examination of the departed soul by a great spirit appointed by God to judge souls. The respective rewards and punishments due are described at length.

What its Christian readers made of the originally pagan Egyptian justification for the cult of images and eschatological polemic against its destruction (68.20–73.22) is difficult to say. Perhaps they simply saw in themselves the fulfillment of its prophecies, much in the same way as other contemporary Christians adduced pagan oracles as witnesses, however grudging or unwitting, to the truth and power of Christianity. It is readily understandable, on the other hand, that contemporary Christian readers, in particular ascetics, would find the discussion of saving *gnosis,* elimination of the passions, kinship to God, the destruction of a sinful world and the judgment of souls (65.34–68.19; 73.22–78.43) attractive reading. *Asclepius* attests, at any rate, the free exchange of literature among various religious groups, Christian and non-Christian alike, in late antique E Roman settings.

Bibliography

Doresse, J. 1956. Hermès et la Gnose: A propos de l'Asclepius copte. *NovT* 1: 54–69.
Krause, M. and Labib, P. 1971. *Gnostische und hermetische Schriften aus Codex II und Codex VI.* Glückstadt.
Mahé, J. P. 1974. Remarques d'un latiniste sur l'*Asclepius* copte de Nag Hammadi. *RevScRel* 48: 136–55.
———. 1978. *Hermès en Haute-Égypte I: Les textes hermétiques et leurs parallèles grecs et latins.* Québec.
———. 1981. Le fragment du *Discours parfait* dans la Bibliothèque de Nag Hammadi. Pp. 304–27 in *Colloque international sur les textes de Nag Hammadi,* ed. Bernard Barc. Québec.
———. 1982. *Hermès en Haute-Égypte II: Le fragment du* Discours parfait *et les* Définitions *hermétiques arméniennes.* Québec.
Parrott, D. M. 1979. *Nag Hammadi Codices V, 2–5 and VI with Papyrus Berolinensis 8502,* 1 *and* 4. Leiden.

Tröger, K.-W. 1978. On Investigating the Hermetic Documents Contained in Nag Hammadi Codex VI: The Present State of Research. Pp. 117–21 in *Nag Hammadi and Gnosis. Papers read at the First International Congress of Coptology,* ed. R. McL. Wilson. Leiden.

HOWARD JACKSON

ASCLEPIUS, CULT OF. Asclepius was the most important god of healing in the Greco-Roman world. In the 1st century C.E. and even more in the 2d, his benefactions as a miraculous healer and divine guide were celebrated in hundreds of temples across the Roman empire. Inevitably, as Christianity emerged proclaiming traditions of Jesus as a miraculous healer, Jesus' virtues were compared with the powers and widely attested wonders of Asclepius.

Asclepius was probably originally an earth deity worshiped before the Greek migrations in the town of Tricca in Thessaly (Hom. *Il.* 2.729–31), though later Epidaurus claimed to be his birthplace (Paus. 2.26.1–27.6). His name was spelled in a variety of ways in its earliest Greek forms, including Aiskalapios, which gave rise to the Latin form, Aesculapius. The etymology of the name is obscure, but by the 4th century B.C.E. a tradition of interpretive wordplays had begun to emerge (Plut. *Mor.* 845B). In the 1st century C.E., for example, Cornutus says that "Asclepius derived his name from healing soothingly *(epios)* and from deferring the withering *(aposklesis)* that comes with death" (*Compend.* 33).

Asclepius was incorporated into Greek mythology with characteristics of both hero and deity. He was the son of Apollo and the mortal Coronis, according to the most common myth. In a jealous rage Apollo killed Coronis but saved Asclepius from her womb, and gave him to the centaur Chiron, who taught him all the healing arts (Pind. *Pyth.* 3; Ov., *Met.* 2.542–648). Asclepius had a family, which included the heroic sons Podilarius and Machaon, whom Homer identified as physicians among the Greeks at Troy (Hom. *Il.* 2.729–33; 11.833–36). His wife and daughters were his familiar companions in his various sanctuaries and were believed to personify aspects of the healing arts: Epione, his wife; Hygieia, his most prominent daughter; and other daughters, Panaceia, Akeso, Iaso, Aigle, and others. Asclepius' skill was such, according to the myth, that he even raised a mortal from the dead and might have done the same for all humankind, but Zeus forestalled granting humanity such salvation from death by striking Asclepius down with a thunderbolt. In his death, however, Asclepius was elevated to the status of a god, and it is as a full deity with both chthonic and celestial characteristics, that he functions in the historical Asclepius cult centers. He was always closely linked to Apollo, sharing the epithet "Paean," and in the imperial period sometimes even identified with Zeus.

The expansion of the Asclepius cult began in the 5th century B.C.E., especially from Epidaurus, where Asclepius was associated with the ancient cult of Apollo Maleatas. Epidaurus actively promoted the cult and established branch sanctuaries in numerous cities. Perhaps most important was the introduction of the cult into Athens in 420 B.C.E., under the patronage of the aged Sophocles, who was said to have provided his home as a sanctuary of the god until his temple on the S slope of the Acropolis was finished (*IG* II^2, 4960a; *Etym. Magn.* s.v. *dexion*). Sophocles composed a paean to Asclepius that continued in use at least into the 3d century C.E. Athenian influence may have contributed to the expansive building program that enhanced the sanctuary at Epidaurus throughout the 4th century. In the early 4th century Epidaurus fostered a branch sanctuary in Pergamon and later in the century sponsored another just inside the city walls of Corinth.

In 293 B.C.E., when a plague struck Rome, the Sibylline Books—perhaps supported by an oracle from Delphi—instructed the Romans to bring Asclepius from Epidaurus to Rome. He was brought, according to legend, in the form of a sacred serpent and chose the Tiber Island for his sanctuary (Livy 10.47; Ov. *Met.* 15:622–745). The only major sanctuary of Asclepius that tried to maintain independence from Epidaurus was that at Cos, the home of Hippocrates, which claimed to have been established directly from Tricca in the 6th century B.C.E. In Ptolemaic Egypt, Asclepius flourished through his identification with the legendary deified physician Imhotep (Imuthes).

The Asclepius cults went through major periods of expansion in the 4th and 3d centuries B.C.E. and again in the 2d century C.E. During the earlier period, Epidaurus, as the god's greatest center, not only expanded its role as place of pilgrimage for healing—promoted in official inscriptions recounting scores of the god's miracles—but also strove to become a Panhellenic center like Delphi or Olympia. In addition to buildings directly related to the cult, Epidaurus added a gymnasium, stadium, baths, and its justly famous 14,000–seat theater. Its wealth was attested in the excellent construction of such buildings as the round Tholos and in the colossal gold and ivory cult statue of the seated Asclepius by the Parian sculptor Thrasymedes. The god's Zeus-like visage expressed grandeur and benevolence; he held a staff in his left hand and extended his right over the head of his sacred serpent (Paus. 2.27.2). In the Roman period, Epidaurus again expanded, adding Roman baths, a music hall, and hotel facilities with 160 rooms.

Epidaurus early developed the regimen of incubation in the sanctuary that was widely used throughout the history of the cult. Typically a pilgrim might undergo a 3-day period of purification with baths and abstinence from sexual intercourse and certain foods such as goat meat and cheese. Afterward, he brought an animal sacrifice to Apollo and offerings of honey cakes to other divinities. He then might sacrifice a piglet to Asclepius and give an offering of money appropriate to his own wealth. As he entered the sleeping chamber (*abaton* or *enkoimeterion*), where he hoped and expected to receive either immediate healing or some helpful prescription from the god in a dream, he would bring offerings of cakes to Fortune, Memory, and Law. The person slept wearing a sacred laurel wreath and left it behind on his bed in the morning (Burkert 1985: 267–68). What followed depended on the dreams experienced by the pilgrim and might vary from an instant cure to a prescribed dietary regimen to an extended period of apparently nonsensical treatments. In any case, the pilgrim was expected to complete his visit to the sanctuary by bringing a thank-offering to the god.

The effectiveness of Asclepius' ministry throughout the Greco-Roman world is attested by the archaeological discovery of hundreds of votive tablets and graphic representations of portions of the body healed by the god. The cult gave emphasis to the needs of the individual and promoted a personal devotion to the god. Such attachment is apparent in numerous inscriptions, but appears most vividly in *Sacred Tales* of orator Aelius Aristides, who was incapacitated by a variety of maladies and spent many months at the Asclepieion in Pergamon during the 2d century C.E. In that period the sanctuary at Pergamon reached its greatest prosperity. Like Epidaurus it had grown with the affluence of the times and the popularity of its deity to be a large health spa complex, and supported a school of medicine led by Galen, the leading physician of the period.

In pagan debates with Christianity, Asclepius as savior and healer played a distinctive role. Both Celsus and later Julian portrayed his activity as clearly parallel to Christ. Christian polemic disparaged many details of the myths attached to Asclepius, and even when powerful deeds were conceded to him (such as driving the plague out of Rome), these were attributed to the power of the devil, since Asclepius himself was a demon. In spite of Christian persecution, the cult continued until the 5th century C.E.

Bibliography

Behr, C. A. 1968. *Aelius Aristides and the Sacred Tales.* Amsterdam.

Burford, A. 1969. *The Greek Temple Builders at Epidauros.* Liverpool.

Burkert, W. 1985. *Greek Religion.* Cambridge, MA.

Deubner, O. 1938. *Das Asklepieion von Pergamon.* Berlin.

Edelstein, E. J., and Edelstein, L. 1945. *Asclepius.* 2 vols. Baltimore.

Habicht, C. 1969. *Die Inschriften des Asklepions.* Altertuemer von Pergamon. 8/3. Berlin.

Herzog, R. 1931. *Die Wunderheilungen von Epidauros.* Philologus, Suppl. 22/3.

Horst, Van der, P. W. 1980. *Aelius Aristides and the New Testament.* SCHNT 6. Leiden.

Kee, H. C. 1982. Self-Definition in the Asclepius Cult. Pp. 118–36 in *Jewish and Christian Self-Definition. Vol. 3: Self-Definition in the Greco-Roman World,* ed. B. F. Meyer and E. P. Sanders. Philadelphia.

Kee, H. C. 1983. *Miracle in the Early Christian World.* New Haven.

Kerenyi, C. 1959. *Asklepios: Archetypal Image of the Physician's Existence.* New York.

Schazmann, P., and Herzog, R. 1932. *Kos, Vol. I, Asklepieion.* Berlin.

Walton, A. 1894. *The Cult of Asklepios.* Cornell Studies in Classical Philology, 3. New York. Repr., 1965.

Weinreich, O. 1909. *Antike Heilungswunder.* Giessen.

THOMAS L. ROBINSON

ASENATH

ASENATH (PERSON) [Heb *ʾāsĕnat*]. Egyptian daughter of Potiphera, priest of On, given by Pharaoh to the patriarch Joseph as wife, and mother of his sons Manasseh and Ephraim (Gen 41:45, 50–52; 46:20). While the Hebrew Bible simply identifies Asenath as Joseph's Egyptian wife and mother of his sons, later Jewish traditions sought to explain how one of the most revered patriarchs could marry the foreign daughter of a pagan priest (Aptowitzer 1924:239–306). By far the longest of these traditions is an anonymous Gk work, JOSEPH AND ASENETH, *(Jos. Asen.)* composed between the 1st cent. B.C.E. and the 2d cent. C.E., probably in Egypt (*OTP* 2: 177–201). What is striking about this work, vis-à-vis the biblical narrative, is that the female character is as fully developed as that of the patriarch Joseph, if not more so. Asenath is the beautiful 18-year-old virgin daughter of Pentephres, priest of Heliopolis and satrap of Pharaoh. A willful and headstrong woman, Asenath spurns all her suitors, preferring the seclusion of her tower to worship her many idols. After rejecting her father's request for her to marry Joseph, Asenath later falls in love with Joseph upon seeing him. Joseph, however, refuses Asenath's love, insisting that he cannot kiss a foreign woman who worships dumb idols and eats at their table. Asenath then repents of her idols and her arrogance and converts to the God of the Hebrews. She can now become a suitable mate for the most pious and chaste of the patriarchs, Joseph.

The name Asenath is characteristically Egyptian. The first 2 consonants have the meaning, "she belongs to. . . ," followed probably by the goddess Neit. This is a common name of the Middle Kingdom and first Intermediate (2000–1500) (*ISBE* 1: 314; Kidner *Genesis* TOTC, 197).

Bibliography

Aptowitzer, V. 1924. Asenath, the Wife of Joseph. *HUCA* 1: 239–306.

GALE A. YEE

ASHAN

ASHAN (PLACE) [Heb *ʿāšān*]. Var. BOR-ASHAN. A city which was originally part of the allotment of the tribe of Judah (Josh 15:42, but see below) and which was later given to the tribe of Simeon (Josh 19:7, 1 Chr 4:32). The site has been associated with Khirbet Asan, NW of Beersheba (see *IDB* 1:248). This site remains unknown archaeologically (Boling and Wright *Joshua* AB, 438). A variant, Bor-Ashan ("well of Ashan"), occurs at 1 Sam 30:30 as one of the cities to which David sent spoil after his defeat of the Amalekites.

Ashan served as a Levitical city according to 1 Chr 6:44—Eng 6:59. A difficulty arises when one notices that some mss of the LXX have *asan* (the Gk form of Ashan) at Josh 21:16 rather than Ain as in the MT. Since Joshua 21 lists the cities given to the tribe of Levi, this would reinforce the placing of Ashan with the Levitical cities. The relationship between Ain and Ashan in the other city-lists, however, is unclear.

Another problem arises when one compares the Simeonite city-lists of Joshua 19 and 1 Chronicles 4 with the Judahite list of Joshua 15. The terms of the scholarly debate on this comparison center on whether Ashan rightfully belongs at Josh 15:42 (it is missing from the LXX at this point) or at Josh 15:32 on the basis of comparisons with the Simeonite lists. In favor of the first position, see Kallai-Kleinman 1958:159 n. 1. The case for the second position is made by Cross and Wright 1956:214. This debate has implications for the administrative location of Ashan. If Ashan belongs at Josh 15:42, then it was grouped with the cities of the Shephelah, or Lowland, region (cf. Josh 15:33). If Ashan belongs at v 32, however, one would place its administrative district further S (cf Josh 15:21).

Bibliography

Cross, F. M., Jr., and Wright, G. E. 1956. The Boundary Lists and Province Lists of Kingdom of Judah. *JBL* 75:202–26.

Kallai-Kleinman, Z. 1958. The Town Lists of Judah, Simeon, Benjamin, and Dan. *VT* 8:134–60.

JEFFRIES M. HAMILTON

ASHARELAH (PERSON) [Heb *ʾăśarʾēlâ*]. Var. JESHARELAH. One of the 4 sons of Asaph who were appointed to prophesy with musical instruments under the direction of their father and the king (1 Chr 25:2). The KJV reads Asarelah in accordance with the dominant MT tradition, while the RSV reads the name according to the Heb variant tradition *ʾăšarʾēlâ*. Williamson (*1 and 2 Chronicles* NCBC, 186) and others suggest that *ʾăšarʾēlâ* is a conflation of the words *ʾăšarʾēl* and *ʾēlleh*, "Asharel. These (are) . . ." Such a scribal error may also have included the omission of the word "four," thus explaining why the sons of Asaph are not explicitly numbered as are the sons of Jeduthun (1 Chr 25:3) and Heman (1 Chr 25:4).

A comparison of the lists of names in 1 Chr 25:2–6 and 1 Chr 25:9–31 reveals that the three brothers of Asarelah in 1 Chr 25:2 receive the 1st, 3d, and 5th lots which were cast to determine duties (1 Chr 25:8–12). The 7th lot fell to Jesharelah (1 Chr 25:14), and the resulting pattern suggests that Jesharelah and Asharelah are names for the same person. While most scholars suggest that 1 Chr 25:9–31 is either literarily dependent upon or historically later than 1 Chr 25:2–6 (Williamson 1979: 255–7), Petersen (1977: 67) contends that 1 Chr 25:9–31 contains the more-original forms of the variant names. Such a view opposes the conflation theory mentioned above. Petersen (1977: 68) suggests that 1 Chronicles 25 originally dealt only with the sons of Asaph, thus explaining the lack of explicit numbering of the sons of Asaph in 1 Chr 25:2.

Bibliography

Petersen, D. L. 1977. *Late Israelite Prophecy: Studies in Deutero-Prophetic Literature and in Chronicles.* SBLMS 23. Missoula, MT.

Williamson, H. G. M. 1979. The Origin of the Twenty-Four Priestly Courses, A Study of 1 Chronicles xxiii–xxvii. Pp. 251–68 in *Studies in the Historical Books of the Old Testament,* ed. J. A. Emerton. VTSup 30. Leiden.

J. CLINTON MCCANN, JR.

ASHBEA (PLACE) [Heb *ʾašbēʿa*]. See BETH-ASHBEA (PLACE).

ASHBEL (PERSON) [Heb *ʾašbēl*]. ASHBELITES. One of the sons of Benjamin and head of the Ashbelites, according to 3 genealogies of Benjamin (Gen 46:21; Num 26:38; 1 Chr 8:1). A 4th Benjaminite genealogy replaces Ashbel with "Jediael" (1 Chr 7:6), a substitution made perhaps to remove the heathen sounding "Ashbel" (man of Baal?), replacing it with the more acceptable sounding "Jediael" (known to God?). The Syr and Ar read "Ashbel" in 1 Chronicles 7:6 instead of "Jediael." Two of the Benjaminite genealogies which include Ashbel speak of him as Benjamin's 2d son (1 Chr 8:1; Num 26:38), while the other (Gen 46:21) lists him as Benjamin's 3d son. In Genesis 46:21, the 2d son is "Becher." Johnson *IDB* 1:248 suggests that Becher can be restored to both Numbers 26:38 and 1 Chronicles 8:1, rendering Ashbel as Benjamin's 3d son in all 3 genealogies. He does this by suggesting that Becher was misplaced in Numbers 26:35 among the sons of Ephraim (the LXX does omit Becher from Numbers 26:35), and that Becher (Heb *beker*) was mistakenly treated as "his first-born" (Heb *bĕkōrô*) in 1 Chronicles 8:1. Williamson is critical of attempts to emend 1 Chronicles 8:1 to read "Becher" as a 2d son, pointing out that the series of ordinals, "the second, the third, etc.," continue through all 5 of Benjamin's sons, making a harmonistic emendation unlikely in this text (*Chronicles* NCBC, 83). See BECHER.

SIEGFRIED S. JOHNSON

ASHDOD (PLACE) [Heb *ʾašdôd*]. Var. AZOTUS. An important Philistine city mentioned in several passages in the Bible. The ancient city is identified with modern Tel Ashdod (M.R. 117129), 15 km N of Ashkelon and ca. 4 km inland from the Mediterranean Sea. The main coastal road from Gaza to Jaffa runs just E of the tell; in antiquity this was known as the "Way of the Philistines" or the "Via Maris." The Lachish river in the region of Ashdod was navigable until recently; at its outlet stands Tel Mor, which most probably served as Ashdod's harbor (Dothan 1960; 1973b).

A. Textual References

The people of Ashdod are first mentioned in Ugaritic, both in cuneiform and alphabetic texts from the 14th–13th centuries B.C. These texts deal mainly with Ashdod textile merchants who brought both purple wool and garments from Ashdod probably to Ugarit. The Ashdod merchants living in Ugarit and in its port Maʾhadu (Minet el-Beideh) bear mostly W-Semitic names.

Ashdod, its inhabitants, and its surrounding territory appear in the Bible many times. In Josh 11:21–22, which recounts how Joshua wiped out the Anakim, there is a note indicating that some Anakim remained in Ashdod. Although Ashdod was assigned to the tribe of Judah (Josh 15:47), it does not seem to have been conquered by the Israelites. After the battle of Ebenezer, Ashdod became the scene of the story about the temple of Dagon to which the ark of the covenant was brought by the Philistines (1 Sam 5:1–7). After the Philistines suffered several more disasters during its stay, the ark was moved to Gath.

Ashdod is not mentioned in the Bible again until the reign of Uzziah, king of Judah, who "broke down . . . the wall of Ashdod and built cities about Ashdod and among the Philistines" (2 Chr 26:6). The conquest of the city in 712 B.C. (Isa 20:1) and its relations with Assyria are well-known from the inscriptions of Sargon II (cf. *ANET,* 284–287). From these sources we know that in 713 B.C. the city, under Azuri, revolted against Assyria. Consequently, Sargon placed Ahimetu on the throne, quelling the revolt while Yamani, who had made himself the king of Ashdod, fled to Egypt. The destroyed city and its territory were annexed by the Assyrians and became a province under an Assyrian governor. In the period of Sennacherib the city did not participate in the revolt of other Philistine cities, and the territory of Ashdod was restored to an independent monarchic status under Mitinti (*ANET,* 287–88). The next vassal king, Ahimilki is mentioned in Assyrian sources under Esarhaddon and Ashurbanipal (*ANET,* 291, 294). According to Herodotus, during Ashurbanipal's reign Ashdod withstood an Egyptian siege for 29 years, until it was conquered by Psamtik I. After Nebuchadnezzar's conquest, the king of Ashdod is mentioned as a captive at the Babylonian court (*ANET,* 307–8), while Ashdod and its territory became a Babylonian province. Some of these and later events of Ashdod's history are also mentioned in the Bible (Zeph 2:4; Zech 9:5–6; Neh 4:1–2). During the Persian period Ashdod is mentioned in the book of Judith (2:28).

Our primary sources for the history of Ashdod during the Hellenistic and Roman periods are 1 Macc (5:69; 10:77–78; 13:34; 16:10) and Josephus' *Antiquities,* which contains many references to Ashdod, some of which do not occur in the Bible (*Ant* 5.87; 5.128; 13.395). The city is mentioned only once in the NT (as Azotus; Acts 8:40). In the Roman period, Pompey returned Ashdod, among other cities, to its former inhabitants, and Gabinius restored it (*JW* 1.156, 165f). Later, Ashdod belonged to the Herodian dynasty, until it fell into the hands of the Romans (*JW* 4.130). Strabo and Pliny are among the Roman writers who refer to Ashdod. Eusebius' *Onomasticon* records that *Azotus* (i.e., Ashdod) was a "notable small town," and Hieronymus writes that Ashdod, described as *insigne oppidum* in his time, was the oldest of the 5 Philistine city-states.

B. Excavations

The city of Ashdod consisted of 2 parts: an acropolis of at least 20 acres, and a lower city, the exact limits of which have not yet been determined since it is still covered with dunes (but which certainly extended over more than 100 acres). The excavations were carried out in 10 areas. On the acropolis 23 strata were uncovered; in the lower city only the 10 uppermost strata were excavated.

Seven seasons of excavations were conducted between 1962–70. The first 2 were sponsored by a joint project of the Pittsburgh Theological Seminary, the Carnegie Museum of Pittsburgh, and the Israel Department of Antiquities, while the last 2 seasons (1971–72) were conducted by the Department of Antiquities alone.

1. Middle Bronze Period. The acropolis was first settled at the end of the MB III period (stratum XXIII). The most significant discovery is a city gate in area G at the N end of the tell. The brick gate has a straight entrance and two pairs of pilasters. Remains of an earth rampart were traced on both sides of the gate. The join between the gate and the rampart is reinforced by short, tongue-like walls. The plan is similar to that of the E gate at Shechem. The pottery is mostly of the second half of the 17th century B.C., indicating that the fortified city was built during the early part of the 15th (Hyksos) Dynasty (1674–1567 B.C.), possibly during the reign of Apophis I. A cylinder seal (Kassite?), though unstratified, is evidence for contacts with Mesopotamia, while some early black-on-red pottery testifies to contact with Cyprus. The earlier gate was destroyed and a new fortification line and probably also a gate—of which little was preserved—were built N of it in the later phase of stratum XXII. In stratum XXI some walls and a paved floor were found in this area. The pottery, including some Cypriot imports, dates from the time between MB III and LB I.

2. Late Bronze Period. In the later stage (stratum XX) a section of a thick brick wall with an adjoining pavement may have been part of a defensive structure (gate?) in area G. Bichrome ware now appears in quantity and the Cypriot pottery imports grow. At least two small early LB buildings were uncovered. The most prominent feature of stratum XIX is part of a complex including three parallel walls, a wall perpendicular to them, and a courtyard. The pottery, both local and Cypriot (base ring I) and some Mycenaean wares, testify that this stratum belongs to the last stage of LB I. A great stretch of paving (stratum XVIII) was unearthed in area G, enabling a clearer separation between the strata below and above it. This stratum was also attested in area B, the earliest in the E part of the tell. One of the trenches revealed a foundation laid down for the construction of the city wall protecting the S edge of he acropolis; the wall itself was almost completely washed away. The finds include imported base ring I and bichrome wares and suggest dating of stratum XVIII to the transition between LB I and early LB II.

The building remains above the site of the gate in area G indicate that the area again became important. The first substantial structures encountered since stratum XX were found here. The walls, pavement, and floors associated with a large fortified building (probably constructed already in stratum XVIII) may best be followed in the remains of strata XVI–XIV. Its 1.5 m thick walls were made of bricks resting on a ca. 1-m-high stone foundation. According to one possible reconstruction, this was a rectangular fortified building (ca. 34 × 27 m), with 8 rectangular rooms and halls in parallel rows, as well as a plastered pool and a cistern. Two circular stone column bases probably supported columns at the entrance to the building. A plastered cistern in one of the courts collected rainwater from the roofs and transferred it through a channel to another cistern. The building was damaged at the end of stratum XV; the finds, however, which included LB II local, Cypriot, and Mycenaean pottery, indicate the continued prosperity of the LB II city. Sporadic murex shells found in this and in other LB strata point to the significance of the purple industry at Ashdod and its anchorage at Tel Mor. Some of the finds also come from the debris used as a fill for the later settlements (strata XIII–XII). These include a glass fragment with a cartouche of Rameses II, an Egyptian stone palette, and a large fragment of a stone doorjamb with part of a hieroglyphic inscription: "Fanbearer (on) the Right Hand of the King." This inscription, which may be attributed to the 18th–19th Dynasties, is the first found in Canaan mentioning one of the highest

Egyptian officials. The building thus seems to have been an Egyptian stronghold palace. In the same period (strata XVI–XIV), on the S side of the tell (area B), a large brick building was uncovered; it may have been a farmhouse, consisting of a central courtyard flanked by rooms. Finds, including Mycenaean pottery, figurines, and scarabs, indicate the prosperity of the city during the Amarna and 19th Dynasty periods.

The end of the LB, though well-attested all over the site, was especially evident in area H. A destruction layer ca. 1 meter thick covered the remains of a brick building with LB and Mycenaean IIIB sherds still on the floors. The destruction of stratum XIV all over the site (and specifically the destruction of the palace in area G) seems to end the Egyptian domination of Ashdod towards the late 19th Dynasty.

3. Iron Age Period. a. Stratum XIII. Though the impact of the destruction is evident throughout the site, the transition from the LB city (stratum XIV) to the Iron Age city (stratum XIII) can best be demonstrated in area G. The new inhabitants reused some parts of the stronghold palace for completely different purposes. Some small, poorly constructed rooms were constructed in one of the yards, including a potters' workshop and storerooms. A large number of whole vessels found there show a new style of pottery belonging to the new inhabitants, who came with the 1st wave of the Sea Peoples. These people brought with them a different cultural background expressed, e.g., in the forms and decorations of their pottery, some of which had monochrome decoration very close to the Mycenaean IIIcI pottery in Cyprus. Near the potters' quarter was a square structure of plastered bricks, covered with ashes mixed with small bones and potsherds and with a reused round stone pillar base blackened by fire. This was probably an altar used by the new settlers. The most interesting of the other finds was a cylinder seal with seated figures, having bird-like heads in Aegean style, and undeciphered signs (letters?).

In area H a large residential quarter was uncovered with two complexes of buildings separated by a wide street. A large rectangular building (17 × 13 m) N of the street had a courtyard and a few rooms bounded on one side by a double wall. Some of the pottery was still made in the Canaanite tradition; however, the most distinctive group was of the Mycenaean IIIc1 type. This pottery appeared at Ashdod before the typical Philistine pottery and may have been brought by some as-yet-unidentified group of the Sea Peoples prior to the arrival of the Philistines proper (stratum XII).

b. Stratum XII. The Philistine settlement is represented best in this stratum in area G. The new inhabitants used the remains of the Canaanite-Egyptian palace as part of their defensive line, creating a kind of "casemate" wall (two parallel walls with regular partitions between them). Some of the empty areas of stratum XIII now became industrial centers. In one of the rooms was found a clay bathtub-like basin containing some sherds and a glass ingot. Nearby, a stone bench, a few crushing stones, and remains of a brick structure indicate some sort of an installation (perhaps a glass kiln). The pottery included typical Philistine bichrome ornamented vessels.

In area H the residential quarter with the dividing street continued to utilize the stratum XIII plan, with some changes. However, a significant addition was found in the N complex of the buildings: an apsidal-like brick structure built above a rectangular base. On the N-most part of this complex a large hall included stone column bases, which might have supported a roof and a rectangular structure (altar?). At a short distance from the apsidal (cultic?) structure was found a figurine of a seated woman, shown as part of a throne. It probably represents a Philistine goddess (nicknamed "Ashdoda"). Fragments of such figurines, whose prototype seems to have been the Mycenaean "Great Mother," were found on the acropolis throughout strata XII–X. The finds in the rooms of this complex—which contained Philistine pottery, scarabs, beads, cosmetic ware, and ladies' jewelry made of gold, faience, bone, and ivory, as well as gold discs ornamented with Aegean patterns and a seal engraved with enigmatic signs—indicate that this residence may have belonged to high-status women.

In area A remains of a well-built brick structure were uncovered. One of the walls was a double one (1.25 m thick). This structure, most probably part of a tower, served as a part of the defense line of the acropolis and continued this function into strata XI and X; it subsequently lost its importance when a new line of defense, the city wall, was constructed also encompassing the lower city.

c. Stratum XI. The increasing prosperity of the city and the growth of its population led to the expansion of the acropolis, N of the casemate city wall of stratum XII (area G). The casemate wall, as well as the courtyards and rooms S of it were rebuilt on a plan similar to that of stratum XII, but with some changes. In the open area to the N of this fortification, a new building complex, made of bricks, was built. The pottery, mainly Philistine, also included a *lekane* bowl known from Greece (Mycenaean IIIcI period) and a large fragment of a pithos decorated with wavy molded application, certainly of foreign origin. In one area a large number of slags and lumps of bronze may suggest a metal industry.

In area A the tower from the previous stratum was still in use. The walls, however, were preserved only on its N side. On the floor, sherds characteristic to the 11th century, mostly Philistine, were found. In area H, a part of a city(?) wall at least 4 m wide was discovered. In addition to the usual Philistine vessels, some sherds of the Mycenaean IIIcI type were still found.

d. Stratum X. In this stratum the expansion of the Philistine city reached its climax. The settling of the lower city probably progressed in all directions outside the acropolis. Its excavated section (area M) reached as far as ca. 400 m to the SE of the acropolis. This enormous expansion was certainly due to the increase of population and wealth in the 11th century. This led to the establishment of a new defense line, which had to secure both the upper and the lower city from a possible enemy attack from the E.

The "casemate" wall in area G was demolished and a residential quarter was built above it. To the N was found a wall (4.5 m wide), probably part of the above-mentioned wall in the lower city (area M). Under its foundation a "foundation deposit," consisting of vessels characteristic to the 2d half of the 11th century, was found. A seal in the form of a seated lion with an incised "Ashdoda"-like figure of a seated musician also helped to date this stratum.

The first settlement in the lower city in area M—stratum Xb—was most probably unwalled; a few trenches revealed a kind of "pioneering" settlement of the early 11th century with few pottery kilns and foundations of some walls. The pottery still exhibited Philistine elements. Only after a generation or so, in stratum Xa, was the settlement fortified. An excavated section of this fortification revealed a city gate and a wall attached to its S and N. The gate consisted of 2 towers, each containing 2 chambers on the W and a solid watchtower in front with a passageway 4.2 m wide. The gate area was 13.75 m long and 16.5 m wide, and it was built of bricks with some stone foundations. The partly exposed city wall is ca. 4.5 m wide. This fortification, which is not unlike some of the early Iron Age fortifications in the Israelite hill country, suits the period of the climax of Philistine power and expansion, which continued during Saul's reign and may have been established as a defense against the Israelites. This is probably the city associated with the biblical story of the capture of the ark (1 Sam 5: 1–7). In a silo and kiln beside the gate a few complete storage jars provide a probable dating for the end of this stratum. Both the typical "Ashdod ware" with a red hand-burnished slip and a black decoration and the black-on-red decoration are first attested in this stratum. The fortifications of stratum Xa in Ashdod were destroyed in the first half of the 10th century, probably by Siamun (ca. 967 B.C.), though a possible conquest of Ashdod by David should not be excluded. There are no building remains from the transition period between the destruction of this and the construction of the next gate a generation or so later (stratum IX; see below).

Stratum X in area H/K is likely to correlate with its later phase (Xa) in other areas. The finds show a mixture of Philistine and other elements in pottery (e.g. red, irregularly burnished pottery). One outstanding find from this area was an incense pottery stand, which shows 5 figurines of musicians playing different instruments. Above them is an incised procession of domestic animals. Such musicians (as depicted in this cult stand) probably served in a local cult place not yet discovered. The scene recalls the story of Samuel foretelling Saul's encounter with the band of prophets coming down from the high place and playing musical instruments, an incident associated with the Philistine fortress at Gibeath-elohim (1 Sam 10:5). It seems that Dagon's cult in Ashdod as described in the Bible and represented probably also by this stand fits the city of stratum X, in contrast to the female-oriented (probably Aegean-inspired) cult of Ashdod in the early Philistine strata XII–XI.

e. Stratum IX. The lower city wall and gate (area M) were destroyed sometime in the 1st half of the 10th century B.C. Only about a generation later a new fortification was built to the S of the earlier (stratum X) gate. The new gate (20.5 m by 18.5 m) was much larger than the former one; made of bricks with rubble foundations and ashlar at the front and rear, it consisted of 2 watchtowers with 3 rooms each. The gateway, 5 m. wide and paved with crushed kurkar, passed between the 2 towers and led into the city. The city wall, 8.7 m wide, narrows after 40 m to a width of 5 m on the S. On both sides of the gate, several storerooms were uncovered with bronze and iron tools, a pair of scales, and other finds. This was the largest gate in the history of Ashdod and was of the "Solomonic" type and period, which has occasioned some debate. Evidence of subsequent repairs in the gate indicates its use over a long period of time. It was partly destroyed ca. 760 B.C., possibly by Uzziah (2 Chr 26:6).

The expansion of the lower city in this period is well represented in area D, located to the S of the acropolis. The early remains included a large building of which brick foundations and several floors were uncovered. In the S the area was surrounded by a 3-m-thick wall which may belong to the city wall of this period. Among the finds the typical Ashdod Ware (red burnished with black decoration, which had already been attested in stratum Xa elsewhere on the site) was predominant, completely replacing the Philistine ware.

f. Stratum VIII. In this stratum a group of large houses consisting of courtyards surrounded by rooms was excavated in Area D. In one of these buildings 7 kilns were established, indicating a potters' quarter; each of these kilns was rebuilt and reused many times. In the S part of area D a building was excavated, a part of which at least served as a temple. To one of the walls was attached a rectangular altar made of white-washed bricks. Both in this room and in adjacent areas was found a large quantity of small figurines (both male and female) belonging to clay offering-tables. With them was also found a large number of domestic animal figurines belonging to the *Kernoi* type of round, hollow libation vessels.

In some of the rooms, secondary mass-burials were found, and a very large amount of human remains was uncovered beneath the floors. It seems that this is probably the city destroyed during the Assyrian conquest by Sargon II in 712 B.C. Three fragments from an inscription on a basalt stele, erected in Ashdod and found in a dump, corroborate this evidence. They belong to a stele which is a copy of a victory stele erected in Khorsabad, where the names of Sargon and the conquered cities, including Ashdod, are preserved. Ashdod seems to be a unique site insofar as the archaeological, the biblical (Isaiah 20), and the Assyrian evidence all corroborate this same event.

Following the destruction of the stratum IX gate complex in area M (see above), the gate complex was repaired, probably by Azuri (ca. 730 B.C.) after Tiglath-pileser III's compaign. The new gate tower was similar to the one of the previous stratum, but the chambers were larger than in the previous gate and a new defensive element was added to its N tower. The plan of the N storerooms was also changed. New floors covered the remains of stratum IX. Part of a wall, which belonged to a large structure, was uncovered outside the N tower. A passage probably served either to house a staircase or as a postern. The finds scattered on the floors, in addition to pottery and other objects, also included fragments of a crucible and tuyere. The gate and the whole vicinity were destroyed by Sargon II; the signs of the breached gate tower are still visible.

g. Strata VII–VI. Even after the destruction of most of the excavationVIII city, the potters' section in area D was still active in stratum VII. Several large pits full of ashes and refuse were found near the kiln area with additional figurines, which belonged perhaps to the discarded temple of stratum VIII. Some of the kilns were found with their air vents still intact, and a number of finished vessels were also there.

The few inscriptions in Hebrew characters found (not in situ) may be ascribed to stratum VII or VI. Among these are *(h)phr,* "(the) potter," the denominations *nṣp, bqᶜ,* and *pym* on weights, and a *lmlk* stamp on a jar handle. The Hebrew script indicates trade relations between Ashdod and the kingdom of Judah. Perhaps Ashdod was even conquered by Judah in the days of Josiah who, according to some scholars, probably expanded his kingdom as far as Mesad Hashavyahu, N of Ashdod.

The gate of stratum VIII (area M) was reconstructed, perhaps as Sennacherib's reward to Mitinti, king of Ashdod, for his loyalty to Assyria. No major alterations could be observed in the plan of the gate of stratum VII, but at least two phases of settlement were recognized. Few burials found in the area, both human and animal, belong to the earlier phase. The final destruction of the gate area (by Psamtik I or Nebuchadnezzar) took place most probably around 600 B.C.

The scanty remains of the Babylonian period (stratum VI) indicate the decline of the city. The fortifications of Ashdod (area M) do not seem to have ever been used again, and some buildings covered the ruins of the gate. There are few remains of buildings, but the few pottery kilns and traces of metalworking suggest that the area became primarily an industrial site.

4. Persian Period. In this period (stratum V) a partial revival could be detected, at least on the acropolis (area A). Although most of the remains in this area were destroyed during the Hellenistic period, the Persian occupation is still well-represented here. Foundations of 2 buildings and a deep fosse were discovered. The large quantity of pottery characteristic to the whole Persian period found here suggests a long period of settlement in this area. A small ostracon with Aram cursive script was found describing the quantity of wine delivered in the name of a man called Zebadia. Dated to mid-5th century B.C., this Aram inscription might be in "the language of Ashdod" mentioned in Neh 13:24, the dialect probably spoken by the Philistines.

The Persian period is best represented in area K by the remains of a large building of which 4 of its halls were excavated; it seems to have served as an administrative center for the Persian governor. Although its exact dimensions have not been determined, the building was certainly not smaller than the "governor's palaces" of this period excavated in Lachish and Qasile. Remains of 2 buildings were found in the former gate area (area M). The walls, ca. 1 m wide and made of bricks, were preserved to a height of 2 courses. In addition to the pottery characteristics of the Persian period (such as the mortaria and lamps), there was also the earliest import of the Attic black-glazed ware. In a number of oval pits some burials of dogs were found.

5. Hellenistic Period. Town planning is obvious in the Hellenistic strata (IV–III) in area A, though no remains of fortification were found. Streets were laid out between groups of well-constructed buildings. A special technique, combining brick foundations and stone walls, was employed in these buildings, as well as in a public building which was probably part of the agora of the city. In one of its rooms was a small cult place, on the floor of which was found a stone offering-table. In Stratum IIIb the courtyard of the building was used for storage. The finds included large Rhodian wine jars and black-glazed Attic vessels. A lead plaque, probably representing a deity with a fish tail (Atargatis?), as well as 2 miniature stone altars—one incised with the letter M (Marnas?)—and some weapons were found in a thick layer of ash from stage IIIb of the cult place. A coin of Ptolemy II (271–246 B.C.) found in the IIIb level helps to date this stratum. The latest coin found there was of Antiochus VIII, dated to 114 B.C. This coin establishes a *terminus post quem* date for John Hyrcanus's conquest of Ashdod, which stayed in Hasmonean hands until the time of Pompey.

Very few structures were preserved in the Hellenistic strata (IV–III) of area K. These included a pottery kiln and a large refuse pit containing Hellenistic pottery. Also, the floors provided a very rich repertoire of both local and imported pottery of the 3d and 2d centuries B.C., ending ca. 50 B.C. The only structure which survived in area M was a pottery kiln full of Hellenistic sherds. Among these, a fragment of a bowl with dark reddish glaze dated to the mid-2d century B.C. was found. Several coins were found here, the earliest being a coin of Ptolemy II, minted in Tyre.

6. Roman and Byzantine Periods. The layout of the town changed completely during the period of King Herod (stratum II) and it is obvious that the city by then was much smaller. A large building of at least 3 rooms was uncovered NW of area A. In one of its rooms, paved with stone slabs, were remains of a circular, clay oven. Among the finds were lamps, which have parallels in Corinth, stamped handles of amphorae, and Terra Sigillata bowls. A large pit filled with burned sherds, animal bones, and refuse might be related to the neighboring kilns. The last phase of stratum II came to an end most probably with the destruction of Ashdod by Vespasian during the 1st Jewish Revolt. The only remains in area M are pits with metal slags and kiln refuse. The pottery found in a pit dug into the Iron Age city wall helps to date this stratum to the early Roman period.

The general features of the previous early Roman stratum (II) could still be identified at the first phase (Ib) of stratum I, which dates to the late 1st century A.D. In area A a small pit was dug inside the larger pit from stratum II; it was full of workshaft refuse. A reservoir, probably for water storage, was also uncovered. Among the finds, a peculiar pilgrim flask should be mentioned as well as a few coins of this period. The few area M structures excavated from the late Roman period included a kiln made of brick discovered to the E of the early city-wall. Although Eusebius still referred to Ashdod as a "significant town," it seems that such a description did not apply to *Azotus Mesogaios* (i.e., inland Ashdod) but to *Azotus Paralios* (on the coast). See ASHDOD-YAM (M.R. 114132). By that time the inland Ashdod was inhabited by Jews (as indicated by a synagogue screen found there) and by Samaritans (as indicated by a section of an inscription and a talisman found in the excavations of the uppermost stage of stratum I).

Bibliography

Asaro, F., et al. 1971. An Introductory Study of Mycenean IIIcI Ware from Tel Ashdod. *Archaeometry* 13: 169–75.

Cross, F., and Freedman, D. 1963. The Name of Ashdod. *BASOR* 175: 48–50.

Dothan, M. 1960. Short Report on the Excavations at Tel Mor. *IEJ* 10: 123–25.

———. 1967. *Ashdod I.* Atiqot, English Series 7. Jerusalem.

———. 1970. The Musicians of Ashdod. *Archaeology* 23: 310–11.

———. 1971. *Ashdod II–III.* Atiqot, English Series 9–10. Jerusalem.

———. 1973a. Relations Between Cyprus and the Philistine Coast in the Late Bronze Age. Pp. 51–56 in *Acts of the First International Congress of Cypriot Studies.* Nicosia.

———. 1973b. The Foundation of Tel Mor and Tel Ashdod. *IEJ* 23: 1–17.

———. 1982. *Ashdod IV.* Atiqot, English Series 15. Jerusalem.

———. 1988. The Significance of Some Artisan Workshops along the Canaanite Coast. Pp. 296–303 in *Society and Economy in the Eastern Mediterranean (c. 1500–1000 B.C.),* ed. M. Heltzer and E. Lipiński. OLA 23. Louvain.

MOSHE DOTHAN

ASHDOD-YAM (M.R. 114132). An archaeological site ca. 5 km NE of Ashdod. The city is mentioned (as *ašdud-immu*) in connection with Sargon II's 713 B.C. campaign against Yamani, king of Ashdod (*ANET,* 286). Yamani hastily fortified not only Ashdod, but also Gath and Ashdod-Yam, the latter apparently serving as a rear base for the city in times of danger.

Archaeological surveys were conducted at Ashdod-Yam from 1965 to 1968. Ten cuts were made in the rampart-like structure and at its base, and the city wall was exposed in 3 of these cuts. Two earthen glacis retained the wall on its inner and outer sides. The 3.1-m-thick wall was built of reddish sun-dried brick, and the outer glacis was mainly made of local sand and kurkar. It was evidently designed to prevent assaults by siege engines and battering rams. The inner glacis served to counter the pressure of the outer one. Two periods of occupation are attested at the site itself. The earlier, which includes the period of construction of the fortifications, dates to the latter half of the 8th century B.C. The later occupation dates to the 7th century B.C., a time when the fortifications were no longer used. Thus, the uncovered wall and glacis are likely the ones built by Yamani (Kaplan 1969).

In Roman-Byzantine times occupation stretched 500 m N of the Iron Age fortifications, along the coast, and the city was then known as *Azotus Paralius.* Here are found the ruins of the Crusader-Mamluk fortress known to the Crusaders as *Castellum Beroardi* and to the Muslims as *Mahûz Isdûd.*

Bibliography

Kaplan, J. 1969. The Stronghold of Yamani at Ashdod-Yam. *IEJ* 19: 137–49.

J. KAPLAN

ASHER (PERSON) [Heb *ʾāšēr*]. ASHERITE. The eponymous ancestor of the Israelite tribe of Asher, reported to have been the 8th-born son of Israel's eponymous ancestor Jacob. The name means "happy one," "righteous one." It may also be the name of a god, the male form of the goddess Asherah (*IPN,* 131).

Asher's secondary status among the Israelite tribes is marked in tradition by his "birth" to Leah's handmaid Zilpah, rather than to one of Jacob's 2 wives (Gen 30:12). As a member of the idealized premonarchic Israel, Asher is included alongside its 11 brethren tribes either implicitly or explicitly in the oppression in Egypt (Exod 1:4); the exodus, the Sinai covenant, and the wilderness wandering (Num 1:40–1; 2:27; 10:26; 26:44–47; Deut 27:13); and the conquest of the land of Canaan (Josh 19:24–31; Judg 1:31–32).

The territory traditionally associated with Asher is located in the W Galilean hills, adjoining the Phoenician coast to the W, Sidon to the N, Naphtali to the E, Zebulon to the SE, and Mt. Carmel to the SW (Josh 19:24–31; *HGB* 204–24). The narrow strip of territory was fertile land, particularly suited to olive orchards (Deut 33:24) and vineyards. Gen 49:20 alludes to Asher's agricultural bounty, referring to the "royal dainties" the region will yield. Judg 5:17 indicates that involvement in maritime activity provided Asher's inhabitants with an additional source of economic prosperity.

The association of the name Asher with the W portion of Galilee tends to be supported by Egyptian texts. The name appears with the determinative for foreign land as early as the reign of Pharaoh Seti I (1291–1272 B.C.E.) (Simons 1937: 147). Two additional occurrences are known from the reign of Rameses II (Simons 1937: 162; *ANET* 475–79), and an additional unpublished reference appears in the Golenischeff collection (Gauthier 1925: 105). The occurrence of Asher in the list of Seti I provides the clearest indication for the name's connection with W Galilee. It appears in a geographical sequence between Kadish, probably representing the Syrian city-state of Kadesh on the Orontes River with its surrounding domain, and Megiddo, the city-state that controlled the NW portion of the Megiddo Plain–Jezreel Valley corridor. Asher seems to represent the hinterland of Phoenicia at the time of Seti I, the W Galilean hills N of Megiddo, as far as Lebanon (Müller 1893: 236).

The Galilean region of Asher did not become part of the Israelite state until the reign of David. Saul did not control Galilee (2 Sam 2:9; see ASHURITES). David was the first Israelite king to have secured the Megiddo Plain–Jezreel Valley corridor by capturing Megiddo and Beth Shean. It is logical to conclude that he was able to gain subsequent control over Galilee. Although no administrative lists from David's reign have been preserved, under Solomon, Asher was joined with Bealoth, probably Zebulon, to form one of the 12 administrative districts of Israel (1 Kgs 4:16). It is likely that Solomon had inherited the pre-established district from his father. Solomon ceded the N portion of Asher, the region of Cabul, to Hiram of Tyre as payment for Tyrian workers and supplies in connection with the building of the palace and temple in Jerusalem (1 Kgs 9:13). Israel's ability to maintain control over Asher and the rest of Galilee during the period after the split of the United Monarchy (ca. 917 B.C.E.) has not been documented, but was probably sporadic.

In addition to the Galilean territory of Asher, there was

a group of Asherite clans located in the S portion of the central Ephraimite hill country (Abel 1937: 219–20; *LBHG,* 244; Edelman 1985: 86; Edelman 1988; see ASHURITES). While it is possible that the two groups were not interrelated but merely shared the same name by coincidence, it is generally presumed that the two groups ultimately shared a common origin and that the more S group had somehow splintered off from the better-known Galilean group (Steuernagel 1901: 31; Abel 1937: 219; Malamat 1962: 146; Yeivin 1957: 99–100; *LBHG,* 244; Edelman 1985: 86).

The detailed genealogy for the tribe of Asher in 1 Chr 7:30–40 pertains to the S Asherite group exclusively. Two analyses of its structure have been proposed. The first considers it to be a homogenous segmented genealogy, containing a few textual corruptions that have obscured its otherwise systematic presentation. Textual errors have crept in vv 35–38 in the listing of the descendants of the 4 sons of Helem/Hotham: Zophah, Imna, Shelesh, and Amal. Thus, Beri and Imrah of v 36 *(bry ymrh)* are not to be seen as additional sons of Zophah, but instead, as corruptions of an original phrase "sons of Imna" *(bny ymnh).* In v 37, the word "sons" *(bny)* should be restored before Shelesh to signal the listing of his offspring, and an additional 3d name is suspected to have inadvertently been dropped from the roster of descendants. Finally, in v 39, a medial *mem* should be restored in the name Ulla, rendering an original Amal rather than Ulla, to list descendants of Helem/Hotham's final son from v 35. According to the second structural analysis, the genealogy contains 3 source strands (vv 30–35; vv 36–37; vv 38–39) that have been combined secondarily to form a single genealogy. The occurrence of name-overlap between the 3 strands (Zophah; Beriah/Beri; Shelesh/Shilshah; Shua/Shual; and Jether/Ithran) indicates that the strands represent enumerations of the same group at different points in its existence (Edelman 1988).

The only names in the Asherite genealogies that can possibly be associated with clans in the N Galilean territory of Asher are Beriah and his siblings Imnah, Ishvah/Ishvi, and Serah. Beriah, Serah, and Imnah also appear as clan groups within the enclave, but it is possible that segments of these clans remained in the Galilean Asherite territory while other portions migrated S. The preservation of the names of Beriah and siblings by the S group may have been motivated by a desire to maintain a record of their founders' positions in the genealogical tree of the parent tribe.

Bibliography

Abel, F. M. 1937. Une mention biblique de Birzeit. *RB* 46: 217–24.

Edelman, D. 1985. The "Ashurites" of Eshbaal's State (2 Sam. 2:9). *PEQ* 117: 85–91.

———. 1988. The Asherite Genealogy in 1 Chronicles 7:30–40. *BR* 33: 13–23.

Gauthier, H. 1925. *Dictionnaire des noms géographiques contenus dans les textes hiéroglyphiques.* Vol. 1. Cairo.

Malamat, A. 1962. Mari and the Bible: Some Patterns of Tribal Organization and Institutions. *JAOS* 82: 143–50.

Müller, W. M. 1893. *Asien und Europa nach altägyptischen Denkmälern.* Leipzig.

Simons, J. 1937. *Handbook for the Study of Egyptian Topographical Lists Relating to Western Asia.* Leiden.

Steuernagel, C. 1901. *Die Einwanderung der Israelitischen Stämme in Kanaan.* Berlin.

Yeivin, S. 1957. The Israelite Settlement in Galilee and the Wars with Jabin of Hazor. Pp. 95–104 in *Mélanges bibliques rédigés en l'honneur de André Robert.* n.s. Travaux de l'Institut catholique de Paris 4. Paris.

DIANA V. EDELMAN

ASHERAH (DEITY) [Heb *ʾăšērâ; ʾăšērâ*]. Asherah appears in the OT both as the name of a Canaanite goddess and of her wooden cult-symbol. She is known in the Ugaritic texts under the name of Athirat *(ʾaṯrt),* where she functions as consort of the chief god, El, and mother of the gods. Prior to the discovery of the Ugaritic texts some scholars denied that Asherah was the name of a goddess while others wrongly equated her with Astarte (Ashtoreth). Since Yahweh is equated with El in the OT, it is understandable that in syncretistic circles Yahweh also appropriated Asherah as his consort.

A. Asherah in Extrabiblical Texts
 1. Akkadian Sources
 2. Ugaritic Texts
 3. Egyptian Representations
 4. Hittite Mythology
 5. Syro-Palestinian Inscriptions
 6. Later Phoenician Sources
 7. Inscriptions from Arabia
B. Asherah in the OT
 1. As a Goddess
 2. As a Cult Object

A. Asherah in Extrabiblical Texts

1. Akkadian Sources. We know from the Ugaritic texts that Athirat was equivalent to the Mesopotamian deity Ašratum. Ašratum is known from cuneiform texts dating from the 1st Dyn. of Babylon (ca. 1830–1531 B.C.), where she appears as the consort of the god Amurru. In the first half of the 14th century B.C. the name of the goddess Asherah appears in the name of the king of Amurru Abdi-Aširta ("servant of Aširta"), who is mentioned a number of times in the El-Amarna letters. It has also been generally supposed that Asherah is mentioned in one of the 15th century B.C. Akkadian texts from Taʿanach, but this has been questioned by A. F. Rainey (1977: 59).

2. Ugaritic Texts. The most complete source of information about the goddess Asherah comes from the Ugaritic texts, discovered at the site of Ras Shamra on the Syrian coast from 1929 onwards. She is there called *ʾaṯrt,* generally vocalized as Athirat, and she is the consort of the supreme god, El. Sometimes she is called *ʾilt* (Elat), lit. "goddess," as befits the wife of El *(ʾil).* She is the mother of the gods and is accordingly called *gnyt ʾilm* "the procreatress of the gods." The gods are referred to in *KTU* 1.4.VI.46 (= *CTA* 4.VI.46) as "the seventy sons of Athirat" *(šbʿm. bn. ʾaṯrt).* The later Jewish notion of the 70 guardian angels of the nations (cf. 1 En 89:59; 90:22–25; Tg. Ps.-J. on Deut 32:8) must ultimately go back to this, via the idea in Deut 32:8 whereby the Most High "fixed the bounds of the peoples according to the number of the sons of God" (so LXX, 4Q Deut).

Her stock epithet is *rbt ʾatrt ym* (e.g. *KTU* 1.4.III.27 = *CTA* 4.III.27), which should be rendered "Lady Athirat of the sea." The view that the expression should be rendered "She who treads on the sea," which is popular in some circles (e.g., Cross *CMHE,* 31), is to be rejected, since (1) the goddess was simply called Ašratum already in the 1st Dyn. of Babylon, which suggests that the shorter form of the name is original, and (2) we know of no conflict between Athirat and the sea. Though certainty is not possible, it may be that the name *ʾatrt* means "sanctuary." One should perhaps compare her epithet *qdš,* which similarly means "holy place" or possibly "holiness" (see below).

Athirat plays an important role in the Ugaritic text involving Baal's desire for a house (palace/temple) in *KTU* 1.4 (= *CTA* 4). Having defeated the sea god, Yam, and assumed the kingship (*KTU* 1.2 = *CTA* 2), Baal is in need of a house. First Anath demands a palace for Baal from El, but without success (*KTU* 1.3.V = *CTA* 3.V). When Athirat, however, intercedes with her husband El, she is successful (*KTU* 1.4.III–V = *CTA* 4.III–V).

Athirat appears again in another Ugaritic mythological text, *KTU* 1.23 (= *CTA* 23), where she is one of 2 women, the other being *rḥmy,* whom El seduces, and this act leads to the birth of Shaḥar (Dawn) and Shalim (Dusk). It is not clear who *rḥmy* is; the common view that she is Anath is improbable, since we have no other evidence that she was a wife of El, and it seems inappropriate for a goddess repeatedly called "the Virgin Anath" to be a mother goddess.

3. Egyptian Representations. Asherah is sometimes called *Qdš* in the Ugaritic texts. *Qdš* is also attested as the name of a goddess in Egypt, where she appears on reliefs and amulets of the New Kingdom (cf. *ANEP,* pls. 470–74), especially the Ramesside period, and is characteristically represented nude, wearing a Hathor wig, standing on a lion, holding snakes in one hand and flowers in the other, and sometimes she holds snakes in both hands. Often she is portrayed together with the deities Resheph and Min and her erotic aspect is emphasized. Most remarkable is the representation on a Theban relief at Winchester College in England (now missing) where the goddess is called *qdš- ʿstrt-ʿnt,* thus indicating a fusion of *Qdš* (Athirat) with the two other important Canaanite goddesses, Astarte and Anath. Figurines and plaques of the *Qdš* type are attested in Syria and Palestine from the period ca. 1700–1200 B.C., which we may confidently regard as depictions of the goddess Athirat. It is noteworthy that the depictions of Athirat/*Qdš* make her role as a fertility goddess abundantly clear. This aspect of her nature is played down in the Ugaritic texts, but emerges again in the OT, where she is constantly associated with Baal and is clearly connected with sacred prostitution in 2 Kgs 23:7.

4. Hittite Mythology. We possess a Hittite myth about a god Elkuniršа, his wife Ašertu, and the storm god, dating from the second half of the 2d millennium B.C. (*ANET,* 519). These deities must correspond to El (more precisely *ʾl qn ʾrṣ* "El creator of the earth"), Athirat (Asherah) and Baal-Hadad, and an underlying Canaanite myth is clearly reflected here. According to the myth the storm god came to Elkunirša's house, and there Ašertu tried to seduce him. Following his refusal, she threatened him with her spindle, but the storm god went off to Elkunirša's tent at the Mala (= Euphrates) river and informed him of Ašertu's attempted seduction. Elkunirša replied by saying, "Go, sleep with her! Lie with my wife and humble her!" The storm god obediently complied but also informed her that he had slain 77/88 of her sons, which led to her lamenting them for 7 years. According to a second fragment, the goddess Ištar (probably = Astarte) overheard a bedroom conversation between Elkunirša and Ašertu and told the storm god about it. Regardless of how the myth ended, we have here evidence of some estrangement between Elkunirša (El) and Ašertu (Athirat).

5. Syro-Palestinian Inscriptions. At Kuntillet ʿAjrud, in NE Sinai, inscriptions have been found referring to 'Yahweh and his Asherah.' One pithos contains the inscription *brkt. ʾtkm. lyhwh. šmrn. wlʾšrth,* "I have blessed you by Yahweh *šmrn* and his Asherah." The word *šmrn* could be rendered "our guardian," but the translation "of Samaria" is more likely (cf. *lyhwh tmn wlʾšrth* "by Yahweh of Teman and his Asherah," which also appears at Kuntillet ʿAjrud). Scholars disagree as to the meaning of "his Asherah," whether it refers to the goddess Asherah, her cult symbol, or a word meaning cella or chapel. It seems most likely to mean the cult-symbol, a wooden pole or suchlike, related to the goddess Asherah. Indirectly, therefore, the allusions probably do imply that Asherah was Yahweh's consort. That it is the goddess Asherah herself who is denoted by 'his Asherah' is syntactically inappropriate, since personal names are not found with a pronominal suffix in biblical Heb. The meaning 'cella' or 'chapel' may also be excluded, since this is not attested elsewhere in Heb, unlike some other Semitic languages.

The pithos mentioning "Yahweh of Samaria and his Asherah" has underneath the inscription a drawing depicting 3 figures: a lyre player and 2 other figures similar to each other, generally thought to represent the goddess Bes. It has been proposed, however, that these latter represent "Yahweh and his Asherah" of the inscription (Gilula 1978–79). But this is unlikely, and the drawings are probably unconnected with the inscription. For example, why should there be 3 figures, if only 2 are mentioned (Emerton 1982:10)? Moreover, the figure claimed to represent Asherah seems to have a square-cut beard, suggesting a god and, indeed, a characteristic of the god Bes (Beck 1982: 27–28).

Curiously, at about the same time as the discoveries at Kuntillet ʿAjrud, another site, Khirbet el-Qom, near Hebron, also yielded a text which seemingly refers to Yahweh's Asherah:

ʾryhw. hʿšr. ktbh
brk. ʾryhw. lyhwh
wmṣryh lʾšrth hwšʿlh
lʾnyhw
wlʾšrth
ʾ??rth

This should most likely be rendered:

Uriyahu the rich wrote it.
Blessed be Uriyahu by Yahweh.

For from his enemies by his Asherah he has saved him.
by Oniyahu
and by his Asherah
his A(she)rah

A. Lemaire (1977: 599, 602) felt forced to emend the text so that *lʾšrth* follows immediately after *lyhwh,* but as the above rendering shows, this may be unnecessary.

It has been claimed that Asherah is mentioned on a plaque from Arslan Tash in Syria, dating from the 7th century B.C., with Aram script and Phoenician orthography. However, since the word in question is *ʾšr,* those who adopt this view either have to emend the text to *ʾšrt,* the form we should most naturally expect, or suppose that we have an anomalous spelling here. It is far more natural to suppose, as most scholars believe, that *ʾšr* denotes the god Asshur (cf. *ʾšr* as the spelling of the place Asshur in *KAI* 24: 8), and since Arslan Tash (Ḫadattu) was an Assyrian province at the time, a reference to the Assyrian god Asshur at this point is not inappropriate.

6. Later Phoenician Sources. It has been argued by F. M. Cross (*CMHE,* 28–34) and others, e.g. W. A. Maier (1986: 96–118), that the goddess Tinnit is to be equated with the goddess Asherah. Tinnit is best known from Punic inscriptions, where she appears as the consort of the god Baal-Ḥammon, but it is now clear that she was already worshiped in Phoenicia quite early (cf. the Sarepta text below). The arguments in favor of her equation with Asherah are, however, open to question.

First, it is claimed that her name means "the One of the dragon," and Ugaritic *ʾaṯrt ym* is compared, understood as "She who treads on the sea (dragon)." However, not only does *ʾaṯrt ym* not have this meaning, but if *tnt* were really related to *tnn* 'dragon' (which is improbable), one would expect it to mean "the female dragon" rather than "the One of the dragon"!

Second, Baal-Ḥammon is commonly supposed to be El, so it is claimed that his consort Tinnit ought to be Asherah. However, Baal-Ḥammon is probably rather a form of the god Baal. The name itself suggests this, and the god is in fact often simply referred to as Baal in Punic inscriptions, and never as El. Latin inscriptions refer to him as *frugifer* and *deus frugum,* suggesting a fertility deity. It is true that classical sources often equate Baal-Ḥammon with Kronos, who usually represents El, but we know that Kronos could also denote Baal, and the fact that Kronos devoured his own children may well have encouraged his equation with Baal-Ḥammon, the god of child sacrifice. Thus, there are not compelling grounds for identifying Tinnit with Asherah. Tinnit is equated with Astarte in a 7th century B.C. Phoenician inscription from Sarepta and associated with (though distinguished from) Astarte in an inscription from Carthage (*KAI* 81:1). She was perhaps a form of the goddess Anath or alternately an independent goddess serving as Baal's consort.

7. Inscriptions from Arabia. It is now known that Asherah is not mentioned as ʾAširā on a 5th century B.C. Aram inscription from Tema (*KAI* 228) as had previously been commonly believed; rather the divine name in question should be read ʾAšimā, as another Tema stele makes clear (Cross 1986: 393). However, the goddess Athirat is attested in S Arabia (Ryckmans 1951: 44). Although the Arabian Athirat has often been seen as a sun goddess, this is not certain.

B. Asherah in the OT

In the OT the Heb word *ʾăšērâ* is used to denote both the name of the Canaanite goddess, well-known from the Ugaritic texts, and also a wooden cult-object that was her symbol.

1. As a Goddess. The ancient versions failed to recognize that OT Asherah was the name of a goddess, and it was only with the discovery of the Ugaritic texts that scholars as a whole were convinced that this was one of the basic meanings of the word in the OT. The places where the name Asherah seems to denote the goddess rather than her cult object are 1 Kgs 15:13; 18:19; 2 Kgs 21:7; 23:4, in addition to Judg 3:7, where the plural form Asheroth appears. In 1 Kgs 18:19 we read of the "four hundred and fifty prophets of Baal and the four hundred prophets of Asherah, who eat at Jezebel's table," who are to confront Elijah on Mt. Carmel. The fact that the prophets of Asherah play no part in the subsequent story in 1 Kings 18 suggests that the reference to them may be a gloss. However, the parallelism with the prophets of Baal makes it natural to suppose that whoever added the gloss about the prophets of Asherah understood Asherah to be the name of a deity. In 2 Kgs 23:4 the name Asherah is likewise paralleled with that of Baal, as well as with the host of heaven, thereby indicating that Asherah is a deity. Referring to Josiah's reformation in 621 B.C. it states, "And the king commanded Hilkiah, the high priest, and the priests of the second order, and the priests of the threshold, to bring out of the temple of the Lord all the vessels made for Baal, for Asherah, and for all the host of Heaven." Both 1 Kgs 15:13 and 2 Kgs 21:7 speak of the image of Asherah, passages in which it is natural to suppose that Asherah is the goddess. In the former passage we read of Asa's removing Maacah, his mother, from the position of queen mother, because of the abominable image for Asherah which she had made. Asa cut down the image and burned it in the Kidron valley. 2 Kgs 21:7 mentions a graven image of Asherah that Manasseh placed in the temple of Jerusalem.

Judg 3:7 uses the plural form Asheroth—"And the people of Israel did what was evil in the sight of the Lord, forgetting the Lord their God, and serving the Baals and the Asheroth." Some scholars wish to emend Asheroth to Ashtaroth, which is paralleled with the Baals in Judg 2:13; 10:6; 1 Sam 7:3,4; 12:10. However, the fact that Asheroth is the *lectio difficilior* inclines one to believe that it is the correct reading here. It is not clear whether "Asheroth" refers to different local manifestations of the goddess Asherah or is a way of referring to Canaanite female deities generally. The same uncertainty applies to the precise meaning of the terms "Baals" and "Ashtaroth."

2. As a Cult Object. The LXX and Vg usually rendered Asherah by "grove," which accounts for the translation in the KJV. The Mishnah similarly understood the Asherim to be living trees that were worshiped, e.g., grapevines, pomegranates, walnuts, myrtle, and willows (cf. *m. ʿOr.* 1:7, 8; *m. Sukk.* 3:1–3; *m. ʿAbod. Zar.* 3:7, 9, 10; *m. Meʿil.* 3:8). It is quite clear, however, from a number of OT references that the Asherim were man-made objects; verbs used in connection with them include "make" (*ʿāśâ,* 1 Kgs 14:15; 16:33; 2 Kgs 17:16; 21:3, 7; 2 Chr 33:3), "build" (*bānâ,* 1 Kgs 14:23), and "erect" (*nāṣab,* 2 Kgs 17:10), which are inappropriate for living trees. It should also be noted that Jer 17:2 speaks of "their Asherim beside every luxuriant tree," which would be odd if the Asherim were themselves actual trees. This makes it impossible to suppose that the Asherim were living trees. The view that they were always living trees is today held by A. Lemaire (1977: 604–7), but some claim more moderately that the Asherim were sometimes living trees. Deut 16:21 might suggest this, often rendered as it is "You shall not plant any tree as an Asherah beside the altar of the Lord your God, which you shall make." However, the word *ʿēṣ* can mean "wood" as well as "tree," and since all the other references to the Asherah in the OT indicate that it is a man-made object, including various references elsewhere in the Deuteronomic corpus, it is more natural to suppose that this is the meaning of *ʿēṣ* here.

That the Asherah cult object symbolized the goddess Asherah in some way is clear from the fact that both are mentioned in similar contexts in the OT. Thus, 2 Kgs 21:3, where we read that Manasseh "erected altars for Baal, and made an Asherah, as Ahab king of Israel had done, and worshiped all the host of heaven, and served them," can be compared with 2 Kgs 23:4, where we read of "all the vessels made for Baal, for Asherah, and for all the host of heaven."

W. L. Reed (1949) has argued that the Asherah was simply an image of the goddess Asherah. However, though symbolizing the goddess Asherah, the Asherah cult object does not appear to have been an image of her, since the Asherim are frequently mentioned alongside *pĕsîlîm* "graven images" (an expression including images of wood) as distinct objects (cf. Deut 7:5; 12:3; 2 Chr 33:19; 34:3, 4, 7; Mic 5:12–13—Eng 5:13–14).

The most likely view is that the Asherah was a wooden pole symbolizing the goddess Asherah. We may compare the statement in Philo of Byblos which declares that the Phoenicians "consecrated pillars and staves *(rhabdous)* after their names (i.e. of their gods)" (Eusebius, *Praep. Evang.* 1.10.11).

In view of the perishable nature of wood and our lack of certain depictions of the Asherah, we cannot be dogmatic about its form. However, it is plausible to suppose that, as a wooden pole, it may also have embodied tree symbolism. If so, this would explain the later misunderstanding that they were actual trees. This interpretation may perhaps claim support from the following consideration. It has been shown (Day 1980) that Isaiah 26–27 appears to be modeled on Hosea 13–14, there being a series of eight parallels which they share, all but one of them coming in the same order. Now the verse corresponding to that mentioning the Asherim in Isa 37:9 is Hos 14:9—Eng 14:8, which alludes to trees; Yahweh declares, "Ephraim, what has he still to do with idols? It is I who answer and look after him. I am like a luxuriant cypress, from me comes your fruit." There may even be a word play on the names of the goddesses Anath and Asherah in the words *ʾanî ʿānîti waʾăšurennu,* "It is I who answer and look after him," though it is probably going too far to accept J. Wellhausen's emendation to *ʾănî ʿanātô waʾăšērātô,* "I am his Anath and his Asherah." Further evidence which might possibly support the equation of the Asherim with stylized trees comes from Pella in Transjordan. Here 2 cult stands were discovered dating from the 10th century B.C., one of which has stylized trees on its sides and the other has depictions of a nude goddess standing on a lioness' head (cf. Asherah/*Qdš*).

The view here adumbrated, namely that Asherah in the OT is the name both of a goddess and of her wooden cult symbol, is the most widely held view, and indeed seems clear enough from the evidence. É. Lipiński, however, supposes that Asherah in the OT denotes variously a sacred grove and a shrine (chapel/cella). It should be pointed out against Lipiński's view that instances which he ascribes to each of these two meanings occur in the same context—cf. 2 Kgs 18:4; 23:14, 15, where Asherah is alleged to mean "grove"; and 1 Kgs 14:23; 2 Kgs 17:10, where it is claimed that it means "shrine." This suggests that Asherah has only one meaning, not two, throughout these passages. Now the former group of passages refers to the Asherah being cut down, and here Lipiński himself agrees that a shrine cannot be intended, while the latter group of passages alludes to Asherim under every luxuriant tree, which makes it unlikely that the Asherim were themselves trees. Since we have seen that the Asherah refers to the same object in both groups of passages, it follows that the Asherah can be neither a shrine nor a grove.

The Asherim, together with *maṣṣēbôt* "pillars," as well as altars, were a regular feature of the local shrines, the "high places" *(bāmôt),* where Canaanite or syncretistic Canaanitizing worship was practiced in ancient Israel. Those who are accused of worshiping Asherah or constructing Asherim include the people in the period of the Judges (Judg 3:7), Jeroboam I (1 Kgs 14:15), Rehoboam (1 Kgs 14:23), Asa's mother Maacah (1 Kgs 15:13), Ahab (1 Kgs 16:32; cf. 1 Kgs 18:19), Jehoahaz (2 Kgs 13:6), the N Kingdom before its downfall in 722 B.C. (2 Kgs 17:10, 16), and Manasseh (2 Kgs 21:3, 7). Those who are said to have removed this cult include Gideon (Judg 6:25–30), Asa (1 Kgs 15:13), Hezekiah (2 Kgs 18:4), and Josiah (2 Kgs 23:4, 6, 7, 14, 15). We do not hear of Asherah or Asherim in later literature, apart from Isa 27:9 (perhaps dating from the 5th century B.C., part of a section which is probably dependent on Hos 13–14).

In the prophets, in addition to Isa 27:9 and Jer 17:2, Asherim are also mentioned in Isa 17:8 and Mic 5:13 (—Eng 5:14). It is possible, though by no means certain, that the Asherah is intended in the reference in Hos 4:12, "My people inquire of a thing of wood, and their staff gives them oracles." The context suggests that we have here an idolatrous practice connected with the Canaanite fertility cult. It is unlikely, however, that Asherah is intended in the allusions in Isa 6:13; Jer 2:27; Ezek 8:3–5; Amos 8:14; or in Gen 30:13.

Bibliography

Beck, P. 1982. The Drawings from Ḥorvat Teiman (Kuntillet ʿAjrud). *TA* 9: 3–68.

Cross, F. M. 1986. A New Aramaic Stele from Taymāʾ. *CBQ* 48: 387–94.

Day, J. 1980. A case of Inner Scriptural Interpretation: the Depen-

dence of Isaiah xxvi.13–xxvii.11 on Hosea xiii.4–xiv.10 (Eng 9) and Its Relevance to Some theories of the Redaction of the "Isaiah Apocalypse." *JTS* 31: 309–19.
———. 1986. Asherah in the Hebrew Bible and Northwest Semitic Literature. *JBL* 105: 385–408.
Emerton, J. A. 1982. New Light on Israelite Religion: the Implications of the Inscriptions from Kuntillet ʿAjrud. *ZAW* 94: 2–20.
Gilula, M. 1978–79. To Yahweh Shomron and His Asherah. *Shnaton* 3: 129–37 (in Heb).
Hadley, J. M. 1987a. The Khirbet el-Qom Inscription. *VT* 37: 50–62.
———. 1987b. Some Drawings and Inscriptions on Two Pithoi from Kuntillet ʿAjrud. *VT* 37: 180–213.
Lemaire, A. 1977. Les inscriptions de Khirbet el-Qôm et lʾAshrah de Yhwh. *RB* 84: 595–608.
Lipiński, É. 1972. The Goddess Atirat in Ancient Arabia, in Babylon, and in Ugarit. *OLP* 3: 101–19.
Maier, W. A. 1986. *ʿAšerah: Extrabiblical Evidence.* HSM. Atlanta.
Meshel, Z. 1978. *Kuntillet ʿAjrud: A Religious Centre from the Time of the Judaean Monarchy on the Border of Sinai.* Jerusalem.
Rainey, A. F. 1977. Verbal Usages in the Taanach Texts. *IOS* 7: 33–64.
Reed, W. L. 1949. *The Asherah in the Old Testament.* Fort Worth.
Ryckmans, G. 1951. *Les religions arabes préislamiques.* 2d ed. Louvain.

JOHN DAY

ASHHUR (PERSON) [Heb *ʾašḥûr*]. According to 1 Chr 2:24, he is the son of Hezron and father of Tekoa. However, the birth of Ashhur after his father's death and the textual confusion of the MT of 1 Chr 2:24 have caused many scholars (e.g., Braun *1 Chr* WBC, 27; Williamson 1979:355) to emend the text on the basis of the LXX, which states that Ashhur is a son of Caleb.

In 1 Chr 4:5 the descendants of Ashhur are incorporated into the genealogy of Judah. This may reflect the later assimilation of the Calebites into the tribe of Judah. The fact that Tekoa is the name of a town in southern Judah has led some scholars to understand the word "father" to mean "settler" or "founder." The similarity between Asshur and Hur, another son of Caleb (1 Chr 2:19), causes some confusion. Curtis (*Chr* ICC) believes the two names actually refer to the same person, Hur being an abbreviated form of Ashhur. Williamson (*Chr* NCBC, 59), on the other hand, prefers to regard Ashhur as the younger brother of Hur. In the LXX, the name Ashhur appears differently in 1 Chr 2:24 and 4:4; in the former passage the name is spelled *Aschod,* while in the latter it appears as *saour.* In Codex Alexandrinus, however, the name is spelled *aschour.*

Bibliography

Williamson, H. G. M. 1979. Sources and Redaction in the Chronicler's Genealogy of Judah. *JBL* 98: 351–59.

H. C. LO

ASHIMA (DEITY) [Heb *ʾăšîmāʾ*]. A god or goddess of uncertain identity, worshiped by the people of Hamath (modern Hama in Syria) who were settled in Samaria by Sargon II after he had deported most of the local population (2 Kgs 17:30). The most widely accepted interpretation of the word Ashima is that it is an Aram form meaning "the Name." As such it would likely refer to one or more of the NW Semitic goddesses Anat, Astarte, or Asherah. Designations such as Face-of-Baal, Name-of-Baal, and possibly Sign-of-Baal are not uncommon for these goddesses, and seem to indicate that the goddess in each case is a particularized manifestation of Baal (*EncRel,* 1: 262–63, 471, 491–92).

A peculiar extension of this type of name formation is encountered at the Aramaic-speaking Jewish community at Elephantine, Upper Egypt, ca. 400 B.C. Bethel, literally "Temple-of-El," is a well-attested divinity in the Levant, but in this rather syncretistic community there are also *ʾšmbytʾl* and *ʿntbytʾl,* Name-of-Bethel and Anat-of-Bethel (*BMAP,* 87–90; *ArchEleph,* 163–79). Some scholars (e.g., Gese in Gese, Höfner, and Rudolph 1970: 189–92) would associate the *ʾšm-* element with the god Eshmun, but this is not a widely accepted view (see also Cogan and Tadmor *2 Kings* AB, 211–12); the suggestion that deities with names compounded with *ʾšm-* are masculine (*ANET,* 491, n. 9a) does not seem to square with the comparative Sem evidence.

The only other possible reference to Ashima in the Bible is Amos 8:14, "those who swear by the *ʾašmat šomrôn,* . . . and say 'as the *derek* of Beer-sheba lives.' " Although many translate "shame of Samaria" and "way of Beer-sheba" in this verse, it seems more likely that the first expression is "Ashima of Samaria." If that is the case, the obscure *derek* is probably not "way," but a garbled reference to the same deity referred to in 2 Kgs 17:31 as *tartaq.*

Bibliography

Gese, H.; Höfner, M.; and Rudolph, K. 1970. *Die Religionen Altsyriens, Altarabiens und der Mandäer,* Vol. 10/2 of *Die Religionen der Menschheit,* ed. C. M. Schröder. Stuttgart.

WILLIAM J. FULCO

ASHKELON (PLACE) [Heb *ʾašqĕlôn*]. A large seaport town located on the Mediterranean coast 20 km N of Gaza and 50 km S of Tel Aviv (M.R. 107119). The city has had a long and eventful history, stretching from at least the latter part of the 4th millennium. Its biblical significance begins in the Conquest narratives as one of the cities of the Philistine Pentapolis (Josh 13:3) and later is the object of one of Samson's outbursts (Judg 14:19). During the prophetic period, Ashkelon was a frequent object of denunciation (cf. Jer 25:20; 47:5, 7; Zeph 2:4, 7; Zech 9:5). Ashkelon's importance as a port city was enhanced by its fertile soils and easily accessible fresh water. Famous in antiquity for its onions, the modern word "scallion" is derived from the name Ashkelon.

Archaeological investigations at Ashkelon were undertaken by John Garstang and his assistant W. J. Phythian-Adams in 1920 (Garstang 1921; 1922; 1924; Phythian-Adams 1921; 1923). Modern archaeological excavations resumed at Ashkelon in 1985 (Stager and Esse 1987). The most-recent excavations have recovered traces of 3d millennium B.C. occupation on the N edge of the site, but the first recorded historical attestation of the name Ashkelon appeared in the Egyptian Execration Texts, in which Ashkelon was vilified as an enemy of Egypt. The city was mentioned in both the Berlin and Brussels texts (Sethe

1926: 53; Posener 1940: 65), and its appearance in the Execration Texts is no doubt a result of its strategic importance as a major city located in the border zone between Egypt and Palestine.

Evidence from modern excavations indicates that at least the N end of the massive ramparts surrounding the city was constructed during the MB, roughly corresponding to the date of Ashkelon's mention in the Execration Texts. If the MB city included the area encircled by the more recent Byzantine and Crusader fortifications, ancient Ashkelon would have been more than 60 hectares in size, one of the largest sites in Palestine in that period.

During the LB Ashkelon was firmly under the control of the Egyptian Pharaoh. Ashkelon's king, Widia, sent at least 7 letters to Akhenaten's court at El Amarna, (EA 320–26, 370), in which he promised loyalty and quantities of food, drink, oil, grain, and oxen for the Pharaoh's troops. In another less-cordial context, however, the ruler of Jerusalem, Abdi Ḫeba, revealed a plot involving Ashkelon, Gezer, and Lachish to supply provisions to the Egyptian king's enemies, the Ḫabiru (EA 287).

Ashkelon, as befits its importance as a border city, remained under direct Egyptian suzerainty throughout the LB. Rebellion was punished swiftly. A relief on the walls of the temple at Karnak, originally ascribed to Ramses II but now re-dated to Merneptah (see Stager 1985; Yurco 1986 for a discussion of the problem), depicts Egyptian troops storming the city of Ashkelon with the legend "the wretched town which his majesty took when it was wicked, Ashkelon. It says: 'Happy is he who acts in fidelity to thee, (but) woe (to) him who transgresses thy frontier!' " (*ANET* 256). Ashkelon was mentioned again by Merneptah in what is often referred to as the Israel stela (1207 B.C.), "Plundered is the Canaan with every evil; carried off is Ashkelon; seized upon is Gezer; Yanoam is made as that which does not exist; Israel is laid waste, his seed is not . . ." (*ANET* 378).

An inscription on a small ivory plaque excavated at Megiddo dating to the time of Rameses III refers to a singer named Kerker who evidently was employed in a Temple of Ptah at Ashkelon (*ANET* 263). By the 8th year of Rameses III (1187 B.C.), a year in which he defeated a coalition of Sea Peoples that included the Philistines, the settling of the S coastal plain of Palestine and its domination by the Philistines was assured. Ashkelon was included, along with Gaza, Ashdod, Ekron, and Gath, as one of the main cities of the Philistine Pentapolis (Josh 13:3; 1 Sam 6:17). These cities would remain linked throughout the biblical period and into classical times. (For recent treatments of the Philistines see Dothan 1982; Mazar 1985.)

During the Iron I period, references to Ashkelon centered on its association with the Philistines and the cities of the plain which could not be conquered by the Israelites. According to biblical tradition, Ashkelon was allotted to the tribe of Judah, which took possession of the hill country but could not drive out the inhabitants of the plain who had chariots of iron (Judg 1:18–19; also Josh 13:3). Ashkelon also shared the miseries that befell its Philistine neighbors when they captured the ark of the covenant after the battle of Ebenezer. To forestall further suffering, the Philistine cities promptly returned the ark with reparations (1 Sam 6:17). In the period of the Judges, the only direct contact, albeit bloody, is related in the story of Samson's riddle. After the Philistines solved his riddle, Samson went down to Ashkelon, killed 30 men, took their garments, and presented them to his tormentors to pay off his bet (Judg 14:19).

During the 10th century B.C., Ashkelon and the other Philistine cities remained a force to be reckoned with by the fledgling Israelite monarchy. David's reaction to the death of Saul and Jonathan in the battle of Gilboa dramatically illustrates the serious conflict that raged between Philistine and Israelite at that time: "Tell it not in Gath, publish it not in the streets (or bazaars) of Ashkelon; lest the daughters of the Philistines rejoice, lest the daughters of the uncircumcised exult" (2 Sam 1:20).

By the 8th century B.C. Ashkelon remained associated with Ashdod, Gaza, and Ekron, and in the Assyrian records is still reckoned as belonging to Philistia. In 734, the Assyrian king Tiglath-pileser III campaigned in Philistia against a coalition that included Aram, Edom, Israel, and Philistia. While on this campaign he forcibly collected tribute from Ashkelon's king, Mitinti. In a 2d campaign to Philistia, Tiglath-pileser III captured Ashkelon and Mitinti's son, Rukibtu, who had succeeded his father on the throne. During this period the prophet Amos referred to the demise of the "remnant" of the Philistines from Ashkelon, Ashdod, and Ekron (Amos 1:8). Rukibtu, as far as is known, remained loyal to the Assyrian kings. The cities of Philistia played an important role as intermediaries between the Assyrian Empire and Egypt. Tribute from Philistia to Sargon included silver, garments of byssus and linen, rolls of papyrus, and elephant hides (Tadmor 1966: 93; Ephᶜal 1984: 87 n. 267). That these exotic items could be sent as tribute to Assyria underscores the active commercial links that existed between Egypt and Philistia during this period.

Loyalty to Assyria was shattered during the reign of Sennacherib, however, as the king of Ashkelon was overthrown by a usurper named Ṣidqia in 701 B.C. Ṣidqia made an alliance with Hezekiah against Assyria, and together they deposed Padi, the ruler of Ekron, who had remained loyal to Assyria along with Mitinti of Ashdod (not to be confused with Mitinti of Ashkelon) and Sillibel of Gaza. Sennacherib's campaign into S Palestine in 701 restored Padi to the throne and stopped Hezekiah's rebellion; Ṣidqia of Ashkelon was deported. The Assyrian monarch replaced Ṣidqia with Sharruludari, the son of the loyal vassal, Rukibtu. Assyrian annals indicate that the territory of Ashkelon was extensive enough to include Jaffa, Beth-Dagon, Azor, and Benei Brak (Tadmor 1966: 96; see also Marcus 1977 for a discussion of the succession from Rukibtu to Sharruludari).

By the mid-7th century B.C. Ashkelon was ruled by another Mitinti, the son of the usurper Ṣidqia. Mitinti sent tribute to both Esarhaddon and Assurbanipal. Ashkelon remained loyal to these Assyrian rulers throughout their reigns and probably served as one of the staging posts for the periodic Assyrian invasions into Egypt.

By the latter part of the 7th century, Assyrian power was faltering, and it is to this period that an enigmatic passage in Herodotus describes an attempted invasion of Egypt by hordes of Scythians sweeping down out of the Caucasus. Although their invasion of Egypt was unsuccessful, the returning Scythian soldiers sacked the Temple of the Celestial Aphrodite in Ashkelon, after which, as Herodotus reports, they were struck with a horrible disease as divine retribution (1.103–6). The prophet Zephaniah referred to this period when he warned Philistia of the fate which would befall it (Zeph 2:4), and suggested that Judah would finally possess the seacoast. His prophecy that Judah would "lie down at evening in the houses of Ashkelon" (Zeph 2:7) should be seen against the background of the expansionist policies of Josiah.

The dissolution of the Assyrian empire in 612 B.C. led to a time of shifting loyalties for Philistia. It is clear from the references in Jeremiah that the Philistine cities were rebellious against the new Babylonian regime and courted destruction by their refusal to pay tribute to Nebuchadnezzar (Jer 25:20; 47:5, 7). By the winter of 604 B.C., Ashkelon was destroyed and its king was deported to Babylonia (Wiseman 1956: 69, see also Porten 1981 and Stern 1984: 1–4 for discussions of the campaign). Exiled Ashkelonites received rations at the Babylonian court. Those specifically mentioned included the sons of Aga, the last king of Ashkelon; sailors; and various nobles (Weidner 1939: 928).

Despite the dire prophesies of the prophet Zechariah (9:5), writing toward the end of the 6th century B.C., Ashkelon once more became a flourishing seaport during the Persian period under the nominal control of Tyre. Pseudo-Scylax in his *Periplus* (2d half of 4th century B.C.), mentions a royal Tyrian palace at Ashkelon (Stern 1984: 10). Ashkelon's temples were known throughout the ancient world. In addition to the Temple of Celestial Aphrodite mentioned by Herodotus, Diodorus Siculus (2.4.2–6) writing in the 1st century B.C. describes a large lake at Ashkelon regarded as sacred to the goddess Derceto (Atargatis), a goddess with the head of a woman and the body of a fish. The legend recounts Derceto's union with one of her mortal votaries which led to the birth of the famous Queen Semiramis. Semiramis was abandoned to die of exposure, but was kept warm and fed by doves, a bird which several ancient authors report as sacred at Ashkelon.

After Alexander's conquest of the Levant and Egypt, Ashkelon fell under the rule of the Ptolemies and later the Seleucids (after Antiochus III's defeat of the Egyptian army in 198 B.C.). Ashkelon remained an independent city throughout the Maccabean period, although the city was threatened by the high priest Jonathan in 147 B.C. after his victory over Apollonius, the governor of Coele-Syria. The ancient tension between highland and lowland, so palpable in the book of Judges, was apparent again as Apollonius taunted Jonathan "do not, therefore, deceive yourself, sitting in the mountains and thinking that you are strong; but if you have confidence in your force, come down to the plain . . . you should know, however, that the best men of each city are in my army, and these are the very men who have always been victorious over your ancestors. And you shall have a contest with us on ground where one cannot fight with stones, but with arms, and where there is no place to which you can flee when defeated" (*Ant* 13.89). Jonathan burned the temple of Dagon at Ashdod, and the Ashkelonites met him outside their city with gifts to prevent a similar calamity in their city. By 111 B.C., Ashkelon asserted its independence from Seleucid rule by minting silver coinage, and by 104 B.C. was minting its own coins according to a new era (Avi-Yonah 1977: 59).

Ashkelon remained a free Greek city throughout the Roman period. In the early 1st century B.C., Alexander Janneaus made Antipas, Herod the Great's grandfather, a general over all Idumea. Antipas established close relations with the Nabateans and the two former Philistine cities of Gaza and Ashkelon (*Ant* 14.10), undoubtedly to control the trade routes across the Negev from the Red Sea to the Mediterranean coast. Ties between Ashkelon and Herod's family were close if one lends credence to Julius Africanus' assertion that Herod's grandfather had spent his childhood as a temple servant in the Temple of Apollo at Ashkelon (Euseb. *Hist. Eccl.* 1.6.2–3). Herod never conquered Ashkelon, preferring that it remain a free city, but Josephus wrote that he built baths, fountains, and colonnades for the populace (*JW* 1.422). Upon Herod's death he bequeathed a palace at Ashkelon to Emperor Augustus who in turn presented it to Herod's sister, Salome (Jones 1938: 165).

With the first significant stirrings of the Jewish revolt in 64 A.D., tensions ran high between the Jews and the inhabitants of the Greek cities. In Ashkelon one riot resulted in the slaughter of 2,500 of the city's Jews (*JW* 2.477). The Jewish revolt against Rome did not directly affect the city, and Ashkelon's sea trade thrived during the Late Roman period. It was known for its agricultural produce, especially wheat, onions (Strab *Geog.* 16.2.29), and a heavy wine that was exported to European markets to be used in celebrating the Eucharist (Avi-Yonah 1977: 195; Riley 1975: 30). The acts of the Council of Constantinople indicate that by 536 A.D. Ashkelon was the seat of a bishop.

With the Muslim conquest of Palestine in the 7th century A.D., Ashkelon became a Muslim city, although Jews and Christians continued to live within its walls. In 940 the Church of *St. Maria Viridis* (St. Mary the Green) was attacked and destroyed, after which the bishop escaped to Ramla. The probable remains of this church were excavated by the recent archaeological expedition to Ashkelon (Stager and Esse 1987: fig. 2). Crusader efforts to capture Ashkelon did not succeed until 1153. Between the Crusader capture of Jerusalem in 1099 and in 1153, Ashkelon served as the main point of contact between the Fatimid government in Cairo and the Crusader kingdom. Jews taken captive in the Holy Land were ransomed at Ashkelon, often with money provided by the Cairene Jewish community (Goitein 1982: 309–15).

By 1187, Ashkelon had surrendered to Saladin after his victory over the Crusaders at the Horns of Hattin. The 3d Crusade, led by Richard the Lion-Hearted in 1191, forced Saladin to abandon Ashkelon, but not before he purposely destroyed it to prevent its falling into Crusader hands. The destruction is vividly recounted by al-Qadi al-Fadil, where Saladin is reported to have said, "I take God to witness, I would rather lose all my children than cast down a single stone from the walls" (Benvenisti 1970: 118–19). Richard partially rebuilt Ashkelon the following year, but Ashkelon was finally surrendered and completely destroyed in an agreement between Richard and Saladin. A castle was built on the site by Richard, Duke of Cornwall, in 1240, but by 1270 the Mamluk sultan, Baybars, destroyed the castle, and Ashkelon was never reoccupied.

Bibliography

Avi-Yonah, M. 1977. *The Holy Land: from the Persian to the Arab Conquest (536 B.C.–A.D. 640).* Grand Rapids.
Benvenisti, M. 1970. *The Crusaders in the Holy Land.* Jerusalem.
Dothan, T. 1982. *The Philistines and Their Material Culture.* New Haven.
Ephᶜal, I. 1984. *The Ancient Arabs.* Jerusalem.
Garstang, J. 1921. The Fund's Excavation at Askalon. *PEFQS* 12–16, 73–75, 162–69.
———. 1922. The Excavations at *Askalon. PEFQS* 112–19.
———. 1924. Askalon. *PEFQS* 24–35.
Goitein, S. D. 1982. Geniza Sources for the Crusader Period: A Survey. Pp. 306–22 in *Outremer: Studies in the History of the Crusading Kingdom of Jerusalem Presented to Joshua Prawer,* ed. B. Z. Kedar, H. E. Mayer, R. C. Smail. Jerusalem.
Jones, A. H. M. 1938. *The Herods of Judaea.* Oxford.
Marcus, D. 1977. Sharruludari, Son of Rukibtu, Their Former King: A Detail of Phoenician Chronology. *JANES* 9: 27–30.
Mazar, A. 1985. The Emergence of the Philistine Material Culture. *IEJ* 35: 95–107.
Phythian-Adams, W. J. 1921. History of Askalon. *PEFQS* 76–90.
———. 1923. Report on the Stratification of Askalon. *PEFQS* 60–84.
Porten, B. 1981. The Identity of King Adon. *BA* 44: 36–52.
Posener, G. 1940. *Princes et pays d'Asie et de Nubie.* Brussels.
Riley, J. 1975. The Pottery from the First Session of Excavation in the Caesarea Hippodrome. *BASOR* 218: 25–63.
Sethe, K. 1926. *Die Ächtung Feindlicher Fürsten, Völker und Dinge auf Altägyptischen Tongefässscherben des Mittleren Reiches.* Berlin.
Stager, L. 1985. Merenptah, Israel and Sea Peoples: New Light on an Old Relief. *EI* 18: 56*–64*.
Stager, L. and Esse, D. 1987. Notes and News: Ashkelon, 1985–86. *IEJ* 37: 68–72.
Stern, M. 1984. *Greek and Latin Authors on Jews and Judaism.* Vol. 3. Jerusalem.
Tadmor, H. 1966. Philistia Under Assyrian Rule. *BA* 29: 86–102.
Weidner, E. F. 1939. Jojachin, König von Juda, in Babylonischen Keilschrifttexten. Pp. 923–35 in *Mélanges syriens offerts a Monsieur René Dussaud.* Bibliothèque archéologique et historique 30. Paris.
Wisemen, D. J. 1956. *Chronicles of Chaldean Kings (626–556 B.C.) in the British Museum.* London.
Yurco, F. 1986. Merenptah's Canaanite Campaign. *JARCE* 23: 189–215.

Douglas L. Esse

ASHKENAZ [Heb *ʾaškĕnāz; ʾaškanaz*]. First "descendant" of Gomer who is the first "offspring" of Japheth in the Table of Nations (Gen 10:2–3). In Jer 51:27, Ashkenaz appears—along with Ararat and Minni—as a kingdom called upon to oppose Babylon. The name is identified with the neo-Assyrian Ishkuza (*iš-ku-za-a-a;* cf. Parpola AOAT 6: 178), who appeared between the Black and Caspian Seas in the 8th and 7th centuries B.C., driving out the Cimmerians (cf. GOMER; this association is reflected in Genesis 10) and threatening the Assyrians. For Herodotus, these people came to be called the Scythians. The correspondence of the consonants in Ashkenaz, Ishkuza, and Scythian is obvious; although the reason for the *nun* in the biblical name is not clear (Westermann *Genesis 1–11 BK,* p. 506; Wenham *Genesis 1–15 WBC pp.* 217–18). The use of a prosthetic *ʾalef* in the Sem forms may suggest an initial consonant cluster in the name which was unacceptable to Sem.

Although cultural associations reach back into the 3d and 2nd millennia B.C., present archaeological evidence for a distinctive Scythian culture begins in the 7th century B.C., especially at Nemirov Gorodische, an agricultural settlement between Odessa and Kiev (Yamauchi 1976: 242; 1982: 63–85). Possible portrayals of Scythians appear on 9th century reliefs of Ashurnasirpal II, but the first neo-Assyrian mention of the Ishkuza occurs during the time of Sargon II in the 8th century B.C. Driving back the Cimmerians, the Scythians were able to push S to dominate "Asia" (E Turkey) and Media in the latter part of the 7th century B.C. (Millard 1979). About this time, a Scythian raid against Egypt was stopped by Psammetichus I (Hdt. 1.105). For the later history of the Scythians and the question of their identification with the enemy from the N mentioned in the first part of Jeremiah, see SCYTHIANS.

Bibliography

Millard, A. R. 1979. The Scythian Problem. Pp. 119–22 in *Glimpses of Ancient Egypt,* ed. J. Ruffle et al. Warminster.
Parpola, S. 1970. *Neo-Assyrian Toponyms.* AOAT 6. Kevelaer and Neukirchen-Vluyn.
Yamauchi, E. M. 1976. Meshech, Tubal, and Company: A Review Article. *JETS* 19: 239–47.
———. 1982. *Foes from the Northern Frontier: Invading Hordes from the Russian Steppes.* Baker Studies in Biblical Archaeology. Grand Rapids.

Richard S. Hess

ASHNAH (PLACE) [Heb *ʾašnāh*]. **1.** A town in the Shephelah, or lowlands, of Judah (Josh 15:33), within the same district as Azekah, Zanoah, and Socoh. The only reference to this settlement occurs in the list of towns within the tribal allotment of Judah (Jos 15:21–62; see also BETH–DAGON). The location of the ancient settlement is uncertain. Suggested identifications include Aslin (Cohen *IDB* 1: 254), on the edge of the coastal plain E of Azekah, and Khirbet Wadi Allin (Boling and Wright *Joshua* AB, 384), just SE of Beth Shemesh.

2. Another town in the Shephelah of Judah (Josh 15:43), located further to the S within the same district as Libnah and Mareshah. Its single occurrence is also in the list of towns within the tribal allotment of Judah. The site cannot be identified with certainty, although modern Idna, located 10 km E of Lachish, has been proposed (*IDB* 1:254; M.R. 148107).

Bibliography

Alt, A. 1925. Judas Gaue unter Josia. *PJ* 21: 100–16.

Wade R. Kotter

ASHPENAZ (PERSON) [Heb *ʾašpĕnaz*]. An important official in the court of Nebuchadnezzar (605–562 B.C.). In Dan 1:3 he is described as the king's chief eunuch who was responsible for the selection and education of members of the Jewish royal family and aristocracy (among whom were Daniel and his 3 companions, Hananiah, Mishael, and

Azariah) who went into exile in Babylon after the fall of Jerusalem (586 B.C.). The etymology of the name has not been satisfactorily explained, but its form points to a Persian origin, possibly Old Persian *ašpinja* "inn," and it has been suggested (Lacocque *Daniel* CAT, 21–22) that originally the text read here *rab ašpinza,* the innkeeper (in the royal palace). Almost the same consonants *(ʾspnz)* are found in an Aram incantation bowl from Nippur dated ca. 600 B.C. Although the name appears only once in the opening chapter of Daniel the descriptive title "chief of the eunuchs" *(śar hassārîsîm)* appears 6 times. The special relationship between Daniel and Ashpenaz (Dan 1–9) has its literary parallel in the association of Joseph and Potiphar, an Egyptian "officer" (lit. "eunuch") of the Pharaoh (Gen 39:4). There is no need to think that Ashpenaz was castrated or that Daniel and his companions were eunuchs. The descriptive title designates a principal functionary employed at the royal court. In the Gk versions Theodotion simply resorts to transliteration *(Asphanez)* and the LXX invents a new name *(Abiesdri)* based on a misinterpretation of the title "steward" in Dan 1:11.

PETER W. COXON

ASHTAROTH (DEITY). See ASHTORETH (DEITY).

ASHTAROTH (PLACE) [Heb *ʿaštārôt*]. ASHTERATHITE. The name of a city in Bashan, situated on a mound known today as Tell ʿAshtarah in Syria (M.R. 243244). According to the OT, prior to its conquest by the Israelites, it was, together with Edrei, the dwelling place of Og, king of Bashan (Deut 1:4; Josh 12:4; 13:12, 31; cf. Josh 9:10, where it occurs without Edrei). Ashtaroth was occupied by the half-tribe of Manasseh (Machir, Josh 13:31) and became a Levitical city, allotted to the Gershonites (cf. Josh 21:27, where MT curiously has *bĕʿeštĕrâ,* and 1 Chr 6:56 [—Eng 6:71]). See BEESHTERAH (PLACE). 1 Chr 11:44 states that one of David's mighty men was Uzzia the Ashterathite, which appears to place his origin in Ashtaroth. Gen 14:5 speaks of a city ASHTEROTH-KARNAIM, inhabited by the Rephaim, which was subdued by Chedorlaomer and his allies. It is disputed whether Ashteroth-karnaim is to be equated with Ashtaroth or with the neighboring site of Karnaim.

Ashtaroth is possibly mentioned in the Egyptian Execration Texts at the end of the 19th century B.C.E. as *ʿs[ ]ʾtm* (Egyptian ʾ can represent Sem *r*). More clearly the place is referred to in the records of Thutmose III (ca. 1479–1425) as *ʿstrt,* in the el-Amarna letters (14th century) as *ʿaš-tar-te,* and in Assyrian inscriptions as *as-tar-tu.* A limestone relief discovered at Nimrud and now in the British Museum depicts Tiglath-pileser III's capture of the city in 732 (*ANEP,* 366).

In two Ugaritic serpent charm texts *ʾṯtrt,* i.e., Ashtaroth, is mentioned as the seat of the god *Mlk,* apparently the prototype of the later Molech and/or Milcom (*KTU* 1.100.41 = *Ugaritica* V 7.41, and *KTU* 1.107.17 = *Ugaritica* V 8.17; Pardee 1988). More controversial is the proposal of B. Margulis (Margalit) (1970: 292–304) who finds that the place-name "Ashtaroth" in the word *ʾṯtrt* in the passage in *KTU* 1.108.2b–3a (= *Ugaritica* V.2.2b–3a) *ʾil. yṯb. bʿṯtrt ʾil ṯpṭ. bhd rʿy,* which he renders as "El sits (enthroned) in Ashtoreth, El rules in Edrei," provides a remarkable parallel to the passage about Og, king of Bashan, dwelling in Ashtaroth and Edrei (cf. Josh 12:4). Though this rendering is ingenious, one can more plausibly translate the passage as "El (or the god) sits next to Astarte, El (or the god) the judge next to Hadad the shepherd." Against Margalit's view stand the evidence (1) that the place-name Edrei begins with ʾ, but *hd rʿy* with *h*; (2) the alternative translation makes better sense in what is clearly a banquet scene; and (3) the text continues *dyšr wydmr bkmr,* "who sings and plays the lyre," suggesting that the preceding *hd rʿy* is a personal rather than a place-name. See also Ferrara and Parker 1972: 37–39.

Bibliography

Ferrara, A. J. and Parker, S. B. 1972. Seating Arrangements at Divine Banquets. *UF* 4: 37–39.

Margulis (Margalit), B. 1970. A Ugaritic Psalm (RŠ 24.252). *JBL* 89: 292–304.

Moore, G. F. 1897. Biblical notes. 1. Ashteroth Karnaim, Gen. xiv. 5. *JBL* 16: 155–57.

Pardee, D. 1988. A New Datum for the Meaning of the Divine Name Milkashtart. Pp. 55–68 in *Ascribe to the Lord,* ed. L. Eslinger and G. Taylor. JSOTSup 67. Sheffield.

JOHN DAY

ASHTEROTH-KARNAIM (PLACE) [Heb *ʿaštĕrōt qarnayim*]. In Gen 14:5, the first locality in the enumeration of the places overrun by the 4 eastern kings (see CHEDORLAOMER) on the route of their invasion. There they defeated the REPHAIM. As with most of the chapter's geography and ethnography, this item follows the historical introduction to Deuteronomy, according to which OG, king of Bashan, lived in Ashtaroth and Edrei (Deut 1:4) and was the last remnant of the Rephaim (Deut 3:11). Ashteroth-karnaim is the same city as ASHTAROTH in Bashan, now Tell ʿAštara in S Syria, near the border with Jordan (M.R. 243244). Its name in Gen 14:5 does not mean "the two-horned Astarte" but indicates that it was located near Karnaim, now Tell Ṣaʿd, 4 km NE of Tell ʿAštara. The route of the 4 kings to the Valley of Siddim reproduces, in the opposite direction, the itinerary of the Israelites in Deuteronomy 1–3. See also ASHTORETH (DEITY); CARNAIM.

Bibliography

Pardee, D. 1988. A New Datum for the Meaning of the Divine Name Milkashtart. Pp. 55–68 in *Ascribe to the Lord,* ed. L. Eslinger and G. Taylor. JSOTSup 67. Sheffield.

MICHAEL C. ASTOUR

ASHTORETH (DEITY) [Heb *ʿaštōret*]. Var. ASHTAROTH. The name by which the Canaanite goddess more commonly known as Astarte is referred to in the OT; Ashtaroth (*ʿaštārôt*) is the plural form of this name. Astarte was a consort of Baal, the great Canaanite storm and fertility god, and is well-attested in many extrabiblical texts.

A. Ashtoreth and Ashtaroth in the OT.

It is generally accepted that the vocalization of the name of the goddess as *ʿaštōret* in the OT is a deliberate scribal distortion of an original *ʿaštart,* which is the form we should naturally expect in light of the extrabiblical parallels (cf. Gk Astarte, Akkadian Ishtar, etc.). It is virtually certain that the distorted vocalization reflects the vowels of the Hebrew word *bōšet* "shame," a term employed in place of the divine name Baal in such references as Hos 9:10 and Jer 11:13 as well as in some personal names (e.g., Eshbaal of 1 Chr 8:33; 9:39 is called Ish-bosheth in 2 Sam 2:10, 12, etc.). The name of the Canaanite god Molech *(mōlek)* is probably likewise distorted.

In the OT we find the singular form Ashtoreth only in 1 Kgs 11:5, 33 and 2 Kgs 23:13. In 1 Kgs 11:5, 33 she is referred to as "the goddess of the Sidonians," an appropriate description since extrabiblical texts make it clear that she was indeed the leading goddess at Sidon. 1 Kings 11 refers to her cult as one of a number of idolatrous practices pursued by Solomon as a result of the influence of his foreign wives. 2 Kgs 23:13 mentions that Josiah defiled the high place which Solomon had set up for Ashtoreth, and this is stated to have been E of Jerusalem, to the S of the mount of corruption.

All the other allusions in the OT are to the plural form Ashtaroth. It has, however, often been supposed that we should emend Ashtaroth to Ashtoreth in 1 Sam 31:10, where we read that the Philistines "put Saul's armor in the temple of Ashtaroth and fastened his body to the wall of Beth-shan," a passage which may imply that the temple itself was in Beth-shan. The emendation is attractive; Astarte among other things was a goddess of war, which makes the placing of armor in her temple not inappropriate. However, it should be pointed out that the parallel in 1 Chr 10:10 says that Saul's armor was placed "in the temple of their gods," which may presuppose the plural reading Ashtaroth already in the Chronicler's *Vorlage.*

All the other references to the Ashtaroth are alongside allusions to the Baals (Judg 2:13; 10:6; 1 Sam 7:4; 12:10) or simply "the foreign gods" (1 Sam 7:3), and are mentioned in connection with the apostate worship of the Israelites during the period of the Judges. When we read of "the Baals and the Ashtaroth," it may be that this is simply a way of speaking about Canaanite gods and goddesses generally, just as in Akkadian *ilāni u ištarāti* means simply "gods and goddesses." On the other hand, it is not impossible that various local manifestations of Baal and Astarte are intended. It has sometimes been supposed that "the Baals and the Asheroth" in Judg 3:7 should be emended to "the Baals and the Ashtaroth," a proprosal supported by 2 Hebrew manuscripts, the LXX, and the Syriac version, but "the Asheroth" should perhaps be preferred as the *lectio difficilior* (i.e., "the more difficult reading," and therefore unlikely to have been corrupted from "the Ashtaroth").

The pairing of the Ashtaroth with the Baals is appropriate, since it is clear from the Ugaritic texts and elsewhere that Astarte was a consort of Baal, as also was Anath. It is actually Anath who plays the preponderant role as Baal's consort in the Ugaritic texts, although Astarte does appear as Baal's spouse in a less dominant role. However, Astarte was apparently more prominent as Baal's consort in the world reflected in the OT (as is certainly also the case in 1st millennium Phoenician inscriptions), and Anath appears only vestigially in OT place names like Anathoth and Beth-Anath. These differences may reflect regional or temporal variations. A further problem is posed by the fact that "Asherah" or "the Asherah" is mentioned alongside Baal a number of times in the OT (Judg 6:25, 28, 30; 1 Kgs 18:18; 2 Kgs 23:4; cf. Judg 3:7), suggesting that she, too, is regarded as Baal's consort, although in the Ugaritic texts she is El's wife. See ASHERAH.

Astarte may be "the queen of heaven" mentioned in Jer 7:18, 44:17, 18, to whom the women made cakes of bread (7:18), burned incense, and poured out drink offerings (44:17, 18). Astarte is referred to as "the mistress of heaven" a number of times in Egyptian texts. On the other hand, it is conceivable that either Asherah or Anath is being referred to in Jeremiah. At any rate, we seem to have here a goddess popular in folk religion, which suggests a local Canaanite cult rather than the Mesopotamian Ishtar, whom some scholars have envisaged.

In addition to the place name ASHTAROTH or ASHTEROTH-KARNAIM ("Ashtaroth of the two horns"), the name of the goddess lingers on in an interesting expression found in the book of Deuteronomy. This is the phrase *ʿaštĕrôt ṣōʾnekā* (Deut 7:13, 28:4, 18, 51), commonly rendered "the young of your flock," and in each case it is mentioned alongside *šĕgar ʾalāpêkā,* "the offspring of your cattle." This expression is clearly a vestige of an earlier belief when the goddess Astarte was thought of as responsible for the fertility of the flocks. Interestingly there is evidence that *šgr,* too, was regarded as a deity by the Canaanites; he is mentioned alongside Astarte as receiving a sheep by way of offering in *KTU* 1.148.31 (= *Ugaritica* V 9, rev. 9). Cf. too the Balaam text from Deir Alla, I.16, where mention is made of *šgr.wʿštr,* "*šgr* and ʿAshtar."

B. Extrabiblical Allusions to Astarte

Precursors of the Canaanite goddess Astarte are to be found in the Mesopotamian Ishtar and the Eblaite Ashtar. In the Ugaritic texts the name of the goddess Astarte is spelled *ʿṯtrt* (probably vocalized ʿAthtart), and there she appears as a consort of the storm and fertility god Baal, though somewhat less prominently than Anath. As such she is referred to as *ʿṯtrt. šm. bʿl* "Astarte-name-of-Baal" in Keret's curse of his son *Yaṣṣib* (*KTU* 1.16.VI.54–57 = *CTA* 16.VI.54–57) and it is generally accepted that the same epithet should be restored in the similar incantation in the Baal-Yam myth in *KTU* 1.2.I.8 (= *CTA* 2.I.8). It is interesting to observe that the identical epithet occurs much later in the 5th century B.C. inscription of Eshmunazar king of Sidon (*KAI* 14.18), and one may also compare the expression "Tinnit-face-of-Baal" *(tnt pn bʿl)* in numerous Punic inscriptions (e.g., *KAI* 78.2).

Since Astarte and Anath were both consorts of Baal, it is appropriate that we find them mentioned together on a number of occasions. Thus, they appear together in the list of deities cited in both of the Ugaritic serpent charms (*KTU* 1.100.20, 1.107.14 = *Ugaritica V*.7.20, 8.14), the former of which names their common dwelling place as *ʾinbh.* They act together in preparing food at El's banquet (*KTU* 1.114.9–14 = *Ugaritica V*.1.9–14) and subsequently go hunting together (lines 22–23), though in another text

Astarte is mentioned hunting alone (*KTU* 1.92 — *PRU* V 1). They unite in attempting to restrain Baal from smiting Yam's messengers (*KTU* 1.2.I.40–42 = *CTA* 2.I.40–42), but later in the story we read of Astarte (alone) rebuking Baal, whether for being too harsh or too lenient towards Yam is not entirely clear (*KTU* 1.2.IV.28–30 = *CTA* 2.IV.28–30). On another occasion (*KTU* 1.108.2 = *Ugaritica V* 2.2) it seems likely that Astarte is referred to as being present at a banquet alongside El or Rpʾu, as well as Hadad and Anath, though some scholars insist that the place Ashtaroth is here intended. In the Keret epic, Astarte's beauty is implied, for it is said of the maiden Huray that her "grace is as the grace of Anath (and) her fairness as the fairness of Astarte" (*KTU* 1.14.III. 41–42 = *CTA* 14.III.145–146).

A common Ugaritic epithet of Astarte is *ʿṯtrt.šd* (e.g., *KTU* 4.182.55, 58 = *PRU* II.106.52, 55), apparently meaning "Astarte of the field," but the precise significance of this has not been properly elucidated. We also read of local manifestations of Astarte, *ʿṯtrt.mrh*, "Astarte in Mari" (*KTU* 1.100, margin line 2 = *Ugaritica V*.7, margin line 2), and *ʿṯtrt ḫr* (*KTU* 1.43.1, 112.13 = *CTA* 33.1, *Ugaritica VII*, RS 24.256, line 13), apparently "the Hurrian Astarte," a deity known in ancient Egypt and in a Phoenician inscription (Cross 1971: 189–95). Presumably these are ways of speaking of Ishtar, the Mesopotamian goddess who is equated with Astarte in the Ugaritic god lists (cf. *KTU* 1.47.25 [*CTA* 29, rev. 3]) and *KTU* 1.118.24 (= *Ugaritica VII*, RS 24.264 + 280, line 24) with *Ugaritica V* 18.24). The identity of Astarte with Ishtar as well as later with Aphrodite in classical times makes it virtually certain that she was equated with Venus. Maybe Canaanite ʿAthtar (*ʿṯtr,* the masculine equivalent form) was the morning star and Astarte the evening star, though explicit evidence for this in Canaanite sources is lacking.

In Egypt, the cult of Astarte, alongside that of a number of other Canaanite deities, was especially prevalent during the period of the New Kingdom, but it also continued into the Late period. For example, from the time of Amenhotep II (ca. 1427–1396 B.C.) to the Late period she was worshiped at *Prw-nfr,* the harbor of Memphis, alongside her consort Baal-Zaphon. Herodotus (2.112) refers to her cult there as that of the "foreign Aphrodite." Astarte is prominent as a goddess of war in Egypt and is depicted a number of times riding a horse, holding in her hands either a spear and a shield, or a bow and arrow (Leclant 1960: 1–67). Further, she is attested as a military patron of the Pharaohs Amenhotep II (ca. 1427–1396 B.C.), Thutmose IV (ca. 1396–1386 B.C.), and Rameses III (ca. 1185–1154 B.C.), and she was also a protector goddess of Pi-Ramesse, the new city of Rameses II (ca. 1279–1213 B.C.). She is sometimes mentioned alongside Anath, as in the Harris Papyrus, where they are referred to as "the two great goddesses who were pregnant but did not bear." (Does this shed any light on the common Ugaritic epithet "the virgin Anath"?) Like Anath she was a consort of Seth (= Baal). Her father is said to be Ptah or Re. A recurring title is "the Mistress of Heaven" and we also find references to "the Hurrian Astarte" (noted above).

Astarte appears in an interesting, although unfortunately fragmentary, Egyptian papyrus of the 18th or 19th Dyn. (ca. 1550–1187 B.C.), commonly dubbed "the Astarte papyrus" (cf. *ANET,* 17–18). The story clearly reflects an underlying Canaanite myth and has at least some points in common with the Ugaritic myth of Baal and Yam. The Sea (called Yam) demanded tribute of the gods, which was brought by Renenut, the harvest goddess. At a later stage, after the Sea had seen Astarte, it demanded Astarte herself as tribute. The end of the papyrus is broken, but probably told how Seth (i.e., Baal) fought and overcame the Sea. Morenz (1962: 307–9) has argued that this myth may well underlie the well-known classical story of Perseus and Andromeda.

The worship of the goddess Astarte was widespread throughout the Phoenician world in the 1st millennium B.C. Thus, she was the chief goddess of Tyre, being worshiped alongside the other main deities Melqart and Baal-Shamem, while at Sidon she was the leading female deity and was worshiped alongside the gods Baal and Eshmun. She is also attested elsewhere in the Phoenician world, e.g., at Kition in Cyprus and at Pyrgi in Etruria. We know from a 6th century B.C. inscription that she was equated with the goddess Tinnit at Sarepta on the Phoenician coast—this is the earliest reference to Tinnit, later famous in Punic inscriptions as the consort of Baal-ḥammon.

In Philo of Byblos' account of Phoenician mythology (ca. 100 C.E.), Astarte, along with Rhea and Dione, is taken by Kronos-El as wife. By Astarte, Kronos had 7 daughters, Titanids or Artemids, and 2 sons, called Desire (Pothos) and Love (Eros). There is a suggestion of Astarte's association with Baal and their subordination to El (cf. Ugarit) in Philo's statement that "Greatest Astarte and Zeus, called both Demarous and Adodos, king of gods, were ruling over the land with the consent of Kronos." Compare also Astarte's epithet "Greatest" with her designation as *rbt* in Phoenician inscriptions. Philo goes on to say that "Astarte placed upon her own head a bull's head as an emblem of kingship," which calls to mind the place name Ashteroth-karnaim (Gen 14:5), lit. "Ashtaroth of the two horns." There seems to be some play on Astarte's name in Philo's further statement that "while travelling around the world she discovered a star *(astera)* which had fallen from the sky. She took it up and consecrated it in Tyre, the holy island." Finally, he reveals that the Phoenicians identified Astarte with Aphrodite, a fact which is well-attested elsewhere.

There was a goddess called Atargatis, the consort of Hadad, whose cult was popular in Syria in the Hellenistic and Roman periods. An important site of her cult was at Hierapolis (Bambyke) and is described by Lucian of Samosata in his *De Syria Dea* in the 2d century C.E. She is there called Hera, and Hadad is named Zeus. It is generally thought that the name Atargatis is a compound of Astarte *(ʿttrt)* + Anath *(ʿnt)* in an Aramaizing form *ʿatta.* (The view that the latter part of the name represents Attis is now rejected.) *ʿtrʿth* is by far the most common Aram form attested, though variants such as *ʾtrʿtʾ* are also found. R. A. Oden (1977: 58–107) has argued that Atargatis combined not only Astarte and Anath but also Asherah, but this is unproven. Whereas Lucian distinguishes Atargatis from Derketo (Lucian, *Syr. D.* 14), other classical sources such as Pliny the Elder (*HN* 5.19) equate the two. Derketo was a goddess who was woman on the top half and a fish on the bottom half.

A number of nude female figurines found in archaeological excavations in Palestine have popularly been known as "Astarte plaques." The emphasized breasts and genitals certainly indicate a fertility goddess, but the close analogy of Egyptian depictions of the goddess *Qdš,* i.e., Asherah (cf. the Hathor hairstyle), suggest that the plaques in question represent Asherah rather than Astarte. Egyptian depictions of Astarte regularly depict her clothed. See ASHERAH.

Bibliography

Cross, F. M. 1971. The Old Phoenician Inscription from Spain Dedicated to Hurrian Astarte. *HTR* 64: 189–95.

Delcor, M. 1976. Various essays reprinted in *Religion d'Israël et Proche Orient Ancien.* Leiden.

Gese, H., Höfner, M., and Rudolph, W. 1970. *Die Religionen Altsyriens, Altarabiens und der Mandäer.* Stuttgart.

Helck, W. 1971. *Die Beziehunden Ägyptens zu Vorderasien.* 2d ed. Wiesbaden.

Leclant, J. 1960. Astarté à cheval. *Syr* 37: 1–67.

Morenz, S. 1962. Die orientalische Herkunft der Perseus-Andromeda-Sage. Ein Rekonstruktionsversuch. *FuF* 36/10: 307–9.

Oden, R. A. 1977. *Studies in Lucian's de Syria Dea.* Missoula, MT.

Perlman, A. L. 1978. Asherah and Astarte in the Old Testament and Ugaritic Literature. Ph.D. diss. University of California and Graduate Theological Union.

Pope, M. 1965. ʿAṯtart, ʿAštart, Astarte. Pp. 250–52 in *Wörterbuch der Mythologie.* Ed. H. W. Haussig. Stuttgart.

Pritchard, J. B. 1943. *Palestinian Figurines in relation to certain Goddesses known through Literature.* AOS 24. New Haven.

Stadelmann, R. 1967. *Syrisch-Palästinensische Gottheiten in Ägypten.* Leiden.

JOHN DAY

ASHURBANIPAL (PERSON). The last great king of Assyria, who ruled from 668–627 B.C. (see MESOPOTAMIA, HISTORY OF for a more complete discussion of his reign). The Assyrian form of his name, *Aššur-bāni-apli,* means "the god Ashur is the creator of an heir." Although Ashurbanipal exercised control over the kingdom of Judah, and his soldiers on more than one occasion marched through Palestine on campaigns against Egypt, he is never specifically mentioned in the Bible.

A. KIRK GRAYSON

ASHURITES [Heb *ʾăšûrî*]. The name of the 2d of 5 districts that comprised the kingdom of Israel during the latter part of Saul's reign, and during Eshbaal's (i.e. Ishbosheth's) brief reign (ca. 1000 B.C.; 2 Sam 2:9). The Syr and Vg read "Geshurites," while the Targum paraphrases with the expression, "house of Asher." The LXX reads *thasiri.* The present spelling of the name is probably best understood as an early corruption of "Asherites" (Edelman 1985: 85–86).

The Ashurite district is the only one designated by a gentilic form, rather than a geographical term. The district list in 2 Sam 2:9 would seem to be organized according to the common ancient principles of boundary descriptions. Limits are set out in terms of the 4 cardinal directions. The Ashurites can accordingly be understood to represent the westernmost district, in contrast to Gilead, the easternmost; Jezreel the northernmost; and Benjamin, the southernmost. Ephraim is an intermediate N-to-S element (cf. Ahlström 1986: 89).

No satisfactory identity can be found for the Ashurites based on the received spelling of their name. They cannot represent the Assyrians, who were not active in Canaan at this time. Neither can they plausibly be identified with the Arab tribe, the Asshurim, the sons of Dedan (Gen 25:3), who would not have been settled within W Canaan at the time of Saul and Eshbaal (cf. Lahav 1982/83; Ahlström 1986: 90). The variant reading "Geshurites" does not yield an acceptable geographical or political answer either, even though it has been adopted by a small group of scholars (i.e. Mauchline *1–2 Samuel* NCBC 6: 204; Ackroyd *First Book of Samuel* CBC, 33; McCarter *1 Samuel* AB, 82–83; 87–88; *HAIJ* 1986: 139–40). As an independent kingdom located in the S Golan (2 Sam 3:3; 13:37), GESHUR could not have formed the W border of Saul's Israel (see SAUL).

The Ashurites are most commonly equated with the Galilean tribe of Asher, and, by extension, are thought to represent the entire Galilee region (for bibliography, see Edelman 1985: 90, n. 4). Recent archaeological survey work in the S area of Issachar has yielded no remains datable to the Iron I period (Gal 1982), so Saul's reported control over the S Issacharite hills north of the Megiddo Plain–Jezreel Valley corridor (1 Sam 31:7; 1 Chr 10:7) can be considered literary fiction. Bearing this in mind, neither Asher nor Galilee could have formed the W limit of Saul's state.

The most plausible identification of the Ashurites would seem to be with some portion of the Asherite enclave that was located in the S region of the Ephraimite hill country (see ASHER). The detailed tribal genealogy for Asher that is found in 1 Chr 7:30–40 appears to enumerate members of this S Asherite group at 3 points during its existence, at times when it was controlled by the Judahite court (Edelman 1988). Perhaps the term in 2 Sam 2:9 designates the W clans of the enclave, including Beriah, Serah, Shomer/Shemer, and Japhlet, who occupied the towns of Aijalon, Upper and Lower Beth Horon, ʾUzzen-sheʾerah, the area N of Lower Beth Horon, and possibly Timnath-Serah.

Bibliography

Abel, F. M. 1937. Une mention biblique de Birzeit. *RB* 46: 217–24.

Ahlström, G. W. 1986. *Who Were the Israelites?* Winona Lake, IN.

Edelman, D. 1985. The "Ashurites" of Eshbaal's State (2 Sam. 2:9). *PEQ* 117: 85–91.

———. 1988. The Asherite Genealogy in 1 Chr 7. *BR* 33: 30–40.

Gal, S. 1982. The Settlement of Issachar: Some New Observations. *TA* 9: 79–86.

Lahav, M. 1982/83. Who is the "Ashurite" (2 Sam. 2.9) and "Ashur" (Ps. 83.9). *Beth Mikra* 28:111–12 (Hebrew).

DIANA V. EDELMAN

ASHVATH (PERSON) [Heb *ʿašwāt*]. The great-great-grandson of Asher mentioned in the abbr. genealogy of Asher (1 Chr 7:33). The complete count of the sons of Asher "enrolled by genealogies, for service in war" numbered 26,000 men. Ashvath, whose name perhaps means "bright," is described in the list as one of the "heads of fathers' houses, approved, mighty warriors, chief of the princes" (7:40).

Perhaps it is because Asher was a tribe of lesser importance, having originated from the Jacob-Zilpah union (cf. Gen 46:17–18), that his lineage received only passing interest. Indeed, one third of the names appearing in Asher's genealogy are found nowhere else in Scripture. The Chronicler is content to give the names of Ashvath's brothers, father (Japhlet), and grandfathers. Beyond this limited information, little or nothing else is known about him.

J. Randall O'Brien

ASIARCHS. The title signifies an office which was associated with the league of Greek cities in the Roman province of Asia. However, the exact nature of the connection has been much debated because of the apparently contradictory information supplied by the sources.

There are 3 main kinds of evidence for asiarchs. The most common are Gk inscriptions dating between the 1st and 3d centuries A.D. These are followed in number by a fairly large group of bronze coins which were issued by the cities in the province between the mid-2d and the mid-3d centuries, and which bear the names of asiarchs. The 3d type of evidence consists of references in diverse literary works, ranging from *The Geography* of Strabo and the Acts of the Apostles in the early imperial period to passages from legal codices of the 5th and 6th centuries.

Despite this wide-ranging evidence, or rather because of it, the nature of the asiarch's role in the province still has not been fully clarified. The information available is so diverse that no single homogeneous explanation taking all into account has been forthcoming so far. Indeed, over the period of more than a century, there have been many different interpretations. In the main, these have centered on whether or not the asiarch should be considered identical with the high priest of the imperial cult of the province, the "archiereus" of Asia. The division of opinion is not simply between those who believe and those who do not that the terms "asiarch" and "archiereus" of Asia are two designations for the one office. Even among those who agree in this respect, significant differences in detail occur.

According to one view, the titles referred to the same office but were used in specialized ways to denote specific functions of the position; for example, the archiereus of Asia only bore the title asiarch in every 4th year when he presided over the provincial festival (Monceaux 1885: 60–62; Merkelbach 1978: 288). An alternative view is that archiereus of Asia was the title used during the term of office while that of asiarch was a life-long designation retained afterwards (Larsen 1955: 119; Rossner 1974: 106–7). A 3rd interpretation is that the two titles, although originally separate, had become completely interchangeable by the 2d century, the existence of 2 different titles for the same office was due to a development during the 1st century A.D. in which the older title, asiarch, gradually became more popular than that of archiereus of Asia. According to this theory, the title archiereus of Asia was virtually out of use by the time of Hadrian, and the term asiarch was used to describe the head of the imperial cult in Asia from that time onwards (Lightfoot 1889: 407–8; Taylor 1933: 261; Deininger 1965: 49–50). This last interpretation of the evidence is the one most widely accepted today.

Yet the argument that the titles are identical has not always been accepted as adequately proved (Chapot 1904: 479–80; Sherwin-White 1973: 404); and some indeed have maintained that the 2 offices were entirely separate. One such view argued that the asiarch functioned only as the president of the festival of the league of cities (Le Bas-Waddington 1870: 245–46), while others have gone further and suggested that the asiarch was primarily linked, not to the league of cities at all, but to individual cities. Two versions of this view exist: (1) that the asiarchs were delegates sent by the cities to the annual assembly of the federation of cities (Brandis *PW* 2: 1577–78); and (2) that the asiarchs were benefactors of the cities, which conferred the title on the occasion of important demonstrations of public spirit, such as a festival or a gladiatorial combat (Magie 1950: 449–50).

The question cannot be considered as settled even today, despite the apparent consensus in favor of the identity of the asiarch and archiereus of Asia in scholarly literature of the last decade and a half. All interpretations of the asiarch proposed so far can still be countered at certain points. For example, it can be argued that imprecise chronology, confusion in distinguishing the local and provincial levels of the imperial cult, and lack of evidence connecting the asiarch with the league of cities in the first 3 centuries render useless some evidence. This applies to the *Martyrdom* of Polycarp and the inscriptions concerning Iulius Reginus of Ephesus, on which the pro-identity view is based (Chapot 1904: 476–77; Magie 1950: 1300). Against those who advocate a separate asiarch and archiereus of Asia it can be argued that insufficient weight is attached both (1) to Modestinus' description of the asiarchs as a national priesthood and (2) to the fact that both asiarchs and the archiereus of Asia sometimes bear qualifying titles referring to the temples of one or other of the major cities of Asia (Deininger 1965: 46–47).

Undoubtedly the controversy over the nature of the "asiarchy" has been complicated by attempts to draw in evidence not only from the province of Asia but also from other provinces in which *-arch* titles are attested (Guiraud 1887: 97–99; Taylor 1933: 256–57; Deininger 1965: 42–43). However, since this question is not yet settled in provinces such as Lycia, Galatia, Bithynia, or Pontus, arguments based on such comparisons are of little value, if any. Moreover, regional differences between provinces, as well as differences in the historical development of the various leagues of cities, make such an approach methodologically unreliable (Chapot 1904: 468–69; Sherwin-White 1973: 442–43). In addition, the broad assumption that all evidence is equally applicable to all periods takes no cognizance of changing political and economic factors (Larsen 1955: 119; Rossner 1974: 111). When these variables are taken into account, it seems unlikely that jurists writing in the first half of the 3d century can be used without extreme caution to throw light on the nature of the asiarchy in the 1st and 2d centuries. The situation demands a comprehensive study of a single, yet representative, body of evidence combined with a strict chronological approach. Such conditions are fulfilled by the inscriptions from Ephesus which now number approximately

5,000; more than 100 asiarchs and archiereis (pl. of archiereus) of Asia are represented over a period of two and a half centuries (*IvEph* 1–8 [1979–84]).

These inscriptions provide the greatest body of direct evidence available at present concerning asiarchs who lived relatively close in time and place to those mentioned in Acts 19:31. In particular, there are 4 asiarchs whose terms of office can be precisely dated between the years A.D. 92/93 and 117/18: P. Vedius Antoninus, Tib. Claudius Aristio, T. Flavius Pythio, and T. Flavius Aristoboulus (*IvEph* 2: 429, 508; 3: 858; 5: 1500). The earliest, Aristio, was asiarch in 92/93, less than 50 years after the events recorded in Acts as taking place in that very city. All 4 asiarchs are documented by 5 or more inscriptions. Aristio appears in more than 20 separate texts and is also mentioned in a letter of Pliny the Younger (*Ep.* 6/31:3).

These 4 asiarchs all held Roman citizenship and belonged to important families of Ephesus. Moreover, the inscriptions reveal a common pattern of participation in the life of the city, including their activities as benefactors: the financing of specific projects such as an aqueduct (*IvEph* 7/2: 4105); the erection of statues to members of the imperial family or to important Roman officials in Ephesus (*IvEph* 7/1: 3033); and the performance of public services such as an embassy to Rome on behalf of the city (*IvEph* 3: 728; Wörrle 1973: 473–74). The standing of the asiarchs at Ephesus is also indicated by the statues erected by the city to them and to their relatives in turn (*IvEph* 2: 425; 3: 638, 728; 7/1: 3064). All this, however, was typical for members of most of the leading families of Asia during the early imperial period and was not limited to the asiarch or archiereus. It therefore reveals nothing specific about these offices except that holders of both titles were frequently drawn from the same families. Nevertheless, this similar family background conceals details of the specific function of each of the two titles which may be extracted by a closer examination of the other aspects of the officeholder's activity.

Aristio, one of the four earliest epigraphically attested asiarchs of Ephesus, is recorded on different occasions with each title, from which it is possible to observe in what circumstances the titles were used. From the various texts in which Aristio appears in an official capacity—as distinct from those inscriptions which are purely honorary—it is clear that each title was used in a different sphere of public life. When Aristio officiated at the dedications made by certain cities of Asia to Ephesus's first provincial temple of the imperial cult in 88/89 and 89/90, he bore the title archiereus of Asia (*IvEph* 2: 234, 235; 5: 1498). But when he bore the title asiarch he was acting as a city magistrate in the capacity of prytanis (chief official) or secretary of the populace, at the same time that he participated in projects of the city not of the provincial league (*IvEph* 2: 427, 461, 508). This close association between the asiarchy and the highest city magistracies of Ephesus, particularly the grammateia, is equally in evidence in the careers of the other 3 early asiarchs, Antoninus, Pythio and Aristoboulus. Each of these was asiarch at the same time as he was grammateus of the populace (*IvEph* 2: 429; 3: 858; 5: 1500). Indeed, the association between these two offices may also be reflected in the Acts of the Apostles since these are the only 2 official positions of the city which are mentioned in the description of the riot of the silversmiths of Artemis (19:28–41).

The available chronological information confirms such an interpretation of the asiarchy's close link with civic magistracies and its individual existence apart from the *archierosynē*, "high priesthood," of Asia. Where proconsular dates are included in the inscriptions, they provide a clear distinction between the occasions on which Aristio held first the provincial *archierosynē* and then the asiarchy (*IvEph* 2: 234, 235, 461, 508). The occurrence of the title asiarch here cannot be interpreted simply as an honorary title retained by Aristio after his term of office as archiereus of Asia had expired; for he, and also Pythio, appear in inscriptions without the title some years after they are known definitely to have been asiarch (*IvEph* 5: 1500; 7/1: 3217b). Furthermore, the features that are commonly taken to imply that the title asiarch was an alternative designation for the provincial priest are lacking, not only in the case of Aristio but also in that of the other 3 asiarchs. There is no evidence, for example, of the so-called temple titles which later appear attached to the names of asiarchs and which, it has been suggested, prove that the titles asiarch and archiereus of Asia were identical (Deininger 1965: 47). Nor is there any indication in the inscriptions relating to the 4 asiarchs that they were in any way connected with the festival of the league of cities of Asia. Although the probability of such a link has frequently been proposed by those seeking to prove that the titles were identical, it is of no relevance here.

The separation in function of the asiarch and archiereus of Asia appears to be confirmed by another inscription from Ephesus (*IvEph* 1a: 27), dating to A.D. 104, which records the details of the perpetual foundation established in that year by Vibius Salutaris. In specifying the benefits and duties under the terms of the endowment, the inscription lists the archiereus of Asia and other sacred officials as a group quite distinct from those described as former asiarchs. The ex-asiarchs are grouped with civic bodies such as the *gerousia* (council of elders) and *boule* in a manner which coincides exactly with the way the inscriptions of Aristio, Pythio, Aristoboulus, and Antoninus link the asiarchy with the *grammateia* (office of secretary) or the *prytany* (presidential office of the senate) (Kearsley *NDIEC* 4 fc.).

When it is recalled that asiarchs are documented by Strabo (14. 649) well before the institution of the imperial cult in Asia, the independence of the asiarchy from the provincial *archierosynē* is not remarkable. Since also there is no evidence at all for a connection between the asiarchs and the league of Asian cities during the Late Republican period, their close relationship with the leading officials of Ephesus under the early Empire is quite credible. Unfortunately, however, it is not yet possible to determine more precisely the function of the asiarch, nor to ascertain whether or not there was more than one at a time. So far no unequivocal epigraphic evidence on this point is available and, although Acts 19:31 refers to "asiarchs," it has usually been argued that the designation there only represents a life-long honorific title applied to wealthy members of society (*contra* Kearsley 1988: 50–51). Moreover, the limited time period to which the evidence of the inscriptions of Aristio, Pythio, Aristoboulus, and Antoninus applies, from the late 1st century until the beginning of the reign of Hadrian, must be emphasized. Any developments which may have occurred subsequently between the asiarchy and the *archierosynē* of Asia remain outside the scope of this evidence.

Bibliography

Chapot, V. 1904. *La province reomaine proconsulaire d'Asie depuis ses origines jusqu'à la fin du haut-empire.* Paris.

Deininger, J. 1965. *Die Provinziallandtage der römischen Kaiserzeit von Augustus bis zum Ende des 3. Jh. n. Chr.* Munich.

Guiraud, P. 1887. *Les Assemblées provinciales dans l'empire romain.* Paris.

Kearsley, R. A. 1988. A Leading Family of Libya and Some Asiarchs of the First Century. *AnSt* 38: 43–51.

Larsen, J. A. O. 1955. *Representative Government in Greek and Roman History.* Berkeley.

Le Bas, P., and Waddington, W. H. 1870. *Inscriptions grecques et latines recueillies en Asie Mineure.* Paris.

Lightfoot, J. P. 1889. *Apostolic Fathers, S. Ignatius and S. Polycarp.* Vol. 3. London.

Magie, D. 1950. *Roman Rule in Asia Minor.* Vols 1–2. Princeton.

Merkelbach, R. 1978. Der Rangstreit der Städte Asiens und die Rede des Aelius Aristides über die Eintracht. *Zeitschrift für Papyrologie und Epigraphik* 32: 287–96.

Monceaux, P. 1885. *De Communi Asiae Provinciae.* Paris.

Rossner, M. 1974. Asiarchen und Archiereis Asia. *Studi Clasice* 16: 101–42.

Sherwin-White, A. N. 1973. *The Roman Citizenship.* Oxford.

Taylor, L. R. 1933. The Asiarchs. Pt. 1, vol. 5 in *The Beginnings of Christianity,* ed. F. J. Foakes Jackson and K. Lake. London.

Wörrle, M. 1973. Zur Datierung des Hadrianstempels an der "Kuretenstrasse" in Ephesos. *AA* 88: 470–77.

R. A. KEARSLEY

ASIBIAS (PERSON) [Gk *Asibias*]. See HASHABIAH (PERSON).

ASIEL (PERSON) [Heb *ʿăśîʾēl*]. **1.** The great-grandfather of Jehu, one of 13 princes or chiefs in the tribe of Simeon during the reign of the Judean king Hezekiah (715–687 B.C. [1 Chr 4:35]th). Jehu was one of only 3 princes whose lineage was traced. Apparently the genealogy in vv 24–43 was intended to update earlier genealogies (Gen 46:10; Exod 6:15; and Num 26:12–14) and to explain the demise of Simeon vis-à-vis Judah (cf. 1 Chr 4:27; Myers *1 Chronicles* AB, 30).

2. An elder ancestor of Tobit from the tribe of Naphtali (Tob 1:1). Asiel transliterates the Heb name *yaḥṣîʾēl* (Jahziel, cf. 1 Chr 7:13), a variant of *yaḥṣĕʾēl* (Jahzeel, cf. Gen 46:24 and Num 26:48). Jahzeel is listed as the eponymous founder of a family within the tribe of Naphtali (Num 26:48). If Jahzeel and Asiel are the same person, Tob 1:1 designates the particular family to which Tobit belonged. Whether the genealogy is genuine cannot be determined. The presence of geographical and historical errors in the book of Tobit (e.g., Tobit claims to have been a young man when the Israelite monarchy divided in 921 B.C. and to have gone into exile in 722) has led many scholars to consider the book fiction.

3. One of the 5 scribes trained to write rapidly (2 Esdr 14:24), who took down the books dictated by Ezra (2 Esdr 14:37–46). Various mss list the total number of books as 94 or over 900. The passage is often interpreted to mean that Ezra dictated 24 canonical and 70 non-canonical books (cf. Myers *Esdras* AB, 320–21; Russell 1964: 85–88), though the nature of the books is not clear from the text. In view of the obscurity of these verses, their import for the understanding of the canonical process is limited.

Bibliography

Russell, D. S. 1964. *The Method and Message of Jewish Apocalyptic.* London.

PAUL L. REDDITT

ASKEWIANUS, CODEX. See PISTIS SOPHIA.

ASMAR, TELL. A site located on the plain of the lower basin of the Diyala, a river that descends from the Zagros mountains and joins the Tigris at the point where Baghdad is situated. Its ancient name, Eshnunna, is the Sumerian form of the Semitic name Ishnou by which it was known in the 3d millennium.

Two extensive archaeological operations, different in nature but complementary, yielded some very precise information on the history of the region. The 1st was a series of traditional campaigns led by the Oriental Institute of Chicago under the direction of H. Frankfort and P. Delougaz to the tells of Tell Asmar, Khafadje, Tell Agrab, and Ischaeli 1930–36—a remarkable undertaking, the results of which for many years formed the basis of our knowledge of Babylonia of the 3d and 2d millennia. The 2d operation was carried out in 1957–58, again under the auspices of the Oriental Institute; this survey by R. McC. Adams indexed 867 archaeological sites. The study of fragments of ceramic pottery collected on these sites allowed for the dating and defining of the major evolutionary phases of the region from the end of the Neolithic period to our day, shedding light on the fundamental role played by irrigation in that period. It established the initial emergence of the first cities in the 4th and 3d millennia B.C., linked to their birth, and their renaissance at the end of the 1st millennium A.D.

Tell Asmar is a good example of the 1st phase of development of the region. The ruins extends more than 1 square km; it is formed by a main tell, approximately 600 by 400 m, and bordered on the W and S by smaller tells. It was on the main tell that most of the research was carried out. It is probably at the end of the 4th millennium B.C. that the beginnings of the site are dated, but practically nothing is known of the city of that era.

A part of an older wall with a gate was found by the excavators on the N and E sides of the N palace. This seems to show that the city in the 1st part of the 3d millennium was rather limited in its dimensions and could have occupied only the central part of the main tell. Judging from what was uncovered by the excavation, the N palace was a long building, approximately 70 by 30 m, separated from the outer wall by a small open space and bound on the E by a passageway that ran N–S with an entrance door leading to it. The most remarkable feature of the building is in the oblong rooms of the E part, where installations of baked bricks coated with bitumen-like little platforms are backed against the wall. Midway a fissure had been cut that was the starting point of an evacuation duct connected to a drainage system, which was also constructed of baked bricks and was closed in by an arch. The main pipe of the sewage system was found under the surface of the N–S passageway. One is tempted to interpret these platforms as toilets, although the number of these installations (7) in a constricted space casts doubt on this supposition. However, certain authors have seen them as unworkmanlike installations. In spite of this uncertainty, the quality of this arrangement emphasizes the attention that the Sumerians gave to the problems of urban sanitation in the middle of the 3d millennium B.C.

A recent analysis of the ruins of this palace points to 2 important conclusions: (1) The existence of a floor over the totality of the discovered edifice has been established and (2) it has been shown that this edifice was the most imposing part of a complex which also developed on the E side of the passageway. This E wing was composed of 2 or 3 main buildings situated next to one another, whose interior arrangements are unfortunately unknown. The whole structure was linked by halls running through the individual blocks. The main hall was placed exactly in the pathway of the door of the older wall and served as the backbone of the complex by giving access to all the buildings. Transversal footbridges on an upper level connected the different architectural units. The palace therefore appears more important in function than it did at the time of its uncovering, revealing the sophisticated aspects of an architecture often poorly perceived.

Dwelling houses were uncovered on the W flank of the palace, and in the middle of these was a small temple, known as the temple of Abu, where excavation has allowed scholars to trace the history and the modifications throughout the ED period (1st half of the 3d millennium). Usually, the temple comprised a single long room with a podium which undoubtedly received the insignia of the divinity; at times, 1 or 2 small rooms for storage or for lodging the priest were added. Nevertheless, one phase was characterized by a building which was more important than the others; it was called the "square temple." Instead of a long room with one podium, this temple contained three podiums, each one occupying part of a square central space in the foyer of the building where the passageways crossed. A stairway situated in the NE corner gave access to either a terrace or an upper floor. This monument became famous because one of the sanctuaries contained a set of small statues which had been buried in the ground during antiquity according to the common practice when sacred or worship-related articles were no longer used. Most of them depict worshipers and generally measure not more than about 30 cm in size; 2 of them are particularly interesting: the taller one measures 72 cm and portrays a person of masculine sex; the 2d measures 59 cm and portrays a woman. Some scholars see them as a divine couple, others as a royal couple—there is no proof to substantiate either interpretation. The sculpture does not possess the fine quality of the one from Mari, but the general outline and the facial features as well as the emphasis laid on the huge eyes, which nearly cover the face, give them an uncommon force.

South of the palace and the temple of Abu was a residential quarter. A level-by-level detailed study yielded precious information on the dwellings and private life of the ED III period and the beginning of the Agade period.

In the late 3d and early 2d millennium B.C. the city may well have known its most splendid period. The new city wall (the Larsa town wall) reveals the great expansion of the area occupied by the city and important monuments constructed 200 or 300 m to the S of the preceding group of buildings. The main block was called the palace of the rulers and the Gimil-Sin temple. That the edifice was the official power center is clear from its plan, centering on the foyer which was also the throne room according to the then-prevailing custom in Mesopotamia. A central corridor leads through a large courtyard to a first long room along one small side; in the back of this was a beautiful suite of rooms, including a very large room where receptions, banquets, and official ceremonies took place. Smaller architectural suites served as apartments for the king and his relatives, or as centers specializing in administrative management and economic reserves. This layout characterized all the palaces of that period. The palace was in use for at least 3 centuries and underwent changes which really did not affect the official residential suites but did remodel the outlying buildings.

The most remarkable added feature, still unique today, was the Gimil-Sin temple (now called the Shu-Sin temple), dedicated to a deified king of the 3d dynasty of Ur which dominated the region for some decades; this was added onto the E facade of the palace. Built according to the common Babylonian plan (a square space in the center surrounded by rooms), this edifice was desacralized at the time that the dynasty disappeared in 2004 B.C., a fact clearly showing the political character of the edifice. This building was then transformed into an annex like any other in the palace. Other monuments of that era (e.g., the building of Azuzum, the S building, the audience hall of Naram-Sin, and living quarters) complete the description of the city. Regaining its independence, Eshnunna played an important political role especially by opposing for a while Hammurabi's hegemonistic intentions; but it finally capitulated, and the region then went into a long decline.

The influence exercised by a regional capital such as Eshnunna can be measured thanks to the excavation of Tell Harmal (ancient Shaduppum). Excavated by T. Baqir in 1946, this small trapezoidal shaped city, lying a little to the S of Baghdad, certainly played an administrative role in the region. The team uncovered a double temple, a group of 2 temples joined side by side, chapels, and a large building where the priests and administrative personnel undoubtedly lived, as well as private houses. But it was the discovery of cuneiform texts which assured the importance of that small site. Tariffs, mathematical texts, literary texts, and above all fragments of a compendium of laws written in Akkadian by King Dadusha around 1790 B.C., clearly show the role of that city as a division of the central administration located in Eshnunna.

Bibliography

Adams, R. McC. 1965. *Land Behind Bagdad.* Chicago.

Baqir, T. 1959. *Tell Harmal.* Bagdad.

Delougaz, P.; Hill, D.; and Lloyd, S. 1967. *Private Houses and Graves in the Diyala Region.* OIP 88. Chicago.
Delougaz, P., and Lloyd, S. 1942. *Pre-Sargonid Temples in the Diyala Region.* OIP 57. Chicago.
Frankfort, H. 1939. *Sculpture of the Third Millennium B.C. from Tell Asmar and Khafajah.* OIP 44. Chicago.
Lloyd, S., and Jacobsen, T. 1940. *The Gimilsin Temple and Palace of the Rulers of Tell Asmar.* OIP 43. Chicago.
Margueron, J. 1982. *Recherches sur les palais mésopotamiens de l'âge du bronze.* Paris.

JEAN-CLAUDE MARGUERON
Trans. Paul Sager

ASMODEUS [Gk *Asmodaios*]. The name of the evil demon that killed the first 7 husbands of Sarah, the daughter of Raguel, each on their wedding night in the apocryphal story of Tobit (Tob 3:8). When Tobit's son Tobias was married to Sarah, however, by following the advice of the angel Raphael he warded off the demon by placing a fish's heart and liver on burning incense. Raphael then captured and bound the fleeing demon.

The derivation of the name is uncertain. It is often taken to come from Aesma Daeva, "the wrath demon," of the Zoroastrian *Avesta.* According to popular Jewish etymology, the Heb name Ashmedai (whence the Gk Asmodeus) was derived from *hismid,* "destroy, exterminate."

For the postbiblical assessment of Asmodeus—a very different one, found in the Talmud and in later Jewish folklore—see Roth, *EncJud* 3: 754–55.

HERBERT G. GRETHER

ASNAH (PERSON) [Heb *ʾasnâ*]. The head of a family of NETHINIM (temple servants) listed among those exiles returning from Babylon to Jerusalem and Judah (Ezra 2:50 = 1 Esdr 5:31). The name is absent from the list as recorded in Nehemiah 7. Galling (1951: 157) prefers to view these lists as registers of the *gôlāh* religious community in Judah. Although Zadok (1980: 113) believes the name remains unexplained by using onomastic criteria, its similarity to ASENATH (Heb *ʾāsĕnat*), the name of Joseph's Egyptian-born wife (Gen 41:45), has suggested that it has an Egyptian theophoric origin.

Bibliography

Galling, K. 1951. The "Gōlā-List" According to Ezra 2 = Nehemiah 7. *JBL* 70:149–58.
Zadok, R. 1980. Notes on the Biblical and Extrabiblical Onomasticon. *JQR* 71: 107–17.

RODNEY H. SHEARER

ASPATHA (PERSON) [Heb *ʾaspātāʾ*]. One of the 10 sons of Haman (Esth 9:7). On problems surrounding this list of names see ADALIA (PERSON). Aspatha (LXX *phasga*) perhaps renders the otherwise unattested Old Iranian name **Aspa-pati,* "master horseman."

Bibliography

Zadok, R. 1986. Notes on Esther. *ZAW* 98: 105–10.

PETER BEDFORD

ASPHAR (PLACE) [Gk *asphar*]. A pool in the wilderness of Tekoa, to which Jonathan Maccabeus, his brother Simon, and their army fled from Bacchides (1 Macc 9:33). Bacchides was one of 2 commanders sent to Judah ca. 160 B.C. by the Seleucid ruler Demetrius I Soter (reigned 162–150). Eschewing retreat, Judas threw himself and his dwindling army into battle against Bacchides and eventually was killed (1 Macc 9:18). When the Jews regrouped under Jonathan, Bacchides sought his life, but Jonathan and his army fled to Asphar. The full name of the place reads in Gk *"to hudor lakkou asphar."* Goldstein (*1 Maccabees* AB, 380) thinks that the LXX translated the Heb word *"bor"* ("cistern") as a common noun *"lakkou,"* missing the fact that *"bor"* was part of the name of the place: Bor-Asphar. Asphar was located "in the wilderness of Tekoa" (1 Macc 9:33). F.-M. Abel (1949: 196–97) identified the site with a place named Bir ez-Zaʿfarān near Tekoa, where a pool or cistern provided water, an identification accepted by Goldstein (*1 Maccabees* AB, 380), but rejected by Simons (1959: 412 §1151–52) on the grounds that the name occurs at several different places.

Bibliography

Abel, F.-M. 1949. *Les Livres des Maccabees.* Paris.
Simons, J. 1959. *The Geographical and Topological Texts of the Old Testament.* Leiden.
Tedesche, S., and Zeitlin, S. 1950. *The First Book of Maccabees.* New York.

PAUL L. REDDITT

ASRIEL (PERSON) [Heb *ʾaśrîʾēl*]. ASRIELITE. The 3d son of Gilead and great-grandson of Manasseh listed in the 2d census taken by Moses in the wilderness (Num 26:31). The Asrielites, along with the other clans of Gilead, received land allotments in Cisjordan (Josh 17:2). The identity of Asriel is confused, however, by the obscurity of 1 Chr 7:14. Rather than Asriel being understood as a son of Manasseh, in the more orderly readings of Numbers and Joshua he is the son of Gilead. Some phrase or understanding, unimportant to the descent of Asriel, has been lost from the Chronicler's reading, which only mentions 2 of the 6 clans, or 3 if Abiezer is taken to be Jeezer. The name Asriel may mean "God is joined."

JOEL C. SLAYTON

ASS. See ZOOLOGY.

ASSAR, TEL (PLACE). See TEL-ASSAR (PLACE).

ASSAYER. See INTEREST AND USURY IN THE GRECO-ROMAN PERIOD.

ASSEMBLY, DIVINE. See DIVINE ASSEMBLY.

ASSEMBLY, GREAT. See GREAT ASSEMBLY.

ASSHUR (DEITY). See MESOPOTAMIA, HISTORY OF (HISTORY AND CULTURE OF ASSYRIA).

ASSHUR (PERSON) [Heb *ʾaššûr*]. One of the sons of Shem and the eponymous ancestor of the Assyrians (Gen 10:22; 1 Chr 1:17). There is debate over whether the reference to Asshur in Gen 10:11–12, which follows vv 8–10 in which Nimrod is associated with the cities of Babylon, Erech, and Accad in S Mesopotamia (Shinar), names a person or a place (either the land or the city). Those who support the former derive it from a literal translation of the passage "from this land (Shinar) went forth Asshur." Those who prefer the latter assume that the context from the previous verses requires that Nimrod, not a ruler named Asshur, be responsible for the construction of the Assyrian cities; they generally translate (although the syntax is awkward) "from this land, he (referring to Nimrod) left for Asshur." For further discussion see *Genesis* AB.

Bibliography

Lipiński, E. 1966. Nimrod et Aššur. *RB* 73: 77–93.

Gary H. Oller

ASSHUR (PLACE) [Heb *ʾaššûr*]. The references to Asshur in the Bible are not to be confused with the references to the tribe of Asher. Also to be distinguished is a certain man called Ashhur who was the son of Caleb and the father of Tekoa who is mentioned in 1 Chr 2:24 and 4:5.

In the Bible the references to Asshur are always to the land, people, and king of Assyria as well as to their patronymic Asshur. In Gen 10:22 and 1 Chr 1:17 Asshur is said to have been a son of Shem. Assyria and Assyrians are frequently mentioned in the books of the Bible and often these references can be fitted into the larger context of Assyrian history and ancient Near Eastern history in general. (See MESOPOTAMIA, HISTORY OF.) However, there are several references, particularly in the prophets, for which no specific date or historical context is known. These references are best considered in the context of the specific book involved.

The god Asshur, the national god of Assyria, is never mentioned in the Bible although there is the rare reference to Assyrian religion. The city Asshur, which was the original capital of the kingdom of Assyria, is also never specifically referred to in the Bible. Nevertheless, it ranked with Nineveh, Calah, and Arbela, as one of the chief cities of Assyria and therefore deserves some further description.

The location of the settlement which developed into the city of Asshur was a logical one from the point of view of social and economic patterns in the region. Asshur was located on the Tigris River at the extreme S limit of the zone of regular rainfall in the Assyrian heartland. Thus it could draw on the rich agricultural resources of the surrounding countryside and at the same time was in proximity to the flourishing Sumero-Babylonian civilization to the S. In other words it was strategically located on the N-S trade route going up and down the Tigris. It was also well situated on a major E-W trade route since it was precisely at the site of Asshur that caravans commonly forded the Tigris river, the reason being that the mountain chain called the Jebel Himrin, which dominated the landscape E of the Tigris, faded into the plain at the site of Asshur. In fact the city of Asshur was built on the final outlying spur of the Jebel Himrin, which circumstance also provided Asshur with natural fortifications, particularly on the N frontier.

Although native traditions, preserved in Arabic sources in medieval and modern times, never forgot where ancient Asshur was located, it was only in the 19th century that Europeans recognized the identification of the site. Systematic archaeological excavation of the site began early in the 20th century with a German expedition led by Walter Andrae. This continued until the outbreak of World War I in 1914. Excavations were not resumed until the late 1970s by an Iraqi Expedition which has been continuing until the present time.

The history of the city of Asshur is intricately involved with the history of Assyria. Only a brief survey need be given here. There is evidence of prehistoric settlement at the site but it is only in the mid-3d millennium B.C. (*ca.* 2400 B.C.) that there is written evidence of a real city-state called Asshur. It was Shamshi-Adad I (1813–1781 B.C.) who usurped the native dynasty at the city-state of Asshur and incorporated the city into a larger political unit which included most of N Mesopotamia. In the 14th century B.C. Asshur became the capital of a land which was for the first time called Assyria, a kingdom which included the cities Nineveh and Arbela. This was the beginning of the period of the Middle Assyrian Empire and the start of major building operations at Asshur. Asshur continued to be the capital until the 9th century B.C. when Ashurnasirpal II (883–859 B.C.) moved the capital to Calah. Then in the 7th century B.C. the capital was once again moved, this time by Sennacherib (704–681 B.C.), to Nineveh. Despite Asshur losing its status as the administrative capital of the Assyrian empire, it remained throughout Assyrian history the spiritual heart of Assyria where her kings were crowned and buried.

Bibliography

Andrae, W. 1938. *Das Wiedererstandene Assur.* Leipzig.

A. Kirk Grayson

ASSHURIM [Heb *ʾaššûrîm*]. A clan name mentioned in the genealogy of ABRAHAM by his wife KETURAH in Gen 25:3. Asshurim is listed as one of the 3 sons of Abraham's grandson DEDAN, the son of JOKSHAN. These 3 sons are not found in the matching, but abbreviated, genealogical clan list in 1 Chr 1:32–33, perhaps reflecting shifts in population or a changing political situation by the time of the Chronicler. Asshurim is not related to Assyria or the Assyrians, but may possibly be identified with Syrians. This group (note the plural form of the name) is one of many obscure ARABIAN tribal groups which inhabited the fringes of the Negev and N Arabian regions. Their very obscurity was used by the biblical author(s) who wished to contrast starkly the importance of the descendants of Isaac, and even those of Ishmael, with the children of this secondary wife.

Victor H. Matthews

ASSIR (PERSON) [Heb *ʾassîr*]. **1.** A Levite, the son of KORAH (Exod 6:24; 1 Chr 6:7—Eng 6:22). The genealogy of Korah recorded in Exod 6:24 may be one of numerous postexilic expansions (compare Noth *Exodus* OTL, 59). The Samaritan Pentateuch reads Assur *(ʾssūr)* for Assir in Exod 6:24.

2. A Levite, the son of EBIASAPH, a descendant of the preceding (1 Chr 6:8, 22—Eng 6:23, 37). Both Assir, the son of Korah, and Assir, the son of Ebiasaph, are mentioned only in the genealogy in 1 Chr 6:1–15—Eng 6:16–30. The genealogy in 1 Chr 6:16–33—Eng 6:31–48 lists only Assir, the son of Ebiasaph, while Exodus 6:16–25 lists only Assir the son of Korah. The differences in the genealogies can be explained 3 ways: (1) There could be 2 men named Assir; one was accidentally dropped or dropped when compressing the genealogy; (2) there is only one Assir; the lists were accidentally expanded during copying; or (3) the differences can be explained by the artificiality of the lists; the 2 lists were constructed for different purposes and have little basis in fact.

TOM WAYNE WILLETT

ASSOCIATIONS, CLUBS, THIASOI. Clubs, guilds, and corporations were a feature of the Greco-Roman world from the 4th century on into the Roman imperial period. Most of the information about these organizations is derived from inscriptions and documentary papyri.

According to Aristotle, the essence of association *(koinōnia)* is friendship (*Eth.Nic.* 8.9.1 [1159b]). Pythagoras is alleged to have founded in the latter half of the 6th century a society of which it could be said that "men who live at distant points count one another friends before they even know or speak with one another" (Iamb. *VP* 237).

Developed out of common interests, all associations were cultically oriented, but other objectives were also frequently satisfied (Arist. *Eth.Nic.* 8.9.5 [1160a]). To achieve honored familial status, numerous Attic groups, whose members called themselves *orgeōnes,* were formed in devotion to deities and local heroes. Broader in outreach and interest were the *thiasoi,* originally associated with Dionysos. Also popular were the *eranoi* or mutual-aid societies, which persisted into Roman imperial times. The names of the associations are many. Frequently mentioned are guilds of artists, who were devoted to Dionysos and the promotion of music and drama. Merchants, who are on occasion linked with shippers in common enterprise, found that cities located on sea routes provided an attractive base for combining business with sociability. In addition, there appears an almost endless variety of guilds that shared a common trade or practice: stone masons, bankers, architects, physicians, tanners, cobblers, producers of linen or woolen goods, dyers, farmers, gardeners, bakers, barbers, fishers, to cite but a few.

Aristotle also notes the close relationship of associations to the state (*Eth.Nic.* 8.9.4 [1160a]), and the accuracy of his observation is borne out by many inscriptions relating to crafts whose proceedings are modelled after official records in the public sector. A decree of a society devoted to Sarapis (Danker 1982: 154–55) is typical not only of the style of formulation but of the subject matter included in such decrees:

> WHEREAS [Zopyros], the treasurer of the Sarapiastai, and the clerk Theophanes, and the trustee Olympichos have time and again proved themselves beyond reproach . . . , be it RESOLVED that the Sarapiastai commend and crown them with a wreath of olive in the temple of Sarapis at the next sacrifice of the Sarapiastai . . . ; and be it further resolved to commend and crown the priestess Nikippe for offering the sacrifices at the appointed times. And be it finally resolved to record this decree on a stone stele and to set it up in the [temple of Sarapis], with expenses for these items to be met by the treasurer Zopyros out of the Association's account.

Luke, who was familiar with Greco-Roman bureaucratic style, uses this type of formulation in Acts 15:22–29 to record the action of the association of Christians at Jerusalem respecting a problem that had originated in Antioch.

Hellenic interest in mental and physical agility encouraged the formation of 2 types of gymnastic associations for men. At Athens, in the 4th century B.C.E., members in the group known as the *epheboi* (ephebes) ranged in age from 18 to 19. The end of the 2d century B.C.E. saw ephebes involved in a variety of cultural activities, including intellectual pursuits and study of literature, mathematics, astronomy, and music, which were in some localities supported by substantial library facilities and visiting professorships as supplements to their gymnastic training (*IG*^{2} 1913: no. 1028 = *SIG*^{3} 1917: no. 717; Danker 1982: no. 17). Alumni from this class of youths formed a substantial membership base for associations called *neoi* or *neōteroi,* whose participants ranged "from a minimum age of nineteen or twenty years to an indeterminable maximum" (Forbes 1933: 2). Their activity was chiefly athletic. The *ephebeia* program spread rapidly from the 4th century on and became especially popular in Asia Minor, where it became a problem especially for Jews (1 Macc 1:14–15; 2 Macc 4:9–15; Josephus *Ant* 12.5.1 §240–41; Schürer *HJP*^{2} 1: 148–49). On the other hand, when Claudius, in 41 C.E., decreed the end of Jewish membership in Alexandria's gymnasium, Jewish aristocrats protested bitterly (*CPJ* 1960: no. 153.88–93). In 1 Pet 5:5, the word *neōteroi* (young men) is part of a common Gk word pair, *presbyteros-neōteros* (elder-younger), and is not used in a technical societal sense.

Roman inscriptions exhibit 2 major classifications of associations, generally termed *collegia:* those sanctioned by the state and a broad range of private associations, many of which were composed of members engaged in a common craft (Kornemann PW 4: 380–480). One of the most exotic was "The Inimitables," whose members' main purpose was to challenge one another in gourmet expenditures (Plut. *Vit.Ant.* 28).

Viability of such private clubs generally depended on their conformity to requirements for public order. Luke's report of the uproar generated by the guild of silversmiths at Ephesos (Acts 19:23–40) captures both the religious factor that was a feature of all associations and the unpredictable nature of their relationship to the Roman state.

For the most part, Rome was inclined to be permissive toward private associations (Pliny 10.33, 34), and Trajan's reply to Pliny's query concerning *eranoi* in the free city of Amisus suggests that policy respected precedent (10.92, 93). Given the whirl of social contacts encouraged by societies, the conversion of a merchant like Lydia (Acts 16:14) and of a craftsperson like Alexander, who is cited in 2 Tim 4:14, would expedite transmission of the Christian message. Similarly, St. Paul's tent-making activity offered generous exposure of the gospel to the gentile world. But as indicated in connection with the affair at Ephesus, political winds could also blow adversely, and Suetonius sums a breadth of imperial viewpoint in his assessment of policies adopted by Augustus: "A number of political parties were formed in the name of a new association, with no other purpose in mind than the commission of every sort of criminal act. . . . Therefore he closed down all associations *(collegia),* except those that enjoyed a long-standing reputation and were not disruptive of public order" (*Divine Augustus* 32.1). Illegal collegia were similarly disbanded after a riot in 59 C.E. at Pompeii (Tac. *Ann.* 14.17).

Some indication of respect for public opinion, and likewise some knowledge of the kind of formalities that were followed in meetings of associations, can be derived from the minutes of a club called the Iobakchoi, whose members were devoted to the worship of Dionysos. So pleased was the membership with the revision of their statutes that with a unanimous vote they had them inscribed on stone (Danker 1982: no. 22). Included in the bylaws are proscriptions forbidding unruliness (cf. 1 Tim 3:3; Tit 1:7), monopolizing the podium (cf. 1 Cor 14:26-33), and publicly litigating internal disputes (cf. 1 Cor 6:6; Jas 5:16), as well as a penalty for lax enforcement (cf. 1 Corinthians 5). In related vein, an association of Ephesian devotees of Demeter assured a proconsul that their annual celebration of the mysteries would be carried on with "due observance of the established customs" (Danker 1988: 288). Ancient and modern generalized allegations of insobriety, promiscuity, and even orgies in connection with guild celebrations and Greco-Roman religious rites in imperial times run the hazard of being libelous. NT broad-brush references to gentile iniquity especially require some discounting.

As Acts 2:9–11 indicates, there was a broad distribution of Jews in the provinces, and inscriptional evidence shows that Luke did not overstate the case (Schürer HJP^2 1: 3–86). The customary term for Jewish cultic associations in the Greco-Roman world was *synagogē* or congregation (Acts 6:9; 9:2 and passim; Schürer HJP^2 2: 429–31). This word, along with the title *archisynagogos* (head of a meeting group), is also used in connection with non-Jewish societies (Poland 1909: 355–58), but most frequently to denote a meeting of the society rather than the society as an entity.

Because Jews enjoyed prestige for their ancient heritage, their associations or synagogues received favorable treatment from the state—*religio licita* is not an accurate description of Jewish status—except when they were alleged to be offenders of public order. Thus, on the one hand, Julius Caesar exempted Jews from his restriction on the formation of religious associations (*thiasoi; Ant.* 14.10.8 §215), and Gallio "looked the other way" at Corinth (Acts 18:5). On the other hand, Claudius at one time suppressed their assemblies at Rome (Dio Cassius 60.6.6), avowedly in the interest of national stability. Jewish and Gentile Christians similarly experienced sporadic local animosities. It is not surprising, therefore, that the writer of 1 Peter emphasized that his addressees were to avoid any conduct that was destructive of public order (4:12–16; cf. Paul's counsel in Rom 13:1–7; 1 Thess 5:14; 2 Thess 3:11; and the passages cited above in connection with the *Iobakchoi*).

Since a festive meal played an important part in Greco-Roman associations, St. Paul could not avoid the subject in his pastoral career at Corinth. The minutes of the Iobakchoi association referred to above include one type of format that would be followed in a meeting, with emphasis on sacrificial rites and distribution of sacrificial meat. Their worship program affords insight into the kind of counsel recorded in 1 Cor 8 and 10 and 2 Cor 6:14–7:1, in which St. Paul discusses the subject of participation *(koinōnia)* in the type of meeting described in the minutes of the Iobakchoi. It is also to be observed that Greco-Roman auditors would have been reminded of their previous cultic experience by his emphasis on commemoration (1 Cor 11:25), which is echoed in Luke 22:19. The social implications for Christians who left their old associations for the new were, as 1 Pet 4:12–16 and Rev 2:20 suggest, formidable.

From the sources hitherto available, it is impossible to define the precision the status of women and slaves in Greco-Roman associations, but the description in Luke 8:1–3 of services rendered by women is in keeping with inscriptional evidence which shows that in collegia of the imperial period women generally took second place to males and were in the main limited in leadership roles to service as benefactors. Thus a number of women, notably Epikteta (*IG* no. 330), founded clubs and gymnasia. Luke's understanding of the role that women of high station played in Hellenic cultural life is apparent from his observations in Acts 17:4, 12, and it is probable that, like Lydia (Acts 16:14–15), Paul's convert at Athens named Damaris became the founder of a house-church (Acts 17:34). It appears that a few clubs, especially those under Roman influence, admitted slaves to their membership. House-oriented groups would naturally include them in some capacity.

The inscription respecting the Iobakchoi probably reflects a common bureaucratic structure. But the differences between their detailed administrative structure and those exhibited in the NT are striking. Indeed, it is improbable that Christians of the 1st century were at all in debt to Greco-Roman structures for administration of their cult. Furthermore, it appears that early Christian communities lacked a fixed-dues structure or rules for admission and made no provision for a priestly office.

Greco-Roman inscriptions offer no evidence of any special interest in meeting the needs of the poor outside of their own associations (Waltzing 1895: 1:145–47; 300–21; Pliny *Tra.* 10.92, 93). Trajan's reply (Pliny 10.93) to Pliny's letter (10.92) shows sympathy for commoners *(tenuiores),* who band together to meet special needs in their midst. In this respect they were like most early Christian groups, which focused on needs within their own religious affiliation (Acts 2:42–47; 4:32–37; 2 Cor 8–9; Gal 6:10). Much other philanthropy in the Greco-Roman world was carried out along other routes and, as inscriptions attest, "both in public and in private" (see BENEFACTOR). In ancient Hellas, care of the deceased was both a public and a private concern, but in the Roman world burial societies became popular, especially as a means of qualifying for legitimate association. Aristotle's view is the sum of the matter: Brothers and comrades have everything in common, yet in varying ways and degrees (*Eth.Nic.* 8.9 [1159b]; cf. 9.2.9 [1165a]).

Bibliography

Danker, F. 1982. *Benefactor: Epigraphic Study of a Graeco-Roman and New Testament Semantic Field.* St. Louis.

Forbes, C. 1933. *Neoi: A Contribution to the Study of Greek Associations.* Philological Monographs of the American Philological Association 2. Middletown, CT.

Humbert, G. 1887. Collegium. Vol. 1, pp. 1292–97 in *DAGR.*

Julian, C. 1896. Fabri. Vol. 2, pp. 947–59 in *DAGR.*

Johnson, A.; Coleman-Norton, P.; and Bourne, F. 1961. *Ancient Roman Statutes.* Austin. (See esp. nos. 49, 94, 109, 125, 151, 171.)

Judge, E. 1960. *The Social Pattern of Christian Groups in the First Century.* London.

Magie, D. 1950. *Roman Rule in Asia Minor to the End of the Third Century after Christ.* 2 vols. Princeton.

Poland, F. 1909. *Geschichte des griechichen Vereinswesens.* Leipzig.

Ramsay, W. 1895–97. *The Cities and Bishoprics of Phrygia.* 2 vols. Oxford.

Robertis, F. M. de. 1955. *Il fenomeno associativo nel mondo romano dai collegi della repubblica alle corporazioni del basso impero.* Naples.

Waltzing, J.-P. 1895. *Étude historique sur les corporations professionnelles chez les Romains.* Vol. 1. Louvain.

Ziebarth, E. 1896. *Das griechische Vereinswesen.* Leipzig.

FREDERICK W. DANKER

ASSOS (PLACE) [Gk *Assos*]. Port city of Assos located in NW Anatolia in the region known as the Troad just N of the island of Lesbos (39°28' N; 26°21' E). In the final stages of the 3d missionary journey Paul went by himself from Alexandria Troas to Assos (cf. Acts 20:5–6 with Acts 20:13), where he then rejoined his companions who came by ship (Acts 20:14). This was a distance of about 20 miles.

It is possible that Paul wanted to be by himself as he contemplated the probability that he would not see his beloved friends in Asia any more (Acts 20:38). Hemer (1976: 105) has suggested that Paul may have lingered behind to instruct the believers at Troas, then left by the more direct land route, perhaps on horseback, to meet his companions at Assos. Burdick (1978: 42) thinks that Paul may have wished to instruct the believers on the way to Assos.

Assos was founded by Aeolian immigrants from N Greece in the early 1st millennium B.C. By 600 B.C. Assos had become the most important city of the Troad with a population of about 12–15,000 according to Clarke (1882: 77). In the 6th century, Assos came under the domination of the Lydians. It fell to the Persians with Cyrus' conquest of Lydia and Ionia in 546. Assos regained its freedom with the victory of the Greeks over the Persians at Mycale in 479. On the basis of the Athenian tribute lists, Cook (1973: 383) estimates that the population of Assos in the 5th century had fallen to 4,000.

In the 4th century B.C., Hermeias, a former slave who had studied under Plato, became the tyrant of Assos. He invited his friend Aristotle to stay at Assos between 347 and 343. It was during his sojourn there that Aristotle began work on his important treatise *Politics.* Cleanthes, the successor of Zeno as the head of the Stoics in Athens, was born in Assos in about 331. It was possibly from Cleanthes' "Hymn to Zeus" that Paul quoted the phrase "For we are also his offspring" in his famous sermon in Athens (Acts 17:28).

Assos was excavated in 1881–83 by J. T. Clarke and F. H. Bacon. This was the very first excavation sponsored by the newly formed Archaeological Institute of America. The city walls, which were erected in the 4th century B.C., are still in a marvelous state of preservation. According to Akurgal (1970: 64), "These walls are the most complete fortifications in the Greek world."

On top of the 700-foot-high acropolis stood the impressive temple of Athena. The trapezoidal agora was flanked by a N Stoa (115 m long) and a shorter S Stoa. The S Stoa was a 3-storied structure with 13 shops on the middle floor and bathrooms on the lowest floor. The mixture of the Doric and Ionic styles reflects the period of Pergamene influence (241–133 B.C.). The S Stoa overlooked the theater, where the spectators would have had a clear view of the harbor.

Like the rest of W Asia Minor, Assos fell to the Romans with the death of the last Pergamene king in 133 B.C. Inscriptions reveal the presence of many resident Romans, and also a devotion to the cult of the emperors.

In 1981–82, Ü. Serdaroğlu excavated in the area of the W gate and in the area of the Athena temple (Mellink 1983; cf. Wescoat-Holtzmann 1981).

Bibliography

Akurgal, E. 1970. *Ancient Civilizations and Ruins of Turkey.* 2nd ed. Istanbul.

Burdick, D. W. 1978. With Paul in the Troad. *Near East Archaeological Society Bulletin* n.s. 12: 31–65.

Clarke, J. T. 1882. *Report on the Investigations at Assos, 1881.* Boston.

———. 1898. *Report on the Investigations at Assos, 1882, 1883.* New York.

Congdon, L. O. K. 1974. The Assos Journals of Francis H. Bacon. *Arch* 27.2: 83–95.

Cook, J. M. 1973. *The Troad.* London.

Ferrero, D. de B. 1970. Teatri Classici in Asia Minore III: Città dalla *Troade alla Pamfilia.* Rome.

Hemer, C. J. 1976. Alexandria Troas. *TynBul* 26: 79–112.

Mellink, M. 1983. Archaeology in Asia Minor. *AJA* 87: 429, 441.

Morton, H. V. 1936. *In the Steps of St. Paul.* London.

Wescoat-Holtzmann, B. 1981. The Temple of Athena, Assos. *AJA* 85: 223–24.

Yamauchi, E. 1980. *New Testament Cities in Western Asia Minor.* Grand Rapids.

EDWIN M. YAMAUCHI

ASSUMPTION OF THE VIRGIN. See VIRGIN, ASSUMPTION OF THE.

ASSYRIA (HISTORY AND CULTURE). See MESOPOTAMIA, HISTORY OF.

ASTARTE (DEITY). See ASTHORETH (DEITY).

ASTROLOGY IN THE ANCIENT NEAR EAST.

Ancient astrology is divisible very roughly into 2 essentially different systems: (1) *Omina,* which studied celestial phenomena as *signs* or indicators of future terrestrial events, and which originated in ancient Mesopotamia, and (2) astrology proper, which studied the *influence* of the heavenly bodies on the course of events on earth, and which originated in the Hellenistic Greek sphere.

In the ancient Near East, prediction of mundane events on the basis of celestial phenomena began in Mesopotamia and was a form of divination *(omina).* Celestial divination shared its underlying rationale and the form of its scholastic tradition with those of the other forms of Babylonian divination, such as extispicy (inspection of the liver). The celestial divination which emerged in the context of Old Babylonian scribal scholarship (ca. 1800 B.C.) was subsequently expanded, codified in a compendium entitled *Enūma Anu Enlil* (hereafter abbreviated EAE) and preserved into the Seleucid period; during the Seleucid period, the 2d major form of ancient astrology developed within the context of Hellenistic Greek science, probably under some degree of influence from Babylonian *omina.* This Hellenistic astrology took a number of forms (see below sub C), but all forms had in common the notion that the situation of the heavens at a given moment were determinative of various aspects of terrestrial life (an individual's life, the fate of a nation, or the propitiousness of an undertaking).

A. Babylonian Celestial Omina

The earliest attestation for the use of celestial *omina* as portents, appears in a number of Old Babylonian tablets. They comprise a purely Akk genre (i.e., no Sum prototypes are known). The Old Babylonian texts are concerned primarily with lunar eclipses (although solar and weather *omina* occur as well) and represent forerunners to the lunar eclipse section of the later EAE (Rochberg-Halton 1988). Textual evidence points to the establishment of the "canonical" series during the Kassite period, but the bulk of surviving sources are those of the Neo-Assyrian version from the library of Assurbanipal at Nineveh (7th century B.C.). Earlier versions of EAE from Middle Assyrian and Middle Babylonian sources with parallels in Hittite sources (Hit and Akk texts from Boğazköy) serve to outline the literary development of the series. While the series provided a standard reference work for the scholars specialized in celestial divination *(ṭupšarrūtu Enūma Anu Enlil),* the textual tradition was not rigidly fixed and it seems that EAE circulated in various recensions.

In its canonical form, EAE numbered some 70 tablets organized into 4 sections according to the phenomena of interest: The 1st section (EAE 1–22) pertains to phenomena of the moon god Sin, such as lunar visibility, halos, eclipses, and conjunctions with planets and fixed stars; the 2d section (EAE 23–36) refers to the phenomena of the sun god Samas, such as coronas, parhelia, and eclipses; the 3d (EAE 37–49/50) contains meteorological phenomena of the storm god Adad, such as lightning, thunder, rainbows, cloud formations and winds; and the 4th section (EAE 50/51–70) contains planetary *omina* such as first and last visibilities, stations, acronychal risings as well as *omina* for fixed star-phases. (Textual sources may be found in Virolleaud 1908–12; Reiner and Pingree 1975 and 1981; Rochberg-Halton 1988.)

The treatment of the phenomena in EAE is predominantly schematic; patterns such as left-right, above-below, or traditional sequences used in noncelestial omen literature, such as the colors white, black, red, yellow, and variegated, are frequently employed. Schematization brought about the introduction of nonoccurring phenomena (i.e., phenomena not observable in nature) for the sake of the schematic symmetries. The schemata also stand in relation to the predictions associated with the phenomena. The techniques for arranging the signs is structurally related to those of all Mesopotamian scholarly divination and to some extent also to the Sum-Akk lexical lists; as such they are determined more by scholastic scribal traditions and conventions than by the natural requirements of the celestial phenomena themselves. It is in this methodological sense that, although EAE comprised a major part of the written corpus of Mesopotamian scribal scholarship, and contributed much to the systematization of astronomical observation, the corpus can in no way be considered scientific in the modern sense, but certainly preliminary to the development of scientific inquiry into nature.

Celestial *omina* are expressed casuistically: if *x* occurs (in the sky), then *y* will occur (on earth). The relationship between *x* the phenomenon and *y* the predicted event was evidently not causative, but one of simple association or correlation. That is to say, the celestial phenomena were indicators, not causes of future events. This rules out astral influence as an underlying rationale for celestial *omina.* The diviners regarded all natural phenomena as comprising a symbolic language of the gods which made possible knowledge of future events. By means of the system of schematic correlation of celestial sign (omen protasis) and terrestrial event (omen apodosis) the divine language was decipherable to the scholars. Because nature was not yet fully separated from divine forces, the correlations of natural phenomena and human concerns in the form of omens made direct and concrete links between human spheres of existence and the divine. The terrestrial events recorded in EAE apodoses are almost entirely public concerns. Uppermost are predictions concerning the prosperity or downfall of the king and his army, or the country as a whole and its enemies. Floods, crop failure, and pestilence also frequently appear. The existence of predictions for private individuals in celestial *omina* should be noted, however, as a rare exception.

In the period of the Sargonid kings, celestial divination seems to have had its most widespread use and took on a status second only if not equal to extispicy. From the Neo-Assyrian period are preserved "astrological" reports from scholars in various Assyrian and Babylonian cities. The Neo-Assyrian reports contain actual observations of celestial phenomena and omens of relevance excerpted from the reference work EAE (Oppenheim 1969; Parpola 1970–1983). It becomes especially clear in this source material that celestial divination was practiced hand in hand with apotropaic magic (*namburbû* rituals), particularly as a means of protecting the king against ill portents. The best example of this is the substitute king ritual *(šar pūḫi)* which was sometimes necessitated by the occurrence of a lunar eclipse.

B. Transmission from Mesopotamia

Scholarly divination was that product of Mesopotamian intellectual history which made the broadest and most profound impact beyond the cultural and temporal spheres of Mesopotamia proper. Celestial divination, liver divination, birth omens (the series *šumma izbu*), and omens about everyday life (the series *šumma ālu*) can be traced both to the E and W of Mesopotamia beginning already in the 2d millennium, and are preserved within non-Mesopotamian contexts well into late antiquity (in India, Egypt, and in the Greco-Roman tradition).

EAE was transmitted during the 2d millennium to other parts of the Near East: to Susa, with an exemplar of EAE 22 in Akk and an Elamite text containing lunar and meterological omens; to Syria, with Akk lunar eclipse omen texts in both Akk and Hit. Also indicative of a widespread 2d millennium interest in celestial *omina* are a few examples of celestial omens in Ug, as well as a Ug text in which a solar eclipse is reported and interpreted by means of liver divination (cf. a lunar eclipse interpreted by extispicy mentioned in a Mari letter, Oppenheim 1969: 132 n.47, for bibliography, see Rochberg-Halton 1988). In many cases of "peripheral" evidence for celestial *omina,* the material is not directly traceable to early Mesopotamian (i.e., pre-1st-millennium) sources. While our extant 2d-millennium Mesopotamian celestial omen texts represent perhaps only a part of a more extensive and varied corpus, it is clear that once the idea of drawing predictions from celestial "signs" was taken over by other cultures and intellectual traditions these individual interests and requirements produced textual traditions within their specific content and construction that do not present exact parallels to texts from Babylonia proper.

Evidence for transmission to India from the 5th century B.C. onward, probably as a result of the Achaemenid occupation of the Indus Valley, comes from Vedic and Sanskrit omen collections that show clear Babylonian parallels: notably the *Gargasaṃhitā* (1st century, but dependent on older sources); the *Pāli Dīghanikāya* (4th or 3d century); *Bṛhatsaṃhitā* of Varāhamihira (ca. 550); the Jaina *Bhadrabāhusaṃhitā* (10th century?); and *Pariśiṣṭas* of the *Atharvaveda* (10th or 11th century?) (Pingree 1973: 119 and 1978: 614–18).

A Demotic papyrus (late 2d or early 3d century A.D.) in 2 books dealing with eclipses of the sun and moon (Book I) and other lunar omens (Book II) attests to the transmission of EAE to Egypt, most likely in the 5th century B.C. (Parker 1959). The dominant features of the omen papyrus—the assignment of months, hours of the day or night, and divisions of the sky to countries—clearly stems from the schematic design of the Neo-Assyrian corpus of EAE eclipse tablets. A Gk astrological work composed in Egypt in the 2d century B.C., under the fictitious authorship of "Nechepso and Petosiris," attests to Egypt's role in the transmission of Babylonian celestial omens (as well as Greek horoscopic astrology) during the Hellenistic period. Other Hellenistic Gk astrological works stemming from Egypt show Babylonian influence: Book II of Ptolemy's *Apotelesmatika,* "Astrological Influences" (also referred to as the *Tetrabiblos*) (ca. A.D. 150), Book I of Hephaestio of Thebes' *Apotelesmatika* (ca. 415), and John Lydus' *Peri semeiōn,* "On Signs" (560).

In the Hellenistic period various W Semitic traditions stemming ultimately from Mesopotamia but representing admixtures of omens and Greco-Roman astrology may be cited: Hermetic texts associated with the Sabians of Harran, e.g. the *Apocalypse* of Daniel (in Gk, Ar, and Syr); the Syr *Book of the Bee;* the Mandaean *Book of the Zodiac* (Sfar Malwašia) (Drower 1949); and a number of omen texts concerning thunder and earthquakes in Gk, Ar, Syr, and Aram (Qumran Cave 4, Milik 1959: 42).

C. Late Babylonian Developments and Greek Astrology

In addition to reliable textual evidence for the transmission of Babylonian *omina* during Achaemenid and Seleucid periods to the Greek sphere, a great many references to "Chaldeans" in connection with astrology are found in Hellenistic Gk writings. This connection between so-called Chaldeans and astrology represents part of a general trend beginning in the 4th century B.C. and persisting throughout the Hellenistic period in which Greeks credited ancients (Babylonians/Chaldeans or Egyptians) with all manner of esoterica, but particularly astrological speculation. While interest in the ancient "scientific" traditions of Babylonia may have intensified during the later Hellenistic period, what the Greeks actually knew about Mesopotamian celestial divination was doubtless not as complete as the many attributions of astrological theories to "Chaldean astrologers" would indicate. These late attributions found in Hellenistic scientific works do not necessarily provide reliable historical sources for the determination of the origins and sources of astrology.

In the Achaemenid period, there appears evidence of the incorporation within celestial *omina* of a number of elements new to this period, namely the zodiac and the derivation of personal predictions from celestial phenomena at the time of birth, which may be seen as the rudiments of what the Greeks developed as personal horoscopy (genethlialogy). The zodiac became the essential tool for Gk astrology. It represents an imaginary band extending about 6° on either side of the ecliptic (the apparent path of the sun with respect to the fixed stars in one year), and was divided into 12 "signs" of equal 30° length. Its invention in Babylonia, ca. 500 B.C., provided a standard reference system for use in astronomy. The earliest evidence for the existence of the zodiac comes from two 5th century cuneiform horoscopes, in which positions of the planets are cited with respect to zodiacal signs. The existence of the zodiac is also suggested in Achaemenid astronomical cuneiform texts, the oldest of which relates longitudes of conjunctions of the sun and moon, computed by a schematic method, with solar eclipses. The phenomena computed in these texts can be dated with relative certainty to 474, although the writing of the tablets could well have been later. (Aaboe and Sachs 1969: 17, Text B obv. col. v with heading *lu-maš* "zodiacal sign".) Another text whose astronomical phenomena are dated to ca. 430 (Neugebauer and Sachs 1967: 193, 197–98, Text C) lists phenomena for Venus and Mars plus a column containing values of "col. ϕ" in the Babylonian lunar theory.

Cuneiform evidence for the prediction of an individual's future by the observation of celestial phenomena at the time of birth seems to be of Seleucid origin (4th and 3d centuries B.C.). These *omina* are in the form "if a child is born *(šerru alid)* when Jupiter has come forth, (his life) will be regular, healthy, he will be rich, will grow old, (his) days will be long" (TCL 6 14:29, see Sachs 1952: 66 and 68), or "a child is conceived *(šerru reḫi)*" followed by celestial phenomena and personal predictions (LBAT 1588 and 1589 passim, see Pinches and Sachs 1955). Zodiacal nativity omens are also known, in the form "if (a child) is born in the middle of Aries" (LBAT 1592 i 16). Although quite late in the history of Babylonian celestial divination, such nativity omens have forerunners in older omen traditions referring to the birth of a child on a certain date, but without consideration of the heavens. For example, "if a child is born in Nisannu" (Labat *Calendrier* 64:1ff. [followed by other months of the year] and duplicate Bab. 1 192ff; TCL 6 12 obv. section 4:18). Hittite parallels confirm the antiquity of this tradition (2d millennium) (KUB 8 35:1–10), as does an Akk text from Boğazköy (KUB 37 118 rev. 6–18). Representing another extension of the traditional omens of EAE, zodiacal omens (often of the moon in various signs of the zodiac) begin to appear in Neo-Babylonian and Late Babylonian texts (Rochberg-Halton 1984).

What may be considered Babylonian precursors to Greek horoscopes begin to appear ca. 400 B.C. and record computed positions of the 7 planets (moon, sun, Jupiter, Venus, Mercury, Saturn, Mars) on the date of a birth. These state the data as follows: "On such-and-such a date a child was born *(šerru alid)*; at that time, the moon was in zodiacal sign *n*, the sun was in . . ., Jupiter was in . . ., etc." The presentation of data always follows the order of planets mentioned above. Additional astronomical events of that month are frequently appended, particularly eclipses (solar and lunar) as well as the lunar datum "NA," which represents the length of visibility of full moon on the W horizon after sunrise, i.e., the time between sunrise and moonset (Sachs 1952). These texts are clearly related to the aforementioned nativity *omina* in that some have predictions which parallel those found in the apodoses of that genre.

The cuneiform horoscopes attest to the continuation and expansion of Babylonian "scientific" traditions; they comprise a genre with affinities not only to (nativity) omen literature, but also, with respect to terminology, to contemporaneous non-mathematical astronomical texts, e.g., the diaries, almanacs, or eclipse reports (published in LBAT). The horoscopes also provide important source material for the study of the transmission of both astronomy and astrology from Babylonian to Gk science.

Another idea of Late Babylonian origin is the micro-zodiac, in which each 30° zodiacal sign was itself divided into 12 parts (Akkadian *zittu* [HA.LA] "share" or "part"). The micro-zodiac had both astronomical and astrological application, and the 12 parts, or *dodekatemoria,* were later integrated into Greek (and Indian) astrology. Other Babylonian elements may be traced (*bīt niṣirti,* which the Greeks termed *hypsoma* "exaltation"; correlation between stars, planets, and stones and plants; zodiacal triplicities) which were adopted and modified for use in Gk astrology and astral magic; but in the main, Babylonian celestial divination had only selective influence on Greek astrology.

As indicated above, the two systems were founded on entirely different theoretical bases. In contrast to Babylonian celestial divination, astrology depended for its existence on the concept of celestial influence and on the geocentric Aristotelian cosmos. The influence of the heavenly bodies on the sublunar region was given physical justification through Aristotelian physics. According to Ptolemy, the motion of the ether, the 5th (celestial) element, through the 8 celestial spheres penetrated to the sublunar elements (earth, air, fire, water) and affected their change. This constituted the mechanism of astrological causation, not the will of gods (Ptolemy Tetr. I.2). Astrology's claim that the motions of the celestial bodies were not only indications but also actual causes of change on earth shows astrology to be antithetical to divination, which depends solely on the will of the deity to provide signs.

The 4 branches of astrology that emerged and became widespread during the Hellenistic period are (1) genethlialogy, (2) general astrology, (3) catarchic astrology, and (4) interrogatory astrology. Pingree gives a summary of the sources and methods of these 4 categories in (1973: 119–25, see also Bouché-Leclercq 1899).

Genethlialogical or horoscopic astrology stems from the notion that the positions of the planets at the moment of an individual's birth directly influence the future course of that person's life. The *horoscopus* or ascendent (the point of intersection of the ecliptic and E horizon) was computed for the moment of birth and the relative positions of planets in the zodiacal signs at the time are interpreted by means of elaborate theories about their relationships. Just when the Greeks adopted the zodiac (and the notion of ecliptic) is not clear. Despite the fact that Pliny (HN 2:31) credits Cleostratus (550–500 B.C.) with its introduction into Gk science, our only irrefutable evidence comes from the fact that the early treatises on spherical astronomy by Autolycus and Euclid, ca. 300 B.C., already assume knowledge of both ecliptic and zodiac.

Gk horoscopes date from the 1st century B.C. and continue to the beginning of the Islamic period, with the bulk of the documents falling within the first 2 centuries A.D. The documents consist of papyri from Egypt, and Byzantine codices which contain the "literary horoscopes" such as those in the *Anthology* of Vettius Valens (2d century A.D., Neugebauer and van Hoesen 1959). Demotic horoscopes are also known, all but one of which fall within the 1st half of the 1st century A.D. (Neugebauer 1943 and Neugebauer and Parker 1968). Gk horoscopes provide evidence of the transmission of astronomy from Babylonia to Hellenistic Greece. Linear or arithmetical methods of Babylonian astronomical computation, as opposed to the geometrical-kinematic methods of the Gk astronomical tradition to which the *Almagest* belongs, are employed in Gk astrological texts. Neugebauer has suggested that a Gk horoscope for the year A.D. 137 has preserved the ancient definition of the linear methods. According to Neugebauer's restoration of the passage, the astrologer says he has computed the position of the sun according to the method of "greatest and smallest (velocity)," an apt description of a linear "zig-zag" function (Neugebauer and van Hoesen 1959: 42 No. 137c col. i lines 11–12). The zig-zag function is a term descriptive of the constantly increasing and decreasing arithmetical progressions used to compute the periodic (synodic) phenomena of the moon and planets in some of the Seleucid Babylonian mathematical astronomical texts. In other words, Babylonian linear methods were discarded in the creation of Gk astronomy, but preserved by Gk astrology.

General astrology brings to bear the situation of the heavens at a significant moment (e.g., at vernal equinox, or at an eclipse, or at some planetary phenomenon) on the public sphere. Predictions are given for countries, cities, populations, etc. (Pingree 1973). Parallels with the emphasis on the public sphere in the apodoses of the EAE tradition are readily found. The method and philosophical underpinnings of general astrology, however, are related to those of genethlialogy, not to *omina*.

Catarchic astrology was also developed by analogy with genethlialogy. If a person's life was influenced by the heavens at the moment of birth, then so could any act or undertaking similarly be influenced by the horoscope of its inception. By means of catarchic astrology, an individual could choose propitious moments for various activities. This form of astrology circumvents the determinism of genethlialogy by providing the possibility of choosing one's own future course of action. Catarchic astrology is attested in the 2d or 1st century B.C. in Hermetic texts applying astrology to medicine and in the work of Serapion. Later, catarchic astrology is found in e.g., Dorotheus of Sidon, "Manetho," Firmicus Maternus, and Hephaestio of Thebes (see Pingree 1973: 124 for further discussion).

A distant parallel worthy of note here occurs in a Neo-Assyrian omen text in which divination by the twinkling of stars *(kakkabu iṣrur)* in various relations to the observer (right, left, behind, in front) determines whether an undertaking will be favorable *(damqu)* or unfavorable *(aḫi)*. The text begins "if someone starts out on an undertaking" *(šumma amēlu ana ṣibûtišu tebīma)* (Bab. 4 116 c [K.139] and p. 125).

Interrogatory astrology enabled the determination of answers to specific questions by the casting of a horoscope for the moment the question was presented. The impulse to learn the outcome of certain events or circumstances is also reflected in a relatively poorly attested branch of Mesopotamian divination in which *omina* were impetrated. In this kind of divination, which Oppenheim termed "operational," the deity was asked by a diviner to respond to a query and was expected to communicate the answer by affecting an object to be observed by the diviner. Such was achieved by throwing lots, observing the action of oil on water, or the movement of smoke from a censer. Operational divination generally yielded binary (yes-no) responses. Celestial divination did not belong to this category, but rather provided signs (changes in natural phenomena) unprovoked by a diviner; however, evidence shows that the techniques were sometimes mixed, so that observation of celestial phenomena, such as shooting stars, at the time a question was posed could be interpreted in a binary (favorable or unfavorable) manner, and these decisions were meant for private individuals. Whether or not such celestial divination techniques were transmitted from Mesopotamia and contributed in any way to astrological interrogations is not ascertainable due to a complete lack of evidence. It is more probable, as Pingree suggests (Pingree 1973: 124), that interrogatory astrology developed out of catarchic astrology and provided another wedge between the determinism of genethlialogy and an individual's desire to exercise free will in making decisions.

Bibliography

Aaboe, A., and Sachs, A. 1969. Two Lunar Texts of the Achaemenid Period from Babylon. *Centaurus* 14:1–22.

Bouché-Leclercq, A. 1899. *L'Astrologie grecque*. Paris. Repr. 1963.

Drower, E. S. 1949. *Book of the Zodiac*. Oriental Translation Fund 36. London.

Milik, J. T. 1959. *Ten Years of Discovery in the Wilderness of Judea*. Naperville, IL.

Neugebauer, O. 1943. Demotic Horoscopes. *JAOS* 63:115–27.

Neugebauer, O., and Hoesen, H. B. van. 1959. *Greek Horoscopes*. Philadelphia.

Neugebauer, O., and Parker, R. 1968. Two Demotic Horoscopes. *JEA* 54:231–35.

Neugebauer, O., and Sachs, A. 1967. Some Atypical Astronomical Cuneiform Texts, I. *JCS* 21: 183–218.

Oppenheim, A. L. 1969. Divination and Celestial Observation in the Last Assyrian Empire. *Centaurus* 14:97–135.

Parker, R. 1959. *A Vienna Demotic Papyrus on Eclipse-and-Lunar Omina*. Providence.

Parpola, S. 1970–1983. *Letters from Assyrian Scholars to the Kings Esarhaddon and Assurbanipal*, Parts 1 and 2. AOAT 5/1, 5/2. Neukirchen-Vluyn.

Pinches, T. G., and Sachs, A. 1955. *Late Babylonian Astronomical and Related Texts*. Providence.

Pingree, D. 1973. Astrology. *Dictionary of the History of Ideas*. 1: 118–26. New York.

———. 1978. Mesopotamian Astronomy and Astral Omens in Other Civilizations. In *Mesopotamien und seine Nachbarn*, ed. H.-J. Nissen and J. Renger. Berliner Beiträge zum Vorderen Orient 1. Berlin.

Reiner, E., and Pingree, D. 1975. *Enuma Anu Enlil Tablet 63: The Venus Tablet of Ammisaduga*. Babylonian Planetary Omens 1. Malibu.

———. 1981. *Enuma Anu Enlil Tablets 50–51*. Babylonian Planetary Omens 2. Malibu.

Rochberg-Halton, F. 1984. New Evidence for the History of Astrology. *JNES* 43: 115–40.

———. 1988. *Aspects of Babylonian Celestial Divination: The Lunar Eclipse Tablets of Enuma Anu Enlil*. *AfO* Beiheft 22. Vienna.

Sachs, A. 1952. Babylonian Horoscopes. *JCS* 6:49–75.

Virolleaud, C. 1908–12. *L'Astrologie chaldéenne*. 12 vols. Paris.

FRANCESCA ROCHBERG-HALTON

ASTYAGES (PERSON) [Gk *Astyagēs*]. The last king of the Medians (585–550 B.C.) before the rise of the Persian

Empire (see MEDES). His name in Old Persian was *Arštivaiga* "Brandishing a Lance," *Ištumegu* in Akk. Astyages married a Lydian princess as part of the peace pact which ended the Medo-Lydian War in 585 B.C. (Herodotus 1.73–74). His daughter Mandane married a Persian, Cambyses I, and gave birth to the famous Cyrus the Great (see CYRUS). This hybrid nature of Cyrus' parentage is reflected in a response from the Delphic Oracle (Hdt. 1.91), which warned the Lydians to beware when a "mule" became king of the Medes. The Persians had developed into a kingdom subordinate to the Medes during the reign of Cyaxares (625–585 B.C.), Astyages' father.

Xenophon's propagandistic *Cyropaedia* "The Education of Cyrus" described Cyrus' perception of Astyages' Median garb: "Then he noticed that his grandfather was adorned with pencillings beneath his eyes, with rouge rubbed on his face, and with a wig of false hair—the common Median fashion."

As in many other examples from Greek folklore, Herodotus tells about a dream which forewarned Astyages that his grandson, if allowed to live, would overshadow him. Later Herodotus narrates the terrible vengeance Astyages took upon Harpagus, the man who failed to see to the death of the child. In a story which recalls the myth of Tantalus and his son Pelops, Astyages served Harpagus with the flesh of his own son (Hdt. 1.110).

When Cyrus came of age, he led the Persians in a revolt against his Median grandfather in 550, as most scholars have interpreted the Nabonidus Chronicle, or, according to Drews (1969), in 553. According to Herodotus (1.127–28) Cyrus overcame the Medes in two battles. Strabo (15.3.8) located the scene of the decisive battle in the plain where Cyrus was to build his new capital: "Cyrus held Pasargadae in honor because he there conquered Asytages the Mede in his last battle, transferred to himself the empire of Asia, founded a city, and constructed a palace as a memorial to his victory."

The Nabonidus Chronicle confirms Herodotus' account (1.127–30) that Cyrus was aided in his victory by the defection of Astyages' own men. Stronach (1971: 4) suggests that Cyrus' half-Median background may explain why the Medes never revolted against him.

Ctesias (König 1972: 50) recounts that Princess Amytis tried to hide her father in the palace. Though he was captured, his life was spared, according to Herodotus 1.130: "As for Astyages, Cyrus did him no further harm, and kept him in his own house till Astyages died."

The apocryphal Additions to Daniel (Bel 1:1; Add Dan 14:1 in the LXX and Vg) asserts: "When King Astyages was gathered to his ancestors, Cyrus of Persia succeeded him" (lit. "received his kingdom"). This is inaccurate on two counts: (1) the Medes did not control Babylon; (2) Cyrus had to wrest the kingdom from Astyages in battle. See the discussion in Moore *Daniel, Esther and Jeremiah: The Additions* AB.

Bibliography

Culican, W. 1965. *The Medes and Persians*. New York.

Diakonoff, I. M. 1985. Media. Vol. 2, pp. 36–148 in *The Cambridge History of Iran*, Cambridge.

Drews, R. 1969. The Fall of Astyages and Herodotus' Chronology of the Eastern Kingdoms. *Historia* 18:1–11.

Grayson, A. K. 1975. *Assyrian and Babylonian Chronicles*. Locust Valley, NY.

König, F. 1972. *Die Persika des Ktesias von Knidos*. Graz.

Olmstead, A. T. 1948. *History of the Persian Empire*. Chicago.

Stronach, D. 1971. Cyrus the Great. *Revue d'archéologie et d'art iraniens* 7–8:4–21.

EDWIN M. YAMAUCHI

ASUR (PERSON) [Gk *Asour*]. A temple servant who was the progenitor of a family which returned from Babylon with Zerubbabel (1 Esdr 5:31). Although 1 Esdras is often assumed to have been compiled from Ezra and Nehemiah, this family does not appear among their lists of returning exiles (cf. Ezra 2:52; Neh 7:53). Omissions such as this also raise questions about 1 Esdras being used as a source by Ezra or Nehemiah. Furthermore, problems associated with dating events and identifying persons described in 1 Esdras have cast doubt on the historicity of the text.

MICHAEL DAVID MCGEHEE

ASYNCRITUS (PERSON) [Gk *Asygkritos*]. A Roman Christian who received greeting from Paul in Rom 16:14 (see PATROBAS). Asyncritus' name occurs only twice according to the epigraphical and literary sources from the city of Rome (Lampe *StadtrChr* 140–42, 148). Since the name was not common there, it probably indicates that Asyncritus immigrated to Rome from the E of the Roman Empire.

PETER LAMPE

ATAD (PLACE) [Heb *ʾāṭad*]. Place "beyond the Jordan" mentioned in Gen 50:10 and 11 where the funeral cortège, bearing the body of Jacob homeward from Egypt to Canaan for burial, stopped and mourned him for 7 days. Since the name occurs in the phrase *"gōren hāʾāṭad,"* some have translated this as "threshing floor of (the place) Atad," while others have preferred to take the whole phrase, Goren-ha-Atad, as a place name meaning "the threshing floor of (or bordered by) thorns." According to v 11, the local Canaanite inhabitants renamed the place Abel Mizraim after observing the great mourning of the Egyptians. This aetiological explanation seems to be based on the wordplay between *ʾēbel* "mourning" and *ʾābēl,* an element found in toponyms and translated earlier as "meadow" but more recently as "watercourse" or "creek."

Problems exist in locating Atad/Abel Mizraim, described as being "beyond," that is, E "of the Jordan." While the 6th century A.D. Madeba mosaic map presents a possibility in locating an Alon Atad (terebinth of Atad) near Beth Agla (Beth Hogla—modern Deir Hajlah) between Jericho and the Dead Sea, this is on the wrong side of the Jordan. Also scholars have questioned why the procession would choose an indirect route to Hebron which apparently took them around the S end of the Dead Sea and northward through the Transjordan. Numerous explanations have been offered, including that it is a prefiguration of what would happen when the bones of Joseph would make the same journey, so that even in death, Jacob showed his descendents the road to the promised land. Finally it has been suggested that 2 different traditions on the burial place of Jacob, one E of the Jordan, the other W in Canaan, have been combined in the text.

Bibliography

Plaut, W. G. 1981. Genesis. Pp. 3–318 in *The Torah, A Modern Commentary*. New York.

Westermann, C. 1986. *Genesis 37–50: A Commentary*. Minneapolis.

GARY H. OLLER

ATARAH (PERSON) [Heb *ʿăṭārâ*]. One of the 2 wives of Jerahmeel and mother of Onam (1 Chr 2:26). From the list of descendants in vv 29–33, one may conjecture that Atarah mothered a more-extended family of Jerahmeelites than did Jerahmeel's 1st wife Hezron. Since Hezron is also a place name, Curtis (*Chronicles* ICC, 93; cf. Myers *1 Chronicles* AB, 14–15) suggests that Atarah derives from the place name Ataroth (Num 32:3, 34; Josh 16:7; also found in various compound place names Josh 16:5; 18:13; and variant compounds Num 32:35; 1 Chr 2:54). He further conjectures that Atarah's position as the 2d wife suggests that Jerahmeel's sons by Hezron were nomad families while the descendants of Atarah represented a settled life. Atarah means "crown" or "wreath" and is derived from the verb meaning "surround."

W. P. STEEGER

ATARGATIS (DEITY). A goddess worshiped in Syria in Hellenistic and later times. Her principal cult center was the city Hierapolis-Bambyke in Syria (modern Membidj), NE of Aleppo. The Hieropolitan temple dedicated to the *Dea Syria* (as Atargatis was widely known) was described with tongue-in-cheek credulity by the satirist Lucian of Samosata in mid-2d century C.E. Details about the identity of the goddess, her iconography, her consort, and the cults celebrated in their honor as given by Lucian in his *De Syria Dea* comport nicely with information derived from other Gk and Latin authors (PW 2/2: 1896) and surviving inscriptions from other sites (see Oden 1977: 47–53).

The name Atargatis is Sem, of Aram origin, and results from the juxtaposition of the names of 2 goddesses of great antiquity in the W Sem-speaking regions of Syria. The name is found in Aram inscriptions (principally Palmyrene) spelled *ʿtrʿth* and in other Aram inscriptions (e.g., Nabatean, Hatran) spelled *ʾtrʿtʾ* (with the initial pharyngeal consonant attenuated to a glottal stop). Gk *Atargatis* is a consensus representation with a number of variants. The 2 elements of the Sem name are *ʿtr-*, the characteristically Aram form of the divine name, best known from Phoenician sources as Astarte, and *ʿt-*, an Aram variant of the divine name Anat, spelled *ʿnt* in Ug texts (on the etymology see *WbMyth* 1/1: 237; Oden 1977: 58–61).

Another important shrine to Atargatis was founded by citizens of the city of Hieropolis resident on the island of Delos in A.D. 128/7. Gk inscriptions from this site make it certain that the consort of Atargatis was the W Semitic god Hadad, also known by the epithet Baal and identified with Zeus. Atargatis was correspondingly identified with Hera (Oden 1977: 55–58). The union of these 2 divinities was celebrated in a ritual of sacred marriage (Gk *hieros gamos*). Among the Nabateans the male consort was Dušara, later identified with Zeus-Hadad.

A temple of Atargatis, called in Greek the *Atargation*, is mentioned in 2 Macc 12:26. The temple was in the vicinity of the Gileadite town of Carnaim (Gk *karnion*), which should be identified with Ashteroth-karnaim of Gen 14:5 (see CARNAIM). It is possible that Carnaim and the *Atargation* were 2 separate places, presumably Seikh Saʿad and Tell ʿAstara. The town of Karnaim was destroyed by Judas Maccabaeus during an expedition into Gilead about 163 B.C. and the inhabitants who fled to the *Atergation* were put to death (2 Macc 12:18–29, 1 Macc 5:24–25; Josephus *Ant* 12.8.4).

While it is certain that *Atargation* means "Temple of Atargatis" (see for example 1 Macc 5:43–44), the Biblical name Ashteroth-karnaim suggests that there was originally a sanctuary of Astarte at the site (see also ASHTAROTH). An Egyptian stele at Tell ʿAstara contains a relief of a goddess with the horns of a cow; Astarte was often depicted as Hathor in Egypt, and the latter's iconography includes bovine features. The link between Astarte and Atargatis is preserved in Strabo's statement that the Syrian goddess was originally called *Athara* (*Geog.* 16.4.27).

Cultic centers for the worship of Atargatis were located throughout the ancient Mediterranean world, with Syrian centers in Baalbek, Caesarea, Ascalon, Khirbet Tannur, Damascus, Palmyra, and Dura Europus. The cult of Atargatis was popularized by Syrian merchants, slaves, and soldiers and by mendicant eunuch priests (Apuleius *Met.* 8.24), spreading the cult to Greece, Macedonia, Egypt, Italy, and the Balkans. The Temple of Atargatis at Baalbek had tame lions, bears, and bulls in its precinct (Lucian *De Syria Dea* 41) and sacred doves were kept at the Temple in Hierapolis (Lucian *De Syria Dea* 14, 41, 54).

Atargatis was depicted as a mermaid or surrounded by dolphins, and her sanctuaries often had sacred pools. According to one legend, the Syrian goddess originated from an egg which fell from the heavens to the Euphrates River. Fish delivered the egg to shore and it was hatched by a dove. Zeus rewarded the fish by making them a sign in the zodiac. Atargatis was also known as Derceto, who was a maiden inspired by Aphrodite with love for a youth who was worshipping at her shrine. Derceto gave birth to a daughter by this youth but was filled with such shame that she exposed the child and attempted to drown herself, at which time she was either miraculously turned into a fish (Diodorus Sic. 2.4) or saved by fish (Hyginus Astron. 2.30). The illegitimate child was saved by a fish and raised in the Temple of Aphrodite and grew up to be the legendary Queen Semiramis. Sacred fish were common to the cult of Atargatis and laws were enacted to punish those who stole or hurt the sacred fish (Lucian *De Syria Dea* 14, 47; compare further with Aelian *De Nat. Animal.* 2.30). The priests of Atargatis ate sacred fish meals according to Lucian (*De Syria Dea* 44), and the image of the goddess at the Temple at Heiropolis was bathed each year in a sacred lake.

Bibliography

Oden, R. 1977. *Studies in Lucian's De Syria Dea.* HSM 15. Missoula, MT.

SCOTT T. CARROLL

ATAROTH (PLACE) [Heb *ʿăṭārōt*]. A name for 2 different places in the OT.

1. A fortified town captured by the tribe of Gad (Num 32:3) from Sihon, king of the Amorites, and Og, king of Bashan, on the E side of the Jordan; it was rebuilt for cattle and sheep (Num 32:34).

Mesha, king of Moab in about 830 B.C.E., boasts on the Moabite Stone of Ataroth's destruction (ANET, 320): "Now the men of Gad had always dwelt in the land of Ataroth, and the king of Israel had built Ataroth for them; but I fought against the town and took it and slew all the people of the town as a satiation (intoxication) for Chemosh and Moab." Ullendorf *(DOTT)* supposes that Mesha captured the "altar hearth of David" *(ʾarʾel dawidum),* but this reference seems to be a proper name for the town chieftan who was replaced by the "men of Sharon and Maharith." *ʾrʾel* might be similar to the biblical *Ariel,* which is often thought to be an altar hearth in Jerusalem; but it appears doubtful that official cultic sacrifice was sanctioned in the 9th century on this side of the Jordan at Ataroth.

Ataroth, meaning *crowns,* is a reasonable metaphor for an ancient dwelling place, designed with height, to protect people and livestock. The modern location for the town is identified by consensus with Khirbet ʿAṭṭarûs (M.R. 213109).

2. A border town shared with Benjamin and belonging to Ephraim on the W side of the Jordan, which was previously controlled by the Archites (Josh 16:2, 7). The Archites are known in the Bible only because king David's loyal diplomat Hushai was an Archite (2 Samuel 15–17).

Noth recognized that Ephraim (Josh 16:1–3) shared the same boundary description as Benjamin (Josh 18:12–13). However, it is not clear from the text that Ataroth in 16:2 is the same as Ataroth-addar in 16:5, since the narrative is also minimizing the confused contours of territory allotted to Ephraim and the W-Jordan Manasseh—both descendants of Joseph (see Seebass 1986: 78). Alt (1953: 9–10) thinks that this W-Jordan Ataroth is the premonarchic name for Mizpah of Benjamin because modern Khirbet ʿAṭarah is found at the foot of the ancient remains of Tell en Naṣbeh, which is ascribed with great controversy to Mizpah. Alt conjectures that the name was changed to Mizpah during Asa's reign. Muilenburg (*IDB* 1: 305) objects that the remains at Khirbet ʿAṭarah do not date earlier than the Roman period, though Alt is merely speculating that Tell en Naṣbeh had an earlier name which is preserved in the local village memory of Khirbet ʿAṭarah.

Bibliography

Alt, A. 1926. Ataroth. *PJ* 22:33.

———. 1953. Neue Erwägungen über die Lage von Mizpa, Ataroth, Beeroth, und Gibeon. *ZDPV* 69:1–27.

Elliger, K. 1930. "Die Grenze zwischen Ephraim und Manasse." *ZDPV* 53: 265–309.

Glueck, N. 1951. *Explorations in Eastern Palestine.* AASOR 25–28/1.

Jenni, E. 1958. Historisch-topographische Untersuchungen zur Grenze zwischen Ephraim und Manassee. *ZDPV* 74: 35–40.

Noth, M. 1935. Die Grenze zwischen Manasse und Ephraim. *ZDPV* 58: 201–15.

Seebass, H. 1986. Zur Exegese der Grenzbeschriebungen von Jos 16, 1–17,13. *ZDPV* 100:70–83.

PAUL NIMRAH FRANKLYN

ATAROTH-ADDAR (PLACE) [Heb *ʿăṭṭārôt ʾaddār*]. A border town between Ephraim and Benjamin on the W side of the Jordan river (Josh 16:5, 18:13). Many critics conclude that the reference to Ataroth in Josh 16:2 has left out *ʾaddār,* but Boling (*Joshua* AB, 402) suggests that the boundary makes more sense if *ʾaddār* is dropped from Josh 16:5. Thus Ataroth would be the NE border town for Ephraim, and Ataroth-addar of Josh 18:13 a S border town of Benjamin.

However, based on LXX (Codex Vaticanus) translations of these verses, Albright notices that rather than the *ʾaddār* of Heb, LXX^B has *erok* (16:5) or *orech* (18:13), which are both misspellings of *erek* (Heb *ʾerek*). Albright proposes that there was an obvious confusion of the Heb *ʾerek* (read *ʾarkî* in 16:2) with *ʾaddar,* since *dalet, reš,* and *kap* are nearly identical in Heb square script. By this reconstruction of a very confused text, all references to Ataroth-addar should actually refer to the same W-Jordan Ataroth of the Archite clan on Ephraim's NE border.

Bibliography

Albright, W. F. 1939. Review of *Geographie de la palestine, II.* by P.F.-M. Abel. *JBL* 58:177–87.

PAUL NIMRAH FRANKLYN

ATER (PERSON) [Heb *ʾāṭēr*]. **1.** Head of a family of Babylonian exiles listed as returnees under the leadership of Zerubbabel and others (Ezra 2:16 = Neh 7:21 = 1 Esdr 5:15). The leader of the clan affixed the family name to the covenant document of Nehemiah in Neh 10:18—Eng 10:17. Since Ater is a Babylonian name, the name Hezekiah (which follows it immediately in the Zerubbabel list and is introduced by *l-,* "namely,") is best understood as the older Heb name for the family (Ezra *IB,* 579). For further discussion see AKKUB.

Many do not regard the list and covenant of Nehemiah 10 as belonging originally in this context. Williamson (*Ezra, Nehemiah* WBC, 325–30) surveys various views about the origins of this list. He concludes that it was compiled from other lists in Ezra and Nehemiah in order to be attached to the terms of an agreement drawn up by Nehemiah following his reforms of Nehemiah 13. This document was then kept in the temple archives until it was inserted into its present position. (See also Clines 1984: 199–200; *Ezra-Nehemiah* AB, 174–75; Jepsen 1954: 87–106.)

2. Head of a family of gatekeepers who are also listed as returnees from Babylonian exile under the leadership of Zerubbabel and others (Ezra 2:42 = Neh 7:45 = 1 Esdr 5:28).

Bibliography

Clines, D. J. 1984. *Ezra, Nehemiah, Esther.* Grand Rapids, MI.

Jepsen, A. 1954. Nehemiah 10. *ZAW* 66: 87–106.

CHANEY R. BERGDALL

ATHACH (PLACE) [Heb *ʿătāk*]. A village in Judah to which David sent gifts after his defeat of the Amalekites (1 Sam 30:30). Most scholars see a connection between this Athach and the Ether in Josh 15:42 and 19:7. In Josh

15:42 some manuscripts of the LXX read *Ithak* and *Athak,* among other variants (see *NHT,* 227). The presence of a village called ASHAN or Bor-Ashan in each of the lists in Josh 15:42, 19:7 and 1 Sam 30:30 alongside Ether/Athach makes the equation of the two all the more tempting, though which spelling should receive priority remains an open question. The presence of Ether in the MT of 2 of the 3 lists tips the scales in its favor in the eyes of many (see McCarter *1 Samuel* AB, 434; for dissenting opinion to the above, see *ISBE* 1: 349). In either case, a location in the Shephelah is likely (cf. Josh 15:33–47, though some scholars dispute the presence of both Athach/Ether and Ashan at Josh 15:42—see the discussion at ASHAN; see *MBA,* 83) McCarter (*1 Samuel* AB, 434) places the site at modern Khirbet el-ʿAter, about 15 miles NW of Hebron.

JEFFRIES M. HAMILTON

ATHAIAH (PERSON) [Heb *ʾătāyāh*]. A Postexilic inhabitant of Jerusalem, the son of Uzziah, and a lay leader from Judah (Neh 11:4). Athaiah is described as the family head of the clan of Perez. He is identified by some scholars with Uthai (Heb *ʿwty*), who is also described as a member of the clan of Perez in a parallel list found in 1 Chronicles 9 (see v 4; Batten *Ezra and Nehemiah* ICC, 268; Brockington *Ezra, Nehemiah, Esther* NCBC, 188). However, the list in Chronicles is a considerably different recension, shaped for other purposes, or, perhaps, by other information (Myers *1 Chronicles* AB, 186). As a result, the description of subsequent generations is completely at odds with that found in Nehemiah (Schumacher *IDB* 1: 306).

FREDERICK W. SCHMIDT

ATHALIAH (PERSON) [Heb *ʿătalyāh(û)*]. Var. GOTHOLIAH. In addition to the name of an infamous queen of Judah (see 3. below), "Athaliah" was also the name of 2 men listed in the Heb Bible. The meaning of the name Athaliah is controversial, since it cannot be traced to a Heb verb root. If derived from Akk, the meaning "Yahweh has manifested his glory" (*IPN,* 191) is conceivable. Assuming an Ar root, a meaning like "Yahweh is just" (Bauer 1930: 78) is possible. J. Gray (*1 and 2 Kings* [3d ed.] OTL, 536) also supports an Ar derivation: "In view of the names *ʿaṯal* and *ʿaṯalan* from the Northern Hejaz, we suggest rather an Arabic derivation *ʿaṯala* ('to be abundant, bulky'), the name referring, perhaps, to a robust child." Given the limits of our current knowledge, the problem cannot be solved. In any case, it is likely that this Heb name represents the oldest documented use of a female (see 3. below) having a name with the theophoric component "Yahweh."

1. The son of Jeroham, and the head of one of the prominent Benjaminite families dwelling in Jerusalem (1 Chr 8:26). The name is part of a longer list of Benjaminites that appears immediately before the note suggesting that the list represents census data taken at the time of the exile (1 Chr 9:1).

2. A descendant of Elam and father of Jesaiah (Ezra 8:7). The parallel list in 1 Esdr 8:33 renders his name Gotholiah (Gk *Gotholias*). His son Jeshaiah accompanied Ezra from Babylonia to the river Ahava, and from there back to Jerusalem.

3. Israelite princess who, through marriage into the Davidic dynasty, became queen mother of Judah and briefly ruled there herself (2 Kgs 8:18 [= 2 Chr 21:6], 26 [= 2 Chr 22:2–3]; 11:1–20 [= 2 Chr 22:10–23:21]; 2 Chr 24:7). The actual dates of her reign are disputed: 845–839 B.C. (Begrich 1929); 845–840 B.C. (Jepsen and Hanhart 1964); 841–835 B.C. (Thiele 1965); 842–837 B.C. (Andersen 1969).

a. Athaliah's Parentage. The exact parentage of Athaliah is as unclear as is the meaning of her name, although her descent from the family of Omri is certain. In 2 Kgs 8:26 (= 2 Chr 22:2) she is called a "daughter of Omri." On the other hand, in 2 Kgs 8:18 (= 2 Chr 21:6) she is called "daughter of Ahab," though without reference to her proper name. The Lucianic branch of the LXX tradition has eliminated the contradiction by also reading 2 Kgs 8:26 as "Ahab" in an obvious attempt at harmonization. Josephus, too, echoes that tradition by regularly calling her "daughter of Ahab" (*Ant* 8.15.3; 9.7.1).

The problem has provoked extended discussion. To smooth out the difference, "daughter" in 2 Kgs 8:26 was often taken as "granddaughter" (i.e., of Omri). But this is just as impossible as interpreting "daughter of Omri" as "belonging to Omri's family" in some broader sense. The OT speaks often of the "house of Ahab" but never of the "house of Omri." Thus, the "daughter of Omri" should be understood in its literal sense.

The better and more numerous arguments favor the likelihood that Athaliah was a daughter of Omri and therefore a sister of Ahab. It would be difficult to reconcile her chronological data with that of Ahab if Ahab had been her father. Furthermore, the value of the two text traditions is unequal: 2 Kgs 8:26 is derived from the Judean royal annals, whereas 8:18 is a later theological judgment of the Deuteronomist redactors; thus, the older and more reliable tradition indicates that Athaliah was a daughter of Omri. The designation "daughter of Ahab" (8:18) may finally be explained as of secondary origin. (The Syr Peshitta, incidentally, reads "sister of Ahab" in its rendering of the parallel passage, 2 Chr 21:6.) "Daughter of Ahab" apparently means "member of the house of Ahab," a phrase also occurring in the same verse. The "house of Ahab" had already become a standard term for the Omridic dynasty. Thus, no textual error needs to be assumed in 2 Kgs 8:18. According to Begrich, the most likely meaning of the biblical phrase is ". . . for it is from the House of Ahab that his wife descended" (1935). It is possible that Athaliah was born shortly before Omri's death, grew up as an orphan at the court of Ahab, and could therefore be termed a "daughter of Ahab" (Katzenstein 1955). But even this speculation is unnecessary in view of the late origin of 2 Kgs 8:18. Therefore, Athaliah was the daughter of Omri and sister of Ahab.

b. Athaliah's Influence on Judah. In the course of the political alliances pursued by Omri and his son and successor Ahab, Athaliah was given in marriage to the Judean crown prince Jehoram. This political marriage, which took place during the reigns of Ahab of Israel and Jehoshaphat of Judah in the year 867 B.C. (*BHH* 1: 144), put an end to the latent hostilities and tensions which had prevailed between the two kingdoms since the death of Solomon. The price Israel paid apparently was the complete withdrawal from those territories of the tribe of Benjamin which Asa of Judah had occupied a few decades before (1 Kgs 15:16–22). On the other hand, Judah was in turn drawn into the political wake of its stronger neighbor to the N. Apparently, however, Judah resisted being lured into the battles on Syrian soil. There was no Judean contingent in the battle of Qarqar (853 B.C.) in which Ahab, together with Hadadezer of Damascus, Irḫulēni of Hamath, and other allied minor states, managed to halt the advance of the Assyrian king Shalmaneser III.

Athaliah's husband Jehoram, apparently regent for his father Jehoshaphat since 852, ruled only a short time: 847–845 (according to Jepsen). Ahaziah, Jehoram's son by Athaliah, then ascended the throne. As queen mother, Athaliah now held the exalted position of "sovereign" (Heb *gĕbîrâ*), which included an extraordinary ceremonial position, and probably also special influence on matters of state (Molin 1954; on Athaliah's role as queen mother, see Donner 1959 and Ihromi 1974). If, during his brief reign, Ahaziah joined Jehoram of Judah in the campaigns against the Arameans at Ramoth-Gilead (2 Kgs 8:28), we must assume that, already at that time, Athaliah wielded much of the power of government. Ahaziah had gone to be with the wounded Jehoram at Jezreel, was there swept up in the overthrow of the Omri dynasty, and was assassinated at Jehu's behest (2 Kgs 9:21–29). Another 42 members of David's royal family, who happened to be in the N kingdom at the time, were also murdered on Jehu's orders (10:12–14).

This monstrous carnage, and even more the slaughter of Omri's royal family (i.e., all of Athaliah's relatives) in Jezreel and Samaria, swiftly ended the alliance between Judah and Israel. The heavy bloodletting suffered by the house of David as a result of the Jehu revolution enabled Athaliah to seize absolute power in Jerusalem. Following the custom of the usurpers in the N kingdom to annihilate completely the overthrown dynasty (1 Kgs 15:29; 16:11; 2 Kgs 10:17), Athaliah had the surviving males of David's house murdered (2 Kgs 11:1 = 2 Chr 22:10). Thus, the "eternal dynasty" almost ended prematurely. Ahaziah's son Joash, however, escaped the massacre (2 Kgs 11:2–3 = 2 Chr 22:11–12).

Athaliah now ruled as absolute monarch for several years, a circumstance unprecedented in all the history of Israel and Judah until the time of the Hasmoneans. She apparently attempted to apply to Judah patterns of Omridic politics, as they had been practiced especially by Ahab in the N kingdom. Thus, it is historically probable that she erected a temple for Baal and granted certain rights to the cult of Baal in order to accommodate the traditionally Canaanite segment of the population. She found support for her rule in certain circles of the court and with the inhabitants of Jerusalem (some of whom possibly continued to be influenced by Jebusite traditions; 2 Kgs 11:20 = 2 Chr 23:21; *IDB* 1: 306). Opposition to her rule, which eventually brought about her downfall, came from the priests of the temple of Yahweh in Jerusalem, from some military circles, and from Judeans with full citizenship.

In the 7th year of her reign, Athaliah was deposed by a palace revolution (2 Kgs 11:4–20 = 2 Chr 23:1–21). The instigator of the conspiracy was Jehoiada the priest. He and the temple guards (these were "Levites," according to the Chronicler) proclaimed the youth Joash king within the temple precincts. Athaliah, who was apparently surprised by the events, had no opportunity for any countermeasures and was slain in the royal palace (2 Kgs 11:16, 20). The temple of Baal in Jerusalem was laid waste by the "people of the land," that is, by the citizenry of the province of Judah (11:18). The attempt to introduce into Judah a royal rule modeled after that of Omri came to a definitive end with Joash's accession to the throne. (See Stade 1885; Rudolph 1950; Liverani 1974; and Levin SBS, 105 for discussions of the narrative about the overthrow of Athaliah in 2 Kings 11.)

The Deuteronomistic redactors of the books of Kings attributes the religious apostacy of Jehoram (2 Kgs 8:18) and Ahaziah (8:26–27) to Athaliah's influence over them. This accusation becomes much more explicit in the work of the Chronicler, which depicts her as responsible for Ahaziah's godlessness (2 Chr 22:3). Chronicles further denigrates the image of Athaliah by a remark that is not contained in the books of Kings, noting that Athaliah allegedly let the temple in Jerusalem go to ruin while favoring the cult of Baal (2 Chr 24:7). The Chronicler uses this (historically uncertain) allegation in order to explain renovations in the temple at the time of Joash (2 Kgs 12:4–16 = 2 Chr 24:4–16).

Bibliography

Andersen, K. T. 1969. Die Chronologie der Könige von Israel und Juda. *ST* 23: 69–114.

Bauer, H. 1930. Die hebräischen Eigennamen als sprachliche Erkenntnisquelle. *ZAW* 48: 73–80.

Begrich, J. 1929. *Die Chronologie der Könige von Israel und Juda.* BHT 3. Tübingen.

———. 1935. Atalja, die Tochter Omris. *ZAW* 53: 78–79.

Donner, H. 1959. Art und Herkunft des Amtes der Königinmutter im Alten Testament. Pp. 105–45 in *Festschrift J. Friedrich.*

Ihromi, 1974. Die Königinmutter und der *ʿamm haʾarez* im Reich Juda. *VT* 24: 421–29.

Ishida, T. 1975. "The House of Ahab." *IEJ* 25: 135–37.

Jepsen, A., ed. 1979. *Von Sinuhe bis Nebukadnezar.* 3d ed. Stuttgart.

Jepsen, A. and Hanhart, R. 1964. *Untersuchungen zur israelitisch-jüdischen Chronologie.* BZAW 88. Berlin.

Katzenstein, H. J. 1955. Who Were the Parents of Athaliah? *IEJ* 5: 194–97.

Levin, C. 1982. *Der Sturz der Königin Athalja.* SBS 105. Stuttgart.

Liverani, M. 1974. L'histoire de Joas. *VT* 24: 438–53.

Molin, G. 1954. Die Stellung der *Gĕbira* im Staate Juda. *TZ* 10: 161–75.

Puech, E. 1981. Athalie, fille d'Achab, et la chronologie des rois d'Israël et de Juda. *Salman.* 28: 117–36.

Rudolph, W. 1950. Die Einheitlichkeit der Erzählung vom Sturz der Atalja (2 Kön 11). Pp. 473–78 in *Festschrift A. Bertholet.* Ed. W. Baumgartner. Tübingen.

Stade, B. 1885. Anmerkungen zu 2 Kö. 10–14. *ZAW* 5: 275–97.

Thiele, E. R. 1965. *The Mysterious Numbers of the Hebrew Kings.* Rev. ed. Grand Rapids.

WINFRIED THIEL

ATHARIM (PLACE) [Heb *hāʾătārîm*]. The name of the route the Israelites were following when they were attacked by the king of Arad (Num 21:1). The Heb word, preceded by the definite article, is obscure, and LXX[A] reads "spies" (Heb *tārîm*?). Aharoni (*LBHG*, 40, 53, 273) identifies it with the road that S of Hebron branches SE to Arad, passes Aroer and Oboda, and proceeds to Kadesh-Barnea. Although there are no LB remains, during the monarchic period a chain of Israelite forts was built along this road (Herzog 1983: map p. 42; Cohen 1985), and it is reasonable to assume that it was a significant route in even earlier periods (Aharoni et al. 1960). See also RAMAT MATRED.

Bibliography

Aharoni, Y. et al. 1960. The Ancient Desert Agriculture of the Negev. *IEJ* 10: 97–111.

Cohen, R. 1985. The Fortresses King Solomon Built to Protect His Southern Border. BARev 11: 56–70.

Herzog, Z. 1983. Enclosed Settlements in the Negeb and the Wilderness of Beersheba. *BASOR* 250: 41–49.

GARY A. HERION

ATHENOBIUS (PERSON) [Gk *Athēnobios*]. A courtier of Antiochus VII Euergetes (Sidetes) (1 Macc 15:28, 32). As Antiochus VII sought to reestablish control over the lands of the Seleucid kingdom, he sent Athenobius, who had the rank of "friend of the king," as envoy to Simon the high priest. Through Athenobius, he demanded either the return of Joppa, Gazara, and the citadel in Jerusalem (all former Seleucid holdings) or 1,000 talents of silver as restitution and tribute. Athenobius interpreted Simon's assumed position and his response as defiance to the king. Simon continued the privileges bestowed on Jonathan by Alexander Balas (1 Macc 10:88, 89) and Antiochus VI (1 Macc 11:57, 58), but not reaffirmed by Antiochus VII, although he had previously led Simon to believe they would be continued (1 Macc 15:2–9). Simon's response that Jerusalem was part of Judea's original inheritance and that Joppa and Gazara were captured only as defensive measures was not acceptable to Athenobius. Simon's counteroffer of 100 talents of silver as restitution further infuriated Athenobius. As a result of his negative report, Antiochus sent Cendebeus to invade Judea (1 Macc 15:35–16:10).

RUSSELL D. NELSON

ATHENS (PLACE) [Gk *Athēnai*]. ATHENIAN. The polis (city-state) of the Athenians which unified the peninsula of Attica at an early date, thereby creating a political entity geographically defined by sea and mountain with an area of approximately 1,000 square miles. The most prominent topographical feature of the city itself (37°59′N; 23°44′E), situated 3–5 miles inland from its harborage on the Saronic Gulf to its W, was the Acropolis, a precipitous mass of rock around which the city spread out in roughly circular fashion. Lower than the Acropolis and a short distance to the NW is the Areopagus, or Mars' Hill, where in A.D. 51 St. Paul preached his sermon on the unknown god (Acts 17:16–34). The city wall, originally built in the early 5th century B.C. with a circumference of 5–6 miles, reached its greatest extent in the 2d century A.D., when the Roman emperor Hadrian added a segment in the shape of a polygon in the W. Only the vine, the fig, and the olive could thrive in the thin soil, rocky terrain, and generally dry climate of Attica, whose chief natural resources were rich supplies of clay and building stone and the mines at Laurium, which yielded a large quantity of silver into Roman times.

A. History

1. Mycenaean and Hellenic Ages. The story of Athens can be told only in broad outline prior to the commencement of her recorded history in the 7th century B.C. The Gk-speaking invaders who ca. 2100 B.C. began moving into the Balkan peninsula and imposing their control over the earlier inhabitants were attracted to the Acropolis. Athens was both a state of secondary importance in the Mycenaean Age (ca. 1600–1200 B.C.) and a center of relative stability during the Dark Ages (ca. 1200–750 B.C.) that followed.

By the early 7th century B.C., 2 gradual political processes were complete: the unification of Attica and the transformation of monarchy into aristocracy. But the Council of the Areopagus, the governing body of nobles named after the hill where it commonly met, proved unable to resolve the social and economic crisis that afflicted Athens (along with the rest of Greece) in the 7th century; and it was probably in 594 B.C. that the aristocrat Solon was appointed archon with power to reform the entire political, judicial, and economic fabric of the polis. He refused to make himself tyrant and instituted a set of extensive but moderate reforms that pointed Athens firmly in the direction of democratic evolution. They nevertheless failed to eliminate the extreme factionalism that was debilitating the body politic, and in 540 B.C. a nobleman named Pisistratus took advantage of the situation to institute a benevolent tyranny that was to last for 30 years. When Pisistratus' son and successor Hippias was deposed in 510 B.C., the old factionalism immediately flared up, only to be extinguished once and for all by another aristocratic lawgiver, Cleisthenes. In the waning years of the 6th century, Cleisthenes enacted a series of constitutional reforms that moved Athens still further in the direction of total democracy and converted sectionalism and aristocratic rivalry into patriotism and constitutionally regulated ambition.

A stern test awaited the new democracy. During the latter half of the 6th century, the Persians had conquered Ionia (i.e., the Greek city-states of coastal Asia Minor and the nearby islands), and mainland Greece soon lay within their designs. A first move was made in 490 B.C., when King Darius sent an expeditionary force to subdue Athens. Its commander encountered the Athenians on the plain of Marathon in NE Attica, and there the Persians suffered their first major defeat at the hands of Greek hoplites. Marathon, however, gave Athens only temporary respite from the threat of Persian domination, for in 480 B.C. Xerxes, Darius' son and heir, personally led a vast army, supported by an armada of comparable size, across the Hellespont and into Greece from the N; the Athenians, whose triremes constituted half the Greek navy, evacuated Athens and joined the allied fleet in the narrows between Attica and the island of Salamis, where the Persian armada was trapped and annihilated. The next year, the allied Greeks destroyed the army Xerxes left behind after his personal departure, and the Athenians turned to restoring their ravished city.

The half century that succeeded the Persian wars witnessed the evolution of Cleisthenic democracy into the radical democracy associated with the name of Pericles, the dominant figure in Athenian public life from the early 450s until his death in 429 B.C. It also witnessed another event of momentous consequence for the future of Greece: Athens succeeded in gradually transforming the Confederacy of Delos, organized on that island in 478 B.C. by the Athenians and the Aegean Greeks for the purpose of liberating the Ionians and driving the Persians out of the Aegean, into its own maritime empire. It was this empire, and the wealth and naval supremacy it entailed, that provoked the grand conflict between Athens and Sparta known as the Peloponnesian War (431–404 B.C.). In the course of this war, Athens' strategic advantages and military successes were mitigated by a plague that reduced her population by a third, by a failure to accept peace at the appropriate time, and above all by a disastrous attempt to conquer the island of Sicily; eventually, there were no more triremes and Athens was blockaded into surrender.

Athens had inflicted mass executions and enslavements on a number of Greek states that had defied its will; and many Athenians reasonably feared that they themselves would suffer similar punishment. But the terms of peace imposed by Sparta in the spring of 404 B.C., though harsh enough for an imperial city, were much more lenient: Athens was to relinquish its empire, limit its navy to a dozen warships, and demolish a goodly portion of its fortifications. Later that year, the democracy was overthrown and the oligarchical regime notorious as the Thirty Tyrants began its bloody career; in scarcely more than a year, however, the Thirty had been deposed and the democracy restored.

Athens quickly undertook to recover what it could of its lost prestige and power, and Athenian maritime fortunes prospered to the extent that in 377 B.C. Athens was able to form a Second Athenian Confederacy. But Athens' imperialist tendencies drove its allies into revolt, and by 348 B.C. the Confederacy had disintegrated. In the meantime, a new challenge to Athenian maritime supremacy had arisen: Philip II of Macedonia, who in the 350s and 340s B.C. methodically extended his hegemony over the N Aegean littoral and into Thessaly and central Greece. The Theban and Athenian hoplites who confronted him on the plain of Chaeronea in Boeotia (338 B.C.) were unequal to the task required of them, and on that day Athens, and the other city-states of Greece, ceased to be a determining factor in the political life of the ancient world. Philip, however, was uncommonly lenient in his treatment of Athens: he refrained from invading Attica, restored without ransom the 2,000 Athenians captured in the battle, and conveyed the Athenian dead to their city under royal escort. Once more, as in 404 B.C. and as would be the case again and again, Athens had been saved by its past, notably its service to Hellas when the Persians had invaded, and by the artistic and intellectual stature it had achieved.

2. Hellenistic Age. The Hellenistic Age was ushered in by the battle of Chaeronea and by the subsequent conquests of Alexander, Philip's son and successor. As it dawned, Athens made a futile attempt to recover its independence by revolting from Macedon in 323 B.C. (at the news of Alexander's death); the following year the Macedonian regent Antipater put down the revolt, replaced the Athenian democracy with an oligarchy, and stationed a Macedonian garrison in Piraeus, the port of Athens. By 272 B.C. the grand struggle for power among Alexander's successors had ended and in its course determined that the Hellenistic world would have 3 centers of power: the kingdoms of Antigonid Macedonia, Seleucid Asia, and Ptolemaic Egypt. For mainland Greece, the age ended in 168 B.C. when the Romans deposed the last of the Antigonids and divided Macedon into 4 separate republics. During the late 4th and 3d centuries, the Athenians had to accept the presence of foreign garrisons in Piraeus and even in the city itself; and the question of whether a citizen was pro-Macedonian or nationalist in his political sympathies gradually became more significant than that of his constitutional preference.

The oligarchy set up by Antipater yielded in 317 B.C. to the rule of the Aristotelian philosopher Demetrius of Phalerum, maintained in power by Antipater's son Cassander. In 307 B.C. Demetrius the Besieger took Athens from Cassander and reinstated democracy. Proclaimed as "savior-god" by the Athenians, he and his seraglio took up residence in the Parthenon. By 276 B.C., Athens had become a more-or-less-permanent dependent of Demetrius' son Antigonus Gonatas, the philosopher king who founded the Antigonid dynasty and treated Athens as the spiritual and philosophical capital of his Macedonian sphere of authority. This privileged position did not, however, prevent Chremonides and his fellow nationalists from once again raising Athens in revolt. Despite Athens' spirited failure in the Chremonidean War (267–262 B.C.), Antigonus was typically lenient when Athens surrendered. But the revolt had exhausted the Athenian yearning for the old freedom, and for the following century and a half, Athens would be content with its role and reputation as the cultural and intellectual center of Hellas. Its reward for acquiescence and political realism came in 228 B.C., 11 years after Antigonus' death, when the Macedonians for a price of 150 talents withdrew their troops from Attic soil.

3. Athens and Rome. Athens remained at peace with the Antigonids until Philip V invaded Attica a few months before the outbreak of the Second Macedonian War (200–197 B.C.), his disastrous conflict with Rome. Athens sided with Rome, endured Philip's repeated devastation of the Athenian countryside, and rejoiced with the other Greek states when the victorious Roman general Flamininus proclaimed their freedom at the Isthmian Games of 196 B.C. Athens was again allied with Rome when the latter defeated Philip's son and heir Perseus in the Third Macedonian War (171–168 B.C.) and then converted his kingdom into republics. On this occasion (166 B.C.), Athens was rewarded more tangibly for its loyalty to Rome, and was given possession of the island of Delos, now a free port.

Athens nevertheless severed its friendship with Rome in 88 B.C., when the nationalists exerted themselves one last time and seized control of the government from the pro-Roman oligarchs. They immediately accepted an alliance with Mithridates of Pontus, who was already in the process of invading Greece and was now able to use Piraeus as his base of operations. The Roman general Sulla soon drove Mithridates out of Greece, but Athens was stubbornly defended by the nationalists and had to be taken by storm (86 B.C.). Given the ancient protocol for dealing with cities so captured, Sulla was benign in his treatment of Athens: his soldiers were allowed to loot and massacre for a while and the ringleaders of the uprising were executed, but no further punishment was exacted; with the oligarchs restored to power, the city was left in possession of its former liberty.

As Athens recovered from the devastation of the Mithridatic fiasco (the city's final attempt at political action independent of the Romans), it became more than ever a cultural center and university town, where the study of philosophy and rhetoric flourished. It became the place to which Roman senators and other wealthy foreigners sent their sons to study (and came themselves to visit and to patronize). Hellenistic kings had done so in the past and so, before long, would Roman emperors. Julius Caesar pardoned Athens for following Pompey in 49–48 B.C., as did Octavian and Antony for espousing the cause of the republican Brutus in 44–42 B.C. The favors with which Antony then courted Athens while he ruled the East came to an end only when Octavian, soon to be Augustus, defeated him at Actium in 31 B.C., ushering in the period of the Roman Empire. Although Octavian deprived Athens of the island of Aegina (which Antony had given to Athens) and imposed some economic restrictions, he did not otherwise penalize the city for supporting his rival; indeed, he even confirmed Athenian possession of Attica and 8 islands, including Salamis and Delos. Athens in fact was never incorporated into the Roman provincial system and enjoyed the privileged status of *civitas foederata,* which gave Athens judicial authority over its own citizens and exempted them from the obligation to pay taxes to Rome.

Athens lost some of its artistic treasures to Caligula and Nero, but the emperors of the 1st century otherwise treated the city with deference, and at the turn of the century (A.D. 98–117) Trajan attempted to rectify the city's fiscal disrepair, which had been initiated by Sulla's depradations and aggravated by the exactions imposed on Athens during the civil wars marking the end of the Roman republic (49–31 B.C.). But the completion of Trajan's task was left to his philhellenic successor Hadrian (A.D. 117–138), who, in the most-favored-city tradition of Antigonus Gonatas, became Athens' grandest patron ever. Hadrian engaged in a monumental building program intended to render the city worthy to be the material and spiritual seat of his Union of the Panhellenes (created for the purpose of revitalizing Greek civilization). Imperial favors continued under Hadrian's successors Antoninus Pius (A.D. 138–161), who endowed a chair of rhetoric, and Marcus Aurelius (A.D. 161–180), who added 4 chairs of philosophy and thereby transformed Athens into a true university.

The deterioration of Athens had already set in before a band of Heruli and other Goths overran Attica and pillaged the city in A.D. 268, the final year of the reign of Gallienus, another Athenian. Athens nevertheless managed to reassert itself, and even to persist as the leading center of Hellenic rhetoric and philosophy during the 2 centuries extending from the conversion of Constantine in A.D. 312 to the reign of Justinian (A.D. 527–565), when paganism, at least as a publicly practiced religion and formally studied system of thought, was gradually (and for the most part benignly) eliminated from the Roman Empire. Athens indeed fared better than other cities at the hands of Christian emperors collecting the artistic treasures of old Greece: Constantine spared Athenian shrines when he assembled art works to adorn his new capital on the Bosporus, and though Theodosius (A.D. 408–450) confiscated famous statues throughout Greece, he did not remove the chryselephantine Athena from the Parthenon. The Visigoth Alaric left the city of Athens unharmed, but the mysteries of Demeter and Core were never revived after he sacked Eleusis in A.D. 397, and at some point, perhaps not until the 6th century, the Parthenon became the Church of the Virgin Mother of God. In A.D. 529 Justinian, as part of his determined effort to eradicate the remaining traces of paganism from the empire, closed the philosophical schools of Greece and thereby officially terminated the intellectual history of classical Athens.

B. Literature and Philosophy

The extant literature of Athens begins at the turn of the 7th–6th century B.C. with the fragmentary poetry of the lawgiver Solon, in which he set forth his moral and political views. After a hiatus of a hundred years, poetic literature resumed under the aegis of the state with the dramas produced in competition at the public festivals honoring the god Dionysus. The overlapping dramatic careers of the great tragic poets (first Aeschylus and then Sophocles and Euripides) span almost exactly the 5th century: of their surviving plays (which with one exception draw their plots from Greek myth and legend), 7 each were written by Aeschylus and Sophocles and 18 (possibly 19) were written by Euripides. The sole extant representative of the Old Comedy, with its fantastic plots and contemporary references, is Aristophanes; 11 of his plays have come down to us, the first produced in 425 B.C. and the last in 388. We also possess one complete play and substantial portions of several others by Menander (died ca. 290 B.C.), the leading poet of the New Comedy—a theater of manners offering its audiences stylized plots and characters derived from daily life.

The city's extant prose, far greater in quantity than its poetry, may be described under the headings of rhetoric, history, and philosophy. Rhetoric was fostered by democracy with its attendant litigation and public discussion, and a large number of speeches on a comprehensive variety of topics has been preserved from a period extending from about the middle of the 5th to the last quarter of the 4th century B.C. Of the Alexandrian canon of ten orators, two perhaps are most worthy of mention. The first is Isocrates (436–338 B.C.), a failed public speaker but influential stylist, who opened a school of rhetoric and in a series of closet orations and open letters published his views on education, ethics, and political matters. The second is Philip II's antagonist Demosthenes (384–322 B.C.), who attacked the Macedonian king in his *Philippics* and other speeches and defended his own political career in his oration *On the Crown.* We possess a substantial historical literature by two Athenians: Thucydides (ca. 460–ca. 400 B.C.), banished for dereliction of duty as a general during the Peloponnesian War, whose monumental but unfinished account of that conflict comes to an end in 411 B.C.; and Thucydides' continuator Xenophon (ca. 428–ca. 354 B.C.), a prolific writer on a variety of historical and quasi-historical subjects whose *Hellenica* records the history of Greece from 411 to 362 B.C.

Athenian philosophy begins with Socrates, put to death in 399 B.C. after being convicted of impiety. Although he wrote nothing, the example of his moral convictions, personal courage, and dialectic methodology inspired and informed the thought of Plato (427–348 B.C.), who was as great a writer as he was philosopher, and who made Socrates the central character and spokesman of his own thought in all but a few of his (later) dialogues. After Plato, Athens produced only a single resident philosopher of permanent significance, Epicurus (341–270 B.C.), who in fact had been born and raised on the island of Samos off the coast of Asia Minor.

The Attic dialect as written by Plato and the orators would long continue to provide the dictional standard of rhetoric and learned discourse in Greece, and by the 4th century B.C. this dialect was spreading widely abroad as the Koine, in which the LXX and the NT would be composed. But by the early 3d century B.C. the literary and philosophic creativity of Athens had been spent. Even so, the influence of Plato and the Academy he founded about 385 B.C., which enjoyed a continuous existence until Justinian's edict in A.D. 529, functioned as a kind of philosophical lodestone, and the intellectual vigor and prominence of Athens was maintained by a constant and abundant influx of immigrant philosophers. The first of these was the greatest: Aristotle of Stagira (384–322 B.C.), who came to Athens at the age of 17 to study under Plato and returned in 335 B.C. to establish his own school at the Lyceum, that of the Peripatetics. Aristotle's successor as head of the school, Theophrastus (died ca. 287 B.C.), best-known in more modern times for his *Characters* (30 sketches of ridiculous character types), came from the island of Lesbos. Another such immigrant was Zeno (335–263 B.C.), who came from the island of Cyprus and was probably not even a Greek; he founded the Stoic school of philosophy and became the admired friend of Antigonus Gonatas.

The permanently altered circumstances of Athens' intellectual and political life, as well as the cosmopolitanism that characterized Hellenistic and Roman Greece, are symbolized by the composition of a political delegation the Athenians sent to Rome in 155 B.C.: its members were the heads of the Academy (Carneades of Cyrene), the Lyceum (Critolaus from Lycia), and the Stoa (Diogenes of Babylon). Foreigners continued to dominate the study of philosophy at Athens until the very end; for example, Proclus (5th century A.D.), a leading representative of the final flowering of Greek philosophy known as Neoplatonism (mid-3d to mid-6th century A.D.), was born in Lycia, even though he spent much of his life at Athens and served as head of the academy.

The study of rhetoric, that other pillar of Athens' intellectual life, was also sustained by immigrants after the 4th century B.C. But perhaps the most illustrious of this discipline's later Athenian masters was a native, the fabulously wealthy Herodes Atticus, consul at Rome in A.D. 143, one of Marcus Aurelius' teachers, and probably his city's most munificent private benefactor.

C. Antiquities

This survey of the material remains of classical Athens will take the perspective of St. Paul (who visited the city in A.D. 51), and will make reference chiefly to those monuments whose state of preservation (or modern restoration) renders them easily identifiable even today (see Fig. ATH.01). Construction dates will be given in parentheses.

If, as is virtually certain, Paul traveled by ship from Berea in Macedonia to Athens (Acts 17:10–15), the Doric-style temple of Poseidon (ca. 444 B.C.) would have come into view on the edge of the cliff as his vessel rounded Cape Sunium at the tip of Attica on its way to the port of Piraeus. After disembarking at Piraeus, Paul would have approached the city passing through the outer Ceramicus, the burial grounds (just outside the W walls) whose streets were lined with graves and cenotaphs surmounted with stone stelae, often adorned with relief sculpture (many still *in situ*). Paul would have entered the city from the NW, through either the Dipylon Gate or the adjacent Sacred Gate. The road from either would have taken him into the Athenian agora where he could have talked with passersby and engaged in discourse with Stoic and Epicurean philosophers (Acts 17:16–18). On a knoll at its W edge stood the Hephaesteum (449–444 B.C.), a Doric temple dedicated to Hephaestus and Athena with metope sculpture

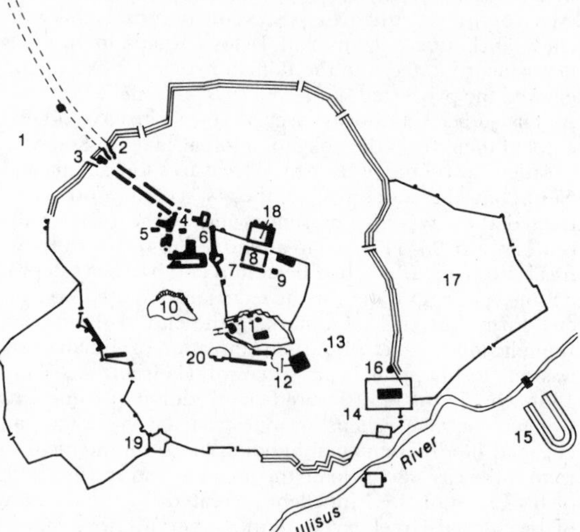

ATH.01. Map of ancient Athens. *1,* Outer Ceramicus; *2,* Dipylon Gate; *3,* Sacred Gate; *4,* Agora; *5,* Hephaesteum; *6,* Stoa of Attalus; *7,* Gate of Athena Archegetis; *8,* Roman Agora; *9,* Horologion; *10,* Areopagus (see Fig. ARE.01); *11,* Acropolis (see Fig. ATH.02); *12,* Theater of Dionysus; *13,* Monument of Lysicrates; *14,* Temple of Olympian Zeus; *15,* Stadium; *16,* Arch of Hadrian; *17,* New Athens; *18,* Library of Hadrian; *19,* Monument of Philopappus; *20,* Theater of Herodes Atticus.

depicting the exploits of Heracles and Theseus. Directly across from the Hephaesteum and running along the E side of the agora was the two-tiered Stoa of Attalus (a gift of Attalus II, king of Pergamum in Asia Minor from 159 to 138 B.C.), fully restored in 1953–56 to serve as a museum for the artifacts from the agora excavations conducted by the American School of Classical Studies at Athens.

Strolling eastward from the S end of the Stoa of Attalus, Paul would have soon reached the gate of Athena Archegetis (erected by Augustus ca. 10 B.C.), the Doric-style propylon that served as the W (and main) entrance to the Roman agora. Had he continued through the agora and exited by its E propylon, he would have observed before him and slightly to his left the Horologion or "Tower of the Winds" (built by the astronomer Andronicus of Cyrrhus shortly after 50 B.C.), a low, octagonal marble tower that functioned as a combination sundial, water clock, and weather vane.

When Paul stood on the Areopagus (Acts 17:19–22), he would have had an excellent view of the Acropolis, about 140 ft. higher and a short distance to the SE, and of the four buildings that were constructed there in the 5th century B.C. These four buildings (see Fig. ATH.02), all in Pentelic marble, sum up the achievement of democratic Athens in the fields of architecture and sculpture. An entrance ramp ascended the Acropolis by its narrow W slope and terminated at the Propylaea (437–432 B.C.), its monumental gateway incorporating an interior Ionic colonnade into a fundamentally Doric design. Atop the bastion that juts out W from the S wing of the Propylaea stood the temple of Athena Nike (427–424 B.C.), a small, graceful Ionic structure screened from the 3 edges of the bastion by a marble parapet with a frieze of Victories and seated Athenas sculpted around its outer face (ca. 410 B.C.). Surmounting the Acropolis as its largest building and rising above all other structures was the Parthenon (447–438 B.C.), a Doric-style temple dedicated to Athena Polias whose proportions and optical refinements bring to its natural Doric sturdiness the gracefulness one associates

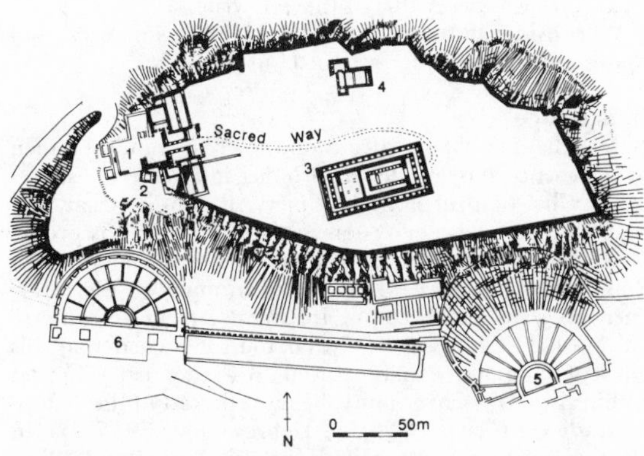

ATH.02. Plan of the Acropolis at Athens. *1,* Propylaea; *2,* Temple of Athena Nike; *3,* Parthenon; *4,* Erechtheum; *5,* Theater of Dionysus; *6,* Theater of Herodes Atticus. *(Redrawn from G. W. Botsford and C. A. Robinson, Jr.,* Hellenic History *[New York: Macmillan, 1956], 246.)*

with the Ionic order; its Doric frieze of triglyphs and sculpted metopes and the statuary of its two pediments were complemented with a continuous Ionic frieze depicting the Panathenaic procession. Near the N rim on the Acropolis, at about its midpoint, Paul would have seen an Ionic temple of unique design, the Erechtheum (421–405 B.C.), where both Athena and Poseidon were worshiped; constructed on two levels, it has a lower N porch looking out toward the Roman agora; on its S (Parthenon) side at the higher level is the small, exquisite porch of the Caryatids, columns sculpted in the form of maidens.

Cut into the steeply rising SE slope of the Acropolis was the theater of Dionysus. Built mostly of wood during the golden era of Athenian drama, it was finally reconstructed with stone in the latter half of the 4th century B.C. and continued to receive modifications throughout antiquity. The space between the upmost level of seats and the Acropolis wall was lined with monuments erected by victorious *choregi,* the wealthy sponsors of the choral and dramatic competitions, to support the tripods they had been awarded as their emblem of victory. The Street of the Tripods, a short distance E of the Acropolis, was similarly lined. There the monument of Lysicrates (334 B.C.) is still *in situ*; it is a splendid structure of fine marble with 6 Corinthian columns describing its cylindrical form, and is the only choregic monument to have survived almost completely intact.

Had Paul journeyed SE as far as the city wall, one monument above all others would have impressed itself on his vision; the unfinished Temple of Olympian Zeus, 16 of whose grand columns remain *in situ* (all but one still standing). Begun in the 6th century by the tyrant Pisistratus as a Doric temple in poros, it was brought to half-completion in 174–165 B.C. as a Corinthian-style marble temple by Antiochus Epiphanes, king of Syria. Beyond the city gates in the SE and on the far bank of the Ilissus lay the stadium; built ca. 330 B.C. for the Panathenaic games and frequently modified and put to other uses in subsequent antiquity. It was fully reconstructed at the turn of the last century and in 1896 was the inaugural site of the modern Olympic Games.

The task of completing the Temple of Olympian Zeus fell to the emperor Hadrian (A.D. 117–38), who also adorned Athens with such additional monuments as the arch and the library which both bear his name. The former, located immediately N of the Temple, is a double-tiered edifice done in the Corinthian manner that functioned as a dividing gateway between old Athens and Hadrian's New Athens. The latter was built just across a major thoroughfare from the N side of the Roman agora; a variety of marbles were prominently displayed in its construction.

Finally, two other post-Pauline monuments require notice, each associated with an illustrious citizen and great private benefactor of Athens. The first is the monument of Philopappus (A.D. 114–16), the remains of which still rise 40 feet above the summit of the Hill of the Muses at what had been the SW corner of the ancient city (before Hadrian's extension of the city walls in the W). Adorned with an elaborate arrangement of columns and statuary, it was erected by the Athenians as a burial vault for Antiochus Philopappus, an exiled prince of Commagene who settled in Athens and became a Roman consul. The second is the Roman-style theater located just off the SW corner of the Acropolis and donated by Herodes Atticus in honor of his wife (d. A.D. 160). It is the last of the grand monuments of Athens still represented by substantial remains, and in recent years it has been restored to regular usage for musical and dramatic performances.

Bibliography

Andrewes, A. 1956. *The Greek Tyrants*. New York.
Bury, J. B., and Meiggs, R. 1975. *A History of Greece*. New York.
Easterling, P. E., and Knox, B. M. W., ed. 1985. *The Cambridge History of Classical Literature*. Vol. 1. Cambridge.
Gomme, A. W., et al. 1945–81. *Historical Commentary on Thucydides*. 5 vols. Oxford.
Guthrie, W. K. C. 1967–81. *A History of Greek Philosophy*. 6 vols. Cambridge.
Hammond, N. G. L. 1986. *A History of Greece*. Oxford.
Hignett, C. 1952. *A History of the Athenian Constitution*. Oxford.
Hill, I. T. 1953. *The Ancient City of Athens*. London.
Jones, A. H. M. 1957. *Athenian Democracy*. Baltimore.
Meiggs, R. 1972. *The Athenian Empire*. Oxford.
Meiggs, R., and Lewis, D., ed. 1969. *A Selection of Greek Historical Inscriptions*. Oxford.
Merrit, B. D., et al. 1939–53. *The Athenian Tribute Lists*. 4 vols. Cambridge, MA.
Rose, H. J. 1960. *A Handbook of Greek Literature*. New York.
Rostovtzeff, M. 1953. *Social and Economic History of the Hellenistic World*. 3 vols. Oxford.
Tarn, W. W., and Griffith, G. T. 1952. *Hellenistic Civilization*. London.
Travlos, J. 1971. *Pictorial Dictionary of Ancient Athens*. New York and Washington.
Wallbank, F. W. 1981. *The Hellenistic World*. Cambridge, MA.

HUBERT M. MARTIN, JR.

ATHLAI (PERSON) [Heb *ʿatlāy*]. A descendant of Bebai and one of the returned exiles who was required to divorce his foreign wife (Ezra 10:28). Athlai is a shortened form of Athaliah—"Yahweh has revealed his loftiness" (*IPN*, 191). In the parallel text of 1 Esdr 9:29, the name Emathis appears in the position Athlai holds in Ezra 10:28. Athlai was a member of a family from which groups of exiles returned with Zerubbabel (Ezra 2:11; Neh 7:16) and later with Ezra (Ezra 8:11). For further discussion, see BEDEIAH.

JEFFREY A. FAGER

ATONEMENT IN THE NT. In discussions about the NT, "the Atonement" is generally understood to refer to the work of Jesus in putting right the human situation in relation to God. Throughout the course of Christian history this has been associated above all with the death of Jesus. Such a view can claim considerable support from the NT (cf. 1 Cor 15:3; Col 1:22; 1 Pet 2:24). However, it should also be noted that the saving work of Christ is just as often associated with the resurrection (cf. 1 Cor 15:17; 1 Pet 1:3; see especially Hooker 1978 in relation to Paul). One should therefore be wary of restricting NT views about the atoning work of Christ to discussions of the meaning of Jesus' death alone.

A. Introduction

One notable feature of NT ideas about the atonement is their variety. Not only are differences found between NT writers but even the same writer can use what appears at times to be a bewildering variety of models and images to describe how the life, death, and resurrection of Jesus have changed the human situation. Sometimes too a writer can combine different images within a single sentence (cf. John 1:29 discussed below). Further, the NT is "more concerned with the nature of salvation than the precise way in which it has been achieved" (Marshall 1974: 169). Thus it would probably be wrong to press any one image too far and claim that this represents the central NT view.

The variety of different descriptions of the atonement is due in part to the variety of ways in which the human situation itself is described. Very different models and categories are used to describe the "lost" condition of the human race prior to Christ, and the corresponding change brought about by the Christ event. Different descriptions of the human situation inevitably lead to different explanations of how this has been altered by the work of Christ. Thus if the human condition is described in terms of (individual) sins, the atonement can be naturally conceived as a sacrifice which deals with sins. If the human situation is described in terms of being under hostile powers, the atonement can be described as a rescue from, or a victory over, those powers. If the human situation is seen as one of ignorance, the atonement can be seen as enlightenment or revelation. Subsequent Christian theology has often fastened on to some of these models of atonement and absolutized one (or more) of them. However, such a restricted view is never that of the NT writers.

We consider in turn some of the various categories used to describe the atoning work of Jesus in the NT.

B. Sacrifice

The claim that Jesus' death on the cross should be seen as a sacrifice has exerted enormous influence on subsequent Christian theology and piety. It is quite clear that such language has deep roots in the NT itself. It is probably reflected in references to Jesus' death as "blood" (e.g., Rom 5:9; cf. Dunn 1974: 133) and in many of the references to Jesus' death being "for many/our sins/us/others" (cf. Mark 14:24; 1 Cor 15:3). Further, it is clear that this kind of language can be traced to a very early period within primitive Christianity, being reflected in the synoptic tradition (Mark 14:24), in Hebrews (cf. 2:9; 7:27), in what are probably pre-Pauline formulations (Rom 3:25f.; 1 Cor 15:3), as well as in the Johannine tradition (cf. John 1:29; 11:50). Moreover, such language is frequently related to an analysis of the human situation in terms of sinfulness: Jesus' sacrificial death enables the sins of the world to be forgiven. Indeed for many contemporary Christians, such an idea is regarded as *the* model of the atonement.

The use of such ideas applied to Jesus' death is not surprising, given the widespread use of sacrifice in the ancient world. However, the precise background of the application of such ideas to the death of Jesus is much debated. Despite the existence of the sacrificial cult in Judaism, it is recognized that the use of sacrificial language to apply to the death of a *person* is rather harder to parallel in pre-Christian Jewish tradition. The idea of people "dying for *(hyper)*" others can be paralleled extensively in non-Jewish Greek thought (see Williams 1975; Hengel 1981: 1–32). Such an idea is less easy to find in Judaism. It appears to surface in the text of 4 Maccabees, which may be extensively influenced by Hellenistic thought (see Williams); it is also present in the famous Suffering Servant passage of Isa 52:13–53:12, and also in later rabbinic traditions about the atoning value of the death of the righteous (though it is not certain how far these ideas would have been current prior to 70 C.E.; see Williams 1975: 121–35).

One must however be wary of making sacrificial language too monochrome. The sacrificial cult within Judaism and elsewhere was very varied and included provision for many different kinds of sacrifice (see Young 1979: 35–70). Some (but *not* all) sacrifices were to do with sins. In the Jewish cult these were the "sin-offerings." But there were also thank-offerings, offered by the worshipper to God in grateful thanks, but with no explicit idea of atoning for sins. Judaism knew of other kinds of sacrifice as well: there was the Passover sacrifice, commemorating God's great act of liberation of Israel at the Exodus; there was also the sacrifice which accompanied the ritual of the making of the covenant. Neither of these had anything to do with sin directly. Thus one should not necessarily subsume every reference to Jesus' death as a sacrifice under the category of a sin-offering.

The rationale of the Jewish sacrificial system has been much discussed, though with no very conclusive results. Judaism provided no explicit rationale for sacrifice: it was simply the God-given way of dealing with sin, and as such was to be accepted gratefully and humbly. Much discussion has also taken place over whether Jewish sacrifice, and/or Christian interpretations of Jesus' death as a sacrifice, should be regarded as "propitiatory" (i.e., averting the anger of a personal deity) or "expiatory" (i.e., nullifying the effects of sin). The idea of appeasing an angry god by sacrifice is certainly present in some non-Jewish ideas of sacrifice. Much hinges on the translation of the word *hilaskesthai* (and cognates) in the NT, and the equivalent OT words (usually *kpr*). In non-Jewish Gk, the word clearly carries ideas of propitiation. However, in a classic essay Dodd (1935: 82–95) argued that Jewish and Christian usage differs from that decisively. Here, almost uniformly, the words are used in such a way that God (or His representative) is always the subject, not the object of the action in question; the object is always sin or its effects. This then demands an interpretation of expiation, not propitiation, since God can scarcely be said to propitiate himself in any very meaningful sense. Dodd's arguments have convinced many that the NT does not think of Jesus' death as appeasing God's anger; rather, God, through Jesus, deals with and nullifies sin and its effects. (Cf. Young 1975: 72 and many others; for the contrary view, see Morris 1955: 125–85; Hill 1967: 23–48.)

The precise way in which an expiatory sacrifice was thought to "work" is never clarified. It has been maintained by some that an element of substitution was always understood and that the sacrificial victim was thought of as enduring the (divine) punishment for the sin committed, thus enabling the sinner to go free. Such a model has of course exerted considerable influence on popular Christian piety as an interpretation of Jesus' atoning death.

This probably reads too much into the rationale of the sacrificial system. It is in fact very unlikely that the sacrificial victim was ever thought of as a substitute in this way. Such a rationale *might* lie behind the ceremony of the Day of Atonement, when the priest laid hands on one of the goats, thereby transferring the sins to the goat (Lev 16:21). However, this goat was not sacrificed: the goat on whom the sins were "laid" was the scapegoat which was driven away into the desert, and it was the other goat which was offered in sacrifice. In fact it was considered vitally important that the sacrificial victim should be *pure* (see Young 1979: 52). Thus it is unlikely that the sacrificial system was ever conceived of in such a substitutionary sense.

Substitutionary ideas have been thought to lie behind much of Paul's language, though many would argue that "representation" rather than "substitution" does far more justice to Paul's thought. (See Hooker [1971 and 1978]. Dunn [1974] argues that this is inherent in the rationale of sacrifice itself, though this probably reads too much into the texts.) Jesus' death is seen as the point at which Jesus joins humanity at its point of final annihilation and lostness; however, through the resurrection, Jesus overcomes death and becomes the source of new life for all who are "in" him. Such a model is well summed up by Irenaeus' summary statement "he became what we are so that we might become what he is." Jesus' life, death, and resurrection are thus "vicarious" in the sense of achieving something for others by taking their place; but it is not "substitutionary" in the sense that Jesus takes the place of human sinners whilst they go free (or elsewhere): human beings are summoned to *join* Jesus.

The importance of other sacrificial language in Paul is debated. Certainly Paul uses a variety of metaphors. Jesus' death can be seen variously as a new Passover sacrifice (1 Cor 5:7), a new covenant sacrifice (1 Cor 11:25), perhaps as a sin-offering (Rom 8:3, though the precise interpretation is disputed), perhaps as the sin-offering of the Day of Atonement (cf. *hilastērion* in Rom 3:25: again the precise reference is disputed, but see Stuhlmacher 1986: 94–109). Some have argued that all such language is pre-Pauline, and that Paul's "real" thought is to be located elsewhere (cf. *BTNT,* 295–306; Käsemann 1971: 39–46). Certainly the importance of the solidarity of Jesus and the Christian is of vital importance for Paul (so Bultmann, cf. also the previous paragraph, though whether such an idea is due to the adoption of Gnostic categories [so Bultmann also] is more debatable). Also the importance of the cross as showing the radical lostness of human beings who cannot save themselves (so Käsemann) is fundamental for Paul (cf.

Romans 1–3). Nevertheless one should perhaps be wary of dismissing sacrificial categories as of no concern to Paul simply because they are taken over from tradition. Paul's use of his tradition presumably implies a measure of agreement with it, and one should perhaps accept a rich variety in Paul's interpretation of the atonement.

Sacrificial language dominates in the exposition of the author of Hebrews. In particular, the writer sees Jesus' death in terms of the great sacrifice of the Jewish Day of Atonement. (See especially Hebrews 9–10.) Here, in a highly suggestive use of imagery, the author sees the Jewish rite fulfilled in Jesus' death whereby Jesus is both the priest and the sacrificial victim so that he offers himself. It is perhaps worth noting, however, that the author does not use this language simply to explain the atonement. Rather, he uses it primarily to show that the whole of the old Jewish sacrificial cult has now been superseded. This then forms a crucial part of the writer's exhortation to his readers not to lapse back into Judaism. The writer never gives any rationale of the sacrificial system: he simply assumes without question that "without the shedding of blood there is no forgiveness" (Heb 9:22; cf. Taylor 1945: 125). As far as the author is concerned, the only question is whether "blood" still needs to be sacrificed or not. Alongside this idea, the writer of Hebrews also develops the idea that Jesus' death inaugurates the new covenant, and hence Jesus' death is to be seen as a covenant sacrifice (cf. Heb 7:22; 8:6; 9:15; and see Young 1979: 149). Again, however, the main point of the discussion is to show that the old covenant has now become outmoded. Thus the whole argument of Hebrews, which is so clearly indebted to sacrificial categories, ends up by being almost antisacrificial in its insistence on the finality of Christ's saving work.

Sacrificial language is also to be found in John, though the highly allusive way in which John writes sometimes makes it difficult to determine his precise meaning. However, it is probable that the words of John the Baptist in John 1:29 ("Behold the Lamb of God") refer to Jesus as the Paschal lamb. This would tie in with the fact that Jesus' death in John coincides with the slaughtering of the Paschal lambs (cf. John 19:14); further, the fact that none of Jesus' bones is broken "fulfills" scripture, and the scripture in question is probably the instruction about the way in which the Passover lambs are to be killed (John 19:36 cf. Exod 12:46). However, the further words of John the Baptist (". . . who takes away the sin of the world") may be introducing quite different sacrificial ideas, since the Passover sacrifice was generally not thought of as expiatory.

The extent to which sacrificial ideas can be traced back to Jesus himself is debated. Many have claimed that Jesus did foresee, and interpret, his own death in terms of a sacrifice for sin, with reference to the prophecy of Deutero-Isaiah about the Suffering Servant. Prime evidence for this would be the two synoptic sayings in Mark 10:45; 14:24. (See, with varying nuances, Taylor 1937; Jeremias 1966: 225–31; Hengel 1981: 65–75; Stuhlmacher 1986: 16–29.) However, the theory that Isaiah 53 was fundamental for Jesus is radically questioned today (see Hooker 1959). The language of Mark 14:24 is more closely connected with the idea of the (new) covenant than with that of expiatory sacrifice. The thought may be as much to do with the establishment of a new (covenant) community as with the forgiveness of sins by a sacrifice. The language of Mark 10:45 is also difficult to relate directly to Isaiah 53. The "ransom" *(lytron)* of Mark 10:45 is not really the equivalent of the Servant's death seen as an *ʾašam* (sin-offering) since the two ideas are quite different (see Barrett 1959; Hooker 1959: 74–79). In any case it is not certain how justified it is to trace these sayings back to the pre-Easter Jesus, and, for example, many would regard the ransom saying in Mark 10:45b as a post-Easter gloss on what may well have been a dominical saying about the importance of serving in Mark 10:45a (cf. Luke 22:27). (Cf. Lohse 1963: 117–22; Williams 1975: 211–12.) However, the category of "ransom" *(lytron)* in Mark 10:45 leads on to the next major category discussed here.

C. Redemption

The language of "redemption" *(apolytrōsis)* would have had a rich background for any 1st-century audience. Slaves could be "redeemed" by paying a suitable ransom price; so too could prisoners of war. The association of this language with freeing slaves made it natural for Jews to use the vocabulary of redemption to refer above all to the great act of liberation by God in rescuing the Israelites from slavery in Egypt (cf. Deut 7:8 and elsewhere). Although the redemption of slaves or prisoners in the secular realm always involved the payment of a ransom price *(lytron),* it is very doubtful if Jews ever thought in such concrete terms in speaking of God's action at the Exodus as a redemption. Rather, God's "redeeming" of Israel simply referred to His rescue, with no idea of a price being paid. (See Hill 1967: 49–81 contra Morris 1955: 9–59.)

NT writers used this language freely, bringing out different aspects of the imagery evoked. Thus texts such as Luke 24:21 simply refer to God's hoped-for intervention in the future in bringing liberation. The same is probably true in Rom 8:23.

Whether NT writers ever conceived of Jesus' death as a "ransom price," a price that had to be paid to secure the release of humanity, is more uncertain. This idea became extremely popular in patristic thought with great discussions about whom the price was paid to (God? or the Devil?) and the nature of the transaction involved. It is however difficult to find such ideas in the NT itself (though see Marshall 1974 for a different view). Texts like Eph 1:7 ("redemption through his blood") and 1 Pet 1:18–19 ("you were redeemed . . . with the precious blood of Christ") can scarcely be made to support the theory of Jesus' death as a ransom price paid, since both texts do not use the Gk construction of a genitive of price. Both are using the language of redemption more generally to claim that the liberation which the Christian can now enjoy has been achieved by means of Jesus' death, without spelling out the means more precisely (see Hill 1967: 70–74).

The related language of Paul, "you were bought with a price" (1 Cor 6:20; 7:23), should also probably not be pressed too far. Paul is simply using the language of the slave market to stress the fact that Christians have now changed their allegiance: they are no longer under their old master (sin or whatever); they are now under a new master in God. The precise nature of the price is not discussed. Similarly Paul's language of Jesus "redeeming" those under the curse of the Law by becoming a curse for us (Gal 3:13; 4:5) can only with difficulty support the view that Jesus' death is being interpreted as a ransom price paid in a substitutionary sense. Far more important for Paul here seems to be the representative nature of Jesus' death (see Hooker 1971). Jesus' becoming a curse for humanity involves his joining humanity; his life of obedience to death, and his vindication by God in the resurrection, annuls the curse of the Law and enables the new life of freedom to be available to all who are "in" him (cf. Gal 3:14). Again, the language of "redeeming" is probably being used in general terms to indicate the liberation (here from the Law) achieved by Jesus, but without pressing the analogy of secular redemption any further to think in terms of specific ransom prices.

The nearest one gets to an idea of a price being paid is in Mark 10:45, where Jesus' death is said to be a *lytron anti pollon,* "a ransom for many." The use of *anti* ("in place of," "for"), if pressed, does suggest ideas of substitution and equivalence, and the ransom idea in *lytron* could be said to reinforce this. However, one should not read too much into this. There is for example no talk of "sin" here and one should not necessarily interpret the verse as implying a view of Jesus' death as an expiatory sacrifice for sin with a substitutionary idea of sacrifice implied. This probably confuses categories unnecessarily. There is a close parallel to the ideas concerned in *4 Macc* 17:22 (see Williams). However, it is as likely that the *lytron* vocabulary is intended to evoke the language of the great act of redemption in the OT whereby Yahweh redeemed the Israelites from Egypt and established them as the chosen nation. The communal, even covenantal, overtones of the language may be just as important as any ideas of precise equivalents in ransom prices paid (see Hooker 1959: 77–78).

D. Victory over Evil Powers

The language of redemption, when used against an OT background, can very easily slide into a rather different model to describe the atonement: that of victory. Yahweh's action on behalf of Israel constituted not only a setting free of the nation, but also a victory over the forces of Pharaoh. This idea of victory is certainly applied to the death of Jesus in the NT. The language assumes a somewhat dualistic view of the universe, with other spiritual powers holding sway over the human race. Jesus' death is then seen as a victory over these powers. Aulen (1931) has shown how influential this view of the atonement was in patristic thought and how it has dropped out of later theological reflection. The *locus classicus* for this view is Col 2:14–15 and it is implied in many other NT passages. Paul sometimes speaks of various other spiritual powers being now subject to Christ (1 Cor 15:24–25; Phil 2:10; Rom 8:35–38); indeed much of Paul's language about the overthrow of the power of sin could be classified in this category, since frequently Paul appears to conceive of sin as a malignant power (cf. Rom 7:7–11) rather than a series of human wrongdoings (cf. also Käsemann 1971: 44).

Elsewhere in the NT, the powers opposed to God are conceived as concentrated in a single Devil figure and Jesus' death is interpreted as the final overthrow of Satan (Heb 2:14; John 12:31; 1 John 3:8; Rev 12:7–12). As with the other categories considered, the precise details of the image are never worked out. It is never stated just how the Devil and/or other powers are defeated by Jesus' life, death, and resurrection. Col 2:14–15 uses the striking imagery of a military victory parade with the disarmed powers actually nailed to the cross. The Johannine tradition appears to be based on a forensic model: Satan's overthrow is his final condemnation in, and eviction from, the divine law court (cf. John 16:11; Revelation 12). All the NT talk of the resurrection as the victory over the powers of death and enabling the Christian to share the consequences of that victory (cf. 1 Cor 15:57) may also be included in this category.

E. Reconciliation

All the categories discussed so far could be considered slightly "impersonal" (God dealing with sin, or achieving victory over other powers, almost *extra nos,* "apart from us"). It is worth recalling that the NT can refer to the work of Christ in a much more personal way, with the language of reconciliation. This language is not common in the NT, being confined to the Pauline tradition. Where sacrificial language conceives of the human situation in terms of sinfulness, reconciliation language thinks in terms of personal relationships, severed and restored. It is also striking that Paul is evidently not bound by any one language of atonement in that he can describe the effects of Jesus' death in heavily cultic and forensic language in Rom 5:8–9, only to follow with a parallel statement in Rom 5:10 using the quite different categories of personal relationships, an initial state of "enmity" being ended by God's act of "reconciliation." This language is developed further in the deutero-Pauline tradition where Col 1:20 speaks of the reconciliation of the whole universe through the cross, and Eph 2:14–16 speaks of the reconciliation of the Jewish and Gentile nations.

F. Revelation

Mention must finally be made of the view that Christ's work is primarily revelatory, both of God and of humanity. This is most characteristic of the 4th gospel. While other models of the atonement relate to human need described in terms of sin, guilt, slavery, or enmity, this model can be thought of in terms of humanity as ignorant or in (mental) darkness. Thus the dominant theme is of Jesus as the one who brings light and knowledge and who reveals the true nature of God. The thought of John is heavily influenced by this idea. The coming of Jesus reveals the glory of God (John 1:14) and Jesus as the only begotten Son is uniquely in a position to be able to "explain" or "make known" God (1:18). Jesus comes as the Light of the world, not to judge the world, for the light simply shows up human beings for what they are (cf. 3:16–21). Similarly the Johannine Jesus can speak of "knowing" as the all-important thing for the disciples (17:3). Much of Jesus' talk about the cross in John is in this vein. The crucifixion is the great "hour" which stands over the whole of the ministry of Jesus. It is the moment when the Son of Man will be lifted up, both physically on a cross, and in glory, so that the cross is the moment at which the full glory of God is revealed (17:1). The cross is thus supremely the moment of revelation.

Such a scheme is characteristically Johannine, but it has close affinities with Mark's presentation as well. In Mark the cross is the moment at which Jesus' true identity is finally and definitively revealed to human beings as that of God's Son (Mark 15:39).

Much of this language in John has affinities with Gnostic thought, although it must be said that John is no Gnostic. *Gnosis* ("knowledge") does not occur in John (perhaps deliberately); and the "knowing" which constitutes eternal life (cf. 17:3) is not the knowing about one's origins, etc., which is so characteristic of Gnostic thought. John's "knowing" is much closer to the biblical idea of "knowledge" as signifying close personal relationships (cf. Hos 6:3; 13:5). Still the idea of Jesus' work as above all revealing the full character of God is an important aspect of NT beliefs about what the life, death, and resurrection of Jesus have achieved.

G. Conclusion

NT views about the atoning work of Christ are many and varied. NT writers use a wide variety of models and images to express their beliefs. Perhaps the very variety itself is indicative of the fact that theories about the atonement were probably of second-order importance. What was primary was the experience of forgiveness and new life which the first Christians claimed to enjoy. NT writers were unanimous in believing that this was the work of God Himself acting in and through the life, death, and resurrection of Jesus. In attempting to describe precisely how this had been achieved, the NT used a variety of ideas based on contemporary models in the 1st century thought world. However, common to all these articulations was the claim that what had happened was of universal significance and was the work of God Himself, acting in love. Any contemporary view of the atonement must take this with all seriousness if it is to be true to the NT.

Bibliography

Aulen, G. 1931. *Christus Victor.* Trans. A. G. Herbert. London.

Barrett, C. K. 1959. The Background of Mark 10:45. Pp. 1–18 in *New Testament Essays,* ed. A. J. B. Higgins. Manchester.

Dodd, C. H. 1935. *The Bible and the Greeks.* London.

Dunn, J. D. G. 1974. Paul's Understanding of the Death of Jesus. Pp. 125–41 in *Reconciliation and Hope. (Festschrift for L. Morris).* Grand Rapids.

Hengel, M. 1981. *The Atonement.* Trans. J. Bowden. London.

Hill, D. 1967. *Greek Words and Hebrew Meanings.* Cambridge.

Hooker, M. D. 1959. *Jesus and the Servant.* London.

———. 1971. Interchange in Christ. *JTS* 22: 349–61.

———. 1978. Interchange and Atonement. *BJRL* 60: 462–81.

Jeremias, J. 1966. *The Eucharistic Words of Jesus.* Trans. N. Perrin. London.

Käsemann, E. 1971. The Saving Significance of the Death of Jesus in Paul. Pp. 32–59 in *Perspectives on Paul.* Trans. M. Kohl. London.

Lohse, E. 1963. *Märtyrer und Gottesknecht.* Göttingen.

Marshall, I. H. 1974. The Development of the Concept of Redemption in the New Testament. Pp. 153–69 in *Reconciliation and Hope. (Festschrift for L. Morris).* Grand Rapids.

Morris, L. 1955. *The Apostolic Preaching of the Cross.* London.

Stuhlmacher, P. 1986. *Reconciliation, Law & Righteousness. Essays in Biblical Theology.* Trans. E. R. Kalin. Philadelphia.

Taylor, V. 1937. *Jesus and His Sacrifice.* London.

———. 1945. *The Atonement in New Testament Teaching.* London.

Williams, S. K. 1975. *Jesus' Death as Saving Event.* HDR 2. Missoula, MT.

Young, F. 1975. *Sacrifice and the Death of Christ.* London.

———. 1979. *The Use of Sacrificial Ideas in Greek Christian Writers from the New Testament to John Chrysostom.* Philadelphia.

C. M. Tuckett

ATONEMENT, DAY OF. See DAY OF ATONEMENT.

ATROTH-BETH-JOAB (PLACE) [Heb *ʿaṭrôt bêt yôʾāb*]. A town in Judah, near Bethlehem, listed in the geneology of Hur (a descendant of Judah) through his son Salma (1 Chr 2:54). Some scholars, rather than accepting Atroth-beth-joab as a place name, choose to translate it "Crowns of the house of Joab," from *ʿăṭārâ,* one of the Hebrew words for crown. They assume this phrase either modifies Bethlehem and Netophath (*ISBE* 1: 349) or refers to a separate town in Judah (Odelain and Séguineau 1981: 46). The LXX transliterates the phrase in question as a place name, *Atarōth oikou Iōab.* While not specifically identifying Atroth-beth-joab, other scholars assume it was located between the 2 towns that surround it in the list: Netophah (tentatively identified as modern Kh. Bedd Fālûḥ, M.R. 171119), which is SE of Bethlehem; and Manahath (modern el-Mâlḥah, M.R. 167128), which is NW of Bethlehem (*LBHG,* 245). If the town was in this area it would have been on the edge of the Judean wilderness. This placement allowed Kallai (*EncMiqr* 6: 168) to propose a connection between this town and Joab, the head of David's army, who was buried in his house in the wilderness (1 Kgs 1:34), a house earlier identified as his inheritance (2 Sam 15:30).

Bibliography

Odelain, O., and Séguineau, R. 1981. *Dictionary of Proper Names and Places in the Bible.* Trans. and adapt. M. J. O'Connell. Garden City, NY.

Susan E. McGarry

ATROTH-SHOPHAN (PLACE) [Heb *ʿaṭrōt šôpān*]. One of several towns built by the descendants of Gad in the Transjordan from territory given them by Moses (Num 32:35). The exact location is unknown (Noth *Numbers* OTL), and scholarly attempts to locate the site are based primarily on textual or topographical evidence. The element *ʿaṭrōt* is lacking from LXX, and the Vg adds *et* ("and") between *ʿăṭrōt* and *šôpān,* thus making 2 place names. In addition, *šôpān* has a variant in both the Samaritan Pentateuch *(špym)* and in the LXX *(sōphar).* This suggests some connection between *ʿaṭrōt* and *ʿăṭārōt* of the previous verse (Num 32:34) since the latter site is specifically mentioned in the Moabite Stone (line 10) as a Gadite city in Moab reconquered by Mesha (see ATAROTH). However, many scholars seem to follow Tristram (1873: 290) who sees the same name repeated for sites barely 2 miles apart, identifying Atroth-Shophan with Jebel (Rujm) ʿAttarus, ca. 2 miles NE of Ataroth, and Ataroth with Khirbet ʿAttarus, ca. 8 miles NW of Dibon. Yet, there are those, like LaSor

(*ISBE* 1: 363), who reject the identification of Atroth-Shophan with either Khirbet or Rujm ᶜAttarus.

Bibliography

Tristram, H. B. 1873. *The Land of Moab.* New York.

C. Gilbert Romero

ATTAI (PERSON) [Heb *ᶜattay*]. The name of 3 individuals in the Hebrew Bible.

1. Mentioned in the genealogy of Jerahmeel in the Hezron clan of the tribe of Judah, he was the son of one of Sheshan's daughters and his Egyptian servant Jarha (1 Chr 2:35–36). Attai in turn fathered a son named Nathan. The Chronicler provides a linear genealogy for 12 further generations down to Elishama, possibly due to the anomaly of his Egyptian ancestry.

2. One of the brave and skillful warriors from the tribe of Gad who joined David prior to his becoming king (1 Chr 12:12—Eng 12:11). By reporting a contingent from Gad, one of the more northern and Transjordan tribes, the Chronicler emphasizes the breadth of support for David.

3. The second son of King Rehoboam by his favored wife Maacah (2 Chr 11:20); the grandson of Solomon. Large families are often used as a measure of divine blessing in Chronicles (2 Chr 11:18–23). The Chronicler includes the note regarding Rehoboam's favoritism toward Maacah as a way of explaining why Rehoboam's eldest son did not attain the throne (cf. 2 Chr 21:3). (For further discussion, see Dillard *2 Chronicles* WBC, 98–99.)

Raymond B. Dillard

ATTALIA (PLACE) [Gk *Attaleia*]. **1.** A city of N Lydia near Thyatira formerly called Agoira.

2. Modern Antalya (Adalia), a city on the coast of Pamphilia in S Asia Minor, modern Turkey, near the mouth of the Catarrhactes (Aksu) river (36°50′N; 30°46′E). Paul accompanied by Barnabas left from this port as he returned to Antioch at the completion of his first missionary journey (Acts 14:25), and he probably landed here when he traveled from Paphos to Perga (Acts 13:13) since the latter is landlocked.

Attalia was founded by Attalus II Philadelphus of Pergamum (159–138 B.C.), hence the name, and it became the chief port of Pamphilia. The city was built on a limestone plateau rising about 37 meters above the Catarrhactes River basin near where it empties into the Mediterranean Sea. The city served as the harbor for Perga, the capital of the province. Today the river has dissipated due to local irrigation procedures. The Romans gained control of the region in 79 B.C. when P. Servilius Isauricus fined the territories of the city as a penalty for their alliance with the pirate Zenicetes. The area was later employed by Augustus for the settling of veterans. It did not become a colony, however, until the 3d century A.D. During the Christian era the city was under the ecclesiastical jurisdiction of Perga until it declined in power and Attalia was declared a metropolis in A.D. 1084.

Attalia has substantial archaeological remains. The ruins of the walls and towers of the outer harbor, originally closed by means of a chain, are still visible. The city was enclosed by a double wall encircled by a moat, and portions of the Hellenistic defensive wall can be seen in this wall of the medieval period. A triple arch built by Hadrian still remains as the most imposing structure of antiquity in the region. See Jones 1971: 130–47.

Bibliography

Jones, A. H. M. 1971. *The Cities of the Eastern Roman Provinces,* 2d ed. Oxford.
Lanckoronski, K. 1890. *Stadte Pamphylien und Pisidiens.* Vienna.

John D. Wineland

ATTALUS (PERSON) [Gk *Attalos*]. Attalus II, king of Pergamum (159–138 B.C.), son of Attalus I and brother of Eumenes II (1 Macc 15:22). He appears in a list of recipients of the letter sent by the consul Lucius endorsing the leadership of Simon. The letter stresses the renewal of friendship and alliance between Rome and Judea, forbids war against Judea by Roman allies, and allows for the extradition of prisoners. Attalus II was the strongest ally of Rome in Asia Minor and would have supported such a decree issued by Rome. His position as 2d in the list following Demetrius II reflects the political situation of the day. In fear of the growing power of the Seleucid king Demetrius I, Attalus II had supported Alexander Epiphanes (Balas), a pretender to the Seleucid throne, against Demetrius I Soter. In so doing he indirectly supported Jonathan (1 Macc 10:46–47).

Bibliography

Hansen, E. V. 1971. *The Attalids of Pergamon.* 2d ed. Ithaca, NY.
Magie, D. 1950. *Roman Rule in Asia Minor.* 2 vols. Princeton, NJ.

Russell D. Nelson

ATTHARATES (PERSON) [Gk *Attaratēs*]. Official who participated in the assembly of the returned exiles when Ezra read the law of Moses to the people (1 Esdr 9:49–52). His prominence among the exiles is suggested by the text recording the blessing he gave to those who responded to Ezra's reading. Although the RSV follows the LXX by treating Attharates as a name, the consensus is that the term is a title the author of 1 Esdras misconstrued. Myers (*1-2 Esdras* AB, 91) and Coggins (*1-2 Esdras* CBC, 72–74) argue that it is a transliteration of the Persian title for governor (Heb *tršt*ʾ). Almost certainly it is a variant of ATTHARIAS in 1 Esdr 5:40 (cf. Neh 8:9). Differences such as this raise questions about the sources of and literary relationship among 1 Esdras, Ezra, and Nehemiah.

Michael David McGehee

ATTHARIAS (PERSON) [Gk *Attharias*]. In 1 Esdr 5:40 this term appears as the proper name of an individual who, with Nehemiah supervised the priests. However, comparison of this passage with the parallels in Ezra 2:63 and Neh 7:65 reveals that this may be a textual alteration in the transmission of the Heb *tiršātā*ʾ (LXX *Athersatha*), the Persian title for a provincial governor. The title may belong to either Zerubbabel, Sheshbazzar, or Nehemiah, depending on when one dates the historical context of this list.

CRAIG D. BOWMAN

AUGURY. See MAGIC (OT).

AUGUSTAN COHORT [Gk *speira Sebastē*]. An auxiliary unit in the Roman army, one of whose centurions guarded Paul on his sea voyage from Caesarea to Rome (Acts 27:1). Acts 27:42 mentions that the centurion, named JULIUS, was accompanied by soldiers who shared responsibility for guarding the prisoners; it is reasonable to assume that these soldiers were also members of the Augustan cohort. Most auxiliary cohorts were infantry units nominally composed of 500 or 1,000 troops, roughly the size of a modern army battalion. Josephus, however, refers to auxiliary cohorts which joined Vespasian's army during the Jewish War and contained 1,000 cavalry, or 600 infantry combined with 120 cavalry (*JW* 3.4.2 §67). As an auxiliary unit, it was not composed of Roman citizens, but during and after the reign of Claudius its soldiers were promised citizenship upon completion of their 25 years service (Webster 1985: 142–43; Grant 1974: 56).

The Augustan cohort mentioned in Acts was probably the *Cohors Augusta I,* which was based in the Roman province of Syria during the 1st century C.E. (*ILS,* 2683). The same cohort was probably stationed in Batanea, E of the Sea of Galilee, during the reign of Agrippa II late in the 1st century (Broughton 1933: 443). The Greek term *Sebastē* translates the Latin *Augusta,* which leads some scholars to ask if Luke may have confused this unit with the Sebastenian cohort, a unit recruited in the city of Sebaste (= Samaria). Josephus mentions several Sebastenian cohorts, all of which were stationed in Syria (*Ant* 19.9.2 §365; *JW* 2.4.2 §58). However, the Sebastenian cohort would have been referred to as the *speira Sebastēnōn,* and there is no evidence that Luke did confuse the two cohorts. Many cohorts were granted the title "Augustan" for honorable service (Cheesman 1914: 46–47), and since there is proof the *Cohors Augusta I* did serve in the area near Caesarea during the first century C.E., it seems wisest to assume Luke's reference to the unit is correct. Gealy (*IDB* 1: 317) believes that Luke mentions the cohort by name because it enhances Paul's prestige to be placed in the custody of a unit carrying the Augustan name. This is possible, but Luke nowhere else emphasizes the unit's name, even when mentioning soldiers presumably from that cohort (Acts 27:31–32, 42).

Bibliography

Broughton, T. R. S. 1933. The Roman Army. Vol. 5, pp. 427–445 in *The Beginnings of Christianity, Part I: The Acts of the Apostles,* ed. F. J. Foakes-Jackson and K. Lake. London.

Cheesman, G. L. 1914. *The Auxilia of the Roman Imperial Army.* Oxford.

Grant, M. 1974. *The Army of the Caesars.* London.

Webster, G. 1985. *The Roman Imperial Army of the First and Second Centuries A.D.* Totowa, NJ.

MARK J. OLSON

AUGUSTUS (EMPEROR). When he composed his brief history of Rome in A.D. 30, the Roman senator Velleius Paterculus portrayed Augustus as the last and most successful in a series of grand figures who dominated Rome in the course of the 1st century B.C. A little less than a century later, the great historian Cornelius Tacitus took a similar line when he wrote that "neither the domination of Cinna nor that of Sulla lasted long; the power of Pompey and the power of Crassus soon gave way to Caesar, the arms of Antony and Lepidus soon gave way to Augustus, who received the whole state, worn out by civil war, under his command with the title of *princeps*" (*Ann.* 1.1.1). Tacitus' contemporary, the biographer Suetonius, saw Augustus as the second in his series of Romans who gave form to the imperial system of government (the first was Julius Caesar); the anonymous author of some lines preserved in the *Sibylline Oracles* placed Julius first, but noted that Augustus passed on power to a successor (*Orac. Sib.* 5.11–20; 12.12–36). The view inherent in all of these authors was that it was difficult to place a firm date on the foundation of that system of government which modern scholars traditionally describe as the principate and associate with Augustus. Indeed, the Augustan principate arose out of the struggle for power among members of the Roman aristocracy in the course of the 1st century B.C. and was moulded by the political circumstances of Augustus' own rise to power after the assassination of his uncle and adoptive father, Julius Caesar on March 15, 44 B.C. He cannot truly be said to have become dominant until his victory over Mark Antony at Actium in 31 B.C., and it was not until 23 B.C. that he found a formula by which he could govern Rome with some security. For this reason, it is essential to understand the political crisis of the Roman state during his rise to power to understand the way that he modified the political system after his victory.

A. The Early Years

Augustus was born on September 19, 63 B.C., the son of Gaius Octavius, a successful politician who was the first member of his family to achieve prominence at Rome, and Atia, the niece of Julius Caesar. Rome was then in chaos because of the severe social disorder within Italy resulting from civil war and changes in the economic structure of the peninsula during the late 2d and early 1st centuries B.C. This disorder was enhanced by the tendency of ambitious aristocratic politicians to exploit social divisions in pursuit of what was then recognized as the proper ambition for any able aristocrat: personal domination over the Roman state.

By the end of 45 B.C. Julius Caesar emerged as the victor in a series of civil wars which began with his invasion of Italy in 49. It was during this time that the young Augustus (still known by his family name, Gaius Octavius) came to his attention. Impressed by his ability, Caesar intended to take him on the campaign against the Persians which he was planning in 44 and included him in his will as his primary heir and adoptive son. It was, in fact, this adoption in Caesar's will which launched the future emperor on his career. The veterans of Caesar's campaigns were devoted to the memory of their general and provided a powerful base of support for the young man when he returned to Rome to take up his inheritance as Gaius Julius Caesar

Octavian (it was customary for Romans to take their adoptive father's name while retaining an adjectival form of their own family name as an additional name, or *cognomen*—hence Octavianus or Octavian, as he is commonly known in English). He found the situation extraordinarily complicated, however. There was a substantial group which supported the assassins, led by Brutus and Cassius, and a serious split among Caesar's remaining supporters as to whether Mark Antony should, as he intended to do, assume Caesar's position. There was an equally important group of generals in W Europe who had decided to wait and see which of the other factions prevailed. At first Octavian appeared to be a convenient figurehead for the group opposing Antony, and when the senate declared war on Antony in 43, as nominal third in command, he accompanied the army under the consuls Hirtius and Pansa that was sent against Antony at Mutina, in N Italy. Two battles were fought outside of Mutina in the spring of that year and, although Antony was defeated, both consuls were killed. Octavian was now in command of a powerful independent force.

At the end of the summer, Octavian made an agreement with Antony and the most important general in S France, Marcus Lepidus, to the effect that they would govern the state as *triumvirs* (essentially 3 dictators—before this a single dictator had occasionally been selected during a time of crisis with absolute power over the state) for a term of 5 years and avenge the murder of Caesar. In part to pay their troops and in part to terrify their political enemies, the *triumvirs* immediately issued an edict of proscription. Any man whose name appeared on the lists they published was thereby sentenced to death and his property was confiscated by the state. This action, for which all 3 partners must have borne an equal measure of responsibility, was long remembered as the bloodiest act of political terrorism in Roman history.

Victory over Brutus and Cassius was won in November of 42 at Philippi in N Greece. After the battle, Octavian returned to Italy and Antony took charge of Rome's E provinces. The next few years were difficult ones. In 41, Octavian had to crush a revolt at Perugia led by Antony's brother, and between 38 and 36 he engaged in difficult naval campaigns against Sextus Pompey, who controlled the seas around Italy. It was only with the victory over Sextus, won by Octavian's close friend Marcus Vipsanius Agrippa, and the subsequent deposition of Lepidus from the triumvirate that Octavian emerged as the dominant figure in the Roman west. It was also at this time that his relations with Antony, who had married his sister Octavia in 40 to seal a treaty between the 2 men after the war around Perugia, began to break down completely.

Antony was estranged from Octavia in 36 and soon married Cleopatra, queen of Egypt. In 33 relations between him and Octavian reached a crisis point; at the beginning of 32 Octavian led a thinly veiled coup at Rome. He forced the senate to declare war on Antony and assumed overall control with the title of *dux,* a position that was essentially that of dictator. The powers which Octavian, Antony and Lepidus had assumed as *triumvirs* in 43 were renewed for a 5-year term in 37; it was the approaching expiration of the 2nd term of the triumvirate that marked the beginning of the crisis at the end of 33 (see Syme 1939: 202–312). On September 2, 31 B.C., the fleet of Octavian, under Agrippa's command, crushed that of Antony and Cleopatra at Actium off the W coast of modern Greece. In the next year Octavian completed his victory by annexing Egypt to the Roman empire. Antony and Cleopatra committed suicide. To honor the victor for his achievements the senate bestowed the name "Augustus" upon him in carefully managed ceremonies between January 13 and 16, 27 B.C. Henceforth Octavian was known as Imperator Caesar Augustus.

B. The Government of Augustus

After his victory, Augustus was faced with administering the empire so as to secure his position and that of his family and to prevent a new outbreak of the chaos of the previous decades. He accomplished this through clever manipulation of the constitution, adroit alliances with leading members of the aristocracy, and skillful selection of commanders for Rome's armies. He also attempted, with less success, to reform what he saw as the moral failings of the Roman state.

The constitutional forms with which Augustus cloaked his autocratic position were many and varied. He felt that these contortions were necessary for a simple reason: There was a long-standing distaste at Rome for the outward forms of monarchy. These smacked of the "degenerate" east or of the tyrant Tarquinius the Proud, the last of Rome's legendary 7 kings, whose expulsion led to the creation of the republican form of government. Moreover, the excessive display of preeminence by one aristocrat was mortally offensive to the sensibilities of others. Caesar's adoption of many of the symbols of monarchy and evident lack of respect for the traditional institutions of government had been the main reason for his assassination.

In the early years Augustus had assumed the powers of a dictator as *triumvir* and then, between 32 and 28, as *dux* or "leader," avoiding the title "dictator" itself because Caesar had adopted it in his later years. In 28 he laid aside these powers and contented himself with one of the two "ordinary" consulships. (These were distinguished from the increasingly common "suffect" consulships because "ordinary" consuls entered office on January 1 and gave their name to the year.) He also became governor of an extended province which included most of the areas in the empire with large garrisons. This state of affairs changed in 23, perhaps because he felt that his constant consulships were offensive to members of the aristocracy who desired the distinction for themselves, and perhaps because he felt that he was strong enough to adopt a new, more powerful position. In that year he laid down the consulship and received the powers of a tribune for life, the proconsulship for life, and the supreme power *(imperium maius)* over all other governors. These powers enabled him to control political life within the city of Rome (as tribune he had the power to bring public business to a halt) and to control Rome's military forces. After receiving these powers and suppressing a conspiracy to murder him, either at the end of 23 or at the beginning of 22, he left Italy to set Rome's eastern frontier in order (Badian 1982; cf. Syme 1986: 387–389). When he returned in 19 he was given the powers of a consul for life and "freedom from the laws." These powers—the consulship, the tribunate of the plebs, and certain other extraordinary powers—served to define the office of *princeps* or emperor for the rest of his reign and for those of his successors.

Augustus' relationship with the aristocracy was summarized by Tacitus as follows: "[T]he most violently opposed had fallen in battle or through proscription, the rest of the nobles, insofar as those who were most readily obedient were raised up with wealth and honor and enhanced with new dignities, preferred the safe present to the dangerous past" (*Ann.* 1.2). The civil wars had had a devastating impact on the governing class of the old Republic; it was indeed true that the majority of those who had not joined Augustus in the course of the wars had been killed. But, even after Actium, Augustus could not depend on the loyalty of the survivors. He carried out revisions of the list of senators, in 29, 18, and 11 B.C. to remove those who he thought were unworthy (or dangerous), and he had a fourth revision carried out by a board of senators in 4 A.D. He also increased the property qualification necessary for entry into the senate and introduced a number of important changes in the way that offices might be held (see Nicolet 1984).

In the course of his reformation of the senate, Augustus concentrated the power of patronage and promotion in his own hands. There were 2 principle features of this control. The first was his power over the provinces in which Rome's main armies were stationed. He therefore had the power to appoint the commanders of these forces; it was virtually impossible for a man of suspect loyalty to obtain one of the military commands that were still cherished by the bellicose members of the aristocracy. The second feature was his virtual control over the electoral process. Tacitus described this as one of the greatest "secrets of power" (*Ann.* 2.36.1). It was very difficult for any man to win office without his approval, and he enhanced this control through the practices of "nomination" and "commendation." For each election, Augustus would publish a list of men whom he supported, or "nominated." These lists would contain fewer names than there were offices, but inclusion on the list meant that a man was virtually assured of election, thus saving him a great deal of stress and presumably a good deal of expense, since running for office often involved tremendous outlays on public spectacles to court public support. A man who was "commended" as a "candidate of Caesar" would receive the office for which he had been "commended" without having to run for it. This was a very special and coveted honor; by the end of Augustus' reign only 4 men would receive it each year. This put a very real premium on Augustus' goodwill; the senatorial ideology which began to emerge in this period stressed service to the state under the emperor's guidance rather than absolute personal dominance (see Mommsen 1887–88: 917–22; cf. Levick 1967; for general discussion see Millar 1977: 299–313; Talbert 1984: 16–27; Eck 1984: 129–67).

The importance of the emperor's guidance was also stressed through Augustus' constant consultations with the senate. It appears that he brought almost all public business before that body. Indeed, there does not seem to have been any important act of state for which Augustus did not seek senatorial approval. Where our sources tell us that Augustus "did" something, their language is masking the process which involved Augustus either making a personal appearance before the senate to make a proposal or writing to the senate asking it to adopt the course that he desired. He may have adopted this approach to cloak the autocratic nature of his regime, but the result was to promote the extreme subservience of the senate to the autocrat. Senators appear not to have been sure why they were consulted on issues ranging from the recognition of an imperial heir to the composition of provincial juries and thus strove all the more to please the emperor whenever he expressed a desire to hear their views—there was no point to risking one's career by crossing the emperor on such occasions. We hear of very few occasions when a debate in the senate in which the issues were not overshadowed by the desire of the speakers to please the monarch or even to anticipate his desires (see Brunt 1984).

The other great problem that Augustus inherited from the Republic was the poverty and unrest rampant among the Italian lower classes. One solution was simply to ensure peace, and this he was able to do after Actium. Another was to change the periodic redistribution of agrarian land to the rural and urban poor and the settlement of veterans on farms in Italy. He did this in the years after Actium by initiating an extensive program of overseas colonization. Such colonization had been attempted from time to time under the Republic and had been a major feature of Julius Caesar's program just before his death, but nothing had been attempted on anything like the scale which Augustus introduced. A great number of new colonies were founded abroad, and they had the effect not only of alleviating problems in Italy and serving as garrisons in newly pacified areas, but also of speeding the spread of Latin culture throughout W Europe as well as into the east. This was one of Augustus' most significant actions (Salmon 1969: 134–44; Brunt 1972: 589–601).

Within the city of Rome itself, Augustus introduced a more regular supply of subsidized grain for the poor and sought to keep better order through the institution of the *vigiles,* Rome's first professional police force and fire department. He engaged in a massive building program which served to beautify the city and celebrate the glory of his achievements. He issued regular distributions of food and money at festivals and to commemorate important moments in his reign. In doing so he not only alleviated the suffering of the poor, but he also bound the lower classes to his house. Preferential treatment of the population of Rome was thus established as one of the foundations of imperial government (Veyne 1976: 557–791; Rickman 1980: 61–66).

Augustus not only sought to refashion the political structure of the Roman state, but also to restore what he thought was Rome's "pristine moral virtue." In 18 B.C. he issued laws that encouraged the upper classes to have more children by giving preferential treatment to fathers of more than 3 offspring and imposing severe penalties upon the childless. He also issued a severe law aimed at curbing adultery. Later in his reign he took strong action to ensure the "racial purity" of the Roman people by limiting the number of slaves that an individual could free and restricting their access to Roman citizenship. He granted new privileges to senatorial and equestrian families, but he also imposed severe penalties upon members of those families who married slaves or engaged in what he regarded as disgraceful professions, such as acting or fighting as gladiators (Last *CAH* 10:425–64; Brunt 1972: 558–66; Levick 1983: 105–15).

The reign of Augustus was also notable as the golden age of Latin literature. Although Augustus himself can take little or no credit for the development of poets such as Vergil, Propertius, Tibullus, and Horace—all of them began writing well before Actium—he did have an active interest in the arts. Vergil's *Aeneid* and Livy's massive history of Rome created images of Rome's past which Augustus found congenial, even though neither, especially Vergil's, can be considered wholly favorable. With the passing of time, however, his attitude towards literature began to harden. His later years were notable for the exile of the one great talent his reign produced, the poet Ovid, whose work Augustus found offensive (Syme 1978: 169–229; Griffin 1984: 189–215).

There were also a number of developments in the overall governance of the empire and its relations with foreign peoples. One of these was the creation of a regular standing army in place of the republican armies which were raised for specific campaigns. This new army engaged in a number of important campaigns carried out by Augustus' lieutenants, often under the overall command of members of his family. The main areas of operation were Germany and the Balkans. Although there were some setbacks—the most important of which was the destruction of 3 legions by the Germans in 9 A.D.—the empire gained much new territory and began to develop fixed frontiers. There is still debate as to whether this was Augustus' intention in beginning these wars; some have argued that he hoped to conquer the world and was only deterred from this aim by problems at the end of his reign. But it is certainly the case that the frontiers developing along the Rhine and Danube at the time of Augustus' death were readily defensible and were to remain, with very few changes, the limits of Roman power down to the fall of the W empire in the 4th century. The administration of the provinces themselves became somewhat more efficient than it had been under the Republic (Syme *CAH* 10:340–81; Brunt 1963: 170–76; Wells 1972). Augustus was able to exercise some restraint over the rapacity of his officials. In addition, he began to create a new bureaucracy, staffed by freedmen and slaves from his own household as well as by members of the equestrian order, to oversee the administration of the grain supply, of certain minor provinces, of his own enormous estates throughout the empire, and of the significant contribution which he made to the finances of the state from his own funds.

C. The Succession

One of Augustus' primary aims was to ensure that the heir to his "station" in the state, as he called it, would be a member of his own family. As he had no sons and only one daughter, Julia, he had to rely upon nephews, stepchildren, and grandchildren to satisfy his ambition. The first heir-apparent was Augustus' nephew, Marcus Claudius Marcellus who married Julia in 25 B.C. He died in 23, and Augustus then turned to his old friend, Marcus Agrippa. Agrippa married Julia, by whom he had a number of children before his own death in 12 B.C. At the same time that Agrippa was marked out for succession, Augustus also promoted his two stepsons, Drusus and Tiberius, an insurance policy against the death of Agrippa. Tiberius, the elder of the two, was the favorite at this time, and after Agrippa's death he married Julia.

Drusus died in 9 B.C. and, as further insurance, Augustus began to promote the careers of two of his grandsons by Agrippa, Gaius and Lucius. This seems to have caused some friction with Tiberius and in 6 B.C. Tiberius retired from public life to live on the island of Rhodes, much against Augustus' will. His retirement soon became little better than an exile, and a dynastic crisis ensued. Gaius and Lucius were too young to succeed, and as Augustus passed the age of 60, it seemed that he might soon die. Julia, who appears to have detested Tiberius, began to conspire with Augustus' nephew Iullus Antonius (the son of Antony and Octavia). This conspiracy was uncovered in 2 B.C.; Iullus was executed and Julia was exiled on the charge of adultery with a number of members of the nobility (Syme 1974: 912–36).

Augustus' hopes for Gaius and Lucius soon foundered. Lucius died of disease at Marseilles in 2 A.D. and two years later Gaius died as the result of a wound he received while on campaign in the east. Tiberius was recalled and formally adopted by Augustus as his heir. At the same time Augustus also adopted his last surviving grandson, Agrippa Postumus—yet another insurance policy. Agrippa Postumus soon proved inadequate (there is some suggestion that he was insane) and was exiled to an estate outside Rome in 6 A.D.; in 7 he was sent into exile on an island. A year later, after yet another domestic scandal, Augustus' granddaughter, the younger Julia, was also exiled. In 13 Tiberius was granted the same powers as Augustus, and when Augustus died on August 19, A.D. 14, Tiberius assumed the sole government of the Roman empire. This succession, without civil war, was Augustus' final political achievement.

Augustus was a brutal and difficult man, given at times to severe delusions, and feared or disliked by those who knew him best. Nonetheless, he proved to be a master politician and administrator and, as a result, his reign marks the great watershed in Roman history. He managed to create a system of government that maintained the unity and peace of the Mediterranean world for centuries to come.

Bibliography

Badian, E. 1982. "Crisis Theories" and the Beginning of the Principate. Pp. 18–41 in *Romanitas-Christianitas. Untersuchungen zur Geschichte und Literatur der römischen Kaiserzeit. Ed. G. Wirth, K. H. Schwarte, and J. Heinrichs.* Berlin.

Brunt, P. A. 1963. Review and Discussion of H. D. Meyer, *Die Aussenpolitik des Augustus und die augusteische Dichtung. JRS* 53: 170–76.

———. 1972. *Italian Manpower 325 B.C.–14 A.D.* Oxford.

———. 1984. The Role of the Senate in the Augustan Regime. *Classical Quarterly* 34: 423–44.

Eck, W. 1984. Senatorial Self-Representation: Developments in the Augustan Period. Pp. 129–67 in F. Millar and E. Segal, *Caesar Augustus. Seven Aspects.* Oxford.

Griffin, J. 1984. Augustus and the Poets: *"Caesar qui cogere posset."*

Pp. 189–218 in F. Millar and E. Segal, *Caesar Augustus. Seven Aspects.* Oxford.
Levick, B. M. 1967. Imperial Control of the Elections under the Early Principate: *commendatio, suffragatio* and *nominatio. Historia* 16: 207–30.
———. 1983. The *Senatus Consultum* from Larinum. *JRS* 73: 97–115.
Millar, F. 1977. *The Emperor in the Roman World.* London.
Mommsen, T. 1887–88. *Römische Staatsrecht.* 2d ed. Leipzig.
Nicolet, C. 1984. Augustus, Government and the Propertied Classes. Pp. 89–128 in F. Millar and E. Segal, *Caesar Augustus. Seven Aspects.* Oxford.
Rickman, G. 1980. *The Corn Supply of Ancient Rome.* Oxford.
Syme, R. 1939. *The Roman Revolution.* Oxford.
———. 1974. The Crisis of 2 B.C. *Bayerische Akadamie der Wissenschaften. Philosophisch-Historische Klasse. Sitzungsberichte.* 7: 3–34.
———. 1978. *History in Ovid.* Oxford.
———. 1979–87. *The Roman Papers,* ed. E. Badian and E. Birley. 5 vols. Oxford.
———. 1986. *The Augustan Aristocracy.* Oxford.
Talbert, R. J. A. 1984. *The Senate of Imperial Rome.* Princeton.
Veyne, P. 1976. *Le pain et le cirque. Sociologie historique d'un pluralisms politique.* Paris.

D. S. POTTER

AURANUS (PERSON) [Gk *Auranos*]. Commander of a temple guard (2 Macc 4:40). After reports circulated that Lysimacchus had stolen gold vessels from the temple and that crowds were forming into a mob, Lysimacchus armed 3,000 men and placed them under the command of Auranus. The attack on the crowd failed, and Lysimacchus himself was killed near the temple treasury as divine retribution (2 Macc 4:39–42). The description of Auranus as "advanced in both age and folly" contrasts with that of the martyr Eleazar, who was "advanced both in age and noble presence/appearance" (2 Macc 6:18). Goldstein heightens the contrast by suggesting that *auranos* is a variant form of *auaran,* the nickname of Eleazar, son of Mattathias (1 Macc 2:5; 6:43). A pious Eleazar (2 Macc 6:18–31) would be contrasted with the impious Hasmonaean Eleazar (Goldstein *2 Maccabees* AB, 242). However, the tentative nature of this identification and the closer contrasts between the martyr Eleazar and Mattathias (Goldstein *2 Maccabees* AB, 282–86) speak against Auranus being associated with Eleazar, son of Mattathias. Further, the omission of the account of Eleazar's noble death (1 Macc 6:40–47) does not automatically suggest that the author of 2 Maccabees would seek a negative episode as a substitution (Goldstein *1 Maccabees* AB, 79–80).

RUSSELL D. NELSON

AURELIUS, MARCUS. See MARCUS AURELIUS (EMPEROR).

AUTHOR OF LIFE [Gk *archēgos zōēs*]. In this expression (Acts 3:15), the word "author" is the rendering of *archēgos* in some English versions (RSV, ASV [margin], NAB, NIV). In 2 other contexts, the word is also rendered "author" in some versions: "author (of salvation)" in Heb 2:10 (ASV, NASB, NIV), and the "author (of our faith)" in Heb 12:2 (KJV, ASV, NASB, NIV). The basic sense here is that of originator or founder (Delling *TDNT* 1: 487–88).

Other renderings in these 3 passages and in Acts 5:31, reveal another line of interpretation of the term *archēgos:* as "leader," "pioneer," "captain," and "prince" (Müller *EWNT* 1: col. 393). For Acts 3:15, examples of this alternative interpretation are evident in such translations as "him who led the way (to life)" (NEB); "the one who leads (to life)" (GNB); and, with less clarity, "the prince (of life)" (KJV, ASV, NASB, JB).

These 4 passages (listed above) constitute all the NT occurrences of the word *archēgos,* and in all of them the reference is to Jesus Christ. By this title he is recognized as the eschatological leader who, by way of the cross and resurrection, leads his followers to faith, salvation, and life, as Moses led God's people in the Exodus (cf. Acts 7:36). This understanding of NT *archēgos* as "leader" is probably preferable to understanding it as "originator" on the basis of Greek and Hellenistic sources.

HERBERT G. GRETHER

AUTHORITATIVE TEACHING (NHC VI,*3*). The 3d tractate of codex VI (pp. 22–35) of the Nag Hammadi codices. The text, a Coptic translation from a Gk original, is well preserved except for lacunas at the top of the first 7 pages (MacRae 1979: 258). The Coptic dialect is Sahidic with some non-Sahidic variations (Krause and Labib 1971: 44–47).

Auth. Teach. offers a highly metaphorical account of the soul's existence from its origin in "the invisible, ineffable worlds," through its encapsulation in a physical body and struggle with the forces of the material realm, to its ultimate salvation and rest. Seams in the narrative structure of the text and changes in person suggest that the present version is dependent upon a collection of originally separate metaphorical accounts (MacRae 1979: 257). In its present form, *Auth. Teach.* is a didactic composition perhaps used as a homily (Ménard 1977: 2; 1978: 288). It belongs to the genre of literature on the soul first identified by Festugière in connection with the Hermetic corpus. Other Nag Hammadi tractates concerned with the soul include *The Exegesis on the Soul* (NHC II,*6*), *The Teachings of Sylvanus* (NHC VII,*4*) and *The Book of Thomas the Contender* (NHC II,*7*) (MacRae 1972: 478–79; Funk 1973: 254).

The anticosmic stance of the *Auth. Teach.* is clear throughout the text. The spiritual soul is described as cast into a body that came from lust, which in turn came from material substance. The material body is the creation of the "dealers-in-bodies," who seek to strike down the invisible soul. The soul is portrayed as a harlot who fell into bestiality, as wheat mixed with chaff. In the body, the soul contests against the wiles of the evil adversaries, who spread hidden nets in order to snare her and draw her down to "man-eaters." An extended metaphor portrays the adversary as a fisherman who baits a hook with various kinds of food (passions). The food is the ruse which draws the soul to the hook by which it is caught and pulled out of freedom into slavery. But the rational soul seeks God and gains salvation and rest through knowledge. She is aided in her quest by her bridegroom, who "applies the word (logos) to her eyes as a medicine to enable her to see with her mind" (22,26–28).

Auth. Teach. offers an important witness to the interest in and speculation on the nature, origin, and fate of the soul in the religious and philosophical cauldron from which Christianity emerged. The language of the text is nonphilosophical (MacRae 1972: 477; Ménard 1977: 3), although its understanding of the soul is thoroughly Platonic (van den Broek 1979). The surviving text contains no clear evidence of a typical gnostic cosmogonic myth (MacRae 1979: 259; Funk 1973: 253), but the strong anticosmic dualism, the dichotomy between ignorance and knowledge, and the various metaphors of salvation (e.g., bridal-chamber and rest) would certainly be at home in a gnostic context (Funk 1973: 254; Ménard 1977: 5–6). While no passage in the tractate betrays certain dependence on Jewish or Christian texts, practices or beliefs (MacRae 1972: 476; 1979: 258–59), various passages do suggest that the author knew the NT and considered it authoritative (Funk 1973: 254; van den Broek 1979: 271–76). The use of the term *logos* in the title, *Authentikos logos,* has no relation to the Johannine use of the term as a title for Christ. It is more closely related to the use of the term in Hermetic literature and/or the role of the *logos* as medicine found in the text itself (MacRae 1972: 476–78; 1979: 257; Ménard 1977: 3–4).

The document supplies no certain internal evidence of provenance or date. Its use of a logos concept, its strong anticosmic stance, and its Platonic doctrine of the soul would be at home in Alexandria by the end of the 2d century C.E. (van den Broek 1979: 281–82).

Bibliography

Arai, S. 1981. Zum "Simonianischen" in *AuthLog* und *Bronte.* Pp. 3–15 in *Gnosis and Gnosticism,* ed. M. Krause. NHS 17. Leiden.

Broek, R. van den. 1979. The Authentikos Logos. A New Document of Christian Platonism. *VC* 33: 260–86.

Funk, W.-P. 1973. "Authentikos Logos": Die dritte Schrift aus Nag-Hammadi-Codex VI; Eingeleitet und übersetzt vom Berliner Arbeitskreis für koptisch-gnostische Schriften. *TLZ* 98: 251–59.

Guillaumont, A. 1975–76 [Untitled note on VI,*3*]. *AEHE V* 85: 250.

Koschorke, K. 1977. "Suchen und Finden" in der Auseinandersetzung zwischen gnostischem und kirchlichem Christentum. *WD* 14: 51–65.

Krause, M., and Labib, P. 1971. *Gnostische und hermetische Schriften aus Codex II und Codex VI.* Abhandlungen des Deutschen Archäologischen Instituts Kairo, Koptische Reihe 2. Glückstadt.

MacRae, G. W. 1972. A Nag Hammadi Tractate on the Soul. Pp. 471–79 in *Ex orbe religionum: Studia Geo Widengren.* Supplements to Numen 21. Leiden.

———. 1979. Authoritative Teaching VI,*3*: 22,1–35; 24. Pp. 257–89 in *Nag Hammadi Codices V,2–5 and VI with Papyrus Berolinensis 8502, 1 and 4,* ed. D. M. Parrott. NHS 11. Leiden.

MacRae, G. W., and Parrott, D. M. 1977. Authoritative Teaching (VI,*3*). *NHL,* 278–83.

Ménard, J. E. 1977. *L'Authentikos Logos: Texte établi et présenté.* BCNHT 2. Quebec.

———. 1978. Gnosis paienne et gnose chrétienne: 1. "Authentikos Logos" et "les Enseignements de Silvain" de Nag Hammadi. Pp. 287–94 in *Paganisme, judaisme, christianisme; Influences et affrontements dans le monde antique: Mélanges offerts à Marcel Simon.* Paris.

James E. Goehring

AUTHORITIES, CITY. See CITY AUTHORITIES.

AUTHORITY OF SCRIPTURE. See SCRIPTURAL AUTHORITY.

AUTHORIZED VERSIONS. See VERSIONS, ENGLISH (AUTHORIZED VERSIONS).

AVARAN (PERSON) [Gk *Auaran*]. Nickname of Eleazar, the 4th son of Mattathias (1 Macc 2:5). His well-known heroic deed was the killing of an elephant at the battle of Beth-zechariah (1 Macc 6:46). There also his nickname is mentioned (1 Macc 6:43). Several suggestions have been proposed for the meaning of Avaran, but none are convincing. Two Hebrew roots are possible: (1) *ʿwr* = "Awake" (i.e., he was not a soundly sleeping baby?); and (2) *ḥwr* = "pale(face)." The suggestion of *ḥwr* as a root may be combined with the feat of killing the elephant which suggests the meaning of "hole" for *ḥor.* However, this assumes a different function of all the nicknames of Mattathias' sons, which does not fit their intention and assumed meanings. For the nicknames of Mattathias' sons see GADDI and MACCABEE. (See also ELEAZAR.)

Uriel Rappaport

AVEN (PLACE) [Heb *ʾāwen*]. A Hebrew word meaning "idolatry," "iniquity," or "nothingness" used by the OT prophets as a derogatory substitute or wordplay in certain place names. Since the Hebrew words *ʾôn* ("power" or "riches") and *ʾāwen* have identical consonants, Aven may be a derisive pun.

1. A place mentioned in the phrase "the high places of Aven" (Hos 10:8). "Aven" has traditionally been understood as an abbreviation of Beth-aven ("House of Idolatry"), Hosea's pejorative name for Bethel ("House of God"). See BETH-AVEN. However, several modern scholars prefer to translate *ʾāwen* as a common noun, i.e., "the high places of transgression" (Mays *Hosea* OTL, 138; Wolff *Hosea* Hermeneia, 171).

2. A valley cited in Amos' denunciation of Syria (Amos 1:5). "The Valley of Aven" may be the plain between Lebanon and Anti-lebanon. Several scholars have attempted to identify Aven more precisely with "Baalbek" (Eissfeldt 1936; Mays *Hosea* OTL, 30–31).

3. A derisive wordplay or misvocalization of the name of the Egyptian city "On" (Heb *ʾôn*) found in the MT (Ezek 30:17). The LXX has *hēliou poleōs* (Heliopolis), the Gk name for On. KJV follows MT with "Aven," while the RSV and NEB render "On." See also ON.

Bibliography

Eissfeldt, O. 1936. Die ältesten Bezeugungen von Baalbek als Kultstätte. *FuF* 12: 51–53.

Carolyn J. Pressler

AVENGER OF BLOOD. See BLOOD, AVENGER OF.

AVESTAN LANGUAGE. See LANGUAGES (ANCIENT IRAN).

AVITH (PLACE) [Heb *ʿăwît*]. The residence of the Edomite "king" Hadad son of Bedad (Gen 36:35; 1 Chr 1:46). See HADAD (PERSON). According to the rules of postexilic Heb and Aram orthography, *ʿwyt* may render Ar *Ghuwaith,* attested as a personal name in Safaitic, S Safaitic, Minaean, and Qatabanian (Harding 1971: 459). *Ghuwaith* is the diminutive of Ghauth, which occurs in Safaitic over 150 times (Harding 1971: 452; note that the vocalizations of the two Safaitic names here differ from those of Harding), and in the Aramaic (Idumaean) ostraca from Tell es-Sebaʾ, ca. 400 B.C. (Knauf 1985: 250, n. 28). Knauf *(ibid)* suggested that *Ghuwaith was the clan or tribe to which Hadad son of Bedad belonged, and that Avith was the more or less permanent encampment of this clan or tribe.

According to Burckhardt (1822: 375), the mountain range which terminates the Moabite plateau to the E was called el-Ghuwaithah. This information is not corroborated by later explorers (cf. A. Musil in Brünnow and Domaszewski 1905: 325). Burckhardt's reference is insufficient evidence to speculate about a Moabite origin for the Edomite "king" Hadad son of Bedad, or to suggest a localization for Avith.

Bibliography

Brünnow, R. E., and Domaszewski, A. von. 1905. *Provincia Arabia.* Vol. 2. Strassburg.

Burckhardt, J. L. 1822. *Travels in Syria and the Holy Land.* London.

Harding, G. L. 1971. *An Index and Concordance of Pre-Islamic Arabian Names and Inscriptions.* Near and Middle East Series, 8. Toronto.

Knauf, E. A. 1985. Alter und Herkunft der edomitischen Königsliste, Gen 36,31–39. *ZAW* 97: 245–53.

Ernst Axel Knauf

AVOT, KHIRBET (M.R. 193276). A site which occupies a small rise on a large hill at the head of Naḥal Avivim, a winding ravine which drains into the Huleh Valley basin to the E. Two short emergency seasons of exploratory excavations were undertaken on one of a series of broad terraces on the W slope of the hillock.

The region is mountainous and well-watered, but with few perennial springs. Adjacent to the site is a seasonal water supply which collects in a natural basalt pool at the SE edge of the hill. It is difficult to establish the economic basis for the early settlements on the site, but it seems likely, despite the rugged nature of the terrain and the somewhat harsh winters, that it was primarily agricultural. A tedious but not impossible journey across the ravine leads to the large expanse of the Yiron plateau, still used for pasturing animals, and the lower slopes of the larger hill on which the site lies still bear traces of agricultural terracing.

The earliest evidence of occupation was found in several places above the basalt bedrock and included fragments of a curvilinear wall and related floor on which were found partial vessels belonging to the EB I or EB II horizon. In two other soundings evidence of human interments, including an infant jar-burial, were accompanied by MB pottery, although nothing of a settlement dating to this period was found.

Major architectural remains of the Iron Age I were uncovered which included a number of successive and distinct building phases. No complete plans of buildings were recovered but the buildings seem to have been large, rectangular, multiroomed dwellings, some with plastered floors and adjacent stone-lined storage pits. The buildings were solidly built of heavy stone foundations, and the sophistication of some of the construction techniques is attested by the discovery of one semisubterranean storage room, the lower floor of what must have been a two-story structure. The plan of these buildings, which seems to follow the contours of the hill, suggests that they may have been built adjacent to each other to create a barrier to the outside.

The Iron I occupation at Kh. Avot could be evidence of the historical process of Naphtali's settlement in the Upper Galilee (cf. Josh 19:32–39). However, on the basis of the archaeological record, there are some real objections to the identification of this site as Israelite.

A distinctive type of pithos at one time identified as a hallmark of Israelite presence (Aharoni 1957) is found at Kh. Avot in quantity and is known from numerous other sites in the region as well as at Stratum XII at Hazor (Yadin et al. 1961: Pl. CLXVII, CLXVIII). Recent excavations of a Canaanite-Phoenician town in W Galilee, TELL KEISAN, have uncovered this same type of vessel (Briend and Humbert 1980: Pl. 68:1–3) making its ethnic identity less viable.

A 2d type of pithos found at Kh. Avot is even more problematic because of what is presently known of its distribution and also what appears to be its foreign pedigree. With its stump base, globular body, tubular neck, and raised wavy-line decoration (see fig. AVO.01), it is totally alien to local ceramic traditional forms and is suggestive of Cypriot forms which can be traced back to at least the 3d millennium B.C.E. Examples of these vessels have been found at the Upper Galilean sites of Sasa, Mt. Adir, Tel Dan V, possibly at Hazor XII (Yadin et al. 1961: Pl. CCII:19), and at the Phoenician coastal city of Tyre (Bikai 1978: Pl. XL) in level XIII; they are dated to the Iron I Period. Despite its Tyrian provenance it does not seem to be a Phoenician type nor could the pottery of Kh. Avot be considered Phoenician.

To what extent these 2 types of pithoi may reflect the ethnic identity of the inhabitants of Kh. Avot is unclear. What seems certain is that there are N and other foreign elements in the material culture of this Iron I occupation which make its identification with an Israelite tribal settlement problematic.

A further obstacle to the "Israelite" identification is the

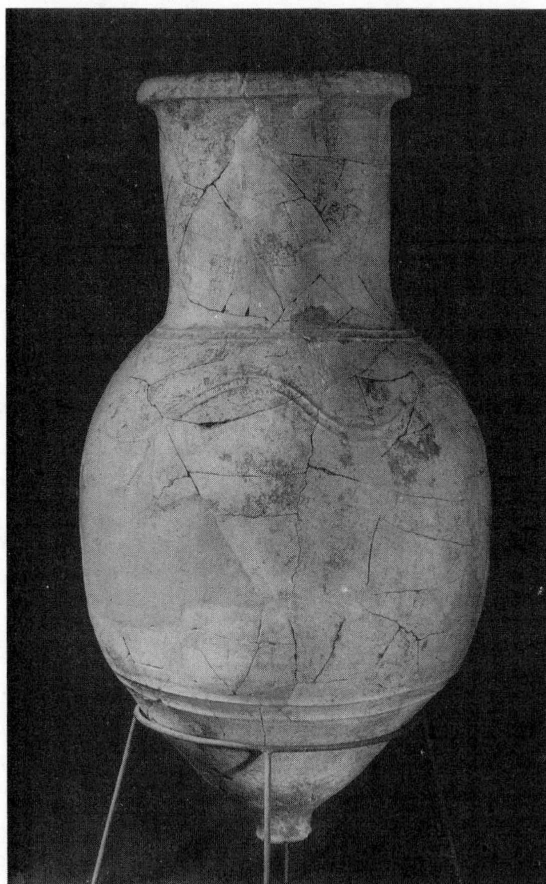

AVO.01. Upper Galilean pithos from Kh. Avot—Iron I. *(Courtesy of Israel Department of Antiquities and Museums.)*

well developed architectural styles at Kh. Avot which are in direct contrast to the squatter occupation of Hazor XII, identified with Israelite tribes (Yadin 1972: 129). While the ceramic repertoires of these two occupations are comparable, sharing many elements, the contrast in the life styles as implied by the architecture or lack of it can not be easily explained. To what, if any extent the Iron I occupation at Kh. Avot reflects the biblical account of the settlement of Naphtali must remain a matter of conjecture.

Directly above some of the walls of the Iron I stratum were found the very poorly preserved remains of a large, multi-roomed structure of the Persian period. Associated pottery suggests a date somewhere in the 4th century B.C.E.

A number of intrusive burials into this stratum and the earlier strata were encountered over large portions of the terrace that were excavated. The style of these burials, the lack of accompanying grave goods, the state of preservation of the bones, and the anthropological data all indicate a Bedouin population of at least several centuries. Excavations have not been conducted on other parts of the now-protected site, and it is unlikely that the entire occupational sequence of the settlement is known.

Bibliography

Aharoni, Y. 1957. *The Settlement of the Israelite Tribes in Upper Galilee.* Jerusalem (in Hebrew).

Bikai, P. M. 1978. *The Pottery of Tyre.* Warminster.

Briend, J., and Humbert, J.-B. 1980. *Tel Keisan* 1971–76. Fribourg, Switzerland.

Yadin, Y. 1972. *Hazor: The Head of All Those Kingdoms.* London.

Yadin, Y. et al. 1961. *Hazor III–IV (Plates).* Jerusalem.

ELIOT BRAUN

AVVA (PLACE) [Heb *ʿawwāʾ*]. AVVITES. A town whose residents were deported by the Assyrians and resettled in Samaria sometime after 721 B.C. (2 Kgs 17:24). A number of mss spell the name *ʿawwâ* (final *he*). Simons (*GTTOT,* 111) proposed identifying Avva with ʿAvvah/ʿIvvah in Syria (modern Tell Kafrʿaya, on the Orontes SW of Homs). However, because the biblical text notes that the people of Avva "made Nibhaz and Tartak" after their resettlement (1 Kgs 17:31), others have suggested that these people were Elamites deported from the city of Ama (Akk *m* is often rendered *w* in Heb) who were successful in reestablishing in Samaria the cults of their native deities Ibnahaza and Dirtaq (Cogan and Tadmor, *2 Kings* AB, 212).

GARY A. HERION

AVVIM (PLACE) [Heb *hāʿawîm*]. **1.** A "place" listed in the 1st city list of the tribe of Benjamin (Josh 18:23) between Bethel and Parah (modern Kh. Abu Musarrah, M.R. 177137). There is general agreement among scholars that Avvim actually represents not a geographical name but a gentilic (*Joshua* AB, 430). Thus, the Avvim were probably the people of either Ai (*HGB,* 401) or Aiath (modern Kh. Haiyân, M.R. 175145; Press 1955: 687).

2. The early inhabitants of the S coastal region who were displaced from some of their holdings by the people of Caphtor (Deut 2:23), and who continued to live S of the Philistines in the time of the conquest (Josh 13:3). While some consider these people to be the autochthonous inhabitants of the S frontier region (*LBHG,* 237), the LXX rendering of these people (Gk *Euaioi*) is that also used for "Hivites." This may indicate that one must look to earlier Sea Peoples for their origins (*Joshua* AB, 338). The text in Deuteronomy indicates that the Avvim dwelt in villages *(baḥăṣērîm)* as far as Gaza. The LXX, however, translates this *en asērōth* (or *en Asērōth*). It is therefore possible that these people occupied the land from Hazoroth (Num 11:35; modern Ar ʿAin Khaḍrā, M.R. 096814) deep in the Sinai to the S coast of Palestine near Gaza. It is more common, however, to translate the place where the Avvim dwelt as "villages" or "enclosures." Speiser (1932: 30–31, n. 67) connected these *ḥăṣērîm* with the terra pisée ramparts that were discovered at Tell el-Farʿah and Tell el-ʾAjjûl in the Negeb. Following Albright (1932: 8), he identified these ramparts with a Hyksos occupation and concluded that the Avvim were part of this Hyksos settlement that was succeeded by the Aegeans. Simons (*GTTOT,* 31) argued that because *ḥăṣērîm* were either small unwalled villages of secondary importance or encampments for nomadic or seminomadic people, they could not be connected with the major fortified cities that were situated on these tells. The Avvim reappear in Josh 13:3 as a S neighbor to the 5 cities of the Philistines (*LBHG,* 237). They probably occupied the land between the Philistines and the Egyptians (*GTTOT,* 111).

Bibliography

Albright, W. F. 1921. A Colony of Cretan Mercenaries on the Coast of the Negeb. *JPOS* 1: 187–94.

———. 1932. The Fourth Joint Campaign of Excavation at Tell Beit Mirsim. *BASOR* 47: 3–18.

Press, I. 1955. *A Topographical-Historical Encyclopaedia of Palestine.* Vol. 4. Jerusalem (in Hebrew).

Speiser, E. A. 1932. Ethnic Movements in the Near East in the Second Millennium B.C. *AASOR* 13: 13–54.

SUSAN E. MCGARRY

AVVITES. See AVVA (PLACE).

ʿAYIN. The 16th letter of the Hebrew alphabet.

AYYAH (PLACE) [Heb *ʿayyâ*]. In 1 Chr 7:20–30, we find a description of the tribe of Ephraim. Their possessions (vv 28–29) included Bethel, Naaran, Gezer, Shechem, Ayyah, Beth-shean, Taanach, Megiddo, and Dor. The traditional tribal allotments include Shechem and the last 4 sites in Cis-Jordanian Manasseh.

For 1 Chr 7:28 several ms traditions (some LXX examplars, Vg, and Targum) support a reading *ʿzh* (Gaza) for MT *ʿyh* (ʿAyyah). If the former reading is correct it would not be the Philistine Gaza, but another site in the hill country (as the context of 1 Chr 7:20–30 demands). The variant name was most probably the result of a confusion between the letter *z* and *y* in the square Jewish script (see Cross 1961: 133–202; Freedman, Mathews, and Hanson 1985: 15–23).

In regard to the identification of Ayyah, Myers (*1 Chronicles* AB, 51) states that the site is unknown. Reed (*IDB* 1: 324), however, suggests equating Ayya with Ai or the nearby Khirbet Haiyan (M.R. 175145). Albright (1924: 144) rejects the equation of Ayyah with Ai, favoring the alternate reading Gaza.

Simons (*GTTOT,* 169; NWBD, 79) proposes Turmus ʿajja (M.R. 177160) as probably Ayyah. It is located in a small fertile plain E of Sinjil between Sinjil and Seilun (Shiloh). Abel (*GP,* 257) notes it was called Turbasaim in the Middle Ages.

Bibliography

Albright, W. F. 1924. *Excavations and Results at Tell el-Fûl (Gibeah of Saul).* AASOR 4. New Haven.

Cross, F. M. 1961. The Development of the Jewish Scripts. Pp. 133–202 in *BANE.*

Freedman, D. N.; Mathews, K. A.; and Hanson, R. S. 1985. *The Paleo-Hebrew Leviticus Scroll.* New Haven.

HENRY O. THOMPSON

AZAEL (PERSON) [Gk *Azaēlos*]. A descendant of Ezora who divorced his foreign wife during Ezra's reform (1 Esdr 9:34). Although 1 Esdras is often assumed to have been compiled from Ezra, Azael does not appear among the list of names in Ezra 10. Omissions such as this also raise questions about 1 Esdras being used as a source by Ezra. Furthermore, problems associated with dating events and identifying persons described in 1 Esdras have cast doubt on the historicity of the text.

MICHAEL DAVID MCGEHEE

AZALIAH (PERSON) [Heb *ʾăṣalyāhû*]. The son of Meshullam and the father of the secretary Shaphan (2 Kgs 22:3). Azaliah's son Shaphan was the state secretary who figured prominently in connection with the discovery and publication of the celebrated book of the law during the reign of King Josiah. "Azaliah" is a verbal sentence-name formed with the perfect conjugation followed by a noun—a type of construction occurring frequently throughout the monarchy. Noth (*IPN,* 193–94) is inclined to link *ʾṣlyh* (i.e., Azaliah) with the Ar *aṣula,* "to be firmly rooted; to be noble," as well as with the Heb *ʾṣyl* (= Ar *ʾaṣîl*), "noble," of Exod 24:11 and to translate the name as "Yahweh has shown himself to be noble." An alternative etymology would produce "Yahweh has set aside." Located in *BMAP* line 44 of papyrus 7 (a Jewish document; pp. 206–7, 222), a possible short form of Azaliah appears in the personal name *ʾṣwl,* father of one of the Jewish witnesses.

EDWIN C. HOSTETTER

AZANIAH (PERSON) [Heb *ʾăzanyāh*]. A Levite and the father of Jeshua, who was a signatory to the code of Nehemiah (Neh 10:10—Eng 10:9). The name is most likely a shortened form of *ʾăzanyāhû* which means "Yahweh has heard" (Fowler 1988: 156, 335).

Bibliography

Fowler, J. D. 1988. *Theophoric Personal Names in Ancient Hebrew.* JSOTSup 49. Sheffield.

FREDERICK W. SCHMIDT

AZAREL (PERSON) [Heb *ʿăzarʾel*]. Var. UZZIEL. A few Heb mss vocalize the name as "Azriel" [Heb *ʿazrîʾēl*]. LXX mss exhibit a wide range of variations on the name [*azarael, azaria, ezerel, ezriel, eliel, esdriel, esriel, oz(e)iel, oziel, ozr(e)iel,* and *ozriel*]. The KJV renders the name as Azareel with one exception: Azarael (Neh 12:36). Interestingly, the NEB has both Azareel (1 Chr 12:6; 25:4; 27:22; Ezra 10:41) and Azarel (Neh 11:13; 12:36). The AB upholds the RSV in its consistent use of the name Azarel in the 6 relevant passages below.

1. One of the men supportive of David during his "outlaw" period (1 Chr 12:7—Eng 12:6). His name occurs in a list of 23 bowmen, archers, and stone-slingers who joined David at Ziklag. If the men were all Benjaminites (1 Chr 12:2), the reference to "Korahites" [Heb *haqqorḥîm*] in 1 Chr 12:7—Eng 12:6 is strange. This might suggest that these Korahite Levites were once resident in the territory of Benjamin, but the greater probability is that the Korahites here have nothing to do with the Levitical Korah, nor even with the Calebite Korah mentioned in 1 Chr 2:43 (Myers *1 Chronicles* AB, 96). Although there can be no certainty, the word may refer to an unattested place in Benjamin or even a place in Judah where these Benjaminites had been living (see Aharoni and Avi-Yonah *MBA,* maps 93–94 and 113). The Chronicler's point in the context (1 Chr 12:1–8—Eng 12:1–7) was to emphasize the loyalty which came to David from outside Judah, from Benjamin, King Saul's own tribe.

2. A Levite, a son of Heman, one of the persons set apart for the service of music and song in the time of David (1 Chr 25:18). He is called Uzziel [Heb *ᶜuzzîʾēl*] in 1 Chr 25:4. The Chronicler reports, somewhat artificially, how each of Heman's 14 sons was assigned by lot a priestly course of temple musicianship; this Azarel is associated with the so-called 11th course out of a grand total of 24 courses, each with 12 members (1 Chr 25:4, 8–31).

3. A Danite, the son of Jeroham [Heb *yĕrōḥām*; LXX *iōram*] (1 Chr 27:22). His name occurs in a list of military and civil administrators in the time of David. The list constitutes an attempt by the Chronicler to show the tribal inclusiveness of David's "Israel" (1 Chr 27:16–22; Coggins *1 and 2 Chronicles* CBC, 134).

4. A Levitical priest, the son of Ahzai and father of Amashsai, descended from Immer (Neh 11:13). Amashsai, his son, was representative of one of the Levitical families serving in the restored Jerusalem temple in the days of Nehemiah. His correspondent in the synoptic parallel, 1 Chr 9:12, seems to be Adiel [Heb *ᶜadîʾel*], father of Maasai (= Amashsai?), likewise a descendant of Immer.

5. Son of a priest, a musician who participated in the procession for the dedication of the wall of Jerusalem in the time of Nehemiah (Neh 12:36).

6. One of the sons of Binnui (RSV), and a contemporary of Ezra (Ezra 10:10, 38, 41). He is included in a list of persons who married foreign women and were induced by Ezra to divorce them along with their children. On the text adopted by the RSV in Ezra 10:38, see the discussion under AMARIAH 10. The parallel, 1 Esdr 9:34, speaks of Azarel [LXX *ezril*] as a son of Ezora [LXX *ezōra*]. See further Braun *1 Chronicles* WBC.

ROGER W. UITTI

AZARIAH (PERSON) [Heb *ᶜăzaryāh, ᶜăzaryāhû*]. Azariah is a personal name (meaning "Yahweh has helped") given to a number of individuals in the books of the Heb Bible and the LXX. Identification of some of the individuals remains tentative because of differences between parallel genealogical texts, differences between the MT and the versions, and questions about the intended function of the genealogical material in the various books.

1. Azariah (1 Kgs 4:2) is listed first in the register of King Solomon's officials. Since his title is given as *hakkōhēn* "the priest"—in contrast to the titles of Zadok and Abiathar (1 Kgs 4:4) who are identified as priests [Heb *kōhănîm*] or Zabud (1 Kgs 4:5) who is called a "priest and king's friend" [Heb *kōhēn rēᶜeh hammelek*]—it is likely that he was the high priest responsible to the king for the supervision of the priests and cult of the Jerusalem temple. Here Azariah is called "son of Zadok"; however, the references to "Azariah son of Johanan" in 1 Chr 5:36–37—Eng 6:10–11 and to an ancestor of Ezra in Ezra 7:3 and 2 Esdr 1:2 ("Azariah son of Meraioth") may refer to the same person. The genealogies given for this family differ (see Braun *1 Chronicles* WBC, 84; Myers *1–2 Esdras* AB, 154), and are probably intended to be only partial (indicating membership in the family of the high priests) rather than complete for the family.

2. Azariah son of Nathan (1 Kgs 4:5) is identified as the official in King Solomon's administration who supervised the 12 officers responsible for securing provisions for the palace. Commentators generally emend the MT of 1 Kgs 4:7–19b; however, since 12 individuals are named in the MT, the "one officer" in 1 Kgs 4:19b could be understood to refer to Azariah and show that the officials listed in 1 Kgs 4:8b–19a were his subordinates.

3. Azariah son of Amaziah and Jecoliah was made king of Judah at the age of 16 following the assassination of Amaziah (2 Kgs 14:19–22; 15:1–2; 1 Chr 3:11; 2 Chr 26:1). 2 Chr 26:7a involves a play on the name Azariah, although the king is called Uzziah [Heb *ᶜuzîyāh, ᶜuzîyāhû* (sic codex Leningradensis); *ᶜuzzîyāh, ᶜuzzîyāhû*] in 2 Chronicles and elsewhere (see 2 Kgs 15:13, 30, 32, 34; 2 Chr 26:1–23; 27:2; Isa 1:1; 6:1; and others). Some scholars hold with Myers (*Ezra, Nehemiah* AB, 149) that Azariah was the king's personal name and Uzziah was adopted as a throne name. Others (Williamson *1–2 Chronicles* NCBC, 333–34; Cogan and Tadmor *2 Kings* AB, 165–66) note that the roots *ᶜzr* and *ᶜzz* are semantically similar and treat Azariah and Uzziah as variants of one name. His achievements included the restoration of Elath to Judah (1 Kgs 14:22). He is credited with a reign of 52 years during which he did "what was right in the eyes of Yahweh" (2 Kgs 15:2–3; 2 Chr 26:3–4). Scholars usually assume that Azariah was put on the throne of Judah when his father was captured by Jehoash, king of Israel; however, chronological reconstructions vary. Both 2 Kings and 2 Chronicles report that Yahweh smote Azariah with leprosy. In 2 Kings the report follows the statement that the high places were not destroyed and the people continued to sacrifice and burn incense at the high places (2 Kgs 15:4–5). 2 Chronicles reports that he entered the temple to burn incense and became angry when the chief priest [Heb *kōhēn hārōʾš*], also named Azariah, and a company of 90 priests challenged him. When he became angry with the priests, a skin disease ("leprosy") broke out on his forehead (2 Chr 26:16–21). His affliction forced him to turn over much of the administration of both the palace and the people of the land to his son Jotham.

4. Azariah son of Ethan (1 Chr 2:8) is identified as a grandson of Zerah and great grandson of Judah.

5. Azariah son of Jehu (1 Chr 2:38–39) is mentioned among the descendants of Judah in 1 Chr 2:3–4:24. He is identified as the father of Helez.

6. Azariah son of Ahimaaz (1 Chr 5:35—Eng 6:9) was a Levite, a descendant of such important priestly figures as Kohath, Aaron, Phinehas, and Zadok; according to the Chronicler, he was the grandfather of the Azariah (see 1. above) who served as priest in the temple of Solomon.

7. Azariah son of Hilkiah (1 Chr 5:39—Eng 6:13) is identified as a Levite and a descendant of the same family as Azariah son of Ahimaaz (6. above) and Azariah (1.

above). He was the father of Seraiah and an ancestor of Ezra (Ezra 7:1; 1 Esdr 8:1; 2 Esdr 1:1).

8. Azariah son of Zephaniah (1 Chr 6:21—Eng 6:36) is identified as a Levite, a descendant of Kohath through Izhar and an ancestor of Heman the singer. Heman and Asaph were appointed by David to be in charge of the service of song for "the tabernacle of the tent of meeting" and later for the temple of Solomon (1 Chr 6:16–17—Eng 6:31–32).

9. Azariah son of Hilkiah (1 Chr 9:11) is identified as one of the priests who returned from the exile to live in Jerusalem. Azariah's name stands out from those of the priests listed in 1 Chr 9:10 because his pedigree is given. Some of the names of Azariah's forebearers are reminiscent of the names of the forebearers of Azariah son of Hilkiah (see 7. above). The title "chief officer of the house of God" [*nĕgîd bêt hāʾĕlōhîm*] properly belongs to Azariah and not to Ahitub, the last name in Azariah's pedigree. Thus Azariah should be understood to be another important figure from the family that included other priests named Azariah (1., 6., and 7. above).

10. Azariah son of Oded (2 Chr 15:1), with the spirit of God upon him, went out to meet King Asa as the king was returning to Jerusalem from a successful campaign against an army of Ethiopians commanded by Zerah and against the cities around Gerar. His message (2 Chr 15:2a–7), directed to the king and the people, stressed that God would be with them when they were with God, and that if they would seek God they would be allowed to find God. Azariah warned them, however, that should they forsake God, God would forsake them. He used an example drawn from the history of Israel to illustrate his point (2 Chr 15:3–6). He exhorted Asa to take courage and not let his hands be weak because there would be a reward for his deeds (2 Chr 15:7). In both the MT and the LXX, 2 Chr 15:8 reports that on hearing these words "and the prophecy of Oded the prophet," Asa continued to remove all the abominable idols from the land. Even the image of Asherah made and worshiped by Asa's mother was removed and destroyed, and she was removed from the office of queen mother. Asa led the people in swearing to enter into a covenant to seek the LORD God of Israel.

11. Azariah [Heb *ʿăzaryāh*] is identified as a son of Jehoshaphat (2 Chr 21:2). King Jehoshaphat had given him and his brothers great gifts of silver, gold, precious stones, and fortified cities in Judah. Jehoram was designated to succeed his father as king, however, because he was the firstborn. When Jehoram gained the throne, he killed Azariah and his brothers as well as some of the officials of Israel.

12. Azariah [Heb *ʿăzaryāhû*] is listed as another son of King Jehoshaphat (2 Chr 21:2) who was killed by Jehoram after Jehoram had gained the throne of their father.

13. Azariah son of Jeroham (2 Chr 23:1) was one of the commanders of hundreds [*śārê hammēʾôt*] who acted with Jehoiada in the crowning of Joash as king, the execution of Athaliah, the making of a covenant declaring that all the people and the new king would be a people of Yahweh, and the destruction of Baal's temple, altars, and priest (2 Chr 23:1–21).

14. Azariah son of Obed (2 Chr 23:1) was another of the commanders of hundreds who cooperated with Jehoiada to depose Athaliah and make Joash king (see 13. above).

15. Azariah (2 Chr 26:17, 20) is identified by the Chronicler as the chief priest [Heb *kōhēn hārōʾš*] who withstood King Azariah/Uzziah (see 3. above) when the king entered the temple to burn incense upon the incense altar. He declared that it was not for the king to offer incense but for the priests, the descendants of Aaron, who were consecrated, and he warned that what the king was doing would bring no honor to him. 1 Kgs 4 lists Azariah (see 1. above) as one of the top level officials of Solomon's administration. He was the chief priest [Heb *hakkōhēn*] but was subordinate to the king. The impression of the relationship between chief priest and king given by the report of the confrontation between Azariah and Uzziah is different, and raises questions about the role of the chief priest or high priest in the period of the monarchy. To what extent might the Chronicler's report reflect the power of the postexilic high priesthood? How might the power of the high priesthood have changed over time during the monarchy?

16. Azariah son of Johanan (2 Chr 28:12) is listed as one of the chiefs of the Ephraimites [Heb *rāʾšê bĕnê-ĕprayim*] who spoke in support of the prophet Oded when the prophet called upon the army of Israel to release the prisoners they had taken when Pekah was at war with Ahaz. Azariah and the other chiefs gave provisions to the captives from the spoil that had been taken and returned the captives to Jericho.

17. Azariah (2 Chr 29:12) is identified as a descendant of Kohath and Zadok. He was the father of Joel, one of the leaders of the Levites who aided in the cleansing of the temple under King Hezekiah. The Chronicler may have held that he was the chief priest during the reign of Hezekiah (see 18. below) and belonged to the important Levitical family of Israel's high priests which included several men named Azariah (see 1., 6., 7., 9., and 15. above).

18. Azariah (2 Chr 31:10, 13) served as chief priest [Heb *kōhēn hārōʾš*] and as chief officer of the house of God [Heb *nĕgîd bêt-hāʾĕlōhîm*] during the reign of Hezekiah. The Chronicler seems to have understood him to belong to the family of Israel's high priests (see 1., 6., 7., 9., 15., and 17. above).

19. Azariah son of Jehallelel (2 Chr 29:12), a descendant of Merari, was one of the Levitical leaders who participated in the cleansing of the temple under King Hezekiah. The emphasis on the role played by the Levites in the cleansing of the temple and in helping the priests to flay the burnt offerings, the inclusion of the names of the Levitical leaders, and the statement that the Levites "were more upright in heart than the priests in sanctifying themselves" (2 Chr 29:34) illustrate the Chronicler's interest in the Levites as an important priestly group in Israel's cult.

20. Azariah son of Maaseiah (Neh 3:23, 24) is identified as one of the people who worked to rebuild the wall of Jerusalem. He restored the section of the wall that was next to his house. The individuals named in Nehemiah 3 should be understood as the leaders of groups of workers presumably including their extended families. This is clear in the cases of Eliashib the high priest (Neh 3:1), Shallum (Neh 3:12), Hanun (Neh 3:13), and Pedaiah (Neh 3:25–

26), instances in which individuals are named with groups. In other cases, groups are mentioned but no individuals are named as leaders: the sons of Hassenaah (Neh 3:3), the Tekoites (Neh 3:5, 27), the priests, the men of the Plain (Neh 3:22), and the goldsmiths and merchants (Neh 3:32).

21. Azariah (Neh 7:7) is identified as a leader of exiles returning to Judah from Babylonian exile. The list of leaders and returned exiles in Neh 7:4–72a differs from those found in Ezra 2:1–70 and 1 Esdr 5:7–42 (Myers *Ezra, Nehemiah* AB, 10–22; *1–2 Esdras* AB, 58–71).

22. Azariah (Neh 8:7) was one of the Levites listed by name who helped the people to understand Ezra's reading of the Torah. Whether their help involved both translation and interpretation or interpretation only is a matter of scholarly debate (Fensham *Ezra and Nehemiah* NICOT, 217–18; Williamson *1–2 Chronicles* NCBC, 277–99).

23. Azariah (Neh 10:3—Eng 10:2) was one of the priests who put his seal on the covenant made by those who had returned from exile. The covenant obligated the people to live by the commandments and ordinances of Yahweh (Neh 10: 29–30—Eng 10:28–29), to avoid intermarriage with foreigners (Neh 10:31—Eng 10:30), to refrain from buying from foreigners on the sabbath or holidays, to observe the sabbatical year and to refrain from charging interest (Neh 10:32—Eng 10:31), to give one-third of a shekel each year for the service of the temple (Neh 10:33–34—Eng 10:32–33), to provide wood for the altar (Neh 10:35—Eng 10:34), and to bring the first fruits, firstborn, and tithes (Neh 10:36–40—Eng 10:35–39).

24. Azariah (Neh 12:33) was one of those who participated in the dedication of the wall of Jerusalem (Neh 12:27–43). He may perhaps be identified with Azariah son of Maaseiah (see 20. above).

25. Azariah son of Hoshaiah (MT Jer 43:2) is named as one of those who refused to heed Jeremiah's warning not to go to Egypt following the assassination of Gedaliah. The MT lists a Jezaniah son of Hoshaiah as a member of the party that had approached Jeremiah to request that he ask Yahweh what they should do (Jer 42:1). The RSV assumes that this was Azariah. In the LXX (Jer 49:1) the 2 named leaders of the party that approached Jeremiah are Johanan and Azariah, but here and in the report of the people's reaction to Jeremiah's warning (Jer 50:2) the LXX identifies this person as Azariah son of Maaseiah.

26. Azariah (Dan 1:6, 7, 11, 19; 2:17) was one of the young Judean men selected to be trained in the "letters and language of the Chaldeans" (Dan 1:4). He was given a new name, Abednego, and along with Daniel, Hananiah, and Mishael ate vegetables and drank water rather than defile himself by eating the food appointed by the king (Dan 1:8–16). At the end of the training period the king found these 4 young men superior to his own magicians and enchanters (Dan 1:17–21). When the king's magicians and enchanters were unable to tell him both the dream he had dreamed and its interpretation (Daniel 2), the king issued a decree that all the magicians and enchanters were to be killed. Daniel called upon Hananiah, Mishael, and Azariah to seek God's mercy that they might not be destroyed with the rest of Babylon's sages, and the mystery was revealed to Daniel in a night vision. When the king made an image of gold and commanded that when everyone heard the sound of music they were to worship the image (Daniel 3), Hananiah, Mishael, and Azariah (here called Shadrach, Meshach, and Abednego) refused to worship the image, even when the king threatened to have them thrown into a fiery furnace. Their faith, courage, and deliverance made them examples for others who faced coercion by foreign rulers (1 Macc 2:59; 4 Macc 16:21; 18:12). The LXX includes a prayer attributed to Azariah and a hymn of praise attributed to the 3 young men (LXX Dan 3:24–90; Pr Azar).

27. Azariah is identified as a "leader of the people" who commanded forces under Judas Maccabeus. When Judas divided the forces, sending Simon and his forces to Galilee while he and Jonathan took their forces to Gilead, he left Azariah and Joseph son of Zechariah with part of the forces, ordering them to guard Judea but not to engage in battle with the Gentiles until the return of the rest of the forces (1 Macc 5:18–19). Azariah and Joseph, wishing to make a name for themselves, disobeyed their orders and led their forces in attacking Jamnia. Their forces were routed with 2,000 casualties reported (1 Macc 5:55–62).

28. Azariah, a descendant of Immer (1 Esdr 9:21), is listed as one of the priests who had married foreign wives and who were required to put away these wives and their children.

29. Azariah (1 Esdr 9:43) is listed as one of those standing at the right side of Ezra at the reading of the law—perhaps to be identified with Azariah the descendant of Immer (27 above).

Bibliography

De Vries, S. J. 1989. *1–2 Chronicles.* FOTL 11. Grand Rapids.

Long, B. O. 1984. *1 Kings: With an Introduction to Historical Literature.* FOTL 9. Grand Rapids.

KEITH L. EADES

AZARIAH, PRAYER OF. See DANIEL, ADDITIONS TO.

AZARIAS (PERSON) [Gk *Azarias*]. The name assumed by the archangel RAPHAEL in the book of Tobit (5:13—Eng 5:12). Tobit, blind and destitute except for money left for safekeeping with a man named Gabael in Rages, prayed for help. God sent Raphael to assist him. The archangel identified himself to Tobit and his son Tobias as Azarias (meaning "God helps"), the son of the great Ananias ("God favors"), one of Tobit's relatives (5:13—Eng 5:12). Zimmermann (1958: 75) argues that the names were chosen to please the reader through word plays. The book appears to be one of a couple of dozen efforts to combine two well-known folk tales, familiar to moderns as "The Grateful Dead" and "The Unlucky Bride" (Dancy 1972: 2–3). As is typical in folklore, neither Tobit nor Tobias recognized that Azarias was an angel in disguise.

True to the meaning of his name, Azarias assisted at every hand. He accompanied Tobias to collect Tobit's money from Gabael and instructed Tobias to take the heart, liver, and gall of a huge fish he had caught (6:5—Eng 6:4). Next (7:10—Eng 7:9), Azarias negotiated the marriage between Tobias and Sarah, a beautiful kinswoman widowed seven times by a jealous demon (Asmodeus) before her marriages could be consummated (3:8). Azarias instructed Tobias to burn the fish's heart and liver on the wedding night to drive away the demon (6:17–18—Eng 6:16–17). During the fourteen-day wedding feast, Azarias took Tobit's receipt to Gabael to secure the money (9:5). Finally, Azarias instructed Tobias to anoint Tobit's eyelids with the fish's gall, thus healing Tobit (11:7–13).

In the intertestamental period, Jewish speculation about ARCHANGELS flourished. Their number varied (principally four or seven), as did their identities. One basic list, which agrees with the book of Tobit (12:15) concerning their number, appears in 1 En. 20:1–7, where they include Uriel, Raphael, Raguel, Michael, Seraqael, Gabriel, and Remiel. Rabinnic commentary on Gen 18:1 *(Gen. Rab.)* attributes their names to Babylonian influence, but modern day scholars contend that the real source was Zoroastrianism (Russell 1964: 258–59).

The Hebrew form of the name, AZARIAH, appears as Abednego in the Hebrew Bible (Dan 1:7). In the addition to Daniel known as The Prayer of Azarias and the Song of the Three Young Men, Azariah offers the prayer on behalf of the three captives and is mentioned again in v 66. Azariah also appears as the name of a Levite who assisted Ezra by interpreting the law (Neh 8:7, 1 Esdr 9:48), and as a general of Judas Maccabeus (1 Macc 5:18, 56, 60).

Bibliography

Dancy, J. C. 1972. *The Shorter Books of the Apocrypha.* Cambridge.

Russell, D. 1964. *The Method and Message of Jewish Apocalyptic.* Philadelphia.

Zimmermann, F. 1958. *The Book of Tobit.* New York: Harper.

PAUL L. REDDITT

AZARU (PERSON) [Gk *Azarou*]. Forefather of an exiled family numbering 432 which returned to Judah with Zerubbabel according to the list in 1 Esdr 5:15. If AZZUR [Heb *ʿazzûr*] (Neh 10:18—Eng 10:17) is accepted as an equivalent variant, then 1 Esdr 5:15 supplements Ezra 2:16b as *BHS* suggests (see Williamson *Ezra, Nehemiah* WBC, 25).

CRAIG D. BOWMAN

AZAZ (PERSON) [Heb *ʿāzāz*]. Name of a Reubenite (1 Chr 5:8), the father of Bela, a kinsman of Beerah (who went into exile under Tiglath-pileser III in the second half of the 8th century according to 1 Chr 5:6). The name Azaz is a hypocoristic form of the theophoric Azaziah, which means "Yahweh is strong." Interestingly enough, although the name is vocalized by the Masoretes as *ʿāzāz* (which would agree with Jerome's *Azaz,* as well as the Ar *ʿazāzun*), the LXX reads *ōzouz,* while the Syr Peshitta reads *ʿûzî.* The Syr is probably explained as being a "Syrianization" of a root which is geminate in Heb, but middle weak in Syr. The LXX may be evidence for a late *ā* > *ō* shift in some dialects of Heb at the time of the LXX, analogous to that which took place in Phoenician, or may simply be an example of the LXX translators not knowing what to do with this name.

H. ELDON CLEM

AZAZEL [Heb *ʿăzā*ʾ*zēl*]. The destination or goal to or for which the scapegoat is sent on the Day of Atonement (Lev 16:8, 10, 26).

A. The Term

The meaning of the term *ʿăzā*ʾ*zēl* is not entirely clear. The main interpretations are: (a) It is the name of a demon (e.g., Delcor 1976: 35–37; Loretz 1985: 50–57; Tawil 1980). (b) It is a geographical designation meaning something like "precipitous place" or "rugged cliff" (*Sipra, Aḥare Mot* 2:8; *Tg. Ps.-J.* Lev 16:10, 22; Driver 1956: 97–98). (c) It is an abstract noun meaning "destruction" or "entire removal" (e.g., *BDB* 736). (d) It is made up of the terms ʾ*ēz* ʾ*ōzēl* "goat that goes (away)" and is a description of the dispatched goat (cf. the LXX, Vg; it is from this interpretation that we get our term "scapegoat").

Of the four views, understanding *ʿăzā*ʾ*zēl* as an epithet of a demonic personality is the most reasonable. The main evidences for this are: (a) Lev 16:8 prescribes that Aaron is to place a lot on each of the two goats provided by the Israelites. One lot designates one goat as being "for *Yhwh*" while the other lot designates the other goat as being "for *ʿăzā*ʾ*zēl.*" As the first lot is for a supernatural being, *Yhwh,* so the second lot should be for a supernatural being of some sort. (b) The goat designated for *ʿăzā*ʾ*zēl* is sent out to *ʿăzā*ʾ*zēl* in the wilderness which is one of the usual abodes of demons (Isa 13:21–22; 34:11–15; perhaps also Lev 17:7; cf. Tob 8:3; Matt 12:43). (c) In pseudepigraphic literature Azazel appears as a full-fledged demonic being (*1 Enoch* 8:1; 9:6; 10:4–8; 13:1; cf. 54:5–6; 55:4; 69:2; *Apoc. Ab.* 13:6–14; 14:4–6; 20:5–7; 22:5; 23:11; 29:6–7; 31:5; on the problems of this tradition, see Hanson 1977: 220–33; Nickelsburg 1977: 397–404; Grabbe 1987: 153–55). (d) While the name could be interpreted as the epithet of a supernatural being while retaining the order of the consonants in the MT (*ʿz*ʾ*zl*), the etymology of the name has been explained as a metathesized form of *ʿzz-*ʾ*l* meaning something like "fierce god" or "angry god" which, if correct, would reveal decisively the demonic character of the being (cf. Tawil 1980; Loretz 1985: 50–57). The *Temple Scroll* and other literature at Qumran contain the form *ʿzz*ʾ*l* (11QTemple 26:13 and see Grabbe 1987: 156).

B. The Character of Azazel

Though Azazel is a demonic personality, caution must be observed in determining his exact character in the Day of Atonement ritual. Just because he is a demon does not automatically mean that he functions like demonic personalities in other religions of the ANE. In fact, there is reason to suppose that in the biblical rite he was to be considered a rather peripheral and impotent figure, hardly more than a place-holder representing the geographical goal of the scapegoat's dispatch (Wright 1987: 21–25). A main reason for believing that the formulators of Leviticus 16 thought of Azazel in this way is the tendency of Israel's monotheistic religion to reject or at least limit any power that would compete with Yahweh (Duhm 1904: 28, 32). Another reason is that the Priestly writings have very little to say about demons. The only other reference to demons besides that to Azazel is in Lev 17:7. But the use of *śĕʿîrîm* ("goat-demons") here seems to be more a pejorative belittling of such beings than an expression of belief in their reality and vitality (cf. similar use of demonic terminology in Deut 32:17; Ps 106:37).

The entirely different treatment of corresponding demonic figures in rites of elimination from the ANE seems to confirm this picture of Azazel (for examples from ancient Anatolia and Mesopotamia, see Wright 1987: 31–74). Many of these rituals speak of offended or angry deities or demons who must be propitiated so that a plague or other evil might be lifted from mankind or an individual. The attacking supernatural beings are addressed with incantations which reveal in some detail the personality of the demonic beings. The human sufferers send offerings of appeasement and substitution to assuage the demonic wrath. For example, in the Hittite ritual of Ashella which seeks to dispel a demon-caused plague among the Hittite army (see Wright 1987: 50–51), leaders of the army decorate rams with colored wools and other materials. They recite: "Whatever god is moving about, whatever god has caused this plague, for you, behold, these rams I have tied up. Be herewith appeased!" The next day the animals are driven into the open country with beer, bread, and perhaps milk as offerings. Before the rams are sent away, the leaders place their hands on the animals and say: "Whatever god has caused this plague—now, behold, the rams are standing; they are very fat in liver, heart, and genital member. Let the flesh of humans be hateful to him. Moreover, be appeased with these rams!" In other rituals, instead of being attacking demons, gods may be custodians of evil. They are called upon to take away and dispose of the evil caused by another source. For their help they receive offerings of thanksgiving. For example, in the Hittite ritual of Ambazzi (Wright 1987: 57), a woman cult officiator removes a bowstring with tin on it from a ritual patient, puts it on a mouse, and says: "I have taken away from you [i.e., the patient] evil and I have put it on the mouse. Let this mouse take it to the high mountains, the deep valleys (and) the distant ways." After this she lets the mouse go, saying: "O Alawaimi [a god], drive this (mouse) forth, and I will give to you a goat to eat." In contrast, Leviticus 16 does not speak of Azazel in any of these terms: he causes no harm, he receives no offerings (the scapegoat is not a sacrifice), prayers are not made to him. Such a laconic treatment of Azazel in view of these other rituals suggests that Azazel is not an active being that is due any sort of veneration or attention.

C. Azazel Before Leviticus 16

Finally, that Azazel appears in repressed form in the Priestly ritual intimates that he is not an invention of that school of thought but comes from a pre-Priestly form of the rite in which he played a more active role, either as an angry deity as one proposed etymology of his name may suggest (*ʿzz-ʾl*) or as merely a beneficent custodian of evil. The reason that he was retained in the Priestly version of the rite may be due to popular belief which would not allow total expunging of the personality.

Bibliography

Delcor, M. 1976. Le mythe de la chute des anges. *RHR* 190: 3–53.

Driver, G. R. 1956. Three Technical Terms in the Pentateuch. *JSS* 1: 97–105.

Duhm, H. 1904. *Die bösen Geister im Alten Testament.* Tübingen and Leipzig.

Grabbe, L. L. 1987. The Scapegoat: A Study in Early Jewish Interpretation. *JSJ* 18: 152–67.

Hanson, P. D. 1977. Rebellion in Heaven, Azazel, and Euhemeristic Heroes in 1 Enoch 6–11. *JBL* 96: 195–233.

Loretz, O. 1985. *Leberschau, Sündenbock, Asasel in Ugarit und Israel.* Ugaritisch-Biblische Literatur. Soest.

Nickelsburg, G. W. E. 1977. Apocalyptic and Myth in 1 Enoch 6–11. *JBL* 96: 383–405.

Tawil, H. 1980. ʿAzazel the Prince of the Steepe [sic]: A Comparative Study. *ZAW* 92: 43–59.

Wright, D. P. 1987. *The Disposal of Impurity: Elimination Rites in the Bible and in Hittite and Mesopotamian Literature.* SBLDS 101. Atlanta.

DAVID P. WRIGHT

AZAZIAH (PERSON) [Heb *ʿazazyāhû*]. The name means "Yahweh is strong." In certain instances, the versions (LXX and Vg) read *ʿuzzîyāhû* (Uzziah) for *ʿazazyāhû* (Azaziah). There are 3 people in the MT who bear this name.

1. A Levite who was appointed to play the lyre during the transfer of the ark of the covenant from the house of Aminadab to Jerusalem (1 Chr 15:21).

2. The father of Hoshea, the chief officer of Ephraim in the reign of David (1 Chr 27:20).

3. One of 12 temple overseers (presumably a Levite) who was in charge of tithes and dedicated contributions. He was appointed by Hezekiah and Azariah the chief temple officer during Hezekiah's reform.

Bibliography

Fowler, J. D. 1987. *Theophoric Personal Names in Ancient Hebrew: A Comparative Study.* JSOTSup 49. Sheffield.

H. ELDON CLEM

AZBUK (PERSON) [Heb *ʿazbûq*]. A Judahite of the time of Nehemiah (Neh 3:16). His son, also named Nehemiah, acted as supervisor of half of the Judean district of Beth-zur during the rebuilding of the wall of Jerusalem. The meaning and grammatical analysis of the name *ʿazbûq* is uncertain (perhaps "[the god] Buk is strong"; cf. *ʿazgad,* "[the god] Gad is strong," Neh 10:16).

NORA A. WILLIAMS

AZEKAH (PLACE) [Heb *ʾăzēkâ*]. A town within the confines of the N Shephelah district of Judah (Josh 15:35).

A. Historical References

Azekah is first mentioned in the story of the 5 Amorite kings whom Joshua defeated at Gibeon and pursued as far as Azekah (Josh 10:10–11). During the encounter of David with Goliath, the Philistines camped in the valley of Elah between Socoh and Azekah (1 Sam 17:1). Rehoboam (922–

915 B.C.) fortified Azekah and included it within the defensive system erected after the division of the United Monarchy (2 Chr 11:9).

An Assyrian inscription mentions Azekah in connection with Sargon II's campaign against Iamani, ruler of Ashdod, in 712 B.C. (Tadmor 1958). Still later, Azekah and Lachish are mentioned as the last remaining fortresses of Judah to withstand the Babylonian onslaught (Jer 34:7). Similar information appears in Lachish letter no. 4 (*ANET,* 322). The town was conquered by Nebuchadnezzar apparently in 588 B.C., a short while before the fall of Jerusalem. With the return from exile, several families of the tribe of Judah resettled in Azekah (Neh 11:30). Fragmentary information from the period following the destruction of the 2d Temple indicates that Azekah was still occupied. Eusebius located Azekah between Eleutheropolis (Beth Govrin) and Jerusalem (*Onomast.* 18:10), a possible reference to Khirbet al-'Almi, E of Tell Zakariya. The Madeba map, which dates from the 2d half of the 6th century A.D., calls the area "Bethzakar," the present-day Kefar Zechariah, which has given its name to Tell Zakariya (Avi Yonah 1954).

B. Site and Identification

Tell Zakariya (M.R. 143123) is located 5.5 miles NE of Beth Govrin. It stands about 117 m above the Elah Valley, which skirts the hill on the N and E. The mound is flat-topped, triangular in shape, and measures 330 by 170 m.

Over a century ago, J. Schwartz identified Tell Zakariya as the site of Azekah on the basis of written sources. F. J. Bliss, who excavated the site (Bliss and Macalister 1902), suggested the name had been transferred later from Azekah to Khirbet Shuweikeh, some 6 km further S in the Elah valley, and that biblical Socoh might conceivably be in the area of Tell Zakariya. However, after the discovery of a large Israelite site at Khirbet Abad (adjacent to Khirbet Socoh), Tell Zakariya has become generally accepted as the site of the town of Azekah.

C. Exploration of the Site

Tell Zakariya was excavated in 1898–99 under the auspices of the Palestine Exploration Fund, and was directed by F. J. Bliss, assisted by R. A. S. Macalister (Bliss and Macalister 1902).

In the SW, building foundations were examined and were found to belong to 3 towers built of rough stones bonded with clay. There were no traces of a wall connecting the towers, which led the excavators to conclude that the towers constituted individual forts intended to protect this side of the mound, which was particularly vulnerable to attack. On the basis of the depth of the foundations and some ceramic finds, the towers were assigned to the Roman-Byzantine period.

A rectangular fortress with towers at each corner was uncovered on the elevated SE section of the mound. Towers also stood along the middle of the E wall. The fortress gate was not discovered, although several doorways were found inside the towers. The entrance levels varied in elevation, and it thus seems that the fortress interior was not of equal height throughout.

Bliss felt that the towers in section I were a later addition to the fortress in section II, while Macalister assumed that they were contemporaneous but constructed by different groups of masons. Both attribute the construction of the fortress to Rehoboam (2 Chr 11:9).

Half of the fortress area was excavated, and bedrock was reached at a depth of approximately 6 m. The excavators were unable to assign periods to the buildings and other remains, nor did they determine the exact number of periods, although they initially distinguished 4 main occupation periods.

Period A is clearly defined by pottery of the type they labeled "Early Pre-Israelite" (see below). Among the objects found was a vessel containing assorted Egyptian jewelry, including two scarabs, one with the name of Thutmose III and the other of Amenhotep II. Period B is a plastered floor slightly above bedrock, with stamped handles containing the word *lmlk* ("[belonging] to the king") and two-winged scarabs. In period C, which the excavators labeled "Jewish" and considered to be later than period B, another plastered floor was discovered, containing four-winged scarab stamped jar handles. Period D has several rock-hewn tombs assigned to the Roman period. Also found were Seleucid, Roman, and Byzantine shards, as well as several graves close to surface level and considered of Arab origin.

A trial pit approximately 30 by 20 m was dug in the center of the mound, where bedrock was reached at no more than 4 m. The pottery consisted mainly of sherds of the so-called Late Pre-Israelite and Jewish periods. Since Seleucid pottery was extremely rare and no Roman-Byzantine shards were uncovered, the excavators concluded that the mound had been deserted by these periods.

All these finds led the excavators to conclude that the settlement had lasted, with short interruptions, from ca. 1500 B.C. until the Byzantine period. However, Albright (1960) subsequently examined the pottery tables published in the excavation reports and suggested the following amended dates:

Period	*Bliss-Macalister*	*Albright*
A	Early Pre-Israelite ca. ?–1500 B.C.	ca. 3000–1800 B.C.
B	Late Pre-Israelite ca. 1550–800 B.C.	1800–1000 B.C.
C	Jewish ca. 800–300 B.C.	1000–587 B.C.
D	Seleucid ca. 300– B.C.	4th–1st cent. B.C.

Today it is possible to introduce additional revisions in the chronology of the various structures on this site. The excavators attributed the fortress to Rehoboam (928–911 B.C.) and dated the 3 towers at the SW extremity of the mound to the Roman-Byzantine period. More recently, S. Yeivin (Avi-Yonah and Yeivin 1955: 289–90; cf. Horowitz 1980) assigned the construction of the fortress to the period of the Judges, and the towers (which in his opinion form part of the city wall) to Rehoboam, who also had the fortress repaired.

Other Israelite fortresses of similar construction have since been found in Judea (Mazar 1982). Also, since the various types of *lmlk* seal impressions can be assigned to the end of the 8th century, it may be assumed that the fortress was in existence at that time.

Bibliography

Albright, W. F. 1960. *The Archaeology of Palestine.* Harmondsworth.

Avi-Yonah, M. 1954. *Madaba Map.* Jerusalem.

Avi-Yonah, M., and Yeivin, S. 1955. *The Antiquities of Israel.* Tel Aviv (in Heb).

Bliss, F. J., and Macalister, R. A. S. 1902. *Excavations in Palestine (1898–1900).* London, 12–27, Pls. 1–5.

Horowitz, G. 1980. Town Planning of Hellenistic Marisa: A Reappraisal of the Excavations after Eighty Years. *PEQ* 112: 100–3.

Mazar, A. 1982. Iron Age Fortresses in the Judaean Hills. *PEQ* 114: 87–109.

Tadmor, H. 1958. The Campaigns of Sargon II of Assur. *JCS* 12: 80–84.

EPHRAIM STERN

AZEL (PERSON) [Heb *ʾāṣel*]. Var. AZALIA(?). A descendant of Saul through the line of Jonathan. His name occurs 6 times in the Heb Bible and twice in the Talmud (*Pesaḥ.* 62b). In the former, the name is part of a list of persons (1 Chr 8:35–36) which cannot be traced to any extant earlier source. When Azel was thought to have lived cannot be determined exactly. The names in the genealogy have been viewed as extending down into late preexilic times or even into the Exile itself. On the whole, it seems reasonable to suppose that Azel lived in the late 7th to early 6th centuries B.C.E. The occurrences of Azel in 1 Chr 9:43, 44, 45 are due to a repetition of the Saulide genealogy in 1 Chronicles 8. This duplication serves to introduce 1 Chronicles 10 which tells the story of Saul's death on Mount Gilboa. Not having chapter and verse divisions by which to cite a biblical text, the writer of the Talmud cites the material from 1 Chr 8:37–9:44 by reference to the name Azel in these verses. The name appears to be a variant form of AZALIAH (2 Kgs 22:3) and may designate "noble" or "laid aside, reserved" in the sense of being protected.

JAMES M. KENNEDY

AZETAS (PERSON) [Gk *Azētas*]. Ancestor of a family which returned from Babylon with Zerubbabel (1 Esdr 5:15). Although 1 Esdras is often assumed to have been compiled from Ezra and Nehemiah, this family does not appear among their lists of returning exiles (cf. Ezra 2:16; Neh 7:21). Omissions such as this also raise questions about 1 Esdras being used as a source by Ezra or Nehemiah. Furthermore, problems associated with dating events and identifying persons described in 1 Esdras have cast doubt on the historicity of the text.

MICHAEL DAVID MCGEHEE

AZGAD (PERSON) [Heb *ʿazgād*]. Head of a family of Babylonian exiles who are listed as returnees under the leadership of Zerubbabel and others (Ezra 2:12 = Neh 7:17 = 1 Esdr 5:13) and later under Ezra (Ezra 8:12 = 1 Esdr 8:38). The leader of the clan affixed the family name to the covenant of Nehemiah in Neh 10:16—Eng 10:15. For further discussion of the exilic name lists and bibliography see AKKUB and ATER. The etymology of the name is uncertain. It has been identified as a theophoric name meaning: "Gad (deity) has proved himself strong" (Noth *IPN,* 190) or "Gad is strong" (Fowler, *TPNAH,* 64). Since these names occur only in the postexilic list, the name may have Persian derivation: *izgad* "messenger" (Fowler, *TPNAH,* 64).

CHANEY R. BERGDALL

AZIEL (PERSON) [Heb *ʿăzîʾēl*]. See JAAZIEL (PERSON).

AZIZA (PERSON) [Heb *ʿăzîzāʾ*]. A descendant of Zattu and one of the returned exiles who was required by Ezra to divorce his foreign wife (Ezra 10:27). Aziza is derived from the verbal root *ʿzz* "to be strong" and probably means "the strong one" (*IPN,* 225). In the parallel text of 1 Esdr 9:28, the name Zerdaiah appears in the position Aziza holds in Ezra 10:27. Aziza was a member of a family from which a group of exiles returned with Zerubbabel (Ezra 2:8; Neh 7:13). For further discussion, see BEDEIAH.

JEFFREY A. FAGER

AZMAVETH (PERSON) [Heb *ʿazmāwet*]. The name of several men in the OT. The name Azmaveth itself means "strong (*ʿaz)* as Death *(māweth)*" or "strong is Death," where Death is the personification of the god of death (cf. Hos 13:14; Hab 2:5; Pss 18:5, 49:5, 116:3; Prov 13:14). The LXX reading, Azmoth, is a legitimate variation on Azmaveth, with the same meaning (see DEATH). See also AZMAVETH (PLACE).

1. One of DAVID'S CHAMPIONS (the *šālišîm;* RSV Mighty Men), called the Barhumite (Heb *habbarḥumî;* 2 Sam 23:31; LXX *ho Barsamites*). 1 Chr 11:33, conversely, lists Azmaveth as the Baharumite (Heb *habbaḥarûmî;* LXX *ho Beermi*), apparently identifying him as a native of Bahurim, a place on the road from Jerusalem into the Jordan valley, and N of the Mount of Olives (see BAHURIM; 2 Sam 3:16; 16:5; 17:18; 19:17, etc.). The disagreement of both parallel texts in the MT as well as the quite different variants in the LXX suggest that the problem here is a corrupt text. Of the available readings, the Baharumite makes the most sense, though the other possibilities are not thereby excluded.

2. The father of Jeziel and Pelet, two archers and slingers of the tribe of Benjamin who were outlaw companions with David at Ziklag (1 Chr 12:3). This Azmaveth may possibly be the same as Azmaveth (1. above).

3. The son of Jehoaddah, a descendant of Saul and Jonathan (1 Chr 8:36, 9:42).

4. The son of Adiel, the treasurer in Jerusalem under David. (1 Chr 27:25).

5. The founder of a house in Israel, father of 42 men who returned from the exile (Ezra 2:24). This verse may, however, refer to 42 men of the city of Beth-Azmaveth (cf. Neh 7:28; see AZMAVETH [PLACE]; *Ezra Nehemiah* WBC, 26).

D. G. SCHLEY

AZMAVETH (PLACE) [Heb *ʿazmāwet*]. Var. BETH-AZMAVETH; BETHASMOTH. A village in the Judean hills N of Jerusalem probably established during the Israelite period (*LBHG,* 108), but remembered in the text from the time of the return from exile. The village is remembered as Azmaveth (Ezra 2:24, Neh 12:29), Beth-Azmaveth (Heb *bêt-ᶜazmāwet,* Gk *Bēthasmōth;* Neh 7:28), and Bethasmoth (Gk *Baitasmōn;* 1 Esdr 5:18). Though these names vary, they each appear in parallel accounts of a census of the people who returned to Jerusalem and Judah from captivity in Babylon. The same number of returnees (42) was recorded for each of them, and they appear in the same place in the list between Anathoth and Kiriatharim. The Azmaveth region is also remembered for providing singers for the dedication of the reconstructed wall of Jerusalem (Neh 12:29). The village has been identified as modern Hizmeh (M.R. 175138), a suggestion first made by Robinson and widely accepted by scholars (Albright 1922: 156). The site near Geba (modern Jebaᶜ, M.R. 175140) and Anathoth (modern Râs el-Kharrûbeh, M.R. 174135), whose patriarch was most likely the Asmaveth who was a descendant of Saul, has provided archaeological remains from the 2d Temple period (*EncMiqr* 2: 95). See also AZMAVETH (PERSON).

Bibliography

Albright, W. F. 1922. Alemeth and Azmaveth. *AASOR* 4: 156–57.

SUSAN E. MCGARRY

AZMON (PLACE) [Heb *ᶜaṣmôn*]. A station named both in the description of the S frontier of Canaan (Num 34:45), and in the delineation of the extreme S border of the tribal allotment of Judah (Josh 15:4). It is the last station W of the BROOK OF EGYPT. Alt (1953) has persuasively argued that the border list of Joshua 15 is derived from an ancient legal document delineating the territorial claims of the tribes during the period of the Judges. The parallel nature of the S border descriptions in Numbers 34 and Joshua 15 suggests that both depend on a single, presumably premonarchical, tradition. Azmon has often been identified with Ain Qoseimeh, a small spring in the vicinity of Ain el-Qudeirat (KADESH-BARNEA[?]), (*IDB* 1:327), but a more plausible possibility is Ain Muweilih (M.R. 085010), where archaeological survey (Rothenberg and Aharoni 1961: 36–37) has revealed a station on the ancient road to S Sinai dating to the Iron I period.

Bibliography

Alt, A. 1953. Das System der Stammesgrenzen in Buche Josua. *KlSchr* 1:193–202.

Rothenberg, B., and Aharoni, Y. 1961. *God's Wilderness.* London.

WADE R. KOTTER

AZNOTH-TABOR (PLACE) [Heb *ʾaznôt tābôr*]. A town that serves as the starting point of the description of the W border of the territory of the tribe of Naphtali (Josh 19:34). Noth (1935: 199–200) has suggested that Josh 19:33 described the N border of the tribal territory; however, the opening phrase of v 34 clearly shows that v 33 actually describes the S border from W to E. Verse 34 opens with the formula "And the border turned back westwards." This formula appears several times in Joshua, indicating that the border description returns to the starting point and then continues in the opposite direction, in this case northwards. The border of the territory of Zebulun is described in opposite directions from one starting point—Sarid (Josh 19: 10, 12); the border of the territory of Asher is described similarly, the starting point being Helkath (Josh 19:25—in LXX "from Helkath"—and in v 27 "And the border turned back eastwards"). It would appear that in the case of Naphtali the starting point is Mt. Tabor; but in order to achieve greater accuracy, *two* starting points appear, HELEPH for the S border (to be sought to the E of Mt. Tabor) and Aznoth-Tabor for the W border (to be sought N of the mountain). Saarisalo (1927: 127) identified the latter at Kh. Umm-Jubeil (M.R. 186237), 4 km N of the mountain, situated on a small hill ideally suited as a starting point for a border description. Saarisalo reported LB pottery from the site, but recent archaeological surveys report only pottery from Iron Age II and later (Zori 1977: 105; Gal 1982: 20).

Bibliography

Gal, Z. 1982. *The Lower Galilee in the Iron Age.* Diss., Tel Aviv (in Heb).

Noth, M. 1935. Studien zu den historisch-geographischen Dokumenten des Josuabuches, *ZDPV* 58: 185–225.

Saarisalo, A. 1927. *The Boundary between Issachar and Naphtali.* Helsinki.

Zori, N. 1977. *The Land of Issachar: Archaeological Survey.* Jerusalem (in Heb).

RAFAEL FRANKEL

AZOR, TEL (M.R. 131159). Tel Azor is situated about 6 km SE of Tel Aviv. The Arabic name Yazur preserves the ancient name of the site, which should probably be identified with "Azor" mentioned in the Vatican edition of the LXX (Joshua 19:45) where it appears as one of the cities of Dan (instead of MT *yhd*). Azor (Azuru) is mentioned in the late 8th century B.C. as a place Sennacherib captured from Sidqa king of Ashkelon (*ANET,* 287).

The site, measuring some 15 dunams, has not yet been excavated. A survey has revealed shards of almost all periods from the Chalcolithic to the medieval. On the summit of the mound stand the ruins of a Crusader fortress (Chateau des Plains). In the Kurkar hills adjacent to the site, many tombs were discovered dating to the Chalcolithic, EB I, MB II, LB, and Iron I–II periods. The extent of this vast cemetery is not known; most of it is now covered by the houses of present-day Azor, as well as by the Holon industrial area. The large number of burials in a relatively small tell suggests that this was a regional cemetery, although this hypothesis still needs to be substantiated.

"Salvage excavations" have been carried out from time to time as necessitated by the current building activity. The following excavators should be mentioned: J. Perrot and M. Dothan (1950s); R. Gophna, A. Druks, and Y. Shapira (1960s); A. Ben-Tor and O. Negbi (1970s). So far only a small part of these excavations has been fully described in published writings.

Since J. Perrot's excavations, Azor has become the type-site for Chalcolithic burials in ossuaries. More than 120 such ossuaries made out of clay were unearthed in a burial cave, in which 9 phases have been observed, including one habitation phase. Most of the ossuaries are house-shaped and some have zoomorphic shapes; others are jars. The house-shaped ossuaries are of major importance since they give some idea of the type of dwelling common in this period. Pottery constitutes the great majority of the funerary offerings: the assemblage is typologically closer to the Beer-Sheba than to the Ghassulian culture.

A large number of burial caves date to this period. They are cut into the Kurkar and all have a similar plan: 3 or 4 steps descending into a kidney-shaped burial chamber of ca. 20 square m. The number of those interred in each tomb may reach 100; burials are usually secondary; an occasional cremation has been observed. Most of the interred are of the local Mediterranean stock, but in several cases African-types (most probably Egyptians) have been noted. This corresponds well to the burial offerings: While most of the ceramic finds are clearly paralleled in other EB I assemblages throughout the country (mainly of the Proto-Urban A family of Kenyon's topology), some of the finds (clay vessels, a slate cosmetic palette, a flint knife, and various beads) are imported from Egypt.

An MB II tomb in which humans were buried side by side with horses is noteworthy. This phenomenon has so far been observed in only one other site in Israel, Tell el-Ajjul. In LB tombs, imported pottery (mainly of Cypriot origin) constitutes an important part of the assemblage.

Several tombs are dated to the 12th or 11th century B.C. Burials in pits, in jars, in brick coffins, as well as some cremations, are among the burial practices observed. In all those tombs, rich assemblages of burial gifts were found: the large variety of Philistine ware is especially noteworthy.

Several communal burials belong to this period: bodies and offerings were placed in successive layers in tombs surrounded by a stone fence. Also noteworthy is a group of burials in typical Israelite jars, one of which bears an inscription of the Hebrew name *šlmy*.

Bibliography

Ben-Tor, A. 1975. Two Burial Caves of the Proto-Urban Period at Azor. Qedem 1: 1–53.

Dothan, M. 1961a. Excavations at Azor. *IEJ* 2:171–75.

———. 1961b. An Inscribed Jar from Azor. *'Atiqot* 3: 181–84.

Ferembach, D. 1961. Les restes humains des tombes Philistines du cimetiere d'Azor. *Bulletin de la Societe d'Anthropologie* 2: 83–91.

Perrot, J. 1961. Une tombe à ossuaires du IVe millénaire à Azor près de Tel Aviv. *'Atiqot* 3: 1–83.

Perrot, J. and Ladiray, D. 1980. *Tombes à ossuaires,* 41–58. Paris.

AMNON BEN-TOR

AZOTUS (PLACE) [Gk *Azotus*]. The name for the Philistine city of ASHDOD in the Apocrypha and the NT. Located halfway between Gaza and Joppa, the ancient city stood less than 3 miles inland. Ashdod was excavated in 1962–72, and its history during the Maccabean and Roman periods is well-documented, particularly in 1 Maccabees and Josephus.

The city of Azotus appears (1 Macc 4:15) as a place of retreat (see Goldstein *1 Maccabees* AB, 265) to which soldiers in the army of Gorgias (one of the officers of Lysias sent to defeat Israel) fled when routed by Judas. Also, Jonathan attacked the city in 147 B.C. (1 Macc 10:78) and burned it along with its villages and its temple to Dagan (10:83–84). Apollonius, the governor of Coele-Syria who was besieging Jamnia, had challenged Jonathan to fight (10:70–73), so Jonathan captured a garrison of Apollonius headquartered at Joppa (10:74–76). Then Apollonius took 3,000 cavalry S to Azotus (i.e. away from Joppa), as though retreating from Jonathan, and left a cavalry of 1,000 behind to catch Jonathan between the two units (10:79; Josephus says [*Ant* 13.4.4 §92] that Apollonius first marched N and then retreated). Apollonius probably chose to fight at Azotus because the level terrain there was better-suited for cavalry than the terrain at Joppa (so Goldstein *1 Maccabees* AB, 422).

Azotus is mentioned again (1 Macc 16:10) in connection with the defeat of Cendebeus, "commander-in-chief of the coastal country" (15:38) under Antiochus VII (reigned 139/8–129/8). John Hyrcanus defeated Cendebeus on a plain outside Modein, sending Cendebeus fleeing to the stronghold at Kedron which he had built (16:9, cf. 15:41). Some of his soldiers fled to the "towers at Azotus." 1 Macc 16:10 reads: "John burned it with fire." The antecedent for "it" is unclear. One might suppose that Azotus was intended, and two Latin MSS read "them," i.e., the towers of Azotus. However, John had followed Cendebeus to Kedron, which is probably the city he torched.

Elsewhere, Azotus appears as the name of a district, rather than a city. In 164 B.C. Judas attacked Azotus (1 Macc 5:68), which was further defined by the appositional phrase "the land of the Philistines" (Goldstein *1 Maccabees* AB, 305). Later (ca. 142 B.C.), Simon fortified Joppa and Gazara (a city on the border of [the territory] of Azotus; 1 Macc 14:34).

One other text mentioning Azotus (1 Macc 9:15) is often considered erroneous. In 160 B.C. Judas fought his last battle, against Bacchides, who had marched from Syria to Jerusalem and then to Berea (9:1–4). Judas was encamped at Elasa nearby (9:5). During the battle Judas attacked the strong flank of the enemy, putting Bacchides' soldiers to flight and pursuing them "as far as Mount Azotus" (9:15). Since Azotus lay approximately 35 miles away, and since the city sits near the coast, and not on a mountain, scholars have often suspected the reading. The *Oxford Annotated Apocrypha* suggests *el-asur,* which lay 6 miles NE of Berea *(el-Bireh).* Goldstein (*1 Maccabees* AB, 373), however, follows the conjecture of Johann David Michaelis (*Deutsche Übersetzung des ersten Buchs der Maccabäer mit Anmerkungen,* 1778) that a copyist misread *ʾšdwt* ("watersheds" or "slopes") as *ʾšdwd* ("Ashdod"). On the other hand, Van Henten (1983: 46) points out that in 3:24, 4:14 and 16:9 the retreating army is also pursued a great distance. In addition, he wants to read the Greek word *orous* not as the genitive singular form *to horos* (mountain) but as an accusative plural of *ho horos,* (boundary) (1983: 47). Thus, the enemy would have fled, not to Mount Azotus (since Azotus is located on the coastal plain), but to the boundary of the territory of Azotus. To the objection that the preposition *heos* takes nouns in the genitive as its object, Van Henten lists examples of its use with the accusative.

Josephus recounts the ensuing history of the city. Alexander Jannaeus held Azotus at the beginning of his reign (*Ant* 13.15.4 §395), and the ruins show evidence of an attack during the Maccabean period, so scholars often assume it was captured by John Hyrcanus. Archaeologists uncovered a coin of Antiochus VIII, dated to 114 B.C., which presumably sets the date after which the city fell into Judaean control. In 63 B.C. Pompey took Azotus away from Judah (*JW* 1.7.7 §156), but Gabinius (governor of Syria from 57–55 B.C.) restored it to Judah under Hyrcanus II (*JW* 1.8.4 §166). Herod's kingdom included the city, which he willed to his sister Salome (*JW* 2.6.3 §98). During the First Revolt the city was captured by the Romans under Vespasian, who stationed a garrison there (*JW* 4.3.2 §130).

In the NT, Azotus is mentioned (Acts 8:40) as the city where Philip the Evangelist was found after baptizing the Ethiopian Eunuch.

Bibliography

Dancy, J. C. 1954. *A Commentary on I Maccabees.* Oxford.

Henten, J. W. van. 1983. Der Berg Ashdod: Uberlegungen zu 1. Makk.9,15. *JSJ* 14: 43–51.

Tedesche, S., and Zeitlin, S. 1950. *The First Book of Maccabees.* New York.

PAUL L. REDDITT

AZRAQ (PLACE). Several oases located at the center of a 12,000-km-square internal drainage basin, 80 km E of Amman. The rainfall over the basin varies from just over 200 mm along the N and W fringes to less than 50 mm in the SE, hence pastoralism is the only viable subsistence activity over much of the area. The N portion of the basin is covered by late Tertiary and Quaternary basalts while the S area comprises early Tertiary limestones and marls, and is covered by a pavement of chert gravel. At Azraq there are a number of copious perennial springs which feed 2 areas of marshland (Biraket el-Ora and Biraket Qeissiyeh). There is also a substantial sabkha (Qa el-Azraq) from which salt is extracted by the villagers. (For further environmental details and modern history see Nelson 1973.)

The springs at Azraq have provided a focus for settlement since the Stone Age. In 1956, mechanical diggers uncovered two impressive late Acheulian/Levallois Mousterian sites at Ain el-Assad and C spring. These were briefly examined by Harding and Kirkbride but have only been recently excavated (Rollefson 1980; 1982; Garrard et al. 1987). Numerous sites of Epipalaeolithic and Neolithic date have been located around the marshes and several were sounded in 1985 (Garrard, Stanley Price, and Copeland 1977; Garrard et al. 1985; 1987). One of these, known as Azraq 31 and dating to ca. 6000 B.C., has produced the earliest evidence of ovicaprid pastoralism from the E desert of Jordan. Betts (1983; 1984; 1985) has found many stone corrals, wheel houses, and "desert kites" in the basalt desert N and E of Azraq. Desert kites are V-shaped structures with a corral at the junction end of the V. They usually open onto areas of good grazing and are thought from historic descriptions, rock drawings, and ethnographic accounts to have been used for capturing gazelle and other large herbivores. Some of these structures are associated with Neolithic artifacts, but from travelers accounts others were still in use in the last century (Mendelssohn 1974).

During the classical and medieval periods, Azraq seems to have been an important watering point on the trade route from the Levant through the Wadi es-Sirhan to central Arabia. Three forts guard the approaches to the oasis—Qasr el-Uweinid, Qasr Aseikhim, and Qasr el-Azraq (Kennedy 1982; Bowersock 1983). Qasr el-Uweinid sits on a basalt bluff overlooking the Wadi el-Uweinid, 13 km SW of modern Azraq ed-Duruz. It is a trapezoid structure with remnants of a tower inside. An inscription at the site refers to it as a *castellum novum Severianum,* suggesting a date of around 200 A.D. A second inscription documents the establishment of a *praesidium Severianum* with a vexillation of the legion Third Cyrenaica. Qasr Aseikhin is located about 13 km NE of Azraq ed-Duruz on the summit of a basalt peak. It is a square fortress with rooms arranged around a central courtyard, and it may also date to the reign of Septimius Severus. Qasr el-Azraq is adjacent to Biraket el-Ora in Azraq ed-Duruz, and seems to have been rebuilt on several occasions. Early aerial photographs show the outline of a large, square encampment which could be of Severan date. The present structure was built inside the encampment before the end of the 3d century A.D., as inferred from an inscription which dates to the period of the Tetrarchy. A later inscription inserted in the castle entrance suggests that the fortress was rebuilt during the governorship of Azz el Dyn Aybak between 1213 and 1238 A.D.

Approximately 5 km S of Azraq el-Duruz are the springs and marshes of Biraket Qeissyeh. Surrounding the springs and enclosing an area of about 10 dunums, is a well-built buttressed wall of either classical or early Islamic date. A second similarly well-constructed wall extends from the first wall around the S and E sides of the marshes. Kennedy (1982) suggests it may have been built to separate the fresh water of the marshes from the more saline water of the sabkha, but recent sondages by Garrard indicate that it was not deep enough to achieve this objective, but that it probably represented an estate boundary. Until the large-scale pumping of water of the last two decades, the Azraq marshes supported a very rich wildlife and was a focus for the spring and autumn bird migrations through the area (Nelson 1973).

Bibliography

Betts, A. 1983. Black Desert Survey, Jordan: First Preliminary Report. *Levant* 15: 1–10.

———. 1984. Black Desert Survey, Jordan: Second Preliminary Report. *Levant* 16: 25–34.

———. 1985. Black Desert Survey, Jordan: Third Preliminary Report. *Levant* 17: 29–52.

Bowersock, G. W. 1983. *Roman Arabia.* Cambridge, MA.

Garrard, A. N.; Stanley Price, N.; and Copeland, L. 1977. A Survey of Prehistoric Sites in the Azraq Basin, Eastern Jordan. *Paleorient* 3: 109–26.

Garrard, A. N.; Byrd, B.; Harvey, P.; and Hivernel, F. 1985. Prehistoric Environment and Settlement in the Azraq Basin. *Levant* 17: 1–28.

Garrard, A. N.; Betts, A.; Byrd, B.; and Hunt, C. 1987. Prehistoric

Environment and Settlement in the Azraq Basin. *Levant* 19: 5–25.
Kennedy, D. L. 1982. *Archaeological Explorations on the Roman Frontier in North-East Jordan.* Oxford.
Mendelssohn, H. 1974. The Development of the Populations of Gazelles in Israel and Their Behavioural Adaptations. Pp. 542–51 in *The Behaviour of Ungulates and Its Relation to Management,* ed. V. Geist and F. Walther. Morges.
Nelson, B. 1973. *Azraq, Desert Oasis.* London.
Rollefson, G. O. 1980. The Palaeolithic Industries of Ain el-Assad (Lion's Spring) near Azraq, Eastern Jordan. *ADAJ* 24: 129–44.
———. 1982. Preliminary Report on the 1980 Excavations at Ain el-Assad. *ADAJ* 26: 5–35.

ANDREW N. GARRARD

AZRIEL (PERSON) [Heb *ʿazrîʾēl*]. A name, the precise meaning of which is uncertain (*TPNAH,* 133). It is borne by 3 persons mentioned in the Bible.

1. In the historical review of the tribes of Israel, the Chronicler mentions Azriel as one of the 7 eponymous leaders of the half-tribe of E Manasseh (1 Chr 5:23–24). Famous for their military prowess, political leadership, and enlightened leadership as the heads of their father's house, they are credited with enlarging their constituency and its territory, so that the territory from the land of Bashan to Mount Hermon became the land of East Manasseh in the early days of the Transjordanian conquest. The addendum in 1 Chr 5:25,26 must be read with the subject understood as the 2½ tribes, not the 7 East Manasseh leaders and their constituency.

2. The father of Jerimoth (so MT) and the tribal head of the tribe of Naphtali in the Chronicler's reconstruction of the officialdom of David (1 Chr 27:16–19).

3. The father of Seraiah who functioned as a member of the court of Jehoiakim (Jer 36:26). In 605 B.C., when the relations between Judah and Babylon were deteriorating, Jeremiah collected his oracles and bid Baruch his secretary read them to the people who would attend a fast to be observed in the 9th month. The revolutionary words of the prophet so disturbed the princes in the audience that they brought word immediately to the king. No doubt in fierce anger, Jehoiakim commanded 3 high officers of the royal court to apprehend Baruch and Jeremiah. These 3 court officials were Jerahameel the king's son, Shelemiah the son of Abdeel, and Seraiah the son of Azriel. Since all other data are absent, one can but speculate about Azriel on the basis of his son's high court position and royal mission.

EDWARD R. DALGLISH

AZRIKAM (PERSON) [Heb *ʿazrîqām*]. **1.** The 3d son of Neriah, a descendant of Zerubbabel. His name appears in 1 Chr 3:23 in an extended genealogy of exilic and postexilic Davidic descendants. Scholars are in disagreement about whether the genealogy from v 21b on—from the phrase "the sons of Hananiah"—should be understood as listing the descendants of Zerubbabel or is composed merely of unconnected lists which have been attached at this point (see Williamson *1–2 Chronicles* NCBC, 58; Myers *1 Chronicles* AB, lxxxviii–lxxxix). If Azrikam is considered a descendant of Zerubbabel then he lived 5 generations later, if v 21b is understood as listing the sons of Hananiah; or if the reading of the LXX for v 21b is adopted (see RSV), he lived 9 generations later. The former is more likely (see Myers, AB, 18–21; Williamson, NCBC, 58).

2. A Levite, a descendant of Merari the 3d son of Levi. Azrikam occurs in Merari's line only in the genealogies given in Neh 11:15 and 1 Chr 9:14. In the partially overlapping lists in 1 Chr 6:19, 29–30 = 6:44–47, only Hashabiah appears from 1 Chr 9:14 = Neh 11:15. This may indicate preservation of different lines of the genealogy in different settings. Azrikam belonged to the house which was given responsibility for the outside work of the House of the Lord (Neh 11:15).

3. A descendant of Jonathan, the son of Saul. In both 1 Chr 8:38 and in the repetition of this genealogy in 1 Chr 9:44, Azrikam is listed as the son of Azel in the extended genealogy of Benjamin (1 Chr 8:1–40).

4. The steward or commander of the royal palace (Heb *nāgîd habbāyit*) of Ahaz, king of Judah ca. 735–715. In 2 Chr 28:7 he is mentioned along with Maaseiah, the king's son, and Elkanah, second in command to the king. All were killed by Zikri the Ephraimite in an incident connected with the Syro-Ephraimite war. Some have suggested that this Azrikam is identical to 3. above, but this is uncertain (*IDB* 1, 327).

RUSSELL FULLER

AZUBAH (PERSON) [Heb *ʿăzûbâ*]. **1.** Mother of Jehoshaphat, king of Judah (1 Kgs 22:42 = 2 Chr 20:31). Azubah's name appears in the regnal formula of her son, Jehoshaphat. She is the daughter of Shilhi, whose place of origin is unknown.

2. Wife of Caleb (1 Chr 2:18). Her name appears in the genealogy of Judah in 1 Chronicles 2, where she is listed as one of the mothers of Caleb's children. Three sons are mentioned specifically in v 18—Jesher, Shobab, and Ardon—but the identity of their mother is unclear (being either Azubah or Jerioth). Upon Azubah's death, Caleb took another wife, Ephrath (1 Chr 2:19).

LINDA S. SCHEARING

AZZAN (PERSON) [Heb *ʿazzān*]. The father of the leader of the tribe of Issachar, Paltiel (Num 34:26). The name is derived from the root *ʿwz,* meaning "strength" (*EncMiqr* 6: 132), and Johnson (*IDB* 1: 327) has translated Azzan as "the deity has shown strength." In LXX, this name appears as *oza,* and, in Syr, as *ʿazor.* The name occurs in both Ug (UT 455, no. 1837), possibly as an abbreviation of *ʿzmlk* (Benz 1972: 165), and in a Phoenician seal from Syria (*PTU,* 378).

Bibliography

Benz, F. 1972. *Personal Names in the Phoenician and Punic Inscriptions.* Studia Pohl. Rome.

RAPHAEL I. PANITZ

AZZUR (PERSON) [Heb *ʿazzûr*]. **1.** The father of Hananiah, the prophet from Gibeon (Jer 28:1). Whether a court prophet or not, Hananiah appears to have been well-known and a leader of a pro-royalist movement in the days of Zedekiah (Jer 28:1–17).

2. The father of Jaazaniah, one of the princes of the people in the days of Ezekiel (Ezek 11:1–25). In a vision experience, the exiled prophet Ezekiel discovers himself at the E gate of the house of Yahweh, where he beholds Jaazaniah and Pelatiah, both princes of the people, sharing in a council of 25 men in the formulation of an undisclosed plot. It appears to be either a plan to seek an alliance with Egypt or to usurp unwarranted power in Judah. Ezekiel is advised of the utter failure of the intrigue; a confirmatory sign followed in the death of Pelatiah. We know nothing about Azzur's relationship to his son's political ambition; since the Judean aristocracy would be disposed to assume the power vacated by the exiled royalty, it is most likely that Azzur would be in general sympathy with the movement. At least, he invested his son with the dignity of a prince.

3. One of the 84 signatories who, as one of the chiefs of the people, confirmed the covenant of Nehemiah (Neh 10:14). Among the several prescriptions of the compact were: (1) avoidance of interracial relationships; (2) strict observance of the sabbath; and (3) provision for the support of the temple establishment (Neh 10:1–39).

EDWARD R. DALGLISH

BAAL (DEITY) [Heb *ba*ˁ*al*]. Canaanite storm and fertility god. The name, which means "lord," is an epithet of the god Hadad (lit. "thunderer"). Well-known from the OT, he is now extremely well-attested in the Ugaritic texts, in addition to being mentioned in other ancient texts.

A. Baal in Extrabiblical Texts

1. The Ugaritic Texts. This deity is first attested in the Ebla texts from the second half of the 2d millennium B.C., where he appears as *ˀa-da,* and in the Egyptian Execration Texts of about 1800 B.C., but it is the Ug mythological texts from Ras Shamra on the Syrian coast which shed the most light on him. He is clearly the most active and prominent of all the Canaanite deities, even though El is technically the supreme god, to whose ultimate authority Baal is subordinate. The Ug texts depict him primarily as the great storm god: the fertility of the land depends on the rain this god supplies. His character is well-represented on a famous stele discovered at Ugarit, which shows him standing (on mountains or clouds?) brandishing a club in his right hand and a lance in his left, the upper part having the form of a tree or stylized lightning (cf. *ANEP,* pl. 490). In one of the Baal myths, the god uses 2 clubs, clearly symbolizing thunder and lightning, to defeat Yam.

While Baal is regularly spoken of in the Ug texts as the son of Dagon, a god who otherwise is only rarely mentioned there (e.g., *KTU* 1.2.I.19; 1.5.VI.23–24 = *CTA* 2.I.19; 5.IV.23–24), he is also referred to as the son of the supreme god Il (cf. *KTU* 1.3.V.35; 1.4.1V.47 = *CTA* 3.VE.43; 4.IV.47). How these statements are to be reconciled is not completely certain. They could reflect divergent traditions, but it is more likely that Dagon is understood to be literally his father, and that Baal was also the "son" of El in the sense that he was a descendant of El (his grandson?), a member of the pantheon of gods which had its ultimate origin in El.

We come now to Baal's consorts. In the Ug texts it is the goddess Anath who appears as Baal's primary consort. It is she who goes searching for him after his descent into the underworld and participates in his conflict with Mot, for example. Astarte also appears as his consort, though she is not so prominent. As we shall see, the situation is reversed in the OT: Anath appears only as the name of Shamgar's father and vestigially in place names (Anathoth and Beth-Anath), whereas Astarte, her name distorted to Ashtoreth or often Ashtaroth (the plural form), appears frequently even though we are not told much about her. Moreover, Asherah is often paired with Baal in the OT, suggesting that she too is considered to be Baal's consort, a point discussed later in greater detail. Returning to Anath, it is curious to note that she is constantly referred to as "the virgin Anath." It is not to be understood from this that she never had sexual intercourse with Baal; rather, the title appears to be explained by an Egyptian reference to her as the goddess who conceives but never bears (Papyrus Harris).

According to the Ug texts, Baal's dwelling was on Mt. *ṣpn,* probably to be vocalized Ṣapān (some scholars call it Zaphon following the Heb vocalization). The mountain in Hittite is called Ḫazzi, whence its classical name Casius. It is located about 40 km N of Ugarit, at Jebel el-Aqraˁ, 1,759 m above sea level—appropriately enough, the highest mountain in Syria. The mountain's location to the N of Canaan accounts for the apparent derivation of the Heb word for "north" *(ṣāpôn)* from its name. Echoes of its mythological sense are found in Ps 48:3—Eng 48:2, where the term is applied to Zion, and also in Isa 14:13. There were also various places in Egypt called Baal-zephon, one of which is mentioned in connection with the Exodus deliverance in Exod 14:2.

The god Baal in the Ugaritic texts has a number of epithets. The most frequently occurring are *ˀalˀiyn b*ˁ*l* "the victor Baal," *rkb* ˁ*rpt* "rider of the clouds," and *zbl b*ˁ*l ˀarṣ* "the prince lord (Baal) of the earth." Suggested echoes of the latter 2 expressions in the Bible are discussed below.

Although the god Baal is mentioned in many Ug texts, one work in particular is of central importance, the Baal cycle on 6 tablets in *KTU* 1.1–6 (= *CTA* 1–6). This is broadly divisible into 3 main sections: (i) the conflict between Baal and Yam ("Sea") in *KTU* 1.1–2 (= *CTA* 1–2); (ii) the building of Baal's house (palace/temple) in *KTU* 1.3–4 (= *CTA* 3–4); and (iii) the conflict between Baal and Mot ("Death") in *KTU* 1.5–6 (= *CTA* 5–6). The following is a summary of the main points made in these 6 tablets concerning Baal.

(i) The god Yam sends messengers to El and the assembly of the gods on Mt. *Ll,* demanding that Baal be given up to him. Baal refuses to be given up, and eventually a battle takes place between Baal and Yam. Yam at first appears victorious, but in the end Baal defeats Yam with the help of two clubs made by the craftsman god Kothar-and-Ḫasis, and Baal is proclaimed king.

(ii) A king must naturally have a palace, and so the 2d main division is to a considerable degree taken up with the building of Baal's palace. Anath first demands a palace for her consort from El, using threats, but is unsuccessful. Subsequently, following the urging of Baal and Anath, Athirat requests El to grant Baal a palace; unlike Anath she is successful. Kothar-and-Ḫasis builds the palace, and particular interest centers on the question of constructing a window for the palace, which Kothar-and-Ḫasis urges on Baal. Baal first declines this but eventually comes round to the idea.

(iii) The 3d section concerns the conflict between Baal and Mot. Mot uses threats to bring Baal, together with his accompanying meteorological phenomena, down into the underworld, which is Mot's realm. This duly takes place and a period of dryness comes over the earth. El and Anath each engage in ritual lamentation over Baal's disappearance. Athtar is nominated to be king in Baal's place by Athirat, but he is not tall enough to occupy Baal's throne, so he descends from it. There is a scene in which Anath destroys Mot, the various verbs employed suggesting that she is treating him as if he were corn. El then has a dream in which he sees the fertility of the earth restored, which gives him confidence that Baal is now alive again. Baal smites the sons of Athirat and ascends his throne. Then we read that in the 7th year Mot complains about his fate at the hands of Baal, and a scene follows in which Baal and Mot struggle with each other. After the intervention of Shapash (the sun goddess), Mot concedes defeat.

One problem concerns the relationship between Baal's conflict with Yam and the creation of the world. In the OT we find the conflict with the waters associated with the creation of the world on a number of occasions (cf. Pss 74:12–17; 89:10–15—Eng 89:9–14, etc.). Similarly in the Babylonian text *Enuma elish,* Marduk's defeat of the sea monster Tiamat is connected with the creation of the world. No such conflict occurs in the Baal-Yam text, but the OT and Babylonian parallels nevertheless cause some scholars to assume this connection. There does not seem to be room in our Ug Baal-Yam text for an account of the creation of the world, although it is possible that there was also a primeval conflict between Baal and Anath, on the one hand, and Yam, Leviathan, etc., on the other, which was a prelude to El's creation of the world. Various Ug texts may allude to this (*KTU* 1.3.III.39–46; 1.5.I.1–3; 1.82.1–3; 1.83.3–10 = *CTA* 3.IIID.36–43; 5.I.1–3; *UT* 1001.1–3; 1003.3–10; cf. *KTU* 1.6.VI.51–53 = *CTA* 6.VI.50–52).

There has been considerable discussion whether the Baal cycle and, in particular, the Baal-Mot cycle reflects the seasonal cycle of an ordinary agricultural year or a 7-year (sabbatical) cycle. The chief proponent of a cyclic seasonal interpretation of the whole of the Baal epic is J. C. de Moor (1971), who compares the allusions in the various sections with current climactic conditions known from Syria today. However, there are a number of objections to the details of de Moor's thesis, as for example his reordering of the tablets so that the first 3 are to be read in the sequence 3, 1, 2. Thus, tablet 3 is related to the autumn, tablets 1 and 2 to the winter, tablets 4 and 5 to the spring, and tablet 6 to the summer. However, de Moor's reordering creates a problem in connection with the building of Baal's house, which de Moor has to suppose was begun, then abandoned, and only later completed. Another problem is that de Moor sometimes advocates novel and debatable translations, e.g. *ṣḥrr* "be dust colored" instead of "be hot."

It would be incorrect, however, to reject all seasonal elements in the work. The crucial passage concerns Anath's destruction of Mot, where she is clearly treating him like corn. Why would a whole series of agricultural images be used if, as some suppose, we simply have a picture of destruction and nothing more? We read that Anath "seized divine Mot, with a blade she split him, with a sieve she winnowed him, with fire she burnt him, with millstones she ground him, in a field she sowed him . . ." (*KTU* 1.6.II.30–35 = *CTA* 6.II.30–35). From this it would appear that Mot symbolizes the corn in some way, clearly indicating a seasonal rather than a sabbatical cycle. There would be no corn to be symbolized in a period of famine as presupposed by the sabbatical-cycle view, and in any case, nothing else in the text suggests a famine. How then are we to understand the reference to "the 7th year" (*KTU* 1.6.V.8–9 = *CTA* 6.V.8–9)? This is not entirely clear, but proponents of a sabbatical rather than a seasonal interpretation of the Baal-Mot cycle appear to overlook the fact that the destruction of Mot and the resurrection of Baal take place only after "months" have passed (cf. *KTU* 1.6.II.26–27 = *CTA* 6.II.26–27) and that the reference to the 7th year occurs *after* this. The text clearly is therefore *not* saying that Baal is in the underworld for 7 years. (Contrast the Hadad text, *KTU* 1.12.II.44–45 = *CTA* 12.II.45–46, and the Aqhat text, *KTU* 1.19.I.42–44 = *CTA* 19.I.42–44, where Baal does disappear for 7 or 8 years.)

One considerably disputed subject is the relation between Baal and El. Is Baal in conflict with El or are the two gods in harmony? The latter would appear to be nearer the truth, though there are signs of tension. The extreme claim, made, for example, by M. H. Pope (1955: 27–32), the Baal deposed El, on the analogy of Zeus' dethroning of Kronos, and that there may be a reference to this in the fragmentary and obscure *KTU* 1.1.V (= *CTA* 1.V) is certainly false. El remains throughout the supreme deity (L'Heureux 1979: 1–108) and there are allusions which make it almost certain that Baal was appointed king by El (cf. *KTU* 1.3.V.35–36 = *CTA* 3.VE.43–44; 4.IV.47–48) just as other deities were. Moreover, although Mot is called "the beloved of El," El does lament when he hears of Baal's death (*KTU* 1.5.VI.11–25 = *CTA* 5.VI.11–25) and rejoices when he has his vision of Baal's resurrection, following the destruction of Mot (*KTU* 1.6.III.4–21 = *CTA* 6.III.4–21). Moreover, Shapash says that El will take away Mot's throne if he goes on opposing Baal (*KTU* 1.6.VI.22–29 = *CTA* 6.VI.22–29). Again, although Yam is called "the beloved of El" and El appears prepared to give up Baal to Yam's messengers, the context suggests that this was due to fear on El's part (cf. *KTU* 1.2.I.21–24 = *CTA* 2.I.21–24). To be sure, there are signs of tension between El and Baal, and open hostility does seem to be present in *KTU* 1.12 (= *CTA* 12), the so-called Hadad text, where El is ultimately responsible for the devouring beasts which lure Baal to his death. This, however, belongs to a work separate from the main Baal cycle: in this latter there are references indicating hostility between Baal and the sons of Athirat (*KTU* 1.6.I.39–43; 1.6.V.1 = *CTA* 6.I.39–43; 6.V.1), though not with El himself.

2. Later Phoenician Sources. In the Phoenician inscriptions, various manifestations of the god Baal are attested, e.g., Baal-Shamem (*KAI* 4.3), Baal of Lebanon (*KAI* 31.1, 2), Baal of Sidon (*KAI* 14.18). In Punic inscriptions the leading deity is called Baal-ḥammon (e.g. *KAI* 102.1; 103.1), and it is widely believed that he is to be equated with El, largely because he was called Kronos by classical writers. However, it seems likely, as the name suggests, that this deity was actually a form of Baal: "Baal of the incense altar" (an incense altar features in a number of depictions of his cult). Sometimes he is simply called Baal in Punic texts (he is never called El), which suggests that Baal is the god's name and that it is not simply an epithet meaning "lord." Moreover, in Latin inscriptions he bears the epithets *frugifer* and *deus frugum* (e.g. *CIL* 8.4581), indicating a fertility god, and his consort Tinnit is equated with Astarte (Baal's wife) in a text from Sarepta in Phoenicia (Pritchard 1978: 105). Finally, there is evidence that Kronos could, on occasion, denote Baal as well as El, and in Hannibal's oath in his treaty with Philip V of Macedon, recorded in Polybius 7.9.2–3, Baal-ḥammon actually appears to be called Zeus. It was probably the fact that Kronos devoured his own children that encouraged his equation with Baal-ḥammon, the god of child sacrifice.

Philo of Byblos in his *Phoenician History* clearly has knowledge of the god Baal, but what he says is far removed from the authentic Baal of the Ug texts. In addition to Beelsamen (i.e. Baal-Shamem), who is equated with the sun, Baal appears in Philo both under the name of Zeus Belos, who is one of Kronos' (El's) children, and also under the name of Demarous (= Zeus = Adodos, i.e., Hadad). We read that "greatest Astarte and Zeus," called both Demarous and Adodos, king of gods, were ruling over the land with the consent of Kronos (Attridge and Oden 1981: 55). We may compare the picture in the Ug texts, where Baal's kingship seems to be exercised under the authority of El. It is also stated that "Demarous advanced against Pontos, but Pontos routed him (Attridge and Oden 1981: 53). This allusion is possibly a reflection of Baal's conflict with Yam (Sea), though it should be pointed out that whereas Baal defeated Yam, Pontos routed Demarous! Although Muth (= Mot) is mentioned, Philo of Byblos displays no knowledge of the Baal-Mot cycle with its account of Baal's death and resurrection.

B. Baal in the OT

1. Israelite Worship of Baal. Prior to the discovery of the Ug texts it was sometimes thought that there were various and quite-separate gods called Baal. This idea was encouraged by the presence in the OT of various compound place names involving Baal, e.g. Baal-peor, Baal-hermon, Baal-meon, Baal-hazor, Baal-gad, etc. However, with the discovery of the Ug texts it became clear that there was one great Canaanite storm-and-fertility deity Baal-Hadad of cosmic stature, so that we must assume that these OT allusions refer to particular local manifestations of this one god. We may compare the variety of local manifestations of the Virgin Mary within Roman Catholicism. The OT itself speaks a number of times of "the Baals" (Judg 2:11; 3:7; etc.). It is not clear whether this is a way of speaking of the different local manifestations of Baal or whether it is speaking of Canaanite deities more generally. We have the same problem over the references to "the Ashtaroth" (Judg 2:13; 1 Sam 7:4; etc.), which could mean local manifestations of Astarte (Ashtoreth) or Canaanite goddesses generally (cf. Akkadian *ilāni u ištarāti*, "gods and goddesses").

Reading the OT, it becomes clear that it was the Baal cult that provided the greatest and most enduring threat to the development of exclusive Yahweh worship within ancient Israel. The fact that the Israelites were settled among the Canaanites, for whom the worship of Baal was so important, and that Palestine is a land utterly dependent for its fertility upon the rain, which was held to be Baal's special realm of influence, accounts for the tempting nature of this cult as well as the strength of the OT polemic against it.

At the time of the entry into the promised land we hear of the temptation to participate in the cult of Baal-Peor at Mt. Peor in the land of Moab (Num 25:1–9; Deut 4:3; Ps 106:28; Hos 9:10). Subsequently, during the period of the Judges, Israel worshiped the Baals (Judg 2:11, 13; 3:7; 10:6, 10; 1 Sam 7:4; 12:10). The text recounts that Gideon pulled down an altar of Baal and cut down an Asherah (Judg 6:25–32). During the Divided Monarchy Ahab married Jezebel, daughter of Ethbaal, king of the Sidonians, and worshiped Baal. He erected an altar for Baal in the house of Baal, which he built in Samaria and made an Asherah (1 Kgs 16:31–33). Ahab's promulgation of the Baal cult provides the background for the famous confrontation between Elijah and the prophets of Baal on Mt. Carmel in 1 Kings 18. Unlike Elijah, Ahab clearly did not see his promulgation of Baal as being incompatible with Yahweh worship; in fact, Ahab's sons Ahaziah and Jehoram bear Yahwistic names. (On the identification of Ahab's Baal, see below.) Ahaziah is said to have worshipped Baal (1 Kgs 22:53)—indeed, we read that he consulted Baal-zebub, the god of Ekron, when he was ill (2 Kgs 1:2–16), a name (lit. "lord of the fly") which looks as though it is a distortion of Baal-zebul ("Baal the Prince," cf. Ug *zbl bʿl* and NT Beelzebul). Ahab's other son, Jehoram, is said to have put away the pillar of Baal which his father had made (2 Kgs 3:2), though he is still regarded by the Deuteronomist as an evil king (2 Kgs 3:2–3). It is clear, however, that Baal worship persisted, for Jehu was later ruthlessly to massacre the Baal priests, prophets, and worshipers in the temple of Baal as well as destroy the temple itself and the pillar of Baal within it (2 Kgs 10:18–27). This act was later to receive the condemnation of the prophet Hosea (cf. Hos 1:4). In addition to the N kingdom (2 Kgs 17:16), Manasseh is singled out as worshipping Baal (2 Kgs 21:3), but Josiah in his great reformation put an end to his cult (2 Kgs 23:4–5). Among the canonical prophets it is Hosea and Jeremiah who seem most exercised by the Baal cult (e.g., Hos 2:10—Eng 2:8; 13:1; Jer 2:8; 23:13).

In the postexilic period we do not hear of Baal, apart from a reference in Zech 12:11 to the Aramean cult of Hadad-rimmon in the plain of Megiddo. Also we need to remember that Antiochus IV Epiphanes rededicated the temple in Jerusalem in 168 B.C. to Zeus Olympios, who was a Hellenistic form of Baal-Shamem. "The abomination of desolation" *(šiqqûṣ šōmēm* or *šiqqûṣ mĕšōmēm)* in Dan 9:27; 11:31; 12:11 is a play on the name of the god Baal-Shamem.

Some discussion of the identity of the Baal propagated by Ahab and Jezebel is necessary. It has often been thought that this is a different god from the one presupposed elsewhere in the OT, and is rather to be equated with the Tyrian deity Melqart. This view, however, is to be rejected (Mulder 1979). It is not until a 2d century B.C. inscription from Malta that we find Melqart referred to as Baal ("the Baal [or lord] of Tyre," *KAI* 47:1). There is every reason to believe that Jezebel's Baal was in fact Baal-Shamem, another Tyrian deity who is in fact identical with the Baal attested elsewhere in the OT. (i) The Baal of 1 Kings 18 is clearly a god who was believed to bring lightning and rain; classical sources, however, reveal that Melqart was thought of as being asleep during the winter months when these phenomena abounded. (ii) The treaty between Baal king of Tyre and Esarhaddon king of Assyria in the 7th century B.C. clearly distinguishes Baal-Shamem and 2 other Baal deities, who manifest themselves in the storm, from the god Melqart (*ANET,* 534). (iii) The god of Carmel, where the contest takes place in 1 Kings 18, was always equated with Zeus. Now it was Baal-Shamem who was regularly identified with Zeus, Melqart being rather equated with Herakles.

Because the god Baal was so detested by the biblical tradition, the word *bōšet* "shame" has sometimes been substituted for the god's name by a scribe. This is the case in Jer 3:24; 11:13; and Hos 9:10. This substitution also occurs in various personal names: cf. Ish-bosheth (2 Sam 2:10) for Eshbaal (1 Chr 8:33; 9:39), Mephibosheth (2 Sam 4:4; 9:6; etc.) for Meribaal (or Meribbaal) (1 Chr 8:34; 9:40), and Jerubbesheth (2 Sam 11:21) for Jerubbaal (Gideon, Judg 6:32). Similarly Astarte (Ashtart) is distorted to Ashtoreth, reflecting the vowels of the word *bōšet,* and Molech is probably a comparable distortion, the original form perhaps being Melek.

The worship of the Baals in the OT is sometimes associated with that of the Ashtaroth (Judg 2:13; 10:6; 1 Sam 7:4; 12:10), which must reflect the fact that Astarte was one of Baal's consorts in Canaanite religion. More curious is the repeated pairing of Baal and Asherah (cf. Judg 3:7; 6:25–32; 1 Kgs 16:32–33; 18:19; 2 Kgs 17:16; 21:3), since in the Ug texts Asherah (Athirat) was the consort of El, not of Baal. Did Baal take over Asherah as his consort? The Hittite-Canaanite Elkuniřsa myth (*ANET,* 519), with its evidence of Asherah's (Ašertu's) flirting with the storm god and alienation from El (Elkuniřsa), might possibly lend support to this. Alternatively, the pairing of Baal and Asherah may be a sign of confusion on the part of the OT; or again, perhaps this pairing is not intended to imply that one was the consort of the other. Certainty is not possible. As for Anath, who appears prominently as a consort of Baal in the Ug texts, she appears in the OT only vestigially in the place names Anathoth and Beth-Anath, and as the name of Shamgar's father.

There is evidence from the OT that Yahweh and Baal could be equated in syncretistic circles. One may compare the personal name Bealiah, lit. "Yahweh is Baal" (1 Chr 12:6—Eng 12:5), and Hosea's declaration, "And in that day, says the Lord, you will call me 'My husband,' and no longer will you call me 'My Baal' " (2:18—Eng 2:16). This syncretism made the Baal cult all the more insidious from the point of view of the Yahweh purists. The Baal cult or Baalized Yahweh cult is associated in the OT with the high places *(bāmôt),* whose characteristic appurtenances include pillars *(maṣṣēbôt),* i.e., symbols of the male deity, Asherim (wooden cult symbols of the goddess Asherah), and altars. These are sometimes spoken of as being situated "on every high hill and under every luxuriant tree" (cf. 1 Kgs 14:23).

Although there are no indications of this in the Ug texts, it seems likely from a number of OT allusions that sacred prostitution formed part of what was involved in the fertility cult of Baal. That sacred prostitutes existed in Israel is clear from a number of allusions, cf. Hos 4:14, where *hazzōnôt* "the prostitutes" are mentioned parallel with *haqqĕdēšôt* (lit. "the holy ones") in a cultic context, and Gen 38:21–22, where Tamar is described as a *qĕdēšâ,* whereas in v 15 she is called a *zōnâ.* This makes it clear that the word *qĕdēšâ* refers to a sacred prostitute. The masculine form *qādēš* "male cult prostitute" occurs in 1 Kgs 14:24; 15:12; 22:46; 2 Kgs 23:6–7; and Deut 23:17. The fact that "harlotry" and "adultery" constitute such a common metaphor for apostasy to Canaanite worship in the OT is perhaps accountable for in the light of sacred prostitution's role within the Baal cult—cf. Hos 5:3–5; 6:10; 7:4; Jer 2:20; 3:2–4, 9:1(—Eng 9:2); Ezekiel 16 and 23. In fact it is not always clear whether the terminology is literal or metaphorical.

2. OT Use of Baal Motifs. That Yahweh was seen as Baal in some circles is shown by Hos 2:18—Eng 2:16, which criticizes those who refer him as "my Baal," and by the personal name Bealiah (1 Chr 12:6—Eng 12:5), as noted above. However, the OT opposes the equation of Yahweh with Baal (Hos 2:18—Eng 2:16), in contrast with its attitude to El, whose identification with Yahweh is admitted (Exod 6:3). But it is clear that the OT does nevertheless ascribe certain Baalistic functions to Yahweh. For example, there are a number of references in the OT to Yahweh's conflict with the dragon and the sea (e.g., Ps 74:12–15; Isa 27:1; Job 7:12). As at Ugarit the sea conflict is associated with the deity's kingship (cf. Ps 74:12–15; Isa 27:1; Job 7:12). Following Baal's victory over the sea his palace/temple was built for him, and similarly in Exod 15:17 we read of the establishment of Yahweh's sanctuary, described in terms reminiscent of Baal's, following his victory at (rather than with) the sea. In Daniel 7 the imagery of the one like a son of man coming with the clouds of heaven, enthroned by the Ancient of Days and victorious over the beasts of the sea, ultimately derives from the figure of Baal, "rider of the clouds," whose kingship resulted from his victory over the sea, and was subordinate to the supreme god El, "father of years."

Yahweh's manifestation in the storm is sometimes depicted in terms reminiscent of Baal. Thus, in Psalm 29 we find not only the theme of Yahweh's kingship and his conflict with the waters (vv 3, 10), reminiscent of Baal, but also a glorious theophany in the thunderstorm, with seven thunders (vv 3a, 4a, 4b, 5, 7, 8, 9) which are doubtless related to Baal's "seven lightnings . . . eight storehouses of thunder" (*KTU* 1.101.3–4 = *Ugaritica* V.3.3–4) ("seven/

eight" appears to mean "seven"). It is doubtful, however, whether the expression *rōkēb bāʿărābōt* used of Yahweh in Ps 68:5—Eng 68:4 is to be rendered "rider on the clouds" on the analogy of Baal's Ugaritic epithet *rkb ʿrpt,* contrary to a widely held view. The expected translation of the Hebrew expression would be "rider through the deserts," since *ʿărābâ* regularly means "desert" in the OT, and it should be noted that this fits the context in the Psalm, dealing as it does with the wilderness wanderings. (Cf. too Isa 40:3, *bāʿărābâ mĕsillâ* "a highway in the desert" with Ps 68:5—Eng 68:4, *sōllû lārōkēb bāʿăbōt* "raise a highway for him who rides through the deserts.") Probably the Hebrew expression is to be understood as a deliberate distortion of Baal's epithet *rkb ʿrpt.*

Various other imagery ultimately related to Baal has also been taken up in the OT. Allusion has already been made to the use of the term *ṣāpôn* to denote Yahweh's dwelling place in Ps 48:3—Eng 48:2 and Isa 14:13, though the context of the latter passage possibly indicates mediation of the imagery through the Jebusite cult of El-Elyon (cf. Isa 14:14). The imagery of Baal's death and resurrection appears to have left its mark on the book of Hosea. It has long been noted that the imagery of the death and resurrection of Israel (a metaphor for its exile and restoration) in Hos 5:12–6:3 appears to reapply the imagery of a dying and rising fertility deity, in view of the reference to the coming of the rain in the context of resurrection in Hos 6:3. What appears not to have been noticed is the relevance of the parallel imagery of death and resurrection applied to Israel in Hosea 13–14, which is introduced with the words "but he (*sc.* Israel) incurred guilt through Baal and died" (Hos 13:1). This strongly suggests that the imagery of Israel's death and resurrection has been consciously appropriated from the Baal cult, against which the prophet is clearly polemicizing throughout his preaching. In these and other ways Baalistic imagery is appropriated by the OT. (For further discussion see Mulden and de Moor, *ba'al, TDOT* 2: 181–200).

Bibliography

Attridge, H. W., and Oden, R. A. 1981. *Philo of Byblos: the Phoenician History.* CBQMS 9. Washington.

Day, J. 1985. *God's Conflict with the Dragon and the Sea: Echoes of a Canaanite Myth in the Old Testament.* Cambridge.

Eissfeldt, O. 1932. *Baal Zaphon, Zeus Kasios und der Durchzug der Israeliten durchs Meer.* Beiträge zur Religionsgeschichte des Altertums 1. Halle.

Habel, N. C. 1964. *Yahweh versus Baal: a Conflict of Religious Cultures.* New York.

Kapelrud, A. S. 1952. *Baal in the Ras Shamra Texts.* Copenhagen.

L'Heureux, C. 1979. *Rank among the Canaanite Gods: El, Ba'al, and the Repha'im.* HSM 21. Missoula.

Margalit, B. 1980. *A Matter of "Life and Death": A Study of the Baal-Mot Epic (CTA 4-5-6).* AOAT 206. Neukirchen-Vluyn.

Moor, J. C. de. 1971. *The Seasonal Pattern in the Ugaritic Myth of Ba'lu.* AOAT 16. Neukirchen-Vluyn.

———. 1972. *New Year with Canaanites and Israelites.* 2 vols. Kamper Cahiers 21–22. Kampen.

Mulder, M. J. 1962. *Ba'al in het oude Testament.* The Hague.

———. 1979. *De naam van de afwezige God op de Karmel. Onderzo ek naar de Baäl van de Karmel in 1 Koningen 18.* Leiden.

Pope, M. H. 1955. *El in the Ugaritic Texts.* VTSup 2. Leiden.

Pritchard, J. B. 1978. *Recovering Sarepta, a Phoenician City.* Princeton.

Smith, M. S. 1986. Interpreting the Baal Cycle. *UF* 18: 313–39.

Zijl, P. J. van. 1972. *Baal. A Study of Texts in Connexion with Baal in the Ugaritic Texts.* AOAT 206. Neukirchen-Vluyn.

JOHN DAY

BAAL (PERSON) [Heb *baʿal*]. This name is shared by 2 people in the Hebrew Bible, both preexilic figures mentioned only in 1 Chronicles. The name's interpretation is debated: some understand it as a reference to the Syro-Canaanite deity Baal (*IPN* 120–22), while others claim that *baʿal* is "master," and is an appellation of YHWH (Gray 1896: 141–46). Each of these interpretations is based on different understandings of preexilic Israelite religion, especially the extent to which it was monotheistic, polytheistic, or syncretistic. The evidence is inconclusive; according to 2 Sam 5:20 a place was named Baal-Perazim, "Baal has broken through" because "the LORD has broken through my enemies before me, like a bursting flood," and according to 1 Chr 12:6—Eng 12:5 one of David's heroes was named Bealiah *(bĕ ʿalyâ)* which may fit either "Baal is Yah(weh)" or "Yahweh is the master." The name of one of David's heroes alternates between Beeliada, *bʿlydʿ* "Baal knows" or "attends to" (1 Chr 14:7) and Eliada, *ʾlydʿ* "God knows" or "attends to" (2 Sam 5:16; 1 Chr 3:8). This interchange could either suggest that Baal is being used as an appellation of YHWH, who is "master," or that among certain groups, the deities Baal and YHWH were syncretistically identified, a process that is strongly suggested by Hosea, especially 2:18—Eng 2:16 ("And in that day, says the LORD, you will call me, 'my husband,' and no longer will you call me, 'my Baal.' "). Whether or not the personal name Baal is a pagan theophoric name depends on the extent to which ancient Israel was polytheistic; Kaufmann (1972) and more recently Tigay (*AIR,* 157–94) claim that preexilic Israel was not polytheistic, while Smith (1971: 13–56) and others (e.g., Freedman *AIR,* 315–35) claim that it was.

Other biblical names have the element Baal in them (*TPNAH,* 54–63). These names are from the period of Saul and David, and one of the editors of the book of Kings has changed the Baal element in them to *bōšet,* "shame." Names with the element Baal are also attested to 5 times for the later preexilic period in the extrabiblical epigraphic corpus, 4 times in the Samaria ostraca, and once in an inscription from Mesad Hashavyahu (Tigay 1986: 65–66). None of these attestations clarify whether the element *baʿal* refers to the divinity or should be rendered "master," as an appellation for *YHWH.*

1. A Reubenite according to the genealogy of 1 Chr 5:5. This genealogy lists the descendents of Joel, whose exact relationship to Reuben is not known. According to v 6, Baal's son Beerah was exiled to Assyria by Tiglath-pileser III, in the 2d half of the 8th century B.C.E. However, "son" in these genealogies often indicates a linear descendent, rather than a "son" of the next generation, so it is difficult to date when this Baal lived. The presence of the potentially problematic name Baal within this genealogy probably attests to its antiquity (Williamson *Chronicles* NCBC, 85). The genealogy in vv 4–5 shares the names Joel and

Shimaiah/Shimei/Shema with the Reuben genealogy in v 8. Verse 8 also contains the name Bela *(belaʿ)*, which is nearly identical with Baal *(baʿal)*. Furthermore, the Peshitta to v 5 reads Bela *(blʿ)* for Baal *(bʿl)*, and this reading is favored by some scholars (Richter 1932: 130). Thus, the genealogies in vv 4–5 and in v 8 are variants of each other, and, as is typical of genealogical fluidity (Johnson 1969; Wilson 1977), one tradition records the name of the descendent of Joel as Baal, while another lists him as Bela.

2. According to 1 Chr 8:30 and 9:36, a Benjaminite who was not the firstborn son of Gibeah and whose descendents later moved to Jerusalem (8:32 and 9:38; Demsky 1971: 17). The use of a Baal name with a Benjaminite is especially interesting because the relatively infrequent names compounded with Baal are found with three members of the family of Saul, a Benjaminite. On the repetition of the Benjaminite genealogy in 1 Chronicles 8 and 9, see AHAZ.

Bibliography

Demsky, A. 1971. The Genealogy of Gibeon (1 Chronicles 9:35–44): Biblical and Epigraphic Considerations. *BASOR* 202: 16–23.

Gray, G. B. 1896. *Studies in Hebrew Proper Names.* London.

Johnson, M. 1969. *The Purpose of the Biblical Genealogies.* Cambridge.

Kaufmann, Y. 1972. *The Religion of Israel from Its Beginnings to the Babylonian Exile.* Trans. Moshe Greenberg. New York.

Richter, G. 1932. Zu den Geschlechtregistern 1 Chronik 2–9. *ZAW* 50: 130–41.

Smith, M. 1971. *Palestinian Parties and Politics that Shaped the Old Testament.* New York, NY.

Tigay, J. H. 1986. *You Shall Have No Other Gods.* HSS 31. Atlanta.

Wilson. 1977. *Genealogy and History in the Biblical World.* New Haven.

Marc Z. Brettler

BAAL (PLACE) [Heb *baʿal*]. In 1 Chr 4:33, an alternative form of the toponym BAALATH-BEER.

BAAL-BERITH (DEITY) *[baʿal bĕrît]*. The phrase Baal-berith, "lord of the covenant," which appears only in Judg 8:33 and 9:4 (a similar form "El Berith" occurs in Judg 9:46) has attracted many different interpretations. Albright, in his 1941 Ayer Lectures (*ARI* 110), thought that Baal-berith was an appellation of the god Haurôn, yet this proposal has found few adherents. While no other proposal has met with consensus among scholars due primarily to the scant evidence, there is a good deal of speculation centering around the identity of Baal-berith of Shechem and any connection between this deity and the development of covenant theology in ancient Israel.

Many scholars have speculated on the relation between Baal-berith and El Berith. Some favor 2 separate deities. Soggin (*Judges* OTL, 170–71, 186) sees 2 different deities corresponding to the 2 sanctuaries at Shechem (cf. *TDOT* 2: 194). Others (Good *HBD,* 84) have argued that Baal-berith and El Berith are one and the same. Clements (1968: 26 n.3) believes that "the title El-Berith was simply an alternative for Baal-berith, with El used in a purely appellative sense." Cross (*CMHE,* 49) has argued that what we have here is an original epithet of the Canaanite deity El who was known at Shechem as both *ʾēlʾĕlōhê yiśrāʾēl,* "El, the god of (the patriarch Jacob) Israel" and *ʾēl baʿl bĕrît* "El, the lord of the covenant." Cross (*CMHE,* 39) also pointed out that *ʾil brt* (= El Berith) occurs in a Hurrian text (RS 24.278) published in Ugaritica V (so too Lipiński 1973: 50–51).

Another topic of discussion is the relation of Baal-berith and El Berith to Yahweh. Most scholars (e.g. Cooke *Joshua* CBSC, 221) describe a process whereby as the Israelites took over the LB Canaanite sanctuary at Shechem (cf. Dever's remarks on Migdal Temple I [1987: 232]), the Canaanite god Baal-berith/El Berith came to be regarded as a manifestation of Yahweh. Kaufmann (*KRI,* 138–39, 260) argues that *baʿal* was an epithet for Yahweh in early times which fits with his theory that "during the age of the judges . . . there are no Baal priests or prophets, nor any other intimation of a vital effect of polytheism in Israel's life." Tigay, who has followed up on Kaufmann's work, holds out the possibility that we have polytheism in Judges 9:4, 46 (Tigay 1986: 41 n.13). See also the discussion of the relation of Yahweh and El in Cross (*CMHE,* 44–75) who suggests that Yahweh was "recognized as originally a cultic name of ʾEl." It is further advocated by Cross that El may have borne the epithet *d̠ū yahwī sabaʾôt,* "He who creates the heavenly armies" (*CMHE,* 71).

In later biblical tradition, as evidenced by the Deuteronomistic editing in Judg 8:33, *baʿal bĕrît* was seen to be a pagan deity. Mulder (*TDOT* 2: 194) has pointed out the association of this deity with wine festivals in Judges 9:27, which would support the notion that Baal-berith was "a god of vegetation and a local manifestation of the Baal par excellence."

Baal-berith has also attracted a good deal of attention by those who have speculated on the origin of the idea of covenant in ancient Israel. How did Baal-berith, "the lord of the covenant," function in the treaty itself? Two viable options have been proposed. Outside of the Bible, there are few parallels in the ancient Near East to deities entering into covenant relationships with peoples. Weinfeld (*TDOT* 2: 278) says that "the idea of a covenant between a deity and a people is unknown to us from other religions and cultures" yet compare the inscription from Arslan Tash (*KAI* 27; see Zevit 1977: 110–18) and *ʾil brt* mentioned above. Baal-berith and El Berith could be seen as rare examples of a deity in the role of a divine partner or suzerain in the covenant. The Shechemites, who would be seen as the vassal party, are referred to as *bĕnê hămôr,* "sons of the ass," which seems to be a covenantal designation to judge from parallel Mari texts (*ARI,* 110; Noth 1984: 108–17). Some who follow this line of interpretation have gone so far as to suggest that the Israelites' development of covenant theology was influenced by the cult of Baal-berith which they encountered when they came to Shechem. Clements (1968: 31–32), however, argues that though Baal-berith played the role of divine partner, this does not imply that there was any profound influence on the Israelite notion of covenant.

Alternatively, Baal-berith could refer not to a deity in the role of a divine partner (parallel to "unique" biblical usage) but rather to a deity in the role of witness or guardian to the treaty. Here there are abundant parallels in ANE treaties where this was the normal role of the gods. Following this line of interpretation, Baal-berith's function would be as the witness or guarantor of the covenant between two peoples. There is no reference to any battle or conquest of Shechem and most scholars agree that this is due to a covenant which was made between the Israelites and the Shechemites. In fact, every fragment of Shechemite tradition which has come down to us refers to some type of treaty. See SHECHEM (PLACE); COVENANT.

Bibliography

Campbell, E. F., and Ross, J. F. 1963. The Excavation of Shechem and the Biblical Tradition. *BA* 26: 2–27.

Clements, R. E. 1968. Baal-Berith of Shechem. *JSS* 13: 21–32.

Dever, W. G. 1987. The Contribution of Archaeology to the Study of Canaanite and Early Israelite Religion. Pp. 209–47 in *AIR*.

Lipiński, E. 1973. Recherches Ugaritiques. *Syr* 50: 35–51.

Noth, M. 1984. Old Testament Covenant-making in the Light of a Text from Mari. Pp. 108–17 in *The Laws in the Pentateuch and Other Studies*. Trans. D. R. Ap-Thomas. Philadelphia.

Tigay, J. H. 1986. *You Shall Have No Other Gods: Israelite Religion in the Light of Hebrew Inscriptions*. HSS 31. Atlanta.

Zevit, Z. 1977. A Phoenician Inscription and Biblical Covenant Theology. *IEJ* 27: 110–18.

THEODORE J. LEWIS

BAAL-GAD (PLACE) [Heb *baʿal gād*]. A Canaanite city in the valley of Lebanon below Mount Hermon (Josh 11:17). It was the N point of the territory conquered by Joshua, beyond which lay the land that remained unconquered (Josh 13:5). When describing this same region, Judges uses the name Mount Baal-Hermon in place of Baal-gad (Judg 3:3).

According to the descriptions in the Bible, Baal-gad must be located in the region of Laish, a beautiful, lush area which has been hallowed ground from time immemorial. In fact, it is possible that the present-day Banias could be the ancient Baal-gad. It would be no wonder that such a fertile region would be a major seat of Baalism. In later times, the Greeks worshiped Pan in a cavern there, and called the sanctuary-town Paneion and the district Paneas. Later, Philip the Tetrarch beautified the town and called it Caesarea Philippi, while Agrippa II renamed it Neronias.

Baal-gad may have had an important theological function in the biblical text. The Deuteronomistic theologian, by referring to it, shows that a significant part of Yahweh's promise to Israel (Josh 1:4; 11:23) was fulfilled. Moreover, just as the land from Mount Halak in the S to Baal-gad in the N was given by the Lord to Israel under the leadership of Joshua, who observed all the words of the commandment, the land from Baal-gad to Lebo-hamath was also subsequently given to Israel under the leadership of David (2 Sam 8:9–10), yet another obedient leader according to the Deuteronomist (1 Kings 11:38). For further discussion see *GB*.

PAUL BENJAMIN

BAAL-HAMON (PLACE) [Heb *baʿal hāmôn*]. A city or district mentioned in the Song of Songs (8:11). It was the location of a plantation of Solomon's that he granted to planters who made it highly profitable. The name is not attested elsewhere in the MT; it may correspond to the place *Balamōn* mentioned (in Greek) in Jdt 8:3 (see BALAMON). Tell Belʿame (M.R. 177205) has been suggested as the site (Gordis 1974; Pope *Song of Songs* AB, 686), but this is more likely Ibleam (so *LBHG,* 148).

Paul Haupt (1902: 223; 1903: 6) suggested that the spelling of the second element with initial *he* was an intentional alteration of an original name **baʿal ḥammôn* (with initial *ḥet*), avoided because it was the name of a Phoenician god (on the name of this deity, see Schmitz 1990: 255–57). The suggestion was furthered by Pope (*Song of Songs* AB, 686-87) with citations of a Phoenician inscription (*KAI* 19.3–4) mentioning the city *Ḥammôn* and allegedly showing the biblical passage to allude to an ancient ritual or myth associated with the goddess Astarte. This, and the interpretation of a Palmyrene text mentioning the divinity *bʿl ḥmn,* are highly speculative and of doubtful relevance. There is no cause to link the name Baal-hamon with the Phoenician divine name.

Interpreted literally, Heb *baʿal hāmôn* means "possessor of a crowd," reflected in the Vulgate's *quea habet populos* (Cant 8:11), or "possessor of wealth" ("Ownalot:" Goulder 1986: 69), implicit in Syr *weʾinbê saggîʾ* "and its fruit (was) plentiful" (on the word *hāmôn, TDOT* 3: 414–18). The transparency of the name has led to speculation that it is an imaginary site in the imagistic world of the supreme song (suggested by Gordis 1974; assumed by Goulder 1986: 69). Others (e.g., Robert 1948) understood the term as a particular application of the image of the vineyard used broadly in biblical language as a metonymy for all of Israel. It seems best, however, to interpret Baal-hamon as an actual site, even if its location cannot be established.

Bibliography

Gordis, R. 1974. *Song of Songs and Lamentations.* Rev. ed. New York.

Goulder, M. D. 1986. *The Song of Fourteen Songs.* JSOTSup 36. Sheffield.

Haupt, P. 1902. The Book of Canticles. *AJSL* 18: 193–241.

———. 1903. The Book of Canticles. *AJSL* 19: 1–32.

Robert, A. 1948. Les appendices du Cantique des Cantiques (viii, 8–14). *RB* 55: 161–83.

Schmitz, P. 1990. Epigraphic Contributions to a History of Carthage in the Fifth Century B.C.E. Ph.D. diss., University of Michigan.

PHILIP C. SCHMITZ

BAAL-HANAN (PERSON) [Heb *baʿal ḥānān*]. This name, meaning "Baal has shown mercy" (*IPN,* 187), belongs to 2 persons in the OT (see below). Outside the OT, the name occurs for the ruler of Arwad at the time of Ashurbanipal (Phoenician **Baʿalḥanōn,* in Akkadian transcription *Ba-ʾ-al-ḫa-nu-nu,* Asb. Prism A II 84; 91).

1. In Gen 36:38–39 = 1 Chr 1:49–50, Baal-Hanan is the 7th ruler in the list of "the kings who ruled in the country of Edom before there was a king of the Israelites," Gen 36:31. Opinions vary about the date of the "Edomite King List," ranging from the 11th century B.C. (Weippert 1982: 155), through the 8th to 6th centuries (Bennett 1983: 16), to the 6th/5th centuries (Knauf 1985a). Scholars tend to agree, however, that the succession scheme of this list is artificial, and that in all likelihood the rulers listed in it were contemporaries (Bartlett 1972: 27; Weippert 1982: 155). The name Baal-Hanan is Canaanite, as is the name of the father of this Edomite "king," *ᶜAkbōr* "Jerboa" (Knauf 1985a: 248).

2. According to 1 Chr 27:28, a certain "Baal-Hanan of Geder" was King David's "commissioner for the olives and sycamores in the lowlands." The list of David's officials 1 Chr 27: 25–31 can be regarded as fictitious (Knauf 1985b: 13). In this case, this Baal-Hanan might refer to an Idumaean of the postexilic period.

Bibliography

Bartlett, J. R. 1972. The Rise and Fall of the Kingdom of Edom. *PEQ* 104: 26–37.

Bennett, C.-M. 1983. Excavations at Buseirah (Biblical Bozrah). Pp. 9–17 in *Midian, Moab and Edom. The History and Archaeology of Late Bronze and Iron Age Jordan and North-West Arabia,* ed. J. F. A. Sawyer and D. J. A. Clines. Sheffield.

Knauf, E. A. 1985a. Alter und Herkunft der edomitischen Königsliste Gen 36, 31–39. *ZAW* 97: 245–53.

———. 1985b. *Ismael. Untersuchungen zur Geschichte Palästinas und Nordarabiens im 1. Jahrtausend v. Chr.* Wiesbaden.

Lemaire, A. 1988. Hadad l'Édomite ou Hadad l'Araméen? *BN* 43:14–18.

Weippert, M. 1982. Remarks on the History of Settlement in Southern Jordan during the Early Iron Age. Pp. 153–62 in *Studies in the History and Archaeology of Jordan I,* ed. A. Hadidi. Amman.

ERNST AXEL KNAUF

BAAL-HAZOR (PLACE) [Heb *baᶜal ḥāṣôr*]. A location near the town of EPHRAIM (2 Sam 13:23) where ABSALOM held a sheepshearing celebration at which he had his brother AMNON murdered for having raped his half-sister TAMAR (2 Sam 13:24–29). The generally accepted location of the place is Jebel el-ᶜAṣur (M.R. 177153), a remote place of rugged Cenomanian limestone slopes 3,332 feet above sea level (*GB,* 174; Simons *GTTOT,* 30). It may be the same site as the Hazor mentioned in Neh 11:33 (*LBHG,* 410), though Simons (*GTTOT,* 390) identifies this Hazor differently.

Baal-hazor is not to be confused with the fortified city Hazor N of the Sea of Galilee. Absalom's mountain home was 15 miles N of Jerusalem and about 5 miles S of Shiloh. Simons (*GTTOT* 334) points out that there is no *tell* at Jebel el-ᶜAṣur that would indicate the ruins of a formerly inhabited city. The Genesis Apocryphon calls the place where God appeared to Abraham after his separation from Lot (Gen 13:14) by the name Ramath-hazor. A late tradition identifies Ramath-hazor as another name for Baal-hazor (*IDB* 1: 331).

HENRY O. THOMPSON

BAAL-HERMON (PLACE) [Heb *baᶜal ḥermôn*]. A border point on the land inhabited by the Hivites (Judg 3:3) and intended for the half-tribe of Manasseh on the E side of the Jordan River (1 Chr 5:23). The Deuteronomistic historian concludes that the sons of Manasseh failed to conquer the Hivite lands, including Baal-Hermon, so that Yahweh could test Israel's rebellion in future generations. By this explanation the historian can rationalize Israel's inability to fulfill the potential of completely possessing the promised land.

Baal-Hermon belongs to the mountains of the Anti-lebanon (see Josh 11:17) range at the edge of ancient Hivite territory, and it is most likely a place on the top of Mt. Hermon, if not one of the 3 peaks comprising Mt. Hermon. The half-tribe of Manasseh is located by 1 Chr 5:23 in 3 places (Baal-Hermon, Senir, and Mt. Hermon). Senir is one of the peaks (see Cant 4:8 and the dual *hermônîm* in Ps 42:7—Eng 42:6) and Mt. Hermon is the name of another. Baal-Hermon is possibly the third peak, which means that the E-Jordan tribe of Manasseh is restricted by the Chronicler to the base of this mountain.

Bibliography

Dar, S. 1988. The History of the Hermon Settlements. *PEQ* 120: 26–43.

PAUL NIMRAH FRANKLYN

BAAL-MEON (PLACE) [Heb *baᶜal məᶜôn*]. Var. BETH-BAAL-MEON; BETH-MEON. A locality listed among the towns and villages of the tribe of Reuben (Num 32:28) which originally belonged to Moab. It is also known as Beth-baal-meon (Josh 13:17) and Beth-meon (Jer 48:23).

Mesha's reference on the Moabite Stone (*ca.* 830 B.C.) to having built a reservoir for Baal-meon implies that the city reverted to Moabite control (cf. *ANET,* 320, line 9). It may have come back under Israelite control (*ca.* 770 B.C.) as inferred from a reference to "Baala the Baal-meonite" on Ostraca 27 from Samaria (assuming that this is the same city). The Jeremiah passage (48:23) clearly indicates Moabite possession of the town (*ca.* 600 B.C.).

Eusebius (*Onomast.* 44.21) identified Baal-meon with "the big village in the environs of (the hot springs of) Baaru . . . with the name of Beelmaus, distant nine miles from, Esbous, place of origin of the prophet Elisha." In 1807, Seetzen identified it with the ruins of Khirbet Maᶜin (M.R. 219120), 9 km SW of Madaba. The ruins were carefully studied by Musil in 1902.

The investigations have revealed no Iron Age remains, but in 1934 the mosaic floor of a church on the acropolis was unearthed. Two other churches were excavated in 1973 and 1977.

The main feature of the mosaic floor in the church on the acropolis, dated A.D. 719/720, are 11 city plans of Palestine and Jordan: Nikopolis, (Eleuthero)polis, Ascalona, Maioumas, (Ga)za, Od(roa), (Charach M)ouba, Areopolis, Gadara, Esboun(ta), Belemoun(ta). North of the W church a *xenion* (a hostel for pilgrims) and a room of a pribaton (bath) were found—two buildings associated with the public assistance for pilgrims, particularly necessary in a village like Maᶜin, which was near the hot springs of Baaru. Among the ruins were stone inscriptions, fine Nabatean sculptures, together with several Byzantine capitals which were richly decorated with geometrical, floral, and figurative motifs. See also MAON; MEUNIM.

Bibliography

Piccirillo, M. 1985. Le antichità bizantine di Maᶜin e dintorni. *LASBF* 35: 339–64.

MICHELE PICCIRILLO

BAAL-PEOR (PLACE) [Heb *baʿal-pĕʿôr*]. The place associated with the idol of Moab that tempted Israel while in the wilderness (Deut 4:3; Hos 9:10). According to the narrative account (Numbers 25), while Israel was encamped at Shittim, the men of Israel engaged in immorality with women of Moab. This activity was linked to the idolatrous worship of Baal of Peor. As a result God brought a plague on Israel in which 24,000 died, and this was only stayed when Phinehas, the son of the high priest, killed Zimri, a Simeonite man, and Cozbi, a Midianite woman with whom Zimri violated the covenant (Num 25:18). According to Mendenhall (1973: 105–21) it was an act of ritual intercourse that yoked this Israelite man to the pagan god; thus he broke covenant with the God of Israel.

Baal-peor or Baal of Peor was one of the leading gods of the Moabites, Midianites, and Ammonites, but akin to the Canaanite Baal and Moloch. The sensual rites of worship indicate a connection with the Phoenician Baal and the Moabite Chemosh. The Baal-peor incident carried this sensual aspect in the history of biblical interpretation as well. In particular, Marvin Pope (*Song of Songs* AB, 217–20) points out how sacral sexual intercourse in the Baal-peor festivals relates to interpretation of the biblical Song of Songs. From Jerome's time, writers have commonly associated Baal and Chemosh with the Roman Priapus. Rather than associating Peor, as the rabbis thought, with Heb *pāʿar* "to fracture," and thus to deprive of virginity, it is best understood as a form of worship in this locality, Baal-peor or Beth-peor, in the mountains of Moab (Deut 3:29, 4:45). For further discussion, see Budd *Numbers* WBC, 274–83 (and bibliography there); Andersen and Freedman *Hosea* AB, 537–38, 540–41; Albright *ARI, YGC.*

Bibliography

Glueck, N. 1943. Some Ancient Towns in the Plains of Moab. *BASOR* 91: 13–18.

James, E. O. 1960. *The Ancient Gods.* New York.

Mendenhall, G. E. 1973. *The Tenth Generation: The Origins of the Biblical Tradition.* Baltimore.

JOEL C. SLAYTON

BAAL-PERAZIM (PLACE) [Heb *baʿal pĕrāṣîm*]. The place where David had his first victory over the Philistine army after moving his capital from Hebron to Jerusalem (2 Sam 5:18–20; 1 Chr 14:9–11). It is identified with "Mount Perazim" (Heb *har Pĕrāṣîm*) in Isa 28:21. Thus Baal-perazim must be a mountain from where David's army could attack Philistines who "spread themselves out in the valley of Rephaim." The Greek name *Epánō Diakopōn* means "upper breaches," but the first element of the Heb name *Baʿal* "lord" may be understood as the noun of relation. So the meaning of *Baʿal Pĕrāṣîm* is literally "lord of breaches," but idiomatically "breach-maker," like the "dreamer" in Gen 37:19 ("the lord of dreams"), the "destroyer" in Prov 18:9 ("the lord of destruction"), and the "archer" in Gen 49:23 ("the lord of arrows"). The second element of the Heb name *Pĕrāṣîm* figuratively means the "outburst" of Yahweh's wrath in 2 Sam 6:8. So the Heb name *Baʿal Pĕrāṣîm* here may mean "(divine) Outburster" which is supported by the expression in 2 Sam 5:20: "Yahweh has broken through my enemies before me like the breakthrough of waters." The use of this place name in 2 Sam 5:20 ("So David came to Baal-perazim") is an example of a biblical practice to modernize geographical names. Here, the place name Baal-perazim was used in the context when this name had not yet been given to the place, like "Dan" in Gen 14:14, "Eben-ezer" in 1 Sam 4:1 and 5:1, and "Lehi" in Judg 15:9, 14.

YOSHITAKA KOBAYASHI

BAAL-SHALISHAH (PLACE) [Heb *baʿal šālīšâ*]. A town (or region) from which a man came bringing "bread of the first fruits, twenty loaves of barley, and fresh ears of grain" to feed Elisha and the sons of the prophets during a famine (2 Kgs 4:42). The Talmud reinforces Baal-shalishah's reputation for agricultural productivity and fertility (*Sanh.* 12a).

The location of Baal-shalishah is tied in with the location of Gilgal, where Elisha and the sons of the prophets were staying. On the one hand, Gilgal here is often assumed to refer to the place near Jericho. Thus, Kallai (1972) identified Baal-shalishah with Kh. el-Marjameh (M.R. 181155) along the upper course of the wadi Samiya (its lower course enters the Jordan valley about 10 km N of Jericho). This identification is problematic, however, insofar as el-Marjameh lies in the wilderness of Ephraim, where the rain-shadow limits annual rainfall and where one would not expect to find a site noted for abundant harvests. On the other hand, because Elisha had been in Shunem and Mt. Carmel immediately before this, it is likely that this "Gilgal" lies somewhere in the N part of the central hill country, probably Jiljulieh (M.R. 171159), 12 km N of Bethel. See GILGAL (PLACE) #2. Eusebius had identified it with "Bethsarith/Bathsarisa" (Jerome rendered "Bethsalisa"), locating it 24 km N of Lydda/Lod. Thus, Baal-shalishah may be identified with Kh. Sirisya (M.R. 151168), overlooking the Sharon plain. The name of Kefr Thilth (M.R. 154174), a village 5.5 km N of Kh. Sirisya, contains the Arabic equivalent of Heb *šalīšâ.* The famine recorded in 2 Kings 4 therefore must have been localized, so that a man from Baal-shalishah about 25 km away could bring surplus food for Elisha and the sons of the prophets.

Bibliography

Kallai, Z. 1972. Baal-shalishah and Ephraim. Pp. 191–204 in *Liver Memorial Volume,* edited by B. Oppenheimer. Tel Aviv (in Hebrew).

GARY A. HERION

BAAL-TAMAR (PLACE) [Heb *baʿal tāmār*]. The place on the highway between Gibeah (modern Tell el-Ful, M.R. 172136) and Bethel (modern Beitîn, M.R. 172148) where the soldiers of Israel mustered to fight against the Benjaminites who were pursuing them from their garrison at Gibeah (Judg 20:33). The 2 main armies fought here while a second portion of the army of Israel that had been encamped W of Geba (modern Ar Jebaʿ, M.R. 175140) attacked Gibeah and secured the victory over the Benjaminites. Baal-tamar was one among many locations in Israel bearing a divine name. It is possible that it was connected with a temple (*LBHG,* 108). Its site has not been conclusively identified, though several possibilities have been mentioned. Press (1951: 115) connected Baal-tamar with the palm *(tōmer)* of Deborah (Judg 4:5) on Mount Ephraim. He proposed that Baal-tamar was at the site, upon which the later Judean city of Ataroth was built (modern Kh. Atārāh, M.R. 170142), that was called Beth-tamar in the Byzantine period. Other possibilities are Ras et-Tavil (M.R. 174137) which is NE of Givat Šāʾul, and Ṣahre al Gibiyeh 500 m E of Tel el-Ful (*EncMiqr* 2: 293).

Bibliography

Press, I. 1951. *A Topographical-Historical Encyclopaedia of Palestine* vol. 1. Jerusalem (in Hebrew).

SUSAN E. MCGARRY

BAAL-ZEBUB (DEITY) [Heb *baʿal zĕbûb*]. A god of Ekron, whom King Ahaziah wished to consult to learn if he would recover from a sickness he was experiencing as a result of a fall (2 Kgs 1:2, 3, 6, 16). However, Elijah pronounced Yahweh's judgment of death on the king for failing to inquire of Yahweh and instead seeking a word from Baal-zebub of Ekron.

The word *baʿal,* "lord," can be understood as the name of Baal, the great Canaanite deity, or as a generic title which could be used for Baal or for any other male divinity. Most scholars are of the opinion that the cult of Ekron mentioned in 2 Kings 1 was a localized form of Baal worship. Nevertheless, the main debate concerning "Baal-zebub" involves understanding the 2d element in the name, with 2 major positions being taken: (a) *zĕbûb* is the original form, and (b) *zbb* is a deliberate distortion of an original *zbl* by Hebrew copyists. The majority of those holding to the 1st position translate *zĕbûb* as "fly" or "flies" (cf. Isa 7:18; Eccl 10:1), interpreting the full name as "lord of the fly/flies." This name, it has been proposed, signifies that the deity of Ekron had control over flies, having the power to send or repulse these noxious disease-bearing insects (and other pests). Comparisons are made with the Greek god Zeus Apomuios ("averter of flies") and the Roman god Myiagrus (on the weakness of these comparisons see Gaster *IDB* 1: 332). By extension, Baal-zebub, "lord of the fly/flies," is viewed as a health god warding off pestilence. The question arises, though, as to why Ahaziah, whose "illness" (or injury) was due to a fall and not a disease, would want to consult specifically this divinity of Ekron, supposedly revered for averting disease-bearing flies and pestilence (Gaster *IDB* 1: 332). A 2d suggestion, that "Baal-zebub" sent oracles by means of flies, lacks reliable supporting evidence. Gordon (*UT,* 388) explains that "lord of the fly" should be compared with the fly ("= divine symbol?") on cylinder seals. Yet on the example cited the representation, if it is a fly, is of undeterminable significance, its relationship to the seal's other images being problematical. Fensham (1967: 361–63), noting the fire motif in the Elijah narratives (including 2 Kings 1), thinks *zĕbûb* may be "flame" (thus "Baal the flame"), on the basis of *ḏbb* (Ug *ḏ* changed to *z* in Heb) in *CTA* 3.3.43. However, the meaning of *ḏbb* in the Ug passage remains uncertain.

The other major position, again, sees *bʿl zbl* as the original name of the god, which was intentionally distorted by scribes to show contempt for the deity and to mock his worshipers (*bʿl zbb* meaning "lord of the fly/flies"). Examples (inexact parallels) from the Heb Bible are mentioned where the theophoric element "Baal" in personal names is known to have been deliberately changed. As to the meaning of *zbl,* the Heb *zĕbûl,* "lofty abode," "exalted dwelling," has been cited (thus: "lord of the lofty abode"). A *zbl,* which can be translated "sick (one)," appears in the Ug literature, but it is doubtful that this word is involved in 2 Kings 1 (i.e., "lord of the sick one"), since it carries connotations of disease or plague. Another proposal interprets *zbl* as "prince." In the mythology of Ugarit Baal several times is referred to as *zbl bʿl ʾarṣ,* "the prince, the lord of the earth." Baal is also called simply *zbl bʿl,* "Prince Baal," as are other deities (e.g., *zbl ym,* "Prince Yam"). Further, the word order of a divine name preceding *zbl* occurs in the Ug texts; e.g., *ršp zbl* and *yrḫ zbl,* which in context are translated "Prince Resheph" and "Prince Yarikh." Thus, *bʿl zbl* could be "Baal the prince," "Prince Baal," or "Baal is prince" (cf. the name Beelzebul in Matt 10:25 and 12:24, 27; Mark 3:22; Luke 11:15, 18, 19).

In summary, on the basis of the available evidence, one cannot reach a proper understanding of "Baal-zebub." Nevertheless, in light of the context of 2 Kings 1, the Ug evidence, and the tendency of Heb scribes at times to distort certain names, it seems best at present to regard "Baal-zebub" as a caconymic ("lord of the fly/flies") for an original "Baal-zebul," "Baal the prince." Why Ahaziah wanted to consult this Baal of Ekron remains unknown. See also BAAL; BEELZEBUL; and *RE* 2: 514–16.

Bibliography

Fensham, F. 1967. A Possible Explanation of the Name Baal-Zebub of Ekron. *ZAW* 79: 361–64.

WALTER A. MAIER III

BAAL-ZEPHON (PLACE) [Heb *baʿal ṣĕpōn*]. A site in the Egyptian E Delta that is mentioned together with Migdol to help locate Pi-hahiroth, near the place where the Israelites crossed the sea (Exod 14:2, 9; Num 33:7). The precise location of Baal-zephon (and of Migdol and Pi-hahiroth as well) is uncertain, but the question is important for the debate regarding the location of the sea crossing and the route of the Exodus. Baal-zephon, after whom the biblical site was named, was a Canaanite god who is well known from the Ugaritic texts. His dwelling place was on Jebel el-Aqraʿ, about 40 km north of Ugarit, which the Semites called *ṣapānu* (Heb *ṣāpôn*) and the non-Semites called *ḥazi,* later Kasios (*TDOT* 2: 186).

At least 3 sanctuaries of Baal-zephon in N Egypt are known: Memphis, Tahpanhes (Tell Defneh), and Mt. Casius at Ras Qasrun. Possibly one of the temples at Tell el-Dabʿa, located 2 km south of Qantir, was dedicated to Baal (Bietak 1981: 253). A *migdol* that is probably called "of Baal-zephon" is mentioned in the Cairo papyrus 31169. Its location seems to have been near Wadi Tumilat (Davies 1979: 81). There were probably additional Baal-zephon sites in N Egypt, since the Canaanite religion was popular there at various times (Helck 1962; Stadelmann 1967).

Four locations for biblical Baal-zephon have been proposed: two N, one central, and one S. (1) Some posit its location at the Egyptian Mt. Casios near Lake Sirbonis. Eissfeldt (1932) argued that Mt. Casios was located at Mahammidiye on the Mediterranean coast, about 13 km E of Pelusium, but Cazelles (1955) has demonstrated that it was located at Ras Qasrun on the N strip separating Lake Sirbonis from the Mediterranean. (2) The other suggested location in the N is Tahpanhes, modern Tell Defneh near the S tip of Lake Menzaleh (Albright 1950; Wright 1962: 62). (3) Others propose a central location near the Bitter Lakes (Simons 1959: 248–51; Davies 1979: 82). (4) The traditional view located the site near the head of the Gulf of Suez (Servin 1948–49). To a great extent one's view regarding the location of biblical Baal-zephon is tied in with one's view regarding the route of the Exodus. The 2d and 3d options appear to be the most plausible. For persuasive arguments against the 1st and 4th options, see Davies (1979: 81–82).

Bibliography

Albright, W. F. 1950. Baal-zephon. Pp. 1–14 in *Festschrift Alfred Bertholet zum 80. Geburtstag*, ed. W. Baumgartner, O. Eissfeldt, K. Elliger, and L. Rost. Tübingen.

Bietak, M. 1981. *Avaris and Piramesse: Archaeological Exploration in the Eastern Nile Delta.* London.

Cazelles, H. 1955. Les localisations de l'Exode et la critique littéraire. *RB* 62: 321–64.

Davies, G. I. 1979. *The Way of the Wilderness.* Cambridge.

Eissfeldt, O. 1932. *Baal Zaphon, Zeus Kasios und der Durchzug der Israeliten durchs Meer.* Halle.

Helck, H. W. 1962. *Die Beziehungen Ägyptens zu vorderasien im 3. und 2. Jahrtausend v. Chr.* Wiesbaden.

Servin, A. 1948–49. La tradition judéo-chretienne de l'Exode. *Bulletin de l'Institut d'Égypte* 31: 315–55.

Simons, J. 1959. *The Geographical and Topographical Texts of the Old Testament.* Leiden.

Stadelmann, R. 1967. *Syrisch-Palästinensische Gottheiten in Ägypten.* Leiden.

Wright, G. E. 1962. *Biblical Archaeology.* Philadelphia.

PAUL R. RAABE

BAALAH (PLACE) [Heb *baᶜălâ*]. **1.** City on the N border of Judah (Josh 15:9, 10; 1 Chr 13:6). Owing to its biblical identification with Kiriath-Jearim (Josh 15:9; 1 Chr 13:6), it is to be located at Tell el-Azhar (Boling *Joshua* AB, 369), alongside one of the major routes leading through the Judean hill country E to Jerusalem (*LBHG*, 59). Noth considers the identification of Baalah and Kiriath-Jearim to be a redactional error, although he concedes that Baalah, which in his opinion may have been no more than a cultic site, lay in the vicinity of Kiriath-Jearim (*Josua* HAT, 88–90, 110). He further views variant names for Baalah/Kiriath-Jearim, such as Kiriath-Baal (Josh 15:60, 18:14) and Baale-Judah (2 Sam 6:2), as artificial constructions. He bases his argument on the putative antiquity of the name Kiriath-Jearim and denies the possibility of multiple concurrent names. Boling (*Joshua* AB, 369), reflecting the view of most modern scholarship, views Baalah as an ancient Canaanite name (meaning "wife" or "lady"), reflecting the worship of one of the Canaanite goddesses (Asherah, Astarte, or Anath). He further speculates that the name Baalah was demythologized by the Israelites into Kiriath-Jearim "Woodsville."

2. One of the towns of Judah (Josh 15:29). It was located in the Negeb toward the Edomite border (Josh 15:21). Abel (*GP* 258) located it at Tulul el-Medbah, near Tel Masos (Khirbet el-Meshash). In the lists of the Simeonite tribal allocations within Judah's territory it is called Balah (Josh 19:3) and Bilhah (1 Chr 4:29). Although most scholars do not commit themselves on the question of the original form of the name, Noth (*Josua* HAT, 88) supported Balah, which Albright (1924: 150 n. 4) viewed as secondary, choosing what in his view is the most difficult reading, namely Bilhah.

3. A point on the NW border of Judah, called Mount Baalah [Heb *har-habbaᶜălâ*] (Josh 15:11). It is commonly identified with the ridge of Mughar, NW of Ekron (Kallai-Kleinmann 1958: 145).

Bibliography

Albright, W. F. 1924. Egypt and the Early History of the Negeb. *JPOS* 4: 131–61.

Kallai-Kleinmann, Z. 1958. The Town Lists of Judah, Siemon, Benjamin and Dan. *VT* 8: 134–60.

CARL S. EHRLICH

BAALATH (PLACE) [Heb *baᶜălāt*]. A town in the W part of the territory of Dan (Josh 19:44), within the lowland regions which that tribe failed to inherit from the Canaanites (Judg 1:34). Baalath appears to have come under Israelite control only in the days of Solomon, when it was fortified (1 Kgs 9:17–18; 2 Chr 8:5–6), along with recently annexed Gezer and with Lower Beth-horon, in order to guard the roads leading to Jerusalem from the plain. Baalath is apparently to be equated with Mt. Baalah (Josh 15:9), on the W boundary of Judah. It has been identified with the site of el-Maghar (M.R. 129138), where sherds of the Bronze and Iron ages have been collected (Kaplan 1953: 140–41).

Bibliography

Kaplan, J. 1953. Researches in the Gederah—el-Mughar Area. *BIES* 17: 138–43 (Hebrew).

Mazar, B. 1986. The Cities of the Territory of Dan. Pp. 104–12 in *The Early Biblical Period.* Jerusalem.

RAPHAEL GREENBERG

BAALATH-BEER (PLACE) [Heb *baᶜalat bĕʾēr*]. A site mentioned in the list of towns purportedly assigned to the patrimony of the tribe of Simeon by Joshua after the conquest (Josh 19:8) and called Baal in a later version of this list (1 Chr 4:33). The list, widely believed to derive from administrative documents of the monarchy, locates Baalath-beer at an indeterminate distance and direction from the vicinity of 4 other towns: Ain, Rimmon, Ether, and Ashan. If Rimmon (En-rimmon?) is to be identified with Tel Halif, then Baalath-beer might be sought in the S Shephelah or N Negeb. Alternatively, the list's vague association or identification of Baalath-beer with Ramath-Negeb might place the site in the Negeb E of Beer-sheba (*HGB*, 358–59), a location which might suggest the site's identification with the BEALOTH mentioned in Josh 15:24. In any case, any modern location of Baalath-beer is clearly a matter of conjecture. The meaning of the toponym "lady of the well" suggests that the patron deity of Baalath-beer may have been a local goddess related to the Canaanite fertility god Baal.

Patrick M. Arnold

BAALBEK (PLACE). A Canaanite, Phoenician, and Greco-Roman town and cult center in Lebanon, 53 miles (85 km) ENE of Beirut in the N part of the fertile Beqa valley, between the region's 2 major mountain ranges. The cultus was dedicated chiefly to the Semitic god Baal (Hadad/Adad) in his capacity as a deity of sky, storm, and fertility of the land. Although excavations have shown occupation of the site as early as the 3d millennium B.C. (Ragette 1980: 16), little is known of the pre-Roman development of Baalbek. Attempts to identify the town with a biblical site, such as Baal-gad, have not been successful.

During the 3d or 2d century B.C. the shrine and town were renamed Heliopolis "City of the Sun" echoing the name of an Egyptian sacred city. From the time of this renaming (if indeed not earlier) until the Islamic conquest in the 7th century A.D., a triad of deities was venerated at the site: Zeus/Jupiter, who may have assumed solar characteristics along with the traditional attributes of Baal; the goddess Aphrodite/Venus (the Syrian Anath/Atargatis); and the youthful god Hermes/Mercury. The assumption that Dionysus/Bacchus was the 3d member of the triad has been shown to be erroneous.

In spite of earthquakes and human destruction, the site has extensive remains dating largely from the 1st through the 3d centuries A.D.; the most important are 6 immense standing columns and other remnants of a temple of Jupiter, a remarkably well-preserved temple popularly known as that of Bacchus, and a small circular temple that has been taken, perhaps mistakenly, to have been dedicated to Venus. Major archaeological excavations were conducted by a German expedition during 1898–1905 (Wiegand); since that time further excavation, along with considerable consolidation and restoration, has been carried out by the Department of Antiquities of Lebanon. Guidebooks to the site include Alouf and Harding; fuller analysis as well as numerous excellent photographs will be found in Jidejian (1975), while Ragette (1980) is helpful for its numerous line-drawings depicting the major temples of Baalbek as they are today and as they may have looked in the past.

Bibliography

Alouf, M. M. n.d. *History of Baalbek.* 25th ed. Beirut.

Harding, G. L. 1963. *Baalbek.* Beirut.

Jidejian, N. 1975. *Baalbek: Heliopolis, City of the Sun.* Beirut.

Ragette, F. 1980. *Baalbek.* London.

Wiegand, T. 1921–25. *Baalbek.* 3 vols. Berlin.

Robert Houston Smith

BAALE-JUDAH (PLACE) [Heb *baʿălê yĕhûdâ*]. See KIRIATH-JEARIM (PLACE).

BAALIS (PERSON) [Heb *baʿălîs*]. An early 6th-century B.C. Ammonite king mentioned only in Jer 40:14. The context indicates that Baalis was either: (1) anti-Babylonian in his foreign policy, seeking to restore the Davidic throne under Ammonite control, and collaborating with and harboring Judean royalty involved in the murder of Gedaliah, the Babylonian-appointed governor residing in Mizpah; or (2) at least disruptive of a stable Judean government in an effort to serve his own ends, perhaps being jealous of any neighbor who had the potential of rivaling his own power.

This king has been identified with the Baʿal-yishʿa mentioned on a seal impression found in 1984 at Tell el-ʿUmeiri, just S of Amman in Jordan (Geraty 1984; 1985). It was found in the sift from topsoil excavated near the W rim of the mound about 50 cm above the remains of a major public structure termed the Ammonite Citadel by the excavators. The seal impression itself (19 mm in diameter) was on the flat end of a fired ceramic cone (21 mm in length) which may have served as a stopper with identification for a juglet of unknown contents.

The finely conceived and executed seal impression is divided into 3 panels. The top and bottom panels contain the Ammonite inscription, dated paleographically to *ca.* 600 B.C. (Herr 1985b and fc.). The middle panel depicts typically Ammonite iconography (Younker 1985): a 4-winged scarab beetle pushing a solar ball flanked by standards, solar discs, and crescent moons in an assemblage reminiscent of Zeph 1:4–6. The inscription reads *lmlkm-ʾwr ʿbd bʿl-yšʿ*, "belonging to Milkom-ʾur, servant of Baʿal-yishʿa (or Baʿal-yashaʿ)." Both of the personal names, that of the owner of the seal and that of the king he served, constitute "firsts." Milkom-ʾor ("Milkom is light") or Milkom-ʾur ("Milkom's flame"), represents the first-known occurrence in which Milkom, the well-known Ammonite divine name, appears as one of the elements in an Ammonite proper name. According to his title, "servant," this individual would have been a prominent government official in the service of the Ammonite king, Baʿal-yishʿa ("Baal is salvation") or Baʿal-yashaʿ ("Baal saves"). The latter is identified with the Baalis of Jer 40:14, and this reference to him is his first extrabiblical confirmation—despite Wright's (1974: 3) claim about "Baʿlay" being on the Tell Siran bottle (a misunderstanding of Cross 1973), misinformation perpetuated by Feinberg (1982: 272).

The spellings for the name of the Ammonite king preserved in Jer 40:14 *(bʿlys)* and in the seal impression *(bʿlyšʿ)* are different enough that one may legitimately question the identification. The following points argue in its favor (Shea 1985: 112):

1. Of the 9 Ammonite kings now known from the Bible, Assyrian texts, and Ammonite inscriptions (cf. Cross's listing in Herr 1985b: 171), the Baalis of Jeremiah is the only one containing "Baal" as a theophoric element.
2. In the more than 100 names assembled thus far in our Ammonite onomasticon, Baalis is the only name containing "Baal" as its theophoric element. Thus the use of "Baal" in an Ammonite king's name is exclusive to the king of the ʿUmeiri sealing and the king mentioned in Jer 40:14. Even though the verbal ele-

ment in the names differ, it is reasonable to conclude that the 2 references are to the same Ammonite king.

The spelling difference in the verbal element of the name thus requires an explanation. Before the discovery of the seal impression, both Cross (1973: 15) and Landes (*IDB* 1: 112), recognized that the name Baalis makes no sense as it stands in the MT, so suggested it could be hypocoristicon. Subsequent to the find, Shea (1985) has argued an intentional pious change in the Bible to avoid heathen theology, a view disputed by Herr (1985a). It is also possible that it could be an unintentional change reflecting the way Judeans heard the name pronounced in Ammonite, partially preserved, perhaps, in Jer 47:14 LXX, as Belisa, where the final vowel would reflect the presence of a final *ᶜayin* which would, of course, not have been written in Greek (Geraty 1985: 100). That Transjordanian *šin* was pronounced *śin* in Cisjordan is well known from the Shibboleth story in Judg 12:6. Whatever the reason for the difference in spelling, it was accurately hypothetically reconstructed by Puech (1985: 10) before the archaeological discovery.

Bibliography

Cross, F. M. 1973. Notes on the Ammonite Inscription from Tell Siran. *BASOR* 212: 12–15.

Feinberg, C. L. 1982. *Jeremiah* NICOT. Grand Rapids.

Geraty, L. T. 1984. A Preliminary Report on the Madaba Plains Project's 1984 Season at Tell el-ᶜUmeiri. *Newsletter of the Institute of Archaeology*. [Andrews University]. 5: 3–4.

———. 1985. A Preliminary Report on the First Season at Tell el-ᶜUmeiri. *AUSS* 23: 85–110.

Herr, L. G. 1985a. Is the Spelling of "Baalis" in Jeremiah 40:14 a Mutilation? *AUSS* 23: 187–91.

———. 1985b. The Servant of Baalis. *BA* 48: 169–72.

———. fc. The Inscribed Seal Impression of the Servant of Baalis. In *Tell el-ᶜUmeiri 1984*, ed. L. T. Geraty et al. Berrien Springs, MI.

Puech, E. 1985. L'inscription de la statue d'Amman et la paléographie ammonite. *RB* 92: 5–24.

Shea, W. H. 1985. Mutilation of Foreign Names by Bible Writers: A Possible Example from Tell el-ᶜUmeiri. *AUSS* 23: 111–15.

Wright, G. E. 1974. Annual Report to the Trustees, the Corporation, Members and Friends. *ASOR Newsletter* 9: 1–2.

Younker, R. W. 1985. Israel, Judah, and Ammon and the Motifs on the Baalis Seal from Tell el-ᶜUmeiri. *BA* 48: 173–80.

Lawrence T. Geraty

BAALSAMUS (PERSON) [Gk *Baalsamos*]. See MAASEIAH.

BAANA (PERSON) [Heb *baᶜanāʾ*]. Three persons in the OT. Baana and Baanah are apparently variant spellings of the same name, as are *uzzāʾ* (2 Sam 6:3) and *uzzâ* (6:7–8), *mîkāʾ* (2 Sam 9:12) and *mîkâ* (1 Chr 8:34–35). There are 2 main approaches to the meaning of Baana(h). The 1st sees it as deriving from *ben-* "son of" plus a 2d element. The loss of *nun* in *bn-* is known, for example, from 10th–9th century B.C. inscriptions from Byblos (*KAI* 6.1; 7.3; 8). The interpretation "son of distress," from *bn-ᶜnh* (BDB, 128) founders mainly on the lack of a noun *ᶜānâ* "distress." Somewhat more likely is the view that the 2d element is the name of a deity ᶜAn (perhaps the masculine counterpart of ᶜAnath), believed to be referred to in personal names from Ug (e.g. *bn. ᶜn*), Amarna (DUMU *[Bin]-a-na*), and elsewhere (Hoffmon *APNM*, 199; cf. 168–69).

The 2d approach understands Baana(h) to begin with the element *bᶜl* "Baal/the Lord" (with *lamed* dropped; Noth (*IPN*, 40; cf. *TPNAH*, 56) adduces a Phoenician example of *bᶜsmm* for *bᶜlsmm*). Noth saw the name as *bᶜ(l) + n +* hypocoristic *-ā*, the *nun* being the first radical of the name's 2d element; the apparently analogous names Baasha and Baara may also be analyzed in this fashion. Alternately, Baana(h) may derive from *baᶜalᶜānâ* "Baal has answered" (Montgomery *Kings* ICC, 125).

Possibly related names in extrabiblical sources include Palmyrene *bwnʾ* (*IPN* 40), Minean *bᶜn* and Safaitic *bᶜnh* (Ryckmans 1934: 54, 257).

1. Son of Ahilud and a prefect over Solomon's 5th administrative district (1 Kgs 4:12). Baana was charged with supplying provisions for the palace during 1 month of each year (1 Kgs 4:7). His district corresponded roughly to the Jezreel and Beth-Shean valleys, areas dominated until David's time by major Canaanite cities such as Taanach and Megiddo. More precise boundaries cannot be delineated with confidence due to the uncertainty of site identifications (notably Zarethan and Jokmeam, which some read as Jokneam) and difficulties in the text of 1 Kgs 4:12, parts of which appear to have been transposed. See further Wright 1967: 59*, 60*, 66*; *LBHG*, 308, 313; Naʾaman 1986: 187–90. Baana may have been the brother of Jehoshaphat son of Ahilud, a high official (*mzkyr* "Recorder") under David and Solomon: 2 Sam 8:16, 1 Kgs 4:3.

2. Son of Hushai and a prefect over Solomon's 9th district (1 Kgs 4:16; for his duties see Baana #1 above). Baana's district is described as *bʾsr wbᶜlwt*, either "in Asher and in Aloth" or "in Asher and Bealoth." Both alternatives are problematic inasmuch as no town Aloth, or N town Bealoth, is known, and it seems unusual for the name of a well-known tribe to be paired with that of an obscure locale. Reading Maaloth (*mᶜlwt*) or the like (unconvincingly connected with the Ladder of Tyre, see Montgomery *Kings* ICC, 126) with some Gk witnesses merely exchanges one unknown for another. A conjectured reading "in Asher and Zebulon" is supported by Cross' demonstration (Wright 1967: 59* fig. 1 and n. 8) that *zbwlwn* could have been misread as *wbᶜlt* in some scripts. The conjectured reading remains viable in spite of objections which have been raised (Montgomery *Kings* ICC, 126; Ahlström 1979), notably on the grounds of *lectio difficilior*, although, the lack of versional support for the reading "Zebulun" is surprising in view of the lateness of Cross' examples. See further *LBHG*, 308, 315; Naʾaman 1986: 192–94.

It is quite possible that Baana's father was Hushai the Archite, David's loyal advisor (2 Sam 15:32–37).

3. The father or ancestor of Zadok, one of those who repaired a section of Jerusalem's walls in the days of Nehemiah (Neh 3:4). Possibly identical to BAANAH #3 or #4.

Bibliography

Ahlström, G. W. 1979. A Note on a Textual Problem in 1 Kgs 4:16. *BASOR* 235: 79–80.

Na'aman, N. 1986. *Borders and Districts in Biblical Historiography.* Jerusalem Biblical Studies 4. Jerusalem.

Ryckmans, G. 1934. *Les noms propres sud-semitiques.* Tome 1. Louvain.

Wright, G. E. 1967. The Provinces of Solomon. *EI* 8: 58*–68*.

FREDERICK W. KNOBLOCH

BAANAH (PERSON) [Heb *baʿănâ*]. **1.** One of the murderers of King Saul's son Ishbosheth (2 Sam 4:2–12). Baanah and his brother Rechab were both company commanders under Ish-bosheth (2 Sam 4:2), who had succeeded Saul as king of Israel. Having slipped into Ishbosheth's house as he rested at midday, the two killed the king in his bed and brought his head to David, then king of Judah and Ish-bosheth's rival, in anticipation of a reward. David, however, denounced the deed, had the two executed, and had their severed limbs hung beside the pool in his capital Hebron—no doubt powerful deterrents to further regicide and vivid reminders that David denied any involvement in the assassination.

There is no consensus as to whether Baanah was an Israelite, an important issue in understanding Ishbosheth's murder. According to one reading of 2 Sam 4:2–3, Baanah's father Rimmon was a Benjaminite *(mbny bnymn)* who lived in Beeroth *(hbʾrty)*. The passage goes on to tell how Beeroth came to be populated by Benjaminites, *viz.* as a result of the flight of the (native) Beerothites to Gittaim, which presumably allowed Benjaminites to move in. This reading involves taking *bʾrty* "Beerothite" in a geographical sense in v 2 ("one who lives in Beeroth") but in an ethnic sense in v 3 ("Beerothite"). In this view Baanah and Rechab were motivated solely by the expectation of a reward from David (McCarter *2 Samuel* AB, 127–28).

Alternately, Baanah was the son of "Rimmon the Beerothite *(hbʾrty)* from (among) the Benjaminites *(mbny bnymn),*" and was therefore of Gibeonite extraction, Beeroth being one of the 4 Gibeonite cities (Josh 9:17). Verse 2 goes on to explain why a foreign Beerothite is associated with the Benjaminites: because Beeroth was located within Benjamin's borders. (Verse 3, loosely connected to the foregoing, adds an explanation of why there were Beerothites living in Gittaim.) If Baanah the Gibeonite killed Saul's son, one cannot fail to connect the episode to the well-known Gibeonite hatred of Saul, even though the biblical narrative does not stress the point. Saul, the Gibeonites said, attempted to exterminate them (perhaps the occasion of the Beerothite's flight to Gittaim); in retaliation the Gibeonites, after Saul's death, demanded and received permission from David to execute 7 of Saul's sons (2 Sam 21:1–9). In this view Baanah and Rechab were motivated by revenge as well as profit (Yeivin 1971: 150–54; see references in McCarter *2 Samuel* AB, 127).

2. Man from Netophah in Judah, the father of one of The Thirty, an honor roll of David's warriors (see DAVID'S CHAMPIONS). Baanah's son was named Heleb (2 Sam 23:29), Heled (1 Chr 11:30), or Heldai (McCarter *2 Samuel* AB, 492).

3. Leader of the exiles who returned from Babylon with Zerubbabel (Ezr 2:2; Neh 7:7; 1 Esdr 5:8). Possibly the same as BAANA #3.

4. One of the leaders who, in the days of Nehemiah, set his seal on a pledge to observe the law of Moses (Neh 10:28—Eng 10:27).

For the meaning of the name BAANAH, see BAANA.

Bibliography

Yeivin, S. 1971. The Benjaminite Settlement in the Western Part of their Territory. *IEJ* 21: 141–54.

FREDERICK W. KNOBLOCH

BAARA (PERSON) [Heb *baʿărāʾ*]. One of the 4 women mentioned in a very detailed genealogy of Benjamin in 1 Chr 8:1–40 (v 8). Her name appears nowhere else in the MT (LXX *Baada*) and is not found in the Apocrypha or the deuterocanonical literature. Baara means "coarse" or "brutish one." Three of the 4 women mentioned in 1 Chr 8:8–9 are wives of the Benjaminite, Shaharaim—Baara, Hushim, and Hodesh. Baara, along with Hushim, was divorced by Shaharaim. No children are indicated for Shaharaim by Baara, whereas such is the case with the other two. Perhaps this contributes to the divorce. The genealogy in which Baara appears seems to conclude the major genealogical emphases of the Chroniclers (other emphases being Judah and Levi). Shaharaim appears for the 1st time in v 8, which supports scholars such as Williamson (*Chronicles* NCBC, 82) in pointing out that there is no apparent structure to the extended Benjaminite genealogy. Rudolph (*Chronikbücher* HAT, 77) emphasizes certain geographical breaks in the genealogy which seem to show parallel lists of Benjaminite families and their dwelling locations at a particular time, probably either during the reign of Josiah or the postexilic period. However, the fact that v 9 locates the family of Shaharaim, and thus of Baara, in Moab might point to a relationship that goes back to earlier times. Certainly Israelites resided in Moab as indicated in Ruth 1 and 1 Sam 22:3, 4. This would have been more likely prior to the time that Moab regained its independence from Israel. Myers (*1 Chronicles* AB, 60) states that while Moab was under Israel's control the Benjaminite association could clearly have been accurate.

G. EDWIN HARMON

BAASEIAH (PERSON) [Heb *baʿăśēyâ*]. A Levite, ancestor of Asaph the musician (1 Chr 6:25—Eng 6:40). The name Baaseiah is found only once in a genealogical list of levitical singers which attempts to trace ancestry back to the time of David. The list is secondary, perhaps based upon the preceding list (1 Chr 6:1–15—Eng 6:16–30). The name should probably be read Maaseiah with several mss, LXX^{BL} and Syr.

TOM WAYNE WILLETT

BAASHA (PERSON) [Heb *baʿšāʾ*]. King of the N kingdom of Israel ca. 900–877 B.C. (1 Kings 15–16). Baasha was the son of Ahijah of the tribe of Issachar and of common birth (1 Kgs 16:2). Baasha is first mentioned abruptly and without introduction in 1 Kgs 15:16 as the opponent in a border war against King Asa of Judah. This border dispute between the N and S kingdoms in 1 Kings 15 represents a literary crossing of the border from stories predominantly about kings of Judah in the Deuteronomistic History (1 Kings 1–14) to stories about kings of N Israel (1 Kings 16—2 Kings 17).

Baasha was the 3d in the series of kings of the N kingdom, following the reigns of Jeroboam and Jeroboam's son Nadab. Baasha gained his kingship by assassinating Nadab in the field in a battle against Israel's archenemy the Philistines after Nadab had ruled for only a few months. Baasha then killed the whole family of Jeroboam and Nadab in order to avoid any rival claims to the kingship. The Deuteronomistic History interprets Baasha's devastation of the house of Jeroboam as a fulfillment of a previous prophecy against Jeroboam (1 Kgs 15:25–30). On a sociopolitical level, the action illustrates the climate of competing rivalries in N Israel with its 10 tribes and their several competing tribal centers and groups. In contrast, the S kingdom was essentially one tribe with one center in Jerusalem, which made for a less tumultuous political atmosphere.

The border war between Baasha and the S king Asa was of long-standing (1 Kgs 15:16, cf. Jer 41:9). The conflict apparently had to do with the position of the boundary between the two kingdoms in the central hill country which was a strategic link in the main transportation route running from S to N. Initially, Baasha gained the upper hand with his control of the town of Ramah which was only 5 miles from the S capital of Jerusalem (1 Kgs 15:17). However, the S king Asa shrewdly used expensive gifts to entice the Syrian king of Damascus Ben-hadad into breaking his covenant of peace with N Israel and invading Israel along its N border. Baasha was thus forced to abandon the border dispute on his S flank in order to deal with the threat from Damascus. Asa then immediately seized the border town of Ramah and pushed a few miles further N to Mizpah where he used building material left by Baasha for his own fortifications (1 Kgs 15:18–22).

Baasha was told by the prophet Jehu that because of his sinful reign the fate of his house would be like that of Jeroboam. Baasha reigned for nearly a quarter of a century and died a peaceful death, but Baasha's son Elah, who succeeded him as king, was promptly assassinated by a usurper to the throne named Zimri (1 Kgs 16:1–7; cf. 2 Chr 16:1; 1 Kgs 21:22; 2 Kgs 9:9). According to 1 Kgs 16:7, Baasha thus came under judgment not only for destroying the house of Jeroboam but also because Baasha was no better as a ruler than the evil Jeroboam. See Gray *Kings* OTL; Jones *Kings* NCBC.

DENNIS T. OLSON

BAB EDH-DHRAᶜ (M.R. 202074). One of several EB settlements in the SE Dead Sea plain (Rast and Schaub 1974), situated on the E edge of the Lisan peninsula. Its importance, among other reasons, lies in being continuously occupied through most of the EB Age (*ca.* 3300–2100 B.C.), and thus it serves well as a type site for developments during the various phases of this period.

The name for the ruins, Bab edh-Dhraᶜ ("gate of the arm"), is apparently not very old. Irby and Mangles (Schaub and Rast 1989) referred to this site by the same name in connection with their explorations in the area in 1818. Unlike es-Safi, however, whose ancient name is now commonly accepted to have been Seghor (Roman) and Zoora (Byzantine), that is, the biblical Zoar, the ancient name of Bab edh-Dhraᶜ has passed completely from memory.

Although visited by a number of 19th century explorers, Bab edh-Dhraᶜ was unrecognized as a significant archaeological site until a 1924 survey in the SE Dead Sea plain led by Albright and Kyle who identified it as an EB Age site (Albright 1924–25: 56–62; Kyle 1928; Mallon 1924; Albright, Kelso, and Thorley 1944).

The 1st excavations at the site were conducted by P. W. Lapp between 1965 and 1967. Lapp's excavations determined that the cemetery contained a variety of tomb types of the different phases of the EB. Lapp also determined that during EB II and III a sizable walled city existed at the site. Since 1973, W. Rast and R. T. Schaub have followed up on Lapp's work, adding new interdisciplinary objectives to the expedition, which grew out of the survey of the entire SE plain (Rast and Schaub 1974). As a result of this work, the site is being studied within the regional framework of the SE Dead Sea plain as a whole.

The earliest EB phase, IA, is known almost exclusively from tomb evidence. These tombs exemplify the widely practiced tradition of shaft-tomb interment, best known from the EB IV phase a millennium later. Vertical shafts, which provided access to the tombs, average somewhat less than 2 m in both depth and diameter. At the base of the shafts a stone-blocked doorway opened into the tomb chamber (average diameter 2 m). A pile of human bones, always toward the center of the chamber, contained small bones in the lower levels surmounted by long bones (humeri and femora) stacked in parallel over the pile. Skulls were normally arranged in a line left of the bone pile. The number of those buried varied between 2 and 10, with both sexes represented, and occasionally adolescents, preadolescents, and even infants. Pottery was typically clustered around the edges of the bone pile on the left and right, and sometimes toward the rear of the chamber. Additional objects in some of the tombs were basalt bowls, mace-heads, basketry, shell bracelets, and clay figurines. In 1 or 2 chambers, remains of what must have been wooden staffs used for herding animals were found. The bone piles were normally placed on reed matting made from plants which still grow in the marshy areas of Wadi Kerak today.

Lapp's interpretation, followed by Rast and Schaub, is that the EB IA occupants were non-sedentary, and that their relation to the site was for the purpose of burial. The few cases of primary burial during the EB IA were probably accounted for by the deaths among members of a group temporarily at the site. Campsite remains are all that have been found in the way of settlement by the EB IA people.

The EB IA population seems not to have been large at any one time, despite early projections of extraordinarily high numbers of burials. Lasting perhaps for little more than a century, the EB IA society consisted of nuclear and extended family groups. Their larger social organization was more in the nature of a "band" than a large tribe. Endogamy was apparently practiced, but exogamy is also indicated by the coexistence of 2 EB IA burial plots, each with its own tradition (Cemeteries A and C).

Schaub and Rast (1984: 34–35) have proposed that the dynamics leading to permanent settlement at Bab edh-Dhraᶜ are to be sought in the EB IB. Since no substantial settlement remains have appeared in association with the EB IA yet are attested for the following phase, it was during EB IB that year-round settlement began. The EB IB phase is easily recognizable by its decorated pottery, with a line-group painting technique applied to various vessel types. The earliest mudbrick structures, found at the lowest levels of the town site, date to the EB IB.

Along with the beginning of a permanent settlement, a new type of burial tradition consisting of circular houses also occurs. The funerary buildings (or charnel houses) were made from plano-convex mudbricks. The doors of these buildings were flanked by stone slabs, and the entries were also sealed by large stones. The burials in these houses were primary interments, with as many as 20 to 30 interments in a single house. As new burials were deposited, earlier ones were moved against the walls following decarnation.

Urbanization thus did not occur at once at Bab edh-Dhraᶜ, but was a gradual development from the EB IB village settlement to the walled city of EB III. The developing town of the EB II phase was an intervening stage between these two. EB II witnessed the establishment of large numbers of rectangular brick houses of the type found at Arad, Jericho, and elsewhere during the EB Age. During this phase as well, the 1st of two sanctuaries was constructed, succeeded in EB III by a later sanctuary of nearly identical proportions directly above it. In the cemetery the circular charnel houses became elongated and rectangular, making it possible to receive an even larger number of burials. The charnel houses of the EB II and EB III phases continued in use until they became overloaded, at which time they were permanently closed.

The EB civilization in the SE Dead Sea plain reached its zenith during EB III. Encompassing more than 10 acres during this phase, a 7 m wide defensive wall girdled Bab edh-Dhraᶜ, and a gateway on the W provided access to the Mazra'a plain, where barley, emmer wheat, and other products were cultivated. As in EB II, the interior of the city was densely built up with brick structures, the most prestigious building being the sanctuary with its courtyard and altar. The EB III occupation was the most long-lasting of all the EB phases, as evidenced by cultural residue found to a depth of 4 m in some excavated areas. This phase lasted approximately 350–400 years. The EB III settlement expanded beyond the walled settlement, so that the population numbered perhaps 1,000 people. The nearby site of Numeira was an offshoot of the flowering EB III city at Bab edh-Dhraᶜ.

Several of the EB II charnel houses were reused during the EB III, and new buildings were constructed. Two of the largest tombs of this type (A 51 and A 52), however, were mainly used during the last phase.

Two important historical questions at Bab edh-Dhraᶜ are how the EB III city came to an end and what the relation of the succeeding EB IV settlement was to that of the previous EB III city. At approximately 2350 B.C., the EB III city suffered some sort of trauma, leaving it in ruins. In fields XIII and IV the upper part of the defensive wall made of brick fell onto the natural slopes of the site. The mudbrick superstructure of the sanctuary also collapsed, apparently after burning. The charnel houses that were still in use were burned. Their brick walls either fell in, or as seems to be indicated by their position, were pushed in. Many of the charnel house bricks were also burned in the conflagration.

Although a natural disaster such as an earthquake may have been responsible for these events, an external attack against the city, as also at Numeira, cannot be ruled out. However the EB III city met its demise, the following EB IV occupants chose for the most part not to reoccupy the area of the earlier city. Their main areas of settlement were found NE and S of the previous city, in fields IX and X. The one exception was what appeared to be a cult area in field XVI on the N edge of the EB III site. EB IV tomb construction abandoned the use of charnel houses, making use rather of shaft tombs reminiscent of those 1,000 years earlier. The EB IV tombs, however, contained mostly primary rather than secondary burials, which also suggested that the EB IV occupation at Bab edh-Dhraᶜ was more permanent than transient.

Most recently, survey and excavation have discovered further evidence for EB IV near Khanazir in the SE Dead Sea plain. Consisting of numerous shaft tombs enclosed within rectangular structures, these tombs and the lack of evidence for settlement nearby suggest, in contrast to Bab edh-Dhraᶜ, a pastoralist population. The EB IV phase in the SE Dead Sea plain lasted approximately 2 centuries until, at about 2150 B.C., the plain was abandoned altogether, perhaps for ecological reasons. Thereafter the region was largely unoccupied until the Iron Age, and more extensively during Roman and Byzantine times. Bab edh-Dhraᶜ itself, however, was permanently abandoned following the EB IV.

In addition to its cultural and historical importance, Bab edh-Dhraᶜ also figures into discussions regarding the location of biblical Sodom and Gomorrah. The question is whether Bab edh-Dhraᶜ (specifically its EB III city) can be related in any way to the biblical city of Sodom, which biblical (Gen 13:10–13; 14; 19) and postbiblical (cf. Philo *Somn* 2.192; *Abr* 140–41) traditions place in the general region of the Dead Sea. Although certain scholars earlier in this century argued to locate Sodom and its related cities at the N end of the Dead Sea, recent scholarship has generally placed the cities at the S end of the Dead Sea valley. Both Albright and Lapp concluded that Bab edh-Dhraᶜ was indirectly connected with ancient Sodom. Albright considered the site as a cultic center for the "cities of the plain" which he concluded were buried irrecoverably beneath the waters of the S basin. Lapp (1968: 25) concluded that the Bab edh-Dhraᶜ necropolis was the cemetery of the "cities of the plain," and he also assumed that Sodom and the related cities in the biblical accounts lay buried below the waters of the S end of the Dead Sea.

Good reasons now seem to exist to place Bab edh-Dhraᶜ more directly into the discussions about the biblical traditions of these cities (Rast 1987). The accounts in Genesis, and references to them in prophetic threats and judgments, show that the location of Sodom was only generally perceived by the Israelites as lying somewhere in the Dead Sea region. Two possibilities exist for explaining the uncertainties in their perceptions of the location. One is that

Sodom was a fictional place name to begin with, that a city by this name never existed, and that the name came into being as an element in a local story or tale stressing a destruction severe enough to account for the startling physiography of the Dead Sea region. Those who have taken this approach to the Sodom accounts have tended to see the account of Sodom's destruction as a story similar to that of the great flood.

A 2d and different approach to the problem, however, assumes that an ancient city did exist in the Dead Sea region during antiquity, and that its name was remembered but the location of its ruins was forgotten. The latter came about partly because the SE plain was so sparsely inhabited between the end of the EB and the Iron Age (1200–600 B.C.) that local memory scarcely managed to preserve the recollection. Associated with this were also traditions of destruction of the cities which took various forms, all based on something only dimly remembered. Perhaps the disturbances at the end of EB III are at the heart of these recollections.

If the 2d of these approaches is followed, the evidence from Bab edh-Dhra[c] and Numeira becomes important as the only ancient sites in the Dead Sea region with remains which can possibly be tallied with the biblical accounts. The theory of buried cities beneath the sea seems more tenuous, given our new understanding of ancient settlement patterns in the region. Biblical scholarship may therefore find that Bab edh-Dhra[c] is more immediately related to the formation of the traditions about Sodom than earlier recognized.

Bibliography

Albright, W. F. 1924–25. The Jordan Valley in the Bronze Age. AASOR 6: 13–74. New Haven.

Albright, W. F.; Kelso, J. L.; and Thorley, J. P. 1944. Early-Bronze Pottery from Bab ed-Dra[c] in Moab. *BASOR* 95: 1–13.

Kyle, M. G. 1928. *Explorations at Sodom.* New York.

Lapp, P. 1968. Bâb edh-Dhrâ[c], Perizzites and Emim. Pp. 1–25 in *Jerusalem Through the Ages.* Jerusalem.

Mallon, A. 1924. Voyage d'exploration au sud-est de la Mer Morte. *Bib* 5: 413–55.

Rast, W. E. 1987. Bab edh-Dhra[c] and the Origin of the Sodom Saga. Pp. 185–201 in *Archaeology and Biblical Interpretation,* ed. L. G. Perdue; L. E. Toombs; and G. L. Johnson. Atlanta.

Rast, W. E., and Schaub, R. T. 1974. Survey of the Southeastern Plain of the Dead Sea, 1973. *ADAJ* 19: 5–53.

Schaub, R. T., and Rast, W. E. 1984. Preliminary Report of the 1981 Expedition to the Dead Sea Plain, Jordan. *BASOR* 254: 35–60.

———. 1989. *Bab edh-Dhra[c]: Excavations in the Cemetery Directed by Paul W. Lapp (1965–1967).* Winona Lake, IN.

WALTER E. RAST

BABEL (PLACE) [Heb *bābel*]. The name given to a city in the plain of Shinar whose completion was thwarted by Yahweh's intervention (Gen 11:1–9). Conventionally known as the "Tower of Babel" story, Gen 11:1–9 is actually about a city that features a tower (Heb *migdāl*), which was perhaps a fortress or more likely a temple. The episode took place when humankind possessed one common language and had migrated to a single region: Shinar (vv 1–2). There the people decided to make bricks for the construction of a city. Such a city, it was hoped, would establish a reputation for its inhabitants and therefore prevent their dispersal (vv 3–4). On seeing what was taking place, Yahweh confused their language and scattered them over the face of the earth in the belief that inhabiting the same locale and possessing one language would allow human beings to do anything they desired (vv 7–8). This divine act explains the name *bābel,* which sounds like the Heb word for "confuse" *(bālal;* Gk *synecheen).*

Scholars have been divided over the question of the literary makeup of this story as well as over what inspired the account. There is general agreement that the narrative is part of the Yahwist (J) source, but that is the extent of the consensus. Some argue that the Yahwist inherited a single unified tradition, or at least one which had already been combined from multiple sources in the course of oral transmission. Others contend that the Yahwist himself fused the various traditions.

Those who hold that discrete traditions were at some stage combined point to the separate motifs of dispersion, erecting a tower to storm the realm of the gods, and the confusion of tongues found in extrabiblical sources (Kramer 1943; 1968; Westermann 1984: 539–40). In their original form, such narrative motifs emphasized either: (1) an important etiology, e.g., why humankind speaks more than one language; or (2) a significant religious teaching, e.g., the danger of encroaching upon the habitat of the gods. Scholars who argue that the Yahwist reworked a fixed tradition or composed a story from separate strands of traditional materials suggest simple literary dependence, citing, for example, the building of the sacred precinct (the Esagila) in Babylon as recorded in the Enuma Elish (Tablet 6: 60–62 in *ANET*: 69; Speiser *Genesis* AB, 75–76).

Some believe that the inspiration for the Babel story was provided by actual temple ruins in Mesopotamia. According to this view, the tower refers to the famous ziggurat architectural form (a kind of pyramid structure in which each successively higher layer is smaller than the one below it) and possibly to the Entemenanki, the great ziggurat temple of Babylon (Borger 1956: 24, 29; *AHW,* 1531–32; *LAR* 1: 58, 194, 252; *LAR* 2: 111, 252–53, 309–10, 390, 405; Hammond 1972: 38–40; Oppenheim 1944). Adherents of this interpretation (cited by Westermann 1984: 540) posit a Mesopotamian provenance for the account. Given the highly polemical and obviously anti-Babylon slant of the story, however, a Mesopotamian origin seems unlikely, unless one posits that it was written by a citizen of a Mesopotamian city which saw itself as a rival of Babylon. If the story were indeed inspired by actual ruins, it appears more plausible to postulate the original composition of an anti-Babylon tale by an Israelite as opposed to the reworking of an already existent Mesopotamian story. The putative Israelite polemicist, playing on likeness between two words, may have wanted to say that although in the Babylonian language (Akkadian) "Babel" means the "gate of god" *(Bab-ilu),* in our language (Hebrew) it means "confused." Logic would locate such an Israelite composition sometime during the Babylonian exile (after 587 B.C.E.), but this raises the problem of the story's relationship to the Yahwist Source (J), which is usually dated much earlier (Ellis 1968: 40–42).

Some scholars believe that this account is historical, arguing not only that it contains allusions to authentic architectural or cultural realities (a viewpoint with which many scholars would concur) but also that it narrates an actual event (DeWitt 1979; Livingston 1974: 145–50; Aalders 1981: 251–55; Harrison 1969: 559–60). Such scholars range from those who suggest that the account is generally and broadly historical (Livingston; Harrison) to those who insist that historicity extends even to the details (Aalders). While marshaling whatever evidence is available to support their contention, these scholars also reveal that their insistence on the Bible's historicity generally is based on a particular theological construal of divine inspiration and the nature of biblical truth.

Other interpreters direct attention to the theological role of the story. Von Rad (*Genesis* OTL, 148–50) views the account as part of the sin-judgment-grace theme which he believes characterizes the Primeval History (Genesis 2–11). Clines (1978: 61–79), however, thinks that von Rad underestimates the fact that, unlike the previous episodes (e.g., Adam/Eve, Cain/Abel, Noah/Flood, etc.), there is no direct message of grace in the Babel story. Thus, the story poses a haunting question: "Is humankind doomed to the punishment of being scattered and confused?" If the Primeval History concluded with the Babel episode the answer to that question would have to be affirmative. Since, however, the subsequent genealogy (Gen 11:10–26) connects the Primeval History to the Ancestral History (Gen 11:27–50:26) by pointing out that Shem (Gen 6:10; 9:18–19; 10:21–31) was the ancestor of Abraham, a negative answer is possible. The punishment inflicted in the Babel story is mitigated by God's renewal of the grace extended to humankind through Abraham, Sarah, and the other ancestors (Clines 1978: 76–79; de Pury 1978: 80–82).

Others explain the narrative as an explicit 10th century criticism of Solomon, referring either to the hubris underlying the desire for a "name," or to the failure to see that one's "house" and "name" consist of a people and not a temple (Brueggemann 1968: 173–74; Lundbom 1983: 203–9).

The story may also be interpreted in terms of its final canonical shaping, i.e., one may focus on the effect of the present composite text rather than its constituent parts. Thus, the message of Gen 9:1, 7 that humankind after the Flood was to increase and fill the earth (J) accords with God's original purposes expressed in Gen 1:28 (P = Priestly Source). Genesis 10 (P; cf. 10:32) demonstrates that God's will was being achieved again when humankind once more obstructed the divine plan by regathering in the plain of Shinar. Because of their sin, God once again scattered them (cf. Gen 10:5, 18, 20, 32), this time an act not of blessing but of judgment (Brueggemann *Genesis* IBC, 99–102).

Similarly, the acts of naming provide a clue to canonical significance. Throughout the Primeval History, naming is positive, whether done by God or humankind (cf. Gen 2:19–20, 23; 3:20; 4:25–26; 5:29; 9:26). There are, however, two possible exceptions. One involves the sin committed by the "sons of God" (Gen 6:1–4), who as divine beings or corrupt human beings (Eslinger 1979: 65–73) cohabited with the "daughters of men" to produce an extraordinary race. This prompted divine judgment (Gen 6:3). If, as seems likely, the offspring of this union are to be associated with the Nephilim mentioned in Gen 6:4, who are known also as "mighty men" and perhaps more significantly as "men of renown" (Heb "men of the name"), and if the extremely negative appraisal in Gen 6:5–7 is to be understood as Yahweh's further reaction to what has just transpired, then the final canonical shaping may actually be calling attention not only to the fame of these "men of the *name*" but to their infamy as well.

The other exception is in the Babel story itself, where the attempt to "make a name for ourselves" (v 4) is seen as resistance to God's will for populating the earth (Brueggemann *Genesis* IBC, 99), which prompts God's judgment. This is tied to what follows by the subsequent genealogy which proceeds from Shem (= "Name"!) to Abraham (Gen 11:10–26 [P Source]) and by the allusion to the "great name" in Gen 12:2 ([J Source]; cf. von Rad *Genesis* OTL, 148–50). Indeed, from the point of view of canon, all divine actions subsequent to the Babel incident constitute God's gracious attempts to reverse its effects, thus the theologically strategic placement of the story. In the context of the Hebrew canon, the consequences of Babel are initially reversed in God's involvement with the Hebrew ancestors (Genesis 12–50). Ultimate reversal occurs when God makes David's name great and blesses him (2 Sam 7:9, 29).

Finally, within the Christian canon, the account of Pentecost (Acts 2:5–13) may be understood as a NT version of God's gracious reversal of the "Babel condition" (Bruce *Acts* NICNT, 64; Davies 1952: 228–29). In the LXX version of the story, God decided to confound (Gk *sygcheōmen*) the people's language (Gk *glōssan*) so that they could not understand one another's speech (Gk *phōnēn*). Conversely, in Acts the disciples "began to speak in other tongues" (2:4; Gk *glōssais*). This in turn produced a "sound" (2:6; Gk *phōnēs*) at which the multitude was "bewildered" or "confused" (2:6; Gk *synechythē*). At Babel, God transformed a single language into many, creating confusion; at Jerusalem the Holy Spirit made it possible for many languages to be understood as one, creating unity. At Babel, language was used to promote a human agenda ("Let us make a name for ourselves."); at Jerusalem, the "new" language was used to announce the "mighty works of God" (Acts 2:11). At Babel, God scattered the people in judgment (Gen 11:9; Gk *diespeiren*); at Jerusalem, God scattered (Acts 8:1, 4; Gk *diesparésan; diasparentes*) the people to spread the news which would eventuate in worldwide unity (Davies 1952: 229).

Bibliography

Aalders, G. C. 1981. *Genesis.* Trans. W. Heynen. Grand Rapids.

Borger, R. 1956. *Die Inschriften Asarhaddons.* AfO. 9. Graz.

Brueggemann, W. 1968. David and His Theologian. *CBQ* 30: 156–81.

Cassuto, U. 1964. *A Commentary on the Book of Genesis.* Trans. I. Abrahams. Jerusalem.

Clines, D. J. A. 1978. *The Theme of the Pentateuch.* JSOTSup 10. Sheffield.

Davies, J. G. 1952. Pentecost and Glossolalia. *JTS,* n.s. 3: 228–31.

DeWitt, D. S. 1979. The Historical Background of Genesis 11:1–9: Babel or Ur? *JETS* 22: 15–26.

Ellis, P. F. 1968. *The Yahwist: The Bible's First Theologian.* Notre Dame.

Eslinger, L. 1979. A Contextual Identification of the *bene haʾelohim* and *benoth haʾadam* in Genesis 6:1–4. *JSOT* 13: 65–73.

Hammond, M. 1972. *The City in the Ancient World.* Harvard Studies in Urban History. Cambridge, MA.

Harrison, R. K. 1969. *Introduction to the Old Testament.* Grand Rapids.

Jenkins, A. K. 1978. A Great Name: Genesis 12:2 and the Editing of the Pentateuch. *JSOT* 10: 41–57.

Kramer, S. N. 1943. Man's Golden Age: A Sumerian Parallel to Genesis 11:1. *JAOS* 63: 191–93.

———. 1968. The "Babel of Tongues": A Sumerian Version. *JAOS* 88 (= *AOS* 53): 108–11.

Livingston, G. H. 1974. *The Pentateuch in Its Cultural Environment.* Grand Rapids.

Lundbom, J. R. 1983. Abraham and David in the Theology of the Yahwist. Pp. 203–9 in *WLSGF.*

Oppenheim, A. L. 1944. The Mesopotamian Temple. *BA* 7: 54–63. Repr. *BAR* 1: 158–69.

Pury, A. de. 1978. La Tour de Babel et la vocation d'Abraham: Gn 11/1–9. *ÉTR* 53: 80–97.

Rendtorff, R. 1977. *Das Überlieferungsgeschichtliche Problem des Pentateuch.* BZAW 147. Berlin.

Skinner, J. 1930. *Genesis.* ICC. 2d ed. Edinburgh.

Westermann, C. 1984. *Genesis 1–11.* Trans. J. J. Scullion. Minneapolis.

FRANK ANTHONY SPINA

BABYLON (PLACE) [Heb *bābel*; Gk *Babylōn*]. A major city in central Mesopotamia, located on the Euphrates (32°33′N; 44°24′E). It played an important role in the history of the ANE during the 2d and 1st millennia B.C. Its present name comes from the Hellenized form of the Akk *Bab-Ilu,* literally meaning "the gate of god" which appears in the Bible in the usual form as "Babel." Undoubtedly, it was the most famous E city of antiquity, and also the most fascinating one—for many people it symbolized the whole Mediterranean civilization.

Two different sources explain this exceptional fame. It was first through the writings of Herodotus, who visited the city in the 5th century B.C., that the West became aware of the metropolis. The other source is the biblical writings, both OT and NT. This source does not treat the city with admiration as the Greek writers did, but in a negative manner based on the memory of conflicts between the great Mesopotamian empires and the kingdoms of Israel and Judah. Indeed, "Babylon" became symbolic of wickedness in many biblical writings.

A. Babylon in the OT

In the 11th chapter of Genesis, Babylon first appears as the location of the mythical Tower of Babel. However, it is only in the books of Kings and Isaiah that historically useful material is to be found: The Babylonian king Marduk-apal-iddin II (722–711 B.C.) sent an envoy to Hezekiah (2 Kgs 20:12–13 and Isa 39:1), with the intention of fighting against Sargon of Assyria, who however defeated him. During the time of the Neo-Babylonian Dynasty (founded by Nabopolassar in 626 B.C. and continued by Nebuchadrezzar his son), Babylon first destroyed Nineveh (612 B.C.) and then built up an empire that was to overturn the kingdom of Judah. In 597 B.C. the Babylonians captured Jerusalem, exiled thousands of Israelites including the prophet Ezekiel, and installed Zedekiah on the throne (2 Kings 24; 2 Chronicles 36). Jerusalem was finally destroyed in 586 B.C., Zedekiah was blinded, and much of the population was deported to Babylonia. The fall of Babylon to Cyrus of Persia in 539 B.C. marked the end of the contentions between Babylon and the Hebrews; but it is clear that that century of difficult relationships greatly influenced the people of Israel and their writings. Consequently, one can understand how the biblical and Greek traditions joined together to confer on Babylon a place of exceptional importance in western thought.

B. The Present Ruins

The ruins of Babylon lie within the suburbs of modern Baghdad. On entering the field of the present ruins one is struck by how widely scattered the tells are. To the N is Tell Babil, which is 22 meters high—an imposing presence in the countryside. It was not a part of the city proper, but constituted the summer palace of Nebuchadrezzar II. It is with the Qasr (fortress) that the ruins of the city really begin, and they extend for nearly 2 km N-S and 1.2 km E-W. However, because the topography is very rugged, the mass of tells does not give a clear idea of the limits of the ancient city. Yet the shape of certain features permits identification. Long, narrow hills which run in a straight line for hundreds of meters are clearly what is left of the 2 city walls; the 1st starts to the N at Tell Babil, runs for about 4 km toward the SE, and then turns toward the SW in the direction of the Euphrates which it meets 3 km further on. A gigantic triangular-shaped space is thus circumscribed by this outer city wall on the E bank of the river; within it, marked off by another chain of hills which formed the inner city wall, is a trapezoidal section whose side measures 1.5 km; it is located along the edge of the river and represents the heart of the city. Finally, a last chain of these distinctive hills encloses a quadrilateral area of 1 km by 1.5 km, which forms the inner city area on the right bank of the river. Thus the limits of the ancient city are still well marked on the ground and testify to the vastness of the city. It is inside the inner city wall that the most important ruins are found, but they do not portray any clear cut plan or design.

C. The Stages of the Excavations

Despite the prestige and infamy surrounding the name of Babylon, none of the 19th century excavators was interested in the city. Yet the reliefs in glazed, baked bricks which were still emerging from the superstructures of the Ishtar gate were the decisive element which finally convinced the Germans Sachau and R. Koldewey to choose Babylon as the inaugural excavation when the Deutsche Orient-Gesellschaft was founded in 1897. On March 26, 1899, the excavation began and continued nonstop until March 7, 1917, when the approach of the British troops led to the departure of the German team and the closing of the work site. Thus for 18 years R. Koldewey directed a team in which the greatest German names in the archaeology of Mesopotamia took their first steps in excavating—

W. Andrae, J. Jordan, A. Nöldeke; they worked without ceasing in order to resurrect the best-known city in Mesopotamia.

Starting from Qasr, the 1st excavation involved the N and S Neo-Babylonian palaces, located on either side of the rampart. Following that the work site was expanded to embrace the temple of Ninmah. They then excavated along the processional way from the Ishtar gate to the temple of Marduk and to the ziggurat, pausing to investigate the temple of Ninurta as they progressed (1899–1904). From 1904, it was the discovery of the theater of the Hellenistic period connected to a pilaster and the systematic research on the ramparts which caught their attention; 1907 marked the beginning of the study of a residential area where domestic architecture was the object of a systematic analysis and also where the temple of Ishtar of Agade was uncovered. This was a gigantic task, unrealistic in many respects, and its results may not have been up to expectations. Koldewey himself recognized this when he said that he had not accomplished half of the tasks he had set for himself, for the study of a city of that magnitude was beyond the possibilities of any one team. Furthermore, the collection of materials has not been what one would expect in light of the renown of the capital. Finally it was only the neo-Babylonian city of Nebuchadrezzar which was revealed by all the excavating. With the exception of a deep sounding, practically nothing has been found of the city of Hammurabi, the founder of the 1st Babylon empire (1950–1892 B.C.). Unfortunately the rising of the level of the water table has blocked all the ancient periods of the site.

After that long period of intense archaeological activity, Babylon experienced a period of relative calm; occasionally, a mission accomplished a specific research task such as that conducted by the Warka team, which unsuccessfully attempted to find the house of festivals (Akk *bīt akīti*) to the N of the Ishtar gate. The Department of Antiquities had heavily stressed the conservation or even the restoration of ancient monuments such as the temple of Ninmah immediately to the E beyond the Ishtar gate or the processional way itself, but for the past 15 years, the policy has been even more ambitious: besides new excavations, such as the temple of Nabu, which was immediately restored after its uncovering, the Department of Antiquities has envisaged a general rescue of the site with a network of systems designed to protect the monument. Although this is an undertaking which ought to be supported, one may wonder if it is entirely realistic. As of the moment, the amount of work which has been carried out helps one to grasp the organization of the city, to become acquainted with the large categories of monuments, and to define those aspects which have made the capital of the Neo-Babylonian empire so original.

D. The City

The city proper was enclosed by a double wall which ran along the edge of a canal bordering a quay made of baked bricks and bitumen and fed by the Euphrates. Nearly a quarter of the surface was occupied by royal or religious buildings located along the river: the great S palace or Nebuchadrezzar's palace, protected at the NW corner by a fortress, the ziggurat called Etemenanki and its immediate buildings—Esagila, the great temple of Marduk, as well as the temples of Nabu, Gula, and Ninurta. There, between the Euphrates and the axis formed by the processional way, was indeed the heart of the capital, even if it is exposed in a disjointed fashion by the excavations. The E part of the inner city, divided by main roads which split up the space into large separate sections, seems to have been occupied by big private dwellings. However, one also finds temples (those of Ishtar of Agade and Ninmah) near the processional way. Judging from the excavated areas, this part was occupied mostly by public buildings and the dwellings of the upper class.

The 2d section of the city extended along the right bank of the river opposite some large religious monuments. It was connected to the main section by a bridge spanning the Euphrates upon 7 piers of brick joined with bitumen and capped with paving stones. It seems that this section was occupied by the common people, no great monuments having as yet been found there. The 3d section of the city, triangular in shape, extended between the right bank of the river and the outer city wall built by Nebuchadrezzar, which was actually 2 parallel walls that encompassed the entire city. Although at present it is impossible to describe the exact nature of what was found to the E and the S, the N appears to have had official buildings. Against the inner city wall, between the river and the Ishtar gate was the N palace; further on there was undoubtedly a festival house which is known from the writings but which the excavations have not succeeded in identifying. To the extreme N, at the place where the outer city wall joined the Euphrates, stood Nebuchadrezzar's summer palace. Nothing is known about the gates of the outer city wall; there were 9 huge gates in the inner city and the right bank called Ishtar, Sin, Marduk, Zabada, Enlil, Urash, Shamash, Adad, and Lugalgirra. The Ishtar gate, the only one that has been excavated, is justly famous for the quality of reliefs in baked, glazed bricks, displaying lions and dragons in interminable lines continuing along the walls of the processional way. This gate has been moved and reconstructed in the Berlin Museum.

E. The Palaces

Of the 3 palaces found, the S palace and the summer palace have been excavated. While they have features in common, the S palace, which is of trapezoidal shape, is the most remarkable. It comprises blocks of buildings round a large courtyard juxtaposed with still other buildings doubtless devoted to economic or administrative functions; on the N side are officials' quarters, sometimes with apartments, and on the S side is a large reception room leading to a courtyard. Five blocks of buildings have been located. The 1st has usually been considered as the headquarters of the garrison. The 2d was used for the administration and its staff. The 3d was for official receptions; the throne room was found there, and the structure was superbly decorated with blue-glazed bricks on which small columns with capitals crowned with half rosettes hung together by garlands of palmettes. The 4th building was the king's apartments and the 5th housed the harem. On discovering a beautiful series of arched rooms at the NE corner, the German excavators thought they had come upon the substructures of the famous hanging gardens of Queen Semiramis; but they turned out to be only the rooms used for storage—thus the location of one of the Seven Wonders of the World is still unknown.

F. The Houses and Temples

The dwellings in the domestic quarter were complex edifices normally composed of a major block of buildings with a large courtyard. This was entered through a reception room. The whole structure was surrounded by rooms with annexes and other blocks of buildings were often built up around this foyer.

Religious architecture of Babylon is particularly well known and is seen as very typical of the city and of Babylonian civilization in general. The layout of temples is never stereotyped, but one always finds the same basic organization, namely a square or rectangular courtyard usually embellished with pilasters or redans. On one of the short sides is a lopsided room with a central entrance followed by a 2d room (and occasionally a 3d one) with exactly the same axis. It was in the last of the group of temples that the podium stood which served as the base of the divine statue. The entrance to the temple was often found opposite the cella and long rooms which at times seem to have given access to an upper level. Outlying buildings which undoubtedly accommodated the clergy were sometimes added to this initial block. The temple of Marduk, which has not been fully excavated, is the largest of these sanctuaries and may be considered as fully representative of this series of temples which includes the temples of Ninmah, Gula, Ninurta, Ishtar of Agade, and Nabu.

G. The Ziggurat

It is surely the ziggurat which has been the focal point of scholarly attention because of its ties with the Tower of Babel. Unfortunately, there is hardly anything left of the ancient monument due to the common practice of reusing mud bricks; excavators have found only the quadrilateral base on a few courses of bricks. The numerous restorations proposed have relied until recently on the scanty archaeological remains, the description by Herodotus, and on a scribe's tablet dating from the Seleucid era which gave a rather obscure description of the monument. These facts led to the restoration of a very tall and straight ziggurat which had little in common with the monuments of this kind discovered at other Mesopotamian sites. However, very recently, J. Vicari has studied the Seleucid tablet and has furnished the basis for a very reasonable restoration of that famous edifice.

Bibliography

Koldewey, R. 1925. *Das wiedererstehende Babylon.* Leipzig.

Lloyd, S. 1984. *The Archaeology of Mesopotamia.* London.

Saggs, H. W. 1962. *The Greatness that was Babylon.* London.

Unger, E. 1931. *Babylon.* Leipzig.

Vicari, J. 1985. Les ziggurats de Tchoga-Zanbil (Dur-Untash) et de Babylone. Pp. 47–57 in *Le dessin d'architecture dans les sociétés antiques.* Leiden.

JEAN-CLAUDE MARGUERON
Trans. PAUL SAGER

H. Babylon in the NT

Babylon is used in the NT in a variety of senses: literal, symbolic, or both. All of these categories have been subject to debate.

1. Literal Sense. Babylon used as the name of the ancient Mesopotamian capital and empire which took Judah captive into exile in the 6th century B.C.E. or as a pivotal epoch in Israel's history is found in the Matthean genealogy (1:11, 12, 17) and in Stephen's defense (Acts 7:43). In the latter, the MT and LXX of Amos 5:27 is changed in light of historical events from "beyond Damascus" to "beyond Babylon" as the specific place of Israel's captivity.

2. Literal or Symbolic Sense. In 1 Pet 5:13 greetings are sent from "she who is at Babylon." Babylon has been taken literally as the Mesopotamian Babylon or the Egyptian Babylon. Mesopotamian Babylon was still inhabited in the 1st century C.E. and Peter could have visited it (Erasmus and Calvin). However, it is difficult to believe that Mark and Silvanus, who accompanied Peter, would also go to Mesopotamian Babylon (5:12–13). There is no church tradition linking Peter, Mark, or Silvanus with Mesopotamian Babylon. Neither is there evidence of a church there in the 1st century (but cf. Acts 2:9). In fact the Jews were driven out of Babylon in the reign of Claudius (41–54 C.E.; *Ant* 18 §371–79), a situation which would have limited the possibilities of missions in the city. Dio Cassius (68.30) records that Trajan found Babylon mostly deserted when he visited in 115 C.E. The fact that the Eastern church claims Peter for itself is of little import because it is a recent tradition based upon 1 Pet 5:13.

Egyptian Babylon was a settlement in Egypt near Old Cairo, possibly founded by a portion of Nebuchadnezzar's army and still inhabited in the 1st century (*Ant* 2 §315; Strabo 17.1.30; Diod. Sic. 1.56.3). Clement of Alexandria (*Strom.* 7.17) states that the Alexandrine heretic Basilides claimed to hold Peter's apostolic tradition through Peter's interpreter Glaukias. A strong tradition links Mark with the Alexandrian church and Mark as the companion of Peter. However, Babylon was little more than a Roman military outpost, providing little reason for Peter to have gone there, and there is no evidence that he ever went to Egypt.

Babylon has also been interpreted as a symbol of the church using feminine imagery. It has been suggested that Babylon is a cryptogram used for reasons of security against the Romans, but the content which exhorts obedience to the state (2:13–17) and adherence to moral virtues makes such measures unnecessary. It has also been suggested that Babylon is a symbol of Christians' earthly exile as opposed to their heavenly home, and recalls the language of exile and dispersion in 1:1, 17; 2:11. However, since all Christians are exiles, there is no reason for Peter to refer to writing from exile. The very particular greetings which conclude 1 Peter (5:12–14) indicate that a particular church is in mind.

The general consensus of the church from earliest times is that Babylon in 1 Peter is a symbol for Rome. Two early cursives add *en Romē* as an explanatory addition to 5:13. Early church tradition claims that Babylon in 5:13 is a metaphor for Rome and 1 Peter was written from Rome (Clem. Al. *ap.* Eus. *Hist. Eccl.* 2.15.2). Strong tradition links

Peter to Rome, a tradition virtually unchallenged until the Reformation when efforts were made by Erasmus and Calvin to dissociate Peter from the Roman Papacy. Mark is also strongly linked to Rome (Col 4:10; 2 Tim 4:11; Phlm 24) and to Peter as his companion and interpreter in Rome (Papias *ap.* Eus. *Hist. Eccl.* 3.39.5–7; Iren. *Haer.* 3.1; Clem. Al. *ap.* Eus. *Hist. Eccl.* 2.15.2; 6.14.5–7). A comparison of the contents of 1 Peter and *1 Clement* strongly suggests a common background in Roman Christianity.

3. Symbolic Sense. In the book of Revelation, all references to Babylon are symbolic of either a place or a place and an idea (14:8; 16:19; 17:5; 18:2, 10, 21). This is indicated in 17:5 (cf. v 7) where the name Babylon is said to be a *mysterion,* a name to be understood figuratively (cf. names in 2:14, 20; 11:8). As a place, Babylon has been understood as a symbol for Jerusalem, an interpretation based on two questionable assumptions: (1) the prophecies of Jesus in the Gospels have Jerusalem as a central focus. Although this is true, these same prophecies have a worldwide impact and those of Revelation need not be restricted to Jerusalem; (2) Jerusalem persecuted the prophets and Christians as here in Revelation 17–18. However, Rome is better known in the late 1st century for this characteristic.

As a place and an idea, Babylon is symbolic of the power, influence, idolatry, and wickedness of Rome. This was the position of the early church (Tert. *Adv. Marc.* 3:13; *Adv. Jud.* 9; Jerome; Augustine) and has remained the majority opinion. Rome is identified with Babylon in early Judaism, for like Babylon it overthrew Jerusalem and destroyed the temple (*2 Bar.* 11:1–2; 67:7; 2 Esdr 3:1–2, 28; *Sib. Or.* 5.143, 155–61, 434, 440; Str-B 3.816). The similarities between Babylon and Rome as capitals of great empires led naturally to their pairing in symbolism. Like Babylon, Rome ruled the kings of the earth (14:8; 17:1–2, 15, 18), was a center of world trade (14:8; 18:2–3; 11–19, 23), reveled in luxury (18:7, 11–17, 22–23), was a persecutor of God's covenant people (17:6; 18:24; 19:2), and was destined to fall (14:8; 18:2, 10, 21). The portrayal of Babylon in Jer 51:6–10 as a cup in God's hand making all the nations drunk seems to have had considerable influence upon the symbolism of Rome as Babylon in Revelation. Rome is clearly indicated by particular details such as its location on the seven mountains (17:9; cf. vv 3, 7).

As a symbol, Babylon embraces more than the empire, city, and culture of Rome. It is the sphere of idolatry and worldliness under the temporary control of Satan, a worldliness in opposition to the people and work of God, a worldliness epitomized first by Babylon and then by Rome. Babylon as the mother of harlots and abominations in opposition to God (17:5) is the antithesis of the Church as the Bride of Christ, the New Jerusalem, and the Kingdom of God.

Bibliography

Beauvery, R. 1983. L'Apocalypse au risque de la numismatique: Babylone, la grand prostituée et le sixième roi Vespasien et la déesse Rome. *RB* 90: 242–61.

Carrington, P. 1931. *The Meaning of Revelation.* New York.

Hunzinger, C. H. 1965. Babylon als Deckname für Rom und die Datierung des 1.Petrusbriefs. Pp. 67–76 in *Gottes Wort und Gottes Land,* ed. H. Reventlow. Gottingen.

Manley, G. T. 1944. Babylon on the Nile. *EvQ* 16: 138–46.

Thiede, C. P. 1986. Babylon, der andere Ort: Anmerkungen zu 1 Petr 5,13 und Apg 12,17. *Bib* 67: 532–38.

DUANE F. WATSON

BABYLONIA (HISTORY AND CULTURE). See MESOPOTAMIA, HISTORY OF.

BABYLONIAN JUDAISM. See JUDAISM (BABYLONIAN).

BACA, VALLEY OF (PLACE) [Heb *ʿemeq habbāḵāʾ*]. The "valley of Baca" (Ps 84:1—Eng 84:6) is either a historical place name or a symbolical expression for "deep sorrow." The first part of Ps 84:6 seems to mean that by "passing through the experience of deep sorrow, righteous ones can make it the source of life." The Septuagint translated the phrase into Gk as "the valley of weeping." The word *ʿemeq* "valley" has the root meaning of "deep," so the expression may mean "deep sorrow."

However, some have considered it as the "valley of the balsam tree" from the same word in plural form found in 2 Sam 5:24. This is based on the assumption that *bāḵāʾ* may be a "gum-exuding [weeping] tree" (Morton *IDB* 1: 338). Another possibility is that the word *bĕḵāʾîm* (pl. of *bāḵāʾ*) may mean "weeping rock-walls" in the valley of Rephaim on whose tops David and his troops were waiting for the coming of the Philistine army passing through the valley below (2 Sam 5:24). It seems safe to seek the meaning of *bāḵāʾ* in relation to the dripping water, since we often find this word in the names related to rivers and wadis, such as Wadi el-Baka in the Sinaitic district and Baca on a wadi in the central Galilee area, W of Meroth. It is also possible to understand *Bĕḵāʾîm* as the place of "weepings" of the Philistine army for their defeat by David. After all these considerations, the expression the "valley of *bāḵāʾ*" can best be taken as a symbolical expression "weeping" or "deep sorrow" which fits well in the context of Ps 84:6.

YOSHITAKA KOBAYASHI

BACCHIDES (PERSON) [Gk *Bakchidē*]. An important supporter of Demetrius I (162–50 B.C.E.). He was ranked as a "friend of the king" and may have held this position already under Antiochus IV (Joseph *Ant,* 12. 393). In the first stages of Demetrius I's reign he was entrusted with the governorship of the Trans-Euphrates province (1 Macc 7:8).

The exact position of Bacchides and the extent of his province are debated among scholars. Some think that he was governor of Coele-Syria, called "beyond the river." Others suggest that all the Trans-Euphrates region was assigned to him temporarily at the time Demetrius was occupied with war on his E frontiers.

The name Bacchides is first mentioned in 2 Macc 8:30 as one of the officers outside Judea, with whom Judas fought. But it remains uncertain whether it is the same person with whom we are concerned here.

Our Bacchides is mentioned for sure first in 1 Macc 7:8

as the person who was sent by Demetrius I to help the reinstallment of Alcimus as high priest. Afterwards Bacchides was involved continuously in the events in Judea. As the highest officer in charge he took the field against Judas Maccabeus, after the latter's victory over Nicanor. Bacchides arrived in Judea with a considerable army, and after some movements he met with Judas at Elasa. After a long and fierce battle Judas fell and his army dispersed (1 Macc 9:1–18). It is difficult to ascertain the details of this engagement (see MACCABEAN REVOLT). Yet it is evident that Bacchides generalship was good and professional.

After his victory as Elasa (160 B.C.E.) Bacchides pursued his foes. Though it may be that some truce was achieved for a while, in which Judas' brothers took his body for burial, the conflict continued. Bacchides drove the rebels, now under Jonathan's leadership to the outskirts of Judea (1 Macc 9:32–49) and tried to stabilize the situation under Alcimus. For that aim he fortified various strategic places in Judea, and took hostages (1 Macc 9:50–53).

Yet, in spite of this considerable effort the internal conflict in Judea went on, and Bacchides was called again to interfere in favour of the "Hellenizers" (Alcimus died about May 159 B.C.E.). He got involved in indecisive battles with the rebels at the borders of the Judean desert and being unsuccessful he spent his anger on the Hellenizers, who involved him in this war. Then in negotiations between him and Jonathan a peace treaty was agreed upon. From this moment the Hasmonean regime progressed continuously.

Summarizing Bacchides's activity and policy in Judea (and this is all we know about him), it may be said that he was an able and efficient officer both militarily and administratively. He did not involve himself with religious affairs, but mainly concerned himself with the political and military aspects of the situation. As with Lysias, when Bacchides became convinced that the material (military and political) investment of the Seleucid government in supporting the Hellenizers was not worthwhile, he changed his policy and came to terms with Jonathan.

Bibliography

Bengtson, H. 1964. *Die Strategie in der Hellenistischer Zeit.* vol. 2. Munich.

URIEL RAPPAPORT

BACENOR (PERSON) [Gk *Bakēnōr*]. A military commander of Dositheus (2 Macc 12:35). According to 2 Macc 12:32–35, Dositheus captured Gorgias during a battle. While attempting to bring Gorgias back alive, a Thacian horseman cut off Dositheus's arm, allowing Gorgias to escape to Marisa. The name Bacenor occurs nowhere else and is supported here only by texts AqLa[v]. Bacenor may be used to distinguish this Dositheus from a captain of Judas Maccabeus of the same name (2 Macc 12:17–25). An alternative is to read with texts La[a′] and the Armenian *toubiakēnōn,* "one of the Toubiankenoi." In this case Dositheus would come from the region of the Tobiads mentioned in 2 Macc 12:17. (See Goldstein *2 Maccabees* AB.)

Bibliography

Goldstein, J. A. 1975. The Tales of the Tobiads, Pp. 85–123 in *Christianity, Judaism and Other Greco-Roman Cults,* Part 3, ed. J. Neusner. Leiden.

RUSSELL D. NELSON

BAEAN (PLACE) [Gk *Baian*]. According to 1 Macc 5:1–2, when the Gentiles in the cities surrounding Judah heard that the Jews had restored the temple (164 B.C.), they began to murder Jews. Judas Maccabeus, however, waged war against the Idumeans and (v 4) "He also remembered the wickedness of the sons of Baean," besieging them in their towers, which he burned (v 5). 2 Macc 10:15–23 sets these events in the context of Gentile oppression against Jews in Judah, but clearly describes the same campaign. The phrase "the sons of Baean" has presented scholars with at least two problems: (1) the derivation of the name and (2) its referent.

Num 32:3 lists a city named Beon among the cities of Gilead requested by Gad and Reuben, and scholars often suppose that Baean refers to Beon (cf. Tedesche and Zeitlin 1950: 110). However, Simons (1959: 405) suggests that the term derives from the Heb name *bhn* in "sons of Bohan" (cf. Josh 15:6, 18:17). Goldstein (*1 Maccabees* AB, 295) argues instead that Baean derived from the Heb *ṣbʿn* (Sabaanites), but so little detail is given in 1 and 2 Maccabees that one cannot choose the best among these options.

Also debated is whether Baean represents a tribal or a place name, or perhaps both. Simons (1959: 405) thinks that the term probably refers to a clan and not—at least primarily—to a region. He cites similar phrases in the context: "sons of Esau" (5:3) and "sons of Ammon" (5:6). Dancy (1954: 103) agrees with earlier scholars who understood Baean as the name of a tribal ancestor. Tedesche, however, understands the term as a place name (1950: 110). On the whole, Simons' reading of Baean as a clan or tribal name seems best. This tribe lived in Transjordan near the river, and likely operated as highway robbers. It is possible that they lived near the stone of Bohan, though one might hold open the option that they moved around in a region.

Bibliography

Dancy, J. C. 1954. *A Commentary on I Maccabees.* Oxford.

Simons, J. 1959. *Geographical and Topographical Texts of the Old Testament.* Leiden.

Tedesche, S., and Zeitlin, S. 1950. *The First Book of Maccabees.* New York.

PAUL L. REDDITT

BAGOAS (PERSON) [Gk *Bagōas*]. The eunuch in charge of Holofernes' personal affairs (Jdt 12:11). Bagoas is a Persian name, and according to Pliny (*HN* 13.41), eunuchs were regularly called "Bagoas." Therefore, this may not be a personal name but a title. The name occurs frequently in extrabiblical sources. Josephus (*Ant* 11.7.1) describes a certain Bagoas as a general of Artaxerxes II Mnemon, who later became the governor of Jerusalem. A Bagoas appears in Diodorus Siculus (*Hist* 31.19.2–3; 16.47.4) as an adviser of Artaxerxes III Ochus in his campaign against Phoenicia and Egypt. In the Elephantine papyrus #30 *(CAP)*, the name Bagoas appears in Aramaic as *baggōhî* (this is the Bagoas who was the governor of Jerusalem). Either of these figures may have been in the mind of the author of the book of Judith when he called the servant of Holofernes "Bagoas" (see JUDITH for a discussion of the genre of the book of Judith).

Bibliography

Cross, F. M. 1966. Aspects of Samaritan and Jewish History in Late Persian and Hellenistic Times. *HTR* 59: 201–11.

SIDNIE ANN WHITE

BAGPIPE. See MUSIC AND MUSICAL INSTRUMENTS.

BAHURIM (PLACE) [Heb *baḥûrîm*]. Var. BAHARUM. A Benjaminite village on the road from Jerusalem into the Jordan valley, north of the Mount of Olives. Bahurim has been identified tentatively with the site of Ras eṭ-Ṭmim (M.R. 174133) or Khirbet Ibqeᶜdan. It is mentioned as the place on the road from Mahanaim to Jerusalem where Abner compelled Paltiel to turn back from following his wife Michal, the daughter of Saul; when she was being taken back to David, her first husband (2 Sam 3:16). Bahurim is also given as the domicile of Shimei ben Gera, who came out cursing David and his men as they fled Jerusalem before the onslaught of Absalom (2 Sam 16:5; 19:17[—Eng 16]; 1 Kgs 2:8). Two of David's spies, Jonathan and Ahimaaz, hid from Absalom in the well of a man of Bahurim (2 Sam 17:18). One of David's champions, Azmaveth, was probably from Bahurim as well (1 Chr 11:33; cf. 2 Sam 23:31).

D. G. SCHLEY

BAITERUS (PERSON) [Gk *Baitērous*]. Ancestor of a family which returned from Babylon with Zerubbabel (1 Esdr 5:17). Although 1 Esdras is often assumed to have been compiled from Ezra and Nehemiah, this family does not appear among their lists of returning exiles (cf. Ezra 2; Nehemiah 7). Omissions such as this also raise questions about 1 Esdras being used as a source by Ezra or Nehemiah. Furthermore, problems associated with dating events and identifying persons described in 1 Esdras have cast doubt on the historicity of the text. The Vg contains the textual variant *Gebbarus.*

MICHAEL DAVID MCGEHEE

BAKBAKKAR (PERSON) [Heb *baqbaqqar*]. One of the Levites who lived in Jerusalem after the return from Babylonian exile (1 Chr 9:15). Bakbakkar was one of 4 Levites in Jerusalem at that time who could trace his ancestry back to Asaph, the head of one of three families of Levitical singers appointed by David (1 Chr 15:16–17, 25:1–8) and the author of several psalms (Pss 50, 73–83). It is likely that Bakbakkar continued in his ancestor's footsteps as a Levitical singer. The parallel passage in Nehemiah (Neh 11:15–18) does not mention Bakbakkar but does list a Bakbukiah (Neh 11:17). Curtis and Madsen (*Chronicles* ICC, 172) suggested that these 2 names might refer to the same person. This is possible, but another plausible explanation is that the author of 1 Chronicles 9 simply employed different traditions than did the author of Neh 11 (Braun *1 Chronicles* WBC, 136).

ROBERT C. DUNSTON

BAKBUK (PERSON) [Heb *baqbûq*]. The head of a family of Netînîm (temple servants) listed among those exiles returning from Babylon to Jerusalem and Judah (Ezra 2:51 = Neh 7:53; 1 Esdr 5:31). The name is a *qatqût* formation of the Heb root *bqq* which means "empty (out)" (Zadok 1980: 113). The noun *baqbuq* denotes a "flask/bottle" (Jer 19:1, 10; 1 Kgs 14:3). The name could be a shortened form of the name *baqbuqyāh* (Neh 11:17; 12:9, 25) where *yāh* is to be understood as an emphatic rather than a theophoric afformative (Noth *IPN,* 105). In 1 Esdr 5:31 the name is rendered *Akouph, Akoum,* or *Akoub.*

Bibliography

Zadok, R. 1980. Notes on the Biblical and Extra-Biblical Onomasticon. *JQR* 71: 107–17.

RODNEY H. SHEARER

BAKBUKIAH (PERSON) [Heb *Baqbuqyāh*]. A Levite known for singing who is found in the list of priests and Levites (Neh 11:17; 12:9; 12:25). Bakbukiah is likely to be the same person in all 3 places, but some problems exist.

First is the problem related to Nehemiah 12:25. In the Heb text, Bakbukiah is listed as the gatekeeper while Mattaniah, Bakbukiah, and Obadiah are grouped as singers in other related texts (Neh 11:15–18; 12:8–11; 1 Chr 9:14–16; 25:1–8). The last 3 names in Neh 12:25, Meshullam, Talmon, and Akkub, are noted in other lists of gatekeepers (1 Chr 9:17; Ezra 2:42; Neh 7:45; 9:19). Williamson (*Ezra-Nehemiah* WBC, 16) asserts Mattaniah, Bakbukiah, and Obadiah, listed in v 25, actually complete v 24. Myers (*Ezra-Nehemiah* AB, 195) suggests that in v 25 the proper name Meshullam has been mistaken for the Heb word singer. Both agree that the 3 singers appropriately fit with the description of musicians and singers in v 24.

Second, Bakbukiah is not found in the Septuagint, suggesting that Bakbukiah may be a late addition to the Heb text. This agrees with problems that parallel chronologies found in 1 Chr 9:15 and 25:4. In each of these places, Mattaniah is listed with families of Levites who are singers. However, in 1 Chr 9:15, Bakbakkar is paired with Mattaniah, and in 1 Chr 25:4, Bukkiah is paired with Mattaniah. Ward (*IDB* 1: 340) and Myers (*Ezra-Nehemiah* AB, 187), suggest that these other 2 names may be variants or misspellings of Bakbukiah.

Bibliography

Kaufmann, Y. 1977. *History of the Religion of Israel. Vol. 4: From the Babylonian Captivity to the End of Prophecy.* Trans. C. W. Efroymson. NY.

GARY C. AUGUSTIN

BAKER'S STREET (PLACE) [Heb *ḥûṣ hāʾōpîm*]. Street in Jerusalem referred to in Jer 37:21. At the order of King Zedekiah, Jeremiah was placed in the courtyard of the guard and given bread from the area called the Baker's Street. It was customary in ancient times in Near East cities for trades and crafts to be grouped together in one street or area—compare the gold shops located in one area of modern Amman. In the OT, baking was highlighted in

Gen 40:1–41:13 in the story of Joseph; in 1 Sam 8:13, bakers are listed along with perfumers and cooks as important for governmental service; and in Hos 7:4, the baker and his oven are a fitting metaphor for wayward Israel. In 1 Kgs 20:34, the markets in Damascus which Ben-Hadad offered King Ahab may have included bakeries along with other trades as well as offices for international trade. Later in NT times, besides the foreign trade in luxury garments, precious ointments and jewelry, etc., the baker's trade was important among the local industries of weaving, leather working, dealing in sheep and cattle, woodworking, pottery making, etc. (Jeremias 1967: chaps I and II). Josephus (*Ant* 15. 309) makes reference to the need of professional bakers in a time of famine. No doubt the individual baker's establishment included his living quarters, ovens, and selling area.

Bibliography

Jeremias, J. 1967. *Jerusalem in the Time of Jesus.* Philadelphia.

W. Harold Mare

BALAAM (PERSON) [Heb *bilʿam*]. A seer summoned by Balak, king of Moab, to curse Israel prior to its entrance into Canaan.

A. Appearances in the OT

Our sources for the story of Balaam are varied and often conflicting. In the Heb Bible, we have first the famous and, in their present form, largely positive stories in Numbers 22–24, of Balaam son of Beor, the intermediary called by Balak son of Zippor, king of Moab, to curse Israel and therefore give Moab the advantage in any hostilities between the two peoples. Then there are the negative Priestly notices in Num 31:8, 16 that tie Balaam to the apostasy at Peor and maintain that he was killed by the Israelites in a battle against Midian (and the reflex of that tradition in Josh 13:22). Next, the implication in Deut 23:5b–6—Eng 23:4b–5 (cited in Neh 13:2) and the Hebrew of Josh 24:9–10 is that Balaam tried to curse Israel, but that Yahweh would not listen to him, and so Israel was blessed instead. Finally, the mention of Balaam in Mic 6:5 can be interpreted either positively or negatively, i.e., as reflecting the point of view of the Numbers 22–24 stories or the more negative tradition in Deuteronomy 23 and Joshua 24. Balak is mentioned in Judg 11:25, but no reference is made there to Balaam or to the connection between Balak and Balaam reported in Numbers 22–24. The incident at Peor also appears in Deut 4:3; Josh 22:17; Hos 9:10; and Ps 106:28–31, but Balaam is not mentioned in these passages.

The relationship between the character Balaam and the Edomite king Bela son of Beor from Gen 36:32–33 (and 1 Chr 1:43–44) is unclear, but the similarities in their names and even their patronymics suggests either that they both represent reflexes of the same character, or else that the tradition of one character has been conflated with that of another.

B. Source Criticism, Numbers 22–24

The doublets and inconsistencies in the Numbers 22–24 account of Balaam have long led scholars to posit evidence of the J and E sources in these chapters, even though use of the divine names does not correspond perfectly to the expected pattern. It is certainly possible to see that even these "positive" stories can be further divided between a "southern" picture of an intermediary and a "northern" or "Ephraimite" one (to use Robert Wilson's [1980] terms). The following represents something of a consensus: *southern/J*—at least Num 22:3b, 4, part of 5, part of 6, 7a, 11, 22–34, 37, 39, 40a; 23:7a, 18a; 24:1, 2b–3a, 10a, 11b, 15a; *northern/E*—at least Num 22:2–3a, part of 5, part of 6, 7b–10, 12–21, 35–36, 38, 40b–41; almost all the prose in chapter 23; 24:10b–11a, 12a–14a, 25. In the verses that many commentators assign to the J source, Balaam is a diviner, a form of intermediary apparently acceptable in court circles in preexilic Judah, as elsewhere in the ANE; the elders of Moab take "fees for divination" *(qĕsāmîm)* to Balaam (22:7); Balaam is one who as a rule looks for omens *(nĕḥāšîm)* before pronouncing (24:1). The introductions to the oracles, and particularly to the 3d and 4th oracles, could also be a reflex of a southern view of prophecy. We read (Num 23:7, 18; 24:3, 15, 20, 21, 23) that Balaam "took up his discourse" *(way-yiśśāʾ mĕšālô),* and the pairing of the verb *nśʾ* with *māšāl* turns up (besides Job 27:1 and 29:1) also and only in Isa 14:4; Mic 2:4; and Hab 2:6. Furthermore, in Num 24:4 and 16 Balaam "sees the vision of *šadday,*" and the description of a prophet as one who sees visions (with derivatives of the root *ḥzh*) is one of the hallmarks of the southern view of prophecy. (The mention of the *rûaḥ ʾĕlōhîm* in 24:2 is perhaps another connection with southern prophecy: cf. the role of the "spirit" in Ezekiel.) Most would place the episode involving Balaam's she-ass within this southern strand, although many consider the ass pericope to be a completely independent story only secondarily connected to the rest of Numbers 22–24.

In those verses generally called E, however, we see in Balaam a typical Yahweh-prophet, one who can only speak the word that Yahweh puts in his mouth, a phrase reflecting the paradigmatic description of a prophet in Deut 18:18 (see Num 22:38; 23:5, 12, 16; similarly 22:8, 18, 19, 20, 35, 38; 23:3, 15, 17, 26; 24:13). Such a description marks this picture of Balaam as issuing from northern, i.e. Ephraimite circles. It is this strand of the Balaam material that includes the familiar picture of elaborate sacrifices provided by the king, and Balaam's conferences with Yahweh wherein Balaam is given the substance of the first two blessings that so disappoint Balak. Further connections with northern concerns are the names of the hills from which Balaam pronounces his oracles in chaps. 22–23; Bamoth-baal, Pisgah, and Peor describe the area of the same Transjordanian mountain range where Deuteronomic tradition records that Moses delivered his final discourses, died, and was buried (note Beth-Peor in Deut 3:29 and 34:6, and the addition of Pisgah to P's Nebo in 34:1). The mountain range where Balaam delivers his oracles is a sacred place, then, to the northern circles that produced Deuteronomy.

C. History of the Traditions

In terms of their tradition history, the biblical passages concerning Balaam son of Beor divide neatly into two groups: (1) those related to the P traditions that Balaam was responsible for the apostasy with the Midianites at Peor, for which he was killed in Israel's battle against the Midianites reported in Numbers 31; and (2) all the rest, which maintain in some form that Balaam son of Beor, a non-Israelite intermediary, was called by the Moabites (at least) to curse Israel but instead blessed them in the end.

1. The Priestly Account of Balaam. According to the P passages, Balaam was responsible for the apostasy of the Israelites at Peor and was killed by the Israelites in a battle against Midian (Num 31:8, 16); this source lumps Balaam together with Moses as the objects of an Aaronid polemic surrounding the incident at Peor and directed also at the Midianites (cf. 25:6 and 10 for suggestions of Moses' complicity with the apostasy and 25:7–8 and 11–13 for the elevation of Phinehas the Aaronid because of his opposite reaction). This seems to be a completely separate Balaam tradition, but one that did apparently influence the final form of the earlier stories with the insertion of the extraneous "elders of Midian" in 22:4, 7. This Aaronid tradition has also made its mark on Josh 13:22, where Balaam's demise along with the Midianite leaders is reiterated, this time not because of his association with the apostasy at Peor, but simply, it would seem, because he was a diviner, a *qōsēm.* Josh 13:22 shows evidence of familiarity: (1) with the anti-Balaam, anti-Midianite P-tradition in Numbers 31; (2) with the southern/J tradition in Num 22:7 to the effect that the elders of Moab (and the elders of Midian) took *qĕsāmîm,* divination fees, Balaam's acceptance of which would have made him a *qōsēm*; and finally (3) with the Deuteronomic description of diviners (along with several other types of intermediaries) as abominations (Deut 18:10–14), and therefore sentenced to die.

2. The Second Grouping. Those passages where a potential curse is turned into a blessing can be further divided into 3 subgroups, according to the reason supplied for this substitution of a blessing.

a. The Northern Tradition. In Numbers 22–24 the change from curse to blessing is attributed to Balaam's inability to do or say anything that Yahweh has not commanded him. The blessing comes about because of Yahweh's desire that Israel be blessed and because of Balaam's position as a true Yahweh-prophet.

b. The Southern Tradition. In Numbers 22–24 the hoped-for curse is again thwarted by Yahweh's desire to bless and power to sway Balaam, this time not because Balaam is a typical Yahweh-prophet, but because of the display of power Balaam encounters on the road (the ass episode, 22:22–34, generally attributed to J). In this version, Balaam had not consulted any deity before leaving on his journey to Balak, but is impressed with the deity who can send an invisible messenger *(malʾāk)* with the power to reveal himself to a donkey, in order to convey his wish that Balaam not go to curse Israel. In response to that wish, Balaam abandons his usual procedure of looking for omens (24:1) and simply pronounces his oracles under the influence of the "spirit of God" *(rûaḥ ʾĕlōhîm).* The result is a blessing.

It has been suggested that the original ending of the ass story has been lost in the combining of the 2 sources, and that the story would have ended either with Yahweh's permission for Balaam to proceed (something like the present v 35, but without the Deuteronomic language), or else with Balaam simply returning home. In the latter case, v 37 of the same chapter could be excised from its present position and interpreted as a continuation of the southern story. The verse could be read literally to mean that Balaam had not gone to Balak at that point but that Balak had, in fact, found it necessary to travel to Balaam. V 37 would be continued by v 39, which describes Balaam's going with Balak, finally, to Kiriath-huzoth.

c. The Tradition in Deuteronomy 23, Joshua 24, and Nehemiah 13. According to these texts, Balaam made an attempt to curse Israel, but Yahweh turned the curse into a blessing. This time there is no indication that Balaam was a Yahweh-prophet or that he was a diviner who knew a powerful deity when he saw one. The implication is rather that Balaam was inclined against Israel, up to and including the pronouncing of a curse, and that Yahweh simply closed his ears to Balaam's speech. Note that all 3 of these passages relate the Balaam episode in contexts where current fears of pollution from foreigners are clear-cut issues of the author's day: who can enter the sanctuary, whose worship is appropriate, who is an appropriate marriage partner. Therefore, the appearance of a foreigner as a Yahweh-prophet or even as a diviner who could recognize Yahweh's power and pronounce Yahweh's oracles would be unacceptable.

These 3 notices are either representative of a completely different strand of tradition, or else they are creative expansions of the traditions already outlined from Numbers 22–24, perhaps reflecting the tendency that we have noticed in the Priestly tradition to denigrate Balaam. This tendency may be present even in the narrative of Balaam's she-ass, who "sees" the messenger from Yahweh when Balaam the "seer" is blind to the appearance, surely not a good advertisement for Balaam's powers as an intermediary. If the ass episode was meant to poke fun at Balaam, then its use in the story as we have it would portray Yahweh's blessing in the following chapters as even more extraordinary—not only coming from a famous, non-Israelite intermediary, but even from one who is on his own somewhat inept.

3. Oracles 3 and 4. Even within Numbers 22–24, oracles 3 and 4 seem to represent a tradition separate from oracles 1 and 2, and from the prose that surrounds the oracles. (Most commentators would leave 24:21–23 out of consideration here as later additions to the 4th oracle, and some would excise v 20 also.) Whereas oracles 1 and 2 depend on the prose setting for any meaningful interpretation, oracles 3 and 4 can be read and appreciated without any reference to the prose story. Furthermore, Balaam is introduced at the beginning of each of these oracles (24:3–4 and 15–16); such an introduction would not have been necessary had the oracles been composed along with the prose and transmitted originally in anything like their present context. The 3d and 4th oracles, then, are generally thought to have originated separately from the prose story and from oracles 1 and 2, and to have been transmitted separately for some time before being combined with the narrative of the curser-turned-blesser summoned by the Moabite king. It has even been suggested that the rest of Numbers 22–24 was composed specifically to provide a context for the traditional Balaam oracles now in chapter 24, the theme of blessing and cursing suggested by 24:9. If one reads only oracles 3 and 4, one sees nothing of the call from Balak for Balaam to curse Israel, but only clear blessings, in the natural and military realms, so that if we give these poems priority over the rest of the Balaam traditions, we would have to assign them to yet a 3d category, besides C.1 and C.2 above, carrying the simple theme that a foreign seer was the bearer of blessings for Israel. The plausibility of such a tradition concerning Balaam son of Beor has increased recently since the discovery of a non-Israelite (or at least nonorthodox) Balaam tradition in the plaster text from Tell Deir ʿAllā in Jordan (see below).

The 3d and 4th oracles might date from the time of the early monarchy, since 24:17–18 can be interpreted to refer to David's defeat of Edom and Moab (with the *bĕnê-šēt,* children of Sheth, identified with the Palestinian tribal name Shutu known from 2d millennium documents). Moreover, 24:7, as well as v 20 and the LXX reference to Agag (?) in v 23, if these be admitted to the 4th oracle, could plausibly refer to Saul's defeat of Agag and the Amalekites. (Albright's attempt to date the oracles even earlier, based on orthographic typology, has not met with much approval; neither has von Gall's proposal [1900] that they were composed in the Maccabean era.)

D. Literary Relationships

The 3d and 4th oracles have literary connections with the well-known lists of tribal features that occur in early Israelite poetry: the leonine characteristics in Gen 49:9 referring to Judah and in Deut 33:20, 22 referring to Gad and Dan (cf. Num 24:9); the horns of an ox in Deut 33:17 (cf. Num 24:8); and the scepter and predominance of Judah in Gen 49:10 (cf. Num 24:17). The introductory phrase in 24:3, 15 describing each oracle as *nĕʾum haggeber šĕtûm hā-ʿāyin,* "oracle of the man whose eye is perfect," is remarkably similar to what is said about the "Last Words of David" in 2 Sam 23:1, *nĕʾum haggeber huqam ʿāl,* "oracle of the man who was raised on high" (if not "established by God," reading 4QSam[a]'s *hqym ʾl*), and to the obscure *nĕʾum haggeber lĕʾîtîʾēl* in Prov 30:1. Once the separateness (and perhaps even priority) of oracles 3 and 4 is established, it is logical to propose that the similarities between the 2d and 3d oracles arise from deliberate imitation in composition, probably of the 2d in imitation of the 3d: so, 23:22 is a reference to 24:8 and 23:24 plays with 24:9.

E. Balaam's Homeland

The location of Balaam's homeland has occasioned much discussion in the scholarly literature. There are several choices offered in the biblical tradition. Pethor, Heb *pĕtôrâ,* "on the river," in Num 22:5, has been plausibly identified with Pitru on the upper Euphrates, known to us from Assyrian inscriptions. The ancient versions are divided as to whether to interpret this word as a geographic reference with locative *-â,* or to read it as a description of Balaam himself as a dream interpreter, from the Heb root *ptr.* A home for Balaam on the upper Euphrates would also bring together the references in Num 23:7 and Deut 23:5—Eng 23:4 that he had come from Aram (Naharaim) and the suggestion that he was operating with the knowledge and methods of a Mesopotamian *bārû*-diviner (Daiches 1909). The upper Euphrates is too far for the southern tradition, however, where Balaam sets off (Num 22:22) riding on a donkey, with just 2 servants to accompany him, hardly preparations for a journey from Pitru to the Arnon. Num 22:5 goes on to say that Balak sent to Balaam in the land of *bĕnê-ʿammô,* which phrase has been variously interpreted as the land of "his people," of "Amaw," or as a scribal error for "the Ammonites." The S tradition would fit more comfortably, certainly, with either the noncommittal "his people" or with "Ammon," to which several of the ancient versions also attest, categorizing "on the river (Euphrates)," at least, and even better "Pethor on the river (Euphrates)," as glosses. It must be pointed out that *ʾereṣ bĕnê-ʿammô* never occurs elsewhere in the Bible as a phrase for "his homeland," but in favor of this translation is Balaam's statement in 24:14 that now that Balak has banished him, he will go to his "people," indicating that that is a reasonable description of his situation when Balak called him.

F. The Balaam Text from Tell Deir ʿAllā

Contemporary with these biblical Balaam traditions, but from a separate source, is the plaster inscription discovered at Tell Deir ʿAllā in the E Jordan Valley dating to the end of the 8th century B.C.E. Like the passages usually assigned to J in Numbers 22–24, the Deir ʿAllā inscription offers a picture of Balaam as a southern intermediary, referred to as *ḥzh ʾlhn,* "seer of the gods," in the first line of the inscription, and sees a vision *(wyḥzh mḥzh)* like an oracle *(msʾ)* from El (I, 1, 2). (The reference to the intermediary as *ḥōzēh* and the description of the oracle as *maśśāʾ* are 2 of the hallmarks of Wilson's southern intermediary.) The extant lines of this inscription have no connection with the content of the Balaam traditions in the Heb Bible, although their language is often reminiscent of the more familiar Balaam story: *wyʾtw ʾlwh ʾlhn blylh* in I, 1, corresponds nicely to *wayyābōʾ ʾĕlōhîm ʾel-bilʿām laylâʾ* "and God came to Balaam at night," in Num 22:20 (without *laylâ* in v 9); and *wyqm blʿm mn mḥr* in I, 3, of the Deir ʿAllā text is close to *wayyāqom bilʿām babbōqerʾ* "so Balaam rose in the morning," in Num 22:13, 21.

Yahweh is nowhere mentioned in the extant (very fragmentary) text, although several other deities are: at least El and the plural *ʾlhn, šadday*-gods, and a goddess whose name begins with *š-*. The existence of a (presumably non-Israelite) sanctuary in the E Jordan Valley in the 8th century, where Balaam is revered as prophet, must have influenced the redaction of the biblical Balaam stories: It might, for instance, have been offensive to the Aaronid priestly group as a rival to their Jerusalem sanctuary and traditions, and so have contributed to the negative attitude toward Balaam in Numbers 31 and Joshua 13. See also DEIR ʿALLĀ.

G. Later Literature

Philo, Josephus, and Pseudo-Philo all mention Balaam in a more or less negative light. Philo, particularly in his *De vita Mosis* and *De migratione Abrahami,* deals with the thorny problem of a foreigner and an evil man who was said to be a prophet. Philo concludes that he was indeed a soothsayer, but not a true prophet.

Josephus (*Ant* 4), in line with some of the biblical passages discussed above, sees in Balaam a diviner who wanted to curse Israel, but could not because it was not God's will that they be cursed. He found a way to harm Israel, however, in advising Balak to have Midianite women entice Israelite men away from their true worship.

Pseudo-Philo is more forgiving toward Balaam in the *Liber Antiquitatum Biblicarum* (18). Here Balaam understands that Balak is wrong to want to curse Israel, but goes to him anyway. He gives Balak the counsel that led to the Baal-Peor incident after he realizes that in going to Moab he has forfeited divine favor.

Rabbinic commentators generally saw in Balaam a representative of all that was bad in "the nations." He was greedy and he was a sorcerer. He is acknowledged to have prophetic powers, but is seen as all the more dangerous because of his powers. It has been suggested that Balaam's portrayal became more and more derogatory as rabbinic sources used him as an example of a gentile seer in order to comment on the Christian exegetes of their own time.

Balaam is mentioned 3 times in the New Testament: 2 Pet 2:15–16; Jude 11; Rev 2:14. In each case the tendency toward a negative appraisal of Balaam noticeable in the later Heb Bible traditions is carried on, although the authors are not always negative for the same reasons. In the first 2 passages, Balaam is used as an example of someone who took money for wrong purposes, and the obvious interpretation is that they refer to the tradition that Balaam indeed tried to curse Israel (and was presumably paid for it, despite Num 24:11). This interpretation may also proceed from a belief that Balaam was wrong to ask God a 2d time for permission to travel with Balak's messengers, but that he did so out of a desire for the money Balak might pay him. It is possible, however, given the references to lust and animal passions in the 2 Peter and Jude passages, that they, like Revelation 2:14, have combined several of the Hebrew Bible traditions about Balaam and are also referring to the Priestly version of the apostasy at Peor where there is the suggestion of sexual immorality (Num 25:6–8) instigated by Balaam (Num 31:15–16). The food sacrificed to idols of Rev 2:14 is clearly an interpretation of the J version of the Baal-Peor apostasy (cf. Num 25:2 and Ps 106:28), for which Balaam is here also blamed.

The statement in Balaam's 4th oracle that "a star shall come forth out of Jacob/and a scepter rise out of Israel" was widely interpreted in the early church as a messianic prediction, as it had been at Qumran and in the Bar Kokhba movement. A non-Israelite sorcerer or magician himself, Balaam was regarded as the founder of the order that produced the Magi of Matthew, the first Gentiles who recognized Jesus as messiah.

Bibliography

Albright, W. F. 1927–28. The Name of Bildad the Shuhite. *AJSL* 44: 31–36.

———. 1944. The Oracles of Balaam. *JBL* 63: 207–33.

Baskin, J. R. 1983. *Pharaoh's Counsellors: Job, Jethro, and Balaam in Rabbinic and Patristic Tradition.* BJS 47. Chico, CA.

Coppens, J. 1964. Les oracles de Biléam: leur origine littéraire et leur porté prophétique. Pp. 67–80 in vol. 1 of *Mélanges Eugène Tisserant.* Studi e Testi 231. Vatican.

Daiches, S. 1909. Balaam—a Babylonian *bārū.* Pp. 60–70 in *Assyriologische und Archaeologische Studien.* Chicago.

Gall, A. F. von. 1900. Zusammensetzung und Herkunft der Bileam-Perikope in Num. 22–24. Pp. 3–47 in *Festgruss für Bernhard Stade,* ed W. Diehl et al. Giessen.

Gross, W. 1974. *Bileam: Literar- und formkritische Untersuchung der Prosa in Num 22–24.* SANT. Munich.

Hackett, J. A. 1986. Some Observations on the Balaam Tradition at Deir ʿAllā. *BA* 49: 216–22.

Mowinckel, S. 1930. Der Ursprung der Bileamsage. *ZAW* 48: 233–71.

Schmidt, L. 1979. Die alttestamentliche Bileamüberlieferung. *BZ* 23: 234–61.

Vermes, G. 1973. *Scripture and Tradition in Judaism: Haggadic Studies.* 2d ed. SPB. Leiden.

Wilson, R. R. 1980. *Prophecy and Society in Ancient Israel.* Philadelphia.

JO ANN HACKETT

BALADAN (PERSON) [Heb *balʾădān*]. According to 2 Kgs 20:12 (= Isa 39:1), the father of Merodach-baladan, a ruler of Babylon who sent a diplomatic delegation to King Hezekiah of Judah. However, it is very uncertain whether this name is actually that of Merodach-baladan's father. Merodach-baladan [Heb *mĕrōdak balʾădān*] was a Chaldean ruler of the Bit-Yakin tribe who fomented rebellion against the Assyrians at the end of the 8th century B.C.E. He twice succeeded in wresting control of Babylon from the Assyrians, where he ruled from 721–710 B.C.E. and again for 9 months in 703 B.C.E. (*IDB* 3: 355; Wildberger *Isaiah 1–12* BKAT, 1474–75). See MERODACH-BALADAN. The name Merodach-baladan (Akk *marduk-apal-iddina*) means "Marduk has given a son." While it has been suggested that Baladan might be an abbreviated form of the father's name without the name of the deity (X has given a son), it appears more likely that the phrase "son of Baladan" is simply an attempt at some stage of the Biblical text to fill out the name of this king by interpreting the 2d part of his name as a patronym. Merodach-baladan himself claims descent from Eriba-Marduk, a king of Babylon from 782–762 B.C.E. It is possible, but not certain, that this is the true name of his father (Kaiser *Isaiah 1–12* OTL, 409). In Babylonian sources Merodach-baladan is called son of Yakin, but this is surely a reference to membership in his tribe or dynasty and not the name of his father (Hobbs *2 Kings* WBC, 294).

Bibliography

Brinkman, J. A. 1964. Merodach-Baladan II. Pp. 6–53 in *Studies Presented to A. Leo Oppenheim.* Chicago.

JOHN H. HULL, JR.

BALAH (PLACE) [Heb *bālâ*]. Town allotted to Simeon in the Negeb within the tribal territory of Judah (Josh 19:3). See BAALAH.

BALAH, DEIR EL- (PLACE). See DEIR EL-BALAH.

BALAK (PERSON) [Heb *bālāq*]. A king of Moab, the son of Zippor, whose encounter with Balaam is described in Numbers 22–24. After the Israelites had defeated the Amorites and were camped in the plains of Moab opposite Jericho, Balak and the elders of Moab and Midian decided to protect themselves from the Hebrews with supernatural power. Acting out of great fear and willing to pay a large fee, Balak sought the assistance of Balaam, a Mesopotamian diviner; Balak was convinced that Balaam's curse on Israel would guarantee a Moabite victory in some future conflict (22:1–7).

After meeting Balaam on the border of Moab (22:36), Balak made every effort to invoke the seer's efficacious pronouncement. Balaam was taken to 4 different locations, including several mountaintops where he could look down upon the people he was expected to curse (22:39, 41; 23:14, 28). Acting as priest, Balak assisted the diviner in sacrificial rituals (22:40; 23:1–4, 14–17, 29–30). As is well known, Balak was frustrated and greatly disappointed, since Balaam could pronounce only blessings on the Moabite king's enemies (23:23).

Balak is virtually unknown in the Bible outside of Numbers 22–24. Balak is mentioned in passing elsewhere in the OT as an example of a futile attempt to thwart God's plans (Josh 24:9–10; Judg 11:25; Mic 6:5). Rev 2:14 discusses Balak and Balaam because of their involvement in the incident at Shittim, the matter of Baal of Peor (Numbers 25; cf. Mic 6:5). While there is much debate concerning the date of the Balak-Balaam traditions, it is obvious that these figures were etched in the memories of later generations.

Gerald L. Mattingly

BALAMON (PLACE) [Gk *Balamōn*]. One of two settlements marking the location of a field in which Manasseh, the husband of Judith, was buried (Jdt 8:3), the other location identified being Dothan (Gk *Dothaim*). Although its precise location remains unknown, the text of Judith makes it clear that Balamon, like Dothan, was to be found approximately 8 miles north of Samaria. This is the only reference to Balamon unless, as Stummer (1947: 7), Enslin (1972: 110), and Moore (*Judith* AB, 44, 180) have conjectured, the word is a corruption of other place names, such as Belmain (4:4) or Belbaim (7:3). Without explanation, but (presumably) on the same basis, Reed (*IDB* 1: 378) and others suggest that Balamon might be identified with the villages of Bebai (15:4), Bileam (1 Chr 6:55—Eng 6:70), Ibleam (Josh 17:11–12), and Abel-beth Maacah (2 Sam 20:14–15). Located 20 miles north of Lake Hula, the last of these would appear an unlikely location for Balamon, given the circumstances described in Jdt 8:3. The possibility of corruption, then, remains a real one, given the large number of place names in Judith which remain unidentified (Moore *Judith* AB, 39–44) and the difficulties inherent in any attempt to reconstruct the book's Heb original. Its clearly fictional character and the general unreliability of the book's geography may, however, preclude any identification (Pfeiffer 1949: 296–97; Nickelsburg 1981: 106–7). See also BAAL-HAMON.

Bibliography

Enslin, M. 1972. *The Book of Judith.* Jewish Apocryphal Literature. Leiden.

Nickelsburg, G. 1981. *Jewish Literature Between the Bible and the Mishnah, A Historical and Literary Introduction.* Philadelphia.

Pfeiffer, R. 1949. *History of New Testament Times.* New York.

Stummer, F. 1947. *Geographie des Buches Judith.* BR 3. Stuttgart.

Frederick W. Schmidt

BALAS, ALEXANDER (PERSON). See ALEXANDER (PERSON).

BALBAIM (PLACE) [Gk *Belbaim*]. A site mentioned in the book of Judith, whose exact location is unknown (Jdt 7:3). It is often assumed to be identical with the BELMAIN in 4:4 and the BALAMON in 8:3. If this is the case, it may be identified with Abel-maim (M.R. 204296) some 13 miles south of Scythopolis (so Aharoni and Avi-Yonah *MBA*). Of course, given the genre of the book of Judith, it is entirely possible that the town is fictitious.

Sidnie Ann White

BALDNESS. See SICKNESS AND DISEASE.

BALM. A historically convenient English translation of the Heb word *ṣŏrî,* found in the OT just 6 times, all with reference to a plant or a derived plant product. The modern botanical identification cannot be established precisely. The LXX translated the Heb word as the Gk *rhētinē* "resin of pine." For the Hellenistic botanist Theophrastus (*Hist. Pl.* 9.2), *rhētinē* was the resins or saps extracted from Aleppo pine and silver fir, the terebinth of Syria, and Phoenician cedar. If the Gk *rhētinē* of Theophrastus and the LXX is an accurate translation of the Heb *ṣori,* then "balm" was a resinous substance harvested from one or several of these few trees which grew in the regions of Palestine and Transjordan, not one of the resinous aromatic spices or incenses imported into Palestine from Arabia or Abyssinia.

In the past, scholars have often placed balm (*ṣŏrî*) within a somewhat larger group of aromatic plants and plant products which included other plant substances such as *bośem* (balsam) and *nāṭāp,* as some references to them occasionally overlap in meaning, description, or usage. This confusion has been retained even in modern translations of the OT; for instance, in the NEB, Ezek 27:17, *ṣŏrî* is translated "balsam" not "balm," and there are many other examples.

It seems necessary to regard balm (*ṣŏrî*) as a distinct substance in biblical study for several reasons. Balm (*ṣŏrî*) appears to have been native to Palestine or Transjordan and specifically produced in this area, whereas balsam *(bośem)* was imported into Palestine from Arabia or Abyssinia (Miller 1969: 101–2; Groom 1981; cf. 1 Kgs 10:2; Ezek 27:22). Famous as a product of Gilead, balm is said to have been exported from there to places like Egypt and Tyre (cf. Gen 37:25, 43:11; Ezek 27:17), but the Hebrew *bośem* is never mentioned as having a special association with Gilead. Balm *(ṣŏrî)* is mentioned as a medicinal product, whereas other incenses or spices such as *bośem* and *nāṭāp* have no such specific distinction and use. In contrast, *bośem* was refined and compounded as a fragrant ingredient of the priestly anointing oil (Exod 25:6; 1 Chr 9:29), of which *ṣŏrî* is never mentioned as a component. Further, *bośem* is often mentioned as a spice with qualities which made it suitable for use by women as a fragrance (Cant 4:10, 4:16, 5:13; Esth 2:12; Isa 3:24), but *ṣŏrî* is never described as such (see also PERFUMES AND SPICES). *Bośem* also had other uses. It was among the fragrant garlands on funeral biers (2 Chr 16:14), but there is no evidence that *ṣŏrî* had such versatile applications. Indeed, it is difficult to see any clear synonymity between *ṣŏrî* and other substances such as *bośem* (balsam) or *nāṭāp*. *Nāṭāp* has been associated in the past with both of the above, but is too poorly attested to be considered here.

A number of proposals for the identification of *ṣŏrî* (balm) have been made previously, some of which, however, assumed the erroneous identification of *ṣŏrî* with other plant products such as *bośem* and *nāṭāp*. Previous botanical identifications have included *Commiphora opobalsamum, Pistacia lentiscus, Balanites aegyptiaca,* and others (see also FLORA). These must be rejected in favor of one or several of the aromatic tree resins mentioned in the Greek botanists. Indeed even today, remnants of the ancient forests of Gilead (the district of Ajlun in modern Jordan) still contain the ancient sources of *rhētinē* mentioned in the classical writers—Aleppo pine *(Pinus halepensis)* and Phoenician cedar *(Juniperus phoenicia)* (Rushbrooke 1943: 427).

In the OT, at least half of the references to balm are to a healing medicinal ointment of some sort, probably made of resin which had been compounded with oil (compare the parallelism of Ugaritic *ẓrw* and *šmn,* and possibly a similar Heb parallelism in Job 29:6 as well if one allows a slight emendation of the text [see Fisher 1972: 359]). In Jer 8:22 and 46:11, balm is some sort of salve or ointment which was applied to wounds where there was a loss of skin: "Why has not skin grown over their wound?" Further, Jer 51:8 suggests that balm was a medicine applied to wounds apparently as a soothing salve. It is important to note, however, that our knowledge of the medicinal use of balm is derived from Jeremiah alone, who speaks allegorically of societal and national healing. From passages in Jeremiah it can be inferred that *ṣŏrî,* the "Balm of Gilead," was regarded with high esteem as the healing salve specific to the region of Gilead ("for which our country is famous," see Gen 43:11), or was an ingredient of this product. There seems to be no reason as yet to reject the current English translation of *ṣŏrî* as "balm," as the English word balm implies both a soothing medicament as well as a pleasant odor.

Bibliography

Fisher, L. R., ed. 1972. *Ras Shamra Parallels I.* Rome.
Groom, N. 1981. *Frankincense and Myrrh.* London.
Miller, J. 1969. *The Spice Trade of the Roman Empire 29 B.C. to A.D. 641.* Oxford.
Rushbrooke, E. G. N., ed. 1943. *Palestine and Transjordan.* Geographical Handbook Series B. R. 514. British Naval Intelligence Division.

RICHARD N. JONES

BALSAM. See BALM.

BAMOTH

BAMOTH (PLACE) [Heb *bāmôt*]. One of the Israelite encampments in N Moab E of the Shittim Valley near Mt. Nebo (Num 21:19–20). Many scholars (e.g., Gray *Numbers* ICC, 291) identify Bamoth with BAMOTH-BAAL (Num 22:41; Josh 13:17) and with the *bt bmt* ("Beth-bamoth") of the Moabite Stone (line 27 [*ANET,* 320]). Noth (*Numbers* OTL, 182) rejected the interpretation of MT *bāmôt-baʿal* as a geographic name in spite of Josh 13:17, but his view is not typical. Boling (*Joshua* AB, 342) has reaffirmed the identification of Bamoth with Bamoth-baal, and proposes Khirbet el-Qeiqiyeh S of Mt. Nebo as the probable ancient site.

The Moabite itinerary of the Wilderness/Conquest narratives is problematic (see Meek 1960: 41–48; Walsh 1977; Briend 1986), and the text of Num 21:10–20 is arguably conflated (see Miller 1989: 585–87, citing earlier studies). Conclusions regarding the identity of sites must therefore remain open to revision.

Bibliography

Briend, J. 1986. La Marche des tribes d'Israel en Transjordanie. *MB* 46: 41–42.
Meek, T. J. 1960. *Hebrew Origins.* New York.
Miller, J. M. 1989. The Israelite Journey through (around) Moab and Moabite Toponymy. *JBL* 108: 577-95.
Walsh, J. T. 1977. From Egypt to Moab: A Source Critical Analysis of the Wilderness Itinerary. *CBQ* 39: 20–33.

C. GILBERT ROMERO

BAMOTH-BAAL

BAMOTH-BAAL (PLACE) [Heb *bāmôt baʿal*]. One of the stopping points in the Hebrew migration through Moab (Num 21:19–20, where the place is listed by its shorter name of Bamoth). It is most likely that Bamoth-baal and Bamoth are identical because the names are similar and the geographical information in the OT that relates to these place-names localizes both to the same region. This settlement was assigned to the tribe of Reuben and was counted among the towns in the tableland of Heshbon (Josh 13:17). Although the identification is not certain, it is possible that Bamoth-baal/Bamoth is the same as Beth-bamoth, mentioned in the Mesha Inscription (line 27).

The Num 21:10–20 narrative on Israel's journey around S Moab and through N Moab names Bamoth in a series of 4 locations: Mattanah, Nahaliel, Bamoth, and "the valley lying in the region of Moab by the top of Pisgah" (Num 21:19–20). While the 1st 2 sites are unknown, the 4th place is clearly in the NW corner of Moab, near Mt. Pisgah and Mt. Nebo, in the mountains of Abarim. The 3d place, therefore, Bamoth, is in the same general direction as

Pisgah and Nebo and is some distance to the N of the Arnon. The edge of the Transjordanian plateau in NW Moab is also the appropriate setting for the episode involving Balak and Balaam (Numbers 22–24).

More specifically, the RSV text of Num 22:41 says that a place called Bamoth-baal was one of several peaks to which Balak took Balaam. This elevated locale was chosen by the Moabite king so that Balaam could see the people whom he had been hired to curse, the Israelites who were encamped in the plains of Moab, opposite Jericho. While the RSV regards Bamoth-baal as a proper name, the KJV translates these Hebrew words in 22:41 as "the high places of Baal." This is, of course, a literal rendering of the Hebrew, but there are many biblical place-names with significant meanings that are not translated. Furthermore, the other 3 places to which Balak took Balaam had specific designations, proper names. It is likely that many of the hills on the Abarim ridge provided the setting where a number of deities were worshiped (e.g., Baal, Nebo/Nabu, Peor). Some of these hills were probably crowned with cultic installations of some sort, including high places. There is every reason to believe that a specific place named Bamoth-baal could have served such a function, as is indicated in the description of the sacrificial ritual performed by Balak and Balaam (cf. Num 23:1–6).

The exact location of Bamoth-baal is unknown, but it was undoubtedly on one of the heights of Abarim, in the vicinity of Pisgah and Nebo. One specific site is usually mentioned by those inclined to localize Bamoth-baal, a place called Khirbet el-Quweiqiyeh. Musil (1907–8) referred to this site as el-Quēziǰe (or Qweiziyeh), which is located ca. 3 miles northwest of Medeba and 1½ miles S of Khirbet el-Mekhaiyet, which is often identified as the town of Nebo. Archaeological confirmation is lacking, but the location fulfills all of the geographical requirements of the Bible and the place is revered by the local population.

Bibliography

Musil, A. 1907–8. *Arabia Petraea*. 2 vols. Vienna.

GERALD L. MATTINGLY

BAN (HEREM). See DEUTERONOMY, BOOK OF.

BANDITRY. Robbery, outlawry, and related resistance movements were elements of the social world of early Judaism and formative Christianity.

A. Studies of Banditry
B. Banditry in Lebanon
C. Banditry in Trachonitis
D. Banditry in Judea
   1. Before A.D. 66
   2. A.D. 70–132
   3. After Bar Kokhba

A. Studies of Banditry

Banditry has attracted the attention of social historians (e.g., Hobsbawm 1985) in recent years for several reasons. First, from a distance banditry has a certain air of romance. Second, it is a phenomenon of great complexity which can assume various forms, some of which involve resistance against the existing social order. Third, the extent to which banditry occurs in a society is often considered a reflection of the degree of internal control and social stability achieved by the system.

Banditry was frequent at least in some periods and some areas of the Roman empire. For Judea and its vicinity there is a good deal of evidence from various periods. Here too it assumed various forms. In the mountains of the Lebanon and in Trachonitis in S Syria an impoverished population harassed the farmers in the plains and the traders traveling along the roads through the area. These forms of robbery were sometimes condoned by local dynasts who shared in the profits. In Judea banditry had often strong ideological roots and some of the bandits might be called guerilla fighters by those sympathetic to their cause, for the prime target was the Roman authorities whose rule some considered illegitimate.

Banditry did not come to an end with the suppression of the 1st Jewish Revolt (A.D. 66–70) or the Bar Kokhba war (A.D. 132–135). In fact there is a good deal of evidence from the Byzantine period which cannot be considered here (Isaac 1984; fc. chap. 2). What follows is a brief survey of the evidence in roughly chronological and geographical order.

B. Banditry in Lebanon

At the time of Pompey's E campaign in 63 B.C. several regions are known to have suffered from brigandage. One people well known for their bellicose nature were the Ituraeans who lived in the Lebanon mountains and the Beqa^{c} Valley. In the reign of Augustus, the geographer Strabo writes in his description of the Lebanon:

> Now all the mountainous parts are held by Ituraeans and Arabians, all of whom are robbers, but the people in the plains are farmers; and when the latter are harassed by the robbers at different times they require different kinds of help. These robbers use strongholds as bases of operation; those, for example, who hold Libanus possess, high up on the mountain, Sinna and Borrama and other fortresses like them, and down below, Botrys and Gigartus and the caves by the sea and the castle that was erected on Theuprosopon. Pompey destroyed these places; and from them the robbers overran both Byblus and the city that comes next after Byblus, I mean the city Berytus, which lie between Sidon and Theuprosopon. (Strabo 16.2.18 §756; trans. H. L. Jones, Loeb.)

C. Banditry in Trachonitis

Further E there were similar problems. In the same work, Strabo claims that the Roman army had taken effective measures following the annexation of the area into the province of Syria. The lava plateau between Damascus and Bostra, modern El Leja (= "a refuge"; a place in which to hide), was known in antiquity as Trachonitis. Strabo has the following to say:

> And then, toward the parts inhabited promiscuously by Arabians and Ituraeans, are mountains hard to pass, in which there are deep-mouthed caves, one of which can

> admit as many as four thousand people in times of incursions, such as are made against the Damasceni from many places. For the most part, indeed, the barbarians have been robbing the merchants from Arabia Felix, but this is less the case now that the band of robbers under Zenodorus has been broken up through the good government established by the Romans and through the security established by the Roman soldiers that are kept in Syria. (Strabo xvi 2,20 [756]; trans. H. L. Jones, Loeb)

In 23 B.C. Augustus gave Trachonitis, Batanaea (Bashan), and Auranitis (Hauran) to the allied king Herod of Judea. His task here was to suppress the robber bands in Trachonitis who had operated in Damascus with the support of a local ruler, Zenodorus the Tetrarch (Joseph. *Ant* 15. 10.1 §§343–48; *JW* 1.20.4 §§398–400; concerning Zenodorus see *HJP*² 1.565–66). Zenodorus received a share of the profit, according to Josephus.

> It was not easy to restrain people who had made brigandage a habit and had no other means of making a living, since they had neither city or field of their own but only underground shelters and caves, where they lived together with their cattle. They had also managed to collect supplies of water and of food beforehand, and so were able to hold out for a very long time in their hidden retreat. Moreover, the entrances (to their caves) were narrow, and only one person at a time could enter, while the interiors were incredibly large and constructed to provide plenty of room, and the ground above their dwellings was not high but almost level with the (surrounding) surface. The whole place consisted of rocks that were rugged and difficult of access unless one used a path with a guide leading the way, for not even these paths were straight, but had many turns and windings. (Joseph. *Ant* 15.10.1 §§346–47)

It is worthwhile to consider these passages in full because they are independent sources which agree and supplement each other. Strabo and Josephus both mention that the major problem was the fact that the territory of Damascus and the roads there suffered from bandits. Both say that the bandits hid in caves. These caves have been identified by archaeologists working in the region. In Israel numerous artificial caves have been found in recent years, clearly used as hiding places in the Roman period. Strabo adds that the banditry was of special concern to the Romans because both the rural population around Damascus, and traders were attacked. Josephus, on the other hand, insists on the economic cause of brigandage, and there can be no doubt that economic hardship lay at the root of the difficulties in the region. (It may be added that the lava fields of Trachonitis were a dangerous area as recently as the beginning of this century.)

Wetzstein, who knew the area in the 1850s, alleges that the Turkish authorities never dared to act against the inhabitants of the region, no matter how much the villagers around Damascus suffered from their depredations. He notes that they might be controlled only by a permanent garrison in their land. The caves described by Josephus were famous in Wetzstein's time as well. We may note the expression "a robbers' cave" used as a matter of course in the NT (Matt 21:13).

In the 19th century, as in antiquity, brigands used to hide in caves in Trachonitis, and, as in Josephus, there was the need for a guide to lead the way. According to Josephus, who presumably relied on his source Nicolaus of Damascus, Herod pacified the region. However, 14 years later the inhabitants rebelled. Herod (according to Josephus) prevented them from practising banditry and forced them to till the soil and live quietly. This they did not want to do, and even had they been willing the land was too poor, so they again attacked their neighbours. Here again the economic roots of the problem become apparent. Herod's army took action and some of the robbers fled to Arabia. There they were provided with a base of operations against Judea (i.e., Galilee) and Coele-Syria (i.e., the territory of Damascus). This is another instance of support and involvement on the part of local rulers. Herod first attacked the home base of the bandits in Trachonitis, but the foray was ineffective because the brigands had a base of operations in Nabatean territory. There "they numbered about a thousand" (*Ant* 16.9.1–2 §§271–85). Herod attacked them there and destroyed their base, which led to conflict between Herod and the Nabataeans. As a supplementary measure in his efforts to suppress banditry, Herod settled 3,000 Idumaeans, his own countrymen, in Trachonitis. This got Herod into difficulties with the emperor Augustus, for allied rulers were not allowed to interfere independently in the affairs of other allies. He was reprimanded, following which the inhabitants of Trachonitis and the Nabateans returned to brigandage and attacked the Idumaean settlers in Trachonitis.

Herod obviously failed to gain control of Trachonitis, for afterward he planted Jewish settlers at Bathyra in Batanaea (perhaps to be identified with Baṣīr, E of aṣ-Ṣanamein [Aere]) (Joseph. *Ant* 17.2.1 §§23–30; for the identification see Dussaud 1927: 331; *HJP*² 1.565). The settlement in itself was successful. The presence of Jewish settlers is attested by carvings found at Nava, which is a site on the route from Damascus to Scythopolis used by Jewish travelers to and from Babylonia. The Jewish settlements were intended to serve as a buffer between Trachonitis and Galilee (Joseph. *Ant* 17.2.1–2 §§23–31). This implies that Herod had given up attempts permanently to subdue the population of Trachonitis itself.

A well-known but fragmentary Gk inscription set up at Canatha on the slopes of Jebel Druze SE of Trachonitis in the reign of either Agrippa I or Agrippa II mentions people who hide in holes like animals (*OGIS* 424; *IGRR* iii 1223; Waddington and Le Bas 1870, no. 2329, with extensive comments).

The ancient sources make it clear that Trachonitis was a poor region which did not allow of profitable cultivation, and the very factors which contributed to its poverty made it suitable as a shelter for brigands. This had consequences not only for the region itself, but also for neighboring fertile lands which suffered depredations. Because important trade routes passed through and near by the region, international trade also suffered from such insecurity. At first Augustus gave his client Herod instructions to solve the problem, but this resulted in armed conflict with another client, a state of affairs that the Romans would not tolerate. The system failed to function. Local problems such as these, often not mentioned in literary sources, might convince the Romans that it was preferable to annex a region. Eventually the Roman army took the matter in hand. However, arms alone cannot solve such problems for good. The factors of geography which cause instability, poverty, and inaccessibility, do not change. Hence we learn that Samaritan rebels fled to Trachonitis in the 6th century (Theophanes *A.M.* 6048; *Historia Miscella* xvi, PL 16.991).

The information regarding banditry in Trachonitis is important, for the situation there had nothing to do with the specifically Jewish resistance to Roman rule in Judea. It was a state of insecurity with social and economic causes in which ideology played no major role. Yet we know of this only thanks to the diligence of 2 good sources, Strabo and Josephus. The possibility must be considered that there was banditry in Trachonitis in other periods of antiquity when there was no author interested in writing about it. Further it is quite possible that there were other areas with endemic unrest of which we know nothing. The complexities which the Romans faced in Syria-Palestine will have occurred in other areas and other times as well.

D. Banditry in Judea

Several sources accuse the Jews in Judaea of brigandage before the Roman conquest. Josephus represents the Hasmonean Hyrcanus as accusing Aristobulus before Pompey of instigating raids against neighboring peoples and acts of piracy at sea (*Ant* 24.3.2 §43). Strabo says that

> the tyrannies (scil. of the Hasmonaeans) were the cause of brigandage, for some rebelled and harassed the countryside, both their own and neighbouring lands, while others collaborated with the rulers and seized the possessions of others and subdued much of Syria and Phoenicia. (Strabo 16.2.37 §761)

Again, in his description of the coast of Sharon from Joppe (Jaffa) to Mt. Carmel, Strabo says that "the ports of robbers clearly are merely robbers' dens" (16.2.28 §758). Similar accusations are found in the *Historia Philippica* in Justin's epitome of Pompeius Trogus (Prologus, L. xxxix; 11.2.4). There it is stated that the Jews and the Arabs harassed Syria by brigandage. It is difficult to say whether this refers only to the Hasmonean conquests of territory outside Judea proper, or also to armed clashes or raids of which we possess no written record.

Statements like these must be distinguished from the information on banditry in Trachonitis. Accusations of Jewish state-sponsored brigandage, like those levelled by Strabo against Zenodorus and by Josephus against the Nabateans, may not be true. Their intention was to justify armed intervention by a third party. The alleged purpose of Pompey's E campaign was the suppression of piracy, and accusations of robbery and piracy clearly served as justification for the subjugation of various peoples. However, it is possible as well that there really was a good deal of banditry in the region in the period of Seleucid decline and before the Roman takeover.

In Judea and Arabia there is much evidence of internal problems. For some periods the sources regarding Judea-Palestine are relatively good as compared with other provinces. Banditry was a problem in periods other than those well known through Josephus' work. In the period which he covers, before and after the Roman conquest, various forms of banditry described by him were endemic.

1. Before A.D. 66. It has been shown that the Roman army was faced with problems of banditry in Lebanon and S Syria. According to ancient sources, banditry was frequent in mountainous and inaccessible areas where the population could not and would not maintain itself at subsistence level by means of agriculture. Judea, and particularly Galilee, were relatively rich countries, but there, as is seen in the next section, banditry of a different kind undermined security.

Josephus provides a good deal of information on unrest in Judea from Herod's death until the outbreak of the 1st Jewish Revolt. Josephus is extremely hostile toward those who physically resisted Roman rule. Moreover, for his account the early part of the 1st century, he relies on a source close to Herod which accordingly was hostile itself.

It was Herod's task as client king to suppress banditry. His first act as governor of Galilee in 47–46 B.C. was an attack on a bandit leader Ezekias who harassed Tyrian villages, a symptom perhaps of tension between ethnic groups in the region. Many of Ezekias' followers were killed, the Syrians were satisfied, and so was the governor of Syria, Sextus Julius Caesar (*Ant* 14.9.2 §159; *JW* 1.10.5 §204). Herod, however, was called to account before the Sanhedrin in Jerusalem because he had killed Jews. We have no further information on Ezekias and his followers, but it is significant that his son Judas was one of the first Zealots, and many of his descendants were active in the resistance to Rome before and during the 1st Revolt, all of them called *leistai* (bandits) by Josephus. The last was Eleazar ben Yair, commander of the defendants of Masada. The manner in which Josephus describes these men and their followers leaves no doubt that the primary motive for their resistance to Rome was religious commitment. It is therefore possible that the banditry practised by Ezekias had other motives besides purely economic ones (see also ZEALOTS).

In 38 B.C. Herod led a campaign against (what Josephus calls) bandits in caves near Arbela in Galilee. There is no information on the nature of the bandits' activities (*Ant* 14.15.4 §415–16; 15.5 §420–30; *JW* 1.16.2 §304–5; 16.4 §309–13). However, an old man who killed his family and jumped down a cliff himself, "submitting to death rather than slavery," apparently was motivated in his struggle by religious ideology rather than economic misery. Martyrdom and suicide by those resisting the foreign tyrant go back at least to 2 Maccabees (see SUICIDE).

The militants are described by Josephus sometimes with admiration, more often with animosity. He recognizes the force of their convictions. They have "an invincible passion for liberty and take God for their only leader and lord" (*Ant* 18.1.6 §23). Their willingness to die for their way of life was an integral part of their ideology, connected with a belief in recompense in the world to come (*JW* 1.33.1 §650; cf. *Ant* 17.6.1 §152; *JW* 1.16.2 §311). Josephus does not hide the fact that he was expected by his comrades to commit suicide rather than surrender at Jotapata (*JW* 3.8.4 §355). The speech of Eleazar ben Yair, commander of the defendants of Masada, is Josephus' eloquent statement of their determination "neither to serve the Romans nor any other save God" (*JW* 7.8.6 §323). More often, however, Josephus describes the rebels as plain criminals. It is also impossible to distinguish resistance against Rome as the foreign power from resistance against the Jewish ruling class which represented the Roman authority in Judea.

The extant information is scanty and colored by the hostility of the sources. There is no basis in the evidence which would justify distinguishing between social and revolutionary banditry (if such a distinction should be made), but it is clear that Judea, from Herod's rise to power until the outbreak of the 1st Jewish Revolt, saw the emergence of groups which refused to accept the order which Rome generally imposed on clients and new provinces. Whenever the sources speak of bandits or murderers, the possibility exists that these are not merely economic or antisocial elements, but Jews motivated by ideology and religion.

It is therefore important to note that there are instances of popular support for, or collaboration with, brigands. The Barabbas released upon popular request at the time of Jesus' trial was, according to Mark, "among the rebels [Gk *stasiastōn*] who had committed murder in the insurrection" (Mark 15:7; cf. Luke 23:19), but John calls him a bandit (Gk *lęstēs*; John 18:40). Around the middle of the century there was serious trouble between Jews and Samaritans. "The masses . . . took up arms and invited the assistance of Eleazar ben Dinai—he was a brigand who for many years had had his home in the mountains" (*Ant* 20.6.1 §121; *JW* 2.12.4 §235). Eleazar is also known from Talmudic sources. He is said to have inspired so many murders that the regular sacrifice of atonement for an unknown murderer was discontinued. He began to be called Ben Harazḥan, son of the murderer (*m. Soṭa* 9:9). However, elsewhere in Talmudic literature he is described as "one who prematurely tried to free the Jews" (*Cant. Rab.* 2:18). Here we have one and the same man seen from the perspective of local, non-Roman sources, as either a murderer or a premature freedom fighter. Even at the stage when these sources were composed, there were differences of opinion about those who practiced armed resistance to Rome.

The Romans held the local population collectively responsible for guerilla attacks in the countryside. These were followed by massive retaliation. When a Roman company was attacked near Emmaus, the town was burned at the orders of Varus (*Ant* 17.10.9 §291; *JW* 2.5.1 §71). In 4 B.C. the arsenal of the royal palace at Sepphoris in Galilee was attacked and the arms stored there were seized. Varus burned the city and reduced the inhabitants to slavery (*JW* 2.5.1 §68; *Ant* 17.10.9 §289). On the road from Emmaus to Jerusalem a slave of the emperor was once attacked and robbed. The governor Cumanus then sent troops to the neighboring villages to bring the inhabitants to him and reprimanded them because they had let the bandits escape (*Ant* 20.5.4 §113; *JW* 2.12.2 §228). These incidents also give an impression of the tactics followed by the rebels. They would attack small groups of soldiers or officials on the move and attack arsenals in order acquire arms, supplies, and money for themselves. From an incident told by Josephus it is clear that the villages were often searched in a manner which could easily lead to violence. This was in fact standing procedure established by law, as later formulated by Ulpian on the duties of the proconsul: "He must besides pursuing temple robbers, kidnappers and thieves, mete out to each of them the punishment he deserves and chastise people sheltering them; without them a robber cannot hide for very long" (*Digest* 1.18.13, Praef.). Such practices, however, could easily be accompanied by acts of provocation which would aggravate tension and hostility.

As a commander of the Jewish insurgents in Galilee, Josephus incorporated into his army 4,500 so-called brigands, which he then proceeds to call mercenaries because he paid them (*Life* 14 §77; cf. *JW* 2.20.7 §581). These were the troops in whom he placed most confidence (*JW* 2.20.7 §583). It is clear also that these were ideologically motivated bandits. They might rob anyone, Jew or gentile, poor or rich, but they would never support the Romans.

It is typical of their attitude toward the empire that Talmudic sources, which all belong to the period after the major wars with Rome, often describe representatives of the Roman government as bandits (Heb/Aram *lîsṭîm*). Many sources describe tax collectors and customs officials in such terms (e.g., *t. B. Meṣ* 9:25; *t. Šebu.* 2:14). The Roman occupation is depicted as a direct cause of instability and banditry. In the words of R. Aha: "Where the empire takes over government, there appear bands and bands of *lîsṭîm*" (*Lev.Rab.* 9:8). It is not clear whether the implication is that Roman rule causes impoverishment and hence banditry among the population, or whether Roman officials and tax collectors are themselves bandits. Josephus recognized the connection between maladministration and the breakdown of security. During the crisis in A.D. 39/40, Jewish leaders asked the governor of Syria to point out to Caligula "that, since the land was unsown, there would be a harvest of banditry because the requirements of tribute could not be met." This is a clear expression of the realization that banditry could be the result of poverty and oppressive taxation. Yet, the occasion for this statement was a conflict about a purely religious affair which nearly led to revolt. Elsewhere Josephus says that famine strengthened the zealots (*Ant* 18.1.1 §8).

These pronouncements show again that social and economic factors could reinforce banditry and insecurity in Judea as elsewhere, but it does not justify a denial of the obvious conclusion: that resistance to Roman rule was particularly fierce in Judea, as a result of the single feature which distinguished the Jews from other peoples, namely their religious attitudes.

2. A.D. 70–132. Banditry with ideological overtones did not come to an end with the suppression of the 1st Jewish Revolt. This appears from Talmudic sources. For instance, a source relating to the 2d century tells of the arrest of a member of a band of *lîsṭîm* (bandits) in Cappadocia (*t. Yebam.* 5:5; cf. *y. Yebam.* 2:4b; *b. Yebam.* 25b). The *Palestinian Talmud* says he was arrested in Caesarea in Cappadocia; the *Babylonian Talmud* mentions Magiza, i.e. Mazaca. Before he was executed he had a last request: "Go to the wife of Shimon ben Cahana and tell her that I killed him as he entered the town of Lydda." Shimon ben Cahana was a pupil of R. Eliezer ben Hyrcanus (*ca.* 100–130), who taught at Lydda, and a teacher of Raban Simeon ben Gamaliel, *ca.* 130–160 (cf. *t. Para* 12:6.). This establishes a rough chronology: Shimon ben Cahana belongs to the period between the 1st Revolt and the revolt of Bar Kokhba. The sources discuss when a confession of murder may serve as evidence which would allow the widow of the victim to remarry. The murderer of Shimon ben Cahana, by his declaration, saw to it that his victim's wife was legally declared a widow and so could remarry. This is remarkable behavior for the murderer of a well-known scholar and can be accounted for by the hypothesis that this was a case of political murder.

Another case also refers to a well-known scholar in the same period, R. Ḥanania ben Teradion, one of the wealthiest men in Galilee and treasurer of a fund for the poor (*b. B. Bat.* 10b). His son first joined a band of *lîsṭîm* and then proceeded to betray them (*Lam. Rab.* 3:6; cf. *Ṣem.* 12.13). This was discovered and he was killed by his former comrades. After 3 days they gave his body up for burial out of respect for the father. However, instead of mourning him in the usual manner, his father, mother, and sister vehemently cursed the son. The father, R. Ḥanania, was executed by the Romans after the revolt of Bar Kokhba (cf. *b. ʿAbod. Zar.* 17b–18a). It is obvious that his son would not have joined a band of robbers for economic reasons, nor would one expect simple bandits to have particular respect for a wealthy scholar—as expressed by the return of the body. The behavior of the family can be explained by the assumption that (1) the term *lîsṭîm* here stands for "guerrilla fighters" and (2) the scholar and the fighters supported a common cause.

A 3d source describes *lîsṭîm* who met with pupils of R. Akiba making for the S on their way to Acco. They made their way together for a distance, and when they separated the bandits expressed their admiration for R. Akiba and his pupils (*b. ʿAbod. Zar.* 25b; cf. Alon 1984: 570–72). This again is evidence of a relation of respect and even warmth between a distinguished scholar and people described as bandits. The scholar was one of the leaders of the revolt of Bar Kokhba, and the obvious explanation is that the "bandits" were guerilla fighters who maintained good relations with Jewish leaders.

To the same period belongs a story of some Galileans who had killed a man. They fled to Lydda and there appealed to R. Tarphon to hide them. R. Tarphon, influential in the years before the Bar Kokhba revolt, did not help them, but he did not betray them either (*b. Nid.* 61a; cf. Alon 1984: 570–72). Two points are significant: first, the fact that the murderers thought an influential rabbi might be prepared to help them, and second, the circumstance that R. Tarphon did not hand over murderers to the authorities. It is likely that the murder again was a political execution.

In recent years remarkable material evidence has been found of the methods used by the guerilla fighters in Judea in the form of numerous subterranean hiding places. Most are found in ancient settlements, their entrances masked by cisterns or innocent-looking cavities in the rock (Gichon 1982: 30–42; Kloner 1983: 210–21). The evidence has now been published fully in a book with copious illustrations but questionable conclusions regarding the dating (Kloner and Tepper 1987).

3. After Bar Kokhba. Jewish sources give the impression that banditry remained endemic in the 2d century and afterward. Talmudic sources rarely provide explicit or unambiguous statements. It is not uncommon for each source to be analysed in isolation and interpreted in a different manner, but this ignores the historical reality which the sources, taken together, indicate in outline (see Schäfer 1981).

A source of the 2d century mentions a hypothetical case in which a Nazirite (who is not allowed to shave) is shaved by *lîsṭîm* (*m. Nazir* 6:3; cf. *Sipre Num.* 25). That probably would not be the work of ordinary robbers. To the same period belongs the rule concerning payment of ransom for a wife taken captive. If she was imprisoned by the authorities, the husband was not obliged to pay ransom; if she was taken by *lîsṭîm,* he was (*t. Ketub.* 4:5; cf. *b. Ketub.* 51b). The reason for this distinction was that a wife in the hands of the authorities might be expected to consent to having sexual relations with her captors. When she was the prisoner of *lîsṭîm* there was no such risk. It is an implicit assumption which says much about the sort of people *lîsṭîm* are taken to be.

It is generally assumed that Judea essentially became a quiet province in the later 2d century. The evidence on *lîsṭîm* in Talmudic sources, however, relates to the 3d century as well. In the 3d century R. Jose ben R. Bun predicted that *lîsṭîm* would occupy the throne of Israel "in the fourth generation." (*y. Hor.* 3:7c) The source ostensibly discusses the biblical period, but it is improbable that R. Jose here refers to a tradition from biblical times. The statement reflects the realities of his own time, the 3d-century period of crisis marked by anarchy and various forms of banditry.

Another source of the early 3d century reminds one of the episode, described above, concerning the murderers who appealed to R. Tarphon. Here it is a conspirator sought by the authorities who actually was hidden by R. Judah ben Levi. (*Gen Rab.* 94:9; *j. Ter.* 8:6b). It is significant that there is no indication in any of these cases of moral condemnation of the bandits as such.

There are many more references to *lîsṭîm* in Talmudic sources. They appear 12 times in the Mishnah, 17 times in the Tosephta, 20 times in the Jerusalem Talmud, and 40 times in the Babylonian Talmud. Often they cannot be dated accurately, and it is not always possible to determine whether the examples reflect historical reality of purely academic dispute. Where this is not in doubt it is not always clear whether the *lîsṭîm* mentioned in the sources were regular robbers and, when they were not, whether they were part of the imperial establishment or belonged to its enemies, as observed above. Since the Roman authorities were not considered a legitimate government by the Jews, any representative of the occupying forces could be called a bandit by the Jews. The term "bandit" might be applied to anyone who used force to achieve his aims, whether on behalf of the Romans or in the struggle against them. The sources discussed above as well as the great number of other references to bandits in Talmudic sources leave no doubt that guerrilla fighting, terrorism, and ordinary brigandage were a chronic problem in Judea throughout the 2d and 3d centuries.

This impression is strengthened by a story in the *History* of Cassius Dio. In the reign of Severus, according to Dio, a remarkable event took place: "While Severus was very proud of his achievements [in the East], as if he had surpassed all people in insight and courage, . . . a certain bandit named Claudius was overrunning Judea and Syria and was therefore being chased with great ardour. And once he came to Severus with some cavalry, as if he were a tribune, and greeted him and embraced him, and he was not found out then nor caught afterwards" (Dio 75.2.4). There is no reason to believe that these bandits were Jews. The story resembles another recounted by Dio regarding the Italian bandit named Bulla (76.10). Dio tells the story of Claudius with relish, for his point is that Severus was engaged in futile foreign wars while he could not control banditry at home, right under his nose. We know of these events simply because a senator disliked imperial policy at the time, but that cannot lead to the conclusion that there was no banditry at other times. In fact, the Severan period is usually considered a time of relatively good relations between the Jews in Judea and the imperial authorities.

Bibliography

Alon, C. 1984. *The Jews in their Land in the Talmudic Age (70–640 C.E.).* Vol. 2. Trans. G. Levi. Jerusalem.

Applebaum, S. 1971. The Zealots: The Case for Revaluation. *JRS* 61: 156–70.

Dentzer, J.-M., ed. 1985. *Hauran I, Recherches archéologiques sur la Syrie du sud à l'époque hellenistique et romaine.* Paris.

Dussaud, R. 1927. *Topographie de la Syrie antique et médiévale.* Paris.

Gichon, M. 1982. The Military Aspects of the Bar Kokhba Revolt in the Light of the Exploration of Underground Hiding Places. *Cathedra* 26: 30–42 (in Hebrew).

Hengel, M. 1961. *Die Zeloten.* Leiden and Cologne.

Hobsbawm, E. J. 1985. *Bandits.* 2d ed. Harmondsworth.

Horsley, R. 1979. Josephus and the Bandits. *JSJ* 10: 37–63.

Horsley, R., and Hanson, J. S. 1985. *Bandits, Prophets and Messiahs.* Minneapolis.

Isaac, B. 1984. Bandits in Judaea and Arabia. *HSCP* 88: 171–203.

———. fc. *The Limits of Empire: The Roman Army in the East.* Oxford.

Kloner, A. 1983. Underground Hiding Complexes from the Bar Kokhba War in the Judaean Shephelah. *BA* 46: 210–21.

Kloner, A., and Tepper, Y. 1987. *The Hiding Complexes in the Judean Shephelah.* Tel-Aviv (in Hebrew).

Oppenheim, M. von. 1899/1900. *Vom Mittelmeer zum Persischen Golf.* Berlin.

Peters, F. 1977. The Nabateans in the Hawron. *JAOS* 97: 263–75.

Poidebard, A. 1928. Reconnaissance aérienne au Ledja et au Safa. *Syria* 9: 114–23.

Rhoads, D. M. 1976. *Israel in Revolution: 6–74 C.E.* Philadelphia.

Rougé, J. 1966. L'histoire Auguste et l'Isaurie au IVe siècle. *REA* 68: 282–315.

Schäfer, P. 1981. *Der Bar Kokhba Aufstand.* Tübingen.

Shaw, B. D. 1984. Bandits in the Roman Empire. *Past and Present* 105: 3–52.

Syme, R. 1987. Isaura and Isauria. Some Problems. Pp. 131–47 in *Sociétés urbaines, sociétés rurales dans l'Asie Mineure et la Syrie hellénistiques et romaines,* ed. E. Frézouls. Strasbourg.

Waddington, W. H., and Le Bas, P., eds. 1870. *Inscriptions grecques et latines recueillies en Grèce et en Asie Mineure.* Vol. 3/1. Paris.

Wetzstein, J. C. 1860. *Reisebericht über Hauran und die Trachonen.* Berlin.

BENJAMIN ISAAC

BANGLES. See JEWELRY.

BANI (PERSON) [Heb *bānî*]. The name of several persons found especially in the postexilic literature of Chronicles and Ezra-Nehemiah. *Bānî* is a short form of the more recognizable name BENAIAH [Heb *bĕnāyāh, bĕnāyāhû*], meaning "Yahweh has built" (from the root *bānâ,* "to build").

1. Bani the Gadite is listed as one of David's champions in 2 Sam 23:36. The corresponding reference in 1 Chr 11:38, however, reads Mibhar the son of Hagri (Heb *hagrî,* "Hagri"; instead of Heb *haggadî,* "the Gadite"), suggesting a corrupt text. The LXX references, which read "the son of Gaddi" (2 Sam 23:36) and "the son of Agari" (1 Chr 11:38) confirm this conclusion. It is thus impossible to know whether the mention of Bani here is in fact accurate.

2. Bani, the father of Azmi, was the 5th ancestor removed from Levi in the clan of Merari (1 Chr 6:31—Eng v 46). His descendant, Asaph (to whom many psalms are attributed), served in the cultic services under David.

3. Bani, from the sons of Perez, the son of Judah, was an ancestor in the family line of Uthai, one of the exiles who returned to dwell in postexilic Jerusalem (1 Chr 9:4), according to the conjectural RSV reading based on the LXX. The MT, however, reads "the son of Benjamin (Heb *bnymn*), of the sons of Perez." The name Bani here is without substantial textual support, and the MT reading of Benjamin should be preferred.

4. According to Ezra 2:10, the ancestor of one of the large family groups returning from the Exile: the sons of Bani, numbering 642. The parallel text in 1 Esdr 5:12 records the sons of Bani as numbering 648, while the parallel reading in Neh 7:15 lists "the sons of Binnui," numbering 648. Inasmuch as Bani and Binnui are short forms of the same name (see BINNUI) and that the Heb *šĕmōnâ* (eight) is easily corrupted to *šĕnayim* (two)—or *vice versa,* it is likely that the text of the lists has been corrupted. The parallel list in 1 Esdr 5:8 names one Baanah as a clan leader returning from the Exile, while 1 Esdr 5:26 lists the line of Bannas returning with the Levites. Since the names Bani, Binnui, Baanah, and Bannas are all variations on the name Benaiah, the parallel references in Ezra 2:10 and Neh 7:15 probably refer to the same person. It is not clear, however, that 1 Esdr 5:8, 26 refer to the same person listed in Ezra 2:10 and Neh 7:15. A proposed deletion of Bani in Ezra 2:10 and its reinstatement in Ezra 2:40 and Neh 7:43 lacks textual support.

5. On the other hand, Bani may have been dropped from the list in Ezra 8:10, as is suggested by several LXX variants, as well as 1 Esdr 8:36 ("and from the sons of Bani, Asalimoth, the son of Josaphias, and with him one hundred sixty men;" cf. MT [Ezra 8:10]: "and from the sons of Shelomith, the son of Josipiah, and with him one hundred sixty men"). The name Bani appears to have been dropped inadvertently from the MT at this point on account of its similarity to the preceding *mibbĕnê.* If this deduction is correct, Bani was another clan chief who accompanied Ezra back from Babylon.

6. According to the lists (Ezra 10:29, 34 = 1 Esdr 9:30 [Gk *mani*], 34) of those who had married foreign wives, several of the sons of Bani were among the accused. The MT reading of Ezra 10:38—"and Bani and Binnui: Shimei"—is probably a corruption of "and from the sons of (Heb *ûmibbĕnê*) Binnui: Shimei" (the difficulty the scribes had in distinguishing the Heb *bānî* from *mibbĕnê* has been noted above (#5).

7. Bani occurs twice in the list of those who set their seal to Nehemiah's covenant: once as a Levite (Neh 10:14—Eng v 13), and once as a chief of the people (Neh 10:15—Eng v 14).

8. Bani was one who helped Ezra the scribe instruct the people in the law (Neh 8:7).

9. Bani, the father of one Uzzi, an overseer of the Levites and a singer of the order of Asaph under Nehemiah (Neh 11:22).

10. Bani, the father of one Rehum, a Levite under Nehemiah charged with repairing a section of Jerusalem's wall adjoining that repaired by Nehemiah (Neh 3:17).

11. Bani is listed 3 times in Neh 9:4–5, twice in the series "Jeshua, Bani, Kadmiel," as one of the Levites calling out the liturgy at the Feast of Tabernacles under Ezra. The 3d instance, following the name Sherebiah in Neh 9:4, may be a dittography of the previous occurrence.

D. G. Schley

BANKING. See INTEREST AND USURY; TRADE AND COMMERCE.

BANNAS (PERSON) [Gk *Bannos*]. Possibly a variant of BANI or BINNUI, Bannas is found in 1 Esdr 5:26 as the levitical ancestor of some of the exiles who returned to Jerusalem.

D. G. Schley

BANQUET, MESSIANIC. See MESSIANIC BANQUET.

BANQUETING HALL/HOUSE [Heb *bêt hayyāyin; bêt mišteh; bêt marzēaḥ*]. In the ANE, banqueting was common among humans and gods (cf. Judg 9:13). While a "house of banqueting" may certainly refer to any place where drinking takes place, the frequent occurrence of a "house" in ceremonial and ritual contexts (cf. especially *bêt marzēaḥ* below) suggests that specific meeting places were built which functioned specifically for these banqueting purposes. Even the gods could own such "houses" (cf. *KTU* 1.114).

A. House of Wine

The expression "house of wine," *(bêt hayyāyin),* which occurs only in Cant 2:4, has occasioned a good deal of discussion. Some scholars have proposed meanings such as a wedding banquet hall, a ritual banquet house, a wine cellar, and a tavern, while others have stated that nothing more is intended than simply a house in which wine is drunk (cf. Pope *Song of Songs* AB, 374–75). The latter is more probable in the present context (cf. Cant 1:16b–17). Fox (1985: 108, 283–84) has pointed out similar booths for lovers' trysts in the Egyptian love songs.

B. House of Drinking

A more common term for a banqueting house is *bêt mišteh* which literally means "house of drinking." Jeremiah was forbidden a normal life as a sign of the impending disaster about to befall the nation. He was commanded not to enter a *bêt mišteh* which may refer to a wedding celebration (Jer 16:8–9). Alternatively, some (e.g. Pope *Song of Songs* AB, 216) have argued that the *bêt mišteh* here is roughly synonymous with a banquet house by another name mentioned in Jer 16:5, the *bêt marzēaḥ* (see below). Similarly, Qoh 7:2 contrasts the "house of feasting" with the "house of mourning."

A similar term *bêt mišteh hayyāyin* is used in Esth 7:8 to refer to the place where Esther had prepared the "wine feast," *mišteh hayyāyin.* In Daniel 5, Belshazzar holds a feast in his banquet hall *(bêt mištĕyāʾ)* and invites his lords, wives, and concubines to drink wine from the vessels which Nebuchadnezzar had stolen from the Jerusalem temple.

C. The *Marzēaḥ*

The Semitic institution known as the *marzēaḥ* has generated a considerable number of studies (for up-to-date bibliography, see Lewis 1989: 80 n.1). Although the word is spelled differently in the various languages (e.g. Akk *ma-ar-zi-ḫi, mar-ze-i, mar-zi-i, mar-za-i;* Ug *mrzḥ* and presumably *mrzʿ*), most scholars have, for the sake of discussion, adopted the convention of using the Hebrew term *marzēaḥ*. Suggestions for a possible etymology for the word *marzēaḥ* date back to Joseph Qimḥi, yet no proposal has found wide acceptance among scholars (Lewis 1989: 93). References to the *marzēaḥ* are widespread in the literature of the ANE and span nearly 2 millennia, as evidenced by Ug and Akk texts from Ugarit; passages in the books of Amos and Jeremiah; an unpublished Transjordanian settlement text of the late 7th century; Phoenician texts from Carthage and Piraeus; Aram texts from Elephantine, Palmyra, and Nabatea; rabbinical references by both the Tannaim and the Amoraim; and the mosaic map at Madeba (6th century A.D.). For convenient collections and analyses of the relevant texts see Bryan (1973), Porten (1968: 179–86), and Lewis (1989: 80–94).

Pope (*Song of Songs* AB, 210–29; 1981: 176–79) is the best example of scholars who have argued that the *marzēaḥ* was a feast for and with the departed ancestors. On the other hand, scholars such as Bryan (1973) feel that such interpretations go beyond the evidence. The question of whether the *marzēaḥ* was associated with the dead has recently been reexamined (Lewis 1989: 80–94).

1. At Ugarit. The *marzēaḥ* at Ugarit was a socioreligious organization whose leader was called a "chief," *(rb),* and whose members were called "the men of the *marzēaḥ*," *(mt mrzḥ).* The property of the *marzēaḥ* organization included vineyards, fields, storerooms, and most notably a "house." The *bêt marzēaḥ* occurs in almost every text and seems to designate the meeting place for the organization. It was presumably owned by the organization and paid for out of membership dues. It seems that the "house" could be leased as well (*KTU* 3.9). The most conspicuous activity of the *marzēaḥ* is its association with drinking (cf. El's behavior in *KTU* 1.114 and the organization's ownership of vineyards). The *marzēaḥ* organizations could grow quite powerful as evidenced by their participation in large transactions requiring many witnesses (RS 14.16) and their property-owning status. Greenfield (1976: 451–55) has noted that the organization "had state sanction since the king transferred and confirmed the ownership of *marzēaḥ* property." A notable religious feature is the association of the *marzēaḥ* organizations with a particular patron deity (cf. Šatrana in RS 15.70; Hurrian Ishtar in RS 18.01; and most likely Anat in *KTU* 4.642).

2. In the Hebrew Bible. The *marzēaḥ* occurs twice in the Heb Bible. In Amos 6:7 it is vocalized *mirzaḥ* (< **marzaḥ* < **marziḥ*) and occurs in a context where the prophet is denouncing the complacent and self-sufficient in Zion. In an elaborate woe-oracle he cries out against those living a life of luxury, sprawled on their ivory beds and taking their fill of food, drink, and music. The *marzēaḥ* described here (usually translated as "revelry") is a luxurious banquet with no hint of funerary imagery.

Jeremiah 16:5 provides the strongest evidence for the *marzēaḥ* as a funerary banquet. The context is undeniably one of mourning and bereavement over the dead. Jeremiah is commanded not to enter the *bêt marzēaḥ* (cf. the same architectural entity in the Ug texts) nor to go there to lament or grieve. In Jer 16:8 we have mention of a *bêt mišteh,* "a drinking house," which seems to be roughly synonymous with *bêt marzēaḥ*. Some scholars have argued that *bêt mišteh lōʾ tābōʾ* in v 8 forms an inclusio with *ʾal tābōʾ bêt marzēaḥ* in 16:5 (note also the chiasm).

The common denominator between the *marzēaḥ* of Amos and Jeremiah is not its funerary characteristics but its association with drinking. This is similar to the picture we get from the Ug texts. The *marzēaḥ* was an organization known for its drinking festivals which in some cases came to be associated with funerary feasts, perhaps due to the large quantity of beer which was consumed by mourners to console themselves.

3. Elsewhere. The *marzēaḥ* is mentioned in the following: (a) an unpublished Transjordanian "deed of removal" *(spr mrḥq)* from the late 7th century B.C.E.; (b) 3 Phoenician texts including the Marseilles Tariff (*KAI* 69.16), the Piraeus inscription (*KAI* 60.1) and a recently published 4th century dedicatory inscription inscribed on a bronze *philaē* (Avigad and Greenfield 1982: 118–28); (c) an ostracon from Elephantine (Sayce 1909: 154–55; Lidzbarski *Ephem* 3: 119–21), (d) a Nabatean text referring to "the *marzēaḥ* of Obodas the god" (Dalman 1912: 92–94) and a series of fragmentary Nabatean inscriptions (Negev 1961: 127–38; 1963: 113–17), (e) a large body of Palmyrene material (du Mesnil du Buisson 1962; Milik 1972; Bryan 1973: 170–97, 213–25); (f) two rabbinic texts (*Targum Pseudo-Jonathan* and *Sifre Numbers*) referring to the Baal-peor incident in Numbers 25; and (g) the phrase *BĒTOMARSEA* [= *bêt marzēaḥ*] *Ē K(AI) MAIOUMAS* on the Madeba Map.

D. Conclusions

Four features appear quite consistently throughout much of the *marzēaḥ* material: the reference to a banquet "house" belonging to the *marzēaḥ* organization or guild; the reference to a leader *(rb mrzḥʾ* or *symposiarchēs);* devotion to a deity or deities; and a good deal of drinking. The LXX of Jer 16:5 translated *marzēaḥ* to *thiasos* which evokes images of Bacchic revelry. The strongest evidence for the association of the *marzēaḥ* with the deceased is the Nabatean text referring to "Obodas the god." Nabatean kings, starting with Obodas I were regularly deified. As a social institution, the *marzēaḥ* was an organization focused on the more affluent of the various societies (Greenfield 1976: 455).

In conclusion, banqueting halls were commonplace in the ANE as evidenced by the textual and archaeological material (see Stager 1985: 172–87; King 1988: 137–61). One can only wonder whether drinking was used as a means of entering into communion with the dead. Compare the 3 parts of the Anthesteria ("opening of jars" *[pithoegia],* "beakers" *[choes],* "kettles" *[chytri])* which was the collective name for the 3-day feast of Dionysus during the Anthesterion, the month when people thought that the ghosts of the dead returned (Burkert 1985: 238).

Bibliography

Avigad, N., and Greenfield, J. C. 1982. A Bronze *phialē* with a Phoenician Dedicatory Inscription. *IEJ* 32: 118–28.

Bryan, D. B. 1973. *Texts Relating to the Marzēaḥ: A Study of an Ancient Semitic Institution.* Diss. Johns Hopkins.

Burkert, W. 1985. *Greek Religion.* Trans. John Raffan. Cambridge, MA.

Dalman, G. 1912. *Neue Petra-Forschungen und der heilige Felsen von Jerusalem.* Leipzig.

du Mesnil du Buisson, R. 1962. *Les tessères et les monnaies de Palmyre.* Paris.

Fox, M. V. 1985. *The Song of Songs and the Ancient Egyptian Love Songs.* Madison, WI.

Greenfield, J. C. 1976. The *Marzēaḥ* as a Social Institution. Pp. 451–55 in *Wirtschaft und Gesellschaft im alten Vorderasien,* ed. J. Harmatta and G. Komoróczy. Budapest.

King, P. J. 1988. *Amos, Hosea, Micah—An Archaeological Commentary.* Philadelphia.

Lewis, T. J. 1989. *Cults of the Dead in Ancient Israel and Ugarit.* HSM 39. Atlanta.

Milik, J. T. 1972. *Dédicaces faites par des dieux (Palmyre, Hatra, Tyr) et des thiases sémitiques a l'époque romaine.* Paris.

Miller, P. D. 1971. The *Mrzḥ* Text. Pp. 37–48 in *The Claremont Ras Shamra Tablets,* ed. L. R. Fisher. AnOr 48. Rome.

Negev, A. 1961. Nabatean Inscriptions from ʿAvdat (Oboda). *IEJ* 11: 127–38.

———. 1963. Nabatean Inscriptions from ʿAvdat (Oboda). *IEJ* 13: 113–24.

Pope, M. H. 1972. A Divine Banquet at Ugarit. Pp. 170–203 in *The Use of the Old Testament in the New and Other Essays,* ed. J. M. Efird. Durham, NC.

———. 1981. The Cult of the Dead at Ugarit. Pp. 159–79 in *Ugarit in Retrospect,* ed. G. D. Young. Winona Lake, IN.

Porten, B. 1968. *Archives from Elephantine.* Berkeley.

Sayce, A. H. 1909. An Aramaic Ostracon from Elephantine. *PSBA* 31: 154–55.

Stager, L. E. 1985. The Firstfruits of Civilization. Pp. 172–87 in *Palestine in the Bronze and Iron Ages,* ed. J. N. Tubb. London.

THEODORE J. LEWIS

BAPTISM. A rite of incorporation employing water as a symbol of religious purification.

A. Introductory

1. Greek Terminology. The Gk verb for "baptize," *baptizein,* is formed from *baptein,* "dip," and means "dip frequently or intensively, plunge, immerse." By Plato's time and onwards it is often used in a figurative sense (e.g., in the passive, "soaked" in wine, Plato *Symp.* 176 B). It appears 4 times in the LXX: 4 Kgdms 5:14 (Naaman in the Jordan), Jdt 12:7 (purification), Sir 34:30—Eng 34:25 (purification after touching a corpse), Isa 21:4 (figuratively of lawlessness). The noun *baptisma* is only used in Christian literature, where it refers to the baptism of John or to Christian baptism. The word *baptismos* is used in a wider sense for dipping, washing (of dishes Mark 7:4), of ritual washings (Heb 9:10; John's baptism, Joseph. *Ant.* 18.117; Christian baptism, Col 2:12 [variant]. A synonymous noun is *loutron* "bath" used of both ordinary and ceremonial baths, but in the NT only with reference to baptism. The corresponding verb *louein* "wash, bathe" is encountered in its everyday use in, e.g., 2 Pet 2:22 and John 13:10. It refers to ceremonial baths in Lev 15:11 and to Christian baptism (probably) in the compound form *apolouein* in 1 Cor 6:11.

2. Phenomenology. Rites of immersion were not uncommon in the world in which early Christianity developed. One type of symbolism with which they were frequently connected was that of purification: from sin, from destruction, from the profane sphere before entering an holy area, from something under a taboo, etc. See, e.g., Lev 16:4, 24 (the high priest before and after the rites of atonement); Leviticus 15 (on menstruating women); 1 QS 3:5–9 (cleansing from sins); *Sib. Or.* 4.165 (a baptism of repentance); Joseph. *Ant.* 18.117 (on John's baptism); Joseph. *Life.* 11 (on Bannus' ablutions for purity's sake); Apul., *Met.* 11.23 (purification at the initiation into the Isis mysteries); *b. Yebam.* 47 ab (on proselyte baptism).

Such cleansings can take place when one stands on the verge of a new state in life or is entering into a new community or upon a new phase of life, etc. Thus they can function as rites of initiation or as rites of passage. Depending on the way in which one regards the situation being left behind and the one being entered, such rites can be connected with ideas of a new birth, of a new life, or of salvation as contrasted to nothingness, chaos, death, or destruction.

3. General Orientative Remarks. In this article attention is concentrated on the ideas of baptism conveyed by the different existing NT texts from the perspective of their historical situation. This does not mean that questions of "history of tradition" are totally left aside or that problems of the prehistory of motifs, etc., are not touched upon, nor that issues of origin are not dealt with. Such problems, however, play a less important role in this presentation. Although one's way of assessing them often has consequences for one's work on the Pauline material, for example, the NT passages themselves will occupy the center of interest. While the results of such exegetical work are subject to the same lack of security as those of all historical research, attempts at reconstructing backgrounds, origins and hidden developments and changes in a history of tradition—legitimate and necessary as they are—take place on even shakier ground.

The reader should be prepared to allow for different understandings of our material. Insofar as texts are part of the communication process, it is normal to try to take into account the situation in which somebody said something to somebody in order to achieve something. But that does not necessarily mean that the author's basic ideas behind the text and their connotations were the same as those of the reader or audience even in the original situation. If, for example, Paul himself, when writing Romans 6, was not inspired by ideas concerning the initiates' dying and rising with a divinity celebrated in some mystery religion, the readers of his epistles in antiquity might very well have had their understanding colored by such associations or experiences (cf. Tert. *De Bapt.* 5, accusing the cults of Isis, of Mithras, and of Eleusis of imitating the Christian rite).

4. History of Religions Background. As already intimated, many religions in antiquity practised different washings and baths. This holds true for the mysteries of Eleusis, of Mithras, and of Isis; the OT prescribed several ablutions to be performed, rules which were observed by Jews also in NT times (John 2:6); the Qumran community laid a particular stress on them, and Bannus (Joseph. *Life.* 10) and John the Baptist were not alone in practising baptisms outside of mainstream Judaism; other baptismal movements also appeared in the Transjordanian/Syrian area. Sometime during the 1st century C.E. proselyte baptism was introduced in Judaism, and when baptism received a central place in Mandeism, the rite as such was certainly no novelty, regardless of whether it should be regarded as pre-Christian or not.

One should beware of assigning the same or even similar meanings to these rites. As rites they are open to several interpretations; in each case it is to be expected that the meaning of the rite is provided by the ritual context or otherwise through instruction or tradition.

B. Baptism of John

1. The Rite and Its Significance. The sources for our knowledge of John's baptism are the notices in the NT and a brief passage in Josephus (*Ant* 18.116–18). The baptism he performed was closely bound to his preaching, which looked forward to God's coming for judgment. He summoned his audience to repentance from this perspective, and in view of the coming judgment one underwent the baptism "unto the remission of sins" (Mark 1:4; cf. Joseph., *Ant* 18.116–18).

Although a scholarly consensus holds that John did not take over or adapt any particular baptism from his milieu, his appearance and preaching, as well as his baptism, can be regarded as one expression of expectations and ideas concerning the *eschaton* which are reflected in, among others, OT pseudepigrapha and Qumran texts. In addition, passages of such contents often contain echoes of OT passages such as Deuteronomy 30–31, Isaiah 40, Ezekiel 36, or Jeremiah 31. Thus, e.g., *Jub.* 1:22–25 and 1 QS 4:18–23 look forward to a time of repentance, when God will cleanse his people from evil through holy spirit, or give them a holy spirit and cleanse them so they do not turn away from him any more. Furthermore, when NT passages apropos of the Baptist (Mark 1:2; Matt 11:3, 10, 14; Luke 1:17, 78, etc.) indirectly refer to Malachi 3–4, this means adducing a text which illustrates the spiritual climate in which John appeared. There, in the perspective of the coming Day of Yahweh, we encounter the following motifs: a messenger sent before God (3:1), God's coming (3:1–2, 5), the coming of the Day (3:2; 4:1, 5), purification through fire (3:2–4), burning (4:1), returning to God (3:7) from sins against fellowmen (3:5) and against God (3:8–9, 13–15), the sending of Eliah before the Day comes (4:5).

John's baptism took place in view of the "coming one," who was to "baptize with the Holy Spirit and fire" (Matt 3:11–12 = Luke 3:16–17; to be preferred to Mark 1:8: "the Holy Spirit" only). The fire baptism is almost certainly an instance of judgment imagery (cf., e.g., Dan 7:10; Rev 20:10; *4 Esdr* 13:10; *Mek. Exod.* to 18.1; ed. Lauterbach vol. 2, p. 163); if we assume that "the spirit" is not a Christian interpretation, it may originally either have meant something like Isa 4:4 "a spirit of judgment and a spirit of burning"; or it may have referred to the positive outcome of the Day, which is more probable with regard to material like the passages from 1 QS and *Jub.* just mentioned.

The same background material also gives a reasonable context for distinguishing John's baptism from most other ritual baths and washings in that one most likely underwent it but once and did not perform the rite on oneself but received the baptism passively. These features, understood in the light of the Jewish material cited above, indicate that John's baptism meant that prior to the approaching divine judgment the repentants who had confessed their sins received the gift of remission. (This seems more probable than interpreting the baptism as meaning an assurance or a hope of being remitted in the coming judgment.) In contrast to the Qumran community, John directed his call for repentance and baptism to all the people, notwithstanding which the rite came in fact to function like a rite of initiation into a group of people who, being pardoned, expected "the stronger one" to come. They also probably followed an ethic which was inspired by John's preaching and its eschatological outlook (Mark 2:18; Luke 3:10–14; 11:1). John's appearance in the wilderness and baptizing in the Jordan point to some sort of Exodus typology, meaning that here a renewed Israel was being created. The group hardly formed anything like a community or a sect, but NT passages (Mark 2:18–19; 6:29; Matt 11:2; Luke 11:1; John 1:35–37; 3:22; 25; Acts 19:1–7; see also *Ps. Clem. recogn.* 1.54, 60; ed. Rehm), as well as certain traces in the Mandean material, point to the existence of groups that regarded themselves as "disciples of John," both in his lifetime and after.

In the NT gospels, John and his baptism are given a two-sided treatment. On the one hand, they are seen as the necessary preparation for Jesus, the Messiah; on the other, their importance is played down. For Mark, John and his baptism certainly belong to "the beginning of the gospel of Jesus Christ, God's son" (Mark 1:1), but his baptism is contrasted with that of him who follows after, "the stronger one," viz., Jesus, who will baptize "with the Spirit." (Consequently, Jesus does not begin his public preaching until "after" John has been arrested; Mark 1:14). Mark does not return to the topic of baptism, but presumably his readers have had the common early Christian conviction of being equipped with the Holy Spirit, and consequently have associated John's words with Christian baptism.

Matthew (3:5–6) does not say that John's baptism was for the remission of sins—perhaps the evangelist was of the opinion that remission was only given through Jesus (Matt 1:21; 26:28). That the coming one was to baptize "in Holy Spirit and fire" (3:11) may possibly have been understood as saying 2 things: the "fire" probably refers to the judgment (3:10, 12; 7:19; 13:40, 42, 50; 18:9; 25:41), a judgment held by the Son of Man (13:40–43; 25:31–46). On the other hand, the Matthew context suggests that the baptism "in the Holy Spirit" is the baptism in the name of the Trinity (28:19), ordered by the risen Son of Man.

In Luke the baptism with the Spirit clearly is the one described in Acts, through which "the coming one" gathers his people (Luke 3:17); since the author repeats John's saying in Acts (1:5) without mentioning the fire (in spite of Acts 2:3!), it seems that by baptism "in fire" (Luke 3:16) he refers to the future burning of the chaff, i.e., the annihilation of the evil in judgment. John's water-baptism is contrasted to the Christian community's receiving of the Spirit (Acts 1:5; 19:1–7).

In the Gospel of John, finally, John's water-baptism is still seen as ordered by God (1:33), but John's role is only that of the precursor. He must "diminish" (3:30) at the arrival of him over whom the Spirit descends and who baptizes with the Holy Spirit (1:33). Thus, the importance of John's baptism is further played down and contrasted with Christ's Spirit-baptism. In the context of John, the latter means that through the completion of the work of the Son, leading to his "glorification" (cf., e.g., 7:39), the life-giving effects of this work are given to men (see further below, on John 3:5).

2. Jesus' Baptism by John. That Jesus was baptized by John is historically certain. It must have been embarrassing to the early Church that its Lord had taken on the ritual sign of repentance, and thus, in some way or another, regarded himself in the light of John's preaching of confession of sins and a return to God in view of the approaching final crisis, including the coming of the stronger one. The history of tradition of the story is problematic (Mark 1:9–11; the "Q" version, distinguishable in Matt 3:13–17 = Luke 3:21–22, is rather similar; see also John 1:32–34).

As presented finally in all 3 of the Synoptic Gospels, the story has a Christological accent.

Thus, in Mark (1:9–11) the brief mention of Jesus' baptism (v 9b) is immediately followed by a report of a combined vision and audition by Jesus, which make evident to the reader who the main character of the Gospel is, viz., the divinely authorized messianic Son. In Matthew a dialogue between John and Jesus is added (3:14-15), which explains that Jesus is baptized, not because he—the stronger one—needs it, but because both of them must "fulfill (5:17) all righteousness," i.e., the baptism belongs to that which God wants. This motif of righteousness is related to the sonship (in 3:17 proclaimed to others than Jesus): in Matthew divine sonship means radical obedience to God's will (4:1–11; 26:39; 27:43). Thus, Matthew's baptism story presents Jesus as an example in humility and obedience (Matt 5:9, 45). For Matthew's reader, Jesus' baptism may also have been taken to indicate that he became a model: as he was baptized, so were the Christians of later times (28:19), and as he fulfilled all righteousness, so righteousness was demanded from them (5:20; 28:20).

In Luke's version (Luke 3:21–22), the baptism itself is pushed even further aside and separated from what follows through a reference to Jesus' praying; in this way the language of the story moves it rapidly towards the public presentation and proclamation of Jesus as God's son, working under God's Spirit (3:38; 4:1, 14, 18). Finally, in John knowledge of Jesus' baptism seems to be presupposed (1:32–34; 3:26), although it is not explicitly mentioned.

We have seen that in their redaction Mark and Luke have not connected Jesus' baptism with that of the Church, but given it a Christological function. So has Matthew, but in such a way that Jesus can be seen also as an example in baptism. On the other hand, Christian readers of Mark and Luke who believed that their baptism was combined with the receiving of the Spirit and who were wont to see themselves in some sense as God's sons or children (Rom 8:14; Gal 3:26)—or who at least knew to turn to God as "Abba" (Luke 11:2; cf. Mark 11:25; Rom 8:15; Gal 4:6)—might naturally have seen their own baptism prefigured in Jesus' baptism by John.

C. Baptism of the Early Church

1. The Beginnings. a. Origin of Christian Baptism. Several reasons favor the assumption that baptism was practised from the very beginning in the early Church as some sort of initiatory rite. Not only does Luke take it for granted in Acts, but so do authors who represent other strands of the early Church and as far as we can see they do so independently of each other (Paul, "John," "Matthew"). Indications that in some place there was no baptizism from the beginning fail to convince most NT scholars. Thus, the lack in Matthew 10 of a commission to baptize is usually explained in other ways. The case is similar to that of the prohibition to go the Gentiles (10:5): In both instances Matthew has his reader wait until 28:17–20. Luke takes care of baptism as the initiatory rite in Acts 2. (It seems to have been an impossible thought to the synoptists to insert a commission to baptize into the story of Jesus' public ministry.) Acts 18:24–19:7 certainly raises some questions for anyone who assumes that baptism was generally practised in early Christianity from its beginning. But it seems that the difficulty is rather the result of Luke's redaction in combining the 2 passages than an indication that in the A.D. 50s there were Jesus-disciples who did not know of Christian baptism.

Thus, if the practice of baptism was general from the beginning of the early Church, all the more intriguing is the question of its origin. John 3:22 and 26 suggest that Jesus had been involved in baptizing, but this is corrected in 4:2 which says that it was his disciples who baptized. Should this be a case in which John provides us with more and better historical knowledge than the Synoptic Gospels, it would point only to such an activity occurring at the very beginning of Jesus' career. Jesus himself apparently did not baptize, and thereafter, in the main part of his public ministry, baptizing apparently had to give way to his preaching and disappeared. Thus, the Jesus who preached the gospel of the Kingdom and summoned people to conversion and belief, did not combine this proclamation with a demand for or invitation to baptism.

The historical riddle is not solved by Matt 28:19, since, according to a wide scholarly consensus, it is not an authentic saying of Jesus, not even an elaboration of a Jesus-saying on baptism. Jewish proselyte baptism has been proposed as the usage the early Church took over and christianized. The practice did exist in the 1st century C.E. and therefore early enough to be adopted by the Christians. Certainly it was more of an initiation rite than the purification baths and the sprinklings prescribed in the OT, and thus invites a comparison with Christian baptism. But it was not associated with any remission of sins or with any other eschatological meanings, nor was it a passive rite: one immersed oneself, although in the presence of 2 men learned in the Law (*b. Yebam.* 47a). Thus, proselyte baptism was hardly the occasioning factor behind Christian baptism, nor for that matter behind John's baptism.

Instead, according to a rather common scholarly opinion, John's baptism is the point of departure of Christian baptismal practice. We have already seen that John's baptism was connected with eschatological expectations, and so was the baptismal rite of the early Church (Acts 2:38–40; John 3:5; Rom 6:4–5; Tit 3:5–7). Both were associated with an act of conversion and were performed "unto the remission of sins" (Mark 1:4; Acts 2:38 etc.). Repentance opened the door to a community which in some respect or another formed a preparatory stage for the *eschaton*. Thus each of the two rites also became a kind of initiation rite, which was only performed once. (This is certain in the case of Christian baptism and probably in that of John). Last, but not least, as already mentioned, both rites were received passively, in that someone else immersed the person being baptized or poured water on him. That Jesus and (some of) his disciples had been baptized by John should have favored the adoption of a baptismal rite, but as we now have them, the versions of the baptism of Jesus show no traces of its having been an etiological story with the function of explaining the adoption of the rite.

If the early Church thus inherited its baptism from John, we would like to know the reason why but are only left with the impression that it was a natural practice—one did not have to defend or to explain it, at least not in such a way as to be visible in the documents left behind. But the conviction of Jesus' followers that his resurrection brought about a decisive shift in eschatological perspective (Acts 17:31; 1 Cor 15:20–21; 1 Thess 1:10) is most likely to have been an important factor that made it natural to take up John's baptism, loaded as it was with eschatological associations. But the role of Jesus Christ and the Christ-event necessitated its becoming a baptism "into the name of the Lord Jesus" or something similar.

b. "Into the name of the Lord Jesus." It is relatively certain that in the early Church one commonly referred to baptism as being done "into the name of the Lord Jesus" or something similar. One strange thing with this phrase is that the construction in what seems to be its earliest form, viz. "into the name of . . ." (Gk *eis to onoma*) was not otherwise used in normal Gk, except for the language of banking, in which it referred to the account/name "into" which a sum of money was placed. It does not occur in the LXX.

NT scholarship has generally assumed that the phrase meant that the baptized person was dedicated to the heavenly *kyrios.* One has either assumed (with W. Heitmüller) that the one baptized was compared with a sum of money added to somebody's bank account, or one has adduced a Mishnah passage quoted by P. Billerbeck, *m. Zebaḥ.* 4.6, which states that a sacrifice has to be offered "into the name of the Name." This expression is then understood as saying that the sacrifice must be offered to God. The difficulty with the first explanation is that it is hard to imagine how one came upon the idea of using such odd imagery. The second one certainly explains the Gk phrase: it is a literal translation of Heb-Aram *lšm/lšwm.* The suggested meaning of the phrase has not enough support, however, in the material adduced. The context of the cited *m. Zebaḥ.* 4.6 rules that the sacrifice also has to be offered "into the name of the offerer," i.e., that one should bear in mind who it is that presents the offering. This observation shows that the Heb-Aram phrase does not have anything to do with dedication. Nor does the Gk phrase insofar as it would be a literal translation of the Sem wording.

In this situation the present writer has suggested that the phrase was coined by the Palestinian Church in Heb (or Aram) and that it was then translated literally into Gk. One should look, however, for a different meaning of the phrase than the ones noted so far. Among other usages of the *lšm/lšwm* there was also one which is found in ritual contexts. Thus we hear of gatherings "into the name of Heaven" (*m. ʾAbot* 4.11), of sacrifices slaughtered "into the name of the Name" (*m. Zebaḥ.* 4.6), or "into the name of the mountains" (*m. Ḥul.* 2.8), of circumcision "into the name of Mount Gerizim" (*t. ʿAbod. Zar.* 3.13), and of knowing "into whose name" one vows (*m. Nid.* 5.6). In these and similar examples the phrase indicates what the fundamental reference of the rite in question is. It is reasonable to assume that early Christianity characterized its baptism using this halfway technical language, and that the formula followed the rite also into Gk-speaking circles. Matthew is witness to the usage of the expression also in other contexts (10:41–42; 18:20), as well as applied to baptism (28:19). In Acts, Luke reveals that "into the name of the Lord Jesus" (Acts 8:16; 19:5) was the formula that he had learned. It is also known by Paul, perhaps as connected with another way of naming Christ (1 Cor 1:13, 15 say only "Christ," Gal 3:27 "into Christ," and Rom 6:3 "into Christ Jesus."

Applying baptism to the analogies mentioned in the preceding paragraph should indicate that baptizing "into the name of Jesus" (etc.) meant that one saw Jesus as the fundamental reference of the rite. This could involve a negative and a positive definition. Negatively it distinguished Christian baptism from other similar rites (not least the baptism of John, as in Acts 19:1–7). Positively it should suggest what baptism meant with Jesus as its fundamental reference, viz., there should be some sort of Christology behind it. But the more specific implications of the expression are likely to have been different in different times and places. If it meant one thing in its first context, this would not preclude its being understood or interpreted in a different manner in another situation or by other early Christian theologians.

In Acts 2:38 and 10:48 the phrase is "in the name . . ." (the Gk prepositions being *epi* and *en* respectively). It has been assumed that they represent variant traditions. In the opinion of the present writer they should rather be explained as examples of Luke's technique as an author of letting the characters in his book speak in a way that suited them. Thus Peter, the revered apostle, is made to express himself in a biblical style when talking of baptism in 2:38 and 10:48: The prepositional phrases in these cases are common in the LXX (which Luke also imitates elsewhere), whereas, as we have seen, the Gk "into the name . . ." *(eis to onoma)* is both unbiblical and a bit strange as compared to normal Gk.

It should also be mentioned, however, that both in Biblical Gk and in rabbinic traditions the "name" phrases could be rather loose and have relatively small weight. Thus, in a rabbinical discussion one could slip from "into the name of x" to "into x" without changing the sense of the phrase (e.g., *m. ʿAbod. Zar.* 3.7; cf. *b. ʿAbod. Zar.* 48a). In Luke 21:12, Luke can write "because of my name," where the parallels in Mark and Matthew say "because of me," and the same Luke in Acts 10:43 can write about forgiveness of sins "through his name" and in Acts 13:38 "through him." Similarly in the Psalms, one calls "on the Lord's name" as well as "on the Lord." This flexibility probably is true also of the baptismal formula and would then be the explanation why Paul can switch between "into the name" (1 Cor 1:13) and "into" without "the name" (as in 1 Cor 10:2 etc.). Such a flexibility may have facilitated Paul's finding a particular meaning in the phrase "baptized into Christ,"—viz. that of being put into and united with the body of Christ. Luke's usage of "*in* the name" (*en* or *epi;* Acts 2:38; 10:48), apparently without meaning anything else than do the "into" formulas, is another indication of how the name phraseology was not very fixed. In spite of the normal conservatism of ritual language, one was not totally bound; thus Paul is probably thinking of baptism in 1 Cor 6:11, but there the phrase is "*in* the name of the Lord" instead of "into. . . ."

The repeated use of "into the name" etc., raises the question whether the name of Jesus (etc.) was actually mentioned at the ministration of baptism. In the NT, Jas 2:7 has been cited as support for the supposition that it was. *Herm. Sim.* 8:6, 4 alludes to the passage, but without clear reference to baptism, while Just. *1 Apol.* 61.10–13 refers to such a practice using similar language. The usage of the *lšm* phrase in the rabbinic regulations may possibly add some extra strength to the supposition. It seems that when somebody presented an offering in the temple, he declared what kind of offering he was giving: cf., e.g., *b. Pesaḥ.* 60a: "Behold, I slaughter the Pesah into its name," i.e., "this is a passover sacrifice." The parallel would then intimate that the purpose or the fundamental reference of baptism was mentioned at the rite and that this was done in such a way that Jesus was mentioned. Indirectly Paul's argument in 1 Cor 1:13, 15 also suggests such a practice.

2. Corpus Paulinum. a. Paul. Paul does not present any direct teaching on baptism as such, but several times he argues other matters by making use of ways of thinking of baptism. In order that his argument be accepted by his addressees, he often refers to or quotes opinions on or understandings of baptism which have also been held by other early Christian theologians, including his opponents or those addressees whom he did not know personally. In most of these cases we can feel certain that Paul has agreed with them; in others he may have modified the opinion he cites (Rom 6:3–4) or just quoted it as an argument without sharing it (1 Cor 15:29). Given this place of baptism in Paul's writings, we have to realize that his view on baptism is largely hidden behind his epistles, in which we mostly only perceive what he regards as implications or consequences of his theology of baptism. Consequently any attempt to make a historically based reconstruction of Paul's thinking in these matters runs the risk of stressing wrong aspects and leaving out others which may have been important to him, but did not happen to be needed for his arguments in the letters we have access to. To these cautions should be added the circumstance that one of the more important texts, Rom 6:1–14, places the interpreter before an exceptionally great number of difficulties in terms of language, content, and function with regard to the receivers.

In 1 Cor 1:12–17 Paul says that he is thankful that he baptized only a few of the Corinthians, "for Christ did not send me to baptize but to preach the gospel" (v 17). This remark is generally understood as showing no contempt on Paul's part for baptism. Rather he let his coworkers baptize, and it is probable that baptizing meant not only performing the rite but also taking an active part in preparation for it. This can explain how people came to rally around a teacher like Apollos (1 Cor 1:12).

As noted, Paul knows of the baptismal formula "into the name of. . . ." But in his arguments he may instead write "into (Gk *eis*) Christ" (Rom 6:3; Gal 3:27; cf. 1 Cor 10:2: "into Moses," and 1 Cor 12:13: "into one body"), or "in (Gk *en*) the name of the Lord Jesus Christ" (1 Cor 6:11). In this way Paul connects certain concepts about Christ and his importance with baptism. Thus in 1 Cor 1:12 it seems that the "party" designations ("I belong to Apollos" etc.) make Paul think of one effect of baptism, viz., that one can say "I belong to Christ" (1 Cor 1:12; 3:23; Gal 3:29). Then he immediately ironically states that he himself was not crucified for the Corinthians, nor were they baptized "into Paul's name." This indicates that to Paul baptism somehow made Christ's crucifixion a crucifixion "for" (Gk *hyper*) the one baptized. In other words, one "belongs to Christ" through baptism, which applies Christ's vicarious death to the person being baptized. Thus the soteriological center of Paul's thinking was a central motif in his understanding of baptism.

The preaching which gathered around this center had to be received in faith, a faith that meant that the believer was put right with God (justified), according to the contents of the kerygma. Inasmuch as it also is intimated that one enters this blessed state through baptism, the question arises regarding the relationship between faith and baptism. There is no tension or contradiction to be seen between the two. Thus, according to Gal 3:26–29 men are "God's sons through faith in Christ Jesus," but this statement is explained by the next one, which says "for all of you who were baptized into Christ, put on Christ." One may say that faith is the subjective side of the receiving of the gift of salvation, baptism the objective side. Furthermore, although 1 Cor 6:11 might be traditional, in its Pauline context it interprets the gifts of baptism as not only "you were washed," and "you were sanctified," but also "you were justified," namely "in the name of the Lord Jesus Christ." Here baptism is associated with all the wealth Paul otherwise connects with the salvific gospel which reveals the righteousness of God through faith (Rom 1:16–17; 5:1–2, etc.).

Already the short remark in 1 Cor 1:13 and its implications point to how Paul—and other early Christian theologians—have wrestled, in part unconsciously, with a task that occurs in many religions: how to relate a fundamental divine act in the past to later times, be that act creation, the Exodus, the death and refinding of Osiris, or Christ's death and resurrection. One needs a bridge between past and present, or, to use different language, an actualization of the past in the present or an understanding of the present in the light of the past. In our case, a kind of actualization of Jesus' salvific act was made in the preaching of the gospel and in its reception in faith *and* in baptism as well.

The topic of actualizing Christ's death and resurrection—the fundamental salvific act—reappears somewhat more specifically, in Rom 6:1–14, where it is part of Paul's argument in defense of the principle of justification by faith without following the Law. His real or imagined opponents accuse him of holding that the law-free gospel he preached meant that one had better "remain in sin, in order that grace may abound" (3:8; 6:1, 15). Over against this accusation Paul launches a tightly knit and rather complicated argument, which partly makes use of elements from tradition. His thesis is that "we who died to sin" cannot "live in it" (6:2).

The argument takes its departure in the statement that baptism "into Christ Jesus" means baptism "into his death" (v 3), indeed, being "buried with him" (v 4) (cf. the tradition in 1 Cor 15:3–7: "Christ died, . . . was buried, . . . was raised . . .") The statement in v 3 is something on which Paul and his opponents agree—otherwise the argument would not work. In other words, baptism "actualized" Christ's death for the one being baptized. The dying and burial with Christ also had an aim, namely that, as he was raised, "so also we should walk in newness of life" (v 4b), i.e., here it is Christ's resurrection which is actualized. In v 5 the consequences of baptism are expressed in a slightly different way. The sentence presents them in a protasis-apodosis construction. The protasis (v 5a) "if we are united with the counterpart of his death" is a variation of the statement concerning the sharing of Christ's death (v 3). Also the apodosis varies the preceding argument, viz., that baptism means that one should walk in newness of life: "we shall be (united with the counterpart) to his resurrection" (a literal rendering of a relatively common way of understanding the difficult construction.) It is now noteworthy that, according to Paul, baptism into Christ's death meant life with the raised Christ in an ethical duty to "newness of life" in the present time (v 4b), and also a hope of sharing his resurrectional life in the (personal or cosmic) *eschaton.* (Some, however, take the future in v 5b as hortative.) From v 6 onwards Paul explains, reconfirms and develops his argument: "we (who died in baptism)" is specified as "our old person," who was "crucified with (Christ)," i.e., the former ("adamitic") conditions under the reign of sin in hostility to God (cf. 5:10) or in estrangement from him, were abolished. Step by step, Paul then forces his way through to a conclusion in 6:12–14: "Thus sin must not reign in your mortal body, so that you obey its passions" (v 12). He arrives there via these stepping stones concerning Christ: "somebody who is dead is not accused of sin (lit.: is justified from sin)" (v 7); Christ died, and did so "to sin once for all" (v 10); Christ is alive (v 9); Christ "lives to God" (v 10). Here are the parallel steps concerning Christians: "we died with him" (v 8); "you must consider yourselves dead to sin (v 11a); "we shall live with him" (v 8); "we must consider ourselves alive to God" (v 11b).

This sketchy scrutiny of Rom 6:1–14 has pointed to some negative and some positive consequences of baptism as Paul sees it: It meant a liberation not from sinning, but from sin's reign, from living according to the conditions of its power. Liberation is real but not automatic; it must be realized in a life lived to God, a life that looks forward to its fulfillment in resurrection (v 5, 8) and eternal life (v 22–23).

The baptismal liberation from sin's power is a positive, dynamic factor in the life of the Christian: In Rom 6:4 it is called "newness of life." This can be contrasted to "our old man" (v 6), and stands for new conditions in which one lives in and under Christ (cf. "new creation," 2 Cor 5:17; Gal 6:15). These conditions are described in another picture in Gal 3:27: in baptism one "puts on Christ." In Biblical language, clothes can be a metaphor for life conditions, essential equipment, etc. (2 Chr 6:41 and Isa 61:10: salvation; Ps 93:1: power; Bar 5:1: glory of God, etc.). Thus Christ, what he has achieved, what he is, and what he stands for, is the life-conditioning, decisive basis of a Christian existence.

The same new conditions are also touched upon in 1 Cor 6:11, "you were sanctified," i.e., brought into a realm which more than others belongs to God and where he is present in a particular sense. This "sanctification," together with a "washing" and a "justification" took place "in the name of our Lord Jesus Christ" and "in the Spirit of our God," i.e., the Christ-related blessings of baptism were given through the powerful working in the present by God himself, who stands behind the giving as well as the reception of these blessings. Lastly it must be pointed out that, precisely as in Romans 6, Paul is arguing a case of morality in 1 Cor 6: It is important to his argument that these God-given new life-conditions bring with them a duty to practice them in an ethically responsible life. Once again, the eschatological perspective is present: In the argument Paul says as a warning, "The unrighteous will not inherit the kingdom of God" (6:9).

That the Spirit is the power at work in baptism is also expressed in 1 Cor 12:13. Also here Paul takes a recognized opinion as a point of departure for an argument: "We were baptized in (or: through) one spirit into one body." We need not discuss whether the Spirit is thought of here as the mode or the means of baptism into the one body—it is both. But it is also a gift connected with baptism, as is seen from the next clause "and we were all made to drink of one Spirit" or, better, "we all had one Spirit poured over us" (v 13b). Possibly 2 Cor 1:22 also refers to baptism (as a seal) on which occasion God also gave the Spirit as a pledge—a pledge of the further eschatological gifts, the Spirit itself being one of them (Rom 8:23; cf. Acts 2:16–21).

1 Cor 12:13 also points to another aspect of Paul's thought on baptism: that it brings with it a unity of the ones baptized. This unity is constituted by the one life, which is given from and in community with the one Christ (in his body, the church in Corinth), as well as by the one Spirit. Whereas in 1 Cor this view is a point of departure for an argument concerning how to deal with the different pneumatic gifts, the same theme also appears in Galatians (3:26–29), and there is an argument for the view that Gentile Christians are God's sons through faith and therefore Abraham's seed (see also 1 Cor 1:10–13). In both passages we encounter what may be a traditional formula: "there is neither Jew nor Greek, there is neither slave nor freeman, there is no male and female" (the last clause only in Galatians; cf. also Col 3:11). This means seeing baptism as having rather radical consequences. The common life in Christ, into which one was baptized, implied a unity and a solidarity which questioned religious, cultural, and social conditions of the ordinary world order.

It has been suggested that this close Christ-relationship which, according to Paul, is a consequence of baptism, was also implied in his use of the formula "(baptize) into Christ." Namely, should this expression be understood locatively, so that baptism meant being put into Christ, the New Adam, a kind of corporate personality? As the expression is so vague and, therefore, so capable of several interpretations, such an understanding is not impossible. For the same reason 1 Cor 10:2 ("our fathers . . . were all baptized into Moses") cannot decisively speak against it, although the idea is certainly not that the Israelites were incorporated, so to speak, into Moses, but rather that "Moses" represented the salvation and revelation at the Exodus.

Finally, Paul can also speak of the Christ relationship established through faith and baptism using terms of ownership (1 Cor 1:12; Gal 3:27; cf. 1 Cor 3:23). That a man "belongs to" or is a slave to his god, who is his "master" or "lord," is a common idea in the world of religions (see, e.g., Isa 44:5). Man's god has him at his command and takes care of him. Given the widely spread confession of Jesus as the Lord *(kyrios),* the idea of belonging to him is near at hand (1 Cor 7:22). The metaphor of sealing in 2 Cor 1:22 has a similar meaning and may possibly refer to baptism. As a matter of fact, the idea of being sanctified at baptism (1 Cor 6:11) has similar connotations, for priests, offerings, buildings, etc., are "sanctified" (see, e.g., Exod 28:36; 29:44; Judg 17:3; 2 Chr 29:5) to God, and belong to him for that reason; they are there for his service and are under his protection. We should also remember that an essential aspect in the thinking concerning the covenant between God and his people was that he was their God and they his people (e.g., Deut 29:13; for the new covenant see, e.g., Jer 31:31).

b. Extra-Pauline Understandings of Baptism in Paul's Letters. We have touched upon interpretations of baptism which Paul presupposes are known and accepted by his addressees. Since these addressees in some cases are unknown to him (which is largely true of his Roman addressees) and are sometimes opposed to him (Romans; 1, 2 Corinthians), it is reasonable to assume that these interpretations are also held by non-Pauline theologians in the early Church.

Such "extra-Pauline" interpretations of baptism involve views of entering a relationship to Christ, receiving the remission of one's sins for Christ's sake (1 Cor 1:13; 6:11), dying and rising with him (Rom 6:3–8), becoming his possession or his slave (1 Cor 3:23; 2 Cor 1:22; Gal 3:29). The Spirit was somehow also connected with baptism in other minds than Paul's. Thus, some have been of the opinion that the Spirit was at work in baptism and that Christians then were endowed with it (1 Cor 6:11; 12:13). In Rom 6:3–8 there are good reasons to believe that Paul subjects the more widespread view to adaptation. This view may have been that baptism meant sharing Christ's resurrection (Col 2:12; 3:1), i.e., some sort of "realized eschatology," whereas Paul is anxious to stress that the resurrection belongs to the future. The adaptation may be caused by an enthusiastic understanding of baptism that Paul has met in Corinth, and which he seeks to restrain. It can be discerned behind the overestimation of glossolalia (the language of the angels, 1 Cor 13:1?) and behind the denial of the coming death and resurrection (1 Corinthians 15; 2 Tim 2:18). A belief that baptism ensured life in an almost magic way may also explain the practice of being baptized on behalf of dead people, mentioned in 1 Cor 15:29. A similar attitude of overestimating the effect of baptism (and of the eucharist) in Corinth seems to lie behind 1 Cor 10:1–13. Paul attacks a sense of security that can be built on such an attitude. That "the fathers" were baptized (in the sea), ate the spiritual food, and drank of Christ (the rock) as Paul points out, did not save them from God's wrath when they sinned.

c. The Pauline School. The author of Colossians stands close to Paul and is well versed in his letters. (Note, however, that some exegetes do not think that Colossians is deutero-Pauline.) In using baptismal motifs as a basis for arguing against a certain "philosophy," he differs somewhat from Paul's thinking as seen in Rom 6:4–5: According to Colossians baptism is not only a death and a burial with Christ (2:12, 20), but also a resurrection with him "through faith in the power of God who raised him from the dead" (2:12). The role of faith is natural also to this author, but it is emphasized that it is directed towards a victor: Baptism means, namely, sharing the destiny of Christ who, in his resurrection, triumphed over the cosmic powers (2:15) which were the authorities to which the "philosophy" referred (2:8, 16–23). As united with this sovereign, the baptized Christians are carried—indeed even "filled"—by his divine "fullness" (2:9–10). Entering the flock of this supreme ruler meant being pardoned all previous sins (1:14; 2:13) and being saved from the power of darkness (1:13), and being moved instead by God into the kingdom of his son and becoming an heir of the lot of the holy ones in light (1:12). The life the Christian has "with Christ" after the death "with him" is a "hidden" one, but one which looks forward to glory at Christ's "revelation" (3:4), which is to say that the present participation in Christ's triumph is coupled with an eschatological expectation.

Baptism is mentioned also under the imagery of circumcision (2:11). On the one hand, this is made to signify that in baptism the "body of the flesh" (2:11), or the "old person and his deeds" (3:9), was put away, i.e., the previous conditions were changed in which one's person was dominated by this-worldly, nondivine factors. On the other hand, it also indicated that the hindrance to belonging to God's people was eliminated (cf. 2:13).

The optimistic and empowering aspect of the consequences of baptism in Colossians is balanced by the parenesis in 3:1–4:6. As in Romans 6, it is a principal point that the life given in baptism has to be lived. The new—indeed radically new—conditions of a new humanity united with Christ and sustained by him as the true image of God (3:10–11; Gal. 3:27–28) imply an imperative to strive for their realization in life and may even have been a social challenge.

Ephesians contains many echoes from the author's thought on baptism, so many, in fact, that it has been suggested that the epistle is a baptism homily or represents a baptismal liturgy. This can hardly be regarded as more than conjecture. But given that the epistle stands in the same Pauline tradition as Colossians (although later), one cannot but recognize the indirect references to baptism and its impact. In Ephesians, however, as distinguished from earlier texts in the Pauline tradition, baptism is not brought in to serve an argument concerning something else, but seems to be almost the warp on which the whole letter is woven.

Baptism becomes a focus of God's immense salvific work: He is the one active behind it and in it (1:3–14; 2:4–10), from the election before the foundation of the world and via the work of Christ on to the eschatological goal, the "heritage," of which the Spirit is a pledge (1:14). The pre-Christian state of the addressees was like a death or a darkness or a sleep (2:1, 5; 5:8, 14). More specifically, they were sinful Gentiles, not belonging to God's people (2:1–3, 11–12). But faith in the gospel of salvation, along with receiving baptism (1:13), meant forgiveness (1:7; 2:7; 4:32) and life and light—already now—through Christ (2:5–6; 5:14). They were "sealed" through the Spirit of the promise (1:13), i.e., the Spirit signified that they belonged to God and had the promise of receiving the heritage (cf. Ezek 9:4; Isa 44:5). Given this picture of the pre-Christian situation, baptism is not described as a death or burial with Christ, but as a resurrection with him, indeed, being enthroned with him (Eph 2:6). The Christian is carried by the same divine power as Christ (1:20) and has "access to the Father" (2:18), or using another image, the Christian is joined to a Temple of God, built on Christ, the cornerstone (2:20–22). This ecclesiological perspective of "realized eschatology" is found also in 5:25–26: Christ gave himself up for the Church "in order that he sanctify her, cleansing her by the washing of water, in the word." In individual baptisms, Christ's self-sacrifice is applied, and the rite adds new members to the Church, which is presented as a bride, cleansed by the bridal bath. The phrase "in the word" is difficult: Either it refers to something said at baptism which in some way mentioned Christ and/or his work, or it has to do with Christ's sanctifying the Church through his word. That this Church is one is mentioned in the formula of 4:5–6: Baptism unites all believers in the same faith in the one Lord.

Also in Ephesians the new, real conditions given in baptism are the basis of a duty to live a moral life (4:22–24). The older conditions are certainly left behind (2:1, 5; 5:8, 14), but nevertheless they still make their claims; so "the old man" must be put off and "the new man" must be put on (4:20–24), i.e., the life in Christ has to be realized as exemplified in the parenesis in 4:25–5:14.

Also in Titus (3:5) baptism is the crucial point in the application of God's saving act through Christ to the individual. In imitation of Paul, the author contrasts God's grace behind this means of salvation to man's deeds of righteousness, which did not bring this salvation. The pre-Christian situation is painted in dark colors: foolishness, disobedience, lusts, etc. (3:3). In baptism, however, God saved the Christian from this condition for a life of "righteousness" (1 Tim 6:11; Titus 2:12; 3:7). The effect of baptism is described as "regeneration" (cf. John 3:5; 1 Pet 2:2) and renewal (cf. 2 Cor 5:17; Gal 6:15; Eph 2:15; 4:24). The former imagery can be compared with the Jewish statement that a proselyte is as a newborn child (*b. Yebam.* 48b). The renewal is effected by the Holy Spirit, the gift of which is connected with baptism, and it all gives the Christian the hope of inheriting eternal life (3:5–7). That the admonitions in 3:8–11 follow the utterances on baptism is a sign that also for this author baptismal renewal has to have a counterpart in real life.

3. Gospel of Matthew. It has been noted above that Matthew's version of the story of Jesus' baptism (3:13–17) not only has a Christological point; it also presents Jesus' baptism as a model of the audience's baptism. Matt 28:19 represents the evangelist's conviction that his Church practiced baptism in accordance with Jesus' will and reflects the baptismal formula in use there (cf. *Did.* 7:1, 3). The main verb of the commission in 28:19 is "make disciples." Becoming a disciple in Matthew's view means to cling to Jesus, to whom the Father has given all authority (v 18), listen to his words, and do his will. Baptism is the step into discipleship—faith is not mentioned, but is presupposed (cf. 18:6). Matt 18:20 ("gather 'into' my name") demonstrates that Matthew retains what above was claimed to be the original meaning of performing a rite "into the name of . . .," viz., that the name indicated the fundamental reference of the rite. What is new in Matthew is the mention of the Trinity in the baptismal formula (the actual thought of the Father and the Spirit together with the Son is found also in Ephesians 1–2 and Titus 3, dealt with above). God the origin and goal, whom Jesus called his Father (7:21; 10:32; 26:42 etc.) and whose will he performed (26:42), was also the Father of the disciples (5:16, 45, 48; 6:9 etc.). He turned to man in the words and works of the Son, but also in the Spirit, the power of the present, active God (1:18; 12:28; cf. 10:20). Thus, the rite of baptism had as its basis the salvific work of a God who communicated with man in these ways. Probably the words of John the Baptist in 3:11 ("baptize in holy spirit") are seen as fulfilled in Christian baptism—because of the central position of Jesus Christ for discipleship it can be said that, in a sense, he is the one who baptizes.

4. Acts of the Apostles. It should be borne in mind that Acts is simply a narrative telling how the witnesses of Jesus advanced step by step from Jerusalem to the world with the gospel (1:8). What is said of baptism therefore belongs to the story of this process and should not be isolated from it. The attempts to reconstruct different baptismal rites and/or theologies using Acts as a source rest on rather unstable ground, and will be left aside here.

Luke takes baptism for granted. It is treated as the undisputed initiation rite of the Church, and when mission enters a new, decisive phase, baptism is mentioned as a natural step in connection with people's acceptance of the message about Christ, i.e., becoming believers (or sometimes "repenting," 2:38; 11:18 etc.). Thus, baptism is reported at the following milestones in the narrative: 2:38–41 (Pentecost in Jerusalem); 8:12 (Samaria); 8:35–39 (the Ethiopian eunuch); 9:18 (Paul); 10:44–48 (Cornelius); 16:14–15, 30–34 (Lydia and the jailer in Philippi); 18:8 (Corinth).

Entering the Christian community through faith and baptism means to be "saved" (2:40; 11:14; 16:30–31), and in 2:40 what one is saved from is specified: "this crooked generation" (cf. Deut 32:5), i.e., from those who have turned away from God. In 8:10–13 the magic practices of Simon form a dark background to faith and baptism. One side of this salvation is the remission of sins, which explicitly is one of the gifts of baptism in 2:38; 10:43, 48; 22:16. However, both "salvation" and remission of sins are among the eschatological blessings which, according to Luke, are present already in the Christian community (2:17–21); the final kingdom is not yet there (1:6–8), but God is present in the community bestowing some of the eschatological gifts. To these also belongs the Holy Spirit (2:17–18), the gift of which is connected with baptism (2:38; 8:14–17; 9:17–18; 10:47–48; 19:1–6).

Four times Luke cites something like a baptism formula "in the name of Jesus Christ" (2:38; 10:48) or "into the name of the Lord Jesus" (8:16; 19:5). The differences are probably more a matter of Luke's style than anything else (see "Into the name of the Lord Jesus" above), but the question arises as to what the expression may mean in the context of Acts. A likely suggestion is that the "name" expression indicates that the rite in some way was based on and/or was an objective application of the message about Jesus Christ which lead to faith in him. Basic points in the preaching of the apostles are these, according to the program in Luke 24:44–49: In Christ's name one shall preach repentance and remission of sins to all nations (v 47), a presupposition of which is his (the Messiah's) death and resurrection, predicted by the Scriptures (v 44–46); and, in addition, his glorified status (v 50–51, 26) from which he sends the Spirit (v 49). Thus, the apostolic message, as presented also in the speeches of Acts, has some important items in common with what is said of baptism. The christological basis of baptism is the same: Jesus is the vindicated and glorified one, the promised Messiah, the mighty and generous Sovereign, the Lord. The one who repents and believes is received by him and graciously pardoned (the death of Jesus seems to play but a minor part in this connection; compare, however, Luke 22:20). From his exalted position on the right hand of the Divine Majesty, Jesus sends the Spirit, who is active in the preaching of the gospel and in giving spiritual gifts.

In 2 instances Acts seems to present "irregularities." The first is 8:14–17, where Peter and John are reported to have to come from Jerusalem to Samaria to lay their hands on the baptized converts in order that they should receive the Holy Spirit. The second is 10:47–48, according to which the Spirit falls on Cornelius and those in his house, so as to compel Peter to order their being baptized. When regarded within the framework of the story of Acts as a whole, these irregularities can be explained without serious problems. Precisely as irregularities they become signposts in the development of the Christian mission. In the 1st case the Samaritans' place within the fulfillment of the promises is confirmed, and in the 2d the move into the Gentile world and the reception of uncircumcised Gentiles into God's people are enforced by God's Spirit itself. This is acknowledged by the Jerusalem Christians in 11:1–18); the conclusion is that "God has given the (opportunity of) repentance unto life also to the Gentiles" (v 18).

Lastly, it should be mentioned that in Acts we can surmise some details in the ritual of baptism. A laying on of hands (with prayer for the Spirit) is mentioned in 8:15–17 and 19:6 (cf. 9:17); a question arises whether there is any hindrance that a particular candidate be baptized (8:36; 10:47); there is a mention or invocation of the name of the "Lord Jesus" (22:16) in such a way that the rite could rightly be called a baptism "into the name of the Lord Jesus" (or something similar). Finally, the designation "the believers" for the Christians may possibly indicate that the rite included a question as to whether one believed in Jesus the Lord (etc.), which received the answer "I believe" (cf. Hipp., *Apost.* 21.12–18, ed. Dix, and the variant reading in Acts 8:37).

5. First Peter. Although baptism is mentioned only once in 1 Peter (3:21), it plays an important role as a basic presupposition for the presentation in the epistle. In fact, it is so important that scholars have suggested that it represents (parts of) a baptismal liturgy or a baptismal homily. Even though such a supposition may go somewhat too far, there is a wide consensus that 1 Peter makes substantial use of ideas associated with baptism. Furthermore, such ideas, to a large extent, seem to be expressed in more or less established turns of phrase.

The writer does not really argue a case in a progressive chain of reasoning, and thus the logical relationships between the ideas are not always explicit. This is also true of the passages where baptism appears to be of some importance to the contents. He seems, however, to want to strengthen and comfort his addressees in leading a faithful and moral Christian life in the face of pressures from the surrounding world. He does so by affirming that suffering as Christ's disciple is part of the discipleship and, not least, that the Christians also have a hope of glory—"an inheritance imperishable and undefiled and unfading, kept for you in heaven" (1:4).

Baptism is obviously a decisive part of the Christian initiation, to which the author refers repeatedly, although not explicitly, as a foundation of his exhortations. It is called a rebirth (1:3, 23; cf. 2:2); it means a new human existence, one brought about by God himself (1:3, 23) through his living word, the gospel (1:23–25). This new existence is sustained and guarded by God (1:5) and looks forward in hope to the coming salvation when Christ is "revealed" (1:4–5, 7, 9, 13, 21; 3:15). The Christ-relationship of the Christian initiation means, not least, that it is his resurrection that is the reason for the hope (1:3, 21) and for the salvific effects of baptism (3:21). His vicarious and redemptive passion and death are mentioned (1:2, 18–19; 2:24; 3:18); they are apparently a presupposition for the possibility of being reborn, but are not brought into any explicit connection with baptism. In the present time, awaiting faithfully the coming glory, the Christians are tested (1:7) and may have to suffer as Christ had to (2:19–23; 3:14–18; 4:1–2, 12–14, 19). Being a minority (3:20), the addressees may feel tempted to conform to their old existence marked by Gentile vices (1:14; 4:2–4), but their new life means that they are holy, belonging to God (1:15–16, 22–25); so they are called instead to live this holiness in obedience in communion with Christ (1:13–14, 22; 2:1–10).

In 3:20–21, the only passage in 1 Peter which explicitly mentions baptism, there are a couple of linguistic difficulties which complicate its understanding. Much, however, is clear enough. Thus, the OT story of Noah and the Flood (Genesis 6–9) is made to prefigure what baptism means to the addressees. Like Noah's family they are few, living in a world which deserves judgment from a patient God. And as Noah and his family were saved in the ark, in a corresponding way the addressees are saved (present tense) "through water" in baptism. One of the linguistic difficulties occurs here, but regardless of how one tries to solve it, the meaning should be something like the one just intimated. The author's explanatory comment does not make matters easier: Baptism is said to mean "not the removal of dirt of the flesh, but an appeal to God for a good conscience through the resurrection of Jesus Christ," or ". . . but a pledge to God of a good conscience through the resurrection . . .". There is a tendency in modern translations and commentaries to favor the latter understanding. Actually, it is in harmony with that which the author otherwise indicates as being one of the aspects of Christian initiation: namely, an upright entering into a covenant with God, a pledge to be holy and obedient (1:13–16; 22–23; 3:8–12), with divine salvation also implied. According to 3:21 this salvation is something taking place in baptism, and according to 1:5, 9 it is a goal, owned in hope. Its foundation, both in 1:5, 9 and 3:21, is Christ's resurrection, the Christ who is now enthroned in glory (3:22). Thus also in 3:19–22 baptism means being brought by God into a new existence, different from the former one, and, because of Christ's resurrection and glory, one can look forward to the glorious fulfillment. On the other hand, the new existence means engaging in a life that demands to be realized, even under pressure.

6. The Johannine Writings. In the 4th gospel as we now have it, 3:1–21 is the only passage which, with some certainty, deals with Christian baptism. (John 13:8–10 and 19:34 are debatable as witnesses and, for that matter, hardly give more information than we already have in 3:1–21).

It is important to take the whole of the dialogue of 3:1–21 into account when assessing 3:3, 5, where baptism is almost explicitly mentioned ("reborn" and "reborn of water and Spirit," respectively). The dialogue is constituted by 3 phases, each leading to a statement of Jesus, introduced by a repeated "amen" (3:3, 5, 11). The 1st phase states the precondition of seeing the kingdom of God: being born anew and/or from above (the Greek word *anōthen* having both meanings; 3:3). The 2d statement specifies the 1st: in order to enter the kingdom of God one must be born of water and Spirit (3:5). In the 3d and prolonged statement, the conditional clauses of the 1st and 2d phases are changed into a semantically equivalent construction: "Whoever believes in him (i.e., the Son), will . . . have eternal life" (3:15). Thus, the basic question is how to attain eternal life, which puts this term in its specifically Johannine context, i.e., it is owned already in this life (cf. 3:36; 5:24; 17:3, etc.). It is not this-worldly, limited and conditioned by "flesh" (3:6; cf. 6:63) or death (the implicit background of 3:14), but has its ultimate source in God (3:3, cf. 1:13) and depends on God's loving initiative (3:16–17). It has come to this world through the Son, whose life-giving activity in word and deed culminated in his "exaltation" on the cross (3:14) and his ascension (3:13). This "going to the Father" was the presupposition for the giving of the Spirit, which pursues the work of the Son. Thus, though in its own way, the 4th gospel works out the Christ-connection of baptism. Christ's death-exaltation makes its life-giving "possible" (3:9), viz., through the activity of the inscrutinable Spirit (3:8). On the other hand, faith on man's side is the necessary disposition for accepting this life (3:15–18; cf. 1:12; 3:36; 5:24; 11:25; 20:31, etc.).

There is no clear mention of baptism in 1 John, although 5:7–8 (the 3 witnesses, Spirit, water, blood) may refer to it as one testimony to the life-giving death of Jesus. At the same time, ideas which occur in baptismal contexts in other NT books are so numerous that there have been suggestions that the epistle cites parts of a rite of initiation, including baptism; that it reflects a baptismal homily; or, less specifically, that it contains echoes from instruction in connection with entrance into the Christian community. In any case, a central concept is the one of being born of God (2:29; 3:9; 4:7; 5:1, 5, 18; cf. John 3:5) and this out of his love (3:1; 4:9, 10, 16). Thereby Jesus Christ is of central importance (3:5; 4:9–10, 14). Sinless, he took away sin (1:7; 2:2; 3:5; 4:10). When the Christian life of the addressees "began" (2:24; 3:11), they received the remission of their sins (2:12) and obtained life in the name of Jesus Christ (3:14; 4:9; 5:12); they were instructed not to love the world but to overcome it (2:15–17; 5:4–5) and to live under the Spirit (3:24; 4:13) in love for one another (2:7–11; 3:18, 23; 4:7–11, 17–21), confessing Jesus as Christ, God's Son (3:23; 4:2, 15; 5:1). This complex is the frame of reference for the warnings and the admonition of the epistle: Being pure and holy they should live accordingly (2:1, 5–6; 3:3). It is quite likely that it reflects essential features in the author's thought on baptism.

7. Other NT Writings. Heb 10:19–25 probably contains an allusion to baptism and baptismal practice: Using priestly imagery, the author summons his audience to "draw near," "with the hearts sprinkled from an evil conscience and with the body washed with pure water" (v 22). This should refer to the remission of sins as a gift of baptism. In 9:9–10, 13–14, etc., the remission is brought about by Christ's self-sacrifice, which, then, would be "applied" in baptism. There is a homology connected to baptism, a confession to Christ which gives hope (10:23; see further 3:1; 4:14). A 2d conversion for the one who willfully turns away, is declared to be impossible in 6:4–6 and 10:26–29. The idea is probably also associated with baptism, which meant "enlightenment," "tasting a heavenly gift," "partaking of the Holy Spirit," and of "the power of the coming age" (6:4–5). Given the short eschatological perspective of the author (10:37), he has no hope for the renegade. The same Hebrews 6 seems to start with a reference to the instruction given to the catecumens (v 1–2).

If 2 Pet 1:9 refers to baptism, it represents a widely spread early Christian conviction in its understanding of it, when it mentions cleansing from previous sins.

Mark 16:16 does not belong to the original gospel of Mark, but to a secondary, though canonical ending, dating from the 2d century (16:9–20). Verses 15–16 contain a commissioning of the disciples to preach the gospel to the whole world. This proclamation is received in belief or unbelief, and as usual belief is combined with baptism. As in Tit 3:5 and 1 Pet 3:21, it means salvation. Here it means the salvation at the *eschaton* and is contrasted to condemnation, the lot of those who have not accepted the proclamation.

8. "One baptism"—Many Interpretations? The presentation above has investigated the different ways in which some early Christians have thought about baptism. The differences are great enough to justify the conclusion that one can hardly add all the views together, call the result "The NT Doctrine of Baptism," and assume that one has done justice to the NT authors by doing so. This is so, even when taking into consideration that Paul is the author who beyond comparison delivers the most material on the topic and easily may dominate such an additive presentation. Given the differences, there are, however, more resemblances between the different witnesses than one might expect in view of the foregoing exposition. It may therefore be justified to conclude with a few words on this aspect.

At the very beginning of Christian baptismal practice there were some aspects and circumstances pertaining to it which seem, somehow, to have been determinative for the ways in which different theologians and traditions in early Christianity came to think of baptism. In all probability, the rite was taken over from John the Baptist, which has an important implication: that eschatological expectations similar to those of the Baptist were associated with Christian baptism. Another decisive element was the conviction that Jesus had risen from the dead and that his resurrection meant a new situation in man's relationship to God, notably as seen in the (short) eschatological perspective. Furthermore, baptism was connected with the Christian preaching to Jews and Gentiles; it had the Christ-event at its center and demanded conversion and/or faith. Lastly, the ones who believed were baptized "into the name of the Lord Jesus" (etc.), which presumably meant that Jesus the Lord—his person and his work—was the fundamental reference for the rite.

NT interpreters of later times easily overlook the constancy with which the eschatological outlook reappears in baptismal passages in the NT. It is realized in different ways: in demand for ethical responsibility in view of the approaching judgment; in references to the hope which looks forward to the final salvation or to the promised heritage; in the question how one enters the kingdom of God or receives eternal life.

But the eschatological perspective does not only mean looking forward. It also means an inaugurated eschatology, in that the salvific gifts of the *eschaton* are regarded as already present, although in varying degrees and in different ways by different authors. The Christ-event, especially the resurrection of Christ, is the beginning of this inaugurated *eschaton*; the preaching of the gospel continues this inauguration; and baptism is the door through which men enter it in connection with faith and/or conversion. It means leaving behind sin, alienation from God, etc., and entering a new, trusting, and sound relation to God. The remission of sins and the activity and presence of the Holy Spirit thus belong to the gifts of this inaugurated *eschaton*. These radically new life-conditions are described in different ways, often in terms from Jewish eschatological expectations. They imply a duty to lead a Christian life which deserves this designation. The degrees in which one believes eschatology to be "realized" vary, and we encounter a relatively wide range of views. On the one hand, there is the eschatology behind 2 Tim 2:18 which is "over-realized" according to Pauline standards, and several scholars suggest that the case is the same with some enthusiasts in Corinth. On the other hand, there are the more tempered views of the authors of Acts or of the Epistle to Titus.

When baptism is performed "into the name of the Lord Jesus" (etc.), this indicates the key position held by Christ in relation to this inaugurated *eschaton*. It was inaugurated through his life, death, and resurrection. And though he was also the extramundane guarantee and point of orientation of the new life-conditions, he was nevertheless not distant.

It seems fair to suggest that the general ideas concerning early Christian baptism, intimated in the preceding few paragraphs, form what appears to be a common ground on which different theologians and traditions of the early Church have developed their understandings of baptism in keeping with their respective theological outlooks. This is not to say that this common ground should be something like an abstraction or generalization of NT statements on baptism which one could call the NT doctrine of baptism. But in so far as such a "doctrine" is to have a basis that is historically motivated, it should do justice to the general aspects of baptism found on this common ground. However, such a statement already means starting to ask hermeneutical questions which need to be dealt with when wrestling with such a "doctrinal" problem, but which cannot be taken up here.

Bibliography

Åland, K. 1972. Zur Vorgeschichte der christlichen Taufe. Pp. 1–14 in *Neues Testament und Geschichte,* ed. H. von Baltensweiler and B. Reicke. Zürich.

Barnikol, E. 1956–57. Das Fehlen der Taufe in den Quellenschriften der Apostelgeschichte und in den Urgemeinden der Hebräer und Hellenisten. *WZ* 6:593–610.

Barth, G. 1981. *Die Taufe in frühchristlicher Zeit.* Biblisch-Theologische Studien 4. Neukirchen-Vluyn.

Beasley-Murray, G. R. 1962. *Baptism in the New Testament.* London.

Bieder, W. 1966. *Die Verheissung der Taufe im Neuen Testament.* Zürich.

Böcher, O. 1972. *Christus Exorcista.* BWANT 96. Stuttgart.

Böcher, O. 1970. Wasser und Geist. Pp. 197–209 in *Verborum Veritas,* ed. O. Böcher and K. Haacker. Wuppertal.

Boismard, M.-E. 1961. *Quatre hymnes baptismales dans la Première Epître de Pierre.* LD 30. Paris.

Chevallier, M.-A. 1986. L'Apologie du Baptême d'Eau à la Fin du Premier Siècle. *NTS* 32: 528–43.

Cullmann, O. 1950. *Baptism in the New Testament.* Trans. J. K. S. Reid. SBT 1. London.

Cuming, G. J. 1980–81. *epotisthēmen* (1 Corinthians 12.13). *NTS* 27: 283–85.

Delling, G. 1961. *Die Zueignung des Heils in der Taufe.* Berlin.

———. 1963. *Die Taufe im Neuen Testament.* Berlin.

Dinkler, E. 1972. Die Taufaussagen des Neuen Testaments. Pp. 60–153 in *Zu Karl Barths Lehre von der Taufe,* ed. Fr. Viering. 2d ed. Gütersloh.

Dunn, J. D. G. 1970. *Baptism in the Holy Spirit.* SBT n.s. 15. London.

Edsman, C.-M. 1940. *Le baptême de feu.* ASNU 9. Uppsala.

Flemington, W. F. 1948. *The New Testament Doctrine of Baptism.* London.

Frankemölle, H. 1970. *Das Taufverständnis des Paulus.* SBS 47. Stuttgart.

Frid, B. 1986. Römer 6.4–5. *BZ* 30: 188–203.

Halter, H. 1977. *Taufe und Ethos.* FTS 106. Freiburg.

Hartman, L. 1973–74. "Into the Name of Jesus." *NTS* 20: 432–40.

———. 1985. La formule baptismale dans les Actes des Apôtres. Pp. 727–38 in *A cause de l'évangile.* LD 123. Paris.

Haufe, G. 1976. Taufe und Heiliger Geist im Urchristentum. *TLZ* 101: 561–66.

Heitmüller, W. 1903. *Im Namen Jesu.* FRLANT 1/2. Göttingen.

Jeremias, J. 1960. *Infant Baptism in the First Four Centuries.* Trans. D. Cairns. London.

Kaye, B. N. 1973. *baptizein eis* with Special Reference to Romans 6. Pp. 281–86 in *SE* 6, ed. E. A. Livingstone, = TU 112. Berlin.

Kirby, J. C. 1968. *Ephesians, Baptism, and Pentecost.* Montreal.

Kretschmar, G. 1970. Die Geschichte des Taufgottesdienstes in der alten Kirche. *Leiturgia* 5: 1–348, esp. 1–58.

Kuss, O. 1963. Zur vorpaulinischen Tauflehre im Neuen Testament. Vol. 1, pp. 93–120 in *Auslegung und Verkündigung.* Regensburg.

Lamarche, P., and Le Dû, C. 1980. *Épître aux Romains V–VIII.* Paris.

Larsson, E. 1962. *Christus als Vorbild.* ASNU 22. Lund.

Leipoldt, J. 1928. *Die urchristliche Taufe im Lichte der Religionsgeschichte.* Leipzig.

Lentzen-Deis, F. 1970. *Die Taufe Jesu nach den Synoptikern.* Frankfurter theologische Studien 4. Frankfurt am Main.

Lindeskog, G. 1983. Johannes der Täufer. *ASTI* 12: 55–83.

Lorenzi, L. de, ed. 1974. *Battesimo e Giustizia in Rom 6 e 8.* Serie

Monografica de "Benedictina," sezione biblico-ecumenica 2. Rome.

Pedersen, S., ed. 1982. *Dåben i Ny Testamente.* Teologiske studier 9. Aarhus.

Pokorný, P. 1980–81. Christologie et Baptême à l'Époque du Christianisme Primitif. *NTS* 27: 368–80.

Quesnel, M. 1985. *Baptisés dans l'Esprit.* LD 120. Paris.

Rissi, M. 1962. *Die Taufe für die Toten.* ATANT 42. Zürich.

Rudolph, K. 1981. *Antike Baptisten.* Sitzungsberichte der sächsischen Akademie der Wissenschaften zu Leipzig, phil-hist. Kl. 121/4. Berlin.

Schille, G. 1965. *Frühchristliche Hymnen.* 2d ed. Berlin.

Schnackenburg, R. 1964. *Baptism in the Thought of St. Paul.* Trans. G. R. Beasley-Murray. New York.

Schnelle, U. 1983. *Gerechtigkeit und Christusgegenwart.* GTA 24. Göttingen.

Segelberg, E. 1958. *Maṣbutā.* Uppsala.

Tannehill, R. C. 1966. *Dying and Rising with Christ.* BZNW 32. Berlin.

Thiering, B. E. 1979–80. Inner and Outer Cleansing at Qumran as a Background to New Testament Baptism. *NTS* 26: 266–77.

———. 1980–81. Qumran Initiation and New Testament Baptism. *NTS* 27: 615–31.

Thomas, J. 1935. *Le mouvement baptiste en Palestine et Syrie.* Gembloux.

Thyen, H. 1970. *Studien zur Sündenvergebung im Neuen Testament und seinen alttestamentlichen und jüdischen Voraussetzungen.* FRLANT 96. Göttingen.

Wagner, G. 1967. *Pauline Baptism and the Pagan Mysteries.* Trans. J. P. Smith. Edinburgh.

Wedderburn, A. J. M. 1983. Hellenistic Christian Traditions in Romans 6? *NTS* 29: 337–55.

Wedderburn, A. J. M. 1987. *Baptism and Resurrection.* WUNT 44. Tübingen.

Ysebaert, J. 1962. *Greek Baptismal Terminology.* Graecitas christianorum primaeva 1. Nijmegen.

LARS HARTMAN

BAPTIST, JOHN THE. See JOHN THE BAPTIST.

BAQᶜAH VALLEY (JORDAN). A valley 15 km NW of Amman and 625 meters above sea level on the Transjordanian plateau which has been the focus of a University Museum (Univ. of Pennsylvania) expedition since 1977. The project is under the general directorship of P. E. McGovern and has been jointly funded by the Museum and its Applied Science Center for Archaeology (MASCA), the National Geographic Society, the Jordanian Department of Antiquities, and several private foundations. A major goal of the project, in addition to recovering stratigraphic sequences of poorly known periods, has been to demonstrate how scientific techniques can be integrated into archaeological investigations, especially salvage operations where constraints of time, manpower, and money exist.

A. General Description

The Baqᶜah (derived from the ancient Semitic root for "valley") is a unique geomorphological feature on the plateau at the juncture of three flexures in the earth's crust. Its elliptical, self-contained area of 10 x 5 km stands in marked contrast to the surrounding terrain of hills and deep wadies cutting down to the Jordan Valley. The almost continuous human occupation of valley from the late Middle Paleolithic (*ca.* 50,000 years ago) to the present is a consequence of several factors: its centralized position on the plateau (the ancient King's Highway probably ran through the middle of the valley); the rich soil *(terra rossa)* suitable for agriculture; one of the highest concentrations of perennial springs on the plateau; a moderate upland climate sustaining diverse plant and animal species; and other natural resources (e.g., large clay deposits).

B. Archaeology of the Valley

Based on the data recovered in four seasons of survey and excavation (1977, 1978, 1980, and 1981), five periods in particular stand out: (1) the Early Bronze Age; (2) the Late Bronze Age; (3) the Early Iron Age; (4) the Late Iron Age, extending into the Persian period; and (5) the early Roman period.

Archaeological investigation has focused on the NW (Umm ad-Danānīr) region of the Baqᶜah, which has more springs and visible ancient remains than any other sector of the valley. See Fig. BAQ.01. A 52.5-hectare area was systematically traversed, and based on artifact clusters, architectural remains, and specific research problems, several sites were chosen for geophysical prospecting. With the additional subsurface data from the latter surveys, certain areas were then targeted for test excavations. The

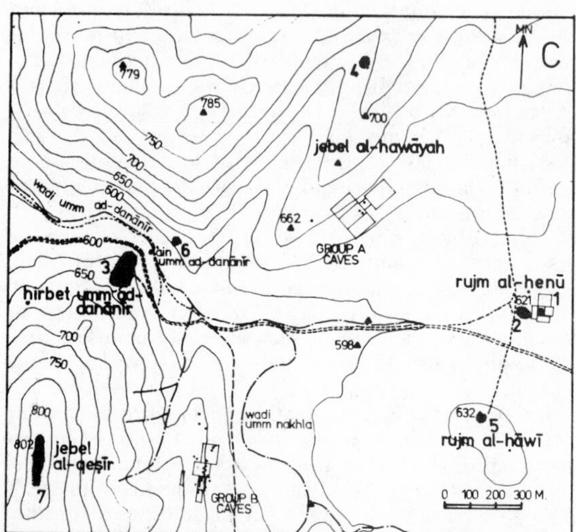

BAQ.01. Area map of Umm ad-Dananir region of the Baqah Valley. *(Courtesy of P. E. McGovern.)*

archaeological results of such an approach attest to its value. Other areas of the valley, according to a preliminary assessment, would appear to have had much sparser occupation, apart from Tell Ṣafūṭ on the SW periphery of the valley; the stratigraphic sequence of this site is comparable to that of Khirbet Umm ad-Danānīr (below).

1. Early Bronze Age. Urban settlement began in the Baqᶜah at least by EB II (*ca.* 2900 B.C.). The impressive site of al-Qeṣīr ("the fortress"; site 7 on Fig. BAQ.01) covers the 5-hectare summit of the hill of the same name at an elevation of about 800 m above sea level (200 m above the valley floor). An encircling stone fortification wall further enhanced the site's defensive position. Al-Qeṣīr is one of a number of large hilltop EB settlements in central Transjordan, none of which has as yet been excavated.

Aerial photography revealed the ground plans of many circular and rectangular stone buildings. Cisterns up to several hundred meters in diameter, hewn out of the bedrock, were located on four sides of the summit. Systematic sharding of the area within the walls showed that the site had been most intensively settled during EB II–III (ca. 2900–2300 B.C.). A marked decrease in occupation occurred in the subsequent transitional period of EB IV (*ca.* 2300–1950 B.C.), after which the site was abandoned.

2. Late Bronze Age. LB remains are exceptionally well represented in the Umm ad-Danānīr region, considering that no earlier survey had found evidence for the period and that the traditional hypothesis (see Glueck 1970, which is a later modification of his 1940 hypothesis) maintained that Transjordan S of the Wadi Zarqa had been occupied primarily by nomads or "semi-nomads," with urban centers confined to a few larger sites, throughout the MB and LB Ages. The archaeological findings from the Baqᶜah over the past eight years conflict with this hypothesis (McGovern 1986a), and in conjunction with investigation elsewhere on the central plateau, it now appears more reasonable to posit a settlement pattern of variously sized LB communities, at least in the area from the Wadi Zarqa S to Madaba (cf. Harding 1967: 32–34; Zayadine 1973: 19–21).

A large LB cemetery of 20 burial caves on the lower slopes of Jebel al-Qeṣīr and Jebel al-Hawāyah (Fig. BAQ.01) were located and investigated. Many of these had been fully or partly robbed out, but it was possible to obtain details about the sizes and shapes of LB caves (circular, elliptical, and two-chambered, with maximum dimensions varying from 1 to 10 m) and their phases of use. The location of undisturbed caves and burial deposits was achieved using a highly sensitive magnetic detecting device, a cesium magnetometer. The burial features were generally silted-up features, and the greater accumulation of soil was more magnetic than the surrounding bedrock; consequently, they showed up as magnetic highs, even where there was no visible evidence of tombs on the surface.

The two most important LB burial deposits were recovered from Caves A2 and B3, belonging to LB I (*ca.* 1550–1400 B.C.) and LB II (*ca.* 1400–1200 B.C.), respectively. From a sounding confined to a 20-m area of Cave A2 (about a quarter of the tomb) came over fifty whole vessels, numerous small finds (including 4 scarabs, 4 cylinder seals, and 75 glass beads), which had been buried with 22 individuals of both sexes and various ages (infants, children, adolescents, and adults). The burial assemblage, which was similar to that of urban communities elsewhere in Palestine (e.g., Tomb 1145 at Megiddo [Guy 1938: 94–99] and Tomb 1 at Pella [Smith 1973]), testified to a sedentary lifestyle and well-developed trade connections. This was also borne out by the local origin of the majority of the pottery; it derived from a clay deposit in the wadi near the spring of ᶜain Umm ad-Danānīr as confirmed by neutron activation analysis.

The urban character of the LB Baqᶜah community was further emphasized by the finds from Cave B3, including about 300 vessels (most of which were made from the local clay), 4 Mycenaean IIIB/IIIA(2) stirrup jars (from central mainland Greece, according to their chemical profiles), a Cypriot White Slip II "milk bowl" and Base Ring II juglet fragments, and a large collection of jewelry (including an iron anklet/bracelet fragment comparable to Iron IA examples, a cylinder seal, an Egyptian signet ring, and glass and faience beads). The burial goods were associated with a minimum of 64 individuals of all ages and both sexes. The principal paleopathologies (arthritis and dental caries), which were also observed in the Cave A2 population, are characteristic of sedentary groups, and two cultivants (emmer wheat and bread or club wheat) from Cave B3, along with the remains of large herding animals (cattle) in both LB burial caves, supported this interpretation.

The LB settlement at Khirbet Umm ad-Danānīr (site 3), although thus far excavated only to a limited extent, provided the remaining piece of the puzzle posed by the burial cave evidence. The site was strategically situated on a cliff overlooking the pass into the Baqᶜah through the S branch of the Wadi Umm ad-Danānīr, along which an ancient route to the Jordan Valley probably ran. It was located downhill from the EB settlement of al-Qeṣīr (above) on the same hill and closer to the strongest spring in the region, ᶜain Umm ad-Danānīr.

Detailed mapping of visible surface remains showed that an area of approximately 2.5 hectares had been enclosed by a wall comprising two lines of boulders (1–1.5 m in length). The size and stratification of the site, as revealed by subsequent excavation, are considerable by Transjordanian standards.

A major discovery was made in the one excavation square where LB levels were reached. More than 3 m from the surface, beneath primarily Iron Age and Roman remains, an LB II refuse pit, about 1 m in diameter and 0.5 m deep, was exposed and half excavated. It was found to contain the charred remains of a variety of animals (sheep/goat, *Equus*, cattle, and some kind of carnivore, possibly a mountain lion), half of a hollow bull rhyton (almost identical to an example from Cave A2), and several large pottery vessels (kraters, jugs, bowls, a storage jar, and a cooking pot), which were all made from the local clay and, except for their larger sizes, were identical to pottery types from Cave B3. Further, the clay lining of the pit merged with a floor that was attached to a boulder wall similar to the proposed city wall. The pit can be compared to refuse pits in the vicinity of buildings at other LB sites (e.g., the Lachish Fosse temple). Its contents and association with a massive wall point to a well-established sedentary community during this period.

Rujm al-Ḥenū East (site 1), which is more than 500 m SW of Khirbet Umm ad-Danānīr, near the middle of the valley, was most probably constructed in the LB Age (McGovern 1983), as evidenced by the discovery of over 20 LB sherds from a surface survey and five test soundings. However, the deposition on the inside was less than 1.0 m thick and only several courses remained of the structure, most of whose large boulders (over 1 m in length) had most likely been used to construct the corners and towers of Rujm al-Ḥenū West (site 2) in the Iron IIC/Persian period. Moreover, the LB sherds all derived from mixed loci containing Roman, Byzantine, and Islamic material, and may represent only robbing and dumping activity sometime between the Roman period and the present.

The surface ground plan of Rujm al-Ḥenū East resembles that of the LB Amman Airport Building (Hennessy 1966: figs. 1 and 2, pl. 33A), 15 km to the SE. The latter is of the *Quadratbau* architectural type, which, as the name implies, has a square layout with a central unit ("courtyard") surrounded by outer rooms. Because of the rich deposits within the airport building and the minimal evidence of a permanent settlement in that vicinity (Hennessy 1966), it was proposed that the building might have been a tribal shrine, possibly a temple or mortuary cult structure of a nomadic group such as the Israelites (Campbell and Wright 1969). Rujm al-Ḥenū East provided the opportunity to test this hypothesis at another building of a similar type.

Rujm al-Ḥenū East differed from the airport structure in being rectangular (*ca.* 24 x 31 m) and in not having any surface remains of crosswalls that defined the central courtyard and rooms on the north. An electrical resistivity survey was first carried out to locate additional crosswalls and to determine the extent of buried structures in the vicinity, which might constitute a settlement. This geophysical technique takes advantage of the fact that dense materials (such as the stones of a wall) will block an applied electrical current and give higher resistivity readings than the surrounding soil.

The follow-up test excavations revealed that most of the high anomalies were due to irregularities in the near-surface bedrock. An undated wall, found extending several meters westward, along the same line as one of the interior walls, might belong to a pathway boundary, an addition to the building, or a separate structure. No additional interior crosswalls, however, were discovered; indeed, several crosswalls on the E and S sides of the building proved to be secondary. Thus, it is likely that the original layout completely lacked crosswalls, which would represent a major departure from the classical *Quadratbau* type. On the other hand, there might well be variant architectural traditions of the same general type, especially in the Amman area, where boulder construction was common (e.g., the Iron IIC/Persian *qasr* type buildings could be rectangular or square and did not adhere to a fixed pattern). Possibly, Rujm al-Ḥenū East served as an agricultural villa (cf. *ArchPal* 36, 92–93 on the interpretation of the MB III–LB I *Quadratbau* structure on Mt. Gerizim). It was built on a bedrock outcrop in the midst of rich agricultural fields, like the Iron IIC/Persian structures which probably functioned as farmsteads (below); and as the nearby primary settlement at Khirbet Umm ad-Danānīr increased in population, it would have been an obvious area in which to expand.

3. Iron IA. An early Iron Age burial cave (A4), which was located by the magnetometer survey, turned out to be one of the largest tombs of this period ever discovered in Palestine. Into a circular cave only 4.5 m in diameter, 227 individuals of all ages and both sexes had been crammed. Most of the burials had been secondarily disturbed and commingled as a result of moving older skeletons to make space for new interments. The cave had two entrances: the main one, which was blocked by five boulders and which faced onto a 20 m^2 "forecourt," entered by a sloping ramp; and a back entrance, with a single boulder wedged into it and with a series of bedrock steps leading down from it into the cave.

The associated burial goods attested to a lower standard of living and fewer foreign contacts in Iron IA than in the LB Age. Thus, the pottery vessel–to-burial ratio (70:227) for Cave A4 was approximately the inverse of that for the LB burial groups. Imports were limited to marine mollusks, most of which were cowries from the Red Sea. Even more notably, marked changes were apparent in the three basic industries: pottery, metals, and silicate technology.

In the case of the pottery, some of these changes could be traced back to LB II. The amount of inclusions (quartz and especially calcite) gradually increased from LB I through Iron IA, even though the same clay source at ʿain Umm ad-Danānīr was exploited throughout this period. Perhaps to avoid calcite disintegration, lower firing temperatures became the rule in the early Iron Age.

A similar trend can be traced in fabrication techniques. Whereas most vessels were made on the wheel in LB I, coil building of medium-sized vessels was the preferred method in LB II. Coil building became the exclusive technique in Iron IA, often with a greater appreciation for the advantages and limitations of the materials and method. Rather than representing a low point in the Palestinian potter's craft, coiling, turning, surface wet-smoothing, trimming, and firing were now directed toward making pottery well suited to the admittedly poorer clay body. Well-contoured forms whose walls and bases were trimmed to a uniform narrow thickness were the result. Some of the changes in traditional pottery styles and the introduction of new forms in Iron IA may reflect this transformation in the pottery industry. Similarly, the relative lack of paints and slips in the early Iron Age may well be more a function of the reduced availability of fine clay fractions than of a deliberate change or the introduction of a new tradition from the outside.

One of the most important discoveries in the Iron IA burial cave was a group of 11 complete mild steel jewelry artifacts (anklets, bracelets, and rings), which more than tripled the number of published iron objects from early Iron Palestine. Some continuity between the Bronze and Iron Ages was evident from the discovery of a similar iron anklet or bracelet in LB II Cave B3. However, the number of Iron IA artifacts and their very uniform carbon composition demonstrated an especially well-developed metallurgical expertise in smelting and working iron (steel) in Iron IA. The 78 copper-base artifacts, again only jewelry and of essentially the same types as those in iron (steel), exhibited similarly high technological standards; they were exclusively tin-alloyed bronzes which had very consistent and high levels of tin, averaging 11 percent.

Glass/frit technology, which probably developed locally on the central Transjordanian plateau in the LB Age (McGovern 1985b), had virtually disappeared by Iron IA in the Baqᶜah. Only one faience, two frit, and five beads of a dark red glass were found in Cave A4. The high amounts of iron oxide in the red glass (up to 50 percent by weight in contrast to the 5–10 percent content in LB red glass) suggested that they were reworked iron ore slag, which constituted a by-product from the contemporary iron (steel) industry.

By the early Iron Age, a very obvious shift was apparent in the three basic industries. The specific changes leading up to the transformed industries, however, had already begun to occur in the LB Age, and presumably some of the underlying causes of change were to be found in the earlier period as well. Moreover, the lack of traumatic injuries in the LB and early Iron populations, as well as the total lack of weapons in Cave A4, suggested that these changes had come about peacefully. Cultural continuity between the LB and early Iron periods was clear from the uninterrupted use of the same cemetery and the continuous occupation of Khirbet Umm ad-Danānīr into Iron IA (numerous surface sherds of the latter period were recovered, although excavated evidence is yet to be recovered, possibly because the Iron IA settlement was small in size).

The changes in the three basic industries (pottery, metals, and silicates) on the central Transjordanian plateau can best be understood within a framework of indigenous socioeconomic transformation (in contrast to the standard hypotheses for understanding the LB/early Iron transition: invasion, peaceful infiltration, or peasant revolt). The very isolation of the central Transjordanian plateau and the availability of certain raw materials there (e.g., copper, iron, and manganese ores) might account for some of the changes. Well-documented invasions elsewhere in Palestine, particularly along the coast toward the end of the LB Age, would also have had serious repercussions on the socioeconomic structure of city-states in the interior of the country. An even more general circumstance contributing to change would have been a gradual climatic deterioration with lower precipitation levels, beginning in LB II (Horowitz 1978; for Greece, see Betancourt 1976). With a contracting subsistence base, the symbiotic relation between transhumant and sendentary groups would have been seriously threatened.

If this reconstruction is correct, at least in its general outlines, then the LB city-state could not have survived. Many of those in the urban population, who would have been thrown out of work by economic dislocations, would have needed to seek out alternative means of support. The establishment of small outlying village communities, which have been documented in other parts of the hill country, and the contraction of larger settlements would be anticipated. The consolidation of technological advances in a frontier setting, even its accentuation as a manifestation of the "new culture," especially after the collapse of hierarchical control in the urban centers, would also be expected. For example, in the case of the highly innovative iron (steel) industry, one of the few known sources of iron ore in the Levant is located a short distance N of the Baqᶜah in the Wadi Zarqa-Ajlun area, which appears to have been a hinterland in most periods. It may be hypothesized that native metalsmiths began to exploit some of the deposits in this area on a larger scale as a result of the disintegration of LB urban culture and the dispersal of the population (the large tracts of oak forest there could also have met the extensive fuel requirements of iron smelting).

4. Iron IIC/Persian. Numerous Iron IIC/Persian structures are scattered throughout the Baqᶜah. Some of these are isolated buildings, primarily circular towers *(rujūm malfūf);* others form extensive complexes of large rectangular and square enclosures (*qasr* type) and *rujūm malfūf.*

Five Iron IIC/Persian sites were located by intensive surveying of the Umm ad-Danānīr region (sites 2, 3, 4, 5, and 6 on Fig. BAQ.01). Apart from Khirbet Umm ad-Danānīr, all were constructed on bedrock outcrops in proximity to arable land. This accords with an interpretation of the buildings as primarily habitation quarters for the rural Ammonite population (Glueck 1939: 163). The Iron IIC/Persian period appears to have been an especially prosperous one in Transjordan, and the spatial distribution of the sites implies a settlement pattern that maximally exploited available agricultural land and accommodated a growing population (McGovern 1985a).

The standard interpretation of the *qasr* and *rujūm malfūf* buildings as watchtowers or fortresses that protected approaches to Amman (Glueck 1970: 183) does not rule out their use as farming communities or villas. Rujm al-Ḥenū West and Rujm al-Ḥāwī (sites 2 and 5) are virtually mirror images of one another, with circular towers facing the western pass and rectangular bastions opposite one another. They are equidistant from the main road, which probably follows the line of an ancient route, and as such are ideally situated to have served as border posts.

5. Early Roman III. Extensive building projects were carried out at Khirbet Umm ad-Danānīr during the Early Roman III period. In a 4 × 20 m area on a middle terrace of the site, a large structure of this period emerged immediately below the surface. A central room of the building was characterized by a northern wall with seven orthostats, placed about 0.5 m apart and several still having the overlying stretchers in place. A representative collection of Early Roman III pottery and artifacts (including glass vessel and bracelet fragments, iron pins and rods, and limestone vessels of Herodian design) were recovered. Large Roman architectural elements were discovered further down the slope, and most of the visible remains on the lower terraces probably belong to this period (4 B.C.–A.D. 73).

Bibliography

Betancourt, P. 1976. The End of the Greek Bronze Age. *Antiquity* 50: 40–47.

Campbell, E., and Wright, G. E. 1969. Tribal League Shrines in Amman and Shechem. *BA* 32: 104–16.

Glueck, N. 1939. *Explorations in Eastern Palestine, III.* AASOR 18–19. New Haven.

———. 1970. *The Other Side of the Jordan.* 2d ed. Cambridge, MA.

Guy, P. L. O. 1938. *Megiddo Tombs.* OIP 33. Chicago.

Harding, G. L. 1967. *The Antiquities of Jordan.* 2d ed. New York.

Hennessy, J. B. 1966. Excavations of a LB Age Temple. *PEQ* 98: 155–62.

Horowitz, A. 1978. Human Settlement Patterns in Israel. *Expedition* 20: 55–58.

McGovern, P. E. 1979–82. The Baqʿah Valley, Jordan. *MASCA Journal* 1: 39–41, 214–17; 2: 8–12, 35–39.

———. 1980. Explorations in the Umm ad-Danānīr Region of the Baqʿah Valley. *ADAJ* 24: 55–67.

———. 1981–83. The Baqʿah Valley Project. *BA* 44: 126–28; 45: 122–24; *LA* 31: 329–32; *AJA* 87: 186; *AfO* 29–30: 271–74.

———. 1983. Test Soundings of Archaeological and Resistivity Survey Results at Rujm al Ḥenū. *ADAJ* 27: 105–41.

———. 1985a. Environmental Constraints for Human Settlement in the Baqʿah Valley. Pp. 141–48 in *The History and Archaeology of Jordan, II.* Ed. A. Hadidi. Amman.

———. 1985b. Silicate Industries of LB–Early Iron Age Palestine. Pp. 91–107 in *Early Vitreous Materials,* ed. M. Bimson and I. C. Freestone. London.

———. 1986a. *The Late Bronze and Early Iron Ages of Central Transjordan.* Philadelphia.

Smith, R. H. 1973. *Pella of the Decapolis.* Wooster, OH.

Zayadine, F. 1973. Late Bronze Age. Pp. 19–21 in *The Archaeological Heritage of Jordan.* Part 1. Amman.

PATRICK E. MCGOVERN

BAR KOKHBA. The name given to Simon bar Kosiba, leader of the unsuccessful Jewish revolt against Rome ca. 132–135 C.E. Today the name is often used as an adjective to modify this "Second Jewish Revolt" or "Bar Kokhba Revolt" (the first being the Jewish War of 66–70 C.E.), as well as a cache of documents discovered in the Judean desert that were written at the time of this war, including some letters written by Simon himself (i.e., "Bar Kokhba Letters"). Rabbi Akiba, who considered Simon bar Kosiba to be the Messiah, called him "son of the star" (Aram *kôkbāʾ*), perhaps suggesting a messianic interpretation of Num 24:17. In rabbinic writings the *s* in the name is usually changed to a *z* (bar Koziba), implying in derogatory fashion that Simon was regarded as "the son of a lie" (i.e., a liar).

BAR KOKHBA REVOLT

Jewish armed resistance against Roman rule in Judea reached its culmination and exhausted itself in the Revolt of Bar Kokhba (132–35 C.E.). Great numbers of rebels participated in the insurrection, employing guerrilla tactics, and large reinforcements were needed to suppress it. The rebels were united under the leadership of one man: Simeon Bar Kokhba. The revolt resulted in the emergence of a short-lived independent state marked by the organization of local authorities, the issue of coinage, and the leasing of state land.

A. Evidence

1. Talmudic Sources. The revolt of Bar Kokhba is mentioned rather extensively in Talmudic literature. Most references to the revolt are found in three groups: *j. Taʿan.* iv 68d–69b; *Lam. Rab.* ii 4; and *b. Giṭ.* 57a–58a. They focus on (1) Bar Kokhba's leadership; (2) the attitude of the sages toward the rebellion and Bar Kokhba himself; (3) the fall of Bethar; and (4) the aftermath of the revolt. Talmudic sources must be taken into account especially when considering the geographical scope of the war and the possible conquest of Jerusalem and the reconstruction of the temple by the rebels. For discussion see Alon 1980–84: 430–60, 570–637; Schäfer 1981; Isaac and Oppenheimer 1985.

2. Greek and Latin Sources. The account of Cassius Dio forms the only consistent survey of the war, but the text is preserved only in the medieval epitome of Ioannes Xiphilinus, a monk of the 11th century (*D.C.* lxix 12.1–13, 111 15.1). It is to be noted also that this is a general description of the war, not a chronological account. It must also be noted that Xiphilinus produced not so much a *précis* of Dio's work as a selection usually but not always keeping to the original order and retaining much of Dio's wording. It is therefore quite likely that we have most of what Dio wrote on the subject. The *Historia Augusta* is the only source to mention a ban on circumcision preceding the revolt as the cause of the revolt (*Scriptores Historiae Augustae, vita Hadriani* 14.2). There are altogether four contemporary references to the war: Appianus, *Syriaca* 50.252; Fronto, *de bello Parthico* 2; Pausanias, *Graeciae descriptio* 15.5; and Apollodorus of Damascus 8.10. The last does not even refer to the revolt specifically. Christian sources, remote in time and antagonistic toward the Jews, yet have features in common with the Talmudic sources: references (1) to Bar Kokhba as leader of the revolt, (2) to Tineius Rufus the legate of Judea, and (3) to the fall of Bethar (for the Greek and Latin sources see Stern 1980, nos. 332; 342; 353; 340).

3. Samaritan Chronicles. The Samaritan Chronicles have not been discussed systematically. They date to the Middle Ages and are very probably influenced by the relationship between Jews and Samaritans as it developed in the period after the revolt. See discussion by Alon 1980–84: 603–7.

4. Archaeological Exploration. Archaeological evidence is immediately relevant for the study of the Bar Kokhba revolt, the more so given the paucity of literary sources. Particularly important is the coinage, now fully treated by L. Mildenberg (1984). Coin hoards help to determine the geographical scope of the revolt (Barag 1980: 30–3). The great size of the Bar Kokhba coinage, and the quantities of coins issued, give an impression of the organization of the rebel government and of the population and the economy of Judea at the time of the revolt. The legends and symbols on the coins embody the only extant contemporary pronouncements of the values and objectives of the insurgents. Among the most spectacular discoveries are the hiding places in the Judean desert with personal belongings and documents of insurgents (see Bar Kokhba Letters below). Also of interest are the numerous subterranean hiding places, some of which were certainly used during the revolt of Bar Kokhba.

B. Causes of the War

The modern literature disagrees on the origins of the war. The following causes or combination of causes are found in recent publications:

(1) The revolt was caused by Hadrian's decision to transform Jerusalem into a pagan city, as stated by Cassius Dio.
(2) It was caused by a ban on circumcision as indicated in the *Historia Augusta.*
(3) These sources are combined. The revolt was then caused by the decision to found Aelia Capitolina and by a ban on circumcision.
(4) Hadrian declared, or was believed to have decided, that the temple in Jerusalem might be rebuilt. When it appeared that he would not permit this the Jews rebelled.
(5) Various scholars have suggested that the destruction of the temple created a psychological climate which led to renewed violence, irrespective of any decisions which may have formed the immediate cause of the revolt.
(6) It has been suggested that the economic situation contributed to the outbreak of the revolt (Alon 1980–84: 572–77; Applebaum 1976: 385–95).

Most scholars advocate the third alternative in one form or another. Several consider the foundation of Aelia Capitolina the sole cause of the revolt. The various opinions are listed in Isaac and Oppenheimer (1985: 44–46). The alleged permission given by Hadrian to rebuild the temple, subsequently withdrawn, is not now ever considered a primary cause of the revolt, but some contemporary studies are not prepared to reject the theory absolutely and assume there may be some truth in it. In this connection the importance of the coinage must be emphasized. The coin legends "Jerusalem" and "For the Freedom of Jerusalem" and the design of the temple on the coinage are to be considered progammatic declarations (Mildenberg 1980: 325; 1984: 29–31). This evidence does not allow a determination as to whether Jerusalem was taken by the insurgents, but the coins are the only extant contemporary pronouncements regarding the values and objectives of the rebels. They provide clear evidence of the central importance of Jerusalem in the war.

Far more obscure is the testimony of the fifth Sibylline Oracle, composed by a Jew before the end of Hadrian's reign. Lines 46–50 contain praise of Hadrian which has been variously interpreted (1) as confirmation that Hadrian was popular among the Jews early in his reign (Alon 1980–84: 453) or (2) as an indication of the attitude of the Jews toward Hadrian at the time of his visit in Judea in 130 C.E. (Bowersock 1980: 134). Note also the different view of Schäfer 1981: 48–50.

The date of the formal foundation of the Roman colony of Aelia Capitolina before the outbreak of the war can still be inferred only from the testimony of Cassius Dio. Archaeological excavations in Jerusalem have so far produced few remains of the Roman city and certainly do not allow any chronological conclusions as regards the foundation of the colony. Attempts to resolve the problem once and for all with the help of numismatic evidence are unconvincing (Mildenberg 1980: 333). The lack of proof naturally does not justify conclusions to the contrary, for Cassius Dio still contains the only explicit pronouncement on the subject.

It may be added that the various opinions expressed in the modern literature on the causes of the revolt often reflected and still reflect varying attitudes toward the Roman empire, the Jewish people, and resistance to imperial authority. Another factor which often determines interpretations is the evaluation of Talmudic sources, considered by some unsuitable as historical source material, by others valuable if judiciously interpreted.

C. Prior Unrest

There is no historical source which offers a running account of the period between the first revolt in 70 C.E. and the Bar Kokhba war, and recourse must be had to Talmudic literature and isolated items such as inscriptions and archaeological material. It is likely that there existed a connection between the activities of the Jewish authorities at Jabneh and the outbreak of the revolt, notably their emphatic expectations of the speedy reconstruction of the temple and the unity of the Jewish people (Alon 1980–84: 111–8; 253–65; 288–307). The fierce rebellion of the Jews in the Diaspora in 115–117 C.E. is well attested, but it is a matter of debate to what extent the Jews in Judea participated (Isaac and Oppenheimer 1985: 50, n. 70). One Roman action is certain and may be relevant: the Roman garrison was strengthened well before the outbreak of the revolt, possibly in or after 117 C.E. (Isaac and Roll 1979: 54–66). This definitely shows that the garrison left by Titus in 70 C.E. was insufficient after several decades and that there was serious unrest in Judea.

The only explicit statement in any historical source is again found in the work of Cassius Dio, who tells that preparations for the war were made during the period between Hadrian's visit to Judea (in 130 C.E.) and the outbreak of the revolt. The latter is dated 132 according to Eusebius' *Chronicle* (see Schürer *HJP*[2] 1: 542, n. 126).

D. Course of the War

Given the paucity of literary sources, any attempt to describe the course of the war is speculative. We know nothing of the first stage of the revolt beyond the fact that it was successful enough for a provisional administration to function, as reflected in the documents discovered in the Judean desert. Another major project realized by the rebel government was the reissue of great quantities of local city coinage (Mildenberg 1984).

1. The Geographical Scope of the Revolt. The available evidence relates almost exclusively to Judea in the narrow and proper sense. A number of references in Talmudic sources may point to incidents in Galilee, but otherwise there is no clear proof that the war spread to that region. There is, however, no consensus on these matters (various opinions cited in Isaac and Oppenheimer 1985: 53, n. 88). Nevertheless it is indisputable that all hoards containing Jewish coins of the revolt were discovered in Judea, notably in the Hebron mountains, west of Jerusalem, and in the Judean desert (Barag 1980). Further confirmation of the fact that the focus of rebellion was in Judea is found in Talmudic sources which contain enactments dealing with the acquisition by Jews of landed property, confiscated by the Romans *(siqārîqôn)*. These were temporarily annulled in Judea, but not in Galilee. This is best explained by assuming that it was a response to large-scale land expropriations by the Romans. The intention was to preserve Jewish occupation of the land in Judea, while there was apparently no need for such measures in Galilee (*j. Giṭ.* v 47b).

After the revolt the focus of Jewish life was transferred to Galilee and the authorities established themselves at the village of Ushah (Alon 1980–84: 663–80). The movement of refugees from Judea to Galilee is illustrated by the organization in settlements in Galilee of priestly courses which were in Judea in the period of the Second Temple (Klein 1967: 62–68; Avi-Yonah 1962: 137–9; Kahane 1978–79: 9–29).

2. Conquest of Jerusalem. There is no decisive evidence to show whether Jerusalem was captured by the Jews in the revolt. The best source, Cassius Dio, is silent on the subject. Appianus and Christian authors lend support to the view that the city fell into Jewish hands and was reconquered by Roman troops (Appianus, *Syriaca* 50.252; Eusebius, *d.c.* vi 18.10; *h.e.* iv 5.2; v 12.1). The coin legend "For the Freedom of Jerusalem" has been explained as celebrating the capture of the city, and the legend "Jerusalem" has been interpreted as a mint indication. Both, however, may equally well be considered programmatic statements, expressing hopes or aims rather than achievements (Mildenberg 1984: 29–31). Serious doubts are raised by the archaeological evidence, for in the excavations carried out in the Old City of Jerusalem since 1967 almost no coins of the Bar Kokhba revolt have been found (Applebaum 1976: 27; more recent publications have not altered the validity of this observation).

3. The Roman Forces. Since there is no literary source which gives a full list, at least of the legions involved in the suppression in the revolt, we must have recourse to random information derived from epigraphic discoveries. As a result it is impossible to estimate the numbers of troops in Judea at any stage of the war (Schürer *HJP*^{2} 1: 547–9, n. 150; further references in Isaac and Oppenheimer 1985: 56, n. 102). The governor of Judea at the outbreak of the war was Tineius Rufus (Eusebius, *h.e.* iv 6.1; *Chron. Hadr.* xvi; see also the Talmudic sources). He was a consular by that time (*HJP*^{2} 1: 518). Fronto, *de bello Parthico* 2, refers to great numbers of Roman soldiers killed under Hadrian in Britain (ca. 118 C.E.) and in the Jewish rebellion. Pausanias, *Graeciae descriptio* 15.5, another contemporary author, mentions the Jewish war as the only event to disturb the peace in Hadrian's reign. Cassius Dio states that Hadrian sent his best officers to Judea under the supreme command of Julius Severus (lxix 13.2; cf. the career inscription *ILS* 1056) and also notes the great number of Roman casualties (14.3). Finally it may be considered certain that Hadrian himself traveled to Judea during the war. This may be inferred from Dio *(loc. cit.)*, Hadrian writing to the Senate, and from a letter written by Appollodorus of Damascus to Hadrian about siege implements (Stern 1980: 136, no. 322; also: Jerome, in *Joel* i 4; *Chronicon Paschale* i). It is proved by several inscriptions: *ILS* 1065, which mentions Q. Lollius Urbicus as legate of Hadrian; and *CIL* vi 974, which refers to Hadrian himself. Finally there is evidence of the participation of praetorian cohorts in the war which presumably indicates that these accompanied the emperor to Judea (*ILS* 2081).

E. Bar Kokhba, Leader of the Revolt

It is no coincidence that the revolt of Bar Kokhba was the only Jewish war fought against foreign rule in antiquity to have been named after one leader (for instance: *S. Olam Rab.*: "the war of Ben Koziba"). In Talmudic sources he is given the titles *nāśîʾ* ("ruler" or "prince") and "Messiah," and the years of his reign are described as "kingship" (for instance, *b. Sanh.* 97b). In his letters he assumes the title *nĕśîʾ yiśraʾēl,* and on coins he appears as *"šimʿôn nĕśîʾ yiśrāʾēl."* The title *nāśîʾ* has been interpreted in various ways. It has been explained as denoting a limited form of authority, lower in status than that of king and comparable to that of ethnarch, the title of the first Hasmonaean rulers (Alon 1980–84: 622). Others assume that it refers to the ideal king as in Ezekiel's vision of the end of Days (Oppenheimer 1982: 51).

R. Akiba declared of Bar Kokhba, "This is the King Messiah" (*j. Taʿan.* iv 68d; cf. *Lam. Rab.* ii 4). The role of messiah, attributed to him, has also been variously interpreted as a divine and supernatural savior and redeemer, and as a general and leader of ordinary human stature whose title merely emphasizes his royal rank (see Oppenheimer 1983, with further references).

Bar Kokhba is not mentioned by Cassius Dio or in the *Historia Augusta.* In literary sources he appears only in Talmudic literature and in Christian sources. These describe him as a murderer and a bandit, but at the same time they attribute to him miracles and supernatural signs (Eusebius, *h.e.* iv 6, 2; Jerome, *Apol.* in *Libr. Rufini* iii 31; and Alon 1980–84: ii.34).

Talmudic sources refer to Bar Kokhba ambivalently. On the one hand they emphasize his legendary strength, R. Akiba's admiration for him, and even his obedience to the sages. On the other, they criticize his addresses to God, "Do not help and do not humiliate," and it is said that he was put to death by the sages when it appeared that he was a false messiah. The Talmud recalls him as Ben Koziba, "son of a lie," a pejorative play on his actual name, Bar/Ben Kosiba (as found in the Bar Kokhba letters). He apparently was designated Bar Kokhba, "son of a star," (a messianic designation) by his supporters.

Bar Kokhba's letters, discovered in the Judean desert, give a partial but genuine impression of his personality. He seems to have been a forceful general and ruler who dealt in person with details of discipline and daily life in his army units. His leadership extended beyond the sphere of military matters, for part of his letters are concerned with the leasing of lands on his behalf. It can be seen that he insisted on the observance of religious commandments such as those of the Sabbath, the four types of tree branches for *sŭkkôt* (the Feast of Tabernacles), and precepts connected with the produce of the land.

F. The Aftermath

Talmudic literature gives vivid and extensive descriptions of the horrors of the Jewish defeat, and much is written about the bitter fate of the besieged at Bethar (*j. Taʿan.* iv 69a; *Lam. Rab.* ii 4; archaeological evidence from the "Cave of Horrors," Aharoni 1962: 186–99). Cassius Dio emphasizes the extent of the destruction in Judea, the numbers of those fallen in battle and the destruction of forts and settlements. After the revolt the Romans issued a series of disciplinary decrees, the nature of which has been much debated (Herr 1972; Lieberman 1939–44; 1975; Schäfer 1981: 194–235).

Bibliography

Aharoni, Y. 1962. Expedition B—The Cave of Horror. *IEJ* 12: 186–99.

Alon, G. 1980–84. *The Jews in Their Land in the Talmudic Age (70–640 C.E.).* 2 vols. Jerusalem.

Applebaum, S. 1976. *Prolegomena to the Study of the Second Jewish Revolt.* Oxford.

Avi-Yonah, M. 1962. A List of Priestly Courses from Caesarea. *IEJ* 12: 137–39.

Barag, D. 1980. A Note on the Geographical Distribution of Bar Kokhba Coins. *INJ* 4: 30–33.

Ben-Shalom, I. 1983. The Support of the Sages for Bar Kokhba's Revolt. *Cathedra* 29: 13–28.

Bowersock, G. W. 1980. A Roman Perspective on the Bar Kochba War. Pp. 131–41 in *Approaches to Ancient Judaism.* Vol. 2, ed. W. S. Green. Brown Judaic Studies 9. Missoula, MT.

Herr, M. D. 1972. Persecutions and Martyrdom in Hadrian's Days. *ScrHier* 23: 82–125.

———. 1978. The Causes of the Bar Kokhba War. *Zion* 43: 1–11.

Isaac, B. 1980–81. Roman Colonies in Judaea: The Foundation of Aelia Capitolina. *Talanta* 12–13: 31–54.

———. 1984. Bandits in Judaea and Arabia. *HSCP* 88: 171–203.

Isaac, B., and Oppenheimer, A. 1985. The Revolt of Bar Kokhba: Ideology and Modern Scholarship. *JJS* 36: 33–60.

Isaac, B., and Roll, I. 1979. Judaea in the Early Years of Hadrian's Reign. *Latomus* 38: 54–66.

Kahane, T. 1978–79. The Priestly Courses and Their Geographical Settlements. *Tarbiz* 48: 2–29.

Klein, S. 1967. *Galilee; Geography and History of Galilee from the Return from Babylon to the Conclusion of the Talmud.* Jerusalem.

Liebermann, S. 1939–44. The Martyrs of Caesarea. *Annuaire de l'institut de philologie et d'histoire orientales et slaves* 7: 395–446.

———. 1975. Religious Persecution of the Jews. Pp. 213–45 in *Studies in Honor of Salo Baron,* ed. S. Lieberman. New York.

Mildenberg, L. 1980. Bar Kokhba Coins and Documents. *HSCP* 84: 311–35.

———. 1984. *The Coinage of the Bar Kokhba War,* ed. P. E. Mottahedeh. Aarau.

Oppenheimer, A. 1982. The Bar Kokhba Revolt. Pp. 40–74 in *Eretz Israel from the Destruction of the Second Temple to the Muslim Conquest.* Vol. 1, ed. Z. Baras et al. Jerusalem.

———. 1983. The Messianism of Bar Kokhba. Pp. 153–65 in *Messianism and Eschatology,* ed. Z. Baras. Jerusalem.

Schäfer, P. 1981. *Der Bar Kokhba-Aufstand.* Tübingen.

Stern, M. 1980. *Greek and Latin Authors on Jews and Judaism.* Vol. 2. Jerusalem.

Benjamin Isaac
Aharon Oppenheimer

BAR KOKHBA LETTERS

The Bar Kokhba Letters are autograph letters and documents written in Hebrew, Aramaic, and Greek, which were discovered in caves W of the Dead Sea between 1950 and 1965. Some were actually written by Simon bar Kosiba, leader of the Second Jewish Revolt (*ca.* 132–135 C.E.), and all constitute important sources for this historical event.

A. Introduction and History of the Finds

It is a rare and transporting occurrence in the study of the ancient world when one comes face to face with new and unquestionably genuine material written by a known historical figure. Yet that is what has happened in the case of the legendary leader of the Second Jewish Revolt against Rome, Bar Kokhba—and not just once, but several times. Classical and rabbinic sources had provided some information on this man and the war, usually dated 132–135 C.E. But the Greek and Latin authors had no interest in the details of the conflict, about which they were silent. The rabbinic sources added little in the way of solid historical facts; they incarnated a minimal skeleton of fact with the flesh of fantasy and legend. Thus there was tremendous excitement when, beginning in the early 1950s and continuing for about a decade, documentary materials from the time of Bar Kokhba came to light. It is necessary to consider the letters in the context of all of these materials for reasons which will become clear.

Written materials from caves in the Wadi Murabbaʿat began to turn up in Jerusalem late in 1951. An archaeological expedition was mounted to explore four caves between 21 January and 21 March 1952. Along with significant biblical manuscripts, documents written in Hebrew, Aramaic, Greek, and Arabic were discovered. These documents spanned the period from the 1st century C.E. to about the 10th century, but by far the most important ones date to the time of the Second Revolt. In addition to a number of letters from Bar Kokhba to his lieutenants, contracts written during his regime or just prior to it shed significant light on the situation at the time of the war. Without them the already enigmatic letters would be even more difficult to interpret.

At this same time, Bedouin had discovered and now offered for sale additional materials related to the revolt. The find spot for these materials was for long a mystery, but it later was discovered that Bedouin had pilfered one or more caves in the Wadi Seiyal (Naḥal Ṣeelim). They apparently also had found materials in the nearby caves of Wadi Ḥabra (Naḥal Ḥever). Naḥal Ṣeelim was explored by Israeli archaeologists between 24 January and 2 February 1960, but the documentary finds were extremely fragmentary. Archaeologists also investigated Naḥal Ḥever during a two-week campaign in 1960 and again in the spring of 1961. The discoveries here were spectacular. One of the caves, known as the "Cave of Letters," yielded three separate collections of documents. The first was a packet of fifteen letters, many from Bar Kokhba himself but some from subordinates, to military leaders in charge at En-Gedi. This was an important military site in the Second Revolt located four and one-half km N of the caves. A second group of materials, the "Archive of the En-Gedites," comprises a group of six contracts concerned with the leasing of state lands. These are written in Hebrew and Aramaic. The third group of documents from the Cave of Letters was the archive of Babatha daughter of Simeon. This group numbered 36 or 37 (the number is uncertain because of unplaceable fragments), and deals with property and litigation concerned with Babatha and her family. The dates span the years 93/94–132 C.E., and the documents are in Nabatean, Aramaic, and Greek. Although Babatha lived most of her life in Maoza, in the Roman province of Arabia, at the outbreak of the war she evidently fled to En-Gedi and, eventually, to the cave where her archive was unearthed.

Many of these materials are still not fully published. All the Murabbaᶜat texts were published in volume two of the series *Discoveries in the Judaean Desert.* Texts 42–48 are Bar Kokhba letters, and numbers 49–52 may be also, but are so fragmentary that a certain identification of their genre is not impossible. The fifteen letters from Naḥal Ḥever have not been published. One must rely on prepublication descriptions, which contain significant excerpts. The Greek materials of the Babatha archive are now available, while the Semitic materials from that group are expected to be published by 1992.

B. Description and Contents

The Bar Kokhba letters thus derive from two different find spots, the caves of Murabbaᶜat and Naḥal Ḥever. They number 22 (or perhaps as many as 26 depending on the identification of Mur 49–52) and are written in three languages, Hebrew eleven, Aramaic eight, and Greek two (Ḥev 13 is so fragmentary that it is uncertain whether it is in Hebrew or Aramaic). With one exception, where an addressee is identifiable, those from Murabbaᶜat involve a man named Yeshua b. Galgula, who is designated by Mur 42 as "camp commander." The only missive which does not concern him is Mur 46, addressed to one Yose b. x (patronym lost) from Yonatan b. MḤNYM (vocalization of patronym unknown). It may be that Yose was an underling of Galgula's, for it seems likely that the letters of the Murabbaᶜat cave were brought there by Galgula or his family. The letters from Naḥal Ḥever, again with one exception, also have an obvious common denominator in their addressee, Yehonatan b. Baᶜyan (also spelled Baᶜyah). Most of the letters also mention Masabala b. Shimon, but as Ḥev 4, 5, 6 and 9 omit his name, it seems likely that this collection is Yehonatan's rather than Masabala's. These two men were co-commanders of the military forces centered in En-Gedi; perhaps Yehonatan was the senior officer, thus explaining why some matters did not involve Masabala. In the case of both groups of letters, from Murabbaᶜat and from Naḥal Ḥever, the great majority were sent by Bar Kokhba or, as the letters reveal, Shimon b. Kosiba (his real name). Mur 42, 46, and 48 are exceptions to this generalization, as are Ḥev 6 and perhaps Ḥev 3. The latter was sent by a man called Soumaios, a Hellenized form of the Hebrew name *Shimon.* The doubt as to the sender's identity arises because in another Greek letter Bar Kokhba's name is simply rendered Simon (a second way in which Greek could handle the Heb *Shimon*). Since Ḥev 3 is addressed to Yehonatan and Masabala in the manner of superior to inferior, however, and since a position of superiority is one that a "Shimon" other than Bar Kokhba is unlikely to have occupied given the considerable authority of the addressees, it is probable that "Soumaios" was simply one scribe's way of rendering his leader's name. Ḥev 3 is therefore likely to be from Shimon b. Kosiba.

The letters for the most part concern relatively trivial matters; there is no clear mention of a specific battle, for example, in a way which would enable scholars to coordinate the letters with information from classical and rabbinic sources. Further, not a single letter bears a date. The relevance of the matters which are raised to the course of the war will be considered below. The following table schematizes the addressee, sender, concerns, and language of each letter.

Table 1. An Overview of the Bar Kokhba Letters

Designation	*To*	*From*	*Language*	*Concerns*
Mur 42	Yeshua b. Galgula Camp commander	Yeshua b. Eleazar Eleazar b. Yehosef	Heb	Ownership of cow
Mur 43	Yeshua b. Galgula	Shimon b. Kosiba	Heb	Treatment of "Galileans"
Mur 44	Yeshua b. Galgula	Shimon	Heb	Shipment of wheat
Mur 45	—	—	Heb	Food shortage; death in fighting
Mur 46	Yose b. [ ]	Yonatan b. MḤNYM	Heb	Difficulties of [ ] bar Eliezer
Mur 47	—	—	Heb	A matter in Tekoa (?)
Mur 48	—	[ ] b. Yohanne	Heb	Uncertain
Ḥev 1	Yehonatan Masabala	Shimeon b. Kosiba	Aram	Confiscation of wheat; punishment of Tekoans for repairing homes; arrest of Yeshua b. Tadmoraya
Ḥev 2	Yehonatan (?) Masabala (?)	Shimon b. Kosiba	Aram	Uncertain
Ḥev 3	Yehonatan b. Baᶜyan Masabala	Soumaios	Gk	Gathering of citrons by one Agrippa
Ḥev 4	Yehonatan b. Baᶜyan	Shimon b. Kosiba	Aram	Yehonatan is to assist one Elisha in all he does
Ḥev 5	Yehonatan	—	Heb	Mentions the "people of En Gedi"
Ḥev 6	Yehonatan	Ananos (Hanan)	Gk	Sending of supplies to troops; Hanan transmits order from B. Kokhba
Ḥev 7	(very badly preserved)	Shimon b. Kosiba	Heb	Uncertain
Ḥev 8	Yehonatan b. Baᶜyan Masabala b. Shimon	Shimon b. Kosiba	Aram	Sending of Eleazar b. Hitta to B. Kokhba immediately
Ḥev 9	Yehonatan	Shimon b. Kosiba (?)	Heb	Uncertain

Ḥev 10	Yonatan Masabala	Shimon	Aram	Sending supplies to camp(s)
Ḥev 11	Yehonatan b. Baᶜyan Masabala	Shimon b. Kosiba	Aram	Mentions Romans; requires the two to come to Shimon and bring Thyriss b. Tinianus; mentions a rabbi, Bitniya b. Mesa
Ḥev 12	The men of En Gedi Masabala Yehonatan b. Baᶜyan	Shimon b. Kosiba	Heb	Negligence of addressees; mentions a ship
Ḥev 13	Masabala (?) + (?) very fragmentary	——	?	——
Ḥev 14	Yehonatan Masabala	Shimon b. Kosiba	Aram	Mobilization or punishment of Tekoans refusing to fight
Ḥev 15	Yehudah b. Manasseh	Shimon	Aram	Gathering of the four "kinds" for Feast of Tabernacles

C. Historical Significance

It is commonly remarked that the Second Revolt lacked a historian such as the First Revolt possessed in Josephus, author of *Bellum Judaicum.* This remark may be a little naive if it means to suggest that by virtue of Josephus the course of events in the First Revolt (66–74 C.E.) is entirely clear, but it contains a basic truth: we are almost entirely ignorant about the Bar Kokhba rebellion. Basic questions such as the causes of the outbreak, the geographical extent of the conflict, and even the dates of the war are impossible to answer definitively because of lack of evidence. The Bar Kokhba letters are teasers in regard to these questions: scholars may feel that by reading between the lines, it will be possible to deduce something more than the immediate exigencies which provoked their composition.

Thus the scholarly literature on the war is replete with speculations of varying plausibility. The fact remains that in spite of the discovery of the letters and the contracts which often help in their understanding, it is not possible to write a history of the Second Revolt. Still, the letters and accompanying documents do shed considerable light on certain limited aspects of the situation. Among other things they illumine the course of the war, the administration under Bar Kokhba, and the prosopography of those involved in the conflict—but even here scholars are often divided on how to understand the new evidence.

1. The Course of the War. According to the ancient historian Cassius Dio, the war between Rome and the Jews was the result of the Emperor Hadrian's attempt to build a shrine to the Roman god Jupiter Capitolinus on the site of the ruined Jewish temple to Yahweh. The effort was in connection with the emperor's rather aggressive policy of building Hellenistic cities throughout the eastern portions of the empire. The *Life of Hadrian,* on the other hand, attributes the outbreak of the conflict to Hadrian's prohibition of castration which, in Roman eyes, included "half-hearted" efforts such as circumcision. Many scholars think that these two suggested causes ought to be understood as complementary rather than mutually exclusive; indeed, this seems a reasonable interpretation. Typically, Greco-Roman sources do not mention another aspect of the Jewish situation which may well have been equally significant in provoking conflict: messianic speculation and eschatological calculations. It is said in rabbinic literature that Rabbi Akiba, one of Bar Kokhba's principal supporters, was among the *mĕḥaššĕbê ʾittōt,* "calculators of the (end) times." In other words, he was taken up with messianic speculations and the attempt to calculate when the Messiah would appear based on hints in the Scriptures. The pseudepigraphic work *Apocalypse of Baruch,* now extant only in Syriac, is a writing from the period immediately after the destruction of the temple in 69 C.E., one with many connections to rabbinic Judaism in terms of concept and legal interpretations. It is therefore not unreasonable to suggest that it represents the type of thinking which was going on in some circles of nascent rabbinic Judaism in the period between the revolts. The dominant typology of *Baruch* involves the temple: it draws parallels between the destruction of the first temple at the time of Jeremiah and that of the second in 69 C.E. Just as there was a rebuilding of the first temple under Ezra and Nehemiah 70 years after its destruction, *Baruch* promises a future rebuilding, a third temple, to inaugurate messianic times. For a people saturated in scriptural knowledge such as these circles of ancient Jewry, who were convinced of such typologies, it was natural to think that another seventy-year period would be involved. And thus the date of the outbreak of the revolt is perhaps connected to an understanding of its causes: here the Bar Kokhba material may be helpful.

Scholars usually prefer the dates Cassius Dio supplies for the revolt, 132–135 C.E., to those of other ancient sources. Mur 24 appears to confirm the first date. This document belongs to the genre of lease contract known in Greek as *diastrōma;* examples have long been known from the Oxyrhynchus papyri of Egypt. Mur 24 specifies in lines 9 and 10 that the lease is to last "until the end of the eve of Remission, which is five full fiscal years." Since the document is dated "the twentieth of Shebat, the second year of (the era of) the redemption of Israel by Shimon b. Kosiba, Prince of Israel," it must have been composed in the second year of the seven-year sabbatical cycle. Earlier sabbath years are known, making it possible to affirm that 131/132 C.E. was the first year of the cycle and, therefore, this document was written in early February 134; concomittantly, the revolt must have begun in 132/133. It is not known whether the years of the revolt were dated from Nisan, the first month of the Jewish year for some functions, or from Tishri, the seventh month but considered the first for other functions. Mur 24 is not the earliest dated document among those of Bar Kokhba's era—that honor belongs to Ḥev 42, which dates to April 132 C.E.

Given that the temple in Jerusalem had been destroyed in 69 C.E. and that, on the basis of a "seventy-year" typology, the next would be built in 139 C.E., it appears that the revolt broke out seven years prior to what some expected to be the dawn of the messianic era. Seven is, of course, a number pregnant with significance in eschatological speculation, and one might suspect that such passages as Dan 9:24–27 and the prophecy of "Seventy Weeks" helped guide those calculating the end. The Bar Kokhba materials thus support the suggestion that eschatological fervor fueled the outbreak of the war, confirming the possible relationship between the war's outbreak and the expected dawn, after a seven-year period of "tribulation," of messianic peace.

With regard to the end of the war, Greco-Roman evidence is not specific. The few known facts seem to require that it ended in late 135 C.E. The Bar Kokhba materials accord with such a date. The latest dated document is Mur 30, written in October 135. The place where it was written is not fully preserved, but what can be read fuels another debate about the Second Revolt for which the Bar Kokhba materials are relevant: whether the rebels ever succeeded in capturing Jerusalem.

Little doubt attaches to the question whether the rebellion aimed at the conquest of Jerusalem. Coins minted by the rebels amply demonstrate the significance of the city in contemporary ideology. They picture numerous images connected with the sacrificial cultus, which had apparently ceased with the defeat of the First Revolt. Some coins bear the inscriptions *yršlm,* "Jerusalem," or more fully *lḥrwt yrwšlm,* "of the freedom of Jerusalem." That they sought to capture the city, indeed, that its capture from the Roman occupiers was perhaps the preminent goal of the warriors under Bar Kokhba, is not at issue. But did they succeed? On this point scholarly opinion is divided.

Against the possibility of conquest is the silence of the best ancient authority, Cassius Dio. Also weighing on the side of the negative is the numismatic evidence. Almost no coins of the Bar Kokhba period have been discovered in Jerusalem, in face of the relatively numerous hoards known from elsewhere in Judea. But this negative evidence, significant as it is, may not be enough to decide the issue. Christian authors of the patristic period are unanimous in asserting that Jewish forces took the city and that the Romans eventually won it back. And two of the Bar Kokhba documents seem to confirm this assertion.

Mur 29, inscribed in August/September 133, says that it was transacted *b[ ]šlym.* Apparently only two letters are missing, probably spelling *byršlym,* "in Jerusalem" (similarly Mur 30, dating as noted to October 135). The reading is unfortunately broken, but it is not apparent what toponym could fit the letters which remain, other than "Jerusalem." (One must be cautious about being overly assertive on this point, however, for the documents under discussion have revealed quite a few previously unknown toponyms.) Also in favor of the view that the rebels held Jerusalem at some point in the war is the evidence of the dating formulas used in the Bar Kokhba contracts and, in modified form, on the coins.

The full form of the standard dating formula was seldom used. Usually contracts would abbreviate by dropping one or more elements. All the contracts would begin, however, with a notation of the day, month, and year of the Bar Kokhba era. A contract from Kefar Baru may provide the best example of the full form. After noting day, month, and year it reads "of the Freedom of Israel at the hands of Shimon ben Kosiba, Prince of Israel." Other contracts, and coins, read "of the Redemption of Israel." The coins and contracts use either "redemption" or "freedom" capriciously, so that, contrary to what was once believed, nothing can be inferred from these terms as to the ideology or progress of the war. One contract, Mur 25, reads "year three of the Freedom of Jerusalem." Taking all this evidence together, it appears that the Bar Kokhba era was dated alternately by "the Freedom of Jerusalem," the "Freedom of Israel," or "the Redemption of Israel." (The dated contracts so far known are, from earliest to latest, Ḥev 42, Mur 22, Mur 23, Mur 24, Mur 29, Kefar Baru, Mur 25, Ḥev 44, Ḥev 45–46, Ḥev 47, "Kefar Bebayu" [now known to come from Kefar Baru], and Mur 30.) The implication of this prosaic dating phraseology is therefore that there existed an equivalence between the freedom of Israel and that of Jerusalem. The formulas thus suggest that the war began with an uprising led by Bar Kokhba which liberated Jerusalem and began the new era by occupying the city. If the readings in Mur 29 and 30 are indeed referring to Jerusalem, then it would seem that the city was in the hands of the rebels for a substantial portion of the war. It is possible, of course, that this period was punctuated by one or more Roman reconquests of the city. But it would seem that, toward the end of the war, the city was under rebel control for long enough to provide some feeling of security. This impression arises from two of the Bar Kokhba letters, Ḥev 3 and Ḥev 15, which apparently belong together.

Ḥev 3 is written in Greek and follows Greek epistolographic conventions. It reads in full:

> Soumaios to Jonathan son of Baianos and to Masabala, greetings: I already sent Agrippa to you. Make haste to send me . . . and citrons. And he [Agrippa] will transport these things back to the headquarters of the Jews. And be sure you do so! It was written in Greek because no one was found [was able?] to write it in "Hebrew." Dismiss him very speedily in view of the festival. And be sure you do so! Soumaios. Farewell. [author's translation]

Ḥev 15 is written in Aramaic and, accordingly, follows the conventions then governing Hebrew and Aramaic letters. It reads:

> Shimon to Yehudah bar Menasseh, at Qiryat Arabayah. I have sent to you two donkeys that you should send with them two men to Yehonatan bar Baʿyan and Masabala. They are to load them with branches and citrons and send them to the camp, to you. As for you, send other men to bring to you myrtles and willows. Prepare them (= tithe them?) and send them to the camp (i.e., to Shimon) because the men comprising the forces are numerous. Be well. [author's translation]

It is impossible to be certain of the relation of these letters to one another, if indeed they are referring to the same situation. One scenario which seems to make sense is to assume that Shimon wrote the Greek letter first. Yehonatan and Masabala carried out their orders and sent branches and citrons to the main camp of the Jews located, perhaps, at Jerusalem. There the forces were about to celebrate the Festival of Tabernacles—those who could be spared and could disengage the Romans for a week or so. Shimon had previously arranged to get myrtles and willows, the other two of the "four kinds" used in the celebration, elsewhere. As men (with their families?) continued to arrive, however, it became evident that not enough of the four kinds had been gathered, so Shimon sent a letter to Yehudah b. Menasseh to arrange for more to be sent. Other interpretations are equally cogent, but the important point is this: Shimon b. Kosiba, a man known from other letters as a Jew who adhered strictly to the legal requirements of Jewish observance, was about to celebrate the Festival of Tabernacles.

In addition to the procession bearing the four kinds, the Feast of Tabernacles was distinctive in two regards: like Passover and Pentecost, it was a pilgrimage festival; adult males were required to journey to Jerusalem. Second, it required the most burnt offerings of any occasion of the religious calendar. While by the time of Bar Kokhba it was perhaps not always legally necessary to journey to Jerusalem, it was always desirable. If offerings were to be made, they, of course, could be made nowhere else. Thus it is likely that at the time of these two letters Jewish forces controlled Jerusalem, although, as noted, it is not absolutely certain. We are ignorant of precisely how the feast was to be celebrated.

Assuming the reading of Mur 30 is indeed "Jerusalem," then it is clear that Bar Kokhba was in control of the city at the time of the Feast of Tabernacles (Tishri 15–22) in the year 135. Do the two letters date from that year, the only year in which there is direct evidence of Jewish control of the city at the time of the festival? Again, the data are of uncertain interpretation, but it appears that the answer is no.

Both letters come from Naḥal Ḥever and, presumably, the "papers" of Yehonatan b. Baᶜyan. It appears that b. Menasseh had sent his letter on to Yehonatan and Masabala as an explanation of his requirements from them. Now, among the Ḥever materials no document thus far published postdates Ḥev 47, a contract of January 135, some eight months before Tabernacles of that year. During this year, the last of the revolt, Roman forces were presumably wiping out the last centers of Jewish resistance. Thus it seems likely that En Gedi, Yehonatan's village, had already been conquered before Tabernacles of 135—a date which is, after all, at most two months prior to the end of the revolt.

Thus, from this rather lengthy excursus, it would seem that the letters pertain to the year 134 or perhaps earlier. Since according to Mur 29, rebel forces apparently held Jerusalem in late August of 133—only a short time before the Festival of that year—the letters may refer to that occasion. The problem with that hypothesis is that the other Bar Kokhba letters addressed to En Gedi seem to presuppose a deteriorating situation in which the men of Tekoa, for example, have lost heart and refuse to support the now clearly failing rebellion. If this intuition is correct, and if the En Gedi letters all date to the last months before it fell to the Romans, then once again we are back to the year 134. And if so, then we may perceive Jewish control of Jerusalem at the beginning of the revolt in 132, in August 133, in October 134, and in October 135. The implication is of a rather lengthy Jewish control of the capital city whose loss signaled the ultimate failure of the revolt.

The Bar Kokhba materials also indicate something of the geographical extent of the war. Taken together with the findings of archaeology and the numismatic evidence, it appears that the revolt was very largely, if not entirely, confined to Judea. Thus the mention of "Galileans" in Mur 43 should not be understood to imply any large-scale hostilities to the north. The reference is probably to Jews from Galilee who had joined the efforts in the south and who now required discipline.

2. Administration of Israel. Indirectly, and if one or two reasonable assumptions are admitted, the Bar Kokhba materials reveal a considerable amount about the political administration during the period 132–135 C.E. It is perhaps fortuitous that among the names which are prominent either in these materials or in the little evidence we possess from classical sources, there are several which served as the capitals of toparchies in the time of the First Revolt and, apparently, in the period which led up to the Second Revolt. Josephus, in *JW* 3.54–55, provides a list of the toparchies in his time, and there one finds, among others, Jerusalem, the central toparchy; Acraba; Herodium; Beth Gubrin (very near Betar, the site of the final battle of the war); and En Gedi. One of the two toparchies of Peraea, Livias, is mentioned prominently in Papyrus Yadin 37 (part of Babatha's archive). In addition, new discoveries in the caves at Ketef Jericho from the time of the revolt may suggest that Jericho, another toparchy mentioned by Josephus, was still functioning as such under b. Kosiba.

Of course, the mere mention of these localities in the Bar Kokhba materials does not alone indicate that he had taken over the administrative machinery he found operating under the Romans. But the evidence that he did so consists of more than mere names. He appears to have taken over imperial lands which had belonged to Hadrian and to have continued the system of leasing them which the Romans employed. For example, in Mur 24, several men lease lands from the administrator in Herodium, a man named Hillel b. Garis. These lands were in a village by the name of ᶜIr Naḥaš of uncertain location. It is clear that the men had to travel to Herodium in order to transact the lease and, therefore, it would seem that it was the capital of a toparchy for at least a part of the war. Later it may have fallen, for while Mur 47, presumably addressed to Yeshua b. Galgula, appears to require him to act in Tekoa (as one would expect the commander of nearby Herodium to do), both Ḥev 1 and 14 direct the attention of the commanders of En Gedi to matters there. Presumably such would not have been necessary if Herodium still functioned. We know from Mur 24 that it was still in Jewish hands in February 134, but later in that year Tekoa was administered from En Gedi. In addition to larger capitals of toparchies, there were smaller centers of bureaucracy as well.

At each administrative center b. Kosiba appears to have appointed one or more "civilian" administrators to lease the state-held lands. These were designated in Hebrew by the term *parnās,* and in Aramaic, if our inference is correct, by *šāṭĕrâ.* The names of a number of such officials are known from the letter and contracts. The administrators of Beth Mashiko near Herodium (?) were Yeshua b. Eleazer and Eleazer b. Yehosef, the men who sent Mur 42 to b. Galgula. In the first year of the revolt the administrators of state lands in En Gedi were Yehonatan b. MḤNYM and Ḥorin b. Ishmael. By the third year only Yehonatan is mentioned in Ḥev 44–46. It appears that Ḥorin was removed or killed in battle. Ḥev 1 mentions a Ḥanun b. Ishmael who is in trouble with b. Kosiba because of some dealings involving wheat. If the two men were brothers—an uncertain point, since about two percent of Jewish men bore the name Ishmael—then perhaps Ḥorin was guilty, with his brother, of malfeasance. At Herodium Hillel b. Garis apparently functioned as *parnās,* although he is not so called. At Kefar Baru, located perhaps in Transjordan near Machaerus, Eleazer b. Eleazar is called a *šāṭĕrâ,* and sells a house (his own, not one belonging to the state). Just north of Beth Gubrin, an archaeological survey has discovered a lead plaque which reads, "Bar Kosiba, Prince of Israel, and his administrator, Shimon DSWY, one half."

In addition to these civilian administrators who leased out the vast estates to which b. Kosiba had fallen heir, there were military commanders in charge of "camps." Yeshua b. Galgula was one such, apparently stationed at Herodium. Yehonatan and Masabala were the two in En Gedi. Yehudah b. Menasseh of Ḥev 15 was apparently another, as may have been Ananos of the Greek letter Ḥev 6 (= Ḥanun b. Ishmael of Ḥev 1?). These men were in charge of military operations; from the surviving letters they seem to have been greatly involved with problems of supplies, especially of wheat. En Gedi served as b. Kosiba's port, wheat coming thence across the Dead Sea. Yehonatan and Masabala saw to it that it was sent where it was needed. From Mur 42 one may deduce that civilian administrators were subordinate to the military commanders of camps.

3. Prosopography. Space permits only a brief indication of the application of the Bar Kokhba finds to this aspect of 2d century Palestine. Actually, prosopographical analysis of these texts is difficult and risky because of the fact that so many Jews of both sexes bore the same overwhelmingly common names. It is comparable to a situation in which seventy or eighty per cent of all male Americans would be named Tom, Dick, Harry, Mike, John, or Jim. How can one decide which Tom is the one in question in a given text? In spite of this obstacle, some insights are possible.

First, we now know, as indicated, the real name of the leader of the revolt. From Christian texts we had known him as Bar Kokhba, "the son of the star." Rabbinic texts call him Bar Koziba, "the son of the Liar." It is now clear that both these appellations are puns on Bar Kosiba's given name. "Bar Kokhba" refers to his messianic claims, which are evident, for example, in the star depicted on some of his coins. The reference is to Num 24:7, "a star shall arise from Jacob," a traditional messianic text. The rabbinic pun is, of course, reaction to the failure of the revolt.

His letters reveal b. Kosiba as a man involved in the small details of affairs in the various camps. They show him to be a man of piety in the sense of legal observance, and of harsh threats. The degree to which this messianic claimant had to resort to threats to get his own men to carry out his orders is both surprising and revealing. He seems to have commanded little awe from his peers, although ordinary soldiers may have been more impressed. And, of course, it must be remembered that most or all of the letters date from a period in the revolt when it was becoming clear to all but the most idealistic of the faithful that the war could not be won.

From the Babatha materials it seems that she was related to the military commander of En Gedi, Yehonatan b. Baᶜyan. Babatha was married twice in her short life (she probably did not live to be older than 30), and the second of her husbands came from En Gedi. Upon his death she inherited property there, and the descriptions of those holdings give us some insight into the topography of the village. The legal materials belonging to her also reveal her to have been a woman of some wealth. Given her relation to Yehonatan b. Baᶜyan, one may hazard that he, too, was a relatively wealthy individual and that their family was one of the leading families of En Gedi. Yehonatan could apparently read all three languages—Greek, Hebrew, and Aramaic—which were in common use among the Jews of Palestine. If his appointment as camp commander is paradigmatic, then we may conclude that b. Kosiba drew his administrators and highest military officers from the village upper classes and families of elders. The ordinary soldiers of his army may have been more like Eleazar b. Hashiloni, Ḥalifa b. Yehosef, and Naqalah b. Yehonatan, three illiterates who leased land in Mur 24 but were unable to sign their own names.

In addition to the aspects of their study here discussed, the Bar Kokhba letters and related materials contain precious information on many other areas of ancient Palestinian life which space precludes discussing. These areas include sociolinguistics, legal and religious practice, Roman administration, and the economics of early 2d century Palestine. While they leave many questions unanswered and frustrate scholars who wish to pull the veil back a little further, they are a priceless legacy of the ancient world.

Bibliography

Benoit, P.; Milik, J. T.; and de Vaux, R. 1961. *Les Grottes de Murabbaat.* DJD 2. Oxford.

Fitzmyer, J. A. 1962. The Bar Cochba Period. Pp. 133–68 in *The Bible in Current Catholic Thought: Gruenthaner Memorial Volume,* ed. J. L. McKenzie. New York.

Goodblatt, D. 1987. A Contribution to the Prosopography of the Second Revolt: Yehudah bar Menasheh. *JJS* 38:38–55.

Isaac B., and Oppenheimer, A. 1985. The Revolt of Bar Kokhba: Ideology and Modern Scholarship. *JJS* 36:33–60.

Kloner, A. 1988. *Lwḥyt-mšql mᶜwprt šl mynhl bn-kwsb* ʾ? *Qadmoniot* 21: 44–48.

Lehmann, M. 1963–. Studies in the Murabbaᶜat and Naḥal Ḥever Documents. *RevQ* 4: 53–81.

Lewis, N.; Yadin, Y.; and Greenfield, J. C. 1989. *The Documents from the Bar Kokhba Period in the Cave of Letters: Greek Papyri; Aramaic and Nabatean Signatures and Subscriptions.* Jerusalem.

Lifshitz, B. 1961. The Greek Documents from Naḥal Ṣeelim and Naḥal Mishmar. *IEJ* 11: 53–62.

———. 1962. Papyrus grecs du désert de Juda. *Aegyptus* 42: 240–58.

Mildenberg, L. 1984. *The Coinage of the Bar Kokhba War.* Aarav.

Yadin, Y. 1961. Expedition D. *IEJ* 11: 36–52.

———. 1962. Expedition D—The Cave of the Letters. *IEJ* 12: 227–57.

———. 1971. *Bar Kokhba.* London.

Michael O. Wise

BAR KOSIBA. See BAR KOKHBA.

BAR-JESUS (PERSON) [Gk *Bariēsoûs*]. A magician, also called a "Jewish false prophet" (Acts 13:6), in the court of Sergius Paulus, proconsul of Cyprus at Paphos. When Sergius Paulus requested to hear Paul and Barnabas, Bar-Jesus opposed them, which resulted in his being struck blind at Paul's denouncement. He is called a false prophet because of his opposition to the message of Paul and Barnabas rather than his association with the practice of magic. In his denunciation, Paul called Bar-Jesus "son of the devil," a play on his name, "son of Jesus." The element *bar* is Aramaic for "son" (Acts 13:10). Bar-Jesus was also known as ELYMAS, a name sometimes interpreted to mean "magician," based on the statement in Acts 13:8. The awkward phrasing in 13:8, however, is likely meant to identify Bar-Jesus with Elymas rather than suggesting Elymas means "magician."

FRANK E. WHEELER

BARABBAS (PERSON) [Gk *Barabbas*]. The name "Barabbas" occurs in all four Gospels for the criminal chosen by the crowd—at the prompting of the priests, in preference to Jesus Christ—for Pilate to release on the feast of the Passover. His name does not occur elsewhere in the NT, and there is no extra-biblical account of his activities leading up to the biblical account, nor of his subsequent history.

"Barabbas" is evidently the Gk rendering of an Aram name, although the precise origin is debated. Most scholars suggest that it is a patronymic derived from Bar Abba, "son of Abba." Some suggest that Barabbas' father was named "Abba." Although no written evidence exists for the use of Abba as a personal name in Jesus' day, a contemporary of Johanan ben Zakkai (*ca.* A.D. 75) was so named (*m. Peʾa* ii. e), and thereafter the evidence for the use of Abba as a personal name is quite conclusive (Abrahams 1924: 201–2). Others suggest that Barabbas was the son of a well-known rabbi, because "Abba" was used for esteemed scholars and rabbis. There are even some codices with a double "*r*" in the name, suggesting the possibility that Barabbas is derived from Bar Rabba(n), meaning "son of a teacher." A less likely suggestion is that Barabbas finds its origin as a disguised abbreviation for the venerated name Abraham ("son of Abraham").

An interesting variant occurs in Matt 27:16–7, where he is called "Jesus Barabbas." While extant manuscript evidence is weak, Origen implies that most manuscripts in his day (*ca.* A.D. 240) included the full name. Many scholars today accept the full name in Matthew as original and suggest that it was probably omitted by later scribes because of the repugnance of having Jesus Christ's name being shared by Barabbas (*TCGNT,* 67–8). It is not improbable for Barabbas to have the very common name *Jesus.* Matthew's text reads more dramatically with two holders of the same name: "Which Jesus do you want; the son of Abba, or the self-styled Messiah" (cf. Albright and Mann *Matthew* AB, 343–4). There is some evidence that the full name "Jesus Barabbas" also originally appeared in Mark's gospel (Mann *Mark* AB, 637).

Barabbas is called "one of those among the rebels who had committed murder in the insurrection" (Mark 15:7; Luke 23:19; cf. Acts 3:14), a "notorious prisoner" (Matt 27:16), and a "robber" (John 18:40). These terms closely resemble the characteristics of social banditry uncovered in recent studies of the social history of 1st century Palestine (e.g., Horsley and Hanson 1985: 48–87). As a bandit (*lēstēs,* the same term used of the two criminals between whom Jesus was crucified [Mark 15:27]), Barabbas may have belonged to one of the rural brigands. These brigands were popular with the common people because they preyed upon the wealthy establishment of Israel and created havoc for the Roman government. Barabbas was being held prisoner by the Roman authorities at the time of Jesus' trial and was released by Pontius Pilate to carry out the customary paschal pardon (Mark 15:6–15). The reason given for the crowd choosing Barabbas over Jesus is said to be the instigation of the chief-priests and elders (Matt 27:20; Mark 15:11), but quite likely the Jerusalem crowds also preferred Barabbas's active methods of Roman resistance to Jesus' way of nonresistance.

The absence of extra-biblical historical verification for the paschal pardon custom remains a problem. Some scholars have attempted to resolve the difficulty by suggesting that the entire incident, including Barabbas himself, is an apologetic creation of the evangelists (e.g., Rigg 1945; Maccoby 1970; Davies 1980). But recent studies have produced evidence of widespread customs of prisoner releases at festivals in the ancient world (e.g., Merritt 1985: 53–68). The gospel account of a custom of reprieve of a prisoner at the Passover echoes the practice of the ancient world.

The portrait of Barabbas in the gospel account remains hazy. In contrast, the portrait of the innocently charged Jesus is thrown into sharp focus. Such appears to be the purpose of the evangelists.

Bibliography

Abrahams, I. 1924. Barabbas. Pp. 201–2 in *Studies in Pharisaism and the Gospels.* 2d Series. New York. Repr. 1967.

Bruce, F. F. 1969. *New Testament History.* Anchor Books. Garden City.

Davies, S. L. 1980. Who Is Called Bar Abbas? *NTS* 27: 260–2.

Horsley, R. A., and Hanson, J. S. 1985. *Bandits, Prophets, and Messiahs.* Minneapolis.

Maccoby, H. Z. 1970. Jesus and Barabbas. *NTS* 16: 55–60.

Merritt, R. L. 1985. Jesus Barabbas and the Paschal Pardon. *JBL* 104: 57–68.

Rigg, H. A., Jr. 1945. Barabbas. *JBL* 64: 417–56.

MICHAEL J. WILKINS

BARACHEL (PERSON) [Heb *barakʾēl*]. The father of Elihu from the land of Buz (Job 32:2). Barachel is not otherwise attested, whereas Berechiah is attested as a Jewish personal name both epigraphically and in the MT (see BERECHIAH). The name does, however, occur in Safaitic (Harding 1971: 102). Although the speech of Elihu (Job 32–37) most probably is an early orthodox addition (and commentary) to the original book of Job, the Elihu-author obviously took pains to accommodate his hero to the Arabian locale of the book of Job by means of Elihu's patronym and country of origin. The Masoretic tradition, as represented by the Leningrad Codex, may acknowledge the Arabian context of Barachel by its peculiar vocalization, which does not accord to the rules of classical Hebrew word formation (one might expect *bĕrakʾēl or bārakʾēl).

Bibliography

Harding, G. L. 1971. *An Index and Concordance of Pre-Islamic Arabian Names and Inscriptions*. Near and Middle East Series, 8. Toronto.

ERNST AXEL KNAUF

BARAITA [Aram *bāraytāʾ* = Heb *ḥîṣônâ*, "outside"]. The Babylonian Talmud often (and the Jerusalem Talmud once) uses this term in reference to a text that is to be distinguished from the Mishnah of R. Judah Hanasi. Thus, a baraita is a "mishnah" that is "outside" the recognized Mishnaic canon. More correctly, a baraita is any text or tradition not included in the Mishnah for which tannaitic status is claimed (the Tannaim were religious leaders of the Mishnaic period).

Baraitot (pl. of baraita) are preserved in independent collections and in both Talmuds. Collections of baraitot include the Tosefta and the legal midrashim *(Mekilta, Sifra, and Sifre)*. See also MIDRASH. The Talmuds preserve thousands of individual baraitot. The Babylonian Talmud generally introduces them with technical terms, including *tĕnô rabbānān* ("our teachers taught"), *dĕtanyāʾ* ("from the teachers"), etc.; in the Jerusalem Talmud there is often no such introduction.

Baraitot originated in various ways. In addition to tannaitic traditions that were preserved independently of R. Judah Hanasi's Mishnah, there are others that, given their dependence on Judah's Mishnah, were clearly composed later (Albeck 1960: 32–33). The Babylonian Talmud preserves Babylonian baraitot (Higger 1948: 36–41), some of which may have been composed by tannaim who settled there in the 2d century (Neusner 1962) but others of which were authored by Amoraim (religious leaders of the Talmudic period). In addition, baraitot of all kinds were transformed by the Babylonian rabbis (Jacobs 1971; Hauptman 1988).

The form in which baraitot circulated in the talmudic period is subject to question. For example, Albeck (1969: 58–72) claims that the Tosefta (a standard collection of baraitot) was not yet present before the authors of the Babylonian Talmud; Neusner widely assumes that it was. Hauptman (1988) shows that there were at least organized collections of baraitot at this time.

The authority of baraitot among rabbinic traditions is second only to the Mishnah. An Amora could (theoretically) dispute a Mishnah or baraita only with the support of another baraita. Thus, the presence of such a wide variety of baraitot in the talmudic tradition provided for immense flexibility in the developing system.

Bibliography

Albeck, H. 1960. *meḥqarîm bĕbāraytāʾ wĕtôseptāʾ wĕyaḥăsan lĕtalmûd.* Jerusalem.
———. 1969. *mabôʾ lattalmûdîm.* Tel Aviv.
DeVries, B. 1971. Baraita, Beraitot. *EncJud* 4: 189–93.
Hauptman, J. 1988. *Development of the Talmudic Sugya: Relationship between Tannaitic and Amoraic Sources.* Lanham, MD.
Higger, M. 1948. *ʾôṣar habbĕraytôt.* Vol. 10. New York.
Jacobs, L. 1971. Are There Fictitious Baraitot in the Babylonian Talmud? *HUCA* 42: 185–96.
Neusner, J. 1962. Studies on the Problem of Tannaim in Babylonia (ca. 130–160 C.E.). *PAAJR* 30: 79–127.

DAVID KRAEMER

BARAK (PERSON) [Heb *bārāq*]. The son of Abinoam and military commander from Kedesh, located in Naphtali, north of lake Huleh (Judg 4:6). His name (meaning "lightning") is widely attested among the Semitic peoples (*HALAT* 155). Barak was summoned from the north by DEBORAH in Ephraim to fight against a coalition of forces commanded by Sisera (note the plural *mĕlākîm* "kings" in Judg 5:19; *Judges* AB, 94). Not all the tribes of Israel were enthusiastic about the mobilization (Judg 5:16–17), but contingents from Benjamin (probably brought by Deborah), Issachar, Zebulun, and Naphtali were led to battle near Meggido by Deborah and Barak. Sisera's army was routed all the way to his home town of Harosheth Haggoyim and was murdered by Jael as predicted by Deborah (Judg 4:15–21). The story contrasts the role of Barak with Deborah. The narrator named Deborah the judge, not Barak. It is possible that he occupied a similar position in the north by virtue of his military stature, but the texts do not say so. It is Deborah who manifests a greater faith in Yahweh than Barak. And Barak loses the opportunity to personally humiliate his foe. Yet ironically it is Barak and not Deborah who is cited by the New Testament writer of Hebrews for his faith (Heb 11:32). If we read with the LXX and Peshitta *bārāq* instead of the MT *bĕdān* in 1 Sam 12:11, then Barak has once again usurped Deborah's place in the tale of heroes.

Bibliography

Clines, D. J. A. 1972. X, X BEN X, BEN Y: Personal Names in Hebrew Narrative Style. *VT* 22: 266–87.

KIRK E. LOWERY

BARDAISAN OF EDESSA (PERSON). A nobleman of Edessa (ca. A.D. 155–222) and associate of its ruler King Abgar VIII (d. A.D. 212; Drijvers *ANRW* 8:2.876; not Abgar IX as Duval 1891–92: 212). Bardaisan was reputed to be of Parthian or Armenian origin, skilled in archery and schooled in Greek philosophy and rhetoric (Sextus Julius Africanus, *Kestoi*, cf. *PG* 10.45–46; Eusebius *h.e.* 4.30; *p.e.* 6.9; Hieronymus *vir. ill.* 33; Epiphanius *haer.* 56). The earliest known Syriac author, Bardaisan invented the *madrāšâ* (Syr), a hymn composed in isosyllabic verse which uses parallelism, rhyme, alliteration, and a variety of wordplay to achieve its effects. Later Greek tradition erroneously attributes this accomplishment to his son Harmonius (Sozomenus *h.e.* 3.16; Brock 1980: 6). According to Ephrem Syrus (d. A.D. 373), in imitation of David's Psalms, Bardaisan composed 150 such hymns, fragments of which are preserved by later Syriac authors (Beck 1957: 203 = Ephrem *HCH* 53.6; cf. Drijvers 1966: 165). Also extant is a dialogue, composed on the Platonic model by his disciple, Phillip, entitled in the Syriac manuscript *The Book of the Laws of the Countries* (Nau 1907 = *BLC;* cf. Drijvers 1965) but known by Eusebius as *On Fate.* Substantively and formally influenced by Carneades' *nomima barbarika,* it sets forth as Bardaisan's view a subtle reconciliation of natural law, astrological determinism, and free will (Eusebius *h.e.* 4.30; *p.e.* 6.10.6 and *Clem. recogn.* 9.19; Schaeder 1932: 32–41; Drijvers 1966: 60–95). Later sources attribute to him works on astronomy, astrology, chronology, and ethnography, particularly on Indian customs, and a history of Armenia.

A clear and unbiased view of Bardaisan's teaching is virtually impossible since all relevant information is mediated by later sources originating with either his followers or their opponents. The formulation of the content of his doctrine depends which of diverse and often conflicting sources are seen as most reliable. Having distinguished three distinct cosmogonic traditions preserved in the later Syriac sources, Drijvers (1966: 96–152) harmonizes the earliest with *BLC* and Ephrem. By contrast, Jansma (1969; cf. Davids 1971) argues that "catholicising" and "manichaeicising" tendencies among the later Bardaisanites militate against this approach; in his view, *BLC* and Ephrem *HCH* 55 best represent the two later tendencies and should be distinguished both from one another and from Bardaisan's views. Essentially following the method of Drijvers produces the following cosmogony: There are four entities (Syr *ʾîtyê* = Gk *ousiai*), water, fire, light, and wind, arranged horizontally according to the cardinal points of the compass, as N, E, S, and W, respectively. Each entity has characteristics associated with each of the five senses, producing in the case of sight a correspondence between the entities and the colors: water with green, fire with red, light with white, and wind with blue (Mitchell, Bevan, and Burkitt 1921 = Ephrem *Pr. Ref.* 2.223–24). Above them is God and below them darkness (Syr *hešôkâ*). A chance movement causes the mixing of the pure entities with darkness, resulting in the creation of matter (Syr *hûlê* from Gk *hyle*). The entities call upon the Most High, Who Sends the Primal Word (Syr *mêmrâ* = Gk *logos*) to order the matter. The four entities and the darkness are repurified and returned to their places through the "mystery of the cross" (Mitchell 1912 = Ephrem *Pr. Ref.* 1.52–60, 138–40, 2.220.29–33; Nau 1932: 191–92 = Barhadbesabba *Arb.* 1.5). Bardaisan's tripartite anthropology of body (Syr *pagrâ* = Gk *sōma*), soul (Syr *nafšâ* = Gk *psyche*), and mind (Syr *madʿâ* or *reʿyanâ* = Gk *nous*) corresponds to three realms in the cosmos, the natural world, the planetary, and the spiritual, which are ruled respectively by Nature (Syr *kyanâ*), Fate (Syr *ḥelqâ*), and Freedom (Syr *ḥerutâ*). The body, subject to the law of Nature, is determined by biological needs; economic and social status are determined by the rules of astrology; moral life and therefore eternal destiny are ruled by freedom of the will (Drijvers 1966: 76–95, 152–61). Consequently resurrection of the body is rejected (Ephrem *Pr. Ref.* 2.143–69; cf. *Pr. Ref.* 1.146; Beck 1963 = Ephrem *Car. Nis.* 46:8, 51:2–3), and the Bardaisanites are said to hold a docetic Christology (Adamantius *dial.* 5.8–10). Mythological elements emerge more strongly in some doctrines attributed by Ephrem to the Bardaisanites if not to Bardaisan himself: Wisdom (Syr *hekmeta* = Gk *sophia*), appearing before the archons and governors, stirred them up to produce the human body (Ephrem *Pr. Ref.* 1.122.45–123:14). "Something flows and comes down from the living Father and the Mother conceives and gives birth to him in the mystery of the fish and he is called the living Son" (Ephrem *HCH* 55.1.3–5). The Holy Spirit has two daughters, one of whom is the reflected image of her sister (*HCH* 55:3–5).

As a whole Bardaisan's work consists of a blend of ideas and imagery with parallels in the NT, Odes of Solomon, Philo, the Hermetic literature, the literature of various Gnostic sects, Aramaean paganism, astrology, Stoicism, and later Platonism. Some scholars argue that his is an independent syncretism without special affinities to Gnosticism of any sort (Schaeder 1932; Drijvers 1966: 166–228; de Halleux 1968; Brock 1970). Some, beginning with Hippolytus, have considered Bardaisan a Valentinian, Ophite, or Saturninian Gnostic (Hippolytus *haer.* 6.35; cf. Ephrem *HCH* 21:10; Ehlers 1970). Other early Greek and Latin writers thought him a Valentinian who converted to orthodoxy or vice versa (Eusebius *h.e.* 4.30.3; Hieronymus *vir. ill.* 33; Epiphanius *haer.* 56.2). Notably, although they consider him a heretic, neither Ephrem nor any later Syriac writer alludes to ties with Valentinianism. Ephrem frequently associates him with Marcion and Mani from whose views, however, he carefully distinguishes those of "the Aramaean philosopher" (Ephrem *Pr. Ref.* 2.7.48–8:1, 225.25–26). There is substantial scholarly agreement with Ephrem's remark that "unwillingly, Mani entered by the door Bardaisan opened," i.e., that Mani's cosmological and anthropological notions were based on Bardaisan's views pushed in a strongly dualistic direction (Ephrem *Pr. Ref.* 1.122.25–31; cf. 123.15–22; Schaeder 1932: 63–73; Aland 1975; Drijvers 1975; but cf. Jansma 1969). Bardaisan's followers survived in the Syriac speaking Christian environment at least until the episcopate of Rabbula of Edessa (d. A.D. 435), and perhaps as late as the 8th century.

Bibliography

Aland, B. 1975. Mani und Bardesanes—Zur Entstehung des manichäischen Systems. Pp. 123–43 in *Synkretismus im syrisch-persischen Kulturgebiet,* ed. A. Dietrich. Abh. Akad. Wiss. Gött. phil.-hist. K1. 96. Göttingen.

Beck, E. 1957. *Des Heiligen Ephraem des Syrers Hymnes Contra Haereses.* CSCO 169. (Trans. CSCO 170). (= Ephrem *HCH*). Louvain.

———. 1963. *Des Heiligen Ephraem des Syrers Carmina Nisibena.* CSCO 240. (Trans. CSCO 241). (= Ephrem *Car.Nis.*). Louvain.

Brock, S. P. 1970. Review of *Bardaisan of Edessa. JSS* 15: 114–15.

———. 1980. An Introduction to Syriac Studies. Pp. 1–33 in *Horizons in Semitics Studies: Articles for the Student.* ed. J. H. Eaton. Birmingham.

Davids, A. J. M. 1970. Zur Kosmogonie Bardaisans: Textkritische Bemerkungen. *ZDMG* 120: 32–42.

———. 1971. Review of *Natuur, lot en vrijheid. OrChr* 19: 233–35.

Drijvers, H. J. W. 1965. *The Book of the Laws of the Countries: The Dialogue on Fate of Bardaisan of Edessa.* Assen.

———. 1966. *Bardaisan of Edessa. SSN* 6. Assen.

———. 1967. Bardaisan, die Bardaisaniten und die Ursprünge des Gnostizismus. Pp. 307–14 in *The Origins of Gnosticism,* ed. U. Bianchi. Studies in the History of Religions 12. Leiden.

———. 1969–70. Bardaisan of Edessa and the Hermetica: The

Aramaic Philosopher and the Philosophy of His Time. *JEOL* 21: 190–210.
———. 1975. Bardaisan von Edessa als Repräsentant des syrischen Synkretismus im 2. Jahrhundert n. Chr. Pp. 109–22 in *Synkretismus im syrisch-persischen Kulturgebiet,* ed. A. Dietrich. Abh. Akad. Wiss. Gött. phil.-hist. Kl. 96. Göttingen.
Duval, R. 1891–92. Histoire politique, religieuse et littéraire d'Édesse jusquà la première croisade. *JA* 18: 87–133, 201–78, 381–439; 19: 5–102.
Ehlers, B. 1970. Bardesanes von Edessa—ein syrischer Gnostiker. *ZKG* 81: 334–51.
Halleux, A. de. 1968. Review of *Bardaisan of Edessa. Mus* 81: 273–74.
Jansma, T. 1969. *Natuur, lot en vrijheid. Bardesanes, de filosoof der Arameeers en zijn images.* Cahiers bij het Nederlands Theologisch Tijdschrift 6. Wageningen.
Mitchell, C. W. 1912. *Saint Ephraim's Prose Refutations of Mani, Marcion, and Bardaisan* I. *The Discourses Addressed to Hypatius.* London. (= Ephrem *Pr. Ref.* 1)
Mitchell, C. W.; Bevan, A. A.; and Burkitt, F. C. 1921. *Saint Ephraim's Prose Refutations of Mani, Marcion, and Bardaisan* II. *The Discourse Called 'Of Domnus' and Six Other Writings.* London. (= Ephrem *Pr. Ref.* 2).
Nau, F. 1907. *Bardesanes: Liber Legum Regionum.* Patrologia Syriaca 1.2. Pp. 490–658. (= *BLC*). Paris.
———. 1932. *La première partie de l'histoire de Barhadbesabba Arbaia.* PO 23.2. (= Barhadbesabba Arb.)
Schaeder, H. H. 1932. Bardesanes von Edessa in der Uberlieferung der griechischen und der syrischen Kirche. ZKG 3. 51: 21–74. Darmstadt.

KATHLEEN E. MCVEY

BARIAH (PERSON) [Heb *bārîaḥ*]. The third son of SHEMAIAH in the list of postexilic Davidic descendants in 1 Chr 3:22. The text of MT is problematic, however: the phrase which appears earlier in v 22, ". . . and the sons of Shemiah . . .," is probably best deleted as a dittography (see Williamson *Chronicles* NCBC, 58). This makes Bariah not the third son of Shemiah, but rather the fourth son of Shecaniah, who then had a total of six sons, which agrees with the tally at the end of v 22. The name "Bariah" means "fugitive."

RUSSELL FULLER

BARKOS (PERSON) [Heb *barqôs*]. The head of a family of *nĕtînîm* (temple servants) (see NETHINIM) listed among those exiles returning from Babylon to Jerusalem and Judah (Ezra 2:53 = Neh 7:55; 1 Esdr 5:32). It is a theophoric Aramaic name meaning "son of *Qōs*" (Zadok 1980: 114). Although *Qōs* appears in Edomite names, evidence from the Arab world suggests that the deity is Arab in origin and, with the westward tribal movements of the 8th and 7th centuries, entered Edom and gave his name to a deity long established there (Rose 1977: 29–30).

Bibliography

Rose, M. 1977. Yahweh in Israel—Qaus in Edom? *JSOT* 4: 28–34.
Vriesen, Th. C. 1965. The Edomite deity Qaus. *OTS* 14: 330–353.
Zadok, R. 1980. Notes On The Biblical and Extra-Biblical Onomasticon. *JQR* 71: 107–117.

RODNEY H. SHEARER

BARLEY. See AGRICULTURE; FLORA.

BARNABAS (PERSON) [Gk *Barnabas*]. An apostle, an associate of Paul, prominent in the church of Antioch-on-the-Orontes in Syria, and an early leader in the mission to gentiles. According to Acts, his name was Joseph, but he was called Barnabas by the apostles. Luke, the author of Acts, translates Barnabas to mean "son of encouragement," (from Aram *bar nĕbûʾâ*) but it may simply mean "son of (the god) Nebo," or something similar. Acts reports that Barnabas was a Levite whose family came from Cyprus; hence he was a Diaspora Jew. He is first mentioned as a man who sold some land and donated the proceeds to the apostles in Jerusalem (4:36–37). Thus in vivid contrast to Ananias and Sapphira, who withheld a portion of their property (5:1–11), Barnabas is shown to typify the spirit of communal sharing which Luke emphasizes in the earliest Jerusalem community.

A. Association with Paul

In Acts, Barnabas receives extensive mention in connection with Saul (later to be known as Paul) and with the emergence of a mission to gentiles. When the disciples in Jerusalem were afraid to meet with Saul after his call, Barnabas brought him to them and gave him a favorable introduction (9:27). Later, when the Jerusalem church received reports that believers from Cyprus and Cyrene were making converts of Greeks in Antioch (11:20–22), Barnabas was sent to investigate. He encouraged them in this missionary activity, then brought Saul with him from Tarsus to Antioch, where they taught together (11:25–26). As leaders in the Antioch community, Barnabas and Saul were sent to deliver a contribution for famine relief to the community in Jerusalem (11:27–30). Collecting contributions of gentile communities for "the poor" in Jerusalem was evidently an arrangement agreed upon between the missionaries to gentiles—Paul and Barnabas, and the leaders of the Jerusalem community (Gal 2:9–10). Such contributions continued to be of great concern in Paul's later work (Rom 15:25–28; 1 Cor 16:1–4; 2 Cor 8–9).

Next, Acts recounts that Barnabas and Saul were commissioned by the Antioch community for a missionary journey to Cyprus, bringing as an assistant John Mark, who had joined them in Jerusalem (12:25–13:3). That Barnabas was Paul's senior partner in the relationship is evident from the fact that Barnabas' name is mentioned before Paul's name in all Acts accounts thus far. But while recounting their stay in Paphos, Luke shifts to the name Paul for Saul just as he performs a miracle to effect the conversion of the Roman proconsul Sergius Paulus (13:8-12). At this point Luke begins to give Paul greater prominence than Barnabas in the mission narrative, calling their party "Paul and his company" (13:13) and mentioning Paul's name several times before that of Barnabas (13:43, 46, 50). Upon leaving Cyprus, Paul and Barnabas traveled without John Mark through the southern regions of central Asia Minor, visiting the cities of Pisidian Antioch, Iconium, Lystra, Derbe, Perga, and Attalia. Acts reports that they conducted their mission through preaching in synagogues and performance of miracles. In Lystra Paul's miraculous healing of a crippled man led the crowd to call Barnabas "Zeus" and Paul "Hermes" (14:8–18). Despite threats from Jews and gentiles (14:5) and physical violence against Paul at the hands of some Jews (14:19), Acts states that the mission of Paul and Barnabas met with success in several cities among Jews, recent converts to Judaism (13:43), gentiles (13:48), and Greeks (14:1). But the summary of their activity reported to the church at Antioch makes it clear that the success of Barnabas' and Paul's pioneering work among gentiles is what Luke wishes most to stress (14:27).

However in Antioch the question of how a gentile mission ought to be conducted came to be hotly debated. According to Acts "some" from Judea were teaching there that circumcision according to the custom of Moses was a prerequisite for salvation. Paul and Barnabas argued against requiring circumcision for gentiles and were appointed to a delegation which brought the question before apostles and elders in Jerusalem (15:1–3). During the debate at this Jerusalem Council, Barnabas and Paul reported on their success among gentiles (15:12), and the council eventually adopted a position which must have been largely favorable to them, since it did not require gentile circumcision. Paul and Barnabas returned to Antioch together with delegates appointed from Jerusalem who carried a letter detailing the decision of the Council (15:22–32).

B. Separation from Paul

After resolution of the question of required gentile circumcision, Paul and Barnabas made plans in Antioch to revisit the cities of their previous mission together, but there arose between them what Luke terms a "sharp disagreement." According to Acts, Barnabas wished to bring John Mark along, but Paul did not (15:37). Consequently Paul left without Barnabas, bringing Silas with him through Syria and Cilicia to the cities of Asia Minor; Barnabas took Mark with him to Cyprus (15:38–40). That there was a close association between Barnabas and Mark is corroborated in Col 4:10, where Mark is called Barnabas' "cousin."

But the parting of ways between Barnabas and Paul may well have been occasioned by more than the personal disagreement mentioned in Acts. Although Acts hints at no disagreement between Barnabas and Paul on the conduct of a mission to gentiles, Paul's letter to Galatia indicates that the two did not share identical views on the observance of Jewish dietary laws. Paul writes that at Antioch he was distressed when Peter refrained from eating with gentiles out of deference to representatives from James. Paul objected to Peter's abrupt withdrawal from his practice of table fellowship and writes that "even Barnabas" sided against Paul (Gal 2:11–13). On this occasion Barnabas, like Peter, took a moderate position between those associated with James, who advocated a strict separation of Jews from gentiles, and Paul, who strongly opposed such separation. Because Paul does not claim to have persuaded Barnabas and the others, it may be inferred that he lost this debate in Antioch and consequently left. Galatians suggests, then, that the split between Barnabas and Paul arose over different views of proper social practice in Christian communities, perhaps due to a theological disagreement about the continuing validity of Jewish laws. It is uncertain how bitter the rift remained because Paul's reference to Barnabas in 1 Cor 9:6 seems to reflect a sympathetic attitude toward his former mentor. Here Barnabas is mentioned as an apostle who, like Paul, practiced a trade and earned his own living while a missionary. It is possible that they had established this practice as a joint policy during their early mission work together.

C. Mention of Barnabas in Extra-Canonical Sources

Concerning Barnabas' career after separating from Paul and journeying to Cyprus, we have no early information. Later Christian writers make legendary claims about Barnabas: e.g., that he preached in Rome during Jesus' lifetime and introduced Clement of Rome to Christianity (*Ps.-Clem. Recogn.* 1.7–13), and that he was one of the seventy (Luke 10:1) sent out by Jesus (Clement of Alexandria *Str.* 2.20). The 5th- or 6th-century *Acts of Barnabas* purports to describe his later mission and martyrdom in Cyprus. Barnabas is also named as the author of some early Christian texts. Clement of Alexandria credits him as the author of the *Epistle of Barnabas,* a treatise which was included in some early biblical manuscripts, e.g., Sinaiticus. Some Western traditions regard Barnabas as the author of Hebrews, and he is also listed (in the *Decretum Gelasianum*) as the author of a gospel.

Bibliography

Koester, H. 1982. *History and Literature of Early Christianity.* 2 vols. Philadelphia.

Meeks, W. A., and Wilken, R. L. 1978. *Jews and Christians in Antioch in the First Four Centuries of the Common Era.* Missoula, MT.

Meeks, W. A. 1983. *The First Urban Christians.* New Haven.

JON B. DANIELS

BARNABAS, EPISTLE OF. An early Christian writing, the significance of which lies not so much in its later influence as in what it preserves of earlier traditions, both Jewish and Christian. The anonymous Christian teacher who wrote *Barnabas* passed on traditional instruction regarding "spiritual" understandings of the Jewish scriptures and God's requirements. Many issues concerning *Barnabas* are problematic and must remain unresolved.

G. Provenance
H. Date, Occasion, and Significance

A. Form, Structure, Style

Although *Barnabas* has several characteristics of an epistle, it is probably best understood as a tractate in epistolary dress. Its contents may be outlined as follows:

I. Introduction (framework), chap. 1
II. First major section: correct understanding of scripture, 2:1–16:10
   A. What the Lord requires: not sacrifice and fasting, 2–3
   B. Warnings in a lawless age facing judgment, 4
   C. Why the Lord endured suffering in the flesh, 5–6
   D. The Lord's suffering foreshadowed in scapegoat and red heifer, 7–8
   E. Circumcised understanding, 9–10
   F. Baptism and cross foreshadowed, 11–12
   G. Correct understanding of the Covenant and its heirs, 13–14
   H. Correct understanding of the Sabbath, 15
   I. Correct understanding of the Temple, 16
III. Transition (framework), 17:1–18:1a
IV. Second major section: The "Two Ways" tradition, 18:1b–20:2
   A. Introduction, 18:1b–2
   B. The Way of Light, 19
   C. The Way of Darkness, 20
V. Conclusion (framework), 21

Barnabas 17:1–18:1a explicitly divides the tractate into two major sections of teaching. The two sections are set into an epistolary framework (Wengst 1971: 5–14; cf. Scorza Barcellona 1975: 14–21).

The tractate's stylistic norms resemble those of Jewish literature. Its rough transitions and awkward arrangement have the benefit of making it easier to isolate its sources.

B. Text

The Gk text of *Barnabas* is relatively well preserved. The chief witnesses to the text are Codex Sinaiticus, Codex Hierosolymitanus, a family of late Gk manuscripts, and an OL translation in Codex Corbeiensis. There are also fragments of a Gk papyrus and of a Syr translation, and several quotations by Clement of Alexandria and later church writers. Although there may have been a "first edition" which lacked the Two Ways tradition, the "final form" presumably consisted of chapters 1–21. The critical edition by Prigent and Kraft (1971) provides a carefully researched eclectic text.

C. The Author and His Circle

Barnabas is anonymous. Clement of Alexandria, Origen, Jerome, Serapion of Thmuys, Codex Sinaiticus, and later manuscripts attribute the work to "Barnabas," but few contemporary scholars accept this attribution. Most scholars consider it unlikely that the Barnabas described by Paul as participating in a literal observance of Jewish cult (Gal 2:13) could write the anti-cultic polemics of *Barnabas*.

It appears that the work as a whole is produced by one person, a male, and that he primarily uses traditional materials to which he contributes little more than a framework within which he arranges them and makes simple transitions between them. He is a teacher who wants his readers to see him not as a teacher but as a friend and peer (1:4; 1:8; 4:6, 9; 9:9). He describes himself with conventional modesty (4:9; 6:5), but he participates as one "who is wise and understanding, and who loves his Lord," in a community which God has allowed to understand secrets (6:10). In the face of the impending final scandals (4:3, 9), he is concerned to pass on some of the traditional teachings of his circle (1:5; 4:9).

Because many of his traditions retain both the style and the substance of Judaism, a significant number of scholars see him as a Jewish Christian (Barnard 1978: 54–58; Manns 1981: 125–146). In view of *Barnabas* 16:7, it probably makes more sense to see him as a Gentile who had access to Jewish traditions in Gk (Kraft 1965: 39; Prigent and Kraft 1971: 28; Wengst 1984: 119).

It is often quite difficult to distinguish the teacher from his sources, many of which are much older. He does not rise above his tradition as a clearly defined individual creator; he is primarily a spokesman for a living tradition, even if he has shaped it here and there. In the case of "evolved literature" such as this, it may be preferable to focus on the tradition rather than on the individual through whom the tradition speaks. The circle that preserved this tradition was a "school" in the sense that it had teachers who developed and transmitted teaching materials concerned with exegesis and moral instruction (Kraft 1965: 19–22; Wengst 1971).

D. Use of Tradition

The teacher indicates in 1:5 that he is passing on traditional materials (see 4:9; 19:1; 21:1). Kraft (1961), Prigent (1961), and Wengst (1971) have examined the sources of these materials in detail.

The traditions in *Barnabas* 2–16 are concerned with understanding the (Jewish) scriptures. Analysis of the quotations show that the tradition represented by *Barnabas* did not use the Heb text (Kraft 1961: 57; Wengst 1971: 69). Apparently the teacher had access to OG translations in a variety of oral and written forms: complete OG scrolls of a few books of scripture (Isaiah; perhaps Psalms, Genesis, and Deuteronomy), individual sayings, independent collections of extracts, free renderings of narratives, and quotations already associated with midrashic commentary (Kraft 1961: 69; Wengst 1984: 129).

The Two Ways section (chapters 18–20) is the largest block of tradition in *Barnabas*. It presents ethical teachings under the rubrics of the way of light and the way of darkness. *Barnabas* 21:1 shows that the teacher considered the Two Ways teaching an authoritative written form of God's requirements. This tradition is found in similar forms in other church writings, notably in *Didache* 1–5. Most contemporary scholars agree that the Two Ways sections in *Barnabas* and *Didache* derive directly or indirectly from a common source. Two Ways concepts in the *Manual of Discipline* show that some form of the tradition existed in a Semitic-speaking Jewish environment. After being translated into Gk and passing through various recensions, it is used independently by *Barnabas* and *Didache*. The teacher incorporates the Two Ways tradition into his writing with relatively few changes (Prigent 1961: 20; Wengst 1971: 66–67).

The themes of the two ways of darkness and light also pervade the whole tractate. Parallels between *Barnabas* 4:9–10 and *Didache* 16:2 suggest that certain forms of the Two Ways tradition may have had an apocalyptic appendix (Kraft 1965: 12–16).

E. Thought

The teacher and his circle are not systematic thinkers, and their traditions are occasionally in tension. Whether or not *Barnabas* has a central theological perspective, the following concepts characterize the tract (Kraft 1965: 22–39; Wengst 1971: 71–99).

1. Gnosis. One explicit purpose of *Barnabas* is to supplement its readers' faith with "perfect knowledge" (*Barnabas* 1:5). This knowledge *(gnōsis)* is a central concept for *Barnabas.* The circle seems to use the term in an exegetical sense and a related ethical sense. Exegetical gnosis is the insight God gave to Abraham, Moses, David, and the prophets, and now gives to believers. This gift enables its recipients to understand the secrets of scripture and of past, present, and future events. Ethical gnosis enables its recipients to understand the conduct required by God (5:4; 21:5).

2. Ethics and Eschatology. Ethical concerns pervade *Barnabas,* as do apocalyptic eschatological imagery, expectation, and motivation. Salvation is primarily a future reward for obeying God's requirements in this lawless age. The day of judgment is near (21:3). At that time, the obedient will be made holy and will receive the promised inheritance: the end of lawlessness and the renewal of the universe (6:13; 15:5–9). Believers should not live as if they were already justified (4:10; 15:7). Instead, they must make use of the evil days before the judgment to perform the will of God, because they will be judged according to their conduct and Satan can use his power to drive them from the Lord's kingdom (2:1, 10; 4:9–14; 19:10; 21:6, 8).

3. Israel. According to *Barnabas,* God promised the patriarchs that he would give a Covenant to "the people" but Israel proved unworthy to receive it (4:6–8; 14:1–4). Instead, Jesus gave it to a "new people" (5:7), made worthy to receive it by his suffering and death (14:4–6). In contrast, an evil angel (9:4) misled Israel into interpreting God's requirements in a literal, external fashion rather than in the intended spiritual manner. *Barnabas* criticizes major aspects of Jewish ritual observance (sacrifice, fasting, circumcision, food laws, the sabbath rest, and the temple) as resulting from this misunderstanding of scripture. Christians, the true heirs of the Covenant, understand the scriptures in their intended spiritual sense.

There is a tension in the circle's relation to Judaism. On the one hand, it defines itself in contrast to Israel, who never received the Covenant and who err in their understanding of what God wants. On the other hand, the circle has taken its ethical teachings, its citations of scripture, its hermeneutics, and even its criticisms of Jewish ritual observance *from Jewish sources.*

4. Christology. *Barnabas* refers to Jesus as Son of God, the Beloved One, the Beloved Heir, and most frequently, the Lord. Preexistent, he participated in creation (5:5, 10; 6:12). The circle denies that he is a son of David or a son of man (12:10–11), but he suffered in the flesh to purify a once-sinful people ("us") for the Covenant and to fill up the measure of "their" sins (5:1–14; 6:7; 7:2; 14:4–5). He will soon come to end this evil age, judge the living and the dead, and recreate the universe (5:7; 7:2; 15:5; 21:3).

Barnabas is concerned to interpret the suffering and death of Jesus by means of scripture. Apart from his suffering in the flesh, the circle shows little interest in the earthly Jesus' words and works as found in written gospel traditions. It looks to scripture rather than to Jesus' sayings for authority in teaching.

5. Interpretation of Scripture. The interpretive method is closely related to what is known of Christian and Jewish schools of Alexandria. The "spiritual" (rationalistic, allegorical) understanding of ritual law appears more radical than that of Philo when it excludes a literal understanding. For example, *Barnabas* 9–10, except for the gematria in 9:8–9, resembles the position of those Philo (*Migr.* 89.92–93) opposed for neglecting the literal meaning of circumcision.

F. Recipients

Barnabas is addressed to both men and women (1:1; see 10:8). The recipients are Christians, probably uncircumcised but not necessarily from the teacher's own sect.

Barnabas gives clues about their community—or at least about his own circle's ideals for a community of believers. The teacher admonishes his readers not to live as hermits but to assemble together (4:10) and to share their possessions (19:8). He mentions no church functionaries other than teachers, "those highly placed" (21:2), and those "who proclaim the Lord's word" (19:9). The community celebrates Sunday, "the eighth day" (15:8–9). They practice baptism (by immersion) as a means of receiving remission of sins and new life (11:1–11). They experience inspired speech (16:9–10).

G. Provenance

Barnabas does not give enough indications to permit confident identification of either the teacher's location or the location to which he writes. His thought, hermeneutical methods, and style have many parallels throughout the known Jewish and Christian worlds. Most scholars have located the work's origin in the area of Alexandria, on the grounds that it has many affinities with Alexandrian Jewish and Christian thought and because its first witnesses are Alexandrian. Recently, Prigent (Prigent and Kraft 1971: 20–24), Wengst (1971: 114–18), and Scorza Barcellona (1975: 62–65) have suggested other origins based on affinities in Palestine, Syria, and Asia Minor. The place of origin must remain an open question, although the Gk-speaking E Mediterranean appears most probable.

H. Date, Occasion, and Significance

Since *Barnabas* 16:3 refers to the destruction of the temple, *Barnabas* must be written after 70 C.E. It must be written before its first indisputable use in Clement of Alexandria, ca. 190. Since 16:4 expects the temple to be rebuilt, it was most likely written before Hadrian built a Roman temple on the site ca. 135. Attempts to use 4:4–5 and 16:1–5 to specify the time of origin more exactly have not won wide agreement. It is important to remember that traditions of varying ages have been incorporated into this work.

Barnabas does not provide sufficient clues to identify an occasion for its writing. Neither the view that it is a polemic in response to Jewish rivals (Lowy 1960: 32) nor the view that it is propaganda to persuade Christian opponents (Wengst 1971: 100–105) accounts for its ethical orientation.

The work appears to have had little impact in the West, although it was translated into Latin in N Africa (or possibly Rome), probably during the 3d century. Clement of Alexandria quotes it as the epistle of the apostle Barnabas, and Origen refers to it as the catholic epistle of Barnabas. Its inclusion in Codex Sinaiticus suggests that it was sometimes considered canonical in 4th century Egypt. Other church writers who mention it (e.g., Eusebius, Jerome, Mkhitar) categorize it with disputed writings or apocrypha.

Although *Barnabas* 4:14 appears to quote Matt 22:14, it must remain an open question whether the *Barnabas* circle knew written gospels. Based on Koester's analysis (1957: 125–27, 157), it appears more likely that *Barnabas* stood in the living oral tradition used by the written gospels. For example, the reference to gall and vinegar in *Barnabas* 7:3, 5 seems to preserve an early stage of tradition that influenced the formation of the passion narratives in the *Gospel of Peter* and the synoptic gospels.

Barnabas is also significant for preserving early stages of Jewish tradition. It preserves halakhic traditions about atonement and red heifer rituals from a century before the Mishnah was compiled. It contains midrashic material and the Two Ways tradition in forms not greatly removed from their Jewish antecedents. It also quotes fragments of Jewish religious literature otherwise unknown (Kraft 1965: 182–84).

Bibliography

Barnard, L. W. 1978. The Epistle of Barnabas in its Jewish Setting. Pp. 52–106 in *Studies in Church History and Patristics*. Thessaloniki.

Koester, H. 1957. *Synoptische Überlieferung bei den Apostolischen Vätern*. TU 65. Berlin.

Kraft, R. A. 1961. *The Epistle of Barnabas: Its Quotations and their Sources*. Diss. Harvard University.

———. 1965. *The Apostolic Fathers*. Volume 3: *Barnabas and the Didache*. New York.

Lowy, S. 1960. The Confutation of Judaism in the Epistle of Barnabas. *JJS* 11: 1–33.

Manns, F. 1981. Les rapports synagogue-eglise au début du IIe siècle après j.-c. en palestine. *SBFLA* 31: 105–46.

Prigent, P. 1961. *Les testimonia dans le christianisme primitif: l'Épître de barnabé I-XVI et ses sources*. EBib. Paris.

Prigent, P., and Kraft, R. A. 1971. *Épître de barnabé*. SC 172. Paris.

Scorza Barcellona, F. 1975. *Epistola di Barnaba*. Corona Patrum. Torino.

Wengst, K. 1971. *Tradition und Theologie des Barnabasbriefes*. Arbeiten zur Kirchengeschichte 42. Berlin.

———. 1984. *Schriften des Urchristentums. Didache (Apostellehre), Barnabasbrief, Zweiter Klemensbrief, Schrift an Diognet*. Munich.

Windisch, H. 1920. *Die Apostolischen Väter III: Der Barnabasbrief*. HNT Ergänzungsband. Tübingen.

JAY CURRY TREAT

BARODIS (PERSON) [Gk *Barōdis*]. A servant of Solomon whose descendants returned from Babylon with Zerubbabel (1 Esdr 5:34). Although 1 Esdras is often assumed to have been compiled from Ezra and Nehemiah, this family does not appear among their lists of returning exiles (cf Ezra 2:57; Neh 7:59). Omissions such as this also raise questions about 1 Esdras being used as a source by Ezra or Nehemiah. Furthermore, problems associated with dating events and identifying persons described in 1 Esdras have cast doubt on the historicity of the text.

MICHAEL DAVID MCGEHEE

BARSABBAS (PERSON) [Gk *Barsabbas*]. Name of 2 persons in NT. The name *Barsabbas* most probably represents the Aram *Bar-Shabba*, "son of the sabbath."

1. A surname of Joseph, who also had the Lat surname Justus (Acts 1:23). He was considered, but not chosen, for the place among the twelve disciples left vacant by the treachery of Judas Iscariot. Evidently, he had been a disciple of Jesus, for the one to take Judas' place was to be a personal witness to the ministry, resurrection, and ascension of Jesus (Acts 1:21–22). Joseph Barsabbas reportedly was one of the seventy disciples (Eus. *Hist. Eccl.* 1:12; see Luke 10:1). He allegedly drank snake venom in the name of Jesus without suffering any ill effects (Eus. *Hist. Eccl.* 3:39; see Mark 16:18).

2. A surname of Judas, one of two leading Christians in the church at Jerusalem who were sent to the churches of Antioch, Syria, and Cilicia to convey the church council's decision on the acceptance of gentile believers (Acts 15:22–33). Judas and Silas, his companion, preached at Antioch for some time until the church dismissed them (v 33). According to v 34, a spurious text, Judas returned to Jerusalem, but Silas remained in Antioch. This verse probably was originally a marginal note that explained how Silas was in Antioch for Paul to choose him as a companion (v 40).

VIRGIL R. L. FRY

BARTACUS (PERSON) [Gk *Bartakos*]. Bartacus, who has the epithet "the Illustrious," was referred to once in 1 Esdr 4:29 as the father of Apame, the concubine of Darius. While nothing is known of Bartacus outside of this single reference, names similar to his own appear in other literature. For instance, the name "Artachaeas," a high-ranking official in Xerxes' army, was mentioned by Herodotus (7.22.117). The name of Bartacus' daughter, "Apame," is identical with the name of the Persian princess who married Seleucus I and became the mother of Antiochus I. Apamea, a city in Asia Minor, was established by Seleucus I in honor of his wife by the same name.

There are several ways to interpret the phrase "the Illustrious" *(Tou thaumostou)* appended to Bartacus' name. The name may have been an epithet, implying that Bartacus was a man of renown or even perhaps a wonder-worker. It is unlikely that the epithet was a second name for Bartacus because the Persians normally used only one name. There is also no evidence that "the Illustrious One" was an official title in the Persian state. The appendage may have been the proper name of his father. The similar Greek name "Thamasios" appears in Herodotus 7.194, and "Themasios" occurs in Josephus *Ant* 11.3.5.

SCOTT T. CARROLL

BARTHOLOMEW (PERSON) [Gk *Bartholomaíos*]. Bartholomew appears in all four lists of the twelve disciples of Jesus (Matt 10:3; Mark 3:18; Luke 6:14; Acts 1:13), but he is otherwise unmentioned in the NT. Bartholomew is quite likely an Aram patronymic *[Bar-Talmai]* for "son of Tholami" (cf. LXX Josh 15:14) or "son of Tholomaeus" (cf. Jos. *Ant.* 20.1.1§5), a name found in several forms in the Gk OT and Josephus.

From the 9th century onward Bartholomew generally has been identified with NATHANAEL. This is based on the conjecture that Nathanael is a surname of Bartholomew, so that his full name would have been Nathaneal Bar-Tholami (cf. Simon Bar-Jonah). Several factors point in this direction. (1) Since the synoptic gospels never mention Nathanael, while John never mentions Bartholomew, the juxtaposition of the names Philip and Bartholomew in the synoptic lists of the Twelve (not in the list in Acts) suggests the close relationship between the two depicted in John 1:43–51. Study of the apostolic lists indicates pairing and grouping into fours; this suggests that Bartholomew and Philip were companions in the second group headed by Philip. (2) John's gospel treats Nathanael as an apostle. All of the companions of Nathanael are apostles (John 1:35–51) and Nathanael appears as a member of a group of apostles (John 21:1–2). Christ's promise to Nathanael, that he would be a witness to the central role of the Son of Man in God's revelation to men, suggests an apostolic function (John 1:50–1). (3) Since Bartholomew is quite likely a patronymic, its bearer would be expected to have another name as well.

Arguments have been raised against each of the above factors. (1) The juxtaposition of Philip and Bartholomew in the synoptic lists may be fortuitous, because in the Acts list they are not together. (2) Since there is no mention of Nathanael during Jesus' ministry, his interaction with Jesus in John 1:43-51 does not necessarily imply a formal call to apostleship. (3) The name "Bartholomew" may stand by itself in the apostolic lists as a proper name. It is not necessarily a patronymic. The patronymic is normally expressed in the lists by the Greek genitive, not by the Aramaic *bar.*

If the identification of Bartholomew with Nathanael is correct; Philip brought Bartholomew (Nathanael), a native of Cana of Galilee (John 21:2), to acknowledge Jesus as the Messiah (John 1:45–46). The description of his encounter with Jesus is found in John 1:47–51. A true Israelite, without guile, Nathanael gave a profound declaration of the messianic identity of Jesus. Jesus, in turn, stated that Nathanael would see even greater demonstrations of messianism. If the identification of Bartholomew with Nathanael is incorrect, then we have no NT information about Bartholomew other than the four lists.

Since the identification of Bartholomew with Nathanael is not conclusive, to assume it without question is to go beyond the evidence. Certainty is unattainable with the present evidence, but to reject categorically the identification is likewise unwarranted.

Traditional stories about Bartholomew abound, but few appear to be trustworthy. According to the "Genealogies of the Twelve Apostles," Bartholomew was of the house of Naphtali, and his name was formerly John, but Jesus changed it because of John the son of Zebedee, the beloved. Eusebius (*Hist. Eccl.* 5.10.3) reports that Bartholomew preached the gospel in India and left behind the Gospel of Matthew "in the actual Hebrew characters." Traditions also claim that Bartholomew ministered in Armenia, Phrygia, Lycaonia, Mesopotamia, and Persia. Several traditions are also associated with his death. One tradition states that Bartholomew brought the Gospel to India and to Greater Armenia, where he was flayed alive and beheaded. The *Martyrdom of Bartholomew* states that he was placed in a sack and cast into the sea.

A few apocryphal works are also traditionally associated with Bartholomew. Jerome, in the preface to his commentary on Matthew, mentions a *Gospel of Bartholomew.* Apart from its condemnation by the Decretum Gelasianum we know little about this work. A later work, "The Questions of Bartholomew," extant in five recensions, may be based in part on this earlier work. A Coptic "Book of the Resurrection of Christ by Bartholomew the Apostle" is extant in several fragments. Authentic association of these works with the apostle Bartholomew is highly doubtful.

Bibliography

Brownrigg, R. 1974. *The Twelve Apostles.* New York.
Budge, E. A. W. 1901. *The Contendings of the Apostles.* 2 vols. London.
Leidig, E. 1980. Natanael, ein Sohn des Tholomäus. *TZ* 36: 374–75.

MICHAEL J. WILKINS

BARTHOLOMEW, GOSPEL (QUESTIONS) OF. A writing mentioned by Jerome in the prologue of his commentary on Matthew (which reference may derive from Origen), and by Epiphanius the Monk (*vita virg.* 24–25). A reference by the venerable Bede (*Luc. ev. expos.* 1) probably stems from Jerome, as does one in the *Decretum Gelasianum,* which lists "gospels in the name of Bartholomew" as ones to be avoided. A *Gospel of Bartholomew* may be quoted by pseudo-Dionysius Areopagita (*myst.* 3), who attributes two sentences to "the blessed Bartholomew." The Syr *Book of Hierotheos* also contains a one-sentence quotation written by "the divine Bartholomew."

There are no extant texts of a *Gospel of Bartholomew,* but two works associated with the name Bartholomew are preserved: *Questions of Bartholomew* is preserved in Greek, Latin, and Slavonic manuscripts; the *Book of the Resurrection of Jesus Christ, by Bartholomew the Apostle* is preserved in one complete Coptic manuscript and in several other Coptic fragments. Both works stem from Greek originals, and they share affinities with one another, such as Jesus' descent into hell and deliverance of Adam, in addition to the prominence of Bartholomew as the guarantor of the traditions. It is possible that "both streams of tradition go back to a special Bartholomew tradition of the 3d or 4th centuries" (*NTApocr* 1.508), but it is unclear whether they derive from an underlying *Gospel of Bartholomew.*

Questions of Bartholomew. This work, perhaps a 5th-century composition of Egyptian provenance, is a collection of revelatory dialogues. Bartholomew is featured as the bold main questioner, seeking knowledge from the risen Jesus, from Mary, and from Beliar, particularly about heaven and the underworld. The contents of the book may be described according to the five chapters into which it has been divided. (1) At the request of Bartholomew, the risen Jesus recounts how he vanished from the cross in order to descend into the underworld. He reports a conversation there between a fearful Hades and Beliar (the devil) and briefly describes how he bound Hades and brought up the patriarchs and especially Adam. The dialogue ends with a brief exchange about the sacrifices and the souls that Jesus receives in paradise. (2) At the behest of the other apostles, Bartholomew asks Mary how she "conceived the incomprehensible," or how she "carried him who cannot be carried." After a prayer, she directs the apostles to restrain her while she reveals that she was visited in the temple by an angelic figure. She receives a baptism from heavenly dew and partakes in a Eucharist when the angelic figure miraculously produces a loaf and cup. She is then promised that after three years she will conceive his son. But her tale is interrupted: fire comes from her mouth and the world is about to be consumed when Jesus silences her. An account of the conception itself, about which Bartholomew had inquired, is therefore prevented. (3) Seven days before his ascension the risen Jesus grants the apostles a brief glimpse of the abyss. They are overwhelmed at the sight, but it is not described. (4) Peter entreats Mary to ask for a revelation of "all that is in the heavens." In a brief exchange Mary declines, but reveals that in her the Lord restored "the dignity of women." Jesus then grants Bartholomew's request to see and to question Beliar, whose dreadful appearance is described. Bartholomew, with his foot upon Beliar's neck, then learns about numerous angels and punishments for the wicked. The devil also recounts how he and his angels had refused Michael's command to worship Adam, the image of God, and how he made Eve susceptible to disobedience by defiling her drinking water with sweat from his body. The dialogue is interspersed with three reverent prayers by Bartholomew. In the end Jesus admonishes Bartholomew that the revelations should be kept secret, and Bartholomew concludes with a doxology. (5) When Bartholomew asks Jesus to name the worst of sins, he names hypocrisy, slander, "the sin against the holy spirit," i.e., speaking ill of any one who serves the Father, and swearing an oath by the head of God. Bartholomew then receives a commission to preach and raises a final question about the consequences of sins of lust. Jesus' reply praises celibacy and also allows for the validity of marriage. But he adds that "he who sins after the third marriage is unworthy of God."

In terms of genre the *Questions of Bartholomew* may be compared with other early Christian post-resurrection dialogues between Jesus and his followers, e.g., *Epistula Apostolorum, Dialogue of the Savior, Sophia Jesu Christi,* and *Pistis Sophia.* In terms of content, scholars have noted affinities to the *Acts of Pilate,* the *Gospel of Gamaliel,* and the *Gospel of Nicodemus,* especially in the descent into the underworld. The depictions of the underworld may draw upon motifs of Egyptian popular religion. The text also may reflect knowledge of the *Protevangelium of James* and the *Infancy Gospel of Thomas.* The recommendation on marriage is paralleled in the *Apostolic Constitutions.* Parallels to gnostic texts have been noted in an early study by Bonwetsch, but Beeston denies any gnostic proclivities in Mary's account of the Annunciation (2) and stresses the account's development of a Catholic doctrine of the Eucharist (Beeston 1974: 127; see also *TRE* 3: 316–62).

Bibliography

Beeston, A. F. L. 1974. The *Quaestiones Bartholomae. JTS* 25: 124–27.

Bonwetsch, N. 1897. "Die apokryphen Fragen des Bartholomaus." *NGWG* Phil.-hist. Kl. 1–42.

James M. R. 1924. The Gospel of Bartholomew. Pp. 161–81 in *The Apocryphal New Testament.* Oxford.

JON B. DANIELS

BARTIMAEUS (PERSON) [Gk *Bartimaios*]. A blind beggar whom Jesus healed while on his last journey to Jerusalem (Mark 10:46–52). Throwing his outer garment aside, leaping to his feet, and rushing to Jesus when called demonstrated his faith in Jesus and his eagerness to be healed. Since Mark records the name of only one other person whom Jesus healed (5:22), the occurrence of the name "Bartimaeus" here implies that he became a full-fledged disciple who was well known in the early church (Cranfield *Mark* CGNT, 346).

As the title "Son of David" suggests, Bartimaeus thought of Jesus in messianic terms. This title expressed Jewish nationalistic hopes for a Davidic king to come as the deliverer of the Jews from foreign domination (see *Pss. Sol.* 17:21; Ezek 34:23–24; Taylor 1966: 448). This interpretation of the address fits well with the multitude's association of Jesus with the coming Davidic kingdom in his triumphal entry into Jerusalem (see Branscomb *Mark* MNTC, 192).

Accounts of restoration of sight occur also in Matt 20:29–34 and Luke 18:35–43 with some differences. Matthew and Mark agree that the miracle occurred as Jesus left Jericho, but Luke places it as Jesus approached the city. Matthew says Jesus healed two blind men. Mark and Luke mention only one. Yet more than one miracle is unlikely because the accounts are so similar and consistent in most details. The main event is so clear and the differences in detail are so insignificant that any attempt at harmonization seems unnecessary.

Mark usually introduces the Aramaic word first and then the Greek translation (3:17; 7:11, 34; 14:36). The reverse order in v 46 may be the result of a scribal insertion into the text of a comment in the margin of an early manuscript (Branscomb *Mark* MNTC, 192). Although the derivation of the name Bartimaeus is a matter of controversy, it is most likely from the Aramaic *bar,* "son," and *timʾai,* "Timaeus" (see Taylor 1966: 447–48).

Bibliography

Taylor, V. 1966. *The Gospel According to St. Mark.* New York.

VIRGIL R. L. FRY

BARUCH (PERSON) [Heb *bārûk*]. **1.** A scribe in Jerusalem during the years just prior to the Babylonian destruction of 587 B.C. and a close friend of the prophet Jeremiah. The book of Jeremiah recognizes his professional status as a "scribe" (Heb *sōpēr;* 36:26, 32). The earlier supposition that he was a royal scribe (Muilenburg 1970: 231) is now all the more likely following the discovery of a seal impression in a royal archive which reads, "Belonging to Berechiah, son of Neriah, the scribe" (Avigad 1978 ["Berechiah" is the long form of "Baruch"]). The mention here and in the book of Jeremiah of Baruch with his patronym (double patronym in 32:12) suggests that he comes from a prominent scribal family (Gevaryahu 1973: 209). Baruch's brother, Seraiah, was "quartermaster" [Heb *śar mĕnûḥâ*] under Judah's last king, Zedekiah (Jer 51:59); he, too, was no doubt a professionally trained scribe. It was not only in Masoretic times, but much earlier, even as far back as the Old Babylonian period, that scribes were known to cluster in families (Lundbom 1986).

Baruch had an important role in preserving the Jeremiah legacy. In chapter 36 of the book of Jeremiah he is reported to have written the first Jeremiah scroll at the prophet's dictation (v 4). Then, on a fast day in the year following, 604 B.C. (or 601 B.C. if the LXX reading of 36:9 is accepted), Baruch read this scroll to a large temple gathering and again to a group of the king's ministers. The scroll was read a third time to King Jehoiakim, though not by Baruch, and the king responded by burning the scroll in the fireplace. Jehoiakim ordered the seizure of both Baruch and Jeremiah, but they were duly warned and managed to escape. Baruch was then instructed by Jeremiah to write a new scroll to replace the one which had been destroyed. To this scroll was added more material of like substance (Jer 36:32). At the time the first scroll was written, Baruch had received a personal word of prophecy concerning his disappointment about not having the opportunity to achieve distinction in his career (Jeremiah 45). In this prophecy Jeremiah informed him that the whole nation was doomed; nevertheless, Baruch would escape with his life.

During the final siege of Jerusalem, when Jeremiah was under house arrest, Baruch served as a witness to the purchase of a piece of family real estate which Jeremiah had made in order to symbolize the nation's future restoration (Jeremiah 32). Baruch was entrusted with the deed of purchase and told to place it in an earthenware jar for safekeeping. He was very likely a signatory to the deed and also the one who affixed the seal (Avigad 1978: 55; Lundbom 1986). Baruch survived the fall of Jerusalem and, like Jeremiah, was apparently released by the Babylonians and allowed to remain in the land. His close association with Jeremiah continued, as can be seen from a charge made against him that he had convinced Jeremiah to dissuade a group from going to Egypt after the assassination of Gedaliah, the Babylonian-appointed governor of Judah. In the end, however, both Jeremiah and Baruch went to Egypt and settled with this group at Tahpanhes (Jer 43:1–7).

Many scholars believe Baruch was responsible for the eyewitness accounts in the book of Jeremiah and was, in fact, Jeremiah's biographer. Some go even further and attribute to him the bulk of the book's prose (Muilenburg 1970: 237; Gevaryahu 1973; Lundbom 1986). Baruch is known to be the person who wrote the first of the Jeremiah scrolls (Jeremiah 36); his close association with the prophet over a period of years would seem to preclude his being simply a one- or two-time amanuensis. Also, the colophonic nature of 36:1–8 and chapter 45 points to Baruch as the scribe who wrote large portions of the Jeremianic text. In the LXX, the latter colophon concludes the entire book (less chapter 52) at 51:31–35. This passage was at one time Baruch's colophon to the "first edition," i.e., chapters 1–20 (Lundbom 1986). The LXX contains the shorter and generally earlier text of Jeremiah, with its provenance in Egypt, where the biblical tradition also last locates Baruch (and Jeremiah).

The notoriety denied Baruch during his lifetime is more than compensated for in later Jewish literature and tradition, where he appears bigger than life (Muilenburg 1970: 237–38). An apocryphal letter is attributed to him (2d century B.C. with later additions), as well as several apocalypses (Grintz *EncJud* 4: 266–67; for texts see Charlesworth *OTP* 1: 615–79). See also BARUCH, BOOK OF.

Bibliography

Avigad, N. 1978. Baruch the Scribe and Jerahmeel the King's Son. *IEJ* 28: 52–56. (Repr. *BA* 42: 114–18.)

Gevaryahu, H. 1973. Baruch ben Neriah the Scribe. Pp. 191–243 in *Zer Ligevurot.* Jerusalem (in Hebrew).

Lundbom, J. R. 1986. Baruch, Seraiah, and Expanded Colophons in the Book of Jeremiah. *JSOT* 36: 89–114.

Muilenburg, J. 1970. Baruch the Scribe. Pp. 215–38 in *Proclamation and Presence,* ed. J. I. Durham and J. R. Porter. Richmond, VA.

JACK R. LUNDBOM

2. Son of Zabbai and a contemporary of Nehemiah (Neh 3:20). He shared with his fellow Levites in the reconstruction of the walls of Jerusalem laboring in the section described as "from the Angle to the door of the house of Eliashib," the high priest (Neh 3:17, 20).

3. One of the 22 signatories of the priestly contingent who ratified the covenant of Nehemiah (Neh 10:6). Besides these, 17 Levites, 44 chiefs of the people, and Nehemiah the governor entered into this compact, which provided for an abstinence from interracial relations and the more scrupulous observance of the Sabbath and other religious duties (Nehemiah 10).

4. Son of Colhozeh and the father of Maaseiah (Neh 11:5). In the three censuses of the returned exiles (Nehemiah 7; 11, and Ezra 2), this Baruch is mentioned but once. His son Maaseiah was among the chiefs of the province who lived in Jerusalem, a commendatory example in view of the incessant danger within the capital. Two Judahite leaders are singled out for particular notice in Nehemiah 11: Athaiah of the Judahite family of Perez, and Maaseiah the son of Baruch of the family of the Shelanite, that is, presumable from Shelah (Gen 38:5; Num 26:20). Since both have their ancestry traced for seven generations, it suggests their importance. Not only did they share the plaudits of the people for their courage (Neh 11:2), but they were accounted as "chiefs of the people" and "valiant men" (Neh 11:2, 6). Since Baruch is the father of Maaseiah, it seems reasonable to believe that he, too, was of statesmanlike character and a revered leader of the Judean repatriates. (See Myers *Ezra-Nehemiah* AB, 181–86, 254; Gunneweg *Nehemia* KAT, 64–76, 180–94.)

EDWARD R. DALGLISH

BARUCH, BOOK OF. An apocryphal text containing five chapters (in the Vulgate and Authorized Version, the Epistle of Jeremiah is added as a sixth chapter) attributed to Baruch, the son of Neriah, Jeremiah's secretary and amanuensis (Jer 36:1–32; 43:1–7). This is one of three compositions among the Apocrypha and Pseudepigrapha attributed to him (cf. *2 Baruch, 3 Baruch*). There is virtual unanimity among scholars that the book was not composed by Baruch the son of Neriah (who, according to biblical tradition, never reached Babylon). Some pseudepigraphic works may well have been attributed to him because in biblical tradition he occupied a position between prophet and scribe, and could therefore become a symbol for the transition from prophets to scribes. The earliest preserved text of Baruch is in Greek, in the Septuagint (cf. in LXX^A and LXX^B, but not in Codex Sinaiticus), and in most Greek manuscripts it appears between Jeremiah and Lamentations. The later versions, i.e., Latin (in the oldest known mss. of the Vulgate, Amiatinus, both Baruch and the Epistle of Jeremiah are omitted), Syriac, Arabic, Ethiopic, and others are based on the Greek version, and already in Origen's time (A.D. 185?–254) there was no Hebrew text available. No text of Baruch has as yet been identified among the fragments from Qumran. The date and place of composition are uncertain; it may have been composed in the Diaspora, but Palestine cannot be entirely ruled out. See also JEREMIAH, ADDITIONS TO.

A. Contents and Literary Genre

The book is a collection of three compositions of different literary genres, linked by one common motif: Sin–Exile–Return.

1. Historical Introduction. In this section (1:1–14) the purpose of the book is stated, and its fictitious date is given. We are told that Baruch wrote a letter in Babylon in the fifth year, on the seventh day of the fifth month, the date on which the Chaldeans captured Jerusalem and set the temple and city on fire (i.e., 582/581 B.C.). Baruch read out the letter to Jeconiah son of Jehoiakim, king of Judah, and to a general assembly of the Diaspora, including nobles, princes, and elders, gathered in Babylon by the river Soud (perhaps Ahava). Money was collected to be sent to the (High) Priest Joakim son of Hilkiah in Jerusalem together with the silver vessels which Zedekiah had made in place of the temple vessels that had been taken away by Nebuchadnezzar. According to Baruch's letter, the message of the Diaspora to the Jews of Jerusalem consisted of four main points. First, they should sacrifice on the altar in Jerusalem, the sacrifices to be bought with the money sent by the Diaspora Jews. Second, they are asked to pray for Nebuchadnezzar and "his son" Belshazzar (an error also found in Dan 5:2, 13, 18, 22; Belshazzar was the son of Nabonidus) that "their days may be as long as the days of heaven are above the earth." Third, they should pray for the Diaspora, because the Jews living there have sinned against God, and God is still angry with them. Fourth, the Jerusalemites should read Baruch's letter sent to them and use it as a liturgy in the temple during the feasts and festivals. This first section of the book is in prose and sets its purpose as being a collection for liturgical purposes. The use of a letter to comment on liturgical matters is known elsewhere in the Apocrypha (2 Macc 1:1–2:18).

2. Confession of Sins. The prayer (1:15–3:8) is repetitive and at first sight seems unorganized. However, an inner logic can be traced and it can be divided into four parts.

a. 1:15–2:5. In these verses the Palestinian Jews are the ones who confess. They declare that the "men of Judah and the inhabitants of Jerusalem" have transgressed against the Torah and God's word ever since God led them out of Egypt and "until this day." They were therefore punished and subjected to all the disasters which Moses predicted when he promised them the Holy Land (Deuteronomy 28–32). Nevertheless they did not follow God's prophets and continued worshiping other gods, and even ate their own offspring, although God had already carried out his threats against the "judges, kings, nobles and the men of Israel and Judah." They were then dispersed among the nations.

b. 2:6–2:30. This section of the prayer is partially parallel to 1:15–2:5. This time, it is probably formulated from the standpoint of the Diaspora Jews (2:13–14, 30). Again we hear a confession about past sins and transgressions against Mosaic Law. The wish is expressed that God should save his people because "only a few of us are left among the nations" (2:13). A reminder is given of God's words through his prophets, and a summary of Jeremiah's words (25:8–11; 27:11–12; etc.) is condensed into three verses: God requested his people to serve the king of Babylonia; the people of Israel ignored his words; thus, they were punished in the Diaspora and their temple is desolate.

c. 2:31–2:35. A turning point will arrive, and the people of Israel will repent through remembering their fathers' sins. Then God will return them to the promised land, and will renew his covenant with them "and never again will I drive my people Israel out of the land."

d. 3:1–3:8. Another prayer for salvation. Although the Jews in exile have repented, they still suffer in the Diaspora.

The prayer shares much of its language and ideas with Dan 9:4–19, Jeremiah, and Deuteronomy 28–32, but Bar 1:15–3:8 is 47 percent longer than Dan 9:4–19 and differs from it in mood. Both prayers have the elements of confession and repentance in common and show a resemblance to liturgical texts from Qumran (4QDibHam). See also WORDS OF THE LUMINARIES. Whereas in Daniel 9 the desolate temple and the deserted city are central, in Bar 1:15–3:8 this is not the case. Moreover, it seems that Daniel prays in Palestine, whereas Baruch prays in the Diaspora. There are two significant additions in Baruch's prayer: first, an emphasis on the transgression of God's command to serve the king of Babylonia; second, God's forgiveness and the Return motif (2:30–35). It is difficult to decide which prayer derives from the other. Possibly there may have existed two versions of a well-known prayer, one in the Diaspora (Bar 1:15–3:8), and the other in Palestine (Dan 9:4–19). The core of these prayers can already be discerned in Ezra 9:6–10 (and Nehemiah 9). Significantly, in both prayers (Daniel 9 and Baruch) there is little emphasis on data taken from Israel's past (unlike in Nehemiah 9 and in other prayers of this kind (e.g., *3 Macc* 6:1–15).

3. Eulogy of Wisdom. In these verses (3:9–4:4) the people of Israel were said to have been subjected to tribulations because they had deserted the origins of Wisdom, which is described here as the "way of God." It is often assumed that vv 3:9–13 are a later interpolation, but this assumption appears unfounded. In this poem the author echoes Proverbs (2:4 and elsewhere), Job (28:12–38), and Ben Sira (chap. 24), and asks where Wisdom dwells in the world: "Learn where Wisdom is, where strength, where understanding is, and so learn where longevity and life are, where there is light for the eyes, and peace. Who has found where she lives . . ." (3:14–15). Then comes a list of places where Wisdom can not be found: neither among the rulers of nations, the rich or the young, nor in Canaan or in Yemen. The giants, too, were not chosen by God to be the bearers of Wisdom, and so were destroyed (3:26–28). Only God the Creator possessed Wisdom, and He granted it to His people (3:32–37); only then did it become available to human beings in general (3:38). Wisdom is the Torah which gives life (cf. Deut 30:15–19); those who abandon the Torah will die. This section ends on a felicitous note: "Israel, we are happy because we know the things that please God" (4:4; cf. Deut 33:29). Unlike Ben Sira (chap. 24) who deals with the same theme, Baruch adopts the more general approach to the abode of wisdom (found in Job and Proverbs). He identifies Wisdom with the Torah (Deut 30:11-13), and emphasizes its place among the people of Israel, whereas Ben-Sira stresses the link between Wisdom, Jerusalem, and the land of Israel.

4. A Psalm of Solace (Zion Poem). The final part of the book (4:5–5:9) ends with the presentation of an antithesis between present and future against the background of the calamities of the past. True, the people of Israel are dispersed among the nations, Zion is deserted, and her enemies rejoice. However, this will change: the people of Israel will return to Jerusalem, which will regain its past grandeur; Jerusalem will once more become a city of "Peace through Righteousness and Glory through devotion" (5:4). The enemies will be destroyed. This part of the book is suffused with thoughts current in both Deutero-Isaiah (chaps. 40–55) and Deuteronomy. Lamentations, which in some of the LXX mss. is the following book, has also influenced this section. Whereas in 4:9–29 Mother Zion recounts her sorrows, in 4:30–5:9 the tone of prayer is again used to express hope for salvation and return. Bar 5:1–9 resembles Psalms of Solomon 11, but is considerably shorter.

B. Unity of the Book

The unity of the book has been questioned by many. It has been attributed to two (1:1–3:8; 3:9–5:9), three (1:1–3:8; 3:9–4:4; 4:5–5:9; but also other divisions have been claimed), or even four authors (1:1–3 + 3:9–4:4; 1:4–14; 1:15–3:8; 4:5–5:9). Many scholars identify the author of Baruch with the final editor of this pseudepigraphic collection, who may also have been the author of one of its constituent parts. The possibility of a later editor is not ruled out and the entire question remains unresolved. However, it is clear that the book contains an unusual collection of compositions of different literary genres which draw on different source material. Whereas 1:1–3:8 draws heavily on Jeremiah and Deuteronomy, 3:9–4:4 show a strong dependence on wisdom literature, while 4:5–5:9 echoes Deutero-Isaiah, Deuteronomy, and to a lesser extent, Lamentations. In this respect the three different sections of the book are almost independent of each other. Many thematic differences can also be detected. For instance, the attitude towards the Babylonians in 1:1–3:8 is positive, but is not so toward the enemies in 4:5–5:9, while the Wisdom Psalm is indifferent about the conqueror. The first section (1:1–3:8) emphasizes the four pillars on which the people of Israel's life rests: the Temple (2:26), the Torah (2:28), the land of Israel (2:34), and the People (2:35, and 2:23, where they are called "the People of Judah and Jerusalem"). The second section (3:9–4:4) emphasizes only the Torah and the people of Israel, and 4:5–5:9 is centered on Jerusalem and its people (and much less on the Torah, 4:12–13). Another difference is that in the first and third sections there is a strong awareness of the Sin–Exile–Return theme, while this is not the case in the second section. In addition, whereas the second section commonly uses *theos,* the two other sections prefer either *kurios* (1:1–3:8) or *ho aionios* (4:5–5:9).

C. Language

There is a virtual concensus since Kneucker (1879) that the original language of 1:1–3:8 was Hebrew. Concerning the second part (3:9–5:9) views are still divided between either a Hebrew or Greek original. Already Thackeray (1902–3) argued that the Semitic texts of Baruch had been translated into Greek by two different translators. The first translated Jeremiah 29–52 through Bar 3:8; the second was responsible for Bar 3:9–5:9. Whitehouse and others thought that Baruch used the Greek of Jeremiah, whereas Schürer (*RE,* 642) and Thackeray (1923) were of the opinion that the translator of Baruch merely imitated the style of Jeremiah. A good case has been made in recent years by E. Tov (1975; 1976) for the following solution: the LXX version of Jeremiah 29–52 (Jer b) shows that a revision was made in an earlier Greek translation (called the Old Greek translation), which is still preserved in Jeremiah 1–28 (Jer a). This section of Jeremiah did not undergo such a revision. Bar 1:1–3:8, which draws heavily on Jeremiah 29–52, shows that the same hand which revised Jer b also revised Bar 1:1–3:8. This argument is supported by instances where Baruch draws on Jer a, but where the reviser changed the style in line with his style in Jer b. Because Bar 3:9–5:9 quotes neither Jeremiah nor Bar 1:1–3:8 it is impossible to establish in terms of vocabulary whether the reviser of Bar 1:1–3:8 also revised Bar 3:9–5:9.

D. Date

The date of composition of Baruch is unknown, and the issues become even more complicated if one accepts the disunity of the book. In fact, many suggestions have been put forward regarding the date of the book (or its constituent sections). These range from the 6th century B.C. to A.D. 70–135. There is no internal evidence which points decisively to some specific date. Even some of the potential clues are not very helpful. The sayings of Jeremiah were popular in Judaism at several junctures. The references to Nebuchadnezzar's "son" Belshazzar is a common error shared by both Baruch and Daniel. Originally it may have been made by Baruch, or else its author may have copied it centuries later from Daniel or some other source. Although in Baruch, Nebuchadnezzar and Belshazzar can be identified either with Antiochus IV and his son or with Vespasian and Titus, alternatively they can be accepted as authentic figures. The theme of the return of the sacred vessels is borrowed from Ezra 1:7–11, and the name of the high priest Joakim is only known from Neh 12:10, 26. The dependence of Baruch on these facts does not provide any clue to a later date. The resemblance of Baruch 1:15–3:8 to Dan 9:4–19 does not take us much further, since Daniel 9 could be an interpolation into Daniel 7–11 (composed circa 164 B.C.). Both prayers may derive from a common source, rather than being interdependent. Baruch could have used Daniel 9 (or vice versa) at a time much later than 164 B.C. The same holds true of the similarity between Bar 5:1–9 and Psalms of Solomon 11; the latter may have been composed after 67 B.C. The psalms may be based on one another, or derive from a common source. Scholars are inclined to the view that the related verses of Psalms of Solomon 11 are secondary to Baruch 5 (Pesch). Even if 3:9–5:9 (or any other part of the book except 1:1–3:8) are by a different author, the dating of the entire book still remains uncertain.) The absence of the theme of resurrection (even where one expects it, Bar 2:17), and the silence of the text regarding angelology, messianism, etc., does not necessarily point to a particular date of composition. The author of Baruch imitated biblical themes and style, and this could be done at any time from the Return until A.D. 135 or later. According to 1:10–14 (but perhaps not according to 2:26), the temple appears to be in operation. Jer 41:5 and Lam 1:4 maintain that worship in the burnt temple (2 Kgs 25:9) continued even after the conquest of 587 B.C. The question whether Baruch borrowed from these data to allude to his own times remains open.

Four positive determinations can be made concerning the date of Baruch. First, if the LXX of Jeremiah can be approximately dated, then at least Bar 1:1–3:8 can be fixed to some point before the end of the 2d century B.C. (116 B.C.). Second, throughout the book the Jews seem to have religious freedom, but not political independence. Moreover, the mood of the entire book excludes the possibility of dating it to the Hasmonean independent state (140–67 B.C.). Third, despite the prevalent mood of desolation and despair, hope is expressed for redemption and complete return of the people of Israel to their land. Fourth, the insistent plea to serve the Babylonian king and his 'son" may refer—taken together with the other points mentioned—either to the period of ca. 200 B.C., when much hope was placed in Antiochus III (who had conquered Palestine from the Ptolemies), or to the period after A.D. 70, when it was hoped that many would return to the land of Israel from all parts of the Roman Empire (4:37): "See, your sons whom you sent away are coming! They are coming, gathered from east and west at the Holy One's command, rejoicing in God's glory." At the present stage of research, the question of dating must remain open.

Bibliography

Burke, D. G. 1982. *The Poetry of Baruch.* Chico, CA.

Goldstein, J. 1980. The Apocryphal Book of 1 Baruch. Pp. 179–99 in *American Academy of Jewish Research Jubilee Volume,* eds. S. W. Baron and I. E. Barzilay. New York.

Kneucker, J. J. 1879. *Das Buch Baruch.* Leipzig.

Nickelsburg, G. W. E. 1984. Baruch. Pp. 140–46 in *Jewish Writings of the Second Temple Period,* ed. M. E. Stone. CRINT. Philadelphia.

Pesch, W. 1955. Die Abhängigkeit des 11. salomonischen Psalms vom letzten Kapitel des Buches Baruch. *ZAW* 67: 251–63.

Pfeiffer, R. H. 1949. *History of New Testament Times.* New York.

Schmitt, J. J. 1985. The Motherhood of God and Zion as Mother. *RB* 92: 557–69.

Thackeray, H. St. J. 1902/3 The Greek Translators of Jeremiah. *JTS* 4: 245–66.

———. 1923. *The Septuagint and Jewish Worship.* 2d ed. Oxford.

Tov, E. 1975. *The Book of Baruch Also Called I Baruch (Greek and Hebrew).* SBLTT 8. Missoula, MT.

———. 1976. *The Septuagint Translation of Jeremiah and Baruch.* HSM 8. Missoula, MT.

Wambacq, B. N. 1959. Les prières de Baruch (i 15 – ii 19) et de Danel (ix 5–19). *Bib* 40: 463–75.

Ziegler, J. 1957. *Ieremias, Baruch, Threni, Epistula Ieremiae.* Septuaginta, Vetus Testamentum Graecum auctoritate Societatis Göttingensis editum 15. Göttingen.

DORON MENDELS

BARUCH, BOOK OF 2 (SYRIAC). Approximately 30 to 50 years after the destruction of the temple by the Roman soldiers in 70 C.E. a gifted Jew, using old traditions, many of which antedate 70, struggled to assert that Judaism is a religion based on Torah—Law—and that the loss of the temple was due to the failure of the chosen nation to be obedient to God and his Law. His central message is the continuing obligation to obey the Law (note 44:5–7; 51:3; so also Collins 1984, contra Murphy 1985). In many ways the concerns and expressions in *2 Baruch* indicate how Early Judaism was moving toward Rabbinic Judaism. Some scholars speculate that the author may have been Akiba (Rosenthal 1885) or belonged to Akiba's group at Jamnia (Violet 1924); Bogaert (1969) suggests that he may have been Rabbi Joshua ben Ḥananiah (ca. 40–125).

The document, which is a full-blown apocalypse (contrast *4 Ezra*), is extant in only the following corrupt or partial manuscripts: one 6th- or 7th-century Syriac manuscript (Milan, Ambrosian Library, MS B.21 Inf. fols. 257[a]–265[b]), which is sometimes meaningless and is based on a lost Greek text; one 10th- or 11th-century Arabic manuscript (St. Catherine's Monastery, Arab. MS no. 589), which is defective and based on a late Syriac text; two 4th- or 5th-century fragments among the Oxyrhynchus Papyri (*P.Oxy.* 403); and three late excerpts in Jacobite lectionaries (BM Add. MS 14686 [13th cent.], BM Add. MS 14687 [13th cent.], Kerala, India, A. Konath Libr. MS 77 (4) [16th cent.]). Without a doubt the major witness to this document is the Syriac manuscript in the Ambrosian Library, but emendations are sometimes necessary.

Although not obvious, it is possible that the apocalypse was intended to have seven sections: the destruction of Jerusalem (1–12); the impending judgement (13–20); retribution and the messianic era (21–34); Baruch's lament and an allegory of the vine and the cedar (35–46); the endtime, the resurrected body, paradise (47–52); Baruch's vision of a cloud (53–76); and the epistle of Baruch (77–87). Some scholars think the epistle was later added to the apocalypse (Sayler 1984), others (Bogaert 1969; Klijn *OTP* 1: 615–52) rightly see it as an original part of the document, as a kind of epilogue (Collins 1984).

While there is a consensus that the document was probably composed in Palestine, there is no agreement on whether it was composed in Greek (Bogaert 1969), Hebrew or Aramaic (Denis 1970a, b), or Hebrew (Charles 1896; Klijn *OTP* 1: 615–52). Earlier in this century, scholars concluded that the work is a combination of sources (Charles isolated six), but today most scholars (Bogaert 1969; Sayler 1984; Murphy 1985) are rightly impressed with the unity of the work. Brockington thinks that *2 Baruch* is roughly contemporaneous with *4 Ezra* and *Pseudo-Philo,* but there is sufficient evidence to conclude, with many specialists, that the chronological order seems to be *Pseudo-Philo, 4 Ezra,* then *2 Baruch* (cf. Klijn *OTP* 1: 615–52. No literary dependence, however, proves this sequence; but in view of the numerous and striking parallels between *4 Ezra* and *2 Baruch* (viz. cf. *4 Ezra* 7:118 with *2 Bar.* 48:42 and 54:19) it is possible that the author of *2 Baruch* attempted to correct the pessimism of *4 Ezra* (cf. Collins 1984).

The brilliant mind of the author is readily apparent. He claims apologetically that Israel's enemies were allowed to enter Jerusalem only after "all the sacred vessels" had been removed and the angels had destroyed the walls (7:1–8:5). He thereby removes the Romans' reason for boasting (7:1). Eschewing the explanation that evil derives from fallen (1 Enoch) or evil angels (cf. 1QS), the author of *2 Baruch* puts the blame on humankind, lamenting in poetic language that insinuates some free will: "Adam is, therefore, not the cause, except only for himself, but each of us has become our own Adam" (54:19; Klijn *OTP* 1). His explanation for the delay in the consummation of the ages is that the endtime will not come until the number of those to be born is fulfilled (23:4–7). One of the most beautiful eschatological passages in the history of the Jewish apocalypses is the following: "For the youth of this world has passed away, and the power of creation is already exhausted, and the coming of the times is very near and has passed by. And the pitcher is near the well, and the ship to the harbor, and the journey to the city, and life to its end" (85:10; Klijn *OTP* 1: 615–52; this passage is truncated in the Arabic version).

Bibliography

Bogaert, P.-M. 1969. *L'Apocalypse de Baruch: Introduction, traduction du syriaque et commentaire.* SC 144, 145. Paris.

Brockington, L. H. 1984. The Syriac Apocalypse of Baruch. Pp. 835–95 in *The Apocryphal Old Testament,* ed. H. F. D. Sparks. Oxford.

Charles, R. H. 1896. *The Apocalypse of Baruch.* London. repr. London, 1917, 1929.

Charlesworth, J. H. 1981. *The Pseudepigraph and Modern Research with a Supplement.* SBLSCS 7S. Chico, CA.

———. 1985. The Triumphant Majority as Seen by a Dwindled Minority: The Outsider According to the Insider of the Jewish Apocalypses, 70–130. Pp. 285–315 in *"To See Ourselves as Others See Us": Christians, Jews, "Others" in Late Antiquity,* ed. J. Neusner and E. S. Frerichs. Chico, CA.

Collins, J. J. 1984. *The Apocalyptic Imagination: An Introduction to the Jewish Matrix of Christianity.* New York.

Dedering, S. 1973. Apocalypse of Baruch. Part 4.3, pp. i–iv + 1–50 in *The Old Testament in Syriac.* Leiden.

Denis, A.-M. 1970a. Apocalypsis Syriaca Baruch. Pp. 118–20 in *Fragmenta Pseudepigraphorum quae supersunt Graeca.* PVTG 3. Leiden.

———. 1970b. *Introduction aux pseudépigraphes grecs d'ancien testament.* SVTP 1. Leiden.

Hadot, J. 1987. Apocalypse Syriaque de Baruch. Pp. 1471–1557 in *La Bible: Écrits intertestamentaires,* ed. A. Dupont-Sommer and M. Philonenko. Paris.

Harnisch, W. 1969. *Verhängnis und Verheissung der Geschichte.* Göttingen.

Leemhuis, F.; Klijn, A. F. J.; and Gelder, G. J. H. van. 1986. *The Arabic Text of the Apocalypse of Baruch.* Leiden.

Murphy, F. J. 1985. *The Structure and Meaning of Second Baruch.* SBLDS 78. Atlanta.

Rosenthal, F. 1885. *Vier apokryphische Bücher aus der Zeit und Schule R. Akiba's.* Leipzig.

Sayler, G. B. 1984. *Have the Promises Failed? A Literary Analysis of 2 Baruch.* SBLDS 72. Chico, CA.

Violet, B. 1924. *Die Apokalypsen des Esra und des Baruch in deutscher Gestalt.* GCS 32. Leipzig.

JAMES H. CHARLESWORTH

BARUCH, BOOK OF 3 (GREEK). Attributed to Baruch and extant in two Slavonic versions (both probably derived from Greek manuscripts) and in Greek, this work is an apocalypse in which Baruch, Jeremiah's scribe, laments over the destruction of Jerusalem until an angel sent by the Lord leads him through five heavens and reveals to him the mysteries of this world and time.

It is possible that Greek is the original language (Gaylord *OTP* 1: 655). The date of composition is uncertain; it obviously must postdate 70 C.E. since the author knows about the destruction of Jerusalem by the Romans, and probably antedates 231 C.E., if Origen alludes to it in *Princ.* 2.3.6 (James 1897). Since the pseudepigraphon is closely linked with the apocryphal Baruch literature, especially 2 and 4 Baruch, which were written in the early 2d century C.E., it is either subsequent to or contemporaneous with them (Argyle 1984: 898). Diez Macho (1984: 295) concluded that *3 Baruch* was composed near the end of the 1st century C.E. in Egypt. A non-Palestinian provenience seems probable (*APOT,* 527–32; *JSHRZ* 5/1: 15–44).

The document was drawn to the attention of modern scholars in 1896 (by E. Cuthbert Butler), and M. R. James concluded soon thereafter that the work was composed in the 2d century C.E. by a Christian. Most scholars now contend that the document is Jewish (Ginsberg, Hughes, Picard, Rost, Hage) and has been redacted by a Christian (but many of the Christian passages in the Greek version are absent in the Slavonic). Thus, while the work is originally Jewish the extant versions are the result of Christian redaction.

The author struggles with many questions, including the relation between the human and the divine since the sacrifices in the temple have been abolished. The author explains that the oil of mercy and glory of God will still be available, because there is a heavenly temple in which Michael offers to God the prayers and virtues of humans. In the fifth heaven Baruch sees "Michael take hold of a very large bowl, its depth being so great as from heaven to earth, and its width so great as from north to south. And I [Baruch] said, 'Lord, what is it that Michael the archangel is holding?' And he said to me, 'This is where the virtues of the righteous and the good works which they do are carried, which are brought by him before the heavenly God' " (11:8–9). See also *OTP* 1: 653–79; *APOT* 2: 527–41.

Bibliography

Argyle, A. W. (with a revision of H. M. Hughes' translation). 1984. The Greek Apocalypse of Baruch. Pp. 897–914 in *The Apocryphal Old Testament.* Oxford: Clarendon.

Denis, A.-M., and Janssens, Y. 1970. *Concordance de l'Apocalypse grecque de Baruch.* PIOL 1. Louvain.

Diez Macho, A. 1984. Apocalipsis Griego de Baruc. Pp. 292–95 in *Apocrifos del Antiguo Testamento,* vol 1. Madrid.

James, M. R. 1897. The Apocalypse of Baruch. Pp. li–lxxi and 84–102 in *Apocrypha Anecdota II.* Texts and Studies 5.1. Cambridge.

Picard, J.-C. 1966. *Apocalypsis Baruchi Graece.* PVTG 2. Leiden.

Riaud, J. 1987. Apocalypse Grecque de Baruch. Pp. 1141–64 in *La Bible: Écrits Intertestamentaires,* ed. A. Dupont-Sommer and M. Philonenko. Paris.

JAMES H. CHARLESWORTH

BARUCH, BOOK OF 4. The pseudepigraphon generally designated as *4 Baruch* is actually entitled in Greek *Paraleipomena Ieremiou,* "Things omitted from the Prophet Jeremiah," and in the Ethiopic mss "The Rest of the Words of Baruch." The document represents itself as an account of the events surrounding the conquest of Jerusalem and the destruction of the temple by the Babylonians in 587 B.C.E.

According to this narrative, the night before the catastrophe, the Lord revealed to Jeremiah that because of the sins of the people, the holy city was about to be attacked by his angels and then delivered into the hands of the Chaldeans, who could not otherwise have prevailed over Jerusalem. Jeremiah is instructed to entrust the vessels of the temple to the earth and the keys of the sanctuary to the sun. The Lord further instructs him to accompany the exiles to Babylon, but to leave Baruch the scribe behind in Jerusalem until the return of the people.

Jeremiah asks the Lord if his faithful servant Abimelech might not be spared, and the Lord agrees, instructing Jeremiah to send Abimelech out of the city early in the morning to gather figs at the farm of Agrippa. There Abimelech takes a nap under a tree and sleeps for 66 years.

When Abimelech finally awakens from his slumber, the figs in his basket are still fresh, but he is disoriented and unable to recognize the city or other landmarks. At last an old man deduces what has happened and tells Abimelech about the destruction and subsequent events. When Abimelech is reunited with Baruch, the scribe takes his awakening as a sign that the return of the exiles is imminent and interprets Abimelech's still-fresh figs as tokens of personal and national resurrection. Baruch then sends a letter to Jeremiah along with some of the figs, instructing the prophet to prepare the exiles for their return.

Jeremiah returns to Judea with the exiles, but as they are crossing over the Jordan river, those who will not put away their Babylonian wives are turned back. Eventually these settle down in Samaria, the progenitors of the Samaritans. In Jerusalem, Jeremiah has another marvelous vision in which he sees many divine mysteries. Following this vision, Jeremiah preaches about the future coming of Jesus Christ the Son of God, and is finally stoned to death by the people.

The date of the final form of *4 Baruch* must certainly be after the middle of the 1st century C.E., as witnessed by the reference to the farm of Agrippa and the resurrection of Jesus. Because Herod Agrippa I didn't come into control of Judea until 41 C.E., the text must date after that time. Moreover, most scholars believe that the concern for the destruction of the city and temple and for the restoration of the nation reflects a period after the destruction of the Jerusalem temple by Titus in 70 C.E. and before the Bar Kokhba revolt. Indeed, if this line of reasoning is correct, the document ought to be dated to the first third of the 2d century since an upper limit of 136 C.E. is obtained by adding the 66 years of Abimelech's sleep, the maximum period envisioned by the author before restoration, to the date of the destruction in 70. The knowledge apparently displayed in the text about Jerusalem landmarks such as the farm of Agrippa or the marketplace of the gentiles suggests, but does not prove, that *4 Baruch* was written in Palestine, or perhaps even in Jerusalem itself.

4 Baruch contains three redactional levels, two Jewish and one Christian. In the oldest portion of the text, chaps. 1–4, the central figure is Jeremiah the prophet; Baruch the scribe is either a subordinate or not present at all. This agrees with traditions preserved in canonical Jeremiah, 2 Maccabees, and *Lives of the Prophets.* The later Jewish redactor, particularly in chaps. 7 and 8, elevated the figure of Baruch the scribe above that of Jeremiah the prophet, and otherwise gave the document a distinctly Pharisaic character. This fits well the historical developments in Judaism during the early 2d century B.C.E. Finally, a Christian redactor made a few interpolations in the body of the text and added the prophecy of Christ in chap. 9.

After the Bar Kokhba revolt, Judaism repudiated much of its apocalyptic tradition and the literature it produced, including *4 Baruch.* This left only the Christianized redaction preserved in Greek, Ethiopic, Armenian, Old Church Slavonic, and the Romanian versions. However, the linguistic evidence strongly supports a Semitic original, probably Hebrew, behind these later versions (see *OTP* 2: 413–25).

Bibliography

Denis, A. M. 1970. *Introduction aux pseudepigraphes grecs d'Ancien Testament.* SVTP 1. Leiden.

Kraft, R. A., and Purintun, A. E. 1972. *Paraleipomena Ieremiou.* T/T 1, Pseudepigrapha Series 1. Missoula, MT.

STEPHEN E. ROBINSON

BARZILLAI (PERSON) [Heb *barzillai*]. The name of three men in the OT.

1. A Gileadite who supported David during his difficulties with Absalom (2 Sam 17:27–29). When David, hounded from Jerusalem by Absalom, camped at Mahanaim, Barzillai supplied him with materials and food from his own considerable wealth. David's refreshed and strengthened troops then defeated Absalom's army. Barzillai's kindness made him the object of David's peculiar favor: David invited him to Jerusalem for permanent residence, proximate to the palace where he might enjoy the privileges of royal friendship. Barzillai declined, however, because of the debilities of his advanced age which would inhibit such enjoyment. Instead he sent his son, Chimham, whom David received as his surrogate. After a solemn and ceremonious benediction pronounced upon his benefactor, the king proceeded toward Jerusalem, accompanied by Chimham; Barzillai returned to his home in Gilead (2 Sam 19:31–40). David rewarded Barzillai's kindness, generosity, and loyalty by instructing Solomon to extend to Chimham and his sons a continuing royal friendship together with its accompanying privileges (1 Kgs 2:7).

2. A resident of Abel-Meholah in Gilead (2 Sam 21:8). His son Adriel married Merab, King Saul's daughter, though she had been promised to David. From Adriel he gained five grandsons, but he suffered the shameful loss of those grandsons to the hostilities between Saul and David. David surrendered them to the Gibeonites, whom he knew to be hostile to Saul; the Gibeonites hanged the five, exposed on a mountain (2 Sam 21:8–9).

3. The father of a family of sons who lived in Jerusalem during the postexilic period (Ezra 2:61 = Neh 7:63). He derived his name from #1 above when he took a wife from his progeny and took the name with the wife. His name is given as "Jaddus" ("Jaddous" in one manuscript) in 1 Esdr 5:38, a passage in which his wife's name is given as "Augia." But these names are both doubtful for reasons which Bewer (1922: 31) summarized already in 1922 and which subsequent students of the passage have found persuasive. "Jaddus" is the corrupted Gk transliteration of the Heb *zlly,* from which the preceding syllable *br* was lost. "Augia" is a corruption of the Gk *Agiliadi,* which was the transliteration of the Heb *hglydy,* "the Gileadite." If his sons' claims were legitimate, he was a priest. His sons claimed the privileges and duties of priests in postexilic Jerusalem, though they were unable to establish their claim when they sought, in vain, their registration in the priestly genealogies. This lack marked them as unclean and excluded them from the priesthood (Ezra 2:62–63 = Neh 7:64–65). Kidner (*Ezra Nehemiah* TOTC, 42) suggests that when Barzillai appropriated a name from a non-priestly family, he compromised his status as a priest; subsequently, his and his sons' names were deleted or excluded from the priestly registers.

Bibliography

Bewer, J. 1922. *Der Text des Buches Ezra.* Göttingen.

GERALD J. PETTER

BASEMATH (PERSON) [Heb *bāśĕmat*]. Derived from *bośem/beśem* "balm (tree)," the name belongs to two women in the OT (see below). Outside the OT, the name bs_2mt occurs in Minaean for a women from Gaza married to a Minaean merchant (M 392 C 47; 3d century B.C.) and in Sabaic for a man (CIS IV 725); the Sabaic reference may be vocalized according to classical Arabic *Bašâmah,* which is a man's name as well (Caskel 1966: 225; Knauf 1985: 93, n. 509).

1. One of the wives of Esau, the legendary ancestor of Edom (Gen 26:34; 36:3, 4, 10, 13, 17). According to Gen 26:34, she was the daughter of "Elon the Hittite." In the 1st millennium B.C., "Hittite" could denote any native of Syria/Palestine (the name "Elon" is Canaanite). In the perception of the priestly source (or layer), to which this verse is generally attributed, it could denote any non-Jewish inhabitant of Syria/Palestine.

According to Gen 36:3, Basemath was the daughter of Ishmael and sister of Nebaioth. This contradicts Gen 28:9 (P), where the daughter of Ishmael married to Esau is called Mahalath. Most probably, Gen 36:1–5 is a redactional addition to Genesis 36 which is more recent than 36:6–9, 40–43 (P) and 36:10–14, 20–28 (from the geographical source of P?). For this geographical source and its date, see Knauf 1985: 61–63, and for the stratigraphy of Genesis 36, Weippert 1971: 437–46. The redactor may have realized that "Basemath" sounds more "Arabic" than "Hittite." The "sister of Nebaioth" probably refers to the immigration of the Qedarite clan or subtribe *Nabaṭ* (the later Nabataeans) into Edom, which may have occurred as early as at the end of the 6th century B.C. (Knauf 1985: 108f).

According to the old (7th century B.C.?) and probably Edomite tradition in Gen 36:10–14, Basemath is the mother of the major Edomite tribe Reuel. This information is copied from Gen 36:10, 13 into Gen 36:4 and 17 (Weippert 1971: 437–46). Judging from the parallels to the name, it is conceivable that the legendary ancestor of the Reuelites could have been either male or female. Only with the incorporation of Reuel into the Edomite state, or even later with the compilation of the biblical lists concerning Edom, Basemath became a wife of Esau.

2. According to 1 Kgs 4:15, Basemath was a daughter of King Solomon and married to one of Solomon's twelve provincial governors. The authenticity of the list in 1 Kgs 4:7–19 is generally accepted.

Bibliography

Caskel, W. 1966. *Gamharat an-nasab. Das genealogische Werk des Hisam ibn Muhammad al-Kalbi,* vol. 2. Leiden.

Knauf, E. A. 1985. *Ismael.* Wiesbaden.

Weippert, M. 1971. *Edom. Studien und Materialien zur Geschichte der Edomiter auf Grund schriftlicher und archäologischer Quellen.* Diss. Tübingen.

ERNST AXEL KNAUF

BASHAN (PLACE) [Heb *bāšān*]. The fertile area of upper Transjordan east of the Sea of Galilee and mainly north of the Yarmuk river. The ancient boundaries of Bashan, although impossible to determine exactly, appear to be the area north of Gilead, west of Salecah and the Jebel Druze Mountains (though some biblical texts appear to include Jebel Druze; see *GB,* 222), south of Mount Hermon, and east of the Jordan and the Sea of Galilee. Its southern boundary was apparently not far from the present border of Syria and Jordan which coincides with the lower Yarmuk River. One of Bashan's early capitals, Edrei (Num 21:33, Deut 3:10), was situated on a tributary of the Yarmuk. Other cities located in Bashan included Karnaim, Ashtaroth (Deut 1:4, Josh 9:10), and Salecah (Deut 3:10) in the regions of Argob (Deut 3:4), Golan (Deut 4:43), and Hauran. The ancient capital of Bashan was Ashtaroth, replaced later by Karnaim.

Bashan always appears with the definite article as "the Bashan," meaning "smooth" or "stoneless plain," or "fertile, fruitful." It was a broad, fertile plateau surrounded by basaltic, volcanic mountains, and hills. The plateau, at an altitude of 2000 feet above sea level, was perfectly suited for agriculture and cattle. The area was well known for its cattle (Ps 22:12; Amos 4:1–3) and timber (Isa 2:13; Ezek 27:6). Because of its fertility and productivity, Bashan was the prize in wars between Syria and Israel.

Bashan was inhabited as early as the late 4th millennium B.C. by whom the Bible calls the Rephaim. By the time of Moses, a prosperous agricultural area had been built around sixty cities (Deut 3:4–6). All of Bashan's cities were defeated by Moses at Edrei (Num 21:33–35; Deut 3:1–9). After the area was subdued, Moses assigned it to the half-tribe of Manasseh and even set aside Golan to be one of the cities of refuge east of the Jordan. Some of the families of Gad settled in Bashan (1 Chr 5:11–12). Ultimately, Israel was removed from Bashan by Tilgath-pileser III (745–727 B.C.) of Assyria.

In the Greco-Roman period, the area was known as Batanea. Its cities included Seleucia, Hippos, Gamala, Decapolis, Abila, and Dion. The district of Hauran became well developed in the centuries following Christ, as evidenced by the construction of aqueducts, reservoirs, temples, theaters, and basilicas. From the period following Trajan (A.D. 117–38), inscriptions abound in the area.

JOEL C. SLAYTON

BASILIDES. Basilides, active in the first half of the 2d century, was a highly influential Christian gnostic philosopher who established his own philosophical school in Alexandria (see GNOSTICISM). Also influential were the early followers of Basilides, like his most popular disciple and "son" Isidore and possibly the great gnostic reformer VALENTINUS. The school of Basilides was apparently still active in the mid-4th century. The present writer is indebted to text anthologies and studies by W. Völker (1932), K. Rudolph (1977), R. Grant (1979), and B. Layton (1987).

A. Patristic Sources

As in the case of most original gnostic literature, the intense heresiological polemic against Basilides and his followers resulted in the effective censorship and eventual elimination of their writings from the medieval manuscript tradition. What we know of Basilides and his teaching comes down to us in the form of incomplete descriptions and quotations by the patristic heresiologists (Grant 1979: 201–16). As yet, there have been no genuine Basilidean texts identified among the papyri including the Nag Hammadi codices (see NAG HAMMADI [CODICES]).

The most important patristic evidence is the description by Irenaeus (ca. 180; *Haer.* 1.24.3–7), possibly based on a now lost writing of Justin Martyr (ca. 160; Layton 1987: 418), which was later reused in summary form by the 4th and 5th century heresiologists Epiphanius of Salamis (*Haer.* 24.1.1–24.10.8) and Theodoret of Cyrrhus (*Compendium* 4; Layton 1987:420–25; Rudolph 1977:309–12). Irenaeus transmits a descriptive summary of Basilides' mythological system which is in line with the contents of the fragments quoted by Clement and Origen (below) and other extant early evidences of the classic gnostic myth (see GNOSTICISM). The myth begins with the "unengendered parent" (first principle) who expands into a complex spiritual universe. This is followed by the creation of a material universe of 365 concentrically nested heavens, each of which is controlled by its own rulers (archons), and at the core center of which is the lowest point of creation: humankind's material world. The lowest heaven, that visible to humans, was created by the evil angels who populate it. According to the myth, their ruler was the minor but effectively evil creator-god of the Jews who rules over a material world and is at odds with the spiritual aspirations of humankind. Humans, whose true home is the spiritual universe, are thus spirits trapped in the material world and can only escape by bodiless spiritual ascent through the 365 levels of dominating authorities if they *know* (i.e., if they are gnostic) that the way has been opened by the descent and ascent of Christ the spiritual Savior. The Christ was not truly incarnate and did not suffer but instead escaped as Simon of Cyrene died on the cross. This Christ (the laughing Savior), having overcome the shackles of the evil god, thus ascends back to the unengendered father and so prepares the way through the heavens for human spirits to ascend. It is clear that the gnosticizing spirit-matter dualism, the inverted interpretation of Gen 1–3, and the denigration of biblical history with its good creator god, certainly put Basilides' teaching at odds with developing orthodox positions (Rudolph 1977:310–12; Layton 1987:420–25).

Clement of Alexandria (*ca.* 200) quotes and comments on seven sections from unknown works of Basilides in Clement's famous *Stromata* 4–5 (cf. frags. A through E, G and H in Layton 1987:427–37, 440–44). Two of the fragments focus on cosmological issues (Layton 1987:428–31): the first is a quote (frag. A; *Strom.* 4.162.1) which refers to two of the constituent members of the octet in the godhead and is in agreement with Irenaeus' description (*Haer.* 1.24.3), while the other is a quote and discussion (frag. B; *Strom.* 5.74.3) refering to the Stoic concept of the uniqueness of the world. The five remaining fragments focus on ethical issues (in line with Stoic ethics; cf. Layton 1987: 418, 432–44): the first (frag. C; *Strom.* 5.3.2–3) refers to Basilides' teaching on election in relation to faith and virtue; the second (frag. D; frag. 4 in Völker; *Strom.* 4.86.1) describes Basilides' teaching on the will of god (fate) to which the virtuous person aspires; the third (=frag. E; *Strom.* 4.165.3) describes Basilides' teaching that human souls retain their identity through their various incarnations and so transcend the world; the fourth (frag. G; frag. 2 in Völker; *Strom.* 4.81.2–4.83.2) is a series of lengthy quotes introduced by Clement with the statement that they are from Book 23 of Basilides' now lost *Commentaries* (the *Exegetica*), quotes which seem to be from a commentary on

1 Pet 4:12–19 in which he argues that the will of god (fate) is "all-powerful and all good" (Layton 1987: 440–43); the fifth (frag. H; *Strom.* 4.153.3) is a single sentence referring to forgivable sins.

Origen, in his commentary on Romans (*ca.* 244), quotes a Basilidean text (frag. F; frag. 3 in Völker; Origenes, *Opera Omnia* 4) in which Basilides interprets Rom 7:7 to refer to incarnation (which Origen accepted) and a certain gnostic cosmology (which Origen rejected). This text may also come from Basilides' *Commentaries* like frag. G in Clement, suggesting that Basilides and the eastern Valentinian gnostic Heracleon (*ca.* 150; Rudolph 1977:323–24) are the first known authors of commentaries on NT texts.

Other early and descriptive patristic refutations of Basilides' teachings are known. One is found in an extant heresiology by Hippolytus of Rome (first half of the 3d century; *Haer.* 7:20–27). But Hippolytus' report is not in tandem with the descriptions and quotations of Basilides' system which we find in the summaries and quotations in Irenaeus, Clement of Alexandria, and Origen (see discussion in Layton 1987:418 n. 2; Rudolph 1977:310). Another is the now lost *Refutation of Basilides* by the heresiologist Agrippa Castor (*ca.* 135) mentioned by Eusebius (*Hist. Eccl.* 4.7.6–8) at the beginning of the 4th century (Rudolph 1977: 309–10).

B. Basilides' Gnostic System and its Development

It is clear from the preceding survey of patristic quotes and discussions that Basilides' system was eclectically based on a variety of sources including classic gnostic teaching, Stoic ethics, and Platonic-Pythagorian soteriology. Yet through it all he employed traditional Christian scripture, language, and terminology (Rudolph 1977:310–12). This eclectic mix was quite common in Christian philosophies of 2d century Alexandria and is also found, on the more orthodox side, in Clement of Alexandria (Layton 1987:417–18).

Basilides was careful to base his teaching on broadly accepted apostolic authority like most innovative theologians of his day. While Valentinus was to base his authority on Paul (through a certain Theudas), Basilides based his authority on Peter (through a certain Glaucias), further strengthening the suggestion that the quote from Basilides' exegetical commentary (frag. G) was from a text in the Petrine tradition (1 Peter; Layton 1987:417, 440–43; Rudolph 1977:309–10).

After the death of Basilides, and in contrast to the popular reception of Valentinus' teachings, his school spread little beyond Egypt. His disciple and "son" Isidore was his most well-known disciple, developed Basilides' teachings independently, and produced at least three works *(On the Grown Soul, Ethics,* and *Expositions of the Prophet Parchor)* which are preserved only in fragmentary form in Clement of Alexandria (Rudolph 1977:309–13; cf. 258–59). At least two centuries after Basilides' death, the heresiologist Epiphanius (*ca.* 375, *Panarion*) seems to know the movement as a relatively small gnostic group still confined to Egypt.

Bibliography

Grant, R. 1979. Place de Basilide dans la théologie chrétienne ancienne. *Revue des études augustiniennes* 25:201–16.

Layton, B. 1987. *The Gnostic Scriptures.* ed. B. Layton. New York.

Rudolph K. 1983. *Gnosis.* San Francisco.

Völker, W. 1932. *Quellen zur Geschichte der christlichen Gnosis.* SQAW n.s. 5. Pp. 38–44 Tübingen.

PAUL ALLAN MIRECKI

BASKAMA (PLACE) [Gk *Baskama*]. The town in Gilead where Jonathan Maccabeus was executed by Trypho, the commander of the Seleucid army *ca* 142 B.C. (1 Macc 13:23). Josephus (*Ant* 12.6.6 §210) refers to this location as Baska.

The Maccabees after leading an extended rebellion against Seleucid control of Palestine, had come to be recognized by the parties which struggled for control of the Seleucid empire. Jonathan had been affirmed as the religious and secular leader of Judea by the faction that Trypho supported (1 Macc 11:57) and as a result militarily opposed and defeated the advance of Demetrius' forces (1 Macc 12:25–30). Trypho however, realizing the increasing independence of Jonathan, sought to depose him. Unable to defeat Jonathan militarily Trypho resorted to subterfuge. Jonathan was taken hostage in Ptolemais where he had expected to receive additional territory as a reward for his allegiance (1 Macc 12:43–45). Trypho's subsequent efforts to regain control of Judea, however, were thwarted by Simon Maccabeus, and Trypho was forced to retreat in the face of inclement winter weather via the sheltered Rift Valley route to the N. When the Seleucid forces approached firmly held Seleucid territory and Jonathan's value as a hostage was reduced, he was executed.

Baskama was located within territory where the Hasmonean forces could be effective. This is demonstrated by the fact that Simon was able to retrieve his brother's body (1 Macc 13:25).

Baskama has not been identified through archaeological research. Possible locations include Tell Bazuk and Wadi Jummeimeh (M.R. 211256) which are both located NE of the Sea of Galilee.

ROBERT W. SMITH

BASTION. See FORTIFICATIONS.

BAT. See ZOOLOGY.

BATASHI, TELL EL- (M.R. 142132). A site located in the alluvial Sorek valley 7 km W of Beth-shemesh and 9 km S of Gezer. The site is often identified with TIMNAH, the city that figures predominantly in the Samson story (Judges 14). This identification is based on the identification of Ekron with Tel Miqne to the W and of Beth-shemesh with Kh. Rumeila to the E, since Timnah is listed between the two in Josh 15:10–11 and since Tell el-Batashi is the only important mound along this line.

Excavations around the tell in 1955 revealed Neolithic, Chalcolithic, EB, and MB remains (see BATASHI, TULEILAT EL-). Excavations on the mound itself, however, began in 1977 and have clarified the history of the mound from the MB Age until the Persian period. Located in the center of a fertile valley, near the brook of Sorek, where wells easily could be dug, Timnah controlled a main road linking the region of Jabneh and Ekron in the coastal plain to the inner Shephelah near Beth-shemesh. Timnah thus was ideally situated for agriculture and as a cultural and commercial link between the coastal plain and the hill country.

The tell itself is a 200 m square mound. The construction of a massive earthen rampart inside a protective moat during the MB Age established its symmetrical shape. This rampart created a central crater-like depression which the site retained through its final occupation at the end of the Iron Age.

Stratum	*Period*
I	Persian (6–5th cent. B.C.)
II	Iron IIC (7th cent. B.C.)
III	Iron IIB (8th cent. B.C.)
IV	Iron IC (10th cent. B.C.)
V	Iron IA–B (12–11th cent. B.C.)
VI	LB IIB (13th cent. B.C.)
VII	LB IIA (14th cent. B.C.)
VIII	LB IB (late 15th cent. B.C.)
IX	LB IA (early 15th cent. B.C.)
X	Transitional MB–LB (16th cent. B.C.)
XI	MB

The MB fortifications have been exposed in 2 sections. The massive rampart was constructed of layers of alluvial earth and pebbles and support a huge mud brick city wall on its crest. During the LB Age (strata X–VI) an unwalled Canaanite town flourished at Tell el-Batashi. The outer walls of large buildings exposed in the NE corner of the mound appear to have created a defensive line. The town appears to have suffered from continuous attacks, since each of the 5 LB strata provided evidence of extensive burning. The destruction levels contained an abundance of finds, including seals, scarabs, metal objects, and various local and imported pottery vessels. Of particular importance is a large building of stratum VII (mid-14th cent. B.C.), with its ground floor divided by two rows of wood pillars supporting its ceiling and the 2d floor. This is a unique example of the use of pillars in Canaanite architecture and may be a forerunner of the later Iron Age pillared buildings.

Exposure of the Philistine town of Timnah (stratum V) has been limited. Brick and stone structures from this period as well as wide open areas containing baking ovens and silos have been excavated. Typical Philistine pottery together with other artifacts such as seals and seal impressions have been found in this level. The site was abandoned in the late 11th century. During the period of the United Monarchy (10th century B.C.) the town was partially rebuilt. Architectural remains covered limited sections of the excavated areas. A large public building partially excavated in the S part of the mound may have been a palace of that period. In the city gate area (Area C), two massive square towers may have been built during this phase. Red-slipped and hand-burnished pottery found in this level is of types characteristic of Israelite sites in the Shephelah.

The 10th-century town may have been destroyed during the Egyptian invasion by Shishak 5 years after the division of the kingdom. After an occupational gap, probably lasting most of the 9th century B.C., the town was rebuilt in the 8th century B.C. (stratum III), perhaps when the region was part of the Kingdom of Judah during the reign of Uzziah. The newly planned city was surrounded by a massive stone city wall and was entered through a double gate consisting of outer and inner gate structures. The exterior gate was composed of a massive outer tower and inner tower flanking a well-defended approach ramp. The interior gate was composed of two pairs of guard chambers. The city suffered violent destruction which safely may be attributed to the Assyrian conquest of 701 B.C. One of the most important discoveries in this city was a store building containing over 30 storage vessels of the *lmlk* type, characteristic Judean jars with handles stamped with the Judean royal seal. One of the handles was sealed with a private impression of Safan son of Abimaas, identical to seals found at Jerusalem and Azekah. The other seals are of either the "four-winged" or the "two-winged" type. These jars are evidence of Judean activity in Timnah, probably during Hezekiah's preparations for the war against Sennacherib.

During the 7th century B.C. (stratum II) the city was rebuilt on a grander scale. The city wall and gate were reconstructed, and new buildings were erected in the town. The use of monolithic pillars to divide courtyards of buildings is characteristic of this phase, though it probably started already in the earlier period. The buildings, forming well-defined architectural units, reflect superb urban planning. A large fort or public building in the NE quadrant of the mound and a series of houses to its W were excavated. One of these units contained a complete oil-press installation, with a large stone trough or crushing basin, two adjoining pressing vats, and stone weights and stone rollers in various sizes used to crush the olives. Parts of another oil press found nearby suggest that, as in nearby Ekron, oil production was one of the main industries of the town during this period. The houses were destroyed by intense fire *ca.* 600 B.C., most probably during Babylonian military campaigns in the region. Rich assemblages of pottery and other finds throw light on the material culture of Timnah during that period. This culture was characterized by the combination of coastal (late "Philistine") and Judean cultural traditions. The identity of a local pottery, similar to that of Ekron, is particularly interesting, and points to the existence of a local regional culture.

Pits and some poor structures are evidence for a limited settlement during the Persian period.

Bibliography

Kelm, G. L. and Mazar, A. 1982. Three Seasons of Excavations at Tel Batash—Biblical Timnah. *BASOR* 237: 1–36.

———. 1985. Tel Batash (Timnah) Excavations. *BASORSup* 23: 93–120.

———. 1989. Excavating in Samson Country. *BARev* 15/1: 36–49.

———. Forthcoming. Seventh Century B.C.E. Oil Presses at Tel Batash, Biblical Timnah. Pp. 121–25 in *Olive Oil in Antiquity*, edited by M. Heltzer and D. Eitam. Haifa.

AMIHAY MAZAR
GEORGE L. KELM

BATASHI, TULEILAT EL- (M.R. 142132). A site on the N bank of Wadi Sorek, about 7 km NW of ancient Beth-shemesh and about 750 m from Tell el-Batashi (biblical Timnah?), which lies on the opposite bank of the wadi and contains remains from the Israelite period onward (see BATASHI, TELL EL-). The Tuleilat el-Batashi site, however, is characterized by two barrows (or tumuli) around which have been found remains dating to the Neolithic, Chalcolithic, EB, and MB periods, reinforcing the assumption that occupation first started in this location and then later shifted S to the site of the mound.

Excavations were conducted in three areas around the barrows during March and July–August of 1955. Area A, to the S of the larger barrow (T-1), yielded two Neolithic shelter pits, each distinguished by the same two occupation levels (IVa and IVb). The pottery of the upper level (IVa) is identical with that of Jericho IX and Kenyon's Pre-Pottery Neolithic A. The pottery of level IVb differs from that of IVa mainly in its decoration; especially common are shards of the "dark-faced burnished ware" first noted in the Amuq plain and at Mersin (Hole 1959: 154; Kaplan 1969). Level III, which is above level IVa and dates to the Chalcolithic period, can be correlated with the culture of Wadi Rabaḥ stratum II (see RABAH, WADI). The artifacts of this level included several Neolithic Yarmukian shards, thus confirming that Jericho IX preceded the Yarmukian culture, as already established by Garstang and Kenyon. Level II, dated to the EB Age, was exposed only in the NW part of area A. Level I is represented by the remains of a MB pit which had penetrated into level II.

Three Chalcolithic occupation levels were exposed in area B, also near barrow T-1. The upper two levels (IIIa and IIIb) contained Ghassulian pottery, while the lowest (IIIc), resting on virgin soil, included pottery identical to that of Wadi Rabah stratum II. This is significant insofar as it provides evidence that the Wadi Rabah culture preceded the Ghassulian.

The excavations in area C cut across the T-1 barrow and exposed two chambers (each measuring 1.7 × 1.9 m), and behind them to the S was uncovered part of a third chamber. MB II–III pottery was found on the floor, as were other artifacts including round ovens of baked clay and a Hyksos scarab. To the E of the chambers were concentric walls which decreased in height toward the edge of the barrow, the space between the walls tightly packed with small stones. This type of barrow is otherwise unattested in Israel, although it is common in W Europe, where it is known as the "long barrow" type. Thus, in addition to the various burial types already attested for this period in Palestine must be added this "long barrow" type. The barrow is not far from area A, whose level I remains (an MB pit) are linked with the MB remains from this T-1 barrow.

Bibliography

Hole, F. 1959. A Reanalysis of Basal Tabbat al-Hamman. *Syria* 36: 149–83.

Kaplan, J. 1958. The Excavations at Teluliyot Batashi in the Vale of Sorek. *EI* 5: 9–25 (in Hebrew, with Eng summary, pp. 83–84).

———. 1959. The Neolithic Pottery of Palestine. *BASOR* 156: 15–22.

———. 1969. A Suggested Correlation Between Stratum IX, Jericho, and Stratum XXIV, Mersin. *JNES* 28: 197–99.

J. KAPLAN

BATH [Heb *bat*]. See WEIGHTS AND MEASURES.

BATH-RABBIM (PLACE) [Heb *bat rabbîm*]. The name of a gate of Heshbon, located near the famous pools, mentioned in Cant 7:4. Although no evidence for this gate was found during the recent excavations of Hesban (biblical Heshbon), the excavators have wondered whether or not a large 2,000,000-liter reservoir built on the S shelf and associated with Stratum 17 (9th–8th centuries) could be one of the pools referred to in this text (Geraty and Willis 1986: 31). If so, the gate would probably have been located nearby.

Bibliography

Geraty, L. T., and Willis, L. A. 1986. The History of Archaeological Research in Transjordan. Pp. 3–72 in *The Archaeology of Jordan and Other Studies*, ed. L. T. Geraty and L. G. Herr. Berrien Springs, MI.

RANDALL W. YOUNKER

BATHING. See UNCLEAN AND CLEAN.

BATHSHEBA (PERSON) [Heb *bat-šebaᶜ*]. The daughter of Eliam and wife of Uriah the Hittite (2 Sam 11:3), who became one of David's wives (2 Sam 11:27) and mother of his son and heir, Solomon (2 Sam 12:24–25). The name may mean "daughter of abundance" (*IDB* 1: 366). The story of David's adulterous affair with Bathsheba, resulting in her pregnancy, and David's stratagem to cause her husband's death and take her as wife (2 Sam 11:1–27) is one shrouded in ambiguity (Yee 1988:240–253). The character of Bathsheba and her motivations are particularly puzzling. The author gives no clues to the emotions of a woman who commits adultery, becomes pregnant, loses her husband, and marries her royal lover. From a literary perspective, according to Berlin (1983:25–27), Bathsheba is simply an agent, a person necessary for the plot, and not a full-fledged character. Since 2 Samuel 11 is a story about David's adultery, and since such a story requires a married woman, Bathsheba fulfills this function.

However, according to Bailey (1989), David and Bathsheba are co-conspirators in a political scheme to marry. Their nuptial union is similar to David's other political marriages, where he weds a woman from an influential family who will assist in either his rise to or his maintenance of power (Cf. also Levenson and Halpern 1980). In this view, Bathsheba is no longer an innocent victim, but a willing partner in the affair who wishes her own son to become David's royal successor. Her claim in 1 Kgs 1:17, that David had swore that Solomon would rule after him, suggests that David was able to convince Bathsheba to marry him by promising that her son would be his heir to the throne.

One finds a portrayal of Bathsheba in 1 Kings 1–2 which

would support the view of her as a co-conspirator in the adultery. Here she a key figure in the ruthless political intrigue surrounding her son Solomon's rise to power. With the prophet Nathan, she holds David to his oath that Solomon would succeed him as king (1 Kgs 1:11–31). Moreover, she plays a vital role in Adonijah's death by personally bringing his request to Solomon to marry David's concubine, Abishag. Since such a request is equivalent to a claim to the throne, Solomon is provided with grounds to eliminate his rival (1 Kgs 2:13–24, Berlin 1983:27–30).

Bathsheba is called BATHSHUA 1 Chr 3:5.

Bibliography

Bailey, R. C. 1989. *David in Love and War: The Pursuit of Power in 2 Samuel 10–12* JSOTSup. Sheffield.

Berlin, A. 1983. *Poetics and Interpretation of Biblical Narrative.* Sheffield.

Levenson, J. D., and Halpern, B. 1980. The Political Import of David's Marriages. *JBL* 99:507–18.

Yee, G. A. 1988. "Fraught With Background": Literary Ambiguity in II Samuel 11. *Int* 42:240–53.

GALE A. YEE

BATHSHUA (PERSON) [Heb *bat-šûaᶜ*]. The name of two women in the OT.

1. The Canaanite wife of Jacob's fourth son, Judah, and the mother of his sons Er, Onan, and Shelah (1 Chr 2:3). In Hebrew, Bathshua literally means "daughter of Shua." Hence, Bathshua may not be a proper name, but rather the familial designation of an unnamed woman (Cf. Gen 38:2). It may, however, also mean "daughter of error" (*IDB* 1:366).

2. Daughter of Ammiel, wife of David, and mother of his sons Shimea, Shobab, Nathan, and Solomon, according to 1 Chr 3:5. The LXX and Vg of this text read "Bathsheba." The change of name may be due to the phonetic similarity of the consonants *bet* and *waw* in *bt-šbᶜ* and *bt-šwᶜ*. According to 2 Sam 11:3, the father of Bathsheba is ELIAM, which may have become Ammiel in the transposition of the consonants *lamed* and *mem.* The name changes of Eliam to Ammiel and Bathsheba to Bathshua may be due to the Chronicler's systematic efforts to eliminate any references to the David-Bathsheba-Uriah affair which he found in his sources. If the "daughter of error" translation is accepted, however, the name change becomes a moral statement.

GALE A. YEE

BAVVAI (PERSON) [Heb *bawway*]. A Levite, the son of Henadad, and ruler of half the territory of Keilah, who was charged by Nehemiah with repairing a section of Jerusalem's walls (Neh 3:18). The evidence from various manuscripts suggests that Bavvai may be a corruption of Binnui, and therefore the same individual recorded in Neh 3:24 (see BINNUI #4).

D. G. SCHLEY

BAWDLERIZATION. See BIBLE, EUPHEMISM AND DYSPHEMISM IN THE.

BAZAAR. See TRADE AND COMMERCE (ANE).

BAZLITH (PERSON) [Heb *baṣlît*]. Var. BAZLUTH. Head of a family of *nĕtînîm* (temple servants) (see NETHINIM) listed among those exiles returning from Babylon to Jerusalem and Judah (Neh 7:54 = Ezra 2:52; 1 Esdr 5:31). While the Greek in all three occurrences is *Basalōth,* Ezra employs the variant Heb form *baṣlût.* Noth (*IPN,* 231) believes the name derives from a plant designation, i.e., Heb *bṣl,* "onion." Zadok (1980: 113) agrees by suggesting the name may be formed from the root *baṣl* (Biblical Heb plural *bĕṣālîm*—Num 11:5; late Heb *bāṣēl* or *beṣel;* Ar *baṣal;* Aram *buṣlāᵓ*) and the hypocoristic suffix *ît* or *ût,* which Jastrow (1926: 158a, 1384b, and perhaps 290a, 324a) shows is attached to other post-biblical names some of which may derive from vegetarian foods.

Bibliography

Jastrow, M. 1926. *A Dictionary of the Targumim, The Talmud Babli and Yerushalmi, and the Midrashic Literature.* Vol. 1. New York.

Zadok, R. 1980. Notes On The Biblical and Extra-Biblical Onomasticon. *JQR* 71: 107–117.

RODNEY H. SHEARER

BDELLIUM. See PERFUMES AND SPICES.

BEADS, BEADWORK. See JEWELRY.

BEALIAH (PERSON) [Heb *bĕᶜalyāh*]. One of the ambidextrous warriors from the tribe of Benjamin, a kinsman of Saul; he supported David before he became king (1 Chr 12:6—Eng 12:5). The inclusion of the element baal *(bᶜl)* in his name suggests that this name and the list in which it occurs come from an early date; compounds with baal are unlikely for later periods in the history of Benjamin. (For further discussion, see Williamson *1 and 2 Chronicles* NCBC, 85, 106.)

RAYMOND B. DILLARD

BEALOTH (PLACE) [Heb *bĕᶜālôt*]. A town in the S reaches of the territory of Judah in the Negeb (Josh 15:24). This is the sole reference to the town of this name in this geographical area, so its exact location is in doubt. Identification of the place with the similar name Baalah found in the same literary context (Josh 15:9, 10, 11, 29) is not satisfying. The latter is identified with Kiriath-jearim (M.R. 159135) and is located on the N side of Judah's holdings rather than the S (*MBA,* 73).

Another suggestion which is more attractive geographically is the identification of Bealoth with Baalat-beer (Josh 19:8; Woudstra *Joshua* NICOT, 244; M.R. 138043). This town is within the allotment of Simeon, which itself is included within and lies to the S of Judah's holdings (*MBA,* 82).

Some translations suggest a town of Bealoth further N in Israel. In the list of Solominic district governors and their jurisdictions, the ninth, Baana, governs "in Asher and Bealoth" (1 Kgs 4:16; RSV; NASB; *HGB*, 66). The Heb grammatical structure would favor a reading of "in Asher and in Aloth" (KJV; NEB; NASB margin), or, translating the last term, "in the highlands" (JB). The reading of LXX[A], "Maaloth," could also be so translated. It is probable that this verse does not indicate a second location called Bealoth.

David W. Baker

BEAM. See PLANK.

BEAN. See FLORA.

BEAR. See ZOOLOGY.

BEATITUDES. Although "beatitudes" is frequently used as a proper noun to denote a collection of eight dominical logia at the beginning of the Matthean Sermon on the Mount (Matt 5:3–10; par. Luke 6:20b–21), the term "beatitude" properly designates a whole body of sayings with a similar literary form. Such sayings, found in Egyptian, Greek, and Jewish literature, are technically known as macarisms (from the Greek *makarios,* "blessed" or "happy"). Matthew's collection of sayings is nonetheless known as the Beatitudes, a term derived from the Latin *beati* (similarly, "blessed" or "happy"), the word with which each of the eight sayings begins in the Latin Bible.

A. Literary Form
B. Jewish Beatitudes
C. New Testament Beatitudes
  1. Jesus
  2. Matthew
  3. Luke
  4. Johannine Literature

A. Literary Form

In form, the macarisms begin with the adjective *makarios,* followed by a relative or personal pronoun introducing a clause which describes a particular conduct or quality which prompted the praise of the person who is pronounced blessed. Typically, macarisms are formulated in the third person, and more commonly in the singular than in the plural. The oldest known example of a macarism is found in the *Homeric Hymn to Demeter* (480–83), "Happy is he among men upon earth who has seen these mysteries."

Macarisms or beatitudes are to be distinguished from blessings, an effective pronouncement in which God himself is deemed to be the real agent. In the LXX, blessings are frequently expressed in the formulation "blessed be . . . ," but the pertinent term is the verbal adjective *eulogētos* or the participle *eulogēmenos,* not the adjective *makarios.* In the Jewish tradition the latter term is not used of God, even though, in the Greek world, the gods were deemed to be supremely happy (*makares;* Homer, *Od.* 5, 7).

Beatitudes are expressions of praise or congratulation. As such they belong to the literary subgenre known as ascription. Four types of macarism have been identified: the secular macarism (in which one is praised on account of wealth, beauty, etc.), the macarism of the wise man (in which one is praised on account of wisdom or virtue), the satirical macarism (*1 Enoch* 103:5–6, "Blessed are the sinners; they saw all their days. And now they have died in prosperity and wealth . . ."), and the religious macarism (Ps 1:1, "Blessed is the man who walks not in the counsel of the wicked."; [Betz 1985:25]).

B. Jewish Beatitudes

In the Hebrew Bible "the man who" (*ʾaśrē hāʾîš*), an expression reflected in the LXX *anēr hos* or *anthrōpos hos,* is commonly cited as the object of praise. The Hebrew Bible contains 45 beatitudes, most of which are found in the wisdom literature: Deut 33:29; 1 Kgs 10:8 (twice); Isa 30:18; 32:20; 56:2; Ps 1:2; 2:12; 32:1, 2; 33:12; 34:9; 40:5; 41:2; 65:5; 84:5, 6, 13; 89:16; 94:12; 106:3; 112:1; 119:1, 2; 127:5; 128:1, 2; 137:8, 9; 144:15 (twice); 146:5; Job 5:17; Prov 3:13; 8:32, 34; 14:21; 16:20; 20:7; 28:14; 29:18; Qoh 10:17; Dan 12:12; 2 Chr 9:7 (twice). To these the LXX adds an additional 15: Sir 14:1, 2, 20; 25:8, 9; 26:1; 28:19; 31:8; 34:15; 48:11; 50:28; Tob 13:14 (twice); Wis 3:13; and Isa 31:9. Of the 45 beatitudes in the Hebrew Bible, all but 4 (Deut 33:29; Ps 128:2; Qoh 10:17, in the 2d person singular; and Isa 32:20, in the 2d person plural) are in the 3d person.

Scholars have long been debating about the original form and life setting of the beatitudes in the Hebrew tradition. Some (Käser 1970) think that the original form of the beatitude was a simple propositional statement (e.g. Ps 2:12; 34:9; 41:2; 84:13; Job 5:17; Dan 12:12), while others (Kähler 1974) think that an expanded form of the beatitude, certainly more common in the extant literature, is more faithful to the original form.

E. Lipiński (1968) argued for a cultic setting for the beatitudes, noting that the oldest biblical beatitudes are in some of the early Psalms, that many have a national and collective character (Ps 33:12), that Prov 16:20; 28:14; 29:18 are dependent on the Psalms, and that parallel Egyptian beatitudes are found in religious contexts. The dominant opinion is, nonetheless, that the biblical beatitudes are essentially wisdom sayings. Scholars who advance this view note the preponderant appearance of beatitudes in the biblical wisdom literature and often cite Job 5:17 as a significant example. In any case, the biblical beatitudes frequently assume religious or paraenetic overtones. Although the beatitude is essentially a declarative statement, its content is such that it readily functions as an implicit exhortation.

The specifically religious beatitude is typically found in apocalyptic literature (*1 En.* 58:2; 81:4; 82:4; 99:10; 103:5; *2 En.* 41:1; 42:6–14; 44:4; 48:9; 52:1–14; 61:3; 62:1; 66:7; *Sib.Or.* 3:371–372; cf. *Pss.Sol.* 4:26; 5:18; 6:1; 10:1; 17:50; 18:7; *4 Macc.* 18:9). These religious beatitudes frequently assume eschatological overtones. Typically a seer pronounces a beatitude because of his visionary experience. Prophetic knowledge enables judgment to be brought to bear upon present conditions. Apocalyptic beatitudes can occasionally function as "anti-macarisms" (Betz: 33), insofar as praise is extended to those who do not measure up to traditional values.

Beatitudes typically appear as isolated sentences. The use of the isolated beatitude passed over into rabbinic literature: e.g., "Blessed are thou Aqiba, because thou wast arrested for words of Torah" (*Ber.* 61b). The collection of beatitudes (9 in *2 En.* 42: 6–14; and 7 in 52:1–14) is a distinctively literary phenomenon. Although collections as such are relatively rare, isolated beatitudes frequently appear at the beginning or end of a longer body of material (Psalm 1 or Sirach 25, where 9 types of persons are praised).

Beatitudes are sometimes to be found in a variety of antithetical formulations. The one who is praised for his qualities or conduct is contrasted with one who is not to be so praised (Ps 1:1, 4; Tob 13:12, 14). Qoh 10:16 contrasts a woe with the beatitude of v 17. Because the content of some conditional sentences in Jewish literature corresponds to the content of some beatitudes (Ps 32:10; Wis 28:25), it has been occasionally suggested (Kahler 1974) that the origin of the beatitude lies in the conditional sentence. A consequent distinction can be made among Jewish beatitudes, i.e., between the beatitude which pronounces someone blessed because of a given condition or situation (Ps 33:12) and the beatitude which is conditional and thereby serves as an implicit exhortation (Ps 32:2).

C. New Testament Beatitudes

The NT contains 37 beatitudes (Matt 5:3, 4, 5, 6, 7, 8, 9, 10, 11; 11:6; 13:16; 16:17; 24:46; Luke 1:45; 6:20, 21 (twice), 22; 7:23; 10:23; 11:27, 28; 12:37, 43; 14:15; 23:29; John 20:29; Rom 4:7, 8; 14:22; Jas 1:12; Rev 1:3; 14:13; 16:15; 19:9; 20:6; 22:7). Since seven of Matthew's beatitudes have parallels in Luke (Matt 5:3 = Luke 6:20b; Matt 5:4 = Luke 6:21b; Matt 5:6 = Luke 6:21a; Matt 5:11 = Luke 6:22; Matt 11:6 = Luke 7:23; Matt 13:16 = Luke 10:23; Matt 24:46 = Luke 12:43) and two of the Pauline beatitudes are a biblical citation (Rom 4:7–8 = Ps 32:1–2), the NT adds 28 new beatitudes to the biblical collection.

1. Jesus. Seventeen of the gospel beatitudes are sayings of Jesus. Among the evangelists, Luke alone attributes a beatitude to a spokesperson other than Jesus (Luke 1:45; 11:27; 14:15). The attribution of beatitudes to Jesus represents a venerable Christian tradition. The seven beatitudes found in both Matthew and Luke undoubtedly derive from the Q source (*ca.* 50 AD). Luke 12:37 seems to have been adopted by the evangelist from his unique material. Six of the NT beatitudes, including that pronounced by the woman in the crowd, appear, in a modified form, in the 2d century *Gospel of Thomas,* dated by many into the 1st century (Matt 5:3 = *Gos.Thom.* 54; Matt 5:6 = *Gos.Thom.* 69b; Matt 5:11 = *Gos.Thom.* 68–69a; Luke 11:27–28 = *Gos.Thom.* 79a–b; Luke 23:29 = *Gos.Thom.* 79c), a text which cites an additional six beatitudes as sayings of Jesus (*Gos.Thom.* 7, 18, 19, 49, 58, 103).

Given the antiquity of the tradition and the widespread distribution of beatitudes throughout the gospel material (although none are found in Mark), scholars frequently ask whether the gospel beatitudes represent authentic sayings of Jesus. The question is raised most often with regard to the beatitudes which have received a classic formulation as the beatitudes of Matthew's Sermon on the Mount (Matt 5:3–12), with a parallel in Luke's Sermon on the Plain (Luke 6:20b–23).

Although both Matthew and Luke have modified the beatitudes taken over from the Q source, it is quite likely that the substance of the four common beatitudes (Matt 5:3 = Luke 6:20b; Matt 5:4 = Luke 6:21b; Matt 5:6 = Luke 6:21a; Matt 5:11 = Luke 6:22) goes back to the proclamation of the historical Jesus. Since the Q formulation can only be reconstituted on the basis of a comparative study of the two extant gospel texts, and the Matthean beatitudes are in the third person while the Lukan beatitudes are in the second person, scholars disagree among themselves as to whether Jesus' proclamation used the form of direct address (thus akin to the Lukan form) or the form of declarative sentence (thus akin to the Matthean form).

The Q collection of four beatitudes is the result of an earlier collection of three beatitudes, similar in form, to which the longer double beatitude of Matt 5:11 = Luke 6:22 was added. These three beatitudes (Matt 5:3 = Luke 6:20b; Matt 5:4 = Luke 6:21b; Matt 5:6 = Luke 6:21a) represent a terse formulation of the gospel proclamation. They proclaim salvation, in the form of an eschatological reversal of conditions *(peripeteia)* for the dispossessed. The poor, the hungry, and those who mourn represent the entire range of the needy. The concepts are not spiritualized, nor are poverty, hunger, and sadness extolled per se. If the poor, the hungry, and those who mourn are called happy, it is because the Kingdom of God will be offered to them in their helplessness.

As proclaimed by Jesus, the Kingdom of God is an eschatological concept. God's initiative and decisiveness are the primary elements. He is to reign as king. According to the oriental understanding, the righteousness or justice of a king is manifest in his action on behalf of the weak and oppressed; thus God as the king par excellence must necessarily act on behalf of the poor, the hungry, and those who mourn. Jesus' availability to them is a sign of the future kingdom of God. Accordingly, the three common beatitudes proclaim God's initiative on their behalf and the gratuity of his grace. They constitute "an unconditional promise of salvation" and thus epitomize Jesus' good news.

The fourth beatitude of the Q collection (Matt 5:11 = Luke 6:22) derives from a time when the church was undergoing persecution and most likely received its Q formulation (a community formulation) as a result of that experience. Its appearance in Q as an appended saying supports the contention that the beatitudes spoken by Jesus were originally isolated statements.

2. Matthew. Differences between the Matthean and Lukan versions of the beatitude point to the editorial activity of the respective evangelists. Editorial activity is particularly apparent in the Matthean collection of "The Beatitudes." His eight—Matthew seems not to have considered Matt 5:11 as an integral part of the series—are formed into a unified whole by means of ring construction, i.e. the opening and closing formula, "for theirs is the kingdom of heaven." "The kingdom of heaven" is a typical Matthean expression (Matt 3:2; 4:17) as is the "righteousness" of Matt 5:6, 10 (3:15; 6:33). Isa 61:1–2 seems to have influenced the Matthean formulation of the first two beatitudes and Ps 107: 5, 8–9 to have influenced the fourth, all of which begin with the letter "p" in the Greek text. Since Matthew has a predilection for seven-part compositions and Matt 5:5 has no constant position in the manuscript tradition, many scholars think that the third beatitude, influenced by Ps 36:11, is a later addition to the Matthean text. The eighth beatitude, formulated in such a way as to bring the series to a close, appears to be a Matthean adaptation of the ninth, originally independent beatitude.

Matthew's spiritualization of the traditional first and fourth beatitudes and his formulation of the fifth, sixth, and seventh, more active beatitudes, imparts to the entire collection the character of an ecclesial exhortation. Those who are praised in the Matthean beatitudes are those whose lives reflect authentic Christian existence from the viewpoint of continuing church life.

3. Luke. Luke's Sermon on the Plain has only the four beatitudes of Q (Luke 6:20b–23). The people praised in the Lukan collection of three similarly formulated beatitudes (6:20b–21) are the physically and materially deprived. Luke accentuates the social referent by the juxtaposition of parallel woes (6:24–25). The fourth woe (6:26) highlights the blessedness proclaimed for the persecuted (6:22–23). In the Lukan collection, the evangelist's editorial work is apparent in his emphasis upon the present (the sapiential "now" of 6:21a, b and "in that day" of 6:22) which stands in contrast to the eschatological future.

Among the five beatitudes proper to Luke (1:45; 11:28; 12:37; 14:15; 23:29), two emphasize the importance of belief in God's word (1:45; 11:28), and are both within a context of reflection on the mother of Jesus.

4. Johannine Literature. Faith is also the basis for praise in the Johannine beatitude (John 20:29), the final proclamation of John's Easter Jesus. In context, the beatitude extols believers of the second and subsequent Christian generations. As such, it functioned as a proclamation of praise of those who belonged to the Johannine community.

Six beatitudes appear in the Book of Revelation, in the form of isolated sayings. Two of them form a distinct pair (Rev 1:3; 22:7), lauding those who keep the words of the book. The parallel sayings function as a sort of *inclusio* unifying Revelation's collection of disparate materials. The other four beatitudes bear a distinctively eschatological stamp. Those formulated in the plural praise those who die in the Lord (Rev 14:13, with pertinent commentary in v 13b) and those invited to the marriage feast of the Lamb (Rev 19:9), while those formulated in the singular laud the vigilant (Rev 16:15), and those who share in the first resurrection (Rev 20:6). Their literary form is clearly that of the religious beatitude.

Bibliography

Betz, H. D. 1985. The Beatitudes of the Sermon on the Mount (Matt. 5:3–12). Pp. 17–36 in *Essays on the Sermon on the Mount.* Trans. L. L. Welborn. Philadelphia.

Broer, I. 1986. *Die Seligpreisungen der Bergpredigt.* BBB 61. Bonn.

Dodd, C. H. 1968. The Beatitudes: A Form-critical Study. Pp. 1–10 in *More New Testament Studies.* Grand Rapids.

Dupont, J. 1969–73. *Les béatitudes.* 3 vols. EBib. Paris.

George, A. 1957. La "forme" des béatitudes jusqu'à Jésus. Pp. 398–403 in *Mélanges Bibliques rédigés en l'honneur de André Robert.* Travaux de l'Institut Catholique de Paris 4. Paris.

Guelch, R. A. 1982. Pp. 62–118 in *The Sermon on the Mount: A Foundation for Understanding.* Waco, TX.

Kähler, C. 1974. *Studien zur Form- und Traditionsgeschichte der biblischen Makarismen.* Diss. Jena.

Käser, W. 1970. Beobachtungen zum alttestamentlichen Makarismus. *ZAW* 82: 225–50.

Lambrecht, J. 1985. Pp. 45–79 in *The Sermon on the Mount: Proclamation and Exhortation.* Good News Studies 14. Wilmington, DE.

Lipiński, E. 1968. Macarismes et psaumes de congratulation. *RB* 75: 321–67.

Schweizer, E. 1972–73. Formgeschichtliches zu den Seligpreisungen Jesu. *NTS* 19: 121–26.

RAYMOND F. COLLINS

BEATTY, CHESTER (PAPYRI). See CHESTER BEATTY PAPYRI.

BEAUTIFUL GATE (PLACE) [Gk *hē hōraía pýlē*]. Gate of Herod's temple where John and Peter healed a lame man (Acts 3:2, 10). The gate is not mentioned by its NT name in any of the Jewish sources. Christian tradition, and some modern scholars, identify it with the Golden or Susa (Shusan) Gate. "Golden is derived from a mistranslation of Gk *hōraia,* "beautiful", and the Latin *aurea,* "golden." The Susa Gate is on the eastern wall of Old Jerusalem facing the Mount of Olives. Today it is marked by the now-closed Byzantine gate. Excavations in 1971 and 1972 revealed an earlier gate 7 to 8 feet beneath the Byzantine Gate (Mare, 1987:158). The lower gate, equal in size to the latter, was in use during Christ's time, and it would have been the very gate mentioned in Acts 3. However, the Nicanor Gate, funded by a wealthy Alexandrian Jew of that name, is a more likely candidate for the Beautiful Gate. But even the location of the Nicanor Gate cannot be identified with certainty. If its location was the gate on the east side of the Court of Women leading from the Court of Gentiles, this would have been the ideal location for beggars. The other leading candidate for the Nicanor, and possibly the Beautiful Gate, is on the west side of the Court of Women at the entrance to the Court of Israel. The designated corner for lepers was nearby—in the NW corner of the Court of Women, and it was highly likely that beggars would have frequented the facility. Also, both of the suggested locations for the Nicanor Gate coincide with *to hieron,* the NT Gk usage of "the temple." Strong support for the Nicanor Gate being the Beautiful Gate, whether on the E or W side of the Court of Women, comes from Josephus (*JW* 5.201). He describes the inner gate (on the E side of the Court of Women) as being more valuable "than those overlaid with silver or even with gold," for it was made of Corinthian bronze. But the gate on the W side was much larger, and "the decoration was more magnificent, the gold and silver plates being extremely thick." The Mishna infers that the Nicanor Gate was the inner of the two gates, and the current majority of opinion places the Beautiful Gate on the outer W wall (Mid. i.4; ii.3–6).

Bibliography

Comay, J. 1975. *The Temple of Jerusalem.* New York.

Mackowski, R. M. 1980. *Jerusalem: City of Jesus.* Grand Rapids, MI.

Mare, W. H. 1987. *The Archaeology of the Jerusalem Area.* Grand Rapids, MI.

Parrot, A. 1955. *The Temple of Jerusalem.* New York.

Smith, G. A. 1908. Vol. 2 of *Jerusalem: The Topography, Economics and History From the Earliest Times to A.D. 70.*
Wilkinson, J. 1978. *Jerusalem as Jesus Knew It.* London.

JERRY A. PATTENGALE

BEBAI (PERSON) [Heb *bēbāy*]. The name of two individuals in the Hebrew Bible.

1. The eponymous ancestor of a group of returning exiles from Babylon (Ezra 2:11). Under Zerubbabel, the number of Bebai's descendants varies from 623 (Ezra 2:11) to 633 (1 Esdr 5:13, Codex Vaticanus) to 628 (Neh 7:16). In the reign of Artaxerxes, more of his descendants are said to have returned with Ezra (Ezra 8:11, 1 Esdr 8:37); these included ZECHARIAH, the chief of the family. Zechariah's father is also named Bebai; in 1 Esdr 9:37 his name reads Babi (*babi;* Var. Baier, Bemai, and Bokchei), but the underlying Hebrew name is clearly Bebai (see Ezra 8:11). Besides Zechariah, Bebai's descendants included twenty-eight other males (Ezra 8:11, 1 Esdr 8:37; LXX of Ezra 8 reads 78). Some of his family intermarried with foreign women, e.g., JEHOHANAN, HANANIAH, ZABBAI, ATHLAI (Ezra 10:28), and Emathis (Ezra 10:28 [LXX], 1 Esdr 9:29).

2. One of the individuals who set his seal to the document of covenant renewal under Ezra and Nehemiah (Neh 10:16—Eng 10:15). He is listed as one of the "leading men" who pledged among other things to obey the Law and to keep their families from intermarriage (Neh 10:30). It is likely that the head of Bebai's descendants signed in the name of his ancestral clan; the names in Nehemiah 10 roughly coincide with the names of the clans originally returning from exile in Ezra 2:1–60 and Neh 7:6–62. There has been much discussion concerning the timing and nature of the agreement in Nehemiah 10 and the sources of the list of names (see Williamson *Ezra, Nehemiah* WBC, 325–31).

GARY S. SHOGREN

BEBAI (PLACE) [Gk *Bēbai*]. Town in the book of Judith which participates in the destruction of the "Assyrian" army after the death of Holofernes (Jdt 15:4). It has not yet been identified. According to the author of Judith, it is adjacent to Betomasthaim, a town which is placed in the north of Palestine, although its exact location is unknown. Although there is mention of a "Bebayou" in an Aramaic contract of the 2d century C.E., it throws no light on the location of Bebai, for, according to J. T. Milik, "Bebayou" was located in southern Palestine. It is probable that, like most geographical names in the book of Judith, Bebai is fictitious. See Moore *Judith* AB.

Bibliography

Milik, J. T. 1955. Note additionnelle sur le contrat juif de l'an 134 aprés J.C. *RB* 1955: 253–54.

SIDNIE ANN WHITE

BECHER (PERSON) [Heb *beker*]. BECHERITES. The second son of Benjamin, according to two Benjaminite genealogies (Gen 46:21; 1 Chr 7:6,8). Efforts have been made to restore Becher to the two other Benjaminite genealogies of the OT (Num 26:38; 1 Chr 8:1). Johnson (*IDB* 1:248, 372) suggests that Becher was misplaced in Numbers 26 from the Benjaminite genealogy of v 38 to the Ephraimite genealogy of v 35. In the MT he is listed as the second son of Ephraim and head of the Becherites. The LXX omits this reference to Becher among the sons of Ephraim, and the inclusion of a "Bered" as Ephraim's second son in the Ephraimite genealogy of 1 Chr 7:20 has caused some to conclude that "Becher" is a mistake for "Bered." In 1 Chr 8:1, Johnson suggests that Becher (Heb *beker*) was mistakenly treated as "his firstborn" (Heb *bĕkōrô*). Williamson is critical of attempts to emend 1 Chr 8:1 to read "Becher" as Benjamin's second son, pointing out that the series of ordinals, "the second, the third, etc.," continue through all five of Benjamin's sons, making a harmonistic emendation unlikely in this text (*Chronicles* NCBC, 83). See ASHBEL.

SIEGFRIED S. JOHNSON

BECORATH (PERSON) [Heb *bĕkôrat*]. An ancestor of Saul son of Kish (1 Sam 9:1); likewise, the son of Aphiah and father of Zeror. The name, meaning "firstborn," is feminine in form, suggesting that the individual may have been the daughter of Aphiah, rather than his son, although the LXX reads "Bakir," a masculine name formed from the same Hebrew root. The variant reading "Machir" in G^L has mistaken the initial *bet* as a *mem.*

The narrator has begun the story of Saul in 1 Sam 9:1 by employing a seven-generation genealogy as a literary device to indicate that Saul was destined to greatness from birth (Sasson 1978:185). Becorath represents the third generation in the genealogy. See also APHIAH. While meant to represent an individual in the Saulide genealogy, the name also was associated with a Benjaminite clan, and the two may ultimately be related (Luther 1901: 55;-Caspari *Samuelbücher* KAT, 105; Malamat 1968: 171). The gentilic form *Bichri* is used as a designation of the clan to which Shimei (2 Sam 20:1), the instigator of the northern revolt against David, belonged, while the masculine form *Becher,* displaying slightly different vocalization, appears as a clan name in the tribal genealogies for Benjamin in Gen 46:21 and 1 Chr 7:6, 8. Becorath may be the eponymous ancestress of the clan or lineage group of the same name. See also BICHRI; BECHER.

The name's absence from the Saulide genealogy in 1 Chr 8:33–40 and 1 Chr 9:39–44 can be explained in three ways. One possibility would be to argue that the name was dropped when competing factions for royal succession within the larger family no longer found it necessary to trace descent through this particular ancestor (Flanagan 1981: 59). A second approach would be to posit that Bakir appears in the Chronicles' lists in 8:30 and 9:36 in the reference to the "firstborn" son of Jeiel, Abdon, and that Abdon somehow dropped out of the corresponding list in 1 Samuel (Dhorme *Samuel* EB, 74, n. 1). A third approach would be to suggest that the name was eliminated by the Chronicler along with Abiel, Zeror, and Aphiah so that he could artificially graft the Saulide family tree onto the postexilic genealogy of the inhabitants of Gibeon (see NER).

Bibliography

Flanagan, J. 1981. Chiefs in Israel. *JSOT* 20: 47–73.

Luther, B. 1901. Die israelitischen Stämme. *ZAW* 21: 1–76.

Malamat, A. 1968. King Lists of the Old Babylonian Period and Biblical Genealogies. *JAOS* 88: 163–73.

Sasson, J. M. 1978. A Genealogical "Convention" in Biblical Chronology? *ZAW* 90: 171–85.

DIANA V. EDELMAN

BECTILETH (PLACE) [Gk *Bektileth*]. Unidentified plain in or near northern Cilicia (Jdt 2:21). According to the author of the book of Judith, it is located a three-days' march W of Nineveh. It is sometimes identified with Bakataïlloi, located to the south of Syrian Antioch, or with Beqʾah, a valley between Lebanon and Anti-Lebanon. The problem with these identifications is that they place Bectileth some three hundred miles from Nineveh, a rather long distance for a three-day march. Given the genre of the book of Judith, it is entirely possible that the place is fictitious.

SIDNIE ANN WHITE

BEDAD (PERSON) [Heb *bĕdad*]. The father of the Edomite "king" Hadad (Gen 36:35; 1 Chr 1:46). The root *bdd* "to separate; to be separated, isolated" produced personal names in Ugaritic (*bddn;* Gröndahl 1967: 380), Epigraphic Arabian (Safaitic and Thamudic *bd,* Safaitic *bdʾl,* Thamudic *bddt;* Harding 1971: 96–97; note, however, that the name *bddh,* frequent in Safaitic, does not belong to *bdd—pace* Harding; read **Bi-Dādih* "by his uncle"), and Arabic (*Budaid;* Caskel 1966: 228).

Bibliography

Caskel, W. 1966. *Gamharat an-nasab. Das genealogische Werk des Hisam ibn Muhammad al-Kalbi, II: Erläuterungen zu den Tafeln. Das Register.* Leiden.

Gröndahl, F. 1967. *Die Personennamen der Texte aus Ugarit.* Studia Pohl 1. Rome.

Harding, G. L. 1971. *An Index and Concordance of Pre-Islamic Arabian Names and Inscriptions.* Near and Middle East Series, 8. Toronto.

ERNST AXEL KNAUF

BEDAN (PERSON) [Heb *bĕdān*]. The name of two men in the OT.

1. The son of Ulam of the tribe of Manasseh (1 Chr 7:17). He was a member of the fifth generation of that tribe through Machir, Manasseh's son. His heredity was mixed, for he was the product of Manasseh's union with an Aramean concubine (1 Chr 7:14). A corrupt text in 1 Chr 7:14–17 renders his genealogy uncertain between Machir and his father, Ulam; for v 16 traces him through either Peresh or Sheresh, both Machir's sons, while v 17b traces him through Machir's son, Gilead. Rudolph (*Chronicles* HAT, 69–71) has attempted a reconstruction of the corrupt text based on Num 26:29–34; his results have gained considerable, though not universal, approval. If his reconstruction is correct, it illumines an obscure portion of Bedan's genealogy.

2. A judge of Israel according to the MT of 1 Sam 12:11. But his identity is unclear; the Bible contains no other reference to him. In 1 Sam 12:11 his name occurs in a list of four judges of which the other three are prominent, significant persons, familiar from the Book of Judges. The presence of the name of an unknown judge among three well-known ones has attracted the attention of students of the text. The LXX, apparently questioning the correctness of "Bedan" and treating it as a textual error, replaced "Bedan" with the familiar "Barak." One ancient version replaced it with "Deborah." An ancient interpretation contended that "Bedan" derived from "Ben-Dan" (= son of Dan) and understood it as a reference to Samson, who was from the tribe of Dan. Another more modern correction replaced "Bedan" with "Abdon." The RSV has adopted the reading of the LXX. All these corrections presuppose that "Bedan" is a textual error. But recently Zakovitch (1972: 123–25) has offered an explanation which does not presuppose a textual corruption in the word "Bedan." Recalling that Bedan in #1 above is, according to 1 Chr 7:14–17, of the tribe of Manasseh, and that Jephthah is also from Manasseh, Zakovitch suggests that, like "Jerubbaal" and "Gideon," "Jephthah" and "Bedan" are two names for the same person. Accordingly, 1 Sam 12:11 originally read: "the Lord sent Jerubbaal, Bedan, and Samuel." "Jephthah" was inserted as a gloss, and a later scribe, not recognizing it as a gloss, inserted the conjunction and the object marker, *wĕʾet.* In his quotation of 1 Sam 12:11, Josephus (*Ant* 6§90) names only Gideon and Jephthah; this supports Zakovitch's suggestion that Jephthah and Bedan are the same person. Helpful discussions of the problem and the history of suggested solutions are found in McCarter (*1 Samuel* AB, 211), and Klein (*1 Samuel* WBC).

Bibliography

Zakovitch, Y. 1972. *bdn = ypt. VT* 22: 123–25.

GERALD J. PETTER

BEDEIAH (PERSON) [Heb *bēdĕyāh*]. A descendant of Bani and one of the returned exiles whom Ezra required to divorce his foreign wife (Ezra 10:35 = 1 Esdr 9:34). *Bedeiah* might mean "Branch of Yahweh," or it might be an abbreviated form of *ʿăbēdyāh,* "Servant of Yahweh." Bedeiah was a member of a family from which a group of exiles returned with Zerubbabel (Ezra 2:10). The three-month investigation of the men who had married foreign women (Ezra 10:16–17) produced a relatively short list of names, leading some scholars to believe that it includes only prominent members of the community (see discussion in Myers, *Ezra, Nehemiah* AB, 87–88). Bedeiah's position in the community, however, remains a mystery. While it seems probable that Bedeiah divorced his foreign wife (note the prior oath taken by the people [Ezra 10:2–5]), that is not certain. There is some debate whether v 19 may originally have been reported after each group. 1 Esdr 9:36 clearly states that everyone on the list did indeed divorce his foreign wife and put away his children; however, Ezra 10:44b is so corrupt that the final outcome of the investigation is left in doubt. For further discussion, see Williamson, *Ezra, Nehemiah* WBC, 157–59.

JEFFREY A. FAGER

BEDOUIN AND BEDOUIN STATES. The word "bedouin," as used in this article, comprises the notion of a stratified society of non-sedentary camel breeders. As such, bedouin are first attested in the Near East in the Iron Age. Although various features that contribute to the definition of "bedouin"—e.g., pastoral nomadism and "tribes" (versus "states")—can be traced back several millennia before the 1st millennium B.C., the emergence of the bedouin in the 1st millennium B.C. changed drastically the sociopolitical environment for pastoral tribes. Therefore, reconstructions of pastoral nomadism before 1000 B.C. should use with great care recent or contemporary ethnographic data on Near Eastern nomadism. "Being a bedouin" involves specific attitudes towards political power, which, from the very beginnings of bedouin history, lead to supra-tribal political formations, "bedouin states." The bedouin states did not, however, acquire all the attributes of real states; at best they were ephemeral, unstable, and short-lived organizations.

A. Terminology

Traditionally, the social landscape of the Near East is characterized by a tripartite division into "city dwellers," "peasants," and "pastoralists" (Wagstaff 1985: 48–81). Within this traditional tripartite model, "pastoralists" are generally assumed to form ethnically and politically separate social organizations, i.e. "tribes" (as opposed to the states of the settled population). It is argued in this article that the emergence of such separate pastoralist tribes presupposes the formation of a class of *specialized* pastoralists, i.e., the camel-breeding bedouin. Therefore, this tripartite division—with its double exploitation of the peasants by both the urban settlements and a specific nonsedentary element, i.e., the bedouin—cannot be uncritically assumed to have applied to the pre-Islamic period (de Planhol 1975: 24–68).

The Arab bedouin described by Near Eastern travelers of the 19th century provided most biblical scholars of that time with an attractive model in terms of which the lifestyle of the patriarchs in Genesis could be viewed. At the same time, the notion of waves of bedouin nomads migrating into the wealthy and fertile centers of civilization from their desert homeland served as an explanation for cultural and linguistic change in the ANE, a notion that biblical scholars adopted to explain the emergence of Israel in the land of Canaan. Even though this appeal to bedouin nomadism has now been almost completely rejected by scholars, the romantic notion that the earliest Israelites were bedouin nomads still lingers behind notions that the "semi-nomadic" or "semi-bedouin" Israelites entered Canaan from the outside at the end of the Late Bronze Age (a concept still upheld by some pupils of Albrecht Alt; Thiel 1985).

1. Nonsedentary Ways of Life. Because the terms "nomad," "bedouin," and "pastoralist" are frequently used as synonyms in discussions of ANE history and society, it may be helpful to outline briefly the basic categories of nonsedentary life.

a. "Nomads." If "nomad" is understood to cover every aspect of nonsedentary life, then hunter-gatherers, migrating laborers without a permanent home, vagrant craftsmen and artists, etc., would qualify as "nomads," whereas the city-based caravan merchants of the ANE and the soldiers of all times may properly be called "semi-nomads." Although these may have spent most of their life on the roads and in tents, they usually had a permanent address. Therefore, it is best to limit our scope to those nonsedentary phenomena of the ANE that apply only to people involved in pastoral and/or agricultural production. (The term "semi-nomad" is too imprecise to be employed at all).

b. Nonsedentary Agriculturalists. The basic livestock—sheep, goat, and cattle—were domesticated by settled agricultural communities in the Pre-Pottery Neolithic period (8th and 7th millennia B.C.). With the seemingly complete breakdown of settled life in Palestine *ca.* 6000 B.C., these sedentary agriculturalists became non-sedentary agriculturalists. As opposed to the large villages of the Pre-Pottery Neolithic, their camps were rather small. Though unsettled, they continued to grow cereals and to herd goat and sheep (Betts 1987). Unlike pastoralists, however, these nonsedentary agriculturalists are self-sufficient in meeting their basic needs. This, for example, was the way of life that recommended itself most readily in later periods, whenever a group of peasants wanted to withdraw from the restrictions of the state. This kind of "nomadism" is either attested or assumed for the "Amorites" of EB IV Palestine and the Shasu of the LB period, most of whom never dwelt in permanent structures. In contemporary reconstructions of their respective origins, both populations are believed to have derived from the villagers of Palestine in the preceding period who had given up their sedentary way of life in the course of a natural, economic, and/or political crisis (Richard 1987; Finkelstein 1988: 338–45). Furthermore, both the "Amorites" and the Shasu were not pastoralists; according to the story of Sinuhe (20th century B.C.) and Ramesside inscriptions, they practiced *both* farming and herding (Weippert 1974). (It is purely for ideological reasons that non-sedentary agriculturalists in the modern Near East—such as the people studied by Banning and Köhler-Rollefson [1986]—claim to be "bedouin.")

c. Transhumance. Part-time nomadism, or transhumance, is a common Mediterranean cultural phenomenon. Transhumance is village-based pastoralism with summer camps set up away from the village (Braudel 1972: 85–102). The pastoral segment of the settled community may be recruited from an age cohort (i.e., the youth from every family), whole families or clans from the community, or even hired laborers. In the 19th century A.D., a type of such village-based transhumance was practiced by the inhabitants of northern and central Transjordan (e.g., at Umm Qais and on the Kerak plateau; Mershen and Knauf 1988). Many travelers at that time (and most archaeologists subsequently), when observing their material culture and its remains, referred to these summer camps loosely as "bedouin" or "nomadic" encampments. But tax records, contemporary oral history, and more detailed descriptions by some observers have helped to correct this misconception. The misinterpretation, however, serves to illustrate how difficult it is to identify nomads in the historical and/or archaeological record, which usually provides scant data.

d. Pastoralists. Agriculture led to the domestication of most familiar domestic animals (with the exception of the camel) already in the course of the Neolithic. Pastoralists are people specializing in stock raising. However, they are not necessarily nomads. Judean landlords in the Iron Age, like Nabal (1 Sam 25:2, 11) or Amos (Amos 1:1; 7:14), can well be called "pastoralists" because herds seemed to have formed the major part of their wealth. Although they spend part of the year with their four-legged capital, they considered their "homes" to be towns like Maon or Tekoa (cf. also Gen 13:12). As a specialized occupation, pastoralism presupposes surplus production from both the pastoralist and the agriculturalist, and therefore a market economy. Unlike the non-sedentary agriculturalists mentioned above, pastoralists are not self-sufficient. Exploiting agriculturally marginal areas of the Near East which provide only scant nourishment for their flocks, pastoralists are forced to move frequently and therefore lead a non-sedentary or part-time sedentary life. Specialized pastoralism can be traced back to the Chalcolithic (Levy 1983), but only in the form of transhumance. From the Chalcolithic through the Bronze Age, pastoralists formed a social stratum within a society of village farming communities, or non-sedentary agriculturalists. There is no evidence of pastoral nomadic *tribes*—i.e., of a sociopolitical and/or ethnic cleavage between peasants and pastoralists—before the emergence of the bedouin. A term for "pastoral nomad" occurs only once in the Hebrew Bible, in a literary context dating to the Persian or Early Hellenistic period: *ʾohŏlê miqneh* "people of herds" (2 Chr 14:14). In this expression, *ʾhl* must be translated as "people" rather than "tent" and, therefore, regarded as an Early Arabic loanword.

e. Bedouin. Bedouin are pastoralists specialized in camel breeding. From the beginnings of bedouin life in the 1st millennium B.C., the bedouin formed a stratified society of pastoral nomads. Camel breeding was operative for the emergence of bedouinism on the sociopolitical level insofar as it facilitated the formation of purely nomadic tribes not depending upon peasant villagers. Camel breeders themselves are nearly self-sufficient: the camel provides them with food (milk, and on festive occasions, meat), fuel (dung), clothing (hair), housing (leather for round huts, which were later replaced by the "black tents" woven from goat hair), and even hair-washing lotion (urine). Furthermore, the camel provides a marketable commodity which one can trade without giving up possession of the animal: transport. Because the camel allows control over desert areas that are impenetrable by other animals or humans, it even provided their owners with power once these remote areas became commercially and/or politically important. Whereas the camel's secondary products (milk, hair, dung) provided the bedouin with the opportunity to exist somewhat independent of the settled communities, the animal's "tertiary product," transportation, increasingly became a valued commodity for those in the urban centers, who therefore had a vested interest in the incorporation of the bedouin. The camel thus constituted the bedouin's link with the urban societies of the ANE in both peaceful and belligerent ways. The influx of capital from the urban trading communities into the desert led to the social stratification and political leadership that made the bedouin increasingly aggressive and predatory. But before there can emerge a predatory society on the periphery, there must be enough surplus in the core area to be preyed upon. The more powerful, effective, and extensive the state became in controlling this core area, the more powerful, effective, and extensive the competing political organizations outside the state had to become. In terms of political evolution, the bedouin are a consequence of and reaction to the emergence of the first empire that tried to encompass the whole ANE: the Assyrian empire in the 8th and 7th centuries B.C.

As the camel herders rose to heights of power and prestige unprecedented among the nomads of earlier times, both nonsedentary agriculturalists and pastoralists who did not herd camels were affected by "bedouinization"; they either joined bedouin tribes, or organized themselves in tribes in imitation of the bedouin. From the Persian period through the Crusades, the population of Palestine appears to be ethnically and politically divided into Aramaic-speaking peasants and Arabic-speaking pastoral nomads. Even today, after modern development has reduced to nothing the significance of the camel, it still remains a common feature among the non-sedentary and the transhumant tribes of Jordan to claim to be "bedouin"—a claim that usually is flatly rejected by the descendants of former camel breeders.

2. "Tribes" and "Tribal Organization." The notion of tribal organization is part of the concept of "bedouin." It is understood—with Fried (1967: 170–74) and Price (1978: 179–82)—that tribalism is one of the possible responses by a nonstate society when confronting an expansionist state. It therefore has nothing to do with nomadism *per se,* since settled villagers can also organize themselves as "tribes" to counter the power of a neighboring state organization. This can be perfectly demonstrated by the emergence of the Mari tribes (Buccellati 1988), and probably applies equally well to the Israelite tribes of the early Iron Age: in order to be politically influential (which usually entails an ability to muster a sufficient number of warriors), a tribal society needs (1) a class of potential political leaders, competing against one another for success, and (2) a functioning system of alliances between the tribal segments (usually expressed by means of a genealogy).

However, among pastoral nomads, these two features are first encountered only with the bedouin of the 1st millennium B.C. In contrast, the Shasu of the LB Age occupy the lowest order within Dostal's scheme of political evolution within pre-urban societies (Dostal 1985): local lineages without any genealogical superstructure (Weippert 1974; Fischer-Elfert 1986: 168). Thus, the Shasu lacked an essential component of "tribal societies," and as such, they were politically insignificant. "Shasu" is a generic term, not an ethnonym. In the Egyptian sources, Shasu are specified by the various areas of their abode, not by tribal names. Tribal/ethnic names do not occur before the emergence of peasant tribes in the highlands of Canaan, such as Israel.

The agricultural tribes of early Iron Age Palestine, and before them the herding and farming lineages of the Shasu, were to a high degree economically independent from the outside world. Maintaining such independence is one of the major political aims of tribalism (Dostal 1985: 347–49), i.e., the ideological expression for the withdrawal of population groups from the exchange network and suppressive hierarchy of state societies. Although "tribalism" may have contributed to the Shasu's abandonment of their villages in the 16th century B.C., the withdrawal does not necessarily (or immediately) lead to the formation of tribes, i.e., stratified societies with an egalitarian ideology in their upper class. The Shasu remained on the level of "ranked society" or local lineages (for these categories, see Fried 1967 and Dostal 1985). After the emergence of the camel-herding tribes, the bedouin had two possible ways of access to those basic commodities which they did not produce: trade or violence (by plunder or extortion). Thus, while the emergence of the pastoral nomad presupposes the emergence of a market economy, the emergence of the bedouin tribe (in which the tribal elite may own 10,000 camels or more) presupposes the emergence of an empire which at one time or another could use (and pay for) a large camel corps.

To summarize this lengthy excursus on terminology: "nomads" are not necessarily "pastoralists," and they are not necessarily organized as "tribes." "Tribal societies" are not necessarily "nomadic." "Bedouin" are camel herding non-sedentary tribes, pastoral nomads whose basic livestock commodity is the camel.

B. Emergence of the Bedouin

1. Early Iron Age Antecedents. The camel had been domesticated and used by sedentary farming communities in East and South Arabia in the course of the 3d and 2d millennia B.C. (Bulliet 1975; Knauf 1988: 9–15). At the end of the LB Age, camels had been used both for transport, as attested at Tell Jemmeh (Wapnish 1981) and at Tell Deir ᶜAllah (Knauf 1987), and as a source of meat, attested at Timnaᶜ/el-Meneᶜiyeh (Knauf 1988: 14–15, 113–14). There can be no doubt that the Midianites (i.e. the inhabitants of NW Arabia in the LB Age) herded camels for these two purposes; at the same time it is clear that they were not pastoralists, since pastoralists prefer the by-products of their animals (their only capital and basic means of subsistence) instead of their meat (Sherratt 1983). It is unlikely that there were camel-herding tribes among the Midianites; however, camel herders may have been integrated into the existing Midianite clans or tribes as were potters, metallurgists, and traders: as specialists in a certain occupation. Undoubtedly, most Midianite tribesmen were farmers.

Like the Kenites, the Midianites became increasingly important for the economy of Palestine in the early Iron Age, when the Cyprus copper supply was interrupted and Palestine became dependent on the copper mines in Wadi Arabah (which in all likelihood were controlled by local clans and tribes; Knauf and Lenzen 1987). With the reemergence of sea trade at the end of the 11th century B.C., both Kenites and Midianites disappeared from the historical record.

The first predatory camel herders mentioned in the literary sources are the Amalekites (1 Samuel 30). It seems that the camel-herding population of the Amalekites did not exceed 400 men (1 Sam 30:17)—still a significant number for military action in the late 2d millennium B.C. (as compared to the contingents of 10 to 200 which the Egyptians sent as support to individual kings in the Amarna period; cf. Gideon's 300 and David's 600). 1 Sam 30:17 indicates why the camel had such an impact on the history of nomadism: it carried its herders beyond the political and military reach of the states they encountered. Distance and the desert (impenetrable without the camel) protected them from the villagers as efficiently as (on the other side of the social spectrum) fortified walls protected the city dwellers. If the Amalekites could already be classified as proto-bedouin, their emergence coincides with the emergence of the territorial state in Israel and Judah, which incorporated those hill country areas previously beyond the control of the Canaanite city-states. The hill country was no longer an area of retreat for populations which did not want to submit to the (often costly) claims of the state; therefore, for tribalism to survive the encroachment of the state, the desert offered a new frontier in an otherwise shrinking world.

Archaeologically, the emergence of the Amalekites in the Negeb can be dated to the very end of the 11th century B.C. Their emergence is reflected by the disappearance of the unfortified settlements which had characterized the Negeb in the early Iron Age, some of which were hamlets and farmsteads used by semi-sedentary agriculturalist and pastoralist populations that moved between the Judean hills and the central Negeb mountains (Finkelstein 1984); e.g., the Jerahmeelites, Kenites, and Calebites. With the emergence of the state on one side and of the bedouin on the other, this social structure, typical for the non-urban societies of the 3d and 2d millennia B.C., disappeared, giving way to towns and fortresses, the architectural appurtenances of the state.

2. The Neo-Assyrian Evidence. Large, powerful, and belligerent bedouin tribes are attested in the Assyrian royal inscriptions and reliefs of the 9th through the 7th centuries B.C. (see ISHMAELITES). It was not, however, before the Persian period that Arabs were wealthy and influential enough to acquire first-class weaponry (Knauf 1989: 22–23). Except for some technical details in riding styles (i.e. the use of a cushion saddle instead of the later *šadâd* saddle), these bedouin exhibit the basic characteristics of the later (full) bedouin. Their tribes must have comprised up to 10,000 people (even if the Assyrian tribute lists exaggerate). A thousand Arab camel riders participated in the battle of Qarqar in 853 B.C. (as opposed to the 400 which fled David); in the following century, Tiglath-pileser III on one occasion received 10,000 camels as tribute. The management of herds this size required slaveholding. Bedouin society, therefore, unlike earlier forms of pastoral society, was a *class society* in which wealth (in herds and in slaves) was one of the basic qualifications for leadership.

Although in theory all freeborn male members of the tribe were equal, only the tribal elite actually qualified for leadership functions. The other basic qualification is *muruwwa, virtus,* manlihood (Meeker 1979; Müller 1981). The ideology of "being a bedouin" with its knightly code of conduct was fully developed only in the last centuries before Islam, when the Arabian tribal elite borrowed the garments, weapons, and attitudes of prestige from Persian (Sassanian) feudalism (Dostal 1979). However, the class structure, i.e., the differentiation of tribal lords and tribal followers, existed earlier and facilitated this later borrowing (for tribal class societies with an egalitarian ideology upheld by the ruling class, see Dostal 1985).

According to Dostal (1959) and Bulliet (1975), the transition from "proto-bedouin" to "full bedouin" is marked by the replacement of the cushion saddle with the so-called *šadâd* saddle. The new saddle provided the rider with a firm seat and enabled him to use long swords and lances. Iconographically, the *šadâd* saddle is first attested at the end of the 5th century B.C. (Knauf 1988: 13, fig. 2:3). However, M. Macdonald (fc.) cautions against the overestimation of this technical development. It did not affect the social and political structure of bedouinism that resulted from large-scale camel herding. The new saddle may still have enhanced the bedouin's belligerence which, according to the Assyrian inscriptions and Gen 16:12, barely needed enhancement.

C. Bedouin States

Since bedouinism is a political program (resisting submission to outside power while simultaneously encouraging the bedouin on both the individual and the communal level to enhance their status by exercising power against the outside world; Meeker 1979) as much as a socioeconomic way of life, we should not be surprised that by the time bedouinism had fully emerged (i.e. by the 8th and 7th centuries B.C.), we also witness the first bedouin state. According to the Assyrian annals, the central North Arabian tribal confederacy led by the tribe of Qedar had its political, economic, and religious center in the oasis city of Dûmat al-Jandal (el-Jauf; 29° 50 ′N; 39° 52 ′E). See ISHMAELITES. (The final and most recent bedouin state was the dominion of the Ibn Rashîd and the Shammar tribe around Ḥâʾil, which succumbed to the Saudis shortly after World War I; Rosenfeld 1965.)

On an internal level, the bedouin state can be defined as being based *militarily* on a bedouin tribe (or a group of tribes, which may or may not be ranked) and *economically* on a city engaged in long-distance trade (for which the camel was a prerequisite). The two would be unified by a ruling family that managed effectively to control the city and to maintain the loyalty of the tribe. The main instrument for resolving the inherent tension between the anti-urban world of the bedouin and the cosmopolitan world of the urban trader seems to have been religion, the ruling family usually assuming a leading role in religious affairs (the first Arab queens attested in history were priestesses; the Ibn Rashîd conducted their campaigns into the territory of neighboring tribes and towns in the name of wahhabism). Religion and personal loyalty to their tribal chief allowed the bedouin to overcome their ideological opposition to the city (on which, economically, their wealth and power depended). The bedouin state thus occupies an intermediate position between complex chiefdom and early state (Rosenfeld 1965).

Bedouin states tended to be unstable, and they seldom lasted for more than three generations of the ruling family. Whenever their institutions approached the point of effectiveness that may have led to the formation of a true state, the bedouin element was either forced to abandon its tribal ideology (as happened in the formation of the Islamic state, although for a limited period only, and more effectively in the formation of the Saʿûdi state), or break loose from its symbiosis with the city. The Nabataeans, who made the transition to statehood *ca.* 80 B.C., lasted unusually long (nearly 200 years). Political conflict was not, as one may expect, primarily expressed by rebellions of either the tribal or the urban element, but rather by revolt and murder within and among the members of the ruling family. This is attested in the history of the Arabs in the 7th century B.C. (see ISHMAELITES), the history of the Nabataeans (see ARETAS #4), and especially the history of the Ibn Rashîd.

On an external level, the bedouin state was an example of a peripheral polity which nevertheless managed to direct the flow of capital and supplies from the urban core of the fertile crescent to its desert periphery. The steady increase in the number of camel herders as well as their increasing political complexity and power from the time of David to the time of Tiglath-pileser III coincided with the establishment of a Mediterranean-based (and soon Assyrian-controlled) world economy in which there was a rising demand for specific luxury goods such as incense. The extensive trade routes associated with the transportation of these goods were controlled by the emerging bedouin (similarly, the principality of Ḥâʾil in the 19th century drew most of its revenues from the Iraqi pilgrims' caravan to Mecca). The emergence of the bedouin and the bedouin state is, in this view, a by-product and consequence of the emergence of the large imperialistic state which alone could afford the luxury of incense, gold, and myrrh (or, in Islamic times, the luxury of a pilgrimage to Mecca).

In the Persian period the Achaemenids seem to have carefully prevented the emergence of bedouin states, preferring to deal with isolated tribal leaders, like Geshem the Arab (see KEDAR), or similar tribal leaders in Mesopotamia. They strengthened the position of the city as opposed to its surrounding tribes (as was the case with Taymâʾ; see TEMA).

The rise of the Nabataeans with their religious, political, and economic center at Petra and el-Jīʾ (see WADI MUSA) on the periphery of Roman Syria furnishes another classic example for the economic and cultural dependence of a bedouin state on an empire. The bedouin domination of Nabataean politics and administration surfaces in the title of the Nabataean king's representative at Damascus, who is called an *ethnarches* in 2 Cor 11:32. The title means "tribal chief" and does not imply that the city of Damascus was under Nabataean rule by the time of St. Paul's visit; quite the contrary, it implies that the Nabataean envoy (we may call him a consul) came from a non-urban social background (Sartre 1982: 123–26; Knauf 1983).

Nabataea, subject to increasing agricultural investment by the Nabataean tribal elite in the course of the second half of the 1st century A.D., and being situated on the border of Roman Syria, did not return to anarchy after the demise of its ruling family, but was annexed into the empire, much to the benefit of all her inhabitants. For the following 200 years, the area experienced the greatest level of prosperity it ever reached. Nothing demonstrates better than the fate of Nabataea, the most long-living, culturally advanced, and amiable bedouin state, that a society ultimately has to cease being "bedouin" in order for it to become fully a "state."

Bibliography

Banning, E. B., and Köhler-Rollefson, I. 1986. Ethnoarchaeological Survey in the Beda Area, Southern Jordan. *ZDPV* 102: 152–70.

Betts, A. 1987. 1986 Excavations at Dhuweila, Eastern Jordan. A Preliminary Report. *ADAJ* 31: 121–28.

———. 1989. The Solubba: Nonpastoral Nomads in Arabia. *BASOR* 274: 61–69.

Braudel, F. 1972. *The Mediterranean and the Mediterranean World in the Age of Philip II.* 2 vols. London and New York.

Briand, P. 1982. *État et pasteurs au Moyen-Orient ancien.* Series: Production pastorale et société. Cambridge and Paris.

Buccellati, G. 1988. The Kingdom and Period of Khana. *BASOR* 270: 43–61.

Bulliet, R. W. 1975. *The Camel and the Wheel.* Cambridge, MA.

Dever, W. G. 1985. From the End of the Early Bronze Age to the Beginning of the Middle Bronze. Pp. 113–35 in *BibAT.*

Dostal, W. 1959. The Evolution of Bedouin Life. Pp. 11–34 in *Lʾantica società beduina,* ed. S. Moscati and F. Gabrieli. Rome.

———. 1979. The Development of Bedouin Life in Arabia seen from Archaeological Material. Pp. 125–44 in *Studies in the History of Arabia* I/1, ed. A. H. Masri. Ar-Riyadh.

———. 1985. *Egalität und Klassengesellschaft in Südarabien. Anthropologische Untersuchungen zur sozialen Evolution.* WBKL 20. Horn-Wien.

Finkelstein, I. 1984. The Iron Age "Fortresses" of the Negev Highlands: Sedentarization of the Nomads. *TA* 11: 189–209.

———. 1988. *The Archaeology of the Israelite Settlement.* Jerusalem.

Fischer-Elfert, H.-W. 1986. *Die satirische Streitschrift des Papyrus Anastasi I. Übersetzung und Kommentar.* ÄA 44. Wiesbaden.

Fried, M. H. 1967. *The Evolution of Political Society.* New York.

Knauf, E. A. 1983. Zum Ethnarchen des Aretas 2 Kor 11,32. *ZNW* 74: 145–47.

———. 1987. Supplementa Ismaelitica 12. Camels in Late Bronze and Iron Age Jordan: The Archaeological Evidence. *BN* 40: 20–23.

———. 1988. *Midian. Untersuchungen zur Geschichte Palästinas und Nordarabiens am Ende des 2. Jahrtausends v. Chr.* ADPV. Wiesbaden.

———. 1989. *Ismael. Untersuchungen zur Geschichte Palästinas und Nordarabiens im 1. Jahrtausend v. Chr.* 2d expanded edition. ADPV. Wiesbaden.

Knauf, E. A., and Lenzen, C. J. 1987. Edomite Copper Industry. Pp. 83–88 in *Studies in the History and Archaeology of Jordan,* vol. 3, ed. A. Hadidi. Amman and London.

Levy, T. E. 1983. The Emergence of Specialized Pastoralism in the Southern Levant. *WoAr* 15: 15–36.

Macdonald, M. fc. *The Bedouin Warrior Saddle.* ADPV. Wiesbaden.

Meeker, M. E. 1979. *Literature and Violence in North Arabia.* Cambridge Studies in Cultural Systems 3. Cambridge.

Mershen, B. and Knauf, E. A. 1988. From Gadar to Umm Qais. *ZDPV* 104: 128–45.

Müller, G. 1981. *Ich bin Labid und das ist mein Ziel.* Berliner Islamstudien l. Wiesbaden.

Planhol, X. de. 1975. *Kulturgeographische Grundlagen der islamischen Geschichte.* Zurich and Munich.

Price, B. J. 1978. Secondary State Formation: An Explanatory Model. Pp. 161–86 in *The Origins of State,* ed. R. Cohen and E. R. Service. Philadelphia.

Rosenfeld, H. 1965. The Social Composition of the Military in the Process of State Formation in the Arabian Desert. *JRAI* 95: 75–86, 174–94.

Richard, S. 1987. The Early Bronze Age: The Rise and Collapse of Urbanism. *BA* 50: 22–43.

Sartre, M. 1982. *Trois études sur l'Arabie romaine et byzantine.* Brussels.

Sherratt, A. 1983. The Secondary Exploitation of Animals in the Old World. *WoAr* 15: 90–104.

Thiel, W. 1985. *Die soziale Entwicklung Israels in vorstaatlicher Zeit.* 2d ed. Neukirchen-Vluyn.

Wagstaff, J. 1985. *The Evolution of Middle Eastern Landscapes. An Outline to A.D. 1840.* London.

Wapnish, P. 1981. Camel Caravans and Camel Pastoralists at Tell Jemmeh. *JANES* 13: 101–21.

Weippert, M. 1974. Semitische Nomaden des zweiten Jahrtausends. *Bib* 55: 265–80, 427–33.

ERNST AXEL KNAUF

BEE. See ZOOLOGY.

BEELIADA (PERSON) [Heb *bĕʿelyādāʿ*]. One of thirteen sons of David listed as having been born in Jerusalem (1 Chr 3:5–9; 14:3–7; cf. 2 Sam 5:13–16). His mother was among the several wives and concubines whom David took in Jerusalem, but she is not named. His name—found in this form only in 1 Chr 14:7—is usually taken to mean "Baal knows." It was changed to "Eliada," meaning "God knows," in 2 Sam 5:16 and 1 Chr 3:8. Most scholars have taken this to reflect the common distaste in Israel for names incorporating that of the Canaanite deity, seen in such name pairs for the same person as Jerubbaal/Jerubbesheth, Eshbaal/Ishbosheth, or Meribbaal/Mephiboshet (e.g., Noth *IPN,* 119–22). However, the element *baʿal* may not always have been understood offensively (Fowler *TPNAH,* 54–63); rather, in some cases, it may have had the generic meaning of "lord" (McCarter *2 Samuel* AB, 85–87). It seems odd for David to have named a son after a foreign god; the name could simply mean "the Lord knows." In 1 Chr 14:7, his name is rendered in Gk as *Balliada* in Codex Alexandrinus and *Baaliada* in Codex Venetus, but as *Balegdae* in Codexes Vaticanus and Sinaiticus.

DAVID M. HOWARD, JR.

BEELZEBUL [Gk *Beelzeboul;* Heb *baʿal zĕbûb*]. Var. BEELZEBUB; BAALZEBUB. According to the synoptic accounts, Jesus was accused of expelling demons by the power of Beelzebul, a name for the "prince of demons" *(ho archōn tōn daimoniōn),* that is, SATAN (Mark 3:22–26; Matt 12:24–27; Luke 11:15–19). Matt 10:25 is the only instance of Jesus using the name *Beelzebul.* Elsewhere the gospel writers record Jesus as using the name "Satan" rather than *Beelzebul.*

Scholars have been fascinated with trying to find an etymology for this preeminent satanic being. The etymology of Beelzebul has proceeded in several directions. The variant reading *Beelzebub* (Syriac translators and Jerome) reflects a long-standing tradition of equating Beelzebul with the Philistine deity of the city of Ekron mentioned in 2 Kgs 1:2, 3, 6, 16. Baalzebub (Heb *baʿal zĕbûb*) seems to mean "lord of flies" (*HALAT,* 250, but cf. LXX^B *baal muian theon akkarōn,* "Baal-Fly, god of Akkaron"; *Ant* 9:2,1 *theon muian*). Prior to the discoveries at Ras Shamra (Ugarit) the elucidation of this deity came through finding parallels in the Greek world which mentioned deities in the role of "the Averter of flies" (e.g. *Zeus Apomuios, theos muiagros;* Nilsson 1967: 213). The decipherment of the Ugaritic texts brought to light the frequent epithet "Prince Baal" or "Exalted Baal" *(zbl bʿl)* or "The Prince, the Lord of the earth" (*zbl bʿl arṣ)* (Albright 1936: 17–18). Armed with this new information from Ugarit, scholars almost unanimously saw in 2 Kings 1 another example of a pejorative rendering of an original *baʿal zĕbûl* with *baʿal zĕbûb,* "Lord of *flies,*" similar to the well-known euphemistic substitution of *bōšet,* "shame," for an original *baʿal* in such personal names as Mephiboshet and Ishboshet (McCarter *2 Samuel* AB, 124–25, 128). Some scholars have also suggested that *zbl bʿl* may underlie the tribal name ZEBULUN (Ringgren 1966: 21), the personal name ZEBUL in Judg 9:28, and JEZEBEL (cf. the Phoenician PN *bʿlʾzbl* in *CIS* I 158), the daughter of Ethbaal (1 Kgs 16:31).

An alternative suggested by many is to connect *zĕbûl* with a noun meaning "(exalted) abode." Prior to the discoveries at Ugarit and Qumran, Aitken argued that the four biblical occurrences of *zĕbûl* (1 Kgs 8:13; Isa 63:15; Hab 3:11; Ps 49:15) as well as the respective rabbinical and medieval commentaries proved that the meaning of *zĕbûl* was "dwelling" and often the exalted dwelling of *par excellence* of God, i.e., heaven. Aitken (1912: 34–53) suggested that Beelzebul as "lord of the heaven" was in fact a sky god. Gaston (1962: 247–55), who had the advantage of working with the new material from Ugarit as well as the four occurrences of *zĕbûl* in the Dead Sea Scrolls (1QM 12:1–2; 1QS 10:3; 1QpHab 3:34), arrived at a similar conclusion stressing that *zĕbûl* can mean either "the temple" or "heaven." Gaston (1962:252) further noted that the chief rival of Yahweh in the Hellenistic period was the heavenly Baal (Gk *Zeus Olumpios,* Aram *bʿlšmyn*). The word *zĕbûl,* argued Gaston, was used in place of the more common synonyms for heaven because Christians were most likely included in the group of those who "stretched out their hands against the temple *(zĕbûl)*" (*t. Sanh.* 13:5; Gaston 1962:253–54).

Matthew 10:25 refers to "the master of the house *(ton oikodespotēn)* Beelzebul." Aitken (1912: 51) pointed out what seems to be a wordplay in which *ton oikodespotēn* could be a translation of the Semitic word *Beelzebul* which follows. This has been the favored view of the majority of NT scholars (cf. the various commentaries on the synoptics as well as MacLaurin 1978: 156–60). This wordplay is also clearly reflected in the Hebrew Matthew extracted from Shem-Tob ben-Shaprut's *Even Bohan* which has *bʿl hbyt—bʿl zbwb* (Howard 1987: 46, 195). On the other hand, a wordplay, like a folk etymology, may not reflect a historically accurate etymology.

A third alternative analysis has seen Beelzebul as "lord of the dung" based on conjectural cognates in postbiblical Hebrew, Aramaic/Syriac, and Arabic. While this view may have been popular in the past, it finds few adherents among modern scholars (see Gaston's critique 1962: 251–52). Albright went so far as to say that "it has been given up by most competent scholars" (1932: 191 n.20).

Some scholars have argued that *Beelzebul* should be connected with the Aram *bĕʿēl dĕbābāʾ* "enemy, adversary" (cf. Matt 13:39, where the *diabolos* is called the *ekthros*). This etymology has not found many adherents in the past (e.g. Schlatter: 1957:343), yet it has recently been advocated by Day (1988:151–59), who argues that it provides a more plausible reason for the equation of Beelzebub/ Beelzebul with Satan. Day (1988: 157) would see another wordplay going on between Aram *bĕʿēl dîbābāʾ* "lord of flies," and Aram *bĕʿēl dĕbābāʾ* "enemy, adversary." On the connection of this expression with Akk *bēl dabābi* see Day (1988: 158), who argues that the accuser role of this expression is primitive. In contrast, see Kaufman (1974: 42–43) who argues that Akk *bēl dabābi* has to do with an adversarial role, which is to be kept distinct from the role of an accuser in court, which was expressed by *bʿl dynʾ*. Aram *dîbābāʾ* and Akk *dabābi* reflect Proto-Semitic **d* which would come into Heb as *d* and not *z.* Thus Heb *zĕbûb* cannot be cognate with these two words. A folk etymology is another question.

Fensham (1967: 361–64) suggests that Baalzebub should be translated "Baal, the Flame." This suggestion would fit nicely with the fire motif in the Elijah narratives, as Fensham points out, yet it rests on the scanty evidence of only one text (*CTA* 3.3.43 = *KTU* 1.3.3.46) where *d̲bb* parallels *išt,* "fire." It may even be that we are dealing with a scribal error of *d̲bb* for *šbb* (cf. Heb. *šābîb* "spark") in the Ugaritic text.

Finally, de Moor (1987: 179, 183) argues that *Baalzebub* "Fly Lord" recalls Baal's victory over monstrous flies (= demons) and compares the "flies of death" in Qoh 10:1. Both de Moor and Saracino (1982: 338–43) interpret an extremely difficult text from Ras Ibn Hani (78/20) to be an apotropaic ritual where Baal drives out "harmful agents (demon-flies)" called *dbbm* which are causing a patient's illness (cf. also the connection of Ugaritic *zbl* with sickness as noted by Held 1968: 93). These scholars suggest that *Baalzebub* need not have been a pejorative change from an original *Baalzebul.* In fact, de Moor argues that this description of Baal's exorcism of evil spirits is directly parallel to Matt 12:24 (=Mark 3:22; =Luke 11:15) which has the Pharisees stating that it is only through Beelzebul that Jesus casts out demons. Yet so far, the divine name *Baalzebub* is unattested in extrabiblical documents, including the Ugaritic texts (cf. the god named *d̲bb* mentioned above in *CTA* 3.3.43 = *KTU* 1.3.3.46).

Bibliography

Aitken, W. E. M. 1912. Beelzebul. *JBL* 31: 34–53.

Albright, W. F. 1932. The North-Canaanite Epic of ʾAlʾêyân Baʿal and Môt. *JPOS* 12: 185–208.

———. 1936. Zabûl Yam and Thâpit Nahar in the Combat Between Baal and the Sea. *JPOS* 16: 17–20.

Day, P. L. 1988. *An Adversary in Heaven. śāṭān in the Hebrew Bible.* HSM 43. Atlanta.

Fensham, F. C. 1967. A Possible Explanation of the Name Baal-Zebub of Ekron. *ZAW* 79: 361–64.

Gaston, L. 1962. Beelzebul. *TZ* 18: 247–55.

Held, M. 1968. The Root ZBL/SBL in Akkadian, Ugaritic, and Biblical Hebrew. *JAOS* 88: 90–96.

Howard, G. E. 1987. *The Gospel of Matthew according to a Primitive Hebrew Text.* Macon, GA.

Kaufman, S. A. 1974. *The Akkadian Influences on Aramaic.* Chicago.

MacLaurin, E. C. B. 1978. Beelzeboul. *NovT* 20: 156–60.

Moor, J. C. de. 1987. *An Anthology of Religious Texts from Ugarit.* Leiden.

Nilsson, M. P. 1967. *Geschichte der griechischen Religion.* 3d ed. Vol. 1. Munich.

Ringgren, H. 1966. *Israelite Religion.* Trans. David Green. Philadelphia.

Saracino, F. 1982. Ras Ibn Hani 78/20 and Some Old Testament Connections. *VT* 32: 338–43.

Schlatter, A. 1957. *Der Evangelist Matthaüs.* Stuttgart.

THEODORE J. LEWIS

BEER (PLACE) [Heb *bĕʾēr*]. **1.** An unidentified site in Moab N of the river Arnon (Num 21:13) at which the people of Israel encamped before traveling to Mattanah (Num 21:16). At Beer, which means "well," the princes and nobles dug a well. The ease with which the water was obtained may have inspired the couplet of Num 21:17–18. The prevailing opinion is that Beer should be located in NE Moab in the *Wâdī eth-Themed,* a tributary of the *Wâdī el-Wāle* where there is an adequate water supply for a large number of people close to the surface (e.g. *GP,* 461; Glueck 1933–1934: 13; *GTTOT,* 262; van Zyl 1960: 85–86). It is commonly assumed that Beer-elim mentioned in Isa 15:8 is identical with the Beer of Num 21:16 (see also BEER-ELIM).

2. The locality to which Jotham, youngest son of Jerubbaal (i.e. Gideon) fled from his brother Abimelech after reciting a parable from the top of Mount Gerizim to the citizens of Shechem (Judg 9:21). In antiquity Eusebius (Lagarde 1966: 238, 73) identified Beer with a village in the S named *Bēra* (Gk) about 7.5 miles N of Eleutheropolis in the neighborhood of Beth-shemesh (cf. *RNAB,* 84). Though the position of Beer remains uncertain some modern scholars suggest a N location and tentatively identify it with *el-Bîreh* in the vicinity of Ophrah about 7 miles NW of Beth-shean (e.g., *GTTOT,* 581; *RNAB,* 129).

Bibliography

Glueck, N. 1933–1934. Explorations in Eastern Palestine, 1. *AASOR* 14:1–113.

Lagarde, P. de. 1966. *Onomastica Sacra.* Hildesheim.

Zyl, A. H. van. 1960. *The Moabites.* Pretoria Oriental Series 3. Leiden.

ARTHUR J. FERCH

BEER-ELIM (PLACE) [Heb *bĕʾēr-ʾēlîm*]. An unidentified site in Moab (Isa 15:8) which has been tentatively equated with Beer of Num 21:16 (e.g. Kaiser *Isaiah 13–39* OTL, 69). Beer-elim, meaning "well of chiefs" or "well of terebinths," may be an abbreviated form of Beer, which has been located north of the river Arnon in the *Wâdī eth-Themed* (see also BEER). The equation of these two locations is based on the notions that (1) *Themed* means "waterhole," as does Beer; (2) terebinths grow in this *Wâdī;* and (3) this is the only location north of the Arnon where water is close to the surface as described in Num 21:16–18.

Objections to the identification of Beer-elim with Beer include the facts that there are other sites prefixed by the name Beer and valleys in which terebinths grow (Wildberger *Isaiah BKAT,* 617). Wildberger suggests that Beer-elim may have been south of the Arnon in the vicinity of *el-Kerak.*

ARTHUR J. FERCH

BEER-LAHAI-ROI (PLACE) [Heb *bĕʾēr laḥay roʾî*]. A location in S Palestine associated with the birth of Ishmael (Gen 16:14) and mentioned twice (Gen 24:62; 25:11) as a residence of the patriarch Isaac. The name is introduced in an etiological narrative of a vision experienced at the site by the pregnant HAGAR, who is promised the birth of a son whom she is told to name ISHMAEL (Gen 16:7–12). In response to the vision, Hagar names the deity who appeared to her "a God of seeing" (Heb *ʾel rŏʾî;* Gen 16:13), and utters another statement concerning seeing. The name of the site is referred to Hagar's utterance (16:14).

Both Hagar's statement and the name of the site Beer-lahai-roi are difficult to interpret, and have engendered speculative solutions of various kinds. The LXX rendering of Gen 16:14, *phrear hou enopion eidon* "well of him whom I have plainly seen," is a midrashic interpretation rather than a translation. The Vulgate's Latin, *Puteum Viventis Videntis me* "Well of the Living One, the One who Sees me," has the semblance of a literal translation. Rabbinic interpretations are variations on the theme of seeing and living. Many modern interpreters separate the toponym from the etiology in which it is embedded. Thus Wellhausen (*WPHI,* 326) interpreted the Hebrew consonants *l-ḥ-y* as the word "jawbone" and *r-ʾ-y* as a kind of antelope (not attested in Hebrew).

The location of Beer-lahai-roi is placed between KADESH and BERED (Gen 16:14), that is, in the Negeb (so Gen 24:62). The water source which gave rise to the name was located "on the way to Shur" (Gen 16:7; see SHUR, WILDERNESS OF).

HENRY O. THOMPSON

BEER-RESISIM (M.R. 109206). A small EB site of ca. 3 acres situated on the S bank of the Naḥal Resisim, a tributary of the Naḥal Niṣṣana, in the W Negeb highlands near Beerotayim on the Israel-Sinai border. Lying at an altitude of 1500 feet, the site receives less than 4 inches of annual rainfall and is in an area suitable only for pastoralism. Even marginal dry farming is possible only with some form of runoff irrigation.

Beʾer Resisim (Arabic *Bîr er-Resīsiyeh,* "Well of the Morning Dew") was discovered by kibbutzniks in the 1950s.

Excavations were carried out for three seasons in 1978,

1979, and 1980 by William G. Dever and Rudolph Cohen. The project was multidisciplinary and designed to carry out newer experimental techniques in order to study the site in its larger regional context and environmental setting. Specialists in the natural sciences therefore conducted geological and geomorphological surveys, palynological and paleozoological analyses, and climatic investigations, in addition to the more traditional stratigraphic and ceramic studies. At the time no site of the period had yet been excavated extensively or with modern multidisciplinary methods.

Beʾer Resisim is one of a group of several hundred known one-period villages and encampments in the Negeb largely belonging to the EB IV period (ca. 2400–2000 B.C.). These sites are related in turn to an even larger complex in the semiarid marginal zone extending from S Transjordan clear across the Negeb into the W Sinai. They represent the maximum extent of the non-nucleated, seminomadic culture that replaced the urban EB I–III culture of Palestine after its collapse ca. 2600–2400 B.C. Many of these sites, however, reveal a scattering of EB II shards (ca. 3200–2600 B.C.), indicating sporadic earlier use by pastoral nomads (Dever 1980).

Nearly all of the builtup area of Beʾer Resisim—the second largest EB IV site in the Negeb—was investigated or cleared. The excavation revealed about 80 small, circular stone sleeping huts, several open-air communal food preparation areas, and several animal enclosures. The nearly complete village plan thus recovered is the only such yet published from any EB IV site in Palestine or Transjordan. There was no trace of an enclosure wall, cult installations, or elite structures of any kind. Based on the usual methods of calculation, the population may have numbered about 100 or so. The form and layout of the structures strongly suggest a small clan or tribal unit, probably polygamous, and socially unstratified. The paleobotanical and paleozoological investigations showed that the subsistence system was based on a mixed economy, principally the herding of sheep and goats (over 90 percent of all bones), with some possible dry farming in good years. In addition, small-scale trade in copper and exotic raw materials from the Sinai seems to have played a minor role in the economy (Dever 1985).

The overall picture at Beʾer Resisim, as elsewhere in the EB IV settlements of the Negeb, is that of seasonal encampments of pastoral nomads. The pottery and copper implements are closely related to "Family S," typical of the Hebron hills (Dever 1980). Since there are numerous EB IV shaft-tomb cemeteries but very few settlements there, we may reconstruct a seasonal pattern of pastoral migrations between winter pasturages in the Negeb and summer pasturages and burying grounds in the higher and cooler altitudes in the hill country (see QAᶜAQĪR, JEBEL). All these arid-zone Negeb encampments disappear with the beginning of the reurbanized MB Age, ca. 2000 B.C., and most are never again occupied.

Bibliography

Cohen, R., and Dever, W. G. 1978. Preliminary Report of the Pilot Season of the "Central Negev Highlands Project." *BASOR* 232: 29–45.

———. 1979. Preliminary Report of the Second Season of the "Central Negev Highlands Project." *BASOR* 236: 41–60.

———. 1981. Preliminary Report of the Third and Final Season of the "Central Negev Highlands Project." *BASOR* 243:57–77.

Dever, W. G. 1980. New Vistas on the EB IV ("MB I") Horizon in Syria-Palestine. *BASOR* 237: 35–64.

———. 1985. Village Planning at Beʾer Resisim and Socio-Economic Structure in Early Bronze Age IV Palestine. *EI* 18: *18–*28.

William G. Dever

BEER-SHEBA (PLACE) [Heb *bĕʾēr šebaᶜ*]. A town in the S Judean desert best known for its association with the biblical patriarchs, and as the S extreme of Israelite territory as delineated in the formula "from Dan to Beer-sheba" (Judg 20:1; 1 Sam 3:20; etc.). The Hebrew name means "well of seven" or "well of oath." Both Hebrew words, "to swear" and "oath," are derived from the word "seven."

The Bible offers two patriarchal traditions to explain the significance of the name. One describes a conflict between Abraham and Abimelech over water rights to a well, which is resolved when Abraham gives Abimelech seven ewe lambs as witness of Abraham's rights to the well (Gen 21:28–31). Another account similarly involves disputes over water rights, but between Isaac and Abimelech: after an agreement is struck between the disputants, Isaac's servants successfully dig a new well, which Isaac named, *šibᶜâ*, a form of the number seven. This account concludes by noting that the city was consequently named Beer-sheba (Gen 26:33).

A. Identification

The ancient name is preserved in the Arabic Bîr es-Sebaᶜ, which referred to the area near the bend of Wadi es-Sebaᶜ (located in the industrial center of modern Beer-sheba). G. L. Robinson (1901) reported seeing seven wells at the site. The *SWP* mentions Bīʾâr es-Sebaᶜ, "the wells of Sebaᶜ," and gives the name of the accompanying ruins as Kh. Bîr es-Sebaᶜ; it also notes Tell es-Sebaᶜ, a mound 4 km to the E at the junction of Wadi el-Khalil (Nahal Hebron) and Wadi es-Sebaᶜ, although the surveyors did not identify it as biblical Beer-sheba. Apparently E. W. G. Masterman (*ISBE* [1929 ed.] 1: 424–25) was the first to propose identifying Tell es-Sebaᶜ with the OT town.

Modern understanding of tell formation and site location led to the assumption that the mound of Tell es-Sebaᶜ (M.R. 134072) was the ancient Israelite town, and that Bîr es-Sebaᶜ to the W (M.R. 130072) was the site of the Roman-Byzantine city of Berosabe, although Glueck (1968: 40–41), among others, disagreed. Excavations in the 1960s at Kh. Bîr es-Sebaᶜ revealed an Iron Age occupation in addition to the Roman-Byzantine ruins, but the topography is ill suited for a fortified center, and no significant fortifications were uncovered (Gophna and Yisraeli 1973).

Alternatively, the excavations at Tell es-Seba^c from 1969–1974, and in 1976 (under the direction of Y. Aharoni and Z. Herzog, respectively) have uncovered a well-planned administrative center with several strata spanning the 10th through the 8th centuries B.C. A letter found at Arad (ca. 7th century) refers to Beer-sheba, but probably does not refer to the fortress, which then lay in ruins (if the chronological attribution of the Arad ostraca is accurate); the letter may instead refer to the settlement at Bîr es-Seba^c 4 km W of the tell. Beer-sheba may have been a dual site consisting of the royal city (i.e., the tell) along with a civilian settlement further W on the banks of the wadi (where the modern city now stands). This could explain the doublet in the ledger of Simeon's towns: Beer-sheba and Sheba/Shema (Josh 19:3; cf. also Josh 15:26 and 1 Chr 4:28).

B. Chalcolithic Sites

A significant and flourishing Chalcolithic culture (*EAEHL* 1: 153–58) has been discovered along the banks of the wadi—Abu Matar (Perrot 1955a), Bîr es-Ṣafadi (Perrot 1955b; 1956; 1959; 1960), and Kh. Beitar (Dothan 1959). These sites show 3 to 4 phases of occupation spanning the early- to mid-4th millennium B.C. Since the discovery of these sites in the 1950s, other sites with similar assemblages have been discovered further afield along the banks of the wadi (e.g., Shiqmim, Ze^{c}elim, Nevatim), indicating the existence of a regional Beer-sheba basin culture (Levy 1986). This cultural horizon, in turn, exhibits similarities with the remains of Tuleilat Ghassul. See GHASSUL, TULEILAT EL-. Some of the Beer-sheba settlements seem to have engaged in craft specialization, such as metalworking (e.g., Abu Matar) and ivory/bone carving (e.g., Bir es-Ṣafadi). These early sites, however, have no association with events recorded in the Bible.

C. Iron Age Sites

1. Bîr es-Seba^c. Alt's (*KlSchr* 3: 409–35) and Glueck's (1968: 40–41) suggestion that biblical Beer-sheba should be sought at Bîr es-Seba received some corroboration with the discovery of Iron Age remains directly beneath the floors of the Roman/Byzantine occupation (Gophna and Yisraeli 1973). Most of the evidence is from the Iron Age IIC, with some from the 10th century (Iron Age IC).

2. Tell es-Seba^c. In 1969, Aharoni initiated eight seasons of excavations which have identified nine Iron Age strata, with additional evidence for the Persian, Hellenistic, and Herodian periods. The presentation here generally follows the major summary of the expedition team, but strives to point out along the way some of the questions and issues that have been raised by others.

Stratum IX. The earliest strata were located only on the SE section of the tell (these occupational levels probably existed in other areas, but were apparently obliterated in the stratum V leveling and construction operations). The earliest settlement consisted of caves and pits dug into the hill. These pits were not of uniform shape, and some apparently were used for grain storage, while others were for occupation (as inferred from the presence of beaten earth occupational surfaces). Some of these pits and caves have subdividing walls, and terraces indicating specific activity areas. The ceramic collection associated with this level (including some shards of Philistine pottery, and red-slipped and hand-burnished wares) implies a date at the end of the 12th century or early 11th century B.C. (Herzog 1984: 42–43).

Stratum VIII. While the ceramic collection of stratum VIII is small, the wares appear more closely related to those of stratum IX than to those of the later periods (Herzog 1984: 46). The excavators therefore date this stratum to the mid-late 11th century B.C. The inhabitants began to build more substantial buildings on stone foundations (actually only one building and part of another have been found from this stratum), but most of the remains show a continued use of the pits and caves from the earlier period.

Stratum VII. A significantly larger area of stratum VII was uncovered and shows evidence of an organized site plan—the buildings (typically four-room house variations) were built encircling the perimeter of the mound with their rear walls connected and facing outward to form a basic security system. The houses opened inward toward an open area where the flocks and herds might be penned at night (Fig. BEE.01). Other buildings surrounded a well shaft outside the gate and perimeter wall. The direct-access gate consisted of two chambers attached to the corners of the houses on either side, and a drainage channel passed through the gate, but there is no evidence that it directed waters toward the well (cf. Herzog 1984: 26). The pottery suggests a date in the late 11th or early 10th century B.C.

It is not possible to determine when the well was dug, although it appears from the building that surrounded the well in stratum VII, and the fact that the well stood almost exactly in the center of the courtyard of this building, that the well existed during stratum VII. Because the stratigraphy of the well area has been disrupted in antiquity (due to the collapse of the upper walls of the shaft), it is impossible to determine stratigraphically the date of the

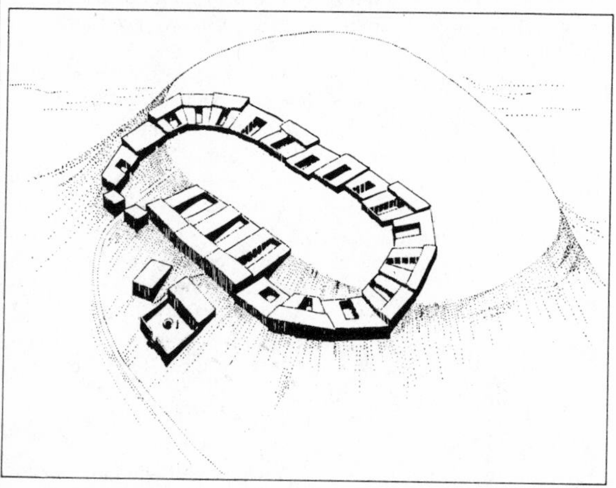

BEE.01. Isometric reconstruction of enclosed settlement at Beer-sheba—Stratum VII. *(Redrawn from Herzog 1984: 80.)*

well. The only possibility available to determine its date is to excavate to the bottom of the well, but after excavating through 28 m of accumulation without reaching bottom, it was deemed necessary to abort the operation. On the basis of the orientation of nearby stratum IX architectural features, the excavators suggest that the well was dug in stratum IX (Herzog 1984: 4–6). There is, however, no evidence to attribute any part of this well to the patriarchal period.

Stratum VI. This stratum differs significantly from the previous one. The four-room house plan is evident in only one building of the excavated area. Otherwise the buildings are poorly built, and look as if they were arranged randomly. Some of the buildings reused portions of the ruins from the earlier stratum. The fairly large ceramic collection of stratum VI indicates a date in the 10th century.

Stratum V. Major changes in stratum V consisted of a leveling operation on the tell and the construction of a solid, 4-m thick, offset-inset city wall. The wall stood on a stone foundation (preserved in places 1.5 m high) on top of which the mud-brick superstructure rested. The wall system was protected with a glacis constructed of layers of soil, small stones, and soil mixed with ash and shards, which was then stabilized with a 1.5–2.0-m thick layer of brick material mixed with ash. The slope of the glacis was ca. 20°. At the foot of the system, a fosse was dug at least 3–4 m deep (it was not fully excavated). The three-entry city gate (similar to the gate at Dan) was located on the SE side and measured ca. 21 by 21 m. On the basis of the ceramic collection, Aharoni parallels this stratum with Megiddo V–IV and therefore dates the stratum to the 10th century. This stratum was destroyed by fire, which Aharoni suggests occurred during Shishak's campaign into S Judah (1973: 106).

The absence of reference to Beer-sheba in the Karnak inscription listing the cities that Shishak conquered may result from the fact that the inscription is damaged in the sections referring to the Negeb. However, the reconstruction by the excavators poses some intriguing questions. Two architectural features that Aharoni dates to the 10th century seem unusual for this period—namely, the solid fortification wall and the three-entry gate. The normal fortification system in the Solomonic period consisted of a casemate wall and a four-entry gate (cf. Hazor X, Megiddo VA-IVB, Gezer VIII). After the discovery of the three-entry gate at Beer-sheba, Aharoni (1974) redated the defensive system at Beer-sheba V (as well as the gate at Dan) to the time of David. While the normal pattern in the United Monarchy does not preclude the use of a different system at Beer-sheba, the features that Aharoni describes are typical of 9th-century defensive systems in Israel and Judah. Furthermore, Biran (*EAEHL* 1: 320) dates the construction of the city gate at Dan (to which Aharoni appeals as a parallel) to the reign of Jeroboam I (for further discussion see Yadin 1976; and Herzog, Rainey, and Moshkovitz 1977).

Stratum IV. A new city was soon rebuilt on the ruins of stratum V, which reused the solid fortification walls. Aharoni suggests (1973: 106) that because of the similarity of the ceramic collection of stratum IV with that of stratum V, stratum IV was destroyed soon after the end of V. This he dates to the beginning of the 9th century, and places it in the historical context of the middle of Asa's reign (ca. 910–865 B.C.).

Strata III–II. The last major city consisted of two phases—stratum III, with isolated areas of repair and rebuild in stratum II (see site plan in CITIES, Fig. CIT.08). No severe destruction separated them. The fortress of strata III–II consisted of a casemate wall on the ruins of the earlier solid wall. The wall thicknesses were ca. 1.6 m for the outer wall and ca. 1.4 m for the inner wall. The increased elevation of the city wall required also that the glacis be raised, however, a level area ca. 3.0–3.5 m wide extended from outside the wall to the top of the downward slope of the glacis.

A new three-entry city gate (ca. 17 m wide × 14 m deep) stood above the ruins of the earlier one. The access through the gate was 4.2 m wide. Benches (ca. 30 cm high) lined the inside of one of the chambers in the stratum III gate, but these were eliminated in stratum II. A new drain channel (associated with strata III–II) collected water from the interior of the city and directed it through the gate to the well which had existed in the earlier strata (Herzog 1984: 4–5).

Since a well is usually a preferred water source because it is relatively free of surface contaminants, it is curious that the people of the city would channel contaminated waters from inside the city to the well. It is therefore possible that the shaft by this time functioned more as a cistern than as a well, especially if an alternative independent water system existed. Indeed, the expedition discovered in the NE corner of the city what appears to have been such a system (although it has not yet been completely excavated).

A plaza area (ca. 12 × 20 m) stood inside the gate from which a street concentric with the city wall circled through the town. This street was flanked on each side by buildings. At least two other streets passed directly from the plaza across the site to the other side where they again intersected the concentric street. The predominant building plan was of the four-room house variety. Immediately to the left after entering the gate were apparently administrative buildings, while three storehouses stood just to the right. The plan and construction of these storehouses are similar to the stables found at Megiddo and Hazor, but the ones at Beer-sheba had huge collections of ceramics, including storage jars, pithoi, holemouth jars, and an array of domestic vessels—cooking pots, kraters, dipper juglets, jugs, lamps, flasks, etc.

Integrated into the walls of the storehouses of stratum II were stones clearly in secondary use. Some of these were of calcareous sandstone, in contrast to the typical limestone otherwise used. Three of the sandstone blocks preserved the shape of large horns typical of four-horned altars, while a fourth showed evidence that the horn had been broken off. The other sandstone blocks apparently had been originally associated with the altar which had been dismantled and its stones reused in the construction of the storehouses. Another of the stones bore the image of a deeply incised serpent. Additional stones, which also had apparently been part of the altar, were later found in a fill associated with the repair of the glacis of stratum II; some of these had evidence of fire on their surfaces (Herzog, Rainey, and Moshkovitz 1977: 57, fig. 4). The postulated reconstruction of the altar (see Fig. BEE.02) measures ca. 63 inches high (from bottom to top of a horn; it is unclear what the length and width were, but Aharoni [1974a: 4] suggests that it conformed to the 5 × 5 cubit dimensions of the Arad altar).

A significant element in Aharoni's plan to excavate Beer-sheba had been to find a temple similar to the one he had earlier discovered at Arad (Aharoni 1968: 32; 1973: 14), and the discovery of a dismantled altar naturally fueled his efforts to locate where the altar had originally stood. See ARAD. An area in the NW section of the town has been suggested as the location of the temple, even though it has yielded no architectural remains from stratum III (except a chalk pavement, which the excavators suggest was part of the temple courtyard; Herzog, Rainey, and Moshkovitz 1977: 58). Several other factors have been offered to substantiate the claim that the NW corner was the site of a temple: (1) the area is easily accessible from the gate and plaza; (2) it is a prominent section in the town; (3) it is the only area (thus far excavated) where a large building could be built with a E–W orientation; (4) a subterranean passage extends from the area to the outside of the city; and (5) numerous cultic objects from later periods have been found in the area, perhaps continuing the reverence for the site (Herzog, Rainey, and Moshkovitz 1977: 56–57; Aharoni 1974b: 271). The failure to find architectural features is explained by postulating that the building had been totally dismantled (similar to the fate of the altar) and "razed to its foundations" (Herzog, Rainey, and Moshkovitz 1977: 57; cf. Aharoni 1974b: 271).

Recognizing that this proposal is largely an argument from silence supported by relatively circumstantial evidence, Yadin (1976) postulated an alternative location for the altar based largely on the statement in 2 Kgs 23:8 which describes the existence of an altar just inside and to the left of the city gate (which he suggests applied to Beer-sheba and not Jerusalem). He argued that the altar originally stood in the courtyard of the building just to the left of the gate and that the rooms associated with it were intended to house animals that were to be offered. The excavators have responded that the placement of an altar in this location would restrict access to the rest of the building, and that the building in which Yadin proposed to place the altar was built in stratum II, *after* the altar had been dismantled (Herzog, Rainey, and Moshkovitz 1977: 56, 58).

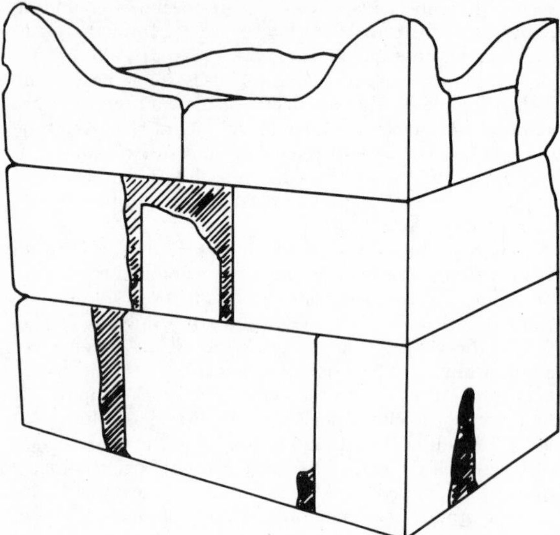

BEE.02. Reconstruction of horned altar from Beer-sheba.

Aharoni contends (1974a: 6; 1974b: 271) that the altar and temple were dismantled as part of the reforms of Hezekiah (i.e., 8th century; cf. 2 Kgs 18:22; Isa 36:7; 2 Chr 31:1; 32:12), and Amos 5:4–5 implies some sort of cultic significance connected with Beer-sheba in the decades prior to Hezekiah (see also Amos 8:14). The excavators point out parallels between stratum II pottery and the pottery from Lachish III and Arad VIII and argue that Beer-sheba II was destroyed by Sennacherib (ca. 701 B.C.). In the ruins of the stratum II gate was found a royal stamped store jar handle *(lmlk zyp).* One should not necessarily expect a reference in the annals of Sennacherib to the capture of Beer-sheba, since he summarizes his campaign by saying that he captured 46 fortified cities in Judah (*ANET,* 288), most of which remain unnamed.

Yadin, however, dates the end of stratum II a hundred years later. He points out some significant similarities between the Beer-sheba II ceramics and those of Lachish II (but see M. Aharoni 1977), which is attributed to the campaigns of Nebuchadnezzar in 586 B.C. (cf. also Holladay 1977). Kenyon (1976) suggests stratum II was destroyed sometime *between* the campaigns of Sennacherib and Nebuchadnezzar.

While it seems likely that Aharoni is correct in attributing the dismantling of the altar to the reforms of Hezekiah, a tension exists between the treatment of the temples at Beer-sheba and Arad. Aharoni describes an extensive dismantling operation in association with a temple at Beer-sheba, while for Arad, he (*ISBE* 1: 229) and others (Herzog, Aharoni, Rainey, and Moshkovitz 1984) affirm that only the sacrificial altar was buried—not only did the temple building at Arad escape a systematic dismantling in stratum VIII, but the "main hall and the 'Holy of Holies' of the temple continued to exist" (Herzog, Aharoni, Rainey, and Moshkovitz 1984: 19). One explanation might be that the "regional" site of Beer-sheba would deserve a more thorough reform than the site of Arad with its more localized shrine/temple. Another explanation might be that the Beer-sheba altar was not necessarily associated with a temple: it may simply have been an altar standing inside the city gate (similar to Yadin's suggestion) or elsewhere. It is of course possible that the temple with which the altar was associated was located elsewhere on the site and has simply not yet been discovered.

Regardless of the date and the agent, the Israelite city ended with a massive conflagration in which the buildings collapsed, burying hundreds of whole vessels and objects in the debris.

Stratum I. After its destruction, the site was refortified by repairing part of the casemate wall with a wall consisting of alternating layers of soil and small stones. Since no interior buildings have been found whose floors or walls join the wall system, questions are raised as to why the site was refortified. The excavators date this to the 7th century B.C. (Aharoni, ed. 1973: 8). Perhaps the main elements of the settlement at this time had moved W to the site along the wadi (i.e., Bîr es-Sebaᶜ), to which the Arad ostracon may refer (see above).

3. Post–Iron Age. The remains of Persian period Beer-sheba, as with most sites in Palestine, consisted of pits and silos, which have yielded some Aramaic ostraca dating from the mid-4th century. These refer to staple grains, while some also list Jewish, Edomite, and Arabic names.

Two centuries later, a small Hellenistic fort was constructed on the site. During the Herodian period, a large palace-like structure with accompanying service buildings (e.g., bathhouse) were built on the site. In the resurface of a courtyard of one of these Herodian buildings was found a coin of Caesar Augustus. During the 2d century A.D., a Roman fortress measuring ca. 30 by 30 m occupied the center of the tell. The site was essentially abandoned after the Roman period.

Bibliography

Aharoni, M. 1977. Some Observations on the Recent Article by Y. Yadin in *BASOR* 222. *BASOR* 225: 67–68.

Aharoni, M. and Aharoni, Y. 1976. The Stratification of Judahite Sites in the 8th and 7th Centuries B.C. *BASOR* 224: 73–90.

Aharoni, Y. ed. 1973. *Beer-sheba I.* Tel Aviv.

Aharoni, Y. 1968. Arad: Its Inscriptions and Temple. *BA* 31/1: 2–32.

———. 1972. Excavations at Tel Beer-sheba. *BA* 35/4: 111–27.

———. 1973. *Beer-sheba: The Excavation of a Biblical City.* New York.

———. 1974a. The Horned Altar of Beer-sheba. *BA* 37: 2–6.

———. 1974b. Notes and News: Tel Beersheba. *IEJ* 24: 270–72.

———. 1975. Excavations at Tel Beer-sheba. Preliminary Report of the Fifth and Sixth Seasons, 1973–1974. *TA* 2: 146–68.

———. 1976. Nothing Early and Nothing Late: Rewriting Israel's Conquest. *BA* 39: 55–76.

Dothan, M. 1959. Excavations at Horvat Beter (Beersheba). *ᶜAtigot* 2: 1–42.

Glueck, N. 1968. *Rivers in the Desert.* New York.

Gophna, R., and Yisraeli, Y. 1973. Soundings at Beer Sheba (Bir es-Sebaᶜ). Pp. 115–18 in *Beer-Sheba I,* ed. Y. Aharoni. Tel Aviv.

Herzog, Z., ed. 1984. *Beer-sheba II.* Tel Aviv.

Herzog, Z.; Rainey, A. F.; and Moshkovitz, S. 1977. The Stratigraphy of Beer-sheba and the Location of the Sanctuary. *BASOR* 225: 49–58.

Herzog, Z.; Aharoni, M.; Rainey, A. F.; and Moshkovitz, S. 1984. The Israelite Fortress at Arad. *BASOR* 254: 1–34.

Holladay, J. S., Jr. 1977. Review of *Beer-Sheba I,* ed. Y. Aharoni. *JBL* 96/2: 281–84.

Kenyon, K. M. 1976. Review of *Beer-Sheba I,* ed. Y. Aharoni. *PEQ* 108: 63–64.

Levy, T. E. 1986. The Chalcolithic Period. *BA* 49/2: 82–108.

Perrot, J. 1955a. The Excavations at Tell Abu Matar, near Beer-sheba. *IEJ* 5: 17–40.

———. 1955b. Notes and News: Beersheba, Bir es-Safadi. *IEJ* 5: 125–26.

———. 1956. Notes and News: Beersheba, Bir es-Safadi. *IEJ* 6: 126–27.

———. 1959. Notes and News: Bir es-Safadi. *IEJ* 9: 141–42.

———. 1960. Notes and News: Beersheba, Bir es-Safadi. *IEJ* 10: 120–21.

Rainey, A. F. 1974. Dust and Ashes. *TA* 1: 77–83, Pl. 16.

Robinson, G. L. 1901. The Wells of Beersheba. *Biblical World* 17: 247–55.

Yadin, Y. 1976. Beer-sheba: The High Place Destroyed by King Josiah. *BASOR* 222: 5–17.

Dale W. Manor

BEERA (PERSON) [Heb *bĕʾērāʾ*]. One of the descendants of Asher listed in the select genealogy which appears in 1 Chr 7:30–40. He is not included in the abbreviated genealogy of Asher found in Gen 46:17 and Num 26:44. Beera, whose name means "well" or "fountain," is mentioned nowhere else in Scripture. In fact, one-third of the names listed in Asher's genealogy in 1 Chronicles 7 are found only here, perhaps since Asher was a lesser tribe originating from the Jacob-Zilpah union. The Chronicler is content to give the names of Beera's brothers, father (Zopha), and grandfathers. Beyond this limited information little is known except that he is described as one of the "heads of fathers' houses, approved, mighty warriors, chief of the princes," in the line of Asher (7:40).

J. Randall O'Brien

BEERAH (PERSON) [Heb *bĕʾērâ*]. A Reubenite leader who was exiled by the Assyrians under Tiglath-pileser III (1 Chr 5:6). His name is cognate with a Hebrew word for "well" or "pit" *(bĕʾēr).* The genealogy in 1 Chr 5:1–10 begins with the names of Reuben's four sons, just as they are listed elsewhere (Gen 46:9; Exod 6:14; Num 26:5), but then it extends the genealogy with the names of Reubenites who are not mentioned elsewhere in the Bible. The additional names are set in two groups, and both are traced to Joel, whose relation to Reuben is not specified. In the Syriac and Arabic versions, however, this problem is resolved by replacing "Joel" with "Carmi," the name of one of Reuben's four sons.

The first list of names ends with Beerah, who occupies the seventh place in the sequence of Joel's descendants. This position in biblical genealogies is an important one (Sasson 1978), and in the present list Beerah is distinguished from the others by the comment that he was a leader in the tribe and was carried into exile by the Assyrians. The contrast between Reuben and Judah is striking in this passage: a "ruler" *(nāgîd),* viz., David, came from Judah (5:2), the favored tribe in Chronicles, but a "prince" *(nāśîʾ)* went away (into exile) from Reuben (5:6).

The kinsmen ("brothers") of Beerah comprise the second list of Joel's descendants (1 Chr 5:7–8), and it may be that the last of them (Jeiel, if not Zechariah and Bela as well) was regarded as a contemporary of Beerah. If this is the case, however, it is unclear why Jeiel was called "the chief" *(hārōʾš),* but Beerah "the prince" *(nāśîʾ).* Rudolph (*Chronikbücher* HAT, 44) resolves this difficulty by emending "his brothers" (*ʾeḥāyw*) to "later" *(ʾaḥar)* in v 7. It is also unclear, however, why the list of generations between Joel and Jeiel (5:7–8) is so much shorter (perhaps by as much as one-half) than that from Joel to Beerah (5:4–6).

Those who argue for the historical accuracy of the genealogy in 1 Chr 5:4–8 point to three considerations. First, the appearance of "Baal" as the name of Beerah's father (5:5) indicates an early date (8th century B.C.E.) and possibly an Israelite provenance for the genealogy. Second, the statement that Beerah was exiled by Tiglath-pileser III (5:6) is consistent with what is known about the history of the region during the Syro-Ephraimite War. Since Reubenite tribal lands were in Transjordan, probably extending north into Gilead, it is reasonable to believe that they were affected by the Assyrian capture of Galilee and Gilead ca. 733 B.C.E. (2 Kgs 15:29; 1 Chr 5:26). Third, the claim that Reubenites dwelt "in Aroer, as far as Nebo, and Baal-meon" reflects accurate knowledge of the period before Moab's conquest of the area, viz., before 850 B.C.E. (Myers *1 Chronicles* AB, 36–37).

Nevertheless, it should be remembered that Beerah's genealogy is fragmentary (it goes back only to Joel and is not attached to Reuben or his sons), has internal inconsistencies (Beerah's relationship to Jeiel), and may reflect more of the author's theology than accurate historical recollection (the reference to the exile of Beerah and the Reubenites by the Assyrians may be an expression of the later idea that all ten northern tribes were exiled [Coggins *1 and 2 Chronicles* CBC, 36; Braun *1 Chronicles* WBC, 70–75]).

Bibliography

Sasson, J. M. 1978. A Genealogical "Convention" in Biblical Chronography. *ZAW* 90: 171–85.

M. PATRICK GRAHAM

BEERI (PERSON) [Heb *bĕʾērî*]. The name of two men mentioned in the OT. "Beeri" is most often understood to mean "of a well" or (taking the ending as a pronominal suffix) "my well" (*IPN,* 224).

1. The Hittite father of Esau's wife Judith (Gen 26:34).

2. The father of the prophet Hosea (Hos 1:1). The Rabbis identified him with Beerah, a Reubenite chief whom Tiglath-Pileser sent into exile (1 Chr 5:6). However, there is no evidence to support the identification, nor do we have any other information about Hosea's father.

CAROLYN J. PRESSLER

BEEROTH (PLACE) [Heb *bĕʾērôt*]. BEEROTHITE. A town in the territory of Benjamin (Josh 18:25). Beeroth was one of the four Hivite cities whose inhabitants deceived Israel, making peace with Joshua on the pretense that they were from a distant land (Josh 9:17). The inhabitants of Beeroth and the other three Hivite towns (Gibeon, Kiriath-jearim, and Chephirah) were thus spared annihilation and were allowed to live among the Israelites as woodcutters and water carriers (Josh 9:26–27). All four towns were incorporated into the tribal territory of Benjamin (Josh 18:25–28; 2 Sam 4:2). Later, Saul, a Benjaminite himself, attempted to eliminate the non-Israelite population living within the territory of Benjamin, specifically the Gibeonites, and presumably the inhabitants of Beeroth as well (2 Sam 21:2, 5). It was probably at this time that many of the people of Beeroth fled to Gittaim (2 Sam 4:3). This persecution may explain why it was two Beerothites, Recab and Baanah, who assassinated Saul's son Ish-bosheth (2 Sam 4:2–7; contra McCarter, *2 Sam* AB, 127–28). Another Beerothite, Naharai (perhaps one of those who were "in distress or in debt or discontented" under Saul's oppressive rule; 1 Sam 22:2), joined David and became a soldier in David's elite unit of fighting men, "The Thirty," serving as Joab's armor bearer (2 Sam 23:37; 1 Chr 11:39). The inhabitants of Beeroth and the other Hivite cities appear to have eventually assimilated into the population; they represent a significant percentage of the Jews who returned from exile (Ezra 2:25; Neh 7:29).

Whether biblical Beeroth is identical with the site known from 1 Macc 9:4 and from later Arabic and Crusader sources as Bereth, Berea, and el-Bireh is uncertain (see Goldstein *1 Macc* AB, 372–74; Avi-Yonah 1949: 89 and map; 1977: 123; ed-Dîn, 1897 ed. 394; Le Strange 1965: 423).

The location of Beeroth is disputed. The confusion goes back at least as early as Eusebius, who in his *Onomasticon* (48.9–10) mentions a village of his day named Beeroth, which he identifies with the OT town that was "under [Gk *hypo*] Gibeon." He states that the village is reached from the 7th milestone on the road from Jerusalem to Nicopolis (Emmaus). This statement would seem to place Beeroth either in the general vicinity of Kiriath-jearim, W of Jerusalem, or near el-Jib, NW of Jerusalem. Jerome, however, in his Latin translation of the *Onomasticon* (49.8–9), records "Neapolis" instead of "Nicopolis," which would place Beeroth between Ramah and el-Bireh, N of Jerusalem. He also renders Eusebius' description *sub colle Gabaon* "under the hill of Gibeon," which seems to miss the political intention of Eusebius' expression (cf. the same phrase under *Chepheira, Chefira* [172.15; 173.22], which Jerome renders *vicus ad civitatem pertinens Gabaon;* see Abel *GP* 2, 262).

Edward Robinson (1867: 452–53) was the first modern scholar to propose that Beeroth be identified with el-Bireh (M.R. 170146), the town E of Ramallah dominating the road from Jerusalem to Nablus at the point where the road reaches the N ridge of the Benjamin plateau. He argued that this site not only has toponymic support but fits Eusebius' description: "el-Bireh can be seen on the right at about 7 miles distance from Jerusalem as one travels to Emmaus via el-Jib." Albright (1923: 114ff.; 1924: 90–111) suggested that T. en-Nasbeh (M.R. 170143), S of el-Bireh, is a better candidate because it is closer to Jerome's mileage from Jerusalem. After Elihu Grant (1926: 187ff.) found walls and pottery from the Bronze Age at el-Bireh (at Ras et-Tahuneh, in the center of town), however, scholars returned to Robinson's identification despite the fact that el-Bireh is 9 Roman miles, not 7, from Jerusalem (Alt 1926; Beyer 1930; Elliger 1935: 62; O'Callaghan 1951; cf. Avi-Yonah 1949: 89 and map; *EncMiqr* 2: 8–9; 1977: 123). Subsequently, the 1967–68 survey (Kochavi 1972: 178) confirmed the archaeological significance of el-Bireh, finding EB, MB, and much Iron Age I–II pottery there.

Aharoni (1962: 183), still troubled by the discrepancy with Eusebius' mileage, suggested (and then abandoned) an identification with Nebi Samwil (M.R. 167137), NW of Jerusalem. Noth (1971: 143–44), on the other hand, placed Beeroth at el-Jib (M.R. 167139), thus satisfying Eusebius' specifications, and then transferred Gibeon to el-Bireh.

Yeivin (1971: 142–44) has suggested an identification at Kh. el-Burj (M.R. 167136), a small site just S of Nebi

Samwil. His main argument is topographical and geometrical: with Beeroth here, the four Hivite cities would form an almost perfect rectangle situated on the border between Benjamin and Judah (the latter part of this assertion is not actually correct). Yeivin found Iron Age (but no Bronze Age) pottery at the site. He suggests that the name *Beeroth* is preserved at nearby Kh. el-Biyar (M.R. 169137), a later Roman and Byzantine site about a mile E of Kh. el-Burj (Arabic *biyar,* like Hebrew *bĕʾērôt,* can mean "wells"); instances of Arabic place names that are translations of earlier Hebrew toponyms, though rare, are attested elsewhere. Yeivin's identification has been accepted by a number of scholars (Aharoni *LBHG,* 431; McCarter, *2 Sam* AB, 123; et al.).

The most serious weakness of this latter identification is that it does not conform to Eusebius' description; Kh. el-Burj and Kh. el-Biyar are located about 4 Roman miles from Jerusalem, not 7. The 7th milestone would have been in the area between el-Jib and the top of the Beth-horon descent, far beyond any logical turnoff for Kh. el-Biyar (although this might be explained by the fact that Eusebius was working with a schematized and thus partially distorted road map). Moreover, Kh. el-Burj is a surprisingly small ruin (just over an acre) to represent a relatively important Iron Age town. Additionally, the nearby place name "Khirbet el-Biyar" is not necessarily significant; it is a very common designation for ruins throughout Palestine. *Yalqut Hapirsumim* (Biran 1964) lists at least six ancient sites so named within pre-1967 Israel alone; and in fact the British surveyors (Conder and Kitchener 1880) recorded a site by the same name E of el-Jib (and none in the vicinity of Khirbet el-Burj).

A number of other sites have been proposed but have not received a wide following (see the list in Press 1951, I: 59–60, n. 2).

At present, therefore, the site of biblical Beeroth remains a matter of dispute. The most likely candidate would still seem to be the one originally proposed by Robinson, i.e., el-Bireh.

Bibliography

Abel, F. M. 1924. Topographie des Campagnes Machabéennes. *RB* 33: 371–87.

Aharoni, Y. 1962. *The Land of Israel in Biblical Times.* Jerusalem (in Hebrew).

Albright, W. F. 1923. The Site of Mizpah in Benjamin. *JPOS* 3: 110–21.

———. 1924. Mizpah and Beeroth. *AASOR* 4: 90–111.

———. 1929. New Israelite and Pre-Israelite Settlements. *BASOR* 35: 1–14.

Alt, A. 1926. Gibeon und Beeroth. *PJ* 22: 11–22.

Avi-Yonah, M. 1949. *Historical Geography of Eretz Israel from the End of the Babylonian Exile up to the Arab Conquest.* Jerusalem (in Hebrew).

———. 1977. *The Holy Land from the Persian to the Arab Conquests (536 B.C. to A.D. 640).* Rev. ed. Grand Rapids.

Beyer, G. 1930. Eusebius über Gibeon und Beeroth. *ZDPV* 53: 209–11.

Biran, A., director. 1964. *Yalqut Hapirsumim* (No. 1091). Registry list of antiquity sites in Israel. Jerusalem.

Conder, C. R., and Kitchener, H. H. 1880. *Map of Western Palestine in 26 Sheets.* London.

ed-Dîn, Behâ (Yusuf ibn Rafi). 1897 ed. *The Life of Saladin.* London.

Elliger, K. 1957. Beeroth und Gibeon. *ZDPV* 73: 125–32.

Grant, E. 1926. Ramallah: Signs of the Early Occupation of This and Other Sites. *PEFQS* 58: 186–95.

Kallai-Kleinmann, Z. 1954. An Attempt to Determine the Location of Beeroth. *EI* 3:111–15 (in Hebrew).

Kochavi, M. ed. 1972. *Judaea, Samaria and the Golan: Archaeological Survey 1967–1968.* Jerusalem (in Hebrew).

Le Strange, G. 1965. *Palestine under the Moslems.* Beirut.

Noth, M. 1971. *Das Buch Josua.* Tübingen.

O'Callaghan, R. 1951. Is Beeroth on the Madeba Map? *Biblica* 32: 57–64.

Press, I. 1948–55. *Eretz Israel: A Topographical-Historical Encyclopedia.* 4 vols. Jerusalem (in Hebrew).

Robinson, E. 1867. *Biblical Researches in Palestine and the Adjacent Regions.* 3d ed. 3 vols. London. Repr. 1970.

Yeivin, S. 1971. The Benjaminite Settlement in the Western Part of Their Territory. *IEJ* 21: 141–54.

David A. Dorsey

BEEROTH BENE-JAAKAN (PLACE) [Heb *bĕʾērōt bĕnê yaʿăqān*]. Translated as the "wells of the sons of Jaakan," this is a place where the people of Israel camped during the wilderness period (Deut 10:6). The claim to water rights for a particular clan is not unusual among tribesmen in the arid zone. This site is said to be near the border of Edom (Jaakan's appearance in the genealogical clan list of Seir the Horite in 1 Chr 1:42 strengthens this identification) and may possibly be associated with Birein, about 6 miles S of el-ʿAuja (or Nessana, M.R. 095031). Aaron is said to have died and been buried while they camped here. An orderly succession of the priesthood is also noted with Aaron's son Eleasar ministering "in his stead." The site is simply referred to as Bene-Jaakan in Num 33:31–32.

Victor H. Matthews

BEESHTERAH (PLACE) [Heb *bĕʿĕstĕrâ*]. Var. ASHTAROTH. A town located in the tribal territory of Manasseh, listed as one of the Levitical cities (Josh 21:27). However, in the parallel passage in 1 Chr 6:56 (—Eng 6:71) there is a city named Ashtaroth (Heb *ʿaštārôt*), which may perhaps have been the same place as Beeshterah. See ASHTAROTH (PLACE). The discrepancy between the Joshua list and the Chronicles list must be interpreted as variations on the same name. The *ʿštr* element is common to both, and there is little doubt that the Chronicler has correctly preserved the name of this Levitical city, which was named after the Canaanite fertility goddess, Ashtart.

Beeshterah/Ashtaroth has been identified with Tell ʿAshtarah (M.R. 243244), although there are some difficulties with this identification. About 6 km to the S of Tell ʿAshtarah is Tell el-Ashʿari. Albright (1925) argued that there was no connection between the names ʿAshtaroth and Ashʿari; however, there continue to be suggestions of possible identity.

Tell ʿAshtarah is located on the King's Highway, known in the N as "The Way of Bashan." Another great trade route, the Via Maris, joins the King's Highway at Tell ᶜAshtarah. They have been no excavations at Tell ᶜAshtarah, and only a surface survey was conducted by Albright in the 1920s. He identified there pottery from the EB, MB, LB periods, as well as from the first two phases of the Iron Age (1200–900 B.C.). In the 1930s A. Biran applied the principles of textual criticism to the problem of the identification of the site, and argued that even at the height of the Solomonic empire, the N boundary in Transjordan did not extend beyond the Yarmuk (Bergman 1936). While the 9th-century Israelite king, Ahab, did not rule any further N than Ramoth-gilead (1 Kings 22), Jeroboam did control the N Transjordan area (2 Kgs 14:23; Amos 6:13) during his reign in the 8th century.

Bibliography

Albright, W. F. 1925. Bronze Age Mounds in Northern Palestine and the Hauran: the Spring Trip of the School in Jerusalem. *BASOR* 19: 5–19.

———. 1945. The List of Levitic Cities. Pp. 49–73 in *Louis Ginzberg Jubilee Volume on the Occasion of His Seventieth Birthday.* New York.

Bergman (Biran), A. 1936. The Israelite Tribe of the Half-Manasseh. *JPOS* 16: 224–54.

JOHN L. PETERSON

BEIT MIRSIM, TELL (M.R. 141096). An 8-acre mound in the S Hebron hills, just at the juncture of the hill country and the N Shephelah, 15 miles SW of Hebron. It lies at almost 500 m above sea level, rising steeply to dominate the small wadi.

Tell Beit Mirsim was identified by Albright with biblical Debir/Kiriath-sepher, largely on the basis of the reference in Josh 15:16–19 (= Judg 1:11–15), especially the mention of *gullôt mayîm.* Albright rendered this not as "springs," much less "wells," but as "water basins," i.e., underground reservoirs, which he thought characterized Tell Beit Mirsim, but no other site in the vicinity (cf. Albright 1967; *EAEHL* 1:171–78). When his own excavations in the years 1926–1932 revealed a late 13th century B.C. destruction, he connected this with Joshua's conquest of Debir (Josh 10:38) and regarded this as confirmation of his identification. More recently, however, M. Kochavi, A. Rainey, Y. Aharoni, and others have revived Galling's proposal that Khirbet Rabûd (M.R. 151093), seven miles SW of Hebron, is a better candidate for Debir/Kiriath-sepher (Kochavi 1974). Not only does Khirbet Rabûd suit the biblical references to the Judaean hill country better, it also has *gullôt* (i.e., "cisterns," contra Albright) in abundance. Finally it was a major LB Canaanite site, with an Israelite reoccupation (although no destruction) in the Iron Age. If Tell Beit Mirsim is thus not Debir/Kiriath-sepher, its identification remains unknown.

Albright's excavations at Tell Beit Mirsim, although small-scale, were far in advance of most archaeological fieldwork in Palestine up to that time, due largely to his own unparalleled mastery of ceramic chronology and the breadth of his scholarship. The prompt publication of the final reports volumes (Albright 1932, 1933, 1938, 1943) made Tell Beit Mirsim the "type-site" for both Palestinian and "biblical" archaeology from the 1930s well into the 1980s. Although later advances in stratigraphic methods revealed that Albright's excavation techniques were more intuitive and more ceramically influenced than formerly supposed, the chronological scheme that he worked out at Tell Beit Mirsim was amazingly precise for that period. Indeed, it still provides our basic framework for Palestinian archaeology.

Since the Tell Beit Mirsim excavations were relatively well done, and the results have been summarized elsewhere many times (i.e., Albright 1967; *EAEHL* 1:111–78), we shall focus here only on the highlights and on more recent scholarship.

Albright had dated the site's founding in stratum J to his "Early Bronze IIIB" period, ca. 2300 B.C. (our current EB IVA). Thus he thought it a unique settlement site in an otherwise non-urban period when most Palestinian tells were abandoned. However, more recent analysis of the unpublished pottery (Dever and Richard 1977) has shown that the basal stratum J materials are mixed and that the earliest occupation must extend from our present EB II into EB III, ca. 3000–2400 B.C. However, the later phase of our EB IV period, phase C (Albright's old "Middle Bronze I"; cf. Dever 1980; now ca. 2200–2000 B.C.), is well represented in strata I–H. Two occupied caves in area H produced good quantities of EB IVC pottery (Dever's "Family S" repertoire; 1980). Albright's claim that a city wall must have existed, even though he had not found one, must be rejected in light of our current knowledge of the overwhelmingly non-urban EB IV period. He was undoubtedly influenced by the notion that his "Middle Bronze I" was the precursor of the Middle Bronze Age proper.

The true Middle Bronze Age (Albright's MB IIA–C, our current MB I–III) is well documented in three main phases at Tell Beit Mirsim, strata G–F, E, and D. Albright had originally placed the *terre pisé* embankment and subsequent(?) masonry "battered wall" in strata G–F, which he dated ca. 1900–1750 B.C. (see Albright 1967). This has been challenged by Yadin, who sought to place *all* the characteristic Middle Bronze defenses in the second phase, Albright's Middle Bronze IIB (i.e., stratum E at Tell Beit Mirsim; Yadin 1973). Most authorities of today nevertheless hold that city walls and gates begin at many sites early in the period, in our MB I, but the exact date of the Tell Beit Mirsim fortifications remains a problem. In his last treatment (EAEHL 1, published 1975, written before 1971), Albright seems to hesitate between a strata G–F and an early stratum E assignment.

In any case, the MB strata, especially stratum D (the latest), exhibit a strongly urban character, with a well laid-out town plan, successive phases of building and rebuilding, and several fine "patrician villas." The cemetery of this (and other periods) has not been located, but good quantities of domestic pottery and other objects testify to a significant degree of technological and aesthetic sophistication. A destruction marks the end of stratum D, as at most sites, no doubt connected with the Egyptian campaigns following the expulsion of the Hyksos from Egypt ca. 1540 B.C. Albright's date of ca. 1540 needs to be lowered only slightly. A gap in occupation follows throughout LB I.

Stratum C_{1-2} belongs to the LB II, ca. 1400–1200 B.C. Albright's reconstruction of a town in decline, destroyed toward the end, needs no major revision. The city wall is poorly rebuilt. Mycenaean and Cypriot imports are attested in the pottery but cease at the end of the period, as elsewhere in Palestine. Albright posited an Israelite destruction at the end of stratum C, dating it ca. 1220 B.C. on the basis of what he held was the contemporary fall of Lachish just after the "fourth year of Merneptah." But today the destruction of Lachish VI must be dated to the time of Rameses III or later (ca. 1150 B.C.); and if Tell Beit Mirsim is not Debir/Kiriath-sepher (above) the biblical tradition of destruction there is irrelevant. Information on the destruction is scant, in any case.

It is clear, however, that stratum B, with three successive phases (B_1, B_2, B_3), belongs to Iron I, ca. 1200–900 B.C. Albright always made much of this sequence and adopted it for nearly the whole of Palestine. He understood the Tell Beit Mirsim phasing as follows:

Str. B_1: Brief "squatter occupation," marked only by pits and silos, with degenerate local LB/Iron I pottery, ca. 1225–1175 B.C.; *early Israelite* occupation following the destruction.

Str. B_2: Quantities of Philistine Bichrome ware; *Philistine occupation,* ca. 1175–1020 B.C., during their rise to power.

Str. B_3: Casemate city wall, predominance of red-slipped and hand-burnished pottery; *Israelite reoccupation,* ca. 1020–920 B.C., specifically Davidic-Solomonic; possibly destroyed by Shishak ca. 918 B.C.

It seems obvious that this reconstruction is largely based on presuppositions regarding ceramic sequences and distributions, notions of biblical tradition and early Israelite history, and factors in cultural change, all of which might be (and have been) challenged more recently (Greenberg 1987). Few scholars would be so sanguine today, and Albright himself made some adjustments in his last résumé (i.e., 1975). All that is clear is that by the mid–late 10th century B.C., Tell Beit Mirsim was a rather typical Israelite site. Certainly the B_1–B_3 sequence is no longer adaptable to the majority of Iron I sites in Palestine.

Stratum A_{1-2} dates to the period of the Divided Monarchy, ca. 918–587 B.C. Albright thought that stratum A_1, poorly attested because of the continuous occupational buildup into A_2, might have been destroyed in the raid of Sennacherib in 701 B.C. Str. A_2, the surface stratum, was cleared extensively in the W and SE quadrants, so that we have a substantial town plan, with many "four-room" houses, a casemate wall, and (apparently) an offset-entrance two-entryway gate. A "west gate and tower" structure has been compared to the Assyrian-style *bit ḫilani,* although this is uncertain. Also found were several buildings containing pierced stone drums that Albright interpreted as "dying vats" and took as evidence for a local textile industry, but they might as easily be connected with olive oil pressing.

Albright dated the destruction of stratum A_2 to the Babylonian conquest in 587 B.C., citing in particular a seal impression of "Eliakim, Steward of Yaukin" and assuming that this was the same person as Jehoiachin the penultimate king of Judah. He also compared the pottery to stratum III at Lachish, which he dated not to ca. 701 (with Tufnell and others) but to ca. 598 B.C. Today, however, the almost universal consensus is that Lachish III was indeed destroyed by Sennacherib (Ussishkin 1977). So presumably the date of Tell Beit Mirsim A_2—and therefore all other "late Judean" levels dated by comparisons with Tell Beit Mirsim A_2—must be raised by about a century, even though that leaves the 7th century B.C. largely unattested on present evidence. As though to corroborate the higher date, Cross has now shown that the proper context of the famous "Yaukin" impression is during the reign of Hezekiah in the 8th century B.C.

In conclusion, many of Albright's confident assertions about Tell Beit Mirsim's history and its implications for Palestinian archaeology and biblical history (thus 1967: 218, 219; *EAEHL* 1: 178) have had to be modified. That does not, however, lessen the importance of the site or minimize Albright's pioneering achievements there.

Bibliography

Albright, W. F. 1932. *The Excavation of Tell Beit Mirsim I. The Pottery of the First Three Campaigns.* AASOR 12. New Haven.

———. 1933. *The Excavation of Tell Beit Mirsim IA. The Bronze Age Pottery of the Fourth Campaign.* AASOR 13. New Haven.

———. 1938. *The Excavation of Tell Beit Mirsim II. The Bronze Age.* AASOR 17. New Haven.

———. 1943. *The Excavation of Tell Beit Mirsim III. The Iron Age.* AASOR 21–22. New Haven.

———. 1967. Debir. Pp. 207–20 in *Archaeology and Old Testament Study,* ed. D. W. Thomas. Oxford.

Dever, W. G. 1980. New Vistas on the EB IV ("MB I") Horizon in Syria. Palestine. *BASOR* 237: 35–64.

Dever, W. G., and Richard, S. 1977. A Reevaluation of Tell Beit Mirsim J. *BASOR* 226: 1–14.

Greenberg, R. 1987. New Light on the Early Iron Age at Tell Beit Mirsim. *BASOR* 265: 55–80.

Kochavi, M. 1974. Khirbet Rabûd = Debir. *TA* 1: 2–33.

Ussishkin, D. 1977. The Destruction of Lachish by Sennacherib and the Dating of the Royal Judean Storage Jars. *TA* 4: 28–60.

Yadin, Y. 1973. The Tell Beit Mirsim G–F Alleged Fortifications. *BASOR* 212: 22–25.

WILLIAM G. DEVER

BEIT RAS (M.R. 230222). One of the cities of the DECAPOLIS, known in Roman times as Capitolias.

A. Name and Identification
B. History of Research
C. History of Settlement

A. Name and Identification

The modern village of Beit Ras, Roman Capitolias, is located five km N of Irbid in Jordan. The *ras* ("peak," "hilltop") is the highest point (ca. 600 m above sea level) N of the ʿAjlun mountain range. From the *ras,* the Wadi ʿArab, its tributaries, and fertile agricultural lands are clearly seen to the W. The Romans founded a city around the *ras* and named it after Jupiter Capitolinus. The Latin name is a Roman adaptation of the Semitic name which already existed and matched the geographical situation of the settlement: *Bayt Râs,* the "settlement on/of the hilltop." The Semitic name is not attested before the middle of the

6th century A.D. (Lenzen and Knauf 1987). It is inconceivable that the site had no name prior to the foundation of Capitolias—the two words *bayt* and *ras* are Aramaic as well as Arabic.

The identification of Beit Ras with the Decapolis city of Capitolias was established by F. Kruse and H. L. Fleischer (1859: 185–87). U. J. Seetzen, one of the earliest 19th-century explorers in N Jordan, visited Beit Ras in 1806. While he was specifically looking for the ruins of Capitolias, he failed to identify Beit Ras with Capitolias.

B. History of Research

After Seetzen (1854: 371), Beit Ras was visited by Buckingham (in 1816), who described it as a permanently occupied settlement (1827: 350). The first plan of the site and its ruins was drawn and published by Schumacher in 1878–79 (1890: 154). S. Merrill, N. Glueck, and S. Mittmann each visited the site and recorded inscriptions and surface finds (Merrill 1881; Glueck 1951; Mittmann 1970). Archaeological excavations have been conducted at the site since the 1960s by the Department of Antiquities of Jordan, and are currently being conducted by a joint group (Lenzen fc.; Lenzen and Gordon fc.; Lenzen, Gordon, and McQuitty 1985; Lenzen and Knauf 1986; 1987; Shraideh and Lenzen 1985).

C. History of Settlement

There is minimal archaeological evidence for occupation before the 1st century A.D. The 1984 survey produced only two shards which could be dated to the 2d–1st centuries B.C. Excavations have provided some body shards which may date to pre-300 B.C.; i.e., the end of the Iron Age. However, all these shards have been found in post-Iron Age contexts. It is unlikely that there was an earlier city, but it may have been used as a lookout.

According to coins issued from 165/6 through 218/19 A.D., it can be calculated that the city was founded in 97/98. It is unclear, however, whether Nerva or Trajan was responsible for its establishment. The main temple of the city, which is represented on coins, was dedicated to Jupiter Capitolinus (Piccirillo and Spijkerman 1978: 96–97). Claudius Ptolemaeus, a mid-2d century A.D. Alexandrian geographer, mentioned Capitolias as belonging to the Decapolis (Lenzen and Knauf 1987). With the establishment of Provincia Arabia in 106 A.D., Capitolias was included in Palaestina Secunda. This did not change until the end of the 6th century.

The Roman city was walled and, according to the numismatic and epigraphic evidence, reached the peak of its prosperity in the 2d–3d centuries. A Nabatean inscription attests to the presence of a non-Greek acculturated population group. Archaeological evidence of Roman occupation includes massive foundation walls for large public buildings (at least one of them a temple), vaults, and a large cistern system surrounding the site.

From ca. 300 to 525, Beit Ras/Capitolias grew in importance within its own region as well as within the larger Byzantine world. The city was represented at the Council of Nicea (325) and at the Council of Chalcedon (451). The complex identified as a "church" by Schumacher was, based on the 1985 excavations, a market area *(suq)*. Archaeological data points to an intensive buildup of the central part of the village from the 4th century through the present, with a possible hiatus in the mid-9th to mid-10th centuries.

According to Hierocles (535) and Georgius Cyprius (575) Beit Ras remained part of Palaestina Secunda. But according to the deacon or archdeacon Theodosius, who compiled a Latin pilgrim's guide to Palestine during the reign of Anastasius (491–518 A.D.) or shortly after that, it belonged to Arabia (Lenzen and Knauf 1987). Beit Ras/Capitolias was integrated into Arabia in the course of the 6th century. It is tempting to identify the *suq* mentioned by the poet an-Nabigha adh-Dhubyani (569) with the recently excavated vaulted area, used as a center of commerce from the 6th through the 9th centuries. The special quality of the Beit Ras wine was well known in Medinah in the days of Mohammad, as is attested by two lines from Mohammad's poet laureate, Hassan b. Thabit. The integration of the Jadar-Beit Ras region into Arabia at the end of the 6th and the beginning of the 7th century meant that the Islamic conquest was not a major affair from the point of view of the inhabitants. According to tradition Beit Ras capitulated to Shurahbil b. Hasana at the beginning of the conquests (Hitti 1914). The flourishing economy of the city continued throughout the Umayyad period.

Bibliography

Buckingham, J. S. 1827. *Reisen durch Syrien und Palaestina.* Vol. 45. Weimar.

Glueck, N. 1951. *Explorations in Eastern Palestine IV.* AASOR 25–28. New Haven.

Hitti, P. K. 1916. The Origins of the Islamic State. Ph.D. diss., Columbia.

Kruse, F., and Fleischer, H. L. 1859. *Commentare zu Ulrich Jasper Seetzen's Reisen durch Syrien, Palästina, Phönizien, die Transjordan-Länder, Arabia Petraea und Unter-Aegypten.* Berlin.

Lenzen, C. J. 1986. Tell Irbid and Bait Ras. *AfO* 33: 164–66.

———. fc. Food Processing and Its Pottery: Two Case Studies from Northern Jordan. *ZDPV.*

Lenzen, C. J., and Gordon, R. L. fc. Rescue Excavations at Beit Ras, 1986. *ADAJ.*

Lenzen, C. J.; Gordon, R. L.; and McQuitty, A. M. 1985. Excavations at Tell Irbid and Beit Ras, 1985. *ADAJ* 29: 151–59.

Lenzen, C. J., and Knauf, E. A. 1986. Tell Irbid and Beit Ras, 1983–1986. *LA* 36.

———. 1987. Beit Ras-Capitolias. A Preliminary Evaluation of the Archaeological and Textual Evidence. *Syr* 64: 21–46.

Merrill, S. 1881. *East of the Jordan.* London.

Mittmann, S. 1970. *Beiträge zur Siedlungs- und Territorial geschichte des nördlichen Ostjordanlandes.* Wiesbaden.

Piccirillo, M., and Spijkerman, A. 1978. *The Coins of the Decapolis and Provincia Arabia.* Jerusalem.

Seetzen, U. J. 1854. *Ulrich Jasper Seetzen's Reisen durch Syrien, Palaestina, Phoenicien, die Transjordan-Laender, Arabia Petraea und Unter-Aegypten.* Vol. 1. Ed. F. Kruse. Berlin.

Schumacher, G. 1890. *Northern ʿAjlun "Within the Decapolis."* London.

Shraideh, S., and Lenzen, C. J. 1985. Rescue Excavations at Beit Ras. *ADAJ* 29: 291–92.

C. J. LENZEN

BEITIN, TELL (M.R. 172148). Since Edward Robinson's proposal in 1938 (based both on linguistic grounds and biblical references [Gen 12:8; Judg 2:19; etc.]), biblical Bethel has been identified with Beitin, 8 miles N of Jerusalem.

The full extent of the ancient site, now largely covered by the modern village, is unknown, but some four acres were available for soundings when the site was first investigated by W. F. Albright in 1927. Following that, Albright directed excavations in 1934, followed by campaigns under James L. Kelso in 1954, 1957, and 1960.

The preliminary reports (Albright 1934a, 1934b, 1935, 1939; Kelso 1955, 1958, 1961) and final reports (Kelso 1968), the final volume in particular, offer some far ranging conclusions, but little of the evidence on which they are presumably based. There are, for example, few complete plans, no usable sections, no stratum numbers—in short, little real data. Therefore the following summary must be brief and very tentative.

Although there are scattered Late Chalcolithic-EB I–III sherds, the real occupational history of Bethel begins in the EB IV, ca. 2200–2000 B.C. (Albright's "Middle Bronze I"). The published pottery is rather late in the period, belonging to Dever's "Family S" (= southern/sedentary; 1980). Kelso (1968: 20–23) claimed to have found a "temple" belonging to the EB IV, associated with "butchering flints" and "bloodstains"; he even ventured to connect this with the biblical traditions concerning the Patriarchs at Bethel. Yet a closer examination of the evidence as published shows that the EB IV "temple" is nothing other than the foundation courses of an MB structure described as a "city gate" (below), the "butchering flints" are simply typical degenerate Canaanean blades of the period. In fact, Bethel was no more than a typical pastoral nomadic encampment in EB IV (Dever 1971; 1980).

The MB (ca. 2000–1500 B.C.) is said to be represented by a city wall and gate, but the details of both are unclear. The published plan of the "gate" is incomprehensible, and the city walls are scarcely even described. A so-called "sanctuary" and "temple" are obviously well-constructed buildings, but their function is far from certain. The range of MB occupation seems to extend throughout MB I–III (Albright's MB IIA–C), but the published pottery is mostly from the last phase of the period, suggesting that most of the structures should be placed there. A destruction is claimed at the end of the MB, ca. 1550 B.C., but again little evidence is presented.

After a gap in occupation in LB I, Bethel was reoccupied in LB II (ca. 1400–1200 B.C.). The final reports and summaries describe "patrician houses," flagstone pavements, and elaborate drainage systems—"the finest architectural phase in the city's history" (Kelso *EAEHL* 1: 192). A severe destruction at the end of the LB is attributed to the Israelites (based on the biblical tradition), but no justification for this conclusion is offered. Indeed, the published description (Kelso 1968: 30, 31; 47–49) does not offer much direct, detailed evidence for such a destruction, beyond such unsupported statements as "a terrific conflagration completely wiped out the Canaanite city . . ."; or "points where the Israelites had breached the walls"; or "the thickest ash levels yet reported in Palestine." Much has been made of the "Israelite destruction" at Bethel, perhaps now one of only two possible candidates for evidence of an Israelite invasion (the other being Hazor; see ISRAEL, HISTORY OF [ARCHAEOLOGY AND THE ISRAELITE "CONQUEST"]). But the historian or biblical scholar seeking to check the evidence will find the final report unuseable (indeed almost a parade example of the interpretative problems typical of the "Biblical archaeology" movement, especially Kelso 1968: 47–49).

The four Iron I levels are said to represent a cultural decline compared to the LB period. The most characteristic feature is probably the typical "four-room" or pillar-courtyard house, but no complete structure is published, much less any indication of the village plan. The Iron I village appears to have been unfortified and possibly built over part of the abandoned Bronze Age city wall. The pottery as published suggests that phases 1–4 date to the 12th–late 10th centuries B.C. The earliest phases have few Philistine shards, the ceramic repertoire being more typical of what we would now regard as the initial "Israelite occupation" of the central hill country. Particularly diagnostic are collar-rim storejars, cooking pots with short triangular rims, carinated bowls, and everted-rim kraters.

The full range of the Iron II period (ca. 900–600 B.C.) is apparently represented, but the few published building remains of phases 1–3 are unexceptional. No defenses are reported. A 9th century B.C. "South Arabian" stamp impression is used as evidence for trade, but questions have been raised as to its authenticity (cf. Van Beek and Jamme 1970, and references there). Bethel seems to have escaped destruction in the early 6th century B.C. Babylonian campaigns. Indeed, its relatively large quantity of 6th century B.C. pottery constitutes a rare corpus for the "Iron III" or early Persian period in Palestine (see L. A. Sinclair in Kelso 1968: 70–76; and cf. J. S. Holladay in Dever 1971).

The Hellenistic, Roman, and Byzantine periods are known from literary sources. Three phases of Hellenistic occupation were found in the excavations, said to range from the late 4th–2d centuries B.C. But P. W. Lapp's publication of the pottery (in Kelso 1968: 77–80) narrows this to late 3d–2d centuries B.C. Ptolemaic and Seleucid coins confirm these dates in general.

For the Roman period, Herodian shards, but no coins, provide evidence, as do domestic remains and numerous cisterns. Byzantine and Islamic shards attest to still later occupation, but only the former is characterized by substantial architecture, including a street, a city gate, a church, and a large reservoir. Bethel's occupation seems to end early in the Islamic period.

Bethel was probably one of the more prominent Bronze-Iron Age towns in central Palestine, and it is also significant in biblical history. Yet the excavations as carried out and published allow us to do no more than sketch the archaeological history of the site, and even that with little precision or confidence in any single detail. The exposure was inadequate, the results of the various seasons are poorly coordinated (there are no stratum numbers), and the description of the successive phases is minimal and sparsely illustrated. Still more serious is the lack of any research design, save the apparent notion of "illuminating the Bible" in some way or another. Albright's early work in 1934 may have been adequate for the time, but the later excavations (and the final publication) are marred by transparent biases, as well as by an embarrassing naïveté. Fact and interpretation are so entangled throughout the final report that few real data emerge for the archaeologist, historian, or biblical scholar (cf. Dever 1971).

Bibliography

Albright, W. F. 1934a. The First Month of Excavation of Bethel. *BASOR* 55: 23–25.

———. 1934b. The Kyle Memorial Excavation at Bethel. *BASOR* 56: 37–43.

———. 1935. Archaeology and the Date of the Hebrew Conquest of Palestine. *BASOR* 58: 10–17.

———. 1939. The Israelite Conquest of Canaan in the Light of Archaeology. *BASOR* 74: 11–23.

Dever, W. G. 1971. Archaeological Methods and Results: A Review of Two Recent Publications. *Or* 40: 459–71.

———. 1980. New Vistas on the EB IV ("MB I") Horizon in Syria-Palestine. *BASOR* 237: 35–64.

Kelso, J. L. 1955. The Second Campaign at Bethel. *BASOR* 137: 5–10.

———. 1958. The Third Campaign at Bethel. *BASOR* 151: 3–8.

———. 1961. The Fourth Campaign at Bethel. *BASOR* 164: 5–19.

———. 1968. *The Excavation of Bethel (1934–1960).* AASOR 29. Cambridge.

Van Beek, G. W., and Jamme, A. 1970. The Authenticity of the Bethel Stamp Seal. *BASOR* 199: 59–65.

William G. Dever

BEKA [Heb *bekaʾ*]. See WEIGHTS AND MEASURES.

BEL (DEITY) [Heb *bēl*]. Essentially a title: "lord" or "master". Akk *bēlu,* "lord," when applied to the gods, was fairly synonymous with the Hebrew. The Akkadian term might also be a theophoric element in divine names, or even a DN itself; it may have reference to the potencies and functions of deity (CAD B 191b–194a; *WbMyth* 1:46).

A. The Title Bel

The honorific title *Bēlu* is of ancient vintage and was used as an exalted appellation in regard to a number of Akkadian deities. However, it concentrated upon the Sumerian god Enlil until this patron deity of Nippur, who was recognized by the Akkadians as the king of the pantheon, became *de facto* the *bēlu,* eclipsing even the theoretical ultimacy of father Anu. Enlil assumed the role as the lord of heaven and earth, the determiner of the destinies of the land, so that all other gods paled before him (Kramer 1963: 118; Streck 1916/3: 740, 742).

B. The Emergence of Bel Marduk

The foregoing situation continued until the beginning of the 2d millennium B.C., when Marduk, the patron deity of Babylon, succeeded Enlil as the supreme deity of the pantheon. Two important texts will substantiate this rise to power. The first is the *enuma eliš,* a composition dated to the early 2d millennium (so *ANET,* 60; but see also Lambert 1964), wherein the investment of Marduk as the lord of the pantheon is graphically portrayed. When Tiamat threatened the assembly of the gods with chaos, and bestowed upon her deputy Kingu the control of the tablets of destiny, Marduk alone of all the gods challenged and utterly defeated the frightful opposition. For this he was unanimously acclaimed king of the gods by the appreciative assembly of the deities and duly invested in that regal office. The fifty gods of the assembly granted to him their authority (*lit.,* name), and Enlil, in a dramatically staged climax, acknowledged Marduk to be his legitimate successor by naming him *Bēl mātāti,* "Lord of the Lands" (7.136).

The second text to indicate the transfer of the title and power from Enlil to Marduk is the Prologue of the Code of Hammurabi (ca. 18th century B.C.; *FSAC,* 15), where a portion of the prelude reads: ". . . the lofty Anum . . . and Enlil, lord of heaven and earth, the determiner of the destinies of the land, determined for Marduk, the first-born of Enki (=Ea), the Enlil functions [the Enlilship] over all mankind . . ." (*ANET,* 164a). The rise of Marduk as the head of the pantheon was concomitant with the supremacy of the city of Babylon, where Marduk was titular deity, until many of the predicates of Enlil were absorbed by Bel Marduk or, simply, Bel.

C. The Spread of the Cult of Bel

The prestige of the universal implication of Marduk's acts as creator of the universe, maker and sustainer of mankind, controller of the destinies of the world, of history, of the individual, of fate locked tightly in his hands, quite transcended the contemporary religious scene and endured and survived with amazing attraction the fortunes of history from the OB regime through the Assyrian and NB eras and Hellenistic period until well into the Roman world. The tenacity of Belism to endure was equally manifest in its appeal to the whole of the Fertile Crescent.

Bel Marduk was well received by the Assyrian regime and accorded honor shared only with Asshur. Personal names in Assyria during this period, compounded with the element of Bel, were legion (Tallqvist 1914: 53–63). As may be anticipated, Bel was supreme in the NB era with Nabu, his son, the city god of Borsippa, augmenting the supremacy of Belism (Stamm 1939: 330–31; Unger 1931: 207–11).

In the far distant Egyptian colony of Elephantine, in the 5th century B.C., it appears that Bel had accompanied the mercenary colonists from Syria. In the surviving texts Bel is included as a litigant with three other prominent Mesopotamian gods; in a letter of that period Bel is coupled with Nabu, Shamash, and Nergal in a prefatory invocation (*ArchEleph* 159; *ANET,* 491).

In Syria the cult of Bel flourished. The treaty between KTK and Arpad (ca. 750 B.C.) indicates that in the region of Harran Marduk was one of the deities used to witness treaty negotiations (*ANET,* 659). This is confirmed by the presence of Bel at Palmyra, an oasis trade outpost some 376 miles WNW of Babylon. Here it appears that the pre-Hellenistic god Bol was transformed to Bel sometime before the 3d century B.C. (Teixidor 1979: 1–18 *et passim*). The considerable archaeological evidence including eikons and expansive ruins of a temple indicates how firm the Bel cult had been adopted by the Palmyrians (*ibid.,* 128). This religious devotion continued unto the early Christian centuries.

D. Bel in the Biblical Data.

There are three instances in the prophetic literature where the name Bel occurs. (1) In Isaiah 46:1 the Judean prophet of the Exile issued, no doubt to the underground exiles, his satire on the Bel processions in Babylon. The prophet predicts that these elaborate displays of religious icons, the procession of the kingly vested gods and priestly officials, will have their nemesis when the same servitors and religious divinities strive frantically to effect an escape with their chief gods, Bel (Marduk) and his son Nabu from the enemy storming at the Babylonian gates. The attempt to elude the foe is vain hope; the weary beasts stumble and are overloaded with the weight of the gods; the very gods sway back and forth on the trotting beasts. A superb satire, a daring prophecy, a questionable hope to the exiles. (2) In the tradition of Jeremiah a kindred prophet forecasts the fall of Babylon and the shame and dismay that will be the lot of the chief god of the pantheon, Bel and Marduk (Jer 50:2). The date of the composition (Jer 50:2–3) would appear to be in the late years of the Babylonian exile, when the internal strength of the empire was rapidly waning and when the external foes were rapidly gaining frightening victories surrounding Babylon. (3) The third occurrence of Bel is Jer 51:44 in the long multiform composition with prophecies of woe mingled with promises of hope with imprecatory passages and satire. In a section of this long composition a prophet forecasts in the language of the lament the capture of Babylon and the praise of the whole earth (Jer 51:41), and immediately indicates that it is Yahweh who is about to punish Bel in Babylon and release those whom he has devoured. The imminent fall of Babylon is the sign for the Judeans to make good their escape from the city under besiegement.

It is true that Bel-Marduk must have suffered the degradation of being defeated by the foe, but it is also true that the Persian conqueror dealt kindly with religious concerns so that Bel, though shamed by his impotence in the Babylonian debacle, survived and passed his legacy on to the Hellenistic and Roman world. But the overthrow of Babylonian idolatry signified to perceptive Israel an unmistakable sign that anaconic Yahweh was truly lord of all.

In the Apocrypha of the OT, Bel appears once in the Letter of Jeremiah (v 41; in the Vulgate and KJV: Baruch 6:40). The Letter of Jeremiah has the literary form of a constructive satire in which idolatry is rationally examined as a worthless pursuit, yet the subject is not handled offensively so as to irritate the idolater. The satire has such parallels as Jer 10:25, 8–11, 13b–15; 11; Psalm 115:3–8, and 125: 6,7,15–17. Such compositions are not tirades, they are didactic, written for a purpose, reasonable, and negatively persuasive. The same analysis will generally fit the apocryphal Story of Bel (vv 3–22) and the Story of the Snake (Beast?) (vv 23–42) in the additions to the Hebrew Book of Daniel. The Story of Bel relates the disclosure of the deceitful servants of Bel who represented the god Bel as the one who consumed the rich quantity of food set daily before him. The seer Daniel exposed this fraud to the shame of Bel, but to the glory of the God of Daniel. The Story of the "Dragon" is another fictional tale designed to expose the fallacious nature of the cult of the "dragon," and to exalt the worship of the god of Daniel. The story borrows some of its motifs from chapter 6 of the Book of Daniel and has the same general didactic purpose as its object. Both of these apocryphal stores are tracts for the times when idolatry had a fascination for many Jews, say, in the last centuries before the Christian era. These three booklets witness the temptation of idolatry among the scattered Jews of the exile, but equally strong is the testimony to a staid orthodoxy that totally rejected idolatry in its contemporary forms and had studied reasons for such a repudiation.

Bibliography

Drijvers, H. J. W. 1976. *The Religion of Palmyra.* Leiden.

Kramer, S. N. 1963. *The Sumerians: Their History, Culture, and Character.* Chicago.

Lambert, W. G. 1964. The Reign of Nebuchadnezzar I. Pp. 3–13 in *The Seed of Wisdom,* ed. W. S. McCullough. Toronto.

Stamm, J. J. 1939. *Die akkadische Namengebung.* Leipzig. Repr. 1968.

Streck, M. 1916. *Assurbanipal.* Leipzig.

Tallqvist, K. L. 1914. *Assyrian Personal Names.* Hildesheim. Repr. 1966.

Teixidor, J. 1979. *The Pantheon of Palmyra.* Leiden.

Unger, E. 1931. *Babylon.* Berlin. Repr. 1970.

EDWARD R. DALGLISH

BEL AND THE DRAGON. See DANIEL, ADDITIONS TO.

BELA (PERSON) [Heb *belaʿ*]. The name of three persons mentioned in the OT.

1. Bela the son of Beor (Gen 36:32 = 1 Chr 1:43) is the first ruler listed in the Edomite King List, Gen 36:31–39. Opinions vary as far as the date of the "Edomite King List" is concerned. Suggestions range from the 11th century B.C. (Weippert 1982: 155) through the 8th to 6th centuries B.C. (Bennett 1983: 16) to the 6th–5th centuries B.C. (Knauf 1985a). Scholars tend to agree, however, that the succession scheme of this list is artificial and that in all likelihood the rulers listed in it were contemporary with each other (Bartlett 1972: 27; Weippert 1982: 155). The name of this king and his father's name can be Canaanite or Arabic (Knauf 1985a: 246). Since names from both *BLʿ*, "to spoil, devour," and *BLĠ*, "to be eloquent," do exist in Arabic, the name Bela can be explained by both roots. Bela son of Beor has been equated with the prophet Balaam ben Beor in *Targum Yerushalmi II* and by some modern authors (Weippert 1971: 595f., n. 812). This was never very likely (if one does not choose to regard Gen 36:31–39 as wholly fictitious) and is finally disproven by the Balaam texts from Tell Deir ʿAlla, which attest the seer as a local figure of N Transjordan prior to ca. 700 B.C. (Knauf 1985b). The capital of Bela, Dinhabah, has not yet been identified (Knauf 1985a: 250, n. 27).

2. Bela son of Azaz is an ancestor of Beerah from the clan of Joel (1 Chr 5:8), living four generations before Beerah, who was exiled by Tiglathpileser (1 Chr 5:6), obviously when the Assyrian province of *Galʾadda*/Gilead was established in 734 B.C. It can be assumed, then, that the "clan of Joel" was one of the major landowning families in Israelite Transjordan in the 9th and 8th centuries B.C. Its incorporation in Reuben in 1 Chr 5:4–8 is, of course, fictitious, since the tribe of Reuben does not figure in the historical record after the 10th century B.C. and did not inhabitate those parts of Israelite Transjordan that remained Israelite after King Meshaᶜ of Moab conquered "the land of Medaba" in the middle of the 9th century B.C. (Wüst 1975: 244–46). This, however, does not discredit this peculiar piece of information about the clan of Joel in Transjordan.

3. According to Gen 46:21; Num 26:38, 40; 1 Chr 7:6f; 8:1, 3, Bela was one of the Sons (i.e., clans) of the tribe of Benjamin.

Bibliography

Bartlett, J. R. 1972. The Rise and Fall of the Kingdom of Edom. *PEQ* 104: 26–37.

Bennett, C.-M. 1983. Excavations at Buseirah (Biblical Bozrah). Pp. 9–17 in *Midian, Moab and Edom.* Ed. J. F. A. Sawyer and D. J. A. Clines. Sheffield.

Knauf, E. A. 1985a. Alter und Herkunft der edomitischen Königsliste Gen 36, 31–39. *ZAW* 97: 245–53.

———. 1985b. Review of J. A. Hackett, The Balaam Text from Deir Alla. *ZDPV* 101: 187–91.

Lemaire, A. 1988. Hadad l'Édomite on Hadad l'Araméen? *BN* 43: 14–18.

Weippert, M. 1971. *Edom. Studien und Materialien zur Geschichte der Edomiter auf Grund schriftlicher und archäologischer Quellen.* Ph.D. diss. Tübingen.

———. 1982. Remarks on the History of Settlement in Southern Jordan during the Early Iron Age. Pp. 153–62 in *Studies in the History and Archaeology of Jordan I,* ed. A. Hadidi. Amman.

Wüst, M. 1975. *Untersuchungen zu den siedlungsgeographischen Texten des Alten Testaments. I: Ostjordanland.* Wiesbaden.

ERNST AXEL KNAUF

BELA (PLACE) [Heb *belaᶜ*]. One of the "five cities of the plain," identified with Zoar (Gen 14:2, 8). This identification is clearly a later gloss. Zoar (Byzantine Zoara, Arabic aṣ-Ṣughar) is an historical city; however, it is doubtful whether any of the "five cities" (Sodom, Gomorrah, Admah, Zeboiim, and Bela) ever existed. The nature of the biblical texts dealing with those cities (Genesis 14, 18–19) does not speak in favor of their historicity (Weippert 1971: 93–101). However, as a toponym, Bela has a parallel in Arabia: *Bulaᶜ* (Yāqūt n.d., I: 485).

Bibliography

Weippert, M. 1971. *The Settlement of the Israelite Tribes in Palestine.* London.

Yāqūt ar-Rūmī. n.d. *Muᶜjam al-buldān.* 4 vols. Beirut (reprint of the 1955–57 edition).

ERNST AXEL KNAUF

BELIAL [Heb *bĕliyyaᶜal*]. *Bĕliyyaᶜal* in Hebrew means wickedness and is often found in compounds expressing evil people (e.g., "man of *bĕliyyaᶜal,*" "sons of *bĕliyyaᶜal*"). The use of *bĕliyyaᶜal* as a proper name for Satan is not found in the Hebrew Bible, but Belial as the leader of the forces of darkness is ubiquitous in the pseudepigraphic and Qumran material. The term (Gk *belial/beliar*) is also found once in the New Testament as a term for the devil (2 Cor 6:15).

A. Etymological Considerations
B. In the Hebrew Bible
C. In the Pseudepigraphic Literature
D. At Qumran
E. In the New Testament

A. Etymological Considerations

According to the rabbis, the corrupt individuals known as *bĕliyyaᶜal* had cast off the yoke *(ᶜôl)* of God and, being yokeless *(bĕlî ᶜôl),* they were uncontrollably lawless *(Sanh.* 111b; cf. *paranomos, anomia, anomos* LXX Deut 13:14; 2 Sam 22:5 = Ps 18:5; Ps 41:9; 1 Sam 25:17; 30:22). Since then many wide-ranging etymologies have been proposed for Heb *bĕliyyaᶜal.* Discussions of the various proposals are provided by Otzen (*TDOT,* 2.131–33) and Thomas (1963: 11–17). Of the numerous suggestions, two avenues of research have gained the most favor among modern scholars.

One approach favored by scholars is to analyze *bĕliyyaᶜal* as being made up of Heb *bĕlî* (a negative) plus one of two roots. The traditional folk etymology found in many lexica renders *bĕliyyaᶜal* as "worthlessness" (*bĕlî* plus the root *yaᶜal,* "to profit, to be of worth;" cf. *Hipᶜil*). Pedersen (1926: 539) found this etymology so agreeable that he asserted "there is no reason to look for other explanations." Yet folk etymologies may not accurately reflect historically correct etymologies. Compare Heb *ṣalmāwet,* "darkness," which was most likely vocalized differently (*ṣalmût* < *ẓlm,* "to be dark") in its original form before the folk etymology "shadow of death" *(ṣēl + māwet)* arose (Lewis 1989: 11–12). The other proposal incorporating Heb *bĕlî* is to combine it with some form of the Heb root *ᶜālâ,* "to go up." This proposal has long been suggested by earlier scholars with the implication that "that which does not come up" = "unsuccessful" (cf. Qimḥi *bal yaᶜăleh ûbal yaṣlîaḥ*). The best formulation of this proposed analysis is that of Cross and Freedman (1953: 22 n.6) who argue that Heb *bĕliyyaᶜal* = **bal(i) yaᶜl(ê),* "(place from which) none arises, a euphemism for Hades or Sheol." Compare Job 7:9 *yôrēd šĕʾôl lōʾ yaᶜăleh,* "he who goes down to Sheol does not come up." A well-known Akkadian expression for the underworld is *māt la târi,* "the land of no return." Hence Cross and Freedman state that "*bny blyᶜl* are simply 'hellions'." Compare Boling's (*Judges* AB, 276) translation of *bĕnê bĕliyyaᶜal* in Judg 19:22 as "the local hell raisers." However, Emerton (1987: 214–17) correctly cautions against implying that Sheol is the abode of only the wicked.

The second approach to solving the etymology of *bĕliyyaᶜal* which has found favor with modern scholars associates it with the root *blᶜ*. The word *blᶜ* means "to swallow" in Heb and is well attested in the comparative Semitic languages (cf. Ar, Aram, Akk, Eth, etc.). Several scholars (e.g., Thomas 1963: 18–19; Dahood *Psalms* AB, 105; Tromp 1969: 125–28) have emphasized how the notion of Belial as "the swallower" or "the swallowing abyss" would fit nicely with what we know of the underworld and the descriptions of Sheol and Mot (cf. Ps 18:5—Eng 18:4).

Driver's (1934: 52–53) argument that Heb *blᶜ* can mean "to be confused" (< Arb *balaġa* = "slander"?) and hence *bĕliyyaʿal* with a suffixed *lamed* = "confusion" is very unlikely.

In the Gk *beliar* is the equivalent of *belial* being the result of a dissimilation of the two liquid consonants (2 Cor 6:15; see P. E. Hughes *2 Corinthians* NICNT, 248–50 n.12; W. Foerster *TDNT,* 1.607).

B. In the Hebrew Bible

The word *bĕliyyaʿal* occurs 27 times in the Hebrew Bible (see Thomas 1963: 14 for suggested additional occurrences resulting from conjectural emendations). Scholars have long recognized the mythological background underlying references to *bĕliyyaʿal* often citing Ps 18:5–6—Eng 18:4–5 (= 2 Sam 22:5–6) where the "torrents of *bĕliyyaʿal*" (cf. Ps 41:9—Eng 41:8) are used in parallelism to the "cords/snares/breakers of Death" (see MOT) and the "cords of Sheol" (see DEAD, ABODE OF THE). It is easy to understand how the association with Sheol and Death colored *bĕliyyaʿal* as it was used to describe "hellions" in biblical narrative. Parallel terms include "man of iniquity" (*ʾîšʾāwen* in Prov 6:12), "evil person" (*ʾîš rāʿ* in 1 Sam 30:22), "man of blood" (*ʾîš haddāmîm* in 2 Sam 16:7, cf. 2 Sam 12:5), and "the wicked" (*rĕšāʿîm* in Prov 19:28). Yet, more specifically, Maag (1965: 294–95) and Otzen (*TDOT,* 2.134–35) have pointed out how the chaotic nature of *bĕliyyaʿal* was often used to denote those who played roles which were detrimental to the maintenance of social order. Graphic examples of this type of unrestrained behavior would include the wicked men responsible for the tragic crime at Gibeah (Judg 19:22; 20:13) and the two "scoundrels" who gave false witness against Naboth (1 Kgs 21:10–13; cf. the *ʿēd bĕliyyaʿal yālîṣ mišpāṭ,* "the *bĕliyyaʿal* witness who mocks justice" in Prov 19:28). *bĕliyyaʿal* type individuals subverted the institution of the monarchy (cf. 1 Sam 10:27; 2 Sam 20:1; 2 Chr 13:7). According to royal ideology, the Davidic king stood as the very antithesis to such behavior (*TDNT,* 2.135; cf. 2 Sam 23:6; Ps 101:3). The expression "sons of *bĕliyyaʿal*" is also attested, albeit briefly, with reference to the cult. The wicked who seduce Israel away to worship other gods are described as "sons of *bĕliyyaʿal*" (Deut 13:14—Eng 13:13) as are the evil sons of Eli "who do not know Yahweh" (1 Sam 2:12).

C. In the Pseudepigraphic Literature

Belial (Beliar) is amply attested in the pseudepigraphic material. The many occurrences include *Jubilees* (1:20; 15:33), the *Testament of the Twelve Patriarchs* (Reuben 4:7,11; 6:3; Simeon 5:3; Levi 3:3; 18:12; 19:1; Judah 25:3; Issachar 6:1; 7:7; Zebulun 9:8; Dan 1:7; 4:7; 5:1, 10–11; Napthali 2:6; 3:1; Asher 1:8; 3:2; 6:4; Joseph 7:4; 20:2; Benjamin 3:3–4,8; 6:1,7; 7:1–2), the *Sibylline Oracles* (3:63–74); the *Martyrdom* and *Ascension of Isaiah* (1:8–9; 2:4; 3:11, 13; 4:2,4,16,18; 5:1, [4],15) and the *Lives of the Prophets* (Daniel 4:6,20; Nathan 17:2). For translations and introductions to these texts, see *OTP.*

Belial is called the angel of wickedness, the ruler of this world (*Mart. Is.* 2:4; 4:2). He is the head of the demonic powers (*Mart. Is.* 1:8). In dualistic fashion, his law and will are described as being set over against the law and will of the Lord (*T. Naph.* 2:6, 3:1). His way is one of darkness as opposed to light (*T. Levi* 19:1; cf. *T. Jos.* 20:2). Belial's angels are set over against the angels of the Lord (*T. Ash.* 6:4). He is master of the spirits of error (*T. Jud.* 25:3; *T. Zeb.* 9:8; *T. Levi* 3:3; cf. the spirit of truth and the spirit of error in *T. Jud.* 20:1).

Belial accuses and ensnares people from the path of righteousness (*Jub.* 1:20) causing them to stumble (*T. Reu.* 4:7). Those who belong to him become "like an ox under the yoke" (*Liv. Pro.* 4:6). Chief among his works is sexual promiscuity, "the plague of Belial," which separates one from God (*T. Reu.* 6:3; *T. Sim.* 5:3). Belial is associated with the most wicked of humanity. Being angry at Isaiah due to his prophecy (*Mart. Is.* 3:13; 5:1), he is said to have dwelt in Manasseh's heart and was ultimately responsible, according to tradition, for Manasseh's sawing the prophet in half (*Mart. Is.* 1:8–9; 5:1–16). *Sibylline Oracles* 3:63–74 records a description of the advent of Belial, the signs he will perform (e.g., raising the dead, leading men astray), and his ultimate demise. Belial here seems to be a reference to Nero (cf. *Mart. Is.* 4:1–2; Collins in *OTP,* 1.360; Knibb in *OTP,* 2.161 n.4d). In addition, Belial is said to have tempted Dan to kill Joseph with a sword (*T. Dan* 1:7), hindered the prophet Nathan on his way to David (*Liv. Pro.* 17:2), troubled Potiphar's wife (*T. Jos.* 7:4), etc. In eschatological imagery, Belial's slaughter is described as taking place on the earth when blood pours forth from a mountain (*Liv. Pro.* 4:20).

Moses intercedes in *Jub.* 1:19ff. with a prayer that the spirit of Belial may not rule over God's people to accuse them and ensnare them from every path of righteousness. In *T. Benj.* 7:1, the faithful are instructed to flee from Belial because he offers a sword which turns out to be the mother of the seven deadly sins. Yet even though Belial may be the ruler of the world, the righteous can resist him in the present age (*T. Reu.* 4:11). *T. Dan* 5:1 exhorts, "Observe the Lord's commandments . . . that Belial may flee from you" (cf. *T. Iss.* 7:7; *T. Ash.* 3:1–2).

The length of Belial's reign has been predetermined (*Mart. Is.* 4:12; see comment on Nero above). He will be overcome in the last days by God's anointed agents (*T. Levi* 3:3; 18:12; *T. Dan* 5:10–11). His demise is described in various ways including being trampled down (*T. Zeb.* 9:8), bound (*T. Levi* 18:12), and cast into the fire (*T. Jud.* 25:3; cf. *Sib. Or.* 3:71–74). Those who have been captives of Belial will be liberated by God (*T. Zeb.* 9:8; *T. Dan* 5:10–11).

D. At Qumran

Belial is the most frequently used title for the leader of the forces of darkness in the Qumran material, occurring especially often in the *War Scroll* (1QM; Yadin 1962: 232–34) and the *Thanksgiving Hymns* (1QH). The references to Belial in the Qumran material parallel what we have seen in the pseudepigraphic literature. Similar to the titles used in the pseudepigraphic material, he is called the angel of enmity (CD 16:5; 1QM 13:11) who is the prince of the kingdom of wickedness (1QM 17:5–6). He heads the forces of darkness, often called "the army/troops or lot of Belial," against the Sons of Light or "the lot of God" (1QM 1:1, 13; 11:8; 15:3; 1QS 2:2, 5; Collins 1984: 127–32). "All the spirits of his lot, the angels of destruction, walk according to the precepts of darkness, and towards them is their desire all together" (1QM 13:12). As in the pseudepigraphic sources mentioned above (e.g., *Jub.* 10:8), the word *maśṭemah,* "hatred, malevolence," is often associated with Belial and his purposes (1QM 13:4, 11; 14:9; CD 16:5; 1QS 3:23).

1QM 13:11 points out that it was God who appointed Belial for the task of corruption. It is because of the angel of darkness that all sons of righteousness go astray (1QS 3:21). It was Belial, according to CD 5:18, who raised up Jannes and Jambres, the names of the Egyptian magicians, in order to oppose Moses and Aaron (cf. Exod 7:11; 2 Tim 3:8). Several times we find references to the cursing of Belial and his lot for the wicked plans of hatred which they engender. This cursing is carried out by the levites in 1QS 2:4b–10 (cf. Deut 27:14) and by the priests, levites, and elders in 1QM 13:1–6 (cf. 4Q286–87; 4Q280–82; 4Q175:23).

The reign or dominion of Belial *(mmšlt blyʿl)* occurs frequently in the Qumran material (e.g., 1QM 14:9; 18:1; 1QS 1:18, 24; 2:19; 3:21–22; CD 12:2). It was believed that the present age was under his control (cf. 1QS 2:19 "year by year as long as the dominion of Belial endures"). This is also supported by CD 4:12–19 which describes the loosening of Belial against Israel. Mention is also made in this same passage of the three nets of Belial with which he ensnares humans (cf. Kosmala 1965: 91–113; Knibb 1987: 40–43).

The present age of wickedness brought about trials which would test the faithful members of the community (1QS 1:17–18a). Yet this age was not to continue for long. In the near future God would intervene and destroy the forces of Belial, as foretold by the seers (1QM 11:8). The great eschatological war will be fierce, with the tide of battle swaying back and forth between the Sons of Light and the Sons of Darkness, the army of Belial. Yet in the end, at the appointed time, the great hand of God will subdue and totally annihilate Belial and all the angels of his dominion and all the men of his lot (1QM 1:4–5, 13–16; 18:1–3; cf. 4QFlor 1:7–9). The divine inauguration of the new age follows where injustice will be no more (1QS 4:18b–23a).

The *Thanksgiving Hymns* are known for their characteristic use of material from the Hebrew Bible, and this is true of the Belial imagery as well. This is most clearly seen in 1QH 3:28b–32 which uses the imagery of the fiery "torrents of Belial" from Ps 18:5–6—Eng 18:4–5 (= 2 Sam 22:5) to describe his personal sufferings which are likened to the eschatological battle at the final consummation ("the period of wrath for all Belial"). On the ambiguity of this eschatological language, see Collins (1984: 137–38).

E. In the New Testament

In light of the extensive use of Belial above, it is surprising to find only one occurrence of Belial in the NT. "What accord has Christ with Belial?" occurs in 2 Cor 6:15. Interestingly, this phrase is preceded by the expression "what fellowship has light with darkness" which reminds us of the dualistic use of Belial and the forces of Darkness fighting God and the forces of light mentioned above in both the pseudepigraphic and Qumran material. The use of Belial here as well as other vocabulary and concepts has led some to conjecture that 2 Cor 6:14–7:1 was taken over by Paul from Qumran or some other form of Jewish Christianity (see Kümmel 1975: 287f.).

Bibliography

Baudissin, W. von. 1897–98. The Original Meaning of "Belial." *ExpTim* 9: 40–45.

Cheyne, T. K. 1896–97. The Origin and Meaning of "Belial." *ExpTim* 8: 423–24.

Collins, J. J. 1984. *The Apocalyptic Imagination.* New York.

Cross, F. M., and Freedman, D. N. 1953. A Royal Psalm of Thanksgiving: II Samuel 22 = Psalm 18. *JBL* 72: 15–34. Repr. 1975, pp. 125–58 in *Studies in Ancient Yahwistic Poetry.* Missoula, MT.

Driver, G. R. 1934. Hebrew Notes. *ZAW* n.s. 52 11: 51–56.

Emerton, J. A. 1987. Sheol and the Sons of Belial. *VT* 37: 214–17.

Galling, K. 1957. Belial. Vol. 1, p. 1026 in *RGG.* Tübingen.

Hommel, F. 1896–97. Belial and Other Mythological Terms. *ExpTim* 8: 472–74.

Huppenbauer, H. 1959. Belial in den Qumrantexten. *TZ* 15: 81–89.

Joüon, P. 1924. *bĕliyyaʿal* Bélial. *Bib* 5: 178–83.

Knibb, M. A. 1987. *The Qumran Community.* Cambridge.

Kosmala, H. 1965. The Three Nets of Belial. *ASTI* 4:91–113.

Kümmel, W. G. 1975. *Introduction to the New Testament.* Trans. H. C. Kee. Nashville.

Lewis, T. J. 1989. *Cults of the Dead in Ancient Israel and Ugarit.* HSM 39. Atlanta.

Maag, V. 1965. Beliјaʿal im Alten Testament. *TZ* 21: 287–99.

Pedersen, J. 1926. *Israel Its Life and Culture.* 2 vols. London.

Thomas, D. W. 1963. *bĕliyyaʿal* in the Old Testament. Pp. 11–19 in *Biblical and Patrisitc Studies in Memory of R. P. Casey,* ed. J. N. Birdsall and R. W. Thomson. Freiburg.

Tromp, N. 1969. *Primitive Conceptions of Death and the Nether World in the Old Testament.* BibOr 21. Rome.

Yadin, Y. 1962. *The Scroll of the War of the Sons of Light Against the Sons of Darkness.* Trans. B. and C. Rabin. Oxford.

THEODORE J. LEWIS

BELIEF, BELIEVERS (NT).

In Christian history "believer" is one of the most common terms used to designate individuals who have "believed" in Jesus Christ as their Savior and Lord. In response to the Philippian jailor's query "What must I do to be saved?" Paul and Silas replied, "Believe in the Lord Jesus, and you shall be saved" (Acts 16:30–31). NT Greek does not have a separate noun for the word "believers"; rather, "believers" is the rendering given by various translations for (1) substantival participial constructions formed from the verb "believe" (*hoi pisteuontes,* e.g. Acts 5:14; Rom 1:16; 1 Thess 1:7,2:10; cf. *Herm. Sim.* 9:19, 1–2) or (2) substantives formed from the adjective "faithful, reliable" (*hoi pistoi,* Acts 10:45; 2 Cor 6:15; 1 Tim 6:2).

The use of "believer" is especially prominent in the post-resurrection community. During the earthly life of Jesus the primary term used to designate his followers was "disciple" (Gk *mathētes*). While there were many different forms of master/disciple relationships in Israel, Jesus' disciples were distinguished from others by their response to his call, by following him only, and by listening to and obeying his teaching (Hengel 1981:61). Once Jesus passed from the scene his disciples could no longer physically follow him. The term "disciple" began to recede in usage, so that in the epistolary literature, "disciple" does not occur at all. Other terms were used to describe the followers of the risen Christ (e.g., "Christians," "brothers/sisters" "saints," "imitators"). For the early church, one phrase which naturally expressed the new relationship with the risen Lord was "believer." Since they could no longer physically follow Jesus, the early church now focused on "belief" as one of the chief characteristics of their relationship with him in the new age.

This transition is recognized in the conclusion to the gospel of John. Thomas, who had followed Jesus as his disciple, gives a great confession upon seeing the risen Lord (Jesus is "Lord and God"), but Jesus pronounces blessing on those who will believe without seeing (John 20:24–30). Paul also recognizes "belief" to be the chief characteristic of the new age. In the oft-disputed phrase where Paul says that he no longer knows Christ "after the flesh" (2 Cor 5:16), Paul decries his former "worldly" attitude toward Jesus, which has now passed away by being "in Christ" (Martin 1981: 59–60). The transition from "disciple" to "believer" may be one indication of the way in which the developing Christian tradition allowed room for both the tradition of the historical Jesus and Paul's proclamation of the risen Christ: the follower of Jesus has passed from being a "disciple" who follows Jesus in a physical sense to being a "believer" who is a new creation in Christ (2 Cor 5:17).

Paul also expands the focus from "belief in Jesus" to "belief of the truth" (2 Thess 2:13), which for him essentially means belief in all that comprises apostolic Christianity. Elsewhere the noun "faith" *(pistis)* has the additional objective nuance "belief" and means simply "Christianity" (1 Tim 4:1, 6; Tit 1:4; *BTNT* 1:90; Guthrie 1981: 593–94). Hence the true believer is one who, although no longer able to follow Jesus physically, focuses belief on the reality of a risen Lord and Savior, exercises personal faith unto salvation, and is characterized by a lifestyle consistent with apostolic teaching concerning the Christian life.

Bibliography

Guthrie, D. 1981. *New Testament Theology.* Downers Grove, IL.

Hengel, M. 1981. *The Charismatic Leader and His Followers.* Trans. J. Greig. New York.

Martin, R. P. 1981. *Reconciliation: A Study of Paul's Theology.* Atlanta.

Wilkins, M. 1988. *The Concept of Disciple in the Gospel of Matthew.* NovTSup 59. Leiden.

MICHAEL J. WILKINS

BELLS [Heb *paʿamōn; meṣillôt*]. Hollow, cup-shaped or conical objects made of metal that produce a sound when struck by a metal clapper suspended within (mentioned in the tabernacle texts of Exodus [28:33–34; 39:25–26] and in Zech 14:20). The sound is produced by the movement of the object itself. Bells, like rattles, therefore belong to the class of musical instruments known as idiophones.

Most of the bells found in archaeological contexts are quite small, some under 2 cm in height and others 4 to 5 cm in height (see catalog in Bayer 1963: 8–12). They are typically made with small metal rings or loops placed on the top and often connected to the inside attachment for the clapper. The small size of the bells and the fact that they nearly all have rings or loops indicates that they were not hand-held bells but rather were meant to be fastened to an item of clothing or jewelry, or even to animal trappings. Most examples of bells are made of bronze, with iron clappers. Presumably they could also be made of iron or of precious metals.

"Bells" as used in Exodus (Exod 28:33–34; 39:25–26) refer to small objects made of "pure gold" and attached alternately with pomegranates made of dyed wool and linen around the skirts of the "robe of the ephod," which is one of four special overgarments worn only by the high priest. These items of high priestly apparel were not garments in the usual sense. Rather, they had ritual significance in their own right; they were part of a complex of ritual acts performed by the chief priest "before Yahweh," that is, within the tabernacle itself and not in its outer precincts (Haran 1978: 214–18). Those ritual acts consisted of two sets: three acts the priest performed with incense, lamps, and "show bread," and three acts represented by three special items of high priestly apparel, with the bells attached to one of these.

The meaning of the bells' sound, to be heard when the priest entered and exited the sanctuary, cannot be determined exactly. In many cultures the ringing of bells has a prophylactic or apotropaic function, to ward away or drive away demonic spirits. Some scholars feel there is a primitive remnant of such a function in the priestly use, since the phrase "lest he die" follows the injunction in Exod 28:35 for Aaron to wear the robe with bells. However, that warning may also be considered a summation of the seriousness with which all the items in that section of Exodus should be regarded. It is more useful to note that the "bells" garment is sandwiched between two other items of apparel, the diadem and the ephod with breastplate, that have symbolic significance for the priest's role in connecting the people of Israel to their God. In this context, the bells perhaps help stimulate the attention of the deity, which is the object of the other two ritual garments.

The other biblical word for bells, *meṣillôt,* found in Zech 14:20, refers to bells associated with horses, apparently attached to their trappings. While the appearance of bells on royal or priestly garb is virtually unattested in Near Eastern art, examples of horses wearing bells can be seen in Assyrian art. The bells on Zechariah's horses are special in that they carry the inscription "Holy to Yahweh," a standard formula denoting sanctity. The prophet's eschatological vision sees a time when even horses, animals of war, will become holy, thus symbolizing the utter holiness and peace of the new age.

Bibliography

Bayer, B. 1963. *The Material Relics of Music in Ancient Palestine and Its Environs.* Tel Aviv.

Haran, M. 1978. *Temples and Temple Service in Ancient Israel.* Oxford.

CAROL MEYERS

BELMAIN (PLACE) [Gk *Belmain*]. A site mentioned in the book of Judith whose exact location is unknown (Jdt 4:4). The many variant spellings attested in the Greek manuscripts suggest that the name is corrupt. It is also possible that other variants of the name occur at 7:3 and 8:3 (BALBAIM, BALAMON), although this is unclear. Aharoni and Avi-Yonah (MBA) identify the site with Abel-maim (M.R. 204296), some thirteen miles south of Scythopolis. Of course, given the genre of the book of Judith, it is possible that the town is entirely fictitious. See also JUDITH.

SIDNIE ANN WHITE

BELNUUS (PERSON) [Gk *Balnouos*]. See BINNUI (PERSON).

BELOVED DISCIPLE. A distinctive feature of the Gospel of John is the appearance in the later chapters of a character denoted simply as "the disciple whom Jesus loved."

A. Introduction

At the Last Supper the beloved disciple (henceforth BD) has a position of intimacy and privilege close to the breast of Jesus. Through him Peter seeks information from Jesus concerning the identity of the betrayer (John 13:23–25). The disciple stands along with the mother of Jesus at the cross. Both are commended to each other by the Lord, and the disciple takes her to his own home (19:26–27). Following Mary Magdalene's report, the disciple outruns Peter in a race to the empty tomb. Prompted by the distinctive arrangement of the grave clothes, he "sees and believes" (20:2–10). The disciple, involved with Peter in the miraculous catch of fish, recognizes the stranger on the shore as the risen Lord (21:7). He later follows Jesus and hears his fate discussed by Peter and the Lord in a way that gives rise to a false rumor that he was not to die (21:20–23). Though not explicitly mentioned, this disciple is clearly meant in the subsequent reference to the one who "witnesses and has written these things" (21:24). Following the death of Jesus and piercing of his side, there is a similar indication of sure witness given by "one who has seen." This witness must be the BD, since he is the only male disciple indicated as present at the crucifixion. More controversial is a reference in 18:15–16 to "another disciple," who accompanies Peter to Jesus' trial and who, on the strength of being known to the high priest, is able to gain access to the proceedings for himself and Peter. The association with Peter and certain links with 20:2–10 (cf. 20:2: "the other disciple whom Jesus loved"; 20:3: "the other disciple") suggest that here too the BD is meant (Neirynck 1975). Some scholars have also seen a reference to the BD in the unnamed disciple who along with Andrew leaves John the Baptist to become a disciple of Jesus in 1:35–40. However, readers of the gospel could hardly be expected to pick up such an elusive hint of the BD's presence.

Following the indication of authorship apparently provided in 21:24, church tradition saw in the unnamed BD the author of the fourth gospel and identified him as one of the Twelve, John, son of Zebedee, not otherwise mentioned by name in the gospel (note, however, "sons of Zebedee" in 21:2). This apostolic identification, though not uncontested in the early centuries, appears towards the end of the 2d century and undoubtedly played a large role in securing for this controversial gospel a place within the canon.

Since the early 19th century, historical-critical scholarship has increasingly questioned both the traditional identification of the BD as John, son of Zebedee, and the concomitant recognition of this apostle as author of the fourth gospel. Some scholars have seen in the BD a literary fiction, lacking all historical identity and playing a purely symbolic role as representative of perfect discipleship (Loisy), of Gentile Christianity (Bultmann), of the more prophetic, spirit-directed church order of Johannine Christianity, in distinction to the more institutional order represented by Peter (Kragerud 1959), or as the embodiment of the ideal witness (Käseman). That the BD is an idealized figure and has a symbolic function within the gospel is beyond doubt. But a lack of any corresponding historical identity would severely undermine his leading role as witness and guarantor of the gospel. Detached from historical plausibility, the remarks of 19:35 and 21:4, whether written by the evangelist or redactor, lose all force. In fact, the dialogue in 21:20–23 concerning the fate of the BD seems to have been prompted precisely by his recent death. Moreover, the BD is constantly set over against historical figures such as Peter and the mother of Jesus, the latter remaining, like the BD, unidentified by name. These considerations incline contemporary scholarship to hold together both the historical and the symbolic aspects of the BD and to see in this figure a genuine historical personage who is presented in the fourth gospel in a symbolic and idealized way.

Within this basic consensus, discussion concerning the BD has chiefly focused upon the following issues:

1. Identifying the historical personage underlying the symbolic character.
2. Delineating the literary/theological/symbolic role he plays.
3. Clarifying his role and status with respect to Peter.
4. Assessing the stage and nature of his contribution to the composition of the gospel.
5. Determining his position and role within the developing and ultimately divisive history of the Johannine community.

B. Historical Personage Underlying the BD

The external evidence for identifying the BD with the apostle John, son of Zebedee, begins in the late 2d century and centers chiefly on the testimony of Irenaeus. However, critical scholarship has encountered grave difficulties in determining any foundation for this testimony of Irenaeus in an earlier period (Barrett 1978: 100–105). Also, the gospel would hardly have had such a battle for acceptance had its authorship by a leading apostle been widely accepted. The chief internal grounds in favor of John, son of Zebedee, would be the nonappearance otherwise in the gospel of this significant disciple and subsequent Christian leader. Moreover, the constant pairing off of the BD with

Peter corresponds closely to the picture of John in the Synoptic tradition.

Several factors, however, speak strongly against this identification: (1) the whole presentation of the gospel is not such as can easily be credited to a Galilean fisherman; (2) its symbolic nature and tendency to blend narrative and lengthy discourse does not suggest an eyewitness account; (3) it is inexplicable that an eyewitness disciple from Galilee would omit the bulk of Jesus' ministry in that region to concentrate so heavily upon Jerusalem; (4) the gospel omits important incidents of Jesus' life (e.g., the raising of the daughter of Jairus, the transfiguration, the agony in the garden) at which the Synoptic tradition records the presence of John; (5) incidents in which the BD does appear, such as the scene at the foot of the cross and the race to the tomb, are of dubious historical value. There are, then, no compelling grounds for identifying the BD with John, the son of Zebedee (though this does not exclude the possibility of a relationship between the two figures on the literary level of the gospel; see Conclusion below).

Other historical candidates proposed include: (1) *Lazarus* (F. V. Filson, J. N. Sanders), the only other person in the gospel of whom it is specifically stated that Jesus loved him (John 11:3, 11, 36). But it is hard to explain why a significant character mentioned by name in chaps. 11–12 becomes anonymous in the so-called "Book of Glory" (chaps. 13–20, 21); (2) *John Mark* (B. Weiss; L. Johnson) whose family, according to Acts 12:12, had a house in Jerusalem and who on this interpretation is supposed to have acted as host at the Last Supper; (3) *Matthias,* or (4) a *blood brother of Jesus* (J. J. Gunther). But all these identifications remain highly speculative. Most scholars abandon the quest for a name and see beneath the BD a well-educated disciple of Jesus, in all likelihood not one of the Twelve. Further specification, such as Jerusalem provenance (Schnackenburg 1982) or former disciple of John the Baptist (Brown 1979), rests on questionable harmonizations of the Synoptic and Johannine traditions.

From chap. 21 it seems indisputable that the BD was a historical person who had played a significant role in the life of the Johannine community and whose recent death had occasioned widespread dismay (v 23). We should probably see in him the founder and head of the Johannine "school" during the period of its consolidation (Culpepper 1975: 264–66). In this role he comes very close to the similarly unidentified "Teacher of Righteousness" at Qumran (Roloff 1968). Though well recognizable under his epithet to the members of community, the BD may not in fact have been a well-known figure outside the Johannine circle (Thyen 1977). If he had been in fact an eyewitness disciple of Jesus, his testimony as recorded in the gospel has evidently gone through a long process of narrative expansion and development along symbolic lines. Clearly, however, the later community believed that its distinctive faith rested upon his sure witness to the Lord.

C. BD as Literary/Theological Symbol

The BD is present at all the key events of the "Book of Glory"—the supper, trial(?), crucifixion, empty tomb, and appearances of the risen Lord. As the comments in 19:35 and 21:24 make clear, he is there precisely as *witness.* As a sure witness present at all these key events the BD offers the community a guaranteed testimony. Beyond the role of witness, however, his position of intimacy "close to the bosom" of Jesus (13:23–25), which echoes Jesus' own being "in the bosom" of the Father (1:18), suggests a parallel between his role vis à vis Jesus and that of Jesus vis à vis the Father. That is, he is a *medium of revelation* between Jesus and the disciples—as shown by Peter's attempt to solicit through him information from Jesus concerning the betrayal. The presence of the BD in such scenes clearly has proleptic significance with respect to his function in the Johannine community. His later role as witness, teacher, and reminder of what he has seen is thereby foreshadowed and guaranteed. In this respect, as many scholars have noted, there is a notable convergence between the role of the BD and that of the Paraclete as depicted in chaps. 13–17 (Culpepper 1975: 267–70). Indeed, the otherwise curious reference to "another Paraclete" in 14:16 may be explained in the sense that after the departure of Jesus the BD would be "Paraclete" of the community, a role which, after his own death, would be carried on by the spirit (see also PARACLETE).

But, along with this role over and against the community, the BD is clearly also a *paradigmatic and representational* figure, and this too in a proleptic way. His faithful following of Jesus (at the trial, at the cross, in the risen life), a following that contrasts favorably with the flight of the other disciples, sets a pattern of perfect *discipleship* in response to Jesus' intimate love. Moreover, in his coming to faith in the resurrection simply on the basis of the signs of the grave clothes and the miraculous catch of fish, without having seen the risen Lord, the BD foreshadows the *faith* of subsequent believers in that they also believe without having seen and because of this come under the blessing pronounced by Jesus (20:29). In this way the disciple functions for later generations as a *point of insertion* into the pivotal events and experiences connected with the "glorification" of Jesus (Byrne 1985). Though separated in time, the later Johannine community has the same relationship to Jesus as the BD has in the gospel. The replacement of his personal name by the simple epithet functions as an invitation to each member to identify with his status of being specially loved by Jesus, his response in faith and his perfect discipleship (Wilckens 1980). Finally, the community is doubtless intended to understand Jesus' bequest from the cross (19:26–27) as an assurance that the faith of its representative (the BD) is now fused with the perfect faith of Jesus' mother, a faith which at Cana (2:5) prompted the first sign and revelation of Jesus' glory. Henceforth, every believer belongs to the family of Jesus, human and divine (20:17). Thus the figure of the BD sums up and embodies the promise held out by the gospel that believers should receive the power "to become children of God" (1:11–12).

D. BD and Peter

In all passages featuring the BD in the Gospel of John, the scene at the cross (19:26–27) alone excepted, Peter also appears. Moreover, wherever the two appear together there is a constant pattern whereby the BD upstages Peter in some key respect: at the supper (13:23–25) he has a position of closer intimacy with Jesus and it is through him that Peter must request information; he arranges for Peter to have access to the trial (18:15–16); he arrives first at the tomb (20:4) and only of him is it said that he "saw and believed" (20:8); after the catch of fish it is the BD who recognizes the stranger on the shore as the risen Lord and communicates this knowledge to Peter (21:7); the latter's threefold protestation of love (21:15–17) inevitably brings to mind the earlier denial that contrasts so unfavorably with the BD's unsullied loyalty. Finally, Peter receives something of a rebuke in response to his question to Jesus concerning the disciple's fate (21:20–22).

Does this pattern of competition with respect to Peter reflect a real anti-Petrine polemic in the Johannine community and an attempt to replace his preeminence with that of the BD? Or is it simply a vigorous attempt to win recognition and status for the BD and the kind of Christianity he represents within the more established movement that looked to Peter? In the passages occurring in chaps. 13–20 the upstaging of Peter seems deliberate and unrelieved (though the scene at the tomb, [20:2–10] implies some recognition of him as prime resurrection witness). Chap. 21, however, provides a more balanced perspective: the spiritual insight of the BD (v 7) is set in relationship to Peter's acknowledged pastoral role (vv 15–17); his "following" of Jesus has involved a "remaining" rather than a glorious martyr death (vv 18–19, 22). It may well be that chap. 21 represents an attempt on the part of the community to soften an earlier polemic in the interests of gaining wider acceptance following the death of the BD (Maynard 1984). The gospel as a whole leaves the impression of a "defensive rather than an offensive polemic against the Petrine claims" (Culpepper 1983: 122). The dual picture of the BD and Peter in the Gospel of John serves notice that the necessary institutional structures of authority and office in the Christian community must in the end be subservient to the supreme dignity shared by all: that of "belonging to the community of the beloved disciples of Jesus" (Brown 1979: 164).

E. BD and the Composition of the Fourth Gospel

Despite the designation of him as "the one who has written these things" (21:24a), the BD is hardly the literal author of the Gospel of John. That an early Christian leader would write himself into the gospel under such a pretentious title as "beloved disciple" is scarcely to be imagined. It is far more likely that the community, which revered him as founder and guide, conferred the epithet upon him (perhaps posthumously) and that in due course their representative in the shape of the Evangelist wrote him into the gospel. It could be that the BD was responsible for a collection of traditions in distinctly Johannine form which served as the Evangelist's primary source. But the Greek phrase *ho grapsas tauta* need not imply any written activity on the part of the BD, since it can be taken in the causative sense and understood simply as designating the BD's witness as the ultimate source and authority for the written gospel.

Though most striking in the case of the "witness" statements of 19:35 and 21:4, all the passages featuring the BD present an aspect of some intrusiveness in their immediate contexts. It is highly likely that they represent insertions by the Evangelist into more traditional material. Some scholars would ascribe their composition entirely to a Redactor seen as responsible for the addition of chap. 21 and other material to the original gospel. The nature of chap. 21, however, does not so much suggest a separate author as fresh circumstances which might have prompted the original Evangelist to compose an appendix. Central among these circumstances would appear to be the death of the BD, clearly alluded to in 21:20–23. Apart from a more general sense of loss, this event would seem to have caused particular dismay in the community because of a pervasive understanding of a "word" of the Lord to the effect that the BD was not to die before the Parousia. The author of chap. 21 clarifies the matter by distinguishing between "not dying" and "remaining" until the Lord comes. The "remaining" of the BD is not incompatible with his death, since his distinctive witness "remains" in the community's life and in the gospel which he ultimately has caused to be written.

In this respect the Gospel of John represents a distinctive case of pseudonymous NT writing. Whereas other late NT authors wrote in the name of well-known early Christian identities (Paul, Peter, James, etc.), the fourth evangelist, for the representational and symbolic purposes discussed above, chose to rest his authority upon an unnamed yet authoritative disciple of Jesus.

The more recent, literary approach to the gospel steps aside from the historical questions to study the way in which the BD figure operates as a literary device. From this perspective, which pays attention to the role of narrator throughout, 21:24 is understood as designating the BD as "implied author" of the work (Culpepper 1983: 44–48).

F. BD and the History of the Johannine Community

Many attempts have been made in recent decades to reconstruct the history of the community that gave rise to the Johannine literature (the gospel and the three letters). While the gospel reflects the tensions that accompanied the emergence of the community's distinctive self-identity and theology, the letters seem to evidence outright separation and schism. It is not easy to relate the somewhat shadowy figure of the BD to particular reconstructions with any degree of confidence, save that his central founding role must be preserved. In effect there may have been a struggle over the correct interpretation of the BD's inheritance. More precisely, some would see the insertion of the BD's witness into the community tradition, in particular the comment recorded in 19:35, as part of a campaign against the tendencies of a docetic nature which seem to have played a role in the later division (1 John 4:1–3). A recent suggestion wishes to identify the BD with the author of 2–3 John, who names himself "the presbyter" and struggles against the (more institutionalizing?) leadership claims of one Diotrephes (Thyen 1977: 296–99). But an identification with such a late figure effectively excludes the possibility that the BD was both founder and original witness of the community.

G. Conclusion

In the figure of the BD we should see the head of the Johannine school in its formative period, the person chiefly responsible for the distinctive cast of its particular brand of Christianity. Whether he was in fact a disciple of Jesus remains obscure. In any case the BD was not widely known or recognized outside his own movement. Towards the end of his life or shortly after his death the Evangelist sought to guarantee the community's gospel by depicting its founder as an eyewitness disciple of Jesus, in fact, as the disciple *par excellence*. Though this depiction may not have been literally accurate in a historical sense, within the framework of Johannine theology it retained a deeper validity because of the central tenet of the community that in its life and witness it gave immediate access to Jesus in a way completely comparable to the intimacy enjoyed by the historical disciples. Insertion of the BD into the gospel as a literary device served both as guarantee and vehicle of that access.

It may well be that the Evangelist found a place for the BD in the gospel tradition by "suppressing" the figure of John, son of Zebedee, and casting his own mentor, anonymously and with much embellishment, in the now vacant role. If this was in fact the case, then the traditional identification of the BD with that particular disciple of Jesus has, in a roundabout way, a certain justification. In the late 2d century John reentered the role from which he had been removed, thereby, with an irony worthy of the gospel itself, winning for it a place within the Christian canon.

Bibliography

Barrett, C. K. 1978. *The Gospel according to St. John.* 2d ed. London.

Brown, R. E. 1979. *The Community of the Beloved Disciple.* New York.

Byrne, B. J. 1985. The Faith of the Beloved Disciple and the Community in John 20. *JSNT* 23: 83–97.

Culpepper, R. A. 1975. *The Johannine School.* SBLDS 26. Missoula, MT.

———. 1983. *The Anatomy of the Fourth Gospel.* Philadelphia.

Hawkin, D. J. 1977. The Function of the Beloved Disciple Motif in the Johannine Redaction. *LTP* 33: 135–50.

Jonge, M. de. 1979. The Beloved Disciple and the Date of the Gospel of John. Pp. 99–114 in *Text and Interpretation,* ed. E. Best and R. McL. Wilson. Cambridge.

Kragerud, A. 1959. *Der Lieblingsjünger im Johannesevangelium.* Oslo.

Kügler, J. 1988. *Der Jünger, den Jesus liebte.* SBB 16. Stuttgart.

Lorenzen, T. 1971. *Der Lieblingsjünger im Johannesevangelium: eine redaktionsgeschichtliche Studie.* SBS 55. Stuttgart.

Maynard, A. H. 1984. The Role of Peter in the Fourth Gospel. *NTS* 30: 531–48.

Neirynck, F. 1975. The 'Other Disciple' in Jn 18, 15–16. *ETL* 51: 113–41.

Roloff, J. 1968. Der johannischen Lieblingsjünger und der Lehrer der Gerechtigkeit. *NTS* 15: 129–51.

Schnackenburg, R. 1982. The Disciple Whom Jesus Loved. Vol. 3 pp. 375–88 (Excursus 18) in *The Gospel according to St. John.* HTKNT. Trans. D. Smith and G. A. Kon. London.

Thyen, H. 1977. Entwicklungen innerhalb der johanneischen Theologie und Kirche im Spiegel von Joh. 21 und der Lieblingsjüngertexte des Evangeliums. Pp. 259–99 in *L'Évangile de Jean: Sources, rédaction, théologie,* ed. M. de Jonge. BETL 44. Gembloux.

Wilckens, U. 1980. Der Paraclet und die Kirche. Pp. 197–203 in *Kirche: Festschrift für Günther Bornkamm zum 75, Geburtstag,* ed. D. Lührmann and G. Strecker. Tübingen.

BRENDAN BYRNE

BELSHAZZAR (PERSON) [Aram *bēlšaʾṣar;* Akk *Bēl-šarra-uṣur*]. Son of Nabonidus (556–539 B.C.), the last king of Babylonia prior to the Persian conquest, Belshazzar ruled as co-regent for at least three years while his father was in Arabia. This arrangement in itself is important, since it has no parallel in any other period of Mesopotamian history. There is no direct evidence that he altered conditions in southern Mesopotamia in any way during his father's absence. Belshazzar's name occurs in a number of contract tablets and letters datable to the first fourteen years of Nabonidus' reign. These comment on his business dealings with certain prominent banking houses or "families," most notably those of Nur-Sin and Egibi. In addition, they document Belshazzar's rise to power prior to Nabonidus' 11th year and outline some of his official duties as co-regent after 545 B.C. He appears to have had ample authority to give orders to temple officials in Uruk and Sippar and could even lease out temple land. His name disappears from the contract tablets in Nabonidus' thirteenth year; it has been suggested that this coincides with Nabonidus' return to Babylonia from Tema.

Belshazzar turns up in a number of Greek and Latin sources, in the rabbinic commentaries, and (along with Nebuchadnezzar) in the Book of Daniel. The *Gen. Rab.* contains one of the earliest references in any source to Belshazzar as a "cosmocrator," possessed of a kingdom whose boundaries extend from one end of the world to the other. It also characterizes him beside Nebuchadnezzar as one of "two wicked men, two destroyers." The story of Belshazzar's feast in Daniel 5 is generally regarded as an attempt by its author(s) to superimpose source material related to Nabonidus' reign on a hostile image of Nebuchadnezzar. The Jews of the postexilic period were acquainted with both favorable and unfavorable characterizations of Nabonidus and Belshazzar in their contemporary cuneiform sources. They nevertheless placed more emphasis on the negative aspects because they were tailor-made for the didactic materials incorporated into the Book of Daniel.

Belshazzar commanded Babylonian troops in the vicinity of Sippar when Cyrus of Persia conquered Anatolia (545 B.C.). Nothing is known of his activities after 543 B.C.

Bibliography

Dougherty, R. P. 1929. *Nabonidus and Belshazzar.* YOSR 15. New Haven.

Hasel, G. F. 1977. The First and Third Years of Belshazzar (Dan. 7:1; 8:1). *AUSS* 15: 153–58.

RONALD H. SACK

BELT. See DRESS AND ORNAMENTATION.

BELTESHAZZAR (PERSON) [Heb, Aram *bēlṭĕšaʾṣṣar*]. Babylonian name given to Daniel by Nebuchadnezzar's chief eunuch Ashpenaz in the exilic period when a group of Jewish noblemen were similarly renamed (Dan 1:7). See SHADRACH, MESHACH, ABEDNEGO. Belteshazzar is the Akkadian name *balāṭsu-uṣur,* "guard his life," and is a shortened form of a name that originally consisted of an invocation of a god, namely "(may Marduk) guard his life." The Hebrew and Aramaic spellings reflect a faulty vocalization of the original Babylonian and are designed to incorporate the title or name of Nebuchadnezzar's god (Dan 4:5; see BELSHAZZAR, which genuinely contains the name of the god Bel.) A few mss render the name *bēlṭĕšaṣar,* and one ms each gives the name *bēlṭʾaššar* and *bēlṭĕšaṣaʾr.* The bestowal of a new name portended a new destiny *(nomen omen)* and finds a parallel in Pharaoh's renaming of Joseph (Gen 41:45) and Nebuchadnezzar's renaming the last crowned head of preexilic Jerusalem (2 Kgs 24:17). Daniel's new name is found predominantly in Dan 4 and always in close association with the spoken works of Nebuchadnezzar. The ironic overtones in the story of the King's dream of the great tree thus extends to the nomenclature. It is not Marduk who guards Belteshazzar's life as his name implies, but the Most High God (Dan 3:32) who alone has the power to protect those who put their trust in Him (Dan 3:17). For further discussion see *Daniel* AB.

PETER W. COXON

BELTETHMUS (PERSON) [Gk *Beeltethmos*]. In 1 Esdras 2, Beltethmus occurs as the proper name of a Persian official living in Palestine at the time of Artaxerxes (1 Esdr 2:12—Eng v 16; 2:19—Eng v 25). However, evidence from the parallel text in Ezra 4 indicates that this is not a proper name, but a Greek transliteration of *bĕʿēl-ṭĕʿēm,* the Aramaic title of the Persian official REHUM (4:8, 9, 17; LXX *baaltam*). The meaning of the title is debated, variously rendered "chancellor" (Schüpphaus *TDOT* 5: 346), "commander," "commissioner" (Snell 1980: 33), "postmaster," "lord of official intelligence," and "recorder of happenings" (cf. Josephus *Ant.* 11.26). Further indication that the meaning of this term was uncertain to the author of 1 Esdras 2 is indicated by the presence of both the title, *tō graphonti ta prospiptonta* ("the recorder" [RSV]), and the proper name, Beltethmus, together in the same verse (2:19—Eng v 25).

Bibliography

Snell, D. C. 1980. Why is there Aramaic in the Bible? *JSOT* 18: 32–51.

CRAIG D. BOWMAN

BEN-ABINADAB (PERSON) [Heb *ben-ʾabînādāb*]. A Solomonic prefect responsible for supplying provisions for the court for one month per year from the area of Naphath-dor; also the husband of Solomon's daughter Taphath (1 Kgs 4:11). Ben-abinadab's territory included the area of the Sharon Plain surrounding the port city of Dor. It apparently extended the length of the plain to the Yarkon River; some scholars, however, draw its S boundary between Dor and Socoh. The debate hinges on whether the third district (Ben-hesed's) was also in the plain (see *HGB* 57–61 for discussion). Explanations of the word "Naphath-" *(nāpâ),* found only in conjunction with Dor, as "region," "height," or "yoke" are all unsatisfactory. Possibly, since Dor was "a town of the Tjekker" according to the 11th-century Wen-Amun account, *nāpâ* is a "Sea People" term cognate with Homeric Greek *napē,* "wooded valley," a reference to the wooded Sharon (Ben-Dov 1976).

The name Ben-abinadab ("Son of Abinadab"), a patronym, may be a title indicating that its bearer held a hereditary office (Alt 1950: 22). Alternately, the personal names of Ben-abinadab and four other Solomonic prefects may have been lost at an early stage of the text's history. Lucian appears to preserve the oldest form of the Greek corresponding to Ben-abinadab. Beginning with the last word of 1 Kgs 4:10, if the Greek is divided as *(. . . phar) achinanadab*—Heb *([ḥ]pr) [bn] ʾḥyndb*—or *(. . . phara) chinanadab,* both with dittography of Gk *na,* it suggests Heb *ʾḥyndb* as in v 14. One may also divide, however, as *(. . . phara) chin anadab* (Heb *([ḥ]pr) kn ʾ[by]ndb),* reflecting *kap* for MT *bet* (Rahlfs 1911: 228).

Bibliography

Alt, A. 1913. Israels Gaue unter Salomo. Pp. 1–19 in *Alttestamentliche Studien für Rudolf Kittel.* BZAW 13. Leipzig.
———. 1950. Menschen ohne Namen. *ArOr* 18: 9–24.
Ben-Dov, M. 1976. *Nāphāh*—A Geographical Term of Possible "Sea People" Origin. *TA* 3: 70–73.
Rahlfs, A. 1911. *Septuaginta-Studien* 3: 224–239.

FREDERICK W. KNOBLOCH

BEN-AMMI (PERSON) [Heb *ben-ʿammî*]. The son of Lot's younger daughter and ancestor of the Ammonites (Gen 19:38). According to Hebrew tradition, the Genesis narrative (19:30–38) explains the origin of Ammon and Moab, but more accurately it underscores the intense contempt and disdain that Israel had for these two nations. H. Gunkel (1895: 190) suggests that the narrative was originally a Moabite folktale, similar to many ancient deluge stories, that traced the common origin of Ammon and Moab to Lot. Rather than the less distinctive meaning "son of my people," a more distinctive "son of my near kinsman" (i.e., his father being his mother's near relation) is preferred. The meaning of the name in the narrative is not necessarily an attempt to explain the origin of Ammon, but to remind Israel of the Ammonites. According to Sayce (1895: 22), "Ammi" or "Ammo" was the name of the god who gave his name to the nation. The name "ammi" is found in cuneiform inscriptions as part of the title of Ammonite kings and deities. While the common origin of the two nations is generally accepted (Judg 10:6; 11:15, 18, 25; Deut 2:19), the etymology of the name is questionable. For further discussion, see Speiser *Genesis* AB, 144–46; Westermann *Genesis 12–36* BK, 383).

Bibliography

Gunkel, H. 1895. *Schöpfung und chaos in urzeit und endzeit.* Göttingen.
Sayce, A. H. 1895. *Patriarchal Palestine.* New York.
Stamm, J. J. 1950. Zum Ursprung des namens des Ammonites. *ArOr* 18: 379–82.

JOEL C. SLAYTON

BEN-DEKER (PERSON) [Heb *ben-deqer*]. One of Solomon's twelve prefects, Ben-deker was responsible for providing supplies for the king from the second administrative district, which included the towns of Makaz, Shaalbim, Beth-Shemesh, and Elonbeth-hanan (1 Kgs 4:9).

Ben-deker's district consisted of land only recently taken from the Philistines. Its boundaries are thought to correspond in general to those of the original allotment of Dan (Josh 19:40–46), which included Shaalbim (Shaalabbin), Ir-(= Beth-) Shemesh, Aijalon, and Elon. One of the latter two sites is probably merged in the place name Elonbeth-hanan (1 Kgs 4:9), a location otherwise unknown and better read as "Elon/Aijalon [both spelled *ʾylwn*] *and* Beth-hanan" (with some Heb MSS) or "*as far as* Beth-hanan" (LXX). Makaz (Heb *māqaṣ*) does not appear elsewhere in the Bible and may be a defective spelling of *mqṣh* "from the end of" or the like, a phrase used in border descriptions (Naʾaman 1986: 114–15). The Greek reading corresponding to Makaz, *mach(e)mas,* is found elsewhere for Heb *mkmš/s* "Michmas(h)," otherwise known only as a town in Benjamin. Greek *mach(e)mas* here may derive from Heb *mqṣ,* with *chi* standing for Heb *qop* (Rahlfs 1911:226).

Ben-deker's name (meaning "Son of Deker") is patronymic in form and may be a title indicating that he held a hereditary office (Alt 1950:22). The name Bidkar (Heb *bdqr*) in 2 Kgs 9:25 has been seen as a shortened form of Ben-deker (see, however, *IPN,* 149–50 n. 1; and Montgomery *Kings* ICC, 406). The name "Deker" is paralleled by the Ugaritic personal name *dqry,* which appears in census and quota lists (*KTU* 4.63:II:33 and 4.108:4 [probably the same individual in both texts]; *KTU* 4.116:17). The name is apparently related to Heb *dqr* "to stab, pierce." Noth (*IPN,* 241) compares Talmudic Aramaic *dqrʾ* "pick, mattock" from the same root. Possible parallels from cuneiform sources include the names *Bi-in-di-qí-ri* and *Da-qí-ru-um* (Tallqvist 1914:64). However, since *qí* may be read also as *ki,* one or both of these names may be related to Heb *zkr* (Aramaic *dkr*) "remember" rather than to Heb *dqr* "stab."

The oldest extant Greek rendering corresponding to Ben-deker appears to be Lucianic *huios rēchab* (Rahlfs 1911:226), which in 2 Kgs 10:15, 23 and elsewhere reflects Heb *bn-rkb* "Ben-rechab," a well-known patronym. Of the two readings, Heb *deqer* and Gk *rēchab,* the Heb seems preferable since the Gk tradition may be explained as resulting from a confusion of Heb *dalet* and *reš,* with Gk *chi* representing Heb *qop* (as in *mach(e)mas* for Heb *mqṣ,* Rahlfs 1911:226), and with assimilation to the well-known patronym Ben-rechab.

Bibliography

Alt, A. 1913. Israels Gaue unter Salomo. Pp. 1–19 in *Alttestamentliche Studien für Rudolf Kittel.* BZAW 13. Leipzig.

———. 1950. Menschen ohne Namen. *ArOr* 18:9–24.

Naʾaman, N. 1986. *Borders and Districts in Biblical Historiography.* Jerusalem Biblical Studies 4. Jerusalem.

Rahlfs, A. 1911. *Lucians Rezension der Königsbücher.* Septuaginta-Studien 3. Göttingen.

Tallqvist, K. L. 1914. *Assyrian Personal Names.* Acta Societatis Scientiarum Fennicae 43/1. Helsingfors.

FREDERICK W. KNOBLOCH

BEN-DOSA, HANINA (PERSON). See HANINA BEN-DOSA (PERSON).

BEN-GEBER (PERSON) [Heb *ben-geber*]. The officer in charge of the sixth administrative district in Solomon's kingdom (1 Kgs 4:13). This district encompassed central Transjordan with its headquarters at Ramoth-Gilead. Each district was required to supply food for the royal court one month out of the year (1 Kgs 4:6).

A major point of discussion has been the similarities between 1 Kings 4:13 and 4:19. The text in 1 Kgs 4:19 lists Geber, son of Uri, as being in charge of Gilead. Some scholars take v 13 as referring to N Transjordan while v 19 refers to south Transjordan. W. F. Albright and others believe that the two verses originally referred to the same person. According to Albright, a later editor has mistakenly changed a reference to one officer and one district into two people and two separate districts. A third possibility is suggested by a Septuagint reading and is supported by Roland de Vaux (*AncIsr,* 134). In place of Gilead in 1 Kgs 4:19, the Septuagint reads Gad (a change which involves only one consonant in the Hebrew text). If the original reading was Gad, as de Vaux argues, then there is no overlapping of territory, and two distinct references to Ben-Geber and Geber are to be understood.

Bibliography

Albright, W. F. 1925. The Administrative Districts of Israel and Judah. *JPOS* 5:17–54.

PHILLIP E. MCMILLION

BEN-HADAD (PERSON) [Heb *ben-hădad*]. The name of at least two kings of Aram-Damascus in the 9th and 8th centuries B.C.E. The name Ben-Hadad is a Hebraized version of the original Aramaic name, Bir-Hadad, meaning "son of (the god) Hadad." The two certain Ben-Hadads are Ben-Hadad, son of Tab-Rimmon (early 9th century B.C.E., see 1 Kgs 15:18–20), and Ben-Hadad son of Hazael (early 8th century, see 2 Kgs 3:3, 24–25). There are serious questions about whether the Ben-Hadad of 1 Kings 20, 22, and 2 Kings 6–8 is a distinct king. Current studies have argued that this Ben-Hadad should be identified with Ben-Hadad son of Hazael and that these stories have been misattributed to the times of King Ahab of Israel and his sons (ca. 875–842 B.C.E.), when they originally described the times of Kings Joahaz and Joash (ca. 814–782). This article will discuss the known kings of this name first and then turn to the problem of 1 Kings 20–2 Kings 8.

1. Ben-Hadad I, son of Tab-Rimmon, son of Hezion, was king of Aram-Damascus early in the 9th century and is known only from 1 Kgs 15:16–22 = 2 Chr 16:1–6. He is mentioned here in the context of a boundary conflict between Baasha of Israel and Asa of Judah. When Baasha attempted to fortify Ramah, at the border between Israel and Judah, so as to control movement in and out of Jerusalem, Asa sent a substantial gift to Ben-Hadad of Aram-Damascus to urge him to attack Israel on its northern flank. Ben-Hadad did so, conquering several towns of N Israel: "Iyyon, Dan, Abel-Beth-Maacah, and all of Kinneroth, as far as all the land of Naphtali" (1 Kgs 15:20). By invading this area, Ben-Hadad gained control of an important part of the major trade routes to the coastal cities of Tyre, Sidon, Acco, and Achzib. Asa's plan worked, since Baasha was forced to withdraw immediately from Ramah and deal with the Aramaean threat. It is unknown what settlement Baasha and Ben-Hadad reached. However, it does not appear that Aram kept control of the northern region of Israel for long, since Dan and Hazor (the latter located in Naphtali) were certainly back in Israelite hands by the reign of Ahab (ca. 875–853 B.C.E.).

2. Ben-Hadad, son of Hazael, ruled in Damascus at the very end of the 9th and the early years of the 8th centuries B.C.E. The son of Aram's most powerful king (see HAZAEL), Ben-Hadad saw much of the empire of his father crumble in a series of misfortunes known from biblical and extrabiblical sources. Clear references to his reign occur in 2 Kgs 13:3–7 and 22–25, but, as discussed below, 1 Kings 20, 22, and 2 Kings 5–7 may also deal with this king. Two extrabiblical sources are also known: (1) the inscription of Zakkur, king of Hamath and Luash in the early 8th century, and (2) a number of inscriptions of King Adad-nirari III of Assyria (ca. 810–783 B.C.E.), in which Ben-Hadad appears under the name Marʾi ("my lord"). All of these sources concern defeats suffered by Ben-Hadad.

The order in which the known events of Ben-Hadad's reign occurred is not certain, but the general flow of events suggests the severe decline in the political power of Aram-Damascus during his years. The Zakkur inscription describes a coalition that he led against Zakkur, king of the combined lands of Hamath and Luash. The latter was besieged in the city of Hazrak by Ben-Hadad and the armies of several N Syrian states, but the siege was broken, according to Zakkur, by divine intervention (although many scholars [see Pitard 1987: 174] suggest that this may be an oblique reference to intervention by the Assyrian army on Zakkur's behalf). Nothing is said in the stela concerning the cause of this attack, but most scholars suspect that Hamath's pro-Assyrian stance was at the root of the problem. Whatever the case, Ben-Hadad was unsuccessful in overthrowing Zakkur.

The inscriptions of Adad-nirari III describe an Assyrian assault on Damascus itself as a result of which Marʾi, its king, surrendered and Adad-nirari entered the city to receive a heavy tribute at the royal palace. Recent studies of these inscriptions have tended to argue for dating this attack on Damascus in 796 B.C.E., and if they are correct, the king called Marʾi in these texts is certainly Ben-Hadad.

The third source of information is the biblical account of Ben-Hadad's relations with Joash in 2 Kings 13. During the reign of Ben-Hadad's father, Israel had been reduced to the status of a vassal state under Aram (2 Kgs 10:32–33). But 2 Kings 13:25 briefly describes how Joash of Israel fought with Ben-Hadad, threw off Aramaean domination and regained the Israelite cities that Aram had annexed during the reigns of his predecessors, Jehu and Joahaz. This was done in three critical battles, and 2 Kgs 13:17 suggests that the key battle took place at Aphek (probably located E of the Sea of Galilee).

Thus it appears that during his reign, Ben-Hadad suffered a major defeat against Hamath to the N, lost his vassal territories in Israel to the S, and was plundered by the Assyrian army in his capital city. Aram appears to have continued to decline over the decades following Ben-Hadad's reign.

3. The identity of the Ben-Hadad of 1 Kings 20–2 Kings 8 is problematic. 1 Kings 20 and 22 describe a major conflict between Israel and Aram-Damascus during the reign of Ahab, and 2 Kings 5–8 ostensibly concern themselves with various dealings between Aram and Israel during the reigns of Ahab's sons, Ahaziah and Joram. In four of these chapters the name of the king of Aram is given as Ben-Hadad (1 Kings 20; 22; 2 Kgs 6:24–7:20; and 8:7–15), and during the past half-century controversy has raged concerning the identity of this king. W. F. Albright (1942) argued that he was Ben-Hadad son of Tab-rimmon, to whom he attributed a reign of over forty years. Others (cf. Mazar 1962) identified him as a successor to the latter and designated him as Ben-Hadad II (thus making the son of Hazael Ben-Hadad III). Other scholars (cf. Jepsen 1948; Miller 1966; Lipiński 1969; Pitard 1987) have noted a large number of apparent discrepancies between the portrait of Ahab in 1 Kings 20 and what is said about him elsewhere in Kings and in the extrabiblical records of his reign. See also AHAB.

Assyrian and Moabite sources, as well as other biblical passages, suggest that both Omri and Ahab were powerful kings of Israel who were on a political par with Aram-Damascus (see the Monolith Inscription of Shalmaneser III [*ANET,* 278–79] and the Moabite Stone [*ANET,* 320–21]). This view is also supported by archaeological evidence which shows that the Omride period was one of significant wealth and architectural achievement in Israel (cf. Samaria, Hazor, Megiddo, Dan). This is quite at odds with the portrayal in 1 Kings 20, where the king of Israel and his father (1 Kgs 20:34) are depicted as weak and completely dominated by Aram. It has also been noted that while the king of Aram is regularly called Ben-Hadad, literary analysis of the passage shows that the king of Israel was not originally named at all in the text (Pitard 1987: 117–18). In addition, Assyrian sources give the name of the king of Aram who was contemporary with Ahab as Adad-idri (= Aramaic, *Hadad-ʿidr*), never Ben-Hadad. It has become increasingly clear that the later identification of the king of Israel in these chapters with Ahab was a mistake. The position of Israel as a weak vassal to Aram, the account of successful battles against a Ben-Hadad which climax with a victory at Aphek (1 Kgs 20:26), and the return of Israelite cities which had previously been captured by Aram, fit exactly into the preserved information available concerning the reign of Joash of Israel (2 Kgs 13:14–25). If the stories of 1 Kings 20 (and a somewhat different version 22:1–38) are to be redated to the early 8th century, then the Ben-Hadad of these stories must be identified as the son of Hazael. In addition, there is nothing in the stories of 2 Kings 5–7 which would argue against identifying their period as that of the Jehu rather than the Omride dynasty.

The only story in this entire section with a Ben-Hadad that cannot be identified with the son of Hazael is 2 Kgs 8:7–15, the account of Hazael's murder of King Ben-Hadad and his usurpation of the throne. Assuming the correctness of the above proposal, two possible interpretations of this passage can be suggested: (1) the name Ben-Hadad here may be a secondary addition placed in this passage after all the other Ben-Hadad stories had been wrongly attributed to the Omride dynasty. In this case the name of the king assassinated by Hazael should be Hadad-

ʿidr. See ARAM (PLACE). (2) It is slightly possible that Hadad-ʿidr was briefly succeeded by a son, Ben-Hadad, and that this is the person Hazael murdered. The former proposal seems more likely.

If this argument is sound, then there are only two attested Ben-Hadads who ruled over Aram-Damascus, and the Ben-Hadad of 1 Kings 20–2 Kings 7 should be identified as the son of Hazael, and not a distinct king.

4. Brief reference should be made to a stela with a relief of the god Melqart found near Aleppo in the 1930s. It possesses an inscription which identifies the donor of the stela as a Bir-Hadad (= Heb Ben-Hadad), apparently a king of Aram. This Bir-Hadad has usually been identified with the royal house of Damascus, and the stela has been used extensively in attempts to reconstruct the succession to the throne of Aram. Bir-Hadad has been identified with Ben-Hadad son of Tab-Rimmon (Albright 1942), Ben-Hadad "II," the supposed contemporary of Ahab and his sons (Mazar 1962), Ben-Hadad son of Hazael (Dearman and Miller 1983) as well as a son of Ben-Hadad "II" (Cross 1972), and an otherwise unknown brother of Hazael (Lipiński 1975: 15–19). The major reason for the uncertainty in identifying Bir-Hadad has been the difficulty in reading the name of his father, which is badly worn on the stela. A recent reading of the inscription, however, suggests that the name of the stela's donor was Bir-Hadad son of ʿAttarhamek, king of Aram. This reading now eliminates the possibility of identifying Bir-Hadad with either the son of Tab-Rimmon or the son of Hazael, while the evidence discussed above argues against the existence of Ben-Hadad "II". Because the name Aram was used to designate other Aramaean kingdoms in N Syria, and because the stela was found in the N, it now seems best not to relate this stela to Aram-Damascus at all (Pitard 1988). For further discussion see *CAH* 3/1: 372–441.

Bibliography

Albright, W. F. 1942. A Votive Stele Erected by Ben-Hadad I of Damascus to the God Melcarth. *BASOR* 87: 23–29.

Cross, F. M. 1972. The Stele Dedicated to Melcarth by Ben-Hadad. *BASOR* 205: 36–42.

Dearman, A. J., and Miller, J. M. 1983. The Melqart Stela and the Ben-Hadads of Damascus: Two Studies. *PEQ* 115: 95–101.

Jepsen, A. 1941–45. Israel und Damaskus. *AfO* 14: 153–72.

Lipiński, E. 1969. Le Ben-Hadad II de la Bible et l'histoire. Pp. 157–73 in *Proceedings of the Fifth World Congress of Jewish Studies.* Vol. 1, ed. Pinchas Peli. Jerusalem.

———. 1975. *Studies in Aramaic Inscriptions and Onomastics.* Leuven.

Mazar, B. 1962. The Aramaean Empire and its Relations with Israel. *BA* 25: 98–120.

Miller, J. M. 1966. The Elisha Cycle and the Accounts of the Omride Wars. *JBL* 85: 441–54.

Pitard, W. T. 1987. *Ancient Damascus.* Winona Lake.

———. 1988. The Identity of the Bir-Hadad of the Melqart Stela. *BASOR* 272: 3–21.

WAYNE T. PITARD

BEN-HAIL (PERSON) [Heb *ben-ḥayil*]. (Literally "son of strength.") An officer under Jehoshophat who was sent with a team of four other secular leaders, eight Levites, and two priests to teach in the towns of Israel (2 Chr 17:7). The context implies that their mission was to instruct the people in both their religious duties as well as their civic ones as a part of the king's religious reforms (*2 Chronicles* AB, 99; *AncIsr* 2: 344, 394). The LXX and Peshitta read the plural *bĕnê-ḥayil* ("men of strength or valor") and interpret the phrase adjectivally, rather than as a personal name. But while the name is not attested elsewhere, the pattern is found in 1 Kgs 4:9 (*ben-deqer,* "son of chisel [?], spear [?]") and 1 Kgs 4:10 (*ben-ḥesed,* "son of piety"). The Hebrew idiom "son of . . ." denotes the inheritance of characteristics from the father. This is abstracted in the case of Ben-hail to mean "the strong or valorous one."

KIRK E. LOWERY

BEN-HANAN (PERSON) [Heb *ben-ḥānān*]. Individual of the tribe of Judah, the son of Shimon (1 Chr 4:20). His name appears to mean "son of gracious, favored one."

DAVID C. SMITH

BEN-HESED (PERSON) [Heb *ben-ḥesed*]. A prefect charged with supplying provisions for palace use one month per year from Solomon's third administrative district (1 Kgs 4:10).

Ben-hesed's district included Arubboth, Socoh, and the Hepher region. Scholars agree in locating Socoh at Eš-Šuweikeh at the E edge of the Sharon Plain, about 16 km NW of Samaria. Some, however, place Arubboth and Hepher in the Sharon Plain (map, Aharoni *LBHG,* 308), while others place them in the hill country east of Socoh. Evidence from the Samaria Ostraca and recent archaeological work support the latter view (Zertal 1984), so Ben-hesed's area probably corresponded to the core area of Cisjordanian Manasseh.

Ben-hesed means "son of Hesed." Hesed was probably a hypocoristic form of Hesediah (meaning "Yahweh has been true to his own") or the like (*IPN,* 183). The patronymic form of the name Ben-hesed has been variously explained. Alt believed that Solomon's prefects whose names began with "Ben-" corresponded to districts of predominantly Canaanite population; based on parallels from Ugarit and elsewhere, he suggested that these prefects were of Canaanite extraction and filled hereditary posts named for the individual who first held them (1950:22). Alternately, an early mishap may have destroyed part of the text of 1 Kings 4, leaving only patronyms in five cases. In accordance with this theory, some modern translations render *ben-ḥesed* as "[. . .] son of Hesed."

The Septuagint translator appears to have had difficulty at 1 Kgs 4:10, since much of the verse, including common Hebrew prepositions, is transliterated, not translated. The possibility that the translator's Vorlage was corrupt casts doubt upon the text-critical value of the Greek at this point. Opposite Heb *ben-ḥesed* LXX^{B} reads "son of *esōth,*" while Lucian has "*machei* son of *echō(bēr)*" (see further Rahlfs 1911: 227–29).

Bibliography

Alt, A. 1950. Menschen ohne Namen. *ArOr* 18: 9–24.

Lemaire, A. 1972. Le "Pays de Hépher" et les "Filles de Zelophehad" à la lumière des ostraca de Samarie. *Semitica* 22:13–20.

Naʾaman, N. 1986. *Borders and Districts in Biblical Historiography.* Jerusalem Biblical Studies 4. Jerusalem.
Rahlfs, A. 1911. *Lucians Rezension der Königsbücher.* Septuaginta-Studien 3. Göttingen.
Zertal, A. 1984. *Arubboth, Hepher, and the Third Solomonic District.* Tel Aviv (in Hebrew).

FREDERICK W. KNOBLOCH

BEN-HINNOM, VALLEY OF (PLACE). See HINNOM VALLEY.

BEN-HUR (PERSON) [Heb *ben-ḥûr*]. The prefect of the first of Solomon's 12 administrative districts (1 Kgs 4:8), responsible for supplying, from the hill country of Ephraim, the provisions needed by the royal court for one month per year. Ben-hur means "son of Hur"; in view of parallels like the widely attested *bn* ʿ*nt*, "Son of Anath," Hur (re-vocalized as *ḥôr*) could refer to a deity, the Egyptian Horus. More likely, however, is the meaning "free; noble," related to the Heb root *ḥrr;* cf. personal names like Ugaritic *ḥry* and Arabic *ḥurr,* "free(born)."

The fact that Ben-hur and four others in the list of Solomon's prefects (1 Kgs 4:7–19) have names of patronymic form has been explained as resulting from a textual mishap by which the personal names of these individuals were lost. Alt, on the other hand, saw these prefects as filling hereditary posts named for the first officeholder (1950: 22).

Alt (1913: 14) viewed "the hill country of Ephraim" as a geographical term embracing the original core of the tribal territories of both Ephraim and Manasseh. It appears, however, that the third district (Ben-hesed's) corresponded to Manasseh's portion of the hill country, meaning that Ben-hur's district was restricted to the Ephraimite part of the mountains (Zertal 1984).

The earliest form of the Greek text corresponding to Ben-hur is apparently *bainōr* (= MT), although B and Lucian read *baiōr* (Rahlfs 1911: 225–26).

Bibliography

Alt, A. 1913. Israels Gaue unter Salomo. Pp. 1–19 in *Alttestamentliche Studien für Rudolf Kittel.* BZAW 13. Leipzig.
———. 1950. Menschen ohne Namen. *ArOr* 18: 9–24.
Naʾaman, N. 1983. The District-System of Israel in the Time of the United Monarchy. *Zion* 48: 1–20 (in Hebrew).
Rahlfs, A. 1911. *Septuaginta-Studien* 3: 224–39.
Zertal, A. 1984. *Arubboth, Hepher and the Third Solomonic District.* Tel Aviv (in Hebrew).

FREDERICK W. KNOBLOCH

BEN-ONI (PERSON) [Heb *ben-ʾônî*]. The name given by Rachel at the moment of her death to her newborn son (Gen 35:18). Jacob later changed the name to Benjamin, "son of the right hand," which can also mean "son of good fortune" (Westermann *Genesis 12–36* BK, 555). Though the meaning of Ben-oni is somewhat obscure, the context and tradition take "oni" to mean "my misfortune or suffering" rather than "my vigor." (See Speiser *Genesis* AB, 274). The meaning of *yamin,* "son of good fortune", has been complicated by the occurrence of the tribal term *DUMU,* (sons of) *-yamin,* in the Mari documents; there *yamin* as Yemen refers to geographical distribution, "south" or "southerner." However, this distinction, though applied to southern Amorites as opposed to northern dwellers, may be coincidental. The context almost demands that Ben-oni be understood as "son of my suffering or misfortune" from the Heb *ʾānâ,* "to be in sorrow." Therefore, Jacob, to avoid an evil harbinger, changed the name to correspond to the son who now had completed the twelve.

Bibliography

Rabin, C. 1961. Etymological Miscellanea. *Scr Hier* 8: 384–400.
Soggin, J. A. 1961. Die Geburt Benjamins, Gen XXXV 16–20(21). *VT* 11: 432–40.

JOEL C. SLAYTON

BEN-SIRA, WISDOM OF. See WISDOM OF BEN-SIRA.

BEN-ZOHETH (PERSON) [Heb *ben-zôḥēt*]. Individual of the tribe of Judah, the son of Ishi (1 Chr 4:20). The LXX exhibits a variant reading of the text from "Ben-Zoheth" to "the sons of Zoheth" (Heb *bĕnê-zôḥēt*) with the names of those sons left wanting. See ZOHETH.

DAVID C. SMITH

BENAIAH (PERSON) [Heb *bĕnāyāh; bĕnāyāhû*]. The name Benaiah means "Yahweh has made (a child)," with *bānâ* meaning "make" as in Gen 2:22, where God makes Eve from Adam's rib (see also Gen 16:2; Ruth 4:11). Parallels in the Semitic onomasticon include Akk *Ibni-Marduk,* Ug *Ybnʾil,* and Amorite *Ya-ab-ni* ᵈ*Da-gan:* "Marduk/El/Dagan has made (a child)"; cf. also Ashurbanipal (*Aššur-bāni-apli* "Ashur is the heir's Maker"). The name Bani is thought to be a shortened form of Benaiah (*IPN,* 172–73).

1. Son of Jehoiada and commander of Solomon's army. Benaiah's career was marked by unwavering loyalty to David and his successor Solomon. He first appears as commander of the Cherethites and Pelethites (2 Sam 8:18; 20:23), probably mercenaries of Cretan and Philistine background who acted independently of the regular army as David's personal bodyguard (cf. 2 Sam 23:23 = 1 Chr 11:25). By backing Solomon's coronation (1 Kgs 1:32–49), Benaiah and his men played a decisive role in the power struggle between Solomon and his older brother Adonijah. Later (1 Kgs 2:13–46), it was Benaiah who executed Adonijah, Joab (who as commander of the army had supported Adonijah's bid for power), and Shimei the son of Gera, who had accused David of illegitimately seizing the throne from the House of Saul (2 Sam 16:5–14). The result of these executions is summed up by 1 Kgs 2:46: "Thus the kingdom was firmly established in Solomon's hands." Following Joab's death, Benaiah replaced him as commander of the army.

Chronicles contains information concerning Benaiah's duties under David which is not found in Samuel. According to 1 Chr 27:5–6, Benaiah was head of a 24,000-man division of the regular army which served the king in the third month of every year. The last part of v 6, where the text is unclear, perhaps indicates that a son of Benaiah, Ammizabad, also occupied this post.

Many elements in 1 Chronicles 27, however, appear to have had their origin in the Chronicler's own time, not in that of Benaiah. The figure of 288,000 men, 12 groups of 24,000, should be compared to the claim, also found in Chronicles, that David appointed 24,000 Levites for work in the Temple (1 Chronicles 23) and that he organized the priests into 24 divisions (chap. 24) and the 288 musicians into 24 groups of 12 (chap. 25). The term *maḥălōqet* "division (of men)," prominent in chap. 27, is not clearly attested in this sense in preexilic literature. Furthermore, the names of Benaiah and the other 11 leaders could have been taken from the list of David's heroes (1 Chr 11:11–47 = 2 Sam 23:8–39).

Benaiah is credited with heroic deeds and is called *bn ʾyš ḥyl* "a worthy/able man" (2 Sam 23:20, reading *ḥyl* for *ḥy* with the Qere and 1 Chr 11:22, and following Talmon 1960: 165–66 in seeing here the conflation of *bn ḥyl* and *ʾyš ḥyl*). He smote the "two *ʾrʾl*" (2 Sam 23:20; *ʾryʾl* in 1 Chr 11:22) of Moab, which is a difficult expression. A translation of "altar-hearth" (cf. Ezek 43:14–16) for *ʾr(y)ʾl* would leave Benaiah with a deed which seems less than heroic. Taking *ʾr(y)ʾl* as Ariel or Uriel, a personal name (cf. Ezra 8:16; 1 Chr 6:9, etc.), the expression could mean "two [sons] of A/Uriel," with *bny,* "sons", of an original *šny bny* lost via homoioteleuton (cf. LXX *dyo huious ariēl* "two sons of Ariel"). In this case "Moab" would not be a genitive (since it is preceded by a proper noun), but rather a locative accusative "in Moab" (cf. Joüon 1923: § 126h; GKC § 118g); alternately *bmwʾb* should be read. One may also explain the word as "mighty lion" (cf. *ʾrzy ʾl* "mighty cedars," etc.), either literally, as the end of 2 Sam 23:20 suggests, or as a figurative term for "champion." The word *ʾrʾl* appears in line 12 of the Mesha Stela (or Moabite Stone), but there too its interpretation is unsure.

Two other incidents relate to Benaiah's valor. On one snowy day he went down into a pit and killed a lion; on another occasion he fought a better-armed Egyptian warrior, snatched the latter's spear away from him, and killed him with it (2 Sam 23:21). The Egyptian is described as *ʾyš mrʾh* (according to the Qere; Ketib: *ʾšr mrʾh*), perhaps meaning "a handsome man." In 1 Chr 11:23, however, the Eg is *ʾyš mdh,* "a huge man," further described as five cubits tall and (in terms reminiscent of Goliath, 1 Sam 17:7, etc.) carrying a spear like a weaver's beam. Many commentators follow Wellhausen in regarding *ʾîš middâ* of Chronicles as original, with *mdh* corrupted to *mrh* and "corrected" to *mrʾh* (e.g., McCarter *2 Samuel* AB, 491). Some scholars have seen parallels to Benaiah's exploits in Egyptian literature, but the similarities are of dubious import and are far outweighed by differences between the accounts.

Several passages treat Benaiah's relation to David's select rosters of warriors: the Three and the Thirty. Benaiah is not one of the Three named in 2 Sam 23:8–12. He did not attain to membership in the Three according to 2 Sam 23:22–23 = 1 Chr 11:24–25; these same two passages, however, say *wlw-šm bšl(w)šh,* "and he had a name among the Three," (not, as RSV, "beside the Three"). Most commentators have proposed emendations such as *šlšym* "Thirty" for *šlšh* "Three;" *kšlšh* "like the Three" for *bšlšh* "among the Three;" and *wlʾ šm lw* "he didn't have a name" or *wlʾ śm* "he was not placed" for *wlw-šm* "he had a name" (*NHT,* 369; BHS at 1 Chr 11:24).

The position of Benaiah vis-à-vis the Thirty is ambiguous in 2 Samuel 23 = 1 Chronicles 11. He is said to have been honored above (but possibly: "honored among") the Thirty. His name does not appear among the 30 names in 2 Sam 23:24–39, but the section dealing with him immediately precedes this list. It is likely that more than 30 men could claim to have been at some point members of the Thirty (through replacement of dead members, etc.), and it is not impossible that an exceptional member would receive separate treatment, especially if he were the group's leader. This was precisely the case, according to 1 Chr 27:6, which also states explicitly that Benaiah was one of the Thirty. We are given pause, however, by 2 Sam 23:18, which says (if, as it seems, *hšlšym* "The Thirty" should be read for MT Ketib, *hšlšy* or Qere *hšlšh*) that Joab's brother Abishai was the leader of the Thirty. Possibly the two led the group at different times, but it may well be that 1 Chr 27:6 is based only upon an interpretation of 2 Samuel 23, and that Benaiah's status was intermediate between the Three and the Thirty.

The unusual prominence accorded to Benaiah in the list of David's warriors (2 Sam 23:8–39), his placement between two brothers of Joab, and Joab's absence from the lists suggest redactional activity in the time of Solomon, after Joab was replaced by Benaiah (Zeron 1978).

Benaiah's hometown was Kabzeel (2 Sam 23:20; called Jekabzeel in Neh 11:25), a town in S Judah near the Edomite border (Josh 15:21). According to 1 Chronicles 27, Benaiah's father, Jehoiada, was the chief priest (v 5; cf. the Jehoiada mentioned in 1 Chr 12:28—Eng 12:27 as a descendant of Aaron). It mentions a son Ammizabad (v 6), and possibly another son Jehoiada (v 34, thus named for his grandfather), but perhaps this should be read "Benaiah son of Jehoiada," not the reverse.

2. One of the Thirty, an honor roll of David's warriors (2 Sam 23:30 = 1 Chr 11:31). Benaiah was an Ephraimite from Pirathon (1 Chr 27:14). For a discussion of his command of 24,000 men in the 11th month of the year, see Benaiah 1.

3. According to 1 Chr 15:18, 20, and 16:5, one of the Levites commissioned to play the harp before the Ark of the Covenant in the time of David. He is probably to be seen as identical to Benaiah the grandfather of Jahaziel, a Levite and prophet of Jehoshaphat's day (2 Chr 20:14).

4. One of the priests of David's day appointed to blow the trumpet before the Ark of the Covenant (1 Chr 15:24; 16:6).

5. A Simeonite chief of Hezekiah's time said in 1 Chr 4:34–41 to have settled in Gedor (or Gerar; cf. LXX).

6. A Levite overseer who helped to manage contributions to the temple in Hezekiah's time (2 Chr 31:13).

7. The father of Pelatiah, a leader in early 6th-century B.C. Jerusalem (Ezek 11:1, 13).

8–11. Four Israelites who married foreign women in Ezra's day. They include a descendant of Parosh (Ezra 10:25; 1 Esdr 9:26 [Gk *Bannaias*]); of Pahath-moab (Ezra 10:30); of Bani (Ezra 10:35); and of Nebo (Ezra 10:43; 1 Esdr 9:35: [Gk *Banaias*]).

Bibliography

Joüon, P. P. 1923. *Grammaire de l'hébreu biblique*. Rome.

Talmon, S. 1960. Double Readings in the Massoretic Text. *Textus* 1: 144–84.

Zeron, A. 1978. Der Platz Benajahus in der Heldenliste Davids (II Sam 23:20–23). *ZAW* 90: 20–28.

FREDERICK W. KNOBLOCH

BENE-BERAK (PLACE) [Heb *bĕnê-beraq*]. One of the towns included in the inheritance of the tribe of Dan, before the tribe migrated N (Josh 19:45). The annals of Sennacherib indicate that Bene-berak (Akk *banai-barqa*) was located near Joppa, Beth-dagon, and Azor (*ANET,* 287). The town was also known as the home of Rabbi Akiba.

Biblical Bene-berak is currently identified with el-Kheirîyah (M.R. 133160), an Arab village located ca. 4 km S of the modern Israeli town of Bene-baraq. In the center of el-Kheirîyah stood the tomb of the Muslim saint Ibn-Ibraq. Surface pottery finds dating from the Iron II and the Roman period tend to confirm the site's identification with the biblical town.

Five archaeological sites have been excavated further N in the area surrounding modern Bene-baraq (M.R. 134166). These are, from N to S, (1) Tell Abu-Zeitun, (2) Pardess Katz, (3) Givat ha-Radar, (4) the hill of the Weisnitz Yeshiva, and (5) Modi'in Street. The ancient names of these sites are not known.

Tell Abu-Zeitun. This small mound is located in the Yarkon valley on the main route from Joppa via Tell Jarisha to Aphek. Abel (*GP,* 53) suggested that Tell Abu-Zeitun should be identified with the levitical city of Gath-Rimmon, mentioned together with Jehud and Bene-berak in the territory of the tribe of Dan (Josh 19:45; 21:24), but against this Mazar (*IEJ* 1: 63) identified it with Tell Jerisha (M.R. 132166; cf. also *LBHG,* 45). Tell Abu-Zeitun was excavated in 1957, and two occupation levels (Ia and Ib), dating from the Persian period, were uncovered. The finds from level Ia date to the 5th century B.C. and include shards of imported Attic ware and an ostracon with the name "Hasshub" inscribed. This name appears 5 times in the Bible, in contexts related to the postexilic period (1 Chr 9:14; Neh 11:15).

Pardes Katz. In 1961 excavations here uncovered the foundations of a hexagonal structure that could be dated to early in the 1st century B.C. on the basis of a coin of Alexander Jannaeus discovered among the ruins. This structure is similar in design to a larger hexagonal structure partially excavated over a decade earlier on Arlosoroff Street in downtown Tel Aviv (whose finds also dated to the Hellenistic period). The Arlosoroff structure appears to have been related to a rectangular structure (13.5 by 9 m) excavated further W on Hayarkon Street in front of the Hilton Hotel in downtown Tel Aviv (*EAEHL* 4: 1167), which also yielded a coin of Alexander Jannaeus. It appears, then, that the Pardes Katz structure near Bene-Beraq was probably part of a fortification line that, in the W, terminated near the Mediterranean Sea with the two downtown Tel Aviv structures. Presumably the E terminus of this line was Ras el-ᶜAin (biblical ANTIPATRIS), since Josephus (*Ant* 13.390) reports that Alexander Jannaeus built the fortification line "from the mountainside above Antipatris to the seacoast of Joppa" (see map, *EAEHL* 4: 1163).

Givat ha-Radar (Bab el-Hawwah). Excavations on the NW side of this hill were first carried out in 1942, and some 12 caves and pits with Chalcolithic burials in baked clay ossuaries were discovered (Ory 1946). These ossuaries were similar to those found in Hederah and Tel Aviv (*EAEHL* 2: 496; 4: 1163). In 1952, the NE section of the hill was excavated, yielding two more Chalcolithic burial caves. One (2 m in diameter) was completely empty; apparently the inhabitants of the site had no time to make use of it. The ceiling of the other cave (7 m in diameter) had collapsed, crushing most of the pottery and ossuaries inside, although the entrance of the cave was undisturbed. The ossuaries, containing human remains, were placed in the corners of the cave on stone-slab benches, while the pottery and incense burners lay in the center. Most of the ossuaries were shaped like rectangular houses within the opening placed high on the short ends (see *EAEHL,* 185). The largest ossuary was 60 by 25 by 40 cm, while the smaller ones were only 15 cm in diameter.

The Weisnitz Yeshiva. Artifacts were uncovered while the foundations of a modern synagogue were being dug at the Weisnitz Yeshiva on a high hill E of Bene-Beraq. Excavations in 1953 uncovered the remains of four building levels, all dating to the 3d and 2d centuries B.C. and all using dressed kurkar stones, rough stones, and *pise de terre.* Other finds included several bronze coins, potshards, and fragments of lamps. Apparently this had been part of a Hellenistic fort which served as an observation point overlooking the road running E from the Yarkon basin to the Ono valley.

Modi'in Street. Modi'in Street serves as the municipal boundary between the modern towns of Bene-Baraq and Ramat-Gan, and ancient remains have been found scattered over the hills on both sides of the street. Excavations there—first by Ory, then by Kaplan—uncovered a number of burial caves, the remains of a mosaic floor, and the floor of a winepress, all dating between the 1st century B.C. and the 5th century A.D.

Bibliography

Kaplan, J. 1963. Excavations at Benei Beraq, 1955. *IEJ* 13: 300–12.

Ory, J. 1946. *QDAP* 12: 43–57.

J. KAPLAN

BENE QEDEM. See EAST, PEOPLE OF THE.

BENE-JAAKAN (PLACE) [Heb *bĕnê yaᶜăqān*]. A campsite for the people of Israel during the wilderness period (Num 33:31–32). It is described as being near the border of Edom. The name Jaakan is also associated with this region as one of the Horite clans in the genealogy of Seir (1 Chr 1:42). The movements of the people in the Numbers passage suggest a regular migration route with their herds from one grazing area and water source to another. Elsewhere (Deut 10:6) this site is called BEEROTH BENE-JAAKAN.

VICTOR H. MATTHEWS

BENEDICTUS. The prophetic poem in praise of God ascribed to Zachariah in Luke 1:67–79. God's redemptive concern for the people of Israel is the dominant theme, which in turn invites consideration of the people's appropriate response.

Within the total structure of Luke 1, the poem serves as counterpoint to the angel Gabriel's announcement (vv 30–33) and the Magnificat (vv 46–55). The poem is carefully crafted. Although it contains numerous Hebraic features, Luke is conscious of his Greco-Roman public and shapes the poem in a pattern of preamble (vv 68–75), in which he features the goodness of God, and of resolution (vv 76–79), in which he sets forth John's assignment, with vv 74–75 serving as transition.

Linking the beginning and the end is the term *episkeptomai* (visit, vv 68, 78). The theme of rescue is expressed in a variety of ways and pervades the whole, with the specific term *soteria* (salvation) sounding the thematic beat with special force at intervals (vv 69, 71, 77). In a corresponding manner, there is dramatic interplay of people's expectations and apparent delay of divine action, a tension that is relieved by assurance of God's fidelity as exhibited in history's present hour (vv 70, 72–73). A further contributing factor to the dramatic impact of the poem are the two varieties of hostilities. On the one hand, the people are oppressed by their enemies (vv 71–73), and on the other, the people through sin are in opposition to God. Salvation in its deepest reality means that God rescues the people from their sins so that they may serve God "without fear in holiness and righteousness . . . all the days of" their lives (vv 74–75). The implication is that God will in turn resolve hostilities from other directions, and it is the function of John the Baptist to prepare the people for the entrance of Jesus (vv 76–77). The poem therefore appropriately ends on the note of "peace" (v 79), for God offers in Jesus the ultimate definition of peace. Within the total structure of Luke's gospel, echoes of the Benedictus are to be heard (especially at 7:16 and, in dramatic contrast to Jesus' reaction in the face of Jerusalem's negative response, at 19:41–44).

Zachariah's words amplify the promises of the Magnificat (Luke 1:46–55). Among its other functions in Luke's total work are introduction of the principal christological issues, especially in reference to Jesus' role as a Davidide (cf. 6:3; 18:38–39; Acts 2, 4, 13), relation to Abraham and moral responsibility (Luke 3:8; 13:16, 28; 16:19–37), and the mission of the Servant of the Lord, with emphasis on the gift of peace. Since Luke's auditors know how the story of Jesus ends, the optimistic tone of the poem evokes awareness of the bleak reality soon to be expressed in Simeon's warning addressed to Mary (2:34).

The poem appears to have originated in Jewish-Christian Palestinian circles, before the fall of Jerusalem. It is a blend of terms and phrases drawn for the most part from the Old Testament, with themes that are reminiscent of the Psalms of Solomon, and in a form that parallels poems in praise of God from Qumran (1 QM 14). Whether Luke edited a Semitic original or a Greek translation cannot be determined with certainty, but vv 73–75 include Hellenistic chancery phrasing, some of which parallels philosophical terminology ("oath which he swore" [cf. *SIG*[3] 1917: no. 736.135–37]) and "in holiness and righteousness" [*SIG*[3] no. 800.21; Pl. *Prt.* 329c]). That he composed the entire poem is not generally considered probable, but vv 70 and 76–77 may well owe their origin to his editorial pen.

The Benedictus is used in the Office of Lauds in Eastern and Western liturgies. (See Fitzmyer *Luke* AB, 374–90; Pirot *DBSup* 4: 956–62.)

Bibliography

Benoit, P. 1956–57. L'enfance de Jean-Baptiste selon Luc I. *NTS* 3: 169–94.

Farris, S. 1985. *The Hymns of Luke's Infancy Narratives.* Sheffield.

Oro, Maria del Carmen. 1983. Benedictus de Zacarias (Luc 1,68–79) ¿Indicios de una cristología arcaica? *RevistB* 45: 145–77.

FREDERICK W. DANKER

BENEFACTOR. A person or deity who is considered to be of singular merit (Gk *aretē*) because of benefits conferred on others. The infrequency of the term "benefactor" and cognates in translations of the Bible does not adequately reflect the historical context in which especially the Greek NT and the LXX and related literature took shape. As indicated below, the word *euergetēs* (one who does good; Luke 22:25; also Esth 8:12c, n; Wis 19:14; 2 Macc 4:2), is but one of many terms used in reference to benefactors (cf. Pollux 5.140) whether deities or human beings, from heads of state to secretaries of small clubs (see Jessen and Oehler PW 6: 978–81; Willrich PW 6: 981–82).

Literature from the time of Homer attests the prestige enjoyed by those who were noted for their *aretē* and displays a democratizing process from recognition of military prowess (Achilles, Hector) to emphasis on moral virtue. Plato's dialogues are mainly discourses on *aretē* and the essence of beneficence (*Meno* 96e). The truly public-spirited citizen or benefactor is one who aspires to the highest virtues, including, especially, uprightness *(dikaiosynē).* Stoic philosophers encouraged the democratizing process, and some of the terminology they helped popularize became a formulaic element in bureaucratic and sacral documents, principally epigraphic, in praise of benefactors, divine and human. Some of Paul's diction (*dikaiosynē* and *charis* [beneficence]) would be especially meaningful to Greco-Roman addressees.

Recognition of *aretē* and beneficence cuts across boundaries of gender. Luke's recognition of a number of women (Luke 8:1–3), and of Lydia (Acts 16:14) shows accurate cultural awareness (see also ASSOCIATIONS). Women benefactors cited in inscriptions include, for example, Manto, daughter of Bion and wife of Chaireas, who was honored by youth associations for her contributions (*CIG* no. 3101); and at Atalaia a woman gymnasiarch named Kaikilia Tertylla headed elders, young men, and boys (*SEG* no. 696).

Among the terms used in the Greek Bible either to describe those who qualify for special recognition or to express their beneficent actions are: extraordinary merit (*aretē,* Phil 4:8; 1 Pet 2:9; 2 Pet 1:3, 5); a good person (*anēr agathos,* Luke 23:50; Acts 11:24); one who exhibits nobility, "fine and good" (*kalos kai agathos* or *kalokagathos,* 2 Macc 15:12; Luke 8:15); one who serves with total devotion, gives oneself (*didous heauton* and related expressions, 1 Macc 2:50; 11:23; Gal 1:4; Titus 2:14; Acts 15:26; 20:24; 2 Cor 8:5; 12:15; 1 Thess 2:8); one engaged in public service (*leitourgos,* Rom 13:6; 15:16; Phil 2:25; verb, *leitourgeō,* Rom 15:27; *leitourgia,* 2 Cor 9:12; Phil 2:17, 30); one who is generously kind (*chrēstos,* frequently of God in the Psalms; 1 Macc 6:11; 2 Macc 1:24; Luke 6:35; Rom 2:4; Eph 4:32; 1 Pet 2:3; *chrēstotēs,* Rom 2:4; 11:22; 2 Cor 6:6; Eph 2:7; Tit 3:4); one who exhibits goodwill (*eunoeō,* Esth 8:12u; *eunoia,* Esth 2:23; 3:13c; 6:4; 1 Macc 11:33, 53; 2 Maccabees passim; Eph 6:7); one who functions as savior (*sōtēr,* passim); one distinguished "in word and deed" (*logō kai ergō,* Luke 24:19; Acts 7:22); one offering friendly help to people in need (*philanthrōpia,* Esth 8:121; 2 Macc 6:22; 14:9; Acts 28:2; Tit 3:4; adj., 1 Esdr 8:10; Wis 1:6; 7:23; 12:19; 2 Macc 4:11; verb, 2 Macc 13:23; adverb, 2 Macc 9:27; Acts 27:3); one who is noted for righteousness (*dikaiosynē,* passim) or piety (*eusebeia,* passim) or both; one eager to render service (*philotimeomai,* Rom 15:20; 2 Cor 5:9; 1 Thess 4:11; adv. *philotimōs,* 2 Macc 2:21); one who does good works (verbs, *euergeteō,* Ps 12[13]:6; 56[57]:3; 114[116]:7; Wis 3:5; 11:5; 16:2; 2 Macc 10:38; Acts 10:38; nouns, *euergetēs,* Esth 8:12c,n; Wis 19:14; 2 Macc 4:2; Lk 22:25; *euergesia,* Ps 77[78]:11; Wis 16:11, 24; 2 Macc 6:13; 9:26; Acts 4:9; 1 Tim 6:2; *euergetikos,* Wis 7:22; *euergetēma,* 2 Macc 5:20; and one who carries out obligations "freely"; *dórean,* Rom 3:24; 2 Cor 11:7). Of the 22 occurrences of the *euerg-* word family relating to beneficence in the Greek Bible, 14 have God as their referent, directly or indirectly: Ps 12(13):6; 56 (57):3; 77(78):11; 114(116):7; Wis 3:5; 7:23; 11:5; 16:2,11; 2 Macc 5:20; 6:13; 10:38; Luke 22:25; Acts 4:9; 1 Tim 6:2. The balance span a variety of benefactors: Esth 8:12c 2x (unspecified); 8:12n (Mordecai); Wis 16:24 (creation); 19:14 (Jews in Egypt); 2 Macc 4:2 (Onias); 9:26 Antiochos Epiphanes; Luke 22:25 (false claimants to the title).

Apart from conventional terminology, praise for a specific service that has been rendered may identify one as a benefactor. Such is the case in Luke 7:1–10. So also Titus and an unnamed "brother" receive commendation from Paul for their valued services (2 Cor 8:16–24), and Onesiphoros is singled out in 2 Tim 1:15–18.

Since the very notion of deity implies beneficent concern, recitals in praise of such deities as Isis and Sarapis have been called aretalogies, but when used in such a narrow sense the term lacks scientific precision and is therefore best applied to all recitals of exceptional merit, whether of deities or human beings. Much of the Book of Wisdom is an aretalogy of wisdom, and Sirach 24 parallels the autobiographical aretalogy of Isis found at Kyme. Various additions to the Hebrew text of Esther (LXX Rahlfs, 3:13a–g and 8:12a–x, 13) bear the impress of benefactor themes and diction. The version of Jesus' sermon in Luke 6:20–49 is a mosaic of benefactor motifs with emphasis on pandemic divine generosity (6:35). Luke 22:24–27 is not an attack on the term "benefactor," but on distortion of the concept by selfish egotists. Indeed, Acts 4:8–10, with its use of the term *euergesis* in v. 9, shows that Luke approves of the diction when understood properly and shows that the disciples finally absorbed their lesson. Luke also makes effective use of the antonym *kakourgos* (malefactor, Luke 23:32, 33, 39) to highlight the contrasting role of Jesus as the Great Benefactor.

At Lystra, Barnabas and Paul describe God as the "benefactor who bestows rain and fruitful seasons, and in rich measure provides you with food and contentment" (Acts 14:17; cf. Xenophon *Mem.* 4.3). Paul repeats the words in slightly altered form at Athens (Acts 17:25–26). Jesus Christ is identified as "one who went about as a benefactor, healing all who were oppressed by the devil" (Acts 10:38). This description encapsulates Luke's portrayal of Jesus in the Gospel, where the evangelist's editorial treatment of tradition depicts Jesus as the Great Benefactor, with the climactic observation of Kleopas: "powerful in deed and word" (Luke 24:19). Like Greco-Roman heads of state who surmounted a variety of perils in behalf of their constituencies, Jesus is an endangered benefactor who endures even death in commitment to responsibility. Instead of pronouncing Jesus to be God's Son (Mark 15:39), the centurion at the cross in Luke's account declares him to be "upright" (Luke 23:47), an outstanding mark of the benefactor.

The ultimate reward for extraordinary beneficence is immortality. According to Greco-Roman legends, some of the most notable recipients of such honor include Herakles, Asklepios, Empedokles, Alexander the Great, Romulus, Julius Caesar, and Caesar Augustus. Through resurrection Jesus becomes the immortal of immortals, restored to Israel and the world as God's unique gift (Acts 10:39–43).

Invitations to imitate benefactors are common in honorary inscriptions, and Paul makes frequent use of the topic in his ethical appeals and in descriptions of his own lifestyle. Indeed, 2 Corinthians owes much of its dramatic coloration to Paul's projection of himself, occasionally with tongue in cheek, as a person of exceptional merit and benefactor of the Corinthian Christians. Hence he emphasizes his total commitment to the gospel of divine beneficence that he brought to Corinth. A dominant feature is the apostle's use of a formulation known as *peristasis* or recital of personal hardships (2 Cor 4:7–12; 6:3–10; 11:22–29). Greco-Romans prized endurance in their heads of state, and the theme frequently appears in documents honoring benefactors.

In Luke's writings the Isaianic Servant of the Lord is partly interpreted through use of the Greco-Roman benefactor model (see NUNC DIMITTIS). In the Book of Revelation both God and Jesus Christ are the recipients of numerous accolades that display a blend of Semitic and Greco-Roman formulation, with references to creation or salvation (Rev 4:11; 5:9–14; 7:10–17; 11:16–18; 12:10–12; 19:1–8).

Bibliography

Danker, F. 1982. *Benefactor: Epigraphic Study of a Graeco-Roman and New Testament Semantic Field.* St. Louis.

Mott, S. 1971. *The Greek Benefactor and Deliverance from Moral Distress.* Diss. Harvard.

Skard, E. 1932. *Zwei religiös-politische Begriffe: Euergetes-Concordia.* Oslo.
Veyne, P. 1976. *Le Pain et Le Cirque.* Paris.

FREDERICK W. DANKER

BENINU (PERSON) [Heb *bĕnînû*]. A Levite and a signatory to the code of Nehemiah (Neh 10:13). The name may mean "our son," but some scholars have suggested that the names of other Levites, Chenani (9:4), Bani (Ezra 2:10), and Binnui (Ezra 8:33), may have originally stood here in the list, since Beninu receives only a single mention (Brockington *Ezra, Nehemiah, Esther* NCBC, 180).

FREDERICK W. SCHMIDT

BENJAMIN (PERSON) [Heb *binyāmîn; binyāmin*]. BENJAMINITE. **1.** The youngest son of Jacob (Gen 35:18) and, as such, a designation for an Israelite tribe and its territory. Accordingly, the tribe's members or the inhabitants of the tribal region are called Benjaminites.

A. Name

Since all of Jacob's sons should be understood as *heroes eponymi* of the corresponding Israelite tribes, the use of the name Benjamin to refer to Jacob's youngest son should be seen as a secondary application dependent on the tribal name Benjamin. All other instances of Benjamin as a personal name should be understood similarly (1 Chr 7:10; Ezra 10:32; Neh 3:23). Thus the use of the name Benjamin as a tribal designation represents the primary witness to the Israelite name Benjamin.

The tribe of Benjamin and its territory, as well as the personal name based on them, are always designated in the OT by the Hebrew word *bnymyn.* Alongside of this, the construction *bn-ymyny (bny)* serves as a name for the members of the tribe of Benjamin. Appearing occasionally, the word *bnymyn* composed with *bn (bny)* or *ʾyš (ʾnšy)* (Judg 1:21; 1 Sam 4:12; Ezra 10:9) represents a subsequent stage of development, since the word *bnymyn* itself already contains the word *bn.* This composition was created by analogy with the verbal construction *bn-ymyny (bny)* or *ʾyš ymyn (ʾnšy).*

A comparison of the word forms *bnymyn* and *bn-ymyny* shows clearly that both have the same meaning and also that the word *ymyn* ("the right side," "the south side") provides the key word for explaining the name Benjamin. Therefore, this name signifies "son of the right-hand side" or "son of the south," that is, the one dwelling on the right or to the south. This designation for the tribe of Benjamin (or its members) can be understood only from the geographical perspective of this tribe in relationship to another geographical or ethnic entity. It is very probable that this name reflects the close connection between the tribe of Benjamin and the influential tribe of Ephraim settled to its immediate north. Since Ephraim, together with the tribe of Manasseh, was subsumed under the rubric "house of Joseph" during the monarchy, it is also clear why Benjamin usually appears alongside Joseph in the tribal lists (Gen 35:24; 46:19, 21; 1 Chr 2:2) and why the fictive tribal ancestor is Joseph's only full brother who receives special treatment; thus Benjamin plays a special role in the Joseph novella (Gen 42:4, 36; 43:14–16, 29, 34; 44:12; 45:12, 14, 22).

In the story of the birth of Benjamin (Gen 35:16–20), which refers back to the birth of Joseph (30:24) and therefore represents Benjamin as the second son of Rachel by Jacob, Rachel gives this son the name Ben-Oni (Heb *ben-ʾônî*). After her death, Jacob changed this name (which means "son of my pain/sorrow") to Benjamin, understood as "child of happiness/fortune" (compare the same doubling of the Arabic "Yemen" ("land of the south" and "Arabia Felix"). The point of this unhistorical narrative (elucidating an itinerary reference; Westermann *Genesis* BKAT, 675) was to elaborate literarily on the death of Jacob's favorite wife at the time his youngest son was born.

B. Tribal History

1. Premonarchic Period. Often attempts have been made to derive the name Benjamin from the historical situation of nomadic groups in the first half of the 2d millennium B.C.E., which witness both *Banū-śimʿal,* "son of the north," and *Banū-yamīna,* "son of the south" (cuneiform texts of King Zimrilim of Mari). Primarily because of the great temporal and geographical discrepancies between the actual appearance of the tribe of Benjamin and the depiction of this emergence in Canaan, such a connection is quite uncertain. This does not exclude the possibility, however, that clans forming the tribe of Benjamin may have originated outside of the land of Canaan. According to the so-called Benjaminite conquest tradition (Joshua 2–9), which was expanded to form a pan-Israelite presentation only at a second stage, these clans shortly before 1200 B.C.E. forged their way from the E across the Jordan at Jericho into the small land mass between Luz-Bethel and Jerusalem. At this time the old Canaanite city Gibeon (Joshua 9) formed the W boundary. Although the figure Rachel is associated especially with Benjamin in the OT traditions (Gen 35:19 emendation; 1 Sam 10:2; Jer 31:15), it remains an open question whether she was the leader of these clans. In any case, Joshua probably played a leading role in the establishment of the Benjaminite clans in Cisjordan. Since he was an Ephraimite (Josh 24:29–30), one can assume that there was a close connection between the Benjaminite and Ephraimite clans even before the conquest, perhaps in the form of a military coalition. This is impressively confirmed by the boundary line between the Benjaminite and Ephraimite settlements in the area around the sanctuary at Gilgal (Joshua 4–5). The territories of the Benjaminite and Ephraimite clans were divided up so that this initial sanctuary to Yahweh, built by Joshua where an older cultic place had once stood, lay almost exactly on the border between the Benjaminite and Ephraimite regions. The traditions of a Benjaminite-Ephraimite military coalition entering Canaan from the E may be confirmed by the archaeological evidence at Benjaminite sites. For example, the excavations at Gibeah, Mizpah, and Ai attest new, small settlements at the beginning of the Iron I period, and field surveys at Anathoth, Geba, and Ramah confirm this picture. Nevertheless some archaeologists suspect that the Iron Age inhabitants of Ai came there not from the E but from the lowlands to the W and N. See also AI (PLACE).

Because of the small size of the Benjaminite clans and

their territory compared with those of the Ephraimite clans, Benjamin soon became increasingly dependent on Ephraim. This seems to be the case already in the Song of Deborah, which presents a leaderless Benjamin associated closely with Ephraim (Judg 5:14). The smallness of this tribe also explains how King Eglon of Moab could force it to render tribute for eighteen years, until Ehud the Benjaminite again was able to dissolve this dependence (Judg 3:12–30). When, on the other hand, Benjamin is compared in Jacob's blessing with a rapacious wolf that rips up and devours its prey (Gen 49:27), an allusion is being made to attacks on merchant caravanners traveling through the land. No doubt the Benjaminites were very skilled in the use of weapons and were feared for that reason, particularly because many of them were left-handed (Judg 3:21; 20:16) and practiced an unorthodox style of combat. It was this moment of unbridled warfare that led the Benjaminites to the brink of destruction, especially when they turned on members of their own people Israel. In a battle against other Israelite tribes, above all Ephraim (Judges 19–21), Benjamin was almost totally destroyed. Its continued existence was made possible only because the men who were not killed were permitted to acquire new wives from non-Benjaminite areas (Judges 21).

2. The Early Monarchic Period. The tribe of Benjamin achieved its historical zenith, exerting a great influence on the other tribes, in the establishment of the monarchy under King Saul, who was himself a Benjaminite (1 Sam 9:1–2, 21; 10:20–21; 2 Sam 21:14; Acts 13:21). Actions taken by him and his oldest son Jonathan against the Philistines (1 Sam 13:2–4, 15–23; 14:16) in the tribal area of Benjamin, signaled Israel's liberation from Philistine occupation. After consolidating his strong position, he expanded the Benjaminite tribal territory to the west. He did this by conquering the old Canaanite cities Gibeon and Beeroth, and perhaps even Chephirah. When he captured Gibeon, he was probably pursuing the concurrent goal of establishing for the young kingdom a capital that was independent of the other tribes. At the same time he was able to build a royal sanctuary on the "great height" located in the immediate vicinity of Gibeon, which took on a special significance even during the reign of King Solomon (1 Kgs 3:4–15).

After the death of King Saul and his three oldest sons in the Philistine defeat of the Israelites (1 Samuel 31), the tribe of Benjamin acknowledged Saul's youngest son, Ishbaal, as his successor (2 Sam 2:9). Soon afterward, encouraged by Abner, it transferred its allegiance to David (2 Sam 2:19). Since Abner's decision was kindled by entirely personal motives, the majority of Benjaminites continued to reject David. Accordingly, Absalom's revolt against David was probably welcomed, as the behavior of Shimei the Benjaminite in this affair indicates (2 Sam 16:11). The rebellion of the Benjaminite Sheba against David also reveals this as well (2 Samuel 20).

When King Solomon parceled out the tribes N of Judah into twelve districts, the tribal territory of Benjamin became an independent district with its own governor, Shimei (1 Kgs 4:18). The division of the kingdom after Solomon's death again neutralized this action, and Benjamin chose an alliance with Judah, forming a kingdom bearing the name Judah ruled by King Rehoboam (1 Kgs 12:20 [LXX], 21–24). The boundary list in Josh 16:1–3, which should be understood as a document supplementing the list in Josh 15:2–12a from the Davidic period, represents the border that had emerged between the fraternal kingdoms of Israel and Judah. By combining these two lists, a Deuteronomistic redactor probably in the exilic period created the Benjaminite boundary list in Josh 18:12–20.

3. The Later Monarchic Period. As a consequence of the battles that were soon to begin between Israel and Judah, in the subsequent decades the boundary between these two kingdoms was shifted repeatedly. This led at the same time to a division of the tribal territory of Benjamin. Initially, Judah was even able to annex the regions beyond Benjamin's N border, in particular, those of Bethel, Jeshanah, and Ephron (2 Chr 13:19). Then, probably still under Jeroboam I, Israel was able to take the offensive and during the reign of Baasha pushed forward as far as Ramah, where a defensive fortification was installed at the border (1 Kgs 15:17). Even if that might have meant the Israelite occupation of Benjamin's N territory, the Judean king Asa soon afterward effected a withdrawal of the N kingdom beyond Geba and Mizpah (1 Kgs 15:22), thereby regaining almost the entire central section of the tribal territory of Benjamin as a possession of the S kingdom. The NE part of Benjamin remained Israelite territory, however, as Jericho's resettlement by Ephraimites from Bethel shows (1 Kgs 16:34). Also Geba and Parah were probably annexed to the Benjaminite territory in the N kingdom during the reign of King Amaziah of Judah (cf. 2 Kgs 14:8–14). For a short time during the Syro-Ephraimite war, Israel eventually occupied the entire region of Benjamin as far as its S border (cf. Hos 5:8).

After the Assyrian destruction of the N kingdom, King Josiah was the first person able to reunite the N part of Benjamin and the districts of Bethel, Ophrah, and Zemaraim with the kingdom of Judah, as indicated by Josh 18:21–24 (which forms a supplement to the list of Benjaminite place names from this time). This additional listing supplements the list of place names for the Kingdom of Judah (probably compiled already during the reign of King Uzziah or even earlier), according to which the S kingdom was divided into twelve districts and the Benjaminite territory that belonged to Judah formed a separate district (Josh 18:25–28a).

In the years immediately before and after the demise of the Kingdom of Judah in 587 B.C.E., Benjamin took on a special significance once again. Apparently not touched by Nebuchadrezzar's reduction of the Kingdom of Judah in 597 B.C.E. (cf. Jer 32:8; 37:12), Benjamin probably served as a center of opposition to the policies of the last Judean king, Zedekiah. The prophet Jeremiah, who spoke vehemently against the anti-Babylonian policies of Zedekiah, came from Anathoth in Benjamin (Jer 1:1). Undoubtedly, Benjaminite territory remained unscathed in the destruction of 587 B.C.E. because of this disposition within Benjaminite circles. It was therefore only a matter of course that the Benjaminite city Mizpah became the administrative seat of the highest ranking, native official installed by the Babylonians over the annexed area (2 Kgs 25:22–23; Jer 40:6) after the dissolution of the kingdom of Judah. That also had the consequence that other officials, scribes, and priests settled here. The sanctuary at Mizpah acquired a special status (Jer 41:5), and the Deuteronomistic History (Dtr) probably even came into existence here soon afterward.

4. The Postexilic Period. In the postexilic period the tribal area of Benjamin remained in close association with Judah. Along with Judah, Benjamin was initially put under the command of the Persian governor in Samaria. Those returning from Babylonian exile considered their destination to be both Judah proper and Benjamin, and Benjaminites participated in various ways in the subsequent restoration. Perhaps already under the leadership of Zerubbabel, but certainly at the time of Nehemiah, Benjamin and Judah achieved the status of an independent subprovince in the Persian satrapy Beyond-the-River (Neh 5:14). The archaeological record attests to the destruction of numerous Benjaminite towns (Bethel, Gibeon, Gibeah) in the first quarter of the 5th century B.C.E. The precise significance of this is debated, although it seems to indicate some disturbances between the Judaean community in Jerusalem and Samaria to its north, possibly related to the political tensions described in Ezra 4 (Widengren *IJH*, 502, 525–26).

Afterwards both Benjamin and Judah were incorporated as *Youdaia* into the kingdom of Alexander the Great and in the kingdoms of the Hellenistic Diadochi. The postexilic literature knows Benjamin as a completely independent tribe, almost always named along with Ephraim and Manasseh or Joseph. Chronicles provides a plethora of genealogical material (1 Chr 7:6–12; 8; 9:3, 7–9) as well as some special traditions (1 Chr 12:2–7, 16–18; 21:6) on this subject. Furthermore, the knowledge that Benjamin was an independent entity was not lost in the Roman period. Even the apostle Paul is acutely aware of his heritage as a Benjaminite (Rom 11:1; Phil 3:5).

Bibliography

Aharoni, Y. 1959. The Province-List of Judah. *VT* 9: 225–46.

Albright, W. F. 1924. The Northern Boundary of Benjamin. Pp. 150–55 in *Excavations and Results at tell el-fûl (Gibeah of Saul)*. AASOR 4. New Haven.

Blenkinsopp, J. 1974. Did Saul Make Gibeon His Capital? *VT* 24: 1–7.

Cross, F. M., and Wright, G. E. 1956. The Boundary and Province Lists of the Kingdom of Judah. *JBL* 75: 202–226.

Halbe, J. 1975. Gibeon und Israel. *VT* 25: 613–41.

Kallai, Z. 1956. Notes on the Topography of Benjamin. *IEJ* 6: 180–87.

———. 1958. The Town Lists of Judah, Simeon, Benjamin and Dan. *VT* 8: 134–60.

———. 1961. Note on the Town Lists of Judah, Simeon, Benjamin and Dan. *VT* 11: 223–27.

Muilenburg, J. 1956. The Birth of Benjamin. *JBL* 75: 194–201.

Schunck, K.-D. 1962. Bemerkungen zur Ortsliste von Benjamin (Jos. 18, 21–28). *ZDPV* 78: 143–58.

———. 1963. *Benjamin. Untersuchungen zur Entstehung und Geschichte eines israelitischen Stammes.* BZAW 86. Berlin.

Soggin, J. A. 1961. Die Geburt Benjamins, Genesis XXXV 16–20 (21). *VT* 11: 432–40.

Weippert, H. 1973. Das geographische System der Stämme Israels. *VT* 23: 76–89.

Yeivin, S. 1971. The Benjaminite Settlement in the Western Part of the Territory. *IEJ* 21: 141–54.

K.-D. SCHUNCK
Trans. Phillip R. Callaway

2. A son of Bilhan (1 Chr 7:10), which according to the genealogy of 1 Chr 7:6–12 (which was probably based on a postexilic list), was a great grandson of the patriarch Benjamin (#1 above). Some scholars have suggested that this genealogy probably belongs to the patriarch Zebulun, but Williamson (*Ezra, Nehemiah, Esther* NCBC, 78) finds the proposed emendations unconvincing.

3. A son of Harim (Ezra 10:31–32), who is listed among those who had married a foreign woman, possibly the Benjamin of Neh 3:23. Since his name appears in the third list, following the lists of priests (Ezra 10:18–22) and Levites (Ezra 10:23–24), this Benjamin must have been a layman.

4. A man who, along with Hasshub (a man who shared a house with Benjamin), repaired part of Jerusalem's wall (Neh 3:23). Although many involved in the repairs were priests and Levites, it is not clear if the Benjamin named here was of levitical descent. Benjamin is not a priestly name. If he was the Benjamin of Ezra 10:31–32, then he was a layman. (A lay Hasshub is mentioned in Neh 3:11; but it is a levitical Hasshub in Neh 11:15.) Is he the Benjamin mentioned in Neh 12:34? His name is given as one of the "princes of Judah" (Neh 12:31) involved in the dedication of the wall (vv. 27–43). But there is some textual uncertainty. Clines (*Chronicles* NCBC, 231) suspects that Benjamin is a minor corruption of Miniamin (cf. vv 5, 17), but both the Vulgate and the LXX read "Beniamin." However since the LXX, but not the Vulgate, reads Beniamin in v 17 as well, Cline's suspicion may be correct.

CRAIG A. EVANS

BENJAMIN GATE (PLACE) (Heb *šaʿar binyāmîn*). Gate of pre-exilic Jerusalem. In Jer 37: 13, Jeremiah tried to leave the city for the territory of Benjamin by way of the Benjamin Gate; and in Jer 38: 7, King Zedekiah was sitting in the Benjamin Gate. The fact that Jeremiah was heading N for Anathoth (Jer 1: 1) by means of the Benjamin Gate argues that this gate was in the northeast part of the city, not far from the temple courts. This no doubt was the gate of the people described in Jer 17: 19 where the kings of Judah went in and out. In postexilic times, this gate may have been called the Muster/Inspection Gate (Neh 3: 31) located at the N end of the E wall, or, as others suggest, the Sheep Gate (Neh 3: 32), at the upper end of the E wall. Some argue that the Upper Benjamin Gate (Jer 20: 2) leading into the temple, rebuilt by King Jotham (2 Kgs 15: 35), is the same as the Benjamin Gate, while others argue that the Benjamin Gate located in the city wall is to be distinguished from the Upper Benjamin Gate, the "north gate of the inner [temple] court" (Ezek 8: 3).

W. HAROLD MARE

BENO (PERSON) [Heb *bĕnô*]. One of the "remaining Levites" who, according to the Chronicler, casts lots before David, Zadok, and Ahimelek in order to receive his place among the levitical household leaders (1 Chr 24:27). The Chronicler grants Beno a levitical lineage as the son of Jaaziah, a descendant of Merari, along with his brothers, Shoham, Zaccur, and Ibri (1 Chr 24:27). However, complex textual problems abound in the two verses of 1 Chronicles where Beno appears. The LXX contains variations on MT's *benô*, yet its readings are also problematic. Two text-critical solutions seem most plausible. The first solution, based primarily on the MT, asserts that *benô* did not originally represent a personal name; instead, it was meant to convey its literal meaning—"his son" (Myers *1 Chronicles* AB, 163). The second solution, following the LXX, argues that *benô* in 1 Chr 24:27 most likely represents a corruption of BANI (Heb *bānî*), a popular name in postexilic Judah (Curtis and Madsen *Chronicles* ICC, 274). In either case, it seems unlikely that *benô* ultimately refers to an historical person. Instead, its presence in the MT highlights the vicissitudes of the textual transmission of names in the OT.

John W. Wright

BEON (PLACE) [Heb *bĕʿōn*]. A site in N Moab allotted to the tribe of Reuben for pasture (Num 32:3). It is generally identified with BAAL-MEON. The critical apparatus of *BHS* conjectures that MT's *bʿn* is corrupt, and should be read **bt mʿn*, that is, Beth Meon (as in Jer 48:23).

C. Gilbert Romero

BEOR (PERSON) [Heb *bĕʿōr*]. **1.** The father of the Edomite "king" Bela (Gen 36:32; 1 Chr 1:43). See BELA.

2. The father of the prophet Balaam (Num 22:5; 24:3, 15; 31:8; Deut 23:5; Josh 13:22; 24:9; Mic 6:5) also attested in the Balaam Text from Tell Deir 'Alla (Weippert and Weippert 1982; Hackett 1984).

As a personal name, *bʿr* is attested in Safaitic (Harding 1971: 111); Ar *Baʿr* in Ibn Hisham supposedly is a clerical error (Caskel 1966: 224). Safaitic *bʿr,* however, is most easily vocalized **Baʿīr* "camel"; this noun signified "cattle" in more ancient West Semitic languages (viz. Heb and Sabaic). The Heb personal name *bʿrʾ*, Baara (1 Chr 8:8), does not furnish a parallel either, since this can easily be explained as an hypocoristic formation of *bʿl* + *rm/rʾh/rʿh.* Albright's attempt (1944: 232) to explain Beor as a similar formation does not agree with the vowel pattern, and the absence of any hypocoristic ending, in Beor. The Edomite and Transjordanian name Beor is, therefore, best regarded as unexplained (see Knauf 1985 for the language of the Tell Deir 'Allah text).

Bibliography

Albright, W. F. 1944. The Oracles of Balaam. *JBL* 63: 207–233.

Caskel, W. 1966. *Gamharat an-nasab. Das genealogische Werk des Hisam ibn Muhammad al-Kalbi, II.* Leiden.

Hackett, J. A. 1984. *The Balaam Text from Deir 'Alla.* HSM 31. Chico.

Harding, G. L. 1971. *An Index and Concordance of Pre-Islamic Arabian Names and Inscriptions.* Toronto.

Knauf, E. A. 1985. Review of Hackett (1984). *ZDPV* 101: 187–91.

Weippert, H. and M. 1982. Die 'Bileam-Inschrift vom Tell Der 'Alla. *ZDPV* 98: 77–103.

Ernst Axel Knauf

BERA (PERSON) [Heb *beraʿ*]. King of Sodom, Gen 14:2. Elsewhere in the chap (vv 8, 10, 17, 21, 22), he appears simply as "the king of Sodom." Together with four other kings (of Gomorrah, Admah, Zeboim, and Bela, that is, Zoar), Bera served Chedorlaomer for twelve years. In their thirteenth year, these kings rebelled and were defeated in the following year by Chedorlaomer and his allies in the Valley of SIDDIM. As the kings of Sodom and Gomorrah fled, they fell into bitumen pits, which certainly means that they perished. Therefore the verses 17, 21–22, in which the king of Sodom reappears alive and well, must be considered an interpolation (see ANER). The name *Bera,* like those of his allies (BIRSHA, SHINAB, SHEMEBER, and originally Bela), is a "speaking name," as was already perceived by the Targum of Pseudo-Jonathan; it means "in evil," alluding to the wickedness of Sodom.

Michael C. Astour

BERACAH (PERSON) [Heb *bĕrākâ*]. A kinsman of Saul; one of the ambidextrous warriors from the tribe of Benjamin (1 Chr 12:3). In this list (1 Chr 12:1–8—Eng 12:1–7) the Chronicler is emphasizing the extensive support David enjoyed among Saul's kin before David became king.

Raymond B. Dillard

BERACAH, VALLEY OF (PLACE) [Heb *ʿēmek bĕrākâ*]. A valley near Tekoa where Jehoshaphat and his people gathered to bless Yahweh for their marvelous victory over a coalition of invading Moabites, Ammonites, and Meunites (2 Chr 20:26). As prophesied by Jahaziel, the enemy was destroyed when they began fighting among themselves in the wilderness of Jeruel (2 Chr 20:14–23). The sensational nature of this story, however, has raised questions about its historicity (*HAIJ*, 223). Edward Robinson (1941, 3: 275) and other early 19th-century explorers suggested that the biblical name was preserved in the ruin of Kh. Bereikut (M.R. 164117), next to modern-day Migdal ʿOz and adjacent to the main highway between Bethlehem and Hebron. Just S of Kh. Bereikut lies Wadi el-Arrub (= N. Mevorach) with its many springs and fertile valley (M.R. 163114). During NT times, an acqueduct directed water from these springs to Solomon's Pools, and from there on to Jerusalem. The majority of scholars who have noticed the similarity between *bĕrākâ* ("blessing") and *bĕrēkâ* ("pool") have thus preferred to locate the biblical site here, rather than in the small valley where Kh. Bereikut itself sits. Biqʿat Horeqanya (= Buqeiʿah Valley), ca. 6–8 km/4–5 miles NW of the Dead Sea has also been proposed, but this seems too far N to be a likely candidate. A more plausible suggestion is the wide valley of el-Baqʿah (M.R. 170116) NW of Kh. et-Tuqu (Markus and Amit 1989: 124–25). The likelihood of this valley being the biblical one is derived from its proximity to the wilderness of Tekoa (2 Chr 20:20), and from its strategic position adjacent to the ridge route between En-gedi and Bethlehem. The traditional identification with Wadi el-Arrub falls out of line with this more natural route of ascent into the Judean hills. It is possible that the apocalyptic Valley of Jehoshaphat mentioned in Joel 4:12—Eng 3:12 is an allusion to the same valley where Jehoshaphat was delivered.

Bibliography

Markus, M., and Amit, D. 1989. Emeq Berakha. Pp. 124–25 in *Har Hebron.* Jerusalem (in Hebrew).

Robinson, E. 1941. *Biblical Researches in Palestine.* 3 vols. Boston. Repr. Jerusalem, 1970.

Simons, J. 1959. *The Geographical and Topographical Texts of the Old Testament.* Leiden.

R. A. Mullins

BERAIAH (PERSON) [Heb *bĕrāʾyâ*]. One of the sons of Shimei, according to the longer Benjaminite genealogy of the Chronicler (1 Chr 8:21). The name means "Yahweh created." Regarding the list of names of Benjaminites in this section (vv 13–27), Myers (*1 Chronicles* AB, 61) suggests that little historical importance can be derived from them, except that they are described in v 28 as "chief men" (Heb *rāʾšîm*) who dwelled in Jerusalem. This is taken as evidence of the tendency of Benjaminites and Judahites to mix during the period of the divided monarchy. Williamson disconnects v 28 from vv 13–27, understanding it instead as the beginning of the section vv 28–40 (*1 and 2 Chronicles* NCBC, 85). Verse 28 is paralleled at 9:34.

Siegfried S. Johnson

BEREA (PLACE) [Gk *Beréa*]. Var. BEROEA. **1.** A Macedonian town on the Egnatian Way (40°31′N; 22°14′E) which Paul and Silas visited (Acts 17:10–15). Beroea, "a place of many waters," is located near natural springs, 24 miles inland from the Gulf of Thermai, just below Mt. Bermius. The abundance of streams, the 600-ft. altitude, the scenic view of the Haliacmon plains, and its out-of-the-way location (Cic. *Pis.* 36) make Beroea one of the more desirable towns of the district of Emathia in southwestern Macedonia—modern Verria. Acts 17 identifies the Beroean Jews as nobler than the Thessalonicans. And Paul's language implies that his audience was of high social standing. Numerous extant inscriptions attest to the town's ancient prominence. Beroea's role in military engagements is noted by the classicists (Polybius 27. 8; 28. 8; Livy 44. 45; 45. 29). Pompey chose Beroea as his winter home (49–48 B.C.) before the battle of Pharsalus. The city fell for the last time to the Turks in 1374. Beroea's bishopric status also highlights its prominence. Andronicus II (1283–1328) made the town a metropolis after it had already realized bishopric status under the metropolitan of Thessalonica.

2. A town in the vicinity of Jerusalem, most likely on the Nablus-Jerusalem road. Bacchides took 20,000 infantry and 2,000 cavalry to Berea, which was near Elasa (M.R. 169144) 1 Macc 7.8ff; 9. 4–5; *Ant* 12. 10.2). Before being slain by Bacchides' forces, Judah the Maccabee encamped at Elasa (161 B.C.)—probably located on the Sharon-Jerusalem road between the two Beth-horons. Bireth, situated ten miles north of Jerusalem (M.R. 170149) on the road to Nablus, is the best possibility for Berea. Beeroth (Bireth) is a Hivite town in Benjamin (Beeroth in Josh 9: 17; Beroth in 1 Esdr 5: 19). Josephus lists a Beerzetho, thus making a candidate of Beerzeth, located four miles N-NW of Bireth (*Ant* 12. 11.1).

3. Northern Syrian city between the Euphrates and the Orontes rivers, lying about midway between Hierapolis and Antioch (36°10′N; 37°0′E). Originally Aleppo (Halab), later renamed after the Macedonian Beroea by Seleucus Nicator (312–280), and then returned to the Semitic name Aleppo during the Middle Ages, this city became a stop on the important trade route between Persia and Europe. Aleppo houses the Mosque Zakariyah, supposedly the tomb of Zechariah, John the Baptist's father, and it formerly hosted the Aleppo Codex of the OT. It was at Beroea where Antiochus Eupator executed Menelaus, the ex-high priest. A vivid account of Menelaus' death is recorded in 2 Macc 13:1–8: the Beroeans pushed Menelaus into a tower fifty cubits high, "full of ashes, with a rotating device descending steeply from every direction into the ashes. . . . he did not even reach the ground."

Jerry A. Pattengale

BERECHIAH (PERSON) [Heb *berekyāh, berekyāhû*]. Var. BERACAH. **1.** A son of Zerubbabel (1 Chr 3:20) and descendant of David. The list of Zerubbabel's offspring consists of two sections. Berechiah is one of five names occurring after a listing of two other sons and a daughter. Why Berechiah and his four brothers are isolated in this way is not clear. Two possibilities are that they have the same mother or that they were born in Judah upon Zerubbabel's migration there. Berechiah means "Yahweh blesses" and in this case participates in a list of names expressing an optimism centered around the Jews' return to Judah; Meshullam meaning "recompensed," Hasadiah, "Yahweh is loyal," Jushabhesed, "loyalty returns," etc.

2. The father of Asaph, the latter being designated as a musician in the preexilic temple (1 Chr 6:39; 15:17) along with Heman and Ethan. All three are noted as descendants of Levi. In the noted passages the name Berechiah occurs in one of three lists anachronistically placing Heman, Asaph, and Ethan in the time of David. Historically the lists belong to the postexilic era; they presuppose a stage in the temple liturgy when Levites and singers were not distinguished as Ezra 2:41 and Neh 7:44 indicates they once were. Complicated questions concerning identity arise regarding references to Berechiah in 1 Chr 6:39; 9:16; and 15:17, 23. Questions of identity are treated below in numbers 3 and 4.

3. A gatekeeper for the ark (1 Chr 15:23). This Berechiah has been identified with the postexilic Berechiah of number 4 below. Because the cultic figures mentioned in 1 Chronicles 15 are anachronistically portrayed as living in the time of David and are historically more at home in the postexilic period, an identification is possible. The identification should probably be extended to include Berechiah in 1 Chr 6:39 and 15:17. In the light of the close narrative proximity of the references to Berechiah in 1 Chronicles 15, might one assume that if distinction were intended, a patronymic or filial reference would have indicated such a difference in 15:23? The fact that in 1 Chr 15:23 Berechiah is noted as a gatekeeper for the ark while in 1 Chr 6:39 and 9:16 the same is noted as a musician does not militate against an identification. Indeed, 1 Chr 15:21, 24 cities Obededom as both musician and gatekeeper (1 Chr 15:21, 24).

4. A postexilic Levite who is listed as among the first Jews to return to Judah (1 Chr 9:16). Note the possible identifications discussed in number 3 above. If they are correct, then 1 Chr 6:39, 9:16, 15:17, 23 refer to the same Berechiah. Neh 11:15–18 contains a parallel list of Levites, but Berechiah's name does not occur there. Curtis and Madsen (*Chronicles* ICC, 172) views the Chronicles text as corrupt. Neither list is a copy of the other since there are significant differences. Instead of one list being a corruption of the other, they both probably stem from a common archival source (Myers *Ezra-Nehemiah* AB, 185) and were edited with regard to the specific intent of the redactor. Whether Berechiah's name was even part of the original archival source cannot be known.

5. A son of Iddo and father of Zechariah the prophet (Zech 1:1, 7; Matt 23:35). Ezra 5:1; 6:14; and Neh 12:16 list Iddo as Zechariah's father. The proposal that Berechiah was inserted in Zech 1:1, 7 due to the influence of Isa 8:2 lacks a basis. First, Isa 8:2 has the form Jeberechiah whereas Zech 1:1, 7 uses the form Berechiah. Assuming influence from Isa 8:2, the change in form begs an explanation. Second, does the Zechariah tradent identify the two Zechariahs, and if so, what would have led to an identification of two persons who obviously lived some two centuries apart? In short, the nature of the alleged influence is ambiguous and lacks explanation. A further consideration lies in the lack of textual evidence indicating that Berechiah is a later addition in the book of Zechariah. Available data do not admit a solution to the problem. That Berechiah was added to the Zechariah text is less likely than that the name simply was not part of the traditions used by the Ezra-Nehemiah writer or that the latter omitted Berechiah in order to enhance Zechariah's prestige by observing his immediate relationship to the venerable Iddo.

6. One of the chiefs of the Ephraimites (2 Chr 28:12) who supported and assisted in repatriating Judahite captives after the Israelite invasion of Judah during the reign of Ahaz. The Chronicler interpreted Israel's invasion of Judah as Yahweh's punishment on the latter. Berechiah's aid to the Judahite captives is a response to the prophet Oded's warning to Israel not to go beyond Yahweh's intent of chastisement. In this context the term "chief" *(rōʾš)* designates a military leader (Muller *THAT* 2:706).

7. The father of Meshullam and son of Mesheshabel (Neh 3:4, 30; 6:18). His son Meshullam worked on the refortification of Jerusalem under Nehemiah.

8. The name Berechiah occurs on a bulla from the City of David which reads *lbrkyhw // on nryhw // hspr*, "belonging to Berekyahu ben Neriah, the scribe," and is likely a reference to Jeremiah's scribe, Baruch, the latter form being a hypocoristicon for Berechiah.

Bibliography

Avigad, N. 1987. Baruch the Scribe and Jerahmeel the King's Son. *IEJ* 28: 52–56.

JAMES M. KENNEDY

BERED (PERSON) [Heb *bered*]. Grandson (1 Chr 7:20) or son (Num 26:35–36) of Ephraim, the younger son of Joseph. According to the Ephraimite genealogy in 1 Chronicles, Bered is the grandson of Ephraim as well as son of Shuthelah and father of Tahath. The significance of the 1 Chronicles passage is to point toward Joshua (v 27), an Ephraimite, the hero of the conquest. Braun (*1 Chronicles* WBC, 114) speculates that the present list in 1 Chronicles 7 could be a combination of two earlier lists due to the repetition of various names (Shuthelah, Tahath), similarity of others (Bered, v 20 and Zabad, v 21; Eleadah, v 20 and Ladan, v 26; Tahath, v 20 twice and Tahan, v 25), and length of the genealogy.

Num 26:35–36 is the only other OT listing of the Ephraimite clan. However, the LXX has an Ephraimite genealogy in Genesis 46. Based on the Numbers passage, Bered should perhaps be read Becher because it lists three brothers as sons of Ephraim: Shuthelah, Becher (Bered), and Tahan. The Peshitta even has Becher in place of Bered in 1 Chr 7:20.

Hogg (1900–1: 148–49) suggests that Bered should be deleted from 1 Chr 7:20. First, Bered is not found in G^B. Second, Becher (Bered) found its way into the Numbers passage through scribal error. Third, he notes that Greek manuscripts which include the Ephraimite genealogy in Genesis 46 know nothing of Bered-Becher.

Bibliography

Hogg, Hope W. 1900–1. The Ephraim Genealogy. *JQR* 13: 147–54.

M. STEPHEN DAVIS

BERED (PLACE) [Heb *bered*]. A place in the Negeb mentioned in connection with the story of Hagar (Gen 16:14). The well of Beer-lahai-roi is said to be located between Kadesh and Bered, but it is unclear in which direction it is located with respect to Kadesh. On the one hand, Simons (*GTTOT,* 217) identifies it with Jebel umm el-Bared, SE of Kadesh. On the other hand, *Targum Onqelos* here renders *Ḥagrāʾ*, and the *Targum Yerušalmi* renders *Ḥaluṣâ*, each of which are also used respectively for Shur (Exod 15:22). Thus there seems to have been a tradition identifying Bered either with Shur (i.e., NW Sinai) or with the Way to Shur, therefore somewhere N of Kadesh. However, if *Ḥaluṣâ* refers specifically to Elusa—a town that has been identified with el-Khalasa (M.R. 117056) and that was occupied in Byzantine times (*EAEHL* 359)—then there appears to have been a tradition locating Bered ca. 55 km NE of Kadesh (and 20 km SW of Beersheba). See also BEER-LAHAI-ROI.

GARY A. HERION

BERI (PERSON) [Heb *bērî*]. Fourth of the eleven named sons of Zophah of the tribe of Asher (1 Chr 7:36). The genealogical list of Chronicles appears to be extraordinarily full, since Beri's name is not mentioned in the parallel genealogies of Asher (Gen 46:17, 18; Num 26:44–47). In light of this, Rudolf (*Chronikbücher* HAT 1st ser., 74) emends the text from *ûbērî wĕyimrâ*, "and Beri and Imrah," a continuation of the sequence of Zophah's sons, to *ûbĕnê yimnāʿ* "and the sons of Imna," which begins a new list of sons (see 1 Chr 7:35). He has no connection with the

Berites (Num 26:44). Moreover, the Berites of 2 Sam 20:14 can be understood to be Bichrites, by grammatical construction, allies of Sheba who is called "the son of Bichri" (2 Sam 20:1).

JOEL C. SLAYTON

BERIAH (PERSON) [Heb *bĕrîʿâ*]. BERIITES. **1.** The fourth son of Asher and the father of Heber and Malchiel (Gen 46:17; 1 Chr 7:30–31). He went down to Egypt with his father when Jacob and his family migrated from Canaan to Goshen. Beriah was the grandson of Jacob and Zilpah, the maid whom Laban gave to his daughter Leah. Beriah was the ancestral leader of the family of the Beriites (Num 26:44).

2. A man from the tribe of Benjamin. Beriah was the father of Zebadiah, Arad, Eder, Michael, Ishpah, and Joha (1 Chr 8:13, 16). According to Curtis and Madsen (*Chronicles* ICC, 161), Beriah was the son of Shaharaim (1 Chr 8:8) and Hushim (1 Chr 8:11). Curtis believes that 1 Chr 8:12 is a parenthetical explanation of the genealogy of Elpaal and that 8:13 continues the genealogy of Shaharaim and Hushim. According to Hicks (*IDB* 1:386) he was the fourth son of Elpaal. Hicks believes that 8:13 continues the genealogy of Elpaal presented in 8:12 (so RSV). Other scholars (Keil 1950: 147; Myers *1 Chronicles* AB, 57), noting that Beriah is not listed as a son of Elpaal in 1 Chr 8:17–18, believe that 1 Chr 8:13 begins an independent list of Benjaminite leaders (so JB). Thus, Beriah would be neither the son of Shaharaim nor the son of Elpaal. The context, however, seems to favor Curtis and Madsen's view.

Beriah and his brother Shema were two clan leaders who fought against the inhabitants of Gath (1 Chr 8:13). The location of this Gath has been disputed by scholars. Keil (1950: 146) believed that it was the Gath of the Philistines, but Mazar (1954: 227–30) has shown that this Gath should be identified with Gittaim, a city in the Shephelah. Beriah and his brother Shema settled in the city of Aijalon. In 2 Chr 11:10, Aijalon is listed as belonging to both Judah and Benjamin.

3. A Levite from the family of the Gershonites and the fourth son of Shimei (1 Chr 23:10–11). When the Levites were organized for the service in the temple, they were grouped by families (1 Chr 23:2–32). The Gershonites were represented by Ladan and Shimei. Shimei had four sons but had only three representations. Because his sons Beriah and Jeush did not have many male sons, they were counted as one family (1 Chr 23:11).

4. A son of Ephraim (1 Chr 7:23). Ephraim named his son Beriah because of the misfortune that had befallen his family. The sons of Ephraim had raided the city of Gath to take the cattle from its inhabitants and in the struggle the sons of Ephraim were killed. Ephraim mourned the death of his sons for many days. Later, Ephraim and his wife had a son whom they called Beriah, because "evil had befallen his house."

The etymology of the name is doubtful. Some take the name Beriah as coming from a Hebrew word for evil (*BDB*, 140), others from a word for gift (Gesenius 1849:174), and others from a word meaning "prominent" (Noth *IPN,* 224). The explanation of the name should be considered an etiology (Lung 1968: 38) or a midrashic commentary (Mulder 1975: 141–66).

Bibliography

Gesenius, W. 1849. *A Hebrew and English Lexicon of the Old Testament.* Boston.

Keil, C. F. 1950. *The Book of Chronicles.* Biblical Commentaries on the Old Testament. Grand Rapids.

Lung, B. O. 1968. *The Problem of Etiological Narrative in the Old Testament.* BZAW 108. Berlin.

Mazar, B. 1954. Gath and Gittaim. *IEJ* 4: 227–35.

Mulder, M. J. 1975. I Chronick 7:21b–23 und die rabbinische Tradition. *JSJ* 6: 141–66.

CLAUDE F. MARIOTTINI

BERLIN GNOSTIC CODEX. See CODEX (BERLIN GNOSTIC).

BERNICE (PERSON) [Gk *bernikē; berenikē*]. Var. BERENICE. The daughter of Agrippa I and Cypros born in A.D. 28. Bernice was present when the apostle Paul presented his defense to her brother Agrippa II (Acts 25:13, 23; 26:30). Like the other Herods, Bernice had inherited Roman citizenship, as indicated by her full name—Julia Berenice. In A.D. 41 she married Marcus Julius Alexander, son of Alexander the alabarch. Ostraca from Egypt give some insight into Marcus' commercial activities (Fuks 1951). Upon Marcus' death shortly after the marriage, Bernice married her uncle, Herod of Chalcis before the end of A.D. 44; by him she had two sons, Berenicianus and Hyrcanus (Jos. *JW* 2.221; cf. *Ant* 19.276ff.; 20.104).

After the death of Herod of Chalcis in A.D. 48, Bernice lived as a widow for a long time with her brother Agrippa II, who received her husband's kingdom from the emperor Claudius (*Ant* 20.104). Rumors of incest with her brother are said to have led her to marry Polemo of Cilicia (cf., Braund 1984a: 42), who seems to have undergone circumcision and at least superficial conversion to Judaism. Polemo's incentive seems to have been Bernice's wealth (or her dead husbands' perhaps), which later evoked a strong attraction in Vespasian also (*Ant* 20.146; cf. Tac. *Hist.* 2.81). However, Bernice soon left Polemo to return to Agrippa (*Ant* 20.146), and was present when he heard Paul's defense in A.D. 60 (Acts 25:13–26:32). Bernice was in Jerusalem to fulfill a vow when the Jewish revolt began in A.D. 66. She sought to intercede with the Roman procurator, Gessius Florus, on behalf of the Jews, but she was ignored; in fact, she herself barely escaped the ravages of Florus' rampaging troops (*JW* 2.310ff). She wrote to Cestius, the Roman governor of Syria, complaining of Florus' maladministration. In response to her and to others' letters, Cestius sent an emissary who joined Agrippa, who was on his way to Jerusalem from Alexandria (*JW* 2.333ff.). Bernice and Agrippa made strenuous efforts to dissuade the revolutionaries, but their efforts met with only temporary success (*JW* 2.402ff.): their residence in Jerusalem was burnt down (*JW* 2.426).

She and her brother had little choice but to withdraw, and it may have been at this time that they refurbished a building in Berytus which Herod the Great, their great-grandfather, had built (*Année épigraphique* 1928, 82). Bernice subsequently contributed to the financing of Vespasian's bid for power in A.D. 68, while her beauty appealed to his son, Titus, who was some ten years her junior (Tac. *Hist.* 2.81). From the start her relationship with Titus seems to have been the subject of gossip, as was her relationship with her brother. It was even said that Titus' return to the East while en route to Rome was the result of his passion for Bernice, as Tacitus reports and denies (*Hist.*2.2).

Upon the success of Vespasian's cause, Titus finally joined his father in Rome in A.D. 71 after suppressing what remained of the Jewish revolt. But Bernice did not come with him to Rome, and not until A.D. 75 did she and Agrippa arrive in the capital. The delay may have been necessitated by power politics among Vespasian's followers, or Vespasian and Titus may simply have wished to avoid scandal until they had established their control; Vespasian was, after all, the fourth emperor of A.D. 69 and did not want to go the way of his predecessors (Crook 1951; Braund 1984b). Certainly Titus' relationship with Bernice did damage to his reputation at Rome, where queens by nature were suspect (Suet. *Tit.* 7). Rumor held that she was to become Titus' wife, and she already had begun to act as such. Two Cynics denounced Titus in the theater, for which one was flogged and the other beheaded (Dio Cass. 66.15.4–5). It may well have been at this time that Quintilian presented a case before her in which she had some personal interest (Quint. *Inst.* 4.1.9). When Titus became emperor upon his father's death in A.D. 79, people feared that he would be a tyrant. Titus took steps to improve his reputation, including the immediate (if reluctant) dismissal of Bernice from Rome (Suet. *Tit.* 7), though later she seems to have returned before Titus' death in A.D. 81, at no cost to his reputation (Dio Cass. 66.18.1).

Bernice's biography is beset by rumors and gossip of a more or less scurrilous nature. She is even said to have had another lover among Vespasian's followers, who is said to have lost his life on that account (*Epit. de caes.* 10.4). The Romans expected such behavior from queens and would even have created it where it did not exist (Braund 1984b). Bernice is regularly given the title of queen.

Bibliography

Braund, D. C. 1984a. *Rome and the Friendly King.* New York.

———. 1984b. Bernice in Rome. *Historia* 33: 120–23.

Crook, J. A. 1951. Titus and Bernice. *AJP* 72: 162–75.

Fuks, A. 1951. Notes on the Archive of Nicanor. *Journal of Juristic Papyrology* 5: 207–16.

Rogers, P. M. 1980. Titus, Bernice and Mucianus. *Historia* 29: 86–95.

DAVID C. BRAUND

BEROEA (PLACE) [Gk *Berōia*]. Var. BEREA. **1.** A city (modern Verria) located in the SW section of the Roman province of Macedonia (40°31′N; 22°14′E—in modern Greece) in the district of Emathia (Ptolemy 3.12). It is located near the base of Mount Bermius (Strabo 7.26) along a tributary of the Haliacmon river some 50 miles from Thessalonica. It is several miles south of the main road of the region, the Egnatian Way, which may account for Cicero's comment that it is a "town off the beaten track" (*In Pisonem* 36.89).

Paul and Silas traveled by night to Beroea (Acts 17:10–15) after they were driven out of Thessalonica by Jews who were angered by their teachings. Timothy seems to have rejoined Paul and Silas here after a short stay in Philippi. They were well received by the Beroeans, who are described as being "more noble than the Thessalonians." Paul taught them for several days and as a result many Jews and prominent Greeks were converted.

Soon the Jews of Thessalonica heard that Paul and his companions were in Beroea. They traveled to the city and upon arrival they incited the crowds to oppose Paul. Some of the local Christians guided Paul to the coast and on to Athens. Timothy and Silas remained in Beroea and later rejoined Paul in Corinth (Acts 18:5). It is not clear if Paul sailed to Athens from a nearby port (possibly Dium) or followed the road which traced the coastline to Athens. Paul is later accompanied by Sopater of Beroea (Acts 20:4) who may have been converted during Paul's brief stay in the city. It is likely that Sopater was sent as delegate of the local congregation to accompany the money they gave to help the needy of Judea.

It is unclear when the city of Beroea was founded, but it was certainly prosperous by the end of the 4th century B.C. as attested by an inscription (*IG,* 2/5). Polybius mentions Beroea twice (27.8; 28.8) and it was the first city to surrender to Rome after the Battle of Pindar in 168 B.C. It was assigned to the third of the four districts of Macedonia (Livy 44.45; 45.29). According to tradition Onesimus was the first bishop of the city. The bishopric of Beroea was under the metropolitan of Thessalonica and was later assigned its own metropolitan by Andronicus II (1283–1328). The Turks captured the city in 1373/74. Few remains of the ancient city remain except the walls and several inscriptions which have been found at the site. See Jackson and Lake 1965: 206–8; Leake 1835: 290–92.

2. Hellenistic name assigned to the city of Aleppo located (36°10′N; 37°0′E) in northern Syria (2 Macc 13:4). It was renamed in honor of the Macedonia city by Seleucus Nicator (312–280). The Seleucid king Antiochus Eupator, who was marching with a large contingent of soldiers to Judea, had former high priest Menelaus put to death at Beroea (2 Macc 13:1–8). The death sentence was ordered after the king was informed by Lysias of the treason of Menelaus. The execution was carried out according to local customs, with the accused dropped into a lofty tower (about 88 ft high) filled with hot ashes. Josephus records the death of Menelaus but assigns it to the end of the war between Judas and Lysias (*Ant* 12.9.7).

The name of the city reverted to its Semitic origins (Haleb) when it came under Muslim control. The name Aleppo was derived from a distortion of the name Haleb by Venetian merchants. Aleppo grew in importance during the medieval period when it was an important link in the caravan trade route linking Europe with the East. Its prosperity waned when an alternate sea route was discovered. Aleppo, one of the largest cities in Syria today, is noted for its impressive ruins of a medieval castle which sits on top of a steep glacis 150 ft above the center of the city.

3. Berea was the camp of the soldiers led by Bacchides

and Alcimus who moved after encamping against Jerusalem and just prior to the battle with Judas Maccabeus (1 Macc 9:4). The exact location of the city is debated with two possible options: al-Bireh, a city located 8 miles N of Jerusalem; and Bir ez-Zait, a town located 13 miles N of Jerusalem.

Bibliography

Foakes Jackson, F. J. and Lake, K. eds. 1965. *The Beginnings of Christianity.* Pt. 1, *The Acts of the Apostles.* Vol. 4. Grand Rapids. Repr.

Leake, W. M. 1835. *Travels in Northern Greece.* Vol. 3. London.

JOHN D. WINELAND

BEROLINENSIS, CODEX. See CODEX (BERLIN GNOSTIC).

BEROTHAH (PLACE) [Heb *bērôtâ*]. One of the places which mark part of the N boundary of Israel as envisioned by Ezek 47:15–16. The LXX places Berothah at the beginning of the verse and immediately after Zedad. Although it is difficult to determine whether the final *he* is a directional marker or an original part of the name, the place may be identical with the Berothai mentioned in 2 Sam 8:8. Accordingly, Berothah may be located on the site of modern Bereitan (33°55′N; 36°08′N) in the Beqaᶜ Valley of Lebanon. As noted by Zimmerli (*Ezekiel* 2 Hermeneia, 517–543), the extent to which Berothah and other places in Ezek 47:15–16 marked actual boundaries of Israel at some point in its history has provoked much discussion by M. Noth, K. Elliger, and other scholars.

HECTOR AVALOS

BEROTHAI (PLACE) [Heb *bērōtay*]. City from which David took much bronze (2 Sam 8:8), and a principal city of the kingdom of Zobah at the time of its conquest by David. It may be located on the site of modern Bereitan (33°55′N; 36°08′) in the Beqaᶜ Valley of Lebanon. Instead of Berothai, the parallel passage in 1 Chr 18:8 mentions Cun, a place about seven miles to the N. Berothai may be identical with the Berothah mentioned in Ezek 47:16.

Bibliography

Pitard, W. 1987. *Ancient Damascus.* Winona Lake, IN.

HECTOR AVALOS

BERRIES. See FLORA.

BESAI (PERSON) [Heb *bēsay*]. The head of a family of *nĕtînîm* (temple servants) (see NETHINIM) which is listed among those exiles returning from Babylon to Jerusalem and Judah (Neh 7:52 = Ezra 2:49; 1 Esdr 5:31). The Greek spelling of the name differs in all three occurrences: *Bēsi* (Nehemiah), *Basi* (Ezra), *Basthai* (1 Esdras). Although Zadok (1980: 113) believes the name remains unexplained by using onomastic criteria, others, such as Myers (*Ezra-Nehemiah* AB,14) and Clines (*Ezra, Nehemiah, Esther* NCBC, 57), believe it to be Babylonian. It has been suggested that the name is a possible contraction of the name *bĕsôdĕyāh* found in Neh 3:6 (Gehman *NWDB*, 105).

Bibliography

Zadok, R. 1980. Notes On The Biblical and Extra-Biblical Onomasticon. *JQR* 71: 107–17.

RODNEY H. SHEARER

BESCASPASMYS (PERSON) [Gk *Beskaspasmus*]. In 1 Esdr 9:31, this name is possibly an alternate form of Mattaniah.

BESODEIAH (PERSON) [Heb *bĕsōdyāh*]. The father of Meshullam, the latter having assisted in the refortification of Jerusalem under the leadership of Nehemiah (Neh 3:6). This name is made up of a preposition, a noun, and the theophoric element representing Yahweh. It presumably means "in Yahweh's council." Speculation is not out of place regarding the possibility that the name recalls the prophetic experience of being admitted to the divine council (1 Kgs 22:19–23; Isaiah 6; Jer 23:18, 22).

JAMES M. KENNEDY

BESOR, THE BROOK (PLACE) [Heb *naḥal bĕśôr*]. A brook or wadi David and four hundred of his men crossed in pursuit of the Amalekites following the Amalekite raid on the town of Ziklag (1 Sam 30:9, 10, 21). The Brook Besor, Wadi Shalleh, or Ghazzeh, along with the Valley of Gerar, Wadi esh-Shari, has been described as one of the two major wadis of the western Negeb (*LBHG,* 26–27).

Because of the flooding waters during the rainy season and the large area for which the Besor provided drainage, the bed of the wadi was extremely wide, approximately 100–150 meters, a width which started near Beer-sheba and continued to the coast (Orni and Efrat 1973:45). The towns along the Besor from the coast eastward include Tell el-Ajjul, Tell Jemmeh, Tell el-Farah (south), Beer-sheba, and Arad (Oren 1982: 155). Ziklag was located near the wadi (Borowski 1988:24). The numerous ancient mounds in the area provide evidence of the strategic and economic importance of the area in ancient times. In the Middle Bronze Age, the heavily fortified cities along the Wadi Besor and Wadi Gerar provided a defense system for the southern border of the land (Oren 1982: 156–57). The fortifications in this region were responsible for the failure of the Israelites to penetrate the land of Canaan from the south, through the Negeb, at the time of the conquest (*LBHG,* 200–201). The Wadi Besor was the scene of many confrontations in ancient times as the nomads from the south sought grazing lands for their flocks to the north, a region comprised of settled communities (Oren 1982: 157).

Bibliography

Borowski, O. 1988. The Biblical Identity of Tel Halif. *BA* 51: 21–27.

Oren, E. D. 1982. Ziklag: A Biblical City on the Edge of the Negeb. *BA* 45: 155–66.
Orni, E., and Efrat, E. 1973. *Geography of Israel.* Jerusalem.
LaMoine F. DeVries

BESTIALITY. See PUNISHMENTS AND CRIMES; SEX AND SEXUALITY.

BET. The second letter of the Hebrew alphabet.

BETA. The second letter of the Greek alphabet.

BETAH (PLACE) [Heb *beṭaḥ*]. A city belonging to Hadadezer, king of Zobah in Syria, from which David took a large amount of bronze (2 Sam 8:8). The name of this N Syrian town is problematic. The Syriac reads *ṭbḥ* and the Lucianic mss of the LXX read *(ma)tebak,* both apparently referring to the well-attested N Syrian town of TIBHATH (cf. the 1 Chr 18:8 parallel). The MT in 2 Sam 8:8 thus reflects an erroneous metathesis of the first two consonants. See also TEBAH (PERSON).

BETEN (PLACE) [Heb *beṭen*]. A town appearing only once in the Bible, in the opening verse of the description of the territory of Asher (Josh 19:25). Beten is therefore to be sought in the S part of the coastal plain N of the Carmel. Eusebius seems to include a reference to this town in his note that "Batnai [is] today called Bethbeten, at the eighth mile east of Ptolemais" (Kosterman 1904: 52, lines 19–20). Abel (*GP,* 2: 264) pointed out that the name had survived in the modern Kh. Ibtin (M.R. 160241), 18 km SE of Acco. Sherds from the relevant periods have not been found at that site, therefore Beten should be located at one of the sites in the vicinity (*EncMiq* 2:50), probably at Tell al-Far less than a km NW of Kh. Ibtin (*HGB,* 430). The discrepancy with Eusebius' distances is to be explained in that the point where the road to Bethbeten turned off from the Ptolemais-Sepphoris road was at the eighth mile stone.

Bibliography

Klosterman, E. 1904. *Eusebius Das onomastikon der Biblischen ortsnamen.* Leipzig (Repr. 1966).

Rafael Frankel

BETH-ANATH (PLACE) [Heb *bêt ʿanat*]. A Canaanite designation for a city, comprised of Beth, "house of" (in modern Heb *bêt* and in Ar *beit*) and the name of the famous goddess Anath, known also as *btlt ʿnt,* "the virgin *ʿanat*" (*UT* 19.1889). The adoration of the goddess Anath was already popular in Canaan prior to the Israelite conquest and settlement, and her sanctuary is the town's focal point.

Beth-anath, according to the tribal allotments cited in the Bible, is located among the fortified towns under the control of Naphtali (Josh 19:32–39). The Naphtalites settled among the Canaanite inhabitants without driving them out, and the latter became tributaries to the former (Judg 1:33). The precise location of the city, however, has not been determined. Geographical identifications advanced by Guérin (1880: 374), Albright (1923: 18–20), and Alt (1926: 55) are discredited by Aharoni (1957: 70) as lacking suitable archaeological support. The locations do not seem to yield any evidence of a *tell,* nor are they identified with a location resembling a fortified Canaanite city resisting the Israelite incursions. Even Garstang (*Joshua, Judges,* 102; 244–45) who offers a mound as the site of Beth-anath is unable to substantiate it satisfactorily (Aharoni 1957: 97).

Two places remain as possible candidates for the geographical location of Beth-anath, ?Hîneh and ?Safed el-Battikh (M.R. 190289). Klein (1933: 5–7; 1939: 16) stated that the talmudic *byt ʿnh* (*b. Kil.* 2.16) was a border city along N Transjordan, and identified it with the modern town of Hîneh, SW of Damascus. The same city is mentioned in the Talmud as *bʾynh* (j. *ʿOr.* 3.7). It is also assumed that *rwm byt ʿnt* (t. *Miqw.* 6.3) and *rmt bny ʿnt* (*ʾAbot R.Nat.* 27) refer to the same place. The Sages describe it as a city whose population is partly gentile, but which is within Israelite biblical borders (Rashi *mwblʾwt* b. *Giṭ* 4a). Grintz (1964: 67), who accepted Klein's identification, proposed that this city is the biblical Beth-anath. He relied on the account of Josephus (*Ant* 5.86) which depicted the territory of the Naphtalites as extending E to Damascus and thus he placed the city along the E Israelite border of Naphtali.

There is, however, another claimant for the ancient city of Beth-anath, the modern place of Safed el-Battikh (Aharoni 1987: 330; Boling, *Joshua* AB, 406). The city appears in Egyptian inscriptions, perhaps as early as LB I and explicitly in LB II. The topographical lists of Thutmose III cite N locations captured by the great Pharaoh (Simons 1937: 113, 118) and the records of King Seti I enumerate *b-t ʿ-n-t or b-(y)-t ʿ-n-t* (Simons 1937: 144–46) situated along the route connecting Hazor and Tyre, and passing next to Kedesh. The city is mentioned again during the campaigns of Rameses II: "*k-r-p* the town which his majesty obliterated on the mount of *b-t ʿ-n-t*" (Simons 1937: 149, 152–53, 160–61). Beth-anath was apparently in a mountainous region and the area took its name from the city.

Zenon papyri (PSI 554; 594) mention the estate of a Greek officer in Baitanatois which Tcherikover (1933: 234–36) equates with Beth-anath in the Galilee. Aharoni goes one step further and identifies it with the biblical Beth-anath (1957: 71–72) and fixes the geographical location in the region NW of Kedesh (Aharoni, *MBA,* 113, map 177). While analyzing Zenon's itinerary, Aharoni dismisses Klein's identification of the talmudical *byt ʿnh=(ʿnt)* (1957: 72).

The name of *rwm byt ʿnt* in rabbinic sources seems to support Aharoni's view. The terminology resembles the old Egyptian nomenclature, mount *b-y-t ʿ-n-t* identified in the upper Galilee, NW of Kedesh. Moreover, the Sages testify to the mixed population of the city and tell of a permanent pool in which more than two thousand *kor* of water was aggregated, a fact which is substantiated by Conder (SWP 1: 95, 104) who surveyed the region and found a warm spring forming a pool next to Safed el-Battikh situated in the heights. Further, Eusebius (*Ono-*

mast. 52) identifies Beth-anath in the tribe of Naphtali, as the village Batanaia, 15 miles from Caesarea where it is told that healing bathhouses were located. It is possible that the reference of Eusebius parallels the talmudic *rwm byt ʿnh = (ʿnt)*, and Caesarea, as Aharoni suggests, is Caesarea Philippi (1957: 73). This would put Batanaia in the vicinity of Safed el-Battikh in the upper Galilee.

The site of Beth-anath cannot be established unequivocally until an archaeological survey of the region is taken. Many mounds in N Israel still await excavation, and among them, no doubt, will be found the precise location of Beth-anath.

Bibliography

Aharoni, Y. 1957. *The Settlement of the Israelite Tribes in Upper Galilee.* Jerusalem (in Hebrew).

———. 1987. *Eretz Israel in Biblical Times.* Jerusalem (in Hebrew).

Albright, W. F. 1923. Contributions to the Historical Geography of Palestine. Pp. 1–46 in *AASOR* 2–3, ed. W. J. Moulton. New Haven.

Alt, A. 1926. Das Institute in Yahre 1925. *PJ* 22: 5–80.

Grintz, J. M. 1964. Judges Chapter 1. Pp. 42–71 in *Studies in the Bible,* ed. J. M. Grintz and J. Liver. Jerusalem (in Hebrew).

Guérin, V. 1868–1880. *Description Géographique, Historique et Archeologique de la Palestine. La Galilee.* Paris.

Klein, S. 1933. Notes on History of Large Estates in Palestine. *BIES* 1: 3–9 (in Hebrew).

———. 1939. *Sefer ha-Yishuv.* Jerusalem.

Simons, S. J. 1937. *Handbook for the Study of Egyptian Topographical Lists Relating to Western Asia.* Leiden.

Tcherikover, V. 1933. Palestine in the Levant of the Papyric of Zenon. *Tarbiz* 33: 226–47 (in Hebrew).

MEIR LUBETSKI

BETH-ANOTH (PLACE) [Heb *bêt ʿănôt*]. One of the cities in the hill country of the tribe of Judah (Josh 15:59). Beth Anoth is listed fifth in a list of six cities after Halhul (modern Ar Ḥalḥûl, M.R. 160109), Beth Zur (Kh. eṭ-Ṭubeiqeh, M.R. 159110), Gedor (Kh. Jedûr, M.R. 158115), and Maarath, and before Eltekon. The cities in this list that have been identified all lie in a line N of Hebron. Eusebius (Klosterman ed., 24, 94) connected Gk *Bethanin* or *Bethenim* with a place 2 miles from the Terebinthos (Oaks of Mamre—modern Ramat el-Khalil, M.R. 160107) and 4 miles from Hebron. Kallai (*HGB,* 391) connects the LXX[B] (Codex Vaticanus) *Baithanam* and A (Codex Alexandrinus) *Baithanōm* renderings of Beth Anoth with Eusebius' site and with modern Kh. Beit ʿAnûn (M.R. 162107). As with most ancient names containing the word *bêt* (house), Beth Anoth may be related to the temple of a god which gave its name to the locale (*LBHG,* 108). Frank (1972:84) claimed that Beth Anoth, along with Beth Anath and Anathoth, was a place name that was derived from the name Anath, an active goddess of fertility.

Bibliography

Frank, H. T. 1972. *An Archaeological Companion to the Bible.* London.

SUSAN E. MCGARRY

BETH-ARABAH (PLACE) [Heb *bêt hāʿărābâ*]. ARABATHITE. A city on the boundary between Judah and Benjamin, near Jericho. It is mentioned four times in the OT, twice each in the boundary descriptions in Joshua 15 (vv 6, 61) and 18 (vv 18, 22). The name might mean "place of the depression" (BDB, 112) or "House of the Desert Rift" (Boling and Wright *Joshua* AB, 366).

There is a similar discrepancy between each of the two pairs of occurrences of the name. According to Josh 15:6, the boundary of Judah passes N of Beth-arabah, while v 61 includes it as one of six cities of Judah in the wilderness. Likewise Josh 18:18 describes the border of Benjamin as "passing on to the north of the shoulder of Beth-arabah" (MT's *mûl-hāʿărābâ* is regularly emended to *bêt-hāʿărābâ*), while v 22 includes Beth-arabah as one of 12 cities of Benjamin. The discrepancy suggests to some commentators that the city belonged to Benjamin at one time, but later changed hands (see *HGB,* 337, 343, 373). Beth-arabah has been identified with ʿAin el-Gharbeh (M.R. 197139) on the N bank of the Wadi Qelt, about 3 miles SE of Jericho and about the same distance W of the Jordan river. Simons (*GTTOT,* 173) observes, however, that the unemended MT of Josh 18:18 suggests a location further W in the hills (see also the reservations expressed by Kallai *HGB,* 396, 400). One would expect the border to be the bed of the wadi, but this is only one of several uncertainties of this border.

One of the thirty champions associated with King David was Abi-albon the Arabathite (2 Sam 23:31; in 1 Chr 11:32 the name is Abiel). The gentilic "Arabathite" is usually taken to refer to Beth-arabah.

HENRY O. THOMPSON

BETH-ARBEL (PLACE) [Heb *bêt ʾarbēʾl*]. A town razed by Shalman (Hos 10:14). Its defeat must have been particularly brutal (cf. Hos 10:14b) and well known. The prophet Hosea cites Beth-Arbel as an example of the massive destruction facing Israel.

Both Beth-Arbel and Shalman are mentioned only in Hos 10:14; neither can be identified with certainty. Beth-Arbel is most often identified with Arbela of the Transjordan (modern IRBID, M.R. 229218), located near Pella. Arbela, mentioned by Eusebius (*Onomast.* 14:18), was located at an economically and militarily important cross-road (Glueck 1951: 153–54). Its destruction would have been a significant and well-remembered event. However, we do not have records of atrocities at modern Irbid in Jordan (Andersen and Freedman *Hosea* AB, 571). Josephus (*Ant* 12.11.1 §421) and 1 Macc 9:2 refer to a second town named Arbela, located just W of the Sea of Galilee. This Arbela has also been identified as Beth-Arbel. However, it is questionable whether the Galilean Arbela was important enough for its defeat to become a byword for violent and large-scale devastation.

Bibliography

Astour, M. C. 1971. 841 B.C.: The First Assyrian Invasion of Israel. *JAOS* 91: 383–389.

Glueck, N. 1951. *Explorations in Eastern Palestine, IV.* AASOR 25–28. Cambridge, MA.

CAROLYN J. PRESSLER

BETH-ASHBEA (PLACE) [Heb *bêt ʾašbēaʿ*]. Location of a family or guild of linen workers descended from Shelah, son of Judah (1 Chr 4:21). Although older translations (e.g. KJV) understood Ashbea as referring to the family of the linen workers it is now accepted that the name refers to their place of residence and should more properly be called Beth-ashbea (cf. RSV and NJV). It was located in the Shephelah district of Judah's settlement, probably in the region of Mareshah, mentioned in the same verse. Noth (1932: 123) speculated that there may have been some connection between the linen factory (about which term see Demsky 1966: 214) at Beth-ashbea and the weaving and dyeing works found by Albright at Tell Beit-Mirsim. The mention of the linen factory at Beth-ashbea adds greatly to our scanty knowledge of guilds and craftsmen in ancient Israel (see Mendelsohn 1940 and de Vaux *AncIsr* 1: 76–78).

Bibliography

Demsky, A. 1966. The Houses of Achzib: A Critical Note on Micah 1:14b. *IEJ* 16: 211–15.

Mendelsohn, I. 1940. Guilds in Ancient Palestine. *BASOR* 80: 17–21.

Noth, M. 1932. Eine siedlungsgeographische Liste in 1. Chr. 2 und 4. *ZDPV* 55: 97–124.

CARL S. EHRLICH

BETH-AVEN (PLACE) [Heb *bêt ʾāwen; bêt ʾôn*]. **1.** A city of Benjamin located near the Ephraimite border between Jericho and Bethel/Luz (Josh 18:12). 1 Sam 13:5 locates Michmash E of Beth-aven, while 14:23 narrates that Israelites under Jonathan pursued Philistine soldiers from Michmash past Beth-aven, presumably toward their home country to the W. In the late 8th century B.C., Hosea (5:8) seems to have warned Gibeah, Ramah, and Beth-aven of an imminent military invasion.

The modern identity of the site is disputed. M. Noth (1935) argued that the toponym was merely a derogatory term for Bethel (see below). J. Grintz (1961: 212–15) identified Beth-aven with et-Tell, but this location does not match information from the above-mentioned texts. Rejecting Albright's proposal of Burqa, Z. Kallai-Kleinmann (1956) suggested that Tell Maryam (M.R. 175141), a mound in the Wadi es-Swenît 1 km W of Mukhmas, best suits the biblical information regarding Beth-aven for two reasons. First, its location in the valley, almost certainly part of the ancient Benjamin-Ephraim border, fits the requirements of Josh 18:12. Second, Tell Maryam's location to the W of Mukhmas (see MICHMASH) is consonant with the situation of Beth-aven reported in 1 Sam 13:5 and 14:23. A recent archaeological survey (Kochavi 1972) found Iron Age remains at Tell Maryam to support of Kallai-Kleinmann's proposal.

Beth-aven's close proximity to ancient Gibeah (Jabaʿ?) and Ramah (er-Ram) also might suggest that Hosea's war-alarm did not refer to Judah's hypothesized counterattack against Israel along the watershed highway after the Syro-Ephraimite invasion (Alt 1959), but rather to the original Syro-Ephraimite attack itself, cf. 2 Kgs 16:5 and Isa 10:27–32 (Arnold 1987: 241–49).

2. A derogatory term (Heb. *bêt ʾāwen,* "house of wickedness") for the Israelite shrine at Bethel (Amos 5:5; Hos 4:15; 10:5). The Hebrew root *ʾwn* can be vocalized to mean either "wealth" or "wickedness" (Coote 1971: 392–94); Amos and Hosea seem to have ridiculed Bethel by creating a pun on the name of the nearby Benjaminite city of Beth-on. This confusion may explain the gloss on the MT of Josh 7:2, which associates Beth-aven with Bethel/Ai, as well as the entire MT vocalization of *beth ʾwn* to mean "house of wickedness."

Bibliography

Alt, A. 1959. Hosea 5:8–6:6: Ein Krieg und seine Folgen in prophetischen Beleuchtung. Pp. 163–87 in *Kleine Schriften zur Geschichte des Volkes Israel.* Vol. 2. Munich.

Arnold, P. 1987. Gibeah in Israelite History and Tradition. Ph.D. diss. Emory University, Atlanta.

Coote, R. 1971. Hosea xii. *VT* 21: 389–402.

Grintz, J. 1961. Ai which is Beside Beth-Aven: A re-examination of the identity of Ai. *Bib* 42: 201–16.

Kallai-Kleinmann, Z. 1956. Notes on the Topography of Benjamin. *IEJ* 6: 180–87.

Kochavi, M. 1972. *Judea, Samaria, and the Golan: Archaeological Survey 1967–68.* Jerusalem. (in Hebrew).

Noth, M. 1935. Bethel und Ai. *PJ* 31: 13.

PATRICK M. ARNOLD

BETH-AZMAVETH (PLACE) [Heb *bêt-ʿazmawet*]. An alternate form of Azmaveth.

BETH-BAAL-MEON (PLACE) [Heb *bêt baʿal măʿôn*]. A northern Moabite town more commonly called Baal-meon, also known as Beth-meon and, probably, Beon. After the Hebrew victory over the Amorites, this settlement was assigned to the tribe of Reuben (Num 32:3, 38; Josh 13:17; 1 Chr 5:8). The alternative names Beth-baal-meon/Baal-meon appear in the Mesha Inscription (lines 9, 30), where the Moabite king says he rebuilt the town and made a reservoir in it. Jeremiah (48:23) and Ezekiel (25:9) mention this place name in their oracles against Moab. Samaria ostracon 27 contains a reference to "Baala the Baalmeonite." The village of Maʿin (M.R. 219120), located ca. four miles southwest of Medeba, is the probable location of ancient Beth-baal-meon, though archaeological confirmation is lacking. See also BAAL-MEON; MAON; MEUNIM.

GERALD L. MATTINGLY

BETH-BARAH (PLACE) [Heb *bêt bārâ*]. An undetermined location thought to be near the Jordan river (Judg 7:24). Here the Ephraimites, under the direction of Gideon, cut off the fleeing Midianites by seizing the area around the Jordan up to this point. The precise meaning of the place name is obscure, leading some to postulate a textual corruption from an original *bēt ʿăbārâ* (meaning place of ford), which would associate the locale with a river crossing. One might place it among the streams in the

Wadi Far^cah, W of the river, but there is a general skepticism about identifying it with Bethabarah of the NT (John 1:28). See also BETHANY BEYOND THE JORDAN.

JEFFREY K. LOTT

BETH-BIRI (PLACE) [Heb *bêt-birʾî*]. A town in which the sons of Simeon dwelt prior to the reign of David (1 Chr 4:31). Apparently the same place is named BETH-LEBAOTH in Josh 19:6. The name may be preserved in Jebel el-Biri, 10 km SW of el-Khalasa (M.R. 117056).

GARY A. HERION

BETH-CAR (PLACE) [Heb *bêt-kār*]. A village in the territory of Benjamin near MIZPAH where the Israelites defeated the Philistines under the direction of Samuel (1 Sam 7:11). After being thrown into confusion by Yahweh, the Philistines fled and were pursued by the Israelites as far as an area below Beth-Car. The location of the site is unknown, though ʿAin Karim and Beth-horon have been proposed (see McCarter *1 Samuel* AB, 146). Several scholars have noted the similarities between the battle described here and the one recounted in 1 Sam 4 and have suggested that this narrative was written with the intention of wiping out the dishonor created by that earlier defeat (McCarter *1 Samuel* AB, 149–50; Garsiel 1983:41–44). Beth-Car figures into the relationship between these two chapters in that the narrative apparently places the erection of the monument stone called Ebenezer here (cf. 1 Sam 7:12, translating *ʿad-hēnnāh* with McCarter (*1 Samuel* AB, 146–47) as "to this point" rather than "hitherto" with RSV). Ebenezer, in turn, is where the Israelites were defeated and the ark taken by the Philistines in 1 Sam 4. A. Weiser (1959) is the most notable of those who see at least part of 1 Samuel 7 as containing a historical account which predates the composition of 1 Samuel. This means that the parallels with the battle described in chap. 4 are reflections of historical coincidence and not the design of the narrator.

Bibliography

Garsiel, M. 1983. *The First Book of Samuel.* Israel.

Weiser, A. 1959. Samuels "Philister-Sieg": Die Ueberlieferung in 1. Samuel 7. *ZTK* 56: 253–72.

JEFFRIES M. HAMILTON

BETH-DAGON (PLACE) [Heb *bêt-dāqôn*]. **1.** A town situated in the Shephelah, or lowlands, of Judah (Josh 15:41), within the same district as LIBNAH and MARESHAH. The only OT reference to this settlement, whose name apparently means "House/Temple of Dagon," occurs in the list of towns within the tribal allotment of Judah (Josh 15:21–62). The theory that this list is derived from an administrative roster compiled under the Judean Monarchy (Alt 1925) has been widely accepted, although controversy continues over the precise makeup of the districts, the proper context of the town lists of Benjamin and Dan, and the period of the monarchy to which the original roster belongs (Boling and Wright *Joshua* AB, 64–72; see also JOSHUA, BOOK OF). This Judean settlement has often been identified with a town of the same name in the vicinity of Jaffa which the Annals of Sennacherib claim was captured during the campaign of 701 B.C. (*ANET,* 257). If this suggestion is accepted, the ancient settlement is probably to be found in the vicinity of modern Beit Dajan (*LBHG,* 374; M.R. 134156), located approximately 9 km southeast of Jaffa. However, such an identification seems doubtful, considering the fact that the remainder of the identifiable towns in this lowland district are located approximately 40 km to the southeast. The location of the ancient town remains uncertain.

2. A town situated on the southern border of the tribal allotment of Asher (Josh 19:27). The historical and editorial context of the boundary lists of the northern tribes is a subject of continued controversy. One viewpoint suggests that the boundary lists of Joshua 19 are based on ancient documents describing either tribal claims from the period of the old tribal league (Alt 1953), or (excluding Simeon) the official internal boundaries of the Kingdom of Israel (*LBHG,* 233–34). An alternative perspective (Noth 1935) argues that these boundary lists, rather than being authentic border descriptions, are based on a partial list of border stations to which an editor added a series of connecting verbs. That many scholars (*LBHG,* 235–39; Boling and Wright *Joshua* AB, 442–67) have found it possible to trace the path indicated by these connecting verbs with a great deal of precision strongly suggests that they stem from actual boundary descriptions rather than mere editorial approximations. Although the exact location of the ancient town remains unclear, a recent proposal to identify it with Tell Regeb (Boling and Wright *Joshua* AB, 454; M.R. 159240), about 8 km SE of Haifa is attractive in both geographical and archaeological terms.

Bibliography

Alt, A. 1925. Judas Gaue unter Josia. *PJ* 21: 100–16.

———. 1953. Das System der Stammesgrenzen im Buche Josua. *KlSchr* 1:193–202.

Noth, M. 1935. Studien zu den historisch-geographischen Dokumenten des Josuabuches. *ZDPV* 58: 185–255.

WADE R. KOTTER

BETH-DIBLATHAIM (PLACE) [Heb *bêt diblātāyim*]. A town mentioned in Jeremiah's oracle against Moab (48:22). According to this verse, "judgment has come upon the tableland," i.e., God's wrath was unleashed against a number of Moabite settlements, including Beth-diblathaim. The Mesha Inscription (line 30) reports that King Mesha of Moab rebuilt Medeba and Beth-diblathaim, among other towns. The same line of this Moabite text mentions Beth-diblathaim between Medeba and Beth-baal-meon, possibly indicating that this town was positioned on the Moabite plateau in the vicinity of the other two sites.

Beth-diblathaim is perhaps identical with Almon-diblathaim, one of the stops on the Israelites' route between Mt. Hor and the plains of Moab. According to Num 33:46–47, Almon-diblathaim was situated between Dibon and the mountains of Abarim, on the Moabite tableland. Assuming that Beth- and Almon-diblathaim are alternative biblical names, both the OT and the Mesha Inscription allow for identification with a site somewhere in the tableland north of the Wādī el-Mūjib. Many scholars associate the ancient place name in question with Khirbet Deleilât esh-Sherqîyeh (M.R. 228116), located ca. ten miles north-northeast of Dhiban. Recently, Khirbet Libb, which is located on the King's Highway ca. eight miles north of Dhiban, has been linked with ancient Beth- and Almon- diblathaim. Neither of these site identifications is certain.

Gerald L. Mattingly

BETH-EDEN (PLACE) [Heb *bêt ᶜeden*]. Var. EDEN. Aramean kingdom in the upper bend of the Euphrates 200 miles NE of Israel, attested in 9th–8th century B.C. texts (Amos 1:5). It is first mentioned by this name in 884 B.C. in Assyrian inscriptions relating rebellion among other Aramean kingdoms (*GARI* II §547). Although subdued by Assurnasirpal II seven years later (*GARI* II §582–83), the first three years of Shalmaneser III's reign were again occupied with the subjugation of Beth-Eden (857–585 B.C.; *LAR* §559–61, 599–601), after which he renamed the kingdom's major cities (the capital Til-Barsip on the east bank of the Euphrates becoming Kar-Shalmaneser). Because the kingdom does not subsequently figure prominently as an independent political entity, some locate the Beth-Eden of Amos 1:5 elsewhere (written at least a century after the above events), noting that a mid-7th century Aramaic letter (*KAI* 233.14–15) points to a similarly named locale in southern Mesopotamia. But Tiglath–Pileser III in the latter half of the 8th century does refer to certain Syrian cities by the old designation Beth-Eden (*LAR* §821). In later texts the conquered "people of Eden" (2 Kgs 19:12 = Isa 37:12) and simple "Eden" (Ezek 27:23) are probably connected with this formerly independent kingdom, for it is named in conjunction with other Euphrates locales, while Ezekiel associates Eden with Lebanon (Ezekiel 31).

Bibliography

Lemaire, A. 1981. Le pays d'Eden et le Bît-Adini: aux origines d'un mythe. *Syria* 58:313–330.

Sader, H. S. 1987. *Les états araméens de Syrie depuis leurs fondation jusqu'à leur transformation en provinces assyriennes.* Beirut.

Samuel A. Meier

BETH-EGLAIM (PLACE) [Gk *Bēthaglaim*]. A village eight Roman miles from Gaza, according to Eusebius (*Onomast.* 48.19). Beth-eglaim is not mentioned in the Scriptures. By analogy with EN-EGLAIM (Ezek 47:10) it has been Hebraicized as *bêt ᶜeglayim.*

Conder (1896: 235) was the first to suggest identifying Beth-eglaim with TELL EL-ᶜAJJUL (M.R. 093097), about four miles SW of Gaza. Petrie (1931–34) excavated Tell el-ᶜAjjul as ancient Gaza, choosing the name on the basis of the mention of *palaia Gaza* in Diodorus Siculus (19.80) as the site of a battle between Ptolemy and Demetrius in 312 B.C.E. (19.81–84). However after the appearance of Maisler's 1933 article it has been common to equate Beth-eglaim and Tell el-ᶜAjjul (for modern dissenters see below). Major components of the argument for the identification of the two lie in Beth-eglaim's situation at the coast according to Eusebius and in the similarity of their names, Beth-eglaim meaning "house/temple of the two calves" in Hebrew ("cattle farm," according to Kempinski 1974: 146), and Tell el-ᶜAjjul, meaning "mound of the little calf" in Arabic. The name may refer to a temple of Baal or Hadad with an iconography of twin bullocks (see Albright 1938: 337 n. 1 and Stinespring *IDB* 1: 389).

Tell el-ᶜAjjul is a major site of 28–32 acres. It lies on the N bank of Nahal Besor (Wadi Ghazzeh, see BESOR, THE BROOK), near its estuary into the Mediterranean Sea and along the Via Maris, "way of the sea," one of the major routes leading from Egypt into Palestine.

Petrie personally excavated at ᶜAjjul from 1931–1934, while a team under his direction excavated there one additional short season in 1938 (Petrie, MacKay, and Murray 1952). Petrie's interpretation of his finds proved suspect, and most studies follow the lines of interpretation and chronology first laid out by Albright in 1938 (see also Stewart 1974: 9–14, 59–61 and Tufnell *EAEHL* 1: 52–61.

Although earlier periods were represented on the S bank of the Nahal Besor, the earliest finds at ᶜAjjul date to EB IV (Kenyon's Intermediate Early Bronze–Middle Bronze Age; see Kenyon 1956). These consist of two cemeteries, one to the NW (1500) and one to the E (100–200) of the tell.

The earliest remains found on the tell itself come from the Courtyard Cemetery on the N and have been dated to MB I. A number of scarabs bearing the names of Egyptian officials, as well as a small statue and a carnelian bead bearing names found at the S end of the tell, could indicate the presence of a contemporaneous settlement, although no structural remains have been found.

ᶜAjjul became a city of major proportions in MB II–III. This great expansion took place during the so-called "Hyksos" period of Egyptian history (Dyn. 15–16), when Egyptian and Canaanite relations were particularly close. Tell el-ᶜAjjul, situated at the junction of the major N–S route from Egypt into Canaan and of a major inland route along the Nahal Besor, as well as being a port city, was in a perfect position to take advantage of growing international commercial contacts. This finds graphic expression in the wealth of gold objects recovered from the tell. Evidence of Tell ᶜAjjul's position as a center of international trade is also indicated by the early and rich appearance of Bichrome Ware at the site starting with the final phase of Palace I and increasing during the succeeding period (LB I; see Epstein 1966: 174–185; and Artzy, Asaro, and Perlman 1973).

Construction of the MB city appears to have followed a well-thought-out plan. The fosse surrounding the tell on three sides was deepened (presumably the slope on the SW side facing Nahal Besor was sufficient for defensive purposes), and debris from it was used to heighten the slope on the top of the tell. Sandstone from this quarrying was also used to lay the foundations of the large Palace I on the N. Inside the walls, the city was laid out according to careful plan (see Yassine 1974). City III on the S was most probably contemporary with Palace I. Both were covered by a thick destruction layer which Albright dated to the period of the anti-Hyksos campaigns of the 18th Dynasty shortly after 1570 B.C.E.

After a brief interval, the palace was rebuilt. Palace II was a more modest structure constructed entirely of bricks. It was contemporary with the early phase of City II. Palace II was eventually succeeded by the fortress-like Palace III, whose appearance was followed in the construction of

Palaces IV and V. It would appear that ᶜAjjul progressively lost importance as a city and became an Egyptian military outpost (Palaces III–V). This was most likely related to the concurrent rise of the importance of nearby Gaza. Eventually Egypt lost control over the area to the Philistines, and the site was virtually abandoned.

Although Tell el-ᶜAjjul has most often been identified with Beth-eglaim, and indeed that has become the name of the site in modern Hebrew, in recent years strong arguments have been raised against this identification.

Kempinski (1974) has argued that ᶜAjjul should be identified with Sharuhen, the site of the Hyksos' last stand after their expulsion from Egypt. First, Tell el-ᶜAjjul lies too close to Gaza to be the Beth-eglaim mentioned by Eusebius. Second, the finds from the tell do not indicate settlement there at the time of Eusebius. He would therefore seek Beth-eglaim in the vicinity of Deir el-Balah, roughly twice as far from Gaza. Third, he has redated the architectural remains from the tell, pushing their dates back in time from those proposed by Albright. Palace II/City II would then be the one destroyed shortly after 1570, pursuant to which the New Kingdom administrative center in SW Canaan shifted to Gaza. Finally the identification of Sharuhen at Tell el-ᶜAjjul, rather than at Tell Farah (South), is based on ᶜAjjul's being the largest city in the region in the Middle Bronze Age. In Kempinski's opinion also the situation directly on the coastal road, rather than twenty additional kms farther inland along the Nahal Besor, would be more fitting for the great Hyksos stronghold which took three years to conquer. Stewart (1974: 63) had previously arrived at the same conclusion regarding the identification of ᶜAjjul. In this they have been followed by Naᵓaman (1980: 147–48) and Weinstein (1981: 4, 6; who, however, sees no need to redate Palace II/Level II to the end of the Hyksos period rather than to the period afterward).

Aḥituv has argued against the attempt to sever Tell el-ᶜAjjul from its identification as Beth-eglaim and to identify it instead with Sharuhen (1984: 171–73). Although conceding that ᶜAjjul would fit the history of Sharuhen in the Hyksos and New Kingdom periods, Aḥituv feels that it departs from what is known of Sharuhen in its lack of habitation at the time of Shishak's campaign in the late 10th century, if one follows Kempinski's dating of Palace V to the 12th century. As regards the location of the tell, Aḥituv feels that if ᶜAjjul were to be identified as Sharuhen, it would lie too far to the SW to be included in the Simeonite geographical lists (Josh 19:6). Also in his opinion an inland location of Sharuhen at Tell el-Farah (South) would not be inconsistent with its location on the Via Maris. He concludes that ᶜAjjul is to be identified with Beth-eglaim, and that its location at the time of Eusebius is to be sought at one of the small sites in the vicinity, perhaps at Tell es-Sanam, on the S side of Nahal Besor and hence slightly farther from Gaza and more in keeping with the geographical information contained in Eusebius.

Resolution of the identification of Beth-eglaim must await further archaeological investigation.

Bibliography

Albright, W. F. 1938. The Chronology of a South Palestinian City, Tell el-ᶜAjjûl. *AJSL* 55: 337–59.

Aḥituv, S. 1984. *Canaanite Toponyms in Ancient Egyptian Documents.* Jerusalem and Leiden.

Artzy, M.; Asaro, F.; and Perlman, I. 1973. The Origin of the "Palestinian" Bichrome Ware. *JAOS* 93: 446–61.

Conder, C. R. 1896. The Onomasticon. *PEFQS* 229–45.

Epstein, C. 1966. *Palestinian Bichrome Ware.* Leiden.

Kempinski, A. 1974. Tell el-ᶜAjjûl—Beth-Aglayim or Sharuḥen? *IEJ* 24: 145–52.

Kenyon, K. M. 1956. Tombs of the Intermediate Early Bronze-Middle Bronze Age at Tell Ajjul. *ADAJ* 3: 41–55.

Maisler (Mazar), B. 1933. Der antike Name von *tell ᶜaddschūl. ZDPV* 56: 186–88.

Naᵓaman, N. 1980. The Inheritance of the Sons of Simeon. *ZDPV* 96: 136–52.

Petrie, W. M. F. 1931–34 *Ancient Gaza I–IV.* London.

Petrie, W. M. F.; MacKay, E. J. H.; and Murray, M. A. 1952. *City of Shepherd Kings and Ancient Gaza V.* London.

Stewart, J. R. 1974. *Tell el ᶜAjjūl: The Middle Bronze Age Remains.* Studies in Mediterranean Archaeology 38. Göteborg.

Weinstein, J. M. 1981. The Egyptian Empire in Palestine: A Reassessment. *BASOR* 241: 1–28.

Yassine, K. N. 1974. City Planning of Tell el ᶜAjjul. *ADAJ* 19: 129–33.

Carl S. Ehrlich

BETH-EKED (PLACE) [Heb *bêt ᶜēqed*]. A town on the road from Jezreel to Samaria (2 Kgs 10:12–14) where Jehu encountered forty-two kinsmen of Ahaziah, the late king of Judah. Jehu seized the men and had them all killed in a pit at Beth-Eked as a part of his campaign against the rulers of Israel and Judah.

The toponym, which can be translated as "house of binding," occurs once (2 Kgs 10:12) with the appellation "of the shepherds" (Heb *hāro ᶜîm*). The LXX interprets Beth-eked as a proper noun, while the Targum translates the name as "meetinghouse."

Many scholars (*GP,* 271) have located the town at Beit Qad (M.R. 208192) in part due to the similarity between the ancient and modern names. However, as Simons (1959: 363) has pointed out, Beit Qad, which is located about three miles east of Jenin (M.R. 178207), is well to the east of any reasonable route between Jezreel (M.R. 181218) and Samaria (M.R. 168187). Others (*GTTOT,* 363) have suggested the village of Kafr Ro'i (M.R. 165198) as the location of Beth-Eked, based upon both the location of the town on a hill above the disused rail tracks between Jenin and Samaria and the similarity of the name to the appellation *hāroᶜîm,* used in reference to Beth-Eked. While this identification is more in keeping with the context of the story, neither identification is entirely convincing.

Bibliography

Simons, J. 1959. *The Geographical and Topographical Texts of the Old Testament.* Leiden.

Melvin Hunt

BETH-EMEK (PLACE) [Heb *bêt hāᶜēmeq*]. A town that appears only once in the description of the territory of the tribe of Asher (Josh 19:27). Robinson (1857: 134) pointed out the similarity of the name to that of ᶜAmqa (M.R.

166264), eleven km NE of Acco, and Guerin (1880: 23) identified Beth-emek with this site. This is almost certainly the "Kefar Amiko" of Talmudic literature (*t. B. Qam.* 8, 10 = p. 362; *b. Taᶜan.* 21A), but no antiquities of the Iron Age or earlier were found at the site. Saarisalo, who had initially also identified Beth-emek at ᶜAmqa, later suggested Tel Mimas (M.R. 164263), two km SW of ᶜAmqa (1929: 36 n. 1; 1930:6). He found Iron Age pottery at the site, and since then LB pottery has also been found. Consequently, the neighboring kibbutz has been named Beth Ha'emek.

The territory of Asher is, in Joshua, clearly described from south to north, and Beth-emek is listed before Cabul (Josh 19:27). The latter can almost certainly be identified at the modern village of Kabul or in its immediate vicinity. See CABUL. Tel Mimas, however, is not south but north of Kabul. If it is presumed that the place names appear in exact geographical order, the identification with Tel Mimas is untenable; thus, Gal (1985) has recently suggested locating Beth-emek at Kh. Mudawer Tamra (M.R. 169250), five km S of Kabul.

Zadok (1985: 157), however, has shown ᶜAmqa to have the same denotation as Beth-emek. There is also every indication that many of the place names in the description of the territory of Asher are not in exact geographical order, and many scholars regard some of these as part of a town list inserted between sections of the border description (Alt 1927: 68–71), thus allowing for the identification of Beth-emek with Tel Mimas (*LBHG,* 376).

Bibliography

Alt, D. 1927. Eine galilüische Ortsliste in Jos. 19. *ZAW* 4: 59–81.

Gal, Z. 1985. Cabul, Jiphtah-El and the Boundary between Asher and Zebulun in the Light of Archaeological Evidence. *ZDPV* 101: 114–27.

Guerin, V. 1880. *Description Géographique Historique et Archéologique de la Palestine.* Vol. VII. Paris (Reprint 1969).

Robinson, E. 1857. *Neuere Biblische Forschungen in Palâstina, Tagebuch einer reise im Jahre 1852.* Berlin.

Saarisalo, A. 1929. Topographical Researches in Galilee. *JPOS* 9: 27–40.

———. 1930. Topographical Researches in Galilee II. *JPOS* 10: 5–10.

Zadok, R. 1985. Notes on Modern Palestinian Toponyms. *ZDPV* 101: 156–61.

RAFAEL FRANKEL

BETH-EZEL (PLACE) [Heb *bêt hāʾēṣel*]. An unknown location in the Shephelah (Mic 1:11). The LXX Symmachus, the OL versions, and the Vg translated the phrase along the lines of "the house next door" (so van Hoonacker 1908: 360; cf. Zech 14:5). But the substantive *ʾēṣel,* "proximity, conjunction," is otherwise used in the Hebrew Bible only as a preposition, "beside, in proximity to;" and "the house next door" does not help with the sense of the passage. In the paronomastic poem of Mic 1:10–16, the pun stems from the verbal root *(ʾṣl)* meaning "withdraw, withhold, take away," a conceptual wordplay on the "take away from" (Heb *yiqqaḥ min*) in the following colon. Thus, an appropriate translation might be, "mourning in 'Withholdon' (Beth-ezel) will keep its support (Heb *ᶜemdâ*; cf. van Hoonacker 1908: 361–62; Allen *Joel, Obadiah . . .* NICOT, 276) from you."

Bibliography

Hoonacker, A. van. 1908. *Les Douze Petits Prophètes: Traduits et Commentés.* EBib. Paris.

Luker, L. M. 1985. *Doom and Hope in Micah: The Redaction of the Oracles Attributed to an Eighth-Century Prophet.* Ph.D. Diss. Vanderbilt University.

LAMONTTE M. LUKER

BETH GADER (PLACE) [Heb *bêt-gādēr*]. One of the references to a geographical name within a genealogical framework (*LBHG,* 246), Beth Gader is listed as the son of Hareph, son of Hur, within the tribe of Judah (1 Chr 2:51). Though its exact location has not been identified, Beth Gader was probably an important border city in the vicinity of Bethlehem (M.R. 169123) and Kiriath-jearim (modern Dier el-ᶜÂzar, M.R. 159135), which appear with it in the genealogy (*EncMiqr* 2: 70). Aharoni, who claims the name derives from the cities fortifications (from Heb *gādēr,* "wall" or "enclosure"), suggests that Beth Gader, along with the other towns in its genealogical list, lies in the NE section of the Shephelah near the Valley of Elah (*LBHG,* 109, 248) which begins M.R. 149121 and runs to the Mediterranean coastal region.

SUSAN E. MCGARRY

BETH-GAMUL (PLACE) [*bêt gāmûl*]. A town located in Moab's tableland, named in Jer 48:23 along with a number of other settlements in this region that were the objects of God's wrath. Since the town is not mentioned anywhere else in the Bible, it has been suggested that Beth-gamul was founded relatively late in history. Such an explanation is not necessary, however, since it is likely that Jeremiah's list of place names included some that were unimportant. Beth-gamul has been equated with Khirbet el-Jemeil, a site with extensive Iron Age ruins that is located ca. eight miles east of Dhiban, but this identification is uncertain.

GERALD L. MATTINGLY

BETH-GILGAL (PLACE) [Heb *bēt gilgāl*]. A town in the general vicinity of Jerusalem, where levitical singers had been established and from which they were summoned to participate in the dedication of Jerusalem's rebuilt walls (Neh 12:29). It is often suggested that it be identified with the more famous Gilgal situated near Jericho, but since *gilgāl* was a common place name in Israel and the text presumes its proximity to Jerusalem for the Levites functioning in the temple, it is preferable to locate the town in the environs of Jerusalem. See also GILGAL.

JEFFREY K. LOTT

BETH-HACCHEREM (PLACE) [Heb *bêt hakkerem*]. One of five districts, or district capitals, of the province of Judah during the Persian Period. Neh 3:14 indicates it was ruled by Malchijah, son of Rechab. According to Jer 6:1, a fire signal station was located there.

Both 3QInv (3Q15) and 1QapGen mention a Beth-haccherem in conjunction with the King's Valley where the tomb of Absalom was located (2 Sam 18:18). Some scholars believe that the *Karem* which the LXX adds to the list of places in Joshua 15:59 may be the same as Beth-haccherem.

Based on Jeremiah's association of Tekoa with Beth-haccherem (Jer 6:1), as well as Jerome's comment that it could be seen from Bethlehem, the proposal has been made that Beth-haccherem be identified with the Herodium (M.R. 173119), although this view has gained little support. Others have suggested that the village of ᶜAin Karim, ca. 6.5 km W of Jerusalem (M.R. 165130), preserves the name of the ancient site. It has further been suggested that cairns located on top of Jebel Ali, which overlooks ᶜAin Karim, could have served as the beacons for Beth-haccherem. The most recent proposal for Beth-haccherem is RAMAT RAHEL, ca. 4 km S of Jerusalem (M.R. 170127; Aharoni, *LBHG,* 432). This location can be harmonized with the ancient sources, and it also would have been ideal for a fire signal station. The recovery of ancient remains from the last years of the kingdom of Judah would also tend to support such an identification.

Bibliography

Avi-Yonah, M. 1977. *The Holy Land From the Persian to the Arab Conquest (536 B.C.–A.D. 640).* Grand Rapids.

Glueck, N. 1951. *Explorations in Eastern Palestine, IV.* AASOR 25–28. New Haven.

Randall W. Younker

BETH-HAGGAN (PLACE) [Heb *bêt haggān*]. A place toward which Ahaziah king of Judah fled when attacked by Jehu king of Israel (2 Kgs 9:27). Ahaziah was fleeing S from Jezreel (v 15) toward Samaria and Jerusalem. Thus he should have taken the main road going SW from Jezreel to modern Jenin, where the natural pass from the Jezreel valley into the Samaria mountains is located. Knowing the road, Jehu ordered an ambush to kill the king of Judah in the narrow pass of GUR leading to the Dothan valley. After being mortally wounded, Ahaziah abruptly changed direction and headed to Megiddo, where he died.

The identification of Beth-haggan must, therefore, be connected to modern Jenin (M.R. 178207), where the name—lit. "house of the enclosure" *(gan)*—was well-preserved in the Roman period as Ginaea, marking the border between Galilee and Samaria and described as "a village situated in the great plain" (*JW* 3.48). In 1968 Porath discovered in the center of modern Jenin a tell of 30 dunams in area, upon which the central bus station was later built. The pottery collected proved that the site existed in the EB I, MB I, LB I–II, Iron I–II, Persian, Hellenistic, Roman, Byzantine, medieval, and Ottoman periods. This discovery enabled the identification, on the same place, of *Kn* (E7 of the later Execration Texts), as suggested by Mazar (1974: 25). It seems as well that this is "kur-Gina" of EA 250, mentioned in connection to the events which took place after the death of Labayu, prince of Shechem. With the identification of Harabu (EA 250) with el-Hurab in the Dothan valley (Zertal 1984: 59–65), it seems even more probable that "kur-Gina" and Beth-haggan were indeed located at Jenin.

Bibliography

Mazar, B. 1974. *Canaan and Israel.* Jerusalem (in Hebrew).

Zertal, A. 1984. *Arubboth, Hepher and the Third Solomonic District.* Tel Aviv (in Hebrew).

Adam Zertal

BETH-HARAM (PLACE) [Heb *bêt hārām*]. Var. BETH-HARAN. A valley allotted by Moses to the tribe of Gad on the east side of the Jordan (Josh 13:27), which includes the city of Beth-nimrah, among others. However Num 32:36 reports that Beth-haran (modern Beit Harran?) and Beth-nimrah (M.R. 210146) are both specific towns controlled by Gad. The discrepancy between a comprehensive territory and a locality is explained by Loewenstamm (1972) and later Kallai (1983) who define various stages in the report of the conquest of the Transjordan. These places were apparently fortified holding pens for livestock and were useful as staging points for persons crossing the Jericho into Canaan.

After working from surveys made in the nineteenth century, Glueck (1951) concludes that both Beth-haram and Beth-haran refer to the same Tell Iktanu (Ikhtenu, M.R. 214136) on the southern side of wadi er-Rameh. Excavations (Prag 1974: 97) have not determined which biblical town is found during the Middle Bronze Age at Tell Iktanu.

Bibliography

Glueck, N. 1951. *Explorations in Eastern Palestine.* AASOR 25–28/1: 389–95.

Kallai, Z. 1983. Conquest and Settlement of Trans-jordan. *ZDPV* 99: 110–118.

Loewenstamm, S. E. 1972. The Relation of the Settlement of Gad and Reuben in Nu 32:1–38. *Tarbiz* 42: 12–26 (in Hebrew).

Prag, K. 1974. The Intermediate Early Bronze—Middle Bronze Age: Interpretation of the Evidence from Transjordan, Syria, and Lebanon. *Levant* 6:69–116.

Paul Nimrah Franklyn

BETH-HOGLAH (PLACE) [Heb *bêt-hoglâ*]. A village that was on the border between the territories of the tribes of Judah and Benjamin (Josh 15:6; 18:19). It is also listed as one of the cities in the territory of Benjamin (Josh 18:21). The border descriptions place Beth-hoglah and its companion village Beth-arabah just N of the bay on the northern shore of the Dead Sea at the mouth of the Jordan River. Beth-hoglah, one of the villages that may be named after an animal (partridge—Heb *hoglâ; LBHG,* 255), was identified by Eusebius (Klosterman ed., 48) with what was in his time called Agla. Today it is identified as modern Dier Hajlah (M.R. 197136), a site near ᶜAin Hajlah SE of Jericho. Its companion village of Beth-arabah (modern ᶜAin el-Gharabeh, M.R. 197139) lies just to the N. Though the linguistic evidence for this identification is very strong, the artifacts recovered from this area do not preceed the Byzantine period. Beth-hoglah and its companion village

Beth-arabah have played an important part in the study of the historical development of the biblical text. Beth-arabah appears in both the city lists of the tribe of Judah (Josh 15:61) and the lists of the tribe of Benjamin (Josh 18:22). While Beth-hoglah only appears in the list of Benjaminite cities (Josh 18:21), it clearly appears, along with Beth-arabah, S of the border (in Judah) in the border description of the S border of Benjamin (Josh 18:19). Beth-arabah is also clearly S of the border in the description of Judah's N boundary (Josh 15:6). These discrepancies have led scholars to conclude that the borders between the tribes shifted over time and that cities may have belonged to different territories in different periods. Kallai (1960: 48) wrote that the N border description of the tribe of Judah (Josh 15:5–11) represented the border after the conquests of David. He claimed the list of Judean cities (Josh 15:21–61) was part of Solomon's second district (*HGB*, 373) but also showed signs of later editing (Hezekiah's time). He concluded that the list of the cities in Benjamin (Joshua 21–17), dating after the division of the kingdoms, could only represent the historical situation during the period between Abijah's conquest and Judah's expulsion from Mt. Ephraim during Asa's war with Baasha (*HGB*, 404).

Bibliography

Kallai, Z. 1960. *The Northern Boundaries of Judah from the Settlement of the Tribes Until the Beginning of the Hasmonaean Period.* Jerusalem (in Hebrew).

SUSAN E. MCGARRY

BETH-HORON (PLACE) [Heb *bêṯ-hôrôn*]. A levitical city assigned to the tribe of Ephraim. The earliest records indicate that there were two cities known as Beth-horon, the one Lower Beth-horon and the other Upper Beth-horon, each situated on the "ascent of Beth-horon." The later writer of Chronicles reveals that the Beth-horons were built by Sheerah (1 Chr 7:24), the daughter of Beriah, who was one of the sons of Ephraim. According to Joshua Beth-horon came under the control of the Hebrews at the time of the Conquest. In this battle (Josh 10:10–11) many of the Amorites were slaughtered at Gibeon, and the remaining Amorites were chased to the ascent of Beth-horon. At the time of the allotment, Lower Beth-horon was given to the descendants of Joseph, that is to say, the Ephraimites (Josh 16:3), while Upper Beth-horon was on the border between Ephraim (16:5) and Benjamin (18:13–14).

During the Philistine wars when the Israelites had been scattered, one of three companies of Philistine "raiders" assaulted Beth-horon, while Saul and Jonathan stayed in Geba (1 Sam 13:18). Later, as a result of the Egyptian capture and burning of Lower Beth-horon (1 Kgs 9:15–17), this site was one of the rebuilding projects of Solomon along with Jerusalem, Hazor, Megiddo, Gezer, Baalath, and Tamar. In a parallel Chronicles text (2 Chr 8:5–6) both Upper and Lower Beth-horon are mentioned as having been fortified with walls, gates, and bars (cf. Myers *2 Chronicles* AB, 13,48). The final reference to Beth-horon is in the account of a raid by disbanded Israelite troops who killed 3000 in Judah, from Samaria to Beth-horon (2 Chr 25:13).

Outside the OT the only references to the Beth-horons are in the intertestamental literature and in the Church Fathers. During the Maccabean Wars Beth-horon was the site of two revolts under the leadership of Judas (1 Macc 3:16, 24; 7:39). The cities were later fortified by Bacchides after the battle with Jonathan (1 Macc 9:50). In *Jubilees* 34:4 the king of Beth-horon during the time of Jacob is mentioned. Beth-horon was also one of the villages held by the Jews against Holofernes (Jdt 4:4).

Beth-horon is a twin city: Upper Beth-horon has been identified with Beit ʿUr el-Foqaʾ (M.R. 16143), while Lower Beth-horon has been associated with Beit ʿUr et-Tahta (M.R. 158144). These identifications are uncontested. The Beth-horons are located in the mountains of Judah in the valley of Aijalon, the most important of all the routes in the hill country from the coastal plain. Beit ʿUr et-Tahta sits on a hill, not dissimilar in height, size, vegetation, or form from its environs. High hills are visible to the N, E, and S, while the deep valley of Aijalon is preserved in two parallel faults, making an easy approach to the mountains from the W. Beit ʿUr et-Tahta has a commanding view of the coastal plain below; it thus occupies a central position of communication between the hill country and the plain. Beit ʿUr el-Foqaʾ, ca. 2.5 km SE, sits on a hilltop site similar in structure to many others in the area. The most important things about these two sites were their role in the security of Judah and their significant impact on commerce. Beth-horon was one of the major cities on the route from Joppa, Lydda, Bethel, and Jericho crossing over to Rammoth-ammon.

A question regards which Beth-horon is referred to in the Hebrew Bible. This is a debated, unresolved problem. Without presenting any evidence, Simons (*GTTOT,* 204) identifies the Beth-horon of Joshua 21 with Beit ʿUr el-Foqaʾ; but others like Albright (1929: 6) have argued for Beit ʿUr et-Tahta. Central to the question is Ephraim's border. According to Josh 16:5 the border of Ephraim goes as far as Upper Beth-horon, while in Josh 16:3 the allotment to Joseph extends "as far as the territory of Lower Beth-horon." Traditionally geographers have wanted to separate these two cities, but that option is not as attractive as it appears on the surface. In the first place, there are references to the "ascent of Beth-horon" and to the "going down of Beth-horon." Garstang (*Joshua, Judges,* 179) first suggested that this distinction "may possibly trace its origins to the fact that two different routes led from the plains of Gibeon towards the coast, but Aharoni (*LBHG,* 59) has proposed that "ascent" and "descent" simply depend on one's direction. Both points have credibility. When one approaches Beth-horon from el-Jîb, one has the feeling of climbing to Lower Beth-horon and then on to Upper Beth-horon. However, when coming from the coastal plain, the same perception is had; but the approach is from the opposite direction. The biblical narrative often is not clear whether the approach is from el-Jîb (E) or from the coastal plain (W).

Garstang's "two route" theory has been supported by recent surveys at both Beth-horons (Peterson 1977: 281). When Beit ʿUr et-Tahta was surveyed, the tell was sterile with the exception of its N face. The S face was only slightly terraced. However, the N side, facing the valley, was covered with shards. Just the opposite was found at

ʿUr el-Foqaʾ. The only part of the tell not sterile at el-Foqaʾ was the S face toward the deep valley. This suggests that et-Tahta's population overlooked and protected the valley and trade routes along its N side, while the ancient occupation at el-Foqaʾ overlooked and protected the valley and trade routes along its S side. Some communication system could easily have been developed between the fortified cities. Pottery supports occupation at both sites as early as Iron II.

Robinson (1841: 62) presents an examination of all the literature written on Beth-horon until his June 9, 1838 visit. He identified the site as Beth-horon, and all geographers since have accepted Robinson's identification.

Since 1926 there have been many surveys at both el-Foqaʾ and et-Tahta. The surveys have shown that the pottery chronologies at el-Foqaʾ begin with LB, while at et-Tahta the earliest is Iron II. However, what is most interesting is that from Iron II forward each period is represented at both sites, giving more credibility to the "twin cities" thesis. Earlier geographers had failed to recognize the antiquity of the pottery at el-Foqaʾ, perhaps because of the many references to Lower Beth-horon in the Bible. The conclusion that can be drawn from the archaeological evidence is a close occupational relationship between the two cities. It is only when one city is specifically mentioned that the other is excluded. Given the occupational history and settlements of both cities, the Beth-horon of Josh 21:22 and of 1 Chr 6:68 must be *both* Beit ʿUr el-Foqaʾ and Beit ʿUr et-Tahta.

Bibliography

Albright, W. F. 1929. New Israelite and Pre-Israelite Sites: The Spring Trip of 1929. *BASOR* 35: 1–14.

Boling, R. 1985. Levitical Cities: Archaeology and Texts. Pp. 23–32 in *Biblical and Related Studies Presented to Samuel Iwry.* Winona Lake, IN.

Peterson, J. L. 1977. A Topographical Surface Survey of the Levitical "Cities" of Joshua 21 and 1 Chronicles 6. Th.D. diss., Seabury-Western Theological Seminary.

Robinson, E. 1841. *Biblical Researches in Palestine.* Vol. 2. Boston.

John L. Peterson

BETH-JESHIMOTH (PLACE) [Heb *bêt hayĕšimôt*]. A place in the Shittim valley N of the Dead Sea and E of the Jordan River mentioned in four biblical passages (Num 33:49; Josh 12:3; 13:20; Ezek 25:9). The first of these is part of a larger passage (Num 33:5–49) giving the itinerary of the Israelites in their journey from Egypt to the plains of Moab. Beth-jeshimoth is mentioned twice in Joshua, first (12:3) as a point of reference in a delineation of the boundaries of the Amorite kingdom of Sihon, and next (13:20) in Moses' allocation of that defeated kingdom to the Reubenites (on the implied linking of Exodus and Conquest traditions, see Soggin *Joshua* OTL, 154–55; Boling *Joshua* AB, 340–41). In a brief oracle against Moab, Ezekiel (25:9) lists the city as one of the three principal sites of that region.

The second element of the same occurs in Hebrew with the definite article (noted by Aharoni *LBHG,* 109), but the first element (Heb *bêt,* lit. "house") is variously interpreted or omitted by LXX translators (see *LBHG,* 98). The ancient name can be detected in that of Khirbet es-Suweimeh, although the view of Glueck (1943: 23–26) that nearby Tell ʿAzeimeh was the actual ancient site is generally followed (Ottosson 1969: 124; *LBHG,* 113; Miller 1989: 582 n. 8).

Bibliography

Glueck, N. 1943. Some Ancient Towns in the Plains of Moab. *BASOR* 91: 7–26.

Miller, J. M. 1989. The Israelite Journey through (around) Moab and Moabite Toponymy. *JBL* 108: 577–95.

Ottosson, M. 1969. *Gilead: Tradition and History.* ConBOT 3. Lund.

C. Gilbert Romero

BETH-LE-APHRAH (PLACE) [Heb *bêt lĕʿaprâ*]. A town, otherwise unknown, mentioned only in Mic 1:10 within a paronomastic dirge lamenting the fall of the Shephelah cities, which formed the military bulwark for Jerusalem. Through a pun on the following Hebrew word, *ʿapar,* 'dust,' the poet obviously wishes to convey the sense of "house of dust." The grammatical problem is the preposition *l,* which normally does not occur after a construct. The exegete might omit the *l* with the support of the Targum, Syriac, and Theodocian, to find possible reference to one of two attested Ophrahs (Heb *ʿoprâ*), but one of these towns lies in Benjamin and the other in Manasseh, both inappropriate localities for the Micah text. An alternative is to understand the *l* as possessive (Williams 1976: 30, 270; *GKC,* 130a), so that *bêt lĕ* (van Hoonacker 1908: 359 reads *mibbêt lĕ,* but MT *bĕbêt* is better, given the parallelism with *bĕgat,* "in Gath" in 10a; cf. BDB, 110b; *GKC,* 130aN) carries the sense of "within" Ophrah/Aphrah (see Rudolph *Micah* KAT, 9, 12). But simplest, and in this case best, is to accept Beth-le-aphrah and the difficult Beth-ezel alongside Shaphir, Zaanan (v 11), and Maroth (v 12) as currently unknown localities named in the Micah 1 text. Given the ancient Hebrew custom of lamenting in dust and ashes, a plausible translation of v 10 would be, "In Gath, tell it not! Weep not at all! In 'Ashton' (Beth-le-aphrah) roll round in the dust!"

Bibliography

Fohrer, G. 1967. Micha 1. Pp. 65–80 in *Das Ferne und Nahe Wort,* ed. F. Maass. BZAW 105. Berlin.

Hoonacker, A. van. 1908. *Les Douze Petits Prophètes.* EBib. Paris.

Luker, L. M. 1985. Doom and Hope in Micah. Ph.D. Diss. Vanderbilt University.

Williams, R. J. 1976. *Hebrew Syntax.* 2d ed. Toronto.

Lamontte M. Luker

BETH-LEBAOTH (PLACE) [Heb *bêt lĕbāʾôt*]. Var. LEBAOTH. Simeonite town located in the Judean NEGEB and listed between HAZAR-SUSAH and SHARUHEN (Josh 19:6). In the list of towns in the Negeb district of Judah, it appears in its abbreviated form as LEBAOTH, between SANSANNAH and SHILHIM (Josh 15:32). However, in the Simeonite genealogy in 1 Chr 4:31 its place is taken by BETH-BIRI, between HAZAR-SUSIM and SHAARAIM. The relationship between Beth-lebaoth and Beth-biri is unclear. It is possible that they were one and the same place, in which case Beth-lebaoth could have been the site's preexilic and Beth-biri its postexilic name (see "Beth-biri" in *IDB* 1: 389). Or they may have been two separate sites located in the same general area (implicit in Abel *GP 2:* 269, 368). Rudolph (*Chronikbücher* HAT, 38) has conjectured that Beth-biri (Heb consonantal *byt brʾy*) and Beth-lebaoth (Heb *byt lbʾwt*) may be biforms of the same name, drawing on different Heb word roots for lion (*ʾry* and *lbʾ*) respectively (in which case he would emend Beth-biri to Beth-ari *byt ʾry*). The site of Beth-lebaoth has not been identified, although it was probably located in the vicinity of Sharuhen.

CARL S. EHRLICH

BETH-MAACAH (PLACE). See ABEL-BETH-MAACAH (PLACE).

BETH-MARCABOTH (PLACE) [Heb *bêt hammarkābôt, bêt markābôt*]. Beth-marcaboth is listed in Josh 19:5 and in 1 Chr 4:31 as one of the settlements occupied by the tribe of Simeon in the aftermath of the Conquest. Since the tribe of Simeon was assimilated to that of Judah at an early date, and most of the Simeonite towns are listed again clearly in the record of the Judean settlements in Josh 15:21–32, an explanation for its absence there is necessary.

In Josh 19:5–6a the text reads: Ziklag, Beth-marcaboth, Hazar-susah, Beth-lebaoth; the parallel passage in Josh 15:31–32a has: Ziklag, Madmannah, Sansannah, Lebaoth. Since these short sections of the list begin and end with the same towns (Lebaoth being a variant for Beth-lebaoth), it is likely that the towns in between are also to be equated. An explanation for this difference is that Madmannah is the earlier name for the site. The name Beth-marcaboth, meaning "the house of the chariots," may have been given to it under Solomon, who is known to have trafficked in chariots and horses (1 Kgs 10:28–29). The older name of the site may be preserved at Khirbet Umm ed-Deimneh though no Iron Age remains have been found there (Abel *GP 2:* 372). The nearby site of Khirbet Tatrit (M.R. 143084), 18.5 km NE of Beersheba, has yielded Iron Age pottery (Kochavi 1972: 80–81; Aharoni, *LBHG,* 431).

Bibliography

Albright, W. F. 1924. Egypt and the Early History of the Negeb. *JPOS* 4: 131–61.

Kochavi, M. 1972. The Land of Judah, Pp. 80–81 in *Judea, Samaria and the Golan, Archaeological Survey 1967–68,* ed. M. Kochavi. Jerusalem (in Hebrew).

Naʾaman, N. 1980. The Inheritance of the Sons of Simeon. *ZDPV* 96: 136–52.

JEFFREY R. ZORN

BETH-MEON (PLACE) [Heb *bêt măʿôn*]. A N Moabite town more commonly called Baal-meon, also known as Beth-baal-meon and, probably, Beon. After the Hebrew victory over the Amorites, this settlement was assigned to the tribe of Reuben (Num 32:3, 38; Josh 13:17; 1 Chr 5:8). The alternative names Beth-baal-meon/Baal-meon appear in the Mesha Inscription (lines 9, 30), where the Moabite king says he rebuilt the town and made a reservoir in it. Jer 48:23 and Ezek 25:9 mention this place name in their oracles against Moab. Samaria Ostracon 27 contains a reference to "Baala the Baalmeonite." The village of Maʿin (M.R. 219120), located ca. 4 miles SW of Medeba, is the probable location of ancient Beth-baal-meon, though archaeological confirmation is lacking.

GERALD L. MATTINGLY

BETH-MILLO (PLACE) [Heb *bêt millôʾ*]. An otherwise unattested place mentioned together with the "citizens of Shechem" as part of an assembly responsible for the enthronement of Abimelech, king of Shechem (Judg 9:6, 20 [2 times]). The passage seems to be earlier than the surrounding narrative (Richter 1963: 305) and may reflect a secondary interpretation of a traditional description of the environment of Shechem.

Several identifications of Beth-millo have been offered (Soggin 1973). The term has been taken to refer to the acropolis of Shechem, presumed to be identical with the *migdal* "tower" mentioned in Judg 9:46. Most who follow this line of interpretation identify the site as an important part of the urban defense system; others consider it to have been an area outside the city (either connected with or separate from the *migdal*).

If the second element of the name Beth-millo means "filling" (from Heb *mlʾ* 'to fill'), it may refer to the foundation of the upper city (so Boling *Judges* AB, 171). This has generally been presumed to be the meaning of the (identically spelled) word *millôʾ* 'Millo' designating an area of fill on the E slope of the city of David (2 Sam 5:9; 1 Kgs 9:15, 24; 11:27; 1 Chr 11:8; 32:5). See MILLO (PLACE). A *bêt millôʾ* is referred to in this area also (2 Kgs 12:21), perhaps "a prominent building in the Millo" (Cogan and Tadmor *II Kings* AB, 139). Beth-millo would then be related to the later function of the urban acropolis as a part of the defense system which included the priests, other temple personnel, and soldiers who inhabited the area (Soggin 1973).

The etymology of the word *millôʾ* remains rather doubtful. It is possible that the word is a borrowing from Eg *m3rw,* which designates a part of the king's court (Görg 1985: 60). Beth-millo may thus be a term for the residential area of the king at Shechem (and Jerusalem, respectively) and may designate the administrative center of the city.

Bibliography

Görg, M. 1985. Methodological Remarks on Comparative Studies in Egyptian and Biblical Words and Phrases. Pp. 57–64 in *Pharaonic Egypt, the Bible, and Christianity,* ed. S. I. Groll. Jerusalem.

Richter, W. 1963. *Traditionsgeschichtliche Untersuchungen zum Richterbuch.* BBB 18. Bonn.

Soggin, J. A. 1973. Bemerkungen zur alttestamentlichen Topographie Sechems mit besonderem Bezug auf Jdc. 9. *ZDPV* 83: 183–98.

M. GÖRG

BETH-NIMRAH (PLACE) [Heb *bêt nimrâ*]. One of the towns built by Gadites E of the Jordan valley in land wrested from the Amorite king Sihon and given to them by Moses (Num 32:36; Josh 13:27). The name is found at Num 32:3 without the initial element (Heb *bêt*, lit. "house"), and LXX omits it at Num 32:36 (Gk *Nambra*). The name of the site persists at Tell Nimrin (on the Wâdī Nimrin), although the ancient site was Tell Bleibil nearby (Aharoni *LBHG*, 112–14). The "waters of Nimrim" (Isa 15:6; Jer 48:34) are perhaps to be associated with this location. See NIMRIM, THE WATERS OF (PLACE).

C. GILBERT ROMERO

BETH-PAZZEZ (PLACE) [Heb *bêt paṣṣēṣ*]. A town in the territory of the tribe of Issachar mentioned only in Josh 19:21. From the position of Beth-pazzez in the list of tribal towns, it should be located to the E of Mt. Tabor (M.R. 187232). Although Abel (*GP 2:* 62) suggested an identification with Kerm el-Haditeh (M.R. 196232), there is not sufficient evidence to establish an identification with any site.

MELVIN HUNT

BETH-PELET (PLACE) [Heb *bêt-peleṭ*]. A town in Judah located in the extreme S (Negeb) near Beersheba and toward the boundary of Edom (Josh 15:27). It was one of the towns reoccupied by Judeans when they returned from exile (Neh 11:26). Petrie (1930: 15) identified it with the S Tell el-Fara (M.R. 100076), 18 miles S of Gaza, although now that site is identified with Sharuhen. The location of Beth-pelet thus remains unknown.

Bibliography

Petrie, W. M. F. 1930. *Beth-pelet (Tell Fara)*. Vol. 1. London.

GARY A. HERION

BETH-PEOR (PLACE) [Heb *bêt pᶜôr*]. Heb for "house" or "temple of Peor," a Transjordanian site the biblical importance of which is based on events that took place prior to the Hebrew conquest of Canaan. Its theophoric name probably indicates that the god Peor, or Baal of Peor, was worshiped in its environs. This place name, Beth-peor, is, in fact, related to a group of proper nouns that occur in the OT and are sometimes a cause of confusion: (1) Baal-peor, the name of a god, a local manifestation of Baal (i.e., Baal of Peor), who was worshiped in NW Moab; (2) Peor, the name of a mountain in NW Moab and a shortened name for the god of Mt. Peor, Baal-peor, whose name was derived from the mountain's designation; and (3) Beth-peor, the place name under discussion in this entry, a town which probably served as the cultic center of Baal-peor (perhaps known as Beth-baal-peor in antiquity).

According to Josh 13:20, Beth-peor was in the territory assigned to the tribe of Reuben, an area that included the Moabite tableland (i.e., Heb *mîšōr*) and the slopes down to the Jordan. Prior to their invasion of Canaan, the Hebrews camped among these hills above the Ghor, "in the valley opposite Beth-peor" (Deut 3:29); here Moses recounted the journey from Egypt and reminded Israel about their covenant obligations (Deut 4:44–45). Still in the vicinity of Beth-peor, Moses viewed the promised land from "the top of Pisgah," died "in the land of Moab," and was buried "in the valley in the land of Moab opposite Beth-peor" (Deut 34:1–6).

In agreement with the forenamed passages that mention Beth-peor, the biblical references to Peor, including those that narrate Balaam's experience in this area (Num 23:28) and the infamous episode at Shittim (Numbers 25), also point to NW Moab as the location of Beth-peor. Though Deut 34:6 says that the location of Moses' burial was unknown in ancient times, this text indicates that it was somewhere "opposite Beth-peor." The lack of information noted by the biblical writer has been compounded in modern times, because the locations of Peor and Beth-peor remain uncertain (these names could refer to the same locale, of course). Clearly, all of the available evidence points to a location somewhere below the massif on which Mt. Nebo and Mt. Pisgah (Ras Siyagha) are found, probably in Wâdī ᶜAyun Musa, but identification with a particular site must remain tentative for the time being.

Two sites have emerged from the scholarly discussion as possible candidates for ancient Beth-peor. According to Eusebius Bethphogor (biblical Beth-peor) and Mt. Phogor were located 6 Roman miles E of Livias (OT Beth-haram), on the road to Esbus. Furthermore, Egeria said she could see the site of Fogor (Peor) when looking N from Siyagha. This position corresponds to Khirbet el-Meḥaṭṭa on the Mushaqqar ridge, as identified by a survey party from the Heshbon Expedition. While many scholars suggest that Beth-peor was located at the Roman fort of Khirbet esh-Sheikh Jayil, Henke concludes that what Musil identified with the latter actually corresponds to Khirbet el-Meḥaṭṭa. Other scholars identify Khirbet ᶜAyun Musa, located ca. 1 mile N of Mt. Nebo, with Beth-peor.

GERALD L. MATTINGLY

BETH-RAPHA (PERSON) [Heb *bêt-rāpâ*]. Name attributed to an individual from the tribe of Judah mentioned in 1 Chr 4:12. The form of the name is strange, since it is the only time a personal name collocated with *bēt* appears in the OT. This has led some to suggest that a place name was intended (Odelain and Séguineau 1981: 72; Aharoni *LBHG*, 108 [but see the list of persons on 248]). However, both the MT and the versions are unanimous in rendering this as a person, along with the other individuals mentioned. It is quite likely that he was either named after a city, or that the city was viewed as going back to one ancestor/founder. He is said to be one of the men of Recah (which Codex Vaticanus and the Lucianic Recension of the LXX render as Recab). Interestingly enough, in an almost midrashic fashion, the Targum to Chronicles identifies this person, as well as the other individuals mentioned in 1 Chr 4:12, as being "the men of the great synagogue" (my translation). There is some difficulty in identifying the connotation of the word *bêt-rāpâ*. It means either "house of the healer," "house of the ghost," "house of the giant" or "house of Rapha" (a Canaanite deity attested at Ugarit and perhaps in several Heb inscriptions. See REPHAIM.). The latter possibility is rejected by Tigay in his discussion of personal names (1986: 79), but if polytheism was more widespread in Israelite society than many would allow, there may well be a reference to a Canaanite deity here. The LXX represents this name as *bathrephan* (or *bathraian* in Codex Vaticanus), which would mean "daughter of Rephan" (or Raian according to Codex Vaticanus). The Vulgate sides with the MT in rendering *bethrapa,* as does the Aramaic *bayta rāpā* (as would be expected). The Peshitta omits the difficult *bêt* (presumably because it sounded like a place name), rendering the name as *rûpāʾ*.

Bibliography

Aharoni, Y. 1979. *The Land of the Bible.* Rev. and enlarged ed. Philadelphia.

Odelain, O., and R. Séguineau. 1981. *Dictionary of Proper Names and Places in the Bible.* Trans. M. J. O'Connell. Garden City, NY.

Tigay, J. H. 1986. *You Shall Have No Other Gods: Israelite Religion in the Light of Hebrew Inscriptions.* HSS31. Atlanta.

H. ELDON CLEM

BETH-REHOB (PLACE) [Heb *bêt rĕḥôb*]. Var. REHOB. A Syrian town along the S border of Hamath, from which mercenaries came to join the Ammonites in war against King David (2 Sam 10:6–8). Beth-rehob is mentioned in close connection with Zobah, and it is possible that Hadadezer, king of Zobah, was a native of (Beth-)Rehob (cf. 2 Sam 8:3, 12). See also REHOB (PLACE). This town perhaps marked the ideal N border of the promised land; in the days of Moses "Rehob near the entrance of Hamath" marked the N extent of the spies' journey (Num 13:21). In the book of Judges the Israelite city of Dan is said to have been located in the valley, which (at the time of the redactor) belonged to Beth-rehob (18:28). Thus, Beth-rehob should be located somewhere in the region where the Huleh valley connects with the Bekaa valley of Lebanon. Its exact location remains unknown, and Thomson's (1882: 547) identification with Baniyas (M.R. 215294) must be rejected since no pre-Hellenistic remains have been found there. Thutmose III refers to a *rḥbw* in his topographic list (*ANET,* 243, no. 87), but if it is to be identified with the (Beth-)Rehob near Dan and the entrance to Hamath, then it cannot be identified with Tell el-Balaṭ (M.R. 177280) or Tell er-Raḥb (M.R. 180275). See REHOB (PLACE).

Bibliography

Thomson, W. M. 1882. *The Land and the Book.* Vol. 2. New York.

GARY A. HERION

BETH-SAIDA (PLACE) [Gk *Bēthsaida*]. A city mentioned in the NT as the home town of several of Jesus' disciples—Philip, Andrew, and Peter (John 1:44; 12:21).

Beth-saida was already a village on the shores of the Sea of Galilee (M.R. 208255) when Herod Philip, son and heir of Herod the Great, advanced its status to that of a city. He enlarged its population, built it up grandly, and called it Julias to honor the daughter of Augustus Caesar (*Ant* 18.2.1 §28). Philip also built his capital of Paneas-Caesarea Philippi nearly 24 miles to the N, but he decreed that he was to be buried at Beth-saida. Upon his death, which took place at Beth-saida-Julias in 33 C.E., he apparently was buried in the city in his own funeral monument, which he had commissioned beforehand (*Ant* 18.4.6 §108).

Josephus records that Beth-saida-Julias was in the lower Gaulanitis, which would place it in the rich, alluvial plain W of the hills and cliffs of the Golan Heights (*JW* 2.9.1 §168; *Life* 73). He noted that the Jordan passed the city on the way to the Sea of Galilee (*JW* 3.10.7 §57). He implies elsewhere that the Jordan was about one furlong away from Beth-saida, or one-eighth of a mile (*Life* 72). Mark 6:45 adds the detail that Jesus and his disciples sailed from the site of the feeding of the 5000, which Luke 9:10 places in Beth-saida. Therefore Beth-saida had a port or anchorage on the lake (cf. *Life* 73). Josephus also explains that King Agrippa's region of Trachonitis extended to Julias at its S extent (*JW* 3.3.5 §57). Pliny the Elder (*Naturalis Historia* 5.21) and Ptolemy (*Geog.* 5.15.3) also knew its location on the E side of the lake. According to Mark 8:22 the territory of the city of Caesarea Philippi could be reached from Beth-saida-Julias on foot, suggesting the existence of a road between the two cities.

John 12:21 locates Beth-saida in Galilee, but probably that is to be understood as an informal designation for the geographical rather than for the political area; for Pliny says the same thing (*Naturalis Historia* 5.21). Later Eusebius and Jerome also repeated "of Galilee," even though politically Beth-saida belonged to Gaulanitis or Trachonitis (*Onomast.* 58.11; 59.12).

Nineteenth-century scholarship identified Beth-saida with the two sites of et-Tell and el-Araj. El-Araj lies on the shore of the lake, while et-Tell stands about 1.7 miles to the NNE. El-Araj should be Beth-saida, the original fishermen's village on the shore, which had an anchorage still usable early in this century. The ancient anchorage was located during a period of low water level. Julias, on the other hand, was identified with the site of et-Tell, at which have been found an aqueduct, a city wall, a mosaic, and a road connecting with el-Araj.

Recently new surveys in the region of the two proposed sites and the discovery of a third site have rounded out the picture without substantively altering the original proposal. See Fig. BET.01. Et-Tell (also known as el-Amiriyye from the nearby village) is now known to cover about 45,000 m^2 (Urman 1985: 120–21). This is too small for an ancient city, but could be the acropolis of the city. El-Araj (el-Hasel or Beith ha-Beq), SSW of et-Tell and on the shore of the lake, is now largely underwater, but has produced architectural fragments that closely resemble those of synagogues excavated in the region. Furthermore, el-Araj and el-Misʾadiyye, about one-half mile E of el-Araj, feature foundations of buildings and pottery from the Early Roman period to the time of the Arab conquest (Urman 1985: 121; 1971: 14). In 1982, 24 m of paved road or jetty extending into the lake were found at el-Araj. El-Araj and el-Mesʾadiyye may together be regarded as the remnants of the large fishing village of Beth-saida, while et-Tell would form the acropolis of the city of Julias, founded by Herod Philip.

According to John 1:44 Philip, Andrew, and Peter came from Beth-saida. Their origin there helps explain Jesus' relationship to the village or city—he healed a blind man at Beth-saida (Mark 8:22–26) and fed 5000 in a deserted

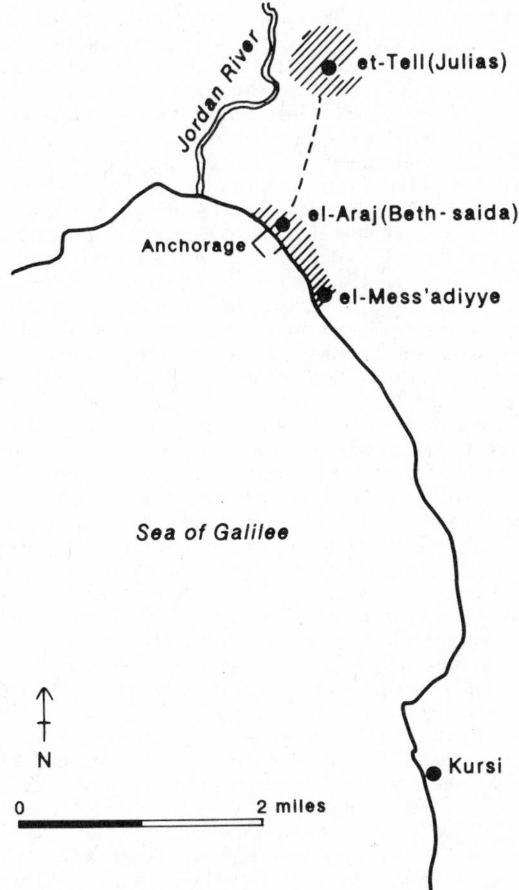

BET.01. Area map of ancient Beth-saida.

place nearby (Luke 9:25). Yet his ministry was evidently not well received, for Matthew 11:21 (cf. Luke 10:13) records his lament over the lack of repentence in Chorazin and Beth-saida.

Bibliography

Avi-Yonah, M. 1976. *Gazetteer of Roman Palestine.* Qedem 5. Jerusalem.

Dalman, G. H. 1935. *Sacred Sites and Ways.* London.

Kochavi, M., ed. 1972. *Judaea, Samaria, and the Golan.* Jerusalem.

Nun, M. 1974. Ancient Harbors and Jetties in the Lake Kinneret. *Nature and Land.* 16: 212–28 (in Hebrew).

Schumacher, G. 1888. *The Jaulan.* London.

Urman, D. 1985. *The Golan.* BAR International Series 269. Oxford.

Urman, D., ed. 1971. *Announcement of Historical Sites (Golan Heights).* No. 1. Headquarters of the Military Government in the Golan Heights (in Hebrew).

James F. Strange

BETH-SHAN (PLACE) [Heb *bêt šan, bêt šĕʾān*]. Var. BETH-SHEAN; SCYTHOPOLIS. An ancient city standing sentinel over the junction of the Jezreel and Jordan valleys (M.R. 197212). The town was given to Manasseh (Josh 17:11), but that tribe was unable to secure the site because of the iron chariotry that the Canaanites had in their arsenal (Josh 17:16; Judg 1:27). It remained in non-Israelite control until after the reign of Saul, and it was at Beth-shan where Saul's decapitated body was put on display in the temple of Ashtaroth (1 Sam 31:10–12). During the reign of Solomon, however, it was listed as part of the administrative district belonging to Megiddo/Taʿanach (1 Kgs 4:12). The site is frequently mentioned in Hellenistic, Roman, and Byzantine times, when it became known as Scythopolis or Nysa Scythopolis. It was reported in the Maccabean conflicts as the scene of some confrontations (1 Macc 5:52; 12:40–42), and its inhabitants were spared massacre because of their hospitality to the local Jewish population (2 Macc 12:29–31). It then became the chief city of the DECAPOLIS, even though it was the only one on the W side of the Jordan river. During the Decapolis period the city expanded beyond the tell to its maximum area of almost 100 hectares, all of which was enclosed with a wall. The significance of Beth-shan is marked by the fact that the Islamic conquest of A.D. 636 was described by the victors as the "day of Beisan." The latter name, Beisan, derived from the ancient one ("house of Shan," Shan being possibly a deity worshiped at the site), continues to be used and now refers to a village SE of the tell.

A. Environmental Setting

Ancient Beth-shan (identified with Tell el-Husn) is strategically located in inland N Palestine where the Jezreel and Jordan valleys meet. The site is at the E terminus of the main route from the coast, the Via Maris, and roads branched out from there to Syria and Transjordan. Arable land, fish and other animal resources nearby, and a perennial water source (from the Wâdī Jalud, biblical Herod, on the S bank of which the site was founded) also encouraged human occupation. Consequently, Beth-shan was almost continuously settled from at least the Chalcolithic period up to modern times.

B. History of Excavations

The tell of Beth-shan, including a large cemetery (the Northern Cemetery) on the N bank of the Wâdī Jalud, was excavated from 1921 to 1933, first under the direction of C. S. Fisher (1921–1923), then under A. Rowe (1925–1928) and G. M. FitzGerald (1930–1931, 1933). This undertaking was one of the large American archaeological expeditions after World War I, a period during which excavation techniques were still in their formative stages. Almost the whole of the top five levels of the highest point of the tell on the SE were cleared; and only by reworking the limited stratigraphic evidence and pottery data, based on current knowledge, can the archaeological sequence be reconstructed (see James 1966; Oren 1973). FitzGerald carried out a deep sounding on the citadel, penetrating to the basal levels, the areal extents of which were so limited that the results were very equivocal and as yet have not been reworked. More recent archaeological work on the tell and in its environs (e.g., Yadin and Geva 1984) has also helped to clarify the findings of the early expedition.

C. Archaeological Sequence

The earliest evidence for occupation on the tell at Beth-shan is represented only by pit deposits in the lowest level (XVIII; above virgin soil) of FitzGerald's deep sounding, which contained pottery dating to the Chalcolithic period (ca. 4500–3300 B.C.) or possibly to the terminal phase of the Neolithic period (Yarmukian). Many other Chalcolithic sites, however, were identified by N. Tzori in the immediate vicinity of the tell.

The Esdraelon culture, which has been identified as either a late Chalcolithic phase or an initial phase of the EB (ca. 3400–3100 B.C.), is attested by gray burnished and "grain wash ware" (i.e., pottery decorated with streaky red paint) from level XVI. Streets and multiroomed structures appeared in the immediately succeeding levels (XV–XI) of the deep sounding, encompassing the main period of urban expansion, down to ca. 2400 B.C. Khirbet Kerak pottery, a distinctive, highly burnished black and red ware with stylistic affinities to E Anatolian types, is very prevalent in level XI (although it was found in mixed contexts with MB material). This pottery is dated to a late phase of EB III and is possibly related to contemporaneous disruptions throughout the Near East that contributed to a weakening of the Palestinian city-state system.

The transitional EB IV period (ca. 2400–1950 B.C.), as elsewhere in Palestine, is primarily attested by shaft tombs in the Northern Cemetery; relatively little evidence for occupation was found on the tell. A reconsolidation of urban life, however, is evidenced by large houses with central courtyards in level X and by tombs with rich deposits (e.g., duckbill-shaped axheads and scarabs) both on the tell and in the Northern Cemetery. Although the stratigraphy of the deep sounding is problematic and has not been reworked, the artifactual material appears to cover most if not the entirety of MB I–III (ca. 1950–1550 B.C.).

Level IX, which also has not yet been reworked, dates primarily to the LB I period (ca. 1550–1400 B.C.); an admixture of earlier and later materials occurs in some contexts. Based on scarabs, Rowe assigned this stratum to Thutmose III, but scarabs of this pharaoh are poor chronological indicators since they continued to be made after his reign and were often retained as heirlooms. The architectural layout of the level on the acropolis is quite different from underlying level X, and included a large, open courtyard bordering a thick-walled rectangular building (possibly a *migdal*-type temple) and a complex of rooms with an altar to the E. A basalt relief showing a lion and dog in combat was a notable find; Palestinian artifacts predominated in the level, although some Egyptian-style artifacts were also recovered.

Egyptian presence was intensified in levels VII and VIII (dating to LB IIB, 13th century B.C., although previously assigned to the late 15th–14th centuries by Rowe on the basis of scarabs), in which the citadel was again laid out on along completely different architectural lines. The buildings (a so-called commandant's house with two large rooms along one side of the structure; a heavily bastioned *migdal;* a large silo; the SE sector with rooms and center hall buildings to either side of a N-S street; and, most significantly, a temple with a columned forecourt and a back altar room approached by a stairway) are analogous to specific Egyptian New Kingdom architectural types. The levels produced more Egyptian-style artifacts than any other LB site in Palestine: scarabs of 19th-Dyn. pharaohs, duck-head bowls, cobra figurines, zoomorphic stands, "flower pots," jewelry, etc., as well as inscriptions (e.g., a stele of Amenemopet the architect, dedicated to "Mekal, the god, the lord of Beth-shan"). The combined evidence leaves little doubt that the Egyptians restructured the site to be a military garrison along the N frontier of Palestine, from which they could protect their interests in the area and participate in trade with major empires to the N. Palestinian artifacts still predominated at the site, and many of the basic industries (pottery, silicates, metals, alabaster, boneworking, goldworking, etc.) continued to function as they had in the past. Nevertheless, as shown by scientific analyses, Egyptian-style artifacts were generally produced locally (one exception being glass and faience vessels); and Egyptian craftsmen must have been present at the site to manufacture such items or to tutor Palestinian craftsmen. A syncretistic Palestinian-Egyptian cult is implied by the representation of Egyptian deities (Hathor and minor gods, such as Bes, Taurt, and Sekhmet) and Palestinian deities (a principal female and male god).

Even though serious disruptions in the Palestinian city-state system occurred at the end of the LB (ca. 1200 B.C.), Beth-shan continued to be occupied by the Egyptians in the early Iron Age. No destruction level was noted between levels VII and VI. With minor refurbishing the level VI temple is identical to that of level VII and located directly above it, and the general layout of the SE sector is the same in both levels; only the commandant's house and *migdal* were totally dismantled, to be replaced by probable storehouses. Egyptian-style artifacts, including scarabs of later Ramesside pharaohs (in particular, Rameses III of the 12th century B.C.), numerous limestone door fragments from central-hall buildings with hieroglyphic inscriptions referring to the "commander of the troops" (Ramesseswes-erkhephesh) during the reign of Rameses III, and pottery and small objects similar to those in level VII are still very prevalent. A group of tombs in the Northern Cemetery contained large anthropoid coffins, several of which had grotesque faces and were shown wearing high head/hairdresses. Because of the similarity of the latter with depictions of the SEA PEOPLES in Egyptian reliefs, it has been proposed that one or more groups of Sea Peoples (the Denyen, Tjekker, and/or Peleset [Philistines]) were resident at the site, perhaps as mercenaries. Although it is possible that some Sea Peoples lived there, their numbers must have been quite small, since very little characteristic artifactual material, such as is common at coastal sites, has been found at the site (only one Philistine shard was recovered from the site). Earlier and later phases of level VI (lower and upper, respectively) broadly date to ca. 1200–1000 B.C. The inscriptional evidence from lower level VI indicates that Rameses III was primarily responsible for consolidating Egyptian control at the site. The possibility of a destruction layer between lower and upper level VI, as well as the sparse remains from the latter phase, suggests that Egyptian power waned during the later Ramesside period.

Architecturally, level V, dated to Iron IC–IIA (ca. 1000–800 B.C.) according to the pottery evidence, represents a significant departure from the plan of the Egyptian garrison. Two long E-W buildings, one in the area of the level VIII–VI temple and another located farther N, have been identified as temples. This interpretation is well supported by the finds from the building's forecourt (a seated statue of Rameses III and monumental steles of Seti I and Rameses II dedicated to Ra-Hamarchis and Amun-Re) and by its interior (a stele dedicated to "Antit," probably the local equivalent of a principal Canaanite goddess). Indeed, the presence of the monumental steles and statue suggests that an imperial cult existed here that had its beginning in the LB (this area in levels VIII–VI was extensively disturbed, but wall lines are directly below those of the level V building). The steles describe in some detail the military defense of the Beth-shan area by the pharaohs against belligerent neighboring city-states and peoples (e.g., the *ʿapiru* [see HABIRU, HAPIRU]; possibly connected with the Hebrews). Since the historical data of the steles accord with other texts of the pharaohs, they most likely originated in their reigns and were moved up from one level to the next as buildings were successively renovated or rebuilt by the Egyptians. Like storehouses of the period, a double row of columns ran the length of the S building. Based on the biblical tradition (I Chr 10:10), Rowe denoted the building the "Temple of Dagon," the primary male deity of the Philistines; no inscriptions, however, were recovered from the building, and it is doubtful that the site was ever controlled by the Philistines. Both N and S temples yielded numerous cylindrical and house-like stands, which were decorated with snakes and birds and which were probably used in the cult. See Fig. BET.02. In the later phase of level V, a gate existed on the NW side of the tell, which was approached by a gentle earthen slope from the valley (earlier gates may have been located here as well). Unfortunately, the gate's overall plan is unclear, but its architectural and masonry style (interior buttresses, header-and-stretcher arrangement of ashlar blocks, and an attached double wall) is similar to that of other gates in N Israel (e.g., Megiddo and Hazor) fortified by Solomon (cf. 1 Kgs 9:15). It is uncertain how the site was taken by the Israelites.

After a possible hiatus in occupation, level IV was rebuilt along different architectural lines from level V. The very poorly preserved stratum is dated according to the pottery to ca. 800–600 B.C.

Another gap in settlement followed level IV, although late Iron Age and Persian period tombs were found by Tzori east of the tell. The site was reoccupied in the Hellenistic (363–332 B.C.) and Roman (63 B.C.–A.D. 324) periods—levels III and II. The Hellenistic structures were extensively disturbed by later Roman buildings, in particular by a large temple on the NW side of the tell (initially assigned to the Hellenistic period, but now dated to the 1st century A.D.). The Roman city spread into the valley below the tell, where a colonnaded street, a hippodrome, a villa with mosaic floors, a theater, and an extensive wall circuit (spanning the Wâdī Jalud) were uncovered. Roman tombs in the Northern Cemetery produced glass vessels, pottery figurines, and portrait busts of the dead; a stone sarcophagus in one tomb was inscribed with the name of Antiochus, son of Phallion, possibly a cousin of Herod the Great.

BET.02. Cylindrical stand with snakes and birds from Beth-shan—Level V. *(Courtesy of P. E. McGovern)*

The uppermost level on the tell (level I) was dominated by a circular Byzantine church, with an ambulatory around an open court. FitzGerald dated the building to the early 5th century because of the similarity between its column capitals and those of the Church of St. Stephen in Jerusalem, which was constructed by the empress Eudocia between 431 and 438. A mosaic in the building was also comparable to one of approximately the same period in the Church of Eleona on the Mount of Olives. Domestic residences surrounded the church, and a paved road led from the latter to the NW gate. A monastery, dedicated to or sponsored by a certain Lady Mary, was constructed N of the cemetery on the opposite bank of the Wâdī Jalud, just outside the Byzantine city wall; inscriptions and a hoard of coins minted under Heraclius I indicate that it was constructed in the early 6th century A.D. and probably stood until the Islamic conquest. Extensive mosaic floors included circular representations of the Labors of the Months grouped around the personified sun and moon. In addition, four synagogues in the vicinity of the tell have been investigated. Near the Monastery of Lady Mary and dating from the 5th through the early 7th century, one synagogue contained mosaics with representations of the ark of the covenant covered by a curtain, ritual vessels, and a seven-branched candelabra, together with four inscriptions (three Greek and one Samaritan). Nearby, the mosaics in a second synagogue of the 6th century also showed ritual vessels and a candelabra, and included Greek, Hebrew, and Aramaic inscriptions. At Farwana (probably ancient Rehob), S of Beth-shan and dating from the 5th–7th centuries, was discovered the longest Hebrew mosaic inscription, detailing halakic laws of the Sabbatical Year and tithing. Byzantine houses, another monastery, and a potter's workshop were also located in the vicinity of the tell. Numerous tombs from the Byzantine period were excavated in the Northern Cemetery.

Bibliography

Bahat, D. 1972. The Synagogue at Beth-Shean. *Qad* 5: 55–58 (in Hebrew).

FitzGerald, G. M. 1930. *The Four Canaanite Temples of Beth Shan.* Vol. 2. *The Pottery.* Philadelphia.

———. 1931. *Beth Shan Excavations, 1921–23: The Arab and Byzantine Levels.* Philadelphia.

———. 1933. Excavations at Beth-Shan in 1933. *PEQ* 65: 123–34.

———. 1935. The Earliest Pottery of Beth Shan. *Museum Journal* 24: 5–22.

———. 1939. *A Sixth Century Monastery at Beth Shan.* Philadelphia.

James, F. W. 1966. *The Iron Age at Beth Shan: A Study of Levels VI–IV.* Philadelphia.

———. 1978. Chariot Fittings from Late Bronze Age Beth Shan. Pp. 102–15 in *Archaeology in the Levant,* ed. P. R. S. Moorey and P. Parr. Warminster.

James, F. W., and McGovern, P. E. 1986. *The Late Bronze II Egyptian Garrison at Beth Shan: A Study of Levels VII and VIII.* Philadelphia.

McGovern, P. E. 1986a. Ancient Ceramic Technology and Stylistic Change: Contrasting Studies from Southwest and Southeast Asia. Pp. 33–52 in *Technology and Style,* ed. W. D. Kingery. Columbus, OH.

———. 1986b. Silicate Industries of Late Bronze-Early Iron Age Palestine: Technological Interaction Between New Kingdom Egypt and the Levant. *British Museum Occasional Papers.* London.

Oren, E. 1973. *The Northern Cemetery at Beth Shan.* Leiden.

Rowe, A. 1927a. The Discoveries at Beth-Shan during the 1926 Season. *Museum Journal* 19: 9–45.

———. 1927b. The Expedition at Beisan. *Museum Journal.* 18: 411–41.

———. 1928. The 1927 Excavations at Beisan. *Museum Journal.* 19: 145–68.

———. 1929a. The Palestine Expedition: Report of the 1928 Season. *Museum Journal* 20: 37–87.

———. 1929b. The Two Royal Stelae of Beth-Shan. *Museum Journal* 20: 89–98.

———. 1929c. Palestine Expedition of the Museum of the University of Pennsylvania, Third Report—1928 Season. *PEFQS,* 78–94.

———. 1930. *Topography and History of Beth-Shan.* Philadelphia.

———. 1940. *The Four Canaanite Temples of Beth-Shan.* Vol. 1, *The Temples and Cult Objects.* Philadelphia.

Thompson, H. O. 1970. *Mekal: The God of Beth-Shan.* Leiden.

Tzori, N. 1962. *The Beth-Shean Valley.* Jerusalem (in Hebrew).

———. 1967. The Ancient Synagogue of Beth-Shan. *EI* 8: 149–167 (in Hebrew).

Vitto, F. 1975. The Ancient Synagogue at Rehov. *Qad* 8: 123–28 (in Hebrew).

Yadin, Y., and Geva, S. 1984. Notes and News. Tel Beth Shean. *IEJ* 34: 187–89.

Patrick E. McGovern

BETH-SHEAN. An alternate spelling for BETH-SHAN.

BETH-SHEARIM (PLACE). See BURIALS (ANCIENT JEWISH).

BETH-SHEMESH (PLACE) [Heb *bêt šemeš, ʿîr šemeš*]. The RSV has three towns with this name and the Heb MT has another.

1. A town located in the NE Shephelah (M.R. 147128) in the Valley of Sorek and which played a small but significant role in Israel's history. It was occupied throughout the biblical period and, as a border town, experienced the varying fortunes of the tribe and kingdom of Judah.

a. Biblical References. Beth-shemesh is mentioned in two geographical lists of Joshua: first as Ir-shemesh (Josh 19:41) within the territory of Dan, and then (Josh 21:16) as Beth-shemesh, a town given by the tribe of Judah to the Kohathite sons of Aaron. However, Beth-shemesh is not mentioned as a town of Judah in the geographical list of Joshua 15. The question of whether Beth-shemesh belonged to the tribe of Judah or Dan may be answered by reference to Dan's 11th-century migration to its N territory, which would have left Beth-shemesh on the NW border of Judah. An equally plausible, though more technical, explanation concerns the second Solomonic administrative district (1 Kgs 4:9), which appears to parallel the territory mentioned in Josh 19:41. The Joshua passage may be a description of 10th-century rather than of 11th- or of 12th-century geography, irrespective of tribal designations.

Beth-shemesh plays a prominent role in the story of the Philistine capture of the ark of the covenant (1 Sam 6:9–15). The ark is carried from Philistine territory to Beth-shemesh, which was a border town just inside Israelite territory.

With the division of the kingdom, Beth-shemesh fell within the borders of Judah. Jehoash of Israel and Amaziah of Judah engaged in a battle at Beth-shemesh in which Jehoash proved the victor (2 Kgs 14:11; 2 Chr 25:21). Not only does this battle emphasize the location of Beth-shemesh as a border town, but the subsequent sacking of Jerusalem by Jehoash also indicates that Beth-shemesh had guarded the Sorek pass from the Philistine plain to Jerusalem. Beth-shemesh later passed from Israelite control when the Philistines captured it during the reign of Ahaz (2 Chr 28:18).

The only other ancient sources to mention Beth-shemesh are the Palestinian Talmud in a geographical context (*Meg.* 1.70a and parallel passages) and Eusebius (*Onomast.*

54.11–13), who identifies it as Bethsamis. The final settlement appears to have been a Byzantine monastery. Between the fall of the Israelite kingdoms and the Byzantine period, only the scantiest remains (Hellenistic coins and Roman ceramics) were deposited at the site. The Beth-shemesh in Judah should not be confused with that associated with Naphtali (Josh 19:38) or that associated with Issachar (Josh 19:22).

b. Archaeological Excavations. The Arab village of ʿAin Shems preserved a reference to the ancient name; and E. Robinson in 1841 identified Tell er-Rumeilah, just W of ʿAin Shems, with biblical Beth-shemesh. The Palestine Exploration Fund began excavations at the site in 1911 under the direction of D. Mackenzie, who identified four strata at the site. The earliest was a Bronze Age stratum containing imported Aegean and Cypriot pottery. The succeeding stratum was characterized by Philistine pottery, which had much in common with Mycenaean IIIC wares. The third stratum was designated "Israelite" and was thought to have been destroyed by Sennacherib in 701 B.C.E. The final stratum was the Byzantine occupation, represented by the monastery on the SE side of the hill. During 1911–1912 Mackenzie excavated the entire monastery and an area on the S side of the mound. He also excavated a Bronze Age fortification system, including a typical MB gate, and a curtain wall with adjoining towers. The wall was followed for its full course around the city. These fortifications may have been reused in the LB, but they clearly went out of use by the beginning of the Iron Age.

A second series of excavations on the W and S sides of the tell were conducted from 1928–31 by E. Grant, assisted by C. S. Fisher and A. Rowe. Although Grant published three reports (1929; 1931–32; 1934), the authoritative volumes on these latter excavations were published by Grant together with G. E. Wright (1939). The following description of the stratigraphy and finds from Beth-shemesh is based largely on that report.

c. Stratigraphy. Six major occupational levels were discovered at Beth-shemesh, some of which were further subdivided (e.g., IVa and IVb). With the improved stratigraphic techniques and ceramic analysis of the last half century, it is apparent that further subdivisions should have been made. However, the published evidence makes it difficult to argue specifically for a more complex stratigraphy.

(1) Stratum VI. The earliest level produced no building remains. Only a collection of flints, ceramics, and some stone objects give evidence of the EB IV–MB I period. It is not known whether this evidence indicates a sedentary occupation, or whether these are simply campsite remains.

(2) Tombs. A series of tombs (9, 17, 13) stratigraphically appear to predate the city wall. Their contents are MB II–III and testify to a preurban phase of the MB occupation at Beth-shemesh.

(3) Stratum V. This stratum represents the first fortification of the site in the MB III period. The fortification consisted of a city wall encircling the tell, three rectangular towers, and a three-chambered city gate. Evidence for a glacis and lower retaining wall, which usually accompany such fortifications, was not found nor was there effort to locate it. The single major house discovered in stratum V was built against the city wall. Called the Herrenhaus by the excavators, this structure consisted of a single courtyard flanked by smaller rooms on three sides. The full extent of this house may not have been excavated. A tower on the SW of the city wall is a later addition to the wall. Although it is possible that this tower was added in the LB, it may indicate a second phase to the MB city. If such is the case, then Beth-shemesh V would have three phases: (1) a preurban phase indicated by tombs; (2) the first urban phase indicated by the city wall, gate, and Herrenhaus; and (3) a later urban phase indicated by additions to the city wall. It seems likely on the basis of the pottery that stratum V spans the period from the middle of the MB II to the end of the MB. An ash layer on the floor of the Herrenhaus and the breaching of the city wall indicate a destruction of stratum V. Wright dates this destruction to the mid-16th century B.C.E.

(4) Stratum IV. During the LB the city's defenses seem to have been repaired on the W side of the mound. However, on the S side of the city, the Herrenhaus was rebuilt above the city wall, indicating the fortifications were not reused. This apparent contradiction may indicate stratigraphic phasing within stratum IV or different uses of the fortifications within the city at the same time. Our present knowledge of Beth-shemesh does not allow a resolution of this issue.

Wright and Grant subdivided stratum IV into two phases: IVA, the earlier spanning the 15th and early 14th centuries; and IVB, which was destroyed in the 13th or early 12th century B.C.E. Stratigraphic differentiation between IVA and IVB was noticeable from a change in building orientation in some areas and from evidence of destruction on the W edge of the tell. Stratum IVB was also burned. A number of large buildings were excavated in stratum IV along with three industrial furnaces and a number of silos and plastered water cisterns.

Wright and Grant have isolated the bichrome pottery from Beth-shemesh into stratum IVA, the Mycenaean imports into stratum IVB, and the Philistine pottery into the subsequent stratum III. Pottery which paralleled that of Tell Beit Mirsim Bl and which is considered characteristic of the early Israelites was found in two silos (551 and 530; stratum IVB). This pottery was buried under destruction debris and the buildings of stratum III.

(5) Stratum III. The Iron Age I (stratum III) probably came to an end in the mid-11th century B.C.E. through another violent destruction. The city may or may not have been fortified at this time. The city wall appears to have been repaired again, but there is no stratigraphic evidence that these repairs did not occur in the previous stratum. The finest building of stratum III, the Hofhaus, consisted of a partially paved courtyard flanked on the W by three smaller rooms.

A significant amount of Philistine pottery was found throughout stratum III as would be expected given the location of Beth-shemesh near the Philistine plain. The occupation of stratum III appears to coincide chronologically with the appearance and disappearance of this distinctive ceramic style.

(6) Stratum II. Stratum II was subdivided into three phases IIA, IIB, and IIC. On the W side of the tell, stratum IIA was characterized by a casemate wall and administrative buildings—one considered a governor's house and another a storage complex. The former building was not fully excavated; the latter consisted of three long rooms. Stratum IIA's occupation was burned in the early 10th century B.C.E. Strata IIB and IIC cover the rest of the Iron Age to the Babylonian destruction of Judah in 587 B.C.E. Mackenzie and Y. and M. Aharoni would date the final destruction of Beth-shemesh to the Assyrian invasion of 701 B.C.E. However, the appearance of some (although not all) 7th-century ceramic forms in the Beth-shemesh collection would seem to contradict that conclusion. The later Iron Age occupation was unfortified. The houses excavated on the W edge of the tell were arranged along the old line of fortifications and were divided by a series of streets. The distinction between strata IIB and IIC is based on ceramic evidence although stratigraphic changes were noted within the unfortified village.

That strata IIB–C at Beth-shemesh were unfortified is reflected in the biblical record. Rehoboam neglected to fortify Beth-shemesh while building defenses at a number of Judean towns including nearby Zorah (2 Chr 11:5–10). Similarly Beth-shemesh is not mentioned in the city list of Judah (Josh 15:33–36), which includes neighboring towns like Zorah and Azekah. It is possible that the site was unoccupied for some time in the 9th century B.C.E.

(7) Stratum I. The Roman-Byzantine period was represented by a Byzantine monastery on the SE side of the tell. Hellenistic, Roman, and medieval pottery were also found in small quantities at Beth-shemesh.

d. Inscriptions. Although Beth-shemesh is not noted for its inscriptional finds, a few significant documents were discovered there. In stratum IV scarabs of Amenhotep III and Rameses I and II were found, along with scarabs of Thutmose II, Seti I, and Rameses III in tomb 11. In room 526 of stratum IVA a cuneiform tablet with an inscription in Ugaritic script was discovered. The signs were written backwards as if to be read with a mirror. A similar mirror-written inscription has been found at Ugarit itself. An ostracon found in area Y31, attributable to either stratum V or IV, bears a proto-Canaanite inscription.

Ten stamped jar handles bearing individualized Hebrew inscriptions typical of the end of the Judean Monarchy were found in stratum II. One reading "To Eliakim, Steward of Yawkin" is identical to two sealings found at Tell Beit Mirsim. Royal stamp seals with either winged scarab or winged scroll decoration typical of the 8th century B.C.E. were also found in stratum II. In most cases these bear the place name "Hebron." A carnelian seal from tomb 14 was also inscribed in Hebrew.

e. Tombs. There were a number of tombs cut in the rock in the area closely surrounding the tell and beneath the earliest dwellings. In the MB these tombs were located within the walled city. Some of the tombs predated urbanization, and some were used while the houses above were occupied. Only two tombs of the LB were discovered—a small tomb within the city walls and a larger one which was extramural. While two skeletons contemporary with stratum III were found with modest grave goods, a considerable series of tombs attributed to stratum II were located outside the city walls. These tombs date primarily to the end of the Iron Age, although some were slightly earlier.

Bibliography

Grant, E. 1929. *Beth Shemesh: Progress of the Haverford Archaeological Expedition.* Haverford, PA.

———. 1931–32. *ʿAin Shems Excavations 1–2.* Haverford, PA.

———. 1934. *Rumeileh.* Haverford, PA.

Grant, E., and Wright, G. E. 1939. *ʿAin Shems Excavations 4–5.* Haverford, PA.

Mackenzie, D. 1911. Excavations at ʿAin Shems. *Palestine Exploration Fund Annual,* I. London.

———. 1912–13. Excavations at ʿAin Shems. *Palestine Exploration Fund Annual,* II. Manchester.

FREDRIC BRANDFON

2. A town belonging to Issachar (Josh 19:22). Its location is uncertain, but Aharoni has suggested *(LBHG,* 432) that it might be identified with Khirbet Sheikh esh-Shamsāwî (M.R. 199232), just SW of the Sea of Galilee. The name preserves some elements of the ancient name (Boling and Wright, *Joshua* AB, 450), and the site is within the described borders of Issachar (Josh 19:17–23).

3. A town given to Naphtali (Josh 19:38) and which from the context of the passage (v 35) appears to have been fortified. This conclusion is strengthened by the statement in Judg 1:33 that Naphtali did not expel the Canaanites from either Beth-shemesh or Beth-anath. The locations of both of these towns are unknown, but Aharoni suggests (*LBHG,* 162, 432) that Beth-shemesh might be identified with Khirbet Tell er-Ruweisi (M.R. 181271) in the far N of upper Galilee. Attempts to locate Beth-shemesh have encompassed both lower and upper Galilee, but it was in the N part of upper Galilee that the Canaanites maintained strong and well-developed towns into the early Israelite period (*LBHG,* 235–36).

The N Galilee Beth-shemesh is likely that mentioned in the Egyptian Execration Texts (Posener 1940: E60) and perhaps is mentioned (No. 89) on the list of Canaanite cities by Thutmose III (*LBHG,* 162).

4. The MT in Jer 43:13 refers to another Beth-shemesh, which was located in Egypt. The RSV renders this site HELIOPOLIS, following the LXX which reads *Hēliou poleōs* (LXX Jer 50:13).

Bibliography

Posener, G. 1940. *Princes et pays d'Asie et de Nubie.* Brussels.

DALE W. MANOR

BETH-SHITTAH (PLACE) [Heb *bêt haššiṭṭâ*]. A site mentioned in Judg 7:22 as one of the locations to which Midianite troops fled to escape the attack of Gideon's band. Beth-shittah appears to be distinct from SHITTIM; it has been identified with Shatta, 2.5 miles E of Harod and 5.5 miles NW of Beisan, although this identification has been doubted (*IDB* 1: 403; *ISBE* 1: 479). Another possible location is Tell Sleihat, E of the Jordan river. The name Beth-shittah means "house of acacia (trees/wood)" (on this important plant and its wood, see FLORA, BIBLICAL).

HENRY O. THOMPSON

BETH-TAPPUAH (PLACE) [Heb *bêt-tappûaḥ*]. A town situated in the central hill country of Judah (Josh 15:53) within the same district as Hebron. This settlement, the name of which perhaps means "house of the apple tree" (from *tappûaḥ* 'apple'), is listed among the towns within the tribal allotment of Judah (Josh 15:21–62; see also BETH DAGON (PLACE). Beth-tappuah is also mentioned in Shishak's inscription on the wall of the Amon Temple at Karnak (Aharoni *LBHG*, 285). The name is preserved in the modern village of Taffuh (M.R. 154105), approximately 5 km W and slightly N of Hebron (*LBHG*, 300). The ancient settlement is no doubt to be found in the immediate vicinity.

Bibliography

Alt, A. 1925. Judas Gaue unter Josia. *PJ* 21: 100–16.

WADE R. KOTTER

BETH-YERAH (M.R. 204235). A city generally associated with Khirbet Kerak (Arabic meaning "ruins of the fortress"), a 50 acre site along the SW shore of the Sea of Galilee. The site is not mentioned in the Bible; primary evidence linking this area with Beth-yerah 'the house of the Moon' comes from the Talmud, which states that the Jordan begins S of Beth-yerah (*b. Talm. Bik.* 55a; *Gen. Rab.* 98.18; cf. Neubauer 1868: 31, 215; Sukenik 1922: 102–3; Maisler, Stekelis, and Avi-Yonah 1952: 165). Sukenik associates the site with Philoteria following Polybius, who depicts Antiochus the Great in 216 B.C.E. marching to Philoteria (Sukenik 1922: 103–4). Polybius states that the city "lies off the shore of the lake into which the river Jordan falls, and from which it issues again to traverse the plains round Scythopolis" (Polyb. 5.70.4). The city had substantial territory so that it, along with Scythopolis, could easily supply Antiochus' entire army (5.70.5).

The name Philoteria suggests a Ptolemaic foundation, possibly by Ptolemy II Philadephus who had a sister by that name (Sukenik 1922: 104–5). The Byzantine chronicler Syncellus places Philoteria E of the Jordan river and lists it as one of the cities captured by Alexander Jannaeus (Syncellus 1984: 355). Avi-Yonah argues that in antiquity Beth-yerah/Philoteria was E of the Jordan because the Jordan's ancient river bed flowed N and W of the site; therefore Philoteria was never part of Galilee (Avi-Yonah 1966: 37, 70, 138). The city may have had a sister city, Sennabris (*j. Talm. Bik.* I.81a; *j. Talm. Meg.* 2a; cf. Sukenik 1922: 106–7; Hestrin 1975: 253), where, Josephus states, Vespasian stationed his troops during the Jewish revolt (ca. 66–67 C.E.) before marching on Tiberias (*JW* 3.447; 4.455).

Excavations at the site indicate a long period of occupation that extended from the Chalcolithic into the Arab period with an apparent occupation break between the MB II and Persian periods. Chalcolithic finds show that inhabitants lived in huts sunk in pits and that they practiced child burial (Maisler, Stekelis, and Avi-Yonah 1952: 167, 229; Hestrin 1975: 255). Major building activity, however, did not occur until EB I, when Beth-yerah became one of the first fortified towns in Palestine. A massive mudbrick wall measuring 8 m in width found at Beth-yerah (Hestrin 1975: 254–55) may reflect increasing rivalry among local townships as well as similar town planning in Mesopotamia and Egypt (Aharoni 1982: 56–58; Anati 1963: 337–41). The discovery of EB I rectangular homes with mudbrick walls, a large courtyard with basalt paving, a tournette for making pottery, and an apsidal house (Hestrin 1975: 255–56) along with the town wall reflects a move toward a walled-town culture with its fixed-plot agriculture and nuclear, closed societies (Hanbury-Tenison 1986: 63, 106; Esse 1982) rather than toward urbanization.

The walled-town culture continues into the EB II period as brick walls, a paved street, and parts of a drainage system have been found. Jars found on the floor of an EB II house are similar to those found in a tomb at Kinneret, 1.25 km W of Beth-yerah and considered a possible burial site for the EB II city (Mazar 1975: 717). Excavation of three levels of EB II burials produced numerous household goods such as jugs, jars, bowls, and platters along with the cremated remains of those buried. The tomb provides a glimpse at the wealth available to some in this period. Numerous beads and jewelry were found including part of a necklace that had two gold and two ruby beads. The city participated in a wider trade network as evident in the composition of the beads, which included copper, faience, ruby, crystal, jasper, quartz, pottery, and mother-of-pearl. In addition, bone plaques with ornamentation and a round plaque of beaten gold were found (Mazar 1975: 717–18; Mazar, Amiran, and Haas 1973: 176–93). Although influenced by its contacts with the Mesopotamian area, Beth-yerah reflects distinctive regional characteristics as evidenced by a locally produced EB II cylinder seal stamp, which was used to make impressions on vessels themselves rather than to seal documents or jars as in Mesopotamia (Ben-Tor 1978: 108–9).

The site flourished in EB III; a paved road with houses on each side (Ussishkin 1968: 267) and a large public building, possibly a granary, indicate increasing centralization and cooperation (Maisler, Stekelis, and Avi-Yonah 1952: 223–28; Hestrin 1975: 257–58; Aharoni 1982: 67). The period is distinguished by the sudden appearance of KHIRBET KERAK WARE, first found at Beth-yerah. This hand-turned and highly burnished ware is found in a number of EB III sites (e.g., Megiddo, Ai, Jericho), although it seems concentrated in N Palestine and Syria. The pottery was apparently brought by peoples moving into the area from Anatolia (Amiran 1952: 101–3; Anati 1963: 359–61). The destruction layers directly below this ware at the EB III layer at Ai and the lack of such a destruction layer at Beth-yerah suggest that the population movement associated with the ware could be violent or peaceable (Kenyon 1979: 99–101).

Evidence of the cultural horizon of the EB III site comes from small figurines of animals, two model mills or houses made of clay, a pottery piece in the shape of a roaring lion (Maisler, Stekelis, and Avi-Yonah 1952: 171), and a rare ivory bull's head found in a large colonnaded structure, possibly a temple (Ben-Tor 1972: 26–27; Tadmor 1986: 98). As yet no clear function can be determined for the ivory bull's head, although two of four EB bull heads found in Palestine appear to have a temple as their provenance, suggesting some cultic purpose (Ben-Tor 1972: 26; Callaway 1974: 60–61). Since no clear parallels can be found in the ANE, the general view is that the head was made locally. The use of ivory, a luxury item at this time, provides further evidence of the larger trade network in which Beth-yerah flourished (Tadmor 1986: 98–99).

The Khirbet Kerak period came to an abrupt end around 2200 B.C.E. when Beth-yerah experienced mass destruction as did other cities such as Jericho, Ai, Megiddo, and Beth-shan (Aharoni 1982: 73). Nevertheless, the city apparently continued through the MB II period as indicated by an MB I potter's workshop and by MB II buildings divided by narrow passages and by a broad street leading from the S gate to industrial kilns (Hestrin 1975: 256; Bar-Adon 1953: 132; Bar-Adon 1954: 128).

Occupation of the site occurs again in the Persian period as evidenced by Perisan pottery in the foundation of a Hellenistic city wall, which extends over 1600 m. In the floors of the wall's towers were found iron arrowheads, Hellenistic pottery, and coins and cooking stoves (Bar-Adon 1955: 273). During the Ptolemaic period certain members of the city apparently flourished as indicated by a large private residence with courtyard. In addition, several excavated houses of the Hellenistic period overlook the Sea of Galilee. One of these houses has colored plaster that imitates black, red, and green marble veneering (Hestrin 1975: 256). Hellenistic culture is evident from a bust of Tyche found at Beth-yerah but in an undatable context; Sukenik dates it to the 1st centuries C.E. (Sukenik 1922: 104–5, 108).

The Roman period is represented by a large Roman fort (60 × 60 m) built in the 2d or 3d century C.E. During the Byzantine period, after the fort went out of use, a synagogue (22 × 37 m) was built within the interior of the Roman fort. A colored mosaic that depicted plants, birds and lions was found as was the base of a column that had a menorah, lulab, ethrog and incense shovel carved in it. Additional finds include a large bath complex of possible 4th–5th century date and a Byzantine church, which dates to 528 C.E. based on a Greek inscription in the mosaic floor (Maisler, Stekelis, and Avi-Yonah 1952: 218–23; Hestrin 1975: 258, 262).

Bibliography

Aharoni, Y. 1982. *The Archaeology of the Land of Israel.* Trans. A. F. Rainey. Philadelphia.

Amiran, R. 1952. Connections between Anatolia and Palestine in the Early Bronze Age. *IEJ* 2: 89–103.

Anati, E. 1963. *Palestine Before the Hebrews.* New York.

Avi-Yonah, M. 1966. *The Holy Land From the Persian to the Arab Conquests (536 B.C. to A.D. 640).* Grand Rapids.

Bar-Adon, P. 1953. Beth Yerah. *IEJ* 3: 132.

———. 1954. Beth Yerah. *IEJ* 4: 128–29.

———. 1955. Beth Yerah. *IEJ* 5: 273.

Ben-Tor, A. 1972. An Ivory Bull's Head From ʾAy. *BASOR* 208: 24–29.

———. 1978. *Cylinder Seals of Third Millennium Palestine.* BASOR Sup 22. Cambridge, MA.

Callaway, J. A. 1974. A Second Ivory Bull's Head from Ai. *BASOR* 213: 57–61.

Esse, D. L. 1982. Khirbet Kerak Publication Project. *The Oriental Institute 1982–83: Annual Report.* Chicago.

Hanbury-Tenison, J. W. 1986. *The Late Chalcolithic to Early Bronze I Transition in Palestine and Transjordan.* Oxford.

Hestrin, R. 1975. Beth Yerah. *EAEHL* 1: 253–62.

Kenyon, K. M. 1979. *Archaeology in the Holy Land.* 4th ed. New York.

Maisler, B.; Stekelis, M.; and Avi-Yonah, M. 1952. The Excavations at Beth Yerah (Khirbet el-Kerak) 1944–1946. *IEJ* 2: 165–73, 218–29.

Mazar, B. 1975. Kinneret. *EAEHL* 3: 717–18.

Mazar, B.; Amiran, R.; and Haas, N. 1973. An Early Bronze Age II Tomb at Beth-Yerah (Kinneret). *EI* 11: 176–93 (in Hebrew).

Neubauer, A. 1868. *La geographié du Talmud.* Paris.

Sukenik, L. 1922. The Ancient City of Philoteria (Beth Yerah). *JPOS* 2: 101–9.

Syncellus, G. 1984. *Ecloga Chronographica.* Leipzig.

Tadmor, M. 1986. *Treasures of the Holy Land.* New York.

Ussishkin, D. 1968. Beth Yerah. *RB* 75: 266–68.

DOUGLAS R. EDWARDS

BETH-ZAITH (PLACE) [Gk *Bēthzaith*].

1 Macc 7:19 identifies Beth-zaith (the "house/place of the olive" from the Heb *bêt zayit*) as the camping place of the Seleucid general Bacchides after his treacherous murder of 60 Hasideans near Jerusalem. Although Beth-zaith was once thought to be Bezeth (or Bethesda) (Meyer 1921: 244 n. 1), the N quarter of Jerusalem, Abel (*GP 2:* 284, 286) identified Beth-zaith with modern Beit Zita (M.R. 161114), 6 km N of Beth-zur. 1 Maccabees indicates that Bacchides had left Jerusalem. That would not have been the case if Beth-zaith were to be identified with Bezeth/Bethesda. Josephus (*Ant* 12.10.2) refers to this place as Berzetho (Gk *bērzēthō*). Schlatter (1896: 225) points out the unreliability of the Josephan text on this point of spelling.

Bibliography

Meyer, E. 1921. *Ursprung und Anfänge des Christentums.* Vol. 2. Stuttgart and Berlin.

Schlatter, A. 1896. Einige Ergebnisse aus Niese's Ausgabe des Josephus. *ZDPV* 19: 221–32.

MICHAEL E. HARDWICK

BETH-ZATHA (PLACE) [Gk *Bēthzatha*].

This pool of Jerusalem is mentioned only in John 5:2 as "a pool, in Hebrew called Bethzatha, which has five porticoes." The name is "Bethsaida" (Gk *bēthsaïda,* house of the fisherman) in the KJV. This reading appears in Papyrus Bodmer (p^{66} and p^{75}), Codex Vaticanus, the supplement to Codex Washingtonus, Codex Psi, two texts of the Old Latin, the Vulgate, the Harclean Syriac, the Coptic, the Ethiopic, the Stuttgart Diatessaron, Tertullian, and Jerome. The name is "Bethzatha" (Aram *bet zathaʾ,* house of olive [oil]) in the RSV, following Codex Sinaiticus, Codex Bezae, Codex Regius, minuscule 33, Eusebius, and many texts of the Old Latin. A third reading is "Bethesda" (Aram *bet ḥesdaʾ* or house of mercy), attested in Codex Alexandrinus, Codex Ephraemi Rescriptus, Codex K, the commentary section of Codex X, at least five other late majuscules, also many minuscules, Byzantine Lectionaries, the Armenian, the Georgian, the Diatessaron, Didymus, Chrysostom, and Cyril. The Editorial Committee of the United Bible Societies Greek New Testament prefers "Bethzatha", because "Bethsaida" may be a scribal assimilation to John 1:44, and "Bethesda" may simply be an edifying etymology. The

Copper Scroll of Qumran refers to *"Beteshdathayim"* in Jerusalem, perhaps Aramaic for "place of poured-out water" (3Q15.xi.12), which some of the committee felt tended to support the reading "Bethesda" (Metzger 1975: 208). Josephus speaks of the "fourth hill" of Jerusalem N of the Temple Mount and calls it "the Bezetha" in Greek (*JW* 5.4.2). The scribal confusion in the textual tradition may be due to the similarity of the name for the NE quarter of the city called "the Bezetha" or "the Beth Zetha" [alt. "Beth Zatha"], where the pool lay and the putative name of the pool (*Bet Ḥesdaʾ* or "house of mercy"). The latter name would derive from the local healing cult that the man in John 5 and his associates at the pool seemed to believe in.

The pool was itself a double pool, as the dual ending on *Betheshdathayim (Bet ʿEshdathayim)* indicates. If the Copper Scroll is to be understood as anything other than a fantasy, then near the pool stood a triclinium with a porch and entry on the W side. The pool underwent excavation from 1863–76 and from 1888–1900 (Yadin 1976: 133), then again after 1956 (Yadin 1976: 24). A bedrock causeway and dam running E-W separated two pools partially cut from the bedrock and partially built of stone and mortar. The five porches mentioned in John 5:2 stood upon this causeway and upon the four sides of the double pool. After 231 C.E. Origen of Caesarea would explain that the porches stood "four around the edges and one across the middle" (*C. Ioan.* 5.2–4.532).

The two pools are of two different sizes and were trapezoids in plan. They extended across at least one city block in the Beth Zatha quarter. The W edge of the two pools was aligned with the N-S street system of the quarter; whereas the E side ran roughly NNW to SSE. Overall length N to S measured about 97 m. The small pool to the N was about 60 m broad on its N side, while the large pool to the S was about 76 m broad on its S side. This comes to about 300 Greek feet N to S by 225 Greek feet E to W on its largest dimension.

Confirmation that a local healing cult continued into the 2d century comes from archaeological excavations at the site (Duprez 1970). Votive offerings characteristic of grateful devotees of Serapis or of Asclepius were unearthed in the debris in the double pool. Thus the local cult assumed Roman dress when Roman cults appeared in the new city of Aelia Capitolina. Aelia replaced Jerusalem under the emperor Hadrian in 135 C.E. after the Second Jewish Revolt against Rome. The site would therefore have become part of the Roman cult, namely, a Serapeum or an Asclepium, which may account for the underground chambers at the site.

Further evidence for the continued importance of the site is the erection of a Christian church in the 5th century just E of the pool. Its courtyard school on arched pillars and buttresses directly over the E end of the double pool. The presence of the church would overthrow and obliterate the local cult, much as the construction of the church of the Nativity in Bethlehem supplanted a cult of Thammuz or Adonis, or the construction of the Anastasis (Holy Sepulchre) in Jerusalem supplanted a temple to Venus (Wilkinson 1978).

Bibliography

Duprez, A. 1970. *Jesus et les Dieux Guérisseurs, à propos de Jean V.* Paris.

Metzger, B. 1975. *A Textual Commentary on the Greek New Testament.* London/New York.

Wilkinson, J. 1978. *Jerusalem as Jesus Knew It.* London.

Yadin, Y. 1976. *Jerusalem Revealed.* New Haven.

JAMES F. STRANGE

BETH-ZECHARIAH (PLACE) [Gk *Baithzacharia*]. 1 Macc 6:32–33 records that Judas the Maccabee and his army met and were defeated by a Syrian force at Beth-zechariah ("the house/place of Zechariah" from the Heb *bêt zĕkaryāhû*). Josephus described Beth-zechariah as a mountain defile (*Ant* 12.9.4; *JW* 1.1.5). Eleazar (or Avaran), brother of Judas, was killed there attacking a Syrian elephant (1 Macc 6:43–46) Abel (*GP* 2, 284) identified Beth-zechariah as the modern *Beit Zekaria* (M.R. 161118) 18 km S of Jerusalem and 10 km N of Beth-zur.

MICHAEL E. HARDWICK

BETH-ZUR (PLACE) [Heb *bêt ṣûr*]. A fortress city in Judah located on the road between Jerusalem and Hebron, about 20 miles S of Jerusalem (2 Macc 11:5); in the Hellenistic period, a S Judean border fortress facing Idumea (1 Macc 4:61). Beth-zur offered a defensible position which could serve to guard the approach to Jerusalem from the S. With an altitude of 3304 feet above sea level it is one of the highest ancient sites in Palestine.

The ancient city has been identified with Khirbet eṭ-Ṭubeiqah (M.R. 159110), although the name of the city survives in the adjacent and newer site Khirbet eṣ-Ṣur (500 yards to the SE), where material remains attest Arab and Byzantine occupation. Two archaeological campaigns have been conducted at Beth-zur under the direction of O. R. Sellers, the first in 1931 and the second in 1957.

Ceramic evidence indicates sporadic occupation of Beth-zur during the EB and MB I ages, but the city first became a fortified stronghold during the MB II period. Excavations at Beth-zur have revealed massive fortifications of a type often attributed to the Hyksos. Beth-zur's fortifications were similar to those of the same period found at Bethel, Tell Beit Mirsim, and Shechem. At the end of the MB age the city was destroyed (it is speculated by the Egyptians), but a less prosperous community continued there during the 1st century of the LB age. The site was abandoned from the 14th to 12th centuries.

The archaeological record attests a reoccupation of Beth-zur during the early Israelite period. Though this settlement apparently used the MB II fortifications, there is also some material evidence to suggest that the new occupants may have reduced the size of the city on the N by building a new wall. By the close of the 11th century the city was again destroyed.

Two biblical texts appear to give information pertaining to the period of Israelite settlement at Beth-zur. In 1 Chr 2:42–50 Beth-zur appears alongside several other cities of Judah including Mareshah, Ziph, Hebron, Tappuah, and Maon in the genealogy of Caleb, signifying that at some time in the history of Judah, Beth-zur was occupied by Calebites (cf. Josh 14:13–15; 15:13–19 in reference to Hebron). Beth-zur also appears in the list of cities allotted to Judah (in Josh 15:20–63 at v 58) at the time when

Joshua apportioned the land to the tribes. However, it is probable that this list of cities, with its organization according to districts, reflects the administrative subdivisions of a much later time in the kingdom of Judah. The time to which it pertains is a matter of dispute. According to A. Alt (1925) the list dates from the time of Josiah, according to F. M. Cross and G. E. Wright (1956) it reflects Jehoshaphat's administrative districts, and according to Z. Kallai (*HGB*, 334–48, 377) it belongs to the time of Hezekiah.

Material remains from the 10th to 9th centuries amount to only a few potsherds indicating only slight occupation during this time. Nothing attributable to Rehoboam has been found. Consequently, a question arises concerning the Chronicler's claim that Rehoboam built up Beth-zur as one of his fortified cities (2 Chr 11:7). Some scholars argue that the Chronicler has incorrectly attributed this defensive measure to Rehoboam and that the cities were actually fortified either by Hezekiah (Na'aman 1986) or by Josiah (Fritz 1981). However, since excavations at Beth-zur offer no evidence of the refortification of the site between the 10th century and the exile, they are unable to offer confirmation for either the hypothesis of Na'aman or that of Fritz.

A significant unfortified occupation of Beth-zur occurred again in Iron Age II. The excavators dated the beginning of this settlement to a time no earlier than 640 B.C.E. on the basis of the pottery (Lapp in Sellers et al. 1968: 28; Funk in Sellers et al. 1968: 8), but Na'aman (1986: 6), using the same evidence, argues that the beginning of the Iron Age II settlement must be moved back to the second half of the 8th century. Especially pertinent for his argument are the 11 *lmlk* jar handles exhibiting the two-winged symbol found in the Iron Age II strata at Beth-zur, because Na'aman (1979) previously contended that the *lmlk* jars belonged to Hezekiah's defensive preparations prior Sennacherib's invasion in 701 B.C.E.

The postexilic city of Beth-zur, according to archaeological evidence, had a sparse population during the 5th and 4th centuries. Yet, according to Neh 3:16 Nehemiah ben Azbuk, governor of half the district of Beth-zur, presumably working with a contingent from Beth-zur, assisted in rebuilding the walls of Jerusalem.

During the Hellenistic period Beth-zur became a thriving community, especially during the 2d century, when it expanded outside the city walls. Significant quantities of coins have been found, and their distribution—9 for the 5th to 4th centuries, 56 for the Ptolemaic period (312–181 B.C.E.), 180 for the Seleucid period (225–96 B.C.E.), and 20 for the Maccabean period (125–78 B.C.E.)—attests to the growth of the community, particularly in the 2d century. Of particular interest is one small silver coin with an inscription the reading of which has occasioned some dispute. Sellers reads, "Hezekiah of Judah" (1968: 2), and takes it as a reference to the high priest Hezekiah, the friend of Ptolemy I (Joseph. *AgAp* 1: 186–87). Funk, on the other hand, reads, "the governor Hezekiah" (*EAEHL* 1: 263–67).

Beth-zur assumed new significance as a stronghold during the conflicts of the Hellenistic period, especially during the Maccabean wars. Three phases of building at the citadel have been distinguished. According to Funk the first phase belongs to the 3d century in the context of the conflict between the Ptolemies and the Seleucids; the second phase was built either by the Seleucids or by Judas Maccabeus; and the third phase was built by Bacchides ca. 161 B.C.E. in the context of the Maccabean wars (Funk in Sellers et al. 1968: 17).

The literary evidence in 1 and 2 Maccabees also gives Beth-zur a prominent place during the Maccabean revolt. Following upon the initial defeat of several Seleucid forces (1 Macc 3:10–4:25), Lysias approached Judah from the S through Idumea and fought Judas at or near Beth-zur in 165 B.C.E. (1 Macc 4:29; cf. 2 Macc 11:5). After his victory over Lysias in this battle, Judas rededicated the temple at Jerusalem, refortified Jerusalem, and also fortified Beth-zur (phase 2 of the citadel? 1 Macc 4:61; cf. 6:7, 26). In 162 B.C.E. Lysias led a second campaign through Idumea. He laid siege to the stronghold at Beth-zur (1 Macc 6:31; cf. 2 Macc 13:19), which was unable to withstand it because of its inadequate food provisions (1 Macc 6:49; cf. 2 Macc 13:22). So Lysias took Beth-zur and stationed troops there. Subsequently Beth-zur remained in Seleucid control for some time, having its fortifications rebuilt by Bacchides in 160 B.C.E. (the third phase of the citadel, 1 Macc 9:52). Finally, in 145 B.C.E. Simon laid siege to Beth-zur and recaptured it for Judea (1 Macc 11:65–66). It remained in Judean control thereafter, but the community slowly declined until the settlement ended about 100 B.C.E.

Bibliography

Alt, A. 1925. Judas Gaue unter Josia. *Palästina Jahrbuch* 21: 100–16. Repr. *KlSchr* 2: 276–88.

Cross, F. M., and Wright, G. E. 1956. Boundary and Province Lists of th Kingdom of Judah [Joshua 13–19]. *JBL* 75: 202–26.

Fritz, V. 1981. The 'List of Rehoboam's Fortresses' in 2 Chr 11.5–12—A Document from the Time of Josiah. *EI* 15: 46–53.

Na'aman, N. 1979. Sennacherib's Campaign to Judah and the Date of the *LMLK* Stamps. *VT* 29: 61–86.

———. 1986. Hezekiah's Fortified Cities and the LMLK Stamps. *BASOR* 261: 5–21.

Sellers, O. R. 1933. *The Citadel of Beth-zur.* Philadelphia.

Sellers, O. R.; Funk, R. W.; McKenzie, J. L.; Lapp, P. and Lapp, N. 1968. *The 1957 Excavation at Beth-zur. AASOR,* 38. Cambridge, MA.

WESLEY I. TOEWS

BETHANY (PLACE) [Gk *Bēthania*]. **1.** Name of a town mentioned in Jdt 1:9, located "beyond the Jordan" but in the vicinity of Jerusalem. The name (Gk *baitanē*) is rendered in the RSV as Bethany, but in the RV as Betane. The expression "beyond the Jordan" in biblical texts may denote areas either E or W of the Jordan river. In this case, however, because the perspective is that of Nebuchadnezzar in "Assyria" and because the list of names (which includes Jerusalem) follows in order moving from Galilee in the N to Egypt in the S, it seems to indicate the region W of the Jordan.

Moore (*Judith* AB) identifies this town with Beth-anoth (M.R. 162107) (modern Beit-ʾAinum), which is located S of Jerusalem, about 7 miles N of Hebron (Josh 15:59) in the highlands of Judea. It is probably not to be identified with the Bethany of Mark 14:3f.

In the legendary story of Judith this city is included in a

list of cities and regions which Nebuchadnezzar conquered and from which he demanded assistance to engage his enemy, Arphaxad. Because they rejected his demands, he mounted a campaign against them which set the scene for the actions of the heroine, Judith. The town did not figure in any of the action of this story.

2. Place where John the Baptist conducted his ministry, situated on the E bank of the Jordan river (John 1:28). See also BETHANY BEYOND THE JORDAN. Because of its location it is doubtful whether it can be identified with the hometown of Lazarus (John 11:18), although Parker (1955) argues for the identity of the two Bethanys.

During his sojourn in Palestine, Origen reports (Comm. G 40) that he visited the area but failed to find any trace of a town with this name on the E side of the Jordan. He concluded that the text should read "Bethabara," a place pointed out to him on the W bank of the Jordan. Etymological factors probably influenced him as well, because it means the "place of crossing over".

The Madaba map mosaic (6th century A.D.), as Schnackenburg (1980) reports, locates a town named Bethabara on the W bank of the Jordan close to the point where the Jordan flows into the Dead Sea. Brown (*John* AB) notes that some modern commentators have accepted this variant, suggesting that the gospel writer is stressing the parallels between Jesus and Joshua. Jesus, like Joshua, crosses over the Jordan after his baptism, leading his people into the promised land.

The discovery of p^{75} (3d century A.D.), which supports the reading "Bethany," leads most scholars to accept this as the original reading. Traditions dating to the 3d century state that John baptized Jesus near the Wâdī el-Ḥarrar, located near the Prodromos Monastery, about 5 miles N of the Jordan's entrance into the Dead Sea. Whether Bethany should be located in this vicinity remains uncertain.

3. Most frequently mentioned town of this name located on the E slopes of the Mount of Olives, 3 km E of Jerusalem (John 11:1). In the Synoptic Gospels Jesus made Bethany his headquarters during his final week of ministry in Jerusalem (Mark 11:11, 12 = Matt 21:17; cf. Luke 19:29). Bethany marked the last station for the pilgrim traveling from Jordan to Jerusalem. Prior to his "triumphal entry" into Jerusalem, Jesus sends some of his disciples to Bethany in order to secure the donkey upon which he will ride into the city (Mark 11:1).

The gospels of Mark and Matthew also note that the anointing of Jesus at Simon the Leper's house took place in Bethany (Mark 14:3 = Matt 26:6). This story may have some relationship with a similar anointing recorded in John 12:1–8 which occurred in Bethany, the village of Lazarus, and in which Mary, Lazarus' sister, is identified as the woman anointing Jesus.

The story of the raising of Lazarus from the dead (John 11:1–44) also occurs in the context of Bethany. The modern town at this site is called El-ᶜAziriyeh (M.R. 174131) by its Muslim inhabitants, reflecting the traditional linkage with Lazarus. The gospel writer stresses the proximity of this town to Jerusalem, just under 2 miles distant (v 18). Eusebius (*Onomast.* 58) places it at the second milestone from Jerusalem on the way to Jericho. Similarly the Bordeaux Pilgrim (CCSL, 125.18), A.D. 333, locates it 1500 paces E of the Mount of Olives.

Luke 24:50 records Bethany as being in the vicinity of the Ascension of Jesus Christ. This Bethany is not mentioned in the OT, although Ananiah (Neh 11:32), associated with Anathoth and Nob, may be the same place. See ANANIAH (PLACE).

Archaeological investigations have taken place at Bethany under the direction of the Franciscans (1949–53). A series of churches dating back to the 4th century A.D. were uncovered. The tomb of Lazarus was also located.

Bibliography

Parker, P. 1955. Bethany Beyond Jordan. *JBL* 74: 257–61.

Saller, S. J. 1957. *Excavations at Bethany (1949–53).* Jerusalem.

Schnackenburg, R. 1980. Vol. 1 of *The Gospel According to St. John.* New York.

L. J. Perkins

BETHANY BEYOND THE JORDAN. Place where John baptized and was questioned by the envoys from Jerusalem concerning his self-claims (John 1:19–28). It was at Bethany that Jesus gained his first disciples from the circle of the Baptist (1:35–51). Following the gospel of John, Bethany is frequently held to be the locus of Jesus' Baptism; however, this view is not cogent, since John 1:32–34 contains only an indirect allusion to the Baptism (Schnackenburg, *John* HTKNT, 1: 283). After Jesus escaped an attempt to lynch him at the feast of Hanukkah in Jerusalem (John 10:22–39) and preceding the Passion, he stayed at Bethany and once more gained a large number of followers there from the circle of the Baptist (10:40–42).

Because Origen could not find a location named Bethany on the E bank of the Jordan, he opted for the reading of *Bēthabara* in John 1:28, though almost all of the mss of his time read Bethany (*Comm. on John* 6. 204). Currently this reading is almost uniformly considered to be original because Bethany is not only extant in codices Vaticanus and Sinaiticus (4th century) but also in a large number of mss with considerable geographical distribution and because it is now possible to trace it back to the 3d century via p^{75}, and as far back as to the 2d century via p^{66}. Further, the transition from John 10:40–42 to 11:1ff. shows that the Evangelist intended the concordance with the name of the location Bethany near Jerusalem (11:1, 18). However, the agreement between Origen and the Syriac version of the Gospels (syr^{c}, syr^{s}) demonstrates that with Bēthabara he followed a genuine local tradition (Burkitt 1904: 308–9, contra Clapp 1907: 75–83). The name, likely derived from the Heb *bêt ᶜabārâ*, "house of crossing," points to one of the fords of the Jordan.

On account of the early ms attestation, all attempts to understand Bethany as a corruption of the text or as an interpolation have failed. This outcome also applies to the assumption that Bethany and Bēthabara are miswritten forms of Baithanabra in Josh 13:27 LXX (B) (*EncBib* 1: 548). Against the hypothesis of a merely fictitious place, (Krieger 1954) is the fact that Johannine references to places have generally proven to be accurate, if they can be verified (Schwank 1981). To parallel Bethany in John 1:28

with the homonymous location on the Mount of Olives (Parker 1955) is grammatically impossible to begin with (Fortna 1974: 67). Furthermore, the Evangelist has deliberately distinguished the two locations (see above).

A modern suggestion lacking the support of tradition or of archaeology (Buzy 1931) is the localization of Bethany at the Tel el-Medesch at the end of the Wâdī Nimrīn on the elevation of the Jordan ford el-Ghōranije (Féderlin 1908; *DBSup* 1: 968–70). The same applies to the search in the Wâdī Gharbe, near Livias, the residence of Herod Antipas (Wiefel 1967: 81). Betonim (Josh 13:26), today's Khirbet Batneh SW of Es-Salt, which was suggested by F. Delitzsch (1876: 602), K. Furrer (1902: 257–58), and T. Zahn (1907: 290–94), is eliminated because of the absence of running water, which is necessary for baptismal practice. C. R. Conder's (1875) assumption that Bēthabara was to be located near a ford by the name of Makhādet ʿAbārah, 5 km NE of Beth-shean was widely accepted in earlier years (Erbes 1928: 82). But the existence of the name could not be verified by later researchers (Lagrange 1895: 510; Rix 1903: 161); the Byzantine tradition locates Bēthabara over against Jericho (see below). Long before Conder, in 1658, J. Lightfoot (reprint 1979: 327–33) equated Bēthabara with the Beth-barah in Judg 7:24 and considered it to be a ford near Beth-shean. Today, however, the search for Beth-barah has moved farther to the S to the vicinity where the Jabbok flows into the Jordan.

Unless one foregoes an attempt at localization altogether (Brown *John* AB, 44–45), the current search for Bethany concentrates mostly on the Wâdī el-Charrār (Mommert 1903; Dalman 1924: 96–102; Kopp 1964: 153–66; Schnackenburg *John* HTKNT 1, 283–84; Keel and Küchler 1982: 527–32), which flows into the Jordan vis-à-vis Jericho. In the Byzantine era a Johannine church which recalled the Baptism of Jesus (Kopp 1964: 158–59; Wiefel 1967: 76–77) was located there at the E bank of the Jordan (Baldi 1982: 172). But this localization dates back to the early 4th century. Since the anonymous Pilgrim of Bordeaux in A.D. 333 (Baldi 1982: 171) also discovered an apparently older Jewish tradition of Elijah's ascension (2 Kgs 2:5–14) at this location, it could indeed be possible that the Baptist himself chose this site in order to point to himself symbolically as the eschatological Elijah (cf. Matt 11:14; 17:11–13 = Mark 9:12–13; Luke 1:17; Schnackenburg, *John* HTKNT 1, 283–84). The map of the Madaba mosaic of the second half of the 6th century marks a Bēthabara over against Jericho, though on the W bank of the Jordan. This name was likely already associated with this region during the time of Eusebius (*Onomast.* 58:19–20) and of Origen. There is no indication in local onomastica, however, of a location Bethany which derived from *bêt ʿaniyyâ*, "house of the boat" = ford.

While the tradition in favor of the place of Jesus' Baptism at the lower course of the Jordan (Matt 3:1; cf. Matt 11:7–9 = Luke 7:24–26) is ancient and reliable (Baldi and Bagatti 1980: 38–46), there are, nevertheless, reasons against an identification of this location with the Bethany of John 1:28. Contemporary researchers have likewise pointed out that the relationship of the distances in John 1–2 and 10–11 require the search for Bethany to take place closer to Galilee than to Judea (Elliger, *BHH* 1: 231; Brownlee 1972: 167–68; Dockx 1984: 14). John 1:35–51 represents a parallel of the Synoptic accounts of the call of the disciples in the vicinity of the Lake of Genezareth (Matt 4:18–22 = Mark 1:16–20; cf. Luke 5:1–11). "Beyond the Jordan" *(peran tou Iordanou)* does not have to carry the political sense of the Perea of Herod Antipas by any means, but simply denotes the land E of the Jordan, and sometimes the more northerly Transjordan (especially so in Matt 4:15). If a parallel is drawn from John 10:40–42 to Matt 19:1 = Mark 10:1 (Brown, *John* AB, 414), the expression "Judea beyond the Jordan" (Matt 19:1) points, against the backdrop of Josh 19:34 (MT), to the N territory E of the Jordan (Riesner fc.).

Hence it is necessary to consider the suggestion of those scholars who claim to see, in Bethany of John 1:28, the name of the region of Batanea (Gk *Batanaia*), the OT Bashan. In the LXX (Num 32:32–33; Deut 3:8; 4:47) and in Josephus (*Ant* 8.37), Bashan is described as "beyond the Jordan" *(peran tou Iordanou)*. An initial reference to this solution appears already in J. Lightfoot (1979: 328). Its first recent defendant was C. R. Conder (1877). Today this theory is espoused especially by K. A. Eckhardt (1961: 168–71) and W. H. Brownlee (1972: 167–73). The change in the forms of the names is feasible philologically, especially if they are compared with the forms in the Targums and in the Jerusalem Talmud (Brownlee 1972: 169). The name of a region would also explain why Origen did not find a location of Bethany. In John 10:40 Bethany is not described as a village or town, but as an undetermined place *(topos)*, in obvious contrast to Bethany near Jerusalem (11:30). Further, this reduces the difficulty presented by the fact that the article one would expect with the name of a region is missing in John 1:28. If Bethany signifies the Batanea, it becomes clearer historically why Jesus withdrew to that place at the end of his ministry (John 10:40). For the time being, Jesus would be secure in the territory of Philip, the tolerant tetrarch, according to Josephus (*Ant* 18.106–7).

The SW part of the Batanea, to which John 1:28 points, later on was not only particularly densely populated by Nazorite and Ebionite Jewish Christians (Epiph. *Haer.* 29.7; 30.2). Under Herod the Great, according to Josephus, this region attracted pious Jews of the most diverse background (*Ant* 17.23–27). Among these seem to have been especially the adherents of Jewish sects, such as the Essenes (Wieder 1962: 1–5; Pixner 1983: 350–58), or the forerunners of the Mandaeans (Rudolph 1960: 248–52). In the area of Mt. Hermon, apparently, those circles resembling the Essenes were settled who considered this mountain, following *1 Enoch* 13 and *T. Levi* 2–5 (cf. Matt 16:13–19), to be a place of special revelation (Nickelsburg 1981). John 1:51 (cf. Gen 28:12–13) is associated with such expectations, and John 10:16, as well as 11:52, may allude to missionary work among Jewish sects.

Jerome (*Comm. on Isa.* 9:1 [130]) knew of a Jewish Christian interpretation of Isa 8:23–9:1 according to which the Messiah would appear in the N because Israel's calamity began there (cf. 2 Kgs 15:29). This expectation is also in the back of Matt 4:13–16 and had Jewish rudiments (Wieder 1962: 3–51). Against this backdrop it may also become clear why John, according to John 10:40, "first" *(to prōton)* began to baptize in the Batanea, that is in the northernmost area of the Holy Land. Together with the baptismal activity in the central Jordan valley (Baldi and Bagatti 1980: 50–52) at Aenon, near Salim (John 3:24), as well as in the lower Jordan valley (see above), we thus obtain a very plausible historical picture of an itinerant preacher (Flusser 1969: 30–31; Riesner 1988: 353–57).

Like other place names in the gospel of John, therefore, Bethany is first of all a concrete geographical designation. But this does not rule out that it also has a deeper theological significance (Mollat 1959: 323; Voigt 1977: 72–75, 93–100). The special prominence of Bethany may indicate the existence of Johannine communities in this area (Scobie 1982: 82). To the degree that Bethany also attributes significance to Transjordan, next to Galilee, Samaria, and Judea, the Fourth Gospel emphasizes the mission of Jesus to all of Israel (Meeks 1966: 163–64). When the evangelist approximates the name of the region (Batanea), which was especially associated with the beginning of the messianic era, with the name of the location Bethany, where Jesus' passion began (cf. John 11:47ff.; 12:1), he merges redemption's beginning and completion into an indivisible unity.

Bibliography

Baldi, D. 1982. *Enchiridion Locorum Sanctorum. Documenta S. Evangelii Loca Respicientia.* 3d ed. Jerusalem.

Baldi, D., and Bagatti, B. 1980. *Saint Jean-Baptiste dans les souvenirs de sa Patrie.* Studium Biblicum Franciscanum, Collectio Minor N. 27. Jerusalem.

Brownlee, W. H. 1972. Whence the Gospel According to John? Pp. 166–94 in *John and Qumran,* ed. J. H. Charlesworth. London.

Burkitt, F. C. 1904. *Evangelion Da-Mepharreshe. The Curetonian Version of the Four Gospels.* Vol. 2. Cambridge.

Buzy, D. 1931. Béthanie au delà du Jourdain. Tell el Medesch où Sapsas? *Recherches de Science Religieuse* 21: 444–62.

Clapp, R. G. 1907. A Study of the Place-names Gergesa and Bethabara. *JBL* 26: 62–83.

Conder, C. R. 1875. The Site of Bethabara. *PEFQS:* 72–74.

———. 1877. Bethany beyond Jordan. *PEFQS:* 184–87.

Dalman, G. 1924. *Orte und Wege Jesu.* BFCT 2/1. 3d ed. Gütersloh.

Delitzsch, F. 1876. Horae Hebraicae et Talmudicae. Ergänzung zu Lightfoot und Schöttgen. *Zeitschrift für die gesammte lutherische Theologie und Kirche* 37: 593–606.

Dockx, S. 1984. *Chronologies néotestamentaires et Vie de l'Église primitive.* 2d ed. Leuven.

Eckhardt, K. A. 1961. *Der Tod des Johannes als Schlüssel zum Verständnis der Johanneischen Schriften.* Berlin.

Erbes, K. 1928. Die Tauforte des Johannes nebst dem Salem des Melchisedek. *ThArb* 24: 71–106.

Féderlin, L. 1908. *Béthanie au delà du Jourdain.* Paris.

Flusser, D. 1969. *Jesus.* Trans. R. Walls. New York.

Fortna, R. T. 1974. Theological Use of Locale in the Fourth Gospel. Pp. 58–95 in *Gospel Studies in Honor of Sherman Eldon Johnson.* Ed. M. H. Shepherd and E. C. Hobbs. ATRSup 3. Evanston, IL.

Furrer, K. 1902. Das Geographische im Evangelium nach Johannes. *ZNW* 3: 257–65.

Keel, O., and Küchler, M. 1982. *Orte und Landschaften der Bibel.* Vol. 2. Zurich and Göttingen.

Kopp, C. 1964. *Die heiligen Stätten der Evangelien.* 2d ed. Regensburg.

Krieger, N. 1954. Fiktive Orte der Johannes-Taufe. *ZNW* 45: 121–23.

Lagrange, M. J. 1895. Origène, la Critique Textuelle et la Tradition Topographique. *RB* 4: 501–24.

Lightfoot, J. 1979. *A Commentary on the New Testament from the Talmud and Hebraica: Matthew—I Corinthians.* Vol. 1. Repr. Grand Rapids.

Meeks, W. A. 1966. Galilee and Judea in the Fourth Gospel. *JBL* 85: 159–69.

Mollat, D. 1959. Remarques sur le vocabulaire spatial du quatrième évangile. *TU* 73: 321–28.

Mommert, C. 1903. *Aenon und Bethania.* Leipzig.

Nickelsburg, G. W. E. 1981. Enoch, Levi, and Peter: Recipients of Revelation in Upper Galilee. *JBL* 100: 575–600.

Parker, P. 1955. Bethany beyond Jordan. *JBL* 74: 257–61.

Pixner, B. 1983. Unravelling the Copper Scroll Code: A Study on the Topography of 3 Q 15. *RevQ* 11: 323–66.

Riesner, R. 1988. *Jesus als Lehrer.* 3d ed. WUNT 2/7. Tübingen.

———. fc. *Bethany beyond the Jordan (John 1,28).* (Vol. 1 of *Jesus als Lehrer.) TynBull* 38.

Rix, H. 1903. Notes taken on a tour in Palestine in the Spring of 1901. *PEFQS:* 159–62.

Rudolph, K. 1960. *Die Mandäer.* Vol. 1. Göttingen.

Schwank, B. 1981. Ortskenntnisse im Vierten Evangelium? *ErbAuf* 57: 427–42.

Scobie, C. H. H. 1982. Johannine geography. *SR* 11: 77–84.

Voigt, S. 1977. Topo-Geografia e Teologia del Battista nel IV Vangelo. *Liber Annuus* 27: 69–101.

Wieder, N. 1962. *The Judean Scrolls and Karaism.* London.

Wiefel, W. 1967. Bethabara jenseits des Jordan (Joh. 1,28). *ZDPV* 83: 72–81.

Zahn, T. 1907. Zur Heimatkundes des Evangelisten Johannes I: Bethania—Bethabara. *NKZ* 18: 265–94.

RAINER RIESNER
Trans. Siegfried S. Schatzmann

BETHASMOTH (PLACE) [Gk *Baitasmōn*]. An alternate form of Azmaveth.

BETHBASI (PLACE) [Gk *Baithbasi*]. A city in the wilderness of Judah to which Jonathan, Simon, and their followers retreated (1 Macc 9:62) from Bacchides, a friend of the Seleucid king Demetrius I Soter, who appointed him governor (7:8) of the province named Beyond the River (i.e. west of the Euphrates). The city is identified with Khirbet Beit Baṣṣi, located SE of Bethlehem about 5 km NE of Tekoa on the Wâdī Umm el-Qalʿah (Simons *GTTOT,* 414).

In 159 B.C. the high priest Alcimus (appointed by Demetrius at the same time as Bacchides, but from outside the legitimate high priestly family) had given orders to tear down the inner wall separating the Court of the Gentiles from direct access to the temple. Alcimus was unable to carry out this plan, however, since he was stricken by paralysis and died. Bacchides returned to Demetrius for two years, then ordered his sympathizers to seize Jonathan and hold him until he returned (1 Macc 9:54–60). When the plan became known, Jonathan killed 50 collaborators and retreated to Bethbasi, refortified it, and waited for Bacchides to besiege the city. Jonathan took a small contingent of his army out of the city and attacked Bacchides. With the rest of the army, Simon attacked

Bacchides' siege weapons and joined the attack on the enemy troops. Bacchides was forced to withdraw, and eventually agreed to peace terms with Jonathan (1 Macc 9:65–73), leaving the Maccabean brothers in charge of all of Judah except for Jerusalem and Beth-zur (*MBA,* map 198).

Bibliography

Tedesche, S., and Zeitlin, S. 1950. *The First Book of Maccabees.* New York.

PAUL L. REDDITT

BETHEL (DEITY) [Heb *bêtʾēl*]. A NW Semitic deity whose presence in the Near East may be traced for more than a millennium, with its greatest attestation in the military colony of Syene-Elephantine in Egypt during the 6th and 5th centuries B.C. See ELEPHANTINE PAPYRI. The divine Bethel may be found in one personal name in the Hebrew Bible (Zech 7:2); other alleged biblical references to the divinity are dubious.

A. The Historical Data

1. Pre-Elephantine History. PHILO OF BYBLOS (116–64 B.C.) in his *Phoenician History,* which purports to be a translation of a work by an early Phoenician historian named Sanchuniathon, has bequeathed a theogony of the Phoenician pantheon. It relates that Uranus and Ge produced four sons: Elus (Kronos), Baitylus (Bethel), Dagon, and Atlas. This exalted status of Bethel indicates the erstwhile importance of the god, being descended from the supreme deities and fraternally related to Elus (El), Dagon, and Atlas (Baumgarten 1981: 15, lines 21–24; cf. pp. 202–3). There is a ring of antiquity in the birth of Bethel in this passage and an implied geographical diffusion of his veneration. It is important to distinguish carefully between the god Baitylos (Bethel) and the *baitylia,* which Uranus devised, contriving to put life into stones (ibid. 202–3), hence "holy stone" (*baitylion,* neuter sing.). Some scholars have attempted to discover the god Bethel in ancient Ugaritic culture (Hyatt 1939: 87f.), but their proposals have been effectively challenged by Marvin H. Pope, who denies any reference to Bethel in the Ugaritic pantheon—at least within our present resources (Pope 1955: 59f.).

The first indubitable reference to the god Bethel appears in an Akkadian tablet embodying the text of a treaty consummated between Esarhaddon of Assyria and Baal, king of Tyre, ca. 675 B.C. (*ANET,* 534a). To preserve inviolate this compact, the great gods of heaven and earth, the gods of Assyria, the gods of Akkad, and the gods of Eber-nari (= Syria) are enjoined. One of the great gods of Eber-nari so implicated was the god Bethel (Akkad). *ᵈBa-a-a-ti-DINGER.MEŠ* = *Bayt-ʾil* = Bethel (Hyatt 1939: 81–84; on the reading, Coogan 1976: 45–47). The relevant imprecation reads: "May Bethel and ʿAnath-Bethel deliver you to a man-eating lion."

2. The Elephantine-Syene Papyri. Although a difficult Aramaic religious text in demotic script of the Persian period has been known for some years to contain the name of the god Bethel (Bowman 1944: 226, lines 8,9; 11,18), the translational difficulties have hindered a satisfactory understanding of the text. The situation is quite the reverse regarding the 108 papyri and some significant ostraca and other inscriptional materials which surfaced largely from the Syene-Elephantine sector (see ELEPHANTINE PAPYRI).

A brief *Sitz im Leben* of the political, ethnological, and religious factors of the Syene-Elephantine community will form a foundation to adjudicate the role of the god Bethel in the military outpost.

a. The Political Situation. Elephantine, known in ancient Egypt as Yeb (Eg *3bw;* Aram *yb;* for the later Greek toponym see *LÄ* 1:1217–24), is one of the larger islands of the Nile. It is elliptical with N-S dimensions of 1 mile with its greatest width one-third of a mile. It embraces an area of some 200 acres (see *ArchEleph,* 35–42). At this strategic location the Egyptian government installed a military garrison composed largely of Jewish mercenaries. On the E bank of the Nile, opposite Yeb, was the counterpart of Yeb; it was the port city and fortress of Syene, populated largely by Syrian Arameans as a complement to the Yeb forces.

b. The Ethnicity of Yeb-Syene. The two fortresses were staffed by foreign mercenaries under the high command of Egyptian officers. With the Persian conquest, the leadership passed to Persian officials. Both Yeb and Syene had populations of Semitic origin, a demographic similarity which at times occasions some difficulty in identifying individuals. Thus in *CAP* 5.2 Koniya b. Zadok and Mahseiah b. Yedoniah are both identified as Arameans of Syene, but in *CAP* 6.3 and 8 they are termed Jews. Both groups seem to have been located in their Egyptian setting as early as the 7th century B.C. When Cambyses invaded Egypt (ca. 525 B.C.), he is reported to have devastated many religious shrines; but he manifested an entirely different attitude toward the Jews and spared their temple at Yeb (*CAP* 30.13; Oppenheim *CHI* 2: 554–59). However, with such plurality of ethnic groups, Egyptians, Babylonians, Persians, Syrians, and Judeans, one can easily forecast that friction would arise. The destruction of the Jewish temple by the instigation of the Egyptians is a case in point (*CAP* 30:14; 31:12, 13).

c. The Religious State of Affairs. Ethnic diversity among the mercenary immigrants, combined with that of the indigenous population, explains the variety of religions in the Yeb-Syene sector. The Egyptians venerated the isle of Yeb as the illustrious site of the temple of the ram headed god Khnum, the giver of rebirth to Hapy, the god of the Nile and the lord of the inundation (*WbMyth* 1: 346–47).

One may forecast that the Aramean garrison at Syene would become a residence of Syrian deities. In four letters destined for Syene, greetings are accorded to "the Temple of Nabu" (BK 1.1), "the Temple of Banit in Syene" (BK 2.1; 3.1), and "the Temple of Bethel and the Temple of the Queen of Heaven" (BK 4.1). In addition, one of the ostraca, dispatched by a certain Yarḥo, invokes Bel, Nabu,

Šamaš, and Nergal for the welfare of Yarḥo's brother Haggai (*ANET,* 491). Aramean personal names composed with a theophoric element such as Nus(h)ku (*CAP* 2.19), Atar (*CAP* 8.27), and Sin (*CAP* 6.19) appear in the documents. The gods are both West Semitic and Babylonian.

The Judean mercenaries may have enjoyed a privileged status in that their temple to Ya'u appears to be the sole foreign religious establishment that shared the island of Yeb with the illustrious Egyptian deity Khnum and the goddess Satet. Their sizable temple to Ya'u had an invested priestly staff and services which, as far as we know, paralleled the operations of the Judean ritual of the temple at Jerusalem, with its sacrifices, sacred calendar, and supportive offerings. Whether it was the offense of the Jewish bloody sacrifices (cf. *CAP* 33; *CHJ* 1: 227–32) or the animosity that developed between the Yahwists and the devotees of Khnum (*CAP* 31.4–11), it was the Jewish opinion that the priests of Khnum instigated an attack upon the temple of Ya'u in 411 B.C. and destroyed it. In 408 B.C. the officials of the temple appealed to Baghoi (Bigvai), the governor of Judea, for permission to rebuild the temple (*CAP* 30; 31). In response the governor, together with Delaiah, one of the sons of Sanballat, the governor of Samaria (Neh 2:10, 19; 13:28), directed that the temple should be rebuilt (*ANET,* 491–92). The Jewish colony seems to have survived until Pharaoh Nepherites I (399–393 B.C.); he is the last king included in the papyri of Yeb (*BMAP,* 13).

In retrospect it may be affirmed that the worship of the Judeans at Yeb favored a Yahwistic conformity, which, though it might not observe the dogma of the Jerusalem cult in regard to exclusive worship at one temple (cf. Deut 12:5–7, 11, 13, 14, 18, 26) and its exclusive sacrificial office, nevertheless comported with the spirit of 5th-century Judaism (*CHJ* 1: 227–31; *ArchEleph* 105–50).

Despite this affirmation there are some unresolved problems that largely concern the place of the foreign deities mentioned in the papyri. In addition to the temples of foreign deities mentioned above, there is a list of donors and their financial contributions for the support of the temple at Yeb, where the beneficiaries included not only Ya'u but the god Eshembethel and the goddess ʿAnathbethel (*CAP* 22.1, 123–25). Again, in an oath of a certain Menahem it is stated that he swore by "[. . .], by the temple and by ʿAnatya'u" (*CAP* 44.22). It is to be noted that the goddess ʿAnat is a component both of ʿAnabethel and of ʿAnatya'u.

In the Aramean documents of the period the god Bethel formed the initial component of 16 different personal names, names severally attached to 31 individuals (*ArchEleph* Appendix V). In the same literary deposit the god Eshem is a component of four diverse names borne by six different individuals, while the god Ḥerem is found in nine instances, including a hypocorisn. Eight of these instances have the divine nominal component in four different personal names.

B. Analysis of the Name "Bethel"

The term *Bethel* (Heb *bêt* "house, temple" + *ʾēl* "God"), meaning "house of God," developed, it is maintained by some scholars, into a pious surrogate for the name of God. This argument has been illustrated by the concept of Pharaoh. This name derives from the Egyptian *pr.ʿ3* "great house." In the New Kingdom it became the custom to address the king of Egypt as "the great house," metonymically to be understood as the dweller within the royal palace. One might roughly compare the name "sublime porte," an English translation of the Turkish *babi aliy,* signifying the chief office of the erstwhile Ottoman government, or the name of the Japanese emperor *mikado* (*mi,* exalted + *kado,* gate), literally, "exalted gate." Similar circumlocutions for a deity are discoverable in Ugaritic, Phoenician, Punic, Egyptian, and Hebrew usage.

C. The Role of Bethel at Syene-Elephantine

The Elephantine-Syene sector was saturated with diverse polytheisms, Egyptian, Babylonian, Aramaic being the dominant types; Judean religious beliefs and practices were in the minority in such a crowded international area. Proselytism, intermarriage, and syncretistic attraction played a significant role within such a society united by a common Aramean tongue. It has been noted that there was such an affinity between the Jews of Elephantine and the Arameans of Syene that it is difficult to differentiate them (*CHJ* 1: 223 n. 6). Accordingly, identifying the various documents as Elephantine Judean or as Syene Aramean is a difficult task. Most of the papyri represent informal correspondence, legal involvements, or a few ecclesiastical exchanges. Much of the material is limited to the concerns of several families. To generalize from these fragments of a centurial culture as though they constituted the total experience of the community is a seduction that must be denied.

The ambiguity of the data fairly prejudices the possibility of a unanimous interpretation of the religion of the Elephantine Judeans and of our particular concern, the role of the god Bethel. Three diverse proposals may now be presented as embodying the most satisfactory approaches to the subject.

The first approach argues that the Judeans were syncretistic or monolatrous: they gave Yaʾu, their ancestral God, preeminence, but accepted in varying degrees the gods and practices of their neighbors. That Israel and Judah repeatedly succumbed to foreign religious practices, the book of Kings, a 6th-century B.C. manifesto of Judean conformity, is frank to admit (2 Kgs 17:29–34; 21:1–7; 23:4–15; Jer 2:28; 7:18; 44:15–21; Ezek 8). By their anomalous priesthood and sacrificial rites the Judeans at Yeb contravened some of the precedents thought normative by the temple officials at Jerusalem. This defection may have occasioned the ecclesiastical officials in Jerusalem to ignore the letter from Yeb petitioning for help to rebuild the temple (*CAP* 30.18, 19). Proponents to this view have a tendency to aggregate the religious evidence given in the papyri. Some have postulated that the religion of 5th-century Judaism was like that of the devotees of the Queen of Heaven (Jer 44:17) or of the diverse foreign cults in Judah from Manasseh to the exile. "It was not a case of falling away from a monotheistic ideal, but a continuation of pre-exilic popular beliefs" (*CAP* xix).

The second proposal carefully separates Syene (and Hermopolis) letters from those thought strictly related to Elephantine. From the ample data regarding the religion of the Judeans at Yeb there has been reconstructed a pattern of worship that indicates a similarity to the temple worship at Jerusalem. An analysis by Porten (*ArchEleph* 133–50) of the Jewish names from Elephantine concludes that they resemble to a large degree the Yahwistic names of the preexilic period. From these, he argues, a solid religious affirmation can be derived. Porten regards the non-Yahwist components found in some names in the Elephantine-Syene sector, theophores containing the names of the deities Bethel, Eshem, Ḥerem, and Anath, as non-Jewish. They are to be attributed to the Syene community.

Some scholars have challenged this view by adducing nomenclature that seems quite opposed: Malkiah, a person possessing a definite Yahwistic name, swears an oath before "Bethel the god" (*CAP* 7:7; on the interpretation, see van der Toorn 1986) even though he is an Aramean (*CAP* 7:2); a number of Arameans, described as such, have Yahwistic names. A rejoinder to these objections may point out that religious inferences from onomastics are a social judgment, not a personal one; the Judeans adapted themselves to the customs of their conquerors while still maintaining their essential religious integrity. If there is any syncretism among the Judeans, it is more apparent than real. In defense of this position a few scholars have interpreted the dual names of the deities as a single unit, considering the first part to be a hypostasis of the second name. To illustrate, Albright proposes to interpret the three names Eshembethel, Ḥerembethel, and Anathbethel to mean respectively "Name of the House of God," (= God), "Sacredness of the House of God," and "Sign (?) of the House of God," names in which the initial deity of the name becomes a "pure hypostatization of the second deity" (Albright 1940: 286). This speculation, which attempts to avoid polytheism in the Judeans' religion at Yeb, has remained generally unconvincing. To identify the Syro-Mesopotamian syncretism described by Ezekiel and observed in the days immediately preceding the Babylonian Exile of 587 B.C. as coincident with the postexilic community at Jerusalem or with the Judeans at Yeb is an impossible religious equation. On the whole the second view assigns the pagan deities mentioned in the Syene-Elephantine papyri to the non-Jewish elements in Syene.

The third view attempts to support a mediating position, to acknowledge the general conformity of the Elephantine Judeans with the postexilic Jerusalem cult, but remains convinced that there are some instances in what appear to be genuine Elephantine correspondence elements which are admittedly tinged with a pagan syncretism. In the document relating the names of the contributors to the support of the temple of Yaʾu at Elephantine, there is the unexpected statement that the total collection was dispersed not only to Yaʾu but to the deities Eshembethel and Anatbethel (*CAP* 22:1, 123–25). Moreover, in the papyri there are in this same list two patronymics whose theophoric element is a pagan deity: [Beth]elnuri and Hadadnuri (lines 4 and 23). In the contemporary period some 32 names have Bethel as the theophoric element: 7 theophores with the name Eshem (cf. 2 Kgs 17:30 and Amos 8:14), and 9 with Ḥerem (*ArchEleph* Appendix V). Other deities mentioned in the Elephantine correspondence are ʿAnatyahu (*CAP* 44:3), Bel, Nabu, Šamaš, Nergal (*ANET,* 491), and the Queen of Heaven (BK 4:1); in the personal names the following gods appear: Nus(h)ku (*CAP* 2:19) Atar (*CAP* 8.27), and Sin (*CAP* 6.19). To relegate all the pagan gods to the Arameans at Syene and to postulate an uncompromised Yahwistic cult at Elephantine seems to suppress evidence to the contrary, however minimal it may be. These discordant data appear to coincide with the cultism practiced by the devotees of the Queen of Heaven (Jer 44:15–25), who brashly justified their cultic adherence by tracing it back to the preexilic practices of their kings, princes, and the Judean people themselves. The view suggested here is that while the greater part of the Elephantine Judeans may have conformed to the contemporary cult in Jerusalem, there were areas where allowances were made and adaptations to the foreign religious cults were tolerated. One may compare the heterodox minority living in an orthodox majority and maintaining their minority convictions with the situation in the days of Ezra (Ezra 10:15) and often elsewhere in the OT.

D. The Diety Bethel and the Old Testament

As the name of a geographical site, some 10.5 miles N of Jerusalem, Bethel appears 71 times in the OT. With the recovery of the Elephantine data, in which Bethel appears as a significant deity, scholars undertook a minute examination of the biblical term *Bethel* to determine whether any of the occurrences involved the name of the god rather than the name of the place. The more significant results of this investigation focused generally on the following passages: the Jacob-Bethel pericope (Gen 28:17, 22; 31:13; 33:20; 35:7, 14–15); 1 Sam 10:3; Amos 3:14; 4:4; Hosea 10:8, 15; Jer 48:13; and Zech 7:12. Some scholars added other passages to these in which the term *Bethel* was conceived to be the NW Semitic deity.

The name Bethel may be applied to three diverse entities: (1) the town some 10 miles N of Jerusalem, prominent in all biblical periods, and the seat of one of the most important religious centers of the N kingdom of Israel (1 Kgs 12:26–33; Amos 7:13); (2) the name of a NW Semitic deity who is identified as one of the sons of Uranus in the Phoenician history of Sanchuniathon (Baumgarten 1981: 15) and became prominent in the Egyptian-Syene papyri of the 6th–5th centuries B.C.; and (3) the name of a stone erroneously conceived as endowed with the vital force by Kronos (Baumgarten 1981: 15, where the text of Philo Byblos is presented). Such was termed *baitýlion* (neuter sing.). It should be remarked that some of the biblical passages indicated above have been considerably emended to arrive at the conclusion that they refer to the deity Bethel. Accordingly, the discussion will be confined to those passages which are more likely to be references to the deity Bethel.

The Jacob-Bethel pericope has occasioned considerable diversity in the interpretation of the naming of Bethel and of the stone which Jacob used as a pillar (Gen 28:11–22; 31:13; 35:1, 6–16). The narrative may be conveniently divided into three parts: the dream of Jacob (Gen 28:10–15; 35:1, 7b); the response of Jacob (Gen 28:16–20; 31:13); and the vow of Jacob (Gen 28:21–22; 35:3, 7, 14, 15). The stone which Jacob used as a headrest was just "one of the stones of the place"; its size would be commensurate with its purpose; it is of secondary importance in the story, a detail that adds realism, since such accommodation was not dissimilar to the Egyptian headrest which relaxes the dorsal neck muscles and promotes slumber (see Sauneron 1962). When Jacob awakened from his awesome dream, his first response was to commemorate the experience by consecrating the headrest stone with oil, then setting it up as a votive stele (Heb *maṣṣēbâ*), no doubt supported by a foundation of other stones (Gen 28:16–20; 35:14; cf. 1 Sam 7:12). In the three instances where Bethel occurs, the focus is the place, not the commemorative stone. There is no suggestion that the stone served as a house for a god; it was to become a *maṣṣēbâ*. This in turn would initiate a *bêt ʾelōhîm* (Hyatt 1939: 97–98). The tense of Gen 28:22 is the Heb imperfect, corresponding to the English future: "shall become the house of God." The vow of Jacob has five components in the protasis specifying the conditions of the apodosis. The apodosis has three responses thereto: Yahweh will be his god; the stone will be the earnest of a house of God, and proper cultic support is epitomized by the tithe (vv 21b, 22). The fulfillment of the vow is noted in Gen 35:1, 3, 7.

The exact nature of the stone of Jacob has caused considerable discussion. No one can deny the widespread worship of holy stones and the identification of the stone as "the seat of a numen" (Moore 1903: 198). Nor would one deny their ubiquity, but general semblance cannot determine particular uniqueness. It may be admitted that "holy stones" appear to be referred to in the OT as deplorable paganism (Jer 2:27; 3:9; Ezek 30:32; Lev 26:1; Isa 57:6), but such are not called *baitylia*, a word that does not appear in the OT.

It has been noted previously that Philo of Byblos clearly distinguishes between *Baitylos* (= Bethel, a NW Semitic deity) and the *baitylia* (animated stones). The statements in Sanchuniathon regarding the god *Baitylus* and the animated stones called *baitylia* assume a new importance. The Semitic data of Sanchuniathon regarding the "Syrian Semitic" deity Baitylus appear to maintain their identity even in a Syrian Greek inscription, dating from A.D. 223, at Kafr Nebo (near Aleppo), where in a dedicatory inscription for an oil press the god Sumbétylos appears with two other gods, jointly named "paternal gods" (Hyatt 1939: 86). The name appears to be the equivalent of Eshembethel, who appears in the papyri of Elephantine.

It may be noted here that in the treaty between Bargaʾyah, king of *KTK*, with Matiʾel, king of Arpad, dated ca. 760 B.C., the place name Bethel occurs (i A 34) and the phrase *batayʾlahayyaʾ* (lit. "houses of the gods") appears three times (ii C 3, 7, 10) and refers not to the temple buildings, but to the stele or steles upon which were engraved the contents of the agreement (*KAI* 262; *TSSI* 2: 44–45). One may postulate that the stone of Jacob, chosen at random and common (profane), was transmuted by the anointing into sacramental object, worthy to be set up publicly as a record of the divine encounter (Gen 28:22).

Two other problems in the Jacob-Bethel pericope, both textual in character, merit some brief comments. The first concerns the initial words of Gen 31:13: *ʾnky hʾl byt-ʾl*. Most scholars translate the compressed words to read: "I am the God of Bethel" (RSV, RV, BJ, NJPS), justifying their rendering from other Hebrew instances, such as 2 Kgs 23:17; Num 21:14 [cf. *GK* §127, Rem. 4]. Others admit the clause found in LXX and T^JP: "I am the God *who appeared to you at Bethel* . . ." (so NEB, Westermann, Speiser, etc.). These renderings are much to be preferred to that which interprets *God* and *Bethel* to be in apposition. That Bethel is a place name and not a divine name is evident from the adverb *where* (Heb *ʾăšer*), twice used modifying Bethel. Of greater weight, however, is the unlikelihood that a foreign Semitic deity would be introduced into a key kerygmatic passage of Israelite tradition.

The second problematic passage is Gen 35:7, where Jacob "built an altar, and called the name El-Bethel." This may be compared with *ʾēl ʾĕlōhê-yiśraʾēl,* the name given by Jacob to another altar he built (Gen 33:20); with *haʾēl ʾĕlōhê-ʾābîkā* (Gen 46:3) and with *ilu-bâyti-īli* (Speiser *Genesis* AB, 244). One notices repeatedly in the 71 or 72 occurrences of *Bethel* in the OT that the term is uniformly geographical. To import by a homonymic accident the Syrian god Bethel into passages in the Hebrew Bible which make excellent sense with a topographical meaning appears to be an invalid approach.

The proponents of the view that the Aramean god Bethel played a significant role in preexilic Israel have had recourse to a wooden apposition in rendering such a passage as 1 Sam 10:3, where Saul is informed of men whom he will encounter as ". . . three men going up to the God Bethel." On the contrary, it appears that the name Bethel is locative, and may admit the omission of the preposition *b-* before a homorganic stop (Andersen and Freedman *Hosea* AB, 406). Hence the more likely translation is ". . . three men going up to God at Bethel" (Heb *šlšh ʾnšym ʿlym ʾl-hʾlhym byt-ʾl*).

It has been further suggested that the god of Bethel appears in the text of Amos and Hosea. The name Bethel occurs seven times in the book of Amos (3:14; 4:4; 5:5 *(bis)*; 5:6; 7:10, 13). Five of these are undisputed references to the city (4:4; 5:5 [both references]; 7:10, 13). The two remaining occurrences (3:14 and 5:6) are likewise allusions to the city Bethel and not to a god. The geographic reference of Bethel in 5:6 is established by its parallelism with the expression "house of Joseph." The threat of destruction of the altars of Bethel (3:13) is best understood as specifying the location of the altars, not the deity to whom sacrifices are offered upon them. While Amos does denounce syncretistic practices elsewhere (8:14), there is no suggestion that a cult of the deity Bethel is the prophet's concern.

In the book of Hosea there are two occurrences of the word Bethel. The first occurrence follows a description of the ravages of war: fortresses destroyed, mothers and children perishing, whereupon the prophet directs its poignant reference to his audience: "Thus it shall be done to you, O Bethel, because of your great wickedness" (Hos 10:15). The MT is perfectly understandable and needs no emendation.

The other use of Bethel refers to the nocturnal wrestling of Jacob with the angel at Bethel (Hos 12:5—Eng 12:4). Here also the prophet uses Bethel as a geographical term, not as a name for the deity Bethel.

The name Beth-aven is sometimes associated with Bethel. Beth-aven was located east of Bethel (Josh 7:2) and figures in the Conquest narrative (Josh 7:2; 18:12) and in the story of Saul (1 Sam 13:5; 14:23). The name Beth-aven was the source of a play on words employed by Amos and Hosea. The element *aven* (Heb *ʾāwen*) of the name appears to be derived from the root *ʾwn* and means "trouble, idolatry" or "wickedness, iniquity." The warning by Amos that "Bethel shall become *Awen*" (5:5; RSV: "Bethel shall come to nought") may be a pun on the name with reference to the Heb word for iniquity. Hosea's three references to Beth-aven (4:15; 5:8; 10:5) may be using the term as a demeaning surrogate for Bethel (so Andersen and Freedman *Hosea* AB, 372). A related pun is also probably the meaning of Hos 10:8.

A strong argument for the appearance of the god Bethel in the OT proceeds from Jer 48:13. The passage is a forecast of woe about to devolve upon the people of Moab and to destroy their confidence in the saving ability of their national god Chemosh. This military disaster, so forcefully portrayed in the preceding verse (Jer 48:12), will shatter the nation's repose in their god and in his ability to save his people. Such fragmentation of their hope in the divine power parallels the unspeakable disaster that the house of Israel suffered when Bethel, the site of the royal sanctuary, proved impotent against the might of Assyria in 722 B.C. It would be strange if the term Bethel in this instance should refer to a god housed in the "temple of the kingdom" (Amos 7:13), when elsewhere, particularly in the contemporary assessment of Bethel by Amaziah its high priest, the term Bethel is topographical.

The final and most likely passage in which Bethel is not used topographically is Zech 7:2, in which a deputation is sent to the priests at Jerusalem in the postexilic period (December 518 B.C.) to inquire whether the fasting practiced during the Exile should still be continued (cf. Zech 7 and 8). Two major interpretations have been proposed regarding the term Bethel in Zech 7:2. The first regards Bethel as a place name and translates the pertinent words thus: "Now *they of* Bethel" (RV, ASV); "now *the people of* Bethel" (RSV, NIV); "Bethel sent" (JB, Dhorme). A variation of this view translates Bethel as "the house of God" and proposes that the deputation went to "the house of God" (LXX, Vulg., KJV). This interpretation needlessly repeats the subject of v 3. In view of the extirpation of Bethel by Josiah (2 Kgs 23:15–20) and the very few Babylonian exiles that returned (Ezra 2:28; Neh 7:32), it may be questioned whether Bethel is a place name in this text.

The second interpretation regards Bethel as the divine element in the name Bethel-sharezer (Heb *bytʾl śr ʾṣr*, "May Bethel protect the king") (NEB/REB, NAB, NJPS). The following considerations favor the identification of the Heb *bytʾl śr ʾṣr* as a single name. The DN *bytʾl* is the theophoric element of a PN of Mesopotamian origin (cf. *ArchEleph*, 328). The theophoric element is in initial position, which is normative. The name in Zech 7:2 is attested in the year 518 B.C. and, accordingly, is situated in a period during which PNs with the theophoric element *bytʾl* are attested epigraphically. The name appears in a Neo-Babylonian text from Uruk datable ca. 541–540 B.C. (Hyatt 1937). The proposed biblical name thus synchronizes with the frequent appearance of theophores compounded with Bethel in the Elephantine papyri. The person bearing the name Bethel-sharezer in Zech 7:2 may have been a Jewish official in Babylon.

Bibliography

Albright, W. F. 1940. *From the Stone Age to Christianity.* Baltimore.
Baumgarten, A. I. 1981. *The "Phoenician History" of Philo of Byblos.* EPRO 89. Leiden.
Beyerlin, W., ed. 1978. *Near Eastern Religious Texts Relating to the Old Testament.* OTL. Philadelphia.
Borger, R. 1950. ʿAnath-Bethel. *VT* 7: 102–3.
Bowman, R. S. 1944. An Aramaic Religious Text in Demotic Script. *JNES* 3: 219–31.
Coogan, M. 1976. *West Semitic Personal Names in the Murašu Documents.* HSM 7. Missoula, MT.
Eissfeldt, O. 1930. Der Gott Bethel. *ARW* 28: 1–30.
Gifford, E. H., ed. 1903. *Preparation for the Gospel.* 2 Vols. Oxford. Repr. Grand Rapids, 1981.
Grelot, P. 1972. *Documents Araméens d'Egypte.* LAPO 5. Paris.
Hyatt, J. P. 1937. A Neo-Babylonian Parallel to Bethel-šar-eṣer, Zec. 7:2. *JBL* 56: 387–94.
———. 1939. The Deity Bethel and the Old Testament. *JAOS* 59: 81–89.
Løkkegaard, F. 1954. Some Comments on the Sanchuniathon Tradition. *ST* 8: 51–76.
Moore, G. F. 1903. Baetylia. *AJA.* 2d ser. 7: 198–208.
Pope, M. H. 1955. El in the Ugaritic Texts. VTSup 2. Leiden.
Porten, B. 1954. *Jews of Elephantine and Arameans of Syene.* Jerusalem.
Sauneron, S. 1962. Headrest. P. 118 in *A Dictionary of Egyptian Civilization,* ed. G. Posener. London.
Toorn, K. van der. 1986. Herem-Bethel and Elephantine Oath Procedure. *ZAW* 98: 282–85.
Vincent, A. 1937. *La religion des Judéo-Araméens d'Elephantine.* Paris.

EDWARD R. DALGLISH

BETHEL (PLACE) [Heb *bêtʾēl*]. The name of two places mentioned in the Hebrew Bible. The name means "house of God."

1. An important town in the central hill country of Palestine, located N of Jerusalem and very close to Ai. Next to Jerusalem, this Bethel is the most frequently occurring place name in the OT, referring both to a city and to a religious sanctuary which was either in or near the city. Two factors, somewhat interrelated, are responsible for the importance of Bethel: (1) it was associated with a religious sanctuary; and (2) it lay along a crossroads and near a physical and political frontier that divided the central hill country of Palestine into two parts.

Bethel became established in the Bible as a sanctuary by association with events in the lives of Abraham and Jacob. When Abram wandered S from Shechem, he pitched his tent and built an altar between Bethel and Ai (Gen 12:8), and on his return from Egypt he revisited this sacred place (Gen 13:3,4). Jacob in his flight from Beersheba to Haran stayed there and had the famous nocturnal vision of angels ascending and descending. In the morning when he awoke, Jacob erected a pillar to mark this sacred place. Jacob called the place Bethel although the city was called Luz (Gen 28:10–22). Many years later Jacob returned to this place on his way home from Haran; he set up another altar and called the place El-Bethel (Gen 35:7). He also set up a pillar and again named the place Bethel (Gen 35:15).

These biblical descriptions of events concerning Bethel are puzzling. Should a distinction be made between Bethel, a name for a sacred place, and Bethel, a name of a settlement? When did the name of the settlement Luz become Bethel?

Some scholars have suggested that, "most of the cultic places in Israel during premonarchic and early monarchic periods were built outside of their respective towns and were called by different names" (Naʾaman 1985). This practice by the Israelites of building sacred places outside the city apparently differed from a Canaanite custom of building sacred places within the settlement and might be indicative of a distinction in religious practice. However, other scholars interpret this matter differently. According to *HGB,* 131 the sanctuary was inside the city, and references to its being outside the city in the Bible are not historical, ". . . but related to the mode of life of the patriarchs." On the other hand, there are indications that Bethel, in certain biblical contexts, could refer to a sanctuary, rather than to a city name. Boling (*Judges* AB) translates Bethel in Judg 20:18 as "sanctuary"—but a sanctuary located in the village of Mizpah. When the Israelites inquired of God at the sanctuary in Mizpah they failed. But when they shifted their battle headquarters and inquired of God in a sanctuary in the city of Bethel, they succeeded. The ark of God's covenant was, at that time, in the city of Bethel, overseen by Phineahas ben Eleazer ben Aaron (Judg 20:26–28). Apparently then, not all "Bethels" are the same—some can be trusted to provide counsel, while others can not.

Bethel is also associated with Deborah, the nurse of Rebekah who died and was buried beneath Bethel under an oak (Gen 35:8), and with Deborah, the Prophetess, who lived near the city (Judg 4:5). Samuel visited this city periodically to judge the people (1 Sam 7:16). However, with the establishment of the United Kingdom by David and the placement of the temple in Jerusalem the importance of Bethel as a sanctuary declined. The fortunes of Bethel improved, however, when the United Kingdom split and Jeroaboam I placed a golden calf in Bethel to serve as a cult center for his people in place of the temple in Jerusalem (1 Kgs 12:29–33). This religious schism aroused opposition among the prophets Hosea (10:15) and Amos, who declared, "Bethel shall come to nought" (3:14). The Judean king Josiah captured Bethel and broke down its altar and defiled the site (2 Kgs 23:15). After that time Bethel lost its importance as a cultic center.

Bethel's historic importance as a sacred place also coincides with its importance as a frontier town. Bethel lies between two separable physiographic provinces: the hills of Ephraim to the N, and the plateau of Judea to the S. Taken together, these provinces constitute the centrally elevated backbone of the land of Canaan between the valley of the Jordan river on the E and the Mediterranean Sea to the W. Throughout much of biblical history this central range was divided politically into N and S tribes, followed by kingdoms of N Israel and Judah, to the S. Later during Roman times these provinces were called Samaria and Judea.

Along the crest of the central range (or more accurately along the water parting) a N-S road ran from Hebron to Shechem, passing through Jerusalem and Bethel. This road provided one of the most important lines of transportation throughout biblical history. Just S of Bethel lay an E-W road leading up from the coast along a ridge overlooking the valley of Aijalon and then down again to Jericho and the Jordan valley along another slope overlooking the Wâdī Suweinit. One would have had to travel beyond Shechem, some 25 miles farther N, to the Wâdī Fari to find a route from the coast to the Jordan river that would have been equally attractive.

Physiographically, the Judean plateau is shielded by a longitudinal valley and an abrupt scarp from easy access from the coastal plain, but routes from the coastal plain to the hills of Ephraim do occur at many places. Climatically, rainfall and agriculture differ between the southerly plateau of Judah and the more verdant Ephraim hills. The dividing line between these provinces can be defined on the basis of physical features; but since more than one criterion can be used, and they do not exactly coincide, one can say that the physical frontier actually lies within a zone—a zone which includes the city of Bethel. The dividing line can be taken at the E-W route a few km S of Bethel, in which case Bethel belongs to the N province. The dividing line can also be taken a few km N of Bethel where the fairly straight N-S road enters a series of switchbacks reflecting the hilly nature of the N province. In this case, Bethel properly belongs to the S province.

This ambiguous geographic relationship is the key to understanding why Bethel is allotted to the tribe of Benjamin (Josh 18:22) but is taken over by the more N tribe of Ephraim (Judg 1:22). Also, although Jeroboam I made Bethel into a N city, Abijah, king of Judah, captured it (2 Chr 13:19). Baasha, king of Israel, however, retook the city, but when Israel fell to the Assyrians, Bethel reverted to Judah (Ezra 2:28; Neh 7:32). Thus Bethel, a frontier town between two provinces, shifted back and forth in political ownership.

The strategic position of Bethel (along the route to Jerusalem coming from the N) figures in later history. During the Hasmonean revolt it was fortified by the Syrian general Bacchides (1 Macc 9:50), and was captured by Vespasian in 69 C.E. (*JW* 4.551). During the Byzantine period Bethel was a village in the territory of "Aelia Capitolina" (Jerusalem) (Eusebius *Onomast.* 192 etc.). It continues to be mentioned in the literature by the Pilgrim of Bordeaux (353 C.E.) and Theodosius (ca. 503 C.E.) and is shown on the Madaba Map (ca. 565 C.E.). Apparently the city was destroyed during the Arab conquest in the 7th century C.E. and remained abandoned until it was repopulated as an Islamic village in the mid-19th century.

Most scholars since the time of Edward Robinson identify Bethel with Tell Beitin (M.R. 172148). See BEITIN, TELL (M.R. 172148). However, Livingston (1989) has suggested that Bethel may actually be el-Bireh, a few km SW of Tell Beitin.

2. A village in Judah to which David sent spoils to his friends and to the elders (1 Sam 30:27). Almost certainly, then, it was a city in Judah and not the more important Bethel N of Jerusalem, and possibly it is the same as Bethul in Josh 19:4 and BETHUEL in 1 Chr 4:30 (and Chesil in Josh 15:30, although this is less likely). Its location is unknown, although the context suggests somewhere generally in the area around Ziklag and Hormah.

Bibliography

Livingston, D. 1989. The Last Word on Bethel and Ai. *BARev* 15/1: 11.

Naʾaman, N. 1985. Bethel and Beth-Aven. *Zion* 50: 15–25.

Smith, G. A. 1931. *The Historical Geography of the Holy Land.* London. Repr. 1966.

HAROLD BRODSKY

BETHEL-SHAREZER (PLACE) [Heb *bêtʾēl śarʾeṣer*]. See SHAREZER (PERSON).

BETHER (PLACE) [Gk *Baithēr, Thethēr*]. A village in one of the districts into which the allotment of land for the tribe of Judah was divided (Josh 15:59a LXX). The list of 11 cities of which Bether is the 10th is found in LXX but not in MT; presumably it was omitted from the Hebrew text by the copyist's error called homoioteleuton (on the textual character of Josh 15:59a LXX, see *HGB*, 392–93). The district lists are variously enumerated; (cf. Bright *IB* 2: 630–33; Soggin *Joshua* OTL, 178; and Boling and Wright *Joshua* AB, 378, 391). Bether is identified with Khirbet el-Yahudi (M.R. 162126) near the modern Bittir, about 7 miles SW of Jerusalem. An archaeological survey showed almost continuous occupation of the site from Iron I through the early Roman period (Carroll 1923–24: 89).

During the Second Jewish Revolt (132–135 C.E.), Bittar (as it was known [Aram *bîttēr;* on the name, see Neubauer 1868: 130]) became Bar Kokhba's capital. See BAR KOKHBA (REVOLT). Some scholars have detected this place name in the name Baiterus found in the list at 1 Esdr 5:17. Eusebius (*Hist. Eccl.* 4.6) refers to the site as *Baithther.* The name is of uncertain derivation. The element *btr* in the name of the location *hārê bāter* (Cant 2:17: "rugged mountains" RSV, but note margin) has been traditionally treated as a contraction of *byt tr* (*Cant. Rab.* to 2:17), but there is no certainty that this name, whatever its derivation, elucidates the meaning of Bether.

Bibliography

Carroll, W. D. 1923–24. Bittir and Its Archaeological Remains. AASOR 5: 77–104.

Neubauer, A. 1868. *La geographie du Talmud.* Paris.

HENRY O. THOMPSON

BETHLEHEM (PLACE) [Heb *bêt-leḥem*]. The name of two places mentioned in the Bible.

A. Bethlehem of Judah

1. Site. Bethlehem of Judah is located 9 km S of Jerusalem and stands at an elevation of 790 m on the E ridge of the watershed. The site lies on the border of the well-watered and fertile region of Beit-Jalah (Giloh) and of the dry district of Boaz—and Shepherds—fields ending in the Judean Desert. The village does not possess any spring, but only cisterns (2 Sam 23:15), some of which are caves on the ridge walled and plastered in the manner common at the end of the Bronze Age.

The site seems to have been inhabited during the lower Pleistocene (*EAEHL* 1: 198–99; Stockton 1967: 129–48, with a survey of the neighboring sites). During the 3d millennium B.C.E. pottery was left in Beth-Sahur, not far from Bethlehem, (Hennessy 1966: 19–40; Saller 1963: 325). Excavations have shown that the Iron Age settlement was not at the top of the spur as was thought before, but on the slope around the church of the Nativity (Saller 1964: 287; 1968: 153–80; Bagatti 1968: 181–237). This observation has been confirmed by the survey of S. Gutman and A. Berman in 1969 (Benoit 1975, with drawings and photos).

2. Name. Place names with *bît* "house, place" are numerous in the cuneiform lists (Groneberg 1980; Nashef *RG* 5; Parpola 1970; *RLA* II: 33–54); in Egyptian sources (Simons 1937: 204); and in the Ugaritic archives (*PRU* 2: 227–28; 3: 265–68; 4: 253–56; 5: 165–67; 6: 146; cf. Astour 1975: 139), but Bît-Lahmu does not appear. Bethlehem may be mentioned in a 14th-century B.C.E. letter of Abdi-Hepa, king of Jerusalem (EA 290: 16; Schroeder 1915: 294–95). In this letter the place is called Bīt-NIN.URTA, and one wonders if the ideogram NIN.URTA should be read as Antum (i.e., Lahama; cf. CT 24: 14–15; see also Honigmann 1938). Other readings have been proposed: Bit-Anat (= i.e., Anatot; Dhorme 1908); Bit-(t)ašmiš = Beth-Shemesh (Lipiński 1973; but see the note by Priestbatsch 1975); or, lastly, Beth-Horon (Kallai and Tadmor 1969), though this latter suggestion has been made more for geographic than for linguistic reasons. The name Lahamu is unknown in the W and is poorly documented in Mesopotamia; the name is related to the subterranean ocean. It is not impossible (though admittedly hypothetical) that before the place name was interpreted as the "house of bread" (Heb *leḥem*), it was the "house of Lahai", the god of a well in the Negeb (Gen 16:14; 24:62, with contraction and mimesis as in Ugaritic).

3. Demography. Bethlehem of Judah (Judg 17:7–9; 19:1, 2, 18; Ruth 1:1–2; 1 Sam 17:12) is called Ephrathah (Mic 5:1—Eng 5:2). This Ephrathah cannot be the Ephrathah of 1 Sam 10:2 (on the border of Ephraim and Benjamin) near Ramah (Jer 31:15, N of Jerusalem), which in a poetic text is set in parallel with Kiriath-Jearim (Ps 132:6; cf. Melamed 1961; Tsevat 1962; Vogt 1975, with reference to Eusebius; Briend 1983). In Gen 35:19 and 48:7 (both P), Bethlehem is related, not to Ephrathah, but to the "way to Ephrathah" or "coming to Ephrathah" (see also *T. Reu.* 3:13).

Such identifications are late (like the identification of Mamre with Hebron) and reveal that the postexilic author felt there was a problem with Mic 5:1. The meaning of Ephrathah is to be determined from 1 Sam 17:12. The father of David is said to be an *ʾeprātî,* i.e., a man of Ephraim (Judg 12:5; 1 Kgs 11:26), just as the two sons of Elimelech and Naomi born in Bethlehem (Ruth 1:2), before Boaz and Jesse. This evidence strongly suggests that at the end of the 2d millennium B.C.E., a clan of Ephraim

(Mic 5:1 speaks of an *ʾelep;* Judg 6:15; 1 Sam 10:19; cf. Neu 1986) was settled in Bethlehem. The Chronicler's genealogies, which are artificial but always have some foundation, treat Ephrathah both as a spouse of Caleb (1 Chr 2:19) and as a woman who became Caleb's wife after the death of Hezron his father; she was "grandmother" of Tekoa (1 Chr 2:24), a village located in the Judean Desert (cf. Myers *Chronicles* AB). The Chronicler admits an extension of the clan as far as Debir near Hebron, where Caleb lived (Judg 1:11–12; Josh 15:13).

The name of the father of David, Jesse (*yišay; ʾiyšay* in 1 Chr 2:13) is not common among Israelites. It may be Aramaic (cf. *ʾšy* in the Daskyleion Inscription; Dupont-Sommer 1966: 47) or simply W Semitic (cf. *yu-šaī* in an Egyptian list of slaves; Hayes 1962), and probably is an abbreviation of Abishai, another member of the clan (1 Sam 26:6).

That the clan of Ephraim moved from the N to the S of Jerusalem is indicated (1) by the travels of Samuel, son of the *ʾeprātî* Elkanah (1 Sam 16:1–12; cf. 1:1–2), (2) by the story of the Levite and his patron Micah (Judg 17:7–9), and (3) by the narrative of the Levite's concubine from Bethlehem (Judges 19). Finally, the elders of Israel recognized David as their kinsman: "We are your bone and flesh" (2 Sam 5:1).

The genealogy of David, inserted at the end of the book of Ruth (4:18–22; Campbell *Ruth* AB), suggests other marital relations which prove that the Ephramite clan of Jesse did not include all the inhabitants of Bethlehem. Amminadab and Nahshon, ancestors of Boaz, are said to be "father and brother of the wife of the Levite Aaron" (Exod 6:23). Through Ram (Amram or Abiram?) they have Hezron as an ancestor. There is a problem with Hezron; he is related either to Reuben (Gen 46:8–9; Exod 6:14; Num 26:6; 1 Chr 5:3), or to Judah through Perez (Gen 46:12; Num 26:21; Ruth 4:18–19; 1 Chr 2:5). Such a double connection can be explained historically by transfer from E (Bohan on the W side of the Jordan is spoken of as the "son of Reuben"; cf. Josh 15:6; 18:17; de Vaux 1953: 541) to W (Perez-uzzah and Baal-Perazim are toponyms between Kiriath-Jearim and Jerusalem). Similarly, the clan of Karmi was transferred from Reuben (Num 26:6) to Judah (Josh 7:1; 1 Chr 2:7). These historical transfers also have a sociological connotation, because Hezron is related to *ḥaṣer,* a Hebrew term that denotes a village with a typical enclosure for herds; one of the Kerioth-hezron (Josh 15:25; cf. 15:3) is the *ḥăṣar-ʾaddār* of Num 34:4. Numerous *ḥăṣērôt* are to be found in the S of Judah, but also beyond the Jordan (1 Chr 2:21–24, with Machir in Gilead and Ephrathah). As suggested by Eissfeldt, the *bên hamišpĕtayim* of Reuben (Judg 5:16) are also related to enclosures for herds (Eissfeldt 1949; 1954).

There were also Arabs in Bethlehem, descendants of Ishmael. David had two sisters, Zeruiah, the mother of Joab (father unknown) and Abigal, the mother of Amasa (2 Sam 17:25; 1 Chr 2:7), whose father was Ithra (Heb *yitrāʾ*) the Ishmaelite; the latter bears a true Arabic name *(watar).* However, the most important connections are with Reuben.

When the tribe disappeared, having been conquered by Moab, David, who was banished from Saul's court, entrusted his father and mother to the king of Moab (1 Sam 22:3–4).

4. Bethlehem in Israelite History. Fighting against the Philistines and the Amalekites, Saul found in Bethlehem-Ephrathah support for his campaigns. He enrolled the sons of Jesse (1 Sam 17:13), along with Elhanan, the son of Dodo (2 Sam 23:24; son of Jaareoregim in 2 Sam 21:19). Afterwards Bethlehem was taken by the Philistines (2 Sam 23:14), remaining in their hands until the victories of David, when it became a dependency of Jerusalem, the new capital city. According to 2 Chr 11:6 Bethlehem was fortified by Rehoboam, but no city walls have been discovered in the excavations of the site. Nevertheless, walls that belong to the same period (Iron I–II) were unearthed in Beit-Jalah (Giloh; Mazar 1981). As Giloh is not mentioned as a fortified city in Chronicles, it may be that the two sites were identified. In the list of Judean towns found in Joshua 15 (established probably under the reign of Josiah), mention is made of Bethlehem only in the LXX and not in the MT. It seems that Bethlehem was very small at the time (Mic 5:1—Eng 5:2, "you . . . who are little to be among the clans of Judah"), and noted only as the origin of the dynasty.

In the 5th century B.C.E. Bethlehem was reoccupied by the returning exiles. The exact figure of returnees varies: 188 men of Bethlehem and Netophah according to Neh 7:26, and 123 "sons of Bethlehem" (and 56 "men of Netophah") according to Ezra 2:21. Bethlehem of Judah was never a priestly town as was Bethlehem of Zebulun (on which see below). It is never mentioned in the Qumran literature, even among the places of the treasures listed in the Copper Scrolls. In the *Martyrdom of Isaiah* (2:7, 8, 12) Bethlehem functions as a stage for the prophet in his flight from Jerusalem to the wilderness, a story line that is possibly built on the pattern of the narrative of Jeremiah and his companions who stopped in Kimham "near Bethlehem" (Jer 41:16–17) during their flight to Egypt. In the martyrdom of Isaiah it is a false prophet who lives in Bethlehem. Elsewhere in the pseudepigraphical literature, Bethlehem was connected with the burial of Rachel (*Jubilees* 32:34), and Ephrathah is located in Bethlehem (*T. Reu.* 3:13).

In the Fourth gospel (John 7:42) Bethlehem was considered by some of those listening to Jesus to be the birthplace of the son of David, but these same people display no knowledge of Bethlehem as the birthplace of Jesus of Nazareth. Elsewhere in the NT Bethlehem is mentioned only in the two Infancy Narratives. Although they are quite different in their traditions and structures, both Matthew and Luke converge on this point. In Luke, Bethlehem is the place where Joseph goes for the census and where the shepherds go "to see the thing that happened" (Luke 2:4, 15). In Matthew 2, Bethlehem is mentioned five times. There Jesus is born (2:1), the Magi are sent there (2:5–7) in accordance with the oracle of Mic 5:1, and it is there that Herod has all the male children who are two years in age or less killed ("in Bethlehem and its boundaries" [*horiois*]) (2:15). Then Bethlehem disappears from the NT (Brown 1985: 177–85, 412–23; Perrot 1983).

5. Bethlehem in Postbiblical Times. After 135 C.E. Bethlehem was occupied by a Roman garrison which exterminated the remnant of the Bar Kokhba army as indicated by Roman inscriptions near Rachel's tomb (*RB* 1901: 107; 1962: 82–83; Vetrali 1967), and perhaps in *Lam. Rab.* 1:15 if we read Bethlehem (instead of Bethel) of Judah (cf. 1:16). It is possible that such a military presence would have led to the establishment of an Adonis cult in the same way as the Roman military presence in Aelia led to an Asclepius/Serapis cult in the caves adjacent to the pool of Bethesda (Duprez 1970: 64–85). The Asclepius cult is attested by Jerome (*Ep.* 56.3; cf. Paulinus of Nole to Sulpicius Severus 3, CSEL 29). Nevertheless, we must be cautious because such a notice is unique in the works of Jerome and the identification of Adonis with Asclepius is not frequent (*mediante* Eshmun). A more direct attestation of a military cult to the Syrian Goddess is known (Birley 1978: 1516). Since Jerome's notice is more concerned with the lamentations over Adonis than with Adonis himself, Welten (1983) thinks there could have been a popular confusion between the tears of the Syrian Goddess (Lucian *Syr.D.*, 6), the *Venus lugens,* and Rachel's mourning for her sons. In the postexilic period Rachel's tomb was venerated in Bethlehem-Ephrathah. If the god Lahmu was really a vegetation deity like Adonis, it is possible that worship of this kind was practiced in a Bethlehem cave; a revival which neither Jews nor Christians wished to remember may have occurred during the Roman occupation.

The Gospels do not speak of a Nativity in a cave; the oldest references are to be found in Justin (*dial.*, 78) and in the *Protoevangelium* of James (18), texts which speak of a Nativity "quite near to Bethlehem," "midway," but not in Bethlehem itself.

Above a cave in Bethlehem, Constantine built an octogon with a basilica and a court enclosed by four porticoes in the front. During the Samaritan revolt of 529 C.E., the building was destroyed. Justinian rebuilt it in its actual shape, which was preserved by the Persian invaders (612). In the crypts the traditional Nativity cave is connected with other caves where the monastic sojourn of Jerome and his community is commemorated (Vincent and Abel 1914; Avi-Yonah *EAEHL* 1: 202–6; Heitz 1983: 6–18; Murphy-O'Connor 1983: 12–13).

B. Bethlehem of Zebulun

A village, located in the N, in the tribe of Zebulun (Josh 19:15), was also known as Bethlehem. It is obviously the place where Ibzan, a minor Judge, was buried (Judg 12:8–10, related to Zebulun in the following verses; cf. Boling *Judges* AB, 215). The village is known to have been the residence of a priestly family (Cesaraea Inscription, 5–6th century C.E.; cf. Avi-Yonah 1962); an Arab village on the Asher-Zebulun border retained the name *(Beit-Laḥm)*.

Bibliography

Abel, F. M. 1962. *Histoire de la Palestine.* Paris.

Avi-Yonah, M. 1962. A List of Priestly Courses from Caesaraea. *IEJ* 12: 137–39.

Astour, M. 1963. Place Names in the Kingdom of Alalah. *JNES* 22: 220–41.

———. 1975. Continuité et changement dans la toponymie de la Syrie du Nord. Pp. 117–42 in *Colloque Strasbourg, La toponymie antique.* Paris.

Bagatti, B. 1968. Recenti scavi a Betlemme. *LÄ* 18: 181–237.

Benoit, P. 1970. Chronique Archelogique. *RB* 77: 583–85.

———. 1975. L'emplacement de Bethlehem au temps de Jésus. *Dossiers de l'Archeologie* 10: 58–63.

Birley, E. 1978. The Religion of the Roman Army. *ANRW* 16/2: 1506–41.

Briend, J. 1983. Bethléem-Ephrata. *MB* 30: 29.

Brown, R. 1985. *The Birth of the Messiah.* New York.

Dhorme, P. E. 1908. Les pays bibliques au tempts d'El-Amarna. *RB* 17: 517–18.

Dupont-Sommer, A. 1966. Une inscription araméenne inédite d'époque perse trouvé à Daskyleion. *CRAIBL* 53.

Duprez, A. 1970. *Jésus et les dieux géréisseurs.* Paris.

Eissfeldt, O. 1949. Gabelhürden im Ostjordanland. *FuF* 25: 9–11.

———. 1954. Gabelhürden im Ostjordanland. *FuF* 28: 54–56.

———. 1966. *KlSchr* 3: 67–70. Tübingen.

Groneberg, B. 1980. *Répertoire Géographique des Textes cunéiformes.* Vol. 5. Weisbaden.

Hayes, W. 1962. A Selection of Tuthmoside ostraca from Dēr el-Bahri. *JEA* 48: 40–41.

Heitz, C. 1983. L'Eglise de la Nativité. *MB* 30: 6–21.

Hennessy, J. 1966. An Early Bronze Age Tomb Group from Beit-Sahur. *ADAJ* 11: 19–40.

Honigmann, E. 1938. Bît-Lahamu. *RLA* 2: 47a.

Kallai, Z., and Tadmor, H. 1969. Bit Niruta-Beth Horon. On the History of the Kingdom of Jerusalem in the Amarna Period. *EI* 9: 138–47.

Lambert, W. G. 1983. Laham-Abzu, Lahmu. *RLA* 6: 430a, 433b.

Lipinski, E. 1973. Beth-Shemesh und der Tempel der Herrin der Grabkammer in den Amarna-Briefen. *VT* 23: 443–45.

Mazar, A. 1981. Giloh: An Early Israelite Settlement Site near Jerusalem. *IEJ* 31: 12–17.

Murphy-O'Connor, J. 1983. *MB* 30: 12.

Melamed, E. Z. 1961. Break-up of Stereotype Phrases. *ScrHier* 8: 122–23.

Neu, R. 1986. Israel von der Entstehung des Königtums. *BZ* 30: 218.

Parpola, S. 1970. *Neo-Assyrian Toponyms.* AOAT 6. Neukirchen.

Perrot, C. 1983. La nativité à Bethlehem? *MB* 30: 34–37.

Priestbatsch, H. Y. 1975. Jerusalem und die Brunnenstrasse Merneptahs. *ZDPV* 91: 23–24.

Saller, S. 1962. Resumé. *RB* 69 82–83.

———. 1963. Bethlehem and its surroundings. *LÄ* 13: 325.

———. 1964. Bethlehem. *LÄ* 14: 287.

———. 1965. Resumé. *RB* 71: 270–72.

———. 1966. *RB* 72: 585s.

———. 1968. Iron Age Remains from Bethlehem. *LÄ* 18: 153–80.

———. 1970. Resumé. *RB* 77: 83–85.

Schroeder, O. 1915. Zu Berliner Amarnatexten. *OLZ* 18: 294–95.

Simons, J. 1937. *Handbook for the Study of Egyptian Topographical Lists Relating to Western Asia.* Leiden.

Stockton, E. 1965. Stone Age Factory Site at Arafa near Bethlehem. *LÄ* 15: 124–36.

———. 1967. The Stone Age of Bethlehem. *LÄ* 17: 129–48.

Strycker, E. de 1961. *La forme la plus ancienne du Protevangile de Jacques.* Brussels.

Tsevat, N. 1962. Studies in the Book of Samuel. *HUCA* 33: 109–11.

Vaux, R. de 1953. Exploration de la region de Qumran. *RB* 60: 541.

———. 1971. *Histoire Ancienne d'Israel.* Paris.

Vetrali, L. 1967. Le iscrizioni dell' acquedo to romano presso Betlemme. *LÄ* 17: 149–61.

Vincent, H., and Abel, F. M. 1914. *Bethléem. Le Sanctuaire de la Nativité.* Paris.
Vogt, E. 1975. Benjamin, geboren 'eine Meil' von Ephrata. *Bib* 56: 341–46.
Welten, P. 1983. Bethlehem und die Klage um Adonis. *ZDPV* 99: 189–203.

HENRI CAZELLES

BETHPHAGE (PLACE) [Gk *Bēthphagē*]. Bethphage was the name of a village on the road from Jerusalem to Jericho meaning literally in Aramaic, "house of the early figs." The village was the place where Christ sent his disciples to find the foal of an ass for his "triumphal entry" and was mentioned together with Bethany in this context in Matt 21:1; Mark 11:1; and Luke 19:29. Both the Mishnah and the Talmud suggest that the town was a suburb of Jerusalem, laying outside the city wall and apparently surrounded by its own wall.

Bethphage was located either beyond Bethany (M.R. 174131) according to Jerome (*Ep.*, 108), or, more likely, W of Bethany toward Jerusalem (M.R. 172131), approximately 1 km E of the summit of the Mount of Olives. The latter site was the location of Bethphage accepted by the medieval Crusaders. A stone with frescoes and inscriptions was found at the latter site, showing two disciples untying a donkey and a colt. The frescoes are preserved in the Franciscan chapel at this location. Archaeological evidence indicates that the site was occupied from the 2d century B.C.E. to the 8th century C.E. Of the many archaeological artifacts found at the occupation site, of particular interest is tomb 21 with its rolling stone, Greek and archaic Semitic inscriptions, and graffiti which include a sign depicting a cross.

SCOTT T. CARROLL

BETHUEL (PERSON) [Heb *bĕtûʾēl*]. Var. BETHUL. A son of Nahor by Milcah (Gen 22:20–22) and the father of Rebekah (24:15) and Laban (28:5). Bethuel played no significant role even in his daughter's betrothal, where her brother was prominent. Rebekah ran to her mother's house (Gen 24:28); Laban prepared the welcome (vv 29–32); then Laban granted consent to the servant to explain his mission (v 33); and gifts were presented to Rebekah, Laban, and her mother (v 53). In the actions of vv 55–60 her brother and mother were the players. Furthermore one notes that peculiar order of names in v 50, where the father's comes after his son's. Perhaps Bethuel had already died. Josephus (*Ant* 1.16.2 §248) does claim that Bethuel was dead and that Laban, with the mother, directed the whole household and was guardian of Rebekah's maidenhood. Such an explanation would require that "and Bethuel" was added by someone who did not realize the narrative assumed Bethuel had died. But it is doubtful that anyone would have inserted the name in the wrong order. Another possible solution is that Bethuel was incapacitated by senility or invalidism or the like. This could account for the reversed order of names in v 50. The most probable interpretation may be that the story assumes a matrilineal family. Jay (1988: 62) points out how in a matrilineal system Laban, as Rebekah's brother, would have authority concerning her marriage; and quite likely only he, his sister, and her mother would receive gifts or be in a position to decide the date of Rebekah's departure. Somewhat more concretely, there are Nuzi texts in which the marriage contract was arranged by a brother for his sister (Pfeiffer and Speiser 1936: 38–39, 104–6).

The meaning of the name Bethuel is uncertain. It might mean "dweller in God"—unless it equals *mĕtûʾēl* (cf. Akk *Muti-ilu*), "man of God." It is similar to Batti-ilu in the Tell el-Amarna letters (EA 650).

Bibliography

Jay, N. 1988. Sacrifice, Descent and the Patriarchs. *VT* 38: 52–70.
Pfeiffer, R. H., and Speiser, E. A. 1936. *One Hundred New Selected Nuzi Texts.* AASOR 16. New Haven.

EDWIN C. HOSTETTER

BETHUEL (PLACE) [Heb *bĕtûʾēl*]. Var. BETHUL; BETHEL. A town in which the sons of Simeon dwelt prior to the reign of David (1 Chr 4:30). It is mentioned in a list along with Hormah and Ziklag. In the Josh 19 list of Simeonite towns, the name is spelled Bethul (v 4; Heb *bĕtûl*), and in an apparent parallel in Josh 15:30 it is replaced with Chesil. In the story of David's exploits in the area around Ziklag and Hormah, a place named BETHEL is mentioned. Given all these variants, Albright (1924: 150) has suggested that Bethuel is the preferred form. The precise location of this town is unknown.

Bibliography

Albright, W. F. 1924. Egypt and the Early History of the Negeb. *JPOS* 4: 131–61.

GARY A. HERION

BETHULIA (PLACE) [Gk *Baituloua*]. City where the events of the book of Judith are located (Jdt 4:6). The author of Judith gives many indications of the location of Bethulia: it is N of Jerusalem (11:19), near Betomasthaim (4:6), over against Esdraelon (4:6), near Dothan (4:6), in the hill country of Samaria (6:11). It is described as having a spring below the city (7:12–13), and it is positioned to hold the narrow mountain pass giving access to Jerusalem from the N hill country (10:10–11). However, the name Bethulia is unknown to modern readers, and its exact location, despite all the descriptive material, is uncertain. Enslin (1972) points out that we do not even know whether the city was actually known to the author. There are 9 Greek variant spellings for the name out of 21 mss collated by the Larger Cambridge Septuagint, indicating confusion in the textual tradition. Many identifications have been proposed for the site: Sānūr, 5 miles south of Dothan; Meseliah, midway between Geba and Jenin; or Kubatje (so Dussaud 1926 and Steuernagel 1943). The name itself has given rise to speculation over the town's location. Is it meant to be a thinly disguised pseudonym for Bethel (Heb *bytʾl/wh*, "house of God")? Priestbatsch (1974) points out in this regard that in the LXX Ezras 2:28 the names Bethel and Ai are corrupted into one word, *baitoliō*. Or is the name itself meaningful, as *bytʾlh*, "house of ascents"? Torrey (1899) follows this hypothesis, saying that according to the book of Judith, Bethulia lay at the head of the most important pass in Samaria and was a large and important city; those facts and his understanding of the name lead him to identify Bethulia with Shechem. None of these locations is definitive. It is possible that the author of Judith modeled his city on one of the major cities in the N hill country (Shechem being the most likely candidate), but that does not lead to an absolute identification. It seems most helpful to follow Craven (1983) when she says, "It seems best to leave the details of the Book of Judith alone as the products of a fertile, creative imagination."

Bibliography

Torrey, C. C. 1899. The Site of Bethulia. *JAOS* 20: 160–72.

Dussaud, R. 1926. Samarie au tempts d'Achab. *Syria* 7: 9–29.

Steuernagel, C. 1943. Bethulia. *ZDPV* 66: 232–45.

Enslin, M. S. 1972. *The Book of Judith.* Jewish Apocryphal Literature 8. Leiden.

Priestbatsch, H. J. 1974. Das Buch Judith und seine hellenistischen Quellen. *ZDPV* 90: 50–60.

Craven, T. 1983. *Artistry and Faith in the Book of Judith.* SBLDS 70. Chico, CA.

SIDNIE ANN WHITE

BETOMASTHAIM (PLACE) [Gk *Baitomasthaim*]. Var. BETOMESTHAIM. Site mentioned in the book of Judith, the exact location of which is unknown (Jdt 4:6; 15:4). The first occurrence of the name in 4:6 gives the variant spelling *baitomesthaim;* however, there seems to be no reason to suppose the author was referring to two different cities. Betomasthaim is set near Dothan, north of Samaria. C. C. Torrey argued that Betomasthaim was a contemptuous pseudonym for Samaria: *byt mśṭmh,* 'house of shame,' or *byt mśṭm,* 'house of the devil.' This is not at all certain. It is entirely possible that the city is totally fictitious; this would be in keeping with the genre of the book of Judith.

Bibliography

Torrey, C. C. 1945. *The Apocryphal Literature.* New Haven.

SIDNIE ANN WHITE

BETONIM (PLACE) [Heb *bĕṭōnîm*]. A border point E of the Jordan river for the land of Jazer, which Moses gave to the families of Gad (Josh 13:26). The location is noted by Eusebius as *Botnia* but has never been verified as *Khirbet Batneh,* 6 miles SW of es-Salt. The location is described briefly by de Vaux (1938: 404) and affirmed by Noth (1938: 26).

Noth suggests that the three place names of Heshbon to Ramath-Mizpeh to Betonim constitute a N-S boundary line between Reuben and Gad. However, Mittmann (1970) dismisses Noth's view as very speculative. In a complex literary study Wüst (1975) concludes that Josh 13:26 is part of a two-step addition to the report, which is intended to support the larger territorial claims of Gad.

Bibliography

Mittmann, S. 1970. *Beiträge zur Siedlungs und Territorialgeschichte des Nördlichen Ostjordanlandes.* Weisbaden.

Noth, M. 1938. Ramath-Mizpe und Betonim (Jos. 13,26). *PJB* 34: 23–29.

Vaux, R. de. 1938. Exploration de la region de salt. *RB* 47: 398–425.

Wüst, M. 1975. Ostjordanland. Vol. 1, pp. 120–32 in *Untersuchen zu den siedlugsgeographischen Texten des Alten Testaments.* Weisbaden.

PAUL NIMRAH FRANKLYN

BEYOND THE JORDAN (PLACE). From the E this would be W of the Jordan, i.e., Cisjordan; from the W, it would be E of the river, i.e., Transjordan. The Talmud refers to Transjordan.

The "Jordan" is usually understood to be the Jordan river but it may be an old word for "river" with the context suggesting which river is involved and thus which area (Aharoni *LBHG* 111; Smick 1973: 26–27). Among the nine references to Cisjordan, Deut 3:20, 25; 11:30 are Moses speaking about the W.

Gen 50:10–11, the burial of Jacob at Atad or Abel-mizraim ("meadow of Egypt"), has been interpreted both ways. For some unknown reason, Joseph carried the body from Egypt through Transjordan and came from the E, so "beyond the Jordan" would designate Cisjordan, with the burial at Hebron (as the usual understanding has it). Perhaps the route was a typology for the Exodus (Ottosson 1969: 37 n. 2). But the reference to burial "beyond the Jordan" has been interpreted as a burial place in Transjordan with Joseph's funeral group making the more obvious and logical trip straight from Egypt to the Jordan. However, the latter could also be a straight, logical trip from Egypt to Hebron if "Jordan" here is the old word for "river," so Joseph's funeral party went "beyond the river," which from Egypt could be the River of Egypt, Wâdī el-ʿArîsh.

Smick (1973: 30–31, 105 n. 72, 111) has pointed out that where Heb *ʿēber* "beyond" or "opposite" refers to the Jordan, the writer specifies the direction. Josh 5:1 refers to the W, while Num 34:15 refers to the E. The word itself also means "a side," hence at the side of, beside, adjacent. Exod 32:15 refers to two sides *(ʿebrêhem)* of the tablets of the law. Smick takes NT *peran* as in John 1:28 as carrying the same range of meaning. Matt 4:15 quotes Isa 8:23—Eng 9:1–2, which seems to put Galilee in Transjordan, if Heb *ʿēber* (and Gk *peran*) are translated "across." But there is no problem if the translation is "beside" or "adjacent to"; Galilee is beside the Jordan, not across (E of) it. Similarly, Matt 19:1 refers to Judea beyond the Jordan. Judea did not extend across the Jordan into Transjordan though rulers like Herod the Great controlled the territory. The reference is usually thought to be Perea, across the Jordan. But "Judea beside the Jordan" makes good sense in this context.

There has been some debate over John 1:28 and the location of Bethany (location unknown) beyond the Jordan. Some manuscripts read Bethabara, SE of Jericho. Finegan (1969: 8–11) suggests that if Jerusalem and Judea went out to John, the place would have been on a main road, at one of the fords of the Jordan river. He notes the Roranije ford, today's Allenby bridge, on the road from Jericho to Amman, 5 miles from Jericho and 9 from the

Dead Sea. There is another ford, 4.5 miles S at the end of the Wâdī el-Charrar and near Mt. St. Elijah (Jebel Mar Elyas) on the E bank and near today's Monastery of St. John (Deir Mar Juhanna) on the W bank. Another mile S is the traditional site of the el-Hajlah ford at the end of the Wâdī Qelt. A half-mile further S is the el-Henu ford. While Finegan notes abundant springs by Mount St. Elijah was a possible site for John's baptisms, the text does not require a location in Transjordan. It could simply mean "beside the Jordan" or "on the banks of the Jordan." See also BETHANY (PLACE).

Bibliography

Finegan, J. 1969. *The Archaeology of the New Testament.* Princeton.
Ottosson, M. 1969. *Gilead: Tradition and History.* Lund.
Smick, E. B. 1973. *Archaeology of the Jordan Valley.* Grand Rapids.

HENRY O. THOMPSON

BEYOND THE RIVER (PLACE) [Heb *ʿēber hannāhār*]. "Beyond the river" (Aramaic *ʿăbar nahărâ;* Gk *peran tou potamou)* can refer to (1) lands E of the Euphrates, (2) the Persian provinces W of the Euphrates including Coele-Syria, and (3) possibly Transjordan. 2 Sam 10:16; 1 Kgs 14:15; and 1 Chr 19:16 use "beyond the River" (RSV, "beyond the Euphrates") from the perspective of those W of the Euphrates to refer to lands on the E side of that river. McCarter (*2 Samuel* AB, 273) surveyed minority opinions to the contrary. The Persians, from their perspective, saw the lands to the W of the Euphrates as "beyond the river" and so named the province which encompassed all the lands from the Euphrates W to the Mediterranean and as far N as the Taurus mountains in Turkey (Shalit 1954: 64–73). Ezra 4:10–20; 5:3, 6; 6:6, 8, 13; 7:21, 25; 8:36; and Neh 2:7, 9; 3:7 follow the Persian use of the term. Josh 24:14–15 refers to "beyond the river" where the patriarchs served Yahweh. This is an obvious reference to Haran in N Mesopotamia (Gen 11:31). Shalit has shown this area to have been included in the province "beyond the river" or Coele-Syria. 1 Macc 7:8 notes that Bacchides was governor of the province "Beyond the River." Shalit (1954: 73–77) demonstrated that under the Seleucids Coele-Syria (or "beyond the river") was limited to the area S of the Orontes to Egypt and from the Mediterranean to the border of the Syrian-Arabian desert. Josephus (*Ant* 12.10.2) misunderstood this and defined "beyond the river" as Mesopotamia. In 1 Macc 11:60, Jonathan traverses "beyond the river." Goldstein (*1 Maccabees* AB, 440) noted that the Greek verb "traverse" *(diaporeuesthai)* takes a direct object ("the province beyond the river") and not a prepositional phrase (implying that the Jordan was crossed). Goldstein further observed that although the absence of the definite article before "beyond the river" appears to argue against this rendering, it should be noted that the LXX of 1 Kgs and of Ezra also lacks the definite article where the meaning is clearly the province W of the Euphrates. Josephus (*Ant* 13.5.5) correctly understands "beyond the river" of 1 Macc 11:60, for he renders it "Phoenicia" (part of Coele-Syria or "beyond the river").

Bibliography

Shalit, A. 1954. *Koilē Syria* from the Mid-Fourth Century to the Beginning of the Third Century B.C. Pp. 64–77 in *Scripta Hierosolymitana,* ed. R. Koebner. Vol. 1. Jerusalem.
Stolper, M. W. 1989. The Governor of Babylon and Across-the-River in 486 B.C. *JNES* 48: 283–305.

MICHAEL E. HARDWICK

BEZAE. See CODEX (BEZAE).

BEZAI (PERSON) [Heb *bēṣāy*]. Head of a family of Babylonian exiles who are listed as returnees under the leadership of Zerubbabel and others (Ezra 2:17 = Neh 7:23 = 1 Esdr 5:16). The leader of the clan affixed the family name to the covenant document of Nehemiah in Neh 10:19—Eng 10:18. For further discussion of exilic name lists and bibliography see AKKUB (PERSON) and ATER (PERSON). The name is likely a shortened form of *bĕṣalʾēl,* "In the shadow of El" (Noth *IPN,* 152; *TPNAH,* 157).

CHANEY R. BERGDALL

BEZALEL (PERSON) [Heb *bĕṣalʾēl*]. The name of two individuals in the Hebrew Bible. It has been suggested that the name Bezalel may mean "in the shadow (protection) of El (God)," consisting of the preposition *b* prefixed to the construct *ṣl* and *ʾl* (*IPN,* 152).

1. The craftsperson responsible for constructing the tent of meeting, the ark of testimony, and the accompanying furnishings (Exod 31:1–11). According to the Chronicler, Bezalel was a descendant of Caleb and a member of the tribe of Judah (1 Chr 2:20). The priestly tradition claims that Bezalel was granted a divine spirit *(rûaḥ ʾĕlōhîm)* which further endowed him with skill *(ḥokmâ),* a faculty of understanding *(tĕbûnâ),* knowledge *(daʿat),* and workmanship *(mĕlāʾkâ)* by which he was able to execute the task (Exod 31:2–3; 35:30–31). Assisting him were Oholiab and "every skilled individual" (Exod 31:6, 36:1–2). The Chronicler states that Solomon brought his bronze altar to the newly constructed temple (2 Chr 1:5), indicating Bezalel's firm position in the tradition. However, Noth suggests that the priests may have added his name to the tradition in order to provide the ancestor of a postexilic family with a prominent place in Israel's sacred history (*HPT,* 187–88).

2. A descendant of Pahathmoab and one of the returned exiles who were required to divorce their foreign wives (Ezra 10:30). He might appear in the parallel list in 1 Esdr 9:31 as Sesthel. Bezalel was a member of a family from which groups of exiles returned with Zerubbabel (Ezra 2:6; Neh 7:11) and later with Ezra (Ezra 8:4). For further discussion see BEDEIAH (PERSON).

JEFFREY A. FAGER

BEZEK (PLACE) [Heb *bezeq*]. The site where the tribes of Judah and Simeon defeated Adoni-bezek (Judg 1:4–5). Bezek is also mentioned in 1 Sam 11:8–11 as the site where Saul took a census of the people during his campaign to save the residents of Jabesh-gilead from Nahash the Ammonite.

To identify the location of Bezek, one must examine the geographical characteristics given in these sources. While no such specifications appear in Judges 1, the second source indicates that one night's march was sufficient for Saul and his army to reach Jabesh from Bezek: Saul promised the residents of Jabesh: "Tomorrow, in the heat of the day, you will have deliverance" (1 Sam 11:9). We may infer from this that the distance between Bezek and Jabesh did not exceed 20–30 km. The site of the census also had to be on one of the convenient roadways which led from the central mountains to the Jordan Valley, since Saul's starting point was Gibeah (11:4). The name of Bezek, according to these criteria, has undoubtedly been preserved at Khirbet Ibzik (M.R. 187197), a large site lying upon the ancient road leading from Shechem and the E valleys of the Manasseh hill country to the Jordan Valley. The prefix "I" in the name "Ibzik" does not deter the identification of the name, since it is typical of later Arabic prefixes (e.g., Chesulloth = Iksal; Bene-barak = Ibn Ibrak). The antiquity of the name is known at least as far back as the Byzantine period: the *Onomasticon* of Eusebius testifies on two villages named Bezek lying on the Neapolis–Scythopolis road, 17 miles from the former.

Khirbet Ibzik is located on the SW slope of Ras es-Salmeh, a high range which encloses the Zebabdeh Valley at the E, and is part of the Far^{c}ah Anticline. This natural passageway, leading from the center of the Manasseh hill country to the Jordan Valley, lies upon the saddle of Ras es-Salmeh, making it the most convenient route for crossing the Jordan and arriving at Jabesh-gilead. (Jabesh-gilead his been identified with the large tell of El Maklub [M.R. 214201] E of the Jordan and approximately 30 km from Khirbet Ibzik, and also with Tel Abu Kh^{c}araz [M.R. 206200] only 16 km from Khirbet Ibziq. Neither site is more than one night's march from the suggested identification of Bezek.)

At least two Roman roads, leading from Neapolis (Shechem) to Scythopolis (Beth Shean), were identified at the passageway of Khirbet Ibzik. The two large sites found on the route were settled mainly during the Roman-Byzantine period. Apparently, Eusebius was referring to these sites, and not to Khirbet Jabrish, located 4 km to the E and not related to the Bezek passageway. In a careful archaeological survey, Zertal found that settlement at Khirbet Ibzik began during the late Iron Age (7th–6th centuries B.C.), and not earlier. Therefore, the double site of Khirbet Ibzik cannot be associated with the place where Saul gathered the people of Israel, nor can it be connected with the ancient tradition of the campaign of Judah and Simeon. According to the principle of names which wandered from site to site in the vicinity, apparently the original site of Bezek should be located somewhere nearby.

During the course of Zertal's survey of the Manasseh hill country, the small tell of Khirbet Salhab (M.R. 185195) was inspected and found to be suitable as the location of ancient Bezek. It lies in the wide Zebabdeh Valley, approx. 2 km W of the narrow Bezek passageway, and near the route of the Roman road. This place is suitable for gathering the people and taking a military census, unlike Kh. Ibzik, which lies in a narrow pass. During the survey of Kh. Salhab, sherds were found from as early as the beginnings of the Iron I period (13th century B.C.), and the site was settled continuously throughout the entire Iron Age. The later site of Kh. Ibzik was founded during the late Iron Age, and the original name was transferred over to it. Possible reference to Salhab is preserved in the Rehob inscription (5th–6th century A.D.), where the name "Palga deShalaf" appears, together with a series of names in the hill country of Manasseh. This source confirms that "Bezek" at that time was in Kh. Ibzik, while the name "Salhab" was already given to this (early Iron Age) site. The reason for this change is unknown; however, it is clear that the name Bezek had already passed to its present location during the Iron Age and was preserved there ever since.

The site of Salhab also seems to suit the ancient traditions preserved in the book of Judges. This tradition apparently preserves a period during which the nuclei of the tribes of Judah and Simeon wandered within the territory of Manasseh. Judah is mentioned as connected to Manasseh by genealogical ties (2 Chr 2:21–22), while the existence of Simeonites in Manasseh is well attested until the end of the existence of the kingdom of Israel and afterward (2 Chr 15:9; 34: 5–6). Further evidence of this phenomenon is found in the book of Judith, dating to the Persian period (8:1).

The historical background of the Bezek battle against the Canaanites is not clear. It is possible that clans of Judah and Simeon moved up from the Jordan Valley to be met at Bezek by the Canaanites, and from there they continued S as a part of an overall movement of Israelite clans from the N mountains to Jerusalem and the Judahite territory.

Bibliography

Welten, P. 1965. Bezeq. *ZDPV* 81: 138–65.

Adam Zertal

BEZER (PERSON) [Heb *beṣer*]. A son of Zophah, from the tribe of Asher (1 Chr 7:37). The name may refer to "gold" (*IPN*, 223). Although it occurs as a personal name, it likely refers to BEZER (PLACE).

BEZER (PLACE) [Heb *beṣer*]. A city of refuge in Transjordan, located "in the wilderness on the tableland for the Reubenites" (Deut 4:43; cf. Josh 20:8). Bezer was one of three cities of refuge established by Moses to the east of the Jordan; the other two places of asylum were Ramoth in Gilead and Golan in Bashan. Bezer was later set apart as a levitical city and assigned to the Merarites (Josh 21:36; 1 Chr 6:63, 78).

Although it pays a relatively minor role in the OT, the Mesha Inscription lists Bezer among the Israelite towns that were taken in Mesha's successful effort to reclaim the Moabite tableland. In fact, line 27 of this text seems to emphasize the severity of the destruction Mesha brought upon Bezer and another town: "I rebuilt Beth-bamoth, for it had been destroyed; and I rebuilt Bezer, for it was in ruins . . ." (*TSSI* 1: 77). It is possible that these two sites were the scenes of heavy fighting because, like Nebo (line 14), they were in northern Moab. At any rate, Mesha rebuilt Bezer in order to consolidate his victory over Israel.

Although its exact location is unknown, Bezer is often identified with Umm el-ᶜAmad (M.R. 235132), which is located ca. eight miles northeast of Medeba. Bezer is perhaps the same town as Bosor (1 Macc 5:36; cf. LXX, *Bosor*), and Moabite Bozrah (Jer 48:24), but it should not be confused with the important Edomite city named Bozrah (modern Buseirah) or still another Bezer, a town in Bashan that is named in Egyptian texts.

GERALD L. MATTINGLY

BIBLE, BISHOPS'. Early in Elizabeth's reign the preparation of the Bishops' Bible was suggested to William Cecil, secretary of state to Elizabeth, in letters of Richard Cox, bishop of Ely, January 19, 1561, and May 3, 1566, in which Cox proposed that one uniform translation be used through the realm. Matthew Parker, Archbishop of Canterbury, then casually stated in a letter to Cecil (March 9, 1565) that a translation was to be done.

Parker seems to have assigned various portions for revision over a period of time, with so many of the revisers either being or later becoming bishops that the effort is known as the Bishops' Bible. Letters collected in the *Parker Correspondence* reveal the progress, and on November 26, 1566, Parker informed Cecil that the work was under way and invited him to review an epistle. It is assumed that Cecil courteously declined.

Parker distributed portions of the Great Bible upon which notes were to be made to the participants, most of whom had been exiles in Mary's reign. It is not likely that the revisers met together. They were instructed to vary from the English translation commonly used in the churches only when Hebrew and Greek demanded it. They were to follow Pagninus and Münster in sections and divisions. No bitter or polemical notes were to be included. Genealogies and unedifying matter were to be marked so that the reader would skip them in public reading. Offensive words in the old translation were to be replaced, and the printer was to use his heaviest paper for the NT since it would have more use.

The initials of the revisers are printed with the books for which they are responsible; unfortunately, there are two lists of names which do not completely agree. Edmund Guest is remembered for having suggested to Parker one of the most asinine procedures for rendering the Psalms ever suggested. He rendered a psalm in the OT as if it was in the NT to avoid offense of "divers translations." It is thought, however, that finally either Thomas Bacon or Thomas Bickley did the psalms. More sensible is the wish expressed by Cox that the revision should use words with which the English were acquainted and should avoid "inkhorn terms." Parker, in addition to some of the revision, did the editorial work, and he explained in the preface to the OT that old copies of Bibles were wearing out and that many churches were lacking Bibles. In his letter to the queen he remarked, without specifically naming it, that the notes of the Geneva Bible were objectionable.

By September 22, 1568, Parker could inform Cecil that the work was completed and that he hoped to be able to make a presentation to Queen Elizabeth; his health did not permit him to realize his wish, however, and on October 5 he again wrote Cecil explaining procedures followed, requesting that Cecil get protection from infringers for Richard Jugge, the printer, and get a license from the queen for use of the Bible in the churches. It seems the license was never granted.

Artistically, the first edition of the Bishops' Bible was the most ornate English Bible yet to appear. Portraits of Queen Elizabeth, William Cecil, and Cecil Burleigh (later Lord Burleigh) were placed in flattering locations. Elaborate woodcuts made up page borders for the five sections of the Bible. Parker's coat of arms was included with his preface, and that of Cranmer for his prologue. The Gospel of Matthew begins with a large T decorated with a scene of Neptune taming the sea horses. At the beginning of the other gospels, Mark is accompanied by the lion, Luke by the ox, and John by the eagle. Illustrations within the text are enclosed in woodcut borders, and the pictures are frequently signed, with the whole making up 143 pictures. The art was not constant through the successive editions. The initial letter G at the Epistle to the Hebrews was decorated with the scene of Leda and the swan, which gave to the 1572 edition the name "The Leda Bible."

The Bishops' substituted "charity" where Tyndale had used "love," had a peculiar rendering not unique to it in Eccl 11:1: "Lay thy bread on wet faces . . . ," and had the misprint at Ps 37:29: "The righteous [for unrighteous] shall be punished." The most famous marginal note is to Ps 45:9: "Orphir is thought to be the Ilande in the west coast, of late founde by Christopher Columbo, from whence at this day is brought most fine golde."

While using verses as the Geneva did, the Bishops,' until 1579, continued to use the older section system of A, B, and C down the margin. The second edition, 1569, is quarto and revealed a number of changes in the OT and some in the NT. A further revision of the NT was done in 1572, and this text appears in all later printings. This third edition in 1572 had both the Bishops' and the Great Bible Psalms in parallel columns and after 1573 all editions but one carry only the Great Bible Psalms.

On April 3, 1571, the Convocation of Canterbury ordered that the Bible of the largest volume as lately published in London be put in the halls of great houses and, as far as possible, in churches. The Great Bible appeared in its last edition in 1569. The 1574 folio edition of the Bishops' carried the words "set foorth by authorities," and by 1589 Whitgift circulated articles stating that the Bible now authorized by the bishops was to be used in the churches. Royal authorization seems never to have come; but parish accounts record purchases of Bibles as well as fines paid for lacking a proper Bible.

Shakespeare in his earlier plays used the Bishops' Bible. There is probability that some early explorers who were loyal churchmen used it in America. There were quarto editions as well as portable New Testaments printed. Alexander Whitaker of Jamestown, who regularly used the Geneva Bible, used a Bishops' phrase in a letter of June 18, 1614. Captain Samuel Argall in 1610 showed the Indians of Patawomek River a picture of creation from a Bible which likely was a Bishops'. However, the days of the Bishops' Bible had passed before the period of colonization, and it was not printed in America until 1962.

There were many critics of the Bishops' Bible. The ninth edition (1577) is quarto, was the last printed by Richard

Jugge, and was criticized by Gregory Martin in the Rheims (1582) marginal notes and in the exchange with Richard Fulke in 1589. The most vocal critic was Hugh Broughton, who hoped in vain to be appointed to do a revision. He faulted many renderings, and of the table preceding the NT said, "The cockles of the sea-shore and the leaves of the forest, and the granes of the Popy may well be numbered as the grosse errours of this Table, disgracing the ground of our one hope."

The Bishops' Bible went through twenty editions in its forty-two years, the last edition being in 1602. The NT was again printed in 1617 and 1633. The instructions to the King James revisers were that they were to follow the Bishops' Bible where it was true to the original. Charles Butterworth (1941: 231) estimated that the King James Bible owes four percent of its wording to the Bishops'.

The text of the Bishops' NT was included in Bagster's *English Hexapla* in 1841 (Herbert 1968, no. 1840) and in Luther A. Weigle's *The New Testament Octapla* in 1962. The text of the Psalms was printed in the *Hexaplar Psalter* of 1911 (no. 2173) and the text of Genesis in Weigle's *Genesis Octapla* of 1965.

Bibliography

Butterworth, C. 1941. *The Literary Lineage of the King James Bible.* Philadelphia.

Dore, J. R. 1888. *Old Bibles.* London.

Herbert, A. S. 1968. *Historical Catalogue of Printed Editions of the English Bible 1525–1961.* London and New York.

Parker, M. 1853. *Correspondence of Matthew Parker, D.D.,* ed. John Bruce and T. T. Perowne. Cambridge.

JACK P. LEWIS

BIBLE, EUPHEMISM AND DYSPHEMISM IN THE.

Reticence with regard to certain subjects—chiefly sexual and excretory functions, death, and matters considered dangerous, numinous, or holy—is notable in varying degrees in many cultures, languages, and literatures; it is also evident in the Bible.

A. Introduction

Measures to reduce offensive language in the Hebrew Bible were applied long before modern movements to sanitize or expurgate literature, both secular and sacred. Rabbinic sages were concerned about "clean language" as well as other kinds of purity, and this had its impact on academic discourse and also on the sacred text and its subsequent translation into other languages. "One should not open his mouth to Satan" or "let an ugly word escape his lips" (*Berakot* 19a; *Pesahim* 3a). Jesus Ben Sira (Sir 23:12) opined that some words merit death and should never be heard among Jacob's heirs, possibly a reference to blasphemy. Ben Sira also considered lewd talk sinful (Sir 23:13): cursing one's birth (as Job and Jeremiah did) dishonored one's father and mother (Sir 23:14), while abusive language was a bad habit and a sign of immaturity (Sir 23:15). Yet Ben Sira seems to have forgotten his own counsel when paying his respects to the wayward woman on whom he lays such epithets as "scorpion" and "dog" (Sir 26:7, 25).

There are various ways of rectifying language deemed improper, apart from simply expunging the offending element. *Euphemism,* the use of mild, delicate, indirect, or negative terms (as "not clean" for "dirty") to hint at an unpleasant matter rather than name it plainly, has been a factor in debasing language by excess refinement. The rabbis early noted and listed some biblical euphemisms and aptly characterized the phenomenon with the locution *kinnāh ha-katûb,* "Scripture has substituted/nicknamed," i.e., euphemized. The opposite tactic, *cacophemism* or *dysphemism,* the use of grossly disparaging terms rather than normal or neutral designations (esp. with reference to enemies or despised activities), is also common in the Bible and elsewhere. Related to euphemism and dysphemism is *antiphrasis,* saying the opposite of what is meant, as when in Akkadian the netherworld was called "clean place" *(ašru ellu),* or when Job's wife urged him to "bless" (i.e., curse) God and die. Another devious rhetorical device is *periphrasis* or *circumlocution,* deliberate evasiveness in speech or writing, i.e., talking around the topic rather than addressing it directly.

Jewish tradition concedes that there are instances where the text of the Hebrew Bible has been altered (see SCRIBAL EMENDATIONS). Such a drastic measure was applied as a last resort to eliminate blasphemy. More common is indirect alteration of the text by vocalizing what is written *(kethib)* as if it were something different and giving the alternative reading *(qere)* in the margin. (The holy name YaHWeH was ineffable and the vowels supplied with the consonants were those of the surrogate *ʾăDoNaY,* "my Lord[s]." Christians unwittingly combined the vowels of the surrogate with the sacrosanct consonants to produce the sonorous sacrilege "JeHoVaH.") Obscene words were also not to be pronounced, and the consonants of the unmentionable term were provided with the vowels of the polite euphemism or circumlocution and the surrogate consonants were supplied in the margin. For example, in Isa 36:12 = 2 Kgs 18:27 the consonants of the plain words for solid and liquid excreta are written but vocalized with the vowels of the polite substitute terms. Since the plain Hebrew word for "piss" is a terse triliteral monosyllable and the polite substitute meaning "water of (the) feet" is somewhat longer, the obscene consonants had to be spaced to make room for the extra vowels of the euphemism, while the consonants of the polite term were supplied in the margin.

B. Treatment of Sexual Subject Matter

1. Genitalia. Sexual terms are the most common objects of evasive language. The use of "hand" *(yād)* for "penis" is attested already in pre-Israelite Northwest Semitic in a mythological poem from Ugarit called "The Birth of the Beautiful Gods" in which the "hand" of the amative sire of the godlings is said to be as long as the sea. In Isa 57:8 it is apparent from the context that "hand watching" refers to phalloscopy (despite RSV's abashed assertion that "the meaning of the Hebrew is uncertain"). The lover's "hand" in Song of Songs 5:4 thrust into or out of the "hole" (some prepositions in Hebrew and Ugaritic may mean both "to" and "from") is suggestive of penile intromission, despite the context evoking the classical motif of the locked-out lover (Pope *Song of Songs* AB, 514–19). Among the sectarian community at Khirbet Qumran, a member was mulcted/fined for exposing his "hand" (1QS 7:13; see Delcor 1967).

"Feet" *(raglayim)* is also used for genitals of either sex, as in the aforementioned circumlocution "feet water" for urine. In Isa 7:20, "hair of feet" refers to pubic hair. Deut 28:57 speaks of the (formerly) pampered woman in famine eating the afterbirth that comes out from between her "feet." Jerusalem, personified as a wanton nymphomaniac (Ezek 16:25), is charged with spreading her "feet" to every passerby. In Isa 6:2 the six wings of the seraphim come in three pairs, one to cover the face (for reverence), one to cover the "feet" (for modesty), and the third pair for flying. Uriah the Hittite, called home on furlough by King David and urged to go home and "wash his feet," protested that while his comrades were still in battle he would not go home to eat and drink and "lie with his wife" (2 Sam 11:8). One who is quick with his "feet" sins (Prov 19:2). The term "soul" *(nepeš)* in this same verse also has sexual meaning, as it has in at least one clear instance in Ugaritic when the impotent hero Danel sought divine help and had his "soul" *(npš)* restored and then went home and sired a son. In Sufi philosophy "soul" *(nafs)* is used of carnal concupiscence which, like a black watchdog, is ever alert to assail a man and make him sin. The proverb (19:2) thus means: "Without knowledge 'soul' *(libido)* is not good. One fast with his 'feet' sins." King Asa, at the end of his long reign, got sick in his "feet" (1 Chr 16:12); whether the ailment was in the pedal extremities or in the urogenital tract is unclear. When the Lord accosted Moses and sought to kill him (Exod 4:25), Zipporah circumcised her son and touched Moses' "feet" with the foreskin. Just where the "blood(y) husband" was dabbed with the son's prepuce we can only surmise, but the best guess seems the area where foreskins are located.

In postbiblical Hebrew, "heels" sometimes referred to the posterior extremities, or arse, as is patently the case in Jer 13:22 where Jerusalem is taunted: "For your great iniquity, your skirts were lifted up and your 'heels' violated." RSV effectively obscured the sense by not mentioning the "heels."

The word for "testicles" *(ʿešek)* is used only once in the Bible (Lev 21:20) where damage to them is listed among the defects which disqualify a man for priesthood. The Ugaritic cognate *(ʿušk)* is used in a torrid love scene in which Baal and his sister Virgin Anat wax warm and begin by grasping each other's genitals. (The action continues and Anat becomes pregnant and gives birth, but still retains her title "Virgin.") In Deut 23:2—Eng 23:1, among conditions that render one unfit to "enter the congregation of the Lord," two words *(pĕṣûaʿ-dakāʾ)* are used for injury to the (paired) organ(s) which are unmentioned but understood. Loss of the adjacent appendage called "spout" *(šopkâ)* also disqualifies a man for entry into the Lord's congregation. Both testicles and "spout" are doubtless included in the term *mĕbûšîm* (pudenda, or private parts) in Deut 25:11, which stipulates that a woman who intervenes in a fight (to save her husband from injury) and grabs his assailant's privates will have her hand severed.

Both male and female genitalia are called "flesh" or "meat" *(baśār)*. The oozing from a man's "meat" (Lev 15:2) may refer to *gonorrhea benigna*. Bloody discharge from a woman's "meat" is normally periodic (Lev 15:19ff.). Israel's Egyptian paramours are characterized as "large of meat" (Ezek 16:26; which RSV renders as "lustful"). The Egyptians' "meat" is compared to that of asses, and their *zirmâ* (ejaculate ?) with that of horses (Ezek 23:20). The term *zirmâ* (which RSV renders "issue") may be a deliberate garbling of the word *zĕmôrāh,* "shoot, twig, or branch," which in Ezek 8:17 figures in an obscene act in the temple (the text has already been emended by the scribes; cf. Greenberg *Ezekiel 1–20* AB, 172). It is probable that in Ezek 23:20 the prominent genitalia of Israel's lovers ("meat" and "branch") were originally compared to those of both asses and horses.

An egregious expression for a human male, *maštîn bĕqîr,* "pisser on a wall" (1 Sam 25:22, 34; 1 Kings 14:10; 16:11; 2 Kings 9:8), was left unaltered by the scribes and was translated quite precisely by Martin Luther and King James' scholars, but is usually explained rather than translated in contemporary versions.

Tools or weapons naturally become sexual metaphors, especially such implements as rod, staff, bow, arrow, and quiver (see *IDBSup* 725–26). The "staff" of Judah between his "feet" (Gen 49:10) suggests more than political power. Joseph's perennially taut "bow" (Gen 49:24) may have sexual as well as martial reference. In 1 Sam 21:6 the "tools" of the young men that are holy by reason of abstinence from women are hardly "vessels." In the midst of his miseries, Job recalls better days when his "root" was open to the water, the dew spent the night on his "branch," his "glory" fresh with him, the "bow" in his "hand" ever ready (29:19ff.). Ben Sira (Sir 26:12) castigates the wanton woman who will squat before any "tent-peg" and open her "quiver" to the "arrow."

The Bible is not bashful with reference to female breasts, but more intimate parts are indicated by indirection. An ancient metaphor for woman was a "well" or "cistern," as seen in the Egyptian hieroglyphic logogram for woman. The youth is advised to avoid the exotic temptress and drink from his own "cistern" or "well" (Prov 5:15). The foreign woman or whore is called a "deep pit" and a narrow "well" (Prov 23:27). In Eccles 12:1, "your Creator" (Heb *bôrʾekā*) may be an alteration of "your pit" *(bôrkā),* which would refer either to one's grave or to one's wife, or to both. The subsequent description of advancing senility (Eccles 12:1–8) bewails the last stage of human existence when all vitality ceases and one goes to his long home. Youth is the time to be mindful of both pits, wife and grave, as well as of the Creator. (For defense of the reading "your grave" in Eccles 12:1, see Scott *Proverbs Ecclesiastes* AB, 254–55; the suggestion of "pit" as "wife" comes from a private communication of B. Zuckerman.)

Poetic allusions to the most intimate of female charms are sometimes overlooked or studiously ignored by translators. In the Song of Songs 2:17 the lady invites her lover to be like a gazelle on the "cleft mount(s)" and in 8:14 the invitation is to "spice mound(s)." Exegetes of the naturalist school, not surprisingly, have taken the "mound" to refer to the lady's *mons pubis/veneris,* much to the distress of more spiritual interpreters. The lady of the Song speaks of her unguarded vineyard (1:6), and there is frequent reference (2:16; 4:5; 5:1; 6:2) to the garden(s) where the lover grazes, not among "lilies" (as traditionally understood), but on the lotus, an ancient and famous sexual symbol. (On lotus eating, see Pope *Song of Songs* AB 406–7, 455.) The body part (Heb *šrr*) praised as a rounded crater (mixing bowl) never to lack mix (7:3—Eng 7:2) is hardly the navel but a receptacle not far below (Pope *Song of Songs* AB, 617ff). The all-spice part(s) of the lady (4:13) are not "shoots" but a "groove" or "conduit" (Pope *Song of Songs* AB, 490–91 on *šalḥ* as a channel and a term for "vagina").

2. Sexual Intercourse, Nudity, and Sexual Innuendo. Various evasive devices are used with reference to sexual intercourse. In four instances the consonants of the transitive verb *šgl* are allowed to remain *(kethib),* but those of the intransitive substitute *škb,* "recline," are to be read *(qere)* despite the logical and syntactic incongruity (Deut 28:30; Isa 13:16; Jer 3:2; Zech 14:2). In 2 Sam 13:14 and Ezek 23:8 *škb* is used as a transitive verb with direct object, as if it were *šgl.* Elsewhere the preposition *ᶜim* or *ʾēt,* "with," is added in the common locution "lie with" which is used for both heterosexual and homosexual copulation as well as for human coupling with animals (despite the unlikelihood that humans and animals would recline in the process).

The verb *b(w)ʾ,* "enter," with the preposition *ᶜel,* "unto," is a common biblical term for coition, and the verbal noun *bîᶜâ,* "entry," though not used in the Bible, became the legal term for consummation of a marriage. (On "know" [Heb *yādaᶜ*] for carnal experience, see Speiser *Genesis* AB, 31–32).

Nudity is generally regarded as shameful in the Bible, as elsewhere. Captives in war were humiliated by being stripped naked (Isa 20:4; 47:1–3). Isaiah himself went naked for three years to dramatize the fate of those who opposed Assyria (Isa 20:2–3). David's emissaries to the Ammonite king were humiliated by having half their beards removed and their clothing lopped off to the buttocks (2 Sam 10:4). "Nakedness" *(ᶜerwâ)* is used to refer to the pudenda of both sexes, and as such is the object of the verbs "see," "cover," and "uncover." Saul rebuked Jonathan's relation with David (1 Sam 20:30) as "shame of your mother's nakedness," perhaps intending to suggest that more was involved than mere filial disloyalty. To uncover a father's "skirt" (Heb *kānāp*) means to have sexual intercourse with one's father's wife, as is clear in Deut 23:1—Eng 22:30 and 27:20. For a man to spread his "skirt" over a woman meant more than merely preventing chill, as is apparent in Ezek 16:8 and Ruth 3:9.

The rabbis were alert to the possibility that nonsexual terms may be used with sexual entente. In Job 31:10 "grind" (Heb *ṭḥn*) refers to pelvic gyrations as confirmed by the poetic parallelism, and was duly noted by the rabbis (*Soṭah* 10b). Samson's "grinding" in prison (Judg 16:21) and captive youths compelled to "grind" (Lam 5:13) was understood by St. Jerome, as well as by the rabbis, in this sexual sense (Pope *Job* AB, 202).

The sexual suggestiveness of "couch" *(mēsēb)* in Song of Songs 1:12a is illuminated by Rab Judah's remark that Jerusalem men were lewd *(ʾănšê šaḥaṣ).* "One would say to his colleague, 'On what did you dine today? On well-kneaded bread or on bread not kneaded; on white wine or dark wine; on a broad couch or a narrow couch; with a good companion or a poor companion?' " "All these (queries)," Hisda explained, (refer) "to fornication *(zĕnût)*" *b. Šabb.* 62b, 63a). The rabbis also perceived sexual entente in the references to eating bread in Gen 39:6 (*Genesis Rabbah* 86:6) and in Exod 2:20 (*Tanhuma* 1:11). In Prov 30:20, "the adulteress eats and wipes her mouth and says 'I've done no wrong.' " References to eating and drinking in the Song of Songs 4:16 and 5:1 have been similarly understood (Pope, *Song of Songs* AB).

The noun *zimmâ,* derived from the verb *zāmam,* "ponder, cogitate, devise, plot," used of human scheming (Deut 19:19) as well as divine planning (Jer 51:12; Zech 1:6; Lam 2:17), in some contexts refers to premeditated sexual misconduct, as in Job 31:11, which relates to seduction of a neighbor's wife characterized as *zimmâ* (RSV "heinous crime") and criminal iniquity. The Ugaritic cognate *tdmmt* is used of indecorum (presumably sexual) by serving wenches at a divine banquet. Just what the girls did is not known because of a break in the text, but it was so repulsive that Baal stood and spat in the assembly of gods and declared that there were three kinds of banquets (sacrifices) he hated and all three were characterized by lewdness *(tdmmt)* on the part of the servant girls.

3. Homosexuality. Homosexual activity is treated fairly frankly, though hardly sympathetically, in the Bible. It was common enough so that strangers were at risk in some towns, as illustrated in the episodes related in Genesis 19 and Judges 19. It was a host's obligation to protect his guests from such abuse and there is a garbled reference to this duty in Job's negative confession (Job 31:31ff.) (Pope *Job* AB, 207–8). Among misconduct condemned in the Wisdom of Solomon 14:24ff. is "change of kind" which RSV renders "sex perversion." The locution "another matter" *(dābār ᶜaḥēr)* in postbiblical Hebrew was applied to homosexuality as well as to other unmentionable activities. Paul in 1 Cor 6:8 uses two different terms presumably to distinguish two types of homosexuals, *malakoi,* i.e., "softies" or effeminates, and *arsenokoitai,* "those who lie (with) males." Moffatt rendered "catamites" (from the name Ganymede) and "sodomites," but RSV took the terms as hendiadys and rendered the two in one as "homosexuals," later revised to "sexual perverts."

It is surprising that nothing was done to the Hebrew text to dysphemize the use of the epithet "holy" for persons elsewhere called "dog" and "whore." Functionaries of the Astarte temple in Cyprus were called "dogs" in a Phoenician inscription (*KAI* 37b, 1. 10); but what relation, if any, these "dogs" had to the male and female hierodules of the Bible is uncertain (*cf. BASOR* 216: 56a). "Dogs" in Rev 22:15 are excluded from the celestial city along with sorcerers, fornicators, murderers, idolaters, and everyone who loves and does falsity. These "dogs" were clearly degenerate human types, whatever their sin. In Rev 21:8

persons "befouled" *(ebdelugmenoi)* are consigned to the lake of fire along with murderers, fornicators, sorcerers, idolaters, and liars. It is a fair guess that the "dogs" and the "befouled" excluded from the celestial city and consigned to fire may have been the same sort of "dogs" and "whores" whose wages were not acceptable in the earthly temple (Deut 23:18–19f.—Eng 23:17–18).

In Deut 23:18–19, the male hierodule of Canaanitish fertility worship, ordinarily called "holy (man)," *qādēš,* is more apparently called a "dog" *(keleb),* while his female counterpart is also called "whore" *(zônâ)* rather than *qĕdēšâ,* "holy (woman)." The wages of both are pronounced unacceptable for payment of a vow or offering in the temple of the Lord. "Dog" and "whore" are presumably dysphemisms for these "holy" functionaries whose activities were officially banned but not eliminated (Gen 38:21f.; Deut 23:18; 1 Kgs 14:24; 15:12; 22:47; 2 Kgs 23:7; Hos 4:14; Job 36:14). The KJV usually rendered *qādēš* as "sodomite" and *qĕdēšâ* as "harlot" or "whore," while RSV made the "sodomite" a "male cult prostitute" and the female a "harlot" or "cult prostitute." In Job 36:14, LXX took the "holy" ones (Heb *qĕdēšim*) for "angels," the Vulgate as "effeminates," the KJV as "unclean," while the RSV dysphemized "in shame" and relegated to a footnote the explanation "among the cult prostitutes." The term *qdšm* occurs several times in Ugaritic lists of professional personnel, but no hint is given as to the sort of services rendered. See also PROSTITUTION.

C. Treatment of Excretory Subject Matter

Terms related to excreta and excretory functions, as noted briefly above, are regularly euphemized. Urine *(šyn)* becomes "water of the feet" *(mêmê raglayim)* and the plain word for excrement *(ḥrʾ)* is changed to "outcome" *(ṣōʾâ).* Earlier, at Ugarit, literary usage was not so polite. The plain words *ṯnt* and *ḫrʾ* were written and presumably spoken with reference to cattle and horses; even the chief god El, head of the pantheon and father of gods and humans, is described as inebriated to the point of delirium and locomotor ataxia, floundering (?) in his own *ṯnt* and *ḫrʾ*. The scene recalls the Ephraimite orgy depicted in Isaiah 28 wherein priest and prophet reel and stagger in vomit and excrement. It seems likely that the word *hrʾ* may have been used in 28:7 and was later deliberately garbled into *brʾh* (Pope *Song of Songs* AB, 217). Ezekiel's aversion to barley cakes (baked) over rolls of human excrement (4:12) moved the Lord to permit substitution of bovine dung (4:15) as fuel for the baking.

The divine title Beelzebub in 1 Kgs 1:12 is a corruption of Beelzebul, i.e., "Baal (the) Prince," which is correctly preserved in the gospels (Matt 10:25; 12:24, 27; Mark 3:22; Luke 11:15, 18–19). This is confirmed by the title of the dying-rising rain god of the Ugaritic myths, *zbl bʿl ʿrs,* "Prince, Lord of Earth." The element *zĕbub,* apparently onomatopoeic imitation of the buzzing of flies or bees (Isa 7:18), has been compared with the fly-repellent god Zeus Apomuios (mentioned by Pausanias). In postbiblical Hebrew, however, the root *zbl* also relates to excrement, and thus there would be no need to change the spelling to *zĕbub* in order to derogate a deity whose ancient title could also be taken to mean "Lord (of) Excrement." The rabbis ridiculed the cult of Baal Peor by connecting *pʿr* with ritual defecation (Pope *Song of Songs* AB, 217).

The biblical circumlocution for defecation is "cover one's feet" (Judg 3:24; 1 Sam 24:3), from the act of squatting with spacious robe spread to cloak the action. The KJV translated the circumlocution literally, but RSV's "relieve himself" offers a dynamic equivalent of the ancient periphrasis.

Piles or hemorrhoids are always uncomfortable and embarrassing, and the biblical term supposed to designate this condition has troubled translators. In Deut 28:27 the word (*ʿŏpōlîm,* cognate with Akkadian *uplu*) occurs along with other chronic ailments which the Lord threatens to lay on his elect if they are disobedient. Among these maladies, variously diagnosed, only the term *ʿplym* is euphemized with the vowels of the word *tĕhōrîm* ("clean/pure [things]") and the consonants of the substitute word are given in the margin. LXX interprets *bʿplym* as localizing the preceding pox of Egypt "in the seat." KJV rendered "emerods," i.e., "hemorrhoids," which RSV changed to "ulcers." However, in 1 Sam 5:6, 9, 12; 6:4, RSV rendered the same term "tumors" (but misgivings have been registered that this suggests cancer (a tumor [swelling] could, of course, be benign). The connection of these swellings with rodents suggests bubonic plague. The LXX of 1 Sam 5:6 mentions an outbreak of plague on ships and increase of mice in the country. The protuberances thus were probably "buboes" (swollen and sore lymph nodes of the groin and armpits) and not anal hemorrhoids (which are caused commonly by constipation). Buboes can be much worse than hemorrhoids, but separation of the tumors from the anal aperture would obviate the need to euphemize.

D. Evasive References to Death

Dying and death are directly mentioned numerous times in the Bible, but there are also devious ways of referring to the same end: "Enoch *walked with* God and *was not,* for God *took* him" (Gen 5:24). Similarly it was announced that the Lord would "take" Elijah (2 Kgs 2:23). When David was about to die, he said to Solomon, "I am about to go the way of all the earth" (1 Kgs 2:2), and Job spoke of going the "way of no return" (7:9–10; 10:21; 16:22). Equation of death with long or eternal sleep is common in many cultures. The psalmist appeals to God, "Give my eyes light, lest I sleep (the sleep of) death" (13:4). The prophet Jeremiah speaks of drunken Babylon that "will sleep eternal sleep and not wake" (51:39). Dan 12:2 announces the awakening of "many who sleep in earth's dust" (some to eternal life and some to eternal shame and contempt). The lover of Song of Songs compares his beloved's kisses to fine wine that goes down straight, flooding (or moving) sleepers' lips (7:10). The Greek, Vulgate, and Syriac read "lips and teeth" rather than "lips of sleepers," but the ancient practice (still extant in Talmudic times, cf. *Ṣem.* 8:4) of piping libations to the dead (to moisten dust-dry lips and throats and enable them to speak) explains the supposedly difficult reading "sleepers," which refers to the dead as guests of the funereal *agapē* or love feast (Pope *Song of Songs* AB, 640–43).

E. Treatment of Sacred Subject Matter

To nullify threats, oaths or self-imprecations, and blasphemy various alterations and substitutions were made in wording. For example, in Num 16:14 Dathan and Abiram defy Moses' order, "Should you gouge out the eyes of these men (to avoid saying "our eyes"), we will not go up." David's self-curses in 1 Sam 20:15f. and 25:22 are redirected to David's enemies. Similarly, in Nathan's rebuke of David for scorning the Lord (2 Sam 12:14) the text was altered to read "enemies of the Lord" to avoid directly accusing David of blasphemy. Naboth was charged with "blessing" (i.e., cursing) God and king (1 Kgs 21:10, 13), and the antiphrasis "bless" for "curse" is similarly used in Job 1:5, 11 and 2:5, 9. This usage survives in contemporary speech: in "Bible Belt" parlance, "he blessed me out" means "he cursed me," while "bad" means "good" in colloquial Afro-American English. A common device to eliminate blasphemy was to turn the derogation back on the speaker. Eli's sons' vilification of God (1 Sam 3:13) was turned back on them by omitting the first letter of the word for God, *ʾlhm,* to make it mean "to them" (see SCRIBAL EMENDATIONS).

1. Avoiding Affront to God. In Jer 2:11, the Lord's original charge, "My people has changed my glory for no profit," was made to read "My people changed his glory." (The letters *y* and *w* representing the first- and third-person suffixes, respectively, are virtually indistinguishable in the oldest Heb mss, i.e., those from Qumran.) In Hab 1:12, the assurance to God "You will not die" was changed to the patently absurd "We will not die," to avoid even the thought that God could die. In Zech 2:12—Eng 2:8, the Lord promises Israel total security: "who touches you touches the pupil of my eye," meaning that any assailant of Israel will get an immediate reaction from the deity as if his (i.e., God's) eye had been poked (cf. Deut 32:10 and Ps 17:8 for the figure of God's guarding of Israel as one would protect his own eyeball). "My eye" was changed to "his eye" (i.e., the assailant's) to avoid blatant anthropomorphism and anthropopathism.

Job's protests about maltreatment by God are sometimes turned back on the complainer by the simple device of changing "his/him" to "my/me," easily done in Hebrew (cf. Pope *Job* AB, 62, 155). The medieval commentator Rashi, averse to Job's accusation against God in Job 9:23b, suggested that the reference must be to Satan. In Job 32:3 the scribes changed "God" to "Job" to eliminate the blasphemous charge.

Concern to preserve divine dignity sometimes resulted in logical absurdity, as in Genesis 18 where the three "men" standing before Abraham included Yahweh. When two of the three departed to go to Sodom and Gomorrah, Abraham went with them a way to start them on their journey (18:16) and then returned to resume conversation with his waiting guest, the Lord. The statement (18:22) that "Abraham was still standing before the Lord" is a circumstantial contradiction. The Lord had been standing alone talking to himself while Abraham was accompanying the departing guests, and the Lord was still standing when Abraham came back. The awkward switch from YHWH to Abraham for the sake of divine dignity shows the urgency of the concern.

To see and converse directly with the deity, as did Abraham in Genesis 18, is rarely done by mortals who are normally seen by or appear before the Lord. Thus the active expression "see the face of the Lord" (Exod 23:15; 34:20, 23; Deut 16:16) was altered by vocalizing the verb as passive, despite the fact that the Lord's face remains the object of the seeing as indicated by the object marker *ʾet* (which was not deleted in Exod 34:23 and Deut 16:16). To see the Lord's face directly was a reward reserved for the righteous in the world to come, called in Catholic theology "Beatific Vision."

2. Disparaging the Foreign. Pious deference to Israel's God of course did not extend to the false gods of enemies or to their foolish and dissolute worshippers. Cacophemisms or slurs were applied especially to items and aspects of foreign worship. The term *ʾĕlîl,* applied disdainfully to foreign gods (Lev 19:4; 26:1; Isa 2:8, 18, 20; 10:10; 19:1, 3; 31:7; Ezek 30:13; Mic 7:1; Hab 2:18; Zech 11:17; Ps 96:5; 97:7; Job 10:15; 1 Chr 16:26) may be related to the common Semitic generic term for deity, *ʾil(u)* > *ʾēl,* as suggested by the reduplicated forms of Old South Arabic *ʾlʾht* and North Arabic *ʾalāʾila-t* applied to deity. Job (13:4) applies the form to his false friends as "quack healers," and Jer 14:4 uses it with reference to worthless divination. Sir 11:3 uses the term of the honey bee as small and insignificant among flying creatures even though it reaps the choicest of all harvests. Whatever its origin, the term is dysphemistic.

The terms *piggûl, tôʿēbâ,* and *šeqeṣ* or *šiqqûṣ,* usually rendered "abomination," are applied to a variety of items regarded as repugnant. The term *piggûl* was used of meat unfit for consumption (Lev 7:18; 19:7; Ezek 4:14). In Isa 65:4 the funerary context mentioning swine flesh in parallelism with *piggûl* broth does not equate the word with pork. The Arabic cognate is used of any kind of decaying meat. The *piggûl* stew meat may have been that of dead relatives eaten in what anthropologists have called "morbid affection."

The term *tôʿēbâ* is applied more than a hundred times in the Bible to a great variety of abhorrent and abominable activities. Eating with a Hebrew was *tôʿēbâ* to Egyptians (Gen 43:32) as was also association with shepherds (Gen 46:34). Among the things deemed "abominable" were forbidden sexual acts (Gen 18:16–23, 30; 20:13), foreign idols (Deut 7:26), eating flesh of "unclean" animals (Deut 14:3), sacrificing defective animals (Deut 17:1), marrying a divorced woman (Deut 24:4), transvestism (Deut 22:5), tainted gifts to the temple (Deut 23:19), cheating with weights and measures (Deut 25:13–16), graven or molten images (Deut 27:15), foreign gods and cults (Lev 18:27; Deut 13:15; 17:4; 18:9; 32:16; Isa 44:19; 1 Kgs 14:24; 2 Kgs 16:3; 21:2; 23:13; Ezra 9:14; 2 Chr 28:3), and other reprehensible acts by Israelites (Jer 6:15; 8:12; Ezek 6:11; 7:20; 16:36; 22:11; 43:8). The scoffer is also proverbially abominable (Prov 24:9).

Various disgusting creatures not to be eaten are termed *šeqeṣ* (Lev 7:21; 11:10–42; Isa 66:17; Ezek 8:10). The so-called "intensive" (actually "factitive") stem *šaqqēṣ* is used in Deut 7:26 with reference to despised or forbidden things. In Ps 22:25—Eng 22:24 the verb *šaqqēṣ* occurs in synonymous poetic parallelism with *bzh,* "despise," and the expression "avert the face." The form *šiqqûṣ* is used of heathen idols (Deut 29:16; 2 Kgs 23:13; 24; Isa 66:3; Jer 4:1;

7:30; 20:7, 30; 37:23; Hos 9:10; 2 Chr 15:8). In Nahum 3:6 it appears that *šiqqûṣîm* can be thrown, and in Zech 9:7 they can be held (as food) between the teeth. Dan 9:27 speaks of a conqueror who will come on the wing(s) of abominations *(šiqqûṣîm),* and this is echoed in Mark 13:14; Matt 24:15 (cf. Luke 21:20) as the "abomination of desolation" (KJV) or "desolating sacrilege" (RSV). It is interesting to note that the term *šeqeṣ* lives on in Yiddish as *sheyqetz* (plural *shĕqatzim*) as an uncomplimentary term for gentile males, while the feminine form *shiqse* has passed into English with an ironic connotation of affection.

The dysphemism *gillûlîm* applied to heathen idols (Lev 26:30; Deut 29:16; 1 Kgs 15:12; 21:26; 2 Kgs 17:12; 21:11, 21, 23, 24; Jer 50:2; Ezek 6:4–13; 14:3–5, 7) is apparently derived from the root *gll,* "roll." The noun *gālāl* in 1 Kgs 14:10 and Zeph 1:17 means "dung," and thus the form *gillûl* presumably also refers to excrement. The precise English translation of *gillûlîm* would thus be "turds," a word that came into English a thousand years ago (from Latin *tord(ere),* "roll") and ought not to be eschewed when apposite.

The word *bōšet,* "shame," is a common biblical dysphemism pronounced in place of proper names of pagan deities, as in the names Ishbaal, Meribaal, Jerubbaal, featuring the theophoron *Baʿl,* meaning "Lord, Husband, Owner," but pronounced *bōšet,* "shame," when the vowels of that word were superimposed on the consonants of the name *Baʿal* and similarly on the names of other pagan deities. The name Ashtart, when provided with the vowels of *bōšet,* may be pronounced "Ashtoreth" or suppressed altogether and pronounced *bōšet,* "shame." The name of the dread god Molech (or Moloch, as in LXX 2 Kgs 23:10) may have been given the *bōšet* vowels, but we do not know for sure the original vocalization of the name; it may be that the traditional vocalization preserves ancient vowels and therefore has nothing to do with the word for "shame."

F. More Recent Expurgations of the Bible

Early scribal efforts to sanitize the biblical text were dilatory because the task was too great. Modern verbal vigilantes from time to time have sought to carry on the battle against crudity and vulgar language. The "authorized" English version of 1611 is replete with earthy language of Elizabethan times which disturbed genteel folk of the Victorian era. Since the text was not copyrighted, it was possible to alter it with impunity. One Dr. Edward Harwood in 1768 produced a Liberal Translation of the NT to "replace the bald and barbarous language of the old version." Harwood thought to allure the "young and gay" by the innocent stratagem of "modern" style, but what he offered was inflated pomposity carried to ludicrous extremes. In America, shortly after the Revolution, Mrs. Sarah Kirby Tremmer, anxious to protect her children and others' from bad language, deleted or obscured indecent expressions in the Sacred History to reduce the text by nearly half. Her commentary and notes made up for the loss by expanding the presentation to six volumes. Beilby Porteus, bishop of London, in 1796 supplied an index to lead the Bible reader to the good parts and away from the unedifying stuff by starring the best passages (sayings of Jesus, parts of Psalms and of Isaiah) and by marking with numerals 1 and 2 other parts fit to read. Unmarked parts, nearly half of the OT and some of the NT, were to be avoided. The Porteusian Index thus, without deleting or changing a word or line, was censorious of half the Bible. There was, of course, the danger that a curious or perverse reader could invert the system and concentrate on the unrecommended parts.

Noah Webster, after achieving fame for his dictionary of decent words, decided that some of the indelicate language of the KJV, especially words like "stink," "stones" (for testicles), and "whoring," required refinement. Webster's sanitized edition was endorsed by the president and faculty of Yale and used for a time by some of the New England clergy, but was gradually abandoned for the old vulgar version.

Recent years have seen a spate of new English translations, some with notable bent toward euphemism and others with more contemporary concern for plain language. There is always the danger that overweening efforts to be frank may conjure up crudities that are imaginary. The most bizarre example of this is NEB's blunder in Josh 15:18 and Judg 1:14, "she broke wind." After the death of the proponent of this impropriety, the deodorized revision "she made a noise" does little to enhance confidence in the judgment of revisers.

The Bible is replete with puns based on assonance and multiple entente and many of them, even when (perhaps only partially) understood, are difficult or impossible to convey in terse translation. Appreciation of this problem increases as more is learned about Semitic languages and literatures. Puns and serious humor, often very earthy, are a vital feature of the Bible and a challenge to coming generations of translators and interpreters. See HUMOR AND WIT.

Bibliography

Delcor, M. 1967. Two Special Meanings of the Word *yād* in Biblical Hebrew. *JSS* 12: 230–34.

Minkoff, H. 1989. Coarse Language in the Bible? *BRev* 5: 22–27, 44.

Perrin, N. 1971. The Assault on the Bible. In *Dr. Bowdler's Legacy. A History of Expurgated Books in England and America.* Garden City, NY.

Ullendorff, E. 1949. The Bawdy Bible. *BSOAS* 42: 425–56.

MARVIN H. POPE

BIBLE, STATISTICAL RESEARCH ON THE.

See STATISTICAL RESEARCH ON THE BIBLE.

BIBLICAL AUTHORITY.

See SCRIPTURAL AUTHORITY.

BIBLICAL CRITICISM.

The word "criticism" comes from the Gk verb *krinein,* which means to distinguish, decide, or judge. Biblical criticism therefore is the practice of analyzing and making discriminating judgments about the literature of the Bible—its origin, transmission, and interpretation. In this context, "criticism" has no negative connotation but, as in other fields, is designed to promote discriminating analysis and understanding. This entry contains two articles: one outlining the history of biblical criticism, and the other surveying specifically recent modern critical approaches to the NT. See also SCRIPTURAL AUTHORITY and THEOLOGY (BIBLICAL).

HISTORY OF BIBLICAL CRITICISM

As soon as oracles, teachings, and sacred narratives are written down in a religious community their authority is fixed and they inevitably become the object of criticism. The members of the community are bound to ask the meaning of obscure passages; they and their leaders are bound to discuss and decide on what the sacred texts entail for belief and practice; and they are bound to show how one sacred text is to be reconciled with another. As such, biblical criticism began even before the Bible was assembled in its current canonical form.

A. Ancient Criticism

The various canons of the OT and the NT are the result of criticism, as are the texts of those canons as they came to be standardized. The "Masoretic" Text of the OT was already fixed by the time the Qumran scrolls were collected (ca. 100 B.C.–A.D. 67), but there existed other texts, fragments of which were also found at Qumran, and the existence of which can be deduced from the LXX. The LXX canon is both longer and (at points) different in content from the Masoretic canon.

The NT canon was fixed as the result of criticism which rejected some gospels and provided reasons for accepting four gospels as sufficiently consistent to be regarded as harmonious. Clement of Alexandria's story that John's gospel provided a "spiritual" complement to the "bodily" Synoptic Gospels (Eus. *Hist. eccl.* 6.14.7) gives us a glimpse of the process of criticism that led to the acceptance of a fourfold gospel canon in opposition to attempts to argue for any one single gospel or a gospel harmony.

The story that Mark wrote down all that he remembered of Peter's discourses about things said and done by the Lord, but not in order, seems to embody a critical hypothesis to explain why Mark's gospel gave events in an order contradicting another authoritative order (probably that of John) (Eus. *Hist. eccl.* 3.39.14, 15). Gaius the Presbyter challenged John's gospel on grounds of its order (Commentary of Dionysius Bar-Salibi).

The authenticity of the Pastoral Epistles must have been discussed, since Marcion does not recognize them as part of his "Apostle" canon, and we know that the authenticity of Hebrews, the Catholic Epistles, and Revelation was disputed, being impugned and defended on the basis of critical arguments about style and content. Eusebius divided the books which claimed to be canonical into Recognized (four gospels, Acts, fourteen epistles of Paul, 1 John, 1 Peter, Revelation[?]), Disputed (James, Jude, 2 Peter, 2–3 John), Spurious (*Acts Paul, Shep. Herm., Apoc. Pet., Ep. Barn., Did., Gos. Heb.,* Revelation[?]), and heretical forgeries (*Hist. eccl.* 3.25.1–7). Both before and after the canonical limits were fixed, critical decisions were taken about a standard text as a result of comparing differing manuscripts or recensions; the "Alexandrian" and "Byzantine" texts of the NT are arguably the result of criticism.

The critical activity that settled standard canons and texts is largely hidden from us, only to be deduced from the results. The critical activity by which the authority of the agreed texts was maintained under questioning from the faithful for enlightenment or in the face of challenges from heretics or opponents is much more visible.

Philo of Alexandria preserved critical theories developed in Alexandria that defended the authority of the Pentateuch against charges that God was presented as though he were a human being with limbs and passions and against charges that he acted immorally and taught immoral actions. These theories conceded the charges and defended the Scriptures on the ground that they were speaking figuratively and allegorically. Christian theologians in Alexandria took over this device and extended it to the NT. The Antiochene school, itself heir to a more literal Jewish school of critics, insisted on the straightforward historical sense of the writings (Theodore of Mopsuestia).

The question of the authority in the Church of the OT and the law of Moses produced critical theories from the beginning. Jesus and Paul must have had theories about the question, and the NT contains both pronouncements on the problem and interpretative comments (Mark 7:19c: "Thus he declared all foods clean"). Paul's position is unclear, and Marcion put forward the critical theory that Paul's genuine writings had been tampered with by the addition of Jewish interpolations.

The Church had to defend the authority of the OT Scriptures against critical theories that argued they contained not only God's laws but laws solely due to Moses and the elders (the Valentinian Ptolemaus, *Letter to Flora,* Epip. *Pan.* 33.3–7; Holl 1.450–53; already labeled a sin in Judaism, *Ps.-Philo* 25.13). It is arguable though unlikely that Jesus had himself introduced this critical principle (Matt 19:8; Mark 10:5–6).

Ancient critics, like their modern counterparts, questioned received opinions about the authorship and integrity of canonical writings and tried to write a history of how they came to be composed and about the relationships in which they stood to each other.

For example, Dionysius, bishop of Alexandria (A.D. 247–65) and a pupil of Origen, argued that John the author of the Apocalypse could not be the apostolic author of the gospel of John and the First Epistle, adducing differences of form, style, syntax, ideas, as well as arguments based on historical probability in support of his case (Eus. *Hist. eccl.* 7.25).

Augustine in his *Harmony of the Gospels* argued that the gospels were written in the chronological order Matthew, Mark, Luke, and John; that only Matthew and John were by actual followers of Jesus; that Matthew was first written in Hebrew, the others in Greek; and that Mark's words are almost the same as Matthew's because he was an epitomizer of Matthew.

B. Renaissance Criticism

The foundations of modern biblical criticism were laid in the Renaissance with the recovery of knowledge of

Greek and the editing and printing of ancient sources. Historians could show that present practices were developments from more primitive customs, and the question was raised as to whether or not the present Church was truly faithful to the beliefs of the primitive Church. The Reformation, both a popular and a nationalist movement, took these humanist questions and turned them into a principle, that the Church should return to the sole authority of the primitive charters as contained in the Hebrew OT and the Greek NT. It rejected the authority of the LXX and the Latin Bible.

Luther used the doctrine of justification by faith alone as an instrument to deny apostolicity to the epistles of James, Jude, and Hebrews as well as to the apocalypse. Zwingli used philological arguments to question the Church's interpretation of the words of institution of the Lord's Supper.

Once the Bible was seen as the sole authoritative basis of the Church's life, biblical criticism designed to maintain and strengthen the position of the various churches that claimed this basis against other churches of the Reformation and against the Roman Catholic Church and heretics became a central and crucial activity. Ten new German universities were founded between 1527 and 1665 to provide for this need. Critics of the Reformed and Lutheran churches from without and within resorted for justification of their position to criticism of received scholarly opinions about the Bible. Unitarians questioned whether the orthodox doctrine of the trinity could be found in the NT, let alone in the OT.

The French Oratorian priest Richard Simon (1638–1712) turned the tables on the Reformation churches by arguing that Scripture alone was far too uncertain a basis for Christianity, unless there should also exist an authoritative teaching office in the Church. He published critical histories of the OT (1678, 1680, 1685), the NT (1689), the versions (1690), and the principal commentaries (1693), together with further observations on the texts and versions of the NT (1695) and a new French translation (1704). He questioned the Mosaic authorship of the Pentateuch. He was expelled from his order for his pains, but continued to press the Roman Catholic case against Protestantism.

Biblical criticism began to move emotionally outside the limits of church controversy after the disaster and devastation of the Thirty Years War in Europe and the Civil War in England. Scholars became disgusted at the seeming hairsplitting disputes about the meaning of Scripture which had, they thought, led to such bloody conflicts. Philosophers like Benedict Spinoza (1632–77) and John Locke (1632–1704) argued that a detached reading of the Bible as a book like any other book, which paid due attention to the original language and historical circumstances, would produce a tolerant and peaceful agreement about the essentials of a moral and spiritual religion.

Heterodoxy and dissent were tolerated in 18th-century Britain, or at least only mildly punished by loss of preferment and university teaching posts (but the universities were not very important, there being only two in England, four in Scotland, and one in Ireland). The ideas worked out and published in Britain were translated into German, where they were developed and refined in the score of Protestant faculties of theology which were to a large extent left free from state censorship so long as the teachers subscribed to the confessions and supported in public the established churches of the kingdoms and principalities the universities were founded to serve. The scholars justified their acquiescence in this restriction on the grounds that Jesus himself had accommodated his teaching about demon possession and the earthly kingdom of God to the false beliefs of his contemporaries. This is the theory of "accommodation" as it was propounded in England by Hugh Farmer (1714–87) and others.

These university scholars were left free to work out in great detail an all-embracing critical hypothesis which also came to them from England. According to this theory, the OT was the religious collection of the Jewish people and had no authority for Christians. Impartial study of the OT would show that an original spontaneous free national religion was cramped and restricted by priests who imposed detailed ceremonial laws on the people in order to get power over them, and who claimed special revelation from God. Similarly the NT, critically examined, showed that Christ preached the old original natural religion, which ecclesiastical authorities had overlaid with dogmas and religious practices. *Christianity* was *as old as the creation; the gospel* was *a republication of the religion of nature,* as the title of Matthew Tindal's famous anonymous treatise had it (1730).

Within this framework Thomas Morgan (d. 1743) put forward an elaborate theory of the history of the NT, which was to exert immense influence on biblical criticism. He argued that Jesus had died renouncing Jewish messianic ideas of the restoration of an earthly kingdom to Israel. Jesus' Jewish followers still adhered to the false conceptions Jesus had renounced. Paul, independently of them, preached Jesus as the savior of the world without distinction between Jew and gentile, and came into head-on conflict with Peter, James, and John. Peter made a pact with Paul, which he could not maintain. The Christian Jews prevailed, introduced angelic mediators, invocation of the saints, and prayers for the dead, and preached the coming violent overthrow of the Roman Empire and the establishment of their own eventual rule in all the earth. Under persecution, the two opposing wings of the Church were gradually reconciled when the gentile Christians found they too were persecuted as Jews. Together they set up a hierarchy in the Church to bind consciences, rule the universal Church, and give supernatural virtue to the two sacraments. Those who remained true to Paul's scheme were branded as gnostics. The NT was corrupted by the addition of passages suggesting Christ, the prophet of the only true natural religion, was the same being with the supreme God, and by the attribution of miracles to him (*The Moral Philosopher, In a Dialogue between Philalethes a Christian Deist, and Theophanes a Christian Jew,* 1737).

Morgan's theory was adopted by Johann Salomo Semler (1725–91), professor at Halle, and the teacher and provider of ideas for generations of biblical critics. The theory was fully worked out and applied to every book of the NT by Ferdinand Christian Baur (1792–1860).

There was endless room for speculation and for discovery once the principle was accepted that the foundation documents of the Jewish and Christian religions were produced in response to the needs of various parts and factions of the nation or Church, the history of which was reflected in the history of the books. The main hypotheses and discoveries can be set out briefly, in roughly chronological order.

The NT was extent in thousands of Greek and Latin manuscripts as well as in manuscripts written in other languages, and it was cited by Church Fathers from the 2d century onward. Johann Albrecht Bengel (1687–1752) suggested that these manuscripts could be sorted into regional recensions, one from Asia Minor and the other from Africa. Semler elaborated the division and laid down the basis of modern study of the text by positing three recensions: the Eastern, the Alexandrian, and the Western.

The Pentateuch of the OT contained palpable parallels, contradictions, and inconsistencies. The French professor of medicine and court physician Jean Astruc (1684–1766), while maintaining Mosaic authorship, argued that Moses had originally composed Genesis and the first part of Exodus in four columns, two of which were the long distinct documents distinguished by the names they used for God, Elohim and Jehovah. Later scribes jumbled the four columns together to make our canonical books (1753). Astruc's book was translated into German at Semler's prompting and provided with new notes (1783).

Johann Gottfried Eichhorn (1752–1827) picked up Astruc's suggestion and proposed that the Pentateuch was compiled from literary sources long after Moses' death. In 1805 Wilhelm Martin Leberecht de Wette (1780–1849) connected the book of Deuteronomy with Josiah's reform, and in 1835 Wilhelm Vatke (1806–82) argued that the Priestly strand (P) in the Pentateuch was later than Deuteronomy and belonged to the Exile. These clues were developed by Eduard Reuss (1804–91) and his pupil K. H. Graf (1815–69), and finally elaborated and canonized by Julius Wellhausen (1844–1918) in the form that two original sources, J and E, had been combined to make JE, to which D (Deuteronomy) was then attached; at the same time a four-covenant source was enlarged to make P (Priestly Codex), which was finally united with JE + D to make up our Hexateuch.

The view that Matthew was chronologically the first of the Synoptic Gospels was first challenged by Johannes Benjamin Koppe (1750–91) in a direct denial of Augustine, *Marcus non epitomator Matthaei* (1782). Eichhorn built on this to establish the two-source hypothesis: there existed one Aramaic source used in various forms by Matthew, Luke, and Mark, and another Aramaic source used by Matthew and Luke. Christian Gottlob Wilke (1786–1854) simplified this theory and argued that our Greek Mark was the source of Matthew and Luke (1838).

The fourth gospel was assumed to have been written by the apostle John until questioned by Edward Evanson (1731–1805) in 1792, and this position was generally accepted after Karl Gottlieb Bretschneider's careful examination of the arguments for and against (1820), despite the author's own later retraction. D. F. Strauss (1808–74) based his *Life of Jesus* (1835) on the assumption that he could disregard the gospel of John.

When the fourth gospel was set aside as a source of information about the historical Jesus, the way was open to exploit the relative silence of Jesus about his own status in the Synoptic Gospels to suggest he did not hold himself to be Messiah. His messiahship was at best implicit (F. C. Baur; Rudolf Bultmann [1884–1976]). The quest of the historical Jesus, brilliantly depicted by Albert Schweitzer (1875–1965), prompted a further quest for the history of the development from what Jesus taught to what was taught about Jesus. Julius Wellhausen in 1894 proposed a theory adopted by Johannes Weiss (1863–1914), William Wrede (1859–1906), and others that Jesus first became and was first confessed as Messiah after the resurrection, citing Acts 10:36; Rom 1:3–4. It was debated whether the titles Lord and Son of God were applied in their highest senses to Jesus by Jewish Christianity, by Hellenistic Jewish Christianity (Ferdinand Hahn; Martin Hengel), or by gentile Christianity (Wilhelm Bousset [1865–1920]). The silence of Jesus, however, may well have been part of his own belief that he was the Messiah.

Edward Evanson, who questioned the authority of John's gospel, also divided the epistles into two groups, the genuine 1st-century epistles (1–2 Corinthians; 1–2 Thessalonians; Galatians; 1–2 Timothy) and the spurious 2d-century ones (Romans; Ephesians; Colossians; Hebrews; James; 1–2 Peter; 1–2–3 John; Jude; the Letters to the Seven Churches in Revelation). University scholars moved more cautiously. Eichhorn observed that the Pastoral Epistles were not Pauline in form and eventually denied that Pauline authorship. By the 1840s the following epistles had been denied to Paul: Ephesians (Usteri and De Wette); Philippians (F. C. Baur); Colossians (Mayerhoff); 1 Thessalonians (Schrader); 2 Thessalonians (J. E. C. Schmidt, De Wette, F. H. Kern); Philemon (F. C. Baur), leaving Romans, 1–2 Corinthians, and Galatians as genuine. Bruno Bauer (1809–82) denied that Paul wrote these either. Christian Hermann Weisse (1801–70), a philospher rather than a professional biblical scholar, held that 1 Corinthians, 1 Thessalonians, and Philemon were genuine, and the rest had been interpolated to a greater or lesser extent.

C. Criticism in the Modern Era

By the end of the 19th century the archaeological discoveries and the recovery and decipherment of religious documents from Egypt and Mesopotamia revived interest in the religion of the Bible and its antecedents in the other religions of the Near East. Hermann Gunkel (1862–1932) showed that a universal religion of cosmic conflict between the forces of light and the forces of chaos and evil had pervasively influenced the religion of the Bible from Genesis to Revelation. He mocked many of the attempts to relate particular features of the books of the Bible to particular historical events. He distinguished various forms of writing, each of which was related to a cultic moment of importance, or to the religious needs of the people. His own work gave the decisive impetus to Sigmund Mowinckel (1884–1965), who in his study of the psalms (1921–24) argued that the psalms were cultic hymns and laments for religious use, a number belonging specifically to the annual New Year festival of the enthronement of Yahweh as king. Gunkel deeply influenced the form criticism of the NT through Martin Dibelius (1883–1947), Karl Ludwig Schmidt (1891–1956), and Rudolf Bultmann. The form critics regarded the gospels as collections of traditions, each of which was shaped according to a limited number of popular forms (parable, conflict story, apothegm, etc.), each form springing from a need in the religious life of the community. Bultmann advanced the study of the fourth gospel by drawing attention to the striking parallels to be found in the Mandaean liturgies translated by Mark Lidzbarski (1868–1928) and in the Syriac *Odes of Solomon*, discovered and published by James Rendel Harris (1852–1941).

The discovery of the Dead Sea Scrolls in 1947 led to renewed interest in Jewish writings of the period. The various theories about the direct influence of the Hellenistic mystery religions on the development of Christianity (Richard Reitzenstein [1861–1931], *Die hellenistischen Mysterienreligionen: Ihre Grundgedanken und Wirkungen* [1910]; Martin Dibelius, *Colossians* [1912]; Hans Lietzmann [1875–1942], *Messe und Herrenmahl* [1926]) and of the Hellenistic cults on christology (Wilhelm Bousset, *Kyrios Christos* [1913]) have always been open to the suggestion, raised by these very scholars, that the undoubted influence was mediated through Judaism. The point had already been made by Gunkel, *Zum religionsgeschichtlichen Verständnis des Neuen Testaments* (1903). Hans Dieter Betz (1931–) has argued for the strong direct influence of contemporary Hellenistic rhetorical forms upon the epistles of Paul (*Galatians* Hermeneia) and upon the epitome-like Sermon on the Mount, but it is open to ask whether here, too, any influence has been mediated through Judaism. The old 16th-century theories that the Essenes provided the soil in which the Christian Church grew up has received a new impulse, despite the sharp contradiction that seems to exist between the Qumran community and the Church on the strict keeping of the law and the rejection of the diseased and handicapped from the community.

Two further important effects of the discovery of ancient documents and inscriptions should be mentioned. Systematic exploration for papyri letters and documents, begun by Flinders Petrie (1853–1942) in 1889–90, made available Greek texts offering contemporary parallels to the Greek of the NT. The results were exploited above all by Adolf Diessmann (1866–1937), and are conveniently gathered up by J. H. Moulton and George Milligan into *The Vocabulary of the Greek Testament illustrated from the Papyri and Other Non-literary Sources* (1930). Papyri are still being found and published. The warm dry sands of Egypt that preserved the secular papyri also preserved papyri copies of books of the NT. The oldest papyrus is P52, a fragment of John 18, from the early 2d century. The existence of long sections of the NT from the 3d century has substantiated the 19th-century view that the Alexandrian text-type was in general more reliable than the other text-types and has led to a revival of the theory of B. F. Westcott (1825–1901) and F. J. A. Hort (1828–92) that this text-type was not so much an "edition" as a good transcript of the original canonical books (Gordon D. Fee [1934–]). However, the confirmation that the editing of the Alexandrian text was good editing does not prove it was not editing. The debate between critics who tend to decide readings on the basis of the text-type to which the reading belongs and "eclectic" critics who believe good and bad readings can be found in all text-types still continues.

The observation that the style of individual authors is stable and can be measured (G. Udny Yule [1871–1951]; W. C. Wake 1947) and the use of computers to make comprehensive and accurate counts of stylistic features like proportions of sentence lengths, variations of sentence length, and position of key words has led to new interest in the authorship of the Pauline epistles. G. H. C. Macgregor (1892–1963) and A. Q. Morton (1919–) defended F. C. Baur's judgment. A. J. P. (Anthony) Kenny (1931–) surveyed all the published tests and concluded no group of the twelve epistles of Paul stands out as containing epistles uniquely comfortable with one another or uniquely diverse from the surrounding context.

The sheer weight of critical scholarship and the seemingly endless theories about all aspects of the biblical texts has led to a sharp reaction, reminiscent of John Locke's reaction against biblical scholarship of the 17th century. The modern reaction has taken the form of "structuralism," based on the work of Ferdinand de Saussure (1857–1913) and Claude Lévi-Strauss (1908–). Structuralism endorses any disciplined and attentive reading of the text that displays the structure of the argument as it appears on the page, without reference to the history of the formation of the text or the history of the community responsible for its production. Structuralism is one facet of a larger movement in literary criticism (I. A. Richards [1893–1979]) to exclude historical considerations from literary appreciation. There is an element of self-deception involved in the enterprise, since we can scarcely exclude knowledge of detailed and specific historical theories from the apparatus we bring to the text. The structuralist answer to this charge is that the structuralist approach (being "synchronic," by which the "significations" of the text are imposed on the reader) can be practiced quite separately from the traditional critical approach (being "diachronic," by which human beings create the "significations") and that the two approaches may be kept in dialectical tension. Yet the structure of the text to which the reader thinks to submit is really the text already interpreted and read according to a critical theory inherited along with the text itself. The structuralist believes that certain basic human patterns form themselves into structures and express themselves in texts—a secularized version of the theory that the text is dictated by God.

There is no doubt that each of the books of the Bible has a history, and it is unlikely that the history of any but the shortest of them is as simple as that they were written by one man at one time to one recipient or set of recipients. Even in the simplest cases, knowledge of the history of the author could be illuminating. But if most books of the Bible are composite, which is widely agreed to be true except for the epistles of Paul (and why are they so different?), a knowledge of their history is all but essential.

Biblical criticism is unavoidable. The story of biblical criticism shows that even those expounders of the Bible who claim to be indifferent to theories about the history of the sacred texts, from the gnostic preachers of the 2d century to the structuralists of the 20th, have their own hidden historical explanations of how their texts came into existence and of how they are to be read. We do well to be conscious of the historical theories we in fact hold, to know something of their history, and to work to make them more adequate to the evidence.

Bibliography

Clements, R. E. 1985. The Study of the Old Testament. Pp. 109–41 in Smart 1985.

Genthe, H. J. 1977. *Kleine Geschichte der neutestamentlichen Wissenschaft.* Göttingen.

Grant, R. M. 1984. *A Short History of the Interpretation of the Bible.* 2d, rev. ed. Philadelphia.

Neil, S., and Wright, T. 1988. *The Interpretation of the New Testament 1861–1986.* 2d ed. New York.

O'Neill, J. C. 1985. The Study of the New Testament. Pp. 143–78 in Smart 1985.

———. 1988. A Sketch Map of the New Testament. *ExpTim* 99: 199–205.

Reventlow, H. Graf. 1984. *The Authority of the Bible and the Rise of the Modern World.* Trans. J. Bowden. Philadelphia.

Rogerson, J. W. 1985. *Old Testament Criticism in the Nineteenth Century.* Philadelphia.

Smart, N.; Clayton, J.; Sherry, P.; and Katz, S. T., ed. 1985. *Nineteenth Century Religious Thought in the West.* Vol. 3. Cambridge.

Wake, W. C. 1947. Sentence-Length Distribution of Greek Authors. *Proceedings of the Royal Statistical Society* 120: 336–47.

J. C. O'Neill

NEW TESTAMENT CRITICISM

Biblical criticism as it is practiced with regard to the NT can be presented according to the following outline:

A. Beginnings in the 18th Century
B. Text Criticism
C. Historical Criticism
D. Literary Criticism
E. Concluding Implications

A. Beginnings in the 18th Century

Modern biblical criticism began in the period of the Enlightenment. At that time the new methods of empirical science were applied to the study of all disciplines, including the Bible.

1. British Deists. Devoted to rationalism and natural theology, the Deists were opposed to supernatural religion. All religious truth, in their view, could be discerned in the order of nature and in accord with human reason. The earlier rationalists, especially John Locke (1632–1704), had believed supernatural revelation to be rational. Indeed, truths disclosed in the Bible could be proved by reason and supported by the evidence of fulfilled prophecy and miracles. The Deists set out to destroy these two foundations of revealed religion.

Anthony Collins (1676–1729) demonstrated that the prophecies of the OT could not be taken literally. Yet, if they were merely allegorical, how could these ancient predictions become solid ground for truth? Thomas Woolston (1669–1733) lampooned the NT miracles, when taken literally, as representing gross absurdity. Even the supreme miracle, the resurrection of Jesus, was a fraud which had been fabricated by the disciples of Jesus.

2. Continental Pietists. On the European continent, the study of the Bible had been dominated by the orthodoxy of the Protestant scholastics. The Bible, according to the orthodox, was a compendium of inerrant truths, taken down as divine dictation by God's inspired "pen men." In the face of this arid orthodoxy, the Pietists called for a vital reading of the Bible, attuned to its spiritual and practical message.

August Hermann Francke, who became the leader of the entire educational system at Halle, published *A Guide to the Reading and Study of the Holy Scripture* (1693). The purpose of this manual was to distinguish between the shell and the kernel of the biblical message—to go beyond the external to the inner meaning of the text. In the first part of the *Guide,* Francke stressed the literal, historical meaning of the Bible, insisting that the study of Scripture required careful attention to linguistic and grammatical detail. In the second part, he presented methods for detecting the deeper meaning. This required the reading of the Bible with a sense of spiritual feeling. The Pietists concluded that only those who possessed the spirit could understand the truth of the text.

Viewed side by side, the Deists and the Pietists represent two ways of interpreting the Bible which have influenced NT criticism ever since: an objective, rational reading; and a subjective, experiential reading. The former focuses on the text and its content; the latter is concerned with the interpreter.

3. Rise of Grammatico-Historical Criticism. In the middle of the century, new methods of linguistic and historical research were applied to the study of the NT. Johann August Ernesti, a noted classicist, published *Institutio interpretis Novi Testamenti* (1761). Like Francke's work, this was a manual of procedures for interpreting the NT. Ernesti, adhering to strict grammatical principles, insisted on the literal meaning of the text in its historical setting. He argued that the same methods used for the interpretation of any other ancient book should be employed in the study of the Bible.

Ten years later, Johann Salomo Semler raised the question of the authority and canonicity of the biblical books. In his *Treatise on the Free Investigation of the Canon* (1771), Semler asserted that the canon was a historical problem. The selection of the canonical books was a gradual historical process, and throughout the history of the Church different views of the content of the canon had prevailed. In Semler's opinion, some parts of the canon, e.g., the book of Ruth, were not relevant for Christians. Using historical research, Semler concluded that Revelation was not written by an apostle, that it did not witness to Christ, and that it should not be recognized as canonical. Semler's work broke the back of the biblicism of the old orthodoxy and opened up the NT for historical investigation.

The investigation of the authenticity of the NT books was pursued by Johann David Michaelis. In his massive *Introduction to the Scriptures of the New Covenant* (4th ed., 1788), Michaelis considered the historical setting of the individual NT documents. Attention was given to such questions as authorship, date and place of writing, recipients, and purpose—the concerns of historical or higher criticism. Using historical method, Michaelis concluded that most of the NT books were written by those to whom they have been traditionally ascribed. He drew a distinction, however, between reliable, nonapostolic writings (like Luke and Acts), and the inspired writings of the apostles. Michaelis concluded that Jude and Revelation were not apostolic and, by implication, neither inspired nor canonical.

4. Bible as Literature. In reaction to the growing historicism of the grammatico-historical method, some scholars approached the writings of the NT primarily as literature, G. E. Lessing (1729–81), the noted poet and dramatist, believed divine revelation to be progressive and continuing. Although revelation came through history, religious truth could not be established by historical argument. Between faith and history there was an unbridgeable chasm; the validity of faith could not be proved by historical fact.

J. G. von Herder (1744–1803), the eloquent court preacher at Weimar, wrote the sweeping *Outlines of a Philosophy of Man,* which traced the evolution of humanity from primitive beginnings. Revelation he saw as the evolutionary process of the education of developing humanity. All revelation was historical, and the Bible was the record of this progressive revelation which reached its zenith in the teaching of Jesus. Although the Bible was a thoroughly human book, it was not to be read the way the historical critics read it. Instead, one should see it as a poetic, aesthetic, literary expression.

5. Emergence of NT Theology. At the end of the century the results of grammatico-historical criticism were incorporated in a theological synthesis. J. P. Gabler, in his inaugural address at the University of Jena (1787), drew a sharp distinction between systematic and biblical theology. The latter he understood to be historical, constant, and normative. The task of systematic theology, on the other hand, was to take the results of biblical theology and translate them into doctrine and ethics. Although the NT spoke in language accommodated to the mythological views of an ancient people, it bore witness to eternal and changeless truths.

G. L. Bauer carried out Gabler's program in the form of his 4-vol. *Biblical Theology of the New Testament* (1800–2). Like his predecessors, Bauer believed the truth of the NT was of an order higher than that of the OT—that it presented the true biblical theology. He interpreted the NT according to empirical and rationalistic methods. The stories of the birth of Jesus he considered to be mythological legends, and the idea of inspiration, since it implied supernatural intervention, was itself a myth. Nevertheless, the NT used mythological expressions to convey universal ethical truths.

The history of NT criticism from the end of the 18th century through the first two thirds of the 20th is largely a recital of the Enlightenment themes with variations. Much of the 19th century, for example, was dominated by the work of F. C. Baur and the Tübingen School. Combining the results of the grammatico-historical method with a philosophy of history which had been articulated by Hegel, Baur proposed a theory of the historical development of early Christian history which could account for the origin and meaning of NT literature. Similarly, in the 20th century, Rudolf Bultmann (1884–1976) could develop a synthesis of historical criticism (including form and history of religions criticism), existentialist philosophy, and dialectical (Barthian) theology so as to provide a hermeneutical key for understanding early Christian literature.

B. Text Criticism

The purpose of text criticism (lower criticism) is to restore the original text. This purpose is problematic, since no autographs are available—no original manuscripts written by the NT authors. Instead, the critic is confronted with a vast collection of handwritten copies, well over 5000 manuscripts and fragments, no two of which are exactly alike.

The materials used in text criticism represent a variety of types. The oldest extant manuscript is a fragment of the gospel of John which can be dated in the early 2d century. Most of the earliest manuscripts are classified as papyri, because of the material (papyrus) on which they were written. These include such important examples as the CHESTER BEATTY and the BODMER PAPYRI. The major NT manuscripts are called uncial manuscripts because they are written in capital letters; these are usually copied on parchment and circulated in book or codex form. Among the most famous are Codex Sinaiticus and Codex Vaticanus, which can be dated in the 4th century. The large body of later Greek manuscripts are called minuscule manuscripts because they are copied in cursive handwriting.

Along with Greek manuscripts, text critics examine other sources. Translations (versions) of the Greek NT into Latin were made as early as the 2d century. The NT was available in other ancient versions, for example, Syriac and Coptic. The Fathers of the Church frequently quoted the NT in their writings; these patristic quotations provide text critics with another source of data. Early Christian lectionaries or liturgical texts include biblical citations which are also useful in the effort to restore the original text.

Although the novice is baffled by the mass of textual variants, the textual expert is able to use them in the classification and evaluation of manuscripts. The presence of common variants may indicate a common source. Variants have occurred through a variety of causes. Unintentional variants are caused by typical visual mistakes—repeating the same word (dittography), skipping to the next occurrence of the word (haplography). Sometimes variants are intentional: a copyist may attempt to "correct" a text or "improve" its theology, grammar, or style.

Modern text critical research was begun in the Renaissance. In 1515, Erasmus produced a Greek text on the basis of a very few manuscripts. Later editions of his text by Robert Etienne (called Stephanus) and Theodore Beza led to an edition produced by the publisher Elzevir in 1624, which became the standard text, the Textus Receptus. In the 18th century extensive collection and collation of manuscripts resulted in texts published by John Mill, J. A. Bengel, and J. J. Wettstein. Although these critics merely reproduced the Textus Receptus, each of them provided a new feature, a critical apparatus, which noted many textual variants. J. J. Griesbach actually published a revised text (1774–75), and carried further the work of Bengel in the classification of manuscripts according to their geographical origin.

In the 19th century text critical work produced significant results. C. Tischendorf was tireless in his search for textual materials. The 8th edition of his Greek NT (1869–72) contains the largest collection of variants available to the modern scholar. The British text critics B. F. Westcott and J. A. Hort published a Greek text (1881) which made use of their classification of manuscripts into geographical families: Western, Alexandrian, and Byzantine. Westcott and Hort also attempted to identify a Neutral Text (represented by Sinaiticus and Vaticanus) which they thought to be very close to the original. Today's student of the Greek NT usually sees a Nestle Text (the result of a series of editions begun by Eberhard Nestle in 1898 and recently carried on by Kurt Aland) or a text published by the United Bible Societies (edited by an international committee of text critics).

C. Historical Criticism

Recent NT criticism can be classified according to analysis which views the NT *either* as a document of history *or* as a body of literature. These two categories can never be completely separated, and some types of criticism make use of *both* historical *and* literary procedures. The difference is largely a matter of point of departure or emphasis.

The original purpose of historical criticism (higher criticism) was to achieve a historical understanding of the NT. To accomplish this, the NT documents had to be viewed in their historical and cultural context. The critics were concerned with historical events, and the literature of the NT was used in historical reconstruction. Actually, the reconstruction had two foci: the historical situation which the text described, and the historical situation of the author and recipients of the NT books. In regard to the former, attention was given to parallels in contemporary literature and the religious environment. Already in the 17th century John Lightfoot had traced the Jewish backgrounds of the NT. In regard to the historical situation of writing, attention was given to the traditional introductory questions: authorship, date, piece of writing, recipients—work already refined in the 18th century by Michaelis and his student, J. G. Eichhorn.

1. Religionsgeschichte. Usually translated "history of religions," this method was developed in the late 19th and early 20th centuries by the members of the *religionsgeschichtliche Schule.* The leading adherents of the "history of religions school" included Johannes Weiss, Wilhelm Bousset, Hermann Gunkel, and William Wrede. These scholars carried on the earlier concern to study the religion of the NT in its historical context; their approach was sometimes called the method of "comparative religion." In the view of these critics, the world of the Bible was a strange and distant world—a world wholly different from the modern world in language, world view, imagery, and symbols. The Lord's Supper, from this perspective, should be understood in the context of the mysterious Hellenistic cult meals, and the Christ of the early Christians should be perceived as the one confessed as the exalted lord of the cult.

Weiss developed the theory of "consistent eschatology." In his view, Jesus was at home in the setting of "late" Jewish apocalyptic religion. Jesus' proclamation of the kingdom of God, therefore, was an apocalyptic message which expected God's imminent, catastrophic intervention in history. Bousset, on the other hand, believed the essential teachings of Jesus to be in sharp contrast to the Jewish apocalyptic thought. The ultimate source of apocalypticism was to be traced to Babylonian mythology. According to Gunkel, early Christianity had been influenced by eastern religion (especially Babylonian) which had been transported through contemporary Judaism. Wrede argued that the historian should not interpret the NT as a document of systematic theology, but as a witness to the religious life and experience of the early Christians.

In later developments, the history of religions school gave increasing attention to Greek religion and the Hellenistic cults. Richard Reitzenstein, for example, thought the Greco-Roman world universally recognized a myth of a heavenly redeemer who descended to earth and returned to heaven, disclosing to humans the way of salvation. This "gnostic myth" was believed to serve as a pattern for expressions of early Christian christology like that found in Phil 2:6–11—a hypothesis important for Rudolf Bultmann's method of "demythologizing." Bultmann believed the message of the NT, the *kerygma,* was communicated through the mythological form of Hellenistic thought. The task of demythologizing was to distinguish the *kerygma* from the myth—to separate the true Christian proclamation from its mythological framework.

2. Form Criticism. Originally termed *Formgeschichte,* this type of criticism attempts to go behind literary criticism to the study of the oral tradition. Literary criticism, which had been investigating the *written* sources of the gospels, had concluded that Mark was the earliest. Wrede had shown, however, that Mark was not a historical record of the life of Jesus but an expression of the theological confession of the author. The quest for the historical Jesus, therefore, would have to go beyond the written material to earlier oral sources which could be identified and isolated in the existing written sources.

Influenced by Gunkel's form critical investigation of oral traditions and oral features of Genesis and the Psalms, three NT critics working independently at the end of World War I arrived at similar results. K. L. Schmidt concluded that the gospels were frameworks upon which smaller, independent units of oral tradition were hung. Martin Dibelius believed the individual units of oral tradition were shaped in accord with the practical needs of early Christian preaching. Rudolf Bultmann saw the origin and development of the units of traditions as related to more specific church concerns—worship, catechesis, paranesis.

All agreed that the earliest memories of Jesus (his sayings and stories about him) were circulated by word of mouth. The earliest identifiable witnesses of the words and deeds of Jesus had already come to confess him as Lord and Christ. As the stories about Jesus were circulated, they were shaped into forms according to principles of oral communication—miracle stories, parables, etc. As these stories were told and retold they took on additional details and emphases, and new stories were created to meet the ongoing needs of the believing community. The intent of the form critic was to find the *Sitz im Leben,* the "situation in life" where such oral forms originated and developed. Although some of the earliest oral units were thought to go back to Jesus himself, many of the traditional forms were created and shaped by the community itself. The evangelists were viewed by the form critics primarily as collectors or editors of these traditional units. The gospels were like a string of beads—a loose collection and arrangement of traditional data which bore little relation to the actual history of Jesus.

In more recent times, form criticism has been applied to other sections of the NT. Here, however, research has been directed toward literary forms, so that form criticism becomes an aspect of literary criticism. In analyzing the Pauline letters, Robert Funk, Nils Dahl, and their students attended to the form and structure of the epistle as a literary genre. Study of the common papyrus letters of the Hellenistic period exhibited a variety of types of epistles (e.g., the letter of introduction)—epistles composed according to patterns prescribed by literary handbooks.

Like these letters, the epistles of Paul largely conform to the Greco-Roman conventions of letter writing. In structure, they follow the order: salutation, opening thanksgiving, paranetic sections, and closing. Within the letters conventional formulae, for example, expressions of exhortation, can be detected. Some scholars have analyzed the NT epistles according to the rubrics of classical rhetoric. H. D. Betz, for instance, identifies Galatians as an "apologetic letter" (letter of defense) which displays the rhetorical patterns of a courtroom defense (Betz *Galations* Hermeneia).

3. Tradition Criticism. Form criticism has been supplemented by tradition criticism or, as it is sometimes called, the history of the transmission of traditions. This type of criticism also considers literary expressions of tradition. Its intent is to analyze the origin and development of units of tradition which are cited within the literature of the NT. For example, Paul presents hymns (Phil 2:6–11), confessions (1 Cor 8:6), and liturgical formulae (1 Cor 11:23–25) which were recited in the pre-Pauline churches. Attention is given to the way NT authors, Paul, for example, use and adapt the traditional material to their own purposes. Some scholars (e.g., J. M. Robinson, H. Koester) trace the course of a unit of tradition as a trajectory moving from its origin through various stages of writing to its final redaction.

4. Concern with Orality. Oral tradition has recently been studied in the light of research applied to oral culture and folklore. From this perspective, the transition from oral to written tradition is seen as a movement not of continuity (as the form critics supposed) but of discontinuity. Oral communication, it is observed, is different from written, since speaking involves presence and immediacy. Written communication, on the other hand, is external, abstract, objective. In applying their method to the study of the gospels, advocates of this theory of orality (e.g., Werner Kelber) note that Jesus taught orally and was heard by a rural, nonliterary people. When oral tradition is put into writing, a fundamental distortion results. As Paul says, "The letter kills."

5. Sociological Interpretation. This modern approach picks up the form critical concern with the *Sitz im Leben* and subjects it to sociological analysis. Sociological interpretation makes use of various methods of the social sciences, especially sociology and cultural anthropology. The method was anticipated in the early 20th century by members of the "Chicago school," particularly S. J. Case and S. Matthews, and in Germany by A. Deissmann.

Critical of a narrow theological reading of the NT, the sociological interpreters note that the early Christians were not university-trained theologians, but ordinary people who lived in families and religious communities. The Hellenistic society in which they participated was largely urban (Meeks) and marked by social and economic stratification. G. Theissen argues that the schisms at the Lord's Supper in Corinth represent economic and social classes in the Church, not factions debating the nature of the eucharist.

Sociological interpretation has two main approaches: the descriptive and the theoretical. According to the descriptive approach, scholars study the customs and institutions of Hellenistic society and detect parallels in the NT. For example, they investigate the status and function of the slave in the Greco-Roman world, and ask how this information illuminates Paul's metaphorical use of the term "slave." According to the theoretical approach, scholars make use of models which sociological thinkers have devised. For example, they ask what Weber's analysis of the "charismatic leader" reveals about Paul's style of leadership.

Especially popular with biblical interpreters is the perspective of the sociology of knowledge. This approach asks how the people of the NT period perceived the social reality in which they lived, that is, their "social world." Moreover, the modern interpreters also share a social world—a perception of reality which determines their own understanding of the NT and its social context. Interpretation of the NT requires modern interpreters to move from their own social world into that of the ancient people whom they are trying to understand.

D. Literary Criticism

In contrast to methods which are primarily concerned with history, literary criticism focuses on the written text. Historical methods are sometimes involved, however, since the NT is an example of ancient literature, and the interpretation of the NT has a history. Early works in literary criticism dealt with vocabulary, grammar, style, and rhetorical figures.

1. Source Criticism. In the 18th century literary criticism was essentially source criticism. Attention was directed primarily to the problem of the sources of the Synoptic Gospels. Two main theories prevailed: the gospels depended ultimately on lost, primitive sources; or the gospels were somehow interdependent. According to the first hypothesis, the lost source(s) consisted of oral tradition, a variety of written fragments (Schleiermacher), or a primitive (usually Aramaic) *Urgospel* (Eichhorn).

According to the second hypothesis, one of the Synoptics made use of at least one of the others. Various possibilities were suggested, but the two most popular solutions advocated either the priority of Matthew or the priority of Mark. According to Owen and Griesbach, the earliest gospel was Matthew, and Mark used both Matthew and Luke in the writing of his "shortened" gospel. The countertheory of the priority of Mark was defended by Wilke and Weisse. Lachmann, who supported this view, also believed Matthew and Luke used a lost written source (Q) as well as Mark.

The resulting "two-document" hypothesis was advocated by noted scholars like Holtzmann and became dominant by the beginning of the 20th century. More detailed analysis resulted in a four-document hypothesis: besides Mark and Q, Matthew and M and Luke used L (Streeter). Recently, the Griesbach hypothesis has been revived and vigorously defended (Farmer), although the majority of scholars continue to support Markan priority.

Source criticism has also been applied to other sections of the NT. In regard to Acts, scholars have given attention to the "we-sections"—sections where the author shifts to the use of first person plural. These are sometimes seen to represent a diary source or perhaps a travel itinerary. Other scholars detect evidence of sources related to important early Christian centers, for instance, an Antioch source. Source criticism in regard to the epistles frequently deals with the problem of integrity. 2 Corinthians, for example, is thought to be a composite of two, or perhaps as many as six, fragments of epistles. The literary dependence of 2 Peter on the epistle of Jude is widely recognized.

2. Redaction Criticism. Assuming the results of form, tradition, and source criticism, redaction criticism is concerned with the final composition; it is sometimes called "composition criticism." Thus, redaction criticism is a type of literary criticism which employs the findings of historical criticism. Assuming form critical results, it asks how Mark used the oral tradition he had received. Assuming the results of source criticism, it asks how later gospels employed earlier gospels. The method was anticipated by F. C. Baur, who noted the *Tendenz,* the theological tendency, which was revealed in the work of a particular NT author. Similarly, Wrede noted that Mark did not simply use his sources to produce a historical record, but employed them in service of a theological expression.

Three scholars working independently developed the method. Willi Marxsen coined the name *Redaktionsgeschichte* (1954). He believed Mark adapted his sources to the situation of the Church in 66 C.E., and used them in support of the expectation of the imminent parousia of Christ. G. Bornkamm investigated Matthew's use of Mark and concluded that Matthew shaped the tradition to present his own christology and ecclesiology. H. Conzelmann believed Luke presented and arranged the traditional material so as to depict a history of salvation consisting of three periods: the era of Israel, the time of Jesus, and the period of the Church.

Redaction criticism directed attention from the small units of tradition to the finished literary product. As a result, the role of the Church in the formulation of the tradition was reduced, and the work of the gospel writers as literary authors and theologians was enhanced.

3. Genre Criticism. Closely related to form and redaction criticism, genre criticism is the study of literary genre, that is, the identification and analysis of the literary type or classification to which a particular text belongs. Sometimes called *Gattungsforschung* (genre research) or *Gattungsgeschichte* (genre history), this method studies the form, style, and content of particular types of literature. In general, the method involves the classification of biblical material in relation to types of literature represented in Hellenistic writings. The method assumes that the classification of a document provides a key to its interpretation. For instance, the recognition that Paul wrote specific letters to particular situations, rather than general epistles, is crucial to interpreting his writings.

In NT research, genre criticism has been most active in the study of the gospels. The fundamental question is: to what genre do the gospels belong? Although some scholars believe the gospel was a new genre created by the early Christians (see GOSPEL GENRE), others find a parallel in the Hellenistic ARETALOGY—the account of the mighty deeds of a heroic miracle worker or divine man. A document like Q, which consists almost wholly of teachings, is often classified as belonging to a genre of literature called the "Sayings of the Sages" (J. M. Robinson and H. Koester).

Acts is widely recognized as an example of Hellenistic historical writing, evidenced, for example, by the author's conventional use of a preface and speeches. However, Acts also displays parallels with the Hellenistic romance, with its fondness for travel narratives involving narrow escapes, like the account of Paul's shipwreck.

In studying Revelation, critics give attention to the genre of the apocalypse. This type of literature, popular in the period of the NT, is marked by typical features: the disclosure of future events by a mediator to a seer (usually the pseudonymous author) who is often taken on a heavenly journey and shown cosmic visions—all presented in symbolic form (cf. Mark 13). According to some recent scholarship, Revelation should be classified as belonging to the genre of the letter or epistle.

4. The New Literary Criticism. This sort of criticism attempts to view the NT exclusively as literature. It represents a revolt against the traditional historical critical method. For the old method, the concern was to reconstruct the history in which the text was written and to discern the meaning the text had in that historical situation. For the new criticism, the text is not to be used as a device for historical or theological reconstruction; the text itself is the sole object of investigation. Once a text has been written, it has a life of its own, independent of its original setting. Thus the text is autonomous; it has its own meaning; it must be interpreted exclusively on its own terms. The original intention of the author, so dear to the historical critics, is for the new criticism unimportant. A Pauline epistle, for instance, may convey meaning which Paul did not intend.

The critic, therefore, is concerned with what is called the "world" of the text. By this term, the new criticism means the perception of reality which the text assumes. A fable, for example, may assume a world in which animals talk. Whether or not the world of the text corresponds to the actual world in which the author lived, or the world in which the interpreter works, is of no moment. According to a favorite metaphor, the text should not be seen as a window which reveals something outside. That is, the text should not be viewed as a means for describing something else, for instance, history or doctrine. Instead, the text must be seen as a mirror which has its meaning locked in. That is, the interpreter must be concerned exclusively with the meaning which is held within the text itself.

Like the older historical critics, the new literary critics believe the Bible is to be understood by the same methods which are used for other literature. They study the text as a whole, and thus are concerned with genre. Consequently, the new criticism has certain affinities with genre criticism, though its concerns are broader. The new critics also analyze style and literary forms within the text—

sentence structure, metaphor, etc. Attention is especially given to the function that the various literary techniques perform within the pattern of the whole literary document. From the perspective of the new criticism, a book like Revelation can be viewed as a work of art—a dramatic presentation, using liturgical and symbolic forms of expression.

5. Rhetorical Criticism. This method is closely related to the new literary criticism. Its origin can be traced to a lecture by James Muilenberg (1968) calling for an approach which would go beyond form criticism. Rather than restricting research to the small units of tradition, rhetorical criticism looks at the work as a whole, the final literary product. In distinction from the new criticism, rhetorical criticism is concerned (as is redaction criticism) with the personal aspects of the author's thought. Moreover, rhetorical criticism is concerned with the context, including those concepts which writer and reader share. Thus, it is interested in the social and cultural relationship between author and reader. The rhetorical techniques and arrangements are analyzed in terms of their function in the author's argument. For example, when H. D. Betz (*Galations* Hermeneia), following classical rhetoric, classifies Galatians as an "apologetic letter," he interprets Paul's account of his call, the Jerusalem conference, and the events of Antioch (1:12–2:14) as "narratio"—the statement of facts upon which the whole defense is to be built.

6. Narrative Criticism. Like the new criticism and rhetorical criticism, narrative criticism is opposed to the historicizing and theologizing of the text. In particular, it intends to restore the narrative features of the Bible. The narrative elements of the gospels and Acts are obvious, yet historical critics have been inclined to sacrifice narrative in the quest for the historical Jesus or in the effort to reconstruct the history of the early Church. Instead, these narratives must be seen as story, with plot, characters, and outcome.

Narrative criticism, however, involves a broader meaning. For some scholars, narrative is a fundamental category of human existence; it has ontological significance. People live in a narrative world, that is, they have a perception of their participation in reality which is story-like. The overarching vision of reality can be described as a symbolic universe—a concept which gives meaning to the smaller stories in which all persons participate.

This larger meaning indicates that narrative criticism is important for nonnarrative or discursive texts. The letters of Paul, for example, assume a narrative substructure, that is, Paul's religious perception is informed by a sacred story—the story of God's action with people which reaches its climax in the story of Jesus (R. Hays). When Paul writes to address the particular problems of churches, he gives expression to this basic narrative. Paul has a story himself, and the relation of this story to the larger story provides his personal meaning. Each of his letters has a story—a plot which involves Paul's previous relation to the recipients of the letter, the expected reception of the letter, and the readers' response.

Narrative criticism does not ignore the importance of historical events. The narrative substructure presupposes the life of Jesus, and Paul's story is related to his own historical experience. The story of each letter is related to a chronological sequence of events, though the poetic sequence by which Paul tells the story within the epistle may be different. Indeed, history is story-like. The writing of history is not the exact reiteration of the past but a process which involves selection, plotting, and interpretation. History is story.

7. Reader Response Criticism. Closely allied to narrative criticism is reader response criticism. See also READER RESPONSE THEORY. This kind of criticism focuses on the role of the reader. The reader, from this perspective, must be differentiated from the critic. The critic reads a text out of the tradition of criticism and views the text as an object for critical analysis. The reader, like a child listening to a story or a person captivated by a novel, is the servant of the text.

Reader response criticism moves beyond these observations to more sophisticated methodology. For instance, it draws a distinction between the real reader and the implied reader. The real reader is the flesh-and-blood person who actually reads a text; the implied reader is the reader the author images when writing the text. Similarly, there is a real author (the actual writer) and the implied author (the writer the reader images when reading the text). In the process of reading, the real reader is manipulated by the implied author to react as, and become, the implied (or ideal) reader. Other participants are envisaged, such as the omniscient narrator, that is, the teller of the story who, in the imagination of the reader, knows everything.

Reader response criticism notes that reading is temporal and linear. Reading is not static but moves through the text in a sequence of time. This temporal, sequential process involves anticipation, reflection, and dialogue. The writer of the text uses devices like repetition for the education of the reader. Thus doublets in a text (for example, the two accounts of miraculous feeding in Matthew) create anticipation and encourage assent. At the same time, minor changes in the second account alert the reader to additional meanings. This temporal and linear quality of reading displays a similarity to oral communication. Just as a participant in a conversation follows a line of discussion through a sequence of time, so a reader follows the words and sentences of a text though an ongoing temporal process.

8. Structuralism. Like the new criticism, structuralism is not primarily interested in history or theology communicated through the text. The object of research is the deep structures which are encoded within the text itself. The concern is with the linguistic structure of the text, not with message the language conveys. According to structuralists, there is no salvation outside the text.

Structuralism is a method of understanding which involves a combination of linguistic theory and anthropological research (Claude Lévi-Strauss). According to the structuralists, human reality is marked by deep structures, that is, unconscious mythic patterns of meaning which have ontological significance. Structuralism believes the human brain operates according to certain structures and these structures correspond to reality. These deep structures are encoded in texts, and the task of structural exegesis is the decoding of texts, the disclosing of the structures. In the main, the structures are binary or dichotomous—contrasting opposites, like life and death.

In the study of literature, structuralism gives attention to the synchronic as well as the diachronic dimensions of the text. The diachronic can be seen as a linear, temporal sequence, while the synchronic structures are vertical, the structures beneath the surface which are present at any moment in the sequence. Like a musical score, texts have both melody (diachronic progression) and harmony (synchronic pattern). These synchronic patterns constitute paradigms of meaning—universal forms of expression which provoke understanding at the deepest level. The structuralists are much concerned with the significance of language (not mere speech) which involves a system of signs (semiotics), that is, patterns of words and sentences which constitute a whole linguistic expression. Applied to narratives, structural exegesis is concerned with narrative structures. The parable of the Good Samaritan, for example, assumes a structure which has such features as an actor or sender (the Samaritan), a recipient (the wounded man), opponents (the robbers), helpers (the innkeeper).

9. Canonical Criticism. Assuming the results of form and redaction criticism, canonical criticism is concerned primarily with the text in its final form. Emphasis is placed on the function of the canon as Scripture in the ongoing community of faith. Like literary criticism, canonical criticism is critical of traditional historical criticism's historicizing of the Bible.

The title "canonical criticism" was coined by J. A. Sanders. According to Sanders, canonical criticism has two main interests: the canonical process, and canonical hermeneutics. The canonical process is the history of the writing and selection of canonical books. The entire process, from oral tradition through writing, editing, and collecting, takes place in the context of the believing community. Study of this process displays both stability (setting boundaries to canonicity) and flexibility (plurality within the canonical boundaries). Throughout the process, the community of faith functions at every stage. What earlier tradition thought to be canonical may be found to be canonical by later tradition for different reasons.

Canonical hermeneutic involves the investigation of how canonical texts are interpreted in the ongoing development of the tradition. This hermeneutic observes the way older traditions are adapted to new situations. According to Sanders, canonical hermeneutic is theocentric. The Bible is a monotheizing literature which witnesses to God's action as creator and redeemer working through human sinfulness.

Brevard Childs dislikes the phrase "canonical criticism," since it appears to present a method alongside other types of criticism. For him, recognition of the centrality of the canon is the essential approach to understanding Scripture. The development of the canon is not a postapostolic achievement; canonicity (the concern with the norm of the gospel) is implicit in the production of the NT from its earliest (oral) beginning. However, the meaning of the NT at the time of its historical origin does not have theological priority, for the canon functions theologically as witness to Christ as Lord, as revelation, throughout the history of the Church. By implication, the Bible can only be fully understood within the community of faith.

E. Concluding Implications

Looking back over this methodological variety, one may wonder what methods are most appropriate. Many contemporary interpreters adopt an eclectic method. Norman Petersen, for example, employs a creative synthesis of social, literary, and narrative criticism in a way which informs the historical aspects of the text. The choice of method(s) can best be made in response to the questions which the interpreters bring. If they are primarily concerned with the history which the text describes, they will use methods effective for reconstructing history. If they are primarily concerned with the literary significance of the text, they will use methods effective for literary analysis. This survey suggests that the Enlightenment model of historical criticism has become increasingly problematic. The variety of critical proposals indicates a current quest for a new paradigm which has yet to be realized.

Bibliography

Baird, W. 1977. *The Quest of the Christ of Faith: Reflections on the Bultmann Era.* Waco, TX.

Beardslee, W. A. 1970. *Literary Criticism of the New Testament.* Philadelphia.

Childs, B. S. 1985. *The New Testament as Canon.* Philadelphia.

Collins, J. J., ed. 1979. *Apocalypse: The Morphology of a Genre.* Semeia 14.

Detweiler, R., ed. 1985. *Reader Response Approaches to Biblical and Secular Texts.* Semeia 31.

Doty, W. G. 1973. *Letters in Primitive Christianity.* Philadelphia.

Farmer, W. R. 1976. *The Synoptic Problem: A Critical Analysis.* Dillsboro, NC.

Funk, R. W. 1966. *Language, Hermeneutic, and Word of God.* New York and London.

Hayes, J. H., and Holladay, C. R. 1982. *Biblical Exegesis: A Beginner's Handbook.* Atlanta.

Hays, R. B. 1983. *The Faith of Jesus: An Investigation of the Narrative Substructure of Galatians 3:1–4:11.* SBLDS 56. Chico, CA.

Johnson, A. M., ed. 1979. *Structuralism and Biblical Hermeneutics.* Pittsburgh.

Kelber, W. H. 1983. *The Oral and the Written Gospel.* Philadelphia.

Kennedy, G. A. 1984. *New Testament Interpretation through Rhetorical Criticism.* Studies in Religion. Chapel Hill and London.

Kümmel, W. G. 1972. *The New Testament: The History of the Investigation of Its Problems.* Trans. S. M. Gilmour and H. C. Kee. Nashville and New York.

Malina, B. J. 1981. *The New Testament World: Insights from Cultural Anthropology.* Atlanta.

McKnight, E. V. 1969. *What Is Form Criticism?* Philadelphia.

Osiek, C. 1984. *What Are They Saying About the Social Setting of the New Testament?* New York and Ramsey, NJ.

Patte, D. 1976. *What Is Structural Exegesis?* Philadelphia.

Perrin, N. 1969. *What Is Redaction Criticism?* Philadelphia.

Petersen, N. R. 1978. *Literary Criticism for New Testament Critics.* Philadelphia.

———. 1985. *Rediscovering Paul: Philemon and the Sociology of Paul's Narrative World.* Philadelphia.

Reventlow, H. Graf. 1985. *The Authority of the Bible and the Rise of the Modern World.* Trans. J. Bowden. Philadelphia.

Robinson, J. M., and Koester, H. 1971. *Trajectories through Early Christianity.* Philadelphia.

Sanders, J. A. 1984. *Canon and Community.* Philadelphia.

Soulen, R. N. 1981. *Handbook of Biblical Criticism.* 2d ed. Atlanta.

Spivey, R. A. 1974. Structuralism and Biblical Studies: The Uninvited Guest. *Int* 28: 133–45.

William Baird

BIBLICAL SCHOLARSHIP, JAPANESE.

This entry consists of two articles surveying scholarship on the OT and NT in Japan.

OT SCHOLARSHIP

A. The Dawn

The period from the late 19th century to 1910 was a time of pioneering work as well as of frustration for Japanese biblical scholars. At least two pioneers earned Ph.D. degrees, but the circumstances did not allow them to continue study in Japan. The only exception was Y. Sacon (1865–1944). Having studied the biblical languages in 1890–1906, he developed a translation of the Bible from the original languages and published his works from 1905 through 1942. Other works in this period included introductions to the OT, OT theology, and a translation of the Apocrypha. With a gifted, strong personality, K. Uchimura (1861–1930) made clear the essential meaning of the Bible through his expositions at his own Non-Church Bible Study group and through a journal. Uchimura not only influenced intellectuals, but he also produced quite a few biblical scholars who in time emerged as leaders.

B. The Formative Period (1920–45)

As early as 1899, the new impact of the Tübingen school of academic OT study was felt in Japan, and the German style of OT analysis gradually prevailed over the Anglo-Saxon type. Having studied the "science of religion" and OT studies in Berlin and Leipzig, T. Ishibashi (1886–1947) published an introduction to the OT (1922) and a history of Israelite religion and culture (1923). Against the background of dialectical theology, Z. Watanabe (1885–1978), who had been an advocate of the critical study of the OT history and literature based on the theories of Wellhausen, after studying at the Pacific School of Religion, Berkeley, California, in the early twenties, began seriously to reconsider the relationship between historical-critical study of the Bible as literature and the canonical claim of the Bible as the word of God in the Church. He had a unique methodology of biblical interpretation which eventually culminated in his trilogy entitled *The Doctrine of the Scriptures* (1949–63). Watanabe first maintained that a sharp distinction should be made between a historical-critical or genetic study of the Bible—how the text developed—and a canonical or holistic study of the Bible—what the text is. He also insisted that an appropriate methodology should be established in accordance with the nature of the Bible as canon, as long as one reads the Bible as the rule of faith and life and not as historical books. Furthermore, he held that the concept of *Gestalt* or configuration can be adapted from phenomenology to canonical interpretation only at the place where the canonicity of the Bible is acknowledged and where one participates in the faith of the historical Church that created the Bible as canon. For him, canonical interpretation should pay due regard to the very location of the books of the Bible within the canon.

In this period, K. Baba (1892–1985) edited the first dictionary of the Bible (1934) and later assumed the editorship of a concordance (1959) and a new dictionary of the Bible (1971). More specific studies were done by several scholars. Y. H. Sacon (1906–   ) was the first to engage in Palestinian field archaeology under W. F. Albright in 1935–36. Having studied in Scotland and Germany, J. Asano (1899–1981) had a keen interest in OT thought and its relevance to Japanese culture and society. The Society for OT Study in Japan was formed in this period (1933).

C. The Period of Establishment and Development

After returning to Japan in 1945 from his study in Germany (1935–45), M. Sekine (1912–   ) broke fresh ground in OT study by introducing the German Alt-Noth-Von Rad school of OT analysis to Japan. With his acute interest in M. Weber's sociology of religion, his gifted intellect, his competent knowledge of jurisprudence and philosophy, and his broad and keen interest in new scholarly developments in the world, M. Sekine is now building his own unique outlook on the OT. His approach can be designated either as "intellectual history" or as the "sociology of literature." Sekine seeks to develop a synthesis of synchronic-literary and diachronic-sociohistorical levels with the aid of such scientific tools as philology, literary studies, sociology, and philosophical-ideological studies.

Along with several other colleagues, Sekine founded the Japan Biblical Institute in 1950 and has been its foremost representative. He is an editor of *AJBI,* which publishes in European languages. K. Nakazawa (1915–   ) has published solid and detailed studies on the Suffering Servant (1954) and Second Isaiah (1962).

The internationalization of Japanese scholarship may be seen in the papers read at the International Society meetings, in increasing number of contributions to international journals, *Festschriften,* and dictionaries, as well as in the books published by A. Tsukimoto. F. Kohata, and S. Sekine. Participation in the international meeting of the Society led to a collection of articles (Ishida, ed. 1982).

On Akkadian and Mesopotamian studies, J. Kikuchi, I. Nakada, A. Tsukimoto, and K. Watanabe are active in international circles. For Ugaritic and Hebrew linguistics, D. T. Tsumura is the most noted and productive. In the historical field, both Y. Ikeda and T. Ishida are noted in the scholarly world. In literary studies, K. K. Sacon and Y. Suzuki are to be noted. The former is developing his own method of literary structural analysis. In the intellectual-historical fields, K. Namiki is producing results comparable with those of M. Sekine. In the historical-theological field, K. Kida is to be mentioned. In 1987, the New Common Bible, a cooperative of Catholics and Protestants, appeared; K. Kida, Sacon, M. Ohta, K. K. Dacon, M. Takahashi, and M. Wada were heavily involved in this project.

Bibliography

A representative sampling of Japanese scholars and their (European-language) works may be found in *AJBI,* ed. M. Sekine and A. Satake. This publication has appeared annually since 1975 and will be sent upon request to those who write to the Japan Bible Society, 5-1, 1-chome, Ginza, Tokyo, 104 JAPAN.

Important books published in Japanese have been reviewed in the Book List since 1974. Selected books and articles have been abstracted in *OTA* since its first volume (1978).

Ikeda, Y. 1977. *The Kingdom of Hamath and Its Relations with Aram and Israel.* Diss. Jerusalem.
———. Solomon's Trade in Horses and Chariots in Its International Setting. Pp. 215–38 in Ishida, ed. 1982.
Ishida, T. 1977. *The Royal Dynasties in Ancient Israel. BZAW* 142. Berlin.
———. 1982. Solomon's Succession to the Throne of David—A Political Analysis. Pp. 175–87 in Ishida, ed. 1982.
———. 1985. Solomon Who Is Greater than David—Solomon's Succession in 1 Kings I–II in the Light of the Inscription of Kilamuwa, King of Y^{c}DY-Sam^{c}al. *SVT* 36: 145–53.
Ishida, T. ed. 1982. *Studies in the Period of David and Solomon and Other Essays.* Winona Lake, IN.
Jouzaki, S. 1956. The Secondary Passages of the Book of Amos. *Kwansei Gakuin University Annual Studies* 4: 25–100.
Kida, K. 1973. *Die Entstehung der prophetischen Literatur bei Amos.* Diss. Munich.
Kumake, F. K. 1980. *The Temple Sermon: Jeremiah's Polemic against the Deuteronomists.* Diss. New York.
Nakada, I. 1974. *Deities in the Mari Texts.* Diss. New York.
———. 1982. Two Remarks on the So-called Prophetic Texts from Mari. *AcSum* 4: 143–48.
Nakazawa, K. 1982. The Servant Songs—A Review after Three Decades. *Orient* 18: 65–82.
Nishimura, T. 1966. *Sagesse et royauté: Les Aspects sapientiels aux origines de la royauté en Israel.* Diss. Strasbourg.
———. 1979. Un mashal de Qohelet 1, 2–11. *RHPR*, 605–15.
Odashma, T. 1985. *Untersuchungen zu den vordeuteronomistischen Bearbeitungen der Heilsworte im Jeremiabuch.* Diss. Bochum.
Sacon, K. K. 1972. Isaiah 40:1–11—A Rhetorical-Critical Study. Pp. 99–116 in *Rhetorical Criticism.* PMTS 1. Ed. J. J. Jackson and M. Kessler. Pittsburgh.
———. 1982. A Study of the Literary Structure of "The Succession Narrative." Pp. 27–54 in Ishida, ed. 1982.
Sekine, M. 1962. Erwägungen zur hebräischen Zeitauffassung. *SVT* 9: 66–82.
———. 1973. The Subdivisions of the North-West Semitic Languages. *JSS*, 205–21.
———. 1977. Wie ist eine israelitische Literaturgeschichte möglich? *SVT* 29: 285–97.
———. 1982. Lyric Literature in the Davidic-Solomonic Period in the Light of the History of Israelite Literature. Pp. 1–11 in Ishida, ed. 1982.
Sekine, S. 1984. *Redaktionsgeschichtliche studie zum Tritojesajabuch.* Diss. Munich.

KIYOSHI K. SACON

NT SCHOLARSHIP

A. Prewar Developments

In 1873 the Meiji government removed the public notices proscribing Christianity. A little more than a decade later, the Japan Bible Society published the first complete Japanese translation of the Bible (1887). This was called the *motoyaku* ("original translation"), and an amended translation of the NT, issued in 1917, was called the *kaiyaku* ("revised translation"). (The second complete translation appeared in 1954 as the *kōgoyaku* ["colloquial translation"], and a third, the *Shin Kyōdōyaku Seisho* [New Interconfessional Translation of the Bible], was published in 1987.) A full-scale Bible dictionary, the *Seisho Daijiten,* was published in 1934 (a revised version appeared in 1971). In 1941, K. Kurosaki produced a NT concordance listing Gk terms with references to the revised NT translation of 1917 (a complete concordance to the Bible appeared in 1959, keyed to the colloquial translation of 1954).

Although they were not NT specialists, several people played important roles in shaping NT biblical scholarship in Japan. Among these were E. Kashiwai, author of *Kirisutokyō Shi* (*History of Christianity* [1914]; K. Ishiwara, whose 1934 *Kirisutokyō Shi* was revised and reissued in 1972 in two separate volumes; K. Sano, author of *Shito Pauro no Shinpishugi* (*The Mysticism of the Apostle Paul* [1935]); and S. Hatano, author of *Genshi Kirisutokyō* (*Primitive Christianity* [1965]).

Following them came trained NT scholars like T. Matsumoto, K. Tominomori. S. Murata, and others who introduced historical and theological studies from the West to seminaries and theological colleges in Japan. Not least among these early scholars was S. Yamaya, the first person whose works ranged over almost the whole field of NT studies. Among his works are an introduction to the NT, a two-volume study of the origin of Christianity, a book on NT theology, and five volumes of translations and commentaries on the Pauline epistles. Also, the influence of Y. Kumano on the Japanese church and its theology has been enormous. Though his primary interest lay in systematic theology, he was an outstanding theological exegete of biblical texts, playing a role in Japan comparable to that of Karl Barth in Europe.

B. Postwar Developments

World War II prevented Japanese NT scholars from keeping up with developments in NT studies in the West, but afterward a number of specialists worked diligently to make up for this lost interaction. Individuals who helped bring Japanese NT studies up to date include I. Takayanagi, author of *Fukuinsho Gairon* (*Introduction to the Gospels* [1951]) and *Iesuden Kenkyū* (*A Life-of-Jesus Study* [1951]), M. Takemori, author of *Shinyaku Seisho Tsūron* (*Introduction to the NT* [1958]) and editor of *Iesuden Kenkyū wo Megutte* (*Life-of-Jesus Research* [1970]), J. Matsuki, author of *Rōmabito e no Tegami, Honyaku to Shakugi* (*The Letter to the Romans: Translation and Exegesis* [1966]) and *Shinyaku Shingaku I* (*NT Theology* I [1972], and G. Maeda, author of *Shinyaku Seisho Gaisetsu* (*Introduction to the NT* [1956]).

In the 1950s and '60s, NT scholars translated the works of many Western scholars into Japanese, especially in the area of life-of-Jesus research (e.g., the works of Bultmann, Dibelius, Stauffer, Jeremias, Cullman, Dodd, Hunter, both Mansons, Taylor, and others). The scholarly distinction between the historical Jesus and Christ of the kerygma became an issue of great importance to the churches, for unless they clung to the historical revelation they would lose not only their Christian identity but also the necessity for mission—an easy temptation in a land where Shinto, Buddhism, and Confucianism have helped to shape a cultured and moral society. In the 1960s, Japanese NT scholars took special interest in redaction criticism, sociological approaches, and neo-literary criticism, methods which led to a number of original approaches to the study of the gospels and their traditions. In the 1970s and '80s, the works of Käsemann, Bornkamm, Conzelmann, Marxsen, Brown, Strecker, Stuhlmacher, Betz, Trocmé,

Theissen, Hengel, Martyn, and others also appeared in Japanese.

The same period saw the beginning of a number of original studies by Japanese NT scholars. Among such studies are T. Hirano's *Iesu to Kami no Kuni* (*Jesus and the Kingdom of God* [1971]) and Y. Magaki's *Yokane Fukuinsho no Kirisutoron* (*The Christology of the Fourth Gospel* [1984]. These works, though published after the 1950s and '60s, reflect the scholarly concerns and methods of those years.

A Japanese synopsis of the first three gospels, the *Fukuinsho Idō Ichiran* (1951), was prepared by T. Tsukamoto, based on his own translation of the Gk texts. A revised edition, a colloquial version of Tsukamoto's translation, was published by his student Y. Hirasawa in 1983.

In connection with NT Greek, T. Kanda wrote an excellent grammar, the *Shinyaku Seisho Girishiago Nyūmon*, published in 1956. This has become the new standard, taking the place of the handy but elementary NT Greek grammars produced at an earlier stage. A full-scale NT Greek dictionary has yet to appear, though there are several concise ones.

T. Hirunuma has been a leader in the field of textual criticism, publishing a monthly journal, *Studia Textus Novi Testamenti*, since September 1966. His recent book, *Shinyaku Honmon Gakushi* (*History of NT Textual Criticism* [1987]), gives a good introduction to the field, and an earlier book, *Shinyaku Seiten no Purosesu* (*The Process of Formation of the NT Canon* [1972]), provides a brief history of how the NT writings were collected and raises some problems with regard to canonization. In the recently published *Shinyaku Seisho Seiten no Seiritsu* (*The Shaping of the NT Canon* [1988]), seven scholars from the fields of NT studies and church history teamed up to describe the process of NT canonization from the days of the earliest church to the period of the church councils. S. Kawashima wrote on the NT; T. Aono on the Apostolic Fathers; S. Arai on the gnostic interpretation of biblical writings; Y. Itani on Marcion and Paulinism; T. Ōnuki on Justin Martyr, Tatian, Irenaeus, and Tertullian; N. Miyatani on canonization in the Western church; and T. Mikoda on canonization in the Eastern church and the decisions of the church councils.

During the last two decades, some excellent commentaries have appeared, striving to match the standard set by publications like HNT and NIGTC. A. Satake published a commentary on Philippians in 1969, another on Galatians in 1974, and his two-volume commentary on Revelation in 1978–89. K. Tagawa issued the first volume of a controversial commentary on Mark in 1972, and S. Arai the first volume of his commentary on Acts in 1977. M. Yamauchi's commentary on Philippians (1987) has also been well received.

C. The Current Situation

Recent work in the field of gospel studies has focused particularly on redaction criticism. For example, A. Ogawa's *Matai*, (a study of Matthew's theology (1984), is a superb example of the application of redaction criticism to Matthew. An earlier popular edition of this work, entitled *Kyūyaku no Kanseisha Iesu* (*Jesus the Fulfiller of the Old Covenant* [1983]), was published as the first volume of a redaction criticism series on the four gospels. The others include S. Kawashima's redaction critical study of Mark, entitled *Jūjika e no Michi Iesu* (*Jesus on the Way to the Cross* [1984]); M. Miyoshi's study of Luke, *Tabizora ni Ayuma Iesu* (*Jesus' Lonely Journey* [1984]); and T. Ōnuki's study of John, *Yo no Hikari Iesu* (*Jesus the Light of the World* [1984]). To this series a fifth volume was added, S. Arai's study of the gospel of Thomas, *Kakusareta Iesu* (*The Hidden Jesus* [1984]). Miyoshi, mentioned above, has produced a number of excellent studies of the Synoptic Gospels, several of which are contained in his *Chiisaki Mono no Tomo Iesu* (*Jesus the Friend of the Least of These* [1987]).

With regard to Johannine studies, there are on the one hand scholars like Y. Ibuki, who is interested in a philosophical and hermeneutical interpretation of the Fourth Gospel. On the other, there are those like K. Matsunaga and K. Tsuchido, who are interested in applying redaction criticism methods to this gospel. Matsunaga made use of redaction criticism methods in his recently published *Hitorigo naru Kami Iesu* (*Jesus the Monogenēs Theós* [1987]) and is currently writing a commentary on John's gospel. H. Kayama has recently published a redaction criticism study of Acts, entitled *Shito Gyōden no Rekishi to Bungaku* (*History and Literature of the Acts of the Apostles* [1986]).

Unfortunately, in comparison with gospel studies, there has not been much published recently in the area of Pauline studies. A. Satake, who made his debut in NT studies with a book on Revelation, has published a substantial work called *Shito Pauro, Dendō ni Kaketa Shōgai* (*The Apostle Paul: A Life Committed to Evangelism* [1981]). Some of his articles on Paul and Paul's writings may be found in his *Shinyaku Seisho no Shomondai* (*NT Issues* [1977]). S. Matsunaga published *Karada to Rinri* (*Body and Ethics* [1976]), a study of the "body concept in the Pauline letters, and T. Aono has written a number of recent articles dealing with Paul's theology.

With regard to other fields of research, A. Kawamura is noteworthy for his ongoing contributions to the study of the letter to the Hebrews, and M. Yamauchi's monograph *Fukkatsu, sono Denshō to Kaishaku no Kanōsei* (*The Resurrection: Its Traditions and the Possibility of Interpreting the Event* [1979]) is a work of considerable importance. In the field of NT history, G. Hata, taking over where H. Niimi left off, has finished translating the complete works of Josephus. These have been published in 20 volumes under the general title *Yosefusu Zenshū* (1975–84). Hata is now working on Eusebius' *Historia Ecclesiastica* and has published three volumes to date (1986, 1987, 1988). Together with L. H. Feldman, Hata is coeditor of a four-volume bilingual Josephus-research series: *Josephus and the Jewish War*, *Josephus and Christianity*, and *Josephus-Hellenism-Hebraism*, vols. 1 and 2. All four volumes appeared in English, and the first two were published in Japanese in 1985. With Feldman, Hata is also coeditor of *Josephus, Judaism, and Christianity* (1987), the Japanese version of which is now in preparation.

Two academic associations should be mentioned. The Japan Biblical Institute was founded immediately after World War II. Its *Annual* has been published regularly in Japanese since 1962 and in a separate English-German version since 1975. Members of the Japan Biblical Institute translated the Dead Sea Scrolls into Japanese under the title *Shikai Bunshō* (1963), and the OT and NT noncanonical writings into Japanese in a 9-volume series called *Seisho*

Gaiten Giten (*Biblical Apocrypha and Pseudepigrapha* [1975–82]). The Japan Society of New Testament Studies has published its own annual journal, the *Shinyakugaku Kenkyū,* since 1973.

Perhaps the most significant issue confronting NT scholars in Japan today is the christological question. In the main, four views compete for attention. K. Tagawa, in his book *Genshi Kirisutokyōshi no Ichi Danmen: Fukuinsho no Seiritsu* (*One Aspect of the History of Early Christianity: The Rise of "Gospel" Literature* [1967]), applied redaction criticism to the gospel of Mark and demonstrated a radical approach to the reconstruction of the historical Jesus. In his view, the Jesus of Mark 1–13 (following Trocmé, he sees these chapters as the original Mark) is a mere man, but a man who befriended the oppressed and sought to liberate them from every kind of demonic oppression, whether social, political, or religious. Angrily opposed to every human authority and establishment, Jesus was basically an anarchist, deliberately seeking the destruction of Judaism as a religious system. The disciples, however, misunderstood his intentions. At the time Mark wrote, they were forming a new religious establishment, this time with Jesus at the center. Mark wrote his gospel to protest against this "rereligionization" of Jesus. The task of the follower of Jesus today, Tagawa maintains, is to "dereligionize" the life and death of Jesus, to live out Jesus' anger, to destroy Christianity.

S. Arai, known for his research on the Nag Hammadi literature, has written two books that relate to the gospels: *Iesu to sono Jidai* (*Jesus and His Times* [1974] and *Iesu Kirisuto* (*Jesus Christ* [1979]. The former focuses on the historical Jesus, the latter on the Christ of faith. In both books he applies a sociological/existential analysis to the gospel traditions. Like Tagawa, Arai holds that the core of the healing miracle traditions is the behavior of Jesus that liberated socially marginal people from social, political, and religious oppression. But what he sees in the miracle stories and in the kerygma of the "death and resurrection of Jesus Christ" is a mythological expression of the response that Jesus' followers made to his existential challenge. Jesus himself was a man who loved the oppressed as his neighbors and treated them without discrimination. He is "savior" in the sense that he challenged his disciples, and challenges his followers across the centuries, to experience the self-understanding that comes from living with love and fairness in all human relationships. In essence, Jesus calls his followers to existential authenticity through social and political commitment. If Christianity offers this same experience today, there is no reason to call for its destruction.

S. Yagi published his *Shinyaku Seisho no Seiritsu (The Formation of the NT)* in 1963, which divides NT thought into three types: (1) Hebraic, a *heilsgeschichtlich* and eschatological interpretation of the life and death of Jesus; (2) Hellenistic-gnostic, a dualistic interpretation; and (3) agape, representing the experience of oneness with God. According to Yagi, the agape type, though found in relatively late NT strata, is actually closest to the orientation of the historical Jesus since this is preserved in his fragmentary sayings or logia. All his activities can be explained by this agape. All NT thought represents, accordingly, some degree of modification of the agape experience that formed the substance of Jesus' relationships with his neighbors and disciples. This agape experience became explicit for them only through the experience of the resurrection. Consequently, the "religiosity" that led to this experience and interpretation is not peripheral but central. It is noteworthy that Yagi indicates in this book the phenomenon of similar interpretations in other religions, particularly Buddhism. Yagi's Jesus appears, therefore, as the bearer of agape to his contemporaries and to those who meet him in the NT. But one must distinguish between agape and its bearer. For Yagi, Jesus is neither agape nor its sole bearer. He is one bearer of agape among others.

K. Matsunaga's *Rekishi no Naka no Iesuzō* (*Jesus in History*) appeared in 1987 (fully revised and enlarged in 1989). He argues that the uniqueness of "gospel" literature, as revealed by redaction criticism, rests on the fact that each evangelist, while relying on received traditions about the Jesus of the past, presents at the same time the Jesus Christ of the present and the Jesus Christ of the future (i.e., in his second coming). The portrayals of Jesus in each gospel are composed, therefore, of these "three-dimensional" pictures. This three-dimensional portrayal, he maintains, belongs to the essential nature of "gospel" literature and derives from the nature of worship in the earliest churches. Through preaching and sacrament, the earliest churches not only recalled *(anamnesis)* the Jesus of the past but also worshipped Jesus Christ as the Lord of the present and as the One who is to come. This raison d'être of the Christian Church was and is repeated orally in worship and verbally in the gospels. The Jesus traditions took shape primarily in relation to this *anamnesis* and therefore retain a certain amount of historical information. Moreover, the overall picture of Jesus attributed to a given evangelist and his milieu by redaction criticism could not have been a free invention either of the evangelist or of his faith-community, for it was controlled by this *anamnesis.* So even after the sayings of Jesus and the so-called Jesus traditions have been examined critically, Jesus remains unique. He was one who not only proclaimed the coming of the kingdom (community) of God but also embodied what it meant for him in his time and place to live the kingdom life. The resurrection of Jesus entailed for his followers a religious experience in and through which it was revealed to them that the Jesus who had spoken so frequently of the kingdom of God was now to be recognized as the one through whose life and death the kingdom had become available. This is the Christ the Church is responsible to proclaim. If its language is partly mythological, this is not necessarily unfortunate, for myth is the symbolic language humans use when they speak of religious reality. Absolute demythologization means absolute dereligionization.

A concise (but dated) list of bibliographic references can be found in Tomonobu Yanagita's *Japan Christian Literature Review* (1958).

KIKUO MATSUNAGA

BIBLICAL THEOLOGY. See THEOLOGY (BIBLICAL), HISTORY OF.

BICHRI (PERSON) [Heb *bikrî*]. BICHRITES. A Benjaminite of the period of the united monarchy, designated eight times as the father of Sheba, a dissident from the hill country of Ephraim who inspired a rebellion against David (2 Sam 20:1–22). This constant reference to Sheba as "the son of Bichri" may serve to connect the Sheba uprising with the line of Saul, also a Benjaminite. While Bichri seems to be understood as a personal name, it is a gentilic formation, making it likely that the phrase "son of Bichri" refers, not to an individual, but to a clan. Dalglish (*IDB* 1: 437) suggests that this clan should be identified with Benjamin's second son, BECHER (Gen 46:21; 1 Chr 7: 6, 8). In v 14 the MT speaks of "the Berites" (*habbērîm;* note the use of the definite article identifying a clan rather than an individual) as a group which followed Sheba in revolt against David. This is probably a mistake for "the Bichrites" and is so translated in the RSV. McCarter (*2 Samuel* AB, 428) suggests that "the Bichrites" *(habbikrîm)* is the correct reading, following LXX[B]. If this is the same group which is everywhere in the chapter related to Sheba, then "Bichri" clearly refers to a clan rather than to a person. This would also serve to indicate the small scale of Sheba's influence, as he is only able to gather support from his own clan.

Siegfried S. Johnson

BIDKAR (PERSON) [Heb *bidqar*]. Officer *(šālîš)* who accompanies Jehu when he slays Joram, king of Israel (2 Kgs 9:25). It is unlikely that a *šālîš* was the third man in a chariot, as has been conjectured in the past. Where the term is used, it seems to suggest an officer of high rank (2 Kgs 7:2, 17, 19; 10:25; 15:25). The term may stem from the root *šlš* (three) to indicate that the officer was "of the third rank." Bidkar is a personal name in spite of the Syr, which translates it "son of stabbing." (See Gray *Kings* OTL; Hobbs *2 Kings* WBC.)

Bibliography

Mastin, B. A. 1979. "Was the *šālîš* the Third Person in the Chariot?" VTSup 30: 125–54.

Pauline A. Viviano

BIGTHA (PERSON) [Heb *bigtāʾ*]. See MEHUMAN; BIGTHAN.

BIGTHAN (PERSON) [Heb *bigtān, bigtānāʾ*]. Guardian of the entrance to King Ahasuerus' private chambers (Esth 2:21, 6:2) (cf. Herodotus 3.77, 118, 120; Loretz 1967; Rüger 1969). With his associate TERESH, he plotted to assassinate Ahasuerus but was exposed by Mordecai (Esth 2:22–23). Such conspiracies by officials close to the king are well attested, Xerxes I (= Ahasuerus?) supposedly having been killed as the result of one (D. S. 11.69.1–2; Ctes. *Persika* 29).

Bigthan (LXX *gabatha*) perhaps renders the Old Iranian name **Bagadāna* "gift of god," a name attested in Aramaic papyri from Egypt in the 5th century B.C.E. (*CAP,* no. 17, 1—*bgdn;* reading uncertain) and in the Persepolis Elamite texts (Hallock 1969: no. 1793, 4). For discussion of this name and other proposed etymologies, see Grelot (1972: 467 sv bgdn); Mayrhofer (1973: §8.192; 8.218); Hinz (1975: 54–55); Kornfeld (1978: 101 sv BGDN). Alternatively, Bigthan may be a form of *bigtāʾ* (Esth 1:10), which is perhaps a short form of the Old Iranian name **Baga-dāta* (Hinz 1975: 59). This name is attested in long form in the Aramaic papyri from Egypt (*CAP,* Nos. 3, 24; 5, 18; 66, 6) and the Persepolis Elamite texts (Hallock 1969: 672 sv Bakadada), as well as in Akkadian, Demotic, and Greek. The supposed short form is attested in the Persepolis Elamite texts (Hallock 1969: nos. 1990,16; 767,2). On the name **Baga-dāta,* "god given," see Mayrhofer (1973: §8.191; 8.192), Hinz (1975: 54–55, 59), Kornfeld (1978: 101 sv BGDT).

Bibliography

Grelot, P. 1972. *Documents araméens d'Egypt.* LAPO. Paris.
Hallock, R. T. 1969. *Persepolis Fortification Tablets.* OIP 92. Chicago.
Hinz, W. 1975. *Altiranisches Sprachgut der Nebenüberlieferungen.* Wiesbaden.
Kornfeld, W. 1978. *Onomastica Aramaica aus Ägypten.* Vienna.
Loretz, O. 1967. *šʿr hmlk*—"Das Tor des Königs (Est 2, 19). *WO* 4: 104–8.
Mayrhofer, M. 1973. *Onomastica Persepolitana.* Vienna.
Rüger, H. P. 1969. "Das Tor des Königs"—der königlische Hof. *Bib* 50: 247–50.

Peter Bedford

BIGVAI (PERSON) [Heb *bigway*]. Etymology uncertain. Noth maintains Persian derivation (*IPN,* 64). From Elephantine (Papyri 30.1; 32.1), a governor of Judah (410–407 B.C.E.) is named Bagohi (Aram *bgwhy*).

1. One of the leaders of the group of returnees from Babyonian exile who is listed along with Zerubbabel in Ezra 2:2 = Neh 7:7 = 1 Esdr 5:18. One name has apparently been dropped from the Ezra list, for those in Nehemiah and 1 Esdras include twelve leaders in what is probably a symbolic representation of all Israel throughout the entire postexilic period (Ackroyd *Chronicles, Ezra, Nehemiah* TBC, 219; Coggins *Ezra and Nehemiah* CBC, 18). For further discussion, see AKKUB.

2. Head of a family of Babylonian exiles who are listed as returnees under the leadership of Zerubbabel and others (Ezra 2:14 = Neh 7:19 = 1 Esdr 5:14) and later under Ezra (8:14 = 1 Esdr 8:40). The leader of the clan affixed the family name to the covenant document of Nehemiah in Neh 10:17—Eng 10:16. For further discussion, see ATER.

Chaney R. Bergdall

BILDAD (PERSON) [Heb *bildad*]. One of Job's three "friends" who had traveled to condole with and comfort him (Job 2:11). On his place of origin, see SHUAH. In the literary cycle of debates that forms the core of the book of Job, Bildad is consistently the second friend to speak in each round: in chap. 8 (round no. 1) he addresses the subject of God's justice, concluding that God will not reject a "blameless man" (v 20; cf. 1:1); and in chap. 18 (round no. 2) he reiterates the conventional platitude that "the light of the wicked is extinguished" (vv 5–6; cf. Job's response in 21:17). In chap. 25 Bildad's speech is surprisingly brief (only 5 verses), leading virtually all scholars to conclude that the present text of Job suffers from some dislocations in round no. 3 of the debate. For example, some scholars suggest that Job's words in 26:5–14 (which echo much of the same imagery in chap. 25) are actually parts of Bildad's now fragmented third speech. See JOB, BOOK OF.

Given the Arabian locale and the Neo-Babylonian setting of the book of Job (see UZ), it seems unlikely that the name is derived from Amorite **yabil-dāda* (Albright 1928) or Nuzi-Akkadian *bil-adad* < *apil-adad* (Speiser 1929). The name Bildad is most probably a *qtll*-formation. Since no names from the root *bld* are known, either in Aramaic, Canaanite, or epigraphic ancient Arabian, it is possibly a corruption or a phonetic variant (due to the frequent *r/l* interchange) of the name **birdād,* attested for Sabaic and among the Qedarites in the 7th century B.C. (Knauf 1985: 6, n.28).

Bibliography

Albright, W. F. 1928. The Name of Bildad the Shuhite. *AJSL* 44: 31–36.
Knauf, E. A. 1985. *Ismael.* ADPV. Wiesbaden.
Speiser, E. A. 1929. On the Name Bildad. *JAOS* 490: 360.

ERNST AXEL KNAUF
GARY A. HERION

BILEAM (PLACE) [Heb *bilʿām*]. A levitical town located in the territory of Manasseh (1 Chr 6:70). It is probably a variant form of IBLEAM, and therefore to be associated with Tell Belʿameh (M.R. 177205).

BILGAH (PERSON) [Heb *bilgâ*] Var. BILGAI. Bilgah appears as a name for an individual only in 1 Chronicles and Nehemiah. 1 Chronicles identifies a priest Bilgah as a contemporary of David. Three priestly Bilgahs appear in Nehemiah. Yet the presence of Bilgah in the reign of David represents an anachronism on the part of the Chronicler. Two of the three references in Nehemiah occur in artificial lists constructed by the editor of the book (see nos. 2 and 4). Historically, the name seems to represent a priestly clan from Judah during the Persian period (see no. 3). Literarily, the name functions to legitimate the Chronicler's portrayal of the history of Judah.

1. A priest who received the fifteenth position in the priestly order of the temple during the reign of David (1 Chr 24:14). Rather than a historical person from the time of David, Bilgah seems to represent a priestly family within the Second Temple period that the Chronicler has projected back into the time of David as an individual (see no. 3 below). The exact date of the priestly list of 1 Chr 24:1–19, where Bilgah appears, remains debated. See GAMUL (PERSON). The stylistic evidence of the list, however, seems to link the list to the time of the composition of Chronicles (ca. 385 B.C.E.).

2. A priest who purportedly returned from exile in Babylon with Zerubbabel (Neh 12:5). The absence of Bilgah from the list of Ezra 2 = Neh 7 and the artificial nature of the list of Neh 12:1–7 (Williamson *Ezra-Nehemiah* WBC, 359–62) suggest that Bilgah arises in Neh 12:5 as a result of the editorial reworking of the Nehemiah Memoir, rather than reflecting a historical person involved in the return. The Chronicler further legitimates the priestly structure of his day by including Bilgah in the return with Zerubbabel, and thereby involved this priestly family in the *golâh* community from the resumption of the cult.

3. The family name of the priest Shammua from the time of Jehoiakim the high priest (ca. 500–450 B.C.E.; Neh 12:18). The presence of Bilgah as a family name for a priestly group most likely originated in an authentic historical source (Williamson *Ezra–Nehemia* WBC, 358–61). The exact provenance of Bilgah remains unknown and conjectural, although he must have lived before 475 B.C.E. His absence from authentic lists of returnees in Ezra–Nehemiah suggests that his inclusion in the *golâh* community occurred after the return of the exiles from Babylon. His presence early in this period may indicate that Bilgah represents either a priestly clan that remained in Judah throughout the 6th century B.C.E. or a clan that began their priestly function after the return. If so, the Chronicler's anachronistic inclusion of Bilgah in other important events of the history of the temple represents the attempt to legitimate the priestly structure of the Chronicler's era.

4. A priest who signed a document that forbade intermarriage between Judeans and other ethnic groups, ensured the observation of Sabbath, and provided for the maintenance of the temple and its staff (Neh 10:9—Eng 10:8). While some commentators have thought the signees reflect authentic historical persons from the time of Nehemiah (Rudolph *Esra und Nehemia* HAT, 173–75), the names of Neh 10:2–27—Eng 10:1–26 seem to represent "an artificial literary compilation, based on other material in Ezra and Neh" (Williamson *Ezra–Nehemiah* WBC, 329). "Bilgah" functions anachronistically in Nehemiah 10 in order to emphasize the involvement of all Judah in reforms initiated by Nehemiah, and thereby legitimates Nehemiah's policy.

JOHN W. WRIGHT

BILGAI (PERSON) [Heb *bilgay*]. A postexilic priest and a signatory to the code of Nehemiah (Neh 10:8). He is identified by some scholars with Bilgah (Heb *blgh*), who is listed as one of the chief priests who returned to Jerusalem with Nehemiah (Neh 12:5, 18; see M. Newman *IDB* 1: 438; Brockington *Ezra, Nehemiah, Esther* NCBC, 179). If this is so, then Bilgai (meaning "cheerfulness") may be a hypocoristic shortening of Bilgah (Brockington NCBC, 179).

FREDERICK W. SCHMIDT

BILHAH (PERSON) [Heb *bilhâ*]. Handmaid of Rachel and mother of Dan and Naphtali (Gen 30:3–8; 1 Chr 7:13). Bilhah was given to Rachel by Laban (Gen 29:29) as a wedding gift. Like Sara some years earlier (Gen 16:2), when Rachel discovered her barrenness, she bestowed Bilhah upon her husband Jacob that she might bear children in Rachel's place. This practice was common and has been verified by the Nuzi documents. There a childless wife gave to her husband a secondary wife who might bear a son, who would become the heir and would be regarded as the son of the true wife (Gordon 1940). Since the Nuzi texts date from the patriarchal period and represent Hurrian customs, it can be assumed it was not an unusual practice for Sara, though quite strange in view of Mosaic law and later practices. For Rachel, Bilhah bore Dan and Naphtali (Gen 30:3–8; 35:25; 46:23–25). Later, Reuben, Jacob's firstborn by Leah, lay with his stepmother Bilhah (Gen 35:22) and consequently lost his father's blessing (Gen 49:3–4). For further discussion, see Speiser *Genesis* AB, 226–27.

Bibliography

Gordon, C. H. 1940. Biblical Customs in the Nuzi Tablets. *BA* 3: 1–12.

Selman, M. J. 1976. The Social Environment of the Patriarchs. *TynBul* 27: 137–47.

Speiser, E. A. 1930. New Kirkuk Documents Relating to Family Laws. AASOR 10: 1–73.

———. 1936. One Hundred New Selected Nuzi Texts. AASOR 16: 7–168.

Weeks, N. 1975. Man, Nuzi and the Patriarchs. *AbrN* 16: 73–82.

JOEL C. SLAYTON

BILHAH (PLACE) [Heb *bilhâ*]. Simeonite town within the Judean Negeb (1 Chr 4:29). See BAALAH #2.

BILHAN (PERSON) [Heb *bilhān*]. The name of two men in the OT.

1. A clan name in the genealogical clan list of Seir the Horite. This person is referred to in Gen 36:27 (where some mss of the Sam. Pent. have *bilʿān*) and in the matching genealogy in 1 Chr 1:42 as the first son of the clan chief EZER, and is thus a grandson of Seir. The ending -an on the name Bilhan and that of his brothers ZAAVAN and JAAKAN may reflect a tribal or clan designation or a dialectical identifier.

2. A son of JEDIAEL, and grandson of Benjamin in the genealogical clan list in 1 Chr 7:10. He is the father of JEUSH, BENJAMIN, EHUD, CHENAANAH, ZETHAN, TARSHISH, and AHISHAHAR. The suggestion has been made, however, that 1 Chr 7:6–11 more properly belongs to the genealogical list of Zebulun. In any case, several sources (genealogies and census lists) may have been used to produce this passage. For further discussion, see ICC and AB commentaries on Chronicles.

VICTOR H. MATTHEWS

BILSHAN (PERSON) [Heb *bilšān*]. One of the leaders of the group of returnees from Babylonian exile who is listed along with Zerubbabel in Ezra 2:2 = Neh 7:7 = 1 Esdr 5:8. The name, etymologically, is possibly an equivalent of Akkadian *Belšunu* (Noth *IPN*, 63). For further discussion, see AKKUB and BIGVAI.

CHANEY R. BERGDALL

BIMHAL (PERSON) [Heb *bimhāl*]. Found in the genealogy of Asher (1 Chr 7:30–40), which preserves the "heads of fathers' houses, approved, mighty warriors, chief of the princes." Listed as a great-great-grandson of Asher, Bimhal, whose name means "son of circumcision," is highlighted as a leader among the sons of Asher, which, "enrolled by genealogies, for service in war," numbered 26,000 men. Since the Chronicler devotes limited attention to the genealogy of Asher, perhaps because the tribe was a lesser one, having originated from the Jacob-Zilpah union (cf. Gen 46:17–18), little is known of Bimhal. That his father was Japhlet and his brothers were Ashvath and Pasach is clear enough. Information regarding Bimhal's family, however, is no more plentiful than that available concerning Bimhal. That Bimhal was a warrior of significant military importance may be safely assumed.

J. RANDALL O'BRIEN

BINDING AND LOOSING. In the gospel of Matthew reference is twice made to a power of binding and loosing: Matt 16:19, where the power is given to "Peter," and Matt 18:18, where it is entrusted to the "disciples," a group identical with the twelve in Matthew. A parallel saying can be found in John where, on the day of the resurrection, the risen Jesus confers the Holy Spirit upon the disciples and says, "If you forgive the sins of any, they are forgiven; if you retain the sins of any, they are retained" (John 20:23). This Johannine logion does not, however, contain the verbs *deo* and *luo,* which appear to have a technical meaning in Matthew.

A. Analogies

Virtually all commentators note that the verbs are the Greek equivalents of the Aramaic *ʾasar* (Heb *ʾasar*) and *šerî* (Heb *hiṭṭîr*), terms commonly found in rabbinic writings. Hence, there has been a tendency among interpreters to find an analogy for the Matthean expression in rabbinic usage. Support for this mode of interpretation can be found in the exceptionally strong Semitic coloration of Matt 16:16–19 (the expressions "flesh and blood," "Bar Jona," "church" [*ekklesia*] with an apparent allusion to the *qahal,* etc).

Apart from confessional disputes apropos the use made of Matt 16:16–19 in Roman Catholicism, where the passage is typically cited as *the* scriptural warrant for the authority of the papacy, the power of binding and loosing is a crux for NT interpretation. In an effort to understand Matthew's terminology, most commentators exploit later rabbinic usage, including that found in the targumic material, where the expressions "to bind" and "to loose" are often found (e.g., *Tg. Ps.-J.* Gen 4:7; *Tg. Neof.* Gen 4:7). Accordingly, binding and loosing are often interpreted (Mantey 1981; Bornkamm 1970; Manns 1983) as declarative authority in doctrinal and disciplinary matters. Christian leadership has the power to interpret and enforce what God has already decreed. By conferring the power to bind and loose upon church leadership, Jesus authorizes it to interpret the Scriptures and establish norms for Christian behavior, the Christian *halakah.* Some authors (e.g., Bornkamm and E. Schweizer) would make a distinction between the meaning of the expression in Matt 16:19 and its meaning in 18:18, interpreting the former as a *teaching* authority and the latter as a *disciplinary* authority.

On the other hand, binding and loosing are often interpreted as the power to ban members from the community and to readmit them. Sometimes this notion is combined with the disciples' authority to establish a Christian *halakah*. Thus church leadership has both the authority to determine forbidden and permitted conduct and to exclude members from the congregation.

Alternatively, binding and loosing are interpreted as the authority to release a person from some sort of vow (Falk 1974) or, especially on the basis of the analogy with John 20:23, as a power either to forgive sins (Emerton 1962) or to affect the consequences of sin (H. W. Basser). R. H. Hiers (1985), drawing attention to NT (e.g., Mark 3:27) and Hellenistic Jewish (e.g., Tob 3:17; 8:3) usage of *delein* ("bind") and *luein* ("loose") in regard to demonic possession, interprets Matthew's expressions of the apostolic commission to exorcise demons (Mark 3:14–16, etc.).

J. D. M. Derrett (1983) has attempted to clarify the NT expression by appealing to a modern Arabic phrase and practice whereby groups of people, capable of being determined *ad hoc* and somewhat independent of the authoritative opinions of the muftis, resolve the doubts troubling a community and exercise a quasi-judicial function by determining what is allowed or forbidden. They are those "who are competent to loose and bind [*mi-man bi yadihim al-ḥall waʾl-rabṭ*]." Such groups would be formed to make decisions with regard to contracts, vows, and banishment, but their competence would not be limited to these matters alone.

B. Matthew

Matthew introduces "binding" and "loosing" in his gospel without further explanation, thereby suggesting that the practice to which these expressions refer was known to his community. Since Josephus writes of the Pharisees' power to loose and bind (*luein kai desmein; JW* 1 §111), it is likely that the primary interpretive analogue is to be sought within contemporary rabbinic practice. Within Matthew's community the Scriptures were midrashically interpreted (e.g., Matt 1:22) and an appropriate *halakah* was established (e.g., Matt 5:21–48). Thus it is probable that the practice to which the Matthean "binding and loosing" refers is the interpretation of the Scriptures and the determination of an appropriate Christian way of life.

Both of Matthew's references to bind and loose are in passages proper to his gospel. There are significant differences between them insofar as the first (Matt 16:19) is formulated in the singular *(ho)* and forms part of a Jesuanic logion addressed to Peter, while the second (Matt 18:18) is formulated in the plural *(hosa)* and is directed to the disciples (cf. Matt 18:1). In its present context, the latter is clearly the work of Matthew, the redactor. Bultmann viewed it as a later variant of the saying in 16:19. The logion of Matt 18:18, appended to a short pericope on church discipline (18:15–17), expresses a significant element of Matthew's ecclesiology, namely, that what is done within the Church, on Jesus' authority, is sanctioned by God (heaven).

The ecclesiastical saying of Matt 16:19 has a postresurrectional provenance. In origin, it belongs to a body of NT sayings in which the risen Jesus commissions his disciples not only to proclaim his message but also to exercise some authority over the faithful. The NT tradition preserves the memory of Peter's role as the first witness to Jesus (1 Cor 15:5; Luke 24:34; cf. John 21:15–17; Mark 16:7). Matthew does not explicitly cite the tradition of an appearance of the risen Jesus to Peter. He does, however, have a tendency to retroject into his sketch of Jesus' ministry elements which are postresurrectional. It is therefore likely that the binding and loosing saying in Matt 16:19—in context, an explanation of the power of the keys—is an element of Matthew's version of the postresurrectional commission of Peter, but scholars dispute among themselves as to the extent to which Matt 16:16–19 represents Matthew's own formulation and the extent to which it represents pre-Matthean tradition.

In the final redaction of the gospel, both uses of the binding and loosing saying are explicitly linked to the Church (cf. Matt 16:18 and 18:17, where the only explicit uses of *ekklēsia*-church in the canonical gospels are to be found). Matthew's Peter somehow represents the Church, but so, too, do the disciples. Hence, the power to bind and loose is attributed both to Peter and to the disciples. The binding and loosing logion ultimately speaks of the authoritative interpretation of the Scriptures within Matthew's community, the Church.

Bibliography

Bornkamm, G. 1970. The Authority to "Bind" and "Loose" in the Church in Matthew's Gospel. *Perspective* 11: 37–50.

Brown, R. E.; Donfried, K. P., Reumann, J., ed. 1973. *Peter in the New Testament.* Minneapolis.

Cullmann, O. 1962. *Peter—Disciple, Apostle, Martyr.* 2d ed. Philadelphia.

Derrett, J. D. M. 1983. Binding and Loosing (Matt 16:19; 18:18; John 20:23). *JBL* 102: 112–17.

Emerton, J. A. 1962. Binding and Loosing—Forgiving and Retaining. *JTS* 13: 325–31.

Falk, Z. W. 1974. Binding and Loosing. *JJS* 25: 92–100.

Grelot, P. 1985. L'Origine de Matthieu 16,16–19. Pp. 91–105 in *A cause de l'évangile: études sur les Synoptiques et les Actes.* LD 123. Paris.

Hiers, R. H. 1985. "Binding" and "Loosing": The Matthean Authorizations. *JBL* 104: 233–50.

Lambrecht, J. 1986. "Du bist Petrus." Mt 16,16–19 und das Papsttum. *SUNT* 11: 5–32.

Manns, F. 1983. La Halakah dans l'évangile de Matthieu: note sur *Mt.* 16,16–19. *BibOr* 129–35.

Mantey, J. R. 1981. Distorted Translations in John 20:23; Matthew 16:18–19 and 18:18. *RevExp* 409–16.

Mathew, P. K. 1985. Authority and Discipline: Matt. 16.17–19 and 18.15–18 and the Exercise of Authority and Discipline in the Matthean Community. *CommViat* 28: 119–25.

Pfitzner, V. C. 1982. Purified Community—Purified Sinner: Expulsion from the Community According to Matthew 18:15–18 and 1 Corinthians 5:1–5. *AusBR* 30: 34–55.

Robinson, B. P. 1984. Peter and His Successors: Tradition and Redaction in Matthew 16.17–19. *JSNT* 21: 85–104.

Schnackenburg, R. 1981. Das Vollmachtswort vom Binden und Losen, traditionsgeschichtlich gesehen. Pp. 141–57 in *Kontinuität und Einheit*, ed. P.-G. Müller and W. Stenger. Freiburg.

———. 1985. Petrus im Matthaeusevangelium. Pp. 107–25 in *A cause de l'évangile: études sur les Synoptiques et les Actes.* LD 123. Paris.

Vorgrimler, H. 1963. Das "Binden und Losen" in der Exegese nach dem Tridentinum bis zum Beginn des 20 Jahrhunderts. *ZKT* 85: 460–77.

RAYMOND F. COLLINS

BINEA (PERSON) [Heb *binʿāʾ*]. Son of Moza, a descendant of King Saul from the family of Benjamin, according to 1 Chr 8:37 and 9:43. The etymology of the name is very unclear. The final *ʾalep* [ʾ] is relatively rare in biblical preexilic names (cf. Amasa [*ʿamasaʾ*]), although its frequent attestations in the Samaria Ostraca (Lemaire 1977: 47–55) and in the El-Jib jar handles (Demsky 1971: 21) indicate that it was in use in the preexilic period. This *-āʾ* ending is used in abbreviated forms of theophoric names (*IPN* 38; *TPNAH,* 159–67). However, if this is the case with Binea, there is no clear etymology from the remaining letters *bnʿ*. Alternatively, the element Bin-[*bin*] may be seen as a prefix for "son of," as in the name Benjamin. This type of name is very rare in the Bible, but is attested to outside the Hebrew Bible (Milik 1956). However, it is difficult to understand the name as "son of *ʿaʾ*, since the meaning of the element *ʿaʾ* is not known. Perhaps the name should be emended with most manuscripts of the LXX to Baana(h) [*baʿănâ* or *baʿănāʾ*] (*Chronicles* HAT, 80), which is well attested to and has a clear etymology. A few mss (Syr, Ar) have *kinʿāʾ*.

In the genealogies, Binea appears after Alemath and Moza, both of which are city names used as personal names (Demsky 1971; see ALEMETH and MOZA), but no city by the name of Binea is known. Perhaps an original Beth Anatot [*byt ʿntt*] became abbreviated and corrupted to Binea [*bnʿʾ*]. Binea appears in the genealogy at a juncture of two types of genealogical formulae; those preceding are introduced by *hôlîd,* "begot," while those that follow use *bĕnô,* "his son," though the exact significance of this difference is elusive. On the doubling of the Benjamin genealogy in 1 Chr 8 and 9, see AHAZ.

Bibliography

Demsky, A. 1971. The Genealogy of Gibeon (1 Chronicles 9:35–44): Biblical and Epigraphic Considerations. *BASOR* 202: 16–23.

Fowler, J. D. 1988. *Theophoric Personal Names in Ancient Hebrew: A Comparative Study.* JSOTSup 49. Sheffield.

Lemaire, A. 1977. *Inscriptions hébraïques. Tome I: Les Ostraca.* Paris.

Milik, J. T. 1956. An Unpublished Arrow-Head with Phoenician Inscription of the 11th–10th Century B.C. *BASOR* 143: 3–6.

MARC Z. BRETTLER

BINNUI (PERSON) [Heb *binnûy*]. Var. BELNUUS. A short form of the name BENAIAH ("Yahweh has built"), often confused with (or substituted for) BANI, another name popular in levitical circles during the postexilic period.

1. Binnui, the father of one Noadiah, a Levite under Ezra charged with weighing in the gold and silver temple vessels as they arrived in Jerusalem (Ezra 8:33). In the RSV, Binnui appears in the parallel text of 1 Esdr 8:62—Eng v 63 as a harmonization of the Greek, which reads Sabannus. Also, in this parallel Greek text, Binnui (i.e., Sabannus) is recorded as the father of Moeth rather than Noadiah (as in Ezra 8:33). For a discussion of this issue, see NOADIAH #1.

2. One of the sons of Pahath-Moab, who had taken a foreign wife (Ezra 10:30). In the 1 Esdras 9 parallel list, the name Belnuus appears instead of Binnui (v 31).

3. The ancestor of a group of men listed in the inquiry concerning those who had married foreign wives (Ezra 10:38; 1 Esdr 9:34). The RSV reading represents a modification of the Hebrew "and Bani and Binnui" on the basis of the LXX reading: "the sons of Banoui."

4. A member of the levitical family group descended from Henadad. To be "son" to someone in Hebrew can mean either (a) the immediate son or male offspring, (b) a descendant, or (c) a member in a larger social group, such as a family, clan, or tribe. Because Binnui is described as "of the sons of Henadad" in Neh 10:10—Eng v 9, it may be better to see him as a member of a larger family group descended from Henadad, rather than as the immediate offspring of Henadad. This Binnui was charged with repairing a section of Jerusalem's wall under Nehemiah (Neh 3:24). This same name has probably been corrupted to BAVVAI, the son of Henadad, in Neh 3:18, as other mss attest. The same Binnui, the son of Henadad, is found in Neh 10:10—Eng v 9 as one of those setting his seal to Nehemiah's covenant.

5. Neh 7:15 reads Binnui in the list of returning exiles where the parallel passage in Ezra 2:10 reads Bani. Either the one is a corruption of the other, or the two names have been used interchangeably for the same person.

6. One of the Levites under Zerubbabel (Neh 12:8). This Binnui may be identical with the Bani of Neh 9:4–5, since both names occur in the series—Jeshua, Bani/Binnui, Kadmiel. The presence of Bunni (another variation on Benaiah) in Neh 9:4, however, confirms the popularity of these shortened variations on the name Benaiah in levitical circles in the postexilic period. The conjectured presence of Binnui in the series Jeshua . . . Kadmiel in Neh 12:24 (Heb: *yēšûaʿ ben-qadmîʾēl*) could as well be Bani: there is no textual reason to prefer the one over the other, and the possibility remains that they were the same person.

D. G. SCHLEY

BIOGRAPHIES, EGYPTIAN. See EGYPTIAN LITERATURE (BIOGRAPHIES).

BIOGRAPHY, ANCIENT. The question of the genre of the gospels has made this topic a matter of interest to modern scholars. A discussion of ancient biography must begin with those writings that call themselves "lives" (Gk *bioi;* Lat *vitae*) and seek to discern what it is that holds them together as a literary group. Modern study of ancient biography may take its cue from what the ancients said about the distinction between history and biography (Polybius 10.21.8; 16.14.6; Cornelius Nepos *Pel.* 16.1.1; Plut. *Vit. Alex.* 1.2–3; *Pomp.* 8) but its conclusions cannot be based upon that alone. Genre is a descriptive, not a prescriptive, category (Perry 1967: 20). Furthermore, ancient theorists are notoriously unreliable from our modern perspective. They did not discuss entire genres, like romance, and when they did theorize, they often violated their theory in practice (Horace is an example). At the same time, therefore, that one is sensitized by the ancients, one must test their descriptive efforts against one's own inductive approach from the extant texts (Vivas 1968: 97–105).

References in ancient literature to biographies not now extant, as well as fragments of numerous "lives" found among the Oxyrhynchus and Herculaneum papyri, show the paucity of the extant remains of the Mediterranean biographical tradition. Nevertheless, a sizable body of such material is available, including Greco-Roman, Jewish, and Christian "lives." Some of these biographies circulated singly, others in collections.

Greco-Roman "lives" circulating alone that are extant in significant portions include: Satyrus, *Life of Euripides* (3d century B.C.E.); Andronicus, *Life of Aristotle* (ca. 70 B.C.E.), the substance of which is probably to be found in the *Vitae Aristotelis Marciana* (Momigliano 1971: 86–87); Nicolaus of Damascus, *Life of Augustus* (1st century B.C.E.); Tacitus, *Life of Agricola* (98 C.E.); the anonymous *Life of Aesop* (2d century B.C.); the anonymous *Life of Secundus* (2d century C.E.); Lucian, *Life of Demonax, Life of Alexander,* and *Passing of Peregrinus* (ca. 180 C.E.); Philostratus, *Life of Apollonius of Tyana* (216 C.E.); Porphyry, *Life of Pythagoras* and *Life of Plotinus* (3d century C.E.); Ps-Callisthenes, *Life of Alexander* (ca. 300 C.E.).

Certain Jewish and Christian "lives" also circulated alone. Philo, *Life of Moses, On Abraham,* and *On Joseph* (ca. 25 B.C.E.) are Jewish biographies circulating outside a collection of "lives." Examples from the numerous Christian "lives" circulating individually include: Pontius, *Life of Cyprian* (259 C.E.); Eusebius, *Life of Constantine* (early 4th century C.E.); the anonymous *Life of Pachomius* (4th century C.E.); Athanasius, *Life of Anthony* (357 C.E.); Jerome, *Life of Paul, the Hermit* (376 C.E.) and *Life of Malchus* (386 C.E.); *Life of Hilarion* (391 C.E.); Sulpicius Severus, *Life of Martin of Tours* (397 C.E.); Paulinus of Milan, *Life of Ambrose* (400 C.E.); Palladius, *Life of Chrysostom* (408 C.E.); Hilary, *Life of Honoratus* (431 C.E.); Ennodius, *Life of Epiphanius* (503 C.E.).

Greco-Roman collections of "lives" include: Cornelius Nepos, *Lives of Great Generals* (1st century B.C.E.); Plutarch, *Parallel Lives* (100 C.E.); Suetonius, *Lives of the Twelve Caesars* (120 C.E.) and *Lives of Illustrious Men* (110 C.E.); Diogenes Laertius, *Lives of Eminent Philosophers* (3d century C.E.); *Scriptores Historiae Augustae* (3d–4th centuries C.E.). The anonymous *The Lives of the Prophets* (1st century C.E.) is a Jewish collection of brief sketches of the "lives" of the prophets. Jerome's *Lives of Illustrious Men* (4th century C.E.) offers an example of a Christian collection.

Although there is no great uniformity in these writings that designate themselves "lives," it is still possible to discern what is essential and what is accidental to ancient biography. It is constitutive of ancient biography that the subject be a distinguished or notorious figure (kings, generals, philosophers, literary figures, lawgivers, prophets, or saints) and that the aim be to expose the essence of the person. Lucian, *Demonax* (67) puts it succinctly: "These are a very few things out of the many which I might have mentioned, but they will suffice to give my readers a notion of the sort of man he was." This constitutive feature becomes clear when biography is compared with history in antiquity. Whereas history focuses on the distinguished and significant acts of great men in the political and social spheres, biography is concerned with the essence of the individual. This difference may be seen at two points where history most nearly approaches biography. The first is the historical monograph which concentrates primarily on one individual. In Sallust's *Catiline* and *Jugurtha* the aim is not to set forth the individuals' essence but to narrate political events with which these two individuals were associated. The second is the incorporation of biographical material into a historical record. In Dio Cassius' *Roman History* (45–56) biographical material about Augustus is incorporated into a history of Rome. The very inclusion of this material in a historical context changes its aim from concern with Augustus' individual essence to his place in a social and political process. The same thing happens when Eusebius incorporates material from his earlier *Apology for the Life of Origen* into his *Ecclesiastical History* (6). Biography is interested in what sort of person the individual is, the subject's involvement in the historical process being important only insofar as it reveals his essence. Whereas history attempts to give a detailed account in terms of causes and effects of events, biography presents a highly selective, often anecdotal, account of an individual's life with everything chosen to illuminate his essential being. Ancient biography consists of information about a significant person, selected so as to reveal what sort of person the subject really was.

Having stated what is essential to ancient biography, it remains to describe what is accidental to it. First, it is incorrect to describe ancient biography as an account of the life of an individual from birth to death. Some biographies begin with the hero's mature life (e.g., Nepos, *Milt., Ar.,* Paus.); others may begin with the subject's birth and stop before his death (e.g., Nicolaus of Damascus, *Life of Augustus,* which ends with Augustus' entrance into the Civil War). How much of a subject's life is described varies. All that is necessary is that enough be given to satisfy the author that the essence of the person is revealed.

Second, the distinctiveness of the hero as an individual was assumed to appear not only in his deeds but also in insignificant gestures or passing utterance (Plut. *Alex.* 1; *Dem.* 11.7). Given this fact, it is difficult to exclude Plutarch's collections of sayings, such as "Sayings of Kings and Commanders," from the *bios/vita* genre. Indeed, in section D, Plutarch says: "their pronouncements and unpremeditated utterance . . . afford an opportunity to observe . . . the working of the mind of each man." In this and his other three collections of sayings one finds a series of materials that look like pronouncement stories, a brief narrative framework within which is set a saying. There is just enough of an event to allow the saying to reveal the individuality of the speaker.

Third, there is virtually no interest in tracing personality or character development. The essence of the person was not examined in its chronological development but only as a fixed constituent in a "life" (Stuart 1928: 178). Consequently, many ancient "lives" are only loosely chronological, being more often than not largely topical or logical in their arrangement (Russell 1973: 115).

Fourth, some biographies have as their aim to affect the behavior or opinions of their readers either positively (Plutarch) or negatively (Lucian, *Alex.*); others seem to have no overtly propagandistic agenda (Laertius). When such "lives" seek to affect the readers' behavior positively, this is often described in terms of imitation (Plut. *Per.* 21.4; Tacitus *Agr.* 46). The imitation of noble examples as understood in ancient biography is not to be regarded as a blind and unthinking repetition of acts performed by some great man in the past. It meant learning from a great exemplar the way to order one's life and then, without necessarily performing the same actions, to emulate what sort of person he was (Plut. *Aem.* 1; *Cim.* 2.3–5) (Gossage 1967: 49).

Fifth, the "life" of a subject may be described in mythical terms (Plut. *Rom.;* Seut. *Aug.;* Philostr. *VA;* Ps-Callisthenes, *Alexander*) or may be devoid of myth. Most biographies that employ myth in the description of their hero treat founders of cities, empires, religions, and schools.

Sixth, the literary form in which "lives" are presented varies. The dominant form is a prose narrative similar to history except that it is anecdotal and unconcerned about cause and effect. Most Greco-Roman, Jewish, and Christian biographies fit into this category. Its roots seem to be in Xenophon's *Memorabilia,* or memoirs of Socrates. This, however, cannot be considered the only form of ancient biography. Satyrus' *Life of Euripides* is in the form of a dialogue with at least three speakers, of whom Diodorus and Eucleia are named. The roots of this form of biography seem to be in the Platonic dialogues that deal with Socrates (e.g., *Phaedo*). Christian adaptations of the same form may be found in Palladius' *Dialogue on the Life of Chrysostom* and in Sulpicius Severus' *Dialogues on the Life of St. Martin* in which a two-day conversation among three friends centers on Martin's life. Yet another form in which biography appears in antiquity is the encomium, a speech praising its subject (Eusebius, *Life of Constantine;* Gregory Thaumaturgos, *Panegyric to Origen;* Hilary, *Sermon on the Life of Honoratus*). The roots of this form may be found in Isocrates, *Evagoras,* and Xenophon, *Agesilaus.* If the collections of sayings like Plutarch's "Sayings of Kings and Commanders" are also granted a place in the ancient biographical tradition, then one finds at least four literary forms in which biography may appear in the Mediterranean world.

Seventh, ancient biographies perform a multiplicity of social functions. Some apparently had only a literary aim (e.g., Laertius). Others seemed to serve a propagandistic purpose of some sort. Within this overall didactic orientation a number of more specific functions can be identified. (1) Certain "lives" portray the subject as an ideal figure so the readers will accept his authority (Nicolaus of Damascus, *Life of Augustus*) or imitate his way of life (Nepos, *Ep., Ag.;* Lucian, *Demon.;* Pontius, *Life of Cyprian;* Athanasius, *Life of Anthony;* Paulinus of Milan, *Life of Ambrose*). Lucian states his aim in an exemplary fashion: "It is not fitting to tell of Demonax . . . that young men of good instincts who aspire to philosophy may not have to shape themselves by ancient precedents alone, but may be able to set themselves a pattern from our modern world and to copy that man, the best of all the philosophers whom I know about" (*Demon.* 2). Although the form is that of a history-like narrative, the spirit of the encomium is felt in these "lives."

(2) Other "lives" aim to defend the subject against misunderstanding either by his followers or by outsiders, so that his true self may be seen and his influence exerted (Tacitus, *Agricola;* Philostratus, *Life of Apollonius;* Palladius, *Life of Chrysostom;* Jerome, *Life of Malchus*). Here three of the examples employ the history-like narrative form while the fourth, Palladius, uses the form of a dialogue. The spirit in all four examples is akin to that in Xenophon's *Memorabilia,* where Socrates is defended, and in Isocrates' *Busiris,* where the king is defended against calumny.

(3) Still other ancient biographies intend to discredit the subject by means of exposé (Lucian's *Alexander the False Prophet* and *Peregrinus;* also in Suetonius' *Lives of the Twelve Caesars* one finds profound censure of men who, far from measuring up to the ideal, exemplify its opposite).

(4) Another social function of didactic biographies in antiquity seems to be to indicate where the true tradition is in the present (Bickerman 1952: 49). This is found first of all in "lives" of founders of philosophical schools that contained within themselves not only a life of the founder but also a list or a brief narrative of his successors and selected other disciples (an "a + b" form). In Diogenes Laertius certain "lives" of philosophers reflect this pattern. There is "a" the life of the founder, followed by "b" a brief list or narrative of his successors and selected other disciples, followed by "c" an extensive statement of the teaching of the philosopher (Aristippus—Life: 2.65–84; Pupils: 2.85–86; Teaching: 2.86–104; Plato—Life: 3.1–45; Pupils: 3.46–47; Teachings: 3.47–109; Zeno—Life: 7.1–35; Successors and other disciples: 7.36–38; Teachings: 7.38–160; Pythagoras—Life: 8.1–44; Successors: 8.45–46; Teachings: 8.48–50; Epicurus—Life: 10.1–21; Successors and other disciples: 10.22–28; Teachings: 10.29–154). Examination of Laertius' references to the sources for these "lives" shows that the material in "c" comes from a different origin than that in "a + b." This permits the inference that Laertius took over individual biographies that were written in terms of the "a + b" pattern and added the "c" component himself.

Such an inference is supported by three strands of early evidence. First, one of the four different works of Aristoxenos, all of which dealt with Pythagoreanism, was "The Life of Pythagoras and His Associates" which contained a biography of Pythagoras and a history of the Pythagoreans in chronological order (Fritz 1940: 22, n.35). Second, Herculaneum papyrus 1018 treats the Stoic succession. At four points the life of a teacher is followed by a discussion of his disciples. This is sometimes just a list of names; at other points it consists of anecdotes about them (Traversa 1952: xiii–xiv). Third, a pre-Christian biography of Aristotle included within itself both a claim that Aristotle was the successor of Plato and an anecdote about Aristotle's selection of a successor to himself (Düring 1957: 465–66; 345–46). Taken together, this evidence establishes the existence of individual "lives" of founders of philosophical schools that contained within themselves not only the biography of the founder but also a narrative, however brief, about his successors and selected other disciples.

Just as Christian biography went to the classical period for its models in other cases, so here as well. In the *Life of Pachomius* one finds a Christian appropriation of this type of ancient biography. It is fitting because this "life" deals with the founder of cenobitic monasticism and with his successors in the community. The early part of the biography deals with the career of Pachomius. In chap. 117 he appoints Orsisius to succeed him, using language that may be regarded as the technical terminology of succession. In the sections that follow the narrative tells what Orsisius did and said (118–129), zealously emulating the life of Pachomius (119). Then Orsisius appoints Theodore (130). In the sections that follow one learns what Theodore did and said.

A second Christian example of this type of biography is Hilary of Arles's *Sermon on the Life of St. Honoratus.* Here is an encomium praising the founder of the monastery that fits into the "a + b" type of "life." In chap. 8, Hilary says he is Honoratus' successor and that his task is to do what the founder had done. In all of these examples, the purpose is to say where the true tradition is in the period after the founder.

(5) Yet another social function performed by some ancient didactic biographies is to serve as a hermeneutical tool, either to legitimate the teaching of the subject by showing that his life corresponded with his profession *(Life of Secundus the Silent Philosopher)* or to furnish an interpretative clue for the reading of his works (Andronicus' *Life of Aristotle,* which served to introduce his edition of Aristotle; Philo's *Life of Moses,* which served as an introduction to Philo's *Exposition of the Law* [Goodenough 1933: 109–25]; Porphyry's *Life of Plotinus,* which served to introduce the *Enneads*).

If our description of what is essential and what is accidental in ancient biography holds true, then it is possible to say that we are dealing with the biographical tradition in antiquity wherever we meet the concern to depict the essence of a significant person, that is, to expose what sort of person it really is. The great variety of the ancient "lives" results from the multiple combinations of what is accidental to the genre: (1) the extent of coverage—whether from birth to death, from birth to mature life, from mature life to death; (2) the types of material used to expose the soul of the subject—whether preponderantly deeds or words or some balanced combination of them; (3) the kind of organizing principle utilized—whether chronology or logic or some combination of both; (4) the degree of detachment or involvement of the author with his readers—whether detached and descriptive or involved and evaluative; (5) the use or disuse of myth—whether the subject is described in divine terms or is depicted without recourse to language about the gods; (6) the literary form employed—whether a prose narrative akin to history or a dialogue or a speech of praise or a collection of sayings; (7) the social function of the "life"—whether didactic or nondidactic and, if the former, whether to hold the hero up as an authority or an example, to defend him against misunderstanding, to ridicule him by means of exposé, to show where the true tradition is to be found in the present, or to furnish a hermeneutical key for proper interpretation. It is crucial that what is essential and what is accidental be clearly understood. When this is done, it is possible to sense what is shared and what is distinctive in each case. For example, it is possible to say about Hilary's *Life of Honoratus* that it is biographical in its aim to set forth what sort of person this noteworthy Christian was, but that it does by using the form of an encomium, or speech of praise, shaped in such a way that it serves the social function of saying where the true tradition is in the speaker's present.

One of the most vexed areas of discussion in the study of ancient biography is the relation of the early Christian gospels, canonical and apocryphal, to this genre. To date, reluctance to view the gospels as a part of the biographical tradition of antiquity has been largely due to misunderstanding either the gospels or ancient biography. If, for example, the gospels are viewed as *Kleinliteratur,* (popular writing without authorial pretensions) and not productions of individual authors, as Schmidt (1923: 76) and Bultmann (*RGG*[3] 2: 418–22) proposed, then obviously they are different from biographies produced by self-conscious authors. This view of the gospels, however, has been discarded ever since the emergence of redaction criticism, by which the evangelists as self-conscious authors is assumed. Or if ancient biography is taken as identical with modern biography, then obviously the gospels are different. The gospels, like ancient "lives," however, do not set their hero against the wider historical background of the time as do modern biographies; like many ancient "lives," the gospels do not adhere to a strict chronological order; like ancient "lives," the gospels are not concerned to trace the personality development of the hero; like many ancient "lives," the gospels do not describe the personal appearance of their subject. The gospels, like some ancient biographies, do tell their story in terms of myth. This tendency to impose upon ancient biographies the qualities of modern ones has been disavowed by all who have worked extensively with ancient "lives." If such misunderstandings are cleared away, then it is possible to view at least some of the early Christian gospels as part of the larger literary scene of antiquity.

Since all of the Christian gospels have as their subject a significant individual and since some have as their aim to indicate what sort of person Jesus is, it is difficult to believe that on first acquaintance the canonical gospels, at least, would not have been considered biographical by Mediterranean readers and hearers (Stanton 1974: 135). What is revealed in the narratives about Apollonius, Pythagoras, Moses, or Jesus is the same—the distinctive nature of each (Smith 1975: 35). Some of the gospels share with the ancient biographies that which is constitutive for them—to set forth the essence of the subject, that is, what sort of person it is. Some gospels, canonical and apocryphal, manifest a biographical interest in depicting what sort of person Jesus was: the canonical four and the apocryphal gospels like the *Gospel of Peter* and the *Infancy Gospel of Thomas.* The *Protevangelium of James* has a biographical concern but it is for Mary, not Jesus. Parts of the *Epistle of the Apostles* also manifest a biographical interest. Other gospels' concern is not biographical: e.g., the gnostic dialogues like the *Sophia of Jesus Christ,* the *Dialogue of the Savior,* the first part of the *Gospel of Mary,* the *Apocryphon of James,* the *Book of Thomas the Contender,* and the sayings collection, the *Gospel of Thomas.*

The variety among the gospels with a biographical interest matches that of the ancient "lives" and for the same reason. It is due to the multiple ways those things that are accidental to biography are combined. For example, as to form, all of the gospels that possess a biographical character are history-like narratives, not dialogues, encomiums, or collections of pronouncement stories. As to the extent of coverage, the biographical gospels vary greatly. Some, like Matthew and Luke, cover Jesus' life from birth to death; others, like Mark, treat Jesus' life from mature manhood to death; still others, like the *Infancy Gospel of Thomas* and the *Gospel of Peter,* deal with more limited periods of Jesus' life. As to social function, all four canonical gospels and the *Gospel of Peter* find it necessary to correct misunderstanding about Jesus at the same time that they set him forth as the expression and the norm of a community's values. In addition, Luke-Acts shares with certain biographies a concern to say where the true tradition is in the present, even if his sense of the radical difference between apostolic and postapostolic times caused him to eschew use of the typical succession vocabulary. Matthew, moreover, has in common with some "lives" the interest in the hermeneutical relationship of the hero's life and teaching. Only the *Infancy Gospel of Thomas* seems straightforward in its praise of the lad in order to reinforce his authority. Regarding the employment of myth, all tell the story of Jesus in mythical terms, although the specific myth may vary: the Synoptics and the *Gospel of Peter* utilize the myth of immortals, John employs the myth of a descending-ascending redeemer, and the *Infancy Gospel of Thomas* expands the traditional theme of the precocious youth so that Jesus becomes a playful divine boy. Like most of the other ancient biographies that utilize myth, the Christian hero of the gospels is a founder. As with them, sacred time is focused around those events which first brought the community or cult into being. Myth becomes the means of designating this sacred time. In this regard, the Christian biographies of Jesus manifest a distinctive difference from all other "lives," Greco-Roman, Jewish, or Christian, that are not constructed in terms of myth and a remarkable kinship with those other biographies, Greco-Roman and Jewish, that do employ myth in their depiction of their hero's life (Moses, Romulus, Augustus, Apollonius, Pythagoras, Alexander). Given these rather obvious links between certain early Christian gospels and the ancient biographical genre, a growing consensus regards certain ancient "lives" as the closest analogy to the canonical four and perhaps a few other early Christian gospels as well (Cartlidge and Dungan 1980; Farmer 1967; Pleissis 1982; Robbins 1984; Schneider 1977; Shuler 1982; Talbert 1977; Toews 1981; *IDBSup,* 370–72).

Bibliography

Bickermann, E. 1952. La Chaine de la tradition Pharisienne. *RB* 59: 44–54.

Cartlidge, D. R., and Dungan, D. L. 1980. *Documents for the Study of the Gospels.* Cleveland.

Cox, P. 1983. *Biography in Late Antiquity.* Berkeley.

Düring, I. 1957. *Aristotle in the Ancient Biographical Tradition.* Göteborg.

Farmer, W. R. 1967. The Problem of Christian Origins: A Programmatic Essay. Pp. 81–88 in *Studies in the History and Text of the New Testament,* ed. B. L. Daniels and M. J. Suggs. Salt Lake City.

Fritz, K. von. 1940. *Pythagorean Politics in Southern Italy.* New York.

Gigon, O. 1962. *Vita Aristotelis Marciana.* Berlin.

Goodenough, E. R. 1933. Philo's Exposition of the Law and His *de Vita Mosis. HTR* 26: 109–25.

Gossage, A. J. 1967. Plutarch. Pp. 45–77 in *Latin Biography,* ed. T. A. Dorey. London.

Hirsch, E. D., Jr. 1967. *Validity in Interpretation.* New Haven.

Leo, F. 1901. *Griechisch-Römische Biographie nach Ihrer literarischen Form.* Leipzig.

Lesky, A. 1966. *A History of Greek Literature.* London.

Momigliano, A. 1971. *The Development of Greek Biography.* Cambridge, MA.

Perry, B. E. 1967. *The Ancient Romances.* Berkeley.

Pleissis, I. du 1982. Die Genre van Lukas se Evangelie. *Theologia Evangelica* 15: 19–28.

Robbins, V. 1984. *Jesus the Teacher: A Socio-Rhetorical Interpretation of Mark.* Philadelphia.

Russell, D. A. 1973. *Plutarch.* London.

Schmidt, K. L. 1923. Die Stellung der Evangelien in der allgemeinen Literaturgeschichte. Pp. 50–140 in *Eucharistērion: Gunkel Festschrift,* ed. H. Schmidt. Göttingen.

Schneider, G. 1977. Der Zweck des lukanischen Doppelwerks. *BZ* 21: 45–66.

Shuler, P. L., Jr. 1982. *A Genre for the Gospels.* Philadelphia.

Smith, J. Z. 1975. Good News Is No News: Aretalogy and Gospel. Pp. 21–38 in *Christianity, Judaism, and other Greco-Roman Cults: Part One—New Testament,* ed. J. Neusner. Leiden.

Stanton, G. N. 1974. *Jesus of Nazareth in New Testament Preaching.* Cambridge.

Stuart, D. R. 1928. *Epochs of Greek and Roman Biography.* Berkeley.

Talbert, C. H. 1977. *What Is a Gospel?* Philadelphia.

———. 1988. Once Again: Gospel Genre. *Semeia* 43: 53–73.

Toews, J. E. 1981. The Synoptic Problem and the Genre Question. *Direction* 10: 11–18.

Traversa, A. 1952. *Index Stoicorum Herculanensis.* Geneva.

Vivas, E. 1968. Literary Classes: Some Problems. *Genre* 1: 97–105.

CHARLES H. TALBERT

BIRᶜAM, KEFAR. See KEFAR BIRᶜAM (M.R. 189272).

BIRDS. See ZOOLOGY.

BIRSHA (PERSON) [Heb *biršaᶜ*]. King of GOMORRAH, (Gen 14:2). Elsewhere in the chap. (vv 8, 10), he appears simply as "the king of Gomorrah." (For the story, see BERA.) The name Birsha, like those of his allies, is a "speaking name" meaning "in wickedness," as befits a king of a sinful city like Gomorrah.

MICHAEL C. ASTOUR

BIRZAITH (PERSON) [Heb K *birzāwit;* Q *birzāyit*]. Found in the genealogy of Asher (1 Chr 7:30–40), which lists the "heads of fathers' houses, approved, mighty warriors, chief of the princes." The name is the first addition to the genealogy of Asher found in Genesis 46 and Numbers 26. However, it is unclear whether the name, which means "well of olives" and appears nowhere else in Scripture, represents a person or a place.

If Birzaith is the name of a person, then he is listed as a son of Malkiel, a grandson of Beriah, and a great-grandson of Asher. However, the construction, "the father of

Birzaith," could be used here as it is in 1 Chr 2:51, where Salma is listed as "the father of Bethlehem." If Birzaith is taken to be a place name, modern Birzeit north of Tyre offers a possible location of the ancient site.

J. RANDALL O'BRIEN

BISHLAM (PERSON) [Heb *bišlām*]. One of several men who were party to a letter written to King Artaxerxes of Persia (Ezra 4:7 = 1 Esdr 2:16). The Heb word is thus understood to be a proper name by 1 Esdras (LXX 2:14)—*Bēlemos*—a transliteration Torrey (1908) suggests resulted from the accidental dropping of the medial *s* by a copyist, and by the Vulgate—*Beselam.* For this proper name various etymologies have been proposed: an abbreviated form of *ben-šĕlām,* "son of peace" (BDB, 122, 143); the Babylonian name *Bel-šallim* or an Aramaic name *Bēl-šalām,* "Bel is peace" (Torrey 1908: 244; Gehman NWDB, 119); a corrupted form of *Belshunu,* a governor of the Persian satrapy of Palestine-Syria whose name appears in a cuneiform tablet dated to Artaxerxes' third year (Rainey 1969: 58). The LXX translation of this word in Ezra 4:7—*en eirēnȩ̄,* "in peace"—rather than understanding *bišlām* as a proper name, perceives it as the Aramaic word *šĕlām* with a *b* prefix. This has given rise to a number of reconstructions and interpretations. Since *šĕlām,* or a form of it, is used elsewhere as a greeting (Ezra 4:17; 5:7; Dan 3:31; 6:26—Eng 6:25) Bowman (*IDB* 3: 599), with reservation, and Newman (*IDB* 1: 441) conjecture that the word constitutes a salutation of the letter which the men wrote. Rudolph (*Esra und Nehemiah* HAT, 34) views it as a truncated form of *bîrûšalēm* which he renders "against Jerusalem" and which Myers (*Ezra-Nehemiah* AB, 31) construes as "concerning Jerusalem." Garbini (1985: 162) reconstructs the word to read *b-śml,* "on the mantel," referring to the covering of a roll (*mtrdd:* Hitqaṭṭel ptcp. from the root *rdd* which he also reconstructs from *mtrdt*) on which the message to the king was written.

Bibliography

Garbini, G. 1985. La Lettera di Ṭabʾel (Ezra IV, 7). *Hen* 7: 161–63.

Rainey, A. F. 1969. The Satrapy "Beyond the River." *AJBA* 2: 51–78.

Torrey, C. C. 1908. The Aramaic Portions of Ezra. *AJSL* 24: 209–81.

RODNEY H. SHEARER

BISHOPS' BIBLE. See BIBLE, BISHOPS'.

BIT. See ZOOLOGY.

BITHIAH (PERSON) [Heb *bityāh*]. A daughter of Pharaoh, married to Mered, a descendant of Caleb son of Jephunneh (1 Chr 4:18—Eng 4:17). It is not sure whether "Pharaoh" should be equated with the Egyptian royal title. The theophoric form of the name, which is made up of *bat* and *yah,* seems to indicate that the person is a worshipper of Yahweh. If so, she could well be a Jewess. See further, *TPNAH,* 115.

H. C. LO

BITHYNIA (PLACE) [Gk *Bithynia*]. A district of NW Asia Minor, which formed a kingdom in the Hellenistic period and subsequently a Roman province. It corresponds approximately to the modern Turkish prefectures of Kocaeli (Izmit), Adapazarı, Bolu, Bilecik, and Bursa, and is mentioned in Acts 16:7 and 1 Pet 1:1.

A. Topography
B. Archaeological Exploration
C. History
  1. The Hellenistic Kingdom
  2. The Roman Province
  3. The Origins of Christianity in Bithynia

A. Topography

Bithynia is a distinctive geographical and climatic region of Asia Minor. East of the river Sakarya (ancient Sangarios) rise the densely forested mountains of the Black Sea coastal region, broken at intervals by well-watered plains such as those of Düzce and Bolu. The rivers Sakarya and Filyos and their tributaries cut deep gorges through the mountains; their courses are characterized by long, trenchlike valleys running parallel to the coast for considerable distances. West of the lower valley of the Sakarya, wooded hills alternate with fertile plains, which support the cultivation of vines, olives, and grain. The whole region lies at the meeting point between the rainy, mountainous Black Sea coastal region, which formed the heartland of the ancient kingdom of Pontus, and the Marmara region, which experiences less heavy rainfall and hotter summers on the plains. The Marmara region itself forms a transitional zone between the climates of the Black Sea and the Mediterranean.

The most important feature of the historical geography of Bithynia is the route linking Istanbul with the interior of Asia Minor, by way of Izmit (ancient Nicomedia), Düzce, Bolu (ancient Bithynium/Claudiopolis), and Gerede. This route was important from the Hellenistic period onward through Roman, Byzantine, and Ottoman times; it is still followed by the main road from Istanbul to Ankara.

B. Archaeological Exploration

The history of the modern archaeological and topographical exploration of Bithynia begins with the journey of the Abbé Boré through the region in 1831, en route for the Lazarist missions in Persia. Subsequent work in the 19th century was carried out by a colorful succession of scientists, antiquarians, consular officials, and "topographers," some of the latter with close links to what would now be regarded as military intelligence. These travelers surveyed and described the resources and topography of the region, recorded antiquities, copied inscriptions, and attempted to identify ancient sites. Their work is surveyed in detail by Louis Robert (1980: 27–60).

Important work was done by Ainsworth, the geologist of the joint Royal Geographical Society—Society for the Propagation of Christian Knowledge expedition to Mesopotamia in 1839, the German travelers, including H. von Moltke, who provided data for Kiepert's map of the area (1844), the French travelers Xavier Hommaire de Hell (1846), Perrot (1861), and Guillaume, the Germans Körte (1895–99) and Von Diest (1886), and by Gustave Mendel, who catalogued the museum at Bursa (ancient Prusa). Major contributions to the collection and study of the Greek inscriptions of the region have been made in our own generation by F. K. Dörner and Sencer Şahın.

Outside Istanbul itself (ancient Byzantium), excavation has mainly been limited to rescue work in towns such as Izmit. The most noticeable traces of the Greco-Roman period are to be found at Uskübü (ancient Prusias on Hypius) and Iznik (ancient Nicaea)

C. History

1. The Hellenistic Kingdom. Bithynia emerged as a separately identifiable political unit in the period of political confusion after the death of Alexander the Great in 323 B.C. In 297 B.C., Zipoetes proclaimed himself king of the Bithynians (Vitucci 1953: 11). Zipoetes was a descendant of a line of local princes who had controlled most of the Izmit Peninsula and lower Sakarya Valley since the late 5th century B.C. and who had never been fully subjugated by the Persians. The Bithynians were a people of Thracian origin with a savage reputation among the Greeks who had planted colonies on the Marmara and Black Sea coasts (Xen. *An.* 6.4.2).

The kingdom of Bithynia lasted until 74 B.C., when Nicomedes IV bequeathed his kingdom to Rome. Detailed narratives are provided by Brandis, Meyer, and Ruge (*PW* 3/1: 507–39) and Vitucci (1953). Bithynia's strategic position astride one of the main roads from Europe into Asia and adjacent to the sea route from the Mediterranean to the Black Sea heavily influenced its history in the Hellenistic period. Certain recurring themes stand out in the kingdom's tortuous political history. Persistent territorial conflict with the Greek cities of the region, notably Chalcedon and Heraclea Pontica (modern Ereğli), was matched by the evident desire of most of the kings to be accepted as part of the progressive Greek world. Nicomedes I (ca. 279–260 B.C.) struck the first Bithynian coinage (on the Attic Greek standard) and founded the city of Nicomedia to be his capital. Nicomedia was a fully fledged Hellenistic city of considerable commercial importance; it succeeded the ancient Greek colony of Askakos, destroyed ca. 301 in a war between Zipoetes and Lysimachus, the Macedonian ruler of Thrace. Nicomedes also returned the Greek cities of Kieros (modern Uskübü) and Tieion (modern Filyos), which had been captured by Zipoetes, to the control of Heraclea. Prusias I (ca. 235–183 B.C.), grandson of Nicomedes I, reannexed the two cities to his kingdom, renaming Kieros as Prusias. He also refounded the two cities of Kios (also later renamed Prusias, modern Gemlik) and Myrlea (later renamed Apamea, modern Mudanya), which had been destroyed by his brother-in-law and ally Philip V of Macedon and handed over to him; at the same time he gained control of Chalcedon, on the strategically vital E shore of the Bosporus. Both Nicomedes I's son, Ziaelas, and Nicomedes III (127–94 B.C.) maintained well-publicized relations with centers of Greek cult, civilization, and commerce, such as Cos and Delos (Magie 1950: 312, 318).

Much of the kings' foreign policy was devoted to warding off threats from the more powerful neighboring kings who controlled central and W Asia Minor, notably the Attalids of Pergamum (modern Bergama). It was Nicomedes I of Bithynia who brought savage Celtic tribesmen into Asia Minor to aid him as mercenaries against his brother (277 B.C.) and probably also in his struggle against the Seleucid monarch Antiochus I (Magie 1950: 311). These Celts, referred to as Galatians by NT (Gal 3:1; [Galatia] 1 Cor 16:1; 2 Tim 4:10, 1 Pet 1:1; [Galatian region] Acts 16:6, 18:23) and other Greek writers, eventually settled in central Anatolia (Galatia).

Prusias I brought Bithynia into the center of the world of Hellenistic power politics. After an unsuccessful attack (in alliance with Rhodes) on the Greek city of Byzantium, he allied with Philip V of Macedon as a counterweight to Attalus of Pergamum, who maintained close relations with the emerging power of Rome. Later, as Philip's fortunes waned, Prusias backed the Romans against the Seleucids in Asia Minor, but was unable to avoid surrendering disputed territory to Pergamum in the settlement of 184 B.C. By then he had acquired the assistance of the exiled Hannibal, but was unable to resist Roman hostility to the latter's presence in Bithynia.

Prusias II (183–149 B.C.) became involved with Eumenes II of Pergamum in a war with the rival kingdom of Pontus to the E. Relations with Pontus and Rome dominated the last century of Bithynian independence. Nicomedes III (127–94 B.C.) attempted to partition Paphlagonia with the king of Pontus, but then incurred the latter's enmity by invading Cappadocia, Pontus' southern neighbor and a Pontic sphere of influence. The last king of Bithynia, Nicomedes IV (94–74 B.C.), was driven from his throne twice by Mithridates of Pontus, being restored on both occasions by the Romans. After Nicomedes died, leaving his kingdom to Rome, Mithridates again invaded the country: the Romans were unable to achieve control over Bithynia until 72 B.C.

In spite of their vicissitudes in the wars of the age, the cities of Bithynia remained centers of Greek language and culture. Nicaea, in particular, was the home of the mathematician and astronomer Hipparchus and the littérateurs Asclepiades and Parthenius; the latter composed poetry as well as a learned handbook on mythology which influenced the Latin poets of the 1st century B.C. The kings were the object of cult in the Hellenistic manner in the cities (Vitucci 1953: 128–29). But native names and cults persisted in the country districts down into the Roman period alongside the gradual spread of more or less Hellenized cults and institutions (Jones 1971: 154). The orator Dio of Prusa (ca. A.D. 40–110) argued that Greek education was essential to "making your city truly Hellenic, free from turmoil and stable" (Dio Chrys. *Or.* 44:10, LCL).

2. The Roman Province. Direct Roman influence was more marked in Bithynia than in other parts of W Asia Minor. The constitutions of the cities display some common features, such as the enrollment of the Council by "Censors" *(timetai)*, of Roman origin. The city of Apamea received a settlement of Julius Caesar's discharged veterans and, with them, the status of Roman colony. Yet a century later Dio addressed a speech on a sensitive political matter to the citizens in Greek (*Or.* 41).

After the Civil War, when Pompey and Mark Antony had levied troops and contributions (Appian, *BCiv.* 2.71; 4.58), Bithynia enjoyed a long period of peace and prosperity. The timber of the mountains and the fertile farmland of the plains were important sources of wealth. Nicomedia was a center of the trade in "prefabricated" marble work and there was also an important trading link with the N coast of the Black Sea (Rostovtzev 1918: 9; Robert 1980: 78–85).

Under the Roman Empire, Bithynia formed the major part of the province of *Bithynia et Pontus.* The province was organized in the usual way, with the principal seat of government and headquarters of the imperial cult in Nicomedia and a number of assize towns, regularly visited by the governor. Assize towns included Nicaea and Prusa. The imperial cult was maintained, as in other provinces, by the "Commonwealth [*Koinon*] of the Greeks of Bithynia," composed of representatives of the various cities. Bithynia was one of the earliest of the E provinces to seek and receive permission for the organization of such a cult in 29 B.C. (Cass. Dio 51.20.6–7). The *Koinon,* with its prestigious priesthoods and opportunities for conspicuous displays of wealth in the organization of ceremonies and games, offered goals for many of the aspirations of the wealthy provincials. It provided something of an institutional focus for expressions of loyalty to the emperors and to pagan, "Hellenic" traditions. As well as organizing the imperial cult, the *Koinon* occasionally provided a focus for political representation of the province in the prosecution of corrupt governors before the State in Rome. Known prosecutions of governors of Bithynia took place in A.D. 103 and 106/107.

Bithynia was governed by proconsuls as a "senatorial" province until early in the reign of Marcus Aurelius (A.D. 161–80), when it was transferred to the control of an imperial legate of consular rank, directly responsible to the emperor. This change probably reflects the growing importance of the strategic military road between the increasingly troubled Danube frontier and the E provinces; this route passed through Bithynia. The proconsul was assisted by a quaestor (senatorial financial official) and legate (assistant governor). The interests of the emperors' treasury were represented by one or more procurators, who managed imperial property, collected the revenues and also certain special taxes from them. The province was never fully garrisoned; in the time of Trajan (98–115), the governor had a small force of about two auxiliary *cohortes* (not more than 2000 men) and there was also a coastal patrol on the Black Sea coast.

The *pax Romana* was rudely interrupted in Bithynia by civil war between Septimius Severus and Pescennius Niger in 193/4, during which Byzantium was besieged and Niger finally defeated in a battle near Nicaea, which had publicly supported his bid for imperial power (Robert 1977). Campaigns by the emperors in the E involved marches by Roman armies through the province in 197, 215, and 219, which placed considerable burdens on the cities lying on or close to the main road, such as Nicomedia and Prusias-on-Hypius. A number of inscriptions from the latter city commemorate the contributions made to easing the passage of the armies by prominent local citizens.

Gothic tribesmen raided Bithynia in 256, sacking Chalcedon, Nicomedia, Nicaea, Kios, Apamea, and Prusa. A few years later, Chalcedon was again destroyed by another Gothic raid and Herculea also attacked. Renewed warfare on the E frontier necessitated the passage of Roman armies through Bithynia several times during the period 242–75. Respite came only with the accession in 284 of Diocletian, who established his capital at Nicomedia. Bithynia now lay in the center of power of the E empire and was a natural setting for the great Council of the Church summoned to Nicaea by Constantine in 325. In 330, Constantine moved the imperial capital to Byzantium, now renamed Constantinople. From then on Bithynia lay at the center of the E empire.

3. The Origins of Christianity in Bithynia. Against this background of a prosperous Greek-speaking Roman province, the first firmly datable evidence for Christianity in the province appears in the correspondence of Pliny with the emperor Trajan in 110 (Pliny, *Ep.* 10.95–96). The legal, political, and religious reasons for the persecution of Christians in the Roman Empire have been exhaustively discussed, with much minute analysis of Pliny's letter and Trajan's reply (Sherwin-White 1966: 691–712, 772–87; Price 1984: 220–22). (It is noteworthy that Price draws an important distinction between sacrifice to the gods and veneration of the emperor's image.) Only a few brief observations on the judicial situation revealed by Pliny's letter are possible here.

The case is a good illustration of the empirical approach of Roman law and administration when confronted with a new situation. Trajan explicitly declines to lay down a general principle. He refuses to allow Christians to be deliberately sought out, but says they must be punished if successfully denounced; at the same time he introduces a novel principle into Roman law by allowing the cessation of a culpable activity as grounds for pardon and what in English legal procedure is called an "unconditional discharge" *(venia ex paenitentia).* Pliny clearly regards the situation created by the spread of Christianity as a public danger *(periculum).* Roman provincial governors had wide powers of discretion, extending to imposition of the death penalty, in dealing with possible threats to public order or local institutions, especially where those responsible were not Roman citizens. Those who appeared before Pliny and refused a direct order, for example to invoke the gods, were in any case liable to punishment for "contempt of court" and insubordination *(contumacia).*

From the point of view of the history of Christianity in Bithynia, the evidence of Pliny for the widespread growth of the new religion in the province is significant. His informants claimed that *until the recent past* attendance at temple ceremonies had fallen markedly and that the trade in the meat of sacrificial victims had been disrupted; he himself reported that Christians were widespread in all age groups and social classes, in the cities as well as the countryside. His letter suggests that the onset of persecution had considerably reduced the growth of the new religion. Sherwin-White argues that Pliny's letter was written in either Amastris (modern Amasra) or Amisus (modern Samsun) in Pontus (1966: 693–94). In the later 2d century it appears that Amastris was the principal diocese of Pontus (Eus. *Hist. Eccl.* 4.33.6).

The other notable piece of literary evidence for the origins of Christianity in Bithynia is the address of 1 Peter. The author identifies his readers as belonging to the "Dispersion," a term with unmistakable Jewish overtones (and so taken by Eusebius, *Hist. Eccl.* 3.4.2). While the contents of the letter are not especially relevant to Christians of Jewish origin, it seems likely that many of the first Christian converts in Bithynia-Pontus were drawn from the Jewish communities of the area. The synagogue of Nicomedia is attested by a series of Greek inscriptions dated to the 2d/3d century A.D. (*TAM* 4.1.375–77). Also from Nicomedia is a probably 3d-century epitaph of a Reader (*TAM* 4.1.374) and another possibly 3d-century epigraph with an incised cross; interestingly, this latter inscription commemorates a man from Aradus in Syria (Robert 1978: 413).

A similar conjunction of Jewish and early Christian material occurs at Nicaea and around Bithynium-Claudiopolis. A group of probably pre-Constantinian Christian epitaphs from Nicaea threaten violators of the tomb with divine vengeance: "He will give an account to God on the Day of Judgment" (e.g., IGSK 9.555–56). The language significantly recalls the Jewish epitaphs of Nicomedia and it is not surprising to find evidence for Jews living in Nicaea (IGSK 9.615). From the countryside near Bolu come the epitaph of a Jew and a lead curse tablet containing a number of garbled Hebraisms and an appeal to the "Lords, Divine Angels," suggesting some magical interest in Jewish religious language (IGSK 31. 9, 180).

The area around Amisus has produced a similar "sub-Jewish" amulet and also a monotheistic epitaph of early imperial date that could be either Jewish or Christian (*CIJud* 802, Anderson; Cumont; and Grégoire 1910: 26). A possibly 3d-century Christian epitaph has also been recorded in Bithynium (IGSK 31. 144). This case is especially interesting as the principal member of the family commemorated had been chief magistrate of the city. While the influence of Hellenized Jewish communities both on contemporary paganism and on the development of a type of Christianity that was relatively well integrated in pagan society is better documented in Phrygia, the indications are that the Jewish communities of Bithynia may have exercised a similar role.

Bibliography

Anderson, J. G. C; Cumont, F.; and Grégoire, H. 1910. *Studia Pontica.* Vol. 3. Brussels.

Jones, A. H. M. 1971. *The Cities of the Eastern Roman Provinces* 2d ed. Oxford.

Magie, D. 1950. *Roman Rule in Asia Minor.* Princeton.

Price, S. R. F. 1984. *Rituals and Power.* Cambridge.

Robert, L. 1977. La titulature de Nicée et de Nicomédie: la gloire et la haine. *HSCP* 81: 1–39.

———. 1978. Documents d'Asie Mineure. VI. Epitaphes de Nicomédie. *Bulletin de Correspondance Hellénique* 102: 408–13.

———. 1980. *A travers l'Asie Mineure.* Bibliothèque des Ecoles Françaises d'Athènes et de Rome 239. Paris.

Rostovtzev, M. 1918. Pontus, Bithynia and the Bosporus. *Annual of the British School of Athens* 22: 1–20.

Sherwin-White, A. N. 1966. *The Letters of Pliny: A Historical and Social Commentary.* Oxford.

Vitucci, G. 1953. *Il Regno di Bitinia.* Studi pubblicati dall' Istituto Italiano per la Storia Antica 10. Rome.

ANTHONY SHEPPARD

BIZIOTHIAH (PLACE) [Heb *bizyôtyâ*]. A town in Judah located in the extreme S (Negeb) near Beersheba: the MT reads "and Hazar-shual and Beersheba and Biziothiah" (Josh 15:28). However, this reading is almost certainly incorrect. First, the parallel list of Neh 11:27 reads "and in Hazar-shual and in Beersheba and its villages" (Heb *bĕnōteyhā,* lit. "daughters"). Second, the LXX of Josh 15:28 reads *kōmai autōn,* "its villages," also presupposing a Heb vorläge reading of *bĕnōteyhā.* Thus, contra the MT (and RSV), there probably was not a village in Judah named Biziothiah.

GARY A. HERION

BIZTHA (PERSON) [Heb *bizzĕtāʾ*]. See MEHUMAN.

BLASPHEMY. See PUNISHMENTS AND CRIMES.

BLASTING/BLIGHT. See AGRICULTURE.

BLASTUS (PERSON) [Gk *Blastos*]. Chamberlain of Herod Agrippa I (Acts 12:20). As chamberlain *(koitōn),* he was in charge of Herod's bedchambers or private quarters. Herod had come to Caesarea in 44 C.E. to see the games. At that time he may have been waging economic war against the cities of Sidon and Tyre, perhaps as an outgrowth of the competition between the ports of Caesarea and Phoenicia. He may have banned grain exports to Tyre and Sidon and effectively cut off their traditional supply of food from Judea (1 Kgs 5:7–12; Ezek 27:17). Probably through a bribe, a Phoenician delegation persuaded Blastus to intervene on their behalf. Through his intervention the people of Tyre and Sidon gained an audience before Herod at Caesarea. There is no reference to Blastus or to this incident in Josephus' account of Agrippa I at the games in Caesarea (*Ant* 19.343–50).

JOANN FORD WATSON

BLESS/BLESSING [Heb *brk*]. The Hebrew root *brk* has diverse but unrelated etymological meanings, just as in other Semitic languages. There are the verbal and nominal forms related to "bless/blessing." A verb "to kneel" and a noun "knee" (Gen 24:11; Ps 95:6; Isa 45:23) also derive from the same root. In addition, there is a noun that Hebrew dictionaries translate as "pool, water reservoir, basin" (Isa 7:3). It is almost unanimously agreed that apart from popular etymologies, which connect these meanings (especially the seeming religious connection between kneeling and praying, praising, blessing), there is in fact no basis in any Semitic language for the etymological tie (Mitchell 1987: 16; *TDNT* 2: 284).

Bless/blessing has been most frequently understood in terms of benefits conveyed—prosperity, power, and especially fertility. This focus on the content of the benefit is now being viewed as secondary. The primary factor of blessing is the statement of relationship between parties. God blesses with a benefit on the basis of the relationship. The blessing makes known the positive relationship between the parties, whether a single individual (Gen 12:1–3) or a group (Deut 7:14–16). The recipient and others become aware of the value of the relationship and hence its desirability (Job 42:12). Human blessings portray the goodwill between parties and find their basis in the human-divine relationship. Just as with God's blessing, they may either convey benediction (Num 6:24–26) or benefaction (Gen 33:11).

The focus on relationship rather than content permits a wide range of lexical meaning, so that *brk* is not always translated in the same fashion. What is conveyed, regardless of translation, is always based on the favorable relationship between parties. The term *brk* is used in the sense of thanking another individual (1 Sam 23:21; 2 Sam 14:22; Job 29:11–13). The thanks are based upon the act done, the relationship established. Of course, there is a vast array of terms for thanks, praise, and even worship that parallel *brk,* and hence *brk* may be translated with one of these terms in English. Most frequently these have God as the object of the praise (Pss 34:2—Eng 34:1; 115:17–18, 145:1–2). The contexts of *brk* found within the Hebrew Bible demand these different translations both because of the diverse relationships out of which blessing occurs and because of the fact that benediction or benefaction may be articulated. Finally, there are seven occurrences where *brk* is used euphemistically to mean "blaspheme" or "curse" (1 Kgs 21:13; Job 2:9; etc.).

The verbal and nominal occurrences of blessing appear approximately 400 times in the Hebrew Bible (88 times in Genesis and 83 times in Psalms with the remaining occurrences fairly evenly divided in the canon). Over half of all occurrences are in the *Piʿel* verbal form. The passive participle, with the so-called *bārûk* formula ("Blessed are you," or "Blessed be . . ." is the only form of the Qal to be used. The subject and object of *brk,* "bless," is evenly divided between God blessing humans, humans blessing other humans, and humans blessing, i.e., "praising" God. While occurrences in other NW Semitic languages employ similar subjects and objects, there is some agreement that the Hebrew usage is both unique (*EncRel* 2: 251) and more wide-ranging (Mitchell 1987: 10). Caution is advised in drawing too many conclusions regarding the peculiarity of the Hebrew occurrences, in part because of the paucity of other NW Semitic texts as opposed to the relative richness of occurrences in Hebrew.

Blessing is a central part of diverse Hebrew Bible traditions, and therefore it has received rather extensive treatment in commentaries, histories of Israelite religion, theologies, and individual studies of selected texts where *brk* occurs. Since *homo religiosus* in all traditions seeks and articulates relationships with the divine or sacred, it is not surprising that blessing is significant in many ancient and modern religious traditions beyond the Hebrew Bible (*EncRel* 2: 247–53). There is promise for an enriched understanding of blessing when it is placed among the analogues outside the Hebrew Bible, although much work needs to be undertaken in these comparative studies.

Specialized *brk* research among Hebrew Bible scholars has been bountiful during the 20th century. The studies focus upon three factors: (1) the history of the concept; (2) the identification of the giver and receiver of blessing; (3) the nature of the transfer that takes place in blessing.

First, much has been written on the history of blessing. The earliest NW Semitic usage is clearly of gods blessing humans with possessions and children. There is considerable difference of opinion regarding whether or not the pre-Islamic concept of blessing, which entailed an animistic understanding of power, influenced the earliest stages of NW Semitic and Hebrew understandings. Assumptions, including what is primitive and the extent of polytheism's influence on monotheism, determine in part the positions taken.

A rather extensive tradition history has been articulated by Wehmeier (1970). Within pentateuchal sources, for example, he is of the opinion that E is void of any blessing theme, that in D God primarily blesses Israel with prosperity in the land, and P utilizes earlier traditions but also spiritualizes the content of blessing. As opposed to Westermann (1978), he does not see much utilization of any blessing tradition among the prophets. Most debated of all the tradition history research is Westermann's contention that blessing and deliverance are quite distinct divine activities. He contends that deliverance concentrates on specific, often miraculous acts of God, whereas blessing deals with the natural processes of God's nurturing creation. Extensive research on the treaty-covenantal understandings of curses and blessings in the ANE and the Hebrew Bible have enriched this dimension of comparative work.

Second, almost every lexical discussion of blessing is divided along the lines of the identification of the giver and receiver of the blessing. The question of what it means for God to be blessed has generated the major disagreements. If one argues that the nature of the referent (God or a human) changes the force of a term, then the translation must change. It would not make much sense for humans to give the same benefits of blessing given by the deity. Therefore translating *brk* in a range from bless to praise preserves the basic factor of relationship in the understanding of blessing. The human response of praise to God's blessing is an entirely understandable development. Human praise is the one benefit which may be given in return for the benefits conveyed by the deity. When referents shift, these kinds of translational shifts are common.

Finally, two interrelated issues, power and magic, continue at the center of understanding what is transferred in a blessing. Here the question surrounds the acquisition of blessing. Can God be coerced into giving a blessing? Can a blessing be obtained unrelated to God's beneficence? Is there any self-fulfilling power residing in words? The earlier studies of Pedersen *(PI),* Mowinckel (1961; originally published in 1924), and Hempel's work of 1925 (1961) understood the ancient world of these texts in a dynamistic perspective and could answer these questions in a positive manner. Wehmeier (1970), Scharbert (*TDNT* 2: 279–308), and Westermann (1978) understand the biblical traditions to have limited the dynamistic perspective at least partially, but not to have obliterated it entirely. Mitchell (1987) strongly opposes any magical understandings in the Hebrew Bible related to blessing.

This last issue needs further work on the individual texts portraying blessing, as well as better perspectives on Israelite religion within its own surroundings. Since there is no comprehensive study of the complex variety of synonyms ("happy," "peace," etc.) and antonyms ("curse") for blessing, we can assume that new perspectives on this important religious term will be forthcoming.

Bibliography

Hempel, J. 1961. Die israelitische Anschauungen von Segen und Fluch im Lichte altorientalischer Parallelen. *BZAW* 81: 30–113.

Mitchell, C. W. 1987. *The Meaning of BRK "To Bless" in the Old Testament.* SBLDS 95. Atlanta.

Mowinckel, S. 1961. *Segen und Fluch in Israels Kult und Psalmendichtung.* Vol. 5 of *Psalmenstudien.* Amsterdam.

Wehmeier, G. 1970. *Der Segen im Alten Testament.* Theologische Dissertation 6. Basel.

Westermann, C. 1978. *Blessing in the Bible and the Life of the Church.* Philadelphia.

KENT HAROLD RICHARDS

BLESSINGS AND CURSES. Scriptures testify to a traditional world in which divine powers (principally the God of Israel, but also "the sons of God," "Satan," "the queen of heaven," and others) are believed to influence, directly and indirectly, the life and destiny of nations and individuals. The course of human events is experienced as neither accidental nor self-directed but as dependent, wholly or in part, on the will of these divine powers. In this setting, blessing and curse, deriving ultimately from the disposition and ability of the gods to further or thwart the "good life," are of crucial importance to human welfare.

A. The Scope of the Discussion

In the Bible, blessing may be understood as a performative utterance (see Austin 1962; 1979), the effective activity of pronouncing and bringing about good for someone. It may be the resultant favor (benefaction) or enablement itself. Blessing may also be an act of greeting or prayer that invokes good for someone or seeks to avert or neutralize evil. Finally, it may be an act of praise by which a benefactor, human or divine, is acknowledged and thanked for benefits received or expected. The meaning of cursing is just the opposite. It may refer to the pronouncement of evil which brings about punishment or harm to someone, the actual harm or punishment effected, or an invocation of the same. It is unthinkable, however, that one would curse the deity (Lev 24:10–16), even for some harm one might attribute to God's neglect or disfavor (Job 2:9–10).

Earlier studies of blessings and curses in the Bible (e.g., Pedersen 1914; PI, 162–212: Mowinckel 1924; Hempel 1961) often dealt with perceived distinctions between "magical" and "religious" conceptions of their efficacy. The "magical" conception would attribute inherent power, for example, to a certain form of pronouncement, so that the benediction or malediction once spoken must automatically bring about its result, barring pronouncement of an equally or more effective counter-curse or -blessing. The "religious" conception, by contrast, would attribute the power and efficacy of a blessing or curse to the cooperative will and action of God or the gods. It was felt that both conceptions could be illustrated from the Bible. Westermann argues that the magical features, still recognizable in some of the Yahwist (J) narratives, are historical leftovers no longer operative in the theological conception of the Yahwist (1978: 57–58). Also, Scharbert (*TDOT* 2: 303) finds little trace of the magical left in the biblical conceptions of blessing and curse.

Closely related to this discussion was a scholarly consensus that the ancient Israelites, along with other contemporary cultures, attributed unusual power to the spoken word (Heb *dābār*); once uttered, the word would practically take on a life of its own and continue in effect whether or not circumstances changed or the original speaker had a change of mind. Thiselton (1974) strongly questions the supposed independent power of words in the Bible. The power of words in general, and of blessings and curses in particular, presumably depends upon the disposition (favorable or unfavorable), power, and status of the person who utters them, the circumstances under which they are spoken, and the expectations and receptivity of the audience for or about whom the words are spoken. The Bible presents blessings and curses as neither automatic nor irrevocable. They are effective only when spoken by authoritative or authorized persons (e.g., God, king, prophets, priests, elders) at what is considered an appropriate time and place, accompanied by the expected gestures or rituals, if any. God willing, they may also be revoked. Recent hermeneutical reflections on the Balaam story by Coats (1982) and Ford (1982) from a "process" perspective interpret blessing and curse in terms of the power of divine persuasion.

B. The Terminology of Blessings and Curses

1. In the Hebrew Bible. The Bible frequently expresses blessings by forms of the verbal root *brk,* "to bless," including *bārûk,* "blessed," and by the related noun *bĕrākâ,* "blessing." Other Hebrew terms belonging to the same semantic field include *ḥnn,* "to act favorably or graciously," *rṣh* and *rāṣôn,* "be favorably pleased," "favor," *ṣlḥ,* "to advance or prosper," *ḥesed,* "loyalty/magnanimity/kindness," and various expressions of the gracious presence or accessibility of God (i.e., God's being "with" *ʿim* or *ʾet* someone). One who has been favored or has experienced blessing may be called Heb *ʾašrê,* "happy," a term found most frequently in the Psalms and Proverbs, while the general state of well-being or security that results from blessing may be termed Heb *šālôm.* In conversation with earlier studies, Mitchell (1983) provides insightful analyses of the semantic relationships between *brk* and many of the other terms cited here.

The terminology of cursing in the Hebrew Bible includes the three principal Heb roots *ʾlh, ʾrr, qll,* and their derivatives. The first carries the basic sense of a vocal or written imprecation, a curse pronounced. The second, frequently encountered in the participial form *ʾārûr* and as an antonym to *bārûk,* seems to have the basic sense of "spell," connoting a sort of banning or barring from benefits. The third has a wide range of meanings, often dealing less with imprecation than with disrespect and verbal or physical abuse (see Brichto 1963: 70–71; 114–15; 176–77). Scharbert (*TDOT* 1: 261–64) adds that Heb *ʾālâ* was commonly used in legal situations as a conditional curse or oath used to prove guilt, protect property, or ratify a treaty. He further notes that the *ʾārûr* formula was the most powerful "decree" expressed by someone in authority to deliver over a transgressor to misfortune (*TDOT* 1: 411). In the Balaam story (Numbers 22–24), the uncommon Heb root *qbb* alternates several times with *ʾrr,* while Heb *zʿm* also occurs once. Also within the semantic field of cursing are the "ban" (Heb *ḥerem*) which singled out persons or groups for extermination (e.g., Joshua 7), the interjections Heb *ʾôy* ("Woe!" e.g., Isa 6:5) and *hôy* ("Ha!" e.g., Jer 22:18), and expressions of divine withdrawal or displeasure such as God's "hiding" or "turning away the face."

2. In the New Testament. The equivalent to *brk* in the LXX, the intertestamental literature, and the NT is Gk *eulogein,* "to bless," and its derivatives, including the divine epithet *eulogētos,* "blessed." The condition of happiness resulting from being favored is expressed by Gk *makarios* (see Matthew 5 and Luke 6). The roots may also be used interchangeably, as in Luke 1:42 and 45, where Elizabeth hails Mary as both *eulogēmenē* and *makaria.*

Cursing in the NT may be expressed by forms of *kataraesthai,* "to curse," *(kat)anathematizein,* "to make anathema," and the related terms; and by Gk *kakalogein,* "to slander or speak evil of." The woeful expression Gk *ouai* appears especially in Matthew, Luke, and Revelation.

There are, of course, many portions of the Scriptures in which blessing and curse are closely discernible in context, even though the expected terminology is not employed.

C. The Efficacy of Blessings and Curses

1. The Power and Authority behind Blessings and Curses. As noted above, blessings and curses derive their efficacy from the power and authority of the one who utters them or serves as guarantor for carrying out their intent. In the Bible, the ultimate source of power is Yahweh, the God of Israel, who is said to finally control all good and evil (Isa 45:6), and who can thwart all other counsel and intentions (Job 12:13–25). In the biblical view, therefore, no blessing or curse can become operative without the assent of this God.

Blessings and curses, once uttered, need not come to pass inexorably, because countermeasures could be taken. For example, when Micah of Ephraim revealed to his mother that he himself had stolen some silver protected by her curse, she immediately responded by pronouncing a blessing in Yahweh's name on her son and consecrating the silver to this God (Judg 17:1–3). When Jonathan brought his father Saul's curse upon himself unwittingly, the people intervened to save him from ritual execution and "ransomed" him (1 Sam 14:24–30, 36–45). Steps could also be taken ahead of time to insure blessing and avert curses. Abram was assured that God would bless those who blessed him but would curse anyone who cursed him (Gen 12:3); Isaac pronounced a similar blessing on his son Jacob (Gen 27:29). Although the specific vocabulary of blessing and curse is not used, the word that came to Jeremiah at the potter's shop indicated that Yahweh is free to reverse blessing-bearing promises ("building," "planting," "good") or curse-bearing threats ("pluck up," "break down," "destroy" if people change their ways (Jer 18:7–10).

2. Accompanying Symbolic and Ritual Acts. Various gestures or rituals may have been expected to accompany the pronouncement of blessings and curses. The laying on of hands (Gen 48:14; Mark 10:16) or the ritual sharing of food and drink (Gen 14:18–20) might accompany a blessing. When Shimei cursed David, he threw stones and dust (2 Sam 16:5–14). A person suspected of adultery was to drink curse-contaminated water which would cause injury if the person were guilty (Num 5:19–28). Jeremiah smashed a pot in the presence of elders and senior priests while delivering a divine message that Jerusalem and its inhabitants were about to be broken by their enemies (Jer 19:1–13) and would become (cursed) objects of hissing (v 8; cf. Jer 29:18). Several variations on another ritual commonly associated with curses, namely, the dismemberment of a person or animals, occur in Gen 15:9–10 (cf. Jer 34:18–20), 1 Sam 11:6–7 and, evidently, Judg 19:29–30. In his discussion of the curse ritual in Deuteronomy 27, Harrelson (1980: 26–33) suggests that the division of the Israelites into two groups facing each other is another variation on this ritual of dismemberment.

D. The Settings of Blessings and Curses

In a wider sense, blessing may be understood as the continuous favorable working of God to bring about good in the world of nature and the life of individuals and families (Westermann 1979: 33, 44–45). The Bible, however, depicts many typical situations in which the mediation of God's favor or disfavor, expressed as a deliberate pronouncement or invocation of curse or blessing, was expected or considered appropriate. These situations often involve a crisis, the onset of a struggle, a time of decision, or the crossing of a threshold into the future.

1. Times of Universal or Cosmic Significance. The crisis or transition may be of universal significance. Thus, in the first story of the creation, God twice directly pronounces blessings on the newly created creatures (Gen 1:22, 28) and also hallows the seventh day, which marks the completion of the "generations of the heaven and the earth" (Gen 2:3–4). By contrast, after the man and the woman have eaten of the fruit and are about to be driven from the garden, Yahweh curses the serpent and the ground (Gen 3:14, 17) and promises pain to the humans in their future production of food and children (Gen 3:16–19).

In the NT, the arrival of the Christ (the Anointed One) and his announcement of the breaking in of the kingdom of God is accompanied by a series of blessings and woes. In Luke, Jesus balances his pronouncement of four "blesseds" with four contrasting "woes" (Luke 6:20–26). As Van Den Doel (1963: 216–20, 224–25) notes, there are several other instances in the gospels where those who are receiving and acting on Jesus' message of the kingdom and the reversal of conditions it represents are called "blessed." He also notes (1963: 151) that, while the many healings and exorcisms performed by Jesus are not designated "blessings" in the text, they carry that meaning for the human beneficiaries.

2. Times of Individual or Family Crisis. Crisis and transition times in individual and family life call for blessings and the averting of curses. The priest Eli blessed Hannah and Elkanah with an invocation for additional children after they had dedicated Samuel to the service of the sanctuary. The text immediately reports Yahweh's fulfillment of this blessing (1 Sam 2:20–21). Indeed, Eli had pronounced a similar benediction over the barren Hannah after her agonized prayers for a first child. That priestly blessing was also quickly answered by Yahweh (1 Sam 1:17–20). When Ruth and Boaz prepared to be married, the elders and people similarly invoked blessings of children and prosperity; and, upon the birth of a son whom they presented to Naomi, the women lauded Yahweh as blessed (Heb *bārûk;* Ruth 4:11–12, 14). Similarly, Raguel blessed his daughter Sarah and her husband Tobias upon their marriage (Tob 7:13).

Blessing may be invoked for someone undertaking an important journey, especially when the future of the family is at stake (Gen 24:7; cf. Tob 5:16). When Rebekah consented to become Isaac's wife, they sent her on her journey with a blessing that she bear innumerable descendants (Gen 24:60). Jacob went to Paddan-aram to find a wife with his father's blessing (Gen 28:1–5). Later, when Laban finally agreed to allow his daughters and grandchildren to go with Jacob, he blessed them (Gen 32:1—Eng 31:55). Finally, the climactic episode wherein Jacob struggles with "a man" at the Jabbok River and subsequently obtains a divine blessing and the new name Israel (Gen 32:22–32) takes place during his sojourn away from Paddan-aram, just before he meets again with the estranged brother he fears, Esau.

Blessings are also appropriate when one generation is about to die and wishes to pass on favor to another. Best known are the blessings bestowed by Isaac and Jacob upon their sons (Genesis 27; 48–49).

Westermann argues (1978: 83–91) that NT accounts of Jesus blessing children (Mark 10:16 = Matt 19:15 = Luke 18:17), speaking the blessing at meals (Luke 9:16; 24:30), and blessing his disciples when he took leave of them (Luke 24:50–51), indicate that he was continuing traditional Jewish practices. Nevertheless, the latter episode also marks a significant moment of transition in the relationship between Jesus and his followers.

In contrast to the usual practice of seeking a blessing during times of crisis, Jeremiah and Job are two individuals who experienced personal crises and such intense suffering that they cursed the day of their birth and wished for death (Jer 20:14–18; Job 3). Also, Jeremiah cursed the person who made the birth announcement (vv 15–17), while Job added a curse upon the night during which he was conceived (v 3; see Alter 1985: 76–83, 96–110). Jonah, in very different circumstances and without actually invoking a curse, also expressed a death wish (Jonah 4:3, 8). It is possible, however, to interpret the actions of all three as desperate attempts actually to motivate God to reverse their fortunes.

The guarantee of one's word was to swear an oath that included a potential curse upon oneself. Saul uttered such an oath which threatened Jonathan's life (1 Sam 14:44), as did Solomon when he doomed Adonijah (1 Kgs 2:23), and the king of Israel who swore to destroy Elisha (2 Kgs 6:31). When Jonathan and David swore loyalty to each other, Jonathan included a self-imprecation to guarantee his fidelity (1 Sam 20:13). Abner, too, uttered this sort of self-imprecation when he publicly switched allegiance from the family of Saul to David (2 Sam 3:9). There are many similar examples in the Hebrew Bible. A striking instance in the NT is Peter's invocation of a curse (once in Mark 14:71; twice in Matt 26:72, 74) when he denied being one of Jesus' followers. In the Sermon on the Mount, Jesus counseled against swearing by anything, but simply to state "Yes" or "No" (Matt 5:33–37).

3. Times of Community or National Decision. Blessings and curses figure prominently in the covenants that Yahweh initiated with the people of Israel. Covenants were believed to be central in determining the nation's fortunes. The rituals renewing or reaffirming covenant included reciting blessings and curses. This is especially clear in the case of the Mosaic covenant as presented in Deuteronomy. At the conclusion of his lengthy exposition of the statutes and ordinances Israel was to keep (Deuteronomy 5–26), Moses instructed the people to observe a ceremony, at Shechem on Mounts Ebal and Gerizim, in which they would declare the curses or blessings that would come upon them for obedience or disobedience to the statutes and commandments just rehearsed (Deuteronomy 27–28). In chap. 30 he reiterates Israel's obligation to choose "life," "good," and "blessing" over "death," "evil," and the "curse" (vv 15, 19) by remaining loyal to their God. The book closes with the song of Moses (chap. 32), which echoes elements of a covenant lawsuit (Heb *rîb*) and the curse-induced evils that would come upon disobedient Israel, balanced and overshadowed by the concluding blessing of Moses on all the tribes of Israel (chap. 33). The latter, set just before Moses' passing in chap. 34, serves as a last will and testament, in some ways similar to the blessing of Jacob in Genesis 49.

The so-called Holiness Code (Leviticus 17–26) also concludes with contrasted blessings (26:3–13) and curses (26:14–39) for observance or nonobservance of Yahweh's statutes. Moreover, the closing words assure the people that, even after the most dire consequences, including exile to enemy lands, genuine repentance and a return to Yahweh would cause him to remember the Abrahamic covenant and the Sinai covenant. For, after all, Yahweh would not abandon them, even in foreign lands, so as to destroy the people completely and break the covenant with them (26:40–45).

Scharbert believes that the blessing formulas in Deuteronomy 28 and Leviticus 26 are briefer and vaguer than the curse formulas (*TDOT* 2: 304–5). He notes that in Deuteronomy there is no formal list of blessings to counterbalance the curses enumerated in chap. 27. Further, blessing plays little role in the preexilic prophets, although curses are present. This may indicate that the blessings were a later insertion into the legal sanctions, which originally were only the curses that would result from covenant-breaking.

Several important studies on covenant (including Mendenhall 1955; Baltzer 1971; and McCarthy 1978) have treated the blessings and curses in Yahweh's covenant with Israel in comparison with curses and blessings found in political treaties now familiar from other nations, notably the Hittites, in the ANE. Hillers (1964: 43–79) usefully correlates some 20 specific curses (e.g., ravaging animals, removal of joyful sounds, breaking of the scepter, dry breasts, contaminated water, etc.) found in various ANE treaties and paralleled in Deuteronomy 28, Leviticus 26, the Prophets, or elsewhere in the Hebrew Bible. Levenson (1985: 35) remarks that it is hardly surprising that the curses in Leviticus and Deuteronomy, so horrific in their detail, are still read in undertones in synagogue worship.

4. In the Cult. Two climactic cultic occasions include David ritually conducting the covenant box into Jerusalem and Solomon's dedication of the temple. On each occasion, the king takes the leading role in the ceremonies, blessing various other participants. David dared to move the covenant box based upon the report that Yahweh had blessed Obed-edom the Gittite, with whom the box had been residing for three months (2 Sam 6:11–12). Upon safely bringing the box to its new residence, David made sacrificial offerings, distributed foodstuffs to the people, and blessed them in the name of the Lord of hosts (vv 18–19). He also intended to bless his own household (v 20), but was met with disdain by his wife Michal the daughter of Saul. Given the context, the laconic report that Michal thereafter became barren for the rest of her life (v 23) strongly implies that, by her actions, Michal exchanged the intended blessing for a curse instead.

Subsequently, when Solomon moved the covenant box to the newly erected temple, the ceremonies of dedication as reported in 1 Kings 8 included prayers, offerings, and shared feasting. In addition, Solomon pronounced blessings on the assembled people (vv 14, 55) and acknowledged Yahweh as blessed (vv 15, 56), while the people, in turn, blessed the king at the conclusion of the week-long festivities (v 66).

The so-called Aaronic benediction or blessing in Num 6:22–27 was probably used in the temple services and has remained in use among Jews and Christians to the present. Yahweh promises Moses that when the priests use this formulaic blessing Yahweh himself will bless the people. The brief formula is dense with the terminology of blessing, including assurance of God's protection (Heb *šmr*), favor (Heb *ḥnn*), and peace (Heb *šālôm*). Noteworthy is the threefold repetition of the Heb root *brk,* once in the formula itself and twice in the accompanying rubrics, as well as the emphatic threefold repetition of the divine name, which, along with the *šālôm* it brings, is being placed (*śym;* vv 26–27) upon the recipients of the blessing. This blessing reaffirms positively the powerful words of Exod 15:26, in which God promised in the negative: "No plague which I placed *(śym)* upon Egypt will I place *(śym)* upon you, for I am Yahweh your Healer."

The book of Psalms contains indications of the use of blessings and curses in the temple liturgy. For example, Psalm 72 speaks of continual prayers and blessings offered on behalf of the monarch (vv 15, 17) and invites people to bless themselves by his name (v 17). Psalms 21 and 22—prayers before and after battle—indicate that victory over enemies was formally requested and acknowledged as a blessing (Pss 21:4, 7—Eng 21:3, 6; cf. Pss 18:47–49—Eng 18:46–48). Many of the psalms were sung as blessings of Yahweh, as is indicated by the formulaic language at the beginning and conclusion of Psalms 103 and 104, the invitation in Pss 134:1–2, and the final verses of Psalm 135. Temple singers or priests are depicted in Psalm 118 as pronouncing "blessed in the name of Yahweh" the one (perhaps the king?) who enters the sacred precincts. Cazelles (*TDOT* 1: 445–48) believes that the frequently encountered expression Heb *ʾašrê,* "happy!" in the Psalms is best understood as a sort of liturgical cry or interjection which found its way into services of the Second Temple, perhaps via Egyptian practice. The solemn pronouncement of curses, evidently, also took place in the temple, as indicated by the lists of imprecations on enemies contained in many of the laments (e.g., Pss 17:13–14; 35:4–6, 26; 58:7–10—Eng 58:6–9). Particularly striking is Psalm 137, which twice calls happy (Heb *ʾašrê*) whoever takes vengeance on Babylon (vv 8–9). Lapide (1982: 166) offers the striking interpretation that these ritualized curses and imprecations helped worshippers to vent emotions of anger and frustration, and thus defused the need for carrying out actual acts of bloodshed.

In the NT Jesus blessed children (Mark 10:13–16) as a sign of their inclusion in the kingdom of God. Many Christian churches have interpreted this story as a sanction of infant baptism and have included its solemn reading or intonation at baptismal ceremonies. In the gospels, Jesus also blesses food (Mark 6:41 = Matt 14:19 = Luke 9:16; Luke 24:30), a practice already well attested at the Qumran community and still widely followed among Jews and Christians. In the new "family" of Christian disciples (Mark 3:31–35; 10:29–31), a central sign and affirmation of the blessing-mediating presence of the risen Christ as the "breaking of bread" together (Acts 2:42, 46–47)—a practice no doubt linked to the tradition of the Last Supper he shared with his disciples at the time of Passover just before his crucifixion (note Mark 14:22–25 = Matt 26:26–29 = Luke 22:15–20; 1 Cor 10:16). Paul, moreover, warns that unworthy eating and drinking of the "Lord's supper" would actually endanger the health of the assembly (1 Cor 11:20–34); the expected blessing, in effect, could be turned into a curse.

The traditional liturgy of St. John Chrysostom celebrated in the Eastern Orthodox churches powerfully presents the continuing mediation of blessing through the risen Christ. Blessing from God to the faithful is both pronounced and effected through the proclamation of the gospel and communing in the eucharistic meal. Surrounding these two climactic activities of blessing, continuous prayers and psalms invoking divine blessing for all people in every imaginable walk of life alternate with repeated ascriptions of glory to the trinity "now and ever and to ages of ages." These ascriptions bear close resemblance to the benedictions honoring God and the divine kingdom in Jewish synagogue worship. The overall mood of the liturgy is reminiscent of the psalmist's exhortation to "bless Yahweh at all times" (Ps 34:2—Eng 34:1) in acknowledgment of the saving strength of the All-Powerful One. This ancient Christian liturgy also draws together in a single cultic celebration the three lines of blessing present in the Scriptures: from God to humanity, from humans to other humans, and from humans to God. These lines of blessing were identified by Schenk (1967), whose analysis was criticized and expanded upon by Westermann (1978: 68–101; see also Mitchell 1983). Westermann has also written on the place and function of blessing in worship and in the rituals of the Church and on possible continuities and discontinuities with practices attested in the Scriptures (1978: 103–20).

E. Blessings, Curses, and the Literary Shape of the Bible

Recent studies have turned attention to the artistic use of blessings and curses as organizing devices by those who composed or shaped longer and shorter sections of the Bible. Some examples follow.

1. Judges 5. The so-called Song of Deborah, widely regarded as among the oldest literary compositions in the Hebrew Bible, is shaped by a series of blessings and curses (see Urbrock 1987: 426–27, 432). The naming of Deborah and Jael, both subjects of praise in the song, is carefully framed by words of blessing (v 2—blessing, vv 6–7—naming, v 9—blessing; "Most blessed . . . Jael . . . most blessed," v 24). Further, the name of the Israelite commander, Barak (Heb *bārāq*), sounds like Heb *brk*, "to bless," and its repetition in vv 12 and 15 nicely balances the double invitation to "Bless Yahweh" in vv 2 and 9. By contrast, mention of the village of Meroz is framed by a double curse in v 23. Similarly, the Canaanite commander Sisera and his mother literally stand outside the blessing-frames in the text and are named only in an ironic context where food (v 25), a sign of blessing, is exchanged for violent death (vv 26–27), sign of a curse, and where those who expected to take spoil actually have been despoiled themselves (vv 28–30). The song ends with the invocation of a curse on the enemies and a blessing on the allies of Yahweh (v 31). This closing invocation, along with the invitation to "Bless Yahweh" in v 2, serves as a clear inclusion or envelope for the entire composition.

Juxtaposition of blessing and curse, used so effectively as a literary device in Judges 5, occurs frequently elsewhere in the Bible, also. The balancing of blessings and woes in Luke and the covenant blessings and curses in Deuteronomy 27–28 and Leviticus 26 have been mentioned above (secs. D.1. and D. 3.) In Jer 17:5–8, one whose heart is turned away from Yahweh is described as cursed, like a shrub in a desert; but blessed like a tree by water is the one who trusts Yahweh (see also Psalm 1). The book of Proverbs contains many maxims that contrast the cursed existence, influence, and fate of the wicked/selfish/fools with the blessed status of the righteous/liberal/wise (e.g., Prov 10:6–7; 11:11, 26; 22:9; 28:14).

2. The Book of Ruth. Blessing and curse are also juxtaposed in Ruth. Trible (1978: 166–99) has shown how the surface design of the book, which moves from an initial scene heavy with death to an "All's well that ends well" conclusion, is generated by a deep structure in which the human actors move between life and death while their God works between blessing and curse behind the scenes. The story line develops around the gradual removal or reversal of the signs of curse (famine, exile, death) and the appearance, ever more openly, of the kindness (Heb *ḥesed*) of Yahweh (2:20), reflected and mediated in the *ḥesed* of Ruth (3:10) and the favor (Heb *ḥēn*) of Boaz (2:2, 10). The action is punctuated at key points by invocations of divine blessing (1:8–9; 2:4, 12, 19; 3:10; and 4:11–12) and is enclosed at beginning and end by proclamations of divine favor (1:6 and 4:13–14). Ruth's conditional self-imprecation (1:17) and Naomi's complaint (1:20–21), with their intimations of death and affliction and emptiness, are swallowed up by life and fullness and blessing for the two women and their families, even including generations past (4:10) and future (4:18–22).

3. The Book of Psalms. Although many or most of the psalms were originally composed for use in the temple liturgies, their current arrangement into five books suggests that they are intended for study and meditation like the five books of the Mosaic Torah. This intention is underscored in the blessing that opens the book in Ps 1:1–2. The editors of the arrangement have also reminded pious readers to accompany their meditation on the collected psalms with prayer and ascriptions of blessing and praise to Yahweh. Thus, each of the first four books now concludes with such a blessing (41:14—Eng 41:13; 72:18–19; 89:53—Eng 89:52; 106:48), while the fifth book concludes with a crescendo of blessing and praise in Pss 144–50. Cazelles (TDOT 1: 446) draws attention to the placement of psalms identifying "happy" (Heb *ʾašrê*) readers and worshippers precisely at the beginning or close of the various divisions (see Pss 1:1; 41:2—Eng 41:1, 89:16—Eng 89:15; 106:3). One may add that Psalm 72, while lacking an *ʾašrê* identification, contains prayers of blessing for the king accompanying a description of the ideal, blessed kingdom. Overall, then, despite the many laments contained in the Psalter and the frequent cursing of enemies, the mood fostered by the blessings which frame the whole and its major subdivisions is one of confidence, praise, and thanksgiving.

4. The Tetrateuch, Pentateuch, and Deuteronomistic History. Wolff (1975) identifies Gen 12:1–4a, with its fivefold play on the central idea of blessing *(brk)*, as the key passage for understanding the message of the Yahwist (J) in the Tetrateuch (Genesis through Numbers). This idea has influenced the shape of the narrative. Before the appearance of Abra(ha)m, J does not use *brk* in reference to humanity; rather, *ʾrr* appears five times (Gen 3:14, 17; 4:11; 5:29; 9:25) and *qll* once (8:21), the latter in a positive passage that points ahead to Gen 12:1–3. As Wolff sees it, the rest of J's contributions to episodes in the Tetrateuch may be understood in terms of the thematic question: how does the blessing reach the peoples through Abraham? For example, the plague narrative in Exodus is shaped by J to emphasize the pharaoh's request that Moses entreat Yahweh to remove the curse, as it were, and effect a blessing even for Egypt (Exod 12:32). The last large J complex in the Tetrateuch is the Balaam narrative in Numbers, with its dramatic portrayal of God's use of a foreigner to bless Israel several times over, although he was paid to curse them. A climactic concluding couplet in Balaam's third oracle is reminiscent of the promise to Abra(ha)m (Num 24:9; cf. Gen 12:3). Nevertheless, J's work ends with a sense that the blessing that is to come to the world through Israel still remains a task and promise to be fulfilled. Moab does not yet share the blessing, and Israel is still prone to apostasy (Num 25:1–5). Wolff sees a schematic arrangement here: a sober episode of warning follows upon pronouncements of blessing, just as the episode of affliction for the pharaoh follows the blessing on Abra(ha)m in Genesis 12.

In a companion article to Wolff's, Brueggemann (1975) suggests that the focus for understanding the message of the Priestly circle (P) in the Tetrateuch is the fivefold blessing declaration of Gen 1:28, "Be fruitful . . . multiply . . . fill the earth . . . subdue it . . . have dominion." Variations on this formula recur often in Genesis (9:7; cf. 17:2, 20; 28:1–4; 35:11; 47:27; and 48:3–4) and in the important story transition at Exod 1:7.

Overall, the Pentateuch (Genesis through Deuteronomy), now long hallowed by tradition as belonging together as the Mosaic Torah, also exhibits an envelope structure that emphasizes blessing and curse at beginning and end. The stories of the primeval times and of the Abrahamic family in Genesis, arranged to reflect the J and P schemata of blessing, are balanced by the repeated Deuteronomistic invitations to choose life and blessing rather than curse and death in Deuteronomy 27–33. Scharbert (TDOT 2: 306–7) comments that the Pentateuch as finally redacted has passed on to Judaism and Christianity an enduring belief that blessing and curse, powers that emanate from God and that become effective through human behavior in relationship to divine law, "finally determine the destiny of all mankind, the nations, and the individual."

In modern scholarship, Deuteronomy is widely regarded as actually having originated not as the conclusion to the Pentateuch but as the introduction to the so-called Deuteronomistic History, which includes the books of Joshua, Judges, Samuel, and Kings. The blessings and curses that figure so prominently in the closing chapters of Deuteronomy are picked up at key points in the ensuing history. Ceremonies of covenant renewal culminating in warnings of possible good and evil for covenant observance and neglect are described as taking place at the time of Joshua's death, after the tribes of Israel had been allotted their lands (Joshua 24), and at the time of transition from tribal league to kingship under Saul (1 Samuel 12). In both instances, leaders of the people—Joshua and Samuel—are about to leave the scene, just as Moses departs at the close of Deuteronomy. When Solomon dedicates the new temple in Jerusalem, he blesses the assembled people, and blesses Yahweh at the beginning and conclusion of his great dedicatory prayer (1 Kgs 8:14, 55). The prayer itself is couched in Deuteronomistic language, acknowledging that such disasters as defeat in war (v 33), drought (v 35), famine and pestilence (v 37), and even exile (v 46) are caused by disloyalty. In a final hortatory prayer, not dissimilar to the addresses of Moses in Deuteronomy, Solomon exhorts the people to keep the commandments, statutes, and ordinances with a heart completely true to Yahweh (1 Kgs 8:58, 61; cf. Deut 6:2, 5; 30:1–2, 15–17). Centuries later, the discovery of the lost "book of Torah," perhaps an early version of Deuteronomy, caused King Josiah to tear his clothes in consternation, evidently at the possibility of the covenant curses taking effect (2 Kgs 22:11–13), and to institute a major reform of cultic practices in Judah and Jerusalem (2 Kgs 23:1–25). Not only does the theology of blessing and curse clearly pervade the Deuteronomistic History, but a pattern of ceremonial recitation of the blessings and curses at crucial points in the nation's history also helps give literary shape to this major work in the Hebrew Bible.

5. The Christian Bible. In his helpful analysis of the differing shapes of the Hebrew and Christian Bibles, Josipovici (1988: 29–49) notes how the books in the Christian OT and NT have been arranged so as to achieve both a correspondence between the major parts of each Testament and "a continuous forward drive from Creation to the end of time" (1988: 42). The design conveys an overall sense of wholeness and completion. It hardly seems surprising, then, that Revelation, the last book in the Christian arrangement, contains seven beatitudes (see Aune 1983: 283–84), two of which appear in the closing verses of the book (Rev 22:7, 14) alongside a conditional curse and a reference to the tree of life (Rev 22:18–19). Along with those uttered by Jesus in Matthew, the beatitudes in Revelation serve as an excellent inclusion scheme for the NT books. But in a more inclusive sense, the blessings and curse in chap. 22 complete a ring around the entire Christian Bible by reversing the prohibition of Genesis (Gen 3:22) and alluding to the solemn warning and invitation of Deuteronomy (Deut 4:2; 30:19).

Bibliography

Alter, R. 1985. *The Art of Biblical Poetry.* New York.

Aune, D. 1983. *Prophecy in Early Christianity and the Ancient Mediterranean World.* Grand Rapids.

Austin, J. L. 1962. *How to Do Things with Words.* Oxford.

———1979. Performative Utterances. Pp. 220–39 in *Philosophical Papers.* 3d ed. Ed. J. O. Urmson and G. J. Warnock. Oxford.

Baltzer, K. 1971. *The Covenant Formulary.* Trans. D. E. Green. Philadelphia.

Blank, S. 1950. The Curse, Blasphemy, the Spell and the Oath. *HUCA* 23/1: 73–95.

Brichto, H. C. 1963. *The Problem of "Curse" in the Hebrew Bible.* SBLMS 13. Philadelphia.

Brueggemann, W. 1975. The Kerygma of the Priestly Writers. Pp. 101–13 in *The Vitality of Old Testament Traditions,* ed. W. Brueggemann and H. W. Wolff. Atlanta.

Coats, G. W. 1982. The Way of Obedience: Traditio-Historical and Hermeneutical Reflections on the Balaam Story. *Semeia* 24: 53–79.

Ford, L. S. 1982. The Divine Curse Understood in Terms of Persuasion. *Semeia* 24: 80–87.
Harrelson, W. 1980. *The Ten Commandments and Human Rights.* Philadelphia.
Hempel, J. 1961. Die israelitische Anschauungen von Segen und Fluch im Lichte altorientalischer Parallelen. *BZAW* 81: 30–113.
Hillers, D. R. 1964. *Treaty-Curses and the Old Testament Prophets.* BibOr 16. Rome.
Josipovici, G. 1988. *The Book of God: A Response to the Bible.* New Haven.
Lapide, P. 1982. *Mit einem Juden die Bibel lesen.* Stuttgart and Munich. Pp. 161–73: Schimpfen in der Bibel.
Levenson, J. D. 1985. *Sinai and Zion.* Minneapolis.
McCarthy, D. J. 1978. *Treaty and Covenant.* 2d ed. AnBib 21. Rome.
Mendenhall, G. E. 1955. *Law and Covenant in Israel and the Ancient Near East.* Pittsburgh.
Mitchell, C. W. 1983. *The Meaning and Significance of BRK "To Bless" in the Old Testament.* Ph.D. diss., University of Wisconsin.
Mowinckel, S. 1924. *Segen und Fluch in Israels Kult und Psalmendichtung. Psalmenstudien 5.* Kristiana. Repr. Amsterdam, 1961.
Pedersen, J. 1914. *Der Eid bei den Semiten.* Strassburg.
Schenk, W. 1967. *Der Segen im Neuen Testament. ThArb* 25. Berlin.
Schottroff, W. 1969. *Der altisraelitische Fluchspruch.* WMANT 30. Neukirchen-Vluyn.
Thiselton, A. C. 1974. The Supposed Power of Words in the Biblical Writings. *JTS* 25: 283–99.
Trible, P. 1978. *God and the Rhetoric of Sexuality.* Philadelphia.
Urbrock, W. J. 1987. Sisera's Mother in Judges 5 and Haim Gouri's *ʾimmô. HAR* 11: 423–31.
Van Den Doel, A. 1963. *Blessing and Cursing in the New Testament and Related Literature.* diss., Northwestern University.
Westermann, C. 1978. *Blessing in the Bible and the Life of the Church.* Trans. K. Crim. Philadelphia.
———. 1979. *What Does the Old Testament Say About God?* Atlanta.
Wolff, H. W. 1975. The Kerygma of the Yahwist. Pp. 41–66 in *The Vitality of Old Testament Traditions,* ed. W. Brueggemann and H. W. Wolff. Atlanta.

William J. Urbrock

BLIGHT. See AGRICULTURE.

BLINDNESS. See SICKNESS AND DISEASE.

BLOOD [Heb *dām*]. Biblical authors identified the liquid, blood, and the solid, fat (Heb *ḥēleb*), as the body substances essential for all animal life. When David eulogized Saul and Jonathan (2 Sam 1:22) for bringing death to the foe, he sang: "From blood of slain, from fat of heroes—the bow of Jonathan never turned back. The sword of Saul never withdrew empty." The deduction that blood and fat were vital substances was arrived at by observing violent death by the sword or by beasts, accompanied by bloodshed and disembowelment. Blood was considered more significant to life than fat. Indeed "blood" and "life" are attested as lexical pairs in Hebrew, Ugaritic, and Akkadian poetry (Avishur 1984: 559, 577). The alternation of phrases in Gen 37:21–22 demonstrates that, in biblical Hebrew, "shed blood" (Heb *šāpak dām*) was synonymous with "struck the life" (Heb *hikkâ nepeš*). Explicit identification of blood with life is made in Deuteronomy (12:23): "For the blood is the life *(nepeš)* and you must not consume the life along with the flesh *(bāśār)*." Similarly, the Priestly writer (P) locates animal life in the blood and equates the value of blood with that of life: "For the life *(nepeš)* of the flesh *(bāśār)* is in the blood. I have consigned it to the altar in your behalf to atone for your lives, because the blood, in its value as life, makes atonement" (Lev 17:11; Levine 1974: 68). According to P, the atoning value of the blood accounts for the efficacy of the sacrificial system. By placing (Heb *sāmak*) a hand on the animal (Lev 1:4; 3:2, 8, 13; 4:4, 15, 24, 29), sinners passed their essence on to it (cf. Num 27:18–23). Once the blood of the victim had been dashed on the sides of the altar, or in some cases applied to its horns, and the fat of the victim turned into smoke, substitution was effected for the two vital substances of the human sinner. The animal's death had brought life to the sinner.

As the primary vital substance, blood was occasionally believed to be present in life-giving objects considered inanimate by moderns. Wine was "blood of the grape" (Deut 32:14; for Ugaritic, see Gordon *UT,* 385) and the Nile together with all of Egypt's sources of water bled when struck (Exod 7:17–24). The vital significance of blood is reflected in the word's special treatment in the Hebrew language. Blood consumption was most often described by the verb "eat" (Heb *ʾākal*), normally said of solids, although "drinking" (Heb *šātâ*) of blood is attested (Num 23:10; Ezek 39:17, 19), as is "get drunk" (Heb *šākar;* Isa 49:26; cf. Rev 18:6).

Because they embodied life, both blood and fat were allotted by biblical legislation to God (Lev 3:2–4, 8–10, 13–15), who was popularly believed to require them as food (Isa 1:11; Ezek 44:7; Ps 50:13). As such, they were forbidden to Israelites (Lev 3:17; 7:22–26). The primacy of blood over fat was reflected in biblical legislation. It was permissible (Lev 7:24) to put to any nonfood use the fat from animals which had died or been torn by beasts. In contrast, blood of a slaughtered animal which had not been sacrificed had to be discarded (Deut 12:24). In addition, only Israelites were prohibited from eating fat, just as they were forbidden other comestibles permitted gentiles, whereas even gentiles were restricted in their consumption of blood. According to Gen 1:29–30 (P), antediluvian humans had been permitted to eat seed-bearing plants and trees with seed-bearing fruit. All other animals were permitted green plants. After the Flood, God (Elohim) expanded the category of permitted comestibles so that all humans might lawfully eat the flesh of the other animals (Gen 9:1–7 [P]), with the provision that they not consume the blood of living animals. "But as regards living flesh *(bāśār bĕnapšô),* its blood *(dāmô)* you shall not consume" (Gen 9:4). Although the entire pericope is theoretical in that it legislates for gentiles and holds beasts accountable for shedding human blood (Gen 9:5), the prohibition against consuming the blood of a living animal is realistic. Experience had demonstrated to the ancients the nutritional value of blood, which is high in protein and low in fat. Blood's accompanying symbolic potency made it even more desirable. Keeping the animal alive after eating of its blood is economical and in modern times has been documented among the Masai (Brichto 1976: 21). For the legislator, however, practical considerations were overridden by the biblical conception that jurisdiction over the most vital substance must be divine.

For Israelites the Bible adds two additional restrictions to the consumption of blood. They may not eat the blood of a slaughtered animal (Lev 17:10, 14; Deut 12:23–25), nor may they eat "with the blood" (Heb *ʿal haddām;* Lev 19:26; 1 Sam 14:32–35), that is, eat the flesh of a slaughtered animal with blood still in it. Doubtless the putative Israelite audience shared with the biblical authors the belief that the life of the flesh was in the blood. For that very reason consumption of blood might be especially attractive when the need for invigoration was felt (Gaster 1975: 65–66). It may be observed that Saul's soldiers consumed meat with the blood in it when they were weary (1 Sam 14:31–32) and that Ashurbanipal's weary enemies slit open the stomachs of their camels (*ANET*, 299) and drank the blood. Possibly the charge "only be strong (Heb *ḥazaq*) not to eat the blood" (Deut 12:23) is a pun based on the belief that eating blood would bring strength. If animal blood was potent, human blood would be more so. Herodotus' well-known account (4.65) that the Scythian warriors drank the blood of their first victims finds a parallel in Balaam's description of Israel drinking the blood of the slain (Num 23:24).

The biblical sources agree that consumption of animal blood by Israelites and the strangers in their midst, even when incidental to eating meat, is a heinous crime equivalent to homicide (Lev 17:4), and constitutes "treachery" (1 Sam 14:33) against God. Biblical legislators differed, however, as to how one might eat meat without unlawfully consuming the blood. The solution of Leviticus 17 (P; cf. 1 Sam 14:34–35) was to make all slaughter of domestic animals sacrificial, thus giving the blood to God (given the nature of the ancient Israelite economy whereby the average individual would not have eaten meat other than fish or fowl more than ten times a year, the requirement was not excessive). Animals from flock and herd were to be brought to the tent of meeting and sacrificed as "tribute-offerings" (Heb *šĕlāmîm;* Levine 1974: 15–52). Only after the blood had been dashed against the altar, the fat turned to smoke, and the altar and the priests had taken their share, was the sacrificer permitted to eat the meat. Profane slaughter (Milgrom 1976: 1–17) was allowed only for clean wild animals such as deer and clean wild birds. Their blood was to be covered with earth (Lev 17:13), in keeping with the notion that what offends God should be hidden from his sight (Gen 37:26; Deut 23:14; 1 Sam 26:20; Isa 26:21; Ezek 24:7–8; Job 16:18). Deuteronomy 12, in contrast, permits profane slaughter of clean animals, both domestic and wild, so long as one is careful not to eat the blood, but instead pours it "out on the ground like water." Obviously, neither of the procedures described above actually removed all of the blood from the flesh, but each avoided its unrestricted human consumption.

Because of its vital power, blood could be employed in rites designed to protect the living against the forces of death. In Exodus 12 the Israelites are instructed to slaughter the Passover offering, collect its blood, and smear some of it on the lintel and the doorposts of their homes. When Yahweh sees the blood he will protect (Heb *pāsaḥ*) the door and not permit the destroyer to enter and smite the home. The apotropaic function of blood is likewise evident in the rites by which the high priest was enabled to enter and exit the inner sanctum "without dying" (Lev 16:2). Among the prescriptions is the threefold sprinkling of blood seven times (Lev 16:14, 15, 19).

The vital power of blood serves to explain its related ritual uses in purification and consecration. Blood is employed to cleanse the altar (Ezek 43:20), the incense altar (Exod 30:10), the sanctuary, and the temple (Lev 16:15–16; Ezek 45:18–20). Blood is especially important in purification of persons who have recovered from the skin disease traditionally translated "leprosy" (Heb *ṣāraʿat*). In the first stage of the ceremony, the blood of a slaughtered bird is mixed with water and sprinkled on them. Eight days later the lepers' extremities are smeared with blood from two sacrificial offerings and with oil (Leviticus 14). The ritual installation of Aaron and his sons in the priestly office contains elements similar to the purification of lepers. The new priests are smeared with sacrificial blood on their ears, thumbs, and big toes. In the climax of the rite, blood from the altar together with anointing oil is sprinkled on the consecrants and their vestments in order to render both priests and vestments holy (Exod 29:9–21; Lev 8:24). The similarities in the two rites stem from their common purpose, which is to change the status of the affected persons and thus confer on them new life. The principle articulated in rabbinic literature that the leper is reckoned dead is already found in Num 12:10–13 and 2 Kgs 15:5 (Cassuto 1972: 36, 238). Accordingly, the fresh water, literally "living water," together with the blood, serves to return the leper to life. The oil in both ceremonies is part of the same complex. Note that elsewhere in the Bible oil confers royal status on commoners (1 Sam 10:1, 16:13) and sacred status on vessels (Exod 40:9–11).

Blood that had been employed in purification rituals would, like any other "used detergent," become unclean; similarly, blood dashed on the altar (Wright 1987: 146–59). In only two categories is blood in itself a source of contamination rather than of purification. Unjustified homicide, termed "innocent blood" (Deut 19:10; 2 Kgs 4:24; Jer 7:6; Heb *dām nāqî*) or, alternatively, "blood of the innocent(s)" (Deut 19:13; Heb *dam hannāqî;* cf. Heb *dam neqîyyîm* in Jer 19:4) brings about BLOODGUILT, which pollutes (Lev 35:33; Heb *yaḥanîp*) and contaminates (Lev 35:34; Heb *ṭimmê*) the land. The second category is menstruation. Indeed, menstrual blood could serve as the epitome of impurity (Ezek 36:17; Ezra 9:11). A menstruating woman was considered to be ill (Heb *dāwâ;* Lev 12:2; 20:18). The flow of blood accompanying the birth of a male child rendered the mother menstrually unclean for a week. Following the boy's circumcision on the eighth day, the woman spent thirty-three additional days in a state of "blood purification" (Heb *dĕmê ṭohŏrâ*). The birth of a girl, presumably because it brought into existence a potential source of menstrual and parturient blood, initiated a two-week period of menstrual uncleanliness, followed by sixty-six days in a state of "blood purification" (see Lev 12:1–8).

Although biblical covenants often describe the slaughter of animals, they generally do not make specific mention of blood. Of special interest therefore is the pericope of Exod 24:4–9 in which Moses concludes a covenant between

Yahweh and Israel. He sacrifices twelve bulls and dashes part of their blood on the altar and part of it on the people. The blood is termed "blood of the covenant" (cf. Zech 9:11; Matt 26:28; 1 Cor 11:25). As is evident elsewhere in the Bible, covenants were concluded in order to create quasi-familial relations. Parties bound by covenant regularly employed family terminology. The role of blood was to create an artificial tie of consanguinity (Gaster 1975: 151). It will be recalled that in Hebrew one refers to a biological relative or a spouse as one's "bone and flesh" (Gen 2:23; 29:14; 2 Sam 19:13, 14) or simply as "flesh" (Lev 21:2). But it was not feasible physically to mingle the bone and flesh of persons who wished to effect ceremonially a social or political kinship.

The role of blood in ceremonial kinship explains the tale in which Zipporah the wife of Moses (Exod 4: 25–28) saves his life after Yahweh's attack by circumcising her son and touching the bloody foreskin to Moses' genitals (Heb *raglayim;* cf. Judg 3:24; 1 Sam 24:4). By this procedure Zipporah transformed Yahweh from an adversary into a "blood kinsman" (Heb *ḥatan dāmîm*), who was required by the newly established kinship to let Moses alone (Gaster 1975: 234).

Murder was particularly heinous when accompanied by bloodshed. Synonymous with the term "murderer" (Heb *roṣeaḥ*) is "man/men of blood" (2 Sam 16:8; Pss 5:7, 26:9; Prov 29:10). A city of murderers (Isa 1:21) might equally be termed "city of blood" (Ezek 22:2; 24:6, 9). Blood shed by a murderer cried to God out of the earth (Gen 4:10). Therefore, persons who felt compelled to commit murder might prefer to mitigate their deed by not physically spilling the blood of the victim. Accordingly, Reuben (Gen 37:21–22) was able to persuade his brothers that casting Joseph into a cistern would accomplish their purpose without shedding his blood. At the very least it was expected that an effort be made to conceal the blood of the victim (Gen 37:26; Ezek 24:7–8) and to hide it from the sight of God (1 Sam 26:20). According to the Chronicler (1 Chr 22:8), even the just warfare waged by David disqualified him from building a temple to Yahweh because he had shed much blood on the earth in Yahweh's sight.

Bibliography

Avishur, Y. 1984. *Stylistic Studies of Word-Pairs in Biblical and Ancient Semitic Literatures.* Kevelaer.

Brichto, H. 1976. On Slaughter and Sacrifice, Blood and Atonement. *HUCA* 58: 1–17.

Burkert, W. 1983. *Homo Necans: The Anthropology of Ancient Greek Sacrificial Ritual and Myth.* Berkeley.

Cassuto, U. 1972. *Studies on the Bible and Ancient Orient.* Vol. 1, *Biblical and Canaanite Literature.* Jerusalem.

Gaster, T. 1975. *Myth, Legend, and Custom in the Old Testament.* New York.

Levine, B. 1974. *In the Presence of the Lord: A Study of Cult and Some Cultic Terms in Ancient Israel.* Leiden.

Milgrom, J. 1976. Profane Slaughter and a Formulaic Key to the Composition of Deuteronomy. *HUCA* 58: 1–17.

Wright, D. 1986. The Gesture of Hand Placement in the Hebrew Bible and in Hittite Literature. *JAOS* 106: 433–46.

———. 1987. *The Disposal of Impurity.* Atlanta.

S. David Sperling

BLOOD, AVENGER OF

BLOOD, AVENGER OF (Heb *gôʾēl haddām*). An individual responsible for avenging the death of a relative. Biblical legislation refers to the blood avenger in connection with the cities of asylum (Num 35:11–28; Deut 4:41–43, 19:1–13; cf. Josh 20:1–9). From these texts as well as from biblical narrative (2 Sam 14:5–11) and extrabiblical parallels it is clear that the legislators were attempting to accommodate an existing institution to the biblical notion that only God had absolute disposition over human and animal life and over BLOOD, in which life was embodied.

In biblical law, one who slew another through "an act of God" (Exod 21:13; Heb *hāʾelohîm ʾinnâ leyādô*), by accident (Num 35: 11; Heb *bišĕgagâ*), without intention (Deut 19:4; Heb *biblî daʿat;* cf. Josh 20:3), or without malice (Num 35:22; Heb *ʾêbâ*), was not guilty or a capital crime (Deut 19:6; Heb *mišpaṭ māwet*), and his was "innocent blood" (Deut 19:10; Heb *dām nāqî*). Nonetheless, that manslayer could be killed with impunity by an avenger of blood unless he found asylum at an altar (Exod 21:13) or at a city of asylum. If, however, malice could be demonstrated, then it was permissible to remove the manslayer from the altar (Exod 21:14). If the killer had fled to a city of asylum, the elders of his native city were to demand his extradition from the city of asylum and to turn him over to the avenger of blood for execution (Deut 19:12). The Priestly legislation (Num 35: 24–25) restricts the blood avenger somewhat by empowering the assembly *(ʿēdāh)* to decide whether a manslayer qualified for asylum and to provide him safe conduct there. The death of the high priest, which atoned for the original homicide, permitted the manslayer to leave asylum without fear of reprisal by the avenger.

The key to understanding the biblical notion "avenger of blood" is the noun translated "avenger" but perhaps more accurately rendered "restorer." Heb *gôʾēl* is derived from the verb *gaʾal,* "restored," a synonym of *pādâ,* "redeemed," "ransomed" (Lev 27:27; Jer 31:11; Hos 13:14); *hošîʿa,* "saved," (Isa 61:16); and *râb,* "interceded legally in one's behalf" (Isa 49:25; Jer 50:34; Ps 119:154). Indeed, as awkward as it sounds in English, the redundancy "returns its restoration" (Heb *yāšîb gĕʾullātô;* Lev 25:51, 52) succinctly demonstrates that *gāʾal* primarily means "restored to an original state." A *gôʾēl* therefore was one who effected restoration to an original, sometimes ideal, state. Such a restorer, usually a close relative (Ruth 3:12), was expected to regain land sold by a family member (Lev 25:25; Jer 32:7–8; Ruth 4:3–4) and to redeem a relative from slavery (Lev 25:47–49). The "blood avenger" was literally "taker back of the blood," that is, a redeemer with a specialized function. The killing of one clan member was construed by the remaining members not only as a shedding of the group's blood (de Vaux 1965: 11) but as misappropriation of blood which properly belonged to the entire group. The responsibility of the blood avenger was to win back that misappropriated blood by killing the original blood shedder (Daube 1969: 123–24). Although blood vengeance for a relative slain in battle was not justified (2 Sam 3:27–30), return of other blood was required by the clan (Heb *mišpāḥâ*), or by an agent acting on its behalf even when both slayer and victim were clan members (2 Sam 14:6–7). It appears that the rise of the monarchy limited blood vengeance in that the king could, in effect, pardon the slayer by restraining the avenger of blood (2 Sam 14:5–11).

The notion that a killer was guilty of misappropriating his victim's blood, which was to be returned, if not to the victim personally, then to his kin through the killer's death, was known in the ANE outside of Israel. The 8th-century Aramaic royal treaty from Sefîre (III:1–19; Fitzmyer 1967: 97–99; Lemaire and Durand 1984: 119) requires that blood be rescued from the hand of the enemies responsible for the king's assassination (Aram *tqm dmy mn yd šnʾy;* cf. 2 Kgs 9:7 and EA Akk *naqāmu*) by putting them to the sword. Similarly, in a 14th-century B.C. letter from King Burnaburiash of Babylon to Pharoah Amenophis IV, the Babylonian demands that bandits who have killed Babylonian merchants in Egyptian territory must be apprehended and executed so that the blood of the slain may be returned (EA 8: 26–29; Akk *damīšunu tēr*). The same notion of misappropriation explains why in Mesopotamia "master of the blood" (Akk *bēl damē*) in the Neo-Assyrian period referred both to the killer and to the kinsman of his victim (Roth 1987: 363–65). The manslayer who had taken the blood had unlawfully become its master. It was the deceased's relative who was bound to reclaim that same blood.

It is of interest that, although God "avenges/rescues blood" (Deut 32:43; 2 Kgs 9:7; Heb *nāqam*) and requires it of those who shed it wrongly (Gen 9:5; 42:22; Ps 9:13; Heb *dāraš*), he is never referred to as *gôʾel haddām.*

Bibliography

Daube, D. 1969. *Studies in Biblical Law.* New York.
Fitzmyer, J. 1967. *The Aramaic Inscriptions of Sefîre.* Rome.
Lemaire, A. and Durand, J.-M. 1984. *Les Inscriptions araméennes de Sfiré et l'Assyrie de Shamshi-Ilu.* Paris.
Mendenhall, G. 1973. *The Tenth Generation.* Baltimore.
Roth, M. 1987. Homicide in the Neo-Assyrian Period. Pp. 351–65 in *Language, Literature, and History: Philogical and Historical Studies Presented to Erica Reiner,* ed. F. Rochberg-Halton. AOS 67. New Haven.
Sperling, D. 1982. Bloodguilt in the Bible and in Ancient Near Eastern Sources. Pp. 19–25 in *Jewish Law in Our Time.* ed. R. Link-Salinger. New York.
De Vaux, R. 1965. *Ancient Israel.* New York.

S. David Sperling

BLOOD, FIELD OF (PLACE). See AKELDAMA (PLACE).

BLOOD, FLOW OF. See UNCLEAN AND CLEAN.

BLOODGUILT. The pollution or guilt incurred when life is taken outside of the legal prescriptions defined in the Hebrew Bible. "Bloudgyltynesse" entered the English language through Coverdale's 1535 translation of Ps 51:16, but the notion that blood wrongly shed makes for guilt as indelible as blood itself is known from antiquity through modern times (Gaster 1975: 56–73). The earliest example from the ANE is in an 18th-century B.C. text from Mari (ARM III: 18) referring to a criminal who is "like a mad dog" and is "polluted with that blood (shed in murder)."

Although biblical Hebrew possesses words for "guilt" and "culpability," there is no Hebrew term corresponding exactly to English "bloodguilt." Because BLOOD has a life of its own (Ezek 35:6) and, in biblical thinking, embodies the life force, the biblical writers found it sufficient simply to employ the word *dām,* "blood" (Num 35:27; Deut 17:8; Josh 2:19; Judg 9:24; 2 Sam 3:27; 1 Kgs 2:37; Hos 6:8), or its plural *dāmîm* (Exod 22:1, 2; Lev 20:9; Deut 19:10, 22:8; 2 Sam 3:28; Ezek 18:13; 1 Kgs 2:23), both for the substance itself and for the consequences of its improper disposition. Justified homicide, such as the tunneling thief killed by a homeowner in darkness, does not incur bloodguilt (Exod 22:1). Unjustified killing, ranging from premeditated murder (1 Kgs 2:32) through killing a tunneling thief in daylight (Exod 22:2), to slaughtering a domestic animal without proper sacrificial rites (Lev 17:4), entails bloodguilt. Bloodguilt may also be incurred through negligence, such as that of a watchman whose failure to sound a horn results in another's death (Ezek 33:6) and that of a prophet who fails to warn his people (Ezek 33:7–9). Persons are sometimes said to bear bloodguilt for their own deaths, even when they have not committed homicide or contributed to the death of another. In this category are the mandated death penalties for the prohibited sexual acts of intercourse with one's father's wife or one's daughter-in-law, male homosexuality, and bestiality (Lev 20:11, 12, 13, 16). Regarding the executed offenders, including the beast, the biblical passages declare: "their bloodguilt is in them" (Heb *dĕmēhem bām;* cf. Ezek 33:5), that is, they and not their executioners bear the responsibility for the blood shed in carrying out the death sentences. The same is said (Lev 20:27) of persons who divine by means of ghosts (Heb *ʾôb*) or familiar spirits (Heb *yidʿōnî*). Alternatively, responsibility for bloodshed is expressed by blood "on" one's "head" (2 Sam 1:16; Heb *ʿal rôʾšĕkâ*) or "at" one's "head" (1 Kgs 2:37; Heb *bĕrôšekâ*). Rahab was told that the Israelite spies would bear on their heads the bloodguilt for any of her family killed by the invading Israelites, so long as they stayed indoors. In contrast, if they ventured outside during the Israelite attack on Jericho their bloodguilt would be on their own heads (Josh 2:19). Note that the phrase "blood at his head" alternates synonymously with the phrase "his bloodguilt is upon himself" (Ezek 33:4–5).

In some ways similar to the Greek notion of *miasma* (Pedersen 1926: 420–25; Gaster 1975: 69–73), the stain or defilement brought about by a crime, illicit bloodshed pollutes the earth. Such contamination can be expunged only by shedding the blood of the killer (Num 35:33–34).

Bloodguilt incurred by a king could cling to his country even when the royal successor came from a new dynasty, so long as the members of the original royal family were themselves not avenged by the offended parties (1 Sam 21:1–11). See BLOOD, AVENGER OF. Likewise, unwarranted bloodguilt (1 Kgs 2:31; Heb *dĕmê ḥinnâm*) that had clung to a royal associate could be removed from the royal family and "returned to the head" (Reventlow 1960: 311–27) of the perpetrator by executing him.

Bibliography

Gaster, T. 1975. *Myth, Legend and Custom in the Old Testament.* Evanston.

Pedersen, J. 1926. *Israel, Its Life and Culture I–II.* London.
Reventlow, H. 1960. Sein Blut komme über sein Haupt. VT 10: 311–27.
Sperling, S. D. 1982. Bloodguilt in the Bible and in Ancient Near Eastern Sources. Pp. 19–25 in *Jewish Law in Our Time,* ed. R. Link-Salinger. New York.

S. David Sperling

BOAR. See ZOOLOGY.

BOARD. See PLANK.

BOAZ (PERSON) [Heb *bōᶜaz*]. A descendant of Judah who married Ruth the Moabitess and fathered Obed, the grandfather of David (Ruth 4:13, 18–22). Many have suggested that the etymology of Boaz is *beᶜōz,* "in the strength of," or *bōᶜōz,* "in him (is) strength," from the root *ᶜzz,* "to be strong." Noth, however, prefers "of sharp mind" (*IPN* 228; also the Ar *baṛzun,* "mental keenness").

Boaz was an influential landowner in Bethlehem and relative of Elimelech, whose family had migrated to Moab (Ruth 2:1; 3:2; 4:3). When Elimelech and his sons died, his wife Naomi and his daughter-in-law Ruth returned to Bethlehem, where they learned of Boaz and his relationship to the Elimelech family. See ELIMELECH; MAHLON; CHILION; ORPAH. Boaz agreed at Ruth's request to act as the family's *gōʾēl* (i.e., kinsman-redeemer) by purchasing the land offered for sale by Naomi (4:3) and by marrying Ruth to "perpetuate the name" of her deceased husband Mahlon (4:10). See FAMILY; LEVIRATE LAW. However, there are several legal problems associated with Boaz' transaction that remain unresolved. See RUTH.

Boaz functions in the story as an example of covenant fidelity and God's reward for faithfulness. A relative closer to Elimelech, who refuses to marry Ruth, serves as a foil for Boaz, but Boaz' supreme act of virtue is not his marriage to Ruth, but rather his willingness to inform the nearer kinsman of his rights. By this gesture Boaz was setting aside his personal desires for the requirements of the covenant law (Berlin 1983; 86). Boaz was a man advancing in years (3:10) who probably had no progeny (cf. the response of the nearer kinsman, 4:6); the story shows that he was rewarded with wife and son for his commitment.

Boaz' name appears in the honored seventh place in the ten-name royal line of David (Ruth 4:18–22). He is also listed in the royal lineage of David by the Chronicler (1 Chron 2:11–15). Because of his relationship to the Davidic house, he is in the ancestral line of Jesus (Matt 1:5 [*Boes*]; Luke 3:32 [cf. LXX *Boos, Booz*]). There is no OT support for Matthew's comment "Salmon begat Boaz by Rahab." Because Matthew presents a schematic, incomplete genealogy he probably means that Boaz is a descendant of Rahab.

The historicity of Boaz and his connection with David have been widely challenged. It is believed that the Ruth genealogy is borrowed from Chronicles and therefore is secondary; furthermore, discrepancies are pointed out between the narrative and the genealogy. However, a growing number of scholars have argued that the genealogy is part of the original composition by showing (1) that the story is not *novelle* (folk story) but an early example of Solomonic historiography and (2) that there are features of the narrative which assume a knowledge of the genealogy.

"Boaz" is also the name of one of the two bronze pillars erected at the N (or "left" facing E) of the entrance to Solomon's temple (1 Kgs 7:21–22; 2 Chron 3:15–17). The LXX of 2 Chron 3:17 translates Boaz *ischus* ("strength") and Jachin *katorthosis* ("a setting right"), which further supports a "strength"-related etymology of the Heb. The meaning and the function of the pillars are disputed. See JACHIN AND BOAZ.

Bibliography

Berlin, A. 1983. *Poetics and Interpretation of Biblical Narrative.* Sheffield.
Campbell, E. F. 1974. The Hebrew Short Story: A Study of Ruth. Pp. 83–101 in *A Light unto My Path,* ed. H. N. Bream; R. D. Heim; and C. A. Moore. Philadelphia.
Davies, E. W. 1979. Ruth IV 5 and the Duties of the GO'EL. VT 33: 231–34.
Levine. B. A. 1983. In Praise of the Israelite *Mispaha:* Legal Themes in the Book of Ruth. Pp. 95–106 in *The Quest for the Kingdom of God: Studies in Honor of George E. Mendenhall,* ed. H. B. Huffmon; F. A. Spina; and A. R. W. Green. Winona Lake, IN.

Kenneth A. Mathews

BOCHERU (PERSON) [Heb *bōkĕrû*]. A Benjaminite descendant of Saul and Jonathan, listed as the second of Azel's six sons (1 Chr 8:38; 9:44). The LXX and Syr read the word as if it were vocalized *bĕkōrô,* meaning "his firstborn" (e.g., LXX *prōtotokos autou*). This reading would render the word as an adjective describing Azrikam, Azel's firstborn son. This is a strong possibility, in that the two words have identical Hebrew consonants and that the position of the word in both lists of Azel's sons is immediately following Azrikam. A similar situation exists with another Benjaminite, BECHER (Heb *beker*), the second son of Benjamin (Gen 46:21; 1 Chr 7:6, 8).

Siegfried S. Johnson

BOCHIM (PLACE) [Heb *bōkîm*]. A place W of the Jordan River near Gilgal and Bethel, where the Israelites wept for their disobedience at the time of Joshua (Judg 2:1–5). The Hebrew and Greek names both mean "Weepers." After entering the land of Canaan the people of Israel disobeyed God's command of *ḥerem,* "total destruction," so that "the angel of Yahweh came up from Gilgal to Bochim" to point out their disobedience. "When the angel of Yahweh spoke these words to all the sons of Israel, the people lifted up their voices and wept" (Judg 2:4). The naming of the place Bochim became a memorial for this repentance, where "they offered sacrifice to Yahweh." The location of Bochim has not been identified.

Yoshitaka Kobayashi

BODMER PAPYRI. Ancient manuscripts named after Martin Bodmer (1899–1971), Swiss humanist and collector of rare books, who founded his "library of world literature," the Bibliotheca Bodmeriana, in Cologny near Geneva. Just prior to his death, Bodmer established the Foundation Martin Bodmer, in order to ensure that his library would remain intact and open to the public.

1. The Bodmer Papyri

In its widest application the term includes not only ancient Greek and Coptic mss in the possession of the Bibliotheca Bodmeriana but also documents of shared provenience at other locations. More commonly, as here, Bodmer papyri refers to mss acquired by Martin Bodmer and in the process of being published in the series *Papyrus Bodmer,* launched in 1954. Not all of the Bodmer papyri are actual papyri, however (XVI, XIX, and XXII are parchment), nor do all derive from the discovery in 1952 (XVII).

2. The Discovery

Though Panopolis (Achmim) was once thought to have been the place of discovery, it is now believed to have been somewhat farther S in the Panopolite nome, namely at Pabau (near Dishna), the ancient headquarters of the Panchomian order of monks. The bulk of the find was bought by Bodmer, but a variety of items came into the possession of Sir Chester Beatty (see CHESTER BEATTY PAPYRI), the Universities of Mississippi and Cologne, and the Fundacio "Sant Lluc Evangelista" in Barcelona. Bodmer's share numbered in excess of the sixteen codices and three rolls which have thus far been published (excluding P. Bodmer XVII). Pap. VIII (1–2 Peter), belonging to a codex of heterogeneous materials, was presented to Pope Paul VI during his visit to Geneva in 1969. Consequently it is now housed in the Vatican Library.

3. The Library at Pabau

The evident composition of the ancient monastic library has received some attention. Of interest is the inclusion of three kinds of texts: Classical Greek, Greek biblical and Christian, and Coptic biblical and Christian. Though it has been disputed that all of the Classical texts are from Pabau, one codex makes a mixture of texts indisputable: XLV (Susanna) + XLVI (Daniel) + XXVII (Thucydides) + moral maxims. That the library can be seen as a monument to the gradual triumph of Coptic over Greek in the Christianity of Upper Egypt is perhaps not confirmed by the fact that it is the majority of OT (not NT) texts that is in Coptic. The bulk of NT mss is in Greek. Not least among the library's points of interest is the virtual absence of biblical (OT) historical books. The lone exception is P. Bodmer XXI, a Coptic papyrus codex of Joshua, minus chaps. 12–21, which never formed part of the ms.

4. The Manuscripts

Dates for the entire ancient library range from the 2d century A.D. (P. Bodmer XXVIII) to the 4th/5th century (VI, XIX, XXII, XXIX–XXXVIII), with the majority of texts falling in the 4th century. P. Bodmer XVII (7th century) does not derive from Pabau. For Coptic studies in particular, the Dishna find must rank as one of the most outstanding discoveries to date. The mss are all of early date and represent Coptic in a considerable variety of forms.

a. Biblical and Related Texts. 1. Greek. All of the published mss are on papyrus and in codex form.

P. Bodmer II = P66: containing John 1:1–21:9 (= fragment at Chester Beatty: John 19:25–28; 30–32). Date II/III century.
P. Bodmer V: Nativity of Mary, also called in the ms Apocalypse of James. Date IV. Same codex as X, XI, VII, XIII, XII, XX, IX, VIII.
P. Bodmer VII = P72: Jude 1–25. Date IV. See P. Bod. V. above.
P. Bodmer VIII = P72: 1–2 Peter. Date IV. See P. Bod. V above.
P. Bodmer IX = 2113: Psalms 33–34. Date IV. See P. Bod. V. above.
P. Bodmer X: Corinthian Correspondence (contains response of the Corinthians to Paul's second letter, and Paul's third letter). Date IV. See P. Bod. V above.
P. Bodmer XI: Ode of Solomon 11. Date IV. See P. Bod. V above.
P. Bodmer XIV = P75: Luke 3:18–18:18; 22:4–24:53. Date III. Same codex as XV.
P. Bodmer XV = P75: John 1:1–15:8. Date III. See P. Bod. XIV above.
P. Bodmer XVII = P74: Acts 1:2–28:31; Jas 1:1–5:20; 1 Pet 1:1–3:5; 2 Pet 2:21–3:16; 1 John 1:1–5:17; 2 John 1–13; 3 John 6, 12; Jude 3–25. Date VII.
P. Bodmer XXIV = 2110: Pss 17:46–117:44. Date III/IV.
P. Bodmer XLV: Sus (Theodotionic text). Date IV. Some codex as XLVI, XXVII, XLVII.
P. Bodmer XLVI: Dan 1:1–20 (Theodotionic text). Date IV. See P. Bod. XLV above.
P. Bodmer? = P73: Matt 25:43; 26:2–3 [ined.]. Date VII. Fragment found in P. Bod. XVII and probably in same hand.

2. Coptic. Of the published mss all but P. Bodmer VI, XVI, XIX, XXII are on papyrus. All are, however, in codex form. Unless otherwise indicated the dialect is Sahidic.

P. Bodmer III: John 1:1–21:25; Gen 1:1–4:2. Date IV. Bohairic.
P. Bodmer VI: Prov 1:1–21:4. Date IV/V. Paleo-Theban ("Dialect P").
P. Bodmer XVI: Exod 1:1–15:21. Date IV.
P. Bodmer XVIII: Deut 1:1–10:7. Date IV.
P. Bodmer XIX: Matt 14:28–28:20; Rom 1:1–2:3. Date IV/V.
P. Bodmer XXI: Josh 6:16–25; 7:6–11:23; 22:1–2; 22:19–23:7; 23:15–24:2 (= P. Chester Beatty 2019). Date IV.
P. Bodmer XXII: Jer 40:3–52:34; Lamentations, Epistle of Jeremiah, Bar 1:1–5:5 (= Mississippi Coptic Codex II). Date IV/V.
P. Bodmer XXIII: Isaiah 47:1–66:24. Date IV.
P. Bodmer XL: Song of Songs [ined.].
P. Bodmer XLI: Acta Pauli. Date IV. Sub-Achmimic.
P. Bodmer XLII: 2 Corinthians [ined.].

P. Bodmer XLIII: An Apocryphon [ined.].
P. Bodmer XLIV: Daniel [ined.]. Bohairic.

b. Christian miscellanea. 1. Greek.

P. Bodmer XII: a liturgical fragment (Melito?). Date IV. See P. Bod. V above.
P. Bodmer XIII: Melito of Sardis, *Peri Pascha.* Date IV. See P. Bod. V above.
P. Bodmer XX: Apology of Phileas (= fragment at Chester Beatty: 135, 13–16 and 136, 14–17). Date IV. See P. Bod. V above.
P. Bodmer XXIX–XXXVIII: Codex Visionum. Date IV/V. [XXX–XXXVIII ined.].
P. Bodmer XLVII: Moral Maxims. Date IV. See P. Bod. XXVII above.

2. Coptic.

P. Bodmer XXXIX: Pachomius' Letter 11b [ined.].

c. Classical texts.

P. Bodmer I: *Iliad* 5 and 6. Date III/IV. 2 papyrus rolls.
P. Bodmer IV: Menander, *Dyskolos.* Date III. Same codex as XXV and XXVI.
P. Bodmer XXV: Menander, *Samia* (= P. Barc. 45). Date III. See P. Bod. IV above.
P. Bodmer XXVI: Menander, *Aspis* (= P. Robinson inv. 38 + P. Köln 3 [inv. 904]). Date III. See P. Bod. IV above.
P. Bodmer XXVII: Thucydides Bk 6. Date IV. See P. Bod. XLV above.
P. Bodmer XXVIII: Satyr play. Date II. Papyrus roll.
P. Bodmer XLVIII: *Iliad* [ined.].
P. Bodmer XLIX: *Odyssey* [ined.].

The number of Bodmer papyri has to date reached L (= business documents of Panopolis on recto of P. Bodmer I).

Bibliography

Part 4.a.1

Carlini, A., and Citi, A. 1981. Susanna e la prima visione di Daniele in due papiri inediti della Bibliotheca Bodmeriana: P. Bodm. XLV e P. Bodm. XLVI. *Museum Helveticum* 38: 81–120.
Kasser, R. 1961. *Papyrus Bodmer XVII: Actes des Apôtres, Epîtres de Jacques, Pierre, Jean et Jude.* Cologny-Geneva.
Kasser, R., and Testuz, M. 1967. *Papyrus Bodmer XXIV: Psaumes XVII–CXVIII.* Cologny-Geneva.
Martin, V. 1956. *Papyrus Bodmer II: Evangile de Jean chap. 1–14.* Cologny-Geneva.
———. 1958. *Papyrus Bodmer II: Supplément. Evangile de Jean chap. 14–21.* Cologny-Geneva.
Martin, V., and Barns, J. W. B. 1962. *Papyrus Bodmer II: Supplément. Evangile de Jean chap. 14–21.* Rev. ed. Cologny-Geneva.
Martin, V., and Kasser, R. 1961. *Papyrus Bodmer XIV: Evangile de Luc chap. 3–24.* Cologny-Geneva.
———. 1961. *Papyrus Bodmer XV: Evangile de Jean chap. 1–15.* Cologny-Geneva.
Testuz, M. 1958. *Papyrus Bodmer V: Nativité de Marie.* Cologny-Geneva.
———. 1959. *Papyrus Bodmer VII–IX. VII: L'Epître de Jude; VIII: Les deux Epîtres de Pierre; IX: Les Psaumes 33 et 34.* Cologny-Geneva.
———. 1959. *Papyrus Bodmer X–XII. X: Correspondance apocryphe des Corinthiens et de l'apôtre Paul; XI: Onzième Ode de Salomon; XII: Fragment d'un hymne liturgique. Manuscrit du IIIe siècle.* Cologny-Geneva.

Part 4.a.2

Kasser, R. 1958. *Papyrus Bodmer III: Évangile de Jean et Genèse I–IV, 2 en bohaïrique.* CSCO 177–78. Scriptores Coptici 25–26. Louvain.
———. 1960. *Papyrus Bodmer VI: Livre des Proverbes.* CSCO 194–95. Scriptores Coptici 27–28. Louvain.
———. 1961. *Papyrus Bodmer XVI: Exode I–XV, 21 en sahidique.* Cologny-Geneva.
———. 1962. *Papyrus Bodmer XVIII: Deutéronome I–X, 7 en sahidique.* Cologny-Geneva.
———. 1962. *Papyrus Bodmer XIX: Evangile de Mathieu XIV, 28–XXVIII, 20; Epître aux Romains I, 1–II, 3 en sahidique.* Cologny-Geneva.
———. 1963. *Papyrus Bodmer XXI: Josué VI, 16–25 VII, 6–XI, 23, XXII, 1–2, 19–XXIII, 7, 15–XXIV, 23 en sahidique.* Cologny-Geneva.
———. 1964. *Papyrus Bodmer XXII et Mississippi Coptic Codex II. Jérémie XL, 3–LII, 34; Lamentations; Epître de Jérémie; Baruch I, 1–V, 5 en sahidique.* Cologny-Geneva.
———. 1965. *Papyrus Bodmer XXIII: Esaïe XLVII, 1–LXVI, 24 en sahidique.* Cologny-Geneva.
———. 1960. Acta Pauli 1959. *RHPR* 40: 45–57.

Part 4.b.1

Hurst, A.; Reverdin, O.; and Rudhardt, J. 1984. *Papyrus Bodmer XXIX: Vision de Dorothéos.* Cologny-Geneva.
Martin, V. 1964. *Papyrus Bodmer XX: Apologie de Philéas évêque de Thmouis.* Cologny-Geneva.

Part 4.c.

Carlini, A. 1975. Il Papiro di Tucidide della Bibliotheca Bodmeriana (P. Bodmer XXVII). *Museum Helveticum* 32: 33–40.
Kasser, R., and Austin, C. 1969. *Papyrus Bodmer XXV: Menandre: La Samienne.* Cologny-Geneva.
———. 1969. *Papyrus Bodmer XXVI: Menandre: Le Bouclier.* Cologny-Geneva.
Kramer, B. 1976. Menander, Aspis 482–97; 520–35. *Kölner Papyri (P. Köln)* 1. Papyrologica Coloniensia 7. Opladen.
Martin, V. 1954. *Papyrus Bodmer I: Iliade, chants 5 et 6.* Cologny-Geneva.
———. 1958. *Papyrus Bodmer IV: Menandre: Le Dyscolos.* Cologny-Geneva.
Roca-Puig, R. 1968. Un Fragmento de La Samia de Menandro: P. Barc. 45. *Estudios Clásicos* 12: 375–83.
Turner, E. G. 1976. Papyrus Bodmer XXVIII: A Satyr-Play on the Confrontation of Heracles and Atlas. *Museum Helveticum* 33: 1–23.

Albert Pietersma

BODY. The word for body (Gk *sōma*) appears in a number of theologically significant contexts in the NT. Consequently, it is important to note this usage and to seek its antecedents in the Jewish and Hellenistic world of the time.

A. OT and Judaism

The OT speaks of the human being in terms of "flesh" and "soul." It uses *gĕwiyyâ* ("body") a few times referring to the body of an angel where "flesh" would be inadequate (Ezek 1:11, 23; Dan 10:6); to a slave in the sense of persons as "manpower" (Gen 47:18; Neh 9:37), and to a corpse or carcass (Judg 14:8, 9; 1 Sam 31:10, 12; Nah 3:3; Ps 110:6; also *gûpâ* 1 Chr 10:12). The OT shows little interest in distinguishing the "body" as one part of a man from the rest of his personality, his "soul." To speak of man's "body" (as distinguished from man as a whole) makes sense only when describing him in his capacity as a worker at the disposal of his master, or as a mere dead substance to be buried. What man is can only be understood in a wholistic way. Man does not possess a soul and a body, rather he is both soul and flesh, full of life and potential activity, while at the same time threatened by illness, transitoriness, and death. Soul without flesh is like a ghost without real existence, while flesh without soul is but a corpse (or, at most, the manpower of a slave). Nor is the OT interested in a conception of the human being as an individual person, either as distinguished from other persons or as a small universe complete in himself/herself. Wherever a person is prominent in the OT, he/she is elected by God to serve God's whole people. The idea of an individual developing to a more and more perfect specimen of human being is foreign to the OT.

Death, therefore, is not understood as a separation of the divine soul from the mortal body, or as the ultimate perfection of a person in his/her "dying beautifully," or as the natural biological goal of life. Death remains a person's enemy, and only God himself is more poweful: "My flesh and my heart may fail, but God is the rock of my heart and my portion forever" (Ps 73:26).

In Aramaic, the language of Jesus, the above view is slightly altered as a result of Hellenistic influence. Aramaic *gĕšēm* appears in Daniel in the sense of corpse (4:30; 7:11), and in the sense of a man exposed to fire or water (3:27–28; 5:21), while in rabbinic literature *gûpāʾ* signifies a "person" (*Qidd.* 37a; *t. Sanh.* 13:4(434); *j. Taʿan.* 1:64d.6) as opposed to the members or the head (*m. Pesaḥ.* 10:3; *t. Taʿan.* 2:5) or even the soul (*Lev.Rab.* 34). This usage illustrates the extent of Greek influence in the first centuries of the Christian era.

B. Greek/Hellenistic World

The situation is quite different in the Greek-speaking world. With Homer, *sōma,* "body," is primarily a "corpse," that is, something different from the ego of the speaker, an object that he observes as lying outside himself. Later, the word denotes a living human or animal body, and a physical (e.g., a celestial) body (so also in English, which lacks the distinction of German *Leib* and *Körper*). During the NT period, *sōma* was also used of a "slave" (Polyb. 2.6.6; 18.35.6, etc.). It could also designate a unity, e.g., the *ekklēsia* ("assembly," the same term designating the "Church" in the NT), as a body of citizens (Chrysipp. *Fr.* 367). Two countries that became united after a war are now "one body" (Plut. *Phil.* 8[I 360c]). All the parts of the universe form such a unity; it is, therefore, possible to speak of the cosmos as a (divine) body (see C.5 below).

The original usage of *sōma* in the sense of "corpse" illustrates one line of development in which the body is seen merely as matter, either dead (as a corpse or a star), as a kind of machine, or as an object at the disposal of its owner (e.g., a slave). This leads to Plato's view, especially in his middle period, of the body as a mere "tomb" (*sōma-sēma, Grg.* 493a, originally a Pythagorean pun; cf. Orph. *Fr.* 228d), a "prison" (*Cra.* 400bc), or an "oyster shell" (*Phdr.* 250c; *Phd.* 66b). Death is, therefore, liberation of the soul. During a later period, Plato also spoke of a beautiful body as a kind of (imperfect) image of the beauty of the heavenly ideas (*Ti.* 29a; *Resp.* 8.591d; *Symp.* 211c).

Plato's student, Aristotle, still valued the soul, though he did not share his teacher's conviction of its heavenly origin as the principle of life higher than the body. For him it was the soul that molds the matter of the body into a piece of art, a living man. The Stoics combined this view with another line of development in which "body" became a designation of unity. The old idea of the human body as a small world *(mikrokosmos),* parallel and related to the great body *(makrokosmos),* the universe, was revived. The soul belongs to the body and is part of it as the power of life within it. Within the great body of the universe, it permeates everything; initially faintly present in the rocks, with gradually increasing concentration in the plants, animals, and men. Thus, man is part of the universe; the same life-spirit that permeates the whole world is, in its most concentrated form, to be found in the human mind. Conversely, the universe is a body governed by Zeus, the highest god, or heaven, or the divine mind or *logos* (Cornutus, *Theol. Graec.* 20; Orph. *Fr.* 21a; Philo *Fuga* 108–13; *Somn* 1.144; *Quaes Ex* 2.117). A heroic or otherwise impressive death would be the last touch of the artist perfecting his piece of art. Epicurus shares with the Stoics the conviction of the bodily quality of the soul. He, therefore, prefers to speak of "flesh" instead of "body," since "the desire of the belly is the first impact and root of every good" (*Fr.* 409), though the pleasures of the soul are higher than those of the flesh (D.L. 10.137). For him, death is the natural biological end of life.

C. The NT

1. Body and Soul. In the NT, the OT wholistic view of man continues to dominate, though the Greek word *sōma* is now used. "Body" designates in the same way the whole man who can be raised after death (Matt 27:52; Acts 9:40; John 2:21; Rom 8:11; 1 Cor 6:14). The "soul" is its life-power, continually renewed by eating and drinking (Matt 6:25). Matthew 10:28 speaks, in a unique way, of those who are able to kill the body but not the soul (the latter phrase is lacking in Luke 12:4), though man remains soul and body after his death. This is understandable when we consider Paul's concept of a "spiritual body" over against a "psychic" (earthly) one. It is the body that will be raised, though it will be changed and not remain "flesh and blood" (1 Cor 15:50–51; Phil 3:21). Once (2 Cor 5:8), Paul speaks of the believers' wish to "emigrate from the body," and of the destruction of "the earthly tent" (5:1). V 3 may be interpreted "so that by putting it on, we may not be found naked"; however, a more probable reading is "provided that, stripped [of earthly body] we shall not be found naked." Be this as it may, it is clear that Paul does not expect any "nakedness" of a pure soul, not even for the interim between death and parousia, but a new "clothing" that will be "life swallowing up what is mortal" (v 4). Most surprising is 2 Cor 12:3, where Paul relates, in a sarcastically boastful manner, a most extraordinary experience of being taken up to paradise and seeing unspeakable things. Moreover, he is not even interested in the miracle as such; whether he ascended to heaven "in the body" or not is of little concern to him. Only the fact that he had been there has meaning for him; whether or not this might be something like a soul that is able to leave the body (as Platonists would think) is insignificant. Rather, Paul states that after the resurrection God's spirit takes the place of the former soul (1 Cor 15:44). Strictly speaking, the soul is the life of the earthly body and, hence, is limited by the body's existence (as with the Stoics or Epicureans). As such the soul can, in one respect, be negatively contrasted to the spirit, since it is open to the influence of demons or any kind of desires (Jas 3:15; Jude 18–19). As such the soul is, according to Philo (*Leg All* 3.246–47), equivalent to the earth cursed by God (Gen 3:17). In another respect, it is also the place of listening to and trusting in God. Thus, God's spirit is already living in earthly men, if and when they do not remain merely "psychic" (literally "soul-ish") men (1 Cor 2:14). That means that God's spirit, and with it the life that is no longer perishable, is, up to some degree, already found within the earthly body. This is the view of John 11:25–26. In Jesus, the resurrection and the life are already present. Certainly the body will die, but the new life that the spirit of God has begun to build in each person individually will live on.

2. The Physical Body of Man. Since there is no word for "body" in the OT (except when designating a corpse or a slave), it is not surprising that the term rarely occurs in Jesus' teachings. Nonetheless, there is some emphasis on life in its bodily form; e.g., Jesus' healing restores the "body" of a sick person (Mark 5:29), and the disciples' obedience concerns their bodies, i.e., that they should not commit adultery (Matt 5:29) or become the cause of anxiety (6:25) or fear (10:28). This becomes central in Paul's letters: to present one's body as a living sacrifice (but not in martyrdom as in 1 Cor 13:3) is one's spiritual worship (Rom 12:1). Even Paul himself must "pommel and subdue" his body in the service of his Lord (1 Cor 9:27). It is the body, not the soul, that is the temple of the Holy Spirit (1 Cor 6:19–20). In the apostle's body, i.e., in his "mortal flesh," the death and the life of Jesus are manifest, as, for instance, in the marks of many whippings (2 Cor 4:10–11; 11:24–25; Gal 6:17). In the last judgment, one is to be responsible for what he/she has done "in the body" (2 Cor 5:10). Thus, "body" is much more than a mere physical instrument (like, e.g., the stomach); it always belongs either to Christ or to other powers (e.g., to sin and death, or to a prostitute; Rom 6:6; 7:24; 1 Cor 6:13, 15). In this body the grace of God transforms the new life of man. Because the believers were "bought with a price" by God's grace, it is in their bodies that God will be glorified (1 Cor 6:20). Hence, all who have been baptized into Christ Jesus' death can no longer allow sin to reign in their mortal bodies (Rom 6:3, 12).

3. The Lord's Supper. The words of institution during the Last Supper of Jesus are handed down in mainly two different versions. Paul writes to the Corinthians (ca. A.D. 50), "I received from the Lord what I also delivered to you, that . . . he . . . took bread . . . and said, 'This is my body which is for you. . . .' In the same way also the cup, after supper, saying, 'This cup is the new covenant in my blood . . .' " (1 Cor 11:23–25). In Mark 14:22–24 these words of institution are rendered differently: "Take, this my body," and "This is my blood of the covenant, which is poured out for many" (written around A.D. 70). Paul's version seems to be, on the whole, the more ancient one. It shows that the first word was separated from the second by a whole meal ("after the supper"). It is, therefore, not surprising that the two sayings are, originally, not perfectly parallel. It is to be expected that gradually they would have been harmonized during the tradition in the NT and especially in modern liturgies. If Mark's version, in which the first statement, "This is my body," runs parallel to the second, "This is my blood," was the original, then we should expect the constantly recurring combination "flesh" and "blood," because "body" and "blood" are never combined in Hebrew or Greek (except, perhaps, in Job 6:14), and "body" does not designate an offering except in Gen 15:11 (referred to in *Apoc. Ab.* 13:3). Differently, the cup in 1 Chr 11:25 (the wine is never mentioned!) is identified with the new covenant, not with the blood, which excludes the idea of drinking blood, horrifying for a Jew. Some scholars argue that this proposed original Markan formula (according to which the disciples drank before Jesus spoke his word of institution, identifying the cup with his blood) was changed to the less offensive form found in Paul's tradition. But would Jesus ever have identified the cup with his blood without pointing in some way to the scandalous character of drinking it (as in the passage of John 6:52–56, probably part of a later church liturgy)? The phrase "which is for you" (1 Cor 11:24) may have been originally lacking (as in Mark 14:24). However, the idea of a vicarious death is implied in 1 Cor 11:25 ("in my blood," cf. Exod 25:8–11), since in the time of Jesus the sacrifice of the covenant was also regarded as being expiatory. Since the Aramaic word for "body" (*gûpā*ʾ) can designate the "I" of a person, Jesus may have meant that he himself would be present with his disciples whenever they ate the bread. The implication of the second formula would then have led to greater emphasis on Jesus' readiness to give up his life ("in my blood"). In the Pauline tradition, the latter was made explicit by combining the words "which is for you" with "body" (cf. Luke 22:19; Heb 10:5, 10; 1 Pet 2:24), and in the Markan tradition by the combination of the "blood" with "poured out for many." Thus, the Lord's Supper reenacts the new covenant in the present communion of the participants with God and their fellow disciples (especially in Paul). This communion is based on the past sacrifice of Jesus (especially in Mark) and is the pledge for the future eschatological fulfillment of the meal in the kingdom of God and the parousia of Christ (1 Cor 11:26; Mark 14:25; Matt 26:29; with special emphasis in Luke 22:15–18). All reports contain this threefold orientation toward the past, the present, and the future.

4. The Body of Christ. When, according to the eucharist tradition, Jesus spoke of "my body," he spoke of his future presence with his disciples as a presence "for you" (added in the Pauline tradition and implied from the beginning in the word about the cup). Hence, "body" is not so much used as a designation of an individual person in and of himself/herself, but rather points to someone's being, living, and acting in relationship with others. Any body is in one sense limited by its form and contour (e.g., a human body by its skin); in another sense it is a means of contact and communication (e.g., seeing through the eyes, hearing with the ears, touching with the hands, walking with the legs). It is in this latter sense that Jesus uses the term in the Last Supper, and that Paul uses it generally. Thus, the "body of Christ" is, primarily, Christ himself crucified for the sake of his disciples (Rom 7:4; Col 1:22). In the Lord's Supper, "participation in" (or "communion with") the body of Christ takes place in such a way that it transforms the "many" into "one body," since all partake of the same bread. In order to emphasize this interpretation of the oneness of the Church, the apostle speaks in 1 Cor 10:16–17 first of the cup, and then of the bread, reversing the usual order. "In Christ" they all become "one body" (Rom 12:5).

As far as this expression goes, Paul's wording is not unusual linguistically. A Greek would have easily understood the phrase "a body of believers" or "all believers becoming one body." However, Paul intends to say more than that. The Christians do not simply become unified by a common belief (e.g., in Jesus giving his body for them). Rather, they become "the body of Christ" (1 Cor 12:27) because they are "baptized into one body" (v 13). This "one body" is Christ's body, as the preceding verse illustrates: "As the body is one and has many members . . . so is Christ." In baptism, the believers are actually brought into Christ himself. Therefore, they did not call themselves "Christians" (as those outside of the Church would do; Acts 11:26; 26:28; 1 Pet 4:16), as if the newness were their own attribute; rather, they call themselves "those in Christ," because what distinguishes them from others is Christ himself, whom they had "put on" in baptism like a garment and in whom they are now living (Gal 3:27–29). This is why Paul, when using the term of the body of Christ (or in Christ) always speaks collectively of the communion with God or Christ as opposed to that of an individual believer. In 1 Cor 6:15–17 he states that an individual man "becomes one body with a prostitute," but when speaking of "becoming one with the Lord," he replaces "body" by "spirit." As members of the Church, "the body of Christ" is of primary importance, whereas its "individual members" are secondary. This is also typical of Jewish thinking which (according to M. Buber) sees a forest not as a sum of many trees (the typical occidental perspective) but the individual trees always as part of the whole forest (see also H. W. Robinson [1936]).

Nonetheless, there is no doubt that Christ also remains the lord of his Church (Rom 10:9; 1 Cor 12:3; etc.). Unity with Christ becomes effective in an event which creates a new relationship, not in a unity of substance shared by Christ and his Church. Thus, it is a dynamic unity of life, not a static one of unchangeable quality. This is what the Corinthians, who attached an almost magical effectiveness to the sacraments (1 Cor 15:29; 10:1–13), could not understand. The difficult saying of 1 Cor 11:27, "Whoever eats the bread or drinks the cup in an unworthy manner will be guilty of the body and blood of the Lord" means basically the same as 8:11–12: whoever becomes "a stumbling block to the weak" (v 9), i.e., "the brother for whom Christ died . . . sins against Christ." According to 8:11–12 this happens when "knowledge puffs up in the congregation" (8:1); according to 11:27, it happens when the congregation does not wait for the latecomers (11:22, 33). In the context of the Lord's Supper, Paul uses the term "body and blood of the Lord" instead of "Christ who died for him/them." In the same way "my body which is for you" (1 Cor 11:24) means "I myself dying for you." Thus 11:27 declares that sinning against the brothers/sisters is sinning against Christ himself. Hence, the unity of the body of Christ ceases to exist for those who, by their actions, place themselves outside the realm of the living Christ. Therefore, Paul uses the term "body of Christ" only within the context of parenesis (see the works of Daines; Guénel; Gundry; Jewett 1971: 201–304; and Wedderburn). This is not the case in Colossians and Ephesians (see below); however, the identification of Christ with the head of the body (Col 1:18; Eph 1:22–23; 4:15–16; 5:23) implies his authority over all the actions of his congregation.

The origin of the phrase "body of Christ" is difficult to determine. Four sources have been suggested: (1) a gnostic myth of a primeval man; (2) the Hellenistic idea of the universe as a divine body; (3) a Stoic parable; and (4) the Jewish view of a patriarch representing the whole present and future tribe. Gnosticism (1) is out of the question since the idea of a savior's "body" including the saved ones as its members is totally lacking up to the 3d century A.D., except in some occasional reminiscences of a Pauline phrase in Christian Gnosticism (Fischer 1973: 62–68). The view of the universe as a (divine) "body" (2) and the corresponding designation of powers (in Christian writings: of believers) as "members" is, however, present in Hellenistic text (Plato, *Ti.* 30b, 31b, 32a,c, 39e; Philetaer. 30a; Diod. Sic. 1, 2, 6; Orph. *Fr.* 21a; Orph. *H.* 11.3; 66. 6–9; etc.). In Stoic texts (3), one also encounters the parable of a body whose members are dependent upon one another. This parable was first used to illustrate how working labor needs the idle nobility in the same manner as the working members of the body need the stomach to digest food (Titus Livius, *Ab urbe condita* 2.32; Dio Chrys. *Or.* 33.16). In 1 Cor 12:14–26 the term "body [of Christ]" is also used parabolically to show that neither inferiority nor superiority complexes are able to endanger the unity of the congregation. This is certainly parallel to and influenced by the Stoic usage. However, Paul says more than that (see above).

Two possible roots of a nonparabolic usage (or parallels to it, which make it linguistically possible) should be noted. First, the contemporary Hellenistic view of the universe (2) was that of a body permeated and governed by God (or heaven, or Logos). Since Plato, this body was regarded as a divine one, though probably not explicitly as a "body of God." This is the understanding of the body of Christ in Colossians and Ephesians, and it is possible that Paul "decosmologized" the Greek conception, reducing it to a description of the Church (not of the world) and coining the unusual phrase "body of Christ." Colossians and Ephesians would, in this case, have reverted to the original view.

Secondly, the Jewish background (4) may be important. John 15:1 identifies Christ with the true vine, the constant symbol of Israel, which even in Jesus' time was seen as a vine of cosmic dimensions reaching from the abyss to heaven, where the vine becomes the "house of God" *(L.A.B.).* In John 15:1 the Son of Man (identified in Ps 79:12 LXX with the "vine" of God) is the new Jacob, and Jacob, according to Gen 35:10, is Israel. The patriarch qualifies his people; it is through Abraham that Israel is the holy people of God, through Jacob that Israel is blessed (*Jub* 2:20; 19:27–29), and through Adam that all humankind has become sinful (2 Esdr 7:118; cf. Wis 10:1, 4); also to his (Adam's) glory part of Israel will be restored (1QS 4:23; 1QH 17:15; CD 3:20; 4QpPs 37 3:1). Thus, in many texts, the patriarch is identical to his tribe or nation: "Adam" (in Hebrew) means "humankind," and Jacob is called "Israel" by God himself. In the same way, Jesus is the new Israel in John 15:1. The vine, apart from which they can do nothing (v 5), includes all its branches, just as the body, apart from which they can do nothing, includes all its members. However, while John 15 sees Jesus as the true vine or Israel, Paul views him as the one "offspring" of Abraham in whom all become one (Gal 3:16, 28), or even the Adam of latter times, "in whom" all are made alive (1 Cor 15:22, 45; cf. Rom 5:12–19). The idea of a patriarch determining the future tribe is originally temporal. It is still alive in the reference to Jacob's experience which is fulfilled in the Son of Man (i.e., Jesus), and in the Church being the offspring of Abraham. However, it is converted by John and Paul to a rather spatial imagery of the vine with its branches or the body and its members. The same can be seen in Gal 4:25–26, where the temporal term "the present Jerusalem" is replaced by a spatial one, "the Jerusalem above." Perhaps it is not possible to decide definitively for either a Hellenistic or a Jewish background, since there was so much cultural interaction between the Jewish idea of a patriarch determining the destiny of humankind and the Hellenistic idea of God's spirit or Logos ruling and permeating the world.

5. Colossians and Ephesians. The hymn in Col 1:15–20 praises Christ's lordship over the whole creation and adds, "He is the head of the body." Compared with earlier Pauline passages, two anomalies are obvious. First, we find "the body," not "the body of Christ" or "his body." Secondly, the hymn speaks of "the body" three times in terms of "all [created] things," and suggests that Christ is the head of the principalities and authorities (1:16; cf. 2:10). Both of the above points are typical of the Hellenistic conception of the universe as "the body" whose "head" is Zeus or Logos. This is indeed what "body" must have originally meant in the context of the hymn, since the Church enters the chain of thought only from v 18b on. The author of the letter, a disciple of Paul (or possibly Paul in a later stage of his life), adapted the phrase to a theological context with the explanatory addition "the Church" (cf. 1:24; 3:15). This transfer of the Greek view of the world to ecclesiology guards the Pauline understanding of the Church as the body of Christ from an abusive identification of the Church with Christ himself (the Church as a "prolonged Christ") by emphasizing Christ's role as the head (2:19). Thus, Christ is head over all creation (2:10, 15) for the Church, which is his body and derives all its strength and growth from him (2:19). In Eph 1:22–23 both statements are combined (cf. 4:15–16), while in Eph 2:16 it is difficult to decide whether the "one body," through which Jews and gentiles are reconciled, means the crucified body of Christ, as suggested by the parallel phrase "in [or by] the blood of Christ" in v 13 (cf. Col 1:22), or, more probably, the Church as Christ's body, as suggested by the images of "one new man" (v 15) and "the whole structure" of "the holy temple" (v 21), into which Jews and gentiles have been brought.

The headship of Christ is certainly no authoritarian power; he rules by filling his body with his own spirit (1:23; 4:10; cf. Col 2:19). Thus, as the head he is the savior of his body (Eph 5:23). In the same way, the husband is the head of his wife, who in turn is his body (Eph 5:23, 28). Even a modern interpreter, critical of this phrase, would note that the Greek text of v 22 says merely "the wives to their husbands," because their behavior is only one example of what is expected from all members; i.e., "Be subject to one another out of reverence for Christ . . ." (v 21). Furthermore, the unity of husband and wife is taken so seriously that "loving his wife as he would his own body" involves "loving himself," because both are "one flesh" (vv 28, 31). The traditional formula of the wife being her husband's "own flesh" (see Sir 25:26; *L. A. E.* 3) emphasizes her status as his property. In Ephesians 5, though still within the context of the patriarchalism of that time, it has been transformed into an image of the oneness of a most intimate love, which is demonstrated through the readiness of the one partner to live for the sake of the other.

D. Summary

Through the Greek language Judaism acquired the word *sōma,* "body." The middle Platonism of the NT period would have strongly suggested a view of man as principally soul, and an understanding of life as a gradual separation of the ego (the soul) from the body and its physical impediment, where death becomes the final liberation. It was, however, the OT background and especially the life and teaching of Jesus that provided the NT with an understanding of the body as a means of communication and mutual help and love among members of the body of Christ (and even beyond to nonbelievers). The climax of this view is manifest in Jesus' body, always open to God's spirit and willing to become the final sacrifice on the cross for the sake of all people.

The Stoicism of the 1st century A.D. would have suggested with equal strength a view of man as part of a harmonious universe where God's spirit could be found everywhere. Again it was the OT and Jesus that made it impossible to equate God and the world. God's spirit is not merely a life power in creation; it is the spirit manifested in Jesus' service and given to his disciples at Pentecost. Therefore, the "divine body" is not simply the totality of nature with its beautiful and beneficial forces (but also with its cruel and destructive forces), but rather "the body of Christ," i.e., the unity of all individuals who allow themselves to be helped, loved, and permeated by Jesus, who gave his earthly body "for many." Every Lord's Supper reminds his Church that it is only in this body that his believers will find real life forever. Through his promise at the Last Supper, the body and blood of Jesus, offered as a sacrifice, become present and real again for the participants in every Lord's Supper, granting them the quality of the one people of God and, at the same time, obliging them to live this oneness of Jew and Greek, lord and slave, man and woman realistically time and again, to be and to become the "body of Christ," until he comes.

Bibliography

For a more extensive bibliography, see *EWNT,* 3771.

Altermath, F. 1977. *Du corps psychique au corps spirituel.* BGBE. Tübingen.

Bouyer, L. 1970. *L'Eglise de Dieu, corps du Christ et temple de l'esprit.* Paris.

Daines, B. 1978. Paul's Use of the Analogy of the Body of Christ. *EvQ* 50: 71–78.

Fischer, K. M. 1973. *Tendenz und Absicht des Epheserbriefs.* FRLANT 111. Göttingen.

Guénel, V., ed. 1983. *Le Corps et le corps du Christ dans la première épître aux Corinthians.* LD 114. Paris.

Gundry, R. H. 1976. *Sōma in Biblical Theology with Emphasis on Pauline Anthropology.* SNTSMS 29. Cambridge.

Jewett, R. 1971. *Paul's Anthropological Terms.* Leiden.

Meeks, W. A. 1977. In One Body. Pp. 201–21 in *God's Christ and His People: Festschrift N. A. Dahl.* Oslo.

Robinson, H. W. 1936. The Hebrew Conception of Corporate Personality. Pp. 49–62 in *Werden und Wesen des Alten Testaments,* ed. P. Volz; F. Stummer; and J. Hempel. *BZAW* 66. Berlin.

Robinson, J. A. T. 1977. *The Body.* 2d ed. SBT 5. London.

Wedderburn, A. J. M. 1971. The Body of Christ and Related Concepts in 1 Corinthians. *SJT* 24: 74–96.

R. Eduard Schweizer

BOHAN, STONE OF (PLACE) [Heb *ʾeben bōhan*]. A site located on the N border of the territory of Judah (Josh 15:6) and consequently the S boundary of Benjamin (Josh 18:17). It is apparently near the top of the descent from the highlands down to the Jordan River, just a few miles N and W of the Dead Sea.

By its name, it is a topographical feature which was known in the period, and not necessarily a settlement. The exact location of the stone is debated, and the lack of any further reference to a son of Reuben named Bohan does not aid the process of identification. The tribe of Reuben was allocated land in Transjordan (Josh 13:8), so a site in this area has been proposed (*GTTOT,* 405). Since the OT description of the boundary between the two tribes of Judah and Benjamin starts at one end of the confluence of the Jordan and the Dead Sea, and runs W from there based on the identifiable sites (Josh 15:5), a location to the W rather than the E of the Jordan is indicated. The association with Reuben could simply be the memory of an undetermined influence of the tribe on the W bank as well as in Transjordan (Woudstra *Joshua* NICOT, 236).

Bohan could be a Heb noun, "thumb," and not a proper name at all (Noth 1966: 69). It would then most probably describe a rocky outcrop or pillar of the period that in some way resembled a thumb. This does not treat the present Heb text with integrity, however, since the biblical description "son of Reuben" indicates that, for the author at least, Bohan was a proper name.

Some currently existing topographical features have been proposed as the location of the stone (Boling *Joshua* AB, 366; *HGB,* 119), but none of the proposals are compelling.

Bibliography

Noth, M. 1966. *The Old Testament World.* Philadelphia.

David W. Baker

BOIL. See SICKNESS AND DISEASE.

BOND. A biblical word often referring to something that restricts one's freedom.

A. Old Testament

In the OT the word "bond" is used to refer to a state of servitude, or "bondage." Thus "bondmaid" (Exod 23:12) and "bondwoman" (Deut 15:17) are used for the Heb *ʾāmāh,* generally "maidservant" as in their parallel texts (Exod 23:12 = Exod 20:8; Deut 15:17 = Exod 21:6). Similarly, "bondman" is used for Heb *ʿebed* (Deut 15:17; Ezra 9:9), usually "slave" or "servant."

A like interpretation is warranted for the phrase "bond or free" (Heb *ʿāṣûr wĕʿāzûb;* Deut 32:36; 1 Kgs 14:10; 21:10; 2 Kgs 9:8; 14:26). The pairing of *ʿzb* with *ʿbd* in Ezra 9:9 would seem to support the implications of servitude. The repeated threats to destroy "every male" of the royal houses of Jeroboam I and Ahab of Israel, "both bond and free," however, imply a broader sense of the phrase, because members of the ruling family did not likely continue in slavery. In these cases, "bond and free" designates those still under the bond of parental authority and especially sustenance, along with those who had been freed from the protection and authority of their parents. The phrase is a merism denoting opposing extremes in the designated group and encompassing all members of it.

In both the singular and the plural, the noun *môsēr* serves as a general term for "chains," "fetters," or the like, as both the symbol and reality of servitude. Isa 52:2 and Jer 30:8, for instance, refer to the bonds or chains of the neck. Expressions of liberation include "to loose the bonds" (Job 12:18; 39:5; Ps 116:16) and "to burst/break bonds asunder" (Pss 2:3; 107:14). Conversely, *môsēr,* "bond," also functions as a positive metaphor for the law (Jer 2:20; 5:5; 30:8) as that which binds the people to Yahweh. As punishment for breaking these "bonds," Yahweh will subject both people and leaders to foreign servitude. Later, however, he will "break the bonds" of their foreign masters, and Israel will return to "serve" Yahweh and the Davidic king.

The noun *ʾāsûr* is used literally of the restraints with which Samson was bound by his Philistine captors (Judg 15:14), and the cognate adjective *ʾāsîr* as a figure of captives not forgotten by their God (Ps 69:33). To "loose the bonds [*rĕṣubbôt*] of wickedness" is the "fast" which God desires of Israel (Isa 58:6).

Bibliography

Willi, T. 1977. Die Freiheit Israels. Pp. 531–46 in *Beiträge zur alttestamentlichen Theologie,* ed. H. Donner; R. Hanhart; and R. Smend. Göttingen.

D. G. SCHLEY

B. New Testament

Two words in the NT can have the meaning "bond": *sundesmos* and *desmos* (BAGD 1957: 175, 793). Col 2:19 uses *sundesmos* to refer to the sinews of the body (for comparative Hellenistic usage, cf. LSJM, 1701; Fitzer *TDNT* 7: 857). In accordance with other Hellenistic usage (Plut. *Num.* 6.3 where Numa is the Sabines' "bond of good will and friendship" with Rome; Simplicius *in Epict.* 30/89.15, "the Pythagoreans . . . called friendship the bond of all the virtues"), Col 3:14 uses the word metaphorically to speak of love as the bond *(sundesmos)* of perfection. This could be understood as the bond of all the virtues or as the bond that leads to perfection or perfect harmony (Lohse *Colossians and Philippians* Hermeneia, 148–49). To keep the unity of the spirit the Ephesians are called to the bond *(sundesmos)* of unrighteousness (unrighteousness is the bond) in Acts 8:23 (cf. Isa 58:6).

Jesus releases the bond *(desmos)* from a deaf mute's tongue (Mark 7:35). A. Deissmann understands it to be a demonic bond (1978: 304–7) by using ancient magic texts and by referring to Luke 13:16, where Satan's bond kept a woman bent over for eighteen years. But nature could place a bond on the tongue in Hellenistic thought (Nonnus *Dion.* 26.261; Bacchus heals it in 26.287). Wettstein (*NovTG*[26] on Mark 7:35) gives uses of *desmos* as a term for mute tongues. "Bond" can refer to physical objects used to bind persons as in Acts 16:26 (stocks for feet: for a description of one kind with five holes, cf. Eus. *Hist. Eccl.* 5.1.27). The word refers to head and foot chains in Luke 8:29 and to eternal chains in Jude 6. An ambiguity occurs because the word can be used to refer to prison (and not physical bonds) as in LXX Isa 42:7; 49:9. Bonds were the rule in Roman imprisonment (Hitzig 1899: 1581) but not in every case (see two laws in Ulp. *Digest* 50.16.216 and Sever. *Codex Iust* 2.11.1). Whether texts such as Phil 1:7, 13 should be translated as "imprisonment" or "bonds" [in a physical sense]" is an unsolved question since the context does not clearly indicate which meaning is present. (See the varying interpretations in BAGD [175] and Gnilka *Philippians* HTKNT, 47, 56).

Bibliography

Deissmann, A. 1978. *Light from the Ancient East.* Grand Rapids.
Hitzig, F. 1899. *Carcer. PW* 3: 1576–82.

JOHN G. COOK

BOOTHS, FEAST OF. One of ancient Israel's three giant annual feasts, celebrated in autumn. See CALENDARS. ANCIENT ISRAELITE AND EARLY JEWISH.

BOR-ASHAN (PLACE) [Heb *bôr ʿāšān*]. See ASHAN.

BORITH (PERSON) [Lat *Borith*]. See BUKKI.

BOSOR (PLACE) [Gk *Bosor*]. One of five sites in Gilead in which Jews were taken captive by gentile inhabitants (1 Macc 5:25, 36). The city is usually identified with Buṣr el-Ḥarīri, approximately 70 km E of the Sea of Galilee, perhaps the same site as "Bezer in the wilderness" mentioned in Deut 4:43 (Tedesche and Zeitlin 1950: 115). Goldstein (*1 Maccabees* AB, 301) argues cogently that ALEMA is the district within which Bosor lies, rather than being a separate city.

Judas Maccabeus' early successes, including retaking the temple in 164 B.C., led to gentile reprisals. Many Jews in Gilead fled to a stronghold at the city of Dathema, from which they sent word to Judas for help. En route to rescue the refugees, Judas encountered Nabateans, who told him that Jews were under attack in the cities of Bozrah, Bosor-in-Alema, Chaspho, Maked, and Carnaim, as well as other cities (1 Macc 5:24–27). Judas detoured from Dathema to rescue Jews in Bozrah first, then in Dathema, and finally in the other cities.

Bibliography

Abel, F.-M. 1923. Topographie des campagnes Machabéenes. *RB* 32: 495–521.
Tedesche, S., and Zeitlin, S. 1950. *The First Book of Maccabees.* New York.

PAUL L. REDDITT

BOUGAEAN (PLACE) [Gk *Bougaios*]. An epithet used to describe Haman in Add Esth 12:6, by the LXX in Esth 3:1 (for the Heb *hāʾagāgi*), and as an addition in 9:10. The precise significance of the designation is disputed. Because the meaning of the term is obscure, some scholars have argued that the term is simply a corruption of the Gk *agagaios* or "agagite" (Gregg *APOT,* 673–74; Newman *IDB* 1: 458). Noting that the term is replaced by the word "Macedonian" in Esth 9:24, some scholars have argued that it is simply a Homeric term of reproach (*Iliad* 13.824; *Odyssey* 18.79), meaning "bully" or "braggart" (Haupt 1908: 141). A third view has been advanced by Hoschander (1923: 23–27) and Lewy (1939: 134–35), who argue that the term *bougaios* is derived from the word *baga.* A West Iranian religious term, meaning "god," these scholars have argued that it refers specifically to Mithra and that, therefore, the designation *bougaios* means "worshipper of Mithra" (Lewy 1939: 135). If this is so, then the use of the word may be one small piece of evidence favoring the argument that the book of Esther, as well as the festival of Purim, is of non-Jewish origin (Moore *Esther* AB, xlviii–xlix). Owing to the limited amount of evidence available, however, it may be impossible to choose between the options (Moore *Esther* AB, 36; *Daniel, Esther, Jeremiah: The Additions* AB, 178).

Bibliography

Haupt, P. 1908. The Book of Esther: Critical Edition of the Hebrew Text with Notes. Pp. 97–186 in *Old Testament and Semitic Studies in Memory of William Rainey Harper,* ed. R. F. Harper; F. Brown; and G. F. Moore. Chicago.

Hoschander, J. 1923. *The Book of Esther in the Light of History.* Philadelphia.

Lewy, J. 1939. Old Assyrian *puruʾum* and *pūrum. RHA* 5: 117–24.

Frederick W. Schmidt

BOWL. See POTTERY (CHRONOLOGY).

BOX TREE. See FLORA.

BOZEZ (PLACE) [Heb *bôṣēṣ*]. An outcropping of rock in the pass between GEBA and MICHMASH (1 Sam 14:4). This outcropping figures in the story in which Jonathan, the son of Saul, initiates the defeat of the Philistines at Michmash. Bozez apparently occupied the N side of the pass, while an outcropping named SENEH stood on the S side. The names of the two outcroppings reflect their formidable appearance. Seneh means "The Thorny One" while Bozez means either "The Gleaming One" or "The Miry One" (see McCarter *1 Samuel* AB, 239). The exact location of these two outcroppings has not been mapped with precision, though it is generally agreed that they must lie upon the Wadi eṣ-Ṣuweinit, which runs between Geba and Michmash, in the middle of the triangle defined by Jerusalem, Bethel, and Jericho (see *NHT,* 106; *MBA,* 60).

Jeffries M. Hamilton

BOZKATH (PLACE) [Heb *boṣqat*]. A town situated in the Shephelah, or low country, of Judah (Josh 15:39), within the same district as Lachish and Eglon. This settlement is listed among the towns within the tribal allotment of Judah (Josh 15:21–62; see also BETH-DAGON). Jedidah, mother of Josiah, was the daughter of Adaiah of Bozkath (2 Kgs 22:1). The location of the ancient settlement is unknown.

Bibliography

Alt, A. 1925. Judas Gaue unter Josia. *PJ* 21: 100–16.

Wade R. Kotter

BOZRAH (PLACE) [Heb *boṣrâ*]. Three sites of antiquity possessed this name. Two are mentioned in the Hebrew Bible and the third is mentioned in the apocryphal writings and secular sources.

1. Bozrah in Edom. According to Gen 36:33 and 1 Chr 1:44, Bozrah was associated with Jobab the son of Zerah, one of the Edomite kings (whether his place of origin or his residence is unclear), and periodically it was the capital and administrative center of the Edomite state. Apart from these, the only other references to Bozrah in the OT are all in the woe-oracles against the nations (Isa 34:6; 63:1; Jer 49:13, 22; Amos 1:12; and perhaps Mic 2:12 [read **baṣṣirâ*]). These defy concrete historical evaluation and their authenticity and dating are uncertain. Because of their apocalyptic character (Isa 34:6, 63:1) they can probably be dated to the postexilic period.

Bozrah, the ancient capital of Edom, is without a doubt to be identified with the modern village of Buseirah, which is located in N Edom (M.R. 208018). It guards both the Kings' Highway (the major N–S route through Transjordan) and a major route W to the Wadi Arabah and thence to the Negeb and S Judah. It is also within striking distance of the Edomite copper mines in the Wadi Dana and Wadi Feinan some 10–15 km SSW.

It is situated W of the Kings' Highway on a projecting spur, steep on the N, W, and E sides, with easy access only from the S. In addition to this natural defensive position, strong walls enclose a site of some 3200 m². No water source has been found within the site, the main supply probably being the spring at ʿAin Jenin, about one km E, which until recently was also the source for the modern village.

Excavations at the site have been undertaken by C.-M. Bennett (1971–74) and the British Institute at Amman for Archaeology and History (1980). These have revealed a large, fortified site with monumental public buildings, far larger than any other site in the region. Two major phases of occupation have been found in all the excavated areas, with numerous rebuildings and subphases. Exact dating has not yet been determined, but both phases would appear to fall within the confines of the 7th–6th centuries B.C. There is no evidence for occupation earlier than the 8th century B.C.

Four main areas have been excavated. See Fig. BOZ.01. Area A, the highest point on the site and the so-called "acropolis," contains large public buildings. Areas B and D, to the SW and NE of Area A respectively, contain private dwellings. Area B also contains a postern gate. Area C, to the S of Area A, contains more monumental buildings, probably residential but of higher quality than those in B or D. Thick plaster floors are in use in all areas.

Two successive large buildings occupy the acropolis (Area A). Building A, the later, measures 48 m N–S and 36 m E–W and is "winged," i.e., the corners curve outward. It is similar to the Assyrian courtyard building and hence has usually been assigned to the Neo-Assyrian period (734–610 B.C.), but Bennett notes (1977: 3) that "the discovery of stratified Persian pottery in a late phase in a

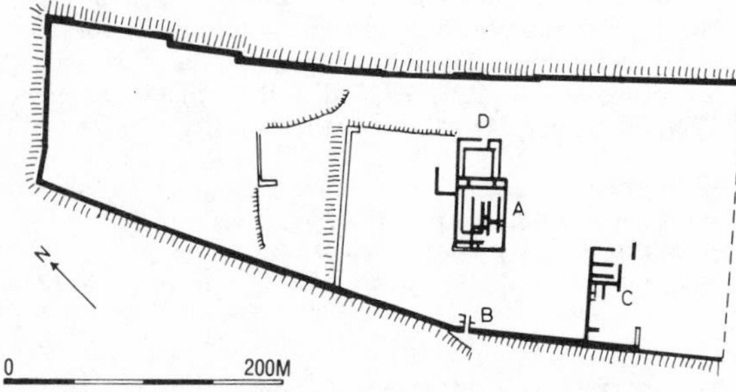

BOZ.01. Site plan of ancient Bozrah (Buseirah), indicating Areas A–D. *(Redrawn from C.-M. Bennett 1974: 2, fig. 1)*

similar building in Area C has given rise to doubt." Building A overlies the S part of Building B.

The plan of the N part of Building B is clear, consisting of a large courtyard (ca. 10 × 15 m), a central cistern, rooms on the N, E, and W sides, and external access in the NW corner. A monumental entrance, consisting of shallow steps flanked by a column plinth on each side, leads to the S part of the building, the plan of which is mostly obscured. It would seem, however, that this is the more important part of the building for which the courtyard was an entrance or antechamber. Bennett (1977: 6) suggests that this might be a temple, the outer area being for purification. A palace or governor's residence would also be a plausible interpretation with the outer area being for general admission.

Area B is a section of the outer defensive wall with a postern gate. The defensive wall is approximately 3.5 m thick at the base and still stands to a height of 3.8 m. At some points the wall was strengthened by the addition of casemates. Domestic houses of rough stone were built against the casemates. A narrow gateway provided access during the main phases of the site. It was blocked in the final phase and the whole area used as a pottery dump.

Area C lies S of the acropolis and covers an area of approximately 67 × 105 m. It contains a large residential complex, not dissimilar in plan to Building A in Area A. Persian pottery was found in the latest phase of Area C. A bath complex suggests the residence of a very important official.

Area D is a small area of domestic houses built on rough stone construction. Several phases of occupation have been identified, some utilizing mudbrick.

All the excavations at Buseirah have taken place in the upper town, which is isolated from the lower town by a battered enclosure wall (see Fig. BOZ.01). It is unclear whether the lower town was residential or mainly open.

Dating for the two main phases at Buseirah has so far not been determined. The earlier phase is probably Assyrian, the later Babylonian/Persian, but there is no evidence to attribute the transition to the Babylonian campaign of 587/586 B.C., which had such a devastating effect on Jerusalem and the cities W of the Jordan. Edomite relations with Babylon at this point appear to have been cordial. The transition is likely to have occurred (supported by the late pottery from Area C) ca. 550 B.C. when the Babylonian king, Nabonidus, passed through Edom on his way to the N Arabian oasis of Teima.

Bibliography

Bartlett, J. R. 1965. The Edomite King-list of Genesis XXXVI 31–39 and I Chron. I 43–50. *JTS* 16: 301–14.

Bennett, C.-M. 1973. Excavations at Buseirah, Southern Jordan, 1971: A Preliminary Report. *Levant* 5: 1–11.

———. 1974. Excavations at Buseirah, Southern Jordan, 1972: Preliminary Report. *Levant* 6: 1–24.

———. 1975. Excavations at Buseirah, Southern Jordan, 1973: Third Preliminary Report. *Levant* 7: 1–19.

———. 1977. Excavations at Buseirah, Southern Jordan, 1974: Fourth Preliminary Report. *Levant* 9: 1–10.

Oakeshott, M. F. 1978. A Study of the Iron II Pottery of East Jordan. Diss., University of London Institute of Archaeology.

STEPHEN HART
ULRICH HÜBNER

2. Bozrah in Moab. The Moabite town, situated on the Mishor *(mîšōr),* is mentioned in a list of geographical places, which are the objects of the woe-oracles against Moab (Jer 48:21–24). This list can hardly be accredited to Jeremiah and is probably a secondary addition. Bozrah may be identical with Bezer *(beṣer),* with which it is etymologically related (Deut 4:43; Josh 20:8; 21:36; and 1 Chr 6:63—Eng 6:78; one of the cities of refuge belonging to Reuben), and *bṣr* of the Mesha Inscription (*ANET,* 320–21; line 27; cf. Euseb., *Onomast.* 46.8.11, Bosor; Josephus, *Ant* 4.173). Although Barāzēn and Umm el-ʿAmed E of Heshbon have been suggested, the exact location of Bozrah is unknown.

3. Bozrah in Ḥaurān. Bozrah lies on one of the fruitful and water-rich plains of S Ḥaurān at the important intersection of the N–S route, which leads from Damascus through the Transjordan to the Hejaz, with the E–W route, on which one could travel from the Mediterranean to Mesopotamia. The ancient site is identical with the modern village Buṣra ash-Shām (32°31′N; 36°29′E), which lies E of Adraa (Derʿā) (cf. Euseb., *Onomast.* 12.14; 13.14; 84.9; 85.8–9). The earliest attestations of Bozrah are in an Egyptian Execration Text as *bw d̄*³*nw* (Posener 1940: E 27) and in the list of conquered Palestinian cities, compiled under Thutmose III, found at Karnak, as *b*³*d̄*³*rwwn*³ *(bd̄rwn).* The literary evidence of the place name ceases after two attestations in the Amarna Letters (197:13 and 199:13; *Buṣruna*). (The Ugaritic site *bṣry* cannot be identified with any of the Bozrahs discussed here. It ought, rather, to be located in the environs of Ugarit. The site of *URU Ba-as-re-e* mentioned in the Assyrian sources is unknown.)

Little is known about pre-Nabatean Bozrah since archaeological excavations (apart from the reconstruction of visibly preserved architectural remains) have only begun. The only settlements (excluding those from prehistory) which can be archaeologically verified are from the LB and from the 2d century B.C.

Bozrah's history is again attested in written sources beginning in the Hellenistic age when Judas Maccabeus conquered Bozrah (1 Macc 5:26, 28; probably Bosorra instead of Bosor, cf. Jos., *Ant* 12.336). It is not known if the town was ruled by the Seleucids, was independent, or was perhaps autonomous. It is likely that Bozrah gradually came under Nabatean control, was slowly incorporated into the state, and soon became its most important city (Bostra Dousaria) except for Petra. This development paralleled the decline of the Seleucid empire. Bozrah's importance remained unchanged from approximately 25 B.C. to A.D. 93. During this time Herod the Great (*JW* 1.398; 2.215), Philip (*JW* 2.95; *Ant* 17.319), and Agrippa I and II (*JW* 2.215) reigned over Aurantis, which was briefly incorporated into the Roman province of Syria (A.D. 34–37).

Following Trajan's annexation of the Nabatean empire, Bozrah became the capital of the newly created Roman province of Arabia in A.D. 106 and remained such throughout all of the expansions and divisions of this province. The status of a *polis,* with its own era (22 March 106) along with the right to mint its own coins, was bestowed upon Bozrah. It also became the garrison of the Legio III Cyrenaica. The city prospered from the construction and enlargement of the Via Nova Traiana. Two

Safaitic inscriptions divulge that the city *(bṣry),* which was promoted to the status of a colony by the Severans (Nea Traiana Alexandriana Colonia Bostra) and to a metropolis *(Mētropolis tēs Arabias)* by Philippus Arabs, had to subject itself to an invasion by the Sassanians (A.D. 253 or 256).

The city's prosperity was due to its important commercial and political position, which enabled it to export grain, wine, and other commodities and to profit from commission and caravan trade with the rest of Syria, Mesopotamia, the Mediterranean coast, and especially N Arabia. Monumental buildings such as the theater, the thermal bath, the avenues flanked by colonnades, the gateways, and the tetrapylons testify to the prosperity of the city in Roman times. The colorful, multiracial population included not only Arabs (Nabateans and Sassanids), Romans, Greeks, Jews, and Christians but also merchants from Palmyra, a Safaitic colony, and, among the soldiers, foreigners of mixed extraction (Carthaginians, Thracians, Persians, Britons, and perhaps even Goths).

Nothing is known about the inception of Christianity in Bozrah, yet Christianity cannot have appeared much later in Bozrah than in Damascus. At any rate, Bozrah was already the seat of a bishop in the 3d century A.D. and shortly thereafter became the metropolitan seat subject to the patriarch of Antioch. Origen sojourned in Bozrah twice. During his first stay he was employed as a teacher by the governor of the province and during his second visit he attended a synod at which he rebuked the residing bishop Beryll, who had uttered heretical views (Euseb., *Hist. Eccl.* 6.19.15; 33.1–3).

Bibliography

Abel, A. 1960a. Baḥhīrā. *Encyclopaedia of Islam.* 2d ed. 1: cols. 922–23.

———. 1960b. Boṣrā. *Encyclopaedia of Islam.* 2d ed. 2: cols. 1275–77.

Campanati, R. F. 1986. Die italienischen Ausgrabungen in Bosra (Syrien). Der spätantike Zentralbau der Kirche der Heiligen Sergius, Bacchus und Leontius. *Boreas* 9: 173–85.

Creswell, K. A. C. 1932. *Early Muslim Architecture.* Vol. 1. Oxford.

Edel, E. 1966. *Die Ortsnamenlisten aus dem Totentempel Amenophis III.* BBB 25. Bonn.

Gaube, H. 1978. *Arabische Inschriften aus Syrien.* Beiruter Texte und Studien 17. Beirut.

Görg, M. 1979. Identifikation von Ortsnamen. Das methodische Problem am Beispiel einer Palimpsestschreibung aus dem Totentempel von Amenophis III. *Ägypten und Alten Testament* 1: 152–73.

Khalil, I., and Mougdad, S. 1983. A Report on the Clearing and Preliminary Excavation of Part of a Christian Basilica in the City of Busra. *Annales archéologiques arabes syriennes* 33/1: 267–80.

Knauf, A. E. 1984. Als die Meder nach Bosra kamen. *ZDMG* 134: 219–25.

Lenzen, C. J., and Knauf, E. A. 1987. Notes on Syrian Toponyms in Egyptian Sources I. *Göttinger Miszellen* 96: 59–64.

Mougdad, S., and Makowski, C. 1983. Nymphée de Bosra en ses abords. *Annales archéologiques arabes syriennes* 33/1: 35–46.

Posener, G. 1940. *Princes et pays d'Asie et de Nubie.* Brussels.

Seeden, H. 1983. Busra 1983: An Umayyad Farmhouse and Bronze Age Occupation Levels. *Annales archéologiques arabes syriennes* 33/2: 161–73.

Wenning, R. 1987. *Die Nabatäer-Denkmäier und Geschichte.* NTOA 3. Göttingen-Fribourg.

ULRICH HÜBNER

BRACELETS. See JEWELRY.

BRAMBLE. See FLORA.

BRANCH [Heb *ṣemaḥ*]. Branch (Jer 23:5; 33:15; Zech 3:8; 6:12) refers to the legitimate Davidic scion who is associated with Yahweh's postexilic restoration of Israel and Judah.

Debate about the exact meaning of branch has focused upon possible messianic connotations of the word. In Jer 23:5 and 33:15 branch refers to an unspecified future Davidic scion whose reign Yahweh would establish in the postexilic restoration of Israel and Judah. In Zech 3:8 and 6:12 branch refers specifically to Zerubbabel as the Davidic scion (Patterson *Haggai Zechariah 1–8* OTL, 273–78), though the difference between the Zechariah and Jeremiah texts is only the degree of specificity. On the basis of these texts, it has been proposed that branch was a technical term for the Messiah in later Judaism (Baldwin 1964: 93–97; cf. Mowinckel 1956: 119–22, 160–65). Yet, while the expectation of a Davidic branch in both Zechariah and Jeremiah may have contributed to the development of a messianic expectation in Judaism, uses of the term in other Northwest Semitic languages make it unlikely that the term was originally a messianic designation.

The phrase *ṣmk ṣdk* has been found in a 3d-century B.C.E. Phoenician inscription where it refers to the legitimate king of the Ptolemaic dynasty (Beyerlin 1978: 232–34). Holladay (*Jeremiah 1–25* Hermeneia, 617–8) concludes that branch is the usual Northwest Semitic word to designate the legitimate king. At the same time, there seem to be several other Hebrew synonyms which convey the same idea: for instance, shoot *(ḥōṭer)* and sprout *(nēṣer),* both in Isa 11:1 (cf. IDB 1: 460–61).

The sense of branch as the legitimate scion is reinforced by studies of *ṣedek* (McKane *Jeremiah 1–25* ICC, 568), which modifies branch in Jeremiah and Semitic occurrences (though in Jer 23:5, cf. Holladay *Jeremiah 1–25* Hermeneia, 616). While *ṣedek* is usually translated "righteous," these studies have suggested numerous Northwest Semitic occurrences where *ṣedek* implies rightful or lawful as a particular nuance of righteous.

Thus, branch, or more specifically righteous branch, should be understood as the legitimate or rightful Davidic scion to the throne of Israel. Especially in Jer 23:5, the legitimacy of this future king contrasts with Zedekiah, whose name suggests legitimacy but who is in fact a Babylonian vassel (Swetnam 1965: 29–40).

Bibliography

Baldwin, J. 1964. Semah as a Technical Term in the Prophets. VT: 93–97.

Beyerlin, W. 1978. *Near Eastern Religious Texts Relating to the Old Testament.* Philadelphia.

Mowinckel, S. 1956. *He That Cometh.* Oxford.

Swetnam, J. 1965. Some Observations on the Background of saddiq in Jeremias 23:5a. *Bib* 46: 29–40.

JOHN M. BRACKE

BRAND, CAMEL. See WASM (CAMEL BRAND).

BREAD. Bread includes various kinds of food such as unleavened and leavened bread, porridge, and gruel prepared from cereal grains such as wheat and barley. The term "bread" was also used for solid food in general. In the Bible, bread is a polyvalent symbol, being used both in everyday life and for metaphoric and symbolic purposes.

A. General Introduction

Many civilizations have developed around the successful cultivation of one main cereal crop such as wheat, rice, or maize. The particular crop raised greatly shaped political, economic, and religious institutions. A large portion of everyday life revolved around the production, distribution, preparation, and consumption of this crop.

Various technologies and tools were necessary for producing different kinds of food from cereals. After the grain was harvested, the husk or bran was removed from the seed. Various means of milling or pounding were used to atomize the endosperm. Different cooking methods, skills, recipes, and utensils were used to produce different kinds of bread.

Humans generally eat only the seeds of cereals, since the outer husk or bran is indigestible. Most of the nutrition of a seed is located in the endosperm. Since the starch in seeds is not easy to digest, humans generally prepare them for consumption. They can be simply parched, toasted, or soaked in water, though more often they are first milled or ground, mixed with liquid, and heated. If the grain is only roughly crushed and the bran is not separated from the rest of the kernel, the product is "meal." If only the kernel, separated from the bran, is very finely ground, "flour" is the result. Heating a mixture of liquid and meal produces porridge (see Moritz 1958: xix). To bake bread, a mixture of liquid and flour is usually heated at least to 450° F. Leaven added to dough produces a light and aerated loaf. Because of the gluten content of cereals, wheat makes the best leavened bread, rye is second best, and barley can only be used for unleavened bread.

B. Bread in the Ancient Near East

1. General Background. Early hunting and gathering societies in the ANE gathered the seeds of wild cereals for food. These native plants were later domesticated. The cereals that were raised and the food products made from them varied regionally and historically. Both climate and soil type shaped people's diets.

Since wheat and barley have different growing requirements, they are often found in different regions. Oppenheim states: "Since barley can be grown in poor and alkaline soils, it was preferred to wheat in Mesopotamia; Egypt became the wheat land, and the regions in between used the cereal which best responded to local conditions" (1977: 314).

In the lands around the Mediterranean, bread was the staple food which provided most of the proteins and carbohydrates for humans for centuries and even millennia. The high costs of transportation kept both imports and exports to a minimum. Therefore, the amount of grain an area produced was a key factor for how large a population could be supported (Broshi 1979: 7). Similarly, within any given community, social and economic differences were reflected in cuisine—bread of the poor and bread of the rich.

Bread played a major role in the civilizations of Mesopotamia, Asia Minor, Syria, Palestine, Egypt, Greece, and Italy. Here only a few brief comments concerning bread in Mesopotamia and Egypt will be made. (For more details, see Hoffner 1974; Darby 1976; Währen 1964; Dalman 1935.)

2. Mesopotamia. Some 300 kinds of bread are mentioned in Mesopotamian vocabulary lists. These breads were made from a variety of ingredients such as flours, spices, and fruit fillings and came in a variety of shapes and sizes. After grain was crushed on a grindstone to make meal and flour it could be used for porridge, mush, leavened and unleavened bread, and beer. Unleavened bread was made by a method called *tinûru.* "A fire was built inside an upright clay cylinder, resulting in very hot exterior walls, upon which loaves of unleavened bread were placed and baked" (Bottéro 1985: 39). Dome ovens, which were available by the 3d millennium B.C.E., were necessary for making leavened bread.

3. Egypt. On the walls of Egyptian tombs one finds depictions of various activities related to the production of bread and beer. Three-dimensional sculpture and wooden models depict people grinding grain, making dough, and baking bread (Filce Leek 1972: pls. 29–32; Darby 1976: 501–28). Breads were made in numerous shapes: conical, circular with slashes, triangular, semicircular, flat and curved, rolled into spirals, and even shaped into animal and human figures.

Archaeologists have found loaves and pieces of bread at grave sites. While the origin of leavened bread is unknown, samples of bread found at Neolithic El-Badari appear to have been leavened (Darby 1976: 515–16). Most specimens of bread examined were made from emmer but this may have been because offering breads had to be made from the best cereal. Most of the samples of the abdominal contents of prehistoric Egyptian mummies that were examined by Netolitzky contained husks of barley (Filce Leek 1973: 200–1).

C. Bread in the Bible

1. Introduction. Biblical texts do not present an extensive treatment about bread. Aspects related to the production and eating of bread were so commonplace that writers did not go into much detail about them. Here only bread in the OT and NT will be examined. Data from other literary works such as the Mishnah, intertestamental literature, and secular sources, as well as material evidence from archaeology, still needs to be collected, sorted, and assimilated.

2. Bread in the OT. a. Etymology. The term *leḥem,* "bread," occurs nearly 300 times in the OT. In Semitic languages *leḥem* was used for "solid food." Ullendorff (1956: 192) contends that the "root *lḥm* expressed in Semitic simply the staple-diet and would, therefore, vary in the different regions." In Arabic one has *laḥm,* "meat," in Ethiopic *laḥm,* "cow," and in the South Arabic language of Soqoṭra *leḥem,* "fish." In Ugaritic, Phoenician, Hebrew, Aramaic, Syriac, and Mandaic *lḥm* referred to bread specifically and food generally (*TWAT* 4:538).

b. Basic Components. Grains such as wheat and barley are used to make porridge, mush, leavened bread, and unleavened bread. Bread is generally made from barley (2 Kgs 4:42) or wheat (Exod 29:2). Ezekiel is told to make bread from wheat, barley, beans, lentils, millet, and spelt, and eat it like a barley cake (Ezek 4:9). The mixture was not typical but reflected the scarcity of food during the siege of Jerusalem.

While wheat bread was probably tastier than barley cakes and therefore more desirable, not all bread was made from wheat. Wheat was more expensive than barley (2 Kgs 7:1–twice as much; Rev 6:6–thrice as much) and may have been too expensive for the average Israelite. Furthermore, it was not advisable or even possible for the farmer to plant only wheat and not barley. Planting both crops allowed for diversification, enabled the farmer to utilize the different types of soil available, and spread out the harvest time (Hopkins 1985: 242). In premonarchic times most people ate barley bread; however, by the 8th and 7th centuries, Silver argues, more of the population ate wheat bread (1983: 93–98).

c. Preparation of Bread. Borowski mentions three stages of cereal ripening during which grain could be picked, processed, and eaten (1987: 88). Grain could be eaten raw, parched (Ruth 2:14), crushed (Lev 2:14), or it could be ground to flour and used in various kinds of leavened and unleavened bread.

While the term *leḥem* can refer to grain in general (Isa 28:28), most often it refers to food processed from grain. It is distinguished from raw grain in 2 Kgs 4:42 and from roasted and new grain in Lev 23:14. The general term for flour or meal from wheat or barley is *qemaḥ,* whereas *sōlet* refers to very fine flour of wheat. Borowski reports that a jar of semolina which is a "by-product of grinding and sifting flour" was found "in Beth-shemesh in an early Iron Age context" (1987: 90). Either a mortar and pestle or grinding stones were used to grind the grain into flour (Num 11:8). Grinding stones and saddle querns are richly represented in archaeological reports (Borowski 1987: 89–90).

Flour and/or meal could be stored in jars (1 Kgs 17:12). Flour which had water added to it was kneaded into dough. Then the dough was shaped (2 Sam 13:8; Gen 18:6) into a form which could be baked. Leaven was sometimes added before baking took place (Exod 12:39). One finds frequent mention of the baking of bread (Lev 23:17; 2 Sam 13:8; Ezek 4:12).

Particular types of bread include *ṣappîḥit,* "flat cake, wafer" (BDB, 860; Exod 16:31); *niqqūdîm,* "hard bisquit or cake" (BDB, 666; 1 Kgs 14:3); *kikkār,* "(disk-shaped, round, thin) loaf of bread" (*CHAL,* 156; 1 Sam 2:36); *ḥallâ* "(ring-shaped) bread" (*CHAL,* 104–5; 2 Sam 6:19); *rāqîq,* "thin cake, wafer" (BDB, 956; Exod 29:23); *lĕbibâ,* "heart-shaped cake" (*CHAL,* 172; 2 Sam 13:6); *ʿugâ* "(circular, flat) bread cake" (*CHAL,* 264; Gen 18:6); *maʾăpeh* "thing baked" (BDB, 66); Lev 2:4); *maṣṣâ* "unleavened bread, or cake" (BDB, 595; Lev 2:5); *ḥāmēṣ,* "that which is leavened" (BDB, 329; Exod 12:15). A loaf of bread which had been preserved by a fire was found at Gezer dating from 1800–1400 B.C.E. (Silver 1983: 92).

While men and women reportedly baked bread (Gen 19:3; 1 Sam 28:24), baking was probably largely the work of women (Lev 26:26). Bread for cultic usage was made by priests (Lev 24:5). While the king could afford to have professional bakers who were women (1 Sam 8:13) or men (Gen 40:1), most families baked their own bread. References to the bakers' street (Jer 37:21) and the tower of the ovens (Neh 3:11) might indicate a quarter of bakers in Jerusalem.

Three methods are mentioned for cooking grain offerings: baked in an oven, made in a pan, or made on a griddle (Lev 7:9). Similar means of making bread were probably used outside the temple: in an oven (Lev. 26:26) or on hot coals (Isa 44:19; 1 Kgs 19:6).

d. Bread as Food or Nourishment. The term "bread" can refer to food in general. The importance of bread is indicated by the expression "staff of bread" (Ps 105:16). Holladay (*CHAL,* 192) suggests that this phrase refers to "a bread-pole, stick on which ring-shaped bread is stacked (to keep it away from mice, etc.)." Other scholars think the expression refers to the support that food provides for humans. When Yahweh breaks this staff of life, he brings famine upon people (Ezek 5:16).

While bread usually is food for humans, it can also be food for all living beings (Pss 136:25; 147:9). Bread offerings are sometimes designated as food for God (Lev 21:6). While some texts indicate that God does not need food for sustenance (50:12–13), sacrificial rites are partly modeled around activities associated with a meal.

Along with water (Neh 13:2) or wine (Gen 14:18), *leḥem* refers to solid food. Bread occurs in lists of food items in such contexts as agricultural products of Israel (Ps 104:15), travel provisions (2 Sam 16:1), food supplies (1 Sam 25:18), gifts to the king (1 Sam 16:20), and sacrificial offerings (1 Sam 10:3).

Bread is a basic part of a meal. The expression "to eat bread" meant to share a meal (Gen 31:54; 37:25). Even the prisoner must have rations of bread and water (1 Kgs 22:27). The author of Proverbs wisely prays not for poverty or riches but rather for the proper portion of bread necessary for daily existence (Prov 30:8–9). The virtuous person shares bread with the hungry (Isa 58:7).

e. Special Usages and Expressions. To show his displeasure, God could send "bread of adversity" (Isa 30:20) or "bread of tears" (Ps 80:5). Tears (Ps 42:4) or ashes (Ps 102:10—Eng. 102:9) are the figurative bread of those who mourn. At some point during mourning rites, others encouraged the mourners to break their fast and eat (1 Sam 28:22; 2 Sam 3:35). This food was called the "bread of mourners" (Hos 9:4).

The idioms "bread of idleness" (Prov 31:27), "bread of deception" (Prov 20:17), and "bread of wickedness" (Prov 4:17) refer to improper means by which people gain bread. They all deal with a characteristic lifestyle which should be avoided.

The idiom "to eat people like bread" (Ps 14:4) or that people are "bread" for others (Num 14:9) refers to oppression. The figurative usage of cannibalistic imagery portrays the horror of oppression.

Manna can be called *leḥem* (Exod 16:8) because it was the daily food of the Israelites in the wilderness. It was prepared for eating like bread from grain (Num 11:8) and was perishable and spoiled much like regular bread (Exod 16:20; cf. Josh 9:12).

f. Theology of Bread. Bread is seen as a gift of God. Westermann (1982: 38) makes a distinction between bread of blessing and bread of deliverance: "Israel learned to differentiate between 'bread of blessing' growing during the yearly cycles, bread in which man's own work participated, and the 'saving bread' received as the preserving gift of the saving God during the distress of hunger."

The Israelites knew that land, fertility, rain, and productive labor were all essential for the production of grain (Genesis 3; Isa 30:23). They also knew that they themselves could not control all of these factors, and therefore depended upon God's blessing (Ps 127:1–2). The bounty of the basket and kneading trough was a result of his blessing or his curse upon their actions (Deut 28:5, 17).

g. Cultic Usages of Bread. This close connection between Yahweh and bread meant that the people needed to maintain a proper relationship with Yahweh. Gerstenberger points out that "The purpose, then, of most ritual activity is to secure and maintain the means of survival: food, shelter, medicine, rain, etc." (*Psalms-Part 1* FOTL, 5–6). Gifts of food were offered to God with the expectation that God would continue to provide food for them.

Bread is frequently part of offerings and sacrifices. Both leavened (Lev 7:13) and unleavened bread (Exod 29:2) could be used. As part of the first fruits of the harvest, bread was offered to God during the Feast of Weeks (Lev 23:15–20). During the Feast of Unleavened Bread, only unleavened bread was eaten (Lev 23:4–6).

Bread was widely used in the ANE and around the Mediterranean for religious purposes (Haran 1985: 221–23), and was probably originally understood to be nourishment for gods. Such an anthropomorphic depiction of a deity was considered crude by some in ancient times and was countered by various polemics (Ps 50:12–13; Bel and the Dragon; editing of the Gilgamesh Epic [Tigay 1982: 224–28]). Even if the deity could not physically consume the food, it was assumed that in some sense the deity was pleased with it. Bread also served as a means for the provision of the daily needs of the priests, and when eaten as part of a religious meal it provided fellowship among community members and the deity.

3. Bread in the NT. a. Bread in Everyday Life. In Classical Greek *artos* is used for a "cake or loaf of wheat-bread" and for bread in general, and is distinguished from *maza,* "porridge" or "barley-cake" (*LSJM*, 250, 1072). In Koine Greek *artos* is used as the general word for bread (*TDNT* 1: 477). In other Koine texts one frequently finds the term with *katharos* referring to "pure" or "white bread" (MM, 1930: 80).

The term *artos,* "bread," occurs nearly 100 times in the NT. Louw and Nida (1988: 50) describe this bread: "a relatively small and generally round loaf of bread (considerably smaller than present-day typical loaves of bread and thus more like 'rolls' or 'buns')."

Barley bread is only mentioned twice (John 6:9,13). The poor may have eaten unleavened barley bread because wheat was expensive. While there is a special term for unleavened bread *(azumos), artos* by itself can be used for both leavened and unleavened bread. The bread eaten at the Last Supper (Mark 14:22) and on the road to Emmaus (Luke 24:30) probably was unleavened since these meals took place during the Passover week (Jeremias 1966: 66).

There is a rich vocabulary related to the production of bread. Mention is made of mills, millstones, and grinding grain (Matt 24:41; Luke 17:2; Mark 9:42). The sound of the grinding of grain was a sound of normal everyday existence in a city (Rev 18:22). References are made to the sifting of flour (Luke 22:31), a batch of dough (1 Cor 5:6–7), yeast and the process of fermentation, regular flour (Matt 13:33), and fine wheat flour (Rev 18:13).

The opening of a meal by giving thanks often focused upon bread (Matt 14:19; 15:36; Luke 24:30). "The father of the household opened a meal by taking a loaf of bread, giving thanks, breaking it, and distributing it" (BAGD, 110). Abbreviated expressions such as "to take bread" (John 21:13) or "to break bread" (Luke 24:35) often referred to the onset of a meal. A common practice of Jesus before meals, including the Last Supper (Matt 26:26 = Mark 14:22; Luke 22:19 = 1 Cor 11:24), this was continued by the early Christians in their daily fellowship (Acts 2:46).

b. Bread as Food in General. The term *artos* can be used for food in general (Matt 4:4). The idiom "to eat bread" meant to have a meal (Mark 3:20). To eat no bread or drink no wine meant to fast (Luke 7:33). "To eat one's own bread" meant to make one's own living (2 Thess 3:12).

The petition for bread stands at the heart of the Lord's Prayer and is the first of a series of requests for human needs (Matt 6:11). The expression with *artos* and *epiousios* has been variously rendered as "bread for subsistence," "bread for today," and "bread for the future" (*Luke 10–24* AB, 900–6; cf. BAGD, 296–97). While there is no consensus, the expression "daily bread" is still useful. Yamauchi (1964–65: 148) states: "In antiquity much of the food, such as bread, was prepared daily, and would be apportioned daily. This daily bread was the very symbol for subsistence, representing the minimal need for existence."

c. Symbolic Usages of Bread. Bread was used in Jewish religious ceremonies including the Feast of Unleavened Bread (Exod 12:17) and the bread of the Presence in the temple (Exod 25:30; Lev 24:5–9). In the Christian eucharist, bread and wine were the elements (1 Cor 11:23–26). In these cases bread had symbolic and religious functions, but it was also eaten and served as food.

By the 1st century a rich midrashic treatment of manna had developed (Borgen 1981). Vermes (1969: 262) summarizes: "in rabbinic tradition Moses is associated with manna and Torah, and manna is accepted as an allegorical Torah. In Philo, manna is connected with Logos, wisdom and Torah, and Moses is presented as Logos and Torah incarnate." Gärtner (1959: 20–25) refers to the Jewish view of the three ages and the bread which is associated with each of them. In the Passover Haggadah a distinction is made between bread of the Mosaic age, bread of the present meal, and bread of the world to come.

Jesus is called the "bread of life" (John 6:35) and the "bread which comes down from heaven" (John 6:41). In John a distinction is made between manna in the desert for the Mosaic age, Jesus' feeding of the people in the wilderness, and the eucharistic bread for the feast in God's kingdom. Borgen suggests that John contrasts the external bread of the past given through Moses with the spiritual bread of the present that is available in Jesus (1981: 172–79). In Luke 14:15 a blessing is pronounced upon those who will eat bread in the kingdom of God. This refers to an eschatological banquet. The idea of such a banquet can already be found in Isa 25:6–8 and continues to develop in the following centuries.

Bibliography

Borgen, P. 1981. *Bread from Heaven: An Exegetical Study of the Concept of Manna in the Gospel of John and the Writings of Philo.* Leiden.

Borowski, O. 1987. *Agriculture in Iron Age Israel.* Winona Lake, IN.

Bottéro, J. 1985. The Cuisine of Ancient Mesopotamia. *BA* 48: 36–47.

Broshi, Magen. 1979. The Population of Western Palestine in the Roman-Byzantine Period. *BASOR* 236: 1–10.

Dalman, G. 1935. *Brot, Öl und Wein.* Vol. 4 of *Arbeit und Sitte in Palästina.* Gütersloh.

Darby, W. J.; Ghalioungi, P.; and Grivetti, L. 1976. *Food: The Gift of Osiris.* Vol. 2. London.

Filce Leek, F. 1972. Teeth and Bread in Ancient Egypt. *JEA* 58: 126–32.

———. 1973. Further Studies Concerning Ancient Egyptian Bread. *JEA* 59: 199–204.

Gärtner, B. 1959. *John 6 and the Jewish Passover.* Lund.

Haran, M. 1985. *Temples and Temple-Service in Ancient Israel.* Winona Lake, IN.

Hoffner, H. A., Jr. 1974. *Alimenta Hethaeorum: Food Production in Hittite Asia Minor.* New Haven.

Hopkins, D. C. 1985. *The Highlands of Canaan: Agricultural Life in the Early Iron Age.* SWBA 3. Decatur, GA.

Jeremias, J. 1966. *The Eucharistic Words of Jesus.* 2d ed. Trans. N. Perrin. Philadelphia.

Louw, J. P., and Nida, E. A., ed. 1988. *Greek-English Lexicon of the New Testament Based on Semantic Domains.* New York.

Moritz, L. A. 1958. *Grain-Mills and Flour in Classical Antiquity.* Oxford.

Oppenheim, A. L. 1977. *Ancient Mesopotamia: Portrait of a Dead Civilization.* Rev. ed. by E. Reiner. Chicago.

Reed, S. A. 1986. *Food in the Psalms.* Diss., Claremont.

Silver, M. 1983. *Prophets and Markets: The Political Economy of Ancient Israel.* Boston.

Tigay, J. 1982. *The Evolution of the Gilgamesh Epic.* Philadelphia.

Ullendorff, E. 1956. The Contribution of South Semitics to Hebrew Lexicography. VT 6: 190–98.

Vermes, G. 1969. He Is the Bread. Pp. 256–63 in *Neotestamentica et Semitica,* ed. E. E. Ellis and M. Wilcox. Edinburgh.

Währen, M. 1964. *Brot und Gebäck im Leben und Glauben des Orients.* Bern.

Westermann, C. 1982. *Elements of Old Testament Theology.* Trans. D. W. Stott. Atlanta.

Yamauchi, E. M. 1964–65. The "Daily Bread" Motif in Antiquity. *WTJ* 27: 145–56.

STEPHEN A. REED

BREAD OF THE PRESENCE. The bread of the Presence consists of twelve loaves of unleavened bread that are displayed in the temple sanctuary. Since the sanctuary is next to the holy of holies, the bread is separated only by a curtain from Yahweh's immediate presence. In this important location, the loaves symbolize the covenant between God and his people Israel (Lev 24:5–9).

Although the purpose of the bread of the Presence is to be on display before Yahweh, the Priestly source (P) directs its attention to the stages of preparation and disposal. (This is not surprising, for, unlike preparation and disposal, the week-long display requires no human intervention.) Preparation begins prior to the Sabbath's onset with the baking of the loaves, each of which contains two tenths of an ephah of flour. Then, on Sabbath morning, the high priest enters the sanctuary with the bread, removes the old loaves, and sets out the new ones. He arranges them—with accompanying pieces of frankincense—into two rows of six on a golden table on the N side of the sanctuary (Lev 24:5–9; Exod 26:35).

Once the bread of the Presence enters the sanctuary, its nearness to Yahweh renders it holy. After the high priest removes the loaves from the sanctuary, therefore, he must properly dispose of the holy bread. To accomplish this, he gives the bread to other priests who in turn must eat it in a holy place—namely, within the temple complex. The frankincense cannot be reused, so it is burned on the sacrificial altar in the priestly court.

The sanctuary constitutes the location for two further rites beside the bread of the Presence: burning lamps every night, and burning pure frankincense at morning and evening. The three observances have the same status, for they all take place on a golden piece of furniture. The bread rests on a golden table (Exod 25:23–30), the lamps are on a golden seven-branched lampstand (Exod 25:31–39), and the frankincense is burned on a golden altar (Exod 30:1–10). Furthermore, each observance is tended by the high priest, who, according to P, is the only priest allowed to do so. Of the three rites, though, only the bread of the Presence is continual, for the lamp burns only at night and the incense burns only a few hours after it has been lit.

The significance of the bread of the Presence within the temple cult is revealed by its location, the sanctuary. Indeed, only one act of worship occurs in a more important area of the temple, namely, the high priest entering the holy of holies on the Day of Atonement. Most temple observances—those involving, e.g., animal sacrifices and grain offerings—take place in a less important area, that is, the priestly court and the sacrificial altar in it. This hierarchy can be seen in several ways. To begin with, the sanctuary is more holy than the court, because the closer an area is to Yahweh, the more holy it is. Since the sanctuary is separated from Yahweh in the holy of holies by only a curtain, it is more holy than the priestly court outside. This difference in status is reinforced by the furnishings and the personnel of the two locations. The sanctuary's furniture is gold, while the court's is primarily of bronze. Similarly, the sanctuary rites must be performed by the high priest, while the sacrifices are usually done by regular priests. Most importantly, however, the purposes of the rites carried out in the two locations differ. Those in the sanctuary maintain the continual relationship between God and his people Israel. Indeed, Leviticus (25:5–9) specifically states that the bread of the Presence symbolizes the covenant. The rites at the altar, by contrast, primarily concern the relationship between individuals and Yahweh. The animals and other offerings brought by private individuals are sacrificed on the altar or distributed in the priestly court around it. P's emphasis on the different locations within the temple complex thus reveals the importance of the bread of the Presence in the worship of Yahweh.

Outside of P, the bread of the Presence is frequently associated with Israelite temples to Yahweh. Most references assume P's description, while occasionally adding a new detail (1 Kgs 7:48; 1 Chr 9:32; 23:29; 28:16; 2 Chr 2:4; 13:11; 29:18; Neh 10:33). Others merely mention the existence of the bread or its table. For example, in 1 Sam 21:5–7, the Deuteronomic historian mentions that the temple at Nob has this bread as part of its rites. Similarly, 1 Maccabees (1:22 and 4:49) states that Antiochus Epiphanes carried off the table in 170 B.C.E. but that Simon the Maccabee later replaced it. Josephus mentions the bread of the Presence (*Ant* 3.6.6; 3.10.7), as do the Temple Scroll (cols. 3, 8), the gospels (Matt 12:4 = Mark 2:26 = Luke 6:4), and Hebrews (9:2). Finally, the Arch of Titus in Rome depicts the golden table being carried in Titus' triumph after he conquered Jerusalem in 70 C.E.

The name bread of the Presence (sometimes mistranslated as "showbread") is based on the Hebrew *leḥem pānîm* (LXX: *artos enōpion*), which literally means "the bread which is in the presence of . . ." (e.g., Exod 25:30). It is also referred to as *leḥem hammaʿăreket* (LXX: *artos tēs protheseōs*), "the arranged bread," presumably because it is arranged (*ʾrk*) in two rows (e.g., 1 Chr 9:32). Num 4:7 calls it *leḥem hatāmîd* (LXX: *prokemai*), the "regular bread" or the "continual bread."

Bibliography

Driver, G. R. 1957. Presidential Address. *VTSup* 4: 1–7.

Haran, M. 1961. The Complex of Ritual Acts Performed Inside the Tabernacle. *ScrHier* 8: 272–302.

———. 1978. *Temples and Temple Service in Ancient Israel: An Inquiry into the Character of Cult Phenomena and the Historical Setting of the Priestly School.* Oxford.

Haupt, P. 1900. Babylonian Elements in the Levitic Ritual. *JBL* 19: 55–81.

Vaux, R. de. 1961. *Ancient Israel: Its Life and Institutions.* New York.

PAUL V. M. FLESHER

BREASTPIECE [Heb *ḥōšen*]. An item made of fabric that constituted part of the high priest's apparel. A different term, "breastplate" [Heb *širyôn*], refers to a type of metal armor worn by soldiers.

The breastpiece of Aaron's priestly wardrobe is described in great detail in the tabernacle texts of Exodus (see esp. 28:5–30 and 39:8–21) and is also mentioned in one passage in Leviticus (8:8) dealing with the tabernacle. The breastpiece was made of the same kind of material as the ephod: gold, blue, purple, and scarlet woolen threads interwoven with fine linen. The workmanship was of a certain skillful type (*ḥôšēb*) also used for the ephod. The woven fabric formed a double piece of material, a span 9 or 10 inches square when folded over. The reason for the doubled fabric was that the breastpiece, in addition to its symbolic ritual value, also served as a container for the Urim and Thummim.

Once fashioned, the breastpiece was set with 12 precious stones, in four rows of three stones, with each stone set in gold filigree. These stones were set into the fabric and evidently did not protrude. Each stone represented one of the twelve "sons of Israel." A series of golden fittings (rings, chains, or cords) and also a blue ribbon were then used to attach the breastpiece to other items of the high priest's garb: at the top to the shoulder of the ephod, and at the bottom to the woven band or girdle of the ephod.

As one of four special overgarments fashioned for the high priest and worn by no other priest, the breastpiece was part of a carefully designed complex of ritual acts associated with the priest's role within the tabernacle, as opposed to the outer courts. Several of the inner rituals involved sacral acts; others were carried out by the wearing of the Aaronic ritual garb, each item having symbolic significance so that the wearing of the item was tantamount to the performing of a ritual (see Haran 1978: 212). Known as the "breastpiece of judgment," the stone-studded breastpiece signified the sons of Israel to God and also contained mantic devices by which God's decisions were rendered. Along with the bells of the ephod coat and the diadem, it aroused the attention of God toward the people of Israel.

The priestly "breastpiece" shares with the "breastplate" the fact that it was worn across the chest. However, the word rendered as breastplate is sometimes translated by the more inclusive term "coat of mail" (as in 1 Sam 17:5, 38). The breastplate as a piece of military garb is used literally in reference to soldiers' clothing (1 Kgs 22:34 = 2 Ch 18:33) and also figuratively to represent righteousness (Isa 39:17; cf. Eph 6:14; 1 Thess 5:8).

Bibliography

Haran, M. 1978. *Temples and Temple Service in Ancient Israel.* Oxford.

CAROL MEYERS

BREASTPLATE. See WEAPONS AND IMPLEMENTS OF WARFARE.

BREECHES. See DRESS AND ORNAMENTATION.

BRIDAL JEWELRY. See JEWELRY.

BRIDE. See MARRIAGE.

BRIDE OF CHRIST. Although the specific phrase "bride of Christ" does not appear in the NT, the concept is found in several NT works as a description of the Church. Paul describes the Corinthian believers as having been betrothed to Christ and presented as a bride to her husband (2 Cor 11:2; cf. Rom 7:1–6). In Eph 5:21–33 the relationship between husband and wife is explained in terms of the relationship that exists between Christ and the Church. The author of Revelation applies the metaphor of the bride of the Lamb (Christ), not only to the Church (19:7), but also to the new Jerusalem, the heavenly city, which is the eschatological manifestation of the people of God (21:2, 9). The source for this imagery is found in the OT where the relationship between Israel and God is often spoken of in marital terms (Isa 54:1–6; Jer 31:32; Ezek 16:8; Hos 2). The transference of this imagery to Christ and his Church was natural for the NT writers who viewed the Church as the new Israel.

MITCHELL G. REDDISH

BRIDLE. See ZOOLOGY.

BROAD PLACE. The RSV translation of *raḥab* in Job 36:16 and *merḥab* in 2 Sam 22:20 = Ps 18:20 (—Eng v 19); Ps 31:9 (—Eng v 8). Both words come from a root *(rḥb)* that means to be wide, spacious, roomy. Because it is geographically descriptive, the root was often used in place names such as Beth-rehob, Rehob, and Rehoboth. However, the root seems to be used metaphorically for salvation in the passages cited above: someone located in the middle of a "broad place" is relatively secure and safe from a surprise attack.

BROAD WALL (PLACE) [Heb *haḥômâ hārĕḥābâ*). Wall of postexilic Jerusalem mentioned in Nehemiah. After repair of the Jeshanah Gate (RSV: "Old Gate," Neh 3: 6), evidently in the NW corner of Jerusalem, repairs were made as far as the Broad Wall (Neh 3: 8), which was reached by going past the Tower of the Ovens (Neh 12: 38), which seems to have been on the W wall. This description would suggest that the Broad Wall was somewhere on the western hill, the Upper City. In 1969–71 N. Avigad (1970; 1972) uncovered a section of a massive Broad Wall in the modern Jewish Quarter of the Upper City, a wall of large unhewn, unmortared stone, 23 feet (7 m) broad and ca. 140 feet long, preserved in part to the height of ca. 11 feet; the foundation section of this massive city wall running NE–SW and ending ca. 917 feet W of the temple platform may have been part of the city wall built by Hezekiah (2 Chr 32: 5) to enclose the Mishneh (Second) Quarter and, according to Avigad, is continued around to the walls of the City of David and enclosed the Siloam Pool. See Mazar 1975: 176–78; CORNER GATE.

Bibliography

Avigad, N. 1970. Excavations in the Jewish Quarter of the Old City of Jerusalem, 1969/70. *IEJ* 20: 1–8, 129–40.

———. 1972. Excavations in the Jewish Quarter of the Old City of Jerusalem, 1971. *IEJ* 22: 193–200.

Mazar, B. 1975. *The Mountain of the Lord.* Garden City, NY.

W. HAROLD MARE

BROOCH. See JEWELRY.

BROOM TREE. See FLORA.

BROTHER, BROTHERHOOD (NT) [Gk *adelphos, adelphotēs*]. *Adelphos* is a compound term formed from the copulative prefix *a* and from *delphus,* "the womb," which gives the meaning "one born from the same womb." *Adelphos* and the feminine form, *adelphē,* are used first to speak of physical relationships, but approximately half of the occurrences in the NT use the figuratively/spiritually, primarily to speak of relationships between the people of Israel or between Christians. All of the derivatives and compounds *(adelphotēs, philadelphos, philadelphia, pseudadelphos)* bring out the figurative significance of the basic term.

Adelphos was used for the male and *adelphē* for the female members of the same physical family. The masculine plural could cover all the children of a family. *Adelphos* was also used to signify near relatives, whether joined together by bloodline (e.g., nephew) or marriage (e.g., brother-in-law). Plato uses it for compatriots (*Menex.,* 239a), Xenophon for friends (*An.,* 7.2.25; 38), and Plotinus calls all the things in the world *adelphoi* (*Enn.,* 2.9.18). It is often used for members of a religious society, both in the papyri and inscriptions and also in literature (Moulton and Milligan 1930: 8–9).

In the LXX *adelphos* is the usual term to render Heb *ʾāḥ,* and only occasionally for *rēaʿ* (Gen 43:33; Jer 31[38]:34). *Adelphos* was used originally for a physical brother and *adelphē* for a physical sister, but *adelphos* could also be used for other relatives as well (e.g., Gen 29:12ff.). The figurative use of the term naturally arose within the nation of Israel because the twelve tribes were descended from the twelve sons of Jacob. This is clearly seen in Ps 22:22[23] where "brothers" are in parallelism with the "congregation" and are synonymous with the descendants of Jacob/Israel in the following verse. A related feature is found in the use of the terms "son" and "brother" in the picture of God's relationship to his people (e.g., Hos 2:1–3 [—Eng 1:10–2:1]).

Judaism also uses "brother" with both a physical and a figurative sense. The term designates physical relationships (4 Macc 9:23; 10:3, 15; 13:19, 27) and also the brotherhood established by covenant fellowship (1 Macc 12:10, 17). The compound term "love of the brethren" *(philadelphia)* also occurs (cf. 4 Macc 13:23, 26; 14:1). Josephus uses *adelphos* figuratively to speak of relationships between members of the Essenes (*JW* 2.122), and in the Qumran texts "brother" is a common term to designate the relationship between members of the community. Indeed, brotherhood was significant for the community because they saw themselves as the true remnant of Israel, the true people of God (Urbach 1979: 584–85; Schilling 1967: 211–12). The Heb term *ḥābēr* ("companion, brother"), although used to designate scholars, was also used to describe the associates of the Pharasaic sect during the Second Temple period up to the time of Jesus (Wilkins 1988: 123; *HJP*[2] 2: 583–89; Aberbach 1967: 19–20).

NT use of *adelphos/adelphē* is consistent with usage in the surrounding milieu, but it has unique characteristics as well. *Adelphos* occurs at least 343 times in the NT, 13 of which are in Acts in conjunction with *anēr* ("man") as an address (e.g., Acts 1:16–*andres adelphoi*). *Adelphē* is used 25 times. As was true with the history of the terms, so also is true of their use in the NT: *adelphos/adelphē* designate both biological and figurative brothers/sisters.

Adelphos/adelphē are used to describe several different literal family relationships, the most famous among them being Peter and his brother Andrew (Mark 1:16 par.), John and his brother James (Mark 1:19 par.), Lazarus the brother of the sisters Mary and Martha (John 11:1–2), and the brothers and sisters of Jesus (cf. Mark 3:31–35; 6:3).

The OT figurative use is carried over to the NT when the apostles addressed Jews as *adelphoi* in Acts (2:29; 3:17; 7:2; 13:15, 26, 38; 22:1; 23:1ff.; 28:17), and are themselves addressed in the same way (2:37).

But the terms come to have a distinctive emphasis in the NT. In Matt 12:46–50 Jesus gives a definition of those who would be his spiritual *adelphoi/adelphai.* While his physical mother and brothers wait outside to see him, Jesus stretches out his hand toward his disciples and says, "Behold my mother and my brothers. For whoever does the will of my Father in heaven, this one is my brother and sister and mother." With this definition Jesus declares that spiritual union in the family of God takes precedence over national or blood-family lines (cf. also Luke 14:26). Here Jesus unites discipleship with a familial emphasis. See also JESUS, BROTHERS AND SISTERS OF.

The early Church understood the family nature of the new community. *Adelphos* was one of the first terms for their self-designation (cf. Acts 1:15, 16; 6:3). The decision of the apostolic council explicitly applied the term to gentile Christians, giving them assurance that they were also part of the family of God (Acts 15:23). In 1 Cor 5:11 Paul calls the immoral person who postures as a believer a "so-called brother," and calls the Judaizers who attempt to bring believers into bondage to law "false brothers" (*pseudadelphoi;* 2 Cor 11:26; Gal 2:4).

But the family relationship is not merely figurative. It is based on a spiritual birth. Jesus is the only begotten, firstborn, beloved Son of God, and through faith in him believers are born into a new life (2 Cor 5:17; 1 Pet 1:3–5) where they are called Jesus' brothers (Rom 8:29; Heb 2:11ff.). To believe in Jesus as the Christ causes one to be born of God, and to love marks the relationship of the members of the family (1 John 5:1–2). The derivative term *adelphotēs* (found only in 1 Pet 2:17; 5:9) conceives of a "brotherhood" of believers throughout the world. Members of the brotherhood are urged to exercise "brotherly love" toward one another (*philadelphos* only in 1 Pet 3:8; *philadelphia* in Rom 12:10; 1 Thess 4:9; Heb 13:1; 1 Pet 1:22; 2 Pet 1:7). Indeed, love is to be so characteristic of the believer's relationships that to hate one's brother is to give evidence that one does not love God (1 John 5:19–21), which means that one is not truly a member of the family of God.

Bibliography

Aberbach, M. 1967. *The Relations Between Master and Disciple in the Talmudic Age.* Ed. H. J. Zimmels; J. Rabbinowitz; and I. Finestein. Vol. 1. Jew's College Publications New Series, 3. London.

Günther, W. 1975. Brother, Neighbor, Friend; *adelphos. New International Dictionary of New Testament Theology.* Vol. 1. Trans. C. Brown. Grand Rapids.

Moulton, J. H., and Milligan, G. 1930. *The Vocabulary of the Greek Testament Illustrated from the Papyri and Other Non-Literary Sources.* Grand Rapids.

Schilling, O. 1967. Amt und Nachfolge im Alten Testament und in Qumran. *Volk Gottes: zum Kirchenverständnis der Katholischen, Evangelischen, and Anglikanischen Theologie. Festgabe für Josef Höfer.* Ed. R. Bäumer and H. Dolch. Freiburg.

Urbach, E. E. 1979. *The Sages: Their Concepts and Beliefs.* Trans. I. Abrahams. 2 vols. 2d ed. Jerusalem.

Wilkins, M. 1988. *The Concept of Disciple in Matthew's Gospel: As Reflected in the Use of the Term Mathētēs.* NovTSup 59. Leiden.

MICHAEL J. WILKINS

BRUCIANUS. See CODEX (BRUCIANUS).

BUCK. See ZOOLOGY.

BUCKLER. See WEAPONS AND IMPLEMENTS OF WARFARE.

BUDDE HYPOTHESIS. In 1882 Karl Budde first described in detail his hypothesis on the structure of ancient Hebrew poetry. Qina meter, or falling rhythm, is a succession of lines of two colons, unequally divided in terms of syllables or accents, so that the first exceeds the second, as in Lam 1:5, Line 1: "Her foes have become the head, her enemies prosper," where in the Heb the syllable pattern is 7:6 and the stress pattern is 3:2. Normally in the Heb the longer colon consists of three words and the shorter is two words, with some recognized variations. Budde held that the line is never equally divided. He described the falling meter as a rhythm that always dies away and he attempted to establish rules for its structure. He associated the rhythm with the lament or funeral song. Like many other scholars of his time and since, Budde accepted the possibility that exceptions to the qina pattern might be due to a faulty text. It is, however, to be noted that Budde accepted the possibility of some overarching principle that would allow for the exceptions found in the text.

The concept of Budde's falling rhythm has attracted scholarly attention up to the present time. The paradox is that, while one can find classic examples of the falling rhythm in Lamentations and elsewhere in the Hebrew Bible, there has been no agreement on a rationale for the numerous exceptions found in the same poems. There are clearly many examples of the qina meter in Hebrew poetry that have nothing to do with lament, and some laments are not written in that pattern. Perhaps the only consensus is that great caution is in order when characterizing falling rhythm.

Conventional statistical tests have the ability to distinguish patterns, differences, or relationships that may not reasonably be attributed to chance. Thus it is possible to analyze Budde's hypothesis by means of statistics in order to determine which patterns of syllable or stress structure may be attributed to the freedom of the poet to express each thought without regard to structure, and which patterns may fairly be laid to nonchance factors, technically called significant differences. A nonchance pattern would imply the presence of design crafted into the structure of the poem under study in terms of line length, colon length, and stress pattern. If all fluctuations and exceptions are nothing more than chance factors, the argument for design could not be sustained. The advantage of such analysis is that it examines only the overall design, rather than the usual practice of stanza-by-stanza analysis.

The acrostic poems of Lamentations 1 through 4 are especially valuable for analysis because a clear structure is built into the text. Because of the alphabetic pattern, we can be certain about where the line or the verse begins, which at least removes one aspect of the uncertainty in approaching the analysis of Hebrew poetry (see Hillers *Lamentations* AB).

The following is a summary of research of David Noel Freedman and Erich A. von Fange to explore aspects of Budde's hypothesis. Stress counts and two methods of syllable counts (A and B) were provided by Freedman.

Analyses of colons according to syllable counts. The first line of each of the 22 stanzas of Lamentations 1, taken as a group, was analyzed according to the extent to which the sum of syllables of all the first colons (163) exceeded that of the second (136). Similar analyses were conducted for second (154 and 120) and third lines (154 and 128) of Lamentations 1, and the same procedure was followed for the other chapters of Lamentations. For this analysis Lamentations 3 was treated as though it consisted of 22 stanzas of 3 lines each. Lamentations 5 (also 22 stanzas) was included in the analysis despite the fact that it is not an alphabetic acrostic. Of 12 analyses each for the A and B syllable counts, nonchance differences occurred for every comparison made in Lamentations 1 through 4, a total of 22 tests for differences. In every case, the first of the two colons under comparison for a given line significantly exceeded the second in length, thus strongly supporting Budde's hypothesis. No significant differences were found for the 2 analyses of Lamentations 5, which clearly does not have a falling rhythm, but one in which parallel colons are equal in length.

Analyses of stress patterns. Stress counts for colons were analyzed following the same pattern as above, e.g., the sum of stresses for the first and second colons of the first lines of Lamentations 1 was 66 and 49 respectively. Similar analyses were made for second and third lines of Lamentations 1, and the same procedure was also followed for the other chapters of Lamentations. In all colon comparisons of total stress counts, a total of 12 tests, the first exceeded the second to a significant degree. The surprising finding was that in Lamentations 5, where the syllable counts of first colons do not differ significantly from the second, the stress counts do differ in the expected manner to support what Budde perhaps felt intuitively when he stated that when the first unit equals the second the first is "heavier."

In sum, statistical analysis provides substantial support for the structural aspect of Budde's hypothesis when the colons and stresses of the poems are taken as a whole. One possible interpretation of this evidence is that the poems were sung in ancient times in such a way as to emphasize the qina pattern, and that the chanter had ways analogous to modern liturgical chanting of accommodating to those lines which did not conform to that pattern.

Bibliography

Budde, K. 1882. Das hebraische Klagelied. *ZAW* 2: 1–52.

Freedman, D. N. 1986. Acrostic Poems in the Hebrew Bible: Alphabetic and Otherwise. *CBQ* 48: 408–31.

Erich A. von Fange

BUKKI (PERSON) [Heb *bukkî*]. Var. BORITH. The name of two people mentioned in the Hebrew Bible, Bukki seems to be a shortened version of the name BUKKIAH (1 Chr 25:4, 13). This is supported by the LXX translation *bōkai* (1 Chr 5:31—Eng 6:4; 6:36—Eng 6:51). However, contrary evidence is supplied by the LXX of 1 Esdr 8:2 (Gk *bokka*) and 2 Esdr 1:2 (Rahlfs ed., 7:4; Gk *bokki,* or *borith,* see Myers *1–2 Esdras* AB, 154), and the LXX of Num 34:22 (Gk *bakchir*). The name may be related to the root *bqq,* "luxuriant," as in Hos 10:1, "the luxuriant vine" (Heb *gepen bôqēq*). Guthrie (*IDB* 1: 473) suggests "proved of God," which relates the root *bqh* to Aram *bqʾ,* "to test, prove" (see *IPN,* 226).

1. The son of Jogli, a leader (Heb *nāśîʾ*) of the tribe of Dan (Num 34:22), when the land of Canaan was allotted to the Israelites.

2. The son of Abishua, and a priest in the line of Eleazar, the high priest (Ezra 7:4; 1 Chr 5:31—Eng 6:4; 6:36—Eng 6:51). His name appears also in a genealogy linking the postexilic leader Ezra with this same original Israelite priestly family (Ezra 7:4 = 1 Esdr 8:2; see Myers *1–2 Esdras* AB, 154 for a comparison of these lists). In noncanonical uses of this same genealogy, Josephus (*Ant* 5.10.5; 8.1.3) employs the priestly lineage, which includes Bukki (Gk *bokki, bokkias*), to establish the period during which Eli, the priest who raised Samuel, lived.

Raphael I. Panitz

BUKKIAH (PERSON) [Heb *buqqîyāhû*]. One of the fourteen sons of Heman who were appointed to prophesy with musical instruments under the direction of their father and the king (1 Chr 25:4). Bukkiah received the sixth lot which was cast to determine duties (1 Chr 25:13). Scholars continue to debate the relationship between the two lists (1 Chr 25:2–6, 9–31) which contain the name Bukkiah. For a summary of the discussion and bibliography, see ASHARELAH. The etymology of the name is uncertain. Suggested meanings include "proved of Yahweh" (from a hypothetical Heb root *bqh,* perhaps related to Aram *bqʾ*) and "flask of Yahweh" (from Heb *bqq;* see the noun *baqbuq* in Jer 19:1, 10; 1 Kgs 14:3).

J. CLINTON MCCANN, JR.

BUL [Heb *bûl*]. The eighth month of the Canaanite calendar, roughly corresponding to October–November. See CALENDARS.

BULL/BULLOCK. See ZOOLOGY.

BUNAH (PERSON) [Heb *bûnâ*]. Individual of the tribe of Judah, the son of Jerahmeel (1 Chr 2:25).

BUNNI (PERSON) [Heb *bunnî*]. Like Bani and Binnui, Bunni is another short form of the name Benaiah (see BANI; BINNUI), found among the Levites at the time of Ezra and Nehemiah.

1. A Levite in attendance at Ezra's reading of the Law (Neh 9:4).

2. The levitical ancestor of Shemaiah, the son of Hasshub, one of those who volunteered to live in Jerusalem at the time of Nehemiah (Neh 11:15). This ancestor was five generations removed from Shemaiah, the contemporary to Nehemiah, and is therefore not to be confused with the Bunni in Neh 9:4.

3. One of the chiefs of the people who set his seal to Nehemiah's covenant (Neh 10:15).

D. G. SCHLEY

BURIALS. Biblical references to burial are descriptive rather than prescriptive. Descriptions often include the formulas, "he lay with his fathers" (mainly in Kings and Chronicles, cf. 1 Kgs 14:31; 2 Chr 12:16), indicating a natural death, or "he was gathered to his people" (used by P, cf. Gen 25:8; Deut 32:50), denoting appropriate burial, apparently thought to ensure reunion with the ancestors. Proper burial required interment in a *geber, geburâ,* or *bayit,* words meaning "burial" and "dwelling." Interment was accorded all who served Yahweh; sinners were cursed with lack of burial or exhumation (Deut 28:25–26; 1 Kgs 14:10–11; Jer 16:4).

ISRAELITE

A. Patriarchs and Matriarchs

From the patriarchal period, with the exception of Rachel, the patriarchs and matriarchs were interred in the Cave of Machpelah purchased by Abraham (Gen 49:29–31). In accordance with their wishes to be buried with family, the embalmed remains of Jacob and Joseph were transported from Egypt to Canaan (Gen 47:29–30; 50:13; Exod 13:19; but cf. Gen 50:5).

Interment at the location of death and in proximity to a tree were also attested in this period and later. Rebekah's nurse, Deborah, was interred where she died near Bethel under an oak tree (Gen 35:8) and the people of Jabesh-gilead cremated the bodies of Saul and his sons and then buried their bones under a tamarisk tree (1 Sam 31:12–13). The tree signified divine presence as demonstrated by Abraham planting a tamarisk tree and calling on the name of God at a treaty site (Gen 21:32–33). Burial under a tree also expressed the desire to propagate and to perpetuate the memory of the individual. The tree was long associated with immortality as illustrated by the "tree of life" in the Garden of Eden (Gen 2:9; cf. Isa 56:3, the eunuch as a "withered tree"). Rachel was also buried where she died. Variant traditions locate her burial on the way to Ephrath where a *maṣṣēbâ* was erected (Gen 35: 19–20) and in Zelzah in Benjaminite territory near the Ephraim border (1 Sam 10:2). The tradition locating her burial in the Bethlehem vicinity has been explained as a later attempt to associate her burial with Ephrathah in Judah, the ancestral home of David and the site of the present-day "Tomb of Rachel" (McCarter *1 Samuel* AB, 181).

In the patriarchal period, usually dated to the MB II from ca. 1750 to 1600 B.C.E. (*IJH,* 142–48), it is impossible to distinguish Israelite from Canaanite burials. The prevalent practice in the highlands was multiple burial in caves, as described for Abraham and his descendants. Typical tombs were cut at the highland site of Gibeon, located 9 km N of Jerusalem. At the bottom of a vertical, cylindrical shaft, a doorway blocked with stones provided access into a circular chamber with lamp niches cut into the walls. Tomb 15 exhibited three phases of use probably representing two generations. The skulls and bones of fourteen individuals were found along the sides of the chamber. Toggle pins used to secure wraps and jewelry demonstrate that the individuals were clothed and adorned at burial. The most common burial provisions were bowls and platters for foodstuffs, jugs for liquids, and juglets for oil and perfume. Additional gifts included a knife, a dagger blade, two limestone pommels for daggers, fragments of bone inlay probably from a box, and four sheep skulls (Pritchard 1963: 22–33). These provisions demonstrate that the deceased were thought to need nourishment and the protection afforded both by weapons and symbolically by colored and metal jewelry.

B. Exodus and Conquest Generations

Like Rachel and Deborah, members of the Exodus generation were interred at the location of their death: Miriam in Kadesh (Num 20:1), Aaron on Mt. Hor (Num 33:39, but see Deut 10:6), and Moses in Moab (Deut 34:6). Burial at the death locale deviates from the patriarchal practice, for just as the bones of Jacob and Joseph were carried from Egypt for burial on family land (Josh 24:32) so could the remains of Miriam, Aaron, and Moses have been transported.

Beginning with the Conquest generation, family burials established a visible, perpetual claim to the patrimony *(naḥălâ),* which sometimes functioned as a territorial boundary marker as in the cases of Rachel (1 Sam 10:2) and Joshua (Josh 24:30). Joshua was buried on the border of his inheritance in the hill country of Ephraim (Josh 24:30), Joseph on family land in Shechem (Josh 24:32), and Eleazar the son of Aaron at Gibeah in the hill country of Ephraim (Josh 24:33). The only other burial from this period was that of the five Amorite kings killed by Joshua. After being hanged from trees, their bodies were thrown into a cave the mouth of which was sealed with stones (Josh 10:26).

The Exodus and Conquest are usually dated to the LB and beginning of the Iron Age, from the 16th through the early 11th century B.C.E. As in the preceding MB, through the LB, the most common mode of burial in the highlands was multiple (family) burial in caves (Gonen 1979). In the highlands of Israel and especially Judah, the conception of the burial dwelling, the treatment of the corporeal remains, and the categories of provisions for the deceased continued unchanged from the MB through the Iron Age. Gibeon tomb 10A–B contained the remains of eleven individuals provided with ceramic lamps, bowls, jugs, dipper juglets, and seven scarabs (an Egyptian amulet signifying birth and renewal which was a standard Egyptian funerary provision) (Pritchard 1963: 11–17). Lachish Tomb 216, dated from ca. 1450 to 1300 B.C.E., consisted of a shaft leading into a circular pit with plastered walls and floors. Buried in the pit were numerous individuals supplied with more than 200 vessels. As at Gibeon, bowls predominated with lamps, jugs, and dipper juglets. There was also a sizable collection of Cypriot and Mycenaean imported pottery. Metal knives, arrowheads, and a dagger, scarabs, beads, toggle pins, and playing pieces provided protection, adornment, and amusement (Tufnell 1958: 232–35, pls. 52–54).

C. Period of the Judges

By the period of the Judges, family tombs of inherited lands were well established and so individuals were interred "in their father's tomb" or "in their hometown." For Gideon, Samson, and Asahel the record specifies that they were buried in their father's tomb on family land (Judg 8:32; 16:31; 2 Sam 2:32). Only the fact of burial locale is given for the remaining judges: Tola in the Shamir hill country of Ephraim (Judg 10:2), Jair in Kamon, Gilead (Judg 10:5), Jephthah in the cities of Gilead (Judg 12:7), Ibzan in Bethlehem, Zebulun (Judg 12:10), Elon in Aijalon, Zebulun (Judg 12:12), Abdon in Pirathon, Ephraim (Judg 12:15), and Samuel in Ramah (1 Sam 25:1; 28:3). Ramah may refer to this city Ramathaim-Zophim as well as to an elevated place, for important individuals were buried in prominent places where their tombs would be visible and accessible. For some of these individuals little is known except for their burial location. Men who enjoyed a special relationship with Yahweh during their lifetimes were thought to continue that relationship after death and so it was important to know where they were buried.

D. Monarchic Period

1. Textual Witnesses. Beginning with David's reign, kings and religious and administrative high functionaries (2 Chr 24:15–16; Isa 22:15–16) were buried in their capital cities. David initiated burial in the City of David (1 Kgs 2:10) and was joined by his son Solomon (1 Kgs 11:43; 2 Chr 9:31). Other recorded family burials from the period of the united monarchy include Abner and the head of Ishbaal (Ishboshet) in Hebron (2 Sam 3:32; 4:12), Ahitophel (2 Sam 17:23), Barzillai in Gilead (2 Sam 19:38), and Joab in the wilderness (1 Kgs 2:34).

Following the death of Solomon and the division of the country into Israel in the N and Judah in the S, monarchs were buried in their capital cities of Tirzah or Samaria and Jerusalem respectively. Of kings and prophets it is recorded that they were sometimes interred in proximity to holy sites: prophets of Judah and Bethel near the Bethel altar (2 Kgs 23: 17–18) and later Judahite kings adjacent to the Jerusalem temple (Ezek 43:7–8). The deaths and burials of the kings of Israel were recounted solely in Kings. The books of Kings present royal interment in a formulaic, consistent manner, perhaps in an attempt to fabricate a positive record for the Judahite kings in homage to the house of David. Varying accounts of the burials of Judahite kings are preserved in Kings and Chronicles (for a discussion of the reliability of the Chronicler's account, see Japhet 1985). The Chronicler's supplemental information has been discounted as glorifying favored kings and discrediting others. However, the Chronicler may have expressed judgment not through manufacturing new material but in choosing which references to include and which to delete.

Relatively little was written about the burial of the kings of Israel. Of several kings, including Nadab, Elah, Zimri, Ahaziah, Zechariah, and all subsequent kings, no details of burial are given (1 Kgs 15:28; 16:10; 18; 2 Kgs 1:17; 15:10). For most of the remaining kings only the fact of burial in the royal city was mentioned: Baasha in Tirzah (1 Kgs 16:6), and Omri, Ahab, Jehu, Jehoahaz, Joash, and probably Jeroboam II in Samaria (1 Kings 16:28; 22:37; 2 Kgs 10:35; 13:9, 13; 14:16, 29).

In Judah, David and his descendants were buried in the Jerusalem City of David, a small ridge bounded by the Kidron, Hinnom, and Tyropoeon valleys. According to the account in Kings, all kings from Rehoboam through Ahaz were buried "with their fathers in the City of David" (1 Kgs 14:31; 15:8, 24; 22:51; 2 Kgs 8:24; 9:28; 12:22; 14:20, 22; 15:7, 38; 16:20; Neh 3:16). Subsequent kings were buried elsewhere, Manasseh and Amon in the household garden of Uzzah (2 Kgs 21:18, 26) and Josiah in his own tomb (2 Kgs 23:30). There is no reference to burial for Hezekiah or for Josiah's successors.

The Chronicler noted no such harmony in burial arrangements. While commendable kings were buried with their predecessors in the City of David, sinful and ailing kings were denied interment with their fathers. A *kabôd* (honor) was prepared for the righteous king Hezekiah. The honor certainly entailed lamenting (1 Kgs 13:30; Jer 22:18) and offering sacrifices (Isa 57:7; 2 Chr 16:14). Jehoiadah the priest was also accorded burial with the kings in the City of David (2 Chr 24:16). Among the discredited kings, Asa was buried in his own tomb. Mortuary practices included laying the body ". . . in the resting-place [*miškāb*] which was filled with spices of all kinds; expertly blended; a very great fire was made in his honor" (2 Chr 16:14). The "very great fire" probably resembled in appearance and intent the burnt-offering sacrifices of sweet savor presented to Yahweh (Gen 8:20–21; Lev 1:9, 18). Others denied burial in the royal tombs included Jehoram, Ahaziah, Jehoash, Amaziah, Uzziah, Ahaz, and Amon (2 Chr 21:19–20; 22:9; 24: 25; 25:28; 26:23; 28: 27).

Isaiah described rock-cut tombs and mortuary practices in a condemnation of the cult of the dead. Isaiah 57, so-called "Third" Isaiah, is usually dated to the last quarter of the 6th century B.C.E. but the text describes Jerusalem bench tombs which had attained their postexilic form by the 7th century B.C.E. According to Isa 57:7–9, tombs were hewn high in the mountainsides. A door and door post opened into the chamber with a resting-place *(miškāb)* for the deceased and a mortuary stele perhaps in the shape of a phallus *(zikrôn, yād)* near the door. At the tomb sacrifices were offered (cf. also Deut 26:14 and Ps 16:3–4) and the dead consulted (cf. also 1 Sam 28 and Isa 8:19–20). To conclude the diatribe, Isaiah refuted the role of the ancestors in insuring control of the patrimony—true inheritance passes not through the ancestral dead (and the family tomb) but through Yahweh (Isa 57:13).

A variety of mortuary practices existed within Israelite society, not all of which were widely practiced or acceptable to 8th century B.C.E. and later prophets and the Deuteronomistic editor(s). The majority buried their dead in family cave and bench tombs located in proximity to the patrimony. Biblical references and inscriptions on a tomb at Khirbet Beit Lei testify to family burial, but there is currently no osteological evidence. Isaiah rebuked Shebna, an official of King Hezekiah, for having hewn an ostentatious individual tomb in Jerusalem, rather than being buried with his family (Isa 22:15–16). The common burial ground in Jerusalem's Kidron Valley was considered by some an illegitimate form and place of burial as suggested by Josiah's scattering asherah ashes over the ground and Jehoiakim's casting in the body of the assassinated prophet Uriah (Jer 26:23; 2 Kgs 23:6). Both royalty and commoners sacrificed children in the tophet in Jerusalem's Hinnom Valley (and presumably buried them as at Carthage; see Stager and Wolff 1984), demonstrating official sanction during certain reigns of a practice considered abhorrent and unacceptable at other times (2 Kgs 16:3; 2 Chr 28:3; Jer 7:31).

Burial markers preserved the memory of the righteous, the sinner, and men without offspring. A *maṣṣēbâ* and *ṣîyûn* ("pillar" and "monument") marked the graves of the righteous Rachel (Gen 35:20) and the unnamed prophet (2 Kgs 23:17) respectively. A circle of stones served to censure Israel's enemies and those who challenged Yahweh's anointed: Achan, the king of Ai, the five kings of the S coalition, and Absalom (Josh 7:26; 8:29; 10:26; 2 Sam 18:17–18). Monuments serving to perpetuate the memory of men without descendants, literally to "memorialize the name," have been associated with death cult activities (Pitard 1979). During his lifetime Absalom erected a pillar, literally, "hand/phallus [Heb *yād*] of Absalom" (2 Sam 18:18; cf. also Isa 57:8) and Yahweh promised the faithful eunuch through his temple and holy city "a monument and memorial [*yād wāšēm*] better than sons and daughters," a perpetual testimonial which cannot be severed (Isa 56:5; cf. 2 Sam 14:7).

2. Archaeological Witnesses. Multiple (family) burials in caves continued from the Bronze Age into the Iron Age at the sites of Gibeon, nearby Tell en-Nasbeh (biblical Mizpah or Ataroth-Addar), and Dothan. In the Gibeon tomb, ceramic vessels, objects of personal adornment, weapons, household articles, and amulets were present as in the earlier assemblages (Dajani 1951: 48; 1953: 66). Dothan Tomb 1 was in use from approximately 1400 to 1200/1100 B.C.E. It contained the remains of at least 288 individuals and 3146 artifacts in an irregularly shaped chamber with a domed roof, six niches, two crypts, and a window (Cooley 1983; Free 1960: 12).

All the salient features of 8th century B.C.E. and later Judahite tombs appeared by the 12th century in tombs at Tell el-Farah(S), in Shephelah tombs at Gezer, Lachish, and Tel ᶜAitun, and at Sarafend on the coast and Pella in Transjordan. Tel ᶜAitun C1 consisted of steps leading into two chambers equipped with waist-high benches extending along the sides of the tomb on which to repose the dead, lamp niches, and a repository. The repository was a pit hewn in the rear of the chamber or under a bench to accommodate skeletal remains and accompanying objects moved to make room on the benches for additional burials. Fifteen individuals were distinguished in the tomb and the repository was completely filled with bones. One inhabitant lay extended on its back with a copper bracelet on its arm, surrounded by lamps, a flask, a Philistine krater and jar, beads, and two bronze-socketed arrowheads. Other goods in the tomb included large quantities of local and Philistine pottery, many objects of personal adornment, household items, weapons, scarabs, and scaraboid seals (Edelstein et al. 1971: 86–87).

Through the 10th to 8th century B.C.E. both cave and bench tombs were utilized in Israel and Judah. Following the fall of the N kingdom of Israel, "bathtub" coffins and jar burials were introduced by the Assyrians and other foreigners who settled there. Assyrian bathtub coffins are named for their characteristic shape, a deep bathtub-shaped ceramic vessel approximately 1 m long, with one rounded and one straight end, and handles around the sides. In a jar burial, the vessel neck was broken off and the body inserted either in a single jar or two facing jars. In both jar and bathtub coffin burials the deceased were supplied with the same types of goods provided in earlier and contemporary cave and bench tombs. In Judah the bench tomb overwhelmingly prevailed. See Fig. BUR.01. Two of the largest and finest examples of bench tombs were preserved in the N cemetery of Jerusalem, the St. Étienne tombs. One example consisted of a central court around which were symmetrically arranged six burial chambers. Each chamber was equipped on three sides with parapeted benches with horseshoe (or Hathor wig)-shaped headrests and a repository under one of the benches. Stone-carved recessed door frames, right-angled cornices, and imitation sunken wooden panels enhanced the tomb (Barkai et al. 1975). Exceptionally fine tombs were also cut in the cliffs of what is today Silwan Village facing the City of David. These tombs incorporated distinctive Phoenician and Egyptian features such as gabled ceilings, stone coffins, funerary inscriptions carved into tomb facades, and a crowning pyramid atop a monolithic aboveground structure (Ussishkin 1970). These magnificent structures surely

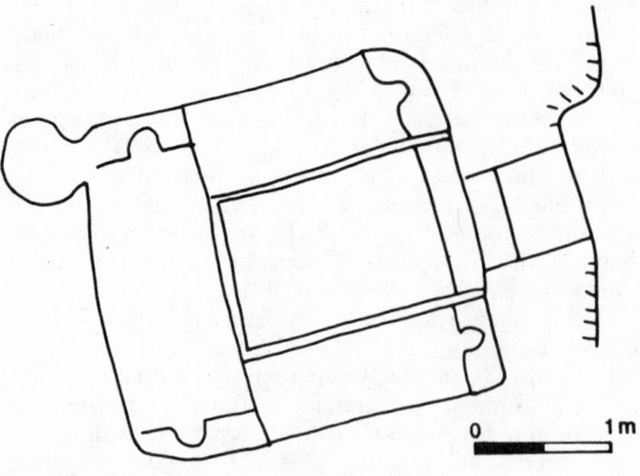

BUR.01. Plan of a typical bench tomb. *(Redrawn from E. Bloch-Smith.)*

housed the wealthy and eminent members of Jerusalem society, such as Shebna (Isa 22:15–16).

Beginning in the 10th century B.C.E. with the settlement of the S highlands of Judah, new objects were added to the standard funerary assemblage. These included additional vessels for the preparation, serving, and storing of foodstuffs and wine: cooking pots, plates/platters, store jars, and wine decanters. Juglets and dipper juglets were more frequently supplied for use as dippers in store jars and as containers of scented oils and perfumes in a period when tombs were repeatedly entered and bodies anointed. Ceramic models of chairs, beds, quadrupeds, and horse and rider figurines were found in Shephelah tombs, and female pillar figurines were recorded from tombs initially in the Shephelah and later from throughout Judah. This figurine has a hollow or solid conical body, pronounced breasts emphasized by arms encircling them, and a hand-fashioned or molded head. The form is evocative of a tree, long depicted in ANE art as a source of nourishment, but identified with different deities at different times. Their presence in Judahite tombs, in conjunction with figurines of the Egyptian god Bes, one of whose roles was to safeguard mothers and their newborn infants and children, indicates widespread concern for adequate lactation to nourish newborns and infants, and an acceptance of the use of figurines for sympathetic magic.

Following the Babylonian conquest, within the region of the former kingdom of Judah, Iron Age burial customs persisted into the 6th century B.C.E. at Khirbet Beit Lei, Gezer, Beth Shemesh, Abu-Ghosh, and Jerusalem. By the end of the 6th century B.C.E. settlement was concentrated along the coast and through the Shephelah where cist tombs with Achaemenid-style metal objects and weapons were succeeded by shaft tombs with Greek and Phoenician pottery and coins (Stern 1982: 68–92). A cist tomb consisted of a rectangular grave which was lined and occasionally floored with fieldstones or stone slabs. In a shaft tomb, a vertical shaft led into a rock-cut chamber of no particular shape.

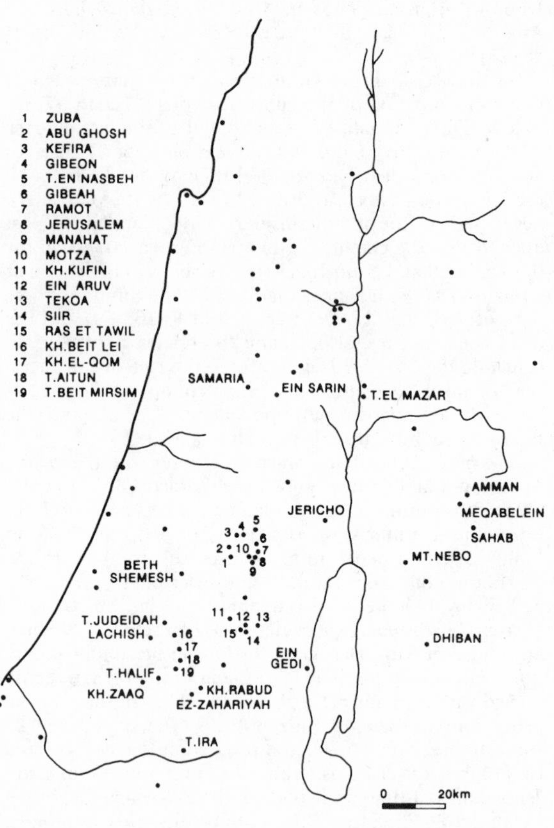

BUR.02. Map of Iron Age burial sites. *(Redrawn from E. Bloch-Smith.)*

Bibliography

Barkai, G.; Mazar, A.; Kloner, A. 1975. The Northern Cemetery of Jerusalem in First Temple Times. *Qadmoniot* 8: 71–76 (in Hebrew).

Cooley, R. E. 1983. Gathered to His People: A Study of a Dothan Family Tomb. Pp. 47–58 in *The Living and Active Word of God: Essays in Honor of Samuel J. Schultz,* ed. M. Inck and R. Youngblood. Winona Lake, IN.

Dajani, A. 1951. Discoveries in Western Jordan, 1949–1950. *ADAJ* 1: 47–48.

———. 1953. An Iron Age Tomb at al'Jib. *ADAJ* 2: 66–74.

Edelstein, G.; Ussishkin, D.; Dothan, T.; and Tzaferis, V. 1971. The Necropolis at Tell ᶜAitun. *Qadmoniot* 4/3: 86–90 (in Hebrew).

Free, J. P. 1960. The Seventh Season at Dothan. *BASOR* 160: 6–14.

Gonen, R. 1979. *Burial in Canaan of the LB as a Basis for the Study of Population and Settlements.* Diss., Jerusalem.

Japhet, S. 1985. The Historical Reliability of Chronicles. *JSOT* 3: 83–107.

Kloner, A. 1982–83. Rock-cut Tombs in Jerusalem. *BAIAS,* 37–40.

Meyers, E. M. 1970. Secondary Burials in Palestine. *BA* 33: 2–29.

Pitard, W. T. 1979. The Ugaritic Funerary Text RS 34.126. *BASOR* 232: 65–75.
Pritchard, J. B. 1963. *The Bronze Age Cemetery at Gibeon.* Philadelphia.
Ribar, J. W. 1973. *Death Cult Practices in Ancient Palestine.* Diss., Ann Arbor.
Stager, L. E., and Wolff, S. R. 1984. Child Sacrifice at Carthage—Religious Rite or Population Control? *BARev* 10/1: 30–51.
Stern, E. 1982. *Material Culture in the Land of the Bible in the Persian Period 538–332 B.C.* Jerusalem.
Tufnell, O. 1958. *Lachish IV, The Bronze Age.* London.
Ussishkin, D. 1970. The Necropolis from the Time of the Kingdom of Judah at Silwan, Jerusalem. *BA* 33: 34–46.

ELIZABETH BLOCH-SMITH

ANCIENT JEWISH

This article will focus mainly on Jewish burial customs and funerary art from the Second Temple period.

A. Burial Customs

Our principal data for funerary customs and art in the Second Temple period come from two cemeteries, one in Jerusalem (Avigad 1950–51; Rahmani 1981, 1982; Kloner 1980) and the other in Jericho (Hachlili 1978, 1979, 1980; Hachlili and Killebrew 1983). They were both located outside their respective town limits, in accordance with Jewish law (*m. B. Bat.* 2: 9). The Jerusalem cemetery consisted of tombs surrounding the walls of the city, in three major areas of concentration to the N, S, and E (Kloner 1980: 259–68) and the Jericho cemetery was located outside the town, on the hills flanking the Jordan Valley.

The Jerusalem necropolis developed as the result of tombs being randomly scattered wherever the rock was soft and could be easily carved. Roads and paths led to the tombs, and plants and trees landscaped the surroundings. Families purchased burial plots presumably according to their means. Several of the loculi tombs have richly ornamented facades, while a group of monumental rock-hewn tombs (the Kidron Valley tombs), probably belonging to prominent Jerusalem families, have a memorial or *nefesh* in the shape of a pyramid or tholus standing above the ground (Hachlili 1981). Despite the lavish ornamentation, burial was probably similar to that of the simpler, undecorated loculi tombs. Apart from two tombs where sarcophagi were discovered, all were found in a disturbed, robbed state. Several crowded burial quarters exist in the present-day areas of Mt. Scopus, Dominus Flevit, and French Hill (Kloner 1980: 268).

A large necropolis at Jericho containing either primary burials in wooden coffins or secondary collected bone burials in ossuaries was excavated and surveyed (Hachlili 1979; 1980).

1. Tomb Types. The tombs found in these two cemeteries may be divided into two types: the first consists of rock-hewn loculi tombs and the second type is a monumental tomb which is rock-hewn and has a memorial or *nefesh* standing next to or above it. Two basic tomb plans exist: one is called the loculi type *(kokhim)* and the other is the arcosolia. Some tombs are equipped solely with a burial room. Both types of plans are found in the Jerusalem necropolis, but the Jericho cemetery consists only of loculi tombs which are hewn into the hillsides. Both serve as family tombs but with provision for separate burial of each individual.

The form of the loculi tomb (see Fig. BUR.03) consists of a square burial chamber, often with a pit dug into its floor to enable a man to stand upright. From one to three arched loculi 1 m high and 2 m long *(kokhim)* are hewn into three walls, the entrance wall excepted. The entrance to the tomb is square; in Jerusalem it sometimes has a forecourt and a molded facade (Avigad 1950–51: 98, fig. 3) or an ornamental facade. It is closed either by a rectangular blocking stone, sometimes in the shape of a large "stopper," or by mudbricks and small stones. Occasionally, single-loculus tombs were constructed.

The evidence from Jericho proves conclusively that loculi tombs were first designed and used for primary—that is, permanent—burial in coffins. This is also indicated by

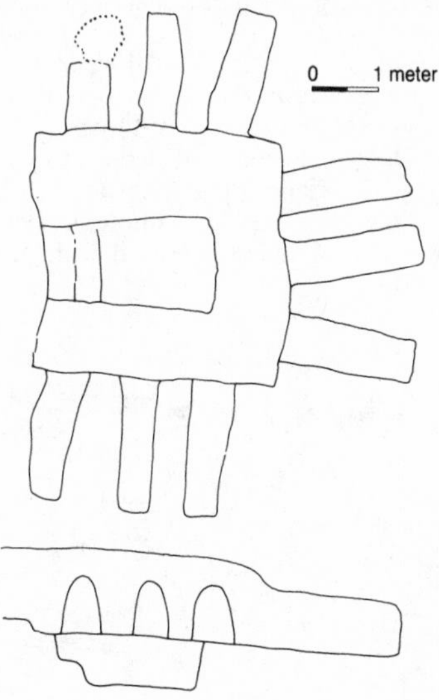

BUR.03. Plan of a loculi type tomb. *(Redrawn from R. Hachlili.)*

the length of the *kokh* (ca. 2 m), which is the length of a coffin. The same tomb plan continued to be used in the case of ossuary burials. In previous research scholars have claimed that the *kokh* was "intimately" connected with secondary burial. If this was the case and the loculi tomb had been designed for 70cm-long ossuaries there would have been no need to dig a 2m-long *kokh.*

The origin of the plan for the rock-cut loculi tomb of the Second Temple period in Judea is to be sought in Egypt, particularly in Leontopolis, from as early as Hasmonean times (*Ant.* 13. 63, 67; 14. 99, 131–33; Hachlili and Killebrew 1983: 110–12).

In some Jerusalem tombs the arcosolium type of burial is found. The arcosolium is a benchlike aperture with an arched ceiling hewn into the length of the wall. The arcosolium is a later type of burial, in use at the end of the Second Temple period. In the Beth-shearim catacombs the arcosolia were usually reserved for more expensive burials. In several cases the deceased was interred in a trough grave hewn in the arcosolium. From the 3d century on, the trough grave became the prevalent type of burial (Avigad 1976: 259).

2. Burial Types. Two distinctly different types of loculi tomb burials, primary and secondary, were discovered during the excavations in the Jericho cemetery. They can be classified typologically, chronologically, and stratigraphically into primary burials in wooden coffins (type 1) and secondary burials of collected bones which were either placed in individual ossuaries or piled in heaps (type 2).

a. Primary Burial in Wooden Coffins. This is the earliest type of burial known from the Jericho cemetery. The coffins were placed in the rock-cut loculi tombs, each loculus holding one wooden coffin; only when all loculi were filled would further coffins be placed on the benches or in the pit.

Coffins took the form of a completely wooden chest, sometimes with a post at each corner, and were constructed by means of mortising and dovetailing. Several types of wood were used in the construction: the most common types were sycamore, Christ-thorn, and cypress. The lid of the chest was usually gabled and consisted of one plank on each side and a pediment at each end. See Fig. BUR.04. One well-preserved example, however, has a hinged lid. Iron nails and knobs found with the coffins were probably used only for decoration or structural support. The coffins were decorated with painted red and black geometric patterns and designs.

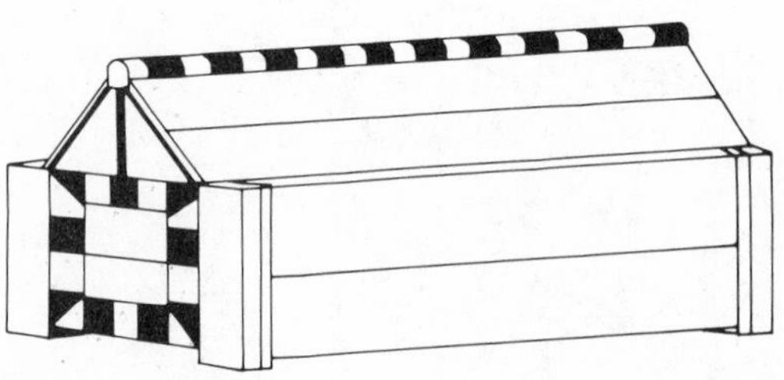

BUR.04. Reconstruction of a wooden coffin from Jericho. *(Redrawn from R. Hachlili.)*

Contemporaneous coffins, different in their construction and decoration, were found in tombs at En-gedi, Jericho, and in the Qumran cemetery (de Vaux 1973: 46–47; Hachlili and Killebrew 1983: 115). Earlier examples of similar wooden coffins dating to the 4th century B.C.E. have survived in Egypt and S Russia (Watzinger 1905).

All the bodies were extended, face upward, in the coffin, usually with the head to one side and hands close to the side of the body. Most coffins contain one individual, but sometimes a mother and a small child (infant or fetus) are found together in a coffin. There are several occurrences where one or two bodies have been added to a coffin that already contained an individual, but no more than three bodies have ever been found in any one coffin.

In most of the coffin tombs, grave goods consisting of both personal possessions and objects of daily use were found in with the deceased, usually placed near the head or feet. Found only with women and children, they include wooden objects such as bowls, spatulas, beads, and a glass amphoriskos. Leather sandals were also commonly found, placed at the head of the deceased inside the coffin. Objects of daily use were found in the floor or in the pit of the tomb, while storage jars were placed outside the entrance to the tomb.

b. Secondary Burial in Ossuaries. This type was at first practiced only in Jerusalem but later became more widespread (Rahmani 1982: 109). From the finds and stratigraphy of the ossuary burials in Jericho it is clear tht they postdate coffin burials. Ossuaries were hewn from one large block of limestone usually in the shape of a small, rectangular box resting on four low legs and measuring ca. 60 × 35 × 30 cm for adults (less for children). A stone lid—flat, slightly curved, or gabled—was placed on top. The ossuaries were often decorated. Only a few pottery ossuaries, but none of wood, have been discovered thus far.

The ossuaries were placed in the loculi or on the benches. Often two ossuaries would be stacked one above the other or placed next to each other. The occupants of ossuaries placed in the same loculus were usually related to each other, as can be concluded from the inscriptions found on the ossuaries. The bodies were prepared for secondary burial by being temporarily buried first to allow the flesh to decay completely, leaving only the bones. It has been suggested that the body was placed in the loculus of the family tomb and that after a year the relatives of the deceased would come to gather the bones and put them in the ossuary (Rahmani 1961: 117–18; Kloner 1980: 226–27; 248–52). The bones were then placed inside the ossuary in a customary order. There are several occurrences of more than one individual being interred in one ossuary.

Grave goods discovered with ossuary burial tombs include unguentaria, bowls, Herodian lamps and cooking pots, and glass vessels, all identical to those used in daily life. No personal objects were found inside the ossuaries themselves, but were usually placed close the ossuaries or in the pit. It is noteworthy that some of the objects in the tombs were defective at the time of their placement; for example, cooking pots were cracked, and pottery was left in fragments. This raises the question whether it was economically preferable to place a defective item in the tomb or whether this had symbolic significance. The practice of placing burial gifts with the dead was widespread throughout the Hellenistic and pagan worlds, but the Jews, although following the custom, gave it their own interpretation by ignoring the connotation of an offering to the dead for their use in the afterlife. Possibly Jews placed personal belongings in the tomb of the deceased because the scene aroused the grief of the onlookers.

Inscriptions were incised, scratched, or written on ossuaries. No particular place was reserved for the inscriptions and they are found on the front, back, sides, and lid. Some were bilingual, written in Jewish and Greek script. The inscription usually included the name of the interred and his position in the family (e.g., father), but in several cases additional information is also given, such as place of origin and age or status, for example, "freedman" (Hachlili 1979: 46).

A unique inscribed funerary bowl, found in an ossuary tomb in Jericho (Hachlili 1978) mentions a three-generation family which originated in Jerusalem but probably lived, died, and was buried in Jericho. In Jerusalem most of the inscriptions consist of names and family relations. Sometimes a profession, such as "Simon the master builder," appears, or an Aramaic inscription appears in archaic Hebrew script (such as the Abba cave inscription). An intriguing aspect of the inscriptions is the identity of their authors: they were probably professional scribes or family members. The latter seems more likely because of the great variety of hands that are evident in the execution of these inscriptions. A consideration of the inscriptions leads us to conclude (1) that ossuary tombs contained at most three generations of a particular family; (2) that the recurrence of names is common in successive generations of a family (Hachlili 1979: 53); and (3) that Jewish families were literate and bilingual in Aramaic or Hebrew and in Greek.

Relatives and friends of the deceased probably performed the more personal duties associated with the burial of the deceased, such as carrying the coffin, placing it properly in the tomb, collecting bones and laying them in the ossuaries, mourning, and writing inscriptions (see *AgAp* 2.205). Contemporary and later sources mention charitable societies, the *hebercir,* who probably dealt with other duties involved in the preparation of the body for burial.

3. Dating. Dates for these burial customs are still the subject of some debate. Rahmani dates the practice of secondary burials in ossuaries in Jerusalem to 30/20 B.C.E.–70 C.E., continuing sporadically either until ca. 135 C.E. or the 3d century. Nevertheless, the Jericho cemetery can provide some chronology for the two different types of burials. Primary burials in coffins can be dated to ca. mid-1st century B.C.E.–10 C.E., while secondary burials in ossuaries followed immediately, dating to ca. 10–68 C.E.

B. Funerary Art

Funerary art of the Second Temple period is a rich and varied art. It consists of ornamentation of tomb facades, ossuaries, and sarcophagi, as well as wall paintings and graffiti.

1. Tomb Decoration. The composite style, an amalgamation of stylistic features influenced by Hellenistic-Roman architecture and by oriental elements, is characteristic of ornamented tombs in Jerusalem, and its execution is typical generally of local Jewish art of the Second Temple period. This composite style is found both on (a) facade-ornamented tombs with either a Doric frieze together with Ionic columns, or an ornate gable (such as the Jerusalem tomb of Zechariah), and on (b) monumental tombs exhibiting a mixture of classical features and Egyptian pyramids and cornices (such as the Jerusalem monument of Absalom, which has a Doric frieze, Ionic capitals, and an Egyptian cornice).

2. Ossuary Ornamentation. Most of the ossuaries found in Jerusalem are undecorated, whereas most of those in Jericho are decorated. The repertoire of motifs decorating ossuaries is quite varied and consists of plant, geometric, and architectural motifs. These motifs are similar to those appearing in other artistic works of the Second Temple period. However, the variation on each motif is greater, probably due to the large quantity of ossuaries found. Stone ossuary workshops and artists probably had a repertoire, presumably in the form of a pattern book, to which reference could be repeatedly made. See Fig. BUR.05.

The ornamentation was carved into the soft stone of the ossuaries with the aid of tools such as a ruler and compass. Few ossuaries were painted. The most common type of ossuary ornamentation is a scheme consisting of a frame of zigzag lines, incised or chip-carved, within two straight lines. This frame is usually divided into two, and sometimes more, metopes which are filled generally with six-petaled rosettes.

The motifs decorating the ossuaries represent actual contemporary funerary art and architecture in Jerusalem. In fact, no symbols are depicted on the ossuaries, neither are there displayed any motifs connected with everyday life or with the temple. Rahmani's contention (1982) seems to be the most acceptable: the repertoire of motifs used to decorate the ossuaries is part of a general ensemble of decorative patterns used in Second Temple period art, several of which are found solely in funerary art.

3. Sarcophagus Ornamentation. A few sarcophagi have been found in tombs in Jerusalem. Made of hard stone, their ornamentation differs from that of ossuaries in both design and execution, although the motifs are similar, consisting of plants, rosettes, vine branches and bunches of grapes, and acanthus leaves. However, differences are noticeable between sarcophagi and ossuary decoration and ornamentation. The sarcophagi are usually depicted in high relief, are skillfully executed, and their design is richer and more elaborate. The richer and beautifully reliefed sarcophagi were probably much more expensive, suggesting that only wealthy families would have been able to afford them.

4. Wall Paintings. Jewish rock-cut tombs of the Second Temple period are not known to have been decorated. However, one wall painting was discovered in the monumental "Goliath" tomb in the Jericho necropolis (Hachlili 1985). Traces of a wall painting enclosed by a painted red

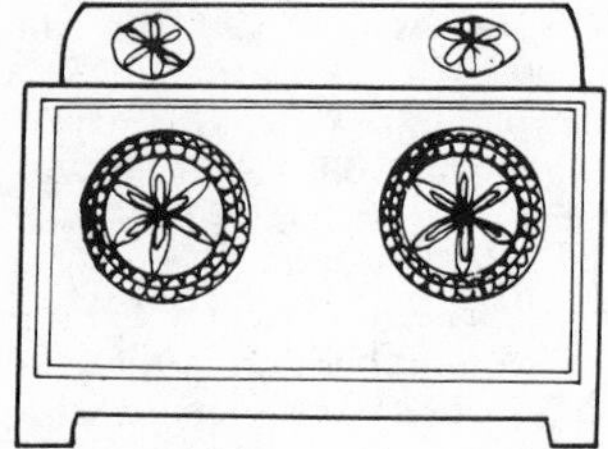

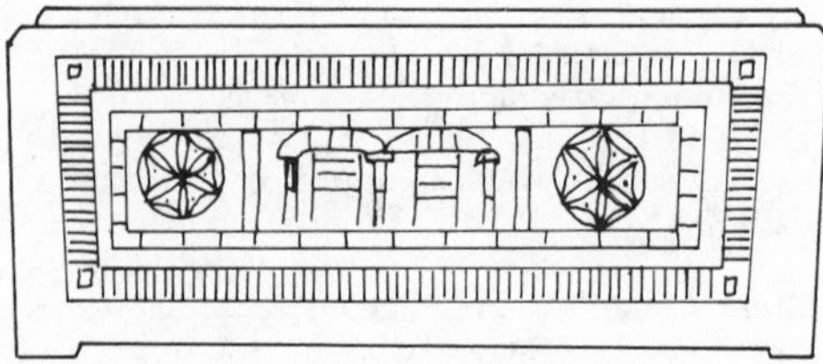
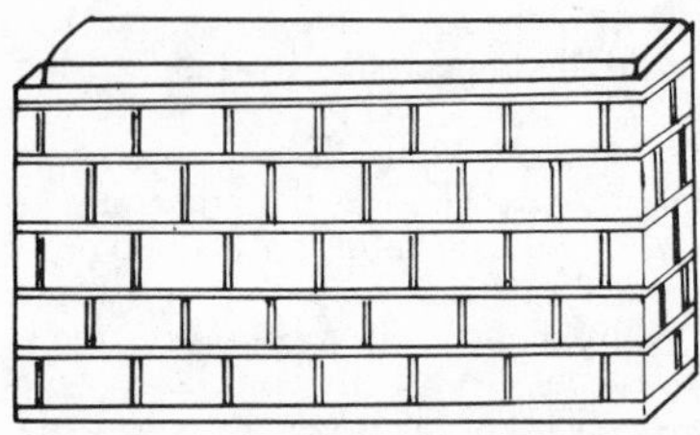

BUR.05. Ornamental ossuaries. *(Courtesy of R. Hachlili.)*

frame appear on three walls of the tomb. The vine motif is the subject of paintings on both N and S walls. Several birds perch on the vines. The Jericho tomb painting was most likely executed at the same time as the tomb itself was hewn, evidently for the benefit of the tomb's visitors and to indicate the family's prominent position.

5. Drawings. Several drawings in charcoal of three ships and a recumbent stag appear on the N and S walls of the porch of Jason's tomb in Jerusalem. They probably were executed by one artist at the same time. On the E wall of the porch graffiti of five menorahs are scratched, probably later than the drawing of the ships, about 30 C.E. A charcoal drawing of a *nefesh,* a column pyramid, was discovered on a tomb wall in the Jericho cemetery. The drawing depicts three columns and part of a fourth.

C. Other Burial Customs

Two completely contrasting Jewish tomb forms and burial customs are encountered in the cemeteries of Qumran and En-el Guweir, (both belonging to the Jewish sect of the Essenes in the Dead Sea area) and in the 2d–4th-century burials in the Jewish necropolis at Beth-shearim.

1. Essene Burial Customs. One sect of Jews during the 1st century C.E., the Essenes, practiced a completely different primary burial in individual graves as evidenced by their cemeteries at Qumran and En el-Guweir. The main cemetery of Qumran is located E of the settlement and contains some 1100 graves (de Vaux 1973). Its organized plan consists of rows of single graves, usually oriented N–S. The graves are marked by oval-shaped heaps of stones placed on the surface. Several graves contained signs of wooden coffins. Most of the excavated tombs contained individual burials; male interments only were found in the main cemetery (de Vaux 1973: 46, pls. XXV–XXVI; Bar-Adon 1977: 12, 16, figs. 19–20). On the outskirts of this cemetery and in the smaller cemeteries of Qumran, a few females and children were interred. The large number of males found in these graves compared to the small number of women and children might point to the importance placed on celibacy in this community.

The Essene burial practices have a few elements in common with those of the Jerusalem and Jericho cemeteries. The coffin burials at Qumran, though later in date, are comparable to those found at Jericho. Grave goods were discovered with women and children at Qumran and En el-Guweir, as well as remains of mattresses and cloth (indicating that the dead had been wrapped in shrouds). Broken storage jars were discovered on top of the graves at En el-Guweir and Qumran, probably a custom parallel to that of placing storage jars outside the tombs at Jericho.

The contrasts in these burial practices indicate differences in religious philosophy toward the dead among the Jews of this time and reflects the separation of the Essenes from more mainstream Judaism. Single-person burials at Qumran and En el-Guweir cemeteries stress the importance of the individual rather than the family.

2. The Beth-shearim Necropolis. The Jewish necropolis at Beth-shearim (M.R. 162234) was the central burial ground for Jews from the land of Israel and neighboring areas. The majority of the catacombs date to the 3d–4th centuries. Beth-shearim was expanded after the death of Rabbi Judah in the latter part of the 3d century. The *terminus ante quem* for the catacombs is the date of their destruction in the year 352 C.E. (Avigad 1976: 260).

The Beth-shearim burial place consists of catacombs, with a frontal courtyard and portals constructed of stone doors imitating wooden doors with nails (Mazar 1973: Plan 1–5; pl. VI; Avigad 1976: figs. 3–5; pls. 25:1; 27:2; 28:1). Several burial halls spaced out along a corridor were hewn in the rock (see Avigad 1976: fig. 31). The graves were mainly loculi or arcosolia types and it is clear that burial customs—that is, primary inhumation in arcosolia, coffins, and sarcophagi—have little in common with those of the Second Temple period. On the walls were carved, painted, or incised decoration, in a popular art style. Decorated marble or clay sarcophagi contained the primary burials of local Jews or the reinterred remains of those returned from the Diaspora (Mazar 1973; Avigad 1976). By this time burial had become a commercialized, public enterprise and was directed apparently by the burial society *(Hebrah Kadisha),* who sold burial places to any purchaser (Avigad 1976: 253, 265).

The Aramaic, Hebrew, and Greek inscriptions found in these tombs mainly record the names of the tomb owners; sometimes a personal note is added. Longer inscriptions are written on the walls. Their purpose was to identify the graves of the deceased for visitors (Schwabe and Lifshitz 1974: 219). The inscriptions found at Beth-shearim indicate that the interred were people of importance, such as rabbis, public officers, merchants, craftsmen, and scribes.

The Beth-shearim tomb walls, sarcophagi, and coffins are adorned with carvings, reliefs, incisions, and drawings. The patterns used are a blend of Hellenistic and oriental elements, with the occasional creation of a new motif. The style in which they are worked is similar to that used in contemporaneous Jewish synagogal art. See ART AND ARCHITECTURE (EARLY JEWISH).

A distinction must be made between the custom of secondary burial in ossuaries and the custom of Diaspora Jews to be reinterred in the land of Israel. Scholars have claimed that ossuaries contained the bones of Diaspora Jews, citing as proof inscriptions mentioning a person's place of origin outside the land of Israel. What the inscriptions actually indicate is that the deceased had belonged to a community of Jews residing in Jerusalem who were of Diaspora origin (Rahmani 1977: 28, and nn. 123–24). Jews did not begin to practice the custom of reinterment in the land of Israel until the 3d century C.E. (Gafni 1981), and especially abundant evidence for this practice can be found in the Beth-shearim cemetery (Schwabe and Lifshitz 1974: 219).

D. Conclusions

The excavations in the extended Jerusalem necropolis and the Jericho cemetery reveal that two completely different burial customs, one chronologically following the other, were practiced by Jews of the Second Temple period. The earlier custom (1st century B.C.E.) is a primary individual burial in a wooden coffin. In Jerusalem indications of such primary burial have been found in many tombs. Jewish burial practices of the late Second Temple period reveal a corresponding importance placed on both the individual and the family. This is reflected in the plan of the loculi tomb, which provided for individual burial of coffins or ossuaries in separate loculi while at the same time allowing a family to be buried together in the same tomb. The entire population and not just the upper classes (as in the Israelite period) were given individual burials. This practice is probably related to the increasing importance played on the individual in contemporary Hellenistic society, and to the Jewish belief in individual resurrection of the body. This belief is reflected in sources dating as early as the 2d century B.C.E. (Rahmani 1961: 117–18, n.6). Similarly, burial in wooden coffins was practiced in En-gedi and in the cemetery of the Qumran sect.

The second type of burial found in Jerusalem and in the Jericho cemetery—chronologically following the coffin burials—is deliberate secondary burial of the bones, placed either in individual ossuaries or in communal burials in loculi or pits, which was also common in burials of the First Temple and Hellenistic periods. This complete change in burial customs occurs during the beginning of the 1st century C.E. simultaneously with a change in the political status of Judea, which now became a Roman province. Up to now no theory has been able to account for this drastic change in burial customs; unfortunately, all sources dealing with ossilegium describe only the custom itself without mentioning the reasons for its sudden appearance.

In summary, what is most extraordinary in the Jewish burial customs of the Second Temple period is the astonishing fact that within a comparatively short span of time burial practices, which are typically among the most conservative customs in a society, underwent rapid changes. Loculi tombs appear with primary coffin burials, and within a century secondary burials in ossuaries in similar loculi tombs becomes the prevalent custom, a practice lacking parallels in any other contemporary neighboring culture. At the same time, these customs were short-lived and show little affinity with either the earlier Israelite customs or the later Jewish rituals of late antiquity which contain only traces of these Second Temple customs. Furthermore, archaeological investigation has been unable to uncover the causes for these ossuary burial innovations. It may be conjectured that the Jews blamed their loss of independence and their state, in 6 C.E., on their sinful behavior; the custom of secondary burial of the bones in ossuaries, after decay of the flesh, may have become a way to expiate sins. The later Beth-shearim necropolis (3d–4th century C.E.) shows the practice of individual burial in various kinds of sarcophagi and was a central cemetery for Jews both in the land of Israel and in the Diaspora.

Bibliography

Avigad, N. 1950–51. The Rock-Carved Facades of the Jerusalem Necropolis. *IEJ* 1: 96–109.

———. 1976. *Beth She'arim III:* Catacombs 12–23. Jerusalem.
Bar-Adon, P. 1977. Another Settlement of the Judean Desert Sect at ʾAin el-Ghuweir on the Dead Sea. *BASOR* 227: 1–25.
Gafni, Y. 1981. Reinterment in the Land of Israel: Notes on the Origin and Development of the Custom. *The Jerusalem Cathedra* 1: 96–104.
Hachlili, R. 1978. A Jerusalem Family in Jericho. *BASOR* 230: 45–56.
———. 1979. The Goliath Family in Jericho, Funerary Inscriptions from a First Century Monumental Tomb. *BASOR* 235: 31–66.
———. 1980. A Second Temple Period Necropolis in Jericho. *BA* 43: 235–40.
———. 1981. The *Nefesh:* The Jericho Column Pyramid. *PEQ* 113: 33–38.
———. 1985. Wall Painting in the Jewish Monumental Tomb at Jericho. *PEQ* 117: 112–27.
Hachlili, R., and Killebrew, A. 1983. Jewish Funerary Customs during the Second Temple Period in Light of the Excavations at the Jericho Necropolis. *PEQ* 115: 109–39.
Kloner, A. 1980. *The Necropolis of Jerusalem in the Second Temple Period.* Diss., Jerusalem (in Hebrew).
Mazar, B., 1973. *Beth She'arim I.* Jerusalem.
Meyers, E. M. 1971. *Jewish Ossuaries: Reburial and Rebirth.* Rome.
Rahmani, L. V. 1961. Jewish Rock-Cut Tombs in Jerusalem. *ʿAtiqot* 3: 93–120.
———. 1977. *The Decoration of Jewish Ossuaries as Representations of Jerusalem Tombs.* Diss., Jerusalem (in Hebrew).
———. 1981. Ancient Jerusalem's Funerary Customs and Tombs. *BA* 44: 171–77, 229–35.
———. 1982. Ancient Jerusalem's Funerary Customs and Tombs. *BA* 45: 43–53, 109–119.
Schwabe, M., and Lifshitz, B. 1974. *Beth She'arim II.* Jerusalem.
Vaux, R. de. 1973. *Archaeology and the Dead Sea Scrolls.* London.
Watzinger, C. 1905. *Griechiesche Holzsarkophage aus der Zeit Alexanders des Grossen.* Leipzig.
Zlotnick, D. 1966. *The Tractate "Mourning" (Semahot).* New Haven.

RACHEL HACHLILI

BUSEIRAH. See BOZRAH.

BUSHEL. See WEIGHTS AND MEASURES.

BUSTARD. See ZOOLOGY.

BUTCHERING ANIMALS. See ZOOLOGY.

BUZ (PERSON) [Heb *bûz*]. **1.** The second son of Nahor (Gen 22:21). See BUZ (PLACE).

2. A "son," i.e., descendant, of Abihail in Israelite Transjordan (1 Chr 5:14). The persons (or rather families?) in 1 Chr 5:12–15 may actually have been "registered" in the reign of Jeroboam II (787–747 B.C.), as 1 Chr 5:17 indicates. In this case, these names may represent the free, landowning, and taxpaying Israelite families in Gilead before it became an Assyrian province in 734 B.C. (cf. 1 Chr 5:6). These Israelites cannot, however, have belonged to the tribe of Gad, as 1 Chr 5:11 claims. Gad did not inhabit Gilead but the region immediately N of the Moabite border and S of Gilead. The attribution of the Gadite territory to Reuben and of Gilead to Gad originated in Israelite historiographic theory after these tribes had disappeared from the scene of history (Wüst 1975: 245f.).

As a personal name, Buz is difficult to explain. Heb *bûz,* "despise," is unlikely to have generated personal names. Perhaps one may compare Arabic *Baus,* "Kissing," already attested in Thamudic and Safaitic (Knauf 1982: 173 and n.16). Buz can be derived from *Baus* by partial assimilation of the voiceless sibilant to the voiced labial.

Bibliography

Knauf, E. A. 1982. Vier thamudische Inschriften vom Sinai. *ZDPV* 98: 170–73.
Wüst, M. 1975. *Untersuchungen zu den siedlungsgeographischen Texten des Alten Testaments. I: Ostjordanland.* BTAVO B 9. Wiesbaden.

ERNST AXEL KNAUF

BUZ (PLACE) [Heb *bûz*]. A country in E Arabia (Jer 25:23; Job 32:2, 6). In 605/604 B.C. (Jer 25:1), the prophet Jeremiah named four polities from the Arabian Peninsula (25:23): the city-states of Dedan and Taima in NW Arabia; "those with cropped hair" (i.e., the Qedarites according to Jer 49:28–33; see KEDAR); and Buz. In Job 32:2, 6, Buz is Elihu's country or tribe of origin. See ELIHU. Buz (*Bauz* in the LXX, i.e., originally **Bôz*) occurs in Assyrian records under the name of **Bâzu* (Knauf 1985: 55, n.267 *pace* Ephʿal 1982: 133). In 677 B.C., Esarhaddon conducted a campaign into *Bâzu* (Ephʿal 1982: 130–37). Two of the conquered cities can be located in E Arabia (Knauf 1985: 55 n.267).

It is highly likely that the "sons of Nahor" (Gen 22:21f.) actually form a list of Syrian and Arabian countries and people from the 1st millennium B.C. The "brothers" of Buz, son of Nahor, are: Uz, a country or tribe in W Arabia (see UZ); Kemuel, the father of Aram (i.e., Syria and/or the Arameans); Kesed, the Chaldeans; and Hazo. The last recalls *Ḫazû,* a mountainous area next to *Bâzu* in the inscriptions of Esarhaddon (Knauf 1985: 55, n. 267). In the Sefire-Inscriptions (KAI 222) B 9, *yʾdy* (Zinjirli; but cf. Lipiński 1986: 85) *bz* denote the extension of the world known to its N Syrian author(s) in the first half of the 8th century B.C.

Bibliography

Ephʿal, I. 1982. *The Ancient Arabs. Nomads on the Borders of the Fertile Crescent, 9th–5th Centuries B.C.* Jerusalem.
Knauf, E. A. 1985. *Ismael.* ADPV. Wiesbaden.
Lipiński, E. 1986. Review of A. Lemaire and J.-M. Durand, Les inscriptions araméennes de Sfire et l'Assyrie de Shamshi-ilu (1984). *BASOR* 264: 85–86.

ERNST AXEL KNAUF

BUZI (PERSON) [Heb *bûzî*]. The father of the prophet Ezekiel (Ezek 1:3). The name means "The man from the land (or tribe) of Buz." See BUZ. Because Ezekiel was of priestly descent, and from Jerusalem, it is highly unlikely that his family originated from this country in E Arabia.

The name may, however, betray links of Ezekiel's family to E Arabia (by way of trade or diplomacy) at the time when his father was given this name.

ERNST AXEL KNAUF

BUZZARD. See ZOOLOGY.

BYBLOS (PLACE). See GEBAL (PLACE).

BYBLOS SYLLABIC. *See* LANGUAGES (BYBLOS SYLLABIC INSCRIPTIONS).

CABBON (PLACE) [Heb *kabbôn*]. A town situated in the Shephelah, or low country, of Judah (Josh 15:40), within the same district as Lachish and Eglon. The only reference to this settlement occurs in the list of towns within the tribal allotment of Judah (Josh 15:21–62; see also BETH-DAGON). It has been suggested (Boling and Wright *Joshua* AB, 386) that Cabbon may be related to MACHBENAH, listed in 1 Chr 2:49 as one of the descendants of CALEB. The location of the ancient settlement is unknown.

Bibliography

Alt, A. 1925. Judas Gaue unter Josia. *PJ* 21: 100–16.

WADE R. KOTTER

CABUL (PLACE) [Heb *kābûl*]. A town in the tribe of Asher (Josh 19:27; 1 Kgs 9:13). Cabul is of great importance for the understanding of the topography of the territory of the tribe of Asher because it is the only place, the name of which has been retained in a modern place name, that is undoubtedly part of the description of the E border of the tribal territory. Other places mentioned in Josh 19:27–28, connected by the conjunctive *waw* ("and"), are generally considered not to belong to the border description but to have been part of a town list later added to it. Literally the phrase in Josh 19:27 reads "and [Asher's territory] went out to Cabul from the left." It has been suggested, however, that "left" should here be understood as "north" (Cooke, *Joshua* CBSC, 180).

The name Cabul has survived in the name of the village Kabul (M.R. 170252) 14 km SE of Acco, situated on a low W spur of the hills of Galilee. This is with little doubt the ancient Chaboulon/Chabolo mentioned by Josephus as having been burnt by Cestius Gallus (*JW* 2.1.9), as his own headquarters (*Life* 43–45), and as the W border of Lower Galilee (*JW* 3.3.1; there "Zaboulon" should be corrected to "Chaboulon"). It is also the "Kabul" mentioned frequently in Talmudic literature (*t. Šabb.* 7:17; *t. Moᶜed Qaṭ.* 2:5; *y. Meg.* 4:78b; etc.).

No evidence of Iron Age occupation has been reported from Kabul, however, and Gal (1985) suggests that biblical Cabul be identified at Kh. Ras ez-Zeitun, 1.5 km NE of Kabul. Excavations there have revealed a town 5 acres in extent from the early Iron Age replaced by a fort from the 9th century B.C.E. Cabul's position between the hills of Galilee and the coastal plain determined its being chosen to demarcate the borders of Asher in Joshua and of Lower Galilee in *JW.* The border of Asher was apparently to the E of Cabul, thus including the foothills in the tribe's territory, while the border of Lower Galilee was probably to the W of Cabul at the foot of the hills.

The "land of Cabul" (Heb *ʾereṣ kābûl*) is mentioned in connection with the episode in which Hiram king of Tyre received "twenty towns in Galilee" from Solomon (1 Kgs 9:10–14; but cf. 2 Chr 8:2). Various attempts have been made to explain the derogatory meaning implied by the text. Josephus explained that it means "unpleasant" in Phoenician (*Ant* 8.5.3), and in the Talmud (*b. Šabb.* 54b) it is explained as "unfruitful." There is, however, little doubt that the Cabul of 1 Kgs 9:13 is to be identified with that of Josh 19:27, and that the explanation in 1 Kgs 9:13 is etiological in character, either unconnected to the Hiram episode (NHI, 212, n.1), or intended to counteract (or at least soften) the negative political implications of the loss of Israelite territory to Hiram.

The biblical text implies that the "land of Cabul" is identical with the "twenty towns in Galilee." These are usually presumed to be the towns of the coastal plain that in Joshua 19 are included in the territory of Asher but that are later Sidonian (*ANET,* 287). However, it is unlikely that this region of important cities would be named after Cabul, a comparatively unimportant town on the periphery. The LXX of 1 Kgs 9:13 renders the MT *kābûl* ("Cabul") as Gk *Opion* ("border"), implying that the original Hebrew was *gĕbûl* ("border") or that the translator interpreted it as such. The "land of Cabul" in 1 Kings 9 has therefore been explained as a smaller region in the vicinity of Cabul/Kabul, and the discrepancy of this explanation with the biblical text has been explained either by presuming that part of the original narrative is missing (Alt 1929: 43–44; *LBHG,* 277) or by separating completely the episode of the land of Cabul from that of the cities in Galilee (*NHI,* 212, n.1).

Bibliography

Alt, D. A. 1929. Das Institut im Jahre 1928. *PJ* 25: 5–57.

Gal, Z. 1985. Cabul, Jiphtah-El and the Boundary between Asher and Zebulun in the Light of Archaeological Evidence. *ZDPV* 101: 114–27.

RAFAEL FRANKEL

CAESAR. Originally "Caesar" was a cognomen used by some of the members of the Julian family, e.g., by the dictator Gaius Julius Caesar. On his death, his heir and adopted son Octavian (later Augustus) added Caesar's names to his own; for it was the custom, according to the historian Dio Cassius, "for a person, when he was adopted, to take most of his name from his adopter" (46.47.6). Subsequently, "Caesar" was transmitted, legally, to those whom Augustus adopted and to their direct descendants, namely, the emperor Tiberius (along with his son Drusus and his two sons), Germanicus (and his five sons, including the emperor Gaius), and the three sons of Marcus Agrippa. But Claudius and Nero (and later emperors as well) used it too, though they were not entitled to do so, or at least had no legal claim to it as a cognomen: neither they nor their fathers had been adopted by Augustus. Presumably, they regarded it as another imperial title. But by the 2d century at the latest it had acquired a new meaning: it was used to indicate the heir to the throne. "Caesar" is first attested in this sense in Hadrian's reign, when he adopted Aelius Verus. Each subsequent heir presumptive was automatically called "Caesar."

Bibliography

Hammond, M. 1959. *The Antonine Monarchy.* Rome.

Syme, R. 1958. Imperator Caesar: A Study in Nomenclature. *Historia* 7: 172–88.

BRIAN W. JONES

CAESAR'S HOUSEHOLD. The extended family of the Roman emperor, including all slaves (*servi*) and freedmen (*liberti*) in his service, constituted the household of Caesar.

The *familia Caesaris* was no different than the *familia* possessed by members of any great Roman clan (*gens*). From the earliest times the Roman *familia* "consisted of the conjugal family plus dependents," and "could in its widest sense, refer to all persons (and property) under the control (*patria potestas*) of the head of the family (*paterfamilias*)" (Rawson 1986: 7–8). Accordingly, the households of wealthy nobles could become very large indeed. Under the empire, by far the wealthiest of Romans was the emperor, and his household was correspondingly greater than any other.

The *familia Caesaris* consisted of thousands of slaves and freedmen of the emperor. Their function was not necessarily servile, though many worked the emperor's estates and properties, while others filled traditional servant roles in caring for the persons of the emperor and his relatives. Quite the contrary, many of the emperor's slaves and especially freedmen functioned as managers of estates, enterprises, or other properties throughout the empire. Others took part in the administration of the government itself, which in the early empire remained attached to the emperor's household in the same way as did his personal property. The first Roman civil service developed out of the secretariats manned by the freedmen of Caesar and headed by a few elite freedmen who thus came to possess power far greater than that of the Roman nobility itself, and ultimately formed in imperial society a new influential class. For their role in the administration and governance of the empire, as well as in the personal service of the emperor, see Weaver 1972.

Bibliography

Rawson, B. 1986. The Roman Family. Pp. 1–57 in *The Family in Ancient Rome: New Perspectives,* ed. B. Rawson. Ithaca, NY.

Weaver, P. R. C. 1972. *Familia Caesaris: A Social Study of the Emperor's Freedmen and Slaves.* Cambridge.

JOHN F. HALL

CAESAR, APPEAL TO. See APPEAL TO CAESAR.

CAESAREA (PLACE) [Gk *Kaisareia*]. A seaport located ca. 50 km N of Tel Aviv and ca. 45 km S of Haifa on the Mediterranean coast (M.R. 140212); also known as Caesarea Maritima or Caesarea Palestinae.

A. Caesarea's History

For millennia before any permanent occupation occurred, the future site of Caesarea Maritima had been used as a roadstead for maritime trade between Egypt and the Levant. The founder of the first known settlement at the site was a Sidonian king named Strato, who lived during the 4th century B.C.E. His trading station came to be known as Strato's Tower.

The original village may have been located ca. 300 m N of the subsequent Crusader fortifications. It probably included a small harbor, private houses, some official buildings, magazines for storage, and perhaps a lighthouse or watchtower that may have given the settlement its name. Adjacent to the fertile Plain of Sharon, the site provided an excellent maritime outlet for the agricultural abundance of the region.

In 259 B.C.E., when the region had passed under Ptolemaic control, an Egyptian official named Zeno arrived at the site to inspect the estates and manage the financial interests of his employer, Apollonius, and his king, Ptolemy Philadelphus. His visit, recorded in the so-called Zeno papyrus, provides the first mention of Strato's Tower or of the site of Caesarea itself.

Near the end of the 2d century B.C.E., a petty ruler named Zoilus seized Strato's Tower and the nearby city of Dor 12 km to the north. He transformed the coastal trading settlement into a fortified port city—a political imperative considering his tenuous hold on these coastal enclaves and the rise of the Hasmonean dynasty. In addition, he expanded his port's harbor capacity by creating an artificial, protected anchorage in the lee (N) of the site's highest promontory. This facility, which was literally carved from the coast and then flooded, augmented a harbor to the north that had served the original settlement. Both basins were now enclosed within the city walls, consistent with the tradition of harbor construction of the Hellenistic age.

Zoilus held Strato's Tower until it was taken by Alexander Jannaeus in 103 B.C.E. Its fate after this date is not clear, although its fortunes clearly declined. It had fallen into a ruinous state by the time of Herod the Great (40–4 B.C.E.).

Having survived the tumultuous last years of the Roman civil wars, Herod continued as Rome's client king of Judea. A successful meeting with Octavian (later Augustus Caesar) led to reconfirmation of his status and to a grant of additional territory which included the coastal region embracing the ruins of Strato's Tower.

Herod decided to build a major international port in his newly acquired land to foster several policy goals. A grand city built in the style of a Roman provincial capital and named for his imperial patron would be a tangible demonstration of his loyalty and would manifest his commitment to the traditions of Rome. In addition, Herod, who was a Jew and who would eventually rebuild the Second Temple in Jerusalem, could show his sympathy and support for his non-Jewish subjects through the construction of a great Greco-Roman urban center complete with pagan temples and other structures (a theater, hippodrome, and amphitheater) that were inimical to his Jewish constituency. This ambitious building program was a gentile counterpoint to his rebuiding of the Jewish temple.

Herod's dream for Caesarea had an economic dimension as well. He hoped that this port, with its great harbor complex called Sebastos, would challenge and perhaps supplant Alexandria as the great emporium of the eastern Mediterranean. Finally, the erection of such an elegant city from the ruins of Strato's Tower would confirm Herod's place in history as a great statesman and master builder. With so much at stake, work on the new city proceeded rapidly. In little more than a decade (ca. 22–10/9 B.C.E.), the city was completed and dedicated with spectacular games, with the Sebastos harbor complex finished perhaps a few years earlier. See Fig. CAE.01.

The primary source for Herodian Caesarea is the ancient historian Flavius Josephus (*JW* 1.408–14; *Ant.* 15.331–41). Although not a contemporary of the king, he knew Caesarea and its history well. We are fortunate to have not only his description of Herod's city at its inception but also an account of the actual building of the Outer Basin of Sebastos as well—a literary description that is unique in ancient texts.

From its inception, Caesarea contained all the principal architectural elements that distinguished contemporary pagan cities—a theater, temples, elaborate sewer and water systems, paved streets installed on the typical orthogonal urban design, etc.—plus some unique features as well. Josephus mentions that Herod erected a grand temple to Augustus and Roma that dominated the harbor and provided a monumental landmark for incoming ships. From archaeological data uncovered, we now know that it was constructed on an artificial podium adjacent to the earlier Inner Basin that itself had been refurbished, perhaps to serve as a limited-use royal harbor or a protected anchorage for Herod's fleet.

Josephus' description of the construction of the Outer Basin, long judged by many scholars as an exercise in inflated prose or even a conscious exaggeration, has been proven largely correct by recent underwater excavations. When completed, this facility was an engineering marvel of the age, incorporating such sophisticated and modern features as a siltation control system that used flushing channels, the extensive use of hydraulic concrete (a building substance that was poured liquid into the sea to harden

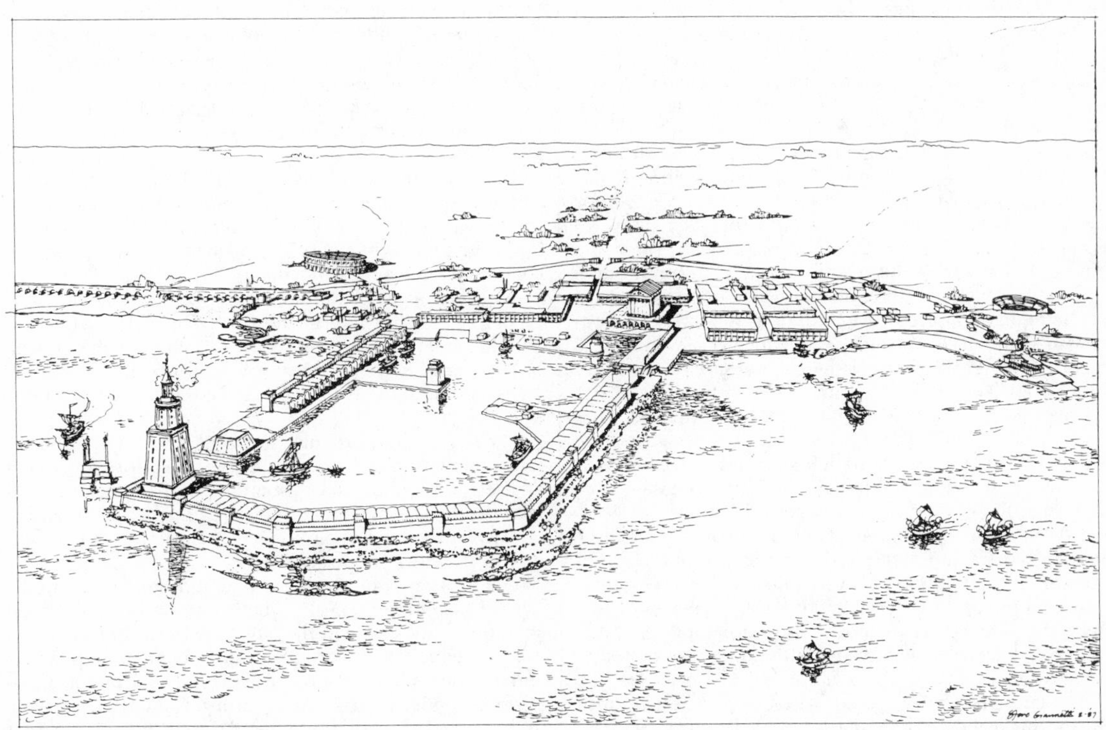

CAE.01. Artist's reconstruction of Caesarea Maritima—Herodian Period. *(Courtesy of R. Hohlfelder.)*

in situ), and certain design elements to mitigate damage from wave energy.

This facility was but one element of the city's elaborate harbor complex known as Sebastos, or *Portus Augusti* (as it is identified on coins from the Roman occupation of Caesarea). Sebastos consisted of four harbors: the Inner Basin and Outer Basin that were connected by a channel, the South Bay anchorage, and the North Harbor (the original Hellenistic facility restored by Herod). Each may have had a distinct purpose. Their total working area was far greater than the immediate economic needs of the city or the Plain of Sharon required. Herod clearly planned for his seaport to assume a premier role in the maritime affairs of the Roman world. Caesarea was intended to be a major transshipment point on the busy maritime trade routes leading to Rome from the east. Although his city never surpassed Alexandria, it did achieve an international prominence and importance commensurate with Herod's dream.

Upon his death in 4 B.C.E., one of Herod's surviving sons, Archelaus, received his throne. Archelaus was judged incompetent by Augustus and was removed from power in A.D. 6. His kingdom, including Caesarea, was then absorbed by the Romans into their empire, and the new province was henceforth known as Judea. Herod's seaport became the new provincial capital. When Judea entered the empire, the Romans took a census in the country, directed from Caesarea, to determine tax liabilities. This was the same census recorded in Luke 2:2 (contrast Matt 2:1).

The city figured prominently in the history of the early Church as recorded in the book of Acts. Philip, a deacon in the Jerusalem church, first brought Christianity to Caesarea (Acts 8:4–40). Pontius Pilate, who presided at Jesus' trial, governed Judea as prefect from this provincial capital. An important step toward fulfilling Christianity's destiny as a world religion occurred at Caesarea when Peter there converted the first gentile, Cornelius the centurion (10:3–48). Paul, who earlier had been safely spirited away to Tarsus from Caesarea (9:29–30), was imprisoned for two years (A.D. 57–59) in Caesarea before being sent to Rome for trial (Acts 23–26). Although incarcerated, he was not isolated from the rest of the Christian community. Caesarea's central position on the major maritime routes of the Roman Empire provided him with ample opportunity to continue his epistolary activities. Following these events, however, our knowledge of Caesarea's Christian history dims until the 3d century.

Caesarea also played an important role in the First Jewish War (A.D. 66–70). Events in the city triggered the onset of hostilities. Nearly 20,000 Jews were slaughtered at Caesarea in one hour. Vespasian, then his son Titus (after Vespasian had been declared emperor of Rome at Caesarea by his legions), conducted the war from there. Over 10,000 soldiers were quartered in the city at one point in the war. When the war was over, Titus held victory games in the amphitheater. There 2500 Jewish prisoners of war were forced to fight to their deaths as gladiators. Vespasian honored Caesarea's loyalty by refounding the city as a Roman colony, *Colonia Prima Flavia Augusta Caesarea.*

The emperor Hadrian, who visited the city at least once during his extensive imperial travels, patronized the city on a grand scale. Among the public works attributed to him are a new temple, a second aqueduct, and possibly the construction of a permanent stone hippodrome. Later emperors favored the city as well. New titles and honors accrued as time passed until the city achieved its most glorious (and ponderous!) recognition under Trebonianus Gallus (A.D. 251–53): *Colonia Prima Flavia Augusta Felix Concordia Caesarea Metropolis Provinciae Syriae Palaestinae.*

Throughout the centuries of Rome's rule, the city prospered on many levels, enjoying the benefits of its role as provincial capital and busy international seaport. Its geopolitical importance, its local prosperity, and its cosmopolitan character as a leading Mediterranean seaport attracted numerous intellectuals and religious leaders. It evolved into one of the leading centers for religious study in the Roman world.

By the beginning of the 3d century, the Jewish population had recovered from the disasters of two wars with Rome (the second in A.D. 132–35) and had grown once again to a considerable size. Prominent rabbis, including Rabbi Hoshaya, Rabbi Abbahu, and Rabbi Isaac Hapaha, taught and issued legal decisions at Caesarea. Their contributions to both the Jerusalem and Babylonian Talmuds loom large. The scholar Origen came to Caesarea in A.D. 231 and almost single-handedly turned the city into a center of Christian learning. During the next two decades he amassed a huge library that attracted serious scholars and students. His efforts were continued by Pamphilus, who educated another generation of Christians at Caesarea.

During the great persecution of Christians (A.D. 303–13), numerous individuals died as martyrs for their faith at Caesarea. Eusebius of Caesarea wrote *On the Martyrs of Palestine* in 311 to describe their sufferings. Slightly earlier, he had written the *Ecclesiastical History,* the first history of the Christian Church. Both works were subsequently revised.

As the Byzantine era dawned with the personal conversion of Constantine and the subsequent Christianizing of the Roman world, Caesarea became an even more important Christian center. As a provincial capital (a role it continued to play during the Byzantine era as well), its bishop, bearing the additional title of *metropolitan,* exercised a leadership role in the Christian Holy Land. This prestige and influence enjoyed by Caesarea's metropolitan bishops engendered a great rivalry with the bishops of Jerusalem until the issue was resolved in Jerusalem's favor in A.D. 451.

The city became a regular stop on Christian pilgrimages to the Holy Land. Numerous imperial visitors, including St. Helena, mother of Constantine, and famous churchmen like St. Jerome, visited Caesarea during its Byzantine era. Jerome's stay was prolonged because he took advantage of the city's famous library.

The prosperity of the city ebbed and flowed during the 4th–7th centuries, reflecting both international and local conditions. Sometime in the late 4th century the city walls were extended to incorporate an expanded population and another aqueduct was constructed. Although its prosperity extended into the 5th century, Caesarea eventually declined, a victim of the general forces at work in that tumultuous century as well as of local drought and religious tensions.

Procopius of Gaza (not to be confused with Procopius of Caesarea, the famous historian of the era of Justinian [A.D. 527–65]), wrote of the restoration of the harbor under Anastasius (probably after A.D. 502) and the subsequent return of prosperity to the city and the region it served. In the reign of Justinian an ambitious rebuilding program was undertaken throughout Caesarea. It is quite likely that the city reached its greatest population during the last years of his reign. Perhaps as many as 150,000 people lived there, making this city one of the largest in the Mediterranean world.

With the dawn of the 7th century, Caesarea's fortunes changed again. The city surrendered without major resistance to the Persians in 614 and was held by them until 627–28 when the emperor Heraclius destroyed the Persian Empire and recovered the occupied territories. Only six years later, the first Muslim army invaded Palestine. Caesarea was first attacked in 634. With its defenses revitalized by Heraclius and its ability to be resupplied by the sea, it withstood Arab attacks until 640 or 641. It only fell then because a Jew named Joseph led the Muslim besiegers into the city through a water "conduit," either the Byzantine aqueduct (described by archaeologists as the low-level aqueduct) or a sewer.

Many inhabitants fled, contributing to Caesarea's decline as a city. In addition, the geopolitical realities of the Mediterranean world changed with the Arab conquest. Caesarea no longer was on the major sea lanes of E–W trade. Its harbors, now allowed to decline because they were no longer required, served only local coastal trade. The economic ramifications were significant.

Caesarea survived, but as a less grand settlement. It lost its international and cosmopolitan urbanity and became an agricultural center on the fringes of a desert empire and a *ribat,* or coast guard station. It gained renown for its produce, its impregnable walls, its fountains, and its Great Mosque, constructed on the same podium where Herod's temple to Augustus and Roma had stood centuries before.

The advent of the Crusades saw another shift of fortunes. Although not taken in the first military actions in the Holy Land, Caesarea soon thereafter came under Western control. In May 1101, Frankish knights under Baldwin I supported by a Genoese fleet assaulted and took the Arab city. One of the prizes of war was a green cut-glass chalice, found in the Great Mosque and thought to be the Holy Grail. It was taken by the Genoese to their city where it still forms part of the treasury of the Cathedral of San Lorenzo.

During the next two centuries the city retrenched again and became a fortified settlement of slightly more than 12 hectares. See Fig. CAE.02. Its history was tumultuous, as it changed hands several times during this period. The fortifications that distinguish the site today were completed in 1252. King Louis IX himself worked on these walls after his failed efforts to take Egypt in the Sixth Crusade. Ultimately, these Crusader fortifications proved insufficient: the Mamluk sultan Baybars, ruler of Egypt, took the city in 1265 after a siege of six days, and the defenders were allowed to evacuate the city. In 1291, as the Crusaders

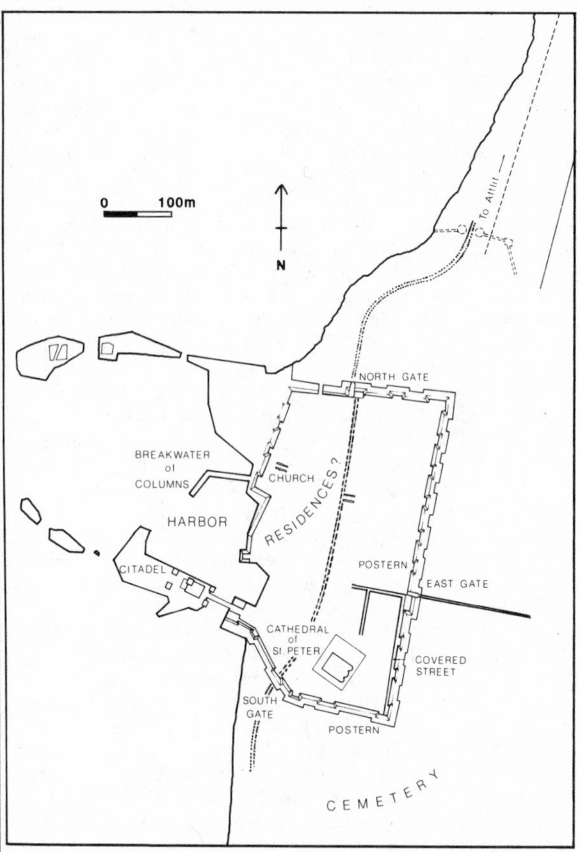

CAE.02. Site plan of Caesarea Maritima—Crusader Period. *(Courtesy of R. Hohlfelder.)*

were finally expelled from the Holy Land, Caesarea, along with other coastal fortresses, was destroyed to prevent any Christians from ever again gaining a foothold in the Holy Land.

From that point to the late 19th century, the site was abandoned. Nature reclaimed much of it, but ancient Caesarea was never forgotten. In 1882 a small village of Bosnian Muslims was settled within its ruins by the Ottoman Empire. A small settlement developed within the precinct of the old Crusader city and survived until the creation of the state of Israel in 1948. Kibbutz Sdot Yam was founded on the site in 1940. Since 1954 the Caesarea Development Corporation has built more than 400 homes on a tract of land NE of the Crusader fortifications. The Department of Antiquities and the National Parks Authority have actively encouraged tourism at this site by promoting excavations by various national and international expeditions and by restoring numerous archaeological monuments. Caesarea annually attracts large numbers of visitors from throughout the world.

B. Archaeology at Caesarea

Various travelers visited Caesarea before the 20th century and left impressionistic records of their observations. The first scientific account of the site, however, was not produced until 1873 by C. R. Conder and H. H. Kitchner, who spent six days exploring the ruins. Actual excavations did not commence until 1951 after agricultural workers from Kibbutz Sdot Yam uncovered an imperial porphyry statue on what is now called the Byzantine esplanade. S. Yeivin, then director of the Israeli Department of Antiquities, conducted that first exploration.

In the next two decades, various excavations were carried out. Beginning in 1959, the Missione Archeologica Italiana, under the direction of A. Calderini, succeeded by L. Crema and A. Frova, carried out six seasons of field work. Several of the site's most important monuments—the aqueduct, the N wall of the Herodian or Hellenistic city, and the theater—were excavated by this team. Their final report was the first significant treatment of the archaeological evidence of Caesarea (Frova 1965).

In 1960, A. Negev and G. Foerster of Hebrew University, assisted by A. Wegman of Kibbutz Sdot Yam, began field work on behalf of the Israeli National Parks Authority. They excavated and restored the Crusader fortifications and many buildings within them. In 1960, one of the first underwater explorations of a submerged terrestrial site, in this case the ruins of the Outer Basin of Sebastos, was conducted by an American-Israeli team headed by E. A. Link. In 1962, M. Avi-Yonah, also of Hebrew University, excavated a synagogue located N of the Crusader fortifications and some adjacent structures.

In 1971, a consortium of universities and colleges known as the Joint Expedition to Caesarea Maritima (JECM), headed by R. J. Bull of Drew University, began field work at various sites in the ancient city. This group has worked at the site intermittently since then (Bull 1982; Bull et al. 1986). Another team from Hebrew University, directed by D. Bahat, E. Netzer, and L. Levine, excavated an important Byzantine building within the N sector of the Crusader fortifications and explored the promontory where Professor Netzer thinks Herod the Great's palace was located (see Levine 1975a; 1975b; Levine and Netzer 1986).

In 1980, another international consortium was formed to carry out maritime excavations at Caesarea. This group, known as the Caesarea Ancient Harbour Excavation Project (CAHEP), is headed by A. Raban of the University of Haifa and codirected by R. L. Hohlfelder of the University of Colorado, R. L. Vann of the University of Maryland, and R. Stieglitz of Rutgers University, Newark. (J. P. Oleson of Victoria University was a codirector until 1985.) CAHEP resumed Link's underwater explorations and began investigating various coastal structures relating to the ancient harbors of Caesarea (see bibliography).

Despite the considerable archaeological effort since 1951, only a small part of Caesarea has been explored. At this writing, JECM has completed its last season of field work and will continue to work on final publication of its explorations. CAHEP is continuing its marine archaeological investigations. In 1989 a new land archaeological team, the Caesarea Land Excavation Project (CLEP), began field work on the temple podium and on the Byzantine fortifications. This consortium, headed by Professor K. G. Holum, plans to conduct field work in these and other areas of the city. In June 1989 the Israel Antiquities Authority announced that it would accelerate its efforts to excavate and restore Herod's city.

Bibliography

Blakely, J. A. 1987. *The Joint Expedition to Caesarea Maritima Excavation Reports Vol. 4.* Lewiston, NY.

Bull, R. J. 1982. Caesarea Maritima—The Search for Herod's City. *BARev* 8/3: 24–40.

Bull, R. J., et al. 1986. The Joint Expedition to Caesarea Maritima: Ninth Season, 1980. *BASORSup* 24: 31–55.

Frova, A., et al. 1965. *Scavi di Caesarea Maritima.* Milan.

Hohlfelder, R. L. 1981. Coin Finds: A Conspectus. *BASOR* 244: 46–51.

———. 1982. Caesarea beneath the Sea. *BARev* 8/3: 43–47.

———. 1983a. The Caesarea Coastline Before Herod: Some Preliminary Observations. *BASOR* 252: 67–68.

———. 1983b. Caesarea Maritima. *AJA* 87/2: 191–92.

———. 1984a. Caesarea Maritima in Late Antiquity: An Introduction to the Numismatic Evidence. Pp. 261–85 in *Ancient Coins of the Graeco-Roman World,* ed. W. Heckel and R. Sullivan. Waterloo, Ontario.

———. 1984b. Caesarea Maritima. *AJA* 88/2: 225–26.

———. 1985. Byzantine Coin Finds from the Sea: A Glimpse of Caesarea Maritima's Later History. Pp. 179–84 in *Harbour Archaeology.* B.A.R. International Series 257. Ed. A. Raban. Oxford.

———. 1987. Herod the Great's City on the Sea. *National Geographic* 171/2: 260–79.

———. 1989. Caesarea Maritima, Israel. Pp. 132–36 in *International Perspective on Cultural Parks.* Mesa Verde, CO.

Hohlfelder, R. L., and Oleson, J. P. 1980. Sebastos, the Harbor Complex of Caesarea Maritima, Israel: The Preliminary Report of the 1978 Underwater Explorations. Pp. 765–79 in *Oceanography: The Past,* ed. M. Sears and D. Merriman. New York.

Hohlfelder, R. L., et al. 1983. Sebastos Herod's Harbor at Caesarea Maritima. *BA* 46/3: 133–43.

Holum, K. G.; Hohlfelder, R. L.; Bull, R. J.; and Raban, A. 1988. *King Herod's Dream—Caesarea on the Sea.* New York.

Levine, L. 1975a. *Caesarea under Roman Rule.* Leiden.

———. 1975b. *Roman Caesarea: An Archaeological-Topographical Study. Qedem* 2. Jerusalem.

Levine, L., and Netzer, E. 1986. *Excavations at Caesarea Maritima 1975, 1976, 1979—Final Report. Qedem* 21. Jerusalem.

Negev, A. 1963. The Palimpsest of Caesarea Maritima. *London Illustrated News.* 2 November, 728–31.

Oleson, J. P. 1984. The Caesarea Ancient Harbor Excavation Project (C.A.H.E.P.)—May 21–June 30, 1984. *Old World Archaeology Newsletter* 13/2: 9–11.

———. 1985. Herod and Vitruvius: Preliminary Thoughts on Harbour Engineering at Sebastos, the Harbour of Caesarea Maritima. Pp. 165–72 in *Harbour Archaeology.* B.A.R. International Series 257. Ed. A. Raban. Oxford.

Oleson, J. P., et al. 1984. The Caesarea Ancient Harbor Excavation Project (C.A.H.E.P.): Preliminary Report on the 1980–1983 Seasons. *JFA* 11: 281–305.

Raban, A. 1984a. Caesarea Maritima, 1984. *RB* 91/2: 246–52.

———. 1984b. Caesarea Harbor Excavation Project, 1984. *IEJ* 34: 274–76.

———. 1985a. Marine Archaeology in Israel. *Oceanus* 28/1: 59–65.

———. 1985b. Caesarea Maritima 1983–1984. *International Journal of Nautical Archaeology* 14/1: 155–77.
———. 1989. *The Harbours of Caesarea Maritima.* Vol. 1. BAR International Series 491. Oxford.
Raban, A., and Hohlfelder, R. L. 1981. The Ancient Harbors of Caesarea Maritima. *Arch* 34/2: 56–60.
Ringel, J. 1975. *Césarée de Palestine.* Paris.
Roller, D. 1982a. The Wilfred Laurier University Survey of Northeastern Caesarea Maritima. *Levant* 14: 90–103.
———. 1982b. The Northern Plain of Sharon in the Hellenistic Period. *BASOR* 247: 43–52.
———. 1983. The Problem of the Location of Straton's Tower. *BASOR* 252: 61–66.
Vann, R. L. 1983. News from the Field: Herod's Harbor Construction Recovered Underwater. *BARev* 9/3: 10–14.

ROBERT L. HOHLFELDER

CAESAREA PHILIPPI (PLACE) [Gk *Kaisareia hē Philippou*]. A town (also called Caesarea Paneas, M.R. 215294) and district 40 km N of the Sea of Galilee along the Nahal Hermon (Wadi Banias), at the SW foot of Mt. Hermon, strategically located between Syria and Palestine. It was in this region that Jesus posed the question to his disciples, "Who do you say that I am?" and Peter answered "You are the Christ" (Matt 16:13–20; Mark 8:27–30; cf. Luke 9:18–22).

Prior to the Hellenistic period, the name of the site is unknown. At the time of Antiochus the Great (ca. 200 B.C.E.), it was called Panion (Polybius 16.18.2). Both the town and the district received this name (later Paneas, Pliny *HN* 5.74) from a cave and spring dedicated to the nature god Pan (widely attested by inscriptional and numismatic evidence; see *HJP*² 2: 40 n.66; also Josephus *Ant* 15.10.3 §364; *JW* 1.21.3 §405–6). Earlier cultic use of this site may be evident in the theophoric element of the toponyms Baal-gad (Josh 11:17; 12:7; 13:5) and Baal-hermon (Judg 3:3; 1 Chr 5:23) which are located in this area. Some have suggested that the transfiguration, which follows Peter's confession in each gospel account (Matt 17:1–8; Mark 9:2–9; Luke 9:28–36), took place in this area of ancient cultic significance (note also the proximity of a mountain near the cave in the Josephus references above). Places identified as "holy" often enjoyed a long history of use in practice and legend. (Miracle stories associated with this spring are recorded in the 4th century C.E. by Eusebius *Hist. Eccl.* 7.17; on the nature of sacred space, see Brereton in *EncRel* 12: 526–28.)

After Zenodorus' death in 20 B.C.E., Augustus gave the district of Paneas to Herod the Great, who subsequently built a magnificent marble temple near the cave in honor of the emperor (called both Paneas and Panium by Josephus, *Ant* 15.10.3 §360–61, 363–64; *JW* 1.21.3 §404–5). The district then passed from Herod to his son Philip, the tetrarch of Trachonitis (*Ant* 17.8.1 §189), who enlarged the city and named it *Kaisereia* to complete the honor to Caesar Augustus (*Ant* 18.2.1 §28; *JW* 2.9.1 §168). The name Caesarea Philippi came to be used in the 1st century C.E. to distinguish it from the other cities named Caesarea.

Agrippa II (ca. 53 C.E.) enlarged the city again and gave it the name Neronias (Gk *Nerōnias*) in honor of Nero (*Ant* 20.9.4 §211; *JW* 3.10.7 §514); however, this use is rare according to numismatic evidence (Benzinger in *PW* 3: 1291). During the First Jewish War, Vespasian and his troops rested at Caesarea Philippi (*JW* 3.9.7 §443–44). After the fall of Jerusalem (ca. 70 C.E.), Titus went to the city, where it is reported by Josephus that some of the Jewish captives were thrown to wild beasts (*JW* 7.2.1 §23–24).

In later Roman and Byzantine times, the name Caesarea Philippi was superseded by the old name Paneas (e.g., Eusebius *Onomast.* 215.82; 217.40; 275.36; see *HJP*² 2: 171 n.465 for its use in rabbinic literature). This ancient frontier city is survived today by the village of Banias (the Arabic form of the name).

For additional bibliography, see *HJP*² 2: 169 n.453; for the most extensive treatment, see Hölscher in *PW* 18/3: 594–600.

JOHN KUTSKO

CAIAPHAS (PERSON) [Gk *Kaiaphas*]. There is not unanimity but rather a consensus among the Gospels that the high priest at the time of Jesus' death was named Caiaphas, and that he played an active role in the proceedings. Each of the presentations amounts to a nuanced portrayal of the events leading up to Jesus' death, and each should be appreciated in its own right before any general statement in respect of Caiaphas may be made. In Matthew, the notice of a conspiratorial meeting of high priests and elders is located in the courtyard of Caiaphas' house (26:3) at the commencement of the passion narrative. In Mark and Luke, there is no such reference to location, and less detail in the description of the conspiracy. The second (and final) reference to Caiaphas in Matthew has scribes and elders gathered with Caiaphas, to whom Jesus, having been arrested, is brought (26:57). The reference marks the success of the conspiracy. The conspirators had "taken counsel, that they might arrest Jesus by stealth, and kill him" (26:4); in 26:57 the "crowd" from the high priests, scribes, and elders (26:47) have succeeded in the arrest, and it is Caiaphas' question and Jesus' response (26:63b–64) which will bring the verdict of blasphemy, and a condemnation to death (26:65, 66). The grounds on which Jesus is found guilty of blasphemy is a vexed question, since no profanation of the divine name appears to be involved (Lev 24:15, 16; *Sanh.* 7:5). But Caiaphas' tearing of his garments in 26:65 (again, cf. *Sanh.* 7:5) supports the reading that a judicial finding is involved.

Matthew's Caiaphas is not explicitly provided with any motivation. Indeed, he is not even named as an active agent of the conspiracy in 26:3. The mention of the courtyard may be more important cartographically than for its owner: in the same place, Peter denies Jesus at the close of the chapter (26:69–75; cf. 57, 58). At the crucial moment of his question, Caiaphas is simply identified as "the high priest" (26:59, 62, 63), the chief representative of "the high priests" generally (26:3, 14, 47, 59), who are primary instigators of Jesus' judgment, and also of his death (27:1, 3, 6, 12, 20, 41, 62). The reference to a plurality of high priests is technically incorrect, although common enough in the Gospels, and presumably is used in respect of the leading families from which the high priest was chosen. The picture of an elite, familial group, intimately associated with hierarchical authority, is supported by Acts 4:6, where Annas is named as high priest, and Caiaphas, John, and Alexander are referred to, along with all who were of high priestly lineage. Matthew's picture, then, is of deadly opposition from those most intimately involved with the temple. Caiaphas is emblematic of the opposition without being an instigator of it. Mark achieves much the same effect with a comparable pattern of diction (particularly "high priest(s)"), but without naming Caiaphas.

Luke does name Caiaphas, but in a peculiar manner (3:2). The ministry of John the Baptist is introduced with what at first sight seems chronological exactitude (3:1), but there is then reference to the time of the high priesthood of Annas and Caiaphas (v 2; Acts 4:6). Because the office was not jointly held, the statement constitutes a puzzle, and one which is complicated by the close relationship between Annas and Caiaphas, as documented by Josephus. *Ant* 18.2.2; 18.4.3 has it that Joseph Caiaphas was appointed high priest around the year 18 by Valerius Gratus and removed from office around the year 36 by Vitellius. Annas was appointed by Quirinius around A.D. 6 and deposed by Valerius Gratus in A.D. 15 (*Ant* 18.2.1, 2). Luke 3:2, and especially Acts 4:6, therefore appear to confuse two quite distinct high priesthoods. S. Sandmel has in fact argued that Luke-Acts mistakenly recognizes only Annas as high priest, and that a careless use of sources caused the name of Caiaphas to intrude (Sandmel, *IDB* 1: 482). But the close relationship between Annas and Caiaphas has simply not been taken into account by Sandmel: Annas' influence survived far beyond his high priesthood, in that five of his sons were to serve in the office (*Ant* 20.9.1), and Caiaphas was perhaps his son-in-law (John 18:13). The fact remains, however, that to single out Annas as high priest after A.D. 15 appears to be an error (Catchpole 1971: 170).

D. R. Catchpole is sufficiently convinced by the tenacity of the Lukan confusion that he understands the reference to the house and courtyard of the high priest in Luke 22:54, 55 in respect of Annas, rather than of Caiaphas (Catchpole 1971: 171). Such an exegesis construes Luke in such a way as to accord strikingly with John, and disrupts any exact parallel with Matt 26:57, 58. Substantially, however, the analogy with Matthew is difficult to explain away, and the latter identifies the house specifically as that of Caiaphas. There are, however, rather clear indications that the Lukan approach to Jesus' condemnation is to focus on "the high priests" as a group. Except for 3:2; 22:50, 54, the noun always appears in the plural in Luke, in order to speak of a judicial proceeding against Jesus (9:22; 19:47; 22:2, 4, 52, 66; 23:4, 10, 13; 24:20). The effect of that pattern is to emphasize the nature and source of opposition to Jesus; the usage of 22:66–71 even puts the fateful question of Jesus' identity in the mouth of the "high priests" generally. Likewise, Luke alone of all the Gospels refers to the *stratēgoi* in 22:4, 52 in connection with Jesus' arrest. The evident reference is to the police of the temple (Jeremias 1969: 180), but Luke uses a word in the plural which appears both in Josephus and Acts as a singular, referring to the "captain" of the temple (*Ant* 20.6.2; Acts 4:1; 5:24, 26). It may be that Lukan usage is somewhat loose at this point; Acts 16:20, 22, 35, 36, 38 employs the plural noun, in respect of magistrates in Philippi. The inference may be drawn that the description of Jesus' arrest and prosecution has been shaped to accommodate a Lukan scheme. Within that scheme, Caiaphas as a personality, or even as an active agent of conspiracy, is not in view. Annas also is little more than a cipher of priestly opposition. What is emphasized is the organization of the prosecuting authorities and their link with the temple.

Caiaphas emerges most clearly as a personality in John, in close association with Jesus' passion, but he does not emerge as an active or willing agent of Jesus' execution. John 11:47–53 presents a gathering of "high priests" and Pharisees, in which Jesus' "many signs," most notably the raising of Lazarus (vv 1–46), provokes the fear that "the Romans will come, and destroy both our place and our nation" (v 48). But Caiaphas is said to have prophesied Jesus' death, being high priest of that year, by pronouncing the dictum that it was expedient for one man to perish for the people, that the whole nation might not be destroyed (vv 49–51). The result is, as in the Synoptics (but not in the context of Lazarus' raising), that counsel is taken to kill Jesus (v 53). Notably, no malice is ascribed to Caiaphas; his prophecy is said to derive from his high priestly office. The reference to "that year" has been taken to mean that, within the Johannine scheme, Caiaphas alternated years in service with Annas. Such a reading is an exegetically desperate maneuver, designed to explain the prominent role of Annas in chap. 18: a less strained understanding would take "that year" as the year in which Jesus died (E. Jacquier *DB* 2/1: 45). Be that as it may, the fact remains that the Johannine portrait of Caiaphas is, so far, respectful of the man and his office.

The 18th chap. of John presents an account of Jesus' arrest and trial which differs substantially from that of the Synoptics. Although Caiaphas is again called high priest of that year (v 13c), the combined forces of "the cohort and the officer and the servants of the Jews" (v 12) take Jesus to Annas first (v 13a). Caiaphas' marital relationship to Annas is also mentioned (v 13b), but that scarcely motivates the session at Annas' house, which is the scene that follows (vv 15–24). Caiaphas until this point is a bystander to the action, and the Johannine presentation heightens the contrast with Annas' activism, by recalling Caiaphas' prophecy in 11:49–52; cf. 18:14. He is more moved by events than he influences them. Consistently, the account of the session at Annas' is punctuated with references to him as the high priest; at one point, his status as such causes Jesus to be struck by a servant for his insolence (v 22; cf. vv 15, 16, 19). Caiaphas, by contrast, is a cipher within the text: Jesus is brought to him in v 24, a final scene of Petrine denial unfolds in vv 25–27, and Jesus is immediately led away from Caiaphas to the praetorium in v 28; cf. 35. Concomitant with this truncation of Caiaphas' role, which denies him any dramatic place in the action, we are left in John with no equivalent to the Synoptic dispute, which involves the temple and Jesus' messianic status. Annas interrogates him regarding his disciples and his teaching (v 19); how the issue comes to be Jesus' royal pretensions, in his confrontation with Pilate (vv 33–38), is not explained. Although Sandmel's theory, that reference to Caiaphas was made in an attempt to clean up Johannine chronology, may be invoked here, it does not actually explain why so very little involvement is attributed to Caiaphas. A possibly more satisfactory explanation is that John's gospel is written on the supposition that the Synoptic catechesis has already been appropriated.

The most striking feature of consensus among the Gospels and Josephus in respect to Caiaphas is his close relationship with the Roman administration. Cordial relations are implicit in his long tenure (some eighteen years) as high priest. Between Herod's appointment of Ananel and the destruction of the temple, Josephus counts twenty-eight high priests (Eppstein 1964: 52; *Ant* 20.10; and Jacquier *DB* 2/1: 44), so that the duration of Caiaphas' high priesthood was exceptional. Removed by Vitellus ca. 36, Caiaphas' exercise of office included the period of Pilate's tenure. The latter was infamous for his insults to the national and religious identity of Judaism, and Caiaphas is notable for his absence from the pages of Josephus which describe objections and rebellions against Pilate's activity (Jacquier *DB* 2/1: 44; *Ant* 18.3.1, 2; *JW* 2.9.24). The same Vitellus who dismissed Pilate also released the high priestly vestments from custody in the Antonia (Jeremias 1969: 149, n.4 and *Ant* 18.4.3), a custody with which Caiaphas had apparently complied. The close cooperation between Caiaphas and the Roman authorities is implicit within the passion narratives of all four gospels. For all the differences between the Synoptics and John, there is a consensus that, following a hearing and high priestly interrogation, it was resolved to dispatch Jesus to Pilate (Matt 27:1–2; Mark 15:1; Luke 23:1; John 18:28). The Johannine version of events may even hint at Roman complicity as early as Jesus' arrest: it speaks of a cohort and an officer in addition to a force associated with the high priesthood (18:1, 12). Catchpole (1971: 149; also Jeremias 1969: 210) rightly points out that "cohort" (*speira*) and "officer" (*chiliarchos*) might refer to a band sent from the Jewish authorities, but probability is against that reading. Both the passages in John speak of the cohort and "servants" of the Jewish authorities; the identity of the two groups does not seem to be implied. Within the NT itself, both "cohort" and "officer" refer straightforwardly to Roman military arrangements. If that usage is also to be understood in the case of John, then the fourth gospel does intensify the portrait of high priestly connivance with the Romans, which is independently attested in the Synoptics and (implicitly) in Josephus.

A single, symbolic, and physical center provided the focus of Roman and high priestly cooperation—the temple. The establishment of a police force to guard the purity of the temple is widely attested, in Mishnah, Philo, and Josephus (Jeremias 1969: 209–10 and *HJP*² 1: 366). From the point of view of successive Roman administrations, the sacrificial cult of the temple was valuable, not merely tolerable, because sacrifices in the emperor's behalf were offered there (*JW* 2.10.4; *HJP*² 1: 379–80; 2/1: 311–12). Custody of high priestly garments, the maintenance of a credibly deterrent force in the Antonia (*JW* 5.6.8), and acceptance of a death penalty against desecrating the temple (*HJP*² 1: 378; 2: 80, 222 n.85, 284–85), together make sense as a coherent policy on the part of the Romans. Provided the cult of the temple proceeded under Roman permission and protection, the Jewish refusal to sacrifice to the emperor's image could be overlooked, and Judaism could be seen as a licit society. The formal outbreak of war with Rome in A.D. 66 is, precisely for that reason, signaled by a refusal to offer sacrifice on the emperor's behalf (*JW* 2.17.2).

Caiaphas would have occupied an important position within this delicate settlement. His interrogation of Jesus, following a series of questions concerning the latter's statement in respect of the temple (Matt 26:57–66; Mark 14:53–64; cf. Luke 22:54–71, which is entirely christological in focus) is quite plausible. Likewise, the suggestion of O. Betz, that Caiaphas' counsel in John 11:49–50 suits a Sadducean theology reflected in Josephus (Betz *ANRW* 2/25/1: 596–98), is speculative but defensible. Josephus calls Caiaphas "Joseph Caiaphas"; attempts to explain the surname have abounded from antiquity until the recent past. The results have been inconclusive, although they eloquently attest the attitudes of the scholars who propose them (cf. *HJP*² 2: 230; Jacquier *DB*, 44; and Jerome's verdict, *"investigator vel sagax, sed melius vomens ore,"* discussed in Kraus *JEnc* 1: 493). No judgment of Caiaphas' character or motivation can make any serious claim on our attention, except as an imaginative exercise. Historically speaking, the available evidence will not permit conclusions of that sort. Nonetheless, Caiaphas' obvious, necessary, and essential link with the temple remains.

A Talmudic tradition has it that, forty years prior to the destruction of the temple, the Sanhedrin was exiled from the chamber of hewn stone in the Jerusalem temple to Hanuth (*ʿAbod. Zar.* 8b; *Šabb.* 15a; *Sanh.* 41a; Jeremias 1969: 210; Eppstein 1964: 48). That momentous reform is naturally placed during the pontificate of Caiaphas, and Eppstein suggests that another innovation should also be attributed to him: the permission for vendors of offerings to set up shop within the precincts of the temple (Eppstein 1964: 55). Eppstein's elaborate reconstruction of a struggle for power between Caiaphas and the "Sanhedrin" (itself a problematic designation) is a tissue of speculation, but he has pointed to what may have been a crucial issue between Caiaphas and Jesus. Within the Gospels, Jesus' expulsion of such vendors and money-changers from the temple is a pivotal event (Matt 21:12–13; Mark 11:15–17; Luke 19:45–46; John 2:13–17). The money-changers are easily presented as villains, but the fact is they served a useful purpose, in that Roman coin, the currency of oppression, was scarcely apposite to achieve atonement. The ancient Tyrean shekel was used instead, and the rate of exchange appears to have been controlled (Eppstein 1964: 43, n.10; *Šeqal.* 1.6, 7). Eppstein suggests that the tables of exchange were knocked over by Jesus in the melee concerning the vendors (Eppstein 1964: 57). That anything accidental or inadvertent can have taken place with furniture as massive as was used in the temple is quite implausible (*Šeqal.* 2.1; 6.5). More probably, the quotation from Jer 7:11 led to the reference to money-changers, whose existence Jesus (or any other Jew of the period) would have taken for granted (*Šeqal.* 1.3). What does stand out as an oddity, however, is that the vendors of animals are placed at the site of the temple instead of at Hanuth.

Naturally, the possibility must be faced, that the reference to both the money-changers and the vendors is the result of a misreading of sacrificial arrangements by Christians who had lost touch with their Judaic heritage. On such an understanding, reflection upon Jer 7:11 alone produced the story as we can read it today in the Synoptics. The fatal flaw in that reconstruction is that Jer 7:11 alone is not what is ascribed to Jesus: rather, a mixed citation of Isa 56:7 and Jer 7:11 is attributed to him. A mixing of scriptural elements in that manner is characteristic of Jesus, not of those who shaped the tradition after him (Chilton 1984). It is theoretically possible that a mixed citation, correctly attributed to Jesus, was then attached arbitrarily to the narrative of the vendors, as it was to that of the money-changers. But the fact is that the vendors appear in the best witnesses of Luke 19:45, without a mention of the money-changers, so that the former appear a more stable element in the narrative than the latter. Moreover, the scriptural citation in John 2:17 (Ps 69:9) is quite unlike the Synoptic allusion (and is not attributed to Jesus), so that the story of Jesus' occupation of the temple does not appear to be a simple expansion of a favorite text into the form of a narrative. As a matter of fact, Jesus would by no means be unique among rabbis in objecting to commercial arrangements related to the cult; Simeon ben Gamaliel is said to have intervened in the matter of pricing doves (*Ker.* 1.7). More generally, complaints of high priestly rapacity are found in *Pesaḥ.* 57a. Even Vitellius, at the time he restored custody of vestments to the temple, also remitted certain taxes; a criticism of financial arrangements during the period of Pilate and Caiaphas may have been implicit in his action (*Ant* 18.4.3). On balance, it would appear that Caiaphas did engineer the installation of vendors in the temple, that Jesus reacted with force, and that the collision of the two was finally adjudicated by Pilate, Caiaphas' protector (Chilton 1984: 18).

Bibliography

Catchpole, D. R. 1971. *The Trial of Jesus.* SPB 12. Leiden.

Chilton, B. D. 1984. *A Galilean Rabbi and His Bible.* GNS 8. Wilmington.

Eppstein, V. 1964. The Historicity of the Gospel Account of the Cleansing of the Temple. *ZNW* 55: 42–58.

Jeremias, J. 1969. *Jerusalem in the Time of Jesus.* Trans. F. H. and C. H. Cave. London.

BRUCE CHILTON

CAIN (PERSON) [Heb *qayin*]. Son of Adam and Eve and father of Enoch (Gen 4:1, 17). Cain appears in Genesis 4 as the murderer of his brother Abel and as the progenitor of a line credited with the initiation of various aspects of culture. The name recurs in the oracle of Balaam at Num 24:22 in a difficult text which associates Cain (*qyn*) with the Kenites (*qyny*). Later references to Cain focus upon him as the murderer of Abel (4 Macc 18:11; 1 John 3:12) or as the one whose sacrifice was not as good as his brother's (Heb 11:4). Jude 11 pronounces judgment upon those who follow the way of Cain. In conjunction with Balaam and Korah, the way of Cain appears to represent an attitude of rebellion against God and the chosen ones of God. In line with other examples of Cain in postbiblical accounts, it may suggest the teaching of others to sin (Bauckham *Jude, 2 Peter* WBC, 79–81; Watson 1988: 59).

The derivation for the name of Cain in Gen 4:1 is the statement by Eve, "I have acquired (*qānîtî*) a man with/from (*ʾet*) Yahweh." A difficulty lies in how to understand the *ʾet,* which regularly serves as a sign of the direct object. On the basis of similar usage of the preposition *itti* in Akk personal names, Borger (1959) argues for a meaning of "from." Claims for divine paternity for Cain (Gordon 1988: 154–55) are not explicit in the present text. Nor do comparative studies prove a divine maternity (Kikawada 1971: 35–37). The association of the name Cain with the root *qnh,* "to create" and "to acquire," leaves open two interpretations for the phrase; either Eve is acknowledging God at work through her in creation (or proudly claiming her own creative act [Cassuto 1961: 201; Westermann *Genesis 1–11* BKAT, 395]) or she is recognizing God as the ultimate source of Cain (Wenham *Genesis* WBC, 102). The verbal root *qnh* associates 4:1 with the genealogy of Cain in 4:17–24. In v 20 Jabal is described as the father of *miqneh* (RSV "[those who have] cattle"), which has a root similar to that of Cain. Cain reappears in the last-named figure of his line, Tubal-Cain. Thematically there is also a connection. Cain and his line create (cities, music, tools, and weapons) and acquire (property, wives, and the fruits of vengeance).

The name of Cain has its etymology in a root, *qyn,* which does not appear other than in proper names and gentilics in biblical Hebrew. A similarly spelled root occurs in South Arabian personal, clan, and tribal names (Beeston et al. 1982: 112; *DOSA,* 454) as early as the 5th century B.C.E. (Ephʿal 1982: 194, 211, 212, 226, 227). A *qyn* root occurs in later Aramaic and Arabic with the meaning of "smith." Furthermore, a similar root appears in the gentilic with which the Balaam oracle associates the name Cain, i.e., the Kenites (Num 24:21–22). These people appear in the biblical text as smiths associated with the desert area of Israel's wanderings. See KENITES. A second etymology for the name may be found in the Hebrew *qînâ,* "song." This has the advantage of appearing in biblical Hebrew but lacks examples of a *qatil* noun formation such as the name Cain possesses. Both interpretations relate 4:1 to the genealogy of 4:17–24. If the former is followed, compare Tubal-Cain, the last-mentioned figure in the line of Cain. He not only possesses Cain's name but also is described as a smith. For the "song" derivation, compare the figure of Naamah in Cain's genealogy. In Ugaritic her name may mean "song." Recent examinations of the line of Cain have led to other connections with the region of the Kenites (Sawyer 1986).

The narrative of Cain and Abel is sandwiched between the naming of Cain and the genealogy of this figure. It also has literary connections with the preceding narratives of chaps 2 and 3 (Hauser 1980). For example, v 16 speaks of the Garden of Eden, mentioned in chap 3. Though brief and clear in its overall plot, the narrative of Cain and Abel bristles with problems. Why was Abel's offering preferred? How did God make known the preference? What is the meaning of the counsel God gave to Cain? What did Cain and Abel say to one another? What is the mark given to Cain? What is the reason behind the story?

As to the preference of Abel's offering before Cain's, see ABEL. The text is silent as to how God made known this preference for Abel's offering. The same is true concerning the conversation of the two brothers, though this has not prevented the ancient versions from filling in this and other "gaps" (*EncMiqr* 7: 119–24). The meaning of the counsel which God gave to Cain hinges on the text of v 7. Westermann's negative assessment of a corrupt text follows other modern commentators, but it is not the only solution (*Genesis 1–11* BKAT, 406–10). The word *śʾt* has been interpreted as "forgiveness," "happiness," and "erect in posture" (Wenham, *Genesis* WBC, 105). The first two seem more likely, given the context. They would then contrast with Cain's fallen countenance in v 6 (Castellino 1960: 443). The word *rōbēṣ* seems to suggest the posture of sin "crouching at the door." However, the Akkadian demon *rābiṣu* may also be intended; and a noun would solve the gender incongruence with the preceding feminine *ḥṭʾt*, "sin." Alternatively, Driver (1946: 158) suggests reading *ḥṭʾt trbṣ*, "sin will crouch," with two *taws* expressed by a single one in an originally continuous Hebrew text without word divisions. Driver goes on to repoint the final phrase as a passive: "And so you shall be ruled by it," (*wĕʾattâ timmešel-bāh*), rather than accepting it as it is and understanding an adversative *waw*, "*but yet* you may/should rule over it." Perhaps, as Huffmon (1985) has suggested, the problem lies in the failure of Cain to investigate the reason for God's rejection of his sacrifice. The sign (*ʾôt*) given to Cain after the murder is not specified, but the narrator intends some means to make public the punishment due to anyone who kills the murderer.

The purpose of the story in its present context remains a matter of dispute. The traditional interpretations have found here a moral tale with lessons to be learned about the consequences of jealousy and anger. Historical approaches have identified a sociological struggle between nomadic shepherds (Abel) and settled farmers (Cain), or they have found an etiology for smiths who travel with nomads, such as the Kenites. Within the present context, the narrative serves to explain the rejection of Cain the firstborn from continuing the line of promise. His own line ends with v 24. It thus prepares the background for the birth of Seth and the continuation of his line. Finally, it introduces the crime of murder, a subject taken up by Lamech and others, but not explicitly forbidden until Gen 9:6.

Bibliography

Beeston, A. F. L., et al. 1982. *Sabaic Dictionary (English-French-Arabic)*. Beirut and Louvain-la-Neuve.

Borger, R. 1959. Gen. iv 1. VT 9: 85–86.

Cassuto, U. 1961. *A Commentary on the Book of Genesis*. Part 1. Trans. I. Abrahams. Jerusalem.

Castellino, G. R. 1960. Genesis IV 7. VT 10: 442–45.

Driver, G. R. 1946. Theological and Philological Problems in the Old Testament. *JTS* 47: 156–66.

Ephʿal, I. 1982. *The Ancient Arabs*. Jerusalem and Leiden.

Gordon, C. H. 1988. Notes on Proper Names in the Ebla Tablets. Pp. 153–58 in *Eblaite Personal Names and Semitic Name-Giving*, ed. A. Archi. Rome.

Hauser, A. J. 1980. Linguistic and Thematic Links between Genesis 4:1–16 and Genesis 2–3. *JETS* 23: 297–305.

Huffmon, H. B. 1985. Cain, the Arrogant Sufferer. Pp. 109–13 in *Biblical and Related Studies Presented to Samuel Iwry*, ed. A. Kort and S. Morschauser. Winona Lake, IN.

Kikawada, I. M. 1971. Two Notes on Eve. *JBL* 91: 33–37.

Sawyer, J. F. A. 1986. Cain and Hephaestus. Possible Relics of Metalworking Traditions in Genesis 4. *Abr-Nahrain* 24: 155–66.

Watson, D. F. 1988. *Invention, Arrangement, and Style: Rhetorical Criticism of Jude and 2 Peter*. SBLDS 104. Atlanta.

RICHARD S. HESS

CAINAN (PERSON) [Gk *Kainam*]. Name of two persons in the NT. The form "Cainan" is a Gk transliteration of the Heb *qênān*. See KENAN.

1. Appears in Luke's genealogy of Jesus as the son of Enos and the great-grandson of Adam (3:37–38). The name occurs in the MT of Gen 5:9–14 and 1 Chr 1:2.

2. Occurs in Luke's genealogy of Jesus as the son of Arphaxad and the father of Shelah (3:35–36). This Cainan is often called the second Cainan. The name appears in the genealogy of Shem in the LXX of Gen 10:24 and 11:12 and in Codex Alexandrinus of 1 Chr 1:18, but not in the MT or in P^{75} and Codex Bezae. The presence of the second Cainan in Luke's genealogy of Jesus suggests that the evangelist used the LXX for this section instead of the MT.

VIRGIL R. L. FRY

CAIRO GENIZAH. See DAMASCUS RULE (CD).

CALAH (PLACE) [Heb *kālaḥ*]. In Gen 10:11–12 it is narrated that Nimrod, who was "a mighty hunter," began his kingdom at Babel (Babylonia) and then went into Assyria where he built cities, among them Nineveh and Calah. This is the only specific reference in the Bible to one of the four great cities of ancient Assyria. Nevertheless, because of this greatness and because Assyrian armies marched from Calah against the kingdoms of Israel and Judah, a brief description and history of Calah are essential. For a fuller description, see MESOPOTAMIA, HISTORY OF (HISTORY AND CULTURE OF ASSYRIA).

The ancient site of Calah was strategically located from an economic and military point of view. It was on the E bank of the Tigris just N of the point where the Upper Zab River flows into the Tigris. From a military point of view this meant that Calah was protected on all but the N flank. From an economic point of view, the site was in the very center of the Assyrian heartland, a region where a rich agricultural economy flourished.

The biblical association of Nimrod with the city Calah has been preserved until modern times in the sense that the medieval and modern name of the site is Nimrud. While native tradition preserved in Arabic literature never forgot the correct identification of the ancient site Calah, it was only in the 19th century that Europeans recognized where the city had been. In fact there was some confusion among Europeans, and Sir Austen Henry Layard, the first excavator of Nimrud, actually thought the site was the location of Nineveh. This error was eventually corrected and his startling discoveries were then viewed in their proper historical context. Since Layard's time, various archaeological expeditions, both Iraqi and foreign, have excavated at this site. Among these was the British expedition led by Sir Max Mallowan during the 1950s and 1960s. Many of the artifacts discovered were removed to the British Museum in London and the museum in Mosul

(Nineveh) but there are still numerous Assyrian stone reliefs to be seen in a museum at the site itself. Of the four great cities of Assyria, the others were ASSHUR, NINEVEH, and ARBELA. In contrast to the other three, Calah was of no significance in the 3d and 2d millennium B.C. It was singled out for importance only in the 9th century B.C. when Assurnasirpal II chose it as his capital. Assurnasirpal totally transformed the insignificant village into a metropolis which was suitable to be the center of the empire he created. The chief god of Calah was Ninurta, the god of war, and Assurnasirpal had an enormous temple and ziggurrat (a temple tower) erected in this god's honor. He also built a splendid palace, the so-called Northwest Palace, for his residence. Many other temples were erected and a huge wall surrounded the city for defense. The waters of the Upper Zab River were partially diverted by an intricate aqueduct in order to provide irrigation inside the walls.

The extensive building program of Assurnasirpal II was continued by his immediate successors and Calah remained the administrative center of Assyria until about 700 B.C. At that time other cities were chosen as capitals, and eventually Nineveh became the chief city. When the Assyrian Empire fell at the end of the 7th century B.C., the site of Calah was abandoned and there has been no major settlement there ever since. See *RLA* 5: 303–23.

Bibliography

Mallowan, M. E. L. 1966. *Nimrud and Its Remains.* 2 vols. London.
———. 1978. *The Nimrud Ivories.* London.
Reade, J. E. 1982. Nimrud. Pp. 99–112 in *Fifty Years of Mesopotamian Discovery,* ed. J. Curtis. London.

A. KIRK GRAYSON

CALAMOLALUS (PERSON) [Gk *Kalamōlalos*]. The name of the ancestor of a family which returned from Babylon with Zerubbabel; included in the RSV as a marginal reading for "of the other Elam" (*kalamō allou*; 1 Esdr 5:22). The identification of Calamolalus is further complicated by the variant Gk text (B) *kalamōkalos,* and is commonly considered a textual corruption. Myers (*1 and 2 Esdras* AB, 65), with the RSV, renders it as "the other Elam" and considers it parallel to Ezra 2:31 and Neh 7:34. However, Turner (*IDB* 1: 482) describes it as a corrupt combination of "Lod and Hadid" (Ezra 2:33 = Neh 7:37).

MICHAEL DAVID MCGEHEE

CALAMUS. See PERFUMES AND SPICES.

CALCOL (PERSON) [Heb *kalkōl*]. A man from Judah, he was the son of Zerah, whom Tamar conceived by her father-in-law Judah (1 Chr 2:4, 6). In 1 Kgs 5:11—Eng 4:31, Calcol is identified as one of the sons of Mahol. Mahol should not be understood as a proper name but, as Albright (*ARI,* 123) and de Vaux (*AncIsr,* 382) have suggested, the title of a guild of musicians, "sons of the choir." See DARA.

Calcol was one of the four wise men whom Solomon excelled in wisdom. According to Albright (*ARI,* 123) the name Calcol appears as *Kulkul* in several inscribed ivories found at Megiddo. According to these inscriptions, written in Egyptian hieroglyphs, which have been dated in the 13th century B.C., *Kulkul* was the name of a female singer of the god Ptah in the Canaanite city of Aijalon (Loud 1939: 11–13). According to Albright, Calcol was the name of a flower or plant. In the ANE that name was applied to musicians.

Bibliography

Loud, G. 1939. *The Megiddo Ivories.* Chicago.

CLAUDE F. MARIOTTINI

CALEB (PERSON) [Heb *kālēb*]. Var. CHELUBAI. CALEBITES. It is possible to distinguish three people with this name, plus one variant form in the name Chelubai (Heb *kelûbāy*). Any discussion of the name Caleb and its variant form must of necessity also entail an investigation of the Calebites, or descendants of Caleb. This gentilic usage is quite important in sorting out the geographical location and genealogical identification of individuals and groups so named; however, these issues are one step removed from an examination of the name itself.

Caleb has most commonly been treated as a form of the root *klb,* "dog," which occurs in virtually every ANE language (*TWAT* 4: 158; Beltz 1974: 116–34). Traditionally, complimentary and uncomplimentary connotations are associated with the literal meaning of Heb *keleb,* "dog." On the one hand meanings like "raving dog" (*IPN,* 230), "dog-faced baboon" (Thomas 1960: 419–23), "dead dog," and the like, all of which are attested in extrabiblical sources (*TWAT* 4: 157–62; Thomas 1960: 410–14), express self-abasement or invective. In one biblical example, Hazael, doubting his own abilities, says to Elisha, "What is your servant, who is but a dog . . ." (2 Kgs 8:13). On the other hand, most scholars agree that Heb *keleb* is used in certain letters, hymns, etc., to express a servant's faithfulness, like that of a faithful watchdog (Thomas 1960: 424–27; *EncMiqr* 4: 106–10; Boling and Wright *Joshua* AB, 356–57). Margalith (1983) contends that these are not two different connotations of meaning for one term, but rather the distinctive meanings of two homonymous terms. Brunet (1985) challenges the traditional view that there are two connotations for the term and concludes that in biblical and nonbiblical occurrences "dog" and its synonyms are almost exclusively terms of self-abasement. Various theophoric names use the root *klb,* i.e., Phoen *klbʿlm,* "dog of the gods" (*PNPI,* 131, 331), and Akk *kalbi-ilsin* and *kalbi-il marduk* (Thomas 1960: 425; see also *TWAT* 4: 158–62). Therefore, the biblical name Caleb appears to be "an abbreviation of a name beginning with the element *kalb-*" (Albright 1941: 47, n.26) meaning lit. "dog," with the primary connotation of self-abasement, and probably also a secondary connotation of "faithful servant."

1. The son of Jephunneh and the representative of the tribe of Judah among the twelve spies sent out by Moses to reconnoiter the land of Canaan (Num 13:6). Caleb (alone in the so-called J source; Num 13:30), together with Joshua the son of Nun (in the so-called P source; Num 14:6), brought back a favorable report of the land and urged the people to go up and take it. In contrast to God prohibiting the people from entering the land because they rejected this recommendation, God singled out "my servant Caleb" and promised to bring him into the land where he had gone, and to give it to his descendants as a possession (Num 14:24; see also Num 26:65; 32:12; Deut 1:36). This promise set Caleb apart from all his peers, even Joshua, and it raises the issues of geographical location and genealogical identification of Caleb and the Calebites.

The land that came to be owned by Caleb, through apportionment (Josh 14:6–15; 15:13), force (Josh 15:14–19 = Judg 1:11–15), or a combination of the two means was associated with Hebron and Debir in S Palestine. 1 Sam 30:14 identifies part of this area as "the Negeb of Caleb." If we identify the cities and boundaries of the tribe of Judah it becomes obvious that the land owned by or associated with Caleb is located within Judah's borders (Josh 15:1–12, etc.; see *KHC,* 115–24, 372–97). Hebron is a key element in this association, in part because of its proximity to other Judahite cities, but in light of the centrality of the Davidic dynasty in the biblical tradition, it was as the first capital city of David that Hebron played an unquestionable and important role. (Note that Nabal, the first husband of David's wife Abigail, was a Calebite who lived in this region; 1 Sam 25:3.) When later tradition identified Hebron as one of Judah's levitical cities, it resolved the problem of Calebite ownership by specifying that the environs, and not the city itself, belonged to Caleb (Josh 21:12; 1 Chr 6:56).

The relationship between the Kenizzite clan of Calebites and its Judahite neighbors was mutually beneficial on political and economic grounds (see Beltz 1974: 64–70), and although the Calebites became part of the tribe of Judah within the Israelite tradition they retained their distinctiveness. Of course, geographical location is not the only basis upon which the Calebites were incorporated into this tradition; there was also a genealogical connection.

In 1 Chronicles several genealogies contain the name Caleb, and these reflect inconsistencies of lineage and raise questions in light of other biblical information about individuals named Caleb. First, Caleb the son of Jephunneh is only explicitly mentioned in a genealogy of sons of Kenaz, or the Kenizzites (1 Chr 4:13–15), which is set within a section concerning descendants of Perez. The daughter of this Caleb is named elsewhere as Achsah (Josh 15:16–17 = Judg 1:12–13), while an Achsah is listed as the daughter of Caleb the son of Hezron, and a grandson of Perez (1 Chr 2:49). Second, the MT never identifies the wife of Caleb the son of Jephunneh. However, Caleb the son of Hezron has several wives and concubines, and his descendants are not easily placed in his genealogy (1 Chr 2:18–24, 42–55). One identifiable descendant, Bezalel (1 Chr 2:20), a great-grandson of Caleb the son of Hezron, was a contemporary of Moses (Exod 31:2; 35:30) and therefore cannot be the great-grandson of Caleb the son of Jephunneh. Third, a Caleb the son of Hur can be identified according to the MT of 1 Chr 2:50, but according to his genealogy (1 Chr 2:42–55), this Caleb appears to be his own grandfather. Fourth, the names of some of Caleb's descendants are place names (i.e., Tekoa, Ziph, Madmannah, and Hebron), which complicates an attempt to understand the purpose of the genealogies (see Noth 1932). Williamson (*1 and 2 Chronicles* NCBC, 48–55) resolves these problems by assuming that the Chronicler pulled together most of the genealogies but was not concerned with the details of genealogical consistency. Rudolf (*Chronikbücher* HAT, 10–25), on the other hand, attributes the inconsistencies to later additions which disrupted the consistency of the Chronicler's composition. It is generally agreed that one section (1 Chr 2:42–50) derives from a tradition which predates the Chronicler, probably from the united monarchy or shortly thereafter (Williamson *1 and 2 Chronicles* NCBC, 55).

The key to resolving the tensions in these genealogies is the fact that Caleb is part of Judah's genealogy. Caleb the son of Jephunneh is a Kenizzite who gained special status through his deeds in the wilderness wandering and conquest stories. On the other hand, Caleb the son of Hezron plays a role only in the genealogies of Judah, and Bezalel the tabernacle builder seems to be the central character in his genealogy. The Chronicler does not attempt to relate Caleb the son of Jephunneh to Caleb the son of Hezron because neither of them is central to his purpose of establishing a royal and cultic origin in the tribe of Judah (Williamson *1 and 2 Chronicles* NCBC, 52). Caleb the Kenizzite is important, rather, because of things he did (Numbers 13–14; Josh 14:6–15) and associations he had (Josh 15:13–19 = Judg 1:11–15; Judg 3:9; see Boling *Judges* AB, 82) outside the Chronicler's framework, although these were not unknown to the Chronicler. Therefore, in addressing the questions raised above, Caleb the Kenizzite who appears in 1 Chr 4:15 within the lineage of Perez is to be identified with the individual so well known from the tradition of Calebites in S Palestine (Numbers 13–14; Joshua 14–15; Judges 1). To ask whether his daughter Achsah is the same as the daughter of Caleb the son of Hezron in 1 Chr 2:49 misses the point of the genealogy there. Furthermore, the complex genealogies of Caleb in 1 Chr 2:18–24, 42–55 serve to highlight the mix of parallel (i.e., a sequence of siblings) and hierarchical (i.e., parent followed by child) genealogies in this chapter. The chiastic structure of the sections of genealogies in 1 Chronicles 2, as discussed by Williamson (*1 and 2 Chronicles* NCBC, 49), focuses the reader's attention on the significance that the Hezron clan had within the tribe of Judah; moreover, this follows the pattern of treating the sons in reverse order as established in 1 Chr 1:5–23, 28–34. Finally, by listing descendants of Caleb who have names associated with geographical locations, the Chronicler reveals both the antiquity of his source material and the close association of persons with places (Noth 1932; see also *EJ* 3: 41–42).

This introduces the final issue of the function of genealogies. According to Wilson (1977: 183), genealogies can be used to delineate social and political ties between two groups, and, in particular, to incorporate marginally affiliated clans into a central group. The genealogy of Caleb is related in this way to the tribe of Judah (Yeivin 1971: 13–14) and was assimilated into the Israelite tribal system thereby (Johnson 1969: 6). Not only the individuals and groups of people but the places associated with them became part of the tribe. Thus, the genealogy provided a means for legitimizing social relations and for defining the geographical domain of the individuals or groups concerned.

It would appear that Caleb the son of Jephunneh is the name of a Kenizzite whose personal exploits became the tradition of the clan which took his name as patronym. This clan existed independently in S Palestine, but through political, economic, and religious ties it eventually became part of the tribe of Judah. Even within the larger Israelite tradition, the distinctive stories of the Calebites were retained into the postexilic period.

2. The son of Hezron and great-grandfather of Bezalel (1 Chr 2:18–20). A variant form of the name occurs in 1 Chr 2:9 as Chelubai (Heb *kelûbāy*), and the LXX interprets the form as *chaleb* and identifies this third son of Hezron with the Caleb who appears in the following verses. The identification is correct because the difference in spelling is a matter of an afformative (Heb *-ay*) which is common (*IPN,* 41), and both persons hold the same position in the genealogy of Hezron (1 Chr 2:9, 18, 42; see Beltz 1974: 38). According to Williamson (*1 and 2 Chronicles* NCBC, 51), the variance may support the view that the Chronicler constructed 1 Chr 2:9 to connect two originally independent sources (1 Chr 2:10–17, and 25–33, 42–50a). As noted above, Caleb is one of three sons of Hezron along with Jerahmeel and Ram, he appears only in this genealogy, and he serves to introduce Bezalel the tabernacle builder into the line of Judah (1 Chr 2:20). Interplay between this Caleb and the tradition surrounding Caleb No. 1 influenced the genealogies. Thus, the names of the region and towns in which the Calebite tribe originally lived came to be so closely identified with the name Caleb (i.e., the Negeb of Caleb) that the town names were included as descendants in the genealogy of this son of Hezron.

3. The son of Hur, according to the MT of 1 Chr 2:50. The textual ambiguity of this verse is correctly resolved in the RSV by reading the accentual pause as a period. Rather than reading with the MT, "These were the sons of Caleb, the son of Hur the firstborn of Ephrathah . . ." the first phrase is taken to summarize the preceding section (vv 42–49) and what follows introduces a new genealogy, ". . . These are the sons of Caleb. The son(s) of Hur the firstborn of Ephrathah . . ." Consequently, this individual should not be differentiated from the Caleb in 1 Chr 2:42 (see Caleb No. 2 above).

Bibliography

Albright, W. F. 1941. Two Letters from Ugarit (Ras Shamrah). *BASOR* 82: 43–49.

Beltz, W. 1974. *Die Kaleb-Traditionen im Alten Testament.* BWANT 5/18. Stuttgart.

Brunet, G. 1985. L'Hébreu Kèlèb. VT 35: 485–88.

Johnson, M. D. 1969. *The Purpose of Biblical Genealogies with Specific Reference to the Setting of the Genealogies of Jesus.* SNTSMS 8. Cambridge, MA.

Margalith, O. 1983. *KELEB:* Homonym or Metaphor? VT 33: 491–95.

Noth, M. 1932. Eine siedlungsgeographische Liste in 1. Chr. 2 und 4. *ZDPV* 55: 97–124.

Thomas, D. W. 1960. *Kelebh* 'Dog': Its Origin and Some Usages of It in the Old Testament. VT 10: 410–27.

Wilson, R. R. 1977. *Genealogy and History in the Biblical World.* YNER 7. New Haven.

Yeivin, Sh. 1971. *The Israelite Conquest of Canaan.* Uitgaven van het Nederlands Historisch-Archaeologisch Instituut te Istanbul 27. Istanbul.

Mark J. Fretz
Raphael I. Panitz

CALENDARS.

A calendar is a system for arranging and calculating the standard divisions of time (days, months, years, etc.). The term is also used to refer to schedules of events such as festivals. This entry consists of two articles, one surveying the use of calendars in the ANE and the other surveying ancient Israelite and early Jewish calendars.

ANCIENT NEAR EAST

A. Introduction

1. The Lunisolar Calendar. In most of the ancient Mediterranean, a civil calendar was developed to regulate the sacred and secular life of the state. The times for religious festivals, agricultural, fiscal, and legal activities were determined with reference to the natural intervals produced by the motion of the sun and the moon. This "lunisolar" calendar reckoned a year as the interval between successive returns of the seasons, usually beginning with spring. The month was defined as the interval between successive first appearances of the moon in its cyclical phases. The beginning of the lunar cycle is defined as the moment when, following the period of invisibility due to nearness to the sun, the lunar crescent appears again briefly on the western horizon just after sunset. The interval which constitutes the lunar month, also termed a lunation, varies in length from 29.26 to 29.80 days, and consequently is experienced as a period never less than 29 days or more than 30 days. The day, in accordance with the use of lunations, was reckoned as the interval between successive sunsets.

The lunar month was taken uniformly throughout the ANE and Mediterranean (by Sumerians, Babylonians, Assyrians, Hebrews, Arabs, and Greeks) to begin with the sighting of the first visible lunar crescent. Only the Egyptians (and later the Romans) did not conform, but instead disregarded the irregular natural time indications in favor of regular arbitrary measures, such as the fixed 30-day month or the 365-day year (see D).

2. Intercalation and the Babylonian 19-Year Cycle. Because the motions of sun and moon are not uniform with respect to one another, a lunisolar calendar, which by definition reckons months by the moon and years by the seasons, faces the problem of maintaining synchrony between the 12 lunar months and the solar year. The effect is that 12 lunations do not divide up the solar year evenly, nor do solar days divide the lunar month into equal parts. Twelve lunar months of an average 29½-day length is 354 days, which is about 11 days less than the average length of the solar year (= 365.2492, or 365¼ days). If no adjustment is made to compensate for the asynchrony, the months will fall 11 days behind each year, and after 3 years the sequence of months will be fully one month out of step with the season or with the activity designated to occur in a particular month, such as the barley or date harvest, or sheep shearing (discussion of seasonal activities reflected in month names may be found in Landsberger 1949: 260–65). The problem would be eminently perceptible, since after only 32½ years a given month would pass through the entire cycle of seasons (as it did in the Middle Assyrian calendar until the time of Tiglath-pileser I; see Weidner 1935–36: 28–29).

To ensure stability in the correspondence between specific months and times of the year, whether defined agriculturally, religiously, or fiscally, an extra "intercalary" thirteenth month was added to the year, not regularly, but whenever necessary to maintain the proper "place" of a month within the solar year. In Mesopotamia, an extra sixth month (ITI.KIN.DIRI = *Ulūlu arkû*) or twelfth month (ITI.ŠE.DIRI = *Addaru arkû*) was intercalated, one or the other being preferred in various periods. Parker and Dubberstein (1942: 3) note that preference for a given intercalary month shifted from *Ulūlu* to *Addaru,* and suggest an early tradition placing the New Year in *Tašrītu* as an underlying reason. Intercalary *Nisannu* (ITI.BARA$_2$.MIN.KAM) is occasionally attested, albeit rarely in economic texts (MUL.APIN 2.18; see also Landsberger 1915: 101; Langdon 1935: 10 and 46–47).

Intercalations were effected by royal decree. Documents from the reigns of Hammurapi, Nabonidus, Cyrus, and Cambyses attest to the procedure (Bickerman 1980: 22; *RLA* 5: 289; YOS 3: 15 and 115, and 196, and further references for intercalary years in the reigns of Samsuiluna and Ammiṣaduqa). The ad hoc intercalation of months represented by the royal letters was the standard procedure for controlling the calendar throughout the ANE from approximately the 3d millennium B.C. until about the middle of the 1st (certainly until 525 B.C.).

Evidence from the 7th century B.C. shows that various procedures were developed for determining in advance whether a given year would be normal (*ešret* or *kīnat,* containing 12 lunar months) or intercalary (*ezbet* or *atrat,* containing 13 lunar months). One such procedure was based on the observation of the relation between the longitudes of the moon and the Pleiades throughout the year. The conjunction of moon and Pleiades (when they occupy the same position in the sky) on particular dates through the year indicated a normal year, while their "separation" (*napalsuhu*) indicated a leap year. Leap years attested in actual documents, however, indicate that the Pleiades intercalation rules were probably not implemented (Hunger and Reiner 1975). In the astronomical series MUL.APIN (Tablet 2.ii.1–6), other rules for predicting leap years using select fixed stars (Sirius, Arcturus, Pleiades) are given. Since the month in which certain fixed stars or constellations had their heliacal rising was known (e.g., Pleiades became visible on the first day of the second month, Aiaru—MUL.APIN 1.ii.38), the delayed appearance of the Pleiades in the third month instead of the second (MUL.APIN 2.Gap A.10–11) signaled the need to intercalate the year in question.

A mathematical scheme producing a regular intercalary cycle was finally introduced into the Babylonian calendar during the Achaemenid period, sometime after 500 B.C. This cycle was based on the good correspondence between the number of days in 19 solar years and 235 lunar months. When and how the nineteen-year cycle was recognized is not precisely known, although on the basis of dated documents from the reign of Artaxerxes II it clearly became the official rule from 380 B.C. Indeed, the exceptions to the rule during the preceding century, going back to 497 B.C. in the reign of Darius I, are rare (a mere two exceptions; see Neugebauer 1975: 354–55). On this basis it is argued that the establishment of the 19-year cycle is to be dated to the 5th century (see Parker and Dubberstein 1942: 1 for the possibility that it was a discovery of the reign of Nabonassar 747 B.C., and Kugler 1924: 362–71; 422–30 contra this date; Neugebauer 1975: 354–57). From 380 B.C. on, the 19-year cycle determined the intercalation of seven months every 19 years ($19^{yr} \times 12^{m} + 7^{m} = 235^{m}$) spaced at conveniently fixed intervals, namely in years 1, 4, 7, 9, 12, 15, and 18. All intercalary years except year 18 had an extra twelfth month (*Addaru arkû*). The eighteenth year in the cycle had an extra sixth month (*Ulūlu arkû*). The 19-year cycle of intercalation, begun under the Achaemenids, remained standard for the succeeding Seleucid and Arsacid periods to the end of the cuneiform tradition.

B. The Babylonian Calendar

The Babylonian calendar was based on the three natural time intervals, the solar year (ultimately defined as the period of the return of the sun to the same fixed star, hence the sidereal year), the lunar month (from one new moon to another, defined above, A.1.), and the solar day (from one sunset to another). Further discussion of each calendaric unit follows.

1. The Year (Akk *šattu*). The Babylonian year began in the spring, with the month *Nisannu* (= March/April in the Julian calendar), and the first of the year fell approximately around the vernal equinox, but actually varied widely. During the Neo-Babylonian period (between years 626–536 B.C.), the first of *Nisannu* could fall between the 11th of March and 26th of April, according to the tables of Parker and Dubberstein (1942). Even after the institution of the 19-year cycle, the New Year could still vary within a 27-day range, but averaged about 14 days following vernal equinox (Kugler 1924: 333–34; *RLA* 5: 298–99).

Evidence is lacking from Babylonian administrative or economic documents for a civil year beginning in *Tašrītu,* whose name means "beginning" (see C.). *Tašrītu,* month 7 in the Babylonian calendar, is generally the month of the autumnal equinox. The possibility of a cultic New Year in *Tašrītu,* based on the performance of an *akītu* festival during that month (Thureau-Dangin 1921: 87; AO.6459 and 6465 contain the New Year's ritual for *Tašrītu,* performed in Uruk), has found further support in letters from the Neo-Assyrian period (Parpola 1970, no. 190 r.2–10; 287 r.2–6; *ABL* 951 r.2; Thompson 1900, no. 16:5). The early preference for intercalary *Ulūlu*'s in the Babylonian calendar (noted by Parker and Dubberstein 1942: 3) is more plausibly explained by such a cultic autumn New Year, although this remains to be finally confirmed or refuted.

Before the articulation of a solar theory in the mathematical astronomy of the late Babylonian period, no value for the length of a year in days can be cited. As a consequence of the lunisolar character of the calendar, the length of the Babylonian civil year varied from year to year, depending on whether an extra lunar month was intercalated. The unit "year" was so defined for all periods of Mesopotamian history. With the development of mathematical astronomy and the derivation of number periods for cyclical phenomena (such as the return of the sun to a particular fixed star), diverse values for the length of the year are seen to underlie various computations (Neugebauer 1975: 528–29). For example, Seleucid astronomical texts from Uruk listing computed solar longitudes on consecutive dates (Neugebauer 1955, nos. 185, 186, 187) use as the value for the mean solar progress $0;59,9^{o/day}$. This produces a year of about $6,5;10,23^d$ (Neugebauer 1975: 529). Such a year length ($6,5;10^d$) has been identified in a procedure text from Babylon (Sachs and Neugebauer 1956: 132:3′ and 4′). Neugebauer 1955, no. 210 sec. 3:11–12 defines the year in terms of an 18-year solar cycle: [1,4]9,34,25,27,18 UD.MEŠ *šá* 18 MU *šá* ^{d}*Šamaš* [*ana* KI-*š*]*ú* GUR *ina* 18 BAL.MEŠ "[1,4]9,34;25,27,18 days of 18 years of the sun, returning [to] its [longitude] in 18 rotations," meaning returns of the sun to the same fixed star (text quoted according to Neugebauer 1955: 272). This value produces a year length of 6,5;14,44,51 days. These and other year lengths (e.g., 6,5;15,36) are found as the periods of functions in Babylonian astronomy. Neugebauer has emphasized (1975: 528–29) that all the "years" underlying Babylonian astronomical computations refer to the so-called sidereal year, as no distinction was yet made between sidereal, tropical, and anomalistic years. Such distinctions presuppose recognition of precession, which has been conclusively shown to lie outside the knowledge of Babylonian astronomy.

2. The Month (Akk *arhu*). Although the Sum logogram ITI, "month," is found in archaic texts from Šuruppak and from Ur, month names do not appear until the ED texts of Lagaš, Adab, and Nippur (*RLA* 5: 299–300; Langdon 1935: 157–58). The month names of the Ur III calendar at Nippur were eventually adopted as standard for all of Babylonia by the early OB (Isin-Larsa) and OB periods. Before this standardization, however, many Sumerian city-states had their own month name systems (Schneider 1936: 80–107). The following are the names that became standard: (1) BARA_2.ZAG.GAR, (2) GU_4.SI.SÁ, (3) SIG_4.GA, (4) ŠU.NUMUN, (5) NE.NE.GAR.RA, (6) KIN.^{d}INNIN, (7) DU_6.KÙ, (8) APIN.DU_8.A, (9) GAN.GAN.E, (10) AB.È, (11) ZÍZ.A, (12) ŠE.KIN.KUD. These Nippur months became the logographic writings for the following Babylonian month names: (1) *Nisannu,* (2) *Aiaru,* (3) *Simanu,* (4) *Duʾūzu,* (5) *Abu,* (6) *Ulūlu,* (7) *Tašrītu,* (8) *Arahsamna,* (9) *Kislīmu,* (10) *Ṭebētu,* (11) *Šabaṭu,* (12) *Addaru.* In other areas of Mesopotamia (e.g., Diyala region, Chagar Bazar, Mari, and Assyria) different names were used, for which, see *RLA* 5: 301–2.

The Babylonian month seems to have been divided, for both fiscal and cultic purposes, into halves (designated as *šapattu* [written UD.15.KAM] *mahrītu* "first 15th day" and *šapattu arkītu* "second 15th day"), and into 7-day units, attested primarily in menologies and celestial omen texts, which make use of a schematic 30-day month (Langdon 1935: 83–84; 90–91).

The length of the true lunar month varied between 29 and 30 days, depending on the (variable) length of the period of the moon's invisibility due to its nearness to the sun. The determination, in advance, of when a month will have 29 or 30 days is a complicated problem solved only in the Seleucid-period Babylonian mathematical astronomy. To predict when the new crescent moon would again appear depended not only on an ability to take into account the motion of the sun and the moon, but also on the recognition of factors affecting visibility, such as the seasonal variation in inclination of the ecliptic to the horizon.

3. The Day (Akk *ūmu*). Several ways of dividing the day may be identified in ancient Mesopotamia, each designed in response to a particular need. For astronomical computation with respect to the period from one sunset to the next, 12 equal intervals of 30° duration (or 120 minutes of time) termed *bēru,* "double-hour," were used. For nonmathematical time reckoning, the periods of daylight and night were divided into 12 intervals termed *simanu.* These were not of equal duration throughout the year but varied seasonally, and so are the equivalent of the "seasonal hours" representing 1⁄12 of the actual period of daylight (or night) attested elsewhere in the ancient world (Rochberg-Halton fc.). Late Babylonian nonmathematical astronomical texts established another system which expressed time as the number of time degrees (UŠ, sometime *bēru* and UŠ) with respect to four divisions of the day that made use of sunset and sunrise as fixed points of reference. Thus the number of UŠ were counted within the four periods (1) from sunset to midnight (GE_6 GIN), (2) from midnight to sunrise (GE_6 *ana* ZALÁG), (3) from sunrise to noon (ME NIM-*a*), and (4) from noon to sunset (*ana* ŠÚ ŠAMAŠ) (Neugebauer and Sachs 1967: 212–14; for the strictly astronomical midnight epoch, see Neugebauer 1955: 79–80).

The determination of the length of daylight through the year was a prominent part of the development both of the calendar and of astronomy. In the early period, before the 5th century B.C., the variation in the length of daylight was interpreted schematically and as a calendaric problem. The ratio of longest to shortest day was determined to be 2:1 (MUL.APIN 2.107, 111, 117, 121). The equinoxes and solstices were placed in schematic fashion in the middle of months 1, 4, 7, and 10, assuming perfect symmetry between the length of the seasons as well as the lengths of days. In fact, however, no symmetry exists in the lengths of the seasons or in the lengths of day and night. The inequality of the seasons due to the irregularity in the sun's motion through the year was not taken into account until the Hellenistic period, at which point the length of daylight was perceived as a function of the sun's longitude and connected with the rising times of the zodiac. The values for daylight length found in the mathematical ephemerides ("Column C"; see Neugebauer 1955: 47) and in the procedure texts (Neugebauer 1955: 187) show the ratio 3:2 for longest to shortest day, which is a useful approximation for the geographical latitude of Babylon (about 32½°).

C. The Assyrian Calendar

The 2d-millennium Assyrian calendar has been reconstructed on the basis of texts from the reign of Šamši-

Adad I (Larsen 1974: 16–17) as well as from the somewhat later archives from Kültepe (Larsen 1976: 192–93). In both periods, the New Year began in the autumn, in Šamši-Adad's time earlier in autumn than in the OA texts from Kültepe level II (=1920–1840 B.C.; see *RLA* 5:299). Fall New Year was also established in the Ebla calendar (Pettinato 1974–77: 33–35). Although no intercalary month is attested in the Old Assyrian calendar, the naming of the year-eponym, by which "solar" years were identified, occurred always at the same time of year. In other words, the solar eponym-year was coordinated with the lunar months (for the exception to this in texts from Kültepe Ib, see Larsen 1976: 53, n. 18). The lack of intercalation and the consequent slipping of the seasons backward through the months in the Middle Assyrian lunar calendar has already been mentioned (above, A; Weidner 1935–36: 27–29). This changed with the Assyrian adoption of the Babylonian calendar in the 1st millennium.

An additional calendaric device was employed in the Old Assyrian calendar. This was the "week"-eponymy, in which the *hamuštum* period of 5 days was also designated by the names of officials. The *hamuštum* system is widely attested in OA commercial documents and is distinctive for the Assyrian calendar. Documents were dated by means of *hamuštum,* month, and year (=eponymy; see Larsen 1976: 354–65 with many references).

D. The Egyptian Calendar

Two developments of major importance in the history of the calendar are contributions from Egypt. These are the Egyptian civil year of 365 days (Parker 1950: 51–56) and the 24-hour division of the day (Neugebauer and Parker 1960: 116–21). The Egyptian civil year consisted of twelve 30-day months with 5 extra "epagomenal" days added at the end of each year. Because the 30-day month was divided into three 10-day "decades," the year contained 36 such decades, plus the 5 epagomenal days. The three seasons of the Egyptian year, each four months long, were defined agriculturally, as is clear from their names: *ʾḫt,* "inundation (of the Nile)"; *prt,* "emergence," which was the season for farming; and *šmw,* "dryness." As such, the Egyptian calendar was practical and constant, needing no intercalation of months (various lunar and cultic calendars were also used, for which, see Parker 1950: 13–50; Parker 1970; also Bickerman 1980: 41 with references).

The Egyptian civil calendar is unique in the ANE for its independence from the complicated astronomical problems endemic to the lunisolar calendars. In establishing a fixed unit for measuring time, the constant 365-day Egyptian civil year had a great advantage over the other ancient calendar years in application to astronomy. Its potential for use in astronomy, however, was not realized until the Hellenistic Greek astronomers adopted this calendar as the standard basis for computing astronomical tables. In this astronomical capacity, the Egyptian calendar remained in use during both the Middle Ages and the Renaissance.

The 24-hour division of the day derives ultimately from the Egyptian practice of counting "hours" at night on the basis of the rising of certain stars called by the Greek term "decan(s)." Around 2400 B.C., Egyptians began to tell time at night by the rising of decanal stars. Originally the decans were defined by their relationship to the 36 decades of the Egyptian civil year, as each successive decade would bring the heliacal rising (first rising of a star just before sunrise after its period of invisibility) of a new decan. The decans indicated the time of night by their risings or, later, by their transits (crossing of the meridian) at 12 intervals during the night. Evidence for the use of rising stars to indicate night hours comes from 12 extant star clocks, which are diagonal diagrams of stars on the inside of coffin lids from the 9th to the 12th Dynasties (Neugebauer and Parker 1960). Although no traces remain of decans in modern astronomy, they continued to play a role in later Hellenistic and medieval astrology, defined as thirds of zodiacal signs (=10° segments of the ecliptic). The 12 intervals between the consecutive rising of one decan and the next, counted from sunset to sunrise, were a direct consequence of the 10-day spacing of the decans. Daylight hours were reckoned on a different basis, one which determined 10 "hours" for the time between sunrise and sunset, plus 2 additional hours for twilight. The resulting division of the day was 12 hours of daylight and 12 of night, or 24 hours whose length varied with the season of the year. Eventually the Hellenistic astronomers replaced these unequal seasonal hours with 24 hours of constant length (equinoctial hours) which were further subdivided, according to the Babylonian sexagesimal system, into 60 minutes. Our present system, in which one day contains 24 60-minute hours, is the historical survival of this development in Hellenistic astronomy.

Bibliography

Bickerman, E. J. 1980. *Chronology of the Ancient World.* London.

Charpin, D. 1982. Mari et le calendrier d'Ebla. *RA* 76: 1–6.

Hunger, H., and Reiner, E. 1975. A Scheme for Intercalary Months from Babylonia. *WZKM* 67: 21–28.

Kugler, F. X. 1924. *Sternkunde und Sterndienst in Babel.* Vol. 2. Münster.

Landsberger, B. 1915. *Der kultische Kalender der Babylonier und Assyrer.* LSS 6/1–2. Leipzig.

———. 1949. Jahreszeiten im Sumerisch-Akkadischen. *JNES* 8: 248–97.

Langdon, S. 1935. *Babylonian Menologies and the Semitic Calendars.* Schweich Lectures 1933. London.

Larsen, M. T. 1974. Unusual Eponymy-Datings from Mari and Assyria. *RA* 68: 15–24.

———. 1976. *The Old Assyrian City-State and Its Colonies.* Mesopotamia 4. Copenhagen.

Neugebauer, O. 1955. *Astronomical Cuneiform Texts.* 3 vols. London.

———. 1975. *A History of Ancient Mathematical Astronomy.* 3 vols. Berlin.

Neugebauer, O., and Parker, R. A. 1960. *Egyptian Astronomical Texts. 1. The Early Decans.* London.

Neugebauer, O., and Sachs, A. 1967. Some Atypical Astronomical Cuneiform Texts. 1. *JCS* 21: 183–218.

Parker, R. A. 1950. *The Calendars of Ancient Egypt.* SAOC 26. Chicago.

———. 1970. The Beginning of the Lunar Month in Ancient Egypt. *JNES* 29: 217–20.

Parker, R. A., and Dubberstein, W. 1942. *Babylonian Chronology 626 B.C.–A.D. 45.* SAOC 24. Chicago.

Parpola, S. 1970. *Letters from Assyrian Scholars to the Kings Esarhaddon and Assurbanipal.* AOAT 5/1. Kevelaer.

Pettinato, G. 1974–77. Il Calendario di Ebla al tempo de re Ibbi-Sipis sulla base di TM. 75.G.427. *AfO* 25: 1–36.

Rochberg-Halton, F. fc. Babylonian Seasonal Hours.

Sachs, A., and Neugebauer, O. 1956. A Procedure Text concerning Solar and Lunar Motion: BM 36712. *JCS* 10: 131–36.

Schneider, N. 1936. *Die Zeitbestimmungen der Wirtschaftsurkunden von Ur III.* AnOr 13. Rome.

Thompson, R. C. 1900. *Reports of the Magicians and Astrologers of Nineveh and Babylon.* Vol. 1. London.

Thureau-Dangin, F. 1921. *Rituels Accadiens.* Osnabrück.

Weidner, E. 1935–36. Aus den Tagen eines assyrischen Schattenkönigs. *AfO* 10: 1–52.

FRANCESCA ROCHBERG-HALTON

ANCIENT ISRAELITE AND EARLY JEWISH

One may assume that the ancestors of Israel and the early Israelites themselves followed some sort of calendar (or calendars), but the extant sources do not permit one to determine what its (their) nature may have been. No part of the Bible or even the Bible as a whole presents a full calendar; information about these matters must be gleaned from occasional, often incidental references to dates, days, months, seasons, and years. The largest amount of biblical calendrical data appears in documents that were written during the exilic or postexilic periods, while an explicit, complete calendar is not found in a Jewish text until approximately the 3d century B.C.E. when the *Astronomical Book of Enoch* (*1 Enoch* 72–82) was composed. The 362-day solar calendar which is described in it may, however, have been nonnormative. The NT has even less to offer in this regard than the Hebrew Bible: it mentions only a few dates and festivals and provides some details about when the day began. In this article the calendrical information in the Bible and in contemporary or nearly contemporary Jewish sources will be surveyed.

A. The Biblical Evidence

Even though more facts about ancient Jewish calendary practices are known from extrabiblical than from biblical texts, it will be useful first to summarize the available scriptural data.

1. The Day. The word *yôm* may be employed to express the general sense of "time," but it was regularly used to refer to "day" in the stricter senses of a period of light and darkness or the time of light alone. In the Hebrew Bible one meets various terms for different parts of the day: *šaḥar* (dawn); *bōqer* (morning); *ṣohŏrayim* (noon); *nešep* (twilight); *ʿereb* (evening); *laylâ* (night); and *ḥăṣî laylâ* (midnight). There are also references to the various watches of the night (e.g., Exod 14:24; Judg 7:19; 1 Sam 11:11; Lam 2:19; Matt 14:25; Mark 13:35), and Matt 20:1–16 and John 11:9 indicate that the daytime was divided into 12 hours.

Scholars have debated but not definitively settled the issue of when the day was thought to begin at various times in biblical history. Before examining the evidence, one should be aware that casual references to "day and night" and "night and day" should not be equated with official calendrical statements. R. de Vaux, for one, has maintained (*AncIsr*) that before the Exile the day was regarded as beginning in the morning while later the evening was considered the point when it began. He was able to adduce various earlier passages in which the order day-night occurs (e.g., Deut 28:67 [but see v 66]; 1 Sam 30:12; Isa 28:19; Jer 33:20) and later ones in which night is mentioned before day (Esth 4:16; Dan 8:14; Jdt 11:17). But texts of this nature are largely irrelevant to the question of when, technically speaking, the day began. Moreover, the order day-night also surfaces in postexilic texts (Neh 1:6). An interesting example is 2 Chr 6:20, which speaks of day and night, while its source (1 Kgs 8:29) displays the reversed order of the two.

A sounder approach is to examine passages which treat the issue more officially. All of them, as it happens, deal with cultic affairs. If there ever was an official, secular position regarding the inception of the day, the sources do not divulge it. (1) Exod 12:6, 8, 10, 18 indicate that the rituals of passover and unleavened bread are to begin the evening of 1/14 (that is, month 1, day 14) and conclude the evening of 1/21. (2) Lev 23:32 mandates that the day of atonement is to be observed "on the ninth day of the month beginning at evening, from evening to evening shall you keep your sabbath." It is evident that the command envisages an evening–evening day, but the underlying calendar (the day of atonement is supposed to be 7/10 [23:27; cf. 16:29]) may have followed a morning–morning sequence. (3) The rules of purity (e.g., Lev 11:24–28; 15:1–12, 16–24; 22:1–9) state that the periods during which one is impure end in the evening. (4) Neh 13:19 relates that the sabbath was beginning as darkness fell. In later sources as well, this is clearly the understanding of when the day commenced (cf. CD 10:14–16; Josephus, *JW* 4 §9, 12; Mark 15:42; Luke 23:54–56; John 19:31–42).

For these texts, then, an evening–evening day is secure, and others are consistent with it (e.g., Gen 1:5, 8, 13, 19, 23, 31; Esth 4:16; Acts 4:3). There are, however, some passages which may, if they are meant to convey exact calendrical information, entail a morning–morning pattern (e.g., Judg 19:4–9; 1 Sam 19:11; 28:19; Lev 7:15–16 [a cultic text]). Perhaps the most that can be said is that in the Second Temple period virtually all cultic texts imply that the day began in the evening. There is insufficient evidence for establishing what preexilic practices may have been. J. Baumgarten has argued that even the author of the book of *Jubilees* (ca. 150 B.C.), who was a staunch adherent of a solar calendar, used an evening–evening day (see 21:10; 32:16; 49:1).

The Hebrew Bible makes it clear that from early times in Israel seven days constituted a week. This week was divided into six days during which work could be performed, and it concluded with a seventh day on which labor was illegal (Exod 34:21; 23:12; 20:8–11; 35:1–3; Lev 23:3; Deut 5:12–15). The familiar creation story in Gen 1:3–2:4a lists the seven days of the first week and refers to them with ordinal numbers. In the Hebrew Bible, only the seventh day receives a special name—the sabbath—but in the New Testament the day before the sabbath is called the day of preparation (Matt 27:62; Mark 15:42; Luke 23:54; John 19:31, 42). Use of this term may, however, be related to the fact that the following sabbath was, on this occasion, also the day of Passover (see John 19:14). Units of seven days are mentioned in the legislation about the festival of weeks which was to be celebrated 50 days after the waving of the barley omer. This 50-day period is divided into seven weeks and one day (cf. Deut 16:9–10; Lev 23:15–16). It should be added that in some texts the word "week" refers to a period of seven years (e.g., Lev 25:8; Dan 9:24–27; and throughout the pseudepigraphic book of *Jubilees*).

2. The Month. The Hebrew Bible mentions months rather frequently but does not name them in a single manner throughout. In fact, it has been argued that there are three distinct systems of month names in the text.

a. The Canaanite Month Names. It is often claimed that the early Israelites used lunar months and called them by names which they borrowed from their Canaanite neighbors. There are indeed some Canaanite month names in the Bible, and the word for month that is found with them is regularly *yeraḥ*. It does not follow, however, that these months were lunar simply because this Hebrew word is etymologically related to the noun for moon (*yārēăḥ*) any more than it does that English-speaking people use lunar months because the term "month" is etymologically related to "moon." It has been maintained that there are four Canaanite month names in the Hebrew Bible: Abib (Exod 13:4; 23:15; 34:18; Deut 16:1 [=the first month]), Ziv (1 Kgs 6:1, 37 [=the second month]), Ethanim (1 Kgs 8:2 [=the seventh month]), and Bul (1 Kgs 6:38 [=the eighth month]). The words "Abib" and "Ziv" have not been identified in Canaanite or Phoenician sources, but the other two have. It is of some interest that the word *ḥōdeš* is used with Abib (always) and with Ziv in one of its two occurrences (1 Kgs 6:1), but it is not found with the remaining two names, which always appear with *yeraḥ*. It is not clear, though, that the presence of two certain Canaanite month names in the Hebrew Bible indicates that the Israelites resorted to a full system of such names in an official calendar. The two undoubted Canaanite names and the name Ziv figure only in the account of Solomon's building and dedication of the temple (which had noteworthy Canaanite connections), and even there the writer always tells the reader the corresponding number of the month. Consequently, one may be dealing with a special source at this point, and these month names may not have been in widespread or official use in Israel. In the parallel passages in 2 Chronicles the names are not given (for 1 Kgs 6:1 [Ziv], see 2 Chr 3:2; for 1 Kgs 8:2 [Ethanim], cf. 5:3). If the ordinals which are added to these months correspond with the time when they occurred in the year, these months would belong to a year which began in the spring.

b. The Numbered Months. Biblical literature which was written just before, during, and after the Exile provides many dates and calendrical hints but again offers no systematic statement about the nature of the calendar(s) employed in Judah. The most noteworthy feature of the calendrical notices in these sources is their use of ordinal numbers to designate the twelve months. References to numbered months are infrequent in 1–2 Kings but are present in the temple-building section discussed above and in the last chapter of 2 Kings which describes the Babylonian capture of Jerusalem (25:1, 3, 8, 25, 27). Some scholars have concluded from their presence in this chapter and in Jeremiah that this system came into use in Judah at approximately the time of the Babylonian Exile. The following works, many of which have undoubted priestly ties, use this nomenclature: the Priestly source; 1–2 Kings (with the exception of the Canaanite month names noted above); 1–2 Chronicles (where the Canaanite month names are eliminated from the temple section); Ezra (with one exception [6:15] in an Aramaic document in which the month when the Second Temple was completed is called Adar); Jeremiah; Ezekiel; Daniel (one example [10:4]); Haggai, and Zechariah (see 7:3–4; 8:19 for the fasts of the fourth, fifth, seventh, and tenth months).

The schedules of holidays in these books are much more precise than in the earlier sources, which give only rather vague indications of dates for festivals. Ezekiel, in his blueprint for the restored temple and community (chaps. 40–48), elaborates a cultic calendar (45:18–25; cf. 46:1) which includes 1/1 (the sanctuary is cleansed through sacrifice of a young bull); 1/7 (the same procedure as for 1/1, but the sacrifice is for "anyone who has sinned through error or ignorance; so you shall make atonement for the temple" [45:20]); 1/14 (Passover, "and for seven days unleavened bread shall be eaten" [v 21]); 7/15 (a seven-day festival begins; it has the same sacrificial prescriptions as the days of unleavened bread [v 25]). Ezekiel also treats the sabbath (46:1–5) and mentions the day of the new moon (46:6; for the new moon celebration, see also 1 Sam 20:5, 18–19, 24–29; Hos 2:11; Amos 8:5). His remarkable calendar of holidays, which fails to mention the festival of weeks and proceeds from spring to autumn, draws no agricultural connections for any of the feasts.

The most detailed schedule of festivals surfaces in the priestly parts of the Pentateuch. In these sections the dates are expressed by numbered months and numbered days within the months, and the first month is in the spring. If one combines the data from the relevant priestly pericopes, one finds a full and precise list of festivals and observances:

1/1–12: a special offering is to be presented on the first of each month (Num 28:11–15);

1/14: Passover. Exod 12:2 specifies that the month of Passover is to be the first one of the year for the Israelites. The Passover lamb was to be selected on 1/10 and sacrificed on 1/14 (Exodus 12; Lev 23:5; Num 9:1–5; Num 28:16; cf. Josh 5:10).

1/15–21: Festival of Unleavened Bread (Exod 12:18–19; Lev 23:6–8; Num 28:17–25). One noteworthy ceremony which is mentioned just after the laws about this festival in

Leviticus 23 is the waving of the omer by the priest (23:9–14). Lev 23:11 dates this ceremony to the "morrow of the sabbath"—a phrase whose ambiguity gave rise to disputes at a later time. The timing of the omer ceremony was especially significant because it determined the date of the festival of weeks.

2/14: The Second Passover. It was meant for those who had become impure through contact with a dead body or who were away on a journey at the time of the first Passover (Num 9:6–14; cf. 2 Chr 30:1–22).

3/?: The Festival of Weeks. Like Deut 16:9–12, Lev 23:15–16 provides for a 50-day count ("fifty days to the morrow after the seventh sabbath" [v 16]) in calculating the date for the festival of weeks; but it names as the starting point for the count "the morrow after the sabbath, from the day that you brought the sheaf of the wave offering [=the omer] . . ." (v 15). It is striking, however, that no date for either the omer ceremony or the festival of weeks is given. In fact, even the month in which this second pilgrim feast occurs must be inferred from other data (cf. also Num 28:26–31; Acts 2).

7/1: According to Lev 23:23–25, a "day of solemn rest" was to be observed on this date; it was to be "a memorial proclaimed with blast of trumpets" (v 24; see also Num 29:1–6). This observance was apparently in addition to what Num 28:11–15 requires for the first of each month. It is never called "New Year" (*rōʾš haššānāh*) in the Bible.

7/10: The Day of Atonement. Leviticus 16 provides the fullest description of the rites for this day; Lev 16:29; 23:27 and Num 29:7 furnish the date.

7/15–21: The Festival of Tabernacles. The date is given in Lev 23:34, 39; and Num 29:12–34. Both of these chapters also mention an eighth day (Lev 23:39; Num 29:35), though they indicate that the festival itself lasts just seven days (Lev 23:34, 36, 39, 42; Num 29:12–34). It was during this festival that Solomon dedicated the temple (1 Kgs 8:2, 65–66 [the eighth day is noted again]; 2 Chr 5:3; 7:8–10 [a "solemn assembly" was held on the eighth day]), and it was this celebration that Jeroboam redated to 8/15 (1 Kgs 12:32–33).

From these books which refer to months by ordinal numbers rather than names one can infer some additional information about them. First, that there were twelve months follows from lists such as those in 1 Kgs 4:7–19 and 1 Chr 27:1–15 and from the fact that no source ever mentions a higher number (2 Kgs 25:27 and Jer 52:31 mention the twenty-seventh or twenty-fifth day of the twelfth month as the date for King Jehoiachin's release; cf. Ezek 32:1; the dates in the book of Esther are discussed below). That is, these texts never mention an intercalary month as nearly as one can tell. Second, the priestly chronological notes which dot the flood story suggest how long these months lasted. On 2/17 the waters begin to come (7:11); they then rise for 150 days (7:24; cf. 8:3). On 7/17 the ark comes to rest on a mountain (8:4), and on 10/1 the summits of the mountains become visible (8:5). By 1/1 the following year the water had disappeared, and on 2/27 the earth was completely dry (8:13–14). It appears that the 150 days of 7:24 and the five months from 2/17 to 7/17 refer to the same span of time. This would imply months of 30 days. It has also been argued that the length of the flood (one year and ten days) may be related to the fact that a solar year is approximately ten days longer than a lunar one, although in a lunar calendar five months would not total 150 days.

The practice of numbering months continued for a long time and is attested in some Jewish writings which postdate the Hebrew Bible. Some examples are Judith (2:1; cf. 4:13); 1–2 Maccabees; *Testaments of the Twelve Patriarchs;* the *Assumption of Moses;* 1 Esdras (14:22, 48); *2 Baruch* (77:18); *Jubilees; 1 Enoch* (72–82); *2 Enoch* (1:1); *Pseudo-Philo* (23:1–3, 14); and the Dead Sea Scrolls (on which see below).

c. The Babylonian Month Names. Yet another practice which appears in the latest OT literature is to employ the Hebrew equivalents of the Babylonian month names. One finds this custom in Ezra (once), Nehemiah, Esther, and Zechariah—all of which are postexilic books. It is well known from later sources that the names which Jewish people gave to the months were borrowed from the Babylonian language: As *j. Roš Haš.* 1.56d says, "They carried the names of the months back with them from Babylonia." These names are used alone at times but they also figure in combination with numbered months. The practice of using the Babylonian month names was a product of the Judeans' exilic and perhaps postexilic contact with the Babylonians and Persians (who borrowed the names from the Babylonians). The Babylonian months were lunar, and the year began in the spring. It is obvious that the Jewish use of the month names entailed that the same features were transferred to the Jewish calendar. The following Babylonian names appear in the biblical sources:

Babylonian Names	*Hebrew Equivalents*
1. Nisanu	1. Nisan (Neh 2:1; Esth 3:7 [=first])
2. Aiaru	2.
3. Simanu	3. Sivan (Esth 8:9 [=third])
4. Duzu	4.
5. Abu	5.
6. Ululu	6. Elul (Neh 6:15)
7. Tashritu	7.
8. Arahsamnu	8.
9. Kislimu	9. Chislev (Neh 1:1; Zech 7:1 [=ninth])
10. Tebutu	10. Tebet (Esth 2:16 [=tenth])
11. Shabatu	11. Shebat (Zech 1:7 [=eleventh])
12. Addaru	12. Adar (Ezra 6:15; Esth 3:7, 13; 8:12; 9:1, 15, 17, 19, 21 [=twelfth])

The twelfth month occurs so frequently in the book of Esther because it was during that month that the events which gave rise to the annual festival of Purim took place. According to Esth 9:21, Mordecai gave orders that all the Jews in the Persian Empire were to "keep the fourteenth day of the month Adar and also the fifteenth day of the same, year by year. . . ."

The Hebrew Bible, then, exhibits at least traces of three methods for naming months: with names, some of which are attested in Canaanite sources; by ordinal numbers; and by Babylonian month names. But in no case does one learn the lengths of all the months, nor is intercalary procedure ever described. It has been held that 1 Kgs 12:32 (Jeroboam dated a festival to 8/15, not 7/15 as in Jerusalem), 2 Chr 30:1–4 (Hezekiah's Passover was celebrated on 2/14 rather than 1/14), and Ezek 4:5 (the prophet lies on his left side for 390 days) point toward intercalation of one month in some years; but these passages are far from making the case even plausible, much less compelling. One also learns nothing about the methods used for determining the beginning of a month.

3. The Year. There is no statement in the Bible about how long a year lasted, and the data about its beginning are confusing. Scholars have argued from different sets of facts that the year was thought to begin in either spring or autumn. A widely held position has been that an autumnal New Year was observed in preexilic times, while a vernal New Year came into vogue in the postexilic age. Some have also maintained (e.g., Thiele) that the kingdom of Judah began the year in autumn but the realm of Israel placed it in the spring. In treating a question of this sort, for which the evidence is sparse and difficult, it is important to remember that simultaneously there could be different inceptions for different sorts of New Years. This point is made abundantly clear by the famous passage in *m. Roš Haš.* 1:1: "There are four 'New Year' days: on the 1st of Nisan is the New Year for kings and feasts; on the 1st of Elul is the New Year for the Tithe of Cattle (R. Eleazar and R. Simeon say: The 1st of Tishri); on the 1st of Tishri is the New Year for [the reckoning of] the years [of foreign kings], of the Years of Release and Jubilee years, for the planting [of trees] and for vegetables; and the 1st of Shebat is the New Year for [fruit] trees (so the School of Shammai; and the School of Hillel say: On the 15th thereof)" (trans. Danby).

a. The Earlier Evidence. As one might expect, there is inconclusive evidence from the earlier biblical literature. The festival calendars of the sources J and E are often cited in this context as indications that the year began in the autumn in preexilic times. The J material is found in Exod 34:18–24. There the first holiday (unleavened bread) is dated to the month of Abib (i.e., the first spring month); the festival of weeks is not dated other than by its association with the wheat harvest; but the "feast of ingathering" is to be observed at the "year's end" (*tĕqûpat haššānāh* [v 22]). The phrase here more literally means the "turn of the year" and clearly expresses the fact that at this point (this must be in autumn) the year has reached a significant juncture. In E (Exod 23:10–17) similar information appears, but the "feast of ingathering" is located "at the end of the year" (*bĕṣēʾt haššānāh* [v 16]). Hence, in the two "epic" sources, the list begins with a vernal and concludes with an autumnal holiday (cf. also Deut 16:1–17). From the two Hebrew expressions just quoted, a number of scholars have inferred that the year ended in the autumn. Here, however, it should be observed that one is dealing with an agricultural cycle which is not necessarily the same as a calendar year. It is obvious that the agricultural year concludes with the fall harvest, but whether one may deduce from that fact that a calendrical year did as well is quite another question. It seems safer to say with D. J. A. Clines: ". . . references to the 'end' (*ṣēʾt*) or the 'turn' (*tĕqûpāh*) of the year in the autumn invariably have to do with the cycle of the agricultural year or of the festival calendar insofar as it is based on the agricultural seasons, and therefore they are irrelevant to the question of the beginning of the calendar year of months" (1974: 29).

In this connection it is interesting to compare the so-called Gezer calendar which undoubtedly dates from preexilic times (ca. 925 B.C. according to Albright). It reads as follows (ANET 320 [trans. Albright]):

> His two months are (olive) harvest [*ʾsp*],
> His two months are planting (grain),
> His two months are late planting;
> His month is hoeing up of flax.
> His month is harvest of barley,
> His month is harvest and *feasting;*
> His two months are vine-tending,
> His month is summer fruit.

As in J and E, the times of the year are identified by agricultural phenomena. The order of the twelve months is from autumn to summer, and the list begins with the process (*ʾsp*) that marks the end of the cycle in J and E. Unfortunately, one does not know what the status of this "calendar" was and what purpose it served.

b. The Later Evidence. The dating systems in which the months are numbered or given Babylonian names place the first month (= Nisan) in the spring as the Babylonians did. It is difficult to determine when the numbered system was first introduced, but there is no clear evidence that it preceded the time immediately before the Babylonian Exile. Jer 36:9, 22 indicate that the ninth month occurred during the winter; this would be true only in a system which began in the spring. But there is other evidence of a conflicting nature. For example, if one pairs the dates in Neh 1:1 (Chislev [= the ninth month] in the twentieth year, apparently of King Artaxerxes) and 2:1 (Nisan [= the first month] in the king's twentieth year) it is apparent that the monarch's regnal years were calculated from some time other than a Nisan inception of the year. If the year began with Nisan 1, this Chislev and Nisan would be in different years. These dates are consistent with a fall inception of the year. But as one is here dealing with the regnal years of a Persian king, it is not clear that these dates indicate anything about a Jewish calendar. It is well known, of course, that in later Judaism 7/1 became the day of New Year, although Nisan continued to be regarded as the first month. To add to the puzzle, Lev 25:8–9 prescribes that the jubilee years were to begin on 7/10. Thus, the practice or practices before the Exile remain unclear, while there is evidence later for both a vernal and an autumnal inception of the year. Depending upon the topic under consideration, the autumnal New Year may have been calculated from different dates.

B. Sources Outside the Hebrew Bible

One encounters fuller calendrical details in Jewish documents which were not included in the Hebrew Bible.

1. The Elephantine Papyri. The earliest of these extrabiblical sources are the Aramaic papyri of the Jewish military colony in Elephantine on the Nile River. There are some 38 papyri that bear dates, and 22 of these have double or synchronized dates (Egyptian and Persian/Jewish). In the papyri one finds all twelve of the Babylonian/Persian month names:

Nisan	(A. E. Cowley, Aramaic Papyri 21)
Iyyar	(Kraeling, The Brooklyn Museum Aramaic Papyri 14)
Sivan	(Kraeling 1; 5)
Tammuz	(Aramaic Papyri 30; Kraeling 6)
Ab	(Aramaic Paypri 14)
Elul	(Aramaic Papyri 5; 20; Kraeling 3)
Tishri	(Aramaic Papyri 15; Kraeling 4; 7; 8)
Marcheshvan	(Aramaic Papyri 17; 30; 31; Kraeling 9)
Chislev	(Aramaic Papyri 6; 8; 10; 13; 25)
Tebeth	(Aramaic Papyri 26)
Shebat	(Aramaic Papyri 28)
Adar	(Aramaic Papyri 61; 67; Kraeling 10)

Horn and Wood (1954) were able to draw no certain conclusions about whether the Jews of Elephantine had fashioned a precalculated, fixed calendar but noted strong similarities with the Babylonian system. There is no evidence among the Elephantine documents for intercalation. Horn and Wood argued that Kraeling's text (*BMAP* 6) implied a civil year that ran from fall to fall, but this has been disputed.

2. The Wâdī ed-Dâliyeh Papyri. Though these mid-4th-century B.C.E. Samaritan papyri have not yet been published in full, the available evidence indicates that the authors used the Babylonian month names. Papyrus 1 reads: "on the twentieth day of Adar, year 2 (the same being) the accession year of Darius the king, in the province of Samaria" (Cross 1974: 19).

3. *1 Enoch* 72–82. The next book in chronological order is the *Astronomical Book of Enoch* (*1 Enoch* 72–82), a work which appears to date from no later than the 3d century B.C.E. It is preserved in Ethiopic, but fragments of the work in the original Aramaic have been found among the Dead Sea Scrolls. These indicate that the original text was probably much longer than the Ethiopic version of it. Here for the first time an extant Jewish document describes a full calendar; or, more precisely, the angel Uriel reveals its details to Enoch. In fact, it sketches two systems: a solar calendar of 364 days (72:32; 74:10, 12; 75:2; 82:4–6) and a lunar one of 354 days (73:1–17; 78:6–17). The solar year of 364 days takes a schematic form (the months are again numbered, not named): months 1, 2, 4, 5, 7, 8, 10, and 11 have 30 days, while months 3, 6, 9, and 12 have 31 (72:6–32). From statements in the book about the relative lengths of day and night at different times in the year, it is obvious that the author thought the year began just after the vernal equinox (which is in the twelfth month). The summer solstice then falls in the third month, the autumnal equinox in the sixth, and the winter solstice in the ninth. Nothing is said about intercalary months, but this calendar, in which each date falls on the same day of the week every year (since 364 is exactly divisible by 7), is compared with a 354-day lunar arrangement (74:12–16; in 74:10–11 a 360-day solar calendar is compared to a 354-day lunar one—that is, the epagomenal days are not considered in these calculations). It is not clear why the author extends the comparison to eight years since in each year the lunar is ten days shorter than the solar year. But for neither the solar nor the lunar year does the writer mention intercalation; every year has the same number of days (cf. also 78:15–17; 79:3–5 where the lunar year is divided into twelve months: 1–3, 7–9 have 30 days; 4–6, 10–12 have 29 [but 78:9 mentions a month with 28 days]).

4. The Book of *Jubilees*. The intriguing solar calendar of *1 Enoch* 72–82 was later advocated by other writers. The most vigorous of these would be the author of the book of *Jubilees* (ca. 150 B.C.) who strongly defended this solar arrangement against any sort of lunar calendar. In it an angel of the divine presence (thus here too it comes by revelation) tells Moses: "Now you command the Israelites to keep the years in this number—364 days. Then the year will be complete and it will not disturb its time from its days or from its festivals because everything will happen in harmony with their testimony. They will neither omit a day nor disturb a festival" (6:32). In the sequel the same angel predicts: "There will be people who carefully observe the moon with lunar observations because it is corrupt (with respect to) the seasons and is early from year to year by ten days" (6:36 [both passages are from Charles' translation]). In other words, the author does not simply compare calendars as in *1 Enoch*; he is decidedly for the solar one and implacably against the lunar arrangement which entails that sacred days are profaned and profane ones are sanctified (6:34, 37). It would be interesting to know the historical background against which the author wrote (see Dan 7:25 for a hint about a change of calendars), but it was apparently a time of calendrical dispute—at least for this writer, who was convinced that the 364-day solar calendar was the divine and anciently revealed system. It seems that *Jubilees,* too, does not deal with the problem of intercalation, although it has been claimed that 6:31, 33, which prohibit "transgressing" the proper year, originally read "intercalate" (the two words would be identical in a Hebrew consonantal text). In whichever way these verses are read, the result is the same: there is no intercalation, so that festivals, which had agricultural ties, would soon be celebrated at the wrong time relative to the agricultural cycle.

Jubilees, with its special calendar (months are again numbered), is able to provide a precise date for the festival of weeks—something not found in any earlier source. The author dates it to 3/15 (15:1 ["in the third month, in the middle of the month"]; 44:4–5) and associates this date with the covenants made with Noah (6:17–22), Abram (14:20), and Moses (cf. 1:1). Though *Jubilees* does not mention the ceremony of waving the omer, its calendar implies that it occurred on 1/26 (that is, the day after the sabbath [= the morrow of the sabbath] which follows the festival of unleavened bread). The book also mentions that the first days of months 1, 4, 7, and 10 were special memorial days (each recalls an incident during the flood [6:23–29]); and it speaks rather vaguely about times for the second tithe of "seed," wine, and oil (32:10–14). Finally, *Jubilees* claims that the day of atonement was instituted to mark the time when Jacob learned of Joseph's "death" (34:17–19); and it, like several biblical works, notes an additional eighth day for the festival of tabernacles (32:4–29).

5. The *Temple Scroll*. The *Temple Scroll* found at Qumran (11QTemple) offers more extrabiblical information about the same calendar of twelve numbered months, the total of whose days was 364. The date of the document is uncertain. The editor Y. Yadin (1983) thought it came from the time of John Hyrcanus (135–104 B.C.E.) or slightly earlier, while others argue that it was written closer to 200 B.C.E. As Yadin has unraveled the cultic calendar (especially in columns 12–29) found in this long but still fragmentary scroll, it can be sketched as follows:

1/1–8	Days of Ordination for Priests
1/14	Passover
1/26	Waving of the Omer (= The Festival of Firstfruits of Barley)
[2/14	The Second Passover (perhaps in a lost part of a column)]
3/15	The Festival of Weeks (= The Festival of Firstfruits of Wheat)
5/3	Festival of New Wine
6/22	Festival of Oil
6/23–29(?)	Festival of the Offering of Wood (cf. Neh 10:34)
7/1	Day of Remembrance
7/10	Day of Atonement
7/15–22	Festival of Booths

A matter of special interest is the series of firstfruits festivals which the author describes and dates. In this system, as understood by Yadin, the day of the waving of the omer (1/26) and the festival of weeks (3/15) are separated, as the Bible prescribes, by seven full weeks. The count begins and ends on a Sunday. The same temporal span separates the festival of weeks (3/15) from the festival of new wine (5/3), and the latter occurs seven full weeks before the festival of oil (6/22). That is, the biblical prescriptions for calculating the date of the festival of weeks from the day the omer was waved have been extended to these other three firstfruits festivals. Indeed, very similar language is used in each case (see 18:10–13; 19:11–13; 21:12–14; compare *Jubilees* 32:10–14). In calculating these exact dates, Yadin was dependent on several bits of data, an important one of which is a fragmentary statement from an unpublished Qumran ms which gives the date 6/22 for a festival of oil (the Hebrew word used for oil—*hšmn*—is not the same as the one in the *Temple Scroll* for this festival—*yṣhr*). If one accepts this date as relevant for the festival of oil in the *Temple Scroll,* and if the last day of one count (i.e., the holiday itself) is also regarded as the first of the next count, every date mentioned fits the *Enoch/Jubilees* 364-day solar calendar.

6. Sectarian Texts. *1 Enoch, Jubilees,* and the *Temple Scroll* may have been written before the Qumran community settled on the shores of the Dead Sea, but the presence of copies of each testifies to the fact that they were used and studied at the Essene settlement. Hence it is not surprising to discover that the 364-day calendar is also attested among the sectarian documents. Indeed, it has been surmised that a calendrical dispute with the priestly establishment in Jerusalem was a precipitating factor in the exodus of the Essenes from Jerusalem to the Dead Sea. Evidence that the group followed a calendar that differed from the mainline one appears in 1QpHab 11:4–9 which indicates that the Wicked Priest—the archvillain for the covenanters and apparently the reigning high priest—appeared (at Qumran?) on the day of atonement. Since the ritual for this solemn day required that the high priest be at the temple, it is highly unlikely that he would have chosen this day for settling accounts with the Teacher of Righteousness. A reasonable inference is that the day of atonement fell on different days for the two protagonists because they lived by different cultic calendars.

It was clear when scholars began studying the scrolls that observance of the festivals at the proper time was a point that the authors considered worthy of emphasis (1QS 1:13–15), but the precise nature of the Qumran calendar was not demonstrated until several other texts were published. The only text which simply states that the year contains 364 days is "David's Compositions"—part of the Cave 11 *Psalms Scroll* which the editor has dated paleographically to the 1st century A.D. It asserts, as it enumerates David's literary output: "And he wrote 3,600 psalms; and songs to sing before the altar over the whole-burnt *tamid* offering every day, for all the days of the year, 364; and for the *qorban* [offering] of the Sabbaths, 52 songs; and for the *qorban* of the New Moons [the phrase should be translated "firsts of the months"] and for all the Solemn Assemblies and for the Day of Atonement, 30 songs" (11QPs[a] 27.4–8; Sanders' translation). The last line (1.11) adds that David spoke all these "through prophecy which was given him from before the Most High."

There are several other indications in the scrolls that the same calendar was known and used. A text named *Songs of the Sabbath Sacrifices* (11QShirShabb) appears to employ it, and the *War Scroll* refers to 26 priestly "heads of courses" (1QM 2.1), whereas 1 Chr 24:7–18 lists just 24 such courses or shifts of temple duty. If there were 26 priestly groups who rotated temple service (and it is known from other sources that each served for two weeks during a year—one week in the first part, one in the second), then the number fits a 52-week year (note the 52 "fathers of the congregation" in 1.1) exactly, unlike the number 24. Further information about the priestly courses comes from an unpublished document, parts of which J. T. Milik quoted in 1957. This text (4QMišmārôt [the term for the priestly shifts]) gives the name of the priestly family which was serving in the temple on the various holidays and also the number of the day within its week on which the festival fell. By using the list of priestly courses in 1 Chr 24:7–18, one can calculate exactly when the feasts were celebrated and every feast fits the dates known from *Jubilees* and the *Temple Scroll.* The available part of the text reads:

The first year, its festivals	
On the third (day) in Maoziah—Passover	[= 1/14]
[On the first (day)] in Jeda[iah]—the waving of the [omer]	[= 1/26]
On the fifth (day) in Seorim—the [Second] Passover	[= 2/14]
On the first (day) in Jeshua—the Festival of Weeks	[= 3/15]
[On] the fourth (day) in Maoziah—the Day of Remembrance	[= 7/1]
[On] the sixth (day) in Joiarib—the Day of Atonement	[= 7/10]
[On the fourth (day) in Jeda]iah—the Festival of Booths	[= 7/15]

One interesting feature of this list is that only names found in 1 Chr 24:7–18 are used. That is, though the year is divided into 26 periods of service, they are filled by 24 groups. Consequently, the time of service for each group would vary from year to year. This appears to be the meaning of the reference to the "first year" in the initial line of the *mišmārôt* text.

Milik has also discussed some texts which evidence a concern to synchronize this 364-day system with a lunisolar calendar which had 354 days in a year, with one 30-day month added every third year. He has mentioned a line from the *mišmārôt* text which reads: "in the sixth (day) in Jehezkel, on the 29th in the 22nd of the eleventh (month)." He has interpreted the extra date (the 29th) as a reference to the same date in a lunisolar calendar, while 11/22 would be its equivalent in the 364-day system. He has also alluded to a six-year priestly roster which he thinks reflects the sect's interest in synchronizing its calendar with this schematic lunisolar one. The two would synchronize every three years, but it would take six years for the time of duty of one's course to return to its original period in the year.

7. Solar and Lunar Calendars. The 364-day calendar was known and perhaps practiced from at least the 3d century B.C.E. to the 1st century A.D. If it was used over such a span of time, the issue of intercalation would have become acute as each year the calendar would deviate another 1¼ days from the true solar year. The earlier sources (*1 Enoch, Jubilees* [though see the comment on 6:31, 33 above], and the *Temple Scroll*) fail to deal with the problem, while some of the scrolls appear to show interest in synchronizing this arrangement with a schematic lunisolar calendar. It should be noted that this dearth of information about intercalation within the 364-day calendar is more than balanced by the complete lack of information in the sources about what may have been the calendar of the "mainline" Jewish community during these centuries. About this no contemporary or near contemporary source supplies any details. It may be that the 364-day calendar was followed only by fringe groups; even so, much more is known about it than about what might have been the calendar of the Jerusalem authorities in different parts of the Second Temple period. The present-day Jewish calendar evolved over several centuries in a process that can be traced in postbiblical texts. A complete list of month names can be found in *Megillat Taʿanit* (perhaps written in the 1st century A.D.), and the Mishnah (edited in approximately A.D. 200) reflects the rabbis' knowledge about the intercalary "second Adar" (*m. Meg.* 1:4; *m. Ned.* 8:5). The 19-year cycle in which an extra month is added to seven lunar years is attributed to Hillel II (ca. 358–59) but may be post-Talmudic.

8. The 364-Day Calendar and the Date of the Last Supper. One additional note should be added about the 364-day calendar. A. Jaubert (1957) has argued that the presence of two calendars in Judaism at approximately the time of Jesus can be used to solve the old problem of when Jesus and his disciples celebrated the Last Supper. The difficulty is as follows: in the Synoptic Gospels, Jesus and his disciples celebrate the Supper as a Passover meal which was eaten near sundown on Friday as Nisan 15 began (Matt 26:17–19; Mark 14:12; Luke 22–7–13); but John implies that the meal was eaten on Thursday as Nisan 14 began (18:28; 19:14, 31, 42) and that Jesus was crucified at the time when the Passover lambs were being slaughtered. Jaubert maintained that the difference reflected use of two calendars—one by the Synoptic writers (the 364-day system), another by John (a lunisolar calendar). Her solution, while it has proved attractive to some, founders on the complete lack of evidence elsewhere that Jesus or his disciples used the 364-day calendar. There is reason to think that the different timing for the meal in the gospel of John may be motivated more by theological than by historical concerns. That is, he wished to present Jesus as the Passover lamb of God whose death symbolized redemption. For further discussions, see *HJP*² 1: 587–601.

Bibliography

Baumgarten, J. M. 1958. The Beginning of the Day in the Calendar of Jubilees. *JBL* 77: 355–60.

Charles, R. H. 1902. *The Book of Jubilees or the Little Genesis.* London.

Clines, D. J. A. 1974. The Evidence for an Autumnal New Year in Pre-exilic Israel Reconsidered. *JBL* 93: 22–40.

Cowley, A. E. 1923. *Aramaic Papyri of the Fifth Century B.C.* Oxford. Repr. Osnabrück, 1967.

Cross, F. M. 1974. The Papyri and Their Historical Implications. Pp. 17–29 in *Discoveries in the Wâdī-ed-Dâliyeh.* AASOR 41. Cambridge, MA.

Finegan, J. 1959. The Principles of the Calendar and the Problems of Biblical Chronology. Vol. 2, pp. 552–98, in *Light From the Ancient Past.* 2d ed. Princeton.

Goudoever, J. van. 1961. *Biblical Calendars.* 2d ed. Leiden.

Horn, S. H., and Wood, L. H. 1954. The Fifth-Century Calendar at Elephantine. *JNES* 13: 1–20.

Jaubert, A. 1957. *La Date de la cène.* EBib. Paris. (ET 1965.)

Milik, J. T. 1957. Le Travail d'édition des manuscrits du désert de Juda. Pp. 17–26 in *Volume du congrès Strasbourg, 1956.* VTSup 4. Leiden.

———. 1976. *The Books of Enoch: Aramaic Fragments of Qumrân Cave 4.* Oxford.

Sanders, J. 1965. *The Psalms Scroll of Qumrân Cave 11.* DJD 4. Oxford.

Stroes, H. R. 1966. Does the Day Begin in the Evening or Morning? VT 16: 460–75.

Talmon, S. 1958. The Calendar Reckoning of the Sect from the Judaean Desert. Pp. 162–99 in *Aspects of the Dead Sea Scrolls. ScrHier* 4. Jerusalem.

Thiele, E. 1984. *The Mysterious Numbers of the Hebrew Kings.* Rev. ed. Grand Rapids.

Yadin, Y. 1983. *The Temple Scroll.* 3 vols. Jerusalem.

JAMES C. VANDERKAM

CALF. See ZOOLOGY.

CALF, GOLDEN. See GOLDEN CALF.

CALIGULA (EMPEROR).

Gaius (Caligula) was born in 12 C.E. and was the third son of the Roman military leader Germanicus and Agrippina the elder (Suet. *Claud.* 8). As a young boy he accompanied his parents on the German frontier and the soldiers nicknamed him "Caligula" for the miniature military boots (*caligulae*) that he wore (Tac. *Ann.* 1.41.69; Suet. *Calig.* 9; and Dio Cass. 47.5).

By his 19th year, his father, mother, and two elder brothers had been murdered. After the fall of Sejanus in 32 C.E., Caligula was adopted by the Emperor Tiberius, with whom he lived on the island of Capreae. Caligula was elected *pontifex* in 31 C.E. and *quaestor* in 33 C.E. When Tiberius died in 37 C.E., Caligula (who had been appointed joint heir in Tiberius' will) was supported by the praetorian prefect Macro and was immediately hailed as *princeps* by the senate. Soldiers who loved the house of Germanicus enthusiastically supported the new emperor and were particularly pleased by the honor he showed to the memory of his relatives who had died treacherously by the hand of Tiberius.

Caligula ruled equitably for his first six months, after which time there was a rapid degeneration in the emperor's character (Josephus *Ant* 18.256). The emperor's insanity, manifesting itself through his inordinate lusts, megalomania, and sadism, appeared to have been precipitated by a grave illness, which was purportedly caused by a reaction in his brain to an aphrodisiac. Caligula's behavioral change was also concomitant with the death of his grandmother Antonia, who may have been a restraining influence in the young emperor's life. Unlike his predecessors, Caligula took his own claims to divinity seriously and rigorously enforced emperor worship.

At the beginning of his principate, Caligula released from prison his friend Herod Agrippa, who had been incarcerated by Tiberius. In addition to his freedom, Caligula gave Agrippa a gold chain supposedly equal in weight to the iron chain that had bound him in prison. Agrippa was appointed by the emperor to rule the territory that his uncle Philip the tetrarch had once governed until his death three years prior, along with Abilene, which had been governed by the tetrarch Lysanias. Caligula also granted the title of "king" to Agrippa (Josephus *JW* 2.181; *Ant* 18.236ff.).

Herodias was Agrippa's sister, and wife of Antipas. Herodias, motivated by envy for her brother's elevation to the station of a client king, urged her husband to petition the emperor for a similar title. Against his will, Antipas complied with his wife's request. Agrippa used the opportunity to accuse his brother-in-law, by letter to Caligula, of treason. Caligula exiled Antipas and Herodias chose to accompany him. Galilee and Peraea, formerly under the rule of Antipas, were added at this time (39 C.E.) to the dominions of Agrippa.

While there is no direct evidence to suggest that Caligula was responsible for any formal persecution of Christians, his short reign was plagued by problems with the Jews. In 38 C.E. a severe anti-Jewish riot occurred in Alexandria which was the result of a combination of factors, including the Greek majority's rejection of the Jews' claim to full citizenship, the Jews' refusal to sacrifice to the emperor, and finally the duplicity of Flaccus, the Roman governor of Alexandria. The two parties sent delegations to Caligula in 40 C.E. Philo, who represented the Jews of Alexandria, has left a vivid account of what transpired.

Eusebius, the early Church historian, states that Philo wrote five books on the troubles of the Jews under the reign of Gaius (Euseb. *Hist. Eccl.* 2.5; see also 2.6 and 2.18). Emil Schürer, the eminent historian of the Jews in the age of Jesus, suggested that Philo's *Contra Flaccum* and the *Legatio* were the third and fourth books, the rest having perished. Other scholars have suggested, on the contrary, that the extant *Legatio* is a mutilated form of the work to which Eusebius referred, originally existing in five books (see PHILO OF ALEXANDRIA).

Another severe incident took place in 40 C.E. when the Jews of the Judaean town of Jamnia destroyed an altar that the Greeks had set up in honor of Caligula. Caligula responded by issuing a decree that the places of worship should be converted into shrines for the imperial cult. Orders were sent to Publius Petronius, the governor of Syria, to erect a statue of the emperor in the guise of Zeus in the Jerusalem Temple. Agrippa realized the potentially devastating consequences of the decree and persuaded Caligula to rescind his order. Not long afterward, Caligula and his family were murdered.

Bibliography

Balson, J. P. V. D. 1934. *The Emperor Gaius (Caligula).* Oxford.

Koeberlein, E. 1962. *Caligula und die Ägyptischen Kulte.* Meisenheim am Glan.

SCOTT T. CARROLL

CALL STORIES (GOSPELS).

Stories of individuals being called to a life of discipleship are a common feature of religious and philosophical biography in antiquity (e.g., Philostr. *VA* 1.19; 4.1, 24; 8.21; Porph. *Plot.* 19–20; and, in general, Bieler 1935–36: 1.122–29). The Gospels contain similar accounts of the miraculous effect of Jesus' call to discipleship. What distinguishes these narratives, however, is the importance placed on the initiative of Jesus and the demand for an immediate and unconditional response on the part of the prospective disciples (Mark 1:16–20; 2:14; 5:18–19; 10:17–22; 10:46–52; Luke 5:1–11; 9:57–62; John 1:35–51). On this the tradition is unambiguous: one can become a disciple of Jesus only on the basis of a call (*TDNT* 4: 444; Schweizer 1978: 394). Indeed, there is not a single instance in all the synoptic tradition of an individual *successfully* volunteering to become a disciple. Nor do the Johannine call stories differ fundamentally in this regard (John 1:35–51; cf. 6:65; 10:3–5, 14, 26–28; 15:16; 21:20–22).

Bultmann classified the call stories of the synoptic tradition under the rubric of "biographical apothegms" and compared them to Elijah's call of Elisha in 1 Kings 19 (1963: 28–29). However, if analyzed strictly on the basis of literary form, these stories are closer to the ancient rhetorical category of the *chreia,* or anecdote, a brief narrative relating a striking saying or deed of some individual. The *chreia* was a popular literary form and became one of the major vehicles of biographical characterization in antiquity (Momigliano 1971: 23, 76). This is shown by the anecdotal nature of Xenophon's *Memorabilia,* Plutarch's *Lives,* Lucian's *Demonax,* and Diogenes Laertius' *Lives of the Philosophers,* to cite only the most well known examples. It should not be surprising therefore if examples of *chreiai* are also to be found in the Gospels (Dibelius 1934: 160).

Bultmann's comparison with Elijah's call of Elisha also stands in need of correction. Although the language and structure of Elijah's call of Elisha appear to be a precedent for the synoptic call stories (3 Kgdms [LXX] 19:19–21 is similar to Mark), a careful reading reveals at least one important difference. Elisha consents to follow Elijah only on the *condition* that he be allowed to return home and bid farewell to his family. It is just this kind of precondition that is explicitly rejected by Jesus in Luke 9:61–62. Jesus instead warns his hearers that the leniency demonstrated by Elijah shall not be extended to his prospective disciples. Unless the response to Jesus' call is immediate and unconditional it is invalid (cf. Luke 9:59–60).

One looks in vain for anything similar to this in the OT or subsequent Jewish literature. Nor are there any rabbinic stories of "calling" and "following after" analogous to those in Mark and Q. Whereas in the Gospels the decisive call comes from Jesus himself, entry into a rabbinic school is based generally on the initiative of the prospective pupil (*TDNT* 4: 444, 447). In contrast, Jesus is portrayed in the gospel call stories much like the wandering philosopher-teacher in Greek tradition who gathers disciples of his own choosing (Robbins 1982: 221–22, 233). A number of analogies can be found in the biographies of various philosophers, as Socrates' call of Xenophon and Crates' call of Zeno illustrate (Diog. Laert. 2.48; 7.2–3). The similarities between these accounts and the gospel call stories are striking. Cast in the form of anecdotes, they describe the sudden call of individuals engaged in the ordinary affairs of life, and their immediate response is characterized by a willingness to follow. These and other examples demonstrate that the gospel call stories exhibit many of the features of the Greek philosophical call story. They show the same typical situations and actions, and often employ the same vocabulary. They also serve the same function, namely, to draw attention to Jesus as the ideal teacher and to give expression to a particular understanding of the nature of discipleship. In other words, a Hellenistic form portraying how the ideal sage gathers disciples was adapted by certain early Christian writers to describe the relationship of Jesus to his disciples.

Not all NT call stories appear in a condensed form. Some, for example, have been expanded so that in place of a terse saying one may find a longer one or even a dialogue. The description of the setting, moreover, may require several sentences and the original saying or deed may be explained or its effects described (Dibelius 1934: 155–56). This is illustrated by the Johannine form of the call of the first disciples (John 1:35–51). Here the author has reworked the call stories of Mark 1:16–20 by elaborating the description of the setting, introducing dialogue, and focusing attention on the divine character of Jesus. In a different way, the author of Luke 5:1–11 has taken over the call stories of Mark 1:16–20 and transformed them into a story about a miraculous catch of fish. The miracle, however, assumes secondary importance, while the essential point of the call story has been retained: the disciples respond to Jesus by leaving everything and following him. The logion about "fishers of men" may have suggested this elaboration. Another example of a call story transposed into a miracle story occurs in the account of the healing of Bartimaeus in Mark 10:46–52 (Achtemeier 1978: 115–45; Steinhauser 1983: 204–6).

In order for a call to succeed, the initiative must come from Jesus himself and the prospective disciple must respond immediately and unconditionally. When either of these components is missing the story inevitably ends in failure. This is illustrated by the collection of three "unsuccessful" call stories in Luke 9:57–62 which are intended to describe inappropriate attitudes about the nature of discipleship (cf. Mark 5:18–19; 10:17–22). Indeed, they function as caricatures of the successful call story insofar as they represent basic misunderstandings of what it means to follow Jesus. The first claimant approaches Jesus with the boast, "I will follow you wherever you go"; the other two also appear willing to follow, but only if certain conditions are met: "Let me first go and bury my father" and "Let me first say farewell to those at my home." All three, however, are rejected by Jesus with an extreme, even bizarre, pronouncement. Jesus counters the heroic gesture of the first claimant by pointing dramatically to the dangers a life of discipleship would entail. In following Jesus, the homeless wanderer, one is even more exposed and vulnerable than the animals themselves (Luke 9:58; cf. Matt. 8:19–20). Similarly, Jesus' call supersedes all ties to an individual's home and family (as well as to occupation and possessions, cf. Mark 1:16–20; 2:14; 10:17–22). Not even the requirement of burying one's father can come between Jesus and his disciple. Examples of "unsuccessful" call stories can also be found in Greek biography (e.g., Diog. Laert. 6:36: Diogenes the Cynic).

Although the gospel call stories do not contain an explicit theory of discipleship, due in large part to their anecdotal nature, they do imply one. First, they presuppose an anthropological dualism. That is, a humanity divided into two camps: in religious terms, the saved and the lost; and in philosophical terms, the wise and the foolish. This dualism, however, is concealed from the eyes of the world. The call story shows us ordinary, indeed disreputable, individuals (e.g., fishermen and tax collectors) who do not appear to enjoy the necessary qualifications for the religious life. The call by a divinely appointed agent functions in such a way as to disclose the true nature of the one called. It is an event which lies beyond human volition. One cannot decide to become a disciple of Jesus; the initiative rests solely with him. This idea is expressed clearly by Jesus in the fourth gospel: "You did not choose me, but I chose you" (John 15:16). And the transformation or conversion occurs instantaneously; there is no notion of preliminary training. In this respect, the synoptic call stories are not far from the Johannine understanding of discipleship.

A second way in which the theory of discipleship implicit in the gospel call stories may be discerned is through the sayings or pronouncements which often form the climax of these accounts, for example: "I will make you fishers of men" (Mark 1:17); "Sell what you have and give it to the poor" (Mark 10:21); "Foxes have holes, birds of the air have nests, but the son of man has nowhere to lay his head" (Luke 9:60); and "No one who puts his hand to the plow and looks back is fit for the kingdom of God" (Luke 9:62). Taken together, these sayings present a picture of discipleship characterized by lack of family, homelessness, poverty, and vulnerability. It is interesting to compare this understanding of discipleship with those collections of sayings which deal explicitly with the theme of discipleship (e.g., Mark 8:34–38; 10:28–31; Luke 14:25–33). Although these collections have some points in common with the call stories, they betray later developments, particularly by (1) stressing the necessity of martyrdom in light of the death of Jesus, (2) introducing the idea of "rewards," and (3) presenting views contrary to those found in the call stories (e.g., the idea of "counting the cost beforehand," Luke 14:28–32).

Bibliography

Achtemeier, P. J. 1978. "And he followed him": Miracles and Discipleship in Mark 10:46–52. *Semeia* 11: 115–45.

Betz, H. D. 1967. *Nachfolge und Nachahmung Jesu Christi im Neuen Testament.* BHT 37. Tübingen.

Bieder, W. 1961. *Die Berufung im Neuen Testament.* ATANT 38. Zürich.

Bieler, L. 1935–36. *Theios anēr: Das Bild des "göttlichen Menschen" in Spätantike und Frühchristentum.* 2 vols. Vienna.

Brun, L. 1932. Die Berufung der ersten Jünger Jesu in der evangelischen Tradition. *Symbolae Osloenses* 11: 36–54.

Bultmann, R. 1963. *History of the Synoptic Tradition.* Trans. J. Marsh. New York.

Butts, J. 1987. The Voyage of Discipleship. *Early Jewish and Christian Exegesis.* 199–219.

Daube, D. 1972. Responsibilities of Master and Disciples in the Gospels. *NTS* 19: 1–15.

Daumoser, I. 1954. *Berufung und Erwählung bei den Synoptikern.* Meisenheim am Galn.

Dibelius, M. 1934. *From Tradition to Gospel.* Trans. B. L. Woolf. New York.

Droge, A. J. 1983. Call Stories in Greek Biography and the Gospels. *SBLSP* 22: 245–57.

Frischer, B. 1982. *The Sculpted Word: Epicureanism and Philosophical Recruitment in Ancient Greece.* Berkeley, CA.

Gigon, O. 1946. Antike Erzählungen über die Berufung zur Philosophie. *Museum Helveticum* 3: 1–21.

Hengel, M. 1981. *The Charismatic Leader and His Followers.* Trans. J. Riches. New York.

Jeremias, J. 1930. Die Berufung des Nathanael (Jo 1, 45–51). *Angelos: Archiv für neutestamentliche Zeitgeschichte und Kulturkunde* 3: 2–5.

Louw, J. P. 1973. Discourse Analysis and the Greek New Testament. *BTrans* 24: 101–18.

Momigliano, A. 1971. *The Development of Greek Biography.* Cambridge, MA.

Pesch, R. 1969. Berufung und Sendung, Nachfolge und Mission. *ZTK* 91: 1–31.

Robbins, V. K. 1982. Mark 1.14–20: An Interpretation at the Intersection of Jewish and Graeco-Roman Traditions. *NTS* 28: 220–36.

Schulz, A. 1962. *Nachfolgen und Nachahmen.* StANT 6. Munich.

Schweizer, E. 1978. The Portrayal of the Life of Faith in the Gospel of Mark. *Int* 32: 387–99.

Schwer, W. 1954. Beruf. *RAC* 2: 142–56.

Steinhauser, M. G. 1983. Part of a "Call Story"? *ExpTim* 94: 204–6.

———. 1986. The Form of the Bartimaeus Narrative (Mark 10.46–52). *NTS* 32: 583–95.

Theissen, G. 1977. "Wir haben alles verlassen" (Mc. X 28): Nachfolge und soziale Entwurzelung in der jüdisch-palastinischen Gesellschaft des 1. Jahrhunderts n. Ch. *NovT* 19: 161–96.

Wach, J. 1924. *Meister und Jünger.* Leipzig.

Wechssler, E. 1936. *Hellas im Evangelien.* Berlin.

Wuellner, W. 1967. *The Meaning of "Fishers of Men."* Philadelphia.

A. J. Droge

CALLISTHENES (PERSON) [Gk *Kallisthenēs*]. A Syrian who helped set fire to the Temple gates in Jerusalem in the time of Judas Maccabeus (2 Macc 8:33). After Judas' victory over the Syrian general Nicanor, Callisthenes and others of the Syrian army who had taken refuge in a small house were burned alive by the Jews for their part in setting fire to the gates of the Temple. This episode may be referred to in 2 Macc 1:7–8, in which case Callisthenes would have been a follower of Jason the Oniad. Goldstein (*2 Maccabees* AB, 338–41) notes that v 33 must continue the description of the victory over Nicanor and Gorgias which has been interrupted by vv 30–33, an account of the victory over Timotheus and Bacchides. The death of Callisthenes and his followers was considered divine recompense, a favorite theme of Jason of Cyrene. Goldstein (*2 Maccabees* AB, 256, 341) cites other examples in 2 Macc 5:9–10; 9:5–6, 28; 13:6–8; 14:32–33. In Psalm 74:3–6 (—Eng 74:4–7) the setting on fire of the sanctuary has been associated with this event. However, most commentators stress that the description of this event in the psalm is too ambiguous to date historically (Anderson *Psalms* NCBC, 537–45; Kraus *Psalmen* BKAT, 514–15; Weiser *Psalms* OTL, 518–20).

Russell D. Nelson

CALNEH (PLACE) [Heb *kalnēh*]. Var. CALNO. A city in Syria in the vicinity of Arpad and Aleppo (Isa 10:9; here Calno, Heb *kalnô*). The conquest of Calneh by Tiglath-pileser III in his 8th year of reign (738 B.C.) was of such significance that it served as the Assyrian eponym designation for that year. This was the same year in which Menahem of Israel gave tribute to Tiglath-pileser III, and it is therefore not remarkable that this crucial conquest is commemorated in the words of both Amos and Isaiah, who perceived Calneh's defeat in recent history as an event which both foreboded the destruction in 722 B.C. of a less significant Israel (Amos 6:2) and prompted Assyria to self-delusions of invincibility (Isa 10:9). Located 300 miles N of Israel in Syria and thus closer to Assyria, it was inevitable that Calneh would experience the Assyrian threat earlier than Israel. The subsequent incorporation of Calneh into the Assyrian empire, with the accompanying payments and supplies which she was required to provide to Assyria, parallels the similar experience of Israel.

The exact location of Calneh remains unconfirmed, possible sites including Kullan Köy and Tell Taʿyinat. In late 8th-century Assyrian texts the name appears as Kulni(a)/Kullani(a) and is probably to be identified with the Ki/unali/ua of earlier Assyrian texts, the capital and most important city of the state of Unqi (see J. D. Hawkins *RLA* 5: 597–8; 6: 305–6). If this identification is correct, then the site of Calneh is to be located somewhere in the Antioch plain on the basis of a 9th-century B.C. itinerary recording an Assyrian march through Syria (*GARI* 2, §584–85). This identification provides further parallels to Israel's experience, for deportees from other Assyrian campaigns were relocated and settled in this the former capital of Unqi. The vocalic fluctuation evident in Assyrian sources (even the reduction of the second vowel) accounts for the different spellings in Amos (*kalnēh*) and Isaiah (*kalnô*), even though the initial *patah* ("a" vowel) in both remains unaccounted for. As elsewhere, the name of the new Assyrian province was derived from the name of the most important city in the province. The Canneh of Ezek 27:23 which some scholars identify with Calneh is probably a different locale.

Although a Calneh appears in the Hebrew text of Gen 10:10 (identical in form to Amos 6:2), the S Mesopotamian context suggests that this city attributed to Nimrod should be located near the renowned cities of Babylon, Uruk, and Agade and not the Syrian location of Amos 6:2. This awareness no doubt generated traditions that the Calneh of Gen 10:10 is to be identified with sites such as Nippur (*b.Yoma* 10a), but there is no Calneh attested in well-documented S Mesopotamia, let alone of significant reputation to match the other three cities. Since a textual corruption is likely, possibly one should revocalize the text to read "and all of them" *wĕkullānâ* (RSV).

Samuel A. Meier

CALVARY (PLACE). See GOLGOTHA (PLACE).

CAMEL. From the order *Artiodactyla* and the family *Camelidae* (even-toed ungulates). In the family there are six living species with two in the Old World: the dromedary (or one-humped camel: *C. dromedarius*) and the bactrian (or two-humped camel: *C. bactrianus*). (For distinctive zoological characteristics, see Clutton-Brock 1981: 121–23.) The family is generally considered to have originated in North America but migrated to Asia by the end of the Pliocene, ca. 2 million B.P., since the earliest recovered fossils from the Siwalik Deposits in India belong to this period (for recent summaries, see Howell et al. 1969; Grigson 1983). It is difficult to determine which modern species inhabited SW Asia or what the early Holocene range and distribution might have been, but for the sake of practicality, most authors have suggested that the dromedary was the species characteristic of SW Asia (Arabian peninsula) as opposed to the Inner Asian range of the bactrian (see Compagnoni and Tosi 1978 for suggested early Holocene ranges). Human association with camel remains in the Levant goes back to the Lower Paleolithic based on sparse finds at Ubeidiya in the Dead Sea area (1 million B.P.) and the Acheulean at Latamne, Syria (ca. 250,000 B.P.). Camel remains are more numerous at selected Middle Paleolithic sites such as Doura Cave in Syria (Takai 1974: 170) and Azraq in E Jordan (Clutton-Brock 1970). (For a summary of Paleolithic finds in general, see Grigson 1983: 312.) Later remains have been reported from a Pre-Pottery Neolithic B context at Ain al Assad in Azraq (Kohler 1984: 201), and from the Pottery Neolithic at Shar-ha-Golan (Stekelis 1951: 16). At no site, however, are the remains particularly numerous or widespread enough to suggest that camels were ever a dietary staple in early human context in the Near East (for overall treatments, see Ripinsky 1975; Zarins 1982). (For rock art depictions from the 7th–5th millennia B.C., showing speared camels from SW Arabia, see Anati 1968: 110 and fig. 74; Anati 1974: 234 and fig. 243; Zarins, Murad, and al-Yish 1981: pls. 36B, 34E, 35F, 11A.) By the advent of the Bronze Age, ca. 3000 B.C., wild camels seem to have disappeared or to have been driven out of their natural habitat into the more inhospitable reaches of the Arabian peninsula and our understanding of their behavior patterns and ecological preference remains unclear (Grigson 1983: 313).

Biblical references to camels are still considered controversial, especially in the Genesis passages. Table 1 lists the occurrences in Old Testament usage:

Table 1

Text	*Person/Period*	*Context*	*Sugg. Date*
Neh 7:69	Iron III	return from exile with camels	c. 530 B.C.
Ezra 2:67	Iron III	return from exile with camels	c. 530 B.C.
Isa 21:7	Iron II/III	camel riders from desert	c. 600 B.C.
30:6		camels among "beasts of the Negev"	
60:6		Midianite camels	
Ezek 25:5	Iron II/III	"People of the East" and Ammonites with camels	c. 600 B.C.
Jer 49:29	Iron II/III	camels of Qedar	c. 600 B.C.
49:32		camels of the inhabitants of Hazor	
2 Kgs 8:9	Hazael/Ben Hadad	camel loads of goods	c. 850 B.C.
1 Kgs 10:2	Solomon	camels of Sheba bearing spices	c. 950 B.C.
1 Chr 27:30	David	camels of Obil the Ishmaelite	c. 1000 B.C.
12:40		camels used as pack animals	
5:21		camels as booty from Hagrites	
1 Sam 30:17	David	the camels of Amalekites	
27:9		camels as booty from Shur	
[Job 1:3, 1:17]		"Chaldeans" raiding Job's camels	
1 Sam 15:3	Saul	camels of Amalekites	c. 1050 B.C.
Judg 6:5	Gideon	camel attacks of Midianites	c. 1150 B.C.
7:12		camel attacks of Midianites	
8:21, 26		camels of Zebah and Zalmunna	

[Lev 11:4 = Deut 14:7]	Mosaic Law	prohibition against eating camel meat	
Exod 9:3	Moses	Pharaoh's camels are plagued along with other herds in Egypt	c. 1250 B.C.
Gen 37:25	Joseph	Midianites/ Ishmaelites going to Egypt with camel caravans	c. 1300 B.C.
Gen 32:15 31:34 30:43	Jacob	Jacob's flocks with Laban include camels as well as herd animals for Esau in the Seir area	
Gen 24:10–67 12:16	Abraham	camels used for trip to Syria, included as bride price; Abraham in Egypt owns camels as part of larger herds	c. ?

From this brief look, we can see that references to camels in the OT fall into three groups. The third period, the latest, corresponds to the Iron Age II–III periods. The occurrence of camels in the greater Near East during this period, 900–400 B.C., is well documented (Ephᶜal 1981). The second period, covering the use of camels from Joseph to Solomon, should fall within the archaeological periods labelled LB III and Iron I (1300–950 B.C.). In the OT, camels are consistently associated with people called Ishmaelites, Midianites, and Amalekites, located to the S and E of Israel and Judah proper. Therefore, it may be the case that domesticated camels were in use in the northwestern portion of the Arabian peninsula sometime in the mid-2d millennium B.C. among pastoral people with whom the Israelites had some acquaintance.

This idea (already noted by Albright *FSAC,* 257, 287; *ArchPal* 206–7), can be affirmed from both independent inscriptional and archaeological data. The earliest mention of the camel as a domesticated animal occurs in the inscriptions of Aššur-bel-kala (1074–1057 B.C.) from Assyria. In an account dated to 1069 B.C., herds of camels are mentioned as if they are curiosities to the people of Assyria (*GARI,* 55). It would appear then that the Assyrians were not familiar with domesticated camels much earlier than the late 2d millennium B.C. This is supported by other lines of evidence. For N Arabia and the S Levant, the occurrence of osteological camel remains follows the development of cultures involved in the S Arabian overland spice trade. This largely supports the pattern derivable from the Biblical references in Table 1. With direct Midianite association, however, we have only a sherd depicting a camel from Qurayya (Ingraham et al. 1981: pl. 79/14); but this sparse attestation is due to the lack of excavation. In the Wadi Arabah at Site 2, at a copper smelting camp dated to the Ramesside period (c. 1350–1150 B.C.), "several camel bones" were found with other faunal remains (Rothenberg 1972: 105; Hakker-Orion 1984: 209). In a later report, the excavators mention that a "large quantity of camel bones" was uncovered at the 13th–12th-century-B.C. sites of Timna (Rothenberg and Glass 1983: 122, n. 50). From Tell Jemmeh on the Gaza Strip, Wapnish identifies only seven camel bones from levels attributable to the 14th–10th centuries B.C. (Wapnish 1982: 2; 1984: 171). Similarly at Heshbon in Jordan, camel remains are very infrequent from the earliest levels, 1230–1150 B.C. (Weiler 1981: table 4). Two early Iron I "fortress" sites (Har Saad, Kadesh Barnea) found in the Negev and northern Sinai dating to ca. 1000 B.C. have been interpreted to represent a fundamental shift among pastoral nomads in the region, perhaps brought on by the advent of domesticated camels (Finkelstein 1984: 200 n. 4). This may be confirmed by Hakker-Orion, who states that camel bones in some quantity were found at Har Saad and Kadesh Barnea (1984: 210).

However, for our first phase, represented by the early Genesis accounts, the evidence for camel domestication remains frustratingly elusive. Part of our problem lies in the attempts to delineate domestic from wild camels on the basis of morphological change in the skeleton alone. This is not yet possible (Hoch 1979: 607; Clutton-Brock 1981: 126; Hakker-Orion 1984: 209). Secondly, the region where this transition may have occurred first is far removed from the S Levant and N Arabia. Our best evidence to date comes from E Iran. From the site of Shahr-i-Sokhta, the excavators recovered not only osteological remains but also hair and dung. Found in a context datable to 2700 B.C., the remains led the excavators to argue that camel domestication began in Turkmenia and spread south (Compagnoni and Tosi 1978: 95–99). The domestic camel was apparently known to the inhabitants of the Indus Valley Civilization by 2300 B.C., although the species utilized remains open to question (Meadow 1984: 134 and references).

From the Arabian peninsula proper, at the site of Umm-an-Nar, analysis of the osteological camel remains suggests tentative steps toward domestication. This idea is based on the unusual number of camel bones found, the age distribution of recovered material, and the cultural context (Hoch 1979: 613). This stimulus toward domestication may well have come from the Indus Valley (Zarins 1978). Camel remains from S Arabia, supporting the thesis that the center of domestication lay in the south, are not common, but again survey and excavation have been limited (Bulliet 1975: 28–56). From Sihi, a shell midden on the S Red Sea coast, camel remains have been recovered in a late 3d–early 2d-millennium B.C. context or earlier (Zarins and Badr 1988; Grigson et al. fc.). The likelihood that camel remains will turn up at other sites of the 3d or 2d millennium B.C. is great with the recent archaeological activity along both the Red Sea coast (Tosi fc.) and highland Yemen (De Maigret 1981, 1984). Several bedouin sites from S Arabia dating to the mid–2d millennium B.C. have also yielded camel remains (Zarins et al. 1981: pls. 43A–B; Zarins et al. 1980: 23 n. 6).

Based on this observed pattern it appears that domesticated camels arrived en masse in N Arabia and the S Levant only by the latter part of the 2d millennium B.C. Essentially, this confirms the biblical evidence outlined above in Table 1. However, the problem of the earlier Genesis accounts is unresolved. Third-millennium B.C. camel remains from the S Levant are very rare. From Arad in an EB I context (ca. 2900 B.C.), a few bones have been found (Lernau 1978: 87); and from Bir Resisim in the N Negev in an EB IV context (ca. 1900 B.C.), several fragments have been reported (Hakker-Orion 1984: 209). It is unlikely that in both of these cases the remains represent domestic camels. Nonetheless, if we hold that the patriarchal stories are essentially historical in outlook, we would not be totally amiss in suggesting that domestic camels may have been known to the inhabitants of Syria-Palestine as early as the turn of the 3d millennium B.C. Conclusions concerning the utilization of the camel within the Arabian peninsula are summarized in Table 2.

Table 2
Suggested Domestication and Developmental Model for Camel Nomads of the Arabian Peninsula (after Zarins 1988)

Phase	*Camel Utilization*	*Date*	*Cultural Evolution*
V	North Arabian saddle (Shadad) Thamudic	500 B.C.	rectangular goat hair tent; minimal use of stone
IV	South Arabic cushion saddle	1000 B.C.	rectangular, stone-outlined structures, tapered structures
III	South Arabic saddle (Hawlani/Hadaja) pack animals; overland incense trade; change in camel status	1500 B.C.	troughs, horseshoe-shaped structures
II	nonriding; herds for milk; little group movement	2200–1500 B.C.	Umm-an-Nar, Subr, Sihi; Phase II rock art in southwest Arabia. Arad and Bir Resisim remains from the Levant?
I	wild camel hunted	6000–2000 B.C.	Phase I rock art in southwest Arabia; osteological remains; Chalcolithic sites in Levant

Bibliography

Anati, E. 1968. *Rock Art in Central Arabia.* Vols. 1–2. Louvain.

———. 1974. *Corpus of the Rock Engravings Sectors J–Q.* Vol. 4 of *Rock Art in Central Arabia.* Louvain.

Bulliet, R. W. 1975. *The Camel and the Wheel.* Cambridge, MA.

Clutton-Brock, J. 1970. The Fossil Fauna from an Upper Pleistocene Site in Jordan. *Journal of Zoology* 162: 19–29.

———. 1981. *Domesticated Animals from Early Times.* Austin.

Clutton-Brock, J., and Grigson, C., eds. 1984. *Animals and Archaeology 3: Early Herders and Their Flocks.* BARIS 202. Oxford.

Compagnoni, B., and Tosi, M. 1978. The Camel: Its Distribution and State of Domestication in the Middle East During the Third Millennium B.C. in Light of Finds from Shahr-i-Sokhta. Pp. 91–103 in *Approaches to Faunal Analysis in the Middle East,* ed. R. M. Meadow and M. Zeder. Cambridge, MA.

De Maigret, A. 1981. Two Prehistoric Cultures and a New Sabaean Site in the Eastern Highlands of North Yemen. *Raydan* 4: 1–13.

———. 1984. A Bronze Age for Southern Arabia. *East and West* 34: 75–115.

Ephᶜal, I. 1981. *The Ancient Arabs.* Leiden.

Finkelstein, I. 1984. The Iron Age "Fortresses" of the Negev Highlands: Sedentarization of the Nomads. *TA* 11: 189–209.

Grigson, C. 1983. A Very Large Camel from the Upper Pleistocene of the Negev Desert. *Journal of Archaeological Science* 10: 311–16.

Grigson, C.; Gowlett, J.; Zarins, J.; and Clutton-Brock, J. fc. The Dromedary in Arabia—A Direct Radiocarbon Date from the Late Seventh Millennium B.C. *Journal of Archaeological Science.*

Hakker-Orion, D. 1984. The Role of the Camel in Israel's Early History. Pp. 207–12 in Clutton-Brock and Grigson 1984.

Hoch, E. 1979. Reflections on Prehistoric Life at Umm-an-Nar (Trucial Oman) based on Faunal Remains from the Third Millennium B.C. Pp. 589–638 in *South Asian Archaeology 1977,* ed. M. Taddei. Naples.

Howell, F. C.; Fichter, L. S.; and Wolff, R. 1969. Fossil Camels in the Omo Beds, Southern Ethiopia. *Nature* 223: 150–52.

Ingraham, M.; Johnson, T.; Rihana, B.; and Shatla, J. 1981. Preliminary Report on a Reconnaissance Survey of the Northwestern Province (with a Brief Survey of the Northern Province). *Atlal* 5: 59–84.

Kohler, I. 1984. The Dromedary in Modern Pastoral Societies and Implications for Its Process of Domestication. Pp. 201–6 in Clutton-Brock and Grigson 1984.

Lernau, H. 1978. Faunal Remains, Strata III–I. Pp. 83–113 in *Early Arad,* ed. R. Amiran. Jerusalem.

Meadow, R. 1984. A Camel Skeleton from Mohenjo-Daro. Pp. 133–39 in *Frontiers of the Indus Civilization,* ed. B. B. Lal and S. P. Gupta. New Delhi.

Ripinsky, M. 1975. The Camel in Ancient Arabia. *Antiquity* 49: 295–98.

Rothenberg, B. 1972. *Were These King Solomon's Mines?* New York.

Rothenberg, B., and Glass, J. 1983. The Midianite Pottery. Pp. 65–124 in *Midian, Moab and Edom,* ed. J. F. Sawyer and D. J. Clines. Sheffield.

Stekelis, M. 1951. A New Neolithic Industry: The Yarmukian of Palestine. *IEJ* 1: 1–19.

Takai, F. 1974. Fossil Vertebrates from the Douara Cave Site. Pp. 169–81 in *The Palaeolithic Site at Doura Cave in Syria* Part 2, ed. H. Suzuki and F. Takai. Tokyo.

Tosi, M. fc. Tihama Archaeological Survey 1986. *East and West* 37.

Wapnish, P. 1982. Camel Caravans and Camel Pastoralists at Tell Jemmeh. *JANES* 13: 101–21.

———. 1984. The Dromedary and Bactrian Camel in Levantine Historical Settings: The Evidence from Tell Jemmeh. Pp. 171–87 in Clutton-Brock and Grigson 1984.

Weiler, D. 1981. *Saugetierknochenfunde vom Tell Hesban in Jordanien.* Diss. Munich.

Zarins, J. 1978. The Camel in Ancient Arabia. *Antiquity* 52: 44–46.

———. 1982. Review of *Domesticated Animals from Early Times* by J. Clutton-Brock. *BA* 45: 251–53.

———. 1989. Pastoralism in Southwest Asia: The Second Millennium B.C. Pp. 127–55 in *The Walking Larder,* ed. J. Clutton-Brock. London.

Zarins, J., and Badr, H. 1988. Archaeological Investigations in the Southern Tihama Plain II. *Atlal* 10.

Zarins, J.; Murad, A.; and al-Yish, K. 1981. Comprehensive Archaeological Survey Program—a. The Second Preliminary Report on the Southwestern Province. *Atlal* 5: 9–42.

Zarins, J.; Whalen, N.; Ibrahim, M.; Morad, A.; and Khan, M. 1980. Comprehensive Archaeological Survey Program. *Atlal* 4: 9–36.

JURIS ZARINS

CAMEL BRANDS. See WASM (CAMEL BRAND).

CAMEL'S HAIR. See DRESS AND ORNAMENTATION.

CANA OF GALILEE (PLACE) [Gk *Kana*]. A village mentioned in the gospel of John. It was called "of Galilee" probably to distinguish it from the Kanah of Asher in the territory of Tyre (Josh 19:28).

1. Cana in the NT. Cana appears only in the fourth gospel. In John 2:1–11 Jesus performed his first "sign" there, turning the water to wine at a wedding feast. From the text we cannot infer any topographical features of Cana, only that the home belonged to an anonymous Jewish family (v 6). However, from the incident of the healing of the son of the "royal man" or "king's man" (*basilikos*) at Cana in John 4:46–54 we can infer that Cana may have been administered by a royal representative (Avi-Yonah 1977: 94). This man petitioned Jesus to come to Capernaum to heal his son, which suggests that Capernaum must have been more or less directly accessible from Cana. Thus, Cana lay on a major road to Capernaum. Yet the father could not get to Capernaum from Cana between 1:00 P.M. (the seventh hour, v 52) and sundown, which suggests that the way to Capernaum was rugged. Nathaniel, one of the Twelve, was from Cana (John 21:2).

2. Identification. Three sites have been suggested as the probable location of Cana of Galilee: *Ain Qana,* 1.5 km N of Nazareth next to the village of Reina (Thomsen 1907: 77); *Kafr Kanna,* also known as Kefr Kenna, a major village about 5 km NE of Nazareth (Bagatti 1971: 42–47); and *Khirbet Qana,* a small ruin on a prominent mountain spur about 14 km N of Nazareth (Robinson 1841: 204; Dalman 1924). Of the three, only *Khirbet Qana* (M.R. 170070) has the consensus of scholarship since Dalman. All the facts of paragraph 1 would fit any of the proposed sites. Yet the name "Cana" means "reed" in Hebrew. *Kafr Kanna* appears to mean "the village of the roof," and has no linguistic connection with the name *qana.* "Reed" fits best the Cana in the Plain of Asochis (today's Beth Netofa valley) mentioned by Josephus: "I spent some time there in a village of Galilee which is called Cana" (*Life* 86, 206). The plain of Asochis favored the growth of reeds during and after the winter rains, as it does to this day, particularly in its eastern lower half. When the Romans destroyed Jerusalem in 70 A.D., the priestly course of Eliashib settled at "*Qana*" (Klein 1909, *Mishmaroth* 11), not "*Ain Qana.*"

3. Cana in Later Tradition. That the priestly course of Eliashib settled in Cana suggests that Cana was a Jewish village, not a gentile or mixed village. By 200 A.D. there was a question of ritual cleanliness about a certain "*Qini.*" ". . . but Rabbi (Judah the Prince) and his law court voted to decide about '*Qini*' [Cana?] and declared it clean" (*m. Ohol.* 18.9; Neubauer 1868: 276). Cana is mentioned in the Jerusalem Talmud (*j. Ter.* 46b) as the village of origin of a famous 3d-century robber, Eli of Cana (Klein 1928: 49). There is no doubt from the citations in the Christian pilgrim literature, which flourished from the 4th century onward, that Cana came to be identified with *Kafr Kanna,* perhaps because it was close to Nazareth. Eusebius in the 4th century A.D. confused Cana of "Sidon the Great of the lot of Asher" with Cana of Galilee (*Onomast.* 116.37r). In the 5th century, Jerome, although he followed Eusebius in this confusion (*Onomast.* 117.3f), seemed to believe that Cana was near Nazareth (Wilkinson 1977: 153). The Pilgrim of Piacenza (570 A.D.) found Cana only 3 miles from Sepphoris-Diocaesarea on the road to Nazareth (Wilkinson 1977: 79), which fits *Kafr Kanna.* This is the town that pilgrims visit to this day.

4. Archaeological Remains at Cana. Visitors to *Khirbet Qana* in the 19th century found the remains of a large village on a low spur of "Mt. Cana" (*Jebel Qana,* apparently modern Mt. Shekhanya) on the N side of the Beth Netofa valley. The records of many visits, including scientific survey in 1982, indicate that Cana was laid out on the points of the compass. An enormous building on the NW side of the village dominated the site. Rock-cut tombs are to be found S and SE of the village on the lower slopes of the hill. The top of the spur is virtually honeycombed with caves and cisterns. The cisterns guaranteed a good supply of water for the village, as there are no remains of an aqueduct. A long wall runs the length of the site on the W side (Bagatti and Loffreda 1969). The entire site is in a very advantageous geographical position to house a "king's man" or "royal man" to administer the royal estates of the Valley of Asochis, as it is situated about 100 m above the valley floor. A major E-W road ran from Ptolemais-Acco in the W through the Valley of Asochis E through the Wadi Hammam to the W shores of the Sea of Galilee. From there it was easy access N and E to Capernaum or S to Tiberius. Pottery and coins from the surface of *Khirbet Qana* suggest occupation from the early Roman to the Byzantine period. A second ruin halfway down the slope on the S side appears to be a more recent ruin built from stones of the Roman-Byzantine village. This latter village was occupied as late as 1838 (Conder and Kitchener *SWP* 2: 313).

Bibliography

Avi-Yonah, M. 1976. *Gazetteer of Roman Palestine.* Qedem 5. Jerusalem.

———. 1977. *The Holy Land from the Persian to the Arab Conquest.* Grand Rapids.

Bagatti, B. 1971. *Antichi Villaggi Cristiani di Galilea.* Jerusalem.

Bagatti, B., and Loffreda, S. 1969. Le Antichità de Khirbet Qana e di Kegar Kanna in Galilea. *LASBF* 15: 251–92.

Dalman, G. 1924. *Orte und Wege Jesu.* 3d ed. Gütersloh.

Klein, S. 1909. *Beiträge zur Geographie und Geschichte Galiäas.* Leipzig.

———. 1928. *Galiläa von der Makkabaerzeit bis 67.* Palestina-Studien. Vol. 4. Vienna.

Neubauer, A. 1868. *La Geographie du Talmud.* Paris. Repr. 1970.

Robinson, E. 1841. *Biblical Researches in Palestine, Mount Sinai, and Arabia Petraea.* Vol. 3. Boston.

Thomsen, P. 1907. *Loca Sancta: Verzeichnis der im 1. bis 6. Jahrhundert n. Chr. erwähnten Ortschaften Palästinas mit besonderer Berücksichtigung der Lokalisierung der biblischen Stätten.* Leipzig.

Wilkinson, J. 1977. *Jerusalem Pilgrims Before the Crusades.* Warminster.

JAMES F. STRANGE

CANAAN (PERSON) [Heb *kĕnaʿan*]. The fourth son of Ham and the father of Sidon and ten other families of the Canaanites (Gen 10:6). When Noah learned what Ham, his youngest son, had done (seeing his father uncovered and telling his brothers of it); Noah cursed Canaan, the son of Ham (Gen 9:18–27). According to the curse, Canaan would be a slave to Ham's brothers, Shem and Japheth. For a discussion of the meaning of the name Canaan, and the peoples and lands encompassed by that term, see CANAAN (PLACE). Two problems emerge from the mention of Canaan in Genesis 9: why is Canaan cursed rather than the apparent perpetrator Ham; and what is the implication of the curse for Canaan and his descendants?

A composite text, in which the narrative and the curse were originally distinct (the "youngest son" of 9:24 would then refer to Canaan, rather than Ham, and would be connected with the curse which follows) and preserved in two separate traditions, might explain origins (Neiman 1966: 133; Westermann *Genesis 1–11* BKAT, 650–51), but does not explain the present text. Some have attempted to solve the problem of why Canaan was cursed by eliminating two Hebrew words in vv 18 and 22 ("Ham, the father of"), so that Canaan, rather than Ham, becomes the principal actor in the narrative (Gunkel *Genesis* HKAT 3: 69–70; Skinner *Genesis* ICC, 182; Schottroff WMANT 30: 148 n. 3; von Rad *Genesis* OTL, 135). But this lacks textual support. The same is true of attempts to portray Ham as involved in incestuous relationships with his mother (Bassett 1971: 235) or with his father (Phillips 1980: 41). Commentators have noted how these (and other similar explanations of sexual misconduct) were intended to symbolize the sinful practices of the Canaanites (Cassuto 1964: 154–55; Wenham *Genesis 1–15* WBC, 201). The emphasis upon the identification of Ham as the father of Canaan has led to the suggestion that Ham learned how to do the evil deed from Canaan (Jacob 1934: 262–65).

Older explanations which observe Noah's blessing upon his sons (Gen 9:1) as irreversible have been used to explain Noah's inability to curse Ham. It has further been suggested that since Ham was the youngest of Noah's sons, the curse would be transferred to the youngest of Ham's sons, Canaan (cf. Cassuto 1964: 153).

Much speculation has centered around the particular circumstances represented in the figures of Japheth, Shem, and Canaan; and reflected in the curse (Schottroff WMANT 30: 149–50). Attempts have been made to date the events (or a desire for their realization) in the pre-Israelite period; e.g., that of Gunkel (*Genesis* HKAT 3: 73), where "Canaan" represents the Amorites and Hittites, who oppose the Hebrews and the Aramaeans, represented by "Shem." Skinner (*Genesis* ICC, 187) also argues for an early period. For him "Canaan" is the Amarna Canaanites, who oppose the Apiru and their allies, represented by Japheth and Shem. Note also Cassuto (1964: 168), who finds the fulfillment of this curse in the account of Genesis 14. Many scholars choose the time period of Joshua/Judges. In this case, "Canaan" (i.e., the Canaanites) oppose the Israelites (= "Shem") and the Philistines/"Sea-Peoples" (= "Japheth" [Speiser *Gen* AB, 62–63; von Rad *ROTT* 137–39; Neiman 1966: 121–33; Bassett 1971: 232; Bastomsky 1977]). The period of the Israelite Monarchy is the one chosen by Hoftijzer (1958). In his view the Israelites, represented by "Canaan," stand against "Japheth," i.e., the Philistines/Assyrians/Babylonians. The underlying assumption in all such theories is that each of the figures mentioned in the curse are intended to represent peoples or groups of peoples, rather than the individuals Canaan, Shem, and Japheth (cf. however Westermann *Genesis 1–15* WBC, 657–60).

Bibliography

Bassett, F. W. 1971. Noah's Nakedness and the Curse of Canaan: A Case of Incest? *VT* 21: 232–37.

Bastomsky, S. J. 1977. Noah, Italy, and the Sea Peoples. *JQR* 67: 146–53.

Cassuto, U. 1964. *A Commentary on the Book of Genesis. Part II: From Noah to Abraham.* Trans. I. Abrahams. Jerusalem.

Cohen, H. H. 1974. *The Drunkenness of Noah.* Tuscaloosa, AL.

Hoftijzer, J. 1958. Some Remarks to the Tale of Noah's Drunkenness. *OTS* 12: 22–27.

Jacob, B. 1934. *Das Erste Buch der Tora. Genesis Übersetzt und Erklärt.* Berlin. New York. Repr.

Neiman, D. 1966. The Date and Circumstances of the Cursing of Canaan. Pp. 113–34 in *Biblical Motifs. Origins and Transformations,* ed. A. Altman. Philip W. Lown Institute of Advanced Judaic Studies. Studies and Texts. Vol. 3. Cambridge, MA.

———. 1972. Canaan, Curse of. Vol. 5 cols. 97–98 in *EncJud.* Jerusalem.

Phillips, A. 1980. Uncovering the Father's Skirt. *VT* 30: 38–43.

Rice, G. 1972. The Curse that Never Was (Gen 9:18–27). *JRT* 29: 5–27.

RICHARD S. HESS

CANAAN (PLACE) [Heb *kĕnaʿan*]. CANAANITES. A term designating the land along the E shore of the Mediterranean encompassing modern Lebanon, part of S Syria, and most of Palestine W of the Jordan. The ethnicon derived from the geographic term designates the indigenous and assimilated inhabitants of the area in antiquity, and, secondarily, the group of related Semitic languages characteristically spoken there. The substantial identity of Canaan with the land occupied by the Israelites is a central theme of the OT. (For a discussion of the prehistory and material culture of this region, see PALESTINE, ARCHAEOLOGY OF.)

The geographic name "Canaan" is spelled *knʿn* in Northwest Semitic alphabetic texts (Ug, Heb, Phoen-Pun). The Masoretic vocalization is *kĕnaʿan,* accented on the second syllable; LXX transliterates *Chanaan,* the Vulgate *Chanaan.* The name is found syllabically written in Akkadian *Ki-na-aḫ-num* (gentilic), with the pharyngeal consonant represented by *ḫ,* and *Ki-in-a-nim,* with the pharyngeal unrepresented. The Egyptian spellings *K-i-n-ʿ-nw* and *K-3-n-ʿ-n-3* consistently represent the pharyngeal consonant. Western peripheral Akkadian texts of the 2d millennium most frequently attest the name with a reduced base *Kinaḫḫ-,* indicating that the final *-n* of the alphabetically written examples is probably an affixational morpheme.

The etymology of the word "Canaan" remains obscure. If it is of W Semitic origin, it probably derives from the root *knʿ* "to bend, to bow" with the afformative *-n;* the meaning "Occident" has been proposed on the basis of such a derivation (Astour 1965: 348). E. A. Speiser (1936) constructed an etymology from a putative word *kinaḫḫu*, designating blue-dyed cloth in cuneiform texts from Nuzi, and probably representing a Hurrian adoption of a Mediterranean term related to Akk *uqnû* and Gk *kyanos*. But the Hurrian word (properly spelled *qinaḫḫu*) has been shown to have an entirely different history than Speiser proposed (Landsberger 1967: 166–67). Improved attestation of 3d-millennium geographic names from Syria-Palestine has lessened the likelihood of a Hurrian etymology for "Canaan"; its meaning should probably be sought in the Semitic lexicon (see Astour 1988).

"Canaan" is first attested as a geographic name in cuneiform texts. The ethnicon "Canaanite" is found in a text from Mari (Dossin 1973; Sasson 1984; [lu]*ki-na-aḫ-num*). The 15th-century autobiographical text of Idrimi (from Alalaḫ) mentions "Ammia in the land of Canaan," (*ANET*, 557; Akk *ki-na-nim*). Ammia is to be identified with modern Ammiun near Tripoli. Later cuneiform texts from Alalaḫ mention Canaan as well. An economic text from Ugarit written in the wedge alphabet (*UT* 311.7; *KTU* 4.96.7) includes a Canaanite (*knʿny*) in a list of foreign merchants. This indicates that Ugarit did not include itself in the Canaanite sphere (so Rainey 1965). The Amarna correspondence refers to Canaan as an Egyptian province (*pī-ḫatu*, EA 36.15) that includes Tyre (EA 148.46), Byblos (EA 109.46; 131.61; 137.76), other coastal cities, and Ḫinnatūni (HANNATHON [PLACE], Josh 19:14) in the Galilee. (The name of the divinity [d]*Be(BAD) ga-na-na* found in 3d-millennium cuneiform texts from Ebla [ARET 3: 31 r. II 13; 42 III 6; VII 6; 769 II 1; ARET 4: 23 v. VIII 4] was alleged by Pettinato [1979: 103] to include the geographic name Canaan, but subsequent study of the texts has not supported this interpretation [*contra* Stolz, *TRE* 17: 540].)

The earliest mention of Canaanites in an Egyptian text is found in a list of booty from the Asian campaign of Amenhotep (Gk Amenophis) II (*ANET*, 246) late in the 15th century. The 13th-century "Israel stela" of Merneptah lists Canaan among the vanquished (*ANET*, 378; *AEL*, 77).

It is generally agreed (following Helck 1971: 246–55) that Egypt administered Syria-Palestine as three provinces: Amurru, Upi, and Canaan (Weinstein 1981; on the history of Upi, see Pitard 1987: 49–80, esp. pp. 59–60; for details see EGYPTIAN RELATIONS WITH CANAAN; Wright 1988; Dever 1987; Leonard 1989). Amurru, the northernmost province, passed to Hittite rule after the Egyptian defeat at Kadesh. Egyptian texts after this period sometimes refer to the area encompassed by Canaan and Upi by the general designation Ḫurru. After the invasion of the Sea People, "Canaan" comes to be used in a more restricted sense to designate S Palestine, and the expression "the city of Canaan" can refer specifically to Gaza (Alt 1944: 4–6; *RLA* 5: 353). The latest Egyptian reference to Canaan, the 22d-Dynasty inscription of an "envoy to the Canaan from Philistia" (so Weippert 1974: 429), has occasioned various interpretations (*RLA* 5: 354 with bibliography).

The word "Canaan" was sometimes transliterated *Chanaan* in Greek sources (PW 3: 2109), and frequently in LXX (e.g., Gen 9:22, 25; Jdt 5:9–10; 1 Macc 9:37). "Canaan" is transliterated twice in the NT (Acts 7:11; 13:9). More frequently, however, Canaan is indicated in Greek by the designation "Phoenicia" and the related ethnicon "Phoenician." The equivalence of the two terms is established by the legends of 3d-century coins from the Beirut mint: the Phoenician text *lʾdkʾ ʾš bknʿn* "Laodicea which is in Canaan" corresponds to Greek *Laodikeia he en Phoinikē* "Laodicea which is in Phoenicia" (*RLA* 5: 354 with bibliography). The equivalence is reflected in the NT, which employs the ethnicon *Chananaia* once (Matt 15:22); the rare word *Syrophoinikissa* is used in the parallel account (Mark 7:26).

A difficult passage in the *Phoenician History* of PHILO OF BYBLOS identifies a certain *Chnâ* as the first to carry the name "Phoenician" (Attridge and Oden 1981: 60–61 and n. 144). Herodianus Grammaticus (2d century C.E.; Lentz 1868: 913) and Stephanus of Byzantium (s.v. *Chnâ*) indicate that the Phoenicians were formerly called *Chnâ*. The reduced form of the name Canaan, written *Kinaḫḫ*- in Akkadian texts of the 2d millennium, may be represented in Gk *Chnâ*.

The distribution of the geographical name "Canaan" in the OT provides some measure of the significance of this word in biblical texts. The word "Canaan" occurs 80 times in the MT. Most frequently (64x, or 80 percent of its occurrences) it is found in the construction *ʾereṣ kĕnaʿan*, "land of Canaan." This construction is most frequent in Genesis, but also occurs in Exodus (6:4; 16:35), Leviticus (14:34; 18:3; 25:38), Numbers (12x), and once in Deuteronomy (32:49). In the Deuteronomistic History, the word "Canaan" is restricted to Joshua and Judges, most often in the construction "land of Canaan." Thus the Primary History accounts for 88 percent of the word's use.

The word "Canaan" is found in passages assigned by literary-critical analysis to the J, E, and P sources. See TORAH (PENTATEUCH). Its concentration in the sections of the Pentateuch which introduce and develop the theme of promise of land to the Patriarchs (i.e., Genesis 12–50; largely in passages attributed to P), and in narratives of the conquest and settlement (Joshua-Judges), which are viewed in the Bible as a fulfillment of the promise to the Patriarchs, shows how closely bound the word "Canaan" is with the theme of promise and fulfillment (Clements 1967; Lohfink 1967). Thus, for example, the divine promise to Abraham that he and his descendants would be given "all the land of Canaan" has been called (by Brueggemann 1977: 21) the "focal verse" of the patriarchal promise theme within the Pentateuch (see also Clines 1978: 36). With the cessation of the settlement theme in Judges, the term disappears from the Primary History.

Reference to Canaan is infrequent outside the Primary History. The name is found in two prophetic books (Isa 19:18; 23:11; Zeph 2:5) and in the Psalms (105:11 [= 1 Chr 16:18]; 106:38; 135:11). In select passages, constructions using the word have been taken (see Maisler 1946) to have the meaning "merchant" (Job 41:6), "trade" (Ezek 16:29; 17:4), or "trader" (Hos 12:7; Zeph 1:11). In the Apocrypha, "Canaan" is a simple geographical name (Jdt 5:9, 10; Bar 3:22; 1 Macc 9:37), but also carries an implicit moral contrast with "Judah" (Sus 1:56). The two references to Canaan in the NT are in recitations of the Joseph story (Acts 7:11) and the conquest theme (Acts 13:19).

The boundaries of the region called "Canaan" undoubtedly changed over time. Num 34:3–12 gives the boundaries of the land that would fall to the Israelites as an inheritance, with the implication (the syntax of v 2 is vague) that it comprehends all of the "land of Canaan." The boundary list must be viewed together with similar lists elsewhere in the OT (*IDBSup,* 922). The S boundary of Canaan listed in Num 34:3–5 (attributed to P) precisely matches the S boundary of Judah given in Josh 15:2–4 (moving E to W): from the S end of the Salt Sea (= Dead Sea) to the ascent of Akrabbim, to the wilderness of Zin, S of Kadesh-barnea, Hazar-addar, to Azmon, along the Brook of Egypt (probably the Wâdī el-ᶜArîsh [see EGYPT, BROOK OF (PLACE)]) to the sea (= Mediterranean). This border is essentially the same as that prescribed in the book of Ezekiel (47:19) as the S boundary of the restored Israel. The N boundary in Num 34:7–9 corresponds to Ezek 47:15–17, and seems to correspond to the boundary implicit in the Idrimi inscription, if the "entrance of Hamath" is identified as modern Lebweh (see HAMATH, ENTRANCE OF (PLACE)), an inland site not far S of Tripoli.

The literary-critical questions raised by the similarity of these lists are difficult to resolve. Josh 15:2–4 was formerly attributed to P (e.g., Eissfeldt 1965: 251); it is part of a section (Joshua 13–22) considered a later addition to the Deuteronomistic history (*NDH,* 40). The essential identity of lists in Numbers 34, Joshua 15, and Ezekiel 47 suggests that the Pentateuchal lists may be retrojected from a later period (for detailed discussion, see Keel, Küchler, and Uehlinger 1984: 1.245–50; Kallai [*HGB,* 279–83] dates them to the period of David and Solomon). A later date is in keeping with the distributional evidence that the word "Canaan" is a theologoumenon in the Primary History.

Some of its uses are, however, early and nontheological. In the archaic poem known as the Song of Deborah occurs the phrase *malkê kĕnaᶜan,* "kings of Canaan" (Judg 5:19), recalling the Akkadian expression *šarrāni ša kinaḫḫi,* "kings of Canaan," from the Amarna letters (EA 30.1; 109.46). This is approximated in the later Hebrew phrase *malkê hakkĕnaᶜăni* "kings of the Canaanites" (Josh 5:1) using the gentilic form of the name. Reflected in this phrase is the movement from a political-geographical reference for "Canaan" to a social and ideological reference for "Canaanite." In Josh 17:16, 18 "Canaanites" are owners of iron chariots and thus a military elite. This is reminiscent of the collocation of Canaanites and *maryanna* (chariot-owning nobility; see Leonard 1989: 8) in a list of booty taken in Palestine by the Pharaoh Amenhotep II (mid-15th century B.C.E.; *ANET,* 246).

In the Pentateuch, the word "Canaanite" is found principally in texts attributed to J (e.g., Gen 10:18, 19; 12:6; 13:7; 15:21; 24:3, 37, etc.; Exod 3:8, 17; Num 13:29; 14:25, 43, 45; 21:1, 3). The word "Canaan" never occurs in D (Deut 32:49 is attributed to P), but "Canaanite" occurs four times in D (Deut 1:7; 7:1; 11:30; 20:17). It serves as a general designation of the pre-Israelite inhabitants of the land (Gen 50:11; cf. Neh 9:24), often in a list of "nations" previously occupying Israelite territory (e.g., Gen 15:21; 34:30; Exod 3:8; 23:23, 28; 33:2; 34:11, etc.). The "Canaanites" are viewed as doomed to expulsion (Exod 33:2) or, from the Deuteronomic perspective, extermination (Deut 20:17). The persistence of Canaanites within Israelite territory was a theological problem variously addressed by biblical writers. The Canaanite elements of the Yahwistic cultus were largely unperceived (see SACRIFICE AND SACRIFICIAL OFFERINGS [OLD TESTAMENT]), and prophetic castigations of the cult arise from ethical rather than ethnic concerns (Amos 5:21–25). Elements of the cult involving Canaanite deities other than Yahweh and practices exceptional to the Judean cult were more openly criticized by biblical writers and actively suppressed by some rulers. See CANAAN, RELIGION OF; PHOENICIAN RELIGION; HEZEKIAH KING OF JUDAH; JOSIAH (PERSON). The essential unity of the Canaanite languages was recognized by their speakers (Isa 19:18), even if regional differences could be the occasion of conflict (Judg 12:6; see also LANGUAGES [INTRODUCTORY SURVEY]).

Bibliography

Alt, A. 1944. Ägyptische Tempel in Palästina und die Landnahme der Philister. *ZDPV* 67: 1–20. Repr. in *KlSchr* 1: 216–30.

Astour, M. 1965. The Origin of the Terms "Canaan," "Phoenician," and "Purple." *JNES* 24: 346–50.

———. 1988. Toponymy of Ebla and Ethnohistory of Northern Syria. *JAOS* 108: 545–55.

Attridge, H. W., and Oden, R. A., Jr. 1981. *Philo of Byblos: The Phoenician History.* CBQMS 9. Washington, DC.

Brueggemann, W. 1977. *The Land.* OBT 1. Philadelphia.

Clements, R. E. 1967. *Abraham and David.* SBT n.s. 5. Naperville, IL.

Clines, D. J. A. 1978. *The Theme of the Pentateuch.* JSOTSup 10. Sheffield.

Dever, W. G. 1987. The Middle Bronze Age: The Zenith of the Urban Canaanite Era. *BA* 50: 148–77.

Dossin, G. 1973. Une mention de Canaanéens dans une lettre de Mari. *Syr* 50: 277–82.

Eissfeldt, O. 1965. *The Old Testament: An Introduction.* Trans. P. R. Ackroyd. New York.

Helck, W. 1971. *Die Beziehungen Ägyptens zu Vorderasien im 3. und 2. Jahrtausend v. Chr.* 2d ed. Wiesbaden.

Keel, O.; Küchler, M.; and Uehlinger, C. 1984. *Orte und Landschaften der Bibel.* Vol. 1, *Geographisch-geschichtliche Landeskunde.* Cologne and Göttingen.

Landsberger, B. 1967. Über Farben im Sumerisch-akkadischen. *JCS* 21: 139–73.

Lentz, A. 1868. *Herodiani Technici Reliquiae.* Vol. 2, pt. 1. Stuttgart.

Leonard, A., Jr. 1989. The Late Bronze Age. *BA* 52: 4–39.

Lohfink, N. 1967. *Die Landverheissung als Eid.* Stuttgart.

Maisler [Mazar], B. 1946. Canaan and the Canaanites. *BASOR* 102: 7–12.

Pettinato, G. 1979. Culto ufficiale ad Ebla durante il regno di Ibbi-Sipiš. *OrAnt* 18: 85–215.

Pitard, W. 1987. *Ancient Damascus.* Winona Lake, IN.

Rainey, A. 1965. A Canaanite at Ugarit. *IEJ* 13: 43–45.

Sasson, J. 1984. The Earliest Mention of the Name "Canaan." *BA* 47: 90.

Speiser, E. A. 1936. The Name *Phoinikes. Language* 12: 121–26.

Vaux, R. de. 1968. Le pays de Canaan. *JAOS* 88: 23–30.

Weinstein, J. M. 1981. The Egyptian Empire in Palestine: A Reassessment. *BASOR* 241: 1–28.

Weippert, M. 1974. Semitische Nomaden des zweiten Jahrtausends. *Bib* 55: 427–33.

Wright, M. 1988. Contacts between Egypt and Syro-Palestine during the Old Kingdom. *BA* 51: 143–61.

Philip C. Schmitz

CANAAN, CONQUEST OF. See ISRAEL, HISTORY OF (PREMONARCHIC PERIOD).

CANAAN, EGYPTIAN RELATIONS WITH. See EGYPTIAN RELATIONS WITH CANAAN.

CANAAN, RELIGION OF. The general geographical limitations of the ancient term "Canaan" are the territories of the modern states of Lebanon, Israel, Jordan, and a portion of S Syria. For a more specific discussion of the geographical range of Canaan, see CANAAN (PLACE).

A. Sources

Prior to the rise of Near Eastern archaeological work, our sources for Canaanite religion were confined to allusions in the OT and various classical authors, especially Philo of Byblos (preserved in excerpts in Eusebius) and Lucian of Samosata. Since then, numerous texts as well as objects have been found which shed direct light on the religion of the Canaanites. Pride of place goes to the mythological texts from Ugarit (modern Ras Shamra), a site on the Syrian coast, which though outside Canaan proper nevertheless shared in the Canaanite culture. More recent discoveries have revealed the nearby site of Ras Ibn Hani, and antecedents of some of the Ugaritic deities have been found in the 3d-millennium texts from Ebla (modern Tell Mardikh). Phoenician and Punic inscriptions reveal deviations from (as well as similarities to) the Canaanite religion attested at Ugarit. Texts from Egypt as well as other countries also shed light on Canaanite religion. In addition to texts, the discovery of temples, images, and other cultic paraphernalia have increased our knowledge of Canaanite religion.

B. The Canaanite Pantheon

1. Second-Millennium Ugarit. Canaanite religion in all its manifestations was always polytheistic. Many of the Ugaritic deities are in the Ugaritic pantheon list, which is attested in both Ugaritic (*Ugaritica* V.18B = *CTA* 29 = *KTU* 1.47) and Akkadian (*Ugaritica* V.18A) versions. The supreme Canaanite deity was the god El. He was the creator of the earth and of man, and was the begetter of the gods (the "sons of El") who are said to be seventy in number. Presumably El was also the creator of the whole universe, though we lack a creation account. He was an aged deity, called "father of years" (*ʾab šnm*), and appropriately had gray hair, and in keeping with this he was noted for his wisdom. Kindness and benignity are also mentioned among his attributes. There is no reason to suppose that the more violent El depicted in the late Philo of Byblos represents an earlier stage of Canaanite religion than the milder El of the 2d-millennium Ugaritic texts. El's dwelling place was "at the source of the rivers, amid the springs of the two oceans." Where this actually was is disputed, though it should be noted that in the Hittite-Canaanite Elkuniřsa myth, El (or Elkuniřsa as he is called, a name deriving from *ʾl qn ʾrṣ*, "El creator of the earth") dwells at the source of the river Euphrates (Mala). One may compare the location of the Garden of Eden at the source of the rivers Euphrates and Tigris in Gen 2:10–14.

El's consort was the goddess Athirat. Her full title was "Lady Athirat of the sea" (*rbt ʾatrt ym*). The popular view that this epithet should be rendered rather "She who treads on the sea" is invalid, since this presupposes the originality of the longer form, whereas the occurrence of the short form (Ašratum) occurs in Akkadian already as early as the 1st Dyn. of Babylon. Athirat was the mother of the gods. She is sometimes called *Qdš* ("holy" or "sanctuary") in the Ugaritic texts, a name which also occurs in connection with Egyptian depictions of a nude goddess wearing a Hathor headdress; Canaanite plaques with similar representations likely represent Athirat. Baal used her as an intermediary in order to get El to grant him a palace/temple, and along with *Rḥmy* she is described as having sexual intercourse with El, thereby giving birth to the gods Shaḥar (Dawn) and Shalem (Dusk). Her cult symbol, a wooden pole of some kind, perhaps a stylized tree, is alluded to a number of times in the OT ("the Asherah"), and this seems to be the point of the reference to the Asherah in the inscriptions from Kuntillet ʿAjrud in N Sinai ("Yahweh and his Asherah"). See ASHERAH (DEITY).

Although El is the chief god in the Canaanite pantheon, as attested at Ugarit, Baal is clearly the most active. He is the bringer of the rain, on which the fertility of the soil depends. He is called "the rider of the clouds" (*rkb ʾrpt*) in Ugaritic, and is responsible for the thunder and lightning, which herald the coming of the rain. Baal ("lord") was originally an epithet of the god Hadad ("thunderer"). Hadad appears already at Ebla under the name ʾAda. In the Ugaritic texts, the Baal cycle (*KTU* 1.1–6 = *CTA* 1–6) consists of three main parts: (1) his conflict with the god of the sea, Yam (*KTU* 1.1–2 = *CTA* 1–2), (2) the subsequent building of Baal's palace/temple (*KTU* 1.3–4 = *CTA* 3–4), and (3) Baal's conflict with Mot ("Death"), in the course of which Baal dies and rises again. There is debate how far the Baal myth should be interpreted in seasonal terms. Although attempts to interpret the Baal myth as a panorama representing a complete year seem too sweeping, it is difficult to deny the presence of seasonal elements in the Baal-Mot cycle. See BAAL (DEITY).

Another question concerns the relation between Baal and El. The extreme view that Baal and El are in conflict is to be rejected, since there is evidence that Baal was appointed king by El, and El clearly regrets Baal's death at the hands of Mot and rejoices at his subsequent resurrection; however, occasions of tensions do exist. More explicit signs of hostility occur between Baal and the sons of Athirat. Baal's dwelling place was on Mt. *Ṣpn* (probably vocalized Ṣapān), the mountain known in classical times as Mt. Casius, and today as Jebel el-Aqraᶜ, a mountain near Ugarit and appropriately the highest mountain in Syria. Ṣapān was itself regarded as a god.

Baal's chief consort is the goddess Anat. She is constantly by Baal's side and is devoted to him. She cuts up Mot like corn, is said to have defeated the dragon (i.e., Leviathan), and in one particularly gruesome scene is depicted wading through blood. See ANATH (DEITY). Also appearing as a consort of Baal in the Ugaritic texts is the goddess Astarte, though she is less prominent in that role than Anat. However, in Phoenician inscriptions and the OT Astarte rather than Anat appears to be Baal's consort, her name having been distorted to Ashtoreth (with the vowels of *bōšet,* "shame") in the OT by later scribes. See ASHTORETH (DEITY).

Baal's father is usually represented as Dagon, but occasionally El is designated as such. Perhaps Dagon was Baal's literal father since Dagon is listed between El and Baal in the Ugaritic pantheon; it is conceivable that Baal was actually the grandson of El. Although Dagon is frequently mentioned as the father of Baal and he appears in a number of sacrificial lists, he does not figure in any mythological texts from Ugarit. However, his dwelling place, Tuttul (in NE Syria), is mentioned in a Ugaritic snake charm text. His name suggests that he was a corn god. This deity is already attested at Ebla and was prominent among the Amorites at Mari and the OT indicates that he was worshiped by the Philistines, who must have appropriated him from the Canaanites. See DAGON (DEITY).

The craftsman of the gods, comparable to the Greek Hephaetus, was Kothan-and-Ḫasis ("skilful and clever"). Among other things he made the magic clubs with which Baal defeated Yam and built Baal's palace/temple. His dwelling place was both Crete and what is probably Egypt. He appeared at Ebla under the name of Kašalu.

At Ugarit the sun was worshiped as a goddess, Shapash. For the unusual spelling of the name at Ugarit we may postulate the development *šamšu* ⟶ *šampšu* ⟶ *šapšu* (employing the form of the name with the nominative ending). Her epithet is *nrt ᵓilm,* "luminary of the gods." Among other things, she scorches the earth during Baal's stay in the underworld (as befits the summer months) but tells Mot to stop struggling with Baal when the time is up. Her nocturnal trip in the underworld is reflected at the end of the Baal myth, where she is found amid the *rpᵓum* (the underworld shades). The moon does not appear to have played a particularly prominent role in Canaanite mythology, though its name is preserved in such place names in Palestine as Beth-yeraḥ and Jericho. From Ugarit we possess a text (*KTU* 1.24 = *CTA* 24) which celebrates the marriage of the moon god, Yarikh, and the goddess Nikkal. Two other deities associated with the sky in some way are Shaḥar and Shalem, whose names mean respectively "Dawn" and "Dusk." *KTU* 1.23 (= *CTA* 23) attributes their birth as a result of El's sexual intercourse with Athirat and *Rḥmy.* Sometimes it has been supposed that Shaḥar and Shalem represent respectively Venus as the morning and the evening star. However, the equivalence of Astarte with Ishtar as well as later with Aphrodite makes it virtually certain that she herself was equated with Venus. Maybe Athtar (the equivalent masculine form) was the morning star and Astarte the evening star, though explicit evidence for this in Canaanite sources is lacking. In the Baal myth Athtar is represented as being appointed to rule in Baal's stead when Baal is in the underworld, but he is said to be too small to fill the throne and so has to step down, though he still becomes king over the earth. It has often been supposed that at this point Athtar represents the waters of artificial irrigation (e.g., Gaster 1961: 127). This may be so, but the Arabic evidence to which appeal is made is ambiguous.

Although Mot is the primary deity associated with the underworld at Ugarit, he is not the only one. Another is the god Resheph, appearing already as Rasap at Ebla. At Ugarit his underworld character is indicated by his equation with Nergal, the Mesopotamian underworld god, and this is fully borne out by other Ugaritic evidence. Thus, he is referred to as the sun goddess' porter at the time of her setting (suggesting a location at the entrance of the underworld). His dwelling place is stated in a serpent charm text to be at *Bbt.*

Various other deities were also worshiped as part of the Ugaritic and wider Canaanite pantheon. A number of the Canaanite deities were worshiped in Egypt, especially during the New Kingdom, including Baal (equated with Seth), Anath, Astarte, *Qdš* (= Asherah), Resheph, and Ḥoron. (The precise function of Ḥoron, also attested at Ugarit and elsewhere, is unclear.)

2. First-Millennium Phoenicia. The name Phoenicia is given to that area N of Palestine where the Canaanites were not dispossessed by the Israelites but maintained their separate identity. The religion is partly known from inscriptions from the 1st millennium B.C. and partly from later classical sources. It shows some continuity with Canaanite religion elsewhere, but also has some distinctive features of its own.

An important god at Tyre and, because of Tyre's supremacy, a leading god of the Phoenicians generally (including Carthage) was Melqart. It has sometimes been supposed that Melqart was a form of the god Baal; however, we have no evidence to equate Melqart with Baal prior to a 2d-century-B.C. inscription from Malta, where he is called "the Baal [or lord] of Tyre" (*KAI* 47:1). The 7th-century-B.C. treaty between Baal king of Tyre and Esar-haddon king of Assyria clearly distinguishes Melqart on the one hand, and Baal-shamem and two other Baal deities on the other, the latter (unlike Melqart) manifesting themselves in the storm. It is possible that Melqart was originally a chthonic deity—he is identified with the underworld deity Resheph in a Punic inscription from Spain and with the Mesopotamian underworld god, Nergal, at Palmyra. In classical times he seems to have taken some attributes of the sun god (he sleeps during winter) and also has connections with the sea. He was commonly equated with Heracles in the classical era (e.g., *CIS* I 122; Eusebius, *Praep. Evang* 1.10.27).

Baal-shamem (lit. "Baal of the heavens") was another

important god at Tyre, as well as elsewhere. The evidence implies that he is simply the well-known Canaanite storm god, Baal, attested in the OT and the Ugaritic texts. Thus, in the 7th-century-B.C. treaty between Esar-haddon and Baal king of Tyre he is associated with the storm and in the 8th-century-B.C. hieroglyphic Hittite version of the Karatepe inscription he is represented by a sign for the Hittite storm and thunder god Tarḫunt.

The chief god of Sidon was Eshmun, but he is also attested elsewhere (e.g., at Carthage). He is first mentioned in the treaty between Esar-haddon and Baal king of Tyre, and was identified by the Greeks with Asclepius, the god of healing. However, not much is known about the character of the god and the meaning of his name remains uncertain.

Adonis was the Greek name of a Phoenician deity, and must be based on the Semitic word *ʾadôn,* "lord," though strangely it has not appeared as the name of a god in Phoenician inscriptions. Classical sources indicate that he was a fertility god and his death (from a boar) and resurrection signified the annual death and rebirth of vegetation. He had to spend half the year in Hades with Persephone and was allowed to spend the other half of the year with Aphrodite. One important center of his worship was at Byblos, and Lucian of Samosata (2d century A.D.) reveals that some believed the reddish color of the river Adonis (Nahr Ibrahim) was due to the blood of Adonis. The "Gardens of Adonis" were a feature of his cult—seed boxes with plants that grew quickly and speedily withered (cf. Isa 17:10–11).

Other deities that the Phoenicians worshiped include other forms of Baal, and El, Baalat, Astarte, and Resheph.

The leading Punic deities (i.e., the deities of the Phoenician colonies in the W Mediterranean such as Carthage) were clearly the god Baal-ḥammon and his consort, the goddess Tinnit. It has been thought that Baal-ḥammon is a form of the god El, but it seems more likely that he is, as his name suggests, a manifestation of Baal. Sometimes in Punic dedicatory texts he is simply called Baal, which suggests that this is his name and not merely an epithet, "lord." Moreover, in Latin inscriptions he is called *frugifer* and *deus frugum,* which suit Baal better than El, and his consort Tinnit is equated with Astarte (Baal's wife) in a text from Sarepta in Phoenicia. But whereas Punic sources refer to the recipient of human sacrifice as Baal-ḥammon, classical texts regularly refer to the recipient as Kronos, the common classical equivalent of El. However, Kronos is occasionally referred to as Baal as well as El, and Baal-ḥammon seems to be called Zeus (the more usual equivalent of Baal) in Polybius (7.9.2–3), which records Hannibal's oath in connection with his treaty with Philip V of Macedon. (On this treaty see Barré 1983.) It seems probable that Kronos' devouring of his own children led to his equation with Baal-ḥammon, the god of child sacrifice. There are two main views as to the meaning of the name Baal-ḥammon: one interpretation understands it to mean "Baal [lord] of the incense altar" (Day 1989: 37–40) while the other takes it as "lord of Amanus" (Cross *CMHE* 24–28, 35–36). The former view is more likely, since a number of depictions of Baal-ḥammon's cult feature an incense altar, whereas Mt. Amanus in N Syria was remote even from the original Phoenician homeland.

Baal-ḥammon's consort, Tinnit, the most prominent Punic goddess, who is sometimes referred to as "the face of Baal," has not been fully explicated. Some have thought that she was of N African origin, but several early attestations in Phoenicia (e.g., at Sarepta) have clarified her E origin. There is, however, uncertainty about her precise relationship to the other Canaanite goddesses and what her name means. On the supposition that Baal-ḥammon was El, it has sometimes been presumed that she was Athirat (Asherah). However, this view of Baal-ḥammon is unlikely, as we have seen. Moreover, Tinnit is known to have been equated with Astarte. We cannot be certain, but possibly she was a variant of Anath or she could have been a completely independent goddess.

Other deities worshiped in the Punic world include Melqart, Eshmun, and Resheph (see above).

One traditional source for ancient Phoenician religion is Philo of Byblos' *Phoenician History* (ca. A.D. 100) which declares itself to be dependent on a much earlier Phoenician author, Sanchuniathon. Excerpts from Philo's work have been preserved by Eusebius of Caesarea in his *Praeparatio Evangelica.* Scholarly evaluation of Philo's work as an account of ancient Phoenician and Canaanite theology has passed through different stages during the course of the last century. See PHILO OF BYBLOS. In the 19th century his work was often denigrated, but with the discovery of the Ugaritic texts, revealing the names of a number of deities mentioned by Philo, he underwent a considerable rehabilitation. In more recent years, as witnessed by the work of such scholars as J. Barr (1974) and A. I. Baumgarten (1981), there has been an increasing awareness that though Philo's work shows acquaintance with Phoenician traditions, these date from a late stage when they were subject to considerable Hellenistic influence. This Hellenistic influence is especially prominent in Philo's cosmogony. It is true that he has knowledge of a fair number of genuine Canaanite/Phoenician deities' names, e.g., Elos (El), Beelsamen (Baal-shamem), Zeus Belos (Baal), Adodos (Hadad) Dagon, Astarte, Chousor (Kothar-and-Ḫasis), and Elioun father of Ouranos (Heaven) and Ge (Earth) (cf. Gen 14:19, 22, where "El-Elyon" is creator of heaven and earth). However, the overall picture which he gives does not correspond closely with genuinely ancient sources—he lacks the important motif of Baal as a dying and rising god who was engaged in conflict with Mot, and his depiction of El as a violent god is quite different from that of the benevolent figure of the Ugaritic texts.

C. Religious Practices and Beliefs

1. Festivals, Sacrifice, Prayer. In spite of the considerable information available about the members of the Canaanite pantheon the details of the various Canaanite festivals and their accompanying rituals and liturgies remain scarce. It appears that the OT feasts of Tabernacles, Unleavened Bread, and Weeks had Canaanite prototypes (cf. Judg 9:27) and that these were essentially agricultural festivals. It is plausible to suppose that Baal's enthronement as king was celebrated at the Canaanite feast of Tabernacles, but detailed reconstructions (e.g., de Moor 1972) must remain speculative.

An important part of Canaanite religious practice consisted of sacrifice to the gods. The beginning of the Aqhat text, which describes Daniel as feeding the gods, indicates that sacrifice could be thought of as food for the gods. A number of Canaanite sacrificial terms are known, many of which are paralleled by similar expressions in the OT, though we cannot be certain that the meaning in every case is identical or that the Israelites appropriated the terms from the Canaanites, although this may be the case. Among the parallel terms are Ugaritic *dbḥ* (Heb *zebaḥ* "sacrifice"), *šrp* (Heb *ʿôlâ,* "burnt offering"), *šlm* (Heb *šelem,* "peace offering"), *šnpt* (Heb *tĕnûpâ,* "wave [or "elevation"] offering") and *ndr* (Heb *neder* and *nēder,* "vow"). Other terms found in Punic may also be compared—cf. Punic *kll* (Heb *kālîl,* "whole burnt offering") and *mtnt* (Heb *mattānâ,* "gift").

There is evidence that human sacrifice was practiced within the Canaanite world, although we have no indications of it at Ugarit. There are a number of references to child sacrifice in the OT, especially in connection with the Canaanite god Molech in the valley of Hinnom outside Jerusalem (see Heider 1985; Day 1989), and classical sources attest child sacrifice among the Phoenicians. The most abundant evidence, however, is in the Punic world: not only do various classical authors attest its practice among the Carthaginians, but archaeological discoveries have revealed cemeteries of sacrificed children (commonly referred to by scholars under the biblical name of "topheth") at Motya (Mozia) in Sicily, Monte Sirai, Nora, Tharros, and Sulcis in Sardinia, and at Carthage, Sousse (Hadrumetum), and Cirta (near Constantine) in N Africa.

Another practice for which we have evidence among the Canaanites but is not certainly attested at Ugarit is sacred prostitution (see below). However, Ugarit has revealed some traces of the practice of divination, where models of livers and lungs probably linked to hepatoscopy have been found (models of livers are known from Hazor and Megiddo). A text written in Ugaritic containing omens based on unnatural births of animals has also been discovered, analogous to the Mesopotamian *šumma izbu* texts. (*KTU* 1.103 + 1.145 = *Ugaritica* VII, RS 24.247 + 24.265 + 24.268 + 24.287 + 24.328A + 24.328B.)

Not surprisingly, prayer was employed as a means of communication with the gods. An interesting example is known from Ugarit requesting deliverance should the city be under attack (*KTU* 1.119.26–36): "If a strong one attacks your gate, a warrior your walls, raise your eyes to Baal [praying]: 'O Baal, please drive away the strong one from our gate, the warrior from our walls! The bull, O Baal, we will consecrate; the vow, O Baal, we will fulfill. The male [animal], O Baal we will consecrate; the sacrifice, O Baal, we will fulfill; the libations, O Baal, we will pour out. Let us go up to the sanctuary of Baal, let us walk to and fro on the paths to the house of Baal!' Then Baal will hear your prayer—he will drive away the strong one from your gate, the warrior from your walls." Clearly this prayer, disregarding Baal's importance as a nature god, sees him as an agent in history.

2. Afterlife and Cult of the Dead. Although we lack precise details, it is clear that the Canaanites envisaged a *post mortem* existence. In the OT the shades of the dead are often referred to as the *rĕpāʾîm,* and they are similarly termed in Phoenician (*rpʾm*) and Punic (*ʾrʾpʾm*). It is now clear that the *rpʾum* in Ugaritic also denote the shades of the dead, and that these are deified. The most explicit text is *KTU* 1.161, where the *rpʾum* are invoked, and these include a number of deceased Ugaritic kings. Again, at the end of the Ugaritic Baal myth, we find the expressions *rpʾim/ʾilnym* in close parallelism with *ʾilm/mtm,* 'gods/dead' (*KTU* 1.6.VI.46–48 = *CTA* 6.VI.45–47), thus supporting the view that they are the deified dead. It now seems that this is the meaning of *rpʾum* in all its occurrences in Ugaritic (Caquot and Sznycer 1980: 19–20) and that it is wrong to seek a temporal reference in certain instances (e.g., the so-called Rephaim text, *KTU* 1.20–22 = *CTA* 20–22, *contra* Gray 1965: 126–30). In one Ugaritic text (*KTU* 1.108.1–3 = *Ugaritica* V.2.1–3) it seems that we have an allusion to *rpʾu* (a shade of the dead) drinking with Hadad the shepherd and Astarte; if this is the correct understanding (see ASHTAROTH [PLACE]), it bears comparison with the 8th-century B.C. Aramaic Panammua text, where the hope is expressed, "May the soul of Panammua eat with Hadad, and may the soul of Panammua drink with Hadad" (*KAI* 214: 21–22).

One institution which has attracted increased attention in recent years (cf. Greenfield 1974) is the *marzēaḥ,* which is attested in the Canaanite world at Ugarit (both in Akkadian and Ugaritic texts), the OT (Jer 16:5; Amos 6:7), at Elephantine, and Piraeus, and in Nabatean, Palmyrene, Punic, and rabbinic texts. It took the form of an association involving banquets and there is evidence from Ugarit (the Rephaim text), Jer 16:5, a Nabatean text, and rabbinic tradition that these could be associated with the cult of the dead. However, other purposes may have been involved. (See DEAD, CULT OF THE; ANCESTOR WORSHIP.)

There is evidence that the Ugaritic kings were thought of as divine after their death, and probably they were also considered divine during their earthly reign. The list of Ugaritic kings (*KTU* 1.113) precedes each name with the word *ʾil* "god," but this could simply allude to their posthumous deification. However, in the Keret text, words are expressed which suggest that king Keret (admittedly not king of Ugarit) was considered divine during his lifetime. A son of his declares, "How can it be said [that] Keret is a son of El, the progeny of Laṭipan and *Qdš*? Or shall gods die? Shall the progeny of Laṭipan not live?" (*KTU* 1.16.I.20–23 = *CTA* 16.I.20–23). Keret's daughter Thitmanat expresses similar sentiments in *KTU* 1.16.II.43–44, 48–49 (= *CTA* 16.II.105–6, 110–11). Furthermore, El says that Keret's (presumably eldest) son "Yaṣṣib . . . will suck the milk of Athirat . . . drain the breast of the virgin [Anath], the suckling nurses of [the gods]" (*KTU* 1.15.II.25–28 = *CTA* 15.II.25–28).

The king's role in the cult included a ritual purification bath (e.g., *Ugaritica* V.12.6; *CTA* 36.10; *KTU* 1.119.5). In addition, Tabnit and Eshmunazar, two kings of Sidon, also served as priests of Astarte (*KAI* 13.1, 2). It is clear that as in ancient Israel, a high ethical ideal was expected of the king, since it was his duty to protect the poor, the widow, and the fatherless (cf. *KTU* 1.16.VI.45–50 = *CTA* 16.VI.45–50).

D. Canaanite Religion and the OT

The relation of the religion of Israel to the religion of Canaan consists of two parts. On the one hand, the OT stands steadfastly opposed to the polytheism and fertility cult practices of the religion of Canaan and firmly in favor of the exclusive worship of Yahweh, the God of Israel. On the other hand, the OT has appropriated elements from the religion of Canaan, baptizing them in a form compatible with Israel's own distinctive faith.

1. El and Yahweh. The chief god of the Canaanites, El, is equated in the OT with Yahweh. Thus, the patriarchal narratives depict them as worshiping various manifestations of El—El-Shaddai in particular, but also El-Bethel, El-Olam, El Elohei Israel, El-Roi, and El-Elyon—and these are understood as revelations of Yahweh (e.g., Exod 6:2–3). It has even been suggested by F. M. Cross (*CMHE,* 68–71) that the name Yahweh derived from part of a cult name of El, *ʾil dū yahwī ṣabaʾôt,* "El who creates hosts." However, against this hypothesis it may be argued: (1) the formula in question is nowhere attested and is highly speculative; (2) the character of El is uniformly benevolent in the Ugaritic texts, whereas Yahweh has a fierce side as well as a kind one; and (3) this view presupposes that the name Yahweh means "he creates" (understood as a *Hipʿil*), whereas it more likely means "he is" (the verb *hyh,* "to be," is nowhere attested in the *Hipʿil* in Hebrew). Perhaps in the time of Moses, as certain biblical references suggest, El was equated with Yahweh, who probably was originally the Midianite god of Mt. Sinai. Whereas the OT abominated Baal, it was happy to equate Yahweh with El, who was the supreme creator god noted for his wisdom, and was not associated with the fertility cult in the way that Baal was.

In his identification with El, Yahweh also appropriated "the sons of El," so that "the sons of God" formed his heavenly court (cf. Job 1:6; 2:1). The notion that they were seventy in number lived on, since Deut 32:8 states that "the Most High . . . fixed the bounds of the peoples according to the number of the sons of God" (so LXX; 4QDeut), from which evolved in Jewish apocalyptic literature the notion of seventy guardian angels of the nations. Thus, as absolute monotheism took over from monolatry in Israel, those who had originally been in the pantheon of the gods were demoted to the status of angels.

In being equated with El, it is not surprising that in syncretistic circles Yahweh also appropriated El's consort Athirat, or Asherah as she is known in the OT. Her cult symbol, known as the Asherah, was a wooden pole, perhaps in the form of a stylized tree. It is mentioned in the OT a number of times and appears to be the point of the inscriptions, "Yahweh and his Asherah" from Kuntillet ʿAjrud in N Sinai.

2. OT Use of Baal Motifs. Although the OT condemns the Baal cult, it nevertheless adopts some of its motifs. Hosea, who is at pains to emphasize that Yahweh, not Baal, brings fertility to the land (Hos 2:10—Eng 2:8), applies the imagery of death and resurrection to Israel's coming exile and restoration (Hos 5:14–6:3; 13:1–14:7). That this imagery is actually derived from the fertility cult of Baal is supported by the allusion to the coming of the rain in connection with the resurrection imagery in Hos 6:3 and the evident irony of the fact that Hosea declares that Israel "incurred guilt through Baal and died" (Hos 13:1).

The OT also appropriates the motif of Baal's conflict with Leviathan (also called "dragon," "twisting serpent") and Yam and applies it to Yahweh. Sometimes the imagery is associated with the creation of the world (e.g., Ps 74:12–17), and this can also be demythologized so that it is simply a case of God's controlling (rather than fighting with) the waters, as in Genesis 1. Sometimes the imagery is historicized, so that the sea becomes a term for the hostile nations (cf. Ps 144:7) and the dragon can symbolize a particular nation, such as Egypt or Babylon (e.g., Isa 30:7; Jer 51:34). Again, the imagery can be projected into the future and eschatologized (cf. Isa 27:1; Daniel 7). A related theme to that of the divine victory over the waters is divine kingship. Just as Baal became king following his victory over Yam, so the OT associates Yahweh's kingship with his defeat of the chaos waters (cf. Ps 74:12; 93:1–2). The name of Baal's sacred mountain, Mt. Ṣapān, is applied to Mt. Zion, the seat of Yahweh's dwelling in Ps 48:3—Eng 48:2, "the heights of Zaphon" (cf. Isa 14:13). Moreover, the description of Yahweh's manifestation in the thunderstorm tends to echo that of the storm god, Baal, and this is particularly striking in Psalm 29.

3. The High Places, Sacred Prostitution, and the Molech Cult. The Asherim formed part of the cultic paraphernalia of the "high places" (*bāmôt*) (see also HIGH PLACE), the local sanctuaries where a Baalized Yahweh cult was practiced in ancient Israel until their abolition by Josiah in 621 B.C. They were frequently located on hills and the cult practices associated with them are described as taking place "on every high hill and under every green tree" (e.g., 2 Kgs 17:10). In addition to the Asherim, stone pillars (*maṣṣēbôt*) symbolizing the male deity, altars, and incense altars were among the characteristic features of these sites. The OT also suggests that rites of sacred prostitution were characteristic of the Baalized Yahweh worship, presumably a form of imitative magic in order to encourage the fertility of the land. That sacred prostitution was a feature of the religion is indicated by the parallelism of the word *zônâ,* "prostitute," with *qĕdēšâ,* lit. "holy one," in Deut 23:18–19 and Gen 38–15, 22–23 and of *zōnôt,* "prostitutes," with *qedēšôt,* lit. "holy ones," in Hos 4:14. The masculine form *qādēš* (Deut 23:18—Eng 23:17; 1 Kgs 14:24; 22:47—Eng 22:46), plural *qĕdēšîm* (1 Kgs 15:12; 2 Kgs 23:7) must therefore allude to male cult prostitution. It is not certain whether the *qdšm* mentioned in the Ugaritic texts were similarly cult prostitutes. Outside the OT, classical allusions confirm the practice of sacred prostitution among the Phoenicians. See PROSTITUTION (CULTIC).

The OT sometimes makes reference to a god called Molech, to whom gruesome rites of child sacrifice are made. Some scholars have denied that Molech is the name of a god, claiming it to be a sacrificial term cognate with Punic *molk* (Eissfeldt 1935), while others maintain that no human sacrifice was involved but simply a dedication in fire (Weinfeld 1972). However, both these views are forced. There is evidence that *mlk* was the name of a Canaanite god (e.g., at Ugarit), and it is most likely that OT Molech is a reference to him, the vowels having been distorted with those of the word *bōšet,* "shame" (cf. how the OT form of Ashtart is likewise distorted to read Ashtoreth; so Day [1989]). Probably he was an underworld god (Heider 1985; Day 1989). Another Canaanite underworld god who has left traces in the OT is Resheph (e.g., Ps 78:48–49; Hab

3:5), who seems to have become a destructive angel in Yahweh's entourage.

4. Israelite Calendar and Kingship. The important dividing line in the agricultural year in Canaan comes with the autumn when the rainy season commences following the months of dryness and summer sun. This must have been the time of the Canaanite new year, just as it was in preexilic Israel (cf. Exod 23:16; 34:22), prior to the adoption of the Babylonian spring new year calendar at the time of the Exile or just before. The festival in the autumn was the feast of Tabernacles, when the corn, wine, and oil were gathered. The Canaanite equivalent of this feast is recorded in Judg 9:27. The other major feasts, those of Weeks and Unleavened Bread, being in origin agricultural festivals, must also have been appropriated from the Canaanites. Some sacrificial practices may well have been adopted (see above).

It was not until about 1000 B.C. that the Israelites adopted the institution of kingship. Since kingship was a new institution for them, it is to be expected that features should be borrowed from the surrounding nations (cf. 1 Sam 8:20). Influence from the Canaanite kingship ideology cannot be denied. The most explicit evidence for this comes from Ps 110:4, where the Davidic king is hailed as "a priest for ever after the order of Melchizedek." Since Melchizedek is represented as a pre-Israelite, Jebusite priest-king in Jerusalem in Gen 14:18–20, it appears that Ps 110 involves a fusion of Israelite with the Jebusite royal ideology. This is most naturally understood as having come about soon after David's conquest of Jerusalem. The Jebusite deity, (El-)Elyon (Gen 14:18, 19, 22), became fused with Yahweh, though it should probably not be supposed that David's priest, Zadok, was originally a Jebusite priest. If he had been, then neither of David's two chief priests (Zadok, Abiathar) would have been a native southern Israelite, which would be surprising. 1 Chr 12:28 may support F. M. Cross' view (*CMHE* 207–15) that Zadok had already been David's priest at Hebron.

In various ways, therefore, it is apparent that Canaanite religion has exerted an influence on the OT, in spite of the condemnation of that religion which the OT often expresses. For further discussion see Albright *ARI, YGC;* Donner and Röllig *KAI;* Eissfeldt *KlSchr;* Gibson *TSSI;* and Gordon *UT.*

Bibliography

Attridge, H. W., and Oden, R. A. 1976. *The Syrian Goddess (De Dea Syria).* Missoula, MT.

Barr, J. 1974. Philo of Byblos and His "Phoenician History." *BJRL* 57: 17–68.

Barré, M. L. 1983. *The God-list in the Treaty between Hannibal and Philip V of Macedonia.* Baltimore.

Baumgarten, A. I. 1981. *The Phoenician History of Philo of Byblos.* Leiden.

Biran, A., ed. 1981. *Temples and High Places in Biblical Times.* Jerusalem.

Bonnet, C. 1988. *Melqart.* StudPhoen 8. Louvain.

Caquot, A., and Sznycer, M. 1980. *Ugaritic Religion.* Leiden.

Clifford, R. J. 1972. *The Cosmic Mountain in Canaan and the Old Testament.* Cambridge, MA.

Craigie, P. C. 1983. *Ugarit and the Old Testament.* Grand Rapids.

Curtis, A. 1985. *Ugarit (Ras Shamra).* Cambridge.

Day, J. 1985. *God's Conflict with the Dragon and the Sea: Echoes of a Canaanite Myth in the Old Testament.* Cambridge.

———. 1986. Asherah in the Hebrew Bible and Northwest Semitic Literature. *JBL* 105: 385–408.

———. 1989. *Molech: A God of Human Sacrifice in the Old Testament.* Cambridge.

Dietrich, M.; Loretz, O.; and Sammartin, J. 1976. *Die keilalphabetische Texts aus Ugarit.* AOAT 24. Neukirchen-Vluyn.

Eissfeldt, O. 1932. *Baal Zaphon, Zeus Kasios und der Durchzug der Israeliten durchs Meer.* Halle.

———. 1935. *Molk als Opferbegriff im Punischen und Hebräischen und das Ende des Gottes Moloch.* Halle.

Fulco, W. J. 1976. *The Canaanite God Rešep.* New Haven.

Gaster, T. H. 1961. *Thespis.* 2d ed. New York.

Gese, H.; Höfner, M.; and Rudolph, K. 1970. *Die Religionen Altsyriens, Altarabiens und der Mandäer.* Stuttgart.

Gibson, J. C. L. 1977. *Canaanite Myths and Legends.* Edinburgh.

Gray, J. 1965. *The Legacy of Canaan.* 2d ed. VTSup 5. Leiden.

Greenfield, J. C. 1974. The *Marzeaḥ* as a Social Institution. *Acts Antiqua* 22: 451–55.

Harden, D. 1971. *The Phoenicians.* Harmondsworth, England.

Heider, G. C. 1985. *The Cult of Molek.* Sheffield.

Hvidberg-Hansen, O. 1979. *La Déesse TNT.* 2 vols. Copenhagen.

Kaiser, O. 1962. *Die mythische Bedeutung des Meeres.* 2d ed. BZAW 78. Berlin.

Kapelrud, A. S. 1952. *Baal in the Ras Shamra Texts.* Copenhagen.

———. 1965. *The Ras Shamra Discoveries and the Old Testament.* Oxford.

———. 1969. *The Violent Goddess: Anat in the Ras Shamra Texts.* Oslo.

Kinet, D. 1981. *Ugarit—Geschichte und Kultur einer Stadt in der Umwelt des Alten Testamentes.* SBS 104. Stuttgart.

L'Heureux, C. 1979. *Rank among the Canaanite Gods.* HSM 37. Atlanta.

Maier, W. A. 1986. *ᵓAšerah: Extrabiblical Evidence.* HSM 37. Atlanta.

Matthiae, P. 1977. *Ebla: An Empire Rediscovered.* London.

Moor, J. C. de. 1970. The Semitic Pantheon of Ugarit. *UF* 2: 187–228.

———. 1971. *The Seasonal Pattern in the Ugaritic Myth of Baᶜlu.* AOAT 16. Neukirchen-Vluyn.

———. 1972. *New Year with Canaanites and Israelites.* 2 vols. Kampen.

———. 1987. *An Anthology of Religious Texts from Ugarit.* Leiden.

Moscati, S. 1973. *The World of the Phoenicians.* London.

Moscati, S., ed. 1988. *The Phoenicians.* Milan.

Mulder, M. J. 1965. *Kanaänitische goden in het Oude Testament.* The Hague.

Negbi, O. 1976. *Canaanite Gods in Metal.* Tel Aviv.

Oden, R. A. 1977. *Studies in Lucian's De Syria Dea.* HSM 15. Missoula, MT.

Ottosson, M. 1980. *Temples and Cult Places in Palestine.* Uppsala.

Pardee, D. 1986. Ugaritic. *AfO* 33: 117–47.

Pettinato, G. 1981. *The Archives of Ebla.* Garden City, NY.

Pope, M. H. 1955. *El in the Ugaritic Texts.* VTSup 2. Leiden.

Pritchard, J. B. 1943. *Palestinian Figurines in Relation to Certain Goddesses Known through Literature.* New Haven.

———. 1978. *Recovering Sarepta, a Phoenician City.* Princeton.

Ribichini, S. 1981. *Adonis: aspetti "orientali" di un mito greco.* Rome.

Ringgren, H. 1973. *Religions of the Ancient Near East.* London.

Schaeffer, C. F. A., et al. 1939–78. *Ugaritica I–VII.* Paris.

Spronk, K. 1986. *Beatific Afterlife in Ancient Israel and in the Ancient Near East.* AOAT 219. Neukirchen-Vluyn.

Stadelmann, R. 1967. *Syrisch-palästinensische Gottheiten in Ägypten.* Leiden.

Tarragon, J.-M. de. 1980. *Le Culte à Ugarit.* CahRB 19. Paris.
Thompson, H. O. 1970. *Mekal: the God of Beth-Shan.* Leiden.
Vaughan, P. H. 1974. *The Meaning of "Bāmâ" in the Old Testament.* Cambridge.
Weinfeld, M. 1972. The Worship of Molech and of the Queen of Heaven and Its Background. *UF* 4: 133–54.
Xella, P. 1981. *I testi rituali di Ugarit.* Vol. 1. Rome.
Yamauchi, E. 1973. Cultic Prostitution. Pp. 213–22 in *Orient and Occident,* ed. H. A. Hofner. AOAT 22. Neukirchen-Vluyn.

JOHN DAY

CANAANITE LANGUAGE. See LANGUAGES (INTRODUCTORY SURVEY).

CANDACE (PERSON) [Gk *Kandakē*]. Title of the person who employed the Ethiopian eunuch converted by Philip (Acts 8:27–39). Candace is not a proper name but a title (like the word "Pharaoh"); in fact, it was one of the first Ethiopic words clearly identified by scholars. It means Queen, though it also seems to have referred to the Queen Mother. Bion of Soli, who wrote a work on Africa probably in the 2d century B.C., says that the Queen Mother, called the Candace, was the real head of the government of the so-called kingdom of Meroe, not in modern Ethiopia proper, but rather along the Nile in modern Sudan. The title Candace may have been a hereditary one, since it is attested in various periods before and after the NT era in the relevant classical literature (cf. Strab. 17.1.54; Dio Cass. 54.5.4–5; Pliny *HN* 6.35.186; Ps.-Callisth. 3.18). Thus, the Candace mentioned only once in the NT (Acts 8:27) cannot be clearly identified because we are not given a proper name (Cadbury 1955: 15–18). Eunuchs were frequently used in ancient Near Eastern courts as guards of the harem or sometimes of the treasury (see ETHIOPIAN EUNUCH).

Bibliography

Cadbury, H. J. 1955. *The Book of Acts in History.* London.
Marshall, I. H. 1980. *The Acts of the Apostles.* Grand Rapids.
Williams, D. J. 1985. *Acts. A Good News Commentary.* San Francisco.

BEN WITHERINGTON, III

CANNEH (PLACE) [Heb *kannēh*]. A N Mesopotamian city with whom Tyre traded in textiles (Ezek 27:23). Assyrian texts of the 8th and 7th centuries B.C. contain numerous references to individuals involved in economic transactions who are from Kannuʾ, a city whose precise geographical location is unknown (see Postgate *RLA* 5: 390). Since this city provides the most likely counterpart to the Canneh of the MT in Ezek 27:23 (once improperly identified with Calneh), one learns from Assyrian sources that it was strategically located on a royal Assyrian highway which facilitated the city's development as a center of trade. Citizens of Canneh are attested long before the time of Ezekiel transporting hundreds of horses for the Assyrian empire (Waterman 1930–36: 529) and engaging in slave sales. Because the city is listed in Ezek 27:23 between the two other well-known locales Haran and Eden (i.e., Beth-eden), Canneh also must have achieved some international stature as a comparable commercial center. The Assyrian evidence indicates that the city was a center for the cult of the god Apladad. The etymology of Kannuʾ/Canneh remains unclear, for a proposed Aramaic etymology from *gannoʾ* "the enclosure" would appear in Hebrew with an initial voiced consonant. The Targum equates Canneh with Nisibis.

Bibliography

Lipiński, E. 1976. Apladad. *Or* 45: 53–74.
Waterman, L. 1930–36. *Royal Correspondence of the Assyrian Empire.* Ann Arbor.

SAMUEL A. MEIER

CANON. The word "canon" comes from the Gk *kanōn,* "measuring stick." By extension it came to mean "rule" or "standard," a tool used for determining proper measurement. Consequently, the word has come to be used with reference to the corpus of scriptural writings that is considered authoritative and standard for defining and determining "orthodox" religious beliefs and practices. Books not considered authoritative and standard are often called "noncanonical" or "extracanonical." Generally speaking, the corpus of authoritative books is called the "Bible," although obviously the Christian Bible (or canon) differs from that of Judaism. This entry consists of two entries: one covering the canon of the Hebrew Bible (i.e., the Christian "Old Testament"), and another covering the specifically Christian writings comprising the "New Testament." See also APOCRYPHA (OT and NT) articles.

HEBREW BIBLE

---

4. Canonical Hermeneutics
5. God and "Powerflows"
E. Canon and Inspiration

A. Introduction

1. Canon in Judaism and Christianity. Some of the religions of the world are "scriptured" such as Judaism, the Samaritans, Christianity, Islam, Confucianism, Taoism, Buddhism, Hinduism, and Zoroastrianism; others are not (W. C. Smith 1977). Judaism and Christianity claim to have Holy Scriptures inspired by God; the Christian includes the Jewish, but the Jewish does not include any of the peculiarly Christian "Second [or New] Testament." That which is common to the two, though in a different order of contents, in most Protestant Bibles is traditionally called the "Old Testament" by Christians but simply the "Bible" by Jews. The Bible of the Samaritans is limited to the Pentateuch. The Bible of the early church before there was a NT canon, that which was most often cited in NT and most Christian literature, was a Greek version of the OT containing many more books than the current Protestant OT or Jewish Bible. The Protestant/Jewish "First Testament" is often inexactly called the Hebrew Bible. In more accurate terms the OT (whether referring to the LXX or the current Protestant OT) may also be called the First Testament. Until recent times the Christian OT, whether Orthodox, Catholic, or Protestant, included more books than the Jewish Bible included; it was not until the late 19th century that Protestants began to exclude the Jewish so-called apocrypha, or deuterocanonical books, which surviving Pharisaic-rabbinic Judaism had excluded from its Bible at least by the end of the 1st century of the common era. Samaritans, also heirs of ancient Judaism, accept only the Pentateuch (Torah) as canon. Muhammad, apparently the single author of the Koran, adapted traditions from both Bibles or testaments into the 7th-century-C.E. Bible of Islam; by contrast, both Judaism and Christianity have accepted the fact of multiple authorship of their canons as well as pseudonymity of some of the books in each. Whereas the Koran is viewed in Islam as a direct revelation from God, the Jewish and Christian canons are viewed as human testimonies to God's revelations (Pokorny 1984: 486–96). When one uses the word "canon" one must specify to which denomination or community of faith it refers even within Judaism and Christianity; within both there is now and was in antiquity more than one canon in the sense of limited lists of sacred books considered canonical. The Church of Latter-Day Saints is perhaps the latest to claim the Christian canon to be open-ended (Davies 1986). And in recent times the word "canon" is used to refer to the rabbinic corpus in addition to the Bible or even instead of the Bible (Neusner 1987: 43–51).

2. Etymology of the Word "Canon." The word "canon" comes from the Greek *kanōn* which was derived from a Semitic root (Hebrew *qāneh,* Assyrian *qanû,* [Sumerian-] Akkadian *qin,* Ugaritic *qn*). It passed into Greek as *kanna* or *kanē,* into Latin as *canna,* and English as *cane.* It originally meant "reed" (English "cannon") and came to mean something firm and straight. In Greek the word was used to indicate a stave, a weaver's rod, a curtain rod, a bedpost, and a stick kept for drawing a straight line or as a constant reference for measuring such as level, plumb line, or ruler. It then took on metaphoric meanings such as model, standard, paradigm, boundary, chronological list, and tax or tariff schedule. In the NT "canon" means rule, standard (Phil 3:16 in some mss; Gal 6:16), or limit (2 Cor 10:13, 15–16). In early church literature it came to be used to refer to biblical law, an ideal person, an article of faith, doctrine, catalog, table of contents, a list of persons ordained or sainted (Metzger 1987: 289–93). Origen (d. 254) may have used the word in the sense of a list of inspired books, but Athanasius (d. 373) was the first known to have done so and the first in his Easter letter of 367 to include the 27 books of the NT.

3. Other Terms Used. The Bible (OT) of the early churches was referred to as "Scripture" (John 2:22; Acts 8:32; 2 Tim 3:16; etc.) or "the scriptures" (Mark 12:24; 1 Cor 15:3–4, etc.). Other terms used were "holy scriptures," "the writings," "the sacred scriptures," "the book," "the sacred books." Use of such terms does not, however, indicate exactly which books were meant beyond the Law and the Prophets in the Jewish tripartite canon (Law, Prophets, and Writings). And doubt has been expressed as to whether the term "Scripture" was synonymous with "canon" (Sundberg *IDBSup,* 137; cf. Metzger 1987: 30).

The same is true of terms used in Judaism where the word "books" (*sĕpārîm*) meant sacred writings but without precise definition (Dan 9:2; Mishnah, etc.). The term "holy books" (*siprê haqqōdeš*), used in medieval commentaries, was also indefinite in reference in that it was used to refer to all Jewish religious literature. In the Greek prologue to Ecclesiasticus (Ben Sira), which was translated (traditionally 132 B.C.E.) by the grandson of the author, the phrases "the other books of our fathers" and "the rest of the books" are also indefinite in reference. In Tannaitic times the term "outside books" (*sĕpārîm hîtzōnîm*) was coined to refer to books not in the Jewish canon (*Sanh.* 10:1), but even then it was used mainly to refer to non-Jewish or nonrabbinic literature, not specifically to refer to Jewish writing outside the Jewish Bible.

More precise in designation, though not content, is the word *miqrāʾ* ("reading"; see Arabic *qurʾan*) referring to Scripture and based on the custom of reading aloud for the assembled faithful in a dominantly oral culture, continued today as oral lectionary readings in most worship services Jewish and Christian; it was and is frequently used to indicate Scripture, as against Mishnah, Midrash, or other Jewish literature.

Another term, "holy writings" (*kitbê haqqōdeš*), is used to refer to holy or inspired writings but not exclusively to the Bible (*Šabb.* 16:1; *B. Bat.* 1: end; *t. Beṣa* 4 [Blau *JEnc,* 141]), another indication of the necessity to distinguish between "inspired" and "canonical" (Leiman 1976: 127; Metzger 1987: 254–57); the term is reflected in Greek in Rom 1:2; John 5:47; 2 Tim 3:15–16; *Ant* 1.13; 10.63; etc.

The word "Torah," like many others in early Jewish literature, has both a narrow (*sensus strictus*) and a broad meaning (*sensus latus*). While it can refer strictly to the Pentateuch it may also refer to the whole Bible; but it may quite broadly refer to all Jewish religious literature, or indeed be used as a virtual synonym of Judaism itself (Sanders 1987: 111–14). Similarly the word *nomos* in the NT and elsewhere may mean "law," or it may mean custom, instruction, or doctrine (Pasinya 1973). The Pentateuch itself is basically a blend of narrative and law (Sanders 1987: 43–60, 115–23); indeed one great Jewish philosopher (Heschel 1972) believed that Judaism itself is made up of *halākāh* and *haggādāh* (law and narrative).

Another term used of Scripture is *hakkātûb,* "that which is written," but the term is usually accompanied by the name of a book of the Bible; "all that which is written" or perhaps "all Scripture" is early and may be reflected in 2 Tim 3:16 (*pasa graphē*). The term "covenant" or "testament" seems to have been principally a Christian term of reference for the OT (2 Cor 3:14), though Sirach apparently used "book of the covenant" (24:23) to refer to the Pentateuch (cf. Exod 24:7; 2 Kgs 23:2, 21 where the same Greek term translates the Hebrew *sēper habberît*).

Other terms used include the expression "those [books] that soil the hands" (*Yad.* 3:5; 4:5, 6), which is as close perhaps as may be found to what is commonly meant by the term "canon"; and yet it is not really clear how the term arose (*JEnc* 1: 141) or even if it was used to mean "canonical" *in sensu stricto* (Leiman 1976: 102–20).

Finally, one of the most common terms used to refer to the Bible in Talmud and Midrash, and perhaps the most common in Jewish speech in any modern language, is *Tanak,* an acrostic made up of the first letters of the three divisions of the Hebrew or Jewish Bible: *T̲ōrāh* (Pentateuch), *N̲ebîʾîm* (Prophets), and *K̲etûbîm* (Writings or Hagiographa).

4. Basic Uses of the Word "Canon." There are two basic uses of the word "canon": the one refers to the shape of a limited body of sacred literature; the other refers to its function. Traditionally it is viewed as both an authoritative collection of books (*norma normata*—shape) and a collection of authoritative books (*norma normans*—function; Metzger 1987: 282–88). The word "shape" refers, however, to more than the number and order of books contained in a community's canon; and the word "function" refers to more than how a community used its canon. Both terms include consideration of pre- and proto-canonical literary and historical factors as well as factors resulting from eventual stabilization of text and canon.

B. External Shape of Canon

1. Extrabiblical References. The designation "Tanak" accurately suggests the basic tripartite shape of the Jewish Bible: Torah, Prophets, and Writings. Beginning in the 2d century B.C.E. the third division was vaguely indicated in the prologue to Ecclesiasticus (Ben Sira) written by the author's grandson in 132 B.C.E. (or 116 [Kahle 1959: 216]; or 110 [Bickermann 1944: 344]). He apparently knew only paraphrastic expressions such as ". . . and the others that followed them," or ". . . the other books of our fathers," or ". . . and the rest of the books." Much has been made by some of the vague expression in Philo's *Vita Cont* 25 which mentions "laws and oracles delivered through the mouth of prophets, and psalms . . ."; or the phrase "They read the holy writings and seek wisdom from their ancestral philosophy by taking it as an allegory . . ." (*Vita Cont* 28). Such expressions can be taken to indicate a closed canon of the third division, the Writings, in pre-Christian times only by inference; the evidence is not clear (cf. Leiman 1976: 131–32; Beckwith 1985: 110–11).

The first two divisions, the Law and the Prophets, are attested to in the Second or New Testament (Matt 5:17; 7:12; 22:40; Luke 16:16; John 13:15; 24:14; Rom 3:21 [see "Moses and the Prophets" in Luke 16:29, 31]), but the third division remained amorphous (without clear shape) in all such designations until the end of the 1st century C.E.; in fact it is not clear when the term "Tanak" itself first appeared (Aicher 1906: 1–53). Recent in-depth study of the function of Scripture in the Mishnah affords no evidence of the tripartite canon in the ways in which Scripture is cited or alluded to beyond the Torah (Pettit 1988). The tripartite division, with the third section clearly not yet having a stable title such as Writings (or Hagiographa), is also indicated in Sirach 39:1; 2 Macc 2:13–14; and Luke 24:44. In Luke 24:44 the phrase ". . . Law of Moses, Prophets and Psalms . . ." is reported said by the resurrected Jesus to the disciples in one of his last meetings with them. The inarticulate *psalmois* in the Lukan phrase could indicate any collection of Jewish religious hymns, but it probably designated a collection of psalms such as we know in the biblical book of Psalms, but not in all probability the stabilized Psalter witnessed in 4th–5th-century-C.E. and later LXX mss or in 10th-century-C.E. and later Masoretic mss, as the various scrolls and fragments of psalms among the Dead Sea Scrolls would suggest. If one took Philo or others as witness to the canon there might be doubt as to how far it extended at the turn of the era beyond the Pentateuch (Barthélemy 1984: 10–14); but if one took the Qumran library or the NT as witness in the same time frame one might wonder if indeed the number of books considered functionally canonical were not still indefinite (Barthélemy 1984: 15–19).

The long encomium to famous men in Ben Sirach 44–49 indicates that the author of Ecclesiasticus knew the Law and the Prophets as we have them, even the title "The Twelve Prophets"; and he seems to cite Mal 3:23. He also apparently knew a good portion of the Writings. He reflects the very old tradition (Amos 6:5) that David was a musician: "In all his works he praised the Holy One Most High with words of glory; with his whole heart he sang (*húmnēse*) and loved Him that made him. He also set singers before the altar . . ." (Sir 47:8–9). He also knew the old tradition that foreigners wondered at David's songs, proverbs, parables, and interpretations (47:17). But he does not thereby indicate, except by the broadest stretch of will (as some have claimed: Leiman 1976: 29; Beckwith 1985: 73), that Ben Sira knew the Psalter as we have it in medieval Masoretic mss.

2 Maccabees explicitly mentions the covenant with Abraham, Isaac, and Jacob (1:2), as well as traditions about Moses and Solomon (2:4–12), and then deals considerably with the work (1:20–2:15), writings, and commentaries of Nehemiah (2:13); it also reflects on the prior prophecies of Jeremiah (2:1–7). The crucial passage states that Nehemiah founded a library collecting literature dealing with official acts or matters "concerning kings and prophets, as well as concerning David, and correspondence of kings concerning sacred gifts"; that Judas Maccabeus recovered the collection scattered because of the war (168–165 B.C.E.); and that it was still extant in the writer's time (2:13–14). To deny double-duty to the earlier preposition *peri* functioning in the expression *ta tou David* in 2:13, and therefore to understand the neuter plural phrase as "the

psalms of David," is unwarranted; 2 Macc 2:13 refers to royal records, probably Samuel and Kings, and quite possibly a Davidic collection of psalms (cf. Beckwith 1985: 150–52). But broad claims about the Psalter and the whole Hagiographa as we know them being already in the shape we have them or already canonical when Judas engaged in his literary restoration (Beckwith 1985: 434–37) cannot be founded on 2 Maccabees.

The stabilized Jewish canon attested to by the end of the 1st century C.E. included 24 books (*4 Esdras* 14:44–46). The textus receptus or early printed editions of Jacob ben Hayyim based on European Hebrew Bible mss of the time (Blau 1902: 141, 144, col. viii) had the following order: the 5 of the Pentateuch; the 8 of the Prophets (Joshua, Judges, Samuel, Kings, Isaiah, Jeremiah, Ezekiel, and the Twelve Minor Prophets); and the 11 of the Writings (Psalms, Proverbs, Job, Song of Solomon, Ruth, Lamentations, Ecclesiastes, Esther, Daniel, Ezra-Nehemiah, and Chronicles).

There is a different order in the third section in earlier Tiberian Masoretic mss on which current printed editions (cf. Yeivin 1980: 38, §71) of the Hebrew-Aramaic Bible are based, as we shall see; but the count of 24 remains the same. Josephus (*AgAp* 1.39), Origen (Eusebius, *Hist. eccl.* 2.25), and Jerome (but only in his preface to Samuel and Kings) counted 22 books, the number of the letters of the Hebrew alphabet; and such a tradition may have been fairly widespread at one time. Such a count would be possible if Ruth were included on the same (Greek translation or even Hebrew) scroll with Judges (or with Psalms), and Lamentations with Jeremiah (*JEnc* 1: 142; Leiman 1976: 133–34). On the other hand, in the case of Josephus there may simply have been only 22 books to count as canonical by the beginning of the fourth quarter of the 1st century C.E. (Talmon 1987: 68). It is clear that too much certainty about Josephus' canon has been drawn from *AgAp* 1.37–43 (Leiman 1976: 31–34; but see n. 155!). The tradition in most Jewish communities after the 1st century C.E. was consistently a count of 24 books except in a very few Midrashim (e.g., *Num. Rab.* 18:21) where the Minor Prophets were separately counted to render 35. Ezekiel, Proverbs, the Song of Songs, Ecclesiastes, and Esther were disputed as late as the early 2d century but eventually won full acceptance in the canon. In the opinion of some (Leiman 1976: 119–20; Beckwith 1985: 318–23; and Talmon 1987: 75–79) the five books were already considered canonical and the passages in rabbinic literature which record the debate assume that they were; the same passages have been read by most others to indicate a genuine debate about their canonical status.

2. Masoretic Text. The order of books beyond 2 Kings has varied to some extent even down to the 20th century as may be noted in the fact that the current student editions of the Hebrew Bible (*BHK* and *BHS*) still place Chronicles at the end of the third division, or Writings, even though the editors claim to use exclusively the Leningradensis ms, the oldest full codex of the Tanak in existence dating to the late 10th/early 11th century, which like its older (though incomplete) mate, Aleppensis (925 B.C.E.), and numerous other mss dating before the 12th century and after, has Chronicles as the first book in that division (see *BHS* xi), as well as a generally different internal order. The third section aside from Chronicles always begins with Psalms and ends with Daniel and Ezra-Nehemiah, no matter whether Chronicles was placed first before Psalms or last after Ezra-Nehemiah.

It is probable that the sequence Genesis through 2 Kings was stabilized in content and order probably by the middle of the 6th century B.C.E. (Freedman *IDBSup,* 131–32), certainly by the middle of the 5th when the Pentateuch or first five books in that sequence was recognized by "all the people as one person," that is, by the whole community, as the "Book of the Torah of Moses" (Neh 8:1) or "The Torah" (Neh 8:2) in what was undoubtedly quite an elaborate ceremony in the Water Gate Square in Jerusalem in the middle (458? B.C.E.) of the 5th century. The Pentateuch (and not the Hexateuch or even Octateuch—that is, Genesis to Deuteronomy and not Genesis to Joshua or even Kings) became the Torah for Judaism for all time because of the triumph of the book of Deuteronomy and the school of thinkers, writers, and editors which its triumph spawned in the exilic 6th-century period (the Deuteronomists and others; Sanders 1972: 9–20). The Torah which was read that day in Jerusalem had been brought there by Ezra from the large exilic community in Persian-occupied Babylonia. But the sequel Genesis to Kings, no matter that Ezra's Judaism needed to break it into two liturgical divisions (called Torah and Early Prophets), was undoubtedly a stabilized written (hi)story fairly much as we now have it in the Tanak by the middle of the 6th century B.C.E. Since that sequence of books, in contrast to all that follows in the Jewish canon, is clearly a story line beginning with creation and ending with the Babylonian destruction of Jerusalem and the exile, the order of the books Genesis to Kings was secured early on even when the text was written on scrolls, well before the invention of the codex in the 1st centuries C.E. Beginning with the Latter Prophets or the Books of the Three, there has been considerable variation. "The order of the Books in the Torah and the Former Prophets has been established from earliest times; however the order of the books in the Latter Prophets and the Writings is not fixed" (Yeivin 1980: 38).

The two great Tiberian mss, Leningradensis and Aleppensis (A), dating to the early 10th and 11th centuries, where A is extant agree on the following order after Kings: Isaiah, Jeremiah, Ezekiel, and the Twelve Minor Prophets (the order indicated already in Sirach 48:22 and 49:6–8); Chronicles, Psalms, Job, Proverbs, Ruth, Song of Songs, Ecclesiastes, Lamentations, Esther, Daniel, Ezra-Nehemiah. By contrast, a Baraita in the Talmud (*B. Bat.* 14b), which at the earliest dates to the 2d century C.E., and a number of mss later than the Tiberian (Blau 1902: 143–44) agree on the order: Jeremiah, Ezekiel, Isaiah, and the Twelve; Ruth, Psalms, Job, Proverbs, Ecclesiastes, Song of Songs, Lamentations, Daniel, Esther, Ezra-Nehemiah, Chronicles.

Even the practice of grouping the Five Scrolls together (Megilloth—Ruth, Song of Songs, Ecclesiastes, Lamentations, Esther) was sometimes abandoned in favor of placing Ruth at the beginning of the Writings. The order of the Five Scrolls varies considerably in the various manuscripts with no apparent pattern evident. With the advent of printing, early editions of the Jewish Bible placed the five in the calendar order of the four feasts and one fast at which each was read: The Song of Songs (Passover), Ruth (Weeks), Lamentations (9th of Ab), Ecclesiastes (Tabernacles), and Esther (Purim) (see *JEnc,* 144 and *IDB* 1: 509); but apparently no medieval mss so ordered them.

Clearly one has to be cautious in constructing theories about "the shape" of the Jewish canon beyond the very secure (hi)story line beginning with the Torah and ending in 2 Kings, and the fact that the books of the three Major Prophets and the Twelve Minor Prophets always followed the record of that (hi)story; but even the order of these within the two categories may have been due as much to lengths of the books as to chronological order or any other factor (*JEnc,* 143; Metzger 1987: 295–300; see the convenient lists in Beckwith 1985: 450–64.)

3. Jabneh. In the past century, since the work of Graetz (1886: 281–98) but especially Buhl (1892: 24), it has been commonplace to refer to the gathering of rabbis at the Palestinian coastal town of Jabneh (Jamnia in Greek) as an authoritative council at which the canonization of the Tanak was completed. For some six decades in the first part of the current century a sort of formula was passed from one student generation to another: the Pentateuch was canonized by 400 B.C.E., the Prophets by 200 B.C.E., and the Writings at Jamnia by about 90 C.E. (Pfeiffer 1948: 64; *IDB* 1: 501–14; Jepsen 1959: 114). The discovery of the Dead Sea Scrolls, both the Qumran literature and other scrolls and fragments from other caves in the area, changed all that.

A pivotal study published in 1964 by J. P. Lewis exposed the misunderstandings and misreadings by Graetz and others of the rabbinic evidence concerning Jabneh. Lewis investigated each passage and came to the conclusion that while there was a gathering at Jabneh it did not function as an authoritative council, in the later sense of the great church councils, which somehow for all time closed the canon. Lewis' work has gained wide acceptance even though it has been used to argue otherwise opposing points of view (Sanders 1987: 9–39; Freedman *IDBSup,* 135; Leiman 1976: 120–24; Barthélemy 1984: 9–45; Beckwith 1985: 276–77; Talmon 1987: 71). For some (Sanders, Barthélemy, Talmon) it means that factors other than conciliar or official decisions must be sought in the sociopolitical realm; for others (Leiman, Beckwith) it has meant that the canon was officially closed up to two centuries earlier and that discussions reported concerning what "soiled the hands" by the end of the 1st century C.E. were about books already canonized.

4. Septuagint. The so-called Septuagint (LXX) presents quite a different picture of the shape of the OT canon. Greek translations of the Jewish Bible seem to have begun in the 3d century B.C.E., first apparently the Torah and then the other books, and some of the others seem to have been in existence by the time of the translation of Ben Sira into Greek (see above). Most Greek First (or Old) Testament mss and most available early lists (see Swete 1902: 201–10) indicate that the (hi)story sequence Genesis through Chronicles was fairly constant. There is little to suggest in the LXX mss or early church lists that the Pentateuch (Torah) was thought of as a separate entity; it was primarily (hi)story in the same sense as the books that followed. Ruth often followed Judges and preceded the four books of Kingdoms (i.e., 1–2 Samuel plus 1–2 Kings), which were immediately then followed by the revisionist (hi)story of all that had been recounted up to that point, supplied by Chronicles (*Paraleipomena*).

In fact, there is no tripartite division in the Greek First Testament, as in the later Hebrew-Aramaic mss and lists noted above, suggesting that such a division after the Pentateuch was either not yet known, or more likely, not of full canonical status by the time of the Roman destruction of Jerusalem and the break of Christianity from Judaism. The further fact that after Chronicles the order of books in the LXX varied widely and without a clear pattern would also indicate that by the time of that break the full canonical process was not yet complete—unless some convincing polemical reasons could be advanced for the varying orders, or for the fact that libertarian variance took place at all; and none has been advanced. All the Greek OT mss were preserved by the churches (Kraft 1978: 225) and might possibly reflect an undetected polemic of order of books. All the principal Greek OT mss were in codex form and hence relatively (though not absolutely) stable in terms of order of books within the mss (Beckwith 1985: 194).

The Twelve Minor Prophets in Hebrew mss were always copied on one scroll; the order of them was fairly stable, usually beginning with Hosea and ending with Malachi in the order found in modern translations. But Greek OT translations and lists show variance within the Twelve; Codices B (Vaticanus) and A (Alexandrinus), e.g., both put Amos and Micah after Hosea before Joel; and the order Hosea, Amos, Joel, Obadiah, Jonah, Micah, Nahum, etc. is also found (Swete 1902: 202); beginning with Nahum the order seems quite stable through to Malachi.

The three Major Prophets with Daniel may appear after the Twelve (B and A) or before them (Sinaiticus); or they may be separated by the Twelve with Daniel and Ezekiel following the Minor Prophets (Melito's list). The (hi)storical books beginning with Genesis may go through *4 Maccabees* (Sinaiticus) before the Prophets, or Maccabees may be put last (Origen). Other such observations could be made, but all would support the view that there was no Alexandrian canon in the sense that the term normally conveys with regard to shape or structure (Sundberg 1964; Freedman *IDBSup,* 135).

5. Dead Sea Scrolls. The so-called Dead Sea Scrolls, discovered between 1947 and 1961 (with perhaps others yet to come in), include the scrolls and tens of thousands of fragments of scrolls found in the eleven caves just N of the Wadi Qumran at the NW end of the Dead Sea, as well as others found in Judean desert caves (Murrabaʿat, Ḥever, Ṣeʾelim, Mishmar) containing literature dating between the two Jewish Revolts (70 to 135 C.E.), in the Palace/Fortress at Masada (68–73), and in caves in the Wadi ed-Daliyeh SE of Nablus (4th century B.C.E.; see Sanders 1973b and Wise 1986a; 1986b). Their discovery has caused a review of nearly every aspect of biblical study including that of questions relating to the canons of Judaism and Christianity and denominations and groups within them. All of the literature emanating from the Qumran caves (except for the few found in caves 3 and 7, and maybe 6) seems to have originally been part of a denominational, theological library belonging to a single Jewish group which treasured them in the period between its founding in the middle of the 2d century B.C.E. until its disintegration and dispersion at the hands of Roman troops in the spring of 68 C.E.

All of the discoveries from all of the areas noted date from before the development of codices; all of it, with the very few exceptions of writing on ostraca and wood, was found or was originally in scroll form whether written on leather or papyrus, and in one case on copper (Cave 3). This makes the question of the shape of the canon at Qumran, even indeed in Judaism during the time of the writing, copying, and reading of the scrolls, difficult to discern; this is the reason, as noted above, that opinions about the shape of the Jewish canon precisely during the period of the scrolls still vary considerably.

Every book of the Jewish Bible with the single exception of Esther has been identified among the scrolls and fragments from the eleven Qumran caves. Some 30 copies of a Psalter or Psalters have been identified, about 25 copies of Deuteronomy, 20 of Isaiah, 15 of Genesis, 15 of Exodus, 8 of Leviticus, 6 of Numbers, 8 of the Minor Prophets, 8 of Daniel, 8 of Numbers, 6 of Ezekiel, 5 of Job, 4 of Samuels, 4 of Jeremiah, 4 of Ruth, 4 of Song of Songs, 4 of Lamentations, 3 of Judges, 3 of Kings, 2 of Joshua, 2 of Proverbs, 2 of Qohelet, and a single fragment each surviving of Ezra-Nehemiah and of Chronicles (cf. Barthélemy 1984: 15).

Caution is in order. One might be tempted to suggest that even the Pentateuch was out of shape at Qumran because of the great popularity, apparently, of Genesis, Exodus, and Deuteronomy, but fewer examples of Leviticus and Numbers. We simply do not know if we have everything they had in their library, probably indeed not. The great interest in laws of holiness and purity evident in their own denominational literature would indicate considerable interest in Leviticus. The complete lack of a representative fragment of Esther may or may not be significant with regard to whether that book was included in the Qumran biblical canon, or yet at the time in the general Jewish canon; even the fact that it was one of the five books disputed after the fall of Jerusalem in 70 may or may not be emphasized now by the lack of Esther at Qumran. Failure to find evidence of the presence of Psalm 110 in any of the many Psalter copies represented is mitigated by the fact that the figure of Melchizedech, important in Psalm 110, was prominent in the angelology of Qumran thinking; yet, Psalm 110 is not needed to deem Melchizedech a canonical figure since he is prominent also in Genesis 14 (cf. Hebrews 6–7). Psalm 111 is also lacking representation.

More interesting is the shape, or perhaps lack of it, of the Psalter at Qumran. Even though there were apparently more copies (30) of the Psalter at Qumran than of any other book, 35 of the 150 psalms in the Masoretic canon are lacking even on fragments (Sanders 1967: 143–49); and there seems to be no pattern to the lack. There is no block of Masoretic psalms missing (Sanders 1967: 146–48). Even more striking is the fact that the longest, most continuous scroll of Psalms, 11QPs[a], contains not only 41 psalms known from the Masoretic (familiar) Psalter, but also contains 8 compositions heretofore either unknown (4) or known in Greek and/or Syriac translations (4). The scroll is about 4.75 m (almost 15.5 ft) long, containing 33 columns, with the order of at least 46 of the 48 compositions contained in the extant leather beyond doubt. This makes the Cave 11 Psalms Scroll one of the longest and best preserved of all the Qumran Scrolls; even though the bottom third of each column is lacking (due to decomposition over the 1900 years in the cave), careful measurement of the lacunae indicates the order and sequence of psalms on the scroll is certain except for the precise placement of one of the fragments of the scroll (fragment E), and even that is virtually certain.

11QPs[b], though surviving in only six fragments, appears to be a copy of the same Psalter; it includes one of the non-Masoretic psalms also in 11QPs[a] and has the same non-Masoretic order as the latter of the traditional psalms preserved in it. 4QPs[f] includes another of the non-Masoretic psalms also in 11QPs[a], though not the same, and has Masoretic psalms as well. 4QPs[b], 11QPs[g], and 11QPsAp[a] also exhibit evidence that the Psalter as we know it was not yet stabilized or that the folk at Qumran had not endorsed it for themselves (Talmon 1987: 73). It is clear that the folk at Qumran knew and used many non-Masoretic psalms of the biblical type (4Q380 and 381 in Schuller 1986: 61–265) as well as others familiar to us now only from Qumran such as the Hodayot (4QH) and the Songs of the Sabbath Sacrifice (4Q400–407 and 11QShirShabb in Newsom 1985: 85–387). It is difficult to know how "canonical" these latter were considered by the folk at Qumran, but they figure in discussions of canon only in a broad sense of what was available to a Jewish denomination in the time before the stabilization of the Masoretic is certain. Those collections, however, like 11QPs[a] and the others noted above, do indeed enter into consideration of stabilization of the proto-MT Psalter. Either they are viewed as evidence of the last stages before stabilization (Sanders 1967: 9–21; 1968: 284–98 [esp. n. 10]; 1973a: 134–48; 1974: 79–99; Meyer 1968: 213–19; Wilson 1985; Wise 1986a: 143–48; Barton 1986: 86), or they are viewed as liturgical collections drawn from an already canonized Psalter with non-canonical compositions mixed in for specific liturgical purposes (Goshen-Gottstein 1966: 22–23; Talmon 1966; Skehan 1973) which are as yet unclear. "The Psalter provides us a sort of revealing microcosm of the fluidity existing on the frontiers of what books were sacred at certain times and for certain members of the community at Qumran" (Barthélemy 1984: 19). Psalters of up to 200 psalms are reported as late as the middle ages (Sanders 1967: 157–58; 1968: 294).

Just as the Psalter at Qumran seems not yet to have been stabilized in terms of content and order, so also the third section of the canon, the Writings, would appear to have been still open, parallel to the witness of the LXX. The Qumran library contained much in the original languages of what are called apocrypha and pseudepigrapha (Sanders 1973a; fc.; Fitzmyer 1977) as well as literary works heretofore unknown. It is simply not possible to be sure how many of these were considered canonical in function in the thinking of the Qumran faithful. Superficial criteria such as care in copying, mode of format in terms of column width and length, practice of using paleo-Hebrew script, whether or not a pesher-type commentary was written only on what was there considered canonical, or any other such, are not determinative. In eastern Christian churches the lengths of canons vary still, up to 81 books in the Ethiopian Orthodox canon (Cowley 1974: 318–23; Kealy 1979: 13–26; Sanders 1984a: 12; cf. Beckwith 1985: 478–505).

6. Sociopolitical Factors and Community Needs. One point on which there is clarity and general agreement is that the gathering of rabbis at the Palestinian coastal town of Jabneh (Jamnia) after the fall of Jerusalem up to about 90 C.E. cannot be considered a canonizing council (Lewis 1964: 125–32; Sanders 1987: 13; Leiman 1976: 120–24; Beckwith 1985: 4–7). The significance of that general conviction, however, varies. For the most part it is taken to mean that such conciliar bodies simply did not exist in early Judaism and that to understand Jamnia as such is a reading back of the hierarchical authority of later church councils. The canonical process was more realistically one of bodies of literature passing the tests of time and space in terms of their value for many scattered believing communities. Canonicity was recognized by communities of faith with common identity as having in effect already taken place because of sociopolitical factors and community needs (Sandmel 1966: 207; Sanders 1987: 125–51; 1984a: 1–20; Barthélemy 1984: 30–37; Talmon 1987: 67–72) and not because of deliberate or conciliar decisions; councils for the most part only ratify what has already happened among the people. But it has also been taken more radically to mean that canonization of the Writings had already taken place either *de facto* (Leiman) or *de jure* (Beckwith) by the 2d century B.C.E., and that variance from that canon, whether in the Dead Sea Scrolls or the LXX, should be taken as benign aberration. It is more likely that surviving Pharisaic-rabbinic Judaism after 70 C.E. trimmed the lush growth of apocalyptic and other literature (Freedman *IDBSup,* 135; Kaestli 1984: 71–102), which had become erratically diverse and in danger of abandoning Judaism's basic monotheizing faith. A part of that lush growth, from the standpoint of Pharisaic-rabbinic Judaism, may have been early Christian literature and practice. Clear evidence for a date earlier than the end of the 1st century C.E. is at best weak and unconvincing (cf. Talmon 1987: 74–79).

7. Stabilization of Text and Canon. Parallel to stabilization of canon was stabilization of the text of books after the Pentateuch. The Torah, whether in text or versions, exhibits remarkable stability in all the witnesses available. Even the some six thousand variants in the Samaritan Pentateuch are, except for a few, largely minor and fall within a range of relative stability. While the actual books of the prophetic corpus may well have been set in an early form about the same time the Torah was being edited, or even perhaps earlier (Freedman 1962: 250–65), the stabilization of the text of the prophetic corpus has been convincingly described as having taken place during the 1st centuries B.C.E. and C.E. (Greenberg 1956: 157–67; *QHBT,* 1–41, 321–400; Barthélemy *IDBSup,* 878–84; Albrektson 1978: 49–65). The variance of texts in the prophets has been understood both as exhibiting distinct families of text types (*QHBT,* 177–95, 306–20; Ulrich 1978) and as simply indicating textual fluidity and variety (Goshen-Gottstein 1965: 17; Sanders 1987: 125–51; Talmon 1987: 45–79; Tov 1988: 28–37) up to what apparently was full stabilization of the text by the middle of the fourth quarter of the 1st century C.E., as witnessed by the proto-Masoretic texts from the Judean desert sites other than Qumran and by the more literal translations into Greek at the end of the 1st century C.E. Stabilization of the Writings in the proto-Masoretic tradition seems to have been complete by the end of the 1st century C.E. (Barthélemy *IDBSup,* 878–84; Tov 1982: 19–27; 1986: 181–85).

C. Internal Shape of Canon

1. Canon as Context. Recent discussions about the shape of the canon have moved beyond issues of fluidity and stability of text and canon to observations about how the shape of a canon provides a context in which to read the individual contributions contained in it. The juxtaposition in the order, where stable, of those contributions, whether sources within a book or the books interrelating among themselves, can influence how each is read. Context influences understanding of text. Canon in this sense is the primary and most authoritative context in which to read the various parts of it (Childs 1978; *IOTS*). There are other contexts in which it is read and these are important as well: these include the community of faith and cultic setting in which a text was and is read, as well as the historical and sociopolitical situation or setting in which a text is composed and in which it is later read and reread; equally important is the hermeneutical context in which a text is heard or read. Whenever a text is read three factors must be kept in mind: the text itself; the sociopolitical situation in which it arose and in which it is read; and the hermeneutics by which it is caused to function when repeated/recited (Sanders 1984a: 77–78). The internal shape of canon focuses on the literary and intertextual chemistry, as it were, of texts in their relation to other texts which had arisen out of different original contexts but are now, in canon, compressed into a canonical-literary whole.

One might contrast the Koran to the Bible. The Koran is the record, supposedly, of a direct revelation of God to a human and to humans; the Bible is the record of human responses to God's revelations. The Bible comes from many different human hands over a 1500-year period of formation from the Bronze Age to the Roman Period. Most of recent biblical criticism has attempted to discern the provenance and source of each literary unit in it as well as the messages of each unit as originally intended. This is in effect a deconstructionist exercise; the original parts are unraveled and examined each in its own right, and only subsequently in the immediate context of the larger literary unit or book to which it belongs. But the Bible is a text in itself. It all hangs together in a larger literary context so that each of the discernible units small and large, including books, may take on new hues and connotations within the whole. Sometimes this resignification of texts may be attributed to an editor, or redactor, who may or may not have altered the sources used to integrate them into a new discernible literary unit; but sometimes it is due to the intertextuality of canonical context (*IOTS,* 46–83).

2. Canon and One God. The (hi)story which begins in Genesis and ends in 2 Kings is made up of a number of ancient sources which are woven together to recount a rather remarkable story focused on the purposes, will, and acts of One God, Creator of heaven and earth and all that in them is. The views in the smaller units of who and what God was or is vary considerably, but they are all woven together in such a way as to present a monotheizing view of the One God who is made up quite clearly of various communities' views of numerous local, tutelary, high, earthly, and heavenly deities, gods, and goddesses, exhibiting their various characteristics and activities (e.g., Gen 6:1–4; Deut 32:8; Hos 2:10—Eng 2:8; etc.). The result is that the God who emerges in the resultant (hi)story is both a high god and a local deity, both a moving and a stationary god, both male and female (e.g., Gen 1:26–28; Jer 31:32), both national and international: creator, sustainer-nurturer, judge, and redeemer. The various surviving names of God in the text become epithets or occasional names; there is a tradition that God has seventy names.

3. Canon and (Hi)story. Beginning with Genesis 12 the story begins to focus on one family, the progenitors of which were Abraham and Sarah. Modern critical study has shown that the stories of the patriarchs and matriarchs in Genesis stem from various ancient sources, but in the Genesis text they are presented as succeeding generations of the Abraham-Sarah family promised in Genesis 12 and 15. Exodus tells of a slave rebellion organized and led by a person named Moses, heir of the same family; in fact the slaves though diverse in background are presented as descendants in the same family. The story as woven incorporates a long stop at the foot of Mt. Sinai and a trek of 40 years in the Sinai desert with efforts to enter the Promised Land of Canaan thwarted until the escaped slaves find themselves on the E bank of the Jordan in the plains of Moab listening to a very long speech by Moses just before his death (most of the Book of Deuteronomy). The (hi)story continues on into the book of Joshua with the settlement in the land, the book of Judges and the Philistine threats to the whole venture, the establishment of a monarchy in Samuel under Saul and David, and then the greatest rise and fall in the Bible of earthly success followed by the split of Solomon's kingdom and the total demise of the Hebrew monarchy at the end of the Book of Kings. The Abraham-Sarah family finds itself at the end of the (hi)story in destitution. That which had started with great promises which indeed were fulfilled in the glorious climax of the reigns of David and Solomon (2 Samuel 5 to 1 Kings 10) ends ignominiously. How so?

The only answer to that question lies in the full canonical text, and that fact was recognized in every shape of the canon noted above. It is still recognizable today but only if all the sources woven together are read as the text is inherited. Scholarship has discerned and tried to name some of the sources which are woven together to make the story: a Jahwist source (J) which was basically southern or Judean; an Elohist source (E) which was northern or Ephraimitic; the book of Deuteronomy (D) and a school of editors and writers which the book spawned, called Deuteronomist (Dtr); perhaps a source or perhaps only editors who seem to have a priestly perspective (P); records from the courts of both N and S; and various other minor sources. Efforts have been made to extricate some of the sources by unraveling the woven canonical text to discern earlier views of the (hi)story (such as Coote and Ord 1988); and they are viable efforts insofar as reconstruction of the sources, or even perhaps the actual history, is concerned. But none of them alone can answer the above question, only the full text as finally shaped.

The answer to the question of the apparent failure lies first in the affirmations found several times but especially in some of the great hymns, such as the Songs of the Sea (Exod 15:1–7), of Moses (Deut 32:39), and of Hannah (1 Sam 2:6–7): that God is the God of the risings and the fallings of the powerful as well as the God of death and of life, of victory and defeat (the same theme is at the heart of the Song of Mary [Luke 1:46–55] in which Luke situates the failure of Jesus as a political messiah). The fulfillment of the promises as well as the demise of the two kingdoms is set in the larger theocentric and monotheizing perspective which no one source alone can provide, not even the most monotheizing book of the Bible, Deuteronomy. The God who emerges from the whole can no longer be identified with any one deity of any of the sources but is the God of all life's experiences, what humans would call good as well as what they would call bad—such as defeats and failings. In the same manner the story that emerges cannot be found in any one of the sources alone. Just as the genre called gospel arose at a later time to explain the apparent failure of the ministry of a wisdom/prophetic teacher from the Galilee in a theocentric monotheizing mode, so the (hi)story which begins in Genesis and moves on through Kings had no exact parallel. And it is difficult to identify one grand, final redactor who did it all because some of the most primitive materials in the story adumbrate the message of the story as a whole. The answer lies in the whole and not in the parts, not even in the intentionality of one final genius, some supposed final redactor.

The answer may be put in the following way: (a) it is not God who let us down in the defeats; (b) it is we by our sins who had let God down in disobedience and polytheistic rebellion; (c) God had in fact sent prophets early and betimes to tell us that is the way it is in the divine economy; (d) but if in destitution we take it to heart that God meant what Moses and the prophets had been saying, then God will be more than pleased to restore Israel, even though in a transformed state if need be.

4. Torah and Prophets. These four points are not stated as such in any one passage in the story (Brueggeman and Wolff 1982: 101–41); they emerge from the whole. The tripartite Jewish canon is shaped in such a way that these four points are celebrated over and over again. After the story is told and the defeat is underscored by the ignominy of the one surviving king of the Davidic dynasty living under house arrest in Babylon (2 Kgs 25: 27–30), then 15 case histories are presented in the Latter Prophets to illustrate the points made: Isaiah, Jeremiah, Ezekiel, Hosea, etc. (i.e., the Books of the Three Prophets plus the Book of the Twelve), which follow the Genesis-to-Kings (hi)story. Israel had indeed been warned often and betimes, and well before it all happened. But even these 15 prophetic messages had been well anticipated by the messages of the prophets who showed up from time to time in the (hi)story itself: Samuel, Nathan, Ahijah, Elijah, Elisha, Micaiah ben Imlah, and others in the Former Prophets (Judges to Kings) anticipated by Samuel's mother's hymn (1 Sam 2:1–10).

Most of the 15 speak both of God's being God of risings and God of fallings, fallings and risings. Most of them end with the fourth point of the answer stressed: God can and will effect restoration if Israel accepts divine discipline, the purging and the cleansing (Sanders 1955: 101–4, 117–19), even the open-heart surgery to be effected by God in the adversity (Hos 5:15–6:1; Jer 30:17; 31:31–34; Ezek 36:26–27). This had been anticipated already in Torah: whereas Jeremiah early in his ministry, and indeed an early level of Deuteronomy, exhorted the people to circumcise their hearts (Jer 4:4; Deut 10:16), Deuteronomy finally says that if the people do indeed in destitution take the whole lesson to heart, God himself will do the circumcising (Deut 30:6) even though the people had failed to do so. Suffering was understood both as God's punishment for sins and as God's restorative and re-creating activity (Sanders 1972: 73–90).

The prophets also make the point time and again that God is the God of the risings and fallings of other peoples as well as of Israel. This is explicitly stated in Amos 9:7, but it is underscored in the so-called oracles against the nations contained in most of the prophetic books. Nahum and Obadiah cannot finally be read in isolation from the rest of the corpus, but should be read on the contrary as oracles against foreign nations in the same sense as the collections of such in the other prophetic books. No one book, especially of the Twelve Minor Prophets, tells the whole story; each must be read in the light of the whole. Amos' great sermon at Bethel (Amos 1:3–3:2) as received in the Amos text starts with oracles against Israel's neighbors and ends with similar indictments and sentences against Judah and Israel, as well as a theological defense of God's being Israel's judge (Amos 2:9–3:2) as well as judge of all God's creation (Amos 9:2–6). None of the points Amos makes, when the book is read in its canonical order (even given the slight variations in order in the Minor Prophets), are a surprise since they have already been made in numerous ways in the basic Torah story. Nahum and Jonah speak in solid canonical cadences of God as both judge and redeemer of Nineveh, the capital of one of Israel's worst enemies. Each can and should be read for itself in terms of the needs of the community doing the reading; but theologically they are complementary.

5. One God and (Hi)story. The Bible comes from differing sources over a 1500-year period ranging from the Bronze Age to the Hellenistic-Roman. This is surely the case with the Christian Bible as a whole, but it is also the case with the LXX and arguably the case with the Jewish Hebrew/Aramaic Bible. It is written in the mores and idioms of the five culture eras of those 1500 years. While it is not strictly speaking a monotheistic literature, the Bible is a monotheizing literature in the sense of exhibiting in all the periods of its formation a struggle against the various forms and expressions, mores and idioms, of the polytheisms of those times. One of the reasons the canonical shapes of the canons, Jewish and Christian, which eventuate from the canonical process are important is that it is only from the whole that we learn how to read the parts. It is important never to absolutize the primary religious language of any of the texts it contains, especially those which exhibit pretty clearly early tribalistic views of the deities (Exod 4:24–26; 1 Sam 15:2–3) in the divine compression called God.

That which the great hymns call the risings and fallings of empires and mighty people, over which God is Lord of history, may also be called "powerflows." For most of Israel's early history Egypt had hegemony over the Palestinian area and the peoples that inhabited it, especially Israel and Judah. Then, about the middle of the 8th century B.C.E., Egypt's power waned while Assyria's waxed in the area. Toward the end of the 7th century, while Egypt tried to reassert hegemony, it was Babylonia which gained the day and remained so until the middle of the 6th century when Persia dominated the whole area, even some of the Greek cities. Persia then had hegemony over the whole area until Alexander the Great came out of Macedonia and conquered the known world. The Greek conquest of the Semitic and non-Semitic worlds of the East created a phenomenon called Hellenism which came to influence Judaism as profoundly as any culture in all its history. Rome then began to assert itself and became the dominant power in Jerusalem from 63 B.C.E. for centuries to come.

The biblical assertion that the one true God is the Lord of history takes on poignant significance when seen in the light of such an overview. All of those cultures contributed to an understanding of the one God (Mendenhall 1973: 198–214) and contributed to attempts to verbalize that understanding through the mores and idioms of those cultures. Such pluralism within a canon provides a self-corrective apparatus within its bounds; no one group of idioms should be absolutized over another. Recognition of this canonical given, or gift, would deter the pervasive tendency to locate a canon within the canon and then to abuse the rest by insisting that it all agrees with the parts chosen. This is one reason it is very important not to decanonize the NT by focusing only on a synchronic understanding of its literature within the Hellenistic culture only. Such a canonical overview of the Bible's shape is also important in understanding its assertions that God is the God of death and life, the risings and the fallings of empires. No government lasts so long, not even the eventual Roman empire, as to escape the observation that the God of the canon is not stumped by the failings nor particularly impressed by the successes.

Judaism as we know it arose (Ezekiel 37) out of the failure of the two kingdoms, and it still exists 2600 years later. And it does so in great measure because of the theological history that is related in Genesis to Kings. The great prophets whose ministries are described in the 15 books of the corpus called Latter Prophets lived, beginning with Amos, when the "powerflows" in the ANE had their greatest effect on the Abraham-Sarah folk. When Persia then became dominant over two centuries later, prophecy reached its zenith with the Isaiah of the exile (Isaiah 40–55) and was believed to have ceased completely with the introduction of the Torah to Jerusalem which Ezra brought back with him from Babylonia (Nehemiah 8) where it had been edited into the short version of the story we call the Pentateuch. It was because of the now-firm belief that God is God in fallings as well as risings, and can wrest life out of death (Deut 32:39), that the story of the settlement in the land of Canaan could be left out of the Pentateuch. One could be an observant, believing Jew without having to live in Palestine, as much a hope as that would always remain (Sanders 1972: 1–53). The function of canon, as we shall see, is to provide ever-new generations with identity (faith) and direction for life (obedience). Hence the practice arose very early in Judaism of reading the Torah in annual (rarely triennial) cycles so that the people could identify with the Abraham-Sarah call and venture. One could indeed continue to live in Babylonia (the largest Jewish community in the world until the Middle Ages, and the community which gave Judaism its official Talmud) and still be a faithful Jew.

6. One God and Hagiographa. The Jewish canon does not end, as does the Christian First Testament, with the prophetic corpus. On the contrary, there is still the third section, the Hagiographa. In the majority of the best Tiberian and Spanish mss, this section begins with Chronicles, a revisionist history of the whole story focusing on the Temple and Temple worship of God, with emphasis on David and Solomon, and with a retelling of many episodes giving hope that one can indeed be obedient. The Genesis to Kings (hi)story had as its major burden its explanation of the failures and defeats and hence gives a fairly pessimistic picture of human efforts at monotheizing obedience and loyalty to God. Chronicles has a quite different perspective on human capacity to obey. Some of the realism of Samuel and Kings is retuned to give hope that Jews, wherever they might be, hopefully in and around Jerusalem, could please God. A Jew is called to the service of God and Judaism is the expression of that service (Neusner 1984: 90–98). The center and heart of Judaism is *ᶜabôdāh,* "service" in both senses: worship and obedience. Many Jews, precisely the remnant that did not assimilate to a dominant non-Jewish culture in which they lived, must have asked many times how they could live so as to serve and please God. One needs to have hope, first and foremost, that it is possible to live a meaningful, that is, an obedient life.

While Judaism, like that of old Israel and Judah, is community- and covenant-oriented, it also is largely family-oriented and considerably more focused on the individual. Jeremiah and Ezekiel had both prepared the remnant for understanding individual responsibility (Jer 31:29–34; Ezekiel 18) and for the hope it could bring; individuals would not have to bear responsibility any longer for all the old sins of the earlier generations (Isa 40:1–3) despite the realism in the old view (Exod 34:7). Chronicles not only offers hope and some examples of obedience, in its review of the old history, it ends on a note of real hope, the edict of Cyrus, King of Persia, that Jews could return to Jerusalem and rebuild the temple (2 Chr 36:22–23). In many of the best mss the Psalter begins immediately after Chronicles with Psalm 1 on the same column as the happy account of Cyrus' edict: "Happy is the person who walks not in the counsel of the wicked . . . but whose delight is in the Torah of God on which he meditates day and night" (Ps 1:1–2). Many of the old royal and community psalms in the Masoretic Psalter are resignified in their canonical context into psalms the individual or the family can identify with no matter their original intent or use.

In those same mss the Psalter is followed by Job and Proverbs, then the five scrolls, and finally (hi)story is resumed with Daniel and Ezra-Nehemiah closing the Jewish canon. In such a shaping there is a return to recounting (hi)story and a closing of the ranks to avoid extinction of Judaism by assimilation, but the emphasis is on hope and the opportunity for individuals and families to live obedient lives. It has been suggested that the Writings in their canonical shape, no matter in what order the individual books are found, provided for Judaism a way to live and exist *in stasis* (Morgan 1990), in community, in whatever locale Judaism was practiced. But its steady assumption is belief in One God. Job takes monotheism more seriously perhaps than any other book dealing with undeserved suffering. The 31 chapters of the Book of Proverbs provide all kinds of suggestions for living obedient lives under One God in all the areas which the laws in the Pentateuch perhaps do not touch.

The five scrolls are read during annual feasts and a fast and deal with ways to understand living under One God (even if God is not mentioned, as in the Book of Esther) on the heights as well as in the dark passages of life. Qohelet says it is normal to question how anyone can believe in One God, and it is important to do so. Doubt is an essential part of faith, otherwise it may be only superstition. The Song of Songs celebrates God's gift of *nepeš* or *eros* and resonates both with the first commandment in the Bible, to be fruitful and multiply (Gen 1:22 and 28), and with the *Shemaᶜ*, in which is the command to love God with all the *nepeš* or self (Deut 6:5). Daniel looks at the larger picture of fortunes rising and falling and how a Jew who truly believes in One God can tolerate living under oppression and even persecution.

7. Septuagint. The LXX provides a quite different context for everything after the Pentateuch. The theological history expressed in the Jewish canon is considerably resignified by the different number and order of books in LXX manuscripts, but there is a strong sense of (hi)story nonetheless. While it is undoubtedly true that there was no Alexandrian canon as such (Sundberg 1964; *IDBSup*, 136–140), codices of the LXX provide interesting contexts for reading the different books in them. Whereas the tripartite Masoretic canon openly stresses a prophetic understanding and perspective on nations' risings and fallings, especially Israel's, under the aegis of the one true God, and then how surviving Jews can live lives of service and obedience, the LXX mss tend to put the historical books together in the order of 1–4 Kingdoms (Samuel-Kings), Chronicles, Ezra-Nehemiah, Esther (Sinaiticus; cf. Vaticanus and Alexandrinus). Ruth is placed right after Judges, or in some just before it. Tobit, Judith, and 1–4 Maccabees are in nearly all LXX mss and extend the sense of history into the Hellenistic-Roman period. It, too, is a theological history in a monotheizing mode but the accents are different and history tends to a speculative perspective with accommodation to the messianic and apocalyptic view of the goals of history. Daniel is grouped with the prophets, often after Ezekiel.

The LXX, while originating in Jewish communities where Greek was the principal language and Hebrew and Aramaic were less well known, was ultimately preserved by Christianity (Kraft 1978). The so-called LXX was the Bible of the early church (Sundberg 1964; McDonald fc.) until the formation of the strictly Christian canon which was by the 4th century C.E. made up of the Greek First (or "Old") Testament (of varying content and order after the Pentateuch) and the peculiarly Christian Second (or "New") Testament (of varying content and order—Metzger 1987: 191–250, 295–300). It was not until Jerome devoted 35 years of his life (d. 420 C.E.) to learning and translating Hebrew/Aramaic mss of the First Testament with a rabbi in Bethlehem that the kind of stability represented by mss of the Vulgate entered the picture, and even then not until well after his death. While Jerome did not adopt the content and order of the Jewish canon but kept those of the LXX as he knew it, by translating a clearly proto-Masoretic copy of the text of the Jewish Bible he in large measure brought the Vulgate into closer textual (though not canonical) relation to what we know as the MT, undoubtedly because of the proto-MT biblical mss of his Bethlehem mentor. From the end of the 1st century of our era up to that point the Greek First Testament was a peculiarly Christian tradition and may well reflect Christian interests if not in the actual texts then in the inclusion and order of books after the Pentateuch (Kraft 1978: 207–26). Jerome not only succeeded in regard to the Roman Catholic Church (though not the Eastern churches), his attitude of pursuing the *Hebraica Veritas* of the text was adopted by the 16th-century Reformers in Europe; in fact Protestantism, while keeping a generally LXX sense of the order of books after the Pentateuch, limited the content to that of the Jewish canon, even bracketing the so-called deuterocanonicals or apocrypha in a kind of appendix. As noted above, it was not until the 19th century that any editions of the Protestant Bible were published with only the content, though still not the order, of the Jewish canon in the First Testament.

D. Canon as Function

1. Canon as Process. The other meaning of "canon," *norma normans,* or "collection of authoritative books," with focus on how the canon functions in the believing communities that find their identity in a canon and base programs of obedience on it, has also received attention in recent study (Sanders 1975; 1984a; 1984b; 1987; Knight 1975; Fishbane 1985). This aspect of study of canon does not totally ignore questions of inclusion/exclusion and the juxtaposition of the contents of a canon, but its focus is on early traditioning processes and the role they played in development of the concept of canon and its function in believing communities, and hence may cut across and challenge readings done in canonical context (see C.1.–C.4. above). Canon understood as process valorizes biblical pluralism and intracanonical dialogue.

It has often been observed that the event of discovery of the scroll of Deuteronomy in 621 B.C.E. and its adoption by King Josiah as the authority for his reformation (2 Kings 22–23) was the beginning of the actual canon (Pfeiffer 1948: 50–70; *IDB* 1: 502–7). There is recorded in the Bible itself royal and official activity by Josiah that suggests a recognition of the authority of the scroll by the community in Jerusalem under Josiah's sponsorship (2 Kgs 22:8–16; 23:1–3); the scroll functioned as legitimizing authority for Josiah's reformation and seems to have been adopted as authoritative at least throughout Josiah's reign, but apparently not thereafter as long as the monarchy lasted, which was almost another quarter century (2 Kgs 23:25). After the kingdom of Judah was destroyed (587 B.C.E.) when those in exile (especially in Babylon) began to reflect on what had happened (Sanders 1987: 18–30), Deuteronomy became the cornerstone of the eventual canon (Sanders 1987: 175–91). Its position as the climax of the eventual Torah with its massive emphasis on belief in One God (Lohfink 1963) gave it pride of place in the whole eventual canon with influence backward to Genesis and forward through the rest of the whole canon, whether MT or LXX (Sanders fc.). But the prehistory of canon as function antedates Deuteronomy. Deuteronomy could function as it did for Josiah and the whole community of Judah because there had been authoritative traditions functioning in a similar manner well before it. When the Pentateuch as Torah came into being on the demise of prophecy in the time of Ezra, with Deuteronomy as its capstone, it functioned as canon (*norma normans*) for Judaism well before canon as an authoritative collection of books came into being (Aicher 1906: 10; Sanders 1972: 1–9).

Canon *as function* antedates canon *as shape.* The function of a written canon has antecedents in the very process by which the concept arose, that is, in the function of authoritative traditions when there was as yet no written literature deemed canonical in the sense of *norma normata,* or shape. One of the results of form-critical study of the First ("Old") Testament has been recognition of the function of early recitals of Israel's early and formative history under God (von Rad *PHOE* 1–78; Wright 1952; Sanders 1972: 1–30; 1975: 75–106; Groves 1987: 7–62). It has long been recognized that most all texts build on earlier texts and traditions. This, too, is properly called intertextuality. We used the term above to refer to how reading a text within an intertextual context such as canon may be different from reading that same text as a totally independent literary unit, as is done in historical, form, and even redaction criticism. But recognition of how a later text "rings in the changes," as it were, on earlier traditions and texts by citing, paraphrasing, alluding to them, or imitating their form, is also intertextuality. In a sense all texts are to some degree intertextual since all new texts in order to be read with understanding presuppose what has gone before in the community's traditions, oral or written. This is recognized as well by others than form critics in the case of the Jewish Bible (Sandmel 1961: 105–22; Fishbane 1985: 91–524).

2. Textual Fluidity. All such observations point to the early function of traditions and texts in nearly all parts and forms of literature within the Bible. One of the most interesting aspects of intrabiblical intertextuality is the fluidity of citation and allusion. Exact quotation is rare such as the verbatim citation of Micah 3:12 in Jer 26:18; attribution is also rare within the Jewish canon (outside the historical books where even so it is not common until Chronicles) such as the mention of Jeremiah's prophecy in Ezra 1:1. But fluid references to earlier traditions abound, and these include reference to the authoritative traditions known from the biblical stories relating the great episodes in the Hexateuch as well as in the Davidic traditions (Sanders 1972: 1–30). When they were alluded to or cited for the most part it was done for the authoritative value in them recognizable by the believing community for which the new speech or text was being composed. They were brought to mind to argue a point. And because a great deal of the Bible in its early forms was oral, fluidity presented a great advantage; the tradition referred to could be shaped to fit the new argument. It did not have to be an exact citation. This situation continues to be the case right on through the literature of Early Judaism, Apocrypha, Pseuepigrapha, Dead Sea Scrolls, even Philo and Josephus, including the Christian Second Testament. It should be clearly understood that the fluidity of citation one sees in all that massive amount of literature is not primarily to be attributed to poor memory, which was not a truly pertinent factor (Balch 1988). Relative fluidity and adaptability were major characteristics of the whole history of formation of the Bible from earliest times through to the stabilization of texts discussed above complete by the end of the 1st century of our era, including citations (Sanders 1987: 9–40; 125–51). Being a written text *and* officially adopted by King Josiah as the foundation of national policy, Deuteronomy began a process of shift from relative fluidity to relative stability that still was not finally complete by the end of the 1st century C.E. (Sanders 1987: 175–91).

3. Adaptability and Stability. Adaptability is a major characteristic of the very concept of canon. Throughout the period of canonical process in antiquity up to stabilization of text and canon, and even to a limited extent beyond it down to today, a canon is marked by its malleability; citations and allusions throughout the literature of Early Judaism including the Second Testament exhibit the relative adaptability of authoritative texts and traditions. Free choice among numerous modern translations of the Bible is an exponent of fluidity of text today. Rewriting of earlier authoritative texts was common, and so was reshaping them a bit to fit the new argument or affirmation of faith. To call a tradition or text "canonical" is to say it will be available for later communities to apply to their new situations. Even when stabilization of text became a major factor, ways were found to get canonical texts to fit later problems, and the need to render the stable adaptable induced hermeneutical regulations to control the exercise (Sanders 1987: 142–51).

But a community's need to adapt what had been accepted as authoritative meant that those texts exhibiting multivalency were appealed to time and again, and thus acquired a special, and eventually a canonical, status (Talmon 1987: 67–69). Another characteristic of canon, at least in the case of both the Jewish and the Christian, in contrast perhaps to the Koran, is the compression, noted above, of various genres and kinds of literature by many different authors over almost 1500 years. Of necessity that very fact of compression of such diverse literature renders the canon pluralistic to a limited extent. The adaptability of canonical literature may therefore be found in its internal contradictions. When the community later needed the challenge of one portion it was there; when it needed the comfort of another, that too was there. When the community needed to settle and build, when it faced the challenges of peace and political stability, there were portions to call on to validate the activity; when the community faced upheaval and disruption and had once more to be uprooted, there were portions to call on to validate the activity. Multivalency of a single passage, and the pluralism of the whole, meant that accuracy of citation, when that became a necessity in itself after full stabilization, did not curtail the ability of a community to adapt the canonical to new phases of life. Even so, if need be, mixing and matching of passages from different portions of Scripture could yield the adaptability needed. The limited pluralism that is in a canon also provides it with a built-in self-corrective, a sort of prophetic, apparatus. For example, a policy or program might be constructed on certain portions of Scripture; then, when it would need modifying, corrections could also be rooted in Scripture (Sanders 1984b: 341–62).

One of the most interesting observations of community use of canon is the pervasive tendency to deny its pluralism. It is supposedly thought that to be honest about a canon's pluralism would be to deny its authority. God cannot be self-contradictory, it is argued (as though limited human experience and intelligence is capable of judging the fullness of the Integrity of Reality, that is the Oneness of God). Canons, precisely because they are human responses to divine revelation, of necessity reflect the ambiguity of reality. Denial of this point, supposedly out of fear of loss of canonical authority, has sometimes led to the danger of idolatry of the Bible, precisely worshiping what is believed to be a gift of God instead of worshiping God the Giver of all gifts; that tendency in some communities of faith has been called bibliolatry. To deny the Bible's pluralism is to deny its prophetic voice when a challenge to what has been constructed on it might later be needed, its built-in self-corrective apparatus.

4. Canonical Hermeneutics. The mid-term between the fluidity or adaptability of traditions and texts and their stability is hermeneutics (Sanders 1987: 61–73). It is always important to ask *how* the text or tradition was being read in the new situation. Jesus is reported to have asked a contemporary, "What is written in Torah and how do you read it [Luke 10:26]?" What is the pertinent text and by what hermeneutic do you read it? What is the conceptuality lying back of the (newer) text being studied and what is the view of reality at play when the older tradition is being called upon? These are crucial questions, and they need to be asked whenever intertextuality is identified in study of a text (Neusner 1983: 43–51). The prophets often surprised, even shocked their contemporaries by the ways in which they caused a tradition to function (Sanders 1987: 87–105) in their arguments and challenges to their people. Study of controversy passages including the disputations between so-called true and false prophets is very revealing in terms of how hermeneutics can cause a text or tradition to be applied to a new situation in two opposing ways.

a. Challenge. Amos' fluid citation of the basic Torah story in 2:9–11 points to a contrast between the people's current activity and what God had done for them in the Exodus-to-Entrance story; in fact, the contrast is highlighted by the Amos text having God refer first to the divine gift of land (v 9), precisely because Amos' indictment of his contemporaries focused on their maltreatment of the poor and the needy in the land which God had given them (2:6–8). The force of God's "remembering" that (as well as God's lifting their heads out of the dust of the earth [cf. 2:7] of Egypt when they were the poor and needy) is poignant indeed. But when then a hearer apparently intervened contradicting Amos' use of those authoritative traditions, Amos agreed with the main point made, namely that they were the only family on earth God knew in the way he knew Israel, but went on to claim that authoritative tradition as the very base of his argument that God would therefore punish them for their iniquities (3:2). The opponent had assumed that the tradition meant that God was their God and would take care of them no matter what. The difference in hermeneutics is that Amos understands God also to be the Creator God of all peoples (9:2–7) and hence free to judge Israel as well as others. The same distinction in hermeneutics, or how the so-called true prophets read Israel's common authoritative traditions, can be traced throughout the prophetic corpus: God is both Redeemer of Israel and Creator of all peoples, hence free to express grace to Israel and to others, and free to judge Israel as well as others (Sanders 1987: 87–105).

Hermeneutics make a difference no matter what tradition is being called on, as Isaiah showed in adducing the Davidic royal traditions in a challenging way in his time (Isa 1:21–27; 28:9–22; et passim). What must be kept in mind is that there are three factors always at play in adapting authoritative traditions, hence canon: (1) the text or tradition called on; (2) the sociopolitical and historical situation to which the text is being adapted; and (3) the implicit hermeneutics used to apply the tradition or text. If one denies the importance of any one of the three the very canonical dimension of the exercise may be missed. This is especially the case when the historical provenance of a text, such as the ones just noted in Amos and Isaiah, is bracketed or reduced in importance (*IOTS*, 56–57); to reduce canonical context to its literary aspect only, as important as that is (see C.1. above), is to reduce the very canonical dimension of the text (Sanders 1987: 153–74), and may indeed reduce its relevance or adaptability to later settings by focusing only on the hermeneutic moves on the literary level. The application of the tradition about the call of Abraham and Sarah and God's promise of land, which the people cited to Ezekiel to offer themselves hope upon receipt of the news of the fall of Jerusalem, is refuted by Ezekiel (33:23–29) but affirmed by the prophet of the exile (Isa 51:1–3). Sociopolitical and historical context has to be carefully discerned as to what the needs of the community are in order to choose a text or tradition to apply and then choose the hermeneutics by which to apply it. The ancient and the new sociopolitical contexts have to be exegeted as carefully as does the text (Gottwald 1985: 301–21).

b. Comfort. The pluralism characteristic of the Bible means that we should be cautious in using the terms "true" or "false" with regard to the prophets in the controversy passages or to their theology, for that which is "false" in one historical setting may well be true in another. There is an ancient, anonymous saying to the effect that the same text may afflict the comfortable and also comfort the afflicted. The prophetic corpus as well as the Gospels are full of passages which indicate that the older text or tradition read or cited or alluded to could be understood by the people as comforting but is applied by the prophet or Jesus so as to challenge (Luke 4:16–30; Sanders 1975: 75–106).

The hermeneutic that emerges from study of the implicit hermeneutics in most passages which exhibit such intertextuality is a theocentric monotheizing hermeneutic, that is, the focus is on what the One God of All has done in given human situations and then what God would yet do in another. There are passages, however, in which God's dominion over all creation is not the view of reality underlying the individual text. There are texts in both testaments which seem to present a tribal view of God; these are often the ones called on by communities of faith when out of fear they feel they need to battle an enemy of some sort or need to feel they are right and others wrong. Judaism and Christianity have often called on such texts in time of conflict; and they are there.

The question then arises as to whether it is canonically legitimate to read such passages with a hermeneutic different from the one implicit in the text. Is it canonically fair to superimpose a hermeneutic that seems to emerge from most biblical passages upon those that do not? Is it canonically legitimate to read the parts in the light of the whole? The answer is Yes (see C.1.–C.7. above). Most of the prophets did so; Jesus did so. The hermeneutical move is first to theologize in reading all passages, using a theocentric monotheizing view of reality, and then only thereafter to moralize, or ask what it means for the new situation in which it is being read. To do so would, in a prophetic manner, turn the passage inside-out, as it were, and expose modern tendencies to tribalize God just as the old text seems to do. The next move would then be to ask if the One God of All was instead commanding the enemy to challenge us. Very important in reading any passage is to be conscious of the particular party in it with which we readers are identifying. Nathan in effect told David that he should identify with the rich man in the mirror of the parable he had told, enabling David to judge himself (2 Sam 12:1–14). Jeremiah castigated the slaveholders in his time for reenslaving their slaves after they had freed them, and he did so by preaching on the tradition we know in Genesis about Abraham and the covenant between the pieces of the carcasses of the sacrificial animals (Gen 15:17–21). Normally the people would, without thinking, use the hermeneutic of God as the covenant God of Israel and hence their God; that is, normally they would identify with Abraham in reading or hearing the tradition. But Jeremiah, on the contrary, said they should identify that time, in that situation (not at all times), with the carcasses cut in two, for that is what would happen to them (Jer 34:17–22). Isaiah agreed with his contemporaries that God had indeed risen as Holy Warrior to assist David in his battles with the Philistines on Mt. Perazim and in the Valley of Gibeon (2 Sam 5:17–25; 1 Chr 14:8–16) and also agreed that God was still Holy Warrior, but in their time (probably 701 B.C.E.) God would instead be at the head of the enemy troops entering Israel (Isa 28:21–22). Jesus agreed that God was sending the messiah to announce good news to the poor and release to captives; but in contrast to the way Isa 61:1–2 was typically understood by his contemporaries (as comfort for their national suffering under Roman oppression), Jesus believed God was free instead to extend grace and comfort to whomever (Luke 4:16–30).

The triumph of the Deuteronomic emphasis on God's being the One God of All, when linked up in the canonical compression of all the Bible with such implicit hermeneutics as seen in the above examples, is also canonical warrant for reading the parts in the light of the whole. This means that the original "intentionality" of individual authors may canonically be overridden in the adaptation of a passage to a new situation. This is in part what is meant by understanding the Bible as canon. It would mean reading the NT not only synchronically in its Hellenistic context, though that is important to do, but also reading it diachronically or canonically in the light of the monotheizing hermeneutic of the canon as a whole.

It does not mean, however, that authorial intentionality is denied altogether. On the contrary, careful exegesis of individual passages is a part of the ongoing canonical process of intrabiblical dialogue; and the one applying a passage may decide that the need of the community for comfort is greater than its need for challenge. Prophetic imagination (Brueggeman 1978) requires that the preacher or teacher doing the adapting ask who, in an increasingly smaller world today, is being threatened when comfort for one's own community is being affirmed. It may indeed be decided that comfort is important, as the Isaiah of the exile knew. One cannot deny the hermeneutics of the so-called false prophets in the preexilic period without denying the very same hermeneutics used by the Babylonian Isaiah (chaps 40–55) when Israel was on the verge of extinction. There is richness in the dialogue between disagreeing colleagues in the same situation, just as there is richness in the pluralism of the canon as a whole.

5. God and "Powerflows." The canon as a whole indicates clearly that God is the God of both the risings and the fallings of life, the victories and the defeats, life and death, the great reversals of which life is made—all the human "powerflows" and all the pluralism of the ambiguity of reality. But in and through it all the Bible as a whole, as canon, celebrates the Oneness of God, that is, the Integrity of Reality. That Integrity is not measurable by any human means (Isa 40:12–26; Job 28). It may not be possible even to comprehend it just as perhaps no one contributor to the whole could understand the full canonical Reality. It may be that only a faith based on these compressed texts as canon can even apprehend it.

God's Oneness or Reality's Integrity is both ontological and ethical. It is a Oneness both in being and in character, and just as there may be no human means of measuring the being so there may be no human means (as the Book of Job seems to say) to affirm, in any one generation, the ethical integrity of God as Reality. A thorough reading of the Bible as canon induces the belief that there is moral fiber to the universe despite all the obvious and evident injustice. God did not just create the world and leave it be. God did not just liberate some slaves from Egyptian bondage and leave them be. God became involved and addressed an assembled community on a mountain, more than once perhaps (Matthew 5–7), with clear suggestions as to how to integrate their own lives with respect to the divine will. God is not only Creator and hence free; God is also Redeemer and hence involved with creation. God made justice the line and righteousness the plummet (Isa 28:17) every bit as much as God made the world in the first place. The Bible as text compressed into canon gives, in multiple and widely varying situations, hermeneutic clues on how to apply those suggestions in ever-new situations as they arise. To call a Bible a community's canon is to say that it continues to be relevant and adaptable to the needs of that community, and of the world.

E. Canon and Inspiration

The traditional view of the inspiration of Scripture holds that God or God's Holy Spirit inspired the individual writers and contributors to the scriptural canon. This seems to receive support in the believed authorship of Moses, first of the scroll found in the Temple in 621 B.C.E. (even though the account in Kings is not clear on the point [2 Kgs 23:25]), and then of the fully compiled Torah Ezra brought with him from Babylonia to Jerusalem (Neh 8:1). Josephus lends credence to the view in his defense of the source he principally used in writing his first work, *The Jewish War.* In the defense he notes that the authors of his source, the 22 books of Jewish Scripture, were prophets inspired by God (*AgAp* 1.37). In this line of thinking tradition developed the view that all the authors of Scripture lived before the demise of prophecy and hence of such inspiration (Leiman 1976: 128; Talmon 1987: 58–59).

It has been recognized, however, that "inspired" and "canonical" are not synonymous terms (Leiman 1976: 127). On the contrary, many in Judaism and Christianity are said to have been "inspired by God," yet their writings are not in any community's canon (Metzger 1987: 254–57); whether or not these can be called Scripture is disputed (Sundberg, *IDBSup,* 139; cf. Metzger 1987: 30). In any case, the concept of inspiration is a broader one than that of canon. Jewish views of the broad concept of Torah, Roman Catholic doctrine, and even such a traditionist as John Calvin insist on a far broader activity of divine inspiration than only on a canon. Even the most traditional statement in the NT on the matter (2 Tim 3:16; cf. John 11:51) is not exclusivist; in fact, it is ambiguous.

Nonetheless, the view persists in many circles, openly in some conservative Protestant groups but also covertly in some scholarship, that inspiration of Scripture means divine inspiration of the individual contributors in antiquity. The image has been that of God or the divine spirit impacting each individual whose words were then more or less accurately heard, understood, transmitted orally, and/or recorded for posterity. This focus on the ancient individuals is even evident in deconstructionist scholarship that unravels the several contributors to various literary units and books, labeling certain portions of the Bible "primary" (or genuine) and "secondary" (or even spurious). This has unfortunately caused otherwise honest, serious (but conservative) students of Scripture to overlook any number of important data in order to continue to sponsor single-person authorship of certain canonical books.

There is nothing, however, in Jewish or Christian Scripture or even tradition to hinder a different, more realistic view of the inspiration of Scripture, particularly of a canon of a given community of faith. That view (Sanders 1984a: xv–xviii; see Knight 1975: 5–54) has its roots in Scripture and tradition, both Jewish and Christian. Taking up the very traditional view of the work of God or God's Spirit (*Shekinah* in Hebrew) being far broader than on a canon only or only on certain individuals, one can just as faithfully affirm the work of the Spirit all along the path of formation of the Bible, or a canon, as on those individuals whose names happen to be recorded (Simon 1685: "Preface de l'auteur").

The broader pneumatic activity would include the so-called secondary passages as well as the so-called primary ones. It would include the work of editors and redactors and scribes. It would include the pseudepigraphic writings now recognized to pervade both biblical testaments (Pokorny 1984: 496; Metzger 1987: 284–85). It would include recognition of how much ancient Israel and the early church learned from others through international wisdom and of the hermeneutics by which such wisdom was adapted into Israel's and Judaism's monotheizing struggles throughout the history of the formation of the canon. It would include recognition of how the traditioning process through that history included dialogue with the wisdom and thinking of others, and celebration of how the same process continues to the present. It would include the canonical process of repeating, reciting, and recommending to the next generation and to neighboring communities certain texts (Sanders 1987: 160–66), the broad acceptance of which favored these for final incorporation in the community's canon (Talmon 1987: 67–68). It would exclude the untenable effort on the part of a believing community to limit the work of God or of God's Spirit, and would challenge the tendency in some so-called fundamentalist circles toward bibliolatry, which is an abuse of the concept of canon, and is itself a form of idolatry.

Understanding canon as having been guided by the Spirit through all its stages of formation permits it to continue functioning for a believing community as paradigm of how that Reality called "God" impacted the vision and thinking of ancestors in the faith—and how it may continue to do so in the present.

Bibliography

Ackroyd, P. 1977. Original Text and Canonical Text. *USQR* 32: 166–73.

Aicher, G. 1906. *Das Alte Testament in der Mischna.* Freiburg im Breisgau.

Albrektson, B. 1978. Reflections on the Emergence of a Standard Text of the Hebrew Bible. VTSup 29: 49–65.

Balch, D. L. 1988. The Canon: Adaptable and Stable, Oral and Written. *Forum* 4/2.

Barr, J. 1983. *Holy Scripture: Canon, Authority, Criticism.* Oxford.

Barthélemy, D. 1984. L'État de la Bible juive depuis de début de notre ére jusqu' á la deuxi ème révolte contre Rome (131–135). Pp. 9–45 in Kaestli and Wermelinger 1984.

Barton, J. 1986. *Oracles of God.* Oxford.

Beckwith, R. 1985. *The OT Canon of the NT Church and Its Background in Early Judaism.* Grand Rapids.

Bickermann, E. 1944. The Colophon of the Greek Book of Esther. *JBL* 63: 339–61.

Blenkinsopp, J. 1977. *Prophecy and Canon: A Contribution to the Study of Jewish Origins.* Notre Dame.

Brueggeman, W. 1978. *Prophetic Imagination.* Philadelphia.

———. 1982. *The Creative Word: Canon as a Model for Biblical Education.* Philadelphia.

Brueggeman, W., and Wolff, H. W. 1982. *The Vitality of OT Traditions.* 2d ed. Atlanta.

Buhl, F. 1892. *Canon and Text of the OT.* Trans. J. Macpherson. Edinburgh.

Childs, B. 1978. The Canonical Shape of the Prophetic Literature. *Int* 32: 46–55.

Coote, R. B., and Ord, D. R. 1988. *The Bible's First History.* Philadelphia.

Cowley, R. W. 1974. The Biblical Canon of the Ethiopian Orthodox Church Today. *Ostkirchlichen Studien* 23: 318–23.

Davies, W. D. 1986. Reflections on the Mormon "Canon." *HTR* 79: 44–66.

Fishbane, M. 1985. *Biblical Interpretation in Ancient Israel.* Oxford.

Fitzmyer, J. A. 1977. *The Dead Sea Scrolls: Major Publications and Tools for Study.* Atlanta.

Freedman, D. N. 1962. The Law and The Prophets. VTSup 9: 250–65.

Goshen-Gottstein, M. 1965. *The Book of Isaiah, Sample Edition with Introduction.* Jerusalem.

———. 1966. The Psalms Scroll (11QPs[a])—A problem of Canon and Text. *Textus* 5: 22–33.

———. 1967. Hebrew Biblical Manuscripts: Their History and Their Place in the HUBP Edition. *Bib* 48: 243–90.

Gottwald, N. 1985. Social Matrix and Canonical Shape. *TToday* 42: 307–21.

Graetz, H. 1886. Der Abschluss des Kanons des Alten Testaments. *MGWJ* 35: 281–98.

Greenberg, M. 1956. The Stabilization of the Hebrew Bible Reviewed in the Light of the Biblical Materials from the Judean Desert. *JAOS* 76: 157–67.

Groves, J. A. 1987. *Actualization and Interpretation in the OT.* Atlanta

Heschel, A. 1972. A Time for Renewal. *Midstream* 18: 46–51.

Jepsen, A. 1959. Zur Kanonsgeschichte des Alten Testaments. *ZAW* 71: 114–36.

Kaestli, J.-D. 1984. Le Récit de IV Esdras 14 et sa valeur pour l'histoire du canon de l'Ancien Testament. In Kaestli and Wermelinger 1984.

Kaestli, J.-D., and Wermelinger, O., eds. 1984. *Le Canon de l'Ancien Testament: Sa formation et son histoire.* Geneva.

Kahle, P. 1959. *The Cairo Geniza.* Oxford.

Kealy, S. P. 1979. The Canon: An African Contribution. *BTB* 9: 13–26.

Knight, D. 1975. *Rediscovering the Traditions of Ancient Israel.* Atlanta.

Kraft, R. 1978. Christian Transmission of Greek Jewish Scriptures. Pp. 207–26 in *Paganisme, Judaïsme, Christianisme,* ed. A. Benoit et al. Paris.

Leiman, S., ed. 1974. *The Canon and Masorah of the Hebrew Bible: An Introductory Reader.* New York.

———. 1976. *The Canonization of Hebrew Scripture: The Talmudic and Midrashic Evidence.* Hamden, CT.

Lewis, J. P. 1964. What Do We Mean by Jabneh? *JBR* 32: 125–32.

Lohfink, N. 1963. *Das Hauptgebot.* Rome.

McDonald, L. fc. *The Formation of the Christian Biblical Canon.* Nashville.

Mendenhall, G. 1973. *The Tenth Generation.* Baltimore.

Metzger, B. 1987. *The Canon of the NT.* Oxford.

Meyer, R. 1968. Bemerkungen zum vorkanonischen Text des Alten Testaments. Pp. 213–19 in *Wort und Welt,* ed. M. Weise. Berlin.

Morgan, D. 1990. *Between Text and Community.* Philadelphia.

Neusner, J. 1983. *Midrash in Context: Exegesis in Formative Judaism.* Philadelphia.

———. 1984. Jacob Neusner Issue. *BTB* 14: 81–125.

———. 1986. *The Oral Torah. The Sacred Books of Judaism: An Introduction.* San Francisco.

———. 1987. *What is Midrash?* Philadelphia.
Newsom, C. 1985. *Songs of the Sabbath Sacrifice.* Atlanta.
Östborn, F. 1950. *Cult and Canon: A Study in the Canonization of the OT.* Uppsala.
Pasingya, L. 1973. *La Notion de* nomos *dans le Pentateuque grec.* Rome.
Pettit, P. 1988. Comparative Study of Torah Citations and Other Scripture in the Mishnah. (Unpublished major paper for Claremont Graduate School doctoral program in biblical studies.)
Pfeiffer, R. 1948. *Introduction to the OT.* New York.
Pokorny, P. 1984. Das theologische Problem der neutestamentlichen Pseudepigraphie. *EvT* 44: 486–96.
Ryle, H. E. 1895. *The Canon of the OT.* New York.
Sanders, J. A. 1955. *Suffering as Divine Discipline in the OT and Post-Biblical Judaism.* Rochester.
———. 1965. *The Psalms Scroll of Qumran Cave 11.* DJD 4. Oxford.
———. 1967. *The Dead Sea Psalms Scroll.* Ithaca.
———. 1968. Cave 11 Surprises and the Question of Canon. *McCQ* 21: 284–98.
———. 1972. *Torah and Canon.* Philadelphia.
———. 1973a. Palestinian Manuscripts. *JJS* 24: 74–83.
———. 1973b. The Dead Sea Scrolls—A Quarter Century of Study. *BA* 36: 109–48.
———. 1974. The Qumran Psalms Scroll (11QPs[a]) Reviewed. Pp. 79–99 in *On Language, Culture and Religions,* ed. M. Black and W. Smalley. The Hague.
———. 1975. From Isaiah 61 to Luke 4. Pp. 75–106 in Part 1 of *Christianity, Judaism and Other Greco-Roman Cults,* ed. Jacob Neusner. Leiden.
———. 1984a. *Canon and Community. A Guide to Canonical Criticism.* Philadelphia.
———. 1984b. Canonical Criticism: An Introduction. Pp. 341–62 in Kaestli and Wermelinger 1984.
———. 1987. *From Sacred Story to Sacred Text.* Philadelphia.
———. fc. Deuteronomy. *Scribner's Books of the Bible,* ed. B. W. Anderson. New York.
Sandmel, S. 1961. The Haggadah within Scripture. *JBL* 80: 105–22.
———. 1966. On Canon. *CBQ* 28: 207.
Schuller, E. 1986. *Non-Canonical Psalms from Qumran.* Atlanta.
Simon, R. 1685. *Histoire critique du Vieux Testament.* Rev. ed. (facsim.), Slatkine Reprints. Genéve, 1971.
Skehan, P. W. 1973. A Liturgical Complex in 11QPs[a]. *CBQ* 35: 195–205.
Smith, J. Z. 1978. Sacred Persistence: Towards a Redescription of Canon. Pp. 11–28 in *Approaches to Ancient Judaism,* ed. W. Green. BJS 1. Atlanta.
Smith, M. 1971. *Palestinian Parties and Politics that Shaped the OT.* New York.
Smith, W. C. 1977. *Belief and History.* Charlottesville.
Sundberg, A. 1958. The OT in the Early Church. *HTR* 51: 205–26.
———. 1964. *The OT of the Early Church.* HTS 20. Cambridge, MA.
Swete, H. 1902. *An Introduction to the OT in Greek.* Cambridge. Repr. 1968.
Talmon, S. 1966. Pisqah Be'emsa Pasuq and 11QPs[a]. *Textus* 5: 11–21.
———. 1967. Review of *DJD* 4. *Tarbiz* 37: 99–104.
———. 1987. Heiliges Schrifttum und Kanonische Bücher aus jüdischer Sicht—überlegungen zur Ausbildung der Grösse "Die Schrift" im Judentum. Pp. 45–79 in *Die Mitte der Schrift,* ed. M. Klopfenstein et al. New York.
Tov, E. 1982. A Modern Textual Outlook Based on the Qumran Scrolls. *HUCA* 53: 11–27.
———. 1986. The Text of the OT. Pp. 156–90 in *The World of the Bible,* ed. A. van der Woude. Grand Rapids.
———. 1988. Hebrew Biblical Manuscripts from the Judaean Desert: Their Contribution to Textual Criticism. *JJS* 39: 5–37.
Ulrich, E. 1978. *The Qumran Text of Samuel and Josephus.* HSM 19. Atlanta.
———. 1982. Inspiration, Normativeness, Canonicity, and the Unique Sacred Character of the Bible. *CBQ* 44: 447–69.
———. 1984. Horizons of OT Textual Research at the Thirtieth Anniversary of Qumran Cave 4. *CBQ* 46: 613–36.
Wilson, G. 1985. *The Editing of the Hebrew Psalter.* Atlanta.
Wise, M. 1986a. The Dead Sea Scrolls: Part 1, Archaeology and Biblical Manuscripts. *BA* 49: 140–54.
———. 1986b. The Dead Sea Scrolls: Part 2, Nonbiblical Manuscripts. *BA* 49: 228–43.
Wright, G. E. 1952. *God Who Acts.* London.
Yeivin, I. 1980. *Introduction to the Tiberian Masorah.* Trans. and ed., E. J. Revell. Atlanta.

JAMES A. SANDERS

NEW TESTAMENT

A. Introduction
B. History of the NT Canon
   1. General
   2. The History of Component Collections
   3. Developments in the 4th and 5th Centuries
   4. Influences in the Formation of the NT Canon
   5. Criteria of Canonicity
C. Theological and Hermeneutical Significance of the NT Canon
   1. The Scope of the Canon
   2. Scripture and Tradition
   3. The Function of the Canon as a Norm
   4. The Hermeneutical Value of the Canon

A. Introduction

In reference to the NT, the term "canon" calls special attention both to its form, that is, a fixed collection of precisely 27 early Christian documents, and to its function, that is, literature that is normative for the faith and life of the Christian community. Both of these connotations belonged to the Greek word *kanōn:* from its fundamental sense, "a tool for measurement," there arose the extended meanings "list," "catalog" (probably derived from the series of calibrations on a measuring tool), and also "norm," "standard." When the term began in the 4th century to be applied to Christian writings it was with the sense of "list": a document was said to be "in the canon" or "canonical" if it was "on the list" of those writings which were read, or were permitted to be read, in Christian assemblies of worship. The word "canon" had previously been used in Christian as in secular circles also in the sense of "norm" or "standard," and though this was not its initial meaning in reference to Christian writings, it followed close behind, since those writings which were used for liturgical reading were certainly regarded as authoritative.

It is customary in modern discussion and necessary for

clarity to observe a distinction between the concepts "scripture" and "canon." "Scripture" signifies writings that are considered religiously authoritative, without regard to their precise number or a fixed collection; "canon," however, is a matter of a definitive, closed list of such writings. Thus the availability of scripture does not imply a canon, but a canon presupposes scripture and delimits its scope. At its inception Christianity inherited from Judaism a rich trove of scripture, including the Law of Moses, the prophetic books, and a great variety of other writings that were authoritative for various groups of Jews, but it did not inherit a canon, for Judaism had not in the 1st century made a list or collection setting limits to its scripture. Christianity, in turn, produced a large body of its own literature (letters, gospels, narratives of apostolic acts, apocalypses, church orders, etc.), much of which became authoritative for various Christian groups, and so came to be regarded as scripture alongside Jewish scripture. But Christianity did not for a long time attempt to create a canon. Not until the end of the 2d century did Christians begin to take an interest in defining the scope of authoritative Jewish writings (Melito, in Eusebius *Hist. Eccl.* 4.26.13–14) and thus begin to think in terms of an "Old Testament" canon, an issue that continued to be debated into the 5th century. And not until the 4th century did Christians begin to draw up lists of authoritative Christian writings and thus attempt to form a "New Testament" canon, the extent of which was not fully agreed even in the 5th century. Hence during most of its first four centuries, the church had scripture, but no set canon.

The designations "Old Testament" and "New Testament" by which the Christian collections of Jewish and Christian scripture came to be known are obviously correlative, implying each other. But originally these phrases had nothing to do with such writings; they referred instead to the covenant (Gk *diathēkē*; Lat *testamentum*) of God, first with Israel, then with the Christian community. Although the "old covenant," by virtue of having a law, could be said to be "written" and "read," the "new covenant" did not have a literary dimension (2 Cor 3:4–18). When in the late 2d century covenant terminology began to be applied to Jewish and Christian scripture (Melito, Clement), the sense was that these were books pertaining to or belonging to the old or the new covenant, not that these books were themselves the covenants.

B. History of the NT Canon

1. General. Although Christianity had recourse from the beginning to Jewish scripture, Christianity was not originally a scriptural religion in the same sense as Judaism. The faith of the earliest Christian community was evoked by and centered on a person, Jesus of Nazareth, and he was apprehended by them not first of all in texts but in preaching, in oral traditions of his words and deeds, and in charismatic experience. Only secondarily were the scriptures of Judaism called into service for the exposition and defense of the Christian faith; they did not constitute its basis. The primary authorities for earliest Christianity were rather "the Lord" (Jesus' teaching and acts, preserved mainly in oral traditions) and "the apostles" (the teachings of the witnesses to Jesus). The appeal to Jewish scripture was made only in the light of these, and consequently the early Christian use of Jewish scripture was selective in both content and method of interpretation, stressing its prophetic and messianic elements.

Christian writings began to be composed by the middle of the 1st century, and gradually increased in number and variety, but none of them was composed as scripture. Though some religious authority might be claimed by their authors (when they were not anonymous) or might lie in their content (when it was traditional), this did not constitute them as scripture for their authors or their readers. Throughout the 1st century and far into the 2d, whenever scripture (*graphe*) was mentioned or cited, it was the Jewish scriptures that were in view. Only very gradually, through their use in worship and teaching alongside the Jewish scripture, did Christian writings acquire the status of scripture in the church. And only after a large number of writings had come to be valued in this way was it necessary to define their number and to fix a canon. The history of the NT canon, then, was a process extending from the composition of Christian literature in the 1st and early 2d centuries, through the spread, use, and progressive esteem of these writings in the 2d and 3d centuries, to the determination of a fixed list of authoritative Christian scripture in the 4th and 5th centuries. This process was not only lengthy but also uneven, moving at a different pace and even in somewhat different directions among the religional constituencies of the ancient church. Further, the process was not always deliberate or self-conscious, but was often influenced simply by historical circumstance. Indeed it is remarkable how little explicit evidence remains about the development of the NT canon. To reconstruct its history it is necessary to rely on (1) the actual use of early Christian documents by Christian writers of the 2d through the 5th centuries, noting the frequency and manner of their citations and inferring the value they attached to them; (2) explicit discussions and judgments by individual writers or ecclesiastical councils about the authority of various documents; and (3) the contents and arrangements of ancient manuscripts, together with the various aids (concordances, prologues, etc.) they include. All of these must be evaluated in the light of what is otherwise known about the history of the ancient church, of which the history of the canon is a part, and to which it is deeply indebted.

2. The History of Component Collections. The NT canon is not so much a collection of individual documents as it is a collection of collections: its major components are a collection of gospels, a collection of letters of Paul, a collection of "catholic epistles." Outside these stand only two documents, Acts and Revelation. Each of these smaller collections had its own distinctive history, and must be treated individually.

a. The Letters of Paul. Paul's letters, the earliest surviving Christian writings, were also the earliest to be collected. They were unlikely candidates for scriptural regard because they are actual letters closely tailored to the particular circumstances of the individual congregations to which they were sent, and their general relevance and value were not clear to all (Dahl 1962). On the other hand, Paul was reputed over a wide area, and his letters did claim the authority of an apostle of Christ. By the early 2d century Paul's letters had been gathered up and were known as a group by Ignatius, Polycarp, and the author of 2 Peter (3:15–16). It is not clear how much this development owed to an informal exchange of the letters among Paul's churches (cf. Col 4:16; Mowry 1944), and how much it was due to the careful efforts of an individual (Goodspeed 1933; Schmithals 1972) or a group of Paul's associates and admirers who after the apostle's death sought to promote Paul's teaching by preserving, collecting, and disseminating his letters (Schenke 1975), but the last possibility gains plausibility from the presence in the collection of pseudonymous writings and evidence of editorial reworking.

The earliest known form of the collection of Paul's letters contained 10 letters, omitting the Pastorals. These 10 letters were presented as "letters to seven churches," letters to the same community being taken together (1–2 Corinthians, 1–2 Thessalonians, Colossians, Philemon). This collection seems to have been available in two different editions, one with the letters arranged by decreasing length, giving the order Corinthians, Romans, Ephesians, Thessalonians, Galatians, Philippians, Colossians (+ Philemon) (Finegan 1956; Frede 1969; Dahl 1978), and the other, apparently attempting to order the letters chronologically, giving the order Galatians, Corinthians, Romans, Thessalonians, Ephesians (=Laodiceans), Colossians [+Philemon], Philippians (Frede 1964; Dahl 1978). The latter order is attested for Marcion (ca. 140) but also for Syrian sources and is presupposed by the prologues to the Pauline epistles that occur in many Latin manuscripts. This order was once thought to be a creation of Marcion, but it is now clear that Marcion simply took over a preexisting edition of the letters of Paul, retaining its sequence (Dahl 1978) as well as many of its peculiar textual features (Clabeaux 1989). The collection of 10 letters was eventually, but already in the 2d century, superseded by a collection of 13 letters, the Pastorals being added. In this edition the "seven churches" rubric was abandoned, and the letters were ordered individually longest to shortest, with the personal letters being placed after the community letters. This resulted in the sequence familiar to modern readers of the New Testament.

In spite of the availability of Paul's collected letters by the early 2d century, most Christian writers of the 2d century show little knowledge or use of them. Only Marcion and the gnostics seem to have relied heavily on them. This circumstance has sometimes been thought to show that Paul became discredited by heterodox appeals to his letters and so was ignored by more traditional writers. But this is not likely. No Christian writers of this period show an animus toward Paul and his letters; the issues and genres of 2d-century Christian literature did not encourage strong dependence on Paul; and there is a progressive tendency in the period to an ever greater use of the letters (Rensberger 1981; Lindemann 1979). By the end of the 2d century Paul's letters were heavily invoked by Clement of Alexandria, Tertullian in North Africa, and Irenaeus in Gaul, and had attained fully scriptural status over a very wide area, a fact which implies their long and broad usage through most of the 2d century.

The Epistle to the Hebrews, which even the ancient church doubted was written by Paul, nevertheless came ultimately to be attached to the collection of Pauline letters, ordinarily at the end, after the personal letters. This document had been respected and used in the Egyptian church from an early time, and it appears within the Pauline collection (standing second after Romans) in the earliest extant manuscript of the Pauline collection, P[46] (which has an Egyptian provenance). In the Western church, however, Hebrews had little popularity, and its authority did not become established there until the 4th century. Hebrews did not belong to the earliest editions of Paul's letters (cf. Anderson 1966; Aland 1979).

b. The Gospels. From the beginning Christianity attributed the highest authority to "the Lord," preserving in memory and transmitting by word of mouth accounts of his teachings and acts. The earliest gospels are partial deposits of this oral tradition, but the oral tradition was so rich in content and established by custom that it persisted well beyond the first written gospels and was respected, and often preferred to written accounts, until about the middle of the 2d century (Koester 1957; Kürzinger 1983). Drawing on it, gospels continued to be written during the 2d century (Koester 1980; Cameron 1982). The composition of written gospels was an effort, on the one hand, to collect and codify Jesus-traditions, but, on the other, also to interpret them for particular situations. No less than the letters of Paul, the gospels are occasional documents, composed in and directed to specific local Christian groups, and so each has a distinctive character. Accordingly, it was at first customary for a given Christian community to know and use only one such document.

It was somewhat contrary to their character as interpretations of Jesus-traditions that the gospels were valued first as historical records, not as scripture. This view became problematic as Christian communities became acquainted with multiple gospels and noticed discrepancies among them that were not easily reconciled. This, together with the custom of using only one gospel and the idea that the Christian message (itself traditionally known as "the gospel") was unitary and coherent, worked against any easy acknowledgment of numerous gospels. Thus the history of gospel literature in the 2d century was governed by two opposing tendencies: the desire for a comprehensive and theologically adequate gospel led to a proliferation of such writings, but the desire for a single, self-consistent gospel worked to reduce the number, either by advocating one gospel against others or by conflating several such documents into one (Cullman 1956; Merkel 1971; 1978). The prime example of this last tendency is the *Diatessaron* of Tatian (ca. 170), which ingeniously weaves together in one narrative most of the contents of Matthew, Mark, Luke, and John, and adds some elements from oral tradition. This effort (and its broad popularity) symptomizes the problem posed by multiple gospels, and shows also that although the gospels were much valued for their contents, they had not acquired sacrosanct status as individual texts. Their texts were not beyond alteration in the earlier 2d century either, as significant additions were clearly made to Mark (the various longer endings after 16:8) and John (chap. 21, and 7:53–8:11).

Justin Martyr (ca. 150) is the first Christian writer to show a knowledge and appreciation of several gospels, which he called "memoirs" (*apomneumonēmata*) of the apostles, thus revealing his historical estimate of them. But he seems not too have known John, and draws often on oral tradition or on other gospels not known to us, and so did not invest exclusive authority in the gospels that ultimately became canonical. John was little known or used by 2d century Christian writers, except among gnostics, who valued it highly (J. N. Sanders 1943; Hillmer 1966). This may explain its unpopularity, but perhaps the strongest reservations about John arose from recognition of its extensive differences in outline, substance, and style from other, more popular gospels. Rather than try to reconcile these, it was easier to neglect John altogether.

The collection of four gospels (Matthew, Mark, Luke, John) which came to be incorporated in the canon arose only near the end of the 2d century, and first in the Western church. Irenaeus (ca. 180) had to argue inventively for it (*Haer.* 3.11.8–9), while in the Eastern church much use was still being made of other gospels (e.g., Clement [Ruwet 1948], Serapion [Eus. *Hist. Eccl.* 6.12.2]). This collection was a compromise among the competing tendencies, resources, and needs of earlier usage, and struck a balance between an indefinite plurality of gospels and exclusive use of one gospel. The collection as such was thought of and entitled as *the* gospel, and each member of the collection was known as the gospel *according to* its putative author. In this "fourfold gospel" the tension between plurality and unity was not resolved, but was perpetuated in manageable form. It is notable that the Gospels acquired their scriptural standing as a group and not individually, and that religious authority was vested in their collective witness.

The collection of four gospels rapidly gained acceptance, and seems to have been broadly established by the middle of the 3d century, but its arrangement varied for some time. The Western church preferred the order Matthew, John, Luke, Mark, thus giving precedence to the two gospels supposedly composed by apostles over those supposedly composed by disciples of apostles. The Eastern church sponsored the order Matthew, Mark, Luke, John, possibly intending a chronological arrangement. The adoption of the Eastern order by Jerome for the Vulgate led to its subsequent dominance also in the West.

c. The Catholic Epistles. The third collection component of the canon was the latest to coalesce. Of the various documents in this collection only 1 Peter and 1 John had much currency in the 2d and 3d centuries. The rest (James, 2 Peter, 2–3 John, Jude) had only local and regional use, and in spite of the claims of some of them, there was no early or strong acknowledgment of their apostolic authorship, and so they remained obscure and questionable well into the 4th century. It is from Eusebius (*Hist. Eccl.* 2.23.25) that we first hear of "Catholic Epistles" as a group of 7 letters, and such a collection probably arose only in the 3d century. It may have been formed in an effort to document a common witness of primitive apostles, perhaps especially of the "pillar apostles" (cf. Gal 2:9; Lührmann 1981), and to balance the imposing collection of Paul's letters.

d. Acts and Revelation. Although the gospel of Luke and the Acts of the Apostles were composed as two volumes of a unitary work, they were early separated and had distinctive subsequent histories. Acts came into general usage later than Luke. Justin Martyr is the first writer to show any knowledge of it, but it was only near the end of the 2d century that real importance began to accrue to Acts, possibly as a result of conflicts with Marcionite and gnostic groups. Acts served to underline the view of mainstream Christianity in the late 2d century that the apostles acted and taught with authoritative consensus, and that Paul was at one with the collective apostolic witness. Thus Acts became useful in documenting the concept of apostolic tradition. The position of Acts among other documents in early canon lists and manuscripts varies considerably. It is often placed with the Catholic Epistles (before or after), often with the Pauline letters (before or after), and sometimes with the four gospels (always after).

The Revelation to John had a controversial career in the ancient church. In the Western church it was well received and by the end of the 2d century was widely cited as scripture. It was also current and respected in the East in the 2d century, but was generally interpreted allegorically. In the 3d century, however, a dispute arose in Egypt as to whether the book should be read literally or allegorically. Dionysius, bishop of Alexandria, defended the allegorists' view, and was led by many acute observations to deny the apostolic origin of the book (Eus. *Hist. Eccl.* 7.25). Subsequently, Eastern Christians tended to reject Revelation. Even in the West the authority of Revelation came into dispute because of its use by Montanists, and both the authenticity and authority of Revelation (as well as the gospel of John) were strongly questioned by the Roman churchman, Gaius, in the early 3d century, but without much effect on Western usage. The full recognition of Revelation in the East did not come about until the late 4th century, and even then with the understanding that it was to be interpreted in nonmillennial terms.

e. Other Writings. Even though the NT canon came to be constituted mainly by bringing together smaller collections that had evolved in the first three centuries, it must be emphasized that the history of the canon was selective as well as collective, and that the canon which finally emerged contained only a fraction of the Christian literature that had been produced in the early period. Many other writings (gospels, acts, letters, and apocalypses) achieved wide currency and attained the status of scripture in some areas without in the end becoming canonical. So, for example, the *Apocalypse of Peter* and the *Shepherd of Hermas* were scarcely less popular than the Revelation to John in the 2d century; the *Gospel of Thomas* and the *Gospel of Peter* were reckoned by some no less authoritative than any other gospel; the letters known as *1 Clement* and *Barnabas* were esteemed and quoted as scripture by many; the *Acts of Paul* also was held in high regard in some areas, as was the manual of church order known as the *Didache.* But any or all of these, and perhaps some others, might have been included in the canon but for various reasons were not.

3. Developments in the 4th and 5th Centuries. By the end of the 2d century a considerable amount of early Christian literature was in broad circulation. The collected letters of Paul were well established, widely used, and considered to have scriptural standing. The collection of four gospels had more recently been formed and was gaining recognition. 1 Peter and 1 John were highly respected as scripture, but belonged to no collection, and many other writings had broad currency and scriptural or quasi-scriptural status. But there was as yet no canon of Christian scripture, for no effort had been made to define the scope of authoritative literature. This situation prevailed throughout the 3d century and into the 4th. Only in the 4th century did attempts begin to evaluate the legacy of early Christian literature as a whole and to determine precisely what documents commanded the authority to be used in the church, and what did not. The 4th and 5th centuries therefore are the period of canon formation proper, when actual lists of authoritative books were drawn up. The most important of these are the following:

a. The Muratorian Canon. The date and provenance of this list are in debate. For a long time the Muratorian Canon was taken to be a Roman (or at least Italian) product of the late 2d or early 3d century, but it would be unique at such an early time, and there are good reasons to consider it an Eastern list of the 4th century (Sundberg 1973; cf. Ferguson 1982). The document is fragmentary and badly translated into Latin, but lists the following books: four gospels, Acts, 13 letters of Paul (omitting Hebrews), Jude, 1–2 John, the Wisdom of Solomon (?), Revelation, *Apocalypse of Peter.* The omission of most of the "Catholic Epistles" is notable, and so is the inclusion of the Wisdom of Solomon in a list of Christian books. Specifically rejected, on the other hand, are the *Shepherd of Hermas,* a pseudo-Pauline letter to the Laodiceans and another to the Alexandrians (both attributed to Marcionites), and some unnamed books of heterodox groups. We have here, then, a list of 24 documents accepted for reading in the church, including two that did not finally become canonical, but excluding five that did.

b. Eusebius. In his *Church History,* written in the first decades of the 4th century, Eusebius variously comments on the uses made of early Christian writings by previous Christian figures, but in *Hist. Eccl.* 3.25 he provides a summary list of these writings in three categories: (1) acknowledged books (*homologoumenoi*), i.e., those accepted without qualification; (2) disputed books (*antilegomenoi*), i.e., those whose genuineness or authority is questioned; and (3) heretical works, i.e., those that are firmly rejected. The acknowledged writings include four gospels, Acts, the (14) letters of Paul, 1 John, and 1 Peter. He also allows that Revelation *may* be placed in this group "if it seem desirable." The disputed books are James, Jude, 2 Peter, 2–3 John, the *Acts of Paul,* the *Shepherd of Hermas,* the *Apocalypse of Peter,* the *Epistle of Barnabas,* and the *Didache.* He also allows that Revelation *may* be classed among these books "if this view prevail," and notes that some would place the gospel of the Hebrews also in this category. Rejected books are the gospels of Peter, Thomas, and Matthias, among others, and the Acts of Andrew, John, and others. The acknowledged books, then, are 21 (22 with Revelation), and the disputed books are 10 (11 with Revelation). This list must reflect what Eusebius took to be the situation obtaining in his time and among the churches of his acquaintance. The ambiguity about Revelation was felt widely in the East, and surely also by Eusebius himself.

c. Other Canonical Lists. Another list is found in codex Claromontanus, a 6th-century Greek-Latin manuscript of the Pauline letters. The list it contains is much earlier than the manuscript itself, and probably derives from the 4th century and an Eastern setting. It contains, in order, the following items: four gospels, 10 letters of Paul (omitting Philippians and 1–2 Thessalonians, certainly accidentally), the seven "Catholic Epistles," *Barnabas,* Revelation, Acts, the *Shepherd of Hermas,* the *Acts of Paul,* and the *Apocalypse of Peter.* Here are 30 documents (if we include the 3 neglected Pauline letters). (Hebrews may also have been unintentionally left out.) Of these 30, four were not ultimately to become canonical.

The so-called Cheltenham Canon, a further list of authoritative Christian books, probably was drawn up in North Africa near the mid-4th century. It offers 24 books, with the claim that "our fathers approved that these books are canonical and that the men of old have said this": four gospels, 13 letters of Paul, Acts, Revelation, 1–3 John, and 1–2 Peter. Thus James, Jude, and Hebrews lack.

Of special note is the list of canonical books given by Athanasius, bishop of Alexandria, in his 39th Festal Letter issued on Easter of 367, for this list is the first to name as exclusively authoritative precisely the 27 documents that finally came to constitute the New Testament as we know it. He was the first Christian writer after Origen to affirm the full authority of Revelation, and must have been influenced in this by his many contacts with the Western churches, especially in Rome.

Athanasius' views were not decisive for the East as a whole, however. Tatian's *Diatessaron* continued to have considerable popularity in the East, especially in the Syrian churches, which tended still in the 4th and 5th centuries to admit in addition only Acts and the Pauline letters, though late in the 4th (Chrysostom) and early in the 5th (the Peshitta, Theodoret) recognition was extended to James, 1 Peter, and 1 John. Even so, the Syrian church typically admitted only 22 books as canonical.

Among the 4th-century lists there was still notable variation, especially in the regard for Hebrews, Revelation, 2–3 John, 2 Peter, and Jude, and other writings occasionally claim attention. It is interesting, for example, that one of the oldest and most important manuscripts of the entire NT, codex Sinaiticus (4th century), contains, along with the 27 books of Athanasius, the *Epistle of Barnabas* and the *Shepherd of Hermas.* So although the four gospels, Acts, the letters of Paul, 1 Peter, and 1 John were almost universally accepted, everything else was to some degree questionable. The resolution of such uncertainties fell largely to ecclesiastical councils of the late 4th and early 5th centuries. The Council of Laodicea (363) held that "the canonical books" were 26 in number (omitting Revelation in the Eastern manner), while the North African councils of Hippo (393) and Carthage (397) named the 27 books of our New Testament, but in accepting Hebrews distinguished it from the letters of Paul. It is worth stating, however, that no *ecumenical* council of the ancient church ever undertook to define the scope of the canon.

4. Influences in the Formation of the NT Canon. A process that extended through four centuries will obviously have been subject to many influential factors. So long as it was (wrongly) supposed that the canon had virtually come to full form by the end of the 2d century, the tendency was to see its chief causes in the conflicts with heterodox movements of the 2d century. It has been held, for example, that Marcion, who based his teaching on an edition of the Pauline letters plus a form of the gospel of

Luke, forced the church to form its own canon in response. It has also been claimed that the gnostics, who produced many writings of their own and appealed to secret apostolic traditions, were opposed by the shaping of a canon that excluded their documents and presented instead a set of broadly recognized and accessible writings containing apostolic and catholic teaching. And it has been maintained that the Montanists, by their claim of charismatic authority and new revelations, provided the motivation for the church to close its canon and restrict revelation to traditional authoritative documents. But none of these arguments is valid: Marcion was not a "first cause" of canon formation, but a case of arrested development, since Paul's letters had previously been collected and were widely valued before him; the gnostic groups tended to value most of the same literature as other Christians, and differed rather in the philosophical assumptions and interpretive methods with which they approached this literature; and in response to the Montanists the church did not deny the continuing activity of the spirit or limit revelation to a limited number of books. Although the heterodox movements of the 2d century threw into relief the question of the resources, authorities, and boundaries of the Christian faith, they do not appear to have had any direct impact on the history of the canon.

The chief determinants of the history of the canon were, rather, the historical origins of the church's faith and the traditional usages of the church's worship and teaching. Since Christianity vested revelatory and redemptive significance in a particular historical person and a specific historical period, the church had always to hark back to Jesus and the events of his life, death, and resurrection. This resource was at first available in the direct testimony of apostles and in a lively and authoritative oral tradition. But with the lapse of time, the demise of the apostolic generation, and the dissipation of oral tradition, it was increasingly necessary to value written materials. This led to the preservation of some early literature (e.g., Paul's letters) and to the composition of additional literature deeply indebted to early tradition, and elevated the importance of these documents as means by which the church sustained its access to the events and to the witness which constituted its *raison d'etre.* The question, however, as to which documents provided this access, and therefore were authoritative, was answered by reference to the actual experience of the church with this literature. Those writings that proved, over time, to be most useful in sustaining, informing, and guiding the church in its worship, preaching, and teaching came to be the most highly valued, and gained a special authority in virtue of their usefulness.

Given this basic impulse and the context in which it played out, there were many specific factors that conditioned the history of the canon. The judgments of respected theologians, for example, Origen and Athanasius in the East, and Jerome and Augustine in the West, were influential, especially for the fates of particular books. Athanasius' sponsorship of Revelation in the East finally overcame the reservations fostered by Dionysius' criticisms, and the acceptance of Hebrews in the West was largely the result of its use by Hilary, Ambrose, Rufinus, and Jerome. Also visible are the effects of the great ecclesiastical centers, Antioch, Alexandria, and Rome. The conservatism of Antiochene Christianity and its tendency to literal-historical interpretation are reflected in the rather narrow collection of scriptures that persisted so long in that region. The open, speculative bent of Alexandrian Christianity and its penchant for allegorical exegesis are mirrored in the expansive body of literature valued as scripture in Egypt. In the history of the canon, as in doctrinal matters, Rome tended to take a middle way between these extremes. Further, particular doctrinal or disciplinary issues sometimes affected the status of certain books. Hebrews, because of its teaching against a second repentance after baptism, was disadvantaged by developing penetential practices in the West; Revelation was called into question in the East and West because of its use by millennialists (*Hist. Eccl.* 7.25; 3.28.1–5); John was once disputed in the West as a result of Montanist appeals to its teaching about the paraclete, and the *Gospel of Peter* was rejected in Syria because of alleged docetic elements (*Hist. Eccl.* 6.12.2). The experience of persecution, which sometimes involved the confiscation and destruction of Christian scriptures, perhaps provided occasion to discriminate between those books held to be sacred and preserved from the authorities, and those that might be surrendered under duress. Even so mundane a matter as the technology of book manufacture may have played a role, for almost from the beginning Christianity made use of the codex (leaf book) rather than the roll in transcribing its scripture (Roberts and Skeat 1983). But it was not until the 4th century that codices were produced that were large enough to encompass most or all of Christian scripture, and it may not be mere coincidence that the canon acquired a relatively fixed content only when it was possible to transcribe the various writings in a single book. And, so far as canonization is understood as a matter of devising a fixed and closed list of scriptures, the decisions of ecclesiastical councils had their effects. No such decisions are known before the 4th century, by which time many documents had secured such established use that councils could only ratify their standing. But ecclesiastical mandates were important in bringing some disputed writings (e.g., Hebrews, Revelation, 2 Peter, Jude) to full canonical regard, and in discounting others. But perhaps the preeminent factor was the actual historic practice of leading churches. The determination of a list of writings which might be read in liturgical assembly was largely a matter of making regulative what had long been merely customary. Only in cases where custom differed were specific decisions required.

All of this indicates that the history of the canon was not an isolated process, but belonged fully to the ongoing life of the ancient church and was in its own ways responsive to the forces broadly operative in the early history of the church.

5. Criteria of Canonicity. Though it was indebted to historical forces, the formation of the canon was not haphazard. The church also reflected critically on its literature and, in setting certain documents apart as peculiarly authoritative, it invoked various principles (Flessemann-van Leer 1954; Ohlig 1972). Prominent considerations were that canonical documents should be apostolic, catholic, orthodox, and in traditional use.

The apostolic character of a writing was often articulated in terms of authorship by an apostle, but it was actually a broader concept than this, and could signify, besides actual authorship, derivation from the time of the apostles, or even simply agreement with what the church took to be apostolic teaching. Even the ancient church did not claim that every authoritative document was written by an apostle, but it did consider that canonical writings should come from the earliest times of the church. For a writing to be catholic, it had to be relevant to the church at large. This criterion embodies the church's preference for broadly accessible and pertinent documents as opposed to esoteric ones. But this preference did not, obviously, exclude documents originally addressed to strictly local churches or even to individuals. It was rather a matter of their availability and their utility to the whole church. The criterion of orthodoxy signified that no document could be acknowledged as authoritative unless it conformed to, or at least did not contradict, what the church took to be its proper teaching. This presumes that the true faith of the church could be known independently of Scripture, specifically in what was known as "the rule of faith" (*regula fidei*), a traditional summary statement of the basic Christian confession. Hence there was no idea that Scripture was the sole repository of authoritative teaching. Rather, the authority of Scripture could be gauged against authoritative but unwritten tradition. No less important was the criterion of traditional usage, that is, whether a writing had been employed from an early time and in most churches. This principle came strongly into play only in the 3d and 4th centuries when the church had a retrospect on its past. But in fact customary usage had been the major force in promoting the authority of various documents before it was articulated as a principle of canonicity.

None of these criteria, however, was absolutely definitive. Thus while Paul's letters were undoubtedly apostolic in the strictest sense, because of their particularity they did not satisfy very well the ideal of catholicity. Or, although there was a persistent uncertainty about the apostolic authorship of Hebrews, it was acknowledged as canonical nevertheless. Or again, although Jude and 2 Peter, for example, had not enjoyed a longstanding tradition of use, this did not finally count decisively against them. Clearly, then, the criteria of canonicity were not applied with great rigor or consistency, and were not narrowly understood. While their use indicates a measure of deliberation and judgment in the history of the canon, it is difficult to regard apostolicity, catholicity, or orthodoxy as the effective reasons why any document gained canonical status. The criterion that was most fully operative was traditional use, and this has reference not to the intrinsic character of a writing but to the church's actual practice.

It remains to be noted that inspiration was not a criterion of canonicity in the ancient church. It was not claimed that the canonical documents were uniquely or exclusively inspired. The reason for this was the conviction that inspiration characterized the church as a whole. Since the concept of inspiration was much broader than the concept of scripture, it provided no basis for distinguishing among writings produced within the church (Kalin 1967; Sundberg 1975).

C. The Theological and Hermeneutical Significance of the NT Canon

The theological and hermeneutical significance of the canon has come under reassessment as a result both of the history of the canon and of modern exegesis of the canonical documents. Of the various issues that have arisen in modern discussion the following are the most prominent.

1. The Scope of the Canon. The traditional contents of the canon are difficult to justify in the light of modern knowledge. The canon as we know it resulted from a complex interplay of contingent factors, and from a historical point of view its limits seem fortuitous. It is easily conceivable that the canon might have been larger or smaller, and that it might have contained other documents instead of or in addition to those that stand in it. Further, the contents of the canon cannot be fully defended on the criteria adduced by the ancient church, for not all of them are apostolic or catholic in any strict sense, and some of them had not enjoyed broad and longstanding use. Finally, the limits of the canon were never officially defined by the ancient church, and have never constituted an article of doctrine. In this situation, two different claims have been made on behalf of the traditional scope of the canon. Protestant scholars have often maintained that the canonical documents possess an intrinsic and self-authenticating authority, and that the canon evolved more or less spontaneously through the religious intuition and experience of the early Christian communities. Catholic scholars, on the other hand, have claimed that the authority of the canonical documents derives from their recognition by the church in accordance with its own tradition and teaching. At issue is the relationship between the authority of the canon and the authority of the church. In fact, this relationship is historically ambiguous. The judgments about the limits of the canon by bishops and councils in the 4th and 5th centuries did not merely ratify a status which the documents had already acquired for themselves, for some of the writings then designated canonical had not previously been widely taken as authoritative. Yet the very high regard in which the gospels or the letters of Paul were held from an early time owed nothing to ecclesiastical decisions, and the church could only acknowledge their authority, not decide it. So, as a closed collection and with a view to its outer limits, the canon is very much a product of the church, but much of the contents of the canon rose to authority by virtue of their self-evident value.

In the interest of maintaining the critical independence of the canon of Scripture over against the church, some Protestant scholars have argued that in principle the canon remains open to revision, even if no change in its scope is actually envisioned. Catholic scholars, however, fully affirm the traditional boundaries of the canon as the authoritative work of the ancient church, and thus conceive the canon of Scripture and the teaching authority of the church to be indivisible. Here it is clear that the theological authority of the canon is differently conceived in different confessional traditions of Christianity.

2. Scripture and Tradition. The same question emerges in a different guise when the relation of Scripture and tradition is explored. The history of the canon shows that the contents of the canon were largely determined by ecclesiastical tradition (traditional usage, traditional ideas of authorship, and the appeal to traditional teaching), such that to acknowledge the authority of the canon is to acknowledge the authority of the tradition which gave rise to it. This point is now freely conceded by Protestant scholars (Cullmann 1956b; Ebeling 1968b). For its part, exegesis has shown further how deeply individual documents of the canon are themselves indebted to earlier kerygmatic, liturgical, parenetic, and exegetical traditions, and indeed exhibit the development of tradition among themselves (e.g., the elaboration of Pauline teaching in the pseudonymous Pauline letters). Thus it can be said that tradition precedes Scripture, is presumed by Scripture, and persists in Scripture. It is appropriate enough, then, to see Scripture itself as "a specific form of tradition" or as "a transcription of tradition at a particular stage" (Ebeling 1968b; Best 1979; Hahn 1980). For these reasons it has become impossible any longer to juxtapose Scripture and tradition as alternatives. Rather, they stand in an organic relationship which precludes the exaltation of either against the other as a theological authority.

3. The Function of the Canon as a Norm. The use of the canon of scripture as a theological norm has required rethinking as a result of exegesis. The historical-critical exegesis of canonical documents has revealed among them a great diversity of theological orientations which are not easily reconciled with each other: Jewish Christianity, various types of Hellenistic Christianity, apocalyptic Christianity, and early Catholic Christianity, to name the most obvious. In this respect the canon seems accurately to reflect theological variegations characteristic of the early church (Dunn 1977). But because it presents no thorough theological consistency, the canon as such, and taken as a whole, cannot serve as a sharply effective theological norm (Käsemann 1964). Once a wholistic, formal conception of the canon is given up in view of its inner diversity, its authority must be conceived in a different way. This is often done, especially by Protestant thinkers, by appealing to a "canon in the canon," that is, a principle or center which is taken as the essential and controlling element within the larger canon, and which may serve as an interpretive criterion of the whole. Efforts to formulate such a principle have been various (Schrage 1976), including, among others, the original preaching of Jesus, the oldest recoverable form of the kerygma, and the Pauline theme of the justification of the ungodly. Other, mostly Catholic, scholars have criticized this approach as reductive, selective, and arbitrary, and have insisted on affirming the unity and coherence of the canon as a whole (Küng 1963). In their view the meaning of Scripture is sufficiently mediated by the tradition and teaching office of the church. But each view is in its own way an assertion that the formal canon cannot of itself function as a theological norm.

What needs special recognition in this debate is that the canon is pluralistic in principle. The effort to discover in it a uniform and coherent norm would seem to be contrary even to the intentions of the ancient church, which canonized no single theological position but a range of theological viewpoints. This is indicated well enough by the repudiation of Marcion's exclusively Pauline canon in favor of a broader but less consistent collection, and the rejection of Tatian's *Diatessaron* in favor of the multiple witness of four gospels. It remains true that every interpreter of the NT and every confessional standpoint within Christianity proceeds, tacitly or explicitly, with an interpretive principle or perspective which elicits from the canon a particular pattern of meaning. This is inescapable if the canon is to inform theological reflection and not remain diffusely meaningless. But just here the importance of the canon as a whole, in all its diversity, can be seen: although it requires a limitation and specification of its meaning to exercise a normative function, it nevertheless resists the absolutizing of any particular appropriation, and thus maintains the potentialities of interpretation against narrow, ideological foreclosures.

4. The Hermeneutical Value of the Canon. The historical-critical study of the canonical documents has customarily approached them in disregard of the canon. Its interest is in individual writings interpreted in terms of the diverse, particular circumstances in which they arose. Their literary context in the canon is not relevant to that aim. But in recent years there has been a growing interest in the relevance of the canon for theological exegesis, and this approach has gained the name "canonical criticism." This enterprise has taken two main forms. One has urged that the theological interpretation of Scripture is properly attentive to the canon when it takes as its basis the "final [canonical] form" of a given text, as distinct from sources that can be identified behind the text or as distinct from an original form of the text, and interprets that text in terms of its "full canonical context," as distinct from its original historical context. Thus the literary and theological context furnished by the canon itself is made the touchstone of interpretation. No document, on this view, should be read in isolation; rather each should be read with a view to the interrelationships established by the canon between it and other canonical documents. What arises from such a reading is the "canonical sense" of the text, which is taken to be the theologically normative meaning of the text (Childs 1979; 1984). Another form of canonical criticism attends not to the final form of a text or its intracanonical relationships, but to the canonical process exhibited within the texts, that is, the hermeneutical dynamics by which authoritative (preliterary) traditions were not only stabilized in writing, but were subsequently and repeatedly revised and adapted, reformulated and rewritten, so as to make them freshly relevant to the changing circumstances and needs of the religious community. The interpretive paradigms that can be observed in this process as it is enshrined in and even continued by the canonical literature may then become useful means for the modern appropriation of the canonical documents themselves (J. A. Sanders 1976; 1984).

It is assuredly true that the formation of the New Testament canon held hermeneutical consequences for the documents that were included in it: new meanings accrued to the texts by their placement in that new context. While this "canonical sense" deserves recognition, it is not usually easy to identify, and is often merely impressionistic. Furthermore, it is not at all clear that the alleged "canonical sense" of a document has or ought to have a better claim to theological authority than the meaning that attaches to an individual document taken by itself or in connection with a smaller group of related documents. For it was these latter meanings that commended the documents to the church and resulted in their incorporation into the canon. An adequate hermeneutic of the canon cannot therefore be indifferent to detailed historical criticism or to the history of the canon. At the same time, the canon is something both more and different than the sum of its parts, and historical criticism cannot fully illumine the NT without reflecting on the hermeneutical significance of the canon.

Bibliography

Aland, K. 1962. *The Problem of the New Testament Canon.* London.

———. 1979. Die Entstehung des Corpus Paulinum. Pp. 302–50 in his *Neutestamentliche Entwürfe.* TBü 63. Munich.

Anderson, C. P. 1966. The Epistle to the Hebrews and the Pauline Letter Collection. *HTR* 59: 429–38.

Best, E. 1979. Scripture, Tradition and the Canon of the New Testament. *BJRL* 61: 258–89.

Cameron, R. 1982. *The Other Gospels: Non-Canonical Gospel Texts.* Philadelphia.

Campenhausen, H. von. 1972. *The Formation of the Christian Bible.* Philadelphia.

Childs, B. S. 1979. *Introduction to the OT as Scripture.* Philadelphia.

———. 1984. *The NT as Canon: An Introduction.* Philadelphia.

Clabeaux, J. J. 1989. *A Lost Edition of the Letters of Paul: A Reassessment of the Text of the Pauline Corpus Attested by Marcion.* CBQMS 21. Washington, DC.

Cullmann, O. 1956. The Plurality of the Gospels as a Theological Problem in Antiquity. Pp. 39–54 in his *The Early Church.* Philadelphia.

———. 1956b. The Tradition. Pp. 59–99 in his *The Early Church.* Philadelphia.

Dahl, N. A. 1962. The Particularity of the Pauline Epistles as a Problem in the Ancient Church. Pp. 261–71 in *Neostestamentica et Patristica: Eine Freundesgabe Herrn Prof. Dr. Oscar Cullmann zu seinem 60. Geburtstag.* NovTSup 6. Leiden.

———. 1978. The Origin of the Earliest Prologues to the Pauline Letters. Pp. 233–77 in *The Poetics of Faith: Essays offered to A. N. Wilder,* ed. W. A. Beardslee. Semeia 12. Missoula, MT.

Dunn, J. D. G. 1977. *Unity and Diversity in the NT.* Philadelphia.

Ebeling, G. 1968a. The NT and the Multiplicity of Confessions. Pp. 148–59 in his *Word of God and Tradition.* Philadelphia.

———. 1968b. "Sola Scriptura" and Tradition. Pp. 102–47 in his *Word of God and Tradition.* Philadelphia.

Farmer, W. R. 1983. *The Formation of the NT Canon* (with D. M. Farkasfakvy). New York.

Ferguson, E. 1982. Canon Muratori: Date and Provenance. *StPatr* 18: 677–83.

Filson, F. V. 1957. *Which Books Belong to the Bible? A Study of the Canon.* Philadelphia.

Finegan, J. 1956. The Original Form of the Pauline Collection. *HTR* 49: 85–103.

Flesseman-van Leer, E. 1954. *Tradition and Scripture in the Early Church.* Assen.

———. 1964. Prinzipien der Sammlung und Ausscheidung bei der Bildung des Kanons. *ZTK* 61: 404–20.

Frede, H. J. 1964. *Altlateinische Paulus-Handschriften.* Vetus Latina: Aus der Geschichte der lateinischen Bibel 4. Freiburg.

———. 1969. Die Ordnung der Paulusbriefe und der Platz des Kolosserbrief im Corpus Paulinum. Pp. 290–303 in *Vetus Latina: Die Reste der altlateinischen Bibel.* Vol. 24/2, *Epistulae ad Philippenses et ad Colossenses.* Freiburg.

Gamble, H. Y. 1985. *The NT Canon: Its Making and Meaning.* Guides to Biblical Scholarship. Philadelphia.

Goodspeed, E. J. 1933. *The Meaning of Ephesians.* Chicago.

Grant, R. M. 1965. *The Formation of the NT.* New York.

Hahn, F. 1980. Die Heilige Schrift als älteste christliche Tradition und als Kanon. *EvT* 40: 456–66.

Hanson, R. P. C. 1962. *Tradition in the Early Church.* Philadelphia.

Harnack, A. 1925. *The Origin of the NT and the Most Important Consequences of the New Creation.* London.

Hillmer, M. R. 1966. The Gospel of John in the Second Century. Diss., Harvard.

Kalin, E. 1967. Argument from Inspiration in the Canonization of the New Testament. Diss, Harvard.

Käsemann, E. 1964. The Canon of the NT and the Unity of the Church. Pp. 95–107 in his *Essays on New Testament Themes.* London.

———. 1970. *Das Neue Testament als Kanon: Dokumentation und kritische Analyse zur gegenwärtigen Diskussion.* Göttingen.

Keck, L. E. 1980. Is the NT a Field of Study? Or, From Outler to Overbeck and Back. *SecondCent* 1: 19–35.

Knox, J. 1942. *Marcion and the NT.* Chicago.

Koester, H. 1957. *Synoptische Überlieferung bei den apostolischen Vätern.* TU 65. Berlin.

———. 1980. Apocryphal and Canonical Gospels. *HTR* 73: 105–30.

Kümmel, W. G. 1950. Notwendigkeit und Grenze des neutestamentlichen Kanons. *ZTK* 47: 277–313. Repr., pp. 230–59 in *Heilsgeschehen und Geschichte: Gesammelte Aufsätze 1933–1964,* ed. E. Grässer, O. Merk, and A. Fritz. Marburger Theologische Studien 3. Marburg, 1965.

Küng, H. 1963. "Early Catholicism" in the NT as Problem in Controversial Theology. Pp. 159–95 in *The Council in Action: Theological Reflections on the Second Vatican Council.* New York.

Kürzinger, J. 1983. *Papias von Hieropolis und die Evangelien des Neuen Testaments.* Regensburg.

Leipoldt, J. 1907. *Geschichte des neutestamentlichen Kanons.* Vol 1. *Die Entstehung.* Leipzig.

Lindemann, A. 1979. *Paulus im ältesten Christentum.* BHT 58. Tübingen.

Lønning, I. 1972. *Kanon im Kanon: Zum dogmatischen Grundlagen-Problem des neutestamentlichen Kanons.* Oslo.

Lührmann, D. 1981. Gal. 2.9 und die katholischen Briefe. *ZNW* 72: 65–87.

Marxsen, W. 1972. *The NT as the Church's Book.* Philadelphia.

Merkel, H. 1971. *Die Widersprüche zwischen den Evangelien.* WUNT 13. Tübingen.

———. 1978. *Die Pluralität der Evangelien als theologisches und exegetisches Problem in der alten Kirche.* Bern.

Metzger, B. M. 1987. *The Canon of the NT.* Oxford.

Mowry, L. 1944. The Early Circulation of Paul's Letters. *JBL* 63: 73–86.

Ohlig, K.-H. 1972. *Die theologische Begründung des neutestamentlichen Kanons in der alten Kirche.* Dusseldorf.

Paulsen, H. 1978. Die Bedeutung des Montanismus für die Herausbidung des Kanons. *VC* 32: 19–52.

Rensberger, D. 1981. As the Apostle Teaches: The Development of the Use of Paul's Letters in Second Century Christianity. Diss., Yale.

Roberts, C. H., and Skeat, T. C. 1983. *The Birth of the Codex.* London.

Ruwet, J. 1942. Les "antilegomena" dans les oeuvres d'Origène. *Bib* 23: 18–42.

———. 1948. Clement d'Alexandrie: Canon des écritures et apocryphes. *Bib* 29: 77–99; 240–68; 391–408.

Sanders, J. A. 1976. Adaptable for Life: The Nature and Function of the Canon. Pp. 531–60 in *Magnalia Dei, the Mighty Acts of God: Essays on the Bible and Archaeology in Memory of G. E. Wright,* ed. E. M. Cross, W. E. Lemke, and P. Miller. Garden City, NY.

———. 1984. *Canon and Community: A Guide to Canonical Criticism.* GBS. Philadelphia.

Sanders, J. N. 1943. *The Fourth Gospel in the Early Church.* Cambridge.

Schenke, H.-M. 1975. Das Weiterwirken des Paulus und die Pflege seines Erbs durch die Paulusschule. *NTS* 21: 505–18.

Schmithals, W. 1972. On the Composition and Earliest Collection of the Major Epistles of Paul. Pp. 239–74 in *Paul and the Gnostics.* Nashville.

Schrage, W. 1976. Die Frage nach der Mitte und dem Kanon im Kanon des Neuen Testaments in der neueren Diskussion. Pp. 415–42 in *Rechtfertigung: Festschrift für Ernst Käsemann zum 70. Geburtstag,* ed. J. Friedrich, W. Pohlmann, and P. Stuhlmacher. Tubingen.

Stendahl, K. 1962. The Apocalypse of John and the Epistles of Paul in the Muratorian Fragment. Pp. 239–45 in *Current Issues in New Testament Interpretations: Essays in Honor of Otta A. Piper,* ed. W. Klassen and G. F. Snyder. New York.

Sundberg, A. C. 1964. *The Old Testament of the Early Church.* HTS 20. Cambridge, MA.

———. 1973. Canon Muratori: A Fourth Century List. *HTR* 66: 1–41.

———. 1975. The Bible Canon and the Christian Doctrine of Inspiration. *Int* 29: 352–71.

Zahn, T. 1888–92. *Geschichte des neutestamentlichen Kanons,* vols. 1–2. Erlangen.

HARRY Y. GAMBLE

CANON, MURATORIAN. See MURATORIAN FRAGMENT.

CANONICAL CRITICISM. The term "canonical criticism" does not adequately convey the range of approaches or the variety of methodologies employed by scholars who are often associated with it. Even scholars who have come to reject the term, e.g., Brevard Childs, may still be regarded by other scholars as its leading practitioners. What is clear is that canonical criticism is less a formal "criticism" than an approach or series of approaches that seeks to raise neglected questions about the form and function of scripture, both Jewish and Christian.

A. Introduction

Approaches currently associated with "canonical criticism," regardless of how it is specifically defined, presuppose the triumph of historical criticism over premodern historical notions about the authorship and formation of biblical books. While many of the proposals associated with a canonical approach rejuvenate traditional questions about the nature and authority of scripture, they do so only through significant innovation and with the hope of a greater degree of historical precision than one could have expected of similar premodern treatments. In this way, biblical fundamentalists find that some subjects neglected by older historical critics are taken up once again, though expressed in the light of critical historical conclusions alien to fundamentalist views regarding the history of the Bible. Canonical criticism, regardless of the theological spectrum that may find it appealing, is a response from within a more liberal, rather than a conservative, assessment of the biblical prehistory.

Canonical approaches in general strive to articulate a perspective on the relationship between biblical studies and the study of religion and theology. In premodern Christian studies of the Bible, both Roman Catholics and Protestants agreed that the "literal sense" of scripture provided the principal authority for Christian doctrine and that this sense, as distinguished from "spiritual senses," could be identified, at least in part, with the "author's intent." Since the 15th century, Nicholas of Lyra and many other Christian exegetes resorted to the idea of a double "literal sense," especially for the OT: one aimed at a grammatical, historical, and religious dimension common to both Jews and Christians; the other based on the role of the OT within Christian scripture as a norm of distinctly Christian doctrines. In the early modern period, biblical scholars frequently sought through a "historical" approach to secure neutral, scientific consensus regarding what a biblical text "meant" distinct from ecclesiastical or sectarian assessments of what it "means." This allegedly neutral meaning of the Bible often became identified with the traditional religious goal of describing the "literal sense" of scripture as a prior step to theological interpretation.

In the past few decades, the confidence that the literal sense of scripture can be equated with the results of historical criticism has been seriously reexamined. At the outset, biblical criticism has convincingly shown that the Bible is a multilayered, editorial composite of diverse texts and traditions. Any effort to describe the "original" historical traditions, as against the "secondary" one now preserved with them in the Bible, is highly speculative and, more significantly, must isolate older traditions away from their context within scripture. Such historical analysis leads properly to an effort to recover the "original" form and function of ancient Israelite traditions and to conjecture about the original prebiblical social settings in which they were once heard or read. If the "literal sense" is identified rigorously with the intent of the first "authors" of such traditions, then the intent will, in most instances, be prebiblical in so far as these authors rarely, if ever, "intended" to write "biblical" traditions. Many of these traditions only became identified as "biblical" at a later time and were publically established as such when they were assigned a place within a scripture by editors. Consequently, the "meaning of the biblical text" cannot be equated uncritically with the historical intent of a modern conception of the "original" authors, without losing precisely what the traditional formulation sought to preserve.

A modern understanding of the form and function of a scripture implies a shift in the semantic import of its antecedent traditions. The canonical context of the Bible exhibits moments of both formal preservation and contextual modification, both historical retention and ahistorical, or topical, reorientation. Just as the semantic force of words is not secured solely by appeal to their etymologies but gains specific import within the context of a particular sentence, so the context of scripture inevitably influences how earlier traditions come to make sense as a part of scripture. This transformation in the meaning of texts and traditions occurs through a complex, sociopolitical process of literary production leading to the public recognition of both a particular religion and the canonization of its scripture. This process is historically serendipitous, but reflects in general terms a dialectical relationship between canon and community, between the formation of a scripture and the identification of the community of faith that treasures it. In sociological terms, a scripture may be considered a social contract between differing groups that assume a common purpose and status before God. While the context of a scripture establishes a restrictive framework in which religious interpretation takes place, the context itself is composed of the favored traditions of different groups, ordered in, at times, a remarkably unharmonized fashion.

In sum, the semantic function of a scripture often exceeds or contravenes the original intent of various historical authors/redactors who can be reconstructed within the prehistory of the canon. In the place of a modern reconstruction of historical authors, Jewish and Christian scripture presents key figures—Moses, David, Isaiah, Jeremiah, Luke, John, Paul—as "biblical" persons whose "intents" can only be found in the canonical context. The very realism of these biographical presentations, together with some degree of modern historical support for their historicity, may tempt interpreters to replace the biblical portrayal with more historically "accurate" biographies. However, such a substitution usually sacrifices the context of scripture and misses the possibility of a biblical anthropology. Only the biblical context warrants such a wedding of word and *persona* that presumes to render the nature of ultimate reality through the reception of scripture as a human witness to divine revelation.

B. "Canon" and Canonical Approaches

As early as the 2d century, Christians could speak of the Bible as "canonical," as well as divinely "inspired." Only later did Athanasius (ca. 350 C.E.) identify *ta biblia* ("the books" of scripture) with the noun *kanon* (a list of normative books). The same usage in Judaism belongs only to the modern period, though, as in Christianity, Jewish scriptures possesses a special normative quality—it is "spoken by God" and "defiles the hands." In both Christianity and Judaism, the identification of books belonging to scripture preceded by several centuries the determination of a *textus receptus,* or fixed textual tradition. Prebiblical uses of the word "canon" reflect well the ambiguities attendant to the formation of a "normative" scripture.

As a Semitic loan word transliterated into Greek and Latin, "canon" can denote (1) an ideal, standard, central criterion, or essential summation and/or (2) a list, catalog, or measure. Something "canonical" may not yet be situated in a fixed list or collection of similar canonical things. So, biblical traditions and even whole books may be viewed as "canonical" long before they belong to a fixed "canon" or list of such books. A scripture is, of course, only one special type of canonical text or tradition. Other canons may include oral Torah, *magisteria,* special exegetical traditions, the inspired interpretation of a rabbi, or a contemporary word of Christian prophecy. These extrabiblical canons may seem more immediately influential for practical religious life than the scripture. The practice of religion is, of course, further subject to still other secular authorities or canons. Nonetheless, scripture is, at least in theory, assigned a superior place as a norm of faith within Judaism and Christianity.

Premodern handbooks or introductions usually began by considering the subjects of text and canon. As the more rigorous historical orientation of the modern period came to dominate, canonical issues seemed to belong only to the last steps in a long process, at great distance from the original historical events upon which the revelatory claims of a religion depends. Therefore, modern scholars, whether conservative or liberal on questions of biblical history, tended to shift the treatment of these subjects to the back of introductions, following the lead of such major orthodox interpreters as J. G. Carpzov (1721). This same priority of biblical history to biblical text informed much of the recent "Biblical Theology Movement" which often focused the theological worth of the Bible to the "acts of God in history" or defined the biblical witness in terms of an "actualized" report about a historical event. The canon could be viewed, according to this model, as merely a late and flawed premodern effort to preserve efficacious "confessions" about history. A canonical approach challenges the assumption that the earliest historical events play such a determinative role in the capacity of scripture to have authority or to render reality. Without denying the value of information gained by means of any critical investigation, a canonical approach seeks to understand a different issue: how a biblical text is normative within religious interpretation, that is to say, how the context of ancient traditions within scripture functions as an arena in which certain religious questions are asked and answered. In this approach, one seeks to recognize the textual warrants and rules whereby a scripture makes specific religious claims, perpetuates paradoxical and ambiguous expressions of faith, engenders the need for repeated interpretation, and imposes upon the reader a vision of the world that God has made.

Though various canonical approaches explore the same neglected perspective on the nature of a biblical text, their chief interpreters do not always agree on terminology, on methods of analysis, or on the practical implications for the future of biblical interpretation and commentary. James Sanders first coined the term "canon criticism" and popularized it through his *Torah and Canon* (1972). Through the study of interpretations within the Bible, which he calls "comparative midrash," Sanders sought to find a "canonical hermeneutic" that would explain why the same normative traditions could properly be interpreted with contradictory implications at different times and places. Later, in *Canon and Community* (1984) he changed the terminology from "canon criticism" to "canonical criticism," stressing its alignment with other critical methods. Brevard Childs, for one, initially used the term "canon criticism" in the 1970s (e.g., *Exodus* OTL) but dropped it as a misleading label for his own approach. It does not occur in either his *Introduction to the Old Testament as Scripture* (*IOTS*) or *The New Testament as Canon* (*NTC*). For Childs, "canon criticism" wrongly suggested a "criticism" parallel to other standard biblical methodologies (e.g., source, form, and redaction criticism).

Childs prefers to speak of a "canonical approach," highlighting how "the canonical shape" of a biblical book established possibilities and limits to its interpretation as a part of Jewish and Christian scripture. He starts with "the final text" of scripture, without uncritically accepting the *textus receptus,* and makes observations about how diverse, even contradictory, traditions share a canonical context together. Rather than allowing the reader to pick and choose what elements of traditions seem the most appealing, this canonical context deepened the demand for interpretation in specific ways and in certain significant theological directions. Leaning more in the direction of Childs than Sanders, Rolf Rendtorff's *The Old Testament: An Introduction* (1983, ET 1986) finds evidence of additional unifying "literary" features in a *Kompositionsgeschichte* ("composition criticism" or "history of composition") for each biblical book. Rendtorff stresses the inability of form criticism to account for how the "literary" dimension of the biblical text extended the audience and often detached traditions from their historical moorings for the purpose of establishing another theological way of receiving these traditions within Judaism and Christianity.

Related studies include I. L. Seeligmann's seminal study of "canon conscious" exegesis within the Bible. Nahum Sarna and Michael Fishbane have elaborated cases of "inner-biblical" interpretation that similarly presume plays upon fixed normative traditions, anticipating in some instances later types of Jewish midrashic interpretation of scripture. More radically, the French school of "anthological midrash" (e.g., A. A. Robert, R. Bloch *DBSup* 5: 1263–81) sought to describe a particular type of inner-biblical interpretation that reemploys words and phrases from canonical traditions in order to compose whole portions (e.g., parts of Proverbs 1–9) of some late biblical books. A number of redaction-critical studies, such as those of Ackroyd, Blenkinsopp, Clements, and Sheppard, have called attention to the special nature of canonical traditions from the perspective of later editors. Certain "canon conscious" redactions tell readers how some biblical books should be read in the context of others (Sheppard *EncRel* 3: 62–69). An editor's use of certain esoteric techniques in the alteration and placement of a tradition suggest self-conscious terms of restriction and freedom in how biblical authors/editors handled the preceding normative traditions. These traditions can be seen to function within the formation of the Bible with a special "semantic depth" (Clements), "vitality" (Ackroyd), "adaptability" (Sanders), or within an implicit "scriptural vision" (Fishbane), or with a special potential for "actualization" (Childs). This highly tendentious sketch of scholarly activities that are often associated with "canon criticism" illustrates some of the diversity in the present debate. In order to convey what is at stake in these newer approaches, a more general discussion of the canonical dimension will be followed by some examples of implications for assessing biblical literature.

1. Canonical Dimension and Biblical Interpretation. The present diversity in canonical approaches has led to a variety of proposals regarding the future of biblical interpretation. Sanders' and Fishbane's concern with "inner-biblical" interpretation suggests a continuity between the prebiblical interpretation of normative traditions and the later postbiblical interpretations of scripture in Judaism and Christianity. As Fishbane finds anticipations of later Jewish midrash, so Sanders detects a midrashic "canonical hermeneutic," already forged among Israel's ancient prophets and continuing into the postbiblical period. Sanders argues that contemporary theological exegesis should employ the same hermeneutic he has found here and there in ancient Israel and throughout the process of canonization. In religious terms he identifies this hermeneutic with "the ancient struggles of our ancestors in the faith to monotheize, to pursue the oneness of God, over against all kinds of polytheisms and fragmentations of truth" (1984: 17). The canonization of scripture represents the freezing of only one imperfect moment within that same process of interpretation. In Sanders' view, this hermeneutical criterion allows one to distinguish true from false prophecy in ancient Israel and can be applied similarly today to discern true and false biblical preaching in Christian churches.

Conversely, Childs, Rendtorff, and Sheppard have emphasized elements of discontinuity between the prescriptural functions of ancient traditions and the new roles they play within "the canonical context" of Jewish and Christian Bibles. While acknowledging different levels of authority and canonicity in the prehistory of the Bible, these scholars start with the canonical context as a way to assess how earlier traditions have been put together to form a new literary entity. Because the historical forces behind the formation of biblical books are so heterogeneous, Childs concludes: "The history of the canonical process does not seem to be an avenue through which one can greatly illuminate the present canonical text" (*IOTS* 67). Only the present "shape" (Childs) or "composition" (Rendtorff) of a biblical book survives as evidence of how the community of faith ordered past traditions as a normative witness to divine revelation. Besides indicating a specific inner-textuality and a unity of subject matter, the canonical context, also, gives permanence to unresolved differences between traditions, delimits functional ambiguities, and perpetuates undecoded symbolism integral to a religion's understanding of divine mysteries yet to be fully revealed. Clearly, many ancient historical features are retained within this later context, though the formation of scripture tends to insure that "texts are less bound up with particular events and situations" (Rendtorff 1986: 125).

The hermeneutical significance of the canonical context of scripture depends partly on how a religion construes the relation between the biblical witness and its revealed subject matter. Rabbinic Judaism sought to interpret the written Torah of scripture chiefly through midrashic methods, honoring the parallel testimony of oral Torah (Mishnah and the Talmud[s]). Christianity moved in another hermeneutical direction. With the addition of a "New Testament" and the transformation of Hebrew scripture into "Old Testament," a new literary horizon emerged. At least by the middle of the 2d century, Christian leaders asserted that priority in dogmatic disputes should be given to a nonmidrashic, "plain" or "literal sense." Similarly, Christians sought to understand the relation of the Torah to the Gospel. A prophetic interpretation often predominated and certain texts lent themselves more readily than others to Christian messianic explication. Though Christianity did not share the oral Torah of Judaism, it did not lack its own extrabiblical authorities in the form of creeds, binding church decisions, local ecclesial laws, and so forth. Though the practice of biblical interpretation differs between Judaism and Christianity, both frequently show a similar concern for warrants implicit within the canonical "shape" of books. In this respect, crucial religious features of the Hebrew Bible are fully retained in Christian scripture in spite of the semantic transformation that takes place when Christians appropriate the Hebrew Bible as the "Old Testament" within the context of the "New." At a minimum, the canonical context is a highly significant factor, but not the only one that may influence the nature of biblical interpretation.

2. "Shape" of Biblical Books. Childs has chosen the term "shape" to describe the distinctive features of biblical books when they are read as scripture. This trope may connote too readily a trait of harmony or full coherence of traditions in books, comparable to geometric symmetry. Nevertheless, Childs uses "shape" carefully to describe the boundaries and orchestration of semantic possibilities of traditions within a biblical book from the perspective of its form and function as scripture. From the 1st centuries of Christianity up to the modern period, Christians have often sought to preserve the same scriptural dimension by an appeal to the "scope" of a biblical book. At times, the "scope" (*skopos*) has pertained to an element in the church's "rule of faith," as in Athanasius' refutation of the Arians' use of Proverbs; at other times, it denoted a more literary appeal to the beginnings and endings of biblical books, to titles, and other transitional markers within a biblical text. The latter usage can be readily seen in the rules of Flacius in the middle of the 16th century and commonly among English Protestants in the late 16th century until the end of the 19th. The indices of the scope of a text were supposed to provide clues regarding the normative "purpose" of the text, coinciding with the "intent" of the inspired author.

In the premodern period, Christian interpreters commonly assumed that the literal sense of scripture was identical with the biblical author's "intent." What becomes obvious is that in these formulations the "biblical author," the central figure associated with a particular book, is not identical with a "historical author" reconstructed by modern historical criticism. A canonical approach can try to express what the older formulation sought to describe in another way, informed by a modern understanding of history and religion. This alternative expression of how the biblical text relates to its subject matter must take into account a different perception of diachronic dimensions and involves a critical awareness of the semantic import of traditions shifted from their origins, through transmission and editing, to their later places among biblical texts. The shape of a biblical book and its canonical context within scripture provide an essential guide as to how the intents of various historical authors and editors pertain to the presentation of a biblical author and a biblical book. Moreover, the canonical context indicates how the presentations of key biblical figures have been linked to the "canonical intention" of the biblical text. In these two ways, the aim of the older identification of literal sense with the author's intent is maintained but expressed in new ways that respond to the impact of historical criticism and the contemporary perception of differences in a biblical text.

3. Examples of a Canonical Approach. The form of the Pentateuch ("the book of Moses," Josh 1:7) corresponds to its function as scriptural "Torah" in various ways. First, as Sanders has eloquently shown, it situates the law of God prior to the actual conquest of the land. The Torah could be received by future readers of the Jewish Diaspora as an address to people who themselves yearn to enter into a promised land. The laws, regardless of what we may say about their original historical settings, refer in this context to a revealed Torah rather than to law codes that reflect merely compromises to the experiences of life at various times in the land.

Second, while "the Torah" denotes a single, coherent instruction from God, it is represented in the narrative form through different Mosaic mediations: as shown in the legal collections of Exodus, Leviticus, Numbers, and, then, those of Deuteronomy. While each of these collections now shares substantially the same Decalog (Exod 20:2–14 and Deut 5:6–18), the other laws contain many disagreements, even within laws governing the same offense. While historical criticism can provide one account for these differences, the canonical context now relates them according to another religious implication. In the context of the Mosaic Torah, the laws found in Exodus, Leviticus, and Numbers belong to the legislation as given to Moses in the region of Sinai, while the laws presented in Deuteronomy belong to Moses' subsequent "interpretation" of them on the plains of Moab to the next generation (Deut 1:5). Based on the role of these laws in scripture, the historical etymology of these traditions is less important than the canonical context which depicts Moses as "interpreting" the earlier laws to the changing circumstances of a later generation. This contextual precedent was recognized by rabbinic Judaism and perpetuated by the acceptance of the oral Torah (the Mishnah and Talmud[s]), that accompanies the interpretation of the written Torah. It was also allegedly perpetuated by Moses through the Elders.

Third, Moses appears in these books as a vivid flesh-and-blood figure with strengths and weaknesses like our own. Genesis elaborates the genealogical record leading to his birth in Exodus, and the five-book Torah concludes in the last chapters of Deuteronomy with an account of his death. This presentation of his life provides a key unifying feature corresponding to the unity of the revealed Torah which this five-book collection mediates. Moses' unique status as the prophet par excellence (Deut 34:10–12) indicates the special role these books play within the scripture as a whole. Though modern critics suspect correctly that a historical Moses could not have written all of these traditions, the biblical portrayal of Moses and the events of his life belong to the very syntax of these books in their form and function as scripture. Modern critics have often sought to improve on the historical elements in this presentation by searching for the "historical" Moses. If such a search claims to pursue "biblical" faith, then it has confused uncritically the mode of understanding congruent to the realism of a scripture with the mode of understanding congruent to a realism pertaining to conceptions of a modern "history."

As Judaism now finds in scripture and in oral Torah different literary manifestations of law as inspired human witnesses to the one Torah that God has given to a chosen people, so Christianity possesses in the NT four different Gospels, as well as Romans and James, despite the confession that there is actually only one Gospel of Jesus Christ. From this perspective the biblical canons do not end interpretation by harmonizing as much as they ground and perpetuate the need for fresh interpretation of the Bible by each generation of believers. Though both Judaism and Christianity resist the expansion of scripture by new revelation, each generation seeks to express the Torah or the Gospel, with the aid of scripture, more precisely and in pragmatically more pertinent ways than preceding generations. Therefore, the scripture harbors in its own contextual ambiguities the potential for a criticism of each believer's current ruling metaphors while, at the same time, it delimits a specific arena in which a grand quest for the revelation of reality can take place.

In both the OT and NT, collections of tradition outside of the Mosaic Torah and the Gospels have been assigned a special context and function together as parts of scripture. What might be regarded as historical anachronisms frequently contribute to the canonical context and religious import of ancient traditions. Though the activity of many of the OT prophets precedes historically the period when the present Mosaic Torah was formed, the traditions of the prophets have been edited together as scripture in a manner that allows the prophetic books now to be read as commentary on the Torah of Moses. So, too, the Pauline Epistles, many of which precede the time when the Gospels were composed, now are found after the written Gospels as a part of a collection of "Pauline Letters" and provide a commentary upon the same essential message found in the four Gospels.

The Solomonic books offer a vivid example of how the canonical context alters our vision and reception of ancient traditions when read as scripture. Modern criticism properly questions a direct connection between the historical Solomon and the books of Proverbs, Ecclesiastes, and Song of Songs. Nevertheless, the context of scripture identifies these books in a highly significant manner as Solomonic "wisdom" within Hebrew scripture. Because of its association with Solomon, biblical wisdom cannot be equated uncritically with a strictly historical conception of ancient Israelite "wisdom" in the Near East. The canon-contextual presentation of Solomon delimits some crucial distinctions between the biblical wisdom traditions and those of the Mosaic Torah. For instance, Solomon epitomizes the wisest person who ever lived (1 Kgs 4:29–31), but he must, also, obey the Torah of Moses as did his father (1 Kgs 3:14). Furthermore, by assigning this "wisdom" literature to Solomon, the canonical context provides its own account for why wisdom literature appears to bracket out self-consciously the idiosyncratic language of faith about the Exodus, the giving of the law of God at Sinai, the covenant, and other historical details regarding Israel's faith in Yahweh. Part of the religious genius of biblical wisdom lies in its affirmation of an international collection of sayings that borrows from and rivals that of other nations, without resolving issues of conflict between different religions. It is the sort of knowledge that inspires the Queen of Sheba to travel to test Solomon with riddles. Biblical wisdom lends itself to an international cooperation in understanding territories not explicitly addressed by the Torah but shared by the wisdom of other religions. This demarcation of wisdom in association with Solomon, distinct from other parts of scripture, naturally invited a debate over how the parts of scripture relate to each other as a guide to the obedient life. Prior to Christianity, Judaism overtly affirmed that the Torah and Wisdom complemented one another and that the one could be read as a resource for refinements in the understanding of the other (cf. Sirach 24 and Bar 3:9–4:4). The manner in which wisdom relates to the Torah and to the Prophets, and how wisdom relates to all of these and to the Gospel, becomes part of the vocabulary that continues to inform the response of both Judaism and Christianity to issues of practical knowledge, scientific inquiry, psychology, and many other areas of common life.

C. Conclusion

Canonical criticism has become a popular, though debated, label for a variety of approaches that inquire into the form and function of the Bible as scripture. A canonical approach assumes a particular perspective by which biblical studies can understand the nature of scripture and its relation to the history of religious interpretation and theology. As shown by Childs' commentary on Exodus, this perspective encourages a critical examination of the history of interpretation, both ancient and modern. In my view, attention to the canonical context of scripture is essential for an appreciation of how religions construe reality and how competence in biblical interpretation is recognized in earlier periods. In the larger task of contemporary Christian theological interpretation, canonical approaches offer foundational descriptions of the context of scripture and detect warrants for a reading of the diverse traditions as multiple human witnesses to the same subject matter of faith and revelation.

Bibliography

Blenkinsopp, J. 1977. *Prophecy and Canon.* Philadelphia.

Brown, R. 1981. *The Critical Meaning of the Bible.* New York.

Childs, B. S. 1970. *Biblical Theology in Crisis.* Philadelphia.

———. 1972. The Old Testament as Scripture of the Church. *CTM* 43: 709–22.

———. 1985. *Old Testament Theology in a Canonical Context.* Philadelphia.

Clements, R. 1978. *Old Testament Theology.* London.

Coats, G. W., and Long, B. O., eds. 1977. *Canon and Authority.* Philadelphia.

Fishbane, M. 1980. Revelation and Tradition: Aspects of Inner-biblical Exegesis. *JBL* 90: 343–61.
———. 1985. *Biblical Interpretation in Ancient Israel.* New York.
Metzger, B. 1987. *The Canon of the New Testament.* Oxford.
Neusner, J. 1983. *Midrash in Context.* Philadelphia.
Rendtorff, R. 1986. *The Old Testament: An Introduction.* Philadelphia.
Sanders, J. 1972. *Torah and Canon.* Philadelphia.
———. 1976. Adaptable for Life: The Nature and Function of Canon. In *Magnalia Dei,* ed. F. M. Cross, et al. Garden City.
———. 1984. *Canon and Community.* Philadelphia.
Sarna, N. 1963. Psalm 89: A Study in Inner Biblical Exegesis. Pp. 29–46 in *Biblical and Other Essays,* ed. A. Altmann. Cambridge, MA.
Seeligmann, I. L. 1953. Voraussetzung der Midraschexegese. VTSup 1: 150–81.
Sheppard, G. T. 1974. Canon Criticism: The Proposal of Brevard Childs and An Assessment for Evangelical Hermeneutics. *SBT* 4: 3–17.
———. 1980 *Wisdom as a Hermeneutical Construct.* BZAW 151. Berlin.
———. 1982. Canonization: Hearing the Voice of the Same God Through Historically Dissimilar Traditions. *Int* 34: 21–33.
Smith, W. C. 1971. The Study of Religion and the Study of the Bible. *JAAR* 39: 131–40.

GERALD T. SHEPPARD

CANOPY. Four different Hebrew words are rendered "canopy" in English versions. The first, *sûkkâ,* derives from the root *skk,* which means "to weave together," thus forming a thick material that can be a shelter, as in the "booths" made of boughs that served as temporary dwellings during harvest time. This noun is used in 1 Sam 22:12 and Ps 18:12 [—Eng 18:11] to refer to Yahweh's heavenly shelter and to enrich the dramatic language of divine theophany in these two passages. Another term, *ʿōb,* is found twice: once in an obscure reference to some part of the pillared forecourt (*ʾûlām*) to Solomon's "Hall of Pillars" (1 Kgs 7:6); and once in a description of a shelter in front of the forecourt (*ʾûlām*) of the Temple (Ezek 41:25). The latter reference uses "wood" with *ʿōb,* thus indicating a more solid architectural element than a woven canopy.

A third Hebrew word for canopy, *ḥûppâ,* is from *ḥpp,* meaning "to cover." The act of covering rather than the material itself is basic to this term, which appears in Isa 4:5 to refer to the way smoke and fire by day and night will provide a cover ("canopy") over the restored Mount Zion and its assemblies in the glorious future. Finally, the word *šaprûr* (or *šaprîr,* Qere) which appears only once in the Hebrew Bible (Jer 43:10), apparently denotes a royal pavilion or canopy being spread out by Nebuchadnezzar over his throne. Related to Akkadian *šuparruri,* it might also indicate a carpet being stretched out. In either case, this too appears to be a textile rather than a solid structure.

All the words rendered "canopy," along with "pavilion" and other terms, are part of the rich Hebrew vocabulary dealing with shelters, both temporary and permanent. Such terms designate both actual shelters and are also used symbolically to indicate God's sheltering, protective presence.

CAROL MEYERS

CANTICLES, BOOK OF. See SONG OF SONGS, BOOK OF.

CAPE. See DRESS AND ORNAMENTATION.

CAPERNAUM (PLACE) [Gk *Kapharnaoum*]. A place on the NW bank of Lake Tiberias (M.R. 204254). Josephus renders the Heb *kĕpar naḥum* as *kapharnaoum* (*JW* 3.10.8), as does the NT. The Arabs of the region call the spot Talhum or Tell Hum.

After Jesus began his ministry, he moved to Capernaum (Matt 4:13; Mark 2:1). Capernaum had a synagogue which had been built with the sponsorship of the local centurion (Luke 7:2–5). While in Capernaum, Jesus healed several people (Matt 8:5; Mark 1:21–28; 2:1–12; Luke 7:1–10; John 4:46–54) and taught in the synagogue (Luke 4:31–38; cf. John 6:22–59). The city, however, eventually received a scathing denunciation when Jesus condemned its stubbornness as worse than Sodom's (Matt 11:23–24). Later, during the First Jewish Revolt, Josephus was taken to Capernaum for his initial medical treatment after he was injured in battle (*Life* 72).

After having been abandoned and completely forgotten for centuries, Capernaum reemerged in 1894, when the ruins of the site were acquired by the Franciscan custody of the Holy Land from the As-Samakiyeh Arabs. The first exploratory excavations were conducted in 1905 under the direction of H. Kohl and C. Watzinger. Their probes were in the central and eastern naves of the synagogue, with a number of additional trenches in the western nave; these allowed a reconstruction of the plan of the building. In the same year, other excavations were conducted under the direction of F. V. Hinterkeuser, which continued until the outbreak of World War I. After the war, excavations resumed until 1921 by P. G. Orfali, who not only published a monograph, *Capharnaum et ses ruines,* but also began a restoration of the synagogue; this work, however, was not completed because of his tragic death.

In April of 1968, V. Corbo and S. Loffreda reopened the excavations of Capernaum and conducted 18 campaigns up to 1985; these excavations led to the discovery of many of the insulae of the city and to the rediscovery of the house of Simon Peter. They also led to the discovery of the synagogue of the Roman centurion beneath the foundations of the synagogue of the 4th–5th century.

A. The City

Until 1968, no remains of the city of the time of Jesus were visible; since then many insulae have been excavated. The city was laid out according to the orthogonal, or Hippodamian, urban plan, which consisted of a *cardo maximus* or *via principalis* (e.g., main N–S thoroughfare) and numerous *decumani* (e.g., E–W intersecting streets). Within the grid pattern of the streets, the dwellings were grouped in insulae. The use of this plan, along with the archaeological finds have allowed the excavators to date the origins of this city to the Hellenistic period. The city continued developing along this same plan until its abandonment in the 7th century C.E., when the Islamic invasion occurred. However, under the pavement of the synagogue, there are remains of an LB dwelling which appears to date to the 13th century B.C.E. During the campaigns of 1984–1985 in the lowest levels of the excavation, the archaeologists began to encounter dwellings with ceramics both of the Persian (538–332 B.C.E.) and of the MB Ages (1900–1550 B.C.E.). These dwellings were enveloped in the Hellenistic urban plan.

B. The Dwellings

In the insulae of the Hellenistic city, the archaeologists found dwellings of two types: "clan" dwellings and individual dwellings. The "clan" dwellings were arranged around internal courts, which numbered at times as many as three; around these courts were rooms which faced inward. There was a single entrance to the house, which faced the street and had a threshold and jambs with pins for the wooden door. The windows of the rooms opened onto the internal courts and never on the streets. Family life took place in the courts, where there were hearths, millstones for the grain, and handpresses. Also situated in the courts were stairs which allowed access to the roofs, which were made with wooden beams and covered with a layer of packed mud.

Household furnishings included vases in white stone for holding water; basalt mortars; various basalt containers and vessels of a whole range of forms and sizes, and much ceramic pottery. The ceramics included lamps, plates, bowls, pans, amphorae, pots, and cups.

The houses were constructed with walls made of blocks of basalt dry-set; the interior faces of the walls were finished with ornamental patterns of pebbles. Seldom were there masonry walls, and then they were almost always of late date. The floors were made of basalt pebblework, sometimes covered with a layer of yellowish earth. The windows of the rooms were set in series on stylobate walls, and were formed of jambs supporting architraves which were crudely carved.

C. The House of Simon Peter

The house of Simon Peter at Capernaum is mentioned many times in the Gospels, so much so that in referring to his house, the Evangelists do so with or without the article (Matt 17:25; Mark 2:1; 3:20; 9:33); alternatively they refer to it with the name of Peter (Matt 8:14) or of Simon and Andrew (Mark 1:29).

The house of Simon Peter was found in 1968 in the first campaign of the excavations. It is situated in the SE corner of a vast insula which extends from the shore of the lake to the Hellenistic *decumanus.* Its N side lies under the balcony of the synagogue; its E side faces an open area which adjoins the *cardo maximus* and to which reference is made in Mark 1:33 and 2:2. The archaeological finds show that this house had already been built in the Hellenistic period, and that therefore, Simon Peter must have acquired it when he settled with his clan at Capernaum. The entry to the vast dwelling was from the open space to the E. See Fig. CAP.01. The plan of the house had three courts, around which were arranged the numerous living rooms. Among these rooms were two situated on the S side of the N court, which was the court into which one entered from the street. These two rooms were transformed in the apostolic period into a "house church"; here the excavators

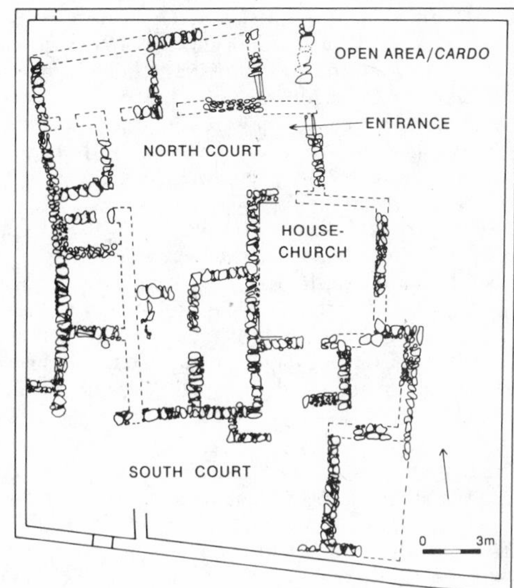

CAP.01. House of Simon Peter showing "house church" at Capernaum. *(Redrawn from Corbo 1975: tav. IX.)*

found part of the paving of the floor, which was surfaced with lime plaster—the same type of paving, in fact, which was found some years later in the triclinia of the palace of Herod at Macheron. The walls of the house–church were likewise covered with plaster and had painted decorations consisting of Judeo–Christian emblems. Christian pilgrims of the first centuries scratched on these plastered walls sacred and devotional graffiti in Greek, Latin, Syriac, and Aramaic (cf. Testa 1972).

The house of Simon Peter underwent a radical restructuring in the 4th century C.E. when, at the initiative of Count Joseph of Tiberias, a friend of Constantine the Great, the house–church was restructured on the interior with the addition of an arch supporting a new roof. The floor was also resurfaced; a new sacristy was added on the N side, while on the E flank a portico was built. The original entrance of the house, which had opened onto the *cardo maximus,* was closed, while there were opened two new entrances in the sacred wall—one on the S toward the shore of the lake and one on the N on the new *decumanus* which had been cut through the insula. This 4th century arrangement was seen by the pilgrim Egeria.

D. The Octagonal Church

In the second half of the 5th century, under the influence of the Gentile church, which, with its clergy of Greek culture, was progressively consolidating its influence in the Holy Land, the house of Simon Peter, including the house–church of the 1st to the 4th centuries, was razed. On the same spot, about 2 m above the earlier house–church, there was erected an octagonal church to mark in perpetuity the spot of the house of Simon. See Fig.

CAP.02. The church consisted in fact of two concentric octagons, with porticos on five sides. The central octagon had eight pilasters which supported a roof covered with tiles. The paving of both octagons was wholly in mosaic: that of the central octagon showed a peacock fanning its tail, while in the large octagon were found the remains of a nilotic mosaic. The portico had mosaics with a woven-reed design laid in circles. This is the church seen by the "Anonymous Placentinus" in 570 C.E.

With the Islamic invasion of Palestine in 638, Capernaum was abandoned, and the two sacred buildings of the city, the church of the house of St. Peter and the synagogue, began to fall into ruin. The later Arab inhabitants who settled within the bounds of the city which had been abandoned in the time of the Omayyads (661–750) had no interest in the Christian and Jewish edifices, and began to despoil them.

E. The Synagogues of Capernaum

The excavations have brought to light two synagogue buildings. In 1905, Kohl and Watzinger partially excavated the later building, which had been seen in ruins by the first explorers in the 19th century. The excavation begun by the two German archaeologists was taken up by the Franciscan custody of the Holy Land. In 1921, Orfali completed the excavation and also tried a partial reconstruction. This synagogue in white stone, the most beautiful and grand of those which have been excavated in the Holy Land, has been variously dated. The two German archaeologists dated it to the 2d and 3d centuries C.E.; Orfali, on the other hand, put it in the time of Jesus. With the reopening of the excavations in 1968, the problem of the dating of this building was addressed once more, and based on remains found under the paving, it was attributed to the 4th–5th century C.E.

1. The Late Synagogue. This building is composed of two edifices—the prayer room, and a vast court. The prayer room is in basilican form without an apse (24.34 × 17.25 m), and has a central nave surrounded by three lateral naves in the form of a horseshoe (on the E, N, and W sides) with Corinthian columns on plinths. On the W and E walls were benches, while on the S side were the ark and the chair of Moses. It probably never had a women's balcony. On the E side, the synagogue adjoined a vast court with a portico on three sides (the S portico was the shortest—11.26 m). On the outside it measures 24.34 × 13.34 m. The portico area faced the *cardo maximus* with three large windows, while on the N and S sides were two or three portals. The court was constructed after the synagogue had already been completed. The synagogue was visited toward the end of the 4th century by the pilgrim Egeria (cf. Petrus Diaconus, Geyer, 112) who referred to it as having "many steps" and walls of "square-hewn stones."

2. The Synagogue of the Roman Centurion. In 13 years of patient research (1969–81), the area under the late synagogue was explored. On the basis of this research, it was possible to ascertain the chronology of the late synagogue; the researchers also discovered the remains of the synagogue constructed by the Roman centurion (cf. Luke 7:5) atop a very ancient dwelling. Under the paving of this earlier synagogue and the adjacent houses were found ceramics of the MB, LB, Persian, Hellenistic, and first Roman periods.

The synagogue of the centurion has a rectangular plan with a slight displacement of the axis with respect to the synagogue of the 4th–5th century. The external perimeter of the first synagogue is the same as that of the later synagogue. The internal area of the synagogue of the centurion, however, is a little smaller, because of the considerable thickness of the wall, which are made of blocks of basalt (120–30 cm). On the inside, on the E wall, there was a sort of atrium, while the wall-bench must have occupied the whole length of the W wall. The paving was of basalt pebblework.

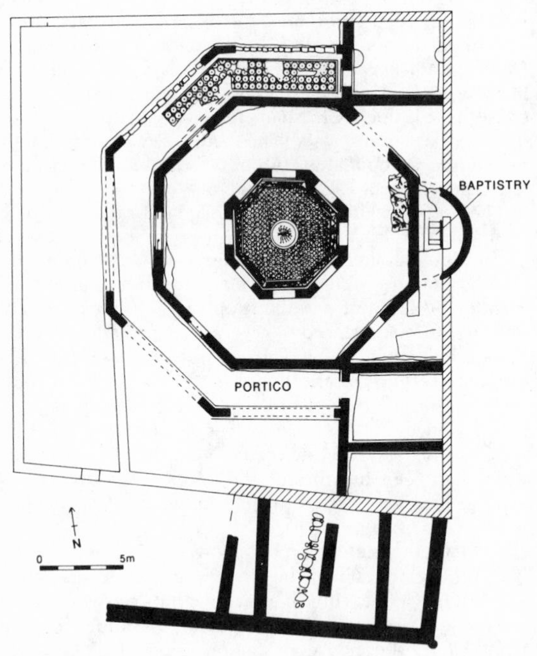

CAP.02. Plan of Octagonal Church at Capernaum—5th Century C.E. *(Redrawn from Corbo 1975: tav. IV.)*

Bibliography

Corbo, V. C. 1975. *Cafarnao I: Gli efifici della Città.* Jerusalem.

———. 1976. Edifici antichi sotto la sinagoga di Cafarnao. *Studia Hierosolymitana* 1: 159–76.

———. 1977. Il Mausoleo di Cafarnao. *LASBF* 27: 145–55.

———. 1982. Ripreso a Cafarnao lo scavo della Città. *LASBF* 32: 427–46.

———. 1983. Gli ultimi giorni di Cafarnao. *LASBF* 33: 373–90.

———. 1984. Le origini di Cafarnao al periodo persiano. *LASBF* 34: 371–84.

Corbo, V. C., and Loffreda, S. 1976. Sarcofago e pietra miliare di Cafarnao. *LASBF* 26: 272–76.
———. 1985. Resti del Bronzo Medio a Cafarnao. Relazione preliminare alla XVIII campagna. *LASBF* 35: 375–90.
Corbo, V. C.; Loffreda, S.; and Spijkerman, A. 1970. *La sinagoga di Cafarnao dopo gli scavi del 1969.* Jerusalem.
Kohl, H., and Watzinger, C. 1916. *Antiken Synagogen in Galilaea.*
Loffreda, S. 1974. *Cafarnao II: La ceramica.* Jerusalem.
———. 1983. Nuovi contributi di Cafarnao per la ceramologia palestinese. *LASBF* 33: 347–72.
———. 1984. Vasi in vetro e in argilla trovati a Cafarnao nel 1984. *LASBF* 34: 385–408.
Orfali, G. 1922. *Capharnaüm et ses ruines.* Paris.
Spijkerman, A. 1975. *Cafarnao III: Catalogo delle monete della citta.* Jerusalem.
Testa, E. 1972. *Cafarnao IV: I graffiti della casa di S. Pietro.* Jerusalem.

VIRGILIO C. CORBO

CAPHAR-SALAMA (PLACE) [Gk *Chapharsalama*]. The location of an ambush of the Seleucid army conducted by Jewish rebels ca. 163 B.C. (1 Macc 7:31). This encounter may be the same as that recorded in 2 Macc 14:16 as occurring at Dessau. The Seleucid army led by Nicanor was sent to Judea upon the request of Eliakim, the Seleucid candidate for high priest. This priest had ordered the execution of 60 pious Jews and as a result of his action, the Maccabees rallied opposition to Eliakim's religious and administrative activities.

Nicanor was an experienced general who had previously confronted the Judean rebels. He safely brought his army to Jerusalem but reportedly lost 5,000 men when he was ambushed at Caphar-salama. Subsequently he was forced to retreat to Jerusalem and to call for additional troops from Antioch to suppress the rebels.

The location of the ambush is not positively identified; however, it clearly took place near Jerusalem which was Nicanor's base of operations. Alternate locations of the battle site have been proposed, but Khirbet Selma (M.R. 167140), located halfway between Jerusalem and the Beth-horon pass, is frequently identified as the site (Goldstein *1 Maccabees* AB, 339–340). This argument is based upon the etymological similarity of the name and the geographic situation. The site is located near Jerusalem and would have provided the context for an ambush.

ROBERT W. SMITH

CAPHTOR (PERSON) [Heb *kaptor*]. CAPHTORIM. The seventh "offspring" of Egypt (Gen 10:13). The Caphtorim are described as originating in Caphtor and as displacing the Avvim along the coast as far as Gaza (Deut 2:23). They are explicitly associated with the Philistines in Jer 47:4 and Amos 9:7. Thus there is conjectured, without textual basis, the association of the phrase in Gen 10:14, "whence came the Philistines," with the Caphtorim rather than its grammatically closer subject, the Casluhim (so *BHS*; *IDB* 1: 534; Skinner *Genesis* ICC, 213; Speiser *Genesis* AB, 68; Strange 1980: 35 n. 132; Westermann *Genesis* BK, 519). Others accept the text as it now stands and apply the phrase to the Casluhim (cf. Cassuto 1964: 206–208; Kitchen 1973: 53; Rendsburg 1987; Wenham *Genesis* WBC, 225). In Jeremiah 47, the prophecy promises the destruction of Tyre, Sidon, and the Philistines from Caphtor. This passage also identifies Caphtor as an island or coastland. The possibility of the relation of the Caphtorim to the Cherethites is strengthened by the latter's association with the Philistines.

A problem associated with Caphtor is its identity. Its traditional identification with Crete (Vercoutter 1956) has been challenged with the proposal of Cyprus (Strange 1980; Merrillees 1982). The issue has been addressed in three areas: archaeology, philology, and geography. As to the archaeology, the absence of Cretan ceramic wares after the mid-15th century B.C. in Egypt and Ugarit, despite the presence of textual citations for Caphtor/Keftiu until the mid-14th century in Egypt and the mid-13th century at Ugarit, has been used to argue against Crete as an identification (Merrillees 1982: 247–48). However, a similar argument could be made for the Cypriote ware in Egypt (exclusive of Amarna) at the same time (Knapp 1983: 285–86; 1985). Further, the textual and pictorial evidence in the chapel of Rekhmire is closely tied together (Vercoutter 1956: 185–88) so that attempts to separate the Keftiu from "the isles in the midst of the sea" and from the Minoan dress worn by the figures (Strange 1980: 44–70) seem strained (Görg 1982; Kitchen 1983).

As to philology, the identifiable "offspring" of Egypt in Genesis 10 appears to reflect place names or people who lived in or near Egypt. The order of the names seems to be according to the number of consonants in the root, beginning with two (LUD) and proceeding to four (NAPHTUHIM and all the names of v 14). Thus the order of the names is probably not intended to follow a geographical sequence (Wenham *Genesis* WBC, 224). Caphtor is also mentioned in Egyptian (*kftiw, kftyw*), Akkadian (*kap-ta-ra*), Ugaritic (*kptr*), and Greek (*kabdēros*) texts (Vercoutter 1956; Strange 1980: 16–112). The 18th dynasty list of names from Egypt, with the title "to make names of Keftiu" has been used to argue a non-Greek, ancient Near Eastern environment more like Cyprus than Crete (Strange 1980: 94–96, 166). However, there can be no certainty as to what the list was intended to reflect (Astour 1982: 395) nor as to the accuracy of the analysis of the names (Vercoutter 1956: 46–47; Kitchen 1983).

A Theban topographical list of Amenophis III (Kitchen 1965: 5–6; Edel 1966: 33–60; Faure 1968) is best identified as a list of cities in the regions of *kftyw* and of *tny*, the latter to be identified with the Danaoi, i.e., Greeks of the Argolid (Faure 1968: 145–47; Helck 1971: 306–7; Kitchen 1973: 54; 1983: 159) rather than Rhodes (Edel 1966: 54–55; Vercoutter 1956: 56) or Adana in Cilicia (Strange 1980: 22). This identification is preferred due to the agreement of the remaining names with places in Crete (e.g., Amnisos, Knossos, and Lyktos) and the Danaoi region (Astour 1966; Edel 1966: 33–60; Kitchen 1966). Thus the text suggests an equation of *kftyw* with Crete.

The remaining issue is geographical. To place Caphtor in Cyprus it is necessary to relocate Alashiya, which has traditionally been associated with that island. Either it becomes a part of the island or it is located near Alalakh (Strange 1980: 172, 183). This latter possibility has been denied by Astour (1982: 395) and Muhly (1972: 202), who find no room for such an important kingdom on the

Syrian coast. Thus the identification of Caphtor with Crete remains a probability.

Bibliography

Astour, M. C. 1966. Aegean Place-Names in an Egyptian Inscription. *AJA* 70: 313–17.
———. 1982. Review of Strange 1980. *JAOS* 102: 395–96.
Cassuto, U. 1964. *A Commentary on the Book of Genesis. Pt. 2.* Trans. I. Abrahams. Jerusalem.
Edel, E. 1966. *Die Ortsnamenlisten aus dem Totentempel Amenophis III.* BBB 25. Bonn.
Faure, P. 1968. Toponymes Créto-Mycéniens dans une liste d'Amenophis III. *Kadmos* 7: 138–49.
Görg, M. 1982. Review of Strange 1980. *BiOr* 39: 533–37.
Helck, W. 1971. *Die Beziehungen Ägyptens zu Vorderasien im 3. und 2. Jahrtausend v. Chr.* 2d ed. ÄA 5. Wiesbaden.
Kitchen, K. A. 1965. Theban Topographical Lists, Old and New. *Or* n.s. 34: 1–9.
———. 1966. Aegean Place Names in a List of Amenophis III. *BASOR* 181: 23–24.
———. 1973. The Philistines. Pp. 53–78 in *POTT.*
———. 1983. Review of Strange 1980. *JSS* 28: 159–60.
Knapp, A. B. 1983. Review of Strange 1980. *Or* n.s. 52: 284–89.
———. 1985. Alashiya, Caphtor/Keftiu, and Eastern Mediterranean Trade: Recent Studies in Cypriote Archaeology and History. *JFA* 12: 231–50.
Merrillees, R. S. 1982. Review of Strange 1980. *RDAC,* 244–53.
Muhly, J. D. 1972. The Land of Alashiya: References to Alashiya in the Texts of the Second Millennium B.C. and the History of Cyprus in the Late Bronze Age. Vol. 1, pp. 201–19 in *Praktika tou Protou Diethnous Kyprologikou Synedriou.* Nicosia, Cyprus.
Rendsburg, G. A. 1987. Gen 10:13–14: An Authentic Hebrew Tradition Concerning the Origin of the Philistines. *JNSL* 13: 89–96.
Strange, J. 1980. *Caphtor/Keftiu. A New Investigation.* ATDan 14. Leiden.
Vercoutter, J. 1956. *L'Égypte et le monde égéen préhellénique.* Cairo.

RICHARD S. HESS

CAPITAL [Heb *kaptôr; koteret*]. Of the two Hebrew terms translated "capital," one always denotes a part of the Tabernacle menorah, except for two uses in prophecy; and the other signifies an architectural element of Solomon's Temple.

The term *kaptôr* is used repeatedly in the tabernacle texts of Exodus in juxtaposition with "flower" (*peraḥ*). The former word may have an architectural meaning, in that it is used twice elsewhere (Amos 9:1; Zeph 2:14) in contexts that suggest a major building element. The ancient versions all indicate a spherical or rounded object, like a kind of fruit (as in the Peshitta and Targums). These renderings may be derived from the rounded shape of a simple capital. However, taken together with "flower," it forms a hendiadys. The two words together denote a floral, or more specifically, a lily capital, since *peraḥ* most likely means "lily" (Meyers 1976: 24–26). This decorative, architectonic element is repeated three times on each of the six branches of the Tabernacle menorah; and the central stand of the menorah features four such arrangements (see Exod 25:33, 35 = 37:19, 21; 25:31, 34 = 37:17, 20; 25:36 = 37:22).

The other word for capital, *koteret,* signifies the elaborate architectural feature surrounding the columns Jachin and Boaz, which were set at the entrance to the forecourt (*ʾûlām*) of the Solomonic Temple (1 Kgs 7:16ff. = 2 Chr 4:12, 13; 2 Kgs 25:17 = Jer 52:22). These capitals, or double capitals, were made of bronze and were exceptionally ornate and large (at least five cubits high). Because they were decorated with floral forms ("lily-work" and "pomegranates"), they can be considered part of the floral capitals that were characteristic features of monumental architecture in the ancient world. The size, material, and decoration of the capitals contributes to the role of Jachin and Boaz as gateposts to the entrance of Yahweh's earthly dwelling (see Meyers 1983).

Bibliography

Meyers, C. 1976. The *Tabernacle Menorah.* Missoula, MT.
———. 1983. Jachin and Boaz in Religious and Political Perspective. *CBQ* 45: 167–78.

CAROL MEYERS

CAPITOLIAS (PLACE). See BEIT RAS (M.R. 230222).

CAPPADOCIA (PLACE). The great plateau which dominated central Asia Minor contrasted markedly with its surroundings. Flat, treeless, ringed by forested mountains, broiling in summer and gelid in winter, it constituted a land apart, difficult to reach but then easy to traverse. Its climatic extremes limited most agriculture to cereals and some fruits; most of its surface lay in pasture.

One long river, the Halys, traversed Cappadocia; another, the Euphrates, formed its eastern boundary; beyond lay Sophene, Atropatene, and the Parthian Empire. The Euphrates came to be regarded as the boundary between Parthia and the Roman Empire, beginning with a dramatic meeting at the Euphrates between Sulla and a Parthian representative of Mithridates II, with the Cappadocian king in attendance.

The Taurus and Antitaurus ranges on the south limited access to and from the Levant; just beyond these ranges lay Cilicia and Commagene. Boundaries to the west and north provided easier passage, leading to struggles with adjacent dynasties, especially in the 1st century B.C.

Cappadocia was notorious for possessing few cities, only two at the time of Christ. In Christian times this resulted in an unusual type of organization, based not on cities but on large districts containing numerous towns or villages.

Persian occupation of Asia Minor for centuries created an Iranian aristocracy ruling the native population. Local kings claimed descent from Darius the Great. After Alexander, the Ariarathid dynasty continued this claim and added Seleucid Greek lineage.

As the Seleucid Empire began to weaken in the mid-2d century B.C., Rome was drawn toward Cappadocia among others. Quarrels with the neighboring Galatians led to Roman mediation in 164 B.C. King Ariarathes IV was described at this time as "one of the true friends to the Romans" (Polyb. 31.7–8). About 160, envoys to Rome from Cappadocia spoke of "the friendly attitude" of King Ariarathes V (Diod. 31.28). The alliance between Rome and Cappadocia bore one unusual feature; instead of being with the king alone, it was "jointly with the Cappadocian king and with the tribe [*ethnos*]" (Strabo 12.2.11.540). That distinction probably arose from the unusual organization of the country into 10 administrative districts termed *strategiai,* one of them controlled by the powerful priest of Comana (Strabo 12.1.2.533). The nobles dwelt in "fortresses" and usually resisted centralized control.

To the north, the kingdom of Pontus arose from territory previously claimed by Cappadocia. By the late 2d century B.C., the expansionist monarch Mithridates VI Eupator of Pontus constituted a clear threat to Cappadocia, which he tried to control through a sister who became queen of Cappadocia, and then through a son who became king.

The Ariarathid line of kings ended early in the 1st century B.C. and Cappadocians elected a new royal house, that of Ariobarzanes I (Strabo 12.2.11.540; Justin 38.2.6–8).

Mithridates continued his interventions and drew Romans into Asia Minor to reinforce Cappadocian resistance. Two Roman allies already bordered Cappadocia, the kingdom of Bithynia and the country of the Galatians. A long struggle began about 95 B.C., which was aimed at adding Cappadocia to the roster of reliable Roman allies.

The Mithridatic Wars between Rome and Mithridates Eupator lasted some 25 years (89/88–63 B.C.) and led to fundamental alterations in the political map of Asia Minor. At the outset of the wars, Mithridates could order massacres of Romans along the Aegean coast and conduct operations as far west as Athens. He could rely on the assistance of his son-in-law, Tigranes the Great of Armenia, and of allies as far north as the Crimea. By the close of the wars, Mithridates was dead, Tigranes defeated, and part of Pontus a Roman province, with an allied king ruling the remainder.

Ariobarzanes I survived some five exiles at the hands of Mithridates or Tigranes, and handed over his kingdom to his apprehensive son about 63 B.C. In the next years, internal disruptions and a new external threat—Parthia—kept Cappadocia unsettled. Ariobarzanes II fell by assassination. His successor required the assistance of Cicero against enemies from within, and his kingdom appeared "stripped bare" by Roman creditors. Invasions were threatened from the directions of Pontus (Pharnaces II), Armenia (Artavasdes II), and Parthia (Orodes II; Pacorus I).

Perhaps against the odds, Cappadocia weathered these political storms and those of the Roman civil wars, too. In 47 B.C., Caesar came through Cappadocia, saw Pharnaces II, and conquered him at Zela. In the aftermath of Caesar's murder in 44 B.C., Cassius killed King Ariobarzanes III (Dio 47.33).

During the reign of his successor, Ariarathes X, a Parthian invasion of Asia Minor in 40 B.C. reminded Cappadocians of their vulnerability. A complicated internal struggle and intervention by Antony replaced this last member of the house of Ariobarzanes with a new king, familiar from Judean history: Archelaus I (Dio 49.32; Sullivan *ANRW* 2/7/2: 1149–61).

Archelaus enjoyed a long reign, over half a century from about 36 B.C. to A.D. 17. His father had held the powerful priesthood at Comana, and his grandfather had served as general in the Pontic army. Antony much admired Archelaus' mother, Glaphyra.

Augustus reconfirmed Archelaus despite his taking Antony's side at Actium (Dio 51.2). Some internal trouble is recorded (Jos. *JW* 1.507; Dio 57.17). However, Archelaus became an important king in the East, receiving additional territory to rule in Cilicia Tracheia and Armenia Minor (Dio 54.9; Strabo 12.2.11.540). Honors given him, his mother, or his son and daughter were recorded on stone in Athens, Olympia, Magnesia, Comana, and elsewhere (*OGIS* 357–63).

To judge from claims exercised by his descendants, Archelaus married a princess from the Armenian royal house. He passed on claims to the throne of Armenia to his grandson, Tigranes V (*ex regio genere Armeniorum* in the words of Augustus, *Res Gestae* 27). His daughter, Glaphyra, boasted of descent on her mother's side from Darius the Great (Jos. *JW* 1.476).

By marrying Queen Pythodoris, widow of Polemo II of Pontus, Archelaus linked two of the East's largest kingdoms (Strabo 12.3.29.556). Under the rule of this pair now fell a large territory in eastern Asia Minor, running from the Black Sea to the Mediterranean off Syria.

Archelaus also became an advisor to the Judean royal house, or a mediator in time of crisis (Jos. *JW* 1.507; 1.538; *Ant* 16.357). Herod came to view Archelaus "as one of his dearest friends" and in fact helped reconcile him with the Roman governor of Syria, Marcus Titius, after an unspecified argument (Jos. *Ant* 16.270).

Ultimately a marriage cemented these good relations. His daughter Glaphyra wedded Herod's son Alexander. Glaphyra's freely stated conviction that she outranked the other women at the Judean court through superior genealogy caused predictable friction. So did the habit Archelaus developed of intervening in Judean politics, as when he assisted two sons of Herod against their father. By 7/6 B.C., after Archelaus executed Glaphyra's husband, Herod returned her and her dowry (Sullivan *ANRW* 2/7/2: 1161–65).

The children of Glaphyra remained in Judea, and both her son Tigranes V and her grandson Tigranes VI attempted to rule Armenia. Her great-grandson, King Alexander (*PIR*[2] J 136), became the last royal ruler of Cilicia under Vespasian.

Glaphyra herself went next in marriage to King Juba of Mauretania (Jos. *Ant* 17.349). She returned once more to her father. Next, Herodes Archelaus, another son of Herod, married her, violating Jewish law. She died soon afterward.

Archelaus fell into disfavor with the emperor Tiberius on a charge of plotting revolution (Dio 57.17). He was summoned to Rome, tried before the senate, and probably condemned; at any rate, he died soon after that, most likely in A.D. 17. (Tac. *Ann.* 2.42). His son, Archelaus II, ruled a portion of Cilicia, at least until A.D. 36 (Tac. *Ann.* 6.41).

Cappadocia itself became a Roman province under Tiberius and remained that way. Vespasian grouped Cappadocia with several other regions in A.D. 72, and Trajan later divided that grouping, joining Cappadocia to Armenia Minor and Pontus. Diocletian divided the group again, leaving Cappadocia in two parts, only the western still called by that name. Late in the 4th century it was subdivided again, and the ecclesiastical boundaries—disputed between the bishops of Caesarea and of Tyana—ceased to coincide with the civil (Jones 1971: 183ff.). The ancient Cappadocian problems of central administration continued at least until Justinian, who complained that public lands there had frequently been alienated by private lessees.

The main lines of royal administration continued to be followed during the first centuries of the province, and the core of the previous kingdom remained permanently bereft of cities, which grew up on the Euphrates and along the trade routes from Cilicia but did not penetrate the interior.

Cappadocia retained a distinctive character for these thousand years (400 B.C.–A.D. 600). Its great size and important location made it a factor in Hellenistic and Roman history, as well as in the early spread of Christianity.

Bibliography

Frank, T. et al. 1939–40. *An Economic Survey of Ancient Rome.* Vol. 4, pt. 4. Baltimore.

Gwatkin, W. 1930. *Cappadocia as a Roman Procuratorial Province.* Princeton.

Jones, A. H. M. 1971. *The Cities of the Eastern Roman Provinces.* 2d ed. Oxford.

Sullivan, R. D. 1989. *Near Eastern Royalty and Rome, 100–30 BC.* Toronto.

RICHARD D. SULLIVAN

CARABASION (PERSON) [Gk *Karabasiōn*]. A descendant of Bani who divorced his foreign wife during Ezra's reform (1 Esdr 9:34). Although 1 Esdras is often assumed to have been compiled from Ezra, Carabasion does not appear among the list of names in Ezra 10. Omissions such as this also raise questions about 1 Esdras being used as a source by Ezra. Furthermore, problems associated with dating events and identifying persons described in 1 Esdras have cast doubt on the historicity of the text. Heltzer (1977: 68) argues that Carabasion is a Gk rendering of the Heb *qrbʿšh.*

Bibliography

Heltzer, M. 1977. Ein Epigraphischer Blick auf das 3. Esrabuch. *Bib* 58: 62–72.

MICHAEL DAVID MCGEHEE

CARAVAN. See TRAVEL AND COMMUNICATION.

CARIA (PLACE) [Gk *Karia*]. Rugged, mountainous region of southwest Asia Minor, bordered on the west by the Aegean Sea, the southwest by the Mediterranean Sea, along the Meander River by Lydia, and to the east by Phrygia and Lycia (1 Macc 15:23). Caria's early political history was dominated by independent cities of which Halicarnassus (the birthplace of Herodotus), Miletus (Acts 20:15–17; 2 Tim 4:20), and Onidus (Acts 27:7) were chief. Caria was ruled successively by Persia and later Rhodes (cf., Ptolemy 5.2), until Rome restored its freedom in 167 B.C.E. (Polyb. 30.5.12–16, 21.3–5, 31; Livy 45.25). In 139 B.C.E., the Carians were granted Roman citizenship (Livy 49.15) and in 129 B.C.E., Caria became part of the Roman province of Asia.

The coastal cities of Caria were populated primarily by Greeks, but the rest of the region had a mixed population which included a high density of Jews, evidenced by a number of Jewish inscriptions, epitaphs and synagogues from the region. According to 1 Macc 15:23, the Roman senate sent a letter in 139–138 B.C.E. favoring the Jews of Caria and the cities of Myndus, Halicarnassus, and Knidos, which, at the time, were independent enclaves within Caria. According to Josephus (*Ant* 14.244–46), the Romans intervened on behalf of the Jews of Melitus, guaranteeing their right to observe the Sabbath and to live according to their customs. The cities of Caria were only mentioned in the NT in connection with Paul's missionary travels at which time they were certainly evangelized. Ignatius of Antioch addressed a letter to a church in the Carian city of Tralles.

SCOTT T. CARROLL

CARITES [Heb *kārî*]. A group of mercenaries loyal to the Davidic house (2 Kgs 11:4, 19). In the account of the revolt against Queen ATHALIAH (2 Kings 11), they were one of the groups called on by JEHOIADA the priest to protect the Davidic scion JOASH, to seize and execute the usurper Athaliah, and to rid the land of the foreign cult of Baal. The Carites are not mentioned in the parallel account in 2 Chr 22:10–23:21. They appear to be mentioned in the Heb consonantal text of 2 Sam 20:23. However the MT marginal Qere "CHERETHITES" (a change from *kry* to *krty*) is followed by the majority of scholars (e.g., McCarter *II Sam* AB, 433; but see Delcor 1978: 415 n. 21) on the basis of its standing in parallel with PELETHITES and of the LXX (B: *cheleththi;* A: *chereththi*).

Attempts have been made to identify the biblical Carites with the Carians, a people of the 1st millennium B.C.E. whose homeland CARIA lay in SW Anatolia. Carians are known to have served as mercenaries in Egypt and Nubia under pharaohs Psammetichus I and II. However, the attempt to link them with the biblical Carites has been called into question on linguistic grounds (see Cogan and Tadmor *II Kings* AB, 126 and Schmitt *RLA* 5: 424). Although the suggestion has been made that the Carites as a royal guard were descended from the Cherethites (e.g., Greenfield *IDB* 1: 557), the evidence for this remains inconclusive at best.

Bibliography

Delcor, M. 1978. Les Kéréthim et les Crétois. *VT* 28: 409–22.

CARL S. EHRLICH

CARKAS (PERSON) [Heb *karkas*]. See MEHUMAN (PERSON).

CARMEL (PLACE) [Heb *karmel*]. A town in the Judean wilderness (Josh 15:55) located approximately eight miles southeast of Hebron (M.R. 162092). Carmel was the site of a monument built by Saul (1 Sam 15:12); the location of the sheepshearing business of Nabal (1 Samuel 25); and the home of Abigail the wife of David, formerly married to Nabal (1 Sam 27:3; 30:5; 2 Sam 23:35; 1 Chr 11:37).

The monument Saul erected in Carmel following the defeat of the Amalekites was probably a victory stela signifying that he claimed authority over the region around Carmel (*HAIJ,* 138). Nabal's response to David's request for supplies (1 Sam 25:9–11) implies that the local inhabitants in the area of Carmel recognized Saul's authority as opposed to David's (*HAIJ,* 166). Aharoni suggested that David made incursions into the area, to Carmel and other sites (1 Sam 23:15, 24b; 25:2), from a base of operation, a fortress, perhaps Masada, a likely candidate because Iron Age sherds have been found at the site (*LBHG* 289–90, n. 9). While the reference to Carmel in the context of Josh 15:21–62 appears to provide information concerning the tribal period, many scholars suggest it reflects the administrative districts and towns during the time of the Judean Monarchy (*LBHG* 347), a period when Carmel was a part of the district of Ziph (*LBHG* 354–55). During the biblical period, Carmel was a fortification and an important part of the defense system of the Judean desert. Though the region appears to be a useless wasteland, on the contrary, in ancient times it was a politically strategic area with an economy based on animal breeding. For these reasons, the Judean desert had two lines of fortifications protecting the highways of the area, one located along the Dead Sea, the other several miles west. Carmel was a part of the western line of fortresses (Har-El, 1981: 13–14). The modern name el-Kirmil, the biblical Carmel, illustrates how the ancient name has been preserved, though the modern Arabic name includes the definite article (*LBHG* 121).

Bibliography

Har-El, M. 1981. Jerusalem and Judea: Roads and Fortifications. *BA* 44: 8–19.

LaMoine F. DeVries

CARMEL CAVES (M.R. 146230). Prehistoric caves in Mount Carmel. The term "Mount Carmel Caves" unmistakably refers to the three which were excavated under the direction of D. Garrod between 1929–34: Tabun, Skhul, and El-Wad. The three are located in a rock cliff on the S bank of Nahal Mearot, or "the River of the Caves," with a fourth one, the cave of Gamal which yielded no ancient remains. The cliff is some 20 km S of Haifa, at the border between Mt. Carmel and the coastal plain. The Tabun excavations were renewed by A. Jellinek between 1967–71, then by A. Ronen (1973–84). A test excavation at El-Wad was carried out by O. Bar-Yosef in 1981.

A. Tabun

The cultural deposits in Tabun were about 25 m thick, a long record with few parallels in the world. Two major units were present: Lower and Middle Paleolithic, each occupying approximately half of the deposits.

The Lower Paleolithic consisted of an Acheuleo-Yabrudian sequence (layers G[?], F, and E) and an Amudian episode located near the top of layer E. The material from layer G was too poor to be indicative. The Acheuleo-Yabrudian had hand axes and sidescrapers as its main tool types, with ratios varying from almost exclusively hand axes to almost exclusively sidescrapers. The dominant technology was flake production, non-Levallois. The Amudian episode was very different: typical tool types were burins and knives—typically *Upper* Paleolithic tools; the technology used in the Amudian was a highly sophisticated blade production, also typical of the Upper Paleolithic. There also appears an original and exclusive phenomenon of reusing older tools for shaping new ones.

The Middle Paleolithic consists of the Mousterian culture (layers D, C, and B), with two main phases. The lower (D) has typically long flakes and long points, the younger (layers C, B) has mainly large flakes and large points. The Levallois technique is widely used throughout the Middle Paleolithic sequence of Tabun.

During layer C, a shaft (or chimney) started to open in the ceiling of Tabun (hence its name, which means "the Oven"); it eventually widened to such a point that it rendered the cave uninhabitable. Afterward (layer B), the cave became a trap into which deer were driven and butchered. The accumulation of layer B may have ended some 40,000 years ago. After that only scattered remains were deposited ranging from the last 10,000 years (layer A), which marks the end of the Paleolithic occupation of the cave.

The Lower Paleolithic levels in Tabun are made of quartz and sand; the Middle Paleolithic levels are silt and clay, with a transitional zone between the two sediments (in layers E and D). The changing sediment probably indicates fluctuations in the sea level, which was probably high during the accumulation of sand, and low during the accumulation of silt and clay. See Fig. CAR.01. These fluctuations are attributed to Isotope Stages 5 and 4 re-

CULTURE	EL-WAD	SKHUL	TABUN	TIME B.C.E.	CLIMATE ← DRY WET →
HISTORICAL PERIOD, NEOLITHIC	A	A	A	9,000	
NATUFIAN	B	GAP	GAP		MEDITERRANEAN WOODLAND
KEBARAN					
ATHLITIAN	C			20,000	
AURIGNACIAN	D				
	E			40,000	
	F				
MOUSTERIAN	GAP	B	B		MEDITERRANEAN WOODLAND
		GAP	C		
	EROSION	EROSION	EROSION		
	G	C_1	D	70,000	
YABRUDIAN AND AMUDIAN	BEDROCK	GAP ?	E	100,000 ?	SWAMP
		C_2 ?			
ACHEULIAN			F		
			G	150,000 ?	

CAR.01. Sequence of cultural deposits in Mt. Carmel caves.

spectively, or the last episode of high sea stand (130,000–80,000 years ago, possibly 20 m above present level), followed by the last glacial period with its very low sea stand (100 or more m below its present level). Some palynological evidence indicates a dry period, with few trees, when the sand accumulated, followed by a wetter climate, and hence a forested landscape, during the silt and clay layers. This theory still needs confirmation.

A Neanderthal burial was found in the Middle Paleolithic of Tabun, a female of 30–40 years of age who was placed in a contracted position. The precise Mousterian layer to which the burial belongs is unclear. Additional fragments of human bones were also found in the Mousterian of Tabun.

B. Skhul

This is the easternmost in the group of Carmel Caves, and had two cultural phases. The lower (layer C2) was a sandy deposit with Acheuleo-Yabrudian(?) remains and was preserved only in small, thin patches with very scanty remains (including hand axes) which do not permit a definite analysis. Above it were some 2.5 m of Middle Paleolithic remains in a reddish silty clay (layers C1 and B). The tools were like those of the younger Mousterian in Tabun, with abundant Levallois technique. The most important find in Skhul was its cemetery (layer B) with 10 fairly well preserved individuals. There were isolated remains of other individuals. These burials contain the remains of anatomically Modern Man, or *Homo sapiens,* as distinguished from the Neanderthal found in the nearby cave of Tabun. The precise chronological relations between these two neighbor populations remains unclear. In Skhul, like in Tabun, the Paleolithic occupation ended with the Mousterian. The upper layer (A) contained the mixed remains of the last 10,000 years.

C. El-Wad

El-Wad is the longest cave in Mount Carmel, penetrating some 50 m into the rock. At its base it contained the remains of Mousterian culture (layer G), overlain by Upper Paleolithic (layers F, E, D, and C) and Natufian (layer B; 12,000–11,000 years ago). El-Wad was then unoccupied except for occasional visitors and shepherds of the last 10,000 years (layer A). The entire sequence is 2–3 m thick.

The Mousterian at the base of El-Wad resembles that of Skhul and the upper part of Tabun, but the precise temporal relations between the three Mousterian occupations is unknown. El-Wad is the only cave among the Mount Carmel classics to have Upper Paleolithic and Natufian cultures.

The Upper Paleolithic starts with an Ahmarian phase, rich in retouched and pointed blades, and poor in grattoirs (end scrapers) and burins (layers F, E). This phase is followed by the Levantine Aurignacian culture, with its typical steep scrapers and abundant burins (layers D, C). In layer B, in a reddish silty clay, the Natufian cultural remains were found. The dominant tools (80–90 percent of the total) are tiny implements called microliths, mainly in the shape of lunates. Besides these there are some burins and scrapers, together with a new invention, the sickle blade, with its typical luster due to grass cutting. The Natufian of El-Wad yielded stone structures, mortars and pestles (in basalt or limestone), and a cemetery containing about 80 burials of anatomically Proto-Mediterranean man. A few individuals had decorations made of bone and seashell. Some had art objects associated with them (i.e., a human head covered in stone and a deer made of bone). The Natufian culture represents the earliest sedentary society in the Near East, and possibly in the world.

As with the other Carmel Caves, the upper layer (A) had mixed remains from the Neolithic period till the present.

AVRAHAM RONEN

CARMEL, MOUNT

CARMEL, MOUNT (PLACE) [Heb *har hakkarmel*]. A range of hills and mountains running SE from modern Haifa on whose promontory occurred the cataclysmic encounter between Elijah and the prophets of Baal (1 Kgs 18). Carmel, a common noun, means "garden," "vineyard," or "orchard" (Isa 10:18; 16:10; etc.). The name may reflect the fertility of Mt. Carmel's slopes which catch the Mediterranean moisture in the westerly sea breezes. Baly gives the annual rainfall as 28 inches (*GB,* 58). The abundance of these mountain slopes is reflected in modern times by the remnants of forests (mentioned by Baly *GB,* 81, see also Isa 33:9; Jer 46:18), by the presence of olives and grain, and by vineyards which produce the famous Mt. Carmel wine. Even today something of the slopes' beauty may be seen in the Bahai garden shrine. Mt. Carmel's beauty is certainly celebrated in the Bible. Cant 7:5 says the loved one's "head crowns you like Carmel, and your flowing locks are like purple." Mt. Carmel is compared to the Plain of Sharon, Lebanon, Tabor, Bashan, and Gilead (Isa 35:2; Jer 50:19). In reversal, a drought makes Mt. Carmel an area of desolation (Isa 33:9; Amos 1:2; Nahum 1:4).

What is usually called Mt. Carmel, Jebel Kurmul or Jebel Mar Elyas, is a headland that juts out into the Mediterranean Sea and helps to form to the N the Bay of Acre together with the modern harbor of Haifa. It appears on maps as a sharply pointed cape on an otherwise mostly smooth coast all the way to Egypt. The headland is the NW end of a 13-mile long, 5- to 8-mile-wide range of hills of hard Cenomanian limestone (formed ca. 55 million years ago). This limestone weathers into a rich red *terra rossa* soil, adding to the areas' fertility. The headland itself rises to ca. 556 feet and the range reaches ca. 1800 feet near its southeastern end. On the N, overlooking the Esdraelon Valley and the Kishon (Mugatta) River (Judg 4:7), the slope tends to be steeper than the S which slopes more gradually toward the Plain of Sharon. The range actually splits Palestine S–N with Sharon and Philistia to the S and Esdraelon and the coastal plain of Acco to the N. Though a narrow beach goes along the sea, traffic of antiquity normally turned inward and went through passes like the ones near Jokneam (Josh 12:22) and Megiddo.

Mountain caves such as those in Wadi el Mugharah (Valley of the Caves) overlooking Sharon, were inhabited from the Lower Old Stone Age through the Middle Stone Age (150,000–10,000 B.C.). Towards the end of this time, the Natufian period included the earliest art found in Palestine—carved animal heads of tool handles, a human head carved in limestone, pendants and beads of dentalium shells, etc. Palestinian Man, *Palaeanthropus Palestinus,* viewed by some as a hybrid of Neanderthal man and modern *Homo sapiens,* inhabited the caves. Others claim there are 10,000 years between the two types. These caves and mountains appear to hold prehistoric significance as the cradle of human development in Palestine (*EAEHL* 1: 290–98; see CARMEL CAVES).

Historically, Mt. Carmel has been mentioned in the writings of both Egypt and Mesopotamia. An indirect reference may be found in the records of the Egyptian pharaoh Pepi, ca. 2350 B.C. They mention a mountain running down to the sea, called "the Nose of the Gazelle's Head," behind which troops landed. Mt. Carmel appears as *Roš Qadeš,* "Holy Head," in the Egyptian records of Thutmose III (1490–1436 B.C.; as No. 48 in his topographical list), Ramses II (1301–1234 B.C.) and Ramses III (1195–1164 B.C.). This suggests that at least in the 2d millennium Mt. Carmel may have been a holy place or sanctuary. Aharoni (*LBHG,* 99, 171) identifies the Egyptian Mount User (e.g., *wsr* "strong, mighty") with Mt. Carmel in Papyrus Anastasi I from the time of Ramses II. In the annals of the Neo-Assyrian King, Shalmaneser III (841 B.C.), Mt. Carmel appears as Ba'li-ra'si (Safar 1951: 19). It is here that Tyre and Jehu, King of Israel, paid tribute to Shalmaneser.

This payment of tribute raises the issue of boundaries. The Mt. Carmel area seems to have formed a natural barrier that placed it in a border region. In the tribal boundaries of Joshua, the forest hills of Mt. Carmel form the southern boundary of the Tribe of Asher (19:26). Some say Mt. Carmel itself was part of Asher while others maintain that it was included in the northern border of western Manasseh (Kallai *HGB,* 176–77; *GTTOT,* 189 n. 173—the borders of Asher "touched" Mt. Carmel). Josephus included it in the tribal territory of Issachar (*GTTOT,* 352). Mt. Carmel may have also marked the border between Tyre and Israel during the period of the divided monarchy. Based on the Neo-Assyrian evidence for the location of the payment of tribute by Jehu and Tyre noted above, Astour (*IDBSup,* 141) maintains (1) that this confirms Mt. Carmel as the border between Tyre and Israel (Sidon and Israel says Simons [*GTTOT,* 87]); (2) that an Assyrian Army crossed Israel as early as 841 B.C. and provides that background for Jehu's seizure of power that year; and that Carmel was a sacred mountain, dedicated to the "Baal of the Promontory" (*IDBSup,* 141).

This evidence together with the Egyptian evidence cited above indicates the religious significance of the mountain and also a possible explanation for the choice of this site by the biblical writers as a background for the Elijah-Elisha cycle. In 1 Kings 18, Mt. Carmel is selected for the famous duel between Elijah and the 450 prophets of Baal and the 400 prophets of Asherah. There Elijah rebuilds an old altar and lifts a challenge to see whose deity would prevail. In this story, as the extrabiblical evidence would suggest, Baal is defeated by Yahweh on Baal's own ground (de Vaux *AncIsr,* 280–81). However, one must note that Baal worship, though dealt a significant defeat in the biblical story, was not eliminated in Israel. The exact location of the subsequent slaughter of the prophets of Baal is not known. One tradition locates it at el-Muragen (Karten Karmel), "the place of burned sacrifices" in the SE, while another refers to Tell el-Qassis, "the mound of Priest" NE of Mt. Carmel. This has become the traditional site. Subsequent to these momentous events, the Elijah cycle narrates the flight of Elijah to Mt. Horeb because of the wrath of Jezebel (1 Kgs 19:1–18). There he discovers a cave (v 9) where he encounters the Lord, the God of Hosts in a "still small voice" (v 12). Some attempts have been made to add to the religious significance of Mt. Carmel by identifying this cave with a grotto on the SW corner of the Mt. Carmel cape. This grotto is part of the antiquities site of Tel Shiqmona (LB–Byzantine period; includes a Byzantine monastery plus later Arab occupation; *EAEHL* 4: 1101–9). The religious significance of Mt. Carmel is perpetuated also with Elisha, Elijah's disciple. In 2 Kgs 2:25 and 4:25, the area seems to serve as a spiritual retreat for Elisha.

Mt. Carmel continues as a religious site into the Hellenistic and Roman periods. Pseudo-Skylax (4th century B.C.) records a temple to Zeus on Mt. Carmel (Aharoni *LBHG,* 361). Pythagoras meditated there. Vespasian and Trajan sacrificed there to the deity, Carmel. Tacitus notes that the priests of the Carmel oracle assured Vespasian that he would become master of the world. The sacredness of the area is indicated by a stone foot, discovered by Avi-Yonah in 1952 while visiting the museum of the Monastery of Elijah. The inscription of the foot reads, "To Heliopoleitan Zeus Carmel from Gaius Julius Eutychas, citizen of Caesarea." The foot was not part of a statue but a votive offering to the deity, Carmel, who is identified with Zeus.

Within the Christian period, Mt. Carmel has been equated with the monastic tradition. Monasteries were located on the summit for centuries and the mountain gives its name to the Carmelite monastic movement originating from a group of hermits who came under the supervision of St. Berthold ca. 1150. A 19th-century monastery of St. Elias continues this ancient tradition.

In modern times, the sacred character of the mountain also continues in the Bahai garden shrine with the tombs of the Bahai leaders Bab-ed-din (d. 1850) and Abdul Baha (Abbas Effendi, 1844–1921). Baly further notes that in the 1930s people still spoke with awe of the "Forty Oaks," a sacred grove still standing on the heights of Mt. Carmel. Subsequently this sacred aura has been lost for "in January, 1970, it was a sorry mess," according to Baly (*GB,* 173 n. 11).

Bibliography

Ap-Thomas, D. R. 1960. Elijah on Mount Carmel. *PEQ* 92: 146–55.

Ritter, C. 1866. *The Comparative Geography of Palestine and the Sinaitic Peninsula.* 4 vols. New York. Repr. 1968.

Safar, F. 1951. A Further Text of Shalmaneser III. *Sumer* 7: 3–21.

HENRY O. THOMPSON

CARMI (PERSON) [Heb *karmî*]. CARMITES. **1.** The fourth son of Reuben. He went down to Egypt with his father when the family of Jacob migrated from Canaan to Goshen (Gen 46:9; Exod 6:14; 1 Chr 5:3). He was the ancestor of the family of the Carmites (Num 26:6).

2. A man from Judah, he was the son of Zabdi (Josh 7:1, 18). Carmi was the father of Achan, the man who violated the religious ban imposed by Joshua upon the city of Jericho (Josh 6:17–19). Noth (*NHI* 64) has identified

Carmi, the father of Achan, with the Reubenite family of Carmi (Num 26:6). In 1 Chr 2:7 the son of Carmi is listed as Achar, "the troubler of Israel." This variation in name was probably a deliberate effort to bring out a play on the Hebrew word for trouble: *ʿākār ʿōkēr yiśrāʾēl*, "Achar, the troubler of Israel."

In 1 Chr 4:1 Carmi, Perez, Hezron, Hur, and Shobal are listed as the sons of Judah. Of these, however, only Perez was Judah's son (1 Chr 2:4). Hezron was the son of Perez (1 Chr 2:5); Hur was the son of Caleb (1 Chr 2:19), who was the son of Hezron (1 Chr 2:18). Shobal was the son of Hur (1 Chr 2:50). Carmi should be reckoned as a descendant of Judah through Zerah and his son Zimri (1 Chr 2:5). The LXX identifies Zabdi, the father of Carmi, with Zimri (see Josh 7:1 where the LXX reads Zambri). For this reason, *BHS* proposes to read Caleb (1 Chr 2:18) or Chelubai (2 Chr 2:9) in place of Carmi in 1 Chr 4:1, thus presenting six generations of Judahites, from Judah to Shobal.

Claude F. Mariottini

CARMONIANS [Lat *Carmonii*]. A people referred to in the apocalyptic visions of war and calamity that constitute chaps. 15–16 of 2 Esdras (15:30). The Carmonians appear in the E, devastate the land of Assyria, and then engage in battle with the "dragons of Arabia." The Carmonians were a people culturally related to the Medes and Persians, who resided in the province of Carmania N of the Strait of Hormuz on the Persian Gulf (cf. Kerman in SE Iran). The vision in 2 Esdras 15:28–33 in all likelihood contains veiled allusions to the A.D. 259–60 campaign of the Sassanian king Shapur I (i.e., "the Carmonians"), who devastated Syria and Cappadocia (i.e., "the land of the Assyrians") and captured the Roman emperor Valerian. The Palmyrene prince Odenathus, husband of the famous Zenobia, then attacked Shapur, apparently in a vain attempt to liberate Valerian. For a detailed discussion of these events, see Myers, *1–2 Esdras* AB, 349–51.

Gary A. Herion

CARNAIM (PLACE) [Gk *Karnaim*]. One of five cities in Gilead in which Jews were taken captive by the Gentile citizens (1 Macc 5:26). The city is widely identified with modern Sheih Sa'ad "because of its ancient city walls and also on account of its especially suitable situation as a place of refuge at the confluence of nahr el-aḥreir (ḥarīr) and wadi ezrāʿ" (*GTTOT,* 425). Goldstein (*1 Maccabees* AB, 303) thinks the site is the same as Ashtoreth-karnaim mentioned in Gen 14:5; Josh 9:10, 12:4; and Amos 6:13, and that the name implies that the goddess Ashtoreth (Ashtaroth) was worshipped in the city's temple in the form of a goddess with horns.

The Maccabean Revolt met with early success, leading to the Jews' retaking the Temple in 164 B.C. Gentiles retaliated in Gilead under a military leader named Timothy. Many Jews in Gilead fled to a stronghold at the city of Dathema, from which they sent to Judas for aid. En route to rescue the refugees, Judas learned from a group of Nabateans that Jews were also under attack in the cities of Bozrah, Bosor-in-Alema, Chaspho, Maked, and Carnaim, as well as other cities (1 Macc 5:24–27). The last of these Jews to be liberated were those living in Carnaim. Judas attacked Timothy and his Arab mercenaries on the bank of a tributary of the Yarmuk River, causing the enemy to retreat to nearby Carnaim (5:43–44; cf. 2 Macc 12:21, 26). There they took refuge in the Temple of Ashtaroth, perhaps thinking the Jews would not attack a temple, even though dedicated to a pagan goddess, or hoping the goddess would save them (Goldstein *1 Maccabees* AB, 303). If so, they were fatally mistaken, for Judas captured the city and burned the temple and Timothy's army.

Bibliography

Abel, F.-M. 1923. Topographie des Campagnes Machabéenes. *RB* 32: 495–521.

Tedesche, S., and Zeitlin, S. 1950. *The First Book of Maccabees.* New York.

———. 1956. *The Second Book of Maccabees.* New York.

Paul L. Redditt

CARPUS (PERSON) [Gk *Karpos*]. A resident of Troas and presumably a Christian, with whom Paul left some of his belongings (2 Tim 4:13). It may have been at the house of Carpus that the Christians of Troas held their gatherings, and perhaps Carpus was Paul's host on the occasion of his visit and preaching when Eutychus fell asleep and tumbled out of the window (Acts 20:7–12). For some reason, before one of his departures from Troas (apparently referred to in Acts 20:13), Paul had left a cloak, books, and parchments with Carpus, items Timothy was later asked to retrieve and bring to Paul in his imprisonment.

In anticipation of winter (cf. 2 Tim 4:21), Paul needed the cloak (called in Greek a *phailonēs,* usually understood as the equivalent of the Lat *paenula*—i.e., a seamless overcoat with a hole for the head and woven to resist rain—Johnson 1950: 8). Such overcoats (and other types) are known to have been made from black glossy wool. This wool, world-famous at the time, came from the region near Laodicea where it was woven, although it is uncertain whether the color's source was a special breed of black sheep or dyes. *Paenulae* later became popular in Rome and eventually developed into the ecclesiastical chasuble.

Paul was also concerned to have "the books, and above all the parchments" (4:13). "Books" (*biblia*) is normally interpreted as the more general term which includes the "parchments" (*membranai*). But Skeat translates: "the books—I mean the parchment notebooks" (1979: 174). The parchments, most likely in scroll form, were made from sheepskin and goatskin and naturally were more expensive than the papyrus rolls which would have made up other types of books. Papyrus was still the usual writing material at the time. Many suggestions have been advanced concerning the contents of Paul's books (e.g., letters to him, copies of his own correspondence, sacred books) and parchments (e.g., OT writings, official copies of the Lord's words, Paul's certificate of citizenship), but there is no way of knowing what they contained. It has been pointed out, however, that while *membranai* means "parchments," it is actually a transliteration into Greek of the Latin term *membrana* by which the Romans meant specifically a parchment notebook (in page form) used for notes, memoranda, or rough drafts (Skeat 1979: 173). Thus, if Paul were using the term in that sense he could have been referring to notebooks he especially valued, perhaps containing lists of Christians in various communities. Whatever their contents, Carpus was trusted by Paul to keep them until he sent for them.

Bibliography

Johnson, S. E. 1950. Laodicea and Its Neighbors. *BA* 13: 1–18.
Skeat, T. C. 1979. "Especially the Parchments": A Note on 2 Timothy IV.13. *JTS* 30: 173–77.

FLORENCE MORGAN GILLMAN

CARSHENA (PERSON) [Heb *karšĕnāʾ*]. One of the seven princes of Persia and Media who were the advisers of King Ahasuerus (Esth 1:14). These men were the most prominent at the court (lit. "sat first in the kingdom") and had the privilege of personal audience with the king (lit. "saw the king's face"). That such a council of seven prominent nobles customarily advised the Persian monarch is well known from extrabiblical sources (for references see Paton *Esther* ICC, 153 and especially *ISBE* 3: 971). Based on the MT form, the name is very likely Persian (see the arguments of Millard 1977: 481–88, who counters the excessive caution of Moore [*Esther* AB, 41–44] regarding the Hebrew spelling) and probably identical with the name *kur-iš-na* (Zadok 1976: 246) occurring in the Persepolis Fortification Tablets (see Mayrhofer 1973: 8.785). The etymology is uncertain. Millard (1977: 485) notes Mayrhofer's analysis into Avestan *Karša* "furrows" plus the patronymic suffix-*ina*. Zadok (1976: 246) offers the alternative explanation that it is from Sogdian *kršn* "(beautiful) form." It would appear that the form of the name in the LXX, *arkesaios,* omits the patronymic (Millard 1977: 485).

Bibliography

Mayrhofer, M. 1973. *Onomastica Persipolitana.* SÖAW 286. Vienna.
Millard, A. R. 1977. The Persian Names in Esther and the Reliability of the Hebrew Text. *JBL* 96: 481–88.
Zadok, R. 1976. On Five Iranian Names in the Old Testament. *VT* 26: 246.

FREDERIC W. BUSH

CARVING. See ART AND ARCHITECTURE.

CASEMATE. See FORTIFICATIONS.

CASIPHIA (PLACE) [Heb *kāsipyāʾ*]. A place in the vicinity of the Ahava River (N Babylonia), where some Jerusalem "temple servants" apparently had been living in exile; Ezra sent a delegation to Iddo, "the leading man at the place of Casiphia" (Heb *hārōʾš bĕkāsipyāʾ hammāqôm*) to solicit volunteers to return with him to Jerusalem where they could presumably resume services as "ministers for the temple of God" (Ezra 8:15–20). Early versions reflect uncertainty about whether Casiphia (mentioned twice in v 17) was a proper (place) name or a common noun related to Heb *kesep,* "silver, money." LXX-A assumes that Iddo was a leading man at "the place of the treasury" (*en tō topō tou gazophylakiou,* 1 Esdr 8:44–45 [—Eng 45–46]), while LXX-B assumes that Ezra sent the delegation to the leaders "with money of the place" (*en argyriō tou topou,* i.e., with money presumably of Ahava, 8:17). The place of Casiphia is unknown, although Winckler (1901: 509–30) suggests that it might be identified with Ctesiphon on the Tigris River ca. 20 miles SSE of Baghdad. See also MERARI (PERSON) and SHEMAIAH (PERSON).

Bibliography

Winckler, H. 1901. *Altorientalische Forschungen.* Ser. 2, vol. 3. Leiden.

GARY A. HERION

CASLUHIM [Heb *kaslūḥîm*]. Sixth "offspring" of Egypt, concerning whom it is said, "whence came the Philistines" (Gen 10:13–14). On the basis of the plural suffix marker, *-îm,* this figure seems to be the name of an ethnic group. The order of the names appears to be according to the number of consonants in the root, beginning with two (LUD) and proceeding to four (NAPHTUHIM and all the names of v 14). Thus the order of the names is probably not intended to follow a geographical sequence (Wenham *Genesis 1–15* WBC, 224).

There are two problems surrounding the Casluhim: who are they, and is the gloss concerning the origin of the Philistines meant to apply to them? As to the first, *Pseudo-Jonathan* identifies the origin as *pentapôliṭî,* i.e., of Cyrene (cf. *pnṭsk(y)nʾy* of two of the fragmentary targums). However, the two problems are related since those who compare Amos 9:7 (as well as Jer 47:4 and Deut 2:23) and transfer the gloss to the following name, Caphtorim, tend to associate the Casluhim with some part of Egypt (cf. Skinner *Genesis* ICC, 213, whose review of the options includes the nomadic Libyans of Herodotus, *nasamōnes* near the oasis of Amon) or provide no identification (Speiser *Genesis* AB, 68–69; Westermann 1984: 519).

On the other hand, those who retain the natural Hebrew grammar and associate the Casluhim with the home of the Philistines, attempt to reconcile the text by: (1) separating the Philistines of Caphtor from an earlier wave of Philistines from Casluhim (Cassuto 1964: 208; Kitchen 1973: 56; Wenham *Genesis* 1–15, 225); or (2) assuming that, by identifying the Pathrusim as Upper Egyptians and the Naphtuhim as Middle Egyptians (or, more likely, "they of the Delta" or "they of the oasis land" as in Kitchen 1980: 1054, since Middle Egypt did not exist as a separate unit in ancient Egypt), the Casluhim must be Lower Egyptians who migrated to Crete before coming to the Levantine coast as Philistines (Rendsburg 1987); or (3) assuming a metathesis from *sklḥ(m),* which is related to the Tjekker of the Egyptian sources, with the addition of a non-Semitic suffix -ḥ (Kitchen 1973: 70 n. 3).

Bibliography

Cassuto, U. 1964. *A Commentary on the Book of Genesis. Pt. 2.* Trans. I. Abrahams. Jerusalem.
Kitchen, K. A. 1973. The Philistines. Pp. 53–78 in *POTT.*

———. 1980. Naphtuhim. *The Illustrated Bible Dictionary* 2: 1054, eds. N. Hillyer et al. Leicester.

Rendsburg, G. A. 1987. Gen 10:13–14: An Authentic Hebrew Tradition Concerning the Origin of the Philistines. *JNSL* 13: 89–96.

Westermann, C. 1984. *Genesis 1–11. A Commentary.* Trans. J. J. Scullion. London.

RICHARD S. HESS

CASPIN (PLACE) [Gk *Kaspin*]. A fortified town in the Hauran Plain captured ca. 161 B.C. by Judas Maccabeus (2 Macc 12:13). Judas' 8,000-man contingent of the Hasmonean army advanced into the region E of Galilee in order to rescue the Jewish populace from the hostilities of the Hellenistic Gileadite forces led by Timotheus. Caspin is equated with CHASPHO in a second account of Judas' Gilead campaign recorded in 1 Macc 5:9–54. The account in 2 Macc 12:10–31 contains fuller detail but is chronologically disjointed and suffers textual difficulties. The account in Josephus (*Ant* 12.8.3 §340) and that in Maccabees vary greatly, probably the result of the name being transliterated from a Semitic dialect into Greek (Goldstein *1 Maccabees* AB, 301).

Caspin was identified by a band of Nabateans as one of the five fortified towns in Gilead where Jews were being held captive (1 Macc 5:24–27). These towns included Bozrah, Bosor in Alema, Chaspho, Maked, and Carnaim. Caspin was the site of one of the earlier confrontations of the Gilead campaign. It was attacked after Judas' army forced Timotheus and his forces to break their siege on a Jewish stronghold at Dathema (1 Macc 5:30–34).

The residents of Caspin were from a variety of ethnic groups and were well-disposed towards Hellenism. They were confident in the ability of their fortifications and provisions to withstand Judas' attack. However, their tauntings and curses were repaid with the slaughter of the residents of the city which was captured when Timotheus' forces were regrouping. A nearby lake reportedly turned red with the blood from the carnage. At the time of Judas' siege there were apparently no surviving Jewish residents in the city.

The location of Caspin has not been substantiated archaeologically. Proposed sites include Khisfin (M.R. 226250), 14 km E of the Sea of Galilee, and El Muzerib in the Wadi Yarmuk.

ROBERT W. SMITH

CASSIA. See PERFUMES AND SPICES; FLORA.

CASTANETS. See MUSIC AND MUSICAL INSTRUMENTS.

CAT. See ZOOLOGY.

CATHOLIC EPISTLES. See EPISTLES, CATHOLIC.

CATHOLIC VERSIONS. See VERSIONS, CATHOLIC.

CATHUA (PERSON) [Gk *Kathoua*]. A temple servant whose descendants returned from Babylon with Zerubbabel (1 Esdr 5:30). Although 1 Esdras is often assumed to have been compiled from Ezra and Nehemiah, this family does not appear among their lists of returning exiles (cf. Ezra 2:47; Neh 7:49). Omissions such as this also raise questions about 1 Esdras being used as a source by Ezra or Nehemiah. Furthermore, problems associated with dating events and identifying persons described in 1 Esdras have cast doubt on the historicity of the text.

MICHAEL DAVID MCGEHEE

CATTLE. See ZOOLOGY.

CAUDA (PLACE) [Gk *Kauda*]. A small island (modern Gozzo or Gaudos) located approximately 23 miles S of Crete (34°50′N; 24°05′E) mentioned in Acts 27:16. Julius the centurion, Paul, and other prisoners boarded a large Alexandrian grain ship bound for Rome at Myra. Strong winds forced the ship to sail to the lee side (E) of Crete, and they set sail for the port of Phoenix where they intended to spend the winter. The ship, however, was forced off of its course by a wind of hurricane force called Euroquiloa or *"northeaster."* The ship could not head into the wind so it was forced to be driven along by the wind. The ship soon came to the lee of the island of Cauda, which provided enough protection for the crew to make some preparations for the storm. The crew stowed a lifeboat which was in tow and hindering steering, undergirded the ship with ropes, and lowered the anchor.

The exact spelling of the name of this island is problematic. Several manuscripts rendered it *Klauda.* The form Cauda is found in many of the most ancient manuscripts, and the Latin Vulgate rendering as *Gaudus* (see also Pliny *HA* 4:12), as well as the modern names, both the Greek Gaudos and the Italian Gozzo, give credence to this spelling.

The small island could only have supported a limited population. Cauda, however, did merit a bishopric during the Byzantine period, but this was undoubtedly due to its association with the apostle Paul. See Smith 1979: 95–96, 110–13; Jackson and Lake 1965: 332.

Bibliography

Jackson, F. J. F., and Lake, K., eds. 1965. *The Acts of the Apostles.* Grand Rapids.

Smith, J. 1979. *The Voyage and Shipwreck of St. Paul.* Repr. Grand Rapids.

JOHN D. WINELAND

CAVALRY. See MILITARY ORGANIZATION IN MESOPOTAMIA.

CEDAR. See FLORA.

CEILING. RSV rendering of the Heb verbal *wayyīspōn,* "to cover/panel over" (1 Kgs 6:9).

CELIBACY. Votive abstention from marriage and sexual relations—unknown unless alluded to in Matt 19:12.

CELSUS (PERSON). Celsus was a late 2d-century Middle Platonist and vigorous opponent of Christianity. Nothing is known about him except what can be inferred from excerpts from his otherwise lost *True Doctrine (TD)* which are embedded in Origen's mid-3d-century work in eight books, entitled *Against Celsus (c. Cel.).* Origen's attempts to identify him with a known historical figure are contradictory and fail under close scrutiny.

A. The True Doctrine
  1. The Trustworthiness of Origen's Quotations
  2. Date
B. Celsus the Person
  1. Identity
  2. Philosophical Views
  3. Scope of His Polemic
C. Celsus and Christian Literature
  1. Old Testament
  2. New Testament
  3. Apologists
  4. Sects
    a. Marcionites
    b. Gnostics
D. Celsus' Picture of Christianity

A. The True Doctrine

1. The Trustworthiness of Origen's Quotations. Although earlier scholarship was mixed on the reliability of Origen's preservation of the original *TD,* more recent studies have concluded in favor of Origen's care and general objectivity in his quotations from the *TD.* He preserved the larger part of the *TD* in some form, most of it in direct quotations. These citations were presented with a remarkable degree of exactness and absence of alteration for apologetic purposes. Further, in almost every instance, the original order of the *TD* is reflected in Origen's quotations.

2. Date. More than a century ago Keim (1873) argued so convincingly that the *TD* was written in the year 178 C.E. that his dating became the scholarly consensus. Certain recent studies, however, have exposed major flaws in Keim's interpretation of key passages and have, in effect, reopened the date question. If, as they should be, Keim's arguments are rejected, the *TD* can be dated no more precisely than the last third of the 2d century.

B. Celsus the Person

1. Identity. A substantial number of men of letters and position in the first two Christian centuries bore the *cognomen* (family name) "Celsus." Unfortunately, Origen, who did not know the identity of his opponent, supplied no information on either Celsus' *praenomen* (first name) or his *nomen* (clan name), so nothing about his nationality or country of residence can be inferred from his name. Celsus' book reflects a broad acquaintance with the Mediterranean world but none of his ideas betray a narrow ethnic or national bias. Efforts to connect him specifically with Rome have failed and little else is known except that he at least traveled in the East. Celsus, thus, cannot at present be identified with any other known 2d-century figure.

2. Philosophical Views. The belief that Celsus was an Epicurean who lived during the reign of Hadrian was first championed (*c. Cel.* 1.8) then abandoned by Origen. In modern times a number of scholars have identified Celsus with the Epicurean to whom Lucian of Samosata dedicated his *Alexander the False Prophet.* This conjecture has rightly been criticized on the basis of the overt Platonism of the author of the *TD,* coupled with the incompatibility of Middle Platonism and Epicureanism during this period. Clearly, Celsus was in the mainstream of 2d-century Middle Platonism. This made him all the more powerful an antagonist of Christianity because he moved in the same intellectual milieu as his Christian apologist adversaries.

3. Scope of His Polemic. Celsus' arsenal contained an impressive array of weapons, from an imaginary Jew (the first two books) to Greek philosophy and mythology. He even pitted competing Christian groups against each other. Almost nothing about Christianity escaped his assault. Celsus attacked the person and teachings of Jesus and his original followers. Subsequent doctrines and practices were no less culpable to him. Christianity was hopelessly divisive, and its underhanded evangelistic methods attracted only the simpleminded. Christians were worthless as citizens and could not be counted on to defend the empire.

Encyclopedic in his knowledge of Christianity, Celsus left no type of Christian group untouched. Jewish Christians, various gnostic sects, and Marcionites were all targets of his scorn. The majority of his polemic, however, including virtually every attack preserved in the first five books of *c. Cel.,* was directed against "orthodox" Christianity or what Celsus characterized as the mainstream ("those of the multitude," *c. Cel.* 5.61). Only in 5.61–64 and 6.24–52 did Celsus focus on the sects, some of which have left no other trace of their existence. Elsewhere their theology surfaces only in scattered fragments in passages that deal predominantly with rather standard orthodox matters.

C. Celsus and Christian Literature

Celsus read widely in Christian writings and, in some cases, especially in biblical books, the literary source of his information can be established with a reasonable degree of certainty. In other passages his comments accurately represent the content of various types of Christian books but definite literary dependence cannot be demonstrated.

1. Old Testament. Although Celsus drew some of his information on the Judeo–Christian cosmogony from Marcionite (6.52–53) and Ophite (6.27–28) sources, in 4.20–53 he exhibited an in-depth acquaintance with the content of the book of Genesis which can only be explained adequately by his having read the book directly. In 4.20–21 he cited examples of divine intervention in the order in which they occur in Genesis and connected one of them with Moses as the source. Celsus' critique in 4.36–47 covers the entire scope of Genesis, beginning and ending where Genesis does and presenting the material in the proper sequence. Celsus' allusions to material found in the rest of the Pentateuch and the prophets, on the other hand, are too brief and commonplace to determine their direct source.

2. New Testament. Celsus never quoted a NT book or author by name, but at several points ample evidence exists to conclude that he was directly dependent on certain NT documents.

Possible allusions to the Gospels present a methodological difficulty, because two thirds of them occur in 1.28–2.79, where Celsus put his anti-Christian argument into the mouth of a Jew. Because of the probable Jewish sources of this section, evidence for direct dependence on the Gospels must be limited to the rest of the *TD*.

While many references to the *TD* are easily explicable on the basis of direct knowledge of all of the four canonical Gospels, rarely can direct dependence be proven. Only in 5.52 was Celsus clearly dependent on Matthew (1:20, 2:13, 28:1–5), but the fact that material was drawn from widely separated passages to support a single line of reasoning suggests more than a casual acquaintance with the book. Similarly, in 7.18 Celsus betrayed familiarity with widely dispersed passages in Luke, thus suggesting that he was conversant with major portions of the work. No demonstrable allusions to Mark or John occur. Numerous additional statements can be explained on the basis of Celsus' having read other NT books but only in the case of the middle portion of 1 Corinthians is the evidence strong enough to suggest direct dependence (8.21–37).

3. Apologists. Celsus was well acquainted with the type of Christianity reflected in the 2d-century apologists. In fact, extensive arguments have been formulated to establish his dependence on Justin (Andresen 1955) and to a lesser extent Aristides (Harris 1893; 1921), the *Kerygma Petrou* (Robinson 1893), and certain other apologists. While all of these efforts fall short of proving a direct literary dependence on any extant 2d-century apologist (Burke 1985), Celsus' knowledge of the religion of the apologists was so extensive and accurate that such a dependence cannot be ruled out and remains a distinct possibility. Ironically, the sole apologetic writing Celsus actually named, the "Dispute Between a Certain Papiscus and Jason" (4.52), has only survived in three late fragments, the largest of which contains a mere seven words.

4. Sects. In 5.61–62, Celsus mentioned by name several sects which he was able to distinguish from what he called "those of the multitude."

a. Marcionites. Elsewhere he alluded to specific Marcionite teachings (5.54 and 6.74) without identifying them as such and in other passages he made possible allusions (6.29, 52–53, 73, 7.2, 18). In no case, however, did Celsus indicate whether or not his sources were Marcionite documents. Two passages, however, are of special interest. In 7.18 the formulation of Celsus' argument so resembles the approach in Marcion's *Antitheses* that he seems to have been familiar at least with Marcion's practice of formulating antitheses, if not with the *Antitheses* themselves. The fact that the quotation from the *Heavenly Dialogue* in 8.15 is consistent with Marcionite thought has led some (Aubé 1878: 374; Patrick 1892: 76) to conclude that it was a Marcionite document, but his citation is too short to make a positive identification. Hence, while Celsus knew Marcionites by name and theology, his direct acquaintance with their literature remains to be established.

b. Gnostics. Celsus treated the gnostic sects primarily in 5.61–64 and 6.24–52. Nowhere did he make any clear references to specific gnostic documents which are now known to exist or to have existed, but there are numerous parallels with statements in the anti-heretical writings of the Church Fathers and in extant Coptic gnostic writings. In 5.61–64 Celsus specifically mentioned by name Gnostics, Sibyllists, Simonians, Helenians, Marcellians, Harpocratians, and followers of Mariamme and of Martha. He seems to have alluded also to Valentinians, Ebionites, and possibly to Carpocratians, assuming that his mention of Harpocratians was not already a reference to that sect. All of this was treated superficially, so no source determination can be made. In 6.24–38 Celsus described a nonextant Ophite diagram which he had seen along with a written explanation of it. Some of his information about the diagram even came from conversations with sect members.

D. Celsus' Picture of Christianity

Celsus is himself a valuable source on certain aspects of late-2d-century Christian life and piety because his knowledge of Christianity was not limited to written sources. He drew much of the standard anti-Christian caricature but also exhibited a sophistication that is best explained by his extensive contact with and observation of Christians. Celsus discussed sectarian documents and theology with Ophites (6.25, 40). He observed Christian evangelistic and group teaching activities (3.72–78; cf. 3.44) and was on occasion even the object of efforts to convert Ophites (1.9, 12).

The following picture emerges from his vast reading of Christian literature and experience with Christians. Christians were, with few exceptions, illiterate members of the lower classes. Their teachers, even the relatively better educated ones (3.44), sought to attract the gullible, uneducated masses by discouraging any kind of rational thought or questions (1.9, 12; 3.49–50, 55; 6.10–14). The fact that such professions as woolworker, cobbler, and laundry worker (3.55) were common was further evidence of Christians' low social status. Because of his philosophical rejection of the notion that people can undergo radical moral change (3.65), Celsus was appalled by the fact that Christians consciously attempted to attract sinners (3.59, 62). Significantly, however, he did not repeat the oft-heard charges of immoral acts and, in fact, treated Christian ethical teaching as commonplace (1.4).

In sum, Celsus portrayed Christianity as a movement with no innate value or status in society. The great masses of Christians were of no consequence whatever and did not deserve to be taken seriously. Yet, Celsus did take them seriously and wrote no small book to discredit the movement. The danger rested precisely in Christianity's appeal to the masses. To the extent Christians could win the great bulk of society, pagan culture as it had been known for more than a millennium was in danger of being eroded. To his credit, Celsus perceived ever so clearly what eventually happened. His is one of the few and most articulate surviving voices from the side of the struggle which ultimately lost.

Bibliography

Editions

Borret, M. 1967–76. *Origène. Contre Celse.* SC 132, 136, 147, 150, 227. Paris.

Koetschau, P. 1899. *Origenes Werke.* GCS 2–3. Leipzig.

English Translations

Chadwick, H. 1953. *Origen: Contra Celsum.* Cambridge.

Crombie, F. 1926. Origen Against Celsus. *ANF* 4: 395–669.

Studies

Andresen, C. 1955. *Logos und Nomos.* Arbeiten zur Kirchengeschichte 30. Berlin.

Aubé, B. 1878. *Histoire des persecutions dans l'Église.* 2d ed. Paris.

Bader, R. 1940. *Der Alēthēs Logos des Kelsos.* Tübinger Beitraege zur Altertumswissenschaft 33. Berlin.

Burke, G. T. 1984. Walter Bauer and Celsus: The Shape of Late Second-Century Christianity. *SecondCent* 4: 1–7.

———. 1985. Celsus and Justin. *ZNW* 76: 107–16.

———. 1986. Celsus and the Old Testament. *VT* 36: 241–45.

Harris, J. R. 1893. *The Apology of Aristides.* TextsS 1: 1. Cambridge.

———. 1921. Celsus and Aristides. *BJRL* 6: 163–75.

Keim, T. 1873. *Celsus' Wahres Wort.* Zurich.

Lods, M. 1941. Étude sur les sources juives de la polémique de Celse contre les chrétiens. *RHPR* 21: 1–33.

Patrick, J. 1892. *The Apology of Origen in Reply to Celsus.* Edinburgh.

Pélagaud, E. 1879. *Un conservateur au second siècle.* 2d ed. Paris.

Robinson, J. A. 1893. Appendix: The Remains of the Original Greek of the Apology of Aristides. Pp. 86–91, 98–99 in *The Apology of Aristides.* TextsS 1: 1. Cambridge.

Rosenbaum, H.-U. 1972. Zur Datierung von Celsus' *Alēthēs logos. VC* 26: 102–11.

Voelker, W. 1928. *Das Bild vom nichtgnostischen Christentum bei Celsus.* Halle.

Welburn, A. J. 1981. Reconstructing the Ophite Diagram. *NovT* 23: 261–87.

GARY T. BURKE

CENCHREAE (PLACE) [Gk *Kenchreais*]. The E seaport of Corinth, located on the Saronic Gulf ca. 11 km E of the city and ca. 4 km S of Isthmia. Two NT references (Acts 18:18 and Rom 16:1) confirm the existence of an early Christian community at the site and the name of one Phoebe, a deaconess of the church. Much later in its history, ca. 4th century C.E., a large Christian complex arose at the S end of the harbor, eventually absorbing and incorporating earlier structures including the Isis sanctuary. It was apparently in use until the port's destruction in the 580s and possibly even beyond. The modern name of the village in the proximity of the ancient site is Kechriais.

A. History

The ancient site of Cenchreae is mentioned infrequently in surviving texts. Its *raison d'être* was to serve as Corinth's E portal to the Mediterranean. Its fate was inexorably linked to the history of the city it served, suffering and enjoying Corinth's changes of fortune.

Little is known of Greek Cenchreae from either extant literary texts or archaeological data, although it was certainly in existence by the Peloponnesian War (Thuc. 4.42). The site may have been in continuous use until its destruction or abandonment following Mummius' devastation of Corinth in 146 B.C.E. When Corinth was revived by Julius Caesar in 44 B.C.E., Cenchreae's situation improved. New harbor facilities were built to accommodate Corinth's rising importance as an emporium of the E Roman empire (Hohlfelder 1976). Two artificial rubble breakwaters were constructed to provide a deep-water anchorage that was available for use during the normal sailing season (approximately April to early October), and that was both larger and more suitable for Roman Corinth's expanded economic role (Hohlfelder 1985).

Its international prominence and prosperity probably peaked in the 2d century C.E. Although damaged by earthquakes and seismic sea waves in 365 and 375 C.E., the port revived and continued to play a significant role until Cenchreae was finally destroyed by marauding Avars and Slavs in the 580s. In the face of these attacks and subsequent vicissitudes, its population apparently fled to safer regions, ending urban life at the site (Hohlfelder 1973; 1975). Thereafter, it may have been occasionally occupied and the ancient harbor area even used intermittently as a fair-weather roadstead, but Cenchreae never again rivaled its earlier glory.

In addition to the artificial breakwaters, which are now submerged because of subsidence and/or a relative sea level rise of ca. 2 m since their construction, the Roman harbor was distinguished by various warehouses and support buildings, monumental statues, and several temples, the most notable being a sanctuary of Isis mentioned in Apuleius' *Metamorphosis.* An apsidal basin of this structure located on the S breakwater was excavated to reveal more than 100 glass *opus sectile* panels, dating from approximately the reign of Julian (361–363 C.E.). They were intended for a renovation that was planned, perhaps started, but never completed (Scranton 1967; Hohlfelder 1976).

B. Archaeology

Excavations were conducted at the site in 1963–1964 under the direction of R. L. Scranton and E. S. Ramage, and in 1965 under Scranton alone. J. W. Shaw led the underwater excavations, one of the earliest ancient harbor explorations and one that pioneered many survey and excavation techniques still in use (Shaw 1967). Fieldwork was conducted from 1963 through 1968 (excepting 1966), but was limited primarily to the Roman site. An adjacent alluvial plain, which has not been excavated, is believed to conceal the earlier Greek harbor. Five volumes of final reports have appeared to date (cf. Scranton, Shaw, and Ibrahim 1978; Ibrahim, Scranton, and Brill 1976; Hohlfelder 1978; Adamsheck 1979; and Williams 1981) with several more in preparation.

Bibliography

Adamsheck, B. 1979. *Kenchreai: Eastern Seaport of Corinth.* Vol. 4, *The Pottery.* Leiden.

Hohlfelder, R. L. 1973. A Sixth Century Hoard from Kenchreai. *Hesperia* 42: 89–101.

———. 1975. Barbarian Incursions into Central Greece in the Sixth Century of the Christian Era: More Evidence from Corinthia. *East European Quarterly* 9/3: 251–58.

———. 1976. Kenchreai on the Saronic Gulf: Aspects of Its Imperial History. *CJ* 71/3: 217–26.
———. 1978. *Kenchreai Eastern Seaport of Corinth.* Vol. 3, *The Coins.* Leiden.
———. 1985. The Building of the Roman Harbour at Kenchreai: Old Technology in a New Era. Pp. 81–86 in *Harbour Archaeology,* ed. A. Raban. BAR International Series 257. Oxford.
Ibrahim, L.; Scranton, R.; and Brill, R. 1976. *Kenchreai Eastern Port of Corinth.* Vol. 2, *The Panels of Opus Sectile in Glass.* Leiden.
Scranton, R. L. 1965. Excavation at Kenchreai. *CJ* 61: 6–8.
———. 1967. Glass Pictures from the Sea. *Arch* 20: 163–73.
Scranton, R. L., and Ramage, E. S. 1963. Explorations at Cenchreae. *Arch* 16: 286–87.
———. 1964. Investigations at Kenchreai, 1963. *Hesperia* 33: 134–45.
———. 1967. Investigations at Corinthian Kenchreai. *Hesperia* 36: 124–86.
Scranton, R. L.; Shaw, J.; and Ibrahim, L. 1978. *Kenchreai Eastern Port of Corinth.* Vol. 1, *Topography and Architecture.* Leiden.
Shaw, J. W. 1967. Shallow-water Excavations at Kenchreai. *AJA* 71: 223–31.
Williams, H. 1981. *Kenchreai Eastern Port of Corinth.* Vol. 5, *The Lamps.* Leiden.

ROBERT L. HOHLFELDER

CENDEBEUS (PERSON) [Gk *Kendebaios*]. Governor of the coastal plain, who attacked Judea, under the orders of the Seleucid king, Antiochus VII Sidetes (1 Macc 15:37–16:10). Cendebeus' name seems to be of Thracian origin. He was a supporter of Antiochus Sidetes. Josephus (*Ant* 13.225) assumed, maybe rightly, that he belonged to the *philoi* (the "Friends" in the court hierarchy). He is one of a line of governors of the coastal plain, the *Paralia,* which existed as a separate province since Antiochos V up to at least Antiochos VII. Cendebeus fortified Kedron, in the S coastal plain and harassed Judea (Bengston 1964: 176–81). Simon, with two of his sons, Judas and John, attacked him and won a battle at the SW corner of Judea, and drove away Cendebeus' forces as far as Kedron. See Goldstein (*1 Maccabees* AB) for new suggestions.

Bibliography

Bengston, H. 1964. *Die Strategie in der hellenistischen Zeit.* Vol. 2. Munich.

URIEL RAPPAPORT

CENSERS. Hand-held devices in which incense was placed along with burning coals; the burning spices would provide a pleasing odor. These devices could be either cup-shaped vessels at the end of a long handle, or bowls set onto an upright pedestal. The former is probably indicated by *maḥtāh* (Lev 10:1, etc.); the latter is called a *miqṭeret* (Ezek 8:11). The term *maḥtāh* can also be used here specifically for various temple vessels that could carry coals and thus be used to burn incense (e.g., RSV "firepans," Exod 27:3, and "snuffers," Exod 25:38). A word in Ezra 1:9 rendered "censer" in RSV probably means something else, but its meaning is uncertain. See also FIREPAN; SNUFFERS.

The cultic use of incense offered in censers may be Egyptian in origin. Its use in Egypt apparently served apotropaic purposes. Worshippers would carry censers in processions to keep away the evil forces associated with impurity (Haran 1978: 239–40). The use of incense in ancient Israel seems to have had similar apotropaic functions, as when Aaron is said to have halted an outbreak of disease by standing, with a censer of burning incense, "between the dead and the living" (Num 17:11–13 [—Eng 16:46–48]).

Most references to censers in the Hebrew Bible are in cultic contexts, and they indicate problems in the proper use of censer incense. Nadab and Abihu (Lev 10:1–3) met difficulties when they used "strange fire," apparently coals from outside the altar area and hence lacking requisite sanctity. Korah's company of 250 (Numbers 16) also apparently used improper incense; but their attempt to take over priestly functions, by using the censers, was an even worse misdeed, for which they were punished by being swallowed up by the earth. Similarly, Uzziah (2 Chr 26:19) contracted leprosy when he tried to take from the priests the right to burn incense in a censer. Finally, the 70 elders holding censers in Ezekiel's vision are called an abomination (Ezek 8:11–13). Clearly, the cultic use of censers was a prerogative of priests—or of angels (Rev 8:3, 5).

Bibliography

Haran, M. 1978. *Temples and Temple-Service in Ancient Israel.* Oxford.

CAROL MEYERS

CENSUS. This entry consists of two articles, one surveying the census in the ancient Near East, and the other exploring the census in Roman times, particularly with reference to the census reported in the gospel of Luke.

ANCIENT NEAR EAST

Census, as we understand it in our day ("an official enumeration of inhabitants, with details as to age, sex, pursuits, etc." or the like) does not find a concrete application in the societies and cultures of the ANE. As is well known, a variety of administrative and economic clay tablets in cuneiform script from Mesopotamia and outlying regions, from the 3d to the 1st millennium B.C., provide partial population listings and counts from various cities and territorial entities. What is lacking, on the other hand, are recordings of the overall size of the population in these places: recordings planned by the central administrations of the ANE in terms of fixed geographical limits and regular spans of time.

In most types of state-formation of the ANE during the Bronze Age, a certain number of contingent and practical needs—from the distribution of rations to fiscal revenues to military levies—constituted the main occasions for drawing up inventories of specific sectors of the population. Thus, e.g., the texts from Ebla (Syria, 24th century B.C.) leave us a list of food provisions for 260,000 people—but it is quite unlikely that this was a "head count" of the local population. On the other hand, the archives of Alalakh (level 4) and Ugarit in Syria (15th–14th century B.C.) present numerous registers of male individuals according to their village of origin and to their social grouping, essentially for the supply of military contingents. And finally, the many interconnecting legal documents from Sippar in lower Mesopotamia allow us to reconstruct the inner organization of this city in full for the period ca. 1900–1600 B.C., from settlement patterns to social mobility, including the career stories of men and women alike—but few, if any, numerical and statistical data and frameworks may be called upon for this picture.

The perspective changes somewhat for the period 1000–500 B.C., when the Mesopotamian states (first Assyria, then Babylonia) engage in the construction of universal empires. Figures on vanquished and deported populations begin to be quoted by the Assyrian kings in order to emphasize imperial might: a statistical study of these data has yielded a sum total of about 4.5 million deportees during the period ca. 930–630 B.C. Great care must be taken, however, in evaluating these materials, as the possibility for fictitious numbers (i.e., numbers inflated for ideological reasons) cannot be ruled out in various cases. On the other hand, partial calculations on these deportees, when proved to be likely, usually refer to an overall count of population—men, women, and children—similar to an actual census appraisal. Thus, e.g., it is of general statistical interest to note that Shalmaneser III (858–824 B.C.) reckoned at 110,610 the total of deportees during 20 years, and that Tiglathpileser III (745–727 B.C.) gives the sum total of 13,520 captives from N Palestine alone.

A group of tablets from the same general period, discovered in the archives of the Assyrian capital Nineveh, comes admittedly closest to a definition of "census" for the ANE, as was stated—with great enthusiasm—by the first editor, C. H. W. Johns: ". . . as a Census, this will bear comparison with the Census in Egypt, or the Roman Census, or the Doomsday Book, which latter it most resembles" (1901). The 21 tablets of the so-called Assyrian Doomsday Book, which are in a fair state of preservation, present divisions in columns and sections. Each section is opened by a list of people in family groups, enumerated in a rigid sequence by age and sex. First come the adult males (whose personal names and professional designations are given), then the "sons" (names but no profession given), followed by the adult women and the "daughters" (no names, no individual listings, just the total for each subgroup given). The sons and daughters are further described by their height in "half-cubits" or "spans," as a marker of their relative age before adulthood. Totals of the type "in all, *n* (people)" end the human enumeration.

The list continues with measurements of land parcels with specified destinations (barley cultivation, vineyard, orchards), and at times with mentions of further commodities forming part of the farm or tied to it (from animals to threshing floors to living quarters). A geographical setting for the plots concludes each section: and all such localizations point to the province of Harran or bordering regions in the NW corner of Mesopotamia. It is also clear, despite the fragmentary character of most texts, that general totals of some type were provided at the end of each document. These totals refer to persons outside of the register itself, at times provided with professional names identifying them as medium-to-high-ranking palace officials.

These clues are sufficient to conclude that not even the well-structured tablets of the Assyrian Doomsday Book may be considered to pertain to a veritable census of population in the modern sense of the word. Rather, it would seem that the interest for listing people and land around the old and famous city of Harran stemmed from a specific policy undertaken by Assyrian kingship: the overall tax-exemption decreed for a few choice sites of the Assyrian empire by Sargon II (721–705 B.C.). The list of villages or other units of settlement, comprising the (servile and forcedly resident) population employed in agriculture, and the land itself with various commodities or fixtures, was drawn up in order to establish the amount of landed property belonging to this or that courtier or official, who was to be exempted from revenues and services otherwise owed to the state. The fact that the archives of Nineveh also yield larger digests, registering all the plots owned by particular officials, validates this theory, and implicitly shows the limits of censual interests in the ANE as consistently tied to here-and-now, practical and ephemeral, perspectives.

Bibliography

Fales, F. M. 1973. *Censimenti e catasti di epoca neo-assira.* Rome.

Johns, C. H. W. 1901. *An Assyrian Doomsday Book or Liber Censualis of the District Round Harran in the Seventh Century B.C.* Leipzig.

Harris, R. 1975. *Ancient Sippar. A Demographic Study of an Old Babylonian City (1894–1595 B.C.).* Leiden.

Heltzer, M. 1982. *The Internal Organization of the Kingdom of Ugarit.* Wiesbaden.

Oded, B. 1979. *Mass Deportations and Deportees in the Neo-Assyrian Empire.* Wiesbaden.

Pomponio, F. 1981. Pp. 270–271 in *Materiali Epigrafici di Ebla 3,* ed. G. Pettinato. Naples.

FREDERICK MARIO FALES

ROMAN CENSUS

The violent transition of Roman government from the late republic to the principate (inaugurated in 27 B.C.E. with Octavian's acceptance of the title Augustus and its attendant imperial prerogatives) was marked by innovations in fiscal policy. Significant among these was the institution of the provincial census. Caesar Augustus began the practice of a regular and periodic count (Lat *census,* Gk *apographē*) of the population of all the provinces of the Roman Empire, and a valuation of individually and corporately held property (Gk *apotimēsis*), for the assessment of tax liabilities. Revenues which the imperial government extracted from the provinces included taxes on land and usufruct (Lat *tributum soli*), variable-rate taxes on chattel and a fixed tax on each liable individual (Lat *tributum capitis*), rents on imperial and public property, percentage taxes on Roman citizens, and extraordinary levies (Neesen 1980). Taxes were variously payable in kind or in cash. In addition to individual liabilities were a variety of communal liabilities incumbent on cities. Public corporations formed for the collection and transmission of taxes became powerful and (at least in reputation) corrupt; but by the time of the principate, tax collection in the province of Judea was administered directly by Rome (see TAX COLLECTOR).

Two NT passages, both of them Lukan, refer to the

Roman census. Both are synchronisms linking events in the narrative of Jesus' life, and its perduring effects, to the larger span of secular history. Both raise difficult questions about the accuracy of the chronological details in the gospel of Luke and the Acts of the Apostles.

The first reference to the census marks a transition from the narrative of the wonders surrounding John the Baptist's conception, gestation, and birth (Luke 1:5–80) to the etiology of Jesus' nativity in Bethlehem (2:1–8). The infancy narrative concerning John (which may derive from a pre-Lukan source, possibly in Hebrew or Aramaic) is set *en tais hemerais Herodou* "in the days of Herod" (Luke 1:5), the latest date for which would be the year of Herod's death, 4 B.C.E. The Bethlehem story is set in motion by a decree of Caesar Augustus *apographesthai pasan tēn oikoumenēn* "that all the world should be enrolled" (Luke 2:1). It is further specified that this census took place while Quirinius was governor of Syria (2:2; on the syntax and related matters see Fitzmyer *Luke I–IX* AB, 399–400).

The distinguished career of P. Sulpicius Quirinius is reasonably well documented from contemporary inscriptions as well as Latin and Greek historical writers (the sources are collected in *HJP*², 259), chief among them Josephus. In all of the five Josephan passages in which Quirinius plays a part, he is associated with a valuation (Gk *apotimēsis*) of the Judeans and its political consequences (see ZEALOTS); the event is called an *apographē* (*Ant* 18.3; *JW* 7.253). In one passage (*Ant* 18.26), Quirinius' administration of the census is set in the 37th year after the defeat of Antony at Actium, and thus in the year 6/7 C.E. The decade separating the death of Herod from the census decreed by Augustus and carried out by Quirinius is the source of the difficulties critical readers have in relating the Baptizer's infancy narrative to that of Jesus, since the pregnant mother of Jesus figures as a character in both. In addition, there are several potential difficulties involved in relating the journey of Joseph and Mary to Bethlehem to reconstructions of how Roman censuses were conducted.

The chronological uncertainties are compounded by the complex synchronism of Luke 3:1 and the reference to Jesus' age in 3:23. These passages imply that Jesus was "about 30 years of age" (3:23) in the 15th year of Tiberius Caesar (26/27 C.E.). This age accords with a date of birth ca. 4 B.C.E., but not with a birth in 6 or 7 C.E.

The apparently incompatible chronologies of these narratives in Luke's "orderly account" (1:3) of the Jesus story have provoked an enormous literature of controversy. Some of the most significant contributions to this literature were made late in the 19th and early in the 20th centuries, at a time when the relevant primary sources were acutely studied (the discussion in *HJP*², 399–427 is fully documented from 1840 to 1972; more recent opinions are voiced by Stern 1974: 372–74; Brown 1977: 547–56; and Fitzmyer *Luke I–IX* AB [1981], 399–405).

Classical scholars are convinced that there is no evidence for a simultaneous census of every province of the empire (Neesen 1980: 39–42; Brunt 1981: 163), and it would be wooden to insist that Luke's use of the phrase "all the world" (2:1) is any less hyperbolic than its use in imperial decrees (*TDNT* 5: 157). The rhetorical concern of the passage is to introduce the census in Judea; Luke did not necessarily understand the Augustan decree to have been carried into effect at once throughout the empire.

Proposed solutions to the chronological problem have attempted to separate Quirinius from the census by means of historical and linguistic arguments. The historical argument posits a census previous to that of 6/7 C.E., at some point late in the reign of Herod. Judea under Herod was a client kingdom (see CLIENT KINGS) not incorporated in the provincial system of the Roman Empire. It is thus unlikely, though not impossible, that a Roman census would have been conducted during Herod's lifetime. Relations between Augustus and Herod deteriorated over time, and Augustus threatened at one point to treat Herod as no friend but a vassal (*Ant* 16.9.3). The ensuing political tensions, it has been argued (e.g., by Stauffer 1960: 31–33), would have provided an opportunity for Roman punitive interference by means of a census and associated taxation; but nothing indicates that Augustus ever carried out his threat (Bammel 1968).

The grammatical argument necessitated by any separation of Quirinius from the census interprets the Lukan clause *hautē apographē protē egeneto* (2:2) adverbially as "this census was the first" (of two made by Quirinius) or "this census was before" (another made by Quirinius) (Turner 1963: 32). It fails to account for the following genitive absolute, and is therefore unsatisfactory.

Yet another approach has been to speculate that Quirinius held an earlier term of office as legate to Syria during which he conducted a census previous to the one with which Josephus concerns himself. Various inscriptions have been appealed to in support of such a reconstruction of Quirinius' career, but classical scholarship remains unconvinced (see CHRONOLOGY (NT); QUIRINIUS).

The census is mentioned again in Acts 5:37 in the course of a speech by Gamaliel to the Sanhedrin. Here it is associated with the uprising instigated by Judas of Galilee, an association made repeatedly by Josephus (see JUDAS (PERSON) #10; ZEALOTS). A revolt by THEUDAS mentioned in the previous verse (Acts 5:36) with the apparent implication that the two were contemporaries has been the source of further questions about Luke's chronological precision.

Bibliography

Bammel, E. 1968. Die Rechtsstellung des Herodes. *ZDPV* 84: 73–79.

Brown, R. E. 1977. *The Birth of the Messiah.* Garden City, NY.

Brunt, P. A. 1981. The Revenues of Rome [review of Neesen 1980]. *JRS* 71: 161–72.

Hayles, D. J. 1973. The Roman Census and Jesus' Birth. *Buried History* 9: 113–32; 10: 16–31.

Hombert, M., and Préaux, C. 1952. *Recherches sur le recensement dans l'Egypt romaine.* Papyrologica Lugduno Batava 5.

Neesen, L. 1980. *Untersuchungen zu den direkten Staatsabgaben der römischen Kaiserzeit (27 v. Chr.–284 n. Chr.).* Bonn.

Sherwin-White, A. N. 1963. *Roman Society and Roman Law in the New Testament.* Oxford.

Smallwood, G. M. 1976. *The Jews under Roman Rule.* Leiden.

Stauffer, E. 1960. *Jesus and His Story.* London.

Stern, M. 1974. The Province of Judea. Vol. 1, pp. 308–76 in *The Jewish People in the First Century*, ed. S. Safrai, M. Stern, D. Flusser, and W. C. van Unnik. CRINT. Philadelphia.

Turner, N. 1963. *A Grammar of New Testament Greek*. Vol. 3, *Syntax*. Edinburgh.

PHILIP C. SCHMITZ

CENTURION [Gk *Kenturiōn*]. See ROMAN ARMY.

CEREMONIAL LAW. See LAW, (BIBLICAL AND ANE).

CERINTHUS (PERSON) [Gk *Kerinthos*].

A gnostic teacher who lived in Asia Minor about 100 A.D. Irenaeus (*Haer.* 1.26.1) says that Cerinthus believed the world was created by a Power separated from and ignorant of the true God. He also taught that Jesus was the son of Joseph and Mary. At baptism the Christ descended on Jesus from the true God. He then proclaimed the unknown Father and performed miracles. Since Christ was a spiritual being incapable of suffering, he left Jesus before the crucifixion. Jesus suffered and rose again.

Hippolytus (*Haer.* 7.33.1–2, 10.21.1–3) differs little from Irenaeus. He claims that Cerinthus was trained in the teaching of the Egyptians (see discussion in Wright, 1984) and that he called the Power that created the world an angel. Pseudo-Tertullian (*Haer.* 3) adds that Cerinthus believed the Law was given by angels. According to Eusebius' sources (*Hist. Eccl.* 3.28.1–6; 7.25.1–3) Cerinthus taught that the kingdom of Christ would be set up on earth with its center in Jerusalem. Several sources associate Cerinthus with SIMON MAGUS or Carpocrates.

Irenaeus also reports that John wrote his gospel against the teaching of Cerinthus (*Haer.* 3.11.1). He quotes Polycarp as saying that one day when John was going to the bathhouse at Ephesus he heard that Cerinthus was there. John rushed out saying he was afraid the bath-house would fall because the enemy of truth was inside (*Haer.* 3:3.4). Eusebius knew some who claimed that Cerinthus wrote the Apocalypse of John (*Hist. Eccl.* 3.28.3–4). Epiphanius refuted those who held that Cerinthus wrote the Apocalypse and the Gospel of John (*Adv. Haeres.* 51.3.6).

Later writers tended to associate Cerinthus with the EBIONITES and describe him in Jewish–Christian terms. Epiphanius (*Adv. Haeres* 28.1–8) says that Cerinthus believed the Law and the Prophets were both given by angels, one of whom was the creator of the world, and that Cerinthus partially adhered to Judaism. He describes Cerinthus as one of the false apostles who promoted circumcision and opposed Paul in the early church. Cerinthus' followers are supposed to have had an edited version of Matthew's gospel which they used to argue that Christians should keep the Law. The reliability of Epiphanius' information is questionable.

Primary sources for Cerinthus with English translation are included in the selections from the Church Fathers in Klijn and Reinink (1973: 101–273). Klijn and Reinink also have a good discussion of these sources (3–19).

Bibliography

Bardy, G. 1921. Cerinthus. *RB* 30: 344–73.

Klijn, A. F. J., and Reinink, G. J. 1973. *Patristic Evidence for Jewish–Christian Sects.* NovTSup 36. Leiden.

Wright, B. G., III. 1984. Cerinthus *Apud* Hippolytus; An Inquiry into the Traditions about Cerinthus' Provenance. *SecondCent* 4: 83–115.

GARETH LEE COCKERILL

CHABRIS (PERSON) [Gk *Chabris*].

One of the elders of Bethulia (Jdt 6:15; 8:10; 10:16). He is also identified as the son of Gothoniel. The name Chabris is confined to the book of Judith, where at least 13 spelling variants are attested in the various Gk manuscripts. Given the number of variants, Moore (*Judith* AB), among others, has suggested that the name has been translated into Greek from a Hebrew name (possibly *ḥbry*?). This is possible but unproven. Chabris always appears with his fellow elder Charmis. He cannot be identified with any historical personage; the author's purpose in using the name appears to have been to add interest and detail to the narrative. This is in keeping with the genre of the book of Judith.

SIDNIE ANN WHITE

CHADIASANS [Gk *Chadiasai*].

A family which returned from Babylon with Zerubbabel (1 Esdr 5:20). Although 1 Esdras is often assumed to have been compiled from Ezra and Nehemiah, this family does not appear among their lists of returning exiles (cf. Ezra 2; Neh 7). Omissions such as this also raise questions about 1 Esdras being used as a source by Ezra or Nehemiah. Furthermore, problems associated with dating events and identifying persons described in 1 Esdras have cast doubt on the historicity of the text. Turner (*IDB* 1: 549) and LaSor (*IDB* 1: 629) suggest that the family's place of origin may have been KEDESH (Josh 15:23).

MICHAEL DAVID MCGEHEE

CHAEREAS (PERSON) [Gk *Chaireas*].

Commander of the city of Gazara, brother of Timotheus (2 Macc 10:32, 37). It is reported that Chaereas was killed with Timotheus and Apollophanes when Judas Maccabeus burned Gazara (2 Macc 10:32–38). This would suggest that Timotheus attacked Judea and then fled W to Gazara (biblical Gezer). However, the parallel account in 1 Macc 5:1–8 describes Judas as attacking Timotheus in his own territory of Ammon. The last city mentioned in this attack is Jazer in Ammon. Goldstein (*2 Maccabees* AB, 393–94) presents a convincing argument that the correct reading behind the text of 2 Macc 10:32 is Jazer and not Gazara. Chaereas would then be the commander of Jazer, a city under Ammonite control. Josephus (*Ant* 12.8.1 §129) also follows 1 Maccabees 5 and supports this conclusion.

RUSSELL D. NELSON

CHALDEA (PLACE) [Heb *kaśdîm*]. CHALDEANS. Biblical name for S Mesopotamia, the area associated with Babylon.

A. The Form of the Name and Its Appearance in Genesis

The distinction between the Heb *kaśdîm* (cf. also Aram) and the Gk *chaldaioi* (cf. also Akk *kaldu*) may be explained linguistically either as the "sibilant + *d*" being assimilated to *ld* in Akkadian (Millard 1977: 70–71), or as an original Arabic(?) consonant "*ḍ*" lying behind both forms (Edzard *RLA* 5: 296). The LXX follows the Akkadian rather than the Hebrew/Aramaic spelling. The Chaldeans are associated with Ur, where Haran, brother of Abram, died, and whence Terah, Abram, and their family set forth for Harran and Canaan (Gen 11:28, 31; 15:7; Acts 7:4). To Nahor, Abram's other brother, was born Kemuel, father of Aram, and Chesed (Gen 22:22; cf. however Saggs 1960: 208–09). The Hebrew consonants of Chesed and *kaśdîm* are identical. The association of Aram and the Chaldeans is also to be found in Jer 35:11, where Nebuchadnezzar's army includes the army of the Chaldeans and the army of Aram.

B. Other Biblical References

The Chaldeans were a people with whom Judah sought an alliance which the prophets condemned using images of lust and harlotry (Ezek 16:29; 23:14–16). The Chaldeans were understood to have been brought against the people of God as a judgment (Job 1:17; Ezek 23:23; Hab 1:6). The term is applied to the Neo-Babylonian army which brought to an end the kingdom of Judah (2 Kgs 24:2; 25: 4, 5, 10, 13; 2 Chr 36:17; Jer 21:4; 22: 25; 32: 4–5, 24–25, 28–29; 33:5, 43; 37: 5, 8–11, 13–14; 38:18–19, 23; 39:8; 43:3; 52:7, 17) and who supervised the land afterward (2 Kgs 25:24–26; Jer 40:9–10; 41:3, 18). On the other hand, in Jer 21:9 and 38:2, the Chaldeans are viewed as a source of life for the besieged inhabitants of Jerusalem who are willing to surrender. Associated with Babylon in the prophetic oracles against that city, the Chaldeans regard Babylon with pride (Isa 13:19).

The land of Chaldea is used in parallelism with Babylon (Isa 47:1, 5; 48:14; Jer 25:12; 50:1; 51:35). It is the land to which the Judeans are sent (Ezek 12:13), where as exiles they reside (Ezek 1:3; 11:24), whose language and culture they are taught (Dan 1:4), and from whence they will return (Isa 48:20; Jer 24:5; 50:8) after God punishes it (Isa 43:14; Jer 50:10, 25, 35, 45; 51:4, 24, 54). In the MT, Isa 23:13 refers to the destruction of Chaldea by Assyria who used it for ships. The Chaldeans appear in Daniel where Darius is made king over Chaldea (Dan 9:1). The Chaldeans are among the royal counsellors of the Babylonian court (Dan 2:2, 4, 5, 10). In the Deuterocanonical narrative of Judith, the Chaldeans are a polytheistic people from whom Israel is descended (Jdt 5:6–7).

C. Chaldean History

As a distinct people, the Chaldeans appear in the 9th century B.C. in the land lying to the S of Babylonia and reaching to the borders of Elam (Oppenheim *IDB* 1:549–550). Although they are already well established when they appear (Brinkman *CAH*³: 287), their earlier origins are uncertain. Neither the possible relationship of Chaldean with a Kassite name for Babylon, Karduniash, nor the presence of West Semitic personal names alongside the Akkadian ones, from the earliest 9th and 8th century sources, have proven conclusive (Brinkman 1968: 265–266). In Assyrian and later cuneiform sources the name appears as *kal-da-a-a; kal-di; kal-du; ka-al-du;* and *kal-da-ni* (Parpola 1970: 188–190; Zadok 1985: 191–192). Like their neighbors, the Arameans of S Babylonia (Dietrich 1970; Brinkman 1977), the Chaldeans possessed a tribal form of social organization, and in the Neo-Babylonian period no clear distinction can be made between the personal names of many of the Chaldeans and those of the Arameans; both may be identified as West Semitic (Zadok 1977: 10). However, the Chaldeans, with only five tribes (each of which was ruled by an individual tribal leader), were distinct from the Arameans (Brinkman 1977: 306–307); the Chaldeans were wealthier, involved in trade and politics, and more urbanized (Brinkman *CAH*³: 288–90; cf. Edzard *RLA* 5: 291–92 for a survey of the opinions on the relationship of these two groups).

During the Neo-Assyrian period, when Babylon was politically and militarily dominated by Assyria, the Chaldeans often found their interests in opposition to the Assyrians. Because of the presence of marshlands, Chaldea, known as the Sealand, made an ideal center from which to wage a guerilla war against the rulers of the Neo-Assyrian empire (Brinkman 1979: 244–25, 235–36). Often allied with Elam, Chaldean leaders were able to rise to positions of leadership in Babylon during periods of Assyrian weakness. One of the greatest of these figures was Merodach-Baladan II, who united the tribes of the Chaldeans and twice occupied the throne of Babylon during the latter 8th century B.C. He was able to lead delegations to other states such as Judah (2 Kgs 20:12–19), probably in order to organize a more widespread revolt against Sennacherib and the Assyrian empire of their day (Brinkman 1964: 33). By this time, the words Chaldean and Babylonian were becoming synonymous in biblical and other texts; indeed, in terms of language and writing, the Chaldeans were not distinct from the Babylonians. The 8th century rise of the Chaldeans, their association with Babylon, and their international policy coincide with their earliest mention in the Hebrew prophets (cf. Saggs 1960: 205–7).

Assyrian dominance in the later 8th century is attested by deportations of nearly 250,000 Chaldeans during the reigns of Tiglath-Pileser III and Sargon II; deportations which continued with Sennacherib (Brinkman 1979: 227). Although Assyria retained the upper hand, the domination was not to outlast the 7th century. With the weakening of the empire following the death of Ashurbanipal, the Chaldeans under Nabopolassar gained the upper hand in Babylonia, allied with the Medes, and drove the Assyrians W to Harran and Carchemish where they were defeated in 605 B.C. Under his rulership, a Chaldean dynasty in Babylon ushered in the Neo-Babylonian empire (Wiseman 1956; 1985). It was this empire that brought about the downfall of the Judean state in 587/586 B.C.

The Chaldeans remained an influence in the administration of affairs in the empire and seemed to have gained a reputation for wisdom and counsel throughout the Persian and even into the Hellenistic periods. We may observe the later tradition of Merodach-Baladan, who was said to have maintained a garden of exotic plants (supported by a contemporary list of 67 plants belonging to his garden) and to have had an observatory in Babylonia for purposes of astronomy (Brinkman 1964: 37, 40). Further, the beginning of careful historical, economic, and astronomical record keeping in Babylon in 747 B.C., roughly coincides with the rise of Chaldean influence, two events which later traditions were to relate to one another (Oates 1979: 112–113).

Bibliography

Brinkman, J. A. 1964. Merodach-Baladan II. Pp. 5–53 in *Studies Presented to A. Leo Oppenheim June 7, 1964,* ed. R. D. Biggs and J. A. Brinkman. Chicago.

———. 1968. *A Political History of Post-Kassite Babylonia 1158–722 B.C.* AnOr 43. Rome.

———. 1977. Notes on Arameans and Chaldeans in Southern Babylonia in the Early Seventh Century B.C. *Or.* n.s. 46: 304–25.

———. 1979. Babylonia under the Assyrian Empire, 745–627 B.C. Pp. 223–50 in *Power and Propaganda: A Symposium on Ancient Empires,* ed. M. T. Larsen. Mesopotamia. Copenhagen Studies in Assyriology 7. Copenhagen.

———. 1984. *Prelude to Empire. Babylonian Society and Politics, 747–626 B.C.* Occasional Publications of the Babylonian Fund, 7. Philadelphia.

Dietrich, M. 1970. *Die Aramäer Südbabyloniens in der Sargonzeit (700–648).* AOAT 7. Kevelaer.

Millard, A. R. 1977. Daniel 1–6 and History. *EvQ* 49: 67–73.

Oates, J. 1979. *Babylon.* London.

Parpola, S. 1970. *Neo-Assyrian Toponyms.* AOAT 6. Kevelaer.

Saggs, H. W. F. 1960. Ur of the Chaldees. A Problem of Identification. *Iraq* 22: 200–9.

Wiseman, D. J. 1956. *Chronicles of the Chaldean Kings (626–556 B.C.) in the British Museum.* London.

———. 1985. *Nebuchadrezzar and Babylon.* The Schweich Lectures of the British Academy 1983. Oxford.

Zadok, R. 1977. *On West Semites in Babylonia during the Chaldean and Achaemenian Periods. An Onomastic Study.* Jerusalem.

———. 1985. *Répertoire Géographie des Textes Cunéiformes VIII. Geographical Names according to New- and Late-Babylonian Texts.* Beihefte zum Tübinger Atlas des vorderen Orients B/7. Wiesbaden.

RICHARD S. HESS

CHALKSTONES. See GEOGRAPHY AND THE BIBLE (PALESTINE).

CHALPHI (PERSON) [Gk *Chalphi*]. Father of Judas, a commander of elite troops under the Hasmonaean Jonathan (1 Macc 11:70). Nothing is known about the ancestry or descent of this family. Even the rendering of this name in Greek and its derivation is uncertain. Josephus (*Ant* 13.5.7.161) renders the name Chapsaios. Scholars have taken the Greek to be derived from the Hebrew root *ḥlp,* meaning a child given in birth as a substitute for another (Swaim *IDB* 1: 551). Another possibility would be a native of the town Heleph in Naphtali (Josh 19:33). It is further debated if the NT name Alphaeus (Gk *alphaios*), applied to the father of either Levi (Mark 2:14) or of James (Matt 10:3; Mark 3:18; Luke 6:15; Acts 1:13), is derived from the same Hebrew root as Chalphi (Swaim *IDB* 1: 551), or a Hebrew root *hlp* (BAGD, 41), or is a purely Greek name (Norris *IDB* 1: 96).

RUSSELL D. NELSON

CHAMPION. See DAVID'S CHAMPIONS.

CHAPHENATHA (PLACE) [Gk *Chaphenatha*]. A name given to part of the wall of the city of Jerusalem on the valley to the E which is the Kidron (1 Macc 12:37). The actual location of the place is uncertain, and the exact derivation of the name is unknown. This opens the topic to speculation and scholars offer various solutions. Torrey (1934: 32–33) reads *caph henatha* as "the bend of the fountains" and identifies the spot with the curved portion of the wall which ran from the Virgin's Fountain to the Pool of Siloam which was commonly referred to as a fountain (Neh 2:14; 3:15). Odelain and Seguineau (1981: 82, 283) think it possibly means a new quarter NW of the temple to which the city expanded (2 Kgs 22:14; Zeph 1:10). In the time of the Maccabean War, Jonathan (160 B.C.E.) sought to fortify Jerusalem and to build a rampart between the city and the citadel to prevent the garrison from having commercial transaction with the city (1 Macc 12:35–37). The suggestion of Goldstein (*1 Maccabees* AB, 465) that Chaphenatha derives from an Aramaic root meaning "hunger," may suggest an attempt to starve out the citadel, but this is purely speculation. Josephus does not speak of this wall by name, though he refers to Siloam as a fountain of sweet and abundant water (*JW* 5.4.1 §140).

Bibliography

Abel, F.-M. 1949. *Les livres des Maccabées.* Paris.

Odelain, O., and Seguineau, R. 1981. *Dictionary of Proper Names and Places in the Bible.* Garden City.

Torrey, C. C. 1934. Three Troublesome Proper Names in First Maccabees. *JBL* 53: 31–33.

BETTY JANE LILLIE

CHARAX (PLACE) [Gk *Charax*]. Ostensibly a town or city located in Gilead. The name appears only in 2 Macc 12:17 as a place where Jews known as Toubiani lived or had sought refuge, whom Judas Maccabeus subsequently transported to Judah for their safety during the early years of the Maccabean revolt (2 Macc 12:13–28; cf. the corresponding account in 1 Macc 5:24–51). The Gk common noun *charax* has the basic meaning of "stake" and, by extension, "palisade;" it was used to designate either a fort or a siege-enclosure (the latter in Luke 19:43, the only occurrence of the word in the NT); and in the LXX *charax* translates any of several Heb words relating to fortifications or siegeworks. In the Greco–Roman world military camps and marketplaces occasionally bore this name (see L. Bürchner et al., PW 3:2121–2124). If the place name had a strictly Greek origin, it may have been a Seleucid fortification that later developed into a regional market town. By coincidence there was, however, a semitic noun *karak(a)* (from the root *krk,* "to encircle, fortify"), meaning "fortification," "city," "capital," or "mercantile center," which occasionally appears as a place name in the Levant, e.g., the Moabite capital of Karak Moab, transliterated in Greek texts as *Charachmōba* (or *Charakmōba*). The similarity of the two terms in both sound and meaning may have given rise to some confusion in antiquity. Abel (1949: 98, 436) identifies the site referred to in 2 Maccabees as the present village of el-Kerak (M.R. 217066). Goldstein (*2 Maccabees* AB, 440) argues that 2 Maccabees does not refer to a place named Charax at all, but erroneously alludes to the "palisaded camp," i.e., fortress palace, at Araq el-Emir, the seat of the Tobiad dynasty in Ammonitis.

Bibliography

Abel, F. -M. 1949. *Les livres des Maccabées.* Paris.

ROBERT HOUSTON SMITH

CHAREA (PERSON) [Gk *Charea*]. See HARSHA (PERSON).

CHARIOTS. Two-wheeled vehicles used throughout the ANE in warfare, hunting, and travel.

A. Egyptian Chariots
B. Levantine Chariots
C. The Origin and History of the Chariot

A. Egyptian Chariots

The basic design of the first chariots mentioned in the Bible, the Egyptian chariots of Gen 41:46; 46:29; and Exodus 14, must have been very similar to that of the chariots of the immediately preceding 18th Dyn.—the only chariots that have been preserved. These are the six from the tomb of Tutankhamen, the chariot box of Thutmosis IV, and the chariot of Yuia and Tuiu, which, although smaller and apparently hand-drawn, is constructed on the same principal. All of them are in the Egyptian Museum in Cairo. To this list should be added a chariot from an unknown tomb at Thebes, now in the Museo Archeologico in Florence, and a wheel hub with fragmentary spokes from the chariot of Amenophis III, in the Ashmolean Museum, Oxford. Further information is furnished by temple and tomb reliefs and wall paintings, showing such vehicles primarily in military or hunting scenes (Littauer and Crouwel 1985: 1–2, 67–69, 69: n. 4). Although there are no actual remains of chariots from the Ramesside period, reliefs of the era depict vehicles identical with the 18th-Dyn. ones, varying only slightly in the armament they carry (Yadin 1963: 232).

These chariots were light, open vehicles, with two spoked wheels; they were drawn by a pair of horses placed under a yoke at the end of the draft pole. There was just enough room for two men—the driver and the archer—to stand abreast. The floor plan was in the form of a capital D approximately 1 m wide by 0.5 m deep (from front to back). The floor was framed by one or two curved, heat-bent members and a straight, rear floor bar. The chariots were entirely open at the rear for ready access and egress. The light breastwork was framed by a rail of heat-bent wood that usually reached hip height.

The wooden axle ran under the rear of the vehicle (although in some representations it was convenient to show it somewhat farther forward). The wheels, which revolved freely on the axle, were of unique construction. The spokes were formed by the two equal sides of an isosceles triangle (with an apex of 60° for a six-spoked wheel or 90° for a four-spoked one). The legs of the angle (the half spokes) were joined back-to-back with those of the adjacent angles to form whole spokes, elliptical in section. The apices of the triangles either formed an integral part of the nave, as in the Ashmolean fragment (Western 1973), or they nestled in the bays of a casing surrounding the nave, as in the chariots in Cairo. The naves were further extended on either side of the wheel by flanges. The spoke ends were morticed into the rim, or felloe, which was composed of two unequal lengths of heat-bent wood, beveled and overlapping at the ends. The nave and spokehead area was consolidated by glue and rawhide; the latter, when applied wet, has a compressing effect as it dries. The felloe ends were bound at their overlaps with rawhide. A rawhide tire, also undoubtedly shrunk on, helped to consolidate the whole, as well as to protect the tread of the wheels. In some cases the latter were also protected by a wooden "tire" in sections, flush with the rim and with a rawhide tire outside it (Littauer and Crouwel 1985: 76–79).

Rawhide again was the material used to lash the parts of the floor frame and the rear floor bar together, and the interwoven thongs formed a light, resilient flooring in an otherwise springless vehicle. This webbing also maintained tension on the bent wood of the floor frame and helped it to keep its shape.

It is noteworthy that such a construction method would have been practical only in a dry climate, since rawhide is susceptible to dampness. Protection against moisture is indeed implied by the birchbark covering of the rawhide bindings on certain chariots, birchbark having waterproofing properties. Since this material is not native to Egypt, the nearest source being E Anatolia, it seems likely that this design of wheel originated farther E and N as did, indeed, the chariot itself.

The wheels were secured on the axle arms by linch pins of wood, boiled leather, or bronze. The latter, the bronze nave hoops on some wheels and the bronze wire sometimes used to bind the ends of felloes with wooden tires, constitute the only metal parts of the chariot itself that were not purely decorative. Thus the vehicle was held together by a tough, resilient bonding material—rawhide—that could not be jolted loose in rough going, as could metal parts.

To compensate for the instability resulting from the lightness of the vehicle, the track was very wide (1.51–1.8 m). This also permitted long naves (0.32–0.44 m). These helped to reduce the tendency of a wooden wheel to wobble on a wooden axle, where it would not fit as snuggly as modern wheels with metal-lined naves can fit on metal axle arms. To help reduce friction and squeaking, the naves were lined with leather and appear to have been greased.

The chariot body had a siding around the front and the two sides; this was fenestrated in a manner that made it resemble a butcher's apron. In the majority of chariots this siding was probably of leather, of which traces remain; in the parade chariots it was of thin wood, which was coated with gesso molded in a design and gilded (two chariots of Tutankhamen) or silvered (chariot of Thutmosis IV) (Littauer and Crouwel 1985: pls 9, 17, 47).

The draft pole ran back all the way under the chariot floor, its flattened end fitting in an open, horizontal, U-shaped socket beneath the rear floor bar. This prevented horizontal movement and the consequent stress on the only area of attachment, which was to the floor frame at center front. Here it was secured by rawhide bindings and, after describing a flattened S curve, ran forward and upward to the yoke. Slender wooden rods joining the front rail to the pole a short distance before the body provided support for the front breastwork and reinforced the attachment of pole to chariot, which was susceptible to stress—particularly in rough going or on turns. Sometimes, however, if we are to judge from representations, the connection was of leather and could have served only the latter purpose.

The pole ran forward diagonally to a yoke, which was secured on top by a peg and lashings. A pair of straps ran out from an area on the pole, one to either arm of the yoke, and kept it from swiveling on the pole. The yoke, originally devised for bovid draft, lay on the neck directly in front of the withers, and was adapted to horses' conformation by yoke saddles (Littauer 1968: 27–31). These were lashed by their "handles" to the yoke arms, and their "legs" lay along the horses' shoulders and took much of the pull. Their ends were joined by a crescentic strap that crossed the front of the neck and kept the saddles in place. A slack strap ran from each outer yoke-saddle end and under the horse's belly to a point near the end of the pole. This served as a backing element, since there was no breaching strap (Spruytte 1983: 28).

The 18th-Dyn. Egyptian chariots carried as armament two bow cases; to these were added under the Ramessides a pair of short spears or javelins—never shown in use. They may have been for close fighting should the chariot be brought to a standstill. The warrior wore a long, protective tunic of lamellar armor; his head was bare. The driver carried a small rectangular shield. In battle, the reins were tied around the warrior's hips, while the driver with one hand held up a small shield to protect his companion's face and, with the other hand, exercised directional control over the reins in front of the warrior. Both, in a sense, "hung on by the horses' mouths." (Metal horse bits—either of plain bar or jointed-shaffle type—begin to be documented in this period.)

B. Levantine Chariots

Levantine chariots, shown in battle or brought as booty or tribute to Egypt, usually appear almost identical to the Egyptian ones. Those of the Hittites or their Levantine allies at the battle of Kedesh (1286/1285 B.C.) are, however, shown as carrying three men: driver, shield bearer, and javelin thrower. They must have been deeper front-to-back than the Egyptian ones and their sidings are not fenestrated but solid.

The close relationship of chariots in the Egyptian/Near Eastern area may be materially supported by a recent find of the remains of a wheel of the unique "Egyptian" construction, in a 13th-century B.C. context at Lidar in SE Anatolia (H. Hauptmann, personal communication). From about the same period we also have evidence of a simpler and more familiar wheel construction. Wheels found in water-logged burials on the shores of Lake Sevan in Armenia had 28 spokes merely morticed into a barrel nave, although their felloes still consisted of two lengths of heat-bent wood. They belonged to light carts in which the occupants apparently sat, and which could not properly be called chariots (Piggott 1983: 95–96).

C. The Origin and History of the Chariot

These superbly designed Late Bronze Age chariots could not have come into existence without a long line of development behind them that stretched back at least to the Uruk period in S Mesopotamia in the later 4th millennium B.C. Here we find our first evidence of wheeled vehicles, in the form of pictographs on clay tablets. The latter show both sledges and what appear to be sledges mounted on four disk wheels (Littauer and Crouwel 1979: 12). More detailed information comes from the ED period (first half of the 3d millennium B.C.) in the form of bas-reliefs, painted pottery, shell mosaics, or models in the round. From this period also come the first remains of buried vehicles (chiefly in the form of impressions in the soil) in tombs at Kish and Ur. The wheel area has furnished the most definite—and certainly the most important—information. It reveals technical advances that suggest an earlier, intensive, trial-and-error period. The wheels already revolve differentially on a fixed axle, instead of being fixed on a revolving axle—the more primitive system. This not only facilitates turning, but helps to cope with uneven terrain. The disk wheels, moreover, were no longer made of single pieces, whether of slices cut across the grain or with it. A disk cut across the trunk would probably have been the first thing to suggest itself. Owing to the nature of tree growth, however, with its spongy heart wood, annual rings, and exterior sapwood and cambium, this method would soon have proven impractical. It would, moreover have limited wheel diameters to the size of trunks that could be worked with the means available. A solid cut lengthwise of the trunk (i.e. with the grain), while quite viable, would have been limited in size for the same reason. Hence a technique was worked out by which the wheel was made from three pieces of wood vertically cut: a wide central plank, through the center of which the axle arm passed, and two quarter moons flanking it on either side, the whole held together by external battens or thongs.

There were four-wheeled vehicles and two-wheeled ones, none of which could yet properly be called "chariots." The four-wheelers are indeed often depicted in battle scenes, but more than one factor must have discouraged this use, and after the middle of the 3d millennium B.C., they are no longer shown in military contexts. Without a horizontally swiveling front axle, the rear wheels of a four-wheeler cannot follow in the tracks of the front ones and are forced to skid, unless the turning is in a very wide arc. To keep the skidding to a minimum, the vehicles were made very short and narrow. There was just room for the driver and warrior to stand one behind the other, the driver necessarily in front. This would hardly make for an efficient instrument of war. Moreover, although the psychological impact of the first use of wheeled vehicles in battle may originally have had a daunting effect on the enemy, this would have worn off with familiarity. The frequently drawn parallel between these four-wheelers and modern tanks is quite invalid. In the tank the personnel and the motive power are both protected, whereas here both men and animals were highly exposed. While the tank can negotiate a variety of rough terrain, these vehicles were limited to smooth and level ground (Littauer and Crouwel 1979: 32–33).

The two-wheelers, of which there were two body types, are never shown in unquestionably military contexts, and since they could carry only one person, this is not surprising (Littauer and Crouwel 1979: 21).

Draft power in the 3d millennium B.C. consisted—apart from bovids—of teams of (usually) four equids under yoke, attached to a central draft pole. These were either domesticated donkeys (of which there is already evidence at this time) or hybrids. The latter are most likely to have been donkey crosses—either with a small local equid, *Equus hemionus* (similar to an onager), or with true horses. The latter animal was beginning to make its way S from the Pontic steppe, where it had been domesticated in the previous millennium (Littauer and Crouwel 1979: 23–28, 41–43).

It was just before and around 2000 B.C. that new types of wheels and vehicles began to appear and to develop rapidly. The first evidence of an attempt to lighten the clumsy disk wheel was found on a cylinder seal from Tepe Hissar in north-central Iran (Littauer and Crouwel 1979: fig. 21). This "cross-bar" wheel was not yet a spoked one, nor did it prove suitable for speed, but it is still in use today with slow-moving, ox-drawn vehicles in several parts of the world (Littauer and Crouwel 1977: 95–105). By about the turn of the millennium, this type of wheel was also used in central Anatolia, along with the first, truly spoked wheel. At the same time, a two-wheeler, with a light, railed body of different design from the previous ones, appeared. It was drawn by a team of only two equids that seemed to be horses rather than donkeys or hybrids. By the 18th–17th centuries B.C. Syrian cylinder seals began to show a variety of such light, horse-drawn vehicles with two-spoked wheels, demonstrating a period of lively experiment and advance—all tending toward the Late Bronze Age chariots we have described. For the first time, a chariot carried a man with a bow—that chariot weapon *par excellence.* And a chariot in which two could stand *abreast*—a requisite for efficient military performance—appeared. These developments took place in the Near East itself; there is no need for the popular theory of an invasion of horse-drawn chariots from the N steppe (Littauer and Crouwel 1979: 68–71).

The light, fast chariots of the period of the Exodus in the Near East and Egypt were used for warfare, hunting, parade, and travel. In warfare, when manned by archers, as they very often were, they constituted a mobile platform from which to fire volleys of arrows—particularly effective in softening up enemy infantry. Javelins or short, light spears could also be used as distance weapons and could serve for thrusting if the chariot were brought to a standstill. In both cases the chariots served as flanking and pursuing arms. It should be emphasized that frontal attacks by squadrons of chariots would have been self-defeating, with easily injured animals and wheels locking with enemy wheels (the long naves here would be a liability). Fairly smooth and level terrain was essential for the deployment of chariots. This limitation also applied to hunting use. Game would be driven by beaters across the path of the chariot over chosen ground. In Egypt, the Pharaoh and royal family were conveyed in chariots in a procession to the temple on a feast day. While travel is implied by various texts (many of them nonbiblical), its practicality, and certainly its comfort, may be questioned for periods before the introduction of the front-to-back division (see below). But to travel on animal back was considered beneath the dignity of members of a privileged class, and man will suffer much to preserve his status and prestige.

Later actual chariot remains in the Near East are scanty or, at best, only fragmentary, and pictorial evidence is largely wanting for something over 200 years after Ramesses III in the early 12th century B.C.

During the tribal period, the Israelites had neither use for nor the means of producing and maintaining chariotry. The rugged interior terrain they occupied would have been as unsuitable for their own chariots as for those of the enemy. Only the important states of the time, with their resources, organization, and technical skills, could have produced and sustained a chariot corps, with its specially trained wheelwrights, drivers, warriors, and draught teams. Hence the first chariots mentioned after the Egyptian ones of Exodus are not Israelite, but the "iron" chariots of Sisera and the Canaanites and their allies (Joshua 11, 17, 24; Judges 1, 4, 5). We would assume that the chariots of this period would still be very like those illustrated under Ramesses III, although there was a development toward what we see in 9th century B.C. Assyria, and perhaps rather rapidly. The repeated stress on "iron" is puzzling, but must reflect some actual iron component of the chariot—no matter how small. This may have seemed remarkable to the Israelites, who had no iron themselves at the time (*CAH* 2/2: 516), and to whom even a small amount might have been sufficient to categorize the whole vehicle.

As we have seen, metal (even bronze) was rarely and sparingly used in Egyptian chariots, and iron was in general use in Egypt only very late. We should look in the opposite direction for this innovation—to the Neo-Hittite states of N Syria and to Assyria, in close proximity to Anatolia, where iron was already mined and used. Unfortunately, our earliest satisfactory chariot representations from these regions do not appear before the early 9th century B.C. The most suitable areas in the chariot for reinforcement by iron were the wheels and the pole-and-chariot-front connection. These were precisely the parts where iron may have been used on chariots under the Assyrian king Ashurnasirpal II (883–859 B.C.). Three wide wooden tires or felloes appear to have been set around a grooved rim so narrow it was more likely to have been of metal than of wood. Its outer face would have been channeled to receive the felloes, just as the surviving wheels of some cult vehicles from W Europe had channeled bronze rims for this purpose. The short, rodlike connection between the chariot front and the pole could also be of iron, adding greatly to its strength in this area of stress. It is doubtful that much more iron than this was employed. Iron was not yet a cheap commodity and its added weight in the chariot might not have been welcome. May we then assume that the chariots of Sisera resembled the 9th-century B.C. Neo-Hittite and Assyrian ones in general? It is impossible to say.

If the Israelites themselves had chariots, it was no earlier than the reign of David; their mention in 1 Samuel may not indicate anything more than the personal chariots appropriate to the status of oriental royalty (Yadin 1963: 284–85). It is clear that Solomon made efforts to build up an important chariotry. However, the discrepancies between the 40,000 "stalls for horses and chariots" of 1 Kgs 4:26, the 4000 of 2 Chr 9:25, and the 1400 chariots of 1 Kgs 10:26 are confusing and certainly point to the hyperbola typical of the scribes of the period. Yadin (1963: 286) suggests a force of 500 chariots, although Schulman (1979: 142) accepts the 1400 in a study that in general tends to deflate the numbers of Egyptian and Near Eastern chariotry. A yet thornier question is that of Solomon's "chariot cities" (i.e. his stables and carriage houses). The building at Megiddo originally identified as "Solomon's stable" is now known to belong to the period of Ahab (Yadin 1963: 286). The same function has been attributed to several smaller buildings of similar construction at other sites, but this hypothesis has been challenged (Pritchard 1970: 268–76, Herzog 1973: 23–30).

The largest body of documentation for 9th to 7th centuries B.C. comes from Assyria. Aside from texts, this consists of extensive bas-reliefs, a few painted murals, several ivory plaques and cylinder seals, all of which are in strict profile view. Thus some of the proportions have to be extrapolated from models in the round or from fragmentary remains of similar vehicles found in Cyprus and elsewhere dating from the 8th century B.C. and later.

The chariots of the reigns of Ashurnasirpal II (883–859 B.C.) and Shalmaneser III (858–824 B.C.) appear in Assyrian reliefs as identical. They preserved the features of the Egyptian chariot listed above, but varied from these in having a solid siding and smaller wheels with wider felloes. Since axles were placed directly beneath the floor, the reduced wheel diameter would have lowered the chariot. The body, to judge from models found in Cyprus, the Levant, and Transcaucasia, was strengthened by a support down the center. This bar ran from the front breastwork back to a vertical post or loop rising from the rear floor bar (Littauer 1976: 221–22), which provided a handhold for mounting and helped to prevent the crew from jostling each other. The loop or post at the rear seems often to have carried an extra shield, which may have provided partial rear closure.

The two-horse team of earlier times had disappeared. These chariots had teams of three or four, with only two horses under yoke, and the extra horse(s) attached loosely as outriggers. The chariots, however, still appear to function as fast, mobile platforms in warfare. Crossed quivers contained bows, arrows, and sometimes axes, and a short spear was carried at the rear of the vehicle; the latter two (close-range) weapons were for use dismounted or from a standing chariot, as was probably the shield carried at the rear. Both crew and horses might have worn protective armor.

By the time of Tiglath-Pileser III (744–727 B.C.), chariot bodies became rectangular and may have been covered with metal. Wheels were larger and usually had eight spokes. The quivers were hung vertically at each front corner of the body, and although the spear was still carried at the rear, there was no sign of the shield. There may have been a door at the rear and the shield may have been carried inside. The chariots had a complement of three—a driver and two warriors.

Chariots of Sargon II (721–705 B.C.), Sennacherib (704–681 B.C.), and Ashurbanipal (668–627 B.C.) were almost identical. They did not differ greatly from those of Tiglath-Pileser III except in having a larger body and an undoubted door closure at the rear. The wheels were larger and their treads were often studded. War and hunting chariots may have carried a complement of four, in the former case consisting of a driver, an archer, and two shield bearers. Although only one horse is shown in some depictions, these were four-horse chariots with a single draft pole and a fitted yoke, as we know from the depictions of unharnessed vehicles.

The Assyrian chariots of the later 8th and 7th centuries B.C. still appeared to be primarily firing platforms for archers in warfare, although less mobile than before as a result of increased size, heavier construction, and the limitations imposed by four horses under yoke. Better armed and protected, they were sometimes depicted as stationary firing platforms. Mounted troops were by now taking over the traditional role of the light, fast chariotry.

Royal chariot hunts were still taking place, with the aid of beaters and even special game parks. Chariots were also used for ceremonial purposes, sometimes carrying a parasol—the prerogative of royalty.

Unfortunately, despite all the references to chariots in the OT, there are not even fragmentary remains from Palestine. And the only representation of a Palestinian chariot is on an Assyrian relief of the conquest of Lachish by Sennacherib. Here, a chariot being carried off as booty by Assyrian soldiers is shown as indistinguishable from the Assyrian chariots. It is impossible to tell how accurately the Assyrian artist rendered a foreign chariot. In periods of active warfare, however, enemies were apt to copy each other's developments in military material. Moreover, there is recent textual evidence that horses from Kush (Nubia) were being imported by Assyria in the late 8th and 7th centuries B.C. via Samaria, where they were being trained specifically for chariot use (Dalley 1985: 43–48).

From the Persian period, the Levant offers only meager documentation in the form of representations of chariots on coins struck at Sidon under the Achaemenid domination. These resemble the Persian chariots on the reliefs at Persepolis and on some Persian cylinder seals. The floor plan is rectangular, the body spacious, the siding solid. The axle is fixed close to the rear and the large wheels are twelve-spoked. From models in the round we know that the front-to-back division down the center still obtained and was indeed broad enough at this time to furnish a seat on which one could sit sideways. The adaptation of this feature to sitting may possibly go much farther back.

There is mention in 2 Kings 5 (among other places) of what seems to be simply traveling in a chariot. This could be very fatiguing if one had to balance standing for hours in a jolting vehicle without the stimulus of battle to keep one alert.

Of the Persian and Seleucid chariots with scythed wheels, mentioned in texts, which have fascinated posterity, there are no representations. Indeed, their role at the time must have been more psychological than practically effective, to judge from accounts of such battles as Cunaxa (401 B.C.) and Gaugamela (331 B.C.). In the former, they faced Greek mercenaries under Cyrus the Younger, and in the latter, Alexander's troops, but being heavy and clumsy, they were easily outmaneuvered and destroyed. These scythed and armored chariots represented an unsuccessful attempt to cope with the greatly increased number and importance of mounted troops. The military chariot was on its way out.

Under the Seleucids, the heirs of Alexander, who occupied Palestine from 199–165 B.C., Greek games were held, and these must have included chariot racing. These games were continued by at least some of the Roman governors, for Herod held them quinquennially. The Roman circus, with its permanent and monumental structure, only came to the Levant in the early 2d century A.D. (Humphrey 1986: 477, 529–33).

Travel by chariot was perhaps more convenient, with a seat when needed, and there were probably better routes. On the other hand, covered two-wheeled carts and four-wheeled wagons are attested in the Near East, dating as far back as the 3d millennium B.C. and seem to have offered an alternative—if slower—travel conveyance (Littauer and Crouwel 1979; Crouwel 1985).

Bibliography

Crouwel, J. H. 1985. Carts in Iron Age Cyprus. *RDAC*, 203–21.

Dalley, S. 1985. Foreign Chariotry and Cavalry in the Armies of Tiglath-Pileser III. *Iraq* 47: 31–38.

Herzog, Z. 1973. The Storehouses. Pp. 23–30 in *Beersheba* I, ed. Y. Aharoni. Tel Aviv.

Humphrey, J. H. 1986. *Roman Circuses: Arenas for Chariot Racing.* Berkeley.

Littauer, M. A. 1968. The Function of the Yoke Saddle in Ancient Harnessing, *Antiquity* 42: 27–31.

———. 1976. New Light on the Assyrian Chariot. *Or* 26: 217–26.

Littauer, M. A., and Crouwel, J. H. 1977. Origin and Diffusion of the Crossbar Wheel? *Antiquity* 51: 95–105.

———. 1979. *Wheeled Vehicles and Ridden Animals in the Ancient Near East.* Leiden.

———. 1985. *Chariots and Related Equipment from the Tomb of Tutᶜankhamun.* Tutᶜankhamun tomb Series 8. Oxford.

Piggott, S. 1983. *The Earliest Wheeled Transport: From the Atlantic Coast to the Caspian Sea.* Ithaca.

Pritchard, J. 1970. The Megiddo Stables: a Reassessment. Pp. 268–76 in *Near Eastern Archaeology in the Twentieth Century: Essays in Honor of Nelson Glueck,* ed. J. A. Sanders. Garden City, N.Y.

Schulman, A. R. 1979. Chariots, Chariotry and the Hyksos. *JSSEA* 10: 105–53.

Spruytte, J. 1983. *Early Harness Systems.* Trans. M. A. Littauer. London.

Western, A. C. 1973. A Wheel Hub from the Tomb of Amenophis III. *JEA* 59: 91–94.

Yadin, Y. 1963. *Art of Warfare in Biblical Lands.* New York.

Mary Aiken Littauer
J. H. Crouwel

CHARISMATA. See HOLY SPIRIT; GIFTS, SPIRITUAL.

CHARITY. See LOVE (NT AND EARLY JEWISH LITERATURE).

CHARMER. See MAGIC (OT).

CHARMIS (PERSON) [Gk *Charmis*]. One of the elders of Bethuliah (Jdt 6:15, 8:10, 10:6). He is also identified as the son of Melchiel. His name is a translation into Greek of the Hebrew name "Carmi" (Heb *karmî*), which appears in, e.g., Gen 46:9, Josh 7:1, Exod 6:14. He always appears with his fellow elder Chabris. Charmis cannot be identified with any historical personage; the author's purpose in using the name appears to have been to add detail and interest to the narrative. This is in keeping with the genre of the book of Judith.

Sidnie Ann White

CHASING. See JEWELRY.

CHASPHO (PLACE) [Gk *Chaspho*]. One of five cities in Gilead in which Jews were taken captive by the Gentile citizens (1 Macc 5:26). The location of Chaspho is not definitely known, but two sites are often suggested: el-Mezerib on the Yarmuk (cf. Simons, *GTTOT,* 423–24; and Abel 1923: 519) or Khisfin, E of the Sea of Galilee (*MBA,* map 189; and Grollenberg 1956: map 31). The city is probably the same as Caspin, whose destruction is detailed in 2 Macc 12:13–16. Goldstein (*1 Maccabees* AB, 301) suggests that the uncertainty over the first letter of the city's name (*kappa* or *chi*) derives from Greek transliterations of the original name *kspw.* Heb and Aram *kap* is usually transliterated by Gk *chi,* but the local inhabitants may not have aspirated the consonant when pronouncing the name of their town, giving rise to an alternate spelling with a *kappa.* The same lack of aspiration may have given rise to differences in transliterating the *pe* as well. The final "-in" of Kaspin may be an Arabic form of the final *waw.*

The Maccabean Revolt met with early success, including retaking the temple in 164 B.C., which led to Gentile reprisals. Many Jews in Gilead fled to a stronghold at the city of Dathema, from which they sent word to Judas for help. En route to rescue the refugees, Judas learned from a group of Nabateans that other Jews were under attack in the cities of Bozrah, Bosor-in-Alema, Chaspho, Maked, Carnaim, as well as other cities (1 Macc 5:24–27). Judas defeated the Gentiles in Bozrah and Dathema before turning his attention to Chaspho. Assuming Kaspin in 2 Macc 12:13–16 to be Chaspho, one finds elaborations upon the defenses of the town and the extent of bloodshed in the battle. That account, however, makes no mention of Gentile persecution in Gilead and moves awkwardly from an account of victories at Joppa and Jamnia to a battle with Arabs and the attack upon Kaspin. The differences in the accounts in 1 and 2 Maccabees may be due to special pleading on the parts of the authors (i.e., 1 Maccabees was written by a Hasmonean propagandist, while 2 Maccabees was more open to contacts with Greeks) or defective accounts received by the author of 2 Maccabees (Goldstein *2 Maccabees* AB, 432–35).

Bibliography

Abel, F. -M. 1923. Topographie des Campagnes Machabéenes. *RB* 32: 495–521.

Grollenberg, L. H., O. P. 1956. *Atlas of the Bible.* Trans. Joyce M. H. Reid. New York.

Tedesche, S., and Zeitlin, S. 1950. *The First Book of Maccabees.* New York.

———. 1956. *The Second Book of Maccabees.* New York.

PAUL L. REDDITT

CHEBAR (PLACE) [Heb *kĕbār*]. A Mesopotamian watercourse mentioned eight times in the book of Ezekiel (1:1, 3; 3:15, 23; 10:15, 20, 22; 43:3). The Hebrew phrase in which it always occurs, *nĕhar kĕbār,* is translated "river Chebar" in RSV, but the Chebar was actually a canal. Its ancient course left the Euphrates River N of Babylon and flowed 60 miles SE through the vicinity of ancient Nippur, rejoining the Euphrates S of Warka (biblical Erech).

It was beside the Chebar canal, as a member of a settlement of Judean exiles there (Ezek 1:1), that Ezekiel had the vision inaugurating the book of his prophecies (1:4–16). This or another settlement of exiles near the Chebar was called TEL-ABIB (3:15). The Chebar was undoubtedly one among the *nahărōt bābel* "waters of Babylon" by which Judean exiles wept (Ps 137:1).

The canal is referred to in cuneiform documents of the 5th century B.C.E. from the Nippur region (see MURASHU, ARCHIVE OF), spelled *ka-ba-ru* (Hilprecht and Clay 1898 [= BE] text no. 9.84; on the texts, see Zadok 1978: 287). Large manors and date palm groves were located along its course, and the names of several settlements near the Chebar are attested. The Chebar is probably the modern Shatt el-Nil, a silted-up watercourse that once ran E from Babylon and merged with a canal coming down from the Sippar region near Baghdad, continuing S to Nippur and Warka (Vogt 1958: 212). It was probably navigable at one time.

The Chebar is not the same as the Ḫabur River (sometimes spelled Khabur), a tributary of the Euphrates in N Mesopotamia (see HABOR).

Bibliography

Daiches, S. 1910. *The Jews in Babylonia in the Time of Ezra and Nehemiah according to Babylonian Inscriptions.* London.

Hilprecht, H. V., and Clay, A. T. 1898. *Business Documents of the Murashu Sons of Nippur.* Babylonian Expedition of the University of Pennsylvania, Ser. A: Cuneiform Texts 9. Philadelphia.

Vogt, E. 1958. Der Nehar Kebar: Ez 1. *Bib* 39: 211–16.

Zadok, R. 1978. The Nippur Region during the Late Assyrian, Chaldaean and Achaemenian Periods, Chiefly according to Written Sources. *IOS* 8: 266–332.

HENRY O. THOMPSON

CHECKER WORK. An English term that translates three Hebrew words. Two of these are apparently derived from the root *šbṣ,* which in Late Hebrew means to decorate something with a pattern. In Exod 28:4 *(tašbēṣ)* and 28:39 (*Piᶜel* perfect verb) "checker work" designates an ornamental aspect of the tunic worn by the high priest. It may indicate some texture-giving process, such as embroidery. In any case, this ornamentation is used only for Aaron's garment and so contributes to the presentation of special priestly garb, of the best quality, reserved only for the high priest, the holiest of the servants of Yahweh in the tabernacle. The third word rendered "checker work" (Heb *śĕbākâ;* 1 Kgs 7:17) also represents an artistic decoration, the exact nature of which cannot be determined. The temple texts in 1 Kings describe the elaborate capitals surmounting Jachin and Boaz at the entry to the temple's forecourt. These large and symbolic architectural features are heavily adorned, including with "checker work with wreaths of chain work."

CAROL MEYERS

CHEDORLAOMER (PERSON) [Heb *kedorlāᶜōmer*]. King of Elam (Gen 14:1, 4, 5, 9, 17) and the leader of a coalition of four kings (the other three were Amraphel king of Shinar, Arioch king of Ellasar, and Tidal king of Goiim). The kings of Sodom, Gomorrah, Admah, Zeboiim, and Bela (Zoar) had served him twelve years before rebelling in the thirteenth year. In the fourteenth year, Chedorlaomer and his three allies came and defeated the Rephaim, Zuzim, Emim, Horites, Amalekites, Amorites, and finally the aforementioned five kings in a battle in the Valley of Siddim. They plundered Sodom and Gomorrah and took away Abram's nephew Lot, but on their way back were defeated by Abram and lost all of their booty.

A. The Name

The very peculiar Genesis 14 has long attracted the attention of biblical scholars and historians of the ANE who have tried to identify the four eastern kings and to clarify the historical background of the narrative. The name "Chedorlaomer" (which, as shown by the form in LXX, *chodollogomor,* was pronounced with a *ġayin*) was found to be genuinely Elamite; both of its elements, *kudur* (Akk rendering of Elamite *kutir*) and the DN *Lagamar,* occur in Elamite royal names. But no king of Elam named **Kutir/Kudur-Lagamar* is attested, nor is there the slightest evidence of Elamite political or military engagement in Palestine at any time in history. The key to understanding this name (as well as the names of his three confederates) is provided by the so-called "Chedorlaomer texts" (or "Spartoli tablets").

B. The "Chedorlaomer Texts"

1. General Description. Th. G. Pinches (1897) published, from a collection of late Babylonian tablets in the British Museum purchased from a dealer named Spartoli, three tablets (Sp. III:2; Sp. 158+II, 962; Sp. II, 987) containing personal names, three of which were in some way reminiscent of three of the four eastern kings in Genesis 14. The tablets date from the Parthian period (after 142 B.C.) but were no doubt copied from earlier (7th or 6th century B.C.) originals. One of the tablets is a prose summary, while the other two are fragmentary poetic presentations of the same events. They are written in a metaphorical, allusive style not unlike that of QL or the Sibylline Oracles.

These texts deal with four kings who, in consecutive turns and according to divine will, sacked, destroyed, flooded, or at least oppressed Babylon and its holiest shrine, Esagila, and carried away the statues of its gods. Afterward, three of them were murdered by their own sons, while the fourth was chased into the sea and died there. The names of these kings were intentionally disguised under pseudonyms or cryptic spellings based on the use of rare ideograms and on the play of polyphones. These names are: (1) [m]KU.KU.KU.MAL (in one tablet) or [m]KU.KU.KU.KU.MAL (in the other two) king of Elam, the only one whose country is plainly spelled out; (2) [m]BÀD.MAḪ-[d]MAŠ (var. [m]DUR.MAḪ-[d]MAŠ, incorrectly read by Pinches [1897] and Jeremias [1917] as *Dūr-maḫ-ilāni*) son of [m]ÌR-[d]É-*a-ku*, var. [m]ÌR-É-*ku-a* (in which ÌR could be read *èri*); (3) [m]*Tu-ud-ḫul-a* son of [m]GAZ.ZA. [..]; and (4) [m]*I-bil-*[d]*Tu-tu*. Pinches tried to read the first name [m]*Ku-dúr-laḫ-mal* or [m]*Ku-dúr-laḫ-ga-mal* and equated it with the Chedorlaomer of Genesis 14. He saw in the patronymic of the second king, [m]*Èri-*[d]*É-a-ku*, the prototype of Arioch; and in the name of the third king, [m]*Tu-ud-ḫul-a*, the prototype of Tidal (Heb *tidʿal*, originally, with LXX, **tadġal*), both of which are also mentioned in Genesis 14. This triple onomastic resemblance, as well as the general tenor of the Chedorlaomer texts (which is somewhat similar to the Deuteronomist historiography [see below]), make it highly probable that the author of Genesis 14 was acquainted with some earlier versions of these Chedorlaomer texts. This raises two questions: (1) what historical characters are hidden behind the cryptic names of the Chedorlaomer texts? and (2) what relationship, if any, exists between the events alluded to in these texts and the story of Genesis 14?

2. The Cryptic Names. Jeremias (1917), proceeding from the ample description of the destructions and atrocities perpetrated by [m]KU.KU.KU.(KU.)MAL in Babylon and other cities of Babylonia, identified him with the Elamite Kutir-Naḫḫunte (Akk Kudur-Naḫḫundu) II, who took part in the conquest of Babylonia by his father, King Shutruk-Naḫḫunte (1185–1155 B.C.), and was left behind as its viceroy (1160–1155). He also defeated and captured the last Kassite king of Babylonia, and deported him to Elam. In the words of a Babylonian historical inscription, he "swept away all the people of Akkad like a deluge, turned Babylon and the other famous shrines into piles of rubble," and carried away to Elam the statue of Marduk along with masses of Babylonians. Kutir-Naḫḫunte succeeded his father in 1155 but died after only four years on the throne. Jeremias read [m]KU.KU.KU.KU.MAL as [m]*Ku-dúr-náḫ-ḫun-*te*, in which only the value of the last sign is hypothetical. This identification was accepted by Cameron (1936: 111), Albright (1942: 34), and Hinz (1972: 127). Earlier, Albright (1921: 71 n. 4 and 1926: 233 n. 8) showed that by a different decoding of the cryptic writing of the name it could be read [m]*Ku-dúr-laḫam-mal*, a decoding from which the biblical form of the name derived.

After Böhl's widely accepted, but wrong, identification of [m]*Tu-ud-ḫul-a* with one of the Hittite kings named Tudḫaliyaš, Tadmor found the correct solution by equating him with the Assyrian king Sennacherib (see TIDAL). Astour (1966) identified the remaining two kings of the Chedorlaomer texts with Tukulti-Ninurta I of Assyria (see ARIOCH) and with the Chaldean Merodach-baladan (see AMRAPHEL). The common denominator between these four rulers is that each of them, independently, occupied Babylon, oppressed it to a greater or lesser degree, and took away its sacred divine images, including the statue of its chief god Marduk; furthermore, all of them came to a tragic end.

3. Relationship to Genesis 14. All attempts to reconstruct the link between the Chedorlaomer texts and Genesis 14 remain speculative. However, the available evidence seems consistent with the following hypothesis: A Jew in Babylon, versed in Akkadian language and cuneiform script, found in an early version of the Chedorlaomer texts certain things consistent with his anti-Babylonian feelings. Among these were the following: (1) the depiction of history as a recurring cycle of sinfulness, divine wrath, and punishment by invasion and destruction, followed by repentance, divine forgiveness, and restoration; (2) stark images of violence and devastations visited upon Babylon, which must have been read with a gloating anticipation of their imminent repetition (compare Isaiah 47; Jeremiah 50–51); and (3) the recurring motif of deluge, flood, and the submergence of Babylon by water. This latter feature of the Chedorlaomer texts evoked the popular legend of the destruction of Sodom and Gomorrah, which was already being associated with the imminent destruction of Babylon in various prophecies of the exilic period (Isa 13:19; 14:22–23; Jer 50:39–40; 51:41–42). The writer of Genesis 14 replaced Babylon with Sodom and Gomorrah, and had them sacked by the same four kings simultaneously (rather than consecutively as in the Chedorlaomer texts). In addition, he depicted the four kings victoriously traversing the territory between Dan and Elath (El Paran), eventually to be defeated by Abram, who received a blessing from Melchizedek, king of Salem. This implies that the land legally belonged to Abram and his descendants, and that Salem (i.e., Jerusalem), in the person of its priest-king Melchizedek, exercised a religious supremacy over the country from the earliest time.

Bibliography

Albright, W. F. 1921. A Revision of Early Hebrew Chronology. *JPOS* 1: 49–79.

———. 1926. The Historical Background of Genesis XIV. *JSOR* 10: 231–69.

———. 1942. A Third Revision of the Early Chronology of Western Asia. *BASOR* 88: 28–36.

Astour, M. C. 1966. Political and Cosmic Symbolism in Genesis 14 and in Its Babylonian Sources. Pp. 65–112 in *Biblical Motifs: Origins and Transformations,* ed. A. Altmann. Philip W. Lown Institute of Advanced Judaic Studies 3. Cambridge, MA.

Böhl, F. M. Th. 1916. "Tudʾalia I, Zeitgenosse des Abraham, um 1650 v. Chr." *ZAW* 36: 65–73.

Cameron, G. G. 1936. *History of Early Iran.* Chicago.

Hinz, W. 1972. *The Lost World of Elam: Re-creation of a Vanished Civilization.* Trans. J. Barnes. London.

Jeremias, A. 1917. Die sogenannten Kedorlaomer-Texte. Pp. 69–97 in *Orientalistische Schriften Fritz Hommel.* Vol. I = *MVAG* 21. Leipzig.

Pinches, Th. G. 1897. Certain Inscriptions and Records Referring to Babylonia and Elam and Their Rulers, and Other Matters. *Journal of the Transactions of the Victoria Institute* 29: 43–89.

MICHAEL C. ASTOUR

CHEETAH. See ZOOLOGY.

CHELAL (PERSON) [Heb *kĕlāl*]. A descendant of Pahathmoab and one of the returned exiles who was required by Ezra to divorce his foreign wife (Ezra 10:30). His name does not appear in the parallel list in 1 Esdr 9:31. While the etymology of the name "Chelal" is not certain, it is probably derived from the root *kll,* meaning "to be perfect." Chelal was a member of a family from which groups of exiles returned with Zerubbabel (Ezra 2:6; Neh 7:11) and later with Ezra (Ezra 8:4). For further discussion, see BEDEIAH.

JEFFREY A. FAGER

CHELLEANS [Gk *Cheleōn*]. An otherwise unknown people mentioned in the book of Judith (Jdt 2:23). It should be noted that the Greek manuscripts show a wide variation in spelling (*chaldiaōn, chellaiōn, chaldaiou,* etc.). The reading "Chaldeans" should be understood as a scribal error. The definite article occurs as both a singular or a plural (*tēs* or *tōn*). Enslin suggests that the singular *tēs* understands an omitted *gēs* ("earth"), while Moore (*Judith* AB) translated the phrase as a place name ("south of Cheleon"), and identifies it with ancient Cholle (modern el-Khalle), located between Palmyra and the Euphrates. If the phrase is translated to refer to a people, they are located to the N of the children of Ishmael, above the desert. This location would still allow them to be connected with ancient Cholle. It is not clear whether or not the author intended them to be related to the site CHELOUS in 1:9.

Bibliography

Enslin, M. S. 1972. *The Book of Judith.* Leiden.

SIDNIE ANN WHITE

CHELOUS (PLACE) [Gk *Chelous*]. A site in the book of Judith, located in the vicinity of Jerusalem (Jdt 1:9). Two possible identifications have been proposed for this site. The first identification is with HALHUL (M.R. 159110) located 4 mi to the N of Hebron. This town is mentioned in Josh 15:58 as one of the towns of the tribe of Judah. The second identification is with Chalutṣa (M.R. 117056), modern Khalasa, which is located to the SE of Beersheba. It should be noted that, given the genre of the book of Judith, the name may be fictitious. It is not clear whether or not the author of Judith intended to relate the site Chelous with the CHELLEANS mentioned in 2:23.

SIDNIE ANN WHITE

CHELUB (PERSON) [Heb *kĕlûb*]. **1.** Brother of Shuhah, father of Mehir, and grandfather of Eshton (1 Chr 4:11). None of these persons are mentioned elsewhere and Chelub's own parents are not identified. In 1 Chr 4:12, the entire group is termed "the men of Recah" (LXX "Rechab," i.e., Rechabites). The LXX, Vg, and Syriac versions read "Caleb" instead of "Chelub" (see Williamson *1 & 2 Chronicles* NCBC, 60; Braun *1 Chronicles* WBC, 55–58). In addition, the LXX reads "the father of Ascha" in place of "the brother of Shuhah," a variation which reinforces the identification with Caleb who in Josh 15:16–17 (= Judg 1:12–13) gives his daughter Achsah to Othniel after he defeated Kiriath-sepher (= Debir). 1 Chr 2:9 mentions a person named Chelubai whose extended family does overlap partially with the extended family of Caleb (2:18, 42). In 1 Chr 4:11, however, the compiler seems to distinguish Chelub from Caleb, for the latter is included subsequently among the references to Kenaz (4:13–15).

2. The father of Ezri, who was a steward of royal property appointed by David (1 Chr 27:26). His name appears in a list of stewards of crown property (1 Chr 27:25–31).

RICHARD W. NYSSE

CHELUBAI (PERSON) [Heb *kĕlûbāy*]. See CALEB.

CHELUHI (PERSON). A descendant of Bani and one of the returned exiles who was required by Ezra to divorce his foreign wife (Ezra 10:35). His name does not appear in the parallel list in 1 Esdr 9:34. The Hebrew text is uncertain (K *klhy,* Q *kĕlûhû*). The LXX *(chelia)* may indicate a corruption of an original *kĕlāyāh,* meaning "Yahweh is perfect" (Williamson, *Ezra, Nehemiah* WBC, 144). Cheluhi was a member of a family from which a group of exiles returned with Zerubbabel (Ezra 2:10). For further discussion, see BEDEIAH.

JEFFREY A. FAGER

CHEMOSH (DEITY) [Heb *kĕmôš*]. The national deity of the Moabites. Like several other small kingdoms, the Moabites lost their independence during the Neo-Babylonian expansion in the early 6th century B.C. The Moabite state never reappeared, and the subsequent mixture of peoples and religions (e.g., Nabatean, Greek, Roman, Christian) led to the extinction of Moabite religion. Some of its features persisted after the kingdom of Moab collapsed, even as some religious elements from the Bronze Age had undoubtedly survived in the beliefs and practices of the Moabites in the Iron Age. The position of the god Chemosh (hereafter Kemosh) remained significant throughout Moab's history; this deity is the fundamental datum in the study of Moabite religion.

Unfortunately, the extant sources that enable us to reconstruct Moabite religion are relatively meager. As in the study of other ANE religions, relevant data come from two kinds of sources, textual and archaeological. Naturally, many of the archaeological data are subject to a broad range of interpretation, and conclusions based on such evidence remain tentative. There is occasional uncertainty in the scholarly interpretations of written sources pertaining to Moabite religion. Few texts relate directly to the religious beliefs of the Moabites, and some of our knowledge about this people's religion is derived from non-Moabite texts.

The most important sources of information on Moabite religion are the OT and the Mesha Inscription. Although the Hebrew scriptures are critical of the religion of Moab, these incidental references should not be dismissed in a cavalier manner. Undoubtedly, the most important source for the study of Moabite religion is the Mesha Inscription, a 34-line text which was written ca. 830 B.C. This inscription is a memorial stele that commemorates Mesha's triumph over Israel, a victory that was attributed to the favor of Kemosh, Moab's principal deity. According to the stele (lines 3–4), Mesha commissioned the inscription to coincide with his dedication of a high place *(bamah)* in honor of Kemosh.

Many scholars have come to assume that Yahweh, Milcom, Kemosh, and Qaus were the leading deities, the national gods, of Israel, Ammon, Moab, and Edom, respectively. Clearly, these peoples held many religious beliefs and practices in common, so much so that the theologies and functions of these various deities were somewhat interchangeable. Even though the Hebrew Bible and the Mesha Inscription indicate that Yahweh and Kemosh and their peoples were in conflict with each other, the similarities in the theology and cult of these two deities are remarkable. Simply put, everything we know about the Moabites' perception of Kemosh finds its parallel in Hebrew religion. Indeed, one scholar has suggested that the Mesha Inscription's treatment of Kemosh reads like a chapter from the Bible.

The logical place to begin any detailed discussion of Moabite religion is with the nature and function of Kemosh. There seems to be little doubt that Kemosh was perceived as the national god of the Moabites, although it is likely that the people of ancient Moab practiced henotheism throughout their history (i.e., they worshiped Kemosh as their leading deity but recognized other deities as well). It is probable that the Moabites were polytheistic in some periods, which could reflect the Canaanite background of this region and the polytheism of Moab's neighbors during the Late Bronze Age and Iron Age.

Kemosh was, of course, very important to the Moabites, but their deity was also worshiped by other ancient peoples before the establishment of the Moabite kingdom and outside of Moab. A god named Kamish (^{d}*ka-mi-iš*) appears in deity lists on tablets from Tell Mardikh (ancient Ebla), the Syrian city-state whose royal archives date to ca. 2600–2250 B.C. There seems to be little doubt that this name "Kamish" is an archaic form of Kemosh. Not only is Kamish listed among the 500 deities acknowledged at Ebla, but he was regarded as one of the principal gods of the city, with his name appearing in the name of a month, in personal names, and in the place name "Carchemish" *(karkamiš)*. There was a temple for Kamish at Ebla; Kamish was also the recipient of offerings. Of great importance is the way in which the Eblaite spelling ^{d}*ka-mi-iš*, or ^{d}*ka-me-iš*, may explain the variant spelling *k*^{e}*miš* in Jer. 48:7, since the other seven appearances of this god's name in the OT are read *k*^{e}*moš*. Textual critics have eagerly amended the consonantal *kmyš* of Jer. 48:7 to *kmwš*, but this is no longer necessary, since the former spelling may reflect the more ancient tradition. The Mesha Inscription spells this god's name *kms*, which is usually vocalized Kemosh.

Even before the recovery of the name "Kamish" at Tell Mardikh, a god with the compound name "mud" or "clay" + *kam(m)ut* (*ṯṯ* or *ṯ* + *kmṯ*) was known from the Ugaritic tablets. A little circular reasoning, based on this reference, allows us to infer that Kemosh was a god of infernal nature. This perception of Kemosh's character is reinforced by the equation between the Mesopotamian deity, Nergal, and ^{d}*ka-am-muš* in an Assyrian god list. Clearly, these ancient and extra-Moabite references to names similar to Kemosh indicate that Kemosh, the leading Moabite deity, was part of an older Semitic pantheon with which a number of Near Eastern peoples were acquainted.

While the etymology of the name "Kemosh" remains uncertain, knowledge about the Moabite understanding of Kemosh's nature and function comes from a variety of sources. The OT mentions this god by name eight times (Num 21:29; Judg 11:24; 1 Kgs 11:7; 11:33; 2 Kgs 23:13; Jer 48:7, 13, 46), always recognizing that Kemosh was the national deity of Moab and that his cult, though similar to Yahweh's, was a rival to the faith of Israel. The one possible exception to the Bible's acknowledgment that Kemosh was the god of Moab exclusively is the puzzling and intriguing reference to this deity in Judg 11:24, a verse that has been interpreted in a variety of ways. In this text, Jephthah makes reference to Kemosh giving land to his (i.e., Kemosh's) people, the *Ammonites.* The problem has been variously solved by assuming that the verse contains a Kemosh-Milcom equation, a Moabite-Ammonite equation, an *ad hominem* argument, an interpolation, a scribal blunder, or an example of diplomatic protocol. Whatever the correct interpretation may be, the important thing to notice is that the text suggests that it was the prerogative of Kemosh to give land to his people.

Another source of information about Kemosh's nature and function is, of course, the Mesha Inscription itself. This Moabite text refers to Kemosh a dozen times, if one includes the theophoric name of Mesha's father, usually restored as Kemosh-yat (line 1), and the compound name of Ashtar-Kemosh (line 17). The precise meaning of the latter remains elusive, though many explanations have been proposed. A number of scholars have suggested that Ashtar-Kemosh is the name of Kemosh's consort, the goddess who was considered the female counterpart of Kemosh; Ashtar-Kemosh has been connected with Ishtar or Astarte. Among other evidence that supports this interpretation is an Aramaic inscription from Kerak that dates to the Hellenistic period; this late text identifies Kemosh's as Sarra. Reference should also be made to the presence of a god and a goddess on the famous Baluʿ Stele, which probably dates to the 12th–11th centuries B.C.

Another group of scholars suggest that Ashtar-Kemosh was simply a compound name for the leading deity of Moab. The element "Ashtar" is associated with the Canaanite god Athtar or ʿAṯtar, the Venus star; the compound name may have been an epithet or hypostasis of ʿAṯtar. Therefore, according to this argument, the Mesha Inscription indicates that the two deities were either identified or assimilated. Since the text refers to Kemosh eleven other times, however, it is likely that Ashtar-Kemosh was simply another name of Moab's national god. In the final analysis, it must be admitted that the unique appearance of this compound name makes it impossible for us to be certain about the meaning of Ashtar-Kemosh.

In addition to the 34-line Mesha Inscription, another reference to Kemosh comes from another inscription from Dhiban, a fragmentary text whose last line can be restored as *bt kmš*, "temple of Kemosh." This text is contemporaneous with the Mesha Inscription and clearly refers to a Kemosh sanctuary in ancient Dibon. A fragmentary text from Kerak, dating to the same period, mentions Kemosh twice. One use of Kemosh appears in the theophoric name of Mesha's father, Kemosh-yat; Kemosh is also mentioned in this text in association with a cultic installation, perhaps a temple.

In addition to the preceding biblical and nonbiblical texts, there are several artistic representations that may (or may not) relate to Kemosh. Because of the description of Kemosh on the Mesha Inscription, it is perhaps natural to view this deity as a god of war. Indeed, this warlike character and the presence of a town named Areopolis (modern Rabba) in the center of Moab have led some scholars to link Kemosh with Ares, the Greek god of war, and to identify the figures on a Greek coin from Areopolis and on the Shihan Warrior Stele as Kemosh. It is possible that some of the small human figurines found in Moab and a recently published seal depict Kemosh, but it must be admitted that there is no representation that can be identified as Kemosh with certainty. It is likely that such artistic representations of Moab's national god were made, however, as may be implied in Jer 48:7.

While the Mesha Inscription was intended to celebrate the achievements of Mesha, there is no doubt that the text also reflects an attitude of loyalty and thanksgiving to the Moabite national god. The OT writers regarded the Moabites as the "people of Kemosh" (Num 21:29; Jer 48:46), a designation that was probably used by the people of Moab themselves. The frequent references to Kemosh in the Mesha Inscription indicate that he was thought to display a wide range of emotions in his control over and involvement with Moab. While it is likely that the Moabites sought Kemosh's favor in many aspects of life, the Mesha Inscription is most emphatic on his intervention and specific guidance in times of war, as is clear in the Moabites' practice of *ḥerem*.

GERALD L. MATTINGLY

CHENAANAH (PERSON) [Heb *kĕnaʿănâ*]. A great-grandson of Benjamin according to one Benjaminite genealogy (1 Chr 7:10). He is one of those Benjaminites described as "mighty warriors . . . ready for service in war," a designation particularly given to the descendants of Benjamin through Jediael. The genealogy in which Chenaanah is found belonging to Benjamin (1 Chr 7:6–12) has been considered by some scholars as mistakenly attributed to Benjamin. Guthrie (*IDB* 1: 556) suggests that the list more likely belongs to Zebulun. This suggestion is made on the basis that 1 Chronicles 8 gives a longer and very different genealogy of Benjamin, while Zebulun is lacking in the genealogies given by the Chronicler. Williamson (*Chronicles* NCBC, 77) calls attention to this and other features of the smaller list which have caused some scholars to view it as a corrupt genealogy of Zebulun, but he concludes that the names are probable in a Benjaminite context, and that the textual emendations proposed by those who wish to attach the list to Zebulun are "too violent to inspire confidence." Myers (*1 Chronicles* AB, 53, 59) likewise sees no reason to attribute the shorter genealogy to Zebulun, stating that it is found in its "proper place" in the Chronicler's arrangement of tribal genealogies.

SIEGFRIED S. JOHNSON

CHENANI (PERSON) [Heb *kĕnānî*]. A Levite present at the public reading of the Law by Ezra (Neh 9:4). A shortened form of a name (Heb *kĕnanyāhû*) meaning "Yahweh has made firm" (Brockington *Ezra, Nehemiah, Esther* NCBC, 171).

FREDERICK W. SCHMIDT

CHENANIAH (PERSON) [Heb *kĕnanyāhû, kĕnanyāh*]. Two individuals in the OT bear this name. It is a theophoric name composed of two elements: *knn* = "be firm/substantial" and *yh* = divine name "*yah*"/"*yahu*" for Yahweh. The name has been translated either "Y. is firm" (Fowler *TPNAH*, 76) or "Y. strengthens" (Noth *IPN*, 179).

1. Leader *(śar)* of the Levites in 1 Chr 15:22, 27. In v 27 Chenaniah is clearly understood as the leader of the singers in the entourage which brought the ark to Jerusalem. Chenaniah's role in v 22, however, is not as clear (for divergent opinions on the relation of vv 22 and 27 and thus the role of Chenaniah, see Rudolph *Chronikbücher* HAT, 125 and Williamson *Chronicles* NCBC, 122). The issue turns on the interpretation of *bammaśśāʾ*, lit., "in the lifting up," in v 22. If its object is understood to be "songs," as in v 27, Chenaniah was an expert in and leader of the music. If, however, its object is the ark, as is clearly the case at 2 Chr 35:3, then his expertise was in the proper manner of carrying the ark (see 1 Chr 15:2, 13–15). If, on the other hand, *maśśāʾ* is to be understood as "oracle," as in 2 Chr 24:27, then Chenaniah was a leader who was learned in the art of giving oracles (Mowinckel 1923: 18).

2. An administrative official in 1 Chr 26:29. His Levitical roots are traced through Izhar, the son of Kohath. He and his "family" were appointed to secular tasks as judges and administrative subordinates to higher officials (van der Ploeg 1954).

Bibliography

Mowinckel, S. 1923. *Psalmenstudien III. Kultprophetie und Prophetische Psalmen.* Kristiana.

Ploeg, J. van der. 1954. Les *šōṭĕrîm* d'Israel. *OTS* 10: 185–96.

J. S. ROGERS

CHEPHAR-AMMONI (PLACE) [Heb *kĕpar hāʿamōnāy*]. A village that was listed among the cities of the tribe of Benjamin (Josh 18:24). The Hebrew text reading tradition (Qere) presented the name of this village as *kĕpar hāʿamōnâ* while the writing tradition (Kethib) presented it as *kĕpar hāʿamōnāy* or *kĕpar hāʿamōnî*. This final presentation supports the conclusion that the village (Heb *kĕpar*) was one inhabited by Ammonites. Press (1952: 482) suggested its founder may have been Zelek the Ammonite, one of David's mighty men (2 Sam 23:37). Although the root *kpr* appears in 1 Sam 6:18 to indicate unwalled villages, Albright (1924: 154) noted that the term was not used in place names in the preexilic period, making it, therefore, unlikely that the name meant "village of the Ammonites." He posited that two cities were indicated by Chephar-Ammoni, Chephirah (a mistaken repetition from Josh 18:26), and Ammoni. Three major Greek versions (Vaticanus, Alexandrinus, and Luciani) do not translate *kpr* as "village," but instead transliterate *kfr* with the place name. Codex Vaticanus separates *kfr* from Moni as if they were separate villages (Gk *Kephira kai Moni*). The Vulgate, however, renders it, *villa Elmona.* Though it has been suggested that the present Khirbet Kafr ʿAna (M.R. 173153) is the site of Cephar-Ammoni (*GP*, 92; Press 1952: 482), this identification is not generally accepted by scholars. Kallai (1960: 33–34) noted that several of the names that are in this part of the list of Benjaminite cities actually lie outside the boundaries of Benjamin as described in the boundary descriptions (Josh 18:12–21). Both Beth-Hoglah and Beth-Arabah lay in the district of Judah. Zamarim, Bethel, Ophrah, and Geba (Geba of Ephraim) lay in the district of Ephraim. Chephar-Ammoni, like its neighbors in the list, probably lay in Ephraim (as does Khirbet Kafr ʿAna). The presence of all of these cities in a Benjamin city list is best explained as reflecting the territorial situation following Abijah's conquests in Mount Ephraim (2 Chr 13:19; *HGB*, 398).

Bibliography

Albright, W. F. 1924. The Northern Boundry of Benjamin. *AASOR* 4: 150–55.

Kallai, Z. 1960. *The Northern Boundries of Judah from the Settlement of the Tribes Until the Beginning of the Hasmonaean Period.* Jerusalem (in Hebrew).

Press, I. 1952. *A Topographical-Historical Encyclopaedia of Palestine.* Vol. 3. Jerusalem (in Hebrew).

Susan E. McGarry

CHEPHIRAH (PLACE) [Heb *kĕpîrâ*]. A town in the territory of Benjamin (Josh 18:26). Chephirah was one of the four Hivite cities whose inhabitants deceived Israel, making peace with Joshua on the pretense that they were from a distant land (Josh 9:17). The inhabitants of Chephirah and the other three Hivite towns (Gibeon, Kiriath-jearim, and Beeroth) were thus spared annihilation and were allowed to live among the Israelites as woodcutters and water carriers (Josh 9:26–27). The town was incorporated into the tribal territory of Benjamin (Josh 18:26), and later its inhabitants were among those who returned from Babylonian Exile (Ezra 2:25; Neh 7:29).

Edward Robinson (1867: 146) was the first modern scholar to identify Chephirah with Khirbet el-Kefireh (M.R. 160137), a 4–6-acre tell located about 1.5 mi N of Kiriath-jearim and 5 mi WSW of Gibeon (el-Jib). Virtually all scholars agree with this identification (*GP* 2:92, 120, 298; Kallai *EncMiqr* 4:228–29; Yeivin 1971: 141, *LBHG*, 433; etc.). Kh. el-Kefireh has not been systematically examined. Garstang (1931: 166, 369) visited the site and found LB pottery there. The site is located on a steep, high spur, bounded on the N and S by two wadies that join just W of the ruin to form Wadi Qotneh, which descends to the Aijalon Valley. During biblical times Chephirah guarded the midpoint of a secondary road that connected the cities of Gibeon and Aijalon, the main connecting road being the famous Beth-horon Ascent, located about 3–4 miles farther N.

Bibliography

Garstang, J. 1931. *Joshua, Judges.* London. Repr. 1978.

Robinson, E. 1867. *Biblical Researches in Palestine and the Adjacent Regions.* 3d ed. 3 vols. London. Repr. Jerusalem, 1970.

Yeivin, S. 1971. The Benjaminite Settlement in the Western Part of Their Territory. *IEJ* 21: 141–54.

David A. Dorsey

CHERAN (PERSON) [Heb *kĕrān*]. A clan name in the genealogical clan list of Seir the Horite. This person appears in Gen 36:26 as well as in the matching genealogy in 1 Chr 1:41. He is said to be the fourth son of the clan chief DISHON and is thus the grandson of Seir. These relationships may reflect tribal affiliation or alliance rather than blood kinship. For discussion of the Horite clans, see JAAKAN.

Victor H. Matthews

CHERETHITES [Heb *kĕrētî; kĕrētîm*]. A people of presumably Aegean origin who settled along the SW coast of Palestine and from whose ranks David drew the core of his personal guard (1 Sam 30:14; 2 Sam 8:18; 15:18; etc.). The term "Cherethite" is first encountered in reference to a region of the Negeb in the account of the sick Egyptian slave abandoned by his Amalekite master and found by David (1 Sam 30:14). The Cherethites are most frequently mentioned in conjunction with the PELETHITES. Together they formed a mercenary unit under the command of Benaiah which was distinct from the regular army (2 Sam 8:18; 20:23 [Qere; about the Kethib *kry* see CARITES] 2 Kgs 11:4, 19; 1 Chr 18:17; see also de Vaux *AncIsr*, 123, 219–22). They owed their allegiance to David and showed him great loyalty in times of crisis.

The Cherethites and the Pelethites accompanied David on his flight from Absalom (2 Sam 15:18); they went out in pursuit of Sheba during his revolt against David (2 Sam 20:7); and they were instrumental in Zadok, Nathan, and Benaiah's efforts to crown Solomon king (1 Kgs 1:38, 44). After the death of David, the Cherethites and the Pelethites disappeared from the biblical record. Albeit there are two references to the Cherethites as a people in poetic parallel with the Philistines in prophetic oracles (Ezek 25:16; Zeph 2:5).

Research on the Cherethites has tended to focus on the

questions of their geographical origin and ethnic affiliation. Although the island of Crete is named Caphtor in the Hebrew Bible (Deut 2:23; Jer 47:4; etc.; Akk Kaptara, Eg Keftiu; see CAPHTOR), most scholars view the Heb *kĕrētî* as meaning Cretan and seek the Cherethites' roots on the island of Crete (Gk *Krētē;* Albright 1920–1921; Delcor 1978; but see Virolleaud [1936: 8–10] who views the Ugaritic hero Keret as the eponymous ancestor of the *kĕrētîm;* arguments against this latter view can be found in Delcor 1978: 414–15).

The exact relationship between the Cherethites and the Philistines is unclear. Since the Hebrew Bible ascribes the Philistines' origin to the island of Caphtor (Amos 9:7), it would appear that the Cherethites and the Philistines came from the same region of the Aegean. In spite of poetic passages such as Ezek 25:16 and Zeph 2:5 in which the Cherethites and the Philistines are juxtaposed, it cannot be determined whether the Cherethites were identical with the Philistines, a subgroup of the Philistines, or a separate ethnic entity. Owing to the absence of their name among the Sea Peoples in the Medinet Habu inscription of Ramses III (*ANET,* 262–63), Albright (1920–21) surmised that the Cherethites were foreign mercenaries already in Egyptian employ before the mass movements of Sea Peoples at the end of the Bronze Age and the beginning of the Iron Age which brought the Philistines to Canaan. Hence they were unrelated to the Philistines and able to enter David's service, in which they presumably fought against the Philistines. Using the same evidence, Delcor (1978: 421) concluded that the Cherethites must have arrived on the scene at about the time of David, or shortly before. In his opinion they either merged with or formed a subgroup of the Philistines. The area of Cherethite settlement was in the Negeb to the S and SE of Gaza (Aharoni 1958: 28–30). It may have been during the time of David's service to Achish, king of Gath, at Ziklag (1 Samuel 27; 29) that he hired the loyalty of the Cherethites and formed them into his personal bodyguard (McCarter *1 Samuel* AB, 435).

Bibliography

Aharoni, Y. 1958. The Negeb of Judah. *IEJ* 8: 26–38.

Albright, W. F. 1920–21. A Colony of Cretan Mercenaries on the Coast of the Negeb. *JPOS* 1: 187–94.

Delcor, M. 1978. Les Kéréthim et les Crétois. *VT* 28: 409–22.

Virolleaud, C. 1936. *La légende de Keret, roi des Sidoniens.* Mission de Ras Shamra 2. Paris.

CARL S. EHRLICH

CHERITH, BROOK OF (PLACE) [Heb *naḥal kĕrît*]. A stream on the E side of the Jordan River where Elijah hid from Ahab and Jezebel during the drought in Israel; he remained there until the spring dried up (1 Kgs 17:2–7).

Ever since the Middle Ages, scholars have been divided as to which side of the Jordan River this stream should be located. Those who have preferred a location on the W side have argued that the Hebrew word *ʿal-pĕnê* should be translated "before" or "toward" the Jordan (e.g., Gen 25:18; 18:16). Scholars preferring this translation include Marinus Sanutus (1321), who suggested ʿAin Fusail (*Phasaelis* of NT times) just N of Jericho, and E. Robinson who preferred the Wadi Qelt near Herodian Jericho. Robinson's argument was based on the idea that the Arabic *Qelt* could have been derived from the Heb *kĕrît.* A major difficulty with this location is that it is hardly an isolated stream, being one of the main routes connecting the two heavily populated centers of Jerusalem and Jericho.

Most scholars have preferred to locate the stream on the E bank, arguing that the most obvious reading of *ʿal-pĕnê* is "east of" the Jordan (e.g., Eusebius in the *Onomast.* p. 174). Although Thenius argued for the *Wadi Rajib or Ajlun,* a number of scholars, beginning with Benjamin of Tudela and including F. Abel (*GP* 1: 484–85) and N. Glueck (AASOR 25–28), have preferred the *Wadi el-Yubis* in the highlands of N Gilead. This suggestion may make the most sense in view of the fact that Elijah was a Gileadite (1 Kgs 17:1). This wadi empties into the Jordan about 8 km S of Pella.

RANDALL W. YOUNKER

CHERUB (PERSON) [Gk *Charaath*]. The leader of a group of exiles returning from two Babylonian locations, Telmelah and Telharsha, who were unable to prove their genealogies (1 Esdr 5:36). While Cherub represents a personal name in 1 Esdras, in the parallel texts (Ezra 2:59 = Neh 7:61 [LXX *charoub*] it is a geographic location. See CHERUB (PLACE). Moreover, in 1 Esdras, Cherub and Addan have been combined in many manuscripts, among them Codex Vaticanus (Gk *charaathalan*) and the Vg (Lat *carmellan*). Variations such as these raise questions about the sources of and literary relationship among 1 Esdras, Ezra, and Nehemiah.

MICHAEL DAVID MCGEHEE

CHERUB (PLACE) [Heb *kĕrûb*]. An unknown Babylonian site from which exiles returned to Jerusalem with Zerubbabel (Ezra 2:59 = Neh 7:61 [LXX *charoub*]). According to Ezra and Nehemiah, those returning from Cherub, as well as from Telmelah, Telharsha, Addon, and Immer, were unable to establish their genealogies, or prove that they belonged to the people of Israel. In the parallel text of 1 Esdr 5:36, however, Cherub (Gk *charaath*), Addan, and Immer appear as the names of the leaders of the people who returned from Telmelah and Telharsha.

MICHAEL DAVID MCGEHEE

CHERUBIM [Heb *kĕrûbîm*]. The terms "cherub" (sing.) and "cherubim" (pl.) occur over 90 times in the Hebrew Bible (and only once in the NT, in Heb 9:5) in reference to fanciful composite beings. Although all of these references are in sacral contexts, there is no uniformity as to the nature of the strange creatures involved except for the fact that they are all winged beings. From a graphic perspective, the biblical description of cherubim can be divided into two major groups: those that were two-dimensional, as they appeared woven into textiles, or in low relief; and those that were free-standing either as modeled, three-dimensional forms or as living, moving creatures.

The two-dimensional or low-relief images of cherubim

were those found in the sacred structure of ancient Israel. In the tabernacle, the inner curtains and the veil that closed off the inner sanctum or holy of holies were adorned with cherubim (Exod 26:1, 31; 36:8, 35). These decorated fabrics, made of a woolen-linen mixture and crafted in special *(ḥôšēb)* workmanship, were part of the innermost and holiest part of the tabernacle complex. The Jerusalem temple, which was constructed of walls and not hangings, featured carved cherubim, covered with gold, on the corresponding elements: the sanctuary walls (1 Kgs 6:29; cf. 2 Chr 3:7 and Ezek 41:18–20) and on the doors separating the internal chambers (1 Kgs 7:32, 35; cf. Ezek 41:25). In addition, the temple had cherubim carved into panels that formed the base and part of the top of the stands for the lavers (1 Kgs 7:28, 36).

Three-dimensional cherubim were also part of the holiest elements of both tabernacle and temple. Two golden cherubim with wings extended were part of the covering of the ark, within the holy of holies of the tabernacle (Exod 25:18–22; 37:7–9). In the Jerusalem temple, two enormous olivewood cherubim, overlaid with gold, virtually filled the innermost chamber (1 Kgs 6:23–28) as a covering for the ark (1 Kgs 8:6–7). In both these instances, the cherubim apparently constituted a resting place, or throne, for God's invisible presence or glory (e.g., 2 Kgs 19:15 = Isa 32:16; 1 Sam 4:4; 2 Sam 6:2). As part of the cultic furniture for God in the divine dwelling place on earth (see Haran 1978: 254–59), these cherubim are to be related to figures attested in several biblical texts which envisage God riding upon living composite beasts (e.g., Ps 18:10 = 2 Sam 22:11) or in which God's glory rests upon the creatures (Ezekiel 10). Finally, the close connection between God and cherubim is present in their appearance as guardians of the garden of Eden (Gen 3:24).

The many variations of cherubim represented in the Bible—examples with one or more faces; with human, leonine, bovine, or aquiline faces; with two or four legs—correspond to various forms of composite beasts depicted in ANE art, particularly the art of Assyria (*TWAT* 4: 330–34). In ancient Israel and its contemporary world, cherubim were characterized by mobility, since they all had wings. By virtue of their combining features of different creatures or having more of such features than real animals or persons, they were unnatural. These characteristics made them apt symbols for divine presence, since deities moved where humans could not and were something other than either animals or humans. The cherubim of the Bible are hardly the round-faced infant cherubim known in Western art.

Bibliography

Haran, M. 1978. *Temples and Temple Service in Ancient Israel.* Oxford.

Carol Meyers

CHESALON (PLACE) [Heb *kĕsālôn*]. One of the towns along the N boundary of Judah, bordering on Dan (Josh 15:10). Eusebius, like LXX A, has *chasalōn,* while LXX B reads *chaslōn.* The imprecision in describing Judah's territory at this point probably stemmed from difficulties encountered by the biblical writer when attempting to define an evidently unsettled region. Eusebius (*Onomast.* 172.16) describes Chesalon in the 4th century C.E. as a large village in the territory of Aelia (Jerusalem), whereas Jerome says it lay in Judah. But neither writer defines its true position. Following the identification of Edward Robinson (1856: 2.30; 3.154), the biblical name is now generally agreed to be preserved in the ruin of *Kesla,* ca. 20 km/12 mi W of Jerusalem (M.R. 154132), and situated at 641 m/1920 ft above sea level. Chesalon was never a fortified town and consequently does not possess a tell. Its bare rock summit, though, is easily detectable in a region inhabited then, as today, by oak forests. A surface survey conducted there revealed pottery from the Iron Age II period and later (Gafni 1984: 26). The Bible locates Chesalon between Mt. Seir and Beth-shemesh, where it is mentioned as an alternative name for the shoulder of Mt. Jearim, meaning a "wooded mountain." When referring to a site in the hills, "shoulder" means the edge of a ridge or a range (*HGB,* 128). According to the biblical description, the border ran seaward from Kiriath-jearim to Mt. Seir. There it turned S, skirting along the edge of the Mt. Jearim range toward Beth-shemesh, including both Mt. Seir and Chesalon within the territory of Judah (*HGB,* 122). A corrupted form of Chesalon may appear in an LXX supplement to Josh 15:59 in the name of *koulon* (*HGB,* 392).

Bibliography

Albright, W. F. 1925. The Fall Trip of the School in Jerusalem: From Jerusalem to Gaza and Back. *BASOR* 17: 4.

Alt, A. 1928. Die Ausflüge—Wäldergebirge. *PJB* 24: 29–40.

Conder, C. R., and Kitchener, H. H. 1883. Kesla. *SWP* 3: 25–26.

Gafni, Y. 1984. *In the Footsteps of Samson.* Jerusalem (in Hebrew).

Robinson, E. 1856. *Biblical Researches in Palestine.* 3 vols. Boston. Repr. Jerusalem, 1970.

R. A. Mullins

CHESED (PERSON) [Heb *keśed*]. The fourth son of Nahor and Milcah (Gen 22:22). Although it occurs only once in the Bible, this name has been associated with the people known in the Bible as the Chaldeans. Chesed is orthographically and phonologically related to the Kasdim (Heb *kaśdîm*), and this group is identified throughout the Bible with the Chaldeans (e.g. Gen 11:28; Job 1:17; and elsewhere). The Old Babylonian term *kasdu,* which became *kaldû* in Assyrian documents, is the equivalent of this term, which the LXX translates *chaldiōn.* A connection could be drawn between the clan of Chesed and these Mesopotamian "Chaldeans," but to do so based on the similarity of terms only is unadvisable.

Joel C. Slayton

CHESIL (PLACE) [Heb *kĕsîl*]. A town in Judah located in the extreme S (Negeb) near Hormah and Ziklag and toward the boundary of Edom (Josh 15:30). In other lists of S Judean towns, it is replaced with Bethul (Josh 19:4) and BETHUEL (1 Chr 4:30). Also, 1 Sam 30:27 refers to a BETHEL in S Judah, in connection with David's exploits in the area around Ziklag and Hormah. Thus, it is impossible to be certain not only about the location but also about the precise name of this town.

Gary A. Herion

CHESTER BEATTY PAPYRI. The papyri named after Sir Alfred Chester Beatty (1875–1968), an American collector who in 1950 settled in Dublin, Ireland. The library which he founded, now called the Chester Beatty Library and Gallery of Oriental Art, was bequeathed to the Irish people at the time of Beatty's death.

A. The Chester Beatty Biblical Papyri

The appellation refers in the first instance to the famous Chester Beatty Biblical Papyri, the largest and most sensational discovery to date of Greek biblical mss written on papyrus, acquired by Beatty in 1930–31.

1. The Discovery. Announcement of Chester Beatty's acquisition was made by Sir Frederic Kenyon, the *Times* (London), November 19, 1931. Though the original announcement mentioned twelve codices, the figure was lowered to eleven when it was found that Pap. IX (Ezekiel, Esther) and Pap. X (Daniel) form part of the same codex. Though the exact place of discovery is unknown, some Christian church or monastery near Aphroditopolis (Carl Schmidt) or perhaps less likely in the Fayum (Kenyon) has gained general acceptance. Although Chester Beatty managed to make a second acquisition from the discovery, in 1935, by no means all parts of the eleven codices found their way to his collection. Substantial segments were acquired by John H. Scheide (Princeton), the Universities of Michigan and Cologne, and the Consejo Superior de Investigaciones Cientificas of Madrid. Fragments are in Barcelona and Vienna. (For all present locations of "Chester Beatty Papyri," consult the Bibliography. In what follows all will be counted as Chester Beatty Papyri).

2. Popular Designation. In spite of the official designation, "Chester Beatty Biblical Papyri," individual Papyri are normally cited as P. Chester Beatty . . . in conformity with standard papyrological practice.

3. The Manuscripts. Since the Papyri must be dated on the basis of paleography, no absolute unanimity among experts has been achieved. Nevertheless, at least the century to which each document was assigned by its chief editor still meets with general approval. Hence the dates range from the 2d (Pap. VI) to the 4th (XI, XII) centuries, with the majority falling in the 3d.

a. Papyrological Importance. At the time of their discovery, prevailing opinion was that the papyrus codex did not gain general acceptance among Christians until the 4th century. The evident date of most of the Papyri altered that opinion. Along with the earlier date for the general use of the codex form, they also supplied an abundance of information on how the papyrus book was constructed. Formats are as numerous as the Papyri. Page size ranges from about 18 by 33 cm (Pap. VI) to 14 by 24.2 cm (III). Similarly, the makeup of individual codices shows much diversity, some being constructed of a single gathering (quire) of papyrus sheets (Pap. II, VII, IX + X), while in others the gathering varies from a single sheet (I) to five (V) or seven (VII). The largest codex among them (Pap. IX + X) must have counted at least 236 pages.

One of the most interesting aspects of scribal practice concerns the *nomina sacra.* In the Papyri we find diversity not only on which names are contracted and how, but also early evidence of sacral treatment of nonsacral names. So, for example, already in the 2d century (Pap. VI) "Joshua = Jesus" was treated as a *nomen sacrum,* suggesting that the sacral treatment of "Jesus" had become routine.

b. Textual Importance. No less than their papyrological significance is the textual importance of the Papyri. Since all but two (Pap. XI, XII) of the eleven codices are dated earlier than the 4th century, they present important evidence for the text of the Greek Bible as it existed in Egypt prior to the *traditio codicum* (the "turning in" of Christian books during the Diocletianic persecutions) and a century or more earlier than the great vellum codices of the 4th century, namely Vaticanus (B) and Sinaiticus (S). Although the Papyri supply a wealth of new information on textual detail, they also demonstrate remarkable stability in the transmission history of the biblical text. In terms of textual affiliation, they can only be described as mixed or unaligned. Only if great latitude is allowed can they be counted as members of textual groups or representatives of particular text types. For the Greek OT, their great significance lies in the fact that their text is pre/nonrecensional, that is to say, their text is untouched by the systematic revisionary activity of Lucian (III–IV) and of Origen (III) as well as other more shadowy or entirely unknown revisers.

(1) OT Papyri. Even though two of the Papyri (VIII [containing Jer 4:30–5:24]; XI [Sir 36:28–37:22; 46:6–47:2]) give relatively little text, so as to make textual analysis precarious, they nonetheless are the most extensive early (3d/4th cent. A.D. and before) witnesses for their respective books.

Pap. IV (Gen 9:1–44:22) and V (Gen 8:13–9:2; 24:13–46:33) between them preserve four fifths of the book of Genesis, a book almost absent from both B and S. Together with the only other substantial papyrus, 911, they are our chief early witnesses to LXX Genesis. Only sporadic corrections to the Hebrew text are in evidence.

Pap. VI (Num 5:12–36:13; Deut 1:20–34:12), though the earliest among the Papyri, postdates P. Fouad 266 (847, 848) and P. Rylands 458 (957) by several centuries. Its text, however, is much more extensive and it exhibits few readings which need have arisen under Hebrew influence.

Pap. VII (Isa 8:18–19:13; 38:14–45:5; 54:1–60:22) has a very low number of unique readings and is an exceptionally good witness to the original text of LXX Isaiah. Its chief claim to fame, however, lies perhaps in its annotations in Old Fayumic. Most interesting among the OT Papyri is Pap. IX–X. Its 3d-century date makes it the earliest substantial witness for all three books it contains: Ezekiel, Daniel-Bel-Susanna, Esther.

Ezekiel (11:25–fin.). Though clearly nonhexapharic, the text of IX–X gives evidence of having undergone correction toward the Hebrew, but whether the equation *kyrios ho theos* = *adonai-yahweh* is to be counted as such is controversial.

Daniel (1:1–12:13)-Bel (c. 4–39)-Susanna (5-subscriptio). Since the popular text in antiquity was not LXX Daniel but the so-called Theodotionic version, the former is extant in but few witnesses, two of which are hexaplaric (88-Syh), while several others are very fragmentary. Pap. (IX–)X is the earliest by at least two centuries and, because of its age and extent, is the most important witness to LXX Daniel. Though not hexapharic, the Papyrus contains sporadic pre/nonhexaplaric corrections to the Hebrew. Uniquely, Daniel 7–8 precede 5–6, and 4:3–6, 5:18–22,

24–25 are lacking as in 88-Syh but against MT. Of considerable interest is the order of the "books" and, according to the subscriptio, that Bel and Susanna were regarded as belonging to Daniel.

Esther (1:1a–8:6). Not unexpectedly, the Papyrus contains the LXX rather than the so-called *L* version which is attested in only a small minority of witnesses. Additions A–D are attested in their usual locations in Greek mss.

The chief importance of Pap. XII lies in the newness of its contents.

Enoch (93:12–13; 94:7–8; 97:6–104:13; 106:1–107:3). The chief text is in Ethiopic translation. For Book V (91–105) and the concluding fragment from the book of Noah (106–107), the Papyrus supplies our only Greek text. Chapters 105 and 108 were never part of the text, and have been regarded as secondary. The former chapter, however, is represented among the Aramaic fragments from Qumran (4QEn[c]). The subscriptio reads "Epistle of Enoch."

Melito of Sardis, *Peri Pascha.* Though at the time of its discovery, Pap. XII constituted the only (original) Greek text of this treatise, it has since been supplemented by P. Bodmer XIII and P. Oxy. XIII 1600.

Apocryphon of Ezekiel. Though cited by Clement of Alexandria (*Paedagogus* I. ix. 84.2–4) Pap. XII supplies the only ms evidence of this work.

(2) NT Papyri. Pap. I (Matt 20:24–Acts 17:7) challenged the prevailing view at the time of the discovery of the Chester Beatty Biblical Papyri that, prior to the 4th century, each Gospel had circulated separately. The order of the individual books in the codex was apparently the so-called Western order: Matthew, John, Luke, Mark, Acts.

Pap. II (Rom 5:17–16:23, Heb, Cor, Eph, Gal, Phil, Col, 1 Thess). The placement of Hebrews among the Pauline epistles at a time when it was widely regarded as uncanonical is remarkable, and its location after Romans is virtually unique. Equally uncommon is that Ephesians precedes rather than follows Galatians. Perhaps the object of greatest textual interest is the doxology of Rom 16:25–27, which in our Papyrus closes chap. 15. That the Pastoral Epistles were not included seems certain but does not necessarily reflect doubts about their Pauline authorship, as some have suggested.

Pap. III (Rev 9:10–17:2). As is the case for most of Genesis (cf. Pap. IV and V), ms B is not extant for Revelation. Moreover, Pap. III is at least a century older than S and, of our early (3d/4th cent. and before) witnesses, is the most extensive.

B. Other Chester Beatty Papyri. Although the Biblical Papyri are the centerpiece of the Library's holdings in early biblical mss, they were neither Beatty's only nor his earliest acquisitions in this field.

1. Coptic Vellums. In 1924–25 Chester Beatty acquired three Coptic (Sahidic) volumes evidently produced in the monastery of Apa Jeremias at Saqqara. (Two more of the same find were bought by the University of Michigan.) All three volumes were in their original bindings, and written, not on papyrus, but on vellum. P. Chester Beatty 2003 (=813) contains the Pauline Epistles (Rom, Cor, Heb, Gal, Eph, Phil, Col, Thess, Tim, Phlm) and the Gospel of John; P. Chester Beatty 2004 (=814) has Acts and the Gospel of John, and P. Chester Beatty 2005 (=815) the first fifty psalms plus Matt 1:1–2:1 (ined.).

2. Manichea. Roughly contemporaneous with the Biblical Papyri was Beatty's acquisition of Manichean mss in Coptic (Sub-Achmimic) translation (ca. 400+ A.D.). Though part of the find of papyrus codices, reputedly from Medinet Madi in the S Fayum, ended up in Berlin (and Vienna), Chester Beatty gained possession of the Homilies and the Psalm Book. Part I of the latter remains to be edited, as well as the Synaxeis Codex now in Berlin.

3. Later Acquisitions. Acquisitions of papyri (and some parchments) continued, notably around the middle 1950s. Not only were some of these materials bought through the same dealer Martin Bodmer engaged, but like the bulk of the BODMER PAPYRI, they were from the discovery near Dishna in 1952. In two instances, a fragment each from Bodmer Papyri was bought by Beatty, namely from P. Bodmer II (John 19:25–28, 30–32) and from P. Bodmer XX (*Apology of Phileas* 135, 13–16 and 136, 14–17). In a third case, a substantial portion was acquired by Beatty: P. Bodmer XXI = P. Chester Beatty 2019. It is not clear which and how many mss in the possession of the Chester Beatty Library also derive from the Dishna discovery.

a. Greek Biblical Papyri. The series of Biblical (but cf. Pap. XII) Papyri launched by Kenyon has been continued for Greek "biblical" papyri acquired at later dates: P. Chester Beatty XIII (Ps 72:6–75:13; 77:1–88:2), XIV (Ps 31:8–11; 26:1–6, 8–14; 2:1–8), XV (*Acts of Phileas* plus Ps 1:1–4:2), XVI (*Apocryphon of Jannes and Jambres* [ined.]), XVII (Luke 14:7–14, XVIII (Job 9:2–3, 12–13. Chester Beatty accession no. (hereafter acc.) 1499 is a Greek grammar, and a Graeco-Latin lexicon on Romans, 2 Corinthians, Galatians, and Ephesians and is being edited.

b. Coptic Texts. (1) Biblical and related. P. Chester Beatty 2018 (*Apocalypse of Elijah*), 2019 (Josh 1:1–6:16; 6:25–7:6; 22:2–19; 23:7–15; 24:23–33 plus Tob 14:13–15), 2021 (John 10:8–13:38 in Sub-Achmimic plus mathematical exercises in Greek), 2023 (Gen 7:13–23, 27:23–25, 27–32, 2024 (Luke 1:63–9:31, 11:1–12:48, 18:8–15, 2 Cor 1:1–12:12 [ined.]), 2025 (lectionary containing at least Ps 31:1–4, 96:3–4, Mark 8:34, Acts 13:28–29, 31–33, 1 John 4:14–16 [ined.]).

(2) Hagiographica: P. Chester Beatty 2022 (Cephalon), 2028 (Herai), 2029 (Phoebammon), 2030 (Hermauo).

(3) Pachomiana: Chester Beatty acc. 1486 (Letter 2 of Theodore [on parchment]), acc. 1494 (Letter 3 of Horsiesius [ined.]), W.145 (Greek trans. of Pachomius' Letters 1, 2, 3, 7, 10, 11[a] [on parchment]), acc. 1495 (Letter 4 of Horsiesius [ined.]), no. 54 (Pachomius' Letters 11[b], 10, 11[a], 9[a], 9[b]).

(4) Miscellanea: P. Chester Beatty 2026 (nonbiblical fragment about Moses and Pharaoh [ined.]), 2027 (nonbiblical fragment about Pilate [Bohairic; ined.]), 2031 (tale featuring Pshoi s. of Jeremiah [ined.]). Various other bits and pieces still await identification.

Bibliography

A. The Chester Beatty Biblical Papyri

Bonner, C. 1937. *The Last Chapters of Enoch in Greek.* London.

———. 1940. *The Homily on the Passion by Melito Bishop of Sardis.* SD 12. London.

Erffa, H. von. 1935. Esai. 19, 3 sqq. *Studi Italiani di Filologica Classica* 12: 109–10 (= *PSI* 12, 1273).

Fernández, G. M. 1971. Nuevas páginas del códice 967 del A. T. griego (Ez 28, 19–43, 9). (P. Matr. bibl. 1). *Studia Papyrologica* 10: 1–77.

Geissen, A. 1968. *Der Septuaginta-Text des Buches Daniel (Kap. 5–12, zusammen mit Susanna, Bel et Draco, sowie Esther 1, 1a-2, 15) nach dem Kölner Teil des Papyrus 967*. Papyrologische Texte und Abhandlungen 5. Bonn.

Gerstinger, H. 1933. Ein Fragment des Chester Beatty—Evangelienkodex in der Papyrussammlung der Nationalbibliothek in Wien (Pap. graec. Vindob. 31974). *Aeg* 13: 67–72.

Hamm, W. 1969. *Der Septuaginta–Text des Buches Daniel* (Kap. 1–2) *nach dem Kölner Teil des papyrus 967*. Papyrologische Texte und Abhandlungen 10. Bonn.

———. 1977. *Der Septuaginta–Text des Buches Daniel (Kap. 3–4) nach dem Kölner Teil des Papyrus 967*. Papyrologische Texte und Abhandlungen 21. Bonn.

Hayes, R. J. 1958. Fasc. 5 and 6 *Numbers and Deuteronomy, Isaiah, Jeremiah, Ecclesiasticus: Plates*. Dublin.

Jahn, P. L. G. 1972. *Der Griechische Text des Buches Ezekiel nach dem Kölner Teil des Papyrus 967*. Papyrologische Texte und Abhandlungen 15. Bonn.

Johnson, A. C.; Gehman, H. S.; and Kase, E. S. 1938. *The John H. Scheide Biblical Papyri: Ezekiel*. Princeton University Studies in Papyrology 3. Princeton.

Kenyon, F. G. 1933–41. *The Chester Beatty Biblical Papyri: Descriptions and Texts of Twelve Manuscripts on Papyrus of the Greek Bible*. London: 1933 fasc. 1: *General Introduction;* fasc. 2: *The Gospels and Acts: Text;* 1934 fasc. 2: *The Gospels and Acts: Plates* [P.Ch.B.I. = P. Vindob. G. 31974; Siglum P45; Date III]; fasc. 3: *Pauline Epistles and Revelation: Text;* 1936 *Revelation: Plates; Supplement: Pauline Epistles: Text;* 1937 *Supplement: Pauline Epistles: Plates* [P.Chb.B.II = P.Mich.inv. 6238; Siglum P46; Date III]; [P.Ch.B.III; Siglum P47; Date III]; 1934 fasc. 4: *Genesis: Text;* 1935 fasc. 4: *Genesis (Papyrus IV): Plates;* 1936 fasc. 4: *Genesis (Papyrus V): Plates* [Sigla 961, 962; Date IV]; 1935 fasc. 5 *Numbers and Deuteronomy: Text* [P.Ch.B.VI = P.Mich.inv. 5554; Siglum 963; Date II]; 1937 fasc. 6: *Isaiah, Jeremiah, Ecclesiasticus: Text* [P.Ch.B.VII = P. Merton I2, PSI 12, 1273; Siglum 965, Date III]; [P.Ch.B.VIII; Siglum 966; Date III]; [P.Ch.B.XI; Siglum 964; Date IV]; fasc. 7: *Ezekiel, Daniel, Esther: Plates* [P.Ch.B.IX (Ezek, Est) + X = P. Princeton Scheide 3, P. Colon, inv.theol. 3–40, P. Matr. bibl. 1, P. Barc. inv. 42, 43: Siglum 967; Date III]; 1941 fasc. 8: *Enoch and Melito: Plates* [P.Ch.B.XII = P. Mich.inv. 5552; Date IV].

Pietersma, A. 1975. The "Lost" Folio of the Chester Beatty *Ecclesiasticus*. *VT* 25: 497–99.

———. 1977. *Chester Beatty Biblical Papyri IV and V. A New Edition with Text-Critical Analysis*. American Studies in Papyrology 16. Toronto.

———. 1987. New Greek Fragments of Biblical Manuscripts in the Chester Beatty Library. *BASP* 24: 37–61.

Roca-Puig, R. 1974. *Daniel. Dos semifolis del còdex 967*. Papir de Barcelona, Inv. no. 42 i 43. Barcelona. *Aegyptus* 56 (1976) 3–18.

Sanders, H. A. 1935. *A Third-Century Papyrus Codex of the Epistles of Paul*. Ann Arbor.

B. Other Papyri

Allberry, C. R. C. 1938. *Manichaean Manuscripts in the Chester Beatty Collection: A Manichaean Psalm-Book Part II*. Stuttgart.

Pietersma, A. 1978. *Two Manuscripts of the Greek Psalter*. AnBib 77. Rome.

———. 1984. *The Acts of Phileas, Bishop of Thmuis (Including Fragments of the Greek Psalter)*. Cahiers d'orientalisme 7. Geneva. [P. Chester Beatty XV; Ps Siglum 2151; Date IV].

Pietersma, A., and Turner Comstock, S. 1982. Cephalon, a New Coptic Martyr. Pp. 113–24 in *Studies in Philology in Honour of Ronald James Williams*, ed. G. E. Kadish and G. E. Freeman. Toronto. [P. Chester Beatty 2022; Date VI/VII].

———. 1986. New Fragments of Genesis in Sahidic. *BASP* 23/24.

———. 1987. Coptic Martyrdoms in the Chester Beatty Library. *BASP* 24.

Pietersma, A.; Turner Comstock, S.; and Attridge, H. 1981. *The Apocalypse of Elijah*. SBLTT 19. Pseudepigrapha Series 9. Chico, CA. [P. Chester Beatty 2018 = acc. 1493; Date IV/V].

Polotsky, H. J. 1934. *Manichäische Handschriften der Sammlung A. Chester Beatty I. Manichäische Homilien*. Stuttgart.

Quecke, H. 1974. Ein neues Fragment der Pachombriefe in koptischer Sprache. *Or* 43: 66–82. [Chester Beatty no. 54; Date VI].

———. 1975a. Ein Brief von einem Nachfolger Pachoms (Chester Beatty Library Ms. Ac. 1486). *Or* 44: 426–33 [Date VI].

———. 1975b. *Die Briefe Pachoms. Griechischer Text der Handschrift W. 145 der Chester Beatty Library*. Textus Patristici et Liturgici 11. Regensburg. [= P. Köln 4, 174 (inv. 3288); Date IV].

Römer, C. 1982. *Kölner Papyri (P. Köln)* 4. Papyrologica Coloniensia 7. Opladen. [= Chester Beatty W 145].

Schmidt, C., and Polotsky, J. H. 1933. Ein Mani-Fund in Ägypten. Pp. 4–90 in *Sitzungsberichte der Preussische Akademie der Wissenschaften*, phil.-hist. Kl. Berlin.

Shore, A. F. 1963. *Joshua I–VI and Other Passages in Coptic, Edited from a Fourth-Century Sahidic Codex in the Chester Beatty Library, Dublin*. Chester Beatty Monographs 9. Dublin. [P. Chester Beatty 2019 (acc. 1389) = P. Bodmer XXI].

Thompson, H. 1932. *The Coptic Version of the Acts of the Apostles and the Pauline Epistles in the Sahidic Dialect*. Cambridge. [= P. Ches. Beatty 2003, 2004; Date VI/VII].

ALBERT PIETERSMA

CHESULLOTH (PLACE) [Heb *kĕsûlōt*]. A town in the territory of Issachar (Josh 19:18). The name is apparently a variant of CHISLOTH-TABOR.

CHEZIB (PERSON) [Gk *Chaseba*]. A temple servant who was the progenitor of a family which returned from Babylon with Zerubbabel (1 Esdr 5:31). Although 1 Esdras is often assumed to have been compiled from Ezra and Nehemiah, this family does not appear among their lists of returning exiles (see Ezra 2:48; Neh 7:51). Omissions such as this also raise questions about 1 Esdras being used as a source by Ezra or Nehemiah. Furthermore, problems associated with dating events and identifying persons described in 1 Esdras have cast doubt on the historicity of the text.

MICHAEL DAVID MCGEHEE

CHEZIB (PLACE) [Heb *kĕzîb*]. A city in S Canaan where Shelah, one of Judah's sons, was born of a Canaanite woman (Gen 38:5). The context of the biblical reference implies that the town was near Adullam (cf. Gen 38:1). The consensus is that the site is the same as ACHZIB [Heb ʾ*akzîb*] in Judah (Josh 15:44; Mic 1:14), which results from the addition of a prosthetic ʾ*alep* to *kĕzîb* (GKC ¶19m). Eusebius' (*Onomast.* 172) identification of Achzib with the town of *Chasbi* further preserves the consonantal tradition. Chasbi is now known as Tell el-Beida (M.R. 145116), which is near Adullam. Saarisalo (1931) visited the site, and although he identified Tell el-Beida as Moresheth-gath, he described a typical tell configuration with early Iron I and II potsherds on its surface; otherwise no archaeological work has been done at the site.

The MT states that "he was" (i.e., Judah) in Chezib when the woman bore Shelah; however the RSV follows the Gk which states "she was" (i.e., the Canaanite woman) in Chezib when she gave birth. Speiser's translation (*Genesis* AB, 295) essentially conflates the two traditions and renders the phrase: "they were at Chezib . . ." The Hebrew text, furthermore, implies that only Shelah was born in Chezib, while the Gk implies ("when she bore them") that there she bore all of the sons—Er, Onan, and Shelah. While the Gk may preserve the more accurate information, the first two sons, Er and Onan, became irrelevant as far as inheritance purposes were concerned, since they both died childless. The descendants of Shelah, however, would need this information (cf. Num 26:19–20). Perhaps the Hebrew text accommodates only the essential information (cf. Keil and Delitzsch n.d.: 339–340).

Bibliography

Keil, C. F., and Delitzsch, F. n.d. *The Pentateuch.* Trans. J. Martin. Repr. Grand Rapids.

Saarisalo, A. 1931. Topographical Researches in the Shephelah. *JPOS* 11: 98–104 [14–20].

DALE W. MANOR

CHI. The twenty-second letter of the Greek alphabet.

CHIASM, CHIASMUS. See PSALMS, BOOK OF.

CHICKEN. See ZOOLOGY.

CHIDON (PERSON) [Heb *kîdōn*]. An alternate form of NACON.

CHIDON (PLACE) [Heb *kîdōn*]. The name of the threshing floor where Uzzah was struck dead for touching the ark of the covenant while it was being transported to Jerusalem by oxcart (1 Chr 13:9). David then renamed the spot PEREZ-UZZAH, preserving it in national memory as the place where God's wrath "broke out" against Uzzah for his irreverant act (1 Chr 13:11 = 2 Sam 6:8). 2 Sam 6:6 calls the place "the threshing floor of Nacon." Josephus, like the LXX A, writes *cheidōn* (*Ant* 7.4.2). LXX B omits "of Chidon." It is not clear from the text whether Chidon was the name of the place or its owner. Some have tried to identify the spot with the threshing floor of Araunah or Ornan the Jebusite (cf. 1 Chr 21:15). In Ugarit, threshing floors were often associated with cultic activity. Thus, Coggins (*1 and 2 Chronicles* CBC, 79) has suggested that the location may have been significant in the earlier form of the story, although it is likely that here the Chronicler was simply following his source. While no name resembling Chidon or Nacon has been preserved, there are two plausible routes for the transport of the ark to Jerusalem. The most direct, but more difficult access would have been to go somewhere along the line of the present Jerusalem–Tel Aviv highway, a distance of about 13 km/8 mi. The easiest, but longer way would have been to go from Kiriath-jearim to Gibeon (el-Jib); and then on to Jerusalem via Gibeah of Benjamin (Tell el-Ful). Thus the ark would have been brought through Benjamin in full view of the local population. Given the political tensions between the Benjaminite house of Saul and the Judean house of David, this would have served as a bold statement by David that he is now the one in charge. This latter route also has the benefit of high ground exposed to westerly winds needed for threshing grain. Several threshing floors still exist in the region today.

R. A. MULLINS

CHIEF. See PALESTINE, ADMINISTRATION OF JUDEAN OFFICIALS (POSTEXILIC).

CHILD, CHILDREN. In the OT, children are a gift from God, instruments of God's activity, and symbolically a guarantee of the covenant between God and the people of Israel. In the NT, children are principally a model or image for the believer to emulate.

A. Children in the OT
B. Children in Mark
C. Children in Matthew
D. Children in Luke
E. Children in John

A. Children in the OT

God's greatest gift and guarantee of the covenant with Israel was that of children. Despite every other gift, Abraham felt at a complete loss without children (Gen 15:1–3). God's promise of a numerous posterity to Abraham and Sarah was at the root of the biblical covenant (Gen 12:1–3). In the creation account, the first woman was called Eve, because she was "mother of all living" (Gen 3:20) and thus source of hope for the fallen first parents. In view of the primacy of children, a favorite image was that of father, mother, and numerous children around a table (Ps 128:3–4). While every birth was considered a divine miracle, those with extreme difficulty or seemingly impossible due to old age were attributed to extraordinary divine intervention (Gen 17:17; 21:6). In the early biblical period, immortality was linked to living on through children who carried on the *name* of their parents (Gen 48:16). When there were no offspring, the Levirate law provided for carrying on this name and for continuity through the nearest relative (Deut 25:5–10). Children were important in worship, prayer, and ritual (Exod 13:8, 14; Deut 4:9;

6:7). The Bible attaches special significance to the blessing of children, especially before the death of parents (Genesis 27, 48, 49). The ancient Jewish custom of blessing children follows the ritual of these texts. The priestly blessing is also used for them (Num 6:24–26).

Despite this special esteem for children, they were the powerless ones on the bottom rung of Hebrew and other ancient societies. Tradition and custom allotted the most important place to older people (Prov 16:31; Job 12:12; Sir 25:4–6). Parents had almost absolute authority over children, who were educated through strict obedience often enforced by severe physical punishment (Prov 13:24; 19:18; 22:15; 23:13; Sir 30:1, 12). The law reinforced parental authority with its own strong sanctions (Exod 21:17; Lev 20:9).

Yet in contrast to human ways, the Bible presents God as acting in a surprising way through children and young people. Wisdom is a special gift from God (Prov 2:6–7) granted even to little ones. God gives the young Joseph the gift of interpreting dreams and ruling the land of Egypt (Gen 41:38). The young Solomon asks God for wisdom through the gift of a listening heart (1 Kgs 3:5–9). The book of Wisdom expands on this story and describes Solomon as asking for wisdom as a child and pursuing it throughout his youth as if searching for a bride (Wis 6:3–7; chaps. 7, 8). In regard to creation, the Psalmist declares that even little children are able to perceive and praise the wonders of God's universe (Ps 8:2).

As if to turn the tables on ordinary human expectations, the Bible focuses on examples where God works through the young and little ones. He favors not Cain the firstborn son of the human race but the younger Abel (Gen 4:4–5). When Rebekah, Jacob's mother, consults the Lord, she receives an answer that the elder shall serve the younger (Gen 25:23). Before death, Jacob blesses his eleven sons, but gives a double blessing to the youngest, Joseph (Gen 48:1–22; 49:22–26). Joseph in turn desires Jacob's special blessing for his older son Manasseh; instead it is granted to the younger, Ephraim (Gen 49:13–20). When the prophet Samuel searches for a new king to replace Saul, he meets Jesse and his seven sons at their home. However, God tells him that despite their impressive strength and appearance none will be the anointed one. Instead, it will be David, a "little one" and shepherd out in the fields doing the work often allotted to children (1 Sam 16:1–13). God enables David, too young even for battle, to overcome the Philistine champion Goliath (1 Sam 17).

The image of a child plays an important part in messianic expectations. The prophet Isaiah announces a future *child* of David's line will be the hope of his people despite much suffering (7:14, 16; 9:16). The same prophet also describes this future in terms of an idyllic return to the childlike innocence of the garden of Eden (11:8–9). The prophet Zechariah has a vision of the messianic era as a time of peace and joy when "the streets of the city shall be full of boys and girls playing in them" (8:5).

B. Children in Mark

Mark writes for an audience oppressed and persecuted by abusive Roman authority. In response, some Christian leaders and prophets proclaimed an imminent powerful return of Jesus and substantiated their message through miracles and signs (13:6, 21–22). To counter these views, Mark presents children as models of discipleship. Two stories about Jesus and children form an important literary frame for illustrating true discipleship in a central teaching section formed around Jesus' three predictions of his passion and death (8:31; 9:31; 10:32–34). As Derrett has shown (1983), these children's stories should not be understood merely as examples of Jesus' compassion for little ones or as a support for the existence of infant baptism in the early church. Instead, they should be studied in light of their context and the importance of Jesus' blessing, which follows OT biblical models (Genesis 48–49).

The first story (9:33–37) follows Jesus' second prediction of death in 9:31 and the connected pericope about the disciples arguing over who would be the greatest among them. (Here Mark's audience would probably think of succession to Jesus in view of the statement about his departure.) There is a direct confrontation with the twelve, who are thinking in terms of power and authority. Jesus illustrates his own response by actions as well as words. He "takes the child in his arms" as again in the literary frame closure in 10:16. Derrett (1983: 5–10) has argued from OT parallels that this is part of an adoption ritual. Jesus then confirms this action by words, and announces that those who receive children receive him, thus introducing a succession motif with words similar to Matt 10:40 and John 13:20. Without a break in the scene, Jesus again confronts John, who wants to forbid someone outside the twelve from working in Jesus' name (9:38). Then Jesus once more gives priority to the child in their midst by stressing the danger of leading little ones into sin (9:42).

The end of the children's literary frame (10:13–16) occurs at a significant point after Jesus has confronted the Pharisees in regard to divorce. Jesus' own disciples also find this difficult and question him in the house. Here there is an even stronger confrontation between Jesus and his disciples, who had rebuked those bringing children to him. Jesus is visibly *indignant* and publicly contradicts the disciples by saying, "Let the children come to me, do not hinder them; for to such belongs the kingdom of God" (10:14). Then Jesus states the necessity of receiving the kingdom as children (10:15). In this second text, children are not only "owners" of the kingdom but models of total childlike reception of Jesus' teaching. The two pericopes end with Jesus' blessing. This is especially significant given the OT parallels Derrett has pointed out and the power of Jesus' concluding blessing as seen in Luke 24:50.

Children and youngsters also play a distinct role in Mark's dramatic sequence. Jesus' greatest miracle is the raising of the twelve-year-old daughter of Jairus (5:35–43). The longest gospel miracle account is that of the young boy afflicted with a life-threatening illness resembling epilepsy (9:14–29). In the passion account, only Mark relates that a young man or youngster "closely followed" (Gk *synēkolouthei*) Jesus after all the other disciples had fled (14:50–51). Yet even this person fled away naked after the soldiers seized him, grabbing hold of the linen cloth around him.

Scholars have not agreed about the relationship of this disciple to the young man at the empty tomb who proclaims Jesus' resurrection (16:6). However, the following textual details suggest an identification as well as a key role in Mark's gospel conclusion. When Mary Magdalene and the other women came to Jesus' tomb, they said to one another, "Who will roll away the stone for us from the door of the tomb?" (16:3). Then the text notes that the women entered the tomb, found the young man sitting there, and were amazed. The sequence suggests that their amazement was due to their perception that the young man was the only one who could have performed the prodigious feat of moving the huge stone.

The following arguments support this view and point to the young man as part of a surprising climax of Mark's gospel: (1) The central importance of the resurrection proclamation needs support by a special sign, as customary in Mark and in prophetic OT proclamations (Mark 11:1–5; 14:12–16; Isa 7:10); (2) The Markan audience would look for an important biblical parallel to such a sign. This is found in the story of Jacob's arrival at the well in Paddan-aram (Genesis 29). Jacob proves God is with him and identifies himself to his future wife Rachel by miraculously rolling a huge stone from the well to water her flocks. The verb "roll away" (in regard to a stone) is found only in the LXX of Gen 29:3, 8, 10. In addition, the same description of a "large stone" occurs in both Gen 29:2 and Mark 16:4. Jacob's feat was really a formative miracle of Israel, for after this we hear about Jacob's marriage and the birth of his children. It would thus parallel a similar formative miracle in Mark announcing a new beginning.

The above considerations would prepare the audience for a final dramatic surprise: the previously weak youngster who had fled away naked (14:51–52) has become the miraculously strong proclaimer of Jesus' resurrection. Thus he summarizes Mark's theme that God reverses human expectations by working through the powerless, children and little ones.

C. Children in Matthew

In the stories of Jesus' birth and childhood, Matthew introduces some of his central gospel themes. Jesus' birth and the following events identify him with the *child* promised through Isaiah the prophet (Isa 7:14, 16). The child Jesus is called Emmanuel to fulfill these prophecies (Matt 1:23). This child will be the hope of the gentile world, as illustrated by the Magi's journey guided by God through a star and by dreams. The child is also one with his suffering people in history, especially in their exile in Egypt. The Jewish king Herod tries to kill the "newly born king," afraid that he himself may be supplanted by another. The experiences of the child Jesus are also remarkably similar to those of Moses, who was saved from death from Pharaoh by God's intervention. Just as Moses liberated his people at the risk of his life, so the child Jesus identifies with his people by suffering, exile, and danger.

Like Mark, Matthew also constructs a literary frame around two stories about children in his discipleship section (18:1–5; 19:13–15). However, unlike Mark, there is no sharp contrast to the twelve, but a simple question addressed to Jesus about who is the greatest in the kingdom (18:1). Yet Matthew enhances the place of children by making this story an introduction to a whole discourse on church discipline (18:1 to 19:1). Thus children will stand as a model for a much larger group in the church. The first image is that of conversion: "Unless you turn and become like little children, you will never enter the kingdom of heaven" (18:3). The second is that of humility: "Whoever humbles himself as this little child is the greatest in the kingdom of heaven" (18:36). The third is that of identification with Jesus: receiving a child in his name (18:5) and the very opposite, causing a little one to sin. Here Matthew emphasizes the identification-with-Jesus theme that is central to his gospel. Jesus then highlights the importance of little ones by declaring that each has a special guardian angel assigned to them by God (18:10).

In this discourse, Matthew expands the image of children or little ones to include first of all lost community members. The audience should search for them like a shepherd looking for a single lost sheep, since it is not the Father's will that a single little one perish (18:14). The evangelist then gives two other examples of the search for little ones: first, the case of a serious transgression within the community where every possible effort should be made to have the transgressor realize what he has done. An initial step is a secret one-to-one talk, then two or three witnesses, and finally the whole community should try to win over the lost person (18:15–20). In regard to the weak backslider, forgiveness must be extended without limit, up to "seventy times seven" (18:22). The children's literary frame ends in 19:13–15. Matthew does not have Mark's significant blessing. However, he has Jesus twice lay his hands on the children. This could have special significance given the importance of the laying on of hands in the early church.

The theme of children/little ones is also important elsewhere in this gospel. Following the OT wisdom motif, Jesus praises God who has hidden things from the "wise and understanding and revealed them to babes" (11:25). When Jesus enters the temple for the last time, Matthew contrasts the indignant attitude of the chief priests and scribes to that of children who saw Jesus' wonderful deeds and cried out to him, "Hosanna to the Son of David" (20:15). When the Jewish leaders objected to the children's words, Jesus replied to them by quoting Psalm 8:2, which describes children as open to the wonders of God's universe. The Last Judgment scene in 25:31 sums up Matthew's theme of Jesus' identification with the little ones and least of the kingdom, who now include the poor, sick, hungry, and homeless in the world. Jesus declares, "Truly I say to you, as you did it to one of the least of these my brethren, you did it to me" (25:40). In contrast, what was not done to "one of the least of these" is not done to Jesus (25:45).

D. Children in Luke

Luke could well be called the "gospel of little children." The stories of Jesus' birth and childhood introduce central motifs found later in that gospel. As in Matthew, the child Jesus is the promised descendant of David. The nativity stories resemble Scripture meditations on the OT. There God directed the prophet Samuel to choose a "little one" as the future king, the youngster David who was out shepherding the flocks (1 Sam 16:1–13). In a similar manner, the promised child is discovered by shepherds in a rustic setting near David's own city of Bethlehem. The shepherds recognize the child through Isaiah's sign of the manger (1:1–2; Luke 2:7, 12, 16). The child's place in a feeding crib symbolizes he will be a shepherd and source of nourishment for his people. This prepares the way for a gospel climax in which Jesus will be recognized in the breaking of bread (24:30–31). The lack of hospitality at Jesus' birth contrasts with the hospitality shown to the mysterious stranger at the end of the gospel who proves to be the risen Jesus (24:28–32). The two childhood wisdom summaries (2:39, 52) are significant in presenting Jesus as a wisdom child in view of the OT wisdom scriptures. Later, Luke will take up the theme of God's gift of wisdom bestowed on little ones, even *infants* (10:21–22). At the Last Supper, Jesus teaches that the greatest of the disciples should be like the youngest (22:26).

Luke's gospel is unique in having a special journey section, beginning in 9:51, where most of his special material is found. He introduces it by focusing on children as the model for the new teachings on discipleship that he will present. J. Kodell (1987) has studied the literary children's framework in the journey section and shown how Luke teaches through opposing pairs based on the model of children and little ones. Jesus teaches that the disciples must receive children as himself and that the least among them is the greatest (9:47–48). The first opposing group is the disciples who argue about first places in the kingdom (9:46–48). The second is the attitude of John forbidding someone outside the twelve from casting out devils in Jesus' name. Connected to this episode is Jesus' opposition to both John and James in their response to Samaritans (9:49–56). The closing children's story is near the end of Luke's journey section (18:15–17). Here the emphasis lies on receiving the kingdom as a child (18:17). Luke expands this to include the least and lowliest in the kingdom. The opposing pairs are the Pharisee and tax collector as well as the rich ruler and Pharisees (18:9–30).

E. Children in John

The gospel prologue announces the Word came down from heaven so that those who believe in Jesus might become children (Gk *tekna*) of God. In the Nicodemus episode, Jesus states the necessity of being born again (or from above) to enter the kingdom of God. While the Synoptic Gospels present children as models for this new birth, John appears to present this model through an actual person (Brown 1979: 31), the beloved disciple, although some scholars consider him to be an idealized disciple or model for the audience.

This beloved disciple (BD) seems to be a youngster, for there was a reported saying of Jesus that he would still be alive when Jesus returned (21:22–23). Also his position at Jesus' bosom at the last supper suggests a young age. His relationship to Jesus seems modeled on that of Jesus to the Father. Jesus reveals his Father's secrets because he is in his Father's bosom (1:18). Correspondingly, the BD at Jesus' bosom learns from him the secret of Judas' betrayal and tells it to Peter. The BD's special place at Jesus' side suggests that he will be his special successor, since chaps. 13–17 treat of Jesus' departure and his continued presence. The gospel presents the BD as the authority behind its views of Jesus' and his teaching. Hence the BD is presented as Jesus' successor either as a favorite disciple or as an adopted son, perhaps modeled on Joseph, the favorite son of Jacob, who receives a double blessing (Gn 49:22–26), and whose children Ephraim and Mannaseh are adopted as Jacob's own (48:1–22).

The following are ways that the BD appears as models for the gospel audience: (1) He is a model for the gospel's emphasis on the Paraclete or Holy Spirit as the inner successor of Jesus (Culpepper 1983: 123–24). As the Paraclete is the Spirit of truth (14:15) so the BD also proclaims the truth (19:35). As the Spirit bears witness, so does the BD (15:26; 19:35). They both teach and bring into remembrance what Jesus has said (14:25; 2:20–22). (2) The "one [or disciple] whom Jesus loved" is the principal designation of the BD in this gospel (13:23; 19:26; 20:2; 21:7, 20). Thus he is a model for every disciple who is likewise loved by Jesus. This love is parallel to and modeled on the love of the Father for Jesus. This is shown in statements like, "the Father loves the Son, and has given all things into his hand" (5:20; also 10:17; 15:9). A prominent example of this love is the "family relationship" of Jesus with Lazarus, Martha, and Mary. The gospel describes each of them as loved by Jesus (11:3, 5, 36). The quality of this love receives special notice, for Jesus risks his life to save Lazarus by being willing to go into Judea (11:8). In response, the family gives a reception for Jesus at Bethany, where Lazarus is seated at table, Martha fulfills her role in serving, and Mary affectionately anoints his feet with oil and dries them with her hair as an extraordinary sign of hospitality (12:1–3). (3) The BD is a model of faith for the audience. On hearing from Mary Magdalene that the tomb was open, the BD ran with Peter, noticed that the tomb was empty, and believed without any accompanying sign or confirmation.

Bibliography

Brown, R. E. 1979. *The Community of the Beloved Disciple.* New York.

Clemens, R. E. 1966. The Relation of Children to the People of God in the Old Testament. *Baptist Quarterly* 21: 195–205.

Culpepper, R. A. 1983. *Anatomy of the Fourth Gospel.* Philadelphia.

Derrett, J. D. M. 1983. Why Jesus Blessed the Children (Mk 10:13–16 par.). *NovT* 25: 1–18.

Kodell, J. 1987. Luke and the Children. *CBQ* 49: 415–30.

JOSEPH A. GRASSI

CHILEAB (PERSON) [Heb *kilʾāb*]. The second son of David, born at Hebron (2 Sam 3:3). He was the firstborn of David and Abigail, the Carmelite, whom David had taken as a wife upon the death of her foolish husband Nabal (1 Samuel 25). Presumably he had died, along with David's first- and third-born sons, Amnon and Absalom, when David's fourth son Adonijah attempted to seize the throne in the last days of his father's life (1 Kings 1–2). He is called "DANIEL" in 1 Chr 3:1, and this—or some form such as "Daluiah" (see McCarter *2 Samuel* AB, 101)—was most likely his correct name. In 2 Sam 3:3, 4QSam[a] has *dl[ ]*, the OG has *Dalouia*, and an OL fragment has *da[ ];* a textual corruption is easily postulated here, since the last three letters of the Hebrew—*lʾb*—are identical to the first three of the next word and since the letters *k* and *d* could have been easily confused.

DAVID M. HOWARD, JR.

CHILIASM. The materialistic and sensual aspect of millenarianism, the belief in an earthly paradise lasting about one thousand years. Illustrative of this belief is *2 Baruch* 29–30, a Jewish work of the early 2d century C.E. It says that the earth will yield "ten thousand fold," the vine will have a thousand branches, one grape will produce a cor (= 55 gallons) of wine, and manna will fall from heaven. This concept is employed and developed by a number of early Christians. Eusebius of Caesarea (ca. 260–ca. 340) states that the gnostic Cerinthus (ca. 100) taught a crude chiliasm which included belief in an earthly kingdom replete with sumptuous banquets, marital bliss, feasts, "sacrifices and slaughter of victims" *(thysiais kai hiereion sphagais):* presumably he means animal sacrifices (*Hist. Eccl.* 3:28; 7:25). Here Eusebius is quoting Dionysius of Alexandria (died ca. 264), who opposed the teaching of Cerinthus. Teaching similar to Cerinthus is attributed to Nepos of Arsinoe (Eus. *Hist. Eccl.* 7:24). He thought that the "divine Scriptures should be interpreted" "after a more Jewish fashion" *(Joudaïkoteron),* that is, according to the model of certain Jewish interpretations which anticipated an earthly paradise. Another exponent of chiliasm was Apollinarius (ca. 310–390). Epiphanius (*anac.* 77:36–38) states that Apollinarius expected persons to rise with resuscitated physical bodies and to observe both male circumcision and the Jewish dietary laws. Chiliasm is found in one of its most crass forms in Lactantius (ca. 224–ca. 320). He states that the righteous will have multiple offspring; celestial bodies will shine seven times more brightly than in this world; mountains will drip with honey; there will be streams of wine and milk and animals will cease to be carnivorous; there will be no need for commerce or agriculture. Dyeing of wool will not be necessary because the sheep will be of different colors (Lactant. *Div. Inst.* 7:24; cf. Verg. *Ecl.* 4:21–45). Commodianus (3d century or later) takes an approach similar to Lactantius and adds that there will be no rain or cold and that Jerusalem will be 12,000 furlongs square and reach as high as the heavens. The righteous shall beget children for one thousand years. Methodius of Olympius (died ca. 311) in *Banquet* 9 views the millennium as the fulfillment of the Jewish feast of Tabernacles. However, he states that there will be no begetting of children. The author of the *Apocalypse of John the Theologian* (von Tischendorf 1966: 70–94) takes a materialistic view of the renewed earth and also argues that there will be neither yellow nor red nor black races, neither Negro nor "different face," and all will be about the age of thirty. However, although his statements refer to a paradise on a renewed earth, he does not mention a thousand years per se.

Bibliography

Bietenhard, H. 1953. The Millenial Hope in the Early Church. *SJT* 6:12–30.

Maier, G. 1981. *Die Johannesoffenbarung und die Kirche.* WUNT 25. Tübingen.

Tischendorf, K. von. 1966. *Apocalypses Apocryphae.* Hildesheim.

J. MASSYNGBAERDE FORD

CHILION (PERSON) [Heb *kilyôn*]. Son of Elimelech and Naomi, husband of Orpah (Ruth 1:2, 5; 4:9). Chilion and his family migrated to Moab, where he married Orpah (4:9–10) and later died with his brother Mahlon and their father (1:4–5). Chilion is always paired with his brother in the story. The initial order of Mahlon followed by Chilion (1:2, 5) is inverted at the gate scene by Boaz (4:9) but not for the reason of chiasmus since 1:5 would interrupt this sequence. The inverted order presented by Boaz has been explained on the basis that the older brother's seniority would require him to be named first in such a commercial transaction and therefore it is assumed that Mahlon is the elder. The reason for the first pairing is unclear. Gordis (1986) attributes it to the symbolic meaning of the names "sickness" (Mahlon) and "death" (Chilion), which together sum up the destitute condition of the family in Moab. See MAHLON.

The etymology of "Chilion" is uncertain, but many relate it to the noun *killāyôn* (masc.) from *kālâ;* thus the name is interpreted "destruction," "annihilation," or "failing" (cf. LXX spellings *kelaion, chelaion,* and *chellaion*). Noth, however, prefers "consumption, a wasting disease" (*IPN,* 11). Those who take the characters as historical point out that the names in the story are plausible, some being attested in ANE onomastica. This is evidenced for "Chilion" in Ug *(klyn),* Phoen *(kly),* and Palmyrene *(kylywn, kyly).*

Bibliography

Friedman, H., and Simon, M., eds. 1977. *The Midrash Rabbah.* Vol. 4. London.

Gordis, R. 1986. Personal Names in Ruth: A Note on Biblical Etymologies. *Judaism* 35: 298–99.

Sasson, J. M. 1979. *Ruth.* Baltimore.

KENNETH A. MATHEWS

CHILMAD (PLACE) [Heb *kilmad*]. A trading partner with Tyre mentioned only in the MT of Ezekiel's lament over that city (Ezek 27:23). The name is last in a list of five places, three of which are well attested: HARAN, EDEN (= Bīt Adini), and ASSHUR; CANNEH is otherwise unattested, but may be the same as CALNEH. Chilmad is obscure, and has given rise to speculative interpretations. LXX reads *Charman,* a puzzling name, and the Vulgate simply transliterates MT to give *Chelmad.* The Targums reanalyzed the consonantal text as *kl md[y]* "all Media," followed by some modern commentators (e.g., Eichrodt *Ezekiel* OTL, 381; Zimmerli *Ezekiel* Hermeneia, 50) and translators (NEB).

The trade with Tyre engaged in by Haran, Canneh, Eden, Asshur, and Chilmad (?) seems to have involved the export of textiles and other woven goods (Ezek 27:24). The three known places are located in Syria and N Mesopotamia, and this has induced suggestions of Mesopotamian and Syrian identifications for Chilmad. Among these are Charmon (Charmande) on the Euphrates near Babylon (Xen. *An.* 1.5.10), Kalwada near Baghdad (Smith 1872: 61; now generally rejected), and Kulmadara in N Syria (Astour *IDBSup,* 145, supposing omission of an *r* by haplography). Simons (*GTTOT* 457) observes that LXX *Charman* may reproduce the name of the Persian province Kirman; if so, the Greek translator may have already made implicitly the analysis of MT as a reference to Media followed by the later Targums. He further notes (Simons

GTTOT, 488) that the "sons of *Cheleoud*" in Jdt 1:6 (RSV: "Chaldeans") have also been associated with Chilmad.

The revocalization *kĕlimmād* "like an apprentice" is at least as old as David Kimḥi (ca. 1160–ca. 1235) and was followed by some critics in the 19th century.

Bibliography

Smith, G. A. 1872. Early History of Babylonia. *Transactions of the Society of Biblical Archaeology* 1: 28–92.

HENRY O. THOMPSON

CHIMHAM (PERSON) [Heb *kimhām*]. Son of Barzillai the Gileadite who resided with King David after the unsuccessful revolt of Absalom (2 Sam 19:38–39, 41—Eng 19:37–38, 40). On David's return to Jerusalem after quelling Absalom's rebellion, he wished to reward faithful Barzillai with a place at the royal residence in Jerusalem. Since he was eighty years old, Barzillai politely declined and, instead, asked the favor for "your servant" Chimham. David complied and Chimham returned to Jerusalem with him.

Although it is not stated that Chimham was the son of Barzillai, this can be reasonably inferred. Some Greek versions and the Syriac add "my son" to Chimham's name in 2 Samuel 19, and Josephus (*Ant* 7.11.4) believed that Chimham was the son of Barzillai. As one of his last requests, the dying David asked Solomon to continue to show favor to Barzillai's "sons" who lived at the royal residence (1 Kgs 2:7). It can be assumed that others had joined their kinsman (lit. brother) Chimham there.

The name also occurs in the place name, GERUTH-CHIMHAM (Jer 41:17). Since the name probably means "lodging place or fief of Chimham," and is located near Bethlehem, some commentators believe that David awarded Chimham a grant of land from his patrimony. For further discussion see Williamson *Chronicles* NCBC.

STEPHEN G. DEMPSTER

CHINNERETH (PLACE) [Heb *kinnāret*]. Var. CHINNEROTH. Chinnereth was identified by W. F. Albright and G. Dalman with Tell el-ʿOreimeh (Tel Kinrot M.R. 200252) on the W shore of Lake Chinneroth, N of the el-Ghuwayer Plain. It comprises a small tell on top of a natural hill clearly visible from the S and the W, and of a lower city covering great parts of the slope extending to the shore of the lake. The primary water source is ʿĒn et-Tine, a spring located at the S foot of the hill underneath a steep cliff.

The identification agrees with the literary sources. Chinnereth is first mentioned in the list of Thutmose III as number 34, the last of four cities in the upper valley of the Jordan, after Laish, Hazor, and Peḥel. The importance of the town during the 18th Dyn. is further documented by the fact that Chinnereth is listed in Papyrus Petersburg 1116 A, together with ten other Canaanite cities, among which are Megiddo, Taanach, Ashkelon, and Hazor. During the later part of the 18th Dyn. no further reference to the town is made. In the Bible, Chinnereth appears one time in Josh 19:35 as one of the cities of Naphtali. However, it must have been an important city in the time of the monarchy, since the lake was named after the town (cf. Num 34:11; Deut 3:17; Josh 12:31; 13:27). In Josh 11:2 and 1 Kgs 15:20, Chinneroth probably designates the region S of Chinnereth, i.e., the el-Ghuwayer Plain. After the Assyrian conquest of the N Kingdom, the city was abandoned, and in Roman and Byzantine times it was replaced by the new settlement called Gennesaret (cf. Matt 14:34), which appears as Ginnosar in the Jewish tradition and can most probably be located in the vicinity of Kh. el-Minya, just .5 km S of Tell el-ʿOreimeh.

At the W edge of the tell, a city wall and part of a house were excavated that can clearly be dated to the EB II. But the pottery from various fills is a mixture of different wares from EB I and II. Common are sherds decorated in the band-slip or grain-washed technique, as well as sherds of red-burnished ware, both typical of EB I, suggesting that a settlement already existed during this period. Not a single sherd of KHIRBET KERAK WARE has been found, suggesting that the site remained unsettled from EB III until MB II.

From the MB and LB ages only scattered remains have been found, so that nothing conclusive may be said about the fortification and extension of the town during the 2d millennium. Habitation during the MB II and LB is indicated by sherds from different loci, including fragments of imported vessels such as Mycenaean bowls and Cypriot milk bowls.

The site was probably not settled during the Iron Age I. A new settlement was founded during the 10th century B.C., replaced by a city covering approximately 6 acres. The earliest city was defended by a massive wall system up to 11 m wide.

At the end of the 9th or the beginning of the 8th century B.C., the city was reduced in size. The city wall encircled only the upper part of the mound, protecting an area of about 2 acres. An entirely new city wall, 3–4 m wide, was built, partly founded on the earlier wall. At the S side, a citadel was separated from the rest of the city, which could be entered from the city in the N. The small two-chambered city gate stood at the E side, and beside it was a pillared building. The whole gate was filled with burnt mudbrick material and ashes to a depth of ca. 2 m, indicating a heavy and sudden destruction. According to the pottery from the rooms adjoining the gate, the destruction can be dated into the second half of the 8th century B.C., and may be attributed to the conquest of Tiglath-pileser III in 733 B.C.

During the Hellenistic period, most of the tell remained uninhabited. Only in the central depression were a few houses erected, and they are badly preserved. They were probably built by local farmers who used the slopes for agriculture. The rooms were entirely empty, with only some scattered fragments of Hellenistic pottery (such as bowls, cooking pots, lamps, and *uguenteriae*) found in the debris. Two bronze coins of the Ptolemaic period indicate that this farming activity started during the 3d century B.C. It probably did not last longer than early Roman times, and most likely came to an end during the war from 66–70 A.D.

Bibliography

Albright, W. F., and Rowe, A. 1928. A Royal Stele of the New Empire from Galilee. *JEA* 14: 281–87.

Darsow, W. 1940. Tell el-ᶜOreme am See Genezareth: Vorläufiger Bericht über die erste Grabung im März und April 1939. *Mitteilungen des Deutschen Archäologischen Instituts. Abteilung Kario* 9: 132–45.

Fritz, V. 1978. Kinneret und Ginnosar. Voruntersuchung für eine Ausgrabung auf dem *Tell el-ᶜOrēme* am See Genezareth. *ZDPV* 94: 32–45.

———. 1983. Tell el-ᶜOreme. *IEJ* 33: 257–59.

Koeppel, R. 1932. Der Tell ᶜOrēme und die Ebene Genesareth. *Biblica* 13: 298–308.

Mader, E. 1930. Archäologisches vom *Tell el-ᶜOrême* auf dem deutschen Besitz et Tabgha am See Genesareth. *Das Heilige Land* 74: 24–47.

V. F.

CHINNERETH, SEA OF (PLACE) [Heb *kinneret*]. See GALILEE, SEA OF.

CHIOS (PLACE) [Gk *Chios*]. A large mountainous island of volcanic origin in the Aegean Sea 8 mi W of Asia Minor (Strabo 14.1.35; Acts 20:15). The island's name was either derived from the Greek word for snow, because its mountains are perennially snow-covered, or from a Syrian word for mastic, because its forests abound with mastic. Chios is situated between the islands of Lesbos and Samos and is a principal island in the Ionian Archipelago.

The island's principal ancient city was named Chios also and had the advantage of a good harbor which could contain 80 ships (Strabo 14.1.35; Herodotus 6.8; Thucydides 8.15). Evidence of Chios exports have been found in large quantity in Naucratis, the Black Sea area, and Massilia, but rarely in the Greek peninsula. The men of Chios made slave trade a chief pursuit. Underwater archaeologists have found a number of amphoras testifying to the significance of the Chios wine trade (Strabo 14.1.15; 14.1.35; 14.2.19).

Emporio was the earliest fortification on the island (C-14 date 2075 B.C.E.) and the site was later settled by the Mycenaean. The site was destroyed by fire about 1100 B.C.E. and was left abandoned until about 750 B.C.E. at which time the population of the island gradually began to grow. The inhabitants of Chios were subject to the Ionians and in 546 B.C.E. fell with Asia Minor to the Persians. The Chians and the Miletians rebelled against the Persians and fought gallantly off the island of Lade with 100 ships only to fall again to the Persians. After the battle of Mycale in 479, the Chians joined the Athenian confederacy and in 412, they sided with the Spartans in the Peloponnesian war against their former allies, the Athenians. The Athenians retaliated by devastating the island of Chios. After the battle of Naxos in 376, the Chians revolted against the Spartans allying themselves again with Athens. In 363, the Chians joined forces with Thebes and successfully defeated the Athenian general Chares in battle. Athens recognized the island's independence in 355. The island later befriended Rome and subsequently had to surrender their ships and 2000 talents to the Pontic king Mithidates. The Romans recognized Chios' independence and probably never made the island part of the province of Asia (Pliny 5.38; 16.6).

Chios was renowned for its red wine (Pliny 14.9; 17.34.22; Horace *Od* 3.19.5; Virgil *Ecloques* 5.7; Athenagoras 4.167; 1.32), mastic (Pliny 12.36; 24.74; Dioscor. 1.90), and marble. The island was also one of the reputed birthplaces of Homer. According to legend, Homer gathered his pupils to himself at the foot of Mt. Epos on the coast of Chios, which was probably the same location of an ancient sanctuary of Cybele.

In Josephus' account of Herod's voyage to the Black Sea to meet Marcus Agrippa (*Ant* 16.2.2), he recorded that Herod was detained for some time by north winds at Chios. During his delay, Herod gave a generous sum of money for the restoration of public works on the island, which had been destroyed during the Mithridatic war.

Paul anchored off the island for a night while returning to Jerusalem after his third missionary journey (Acts 20:15), but never went to shore. Isidorus, an Alexandrian Christian and soldier in the Roman army, went with his fleet to Chios, where he was accused for his beliefs and martyred in 251 C.E. There is evidence of Christianity on the island by the 4th century, with a Bishop of Chios (who was not present at the Nicaean Council) and post-Constantinian basilicas at Chios and Phana (on the southern end of the island).

SCOTT T. CARROLL

CHISLEV [Heb *kislēw*]. The ninth month of the Hebrew calendar, roughly corresponding to November and December. See CALENDARS (ANCIENT ISRAELITE AND EARLY JEWISH).

CHISLON (PERSON) [Heb *kislôn*]. A Benjaminite, and the father of Elidad (Num 34:21). The latter was selected from the tribe of Benjamin to help oversee the distribution of the land of Canaan W of the Jordan among the ten tribes who would occupy that territory.

Several meanings have been suggested for the name "Chislon." Johnson (IDB 1: 562), following Noth (IPN 227), suggested "slow" or "heavy of movement," relating the name to an Arabic cognate. Others have proposed "hope" or "aspiration" and have suggested a derivation from occurrences of the root *ksl* in Ugaritic sources (*EncMiqr* 4:222). There are also several cities mentioned in Scripture whose names recall that of Chislon: Chesalon (Josh 15:10), Chisloth-Tabor (Josh 19:12), and Chesulloth (Josh 19:18).

RAPHAEL I. PANITZ

CHISLOTH-TABOR (PLACE) [Heb *kislōt tābōr*]. Var. CHESULLOTH. A town on the S border of the territory of Zebulun (Josh 19:12). It is apparent that Chesulloth (Heb *kĕsûlōt*) in the territory of Issachar (Josh 19:18) is a variant name of this town. Eusebius states that it is "called Chsalous, a village in the valley by Tabor 8 miles from Diocesarea eastwards" (Klosterman 1904: 28, lines 23–25). Josephus mentions it twice, once as "Xaloth" (*JW* 3.3.1) as the S border of Lower Galilee, and again as "Exaloth" (*Life* 44). In a homiletical interpretation of Gen 49:14, *Gen. Rab.*

(98:12) describes Issachar as a mountain between two valleys, that of "Iksalo" and that of "Jezreel."

As already recognized by Eshthori ha-Parhi (Edelman 1852: 47) and again by Guerin (1880: 108–9) and the Survey (Conder and Kitchener 1881: 365), the village of Iksal (M.R. 180232) 5 km W of Mt. Tabor retains this ancient name. However, no Iron Age sherds have been reported from Iksal, but neither has an alternative site been found in the immediate vicinity. The position of the four places mentioned in conjunction with Chesulloth in Joshua 19—Sarid, Daberath, Jezreel, and Shunem (the names of which having all survived in modern place names)—confirms the identification of Chesulloth/Chisloth-Tabor with Iksal.

Iksal's position shows the border between Issachar and Zebulun to have been at the foot of the hills, and also that in *JW* 3.3 Josephus excluded the Jezreel valley from Galilee.

Bibliography

Condor, C. R., and Kitchener, H. H. 1880. *The Survey of Western Palestine.* Vol. 1. London (Reprint 1970).

Edelman, H., ed. 1852. *Pharchi (Parchi) Caftor wa-pherach.* Berlin (Repr. 1959) (in Hebrew).

Guerin, V. 1880. *Description Géographique Historique et Archëologique de la Palestine.* Vol. 7. Paris (Repr. 1969).

Klosterman, E. 1904. *Eusebius Das Onomastikon der Biblischen Ortsnamen.* Leipzig (Repr. 1966).

RAFAEL FRANKEL

CHITLISH (PLACE) [Heb *kitlîš*]. A town situated in the Shephelah, or low country, of Judah (Josh 15:40), within the same district as Lachish and Eglon. The only reference to this settlement occurs in the list of towns within the tribal allotment of Judah (Josh 15:21–62; see also BETH-DAGON). The location of the ancient settlement is unknown. It has been suggested (Boling and Wright *Joshua* AB, 386) that Chitlish may be the same place as Kentisha of the list of Thutmose III, and *k-n-ti-sa,* mentioned on a hieratic ostracon discovered at Lachish.

Bibliography

Alt, A. 1925. Judas Gaue unter Josia. *PJ* 21: 100–16.

WADE R. KOTTER

CHLOE (PERSON) [Gk *Chloē*]. A woman singled out for mention by Paul in 1 Cor 1:11 because her "people," literally "those of Chloe," had reported to Paul about quarreling among the Corinthians. Chloe's "people" were presumably either family members, or slave or freed member employees of her household. The information they conveyed to Paul, who was in Ephesus, could have been delivered either by a letter from the Corinthians or by word of mouth. It is unclear whether Chloe's people resided in Corinth or in Ephesus at the time. An Ephesian rather than a Corinthian base for the household of Chloe seems more probable since Paul probably would not have been so tactless as to identify his informants in remarks to their local Corinthian brothers and sisters. On the other hand, since Chloe herself is apparently known to the Corinthians, she and her people may well have lived in Corinth. But in view of the conjecture above, it is more likely that they resided in Ephesus where, probably as a person of means, Chloe ran a business which required sending emissaries to Corinth and resulted in her being acquainted with residents there.

Chloe's people were obviously Christian. But the same cannot be said with certainty about Chloe. It has been noted, however, that the Greek phrase describing her people as *hoi tōn chloēs* lit. "those of Chloe" contrasts with references to Christian members of other households, e.g., *hoi ek tōn ʾAristoboulou, hoi ek tōn Narkissou* lit. "those from (of) Aristobulus, those from (of) Narcissus" (Rom 16:10–11). The absence of the Gk preposition *ʾek* (from) in the phrase mentioning Chloe may imply that the whole of her household including Chloe was Christian (Meeks 1983: 217, n. 54). One can also surmise that Paul's identification of his informants by using Chloe's name could reflect some familiarity with her, perhaps acquired through business, but just as likely through membership in the Christian community. Chloe may well have been known to Paul as a believer along with her whole household. In that sense she would be reminiscent of Lydia of Philippi and, together with Lydia, might be cited as one type of woman who belonged to the Pauline communities: female heads of households and businesses, women thus accustomed to social leadership and decision-making roles.

Bibliography

Meeks, W. 1983. *The First Urban Christians.* New Haven.

FLORENCE MORGAN GILLMAN

CHOBA (PLACE) [Gk *Chōba*]. Var. CHOBAI. A site in the book of Judith, located in Israelite territory (Jdt 4:4, 15:4, 15:5). The location of the site is uncertain, and given the genre of the book of Judith, the name may be fictitious. It is even unclear whether 4:5 and 15:5 are referring to the same place (15:4 gives the probable variant spelling *chōbai*). The Choba in 4:4 is located to the N of Jerusalem, but seemingly S of the area of Samaria, while in 15:5 it seems to be a border town. In 15:5 the mention of Damascus has led some to draw a connection with the Hobah in Gen 15:14, the place to which Abraham pursues the captors of Lot. However, that Hobah is located N of Damascus, so the connection does not seem fruitful. Aharoni and Avi-Yonah *(MBA)* have identified Choba with el-Marmaleh (M.R. 196163), which is located 30 mi S of Scythopolis and 3 mi W of the Jordan. Moore (*Judith* AB) suggests an identification with el-Mekhubbi, which is located between Tubas (biblical Thebez M.R. 185192) and Besan. See Abel *GP.*

SIDNIE ANN WHITE

CHORAZIN (PLACE) [Gk *Korazin*]. Chorazin was a Galilean town rebuked by Jesus for its rejection of his message, although it had witnessed his miracles (Matt 11:21; Luke 10:13). Ancient Jewish sources describe it as a medium-sized town (*t. Mak.* 3:8) noted for its remarkable wheat production (*b. Menah.* 85a).

Eusebius (*Onomast.* 174.23) and Jerome (*De Situ et Nom.*

Loc. Hebr. 194) located the ruins of the town 2 mi N of Capernaum. C. W. M. Van de Velde's identification of Khirbet Karazeh (M.R. 203257) as ancient Chorazin in the 1850s has been generally accepted (Yeivin 1987: 24).

Located in the hills overlooking Capernaum and the N shore of the Sea of Galilee, this town thrived in the 2d century A.D. when the population of the region expanded as a result of the Bar Kokhba rebellion. The imposing basalt ruins have been subjected to some architectural clearance by the Department of Antiquities of Palestine in 1926, and more recently Zeʾev Yeivin has conducted excavations for the Israel Department of Antiquities and Museums 1962–65, 1982–86. Domestic complexes, a public building, and a synagogue have been exposed. The well-preserved architectural fragments of the 4th-century synagogue, which include friezes adorned with geometrical, floral, and even anthropoid imagery, make it an important site for the study of post-temple Judaism and synagogue architecture. The discovery of numerous coins on the floor of the synagogue has been interpreted as indicating that the town was a stop on the journey of Christian pilgrims who came to witness the fulfillment of Jesus' reproach and who tossed coins into the ruins.

Archaeological excavations as of yet have not unearthed evidence of occupation prior to the 2d century A.D. at Kh. Karazeh, although Chorazin's earlier existence is attested in the literary evidence. Only a small percentage of the site, which covers over 80 acres, has been excavated. The remains of 1st-century Chorazin remain to be discovered. See also *EAEHL* 1: 299–303.

Bibliography

Yeivin, Z. 1987. Ancient Chorazin Comes Back to Life. *BARev* 13/5: 22–36.

ROBERT W. SMITH

CHORBE (PERSON) [Gk *Chorbe*]. The head of a family in a list of returnees from exile in Babylon (1 Esdr 5:12 = Ezra 5:9; Neh 7:14). This section of the list (5:9–15) identifies laymen by family relationship rather than by town of origin. 1 Esdr 5:7–46 is based on the parallel in Ezra 2:1–70 rather than on Neh 7:6–73. However, both parallel verses in Ezra and Neh give the name "Zaccai," which either means "pure" or is a contraction of Zechariah ("Yahweh remembers"). Since the Gk text of 1 Esdras contains many corruptions of the Hebrew *Vorlage,* W. Rudolph (*Esra und Nehemiah* HAT) considers *Chorbe* to be a corruption of *zobbei,* a Gk transliteration of the Hebrew word *zabbai.* Some manuscripts interchange Zaccai and Zabbai in Neh 3:20, so it is possible for Zaccai to have been corrupted to Zobbei and then to Chorbe. One Gk manuscript of 1 Esdras has Zakchai instead of Chorbe. Nothing is known about this person, though a stamp discovered by Moscati contains the name "Zaccai." (See Myers *Esdras* AB.)

MITCHELL C. PACWA

CHOSAMAEUS (PERSON) [Gk *Chosamaios*]. A name associated with Simon, a son of Annan, who divorced his foreign wife during Ezra's reform (1 Esdr 9:32). Although the RSV follows the LXX by listing Simon Chosamaeus as the last of the five sons of Annan, the apparently parallel account in Ezra 10:31–32 mentions eight sons of Harim, of which the fifth, Shimeon, is often assumed to be a Heb variant for Simon in 1 Esdras. Chosamaeus is lacking in the Ezra parallel. However, Fritsch (*IDB* 1: 563) argues that "the name Chosamaeus probably arose as the result of a scribal error in copying the three Greek proper names following Shimeon" in Ezra 10 (i.e., Benjamin, Malluch, and Shemariah). Differences such as this raise questions about the sources of and literary relationships among 1 Esdras, Ezra, and Nehemiah.

MICHAEL DAVID MCGEHEE

CHREIA [Gk *Chreia*]. Isocrates used to say that the root of education is bitter, but its fruits sweet (Aphthonius in Hock and O'Neil 1986: 224). Diogenes, on being asked why people give to beggars but not to philosophers, said, "Because they think that they might become lame or blind, but they never think that they will take up philosophy" (D.L. 6.56). The forms of these two anecdotes—So-and-so said . . . , and So-and-so, on being asked . . . , said . . . —represent two of the most popular varieties of a literary form known in antiquity as the chreia, itself a very popular form in Greco-Roman literature. Indeed, one estimate of the number of chreiai attributed to Diogenes alone is perhaps a thousand (Fischel 1968: 374), and thousands more, attributed to other philosophers as well as to kings, generals, sophists, even courtesans, are scattered across the pages of Athenaeus, Diogenes Laertius, Plutarch, and Stobaeus, to name only a few writers who made extensive use of this form. In short, preserving the wisdom and wit of an Isocrates or a Diogenes by casting it as a chreia was a widespread habit among ancient writers, one that was learned early on, for the chreia was used in grammatical and compositional exercises in school.

The educational use of the chreia, however, assured more than its popularity; it also assured it of receiving a sustained and sophisticated analysis, as the chreia was taken up, along with a baker's dozen of other literary forms, into those teachers' manuals on elementary composition and argumentation known as *Progymnasmata.* The earliest surviving example of these manuals is that by Aelius Theon of Alexandria in the late 1st century C.E. (Stegemann *PW* 5A: 2037–54; Butts 1986), who was followed in the late 2d century by Hermogenes of Tarsus (Radermacher *PW* 8: 865–77; Rabe 1913), in the late 4th century by Aphthonius of Antioch (Brzoska *PW* 1: 2797–2800; Rabe 1926), and in the 5th by Nicolaus of Myra (Stegemann *PW* 17: 424–57; Felten 1913; see also Hock and O'Neil 1986). These manuals subject each form—fable, narrative, chreia, maxim, encomium, comparison, and so on—to a relatively standard analysis which emphasizes matters of definition and classification, and to various compositional exercises which would allow students who had just finished with their literary studies to learn the compositional skills and techniques necessary for writing speeches and declamations (Bonner 1977: 250–76; Hunger 1978: 92–120; Russell 1983). The terms of this analysis and the techniques of composition in these manuals thus provide a complex as well as a contemporary perspective from which to view these forms and the chreia in particular—a perspective that will organize and inform the following discussion of the chreia.

All the manuals define the chreia—and without substantial disagreement. Aphthonius's definition is: "A chreia is a concise reminiscence aptly attributed to some character" (Hock and O'Neil 1986: 225). The key term is "reminiscence," which Theon says is "an action or saying that is useful for living" (Hock and O'Neil 1986: 83). But since a reminiscence might be quite long according to Theon (Hock and O'Neil 1986: 83), the word "concise" is necessary to distinguish the chreia from its longer relative. In any case, the saying or action must also be attributed to some Gk *prosōpon,* whether to an individual person (e.g., Diogenes) or to an identifiable character (e.g., a defiant Laconian). In either case, however, the attribution must be "aptly" made, be "in character," as it were. For example: A Laconian woman, on being sold into slavery and asked what she knew how to do, said, "Be free" (Stobaeus 3.13.58).

Classifying the chreia according to species and subspecies serves to refine the definition further. All the manuals identify and illustrate the simple classification of three species: sayings-chreia, action-chreia, and mixed chreia (Hock and O'Neil 1986: 85, 175, 225, 255). The point of the chreia, accordingly, is made by a saying, an action, or both. The chreiai quoted at the outset thus become sayings-chreiai. An example of an action-chreia is: In response to the person who said there is no motion, Diogenes got up and walked around (D.L. 6.39). A mixed chreia: When Plato defined man as a two-footed, featherless creature and was highly esteemed for it, Diogenes plucked a rooster, carried it into the school, and said, "This is Plato's man!" (D.L. 6.40).

Only Theon provides a detailed discussion of the subspecies of chreiai and indeed provides two such classifications, though both are largely of sayings chreiai only. In one, he (Hock and O'Neil 1986: 85–87) distinguishes between chreiai whose saying is simply a statement *(apophantikai)* and those whose saying is a response to some remark, usually a question *(apokritikai).* The Isocrates chreia quoted at the outset thus becomes an example of a statement sayings-chreia; he simply said that the root of education is bitter and so on. The Diogenes chreia quoted at the outset is therefore a responsive sayings-chreia, as his saying about giving to beggars but not to philosophers is the response to a question. In the other way of identifying subspecies, Theon (Hock and O'Neil 1986: 89–93) restricts himself to classifying the formal features of the saying: maxim, demonstration, joke, syllogism, enthymeme, example, wish, symbol, figure, double entendre, change of subject, and a combination of two or more of these. Thus a saying with a syllogistic style, i.e., having clauses introduced by *ei men . . . ei de . . .* ("Now if . . . , but if . . ."), is: To the one who asked at what hour lunch should be eaten Diogenes said, "Now if you are rich, whenever you want, but if you are poor, whenever you can" (D.L. 6.40).

John Doxapatres, an 11th-century commentator on Aphthonius, illustrates how a chreia is classified according to species and subspecies. "Plato used to say that the offshoots of virtue grow by sweat and toil. This is a sayings-chreia, with its statement made voluntarily, and it is figurative. It is a sayings-chreia because it discloses its benefit by means of a saying. It is a voluntary statement because Plato was not prompted by some circumstance to utter this saying. And it is figurative because it has metaphorical language" (Doxapatres in Walz 1835: 230). Such then is a brief treatment of the classification of the chreia; more detailed treatments are available in Hock and O'Neil (1986: 27–35) and Robbins (1988).

The placement of the chreia in the series of *progymnasmata* varies. In Theon it holds first position, but by the time of Hermogenes it has moved up to third (Hock and O'Neil 1986: 65–66), and while either position is quite early in the sequence and thus called for rather simple exercises to be performed on it, the move from first to third changed the difficulty of the exercise perceptibly. In Theon the chreia still has grammatical purposes in the exercise known as "declension" *(klisis),* since students were asked to write the chreia by declining the character in it through the various cases and numbers. Thus in the nominative: Diogenes on being asked . . . , in the genitive: The saying of Diogenes on being asked . . . , in the dative: It occurred to Diogenes on being asked . . . , in the accusative: They say that Diogenes on being asked . . . , and the vocative: You Diogenes, on being asked . . . (Theon in Hock and O'Neil 1986: 95–99).

Other exercises with the chreia in Theon are more compositional. Included here are: recitation, or writing an assigned chreia in different words but without changing the meaning; commenting, or adding a single sentence to the effect that the recited chreia is true, noble, advantageous, or in keeping with the opinions of other distinguished persons; and expanding a concise chreia into a paragraph or condensing it back to its concise form (Theon in Hock and O'Neil 1986: 99–103). To illustrate only the last two: In the Gospel of Mark the so-called "Cleansing of the Temple" incident is cast in the form of an expanded chreia. "Jesus, on entering the Temple began to evict those who bought and those who sold in the Temple, and he overturned the tables of the money-changers and the seats of those who sold pigeons. And he taught and said to them, 'Is it not written, "My house shall be called a house of prayer for all nations"? But you have made it a cave for brigands' " (Mark 11:11–15). Luke, however, has condensed this expanded chreia back to a concise one: "Jesus, on entering the Temple began to evict the sellers and said to them, 'It is written, "My house shall be called a house of prayer," but you have made it a cave for brigands' " (Luke 19:45–46).

Once the chreia is in third position, however, as it is in Hermogenes, Aphthonius, and Nicolaus, the compositional skills taught become more advanced. Now the chreia itself is no longer declined, recited, commented upon, or expanded and condensed; instead, it becomes the basis for a short essay explaining the meaning and truth of the saying or action in the chreia. Aphthonius is fullest at this point. He identifies eight "headings" *(kephalaia)* under which the student was to organize the essay: (1) an encomium of the one who spoke or acted in the chreia, (2) a paraphrase of the chreia itself, (3) the rationale for the point made in the chreia, (4) an argument that the opposite or converse point is also true, (5) an analogy from other spheres of life, (6) historical examples which illustrate the truth of the saying or action, (7) a citation from an ancient authority which agrees with the point of the chreia, and (8) a brief epilogue (Aphthonius in Hock and O'Neil 1986: 225). Aphthonius provides a sample essay on the Isocrates chreia quoted at the outset (Hock and O'Neil 1986: 225–29), and many other such essays are extant, especially in Byzantine rhetorical texts (Hunger 1978: 98–100). These all show the decisive influence of Aphthonius's model essay, down to phraseology and figures of speech, but the outline is much older, perceptible already in the 1st century B.C.E. *Rhetorica ad Herennium* (4.44.56–57). Consequently, it is not surprising that the Gospel writers not only expanded and condensed chreiai but also organized longer blocks of teaching material according to this outline (Mack 1988: 161–65; Robbins 1988: 19–21).

Bibliography

Bonner, S. F. 1977. *Education in Ancient Rome from the Elder Cato to the Younger Pliny.* Berkeley.

Butts, J. 1986. *The Progymnasmata of Theon: A New Text with Translation and Commentary.* Ph.D. diss., Claremont.

Felten, J. 1913. *Nicolai Progymnasmata.* Vol. 11 in *Rhetores Graeci,* ed. H. Rabe. Leipzig.

Fischel, H. A. 1968. Studies in Cynicism and the Ancient Near East: The Transformation of a Chria. Pp. 372–411 in *Religions in Antiquity.* ed. J. Neusner. Leiden.

Hock, R. F., and O'Neil, E. N. 1986. *The Chreia in Ancient Rhetoric.* Vol. 1, *The Progymnasmata.* SBLTT 27. Atlanta.

Hunger, H. 1978. *Die hochsprachliche profane Literatur der Byzantiner.* Vol. 5 in *Byzantinishces Handbuch. AW,* ed. H. Bengston. Munich.

Mack, B. 1988. *A Myth of Innocence: Mark and Christian Origins.* Philadelphia.

Rabe, H. 1913. *Hermogenis Opera.* Vol. 6 in *Rhetores Graeci,* ed. H. Rabe. Leipzig.

———. 1926. *Aphthonii Progymnasmata.* Vol. 10 in *Rhetores Graeci,* ed. H. Rabe. Leipzig.

Robbins, V. 1988. The Chreia. Pp. 1–23 in *Greco-Roman Literature and the New Testament,* ed. D. Aune. SBLSBS 21. Atlanta.

Russell, D. A. 1983. *Greek Declamation.* New York.

Walz, C. 1835. *Rhetores Graeci.* Vol. 2 of *Rhetores Graeci,* ed. C. Walz. Stuttgart.

RONALD F. HOCK

CHRIST. The word entered English from Lat *Christus,* which transliterates Gk *christos.* Outside the LXX, NT, and early Jewish and Christian writings, *christos* is an adjective meaning "rubbed on" or "used as an ointment or salve." It modifies the word indicating the substance so applied, as in the expression *to elaion to christon* "the anointing oil" (Lev 21:10, 12 [LXX]).

Elsewhere in the LXX, the term is only used in connection with persons in the meaning "anointed," translating Heb *māšîaḥ.* This is also the case in early Jewish writings. In the books of the NT, *christos* is used generally of the coming "anointed one" ("Messiah") of Jewish expectation or specifically of Jesus, believed to be this "Messiah." In the Greek text of John 1:41—"We have found the Messiah (which means Christ)"—the Greek *messias* and *christos* are used (cf. John 4:25).

The word *christos* occurs about 350 times in the NT (exact figures are difficult because of the many variants in the manuscript tradition, particularly in the case of Jesus). It is often found in the combinations "Jesus Christ" and "Christ Jesus," and sometimes functions as a second name. In a considerable number of cases it cannot be demonstrated that *christos* carries the meaning "Messiah" or has messianic overtones.

A. *Christos* in the LXX and in Early Jewish Sources

In the LXX *christos* is the regular term to translate the Hebrew word *māšîaḥ* in the OT. Anointing was part of the investiture of kings and priests in Israel, and holders of these offices were regularly referred to as "anointed" with reference to this symbolic act. See MESSIAH. The expression is used once of the patriarchs in Ps 105:15 (= 1 Chr 16:22), where Heb *mĕšîḥāy* "my anointed ones," used oddly in parallel with "my prophets," is translated into Greek *ton christon mou* (Ps 104:15 [LXX]).

The expression "the anointed priest" is found in Lev 4:5, 16; 6:15 (RSV 6:22); the Greek term found here is *christos.* In Lev 4:3, the LXX uses the participle *kechrismenos,* with the same meaning. Elsewhere in biblical Hebrew usage, the term "the Lord's anointed" and the corresponding expressions "my/your/his anointed" are used only of kings; compare also the expression "the anointed of the God of Jacob" in 2 Sam 23:1. In the two cases where the Hebrew Bible uses *māšîaḥ* absolutely but without article (Dan 9:25, 26), the two Greek versions give different translations. In v 25 only Theodotion has the phrase "until an anointed one, a leader"; in v 26 both Theodotion and LXX speak of "ointment" instead of "an anointed one," while LXX adds that a gentile kingdom will destroy the city and the whole place *meta tou christou*—either "with the anointed one" (Theod. "with the coming leader") or "with that which was anointed."

In the apocryphal books of the OT *christos* occurs in Sir 46:19 where the expression "the Lord and his anointed" is found in a reference to 1 Sam 12:5. In 2 Macc 1:10 Aristobulus is said to be "of the family of the anointed priests." In the Greek pseudepigrapha we note the expression "an anointed lord" (used of the expected ideal Davidic king) in *Pss. Sol.* 17:32. In view of *Pss. Sol.* 18:5 (and 18:7 with the superscription of this psalm), this passage is probably to be amended to "the anointed of the Lord." In the Testaments of the Twelve Patriarchs we find the word *christos* in *T. Reub.* 6:8 that speaks of "(the times of) the anointed highpriest, of whom the Lord spoke"; the passage in its present form is undoubtedly Christian.

Not only in Greek sources, but also in those preserved in other languages, the term "the anointed one" seldom occurs (see MESSIAH). References to a future royal figure predominate but differ in many details. Only in the Qumran Scrolls do we find the expectation of an anointed high priest in the future, and one reference to a prophetic "anointed one of the Spirit" in 11QMelch 18. The late apocalypses of Baruch (*2 Bar.* 29:3; 30:1; 72:2) and Ezra (*4 Ezra* 12:32) are the only ones that use the term "the anointed" in an absolute sense to denote the expected future king. This use of the term is common in the writings of the NT, also to characterize the central figure in Jewish expectation (Mark 12:35; 15:32; 7:27, 42; 12:34). Discussions between Jews and Christians mentioned in Acts (9:22; 18:5, 28) center around the nature of the expected messiah and whether Jesus is the awaited one. In these instances the designation *ho christos* is used without any further addition.

Josephus uses the expression *ho christos* twice, in two much-disputed passages about Jesus as the Messiah (*Ant.* 18.63–64 and 20.200).

B. The Use of *Christos* in the NT

1. Central Questions. The discrepancy between the frequent Christian use of the term *christos* as a central designation for Jesus and the very restricted use of the term in Jewish contemporary writings is striking. Why was the category "anointed one"/"Christ" considered appropriate to characterize Jesus? Who were the first to use this designation in connection with Jesus? Was Jesus called "Christ" by his followers only after his death and resurrection, or did his disciples apply the title to him during his lifetime? Did Jesus himself accept this title or did he avoid it? Scholars have given many different answers to these central questions, which can only be addressed after a careful and detailed analysis of the occurrences of the term "Christ" in early Christian writings.

2. The Letters of Paul. An analysis of the early Christian use of the word *christos* will have to start with the earliest written evidence, the letters of Paul. In Romans, 1 and 2 Corinthians, Galatians, Philippians, 1 Thessalonians, and Philemon, commonly regarded as genuine, the term occurs 270 times. Thus over half of the instances are found in about one sixth of the NT. Paul uses *christos* alone, with or without the article, but nowhere with a clear difference in meaning. He also uses it in combination with other words: "Jesus Christ," "Christ Jesus," "Jesus Christ the/our Lord" or "the/our Lord Jesus Christ." There does not appear to be a difference in meaning between "Jesus Christ" and "Christ Jesus"; the latter expression is sometimes preferred for grammatical reasons. We may compare here the case of Jesus' disciple Simon, who received the name Cephas/Peter ("man of the rock") and is referred to as Simon, Cephas/Peter and Simon Peter alike. The combination of *christos* with *kyrios* "Lord" is avoided by Paul (though it is found in Luke 2:11). In Rom 16:18 the expression "our Lord Christ" is probably used to contrast between serving the Lord and serving other lords (cf. Col 3:24). When *kyrios* is used by Paul together with "Christ Jesus," it follows that expression (Rom 6:23; 8:39; 1 Cor 15:31; Phil 3:8).

The fact that a direct combination of Christ with Lord is avoided in the Pauline letters shows that Christ is not a proper name. Nor does Paul use *christos* as a general term; it is always and exclusively a designation for one person, Jesus. The word is nowhere used as a predicate. Paul never finds it necessary to state "Jesus is the Christ." Expressions of the type "Jesus the Christ" are not found, nor does the OT expression "the anointed of the Lord" occur. The designation "Christ" receives its semantic content not through a previously fixed concept of messiahship but rather from the person and work of Jesus.

Yet Paul (and his readers) knew very well what the term meant to Jews. In a list of God's privileges for Israel, Paul states: "of their race, according to the flesh, is *ho christos*" (Rom 9:5); the titular use of the term is evident. Use of Christ as a title may also be intended in a number of other passages (Rom 15:7; 1 Cor 1:23; 10:4; 15:22; 2 Cor 5:10; 11:2–3; Gal 3:16; Phil 1:15, 17 and 3:7). We may note in passing that in Rom 1:3–4 Paul quotes a formula that states that Jesus was descended from David. But in all these cases it is not necessary to know that *christos* has "messianic" connotations. Invariably Paul speaks about the one Christ, Jesus, and even in Rom 9:4 his point is equally valid for those readers who do not realize that he is using a "technical" term. In 2 Cor 1:21 the Greek suggests a play of words between "Christ" and "anointing" ("It is God who establishes us with you in Christ, and has anointed us")—but significantly the verb *chriō* is applied to those united with Christ in baptism, not to Jesus himself. Paul also emphasizes that the crucified Christ of whom he preaches is a stumbling block to the Jews (1 Cor 1:23; Gal 5:11). Here and in Gal 3:13 we may detect biographical overtones; a crucified messiah was unacceptable for Paul before he found himself called to be an apostle of the one whom he persecuted. Yet in his letters he regards it as unnecessary to argue explicitly that Jesus is the *christos* whom Israel expected or why this is the case; Paul and his readers were convinced he was. When early Christians spoke about (the) "Christ," they meant Jesus in whom they believed; they did not necessarily intend to convey the "messianic" connotations of the term.

It can be shown that Paul refers to earlier formulas familiar to his readers in which *christos* is used of Jesus. The expression "Christ died for us/you" is such a fundamental statement; it is found (with variations) in Rom 5:6, 8; 14:15; 1 Cor 8:11; 2 Cor 5:14–15; 1 Thess 5:9, 10, and is clearly presupposed in 1 Cor 1:13; Gal 2:21; 3:13. "Christ" is not regularly used in formulas referring to the resurrection, but it occurs in a number of formulas speaking about Jesus' death and resurrection jointly: 1 Cor 15:3–5; 2 Cor 5:15; Rom 8:34; 14:9; "Christ" used absolutely in Paul's disquisition on baptism in Rom 6:3–11.

Introducing the statement in 1 Cor 15:3–5, Paul makes clear to his readers that its message constitutes the heart of the gospel which he preaches and which he himself received. Here and in 15:12–19 it is evident that the word "Christ" (denoting Jesus, who died "for us and for our sins" and was raised again, according to the Scriptures) indicates the core of what is believed and proclaimed as the gospel of salvation. It can be shown that in Paul's letters it is used repeatedly in combination with believing/faith (Gal 2:16; Phil 1:29), preaching (1 Cor 15:11–14; Rom 10:14–16), and gospel (see for the expression "the gospel of Christ" Gal 1:7; 1 Thess 3:2). This, too, may reflect pre-Pauline usage. As to Paul himself, he regularly introduces himself as the apostle or servant of Christ (Jesus), particularly in the prescripts of the letters, and emphasizes that

Jesus Christ died on the cross (1 Cor 1:13, 17–18; 2:2, 8; 2 Cor 13:4; Gal 3:1; 6:12, 14; Phil 2:8; 3:18).

For Paul and the tradition before him, the designation "Christ" was thus linked with Jesus' death and resurrection and their salvific effects. It is relatively seldom found in texts speaking about the *parousia,* which seems to be traditionally linked with the designation "Lord." Only in Philippians does Paul use the expression "the day of Christ" (1:10; 2:16; cf. "the day of Jesus Christ" in Phil 1:6).

Among other instances where Paul clearly prefers the term "Christ" to other designations and titles of Jesus, we may note a number of cases where the term is used in connection with Christ's followers regarded as a close community united with him. In 1 Cor 1:10–16 Paul argues that there is only one Christ crucified for those who believe and in whose name all were baptized (this is implied in vv 13, 15). They now belong to Christ, are "of Christ" (v 12; 3:23; 15:23; 2 Cor 10:7; Gal 3:29; 5:24; Mark 9:41); they therefore form a unity and should live in harmony. Gal 3:26–28, using corporate language, emphasizes the unity of believers in Christ: "for in Christ Jesus you are all sons of God through faith. For as many of you as were baptized into Christ have put on Christ. There is neither Jew nor Greek, there is neither free nor slave, there is neither male nor female; for you are all one in Christ Jesus." Believers are "in Christ Jesus"; they are therefore one. In 1 Cor 12:12–31, Paul, in a plea for unity and diversity within the Christian Community, calls it "the body of Christ." In Rom 6:3–11, "baptism into Christ Jesus" implies being "baptized into his death" and sharing in his new life. "So you also must consider yourselves dead to sin and alive to God in Christ Jesus" (v 11). Similar corporate language is found in Rom 8:9–11; 2 Cor 5:14–15; Phil 3:7–11 (the figure of death and life is also central to Col 2:12–13; 2 Tim 2:11–12). Corporate notions occupy a very important place in Paul's thinking about the present and future effects of Jesus' death and resurrection on those who are united with him. It is not quite clear to what extent he makes explicit here what was experienced by early Christians who underwent the ritual of baptism; it is likely, however, that the term "Christ" was connected with baptism from early times onward.

Baptismal language, with its imagery of death and rebirth, is brought into proximity with the Christian hope of future redemption in the expressions "in Christ Jesus" and "in Christ," both of which occur with some frequency in the Pauline corpus. In many cases the expressions serve to connect the salvation offered by God and experienced by Christians explicitly with the central event of Christ's death and resurrection (as in Rom 3:24 "the redemption which is in Christ Jesus"; Phil 3:14 "the upward call of God in Christ Jesus"; Gal 2:16 "to be justified in Christ"; 1 Cor 15:22 "in Christ shall all be made alive"). In many other cases the terms are connected with the Christian community (Rom 8:1 "there is no condemnation for those who are in Christ Jesus"; Rom 12:5: "So we, though many, are one body in Christ"; Gal 3:26–28; Rom 6:11). It is often difficult to determine the exact nuance of the Greek preposition *en* that is used in these contexts, and generally impossible to choose between an instrumental meaning and a locative one (implying corporate imagery). Essential is the fact that Christians live in close communion with Christ, the effects of whose death and new life determine their existence. With the "we . . . in Christ" corresponds the "Christ in us" (Gal 2:20; Rom 8:10; 2 Cor 13:5; Col 1:27—where "in you" may also mean "among you"; Gal 4:19; 2 Cor 13:3; Gal 2:8).

The other instances where "in Christ (Jesus)" occurs cannot be subsumed under a single heading. The expression is used there to characterize individual persons, specific activities, or situations. In all cases there is again a connection with the central message about Christ, though the term may sometimes be used rather loosely. There is not always a clear distinction between "in Christ" and "in the Lord," an expression used by Paul predominantly in exhortations and commands.

Finally, *christos* is found in parenetical statements which stress that Christ's conduct forms the foundation of the believers' conduct toward others and determines it (1 Cor 8:12; Rom 14:15). Related admonitions use the "conformity pattern" (Rom 15:2–3 and Rom 15:7), the much discussed "have this mind among yourselves which you have in Christ Jesus" (Phil 2:5), as well as the expressions "in accord with Christ Jesus" (Rom 15:5) and "Be imitators of me, as I am of Christ" (1 Cor 11:1). Paul can speak of fulfilling "the law of Christ" (Gal 6:2) and describe himself as one "under the law of Christ" (1 Cor 9:21).

3. The Deutero-Pauline Writings. Of those letters that are commonly regarded as written not by Paul himself but by authors standing in the Pauline tradition, Colossians and Ephesians use *christos* in much the same way as Paul. There are no "messianic" overtones.

In Colossians we find the expressions "apostle/servant of Christ (Jesus)" (1:1, 7; 4:12; cf. 3:24 comparable to Rom 16:18), "peace of Christ" and "word of Christ" (3:15 and 16). Interesting is the expression "to declare the mystery of Christ" (4:2), to be connected with "the knowledge of God's mystery, Christ in whom are hid all the treasures of wisdom and knowledge" (2:2–3). Elsewhere the author speaks of "this mystery, which is Christ in you, the hope of glory" (1:27). This mystery, hidden for generations, had been made manifest to "his saints" to whom in particular Gentiles belong. The mystery of Christ forms the content of the proclamation of the community of believers (1:24–29). They are "in Christ" (1:2); their faith is "in Christ" (1:4; 2:5). They "received Christ Jesus the Lord" (2:6) and live therefore "according to Christ" (2:8) and not according to the rules of the elemental spirits of the universe. The church constitutes the "body of Christ" (1:24, also 1:18 and 2:19 [Christ is the head of the body]). Much attention is paid to the idea of incorporation in Christ, with an emphasis on the present salvation enjoyed in communion with Christ (2:20; 3:1–4, 11; cf. 1:24).

In Ephesians the word "mystery" recurs, again centered around what has been effected by and granted in Christ (1:9; 3:3–13; 5:32; 6:19). Particular emphasis is laid on the unity of Gentiles and Jews in Christ (2:11–22; 3:3–13). Again we find the notion of being raised with Christ (after being dead in sin) and being exalted with him (2:1–6; cf. Col 3:1). In 5:14 the phrase "Awake, O sleeper and arise from the dead, and Christ shall give you light" seems to have been taken from a baptismal hymn. Often the author uses "in Christ" and "in Christ Jesus," and much attention is paid to the life of the community as that of a body of which Christ is the head (1:23; 2:16; 4:4, 12–16). The relation between Christ and the church is an example for relations between husband and wife (5:21–33).

In 2 Thessalonians "Christ" occurs only in the fixed expression "the/our Lord Jesus Christ" with the sole exception of the phrase "the steadfastness of Christ" (3:5). In the Pastoral Epistles (1–2 Timothy, Titus), we find stereotyped language, both in sentences using earlier christological formulas and in free composition. "Christ Jesus" is used twenty-six times, four times together with "the (our) Lord," and three times with "our savior"); five times we find "Jesus Christ" once with "our Lord," and once with "our savior"), and only once "Christ" (1 Tim 5:11). The frequent use of Christ Jesus (in all grammatical constructions) is striking. It may show awareness of the fact that Christ is more than just a name. The author may have been influenced by the earlier formulas he uses; their exact date cannot be determined and may differ from case to case. But 2 Tim 2:8 (which resembles the ancient formula found in Rom 1:3–4) mentions Jesus Christ's descent from David and it is possible that 1 Tim 1:15, 2:5–6, and 6:13 betray earlier formulaic usage of the term "Christ."

4. The Gospel of Mark. In this gospel, commonly regarded as the oldest of the three Synoptics, the word *christos* is used seven times. In 1:1 the evangelist characterizes the story he is going to tell as "the gospel of Jesus Christ." Important manuscripts add "the Son of God," bringing out an essential feature of Markan christology: Jesus, who is called the Christ, and who often refers to himself as "the Son of Man," is God's Son. Demons recognize him as such (3:1; 5:7), as does the Roman officer present at the crucifixion (15:39). Jesus accepts this designation during his trial before the Sanhedrin (14:61, cf. 8:38; 12:6–8; 13:32), and most significantly God himself is introduced in the story twice with a solemn declaration: "you are/this is my beloved son" (1:11; 9:7).

In the expression "gospel of Jesus Christ," Mark uses traditional terminology (cf. the use of "gospel of Christ" and of "Jesus Christ" in the letters of Paul). Also in 9:41, where disciples are characterized as "being of Christ," is conventional language. In the five remaining instances, however, the original titular meaning of the term is evident.

In 8:29 the disciples, through Peter, confess, "You are the Christ." For Mark and his readers, this is a well-known confession and it does not come as a surprise. Peter utters it after having witnessed Jesus' activity in Galilee as preacher, teacher, healer, and exorcist. It is understandable that outsiders regard Jesus, the herald of God's kingdom (1:14), as a revived John the Baptist, or Elijah, or one of the prophets (8:28); his disciples call him "the Christ." At the moment they say this, they do not yet know the whole story. Immediately after, Jesus enjoins his disciples to keep silent about him (8:30). He announces his suffering, death, and resurrection, referring to himself as Son of Man (8:31, repeated in 9:31; 10:32–34). He declares that those who follow him must be ready to lose their lives "for me and the gospel" (8:35); that they will be vindicated when the Son of Man returns "in the glory of his father" to introduce the kingdom of God with power (8:38–9:1). The story of Jesus' transfiguration follows (9:2–8) with God's solemn pronouncement "this is my beloved Son" (9:7) and another command for secrecy (9:9).

In 12:35–37 Jesus introduces the thesis "the Christ is the Son of David" as a typical opinion of the scribes. Similarly, in the crucifixion story the chief priests and the scribes speak about "the Christ, the king of Israel" (15:32). Earlier in the gospel, Jesus is twice addressed as "Son of David" by Bartimaeus (10:46–52), and he is associated with "the coming kingdom of our father David" by those who hail him at his entrance into Jerusalem (11:1–11). In 12:35–37 Jesus quotes Ps 110:1 and remarks that David addresses the one who is said to be his son as "lord." The true son of David—Christ—is different from what the scribes expect.

This becomes very clear in 14:61–62, where Jesus, standing before the Sanhedrin, acknowledges that he is "the Christ, the Son of the Blessed," but adds "you will see the Son of Man sitting at the right hand of Power, and coming with the clouds of heaven (an allusion to Ps 110:1 and Dan 7:13). Jesus the Son of Man will reign as the Son of David/Christ/Son of God when God's kingly rule will be established on earth (8:38–9:1; 13:26). In the story about the trial before Pilate and the crucifixion, the designation "king of the Jews" stands central (15:2, 9, 12, 18, 26, cf. v 32). Its thematic importance is that Jesus is not a king in the political sense; even less is he a bandit like the ones crucified with him, or an insurgent like Barabbas. His royal rule will only be revealed at the *parousia* when the crucified Christ will be shown to be triumphant.

Mark 15 reflects the political tensions before, during, and after the war between the Jews and the Romans, culminating in the destruction of Jerusalem and its temple in A.D. 70. This is also clear in chap. 13, where Jesus' followers are warned against people who say "Look, here is the Christ" or "There he is." False messiahs and false prophets will arise to lead astray the elect (vv 21–22). They need not waver, however, for they know whom they may expect: "the Son of Man coming in clouds with power and glory" (v 26).

5. The Gospel of Matthew. The two other Synoptic Gospels bring out more clearly what Mark wanted to convey. In doing so they could only rely on Mark and on general early Christian usage, but not on Q, the sayings-source commonly thought to have been used by Matthew and Luke. Mark uses *christos* very sparingly, but in the sayings attributed to Q it is not used at all.

Matthew knows Jesus Christ as a double name (1:1, 18 and 1:16; 27:17–22). Straightaway he explains to his readers that Christ denotes the Messiah, Son of David, king of Jews (2:1–6). It is clear, however, that Herod's interpretation of the term is wrong. While Gentiles worship the newborn "king of the Jews" (2:9–12; they are the first to do so), Herod tries in vain to destroy a potentially dangerous political opponent (2:13–18). Chap. 2 prepares the reader for the misunderstandings apparent in chap. 27 (= Mark 15). Matthew also stresses that Jesus is the Son of David (1:1–17; 1:20; 21:9; 22:41–46). He uses this term in particular in stories about healing (9:27–31; 12:22–23; 15:21–28; 21:14–17 plus the Bartimaeus story in 20:29–34).

The title "Christ/Messiah" receives more emphasis in the story of Peter's confession (16:16, "you are the Christ, the

Son of the living God"; and 16:20, ". . . he strictly charged the disciples to tell no one that he was the Christ"). "The Christ" (with the definite article) is significant in 11:2 where "the works of the Christ" refers to Jesus' healings and his preaching of the gospel, as also in 23:10 ("you have one master, the Christ"). In 24:5 and 26:68 Matthew adds the designation in contexts where it was already used by Mark.

6. Luke-Acts. In Luke-Acts we find the phrase "the Lord's Anointed" (Luke 2:26, Acts 4:26) and "the Anointed of God" (Luke 9:20; 23:35); the genitive refers to the One who anoints, as in the Old Testament. Luke specifies that God anointed Jesus with the Spirit (see the quotation from Isa 61:1–2a in Luke 4:18; Acts 10:38; also 4:27). At the same time "Christ" and "Lord" are found as parallels in Luke 2:12 ("a Savior who is Christ and Lord") and Acts 2:36 ("God made him both Lord and Christ"). As Christ/Messiah Jesus is Son of David (Luke 1:32; 2:4, 11; 3:31; cf. 1:69). He is "King of Israel/the Jews," but does not exercise political power (brought out very clearly in Luke 23:3, 39; cf. Acts 17:7). There will be no end to the reign of this Son of David, who is at the same time Son of the Most High (Luke 1:32–33; cf. 1:69). The emphasis is on his reign after his exaltation in heaven (Luke 22:67–69; 23:42–43; Acts 2:36; but see also Acts 3:19–21, which connects the designation Christ specifically with the *parousia*).

Another feature of the Lukan use of *christos* has to be singled out. The word is used in a typical variant of the double formula speaking about Jesus' death and resurrection/exaltation. The first part speaks about "the suffering of Christ" (Luke 24:26, 46; 26:23; Acts 17:3; 26:23; cf. 3:18; 25:19, see also below on 1 Pet 2:21; 3:18). In Acts 17:1–3 it is made clear that this central element in the Christian message forms a special point of debate in discussions with the Jews. In the synagogue of Thessalonica, Paul explains "that it was necessary for the Christ to suffer and to rise from the dead" before testifying that Jesus is the Christ. In the narrative of Acts, the core of Paul's message (and that of Apollos) may be reduced to "Jesus is the Christ" (9:22) or "the Christ is Jesus" (18:5; 18:28). It may also be summed up as "Jesus is the Son of God" (9:20); also elsewhere the designations "Christ" and "Son of God" are closely connected (Luke 1:32–33; 4:41; 8:28; 22:67–69).

Finally it should be pointed out that according to Acts 11:26 (cf. 26:28 and 1 Pet 4:16), the designation "Christians" was first used for the followers of Jesus in Antioch. This implies that they formed a separate group, the identity of which was determined by their allegiance to one who was commonly called *christos* (see CHRISTIAN).

7. The Johannine Corpus. Apart from 1:17 and 17:5, where we find the expression "Jesus Christ," all instances of the use of *christos* in the Gospel of John presuppose the titular use of the term. The Gospel wants to demonstrate what it means to believe "that Jesus is the Christ, the Son of God" (20:31). The confession "Jesus is the Christ" formed the breaking point with the synagogue (9:22), and followers of Jesus should therefore consider very carefully what constituted the core of their faith and what should be kept in mind in ongoing discussions with "the Jews."

John the Baptist, introduced as prime witness for Jesus, denies that he himself is the Christ (1:20, 25; 3:28). Two of his disciples follow Jesus and one of them, Andrew, tells his brother Simon: " 'We have found the Messiah' (which means Christ)" (1:41). Here and in 4:25 the Greek transliteration of the Hebrew term is introduced to illustrate the meaning of the designation "Christ." In 4:4–42 a Samaritan woman, after listening to Jesus, identifies him with the Messiah of Samaritan expectation, who "will show us all things" (4:25; cf. v 29; see also MESSIAH). Jesus answers "I who speak to you am he" (v 26). In a discussion with his disciples, he makes clear that his task is to accomplish the work of God who sent him, in complete agreement with the divine will (vv 31–38). After further contacts with the Samaritans of the woman's city, they declare, "we know that this is indeed the Saviour of the world" (vv 39–42).

In the debates between Jesus and the Jews and the discussions among the people in Jerusalem narrated in John 7, Jesus is called "the Christ" (vv 26, 27, 31) and "the prophet" (v 40, and an important variant reading in v 52). This chapter is important because here, as in 12:34, several aspects of the Jewish expectations concerning the Messiah are mentioned (see MESSIAH). But the Johannine Jesus puts all emphasis on his unique unity in will and work with the Father who sent him. In this light the Davidic descent of the messiah and his birth in Bethlehem are irrelevant (7:40–44). When in 10:24 the Jews ask Jesus, "If you are the Christ, tell us plainly," Jesus answers with a short discourse on the intimate union of the Father and himself, ending with the statement "I and the Father are one" (vv 25–30). Martha therefore confesses Jesus as the Christ, the Son of God (11:27); this is the message the Gospel is intended to bring to its readers (20:31).

The First and Second Letter of John address a different situation. Christians believe in "Jesus Christ, the Son of God" (1 John 1:3; 3:23; 5:20; 2 John 3). Confessing that "Jesus is the Christ" (1 John 5:1) stands parallel with confessing that "Jesus is the Son of God" (1 John 4:15; 5:5, 10, 13). Denying that Jesus is the Christ means denying Father and Son, according to 1 John 2:22 (2 John 9). This implies that the designations "Christ" and "Son of God" have become virtually interchangeable. The false teachers combated in the two Johannine letters believe in the Christ as the Son of God but fail to take seriously that this Christ is a human being of flesh and blood. Hence the emphasis on the part of the authors of the Letters on the confession that "Jesus Christ has come in the flesh" (1 John 4:2,3; 2 John 7).

Jesus Christ, he adds, "came by water and blood" (1 John 5:6). This is the sound "doctrine of Christ" (2 John 9) in which true believers have to abide. The dogmatic emphasis on Jesus' corporeal substance appears to address the beliefs of some groups of "Johannine" Christians who, perhaps by induction from their faith in the Son of God who exists and acts in complete unity with the Father, arrived at a conception of Christ that completely neglected Jesus' human life, work, suffering, and death. The authors of 1 and 2 John want to redress this neglect; in their contribution to the ongoing debate they do not try to explain the background of the term "Christ," but rather stress a more specific confessional statement: "Jesus Christ has come in the flesh."

Interestingly, the authors refer to the expectation that

"Antichrist is coming" (1 John 2:18) to characterize opponents as "antichrists" (1 John 2:18, 22; 2 John 7) or false prophets inspired by the spirit of the Antichrist (1 John 4:3). Specific to 1 John is also the use of the term "anointing" as source of true knowledge of the (true) believers (1 John 2:20, 27; cf. 2 Cor 1:21–22).

8. Other NT Writings. Of the other writings in the NT, the Letter to the Hebrews, the First Letter of Peter, and the Revelation to John require our attention. In the first two writings we find no "messianic" overtones. In Revelation we find a few instances where *christos* is used as a title. Central in the argument of Hebrews is the notion that Jesus Christ, "the same yesterday and today and forever" (13:8), is the eternal Son of God and (high) priest after the order of Melchizedek forever (chap. 7). The eternal kingdom of the Son is emphasized by a citation (Heb 1:8–9) of Ps 45:6–7 (LXX Ps 44:7–8), including the sentence "therefore God, thy God, has anointed thee with the oil of gladness beyond thy comrades." A subsequent concatenation of Psalm quotations (Ps 2:7 and 110:4, cited at 5:5–6) establishes that Christ did not arrogate high priesthood, but was divinely appointed to that office. The designation "Christ" is still used to indicate the central content of the Christian message. In 6:1 the author speaks about "the elementary doctrines of Christ"; he describes the believers as the house of Christ (3:6) and as sharing in Christ (3:14). The special connection between the designation "Christ" and Jesus' death for others comes out clearly in 9:11–28 (see v 11; v 14 "the blood of Christ"; v 24 and v 28 "Christ, having been offered once to bear the sins of many"; cf. 10:10). But to bring out the essential meaning of Christ's death the author, here and elsewhere, sets forth the implications of the fact that he is high priest after the order of Melchizedek.

The use of the word *christos* in 1 Peter shows many similarities with its use in the letters of Paul. The designation occurs in connection with Jesus' suffering and death or with his suffering/death and the following resurrection with an outlook on his present and future glory. At the same time the communion between Christ and the Christians (the term is used in 4:16) is emphasized. By way of example, we may mention 1:18–19 "you were ransomed . . . with the precious blood of Christ, like that of a lamb without blemish or spot" (cf. 1:2); 2:21 "Christ suffered for you, leaving you an example, that you should follow in his steps" (cf. 3:15). The "Spirit of Christ" speaking to the prophet of the old dispensation revealed to them that their message "predicting the sufferings of Christ and the subsequent glory" was intended not for their own, but for the present generation (1:10–12). In 3:18–22 we find a complete confession of faith, consisting of many old elements: "Christ suffered [or: died; because the Greek words are very similar the manuscripts differ here and at 2:21] for sins once for all, the righteous for the unrighteous, that he might bring us to God, being put to death in the flesh but made alive in the Spirit . . . preached to the Spirits in prison . . . , has gone into heaven and is at the right hand of God, with angels, authorities and powers subject to him." Christians, therefore, may live in hope through Jesus Christ' resurrection (1:3), looking out for his final revelation (1:7,13). They share in his sufferings (4:13–16; 5:10; cf. 5:1), but may be confident that they will share in his glory (4:13; 5:1, 10). In the meantime, knowing that Christ "bore our sins in his body on the tree, that we might die to sin and live to righteousness" (2:24, cf. Isa 53:4, 12), maintaining good conduct as aliens and exiles among the Gentiles (4:1–6; 2:11–12; cf. 1:1, 17). Christians are "in Christ" (5:14).

In the Revelation to John the designation "Jesus Christ" is found three times in the introductory verses. The word *christos* alone is found four times, in 11:15 and 12:10 speaking about "his (the Lord's, God's) anointed" and in 20:4, 6 where "his" is not found, but the titular meaning of *christos* is certainly present. In all four cases, Jesus is referred to.

The book contains the revelation of Jesus Christ to John (1:1) "who bore witness to the word of God and to the testimony of Jesus Christ" (1:2). In v 5a Jesus Christ is called "the faithful witness, the firstborn of the dead, and the ruler of the kings of the earth." Verses 5b–6 (perhaps using ancient baptismal terms) praise "him who loves us and has freed us from our sins by his blood and made us a kingdom, priests to his God and Father."

In chap. 5 the seer, after having heard the announcement that "the Lion of the tribe of Judah, the Root of David has conquered" (v. 5, cf. 3:7; 22:16) sees a Lamb standing near God's throne "as though it had been slain" (v. 6; cf. 7:9, 17; 12:5). This Lamb clearly is the victorious Lion of Judah; in hymns, God who sits on the throne and the Lamb are glorified together (5:13; 7:10). In 17:14 the victorious Lamb (accompanied by those who "are called and chosen and faithful" (cf. 3:21) is called "the Lord of lords and King of kings"; the same name is inscribed on the robe and the thigh of the rider on the white horse in (19:11–16), whose victory introduces the last series of eschatological events described in this book. In the first hymn to the Lamb in 5:9–10 we find a clear reference to 1:5b–6: "thou wast slain and by thy blood didst ransom men for God from every tribe and tongue and people and nation, and hast made them a kingdom and priests to our God, and they shall reign on earth."

In 11:15 voices in heaven announce: "The kingdom of the world has become the kingdom of the Lord and his Anointed [RSV: his Christ], and he shall reign for ever." The terminology is influenced by that of Ps 2:2 (cf. v 18, reminiscent of Ps 2:1–2, 5, 12 and Ps 99:1). The emphasis is on God's sovereignty, as vv 17–18, which speak only about God, show. In 12:10 another loud voice in heaven declares, "Now the salvation and power and the kingdom of our God and the authority of his Anointed [RSV: his Christ] have come." Satan no longer has power to accuse "our brethren" (cf. v 9) of whom it is said, "They have conquered him [i.e., Satan] by the blood of the Lamb and by the word of their testimony" for "they were willing to give their lives and die" (TEV). The connection with 5:9–10 (cf. 7:14) is obvious.

The final reign of the faithful who give their lives for their testimony to Jesus and for the word of God is described in 20:4–6. They will come to life ahead of others, and will reign with the Anointed/Christ for a thousand years as "priests of God and of Christ" (cf. 5:9–10). The pericope 20:4–6 describes one of the many episodes of the End; those who have resisted actively in the fierce struggle against Satan and his servants on earth will take part in the first resurrection, and reign with Christ on earth. The final judgment and another resurrection follow (20:11–15). In the new Jerusalem, descending on the new earth, there will be no temple (21:22) and therefore no priests. But "the throne of God and the Lamb will be in it, and his servants shall worship him" (22:3); "they shall reign for ever and ever" (22:5).

The use of *christos* in Revelation is interesting, because it shows that its original messianic meaning was still known. In the time of distress caused by discrimination and persecution in the nineties, Christians in Asia Minor associated this designation with the final triumph of God and the reign of Jesus as "the Lord's Anointed," as Davidic king on earth after the destruction of all hostile powers. At the same time it is made very clear that this future king is Jesus Christ, who redeemed the faithful by his death and rose from the dead; also the close relationship between Jesus Christ and the faithful receives emphasis: They share in suffering in order to share in the final victory.

C. The Use of *Cristos* for Jesus

From the Pauline Letters and the ancient formulas contained in them, it is clear that from a very early period the word *christos* was used in "Christian" circles as the central term to denote Jesus. It is used very often, and it received its content not through a previously fixed concept of messiahship but rather from the person and work of Jesus. The term is especially used in connection with his death and resurrection, the salvation effected by him, and the intimate bond between him and the believers. Although awareness of the original titular meaning "Messiah" persists, there is no longer any need to state explicitly "Jesus is the Christ."

In later writings (the Deutero-Pauline letters, 1 Peter, Hebrews) the same usage prevails. Speaking about Jesus, one uses the word "Christ," especially in specific contexts. Jesus Christ functions virtually as a double name. Yet in Revelation the OT designation of the king as "the Lord's Anointed" returns in connection with the final triumph of God and the reign of Jesus as Davidic King.

At the time the Gospel of Mark was written, it was clearly necessary to remind the readers how their confession "Jesus is the Christ" should be understood. The emphasis is on his impending suffering and death, and on the nonpolitical nature of his kingship. Matthew essentially underlines what is found in Mark. In Luke-Acts, Jesus' messiahship is the central issue in the debate between the early Christians and the Jews, bringing with it a discussion about the true meaning of predictions concerning the Messiah in the Scriptures. Two other features in Luke-Acts are of interest: a certain emphasis on Jesus' reign after his exaltation in heaven, and the explicit statement that God anointed Jesus with the Spirit. The latter is found in Jesus' first public speech, related in the gospel as having taken place in his home town Nazareth (Luke 4:18).

The Gospel of John, a late NT book, presents an interesting picture. On the one hand, it stresses that Jesus the Christ is the Son of God living in a unique unity with the Father; it does so to such an extent that later Johannine Christians have to be reminded that the Son of God in whom they believe really led a human life once. On the other hand, it pictures Jesus in an ongoing debate with Jewish opponents, a debate from which features of Jewish messianic expectation emerge.

Can we explain how the term *christos,* rarely found in contemporary Jewish literature, became so important to early Christians that it could receive a specific Jesus-centered Christian content and meaning very soon? In Jewish sources, the term is mostly used for a royal figure as agent of divine deliverance. The same notion seems to be present or presupposed where the Christian use of the term in connection with Jesus is made explicit. Only in Luke-Acts do we find the notion of "anointing with the Spirit" (also found in 11QMelch 18). The idea of an anointed high priest, very important in the Qumran Scrolls, is not found in the writings of the New Testament. In Hebrews there is no emphasis on the anointing of Jesus as high priest; at the same time it is made very clear that the new high priest is of a completely different order than the Levitical (high) priests before him.

Why, then, was this term with its royal connotations used of Jesus? How did it become a very central designation?

In the oldest pre-Pauline tradition, the designation was especially used in connection with Jesus' death, and according to Luke-Acts it remained necessary to explain, to insiders and outsiders, that his death, followed by his resurrection, was "in accordance with the scriptures" (1 Cor 15:3, 4). In the pre-Pauline formula Rom 1:3, 4 Jesus' Davidic descent receives emphasis, and the motif of Jesus' royal lineage recurs in the latest books of the NT (e.g., 2 Tim 2:8; Revelation). In Mark (12:35–37; 14:61–62), it is made clear that the royal dominion of this Son of David/Son of God/Son of Man only becomes evident after his exaltation to God and will be fully realized with the coming of the kingdom of God in power—that is, God's definitive intervention in human affairs. Yet the Synoptics and John seem to prefer the term "Son of Man" in passages speaking about this future, and in the Letters of Paul the term *kyrios* predominates in such passages. "Christ" is used only seldom in connection with the eschatological rule (Phil 1:6, 10; 2:16; 1 Cor 15:23–28; cf. Acts 2:36; 3:20–21; and Revelation).

It is clear that Mark's story of the trial before Pilate and the crucifixion (chap. 15) combats the misunderstanding that Jesus, the Christ, the king of Israel, wanted to exercise political power. As chap. 13 shows, this misunderstanding will have been particularly acute in the troubles of the sixties when tension mounted in Palestine, finally resulting in the explosive Jewish war.

It is often argued that Mark 15 reflects the historical circumstances preceding Jesus' death on the cross. That Jesus was crucified is beyond doubt, but that he was crucified on the charge that he claimed to be "the king of the Jews" (Mark 15:26) is much more difficult to substantiate. Scholars have pointed out, however, that the story of Jesus' activities in Galilee and Jerusalem shows hardly any royal-messianic features. If we dismiss the unlikely hypothesis that they were there originally but were removed later, it must be assumed that in the events leading up to his crucifixion, accusations by his opponents that Jesus did in fact have royal-messianic claims, and was therefore a dangerous person, played a significant role. Because he was crucified as King of the Jews, his first followers took up the royal designation "Christ," particularly in connection with his death and resurrection.

According to this view, the opponents accused Jesus of royal-messianic pretensions because of the messianic hopes of his followers, his teaching with authority resulting in a sovereign attitude toward the Law and Jewish rules, and perhaps also his behavior in the temple (reflected in Mark 11:15–19). Jesus himself could not deny this charge without putting in question the final eschatological validity of his whole message. Whether he himself would have chosen this designation to express the essence of his mission and did, in fact, use it, remains uncertain.

It is difficult to verify the various constituent parts of this historical reconstruction; an unsatisfactory aspect of it is that it assigns a decisive role to Jesus' opponents in the choice of the term characterizing Jesus' public image. Another approach to the solution of this problem is called for.

It is difficult to believe that the term "Messiah/Christ" came to the fore only at the very last stage of Jesus' ministry because of the accusations of his opponents, and that it was only because of its prominence at the trial and the crucifixion that later Christians used it as the central designation for Jesus. Should we not assume that Jesus' disciples came to regard him as (a special) Messiah already during his lifetime, that this designation was misconstrued in a political sense by his opponents, but that it was taken up again in a nonpolitical manner (with emphasis on his suffering and his death) by his disciples after Golgotha? There is much to be said for this theory.

The Gospel of Mark not only uses the designation "Christ" (with Son of God, Son of Man) in connection with Jesus' future kingship, but it also has Peter confess Jesus as the Messiah in 8:29 on the strength of Jesus' activity as (unique) preacher, teacher, healer, and exorcist. For Mark, Jesus is the Christ: on earth, a charismatic Spirit-inspired figure; at the final realization of his kingdom, king on God's behalf. Looking at Mark 10:46–52; 12:35–37; and 14:61, 62, we may say that his actions are those of a true Son of David.

It has been argued that the Gospel of Luke, which corroborates Mark's picture by explaining that Jesus could be called "the Anointed One" because the Lord anointed him with the Spirit (Luke 4:16–30), reflects Jesus' own opinion. Unfortunately, this hypothesis cannot be substantiated. The related Q-passage (Luke 7:18–23 [= Matt 11:2–6]) does not use *christos,* so that we cannot be sure that the early Christian use of *christos* was connected with the notion of anointing with the Spirit before Luke.

Interestingly, contemporary sources portray David not only as king but also as a prophet. On the strength of 1 Sam 16:13 and the directly following passage 16:14–32, Josephus emphasizes that immediately after the divine Spirit had moved to David, the latter began to prophesy and to exorcize the demons which troubled Saul (*Ant* 6.166–68). We may compare the statement "David was a prophet" in Acts 2:30 (cf. 1:16; 4:25) and 2 Sam 23:1–2, as well as Ps-Philo, *L.A.B.* 59–60 describing David's psalm-singing for Saul after his anointing by Samuel. A Qumran fragment, 11QPs[a] *David's compositions,* attributes 3600 psalms to David and no less than 450 songs, 4 of which were songs for making music over the stricken; it emphasizes that David spoke all these things through prophecy. It should be added that also in texts like *Pss. Sol.* 17 that picture the future Son of David as a king, that king is not simply a military or political figure, but a wise and discerning ruler; Isa 11:1–5 exercised a great influence on Jewish expectations concerning the coming Son of David.

In view of this, it is quite plausible that in the eyes of his earliest followers, if not in his own, Jesus was a true Son of David who could properly be called the Lord's Anointed, not only in view of his future role when God's kingdom would reveal itself in power, but already in the present while God's saving and liberating power manifested itself in Jesus' words and actions. Considering Mark's very restricted use of the designation "Christ," it is probable that the historical Jesus did not widely advertise any christological self-designations. If he used them, he used them creatively, in his own way, and he must have tried to avoid misunderstandings.

Bibliography

Berger, K. 1970–71. Zum traditionsgeschichtlichen Hintergrund Christologischer Hoheitstitel. *NTS* 17: 391–425.

———. 1973–74. Die königlichen Messiastraditionen des Neuen Testaments. *NTS* 20: 1–44.

———. 1974. Zum Problem der Messianität Jesu. *ZTK* 71: 1–30.

Cullman, O. 1963. *The Christology of the New Testament.* Rev. ed. Philadelphia.

Dahl, N. A. 1974. *The Crucified Messiah and Other Essays.* Minneapolis.

Fuller, R. H. 1965. *The Foundations of New Testament Christology.* London.

Hahn, F. 1969. *The Titles of Jesus in Christology.* London and New York.

Hengel, M. 1982. Erwägungen zum Sprachgebrauch von *Christos* bei Paulus und in der "vorpaulinischen" Überlieferung. *Paul and Paulinism: Essays in Honour of C. K. Barrett,* ed. M. D. Hooker and S. G. Wilson. London.

Jonge, M. de. 1972–73. Jewish Expectations about the "Messiah" according to the Fourth Gospel. *NTS* 19: 246–70.

———. 1980. The Use of the Expression *ho christos* in the Apocalypse of John. *L'Apocalypse johannique et l'apocalyptique dans le Nouveau Testament,* ed. J. Lambrecht. BETL 53. Gembloux and Louvain.

———. 1986. The Earliest Use of *christos:* Some suggestions. *NTS* 32: 321–43.

———. 1988. *Christology in Context.* Philadelphia.

Kim, K. H. 1981. *Die Bezeichnung Jesus als (ho) Christos: Ihre Herkunft und ursprüngliche Bedeutung* Diss. Theol. Marburg.

Kingsbury, J. D. 1983. *The Christology of Mark's Gospel.* Philadelphia.

Kramer, W. 1966. *Christ, Lord, Son of God.* SBT 50. Naperville, IL.

Moule, C. F. D. 1977. *The Origin of Christology.* Cambridge.

Unnik, W. C. van. 1961–62. Jesus the Christ. *NTS* 8: 101–16.

MARINUS DE JONGE

CHRIST, BODY OF. The NT usage of the phrase "body of Christ" and its parallel expressions divides naturally into three categories: (1) the physical body of Jesus Christ, (2) the references to the bread in the Last Supper and Lord's Supper, and (3) as a description of the relationship between the resurrected Lord Jesus and His *ekklēsia.*

A. Physical Body of Jesus

This concrete meaning is foundational, serving as the basis of comparison for the other categories (Gundry 1976; Hoehner 1984; Robinson 1952). A study of the Gospels yields a vast and varied amount of data pointing to the true humanity of Jesus (John 1:14; Luke 2:52). There is nothing to indicate that his physical being was other than a normal human body, with its needs and limitations (e.g. John 4:6–7; 19:28). The specific usage of the concept of the "body of Jesus [Christ]," however, is focused on his death and burial (Matt 27:58–59, and par; Col 1:22; Heb 10:10) (Robinson 1952:34–48). Relatedly, passages dealing with Jesus' resurrected body (e.g. John 20:19–29), ascension (Acts 1:9–11), and later appearances (e.g. Acts 9:3–6 = 22:6–8 = 26:12–15) imply both significant continuity and discontinuity with his pre-cross physical state.

B. Bread in the Communion Meal

The Synoptic Gospels record that, at the Last Supper, Jesus made the intriguing assertion "This is my body" after the breaking of the bread (Matt 26:26 = Mark 14:22 = Luke 22:19). This statement has been a notable *crux interpretum,* along with (perhaps) its earliest canonical echo in 1 Cor 11:24. Varied understandings of the relation between Jesus' actual person and the bread of the Eucharist (which He was instituting) have proliferated over the centuries, although such views can be generally categorized as "literal"/physical, metaphorical/spiritual, or some *via media* or combination approach (Küng 1967: 211–24; Ridderbos 1966: 373–76).

Of these historic options, careful exegesis of the 1 Corinthians 11 pericope indicates that the metaphorical, and thus spiritual, understanding of "body of Christ" in relation to the bread of communion is best. The continued Pauline references to "the bread" at the point of the individual's reception of the element (1 Cor 11:26–28) would be strange if there were any physical transformation involved. Certainly there is a close identification here with the physical "body of Christ," as the Corinthian church was urged to properly consider the meaning and significance of Jesus' death (1 Cor 11:27–29). However, such identification clearly stops short of full identity, as a physical understanding requires.

Similarly, in John 6, Jesus refers strikingly to himself as "the bread of life" (6:34, 48, NIV), "the bread that came down from heaven" (6:41), and "the living bread" (6:51). Even though the last usage is said by Jesus to be in reference to "my flesh" (6:51, NIV), there is no clear reference to the Lord's Supper here. It is no more intended for a literal understanding than "I am the light of the world" (John 8:12; 9:5) or "I am the door [of the sheep]" (John 10:7, 9). That is especially seen to be the case in John 6 when it is noted that the receiving of "the bread of life" there takes place by believing in Jesus (John 6:35, 40, 47).

C. Relationship between Christ and His Church

Within the Pauline corpus interpreters encounter a number of powerful expressions that picture the intimate connection between the resurrected Savior and His *ekklēsia.* Notable among these are references to the Church as the bride of Christ (Eph 5:23–32), the temple of the Holy Spirit (1 Cor 3:16; Eph 2:21), and the household of God (Gal 6:10; 1 Tim 3:15).

The most common and well developed of such expressions views the Church as "the body of Christ." The idea is utilized in different ways in different contexts, however. For example, in 1 Cor 12:12–27 and Rom 12:4–8 the emphasis is on the unity of the Church amid the rich diversity of its members. A related, but distinct, usage is seen in passages like Eph 4:4, 12–16 and Col 1:18–22; 3:15. There the focus is on Christ as the "head" of his body, the Church (Ridderbos 1966: 369–87).

Again, there is significant difference of interpretive opinion in regard to whether the idea of the Church as the "body of Christ" should be taken as speaking of virtual identity (the counterpart of the "physical" view of the Supper) or strong identification (Radmacher 1978: 223–37; Küng 1967: 224–41). To view the Church as an extension of the Incarnation might seem the implication of 1 Cor 12:12: "The body is a unit, though it is made up of many parts. . . . So it is with Christ" (NIV; Robinson 1952: 58–59). However, the entire context, including the recapitulatory words "Now you are the body of Christ, and each one of you part of it" (1 Cor 12:27, NIV) argues for a close bond or link that is less than the fullest identification (Best 1955: 95–105; Ridderbos 1966: 369–71).

Thus, since the other passages assume (with minor variations) the same central sense for the imagery of the "body of Christ," it is preferable to understand it in a metaphorical way. The Church is not Christ in the sense of embodying his authority and infallibility. Rather, it draws its direction and empowering from him as its head, as does a human body (Eph 4:15–16).

A final important consideration has to do with the origin of the Pauline phrase "the body of Christ." Various plausible backdrops for the idea have been postulated, arising out of Hebrew, Greek, Gnostic, and Eucharistic contexts (Best 1955: 83–93). However, the likeliest point of origin is the words of the risen Christ on the Damascus Road. "Saul, Saul, why do you persecute me?" (Acts 9:4 = 22:7 = 26:14; Kim 1981). Indelibly etched in Paul's thought patterns, these words best explain the close identification and communion between the Lord Jesus and His church as "the body of Christ" in 1 Cor 12:12, 27.

Bibliography

Barth, M. 1958. A Chapter on the Church—The Body of Christ. *Int* 12:131–56.

Best, E. 1955. *One Body in Christ.* London.

Cole, R. A. 1964. *The Body of Christ.* Philadelphia.

Gundry, R. H. 1976. *Soma in Biblical Theology.* Cambridge.

Hoehner, H. W. 1984. Body, Biblical View of the. P. 166 in *EvDTh* ed. W. A. Elwell. Grand Rapids.

Kim, S. 1981. *The Origin of Paul's Gospel.* Tübingen.

Küng, H. 1967. *Die Kirche.* Frieburg. (ET 1967).

Minear, P. S. 1960. *Images of the Church in the New Testament.* Philadelphia.

Radmacher, E. D. 1978. *What the Church Is All About.* Chicago.

Ridderbos, H. 1966. *Paulus: Ontwerp von zijn theologie.* Kampen. (ET 1975).

Robinson, J. A. T. 1952. *The Body.* London.

Saucy, R. L. 1972. *The Church in God's Program.* Chicago.
Schweizer, E. 1964. *The Church as the Body of Christ.* Richmond, VA.

A. Boyd Luter, Jr.

CHRIST, DAY OF. See DAY OF CHRIST.

CHRIST, DEATH OF. The death of Jesus of Nazareth by crucifixion is generally accepted as historical fact. The circumstances of his execution admit a variety of questions of a historical character, and the centrality of the event in early Christian belief and practice necessitates theological reflection.

A. The Condemnation of Jesus

1. By Roman Authorities. Although many of the circumstances surrounding the trial and death of Jesus are disputed, there is little doubt that Jesus of Nazareth was crucified under Pontius Pilate, the Roman procurator of Judea from 26–36 A.D. Crucifixion was a Roman penalty practiced upon violent criminals, political rebels, and slaves (Hengel 1977:46–63). Tacitus said it was "the punishment usually inflicted on slaves" (*His.* 4.11), and Cicero referred to it as "the most cruel and disgusting penalty" (*Verr.* 2.5.165). The charge on the cross, "the King of the Jews" (Mark 15:26), and the crucifixion of Jesus between two rebels (Gk *lēstas,* Mark 15:27) suggest that Jesus was put to death by the Romans as a political insurgent.

Precisely why Pilate condemned Jesus as a political rebel is more difficult to determine, especially since the Romans do not seem to have arrested and persecuted Jesus' followers after his death. The clearest expression of the charges against Jesus is in Luke 23:2. From the point of view of the Evangelist, these charges are false, but they may provide a clue to how the Romans viewed Jesus. At the heart of Jesus' message was his proclamation that the Kingdom of God was at hand (Mark 1:15), and in the final days of his life Jesus made a triumphal entry into Jerusalem and cleansed its temple (Mark 11:1–19). This action, as well as the proclamation of a kingdom, might well have led the Romans to accept Jewish reports about Jesus, given the volatile atmosphere of 1st-century Palestine.

The Gospels portray Pilate as weak and vacillating during Jesus' trial, seeking a way to release him. But this characterization of the governor does not correspond with what we know of him from other sources (*JW* 2.9.4 §175–77). It is probable that the Gospel portrayal of Pilate is part of a Christian apologetic to place the burden of guilt for Jesus' death upon the Jews, especially their leaders. In all likelihood, Pilate assumed a decisive role in the trial, condemning Jesus as a political insurgent. Consequently, the early Church had to deal with the scandal of the cross (1 Cor 1:23): Jesus was a crucified Messiah, condemned to death as a political rebel.

2. By Jewish Authorities. It is even more difficult to identify the precise reason why the Jewish authorities condemned Jesus and handed him over to Pilate. The events surrounding the Jewish trial of Jesus—if indeed there was a formal trial before the whole Sanhedrin—present one of the most complicated problems of NT scholarship (Blinzler 1969: 15–38). Matthew and Mark report a night trial during which false witnesses testified that Jesus threatened to destroy the temple (Matt 26:61; Mark 14:58), but then the Sanhedrin condemns Jesus on the grounds of blasphemy (Matt 26:65–66; Mark 14:64). In Luke the trial takes place in the morning, the temple charge is not mentioned, and the issue is Jesus' messiahship, but there is no formal condemnation (Luke 22:71). John reports only an informal hearing before Annas during which the former high priest questions Jesus about his disciples and his teaching (John 18:19), passing over the trial reported by the Synoptics and focusing upon the trial before Pilate instead. Given the conflicting nature of the Gospel trial accounts, the reason for the Jewish condemnation of Jesus should be sought in the broader context of Jesus' ministry.

Since Jesus was not a scribe by profession and did not belong to the party of the Pharisees or Sadducees, he stood outside the professional religious establishment. Nonetheless the Gospels portray him as one who taught and acted with supreme authority (Gk *exousia,* Mark 1:22, 27; 2:10; 11:28). In the Sermon on the Mount, Jesus pits his interpretation of the Law against the traditional interpretation (Matt 5:21–48), making himself the mouthpiece of God. On several occasions he apparently violated the Sabbath (Matt 12:1–14) and challenged the traditions of the elders (Mark 7:1–23). He assumed the divine prerogative of forgiving sins (Mark 2:1–11), and on a regular basis he shared table fellowship with tax collectors and sinners (Luke 15:1–2; 19:1–10). It is doubtful that Jesus offered the wicked forgiveness without requiring repentance [as E. P. Sanders has argued (1985: 174–211)], but he may well have given the appearance of doing so. Most importantly, Jesus confidently proclaimed that God's Kingdom was at hand, thereby establishing himself as God's eschatological messenger.

Such activity on the part of Jesus would have inevitably raised the question of his authority. Was Jesus an authentic prophet, or was he a false prophet (Deut 18:20–22; Jer 23:9–40), a rebellious son (Deut 21:18–21), a beguiler who led the people astray (Deut 17:1–13)? On several occasions, it appears that the religious leaders viewed Jesus as a false prophet who led the people astray (Schillebeeckx 1981: 312–18). He is accused of being in league with Beelzebul (Mark 3:22) and of being possessed by an unclean spirit (Mark 3:30). In Matt 11:19 Jesus laments that he is viewed as a rebellious son (cf. Deut 21:18–21). And both in Matthew (27:63) and John (7:12, 47), he is described as one who deceives the people. Some of the religious leaders, therefore, must have viewed Jesus as a false prophet and beguiler who assumed authority to himself.

The proximate occasion for the religious leaders to condemn Jesus, however, is related to his temple ministry. The Synoptic Gospels report that, during the final week of his life, Jesus provoked the religious leaders by cleansing the temple. John transposes this incident to the beginning of Jesus' ministry, but notes its intimate connection with Jesus' death (John 2:17). For Jesus, the cleansing may have been a prophetic action pointing to the coming kingdom and a temple not made by human hands (cf. Mark 14:58) which God would establish. But for the religious leaders his action would have been perceived as an assault upon their authority by one whom some of them already viewed as a false prophet and deceiver. The temple cleansing, then, provided the most important motivation to do away with Jesus.

If this scenario is correct, the religious leaders saw Jesus as a threat to the nation (John 11:45–53) on two counts: deceiving the people and threatening the temple. Since, according to John 18:31, the Jewish leadership did not have the power to inflict the death penalty, they brought him to Pilate as a messianic pretender, who claimed to be the King of the Jews, a political insurgent. It was on the basis of this charge that Pilate condemned Jesus. The Jewish responsibility probably lies with an inner circle of chief priests who viewed Jesus as a false prophet and deceiver rather than with the whole Sanhedrin or people of Israel.

B. Jesus' Understanding of His Death

1. During His Ministry. The writings of the NT provide a comprehensive interpretation of Jesus' death, but the process of interpretation was initiated by Jesus himself. Although he proclaimed the imminent arrival of God's Kingdom, he seems to have reckoned at an early stage with the probability of his own violent death (Léon-Dufour 1986: 49–77). The death of the Baptist must have alerted Jesus that he faced a similar fate. Matthew reports that Jesus withdrew to the wilderness when he heard of John's death (14:13), and Mark narrates a conversation in which Jesus speaks of his death in connection with John's (9:9–13).

The Gospel of John notes that after the feeding of the 5000 in Galilee, Jesus withdrew from the crowd because he knew that they wanted to make him king (6:15). If this remark is correct, it may explain the text of Luke 13:31–33 in which the Pharisees warn Jesus to flee because Herod Antipas, the ruler of Galilee and the murderer of John, sought to kill Jesus as well (Bammel 1984: 211–40). Like John, Jesus attracted large crowds who viewed him as a messianic figure; he was a political threat not only to the Romans but to petty rulers such as Herod. Faced with the growing prospect of a violent death, Jesus seems to have viewed his fate as an inescapable part of his prophetic vocation (Luke 13:32–33; Matt 23:29–36).

Jesus' predictions of his passion, death, and resurrection (Mark 8:31; 9:31; 10:32–34) also witness to a realization on his part that he faced a violent death. Although the predictions, in their present form, were composed in the light of Easter, several authors have convincingly argued that they are grounded in Jesus' own conviction that his death was part of God's plan and that God would vindicate him (Bayer 1986: 149–218; Jeremias 1971: 276–99).

2. In the Face of Death. Jesus' most complete interpretation of his death is given at the Last Supper. The eschatological prospect of Mark 14:25 proclaims Jesus' faith that he will share table fellowship with the disciples in the kingdom of God despite his imminent death. The Eucharistic words, handed down in two different traditions (Matthew and Mark, Luke and Paul) indicate that Jesus attached redemptive value to his death. According to the first tradition (Matt 26:26–29; Mark 14:22–25), the shedding of his blood will establish a covenant on behalf of many (Gk *hyper pollōn*) as was done on Sinai (Exod 24:8). According to the second, the cup is the *new* covenant in Jesus' blood (Luke 22:20; 1 Cor 11:25) promised in Jer 31:31–34. Although scholars dispute Jesus' precise wording, many agree that he understood his death as having redemptive value.

C. Interpretations of Jesus' Death

1. The Gospels. The Gospel passion narratives are the most sustained presentations of Jesus' death. Mark's account appears to be the oldest and Matthew and Luke are dependent upon it. The account of John is remarkably similar to the Synoptics, but not all scholars are convinced that John is dependent upon them.

It is likely that an account of Jesus' passion was composed at an early stage for liturgical usage. Such a composition probably presented Jesus as the righteous sufferer as found in the psalms of lament (e.g., Pss 22, 38, 69) and the book of Wisdom 2:12–20; 5:1–7. By the NT period it was an accepted fact in some Jewish circles that the righteous person is bound to suffer but that God will vindicate him (Ruppert 1972: 23–28). In addition, the servant text of Isa 52:13–53:12 played a role although not as great a role as did the psalms.

In their present form, the passion narratives clearly portray Jesus as more than a righteous sufferer. In Matthew and Mark, Jesus dies as the abandoned Son of God, the crucified Messiah. In Luke, the focus is upon his innocence; he dies as God's righteous Son, and his death leads people to repentance (23:39–43, 48). In John, Jesus' death becomes his exaltation (3:14; 8:28; 12:34), his return to the Father (13:1), and his glorification (17:1–5).

In terms of soteriology, Matthew and Mark view Jesus' death as a ransom (Gk *lytron,* Matt 20:28; Mark 10:45). His death leads to the forgiveness of sins (Matt 26:28). The tearing of the temple veil (Matt 27:51; Mark 15:38) suggests that the Messiah's death replaces the temple cult; there is no need for further sacrifice (Hengel 1981: 47–55). In Luke, Jesus' promise of salvation to the repentant thief (23:43) indicates the salvific aspect of his death. John focuses upon Jesus the Good Shepherd who freely lays down his life on behalf of *(hyper)* the sheep (10:1–18).

2. Pauline Writings. The Pauline corpus focuses more upon the benefits of Christ's death than upon the historical circumstances surrounding it. Employing a number of phrases with the preposition *hyper* ("for," "on behalf of"), the Apostle stresses that Christ died for or was put to death on behalf of us. In two of these texts (1 Cor 15:3; Gal 1:4), he explicitly notes that Christ died or gave himself *for* our sins. In Romans he says that Christ died *for* the ungodly (5:6); he died *for* us while we were still sinners. In Gal 3:13 he notes that Christ redeemed us from the curse of the law, becoming a curse *for* us by being crucified (see

Deut 21:23). And in 1 Thess 5:10 he writes that Christ died *for* us that we might live with him.

At other times Paul speaks of God sending or giving up his Son (Rom 8:3). God did not spare his own Son but handed him over *for* us all (Rom 8:32). God sent his Son, born of a woman "to redeem those who were under the law" (Gal 4:4–5). In other places, Paul speaks of Christ giving himself *for* us (Gal 1:4; 2:20).

In addition to these formulas, Paul describes God as setting forth Christ as an expiatory sacrifice, making him the new mercy seat (Rom 3:21–26). The effect of Christ's death is universal in scope (Rom 5:12–21); it overcomes the power of sin which enslaves the whole of humanity.

In the Deutero-Pauline writings of Colossians, Ephesians, and the Pastorals, there is a subtle shift of emphasis, as A. Hultgren (1987: 91–112) has shown. Whereas Paul concentrates upon the redemption accomplished in Christ, making God the active agent, these writings point to the redemption won by Christ, making him a more active agent of salvation. So the authors of Ephesians says that *Christ* broke down the dividing wall separating Gentile and Jew and reconciled them through the cross (2:14–18). He gave himself *for* the Church (5:25). In Colossians we learn that *Christ* canceled the bond against us by nailing it to the cross, thereby disarming the powers and principalities (2:13–15). And the author of the Pastorals says that *Christ* came into the world to save sinners (1 Tim 1:15), giving himself as a ransom *for* all (1 Tim 2:6), giving himself *for* us to redeem us from all iniquity (Tit 2:14).

3. Other NT Writings. Of the remaining NT writings, the most important for understanding Christ's death are Hebrews, 1 Peter, 1 John, and Revelation. Hebrews offers a profound theological reflection on the death of Christ. Jesus is presented as the great high priest who has entered the heavenly sanctuary (6:19–20). The mediator of a better covenant, he has no need to offer daily sacrifice, since he offered himself as a sacrifice once for all (7:27), obtaining redemption through his blood (9:12). This sacrifice has accomplished purification from sins (1:3), the forgiveness of sins (10:12), and is expiatory in nature (2:17). Most importantly, this sacrifice, universal in scope (2:9), need never again be repeated (7:27; 9:12, 26, 28; 10:10).

The author of 1 Peter also states that Christ's suffering need not be repeated (3:18). Comparing Christ to an unblemished lamb (1:19), he reminds his readers that Christ's death has ransomed them from their past conduct (1:18). The most important statement, however, comes in a hymnlike passage (2:21–25) which compares Christ to the servant of Isaiah 53. Christ suffered on behalf of *(hyper)* us (2:21), bearing our sins in his body on the tree of the cross, so that we are healed by his wounds (2:24).

In 1 John the author makes explicit statements about the atoning nature of Christ's death. The blood of Jesus cleanses us from all sin (1:7); he was revealed to take away sins (3:5) and destroy the devil's work (3:8). Most importantly, Christ died as an expiation *(hilasmos)* for *(peri)* our sins (2:2; 4:10).

Like the three writings mentioned above, the book of Revelation focuses upon the redemptive value of Christ's blood shed on the cross (1:5). Comparing Christ to a lamb *(arnion),* the author states that he ransomed "men for God from every tribe and tongue and people and nation" (5:9), making them "a kingdom of priests to our God" (5:10). As the people of the old covenant washed their garments in preparation for the theophany at Sinai (Exod 19:10, 14), so the people of the new covenant "have washed their robes and made them white in the blood of the lamb" (7:14). The scandal of the cross has become the center of NT theology.

Bibliography

Bammel, E. 1984. The Feeding of the Multitude. Pp. 211–40 in *Jesus and the Politics of His Day,* ed. E. Bammel and C. F. D. Moule. Cambridge.

Bayer, H. F. 1986. *Jesus' Predictions of Vindication and Resurrection.* Tübingen.

Blinzler, J. 1969. *Der Prozess Jesu.* Regensburg.

Hengel, M. 1977. *Crucifixion in the Ancient World and the Folly of the Message of the Cross.* Philadelphia.

———. 1981. *The Atonement: The Origins of the Doctrine in the New Testament.* Philadelphia.

Hultgren, A. J. 1987. *Christ and His Benefits.* Philadelphia.

Jeremias, J. 1971. *New Testament Theology. Vol. 1, The Proclamation of Jesus.* New York.

Léon-Dufour, X. 1986. *Life and Death in the New Testament.* San Francisco.

Matera, F. J. 1986. *Passion Narratives and Gospel Theologies.* New York.

Ruppert, L. 1972. *Jesus als der leidende Gerechte?* SB 59. Stuttgart.

Sanders, E. P. 1985. *Jesus and Judaism.* Philadelphia.

Schillebeeckx, E. 1981. *Jesus: An Experiment in Christology.* New York.

Winter, P. 1974. *On the Trial of Jesus.* Berlin.

Frank J. Matera

CHRISTIAN

CHRISTIAN [Gk *Christianos*]. Although "Christian" is the most common name used today to designate followers of Jesus Christ, it occurs only three times in the NT: Acts 11:26; 26:28; 1 Pet 4:16. Most scholars agree that the formation of this term is Latin in origin. *Christianus* (pl. *Christiani*) is a second declension masculine Latin noun found in Tacitus, Suetonius, and Pliny the Younger. A common practice of the 1st century for identifying adherents was to attach the termination *-ianus* (pl. *-iani*) to the name of the leader or master (e.g., *Pompeiani, Augustiani, Ceasariani*). Early Hellenistic practice paralleled this by attaching *-ianos* (pl. *-ianoi*) to the name of a leader or master (e.g., *Herodianoi,* Matt 22:16; Mark 3:6; 12:13; Joseph. *Ant* 14.15, 10). Hence, whether in Lat *(Christianus)* or in Gk *(Christianos)* the term is formed from Christ and indicates Christ's adherents, those who belong to, or are devoted to, Christ.

The origin of the term, according to Acts 11:26, was in Antioch, dating in the Lukan chronology somewhere between A.D. 40–44: ". . . in Antioch the disciples were for the first time called Christians" (RSV). The infinitive *chrēmastisai* has been interpreted to mean that the disciples first "bore the title" Christians in Antioch (e.g., Bickermann 1949: 355), suggesting that the term was coined by the church to give expression to their own self-consciousness in the new age of the Messiah. But Haenchen has demonstrated that, while possible, usage in Philo and Josephus shows that the infinitive should be rendered "were called," indicating that the name was coined by those outside of the church (1971: 367–68 n. 3). Of those outside, the Jews were not likely to have referred to the disciples as Christians, *followers of Christos,* the Messiah, since this would have validated Jesus' claim to that title (see the disputed passage in Josephus where *Christos* and *Christianoi* are used in this manner [*Ant* 18.63–64). The Jews instead referred to the disciples of Jesus as "the sect of the Nazarenes" (Acts 24:5). Hence, the name "Christian" must have originated within the Gentile population of Antioch. In the large metropolis of Antioch, with its many competing cults and mystery religions, those who spoke so much about *Christos* were soon called *Christianoi,* Christ's people. The term would have then distinguished the disciples from uncoverted Gentiles as well as from Judaism.

The reason for the origin is problematic. The term *Christianoi* may have been coined by the Antiochian governor's staff to indicate official Roman registry. Or the use of the term may have been intended satirically by the Antiochian people to mock those who believed in Jesus as Messiah, paralleling the mockery directed toward the *Augustiani,* the official enthusiasts of Nero (Mattingly 1958). Or more likely, the term may have arisen generally among the populace as a slang term to indicate those who were followers of their God *Christos,* and who were regarded as a sort of mystery fellowship (Grundmann *TDNT* 10: 537). The name *Christos,* Messiah, meant nothing special to the Gentiles, sounding more like a second personal name for Jesus than a religious title.

In all three NT passages the variant *Chrēstianoi* occurs in the uncorrected Codex Sinaiticus; remarkably persistent textual testimony that Gentiles often confused the term *Christos* with the homophone, *chrēstos,* "kind, useful." *Chrēstos* was a common proper name, especially for slaves, and apparently Gentiles tended to think that the disciples were followers of one called *Chrēstos.* This is the likely reason why the Latin historian Suetonius says that Jews were expelled from Rome because of disturbances made at the instigation of one called *Chrēstus* (*Claud.* 25.4). Tacitus, in one of the earliest extrabiblical testimonies to the term (ca. A.D. 115), appears to correct for his readers the common mistake among the Roman populace of A.D. 64 of confusing *Chrēstianoi* with *Christianoi* (*Ann.* 15.44).

While the occurrence of the term in Acts 11:26 indicates, at the very least, the recognition by Gentiles that believers in Christ were an entity separate from both pagan Gentiles and Judaism, the other two occurrences in the NT possibly indicate that elements of contempt (Acts 26:28) and hostility (1 Pet 4:16) were attached to the term by the early use of those outside of the church. There is no NT evidence that the term was commonly used as a self-designation by the early church. Luke's anachronistic reflection in Acts 11:26 implies that the common term for believers at the time of the origin of Christian was "disciples" *(mathētai),* and other terms soon came to be used by the early church, such as "believers" *(hoi pisteuontes; hoi pistoi)* (Acts 5:14; Rom 1:16; Acts 10:45; 1 Tim 6:2), "brothers" *(adelphos)* (Acts 6:3; Jas 2:15), and "saints" *(hoi hagioi)* (Acts 9:13; 1 Cor 1:2).

Christianos appears for the first time as a self-designation in *Did.* 12:4, and is commonly used by Ignatius for a member of the believing community (late 1st/early 2d century), but the name does not occur in abundance elsewhere in the writings of the early church fathers. In the middle of the 2d century, Polycarp calls himself a *Christianos* (*Ep.* 10:1; 12:1), and in the Apologists the term was used as a self-characterization of one who followed Christ into the death of martyrdom. The reason for the scarcity of the term in the early church fathers may be found in a letter by the Roman governor Pliny the Younger to Emperor Trajan (ca. A.D. 112). Those accused of believing in Jesus Christ were asked whether or not they were "Christians." If they admitted to the name, they were put to death, or else, if they were Roman citizens, sent to Rome for trial (*Letters* 10.96). In the days of persecution of the early church, the use of the term was dangerous, because it clearly marked them out in the minds of the Romans as believing in a god who was in opposition to the emperor. But nonetheless, in the church, as early as 1 Pet 4:16, honor was associated with those who suffered because they bore the name of their Messiah, since suffering as a "Christian" glorifies God.

Bibliography

Bickermann, E. J. 1949. The Name of Christians. *HTR* 42: 109–24.

Bruce, F. F. 1969. *New Testament History.* Garden City, NY.

Haenchen, E. 1971. *The Acts of the Apostles: A Commentary.* Trans. R. McL. Wilson. Philadelphia.

Mattingly, H. B. 1958. The Origin of the Name *Christiani. JTS* 9: 26–37.

MICHAEL J. WILKINS

CHRISTIAN ART, EARLY. See ART AND ARCHITECTURE (EARLY CHRISTIAN).

CHRISTIAN ATTITUDE TOWARD ROME. See ROME, EARLY CHRISTIAN ATTITUDES TO.

CHRISTIAN LITERATURE, EARLY. See LITERATURE, EARLY CHRISTIAN.

CHRISTIAN MINISTRY. See MINISTRY IN THE EARLY CHURCH.

CHRISTIAN PAPYRI. See PAPYRI, EARLY CHRISTIAN.

CHRISTIAN-JEWISH RELATIONS. See JEWISH-CHRISTIAN RELATIONS (70–170).

CHRISTIANITY. This entry consists of eight separate articles covering various aspects of the emergence of Christianity in the various regions of the Mediterranean world. The first entry explores the early social life and organization of Christianity, and the second deals with early Jewish Christianity. The subsequent articles generally explore the origin and development of Christianity in Asia Minor, Egypt, Greece, North Africa, Rome, and Syria.

EARLY SOCIAL LIFE AND ORGANIZATION

The movement that emerged around the figure and memory of Jesus of Nazareth did not burst onto the Roman world as a fully developed religious institution, the Church. It began rather as one or more small sects in an out-of-the-way province. Yet within a few centuries the movement would find its way into the very center of Roman society, a process already being recognized, albeit grudgingly, by the Roman historian Tacitus in the early 2d century (*Ann.* 15.44). The course of this growth, viewed by some of the old Roman nobility as a "plague," was seen by Christian apologists and historians as the divinely ordained "triumph of the Gospel" (Eusebius, *Praep. Evang.*) Nonetheless the process was conditioned by the social environment of the Roman world in and through which diffusion and organizational development took place.

A. Early Diffusion of the Christian Movement
   1. Sectarian Origins of the Jesus Movement
   2. Early Diffusion: The Jewish Mission
   3. Phases of Growth and Paths of Diffusion in the Roman World
B. Social Life of Christian Groups
   1. Social Location of Christian Groups
   2. Relations to Society
C. Organization and Development of the Christian Movement
   1. Models from the Environment
   2. The House Church Setting
   3. The Beginnings of Institutionalization: Offices, Orthodoxy, and Heresy

---

A. Early Diffusion of the Christian Movement

1. Sectarian Origins of the Jesus Movement. Jesus did not begin as a founder of a new religion, but rather as a reforming preacher within the apocalyptic environment of 1st-century Palestine, while Rome perceived that Jesus was promoting sedition (Matt 10:34–35 = Luke 12:51–53). The group that originated around Jesus, likewise, appears as one among many reforming sects, or splinter religious groups, within the diverse spectrum of Palestinian Jewish society.

The earliest forms of the Jesus movement must have looked much like other Jewish groups known from the time. Much like the picture of disciples at table with Jesus, there were Pharisaic *haburoth* ("fellowships") which met to study and eat together in piety, often in the upper rooms of houses (*m.Shabb.* 1.4; *b.Menah.* 41b; cf. Luke 22:12, Acts 1:13). At the same time, as a reforming sect, the movement would have offered alternative forms of organization and participation to individuals and groups, including dissidents, women, and marginal groups, that would have felt left out of the traditional power structure. Some references suggest that one early form of the Jesus movement was vested in wandering preachers or prophets of the coming apocalyptic kingdom (Matt 10:9–14 = Mark 6:8–11; Luke 9:2–5; 10:4–11). In these passages an ideal of homelessness and poverty is stressed as a reaction against the normal constraints of society (cf. Theissen 1978: 8–16). While the role of men alone has been preserved in the later form of the mission tradition, it reflects a more fundamental renunciation of family and normal social structures as the center for a new self-understanding (Schüssler Fiorenza 1983: 72–76; 144–49). Reflections of this early form of the movement were still visible in the 2d century, probably still in the Syrian region, in the instructions of the *Didache* on the proper respect as well as caution to be afforded traveling teachers and prophets (*Did.* 11–13). It suggests, therefore, that a fundamental tension persisted from the earliest days of the movement between a traditional familial model of religion and claims to new modes of social relationship based on nonfamilial or antifamilial structures. This tension goes back to early dominical sayings predicated on apocalyptic midrash of Mic 7:6, the shattering of the household (cf. Luke 12:51–53 [Q]).

Initially, at least, the missionary impulse of the Jesus movement was directed toward proclaiming the imminent apocalyptic kingdom exclusively to other Jews (Matt 10:5–6; 22). There was no need for a more firmly established institution apart from the framework of Judaism, it would seem, since the kingdom was expected soon (Mark 9:1 = Matt 16:28). Thus, it was possible for the earliest Christian groups to remain within the bounds of Jewish piety and practice, though they, like the ESSENES and others, might have decried and opposed perceived impiety among other Jews. In the earliest stages there were several different arenas of interaction with the larger Jewish society and its diverse religious spectrum. In addition to the nonlocalized efforts of wandering charismatics, some followers of the Jesus movement maintained traditional temple worship in Jerusalem while at the same time meeting for devotion and study in private homes (Acts 2:46, 5:42, 12:12). Thus, it is likely that there was some tension between the ideals of piety reflected in the homelessness of itinerant prophets and in the localized tradition preserved around the images of women disciples, but tended to be subsumed under household structures (Schüssler Fiorenza 1983: 144–51). In this way they corresponded to the ranges of apocalyptic sectarianism seen elsewhere in Judean society prior to the debacle of the First Revolt (cf. Meeks 1986: 97–107; Cohen 1987: 124–36, 164–68).

In defining the earliest Jesus movement as a sectarian phenomenon, or what some would call a revitalization movement, several cautions must be kept in mind. While Jewish religion and society in the last century of the Second Temple Period were extremely diverse, not all of its groups or currents were sects in the strict sociological definition of the term. A sect, in this sense, refers to a group which separates itself to some degree from the rest of a particular society in order to reform or purify the society from within. Despite passionate denunciation of the ills of society, the sectarian group shares the same basic belief system and values as the parent culture (White 1988: 12–15). This tension over the religious definition of the society produces a conflict of standards, a sense of "two ways" (good and evil, light and dark). They are assumed to determine the fate of the society. From the perspective of the sectarian group, faith, piety, and proper observance are invariable markers of the true "way of God" over against the "way of the world." Within 1st-century Judea, therefore, some groups (like the Essenes) more clearly represent sectarian organization and attitudes, while others (such as the SADDUCEES) do not. Indeed, despite the extreme diversity of religious sympathy and the escalating social and religious protest (cf. Horsley and Hanson 1985: 244–47), the vast majority of Jews would not have been attached to any particular sect. It is also likely that in the earliest period new religious groups, such as the Pharisees or the Jesus movement, might have exhibited greater or lesser sectarian tendencies from cell to cell or time to time. The peculiar features of sectarianism in 1st-century Judea were a result of the dominant apocalyptic milieu, which included, among other things, diverse expectations of an imminent transformation of the present social order and the establishment of a new messianic age on earth (Meeks 1986: 100).

So long as the emergent Jesus sect remained clearly within the realm of Palestinian Judaism, then its message and appeal were determined within this realm as well. Thus, the earliest mission was not to convert the gentiles, but to go instead "only to the lost sheep of the house of Israel . . . saying, 'The kingdom of heaven is at hand' " (Matt 10:5–7). These were messianic Jews preaching Jesus to other Jews. Consequently, conversion and boundary definition must be thought of differently than for Jews proselytizing non-Jews. The rituals by which one was admitted into membership as well as strict standards of behavior were initially ways of marking off the sect from the "world," meaning the larger Jewish society. Yet the basic criterion of membership in the congregation of the faithful, the eschatological community or new Israel, was held by all Jews by right of birth. Conversion, therefore, largely meant coming to a reformed vision or understanding of what it meant, at least within the sect's definition of things, to be a true Jew and conforming oneself to this vision.

A sect's religious vision of the new order arises out of its experiences of tension and protest over the perceived ills of its society. Often, it seems, such groups tend to emerge from conditions of social or economic deprivation or from some experience of political oppression. The particular form of disenfranchisement or deprivation, such as in the marginalized position of certain individuals or classes in society, may then be conceived as the embodiment of evil and the symbol of the abuse that needs reform. The group looks for a remedy to these social ills in terms of religious redefinition of the social order. Far from calling for a radical destruction of the society, however, such sectarian rhetoric tends to preserve some of the basic social structures, but with new means of access or empowerment for the previously downtrodden and powerless. The new image embodies some of the resonant sense of tension with the old order as fundamental to the idealization of the new. Thus the language of radical status reversal (Matt 20:26–27, 23:12; Mark 10:43–44; Luke 22:26, 14:11) may reflect some early expectations of the Jesus sect for new social order in a coming earthly kingdom (cf. Luke 4:14–16). At the same time, the tensions with a "worldly" society would not have prevented substantial areas of interaction with the society, depending upon how far any particular sectarian group went in distancing itself from the world. A total renunciation of the world, such as that at Qumran, was rare. Even so, at Qumran the apocalyptic ideal of the pure community retained very traditional priestly categories (see also ESSENES). It would have been more common to seek new ways of working out a life in the world, while maintaining some sense of tension with it. Stricter social ethics (such as those reflected in Matt 5:17–20 and in the following sections for internalizing and strengthening the commands of the Law) are patently Jewish boundary markers for a particular Jesus sect over against the normal patterns of religiously defined Jewish social behavior. Even the ultimate disciplinary sanctions within the Jesus sects could be framed in terms of Jewish identity, since to be "cast out" of the sect was tantamount to becoming no longer a Jew at all, but rather a "Gentile and tax-collector" (Matt 18:17).

2. Early Diffusion: The Jewish Mission. The original social location of the Jesus movement was as diverse sectarian groups within Palestinian Jewish society. They sought to draw adherents exclusively from among fellow Jews, and they expected an imminent apocalyptic consummation of history and the establishment of a new, messianic social order. Even so, there was considerable diversity of expectation possible within different streams of the Jesus movement. Both the timing and the nature of the coming messianic kingdom were open to varying interpretations. Within a relatively short time, however, one finds that the Jesus movement had begun to spread beyond these original bounds. In part, the initial impulse toward diffusion may have come from the activities of the wandering charismatic prophets, who commissioned localized cells as well (Matt 10:11–13). At the same time, it must be recognized that the traditional picture of a unified, concentric mission based exclusively on the Twelve at Jerusalem is an idealization of Acts (cf. Hengel 1979: 65, 75–77). Other references clearly indicate early centers of the movement, such as the Galilee, that were not derivative from Jerusalem (Mark 16:7 = Matt 28:7–10, 16). The early diffusion of the movement was a product of new impulses operating within the diverse social circumstances of individual groups.

One such impulse toward diffusion might have come from an early sense that the imminent expectations for a new social order had failed. On this suggestion, some early Christian groups would have closely resembled adventist millenarian movements, that is, groups which make predictions of the end of the world (Gager 1975: 20–27). A crisis occurs for such groups when their predictions do not come to pass, and this radical disconfirmation tends to produce heightened activity and new directions of outreach (Gager 1975: 37–41). Increasing agitation over the delay of the eschatological consummation began to produce cognitive anxiety among early Christians, especially in the wake of the failure of the First Revolt (cf. Mark 13) and increasingly so in ensuing decades (2 Pet 3:3). Rethinking their eschatological expectations was perhaps a contributing factor in further diffusion of the movement.

Another impulse toward diffusion might have come from the establishment of cells among Jewish communities in urban settings where contact with gentiles would become more of an issue. A number of cities in the Galilee and the Decapolis were highly hellenized urban centers. In Acts, too, it was among the Jewish communities of Antioch that the disciples first came to be known as "Christians." The name itself seems to reflect a slur on this odd Jewish messianic sect, now promoting a new piety in the syncretistic urban environment of Roman Syria (cf. Meeks and Wilken 1978: 13–15). Paul, too, it would appear, encountered the new directions of the Jesus movement among Jewish communities in Roman Syria, first in Damascus and later in Antioch.

3. Phases of Growth and Paths of Diffusion in the Roman World. By the time Paul began to work out the initial lines of a gentile mission in Antioch, a new phase of diffusion was on the horizon. It would probably be a mistake to try to fix the dates for this change too narrowly, but the circumstances surrounding the so-called Jerusalem Council reflect something of this phase. The greatest danger in using such a dating mechanism lies in the false assumption that all early Christian groups were equally influenced by the circumstances and decisions reflected in the stories of the Council. The accounts of Paul (Gal 2:1–10) and Acts 15 vary sharply regarding the nature of the dispute and its resolution. Clearly, there was great diversity. Yet the accounts of the Jerusalem Council probably do signal a significant parting of the ways in the paths of diffusion for the Christian movement at Antioch. The main question which was being addressed was whether and how gentiles might be brought into the Jesus sect, given its strictures on Jewishness. Some Christians seem to have advocated full proselyte conversion before a gentile could be considered legitimately a Christian, while others began to argue for a less stringent position.

Though he was not likely the first, Paul became one of the chief advocates of the latter position. After a significant falling out with the conservative Jewish faction among the Christians at Antioch, led by Peter (Gal 2:11–16), Paul apparently left Antioch for good to embark on a mission to gentile converts in Asia Minor and Greece. The Council and the beginning of Paul's mission may be dated between 44/45 and 49 C.E., or roughly twenty years after the inception of the sect at the death of Jesus. In his mission preaching to gentile converts in Asia Minor and Greece, Paul did not finally consider the Christian movement as a separate organism from the Jewish religion, even though his synthesis might have helped to induce the rift (cf. Sanders 1983: 207–10). His elaborate use of commonplaces and models from Greek culture and popular philosophy did not force him to abrogate an apocalyptic worldview. Nonetheless, the social location of Christian groups would vary markedly in the urban environment of the Greek east. Paul and others had to begin to work out a synthesis for Jewish and gentile Christians to live within that society. Given this difference, it is better to think of this phase of the Christian movement as a kind of syncretistic Jewish *cult* relative to the larger Greco-Roman culture, while at the same time it maintained its sectarian tensions in relation to traditional Jewish culture (White 1988:16).

The institutional separation of the Christian movement away from Judaism did not really commence until after the failure of the First Revolt against Rome (66–74 C.E.). Simultaneously, then, sectarian tensions with the larger Jewish cultural heritage had continued while Christians (and other Jewish groups) were also forging a cultural synthesis and social self-definition with Greco-Roman culture. The first clear recognition on the part of Roman authorities that Christians marked something of a separate religious group from Jews comes in the letters of Pliny (*Ep.* 10.96) and the histories of Tacitus (*Ann.* 15.44). Both were written after the year 110 C.E. and after recognition of Christian activities in Asia Minor and Rome. Other reflections of this growing tension with its Jewish heritage are found in Christian literature of the post-70 period (including Matthew and Luke-Acts). The tension is also reflected in Jewish traditions concerning the Rabbis of Jabneh (Cohen 1984) and in the introduction of the *Birkhat ha-minim* (or curse against the heretics) into the *Shemonah esre.* Both traditions probably come from the period between 100–150 C.E. in their final form (cf. Schiffman 1981: 115–23; Kimelman 1981: 226–44). In some cases, however, Jewish-Christian groups maintained their place within the Jewish cultural framework much longer, and groups such as the Ebionites were known down to the end of the 4th century. At the very least, it would probably be best to say that the full-scale recognition of a separation of Greek-speaking Christianity from Judaism did not occur until after the failure of the Bar Kokhba revolt (132–135 C.E.), which is in all probability where the Pella tradition (Eus. *Hist. Eccl.* 3.5.3; Epiphanius, *Pan.* 29.7.7, 30.2.7) ought to be dated as well (cf. Lüdemann 1980: 169–73).

This schematic overview of the phases of growth and diffusion suggests that one must keep in mind the diverse nature of Christian groups in the environment of the Roman Levant. In addition to theological areas of self-definition away from Judaism and of synthesis toward Greco-Roman culture, there are several social factors that need to be considered. The first is the diversity itself. The Christian movement was not a unitary religious phenomenon from the moment of inception, and it varied sharply according to the diverse geographical diffusion it enjoyed. Jewish communities, especially in the Greek-speaking Diaspora, were equally diverse both in social location and in social makeup, and relations between Jewish and Christian cells in any given locality would have been determined by a range of local conditions. Second, it must be kept in mind that both Jewish and Christian groups outside the homeland tended to circulate around and settle in major urban centers in the Roman empire. Hence patterns of social life and organization for both groups were largely determined by conditions in the local urban environment.

B. Social Life of Christian Groups

1. Social Location of Christian Groups. While in late Medieval and Renaissance art, the mendicant orders notwithstanding, it was common to portray the 1st-century Christians in Venetian high fashion, since the Enlightenment the vogue has gone in the opposite direction. The Christian movement has typically been portrayed as a movement of the dispossessed, a proletarian revolt, or a social reform. In consequence, the models of institutionalization in the area of church order insinuated the change of social location from a persecuted sect to a state religion and from peasant revolt to aristocratic oligarchy. Most of these have started with the portrayal of Jesus and his disciples as common folk out of the Galilean hills and with the statements of Acts 2–5 that the members of the earliest Jerusalem church sold all their possessions, gave their means entirely to the apostles, and "held all things in common" (Acts 4:32). In addition to such utopian portrayals, older sect typologies tended to portray all such reform movements as located among the dispossessed of society

(White 1988: 7–9). Both types of romanticized portrayals have been used to advance theological interpretations (cf. Malherbe 1983: 4–13). The picture in Acts, however, is highly idealized, likely for various apologetic purposes, and cannot be used to create a historical generalization of the social location of the early Christians. The story in Acts itself (5:42; 12:12) presupposes that at least some of those early Christians retained their possessions and used them for hosting Christian assembly in their homes.

As has been suggested, at least some forms of the earliest Jesus movement adopted an ethos of rejecting home, possessions, and society (Gager 1975: 23–37; Theissen 1978: 8–15). On the other hand, it is likely that these do not represent the whole of the early movement, but only some of its nascent forms. Nonetheless, these various forms persisted and grew up alongside one another in the early generations of the movement.

In recent work, focus has shifted to the diffusion of the movement outside of the original Jewish moorings, and here one gets a slightly different perception of its social location (Malherbe 1983: 31–37). In a key statement, Paul alludes to the social status of members of the Christian community at Corinth in such a way that it is clear that at least some were wealthy, educated, and highborn (1 Cor 1:26–28). It is also likely that such status distinctions are correlated with the leadership by house church patrons, both men and women. Rather than a proletarian movement, the urban Christian communities of the Aegean more likely represented a cross section of the highly stratified society in which they lived (Meeks 1983: 51–63).

This recognition has been used to reconsider a number of the issues in the Pauline letters. Travel, letter writing, and hospitality were functions occasioned out of the geographical and social mobility of Roman society in the 1st century (Malherbe 1983: 35–49, 67–70). The divisive circumstances of the several house churches at Corinth (1 Cor 1:11) may be directly attributable to conflicts over wealth and status among its members (Theissen 1982; Malherbe 1983: 71–83). Areas where such status distinctions likely produced dissension and quarreling were in Christian communal dining (1 Cor 11:17–34), in social interaction (dining) with pagans (1 Corinthians 8–10), and in relations to the gifts of house church patrons to other apostles (2 Cor 11:7–11). It has been suggested that the social pretensions of the wealthier members of the Christian communities were in fact heightened by Paul's own preaching of "freedom" in Christ. Yet in several instances the exercise of individual liberty was at odds with Paul's own sense of solidarity or "fellowship" *(koinonia)* in "the body," that is, the Church (cf. Meeks 1983: 68–73; 157–63).

How far can one go in projecting from the description of Paul's churches onto the general social level of the early Christian movement is problematic. One should guess that local communities faced different socioeconomic circumstances, depending upon the establishment, relations to local Jewish groups, the ability to rely upon or attract wealthy patrons, and competition with other indigenous groups. It is likely that the networks of social interaction by which diffusion occurred had a lot to do with establishing the social placement in the early years for any given locality. For each locality, whether Edessa, Alexandria, Carthage, or Rome, one must attempt to evaluate the social placement and the interaction of Christians on the basis of available evidence for the local conditions. Even the degree of wealth and social pretension at Corinth in Paul's day suggest that the upper reaches were yet below the old Roman aristocracy, the pinnacle of the social pyramid. Christian membership came instead from artisan classes, local entrepreneurs, and at best, the local decurionate, but also contained many from the other end of the social spectrum. Thus, the forms of social organization likely reflect some of this stratified social mix. Ultimately, one does find Christians among the elite segments of Roman society by the end of the 2d century (in provincial cities) and in the 3d century (in Rome itself). The gradual social acceptance of Christians among the population probably did not come from the sheer number of conversions alone, but through a gradual diffusion of Christian affiliations through the networks of power and wealth and a gradual acculturation of Christian practice and social life. At least one area in which such socioeconomic impulses can be seen is in the gradual development of Christian architecture out of the original house church meetings. In such cases patronage continued to play a major role in the process and furthered the public growth and awareness of the Christian movement through the first centuries.

2. Relations to Society. As an apocalyptic sect, the earliest Jesus movement stood in direct tension with its parent culture, since it was viewed as inherently flawed, under the evil forces of Satan and the oppression of outsiders. Being in the "Kingdom of Light" meant preparing to fight (militarily, if necessary) the enemy and removing oneself in some measure from the pollutions of the world, the "Kingdom of Darkness." This sectarian self-consciousness, clearly visible at Qumran, is yet discernible in some of the boundary maintenance language of the early Jesus movement. It may be preserved, for example, in the fragment of apocalyptic exhortation in 2 Cor 6:14–7:1. On the other hand, such sects look toward the moral reformation of society and so seek to enact presently, at least in some provisional way, a future ideal. In the case of the Pharisees, then (though not a sect in all cases in the pre-70 period), democratizing temple purity by making the law livable may be viewed as a sectarian ideal of hasidic reform (see PHARISEES). Likewise, there are vestiges of such an ideal social order in the portrayal of Jesus at table with "sinners and tax collectors" (Matt 9:10 = Mark 2:15 = Luke 5:27) and especially in connection with the wisdom tradition sayings (Matt 11:16–19 = Luke 7:31–35 [Q]). The sense of tension arises in maintaining the proper balance with society, especially as such sects tend, if they survive, to move toward some accommodation to the parent culture (cf. Meeks 1986: 102–4; White 1988: 19).

In the development of the Jesus movement, one sees different attempts to work out such balance depending upon the particular circumstances of each Christian group. For example, the community reflected in the gospel of Matthew, which was probably situated somewhere in the highly acculturated areas of the Galilee or nearer Syria, shows signs of sectarian self-definition over against its pharisaic neighbors (Matt 23:1–36). Part of this debate centers on similarly pharisaic ways of erecting boundaries against the world through patterns of Torah observance, fasting, alms, and prayer (5:17–21; 6:1–8, 16–18). At the same time the Matthean community was attempting to work out the strictures of both an internal church order (18:15–20) and an external gateway for non-Jewish converts (28:18–20) in the period after the First Revolt. Ultimately, the Matthean church retained its essentially Jewish markers of identity and social customs (18:17; 22:1–14).

By way of contrast, Pauline churches situated in the cosmopolitan urban environment of the Aegean effected a different balance with its cultural host. Indeed, the social makeup of Paul's churches moved them more toward a cult-culture self-definition. Thus, at Corinth one finds Paul himself redefining traditional sectarian boundary markers against society to allow some, though not all, interaction (1 Cor 5:9–11; 6:1–6). Of course, a chief factor in this redefinition came in regard to matters of Torah observance for non-Jews; now they were accorded full status within the community without enforcing circumcision. While still retaining a strict sense of community ethics and moral discipline in terms of apocalyptic ideas (5:1–5; 6:9), Paul nonetheless permitted marriage to nonbelievers (7:13–15) and dining in pagan social contexts (8:10; 10:27) as part of the new social order. It is clear, too, that within the house church context new social relations were being explored, as in the status and leadership of women charismatics and patrons (11:3; 16:19; cf. Rom 16:1–2). Nor is it likely that either Jewish or gentile Christians would have recoiled uniformly from these new freedoms. It would appear, however, that Paul at other times backed down from some of the more radical social implications of earlier preaching (7:1, 21), especially in regard to the sense of new order reflected in the so-called *baptismal reunification formula* (12:12; cf. Gal 3:28; Col 3:11).

In many ways Pauline churches were encouraged to enact a moral paradigm that was very close to that of the surrounding culture. So Christians (perhaps like other Diaspora Jewish communities, but in sharp contrast to traditional apocalyptic rhetoric) were to respect the Roman government and pay proper taxes (Rom 13:1–7) and to practice almsgiving and hospitality (12:13). Indeed, many of the typically Pauline exhortations for the ethical life "in Christ" are built around standard catalogs of virtues and vices (Phil 4:8–9; Col 3:5–17) derived from commonplaces in the Hellenistic moral philosophers (cf. Malherbe 1987: 61–95).

In sum, Pauline tradition began to move the center of Christian social identity much closer to a Hellenistic-Roman cultural ideal, even though Paul himself never seems to have conceived of this shift as a move to a non-Jewish self-definition. Later Pauline tradition, however, appropriated even more of the standard social mores from the larger Roman culture. A good example is the introduction of the *Haustafel* (or "household code"), which derives from Greek philosophy (Col 3:19–4:1; Eph 5:22–6:9; 1 Tim 2:8–15, 6:1–2; Tit 2:1–10; 1 Pet 2:13–3:7). In Aristotle (*Pol.* 1,1253b; *Eth. Nic.* 8,1162a), for example, the order of the family is likened to that of the *polis* or state. Already in Philo one finds it appropriated for Jewish ethics in the Greco-Roman world (*Jos.* 38; *Dec.* 165). The overtly hierarchical and patriarchal order of this paradigm may have been intended (as in Joseph. *AgAp* 1) as an apologetic against pagan claims that Christians disrupted households, as seen in older apocalyptic slogans (so Balch 1981: 65–80). As such it probably facilitated the acculturation of the Christian cult to pagan culture. At the same time, it created new hierarchical orders within the church community and a consequent tightening of leadership roles, especially for women (Schüssler Fiorenza 1983: 251–70). It is noteworthy, too, that this move in the area of social ethics corresponds, both in time and in social impact, to the hierarchical ordering of offices under the bishopric in the area of organization.

By the end of the 2d century, one finds that Christians in most urban areas of the Roman empire were moving more and more into the mainstream of social life. The pace of such acculturation would, of course, be different, owing to local conditions and circumstances relative to each Christian community. Even though there were sporadic persecutions and one hears of pagan charges against antisocial behavior, on the whole these were tensions created as the Christian movement became more acculturated to its host culture. Thus, in Origen's refutation of Celsus, one still finds claims that Christians proselytize only those individuals on the margins of society: women, children, slaves, and illiterate yokels (*Cel.* 3.55; cf. Wilken 1984: 95–100). But in Tertullian (*Apol.* 39) and, to an even greater degree, in Clement of Alexandria (*Paed.* 3), one sees the efflorescence of an active Christian social life that would eventually become a prevalent and fully accepted part of the Roman world.

C. Organization and Development of the Christian Movement

1. Models from the Environment. In order to understand the organization of Christian groups, one may consider their appearance within the context of the urban environment of Greco-Roman cities. It has been suggested that local Christian congregations followed or emulated models of other small cells or associations (Meeks 1983: 75–81; 1986: 108–14). Hence, the household or private house associations served as one model for organizing Christian groups alongside Diaspora synagogues, voluntary clubs (or *collegia*), and philosophical schools.

Given the sectarian origins of the movement, the synagogue provided a natural avenue of Christian diffusion, once it had moved to urban Jewish centers of the Diaspora. Thus, too, the organization and social experience of synagogue communities paved the way for Christian groups to establish their own identity in the alien environment of the Diaspora. Diaspora Jewish communities are known from literary, epigraphic, and archaeological remains throughout the Mediterranean, especially in the major cities of Egypt, Asia Minor, and Greece, as well as Italy (including Rome and Ostia) and North Africa. Nonetheless, some caution must be exercised in two regards. First, one should not assume as universal fact the presentation in Acts, that the earliest Christian mission commenced in synagogues only to open out to gentiles after being expelled. Second, one should not assume that all synagogues followed the same organization and plan, especially in the Diaspora, or that there was a normative synagogue structure for the first several centuries of the Common Era (Kraabel 1981: 81–91).

The development of the early synagogue owes in large

measure to the experience of Jews in the alien environment of the Diaspora. The need to preserve their heritage, the sense of belonging to the heritage of Israel, might result in the formation of a closed cultic community against the alien world outside. At the same time, dealings with their pagan neighbors in business and daily life resulted in social interaction and acculturation. The synagogue served as a way of mediating these tensions with the Greco-Roman culture, especially while the temple still stood at Jerusalem. It is significant, therefore, that most of the earliest synagogue buildings were renovated from private homes which had been owned by leading members of the Jewish congregation, while others also reflect considerable social acceptance and support by non-Jewish sympathizers (Kraabel 1981: 87–90). The social structures as well as the worship and architecture of these early Diaspora synagogues was still very much determined by local conditions and cultural relations. So, too, one finds that women and non-Jews often held substantial positions within the life of these Jewish communities (Brooten 1982: 139–48; White 1987: 153–55). Also, there might have been several synagogue cells or congregations in any of the larger cities differentiated by language, socioeconomic status, relations with locals, or theology.

In many cases local synagogue groups were also organized after the fashion of *collegia.* This common form of social club or voluntary association in Greco-Roman city life would have offered a ready legal model for establishing community organization. The clubs themselves, even the smallest ones, often aped the titles and structures of official municipal organizations. Trade guilds and professional organizations up and down the social ladder followed these lines. In the larger cities one could expect that associates would agglomerate on ethnic lines as well as by trade or craft, all reflecting some need for a community tie, a sense of rootedness, within the pluralistic hubbub of the city. Still, it is worth noting that both house cults and foreign religious groups were often organized after collegial models.

Finally, it has been suggested that early Christian groups also followed the model of a philosophical school. While it is a clearer comparison to make by the middle of the 2d century (as in Justin Martyr, cf. Wilken 1984: 72–83) a similar organization has been suggested for the Pauline mission, at least as regards Paul and his immediate circle of "fellow-workers" (Meeks 1983: 81–83). The comparison is more apt when one looks at the tradition of teaching and pastoral care among the moralist philosophers or at the social organization of Epicurean communities (Malherbe 1987: 7–13, 95–105) (see APOSTLE, CONCEPT OF).

Despite the high degree of acceptance of each of these models, there was great diversity and fluidity in the actual form of communal associations. Synagogues and other cults could be organized as *collegia* and most of the voluntary associations had religious affiliations or patron deities. Yet one of the most significant areas of social intersection lies in the fact that all these groups could use the private home setting or the household model either as the locus of its activities or as the core of its communal organization.

2. The House Church Setting. The picture in Acts (2:42) pushes the communal dining and study of Christians at home back to the very beginning of the movement. Acts then pushes forward in its model of the mission by following conversions especially through household lines. Both of these features seem to be Lukan idealizations for apologetic interests, which may color over a more diverse social picture. Nevertheless, by the time of Paul's mission in the Aegean region, a standard form of address was to the "church in the house" *(he kat' oikon ekklesia)* of someone (Col 4:15; Rom 16:5; 1 Cor 16:19). It is likely that household networks and organization were already operative in the initial diffusion through Jewish communities of the Diaspora, since synagogues likewise employed the household setting. Thus, despite a high degree of idealization of the picture in Acts, the basic reflection of the setting in Corinth (18:7–8) may be indicative, since it assumes a synagogue in residential areas and under patronage leadership, contiguous to a house where the Christians began to meet. Within the Pauline letters themselves the assumed setting of Christian assembly is even more firmly rooted in private homes and attendant social conventions (Malherbe 1983: 60–91; Meeks 1983: 75–77; 1986: 110–13; Schüssler Fiorenza 1983: 175–84).

The house church setting provided avenues both for diffusion and social organization of Christian communities. Conventions of hospitality were very important in Greco-Roman society. They could be applied to travelers and to the hosting of guests for dinners and other social functions. Thus, the technical language of hospitality is to be found in Pauline usage, especially in writing letters of recommendation for his traveling co-workers, such as Phoebe (Rom 16:1–2; cf. Malherbe 1983: 94–97). Here, Paul was asking that she be received hospitably within the various house church cells at Rome, just as she, as house church patron, had hosted others (including Paul himself) at Cenchreai. Letter writing, hospitality, and patronage were bound up together in the organization of these house church communities.

In Paul's churches, at least, hosting the assembled congregation seems to have fallen to a few leading individuals who would have owned houses large enough for such a gathering. House church patronage and social mobility were exhibited by the artisan couple Prisca and Aquila as they moved about within the Aegean region and eventually to Rome. Paul was heavily dependent upon the financial support of these house church patrons, who not only hosted the congregation but afforded lodging and assistance for Paul and his co-workers (Rom 16:2, 23; Phlm 2, 22; Phil 4:14–19). The house church setting also meant that there were likely several meetings or cell groups in any of the larger urban centers, such as Corinth, Ephesus, or Rome (even though Paul had not organized the community at Rome). Hence diversity or friction could easily develop within a given locale, partly as a result of these house church relations (1 Cor 1:11–16; 2 Cor 11:7–11). Moreover, the household in Greco-Roman urban life comprised a wider circle than the nuclear family. Members of the household also included other relatives, friends in residence, domestic slaves, and clients or business associates. In the structure of the society at large all were attached and obligated to the head of the household, usually meaning the *pater familias.* In growing numbers during the Roman period women, too, held the property and the status of head of the household. Cultic associations, such as that under the household of Agripinilla at Tusculum, reflect the merging of religious organization also under the patronage of women. Likewise, in Jewish groups one hears of women who served as "mother of the synagogue," meaning its patron both in honorific terms and in functional leadership. In the Pauline churches there were not as yet any leadership offices (such as bishops or elders); therefore, one of the natural lines of organization and authority fell to the house church patrons, both women and men. Paul himself as itinerant apostle was dependent upon the patronal beneficence and authority of individuals such as Prisca, Phoebe, Gaius, or Philemon (Schüssler Fiorenza 1983: 181–82; Meeks 1983: 68–69, 134–36).

Numerous features of church life must be understood in the light of this social setting. Paul himself communicated with his congregations by means of letters and emissaries moving within the house church network. Christian assembly meant gathering in the home of a leading member, usually around the dinner table as the center both for a communal meal (1 Cor 11:17–34) and for mutual exhortation (1 Cor 14:26). It is not likely, however, that all Christians in a large city like Corinth gathered in one place on a regular basis, not even for the eucharist. Women and men, drawn from the wider circles of household networks and other social relations, participated equally in these gatherings, depending upon their sense of spiritual gifts (1 Cor 11:5; 14:23–26). Paul himself resisted the tendency to allow such fellowship to replicate the class structure of the society at large, even though it was based in that structure. This tension could not always be escaped, as Paul had to allow for Christians to continue to associate fully in normal social activities (1 Cor 5:9; 10:24–28), and he did not always go as far as some might have hoped in moving toward radical social change (Gal 3:28; 1 Cor 7:22; 11:27–33; Phlm 17).

3. The Beginnings of Institutionalization: Offices, Orthodoxy, and Heresy. As a sect within the framework and worldview of Judaism, the Jesus movement implicitly held ideas of religious institution from the dominant cultural models, but felt tensions enough to question and in some cases reject them. As a cult phenomenon in the Greco-Roman culture, however, there may have been different impulses at work, since foreign cults tend rather to emulate the organizational models of the host culture and to rationalize assimilation. The Christian movement, in particular cases, likely felt certain internal tensions in this regard, since it maintained much of its basic sectarian attitude toward its Jewish heritage while simultaneously pursuing cultic assimilation toward Greco-Roman culture. Once again, a keynote is the recognition of diversity. In Paul's case there arose several debates over apostolic authority. In the earlier situation at Antioch (Gal 2:11–14), Paul claims to have faced Peter down over issues of communal fellowship with gentiles. Later, the case of the so-called superapostles (2 Cor 11:5–6, 13) further called into question Paul's own apostolic authority in the light of their claims to superlative charismatic gifts and apostolic authority, even though neither party was among the core of original disciples of Jesus (Meeks 1983: 131–34) (see APOSTLE, CONCEPT OF).

While authority questions came out in Paul's day, it is significant that the main sources of debate arose from the power to preach and the governance of Christian ethical behavior. In cases of disciplinary sanctions the extreme action seems to have been focused largely on matters of unsuitable behavior (Matt 18:15–17; Heb 6:4–6, 10:26). As in the case of sexual immorality in 1 Cor 5:1–11, the normal response was to exclude the offender from the communal fellowship. While in later development of penitential discipline this was viewed as a temporary excommunication from the eucharist, in 1 Corinthians it more clearly denotes sanctioning out of the dining context of the house church assembly. There is little or no concern over what could be called orthodoxy in doctrine or liturgy. The need to guard the "deposit of faith" through disciplinary excommunication begins to appear only in the later writings of the New Testament and more consistently in the literature of the 2d century (1 Tim 1:20, 6:3–4; 2 Pet 2:1; 2 John 7–11). Governance over the authority to teach and the power to exercise discipline was viewed in terms of emerging institutional authority structures or "offices" in the communities. Hence apostles, prophets, teachers, *and* patrons in the earliest days gave way to bishops, elders, and deacons by the 2d and 3d centuries (1 Cor 12:28; cf. Eph 4:11; 1 Tim 3:1–13; *Ign. Eph.* 4:1–2; *Ign. Mag.* 6:1).

By focusing on "offices," the traditional pictures of development in early Christian organization have tended to follow one of several straight-line models of development toward hierarchical institutional order. The Great Church model, largely derived from the picture of Jesus commissioning Peter with the "keys of kingdom" (Matt 16:17–19) and preserved in much of Western iconography, asserts the tradition of the twelve disciples as the basic authority structure of the church from the moment of inception. An alternative sociological model, usually associated with Max Weber and Ernst Troeltsch, tries to account for the noninstitutional sectarian origins. It assumes that there was a necessary process of development from the fluid charismatic leadership of the earliest sect toward a routinized leadership in ecclesiastical offices of bishop, elder, and deacon (so von Campenhausen 1969; cf. White 1987b: 209–13). Inherent in both models is an essentially hierarchical and patriarchal notion of authority vested in later notions of ordination and priesthood.

It is possible to suggest that there were really four intersecting lines of authority structures which came into play in diverse combinations depending upon the local circumstances of Christian communities. The first derived from the gradual separation from Judaism in the generations after the First Revolt. Here two factors can be seen. The loss of the temple itself as a central institution created a vacuum in authority structure which had traditionally been lodged in a priestly ideal. The sense of loss called for rationalization, and of course, Judaism itself had to face this same dilemma. Separation from Jewish identity, however, demanded an authority which stood outside of the emerging reconstruction under the Rabbinic academy (cf. Stendahl 1968). The second derives from the lines of patronal authority seen both in the Diaspora synagogue and in the house church setting, especially in the Greco-Roman urban setting. Here it is worth noting that authority was invested after the cultural model of obligation of a client toward a benefactor as regularly applied both in interpersonal bonds and in the organization of clubs and other cults (White 1987b: 218–21). While it derived much of its symbolism from the paterfamilias, nonetheless women increasingly exercised such patronal roles in cults or associations and even in official civic functions or the imperial cult (Schüssler Fiorenza 1983: 180–83). The third is related but distinct in social application and derives from the metaphorical use of the patriarchal family as a model for understanding the order of the state or society, seen most clearly in the later ethical model of the HAUSTAFELN (or "household duty codes," cf. Eph 5:21–6:9; Col 3:18–4:1; 1 Pet 2:18–3:7). The fourth is charismatic leadership and derives from the apocalyptic sectarian consciousness of challenging worldly authority through the idealized image of inspired prophets, who interpreted the divine will against the prevailing social order.

Gradually, over time and in different combinations one sees the Christian movement adopting an amalgam of these four into the various notions of ordained offices and church order. Gradually, too, there was a sharp diminution in the leadership roles available to women and others who had found expression in the earlier generations, just as Jewish heritage itself was restricted. In particular the role of charismatic power was sharply curtailed since it was increasingly difficult to keep under control, and it was replaced instead with the authority of the episcopal offices as a combination of several lines of power. The continued lines are seen in the so-called "New Prophecy" or Montanist movement in 2d-century Phrygia, since it perpetuated an ideal of female charismatic gifts. What would eventually emerge as the dominant form was a hierarchical church order of offices ranging from the bishop (or priest) to the elder (or presbyter) and to the deacon (1 Tim 3:1–13). In earlier usage bishops and elders were interchangeable, but by the early 2d century (especially in the writings of Ignatius of Antioch) there were indications of a further move toward a single bishop at the top of a pyramidal order. Women (in particular the widows) were placed in a special category which removed them from this dominant hierarchical structure.

The sense of order implied in this organizational development also carried over into two other areas of church life. The first was the ordering of worship and, hence, the development of liturgy. By the early 2d century the free-flowing love feasts of the early period seem to have been more formalized and restricted. Eventually it would lead to a complete segregation of the eucharist (or Mass) from the dinner setting by the beginning of the 3d century. The *Didache*, one of the earliest pieces of church order literature dating from the first half of 2d century, makes special provision for the proper conduct of the eucharistic meal and for who could preside. Second, as time went along, the diversity of traditions became increasingly a problem, at least to some. The result was to delimit more narrowly the range of acceptable teaching and belief, or the beginnings of doctrinal formulation (as seen both in the Pastoral epistles and in Ignatius). It is important to note, however, that regional variations in Christian development (depending in large measure on local social circumstances) tended to be treated as heresy. The result was that an imperialist tradition, under the aegis of Roman authority, actively superimposed a notion of orthodoxy and heresy on these local variations (cf. Bauer 1971; Koester 1972). Notions of apostolic succession were used from as early as the 2d century (Hegesippus, preserved in Eusebius, *Hist. Eccl.* 4.22.1) to claim the authority of bishops in a specific line to govern in such matters of orthodoxy and liturgy.

Bibliography

Balch, D. L. 1981. *Let Wives Be Submissive: The Domestic Code in 1 Peter*. SBLMS 26. Chico, CA.

Bauer, W. 1971. *Orthodoxy and Heresy in Earliest Christianity*. Philadelphia.

Brooten, B. J. 1982. *Women Leaders in the Ancient Synagogue*. BJS 36. Chico, CA.

Campenhausen, H. von. 1969. *Ecclesiastical Authority and Spiritual Power in the Early Church*. London.

Cohen, S. J. D. 1984. The Significance of Yavneh: Pharisees, Rabbis, and the End of Jewish Sectarianism. *HUCA* 55: 27–53.

———. 1987. *From the Maccabees to the Mishnah*. Philadelphia.

Gager, J. G. 1975. *Kingdom and Community: The Social World of the Early Christians*. Englewood Cliffs, NJ.

Hengel, M. 1979. *Acts and the History of Earliest Christianity*. Philadelphia.

Horsley, R., and Hanson, J. 1985. *Bandits, Prophets, and Messiahs: Popular Movements at the Time of Jesus*. New York.

Kimelman, R. 1981. *Birkat Ha-Minim* and the Lack of Evidence for an Anti-Christian Jewish Prayer in Antiquity. Pp. 226–44 in Sanders 1981.

Koester, H. 1972. GNOMAI DIAPHOROI: The Origin and Nature of Diversification in the History of Early Christianity. Pp. 114–57 in *Trajectories through Early Christianity*, ed. by J. M. Robinson and H. Koester. Philadelphia.

Kraabel, A. T. 1981. The Social Systems of Six Diaspora Synagogues. Pp. 81–91 in *Ancient Synagogues: The State of Research*, ed. J. Gutmann. Chico, CA.

Lüdemann, G. 1980. The Successors of Pre-70 Jerusalem Christianity. Pp. 161–83 in Sanders 1980.

Malherbe, A. J. 1983. *Social Aspects of Early Christianity*. 2d ed. Philadelphia.

———. 1987. *Paul and the Thessalonians*. Philadelphia.

Meeks, W. A. 1983. *The First Urban Christians*. New Haven.

———. 1986. *The Moral World of the First Christians*. Philadelphia.

Meeks, W. A., and Wilken, R. L. 1978. *Jews and Christians in Antioch in the First Four Centuries of the Common Era*. SBLSBS 13. Missoula, MT.

Sanders, E. P. 1980. *Jewish and Christian Self-definition*. Vol. 1: *The Shaping of Christianity in the Second and Third Centuries*. ed. by E. P. Sanders. Philadelphia.

———. 1981. *Jewish and Christian Self-definition*. Vol. II: *Aspects of Judaism in the Greco-Roman Period*. Ed. by E. P. Sanders, with A. I. Baumgarten and A. Mendelson. Philadelphia.

———. 1983. *Paul, the Law, and the Jewish People*. Philadelphia.

Schiffman, L. H. 1981. At the Crossroads: Tannaitic Perspectives on the Jewish-Christian Schism. Pp. 115–56 in Sanders 1981.

Schüssler Fiorenza, E. 1983. *In Memory of Her*. New York.

Stendahl, K. 1968. *The School of St. Matthew*. 2d ed. Philadelphia.

Theissen, G. 1978. *Sociology of Early Palestinian Christianity*. Philadelphia.

———. 1982. *The Social Setting of Pauline Christianity*. Trans. by J. Schütz. Philadelphia.

White, L. Michael. 1987. The Delos Synagogue Revisited. *HTR* 80:133–60.

———. 1987b. Social Authority in the House Church and Ephesians 4:1–16, *ResQ* 29: 209–28.
———. 1988. Shifting Sectarian Boundaries in Early Christianity, *BJRL* 70: 7–24.
Wilken, Robert L. 1984. *The Christians as the Romans Saw Them*. New Haven.

L. MICHAEL WHITE

EARLY JEWISH CHRISTIANITY

When the qualifying phrase "early Jewish" is applied to Christianity, the temptation arises to contrast it with "early gentile" Christianity. This contrast between Jewish and non-Jewish forms of Christianity seems to have arisen later, and was then retrojected into the earlier periods, resulting in an anachronistic distortion of early Christianity. It is only when we understand the earliest Jesus movement and the first post-Easter Christianity as a phenomenon within Judaism that the historical development of Christianity can be clarified.

A. Definition

There is little doubt that Jesus himself was firmly rooted within the Jewish faith, and that with him arose a movement that was first and foremost an inner-Jewish phenomenon. But Jesus' idiosyncratic attitudes with respect to fundamental Jewish theologumena like law, sabbath, the traditions of the elders, etc., meant that early Jewish Christianity was, after Easter, a broad movement comprised of (about 500? 1 Cor 15:6) people with very different opinions and likely no generally recognized organization. The idea of a homogeneous primitive church ("*Urgemeinde*") from which Christianity arose (as depicted in Acts) is a simplifying Lukan construct. Thus the term "Jewish Christianity" must be used cautiously when discussing the earliest periods. Groups that gradually contracted toward Jewish thought and emerged in later times as an "Ebionitism" (see EBIONITES) are defined here as "Judaistic Jewish Christianity." Groups which practiced baptism are here defined as "Primitive Baptist." The label "Missionary Jewish Christianity" refers to groups with a program of mission. Most of the traditions that became canonized in the NT can be assigned to this early "Missionary Jewish Christianity." But even here there is a great difference between groups which addressed gentiles (Paul, most NT writings) and groups which felt particularly obliged to address mainly fellow Jews (Peter, see also Gal 2:8ff. and Matt 10:5–23 and 15:24).

B. Sources and Methods

The NT is our basic source for the origins of Jewish Christianity, but we must keep in mind that most NT traditions have been handed to us from the "missionary" groups. Strictly speaking, "Judaistic" traditions are often preserved only in fragments, or we have to reconstruct them from sources that sought to refute their claims (e.g., Galatians). Our sources for the groups which eventually emerge as Ebionitism are not very reliable. Previous attempts to ascertain the roots of Jewish Christianity have been hampered because scholars tended either to import subsequent distinctions between Jewish- and gentile-Christianity into the earlier period or to rely largely on the book of Acts for a straightforward account of the evolution of the primitive Church. One could support one's conclusions by appealing to the pseudo-Clementines (Schoeps 1949; 1956) or to specific traditions of the Church concerning the alleged Jewish-Christian sources (Danielou 1964). However, the notion of a vast body of ancient Jewish-Christian writings cannot be verified (Torrey 1952–53: 205ff.).

The isolation of the "Q" source as a product of early Jewish Christianity (see Q [GOSPEL SOURCE]) promises to help correct the deficiencies in our earliest sources, but it must not be forgotten that Q is a "hypothesis," not a real source (and may itself contain various layers). But this appeal to Q constitutes a step in the right direction: if we want to identify the beginnings of Jewish Christianity, we must consider the history of the traditions ("*Traditionsgeschichte*") underlying the NT.

Traditionsgeschichte is a complicated method, often leading at best to conclusions that must be properly qualified as to their level of "probability." Redaction-critical research has demonstrated that in this endeavor the topographical references must be considered carefully (Lohmeyer 1936). Topographical statements sometimes have for an evangelist a highly theological importance (e.g., Galilee in Mark). But not all geographical references are charged in this way. A great many of them are deeply rooted in specific traditions; therefore they must be explained in terms of the history of that tradition. When this is done (Schille 1957), we discover that primitive materials oriented more to the north (Galilee and environs) often have "missionary" tendencies, whereas traditions closer to Judea represent a more static Christianity (distinguished by an emphasis on the Jewish cultic calendar).

This is reinforced by an examination of primitive christology. It is noteworthy that christological titles are used differently in the earlier traditions than in subsequent NT traditions. For example, the christological titles "King of the Jews" (Passion tradition) and "Son of Man" (also in Passion tradition, in Mark 13, and in the sayings of Jesus) are connected to "Judaistic" traditions; "Son of God" (traditions about the baptism and temptation of Jesus) are connected to "Baptismal" traditions; and "Lord" (Gk *kyrios;* in Paul and in the miracles traditions) are connected to "Missionary" traditions.

C. Origins and History

Jesus carried out his preaching and his work within the Judaism of his day. On the other hand, he reserved for himself the freedom to eliminate all possible restrictions to religious community. We can see this, for example, in his selection of companions: tax collectors (Mark 2:14ff.), outcasts (5:2ff.), women, and political radicals (e.g., Simon the Canaanean). Similarly, he had little regard for national or ethnic boundaries (Matt 8:5ff.; Mark 7:24ff.). Also, he invoked as a model the child (Mark 10:15), who was not yet granted permission to participate in the orthodox

Jewish liturgical ceremonies. Jesus' followers seem to have accepted the main features of his teachings and example. Therefore, we have to consider the Jesus movement as an inner-Jewish phenomenon, taking into consideration the probability that it extended beyond earlier Jewish regions into the Hellenistic Decapolis, Samaria, and beyond the Jordan (where a pre-Easter preaching activity had begun).

Jesus' crucifixion certainly failed to destroy this movement (1 Cor 15:6 attests a mass meeting of Jesus' followers at the time of his resurrection). Visions of the risen Lord likely had the effect of reinvigorating the disciples to their task of proclamation, and of converting the uncommitted and even the occasional opponent such as Paul. However, what arose was not a uniform "Christianity" but rather a charismatic movement with diverse preachers and different organizations. Individual charismatics or groups would be proclaiming Jesus as Savior in their respective homelands (cf. Mark 5:20). Thus the movement from the very beginning was very diverse, as is evident in the christological titles. Only gradually did certain titles (e.g., "Lord," "Son of God," "Son of Man") rise to predominate over earlier ones ("King of the Jews," *christos* ["anointed one"]). The very earliest christological terms (e.g., "the holy one of God," "prophet") are often mentioned only obliquely in Scripture. That the earliest Christianity was a self-conscious inner-Jewish phenomenon is evident in the fact that initially the mark of a Christian was not membership in an organized body (the church; against this, see Mark 9:38ff.) but rather being a disciple of Jesus the Messiah. This did not preclude "Baptismal" groups (such as those descended from John the Baptist) from continuing to stress baptism (indeed, John's eschatological dipping did not lead him or anyone else away from Judaism). Similarly, it did not preclude "Missionary" groups from crossing over into regions that were not principally Jewish (e.g., Paul was baptized in Damascus; consequently this boundary had already been crossed earlier). Thus, neither baptizing nor preaching outside "proper" Jewish geographical boundaries distinguished early Christianity from Judaism, as long as the focus of these activities was understood as a concentrated appeal to Israel, the people of God.

The christology which is often invoked as the reason for the separation of Jews and Christians did not initially separate anyone from Judaism, since the earliest christological titles describe the person of Jesus within the accepted framework of Jewish messianism. Thus, anyone who believed himself to live in the "messianic age" could (and was in fact allowed to) believe that the Jewish law had been fulfilled in a way consistent with Jewish notions. Similarly, Paul's belief in freedom from the law would not necessarily be inconsistent with basic Jewish thought of his day.

However, it must be conceded that "Baptismal" and "Missionary" groups initially would be more likely to accept the freedom inaugurated through Jesus than those groups advocating a stricter adherence to traditional Jewish norms. It is possible, however, to suggest a "Christian" theological motive behind this more conservative adherence to Jewish norms. While the "Baptismal" tradition might emphasize the Christian as someone saved in the time of fulfillment ("time of the bridegroom" in Mark 2:18–20) and the "Missionary" tradition might stress the miracles and the proclamations of Jesus as a fulfillment of prophecy (of Isa 35:5, for example; see Matt 11:4–5 and par.), for others the turn of the era would be associated rather with the return of the Son of Man. Thus, one interpreting his own time as a period of apocalyptic world travail could certainly see himself approaching the turn of the era without considering the present moment to be that time of fulfillment. Therefore, such a person could legitimately insist on continued obedience to Jewish norms until that time of fulfillment had actually arrived. Thus, in the beginning, the dispute over adherence to Jewish norms was not between Jewish and non-Jewish Christians, but existed entirely within Jewish Christianity itself (see Galatians), although it was this dispute that eventually led to the separation of Christianity from Judaism. But at this early stage we see here only the primary distinction between "Judaizing Jewish Christianity" and "Missionary Jewish Christianity" (which later was identified with gentile Christianity).

This issue soon embroiled the various parties concerned; in the Jerusalem council (Acts 15) the apostles were forced to deal with it (see Bornkamm 1971). The "Missionary" groups (and only these were represented!) united in order to distinguish their respective tasks (Gal 2:7–10): Peter would himself return to preaching among the Jews (the "circumcised"), and the Antiochenes to preaching among the gentiles (the "uncircumcised"). Not long afterward a dispute broke out among the formerly united missionaries (Gal 2:11–14) centering around the question of the kosher table (a ritual norm that had always been a focal point for theological reflection; see Mark 7; Acts 10). Paul claimed freedom from circumcision and from the Jewish law (Galatians). The letter quoted in Acts 15:23–29 proposed a compromise, recommending the Noachic orders (cf. Gen 9:3–4) of the Diaspora (rather than the Mosaic orders of Judea) to facilitate fellowship between Jews and non-Jews.

Radical Hellenistic groups within the Jesus movement apparently contributed to the growing alienation between "Missionary" and "Judaistic" Jewish Christians. Actually, we know too little about the "Stephen circle" and the "Hellenists" of Acts 6ff. to appreciate fully their historical impact. We cannot be sure whether these groups drew upon religious themes similar to those expressed at Qumran (Cullmann 1955) or upon the traditions of Diaspora Judaism that tended to be more critical of the temple (Simon 1958), if either. The traditions within Acts, however, suggest that these groups tended to proliferate outside the region of Jerusalem (e.g., in Samaria in the south and in Caesarea on the coast; see Acts 8:40 and 21:8ff); only the martyrdom of Stephen is located in Jerusalem.

A Christian enclave was gradually forming within Jerusalem, despite initial difficulties (e.g., the martyrdom at least of James, see Acts 12:1ff.). Owing to the idealized representation of Luke, the size of this Jerusalem enclave has often been overestimated (Paul found in Jerusalem practically nobody except Peter and James, the brother of Jesus, see Gal 2:19). The traditions about Jerusalem contained in Acts are mostly subsequent materials from a later time (although several traditions go back to the time of Peter's leadership; Acts 12:17 describes etiologically the transfer of this leadership from him to James, the brother of Jesus). Here the parish approaches a size (120 people, Acts 1:15) which had allowed the organization its own jurisdiction under Jewish premises. But James, the brother of Jesus, was initially a "Missionary" (see 1 Cor 9:5 for all the brothers of Jesus), and Josephus informs us about his martyrdom in A.D. 62 (*Ant* 20.200). Later, kinsmen of Jesus apparently played a leading role within "Judaizing Jewish Christianity" (Euseb. *Hist. Eccl.* 3.20.6), but this should not be accepted uncritically (Brandon 1957; Elliot-Binns 1956). After the failure of the Bar Kokhba revolt (A.D. 135) there probably no longer existed a Jewish-Christian parish in Jerusalem. Afterward our already deficient data on "Judaizing Jewish Christianity" disappears altogether, and we are left only with marginal notes from the 2d century describing Jewish Christianity, now considered a full-blown heretical movement (see Koester 1982, 2: 86–89, 198–201).

We must regard the earliest theological discussion at the time of Paul as a debate within Christianity. But soon (for the earlier period, see 1 Thess 2:14)—especially shortly before and after the Jewish War (A.D. 66–70)—Judaism itself was influencing developments. A more orthodox Jewish defense was gradually developing against some general Christian theologumena leading finally to the exclusion of Christians from the synagogues (see John 16:1–4). Luke, who retrojected these explanations anachronistically to the earliest days, refers to an original and uncompromising rejection of Christian preaching throughout Judaism. Similarly, the stereotypical opposition of the Pharisees to Jesus depicted in the Gospels probably distorts the facts, reflecting an opposition that existed not so much in the time of Jesus but actually a generation or more later. This finally culminated in the addition of the Christians to the Jewish curse of heretics in the *Shemonah-esre* of the Diaspora.

"Judaizing Jewish Christianity" was devastated by this strong reaction from their non-Christian Jewish brethren, since now one of its essential premises was being denied; i.e., that it was possible to incorporate one's own faith in Jesus within the traditional framework of Judaism (Matt 5:23 presupposes participation in the sacrificial rites of the temple; and Matt 24:20 implies a strong respect for the sabbath ordinances). "Judaizing Jewish Christianity" could only survive by developing its own form of particular norms.

D. Traditions and Theology

In trying to ascertain the traditions and the theology of such a diverse phenomenon as "Jewish Christianity," we must attempt to identify which specific elements derive from which original groups of the Jesus movement. Lohmeyer (1936) tried to distribute the traditions between Jerusalem and Galilee, but now we know that this distribution is overly dependent upon the Lukan view of history. When we move beyond Luke's idealized reconstruction, we can actually distinguish the contributions of the three major groups (see above).

One of these was a "Baptismal" group of Jewish Christians probably located in the Jordan Rift Valley and associated with followers of John the Baptist (John 3:22–30). This group promoted especially the faith in the risen Lord (reflected in the earliest hymns), Christian freedom (rooted in the view that the present age is a time of fulfillment; Mark 2:18), as well as baptism and a few other statements reminiscent of the Qumran beliefs that were being articulated at the same time in the same general area (see, above all, Eph 2:5ff: rising with Christ). The two Jericho narratives (Mark 10:46–52; Luke 19:1–10) possibly belong to this group. There also seems to be some connection with some of the traditions in the Lukan special material (e.g., the prodigal son parable, Luke 15:11–32).

Another of these was a "Missionary" group of Jewish Christians whose traditions are reflected above all in the call narratives (Mark 1:16–20; 2:14; Luke 5:1–11) and in the miracle and exorcism narratives. Traditions such as these deal with the ever-relevant question concerning the right to cross the boundaries delimiting the people of God (Mark 7:24–30; Matt 8:5–13; and many narratives in Acts). It is possible that the meal narratives (Mark 6:35–44; 8:1–8) also circulated primarily among this group.

The other was a "Judaizing" group of Jewish Christians. To this group belonged above all the tradition of Jesus' Passion, a multitude of Jesus sayings, and the apocalyptic consolation sayings (Mark 13). Here Jesus was called "King of the Jews" and the "Son of Man" (i.e., the coming judge of the world, according to Daniel 7). Mark 14 depicts Jesus in his last night as a prophet making several predictions that were fulfilled immediately, and we might wonder whether the christological title "prophet" (already repudiated in Mark 6:15) is ultimately traceable to this group. This "Judaizing" group was probably most successful in establishing an early Christian regiment of cultic observances (see the criticism in Gal 4:10 and Col 2:16). In addition to participation in the traditional Jewish liturgical order, they gradually established their own festivals, mostly rooted in existing Jewish rites (e.g., the Lord's Supper was one of their earliest creations). Prayer was also formulated by this group with respect to existing Jewish customs (cf. later *Didache* 8). The narratives of the empty tomb and of the Ascension (Acts 1:9–11) as well as the narrative about Pentecost (Acts 2:1–4) also came from this group. The development of such etiological tales to explain liturgical celebrations are characteristic of static groups, since ceremonies and celebrations tend to be stabilizing elements in the life of communities.

In summary, this "Judaizing" group not only "Christianized" the Jewish liturgical calendar but also collected and secured important memories about Jesus (especially the logia as derived from elements of Jesus' teachings). It thus becomes clear that this relatively modest group in the immediate area of Judea, soon to be overshadowed by the "Missionary" groups operating abroad, played an integral role in the development of Christian traditions and theology, an insight that often gets underestimated when our research focuses mainly on Paul.

E. Summary

It should be obvious that these early Jewish Christian groups were instrumental in establishing the Christian Church and in arranging important Christian traditions. But if they were asked to evaluate the overall significance of their special contributions (vis-à-vis those of gentile Christians), the answer would be rather complicated. It is certain that the program of mission to the gentiles led to the formation of fellowship groups and, through that, to the question of what constitutes the unity of the movement.

There is little doubt that the NT canon is essentially a Deutero-Pauline work; its supplementation with the Johannine traditions (with its subsequent baptismal tradition) and several "apostolic" writings took place relatively late. There was practically no "Judean" tradition in the NT canon. If we had to reconstruct the developments of early Christianity by means of this canonical end product, we would be forced to conclude that "Judaizing Jewish Christianity" played, at best, an insignificant role in the history of Christianity and Christian tradition.

But on the contrary, this "Judaizing Jewish Christianity" actually mediated the central theological ideas, without loading on to them more novel ideas about mission and baptism. Being an essentially static group, these "Judaizers" created the worship and liturgical orders (Lord's Supper, prayers) and had initiated theological reflection into the death of Jesus (Passion narrative). Furthermore, this group played an important literary role insofar as it nurtured the sayings tradition that became the primary basis for understanding the teachings of Jesus. Strictly speaking, it was a small and sociologically unimportant group (the "poor" in Gal 2:10) within the rapidly expanding Christian movement; nevertheless it played a critical and decisive role.

Gradually, Christians who were not Jewish had to make a decisive break with the stricter norms of those who were Jewish, eventually relegating Jewish Christianity to the (heretical) fringe. There were logical reasons for this. Evidently restricting the Christian proclamation only to God's elect people Israel came to be seen as fundamentally incompatible with the freedom inaugurated through Jesus, indeed a freedom that could be found in the very teachings of Jesus that Jewish Christianity had valued and preserved. Thus, limiting the Christian program to the Jews in the name of Jesus had the effect of diluting or annulling the full force of the gospel message and Christian identity. In the long run, the self-imposed limitations of Jewish Christianity had much more influence on the eventual development of Islam than it did Christianity.

Bibliography

Bornkamm, G. 1971. *Paul.* Trans. D. Stalker. London.

Brandon, S. G. F. 1957. *The Fall of Jerusalem and the Christian Church.* 2d ed. London.

Bruce, F. F. 1979. *Peter, Stephen, James and John: Studies in Non-Pauline Christianity.* Grand Rapids.

Cullmann, O. 1955. The Significance of the Qumran Texts for Research into the Beginnings of Christianity. *JBL* 74: 213ff.

Danielou, J. 1964. *The Theology of Jewish Christianity.* Vol 1. of *The Development of Christian Doctrine Before Nicea.* Trans. London.

Elliot-Binns, C. 1956. *Galilean Christianity.*

Goppelt, L. 1954. Christentum und Judentum im 1. und 2. Jahrhundert. *BFCT* 55.

Johnson, S. E. 1954. The Dead Sea Manual and the Jerusalem Church of Acts. *ZAW* 66: 106ff.

Koester, H. 1982. *Introduction to the NT.* 2 vols. New York and Berlin.

Lohmeyer, E. 1936. *Galiläa und Jerusalem.* Göttingen.

Schille, G. 1957. Die Topographie des Markusevangeliums. *ZDPV* 73: 133ff.

———. 1966. *Anfänge der Kirche.* Munich.

Schoeps, H.-J. 1949. *Theologie und Geschichte des Judenchristentums.* Tübingen.

———. 1956. *Urgemeinde, Judenchristentum, Gnosis.* Tubingen.

Simon, M. 1958. *Saint Stephen and the Hellenists in the Primitive Church.* London.

Strecker, G. 1956. Christentum und Judentum in den ersten beiden Jahrhundert. *EvT* 16: 458ff.

———. 1958. *Das Judenchristentum und die Pseudoklementinen.* TU 70. Berlin.

Torrey, C. C. 1952–53. The Aramaic Period of the Nascent Christian Church. *ZNW* 44: 205ff.

GOTTFRIED SCHILLE

CHRISTIANITY IN ASIA MINOR

Asia Minor, the peninsula of the Asian continent bounded by the Mediterranean Sea, the Aegean Sea, and the Black Sea (and today known as Turkey), was an early center of Christianity. The particular character and history of the churches of Asia Minor is considered in this article.

A. Introduction

Even though the eastern seaboard of the Mediterranean was the birthplace of Christianity, it was in the region of Asia Minor that this fledging religion of the East experienced growth and maturation. For more than a century (50s–200) this region played host to some of the most significant individuals in the history of nascent Christianity. In addition, Asia Minor served as the land bridge over which the Christian movement passed in its westward expansion as its focus shifted from Syria-Palestine to the imperial capital of Rome. During this period of Asia Minor's apogee in early Christian history, certain unique and irreversible historical events were happening which shook the roots of this new religion. Historical events which ripped the roots of early Christianity from the soil of Judaism include the martyrdom of Peter, James, and Paul; the destruction of Jerusalem and the subsequent diminution of the hegemony of Judaistic Christianity and the

Jerusalem church (*pace* Jervell 1984); and the suppression of the Jewish Revolt during Hadrian's reign. This same period also saw the emergence of diverse Christian literary corpora and, as a consequence, a multiplication of theologies and canons. Finally, it was during this time frame that the church became a visible entity to the populace and to Roman administrators and this visibility, in turn, forever changed the State's attitude and behavior toward Christianity.

B. Methods and Sources

1. Methodology. Even though Christian authors provide the greatest number of texts for the study of early Christianity in Asia Minor, these texts are as diverse in occasion, genre, and content as the geography of Asia Minor is in its terrain. Only in recent years have scholars begun to realize the full significance of the fact that all of the documents of the early Christianity are occasional in nature. The necessary consequence of this is that these sources fundamentally defy scholarly attempts to arrange them into homogeneous and well-ordered categories. Complex and often irresolvable issues regarding the dates and authorship of these documents frustrate efforts at exact postulations. In addition, the randomness of the extant corpus of Anatolian texts is so high that this corpus cannot bear the weight of many of the interpretations often foisted upon it by scholars of numerous theological and methodological schools of thought. Methodologies, therefore, which either rely upon anachronistic formulations of later orthodoxy or which project trajectories of evolutionary development in the formation of Christian communities, even by geographical areas, are susceptible to the accusation of subjectivity. Obviously studies of discrete documents or individuals can be quite productive for the reconstruction of various individual facets of Anatolian Christianity. It has been, however, the attempts at a grand scheme or comprehensive synthesis that usually belie the historical evidence and have been, more times than not, guilty of "reconstructing the lion from a single claw."

2. Sources. a. Christian Sources. The majority of the extant primary sources shedding light upon Anatolian Christianity are associated with the names of Paul, John, Peter, Ignatius, and Polycarp. While no scholarly consensus exists regarding the dating, authorship, or occasion of all of the documents associated with these names, most would agree that these documents do shed important light upon Anatolian Christianity, regardless of author. The following table gives, by traditional arrangement, the most prominent texts addressed to individual Christians or Christian communities in Asia Minor.

Paul: Galatians, Colossians, Philemon, Ephesians, 1 and 2 Timothy
Peter: 1 and 2 Peter
John: Gospel of John; 1, 2, and 3 John, Revelation
Ignatius: Ephesians, Magnesians, Trallians, Philadelphians, Smyrnaeans, Polycarp
Polycarp: Martyrdom of Polycarp, Letter to Philippians
Melito of Sardis: Paschal Homily

A corpus of secondary sources related to Asia Minor includes sections of Acts (chaps. 13–14; 16; 19–20) and numerous *fragmenta* of 2d century leaders (conveniently collected in Grant 1946) preserved in Eusebius' *Church History*.

b. Pagan Sources. Unfortunately, there is a dearth of pagan sources for Anatolian Christianity in the early period. The extant sources include the Imperial Rescripts of Trajan, Hadrian, and Aurelius (Coleman-Norton 1966: 1–13). Lucian's accounts of Peregrinus *(Death of Peregrinus)* and Alexander of Abonuteichos explicitly relate to Anatolia (*Alex.* 25; 38), while the comments of Galen (Walzer 1949: 56–74) and Aelius Aristides (*Orat.* 3.671) probably reflect their respective experiences of Christianity in Asia Minor.

C. Contexts

1. Geography. The term "Asia Minor" *(Mikra Asia)* occurs as early as the 2d century A.D. (Ptolemy *Tetrabiblos* 2.3.17). On occasion the word "Asia" was used as a synonym for Asia Minor in both Greek authors (e.g., Strabo Geog. 2.5.24) and in the New Testament (e.g., Acts 27:2). This region was described in some detail by the ancient authors Aristotle, Strabo and Ptolemy. Modern usage of the term "Asia Minor" usually refers to that peninsula of land bounded on the north by the Black Sea, on the south by the Mediterranean Sea, on the west by the Aegean Sea, and on the east by the upper part of the Euphrates River. This region contained an area of approximately 275,000 square miles, most of which was a central plateau with mountain peaks at its extremities attaining 9000 ft. on the north, 5000 ft. on the east, 10,000 ft. on the south, and 2500 ft. on the west. The diversity between the coastal regions and the extensive interior in regard to topography, geology, climate, and natural resources fostered a longstanding condition of cultural and political heterogeneity of the peninsula. Even the inexorable imperialism of Alexander the Great and the later Roman Caesars could not totally overcome the physical realities of nature and geography. As was the case with all the continents surrounding the Mediterranean Sea, the greatest extent of Roman influence upon Asia Minor was on the edges which touched the Mediterranean itself. Even more than the great highways of antiquity, the sea enhanced the possibility of intercourse between Rome and its various provinces and allies, and thereby promoted cultural homogeneity, understood in a broad sense, in seaboard areas. If the survival of indigenous languages is any indication (*ANRW* 2/29/2: 565–70 see also LANGUAGES [INTRODUCTORY SURVEY]), the farther eastward and toward the interior one traveled in Asia Minor, the less the penetration of Greco-Roman influence would be found (Tarn 1952: 160). David Magie's observation that "the veneer of Hellenism tended to grow thinner in proportion to the distance from the Aegean seaboard or from the great routes which led into the interior" (Magie 1950: 120) holds true likewise for Roman influence in Asia Minor at the period of nascent Christianity, though Roman influence was more pervasive than earlier Greek influence had been.

The following is a listing of the names of the Roman provinces, geographical regions and prominent cities located in this peninsula.

Provinces: Asia, Cappadocia, Cilicia, Galatia, Lycia, Pamphylia, and Bithynia-Pontus
Regions: Caria, Commagene, Ionia, Lycaonia, Lydia, Mysia, Paphlagonia, Phrygia, and Pisidia
Important cities: Alexandria Troas, Amastris, Amisus, Ancyra, Apamea, Attaleia, Byzantium, Caesarea, Comama, Cyzicus, Ephesus, Heraclea, Iconium, Melitene, Miletus, Nicea, Nicomedia, Pergamum, Prusa, Rhodes, Samosata, Selinus, Smyrna, Tarsus, and Tyana

Many of these names are well known to the student of early Christianity. It must be kept in mind that the letter to the Galatians, the Revelation of John, and 1 Peter were explicitly designated as circular letters, thereby increasing the number of Christian sites that can be inferred from early Christian literature. In addition to the primary evidence of these documents, there is also the invaluable geographical material preserved in the accounts and sources incorporated into both the Acts of the Apostles and the *Church History* of Eusebius. The tabulation of Anatolian cities available from combining the evidence of both the histories of Luke and Eusebius on the one hand and the letters of Ignatius and the Revelation on the other hand produces an impressive list of cities. In addition, there were scores of cities whose names were never mentioned in the ancient sources even though one could find Christian communities there (e.g., those referred to in Paul's Letter to the churches of Galatia and Pliny's comment to Trajan that Christians had infected the cities, villages, and farms of Bithynia-Pontus [*Ep.* 10.96]). The following is a list of Anatolian cities of the 1st and 2d centuries where Christian communities were established (Meer and Mohrmann 1958, map no. 5).

Amastris	Iconium	Perge
Ancyra	Ionopolis	Philadelphia
Antioch of Pisidia	Laodicea	Philomelium
Apamea	Lystra	Sardis
Byzantium	Magnesia	Scepsis
Caesarea (Cappadocia)	Miletus	Sinope
Chalcedon	Myra	Smyrna
Colossae	Nicomedia	Tarsus
Derbe	Otrus	Thyatira
Ephesus	Parium	Tralles
Eumenea	Pepuza	Troas
Hierapolis	Pergamum	Tymian
Hieropolis		

2. History. In viewing the history of ancient Anatolia, one must not overlook the clear fact that in the 1st millennium B.C., the indigenous alphabets, languages, and cultures of Asia Minor (e.g., Lydian, Lycian, Carian, Neo-Hittite) were as diverse as in any Mediterranean region. In addition to this fact, one must also reckon with the imposition of various immigrant as well as occupation cultures, the most important of which included the Greek, Celtic, Persian, and Roman. Since each of these left its own indelible mark on the character of the area where it dwelt, no one of these cultures can be ignored in tracing the historical and cultural patterns which formed the backdrop of early Christianity in Asia Minor.

Significant Greek influence in Anatolia began with the colonization of the western seaboard in about 1000 B.C. By the 7th century B.C., the most important Greek cities of western Asia Minor (e.g., Miletus) were already sending Greek colonists to other regions to spread Greek culture (Boardman 1980). The Ionian seaboard nurtured outstanding Greek philosophers and littérateurs in the classical period, presaging a similar zenith of rhetoric and erudition in the Sophistic movement of the 1st and 2d centuries A.D. The city of Troy, immortalized in Greek literature by Homer, brought fame to Anatolia by its location on the northwestern coast. The political and military impact of Greece on Anatolia was no less profound than its cultural influence. Not only were the Greeks responsible for the "liberation" of Asia Minor from a Persian occupation, but the later victories of Alexander the Great were to set in place the political structures which were to foster rapid urbanization and to stabilize the new régime of Hellenism until the arrival of the Romans approximately two centuries later in 133 B.C. Although several indigenous tongues were still in use in both the early (Acts 14) and late Empire, Hellenism provided the area with a lingua franca which served all participants of Anatolian civilization, pagan, Jew, and Christian alike. In addition, the veneration expressed toward the political successors of Alexander the Great was to have a strong influence centuries later upon the Roman ideas of emperor worship. The eventual Roman assimilation of these notions of ruler veneration was to set in motion great forces of conflict between Christianity and devotees of the imperial cult.

The true impact of the imposition of Persian rule from 546 B.C., the capture of Sardis, to the advent of Alexander the Great in the early months of 334 B.C. is debated by scholars (*CAH*[2] 4:211–33). Some opine that Persian hegemony consisted of "no more than military and administrative control" (H. Metzger 1969), while others have assembled a rather impressive group of archaeological and literary data that suggests Persian influence was neither superficial nor ephemeral (*CHI* 2:292–391; *CHI* 3/1:100–15). The fact that the residual influence of Persian cult and mythology centuries after Alexander's victory over the Persians in Asia Minor should not be discounted is evident in the remains, from extreme east to extreme west respectively, at Nemrud Dagh (Dörner 1975) and in the early imperial Sardian epigraphy regulating worship in the Persian cult of Ahura Mazda (Robert 1975; *NDIEC* 1:21–23).

The Celtic invasion of Asia Minor in the early 3d century B.C. was a major event in the political history of the region. The Celts' domination of the area was severely curtailed, however, when Attalus I of Pergamum (230 B.C.) defeated them. Thereafter their influence was limited primarily to the central Anatolian region of Galatia. In all probability, this Greek victory over the barbaric Celts provided inspiration decades later for the construction of the magnificent Altar of Zeus at Pergamum in the early 2d century B.C. (Havelock 1981: 192). The eastward expansion of Rome and its ability to consolidate its influence in the east was greatly accelerated by the acquisition of the Pergamene empire in 133 B.C., fully 150 years prior to the advent of Christianity there. The inestimable possession was acquired with little effort at the death of the last king of the Pergamum empire, Attalus III, when he bequeathed his entire nation to the Romans in his will. While this was not by any means Rome's first involvement in Asia Minor, this gift gave the Romans an unquestioned hegemony in the peninsula and a base for further implementation of its manifest imperialism in the East. As is often noted, Rome's unique contribution in the East was its military, legal, and administrative genius, but the spirit and soul of the culture was that of Hellenism. Accordingly, the most important impact of Rome upon Asia Minor was its attempt to administer this culturally and geographically diverse region which was both rich in natural resources and, equally important, served as a strategic buffer between Rome and the ever threatening Parthian Empire to the east. Building upon the efforts of previous Hellenistic urbanization, the emperors established strategically located colonies, e.g., Pisidian Antioch, which were established "primarily for security reasons" (Levick 1967: 187). Consequently, the early generations of Anatolian Christianity transpired in the context of Pax Romana and, historically viewed, relative cultural euphoria (e.g., for Aelius Aristides' praise of Rome see Oliver 1953).

3. Religions. The religious situation of Anatolia was a true microcosm of the entire eastern Mediterranean, with a rich mixture of Greek, Roman, Anatolian, Jewish, Persian, and other Eastern cults represented. Notwithstanding the potential dangers of "parallelomania" (Sandmel 1962; B. Metzger 1955), one may not ignore the analogies and parallels between numerous institutions, values, and formal beliefs of early Christianity and contemporary Anatolian piety. The number of similarities abounds, in part, because nascent Christianity in this region was itself so diverse and, when taken as a whole, possessed a plethora of religious institutions, values, and beliefs. From this multifaceted background to Anatolian Christianity, three components of Anatolian religious life are especially important to highlight, i.e., folk religion, pagan religious associations, and Jewish religion and institutions.

a. Folk Religion. In many ways this term defies precise definition. It connotes an ethos of religious values and beliefs rather than one particular mythology or cult. Moreover, folk religion was not idiosyncratic to any region or to any established social, economic, political, or religious stratum of antiquity. Nevertheless, this folk religion worldview germinated and thrived with special vigor in Asia Minor (*GGR* 2: 578–81). This worldview was frequently designated by ancient writers as *deisidaimonia* (Koets 1929; Theophr. *Char.;* Plut. *De Superst.;* Meijer 1981: 259–62; *GGR* 2: 102–120; Hadas 1972: 182–211). *Deisidaimonia* was a superstitious, even magical, approach to the gods which influenced every religion and cult in the Greco-Roman world, and had had its detractors since Plato's criticism of Orphic evangelists of his own day (*Resp.* 364B–365A). The hallmarks of this religious outlook, particularly in Eastern cults, were its emphases upon the "fear of God" and upon achieving superior religiosity through supererogative rituals and ascetic practices (*Superst.* 166A–B; 168D; 171B; *RAC* 1: 753–58), sometimes in conjunction with long-established shrines, and sometimes not. Spiritual tranquility was predicated upon such things as public confession of sins *(hamartia)* committed against the deity (*Superst.* 168D, 171B; Pettazzoni 1937; Steinleitner 1913; Hermann 1986). Terms such as "ransom" and "sinner" were not unknown in this context (*NDIEC* 1:32–33; 2:90, 100f; 3:20–31) and immersion rites in water abounded (*Superst.* 166A, *baptismous*). Sins often consisted of violating taboos regarding what one ate and drank (*Superst.* 168D; 170D), in lying to the deity (Malay 1988: 150; MacMullen 1981: 58), in sexual immorality (Petzl 1988), or in the failure to worship properly on a holy day (*Superst.* 169D–E). Inordinate, some would say pathological, interest in the performance of punctilious acts of asceticism to prepare one for a mystical experience of the deity were typical (Behr 1968; e.g., glossolalia *Superst.* 166B). The superstitious devotee was especially desirous of prophetic oracles and their correct interpretation. *Deisidaimonia* was also characterized by a concern about the spirit world and attacks from spirit beings and the heavenly hosts (*Superst.* 168C). Divine retribution, threats of eternal punishment (*Superst.* 167A), and punitive miracles from particular gods and goddesses were of the gravest concern to this religious type of personality. Individuals, and their number was legion, caught in the web of *deisidaimonia* tended to be ecumenical in outlook. They were driven by a pragmatist's approach to religion and consequently imbibed the strangest concoctions of syncretism.

b. Religious Associations (Poland 1909: 173–270; 499–513). Anatolia during the Roman era was replete with formal and informal guilds and associations *(synodos, thiasos, collegium).* Typical were the labor guilds which provided comradeship in the midst of the harsh realities of everyday life and offered some social services for its members (Dill 1964: 251–86; Wilken 1971: 279–88; Meeks 1983: 77–80). Beyond the labor unions, there were the religious associations which focused their attention more narrowly on religious ceremonies. They often existed under the tutelage of a particular god or goddess, perhaps related to a common trade (e.g., the Dionysiac guild of performers and entertainers), would use their particular deity as one avenue to the world of Greco-Roman religious life, experiences, and benefits (e.g., safety, morality, answered prayers, protection from Fate). Of special interest in this regard is a religious association that existed in the city of Phildelphia in the Roman province of Asia. The epigraphic testimony of this association is especially didactic in demonstrating the existence of pagan associations which placed an emphasis upon morality. This association was created and regulated by the divinely revealed statutes of Zeus. It met in a patron's house, was open in its membership to both male and female, free and slave, and its members committed themselves by oath to eschew acts of sexual immorality, murder, abortion, etc. (Horsley and Barton 1981). On occasion, these private associations might be viewed as competitors to the longer established public temples where, in some cases, the same deity was worshiped (cf. Serapis on Delos, *SIG* no. 664; cf. Pl. *Leg.* 909e). Like the large temples, these private pagan associations would often have officers such as prophet(ess), deacon(ess), herald, and preacher of the divine story. These *collegia* often maintained a common treasury and held regular gatherings for worship and communal meals. It is not to be overlooked that in many instances a private religious association would assemble in the house *(oikos)* of one of its members. Consequently, matters such as the

Greco-Roman concept(s) of household religion, personal relationships in the family, social functions of homes, etc. (Malherbe 1983) become relevant for the background to the ubiquitous institution of religious "house assemblies" (Klauck 1981).

c. Jewish Religion and Institutions. Recent years have witnessed new and vigorous discussion regarding Judaism and its relationship to Christianity in the Roman era. The points under consideration include the nature and activity of Jewish Christianity, the attraction to synagogues of gentiles who remained uncircumcised, and the existence and extent of pagan anti-Semitism. All of these bear directly upon one's view of Anatolian Christianity since these areas relate directly to issues such as continuing gentile attraction to Jewish Christianity, Jewish-Christian heterodoxy (Klijn and Reinink 1973 for patristic references; Daniélou 1964), Christian evangelism among synagogues, gentile churches drifting from their Jewish roots because of anti-Semitism, and Jewish collaboration with pagans in the harassment of Christians (Frend 1965).

A storm center of current debate centers on the meanings and use of the Greek words *theosebes* and *sebomenoi* (and *phoboumenoi*) and what, if anything, these phrases depict about gentile sympathizers toward Judaism. A. T. Kraabel is a proponent of a new view that is characterized by questioning the very existence of the ancient gentile group known as "God-fearers" (Kraabel 1981). The traditional view maintained that "God-fearers" were gentiles who were not yet proselytes, i.e., circumcised, to Judaism, but who were very sympathetic to many of the beliefs of ancient Judaism. This group, it was said, provided the pool from which early Christianity drew many of its synagogue converts. It is Kraabel's conclusion that such a group was a fiction created by the author of the Acts of the Apostles (MacLennan and Kraabel 1986). This effort to discount both the Lukan view as well as the view traditionally supported by many ancient historians experienced a setback with the recent discovery of an inscription at the Carian site of Aphrodisias (Reynolds and Tannenbaum 1987, esp. p. 47 and text B *l.* 34 *theosebeīs*) that seems to substantiate the more traditional reading of the Greco-Roman literature and archaeological data regarding the existence and vitality of the "God-fearers." Even though this new perspective of Kraabel's is not likely to win the day in completely changing the mind of the majority of those in the scholarly community, it has correctly demonstrated that the traditional view has been naïve at times in both its philological analysis of the terms *theosebes* and *sebomenoi* (and *phoboumenoi*) as well as its monolithic reconstruction of ancient Judaism and its "missiology" (cf. Cohen 1987: 419). Regardless of the precise labels used to refer to these adherents, most scholars will probably continue to agree that the "evidence shows beyond reasonable doubt that Judaism in the Roman Diaspora did win adherents who stopped short of circumcision" (Collins 1985: 183–84; Cohen 1987: 419).

Another important topic that has emerged in recent scholarship relates to the topic of anti-Semitism in antiquity. John Gager (1983), according to whom anti-Semitism was not primarily a pre-Christian phenomenon as has been thought by most scholars, argues that the literary evidence shows that virtually all the pogroms against ancient Jews were isolated and should not be used as a foundation upon which to formulate a widespread anti-Semitism. His conclusion is that it was Christianity, and not paganism, that initiated thoroughgoing anti-Semitism in antiquity. Once again, this attempt to recast the numerous historical sources in a totally new light has not appeared cogent to many scholars (Goldenberg 1985: 335–36). Gager's work has correctly highlighted some of the popular misconceptions regarding the nature and extent of anti-Semitism in the Greco-Roman world, but it has not been able to explain away the fact that the Jewish apologists of antiquity themselves, prior to the advent and dissemination of Christianity, surely thought that they were the object of widespread, though not continual or universal, discrimination (e.g., Josephus *Ant* 14.213–44ff).

The salient facts of Anatolian Judaism (Appelbaum 1974; Tcherikover 1970; Kraabel 1968 must be used carefully since it encompasses evidence two and three centuries later than the period under consideration in this article) for the period of the early empire include the following: (1) what was true of Anatolian Judaism may not have been true of Judaism in its environment at Rome or at Alexandria; (2) the cultural origins of Anatolian Judaism were largely Babylonian and not Palestinian; therefore, one must not read it necessarily in light of ostensibly conservative Palestinian Judaism; for example, certain Anatolian Jewish women served as head of the synagogue (Smyrna *CIJ* 741 = Brooten 1982: 5); (3) its commitment to send the temple tax to Jerusalem evidences a recognition of the hegemony of the Jerusalem cultus; (4) its legal status as an ethnic and religious *collegium* was recognized and protected by the Romans; (5) some Anatolian Jews were participants in urban civic and political institutions, thereby providing evidence of partial assimilation to Greco-Roman culture (Kraabel 1968; Ramsay 1895–97: 621–76); and (6) though certain gentiles were sympathizers and adherents (for a variety of reasons) to Anatolian Judaism, there were, nevertheless, underlying currents of anti-Semitic prejudices in some quarters.

D. General Characteristics of Anatolian Christianity

1. Heterogeneity. Although Paul has often been viewed as the founder of the Christian mission outside Palestine, that could hardly be the case. Neither Acts nor the Pauline Corpus even suggests such. On the contrary, the Pentecost discourse (Acts 2:9–10) states that Jewish pilgrims from Asia Minor were among the first to accept Jesus as the Christ. Moreover, the Acts of the Apostles makes it abundantly clear that Paul was not the first to bring the Gospel to sites such as Ephesus, Corinth, or Rome. The realization that Paul was neither the first nor necessarily the premiere missionary in Asia Minor also affords optional explanations for the existence of "non-Pauline" churches in Asia Minor (e.g., those of Revelation and 1 Peter) without resorting to "early Catholic" theories, which are essentially anachronistic and Protestant (Murray 1982: 197). From the outset the Christian communities of Asia Minor were filled with converts whose beliefs and practices bore the almost indelible imprint of their pre-Christian worldview. One cannot truly understand the genesis of the heterogeneity of early Anatolian Christianity without first recognizing the steadfast influence of the cultural heritage of each convert. This influx of religious variety led the Christian movement, in a quantum step, into a world of new challenges. To be sure, this step was not synchronized throughout Asia Minor, nor was it always a step in the same direction. Some congregations and regions took this step later than others. It was, nevertheless, because of both the frequency and the magnitude of the new challenges that Anatolian Christianity encountered that in the decades of the 50s to 200 this region was without peer in its historic significance.

2. Households. The household was a basic social context for the early Christian communities. This is seen in references to the Anatolian assemblies occurring in the homes of Aquila and Prisca (1 Cor 16:19), Nympha (Col 4:15), and Philemon (Philemon 2). By extension, the entire Christian community was embraced in a metaphorical sense in the phrases "household of faith" (Gal 6:10) and "members of the household of God" (Eph 2:19; 1 Pet 4:17). The *Haustafeln* ethical paradigm (in general Balch 1981; Col 3:18–4:1; Eph 5:21–6:9; 1 Pet 2:18–3:7) points to the same domestic social realities. As a place of Christian instruction the home had to be protected from serving as a channel for the propagation of heterodox teaching (2 John 10; 2 Tim 3:6; Malherbe 1977). In the same line of thought, the properly ruled "household of God" imagery of 1 Timothy is clearly employed as a defensive strategy against unsound doctrine (1 Tim 3:14–15) and is constructed as a metaphor on the basis of the Greco-Roman household (cf. 1 Tim 3:4–5, 12; 5:14; 2 Tim 2:20). The significance of the household stands out in the references to them in the later Ignatian corpus. Among the Smyrnaeans, Ignatius "greets the households of my brethren with their wives and children" (13:1) as well as the "household of Tavia [a woman]" (13:2). In his letter to the bishop of Smyrna (*Polyc.* 8:2), Ignatius greets "the wife of Epitropus with her whole household and her children." Interestingly, the phrase "corrupters of houses" is a designation for false teachers (*Eph.* 16:1), thereby highlighting the household as an important locus for Christian teaching.

3. Heresy. One's knowledge of Anatolian Christianity is primarily dependent on contemporary sources that were written by leaders engaged in battles to correct aberrant views and/or practices. While these early contemporaneous sources are not without difficulties, they are far superior to later heresiological summaries by writers such as Eusebius (Lawlor and Oulton 1954, vol. 2; Grant 1980; Barnes 1981). When one focuses upon the occasion of these documents themselves, it becomes immediately clear that any history of Anatolian Christianity must be conducted in light of the endemic controversies there. The standard works of A. Hilgenfeld (1884), W. Bauer (1934; ET 1971), and H. E. W. Turner (1954) represent significant investigation into ancient issues of orthodoxy and heterodoxy, including those issues as they were manifest in Anatolia. In this century Bauer in particular has set the tone for discussion of heresy and heresiology in Asia Minor. His goals, methods, and general characterizations of the evidence are still attractive to many scholars (e.g., Koester 1971; in general, Strecker and Kraft 1971: 286–316), but clearly not to all (Turner 1954; Hawkin 1976). Unfortunately, the infrastructure of much of Bauer's work belongs to a scholarship of an earlier day, particularly reflecting the presuppositions and schematizations of German Protestant theology of the late 19th and early 20th century. A chief concern of Bauer was to overthrow the naive view of the evolution of the Christian mission and history which affirmed that the "development takes place in the following sequence: unbelief; right belief, wrong belief" (Bauer 1971: xxiii). Most New Testament scholars today would agree that Bauer's conviction at this point could be supported easily by even an elementary reading of the New Testament. A misfortune of Bauer's work was that in order to reach his goal he forced many texts into Procrusteans beds, a procedure which resulted at times in a distorted and truncated reconstruction of Anatolian Christianity (Norris 1982: 365–77 and 1976: 23–44; Robinson 1988). One of the legacies of Bauer's work is the current sympathy, at times apologetic zeal, toward early Christian heterodoxy. Some scholars appear to be "enamored of ancient heresies" (Henry 1982), and others believe that generally the orthodox characterizations of the opponents were, in fact, often only caricatures (Wisse 1971; Karris 1973; Grant 1981).

When examining the matter of orthodoxy and heterodoxy in Anatolian Christianity, it is extremely important to include in one's taxonomy of the "orthodoxy-heresy" phenomenon the matter of whether attacks against heterodoxy by soon-to-be "canonical" writers were primarily defensive or offensive. The epistle to the Galatians is instructive in this point. It was patently Paul's opponents who were the first to invoke the concept of "orthodoxy" against fellow believers. The only plausible explanation for the circumcision of Paul's converts after his departure was that they were convinced by "those from James" that their standing with God and their reception of Abraham's blessings were in doubt because they were failing to carry out the scriptural requirements of circumcision, feast days, Sabbaths, etc. (4:10). It was Paul's opponents who introduced the concept of the imprecation (3:10–14) upon those who disagreed with their own Jerusalem standard of orthodoxy. Like his opponents, Paul held to orthodox convictions, the truth of the Gospel (2:14), as he called it, but thought that orthodoxy excluded, rather than included, the requirements of circumcision, feast days, Sabbaths, etc., for gentile believers. Another example of a defensive concern for orthodoxy is found in Colossians. The internal evidence for this polemical milieu includes the following:

1. The conditionality of salvation: "*If* you continue in the faith . . . *not shifting* from the hope of the gospel which you heard" (1:23).
2. The cluster of pejorative terms used to depict the slogans and views of the heterodox teachers:
   a. Beguiling speech (2:4).
   b. Philosophy and empty deceit (2:8).
   c. Human tradition not according to Christ (2:8).
   d. Elemental spirits of the universe (2:8, 20).
3. Statements of concern.
   a. Warning and teaching every man (1:28).
   b. I say this so that no one may delude you (2:4).
   c. "See to it that no one makes a prey of you" (2:8).
   d. Why do you live as if you still belonged to the world (2:20)?

It is clear that the false teachers were demanding submission to ascetic dietary rules (2:20), viewed by the author as a worldly and carnal demand (2:20, 23). Furthermore, they were making religious judgments against the nonconformists who did not submit to "holy days" religiosity (2:16) and they were denigrating, if not negating, the spiritual status of their nonconformist fellow Christians (2:18). Based upon the historical reconstruction made possible through the details of 2:1–23, it appears that the author's point of departure for attacking the Colossian opponents was a defensive one in response to the opponents' prior offensive initiative when they declared that their own spiritual understanding and devotional practices were the standards for orthodoxy.

A similar pattern of the use of orthodoxy in self-defense is apparent in sections of the Pastorals which either combat asceticism or emphasize confidence in one's salvation in the light of detractors (2 Tim 2:18–19). Similarly in the Johannine epistles (Bogart 1977; Brown 1979), the attacks upon those who both voiced perfectionistic slogans and advanced aberrant Christology were constructed out of a sense of self-defense. It would be a distortion to suppose that the gnostics of the 2d century were only a group of unassuming intellectuals attacked preemptively by orthodox "witch hunters." One ought not forget that even in the 2d century and later, the soon-to-be "orthodox church" was accused by various sectarian and gnostic Christians as being itself heretical (Koschorke 1978). In fact, it may well have been the case that the orthodox canon (Campenhausen 1972; B. Metzger 1987), the ultimate weapon of the Great Church, was in part compiled, particularly in Asia Minor, out of self-defense against Marcion, Montanus, and Gnostic leaders. A frequent topic for research into Anatolian heresiology is the issue of church government, especially the bishopric, and its duties to oppose heresy. While the household supplied the social and liturgical framework for Christian congregations and some of the church's vocabulary for its self-identity, the titles for the congregations' rulers seemed to have originated in other spheres. The information, admittedly sparse, points to the existence of various religious offices in the Christian communities of Asia Minor, some of which may have been modeled, at least in name, on synagogue practice, or on existing urban models of government (Hatch 1882), or upon organizational structures present in Greco-Roman *collegia* (Meeks 1983: 80). Moving beyond the issue of nomenclature to the issue of the matrix of the increasing authority and regimentation in the bishopric, there is renewed effort to locate this development in the social structures of the household (Schöllgen 1988). Since Philippians (1:1) testifies to the early presence of bishops *(episkopos)* and deacons within Pauline communities, there are no grounds for an *a priori* rejection of the Lukan reference to the appointment of elders *(presbuteros)* in the churches of central Asia Minor (Acts 14:23). At Acts 20:17 "The same persons who are here called *presbuteroi* are described in vs. 28 as *episkopoi*" (Lake and Cadbury 1932: 259) and later (20:28) are associated with the ministry of shepherding *(poimaino)*. The charismatic nature of this ruling ministry is attested in the Lukan account (Acts 20:28) as well as in Eph 4:11. In other Anatolian literature a synonymous use of the terms "elder" and "shepherd" is seen in 1 Pet 5:1–5, while *presbuteroi* and *episkopoi* are tightly knit in 1 Timothy's description of the rulers of the community (1 Tim 3:1–7; 5:17–22). J. B. Lightfoot's argument that the terms "elder" and "bishop" were used "in the language of the New Testament" to refer to "the same officer in the Church" is still cogent (Lightfoot 1913: 95). The Apocalypse of John is not particularly informative in this matter. Since the term "elder" in Revelation is used regularly in the idiom "twenty-four elders" (e.g., 4:4; 5:8; 11:16; 19:4), it is not likely that this use mirrors any particular practice within Anatolian Christian communities. With the Ignatian correspondence the use of the terms *presbuteroi* and *episkopoi* undergoes transformation. By the time of the journey of Ignatius from Antioch via Asia Minor to Rome in 110, each church of Asia Minor, at least those addressed by Ignatius, was governed by a single bishop (e.g., *Magn.* 6:1). In the Ignatian hierarchy a council of presbyters served under the single bishop, and below the presbyters served the deacons. In more than one letter Ignatius sets forth a church polity wherein "The bishops are regularly compared with God or Christ" and "The presbyters or elders are regularly compared with the apostles" (Schoedel *Ignatius* Hermeneia, 112).

Scholars have not agreed on how the office of the bishop evolved in relationship to the control of heterodoxy. That is, was the development of the monarchical episcopacy an inexorable process (Hatch 1882: 83–111) or was it a regional ad hoc response to acute heresy? The texts of Acts are extremely difficult to interpret since that work is notoriously silent in general regarding even the existence of heresy in the early communities of faith. There are only two texts in Acts that mention elders in Asia Minor, namely, 14:23 and 20:17–35. The first text is totally silent on the anticipated function of the eldership, but the second text reveals clearly that the bishops are to oppose lupine heretics who will attack the flock. Even the eldership itself will engender errorists who will teach perverse doctrines. Ephesians also portrays the pastor in a role which promotes doctrinal stability in the congregation (Eph 4:11–14). A somewhat different picture is seen in the treatment of the bishops in 1 Timothy. While that text gives numerous qualities for those in the bishopric, there is no mention of their role as preservers of the faith and promoters of sound doctrine (cf. Tit 1:9), though some have suggested that heresy in the Ephesian eldership was the occasion for the writing of 1 Timothy (Fee 1984). In any case, it is Timothy who is given the duty of constraining false teachings (1 Tim 1:3–7). If the rather unique use of the term "elder" in 2 John 1 and 3 John 1 is viewed in light of its milieu of opposing antichrists, then the author may have chosen the word "elder" intentionally because of its authoritative connotations (Smalley *1, 2, 3 John* WBC, 316–18). When turning to Ignatius, his voice is clarion in the matter of the bishop's unique role in achieving unity and attacking heterodoxy (e.g., *Eph* 3:2–6:2; *Mag* 3:1–2, 6:1–2, 7:1–2, 13:1–2; *Trall* 2:1–3; *Phil* 3:1–3; *Poly* 6:1–2). The implication and impact of Ignatius' belief regarding the singular role of the bishop is preserved in the following thoughts: "All of you are to follow the bishop as Jesus Christ follows the Father. . . . Apart from the bishop no one is to do anything pertaining to the church. A valid Eucharist is to be defined as one celebrated by the bishop.

. . . It is not right either to baptize or to celebrate the agape apart from the bishop; but whatever he approves is also pleasing to God, so that everything you do may be secure and valid. . . . It is good to know God and the bishop. He who honors the bishop has been honored by God; he who does anything without the bishop's knowledge worships the devil" (*Smyr.* 8:1–9:1, trans. by Grant 1966, *ad loc.*). These pronouncements mirror Ignatius' strategy of maintaining the churches' orthodoxy by comprehensively controlling its liturgy and activities through an orthodox episcopacy (Wiles 1982). Though not a shepherding office, the ministry of deacons is also documented in various Christian communities in Asia Minor. Deacons (1 Tim 3:8–10, 12–13) as well as deaconesses (1 Tim 3:11; Pliny *Ep.* 10.96) are mentioned.

E. Major Issues Facing Anatolian Christianity

The collection of Anatolian Christian sources reveal at least four salient and recurring issues of conflict. These are: (1) folk religion and superstition, (2) Jewish issues, (3) Christian Gnosticism, and (4) persecution and harassment.

1. Folk Religion and Superstition. The general theme of the epistle to Colossae has been generally summarized as the "all sufficiency of Christ." Although most would fundamentally agree with this summary, the historical background to the occasion of Colossians remains hotly disputed. One scholar has championed the view that there were no false teachers (Hooker 1973), but others, the vast majority, have argued that the opponents were influenced either by the religious outlook of Essenes, or gnostics, or devotees of mystery religions, or Jewish Christian mysticism (O'Brien *Colossians, Philemon* WBC, xxx–xxxviii).

Although the language of Colossians is not as vituperative as Galatians, the letter is clearly concerned to correct heterodoxy and heteropraxy at Colossae, which the author had probably heard about from Epaphras (2:8). The Colossian opponents surely included Christians. It is doubtful that they would have understood and granted Paul's working assumption that their approach to spiritual growth and attainment to the fullness of God encroached upon an orthodox christology. Although the Colossian heresy manifested itself partially in OT acts of piety (2:16), it was clearly not the same cluster of issues which Paul attacked in Romans or Galatians or which Luke depicted in Acts 15. Colossians lacks all of the lexicographic and rhetorical resources necessary to carry out attacks against Judaizers. It lacks, for example, both the usual diatribe and numerous terms such as Law, commandment, covenant, Abraham, Moses, righteousness, to justify, and Israel. Moreover, certain aspects of the opponents' practices and theology were not rooted in Jewish Scripture or in distinctive Jewish practices (2:18). Even the veneration of angels need not be Jewish since it was a part of pagan Anatolian piety in the Roman era (Sokolowski 1960; Sheppard 1980–81). The foundational worldview that animated the ritual and ascetic approach of the Christian heresy at Colossae was neither classic Gnosticism nor the stereotypical Jerusalem Judaizers, but rather *deisidaimonia.* The outline of the opponents in Colossians fits perfectly Plutarch's description of superstition, with its attentiveness to ways to achieve piety and superior religiosity through channels of prescribed rituals, ascetic practices, and divine revelations. It was this punctilious ceremonial approach to spiritual attainment, to purification from sins, to divine wisdom, to revealed knowledge, and to the experience of the fullness of deity which had attacked the Pauline view of the gospel. *Deisidaimonia* could not tolerate the *all sufficiency* of God's work through Christ as affirmed by Paul.

The fight against superstitious asceticism was not limited in Asia Minor to the evidence of Colossians. The Pastoral letters indicate the presence of related issues in the churches where Timothy worked (1 Tim 1:3). In particular, 1 Tim 4:1–10 highlight three areas of asceticism about which Timothy should be concerned. These are: (1) prohibition of marriage and sexual relations in it, (2) dietary asceticism, and (3) ascetic mistreatment of the body under the guise of "training" (cf. Epictetus, *Diss.* 3.12). The first two issues are condemned outright as being demonic in origin, and caution is expressed concerning the third. All three of these approaches to spirituality were evident in the superstition of Greco-Roman Anatolia. An Anatolian Christian leader of the 2d century, noted for his mercurial piety, was Peregrinus Proteus (Lucian *Peregr.*) In light of his abiding interest in piety (some would say notoriety) through asceticism, punishment of the body by flagellation, and Cynic self-denial, it is significant that Proteus, at one time in his life, felt at home among and was a hero to the Christians of Asia Minor. The attitudes and demeanor that served as the common denominator throughout his public life, irrespective of his religious affiliation, were his total commitment to departure from the status quo, his desire for imprisonment, and his demonstration of his indifference to his own physical comforts. His life ended with a suicidal leap onto a pyre shortly following the Olympic Games. Peregrinus' attraction for suicide was not without parallel. Anatolian Christianity of the 2d century was itself involved in the debate over the virtue of a form of suicide, namely, voluntary martyrdom. That a Christian theology of martyrdom could have been influenced by pagan *deisidaimonia* is not beyond probability. Since the veneration of the relics of Christian martyrs began quite early in Asia Minor (*Martyr. Pol.* 18.3) and was very widespread there, this aspect of Christian martyrdom may reflect pre-Christian concepts of superstition and hero veneration (modern discussion given by Baumeister, *RAC* 14:102–35). The martyrdom of Polycarp, bishop of Smyrna, has been investigated in regard to the question of whether his death was voluntary or not (Tabbernee 1985). In the account of Polycarp's death (*Martyr. Pol.* 4), there is an interesting reference to the fact that some Christians, though later changing their minds, pursued martyrdom "of their own free will." The particular group mentioned was from Phrygia. For the author of the *Martyr. Pol.* to mention that "we do not praise those who surrender themselves [for martyrdom], since the Gospel does not teach us this," this question was surely already a matter of theological reflection at the time. Perhaps the physician Galen of Pergamum (ca. 125–200) had ascetic Christians from Asia Minor in mind when he made his remarks about Christians having contempt for death and exercising great self-control in matters of food and drink. The late 2d century (ca. 170, Barnes 1970) Anatolian schismatics known as Montanists (after their founder Montanus) or Cataphrygians (after their Phrygian provenance) have been a constant enigma to modern historians (Klawiter 1975). Consequently, many attempts have been made to locate the religiohistorical matrix of this Anatolian Christian movement. Scholars have sought to discover whether its origins and theology were rooted in Anatolian, specifically Phrygian, pagan cults. Although some scholars continue to look for partial Phrygian influence (Freeman 1950; Daunton-Fear 1982), most have abandoned this perspective based upon the earlier conclusions of Schepelern (1929). Some have seen Montanism as an antagonist to Gnosticism, while others (Froehlich 1973) have viewed it as quite similar to Gnosticism. A Jewish or Jewish-Christian matrix for this movement has also been advocated (Schwegler 1841; Ford 1966). Even though this schism endured several centuries (the most complete collection is that of de Labriolle [1913]; the best critically evaluated and arranged edition is Heine [1989]), it is its first generation that pertains distinctively to an Anatolian situation (Aland 1955). When dealing with Anatolia, it is crucial not to confuse the mutation of Montanism in Rome (Heine 1987–88: 11–16) or its appearance in Tertullian (Powell 1975) with the first generation of 2d century Montanists (Grant 1946: 94–108) who were Anatolian and whose history and beliefs are best reconstructed from quotations and *testimonia* preserved in Eusebius (*Hist. Eccl.* 5.16.1–5.19.4) and Epiphanius (*Haer.* 48.1–13). The so-called "Christians for Christians" inscriptions (Gibson 1978) from Anatolia are both later than the scope of this study and very probably "there is no argument in favour of a Montanist interpretation" (Pleket 1980: 198) of these epigraphical documents. Even though any conclusion about the origins, practices, and beliefs of Montanism ought to be stated with caution, it is necessary to point out that many of the traits and theological convictions that separated later Montanism from the Great Church (e.g., penchant for martyrdom, eschatology, emphasis upon the Paraclete) cannot be reliably documented from the sparse records of 2d-century Phrygian Montanism. What does seem to characterize the early Anatolian Montanists (Heine 1987–88) was their predilection for uncontrolled and ecstatic prophecies and oracles ("abnormal ecstasy, insomuch that he became frenzied and began to babble and utter strange sounds," anonymous in Euseb. *Hist. Eccl.* 5.16.7). The orthodox writers of the time had no problem with prophecy itself, just its misuse characterized by techniques of pagan oracles and prophecy. Another manifestation of the falseness of the prophecies of Montanus was his practice of engaging in this spiritual gift in exchange for remuneration. Finally, the orthodox church attacked the Montanists because they *mandated* spiritual ascetic disciplines ("Montanus taught dissolutions of marriages" . . . and "laid down laws on fasting," Apollonius in *Hist. Eccl.* 5.18.2) rather than allowing or suggesting them. In light of these traits of Anatolian Montanism, it seems that *deisidaimonia* (whether mediated through Jewish, Christian, or pagan media) offers a plausible matrix for the emphases of Montanus and his followers. If the emphases of Montanus (i.e., frenzied oracles, rigid asceticism, and paid thaumaturgy) had been recounted by the pagan authors Juvenal, Lucian, or Plutarch rather than Eusebius, they would have been clearly labeled as superstition and *deisidaimonia* rather than false doctrine or heterodoxy. Modern authors have also noted the similarities (Klawiter 1975: 130–55).

Various documents of Anatolian Christianity reveal a seemingly widespread problem among Christian communities with another component of superstition, namely, magic and the occult. The condemnation of this quintessential dimension of folk religion is evident in the list of the works of the flesh given to the numerous (Gal 1:2) Christian communities in central Asia Minor (Gal 5:20) when Paul mentions *pharmakeia.* Turning to other regions of Asia Minor, the oracles of judgment found with the Revelation of John contain several references to the divine wrath awaiting those who work magic (*pharmakeia* and cognates, e.g., 9:21, 18:23, 21:8, 22:15). The city of Ephesus provides a clear example of a society (Acts 19) where pagan magic had penetrated into Christian faith and practice. It is significant that the generic name for the collection of magical spells and incantations in the Roman period was Ephesian Letters *(Ephesia grammata).* The Pastoral epistles reflect a similar interest in condemning the practice of magic by Christians. Since the names "James" and "Jambres" were associated in Jewish tradition with the magicians who opposed Moses (Exod 7:11), it is highly probable that they were used in 2 Tim 3:8 as a prototypical opponents in order to combat magical practices associated with heterodox teachers. This interpretation is supported by the occurrence of the Greek term *goes* (lit. magician) in the same context (2 Tim 3:13). Acts 19:11–20, esp. 19:18, depicts the strong grip that folk religion had on many believers there, even influencing the interpretation of the Pauline miracles (19:11–12). Moreover, it is noteworthy that the Ignatian collection of letters uses the term *mageia* (magic) only once, and that in his letter to the Ephesians (19:3, Christ destroyed all magic). An indication of the continuing struggle against the influence of *deisidaimonia* among the Christian communities of Anatolia is reflected in the content of the two mid-4th century Anatolian Councils of Gangra and of Laodicea (Hefele 1876). Both of these attest the ongoing belief among Anatolian Christians in ascetic spirituality achieved through dietary and sexual deprivation.

2. Jewish Issues. There is an increasing awareness of the social and theological diversity that existed among Greco-Roman Jews in general and Anatolian Jews in particular (cf. Kraabel 1968; *HJP*[2] 3/1). Judaism did not, even in Palestine, possess only one self-definition (Sanders et al. 1981; Hengel 1974). In all probability the first Christians in Asia Minor lived, worshiped, and studied Torah in the context of Anatolian synagogue congregations. In the case of Paul's efforts as an *apostolos,* his foremost energy was spent in fulfilling an Isaianic missiology that led him to gentiles through restored Israelites (= "converted" Jews). This is the only plausible explanation for the habitual Pauline modus operandi best captured in the phrase "to the Jew first" (Rom 1:16, 2:9–10; 1 Cor 9:20; Acts 17:2). In line with this outlook, there was the conviction that the Israel of God consisted of those who were, by faith, heirs of Abraham, irrespective of their race (Gal 6:16). Regarding the synagogue attitude toward circumcision, which was the essence of the problem among churches in central Anatolia in the mid-1st century, there was no standard practice. The fact that as a Jewish boy Timothy had not been circumcised (Acts 16:1) provides an Anatolian example of a fact already known from Hellenistic Jewish authors, namely, that the issue of the requirement of circumcision for membership in Israel, both for Jews and proselytes, was unsettled among 1st-century Jews. Evidence of diversity in other matters is seen in the coexistence of a Samaritan/Gerizim synagogue and a Jewish/Jerusalem synagogue on the nearby island of Delos in the Hellenistic period (White 1987). It is quite natural to assume that this ubiquitous Jewish theological diversity had an appreciable impact on Christian believers both before and after the major rift between the church and synagogue. For example, this type of Jewish diversity regarding the necessity of circumcision provides a significant context for early Christian struggles with the same issue (e.g., Galatians). It is quite evident that the theology of Anatolian Judaism contributed to the theology of Anatolian Christianity, its offspring. Even after the Jewish faith had reluctantly given birth to the church, the church's umbilical cord to Judaism was never entirely severed, with the possible exception of the Marcionite churches. The most obvious example of this would be in the heavy dependence upon the Jewish Scriptures (e.g., Acts' depiction of the Pauline sermons in Asia Minor, Galatians, Ephesians, 1 and 2 Timothy, Revelation, 1 Peter, Ignatius of Antioch, Justin's *Dialogue with Trypho*). It is equally important to observe the reverse side of this relationship, namely, that many of the schisms, aberrations, and heresies occurring within Anatolian Christianity can be traced to the abiding influence of Jewish faith and practice, especially among gentile converts. The list of Christian authors who deal with this issue of Jewish influence and competition is impressive and reflects the strength of the attraction that Jewish ceremonies and faith had for many gentile converts. The internal debate with stereotypical Judaising Christians in Asia Minor is well known and well documented in the texts of Galatians and Acts 15. The epistle to the Colossians explicitly labels as aberrant the requirement of Sabbath observance by the Christian community there.

1 and 2 Timothy, however, are not as significant in this regard as is often assumed. It is routine for scholars to point out that the epistles of 1 and 2 Timothy contain censure against Jewish intrusions into the Christian community in Ephesus by its reference to those who "want to be teachers of the law, but do not know what they are talking about" (1 Tim 1:7). However, this is not *necessarily* the case. When all the characteristics of the opposition to Paul's gospel are taken from all three Pastoral Letters and are put into one lump, "the effect is to rob each letter of its distinctiveness. Specific and difficult texts are replaced by an easy generalization" (Johnson 1987: 8). Unless one subscribes to a theory of synoptic harmonization among the Pastorals, and thereby harmonizes 1 and 2 Timothy with Titus, even though they are addressed to different geographical regions (Ephesus and the island of Crete), then it is not a foregone conclusion that "teachers of the law" (1 Tim 1:7) should be equated with "those of the circumcision" (Tit 1:10). In fact, 1 Tim 1:8–11 makes it clear that the author's use of the term "law" points to an almost generic moral meaning of the term. Furthermore, even though the genealogies of 1 Tim 1:4 *could* be Jewish, they need not be since the use of genealogies was widespread in antiquity (*RAC* 9: 1145–1268).

Turning to the Johannine materials, it is usually acknowledged that there is cogent evidence for locating the origin of the gospel of John in Asia Minor, at least in its final form (*RGG*³ 3:849; Martin 1975: 282; Robert and Feuillet 1965: 648). It is likewise clear that the fourth gospel reflects, in part, the church-synagogue debate of the late 1st century (Pancaro 1975). This debate is reflected in the gospel's redaction of Jesus' frequent statements regarding the Jews (in the third person, passim) and in the use of the phrase "your Law" and "their Law" (8:17; 10:34; 15:25). The Revelation of John also mirrors the fierce competition between the churches and synagogues of western Asia Minor. When John denounces the Jewish synagogues at Smyrna and Sardis (Noakes 1975) with references to "those who claim to be Jews and are not" and to the "synagogue of Satan" (2:9, 3:9), it is obvious that at least in these two cities the churches' self-identification and survival depended in part on its ideological victory over the local synagogue. Particularly revealing in this regard are the comments of Ignatius that reveal, a decade or so later than the Apocalypse, the abiding influence of Jewish ceremonial practices upon certain Christians in western Asia Minor. In his communication with the Magnesians, one discovers the continuing threat of Jewish ways in remarks such as "It is stupid to speak of Jesus Christ and to practice Judaism. For Christianity did not rely upon Judaism, but Judaism upon Christianity" (10:3; cf. 8:1; 9:1). In another text Ignatius portrays a peculiar situation wherein the presence of both orthodox Jewish Christians and uncircumcised advocates of non-Christian Judaism are mentioned (*Phil.* 6:1). This somewhat enigmatic and provocative text (Barrett 1976) reads, "It is better to hear Christianity from a man who is circumcised (= Jewish Christian) than Judaism from one who is uncircumcised." An equally intriguing text is found later in this Philadelphian correspondence. It is not known whether Ignatius' opponents mentioned in *Phil.* 8:2 are Christians or non-Christians. What is noteworthy is that he admits the hermeneutical problems he encounters when attempting to argue with these individuals from the OT. These people apparently do not accept the presuppositions which allow Ignatius to discover Christ's cross, death, and resurrection in the Jewish Scriptures (cf. *Phil.* 9:1–2).

Melito of Sardis (annotated bibliography, Drobner 1982) castigates with trenchant invective (*Pass.* 72–99) the unbelieving Jews who crucified the Lord. Little is known of the church in Sardis before the writings of Melito, though unquestionably it was significantly smaller than the synagogue community there (Josephus *Ant* 12.147–53). Since, however, Melito is consistent in his pejorative use of the term "Israel" and his belief that Israel had "been replaced by the church, as the Law has been replaced by the Gospel" (Noakes 1975: 249), some argue that the affluence and superior social influence of Sardian Judaism precipitated Christian reaction (and perhaps anti-Christian persecution) which in turn ignited vitriolic Christian fulminations like that of Melito's (Kraabel 1971; Manis 1987). Some, however, have not yet been convinced by what appears to be a "sociopolitical" interpretation that is remiss about Melito's theological concerns (Norris 1986).

The Quartodeciman controversy, which continued for over two centuries in Asia Minor (Canon no. 7 of the Synod of Laodicea, ca. 350), testifies with clarion voice to the perennial desire of many Anatolian Christians to maintain the Jewish heritage of the Christian observance of Easter/Passover. Easter was celebrated in the earliest church at each and every Sunday assembly (*RGG*[3] 4: 1960). While the Sunday liturgical ceremonies from Asia Minor recorded in Acts 20:7 and Pliny's description of Christian worship (*Ep.* 10.96) both point to nocturnal celebrations (Staats 1975), this need not have been the normal procedure on each Sunday. It is in the 2d century that the annual celebration of Easter began. At that time some Christians, primarily from Asia Minor and Syria, believed that they should keep the annual Easter/Passover celebration in accordance with the Jewish reckoning of the Passover, while Christians in Italy and Egypt preferred to celebrate this annual rite on the following Sunday. Moreover, those who preferred the Jewish calculation of the 14th (= *quartusdecimus* = Quartodecimans) of Nisan for Easter also accompanied it with a fast, which caused conflict with those wishing to observe Easter on the following Sunday (von Campenhausen 1974). In this context it is not germane to delve into the intricate arguments concerning the origin, date, literary references, and distinctiveness of the Quartodeciman celebration of Easter in the 2d century (Huber 1969) or whether it was in part "an anti-Marcionite and anti-gnostic institution" (Hall 1984) or if in fact there were distinct groups within the Quartodeciman camp (Richardson 1973). What is noteworthy is the number of significant church leaders and bishops in Asia Minor (e.g., Melito of Sardis; Irenaeus; Apollinarius of Hierapolis; Polycarp, Bishop of Smyrna; and Polycrates, Bishop of Ephesus) who were Quartodecimans and thereby advocated a liturgical calendar which had not yet given in to gentile Christian pressure to jettison older Jewish dimensions of the annual Easter/Passover rite.

In a similar fashion, the widespread advocacy of chiliasm (*RAC* 2:1073–78) in Anatolian Christianity is most likely a reflection of the impact of Jewish apocalypticism upon Christianity there (Daniélou 1964). Although the idea is still undeveloped, the terminology of the 1000-year reign first occurs in Anatolian literature in the Revelation of John (20). Though it later fell into disrepute (e.g., Eusebius's disdain for it), the millennial age concept had among its proponents in Asia Minor the following Christian luminaries: Papias of Hierapolis (Euseb. *Hist. Eccl.* 3.39); Irenaeus (*Haer.* 5.35); Justin Martyr (*Dial.* 80); Cerinthus (Euseb. *Hist. Eccl.* 3.28); John's followers (Iren. *Haer.* 5.33.3); and Montanus (Euseb. *Hist. Eccl.* 5.18.2; Tertullian *Adv. Marc.* 3.4.5). Still in the 3d century traces of this doctrine's influence are seen in Anatolian authors such as Methodius (*The Banquet* 9.5).

Though one cannot be certain, the tone heard in Justin Martyr's extended exegetical arguments and counterarguments, even over textual variants (Skarsaune 1987), with the Jewish Rabbi Trypho *(Dial.)* may reflect the situation in mid-2d century Anatolia. With the passage of time and a shift in the missiological outlook of later Christian leaders, the church's interaction with Judaism had become less and less intramural. Conversions, which were occurring in both directions, took place in an increasingly trenchant context. The active involvement of Jews in the harassment and occasionally in the public clamor against Christians in Asia Minor is incontestably attested in the Christian sources of the 2d century (Wilde 1949: 141–47; Frend 1965). A significant testimony to the enduring influence of Judaism upon the churches of Anatolia is easily seen in the regulations from the 4th-century Council of Laodicea. At this council the Christian leaders of Anatolia believed it necessary, still in ca. 350, to prohibit Christians from keeping the Passover/Easter feast according to Quartodeciman ordinances (Canon 7), honoring the Sabbath rather than Sunday (Canon 29), attending a Jewish festival with a Jew (Canon 37), and accepting unleavened bread from Jews or heretics (Canon 38).

3. Christian Gnosticism. Since the study of Christian Gnosticism is beset with numerous methodological problems regarding definition, sources, and chronology (*TRE* 13: 535–50), it is no wonder that at times speculation (e.g., Bultmann 1956) has outrun the evidence. Even the discovery of the Nag Hammadi texts has not always clarified the issues. In fact, it is not completely clear to all scholars that these texts are even gnostic. As one writer observed, these "individual tractates can no longer be assumed to be Gnostic. . . . Thus a significant number of Nag Hammadi texts can no longer serve as primary evidence of Gnosticism" (Wisse 1983: 138). A more sober estimation of the possible significance of Gnosticism upon the theology of Paul, John, and the documents of the New Testament in general and its supposedly early date (Yamauchi 1983) is now forming among scholars. Since occurrences in the New Testament of the word *gnosis,* or other later gnostic technical vocabulary, are alone no longer regarded as adequate evidence for the presence of Gnosticism understood in its 2d-century sense, scholars are not so ready to posit automatically this phenomenon as the background of the opponents of the Prison Epistles or even the Pastorals. For example, the unsound doctrine of a Hymenaeus and Philetus (2 Tim 2:17–18) which emphasized the present reality of the resurrection can be explained in terms of the similar eschatological error in 2 Thess 2:2 or in terms of a misunderstanding of the resurrection accomplished in baptism (e.g., Eph 2:6) rather than by relying facilely upon later gnostic views of the resurrection (Fee 1984, *ad* 2 Tim 2:17–18). The fact that a later Christian writer such as Irenaeus quotes the Pastorals and assumes that their author was fighting heretics identical to those he was fighting hardly proves the case for 1st-century Gnosticism, unless one wishes to assume that later Christian authors were never guilty of employing anachronisms. With justification, scholars no longer allow later Christian writers, whether it be Marcion, Irenaeus or Heracleon, to pronounce themselves, without cogent demonstration, as the spiritual successors of NT authors.

The evidence for signs of embryonic Gnosticism is stronger, however, when the materials in the Johannine Gospel and epistles are investigated (cf. Yamauchi 1981 with MacRae 1986). The term "docetism" is the most frequently used label to identify the heretical group against which the Johannine author writes, though scholars still debate whether its origins are Jewish or not (Davies 1962). Although docetism is neither a synonym for Gnosticism nor a necessary criterion to establish its presence, this christological heresy is normally regarded as evidence for the presence of certain strains of Gnosticism. In brief, docetic Christology advocated a rather "high" christology, based upon a stark contrast between the Redeemer from heaven and the earthly man Jesus (*TRE* 16: 726–28), while stressing the glorification and divinity of Christ at the expense of his humanity and his full participation in the flesh. Once it has been established that the community which John addressed in the gospel was also among the recipients of the epistles, it is fairly easy to detect polemic against a heretical christology throughout much of the Johannine corpus (Brown 1979; *Epistles of John* AB). This docetic background of the Johannine material makes the best sense out of the unique *logos* christology in the fourth gospel's prologue (1:1–18) and explicitly fits into the doctrinal denunciations of 1 John 4:1–3 and 2 John 7–11 where the bearers of this doctrine, denying that Jesus came in the flesh, are attacked as *antichristoi.* Regardless of whether the vignette regarding the encounter between the "gnostic-docetist" Cerinthus (Iren. *Haer.* 1.26.1) and the Apostle John (Iren. *Haer.* 3.3.4) is factual, the letters of Ignatius, written within approximately a decade of the Johannine letters, document the growing problem the churches of western Anatolia were having with docetic christology. Ignatius' antidocetic polemic is implicit in affirmations such as God's manifestation in humanness (*Eph.* 19:3) and in references to Christ's being *truly* crucified and *truly* partaking of food (*Trall.* 9:1–2; *Smyrn.* 1:2). Explicit indications of the presence of docetism are contained in his allusions to heterodox slogans that Christ only seemed *(dokein)* to suffer (*Trall.* 10:1; *Smyrn.* 2:1; 3:1–3; 4:2). At one point Ignatius argues, "For how is one assisting me, if he praises me but blasphemes my Lord by denying that he is a bearer of the flesh *(sarkophoros)?* And the one who does not make this confession has completely denied him [Christ], and made himself a bearer of a corpse *(nekrophoros).*" Years later the Asian bishop and martyr Polycarp also identified the antichrists as those who did not confess that the Christ came in the flesh (*Phil.* 7:1).

Even though Italy and Egypt provided the context for most of the major Gnostic teachers and schools of the 2d century, the early role of Asia Minor should not be overlooked. Later orthodox authors such as Irenaeus saw Asia Minor as a battleground where the true tradition and gospel of the church were vigorously maintained through the efforts of the apostles and their pupils (Zahn 1900). Irenaeus, whose theological roots were planted deeply in the soil of his native Anatolia (Euseb. *Hist. Eccl.* 5.20.5), is exemplary in his many arguments against the Gnostics (Vallée 1981) that "all the Asiatic churches testify" (*in Asiae Ecclesiae omnes* 3.3.4) to orthodox doctrine and apostolic parentage. Later comments by Eusebius provide little substantive information previously unknown on this matter since he basically knows only what is available in the sources he quotes (e.g., Irenaeus) and was himself "no student of heresy" (Grant 1980: 86–87).

4. Persecution and Social Harassment. Several of the leading personalities associated with Anatolian Christianity were criminals. A list of these offenders would include Paul, the author of the Apocalypse, Ignatius, and Polycarp. Behind these few names stood scores of unnamed Christian convicts whose crimes and capital punishment are mentioned in works such as the Apocalypse of John and the correspondence between Pliny and Trajan. Furthermore, the majority of the literature pertaining to early Christianity in Asia Minor was penned by authors after their arrests (e.g., Prison Epistles, Pastoral Epistles, and Ignatian Epistles). In a less extreme form, Anatolian Christians knew of sporadic outbursts of social and legal harassment which might or might not have eventuated in imprisonment. The Lukan account of Paul's work in Asia Minor (Acts 13–14; 19–20) reflects the presence of opposition and pogroms against the Christian mission through use of phrases such as "through many tribulations we must enter the kingdom of God" (Acts 14:22) and ". . . with tears and with trials which befell me through the plots of the Jews" (Acts 20:19) and through vignettes such as the urban protest against Christianity engendered by a discontented labor union (Acts 19).

The epistle of 1 Peter is directed to Christian communities in Asia Minor (1:1) and gives significant attention to the matter of Christian suffering (2:11–4:19). Scholars are not of one mind regarding this epistle's historical matrix. Contemporary scholarship is less sympathetic with the earlier view of, among others, F. W. Beare (1947), who postulated that the situation depicted by the Pliny-Trajan letters (A.D. 110–15) was one of imperial persecution and that this was the appropriate context in which to interpret the epistle of 1 Peter. It is no longer evident to many scholars (Talbert 1986: 13–14) that the situation depicted in the Pliny-Trajan letters is one of official persecution or that this Christian epistle, whenever penned, should be read against the background of any supposed official persecution, whether instigated at either the imperial or provincial level. Scholars also differ on whether or not 1 Peter was exhorting the Christian communities to maintain themselves in times of harassment through means of sectarian principles such as internal group identity, cohesion, and boundary maintenance (Elliot 1981), or whether 1 Peter represents, at least in its Household Codes, a more open and assimilated posture (Balch 1981). In terms of the development of anti-Christian harassment, several points stand out in 1 Peter, particularly in regard to its place in the history of Anatolian Christianity. Of particular interest is the awareness that the "name of Christ" is a source of animosity and also that individuals are suffering *as Christians* (4:14–16), a situation already present in Rome under Nero. Possible arrests and incarcerations are implied by statements in 1 Peter (4:2:12, 16; 4:15). The rhetoric of the epistle is cast in dualistic e.g., Babylon, 5:13) and eschatological tones (4:17), but there is no general designation of the State or emperor cult as Satanic (*ANRW* 2/23/1: 205), nor are there any allusions to the imperial cult. In fact, both the emperor and his minions are granted the status of authority and honor (2:13–17), and the author indicates that the fiery ordeal and sufferings that the Christians are experiencing are part of the normal Christian life throughout the empire (4:12; 5:9b). The immediate source of the Christians' suffering seems to come from pagan outrage (4:4) at the sectarian lifestyle and ideology that is typified in the Christian demeanor (Goppelt 1978).

Several important developments both in the relationship between "Church" and "State" and in the suffering of early Christians appear for the first time in the Apocalypse of John (*ANRW* 2/23/1: 215–26). Among the new developments is the presence of a large number of martyrs. No longer is it just a matter of tribulations and suffering, but now John refers to those "who had been slain for the word of God" (6:9) and to "the blood of the prophets and of saints" (18:24) and to "the souls of those who had been beheaded for their testimony to Jesus and for the word of God" (20:4). A second development is the explicit evidence that a Christian's impious attitude toward the cult of the emperor (bibliography on imperial cult in *ANRW* 2/16/2: 833–910) was grounds for martyrdom (13:15). This is not at all surprising in light of the long-standing presence in Asia Minor of cults to the goddess Roma (Mellor 1975), in light of the rapid reception of Augustus as a deity in Asia Minor (Bowersock 1965), and in light of the ubiquitous and beneficent presence of the imperial cult in Roman Asia Minor (Price 1984). The architecture, the rituals, the festivals and games, the swearing by the divinity of the emperor (Hermann 1968), and the pledges of allegiance to the imperial family (Weinstock 1962) all make it very clear that in Asia Minor "the imperial cult was not simply a game to be played in public" (Price 1984: 120). Rather, it "was a major part of the web of power that formed the fabric of society. . . . [and] along with politics and diplomacy, constructed the reality of the Roman empire" (Price 1984: 248). Accordingly, the persecution of the Christians was a response not only to their antipathy toward concerns of Roman jurisprudence but also to their violation of matters of Roman religion and piety (*RAC* 2: 1159–1208; Vogt 1962). A third development was the dualistic framework in which the author of the Apocalypse perceived the Roman State and provincial government. Even though contemporary pagan authors could use animal epithets (Pliny *Pan.* 48.3 *immanissima belua,* fearful monster) to describe Domitian or to state that Domitian "was in reality an evil demon" (*daimona poneron,* Dio Chrysostom *Orat.* 45.1), these do not approach the dualism employed in the Apocalypse (chap. 13). Clearly John views the government and imperial cult as a manifestation of Satanic oppression and influence. Of course, the State's estimation of John would not be much higher. In light of the early imperial policy to destroy prophetic books which contained damning and foreboding oracles (e.g., Suet. *Aug.* 31), one can anticipate how the government would look upon the sedition reflected in the prophecies of the fall of Babylon (Revelation 18), especially penned by an exiled dissident (in general MacMullen 1966; cf. Juvenal *Satires* 6.553–564). In order to contextualize more accurately the church's treatment by the Roman State at that period, it must be observed that Christians were not the only group regarded as a counterculture which was to be harassed by Domitian and his policies (Cuss 1974). For example, Domitian's pogroms against individuals, even family members, guilty of adopting "Jewish ways" is well attested in ancient literature (Smallwood 1976: 376–85). Domitian also banished philosophers and moral preachers from Italy, at least those whom he perceived to be seditious, and "put many Senators to death" (Suet. *Dom.* 10). Disdain for Domitian was so intense that after his assassination his name was erased from many Anatolian monuments (Suet. *Dom.* 23; Magie 1950: 1440–41 n. 30). Given the general cruelty and paranoia which characterized Domitian's reign of terror, one should regard the State's active persecution against Anatolian Christianity in the light of numerous barbaric idiosyncrasies of Domitian rather than as a manifestation of constant imperial policy.

In less than two decades after Domitian's pogrom against the churches of western Asia Minor, the Pliny-Trajan *Letters* (10.96–97) detail occurrences of the sufferings and criminal punishment of Christians in the Roman area of Bithynia-Pontus. This official exchange enhances the picture of the State's comportment toward Christianity under Trajan, but reveals little of the attitudes held by the diverse Christian population of north-central Anatolia (Keresztes *ANRW* 2/23/1: 273–87 surveys various schools of interpretation of the Pliny-Trajan *Letters* and their reflection of current Roman law). Pliny reports that the Christians were accused by public detractors, probably on two counts. The first point of accusation was that of crimes associated, at the very least by rumor, with the name of Christian *(flagitia cohaerentia nomini)*. These crimes were in all probability the disgusting and bizarre accusations discussed by the 2d-century apologists (*ANRW* 2/23/1: 579–604; Henrichs 1970) rather than the more mundane crimes of theft and murder mentioned in 1 Peter. The second point of accusation, and one that seemed quite enigmatic to a legal mind like Pliny's (10.96.1), was that the "name of Christian" was illegal. Whether Roman jurisprudence could *legally* approbate such evidence in a court of law was the question which motivated the governor Pliny to inquire of the emperor. No clear answer was given, in part because other legal issues surfaced between the time of the original accusations and the end of Pliny's legal examination of the accused. In particular, criminal contumacy, as Pliny defines the attitude of numerous believers he questioned (10.96.3), was a serious crime (Sherwin-White 1966: 699, 784). The point that Pliny makes to Trajan is that he had these Christians executed, in part, because of their "stubbornness and unshakeable obstinacy" (10.96.4). As in the case of the martyred Christians of the Apocalypse, these Christians were summarily executed by decapitation. Pliny employs the use of oaths to the gods, sacrifices to the cult statue of the emperor (Scott 1932; Kruse 1934), and denunciation of Christ to distinguish between those who were real Christians *(vera Christiani)* and those who were only nominal, or in some cases former, believers (10.96.5). In his response, Trajan supports the governor's previous actions (10.97.1) and also through his counsel reveals his convictions about the potential danger of this depraved religion. The emperor's prime directive to Pliny is that Christians must *not* be sought out by the government *(conquirendi non sunt)*. Moreover, when they are accused, their trials must be conducted within the guidelines of enlightened Roman jurisprudence, a policy not followed by his predecessor Domitian. Moreover, if they repent of their Christian past, all must be forgiven.

Contemporary with Pliny's treatment of Christians in northern Anatolia is the famous journey of Ignatius. Since he was arrested in the province of Syria and not the region of Asia Minor, the details of his arrest are not germane. It is instructive, however, to observe that the Roman guards who were accompanying him had ample opportunity to arrest or accuse numerous Christians en route with whom Ignatius shared fellowship and social intercourse. Even though Ignatius was soon to be martyred, it is patently evident that neither he nor his guards believed that the dozens of Christians whom he calls by name in the numerous Christian communities he addresses are in any danger legally. Clearly, there is no evidence in the Ignatian correspondence to support the idea that it was a crime to be a Christian or that there existed legislation, either in the provinces or in Rome, that outlawed Christianity (Millar 1973: 145–75). A decade following the official exchange between Trajan and Pliny, the emperor Hadrian sent official correspondence about the same matter. Silvanus Granianus, governor of Asia, wrote Hadrian about the "Christian problem" (A.D. 121–22), and the emperor's reply was sent to the governor's successor Minicius Fundanus (A.D. 122–23) and later preserved in Justin's *1 Apology* (68). Hadrian's reply "denounced informers, eager to blackmail their victims, and insisted that charges had to be proved in court, not simply initiated by petitions or popular clamor," while at the same time, it "did not revoke the penalties against convicted Christians but did require orderly procedure" (Grant 1988b: 34).

Fragments of Anatolian Christian writers of the late 2d century depict a new development in the Church's effort to carve out a workable peace with the Roman State. Two prominent apologists who articulated a theology of a synergistic relationship between the Roman State and the Christian Church are Apollinaris, bishop of Hierapolis, and Melito, bishop of Sardis. In approximately 176 both men wrote to the emperor Marcus Aurelius, writings now partially preserved in Eusebius' *Church History* (Apollinaris, 5.5.4; Melito, 4.26.5–11). It was during the Marcomannic Wars that the troops of the emperor engaged the Quadi, a Germanic tribe. The Quadi's siege machine was destroyed by lightning. Later a miraculous rain storm invigorated a fatigued Roman army and helped them become victorious. Virtually every one, except the Germans, regarded these miraculous occurrences as the providential intervention of deity. For example, the pagan miracle worker Alexander of Abonuteichos, an Egyptian priest named Arnuphis, Roman priests, Christian soldiers, and others all claimed some type of credit for these miracles. The Christian bishop of Hierapolis, though partially misrepresented by Eusebius, apparently used this miraculous event a part of an apology. Specifically, he argued that the victory was given to the Roman troops because a legion of Christian soldiers had been prayerful on behalf of the empire. Needless to say, this was also a way to demonstrate to the emperor and his provincial leaders that the church was not seditious. The thrust of the apology of Melito was that the proof of the divine origin of Christianity is demonstrated by the fact that it appeared simultaneously with the advent of Augustus. Christianity, according to Melito, was nursed in the cradle of the Roman Empire. Moreover, the general prosperity and longevity of the Roman Empire can only be attributed to the peaceful coexistence (with a few exceptions) of Rome and the church, both created and protected by the Christians' God. The historical realities of the late 2d and 3d centuries indicate that the apologetic efforts of these two Anatolian bishops was not particularly effective. According to R. M. Grant, the greatest effectiveness of these apologetic pleas was within the Christian community itself as a means to undergird the Christian's theology of culture, morality, and politics (Grant 1988a: 14).

F. Conclusion

Since the content of the historical sources themselves are controlled by specific occasions, one should not expect to arrive at more than a partially distorted reconstruction. Working within the boundaries of this fact, one can, nevertheless, conclude that the first two centuries of Anatolian Christianity demonstrated several important features. An obvious feature is that Christianity in Asia Minor, at least in the eyes of its leaders, was characterized by conflict. The sources of the conflict were at times internal and at times external; there were few times, however, when there was not an open conflict. A second feature was that the conflicts were often accurate reflections of the points of collision between the Christian gospel and various facets of Anatolian culture. Another characteristic of the early history of Christianity in Asia Minor is its dynamic development. Whether it be orthodox or heretical developments, the Christian churches were, though not always consciously, adapting and modifying its message and teaching. The final feature is the dominant role that Anatolia played in providing the regional context for the growth and training of prominent Christian individuals and in setting the stage for the occasions, developments and articulation of most of the important issues and doctrines of early Christianity throughout the Roman world.

Bibliography

Aland, K. 1955. Der Montanismus und die kleinasiatische Theologie. *ZNW* 46: 109–16.

Applebaum, S. 1974. Legal Status of the Jewish Communities in the Diaspora. vol. 1, pp. 431–63 in *The Jewish People in the First Century*, ed. S. Safrai and M. Stern. CRINT. Philadelphia.

Balch, D. 1981. *Let Wives Be Submissive: The Domestic Code in 1 Peter*. SBLMS 26. Chico, CA.

Barnes, T. D. 1970. The Chronology of Montanism. *JTS* n.s. 21: 403–8.

———. 1981. *Constantine and Eusebius*. Cambridge, MA.

Barrett, C. K. 1976. Jews and Judaizers in the Epistles of Ignatius. Pp. 220–44 in *Jews, Greeks and Christians: Religious Cultures in Late Antiquity*, ed. R. Hamerton-Kelly and R. Scroggs. SJLA 21. Leiden.

Bauer, W. 1971. *Orthodoxy and Heresy in Earliest Christianity*. 2d ed. Trans. R. A. Kraft and G. Krodel. Philadelphia.

Beare, F. W. 1947. *The First Epistle of Peter*. Oxford.

Behr, C. A. 1968. *Aelius Aristides and the Sacred Tales*. Amsterdam.

Boardman, J. 1980. *The Greeks Overseas*. 2d ed. London.

Bogart, J. 1977. *Orthodox and Heretical Perfectionism in the Johannine Community as Evident in the First Epistle of John*. SBLDS 33. Missoula, MT.

Bonner, C. 1940. *The Homily on the Passion by Melito Bishop of Sardis*. SD 12. Philadelphia.

Bonwetsch, G. N. 1881. *Die Geschichte des Montanismus*. Erlangen.

Bowersock, G. 1965. *Augustus and the Greek World*. Oxford.

Brooten, B. J. 1982. *Women Leaders in the Ancient Synagogue*. Brown Judaic Studies 36. Chico, CA.

Brown, R. E. 1979. *The Community of the Beloved Disciple*. New York.

Bultmann, R. 1956. *Primitive Christianity in Its Contemporary Setting.* New York.

Campenhausen, H. von 1972. *The Formation of the Christian Bible.* Philadelphia.

———. 1974. Ostertermin oder Osterfasten? Zum Verständis der Irenäusbriefs an Viktor (Euseb. *Hist. Eccl.* 5.24.12–17). *VC* 28: 114–38.

Cohen, S. J. D. 1987. Respect for Judaism by Gentiles According to Josephus. *HTR* 80: 409–30.

Coleman-Norton, P. R. 1966. *Roman State and Christian Church: A Collection of Legal Documents to A.D. 535.* 3 vols. London.

Collins, J. J. 1985. A Symbol of Otherness: Circumcision and Salvation in the First Century, Pp. 163–86 in *"To See Ourselves as Others See Us." Christians, Jews, "Others" in Late Antiquity,* ed. J. Neusner and E. S. Fredrichs. Chico, CA.

Cuss, D. 1974. *Imperial Cult and Honorary Terms in the New Testament.* Paradosis. Contributions to the History of Early Christian Literature and Thought 23. Freiburg.

Daniélou, J. 1964. *The Theology of Jewish Christianity.* The Development of Christian Doctrine before the Council of Nicaea, 1. Chicago.

Daunton-Fear, A. 1982. The Ecstasies of Montanus. *StPatr* 17/2: 648–51.

Davies, J. G. 1962. The Origins of Docetism. *StPatr* 6/4: 13–35. TU 81. Berlin.

Dill, S. 1964. *Roman Society from Nero to Marcus Aurelius.* New York.

Dodds, E. R. 1965. *Pagan and Christian in an Age of Anxiety.* New York.

Donahue, P. J. 1978. Jewish Christianity in the Letters of Ignatius of Antioch. *VC* 32: 81–93.

Dörner, F. K. ed. 1975. *Kommagene. Geschichte und Kultur einer antiken Landschaft.* (Essays by various authors collected in one volume of *Antike Welt. Zeitschrift für Archäologie und Urgeschichte.* Sondernummer 6).

Drobner, H. 1982. 15 Jahre Forschungen zu Melito von Sardes (1965–1980). Eine kritische Bibliographie. *VC* 36: 313–33.

Elliott, J. H. 1981. *A Home for the Homeless: A Sociological Exegesis of 1 Peter.* Philadelphia.

Fee, G. 1984. *1 and 2 Timothy, Titus.* GNC. San Francisco.

Feldmann, L. 1950. Jewish "Sympathizers" in Classical Literature and Inscriptions. *TAPA* 81: 200–8.

———. 1986. The Omnipresence of the God-Fearers. *BARev* 12: 58–63.

Ford, J. M. 1966. Was Montanism a Jewish Christian Heresy? *JEH* 17: 145–58.

Freeman, G. 1950. Montanism and the Pagan Cults of Phrygia. *Dominican Studies* 3: 297–316.

Frend, W. H. C. 1965. *Martyrdom and Persecution in the Early Church.* Oxford.

Froehlich, K. 1973. Montanism and Gnosis. In *The Heritage of the Early Church,* Ed. D. Neiman and M. Schatkin. OCA 195. Rome.

Gager, J. 1983. *The Origins of Anti-Semitism.* Oxford.

Gibson, E. 1978. *The "Christians for Christians" Inscriptions of Phrygia.* HTS 32. Missoula, MT.

Goldenberg, R. 1985. Review of Gager 1983. *RelSRev* 11: 335–37.

Goppelt, L. 1978. *Der erste Petrusbrief.* 8th ed. MeyerK 12/1. Göttingen.

Grant, R. M. 1946. *Second Century Christianity.* London.

———. 1966. *The Apostolic Fathers,* vol. 4. *Ignatius of Antioch.* London.

———. 1980. *Eusebius as Church Historian.* New York.

———. 1981. Charges of "Immorality" against Various Religious Groups in Antiquity. Pp. 161–70 in *Studies in Gnosticism and Hellenistic Religions,* ed. R. van den Broek and M. J. Vermaseren. Leiden.

———. 1988a. Five Apologists and Marcus Aurelius. *VC* 42: 1–17.

———. 1988b. *Greek Apologists of the Second Century.* Philadelphia.

Green, H. A. 1977. Gnosis and Gnosticism: A Study in Methodology. *Numen* 24: 95–134.

Hadas, M. 1972. *Hellenistic Culture: Fusion and Diffusion.* New York.

Hall, S. G. 1984. The Origins of Easter. *StPatr* 15 1:554–67. = TU 128. Berlin.

Hatch, E. 1882. *The Organization of the Early Christian Churches.* 2d ed. London.

Havelock, C. M. 1981. *Hellenistic Art.* 2d ed. London.

Hawkin, D. J. 1976. A Reflective Look at the Recent Debate on Orthodoxy and Heresy in Earliest Christianity. *EgT* 7: 367–78.

Hefele, C. J. 1876. *A History of the Councils of the Church.* Vol. 2 (A.D. 326–A.D. 429). Edinburgh.

Heine, R. E. 1987–1988. The Role of the Gospel of John in the Montanist Controversy. *SecondCen* 6: 1–19.

———. 1989. *The Montanist Oracles and Testimonia.* North American Patristic Society Patristic Monograph Series 14. Macon, GA.

Hengel, M. 1974. *Judaism and Hellenism.* Philadelphia.

Henrichs, A. 1970. Pagan Ritual and the Alleged Crimes of the Early Christians. Some New Evidence. Vol. 1, pp. 18–35 in *KYRIAKON: Festschrift Johannes Quasten,* Ed. P. Granfield and J. A. Jungmann. Münster.

Henry, P. 1982. Why Is Contemporary Scholarship So Enamored of Ancient Hereses? Pp. 123–26 In *Proceedings of the 8th International Conference on Patristic Studies,* Ed. E. A. Livingstone. Oxford.

Hermann, P. 1968. *Der römische Kaisereid.* Hypomnemata 20. Göttingen.

———. 1986. Sühn-und Grabinschriften aus der Katakekaumene im archäologischen Museum von Izmir, *Anzeiger der österreichischen Akademie der Wissenschaften,* Phil.-hist. Klasse 122: 248–61.

Hilgenfeld, A. 1884. *Die Ketzergeschichte des Urchristentums.* Leipzig.

Hooker, M. 1973. Were There False Teachers in Colossae? Pp. 315–31 in *Christ and Spirit in the New Testament,* Ed. B. Lindars and S. S. Smalley. Cambridge.

Horsley, H. G. R., and Barton, S. C. 1981. A Hellenistic Cult Group and the New Testament Churches. *JAC* 24:7–41.

Huber, W. 1969. *Passa und Ostern.* BZNW 35. Berlin.

Irenaeus. 1974. *Irénéé de Lyon. Contre les Hérésies Livre III.* 2 vols. Ed. A. Rousseau and L. Doutreleau. SC 211. Paris.

Jervell, J. 1984. *The Unknown Paul.* Minneapolis.

Johnson, L. T. 1987. *1 Timothy, 2 Timothy, Titus.* Knox Preaching Guides. Atlanta.

Karris, R. J. 1973. The Background and Significance of the Polemic of the Pastoral Epistles. *JBL* 92: 549–64.

Klauck, H.-J. 1981. *Hausgemeinde und Hauskirche im frühen Christentum.* SBS 103. Stuttgart.

Klawiter, F. C. 1975. The New Prophecy in Early Christianity. Ph.D. diss. Chicago.

Klijn, A. F. J., and Reinink, G. J. 1973. *Patristic Evidence for Jewish-Christian Sects.* NovTSup 36. Leiden.

Koester, H. 1971. GNOMAI DIAPHOROI: The Origin and Nature of Diversification in the History of Early Christianity. Pp. 114–57 in Robinson and Koester 1971.

Koets, P. J. 1929. *Deisidaimonia: A Contribution to the Knowledge of the Religious Terminology in Greek.* Purmerend.

Koschorke, K. 1978. *Die Polemik der Gnostiker gegen das kirchliche Christentum.* NHS 12. Leiden.

Kraabel, A. T. 1968. *Judaism in Western Asia Minor under the Roman Empire, with a Preliminary Study of the Jewish Community as Sardis, Lydia.* Diss. Harvard Divinity School.

———. 1971. Melito the Bishop and the Synagogue at Sardis: Text and Context. Pp. 77–85 in *Studies Presented to George M. A. Hanfmann,* Ed. D. G. Mitten, J. G. Pedley and J. A. Scott. Harvard University Monographs in Art and Archaeology 2. Cambridge, MA.

———. 1981. The Disappearance of the "God-Fearers." *Numen* 28: 113–26.

Kruse, H. 1934. *Studien zur offiziellen Geltung des Kaiserbildes im römischen Reiche.* Studien zur Geschichte und Kultur der Altertum 19/3. Paderborn.

Labriolle, P. C. de. 1913a. *La crise montaniste.* Paris.

———. 1913b. *Les sources de l'histoire du Montanisme.* Collectanea Friburgensia n.s. 15. Freiburg. Repr. New York, 1980.

Lake, K., and Cadbury H. 1932. *The Acts of the Apostles.* Vol. 4 in *The Beginnings of Christianity.* London.

Lane, E. 1971–78. *Corpus monumentorum religionis dei Menis (CMRDM).* 4 vols. EPRO 19. Leiden.

Lawlor, H. J., and Oulton, J. E. L. 1954. *Eusebius, Bishop of Caesarea.* 2 vols. London.

Levick, B. M. 1967. *Roman Colonies in Southern Asia Minor.* Oxford.

Lightfoot, J. B. 1913. *Saint Paul's Epistle to the Philippians.* London.

MacLennan, R. S., and Kraabel, A. T. 1986. The God-Fearers—A Literary and Theological Invention. *BARev* 12: 46–53.

MacMullen, R. 1966. *Enemies of the Roman Order.* Cambridge, MA.

———. 1981. *Paganism in the Roman Empire.* New Haven.

MacRae, G. W. 1986. Gnosticism and the Church of John's Gospel. Pp. 89–96 in *Nag Hammadi, Gnosticism and Early Christianity,* ed. C. W. Hedrick and R. Hodgson. Peabody, MA.

Magie, D. 1950. *Roman Rule in Asia Minor, To the End of the Third Century after Christ.* 2 vols. Princeton.

Malay, H. 1988. New Confession-Inscriptions. *Zeitschrift für Papyrologie und Epigraphik* 12, 147–54.

Malherbe, A. J. 1977. The Inhospitality of Diotrephes. Pp. 222–32 in *God's Christ and His People: Studies in Honour of Nils Alstrup Dahl,* ed. J. Jervell and W. Meeks. Oslo.

———. 1983. *Social Aspects of Early Christianity.* 2d ed. Philadelphia.

———. 1986. *Moral Exhortation: A Greco-Roman Sourcebook.* Library of Early Christianity. Philadelphia.

Manis, A. M. 1987. Melito of Sardis: Hermeneutic and Context. *GOTR* 32: 387–401.

Martin, R. P. 1975. *New Testament Foundations: A Guide for Christian Students.* Vol. 1. Grand Rapids.

Meeks, W. 1983. *The First Urban Christians.* New Haven.

Meer, F. van der, and Mohrmann, C. 1958. *Atlas of the Early Christian World.* London.

Meijer, P. A. 1981. IV. *Deisidaimonia,* in Philosophers, Intellectuals and Religion in Hellas. In *Faith, Hope and Worship: Aspects of Religious Mentality in the Ancient World,* ed. H. S. Versnel. Studies in Greek and Roman Religion 2. Leiden.

Mellor, R. 1975. *THEA RHOME. The Worship of the Goddess Roma in the Greek World.* Hypomnemata 42. Göttingen.

Metzger, B. 1955. Methodology in the Study of the Mystery Religions and Early Christianity. *HTR* 48: 1–20.

———. 1987. *The Canon of the New Testament.* Oxford.

Metzger, H. 1969. *Anatolia II: First Millennium B.C. to the End of the Roman Period.* Geneva.

Millar, F. 1973. The Imperial Cult and the Persecutions. In *Le Culte des Souverains dans l'Empire Romain.* Entretiens sur l'Antiquité classique 19. Geneva.

Murray, R. 1982. Jews, Hebrews and Christians: Some Needed Distinctions. *NovT* 24:194–208.

Nilsson, M. P. 1961. *Greek Folk Religion.* New York.

Noakes, K. W. 1975. Melito of Sardis and the Jews. *StPatr* 13 2: 244–49 = TU 116. Berlin.

Norris, F. W. 1976. Ignatius, Polycarp, and I Clement: Walter Bauer Reconsidered. *VC* 30: 23–44.

———. 1982. Asia Minor before Ignatius: Walter Bauer Reconsidered. *SE* 7: 365–77.

———. 1986. Melito's Motivation. *ATR* 68: 16–24.

Oliver, J. H. 1953. *The Ruling Power.* TAPhS n.s. 43/4. Philadelphia. Repr. 1980.

Pancaro, S. 1975. *The Law in the Fourth Gospel.* NovTSup 42. Leiden.

Pettazzoni, R. 1937. Confessions of Sins and the Classics. *HTR* 30: 1–14.

Petzl, G. 1988. Sünde, Strafe, Wiedergutmachung. *Zeitschrift für Papyrologie und Epigraphik* 12: 155–66.

Pleket, H. W. 1980. Review of E. Gibson. *The "Christians for Christians" Inscriptions of Phrygia* in *VC* 34: 197–98.

Poland, F. 1909. *Geschichte des griechischen Vereinswesens.* Leipzig.

Powell, D. 1975. Tertullianists and Cataphrygians. *VC* 29: 33–54.

Price, S. R. F. 1984. *Rituals and Power: The Roman imperial cult in Asia Minor.* Cambridge.

Ramsay, W. M. 1895–97. *Cities and Bishoprics of Phrygia.* 2 vols. Oxford.

Reynolds, J., and Tannenbaum, R. 1987. *Jews and God-Fearers at Aphrodisias.* Cambridge Philological Society Sup 12. Cambridge.

Richardson, C. C. 1973. A New Solution to the Quartodeciman Riddle. *JTS* 24: 74–84.

Robert, A., and Feuillet, A. 1965. *Introduction to the New Testament.* New York.

Robert, L. 1975. Une nouvelle inscription grecque de Sardes. Règlement de l'autorité perse relatif á un culte de Zeus. *CRAIBL* 306–30.

Robinson, J. M., and Koester, H. 1971. *Trajectories through Early Christianity.* Philadelphia.

Robinson, T. A. 1988. *The Bauer Thesis Examined: The Geography of Heresy in the Early Christian Church.* Lewiston, NY.

Sanders, E. P., Baumgarten, A. I., and Mendelson, A., eds. 1981. *Jewish and Christian Self-Definition.* Vol. 2, *Aspects of Judaism in the Graeco-Roman Period.* Philadelphia.

Sandmel, S. 1962. Parallelomania. *JBL* 81: 1–13.

Schepelern, W. 1929. *Der Montanismus und die phrygischen Kulte.* Trans. W. Baur. Tübingen.

Schöllgen, G. 1988. Hausgemeinden, OIKOS-Ekklesiologie und Monarchischer Episkopat. *JAC* 31: 74–90.

Schwegler, F. C. A. 1841. *Der Montanismus und die christliche Kirche des zweiten Jahrhunderts.* Tübingen.

Scott, K. 1932. The Elder and Younger Pliny on Emperor Worship. *TAPA* 63: 156–65.

Sheppard, A. R. R. 1980–81. Pagan Cults of Angels in Roman Asia Minor. *Talanta* 12–13: 77–101.

Sherwin-White, A. N. 1966. *The Letters of Pliny.* Oxford.

Skarsaune, O. 1987. *The Proof from Prophecy: A Study in Justin Martyr's Proof-Text Tradition.* NovTSup 56. Leiden.

Smallwood, E. M. 1976. *The Jews under Roman Rule, from Pompey to Diocletian.* SJLA 20. Leiden.

Sokolowski, F. 1960. Sur le culte d'angelos dans le paganisme grec et romain. *HTR* 53: 225–29.

Staats, R. 1975. Die Sonntagnachtgottesdienste der christlichen Frühzeit. *ZNW* 66: 242–63.
Steinleitner, F. 1913. *Die Beicht im Zusammenhange mit der sakralen Rechtspflege in der Antike.* Leipzig.
Stern, M. 1976–84. *Greek and Latin Authors on Jews and Judaism.* 3 vols. Jerusalem.
Strecker, G., and Kraft, R. A. 1971. Appendix 2. The Reception of the Book. In Bauer 1971.
Streeter, B. H. 1929. Lecture IV. The Church in Asia. Pp. 103–41 in *The Primitive Church: Studies with Special Reference to the Origins of the Christian Ministry.* New York.
Tabbernee, W. 1985. Early Montanism and Voluntary Martyrdom. *Colloquium* 17: 33–44.
Talbert, C. H., ed. 1986. *Perspectives on First Peter.* NABPR Special Studies Series 9. Macon, GA.
Tarn, W. W. 1952. *Hellenistic Civilization.* 3d ed. New York.
Tcherikover, V. 1970. *Hellenistic Civilization and the Jews.* New York.
Turner, H. E. W. 1954. *The Pattern of Christian Truth.* London.
Vallée, G. 1981. *A Study in Anti-Gnostic Polemics.* Studies in Christianity and Judaism 1. Waterloo, Ontario.
Vogt, J. 1962. *Zur Religiosität der Christenverfolger im römischen Reich.* SHAW, phil.-hist. kl. 1. Heidelberg.
Walzer, R. 1949. *Galen on Jews and Christians.* London.
Weinstock, S. 1962. Treueid und Kaiserkult. *Mitteilungen des Deutschen Archäologischen Instituts. Athenische Abteilung.* 77: 306–27.
White, L. M. 1987. The Delos Synagogue Revisited. Recent Fieldwork in the Graeco-Roman Diaspora. *HTR* 80: 133–60.
Wilde, R. 1949. *The Treatment of the Jews in the Greek Christian Writers of the First Three Centuries.* Catholic University of America Patristic Studies 81. Washington, D.C.
Wiles, M. F. 1982. Ignatius and the Church. *StPatr* 17 2: 750–55.
Wilken, R. L. 1971. Collegia, Philosophical Schools, and Theology. Pp. 268–91 in *The Catacombs and the Colosseum. The Roman Empire as the Setting of Primitive Christianity.* Ed. S. Benko and J. J. O'Rourke. Valley Forge, PA.
Wisse, F. W. 1971. The Nag Hammadi Library and the Heresiologists. *VC* 25: 205–23.
———. 1983. Prolegomena to the Study of the New Testament and Gnosis. Pp. 138–45 in *The New Testament and Gnosis,* ed. A. H. B. Logan and A. J. M. Wedderburn, Edinburgh.
Yamauchi, E. M. 1981. Jewish Gnosticism? The Prologue of John, Mandaean Parallels, and the Trimorphic Protennoia. Pp. in *Studies in Gnosticism and Hellenistic Religions,* Ed. R. van den Broek and M. J. Vermaseren. EPRO 91. Leiden.
———. 1983. *Pre-Christian Gnosticism: A Survey of the Proposed Evidences.* 2d ed. Grand Rapids.
Zahn, T. 1900. I. Apostel und Apostelschüler in der Provinz Asien. *Forschungen zur Geschichte des neutestamentlichen Kanons und der altkirchlichen Literatur.* Pt. 6:3–224. Leipzig.

RICHARD E. OSTER, JR.

CHRISTIANITY IN EGYPT

This article is limited to a discussion of the development of Christianity in Egypt to the end of the 2d century, focusing upon the period before the middle of the 2d century.

A. Eusebius on Christian Origins in Egypt
  1. Eusebius' Account
  2. Eusebius' Sources
B. The Mark Legend
C. Miscellaneous Traditions and Allusions
D. Early Alexandrian Christian Literature
  1. Noncanonical Gospels
  2. Miscellaneous Nongnostic Writings
  3. Gnostic Writings
E. Christian Origins in Egypt: Two Theories
  1. Originally "Heretical": Walter Bauer
  2. Originally Jewish: C. H. Roberts
F. Summary and Conclusions

A. Eusebius on Christian Origins in Egypt

The earliest historical treatment of Christianity in Egypt of any consequence is that of Eusebius of Caesarea in his *Ecclesiastical History* (first edition ca. 311 C.E.). To be sure, Eusebius does not concentrate in any way on Egypt; instead he intersperses his discussion of the developments in Egypt with his discussion of events, persons, etc., elsewhere. Even so, one can string together Eusebius' isolated reports so as to get a running account of his version of the origins and development of Christianity in Egypt. That account, tendentious as it is, can be condensed and paraphrased as follows (ending at the beginning of the 3d century):

1. Eusebius' Account. Mark, after recording in his gospel Peter's teaching in Rome (2.15), was sent to Egypt to proclaim this gospel and was "the first to establish churches in Alexandria itself" (2.16; trans. Lake 1926: 145). The ascetic and philosophical lifestyle of Mark's converts is described at length by the Jewish philosopher Philo, who is also reported to have visited Peter in Rome in the days of Claudius (2.16.1–17.1). Philo refers to the Alexandrian Christians as "Therapeutae" (2.17.3–24; cf. Philo *Vit. Cont.*). It is clear from his description that Philo "welcomed, reverenced, and recognized the divine mission of the apostolic men of his day, who were, it appears, of Hebrew origin, and thus still preserved most of the ancient customs in a strictly Jewish manner" (2.17.2).

"In the eighth year of the reign of Nero (62 C.E.) Annianus was the first after Mark the Evangelist to receive charge of the diocese of Alexandria" (2.24). The bishops who succeeded Annianus were Abilius (85–97/98), Cerdo (98–109), Primus (109–20), Justus (120–31), Eumenes (131–44), Mark (144–54), Celadion (154–68), Agrippinus (168–80), Julian (180–89), Demetrius (189–232; Eusebius 3.14, 21; 4.1, 4, 5, 11, 19; 5.9, 22; 5.26). (There are some minor discrepancies in the datings of some of these bishops between Eusebius' *Ecclesiastical History* and his earlier *Chronicle.* The dates are established with reference to regnal years of the emperors.)

During the eighteenth year of Emperor Trajan (115 C.E.), "the tragedy of the Jews was reaching the climax of successive woes." A rebellion broke out in Alexandria and in the rest of Egypt and Cyrene, bringing great devastation to the Jews there (4.2).

"Like brilliant lamps churches were now [in the time of Hadrian, 117–38 C.E.] shining throughout the world," but the devil was also "turn[ing] his devices against the church" by fomenting heresies. From the teachings of Menander (cf. 3.26) there developed in Antioch the sect of Saturninus, and in Alexandria that of Basilides. Basilides' mythology was met with rational refutations on the orthodox side in Alexandria, of which a most powerful example was that of Agrippa Castor (4.7.1–8).

Carpocrates, a contemporary of Basilides, was father of the so-called "Gnostic" heresy. The Carpocratians engaged in shocking obscenities, and it is on their account that calumnies have been spread about Christians among the unbelievers (4.7.9–11).

Valentinus, the founder of a special heresy, came to Rome in the time of Bishop Hyginus (138–41). (Eusebius does not say where Valentinus came from, but he was presumably not unaware of his prior activity in Alexandria.)

In the days of Emperor Commodus (180–92) and Bishop Julian (180–89), the famous Pantaenus was a leader among the Alexandrian faithful in the school of sacred doctrine that had existed there from ancient times. Pantaenus, formerly trained in Stoic philosophy, had gone on a missionary journey as far as India. There he found a copy of the gospel of Matthew in Hebrew, left among the Indians by Bartholomew. Pantaenus was head of the school in Alexandria until his death (5.10).

The famous Clement was a student of Pantaenus (5.11), and succeeded him as head of the school, serving in that capacity into the reign of Emperor Severus (193–211; 6.6). Another student of Pantaenus' was Alexander, who later became Bishop of Jerusalem and was involved in the ordination of Origen to the priesthood (6.8.4, 7; 11.1–2; 14.9). Among Clement's pupils were Origen (6.6) and the aforementioned Alexander, also a student of Origen's (6.14.9). Origen became head of the catechetical school at the age of eighteen (in 204), during a time of persecution (6.3.3).

During the Easter controversy many conferences of bishops were held in various places, including one in Palestine over which Bishop Theophilus of Caesarea and Bishop Narcissus of Jerusalem presided. A letter was formulated in the conference defending the view that Easter should be celebrated only on a Sunday (5.23). In that letter, meant to be read in all the churches, it was reported that the Alexandrian church also celebrated on the same day as the Palestinians, and that letters had been exchanged between Alexandria and the Palestinian churches on the question (5.25).

The persecution of the Church under Severus (203 C.E.) was especially severe in Alexandria, where many martyrdoms took place. "God's champions" were brought there from Egypt and the whole Thebaid for torture and death. Among the martyrs of that persecution was Leonides, father of Origen (6.1).

2. Eusebius' Sources. Where did Eusebius get his information, and how reliable is it? We shall for now skip over the Mark legend (see below). Eusebius' equation of the Jewish Therapeutae with the earliest Alexandrian Christians, and the story of Philo's visit with Peter in Rome, could have been based on his own reading of Philo and/or on a local Alexandrian tradition. In either case there is no real substance to this account.

Eusebius' information on the early bishops of Alexandria is based on a list of Alexandrian bishops probably taken from the lost *Chronographies* of Julius Africanus (Harnack 1897: 123–40). Those named between Mark and Demetrius are mere ciphers; no information is related about them, for none was available to Eusebius. Demetrius (189–232) is therefore the first Alexandrian bishop of whom anything concrete is known. Julius Africanus had visited Alexandria (6.31.2) and presumably got his list of Alexandrian bishops during that visit, either from Demetrius or his successor Heraclas (232–247/48). The original source of the list is unknown, and nothing can be ascertained as to its historicity.

While Eusebius has a good deal of information about Bishop Demetrius, particularly on his stormy relationship with Origen, Eusebius says nothing of the pivotal role apparently played by Demetrius in the development of the Egyptian hierarchy. An interesting detail is provided in a much later source. Eutychius, a Melchite patriarch of Alexandria who wrote in Arabic in the 10th century, reports in his *Annals* that until the time of Demetrius there was no other bishop in Egypt than the one in Alexandria. Demetrius appointed three bishops, and his successor Heraclas (232–247/48) appointed twenty more (*P.G.* 111: 982; cf. Kemp 1955: 138).

Eusebius' account of the Jewish revolt under Trajan (115–17) seems to be based on solid sources. The "Greek authors" he mentions (4.2.5) are now unknown (but cf. Cassius Dio 68.32 and the commentary in Stern 1980: 385–89). The virtual annihilation of the Jewish communities in Alexandria and elsewhere in Egypt must have had a profound effect on the development of Christianity there, but we have no knowledge of what role, if any, was played in the events by Christians, Jewish or gentile.

Eusebius names his sources for his discussion of the heretics: Agrippa Castor for Basilides (4.7.6), Irenaeus for Carpocrates (4.7.8; cf. *haer.* 1.25) and Valentinus (4.10.1; cf. *haer.* 3.4.3). We know nothing more of Agrippa Castor's refutation of Basilides than what is reported by Eusebius, nor do we know when it was written.

It should be noted that Eusebius had at his disposal little reliable information on the Alexandrian church for the period before ca. 180, when Pantaenus was flourishing as head of the Christian school (5.10; cf. 5.9). Of the persons named in the earlier period, it is only the aforementioned heretics concerning which we have any solid information. For the time from Pantaenus on, Eusebius had at his disposal the writings of Clement, Origen, and other Alexandrian churchmen; other sources may have come from the libraries of Caesarea and Jerusalem, such as the letters of the former Alexandrian, Bishop Alexander of Jerusalem, and the letter from the Palestinian churches on the question of Easter.

It is also to be noted that, in his discussion of people and events in Egypt, Eusebius deals exclusively with Alexandria until he comes to the persecution under Severus (203), when suddenly Christian martyrs are named whose home territory includes "Egypt and the whole Thebaid" (4.1.1). That Christianity had expanded as far as Upper Egypt by the end of the 2d century is likely. Unfortunately Eusebius is not able to tell us the story of that expansion. (On the expansion of Christianity in Egypt up to 325 C.E., see Harnack 1924a: 705–29).

B. The Mark Legend

Until the publication of the fragmentary letter to Theodore by Clement of Alexandria (Smith 1973), Eusebius was our earliest extant source for the tradition that connects

Mark with the early history of the Alexandrian church. According to Clement's letter, whose authenticity is widely but not unanimously accepted, Mark came to Alexandria after the martyrdom of Peter. There he expanded the gospel that he had written earlier, during his sojourn with Peter in Rome, producing a "more spiritual gospel" for use in the Alexandrian church (the *Secret Gospel of Mark*). Unfortunately the Carpocratian heretics eventually acquired this gospel and falsified it for their own purposes (text and translation in Smith 1973: 446–52).

Clement's letter says nothing of Mark's role as founder of the Alexandrian church. Indeed, it implies that the church there was already in existence when Mark arrived from Rome after Peter's death. Nothing is said of any earlier sojourn of Mark in Alexandria, though the wording of the fragment does not exclude that possibility. Eusebius, in his *Chronicle,* dated Mark's arrival in Alexandria to the third year of Claudius, i.e. 43 C.E. (Jerome's Latin version, Helm 1956: 179). Did Mark make more than one visit to Alexandria? (cf. Pearson 1986a: 139). In any case, the Mark legend as reflected in Eusebius, who probably got it from Julius Africanus, goes back at least to the 2d century, to the time of Demetrius or earlier.

The Mark legend is filled out in the *Acts of Mark* (*Passio,* April 25). In the *Acts,* which is preserved in two Greek recensions (see *P.G.* 115, 164–69; *Acta Sanctorum* 12: April, 3:xxxviii–xl) and several versions (for an English translation of the Ethiopic version see Haile 1981: 117–34), Mark's first convert was a cobbler named Ananias (Annianus), whom he eventually ordained as bishop. Three presbyters were also ordained by Mark: Milius, Sabinus, and Cerdo (cf. the episcopal succession list: Annianus, Abilius, Cerdo, Primus). According to the *Acts,* the first church in Alexandria was located in a place called Boukolou (later associated with Arius), where Mark was buried following his martyrdom. The *Acts,* which goes back to the 4th century, preserves some local Alexandrian traditions, but the material is essentially legendary (for discussion see Pearson 1986a: 140–44). Whether or not Mark's association with the Alexandrian church is a historical fact remains an open question (cf. Smith 1973: 279–81). The exact nature of that association, if it is a fact, is impossible to ascertain.

C. Miscellaneous Traditions and Allusions

The New Testament provides few hints of a Christian mission to Egypt. One does find references in the book of Acts to persons from "Egypt and the parts of Libya belonging to Cyrene" in the Pentecost narrative (Acts 2:10), and a Jerusalem synagogue of Alexandrians whose members disputed with Stephen (Acts 6:9). There is also, more importantly, the description of Apollos: "A Jew . . . a native of Alexandria . . . an eloquent man, powerfully trained in the scriptures" (Acts 18:24). According to the Western text, Apollos "had been instructed in the word in his home country." Something of the nature of Apollos' teaching can probably be extrapolated from the apostle Paul's comments in the early chapters of 1 Corinthians (Pearson 1983: 81–83; 1986b: 215).

Mark's cousin Barnabas (Col 4:10) is associated with the earliest history of the Alexandrian church in the Pseudo-Clementine literature. In the first *Homily* the young Clement, newly arrived from Rome, is instructed in the Christian faith in Alexandria by a Hebrew from Judea named Barnabas (*Hom.* 1.8.3–15.9). It is possible that this story of Barnabas' preaching in Alexandria is somehow related to the diffusion of the *Epistle of Barnabas,* which is probably of Alexandrian origin (Pearson 1986a: 136–37; cf. Trevijano 1975).

A well-known document bearing upon Judaism in 1st-century Alexandria, Emperor Claudius' letter to the Alexandrians (*PLond.* 1912, dated 10 Nov. 41 C.E.), has sometimes been thought to allude to the coming of Jewish Christian missionaries to Alexandria. In his letter, Claudius prohibits the Alexandrian Jews from inviting into Alexandria "Jews coming from Syria or Egypt." If such Jews included Jewish Christians from Palestine, Claudius' letter would constitute "the first allusion to Christianity in history" (Reinach 1924). However, most scholars reject such an interpretation of the letter (Tcherikover, Fuks, and Stern 1960: 36–55; cf. Pearson 1986a: 134–35).

D. Early Alexandrian Christian Literature

The best possibility for understanding the nature of early Egyptian Christianity in its various manifestations is to examine the literature produced by Christians there. Unfortunately the evidence is ambiguous, for it is not easy to determine the provenience of early Christian writings, and scholarly opinion is in many cases divided. (For more detailed treatments, see the articles on these early Christian writings.)

1. Noncanonical Gospels. The early Christian writings for which an Egyptian (Alexandrian) provenience can be established with relative certainty are noncanonical gospels: the *Gospel of the Hebrews,* the *Gospel of the Egyptians,* and the *Secret Gospel of Mark.* None of these gospels is fully extant; they are known only through quotations by Clement of Alexandria and other writers within the Egyptian church. Another gospel, represented by Papyrus Egerton 2 (see Koester 1982: 181–83; 222), could have been brought into Egypt from somewhere else, as is the case with numerous other canonical and noncanonical writings (e.g. the *Gospel of Thomas*).

The three Alexandrian gospels mentioned represent various traditions and could be taken to reflect the existence, already at the end of the 1st century, of different Christian groups. The *Gospel of the Hebrews* has a strong Semitic flavor and, as its name suggests, circulated among the Jewish Christians (Christian Jews) for whom the symbolic authority of James, brother of Jesus, was an important feature. It contained both narrative and sayings material, the latter representing sayings found also in the *Gospel of Thomas* (cf. Hennecke and Schneemelcher 1963: 158–65; Koester 1982: 223–24).

The *Gospel of the Egyptians* (not the writing with the same title in the Nag Hammadi corpus; cf. Hennecke and Schneemelcher 1963: 166–78), of which only sayings material is preserved, shows a strong encratic flavor and, like the *Gospel of the Hebrews,* contains tradition that overlaps with the *Gospel of Thomas* (cf. Koester 1982: 230). Its name indicates that it circulated among (Greek-speaking) native Egyptians, and it was probably first compiled for Christians living in the Rhakotis district of Alexandria (Pearson 1986a: 150).

Of the *Secret Gospel of Mark,* one complete pericope is preserved, a story about a young man raised from the dead by Jesus. According to Clement's letter, *Secret Mark* was intended to be read "only to those who are being initiated into the great mysteries" (Smith 1973: 446). This "more spiritual gospel" was therefore intended to be understood as a cultic allegory, symbolically associated with the sacramental life of the Christian community (cf. Smith 1973: 167–85). Presupposed in Clement's letter is the public use in Alexandria of canonical Mark, as well as a later heretical expansion of *Secret Mark* by the Carpocratians. Whether or not Clement's understanding of the development of these various "Markan" gospels is historically accurate is still under debate (see e.g. Schenke 1984).

2. Miscellaneous Nongnostic Writings. It should be stressed that, at the same time as the aforementioned gospels were being used in Alexandria, other literature, including literature later canonized in the Catholic church, was being introduced to the Christians in Alexandria. By the time that the heretics mentioned by Eusebius were flourishing in Alexandria during the time of Hadrian (see above), a substantial number of Christian writings were already in use there. The heretics themselves freely used Christian writings later accepted in the Catholic church as canonical. For example, the extant fragments of Valentinus, which presumably stem from his Alexandrian period, reflect not only the use of gnostic mythological writings but also of the epistles of Paul and the gospel of Matthew (cf. Layton 1987: 229–49). Basilides knew and used the epistles of Paul and, perhaps, 1 Peter (fragments in Layton 1987: 427–44).

Returning now to other early Christian writings composed in Egypt, at least two would seem to qualify as coming from the time before (or at least during) the *floruit* of the aforementioned heretics: the *Kerygma of Peter* and the *Epistle of Barnabas.* The former is an apologetic work, pseudonymously attributed to the apostle Peter, which characterizes the people of the "New Covenant" (Christians) as a "third race" (cf. Hennecke and Schneemelcher 1964: 94–102). The latter is charged with apocalyptic fervor and devoted to a specifically Christian reinterpretation of older Jewish exegetical and ethical traditions (Kraft 1965: cf. Pearson 1986b: 211–14).

Other (nongnostic) Christian writings probably composed in Egypt during the first half of the 2d century are *2 Clement* (Koester 1982: 233–36), the *Apocalypse of Peter* (not the writing with the same title in the Nag Hammadi corpus), and the *Protevangel of James.* It is also possible that the canonical epistles of Jude and 2 Peter were written in Egypt (Gunther 1984). It is quite probable, too, that Christian redactions of Jewish pseudepigrapha were already being made in Egypt during this period, e.g. the *Ascension of Isaiah,* the *Testaments of the Twelve Patriarchs,* the *Sibylline Oracles,* the *Apocalypse of Elijah,* and the (lost) book of *Jannes and Jambres.* Of the Christian literature now lost to us, I would mention here especially the *Traditions* (or *Gospel*) *of Matthias* (Hennecke and Schneemelcher 1963: 308–13) and the letter of Paul to the Alexandrians named in the Muratorian canon list (Hennecke and Schneemelcher 1963: 44; cf. 1964: 91). The latter is said to have been forged by the Marcionites, and may have been used in the early states of a Marcionite mission to Alexandria (Harnack 1960: 134*). *Pace* Koester (1982: 236–38) and others, I would regard the *Epistula Apostolorum* as a product of Asia Minor rather than Egypt (cf. Pearson 1986a: 149).

Two writings probably composed in Egypt shortly after the middle of the 2d century should also be mentioned here: the *Sentences of Sextus* and the *Teachings of Silvanus,* two of the nongnostic tractates included among the Coptic papyri discovered near Nag Hammadi in Upper Egypt in 1945. The *Sentences of Sextus* (NHC XII,*1*), a collection of gnomic sayings, is strongly influenced by Greek ethical philosophy and is marked by a mild asceticism (cf. Edwards and Wild 1981). The *Teachings of Silvanus* (NHC VII,*4*) is a book of Christian wisdom akin to the Wisdom of Solomon both in form and content. Explicitly antignostic, it is an important link in the chain of tradition that runs from Philo, and probably Apollos, to the great Alexandrian teachers Clement and Origen (cf. Pearson 1986b: 211–15).

3. Gnostic Writings. Turning now to the writings of the Gnostics, we now have a whole "library" of gnostic works discovered in Egypt, the NAG HAMMADI CODICES. The problem we confront in this case, however, is how to determine which of the tractates, all of them composed originally in Greek, are of Egyptian provenience, and when they were written. Can any of the Nag Hammadi writings be dated to the time of Basilides and Valentinus or before? Were they produced in Egypt, or brought there from somewhere else?

The *Gospel of Truth* (NHC I,*3*; IXX,*2*) is the only Nag Hammadi tractate which can safely be attributed to one of the great heresiarchs, viz. Valentinus (Layton 1987: 250–64). This marvelous work of Christian mysticism could either have been written in Alexandria, or in Rome after Valentinus' departure from Egypt.

Valentinus, as a Christian "reformer" of the gnostic religion, certainly based his mythology on a previously existing gnostic myth (cf. Layton 1987: 5, 217–27). There can hardly be any doubt that the myth found in the *Apocryphon of John* comes closest of any of the Nag Hammadi writings to the one used and modified by Valentinus and his disciples. The same myth is also partially represented in Irenaeus, *haer.* 1.29. However, that is not to say that Valentinus, or even Irenaeus, knew and used the *Apocryphon of John,* which in its extant form is a composite document probably later than Valentinus (cf. Pearson 1986c: 19–25). The myth in question, therefore, is a common source used by the author of the *Apocryphon of John* and by Valentinus.

Where did that myth originate, Egypt or Syria? Syria is often regarded as the birthplace of Gnosticism, and some scholars even locate some of the most important Nag Hammadi texts there, including the *Apocryphon of John* itself (e.g. Koester 1982: 209–14; the others named by him are *Apocalypse of Adam* [V,*5*], *Hypostasis of the Archons* [II,*4*], *First Apocalypse of James* [V,*3*], and *Second Apocalypse of James* [V,*4*]). It should be noted that the system of Saturninus summarized by the heresiologists (Iren. *haer.* 1.24.1–2) evidently presupposes the same myth as that of the *Apocryphon of John* (Layton 1987: 159–62). Saturninus was active in Syrian Antioch. It is therefore likely that the myth used by Valentinus was brought to Egypt from Syria early in the 2d century, if not before.

However, there is also good reason to posit an Alexandrian origin for some of the early Nag Hammadi texts, both Christian and non-Christian. The most important one in the latter category is *Eugnostos the Blessed* (III,*3*; V,*1*), a theological treatise of Jewish gnostic origin. Its version of the Anthropos-Sophia myth probably contributed to Valentinus' doctrine of the Pleroma (van den Broek 1986: 195–201). The Christianized expansion of *Eugnostos,* the *Sophia of Jesus Christ* (III,*4*; BG,*3*), was also, no doubt, produced in Egypt. Another Christian text, the *Apocryphon of James* (I,*2*), preserving valuable gospel tradition, reflects the kind of Jewish Christianity that is also found in the *Gospel of the Hebrews* (Koester 1982: 224–25). Its relationship to Gnosticism is difficult to ascertain, though it is sometimes thought to reflect some Valentinian influence (cf. Williams 1985).

The origins of Egyptian Gnosticism are just as obscure as the origins of Egyptian Christianity, and this is not the place to discuss Gnosticism and the Nag Hammadi texts. (See GNOSTICISM; NAG HAMMADI [Codices].) Suffice it to say here that the Nag Hammadi corpus does not provide us with much information on the origins either of Egyptian Christianity in general or of Egyptian Gnosticism. It does serve as evidence of the proliferation of Gnosticism in Egypt in the 2d century and its persistence into the 4th century in upper Egypt. It is clear from such evidence that definite borderlines between "orthodoxy" and "heresy" were established in Egypt rather late (cf. Koester 1982: 239).

The last observation implies, of course, that no clear borderlines between "orthodoxy" and "heresy" existed in the early period either. The basic question at issue here is the relative strength and antiquity in Egyptian Christianity of those varieties of the Christian religion that later came to be identified as "heretical" or "orthodox." Very different answers have been put forward by scholars in attempting to answer this question.

E. Christian Origins in Egypt: Two Theories

1. Originally "Heretical": Walter Bauer. In his pioneering work, *Orthodoxy and Heresy in Earliest Christianity* (1934, ET 1971), Walter Bauer subjected to vigorous critical scrutiny the ancient and still common view that "orthodoxy" always preceded "heresy" in the history of the church, and was inevitably invincible in theological struggles over belief and practice as they broke out in the church. The method Bauer used was to examine the available evidence for the development of Christianity in various geographical areas. What he found was that "heresies," as later defined in ecclesiastical circles, were often the original and only forms of Christianity in many areas. The "orthodoxy" that eventually came to prevail in such areas did so under the later influence of the Roman ecclesiastical establishment.

While Bauer's views have often been criticized, particularly with regard to certain geographical areas, it is fair to say that they have gained most acceptance in the case of Egypt. Bauer starts with the assumption that the very absence of solid evidence for the earliest history of Egyptian Christianity in ecclesiastical sources is itself suggestive. Evidence there must surely have been. The question is: "What reason could [churchmen] have had for being silent about the origins of Christianity in such an important center as Alexandria if there had been something favorable to report?" (Bauer 1971: 45). Answer: The earliest form of Christianity in Egypt was not "orthodox" but "heretical," specifically "gnostic." The only representatives of early Alexandrian Christianity of which we have any solid knowledge are all gnostic heretics: Basilides and his son Isidore, Carpocrates, and Valentinus (48).

According to Bauer, the ten bishops enumerated by Eusebius after Mark "are and remain for us a mere echo and a puff of smoke" (1971: 45). As for Mark, it was probably the Roman church that lent to orthodox Alexandria the figure of Peter's "interpreter" as a church founder and an apostolic initiator of a succession of bishops (60, 117). The earliest real glimpse that we get of "ecclesiastical" Christianity in Alexandria is with Demetrius, under whose episcopal rule (189–232) an "orthodox" form of Christianity first developed (53–54), and to whom the succession list of Alexandrian bishops must be attributed (55).

In order for him to maintain his theory of the heretical ("gnostic") origins of Egyptian Christianity, Bauer must assess the earliest Egyptian Christian literature consistently with that theory. Thus, the *Gospel of the Hebrews* and the *Gospel of the Egyptians* both become products of "movements resting on syncretistic-gnostic foundations" (1971: 50–53). The *Epistle of Barnabas,* given to "a thoroughly grotesque allegorization," is essentially "gnostic" (47), with a Christology that "seems docetic" (48). These characterizations, when compared with the evidence (the texts themselves!), are enough to cast a large shadow of doubt over Bauer's entire reconstruction of early Egyptian Christianity. (Cf. discussion of these and other texts above.)

2. Originally Jewish: C. H. Roberts. A different approach is taken by C. H. Roberts in his important study, *Manuscript, Society, and Belief in Early Christian Egypt* (1979). Roberts, an eminent papyrologist, bases his study on evidence not taken into account by Bauer, viz. early Christian papyri. Since documentary papyri provide no useful evidence before the 3d century (on the 3d and 4th century documents see Judge and Pickering 1977), Roberts concentrates his attention on the earliest Christian literary papyri.

Roberts' survey of the extant Christian manuscripts discovered in Egypt that date to the 2d century (there are none earlier) yields very significant results. Ten "biblical" manuscripts are listed: seven Old Testament (Genesis, Exodus, Numbers, Deuteronomy, Psalms) and three New Testament (Matthew, Luke, John, Titus). Four "nonbiblical" manuscripts are listed: the Egerton gospel, *The Shepherd of Hermas,* P. Oxy. 1 = *Gospel of Thomas* (possibly early 3d century), and Irenaeus, *Adversus Haereses* (Roberts 1979: 12–14; all are codices, except *Hermas* and Irenaeus). Manuscript finds are, of course, haphazard, but it is worth noting that this evidence provides no support whatsoever for Bauer's view that Gnosticism was the earliest and, for a long time, most dominant form of Christianity in Egypt.

Roberts' most important contribution is his discussion of *nomina sacra* in early Christian manuscripts, i.e abbreviations, with superlineation, of "sacred" words such as *Iesous, Christos, kyrios, theos,* and others (fifteen in all, 1979: 26–27). The starting point for the development of *nomina sacra,* a Christian scribal invention, is the name *Iesous.* Early forms of the *nomen sacrum* are *IE* (a suspended form), and *IES* and *IS* (contracted forms, the latter becoming standard). The form IE occurs in the Egerton gospel and is presupposed in the *Ep. Barn.* 9.8 (35–37). Roberts argues persuasively that the use of *nomina sacra* in Christian manuscripts originated in the Jerusalem church (41–46). The choice of "sacred" words to be specially treated in manuscripts as *nomina sacra* reflects a primitive Jewish Christian theology such as is found in early Alexandrian Christian literature. The conclusions to be drawn from this are that Jerusalem is the source of the earliest Egyptian Christianity, a Christianity which was essentially Jewish. The earliest Christians in Egypt would have been an integral part of the Jewish community of Alexandria (49–73).

Roberts points to the Jewish war of 115–17 C.E. as a watershed in the history of Egyptian Christianity. After 117, "there is good reason to think that the Egyptian Church was assisted from without and looked less to Jerusalem and Syria, as it probably had earlier, and more and more to Rome" (1979: 59). Aside from the regular contacts existing in all areas of life between Rome and Alexandria, Roman Christianity itself, which then was "strongly Jewish," can be expected to have exerted its influence. This observation is reinforced by the 2d-century Fayum fragment of the *Shepherd of Hermas* and the 2d-century fragment of Irenaeus' *Adversus Haereses* found at Oxyrhynchus (59,53).

Roberts has abandoned his earlier view that the adoption of the papyrus codex for Christian literature in place of the scroll was associated with the production and propagation of the gospel of Mark, a view which also took into account the tradition of the founding of the Alexandrian church by Mark (Roberts 1954: 187–89; cf. 1979: 59 n.5; Roberts and Skeat 1983: 54–57). He now looks to Jerusalem or Antioch as the place where the codex was adopted for Christian literature. This development undoubtedly occurred already in the 1st century, and would have spread early to Egypt, where our evidence begins with the 2nd century examples cited. Indeed, the Christian codex and the *nomina sacra* should probably be considered as related developments (Roberts and Skeat 1983: 57–67).

F. Summary and Conclusions

How, then, do we finally assess the evidence for the origins and development of Christianity in Egypt? As we have seen, it is scanty and ambiguous, and has been subjected to diametrically opposed interpretations.

Roberts is undoubtedly correct in stressing the Palestinian and Jewish origins of Christianity in Egypt, something that was intuitively affirmed by Eusebius (2.17.2, above). The earliest Christianity in Egypt was certainly not "gnostic," as Bauer argues. Nor is it useful to apply to earliest Christianity, whether in Egypt or elsewhere, the categories "heresy" and "orthodoxy." Something of the flavor of Jewish Christianity in Alexandria can be extrapolated from *Barnabas* and the *Gospel of the Hebrews*. The writings of Philo were probably utilized early by philosophically oriented Christians, and resulted in the kind of Christianity that is later exemplified by the *Teachings of Silvanus* and Clement of Alexandria. Probably already in the 1st century early Jewish forms of Gnosticism were being adapted to the Christian message by some Alexandrian Christians.

The war of 115–17 resulted in the final break of Christianity from the larger Jewish matrix. From that time on, Gnosticism became a powerful influence in Alexandrian Christianity, as is illustrated especially by the activities of Valentinus and Basilides, who were quite willing to appropriate to their own purposes the Christian books used by nongnostic Christians. It is to be stressed that the very structure of Valentinian and Basilidian ecclesiology presumes the numerical superiority of ordinary, nongnostic Christians. Even so, Gnosticism gained a very strong foothold in Alexandrian Christianity during the 2d century, and certainly dominated its intellectual life until the time of Pantaenus.

Bauer is correct in stressing the pivotal role played by Demetrius in the development of an orthodox ecclesiastical establishment. Properly called "the Second Founder of the church of Alexandria" (Telfer 1952: 2), he was clearly the first "monarchical" bishop of Alexandria. However, it is doubtful that the impetus for this development came from Rome, for the monarchical episcopacy was as late in coming to Rome (with Victor, bishop 189–99) as it was in coming to Egypt (cf. La Piana 1925). The writings of the Gallican bishop Irenaeus (himself a native of Asia Minor) would certainly have served Demetrius well in the promotion of orthodoxy (the Oxyrhynchus fragment of Irenaeus already cited dates to the time of Demetrius), and were probably transmitted to Alexandria via Rome. But there must presumably have been sufficient "orthodoxy" in Alexandria before Demetrius for Irenaeus, writing about 180, to include the church in Egypt among the churches scattered throughout the world that preserve the catholic faith with "one heart and one soul" (*haer.* 1.10.2).

It is probable that the catechetical school of Alexandria played a large role in the development of a theological orthodoxy, at least from the time of Pantaenus. Roberts suggests that it was Pantaenus who purged the school of the influence of the Gnostics (1979: 54). It was, of course, under Demetrius that the school came under the control of the bishop.

Finally, the expansion of Christianity in Egypt outside of Alexandria, implicit in Eusebius' report of the Severan persecution (6.1.1, above), is documented by the 2d-century manuscript evidence already cited. The places where the manuscripts have turned up include, in addition to Oxyrhynchus and the Fayum, Qarara (Hipponon), Antinoopolis, and Coptos in Upper Egypt (in several cases the provenance is unknown; cf. van Haelst 1976: nos. 462, 33, 12, 52, 179, 224, 151, 336 + 403, 534, 372, 586, 657, 594, 671; and Roberts 1979: 13–14). The expansion thus documented applies only to Greek-speaking Christianity. The expansion of Christianity among Egyptian-speaking natives is documented from the 3d century on, though it can be presumed to have begun earlier. The development of a native Egyptian Christianity is coterminous with the development of the Coptic language, the latest form of the tongue of the ancient Pharaohs.

Bibliography

Bauer, W. 1934. *Rechtgläubigkeit und Ketzerei im ältesten Christentum.* BHT 10. Tübingen.

———. 1971. *Orthodoxy and Heresy in Earliest Christianity.* Trans. R. Kraft et al. Philadelphia.

Broek, R. van den. 1986. Jewish and Platonic Speculations in Early Alexandrian Theology: Eugnostos, Philo, Valentinus, and Origen. Pp. 190–203 in *The Roots of Egyptian Christianity,* ed. B. A. Pearson and J. E. Goehring. Studies in Antiquity and Christianity, 1. Philadelphia.

Edwards, R. A., and Wild, R. A. 1981. *The Sentences of Sextus.* Texts and Translations 22: Early Christian Literature Series 5. Chicago, CA.

Gunther, J. J. 1984. The Alexandrian Epistle of Jude. *NTS* 30: 549–62.

Haelst, J. van. 1976. *Catalogue des papyrus littéraires juifs et chrétiens.* Paris.

Haile, G. 1981. A New Ethiopic Version of the Acts of St. Mark. *AnBoll* 99:117–34.

Harnack, A. von. 1897. *Geschichte der altchristlichen Literatur.* Vol. 2/1. Leipzig.

———. 1924a. *Die Mission und Ausbreitung des Christentums in den ersten drei Jahrhunderten.* Vol. 2. Leipzig.

———. 1924b. *Marcion: Das Evangelium vom fremden Gott.* 2d ed. Leipzig. Repr. Darmstadt, 1960.

Helm, R. 1956. *Die Chronik des Hieronymus.* In *Eusebius Werke,* Vol. 7:7. GCS 47. Berlin.

Hennecke, E., and Schneemelcher, W. 1963–64. *New Testament Apocrypha.* Trans. R. McL. Wilson. 2 Vols. Philadelphia.

Judge, E. R., and Pickering, S. R. 1977. Papyrus Documentation of Church and Community in Egypt to the Mid-fourth Century. *JAC* 20:47–71.

Kemp, E. 1955. Bishops and Presbyters at Alexandria. *JEH* 6:124–42.

Koester, H. 1982. *Introduction to the New Testament.* Vol. 2 of *History and Literature of Early Christianity.* Berlin and New York.

Kraft, R. A. 1965. *Barnabas and Didache.* Vol. 3 of The Apostolic Fathers, ed. R. M. Grant. Toronto.

Lake, K. 1926–32. *Eusebius: The Ecclesiastical History.* 2 vols. The Loeb Classical Library. Cambridge, MA.

La Piana, G. 1925. The Roman Church at the End of the Second Century. *HTR* 18: 201–77.

Layton, B. 1987. *The Gnostic Scriptures.* Garden City, NY.

Pearson, B. A. 1983. Philo, Gnosis and the New Testament. Pp. 73–89 in *The New Testament and Gnosis,* ed. A. H. B. Logan and A. J. M. Wedderburn. Edinburgh.

———. 1986a. Earliest Christianity in Egypt: Some Observations. Pp. 132–59 in *The Roots of Egyptian Christianity,* ed. B. A. Pearson and J. E. Goehring. Studies in Antiquity and Christianity, 1. Philadelphia.

———. 1986b. Christians and Jews in First-Century Alexandria. *HTR* 79: 206–16.

———. 1986c. The Problem of "Jewish Gnostic" Literature. Pp. 15–35 in *Nag Hammadi, Gnosticism, and Early Christianity,* ed. C. W. Hedrick and R. Hodgson. Peabody.

Reinach, S. 1924. La première allusion au christianisme dans l'histoire. *RHR* 90: 108–22.

Roberts, C. H. 1954. *The Codex.* Proceedings of the British Academy, 40: 169–204. London.

———. 1979. *Manuscript, Society and Belief in Early Christian Egypt.* London.

Roberts, C. H., and Skeat, T. C. 1983. *The Birth of the Codex.* London.

Schenke, H.-M. 1984. The Mystery of the Gospel of Mark. *SecondCent* 4: 65–82.

Smith, M. 1973. *Clement of Alexandria and a Secret Gospel of Mark.* Cambridge, MA.

Stern, M. 1980. *Greek and Latin Authors on Jews and Judaism.* Vol. 2. Jerusalem.

Tcherikover, V.; Fuks, A.; and Stern, M. 1960. *Corpus Papyrorum Judaicarum.* Vol. 2. Cambridge, MA.

Telfer, W. 1952. Episcopal Succession in Egypt. *JEH* 3: 1–12.

Trevijano, R. 1975. The Early Christian Church of Alexandria. Vol. 12, 471–77 in *Studia Patristica.* TU 115. Berlin.

Williams, F. 1985. The Apocryphon of James (Introduction). Pp. 13–27 in *Nag Hammadi Codex I (The Jung Codex),* ed. H. W. Attridge. NHS 22. Leiden.

Birger A. Pearson

CHRISTIANITY IN GREECE

This article will trace the origins, growth, and development of Christianity in Greece, beginning with the missionary efforts of Paul, recorded in the NT, through the empire-wide decrees of Constantine.

A. Sources
B. The First Century
C. The Second Century
   1. Polycarp
   2. The Greek Apologists
   3. Dionysius of Corinth
   4. Bacchyllus
   5. Melito of Sardis
   6. Theodotus
   7. The Letters of Serapion
D. The Third Century
E. The Fourth Century
   1. The Diocletian Persecution
   2. The Martyrs
   3. The Conversion of Constantine and the Edict of Milan
   4. The Council of Nicea (325)
   5. The Churches in Greece
   6. Constantinople as the "New Rome"

A. Sources

The primary sources which deal with the development of Christianity in Greece are quite limited, especially before the time of Constantine. The scriptural sources which focus almost exclusively on the ministry of Paul in Greece include Acts 16–20, the epistles of Paul to the churches at Corinth, Philippi, and Thessalonica as well as a few brief references in other NT epistles (Rom 15:26; 16:1; Titus 1:5; 3:12). Scholars do not agree on the historical reliability of those sources, especially in the case of Acts and the epistle to Titus, but the chronological sequence of the journeys of Paul in Greece in Acts is not in doubt, nor that he was the first to found churches in the places mentioned in Acts. The epistle to Titus, which in its present form did not come from Paul, nevertheless gives a reliable tradition that Paul had some influence on the starting of the churches in Crete (1:5) and that he spent a winter in Nicopolis in Epirus (3:12). This information is not such that would be fabricated in the ancient sources.

Besides these scriptural references, there are a few brief comments, mostly incidental, from the Church Fathers indicating the presence of churches in Greece before Constantine, but they are not sufficiently detailed to provide a clear picture of the size or impact of those churches. These references, however, do permit us to see that Christianity not only was still growing in Greece in the first four centuries, but also had become fairly widespread among the local people without much opposition from them. It is also clear that the churches had organized themselves into a strong episcopal body which included parts of Macedonia, Thessaly, Epirus, Thrace, most of the southern province of Achaia, and many of the Greek islands. The primary sources for reconstructing the history of Christianity in Greece before the time of Constantine include Eusebius' *Historia Ecclesiastica* (ca. 330–40) and also his *De Vita Constantini,* Hippolytus' *Philosophoumena* (ca. 220–30), the ecclesiastical histories of both Socrates (ca. 439–50) and Sozomen (ca. 435), the various collections of the accounts of martyrdoms in the ancient churches (especially the *Acta Sanctorum*), and Jerome's *De Viris Illustribus* (ca. 392–95). References to the growth and development of the church in Greece are also found in incidental comments from *1 Clement* (ca. 95), the so-called *2 Clement* (ca. 120–70), *The Apostolic Constitutions* (ca. 350), Polycarp's letter to the church at Philippi (117–20), the writings of Origen, especially *Contra Celsum* (ca. 230), and Porphyry, *Philosophy from Oracles* and *Against Christians* (ca. 260–63).

B. The First Century

The Christian proclamation first came to Greece through the missionary activities of the Apostle Paul (Acts 16:9–40; 2 Cor 2:12–13) ca. 50. After landing at Neapolis (Acts 16:11), Paul began his first church in Greece at Philippi (Acts 16:12–40), a Roman colony where Latin was the official language of the courts and the common people. Paul's reception at Philippi was mixed, but an important church was started there which later contributed to his needs while he was ministering elsewhere in Macedonia, especially in Thessalonica (Phil 4:15–16). After a brief imprisonment in Philippi, Paul departed for Thessalonica, passing through Amphipolis and Apollonia (Acts 17:1–9), but again he encountered strong opposition. This time, however, it was the Jews who opposed his ministry and for safety's sake he had to leave the city (Acts 17:5–7, cf. 1 Thess 2:14–16), but not before he started an important church. In a matter of months the Thessalonian Christians were evangelizing the Macedonian province and had even become an example to the churches in Achaia in the south (1 Thess 1:7–8). From Thessalonica he went southwest some forty-five miles to Beroea and enjoyed considerable success before a Jewish contingent of opponents from Thessalonica came and again forced him to leave (Acts 17:10–13). According to the *Apos. Con.* 7:46, the first bishop of Beroea was Onesimus, the runaway slave of Philemon (cf. Phlm 10). After leaving Beroea, Paul went to Athens, but had little success in his mission there (Acts 17:16–34). One of his Athenian converts was Dionysius the Areopagite (Acts 17:34), who later was called the first bishop of Athens by bishop Dionysius of Corinth (Eus. *Hist. Eccl.* 4.23.3). Departing from Athens, Paul went to Corinth (ca. 51–52, depending on the dating of the famous inscription from Delphi which locates Gallio in Corinth for a brief stay, cf. Acts 18:12–17) and founded his most significant and influential church in Greece (Acts 18:1–17). Almost from the beginning this church had problems and even serious divisions (see 1 Cor 1:11–15; 3:1–3), but there was an important response to the Christian proclamation at Corinth. After some eighteen months of ministry in Corinth (Acts 18:11), Paul departed through the seaport village at Cenchreae, where he completed a Jewish vow (Acts 18:18). Acts does not say whether Paul founded a church there, but in the appendix of his letter to the Romans, he commends Phoebe, a deacon in the church of Cenchreae, and encourages the Romans to help her along her way (Rom 16:1–2). According to the *Apos. Con.* 7.46, Lucius was appointed by Paul as the first bishop of Cenchreae.

In Titus 1:5 we read that Paul founded churches on the island of Crete and left Titus behind to give leadership and direction to the churches. Those churches included at least the ones at Knossos and Gortyna. Also in that epistle there is a brief reference to Paul's plans to spend the winter in Nicopolis. It may be that Paul started a ministry there, but it cannot be confirmed. It is also possible that he stayed the winter at Nicopolis in preparation for his ministry in Illyricum (Rom 15:19). If one were to include the impact of Christianity on the whole of the Hellenistic peninsula, then Illyricum on the northwestern part of the Grecian peninsula must also be added to the missionary activities of Paul. The departure of Titus from Paul to the province of Dalmatia in Illyricum (2 Tim 4:10) also implies the presence of a church there, though nothing more is known of either his or Paul's labors in that region.

Besides the Apostle Paul, the most influential companions who were involved with him in his mission in Greece were Timothy, Silas, Luke (probably), Priscilla and Aquila, and Apollos. Dionysius, bishop of Corinth, claimed that the Apostle Peter joined with Paul in founding the church at Corinth and labored side by side with him (*Hist. Eccl.* 2.25.8), but this has no other ancient support. The problem of the division of loyalties in Corinth (1 Cor 1:12) has suggested to some commentators that Peter actually ministered in Corinth; however, this could mean simply that Peter, as a founding pillar of the church, was appealed to for justification for some form of Jewish Christianity present in Corinth. Finally, there is a strong multiple tradition from the 2d to the 6th centuries which points to the ministry of the Apostle Andrew in Scythia, Thrace, Epirus, Macedonia, and Achaia. That tradition also reports that Andrew was crucified in the Achaian city of Patras at the direction of the proconsul Aegeas (see *Acts of Andrew, Passio, AcApos* 56:586; Philasterius *De Haeresibus* 88; Jerome *Ad Marcellum, Breviarium Apostolorum, Martyrologium Romanum;* and Epiphanius *Haer.* 61.1, 63.2). According to Jerome, Andrew's bones were transferred from Patras to Constantinople by Constantius II, Roman emperor 337–61 (*De Vir. Ill.* 7).

At the end of the 1st century, Corinth is mentioned again because there was quarreling going on in the church which led to the expulsion from office of several of its presbyters. Clement of Rome wrote to them encouraging them toward peace, humility, and obedience to their leaders (*1 Clem.* 4–20, 44–46).

It is likely that there were other churches in Greece in the 1st century at Larissa, Patras, and Aegina (according to *Apos. Con.* 4.46, Crispus, presumably of 1 Cor 1:14, was the first bishop of Aegina), and probably elsewhere owing to the evangelistic spirit of the churches in Macedonia (1 Thess 1:7–8).

C. The Second Century

Because the sources for understanding the development of Christianity in Greece in the 2d century are more limited than those for the 1st, even a broad outline of the church's activity in Greece for that era is difficult to produce. The following references, though limited, are essential for any description of the ecclesiastical climate in 2d-century Greece.

1. Polycarp. Around 117–20 Polycarp, bishop of Smyrna, wrote a letter to the Christians at Philippi partly to prepare them for an impending visit of Ignatius of Antioch, who was on his way to Rome for martyrdom, but mostly to warn them against disorders and apostasy *(Ep. Pol.).* He rejoiced with them that their faith had deep roots and that it was still bearing fruit (1:2).

2. The Greek Apologists. At nearly the same time Quadratus of Athens, the first Christian apologist, wrote a defense of the Christian faith to the Emperor Hadrian (ca. 124–25), answering the objections of both Jews and pagans (*Hist. Eccl.* 4.3.1–2). Aristides, also from Athens, sent another apology to Hadrian (ca. 125), defending both the existence and eternity of God as well as the superiority of the Christian understanding of God (*Hist. Eccl.* 4.3.3). Some scholars locate both of these apologists' writing careers ca. 160 during the reign of Antonius Pius (138–61), but that view is difficult to establish. The most distinguished 2d-century apologist from Athens was Athenagoras (ca. 170–80), who set forth the earliest defense of the Christian doctrine of God as three in one. Whether there was a Christian philosophical school in Athens during the 2d century which trained these apologists is not known, but the fact that they all came from Athens in the 2d century is suggestive.

3. Dionysius of Corinth. The most influential bishop in Greece in the 2d century was Dionysius (ca. 170), who wrote letters to several churches and individuals encouraging them in the Christian faith. Among the eight letters referred to by Eusebius, he wrote to the churches at Athens, Lacedaemon, and to Gortyna and Knossos in Crete (*Hist. Eccl.* 4:23). He rebuked the Christians at Athens for their tendency toward apostasy following the death of their bishop (Publius), but rejoiced that their new bishop (Quadratus—not the apologist) had brought them back to the faith. The church in Lacedaemon shows that the Christian message had reached the southernmost part of the Peloponnese by 170. The significance of this city is not known during the 2d century—it may have been a small country community and may also have been an alternative name for Sparta, as some have suggested—but by the 4th century its importance both socially and politically is seen by its inclusion, along with Corinth and Athens, in the request from the emperor Julian to help him in his political reforms. Dionysius' exhortation to Pinytus, the bishop of the church at Knossos in Crete, to cease imposing his strict views of continence on the church there shows an early tendency toward asceticism in the churches of Greece (*Hist. Eccl.* 4.23.7). After mentioning his letter to Soter of Rome, Eusebius calls attention to Dionysius' complaint about the altering of some of his letters by his opponents, possibly the Marcionites, whom he condemned in his letter to the church at Nicomedia (*Hist. Eccl.* 4.24.4).

4. Bacchyllus. Following Dionysius, Bacchyllus became bishop of Corinth (ca. 185–90) and was an active participant in the Easter (Quartodecimian) Controversy, writing an influential letter on the matter (*Hist. Eccl.* 5.22.1; 5.23.4; see also Jerome *De Vir. Ill.* 44).

5. Melito of Sardis. Eusebius tells of a letter from Melito of Sardis (ca. 180) to the emperor Marcus Aurelius, or Antonius Verus, (emperor, 161–80) and his son Commodus, imploring them to send a letter to the magistrates of Asia not to take further actions against the Christians. He reminds the emperor that his father, the emperor Antonius Pius (138–61), had written similar letters to the cities of Larissa, Thessalonica, and Athens directing them to do no further harm to the Christians (*Hist. Eccl.* 4.26.7–11).

6. Theodotus. Among the defectors from the Christian faith during the 2d-century persecutions (probably those of Marcus Aurelius, 161–80), Theodotus of Byzantium was condemned by Hippolytus of Rome (ca. 190) for his denial of the faith (*Philosophoumena* 7:7). He was later excommunicated by Victor of Rome (192–202) for his Arian doctrines about Christ (Epiph. *Haer.* 54.1).

7. The Letters of Serapion. A final witness to the growth and development of the church in Greece in the late 2d and perhaps early 3d centuries comes from Eusebius. While describing the letters of Serapion of Antioch against heresy, he mentions the names of various bishops who signed Serapion's letters, signifying approval of the contents. Among these bishops was Aelius Publius Julius, bishop of Debeltum, a colony of Thrace (*Hist. Eccl.* 5.19.3). This story also provides evidence that a Thracian provincial synod was held toward the end of the 2d century in order to discuss the Montanist controversy, showing the kind of cooperation existing among the various churches both in and outside Greece.

D. The Third Century

The few ancient sources that do exist for the reconstruction of the growth and development of Christianity in Greece in the 3d century are mostly concerned with the persecutions initiated by Decian. About all that is otherwise known is the visit of Origen to Nicopolis near Actium in Epirus (ca. 230), where he found a copy of the Scriptures (presumably the OT). Both his stay there and his finding a copy of the Scriptures obviously suggests that a Christian community was situated in Nicopolis (*Hist. Eccl.* 6.13.2). About the same time, Origen also spent some time in Athens in order to finish his commentary on Ezekiel (*Hist. Eccl.* 6.32.2). He described the church in Athens as a "peaceful and orderly body, as it desires to please Almighty God" (Origen *c. Cels.* 3.30). He also spoke along similar lines about the church at Corinth.

The life of the churches in Greece in the middle of the 3d century was dominated primarily by the Decian persecution. The Roman emperor Decius saw the Christians as a threat to the unity of the empire. They were emerging as an empire within the empire, and they were even referred to as a "nation" (Gk *ethnei*) by Jovius Maximinus Augustus in a letter to Sabinus (see *Hist. Eccl.* 9.9a.1, 4). The text (written ca. 312–13) clearly shows the perceived threat Christianity posed to the Roman Empire. The growing number of Christians and the consequent abandonment of the state religion by many was taken with utmost seriousness. With his edict in January of 250, Decius began the first empire-wide persecution of the Christians, starting with the execution of Fabian, bishop of Rome. The persecution lasted about eighteen months until Decius was killed. Valerian, his successor, resumed the persecutions in August of 257 and they continued until his capture by the Persians in June of 260. His son, Gallienus, reversed the edict of Valerian in July of 260 and for the next forty years the Christians throughout the empire lived in relative peace and freedom to practice their religion (*Hist. Eccl.* 7.11–13). Our information about the persecutions from 250–60 is more complete for cities like Rome, Carthage, and Alexandria, where the full force of the persecutions and executions was felt, but there were many other Christian martyrs throughout the empire during this period of which only a few names have survived. The fragmentary literature that has survived this era is indicative of the severe nature of the persecutions which the Christians endured in Greece and especially in Achaia. Among the Greeks known to have been martyred are Leonides, bishop of Athens, and his eight companions from Corinth (*ActSS* April 2; *Bibliotheca Hagiographica Graeca [BHG]* 2:54–55); Quadratus and his Corinthian companions (*BHG* 1: 119); and Irene and Adrian from an unnamed city in Achaia whose feast day was kept on March 10 (*ActSS* March 2). Unfortunately, there is no surviving evidence that the churches in Greece produced any great leaders, scholars, writers, or spokespersons during this time comparable to those found elsewhere in the Roman Empire in the 3d century (e.g., Origen, Ambrose, Fabian, Dionysius of Alexandria, and Cyprian). Eusebius is usually quite detailed in his descriptions of the most prominent persons in the church, but is silent about church leaders from Greece during this period. See *Hist. Eccl.* 6–7, where he focuses on this period of the church's life, but says almost nothing about the church in Greece or its leaders.

Throughout the 3d century, apart from the period of intense persecution, there was essentially complete freedom to preach the Christian message. It is clear from the catalog of bishops from Greece representing their churches at the Council of Nicea (see the lists below) that significant evangelization had taken place throughout Greece, especially in Achaia. (See Sozomen *Hist. Eccl.* 7.7 for further evidence of numerous well-organized Greek churches in the 4th century.) Eusebius also makes it clear that the period of relative ease for the church also produced a time of moral laxity which, he believes, led to the Diocletian persecution in the early 4th century (*Hist. Eccl.* 8.1.7–8.2.3).

E. The Fourth Century

By the 4th century, much of Greece was already Christianized and evidently without significant opposition from the local residents. The Greeks in the Peloponnese, by and large, had embraced Christianity, and as can be seen from the number of bishoprics there, their churches were well organized. Churches elsewhere in Greece were also apparently numerous and well organized as the large number of bishops at the Council of Nicea in 325 from both prominent and insignificant Greek communities suggests. Sozomen gives evidence of the strong organization of the Greek churches when he describes the Macedonian christological controversy in the 4th century. He relates how the Macedonian bishops rejected the notion that the substance of the Son was the same as that of the Father and they exhorted their churches not to conform to the doctrines of Nicea (*Hist. Eccl.* 7.7).

Probably as a result of the rapid growth of the church both in Greece and elsewhere, the church was set on a collision course with Rome.

1. The Diocletian Persecution. On February 23, 303, after some forty years of peace and prosperity for the church, Diocletian, the Roman emperor, launched the last great empire-wide persecution of the Christians. In a series of four edicts between 303 and 304 Christianity, in effect, became an outlawed religion in the empire. Its Scriptures were destroyed, its properties destroyed or confiscated, and its ministers were imprisoned and forced under penalty of death to offer sacrifices to the pagan gods. The causes for the persecution are not given in the edicts, but the social context of the day gives a major clue.

First, the Christian community had increased considerably in the pagan world in the last quarter of the 3d century. Porphyry wrote fifteen volumes against the Christians because he saw them as a major threat to the empire. He feared that none of the Christian converts could be reconverted to the state-recognized religion (*Philosophy from Oracles,* ca. 263), and he was especially concerned about the influx of educated women into the church. He spoke with alarm and disappointment that the Christians were building up their "great houses" to assemble for prayer (*Against Christians* 2.63–64). Eusebius agrees with such claims and speaks with pride of the growth of the church and its rising prestige in the last decades before the Diocletian persecution. He gives several examples of the many Christians who held high offices in the imperial service (see *Hist. Eccl.* 8.11.2; 8.6.1; and 8.9.7–8).

Second, at the same time that the Christians were improving their image and gaining converts almost everywhere, Rome, its government, and its religion, were clearly on the decline in public sentiment. Disloyalty and disrespect for the government was on the rise. This was due in part to the many foreign invasions in both Britain, Germany, and elsewhere, as well as the consequent need for heavier taxation to support an even larger military necessary to suppress the unrest in the empire. Both the Decian and Diocletian persecutions as well as their reforms had little effect on bringing the necessary changes in the empire. The immorality of the higher classes continued to undermine the people's confidence in Rome. Lack of loyalty for the empire can be seen in the fact that the majority of the Roman army was made up of mercenaries, and neglect of paying one's taxes was praised among the common people. Further, unequal distribution of justice, i.e., the rich were getting richer and the poor poorer, along with a moral laxity especially among the highest leaders of the empire, led to a growing lack of respect for leadership. The opulence of the emperors and their favored lieutenants came at the expense of the already increasingly poor population. (See Finlay 1877: 1.99–114 for a detailed discussion of the social climate of the Roman empire in the late 3d and early 4th centuries.)

The empire was deteriorating and Diocletian was painfully aware of it. Before him, Aurelian (270–75) and Probus (276–82) had tried to reform the empire, but without success. Diocletian, in the same spirit, tried to set the clock backward, and again it did not work. His solution was to return to the stability of the former generations through loyalty to the gods of the state and unity within the empire brought about by a stronger military. Eusebius indicates the Roman concern that the Christians were not loyal citizens (*De Vita Constantini* 2:50), and also that the Christians were excluded from military service at the beginning of the Diocletian persecutions (*Hist. Eccl.* 8.1.7).

The Christians, on the other hand, assumed that the empire would not and could not last because it had stood for evil, unequal justice, promiscuity, and immoral behavior in the upper classes. The Greeks, long imbued with a sense of equality and the feeling of a moral code which applied to both superiors and inferiors, generally embraced Christianity because it enforced the observance of the moral duties on every rank of society without distinction. The general demoralization of women in the empire compared to the morality taught by the Christians with respect for women led many women to convert to Christianity. It is not surprising, therefore, that the Roman emperors should have seen Christianity as a threat. The church stood for the morality that the populace was coming to appreciate. The loyalty and fervency of faith common among the Christians were sorely lacking in the Roman hierarchy and in their religious practice. The church was well established and highly organized in the early 4th century and their political clout was doubtless a key factor in their being persecuted. The fear of the continued growth of the Christians is noted in the letter of Jovius Maximinus Augustus to Sabinus in which he justified the persecution of Christians because "almost all men had abandoned the worship of the gods and associated themselves with the *nation* of the Christians" (*Hist. Eccl.* 9.9a.1). The term "nation" (Gk *ethnei*) suggests the solidarity with which the emperor viewed the Christians and not without reason. The authority of the bishops over the people in their congregations was powerful and effective not only in the church's ministries, but also in daily social discourse.

The exact reason for the Diocletian persecution is not clear, but the hatred for the Christians by one of his closest lieutenants, Galerius, is well known and both were together in Nicomedia at the time of the outbreak of hostility toward the church. At any rate, the Diocletian persecution was quite severe and lasted for some ten years. In Greece especially, where Galerius had a home in Thessalonica and exercised great influence, the persecution was carried out with extreme cruelty as the various accounts of the martyrdoms there show.

2. The Martyrs. Evidence for a strong church in Greece in the early 4th century can be found in its lists of martyrs. One of the most dramatic examples shows that young and even pregnant women were not immune from torture and death by the Roman authorities (*ActSS* April 2: *Agape, Irene, and Chione at Thessalonica* sec. 4). The notices of martyrs in Adrianopolis, Drizipara, Epibata in Thessaly, Buthrotum in Epirus, and Pydna testify to the vibrant faith of the Christians in Greece. These persecutions also included the burning of sacred Christian literature and the destruction of their properties and places of worship (see *ActSS* March 2 and April 2, and *Hist. Eccl.* 8.2.1–5). The destruction of Christian literature no doubt had a severe effect upon the Christians' ability to keep accurate records of the growth of their mission (see the solicitation of Christian books in *Gesta apud Zenophilum* 26), especially in Greece, where Galerius resided and was actively involved in the persecution of Christians until shortly before his death in 311 (*Hist. Eccl.* 8.17.1).

3. The Conversion of Constantine and the Edict of Milan. Without question the most important event for Christians throughout the Roman Empire in the early 4th century was the conversion of Constantine to the Christian religion and his subsequent Edict of Milan in 313, which gave complete religious freedom to the Christians. Even before the edict was issued, Constantine had given Christians freedom to worship in safety in Macedonia and Illyria (Sozomen *Hist. Eccl.* 1:2). After the Edict of Milan, there were only a few months of persecution by Licinius in the East and again just briefly during the reign of Julian (361–63).

4. The Council of Nicea (325). The listing of the names and home cities of the bishops who attended the Council of Nicea offers evidence for the considerable number of churches in Greece by the early decades of the 4th century. According to Sozomen there were three hundred and twenty bishops attending the council (*Hist. Eccl.* 1:17). Those from Greek cities of which we are aware include Bishop Pistus of Athens, Bishop Strategius of Hephaistia on the island of Lemnos in the Aegean Sea, Bishop Claudian of Larissa in Thessaly, Bishop Eustathius of Beroea, who was voted by the other bishops to fill the apostolic throne at Nicea (Sozomen *Hist. Eccl.* 1:2), Bishop Paederus of Heraclea of Thrace, Bishop Budius of Stobi in Macedonia, Bishop Cleonicus of Thebes in Thessaly, Bishop Ballachus of Pele and also of Thessaly, Bishop Dakos of Scupi in Dardania, whose bishopric included Macedonia, and Bishop Marcus from Chalcis on the island of Euboea. Eusebius, commenting on the wide representation at the council, claims that "those in the remotest districts of Thrace and Macedonia, of Achaia and Epirus . . . were in attendance" (*De Vita Constantini* 3:7). There was no mention of representative churches in Crete at Nicea, which was probably an oversight since churches were known to have been established there in the 1st century at Knossos and Gortyna. There were also other representatives from the Christian communities on several Greek islands such as Corcyra, Cos, Lemnos, Rhodes, and presumably Patmos. It is clear that by the 4th century, Christianity had reached the Greek settlements on the northern coasts of the Black Sea and in the Crimean settlements since two bishops from that region (Theophilus of Gothia and Cadmus of Bosphorus) were also in attendance at the council.

5. The Churches in Greece. Both before and following the Diocletian persecutions, the churches in Greece were stable and well organized. That continued to be the case up to the time when the emperor Theodosius I (The Great, 379–75) established Christianity as the religion of the empire. There was solidarity not only within Greece, but also with other churches throughout the empire. The episcopal form of church government also seems to have taken hold throughout Greece, and as is clear from the correspondence of Dionysius to Soter, bishop of Rome, there was a growing appreciation of the value of ancient correspondence in the churches. This was especially so after the edicts to burn this material. The reading of Clement of Rome's letter to the Corinthians in worship as a means of drawing admonition from it, even some seventy years after it was written, was the very practice which led ultimately to the recognition of Christian writings themselves as Scripture (*Hist. Eccl.* 4.23.11).

In the 4th and 5th centuries, Athens continued to be the stronghold of the non-Christian philosophies long after Constantine had declared that the city corrupted the people who continued to flock from all over the empire to its teachers of philosophy. Later, during the reign of the emperor Julian (361–63), pagan sacrifices at Athens were still tolerated, but by the middle of the 6th century, Justinian closed the philosophical schools in Athens and discontinued the pagan sacrifices. The Athenian philosophical schools nonetheless continued to have an important influence on the people centuries later, not only in pagan communities, but also in the Christian church. It is important to note that the Christian doctrine of the Trinity was framed within Platonic philosophical categories. Both Plato and Aristotle had a significant impact on the theologies of the Church Fathers, especially Boethius (480–524) and Thomas Aquinas (1225–74). Although Athens never had a prominent Christian church, it continued to be revered by the Romans and the entire Hellenistic world for its focus on education and philosophy. However, whatever the strength or character of the church in Athens, it had little impact upon the moral and social climate of its day.

Corinth, on the other hand, was the ecclesiastical metropolis of Achaia, having preeminence over the church in Athens well into the 4th century. While Corinth was one of the most flourishing commercial centers of antiquity, the church there was composed primarily of lower-class individuals (1 Cor 1:26–29), at least at first. It was also concerned with the evangelization of the Peloponnese (*Hist. Eccl.* 4.23.1–8).

6. Constantinople as the "New Rome." In the early part of the 4th century, Heraclea, which had been the metropolis of Thrace, was surpassed by Byzantium, which became the capital of the Eastern empire and was renamed Constantinople in 326. The removal of the capital from Rome was an astute move on the part of Constantine. Since Greece was already predominately Christian and Rome was not, the Hellenistic peninsula was a much more favorable climate to relocate the capital of the empire, especially when the emperor wanted to wed the empire with the church. Finlay has rightly observed that "when the emperor, by becoming a Christian, was placed in personal opposition to the Roman Senate, there could be no longer any doubt that Rome became a very unsuitable residence for the Christian court. Constantine was compelled to choose a new capital" (Finlay 1877: 1.139). The power the church had acquired in Greece no doubt influenced Constantine's choice of relocation, but the strategic location of Byzantium must also have influenced his thinking. From there he was able to solidify the Eastern empire and organize the whole of it into four major sectors with the leadership of each reporting to Constantine in Constantinople. The problems of the empire were not fully solved by this move, but to Constantine's credit, there was once again widespread unity in the empire. When he became the recognized head of the church, he also involved himself in its affairs to the point of calling church councils and settling disputes of doctrine. His overriding passion for the empire was unity and conformity and this affected his dealings with the church (see examples of this in Eusebius, *De Vita Constantini* 2.61, 3.6–18, 37; 4.41–43). When Constantinople became the "New Rome," Latin was the official language of the city, but Greek was still the dominant language of the people. Only later when the problem of communication persisted between the two great centers in Rome and Constantinople was the separation between the Eastern and Western empires completed. After Constantinople became the capital of the Eastern empire, it also became the focal point of church hierarchy in the East, which has lasted unto this day.

Elsewhere in Greece, pagan temples were converted by Christians for use in worship and ministry. Many monks also took possession of pagan shrines after Constantine had declared that full restitution be paid to the Christians for their suffering and loss during the persecutions. Nowhere else in the ancient world is there so much evidence of Christians building their churches on the sites of pagan temples and shrines than in Greece. An ancient mausoleum in Thessalonica, for example, which was originally built for the emperor Galerius (d. 311) to entomb his body and to be a pantheon, was converted into a church no later than the last quarter of the 4th century. It is still standing and is now called the "Rotunda" or "Agios Georgios Church."

Bibliography

Baus, K. 1965. *From the Apostolic Community to Constantine.* Vol. 1 of *History of the Church.* New York.

Cruttwell, C. T. 1893. *A Literary History of Early Christianity.* Vol. 1. London.

Finlay, G. 1877. *A History of Greece.* Vol. 1. Oxford.

Frend, W. H. C. 1984. *The Rise of Christianity.* Philadelphia.

Grant, R. M. 1970. *Augustus to Constantine.* New York.

Harnack, A. 1908. *The Mission and Expansion of Christianity in the First Three Centuries.* Vol. 2. New York.

Kidd, B. J. 1922. *A History of the Church to A.D. 461.* Vol. 1. Oxford.

Latourette, K. 1937. *A History of the Expansion of Christianity.* Vol. 1. New York.

Lebreton, J., and Zeiller, J. 1944. *The History of the Primitive Church.* Vol. 1. New York.

MacMullen, R. 1984. *Christianizing the Roman Empire (A.D. 100–400).* New Haven.

McDonald, L. M. 1988. *The Formation of the Christian Biblical Canon.* Nashville.

Musurillo, F. 1972. *The Acts of Christian Martyrs.* Oxford.

Peterson, P. M. 1958. *Andrew, Brother of Simon Peter: His History and His Legends.* Leiden.

Quasten, J. 1950–60. *Patrology.* Vols. 1–3. Utrecht and Antwerp.

LEE MARTIN MCDONALD

NORTH AFRICAN CHRISTIANITY

It is one of the ironies of history that although Christianity in the Roman West is defined by such African luminaries as Clement of Alexandria, Origen, Tertullian, Cyprian, and Augustine, its introduction to and earliest development on that continent remain hidden. The first indications of contact are found in the book of Acts. According to Acts 2:10, the witnesses to Pentecost include "Jews and proselytes" from "Egypt and the parts of Libya belonging to Cyrene." The historicity is questionable for, in addition to the doubtfulness of the event, the list of nationalities presented anticipates the later church universal. Alexandrines and Cyrenians are also mentioned at Acts 6:9, as opponents of Stephen. Acts 18:24 speaks of a certain Apollos, who is called a native of Alexandria; 5th-century Codex Bezae Cantabrigiensis (D) adds an interesting gloss, stating that he was "taught the word of the Lord in his native country." If Bezae's report is correct, then it would mean that Christianity was already winning converts in Egypt by the middle of the 1st century. Philip's baptism of the Ethiopian eunuch (Acts 8:26–40) represents another link (probably symbolic; cf. v. 39b) with Africa. Our survey concentrates on Egypt (centering on Alexandria) and North Africa (centering on Carthage).

No single person is linked with the founding of Egyptian Christianity until the 4th century, when Eusebius (*Hist. Eccl.* 2.16) states that Mark the evangelist was "the first man to set out for Egypt," and was "the first to establish churches in Alexandria itself." In his *Chronicle,* Eusebius says Mark arrived in Alexandria in 43 C.E. The report of Marcan foundation must, however, be read in light of the well-known propensity for important sees to claim foundation by an apostle or evangelist. Mark's connection with Alexandria may be nothing more than another example of this mythmaking. While not linking him with the introduction of Christianity in Alexandria—its existence prior to his arrival is implied—a recently discovered letter (Smith 1973) attributed to Clement of Alexandria (and thus dating from ca. 200 C.E., if genuine) states that after Peter's martyrdom, Mark went to Alexandria. Opinion on the question of Marcan foundation is divided: W. Bauer (1977: 53–58; 60) felt that Eusebius' story was a fabrication, introduced in the late-2d century to support the founding of an "orthodox" monarchic episcopate; recently, B. Pearson (1986: 137–45), while not giving credence to the story, has been reluctant to dismiss it out of hand: *in dubito pro traditio.*

If one probes behind piety and examines the literary remains and theology, one fact emerges from recent studies of earliest Egyptian Christianity: it was dominantly Jewish, essentially another sect within Judaism. Therefore, it seems only natural to assume that the channels through which Christianity first spread beyond Palestine were Jewish. Trade, professional, and family connections would have carried this new Jewish sect of Christianity to the various Diaspora communities. These included, of course, the old, well-established Jewish communities in Africa. Eusebius also supports this analysis, for elsewhere he ascribes the origins of Egyptian Christianity to "the Jews" and states that, "for the greater part," it followed "ancient Jewish customs" (*Hist. Eccl.* 2.17.2–3; cf. Klijn 1986: 164).

Part of the difficulty in discerning traces of early Christianity in Egypt stems to the fact that the earliest Christians still regarded themselves as Jews. The writings of Philo (10 B.C.E.–50 C.E.) evidence the diversity of Jewish thought present in Egypt in the 1st century. As elsewhere, the estrangement between Christian and Jew developed incrementally, and only became final and decisive—manifesting itself in recoverable evidence—after the end of the 1st century. Second-century Egypt yields a rich trove of canonical as well as noncanonical Christian literature: papyrus fragments of Matthew and John (but not Mark!), as well as the "unknown gospel" of the Egerton Papyri (Bell and Skeat 1935), the *Shepherd of Hermas* and portions of the *Gospel of Thomas* (in the Oxyrhynchus Papyri). These findings confirm the pluriformity of early Egyptian Christianity, its eclectic tastes, and its close relationship with Alexandrian Judaism, especially as reflected in Philo. Gnostic currents are evident, probably related to or parallel with similar tendencies within Philonic Judaism. Traditional Jewish motifs, such as the "two ways" teaching, are also evident. Another sign of the link with Judaism is the fact that the two earliest Alexandrian Fathers of note, Clement (*Str.* 2.9.45) and Origen (*Io.* 2.12; *Hom. Ier.* 15.4; cf. Jerome, *de vir. inl.* 2), both know and cite without prejudice the Judaic-Christian *Gospel according to the Hebrews.*

The role of Alexandrian Christianity in the development of Christian literature, thought, and doctrine cannot be overemphasized. Because of its library (founded by Ptolemy Soter I), the literary arts of editing and interpretation reached heights unequaled in the ancient world (Reynolds and Wilson 1974: 5–15). The most polished recension of the NT gospels, the so-called "Alexandrian" text, exemplified in Codex Vaticanus (B) and P^{75}, is the work of Christian scribes of the generation of Clement of Alexandria. Hellenism was the dominant cultural influence in Egyptian life during this period; Greek was the dominant language. Clement himself is a sophisticated, urbane writer, who attempted to meld Greek philosophy and Christianity. His successor in the catechetical school in Alexandria, Origen, became one of the most famous scholars in antiquity. Pagan scholars in Alexandria had developed the art of allegorical exegesis for interpreting portions of Homer and Hesiod deemed "offensive" to current tastes; later, the Jew Philo borrowed the technique and applied it to embarrassing or awkward portions of the OT. Clement and Origen borrowed the technique and applied it to the Gospels (see ORIGEN).

In addition to the likes of Clement and Origen, 2d-century Alexandria also produced Valentinus, Basilides, and Carpocrates, all later deemed heresiarchs. In the 3d and 4th centuries, Alexandria was home to Arius, leader of the Arians, as well as his opponent, Athanasius. This unparalleled crop of theologians represents leaders on both sides of the two major heresies of the early church: Gnosticism and Arianism; it is proof of the diversity and fluidity of early Christianity in Egypt.

Egyptian Christianity is characterized by its intellectual activity, relative openness, and syncretistic speculation. Whether gnostics working with Greek or Jewish ideas, or Clement and Origen adapting Greek philosophy and exegetical methods, it was an intellectual enterprise. Clement reflects that view when he defends philosophy ("it is impossible for a man without learning to comprehend the things which are declared in the faith," (*Str.* 1.6) and disparages those who "demand bare faith alone, as if (it were possible) without bestowing any care on the vine, straightway to gather clusters from the first" (*Str.* 1.9).

Klijn (1986: 170–75) has pointed to certain theological themes which emerge in early Egyptian Christianity: a logos christology, in which Jesus is the intermediary between God and man; the immutability of the *logos;* an interest in the wonders worked by the incarnate *logos,* which demonstrate that his powers are not mitigated by his having taken on flesh. This "high" christology, emphasizing the divinity of the incarnate one of his immutability, distinguished the so-called "Alexandrian School," as opposed to the "Antoichene School," which sought to preserve the humanity of Jesus (Sellers 1954). These differences set the stage for the christological and trinitarian controversies which were to follow, in which Alexandria and its theologians played such key roles.

Moving west from Egypt along the coast of the Mediterranean Sea, one encounters the Roman provinces of Cyrenaica (roughly corresponding to present-day eastern Libya), Tripolitana (western Libya), Africa (Tunisia), Numidia (eastern Algeria), Mauretania Caesariensis (western Algeria), and Mauretania Tingitana (Morocco). Research into the introduction of Christianity in these regions centers on Carthage, the capital of the Roman province of Africa. Here, too, the imprint of Judaic Christianity is found. It seems reasonable to assume that Jewish lines of communication first brought word to Jews that their Messiah had come in the person of Jesus; the large Judaic-Christian community in Rome may well have been the source of this datum.

Documentary evidence begins in the 2d century, with the *Acts of the Scillitan Martyrs.* These twelve martyrs, from the obscure village of Scillium, near Carthage (or, perhaps, Scilli, in Numidia), were executed in Carthage on July 17, 180 C.E. Their Punic and Latin names are taken as indicators of their backgrounds: they are rustics, from the small villages, Latin-speaking, with ethnic ties to the land. Perhaps the most striking detail is that when they are questioned by the Proconsul Saturninus about the contents of a satchel, one of the martyrs, Speratus, states that it contains, "Books and letters of Paul, a just man." Hence, we know that portions of the Pauline corpus had reached North Africa by 180; furthermore, it is presumed that the documents were in Latin, for it is doubtful if the education of a commoner would have included Greek. (It is often argued that one of the first Latin translations of the Gospels was done in North Africa; the "afra" family of mss in the Vetus Latina are representatives of this effort.) Implicit in this first notice of Christianity in North Africa is a period of development: time for converts to be made in rural areas and among the indigenous population, for literature to be translated and disseminated, and for friction to arise with the authorities, necessitating persecution. We have no sources, however, to take us behind these events of July 180.

Already at this date, the Scillitan Martyrs display a Latin practicality and stubbornness which will become a hallmark of North African Christianity. They are absolutely unwavering in their devotion to the faith, and seem almost eager to die a martyr's death. There is no second-guessing, no philosophical hairsplitting or reflection. About twenty years later, Tertullian will echo this stolid piety by asking: "What has Athens to do with Jerusalem? What concord is there between the Academy and the church? . . . Away with all attempts to produce a mottled Christianity of Stoic, Platonic and dialectic composition. We want no serious disputation after possessing Christ Jesus" (*De praescr. haeret.* 7.9–11). Despite such sentiments, the view that North African Christianity was wholly anti-intellectual is confounded by the carefully styled, philosophically slanted writings of scholar-churchmen such as MINUCIUS FELIX (if an African), Augustine, and Tyconius.

If heresy was the plague of the Egyptian church, then schism was the bane of the North African church. The same rigorist tone noted in the *Acts of the Scillitan Martyrs* and Tertullian later manifests itself in the Donatist schism, which split the church in 312. The Donatist party consisted of those who had survived the Diocletian persecution (303–305 C.E.) without recanting the faith. They objected to the readmission of *traditores* into the church, especially the installation of Majorinus, who had allegedly surrendered Scriptures during the persecution, as bishop of Carthage.

Christian inroads in North Africa during Roman times seem to have been limited to the coastal regions—in other words, to the territory within Roman frontiers. Converts seem to have come largely from the two uppermost layers of society, the Greco-Roman population and the Punic "middle class." The lowest stratum, the Berbers, remained largely untouched (Groves 1948: 64–65). The death of Augustine (430) and the establishment of a Vandal kingdom in Africa (442) mark a watershed in the history of North African Christianity. After that point, the transition from the early period to the middle ages has begun. The Vandals were Arian Christians; consequently, the stage was set for new conflicts between the "old" church of Tertullian, Cyprian, and Augustine, and the "new" Arian church brought by the conquering Vandals. After a period of decline under the Vandals, Christianity experienced a renaissance when Byzantium gained control over North Africa in the 530s. This relative calm was shattered by the appearance of Islam, which once again put the church into a period of decline, commencing with the conquest of Egypt in the 640s; Carthage fell in 698. Although the Coptic church survived in Egypt, the North African church appears to have virtually vanished with the arrival of Islam.

The introduction of Christianity into the sub-Saharan regions of the African continent did not commence until the Portuguese voyages south, along the West coast of Africa, on their way to India and the Spice Islands in the 15th century.

Bibliography

Atiya, A. S. 1968. *History of Eastern Christianity.* Notre Dame.

Barnes, T. D. 1985. *Tertullian: A Historical and Literary Study.* Oxford.

Bauer, W. 1977. *Orthodoxy and Heresy in Earliest Christianity.* Trans. R. A. Kraft and G. Krodel. Philadelphia.

Bell, H. I., and Skeat, T. C. 1935. *Fragments of an Unknown Gospel.* London.

Daniélou, J. 1977. The Origins of Latin Christianity. Vol. 3 in *A History of Early Christian Doctrine before the Council of Nicaea.* Philadelphia.

Frend, W. H. C. 1952. *The Donatist Church.* Oxford.

———. 1965. *The Early Church.* Philadelphia.
———. 1984. *The Rise of Christianity.* Philadelphia.
Groves, C. P. 1948. *The Planting of Christianity in Africa.* Vol. 1. London. Repr. 1964.
Harnack, A. von. 1915. *The Mission and Expansion of Christianity in the First Three Centuries.* 2 vol. Transl. London.
Klijn, A. F. J. 1986. Jewish Christianity in Egypt. Pp. 161–75 in *The Roots of Egyptian Christianity,* ed. B. Pearson and J. Göhring. Philadelphia.
Leclercq, H. 1904. *L'Afrique chrétienne.* 2 vols. Paris.
Mesnage, J. 1912. *L'Afrique chrétienne.* Paris.
Monceaux, P. 1901–23. *Histoire littéraire de l'Afrique chrétienne depuis les origines jusqu'a l'invasion Arabe.* 7 vols. Paris.
Pearson, B. 1986. Earliest Christianity in Egypt. Pp. 132–59 in *The Roots of Egyptian Christianity,* ed. B. Pearson and J. Goehring. Philadelphia.
Quispel, G. 1982. African Christianity before Minucius Felix and Tertullian. Pp. 257–333 in *Actus, Studies in Honour of H. L. W. Nelson,* ed. J. den Boeft and A. H. M. Kessels. Utrecht.
Reynolds, L. D., and Wilson, N. G. 1974. *Scribes and Scholars: A Guide to the Transmission of Greek and Latin Literature.* 2d ed. Oxford.
Roberts, C. H. 1979. *Manuscript, Society and Belief in Early Christian Egypt.* London.
Sellers, R. V. 1954. *Two Ancient Christologies.* London.
Smith, M. 1973. *Clement of Alexandria and a Secret Gospel of Mark.* Cambridge, MA.
Thompson, L., and Ferguson, J. 1969. *Africa in Classical Antiquity.* Ibaden, Nigeria.

WILLIAM L. PETERSEN

CHRISTIANITY IN ROME

The presence of Christianity in Rome goes all the way back to the 1st century. Rome eventually became the most significant city for the growth of Western Christianity.

A. Origins

The presence of a sizable Jewish community in Rome made it inevitable that Christianity would appear there quite early. Possibly as many as thirteen synagogues existed in primarily the Trastevere (west across the Tiber River) area of Rome. Presumably the first Christian house churches began in these Jewish sectors. It is not known when this occurred. According to Acts, Jewish visitors from Rome were present at Pentecost, but the narrative does not imply that the new faith was carried back to the Roman Jewish community (Acts 2:10).

Whatever the means by which Christianity was introduced to Rome, it is widely assumed that it was already known there by the middle of the 5th decade. Suetonius (*Claud.* 25) tells us that the emperor Claudius "expelled the Jews from Rome because they were continually rioting *impulsore chresto.*" If *Chrestus* actually refers to Christ, the agitation may have been caused by the incipient Christian community or, perhaps, preaching about Christ. The date of the expulsion of the Jews has minimal attestation, but the relationship of Acts 18:2 with the fairly firm date for the arrival of Gallio in Corinth (Acts 18:12) indicates some time during or prior to the year 49 C.E.

Paul's letter to the Romans reflects the condition of the Roman church about 56 C.E. The church at Rome met primarily in its house churches. Priscilla and Aquila utilized their house for that purpose (Rom 16:3–5). Verse 16:15 may refer to yet another location. It is not clear when, if ever, the local house churches met as a metropolitan unit (note Col 4:16). The house churches involved both Jewish Christians (Rom 4:16) and gentile Christians (Rom 11:13). An onomastic analysis of Romans 16 indicates the presence of all levels of Roman society: slave and/or freed (e.g., Ampliatus [in Roman nomenclature a virtue name, like "ample," usually referred to a slave], Urbanus); Jews, Romans, and Greeks (e.g., Andronicus, Junia, Mary); and male and female.

1. Paul at Rome. The church at Rome claims as its apostolic foundation the two apostles, Paul and Peter. The presence of these two apostles at Rome has become a highly complex problem in which traditional, historical, and archaeological data are intertwined. Paul first came to Rome as a result of the decision of Festus (Acts 25:11–12). Paul must have arrived in Rome about the year 61. Some traditions would have Paul write the so-called Captivity Epistles while imprisoned at Rome and, after a missionary journey to Spain, the Pastoral Epistles during yet another imprisonment. Other sites (Ephesus, Caesarea Philippi) have been suggested for the provenance of the Captivity Epistles. The Pastoral Epistles are not generally considered original letters of Paul. Paul was likely martyred under Nero about the year 63. The first veneration of Paul occurred at the *memoria apostolorum,* "the memorial of the apostles," on the Via Appia (present-day S. Sebastiano). There on the graffiti (east) wall of the *triclinium,* or eating room, can be found numerous prayers to Paul and Peter (ca. 250 C.E.). Whatever happened between 250 and ca. 330, the veneration of Peter shifted to the Vatican site and the veneration of Paul shifted to Via Ostia (S. Paolo fuori le Mura).

2. Peter at Rome. According to tradition, Peter also spent the last days of his life in Rome. Tradition places his martyrdom to the northwest of the city at the circus of Nero, but the apostle Peter also was venerated at the *triclinium* on the Via Appia. Only after the accession of Constantine did the veneration of Peter at the *memoria apostolorum* cease. Yet even prior to the construction of the *triclinium* Peter was honored (with no sign of cultic veneration) at the Vatican site near the Neronian circus. A monument had appeared at the Vatican cemetery (a niche in the red wall of Campo P) about the year 160. Shortly thereafter an *aedicula* or small monument was built into the niche. Its exact date cannot be determined but about 200 a presbyter Gaius wrote, "I can show you the monuments *[tropaia]* of the apostles, for if you will go to the Vatican or to the Ostian Way, you will find the monuments of those who founded this church" (Eusebius, *Hist. Eccl.* 2.25.6,7). Though no signs of Christian cultic activity appear at the Vatican, eventually the emperor Constantine built the edifice S. Pietro over the *aedicula.* In one wall (the graffiti wall) of the *aedicula* was placed a marble box which presumably held the remains of the apostle.

According to tradition, the letters of Peter were written by him from Rome (1 Pet 5:13). More likely 1 Peter comes from a Petrine group in Rome, perhaps the first attempt of certain persons in the Roman church to advise the church catholic. 2 Peter was written much later in the 1st century.

B. Rome in Early Christian Literature

Tradition placed the NT book of Hebrews from Rome (13:24) near the end of the 1st century, though its similarity to Hellenistic Jewish thought makes Egypt attractive as the provenance, or an Alexandrian as the author. About 98 C.E. Clement of Rome wrote to the church at Corinth on behalf of the church at Rome *(1 Clem.,* Salutation). Clement does not claim authority to intervene at Corinth, nor does he evoke the power of the two apostles. See CLEMENT, FIRST EPISTLE OF. But Ignatius, writing to the church at Rome about 117, speaks of the church there as presiding over the Christians of Italy (*Ign. Rom.,* Inscription). Eventually the authority of the capital of the empire shifted to Rome as the central city of the universal church. And apostolic authority fell on the leader, Peter, rather than the theologian, Paul.

Much of the literature emanating from Rome does not actually reflect, it would appear, the condition of the church at Rome. A Gnostic school was formed in Rome before the middle of the 2d century. Its most famous scholar was Valentinus (in Rome ca. 136–60), quoted frequently by Clement of Alexandria and Irenaeus. His (or his followers') *Gospel of Truth* was a key find in the Nag Hammadi Library. Another school was formed by JUSTIN MARTYR. His two Apologies were written in Rome and addressed to the emperor Antoninus Pius (136–61). His description of the sacraments and Christian life in the first Apology (64–67) probably reflect the situation at Rome during the middle of the 2d century. The *anamnesis* or remembrance-style eucharist reflects the urban tradition of Rome in contrast to the more suburban, popular "agape" of Hippolytus *(The Apostolic Tradition).*

Literature from Rome during the first three centuries was written primarily in Greek, but the shift toward Latin can be seen in the writing of Minucius Felix. His remarkable apology, *Octavius,* written in Latin about 240, defends the Christian faith just prior to the Decian persecution (249–59). *Octavius* was used by another Roman, a pupil of Hippolytus, Novatian, in his *de trinitate* (ca. 250). Hippolytus himself, however, the most prolific of Roman writers prior to Constantine, wrote in Greek.

C. Key Issues in the Church at Rome

During the 2d and 3d centuries serious issues of the Christian life were addressed at Rome. In about 140, MARCION of Sinope came to Rome and proposed a radical ethic of love based on an attenuated "New Testament" canon. The church responded with a canon which included the Old Testament, with judgment as well as love. Incorrectly labeled a gnostic, Marcion was expelled from Rome in July 144. By the end of the 2d century the Roman church itself responded with a fuller canon which probably formed the basis for the Muratorian Canon. About the same time the author of the *Shepherd of Hermas* proposed a system of penance and at least a modicum of leniency in the readmittance of repentant apostates to the faith community. The issue of apostasy continued to plague the Roman community. At the end of the 2d century a powerful deacon named Callistus also favored a more lax attitude toward those who sinned or left the faith under pressure (the origin of John 7:53–8:11?). Callistus was opposed by the more demanding Hippolytus (*Philosophumena* 9). The issue was postponed by the failure of the Hippolytan group to elect a dissident bishop once the persecution of Decius had started, though the followers of Novatian continued to oppose leniency for those who apostasized during the persecution. Bishop Fabian (martyred under Decius on January 20, 250) took the opportunity to initiate veneration of the bishops of Rome instead of the martyrs. This shift in power toward the urban, pastoral types vis-à-vis the more unbending, populist type resulted finally, under Damasus, in a hierarchical Roman Christianity centralized under an episcopal authority based on the dual apostolic authority, especially that of St. Peter (*Hic habitasse prius sanctos cognoscere debes; nomina quisque Petri pariter Paulique requiris,* "You who seek the names of both Peter and Paul, you should know that these saints once dwelled here" [inscription of Damasus at S. Sebastiano]).

D. Onomastic Data

The later Roman church understood itself to be the heir of some early well-placed patrons. At the end of Domitian's reign a number of noble families were banished or put to death (ca. 95). A consul, Flavius Clemens, cousin of Domitian, was executed. His wife, Domitilla, was sent into exile. The catacomb of Domitilla is reputedly named for this noblewoman. A former consul, M. Acilius Glabrio, was also executed, and the catacomb of Priscilla reputedly derived from his wife.

It is not known how many house churches were formed in Rome. Eventually the later church claimed twenty-five titular churches which reputedly came from the earlier centuries. For example, the title church S. Clemente presumably evolved from the domicile of the so-called successor of Peter, Clement. These connections have not been proved. Nevertheless onomastic studies of early Christians in Rome do indicate that a broad spectrum of society adhered to nascent Christianity. One sample survey of inscriptions *(StadtrChr)* shows that before Constantine 10.5 percent of Christian men were designated by a tria nomina system; 32 percent of the men and 50 percent of the women were designated by a duo nomina system; and the rest were known only by a cognomen. Persons with two or three names must have been from Roman families, while the single-named persons (ca. 50 percent) must have been slaves or freed. After the "peace," Roman family names nearly disappeared. The Roman church participated in, or perhaps facilitated, an increasing democratization of Roman society. A similar phenomenon is observable with respect to slave names. While 3 percent of Roman inscriptions mentioned the status of slavehood, practically no such inscriptions can be found among Christian collections, even though 50 percent or more of the Christian population either were slaves or had been slaves. Christian or biblical names (e.g., Agape or Paulus) appear late (middle 3d century). Until that time Christians were primarily converts. There was little use of Christian birth names prior to Constantine.

E. Organization

The earliest organization of the church at Rome can only be ascertained obliquely. There are remarkably few references to offices in the inscriptional data. *Shepherd of Hermas* (8.3) refers to presbyters, apostles, bishops, teachers, and deacons (some still living) who formed the foundation of the church. Near the end of the 2d century a system of organization becomes evident. Bishop Victor (189–99) emerged as a very strong monarchical bishop. In the controversy over the date of Easter (Rome and others held to the first Friday through Sunday after the 14th of Nisan; the church of Asia kept the 14th of Nisan regardless of the day of the week), Victor even attempted to excommunicate the Asian churches. The next bishops of Rome, Zephyrinus (199–217) and Callistus (217–22), followed the same pattern.

About the turn of the century the deacon Callistus was given supervision of the catacombs. Underground Christian burials were legally registered by this time, so the Roman organization took on an institutional character. At the same time (ca. 200) the *fossores,* catacomb diggers, formed a legal society. Their insignia can be seen on a number of marble slabs from the catacombs. It was the bishop Zephyrinus, an opponent of Hippolytus (*Philosophumena* 9), who appointed Callistus as bishop of Rome. During that time a few people, likely connected with the suburban cemetery group, elected Hippolytus bishop. The schism continued through Urban (222–30), Pontianus (230–35), and Anteros (235–36). In August 236 or 237 the opponents Pontianus and Hippolytus were buried as martyrs in Rome, apparently reconciled. In any case, a process of replacing sporadic martyrs with church leaders had begun. In addition to presbyters and *fossores* there may have been a women's organization. The *Shepherd of Hermas* (78–110) mentions women Christians as if they performed certain pastoral functions; one Roman inscription (*SICV* no. 166; Snyder no. 3) hints at a nurturing function of women (*nonnae dulcissima* "most sweet nurse").

The church at Rome was much occupied with persecution from the beginning of the Decian attacks in 249 through that of Diocletian (starting February 23, 303). Pressured by a fatal illness, the emperor Galerius issued an edict of toleration in April 311. The churches moved from toleration to acceptance when Constantine received his famous vision at the Milvian bridge on October 26, 312. In June 313 the Edict of Milan, granting full benevolence to Christians, was published under the names of both Constantine and Licinius.

F. Theology

Unlike other urban Christian centers, no distinctive theology appeared in Rome before Constantine. The *Shepherd of Hermas* reflects a popular two-way or, more specifically, a two-spirit theology. In either case, like the authors of *Didache* and *Barnabas*, Hermas calls (*Shep. Herm.* 35–39) for the local Christian to choose between the way of righteousness and the way of evil. Marcion presented a radical ethic opposing grace and love to judgment, while Valentinus held to a sharp gnosticism with its dualistic view of the world. Both Justin Martyr and Minucius Felix defended Christianity in terms of Greek philosophy. At the time of Victor, a theology of Modalism (the trinity represents God the Father in three different historical modes) appeared in Rome, but the great writer Hippolytus described the trinity with an emphasis on function.

The intellectual energy of the church at Rome involved order. Its literature reflects primarily issues of rigidity and laxity in regard to church order. On the other hand, the popular material (such as art) reflects a theme of deliverance from threatening circumstances (Hebrew Scripture scenes such as Noah, Daniel, Jonah, and the three young men in the fiery furnace). The deliverer is portrayed as a young Jesus who functions as wonder worker (New Testament scenes such as healing miracles and the resurrection of Lazarus). There are very few allusions to a kerygmatic theology (death and resurrection of Jesus) or a creation theology (the ordering function of God).

Bibliography

Frend, W. H. C. 1984. *The Rise of Christianity.* Philadelphia.

La Piana, G. 1925. The Roman Church at the End of the Second Century. *HTR* 18: 201–77.

Pietri, C. 1976. *Roma christiana.* 2 vols. BEFAR 224. Rome.

Snyder, G. F. 1985. *Ante Pacem: Archaeological Evidence of Church Life before Constantine.* Macon, GA.

Vielliard, R. 1959. *Recherches sur les origines de la Rome chrétienne.* 2 vols. Rome.

GRAYDON F. SNYDER

CHRISTIANITY IN SYRIA

This branch of the Christian tradition is identified through the predominance of the Syriac language (a form of Aramaic developed primarily at Edessa) in theological and liturgical expression. The geographical boundaries of Syriac-speaking Christianity have varied with the vicissitudes of Middle Eastern history. Centering in what is now northern Iraq and eastern Turkey, Christians with this linguistic and cultural identity were active in areas now denominated by Syria, Lebanon, Iran, India (especially South India), China, parts of Georgia and Armenia, and the Gulf States. This article indicates the early development of Syriac-speaking Christianity with special attention to the history of exegesis.

A. The Mythology of Origins

Theories about the origins of Christianity in Syriac-speaking regions have focused on Edessa. Most scholars suspect that some Christian evangelistic activities were carried out there during the 1st century of the Christian era. Edessa was at that time capital of Osrhoene, a buffer state between the Parthian and the Roman empires. The theory recurring in early Syriac literature is that Edessa and territories to the east (as far as India) were evangelized by the Apostle Thomas. This datum is found in various 4th-century writers including Ephrem of Syria (*Hymn on Nisibis* 42), Cyrillonas (*Hymn of the Huns,* written ca. 396 C.E.), Gregory of Nazianzus (*Oration* 33.11), and Ambrose (*Narration on the Psalms* 45.21). The tradition, which apparently originated at Edessa during the early 4th century when major cities of the Roman Empire were attempting to achieve legitimation and stature by claiming apostolic origins for their Christian communities, is developed most extensively in the anonymous *Acts of Thomas.*

The second theory, not necessarily at odds with the Thomas tradition, is that of Addai, the Thaddaeus of the gospel narratives. In a tradition canonized by Eusebius (*Hist. Eccl.* 1.13), an exchange of letters took place between King Abgar V of Edessa and Jesus. Abgar begged Jesus to visit Edessa and offered him refuge there from his Jewish persecutors. Jesus gave Abgar a portrait and eventually sent Addai to become court evangelist and healer. This correspondence is extant in Syriac, Greek, and Armenian and has been noted by various early historians. This tradition has provoked much scholarly debate. Drijvers (1984) suggested it is a late 4th-century forgery used to fight the Manicheans (see below). Others, especially Chaumont (1988), have suggested there may be some historical basis to the story. The problematic *Doctrina Addai* is at the center of the controversy as are the *Acts of St. Mari the Apostle,* the reputed successor of Addai. At present, there is little contextual material by which to evaluate the claims of the documents or their interpreters. Most probably, both traditions, in the form now extant, are of late 4th-century provenance, written on the basis of oral traditions, and tell us little about the actual origins of Christianity in Syria.

Another theory (Vööbus 1958; Neusner 1971, and others) suggests that Christianity in Northern Mesopotamia first developed within the Jewish community. This theory would appear to find support in the *Chronicle of Arbela* which describes a Christian presence in the city of Arbela from ca. 100 C.E. However the *Chronicle of Arbela* (see below) is of disputed authenticity and one must hesitate to use its contents for information about the early 2d century.

Once again there is little data from earlier than the 4th century with which to test this theory. Probably the position of Edessa and Nisibis as important points on the "Silk Road," the main artery of commerce between the Roman Empire and the East (China, India, Parthia) and the involvement of Arameans in that commerce meant that Christianity traveled with the traders from Antioch toward the East. The demographics of Christianity within the Roman Empire would make it very plausible that the earliest converts were from Judaism. It is also probable that Christianity traversed the "Silk Road" at an early date. It is unclear whether Christianity in the Syriac-speaking areas was first structured in Aramaic (Syriac) or in Greek. Certainly at Dura Europas, the Christian community of this Roman military center appears to have been Greek-speaking; the 3d-century fragment of the *Diatessaron* found there is written in Greek.

B. The Earliest Evidence for Christianity in Syria

There is a paucity of documentation for Christianity in Syria before the 4th century. The most important documents are the Aberkios Inscription, the works of Tatian, the Socratic dialogue attributed to Bardaisan, the *Chronicle of Edessa,* and the problematic *Chronicle of Arbela.* There is some evidence regarding the Marcionites in Northern Mesopotamia.

1. The Aberkios Inscription and the *Life of Aberkios*. The earliest evidence for the development of Christian communities in Northern Mesopotamia is the Aberkios inscription from Asia Minor. This burial inscription, datable from before 216 C.E., recounts the visit of Aberkios to Nisibis where he encountered Christian co-religionists. The text recounts, "My name is Aberkios, the disciple of the chaste pastor who pastures his flock on the mountains and in the plains. . . . I saw the plain of Syria and all the villages, Nisibis across the Euphrates. Everywhere I found people with whom to speak . . . the faith preceded me everywhere" (Abel 1926). This inscription, without doubt authentic, provides no information as to the identity of the Christian groups in Syria, no indication of theological persuasion, and no names of persons met during the journey. On the basis of this inscription, a late 4th- or 5th-century writer composed a *Life of Aberkios* (edited by Nissen 1912) which provides a detailed account of the travels, miracles, exorcisms, struggles, and victories of the peripatetic sage as well as a purported verbatim of a discussion between Bardaisan (see below) and Aberkios. In this dialogue, Bardaisan's words as recorded in *The Book of the Laws of the Countries* are placed in the mouth of Aberkios. Drijvers (1966; 1984) has argued that the account of the meeting between Aberkios and Bardaisan is historically accurate but such an optimistic assessment of the *Life of Aberkios* is clearly unwarranted (Bundy 1990).

2. Tatian. Tatian, author of *Oration to the Greeks* (Whittaker 1982) and compiler/translator of the *Diatessaron,* was born in Assyria (*Oration* 43.10–11). He studied in Rome (*Oration* 37.1) and was active in the church there before returning to Mesopotamia, perhaps to Palmyra or Adiabene, ca. 172 C.E. probably because of a dispute with that church over its disregard for rigorous asceticism (Eusebius, *Eccl. Hist.* 4.9). It is unclear when the *Oration* was written, but its perspective is remarkably congruent with later Syriac thought and with the tendencies of interpretation in the *Diatessaron.* He presents a vision for an intellectual tradition "unmarred by party divisions" (*Or.* 27.3–5). He describes the church: "we reject all that is based on human opinion [and] taboo" (*Or.* 33.4–11). Within the church, the individual must strive to "obey God's word and not dissipate ourselves" (*Or.* 30.20–21), "lest the constitution of wickedness . . . grow strong" (*Or.* 30.18–19). It is the world which "drags us down, and it is weakness which makes me turn to matter" (*Or.* 22.10–11). Mankind is to "advance beyond his humanity towards God himself" (*Or.* 16.14–16). The divine spark in humans, aided by God, disciplined by the free will, arrives at a knowledge of God (*Or.* 14.12–16) as well as of "the precepts and doctrine of a single ruler of the Universe" (*Or.* 30.10–11). The theological analysis is aimed against both Greek pagan and Marcionite theology.

The life which will nurture the spirit is characterized by sexual rectitude (his main critique of Greco-Roman society), by trust in God for all needs, including healing, and by study of the Scriptures. There is to be a rejection of Greco-Roman values and culture in favor of Scriptural values. This rigorous asceticism probably forms the ideological base for "Sons and Daughters of the Covenant," a group of perfectionistic Christians who by their spirituality, celibacy, and asceticism attempted to live the "ideal" Christian life. The celibacy and other encratic practices of self-denial for spiritual development, as expressed in known *Diatessaron* fragments, have been discussed by Vööbus (1951a), Messina (1943), and Leloir (1956).

The *Diatessaron* was Tatian's most influential work. This effort to harmonize the divergent and contradictory accounts of the life of Jesus as recounted in the four canonical Gospels circulated in both Greek and Syriac. Because of later Manichean use of the text, it was first corrected on the basis of the Greek gospels and then abandoned and systematically destroyed. It was translated into Arabic, Persian, as well as Western European languages (Metzger 1977). It provided the early Syriac church with a unique Scripture and certainly aided the process of development of the Syriac-speaking Christian subculture. The only extant remains in Syriac are in Ephrem's *Commentary on the Diatessaron* (Leloir 1963) and occasional citations in early Syriac language writings.

3. Bardaisan. Bardaisan is known from a dialogue recorded by his disciple Philippus, *The Book of the Laws of the Countries* (*BLC*) (Nau 1907), a reference to his skills as an archer by Sextus Julius Africanus (Thee 1984: 147–48), the approbation conferred by Eusebius for his erudite anti-Marcionite texts (*Hist. Eccl.* 4.30.1–2), and the angry diatribes of Ephrem of Syria about Bardaisan's syncretism and expensive clothes and jewels *(Prose Refutations; Hymns against Heresy).*

He was born at Edessa, ca. 155 C.E., into the royal family of Osrhoene. Educated under a pagan priest at Mabbug (Hierapolis), he became the first author of whom it is certain that he composed his writings in Syriac. According to legend, he and his son Harmonius wrote hymns which Ephrem and others felt obliged to counter with hymns of their own. Although writers centuries later would cast aspersion on Bardaisan's orthodoxy, he was presented by Phillipus as an apologist for an understanding of Christianity which stood over against Marcion, regional astrological systems, and Greek theologies.

In *BLC,* Bardaisan argues against determinism and for freedom of the will. This freedom and the dominion of creation constitute the image of God (*BLC* 11). After recounting the divergent customs and laws of various countries to prove their diversity, he characterizes Christians as "the new people . . . that the Messiah has caused to arise in every place and in all climates by his coming" (*BLC* 58–60). They are called Christians after the Messiah, on the first day, "we gather together," on appointed days they fast (*BLC* 60). He provides a list of examples where Christian ethics differ from un-Christian ethics (seven of nine deal with sexuality). "But in whatever place they are . . . the local laws do not force them to give up the law of their Messiah, nor does the fate of guiding signs force them to do things which are unclean for them" (*BLC* 60.12–15). Bardaisan insisted, as did all Syriac writers, that sexual rectitude was essential to the Christian life. However, Bardaisan did not see sex within marriage as illegitimate or indicative of an inferior level of spirituality as did others such as Tatian (*BLC* 34.15–25, see Bundy 1985a).

References to the changes of laws in Edessa after the conversion of King Abgar (*BLC* 58.21–22) suggest that Bardaisan's church was sanctioned by the government. The relatively upper-class nature of the church is evident from Ephrem's attacks on the "worldliness" of the Bardaisanites (*Hymns against Heresy* 1.12) of the late 4th century. After the conquest of Osrhoene by Rome, Bardaisan and others appear to have taken refuge in Armenia.

The interpretation of Bardaisan in Christian history has been prejudiced by his inclusion in early Western lists of heretics and by Ephrem's scathing analyses. Modern discussion has focused on his adaptation of indigenous philosophical structures to articulate Christian doctrine. His syncretistic tendencies have been viewed positively (Drijvers 1966) and negatively (Jansma 1969). However, the question of Bardaisan's intellectual structures has not been definitively resolved.

4. The *Chronicle of Edessa*. This text is a chronological listing, composed sometime during the 6th century from earlier sources, of the most significant events of Edessa and surrounding towns, especially Nisibis. It notes that a "Church of the Christians" was destroyed in 201 C.E. by flood waters. The next reference is to the "foundation of the church in Edessa" by Bishop Kune in 313 C.E. which was completed by his successor, Bishop Scha'ad. Bishop Aithallah who represented Edessa at Nicea is said to have built the cemetery and expanded the east side of the church in 324–25 C.E.

The validity of this data was rejected by Bauer (1934; ET 1971) and accepted at face value by Turner (1954) and Segal (1970). It would appear that Bauer's devaluing of the *Chronicle of Edessa* is too severe. It is probable that, with royal patronage or at least tolerance during the last decades of the Kingdom of Osrhoene, a church building did exist at Edessa before 201 C.E.

5. The *Chronicle of Arbela.* This chronicle is devoted to the city of Arbela in the buffer state of Adiabene, which was ruled by a Jewish monarchy until the invasion of Trajan, 115/16 C.E. It recounts the lives, in later hagiographical form, of the early bishops of Arbela, beginning in about 100 C.E. The second bishop, Bishop Samson, was martyred by the Parthian king Xosroes, during a period of Parthian occupation. The first publication of the text (Mingana 1907) produced a flurry of scholarly activity. Assfalg (1966) and Fiey (1967) argued against its authenticity and suspected it to be a forgery of the editor. Brock (1967) was less certain that it was not a medieval composition. The most recent editors, Kawerau (1985) and Chaumont (1988), believe it to have historical value, as did Neusner (1966) and Sachau (1915).

If the *Chronicle of Arbela* gives an accurate rendition of earlier sources, it may mean that Christianity in Syriac-speaking areas first developed in Arbela and that Syriac (or a related form of Aramaic) began to be used as a liturgical and biblical language there. Even if the dates and names are accurate, the interpretive framework of the *Chronicle* is of a later century, certainly no earlier than the 6th or 7th.

6. Marcionite Christianity. The importance of the Marcionite tradition in the evangelization of Syria is well known. Much of the literature of other Christian groups, from Bardaisan to Ephrem, was written to counter Marcionite influence (Bundy 1988). In many areas of northern Mesopotamia, Christian meant Marcionite. The emperor Julian mentions (*Letter* 41) pogroms by his predecessors against Marcionite villages after the advent of imperial Christianity. Unfortunately, there is no data about the beginnings and development of this tradition.

7. Other Early Documents of Syriac-speaking Christianity. There are a variety of undated (and perhaps undatable) documents which circulated early in Syriac-speaking areas. These include the *Odes of Solomon,* the *Gospel of Thomas* (here the evidence is less than clear), the Pseudo-Clementine corpus, the *Didascalia Apostolorum* (and perhaps the *Didache*), the *Acts of Judas Thomas,* and the intriguing but relatively unexamined *Apology* of Pseudo-Melito. The use of these texts to illumine the early period of Syriac-speaking Christianity is problematic. For example, Murray (1975) suggested the *Odes of Solomon* are the earliest extant Syriac sources. Drijvers (1981; 1984), on the other hand, argues that the present form of these hymns dates from the 3d or 4th century and reflects the struggle with Manichaeism. Lattke (1986) rejects Drijver's theory, arguing for an earlier date. The issues of date and provenance of this collection of hymns (and of the other texts mentioned) are far from settled.

8. The Early Syriac-speaking Church before the 3d Century. The chronological and prosopographical data about the origins of Christianity in Syriac-speaking areas of northern Mesopotamia are uncertain. The religious vision is not uniform, vacillating between the poles of Tatian's rejection of Greco-Roman culture and Bardaisan's acceptance of contemporary science and cosmology. Each text is fraught with interpretive and/or authenticity problems. It is not possible to construct a traditional historical narrative of the early development of Christianity in this region.

C. Early Biblical Texts

The Syriac versions of the Bible have posed many scholarly problems. These concern the relationships between the various translations, their places of origin, and their exegesis. The primary efforts at biblical translations include the Peshitta of the Old Testament, the *Diatessaron,* the Old Syriac *(Vetus Syra),* the Peshitta translation of the NT, the Philoxenian and/or Harklean version, and the Palestinian version. A discussion of the NT versions can be found in Metzger (1977).

1. The Peshitta of the OT. The origin of this translation is unknown. Its connections to Jewish targumic literature suggest that it evolved in a Jewish milieu. Kahle (1959) argued that it was made in Adiabene as an effort to adapt the Palestinian targum for new converts. This theory has been accepted by Murray (1975: 10), *inter alia.* The problem is that there are also readings shared with the *Targum Onkelos* of Babylon. The Adiabene theory is plausible, but with no philological or historical evidence. In addition to the problem of provenance, there is no possibility of dating the translation with any precision. The earliest citations are from 4th-century texts.

The text is remarkably consistent throughout its transmission history as has been demonstrated by Koster (1977) and Dirksen (1972). A definitive critical edition, *Vetus Testamentum Syriace* (1972–), is being published by the Peshitta Institute of Leiden. Later commentators would indicate variant readings with the LXX traditions and occasionally the Hebrew text, but it appears that little emmendation was attempted.

2. The *Diatessaron.* This harmony of the gospel composed by Tatian has been mentioned above. The original language (Greek, Syriac, or Latin), theological tendencies, and function in the churches has been extensively discussed. For a summary of the various points of view, see Metzger (1977). There are witnesses to the text in Old Dutch, Old Italian, medieval German, Persian, and Arabic. In Greek there is only the fragment found at Dura Europas (see above). In Syriac and Armenian, the most extensive witness is the *Commentary on the Diatessaron* attributed to Ephrem of Syria (306–73). Lyonnet (1950) has demonstrated that the earliest translations of the Gospels into Armenian owed much to the Syriac *Diatessaron.* Extensive quotations are found in such writers as Aphraates, Ephrem, Eznik, Marutha Maipherkatensis, Agathangelos, Rabbula, and the author of the *Liber Graduum.* See also DIATESSARON.

3. The Old Syriac *(Vetus Syra).* This version is known primarily from two manuscripts. Both contain only the four canonical Gospels. No Old Syriac of the Pauline or general epistles has been found, although citations of those texts in Armenian translations of Syriac literature suggest these may have existed. The first is in the British Library (B.L. 14451). Discovered by William Cureton, it was definitively edited by F. C. Burkitt (1904) with additional pages of the same manuscript found in the Royal Library of Berlin. The second manuscript was discovered by Agnes Smith Lewis and Margaret Dunlop Gibson at St. Catharine Monastery on Mt. Sinai. The manuscript had been reused, as a manuscript for lives of women saints, by imperfectly cleaning off the biblical text. After two less than adequate efforts by scholars to decipher the manuscript, A. S. Lewis made several trips to Sinai and was able to publish what remains the best edition (1910).

The text of the Curetonian and Sinaitic manuscripts do not agree at all points, although they clearly stand alone and close together in the larger world of Syriac NT translations. Scholars have generally assumed either that the two are revisions of a common source or that they are independent translations made during the same period. Linguistic peculiarities shared by the two manuscripts suggest that they may be the effort of individuals to gain access to the Greek tradition which lay behind the Syriac *Diatessaron.* Matthew Black (1972) argues for dating these efforts to the 4th century. For a detailed survey of the discussion of scholarly work on the Old Syriac, see Black (1972) and Metzger (1977). The effort of Vööbus (1951b; 1951c) to marshal evidence from the *Letter of Aithallah* in support of his theory of early 4th-century prominence of the *Vetus Syra* at Edessa has been demonstrated to be incorrect (Bundy 1987).

4. The Syriac Peshitta. The word "peshitta" has generally been understood as "simple" or "clear," not unlike the term "vulgate" applied to the received Latin translation. This version of the New Testament is used by both East Syrians (Nestorians) and West Syrians (Jacobites) and therefore certainly predates the division of the Syriac church along political, geographical, and theological lines during the mid-5th century. More precise dating of the translation has provoked controversy. Some have dated it as early as the late 1st or early 2d century. Burkitt (1901) argued that it was from the early 5th century and later suggested that it was translated by Rabbula of Edessa (Burkitt 1904). This conclusion has been contested by Vööbus (1951b), who argued that it was much older although slow to achieve dominance in the Syriac-speaking church.

The manuscript tradition is quite uniform. There are remarkably few variants in the Peshitta as compared to the Old Syriac or Greek versions. Its textual tradition is well documented by the hundreds of manuscripts preserved, the earliest manuscript (ca. 460–464) probably being *Paris Syriac 296.1* in the Bibliotheque Nationale which contains *Luke* 6:49–21:37. No adequate critical edition of the entire NT in the Peshitta version has been published despite the fact that the first printed edition was done at Venice as early as 1555. The best text available, based on earlier editions which were themselves only partial collations of the manuscript evidence, is published by the Bible Society as *The New Testament in Syriac.* This printing has no critical apparatus. It also contains the Apocalypse and General Epistles, which were not part of the Peshitta translation, but based on the Philoxenian version.

5. Later Syriac Translations. The Philoxenian version was prepared at the direction of Philoxenos of Mabbug (Hierapolis) by a certain Polycarp in 507–8 C.E. An effort to bring the Syriac more in line with the Greek, it also provided, probably for the first time in Syriac, 2 Peter, 2 and 3 John, Jude, and the Apocalypse. A century later (616 C.E.) the version of Thomas of Harkel, assistant to the famous translator of the OT Paul of Tella, was produced. The Harklean version has been variously considered either a revision of the Philoxenian or a new translation. For a history of this debate, see Metzger (1977).

The Palestinian Syriac version is actually a different version of Aramaic. It is closer to Jewish Palestinian Aramaic than to the Syriac of Edessa and northern Mesopotamia.

6. The Early Versions. Apart from the *Diatessaron,* the early Syriac biblical texts are difficult to date. There is no concrete evidence of their existence before the 4th century, although it is probable that at least the OT was available in Syriac early in the Christian period. The *Diatessaron* exerted a strong influence on the development of early Syriac theology and praxis. The Peshitta displaced the *Diatessaron* slowly at first because of pressure from the Greek church and the problems posed by Manicheans finding readings that lent support to their understanding. The major blow came in the late 4th century when Theodoret of Cyrus, because of Tatian's reputation as a heretic in the Western church, gathered and destroyed over 200 copies after replacing them with copies of the individual Gospels.

D. The Third Century

There was significant sociopolitical upheaval in northern Mesopotamia during the 3d century. Rome continued to push its interests eastward. Trajan had conquered Adiabene in 115/16 C.E. as well as Osrhoene. The local dynasty has been allowed to remain in Osrhoene (Abgar et al.) but as tributary clients of the Roman state. Lucus Verus (165–66) had extended Roman control at least as far east as Nisibis. Dura Europos came into Roman hands and was made a frontier fortress city. Septimius Severus (d. 211), mentor of the Christian scholar Sextus Julius Africanus, married Julia Domna, daughter of the high priest of Emesa.

After 226 C.E., the Sassanid Empire, which replaced the Parthian, began to look westward. Shapur I (240–72) set out to reduce Roman influence in the eastern provinces. A series of campaigns allowed him to incorporate Roman fortifications on the Euphrates (including Dura Europos, 256), Emesa, and parts of Cilicia as well as Antioch, which appears to have been occupied in 256 C.E. Many Greek and Aramean/Syriac-speaking Christians were among the many thousands of civilians deported to weaken the economic and military base of Roman Syria and strengthen that of the Persian Empire. The Christians among the exiles brought with them their ecclesiastical structures, and in several villages, both Syriac and Greek languages churches were organized (Chaumont 1988). From this series of deportations comes one of the traditions of the ecclesiastical identity of Mesopotamian leaders, namely that early on they were ordained by and in submission to the Bishop of Antioch.

Palmyra, a city-province to the south of Edessa, took advantage of the power vacuum in Syria to assert its independence and to expand its influence toward Palestine and Egypt. This brought Palmyra into direct confrontation with Rome and the emperor Aurelian conquered Palmyra in 271 and sacked the city, after a revolt, in 272. Among the advisors *(Procurator Ducenarius)* of Queen Zenobia of Palmyra was Paul of Samosata, Bishop of Antioch from 260 until his removal in 268 by a synod of Antioch for supposed heretical teachings which were later, anachronistically, credited with being foundational to Nestorianism. His civil power was probably the main root of the theological controversy (Eusebius, *Eccl. Hist.* 7.27–30). None of his writings have been preserved.

Probably because of the social and theological turmoil, no Syriac language documents have survived between the writing of Bardaisan (ca. 212 C.E.) and the early decades of the 4th century.

Religious life in northern Mesopotamia was complicated by the arrival of Manichaeism with the Persian armies. See also MANICHEANS. Manichaeism was a result of the "mission" of Mani, who understood himself as the Paraclete promised in the Gospel of John and as an "apostle of Jesus Christ." Mani was apparently part of the entourage of Shapur I and used his travels to spread his religious perspective. He left behind a vigorous movement. From ca. 240 C.E. Manichaeism became a powerful contender for the minds of the inhabitants of northern Mesopotamia. It appealed to people because of its rigorous asceticism with respect both to food and sexuality (not unlike Tatian), a clearly defined cosmology and divinization program (which drew on Bardaisan and popular philosophy), and its carefully crafted hymnody and liturgy which were not unlike the established Christian patterns.

Several of the texts mentioned above including elements in the *Odes of Solomon,* the Abgar correspondence, and the *Doctrina Addai* may be efforts of established Christian groups to use the language, imagery, and history of Manichaeism against it (Drijvers 1984).

Manichaeism was not the only competitor for what would be recognized as imperial Christianity in the 4th century. The Marcionite communities continued to wield influence and attract the attention of apologists (Bundy 1988). Roman, Greek, and regional pagan cults continued to flourish. There was also influence from astrological myths and science.

E. The Fourth Century

At the turn of the 4th century, there is once again evidence of Christian activity in Edessa, Nisibis, and the Persian Empire. The earliest data is of Nisibis. Ephrem (306–73 C.E.), writing at Nisibis, describes the life and work of James of Nisibis, who served as Bishop from 308–38. He attended the Council of Nicea as did Bishop Aithallah of Edessa.

1. Nicea. The Council of Nicea changed the balance of power within Syriac Christianity. Imperial Christianity, that is, one version of Christian doctrine and praxis as the unifying ideology of empire, determined and enforced from the center of political power, authenticated the tradition of Palut (the earliest "orthodox" bishop) rather than that of Bardaisan. The Marcionites were now prescribed. Christian emperors would actually eradicate Marcionite villages in northern Mesopotamia. It is no accident that the *Ecclesiastical History* of Eusebius was almost immediately translated into Syriac.

2. *De Recta Fide* of Adamantius. The earliest text is, probably, the dialogue of Adamantius, *De recta fide* (for centuries mistakenly thought to be by Origen) against two disciples of Marcion, Megethius and Marcus (parts 1–2) and against Marinus, a contrived follower of Bardaisan (parts 3–4). The essay cites Methodios of Olympus (d. ca. 311) and was translated into Latin by Rufinius. It is uncertain that it existed in Syriac but definitely seems to be from northern Mesopotamia. It is possible that parts of Bardaisan's dialogues against Marcion are preserved in this text.

3. The Anti-Marcionite Commentary on the Lukan Parables. Also from the first 3d of the 4th century is the anti-Marcionite apology which is a commentary on the Lukan parables, known as *Pseudo-Ephrem A.* It has been attributed to Ephrem but was definitely not written by him (Bundy 1988). The chosen ground of discussion is the parables found in the Gospel of Luke discussed (with the exception of one reversal) in the order they appear in the *Diatessaron.* The author cites, on occasion, Matthew and John but is aware that they are not in the Marcionite canon. Only Pauline texts accepted by Marcion are cited. The piety, ecclesiology, and spirituality are not attacked. The issue is one of scriptural interpretation (with more than Luke's gospel, one can know more) and belonging to the author's ("true" Christian) community. The tone is respectful and moderate.

4. Aphraates, Persian Theologian. The same can be said of the works *(Demonstrations)* of Aphraates, a Persian writer who wrote in Syriac. An unverifiable tradition recorded in the title of *Demonstration* 23 says he was known as Jacob and that he was from the Mar Mattai Monastery east of Mossul. Nothing is known of his life but he did write a letter on behalf of a Synod (*Dem.* 14). The dates of several of the essays are known: *Dem.* 1–10 (336–37 C.E.); *Dem.* 11–22 (344 C.E.); and 23 (344–45 C.E.) during the persecution of Shapur I. Aphraates is aware of the Marcionite church but is more concerned with Valentinianism, Manichaeism, and Judaism. The latter is viewed as potentially most seductive to his co-religionists. Discussions of Judaism and the Jewish understanding of the OT dominates *Dem.* 11–13, 15–19, 21, and 23. Neusner (1971) has argued that Aphraates' debate with the Jews is remarkably free from anti-Semitism and that the argument is conducted around the focus of arguments about the interpretation of biblical-historical data rather than about theological concerns.

The other *Demonstrations* offer explanations of Christian life and theology. It is a perspective distinct from that found within the church inside the Roman Empire of the period. Christological debates provoked by the Arian controversies are absent. Instead the effort is to argue that the concepts of God and Son are not incompatible with monotheism. The Creed of Aphraates (*Dem.* 1.19) is unique among early Christian creeds: "The faith is, when one believes: in God, the Lord of all, who made the heavens, the earth, the sea and all that they encompass; He made Adam in his image; He gave the Law to Moses; He sent his Spirit upon the prophets; He sent moreover his Christ into the world. Furthermore, that one should believe in the resurrection of the dead; and should furthermore believe in the sacrament of baptism. This is the faith of the Church of God." In addition to this positive statement, there is a series of negative statements which insist the believer avoid astrology, numerology, "Chaldean arts and magic," adultery, fornication, and lying.

Aphraates provides the earliest references to an institutional feature of early Syriac Christianity, the "Sons of the

Covenant" *(benai qyama)* and "Daughters of the Covenant" *(benat qyama)*. The exact nature of these groups of believers within the Church has perplexed scholars. Some (e.g., Vööbus 1958) have wanted to see it, anachronistically, as a precursor to monasticism because of the solitary living, abstinence from sexual relations even within marriage, and ascetic food practices. Others (e.g., Brock 1973) have more plausibly argued that they functioned as diaconal clergy or as ascetics within everyday society. Without doubt, this structure for Christian spirituality antedated Aphraate, but its origins are unknown. It would appear that Ephrem of Syria, our next subject of discussion, was a member of the "Sons of the Covenant."

5. Ephrem of Syria, Theologian at Nisibis and Edessa. a. Nisibis. Nisibis during the 4th century had the dubious advantage of being situated on the frontier between the Roman and Persian empires as the most significant trading center between those two usually hostile states. Situated on the so-called "Silk Road" over which goods and people traveled between the Roman Empire and China and India, there were economic benefits as the anonymous northern Mesopotamian writer of *Expositio totius mundi et gentium* (written ca. 359 C.E.) explains: "They [Nisibeans] are rich and supplied with all goods. They receive from the Persians that which they sell in all of the lands of the Romans and that which they purchase, they in turn sell to them, except bronze and iron, because it is forbidden to give bronze and iron to the enemies."

Ephrem provided an interpretive analysis of life and morality in Nisibis. His *Hymns on Nicomedia,* ostensibly written as reflections on the earthquake of Nicomedia (358 C.E.), are actually a detailed portrait of Nisibis. They provide insights into the nature of the cultural and social pressures which Ephrem and his co-religionists were facing. Ephrem describes the fields, vineyards, gardens and farms, as well as the artisans, weavers, metal workers, and tailors and notes the governmental infrastructure. The prosperity described reflects the observation of the author of *Expositio totius mundi et gentium* that ". . . they lead a good life." Ephrem is less sanguine about the nature of religious life in Nisibis. He condemns the avarice of businessmen and government officials. He discounts the results of pagan science and culture, scorning those Christians who consult magicians and astrologers for help in healing illnesses and sterility. He criticizes the husbands of "pious women" who refuse to accept their wives' vows of celibacy and turn to Arab women as concubines and prostitutes. Socially, Nisibis is portrayed as a quintessential frontier commercial center.

The major drawback to the location is seen in the siege of Nisibis by the Persians in 338. The city resisted the siege. Ephrem attributed this to the prayers and leadership of Bishop Jacob of Nisibis. Jacob became a legend in Syriac, Armenian, and Greek Christianity and paradigmatic of the ascetic, devout, politically active Christian bishop. Little is known of his career except for the fact of his participation at Nicea and the narratives of his pastoral activities and prayers for the deliverance of Nisibis recorded in Ephrem's *Hymns on Nisibis.* The data in Armenian sources and in Theodoret of Cyr are unreliable. Even less is known of the other three 4th-century bishops mentioned by Ephrem: Babou (d. 346), Vologese (346–61), and Abraham (361–?).

b. Who Was Ephrem (306–73)? Ephrem's influence in the Syriac-speaking churches was perhaps the most important factor in their intellectual and spiritual development. His work largely determined the relationships between theological investigation, spirituality, and liturgy. His poetry, written exclusively in Syriac, was translated into Armenian, Georgian, Arabic, Ethiopic, Paleo-Slavic, Latin, and Chinese. No other writer is as extensively represented in the Greek manuscript tradition. Despite his fame and influence, little is known about him. Supposedly a student, a certain Symeon of Samosata, wrote a biography, but if so, it is lost. All we have are the accounts of Palladius and Sozomenos, which have served generations of hagiographers. From the Syriac world, the earliest is a eulogy by Jacob of Serug, delivered more than a century after Ephrem's death and devoid of detail. The only authentic sources are the occasional autobiographical allusions in his own work. The fact that these contradict the traditional stories of Ephrem's life adds credibility to the statements.

From comments in Ephrem's works, it appears that he was born into a Christian family, became a Christian believer at an early age, and was baptized, probably in his early teenage years. He was a participant in the "orthodox" church of Nisibis. He was not ordained, but was a member of the lay order, the *benai qyama* (Sons of the Covenant), which required vows of asceticism, poverty, and contemplative lifestyle. The oft-cited date of his birth, 306 C.E., cannot be verified.

After the surrender of Nisibis to the Persians by the emperor Jovian in 363 C.E., Ephrem became a war refuge. He apparently made his way to Edessa, where he entered the service of Bishop Barses. There he wrote extensively, taught choirs of women to sing his hymns against heresies, and involved himself in relief work. He died in the famine of 373 C.E. on June 9. On Ephrem's life, see Brock (1975) and Bundy (1986).

c. Ephrem as a Writer and Theologian. Ephrem was a prolific author. He used several genre: prose (commentaries on the Bible, sermons, letters refuting heresies); *memre* (verse homilies), and *madrase* (hymns).

(1) Commentaries. Of the prose works, the commentaries are important for our discussion. The *Commentary on the Diatessaron* (Leloir 1963) quotes extensively from the *Diatessaron* and preserves more of the text of the Syriac *Diatessaron* than any other source. Ephrem's commentary was translated into Armenian, probably during the 5th century.

The exegesis of the commentary reflects several of Ephrem's concerns. First, there is both a level of linear historicity and the level of symbolism. In many passages there is the recognition that the basic data of the life of Jesus and others as encountered in the text are phenomena to be examined, systematized, and clarified. However, the focus is on the significance of the Gospel text in what Brock (1985) has described as "sacred time." Second, there is an effort to balance the OT and NT images and symbols to demonstrate the convergence of the OT toward the NT. Third, it reflects Ephrem's conviction that nature is revelatory of God and of God's intention for the world.

The same pattern is seen in the *Commentary on the Pauline*

Epistles. This corpus is preserved only in an Armenian translation. The structure of the commentaries is scholiastic. That is, a Pauline phrase is quoted and then followed immediately by an explanation. Because of the provisional nature of the edition and the linguistic difficulties, this text has been rarely studied.

The *Commentary on Genesis and Exodus* preserved in a single Syriac manuscript from the Vatican Library *(Vat. Syr.* 110) is an important witness to early Christian exegesis. As with Ephrem's other commentaries, it reflects a tradition of exegesis with significant divergences from the Western tradition. It reflects an awareness (probably indirect) of the results of Rabbinic exegesis of *Genesis* and *Exodus.* Hidal (1974) and Kronholm (1978) have demonstrated the congruence of this commentary with the rest of the Ephrem corpus.

Other commentary material attributed to Ephrem preserved in Syriac, Armenian, Ethiopic, Arabic, and Georgian has not been definitively examined, but is probably not directly from Ephrem although it may depend on his work or be part of the production of the so-called "School of Ephrem." This corpus of *dubia* includes commentary on the entire OT and the separate Gospels.

(2) Prose Sermons, the Letter to Publius and Refutations of Heresies. The magnificent, magisterial *Homily on Our Lord* is the only prose homily attributed to Ephrem which is certainly authentic. Other sermons preserved under the name of Ephrem are highly dubious or spurious. Brock (1976), who provided an edition and translation of the *Letter to Publius,* argued that it is probably authentic. It discusses eschatology and judgment and offers surprising divergences with Western views on these subjects.

The prose *Refutations of Heresies,* written in the form of letters, provide insights into the debates in which Ephrem engaged. He argued against four primary competitors: the Marcionites, Bardaisanites, Manicheans, and Arians. Against the Marcionites he contended that their dualism and determinism (Ephrem was a firm believer in freedom of the will) led to an understanding of matter and humanity as inherently evil. This led Marcionites to a docetic christology and denial of the resurrection of the human body, soul, and spirit. The critique of Bardaisan was at two levels. He found their lack of asceticism and confidence in northern Mesopotamian science unfortunate. More serious was the conception of monotheism with attendant ideas of emanations which he felt verged on polytheism.

The Manicheans were radically dualistic and deterministic. Both of these concepts were alien to Ephrem as was the Manichean ascription of a revelatory role to Mani. Ephrem accused Mani of having taken over the Greek understanding of matter and Indian dualism. Arians were criticized for having accepted a Greek philosophical framework for articulating the gospel message and for abandoning faith in scriptural testimony. This resulted, according to Ephrem, in excessive speculation about God, Christ, and the world. The most dire consequence of their "deviation" was understood to be its effect on the mission of the church, the dissension which makes the church appear ridiculous to the "pagans" outside.

(3) Hymns (Madrase) and Metrical Homilies (memre). From Ephrem's pen about 450 *madrase* have been preserved. These were gathered into loosely defined cycles: *On the Nativity* (28 hymns), *On Faith* (87 hymns), *On Virginity* (52 hymns), *On the Church* (52 hymns), *On Nisibis* (77 hymns), *Against Heresies* (56 hymns), *On Unleavened Bread* (21 hymns), *On Paradise* (15 hymns), *On the Fast* (10 hymns), *Against Julian* (4 hymns), and 51 hymns preserved only in Armenian. In many cases the hymn tune name has been preserved, but there is no evidence about the music. Other hymn cycles existed at an earlier date but have been lost through the vicissitudes of northern Mesopotamian history.

The *memre* include at least 27 items which are of reasonable authenticity: *On Nicomedia* (16 *memre*), *On Faith* (6 *memre*), *On Reprehension* (4 *memre*), and *On Nineveh and Jonah* (1 *memra*). Other *memre* attributed to Ephrem are probably inauthentic. The authentic *madrase* and *memre* reflect an exegetical method congruent with the authentic commentary material discussed above. On the theology of Ephrem, see Beck (1949), (1980), (1981), and (1984).

6. Ephrem's Disciples. Works by several disciples of Ephrem are found in the literary fragments of late 4th- and early 5th-century Syriac Christianity. From the pen of Zenobius there are three sermons preserved in Armenian: two on the traditions of the Jews and one in praise of Melitius, the martyr. Fragments of a verse homily or homilies by Aba is preserved in a Sinaitic Syriac manuscript. Six hymns attributed to Cyrillonas have survived. These deal with a variety of topics including the invasion of the Huns (396 C.E.), the conversion of Zacchaeus, the anointing of the feet of Jesus, the passion of Christ (2 hymns), and the "Wise Ones." An anonymous vita of Eusebius of Samosata (d. 380) is dated by Ortiz de Urbina (1965) to this period. The exegetical traditions of Ephrem continued to be used and preserved and expanded as can be seen from the Severian catena. The rest of the writings from what appears to have been a rich literary period have been lost.

F. Subsequent Development of Syriac Exegetical Traditions

After the division of Syriac Christianity into two competing traditions ca. 428 C.E., owing to sociopolitical and theological considerations, the exegetical traditions of East (Nestorian) and West (Jacobite) Syrians developed with different influences. In the West, the main sources were Cyril of Alexandria and Chrysostom translated from Greek with Ephrem of Syria and scholia attributed to him. These have been preserved most extensively in the *Exegetical Catena* of Severus of Edessa, compiled in 861 C.E. The influence of this material would extend into Cilician Armenia. Most notably this catena served as a source for the huge commentary of Gēorg Skewṛacʿi on *Isaiah* (Bundy 1983a). After Ephrem, the most influential West Syrian exegetes included Jacob of Edessa, Moses bar Kepha, Dionysius bar Ṣalibi, and Barhebraeus.

In East Syrian exegesis, the commentaries of Theodore of Mopsuestia, translated from Greek ca. 428, served as models and sources. The East developed a rich exegetical tradition, some of which (e.g., Mar Aba, Seharbokt, Henanišo, Gabriel Qatraya, Daniel bar Tubanita, Sabrišo' bar Paulos) is known only from fragments preserved in the large *Gannat Bussame (Garden of Delights),* a collection of biblical exegetical material organized around the liturgy (Reinink 1979). Significant amounts of material of Theodore bar Koni, Išo' bar Nūn, and Išo'dad of Merv have been preserved. For trends in the development of Syriac exegesis, see Bundy (1983b).

G. Texts

Editions of Syriac texts may be found, usually with translation, in the *Patrologia Orientalis, Corpus Scriptorum Christianorum Orientalium,* and the *Patrologia Syriaca.* Here one can find texts of Aphraates, Bardaisan, and Ephrem mentioned above. Ephrem's *Prose Refutations* are available, with English translation in C. W. Mitchell (1921). Bibliography and articles about personages and events in early Syriac Christianity can be found in Baumstark (1922), Ortiz de Urbina (1965), *Dictionnaire de Spiritualité, Dictionnaire d'histoire et de géographie ecclésiastiques,* and Assfalg and Kruger (1975). For extensive, more recent bibliography see Bundy (1985b), Brock (1981–82), and Brock (1987).

Bibliography

Abel, A. 1926. Étude sur l'inscription d'Abercius. *Byzantion* 3: 221–411.

Assfalg, J. 1966. Zur Textuberlieferung der Chronik von Arbela. Beobachtungen zu Ms. or. Fol. 3126. *OrChr* 50: 19–36.

Assfalg, J., and Kruger, P. 1975. *Kleines Worterbuch des christlichen Orients.* Wiesbaden.

Bauer, W. 1971. *Orthodoxy and Heresy in Earliest Christianity.* ed. R. Kraft, et al. Philadelphia.

Baumstark, A. 1922. *Geschichte der syrischen Literatur.* Bonn.

Beck, E. 1949. *Die Theologie des hl. Ephraem.* Studia Anselmiana 21. Rome.

———. 1980. *Ephräms des Syrers Psychologie und Erkenntnislehre.* CSCO 419, Subsidia 58. Louvain.

———. 1981. *Ephräms Trinitätslehre im Bild von Sonne/Feuer, Licht und Warme.* CSCO 425, Subsidia 62. Louvain.

———. 1984. *Dorea und Charis. Die Taufe. Zwei Beiträge zur Theologie Ephräms des Syrers.* CSCO 457, Subsidia 72. Louvain.

Black, M. 1972. The Syriac Versional Original. *Die alten Übersetzungen des Neuen Testaments, die Kirchenväterzitate und Lektionare,* ed. K. Aland. Berlin.

Brock, S. 1967. Alphonse Mingana and the Letter of Philoxenos to Abū ᶜAfr. *BJRL* 50: 199–206.

———. 1973. Early Syrian Asceticism. *Numen* 20: 1–19.

———. 1975. *The Harp of the Spirit. Twelve Poems of Saint Ephrem.* Studies Supplementary to Sobornost 4. n.p.: Fellowship of St. Alban and St. Sergius.

———. 1976. Ephrem's Letter to Publius. *Le Muséon* 89: 261–305.

———. 1981–82. Syriac Studies, 1971–1980, A Classified Bibliography. *Parole de l'Orient* 10: 291–412.

———. 1984. *Syriac Perspectives on Late Antiquity.* Collected Studies Series 119. London.

———. 1985. *The Luminous Eye. The Spiritual World Vision of St. Ephrem.* Placid Lectures 6. Rome.

———. 1987. Syriac Studies 1981–1985, A Classified Bibliography. *Parole de l'Orient* 14: 289–360.

Bundy, D. 1983a. The Sources of the Isaiah Commentary of Gēorg Skewṙac'i. Pp. 395–414 in *Medieval Armenian Culture,* ed. T. Samuelian and M. Stone. University of Pennsylvania Armenian Texts and Studies 6. Chico, CA.

———. 1983b. The Peshitta of *Isaiah* 53:9 and the Syrian Commentators. *OrChr* 67: 32–45.

———. 1985a. Criteria for Being *In Communione* in the Early Syrian Church. *Aug* 25: 597–608.

———. 1985b. Middle Eastern Christian Studies: Basic Resources. Pp. 102–129 in *Summary of Proceedings, 39th Annual Conference of the American Theological Library Association.* St. Meinrad.

———. 1986. Language and the Knowledge of God in Ephrem Syrus. *Patristic and Byzantine Review* 5: 91–103.

———. 1987. The Creed of Aithallah: A Study in the History of the Early Syriac Symbol. *ETL* 63: 157–63.

———. 1988. Marcion and the Marcionites in Early Syriac Apologetic. *Le Muséon* 101: 21–32.

———. 1990. The *Life of Aberkios:* Its Significance for Early Syriac Christianity. *Second Century,* in press.

Burkitt, F. C. 1901. *St. Ephraim's Quotations from the Gospel.* Texts and Studies 7. Cambridge.

———. 1904. *Evangelion de-Mepharreshe; the Curetonian Syriac Gospels, Re-edited, Together with the Readings of the Sinatic Palimpsest.* Cambridge.

Chaumont, M.-L. 1988. *La Christianisation de l'Empire Iranian des origines aux grandes persécutions du IVᵉ siècle.* CSCO 499, Subsidia 80. Louvain.

Dirksen, P. B. 1972. *The Transmission of the Text in the Peshitta Manuscripts of the Book of Judges.* Monographs of the Peshitta Institute Leiden 1. Leiden.

Drijvers, H. J. W. 1966. *Bardaisan of Edessa. SSN* 6. Assen.

———. 1981. Odes of Solomon and Psalms of Mani. Christians and Manichaeans in Third-Century Syria. Pp. 117–30 in *Studies in Gnosticism and Hellenistic Religions Presented to Giles Quispel,* ed. R. van den Broek and M. J. Vermaseren. Leiden.

———. 1984. *East of Antioch.* London.

Fiey, J. M. 1967. Auteur et date de la Chronique d'Arbeles. *L'Orient Syrien* 12: 267–302.

———. 1977. *Nisibe, metropole syriaque orientale et ses suffragants des origines à nos jours.* CSCO 388, Subsidia 54. Louvain.

Hidal, S. 1974. *Interpretatio Syriaca. Die Kommentare des Heiligen Ephräm des Syrers zu Genesis und Exodus mit besonderer Beruchsichtigung ihrer auslegungsgeschichtlichen Stellung.* ConBOT 6. Lund.

Jansma, T. 1969. *Natuur, lot en vrijheid. Bardesanes, de filosoof der arameers en zijn images.* Cahiers bij het Nederlands Theologisch Tijdschrift 6. Wageningen.

Kahle, P. 1959. *The Cairo Geniza.* 2d ed. Oxford.

Kawerau, P. 1985. *Die Chronik von Arbela.* CSCO 467–68, Syr. 199–200. Louvain.

Koster, M. D. 1977. *The Peshitta of Exodus. The Development of Its Text in the Course of Fifteen Centuries.* (Ph.D.) Diss. University of Leiden. Assen.

Kronholm, T. 1978. *Motifs from Genesis 1–11 in the Genuine Hymns of Ephrem the Syrian.* ConBOT 11. Lund.

Lattke, M. 1986. *Die Oden Salomos in ihrer Bedeutung fur Neues Testament un Gnosis.* OBO 25/3. Freiburg and Gottingen.

Leloir, L. 1956. Le diatessaron de Tatien. *L'Orient Syrien* 1: 208–31.

———. 1963. *Saint Ephrem, Commentaire de l'Évangile Concordant.* Chester Beatty Monographs 8. Dublin.

Lewis, A. S. 1910. *The Old Syriac Gospels, or Evangelion Da-Mepharreshe; Being the Text of the Sinai or Syro-Antiochian Palimpsest, Including the Latest Additions and Emendations, with the Variants of the Curetonian Text.* London.

Lyonnet, S. 1950. *Les Origines de la version Arménienne et le Diatessaron.* BibOr 13. Rome.

Messina, G. 1943. *Notizia su un Diatessaron persiano tradotto dal siriaco.* BibOr 10. Rome.

Metzger, B. 1977. *The Early Versions of the New Testament.* Oxford.

Mingana, A. 1907. Chronique d'Arbeles. *Sources syriaques,* I, 1: *Msiha Zhka.* Mossoul-Leipzig.

Mitchell, C. W. 1917–21. *St. Ephraim's Prose Refutations of Mani, Marcion and Bardaisan.* London.

Murray, R. 1975. *Symbols of Church and Kingdom. A Study in Early Syriac Tradition.* Cambridge.

Nau, F. 1907. *De Libro legum regionum.* Patrologia Syriaca I,2. Paris.

Neusner, J. 1966. The Conversion of Adiabene to Christianity. *Numen* 14: 144–50.

———. 1971. *Aphrahat and Judaism. The Christian-Jewish Argument in Fourth-Century Iran.* SPB 19. Leiden.

Nissen, T. 1912. *S. Abercii Vita.* Bibliotheca auctorum graecorum et romanorum Teubneriana. Leipzig.

Ortiz de Urbina, I. 1965. *Patrologia Syriaca.* 2d ed. Rome.

Reinink, G. J. 1979. *Studien zur Quellen- und Traditionsgeschichte des Evangelienkommentars der Gannat Bussame.* CSCO 414, Subsidia 57. Louvain.

Sachau, E. 1915. *Die Chronik von Arbela. Ein Beitrag zur Kenntnis des altesten Christentums im Orient.* Abhandlungen der Köngl. Preuss. Akademie der Wissenschaften, Jahrgang 1915, Phil.-hist. Kl. 6. Berlin.

Segal, J. B. 1970. *Edessa, "The Blessed City."* Oxford.

Thee, F. C. R. 1984. *Julius Africanus and the Early Christian View of Magic.* Hermeneutische Untersuchungen zur Theologie 19. Tubingen.

Turner, H. E. W. 1954. *The Pattern of Christian Truth.* Bampton Lectures 1954. London.

Vööbus, A. 1951a. *Celibacy, A Requirement for Admission to Baptism in the Early Syrian Church.* Papers of the Estonian Theological Society in Exile 1. Stockholm.

———. 1951b. *Studies in the History of the Gospel Text in Syriac.* CSCO 128, Subsidia 3. Louvain.

———. 1951c. *Neue Angaben über die textgeschichtlichen Zustande in Edessa in den Jahren ca. 326–340. Ein Beitrag zur Geschichte des altsyrischen Tetraevangelium.* Papers of the Estonian Theological Society in Exile 3. Stockholm.

———. 1958. *History of Asceticism in the Syrian Orient. A Contribution to the History of Culture in the Near East. 1. The Origin of Asceticism. Early Monasticism in Persia.* CSCO 184, Subsidia 14. Louvain.

Whittaker, M. 1982. *Tatian, Oratio ad Graecos and Fragments,* ed. and trans. Oxford Early Christian Texts. Oxford.

DAVID BUNDY

CHRISTIANITY, SOCIOLOGY OF EARLY.

See SOCIOLOGY (EARLY CHRISTIANITY).

CHRISTIANS, PERSECUTION OF.

See PERSECUTION OF THE EARLY CHURCH.

CHRISTOLOGY (NT). The main object of NT christology is to trace the emergence of Christianity's distinctive claims regarding Christ as documented in the writings of the NT.

A. Introduction

1. Aim. Prior to Jesus' ministry, we can speak only of a diverse Jewish hope of a new age often involving one or more intermediary or redeemer figures—messiah, prophet, exalted hero, archangel, even God himself. A century later all these categories and more were either superseded or focused in one man, Jesus Christ. Ignatius spoke of Jesus in straightforward terms as "our God, Jesus (the) Christ" (*Eph.* 18:2; *Rom.* 3:3), and showed how Christology was well on the way toward the classical credal statements of the ecumenical councils. "There is one physician, who is both flesh and spirit, born and yet not born, who is God in man, true life in death, both of Mary and of God, first passible and then impassible, Jesus Christ our Lord" (*Eph.* 7:2). In the course of that hundred years, the claims of Christianity appeared and began to take definitive shape. The NT contains that first flowering and enables us to appreciate a good deal of how and why it came about and took the forms it did.

2. Method. Since a transition is involved, at the very least, from Jewish expectations to Christian faith, a developmental approach has been chosen. This assumes that a tradition-history analysis is able to uncover the main outlines of Jesus' own convictions and teaching, and similarly that sufficiently reliable information can be had about the beliefs of the earliest Christian congregations. Thereafter we can trace the teaching and emphasis of the individual NT writers themselves, following consensus dating and location where necessary. This approach, of course, will not reveal all that Christians said about Christ during that period, but the NT writings were obviously regarded as of more than passing significance from the first and therefore can be said to have preserved the most influential material from the foundational epoch.

NT christology could properly confine itself to a description of the christology of each individual document, seeking to demonstrate such correlation and coherence as seems appropriate. Several standard treatments have focused on titles; and though titles cannot tell the whole story, the emergence and use of certain titles can tell us a good deal. Dissatisfaction with an excessive emphasis on titles has more recently resulted in calls for different approaches—motif-centered, transformation of categories, conceptual trajectories, and the like. The following analysis will use all these methods, as seems appropriate.

Most attempts to write a NT christology also use the benefit of hindsight and global perspective to trace the larger patterns and developments of which individuals were a part. They describe the process by which the earliest christological formulations came to expression, as it were, from "outside." The danger of such an approach is that it reads back later developments into the earlier material; it fails to respect the inevitably more limited horizons of the writers themselves. We will attempt the more difficult task of describing the process from "inside." That should not prevent us from recognizing any new or previously unexpressed formulation. On the contrary, we should be better able to distinguish the genuinely new from mere variation or transfer categories.

3. Chief Impulses. The principal stimulus in the formulating of NT christology was threefold: (1) the impact of Jesus, including the impact of his ministry in style and content as well as of his teaching in particular; (2) the impact of his death and resurrection; (3) the experience of (many of) the first Christians in which they recognized further evidence of Jesus' power and status.

The material with which NT christology worked was again primarily the first Christians' memories of Jesus and their own experience. But a principal tributary was the various main features of Jewish hope seen to cohere in Jesus. Also of increasing importance over the hundred-year period under review were various categories of wider currency in the Greco-Roman world.

B. Christological Claims Attributed to Jesus

Did Jesus have a christology? That is, did he make significant claims regarding himself? The Synoptics and John's gospel are most markedly different at this point. Whereas in the latter Jesus' claims for himself are a prominent feature chapter after chapter, in the former he seems on the contrary to want to avoid drawing attention to himself. Since John's christology is so distinctive in comparison with the others, it is best to confine attention here to the Synoptics and treat John separately below.

1. Jesus and Jewish Expectation. At the time of Jesus, Jewish hope embraced a variety of messianic and/or prophetic categories.

a. Royal Messiah. Son of David (as in Isa 11:1–5; *Pss. Sol.* 17:23; 4QFlor 1:10–13). This was probably the figure of the popular hope—a new king to restore Israel's independence and greatness. It is likely that anyone who roused the sort of popular interest and excitement which John the Baptist and Jesus provoked would have been regarded as a candidate for such a messianic role (cf. John 1:20, 6:15). And a basic fact is that Jesus was executed as a messianic pretender—King of the Jews (Mark 15:26 pars.). In the hearing before Caiaphas the question was also probably raised, "Are you the Messiah, son of the Blessed?"—on the basis of the accusation about destroying and rebuilding the temple seen in the light of 2 Sam 7:13–14, interpreted messianically (as in 4QFlor). The distinctive features of Jesus' entry into Jerusalem and of his symbolic action in the temple ("the cleansing of the temple") would almost certainly have raised the same issue in broad (eschatological) or specific (royal messiah) terms. It would hardly be surprising then if his closest followers had themselves raised the question at an earlier stage of his ministry, particularly in the light of the success and popularity it clearly enjoyed (so Mark 8:27–30. pars.).

The key question, however, is how Jesus reacted when this option was put to him. And the answer of the earliest traditions seems to be, not very positively. He never once laid claim to the title on his own behalf or unequivocally welcomed its application to him by others. Mark 6:45 strongly suggests that he rejected the messianic role of popular anticipation (cf. John 6:15), and Mark 8:30–33 and the entry into Jerusalem portray a rather different model. So far as we can tell, he did not reject the title "Messiah" outright when put to him (Mark 8:30, 14:62, 15:2), but as currently understood it was evidently unsuited to describe the role he saw for himself. It needed the events of the cross and resurrection to reshape and fill the title with new content for the first Christians.

b. Priestly Messiah. In one or more strands of pre-Christian Judaism a priestly messiah was accorded greater significance than the royal messiah (e.g., *T. 12 P.;* 1QSa 2:11–22). But apparently this was never seen as an option for Jesus, presumably because he was known to be of a tribe other than the tribe of Levi.

c. The Prophet. Jewish expectation took various forms here—the return of Elijah (Mal 4:5; Sir 48:9–10), the prophet like Moses (Deut 18:15, 18), and an unnamed or eschatological prophet (Isa 61:1–2; 1QS 9:11; 11QMelch). Whether these were different expectations or variants of a single expectation is not clear, and probably was not clear then either. What is clear, however, is that there was a readiness to recognize Jesus as a prophet or the prophet (Mark 6:15 par.; 8:28 pars.; John 6:14; 7:40, 52), though it should not be forgotten that others were accorded the same title in this period (Mark 11:32; John 1:21; Joseph., *Ant* 18:85–87; 20:97f., 167, 169–72, 188).

Jesus himself seems to have accepted the designation in some degree (Mark 6:4 pars.; Luke 13:33) and in particular to have used Isa 61:1–2 as a program for his mission (Matt 5:3–4 = Luke 6:20–21; Matt 11:5 = Luke 7:22; Luke 4:18–19). He also seems deliberately to have engaged in prophetic or symbolic actions (particularly the action in the temple and the Last Supper). But at times there are hints that he saw his role as transcending that of the normal prophetic figure—Mark 12:1–9, the claim, "I came," rather than, "I was sent" (as in Mark 2:17 pars.); and the use of the formula, "But I say," rather than the more typically prophetic, "Thus says the Lord."

d. Healer. Although miraculous restoration of physical faculties was expected to be a mark of the new age (Isa 17–19, 35:5–7), it was not particularly associated with any of the above figures. Healings and exorcisms were widely practiced in the ancient world, by pagans and Jews (Mark 9:38–39, Acts 19:13–19; Josephus, *Ant* 8:45–49). So although it is beyond dispute that Jesus was known as a successful healer and exorcist, it is not clear whether much significance would have been read into this activity by his contemporaries.

Jesus himself, however, seems to have seen in his own ministry clear evidence that God's final rule was already beginning to operate through his exorcisms (Mark 3:23, 27; Matt 12:28 = Luke 11:20; Luke 10:18) and healing (Matt 11:5–6 = Luke 7:22–23). This self-estimate included a claim to a plenary anointing by God's spirit, which marked out his ministry as distinctive and which should have been sufficiently clear to his critical onlookers (hence also Mark 3:28–29 pars.). Also distinctive was his exorcistic technique, since he seems neither to have used physical aids nor to have invoked some higher authority in a formula of adjuration. We may properly infer a consciousness on his part of his own authority or of an immediacy and directness of empowering from God (Mark 11:28–33 pars.).

e. Teacher. Jesus is regularly called teacher in the tradition (Mark 5:35; 9:17, 38; 10:17, 20, 35; etc.), and his characteristic style as a "parabolist," one who spoke in parables and pithy sayings, is clearly enshrined in the Synoptics. This would be relatively unremarkable in itself, except that the authority with which Jesus taught seems to have provoked surprise and question (Mark 1:27 par., 6:2 par., 11:28 pars.). In a large part this must have been because of the same immediacy and directness which his teaching style embodied—the lack of appeal to previous authorities, the typical "Amen" with which he often began a saying, and not least his readiness to dispute established rulings even if given by Moses himself (as in Matt 5:31–42).

As Jesus evidently saw himself as God's ambassador and spokesman (Mark 9:37 pars.) and as the climax of the prophetic tradition, so he may have seen himself not simply as a teacher of wisdom but as the eschatological emissary of divine Wisdom (Luke 7:31–35 par.; 10:21–22 par.; 11:49–51 par.). Such self-understanding must lie behind his pronouncement of sins forgiven without reference to the sacrificial cult (as in Mark 2:10) and the exclusiveness of the claim he made for his teaching and call (Matt 7:24–27, 10:32 pars., 10:37 par.).

In short, none of these various categories available or applied to Jesus seem to have proved entirely suitable to describe the role Jesus saw for himself. Four of the five caught aspects of his work, but only aspects.

2. Jesus' View of His Own Role. The evidence reviewed above indicates that Jesus saw his ministry as having a final significance for his hearers. He saw himself as the eschatological agent of God. This self-understanding seems to have been encapsulated in two modes of self-reference.

a. Son of God. This title, which eventually became *the* title for Christ in the classic creeds (God the Son), at the time of Jesus had a much broader reference and simply denoted someone highly favored by God. Hence it could be used of Israel (as in Exod 4:22), of angels (as in Job 1:6–12), of the king (as in 2 Sam 7:14), of the righteous man (as in Wis 2:13–18), or of (other) charismatic rabbis (*m. Taʿan.* 3:8). The process by which the first Christians commandeered this title and gave it exclusive reference to Jesus is reflected in its increasing significance in the Gospel traditions during the second half of the first century—as indicated by the number of times Jesus speaks of God as his father (Mark 3 times, Q 4, Luke's special material 4, Matthew's special material 31, John over 100).

There is sufficient indication that the process that permitted Christians to call Jesus Son of God had already begun with Jesus himself. The basic data is Jesus' habit, as it appears to have been, of addressing God as "Father" in his prayers (as in Matt 11:25–26 = Luke 10:1–22; the only exception being Mark 15:34). The word used was almost certainly the Aramaic *ʾabbā* (so Mark 14:36), since it was evidently remembered and treasured in the Greek-speaking churches as characterizing the sonship of Jesus (Rom 8:15–16; Gal 4:6). The point is that "abba" is a family word, expressive of intimate family relationship. So the deduction lies close to hand that Jesus used it because he understood (we may even say experienced) his relationship to God in prayer in such intimate terms. And though he evidently taught his disciples so to pray (Luke 11:2), the same Pauline passages clearly indicate that this mode of prayer was seen as something distinctive of the Christians in their dependence on the Spirit of the Son. To that extent at least we can say that the process of narrowing the concept of divine sonship by reference to Jesus did indeed begin with Jesus. Whether Jesus made this a subject of explicit teaching, however, may be doubted, since Matt 11:27 and Mark 13:32 in particular may already evidence some of the christological intensification which comes to full expression in the fourth gospel. But at least we can say that the directness and immediacy of his relationship with God noted above seems to have cohered for Jesus in his "abba" prayer.

b. Son of Man. As our records stand, this seems to be the most obvious example of a self-chosen self-designation (e.g., Mark 2:10, 8:31, 14:62). But the significance of the phrase has been disputed in NT scholarship throughout this century.

Certainly the phrase must go back to Jesus in some form. It belongs almost exclusively to the Gospels (82 out of 86 times), and in the Gospels it appears in effect *only* on the lips of Jesus. Apart from Acts 7:56 we cannot speak of a "Son of Man christology" outside the Jesus tradition. The most consistent explanation is that the usage originated in the Jesus tradition, and that means, in this case, with Jesus himself. That is not to exclude the likelihood that a number of particular examples within the Jesus tradition reflect some editorial reworking of the tradition (as in Matt 16:28). But even that reworking follows what was probably the established and therefore original pattern of a speech usage confined to Jesus' own words. It must have been a firm and clear characteristic of Jesus' speech.

In some instances at least he seems to have used the phrase in the normal Aramaic idiom—"son of man" = man (cf. Ps 8:4), though with something of a self-reference (the polite English style of referring to oneself by the general "one" is a useful parallel). This usage is probably reflected in such passages as Mark 2:10 (the use of the phrase occasions no surprise or offense in the story) and 2:28, and the variant traditions of Mark 3:28–29 pars. are best explained by an ambiguous son of man/man formulation in the original Aramaic. It would also explain why "I" appears in place of "the Son of Man" in other parallel traditions (as in Luke 6:22 = Matt 5:11; Luke 12:8 = Matt 10:32). In such cases, of course, the phrase would not have had a titular significance to start with.

The alternative suggestion that the phrase was already firmly established in Jewish thought as a title for a heavenly redeemer figure is not securely grounded. In Dan 7:13 it is not title: the manlike figure represents Israel over against the beastlike figures which represent Israel's enemies in a creative reuse of the familiar creation mythology—the saints of the most high fulfilling Adam's role of dominion over the rest of creation. Jewish apocalyptic writers certainly interpret the Dan 7:13 vision with reference to a heavenly redeemer, but in each case (Similitudes of Enoch and *4 Ezra*) the implication is that this is a fresh interpretation of the Daniel passage. The date of the Similitudes is disputed but a date prior to Jesus cannot be assumed, and *4 Ezra* is certainly later than A.D. 70 (see ENOCH, FIRST BOOK OF; EZRA, GREEK APOCALYPSE OF). Nor is there any indication whatsoever that Jesus was thought to have identified himself with an already known redeemer figure of Jewish expectation or that such an identification needed to be confessed or defended. The likelihood that it was Jesus himself who first drew upon Dan 7:13 to interpret his own role is part of the larger question which follows.

3. Jesus' View of His Death. It is highly probable that Jesus foresaw the likelihood of a violent or ignominious death. This was the typical fate of prophet and righteous man in Jewish tradition (Wis 5:1–5, Matt 23:29–37 par.), as his immediate predecessor (John the Baptist) showed all too well. The hostility which resulted in his eventual crucifixion must have been evident some time before that (cf. Mark 3:22 pars., 14:8 pars., Matt 23:37 = Luke 13:34), and the prophetic action in the temple certainly invited the retaliation which soon followed. The sayings tradition which can be traced back to Jesus with some confidence suggests that Jesus saw a fuller significance in his death. The "cup" sayings (Mark 10:38 par., 14:36 pars.) evoke the OT image of the cup of God's wrath (as in Isa 51:17–23), and the "baptism" and "fire" sayings (Mark 10:38, Luke 12:49–50) probably take up the Baptist's metaphor of a fiery baptism to represent the final tribulations which would introduce the end. In applying such images to himself, Jesus presumably implied that his death was to have some sort of representative or vicarious meaning.

If, in addition, the Son of Man passion predictions (Mark 8:31, 9:31, 10:34) already contained, in their original form, an allusion to the manlike figure of Daniel's vision, an even more explicit representative significance would be hard to exclude (= "the saints of the most high"). Similar implications are involved in Mark 10:45 and 14:24, though a more direct allusion to the suffering servant of Isa 53 is harder to sustain at the earliest level of the tradition.

It is also highly likely that Jesus expected to be vindicated after his death. The pattern was already well established in Jewish reflection on the suffering of the righteous (Isa 53:10–11; Dan 7; Wis 5:1–5; 2 Macc 7:23), and hope of vindication after enduring the eschatological tribulation would be an obvious way to correlate his expected suffering with his confidence in God's coming reign (as Mark 14:25 confirms). If he did express this hope in terms of resurrection (Mark 8:31; 9:31; 10:34), it would presumably be the final resurrection he had in mind, since the concept of the eschatological resurrection of an individual seems to have emerged as a Christian perception of what had happened to Jesus.

In short, while we cannot say that Jesus placed himself at the center of his own message or called for faith in himself as such, neither can we say that Jesus simply saw himself as the eschatological proclaimer of the kingdom of God. The claim to be the medium of God's rule, the sense of an immediacy and directness in his relation with God, and the expectation of representative death and vindication is well enough rooted in the Jesus tradition. It is also the sort of base we both need and anyway expect if we are to explain the subsequent development of christology.

C. The Beginnings of Christology Proper

Despite what has just been said, it is highly doubtful whether the movement begun by Jesus during his lifetime would have amounted to anything without the resurrection and the experience of the Spirit.

1. The Resurrection of Christ. The belief that God had raised Jesus from the dead was clearly foundational in shaping christology. It is the most prominent feature in the sermons in Acts, reflecting the emphasis both of Luke and of the material he uses (Acts 2:24–32; 4:1–2, 33; 10:40–41; 13:30–37; 17:18, 30–31). The pre-Pauline formula, "God raised him from the dead," may justly be described as the earliest Christian creed (Rom 10:9, 1 Thess 1:10, Rom 8:11 (twice), Gal 1:1, Col 2:12, Eph 1:20, 2 Tim 2:8). The centrality of Christ's resurrection for Paul himself is underlined in 1 Cor 15:12–20, particularly 15:17, and Phil 2:9–11. In all the Gospels the resurrection forms the climax to the whole presentation of Jesus. Its watershed character in determining christology is indicated variously: in Mark it resolves "the messianic secret" (Mark 9:9); similarly it is the hermeneutic key in John (John 2:22); Luke carefully monitors his use of the title "Lord" in reference to Jesus in acknowledgment of the fact that the title only became his by reason of the resurrection; and in Matthew it is only with the resurrection that the commission of Jesus becomes universal (Matt 28:18–20; cf. 10:5–6).

Even where the concept "resurrection" is not prominent, the significance of what happened to Jesus after his death is central in assessments of Christ and his significance, as in Hebrews (e.g., 9:11–12) and Revelation (e.g., 5:5). And elsewhere there seems to be no attempt to distinguish resurrection from exaltation (e.g., Acts 2:32–33; Phil 2:9; 1 Pet 3:21–22; John 12:32). Nevertheless, it remains a striking fact that the concept of "resurrection" became established from the first, rather than what might otherwise have been the more obvious and recognized category of vindication in heaven of the dead hero (see 2:2b above). Indeed the earliest formulations seem to have assumed that Jesus' resurrection was the beginning of "the resurrection from the dead" in general (1 Cor 15:20; cf. Matt 27:51–53).

2. The Experience of the Spirit. That the outpouring of the Spirit expected for the last days was already a factor of their experience seems likewise to have been a basic and unifying claim of the earliest Christians. What is most relevant here is that the perceived influence of the Spirit seems also to have been a determinative factor in shaping christology. The Baptist's prediction that the coming one's ministry would be characterized by baptizing in Spirit is retained by all forms of the Gospel tradition (Mark 1:8 pars.). The Pentecost outpouring is attributed explicitly to the exalted Jesus (Acts 2:33). The identification of the Spirit as "the Spirit of Christ" evidently became soon established (Acts 16:7, 1 Pet 1:11, on Paul see below). So, too, the understanding of the Spirit as witness to Christ (Acts 5:32, Heb 2:4, 1 Pet 1:12, 1 John 5:7, Rev 19:11; on John see below). In Revelation the seven spirits of God (= the Holy Spirit) are depicted as the eyes of the Lamb (Rev 5:6).

3. Other Features of Early Christology. The search for scriptural explanations of what had happened must inevitably have been a primary objective for the first Christians. To show that Jesus was Messiah despite his shameful death would have been an urgent necessity, reflected in such passages as Luke 24:26, 46 and Acts 3:18, in the early formula "Christ died" (Rom 8:34, 14:9; 1 Thess 4:14), and in the established Pauline emphasis on "Christ crucified" (1 Cor 1:23, 2:2, Gal 3:1). Isaiah 53 undoubtedly came early into play (as in Rom 4:25, 1 Cor 15:3, 1 Pet 2:24–25), though allusions in Acts 3–4 highlight the suffering-vindication theme rather than that of vicarious suffering.

On the theme of Jesus' exaltation, Ps 110:1 quickly became a basic proof text (as, e.g., in Acts 2:34; Rom 8:34; 1 Cor 15:25; Heb 1:3, 13; 1 Pet 3:22). Also, to lesser extent, Ps 2:7 (as in Acts 13:33, Heb 5:5). The consequence of such usage was to give what could be later regarded as an "adoptionist" ring to some early formulations (Acts 2:36, 13:33, Rom 1:4). More important, however, was the fact that these texts gave added impulse to the two titles for Jesus which were most capable of providing a bridge of communication for the Gospel from Judaism to the wider Hellenistic world—Jesus as Lord (1 Cor 16:22, Jas 5:7–8, and Acts 11:20, Rom 10:9 = pre-Pauline baptismal confession; Phil 2:9–11), and Jesus as Son of God (Acts 9:20, 1 Thess 1:9–10, Heb 4:14).

The early Christian use of these same texts left its mark on the Jesus tradition itself (as in Mark 1:11, 12:35–37, 14:24, 62, Luke 22:37), obscuring the issue of whether Jesus himself referred to them. The transformation of various "son of man" sayings within the Jesus tradition into full titular self-references with consistent if often implicit reference to Dan 7:13 must also have happened early on.

At the same time the use and reuse of the Jesus tradition throughout this whole period is sufficient indication of a lively desire to recall the words and character of Jesus' ministry because of their continuing relevance. This remains a compelling deduction despite the relative lack of interest shown in the content of the Jesus tradition outside the Gospels. The Q collection, for example, reflects a strong concern to present Jesus as (eschatological) teacher of wisdom (particularly Luke 7:35; 10:21–22, 11:31, 49; 13:34). Besides this, it is inconceivable that substantial elements of the Jesus tradition were not passed on to newly established congregations (cf. Acts 2:42; 1 Cor 11:2; Col 2:6; 2 Thess 2:15). Such traditions must have provided a common ground between writer and readers to which allusion need only be made (e.g. Rom 13:8–10, 2 Cor 10:1, 1 Thess 5:2, Jas 5:12).

A strong feature of the earliest period was also the expectation of the imminent return of Christ. It was the corollary of the belief that Christ's resurrection was the beginning of the final resurrection (see above), and is reflected in such early formulations as Acts 3:19–21, 1 Cor 16:22, and 1 Thess 1:9–10. The Son of Man material used by Q also reflects a keen interest in his coming in glory and judgment (Matt 19:28 par.; 24:27, 37, 44 par.). Such imminent expectation was slow to disappear, as the early letters of Paul demonstrate (1 Thess 4:13–18, 1 Cor 7:29–31), and retained a particular vitality in Jewish-Christian circles (Jas 5:7–8, Rev 22:20).

The short time lag anticipated between Jesus' exaltation and return may be sufficient to explain why no interim function in heaven seems to be attributed to Jesus in the Acts material. On the other hand, the understanding of Jesus as heavenly intercessor must have emerged early, prior to its development in Hebrews (Rom 8:34), since the idea of heavenly intercession was already well established in Judaism (e.g. Tob 12:15; *T. Levi* 3:5, 5:6–7).

While it is impossible then to gain a detailed picture of this earliest stage of christology, a sufficiently clear and coherent outline can be reconstructed.

D. The Christology of Paul

The background of Paul's christology has already in effect been given above. The impact of the Damascus road experience should not be underestimated (in view of 2 Cor 4:6 and Gal 1:16), though it can as easily be exaggerated. Likewise his continuing experience of being "engraced" or "enChristed" was fundamental (see section D.3. below). The most important other influences came through Hellenistic Judaism (see section D.2.). The 20th-century entrancement with the hypothesis that Paul adopted an already widely spread Gnostic redeemer myth is neither justified by the pre-Pauline sources nor necessitated by the Pauline material itself.

The distinctive Pauline contribution can be summarized under three heads.

1. Adam Christology—Christ as Man. It is a fundamental conviction of Paul that in his life and death Jesus was one with humanity in his fallenness and that his resurrection inaugurated a new humanity. The latter is explicit in the passages in which he sums up the whole sweep of human history in the two epochs of Adam and Christ (Rom 5:12–21; 1 Cor 15:20–22, 45–49). The former is implicit in his use of Ps 8:4–6 (1 Cor 15:27, Eph 1:22, Phil 3:21), as its fuller exposition in Heb 2:6–9 indicates. But it also comes to expression in Rom 8:3 ("the actual likeness of sinful flesh"), Gal 4:4 ("born of woman, born under the law"), 2 Cor 8:9 ("his poverty"), and Phil 2:7 ("form of a slave . . . as man"), though the majority of scholars would question whether these last verses are properly to be seen as expressions of Adam christology.

As many of the above references also indicate, this representative function of Christ's life achieves its point particularly in his death; if this one man dies, then all die (2 Cor 5:14). This dovetails with Paul's readiness to interpret Christ's death under the category of "sacrifice" or "sin-offering" (Rom 3:25, 1 Cor 5:7). As several passages clearly imply, Paul saw the "mechanism" of sacrifice in terms of representative "interchange" (2 Cor 5:21; Rom 8:3; Gal 3:13, 4:4–5). That is, the sinless one suffers the full effects of human sin (death) in order, not that death might be escaped (= substitution), but that the finality of death might be broken through a sharing in his death leading to resurrection (Rom 6:5–8, 8:17, Phil 3:10–11).

Since the obedience of his death was primarily an undoing of Adam's disobedience (Rom 5:19, Phil 2:8), a voluntary embracing of the human lot which was the consequence of Adam's folly, it is more accurate to speak of Christ's role as inaugurator of a new humanity as stemming from the resurrection (1 Cor 15:21–22, Rom 8:29, Col 1:18). It is as resurrected, as "spiritual body," that Christ is "last Adam" and pattern of the humanity which at last fulfills the divine purpose in creating humankind (1 Cor 15:45–49).

Somewhat surprisingly, some of Paul's other distinctive emphases can be included under this head. In particular, his intensive use of "Christ" (already established as a proper name) in corporate imagery—the characteristic "in Christ" (about 80 times), "into Christ" (as in Gal 3:27), "with Christ" (as in Gal 2:20), and "through Christ" (more than 20 times), not to mention the "body of Christ" (as in Romans 12 and 1 Corinthians 12). The language refers to the identification with Christ made possible by Christ's identification with fallen humanity—the process of salvation understood as a growing participation in Christ's death with a view to a complete participation in his resurrection as the final goal (Rom 6:3–6; hence also the creation motif of "old nature/new nature" in Col 3:9–11, Eph 4:22–24). The Adam christology corresponds with the understanding of the process of salvation as corporate, more than individual (cf. Eph 2:15, 4:13).

Other facets of Paul's christology also cohere effectively under Adam christology. For obvious reasons this applies to the relatively less important theme of Jesus as God's Son, as the prominence of this title in some of the material reviewed above makes clear (Rom 8:3, 15–17, 29; Gal 4:4–7; Col 1:13)—the risen Christ as the eldest brother in the eschatological family of God. But it applies even more to an important aspect of Paul's most prominent designation for Jesus, that is "Lord," since it is only as risen Lord that Christ fulfills God's original intention in creating the first human—"to put all things under his feet" (1 Cor 15:25–27 referring to Ps 8:6). This may include the "Christus victor" theme of Col 2:15.

2. Wisdom Christology—Christ as Divine. Perhaps the most enduring development was the application of Wisdom categories to Jesus. Divine wisdom had long served as one of the most important bridge concepts for a Judaism seeking to present itself intelligibly and appealingly within the context of the wider religiophilosophic thought of the time. Within Judaism itself, Wisdom (along with Spirit and Word) was one important way of speaking of God in his creative, revelatory, and redemptive imminence (Proverbs, Sirach, Wisdom, Philo). Judaism's distinctive claim was that this wisdom was now embodied in the Torah (Sir 24:23; Bar 4:1).

Already with Paul the equivalent association is being made between Wisdom and Christ (1 Cor 1:30)—that is, Christ as the embodiment of divine Wisdom and thus as the definitive self-expression of God (Col 1:19; 2:9). He uses Wisdom terminology boldly of Christ, particularly in speaking of his role in creation (1 Cor 8:6; Col 1:15–17). Whether he means by this that Christ himself was preexistent, as most conclude, or, more precisely, that Christ has assumed the role of preexistent Wisdom without remainder, is less clear. At all events, he has no doubt that it is Christ crucified who is the definition of divine Wisdom (1 Cor 1:24), the determinative revelation and redemptive act of God (2 Cor 5:19).

The element of ambiguity here is not resolved by other references. The concept of Jesus' divine sonship provides an important bridge between Adam and Wisdom christologies, but the usage in Rom 8:3 and Gal 4:4 seems as close to the imagery of Mark 12:6 as to that of the Fourth Evangelist. Potentially more revealing is the title "Lord," since it was such an important indicator of Christ's status for Paul (note particularly Rom 10:9 and 1 Cor 12:3; well over 200 times in reference to Christ). Its use in Hellenistic religion for the cult god made it an important evangelistic and apologetic tool. Over against Hellenistic tolerant syncretism Paul claimed exclusivity for Christ's Lordship (1 Cor 8:5–6, Phil 2:9–11, 1 Cor 15:25). In so doing he did not hesitate to apply OT texts referring to Yahweh to the Lord Christ (Rom 10:13; 1 Cor 2:16; Phil 2:10–11—using the strongly monotheistic Isa 45:22–23). Yet, at the same time, Paul evidently did not see such usage as an infringement on traditional Jewish monotheism (1 Cor 8:6; also 3:23; 11:3; 15:24, 28). To call Jesus Lord was as much a way of distinguishing Christ from the one God as of attributing him to God's agency. Hence the frequent reference to "the God and Father of our Lord Jesus Christ" (Rom 15:6; 2 Cor 1:3, 11:31; Eph 1:3, 17; Col 1:3).

The question whether Paul called Jesus "God" does not provide much help on this point. For one thing, "God," like "son of God," did not have such an exclusive reference at this stage, even in Jewish circles (cf. Ps 45:6; 82:6; Philo, *Sacr* 9; *Quaes Gen* II. 62). And for another, the only clear occurrence comes in the late or Deutero-Pauline literature (Tit 2:13). In the strongly Jewish context of the earlier Rom 9:5 it is unlikely that any Jew would have read the benediction as describing "the messiah" as "God over all." The fact that Paul evidently offered his prayers to God "through Christ" (Rom 1:8, 7:25; 2 Cor 1:20; Col 3:17) confirms that for Paul Christ's role is characteristically as mediator. In other words, neither Adam christology nor Wisdom christology should be emphasized at the expense of the other.

3. Spirit Christology—Christ as Spirit. Although "Spirit" was virtually synonymous with "Wisdom" in pre-Christian Judaism (as in Wis 9:17), Paul did not take what might have appeared to be the logical step of identifying Christ with the divine spirit in the same way as he had identified Christ and Wisdom. The identification with Wisdom took in Wisdom's role in creation; but the identification with Spirit is dated only from Christ's resurrection (Rom 1:4, 1 Cor 15:45; but not 2 Cor 3:17, where "the Lord" is the Lord of Exod 34:34). Hence the strong degree of synonymity between Christ and Spirit in passages dealing with Christian experience (particularly Rom 8:9–11 and 1 Cor 12:4–6): it is in Christian experience of the divine that Christ and Spirit are one; Christ experienced not independently of the Spirit but through and as the Spirit.

This also means that for Paul christology becomes a controlling factor in pneumatology. Paul takes it for granted that the Spirit of God is known now only by reference to Christ—"the Spirit of sonship" voicing Jesus' prayer, "Abba, Father" (Rom 8:15), the Spirit known by the confession "Jesus is Lord" (1 Cor 12:3), the Spirit who transforms us into the image of Christ (2 Cor 3:18). The Spirit can now be defined as "the Spirit of Christ" (Rom 8:9, Gal 4:6, Phil 1:19), and spirituality must be measured against the pattern of Christ crucified (2 Cor 4:7–5:5, 13:4; Phil 3:10–11). The Spirit is thus redefined as the medium of Christ's relationship with his people (1 Cor 6:17). Beyond that it is much less clear that we can properly speak of an identification between Christ and Spirit. The Spirit is still preeminently the Spirit of God (Rom 8:9, 11, 14; 1 Cor 1:11, 14; etc.) and given by God (1 Cor 2:12; 2 Cor 1:21–22, 5:5; etc.). To speak of Christ as Spirit was evidently not the same as speaking of him as Wisdom and Lord. Judging by the convoluted syntax of Rom 8:11, Paul did not perceive the relation between Christ and Spirit in such clear-cut terms as that between Christ and Wisdom. In other words, even at this early stage, the redefinition of God in his immanent self-revelation, which developing christology was already occasioning, was throwing up factors which were not going to find easy resolution either in simple polytheism or in some more sophisticated "binitarianism" (the worship of two of the persons of the trinity).

E. Varied Emphases in Second-Generation Writings

1. Deutero-Pauline Letters. In Ephesians a distinctive note is struck immediately in the long opening benediction focusing on the theme of Christ as the predetermined redeemer and focus of cosmic unity in "the fullness of time" (Eph 1:3–14). The idea of Christ as the revelation of God's hitherto mysterious purpose, already developed in Colossians (1:26–27, 2:2), is taken further and spelled out in still more emphatic terms (Eph 2:11–3:13). All this is a variation of Paul's Wisdom christology (Col 2:3, Eph 3:10), integrating it more fully with Paul's central concern as apostle to the Gentiles. Note also the fuller confessional material in Eph 4:4–6 and the more elaborate images of the body of Christ (4:15–16) and of Christ as husband of the church (5:23–27).

The Pastorals do not mark much further development in ways of speaking about Christ. The talk is still of Christ's predetermined appearing to fulfill God's purpose of salvation (2 Tim 1:9-10, Tit 1:2–3), and in Tit 2:13 the reference is not to Jesus as a second God but rather to "the appearance of the glory of our great God and Savior"—Jesus' coming as the manifestation of the glory of the one God. The title "Savior" is much more prominent than in the earlier Paulines and is used equally of Christ as of God (especially Tit 1:3–4; 2:10, 13; 3:4, 6). But otherwise the christology is characteristically contained in what are already well-established credal and hymnic formulae (1 Tim 1:15, 2:5–6, 3:16, 6:13; 2 Tim 2:8; Tit 3:5–7), "the teaching which accords with godliness" (1 Tim 6:3). So, too, the talk of the second appearing has already assumed the more measured tones of a hope which no longer expects imminent fulfillment (1 Tim 6:14; 2 Tim 4:1, 8; Tit 2:13).

2. The Wider Circle of Pauline Influence. In 1 Peter we find the same conviction that Christ had been "predestined before the foundation of the world" and "manifested at the end of the times" (1:20)—clearly a widespread christological emphasis at this period. But distinctive of 1 Peter is the continual focus on suffering, and this determines the main christological concern. The Spirit is designated "the Spirit of Christ" as having predicted the prophecies of Christ's sufferings (1:11). Christ was the spotless sacrificial lamb (1:19). In the fullest use of Isaiah 53 in the NT, Christ's patience in suffering is held up as an example (2:21–25; similarly 3:17–18). In echo of the characteristic Pauline emphasis, experience of "the Spirit of glory" is linked with sharing in Christ's sufferings (4:13–14). The vicarious effect of Christ's suffering and death, however, was evidently linked in the author's mind with Christ's resurrection, which he also regards as a medium of salvation (1:3, 3:18–21). At the same time he gives evidence of the earliest speculation about Christ's ministry between death and resurrection—preaching to "the spirits in prison" (3:18–20, 4:6). 1 Peter also contains one of the best examples of a collection of OT texts used for evangelistic or apologetic purposes—the "stone testimonia" (1:6–8).

Next to the Fourth Gospel, Hebrews has the most carefully worked out and sustained christology in the NT. It includes two of the most developed expressions of Wisdom and Adam christologies (1:2–3; 2:6–17). But its main objective is to present Christ as superior to all other potential mediator figures—superior as Son to the prophets (1:1–2), to the angels (1:4–16), and to Moses (3:1–6). The principal thrust, however, comes in the presentation of Christ as High Priest—not of Aaron's line, though sharing the very human characteristics required of a good high priest (5:1–10), but of the order of Melchizedek (Ps 110:4) "by the power of an indestructible life" (7:16). As such he is superior to the Levitical priesthood as a whole.

This central thesis is worked out in 8–10 by means of a magnificent blend of Platonic idealism and Hebraic eschatology. As also in Philo, the earthly world of everyday perception is only a shadow and imperfect copy of the real heavenly world. So the tabernacle with its priesthood and sacrifice is only a shadow of the real heavenly sanctuary, and Christ is the real High Priest and his sacrifice (of himself) *the* sacrifice which alone suffices to purify the conscience and make the worshiper perfect. In the blend with Hebraic eschatology, the shadowy "here below" is identified with the preparatory "then" of the old covenant, and the heavenly real with the eschatological "now" of the new covenant. Thus priesthood and cult are shown to belong to the outmoded age of imperfect and preparatory shadow. Christ has opened the way once for all into the real inner sanctum of God's presence. By such sophisticated means the writer clearly hopes to discourage his readers from harking back to the tangibility of the Jewish cult and to persuade them of the virtues of a Christianity whose only priest and atoning sacrifice is Christ, even if it means social ostracism (13:8–16).

Of the Gospels, Mark most closely shares Pauline concerns. His aim is to present Jesus as Christ, Son of God (1:1, 11). But if this claim is understood in terms simply of mighty works (as in 3:11 and 5:7), it is misunderstood (so also 13:22). Hence the secrecy motif (as in 3:12 and 5:43) and the theme of the disciples' dullness (as in 4:13 and 8:14–21). Hence, too, at what is obviously the center and turning point of the gospel, Jesus responds to Peter's confession, "You are the Christ," by repeating the call for secrecy, and immediately goes on to teach that the Son of Man must suffer and be killed (8:30–31). The second half begins with the heavenly voice once again hailing Jesus as God's Son (9:7), giving the stamp of divine approval to the christology and its consequences for discipleship just expressed (8:31–9:1). Thereafter the movement of the narrative is all toward Jerusalem, with repeated predictions of the imminent passion (9:12, 31; 10:33–34, 38–39, 45; 12:8; etc.). In the climax to the whole, the high priest poses the question of Jesus' messiahship and divine sonship only to reject him (14:61–64), whereas, with supreme dramatic effect, it is the Roman centurion who at last makes the right confession, "Truly this man was God's Son"—speaking of the crucified Jesus who has just died (15:39). In the light of this, several have concluded that Mark wrote his gospel with an object similar to that of Paul in 2 Corinthians 10–13—to correct a christology of glory (a so-called "divine man" christology), which emphasized too much the mighty works of Jesus, by means of a christology of the cross.

3. Luke-Acts. Any study of the theology of Luke must take account of the fact that he wrote two volumes. The significance of this fact is not reducible to the tracing of structural parallels (e.g. the two prologues and inaugural Spirit anointings—Luke 1–2 = Acts 1 and Luke 3:21–22 = Acts 2:1–4; the journey framework for narrative). Rather it implies that there is a continuity and interconnectedness between the two parts of Luke's twofold composition which should prohibit us from drawing conclusions regarding Luke's christology from only one part, or from one part independently of the other. So, e.g., Luke evidently did not think it necessary to include much reference to the ministry of Jesus in the sermons in Acts (only 2:22 and 10:36–39), since he could presume that his readers already knew the gospel.

In particular, the two-volume scope of Luke's theology enables us to recognize the governing claim of his christology: that Jesus Christ is both the climax of God's purpose through Israel and the center of history. Hence the counterpoint themes of continuity and discontinuity by which Jesus both links and separates the epochs which precede and succeed him. On the one hand, the climactic note of fulfillment which marks not least the periods of transition from one epoch to the other (from Israel to Jesus—Luke 1:67–79, 3:4–6, 4:16–22; from Jesus to church—24:26–27, 44–48; Acts 1:16–20; 2:16–21, 25–36). Likewise the subtle evocation of the Exodus theme in Luke 9:31 and 11:20, and the maintenance of a Moses/prophet christology across the divide of his two volumes (Luke 24:19; Acts 3:22, 7:37). With similar effect, and even more marked, his emphasis on the spirit, as both heralding the coming of the Christ (Luke 1:15, 41, 67; 2:25), as distinguishing his ministry in special measure (3:22; 4:1, 14, 18; 10:21; Acts 1:2, 10:38), and as poured out in eschatological fullness on the first believers (Acts 1:5, 8; 2:4, 17–18, 33; etc.).

On the other hand, the period of Israel becomes increasingly superseded. The Jerusalem temple, which provides an important focus of continuity (Luke 1:8–23; 2:22–51; 24:52–53; Acts 2:46; 3:1–10; 5:20–21, 42), is attacked by Stephen as "made with hands" (7:48; cf. v 41) and becomes the occasion for Paul's final rejection and arrest (21:7–36; 26:21), a development complemented by Paul's own increasing turning away from "the Jews" and to the gentiles (9:15, 13:45–50, 22:21–22, 28:25–28). The discontinuity between epochs is also marked christologically, in the depiction of the successive modes of relationship between Jesus and the Spirit—first, as the one whose human life is created by the Spirit (Luke 1:35), second, as the one who is uniquely anointed by the Spirit (3:22, 4:18; Acts 10:38), and third, as the exalted one who in his exaltation has received divine power to bestow the spirit (Acts 2:33), so that, as with Paul, the Spirit can be designated "the Spirit of Jesus" (Acts 16:7). The attempt to mark off the epoch of Jesus from the epoch of the Spirit by limiting the resurrection appearances to forty days so that there is a ten-day gap between ascension and Pentecost (Acts 1) is particularly noticeable.

An important factor in this reshaping of the christological focus of salvation history is the delay of the parousia. The extent of the delay envisaged by Luke should not be exaggerated: he still uses the language of imminent expectation in Luke 10:9, 11, 18:7–8, and 21:32. Nevertheless he does inject clear warnings of delay into the earlier tradition at Luke 19:11, 20:9, and 21:8, and in Acts a longer time scale does seem to be envisaged for the mission (Acts 1:6–8), with the talk of Christ's parousia reading more like a doctrine of the last things than a threat pressingly close (Acts 10:42, 17:31, 24:25). This stretching out of the period between exaltation and parousia reinforces the impression that Acts has an "absentee christology," with no further activity predicated of him other than through his name (Acts 3:6, 16; 4:10–12, 30; 10:43) or in visions (Acts 9:10, 18:9, 22:17–21, 26:13–19), in some contrast to the more intimate "in Christ" and mutual indwelling emphases of Paul and John.

Other distinctive features of Luke's christology include his focus on "salvation." Of the Synoptic Evangelists, only Luke calls Jesus "Savior" (Luke 2:11; in John only at 4:42) and attributes "salvation" to him (Luke 1:69, 2:30, 3:6, 19:9). The same emphasis is continued in Acts, in the use of both nouns (Acts 4:12; 5:31; 13:23, 26; 28:28) and of the verb (particularly 2:21, 4:12, 15:11, 16:31). Equally striking is the surprising lack of any clear atonement theology in Luke-Acts. As already noted, the references to the death of Christ in the Acts speeches, including the allusions to Jesus as "Servant," emphasize the suffering-vindication theme rather than the motif of vicarious suffering (Acts 3:13, 26; 4:27, 30; 5:30; 10:39–40; 13:29–30). The impression that this feature may be indicative of Luke's own theology of the cross is strengthened by the absence of the clearest Markan expression of atonement theology (Luke 22:27; cf. Mark 10:45) and by the textual confusion at the other two most sensitive points in the narrative (Luke 22:19b–20, Acts 20:28). Finally we may note that Luke's depiction of the substantial and objective nature of Christ's resurrection appearances (Luke 24:39–43; Acts 1:3), which in part at least may be simply the result of his own perception of the tangible character of spiritual phenomena (e.g., Luke 3:22; Acts 4:31, 8:18–19,

12:9), enables him to emphasize still further the contrast between the epoch of Christ and that of the Spirit and marks off the ascension from the resurrection in a way that is unparalleled elsewhere in the NT.

4. Outside the Circle of Pauline Influence. James almost seems to lack any christology worth speaking of, Christ being explicitly referred to only twice (1:1; 2:1), though the ambiguous "Lord" of 5:7–8 probably also refers to Jesus. But he does draw directly on the Jesus tradition (e.g., 1:5, 22–23; 4:12; 5:12) and may refer to Jesus as "the righteous one" (5:6) in a fine blend of Jewish wisdom teaching and prophetic fervor against social injustice. This can quite properly be called an implicit christology, since it shows how these emphases of Jesus' ministry were maintained, without necessarily having to be held all the time within a Markan passion framework (as in all the Gospels).

The two-fold emphasis of the birth narratives also provides Matthew with his principal christological themes—Jesus as Son of David and messiah (1:1, 17, 20; 2:4), but also Son of God (1:18, 20; 2:15). Evidently within a more Jewish context the assertion of Jesus' messiahship was still a matter of apologetic importance (hence the redactional insertions at 11:2, 16:20, 23:10, 24:5). Matthew also makes more use of the "Son of David" title than any other NT writer (9:27; 12:23; 15:22; 20:30–31 pars.; 21:9, 15). But "Son of God" is clearly the more important designation. For Matthew not only retains the high points of Mark's presentation (3:17, 8:29, 17:5, 26:63, 27:54) but takes pains to extend the motif (14:33; 16:16; 27:40, 43; 28:19).

On the one hand, this means that Christ recapitulates Israel's history to complete God's purpose for Israel (2:15; 4:3–6 = midrash on Deuteronomy 6–8)—an Israel christology rather like Paul's Adam christology. Hence also the implicit Moses typology (Jesus gives the first of five blocks of teaching on a mountain) and the sustained fulfillment of prophecy theme (1:22–23; 2:15, 17–18, 23; 4:14–16; 8:17; 12:17–21; 21:4; 27:9–10). But even more, this means that Jesus, Son of God, is the divine presence among his people (1:23; 18:20; 28:20). The process whereby "Son of God" gains in christological significance is already well advanced—as reflected also in the marked increase in Jesus' reference to God as "Father" (as in 7:21; 10:32–33; 12:50; 16:17; 18:10, 19). Hence, too, the evidently deliberate Matthean redaction whereby Jesus is presented not merely as the eschatological emissary of Wisdom but as Wisdom herself (11:19, 25–30; 23:34–36, 37–39).

The most striking feature of the christology of the Revelation of John is the relation envisaged between God and the exalted Christ—although the full force of the christology involved remains unclear since the apocalyptic imagery is open to diverse interpretations. The description of the initial vision of Christ is a fascinating mixture of elements drawn from previous apocalyptic visions (particularly Ezek 1:24, 8:2; Dan 7:13, 10:5–6), and is of a piece with the tradition of Jewish apocalyptic (or merkabah mysticism) in which a glorious angel seems to have the appearance of God (as in *Apoc. Abr.* 10). The difference is that elsewhere in the tradition the angel forbids the offer of worship, whereas in Revelation, Christ is as much the object of worship as God (5:13, 7:10).

Christ, initially introduced as the Lion of Judah and Root of David, conqueror of death and lord of history (5:5), is referred to thereafter as the Lamb once slain (5:6, 8, 12–13; 6:1; etc.), whose blood enables his followers to conquer and who is the executor of divine wrath (6:16, 7:14, 12:11). More significant is the fact that the Lamb is also said to be "in the middle of the throne" (5:6; 7:17), whereas elsewhere it is God who is described as "he who is seated on the throne" (4:9–10; 5:1, 7, 13; 6:16; 7:10, 15; 19:4; 21:5). The one throne is evidently shared by both God and the Lamb (22:1). So, too, each can equally be called "the Alpha and the Omega" (1:8, 21:6, 22:13). In other words, Christ has not simply been exalted alongside God as a second divine power in heaven, but in the visionary imagery of the seer is somehow merged with God. This makes the promise of salvation as a being given to sit on the same throne and as a being given in marriage to the Lamb all the more profound (3:21; 19:7–8; 21:2, 9–14).

F. The Christology of John

The Fourth Gospel has the most fully developed christology in the NT. The contrast with the Synoptics is at once apparent in the public roll call of titles which climaxes chap. 1 ("Lamb of God," "Messiah," "Son of God," "King of Israel," "Son of Man"). The style and content of Jesus' teaching is strikingly different: in the Synoptics, Jesus speaks in epigrams and parables, principally about the kingdom of God/heaven and very little about himself; in John, Jesus speaks in long, often involved discourses, principally about himself and very little about the kingdom. Jesus' consciousness of having preexisted, as Son with the Father, as Son of Man descended from heaven, as the eternal "I am," confronts the reader throughout. There is sufficient evidence that John's presentation is rooted in good tradition (cf., e.g., John 6:20 with Mark 6:50; John 6:51–58 with Mark 14:22–24 = Luke 22:19–20; John 10 with Luke 15:4–6), but the above emphases are so consistent in John and so lacking in the earlier Jesus tradition that they have to be attributed to a developed reflection on that earlier tradition.

The chief objectives of the Fourth Evangelist are clearly marked in the Prologue, which must have a programmatic function since it matches the subsequent emphases so closely, and in 20:31.

1. The Word Incarnate. In the Prologue the line of the earlier Wisdom christology is extended. The concept "Word" is given preference over "Wisdom," perhaps simply because the masculine concept seemed more appropriate, but probably mainly because "Word" was the more serviceable concept to provide a bridge of communication between Jewish monotheism and Greek religious philosophy (as with Philo). In the line of Jewish Wisdom theology, the Word is not thought of as being other than God, but as God in his self-revelation, God insofar as he may be known by man. The Word was not a redemptive "afterthought" but was "in the beginning" (1:1–2), God's own power put forth in creation and revelation (1:3–5, 9–10). Jesus Christ is this Word become man, embodying the divine glory (1:14). He alone reveals God (1:18).

Although the concept "Word" disappears after the Prologue, what follows is in effect a massive elaboration of Word/Wisdom christology. In varied ways the message is constantly repeated—Jesus is the one who has finally and definitively revealed God. Nathanael is a "true Israelite" (= "one who sees God") because he will see the Son of Man as the ladder between heaven and earth (1:47–51). No one has ascended to heaven; only the Son of Man who descended from heaven can bear witness to heavenly things (3:11–13). He who comes from above is above all whose witness is from God (3:31–33). Only he who is from the Father has seen the Father (6:46). The "I am" statements unique to John pick up Wisdom language (shepherd, light, etc.) and in echoing the "I am" of Yahweh (Exod 3:14; Isa 43:10; etc.) make the claim even more emphatically—Jesus is the self-revelation of the covenant God (John 6:35; 8:12, 24, 28, 58; etc.), the definitive manifestation of that divine reality (1:14, 17; 14:6). Isaiah saw Christ because he saw God in his glory, God as manifested to man (Isaiah 6; John 12:41). Hence the charge leveled against the Johannine Jesus by "the Jews": he made himself equal with God, made himself God (5:18; 10:33). John does not dispute the charge; rather he makes it an article of faith on his own account (1:18; 20:28); only, Jesus as God must not be understood as another, a second God, but as God himself incarnate, God making himself present and known to man so far as that was possible within the confines of human experience.

This also is the function of the dominant category of John's christology—Son of God. Although the designation "Messiah" is still important (note 1:41 and 4:25), it is clear that he wants the Christ title to be understood in the light of the Son of God title (11:27; 20:31). The reason is also clear from the characteristic Johannine elaboration of the Son language: "Son" expresses well the intimate relation between Jesus and God and the authority of Jesus' revelation of God. As "Son of God," Jesus is unique: he is the *monogenēs,* "one of a kind" (like no other son), (1:14, 18; 3:16, 18); his sonship cannot be shared (he alone is "son"; believers are "children"; contrast Paul). As "the Son," he is not a different divine being from the Father, but God making himself visible to men: he and the Father are one (10:30); to have seen him is to have seen the Father (14:9). Hence also the repeated note usually taken subsequently as emphasizing the Son's subordination to the Father, but better understood as highlighting the continuity between Father and Son and the authority of the Son's witness on the Father's behalf (e.g., 5:19–23, 26–27; 6:35–40, 57; 10:25, 37–38; 14:25–31; 15:26).

With this as the chief emphasis of John's christology, the Christian redefinition of Jewish monotheism can be said to be already well under way. Clearly evident, too, are the strains which caused rabbinic Judaism to reject such redefinition as in effect an abandoning of the unity of God. The danger of an overemphasis on Jesus as God on earth is also evident, but John was aware of it and took steps to guard against it.

2. The Son Glorified. Although the Fourth Evangelist has nothing like the Adam christology with which Paul balanced his Wisdom christology, a somewhat different balance is nevertheless provided by important other strands of the gospel. In particular, John takes pains to exclude the impression that Jesus was simply God in human appearance, not really part of the human species. The Word became "flesh" (1:14), that which constitutes the human born (1:13; 3:6). To have eternal life one must believe in Jesus, that is, must accept his fleshliness in all its earthliness (6:53–56). He really died on the cross, as eyewitness testimony confirms (19:34–35). The emphasis is not prominent, but it does come at critical points in the gospel, and John presumably thought the line was clearly enough drawn.

The subject of Jesus' rejection and death is, in fact, more intensively elaborated, in its own way, than in any other gospel. The theme of the light opposed by the darkness, of the Word rejected by his own, first announced in the Prologue (1:5, 11), becomes a leitmotif of the whole gospel. The light inevitably has a critical or divisive role, since some accept it but many hate it (3:19–21). "Judgment" as a sifting process separating into "for" and "against" is the thread which holds together the central section of the gospel (6–12), with only the inner circle left before Judas, too, goes off into the night (13:30). The mention of "the hour" sounds a steady drumbeat throughout the heralding of the coming passion (2:4; 7:30; 8:20; 12:23, 27; 13:1; 17:1). The soteriological significance of Jesus' death is still prominent (1:29, 6:51, 12:32, 13:10, 19:34), but more prominent is the christological point that his death forms a theological unity with his resurrection and ascension—a single act of being "lifted up" (3:14, 8:28, 12:32), of ascension (3:13, 6:62, 20:17), and particularly of glorification (7:39; 12:16, 23; 13:31; 17:1). As with Paul, the glory of Christ does not come into focus apart from the cross.

As with Paul, the concept of the Spirit is drawn into close correlation with christology. Despite the powerful Word/Wisdom christology, the Spirit is still depicted as given to Jesus at Jordan, but given to "remain on him" and "without measure" (1:32; 4:34). More to the point, the Spirit is now clearly a gift to be given by Christ (1:33; 4:10, 14; 4:34(?); 7:39; 15:26; 16:7; 19:34); and here, too, the unity of the salvation climax of Jesus' ministry is underlined, since Jesus "hands over" the Spirit on the cross (19:30) and the (Pentecostal) bestowal of the Spirit for mission is effected on the day of resurrection (20:21–23). Most distinctive of all, the Spirit is described as the "Paraclete" or Counselor, or more precisely, as "the other Paraclete" (14:16). That is to say, the Spirit is Jesus' successor and takes Jesus' place, so that the promise of Jesus' return to dwell in his disciples can be immediately linked to the coming and indwelling of the Paraclete (14:15–26)—one of the most striking features of John's "realized eschatology." Significantly, the Paraclete's primary role is to maintain and complete the revelation of Christ (14:26; 15:26; 16:7, 10), to glorify Christ by taking what is Christ's and reproclaiming it to his disciples (16:12–15). Yet once again, as with Paul, all this does not mean that John's christology has absorbed the concept of Spirit without remainder, as it has the concepts of Wisdom and Word (see PARACLETE). For distinct functions are still attributed to both—to the Spirit in worship and to Christ apart from the Spirit: despite his realized eschatology, John retains the promise of a still future parousia (14:3); and despite having already given the Spirit and ascended Christ reappears to Thomas a week later (20:26–29).

3. 1 and 2 John—Crisis over Christology. 1 John was probably written after the gospel and reflects a situation of some crisis in the Johannine congregations which the gospel and its presentation of Christ may have helped bring about. A number of erstwhile members had evidently left (1 John 2:19), and the breaking point seems to have been a matter of christology, since they are described as "antichrists" and accused of failing to confess or acknowledge Christ (2:18, 22; 4:3; 2 John 7). In particular, they claimed that Jesus Christ had not come in the flesh (1 John 4:2–3; 2 John 7), a form of docetism which, conceivably, they may have derived from or defended by means of a lopsided reading of the gospel (cf. 6:1 above). Consequently this second member of the Johannine school draws back somewhat from the bolder synthesis attempted in the gospel. The opening verses clearly recall the prologue to the gospel, but they also recall the older idea of Christ as the content of the word of preaching (cf. 1 John 1:1–3 particularly with Luke 1:2 and Acts 10:36). And 1 John 5:20 probably refers to Jesus as "the true God" (cf. particularly John 1:18). But the balancing emphasis is more clearly and sharply drawn: the word of life had a tangible historicity (1 John 1:1); the confession that "Jesus Christ has come in the flesh" is the key criterion for testing the spirits (4:1–2); any suggestion that the Christ did not really die is emphatically ruled out (5:6–8).

In short, 1 and 2 John provide vivid indications of the hazardous frontiers of reproclamation which christology at the end of the first century was beginning to explore.

G. Conclusions

1. Continuity with Judaism. Throughout the various NT writings there is never any slackening of a central claim: Jesus was a Jew and must be understood within the terms provided by Judaism and its sacred scriptures. Most striking is the way in which a range of diverse categories is focused on Jesus—Messiah and son of man, Lord and son of God, Wisdom and Word, atoning sacrifice and priest, Adam and Spirit, Servant and Lamb, Savior and God. Of course, most of the categories are redefined in one degree or other—son of man becomes Son of Man, son of God becomes only-begotten Son of God, Spirit becomes Spirit of Christ, and so on. But the categories remain essentially Jewish, even when they had wider currency in the Greco-Roman world, and it was evidently understood to be important, even if not stated explicitly, that Jesus should continue to be comprehended in Jewish terms—important that Jesus should be seen in continuity with the purposes of God from creation and in the calling of Israel. Clearly then the first Christians felt that Jesus was so much the decisive and definitive fulfillment of Israel's hopes that his significance could not be adequately expressed without pulling in all available categories provided by Jesus' own Jewish faith.

2. Continuity with Jesus' Own Self-Understanding. This second aspect is not so easy to recognize. The important reason is that so much of NT christology turns on the event of the cross and resurrection. That event so decisively reshaped the categories applicable to Jesus that their occurrence on either side of that event is not strictly comparable. For example, it is only as Christ crucified that the Messiah claim can be incorporated into christology. It is only as priest "in the order of Melchizedek," "by the power of an indestructible life," that the category of priest can be taken over. It is only as the man whose obedience in death reverses the disobedience of the first man that the title "Adam" can be given to the exalted Christ. Nevertheless, there are sufficiently clear antecedents within the historical Jesus tradition itself that a continuity can properly be claimed—particularly in Jesus' consciousness of intimate sonship, his premonition of suffering in a representative capacity, and his hope of vindication following death. Consequently the claim can justly be made that the cross and resurrection was not a distortion of Jesus' own claims for himself but an appropriate outworking of them. So also the subsequent claims of NT christology can fairly be seen not as a wholly new departure without foundation in Christ's own ministry, but a fuller insight into the reality of that mission in the light of the cross and resurrection.

3. Unity and Diversity in NT Christology. At the heart of NT christology is the claim that the man Jesus was raised from the dead to a status of supreme exaltation. This is the most constant element throughout all the NT documents. In its more expanded form, it takes on a double aspect—Christ as the culmination of God's purpose for man (and Israel) in creation and salvation, and Christ as the definitive revelation of God to humankind. The latter comes to increasing prominence in the later writings, explicitly as a doctrine of incarnation in John's gospel, but not at the cost of removing the earlier emphasis on Jesus' death and resurrection as a decisive moment not only for Christ's work but also for his person. Neither aspect can be neglected and neither emphasized at the expense of the other in any christology which claims to be rooted in the NT, but consistently in the NT writings it is the fact and character of Christ's death and resurrection which provided the criterion and control for christology.

Particular emphases of the individual writers by no means reflect a uniform expression and weighting of this central core. Even the core itself is something of an abstraction, since no two writers express it in precisely the same terms. The differences of the writers themselves and the differences of the situations they addressed inevitably made for a rich diversity of expression of what nevertheless can be called a common faith in Christ. But beyond that core the range of presentations includes a wide-ranging diversity of motif, form, and image—wide enough to include the differences of Mark and Matthew, the absence of significant christological features in James and Acts, and the idiosyncratic elements in Hebrews and Revelation. Evidently the individual writers felt free to reexpress ("reproclaim" is John's word) the gospel that is Jesus in different ways and with different emphases to speak more pertinently to their own diverse situations. In all cases that included a concern to be true to the insights which had already become established. In some cases that concern dominated largely to the exclusion of all else (particularly the Pastorals). For the most part, however, christology was seen as no mere transfer of set traditions from one church to another, but as a creative response to the exalted Christ and his Spirit, which could sometimes have unpredictable results. But that, too, is part of NT christology.

4. The Foundation for Subsequent Christology. The context-specific and at the same time developing character of so much of NT christology made it inevitable that not all elements within NT christology would be carried forward—particularly the "adoptionist"—like notes in some of the earliest formulations, and idea of Wisdom as created which came in as part of the pre-Christian Jewish Wisdom tradition. Some elements were caught up spasmodically—Paul's Adam christology is taken up in Irenaeus' doctrine of "recapitulation," Luke's schematization of the epoch of Christ followed by the epoch of the Spirit reappears in corrupt form in Montanism and modern dispensationalism, and the visionary magnificence of the Revelation of John retains its impact in the Byzantine Pantocrator. But the main highway into the future was provided by the Wisdom/Word christologies of Paul and John. That way was by no means smooth. The concept of Christ as God's self-revelation not only had to skirt around docetism (already in 1–2 John), but also resulted in an outright breach with Judaism over the question mark it seemed to pose to the unity of God (already foreshadowed in John), and it also gave scope to a modalist interpretation later in the second century. In the event, as it happened, the NT writing contained sufficient safeguards to prevent Christianity from abandoning monotheism (Christ as God incarnate), but also sufficient dynamic in the relationships implied between God, the exalted Christ, and the Spirit of Christ to require redefinition of that monotheism in a trinitarian direction. Whether subsequent formulations managed to take sufficient account of all the balancing elements in NT christology, however, remains an open question.

Bibliography

Balz, H. R. 1967. *Methodische Probleme der neutestamentlichen Christologie.* Neukirchen.

Bauckham, R. 1978. The Sonship of the Historical Jesus in Christology. *SJT* 31: 245–60.

———. 1980–81. The Worship of Jesus in Apocalyptic Christianity. *NTS* 27: 322–41.

Berger, K. 1970–71. Zum traditionsgeschichtlichen Hintergrund christologischer Hoheitstitel. *NTS* 17: 391–425.

Berkey, R. F., and Edwards, S. A. 1982. *Christological Perspectives.* New York.

Black, M. 1971–72. The Christological Use of the Old Testament in the New Testament. *NTS* 18: 1–14.

Boers, H. 1972. Where Christology Is Real: A Survey of Recent Research on New Testament Christology. *Int* 26: 300–27.

Borsch, F. H. 1967. *The Son of Man in Myth and History.* London.

Boslooper, T. 1962. *The Virgin Birth.* London.

Bousset, W. 1921. *Kyrios Christos,* Nashville. 2d ed. 1970.

Braun, H. 1968. The Meaning of New Testament Christology. *JTC* 5: 89–127.

Brown, R. E. 1968. *Jesus: God and Man.* London.

———. 1977. *The Birth of the Messiah.* Garden City, NY.

———. 1979. *The Community of the Beloved Disciple.* London.

Bühner, J. A. 1977. *Der Gesandte und sein Weg im 4. Evangelium.* Tübingen.

Bultmann, R. 1969. The Christology of the New Testament. Pp. 262–85 in *Faith and Understanding.* London.

Burger, C. 1970. *Jesus als Davidsohn.* Göttingen.

Caird, G. B. 1968. The Development of the Doctrine of Christ in the New Testament. Pp. 66–81 in *Christ for Us Today,* ed. N. Pittenger. London.

Casey, M. 1982. Chronology and the Development of Pauline Christology. *Paul and Paulinism,* ed. M. D. Hooker & S. G. Wilson. London.

Casey, P. M. 1980. *The Son of Man.* London.

Cerfaux, L. 1959. *Christ in the Theology of St. Paul.* Freiburg.

Christ, F. 1970. *Jesus Sophia.* Zurich.

Conzelmann, H. 1961. *The Theology of Saint Luke.* London.

Craddock, F. B. 1968. *The Pre-existence of Christ in the New Testament.* Nashville.

Cullmann, O. 1979. *The Christology of the New Testament.* London.

Deichgraeber, R. 1967. *Gotteshymnus und Christushymnus in der fruehen Christenheit.* Göttingen.

Dunn, J. D. G. 1975. *Jesus and the Spirit.* London.

———. 1977. *Unity and Diversity in the New Testament.* London.

———. 1980. *Christology in the Making.* London.

———. 1983. Let John Be John. Pp. 309–39 in *Das Evangelium und die Evangelien,* ed. P. Stuhlmacher. Tübingen.

Dupont, J., ed. 1975. *Jesus aux origines de la christologie.* BETL 40. Louvain.

Ernst, J. 1972. *Anfänge der Christologie.* SBS 57. Stuttgart.

Feuillet, A. 1966. *Le Christ Sagesse de Dieu d'apres les Epitres Pauliniennes.* EBib. Paris.

Foakes-Jackson, F. J., and Lake, K. 1920. *The Beginnings of Christianity Part I: The Acts of the Apostles,* vol. 1. London.

Franklin, E. 1975. *Christ the Lord: A Study in the Purpose and Theology of Luke.* London.

Fuller, R. H. 1965. *The Foundations of New Testament Christology.* London.

Fuller, R. H., and Perkins, P. 1983. *Who Is This Christ?* Philadelphia.

Gnilka, J. 1970. *Jesus Christus nach frühen Zeugnis des Glaubens.* Munich.

Hahn, F. 1969. *The Titles of Jesus in Christology.* London.

Hamerton-Kelley, R. G. 1973. *Pre-existence, Wisdom and the Son of Man.* SNTSMS: Cambridge.

Hanson, A. T. 1965. *Jesus Christ in the Old Testament.* London.

———. 1982. *The Image of the Invisible God.* London.

Harvey, A. E. 1981. *God Incarnate: Story and Belief.* London.

Hay, D. M. 1973. *Glory at the Right Hand: Psalm 110 in Early Christianity.* SBLMS 18. Nashville.

Hengel, M. 1976. *The Son of God.* London.

———. 1983. *Between Jesus and Paul.* London.

Hermann, I. 1961. *Kyrios und Pneuma: Studien zur Christologie der paulinischen Hauptbriefe.* Muenchen: Koesel.

Holtz, T. 1962. *Die Christologie der Apokalypse des Johannes.* Berlin.

Hooker, M. D. 1977–78. Interchange and Atonement. *BJRL* 60: 462–80.

Hurtado, L. W. 1979. New Testament Christology: A Critique of Bousset's Influence. *TS* 40: 306–17.

———. 1981. The Study of New Testament Christology: Notes for the Agenda. *SBLSP* 185–97.

Jeremias, J. 1967. *The Prayers of Jesus.* London.

———. 1988. *Christology in Context.* Philadelphia.

Jewett, R., ed. 1984. Christology and Exegesis: New Approaches. *Semeia* 30.

Jonge de, M. 1977. *Jesus: Stranger from Heaven.* Missoula.

Jüngel, E. 1967. *Paulus und Jesus.* 3d ed. Tübingen.

Käsemann, E. 1968. *The Testament of Jesus.* London.

Kazmierski, C. R. 1979. *Jesus, the Son of God.* Würzburg.

Kehl, N. 1967. *Der Christushymnus im Kolosserbrief.* Stuttgart.

Kim, S. 1981. *The Origin of Paul's Gospel.* WUNT 2/4. Tübingen.

———. 1983. *The "Son of Man" as the Son of God.* WUNT 30. Tübingen.

Kinsbury, J. D. 1975. *Matthew: Structure, Christology, Kingdom.* Philadelphia.
———. 1983. *The Christology of Mark's Gospel.* Philadelphia.
Knox, J. 1967. *The Humanity and Divinity of Christ.* Cambridge.
Krämer, W. 1966. *Christ, Lord, Son of God.* London.
Lampe, G. W. H. 1977. *God as Spirit.* Oxford.
Lindars, B. 1983. *Jesus Son of Man.* London.
Loader, W. R. G. 1981. *Sohn und Hoherpriester.* WMANT 53. Neukirchen.
Lohfink, G. 1971. *Die Himmelfahrt Jesu.* Munich.
Longenecker, R. N. 1970. *The Christology of Early Jewish Christianity.* London.
Marshall, I. H. 1968. *The Origins of New Testament Christology.* London.
Martin, R. P. 1983. *Carmen Christi: Philippians 2:5–11 in Recent Interpretation and in the Setting of Early Christian Worship.* SNTSMS. 2d ed. Grand Rapids.
Marxsen, W. 1960. *The Beginnings of Christology.* Philadelphia.
Meeks, W. A. 1967. *The Prophet-King: Moses Traditions and the Johannine Christology.* NovTSup 14. Leiden.
Meeks, W. A. 1972. The Man from Heaven in Johannine Sectarianism. *JBL* 91: 44–72.
Moule, C. F. D. 1967. *The Phenomenon of the New Testament.* London.
———. 1977. *The Origin of Christology.* Cambridge.
Müller, U. B. 1975. *Die Geschichte der Christologie in der johanneischen Gemeinde.* SBS 77. Stuttgart.
Neufeld, V. H. 1963. *The Earliest Christian Confessions.* Leiden.
Pannenberg, W. 1968. *Jesus—God and Man.* London.
Perrin, N. 1974. *A Modern Pilgrimage in New Testament Christology.* Philadelphia.
Polag, A. 1977. *Die Christologie der Logienquelle.* Neukirchen.
Pollard, T. E. 1970. *Johannine Christology and the Early Church.* SNTSMS. Cambridge.
———. 1982. *Fullness of Humanity: Christ's Humanness and Ours.* Sheffield.
Rahner, K., and Thüsing, W. 1980. *A New Christology.* London.
Rawlinson, A. E. J. 1926. *The New Testament Doctrine of the Christ.* London.
Robinson, J. A. T. 1956. The Most Primitive Christology of All? *JTS* 7: 177–89.
———. 1973. *The Human Face of God.* London.
Robinson, J. M., and Koester, H. 1971. *Trajectories through Early Christianity.* Philadelphia.
Rowland, C. 1980. The Vision of the Risen Christ in Rev 1, 13ff. *JTS* 31: 1–11.
Sanders, J. T. 1971. *The New Testament Christological Hymns.* SNTSMS. Cambridge.
Schillebeeckx, E. 1979. *Jesus: An Experiment in Christology.* London.
———. 1980. *Christ: The Christian Experience in the Modern World.* London.
Schnackenburg, R. 1970. Christologie des Neuen Testaments. *Mysterium Salutis* 3:1. Einsiedeln, 227–388.
———. 1983. Paulinische und johanneische Christologie. Pp. 221–37 in *Die Mitte des Neuen Testaments,* ed. U. Luz and H. Weder. Göttingen.
Schweizer, E. 1960. *Erniedrigung und Erhoehung bei Jesus und seinen Nachfolgern.* 2d ed. Zurich.
———. 1971. *Jesus.* London.
———. 1972. *Neues Testament und Christologie im Werden.* Göttingen.
Scroggs, R. 1966. *The Last Adam: A Study in Pauline Anthropology.* Oxford.
Stanton, G. N. 1974. *Jesus of Nazareth in New Testament Preaching.* SNTSMS. Cambridge.
Stuhlmacher, P. 1977. Zur Paulinische Christologie. *ZTK* 74: 449–63.
Taylor, V. 1958. *The Person of Christ in New Testament Teaching.* London.
Thüsing, W. 1965. *Per Chrisum in Deum.* Münster.
———. 1970. *Erhöhungsvorstellung und Parusieerwartung in der ältesten nachösterlichen Christologie.* SBS 42. Stuttgart.
Tiede, D. L. 1980. *Prophecy and History in Luke-Acts.* Philadelphia.
Vermes, G. 1973. *Jesus the Jew.* London.
Vielhauer, P. 1965. *Aufsätze zum Neuen Testament.* Munich.
Wainwright, A. W. 1962. *The Trinity in the New Testament.* London.
Wengst, K. 1972. *Christologische Formeln und Lieder des Urchristentums.* Gütersloch.

James D. G. Dunn

CHRONICLES OF THE KINGS (ISRAEL/JUDAH), BOOK OF THE

CHRONICLES OF THE KINGS (ISRAEL/JUDAH), BOOK OF THE [Heb *sēper dibrê hayyamîm lĕmalkê*]. A book or books not extant but cited by the author of 1–2 Kings. The term literally means "the daily affairs for [or belonging to] the kings of [Israel/Judah]," but it is most often translated as either the Chronicles of or the Annals of the Kings of Israel/Judah. The Chronicles of the Kings of Judah is mentioned fifteen times (1 Kgs 14:29; 15:7, 23; 22:46—Eng 22:45; 2 Kgs 8:23; 12:20—Eng 12:19; 14:18; 15:6, 36; 16:19; 20:20; 21:17, 25; 23:28; 24:5) in reference to every post-Solomonic ruler except Ahaziah, Athaliah, Jehoahaz, Jehoiachin, and Zedekiah. The Chronicles of the Kings of Israel is mentioned eighteen times (1 Kgs 14:19; 15:31; 16:5, 14, 20, 27; 22:39; 2 Kgs 1:18; 10:34; 13:8, 12; 14:15, 28; 15:11, 15, 21, 26, 31) in reference to every king of Israel except for Jehoram and Hoshea. These citations include a standard formula: ". . . the rest of the acts of ___ how he [or "and all that he did"] ___, behold, they are [or "are they not"] written in the book of the Chronicles of the Kings of Israel [or Judah]."

The author of Kings also refers to a book of the Affairs of Solomon (Heb *sēper dibrê šĕlōmōh*), which is normally translated as the book of the Acts of Solomon (1 Kgs 11:41). Among the numerous sources mentioned in the OT book of Chronicles are "the book of the kings of Israel and Judah" (2 Chr 27:7), "the book of the kings of Judah and Israel" (2 Chr 16:11), "the book of the kings of Israel" (2 Chr 20:34), and "the chronicles of the kings of Israel" (2 Chr 33:18). Most scholars agree that these probably are descriptive terms rather than titles and most likely all refer to the same work. Disagreement exists as to whether these are the same books mentioned in 1–2 Kings. In addition, a book of chronicles (Heb *sēper dibrê hayyamîm*) is mentioned incidentally in Neh 12:23 as being a book in which the heads of Levite families are registered, but few scholars have connected this to the books mentioned in 1–2 Kings. The only other use of a similar term in the OT occurs in Esth 10:2 which, using the same formula used in 1–2 Kings, refers to the book of the Chronicles of the Kings of Media and Persia.

Though the author of Kings specifically refers to the books of the Chronicles of the Kings only as sources for further information, it is widely assumed that he used these books as sources for his own writing (*NDH,* 57). Scholars who do not make this assumption generally conclude, on the basis of the titles, that they were the official court annals of the two kingdoms. For four of the kings of Judah and seven of the kings of Israel, the formula includes amplifying information ("how he ____") which would then be the only basis for judging what might have been their content. Indeed, ten of these eleven cases refer specifically to military campaigns, "conspiracies," or building projects. This corresponds well to known Mesopotamian court annals which typically include brief, highly stylized reports of military campaigns, building projects, and hunting exploits.

The majority of scholars who assume that the author of Kings utilized these chronicles as a primary source for his own writing note that although certain idiomatic phrases suggest derivation from official annals (Montgomery 1934), much of the material in Kings is clearly not of the sort included in official annals. Thus they conclude that the Chronicles of the Kings must have been unofficial histories based on official annals but with substantial amplification.

Prominent hypotheses regarding the Chronicles of the Kings include the following: (1) They were unofficial histories composed by prophets based upon official annals and prophetic writings (Keil 1876: 12–14). (2) The chronicles for both Israel and Judah and the Acts of Solomon were probably a single annalistic work written by a priest of Jerusalem in the time of Manasseh (Jepsen 1956: 54–60). (3) They were unofficial histories based on official annals: the author drew upon the Judean chronicles for information about the temple, royal succession, and political events, but took little from the chronicles of Israel apart from its chronological framework (*NDH,* 63–74). (4) They were the official annals of the court of Jerusalem—a single work in two columns, one for Israel and one for Judah (Mettinger 1971: 36–42). (5) If official annals of the court of Israel ever existed, the author of Kings did not use them. The Chronicles of the Kings of Judah included the core of the material attributed to the Acts of Solomon. These three titles should not be viewed as actual works, but as a literary device representative of the author's historical perspective (Garbini 1981).

Bibliography

Garbini, G. 1981. Le Fonti Citate Nel "Libro Dei Re." *Hen* 3: 26–46.

Jepsen, A. 1956. *Die Quellen des Königsbuches.* Halle.

Keil, C. F. 1876. *The Books of the Kings.* Biblical Commentary. Trans. J. Martin. Grand Rapids.

Mettinger, T. N. D. 1971. *Solomonic State Officials.* ConBOT 5. Lund.

Montgomery, J. A. 1934. Archival Data in the Book of Kings. *JBL* 53: 46–52.

DUANE L. CHRISTENSEN

CHRONICLES, BOOK OF 1–2. Final books in the third major division (Hagiographa, Sacred Writings) of the Hebrew Bible. Its position in English Versions derives from the LXX, where it is placed between Kingdoms and Ezra-Nehemiah.

A. Name

In the Hebrew Bible this work carries the title *dibrê hayyāmîm,* "the events of the days." The title "Chronicles" can be traced back to Jerome, who, in his *Prologus Galeatus* (a preface to the Books of Samuel and Kings), provided a more appropriate title, *Chronicon Totius Divinae Historiae,* or Chronicle of the Entire Divine History. In his German translation of the Bible, Luther called the book *Die Chronik,* which led to the familiar "Chronicles" in English Bibles. In the LXX, Chronicles is called *Paraleipomena* (hereafter *Par.*), that is, "the things omitted" or "passed over." The church father Theodoret interpreted this to mean that Chronicles assembled whatever the author of 1–2 Kings omitted, though this view does not indicate that Chronicles has also omitted much of what is contained in the biblical books of Kings. The division into two books appears first in the LXX and has been standard in Hebrew Bibles since the 15th century.

B. Canonicity

It is frequently asserted (e.g., Curtis and Madsen *Chronicles* ICC, 3), apparently incorrectly, that the position of Chronicles at the end of the Hebrew Bible indicates its late acceptance into the canon. Actually, there does not seem to have been much discussion about canonicity, perhaps because Chronicles included so much material found elsewhere in the canon (Willi 1972: 179); the book may have been granted canonical status at the same time as Ezra-Nehemiah. In some Hebrew manuscripts from Spain it appears as the first book among the Writings, where its worship emphases provide a fitting introduction to the following book of Psalms. Its now standard position at the end of the canon follows the practice of the Jewish community in Babylon. In the Septuagint and associated translations (e.g., Vulgate, Ethiopic), the order is Kings, Chronicles, 1 Esdras, 2 Esdras (= Ezra-Nehemiah).

C. Extent of the Book

1. Relationship to Ezra-Nehemiah. Since the time of Leopold Zunz (1832), Chronicles has been considered by the majority of scholars to be part of the Chronicler's History, consisting of (all or most of) Chronicles and (all or parts of) Ezra-Nehemiah. Because this hypothesis has important implications for the date and meaning of Chronicles, and because it has been sharply called into question in recent years, the arguments for and against it must be reviewed and assessed. Arguments for the unity of Chronicles-Nehemiah include (Japhet 1968: 331–32): (a) The presence of the first verses of Ezra (1:1–3a) at the end of Chronicles (2 Chr 36:22–23). (b) The book of 1 Esdras, which duplicates 2 Chronicles 35–36, Ezra 1–10, and Nehemiah 8. (c) The linguistic resemblance of the three books, e.g., their common vocabulary, syntactic phenomena, and stylistic peculiarities. (d) The common point of view from which the history is treated, the method followed in the choice of materials, and the preference demonstrated for certain topics.

While in argument (a) the overlap may indicate where the story is continued, it does not in itself demand unity of authorship. The overlap can be understood equally well as support for diversity of authorship of Chronicles and Ezra-Nehemiah (Welch 1935: 186).

1 Esdras, as noted in argument (b), is a fragment that breaks off in mid-sentence (= Neh 8:13); it probably once began at a point other than 2 Chr 35:1 as well. Those who argue that it is a translation of an earlier version of the Chronicler's History, to which the Nehemiah Memoirs had not yet been added, posit a beginning at 1 Chronicles 1 (Pohlmann 1970) or at 1 Chronicles 10 (Cross 1975). Williamson (1977b: 12–36; criticized by McKenzie 1985: 20–23) holds that 1 Esdras is both a fragment and a secondary compilation, and he argues that the text of 1 Esdr 9:37 shows knowledge of Neh 7:72—Eng 7:73. Hence the compiler, in his judgment, was following a *Vorlage* in which Nehemiah 8 followed Nehemiah 1–7, not Ezra 10. He also maintains that it is unlikely that *Par.* and 1 Esdras, which derive from the same time (2d century) and place (Alexandria), would both include the entire text of Chronicles. One can, of course, still argue from 1 Esdras that at least a part of Jewish tradition in the 2d century associated Chronicles, Ezra, and Nehemiah 8 with one another and interpreted them along the lines of a Chronicler's History.

Japhet (1968) focused her attention on the linguistic differences between Chronicles and Ezra-Nehemiah while acknowledging general linguistic similarities. She found differences that could be classified as linguistic opposition, variation in technical terms (with Chronicles showing a stage in the use of these terms later even than the latest stratum of Ezra-Nehemiah), and stylistic traits peculiar to Chronicles and to Ezra-Nehemiah respectively. Cross (1975: 14, n. 58) and Polzin (1976: 55), however, hold that much of the linguistic opposition can be accounted for by arguing that the scribal tradition lying behind Chronicles was more consistent than that lying behind Ezra-Nehemiah (Throntveit 1982a: 203–4). Mosis (1973: 215, n. 23) believed that Japhet did not distinguish adequately between the linguistic usage of the *Vorlagen* taken over by the Chronicler, the pieces composed by the Chronicler himself, and secondary additions to his work.

Williamson (1977b: 37–59) investigated a list of 140 items (first drawn up by S. R. Driver [1913: 535–40] and later expanded by E. L. Curtis and A. A. Madsen [*Chronicles* ICC, 27–36]) that show similarities in style between Chronicles and Ezra-Nehemiah (the third argument for the unity of these books) and was able to eliminate all but six of these stylistic features as either irrelevant to the question of unity of authorship or as actually favoring *diversity* of authorship. In a recent study, Throntveit has shown that Polzin was only able to add two additional grammatical or syntactic features to the evidence for similarity of authorship. He concluded, "While Japhet and Williamson have provided strong arguments against the ability of linguistic analysis to prove common authorship, they have not shown separate authorship on these grounds" (1982a: 215).

While the priestly point of view, a focus on the temple and the cult, and a favoritism toward the Levites are among the themes shared by Chronicles with Ezra-Nehemiah, recent discussion has also identified possible theological differences between the two works, among which the following seem most convincing: (1) The concept of retribution and the terms related to it in Chronicles are almost entirely lacking in Ezra-Nehemiah (Braun 1979: 53–56; Williamson 1977b: 67–68). (2) The two works differ in their attitude toward the northern tribes, and in particular the Samaritans (Braun 1979: 56–59; Williamson 1977b: 60–61). (3) Chronicles places a greater emphasis upon the Davidic monarchy (Braun 1979: 63). (4) In Ezra-Nehemiah there is mention of the election of Abraham and the Exodus, while in Chronicles there is a concentration on the patriarch Jacob (who is always called Israel) and a deemphasis on the Exodus (Williamson 1977b: 61–66). (5) The frequent references to prophets in Chronicles make it a prophetic history; in Ezra-Nehemiah, by contrast, the prophetic influence has virtually ceased (Williamson 1977b: 68). (6) The *nĕtînîm* ("temple servants") and the sons of Solomon's servants appear throughout Ezra-Nehemiah, but are absent from Chronicles, with the exception of 1 Chr 9:2 (Japhet 1968: 351–54; Williamson 1977b: 69). (7) In Chronicles, Israel comprises all twelve tribes, whereas in Ezra-Nehemiah Israel is Judah and Benjamin (Williamson 1977b: 69).

Three main positions are held today on the existence of the Chronicler's History: (a) Some affirm it, including all or parts of Ezra-Nehemiah within the history (e.g., Ackroyd *CHJ* 1: 130–61; Clines *Ezra, Nehemiah, Esther* NCB; Cross 1975; Freedman; Mosis); (b) others (most notably Japhet and Williamson) believe that Chronicles and Ezra-Nehemiah are separate works by separate authors; and (c) still others (e.g., Welten, Willi) believe that the books are separate works by the *same* author. The ideological or theological differences between the books are perhaps the most convincing argument for diversity of authorship. While the question is by no means closed, the discussion that follows will assume the diverse authorship of these books.

2. Secondary Elements within Chronicles. Since M. Noth's seminal work in 1943 *(ÜgS)* the dominant opinion has been that one author was responsible for the book of Chronicles with some subsequent glossing of the text (Noth *NCH* 29–42; Rudolph *Chronikbücher* HAT, 1–3). Much secondary Levitical material has also been detected in 2 Chronicles by Willi (1972: 196–204). Major passages still in dispute include the following:

a. The Genealogies in 1 Chronicles 1–9. Welch (1939: 185–86) and Cross (1975: 4–18; cf. McKenzie 1985: 30, n. 32) have proposed that the entire genealogical preface is secondary. Noth and Rudolph argued for the originality of a basic genealogical scheme later enriched with various secondary additions. In Rudolph's case the secondary materials amounted to more than 75 percent of the text. Williamson, however, defends the substantial unity of 1 Chronicles 1–9 as part of the original book of Chronicles, though he does detect a few additions (e.g., 6:35–38—Eng 50–53). These genealogies, like the rest of the book, show a concern for all Israel, for David and his dynasty, for the centrality of Judah and Jerusalem, and for immediate retribution. They call the patriarch Jacob "Israel" and show little interest in Moses and the Exodus.

b. Portions of 1 Chronicles 15–16. Rudolph considers 15:4–10, 16–21, 22–24; and 16:5b–38, 42 secondary (*Chronikbücher* HAT, 2; cf. Noth *NCH,* 35). Williamson (*Chronicles* NCB, 122–32) finds a priestly, secondary redaction in parts of 15:4, 11, 14, 18, 24 and 16:6, 38, 42.

c. 1 Chr 23:3–27:34. Noth (*NCH,* 31–33) and Rudolph (*Chronikbücher* HAT, 3) dismiss all of this material dealing with David's organization of the Levites. Williamson (*Chronicles* NCB, 158) detects a primary stratum in 23:3–6a, 6b–13a, 15–24; 25:1–6; 26:1–3, 9–11, 19, 20–32, assigning the rest of chaps. 23–27 to a pro-priestly reviser who flourished about a generation after the original author.

d. 2 Chr 36:22–23. Japhet retains this doublet of Ezra 1:1–3a, but Williamson declares it secondary (NCB, 419) and so argues that the original book ends with 2 Chr 36:21.

D. Date and Place of Authorship

Jerusalem is clearly the place of authorship. If there was a Chronicler's History, including all or parts of Chronicles, Ezra, and Nehemiah, then the Chronicler must be subsequent to the work of Ezra (458 or 398 B.C.E. [7th year of Artaxerxes I or Artaxerxes II]) and Nehemiah (445–432 B.C.E.). Internal clues in Ezra-Nehemiah, such as the list of high priests in Nehemiah 12, also figure in this argument, unless this list or the Nehemiah Memoirs in general are held to be supplementary to the original Chronicler's History. Those who find the genealogical preface of 1 Chronicles 1–9 secondary (e.g., Welch, Cross), or who find at least chap. 3 secondary, are not bound by the chronological implications of 3:17–24, which includes the exilic and postexilic line of David.

The evidence for dating the books of Chronicles apart from Ezra-Nehemiah rests on the following types of evidence. (1) The mention of the rise of the Persian kingdom (2 Chr 36:20) makes 539 the earliest possible date. (2) *Par.* is cited in Eupolemus, ca. 150 B.C., and the translation of 1 Esdras, containing 2 Chronicles 35–36, also dates to the 2d century. Since some time would elapse between the composition of a book and the need for a Greek translation, a date of composition after 200 would seem to be impossible. Note also that Sir. 47:8–10 (ca. 190 B.C.E.) presupposes Chronicles' description of David. Decisions on the following evidence can narrow this three-century range:

1. Internal Clues. a. 1 Chr 3:17–24. This genealogy of the sons of Jeconiah (= Jehoiachin, exiled in 597 B.C.E.) extends for six generations following MT or eleven following *Par.* (see the commentaries). Depending on how many years one allows per generation, MT suggests a date between 400–350, and the LXX a date about 250. The assumption is that the author recorded the genealogy down to his own day.

b. 1 Chr 29:7. The mention of *darics,* a Persian coin not minted before 515 B.C.E., in the reign of Darius I, is here used anachronistically of contributions for the temple in the time of David. Presumably enough time would have to pass after 515 for an author to employ this anachronism. Mosis (1973: 105–6) and Throntveit (1982b: 128), however, believe this verse is secondary.

c. 2 Chr 16:9. The clause "The eyes of the Lord run to and fro throughout the whole earth" appears to be a citation of Zech 4:10. Since the prophet flourished in 520–518, a date for Chronicles must be somewhat later, though it is a matter of judgment as to how much time would have to elapse before the prophet could be referred to in such an authoritative manner.

d. The Language of the Book. Polzin (1976: 27–75) classifies the language of Chronicles, Ezra, and Nehemiah (exclusive of the Nehemiah Memoirs) as Late Biblical Hebrew, subsequent to P. However, it is doubtful whether the language by itself can be dated precisely within the postexilic period since he has only shown similarity of language, rather than similarity of authorship, in the three documents (Throntveit 1982a: 215). The absence of Greek words and Hellenistic influence might favor an earlier date within this period.

2. Historical or Theological Situation. a. The Schismatic Samaritan Community. Noth believed that the rival Samaritan cult was set up about the time of the fall of the Persian Empire and that the Chronicler's work was a response to this in the 3d century. Recent studies, however, have changed the understanding of the Jewish and Samaritan schism. First, it is now widely held that the decisive break between the Jerusalemite and Samaritan communities did not take place before the time of John Hyrcanus at the end of the 2d century (Cross 1966; Purvis 1968; cf. Coggins 1975). Hence, to call the Chronicler anti-Samaritan is anachronistic. Secondly, the questioning of the unity of Chronicles-Nehemiah has led to the observation that the more exclusivistic claims are contained in Ezra-Nehemiah and not in Chronicles. Coggins has proposed that even in Ezra-Nehemiah we can detect only an anti-Samarian, rather than an anti-Samaritan attitude. Thirdly, the attitude toward the North in Chronicles is positive.

b. The Era of Zerubbabel. Freedman proposed that the Chronicler structured his history around the figure of David and his dynasty and defended the claims of the house of David in its authoritative relationship to temple and cult. The occasion for the book was the return from exile and the rebuilding of the temple under the leadership of Zerubbabel and Joshua (parallel to David and Zadok respectively). Though the exact ending of the Chronicler's History is unknown, according to Freedman, it included at least Ezra 1–3 and possibly Ezra 6:19–22

(1975: 183). The narrative of Zerubbabel and the temple has been supplanted by an Aramaic record (4:6–6:18) in the present work, which brings the picture down to 515 (1961: 441).

Cross (1975) proposed a modified version of this reconstruction, which postulates three editions of the Chronicler's History. The first edition (1 Chronicles 10 through 2 Chronicles 34 plus the *Vorlage* of 1 Esdr 1:1–5:65 [= 2 Chr 35:1–Ezra 3:13]) was composed in support of the restoration of Davidic rule, the building of the temple, and the establishment of the cult shortly after the founding of the temple in 520 and before its dedication in 515. The second (1 Chronicles 10–2 Chronicles 34 plus the *Vorlage* of 1 Esdras [2 Chr 35:1–36:23; Ezra 1–10; Nehemiah 8; and the story of Zerubbabel's wisdom and piety in 1 Esdr 3:1–5:6]), was written after Ezra's mission, in 450. The final edition (1–2 Chronicles; Ezra-Nehemiah), dated to 400 or a little later, incorporated the genealogies of 1 Chronicles 1–9 and the Nehemiah Memoirs, but suppressed the title "servant of the Lord" for Zerubbabel in Ezra 6:7 and the story of Zerubbabel's wisdom and piety (= 1 Esdr 3:1–5:6). The 400 date is established by the Davidic genealogy in 1 Chr 3:17–24, the reference to Darius II (423–404) in Neh 12:22, and the references to the high priests Yohanan II and Yaddua II (late 5th century) in Nehemiah 12–13. McKenzie (1985: 189–206) suggests that the earliest edition (= Chronicles 1) was based on Dtr 1, the preexilic version of the Deuteronomistic History (hereafter DH).

c. Conditions of the 4th Century. Japhet (*EncJud* 5: 533–34) points to the absence of Greek influence in the books of Chronicles, but also holds that they were composed *after* Ezra-Nehemiah. Williamson relates the emphasis on faith in Chronicles to the aftermath of the Persian suppression of the revolt led by the Sidonian Tennes (351–348 B.C.E.), though he admits the dating is only probable. Since he dates the pro-priestly reviser of Chronicles to very late in the Persian period (1979: 268), the original Chronicler may be placed a generation earlier.

d. Conditions of the 3d Century. Welten (1973) and Willi (1972), who believe that Chronicles and Ezra-Nehemiah were written by the same person but not as one work, are forced to a date after Ezra. Welten points to the growing tensions between Jerusalem and Samaria in postexilic times and claims that the time of Ezra and Nehemiah was far in the past when Chronicles was written (1973: 200). The war reports, in his judgment, reflect the conflicts between the Ptolemies and the Seleucids in the first half of the 3d century. His appeal to the use of catapults in 2 Chr 26:14–15 as a war machine first in general use in the 3d century is mistaken since the passage in question refers to a platform on city walls from which stones and arrows could be fired (Williamson *Chronicles* NCB, 338).

The suggested correlations with historical periods either seem tenuous or presuppose highly debatable literary-critical judgments (such as the original connection of part of Ezra with 1–2 Chronicles). The three internal clues from 1 Chr 3:17–24; 29:7; and 2 Chr 16:9 are more specific, suggesting the late 5th or 4th century. This fits well with Chronicles' relationship to the Dtr, which underwent its final redaction in the mid 6th century and must have passed through several manuscript generations before it was used by the Chronicler. Hanson (1975: 270) has argued for a date around 400 to account for the book's evenhanded approach toward the Levites following a period of great hostility in the 6th and 5th centuries.

Though a 4th-century date seems likely, the uncertain nature of the evidence suggests caution when tying one's interpretation to anything more historically specific than the general situation of postexilic times.

E. Text

1. Text of Chronicles. Since only four complete words from Chronicles are preserved in the Dead Sea Scrolls, the primary witnesses to the text, apart from MT, are two Greek translations and their respective daughter versions (e.g., Ethiopic, Bohairic, Old Latin, Armenian, Syro Hexapla, etc.). 1 Esdras contains only chaps. 35–36 from the book of 2 Chronicles and was written in 2d-century Egypt. Though its elegant Greek style is paraphrastic, making reconstruction of the Hebrew *Vorlage* more difficult than elsewhere in the LXX, it bears witness to an older and often shorter form of the text, differing both from the MT and the other Greek translation (Klein 1966).

This second translation *(Par.)* is also now dated to 2d-century-B.C.E. Egypt, primarily because the translation seems to have been known by Eupolemus (ca. 150) and shows Ptolemaic Egyptian coloring (Allen 1974a: 12). This translation is best preserved in the G family of texts (Vaticanus [=B]; cf. Sinaiticus and miniscule c_2), of which the L, R, and O families are revisions (Allen 1974a: 65–108). G itself has been extensively revised (Allen 1974a: 142–74), so that its fairly close approximation to MT may result to a large extent from the recensional process. 1 Esdras may provide more direct access to the state of the Hebrew text in the 2d century. *Par.* does not seem to be a full part of the *kaige* recension since it does not share fully 10 of 19 translation characteristics, and its use of the other characteristics is sporadic and inconsistent (Allen 1974a: 137–41). C. C. Torrey's opinion that *Par.* was written by Theodotion depended almost exclusively on the use of transliterations and is now generally rejected.

In synoptic passages, *Par.* often agrees with Samuel-Kings (Hebrew and/or Greek) against the MT of Chronicles. Allen argues extensively (1974a: 175–218) that *Par.*'s *Vorlage* and, occasionally, *Par.* itself have been assimilated to the Samuel-Kings text, thus removing changes introduced by the Chronicler. He concedes that in some of these cases Chronicles' MT itself may be corrupt, and the proportion of such cases may be higher than he suggests. Allen considers *Par.*'s *Vorlage* to be a popular (vulgar) text (1974b: 167–68).

2. Text of Samuel-Kings Used by the Chronicler. Great text-critical interest has focused on the character of the text of Samuel and Kings that lay before the Chronicler himself (Cross 1961: 188–92; Lemke 1964; 1965; summary in Klein 1974: 42–50). Earlier scholars had assumed that the Chronicler used a text much like the MT of Samuel-Kings, though now it is clear that what he had was the Palestinian text of Samuel-Kings attested by Qumran mss (especially 4QSam[a]), the Old Greek and the proto-Lucianic recensions of LXX, and Josephus. In a number of cases, historical or theological changes ascribed to the Chronicler have been shown to be part of the textual history of Samuel-Kings (examples in Klein 1974: 42–46; Lemke 1965). McKenzie (1985: 119-58) distinguishes between Samuel and Kings, and claims that the Chronicler's *Vorlage* in Kings was a proto-rabbinic text type.

This is not to deny the extensive rewriting of the Deuteronomistic History which the Chronicler undertook. But it does mean that before a change can be credited to the Chronicler, one must be sure of the textual shape of his *Vorlage*. Micheel (1983: 25), for example, detected the theological hand of the Chronicler in the notice in 2 Chr 18:31 that Jehoshaphat's cry was answered by the Lord's saving him since the reference to salvation is not mentioned in 1 Kgs 22:32. This reference, however, is contained in the (proto-) Lucianic text and therefore in the text of Kings that lay before the Chronicler. Many other variations between Chronicles and Samuel-Kings, to which no historical or theological significance has been ascribed, are also now explainable in this fashion (Klein 1974: 47–50).

F. Sources

1. Canonical Sources. The author of 1 Chronicles 1 drew his genealogies from the book of Genesis. Other genealogical notices in 1 Chronicles 2–8 show strong ties to Genesis, Exodus, Numbers, Joshua, Samuel, and Ruth. Psalms 96, 105, and 106 are cited in 1 Chronicles 16. There are also allusions to or evident knowledge of the books of Isaiah (2 Chr 28:16–21), Jeremiah (2 Chr 36:21), and Zechariah (2 Chr 36:9). But clearly the most frequently used canonical source is the Samuel-Kings corpus from the Deuteronomistic History. (For a convenient list of parallels see Myers [*2 Chronicles* AB, 227–31].) A recent attempt by Halpern (1981: 52) and Macy (1975) to show that both Kings and Chronicles were dependent on a common, Deuteronomistic source has not been successful in my judgment. McKenzie's proposal (1985: 189–206) that the Chronicler knew the Deuteronomistic History only in its preexilic redaction (Dtr 1) is also not persuasive. When Chronicles contains parallels to passages commonly assigned to the exilic edition of DH (Dtr 2), McKenzie either denies the exilic date of these pericopes from Kings or alleges that the passages in Chronicles (2 Chr 7:19–22 and 34:22–27) are themselves secondary. His argument, thus, appears to be circular.

The Chronicler's use of Samuel-Kings is, of course, selective. For his depiction of David he utilized those materials from the DH that would enhance David's qualifications as builder of the temple or highlight his position as a victorious and powerful king. Thus he omitted most of the narrative commonly known as the History of David's Rise (1 Samuel 16–2 Samuel 5), in which David gradually gained ascendancy over Saul and kingship over all Israel, and almost all of the Succession Narrative (2 Samuel 9–20; 1 Kings 1–2). The reader of Chronicles is not told about David's adultery with Bathsheba, his murder of Uriah, or the revolt of Absalom. These omissions are probably not the cover-up they are sometimes portrayed to be, since the Chronicler could have presupposed that his readers already knew these stories. Rather, the Chronicler selected only those passages for his account of David that fit his positive agenda. Similarly, passages about the northern kingdom were omitted unless interaction with the south required their inclusion (e.g., 2 Chr 18:2–34, the joint campaign of Ahab and Jehoshaphat).

At times his selective citations ignored the original context. For example, 1 Chr 14:3–7 begins, "And David took yet more wives at Jerusalem" (= 2 Sam 15:13–16), although 2 Sam 3:2–5, to which the "yet more" refers, is omitted by the Chronicler. He also picked up the story of the people of Jabesh-gilead caring for the body of Saul (1 Chr 10:11–12 = 1 Sam 31:11–13), but omitted 2 Sam 2:4b–7, the real goal of this narrative, where David congratulates the people of Jabesh-gilead on their actions and invites them to recognize his kingship (Noth *NCH*, 90, for other examples).

The Chronicler also sometimes rearranged the order of items from Dtr to serve his own interests. For example, the list of David's mighty men was taken from 2 Sam 23:8–39, where it forms part of an appendix to 2 Samuel identifying acts of heroism. In 1 Chr 11:10–47, however, this list is placed within a series of lists of those from all Israel who gave David unanimous support in the early days of his kingdom.

Finally, the Chronicler combined items from his sources in order to avoid the unfavorable implications of the tradition. According to 1 Kgs 3:4–15, God appeared to Solomon at the high place of Gibeon, but the Chronicler added in 1 Chr 16:39 and 2 Chr 1:3 that the Tent of Meeting from the wilderness period stood at that site until the completion of the temple. Hence the possible impression that God had appeared at an illegitimate sanctuary was avoided (Noth *NCH*, 94–95).

2. Noncanonical Sources. a. Explicit Source References. The Chronicler refers the reader to sources at the end of virtually every king's history. Typical references include: (1) 2 Chr 9:29 "The rest of the acts of Solomon, the first and the last, are they not written in the acts of Nathan the prophet, in the prophecy of Ahijah the Shilonite, [and] in the vision of Iddo the seer concerning Jeroboam the son of Nebat?" (cf. 1 Kgs 11:41). (2) 2 Chr 24:27 "Accounts of his sons, and of the many oracles against him, and of the rebuilding of the house of God are written in the Commentary [Heb *midraš*] on the Book of the Kings" (cf. 2 Kgs 12:20). (3) 2 Chr 27:7 "The rest of the acts of Jotham, and all his wars, and his ways, behold they are written in the Book of the kings of Israel and Judah" (cf. 2 Kgs 15:36).

While the names of the recorded sources may vary in Kings and Chronicles in these and other cases, we should probably not suppose that the Chronicler here referred to extant records which were available to him or his readers. Rather, these source references are paraphrases or interpretations of source references from DH. The following four observations may be made:

All of the references are found at the same place in Kings and Chronicles, even when the source reference does not come at the exact end of a king's reign (e.g., 2 Chr 16:11; 20:34; 25:26). This makes unlikely the proposal that these source notices themselves come from sources other than the book of Kings (McKenzie 1985: 174). The unique addition of a source reference for David at 1 Chr 29:29 attributes the materials drawn from the Dtr account of David to the three prophets associated with

David (Samuel, Nathan, and Gad), even though Samuel died before David took office.

Other references to such sources as the acts, prophecies, or visions of a variety of prophets are merely new titles for the source references already contained in DH, indicating that in the Chronicler's judgment the earlier history (DH) was a prophetic history (Nathan, Ahijah, Iddo, 2 Chr 9:29; Shemaiah and Iddo, 2 Chr 12:15; Iddo, 2 Chr 13:22; Jehu ben Hanani, 2 Chr 20:34; Isaiah, 2 Chr 26:22; 32:32). The mention of prophets in the source references occurs only for those kings who play an important role within the dynasty or in fostering the cult, that is, for those kings who are evaluated positively, in whole or in part, by the Chronicler. The source reference at the end of Solomon's reign (2 Chr 9:29) refers to three "prophetic" records instead of "the book of the acts of Solomon" of 1 Kgs 11:41, even though all the materials in 2 Chronicles 1–9 are drawn from 1 Kings 1–11, with no evidence for information from additional sources.

The reference to "the book of the kings of Judah and Israel" (2 Chr 16:11; cf. 20:34; 25:26; 27:7; 28:26; 32:32; 33:18; 35:26; 36:8 with minor variations in the name of the source), instead of "the book of the chronicles of Judah" (1 Kgs 15:23, etc.), shows the Chronicler's interest in pointing out that Judah was part of that inclusive Israel which he maintained before his readers as an ideal (Williamson 1977b: 106–7, 128).

There is no need to think of "the *midraš* of the book of the kings" (2 Chr 24:27) as anything other than a rephrasing of the source reference in 2 Kgs 12:20—Eng 12:19.

b. Implicit Source References. The question of the availability of additional sources is related to, though not identical with, the question of the historical value of the Chronicler's additional information.

Most scholars agree that the genealogies in 1 Chronicles 1–9 came to the Chronicler from a variety of sources. Note the varieties of genealogical genres in these chapters (horizontal and vertical genealogies; some genealogies feature the word "begat," while others link the generations with "his son" or "the sons of," etc.), the varying amount of material for the various tribes, the mention of events (4:41; 5:10) not recorded elsewhere in the Bible, and the general obscurity of many of the names. (The same line of argumentation is probably applicable to many of the other lists of names in the book [e.g., 1 Chronicles 12, apart from redactional elements; chaps. 23–27].) 1 Chr 4:24–5:22 seems to have been drawn from a genealogy that included intertribal history and geography, while chap. 7 was once a military census list.

The reference to Hezekiah's tunnel in 2 Chr 32:30 and to Neco's goal in his battle against Josiah (2 Chr 35:20), though not attested in the parallel passages in Kings, are regarded as historically reliable additional information that could not arise from exegesis of Dtr (Noth *NCH,* 57–58). Again, the reference to the fortifications of Rehoboam in 2 Chr 11:5–10, which fits awkwardly in the context, must have been available in some kind of source. Williamson believes that the descriptions of armies in 2 Chr 14:8; 17:14–19, 25:5, and 26:11–15 are from a source (*Chronicles* NCB, 261–62; contra Welten 1973: 79–114). The interpreter of Chronicles in each case must decide whether the additional material in Chronicles comes from a source, and, if so, what the historical value of that additional information may be. The speeches and prayers of the kings and prophets are best understood as the Chronicler's own compositions (see I. 1 and 2 below).

G. Historical Value of Chronicles

Opinions on this question vary widely in the scholarly literature. Wellhausen remarked: "See what Chronicles has made out of David! The founder of the kingdom has become the founder of the temple and the public worship, the king and hero at the head of his companions in arms has become the singer and master of ceremonies at the head of a swarm of priests and Levites. . . . It is only the tradition of the older source [Samuel-Kings] that possesses historical value" (*WPHI,* 182). Among critical scholars, a quite opposite position was held by W. F. Albright (1950: 66–69). He believed the Chronicler was correct in: (1) attributing a 10th-century origin to the guilds of temple singers; (2) in listing towns fortified by Rehoboam in 2 Chr 11:5–10; (3) in the regnal years assigned to Asa; and (4) in his report of a judicial reform under Jehoshaphat. Albright admitted, of course, that the evidence was not one-sided and that it was "more difficult than ever to accept the stories of the wars of Abijah (II Chron. 13), Asa (II Chron. 14), and Jehoshaphat (II Chron. 15) *'au pied de la lettre'* since we know that the numbers are exaggerated out of all relation to the possible facts" (1950: 68–69). (For examples where the historical value of Chronicles is supported by archaeology and related studies, see Hasel *ISBE* 2: 668–69.)

In recent years, emphasis has focused more on the Chronicler's use of additional material, rather than upon that material's historical value. Although Welten's largely negative historical judgments about the building activities of various kings have not been unanimously accepted, he has found a wide following in his observation that the seven paragraphs dealing with building activities of a king in 2 Chronicles 10–36 are always included for kings whom the Chronicler judges positively (2 Chr 11:5–12 [Rehoboam]; 14:5–6 [Asa]; 17:12–13 [Jehoshaphat]; 27:3–4 [Jotham]; and 32:5–6a [Hezekiah]) or, if a king has both positive and negative periods, within the positive part of his reign (2 Chr 26:9–10 [Uzziah]; 33:14 [Manasseh]).

Welten also evaluated the five reports of successful wars in Chronicles that have no parallel in Kings (2 Chr 13:3–20 [Abijah]; 2 Chr 14:8–14—Eng 9–15 [Asa]; 2 Chr 20:1–30 [Jehoshaphat]; 2 Chr 26:6–8 [Uzziah]; and 27:5–6 [Jotham]). He pointed out that all the kings involved were positively evaluated by the Chronicler, at least for the portion of their reign when the alleged war took place. Welten's own historical judgment is negative, believing that the Chronicler is merely giving a graphic description of the animosities that beset his 3d-century community. The only historical source he allows in these accounts is in 2 Chr 26:6a.

In his recent commentary Williamson also deals with these five war accounts. He notes how these reports of successful wars and/or tribute illustrate a king's faithfulness and complete reliance on God, his self-humbling repentance, or the fact that a king was under God's blessing. He also concedes that the Chronicler has in almost every case expressed the account in his own language, complete with the ideology of Holy War. When it comes to historical judgments, Williamson opts more often than Welten for some kind of historical kernel. On Abijah he cites the authentic-sounding place names in 2 Chr 13:19 (though see now Klein 1983) and wonders whether the Chronicler would have arrived at a favorable evaluation of Abijah had he not had some previous account of his victory over the North. He sees Asa's reported battle against a million Ethiopians as an exaggeration of a local bedouin raid. Jehoshaphat's war is interpreted, following Noth and Rudolph, as the magnifying (for didactic purposes) of an incident that originally was fairly insignificant. He finds the account of Uzziah's war concise, specific, and historical, without the Chronicler's usual lengthy expansions, though he dismisses 2 Chr 26:6b for textual reasons. Finally, on Jotham's war he withholds historical judgment for lack of data.

This comparison of Welten and Williamson indicates that there is a tendency in current scholarship to recognize the extensive theological contribution of the Chronicler, whether the event is historical or not; that archaeological and form-critical judgments are reaching new levels of sophistication (documented more in the works of the two scholars than in the above summary); that in many cases a positive or negative historical judgment reflects in part a given scholar's overall evaluation of the historical value of Chronicles; and that in some cases there is no hard data that justifies a historical judgment one way or the other. Thus, Wellhausen's views on David in Chronicles seem misdirected by today's standards.

The Chronicler's magnification of an account for theological reasons can be seen in his use of large numbers. Abijah, accompanied by an army of 400,000, attacked the army of Jeroboam, which was 800,000 strong and inflicted some 500,000 casualties (2 Chronicles 13). Abijah's successor, Asa, supported by an army of 580,000, was able to stave off an invading horde of one million Ethiopians. These and similar numbers are totally out of line with what we know about ancient military forces, and they are in excess of what could have been mustered from the population of Israel or Judah. There has been a recent attempt to rationalize these numbers by understanding the word *ʾelep* as meaning not 1,000 but a tribal subsection and the military unit that went to war from this subsection (Mendenhall 1958; Myers *Chronicles* AB). In the usual reading of chap. 12 of 1 Chronicles, 340,822 men made their way to Hebron to make David king, but Mendenhall reduced the number through his understanding of *ʾelep* to 15,290. However, this attempt to lend plausibility to the numbers in Chronicles has not been successful, however valid it may be for early Israel. When Chronicles and DH both have large numbers, slight differences between the texts allow us to conclude that the Chronicler understood these figures as true thousands and not as military units (e.g., 1 Chr 19:7 = 2 Sam 10:6; 1 Chr 21:15 = 2 Sam 24:9; 2 Chr 2:1, 16, 17—Eng 2:2, 17, 18 = 1 Kgs 5:29, 30—Eng 5:15, 16). The proposed new understanding of *ʾelep* does not seem appropriate in a monarchical setting, nor does it offer an adequate interpretation of the tribal numbers within Chronicles (e.g., the sons of Bela in 1 Chr 7:7 number 22,034, but it is meaningless to speak of 22 military units with an average number per unit of 1.5 men). Note also the impossibly large numbers for other objects in Chronicles where the tribal/military interpretation of *ʾelep* is irrelevant (1 Chr 22:14—100,000 talents of silver and 1,000,000 talents of gold).

H. Some Characteristic Features of Chronicles

1. Royal Speeches and Prayers. The speeches and prayers of kings and prophets in Chronicles are frequently referred to as Levitical sermons (von Rad *ROTT*). Recent studies, however, have raised doubts about whether the Levites were specialists in preaching and whether these speeches should be classified as sermons (Mathias 1984). Von Rad believed that the Chronicler was using a well-established genre and, apparently, actual sermons that were available. But the theological themes in these speeches are those of the Chronicler elsewhere, and von Rad disparaged unnecessarily the literary ability of the Chronicler (*ROTT*, 277). Perhaps the most significant part of von Rad's work was his observation of the way in which these speeches base their appeal on an authoritative scriptural text (for 2 Chr 15:2–7, cf. Jer 19:14; 31:15; for 2 Chr 16:7–9, cf. Zech 4:10; for 2 Chr 19:6–7, cf. Deut 10:17; Zeph 3:5, etc.).

Throntveit (1982b: 25–63), building on Braun, has distinguished the following genres in the royal speeches: (a) *Edicts*. A specific audience is addressed with an imperative that is to be immediately carried out (1 Chr 15:12–13; 22:5; 29:20; 2 Chr 29:31; 35:3–6). (b) *Rationales*. There is no specific audience, imperative, or reported action, but the speech provides some rationale for a cultic action (1 Chr 15:2; 22:1; 2 Chr 8:11; 23:25–32; 28:23). (c) *Orations*. Similar to edicts, but these speeches make frequent use of historical retrospects (1 Chr 13:2–3; 29:1–5; 2 Chr 2:2–9; 13:4–12; 14:6; 29:3–11; 30:4–9).

The royal speeches and prayers play a significant role in the structuring of Chronicles. The three speeches (22:7–16, 18–19; 28:2–8, 9–10, 20–21; 29:1–5) and the prayer of David (29:10–19) serve to link him with Solomon closely and place great emphasis on the temple as the joint project of the two kings and a united Israel. David's participation in the building of the temple is bracketed at the beginning (1 Chr 17:16–27) and at the end (1 Chr 29:10–19) by prayers. Similarly, the period of the Divided Kingdom is enclosed within speeches calling for repentance by Abijah (2 Chr 13:4–12) and by Hezekiah (2 Chr 30:6–9). Both speeches indicate the Chronicler's openness to Northern participation in the Jerusalem cult.

2. Prophets. The references to prophets, seers, and men of God in Chronicles can be divided into three groups (much of the following is drawn from Micheel 1983). The first group are those taken from parallel accounts in Samuel-Kings (Nathan [1 Chronicles 17]; Gad [1 Chronicles 21]; Shemaiah [2 Chronicles 11]; Micaiah [2 Chr 18:4–27]; and Huldah [2 Chr 34:22–28]).

A second group is part of Chronicles' additional material (Shemaiah in a second appearance [2 Chr 12:5–8]; Azariah [2 Chr 15:1–7]; Hanani [2 Chr 16:7–10]; Jehu ben Hanani [2 Chr 19:2]; Jehaziel [2 Chr 20:14]; Eliezer [2 Chr 20:37]; Elijah active in Judah [2 Chr 21:12–15]; Zechariah [2 Chr 24:20–22]; Oded [2 Chr 28:9–11]; an anonymous man of God and prophet [2 Chronicles 25]; Jeremiah [2 Chr 35:25; 36:22]). With the exception of

Shemaiah, Hanani, Jehu ben Hanani, Elijah, and Jeremiah, these individuals are unknown from other contexts. According to the Chronicler, the attitude shown toward the prophets also reveals one's attitude toward Yahweh: "Believe in Yahweh your God, and you will be established; believe his prophets, and you will succeed" (2 Chr 20:20). These prophets often link the results in a king's domestic or foreign activities with his relationship to Yahweh, although in a few cases success or failure is linked to the whole people's behavior (e.g., Zechariah, Oded).

While some believe that all the words of these prophets were created by the Chronicler (e.g., Micheel), others hold that at least some of them were present in the traditions available to him (e.g., Westermann 1967: 163–68).

A third context is the source references which mention prophets or seers in connection with certain kings (see F.2.a above).

3. Levites. The Levitical genealogies can be described as follows:

a. 1 Chr 5:27–41—Eng 6:1–15. Two sets of Aaronic high priests, from Aaron to Ahimaaz, and from Azariah I (the priest in Solomon's temple) to Jehozadak (who was exiled).

b. 1 Chr 6:1–15—Eng 6:16–30. Each of the three sons of Levi (Gershom, Kohath, and Merari) is provided with a vertical genealogy of seven generations of ordinary Levites that connects to them through their oldest son. A seven-generation genealogy of Samuel and his sons has been inserted into the Kohath genealogy.

c. 1 Chr 6:16–32—Eng 6:31–47. Kohath, Gershom, and Merari are each provided with a vertical genealogy of 14 generations of Levitical singers, ending with Heman, Asaph, and Ethan, the chief singers at the time of David.

d. 1 Chr 6:39–66—Eng 6:54–81. No completely satisfying understanding of this list of Levitical cities or of its date is yet established. Mazar (1960) dated it to the time of the United Monarchy when there was an attempt to strengthen government control by stationing Levites in strategically significant administrative areas. Peterson (1977) proposed an 8th-century date and believed that the Levites in these cities taught the people the Mosaic covenant. According to Spencer (1980), this list is a fictitious composition designed to explain the appearance of the Levites and their secondary role in the postexilic period.

e. 1 Chronicles 23–26. *1 Chr 23:3–6a:* Four types of Levites, whose organization is credited to David; *23:6b–13a, 15–24:* a genealogically based list of those in charge of the work of the house of the Lord; *25:1–6:* a list of singers installed by David; *26:1–3, 9–11, 19:* a list of gatekeepers; *26:20–32:* a list of judges and officers. The Chronicler wanted to give Davidic authority to the role of the Levites in the temple of his day.

In five places (1 Chronicles 25; 2 Chr 20, 29, 34:30, and 35:15) the Chronicler identifies the singers as prophets or as performing prophetic activities. Petersen (1977) argues that the Chronicler hoped through these accounts to substantiate the Levitical singers' claim to cultic authority as prophets in postexilic society. This role is not (contra Mowinckel) a remnant of preexilic cult prophecy.

The standard terminology for cultic personnel in the Chronicler is "the priests and the Levites." The priests are sons of Aaron and descendants of Zadok. The term "sons of Aaron" seems to be used in place of "priests," especially when their rights over against the Levites are being stressed (2 Chr 26:18; 29:21).

The Levites consist of a wide variety of minor clergy, and any group that wanted to be a part of this minor clergy claimed to be a Levite, usually through the Kohathite Korah. Groups like the singers (1 Chr 6:16–24), the gatekeepers (1 Chr 9:17–26; 23:3–5; and 26:1, 19), and even the bakers (1 Chr 9:31–32), which in the sources used by the Chronicler were not identified as Levites, became Levites in the Chronicler's interpretation.

Among the many tasks of the Levites was teaching. The blessing of Moses (Deut 33:8–11) describes them as teaching legal ordinances to Israel. The Chronicler reports their teaching mission in Judah at the time of Jehoshaphat when they took with them the book of the law of Yahweh (2 Chr 17:7–9; cf. also 2 Chr 35:3; Neh 8:7). They also were in charge of various holy objects and prepared things such as the shewbread (1 Chr 9:28–32; 23:29–31; 2 Chr 29:34). Jehoshaphat appointed them to be judges in Jerusalem (2 Chr 19:8–11), and they also served as scribes (1 Chr 24:6; 2 Chr 34:13). In addition, they led in singing and praise (1 Chr 15:16–24; 16:4–42; 2 Chr 5:12–13; 8:14; 20:19–22; 23:13, 18; 29:25–30; 35:15).

I. Theology

1. Monarchy, Cult, and Temple. The Chronicler devotes an extraordinary amount of attention to David and Solomon, and in fact treats the two of them in equal or parallel fashion. David is approved by all Israel right after the death of Saul, with no reference to his conflicts with Saul (cf. 1 Samuel 16–30) or the divided character of Israel early in his reign (2 Sam 1:1–5:3). His first act as king was to capture Jerusalem, the future site of the temple (1 Chr 11:4–9), to which he brought the ark (1 Chr 15:25–16:3). David arranged for the ordering of the priests and Levites, and assigned the latter a role as singers after their requirement to carry the ark had become obsolete (1 Chr 16:4–7, 37–42; 2 Chr 7:6; cf. 1 Chronicles 23–27). He designated the site for the temple (1 Chr 22:1) after Yahweh had indicated his own approval for it by sending fire from heaven (1 Chr 21:26–30). He also made massive preparations for the building of the temple before his death (1 Chr 22:2–5; 29:2–5; cf. 28:12–18, which may be secondary).

Solomon, too, receives unanimous approval, even from the other sons of David (1 Chr 29:23–25). He makes his own preparations for building (2 Chr 2:2–16) and erects the temple on David's site. He puts the ark in the temple (2 Chr 5:2–14) and installs the priests and Levites in their offices (2 Chr 8:14–15). While David had been prevented from building the temple because he had shed blood and waged wars, Solomon was a man of peace and rest (1 Chr 22:8–10). Designated by David, he was also the one chosen by Yahweh specifically for the building of the temple (1 Chr 28:10; 29:1). The Chronicler is the only writer in the OT to designate any king after David as chosen. Solomon's idolatry as reported in 1 Kings 11 is omitted in Chronicles. Braun (1971b; 1976) has made clear that the speeches in 1 Chronicles 22, 28, and 29 tie together the two most significant parts of the history, the reigns of David and Solomon.

The work of David and Solomon centered on the building of the temple, with its completion appropriately noted in 2 Chr 8:16. These two kings alone were recognized by all Israel just as they alone ruled all Israel. The two of them were concerned both with the ark and the temple. Their words and efforts gave legitimacy to the Jerusalem temple as the only appropriate worship site. The North's apostasy, according to the speech of Abijah, consisted primarily in its rejection of the temple (2 Chr 13:4–12). When Hezekiah appealed to Israel and Judah to repent, he called for a return to the sanctuary which God had sanctified forever (2 Chr 30:6–8). Hezekiah, in fact, is a kind of second Solomon. His passover is the first of its kind since Solomon (2 Chr 30:26), and its fourteen-day duration (2 Chr 30:23) echoes the duration of the temple dedication under Solomon (2 Chr 7:8–9). Apparently, the Chronicler was calling on all Israel of his day, including especially the North (see below), to join in recognizing the legitimacy of the Second Temple in Jerusalem, the heir of the temple erected by David and Solomon. The rebuilt temple could be seen as the major fulfillment of God's promise to David through Nathan (2 Chr 6:10–11; cf. 1 Chronicles 17).

Is the significance of the monarchy only to be found in its legitimation of the postexilic theocracy and/or the postexilic temple? Or does the Chronicler hope for a restoration of the monarchy? Note that kingship in Israel is equated with the kingdom of God (1 Chr 28:5; 29:23; 2 Chr 13:8) and that it is inalienably linked to the Davidic dynasty (1 Chr 17:13).

Otto Plöger believes that David and Solomon created for the temple those ordinances on which the acceptable worship of the present community depended, and that the work itself is antieschatological. Freedman, Cross, and Newsome, on the other hand, detect in the Chronicler hope for a restoration of the monarchy under Zerubbabel. For Freedman and Cross, this also entails including parts of Ezra in the original book of Chronicles, an interpretation we have decided not to follow.

Mosis (1973) proposes an alternate eschatological scenario, viewing Saul, David, and Solomon as symbolic representations of the exile, the restoration, and the ideal eschatological future respectively. His case falls, among other reasons, because of the unity between David and Solomon noted above, and also because it presupposes the unity of Chronicles-Nehemiah.

Williamson (1977a) detects a subtle, "royalist" eschatology in 2 Chr 6:41–42 (a modification of the *Vorlage* we know as Psalm 132:8–10). Verse 42 reads: "Remember thy steadfast love for David thy servant." This verse is a reapplication of Isa 55:3, which had broadened the promise to David to include all of Israel. Now this promise is again understood dynastically, suggesting that the prophecy of Nathan was only partially exhausted with the completion of the temple. In the Chronicler's view, the dynastic promise had become unconditional thanks to the promise of God and the carrying out of the conditions of this promise by Solomon, particularly in the building of the temple (cf. 1 Chr 28:7, 9; 2 Chr 6:16; 7:17–18). The Chronicler believed that a brighter future lay in store for an obedient people, and a restoration of the monarchy may well have been part of his future hope. Immediately after Solomon's prayer for God to remember his promise to David, fire came down from heaven and consumed the sacrifices in the temple (2 Chr 7:1). This would seem to be an implicit yes to Solomon's prayer (cf. also 2 Chr 7:21–22; 13:5–8; 21:7).

2. Retribution. The Chronicler often interprets divine punishments or blessings as a retributive response to a king's behavior (Wellhausen *WPHI,* 203–8; cf. von Rad *ROTT,* 348–49). Rehoboam, for example, was attacked by Shishak I in his 5th year (1 Kgs 14:25–26) because he had forsaken the law of Yahweh the previous year (2 Chr 12:1). Asa became seriously ill in his old age (1 Kgs 15:23) because he had not relied on Yahweh in a war with Baasha and had imprisoned a prophet who rebuked him (2 Chr 16:7–10). Afflicted with leprosy, Azariah/Uzziah had to abdicate (2 Kgs 15:5), but it is only in Chronicles that we learn that his illness resulted from his pride and his assumption of the right to burn incense (2 Chr 26:16–21). In each of the above cases, the Chronicler has provided a theological rationale for an event reported in the books of Kings. Retribution is immediate, with the consequences befalling the evil or righteous king during his own lifetime. This threatens to break down the unity of history achieved by Dtr into a large number of single actions of Yahweh (von Rad *ROTT,* 350).

In his descriptions of positive behavior, the writer delights in words like "seek" (Heb *dāraš*) or "rely on" (*šāʿan;* Braun 1979: 53–54). David says to Solomon, "If you seek him, he will be found by you" (1 Chr 28:9). For negative behavior, the Chronicler charges that the person in question forsakes Yahweh, his law, or the temple; acts unfaithfully; engages in foreign alliances; and fails to give heed to Yahweh's prophets (Braun 1979: 54). Faithful royal behavior is accompanied by many children, building projects, a well-equipped army, victory in war, cultic reforms, or tribute from the nations (Welten 1973). A wicked king experienced God's wrath, war, defeat in battle, disease, or conspiracy. Note the Chronicler's summation of Saul's reign: "So Saul died for his unfaithfulness; he was unfaithful to the Lord in that he did not keep the command of the Lord . . . and did not seek guidance from the Lord. Therefore the Lord slew him" (1 Chr 10:13–14). The concept of retribution and the specific terms associated with it are almost entirely absent from Ezra-Nehemiah, an argument noted by those who favor separate authorship.

This retribution, however, is not mechanistic or inescapable. A king like Rehoboam who repents (2 Chr 12:13; cf. 2 Chr 7:14 and its references to humbling oneself, praying, seeking God's face, and turning) experiences some deliverance (2 Chr 12:7) and is not completely destroyed (2 Chr 12:12). Prophets are often sent to warn the king before a judgment falls, sometimes with success (cf. Rehoboam above) but often without (e.g., 2 Chr 16:10–12). Throntveit notes that the ten prophetic speeches between Abijah's sermon in 2 Chronicles 13 and Hezekiah's appeal to the North in 2 Chronicles 30 all enunciate the doctrine of retributive justice (1982b: 163–65). Retribution is more than a grid spread out over Israel's history; it is also a call for faith addressed to the Chronicler's audience. Just as repentance in the past led to divine favor, so faithfulness in the writer's present would have similar positive results. This aspect of his theology seems well summed up in 2

Chr 20:20: "Believe in the Lord your God, and you will be established; believe in his prophets and you will succeed."

3. Attitude toward the North. Earlier scholars (e.g., Torrey, Noth, and Rudolph) found one of the principal themes of the book to be its anti-Samaritan attitude. This has now been called into question because of the late date currently assigned to the Samaritan schism and the distinction between Chronicles and Ezra-Nehemiah. There is also a far more open attitude to the North in Chronicles than was previously recognized (Mosis 1973: 169–72, 200–1, 224, 232). Those willing to return to the Lord and come to his sanctuary are to be welcomed (2 Chr 30:7–8).

Shortly after the division of the kingdom, priests and Levites from the North, together with representatives from all the tribes of Israel, came to Jerusalem for sacrifice (2 Chr 11:13–17). From the very start, therefore, there were people who were willing to repent and acknowledge the Jerusalem sanctuary. While Abijah accuses the North of rebellion against the Davidic dynasty, idolatry, and a generally improper cult (2 Chr 13:4–12)—surely one of the most "anti-Northern" passages in the book—he also admonishes them as if repentance was possible (vv 4, 8, 12). In the reign of Asa, great numbers from Ephraim, Manasseh, and Simeon deserted to the Southern king (2 Chr 15:9) and were part of those who entered into a covenant to seek Yahweh (2 Chr 15:9–15). Prophets were active in the North, including Oded, who persuaded Northerners during the reign of Ahaz to release their Southern prisoners (2 Chr 28:8–15). A number of Northern leaders openly confessed their sin on this occasion (v 13).

Hezekiah, according to the Chronicler, was the first king after the fall of the N kingdom and so was the first since Solomon to rule a united Israel. The king's invitation to the Passover was, to be sure, rejected in parts of the North, but individuals from Asher, Manasseh, and Zebulun did humble themselves and come to Jerusalem (2 Chr 30:11). Hezekiah's description of a merciful God—"For the Lord your God is gracious and merciful, and will not turn away his face from you, if you return to him" (2 Chr 30:9)—is nowhere withdrawn in Chronicles. His united Passover celebration was unique in its inclusion of the North for the first time since Solomon (2 Chr 30:26; cf. the similar celebration under Josiah in 2 Chr 35:17–18). His reform activities broke down cultic institutions not only in Judah and Benjamin but also in Ephraim and Manasseh (2 Chr 31:1). Josiah carried on reforming activities in Manasseh, Ephraim, and as far as Naphtali (2 Chr 34:6), making all Israel serve the Lord (2 Chr 34:33).

The Northerners, therefore, were not a people to be shunned, though they and all others who rejected the sole legitimacy of the Jerusalem temple are criticized by the Chronicler. Even at the division of the kingdom Shemaiah refers to the Northerners as brothers and to the division itself as God's will (2 Chr 11:1–4). From the Chronicler's point of view there were good reasons for Israel's refusal to endure the rule of the Judean king. The Chronicler seems to be inviting Northerners and, perhaps, other unidentifiable groups in Israel to acknowledge the claims of the temple in Jerusalem and participate in its cult.

Bibliography

The best full-length commentaries are those by Braun (WBC), Curtis and Madsen (ICC), Dillard (WBC), Galling 1954, Michaeli (CAT), Myers (AB), Rudolph (HAT), and Williamson (NCB). Also helpful are the shorter, less technical works by Ackroyd (JBC), Coggins (CBC), and McConville 1984.

In addition to the summaries in the commentaries, there are excellent reports on 19th-century research in Graham (1983), dealing especially with historical questions, and in Mathias (1977), dealing especially with the prophetic materials. A history of interpretation throughout the Common Era is found in Willi (1972: 12–47). Synoptic presentations of Chronicles and its counterpart in Samuel-Kings are found in Bendavid 1972 (Hebrew only) and Vannutelli 1931–34 (Hebrew and Greek). An English synopsis is found in Crockett 1951 and Newsome 1986. (Cf. also Ackroyd *Chronicles, Ezra, Nehemiah* TBC; Braun *Chronicles* WBC; Brown *HDB* 1: 389–97; Clines *Ezra, Nehemiah, Esther* NCB; Coggins *Chronicles* CBC; Dillard *2 Chronicles* WBC; Michaeli *Chroniques, d'Esdras et de Nehemie* CAT.)

Ackroyd, P. R. 1967. History and Theology in the Writings of the Chronicler. *CTM* 38: 501–15.

———. 1977. The Chronicler as Exegete. *JSOT* 2:2–32.

Albright, W. F. 1921. The Date and Personality of the Chronicler. *JBL* 40: 104–24.

———. 1950. The Judicial Reform of Jehoshaphat. Pp. 61–82 in *Alexander Marx Jubilee Volume,* ed. S. Lieberman. New York.

Allen, L. C. 1974a. *The Greek Chronicles.* Pt. 1, *The Translator's Craft.* VTSup 25. Leiden.

———. 1974b. *The Greek Chronicles.* Pt. 2, *Textual Criticism.* VTSup 27. Leiden.

Bendavid, A. 1972. *Parallels in the Bible.* Jerusalem.

Braun, R. L. 1971a. The Message of Chronicles: Rally 'Round the Temple. *CTM* 42: 502–14.

———. 1971b. *The Significance of 1 Chronicles 22, 28, and 29 for the Structure and Theology of the Work of the Chronicler.* Diss. Concordia Seminary.

———. 1973. Solomonic Apologetic in Chronicles. *JBL* 92: 503–16.

———. 1976. Solomon, the Chosen Temple Builder: The Significance of 1 Chronicles 22, 28, and 29 for the Theology of Chronicles. *JBL* 95: 581–90.

———. 1977. A Reconsideration of the Chronicler's Attitude toward the North. *JBL* 96: 59–62.

———. 1979. Chronicles, Ezra, and Nehemiah: Theology and Literary History. Pp. 52–64 in *Studies in the Historical Books of the Old Testament.* VTSup 30. Leiden.

Coggins, R. J. 1975. *Samaritans and Jews.* Atlanta.

Crockett, W. D. 1951. *A Harmony of Samuel, Kings and Chronicles.* Grand Rapids.

Cross, F. M. 1961. *The Ancient Library of Qumran and Modern Biblical Studies.* Rev. ed. Garden City, NY.

———. 1966. Aspects of Samaritan and Jewish History in Late Persian and Hellenistic Times. *HTR* 59: 201–11.

———. 1975. A Reconstruction of the Judean Restoration. *JBL* 94: 4–18.

Driver, S. R. 1913. *An Introduction to the Literature of the Old Testament.* 9th ed. Edinburgh.

Freedman, D. N. 1961. The Chronicler's Purpose. *CBQ* 23: 436–42.

———. 1975. Son of Man, Can These Bones Live? *Int* 29: 171–86.

Galling, K. 1954. *Die Bücher der Chronik, Esra, Nehemia.* ATD 12. Göttingen.

Graham, M. P. 1983. *The Utilization of 1 and 2 Chronicles in the Reconstruction of Israelite History in the Nineteenth Century.* Diss. Emory.
Halpern, B. 1981. Sacred History and Ideology: Chronicles' Thematic Structure—Indications of an Earlier Source. Pp. 35–54 in *The Creation of Sacred Literature,* ed. R. E. Friedman. Near Eastern Studies 22. Berkeley.
Hanson, P. D. 1975. *The Dawn of Apocalyptic.* Philadelphia.
Japhet, S. 1968. The Supposed Common Authorship of Chronicles and Ezra-Nehemiah Investigated Anew. *VT* 18: 330–71.
Klein, R. W. 1966. *Studies in the Greek Texts of the Chronicler.* Diss. Harvard.
———. 1974. *Textual Criticism of the Old Testament.* Philadelphia.
———. 1983. Abijah's Campaign against the North (II Chr 13)—What Were the Chronicler's Sources? *ZAW* 95: 210–17.
Lemke, W. 1964. *Synoptic Studies in the Chronicler's History.* Diss. Harvard.
———. 1965. The Synoptic Problem in the Chronicler's History. *HTR* 58: 349–63.
Macy, H. 1975. *The Sources of the Books of Chronicles.* Diss. Harvard.
Mathias, D. 1977. *Die Geschichte der Chronikforschung im 19. Jahrhundert unter besonderer Berücksichtigung der exegetischen Behandlung der Prophetennachrichten des chronistischen Geschichtswerkes.* 3 vols. Leipzig.
———. 1984. "Levitische Predigt" und Deuteronomismus. *ZAW* 96: 23–49.
Mazar, B. 1960. The Cities of the Priests and the Levites. VTSup 7: 193–205.
McConville, H. G. 1984. *I & II Chronicles.* Daily Study Bible. Philadelphia.
McKenzie, S. L. 1985. *The Chronicler's Use of the Deuteronomistic History.* HSM 33. Atlanta.
Mendenhall, G. E. 1958. The Census Lists of Numbers 1 and 26. *JBL* 77:52–66.
Micheel, R. 1983. *Die Seher- und Prophetenüberlieferungen in der Chronik.* BBET 18. Frankfurt am Main.
Mosis, R. 1973. *Untersuchungen zur Theologie des chronistischen Geschichtswerkes.* FTS 92. Freiburg im Breisgau.
Newsome, J. D., Jr. 1973. *The Chronicler's View of Prophecy.* Diss. Vanderbilt.
———. 1975. Toward a New Understanding of the Chronicler and His Purposes. *JBL* 94: 201–17.
———. 1986. *A Synoptic Harmony of Samuel, Kings, and Chronicles.* Grand Rapids.
Petersen, D. L. 1977. *Late Israelite Prophecy.* SBLMS 23. Missoula, MT.
Peterson, J. L. 1977. *A Topographical Surface Survey of the Levitical Cities of Joshua 21 and I Chronicles 6.* Th.D. Diss. Chicago Institute of Advanced Theological Studies and Seabury-Western Theological Seminary.
Plöger, O. 1957. Reden und Gebete im deuteronomistischen und chronistischen Geschichtswerk. Pp. 35–49 in *Festschrift für Günther Dehn,* ed. W. Schneemelcher. Neukirchen.
Pohlmann, K.-F. 1970. *Studien zum dritten Esra.* FRLANT 104. Göttingen.
Polzin, R. 1976. *Late Biblical Hebrew.* HSM 12. Missoula, MT.
Purvis, J. 1968. *The Samaritan Pentateuch and the Origin of the Samaritan Sect.* HSM 2. Cambridge, MA.
Rad, G. von. 1934. The Levitical Sermon in I and II Chronicles. Pp. 267–80 in *The Problem of the Hexateuch and Other Essays.* Trans. E. W. Trueman. New York. ET 1966.
Rehm, M. 1967. *An Investigation into the History of the Pre-Exilic Levites.* Th.D. Diss. Harvard.
Spencer, J. R. 1980. *The Levitical Cities: A Study of the Role and Function of the Levites in the History of Israel.* Diss. Chicago.
Throntveit, M. A. 1982a. Linguistic Analysis and the Question of Authorship in Chronicles, Ezra and Nehemiah. *VT* 32: 201–16.
———. 1982b. *The Significance of the Royal Speeches and Prayers for the Structure and Theology of the Chronicler.* Diss. Union Theological Seminary, Richmond, VA.
———. 1987. *When Kings Speak.* SBLDS 93. Atlanta.
Torrey, C. C. 1910. *Ezra Studies.* Chicago.
Vannutelli, P. 1931–34. *Libri Synoptici Veteris Testamenti seu Librorum Regum et Chronicorum Loci Paralleli.* 2 vols. Rome.
Welch, A. C. 1935. *Post-Exilic Judaism.* Edinburgh.
———. 1939. *The Work of the Chronicler. Its Purpose and Date.* London. Repr. Munich, 1980.
Welten, P. 1973. *Geschichte und Geschichtsdarstellung in den Chronikbüchern.* WMANT 42. Neukirchen-Vluyn.
Westermann, C. 1967. *Basic Forms of Prophetic Speech.* Trans. H. C. White. Philadelphia.
Willi, T. 1972. *Die Chronik als Auslegung.* FRLANT 106. Göttingen.
Williamson, H. G. M. 1977a. Eschatology in the Books of Chronicles. *TynBul* 28: 115–54.
———. 1977b. *Israel in the Books of Chronicles.* Cambridge.
———. 1979. The Origins of the Twenty-Four Priestly Courses. A Study of 1 Chronicles xxiii–xxvii. Pp. 251–68 in *Studies in the Historical Books of the Old Testament.* VTSup 30. Leiden.
Zunz, L. 1832. *Die gottesdienstlichen Vorträge der juden, hist. entwickelt.* Berlin.

RALPH W. KLEIN

CHRONOGRAPHER, DEMETRIUS THE.

See DEMETRIUS THE CHRONOGRAPHER.

CHRONOLOGY.

Numerous problems often arise when one attempts to assign approximate (much less exact) dates to persons and events mentioned in the biblical corpus. This entry attempts to survey those problems. It consists of two articles, one focusing on the chronology of the Hebrew Bible/Old Testament, and the other focusing on the New Testament. For discussions of Mesopotamian and Egyptian chronology, see the articles EGYPT, HISTORY OF (CHRONOLOGY) and MESOPOTAMIA, HISTORY OF (CHRONOLOGY).

HEBREW BIBLE

A. Introduction: Premodern Views
B. Primeval History
C. From the Patriarchs to the Exodus
D. From the Conquest to the Monarchy
E. The Monarchic Period
   1. History of Research
   2. Terminology
   3. The Sources and Their Editing
   4. From the Fall of Samaria to the Fall of Jerusalem
   5. From Jehu until the Fall of Samaria
   6. From the Division of the Monarchy to Jehu
   7. The United Monarchy

A. Introduction: Premodern Views

The generally chronological arrangement of the historical books of the Bible (Pentateuch-Kings) and the calendric superscriptions of most of the prophetic books show that the final redactors of the Hebrew Bible had a sense of chronology; yet, no all-encompassing chronological system is in use throughout the Bible. In some traditions, the Exodus from Egypt served as a pivotal point of reckoning (cf. Num 33:38; Judg 11:26; 1 Kgs 6:2). But it was not until the Hellenistic period, when the method of counting years by "eras" (Lat *aera,* "number") was introduced (Bickerman 1968: 70–77; *CHJ* 1: 60–69; Hallo 1984–85; 1988: 185–90) and the biblical canon was more or less set, that the first steps were taken to integrate the heterogenic chronological data.

In order to show the Bible to be reliable as history and so worthy of respect within Greek circles, its chronological picture was often found to need amplification or clarification. The earliest example is the extant fragments of Demetrius (early 3d cent. B.C.E., Alexandria) who dated events by reference to Adam and the Flood. Several centuries later, Josephus is found complementing the biblical record with information and nonbiblical dates gleaned from the works of other historians (mostly Menander and Berosus) and summarizing historical periods, e.g., the Temple of Jerusalem lay waste for 50 years (*AgAp* 1.154); in some of these matters, Josephus showed an acquaintance with chronological topics which are discussed in later rabbinic sources.

Chronological discussions in the Talmud often associate Rabbi Yose ben Halafta with the work *Seder Olam* ("Order of the World") (e.g., *b. Šabb.* 88a; *b. Nid.* 46b), and it seems that the tanna R. Yose both compiled and authored sections of this major midrashic chronography which treats events from Adam to the Bar Kokhba rebellion. Though often credited with being the first to use the "Era of Creation" (Heb *minyan layyĕṣîrâ;* Lat *anno mundi*), *Seder Olam* in actuality set dates by sabbatical and jubilee cycles (e.g., 11:50; 15:14; 23:83; 24:24; 25:54) and in so doing, adopted a practice already found in Josephus and occasionally in the Talmud. The main concern of *Seder Olam* was "the establishment of a chronological continuum from the beginning of the biblical story until its end" (Milikowsky 1981: 4), achieved by calculating the intervals between events and harmonizing conflicting traditions; its eclectic methodology embodies the essence of rabbinic rationalization of the biblical data (cf. Heinemann 1978). (The "Era of Creation," together with the regulated 19-year cycle of intercalation, the basis for the current Jewish festival calendar, is traceable to the 9th century.)

The reworking of biblical chronology in the book of *Jubilees* is exceptional in the freedom displayed by assigning days, months, and years to recorded events. This sectarian work of the so-called "Enoch circle" (ca. 1st century B.C.E.), known to have influenced the Qumran order, was based upon an essentially solar calendar of 52 weeks with an even number of 364 days in each year (cf. Jaubert 1953); epochs were counted by sabbatical and jubilee cycles; thus, e.g., Jacob arrived in Egypt in the 45th jubilee cycle (since creation), in its 3d sabbatical cycle, in the 2d year of that cycle, on the 1st day of the 4th month (*Jub.* 45:1).

Early Christian writers were the first to synchronize biblical dates with secular calendars, e.g., Julius Africanus used the era of the Olympiads as a frequent reference point, later taken over by Eusebius in his *Chronicle.* Eusebius' opus, best preserved in Jerome's Latin translation, worked through the data from Adam to the rebuilding of the Temple in the second year of Darius, and then through the life of Jesus until the destruction of Jerusalem.

While viewing the biblical text as sacred scripture, some medieval Jewish exegetes took an approach independent of *Seder Olam* and reinvestigated critically several of the numerical calculations which by then had become traditional, cf., e.g., Abarbanel to 1 Sam 13:1 with reference to the length of Saul's reign. In the 12th-century history *Sefer Ha-Qabbalah* ("The Book of Tradition") by Abraham Ibn-Daud, chronology was made to conform to a preconceived notion of the symmetry of history, perceivable in recurring cycles set in time by divine providence. Now and then, the figures given in the biblical text were abandoned in order to save the pattern, e.g.: "Behold how trustworthy are the consolations of our God, blessed be His name, for the chronology of their exile corresponded to that of their redemption. Twenty-one years passed from the beginning of their exile until the destruction of the Temple and the cessation of the monarchy [—contrast the biblical calculation of 11 years—2 Kgs 24:12 and 25:8]. Similarly, twenty-one years passed from the time its rebuilding began until it was completed [—the exact figure is uncalculable from the biblical data]" (Cohen 1967: 10).

In the English-speaking world, the chronological calculations of Bishop James Ussher (published 1650–54) were for centuries the best known biblical dates, due to their publication in the margin of some editions of the KJV of the Bible. Ussher arrived at 4004 B.C.E. as the date of creation by following the Hebrew text and principles not unlike those which guided the author of *Seder Olam.*

A survey of the chronological issues regarding the major periods of biblical history as understood in critical circles follows.

B. Primeval History

Two ages of ten generations each, separated by the great Flood, open the biblical account of primeval history. The first age, the Age of Creation, is presented in two parallel traditions (Gen 4:17–26—"J" tradition; Gen 5:1–32—"P" tradition); the second one contains chronological data embedded within a genealogical table composed in a distinct literary form ("*a* lived *x* years and he begot *b; a* lived *y* years after begetting *b;* the total years of *a* were $x + y$"). The total number of years for this age is 1656, with most of the antediluvians living extraordinarily long lives, e.g., Jared, 962 years (Gen 5:50); Methuselah, 969 years (Gen 5:27). The second age, the Age of the Dispersion (Gen 9:28–29; 11:10–26—both "P"), numbers 290 years, with the lifespans of the postdiluvians gradually diminishing to near "normal" lengths as the age ends (Terah, 205 years; cf. Gen 11:32).

Table 1.
The Age of Creation (Gen 5:1–32)

	Age at Birth of Son	*Total Years Lived*
Adam	130	930
Seth	105	912
Enosh	90	905
Kenan	70	910
Mehalalel	65	895
Jared	162	962
Enoch	65	365
Methuselah	187	969
Lamech	182	777
Noah	500	950
(age at Flood)	(600)	
Total	1656	

Table 2.
The Age of the Dispersion (Gen 11:10–26)

	Age at Birth of Son	*Total Years Lived*
Shem	100	600
Arpachshad	35	438
Shelah	30	433
Eber	34	464
Peleg	30	239
Reu	32	239
Serug	30	230
Nahor	29	148
Terah	70	205
Total	290	

The numerical variants found in the LXX and the Sam. Pent. cannot be taken as more reliable than those given by the MT, because they may be rational corrections of items in the received text considered illogical and/or sectarian doctrinal manipulations made during the postbiblical period (Larsson 1983). E.g., in the Sam. Pent., Jared, Methuselah, and Lamech all die in the year of the Flood; in LXX, the ages of most postdiluvians at the birth of their firstborn is higher by 100 years so that none of them outlive Abraham (as in MT).

Moreover, no systematic pattern has been discovered in these figures. A suggestion to derive the total 1657 years (1656 years + 1 year of the Flood—Gen 8:13) by means of calculations based on the sexagesimal system augmented by the number "seven" (600,000 days = 1643 years of 365 days each + 2 × 7 years = 1657 years), though tempting, remains speculative (Cassuto 1972: 253–62). At the same time, individual lifespans may signal special personages, e.g., the seventh worthy in the list of Genesis 5, Enoch, who "walked with God," lived 365 years (equivalent to the days in a solar year).

The biblical periodization of primeval times seems to derive ultimately from ANE tradition. For example, Sumerian sources record that the world's first rulers lived tens of thousands of years before the Flood destroyed all, e.g., "8 kings [variant: 10] reigned there 241,200 years. The Flood swept thereover." (Jacobsen 1939: 77). In the period following, the rulers still attained long lives, but not those of their ancestors. See also PRIMEVAL HISTORY. As to the dynastic and regnal years in the Sumerian king list, all of which are of extraordinary duration, some seem to be artificial constructions demonstrating the expertise of the ancient mathematicians (Young 1988a); and ultimately may have influenced the figures in the biblical scheme (Young 1988b).

C. From the Patriarchs to the Exodus

The chronological data of this period consists, for the most part, of general statements and schematic numbers—multiples of 5 and 60, plus 7—and thus is of questionable value for historical purposes.

Table 3.
The Patriarchs

	Age at Birth of Son	*Total Years Lived*	*Source*
Abraham	100	175	Gen 17:17; 25:7
Sarah	90	127 (2 × 60 + 7)	Gen 17:17; 23:1
Isaac	60	180 (3 × 60)	Gen 25:26; 35:28
Jacob		147 (2 × 70 + 7)	Gen 47:28
Joseph		110	Gen 50:22

A total of 215 years elapsed from the migration of Abraham (aged 75) to Canaan until the move of Jacob and his family to Egypt (Gen 12:4; 21:5; 25:26; 47:9). The Israelite sojourn in Egypt lasted 430 years (Exod 12:40), a statement that does not accord with the promise to Abraham in Gen 15:13 that his progeny would be enslaved in a foreign land for 400 years, the fourth generation returning to the Promised Land (15:16). The tradition that the "fourth generation" was liberated from Egypt is supported by most of the genealogical lists in the Pentateuch, in which Moses appears as the great-great-grandson of Jacob (Exod 6:16–20; Num 26:57–59). In order to harmonize this with a 400- (or 430-) year enslavement, the entire period from the Covenant with Abraham in Genesis 15 until the Exodus has to be included in the tally. (Thus, LXX and Sam. Pent. read in Exod 12:40: "The time that the Israelites *and their fathers stayed in the land of Canaan* and in Egypt," cf. too, the rabbinic sources, *Gen. Rab.* 63. 3; *Mek.* 1.14.7; *y. Meg.* 1.11.) Note, however, that the genealogies may not be trustworthy as they apparently telescope many generations in a three-member scheme, naming only a person's immediate family, clan, and tribe, so the true number of intervening generations in each stage is incalculable (cf. the ten-member line of Joshua in 1 Chr 7:20–27 for this same period).

No absolute dates for the patriarchal age are available since the events related in Genesis and Exodus cannot be synchronized with extrabiblical fixed chronology. Despite all that is known of the ANE, the E kings who joined battle in the Valley of Siddim/Dead Sea (Genesis 14) cannot be identified with certainty. See CHEDORLAOMER (PERSON). Nor does the tradition concerning the founding of Hebron "seven years before Tanis in Egypt" (Num 13:22), often associated with the 400th anniversary of the cult of the god Seth at Tanis (cf. Haremhab Stele, *ANET,* 252–53), provide a fixed reference point to any biblical event.

Many scholars would place the Patriarchs in the MB I period (2000–1800 B.C.E.), a conjecture based on the putative similarities between their seminomadic lifestyle as described in Genesis and the Amorite movements known from archaeology and the Mari documents. A few place them in the LB Age (1550–1200 B.C.E.), considering the affinities between the social customs in the patriarchal stories and the Nuzi texts (cf. Dever *IJH,* 92–102).

There is also no agreement as to the identity of the Pharaoh of the enslavement. The reference to the garrison cities Pithom and Raamses, built by the enslaved Israelites (Exod 1:11), indicates Rameses II, the resplendent ruler of the 19th Dynasty (1290–1224 B.C.E.). But this oft-proffered identification conflicts with the date in 1 Kgs 6:1: Solomon began to build the Temple "480 years after the Israelites left Egypt, in the fourth year" of his reign. Since Solomon's fourth regnal year is dated ca. 964 B.C.E. (see E.7 below), this would place the Exodus in the year 1444 B.C.E., almost two centuries earlier than the most plausible dating of the Exodus (i.e., the end of the 13th century B.C.E., the age of Rameses II–Merneptah. (On the literary nature of the "480 years," see further below.)

D. From the Conquest to the Monarchy

According to the biblical data, after a 40-year period of wandering (Num 32:13), the Israelites entered the land under the leadership of Joshua, who led them in battle for 5 years (Josh 14:10). This initial stage was followed by the dispersal of the tribes to their territorial allotments throughout Canaan, after which they suffered alternating periods of oppression and deliverance lasting, according to Judges, some 470 years.

Table 4.
The Judges

	Years of Oppression	*Years of Deliverance*	*Source*
Cushan-rishathaim	8		Judg 3:8
Othniel		40	Judg 3:11
Eglon	18		Judg 3:14
Ehud		80	Judg 3:30
Jabin	20		Judg 4:3
Deborah		40	Judg 5:31
Midianites	7		Judg 6:1
Gideon		40	Judg 8:28
Abimelech		3	Judg 9:22
Tolah		23	Judg 10:2
Jair		22	Judg 10:3
Ammonites	18		Judg 10:8
Jepthah		6	Judg 12:7
Ibzan		7	Judg 12:9
Elon		10	Judg 12:11
Abdon		8	Judg 12:14
Philistines	40		Judg 13:1
Samson		20	Judg 15:20
Eli		40	1 Sam 4:18
Samuel		20+	1 Sam 7:2

Innumerable attempts have been made at reconciling the total years recorded in Judges with other data concerning the premonarchic settlement period gleaned from Joshua and Samuel. The years of deliverance, during which the Israelite tribes were ruled by what scholars term the "major" judges, are expressed in typological numbers "20," "40," "80" and are likely to be from the hand of the Deuteronomistic editor of Judges; the uneven years of judgeship of the remaining "minor" tribal chieftains appear to have been drawn from a traditional listing of unknown origin. But while the final edition of Judges may be the work of Deuteronomistic historiographers, there is no explicit indication that the book's chronology was coordinated with any of the other calculations in the overall Deuteronomistic history Joshua through Kings. The round figure of Israel's 300-year settlement in Transjordan (Judg 11:26) is not helpful in this regard. And the 480 years of 1 Kgs 6:1 is too large to cover the years recorded for the period of the Exodus until the founding of the Temple; only by assuming overlapping figures for the Philistine oppression and certain late interpolations can one approach the total given in 1 Kgs 6:1 (so, e.g., *NDH,* 18–25). The figure 480 most likely comprises 12 generations of 40 years each, based on twelve leaders of Israel between the Exodus and the building of the Temple; e.g., Moses, Joshua, Othniel (Judg 3:11), Ehud (Judg 3:30), Deborah (Judg 5:31), Gideon (Judg 8:28), Samson (Judg 16:31), Eli (1 Sam 4:18; cf. LXX: "twenty"), Samuel (1 Sam 7:2, 15), Saul (1 Sam 13:1; cf. Acts 13:21; *Ant* 6.378), David (2 Sam 5:4; 1 Kgs 2:11), Solomon (1 Kgs 11:42) (cf. Rowley 1950: 77–96). Priestly traditions preserved in the book of Chronicles similarly counted 12 generations from Aaron, brother of Moses and Israel's first High Priest, to Azariah, the priest who served in Solomon's Temple (1 Chr 5:29–36).

Because most of the events described for the period down to Samuel's judgeship were local, absolute dating has to reckon with the possibility that a number of judges were contemporaries, though the Deuteronomistic editors portrayed them as ruling "all Israel" in succession. David began his rule in Hebron ca. 1005 (see E.7 below); hence the events depicted in Joshua–Samuel fall during the approximately two centuries which separate the Exodus from David's rise to power.

E. The Monarchic Period

The chronological presentation in the book of Kings is the most systematic of any in the Bible. The editorial framework gives the following data for each king of Judah and Israel: his age at accession, the length of his reign, and a synchronic note concerning the regnal year of his royal contemporary in the neighboring kingdom.

It has often been pointed out that 430 regnal years are recorded for the Davidic kings from the beginning of the construction of the Temple under Solomon until its destruction during the reign of Zedekiah, and that this figure, together with a supposed 50-year exile, constitutes a second 480-year period (cf. 1 Kgs 6:1; and see D above) which marked the epoch from the First to the Second Temple (so, e.g., Koch 1978). But if such indeed was the intention of the ancient chronographer, it is nowhere stated nor is the sum of years ever given (cf. Begrich 1929:

14–16). (Note, though, that Ezekiel counted 430 sinful years for which Israel and Judah would have to do penance; Ezek 4:5–6.)

1. History of Research. Scholars of the late 19th century were skeptical regarding both the historical value of the synchronisms and the fidelity of the textual tradition of the regnal year totals (cf. Wellhausen 1875). A more just appreciation of the biblical data is now possible as ancient Israel's chronological reckoning is illuminated by the practices of its neighbors. Mesopotamian examples of synchronic chronologies have lent credibility to biblical synchronisms (Lewy 1927). Studies by Kugler (1922) and Begrich (1929) treat the Assyrian-Israelite synchronisms as pivotal points in their reconstructions. Though he leaned heavily upon extrabiblical data, Albright was less sanguine about the possibility that the numbers were "handed down through so many editors and copyists without often becoming corrupt," and so "corrected" items in several key reigns (Albright 1945: 17; cf. Mowinckel 1932: 163–64).

Contrariwise, the major work of E. R. Thiele (1983) proceeds from the assumption of the basic soundness of the Hebrew text. This entails an elaborate system of calendrical and regnal patterns which were operative at different times in the two kingdoms. H. Tadmor (*EncMiqr* 4: 245–310) bases his chronology upon considerations similar to those of Begrich and Thiele, but assumes far fewer systemic fluctuations; items which are inexplicable are regarded as late editorial calculations or errors.

Thiele's work has become a cornerstone of much recent chronological discussion (cf. De Vries *IDB* 1: 580–99; *IDBSup:* 161–66); but his harmonizing approach has not gone unchallenged, especially because of the many shifts in the basis of reckoning dates that it requires (e.g., Jepsen 1968: 34–35)—shifts which were unlikely in actual practice. The numerous extrabiblical synchronisms he invokes do not always reflect the latest refinements in Assyriological research (cf. E.2.f below). In many cases, he posits an undocumented event in order to save a biblical datum (e.g., the circumstances surrounding the appointment of Jeroboam II as coregent; Thiele 1983: 109). While also somewhat conservative in his approach to the figures in MT, Tadmor's pragmatic reconstruction delves into the process by which the redactor(s) of Kings compiled their chronological framework from heterogeneous materials, sometimes leaving traces in textual inconsistencies (Tadmor *EncMiqr* 4: 45).

2. Terminology. The key terms in the discussion of monarchic chronology are: (a) regnal year, (b) accession year, (c) accession year (or postdating) system, (d) nonaccession year (or antedating) system, (e) coregency, and (f) absolute dates.

a. Regnal Year. The official "royal year" was reckoned from the start of the New Year. The month of Nisan (March–April) is the first month of the *cultic* year (cf. Exod 12:2; Num 28:16); the month of Tishri (September–October) marks the start of the *agricultural* year with the onset of the rainy season (Exod 23:16; 34:22. Note that the terms used in these verses, *ṣēʾt haššānâ,* "the end of the year" and *tĕqûpat haššānâ,* "the turn of the year," refer to the seasons of the year and are not calendrical terms, as is the synonymous expression *tĕšûbat haššānâ,* "the turn of the year," 2 Sam 11:1; 1 Kgs 20:22, 26; 2 Chr 36:10; cf. Clines 1974). The Mishnah records that the New Year "for kings and pilgrimage festivals" was counted from Nisan (*m. Roš. Haš.* 1:1), as was the practice in Mesopotamia, but this statement has often been taken to reflect postbiblical practice. Some scholars hold that the regnal year ran from Tishri to Tishri (Mowinckel; Thiele); others from Nisan to Nisan (Kugler; Lewy; Tadmor); while still others argue for different calendars in Judah and Israel, with shifts made at certain junctures (Begrich; Morgenstern).

Though the evidence is inconclusive, it appears that a Nisan calendar was in use in S Judah, while in N Israel, a Tishri calendar was used. The posited half-year difference between the two kingdoms can be seen in the notice of the 6-month reign of Zechariah of Israel (2 Kgs 15:8) which is synchronized with the 38th year of Azariah of Judah; while the 1-month reign of his successor Shallum is in the 39th year of Azariah (2 Kgs 15:13). In Judah, the regnal New Year had passed, while in Israel, the regnal year had not yet ended; if it had, Zechariah would have been credited with 2 years (by nonaccession reckoning, see d below).

The counting of N Israel's regnal years from Tishri rather than Nisan may have been prompted by a desire to be independent of Judah's practice. On the other hand, the shift of one month in the celebration of the autumn festival, from the 7th to the 8th month, proclaimed by Jeroboam I (1 Kgs 12:32), looks like an accommodation to local tradition (according to Talmon 1958, based upon climatic considerations), Deuteronomistic editorial criticism notwithstanding.

b. Accession Year. The "accession year" is the period from the king's taking the throne until the start of the New Year (Akk *rēš šarrūti;* Heb *šĕnat molkô;* cf. 2 Kgs 25:27; not equivalent to the nonchronological Hebrew term *rēʾšit mamleket,* "the beginning of the reign," Jer 28:1; cf. Tadmor *EncMiqr* 4: 49).

c. Accession-year (or Postdating) System. This system counts the years of a king's reign only from the first full "regnal year" after his accession year. Assyrian and Babylonian texts employ this system of postdating throughout.

d. Nonaccession-year (or Antedating) System. This system does not recognize an accession year, and so counts the first year of a king's reign from his actual taking the throne; thus, in the antedating system the last year of the deceased king and the first one of his successor, which are the same year, are counted twice. Antedating was employed in Egypt for most of its history.

In Judah and Israel, the chronological data can, for the most part, be understood on the assumption that the nonaccession system in counting regnal years was in use. However, toward the middle or end of the 7th century, under the strong assimilatory pressures of the Mesopotamian empires, Judah apparently adopted the accession-year system.

e. Coregency. This term refers to the designation of a royal heir during the lifetime of the reigning monarch. Coregency seems not to have been the regular practice in either Israel or Judah; generally, unusual historical circumstances led to such an appointment which sought to insure the continuity of the ruling family on the throne (contrast Naʾaman 1986: 83–91). The number of cases of coregency explicitly recorded in Kings is not great; sometimes the synchronisms lead one to suspect a period of coregency—an overlap counted in the total regnal years of both kings. Thus, e.g., Jotham judged the "people of the land" as coregent following Azariah's leprosy (2 Kgs 15:5). Azariah himself was coregent with his father Amaziah (2 Kgs 14:21).

f. Absolute Dates. Absolute chronology can be achieved through correlation of biblical dates with extrabiblical ones that are fixed astronomically. Most reliable are the Assyro-Babylonian dates, preserved in eponym (Akk *līmu*—a high official after whom the year was named) and king lists, and chronicles. Thus, e.g., the three-month reign of Jehoiachin at the end of which Jerusalem was captured by Nebuchadnezzar (2 Kgs 24:8, 12) can be set in December 598–March 597 B.C.E. by reference to the precise dates recorded in the Babylonian Chronicle (see Table 5). (Several of Nebuchadnezzar's regnal years are noted in the concluding sections of Kings, no doubt under the bureaucratic influence of his hegemony over Judah's affairs [2 Kgs 24:12; 25:8, 27; cf. Jer 52:30].)

Egyptian dates, on the other hand, are still in question at certain crucial historical junctures. E.g., the invasion of Shishak in the fifth year of Rehoboam (1 Kgs 14:25), the only recorded Egyptian-Israelite synchronism, is primarily dated by reference to biblical coordinates (Kitchen 1973: 72–76).

A list of absolute dates, indicating their sources follows:

Table 5.
Absolute Dates for Events during the Monarchy

Event	*Date*	*Source*	*Biblical Citation*
Ahab participates in Battle of Qarqar against Shalmaneser III	853	Monolith Inscription 6th year of Shalmaneser III (*ANET,* 278–79)	
Jehu renders tribute to Shalmaneser III	841	Annals: 18th year of Shalmaneser III (*ANET,* 280)	
Joash renders tribute to Adad-nirari III	796	Stele inscription (*Iraq* 30 [1968]: 141–42)	
Menahem renders tribute to Tiglath-pileser III	740	Stele inscription (*BASOR* 206 [1972]: 40–42)	
	738	Annals: 8th year of Tiglath-pileser III (*ANET,* 283)	2 Kgs 15:19
Ahaz renders tribute to Tiglath-pileser III	734	Summary inscription Tiglath-pileser III (*ANET,* 282)	
Pekah removed; Hoshea ascends throne in Israel	732	Summary inscription Tiglath-pileser III (*ANET,* 284)	2 Kgs 15:30; 17:1
Fall of Samaria	722	Babylonian Chronicle: 5th year of Shalmaneser V (Grayson 1975: 73: 27–31)	2 Kgs 17:6aα
Recapture of Samaria and exile of inhabitants	720	Annals: 2nd year of Sargon II (*ANET,* 285)	2 Kgs 17:6aβ-b
Assyrian Campaign to Judah	701	Annals: Sennacherib (*ANET,* 287–88)	2 Kgs 18:13–19:36
Manasseh renders tribute and service to Assyria	ca. 674	Prism B: Esarhaddon (*ANET,* 291)	
	ca. 668	Annals Prism C: Ashurbanipal (*ANET,* 294)	
Battle of Carchemish	605	Babylonian Chronicle: 21st year of Nabopolassar (Grayson 1975: 99: 1–5)	Jer 46:2
Capture of Jerusalem	597	Babylonian Chronicle: 7th year of Nebuchadnezzar (*ANET,* 564)	2 Kgs 24:12
Release of Jehoiachin	561	Accession year of Amel-Marduk (Parker-Dubberstein 1956: 12)	2 Kgs 25:27

Besides pinpointing individual events, these absolute dates determine the limits of scholarly conjecture. Menahem's reign could not have ended in 742, as Thiele supposes (1983: 139–62), if Menahem is listed among the kings who rendered tribute to Tiglath-pileser III four years later in 738. Similarly, a widely accepted interpretation of Assyrian inscriptional data from the days of Tiglath-pileser III which led to the identification of Azariah of Judah with a certain Azriyau has been refuted (cf. Naʾaman 1974); as a result, an absolute date for Azariah's reign is no longer available.

3. The Sources and Their Editing. The précis of monarchic chronology which follows is based upon these premises:

(a) The lengths of reigns and the synchronisms recorded in Kings ultimately derive from king lists and a synchronic chronicle. We cannot say whether the Deuteronomistic editor had access to the original materials or whether the data was already incorporated in "the Annals of the Kings of Judah" and "the Annals of the Kings of Israel"—those composite works he so often refers to (Lewy 1927: 7; Begrich 1929: 173–74). Nothing is known about these "annals," their relation to archival data, or their comprehensiveness. The material concerning the N kingdom likely reached Jerusalem in compiled form soon after the fall of Samaria in 722 B.C.E. The Judean royal archives were accessible at the time the first edition of Kings was prepared, presumably during the reign of Josiah. The editorial attempt to integrate such diverse sources, and at the same time remain faithful to their differences, explains some of the conflicting chronological figures now in Kings.

(b) Some of the Judean synchronisms appear to be late calculations of the Deuteronomist who had no firsthand knowledge of the history of the N kingdom (cf. Aharoni 1950). This explains the synchronization of the reigns of the Judahite kings Jotham (2 Kgs 15:32) and Ahaz (2 Kgs 16:1) and the bloated figure of a 20-year reign for the Israelite Pekah (2 Kgs 15:27), who actually reigned just 2 years (see E.5 below). Similarly, the synchronization of Hezekiah's 6th year, the year that Samaria fell, with Hoshea's 9th year (2 Kgs 18:10) proves to be an erroneous assumption (as shown by the absolute dates for Israel's last decade).

4. From the Fall of Samaria to the Fall of Jerusalem. The number of years between these two landmark events is reckoned in the Bible with respect to the reigns of the kings of Judah (see Table 6).

Table 6.
From the Fall of Samaria to the Fall of Jerusalem

	Total reign	*Source*
Hezekiah	29	2 Kgs 18:2
Manasseh	55	2 Kgs 21:1
Amon	2	2 Kgs 21:19
Josiah	31	2 Kgs 22:1
Jehoahaz	3 mths	2 Kgs 23:31
Jehoiakim	11	2 Kgs 23:36
Jehoiachin	3 mths	2 Kgs 24:8
Zedekiah	11	2 Kgs 24:18

Working from the absolute dates provided above, it appears that the accession-year system was in use during the final decades of Judah. Jehoiachin surrendered to Nebuchadnezzar in March 597 B.C.E. His father Jehoiakim had come to the throne in 609/8 (according to the Babylonian Chronicle and the date in Jer 46:2 for the battle of Carchemish in the king's 4th year = 605/4). In that same year, 609 B.C.E., Josiah met his death at Megiddo and Jehoahaz was deported to Egypt after a short 3-month reign. Accordingly, Josiah reigned from 639–609. Thus, keeping in mind that Samaria was captured in the 6th year of Hezekiah, 83 years had elapsed from the fall of Samaria to the accession of Josiah (722–639). The total for the three kings who reigned during this period, however, adds up to 81 years. The missing two years may be accounted for by assuming that the chronographer disregarded the partial years of these kings, though if the nonaccession-year system were then still in use, he should have included them in his counting.

The datum given in 2 Kgs 18:13 that Sennacherib attacked Judah in Hezekiah's 14th year has generated much controversy. Assyrian inscriptions indicate an attack in 701, thus Hezekiah's reign would have begun in nonaccession year 714 or accession year 715 (Mowinckel; Albright; Thiele). This calculation not only contradicts the synchronism in 18:10 in which the year of Samaria's fall (722) was Hezekiah's 6th year, but the 715/14 date requires extending the reign of Ahaz his father and shortening that of his son Manasseh (Albright 1945: 22) or positing a coregency for Manasseh (Thiele 1983: 174). Preferable is the alternate solution which takes the "14th year" date as belonging to the prophetic story of Hezekiah's illness (2 Kings 20) which tells of the promise to the king of an additional 15 years of life (20:5), thus giving Hezekiah a 29-year reign (cf. 18:2). The present position of the date in 18:13, rather than its original one at the head of 2 Kings 20, is likely due to late editing of all the traditions concerning Hezekiah (cf. Cogan and Tadmor *2 Kings* AB). The mention of the Egyptian Taharqa in 2 Kgs 19:9 as having fought against Sennacherib was once thought to be decisive in restoring a second Assyrian campaign in the second decade of the 7th century (Albright; Thiele); for if Taharqa became king in 690 at age 20, he could not have fought the Assyrians in 701. But this interpretation of the Egyptian evidence is unwarranted (Kitchen 1973: 161–72) and leaves modern historians with a single campaign to Judah in 701 B.C.E.

The date of Jerusalem's fall and the destruction of the Solomonic Temple is also in dispute. According to the Babylonian Chronicle, Zedekiah was appointed king in March 597, Nebuchadnezzar's 7th year; thus Zedekiah's 11th year, the year Jerusalem was taken (2 Kgs 25:2), was the summer of 587 (cf. Freedman). But if Jehoiachin was deported only in Nebuchadnezzar's 8th year (as 24:12), then Zedekiah's accession year would have been 597/96. Whether Zedekiah's 1st regnal year is counted from Tishri 597 (Thiele, Malamat) or Nisan 596 (Tadmor), in both cases Jerusalem fell in 586.

5. From Jehu until the Fall of Samaria. The assassination of Jehoram of Israel and Ahaziah of Judah by the usurper Jehu (2 Kgs 9:21–28) provides a convenient point for calculating the chronology of both kingdoms since new rulers took their respective thrones simultaneously.

Table 7.
From Jehu until the Fall of Samaria

	Total reign	*Source*
ISRAEL		
Jehu	28	2 Kgs 10:36
Jehoahaz	17	2 Kgs 13:1
Joash	16	2 Kgs 13:10
Jeroboam	41	2 Kgs 14:23
Zechariah	6 mths	2 Kgs 15:8
Shallum	1 mth	2 Kgs 15:13
Menahem	10	2 Kgs 15:17
Pekahiah	2	2 Kgs 15:23
Pekah	20	2 Kgs 15:27
Hoshea	9	2 Kgs 17:1
Total	143 yrs 7 mths	
JUDAH		
Athaliah	7	2 Kgs 11:4
Jehoash	40	2 Kgs 12:2
Amaziah	29	2 Kgs 14:2
Azariah	52	2 Kgs 15:2
Jotham	16	2 Kgs 15:33
Ahaz	16	2 Kgs 16:2
Hezekiah	[6]	2 Kgs 18:10
Total	166 yrs	

Jehu paid tribute to Shalmaneser III in 841 (see Table 5), which may have been a year or so after he seized the throne (cf. 2 Kings 9–10). Between 842 and 722, a period of 120 years had lapsed. But the total regnal years listed for both N Israel and S Judah are too high (for Israel: 143 yrs, 7 mths; for Judah: 166 yrs). By assuming a number of coregencies and overlapping reigns, as is explicitly stated of Jotham (cf. 2 Kgs 15:5), most of the figures can be accommodated.

a. Israel. The synchronisms in 2 Kgs 13:1 and 13:10 show that the 17-year reign of Jehoahaz includes a 3-year coregency with his father Jehu. Similarly, Jeroboam had a 4-year coregency with his father Jehoash which is included in the total 41 years of Jeroboam's reign (cf. 2 Kgs 14:17, 23; 15:8). The Judean synchronism in 2 Kgs 15:1 would give Jeroboam a reign longer than listed, 53 years instead of 41 and seems to be an error (cf. Josephus, *Ant* 9 §216, for a different synchronism). Pekah's 20 years (2 Kgs 15:27) are more difficult to explain. He was removed from the throne in a coup led by Hoshea in 732 (see Table 5), and if he took the throne in Azariah's 52d year (2 Kgs 15:27) (= 734/33), then Pekah actually ruled in Samaria for a little more than 2 years. The figure "20" has been thought to include the years he ruled "in Gilead as pretender to the crown of Israel" as well as those of his "official" rule in Samaria (Vogelstein; Thiele; Tadmor). Hoshea, who came to the throne in 732/31 with the approval of his overlord Tiglath-pileser III, ruled for 9 years until the winter of 724, after which Samaria continued without a monarch during the 3-year siege by Shalmaneser III.

b. Judah. Azariah served as coregent for 15 years with his father Amaziah (2 Kgs 14:17), after Amaziah had been defeated and taken captive by Jehoash of Israel (14:13). When Azariah was stricken with leprosy, his son Jotham "judged the people of the land" (15:5) in his stead. All of Jotham's rule (preserved in two conflicting traditions: a 20-year reign in 15:30; a 16-year reign in 15:33), as well as part of the years of his son Ahaz, overlapped with the 52 years credited to Azariah. In one instance, synchronisms show that Jehoash of Judah ruled just 39 years which were rounded off to the typological number "40" (2 Kgs 14:2, 23).

6. From the Division of the Monarchy to Jehu. Upon the death of Solomon, the kingdom split into two (1 Kings 12), and assuming that this event occurred close to the accession of Rehoboam son of Solomon, the period from the secession of N Israel down to the revolt of Jehu is of equal length in both Israel and Judah (since Jehu assassinated both Joram of Israel and Ahaziah of Judah; 2 Kgs 9:24, 27). Yet the total regnal years for the two kingdoms do not bear this out. While some synchronisms show that the totals can be reduced, other synchronisms are contradictory. Furthermore, an excessive number of years emerge from the biblical data for the 13-year period delimited by the absolute dates 853–841 B.C.E. (see E.2.f above).

Table 8.
From the Division of the Monarchy to Jehu

	Total Reign	*Source*
ISRAEL		
Jeroboam	22	1 Kgs 14:20
Nadab	2	1 Kgs 15:25
Baasha	24	1 Kgs 15:33
Elah	2	1 Kgs 16:8
Zimri	7 days	1 Kgs 16:15
Omri	12	1 Kgs 16:23
Tibni		1 Kgs 16:23
Ahab	22	1 Kgs 16:29
Ahaziah	2	1 Kgs 22:52
Jehoram	12	2 Kgs 3:1
Total	98 yrs and 7 days	
JUDAH		
Rehoboam	17	1 Kgs 14:21
Abijam	3	1 Kgs 15:2
Asa	41	1 Kgs 15:10
Jehoshaphat	25	1 Kgs 22:42
Jehoram	8	2 Kgs 8:17
Ahaziah	1	2 Kgs 8:26
Total	95 yrs	

a. Israel. From the synchronisms (1 Kgs 16:15, 23), it can be determined that Omri's 12 years include the 4-year struggle with Tibni over the throne of Israel; the notice of his 6-year residence in the capital Tirzah (16:23) points in the same direction. Ahab's 22 years include a 2-year coregency.

The synchronism in 2 Kgs 1:17 of Jehoram son of Ahab with Jehoram son of Jehoshaphat of Judah belongs to the LXX chronological system (see E.8 below); it contradicts 3:1 which fits the other data in the MT and so would seem to be a posteditorial addition.

The surplus of regnal years for 853–41 (from Qarqar to the death of Ahab at Ramoth-gilead = approx. one year; 2-year reign of Ahaziah; 12-year reign of Jehoram; Jehu's coup = approx. one year) necessitates shortening the reign of Jehoram to about 10 years (cf. Tadmor *EncMiqr* 4: 59; contrast Thiele 1983: 76–77).

b. Judah. The synchronisms for Jehoshaphat show that he served as coregent for 3 years (1 Kgs 22:52) and that Jehoram his son was likewise coregent for 4 years (2 Kgs 8:17).

7. The United Monarchy. The chronological traditions concerning Israel's first three monarchs are all problematic, so that only approximations of the length of their reigns can be offered.

The data on Saul's reign in the MT is corrupt: "Saul was [. . .] years old when he took the throne and he reigned [. . . +] two years" (1 Sam 13:1); the LXX versions are either defective or missing, while Josephus (*Ant* 6 §378; cf. 10 §143) and Acts 13:21 give the paradigmatic "40 years." For David, his 7½ years in Hebron and 33 years in Jerusalem are rounded off to the paradigmatic "40 years" (2 Sam 5:4). Saul's son Ishbaal is said to have ruled for two years in Transjordan over the survivors of the Gilboa debacle (2 Sam 2:10), but this period ostensibly parallels David's early years in Hebron. The 40 years assigned to Solomon (1 Kgs 11:42) looks to be of similar typological origin and there is no way of knowing just how long the overlap between Solomon and his failing father lasted (cf. 1 Kings 1).

Moreover, there are no absolute dates for this period, save perhaps the date for start of the Temple construction in Solomon's 4th year (1 Kgs 6:1) which might be correlated with the 12th year of Hiram I of Tyre, who took the throne 155 years before the founding of Carthage (Josephus, *AgAp* 1.126). But discrepancy among the classical authors prevents exact dating of the founding of Carthage; most scholars date the event to 814 B.C.E.; others, who follow a minor tradition, set it in 825 B.C.E. (Liver 1953). Furthermore, doubts have even been raised about Josephus' reliability altogether (Katzenstein 1973: 80–83). Therefore, the dates offered in Table 9 have a margin of error wider than usual.

8. The Chronology of the Monarchy in the LXX. A major divergence from the chronology of the Divided Monarchy as presented by MT appears in Lucianic manuscripts of the LXX, especially for the period from Omri to Jehu. According to the MT synchronisms of Omri, his 12-year reign includes 4 years during which he contended with Tibni over the throne of Israel (cf. 1 Kgs 16:15, 23). An alternate construing of the text preserved in the Old Greek translation gives Omri all 12 years as sole ruler, and it not only reworks all the succeeding synchronisms with the kings of Judah but it also reorders the sequence of their reigns. It also identifies the king of Judah in 2 Kings 3 as Ahaziah (as opposed to MT's Jehoshaphat). It has been argued that the Old Greek chronology is original and that the MT is a secondary development adjusted to accommodate the prophetic narratives concerning Elijah and Elisha (Shenkel 1968; cf. Miller 1967: 281–84); but several of the Greek calculations (e.g., Zimri is assigned 7 years) and its repositioned textual units (e.g., 1 Kgs 16:28[a–h] [= 1 Kgs 22:41–51]) do not recommend themselves as original (cf. Gooding 1970). The Greek may represent the earliest preserved attempt at revising imagined difficulties in MT's chronology (Thiele 1983: 88–94).

9. The Chronology of the Monarchy in the Book of Chronicles. Chronicles adopts for the most part the regnal data of Kings concerning Judah's monarchs, while shunting that of the N kingdom of Israel. In but a single instance is there any serious discrepancy between the two works: in Asa's 36th year, he was attacked by Baasha of Israel (2 Chr 15:19), who according to Kings was long since dead (in 1 Kgs 15:33 Baasha began his 24-year reign in Asa's 3d year). Crediting the higher figure for Baasha's reign requires assuming that it was calculated on a system which reckoned dates from the rule of Jeroboam I, as well as altering the numbers assigned other monarchs (Albright 1945: 20; cf. Thiele 1983: 84–86).

A number of dates in Chronicles are used in a literary fashion and have no chronological significance. The notice that Hezekiah undertook a cult reform "in the first month of the first year of his reign" (2 Chr 29:1) means only that the king's very first act of state concerned the Temple (cf. Cogan 1985). Similarly, the dates assigned to the Great Reform of Josiah (2 Chronicles 34–35), spread over 10 years, depict the king attending to cultic matters immediately upon reaching his majority (contrast 2 Kings 22–23). Other nonchronological items in Chronicles include the formulaic date "in the third year" (2 Chr 11:7; 17:7).

All of the data pertaining to the monarchic period can thus be synthesized to yield a plausible chronology for the kings of S Judah and N Israel (see Table 9):

Table 9.
Kings of Judah and Israel

Judah		*Israel*	
	Saul	ca. 1025–1005	
	David	ca. 1005–965	
	Solomon	ca. 968–928	
Rehoboam	928–911	Jeroboam I	928–907
Abijam	911–908	Nadab	907–906
Asa	908–867	Baasha	906–883
Jehoshaphat	870–846*	Elah	883–882
Jehoram	851–843*	Zimri	882
Ahaziah	843–842	Tibni	882–878**
Athaliah	842–836	Omri	882–871
Joash	836–798	Ahab	873–852
Amaziah	798–769	Ahaziah	852–851
Azariah	785–733*	Joram	851–842
Jotham	759–743*	Jehu	842–814
Ahaz	743–727*	Jehoahaz	817–800*
Hezekiah	727–698	Jehoash	800–784
Manasseh	698–642	Jeroboam II	788–747*
Amon	641–640	Zechariah	747
Josiah	639–609	Shallum	747
Jehoahaz	609	Menahem	747–737
Jehoiakim	608–598	Pekahiah	737–735
Jehoiachin	597	Pekah	735–732
Zedekiah	596–586	Hoshea	732–724

*Includes years as coregent **Rival rule

F. The Exile and the Restoration

The Judean expatriates in Babylon counted the years of their exile from the deportation of Jehoiachin by Nebuchadnezzar in the spring of 597 (Ezek 1:1, 2; 3:16; 8:1; 20:1; 24:1; 26:1; 29:1, 17; 30:20; 31:1; 32:1, 17; 33:21; 40:1; cf. Greenberg, *Ezekiel 1–20* AB, 8–11). The appended note on the release of King Jehoiachin from prison in 2 Kgs 25:27–30 counts by the same era. According to the Chronicler, when the Persian king Cyrus, in his first year, permitted the rebuilding of the Jerusalem Temple (2 Chr 36:23), it was in fulfillment of Jeremiah's prophecy of a 70-year exile (Jer 25:11–12). But Achaemenid sources count the years of Cyrus' reign from his conquest of Babylon in 539, less than 50 years after the destruction of Jerusalem. Perhaps the end point of the Chronicler's 70-year epoch is the year of dedication of the rebuilt Temple, 515 (Ezra 6:15; cf. Zech 1:12).

In postexilic historic and prophetic literature events are dated by reference to the regnal years of the Persian kings, as was common throughout the empire. The assertion that the native Israelite sabbatical year cycle, known from late Second Temple texts, was in actual calendrical use in the 5th century (Demsky 1985: 43–44), cannot be supported by solid evidence.

Because a distinction is not made in the biblical record between Persian kings bearing the same name, and because the Greek translations and Josephus present a different order of events (especially Neh 7:73–8:12 relating to the activities of Ezra the scribe, which appears in Greek and in Josephus after Ezra 10 [cf. 1 Esdr 9:37–55; *Ant* 11 §154–58]), it is often suggested that, contrary to MT, Nehemiah preceded Ezra. Recent papyrus finds at Wadi Daliyeh, though not providing absolute dates, establish the succession of the contemporary Samaritan governors and confirm the MT sequence (Cross 1975). Perhaps the principle of composition of certain disordered units, e.g., Ezra 4:6–24, was thematic association, rather than chronology.

The identification of the Persian kings in Table 10 assumes that the biblical text is intact (contrast Albright 1963: 93); Ezra preceded Nehemiah (as in MT).

Table 10.
Persian Kings in Postexilic Literature

Cyrus (539–530):	Ezra 1:1; 4:3; 5:13; 6:3, 14
Darius I (521–486):	Ezra 4:5, 24; 5:6; 6:1, 13; Hag 1:1, 15; 2:10; Zech 1:1, 7; 7:1

Xerxes I (485–465):	Ezra 4:6
Artaxerxes I (464–424):	Ezra 4:7, 8, 11, 23; 6:14; 7:1; 8:1; Neh 2:1; 5:14; 13:6
Darius II (423–404):	Neh 12:22

Bibliography

Aharoni, Y. 1950. The Chronology of the Kings of Israel and Judah. *Tarbiz* 21: 92–100 (in Hebrew).

Akavia, A. A. 1953. *The Calendar and Its Use for Chronological Purposes.* Jerusalem (in Hebrew).

Albright, W. F. 1945. The Chronology of the Divided Monarchy of Israel. *BASOR* 100: 16–22.

———. 1953. New Light from Egypt on the Chronology and History of Israel and Judah. *BASOR* 130: 4–11.

———. 1963. *The Biblical Period from Abraham to Ezra.* New York.

Andersen, K. T. 1969. Die Chronologie der Könige von Israel und Juda. *StTh* 23: 69–114.

Begrich, J. 1929. *Die Chronologie der Könige von Israel und Juda und die Quellen des Rahmens der Königsbücher.* Tübingen.

Bickerman, E. J. 1968. *Chronology of the Ancient World.* London.

Cassuto, U. 1972. *A Commentary on the Book of Genesis.* Jerusalem.

Clines, D. J. A. 1974. The Evidence for an Autumnal New Year in Pre-Exilic Israel Reconsidered. *JBL* 93: 22–40.

Cogan, M. 1985. The Chronicler's Use of Chronology as Illuminated by Neo-Assyrian Royal Inscriptions. Pp. 197–209 in *Empirical Models for Biblical Criticism,* ed. J. H. Tigay. Philadelphia.

Cohen, G. D. 1967. *The Book of Tradition (Sefer Ha-Qabbbalah)* Philadelphia.

Cross, F. M. 1975. A Reconstruction of the Judean Restoration. *JBL* 94: 4–18.

Demsky, A. 1985. The Days of Ezra and Nehemiah. Pp. 40–65 in *The Restoration—The Persian Period. WHJP.* Tel Aviv (in Hebrew).

Finegan, J. 1964. *Handbook of Biblical Chronology.* Princeton.

Finkelstein, J. J. 1963. The Antidiluvian Kings: A University of California Tablet. *JCS* 17: 39–51.

Freedman, D. N. 1956. The Babylonian Chronicle. *BA* 19: 50–60.

———. 1965. The Chronology of Israel and the ANE. Section A. OT Chronology. Pp. 265–81 in *BANE.*

Gooding, D. W. 1970. (Review of Shenkel 1968) *JTS* 21: 120–31.

Grayson, A. K. 1975. *Assyrian and Babylonian Chronicles.* TCS 5. Locust Valley, NY.

Hallo, W. W. 1984–85. The Concept of Eras from Nabonassar to Seleucus. Pp. 143–51 in *Ancient Studies in Memory of Elias Bickerman. JANES* 16–17.

———. 1988. The Nabonassar Era and Other Epics in Mesopotamian Chronology and Chronography. Pp. 175–90 in *A Scientific Humanist,* ed. E. Leichty et al. Philadelphia.

Heinemann, J. 1978. The Attitude of the Rabbis to Biblical Chronology. Pp. 145–52 in *Studies in Bible and the Ancient Near East,* eds. Y. Avishur and Y. Blau. Jerusalem (in Hebrew).

Jacobsen, T. 1939. *The Sumerian King List.* AS 11. Chicago.

Jaubert, A. 1953. Le calendrier des Jubiles et de la secte de Qumran. *VT* 3: 250–64.

Jepsen, A. 1953. *Die Quellen des Konigsbuches.* Halle.

———. 1964. Zur Chronologie der Könige von Israel und Juda, Eine Überprüfung. *BZAW* 88: 4–48.

———. 1968. Noch einmal zur Israelitisch-Jüdischen Chronologie. *VT* 18: 31–46.

Katzenstein, H. J. 1973. *The History of Tyre.* Jerusalem.

Kitchen, K. A. 1973. *The Third Intermediate Period in Egypt (1100–650 B.C.).* Warminster.

Koch, K. 1978. Die mysteriosen Zahlen der Jüdaischen Könige und die apokalyptischen Jahrwochen. *VT* 28: 433–41.

Kugler, F. X. 1922. *Von Moses bis Paulus, Forschungen zur Geschichte Israels.* Munich.

Larsson, G. 1983. The Chronology of the Pentateuch: A Comparison of the MT and LXX. *JBL* 102: 401–9.

Lewy, J. 1927. *Die Chronologie der Könige von Israel und Juda.* Giessen.

Liver, J. 1953. The Chronology of Tyre at the Beginning of the First Millennium BC. *IEJ* 3: 113–20.

Mahler, E. 1916. *Handbuch der jüdischen Chronologie.* Repr. Hildesheim, 1967.

Malamat, A. 1975. The Twilight of Judah in the Egyptian-Babylonian Maelstrom. VTSup 28: 121–45.

Milikowsky, C. J. 1981. *Seder Olam, A Rabbinic Chronography.* Ann Arbor.

Miller, J. M. 1967. Another Look at the Chronology of the Early Divided Monarchy. *JBL* 86: 276–88.

Morgenstern, J. 1924. The Three Calendars of Ancient Israel. *HUCA* 1: 13–78.

Mowinckel, S. 1932. Die Chronologie der israelitischen und jüdischen Könige. *AcOr* 9: 161–277.

Naʾaman, N. 1974. Sennacherib's "Letter to the God" on His Campaign to Judah. *BASOR* 214: 25–38.

———. 1986. Historical and Chronological Notes on the Kingdoms of Israel and Judah in the Eighth Century B.C. *VT* 36: 71–92.

Parker, R. A., and Dubberstein, W. H. 1956. *Babylonian Chronology 626* B.C.–A.D. *75.* 3d ed. Brown University Studies 19. Providence.

Pavlovsky, V., and Vogt, E. 1964. Die Jahre der Könige von Juda und Israel. *Bib* 45: 321–47.

Rowley, H. H. 1950. *From Joseph to Joshua.* London.

Shenkel, J. D. 1968. *Chronology and Recensional Development in the Greek Text of Kings.* HSM 1. Cambridge, MA.

Tadmor, H. 1979. The Chronology of the First Temple Period. *WHJP* 4/1: 44–60.

Talmon, S. 1958. Divergences in Calendar-Reckoning in Ephraim and Juda. *VT* 8: 48–74.

Thiele, E. R. 1974. Coregencies and Overlapping Reigns among the Hebrew Kings. *JBL* 93: 174–200.

———. 1983. *The Mysterious Numbers of the Hebrew Kings.* 3d ed. Grand Rapids.

Vogelstein, M. 1957. *Fertile Soil.* New York.

Wacholder, B. Z. 1968. Biblical Chronologies in Hellenistic World Chronicles. *HTR* 61: 451–81.

Wellhausen, J. 1875. Die Zeitrechnung des Büches der Könige seit der Theilung des Reiches. *Jahrbücher für deutsche Theologie* 29: 607–40.

Young, D. W. 1988a. A Mathematical Approach to Certain Dynastic Spans in the Sumerian King List. *JNES* 47: 123–29.

———. 1988b. On the Application of Numbers from Babylonian Mathematics to Biblical Lifespans and Epochs. *ZAW* 100: 331–61.

MORDECAI COGAN

NEW TESTAMENT

Any attempt to reconstruct the chronology of the NT must be tentative at best. The primary intention of the Gospels and other NT writings is not historical or biographical—they are documents of faith intended to proclaim, teach, and encourage the various early Christian communities. Thus, chronological information which may be found in these documents is incidental to their fundamental purpose. In addition to this, secular references to NT happenings are minimal and not without their own ambiguities and the patristic references to these events are often contradictory and based on data which is frequently nonverifiable by the contemporary historian. As a result, what follows is more an introduction to the problematic of NT chronology than a solution to the manifold and complex issues raised.

A. Chronology of the Life of Jesus

1. The Birth of Jesus. a. The Death of Herod. Both Matt 2:1 and Luke 1:5 assert that the birth of Jesus took place during the reign of Herod the Great, king of Judea; according to Matt 2:15, 19–20, Herod died not long after Jesus' birth. Herod died in the 34th year after his assumption of power (Josephus *Ant* 17.8–9), which would be Nisan, 4 B.C. Further, Josephus states that an eclipse of the moon took place in the year of Herod's death, 12–13 March 750 (= 4 B.C.). Herod's death in 4 B.C. provides a relatively certain *terminus ante quem;* accordingly, most scholars place the birth of Jesus in the period 6–4 B.C. As a result of a mistake made by Dionysius Exiguus in the 6th century A.D., the calculation of the Christian era is in error by several years. One should also note that the common assumption that Jesus was born on December 25 stems from the interaction of 3d- and 4th-century Christianity with Roman paganism.

b. The Lukan Census. According to Luke Jesus was born during the time of a census when Quirinius was governor of Syria: "In those days a decree went out from Caesar Augustus that all the world should be enrolled. This was the first enrollment, when Quirinius was governor of Syria. And all went to be enrolled, each to his own city" (Luke 2:1–3). According to Josephus (*Ant.* 17.13.5 and 18.1.1), Quirinius only became governor of Syria after A.D. 6. As a result, many scholars argue that Luke is guilty of an egregious error: he was perhaps correct about the census but wrong about the name of the governor, who was, in fact, not Quirinius but Sentius Saturninus (9–7/6 B.C.; Tertullian *Adv. Marc.* 4.19); his successor was P. Quinctilius Varus (7/6–4 B.C.). Further, it has been pointed out that Luke is involved in another significant chronological error when in Acts 5:36–37 he states that "Judas the Galilean arose in the days of the census" and places this event after the revolt of Theudas. According to Josephus (*Ant.* 20.5.1) the Theudas revolt is dated to the procuratorship of Fadus (A.D. 44–46).

Some who would wish to defend the accuracy of the information about Quirinius presented in Luke 2:1–3 point to the existence of a damaged inscription from Tivoli, the *lapis* or *titulus tiburtinus,* now in the Vatican Museum, which refers to a nameless Roman who was twice governor of Syria. Mommsen, W. R. Ramsay, and others argue that the person in question is Quirinius and that his first reign was in the late years of Herod's reign. Ramsay has also pointed out that there are recorded occasions when two men with the rank of *legatus Caesaris* were appointed to one province and that it is possible that Quirinius was given some type of extraordinary command alongside the regular governor of Syria. Yet there are problems with this defense of Lukan accuracy: (1) there is no evidence that the *titulus tiburtinus* refers to Quirinius; (2) the Latin of the text is wrongly translated. As Fitzmyer and others have shown, *iterum* does not modify *optinuit* but the preceding phrase. Thus, the text reads: as "propraetorial legate of Divus Augustus for the second time, he received Syria and Phoenicia." Further, there is no evidence that a proconsul would become a legate of the emperor twice in the *same* province (Fitzmyer, *Luke* AB, 403).

Some of the factors frequently employed in the debate over these verses include the following: (1) In Acts 5:37, as referred to above, Luke states that "Judas the Galilean arose in the days of the census"; from Josephus (*Ant.* 17.13.5, 18.1.1; *JW* 2.8.1) it is likely that the resistence of Judas was during the census of A.D. 6–7. This would suggest not only that Luke was aware of the census of A.D. 6–7, but also that he was attempting to distinguish the nativity census from this and others about which he may have known. The use of *prote* (first) in Luke 2:2 is cited in support of this view. However, the chronological problem between Theudas (Acts 5:36) and Judas has already been pointed out and it is perhaps the vagueness of this recollection that leads to Luke's false synchronization of the Quirinius census and "the days of Herod." (2) Some have attempted to translate *prote* in the comparative sense of "former, prior," which would govern the following genitive and render Luke 2:2 as "This registration was before Quirinius was governor of Syria." Since the genitive which follows *prote* is a genitive absolute, this interpretation cannot be maintained. (3) Those advocating Luke's chronological accuracy would argue that the sole censorship of Augustus in 8 B.C. coincides with the Egyptian 14-year census pattern as well as with Luke's testimony and that such a reconstruction would provide the years 8–7 B.C. as a *terminus a quo* for the birth of Jesus. This interpretation, however, has fused what must be kept separate. Augustus conducted two types of enrollments in the empire: one for Roman citizens (in Italy and in the provinces) and one for provincial inhabitants. The first type of census, the *census populi,* was conducted in 28 B.C., 8 B.C., and A.D. 14 (Suetonius *Aug.* 27.5). The second type of census, called by the same term Luke uses in 2:2, *apographē,* was administered in individual provinces and therefore could not involve "all the world" as Luke claims. It is known that in Roman Egypt such a census was carried out every 14 years from A.D. 34 to A.D. 258 (*POxy* 2.254, 255, and 256). Similarly, in Gaul such a census was administered in 27 B.C., 12 B.C., and A.D. 14–16; there are also extant references to such enrollments in Lusitania, Spain, and Judea. However, Syria was an imperial province and the emperor appointed the legates, prefects, or procurators to carry out the census of the *provincial* inhabitants, as opposed to the *census populi* in which Augustus was directly involved. The census of the *legatus* Quirinius was administered in A.D. 6–7, following the incorporation of Judea into the province of Syria. (4) It has been suggested that the discrepancies can be resolved by the concept of an *imperium maius* ("greater command"), the argument being that Quirinius would have been given a special imperial commission to carry out a census in Syria while someone else was actually legate there, especially S. Sentius Saturninus (9–6 B.C.). The plausibility of this solution founders on the very ambiguity and confusion found in the source it cites: Tertullian (compare *Adv. Marc.* 4.19,10, with *Adv. Iud.* 8 concerning the birth of Jesus).

A review of this material would suggest that all that can be said with confidence is that Jesus' birth took place in the days of Herod, a fact also mentioned in Matt 2:1. Further, following Matt 2:15–19, one can state that in all likelihood the birth took place shortly before the death of Herod in 4 B.C.

c. The Magi. According to Matt 2:1–12, certain Magi (astrologers) from the East came to Jerusalem searching for Jesus "for we have seen his star in the East, and have come to worship him" (v 2). Several ways of understanding this reference to the "star" have been proposed. (1) In 1606 the astronomer Johannes Kepler fixed the date of Jesus' birth in the year 7/6 B.C. on the basis of the triple conjunction of the planets Saturn and Jupiter in May/June, Sept/Oct and Dec of 7 B.C., with Mars passing shortly after the conjunction of Jupiter and Saturn. Kepler argued that such proximity of Jupiter, Saturn, and Mars occurs only every 805 years. What is intriguing about Kepler's hypothesis is that such a constellation was predicted by Babylonian astronomers and, further, that Jupiter was understood to be the star of kings and Saturn both as the star of the sabbath and sometimes even as the star of the Jews. (2) J. Finegan (1964) and others date the birth in the year 5/4 B.C., identifying Matthew's star with that of an unusual nova or supernova (a faint star which, as the result of an explosion, gives out much light for weeks or months). Although about a dozen novae are noted yearly, there is no record of such a nova or supernova before the birth of Jesus. (3) The comet named after E. Halley (d. 1742) occurs every 76 years and has been dated back to 240 B.C. in Europe, China, and Japan. Astronomical calculation has indicated that Halley's comet made an appearance in 12/11 B.C. Because this hypothesis requires an unusually early dating for the birth of Jesus it has not found many advocates.

Most biblical scholars today recognize the impossibility of reaching firm chronological conclusions on such hypothetical reconstructions, especially if Matthew's references to the star are primarily literary and theological. Even so, there is no compelling reason why one ought not to allow for the influence of such unusual astronomical occurrences in the development of the Matthean account of the visit of the Magi. Such occurrences, together with the popularity of astrology (the Aramaic fragments from Cave IV at Qumran contain fragments of an astrological treatise) and of magi as a professional class in the period (according to the Greek form of Daniel, *magoi* are active in every possible place in the Babylonian kingdom of Nebuchadnezzar) and the fact that many expected a star to attend the birth of a notable person, must be taken into account in understanding the setting of Matthew's assertions. Given the circulation of such prophetic oracles as that of Balaam (Num 24:17) with its promise of a "star coming from Jacob," many, as in the Qumran community, anticipated that a messiah's advent must be accompanied by such a stellar harbinger as Matthew describes.

2. The Beginning of the Ministry. a. John the Baptist and the Baptism of Jesus. Luke makes an extensive chronological statement about the beginning of John the Baptist's preaching activity: "In the 15th year of the reign of Tiberius Caesar, Pontius Pilate being governor of Judea, and Herod being tetrarch of Galilee, and his brother Philip tetrarch of the region of Ituraea and Trachonitis, and Lysanias tetrarch of Abilene, in the high-priesthood of Annas and Caiaphas, the word of God came to John the son of Zechariah in the wilderness" (Luke 3:1–2). Except for the first reference, the strokes are indeed broad: Pilate was governor of Judea from A.D. 26–36, Herod served as tetrarch of Galilee from 4 B.C. to A.D. 39, Philip was tetrarch of Ituraea and Trachonitis from 4 B.C. to A.D. 34, and Caiaphas was deposed from office at a Passover festival not later than A.D. 34. The 15th year of the reign of Tiberius, based on the year of Augustus' death (19 August A.D. 14) and the use of the Julian calendar, would be August A.D. 28 to August A.D. 29.

For those scholars who believe that this date (A.D. 28–29) is too late, one of the most common alternatives is to argue that Luke had in mind the date when Augustus allowed Tiberius to serve as coemperor. If on the basis of Velleius Paterculus (2.121) this date is assigned to A.D. 11 or on the basis of Suetonius (*Tib.* 21) to A.D. 12, the Baptist's activity would then be placed in the period A.D. 25–26. Other variables which affect dating include how Luke was reckoning Tiberius' regnal years (did he distinguish the accession year from the regnal years, or did he consider the partial accession year as the first regnal year?) and the calendar he was using (Julian, Jewish, Syrian–Macedonian or Egyptian).

All these and other factors suggest that since we are uncertain as to Luke's frame of reference one needs to be most cautious in using these materials for an exact dating of the appearance of John or for the beginning of Jesus' ministry. This caution is further underscored by those scholars who hold that many of Luke's chronological references serve more the historical perspective of Lukan theology than exact chronological reckoning. Thus, while Luke 3:21–22 suggests that some time elapsed between the beginning of John the Baptist's preaching activity and the baptism of Jesus, the exact length of that interval cannot be determined. What is clear, however, is that the baptism and ministry of Jesus could not have preceded that of the Baptist.

b. The Age of Jesus. How old was Jesus when he began his ministry? Once again it is Luke who supplies information: "Jesus, when he began his ministry, was about thirty years of age . . ." (Luke 3:23). What is the force of *osei* (about)? Given its use in 1:56; 9:14, 28; 22:41, 59; 23:44 it is evident that Luke is not intending to be precise in his determination of the age of Jesus (adding thirty to the tentative date established for Jesus' birth in Luke one would arrive at the years of A.D. 23–25, which, as will be discussed below, is impossible) and that he is consciously presenting the reader with a round number.

Some have suggested that Luke may be using the number thirty for theological reasons. In 2 Sam 5:3–4 it is stated that David was thirty at the beginning of his kingship; also Joseph (Gen 41:46) and Ezekiel (Ezk 4:1) were thirty when they were called by God. It is possible that Luke is using this number to refer to the age of maturity. There is evidence from the Qumran community (CD 17.5.6) that one had to be thirty in order to serve in a position of leadership.

On the basis of John 8:57, "You are not yet fifty years old . . .?" some (Irenaeus *Haer.* 2.22.5) have concluded that Jesus was in his forties during the ministry. Yet this, too, is intended as a round number and the phrase simply wishes to underscore the great time interval between Jesus and Abraham.

c. The Building of the Temple. In John 2:18 Jesus is in discussion with the Jews and they ask him, "What sign have you to show us for doing this?" Jesus replies: " 'Destroy this temple, and in three days I will raise it up.' The Jews then said, 'It has taken 46 years to build this temple, and will you raise it up in three days?' But he spoke of the temple of his body" (vv 19–20). Josephus (*Ant.* 15.11.1) indicates that the reconstruction of the Temple began in the 18th year of Herod the Great (20–19 B.C.). This date is normally believed to be more reliable than the 15th year of Herod which Josephus records in *JW* 1.21.1. Perhaps this later reference refers to the initial planning for the Temple. Following the reference in *Ant*, 46 years would bring us to the Passover (John 2:13) of A.D. 28, a date which coheres with the date reached above on the basis of the information provided in Luke 3:1.

Some wish to find an exact reference to the age of Jesus in the number 46. However, the evidence for this is slim and even given the approximate references to Jesus' age in Luke 3:23, such a view would allow for a substantial contradiction between Luke and John.

3. The Duration of the Ministry. One looks in vain for a definitive answer to this question. The gospel of John is filled with chronological ambiguity and the synoptic gospels give no precise indication as to the length of Jesus' ministry. In the latter, there is only reference to one Passover (Matt 26:17; Mark 14:1; Luke 22:1). At the minimum one can speak of a one-year ministry or, at most, one that approached two years.

Strong advocacy for a one-year ministry was present during the ante-Nicene period, particularly among Valentinian gnostics (Irenaeus *Haer.* 2.22.1), Clement of Alexandria (*Str.* 1.21), and Origen (*Princ.* 4.5). Key to this interpretation was the chronological interpretation of Luke 4:19 ("the acceptable year of the Lord") as specifying a duration of one year. Most scholars today would doubt that Luke, in citing Lev 25:10 (LXX), has a literal interest in chronology in mind. The same would hold true of the parable of the barren fig tree, found only in Luke 13:6–9: the reference to "three years" is not a subtle indication of the length of Jesus' ministry. Many supporters of the one-year ministry also claim Mark in their support. Mark 2:23–28, the incident of plucking grain on the Sabbath, is said to take place in the early summer, the feeding of the five thousand in the spring (Mark 6:39, "the green grass"), and the death of Jesus during the Passover season. Such a view, however, involves another assumption which runs contrary to most contemporary understandings of Mark, viz., that Mark does not intend to present the reader with a consecutive ordering of the ministry of Jesus. Thus, all the texts cited from the synoptic gospels in support of a one-year ministry do not necessarily exclude other views of the length of Jesus' ministry.

Origen (*Jo.* 4.35) was of the opinion that even the gospel of John could be understood as describing a one-year ministry for Jesus, a ministry that begins (John 2:13) and ends (John 11:55) with a Passover. Presumably Origen had a text of the Fourth Gospel which lacked the reference to *to Pascha* in 6:4 (argued as the original text by Hort), thus allowing Origen to identify this feast with the Feast of Tabernacles referred to in the next chapter of the gospel. For many, however, the gospel of John points in the direction of a minimum length of at least three years. Such a position involves two assumptions: (1) that *to pascha* in 6:4 is the original reading, a reading which is today virtually unanimous; (2) that the Fourth Gospel is chronologically reliable and following a consecutive order, a position maintained by fewer and fewer interpreters today.

The earliest known supporters of a three-year ministry include Melito of Sardis (*ca.* A.D. 165) and Eusebius, who allows the ministry to last "not quite four full years" (*Hist. Eccl.* 1.10). Most who move in this direction place their emphasis on John's gospel. Yet the critical question is whether this gospel is able to carry such a burden of proof. Key to an adequate answer is the evaluation of the historical reliability and intention of John's gospel. Since it is impossible to review in detail all the historical and theological issues related to such an evaluation, one dominant, but not universal, perspective will be described: while the Fourth Gospel has access to reliable traditions, these are recast substantially to fit its theological portrayal of Jesus. One example of this procedure can be found in John's account of the cleansing of the temple (2:13–22). It shares with the synoptic gospels the same account of the cleansing of the temple, but while the synoptics (Mark 11:15–18; Matt 21:12–17; Luke 19:45–46) place this incident at the end of Jesus' ministry in connection with the triumphal entry into Jerusalem, John places it at the outset of the ministry, expands the account, and makes the identification between temple and the body of Jesus (v 20). His reason for doing so is theological: already at the outset of this gospel Jesus is portrayed as the glorified and risen Christ (note, for example, the explicit confession of Andrew in John 1:41, unique to this gospel, "We have found the Messiah").

The supporters of a minimum three-year ministry use primarily those texts in John which make references to feasts. Yet many scholars view the frequent mention of at least some of these feasts as due not to genuine historical reminiscence but rather to literary device: the author of the Fourth Gospel often uses the occasion of a "feast" to bring Jesus to Jerusalem, as for example, in 5:1. In light of this it becomes impossible simply to strip away the theological interpretation of the tradition so that one can arrive at reliable chronological facts; to do so will lead to distortion. The genius of John lies not with the accurate, consecutive presentation of historical detail but rather in the ability to grasp the central meaning of the tradition and, from his perspective, to bring to expression its true meaning.

Other than the references related to the final Passover season of Jesus, the essential Johannine references used in chronological reconstruction of a three-year minimum ministry are found between John 2:13 and 6:4. Mention will also be made of John 7:2 and 10:22, but these are linked with the final Passover to form one liturgical year.

a. John 2:13. It has already been indicated that the Fourth Gospel has transposed a scene found elsewhere in the synoptic gospels. There is also a reference to the Passover in 2:23; however, most interpreters understand this reference as being identical to that referred to in 2:13 in the literary structure of John.

b. John 4:35; "Do you not say, 'There are yet four months, then comes the harvest'?" Sowing took place in Nov/Dec, following the autumn rains. According to the 10th-century-B.C. Gezer calendar, the harvest follows the sowing by four months. If this verse is part of an authentic tradition, it is possible that Jesus related this proverb at a time of sowing; the barley harvest would then follow in April and the wheat harvest in May.

c. John 5:1. Jesus had returned to Galilee in John 4:43; now he comes to Jerusalem again: "After this there was a feast [the majority of manuscripts omit the article] of the Jews, and Jesus went up to Jerusalem." The only specific identification of this feast is as a Sabbath (v 9); anything beyond that is a pure speculation since there is no substantial evidence that a chronological sequence has been preserved. Thus, the possible identification of this feast as Pentecost, since it follows the Passover referred to in 2:13, is without verifiable basis. It is best to take the reference to "*a* feast" as a literary device which enables John to account for Jesus in Jerusalem.

d. John 6:4, "Now the Passover, the feast of the Jews, was at hand." There is no manuscript evidence for the omission of the name of the festival; therefore this conjecture should be eliminated. Given the previous mention of a common Johannine literary technique, it is questionable to read this text as referring to the next Passover following that of 2:13. Once again, the Passover is mentioned not for chronological but for the theological reasons developed in chapter 6: the Eucharist, the Last Supper, can only be understood in a Passover context. That the feeding of the five thousand in John 6 takes place in the spring (near Passover) agrees with the evidence of the synoptics ("grass," "green grass"; Mark 6:39; Matt 14:19).

e. John 7:2, "Now the feast of Tabernacles was at hand." It has already been pointed out that this text and the next (10:22), form, from John's perspective, a common liturgical year with the final Passover mentioned in the Fourth Gospel. In this text the double ceremony of the water pouring and the illumination of the Court of the Women involved in this autumn feast undoubtedly serve as the background for the theological saying of Jesus in 7:37–38 and 8:12.

f. John 10:22. Here one finds another time reference: "It was the feast of the Dedication at Jerusalem." Already in the tradition this scene is bound to the feast of the Dedication for it is hard to believe that this was invented. Yet this fact alone does not necessarily allow us to conclude that the chronological sequence of this feast—or any in the gospel of John—are accurate as presented.

g. John 11:55; 12:1; 13:1; 18:28; 18:39; 19:14. All these texts refer to the final Passover of Jesus, viz., the time of his death, a topic to be analyzed more fully below.

Based on this discussion, there is no unambiguous evidence in the gospel of John allowing the construction of a minimum three-year ministry of Jesus based on the reference to three sequential Passovers in that gospel. In all likelihood these festival references are of a theological rather than of a chronological nature. In light of this review of John and the synoptics and the tentative nature of any conclusion based on documents intended primarily for proclamation of the faith and not of biography or history, the evidence points in the direction of a ministry which may have lasted a minimum of one, or a maximum of two, years.

4. The Conclusion of the Ministry.—The Crucifixion. The basic problem in trying to determine the date of the crucifixion is that the synoptic gospels and the gospel of John disagree. According to John 18:28 and 19:14 the Passover meal was eaten on the Friday evening after the crucifixion. The Jewish day began at 6 P.M. and the Passover was eaten in the early evening of Nisan 15. Therefore, according to the gospel of John, and it is emphatic about this (19:14 and 16: "Now it was the day of Preparation of the Passover . . . Then he handed him over to them to be crucified"), Jesus was crucified on the day before Passover, i.e. Nisan 14. Mark 14:12 (see also Luke 22:11 and Matt 26:18–19), on the contrary, asserts that the Last Supper was the Passover meal. This means that the arrest, trial, death, and burial of Jesus all took place on Passover, Nisan 15.

The Passover account in Mark 14:12–16 is characterized by imprecision. The day of Unleavened Bread belongs to the Passover, viz., Nisan 15, yet Mark apparently understands it as having occurred on the previous day (Nisan 14), the day the Passover lambs are slaughtered. Such ambiguity is an indication that Mark was not well versed in Jewish law and the events of Passover. Further, because the difference in the calculation between Jewish and Greek days is not taken into account, Mark misinterprets Exod 12:18 ("In the first month, on the fourteenth day of the month at evening, you shall eat unleavened bread, and so until the twenty-first day of the month at evening"). Generally speaking, one not familiar with Jewish customs would not be able to reconstruct the flow of events characteristic of the Jewish Passover. Mark, not having an exact knowledge of these customs, confuses a meal Jesus had with his disciples during the Passover season with the Passover meal itself. Aside from these ambiguities in Mark's narrative, there is the further question whether all these events would have taken place on such a high holy day as Passover. In this case, the Johannine chronology of these final events in the ministry of Jesus is to be preferred.

Calendaric explanations have been offered to explain the contradiction between the Johannine and synoptic contradiction concerning the Last Supper. Some suggest that the Jewish priests were following the Sadducean calendar and Jesus the Pharisaic; others urge that the priests followed a Judean calendar and Jesus a Galilean. The most elaborate calendaric proposal is that of A. Jaubert (1965). According to this Jesus prepared for and ate the Passover meal following an Essene solar calendar; however, his death on the eve of Passover, as in the Johannine account, was according to the "official" calendar which was lunar or lunisolar. Her detailed proposal is illustrated in Table 1.

Table 1.
Proposal of Jaubert

Time of Day	*Solar Calendar*	*Lunisolar (Official) Calendar*
Tues—before sundown	13 Nisan: preparation for the Passover (Mark 14:12–16)	
About sundown	15 Nisan: Last Supper (Passover meal, Mark 14:17–25)	12 Nisan
Night	Arrest; interrogation before Annas (Mark 14:53a; John 18:13); Peter's denials; led to Caiaphas (John 18:24)	
Wed—before sundown	15 Nisan: first appearance before the Sanhedrin (Mark 14:55)	12 Nisan
At sundown	16 Nisan	13 Nisan
Thurs—before sundown	16 Nisan: second appearance before the Sanhedrin (Mark 15:1a); Jesus is led to Pilate (Mark 15:1b); Jesus is sent to Herod (Luke 23:6–12); people are stirred up to demand Barabbas' release (Mark 15:11)	
At sundown	17 Nisan: dream of Pilate's wife (Matt 27:19)	14 Nisan
Fri—before sundown	17 Nisan: Jesus is led to Pilate again (Luke 23:13); Barabbas released (Mark 15:15); Jesus delivered to be crucified; death on the cross (Mark 15:15–37)	14 Nisan: Preparation for the Passover (John 18:28)
At sundown	18 Nisan: Sabbath; Jesus in the tomb (Mark 15:42–46)	15 Nisan: Sabbath and Passover (John 19:31)
Sat—before sundown	18 Nisan: Sabbath; Jesus in the tomb	15 Nisan: Sabbath

This resolution of the problem has met with limited enthusiasm. It is pointed out that there is no NT evidence that Jesus followed a solar calendar in opposition to the lunisolar calendar, and, further, that Jaubert often resorts to a pre-form critical harmonization of the synoptic with the Johannine texts.

Working on the hypothesis that in this case the Johannine account is the more accurate and following the Jewish table of true moons, one is presented with two alternatives for the crucifixion of Jesus: 14 Nisan = 7 April A.D. 30 or 3 April A.D. 33 (Fotheringham 1934). Given the previously discussed probable dates and parameters, the first of these is to be preferred.

5. Summary. It is likely that Jesus was born between 8–6 B.C. and began his public ministry about A.D. 28 at the approximate age of 35, a ministry which lasted probably, at the most, not more than two years. Death would have come in the year A.D. 30.

B. The Apostolic and Pauline Period

1. Introductory Comments. The apostolic and Pauline period in early Christian history is presently being reviewed with renewed scrutiny and much vigor. As a result, the chronological options are several, although it is possible to reduce the major options for this period to two: (1) the traditional approach, heavily dependent on the accuracy of the information and chronological framework found in the Acts of the Apostles, which understands Paul's primary apostolic work to have begun in A.D. 47–48, and; (2) the approach pioneered by John Knox and now argued in greater detail by others (Lüdemann 1984), which is skeptical of the uncritical dependence on the chronological material provided by Acts, and suggests that Paul's apostolic work began as early as 37 or at the latest in A.D. 40. It is thus clear that the decisive issue between these two major approaches is the evaluation of the chronological reliability of Acts. But before these methodological considerations are discussed, it may be useful to provide a general overview of the traditional dating of the Pauline period, recognizing, of course, that individual scholars sharing this overall perspective may vary from this outline at some points.

Table 2

Event	*Date (A.D.)*
Conversion of Paul	33
First visit to Jerusalem	36
Famine visit	46
First missionary journey	47–48
Apostolic conference	49
Paul's arrival in Corinth	50
Paul leaves Corinth	autumn 51 or spring 52
Paul's arrival in Ephesus	autumn 53
Paul leaves Ephesus	summer 56
Paul's arrival in Corinth	late 56
Paul in Philippi	Passover 57
Paul's arrival in Jerusalem	Pentecost 57
Paul before Festus	summer 59
Paul's arrival in Rome	spring 60

2. Methodological Considerations. Given the remarks just made and the lack of consensus in evaluating the chronology of the apostolic and Pauline period, careful attention needs to be given to the issue of methodology in attempting to reconstruct the chronology of this period. To begin, it must be recognized that there are essentially only two sources for our knowledge of the Pauline period: the letters of the apostle himself and the events recorded by Luke in the Acts of the Apostles. Most NT scholars today give clear priority to the Pauline letters since Paul himself stands closest to the events he records. It is increasingly recognized that Luke in writing his second volume reshapes many traditions, just as he does in the Gospel, to cohere with his overall theological purpose. Thus, for those scholars who maintain such a view of Luke's purpose, Acts becomes a less useful source for exact chronological information since much of this information has been subjected to a larger theological program. While Acts can still be a valuable source of detailed and accurate information when separated from its programmatic framework, it should never be given priority over the documents stemming from Paul and should only be used when it does not contradict assertions made by the apostle.

Although implementing this critical methodology is, according to its adherents, a requisite of rigorous historical research, its adoption does not make the task of establishing a chronology of the Pauline period easier. If anything, it reveals how tentative and speculative previous attempts have been and how tenuous all reconstructions must be. For when all is said and done, Paul gives us not one specific date. Inevitably, if one is to establish a possible chronology of this period, there will have to be some dependence on Acts. Recognizing this, one should be cautious to use Acts in a way which is both critical and plausible. Yet it must be acknowledged that no matter from what perspective one views the data, *there can be no absolutely definite chronology of this period;* all attempts must be tentative and subject to correction and revision.

All scholars, no matter which chronological option they follow in their reconstruction of Paul's career, find it useful to distinguish carefully between the information found in the Pauline letters and that in the Acts of the Apostles. The first step will be to isolate certain information found in the Pauline correspondence which may have chronological implications.

3. The Pauline Correspondence. The information found in these letters might best be summarized in the following way: (a) the revelation of the Risen Jesus to Paul in Damascus (Gal 1:12–16); (b) the visit to Arabia and the return to Damascus (Gal 1:17); (c) "then *[epeita]* after three years" the first visit to Jerusalem for 15 days (Gal 1:18)—the so-called "acquaintance visit"; (d) then *(epeita)* activity in the regions of Syria and Cilicia (Gal 1:21); (e) then *(epeita)* after 14 years a second visit to Jerusalem (Gal 2:1)—the so-called "conference" visit; (f) activity in the churches of Galatia, Asia, Macedonia, and Achaia with special emphasis on the collection of the offering for Jerusalem (Gal 2:10; 1 Cor 16:1–4; 2 Cor 8–9; Rom 15:25–32); and (g) the final visit to Jerusalem (1 Cor 16:3; Rom 15:25–32)—the so-called "offering" visit. Let us examine these individual pieces of information provided by the Pauline letters more closely.

(a) The revelation of the Risen Jesus to Paul in Damascus (Gal 1:12–16). This is often referred to as Paul's "conversion," yet one should be most hesitant in using this term since it is not found anywhere in the text. In language reminiscent of prophetic imagery, the apostle declares that the God who had set him apart before he was born "revealed his Son to me, in order that I might preach him among the Gentiles." Most accurately we have here a "commissioning" event—the commissioning of Paul as one who is to preach Jesus Christ to the Gentiles.

In order to understand the context in which these remarks about commissioning, travel, and chronology are made, one must remember that Paul is attempting to document the thesis that "I did not receive it [the gospel] from man, nor was I taught it, but it came through a revelation of Jesus Christ" (Gal 1:12). One aspect of the argument that this Pauline gospel is not dependent on any human authority is for the apostle to insist on his independence from Jerusalem. That is exactly the point which follows upon this "commissioning" scene: "I did not confer with flesh and blood, nor did I go to Jerusalem to those who were apostles before me" (Gal 1:16–17). Not unimportant is to observe the word *eutheos* ("immediately, at once") in the text—"I did not confer *immediately* with flesh and blood." To understand very carefully this context is critical for an accurate perspective in interpreting the information which is to follow in the succeeding verses, viz., that Paul is primarily attempting to show his independence from Jerusalem and not to give detailed chronological information.

(b) The visit to Arabia and the return to Damascus (Gal 1:17). To underscore the independence of his gospel and to insist that it came to him through a revelation of Jesus Christ, Paul asserts that following this revelation, he did not go immediately to Jerusalem but rather to Arabia and "again I returned to Damascus" (Gal 1:17). This Pauline description allows one to conclude that the location of the original commissioning was in Damascus, a fact which coheres with the embellished description of this event in the book of Acts (9:3ff.; 22:5ff.; 26:12ff.). How long Paul was in Arabia or why he went there is unknown; how long he spent in Damascus is dependent on how one interprets the "then" of Gal 1:18. From the text before us it is likely to conclude that Paul spent his time in Damascus in the midst of a Christian community, a view that also coheres with the information provided in Acts 9:19–22.

(c) "Then *[epeita]* after three years" the first visit to Jerusalem for 15 days (Gal 1:18)—the so-called "acquaintance visit." To what does the "then" refer—to Paul's commissioning or to his return to Damascus? (Of course, if his stay in Arabia was a brief one, as it probably was, the commissioning event and his return to Damascus might be relatively close in time.) However, since this is not the only occurrence of the adverb "then" in the sequence of events to be described in Galatians, the interpretation of this word assumes great importance. Many interpreters see it consistently as referring back to the commissioning event; many others see it as consistently referring back to the immediately preceding event. The latter interpretation is strengthened by the parallel use in 1 Cor 15:6 and 7. Interpreted in this way, Paul remained with other Christians in Damascus for about three years (either two or three as a result of the ancient method of calculation) before making his first visit in Jerusalem since his call to preach Jesus Christ to the Gentiles. In keeping with his main thesis in this section, the apostle describes that he was only in Jerusalem with Cephas (Peter) for 15 days and saw no one else except James the Lord's brother.

(d) Then *(epeita)* activity in the regions of Syria and Cilicia (Gal 1:21). In light of what has just been discussed, *epeita* ("then") is likely to refer to the immediately preceding event: "I went to Jerusalem, then I went into the regions of Syria and Cilicia." That the *epeita* refers back to the commissioning event is hardly possible.

The critical question with regard to this verse in Galatians is not, then, the referent of *epeita* but rather what is meant by the reference to the activity in Syria and Cilicia. Syria includes Christian centers in Damascus, the place of Paul's commissioning, and Antioch, an area where, by Paul's own description, he had worked (Gal 2:11) and a city extensively referred to in Acts (11:19; 13:1, 14; 15:22; 18:22). In addition, Cilicia includes Tarsus, which according to Acts 22:3 is Paul's native city. Is the intention of this reference to suggest that Paul spent some 11 to 14 years (see (e) below) only in Syria and Cilicia? Or, given the overall context of Paul's desire to distance himself from Jerusalem, does he merely wish to say that "then, after leaving from my 15-day stay in Jerusalem, I did not stay around that area but I began moving as far away as Syria and Cilicia" without in any way wishing to suggest that he worked only in this area? How one interprets this reference to Syria and Cilicia will be crucial for the reconstruction of a chronology of the Pauline period. For those scholars who understand the reference to Syria and Cilicia as not limiting Paul's activity to these regions, the apostle was involved in missionary work as far away as Philippi, Thessalonica, Athens, and Corinth very early in his career. They would urge that the reference in Phil 4:15 to "the beginning of the gospel" literally refers to the beginning of Paul's independent missionary work in Philippi and that 1 Thess 3:1 refers to Paul's continuing work during this period in Thessalonica, Athens, and Corinth. This interpretation, to date not the majority one, allows for an "uncrowding" of Paul's missionary work, for the maturing of his apostolic ministry and the development of his theology. Rather than an extended period of some 11 to 14 years in Syria and Cilicia, this perspective allows for the beginnings of the European mission at a much earlier point in his apostolic career and does not reduce the remainder of his activity to such a severely limited time frame. If one accepts this reading of the evidence then it is probable that 1 Thessalonians stems from this period prior to the conference visit in Jerusalem.

(e) Then *(epeita)* after 14 years a second visit to Jerusalem (Gal 2:1)—the so-called "conference" visit. In Gal 2:1 Paul indicates that he made this second visit to Jerusalem "by revelation" as opposed to being summoned by any human authorities. At the end of this meeting with James, Cephas, and John, Paul relates how they "gave to me and Barnabas the right hand of fellowship, that we should go to the Gentiles and they to the circumcised; only they would have us remember the poor, which very thing I was eager to do" (Gal 2:9–10).

Paul uses *epeita* here for the third time. To what does it refer—back to his commissioning or back to the initiation of his activities in Syria and Cilicia? In view of the remarks made above, the more likely is the latter. Since his work in Syria and Cilicia began so very soon after his brief visit in Jerusalem, the 14-year period can accurately be said to describe the time between the first ("acquaintance") and the second ("conference") visit to Jerusalem.

(f) Activity in the churches of Galatia, Asia, Macedonia, and Achaia with special emphasis on the collection of the offering for Jerusalem (Gal 2:10; 1 Cor 16:1–4; 2 Cor 8–9; Rom 15:25–32). A general review of the Pauline letters suggests that his activities in this postconference period were concentrated in Galatia, Asia, Macedonia, and Achaia and that one important focus of the apostle's work was in collecting the offering for the poor in Jerusalem, which was a request made at the end of the Jerusalem meeting with James, Cephas, and John.

The major center for Paul's activities during this period was Ephesus (1 Cor 16:10–11) and it is from here that Galatians, Philippians, Philemon, and 1 Corinthians were written. From here he traveled to Macedonia with Timothy, making a first stop in Philippi (1 Cor 16:5; 2 Cor 2:13) where they met Titus (2 Cor 7:5). If one sees 2 Corinthians as a composite document then it is possible that much, if not all of it, was written from Philippi. From Macedonia, which may have included a stop in Thessalonica, Paul heads on toward Corinth (2 Cor 9:3ff.; 12:4; 13:1). Finally, from Corinth, where the apostle writes Romans, he makes his final trip to Jerusalem.

(g) The final visit to Jerusalem (1 Cor 16:3; Rom 15:25–32)—the so-called "offering" visit. The last part of Paul's missionary activities that can be documented from his letters is this final trip to Jerusalem, although Acts continues on beyond Jerusalem until the apostle is placed in Rome. Paul's intention in making this last trip to Jerusalem is to "make some contribution for the poor among the saints at Jerusalem" (Rom 15:26). That Paul is anxious about this trip is evident from his request for the prayers of the Romans "that I may be delivered from the unbelievers in Judea, and that my service for Jerusalem may be acceptable to the saints . . ." (Rom 15:31). There is no precise indication from the letters concerning the length of the period between the "conference" visit and the "offering" visit to Jerusalem.

The result of this rapid survey of chronological information provided us by the Pauline letters is that only two (other than the reference to 15 days) references are given: three years between the return to Damascus and the first, acquaintance visit in Jerusalem, and 14 years between the first and second visits to Jerusalem. This is where firsthand information from Paul ceases. From the letters there is no information whatsoever as to the year in which any of these visits or activities take place. The next task is to turn to Acts cautiously and critically to see whether reliable information can be found there which coheres with and does not contradict the primary evidence which has been derived from the Pauline letters.

4. The Acts of the Apostles. The relevant information in Acts having a possible bearing on Pauline chronology may be summarized as follows: (a) the revelation of the Lord to Saul and his subsequent commissioning in Damascus (Acts 9:1ff.—but notice the repetition of this event in 22:5 and 26:12); (b) first visit to Jerusalem to meet with the apostles (9:26); (c) preaching in Jerusalem followed by departure for Tarsus (Cilicia) and return to Antioch (9:28–30; 11:25–26); (d) second visit to Jerusalem to bring relief in time of famine (11:29–30; 12:25); (e) activity in Syria, Cyprus, and Galatia (Acts 13–14; the so-called "first missionary journey"); (f) third visit to Jerusalem for the apostolic council (15:1–29); (g) activity in Galatia, Macedonia, Greece, and Asia (15:36–18:21); the so-called "second missionary journey"); (h) fourth visit to Caesarea to greet the church, Jerusalem(?), Galatia, and Phrygia (18:22); (i) activity in Syria, Galatia, Asia, Macedonia, and Greece (18:23–21:14; the so-called "third missionary journey"); and (j) fifth (final) visit to Jerusalem (21:11ff.).

In order to compare this information with that found in the Pauline letters and to resolve the apparent contradiction concerning the number of visits to Jerusalem, it will be useful to examine this outline of Acts more closely.

(a) The revelation of the Lord to Saul and his subsequent commissioning in Damascus (Acts 9:1ff.; 22:5ff.; and 26:12ff.). Although Luke greatly embellishes the material found in Galatians 1, this event corresponds to item 3.(a) in the Pauline correspondence (see above).

(b) First visit to Jerusalem to meet with the apostles (9:26). This information coheres well with item 3.(c) above.

(c) Preaching in Jerusalem followed by departure for Tarsus (Cilicia) and return to Antioch (9:28–30; 11:25–26). This agrees only partially with item 3.(d) above in terms of the departure, and then differs substantially with the letters in terms of a return to Antioch followed by item (b), the second visit to Jerusalem.

(d) Second visit to Jerusalem to bring relief in time of famine (11:29–30; 12:25). There is no parallel for such a visit in the Pauline letters. This reference to a visit to Jerusalem is one of the two additional visits to Jerusalem which is described by Acts. When we discuss item (j) (below), we will observe that Luke gives no reason for this final visit to Jerusalem, a visit which in the letters is clearly described as the offering visit. One solution to the extra visits in Acts would be to suggest that the final offering visit is moved to this much earlier and likely incorrect position of Acts. Some (Knox, Lüdemann) would argue that although the tension between Jewish and Gentile Christians continued and perhaps intensified even into the last stages of Paul's apostolic ministry, Luke wished to suggest that these differences were essentially overcome at an early date. This is the real motivation for Luke's rearrangement and modification of Paul's visits to Jerusalem.

(e) Activity in Syria, Cyprus, and Galatia (Acts 13–14; the so-called "first missionary journey"). It is difficult to coordinate Acts (c), (d), and (g) with Paul's (d) above. Given our previous discussion that for Paul the reference to Syria and Cilicia was possibly only the starting point for activities that took him as far as Macedonia and Achaia, then it appears that Luke is fragmenting one longer visit into some smaller ones so that the Jerusalem visits can be rearranged according to his schema.

(f) Third visit to Jerusalem for the apostolic council (15:1–29). The majority of NT scholars today would hold that this visit to Jerusalem corresponds with item 3.(e) above, the so-called "conference" visit, although holding that Galatians describes a private meeting between Paul and the Jerusalem authorities, while Acts intends to describe a more public form of this meeting. If this correspondence is abandoned, then one is faced with a "jungle of problems" (Haenchen) as well as a jungle of solutions. These include: (1) Gal 2:1–10 does not describe the same Pauline visit to Jerusalem as Acts 15. Rather, the meeting referred to in Galatians is to be identified with the visit in Acts 11:27–30 (the famine visit) or with 18:22 or with a visit not mentioned in Acts. (2) Gal 2:1–5 and 6–11 represent separate Pauline visits to Jerusalem, which are then identified with any of the three to five visits to Jerusalem by Paul described in Acts.

If one holds to the majority identification of Acts 15 with Galatians 2, then for Luke this is a third visit to Jerusalem while for Paul only a second. In view of the fact that in Acts 18:22 [(h)] that visit to Jerusalem is totally unmotivated and fits into its context very awkwardly, it has been suggested that the original location for this visit was at 18:22 and that Luke retrojected it back to chapter 15 [(f)] for theological reasons: for the sake of the unity of the church this controversy had to be settled early, before he went to Asia Minor, Macedonia, and Achaia. If this suggestion is correct, then after the elimination of (d) and (f), the activities described by Luke in (c), (e), and (g) all fall into place as part of one "missionary journey."

(g) Activity in Galatia, Macedonia, Greece, and Asia (15:36–18:21; the so-called "second missionary journey"). As we have noted, it is possible that (c), (e), and (g) are part of what took place during the 14-year activity described by Paul in item 3.(d) above.

(h) Fourth visit to Caesarea to greet the church, Jerusalem(?), Galatia, and Phrygia. Aside from the fact that no reason whatsoever is given why Paul "went up and greeted the church" (Acts 18:22) it is striking that in Acts 18:21 Paul is in Ephesus and then in v 24, after having traveled to Caesarea, probably Jerusalem (many commentators argue that it is unlikely that the original, pre-Lukan itinerary did not mention a visit to Jerusalem if Paul had already traveled as far as Caesarea), Antioch, and through the region of Galatia and Phrygia (all in three verses!), he is back in Ephesus. It is indeed possible that 18:22 was the original location for the conference visit which is now described in Acts 15:1–29 [(f)].

(i) Activity in Syria, Galatia, Asia, Macedonia, and Greece (18:23–21:14; the so-called "third missionary journey"). This material coheres well with item (f) in the Pauline section (above), although it is noteworthy that Luke eliminates what was so prominent for Paul in this period of his apostolic ministry: the collection. At this point one notes the consistency of Luke: not only does he eliminate the real reason for the final visit to Jerusalem in 21:11ff., viz., to present the collection in Jerusalem, but he also omits the collection as a primary objective during Paul's final activity in the areas described here in (i).

(j) Fifth (final) visit to Jerusalem (21:11ff.) As we have already observed, this final visit is in agreement with Paul's final visit described in item 3.(g), although Luke omits the association with the offering and, as we suggested previously, retrojects this motivation to (d) (Acts 11:29–30; 12:25)—the "famine" visit.

However one resolves the differences between the Acts account of Paul's activities and Paul's own account—and we have suggested only one general possibility here—all scholars will have to acknowledge that these apparent contradictions require explanation. Although a comparison of those events in the Pauline literature and Acts which have possible chronological implications have allowed an overview of their similarities and dissimilarities, one is still not in possession of concrete and precise chronological data. Therefore, it will be necessary to examine Acts to see what other specific data it may provide and whether such evidence may be useful for determining the more exact limits of Pauline chronology, remembering the cautionary remarks already made concerning the transference of such information.

5. Chronological Information Provided by Luke. a. The Gallio Inscription and the Edict of Claudius. Reference is made in Acts 18:12 to Paul's visit to Corinth: "But when Gallio was proconsul of Achaia, the Jews made a united attack upon Paul and brought him before the tribunal . . ." Although the precise details, implications, and context of the events described are disputed, there is little doubt that Paul made one of his visits to Corinth at the time that Gallio was proconsul of the province of Achaia; most scholars place Gallio's term of office in the years A.D. 51–52 in light of the epigraphical evidence now in hand. While at first glance Acts 18:12 appears straightforward, caution must be exercised: was Paul's visit to Corinth in the vicinity of A.D. 51–52 his first visit or does it refer to a subsequent one? Acts 18 may well conflate two or more Pauline visits to that city into one. Among the several factors pointing in this direction is the fact that in Acts 18:8 Crispus is the ruler of the synagogue and in 18:17 the reference is to Sosthenes as the ruler of the synagogue. It is fully possible that if Acts 18 is conflating at least two visits of Paul to Corinth that he may well have been in the city at a much earlier date.

Another piece of information relating to secular history mentioned in Acts and which may be useful in reconstructing Pauline chronology is the reference to the edict of Claudius in Acts 18:2. There it is stated: "After this he left Athens and went to Corinth. And he found a Jew named Aquila, a native of Pontus, lately come from Italy with his wife Priscilla, because Claudius had commanded all the Jews to leave Rome. And he went to see them . . ." It is likely that Suetonius (*Claud* 25) is referring to this edict: "*Iudaios impulsore Chresto adsidue tumultuantes Roma expulit.*" Since Suetonius does not date this edict, one cannot be certain whether it is referring to one issued by Claudius in A.D. 41 or whether it is referring to disturbances later in his reign. Those who would argue against the early dating cite Dio Cassius' reference (60.6.6) that the large number of Jews effectively ruled out their expulsion and point to Orosius' reference (7.6.15) that the edict occurred in Claudius' 9th year (= A.D. 49). Yet these references in themselves do not settle the issue. In the first place, there need not be any contradiction between Dio Cassius' assertions and Luke's characteristically exaggerated use of *pas* (the Lukan "all") in Acts 18:2 and elsewhere. Further, there is the critical issue about the reliability of the information provided by Orosius, a 5th-century church historian.

If the Claudius edict is dated in A.D. 41 then one would have strong evidence for the dating of Paul's first visit to the city at some point after the arrival of Aquila and Priscilla from Italy. If the more usual dating of this edict in the year A.D. 49 is to be accepted, this in and of itself would not speak against an earlier visit of Paul to Corinth, for it is difficult to know how thoroughgoing is the conflation in Acts 18. For example, a case could be made that Acts 18:1 had its original continuation in v 5 and that vv 2–4 are a retrojection made from a later period.

To place Paul's first arrival in Corinth as early as A.D. 41 is possible; yet some flexibility is in order since one does not know how long it took Aquila and Priscilla to travel to Corinth, nor if they went there directly. On this reckoning Paul's original visit to Corinth may have taken place sometime between the approximate period of A.D. 41–44. Additionally, it is most probable that he was also in Corinth during the years that Gallio was proconsul in A.D. 51–52. Some would place a visit by Paul to Corinth, usually his first, just before the Jerusalem Conference (Jewett 1979) and some just after (Lüdemann 1984—an intermediate visit). Thus, the Jerusalem Conference would be dated either in *ca.* A.D. 50–51 or A.D. 52. If his first visit to Jerusalem was 14 years before this conference visit, the date of that first visit would be between *ca.* A.D. 36–38, and his commissioning three years prior to the first visit would then be placed between *ca.* A.D. 33–35. Since in the view of this writer it is more likely that Paul was in Galatia, rather than Corinth, prior to the Jerusalem Conference, the first sequence of dates is preferred: *ca.* A.D. 33, commissioning of Paul; *ca.* A.D. 36, Paul's first visit to Jerusalem; *ca.* A.D. 50, the Jerusalem Conference; *ca.* A.D. 50–52, intermediate visit to Corinth.

b. Aretas. In 2 Cor 11:32–33 Paul states that at "Damascus, the governor [Greek: the ethnarch of] under King Aretas guarded the city of Damascus in order to seize me, but I was let down in a basket through a window in the wall, and escaped his hands." The king referred to is Aretas (Arabic *ḥarita*) IV, who reigned at Petra over the Nabataean Arabs from 9 B.C. to A.D. 40. Although his kingdom extended to the vicinity of Damascus and although this city had been subject to his predecessors until the Romans took control of the city in B.C. 64, there is no definitive way of knowing when Damascus became subject to Aretas. One recent proposal (Jewett) suggests that such control over Damascus was only given to Aretas in A.D. 37. If this is the case, then the *terminus a quo* for the references in 2 Cor 11:32–33 would be A.D. 37 and the *terminus ad quem* would be A.D. 40, the year of Aretas' death. Yet, the text in no way suggests that Aretas controlled Damascus nor is this in any way necessary. 2 Corinthians 11 asserts only that this leader was the representative (*ethnarches*—ethnarch) of King Aretas. In this case no *terminus a quo* can be reached. All that can be asserted is that this event took place before A.D. 40.

The "governor" (ethnarch) to whom Paul refers was, in all likelihood, the leader of the semiautonomous Nabataean community in Damascus, a community which had been organized as an *ethnos* within the city, much as the Jews of Damascus would have been organized following the pattern of the Jews in Alexandria, viz., functioning as an *ethnos* within the city and under the leadership of an ethnarch (Strab. 17.798; Jos. *Ant* 14.117). In Gal 1:17 it is asserted that immediately following his call to proclaim the gospel to the Gentiles, Paul "went away into Arabia" (presumably to evangelize the Nabataeans) and thereafter "returned to Damascus." Presumably the Nabataean community in Damascus and their leader took this opportunity to express their displeasure at the apostle's activity in the territory of the Nabataean Arabs.

A similar account is found in Acts 9:23–25. There is, however, one substantial difference: in Acts it is the Jews, while in 2 Corinthians it is the ethnarch of the Nabataeans, who plots against Paul. Given the well-documented emphasis of Luke to portray the Jews as those hostile to the early Christian mission, the account of Paul is to be preferred.

c. The Great Famine under Claudius. In Acts 11:28 Luke writes that "one of them named Agabus stood up and foretold by the Spirit that there would be a great famine over all the world; and this took place in the days of Claudius." This event is cited as the background of the first collection for the relief of the Jerusalem church. Although both Suetonius (*Claud* 19) and Tacitus (*Ann* 12.43) refer to widespread scarcity under Claudius, there was no famine over "all the world" under Claudius; this phrase is undoubtedly an exaggeration. Either Acts is referring to a more local crisis or it has intentionally retrojected an event which took place after A.D. 51 to this early point in the narrative.

d. The Death of Herod Agrippa I. The death of Herod Agrippa I, which occurred in A.D. 44, is mentioned in Acts 12:23. The narrative continues in v 25 with the reference that "Barnabas and Saul returned from Jerusalem when they had fulfilled their mission . . ." This is certainly redactional and provides no firm chronological information.

e. Sergius Paulus. During the time that Paul and Barnabas were in Paphos on the island of Cyprus, they encountered a certain Bar-Jesus who "was with the proconsul, Sergius Paulus" (Acts 13:7). Unfortunately the extant sources are ambiguous and do not provide a precise date for this proconsul's term of office. It has been shown that the famous inscription from Soli (D. G. Hogarth, *Devia Cypria,* 114) on the north coast of Cyprus, which refers to a certain Proconsul Paulus, should probably be identified with Paullus Fabius Maximus, who was a consul in 11 B.C. Among the various inscriptions which may refer to a Sergius Paulus there is one from Pisidian Antioch with the name L. Sergius Paullus; however it is dated between A.D. 60–100. Another inscription (*CIL* VI 31 545) placed in Rome between A.D. 41–47 also refers to a certain L. Sergius Paullus who was the Curator of the Tiber; however, this reference does not specifically relate him to Cyprus. If he went to Cyprus after serving as one of the Curators of the Tiber, perhaps in the late thirties, this time frame would coincide with what we know elsewhere about Paul's travels.

f. The Trials under Felix and Festus. Acts 23:23–24:27 relate Paul's trial and imprisonment under M. Antonius Felix, procurator of Palestine. According to 24:27 the minimum period of time which elapsed was two years. The continuation of this situation is recounted in Acts 25:1–26:32. Here Porcius Festus has succeeded Felix; in addition, Paul has an opportunity to present his case to King Herod Agrippa II. If the testimony of Josephus (*JW* 2.12.8; *Ant* 20.7.1) is accepted, Felix arrived in Palestine during the summer of A.D. 53 and continued in office until the summer of A.D. 55 when he was succeeded by Festus. This would place the trial of Paul in the year A.D. 55. But once again the evidence is contradictory (cf. Tacitus *Ann.* 12.54) and it is possible that Festus succeeded Felix at a later date and a *terminus ad quem* of A.D. 60–61 has been argued (Jewett 1979). This later dating is supported by Plooij's reading of Eusebius' *Chronicle* where the transfer of the procuratorship is placed in the 10th year of Agrippa II (A.D. 59). If this later dating is accepted, it would cohere nicely with the view that Ananias, the high priest who censured Paul during his appearance before the Sanhedrin (Acts 23:1–5; 24:1), was probably replaced as high priest by Agrippa II in A.D. 59 (Josephus *Ant* 20§179).

6. Summary. Given the range of dates just discussed in Acts and the approach championed by J. Knox and most recently especially by G. Lüdemann, an alternative chronology to that given in Table 2 would be as follows, once again remembering that advocates of a similar approach may vary from another in some details. Since this approach insists on the radical priority of the Pauline correspondence, it is important to follow the sequence of events found in the Pauline letters.

Table 3

Event	*Date (A.D.)*
1. The revelation of the Risen Jesus to Paul in Damascus (Gal 1:12–16)	*ca.* 33
2. The visit to Arabia and the return to Damascus (Gal 1:17)	*ca.* 33
3. "Then *[epeita]* after three years" the first visit to Jerusalem for 15 days (Gal 1:18)—the so-called "acquaintance visit"	*ca.* 36
4. Then *(epeita)* activity in the regions of Syria and Cilicia (and beyond) (Gal 1:21)	*ca.* 36–50
5. Then *(epeita)* after 14 years a second visit to Jerusalem (Gal 2:1)—the so-called "conference visit"	*ca.* 50
6. Activity in the churches of Galatia, Asia, Macedonia, and Achaia with special emphasis on the collection of the offering for Jerusalem (Gal 2:10; 1 Cor 16:1–4; 2 Cor 8–9; Rom 15:25–32)	*ca.* 50–56
7. The final visit to Jerusalem (1 Cor 16:3; Rom 15:25–32)—the so-called "offering visit"	*ca.* 56–57

If one were to assume that the general sequence of the subsequent events outlined in Acts is accurate—two-year Caesarean imprisonment, hearing before Festus, and arrival in Rome—then the dates *ca.* A.D. 57–59 for the first of these and a date of *ca.* A.D. 60 for Paul's arrival in Rome would agree with the parameters of possible dates reviewed above.

While the traditional dating exhibited in Table 2 is still held by many, the chronology itemized in Table 3 is a viable alternative. It has these advantages: it incorporates the recent redaction-critical studies of Luke-Acts in its analysis; it eliminates the long and problematic "silent period" early in Paul's career and intelligently explains the shape of Paul's apostolic activity in that period; it "uncrowds" the entire career of the apostle and provides the context for a ministry that actively spanned a much longer period, thus allowing for the possibility of growth and development both in the apostolic ministry and theology of Paul. Such an approach would allow one to more readily speak of an "early Paul" and a "late Paul," and it would permit placing the concrete, contingent letters of Paul against a broader and wider spectrum of time and activity resulting in a more coherent understanding of the theology of this often complex and paradoxical apostle.

Bibliography

Brown, R. E. 1977. *The Birth of the Messiah.* Garden City, NY.
Finegan, J. 1964. *Handbook of Biblical Chronology.* Princeton.
Fotheringham, J. K. 1934. The Evidence of Astronomy and Technical Chronology for the Date of the Crucifixion. *JTS* 35: 146–62.
Hyldahl, N. 1986. *Die Paulinische Chronologie.* Leiden.
Jaubert, A. 1965. *The Date of the Last Supper.* Staten Island.
Jewett, R. 1979. *A Chronology of Paul's Life.* Philadelphia.
Knauf, E. A. 1983. Zum Ethnarchen des Aretas 2 Kor 11, 32. *ZNW* 74: 145–47.
Knox, J. 1987. *Chapters in a Life of Paul.* Rev. Ed. Macon, GA.
Lake, K. 1966. The Chronology of Acts. Pp. 445–74 in *The Beginnings of Christianity* I. Vol. 5, ed. F. J. Foakes Jackson and K. Lake. Grand Rapids.
Lüdemann, G. 1984. *Paul Apostle to the Gentiles: Studies in Chronology.* Philadelphia.
Moehring, H. R. 1972. The Census in Luke as an Apologetic Device. Pp. 144–60 in *Studies in New Testament and Early Christian Literature: Essays in Honor of Allen P. Wikgren,* ed. D. E. Aune. NovTSup 33. Leiden.
Ogg, G. 1940. *The Chronology of the Public Ministry of Jesus.* Cambridge.
———. 1968. *The Chronology of the Life of Paul.* London.
Plooij, D. 1918. *De Chronologie van het Leven van Paulus.* Leiden.
Suggs, M. J. 1960. Concerning the Date of Paul's Macedonian Ministry. *NovT* 4: 60–68.

KARL P. DONFRIED

CHURCHES, SEVEN. See SEVEN CHURCHES.

CHUSI (PLACE) [Gk *Chous*]. A site mentioned in the book of Judith, whose exact location is unknown (Jdt 7:18). The name "Chusi" appears only here in the biblical literature. It may possibly be identified with the modern village of Quzeh (M.R. 174171), six miles south of Nablus, which, as Torrey points out, is on the direct road to Jerusalem. However, that location ignores the verse's specific reference to the Wadi Makhmur ("near Chusi beside the brook Mochmur"). Taking that into consideration, Aharoni and Avi-Yonah *(MBA)* identify Chusi with modern Kuzi on the Wadi Makhmur, one of the tributaries of the Jarkon river. See MOCHMUR (PLACE). Of course, given the genre of the book of JUDITH, it is entirely possible that the name is fictitious.

Bibliography

Torrey, C. C. 1945. *The Apocryphal Literature.* New Haven.

SIDNIE ANN WHITE

CHUZA (PERSON) [Gk *Chouzas*]. A steward *(epitropos)* of Herod Antipas whose wife, Joanna, followed Jesus and supported him with her means (Luke 8:3). Most likely, Chuza was Herod's business manager, but he may have been some kind of political appointee since the Gk term for "steward" may refer to a political office. The fact that the name "Chuza" occurs in Nabatean and Syrian inscriptions (see Fitzmyer *Luke 1–11* AB, 698) may mean that Chuza was a Nabatean married to a Jewish woman. Chuza may have been the royal officer who, along with his entire household, believed after Jesus healed his son from a distance (John 4:46–53). If this were the case, it might help explain why Chuza permitted his wife to travel with Jesus and minister to his needs. The special knowledge of Herod and his court reflected in Luke may have come through Chuza. Luke's mention of Chuza and his wife offers evidence of Christianity within the aristocracy from the very beginning (Marshall *Luke* NIGTC, 317).

VIRGIL R. L. FRY

CILICIA (PLACE) [Gk *Kilikia*]. A province mentioned in Judith 1:12; 2:21–25 as an object of the ire of Nebuchadnezzar, who dispatched his general Holofernes with the army to punish the inhabitants for their insubordination. It is later mentioned in 1 Macc 11:14 as the location where Alexander Balas had gone to put down a rebellion and in his absence, Ptolemy usurped his throne. In the NT, the province is most noted as the homeland of the apostle Paul (Acts 21:39; 22:3; 23:34), and which was included in some of his evangelistic efforts (Gal 1:21–23; cf. Acts 15:23, 41).

Cilicia is on the SE coast of Anatolia and consists of two major divisions: Cilicia Tracheia (or Aspera) in the mountainous region W of the Lamus River as far as Syedra in Pamphylia, and Cilicia Campestris (or Pedias), the fertile plain S of the Taurus and W of the Amanus mountains. A limestone ridge, Cebilinur, running S from the Taurus to the coast at Karatas, divides the plain into an E section, where are located Misis and Anazarbus, and a larger W section, accommodating Adana, Tarsus, and Mersin.

A. Geography

Cilicia Campestris is a well watered alluvial plain formed by the deposits of the Ceyhan River (ancient Pyramus) in the E and the Seyhan and Tarsus Cay (Sarus and Cydnus Rivers) in the W. The Göksu (Calycadnus) flows through Cilicia Aspera reaching the Mediterranean at Selifke (ancient Seleucia on Calycadnus). These rivers made Cilicia a fertile region for producing grapes, cereals, grain, and flax in ancient times. In ancient times Cilicia had additional economic importance because of its access to rich metal producing areas in the Taurus and Anti-Taurus mountains. The plain also provides a comparatively easy link between Syria-Mesopotamia to the E and Cappadocia-Phrygia on the Anatolian plateau to the N and W. The Bahce and Beilan Passes, the former being more frequently used in ancient times, provided access to Syria through the Amanus mountains. The Anatolian interior is usually reached from Cilicia through the Taurus mountains at the Cilicia Gates, but also from Selifke up the Göksu River, and passes in the watershed of the Seyhan River N into E Cappadocia in the Anti-Taurus mountains. These passes, the fertile plain, and the proximity of metal ores in the surrounding mountains gave Cilicia strategic importance in ancient times. The excavations at Mersin and Tarsus testify to the long and continuous habitation of the Cilician plain. Numerous ancient mounds extending along a trunk line from the Bahce pass westward to the Lamus River with northern branches from Misis along the Seyhan River and from Tarsus toward the Cilicia Gates indicate extensive village occupation as well as the use of Cilicia as a link between Cappadocia and Syria throughout the ancient period (Seton-Williams 1954).

B. Prehistory and Bronze Age

In the Neolithic period, cultural influences from the Konya plain in the N and from Syria in the E are both apparent in the archaeological strata at Mersin and Tarsus. Cilicia appears to have been a cultural and political crossroad for the Bronze Age as well. Sargon of Akkad, the founder of the first Mesopotamian empire (ca. 2370 B.C.) claimed to control the NW regions as far as Cedar Forest and Silver Mountain. The latter could be any one of several rich silver deposits in the mountain perimeter N of the Cilician plain, while Cedar Forest is likely the Amanus mountains. In the 17th century B.C., the Hittite king, Ḫattušilis I (ca. 1650–1620), marched through Cilicia, and may have been responsible for the artificial rock cut which resulted in the present passage through the Taurus mountains at the Cilician Gates. Hittite domination in this region declined following the reign of Muršili I (ca. 1620–1595), and Hurrians pushed into Cilicia.

In the LB Age Cilicia briefly was ruled by independent kings, at least three of whom were allied by parity treaties with Hittite kings who referred to the region of E Cilicia as Kizzuwatna. Finally in the reign of Šunaššrua of Kizzuwatna, Cilicia became a vassal kingdom in the Hittite empire then ruled by Šuppiluliuma (ca. 1375–1335). The Amarna letters from Egypt, as well as the letters from Ugarit, reflect an interest in Cilician. Analysis of ceramic evidence from Tarsus and elsewhere in Cilicia for this period suggests a Mycenaean presence with close contact with the Mycenaean mainland especially in the Late Helladic III C period (Mee 1978).

C. Iron Age

In the early Iron Age, Cilicia appears to have had a cultural and social pattern similar to other small, contemporary Neo-Hittite states which emerged throughout SE Anatolia, Syria, and N Mesopotamia, whose development was triggered by the collapse of the LB Age empires, population migrations, and invasions. The E plain of Cilicia appears to have been inhabited by a mixed population including Hurrian, Luwian, and Phoenician elements.

This condition is illustrated by the bilingual inscription found at Karatepe in the hills NE of the Cilician plain where the Taurus mountains meet the Amanus. The inscription is on stone steles and sculptures which line two gateways to a fortress citadel, and is written in hieroglyphic Hittite (a script used to write the Luwian language) and in Phoenician. Its Phoenician text is the longest Phoenician inscription found to date. The inscription and associated sculptures have been variously dated from the 9th to the 7th centuries B.C. While some of the material found at Karatepe may date to the 9th century, it is most likely that the inscription and its author, Azatiwatas, date to the late 8th or early 7th century B.C. (Winter 1979; Hawkins and Davies 1978).

The independent Neo-Hittite states of Cilicia, like other similar small states in the surrounding regions were eventually annexed into the Assyrian Empire in the 7th century B.C. The Assyrians called the Cilician plain *Que,* and part of the mountain perimeter to the N and W *Ḫilakku.* Shalmaneser III (858–824 B.C.) was the first Assyrian king to subjugate Cilicia after several annual campaigns against its border defenses. Cilicia continued to be a difficult region to control because of local resistance and the interest taken in the area by Phrygia, Urartu, Phoenician, and Greek traders and colonists who wanted to limit Assyria's power. Sargon II (721–705 B.C.) used Cilicia as the base for extensive military campaigns into the Anatolian interior which resulted in the submission of the Phrygian king to Assyria (Postgate 1973).

With the collapse of the Assyrian Empire, a period of political balance ensued between Lydia, Egypt, Neo-Babylonia, and Media. The treaty on the Halys River in 585 B.C. between Lydia and Media which was arbitrated by Labynetus, a Babylonian, and Syennesis of Cilicia illustrates the political balance of this period (Hdt. 1.74). Possibly at this time Cilicia or parts of it became politically independent. But Neo-Babylonian sources indicate that the Cilician plain (*Ḫume* in Neo-Babylonian) was under Babylonian control. From this territory Babylonia obtained high quality iron. Nebuchadnezzar conquered the Cilician plain ca. 592 B.C., and Neriglissar reasserted Babylonian control over the region in 557/556 B.C., not long before Cyrus the Great brought Cilicia into the Persian Empire.

D. Persian Empire and Hellenistic Period

In the 5th century B.C., the Persians controlled Cilicia through a series of semi-independent vassal kings called Syennesis, and this region served as a mobilization area for military expeditions against the Danube region, Ionia, and Greece. The seizure of Cilicia was an important phase of the expedition of Cyrus the Younger in his revolt against his brother, Artaxerxes, in 401. As a result of Syennessis's cooperation with Cyrus, Cilicia was annexed as a province (satrapy) to the Persian Empire. During the 4th century B.C., a series of satrap generals issued coins in Cilicia which were used to pay mercenary soldiers and other military expenses. The legends of these coins are written either in Greek or Aramaic.

The occupation of Cilicia was also a crucial phase of Alexander's conquest of the Persian Empire. In addition to the good fortune of taking the undefended Cilician Gates, Alexander also fought his first battle against Darius III at Issus on the E edge of the Cilician plain in 333 B.C. The Macedonian king established his first imperial mint outside of Macedonia at Tarsus, the site of Persian satrapal mints as well as the capital of this Persian province. During the struggles of the successors of Alexander (Diodochi),

Cilicia often played a military or financial role because of its strategic location between Asia Minor and Syria, its coastal position, and proximity to silver deposits in the surrounding mountains.

In the Hellenistic period, the Seleucids acquired control of the Cilician plain but were challenged by the Ptolemies for possession of Cilicia Tracheia during the 3d century. Antiochus III's naval expedition in 197 eclipsed Ptolemic influence on the W coast of Cilicia. With the Treaty of Apamea, Antiochus retained control of both districts of Cilicia, but had restricted access to Cilicia Tracheia because his naval activity was limited to the coast E of the Calycadnus River. The Cilician plain remained under Seleucid control for the next hundred years. The Seleucid kings pursued a continuous policy of urbanization and hellenization in Cilicia, with many of its towns receiving names in honor of their Seleucid patrons. Antiochus IV Epiphanes (175–164) was especially active in this regard, adding to the already hellenized Tarsus (Antiocheia-on-Cydnus), Mopsuestia (Seleucia-on-Pyramus), and Silifke (Seleucia-on-Calycadnus) the towns of Adana (Antiocheia-on-Sarus), Mallus/Magarsus (Antiocheia-on-Pyramus), Oeniandus (Epiphaneia), and Castabala (Heiropolis). Seleucid control over Cilicia weakened after Antiochus IV, and Cilicia Tracheia came increasingly under the influence of local lords engaged in brigandage who were secure in their mountain fortresses. This region was geographically conducive to outlaws on land as well as by sea (Strabo 14.671). Pirates exploited the timber in the mountains and the numerous small protected coves along the coast with fertile valleys nearby. The region became so infested with pirates that "Cilician" became practically synonymous with "pirate" (Appian, *Mith.* 92).

E. Roman Period

Pompey annexed Cilicia Tracheia into the Roman empire during his campaign against the Mediterranean pirates in 67 B.C. He colonized defeated pirates in Cilicia Campestris at Soloi (refounded as Polpeiopolis), Mallus, Epiphaneia, and Adana, and annexed the Cilician plain at the conclusion of the war against Mithridates VI, king of Pontus. The two regions of Cilicia were joined to the already existing province of Cilicia which consisted of Pamphylia and Isauria. The region E of the Pyramus River remained under control of Rome's friend and ally, the local dynast Tarcondimotus, whose capital was at Castabala (Hieropolis-on-Pyramus).

Roman republican administration of Cilicia was generally corrupt despite the best efforts of the provincial governor, Marcus T. Cicero (51 B.C.), to rectify the maladministration of his predecessor. Conditions in the province worsened during the Roman civil wars which were largely fought in the E. Cassius imposed severe economic penalties on Tarsus in 43 B.C., and political instability, severe requisitions, and taxes followed Mark Antony's gift of Cilicia Aspera to Cleopatra. By the early principate, Cilicia Aspera was joined to the province of Lycaonia while the Cilician plain was linked to Syria. Two client kings ruled portions of Cilicia: the temple state of Olba in the W, while the region E of the Pyramus came under the control of Archelaus, king of Cappadocia, following the death of Tarcondimotus.

The emperor Vespasian joined Cilicia Tracheia and Campestris to form the province of Cilicia. This emperor as well as Trajan improved roads in Cilicia connecting this region to its neighboring provinces. The Flavians and Antonines promoted urbanization and hellenization within the province, and Hadrian and Antoninus Pius enlarged Cilicia with the addition of Lycaonia and Isauria. These policies were probably designed to strengthen Cilicia's military functions within the empire's defensive system. Road improvements in the reign of Alexander Severus (ca. A.D. 230) further strengthened Cilicia as a conduit for troop movements and a source of military provisions. Many of the governors of the province are known from the Flavian through the Severan dynasties, and a study has been made of their previous and subsequent positions in the imperial administration (Pflaum 1966).

Following the capture of Valerian by the Persians, about A.D. 260, this new aggressive enemy of Rome overran the provinces of Syria and Cilicia. These provinces were recovered for Rome as a result of the counterattacks of Callistus (or Ballista) who was in charge of Roman military supply at Samosata. Due to his efforts, the Roman frontier was restored on the upper Euphrates—part of a broader policy of restoration accomplished by the barracks emperors of the late 3d century culminating in the imperial reunification and reforms of Constantine (A.D. 306–37). As part of these reforms, the administration of Cilicia was divided with Cilicia Tracheia becoming part of the province of Isauria, while the Cilician plain constituted the province of Cilicia. Both Isauria and Cilicia belonged to the diocese of Oriens which also included Arabia, Palestine, Syria, and NW Mesopotamia.

References in the NT to Cilicia consistently link it to Syria reflecting the administrative unity of these two areas during the early principate (Acts 15:23, 41; Gal 1:21; also Acts 27:5). The apostle Paul came from Tarsus, and probably belonged to a prominent Jewish family of that city, holding both local and Roman citizenship (Woloch 1973). The fact that he was a tent maker fits with other evidence which indicated that textile manufacturing was an important industry in Tarsus during the Roman period.

Bibliography

Hawkins, J. D., and Davies, A. M. 1978. On the Problems of Karatepe: The Hieroglyphic Text. *AnSt* 28: 103–19.

Mee, C. 1978. Aegean Trade and Settlement in Anatolia in the Second Millennium B.C. *AnSt* 28: 121–56.

Pflaum, H.-G. 1966. Deux Gouverneurs de la Province de Cilicie de l'Époque de Trajan à la Lumière de deux nouvelles Inscriptions de Iotapé en Cilicie Trachée. Pp. 183–95 in *Corolla Memoriae Erich Swoboda Dedicata.* Römische Forschungen in Niederösterreich 5. Graz.

Postgate, J. N. 1973. Assyrian Texts and Fragments. *Iraq* 35: 13–36.

Seton-Williams, M. V. 1954. Cilician Survey. *AnSt* 4: 122–74.

Winter, I. J. 1979. On the Problems of Karatepe: The Reliefs and Their Context. *AnSt* 29: 115–51.

Woloch, M. 1973. St. Paul's two citizenships. *Cahiers des Études Anciennes* 2: 135–38.

J. DANIEL BING

CIMMERIANS [Gk *Kimmerioi*]. The Greek name of a group of Indo-European nomadic people possibly to be identified with the descendants of the biblical Gomer in the "Table of Nations" (Gen 10:2–3) and mentioned as providing part of the forces of Gog (Ezek 38:6). The Cimmerians, as they are called in Classical literature, lived on the steppes of Russia. Josephus wrongly equates the Gomerians with the Celtic Galatians (*Ant* 1.123). Homer indicates that the Cimmerians were from a foggy land possibly located along the northern shore of the Black Sea on the Crimean peninsula (*Od.* 11.13–19; cf. Strabo 7.4.3).

There is much debate over the history of the Cimmerians prior to the 8th century B.C. It is thought that they occupied the steppes north of the Caucasus Mountains from the 18th to the 13th century B.C. Then it is likely that they moved south to the area of the Caucasus mountain range and resided there from the 13th to the 8th century B.C. The Cimmerians were pushed south from the Ukraine region of Russia by the Scythians who, in turn, were being pressed westward by other peoples from farther east.

Several cuneiform texts from the late 8th to the early 7th centuries B.C. record Cimmerian conflicts with Urartu and the Assyrians. The Cimmerians attacked the Urartians twice, once during the reign of Rusa I, king of Urartu (734–714 B.C.) and a second time in 707 B.C. These attacks weakened the Urartians and allowed the Cimmerians to move farther west into eastern Turkey. The threat of the Cimmerians worried the Assyrians and an elderly Sargon II (722–705 B.C.) led an attack against them during his campaign in Tabal. In 679 B.C. Esarhaddon managed to defeat them near Tabal.

The conflict with the Assyrians caused most of the Cimmerians to move further west to central Anatolia. There they attacked Sinope, a Greek colony located along the shore of the Black Sea. In ca. 676 B.C. they destroyed Gordion, the capital of the Phrygian kingdom and home of the legendary King Midas. Strabo records that Midas, distraught over the defeat, committed suicide by drinking bull's blood (Strabo 1.61).

The Cimmerians led three attacks against Gyges, king of the Lydians, the first being between 668 and 665 B.C. It was after this first attack that Gyges pleaded for military aid from the Assyrians. The second Cimmerian attack against Lydia came in 657 B.C. The death of Gyges and the fall of Sardis, the Lydian capital city, came as a result of the third and final Cimmerian attack. The Cimmerians pushed on into Ionia and attacked Smyrna, Magnesia, and Ephesus.

The Cimmerians, under the leadership of Lygdamis (Strabo 1.61; known as Tugdamme in cuneiform sources), then attacked Cilicia in southeastern Turkey. The Assyrian king Ashurbanipal (668–631 B.C.), reportedly killed Tugdamme in battle. Shandakshatru, the son of Tugdamme, then submitted to Assyrian authority and the Cimmerians were no longer an independent entity. The name *Gimmiraia,* however, survives in the Akkadian portion of the Behistun inscription. Cappadocia, later called Gomir by the Armenians, may have been the home of some Cimmerians after their submission to the Assyrians.

Bibliography

Sulimirski, T. 1959. "The Cimmerian Problem," *Bulletin of the Institute of Archaeology* 2: 45–64.

Wiseman, D. J. 1958. *The Vassal-Treaties of Esarhaddon.* London.

Yamauchi, E. 1982. *Foes from the Northern Frontier: Invading Hordes from the Russian Steppes.* Grand Rapids.

JOHN D. WINELAND

CINNAMON. See PERFUMES AND SPICES; FLORA.

CIRCUMCISION. In the ancient Near East circumcision was widely practiced in two distinct forms: certain classes of Egyptian men, especially priests, slit the foreskin to let it hang free; many men from western Semitic groups in Syria and Palestine removed the foreskin altogether. The origins of the practice are irretrievable. Herodotus (5th century B.C.E.) speculated that circumcision had originated in Egypt and then moved E and N around the Mediterranean to Phoenicia. Although his view prevailed among modern scholars until recently, archaeological discoveries have required a reassessment of the evidence. Depictions of Syrian warriors circumcised in the W Semitic manner unearthed in Syria and Egypt date from early in the 3d millennium B.C.E. (Sasson 1966: 473–76). The Egyptian practice of circumcision first surfaces in the 23d century: a stele describes a group rite in which 120 men were circumcised (*ANET,* 326). On the basis of this evidence, Sasson argued that the practice began among NW Semites and moved S where Egyptians adapted it. His assessment accounts for the data currently available.

Hebrews adopted the W Semitic practice of circumcision as they moved into Palestine (Genesis 17; Josh 5:2–9). Because circumcision occupied a central place in the Hebrew sense of cultural and religious identity, each generation had to appropriate and interpret it. As a result, the Hebrew understanding of the rite's significance became extraordinarily rich. The subject divides neatly into three divisions: Hebrew writings, Jewish writings authored between Alexander's conquest (333 B.C.E.) and the Bar Kokhba Revolt (132–35 C.E.), and early Christian writings.

A. Hebrew Writings

The stories concerning circumcision as told in the Hebrew scriptures already show the richness which results from long reflection. Differing conceptions intertwine below the surface of these stories. Although disentangling these conceptions will not suffice to interpret the stories from which they come, it can isolate ideas significant for the Hebrew understanding of circumcision.

1. Circumcision behind the Stories. Circumcision was a marriage or fertility rite. Israelites cannot marry Shechemites until Shechem circumcises himself and all his men (Genesis 34). Zipporah announces that circumcision has made someone a "bloody bridegroom" to her (Exod 4:25). Whatever her enigmatic phrase means, it implies connection between marriage and circumcision even if it loses that significance in the Exodus account. The story of Abraham presupposes a rationale for uniting a marriage with circumcision: Only after Abraham's circumcision can Sarah bear a child or can Abraham have the right child who will be blessed by God. Circumcision is a fertility rite to ensure a goodly number of offspring blessed by God.

Circumcision was also an apotropaic rite, that is, a ritual to ward off evil. In a Phoenician myth El escapes grave danger by sacrificing his only son, then circumcising himself and his confederates (Euseb. *Praep. Ev.* 1.10.33, 44; cf. Flusser and Safrai 1980: 46). Although this passage is late (from Philo of Byblos, ca. 100 C.E.) it probably preserves an ancient Phoenician belief that circumcision turns evil away. In Exod 4:24–26 an act of circumcision turns aside a threat of death. Conversely, uncircumcision delivers kings and armies to the fullest possible experience of death, relegating them to the deepest corner of Sheol (Ezek 28:10; 31:28; 32:19–32; Lods 1943: 271–83). When later Jews, by analogy with Passover blood, attribute to circumcision sacrificial value to thwart the destroying angel (Flusser and Safrai 1980; Vermes 1958), they elaborate ideas long implict in the Hebrew conception of circumcision.

E. Isaac (1965) argues that circumcision served as a knife rite to ratify a covenant. Parties to a covenant, after killing an animal, swore by imprecation: if I fail to keep this covenant may the knife turn on me. The Abraham story associates circumcision with a covenant (Genesis 17). Similarly circumcision is associated with an agreement between Israel and the Shechemites (Gen 34:14–17). Perhaps the circumcisions at Gilgal (Josh 5:2–9) occurred at a covenant renewal ceremony. Yet this motif lies below the surface and was not developed in later Hebrew literature.

Although many of the surrounding nations practiced it (Jer 9:25–26), circumcision gave Hebrews a sense of national identity. This usage peaked when the Hebrews confronted "uncircumcised" nations, the Philistines (Judg 14:3; 15:18; 1 Sam 14:6; 17:26, 36; 31:4 [cf. 1 Chr 10:4]; 2 Sam 1:20), the Babylonians and the Greeks.

The heart (Deut 10:16; 30:6; Lev 26:41; Jer 4:4; 9:25–26), the lips (Exod 6:12, 30), the ears (Jer 6:10, and even fruit trees (Lev 19:23–25) are called circumcised or uncircumcised. What are the connotations on which these metaphors rely?

Passages which use the metaphor of the circumcised heart cluster in the Exile and in the years immediately preceding it. The heart is the thinking, willing part of a human being; hence the passages hold up the ideal of a circumcised mind, one which delights in the obedient love of God (Deut 10:16; 30:6). An Israelite with an uncircumcised heart differs not at all from a Gentile whose nation practices circumcision (Jer 9:25–26). Only those with a circumcised heart can experience the blessings of the covenant of Abraham (Jer 4:4; cf. 4:2) or return from exile (Lev 26:41; Deut 30:6) or enter the rebuilt temple (Ezek 44:7, 9). A circumcised heart is a mind of the right kind, one able to participate in a covenant with God. Human beings ordinarily circumcise their own hearts, but God promises to do so after the exile (Deut 30:6).

Moses complains that he has uncircumcised lips: he delivered God's message to the people and they did not respond (Exod 6:12, 30). Again the metaphor concerns ability for participation in what God is doing; since the problem cannot be with God's word, it must be with Moses' lips. In the subsequent narrative God responds by giving Moses heightened ability for the task: God will make Moses like God to Pharaoh (7:1).

Jeremiah speaks of uncircumcised ears which cannot hear the warning God issues through him (Jer 6:10). These are ears unable to participate in what God is doing; they cannot hear God's message.

Israelites must not eat from newly planted trees for their fruit is uncircumcised (Lev 19:23–25). This injunction is a specific instance of the command, "You shall be holy for I the Lord your God am holy" (19:2). Uncircumcised fruit is unsuitable for a people participating in God's holiness.

In the Hebrew Scriptures the metaphorical use is consistent. Circumcision connotes suitability for participation in what God is doing. It follows that physical, literal circumcision also carried this meaning. Circumcision made Israel fit to participate in God's activity as God's people. This meaning for literal circumcision lies behind the requirement that only the circumcised may eat Passover (Exod 12:43–49).

Hence Hebrews could draw from a plethora of significances when interpreting stories about circumcision. They could emphasize connotations of marriage and fertility, of covenant making, of deliverance from evil, of suitability for participation within God's activity, and of national identity. Of course, few stories make use of all of these ideas. We now turn to several of the more important stories to see how these ideas intertwine.

2. The Bloody Bridegroom (Exod 4:24–26). The most vexing of all stories about circumcision is that of Zipporah, her son, and the "bloody bridegroom" (Exod 4:24–26). The many puzzles of this passage reduce to two: What does the phrase "bloody bridegroom" mean? Does God seek to kill Moses or Moses' son?

The first puzzle stems from the ordinary meaning of the Hebrew word translated "bridegroom" *(ḥātān).* Since Moses and Zipporah have at least one child, "bridegroom" describes Moses poorly. Applying "bloody bridegroom" to Zipporah's son fares even worse. In Arabic *ḥatan* can also denote one who is circumcised. Perhaps Zipporah declares, "You are a blood-circumcised one for me" (Kosmala 1962: 27). Whether or not the story presupposes the meaning "circumcised one," the last verse of the story shows how the final editor wants the reader to understand the phrase: "She said *'ḥātan dāmîm'* concerning circumcision" (Exod 4:26) as if to say "Don't worry about this puzzling phrase; Zipporah was talking about circumcision, nothing more."

The second puzzle concerns antecedents of the pronouns in the passage. Do the masculine pronouns refer to Moses or Zipporah's son? Although the story does not mention Moses by name (the RSV clarifies the text by introducing Moses' name in 4:25), ambiguous masculine pronouns most naturally refer to him. But God has just charged Moses with a message and sent him to deliver it to Pharaoh. Why would God immediately waylay his messenger? If God attacks Moses, the story hardly fits its context.

What if God seeks to kill Moses' son? This requires mental agility from the reader, but, once the reader makes the required leap the story not only fits the context but makes a positive contribution to the argument. The message with which Moses has been entrusted threatens Pharaoh's first born son with death (Exod 4:23). If uncircumcised, Moses' own son is a son of Egypt, unable to live once the prophetic word has gone forth against Egypt's first born. Zipporah wards off the threat of death by circumcising her son and daubing him with the blood. The story not only foreshadows the later events of Passover but also confirms the commission God has just given Moses. The narrow escape of his son is a sign that Moses' message is true: not even Moses' own son is safe apart from the covenant of circumcision; how much less Pharaoh's!

Since the story fits its context better if the pronouns refer to Moses' son than if they refer to Moses, probably this is the intention of the final author. Perhaps the author has made some attempt to narrow the gap the reader must leap. After all the author has most recently been writing not about Moses but about firstborn sons. Perhaps he gave another clue that is now obscured. Changing one letter in the Hebrew phrase "in the way" *(bdrk)* yields "your first-born son" *(bkrk).* The text may originally have read "When his first-born son was at the lodging, God met him and sought to kill him" (Exod 4:23). Other interpretations of this difficult story have been well defended. See Childs (*Exodus* OTL, 90–107), Kosmala (1962), Kaplan (1981), and the literature they cite.

The Zipporah story draws upon a number of the themes discussed above. Circumcision incorporates Moses' son into Israel, God's first born. It wards off death from him as an apotropaic, sacrificial rite. It fits him to partake in what God is doing.

3. Circumcision of Abraham. The authors of Genesis 17 lived in a culture, probably during the Exile, which did not practice circumcision. They had to explain why Israelites should circumcise their children. They drew gladly upon traditions which claimed that circumcision ensured many offspring who would be blessed by God and who would experience what God was doing for his people. Before Abraham's circumcision Sarah is not fertile; afterward she is. Before his circumcision Abraham can only beget Ishmael; afterward he can beget Isaac, the child blessed by God. The chapter generalizes the principle: to experience the promise of many children blessed by God in the land, Abraham's children through Isaac must be circumcised on the eighth day (Gen 17:8, 14). But, since they were uncomfortable with the magical associations these claims had, the authors invented a new mode of operation: circumcision does not bring about these blessings; God has promised them. Circumcision is a mnemonic sign of the covenant with God. It reminds both God and Israelites that they are God's and he is theirs; that he has chosen them and that they are in the sphere of his working (Fox 1974). With circumcision Israelites commit themselves to living in this sphere; hence, to neglect it is to read oneself out of God's people. Since circumcision denotes the beginning of this new sphere of existence, both Abraham and Sarah change names. Although Abraham, like Phoenician El, both circumcises himself and seeks to offer his son as a sacrifice, Genesis no longer assumes that circumcision completes the sacrifice of an only son. However, the stories may be connected at another level (Flusser and Safrai 1980; Alexander 1983).

4. Circumcisions at Gilgal (Josh 5:2–9). Editors of the Joshua story wondered why the Israelites were not circumcised already and gave three answers: (1) Israelites were already circumcised but are circumcised a second time. Sasson (1966) suggests a plausible background for this explanation: They had been circumcised in the Egyptian manner; now they made the incision all the way around, "rolling off" (from the same root as Gilgal) the reproach of Egypt (Josh 5:2, 9). (2) The children of those who had disobeyed God and hence wandered in the wilderness had not been circumcised but were circumcised at Gilgal so they could eat Passover (cf. Exod 12:44–48). (3) The LXX preserves a different explanation: some of them had not been circumcised in Egypt.

The authors may have included the story because it connects circumcision with entering the land. Probably the backdrop is exilic. Why should we circumcise? Because only the circumcised can participate in what God is doing, only they can enter the land and take it. Their parents, who had neglected circumcision, could not.

B. Greek and Roman Periods to the Bar Kokhba Revolt

With the arrival of the Greeks came strong cultural pressure against circumcision. Greek sensibility accepted public nudity but strongly recoiled against removing the foreskin. Greeks considered a bare glans so repugnant, perhaps indecent, that those born with a defectively short foreskin frequently submitted to epispasm, surgery designed to restore the foreskin to its natural shape (Celsus *Med.* 7.25.1; Soranus *Gynecology* 2.34; Dioscorides 4.153; Hall 1988). Even those adequately endowed frequently secured the foreskin in place with a string or a pin (fibula), a practice called *kunodesme* in Greek, *infibulation* in Latin (Kreuls 1985; Celsus *Med.* 7.25.2), lest the glans inadvertently be revealed. Since the Romans shared the Greek repugnance toward circumcision, circumcision became the target of horror, contempt, scorn, and ridicule (Martial *Epigrams* 7.35, 82) throughout the period.

Cultural pressure against circumcision manifested itself in several ways. Since Jews were widely known to be circumcised, they were frequently ridiculed and ostracized. The Greek gymnasium or the Roman bath, both favorite institutions of those who could afford them, presupposed public nudity. The severe social stigma against circumcision discouraged Jews from participating. Greek athletics offered lower class boys of ability one of the readiest avenues for social and economic advancement, but since athletes competed naked, those who were circumcised could not compete. In Alexandria and probably other cities organized on the Greek pattern, citizenship hinged on Greek descent and successful completion of training as an ephebe. Since ephebes regularly exercised in gymnasia, circumcised Jews had to dispense with the privileges of citizenship. After the Jewish War (66–72 C.E.), Rome levied a tax on all circumcised Jews to support the worship of Jupiter Capitolinus. The tax not only imposed a financial burden; it also made it impossible for Jewish men to avoid the stigma of being Jewish by ceasing to practice Judaism. Suetonius tells with sympathy how an elderly man, who for years had not lived as a practicing Jew, was stripped in court, found to be circumcised, and forced to pay (*Dom.* 12.2). Two rulers outlawed circumcision on pain of death: Antiochus IV Epiphanes, a Greek Seleucid ruler (ca. 160 B.C.E.), hurled mothers and their circumcised babies from the walls of Jerusalem (1 Macc 1:48, 60–61; 2 Macc 6:10; *4 Macc.* 4:25); Hadrian, a Roman emperor, considered circumcision the moral equivalent of castration and outlawed both, precipitating or responding to the Bar Kokhba revolt (Smallwood 1959).

This stiff resistance to circumcision produced several responses among Jews. Some consolidated the traditional emphasis on circumcision so that circumcision became even more important than before. Some, educated in the Greek mode, retained circumcision and sought to explain it in ways acceptable to Greek sensibility. Some Jews, abandoning circumcision but not Judaism, allegorized circumcision and practiced a Judaism consonant with the best ideals of Greek culture. Some abandoned Judaism with circumcision and faded entirely into their cultural surroundings. We will examine these groups in turn.

1. Consolidating Circumcision. As *Jubilees,* written shortly after the Hellenizing reforms of Jason the High Priest (175–172 B.C.E.), takes a rigid stance against Greek culture, so it staunchly supports the necessity of circumcision. Those who are circumcised live in the godly sphere of existence; the uncircumcised live in a sphere dominated by evil. After narrating the ancient institution of circumcision by divine command to Abraham, an angel reveals to Moses the necessity of circumcision. Evil spirits rule the nations to deceive and annihilate them, but God rules Israel. Circumcision removes Israelites from the dominion of evil, places them under God's reign, and sanctifies them to experience God's presence with the holy angels who were created circumcised (*Jub.* 15:25–34). Circumcision determines the sphere in which one lives: the uncircumcised are dominated by evil, the circumcised, being ruled by God, experience his blessing. A paraphrase of the Shechem story demands that Israelite daughters not be given to the uncircumcised (*Jubilees* 30). To do so would place them outside the sphere of God's activity. Since not everyone physically circumcised fits in God's sphere, circumcision of the heart is necessary as well. When people repent God will circumcise their hearts and include them in his sphere as his children (*Jub.* 1:23–25).

The community at Qumran, which owned several copies of *Jubilees,* elaborated the doctrine of circumcision found in *Jubilees* and added a thrust of its own. Circumcision removes one from the wicked sphere and places one in the sphere of God: entering the community resembles Abraham's circumcision in that it frees one from the Angel of Enmity (CD 16:4–6). Those ruled by the spirit of truth in the community circumcise the foreskin of inclination (1QS 5:5). From the Qumran writings, metaphorical circumcision signifies the ability to receive or impart revelation. Circumcised ears can hear God speak the truth (1QH 18:20); uncircumcised lips cannot speak God's message truly (1QH 2:7, 18). Because those at Qumran viewed the rest of Israel as apostate, they used circumcision metaphorically rather than literally to define the sphere where God works. Yet in doing so they follow a path blazed by *Jubilees.*

Flusser and Safrai argue that the traditional Jewish blessing for the rite of circumcision praises God for instituting circumcision to save Abraham and his kin from destruction. If so, this blessing draws upon the same circle of ideas: circumcision removes one from the sphere of evil. Levi presupposes the same conception of circumcision when he argues against circumcising the Shechemites since God's wrath burned against them (*T. Levi* 6:3).

The LXX and the Targums interpret Zipporah's circumcision of her son as a sacrifice. The blood of circumcision atones for the guilt of Moses, thus warding off the angel of destruction who seeks to kill him (Exod 4:24–26 in LXX, *Tg. Onq.; Frg. Tg., Tg. Neof., Tg. Ps.-J.;* Vermes 1958). Somewhat later than the period of interest here, the Mishnah and Talmud elaborate the sacrificial significance of circumcision and speak of the blood which ratifies the covenant (for references to circumcision in the later works see Betz's remarks: *TRE* 5: 717–19).

Other books emphasize the necessity of circumcision without offering a rationale. Judith and Esther pointedly mention circumcision of proselytes (Jdt 14:10; Esth 8:17 [LXX]). The Hasmoneans regularly permitted residents of conquered territory to remain only if they submitted to circumcision (1 Macc 2:46; Joseph. *Ant* 13.257, 318–19, 397). As in *Jubilees* Hebrew daughters should only marry circumcised men (Joseph. *Ant* 20.139, 145). In the LXX recension of the book of Esther, the heroine abhors the bed of the uncircumcised (Esth 14:15). Moses is blessed by what the Greeks abhorred; like the angels in *Jubilees,* Moses was born circumcised (*L. A. B.* 9:13).

All of these works counter the Greek threat against circumcision by reasserting its necessity or explaining its significance. Circumcision atones for guilt as a sacrifice, transfers one from the realm of the deceiving, destroying angels to the realm of blessing, and sanctifies one for participation in heavenly worship in God's presence. It is folly to neglect it, folly inspired by the demonic rulers of the uncircumcised.

2. Explaining Circumcision to the Greeks. Jews who wanted to participate in Greek culture as fully as possible had to deal with the Greek prejudice against circumcision. Josephus and Philo, from the 1st century, and Artapanos, who wrote somewhat earlier, probably fit in this category.

Although Josephus projected but did not complete a book on the customs of the Jews, his existing works offer some clues. God gave circumcision to keep Abraham's posterity from mixing with others (*Ant* 1.192). As Jews circumcise on the eighth day to follow Isaac's example, so Arabs follow Ishmael in circumcising in the thirteenth year (*Ant* 1.214). Apion, an Egyptian, abuses the Hebrews for practicing circumcision and teaching the practice to others. Josephus, by pointing out that Egyptians circumcised priests and, according to Herodotus (2.104), taught others to follow their example, turns the tables on him (*AgAp* 2.141–44).

Artapanos claims that Moses originated Egyptian and Ethiopian as well as Israelite customs. Moses established (pagan!) deities for the various nomes within Egypt. When he heads an army against the Ethiopians, his enemies emulate his circumcision (Eus. *Praep. Ev.* 27.10). Artapanos hopes to defend and honor the customs Moses established, especially circumcision. If Egyptians and Ethiopians still obey the customs Moses gave them, why should not the Hebrews obey him as well?

When specifically replying to ridicule against circumcision (*Spec Leg* 1–11), Philo divides his defense of circumcision into two parts. In the first of these, attributed to divinely gifted men of old, Philo lists four reasons justifying circumcision: (1) it renders one less susceptible to disease, (2) it promotes that cleanliness of the whole body is necessary for priestly sanctification, (3) it likens the circumcised member to the heart (since the heart begets thought, the highest excellence to issue from human beings, it is fitting for the member which alone begets sensible things to resemble the heart as much as possible), (4) circumcision, by clearing the way for the seed, enhances fertility (*Spec Leg* 2–7). To these Philo adds two allegorical reasons: since the mating of man and woman is the most imperious of pleasures, circumcision tokens the excision of those pleasures which bewitch the mind. Since human beings readily arrogate to themselves the power to produce children, circumcision shows in the begetting member that the prerogative belongs to God alone (*Spec Leg* 8–11; cf. 304–5; *Migr* 92). Philo further elaborates his ideas in his commentary on Genesis 17 (*Ques Gen* 3.46–62).

3. Neglecting Circumcision. Every religious or cultural tradition has its dropouts. In the face of the severe social pressure against circumcision in the Greco-Roman period, many Jews quietly bowed out and joined the dominant culture, ceasing to practice circumcision. So much cannot be disputed, but dispute does arise over whether some Jews created a Jewish theology capable of offering a rationale for neglecting the practice of circumcision. This dispute, when reduced to the least common denominator, concerns whether a Jew who does not practice circumcision is apostate. Recognizing that "apostate" applies differently within differing confessional groups, we will sidestep this question by applying the term "Jewish" to any theology held by those claiming to live as Jews.

Evidence for compromise with Greek sensibility is strong. Martial twice mentions Jews who have hidden their circumcision by infibulation (*Epigrams* 7.35, 82). Celsus describes an operation (epispasm) to restore the foreskin of those who were circumcised (*Med.* 7.25.1). References to Jews who had submitted to epispasm begin about 150 B.C.E. and last throughout the period of interest here (1 Macc 1:15; cf. Joseph. *Ant* 12.241; *T. Mos* 8.3; 1 Cor 7:18; *m. ʾAbot* 3.16; Epiphanius *Mens.* 16; frequent in Babylonian Talmud; Hall 1988). *Jub* 15:33, written in the middle of the 2d century B.C.E., mentions two ways Israel transgresses circumcision: by cutting off too little of the foreskin, by leaving their sons just as they were born. Removing too little of the foreskin clearly concedes to Greek sensibility; not only would it facilitate infibulation and epispasm, but a sufficiently small cut would hardly show even without these expedients. Both forms of neglect were problems throughout the period. Mattathius forcibly circumcised uncircumcised Jewish boys (1 Macc 2:46) as, perhaps, did Bar Kokhba (*t. Šabb.* 15:9; *b. Yebam.* 72a). *2 Baruch* 66:5, in attributing a similar action to good King Josiah, presupposes that the problem of uncircumcised Jews was ever present. The Mishnah must stipulate removal of the entire foreskin for circumcision to be valid (*b. Šabb.* 137a–b).

Some references to neglect of circumcision presuppose a rationale. Those Jewish parents who cut off a minute portion of their son's foreskins show as much concern for Jewish tradition as they do for Greek sensibility. After all, their quarrel with other Jews concerns not whether circumcision should be done but what constitutes circumcision, a matter of interpreting traditions which were vague when the question first arose.

Some Jews required proselytes to be baptized but not circumcised. *Sibylline Oracle* 4.163–170 pleas for all mortals everywhere to repent and be baptized but does not mention circumcision. Ananius, a Jewish merchant (ca. 50 C.E.), after working hard to convert Izates, Prince of Adiabene, tried to dissuade him from offending his subjects by being circumcised. Ananius argued that, in his case, keeping the ordinances of God in a general way sufficed (Joseph. *Ant* 20.38–48). Although the rabbis staunchly supported circumcision of proselytes, a debate between Eleazer, who maintained that circumcision alone could make a proselyte, and Joshua, who maintained that baptism alone sufficed, may reflect issues raised first by those who thought circumcision of proselytes unnecessary. Philo, although he probably wished proselytes to submit to circumcision (*Migr* 92), says that the real proselyte circumcises not his uncircumcision but his passions (*Quaes Ex* 2.2). Such thinking, in other minds than Philo's, probably justified allowing proselytes to remain uncircumcised.

Philo criticizes Jews who so allegorized the law that they robbed it of its literal meaning. They repudiated sabbaths, feasts, the temple, and circumcision, among many other things (*Migr* 89–93). *ʾAbot* denies a portion in the world to come to those with a similarly defective practice (*ʾAbot* 3.16; cf. a similar list in *b. Yoma* 85b). Ignatius warns the Philadelphians against listening to Judaism taught by those who were uncircumcised (Ign. *Philad.* 6.1). Such passages imply that some Jews dispensed with practices offensive to Greeks by interpreting them allegorically. Since they still valued the law and other Jewish traditions, they represent a Jewish theology which found circumcision unnecessary. (For further consideration of this topic see Collins 1985.)

C. Early Christians and Circumcision

Like Jews of the same period, early Christians differed in their stances toward circumcision. The issue certainly threatened and probably fractured the unity of the early church. One question dominated the dispute: how could Christians inherit the blessings regularly associated with circumcision? This question broke down into several others: Was circumcision necessary for Christians? What does circumcision mean? How does what God is doing in Christ fit with what God did in the past through Abraham's covenant of circumcision? Answers to these questions took several forms: (1) what God has done in Christ is part of the wonderful thing God did in Abraham, hence circumcision is necessary for all (Paul's opponents); (2) what God is doing in Christ surpasses anything he did in the past, hence circumcision, valuable in itself, now is irrelevant (Paul); (3) in Christ the plan of God has widened to include the gentiles; Jews should circumcise, Gentiles should not (Luke-Acts); (4) a proper reading of Scripture shows that literal circumcision is abolished (Ephesians, *Barnabas, Diognetus, 4 Ezra* 1–2); (5) others sidestep the central questions to use the imagery of circumcision to illustrate a point (John, *Odes of Solomon, Gospel of Philip*).

1. Circumcision Is Necessary. Although no early Christian writing advocating circumcision for all Christians has survived, Luke describes a group of Judean Christian Pharisees who find circumcision and observance of the Law of Moses necessary for salvation (Acts 15:1, 5). Paul faces similar opponents in Galatians. Since Paul argues that the decisive move from the sphere of evil to God's sphere occurs in Christ, his opponents probably made a similar claim for circumcision. In analogy with the claims in *Jubilees* and other works, Paul's opponents probably claimed that without circumcision the Galatians belonged in the present evil age (Gal 1:4) enslaved to "elemental spirits" or "beings not gods" (Gal 4:1–11) and that they could not partake of the heavenly blessings belonging to the descendants of Abraham (Gal 4:21–5:1). The opponents in Colossians, whether they have elaborated the spirit world in Essene or Pythagorean directions, adapt similar ideas. In Phil 3:1–21 Paul does not counter a heavenly mythological thrust: those who advocate circumcision are concerned only with earthly things (3:19). Hence some early Christians saw what God was doing in Christ as part of what God had done in Abraham; therefore, they required circumcision. A subset of this group adapted older and current Jewish arguments to explain the necessity of circumcision. Since circumcision removed human beings from the dominion of evil and included them in the rule of God where Christ was, and since circumcision fit them for the heavenly Jerusalem where Christ was at God's right hand, circumcision was necessary for salvation.

2. Circumcision Is Irrelevant. Paul and his followers argue that advocates of universal circumcision have failed to grasp what God is doing. Contrary to the kind of thinking preserved in *Jubilees*, not circumcision but faith in Christ assures acceptance before God. Since the heavenly court reckoned Abraham righteous by faith before he received circumcision, and since God's promise made Abraham father of many nations, not of Jews alone, circumcision does not produce acceptance with God but only signifies it (Rom 4:9–12; cf. 15:8–9). Reliance upon circumcision obligates one to keep the rest of the law; failing that, circumcision becomes uncircumcision (Gal 5:3; Rom 2:25–29; cf. Jer 9:25–26). But the law, only a temporary restraining injunction handed down by the heavenly court, sentences everyone to death (Rom 3:9–19). Justification and acceptance before the heavenly court comes in Christ and is awarded to faith as with Abraham (Rom 3:21–5:5). Hence circumcision, far from assuring acceptance before God, actually condemns anyone who trusts it. Those who exalt circumcision seek salvation from a part of God's plan designed to give condemnation. Not circumcision but Christ makes one fit to stand before the heavenly court.

As Christ, not circumcision, assures acceptance with God, so Christ, not circumcision, assures deliverance from the reign of evil powers. Not those in the covenant of circumcision but those in Christ are children of Isaac through Sarah, born for freedom not slavery (Gal 4:21–5:1). Not those circumcised and keeping the law are free from the "elemental spirits" and "beings not gods" but those in Christ (Gal 4:1–11). It is Christ who delivers from the present evil age (Gal 1:3–4) and makes a new creation (Gal 6:15).

Concern for literal circumcision shows a mind set on the flesh, on the earth, on the old age, not on the Spirit or on heaven (Gal 6:1–13; Phil 3:2–21; Col 3:11). Real circumcision is of the heart; it is spiritual not literal and belongs, in Christ, to Christians (Rom 2:25–27; Phil 3:2–5; Col 2:11–13) who worship God in Spirit, who glory in Christ, and who put no confidence in the flesh (Phil 3:3).

Paul sums up his thinking in a series of allied statements: circumcision is irrelevant: "neither circumcision nor uncircumcision is anything, but a new creation" (Gal 6:15; cf. Gal 5:6; 1 Cor 7:19). A circumcised man should not seek epispasm; an uncircumcised man should not seek circumcision; each should remain as God called him (1 Cor 7:18–19). Circumcision has its place, even its value (Rom 3:1–2), but it neither removes one from the realm of evil nor fits one for God's presence. Only Christ delivers human beings from this present evil age and reconciles them to God.

3. Jews Should Circumcise; Gentiles Should Not. Luke-Acts chronicles the transition in God's plan. Jesus reveals the plan at the climax of the work: Christ must be rejected, suffer, and rise; repentance and forgiveness must be preached to all nations; you are witnesses of this plan (Acts 2:14–42; Luke 24:46–48). The transition in the plan begins squarely within the promise to Abraham: both John the Baptist and Jesus are circumcised, and, like Abraham, receive significant names at their circumcision (the giving of names at circumcision does not appear to be the usual Jewish custom). Stephen's speech makes a crucial transition: Abraham receives the promise along with circumcision (Acts 7:8) and recognizes God's fulfillment of it by circumcising Isaac. But the rest of the speech proves that Israel never recognizes the fulfillment of God's promises. Stephen concludes: despite its circumcision, Israel is uncircumcised in heart and ears; Israelites always resist the Holy Spirit. If resisting the Spirit implies that circumcision has become uncircumcision, receiving the Spirit implies that the uncircumcised have entered the plan of God (Acts 10:45, 11:2–3). This raises a question: Must Gentiles be circumcised to be saved (Acts 15:1, 5)? The council under the Holy Spirit (Acts 15:28) discerns that the plan of God includes Gentiles as the are and Jews as they are. Hence Jews must circumcise and keep the law of Moses; Gentiles must keep only the Noachic commands binding on all human beings (Acts 15:19–29). The principle is illustrated when Paul circumcises Timothy, who has Jewish blood, and when Jerusalem Jews are suspicious of Paul not because he teaches Gentiles not to circumcise but because they erroneously suppose he teaches Jews not to circumcise their sons (Acts 21:21). Luke thus endorses a mediating position: the newly revealed plan of God includes Jews as Jews and Gentiles as Gentiles. Brown (1983) probably does not have quite enough evidence to label this new view "Hellenist"; I would call it Lukan.

4. Literal Circumcision Is Abolished. Ephesians asserts the view of circumcision current among Jews of the

1st century but rigorously limits it to the past. Circumcision once effectively separated Jew from Gentile, uniting the former to Israel, to the covenants, and to God, but denying all hope to the latter (Eph 2:11–12). By abolishing circumcision among other such commands, Christ has included Gentiles and Jews in one new body with access to the Father (Eph 2:13–22). In part because circumcision is nullified, Ephesians readily announces that Gentiles are no longer sojourners (proselytes?) but full-fledged citizens (Eph 2:19).

The *Epistle of Barnabas* indulges in full-blown allegorical interpretation to assert a much less sympathetic view of circumcision. Circumcision of the flesh has been abolished. Not those who are uncircumcised but those who require circumcision are deceived by an evil angel (*Ep. Barn.* 9:4). Christians, however, have received true circumcision of heart and ears which reveals to them what scripture really says (*Ep. Barn.* 9:1–3, 9; 10:12). *Ep. Barn.* presents a mirror image of Qumran: although it equates circumcision of heart and ear with revelation as do the Qumran writings, it assumes that the angel of error inspires the literal practice of circumcision, instead of apostasy from the law.

In the *Gospel of Thomas,* Jesus denies the value of literal circumcision but upholds an unspecified spiritual value of true circumcision (*Gos. Thom.* 53). Later Christian writers view circumcision as silly (*Diognetus* 4.1, 4) or as ineffectual with God (*4 Ezra* 1:31).

5. Circumcision Used Positively. As it is right to circumcise on the Sabbath, so it is right to heal on the Sabbath (John 7:21–24). Though this argument is similar to a rabbinic one (*m. Ned.* 3.11), John invests it with special nuances. The argument presupposes that circumcision retains the connotations of blessing it commonly has in Jewish works and on this basis sets up a typical Johannine contrast between Moses and Jesus. You do not delay the blessings of circumcision, how much less the far greater blessings of what Jesus does. Circumcision from Moses cures in part; healing from Jesus cures completely.

In *Odes of Solomon* 11 circumcision is a metaphor for salvation which opens the odist to God and enables him or her to receive revelation and to experience a heavenly trip. Here common Hebrew notions of circumcision form a complex metaphor with many connotations. As at Qumran or in *Jubilees* circumcision fits the odist for the experience of God and enables the reception of revelation, but the odist speaks of something more than physical circumcision. He speaks of an act of the Holy Spirit which uncovers himself toward God.

A positive use of circumcision persists as late as the Gnostic Christian *Gospel of Philip* (*Gos. Phil.* 82.26–29). As Abraham circumcised himself when he received revelation it is proper for others likewise to destroy the flesh (Jewett 1971: 199, 212).

The use and significance of circumcision in ancient Hebrew and Christian writings is rich with diversity. As common with other religious practices, the meaning of circumcision resists reduction to a least common denominator. The foregoing review illustrates both the consistency and complexity of circumcision as a religious concept in the Judeo-Christian tradition.

Bibliography

Alexander, T. D. 1983. Genesis 22 and the Covenant of Circumcision. *JSOT* 25: 17–22.

Brown, R. E. 1983. Not Jewish and Gentile Christianity But Types of Jewish/Gentile Christianity. *CBQ* 45: 74–79.

Collins, J. J. 1985. A Symbol of Otherness: Circumcision and Salvation in the First Century. Pp. 163–86 in *"To See Ourselves as Others See Us": Christians, Jews and "Others" in Late Antiquity,* ed. J. Neusner and E. S. Frerichs. Chico, CA.

Flusser, D., and Safrai, S. 1980. Who Sanctified the Beloved in the Womb? *Imm* 11: 46–55.

Fox, M. 1974. Sign of the Covenant: Circumcision in the Light of the Priestly *'ot* Etiologies. *RB* 81: 537–96.

Hall, R. G. 1988. Epispasm and the Dating of Ancient Jewish Writings. *JSP* 2: 71–86.

Isaac, E. 1965. Circumcision as Covenant Rite. *Anthropos* 59: 444–56.

Jewett, R. 1971. Agitators and the Galatian Congregation. *NTS* 17: 198–212.

Kaplan, L. 1981. "And the Lord Sought to Kill Him" (Exod 4:24) Yet Once Again. *HAR* 5: 65–74.

Kosmala, H. 1962. The "Bloody Husband." *VT* 12: 14–28.

Kreuls, E. C. 1985. *The Reign of the Phallus: Sexual Politics in Ancient Athens.* New York.

Le Deaut, R. 1982. Le theme de la circoncision du coeur (Deut XXX6; Jer IV4 dans les versions anciennes (LXX et Targum) et a Qumran. *VTSup* 32: 178–205.

Lods, A. 1943. La mort des incirconcis. *CRAIBL* 271–83.

Sasson, J. M. 1966. Circumcision in the Ancient Near East. *JBL* 85: 473–76.

Smallwood, E. M. 1959. The Legislation of Hadrian and Antoninus Pius against Circumcision. *Latomus* 18: 334–47.

Vermes, G. 1958. Baptism and Jewish Exegesis: New Light from Ancient Sources. *NTS* 4: 308–19.

ROBERT G. HALL

CIRCUMLOCUTION. A rhetorical device (often employed in the Bible) involving deliberate evasiveness in speech or writing, talking around a delicate subject rather than using straightforward references. For example, defecation is sometimes referred to as "covering one's feet" (Judg 3:24; 1 Sam 24:3). See BIBLE, EUPHEMISM AND DYSPHEMISM IN THE.

CISTERN OF SIRAH (PLACE). See SIRAH, CISTERN OF (PLACE).

CISTERNS. See AGRICULTURE.

CITIES. There is no single definition of a city. As a cultural phenomenon, the nature of a city depends on the social and historical context within which it evolved (Eisenstadt and Shachar 1987). Generally speaking, however, a city is a permanent settlement which serves as a center for a large region and whose population is engaged in activities additional to agriculture. This entry consists of two articles that treat this subject. The first surveys cities in the Levant, particularly focusing on the emergence of the Israelite city in the Iron Age. The second surveys cities in the Greco-Roman world, focusing especially on the model of the Greek *polis.*

CITIES IN THE LEVANT

Urbanism in the Levant, as in other regions, is a cyclical process that reappeared roughly every millennium: in the Early Bronze Age (ca. 3000 B.C.E.), in the Middle Bronze (ca. 2000 B.C.E.), and in the Iron Age II (ca. 1000 B.C.E.). Each of these urban phases was preceded by a period of village life and pastoral nomadism. Emergence of cities is therefore an adaptive process rather than a result of diffusion of ideas or population.

A. Steps Toward Urban Life: The Chalcolithic Period

Before the Chalcolithic Period, evidence for urbanization is minimal and ambiguous. Pre-Pottery Neolithic Jericho is usually given the status of a city on account of its defensive wall. However, that position needs to be modified in light of Bar-Yosef's convincing demonstration (1986) that the wall was in fact a retaining wall against floods, built only at one side of the village. Therefore the first solid evidence for urbanization is found in the Chalcolithic Period, at which time large communities demonstrated the characteristics of a stratified society, such as the production of prestige goods and the establishment of ceremonial centers. The need for a centralized institution arose, possibly, from the unpredictability of agricultural yields and the deterioration of economic conditions at the end of the Chalcolithic period (Horowitz 1978). The cultic elite, which established itself around ceremonial centers, was the only entity that could control the storage and redistribution of cereals and cope with the difficult economic situation. One city in this period, Tuleilat-Ghassul, appears to be one continuous settlement of about 20 hectares with a temple surrounded by a ceremonial temenos. Other such centers arose, such as Gilat, a settlement of about 10 hectares in the northern Negeb, and En-Gedi in the Wilderness of Judah. A complete picture of the development of a ceremonial center into an urban one is offered so far only at Megiddo; this took place in the next stage, the Early Bronze Age I. A temenos with twin temples was erected above a village in Stratum XIX, followed by a fortified settlement in Stratum XVIII.

B. The First Cities: The Early Bronze Age

1. Early Bronze Age I. The first clear representation of a city in the Levant is Hububa Kabira on the Upper Euphrates dated to the late 4th millennium. See Fig. CIT.01. The city has a preplanned rectangular layout, a developed system of fortifications, a network of streets and, on a raised elevation, separated buildings constructed

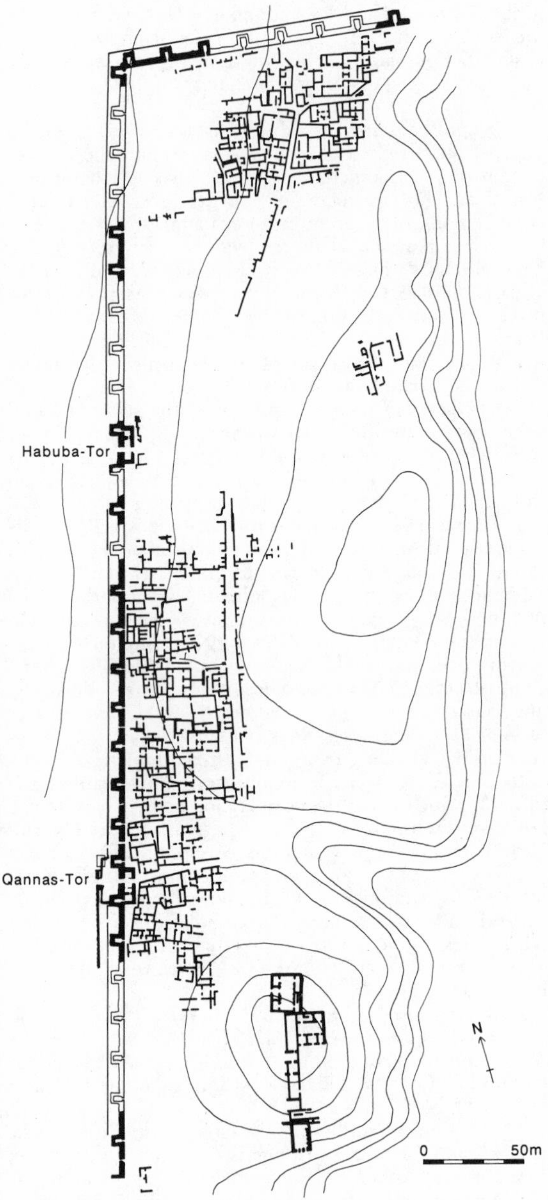

CIT.01. Site plan of Habuba Kabira in Syria—late 4th millennium. *(Redrawn from E. Strommenger,* Habuba Kabira. Eine Stadt vor 5000 Jahren *[Mainz: Philipp von Zabern, 1980], back cover.)*

for the city's elite. The earliest urban center in Israel, roughly contemporary with Habuba Kabira, is found in the Early Bronze Age I at Tel 'Erani, in the Southern Coastal Plain (Kempinski and Gilead 1988). However, very little is known of this city so far. It covered about 15 hectares and contained public structures, a city wall and square towers. The complex process of urbanization seems to have gained momentum during the later part of the EB I, as indicated by the presence of fortifications at sites like Aphek, Tell Shalem, and Tell el-Farᶜah (north) and ᶜAi.

2. Early Bronze Age II. The general nature of an urban center in Israel may be studied from the detailed information on cities of the EB II, such as Arad and Megiddo.

The city of Arad, located at the southern edge of the Judean Hills and bordering the valley of Beer-sheba, is the best preserved and most widely exposed city in Early Bronze Age II. Like previous Chalcolithic and EB I villages at the site, the city occupied several elongated hills in a horseshoe shape around a central depression, in which runoff water was collected and stored. On the crest of the surrounding hills a modest city wall, 2.25 m wide, was constructed, from which semicircular towers projected; the wall was segmented by a main gate and several secondary gates. The excavator's interpretation of "a grid of streets, which includes streets running parallel to the wall and radial streets leading into the city centre" (Amiran 1980: 6) cannot be observed on the plan. The inner urban matrix of Arad is rather determined by the shape of its dwelling units. These are compounds created by the arrangement of the dwellings, storage units and fences encircling a central open space (such compounds are called "Huerdenhaus" by Heinrich (*RLA* 4: 173–220). Each compound covers about 150–200 m^2 and includes at least one broadroom dwelling (the "Arad House") and several working and storage installations. Part of the central courtyard was probably used to pen the flocks. The "streets" are simply the open spaces between the compounds. See Fig. CIT.02. Besides the city wall, the only other public structure is a rectangular "fort" which dominates the central water reservoir. Two of the larger but otherwise unremarkable compounds are interpreted by the excavator as palace and temple units. If this identification is correct, it indicates that the concentration of power at Arad was not extensive.

The limited evidence on the early phase of the city (Stratum III) shows many open spaces and numerous clustered circular stone platforms, which served as bases for silos. It seems, therefore, that the city was erected not as a result of population growth and prosperity, but rather as an adaptation to the economic stress of a sparse population, with the aid of a system of redistribution organized by a central authority.

Cities built in the Early Bronze Age II were uncovered at several sites but, due to later overlying occupation layers, they could be exposed only in limited areas. Fortified cities were excavated at Beth-Yerah, Tell el-Farᶜah (north), Khirbet Makhruk, Megiddo, ᶜAi, Jericho, Tell Yarmut, and Bab edh-Dhraᶜ, to mention the main ones. They are characterized by very thick city walls (4.00–5.00 m), which, when attached to existing walls from the previous phase, could reach a total width of about 10 m or more. Semicircular or rectangular towers offered the defender the possibility of aiming flanking fire over the "dead area" at the foot of the

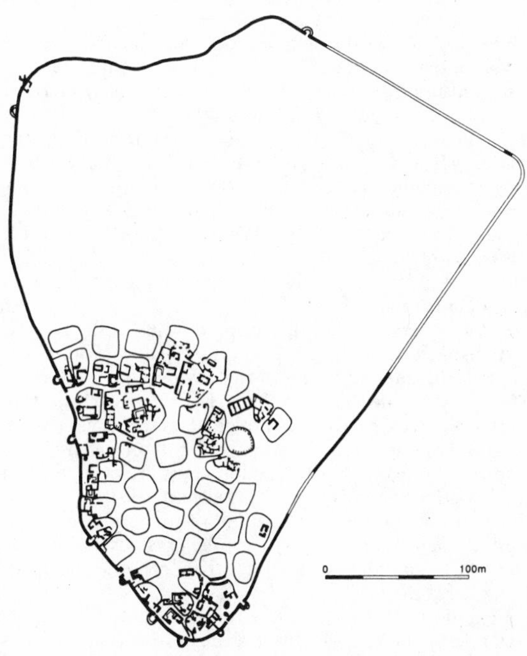

CIT.02. Site plan of Arad—EB II. *(Redrawn from Z. Herzog.)*

wall. In some instances like at Tell Yarmut a large bastion and a stone covered glacis were added.

Two types of gates were used in an Early Bronze Age city: a main gate more than 2 m wide, which allowed the passage of fully laden beasts of burden, and several secondary narrow gates (0.80 to 1.00 m). An example of a main gate is the entrance to Tell el-Farᶜah (north) protected by two impressive towers. Secondary (or postern) gates are known from Arad, ᶜAi, Jericho and Tell el-Farᶜah (north). It is suggested that the multiple passages met the requirements of the farmers who inhabited the large cities of the period, allowing them direct access to their fields.

In addition to fortifications, an important communal concern was the water supply. The cities at Arad and ᶜAi took into consideration the topography in such a way that rainwater within the city was directed into large reservoirs. The water inside the walls was vital in both times of siege and periods of drought. The internal organization of the city shows little attempt at planning. Household units arranged in compounds were typical at Arad, Tell el-Farᶜah and Jericho, but no street networks can be observed.

The only remarkable structures inside EB II cities are ceremonial buildings usually called temples. The importance of temples in the period is clearly attested by the large scale construction, the thick walls, the orthogonal layout and the superb building materials used for these edifices. The temple at ᶜAi, located on the summit of the mound, was shaped as a broadroom with outer measurements of 22.00 by 9.50 m. In the center of the hall were four stone bases for wooden columns which supported the roof. An auxiliary room surrounded it on three sides, probably serving as the storeroom of the temple.

The first clear evidence of a process in which the temple establishment developed into a military-political power base is in the fortified citadel built in Stratum XVIIIB at Megiddo. The citadel was protected by a 4.00-m-wide wall and had a gate guarded by towers. The area inside the citadel, which was only partly exposed and poorly preserved, contained part of a broadroom temple. A broadroom temple was erected also at Bab edh-Dra^{c} in EB II, while its later phase and the city's fortifications date to EB III. A large compound at Arad is interpreted by some scholars as a temenos with twin temples and by others as the dwelling of an affluent family.

3. Early Bronze Age III. During the EB III the process of urbanism reached its peak: fortifications were expanded, the internal layout of the city became more complex and many new cities such as Hazor and Lachish were erected for the first time, although several urban centers, such as Arad and Tell el-Far^{c}ah (north), were abandoned at the end of EB II. These developments are evident from architectural elements related to religious, economic, military and political institutions. The relative importance of these elements in the city reflects the crystalisation of the role of the social elite in the urban centers and their struggle for power.

Megiddo is the best example for illustrating the important role of the temple. In Stratum XVI a new temenos was constructed, to the west of and higher up the mound than the previous one. The new temple is an impressive structure with an innovative plan: a combination of a local traditional broadroom and the northern megaron (Ben-Tor 1973); it consisted of a cult room (13.75 by 8.90 m) with two central bases and a porch with two pillars before it. Behind the back wall of the temple stood a circular stone platform 8.00 m in diameter and 1.40 m high, generally interpreted as an altar. Alternatively, it may be considered the base of a central granary (Herzog 1986a): it is not located, as other altars are, in front of the temple, its size is much larger than that of any known altar, and the fence around it prevented worshippers from participating in the ceremony. On a lower terrace than the temple stood a large building which served as a palace. Although it was not completely exposed, the palace is a neatly planned unit separated into two wings by a narrow corridor and by a street on the three exposed sides. Its inferior topographical position and thinner walls show the lower status of the palace in comparison to the temple, or in social terms, the superiority of the cultic role of the elite—apparently due to control of the central granary—over its political role. In the same phase, the city wall was doubled in thickness and extended over additional lower sections of the city, providing an early example of a separately fortified acropolis.

In Stratum XV at Megiddo, in the latest phase of the EB III period, the city saw an even more dramatic increase in the role of the religious establishment, when in addition to the previous temple, another two identical megaron-like temples were erected. The temenos with three large temples dominated the whole mound and the use of the palace was discontinued. The grandiose appearance of the center was further enhanced by a monumental gateway, built over the dismantled remains of the previous palace. The gateway contained two straight approaches with stairs, set between three rectangular structures. The 15-m-long parallel flights of stairs and the relatively thin walls of the flanking rooms point to a ceremonial rather than a military function.

Important information regarding economic organization on the community level comes from Beth-Yerah, on the southern shore of the Sea of Galilee. A well planned structure covering 1200 m^2 included nine circles, each 8 m in diameter, sunk into a wide stone base. The circles were arranged around a square area divided into a courtyard and a room measuring 11.00 by 4.50 m, the roof of which was supported by two columns. A corridor 3 m wide led into the courtyard. The building is generally interpreted as a public granary and its total capacity was about 2500 m^2, or 1750 tons of grain. Such a large quantity surely had to be gathered from a populous community of farmers, which indicates a complex redistributional economy. The broadroom plan of the central room and the column bases very much resemble the typical temples of the period. The ceremonial function of the central unit is further supported by the presence of several large ovens in the courtyard, in front of the suggested cult room. If this interpretation is correct, then Beth-Yerah is another example of the correlation between the religious and economic social institutions in the EB III city.

Another aspect of urban life, emphasized in some cities, are large bastions incorporated into the fortifications. Their location, size (about 10 by 20 m) and the thickness of their walls show us that the role of the city guard had developed into a powerful and independent institution. The bastions, like those at Jericho and Tell Hesi, were undoubtedly several stories high, and their rooms could accommodate soldiers, weapons, and food.

C. Gap in Urban Life: The Early Bronze Age IV

The decline of urban life was a long and complex process that started already at the end of the Early Bronze Age II with the abandonment of important cities such as Arad, Tell Erani and Tell el-Far^{c}ah (north). However, by the end of the Early Bronze Age III, most cities in Palestine had ceased to exist. It is as yet unclear what the forces were that caused such a drastic social upheaval, forcing large communities to abandon their homes in cities and move into small villages or to convert their way of life to pastoral nomadism. In cases such as Megiddo or Lachish, where some objects date to the Early Bronze Age IV, the poor architectural remains of a rural or nomadic nature demonstrate this great break. The only exception known so far is Khirbet Iskander in trans-Jordan, where a 7.5 acre site surrounded by a 2.50 m wall is dated to this period. Rich urban centers, such as Hama and Ebla, flourished at this same time in northern Syria, indicating that the social change did not influence the entire Levant.

D. Second Urban Period: The Middle Bronze Age

Restoration of urban life in ancient Israel was not a revolutionary event. In most sites the first phase of occupation was represented by an unfortified settlement. This shows that urbanism was reestablished by groups of local farmers and pastoralists who found it worthwhile to live together in towns. Early in the Middle Bronze Age I, fully advanced urban centers emerged, first in the coastal and inner plains and then in the rest of the country.

Megiddo serves again as the key site to illustrate the developmental process. The only element in Stratum XIIIB is the old temple of Early Bronze Age III, reused in Early Bronze Age IV, now used again as a cult chamber with a few poor dwellings around it. In Stratum XIIIA the city is fortified with a buttressed wall, a projecting tower and a city gate with stairs leading into a bent-axis gate entrance. The houses near the cult area are slightly larger and better arranged, but the dramatic development in the acropolis happens in the next phase. In Stratum XII the old temple is finally abandoned and replaced by another small cult chamber with a thin fence, but to the west an impressive palace is now constructed, built with 2.00-m-thick walls over an area of about 1000 m^2. Blocks of houses fill the space between the palace and the city wall. The houses, which are of medium size, uniformly oriented with straight streets, were probably used as dwellings by the city's well-to-do families. The order in which the architectural elements appeared at Megiddo teaches us how the social institutions were consolidated: at first, when the military aspect was of prime importance, the city was fortified, later the political elite expressed its ascendancy with a monumental palace, but in both phases the religious aspect is hardly noticeable.

A similar picture, although less detailed, unfolds in other cities. The dominant structure in MB I fortified sites such as Tell Aphek is a courtyard palace, which in this case covers an area of 750 m^2. Not a single temple is known in the excavated urban centers of the period. This fact, which contrasts so strongly with the importance of the temple in the previous Early Bronze Age II–III, reflects the change of social organization in the cities of the Levant. Clearly the power in this period was no longer in the hands of the theocratic elite but had been taken over by the ascendant political-military class. Like other characteristics of this urban phase, the palaces, arranged around large courtyards, are obviously inspired by the formidable palace complexes in northern Syria, such as those at Mari and Tell Mardikh (Ebla). Large courtyard palaces were constructed also in many of the MB IIB cities such as Hazor, Shechem, Lachish, Aphek and Tel Sera^c.

City walls in the Middle Bronze Age were of modest width (about 2.00 m), but various improvements indicate that protection of cities was based more on the availability and mobility of professional soldiers than on the passive dependence on solid walls. First, towers or bastions were erected along the city walls, at intervals of 20.00 to 30.00 m. These could serve both as accommodations for the garrisons and as firing platforms. Such installations were excavated at Tell Beit Mirsim, Tel Zeror, Megiddo, Gezer, and Tel Poleg. A huge bastion at Tell Mardikh points again to the origin of this defensive feature. A second improvement of the MB I fortifications was the systematical maintenance and repair of the glacis covering the slopes outside the walls. Smooth, steep slopes made any attempt to climb up to the walls very difficult.

But the most important innovation regarding city planning was the erection of very large cities not on previous mounds (which were evidently too small), but on entirely new and flat areas, such as the lower cities found at Qatna (100 hectares) and Tell Mardikh (56 hectares) in Syria and Hazor (60 hectares) in Israel. These new settlements were surrounded by enormous earthen ramparts, which could reach a width of 60.00 m at their base and a height of 15.00 m, as in the western rampart of the lower city at Hazor. In front of this rampart was a moat, 15.00 m deep, from which most of the soil for the construction of the rampart was taken. Since no city walls were found incorporated into the ramparts, they apparently did not serve as fortifications against military attack. Instead, their erection seems to indicate peaceful times, when the large communities that settled the new urban centers were satisfied simply with the demarcation of the city's limits. Unlike city walls which required professional masons and expensive construction materials, earthen ramparts could be piled up by the thousands of unskilled inhabitants within a short period. As such, the ramparts provided fast and cheap means for delimitation of the city's borders, and their steep slopes could prohibit access by thieves or other undesirable elements.

This interpretation of the earthen ramparts is supported also by the unique design of the city gates commonly associated with them. The gates are shaped like strong forts consisting of two large towers and a passageway between them, narrowed down by three pairs of piers. Absence of a city wall is seen here again: no wall was found attached to the gates but instead they were joined into the ramparts by short "anchor walls." Two sets of doors, one on the outer and one on the city side, converted this building from a simple fortified entry into an independent stronghold (Herzog 1986b). The absence of city walls clearly encouraged the introduction of this type of gate. The guards could control the daily traffic through the gate and could repel enemies on either side in times of emergency. Gates of this type, associated with earthen ramparts, were found at Tell Mardikh, Qatna, Carchemish and Alalakh in Syria, where both elements probably originated in the MB I—and at Yavneh-Yam and Hazor in Israel. This gate was eventually adopted in cities fortified by conventional walls in Israel, such as Megiddo, Shechem, Gezer, Beth-Shemesh and Tell el-Far^{c}ah (south). It had the advantage of providing the ruling class protection not only from foreign enemies but also against internal attempts at revolt.

A glimpse at the internal organization of a MB I city is provided at Tell el-^{c}Ajjul. See Fig. CIT.03. The city covers an area of 12 hectares and is demarcated by a 3 m high earthen rampart and a 6 m deep glacis, without a city wall. On a raised elevation of the city, close to the main approach way, stood the Courtyard Palace I covering about 1500 m^2, built contemporaneously with the first erected City III. The excavations of the residential quarter cleared mostly the later City II, which, however, followed the same plan as Stratum III. The area was filled with large blocks of houses, erected along straight streets 3–4 m wide, bisected by narrower lanes. The buildings in the city were not equal in size: it seems that each block included one house occupied by a more affluent family (200–400 m^2) and the rest were smaller dwellings. Towards the end of the Middle Bronze Age II dramatic developments in city planning are apparent, best illustrated by Stratum X at Megiddo. Here a new temple was erected above the re-

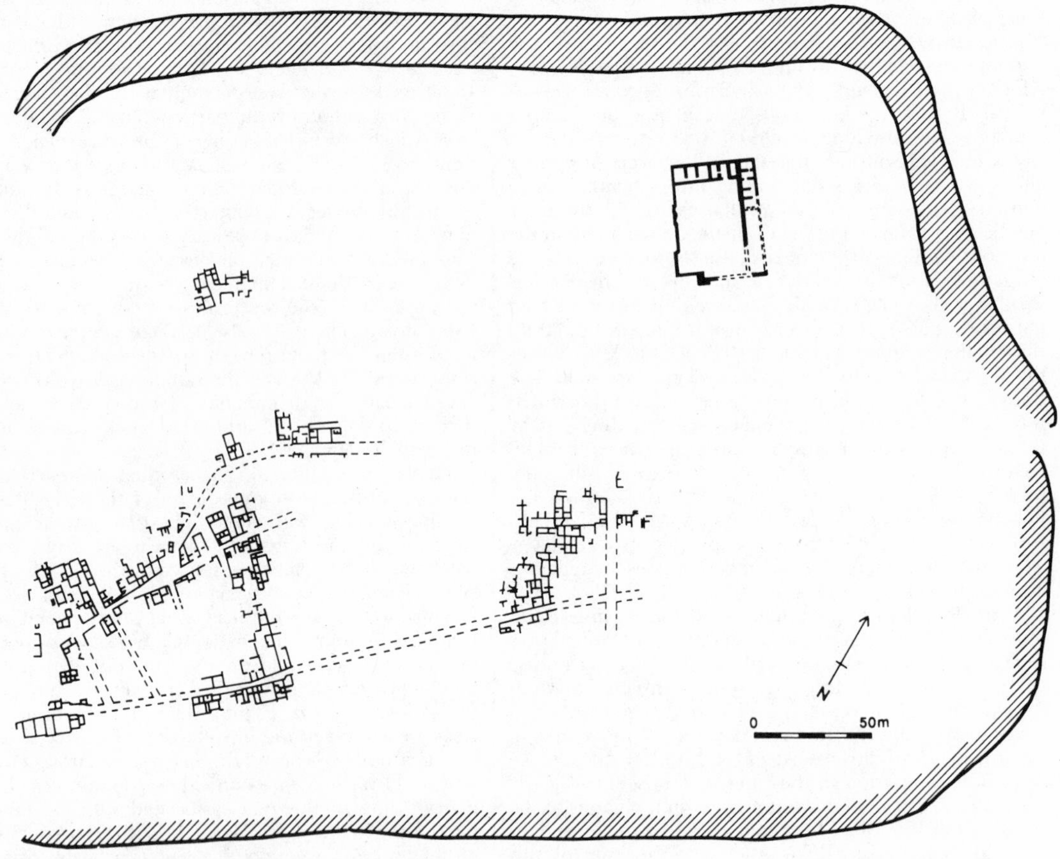

CIT.03. Site plan of Tell el-ʿAjjul—MB II. *(Redrawn from Kempinski 1987: 106.)*

mains of the previous cult place, starting a new tradition of shrines with a long room and thick walls. The temple, which stood inside a large temenos, was joined at its west by a large palace, with an entrance from the temple courtyard. At the same time, a second palatial center was established on the northern side of the mound, an area which gradually developed into the sole location of the city's palaces. Here a 6-pier city gate was built adjoining the new palaces on either side. These changes may be explained as the result of a final split in the structure of the ruling class; at first large palaces were erected near the traditional religious center and later they became completely independent. Another important change first observed at Stratum X at Megiddo is the absence of a city wall; the city was simply encompassed by a belt of houses, a feature that became common in the subsequent Late Bronze Age. Residential areas in all excavated parts of the city were well organized and had a common orientation. In the area east of the temple, a grid of perpendicular streets is observed.

E. The Decline of the Canaanite City: The Late Bronze Age

Cities in the Late Bronze Age show continuation and even elaboration of some aspects of the late Middle Bronze Age, but at the same time there is some deterioration in many other elements of the urban structure. New palaces, designed apparently as enclosed citadels, are constructed next to the city gate and are entirely separated from the temples. Fortification systems, on the other hand, are mostly neglected: often the old city wall or earthen ramparts are reused without any repair, but in other instances, such as Megiddo and Lachish, the city is surrounded solely by a belt of houses with no city wall at all. The religious institution seems to maintain some power, and temples continue the tradition from the MB II period; the reduction of their status within the social structure of the city is indicated by their removal from the area of the royal palace.

These developments are especially clear in Strata IX to VII at Megiddo. In area AA the former temple of Stratum

X was rebuilt and reused throughout the whole period, but the large building on its western side was diminished in size and gradually disappeared. Concurrently, the palaces near the gate constantly grew in size, in width of walls and in the complexity of their design. The excavated part of the palace in Area AA, west of the city gate, covers about 1500 m^2 and the one in Area DD 1200 m^2. In view of the lack of a city wall, it may be suggested that the gate and the two palaces were actually parts of an enclosed royal citadel occupying about 7000 m^2 and separated from the other cultic and residential quarters. This theory is supported by the large palatial citadels found immediately inside the main gates in major urban centers like Alalakh and Ugarit. The desire to erect such enclosed palaces stimulated their transfer into the gate area. In an unwalled city it was essential to provide the palace complex with a defensible entrance. The buttressed outer walls of the palace in Area AA at Megiddo in Stratum VIIB were shaped in the Egyptian style and were intended to serve as a symbolic expression of power and to camouflage the lack of real military strength.

If this interpretation is correct, a separate entry to the "civilian" part of the city might have been necessary; in fact, such a passage may be observed in the plans of Strata IX–VII, immediately west of the palace, where there is a clear gap between the palace and the outer walls of the adjacent structures. In area CC at the southern side of the city a residential quarter was extensively exposed in Stratum VII. The thin walls and small size of units in this area stand out in bold contrast to the luxurious palaces in the N citadel and demonstrate an extreme lack of socioeconomic equality in the social structure of the inhabitants. See Fig. CIT.04.

No site other than Megiddo is so far available for a comprehensive view of a Late Bronze Age city, but similar elements may be recognized even in partly excavated sites. Cities protected by a belt of houses instead of a city wall are known, in addition to Megiddo and Lachish, at Tel Batash, Tell Beit Mirsim and Jericho. Such conditions probably existed in many other sites of the Late Bronze Age where no city wall was found. Large buildings of the Late Bronze Age called forts, fortified palaces or public buildings by their excavators were exposed in otherwise unfortified sites, such as Tell el-ᶜAjjul, Tell el-Farᶜah (south), Tel Seraᶜ, Ashdod, Taᶜanach, and Beth-shean. It is very likely that these structures were also enclosed palaces, separated from the rest of the city occupied by the common people.

The archaeological data on the nature of cities in the Late Bronze Age exposes the degree of exaggeration of the Egyptian records which describe the conquered Canaanite fortified cities; obviously it was merely the enclosed palaces that they had to overcome. One of the exceptional cases of a fortification wall erected originally in the Late Bronze Age is at Tell Abu-Huwam, where a 2-m-wide city wall is attributed to Stratum V. In the 13th century a new type of building, called the "governor's residency," is found in several sites with clear Egyptian influence. These were compact forts of about 200–500 m^2 with a small center courtyard surrounded with rooms on three or four sides. Column bases in some of the courts probably indicate that half of the space was shaded. Governors' residencies were found at Beth-shean, Tel Hesi, Tel Seraᶜ, Tell Jemmeh, Tell el-Farᶜah (south) and Tel Masos and served the Egyptian administration that controlled the country. Stronger Egyptian fortresses were built along the main coastal road: at Haruvit, Deir el-Balah and Tel Mor (Oren 1984). Many of these centers functioned until the termination of Egyptian rule in Canaan, in the middle of the 12th century B.C.E. The intensified activity of the Egyptians was generated not by a sudden flourishing of Canaanite culture but by an attempt to maintain the economic viability of the land despite the collapse of the local system.

F. Emergence of the Israelite City: The Iron Age

1. Variety of Settlement Forms in Iron Age I. In spite of the general decline, urban culture did not totally disappear in the Iron Age I, but survived in several cities such as Megiddo Strata VIIA and VIA and Lachish Level VI, alongside the above-described Egyptian administrative and military centers. The character of the Philistine cities in their initial occupational phases in the late 12th and early 11th centuries is not yet clarified due to the limited extent of the excavations of sites such as Ashdod, Tel Miqne and Ashkelon. It is only from the late 11th century that the site of Tel Qasila is able to provide an indication of the nature of a Philistine town. See Fig. CIT.05. Although relatively small, it has an orthogonal layout with a network of perpendicular streets, parallels of which are known from Cyprus (Negbi 1986). Functional division inside the town of Tel Qasila includes quarters for craftsmen and temple priests. No palace or fortifications were uncovered there.

New settlements founded in the hinterland in Iron Age I, generally attributed to the Israelites, demonstrate different phases of the sedentarization process of pastoral nomads. The sites range from a simple camp of huts with storage granaries (Beer-sheba Stratum IX), through groups of enclosures (Giloh), to densely occupied villages (Beth-shemesh). All these are unfortified sites without any attempt at planning. This concept is first seen in the "enclosed settlements," such as those at Beer-sheba Stratum VII (see Fig. BEE.01) and Izbet Sartah. These settlements are designed with an eliptical belt of dwellings arranged around an open courtyard, which apparently served to pen the flocks (Herzog 1983). The large site of Tel Masos, identified variously as Israelite, Amalekite, or Canaanite, also seems to incorporate one or more enclosed settlements in addition to administrative and commercial buildings.

2. Iron Age II: Criteria of Planning. In Iron Age II, cities developed into full urban systems, organized for the first time under a United Monarchy, which, however, was soon divided into the kingdoms of Judah and Israel. Cities were established in both of these states according to an overall administrative-hierarchical scheme. Several criteria may be applied for the analysis and interpretation of the degree of planning of the city and its role in the system (Herzog 1987; Shiloh 1987).

a. Size of City. Iron Age cities were of medium size, about 3 to 7 hectares, but the capitals at Jerusalem and

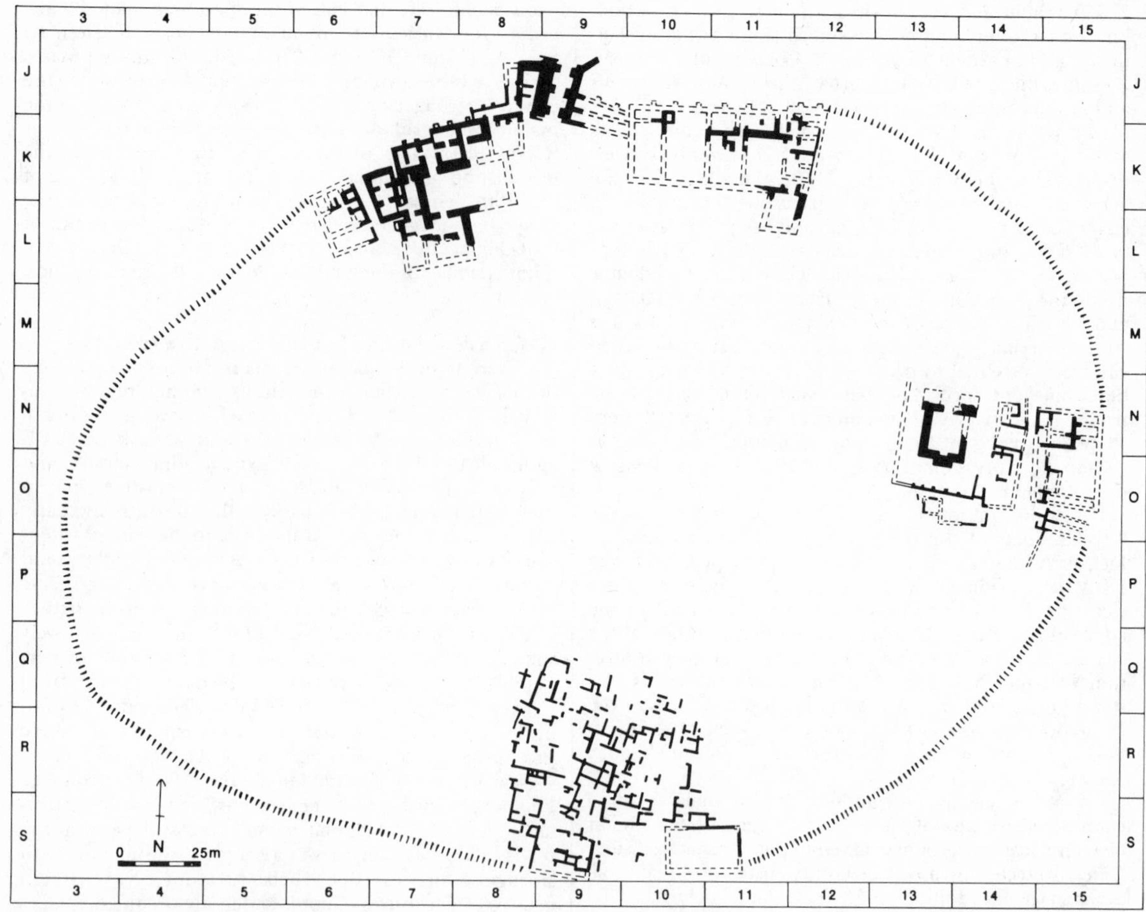

CIT.04. Site plan of Canaanite city at Megiddo—Stratum VIIA, Iron Ia. *(Redrawn from Herzog 1987: 198, fig. 3.)*

Samaria grew to be 30 to 50 hectares, attracting a considerable population.

b. Administrative Buildings. The higher the rank of a city in the hierarchical order, the larger were its administrative buildings. They were also more closely grouped together on higher elevations, and had a more organized layout. Under this heading are included the palace of the king or the city's governor, the temple, storehouses, and open spaces for markets and army encampments.

c. Fortifications and Water Systems. Solid city walls were the most costly. Casemate walls were less effective but much more economic in regard to materials and space. The simplest defense was the outer belt of houses usually found in cities located at some distance from the border. Cities of higher rank were equipped with systems of water supply which enabled them to withstand long periods of siege.

d. Street Networks. In the better planned cities, streets were of constant width and ran in continuous lines, parallel or radial to the city wall. Channels under the streets allowed fast drainage of rainwater and reduced the danger of dampness undermining the foundations of the buildings.

e. Construction Materials. The strongest, most impressive and most expensive construction materials were the ashlar stones widely applied in the monumental architecture of this period (Shiloh 1979). More ordinary materials were the unhewn stones used for foundations and the mudbricks used extensively in the superstructures.

f. Domestic Architecture. In high-ranking cities, dwellings tended to share a common plan in strictly allocated plots of land. In unplanned cities, houses varied in shape and size, resulting in a high percentage of unbuilt and wasted space.

3. Hierarchical Order of Cities. a. Royal Capitals. Of the two capitals of the Iron Age, only the acropolis of Samaria, capital of the N kingdom of Israel, is widely exposed, but it provides a remarkable illustration of the royal quarter of the city. See Fig. CIT.06. The acropolis was a large rectangular area, which extended in its final stage over 2.6 hectares, and necessitated quarrying, leveling, and infilling operations on the summit of the hill. It

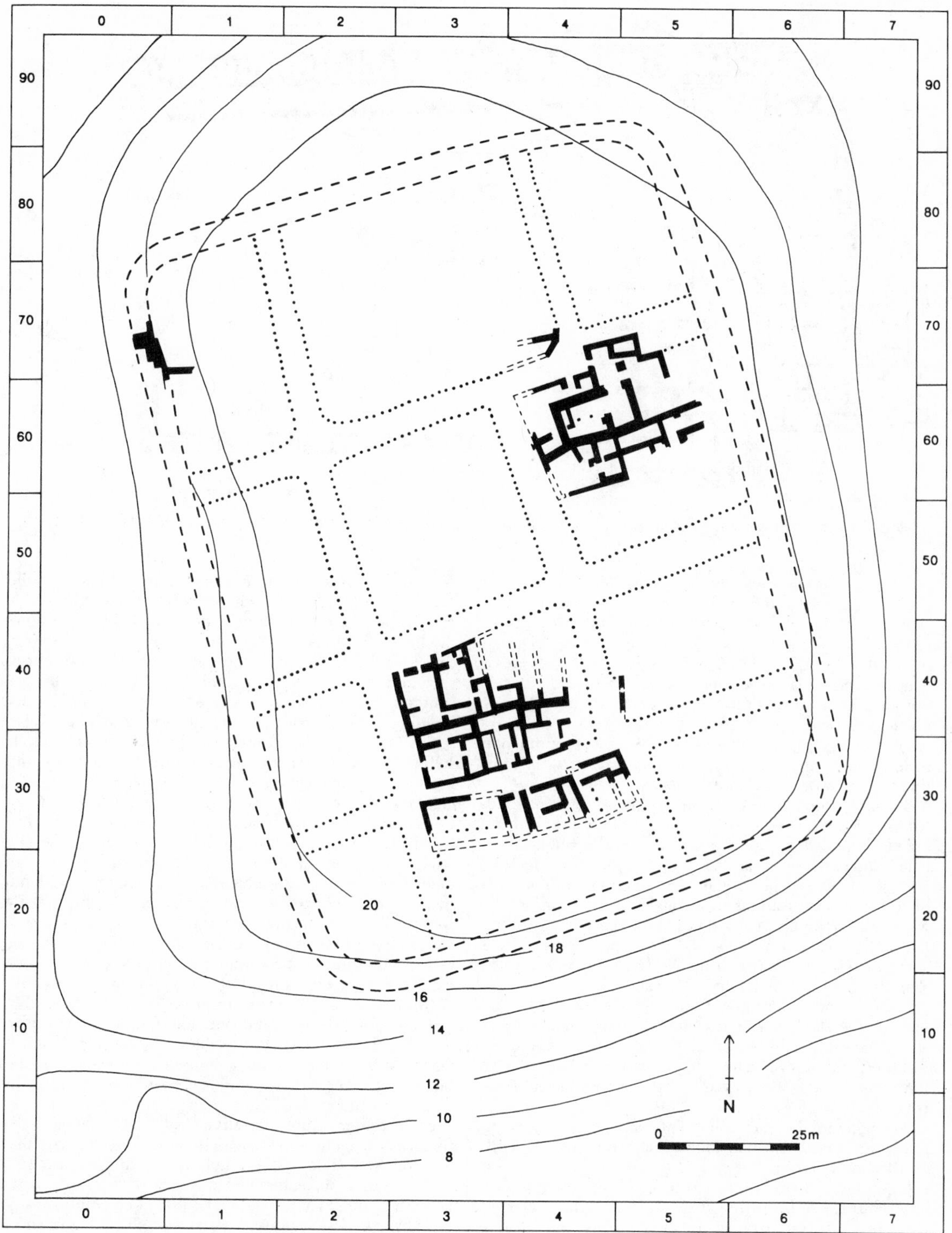

CIT.05. Site plan of Tel Qasila—Stratum X, Iron Ib. *(Redrawn from Herzog 1987: 203, fig. 7.)*

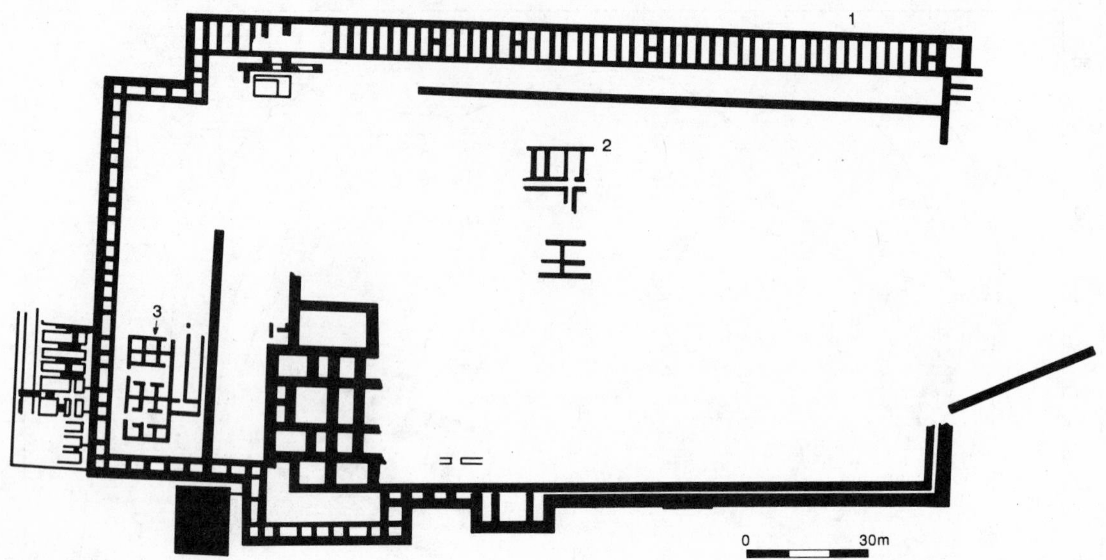

CIT.06. Plan of royal palace on the acropolis at Samaria—Iron IIb. *1,* casemate wall; *2,* "Ivory House"; *3,* "Ostraca House." *(Redrawn from* EAEHL *4: 1033.)*

was surrounded by wide casemate storerooms on most of its circumference and by a solid wall on the rest. On the S side stood the royal palace with an open courtyard in front of it. The N part had a well-planned street grid, occupied by dwellings of the noble families of the court (in one of which the Samaria ivories were found). West of the palace was an administrative office which contained an archive of ostraca. Although not completely preserved, enough remains of the acropolis at Samaria to show its monumental scale, strict planning, and superb ashlar masonry, all befitting the superior social status of its occupants.

Similar features were surely incorporated into the architecture of the acropolis at Jerusalem, which has not been archaeologically explored. In addition to the king's palace it also housed the royal cult center: Solomon's Temple. Part of a huge stepped retaining wall exposed in Area G of the recent excavations probably served to support the wall of the acropolis. Around the raised acropolis, the civic parts of the capital were located. Royal acropolises of the same pattern are known from N Syrian capitals such as Zenjirli, Carchemish and Tell Taʿainat.

b. Major Administrative Centers. Cities of the second level in the state hierarchy, which apparently served to supervise a single district of the kingdom, were only about 5–7 hectares in size. The administrative functions were performed in different sectors of the city and occupied a considerable part of it.

At Megiddo the increasing entrenchment of the bureaucracy is evident when comparing Strata VA and IVB. In the first phase of the early 10th century B.C.E., it was still an unwalled city, protected by a belt of buildings and entered through a simple gate. Two large structures were dedicated to administrative functions. These were Palace 1723 with a large square courtyard and an adjacent building in the S and Palace 6000 near the gate on the N. The rest of the area (about 75 percent) was filled with common dwellings. In the second phase, in the late 10th century, the city was fortified by a solid wall of the offsets and insets type and a large six-room gatehouse. More than 80 percent of the city's area was allocated for administrative buildings. They included: the city wall and gate, Palace 338, 17 royal storehouses (assumed by some scholars to be stables), large open courtyards apparently used as camping grounds for merchant caravans or army units, and an elaborate water system. See Fig. CIT.07. The concentration of administrative functions is even greater at Lachish Level III of the 8th century B.C.E. Here at an elevated palace, two types of storehouses and an immense rectangular courtyard were exposed. The common population was crowded into a few small, miserable dwellings at the foot of the raised palace. As the result of the large section allocated for administrative functions in these Iron Age cities, only limited space was available for dwellings. For example, apparently only 500–700 people lived at Lachish at this time (about 100 per hectare).

These characteristics indicate that, unlike in the Bronze Age, the Israelite city did not have a large population of agriculturalists but rather a limited number of families belonging to the political, military, economic and religious elite of the monarchy.

c. Secondary Administrative Centers. For smaller, economically less important districts another type of city plan was followed. The best example is seen in Stratum II at Beer-sheba, a small fortified city (ca. 1.1 hectare) of the late 8th century B.C.E. See Fig. CIT.08. The administrative units, such as storehouses, water system and governor's

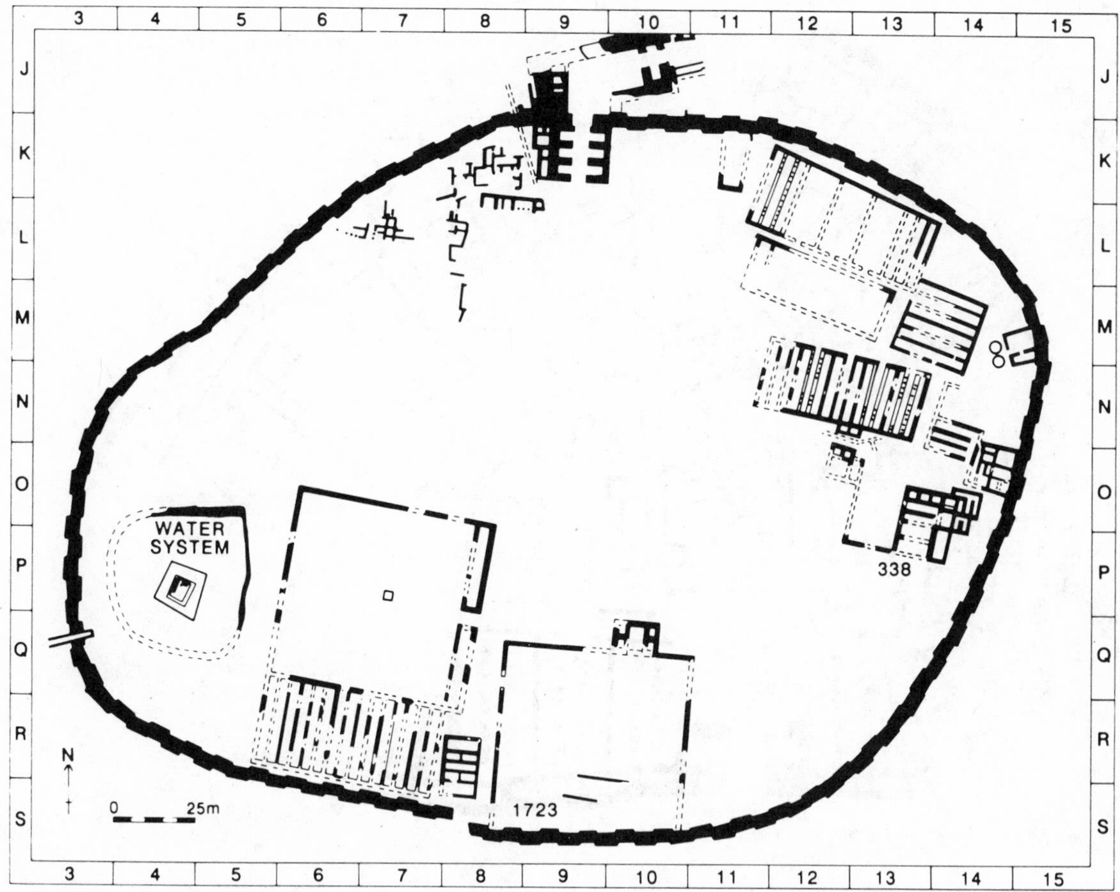

CIT.07. Site plan of Megiddo—Stratum IVB, Iron IIa. *See also* Figs. MEG.04 and MEG.05. *(Redrawn from Herzog 1987: 204, fig. 16.)*

residence, were not confined to a separate quarter but were organically integrated with the dwellings. This is evident most clearly in the association of the houses and the casemate city wall; the casemates served as the rear rooms of the adjoining dwellings. The complete city is neatly planned with two circular streets running parallel to the city wall. Apparently, the entire city was a royal administrative center.

d. Fortified Provincial Towns. In this category are fortified sites in which the city wall is the only clear public element. Dwellings inside the settlement are scattered haphazardly in an agglutinative pattern. Stratum A at Tell Beit Mirsim is typical of such towns, demonstrating a total lack of planning. Instead of streets of equal width as at Beer-sheba, here the spaces between the houses are of uneven size. In the initial phase of the stratum no administrative structures were exposed, not even a proper city gate. Evidence of light industry such as olive presses, looms, dying installations and pottery kilns, apparently related to royal estates, may provide partial explanation of the function of these towns. In addition, the fortifications of the town could have served as part of the regional defense framework of the monarchy.

e. Fortresses. Although these were not cities, they provide an interesting view of a "condensed" city. Fortresses such as that at Arad illustrate all the administrative functions: fortifications for military needs, stores and industrial quarters for economic functions, a royal temple serving the religious needs, and dwellings for the commander and his staff.

4. Assyrian Provincial Capitals. Stratum III at Megiddo offers a view of the layout of such a city. See Fig. CIT.09. It is characterized by an orderly street network, which was, however, more regular for the north-south streets than for the east-west ones. Each block was 65–75 feet deep, and the width of the street was about 8–10 feet. A full one-third of the city was occupied by several large courtyard palaces. Lack of separation between the palaces and the other dwellings may indicate that the whole city

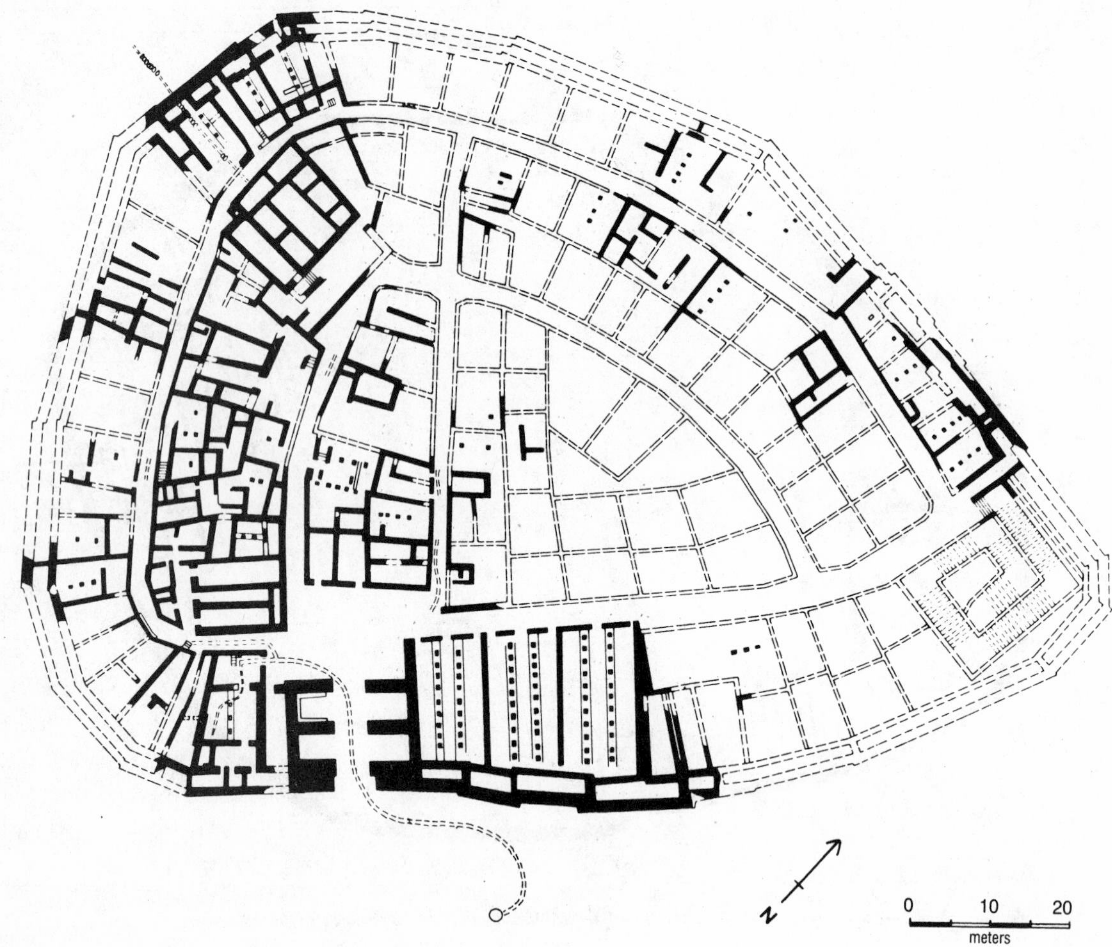

CIT.08. Site plan of Beer-sheba—Stratum II, Iron IIc. *(Redrawn from Herzog 1987: 220, fig. 19)*

was occupied by high functionaires of the Assyrian administration, however, no similarly planned Assyrian center has yet been found in the Levant.

Bibliography

Amiran, R. 1980. The Early Canaanite City of Arad—The Results of Fourteen Seasons of Excavations. *Qadmoniot* 13: 2–12 (Hebrew).

Bar-Yosef, O. 1986. The Walls of Jericho: An Alternative Interpretation. *Current Anthropology* 27: 157–62.

Ben-Tor, A. 1973. Plans of Dwellings and Temples in Early Bronze Age Palestine. *EI* 11: 92–98 (Hebrew).

Eisenstadt, S. N. and Shachar, R. 1987. *Society, Culture and Urbanization.* Newbury Park.

Herzog, Z. 1983. Enclosed Settlements in the Negeb and the Wilderness of Beer-sheba. *BASOR* 250: 41–49.

———. 1986a. Social Organization as Reflected by the Bronze and Iron Age Cities of Israel. In *Comparative Studies in the Development of Complex Societies Volume 2.* Southampton and London.

———. 1986b. *Das Stadttor in Israel und in den Nachbarlandern.* Mainz.

———. 1987. City Planning and Fortifications in the Iron Age. Pp. 195–231 in *The Architecture of Ancient Israel,* ed. H. Katzenstein, a.o. Jerusalem. (Hebrew).

Horowitz, A. 1978. Human Settlement Pattern in Israel. *Expedition* 20: 55–58.

Kempinski, A. 1978. *The Rise of an Urban Culture.* Jerusalem.

———. 1987. Urbanization and City Plan in the Middle Bronze Age II. Pp. 102–6. in *The Architecture of Ancient Israel,* ed. H. Katzenstein. Jerusalem. (Hebrew).

Kempinski, A. and Gilead, I. 1988. Tel ʿErani, 1987. *IEJ* 38: 88–90.

Negbi, O. 1986. The Climax of Urban Development in Bronze Age Cyprus. *RDAC* 97–121.

Oren, E. D. 1984. "Governors' Residence" in Canaan under the

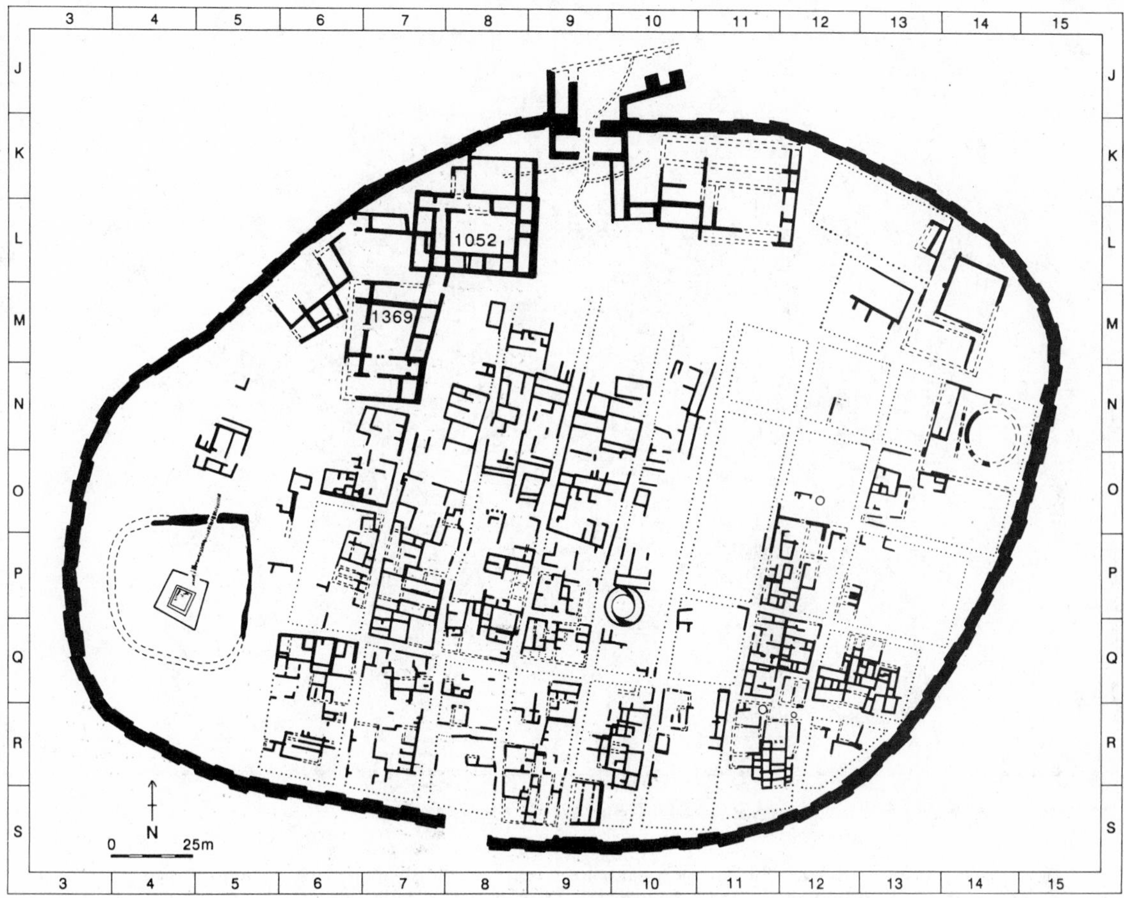

CIT.09. Site plan of Megiddo—Stratum III, Iron IIc. *(Redrawn from Herzog 1987: 216, fig. 17.)*

New Kingdom: A Case Study of Egyptian Administration. *JSSEA* 14: 37–56.

Richard, S. 1987. The Early Bronze Age: The Rise and Collapse of Urbanism. *BA* 50: 22–43.

Shiloh, Y. 1979. *The Proto-Aeolic Capital and Israelite Ashlar Masonry.* Qedem 11. Jerusalem.

———. 1987. The Casemate Wall, the Four Room House, and Early Planning in the Israelite City. *BASOR* 268: 3–15.

Strommenger, E. 1980. *Habuba Kabira, Eine Stadt vor 5000 Jahren.* Mainz.

Zeʾev Herzog

GRECO-ROMAN CITIES

Greco-Roman cities throughout the ancient world were based on the model of the Greek *polis.* The Greek *polis* was a politically and economically independent community centered around one town, usually walled but also including the surrounding countryside.

A. The Classical Greek Polis

The tradition of the *polis,* the Greek city-state, goes back at least to the 7th century B.C., when local tensions between landed aristocrats, poor peasants, and upwardly mobile merchants produced a system of independent political units. On the mainland of Greece, on the west coast of Asia Minor, and in colonies sent out to the Black Sea and the western shores of the Mediterranean (especially Sicily and southern Italy), the geographical boundaries of these *poleis* varied from narrow mountain valleys of uncertain fertility to broad expanses of rich ground.

The citizen body of a *polis* was smaller or larger depending on whether the city had an oligarchic or democratic constitution, and membership in it was tightly controlled.

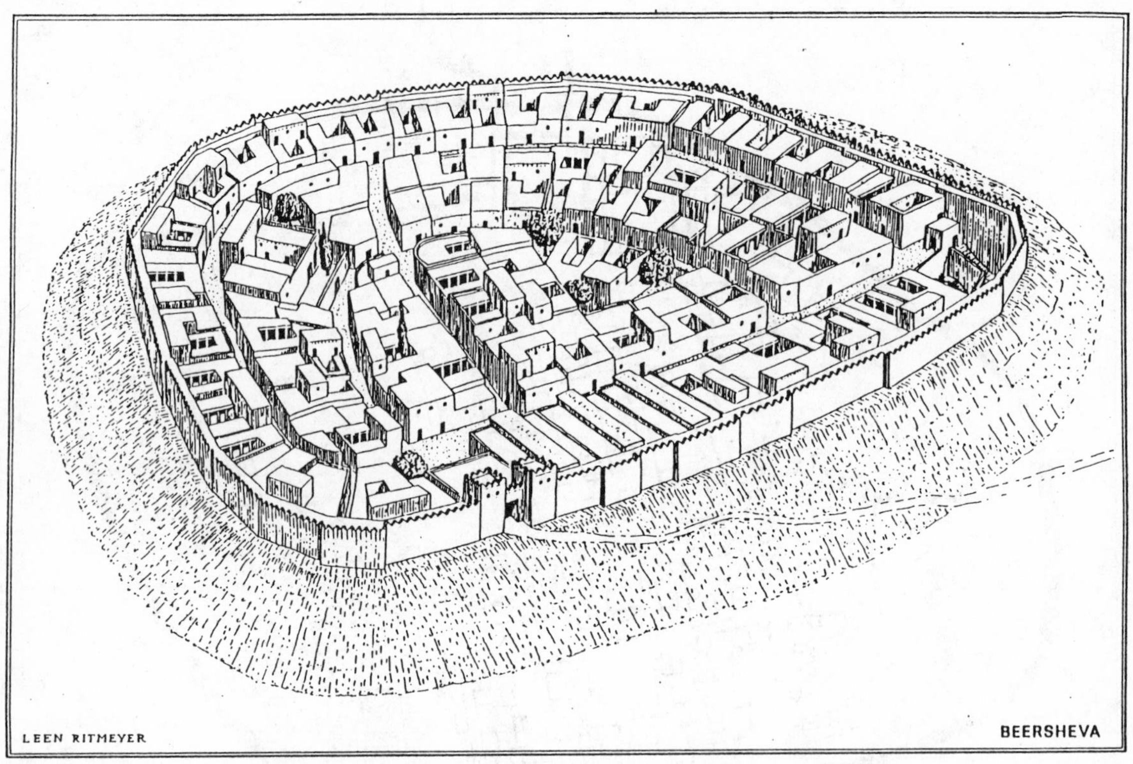

CIT.10. Hypothetical reconstruction of the Israelite city of Beersheba—Iron II. *(Reconstruction by Leon Ritmeyer.)*

The citizens met in an assembly to hear reports and to register their reactions to proposals which normally originated in a *boule,* a council usually composed of members of the old aristocratic families. A small group of magistrates administered the political system and the civic religious rites. They were normally elected or appointed for terms of a year.

Besides the aristocratic elite and the larger group of citizens, the population of most cities included a variable number of free resident foreigners and of slaves. In comparison with a modern city, the *polis* was small—the little island of Keos in the 5th and 4th centuries had four separate *poleis,* the smallest with about 700–800 inhabitants, and represents the lower range of population; Athens, with perhaps 40,000 adult male citizens and a total population of about 200,000 in the 5th and 4th centuries, was the largest *polis* in Greece.

The financial affairs of the *polis* show common collaboration of the population in public work. Large projects were assigned to the wealthy, in the form of "liturgies" [*leitourgiai,* literally "people-work"]. These might include the requirement to outfit a warship, pay for a religious procession, or sponsor a dramatic performance. Public construction was sometimes undertaken by corvee labor. Other expenses of building and maintaining temples and other public structures were paid by income from *polis*-owned farms and mines, and from taxes and tolls (usually levied on foreigners and resident aliens).

The *polis* was the whole community of citizens, and the whole land area they possessed. When the Athenians for example referred to a political or military action of their city they called it, not "Athens," but "the *polis* of the Athenians." The surrounding hinterland was an indispensable part of the *polis.* Citizens regularly owned farms in the country, even if they lived in the town where they practiced their citizen rights, and the economy of the *polis* was inextricably tied up with the agricultural produce of its fields. The army and citizen assembly were both made up, in the classical era, of farmers. Both Plato (*Rep.* 2.369B–372A) and Aristotle (*Pol.* 1.1252a26–1253a3) mention self-sufficiency as a characteristic of the *polis,* though even they recognized that imports enrich city life. Grain was often imported from near or far during a shortage, and luxury items were traded in small quantities by traveling merchants.

The Greeks regularly regarded the *polis* as the natural form of human society. When Aristotle (*Pol.* 7.1328b2–23) in the 4th century B.C. names the essential characteristics of the *polis,* he lists: a supply of food, necessary skills and crafts, military supplies, commerce, religion, and a system of justice. Five hundred years later, in the second century A.D., Pausanias considers similar needs when he writes (10.4.1) that a *polis* is defined by a municipal office, gymnasium, theater, *agora,* and public water supply.

The normal Greek word for the urban sector within the city walls was *asty.* Certain types of buildings, invented to fit the particular needs of *polis* life, became characteristic of the classical Greek city. The *agora,* a market and gathering place, was the center of public life. It was either located physically at the center of town or demarcated by streets and monuments to claim a dominant position. In or near the *agora* stood the essential political buildings: steps or bleachers for the citizen assembly; a *bouleuterion,* an enclosed stepped building to house meetings of the council; and a *prytaneion,* a houselike structure with a symbolic civic hearth, and meeting and eating facilities for the magistrates. Roofed colonnades called "stoas" provided shelter, and allowed the talk, commerce, and legal proceedings of the *agora* to go on no matter how hot the sun or insistent the rain. In the *agora,* and in many other parts of the *polis,* both inside and outside the walls of the *asty,* were sanctuaries. Sanctuaries were usually defined precincts which might be furnished with springs, stoas, statues, commemorative inscriptions, cooking facilities, and temples. Normally the most architecturally elaborate of the city's buildings, temples provided shelter for dedications and cult statues. Another prominent architectural complex was the *gymnasion,* where young men were educated intellectually and physically, and where adults continued their education, exercising, listening to lectures and readings, and visiting with acquaintances. The gymnasium (of which the Academy, Lyceum and Cynosarges at Athens were examples) was frequently located outside the walls where there was more space for its sand-covered open-air exercise court *(palaistra),* its school rooms and changing rooms, its colonnades, its shrines, and sometimes its gardens. A *stadion* also provided place for exercise, and for the athletic contests which were an important part of civic festivals. A theater, arranged on a hillside to face a circular *orchestra* ("dancing floor") where at festivals chorus and actors performed at the bottom of the slope, also provided continuing education in the tradition and myths of the *polis.*

In the *asty,* richly appointed public spaces and two or three main streets often contrasted strongly with crooked, modest, even squalid alleys leading to houses which were, at least in the face they presented to the street, small and unpretentious. In older cities, which had grown organically during the early stages of *polis* development, streets tended to wind casually along the lines of early roads, sheep tracks, and property boundaries. In others, new foundations where surveyors were able to begin with a clear plot of ground, a grid imposed some regularity on the town plan and the surrounding farm land. Colonies in the Greek west (Paestum in Italy, Agrigentum in Sicily, for instance) show a characteristic Greek grid plan: in one direction run three or four parallel, widely spaced avenues, intersected by many smaller, perpendicular, streets. The grid produced was composed of blocks, their narrow ends facing the main streets, their long sides facing the side streets. This rational grid plan was codified in the 5th century B.C. It leaves traces in literature at Thurii in Italy (Diod. 12.10.7), and on the ground at Olynthus in Greece and Miletus in Asia Minor. Later, during the 4th and 3d centuries, it became standard, as at Hellenistic Thessalonica, where the blocks measured 100 × 50 m. At places like Priene in Asia Minor we find it imposed on a steeply sloping, not particularly hospitable hillside site.

This grid plan became identified with the urban theories of Hippodamus of Miletus (Arist. *Pol.* 2.1267b–1268a), who in the 5th century B.C. wrote of a utopian *polis* of 10,000 citizens, composed of craftsmen, farmers, and soldiers. He also provided for a rational legal system, and for democratically elected magistrates, who were to take care of public property, resident aliens, and orphans.

The *asty* was normally bounded by some sort of defensive wall, although Sparta, relying on its soldiers, claimed to need no wall. (Plato *Leg.* 778, recommended Sparta's model, though Arist. *Pol.* 1330–1331, vigorously disagreed, maintaining that a wall was essential for a city's well-being.) From the 8th to the 5th centuries, city walls were usually irregular in ground plan, conforming to the local topography, even when the town inside was oriented to a strict Hippodamian grid. They were also rather casual in construction, since warfare tended toward pitched battles rather than extensive sieges. A change to more highly developed types of warcraft at the end of the 5th century B.C. and through the 4th century brought with it the necessity for more sophisticated city walls, and a writer on 4th-century strategy (Aeneas Tacticus 1–2) discusses arrangements for siege defense which will both protect the walls from direct attack and be alert to the constant danger posed by citizens who sympathize with the enemy.

B. The Hellenistic Greek City

The campaigns of Alexander the Great, who presented himself as a champion of Hellenic culture, marked a turning point in the history of the *polis.* His empire, and the large-scale kingdoms of his successors, helped limit the power of the old individual *polis* to act independently. On the other hand, the traditional *polis* provided the standard setting for Hellenic culture. As Alexander led his armies through Asia Minor, Syria, Palestine, Egypt, Mesopotamia, Persia and Bactria he founded many new cities (Plut. *Alex.* 1.5 gives a probably exaggerated total of seventy), and his successors used the *polis* as the model for new cities throughout the conquered East in the 3d and 2d centuries B.C. These cities attracted Greek settlers, veterans, and traders, as well as natives of the lands in which they were located. They were beacons of Greek civilization with their theaters, gymnasia, statues, and inscriptions. They were also a focus at which Greeks met their oriental neighbors and absorbed features from their cultures. Some served as royal capitals for the kings, others as market centers for an extensive hinterland, still others as military outposts.

Royal capitals, like Alexandria and Antioch, were governed by servants of the king, and from the Attalid capital of Pergamum in the 2d century B.C. we have a detailed inscription (*OGIS* 483—cf. Plato *Leg.* 759–66; Arist. *Ath. Pol.* 50.2) describing the duties of the *astynomoi,* officials in charge of day-to-day urban administration under the supervision of a board of "generals" *(strategoi).* They were in charge of buildings on public land, highways, common walls between properties, and had to keep streets open and accessible, enforce clean water regulations at public fountains and private cisterns, and maintain the public latrines. Older Greek cities tended to keep their traditional constitutions during the Hellenistic period, like the board of *politarchai* typical of Macedonian magistrates mentioned (Acts 17:6–8) as the "city authorities" at Thessalonica. Oligarchical governments flourished, a phenomenon which increased under the Roman empire, since the Romans were used to an aristocracy at home and found it easier to deal with aristocrats in provincial cities. Even at Athens, where the democratic assembly continued to meet and pass decrees throughout antiquity, the real government of the city was in the hands of the aristocratic council of the Areopagus. The text of the NT hints at the Roman presence hovering over the local administration: at Jerusalem for example the presence of Pilate and his soldiers pervades the Passion Narratives, and at Ephesus it is a local magistrate (*grammateus,* "town clerk") who deals with the riot in the theater (Acts 19:38–40), but he reminds the unruly crowd that the Roman authorities feel free to intervene if things get out of hand, and that the courts of the proconsul administer Roman justice. The letters that Pliny the Younger, when governor of the province of Bithynia between A.D. 109 and 111, wrote to the emperor Trajan (*Ep.* 10) also show independent cities like Nicomedia submitting requests for permission to undertake public building and for financial help to the Roman authority represented by Pliny.

The population of Hellenistic cities represented a rich ethnic mix. At Alexandria, distinct quarters were occupied by the ruling Greeks, the Egyptian natives, and the large Jewish population (which was permitted a certain degree of self-government as an autonomous (*politeuma,* always of course subject to the central authority). In other cities too, both in the east and in the west, Greek cities were inhabited by descendants of Greek settlers, by highly mobile merchants and craftsmen (exemplified by Priscilla, Aquila, and Paul—Acts 18:1–3, 18–28; Rom 16:3–5; 1 Cor 16:19), and by members of the original population, attracted to the cities by proximity, business, or the varied opportunities available in an urban setting.

Royal cities were financed from the purse of the kings, who were concerned that their capitals reflect the glory of the king in a way that was evident and easy for all to understand. Auxiliary building projects might well be undertaken by friendly monarchs eager to make an impression: an example is the project which Herod the Great undertook for Antioch in honor of Augustus, paving with marble two Roman miles of one of the city's main streets. Smaller cities relied on traditional means of financing their building and maintenance projects: liturgies, taxes, and tolls. During the age of the Hellenistic kings and into the period of Roman dominance, many cities vied eagerly for the favor and patronage of kings and the Roman senate.

Prosperity came to some cities because of their location or local industries. A good harbor, as at Thessalonica, was important in bringing goods from the roads of the interior to the sea. Dura-Europus, at a junction of a major desert road and the Euphrates River, grew into an important caravan city, as did Gerasa at the junction of several desert routes. Thyatira, in the western part of Asia Minor, and Tarsus, on the south coast, were both known especially for their textile industries.

In physical appearance, Hellenistic cities resembled those of the classical age, except that buildings were often larger, more elaborately decorated, and deliberately sited for dramatic effect. New cities were laid out, usually according to a Hippodamian grid, in plains and on hillsides. The *agora* was often surrounded and enclosed by a formal arrangement of stoas, producing a more regular, symmetrical space. The traditional buildings—*bouleuterion, prytaneion,* theater, gymnasium, stadium—were still built, bearing witness to the continuity of political and cultural ideas. In royal capitals, palaces were placed in dominant positions (on the mountain top at Pergamum, for example, or the riverfront at Antioch, or the main harbor at Alexandria). New large theaters, as at Ephesus, where 24,000 could be accommodated, and temples proclaimed the prestige of important cities, and were imitated on a smaller scale at more modest towns.

The Hellenized cities of Palestine and the Decapolis were in many ways typical. Some were new foundations of the kings, but at most of them the structures and institutions of a Hellenistic *polis* were imposed on earlier non-Hellenic towns and villages. For example, at Samaria, the old capital of the northern kingdom of Israel, Herod the Great rebuilt the city on a grand scale (27 B.C.) and renamed it Sebaste in honor of Herod's patron, the emperor Caesar Augustus [Gk *Sebastos*]. Among its Hellenized features were a new city wall, a temple to Augustus and Rome, a gymnasium, a theater, and a mixed population of Jews and Greeks. Caesarea Maritima, built by Herod the Great between 22 and 9 B.C., was provided with a big harbor from the start, which made it a center of trade. It was also an administrative center, and was eventually a congenial residence for the Roman governors of Judaea (Acts 23:23, 25:6). The city's constitution was along Greek lines, and apparently the Jews who settled there did not enjoy the rights of citizenship (Joseph. *JW* 2.266; *Ant* 20.173). Herod's son Antipas, tetrarch of Galilee and Peraea, continued the policy of building and rebuilding cities. Sepphoris (an easy walk from Nazareth) with its walls, may have been founded as a *polis* under Antipas, even though its population seems to have been predominantly Jewish; later it minted its own coins, a special sign of the status of a *polis.* Its wall, theater, and water supply may well have been built by Antipas. In A.D. 18, he also built a new city, Tiberias (named for the reigning emperor), on the shores of the Sea of Galilee. Its population included both Jews and Greeks, and its administration had such typical Greek features as an *archon* as chief magistrate, a board of ten magistrates *(dekaprotoi),* and a *boule* of 600 (Joseph. *Life* 278, 296; *JW* 2.641). It apparently lacked city walls, as well as authority over its hinterland, which was ruled by the king's ministers. Antipas' brother Philip, tetrarch of Auranitis, Trachonitis, and Batanaea, rebuilt the Hellenistic city Paneas, site of an important shrine to Pan and the Nymphs, as his capital; he renamed it Caesarea Philippi, organized it as a *polis,* and established a mint there.

In the Decapolis, some cities may have enjoyed some form of self-government even under the Roman domination. At Gerasa, for example, inscriptions record activities of local political units ("tribes") which show that an active civic life continued at least into the 2d century A.D. Most, however, like Damascus (2 Cor 11:32–33) were under the control of one or another of the kings and princes. In most of them, Jews lived together with the Hellenized gentiles, and were themselves highly Hellenized (Acts 9:20–22, 11:19–26). The physical remains of most of them show the typical features of a Hellenistic city: walls, fortresses, palaces, temples, theaters, and aqueducts. Jerusalem itself took on these features: the Hellenizing which preceded the Maccabean revolt was recognizable by the building of that most typical Greek structure, a gymnasium (1 Macc 1:14; 2 Macc 4:9–10), and in the time of Herod the Great, Jerusalem boasted such standard Hellenistic features as a grid plan, a careful arrangement of aqueducts, and aristocratic houses of Hellenistic type.

C. The Roman City

The Romans, as they spread their political and military influence throughout the Hellenistic East during the 2d and 1st centuries B.C., planted colonies of their own, which served as bastions of Roman power and civilization, just as the Greek colonies had proclaimed the political and cultural dominance of the Hellenistic kings.

The special characteristics of Roman cities developed during the 4th and 3d centuries B.C., when colonies were sent out to guard the expanding borders of Roman territory. These were of two main types. "Citizen" colonies were settled by Roman citizens, and they were considered extensions of Rome itself. Even political life was dictated by Rome, and citizens had to return there to vote. "Latin" colonies on the other hand were joint ventures of several of the Latin peoples; as Rome's prominence and dominance increased in Italy during the 4th and 3d centuries B.C., it exercised increasing control over such colonies, and dealt with them as it did with other Latin cities. They were politically autonomous, were entitled to the rights of trade and intermarriage with Roman citizens, and their citizens could under some circumstances come to Rome to vote.

The physical layout of newly established Roman or Latin colonies reflected the orthogonal planning learned from the Greeks, including a regular survey of the surrounding farm land into long rectangular plots, delimited by north-south *kardines* ("hinges") and east-west *decumani* ("tenths"). When a flat, unimpeded site permitted it, the junction of the main survey lines (*cardo maximus* and *decumanus maximus*) also served as the center of the walled town. Two main streets followed the line of the survey, and crossed at the central junction. Here, ideally, was the *forum,* which like the Greek *agora* offered space for political and commercial functions. A wall normally surrounded the built-up town site, where only a small portion of the settlers had their houses or shops. The majority of the population lived in farmhouses on their lots in the countryside. By the 1st century B.C., the planting of colonies spread overseas, as Roman generals used them to reward their soldiers with land—normally confiscated from defeated enemies—in a context of Roman civic institutions that would have been familiar to them. Such colonies inevitably displaced native populations, carving up their land into regular plots whose surveyed traces are still visible through aerial photography at, for example, Aurasio (Orange) in S Gaul. Towns which the Romans had destroyed were sometimes refounded as colonies, as was the case with Julius Caesar's new colonies at Carthage and at Corinth. As a special honor, older municipalities sometimes received the status of a Roman colony: examples are Caesarea Maritima under Vespasian, and Antioch under Caracalla.

Colonies expressed their ties to Rome by imitating its civic institutions. A Roman colony was governed, like Rome itself, by a senate-like council of former magistrates (the *curia,* or *ordo decurionum*), and administered by committees of magistrates elected for single-year terms. Most commonly these magistrates were called *duumviri, aediles,* and *quaestores.* The whole citizen body voted for these magistrates, although as at Rome voting power was often weighted heavily in the favor of those with higher social status. The *duumviri* at the head of the colony's government were referred to in Greek as *strategoi,* "generals," as at Philippi (Acts 16:19–39), where they were assisted by the *lictores* (in Greek *rhabdouchoi,* "rod-bearers," Acts 16:35, 38) who normally attended Roman magistrates. In Corinth, the capital of the Roman province of Achaea, Paul is brought before the Roman governor, Gallio, who conducts hearings in the forum of the Roman colony (Acts 18:12–17).

Along with its political structure, a Roman colony took Rome as its model in topographical details. A prominently situated Capitolium housed images of Jupiter, Juno, and Minerva, and recalled the focal temple on the Capitoline hill in Rome. The forum of a colony with certain "Latin" rights was regularly adorned with a statue of the satyr Marsyas, in imitation of a similar statue in the Forum at Rome. Images of the emperor and his family appeared ubiquitously in public places, and certain specific buildings, like basilicas and arches, alluded to similar structures in the capital.

The financial arrangements of Roman colonies were similar to those of other ancient towns. The immediate agricultural hinterland produced food and revenues to finance ordinary expenditures, and rich patrons both inside and outside the colony were expected to pay for festivals, shows, and new construction. When feasible, the local council appealed to the governor of the province, or directly to the emperor. Corinth for example had several monuments dedicated by various members of the imperial family.

As the towns grew, they tended to expand in a fairly haphazard way outside the carefully planned grid of the original colony, as shops, houses, and cemeteries grew up along roads leading to the next town.

The physical features of a typical Roman town are similar to those of the Greek *polis,* but we can make a few generalizations about peculiarly Roman characteristics. Where topography permitted, the city wall tended to be more regularly rectangular than the walls of Greek towns. Inside, the space was divided by streets into residential blocks which generally were more square than their counterparts in Greek towns. Plazas and temple precincts also tended to show a sterner symmetry than Greek counterparts. Where a Greek town might feature two or three parallel main streets, a Roman town usually focused around one main street, and perhaps a single important cross street, the effect of which was to give a stronger axial focus to the whole design. The most important street tended to form a thoroughfare, what MacDonald (1986) calls an "armature," and along its sides the most important monuments were arranged, not necessarily concentrated in one spot but distributed throughout its length across the town. Such monuments as temples, theaters, porticoes, monumental staircases, and fountains were also typical of Greek cities, but during the Roman period they tended to become even more imaginative and elaborate. The decorative Corinthian order dominated, colonnades were added to main streets on one or both sides, and fountains were transformed into elaborate *nymphaea* through several stories of attached and projecting columns.

Among peculiarly Roman types of structures we may mention the commemorative arch, marking a passage with a large structure decorated with statues, inscriptions and reliefs; the *basilica,* a roomy columned hall adjacent to the forum which housed legal and other business; the amphitheater, a major structure near the edge of important towns, to which gladiatorial shows attracted huge crowds; and the public or private bath, to which most free urban residents paid regular visits to exercise, wash, visit, see and be seen, and hear lectures and readings.

Such amenities were particularly characteristic of Roman colonies, but during the Empire, as a more homogeneous Greco-Roman fabric was woven out of the many cultural strands within the empire, even proud, old Greek cities adopted the special features of Roman urbanism. Thus, during the 1st century A.D., the main thoroughfares in Antioch (which had been paved with marble by Herod the Great) received colonnades, and soon cities like Alexandria, Damascus, and Philadelphia also used rows of columns to emphasize their main streets. Technological improvements like aqueducts, roads, masonry drains, and building techniques using concrete were quickly adopted. The correspondence of the governor Pliny (*Ep.* 10) indicates that the cities of Bithynia must have been vying with each other to add Roman-style aqueducts, drainage ditches, theaters, and baths to their urban fabric.

Bibliography

Castagnoli, F. 1971. *Orthogonal Town Planning in Antiquity.* Trans. V. Caliandro. Cambridge, MA.

Glotz, G. 1929. *The Greek City and Its Institutions.* London.

Grimal, P. 1983. *Roman Cities.* Trans. and ed. G. M. Woloch. Madison.

Hopkins, K. 1978. Economic Growth and Towns in Classical Antiquity. Pp. 35–77 in *Towns in Societies,* ed. P. Abrams and E. A. Wrigley. Cambridge.

Jones, A. H. M. 1940. *The Greek City from Alexander to Justinian.* Oxford.

———. 1971. *The Cities of the Eastern Roman Provinces.* 2d ed. Oxford.

MacDonald, W. L. 1986. *The Architecture of the Roman Empire.* Vol. 2, *An Urban Perspective.* New Haven.

MacMullen, R. 1974. *Roman Social Relations.* New Haven.

Osborn, R. 1987. *Classical Landscape with Figures.* Dobbs Ferry, NY.

Stambaugh, J. E. 1988. *The Ancient Roman City.* Baltimore.

Stambaugh, J. E., and Balch, D. L. 1986. *The New Testament in Its Social Environment.* Library of Early Christianity 2. Philadelphia.

Stillwell, R.; MacDonald, W. L.; and McAllister, M. H., eds. 1976. *The Princeton Encyclopedia of Classical Sites.* Princeton.

Ward-Perkins, J. B. 1974. *Cities of Ancient Greece and Italy.* New York.

Wycherley, R. E. 1962. *How the Greeks Built Cities.* 2d ed. London.

John E. Stambaugh

CITIES OF REFUGE. See REFUGE, CITIES OF.

CITIES, LEVITICAL. See LEVITICAL CITIES.

CITIZENSHIP. Before the Hellenistic period citizenship did not have the rather technical political significance in the biblical world that it thereafter acquired. In the ANE citizenship amounted to little more than birth or residence in a particular place; such privileges as it conferred were confined to freeborn males. Special prestige attached to citizenship of an outstanding city: thus in Psalm 87 to have been born in Jerusalem is something to be proud of. From the LXX of this psalm (especially v 5, Gk *mētēr Siōn,* "mother Zion") is derived in part from the NT concept of citizenship in the heavenly city, "Jerusalem above" (Gal 4:26; cf. Phil 3:20; Heb 12:22; Rev 3:12; 21:2, 9–27; 22:1–5).

The city *(polis)* was a political entity among the Greeks, and citizenship involved jealously guarded privileges. Thus in Athens in the 5th century B.C. only the children of two freeborn Athenians ranked as citizens: the child of an Athenian father and a non-Athenian mother was excluded from the register of Athenian citizens (Arist. *Ath. Pol.* 26).

Paul was obviously proud of his status as a citizen of Tarsus, "no mean city" (Acts 21:39). He was evidently born into a family which possessed the citizenship. For inclusion on the Tarsian citizen roll a property qualification of 500 drachmae had been fixed, perhaps ca. 30 B.C. by Athenodorus (Dio Chrys. *Or.* 34.23).

Paul's Tarsian citizenship, however, was not nearly so important in the world of his day as his Roman citizenship by birth, i.e., by inheritance from his father (Acts 22:28).

Roman citizenship, originally restricted to the city of Rome, was prudently extended to selected non-Romans as an honor for services rendered to Roman interests. The possession of Roman citizenship was a high social distinction in the Near East. Once conferred, it remained in the family. Paul's Roman citizenship, amply attested in Acts, has been questioned (cf. Stegemann 1987), but on no sufficient grounds.

Luke reports Paul as claiming the privileges of a Roman citizen on three occasions. In Philippi (a Roman colony) he does so in protest against having been beaten without receiving a fair trial (Acts 16:37). In Jerusalem he appeals successfully against being flogged by the Roman authorities in an attempt to discover the true reason for his being riotously assaulted in the temple precincts (Acts 22:25): a non-Roman might be examined under torture but citizens were exempt (by a series of Valerian and Porcian laws). In Caesarea he exercises the right of a Roman citizen to appeal to Caesar—to have his case transferred from the inferior jurisdiction of the governor of Judaea to the supreme tribunal in Rome (Acts 25:11).

The question arises of the means by which the claim to

be a Roman citizen was validated. The Lex Aelia Sentia of A.D. 4 and the Lex Papia Poppaea of A.D. 9 provided for the registration of Roman citizens at birth. The father or his agent would receive a certified copy of the entry in the register; if the child on coming of age gained personal possession of this copy (a diptych) it may have been carried around and produced when necessary (Schulz 1943: 63–64), but some hold that it was more probably kept in the family archives (Sherwin-White 1963: 149).

The picture of Roman citizenship given in Acts is true to the conditions of the mid-1st century A.D. By the beginning of the 2d century Roman citizens in the provinces, charged with offenses not covered by standard procedure, were sent to Rome almost automatically without formally appealing to Caesar. Thus in A.D. 112 Pliny the Younger, reporting to Trajan on his treatment of Christians in Bithynia and Pontus, mentions some "whom, because they were Roman citizens, I marked down to be sent to the capital" (*Ep.* 10.96.4).

There seems to have been a steady erosion of the citizen's privileges as the 2d century advanced. The Roman citizens arrested with other Christians of the Rhone Valley in A.D. 177 were kept in custody until a ruling could be obtained from the emperor; even after he had ruled that they should be beheaded and not put to death by torture, like the non-citizens, one of them, Attalus, was exposed to the beasts to please the mob (Eus. *Hist. Eccl.* 5.1.44, 50). The special privileges of citizenship lapsed in 212 when Caracalla extended it to all freeborn provincials throughout the Roman Empire.

Bibliography

Jones, A. H. M. 1968. *Studies in Roman Government and Law.* 2d edition. Oxford.

Schulz, F. 1942. Roman Registers of Births and Birth Certificates. *JRS* 32: 78–91.

———. 1943. Roman Registers of Births and Birth Certificates (continued). *JRS* 33: 55–64.

Sherwin-White, A. N. 1963. *Roman Society and Roman Law in the New Testament.* Oxford.

———. 1973. *The Roman Citizenship.* 2d edition. Oxford.

Stegemann, W. 1987. War der Apostel Paulus ein römischer Bürger? *ZNW* 78: 200–89.

F. F. BRUCE

CITY AUTHORITIES. Where Near Eastern cities formed part of a larger political grouping, their internal affairs were normally administered by the "elders" who "sat in the gate" (cf. Deut 21:2, 19; 25:7; Ruth 4:1–2; Amos 5:10, 15). This holds true into NT times, as with the "elders" (Gk *presbyteroi*) of Capernaum who acted as the centurion's messengers to Jesus (Luke 7:3). In a fortified city final authority would lie with the commander of the garrison.

The rulers of independent city-states (like the kings of cities in the Euphrates-Tigris valley) had greater authority. When one such city-state gained power over its neighbor its ruler became a "great king" or "king of kings" (cf. 2 Kgs 18:19; Dan 2:37).

The city as a distinct political institution (Gk *polis*) was a Greek development. Athens, for example, was governed by ten *archons,* democratically elected, and Sparta by two kings and five *ephors.* After the conquests of Alexander the Great (d. 323 B.C.) the *polis,* with its civic administration, became a familiar feature of the whole Near East.

Antiochus IV (168 B.C.) failed in his attempt to reconstitute Jerusalem as a Hellenistic *polis.* Since the return from exile, Jerusalem had enjoyed the status of a holy city, centered upon the temple; the temple staff, from the high priest downward, exercised authority over the city in general, although the judgment of the most influential citizens could not be ignored.

The titles of city authorities in Hellenistic and Roman times varied from place to place. The NT knows of the POLITARCHS (RSV "city authorities") of Thessalonica (Acts 17:6); this title is attested in inscriptions for the chief magistrates of several Macedonian cities. The chief magistrates of cities in Thessaly received the similar designation *poliarchs.* The chief magistrates, even in a free city, were responsible to the Roman administration of the province, and ultimately to the emperor, for the maintenance of public order and the suppression of sedition.

Elsewhere the city authorities are referred to by more general terms, such as "the leading men (Gk *prōtoi,* "first") of the city" in Pisidian Antioch (Acts 13:50), or "the prominent men of the city" *(hoi kat'exochēn)* at Caesarea (Acts 25:23). At Ephesus Luke mentions the town clerk *(grammateus),* the chief executive of the citizen body *(dēmos).* He, in consultation with the chief magistrates *(stratēgoi),* drafted the decrees to be set before the civic assembly and was also principal liaison officer with the Roman government of proconsular Asia.

Roman colonies like Philippi and Corinth were settlements of Roman citizens, and their administrations were modeled on that of Rome. The chief magistrates of Rome from early Republican days were the two collegiate consuls; each Roman colony therefore was administered by two chief magistrates. These were usually called *duumvirs* ("two men"), but in some colonies, such as Philippi, they preferred the more grandiloquent title of *praetors* (Gk *stratēgoi,* RSV "magistrates," Acts 16:20–38). Like the Roman consuls, they were attended by *lictors* (Gk *rhabdouchoi,* "rod-bearers"; RSV "police," Acts 16:35, 38), with their bundles *(fasces)* of rods and axes as badges of office. The ethos of a Roman colony is well illustrated by Acts 16:20–21, where the Philippian citizens are so proud of being Romans, much superior to the neighboring Greeks, not to mention Jews. For further discussion see PWSup 13: 483–500.

Bibliography

Helly, B. 1977. Politarques, poliarques et polito-phylarques. Pp. 531–44 in *Ancient Macedonia,* ed. B. Laourdas and C. Makaronas. Thessaloniki.

Jones, A. H. M. 1940. *The Greek City from Alexander to Justinian.* Oxford.

———. 1971. *Cities of the Eastern Roman Provinces.* 2d ed. Oxford.

Levick, B. 1967. *Roman Colonies in Southern Asia Minor.* Oxford.

Magie, D. 1950. *Roman Rule in Asia Minor to the End of the Third Century after Christ.* Princeton.

Oliver, J. H. 1963. Civic Constitutions for Macedonian Communities. *CP* 58: 164–65.

Ramsay, W. M. 1907. *The Cities of St. Paul.* London.
Schuler, C. 1960. The Macedonian Politarchs. *CP* 55: 90–100.

F. F. Bruce

CITY NAMES. One major division of city names in the Bible (and other areas of the ancient world as well) is the class of cities which have two or more alternate names. Of this group, there is an important distinction between those whose alternate names mean the same thing and those that have no more functional/semantic connection with each other than *New Amsterdam* which became *New York,* due to a change of rulers. The first of these two classes is further divided into names where the homosemic alternates are in one and the same language and names whose etymons are from different languages.

A. Names Involving the Roots *dbr/śwh*

In the modern period some of the earliest proposals were those of A. Wieder and of G. Mendenhall. Wieder (1965: 161–62) saw such an equation in the "gloss" in Gen 14:17 (*ᶜēmeq šāwēh hûᵓ ᶜēmeq hammelek*), " 'The Valley of the Ruler' which is 'The Valley of the King,' " with *šāwēh* as the older and residual NW Semitic word for "ruler" (cognate with Ug *t̠wy* "to rule, to govern," used in parallelism with *dbr* "to lead" in Ug (see UT 3: 641, 2662). Though Wieder's is a valid conceptualization, matters are further complicated by the fact that *šāwēh* itself is a Heb lexeme for "(level) plain" and is a component in the place name *Šāwēh Qiryātāyim,* probably "The Plain of the Two-Cities." De Moor (1973: 89–93) launched a severe attack on Wieder's procedures and, while some of his points are very well taken, it is always possible that Heb preserves in place names two different nouns *šāwēh*[1] "ruler" and *šāwēh*[2] "level plain," with the initial letter *šin* corresponding etymologically to Sem **t̠* and **š* respectively.

Mendenhall (1973: 76, 163, n. 60), with reference to the "gloss" in Josh 15:15 (= Judg 1:11), (*wĕšēm dĕbīr lĕpānîm qiryat sēpēr*) "And the name of Debir was formerly 'City-of-the-Scribe,' " read *sōpēr* "scribe" rather than MT *sēpēr* "book," and ascribed the meaning "marshall, ruler" to *sōpēr,* saying that *dĕbir* represented Hit *dabara* "lord, governor," and that the former was a translation of the latter (see Arbeitman 1988: 10–11, 43). Where Mendenhall appealed to NW Semitic for his analysis, some 1500 years earlier the Rabbis of the Bab. Talm. looked to the east for their interpretation. They explained (*ᶜAbod. Zar.* 2.4b.d) the biblical passage as being based on the semantic equivalency of Aram *sprᵓ* ("scribe," traditionally vocalized as "book") with Pers *dbyr* "scribe." Arbeitman (1988) devotes the entirety of his study to an examination of these two proposals, which employ identical methodology, and of a third proposal: that the equation of the two cited names may involve NW Semitic *spr* and NW Semitic *dbr,* both meaning "to lead".

B. Names Involving the Root *ṣph*

Gen 31:44–53 describes the naming of the site where Laban and Jacob made their covenant. Three names were given to this place, names which all have the covenant as their referent: *Galᶜēd, Yĕgar Śāhădûtāᵓ* and *Miṣpâ.* Arbeitman (1981: 999) suggests that the first two names are mutual translations in Heb and Aram respectively ("Cairn-of-Witness [of the covenant by the respective deities]") with the third name being Heb for "Look-Out[-Point]"/"Observation[-Place]"/"view"/"scope." This passage is the only explicit statement of (a) meaning identity and (b) such identity being in the respective languages of the parties, made in the Bible.

Astour (1975: 319–21), basing his position on (a) Eissfeldt's identification of Mt. *Ṣpn,* Baal *Ṣapun,* etc., with the Classical Mt. *Kasion* (present-day Jebel Aqraᶜ) and (b) Eissfeldt's etymological derivation of Mt. *Ṣpn* from the NW Semitic verb *ṣph* (Heb *ṣāpāh* "to look out"), concludes (p. 321): "Moreover, the same meaning is quite conceivable for its other name," i.e., Mt. *Ha-zi/Ha-az-zi* in cuneiform, *ḫz* in Ug alphabetic spelling. This alternate name is the source of what is represented in classical Mt. *Kasion.* Astour asserts that *Ḫaz(z)i* is from the Semitic root **ḥzy* (Heb *ḥāzāh* "to see").

Grave (1980: 221–26) provides an exhaustive survey of a number of proposals, each of which derives Mt. *Ṣpn* from a different Semitic root. At the same time she discusses other etymological proposals for the name *Ḫaz(z)i.* She then takes up Astour's proposal and suggests that *Ḫazzi* might have been taken as either a passive or a stative formation of *ḥzy* and understood as "(a mountain that is) seen/being sighted" and then this "oronym could have been 'glossed' by means of *Ṣpn* . . . because it was a beacon that was seen/sighted from the sea." In this theory, the "glossing" is based on a folk understanding of the old name *Ḫazzi* (probably of non-Semitic origin). She concludes, however, that the oronym *Ṣpn (Ṣapānu)* does derive from the root *ṣph,* but with a meaning "clearing/visibility" or, preferably, "the Clearer (of the sky and air)," and that the Modern Ar name *Jebel al-Aqraᶜ,* "the Bald Mountain," may refer to the same phenomenon, the mountain "as having been shorn/cleared together with the sky by the northwind . . ." (see also ZAPHON, MOUNT).

Josephus (*Ant* 11.329) remarks concerning Mt. Scopus: "At a certain place called *Saphein.* And this name, rendered into the Greek tongue, signifies *Skopos.*" As noted in the translation and notes by Marcus (Loeb ed.), Josephus' *Saphein* represents Aram *ṣāpîn,* which corresponds to Heb *ṣōpîm. Skopos* (Scopus) is the Gk word for "lookout," while the Heb/Aram words mean "(Mount-of) the Lookouts" or "Those Who Observe." Likewise, Philo of Byblos renders the Phoenician name *Zōphasēmin* by Gk *ouranoû katoptai* (see GesB for suggested meanings). Both the Phoen and Gk mean "those who contemplate the heavens" (as *LSJM,* 929 renders). Josephus wrote the Hebrew words, and Philo of Byblos Phoenician terms, in Greek letters. The current Hebrew form *(Har) haṣṣōfîm* first occurs in the Mishna (*EncJud* 16: 1191–92).

Returning to Gen 31:44–53, throughout this pericope both the pair of "witness" names given in Heb and Aram and the single Heb "lookout" name are repeatedly supplied with etiological explications in the text-intrinsic glosses. In the renderings in the LXX the explications of the "Witness" names work because both the names and the "cause" are rendered with a single Gk root. The "lookout" name fails to work because Gk has several suppletive roots for "see/observe"; and while the site is rendered *horasis* ("Seeing/sight"), the explanatory verbal phrase "May (God) look at us" is rendered in Gk with the root *id-* (in the compound *ep-idoi*). As opposed to the glosses embedded in the texts, which can be called "intrinsic glosses," the translations of place-names are best considered as "extrinsic glosses."

The rest of the occurrences of a set of nouns, *miṣpeh*¹, *miṣpeh*², and *miṣpâ* (all three spelled in Heb *mṣph*) are to be analyzed as follows. The noun *miṣpeh*¹ occurs as a common noun only twice in the Heb Bible, (2 Chr 20:24; Isa 21:8), translated "watchtower" (RSV). In both loci the LXX renders *skopia* "lookout place" as it does in Isa 41:9 (no equivalent in the Heb) and in Sir 37:14. Of the occurrences of *miṣpeh*², the proper noun MIZPEH, a place name, the LXX renders one of them, Judg 11:29, as a common noun: Heb *miṣpeh gilʿād* is translated by *skopian Galaad,* "watchtower of Gilead." Among the numerous places called *Miṣpâ,* the LXX renders 1 Kgs (LXX 3 Kgdms) 15:22 *gebaʿ binyāmīn wĕʾet hammiṣpâ* (RSV: "Geba of Benjamin and Mizpah") by *bounon Beniamin kai tēn skopian* "mound of Benjamin and the watchtower." Similarly LXX renders Hos 5:1 *kî paḥ hĕyîtem lĕmiṣpâ* (RSV: "for you have been a snare at Mizpah") by *hoti pagis egenēthēte tę skopia* "because you were a snare to the watchtower."

The *Qal* masc. pl. act. part. of the verbal root *(ṣph)* of the three nouns of this subsection, *ṣōpîm,* occurs as part of a place name in Num 23:14: *śĕdê ṣōpîm (ʾel rōʾš happisgâ)* (RSV: "the field of Zophim, to the top of Pisgah") and is rendered by the LXX as *eis agru skopian epi koryphēn lelaxeumenu* ("to the watchtower of the field, hewn upon the peak"). Here the note given in the NJPSV displays how the choice of retaining the Heb name in transliteration offers the benefit of recognition of the place name but also the deficit of losing any etiological intention. In contrast to the RSV rendition of the place name Zophim in Num 23:14, the much more effective NJPSV offers in the text: "Sedeh-Zophim, on the summit of Pisgah." NJPSV's alternate rendering, "to the Field of (the) Lookout Point," approximates LXX (with reversal of "field" and "watchtower/Lookout Point").

Similarly, in Gen 31:47–48 the NJPSV gives the text (with marginal notes, here provided immediately following in parentheses) "Laban named it Yegar-Sahadutha (Aramaic for *'the mound [or, stone-heap] of witness'*), but Jacob named it Gal-ed (Heb for *'the mound [or, stone-heap] of witness,'* reflecting the name Gilead, v 23)." The translation continues (Gen 31:49): "Also Mizpah, because he said, "May the LORD watch (Heb *yiṣeph,* associated with Mizpah) between you and me." The comparable translation (and notes) in the RSV goes: "Laban called it Jegar Sahadutha (in Aramaic *The heap of witness*), but Jacob called it Galeed (in Heb *The heap of witness*)"; RSV continues, "And . . . Mizpah (that is, *Watchpost*), for he said, 'The LORD watch between you and me.' " The total translation is also, as we saw in the LXX rendition of Num 23:14, a justified path for comprehension.

As noted above, the LXX renders the word *miṣpeh* in this locus by *horasis;* it renders the two other names similarly: *kai ekalesen auton Laban Bounos tēs martyrias, Iakōb de ekalesen auton Bunos martys* ("And Laban called it 'Mound-of-Testimony/Witnessing' but Jacob called it 'Mound-Witness' "; cf. Speiser *Genesis* AB, 243, 248–49). The use of *Bounos* in the LXX for rendering both Heb *gal* and Aram *yĕgar* here is like the use of the same word to translate Heb *gebaʿ* in 3 Kgdms 15:22.

Another school considers the name-giving pericope in Genesis 31 to be entirely etiological, arising from the creation of stories to explain by folk etymology already existing names, ultimately from different and not always comprehensible sources. In this scenario, certainly the *mṣph* names are common enough. Speiser (*Genesis* AB, 248–49) deems the name *Galʿēd* as such an etiological "event" explicating the toponym *Gilʿād,* the theater of the conflict and covenant with the mound or cairn *(gal)* of the Witness *(ʿēd)* and thus supplying the basis for the regional name Gilead. This part of the etiology is from the "J source," while the alternate Mizpah (Heb *miṣpâ*), a similar connection to the stele (Heb *maṣṣēbâ*) set up, derives from the "*E* source."

A modern lexicon (KB) states that *Galʿēd* is actually only such an etymologically etiological product, created for the tale by revocalization of *Gilʿād* to *Galʿēd* (same Heb consonantal text: *glʿd*) and that the "true" derivation of *Gilʿād* is a root **gʿd,* known from Arab *jaʿuda* "to be wrinkled/lined" (said of cheeks), with a phonetic development **giʿʿad* > *gilʿad* (an *-lʿ-* medial cluster replacing the original geminate *-ʿʿ-). (Similarly, they explain the toponym *Gilbōaʿ* as deriving from **gibbōaʿ* and thus being a "comparative form" to *Gebaʿ,* with a meaning something like "the Hillier Hill." W. Borée had already noted (1930: 34n. 1) the absence of any analogy for this presumed "dissimilation" of geminate *-b-* to *-lb-*.)

C. Names Involving the Root *ḥbr*

Arbeitman (1981), basing himself on (a) Mendenhall's methodology, (b) the covenantal relationship of the three name-giving events in Genesis 31, and (c) Borée's analysis, proposed interpreting the ancient triad of names, *Ḥebrôn, (Qiryat) ʾarbaʿ,* and *Mamrēʾ* in a manner analogous to the interpretation of the three names just noted. Each member of this triad of place names has reference to a covenant or treaty occurrence at that site. This treaty is noted in the Bible, though not in any way so explicitly as the treaty detailed in Genesis 31. It is rather with reference to the implicitly understood treaty between Abraham and Ephron in which the former obtains a burial cave from the Hittites. The name *Ḥebr-ôn* is to be explained as "the One-of [= Place-of-] the [Treaty-]-Ally" in Heb, and *ʾarbaʿ* as an exact Hittite translation (Hit *ara-* "friend, ally"); the third toponym, *mamrēʾ,* fits in as representing Hit *miu-mar* "friendship." The entire triad of names as applied to one and the same place is displayed ineluctably in Gen 35:27: "And Jacob came to Isaac, his father, at *Mamrēʾ, Qiryat ha-ʾarbaʿ,* which [is] *Ḥebrôn* where Abraham sojourned and Isaac [too]." Yet some other scholars (e.g., Mazar [Maisler] 1949) have long believed *Mamrēʾ* to be a section of the *Ḥebrôn* complex, nearby, but separate. This perspective seems to be inescapably tied in with their implicit acceptance of the midrashic (but nonbiblical) explication of *qiryat ʾarbaʿ* as "City-of-the-Four-Quarters/Sections" (Arbeitman 1981: 895–900).

Finally, on the basis of Borée (1930: 58 n. 6), Arbeitman perceived the Arabic name of the city, *el-Khalîl* (traditionally considered as a reference to Abraham as "the Friend of the Merciful" [*ḫalîl ar-raḥmān*]) to fit with the Hit name triad when allowance is made for its original application to Abraham as the Friend (Heb *ḥābēr,* Hit *ara-* [and *miu-*]) of Ephron (Arbeitman 1981: 955–98).

D. Names Involving the Elements *tad-/pal-*

M. O'Connor (1988: 235–54) examines the alternate names of *Tadmōr,* the earlier attested name and the one used in Semitic language sources, together with the later attested name, used in Classical sources, *Palmyra.*

O'Connor notes that the traditional folk etymology, wherein *"Tadmōr"* is deemed to be a derivative from the Semitic word for "date," *tāmār,* while the later attested name, *Palmyra,* is simply a translation/calque on this in Latin, where *palma* "the stretched out 'palm' of the hand" has the secondary meaning "palm tree," runs up against several vitiating factors, both phonological and chronological (1988: 235). He then suggests that both *Tadmōr* and *Palmyra,* far from being respectively Semitic and "classical" (i.e., Latin) names, are both names left by the important Hurrian element of the population in Syria. Following the methodological framework established by Arbeitman (O'Connor 1988: 251 n. 25) and adding a wide survey of various other cities with multiple names, he concludes that the alternate Hurrian names offer a semantically unimpeachable sense when the second syllable of *Tad-mōr* and *Pal-myr(-a)* is separated as representing the well-documented Hurrian suffix *-mVr* (probably /mar/), the meaning of which is unknown, but not likely to be a suffix forming abstract nouns (O'Connor 1988: 249 n. 18). The bases that then remain, *tad-* and *pal-,* are of the semantic sphere of covenant terminology, "to love" and "to know" (O'Connor 1988: 238).

In this last regard they resemble the names in Genesis 31 as well as the triad of ancient names involving *ḥbr.*

E. Dān and Others: Arabic Translations

Rainey (1978: 9) notes: "Examples of pure translation from Heb to Arab are rare. One certain case is that of *Tell el-Qâḍī:* 'the mound of the judge,' representing Dān: 'He (who) judges.' Another may possibly be *Khirbet el-waṭn:* 'Ruin of the homeland,' if its identification with *Môlādāh* should be substantiated." Arabic *qâḍî* translates NW Semitic *dān* in either its "real" meaning or its folk etymological understanding by the Hebrews as "judge." Its actual origin lies with one of the Sea Peoples, the people of (A)daniya in Anatolia, as maintained by Arbeitman and Rendsburg (1981: 147–57). (With reference to the root *ṣph/ṣfw,* examined in Section B above, Rainey [1983: 10] provides a necessary word of caution against using vague semantic similarities for the purpose of site identification: "Many suggestions have been made for the identification of Libnah. One of the most frequent was Tell eṣ-Ṣâfī; but the name of that tell means 'bright, shining' and not 'white.' " For further discussion of place names, see also TOPONYMS AND TOPONYMY.

Bibliography

Arbeitman, Y. L. 1981. The Hittite is Thy Mother: An Anatolian Approach to Genesis 23 (Ex Indo-Europea Lux). Pp. 889–1026 in *Bono Homini Donum: Essays in Historical Linguistics in Memory of J. Alexander Kerns,* ed. Y. L. Arbeitman and A. R. Bomhard. Amsterdam.

———. 1988. Iranian "Scribe," Anatolian "Ruler," or Neither: A City's Rare Chances for "Leadership." Pp. 1–101 in *FUCUS: A Semitic/Afrasian Gathering in Remembrance of Albert Ehrman,* ed. Y. L. Arbeitman. Amsterdam.

Arbeitman, Y. L., and Rendsburg, G. A. 1981. Adana Revisited: 30 Years Later. *ArOr* 49: 145–57.

Astour, M. C. 1975. Place Names. Pp. 249–369 in *Ras Shamra Parallels II,* ed. L. R. Fisher. AnOr 50. Rome.

Borée, W. 1930. *Die alten Ortsnamen Palästinas.* Repr. Hildesheim, 1968.

Grave, C. 1980. The Etymology of Northwest Semitic *ṣapānu. UF* 12: 221–26.

Mazar [Maisler], B. 1949. Qiryat ʾarbaʿ hîʾ Ḥebrôn, in *Sepher Derenburg.* Jerusalem.

Mendenhall, G. M. 1973. *The Tenth Generation.* Baltimore.

Moor, J. C. de. 1973. Ugaritic Lexicography. Pp. 61–102 in *Studies on Semitic Lexicography,* ed. P. Fronzaroli. Quaderni di Semitistica 2. Florence.

O'Connor, M. P. 1988. The Etymology of Tadmor and Palmyra. Pp. 235–54 in *A Linguistic Happening in Memory of Ben Schwartz: Studies in Anatolian, Italic, and Other Indo-European Languages,* ed. Y. L. Arbeitman. Louvain-la-Neuve.

Rainey, A. F. 1978. The Toponymics of Eretz-Israel. *BASOR* 231: 1–17.

———. 1983. The Biblical Shephela of Judah. *BASOR* 251: 1–22.

Wieder, A. A. 1965. Ugaritic-Hebrew Lexicological Notes. *JBL* 84: 160–64.

YÖEL L. ARBEITMAN

CITY OF DAVID.

See DAVID, CITY OF (PLACE).

CITY OF DAVID, STAIRS OF.

See STAIRS OF THE CITY OF DAVID.

CITY OF PALM TREES

(PLACE) [Heb *ʿîr hattĕmārîm*]. An epithet for the city of JERICHO. From the top of Pisgah of Mount Nebo, Moses was shown the land to be possessed, "from the valley of Jericho, the city of palm trees, as far as Zoar" (Deut 34:3). From this text we can assume that Jericho was already called "the city of palm trees" before its destruction by Joshua. The name "City of Palm Trees" was probably given to this city because of the abundance of date-palm trees *(Phoenix dactylifera)* watered by the perennial spring *ʿain es-Sulṭan* located just east of the OT Jericho mound (Tell es-Sulṭan).

The name "City of Palm Trees" can be paraphrased as: "the city near which date-palm trees abound." S. Cohen (*IDB* 1: 638) thought that this term was used for a place which was a part of Jericho, and that after the destruction of the city by Joshua the term probably referred to the "groves of palm trees that flourished nearby." It is inconceivable, however, that the palm grove itself was called by this name because we do not have any reason to call a grove a "city." Rather, the destroyed city must have retained its names Jericho and "City of Palm Trees" which also included the surrounding area.

The Hebrew word for the date-palm is *tāmār* "erect," like a column or post *(tōmer).* This tree has no branches but its top is a large circle of palmate leaves. (RSV's use of the English word "branches" with respect to the palm tree [e.g., Lev 23:40; John 12:13] is imprecise.) So the Heb *tāmār* "palm tree" meant "erect tree" and symbolically represented a righteous man (Ps 92:12). The shape of the palm tree at a distance resembles a woman standing; therefore, in Cant 7:17, a nobleman's daughter is likened to the palm tree: "Your stature is [RSV marg.] like a palm tree, and your breasts are like its clusters."

Since this tree bears abundant sweet dates, the date-palm was a desirable fruit tree. The date-palm can reach a height of about 20 meters; its root is strong and fibrous so that the leaves are always full of sap and very green (Ps 92:14). The shape of the palm tree is graceful. Representations of date-palms ornamented Solomon's temple (1 Kgs 6:29). These excellent qualities may be the reasons why Tamar, "date-palm," was used as the name of some women in the Bible.

Many sorts of palm trees, different from each other in taste and name, were watered by the spring at Jericho. The better types yielded an excellent kind of honey when they were pressed, not much inferior in sweetness to the honey of bees. The Heb *náḥal,* generally translated "valley," may also have been the name of one of the excellent date-palms (Num 24:6; Cant 6:11). Also *ʾêl* "which you have desired" (Isa 1:29) may be a fruit tree like the date-palm. A place south of Judah near the Dead Sea had the name Tamar, "Date-palm" (Ezek 47:19; 48:28) which may be another name for En-gedi, where many date-palm trees now grow, though it must be differentiated from the "City of Date-palms."

Bibliography

United Bible Societies. 1972. Palm. Pp. 160–62 in *Fauna and Flora of the Bible*. London.

YOSHITAKA KOBAYASHI

CITY OF SALT (PLACE) [Heb *ʿîr hammelaḥ*]. A Judean city near the Dead Sea mentioned once in the OT (Josh 15:62). Identification of the site is problematic, and the problems are reflected in the variant readings of LXX mss. LXX[A] agrees with MT in reading *poleis halōn* "City of Salt," whereas LXX[B] reads *poleis Sadōm* "city of Sodom." Sodom has commonly been thought to lie E of the Dead Sea. Conder identified the City of Salt with Tell el-Milḥ (M.R. 152069). The situation of the tell at the upper end of the Valley of Salt (Wâdī el-Milḥ; 2 Sam 8:13; 2 Kgs 14:7) E-SE of Beer-sheba makes this identification attractive, but Tell el-Milḥ has more recently been identified as Moladah (Gk *Malatha*).

There are six cities listed in Josh 15:61–62 as lying "in the wilderness" later known as the wilderness of Judah: (v 61) Beth-arabah, Middin, Secacah, (v 62) Nibshan, the City of Salt, and En-gedi. Of these, the only firmly identified site is En-gedi (the Hazazon-tamar of 2 Chr 20:2) on the W side of the Dead Sea 28 miles S of Jericho. The sites of Middin (Khirbet Abu Tabaq), Secacah (Khirbet es-Samrah) and Nibshan (Khirbet el-Maqari) have suggested locations in the Valley of Achor (although Bar-Adon [1977: 22–23] is among those who disagree with these identifications).

The City of Salt is now commonly identified with Khirbet Qumran (M.R. 193127; Noth *Joshua* HAT[2], 100), although Kallai (*HGB,* 396 n. 143) prefers to identify Qumran with Secacah. Others suggest Ain el-Ghuweir further S as the City of Salt. Qumran is just E of the Valley of Achor, about 14 miles from Jerusalem (on the site, see QUMRAN, KHIRBET).

Bibliography

Bar-Adon, P. 1977. Another Settlement of the Judean Desert Sect at En el-Ghuweir on the Shores of the Dead Sea. *BASOR* 227: 1–25.

HENRY O. THOMPSON

CITY OF THE SUN (PLACE). See SUN, CITY OF THE (PLACE).

CLAMS. See ZOOLOGY.

CLAN. See FAMILY.

CLAROMONTANUS. See CODEX CLAROMONTANUS.

CLAUDIA (PERSON) [Gk *Klaudia*]. A Christian woman who was in contact with Paul during the imprisonment referred to in the Pastorals, probably in Rome, although Caesarea has also been defended (2 Tim 4:21). Claudia, along with Pudens and Linus after whom she is mentioned, sent greetings to Timothy. Her name suggests that she belonged to the imperial household, perhaps as a slave, or possibly as a member of the *gens Claudia.* The *Apos. Con.* 7.46 note that a certain Linus, the son or husband of Claudia (Gk *Linos ho Klaudias*), was the first bishop of Rome after the death of the apostles. Whether this Claudia and Linus are to be identified with those mentioned in 2 Timothy is not certain, although not impossible.

The supposition that the Claudia and Linus of 2 Timothy were mother and son has led some to assume that she was therefore the wife of Pudens. But this leads to the problem of explaining why in the text of 2 Tim 4:21 Linus is named between them. Redlich (1913: 222) has argued that if Claudia was the wife (or sister) of Pudens, she would have been mentioned before Linus and along with Pudens. He concludes that "if the order of names suggests anything, it points to a closer relationship between Linus and Claudia than between Pudens and Claudia." Nevertheless, those who suppose Claudia to have been married to Pudens draw the further inference that the two were identical to a couple with the same names mentioned by the Roman poet Martial (*Epigrams* 4.13) and to Roman couples named in British (*CIL* VII.17) and Roman (*CIL* VI.15.066) inscriptions. But since these names were common, there is no persuasive support for the linking. See a fuller discussion under PUDENS (PERSON).

Bibliography

Redlich, E. B. 1913. *S. Paul and His Companions*. London.

FLORENCE MORGAN GILLMAN

CLAUDIUS (EMPEROR). Claudius (Tiberius Claudius Nero Germanicus), younger son of the elder Drusus and Antonia was born at Lyons on 1 August 10 B.C. and became emperor after the assassination of his nephew, Gaius, on 24 January A.D. 41. Although not a member of the Julian family by birth or by adoption (unlike his three predecessors), he was, on his father's side, the grandson of Livia (who married Augustus after the divorce of her first husband, Claudius' grandfather) and, on his mother's side, grandson of Mark Antony and also of Augustus' sister. He suffered throughout his life from some physical disability (possibly a form of paralysis) and was an object of scorn to many members of his family. "His grandmother Augusta [i.e. Livia] always treated him with the utmost contempt" (Suetonius *Divus Claudius* 3.2); to his mother, he was a "monster" (ibid.). Under the emperors Augustus and Tiberius, he held no public office, even though he was in his mid-forties at the time of Tiberius' death. Augustus had been wary of the public's reaction to his seemingly eccentric behavior—"they might ridicule both him and us" (Suet. *Claud.* 4.2). His first significant office was the "suffect" consulship of July 37: even this was a lesser award since members of the imperial family always received the "ordinary" consulship, i.e., they were the first consuls of the year, serving in January and replaced some months later by "suffect" consuls.

His accession was far from normal. Found hiding in the palace behind a curtain, he was dragged off by the praetorians and proclaimed emperor, while the senators debated whether the imperial "system" should be abolished and the Republic restored. He soon established his ascendancy, however, though his relationship with the senate was never good. Conspiracies against him were many, starting in 42 with that of L. Arruntius Camillus Scribonianus. The full extent of the opposition that existed (or that he believed existed) against him may be assessed by Suetonius' claim (*Claud.* 29.2) that in his reign thirty-five senators and more than 300 knights were executed.

Despite the hostile literary tradition belittling him and accusing him of succumbing to the power and influence of his wives and freedmen, at least some of the substantial administrative achievements of his reign were due to his personal intervention. His speech urging the admission to senatorial status of a number of Gallic leaders has survived: the irrelevancies and awkward expressions must be his. His intentions, though, were sound and consistent with his general belief in the importance of Romanizing the empire—note the new cities he created and the colonies established from Britain to Syria. Of some importance, too, were his efforts to improve Rome's grain supply by building a new harbor (*Dio Cass.* 60.11.1–5) and by establishing greater control over the process of distribution. As well, he was responsible for substantial improvements in roads and aqueducts in both Italy and the provinces. He was extremely interested in legal matters, from the introduction of measures aimed at greater humanity towards slaves to attempts at speeding up the judicial process. However, his preference for trials before the emperor and his advisors (*intra cubiculum*), rather than before the senate, did nothing to lessen his unpopularity with that body. His most powerful ministers included the former slaves Narcissus (responsible for the official correspondence), Pallas (financial minister), and Callistus (in charge of petitions). But the extent of their influence is impossible to assess, especially in view of the sources' hostility not only to Claudius himself but also to former slaves in general. There is no reason to doubt their efficiency; on the other hand, the argument that, through them, Claudius extended and centralized the bureaucracy ought to be regarded with extreme caution, because the evidence for it is slight.

Claudius was a scholar. In his youth, he was encouraged by the historian Livy: later he composed an autobiography, a defense of Cicero, accounts of the Carthaginians and the Etruscans, a history of Augustus' principate from the end of the Civil wars and, as well, tried to have three letters added to the alphabet. His foreign policy was markedly more aggressive than that of his predecessors. A revolt in Mauretania was settled and two new provinces were created there. Thrace became a province in 46. Most expansion, however, occurred in Britain, where Roman influence had been confined to the south-eastern quarter. Claudius' massive invasion force of four legions moved rapidly and before long, the Fosse Way from Exeter to Lincoln marked the limit of their progress. Britain was now a province.

His attitude to the Jews was more enlightened than Gaius'. He posted an edict guaranteeing Jews throughout the empire the right to practice their religion "without let or hindrance" (Josephus, *Ant* 19.290). In Alexandria, where Gaius' policy had led to serious unrest, an edict of A.D. 41 (*British Museum Papyrus* 1912) reprimanded both the Greek and Jewish rioters, urging the former to "act kindly towards the Jews." The reaction of the Greeks in that city is presumably represented in a collection of papyrus documents now known as "The Acts of the Pagan Martyrs" which purport to give, *inter alia,* details of the trials in Rome of Greek nationalist leaders: In tone, they are violently anti-Roman and, at the same time, hostile to the Jews. Later, though, he expelled the Jews from Rome "for constant rioting at the instigation of Chrestus" (Suet. *Claud.* 25.4), where at least the reference to Christianity is unambiguous; the emperor's action is confirmed by an incident recorded in Acts 18:2, where two Jews, Aquila and Priscilla, expelled from Rome, came to Corinth and later met Paul. Finally an inscription said to come from Nazareth records a decree (possibly of Claudius) on the violation of tombs: scholars since 1930 have debated the possibility of an allusion to the burial and resurrection of Christ.

Of his four wives, the last two are the best known. At the time of his accession, he was married to Valeria Messalina: their children were Octavia (whom Nero later married) and Britannicus (whom Nero later poisoned). After Messalina was put to death in 48 following her public "marriage" to Silius, Claudius married his niece Agrippina who already had a son, Domitius Ahenobarbus, some four years older than Britannicus: shortly after the marriage, Domitius was adopted by Claudius and named Nero Claudius Drusus Germanicus Caesar, though his young stepbrother persisted, much to Nero's annoyance, in calling him "Ahenobarbus" (Suet. *Nero* 7). Greater honors came to Nero and greater power to Agrippina, but, fearing that Claudius might regret his promotion of Nero, Agrippina had him poisoned on 13 October 54, thereby ensuring her son's accession. Scholars have attempted to rehabilitate Claudius or at least to moderate the uniformly hostile picture painted by the ancient sources. Yet he remains a paternalistic autocrat and a pedantic administrator. The influence exerted over him by his wives and former slaves has been exaggerated: only in his last years did Agrippina's power become excessive.

Bibliography

Boer, W. den. 1957. Claudius. *RAC* 3: 179–81.

Garzetti, A. 1974. *From Tiberius to the Antonines: A History of the Roman Empire A.D. 14–192.* London.

Levick, B. M. 1978. Antiquarian or Revolutionary? Claudius Caesar's Conception of his Principate. *AJP* 99: 79–105.

Momigliano, A. 1934. *Claudius: The Emperor and his Achievement.* Oxford.

Musurillo, H. A. 1954. *The Acts of the Pagan Martyrs: Acta Alexandrinorum.* Oxford.

Scramuzza, V. M. 1940. *Claudius.* Cambridge.

Weaver, P. R. C. 1979. Misplaced Officials. *Antichthon* 13: 70–102.

BRIAN W. JONES

CLAUDIUS LYSIAS (PERSON) [Gk *Klaudios Lysias*]. A chiliarch and tribune of a cohort of Roman troops in Jerusalem. He was not a Latin, as his Greek cognomen Lysias indicates. Perhaps he took on the nomen Claudius when he purchased his emancipation from slavery and became a Roman citizen while Claudius was Emperor (Acts 22:28). Claudius and his cohort were quartered in the tower of Antonia, northwest of the Temple and connected to the Court of the Gentiles.

Claudius arrested Paul during his struggle with the Jews in Jerusalem (Acts 21:30–23:35). When Paul's life was threatened by the Jews in the Temple, Claudius had Paul bound and carried to the tower of Antonia, thinking initially that Paul was the Egyptian sicarii who had led a recent rebellion against Jerusalem (21:38; cf. Jos. *JW* 2.261–63). See EGYPTIAN, THE (PERSON). When he commanded that Paul be examined by scourging to find out why the Jews made such an outcry against him, he was deterred by Paul's claim to Roman citizenship (22:24–29). Claudius later had Paul examined before the Sanhedrin (22:30–23:10). Informed by Paul's nephew of a conspiracy against Paul's life (23:12–22), Claudius dispatched a full military escort at night to take Paul from Jerusalem to Caesarea, where Felix, the procurator of Judea, was stationed (23:23–35). He sent along a letter to Felix outlining his dealings with Paul (23:26–30). The only reference to his name occurs in the heading of this letter (23:26).

JOANN FORD WATSON

CLAY. See POTTERY (TECHNOLOGY).

CLEAN. See UNCLEAN AND CLEAN.

CLEMENT (PERSON) [Gk *Klementos*]. A Philippian Christian and one of Paul's fellow workers whose names are recorded in the "book of life" (Phil 4:3). The Latin name, Clement, may indicate that his family was among the original, prospering colonists in the Roman colony of Philippi. Clement is named by Paul, along with Euodia, Syntyche and "true yokefellow," as having struggled side by side with him to preach the gospel. "To struggle side by side" (Gk *sunathleō*) is an image taken from the games and suggests that Clement was a "fellow athlete" striving together with Paul in the united effort of preaching the gospel and sharing the suffering involved in that endeavor. Clement is also described as being among those whose names are in the book of life. Just as in the OT reference is made to a "book of life," as a kind of registry of God's chosen people (Exod 32:32–33; Ps 69:28; 139:16; cf. this expression in apocalyptic literature: Dan 12:1; Rev 3:5,20; *1 En* 47:3; and in Qumran: 1QM 12:2), and just as in cities like Philippi there must have been a civic registry that included all the names of citizens, so also, as Paul sees it, the heavenly commonwealth (cf. Phil 3:20) has inscribed in God's book of life the names of believers. Although the phrase "names in the book of life" can indicate in apocalyptic literature that those people so designated have already died, such an assumption regarding Clement is improbable.

Tradition from the ancient church, specifically Origen (*Jo.* 6.36), has identified this Clement from Philippi with Clement of Rome, the author of *1 Clem.* (ca. 96), a view then transmitted by Eusebius (*Hist. Eccl.* 3.4.9) and taken up by later writers. Irenaeus, writing before Origen, had said that Clement of Rome, whom he lists as the third in the list of Peter's successors, was a disciple of the Apostles (*Haer.* 3.3.3), but he did not link him explicitly with the Philippian Clement. Nor did Tertullian, who wrote that Clement of Rome was consecrated by Peter (*De praescr. haeret.* 32), mention any connection between Clement and Paul. It is generally judged, in spite of Origen's statement, that an identification of the Philippian Clement with the Clement of Rome is unlikely because of the geographical and chronological distance that separates these two (Lightfoot 1888: 168–71). Also, Clement was a common name in the 1st century.

Bibliography

Lightfoot, J.B. 1888. *Saint Paul's Epistle to the Philippians.* London.

JOHN GILLMAN

CLEMENT, FIRST EPISTLE OF. An epistle sent in the name of the Apostolic Father Clement from the church in Rome to Corinth late in the 1st century C.E.

A. Tradition and Influence
B. Principal Sources
C. Greco-Roman Context
D. Literary Form
E. Occasion and Purpose
F. Authorship
G. Date

A. Tradition and Influence

The so-called *First Epistle of Clement* was an authority in the early church. For a time, it was part of the canon of the churches of Egypt and Syria. Three of the manuscripts in which it is found contain portions of the Christian Scriptures: Codex Alexandrinus (5th century), a Coptic papyrus codex (5th century), and a Syriac NT (12th century). It appears alongside the Didache in Codex Hierosolymitanus. The Latin translation is to be assigned, on linguistic grounds, to the 2d century (Mohrmann 1949). In ca. 150 A.D., Dionysius, bishop of Corinth, wrote to his Roman counterpart, Soter, that the epistle sent by Clement was still being read from time to time in the Christian assembly (Eusebius *Hist. Eccl.* 4.23). Eusebius attests that the letter was read in the worship services of many churches, in the days of old and in his own time (*Hist. Eccl.* 3.16). Indeed, the letter seems to have been one of the best known writings in the early church. Polycarp makes full, if tacit, use of the work (Lightfoot 1890:1.149–52). Irenaeus praises the letter and summarizes its first chapters (*Haer.* 3.3.3). The epistle is frequently utilized by Clement of Alexandria, who knew the work when he wrote his *Paedagogus* (1.91.2), and filled the *Stromata* with explicit quotations (Grant 1965:5–6). The high esteem in which the letter was held contributed, no doubt, to the legend of its reputed author, to whom anonymous works were subsequently attributed (*2 Clement,* two epistles *De virginitate,* the *Apostolic Constitutions*), making it possible for him to become the hero of a 3d-century romance, the Pseudo-Clementine *Homilies* and *Recognitions,* and glorifying him with a posthumous martyrdom (*Martyrium Clementis,* 4th century). The reading of the work in the worship assembly, the frequent citations in the writings of the fathers, the early translation of the work into three languages, the canonical status which the work sometimes enjoyed—these are so many testimonies to the authority of *1 Clement* in the early church. It is a surprising authority, given the fact that the work made no claim to apostolic authorship. How, then, is one to account for the remarkable authority of this text?

An answer to this question might be sought in the usefulness of the work to the orthodox leaders of the church. *1 Clement* was a weapon in the struggle against the gnostics; it was understood and utilized as an antiheretical writing by Hegesippus and Irenaeus (Bauer 1970: 103–4). Moreover, its teaching on the divine origin of church order and the apostolic succession of ecclesial office (40:1–44:6) seemed to lay the foundation for the concept of the monarchical episcopate and the claim of the Roman church to primacy (Ziegler 1958:102–22). But the usefulness of the work was limited in both respects. For, in fact, Clement's orthodoxy left something to be desired, as Photius quickly pointed out (*PG* 103.408A). It is interesting to note, in this connection, that Clement of Alexandria already omits reference to the mythical phoenix of chap. 25 and the virtuous pagans of 54:1–55:2. Those who wished to assert Roman primacy came, in time, to prefer to cite the Pseudo-Clementine *Homilies* and *Recognitions,* or the *Apostolic Constitutions,* since, in fact, *1 Clement* says nothing about the primacy of Rome or the monarchical episcopate (Peterson 1950: 129–30). The Latin version had to alter the wording of 60:4–61:1 to make it clear that it is to the Roman church that God has given authority. As a result, by the late Byzantine era, *1 Clement* had virtually disappeared from sight, until the first edition was published by Patrick Young in 1633.

If one seeks to comprehend the authority of the text, one must go beyond its function in the struggle for orthodoxy, beyond its influence upon the fathers of the church. In fact, one cannot stop short of the text itself. For the letter makes its own claim to authority, which is altogether surprising at this early period. One is immediately struck by the naturalness with which the Roman church intervenes, all unbidden, in the affairs of another congregation, and not in order to urge both parties to seek peace and reconciliation, but to take sides with the deposed presbyters. The author insists upon strong disciplinary measures: the exile of the younger persons who had raised the rebellion (54:1–4; 1:1; 3:3), and the restoration of the old presbyters to office, apparently against the will of the majority (44:1–6). Astonishing instructions, when one remembers that at this time the Roman church possessed neither the means nor the position to effect such an intervention. That the author did not possess the authority he claims is evident from the rhetorical character of the letter: He must persuade by argument and induce by example; that is, it is not yet his to command.

B. Principal Sources

What is the source of the authority which the letter asserts? Where is the presumption of its author grounded? It is clear that the OT is a warrant for Clement (Wrede 1891: 58–107); it is the book of revelations through which God speaks (22:1). It provides instructions for conduct and examples of nurture (1:3; 3:4; 40:4–5; 50:5; 58:2). More importantly, it prophesies, typologically, the order of the church, the offices of bishop and deacon (42:5, citing Isa 60:17). Like Moses before them (43:1–6), the apostles knew that there would be strife over the title of bishop; thus they decreed that, at the death of the bishops, other approved men should succeed to their ministry, with the consent of the whole church (44:1–3). The presbyters are viewed as cultic officers, on the analogy of the OT priests, and thus are fundamentally distinguished from the laity (40–41). Their task consists, in accordance with the priestly example, in the offering of sacrifices and in service to the community (44:3–4).

Christian tradition is a second source of authority. The lives of Peter and Paul are paradigmatic (5). 1 Corinthians is cited repeatedly (24:1; 35:5–6; 37:5–38:2; 47; 49:5–6). The author calls upon the liturgy to give force to his counsel: doxologies (20:12; 43:6; 45:7–8; 58:2; 61:3; 64), trinitarian formulae (46:6; 58:2), and, above all, the solemn liturgical prayer, with which the work concludes (59:1–61:3), situate the advice in the worshipping community and invite its sanction. Moreover, the letter has a homiletical character; the first long section (4–39), especially, makes the impression of a sermon. It has even been suggested that *1 Clement* is composed of old homiletical pieces. One has no difficulty locating the accustomed elements of Christian paraenesis: household codes (1:3; 21:6; 21:8), catalogues of virtues (62:2; 64), and of vices (30:1; 35:5–6). In keeping with its homiletical character, the epistle makes use of rhetoric to a far greater degree than other early Christian writings. The author is more familiar with the figures of ancient prose, more sure in his use of diatribal style, than Paul, or than the author of the Epistle to the Hebrews. One repeatedly encounters rhetorical questions and imperatives, antitheses, anaphora, alliteration, etc. The panegyric on love in chap. 49 draws upon rhetorical models in its attempt to rival 1 Corinthians 13. Like the synagogue preacher and the political orator, Clement makes frequent use of examples to illustrate his admonitions on jealousy and envy (4–8), faith and hospitality (9–12), humility (16–18), repentance (51–53), and voluntary exile (55). The agon motif (in chaps. 5–7) is taken over from the diatribe (Dibelius 1942: 192–99; Ziegler 1958: 24–37). All in all, the work makes the impression of a sermon, permeated with scripture citations and concluded by a solemn liturgical prayer. There can be little doubt that the work was intended, from the very beginning, for reading in the assembly, and perhaps in churches beyond Corinth (Stuiber *RAC* 19: 192).

These are strong warrants—the OT and Christian tradition. But it is not here that the claim of the text is grounded. For it is not the content of the tradition which is normative for Clement, but a value which he imports from without. For example, the author of the epistle asserts that God saved through Noah the living creatures which entered in concord *(homonoia)* into the ark (9:4). What is peculiar about this formulation is that the emphasis falls not on the salvation of Noah and his family, as in 1 Pet 3:20, but on that of the animals who entered the ark in concord. There is no tradition, Jewish or Christian, in which the animals are said to have entered "in concord." The notion was doubtlessly suggested to Clement by the "two by two" of Gen 6:10. Behind the curious statement lies the desire to tell the Corinthians, as Knopf rightly observed, "the animals were peaceable, the humans were not" (1920: 59). But precisely this purpose is foreign to the text. The same motive is apparent in chap. 11, where the sin of Lot's wife is said to consist in a difference of opinion with her husband, in her failure to remain in concord *(homonoia)* with him (11:2); thus she was changed into a pillar of salt to make it clear to all that "those who are double-minded fall under condemnation" (11:2). But nowhere is it said in the biblical text that Lot's wife held different opinions from her husband, that she was not in concord with him. Precisely what Clement views as essential has been imported into the text from without. So it is everywhere that the OT is cited: the specific regulations are not considered normative, but the principle of order as such. And whence this principle?

Nor is Christian tradition the basis for the obedience which Clement demands; it furnishes the occasion, or, at most, the content for instructions which are grounded elsewhere. Clement's account of the trials of Peter and Paul (chap. 5) reflects no knowledge of the actual events of their lives, no acquaintance with the autobiographical portions of Paul's letters; rather, the description is shaped by the image of the philosophic athlete, who enters the moral arena to fight for virtue, whose mythological prototype is Hercules, the Cynic-Stoic hero (Sanders 1943: 30–31).

Similarly, Clement adds to Paul's hymn on love, from which he quotes in 49:5, precisely what he wishes to say: "Love creates no strife, love does all things in concord *(homonoia)*." When Clement takes up Paul's image of the body (from 1 Cor 12:12–27), he gives it a very different significance: Paul meant to illustrate the relationship between members, despite their differences; but by stressing the contrast of hand and foot, and the collaboration of great and small (37:1–5), Clement preaches subordination, in contrast to Paul. Nor does the tradition of Christian worship provide sufficient warrant for the text. Contrast the solution which Clement recommends to the crisis in the Corinthian church, voluntary exile (chap. 54), with the procedure which Paul directs against the sinner of 1 Corinthians 5. Paul insists upon the removal of the man from the community; judgement is to be pronounced in the name of the Lord, and the sinner is to be delivered to Satan. Paul's advice is modelled upon the process for excommunication from the synagogue. Neither the vocabulary nor the process has anything in common with what Clement suggests. Clement's measures are not based upon Jewish or Christian precedents; the norm must be sought elsewhere.

C. Greco-Roman Context

These observations lead one to search for an external warrant for the text. The influence of popular philosophical conceptions, like the moral athlete, with their Cynic-Stoic character, has long been noted (Sanders 1943: 13). One finds, for example, in Clement's discussion of the resurrection, alongside much that is dependent upon Paul (24:1–5, citing 1 Cor 15:20,36–37), an argument drawn from natural history, the story of the phoenix (chap. 25), in a version which is closely akin to that of Pliny (*HN* 10.2) and Pomponius Mela (*Chorogr.* 3.8). Military obedience as an example of social order (37:1–3) was a favorite topos of the Stoics, as well (Sanders 1943: 82–83). The collaboration of great and small was admired by Plato and Euripides, among others (Sanders 1943: 84). Clement's use of the metaphor of the body (chap. 37) has more in common with Menennius Agrippa (in Livy) than with the purposes of the apostle Paul (Sanders 1943: 85–91). In recommending voluntary exile (chap. 54), Clement follows the precedent of Roman politics, in keeping with Stoic teaching (Sanders 1943: 41–50). Clement's conceptions, illustrations, and figures of speech reflect his dependence upon Greco-Roman models.

But it is not merely a matter of diffuse cultural influence. For the order which Clement seeks to create within the church is that recommended by Roman political philosophy; it is the ideal of "peace and concord," visibly established in the Imperium Romanum and vigorously defended by contemporary orators. At the close of the epistle (63:2), Clement describes his work as "an appeal for peace and concord" (Gk *enteuksis peri eirēnēs kai homonoias*), and expresses the desire that the ambassadors who have accompanied the work will be sent back to Rome quickly, in order that they may report the sooner "the peace and concord which we pray for and desire" (65:1). One notices what a large role is played by "peace and concord" in Clement's account of cosmic order in chap. 20: The heavens are subject to God "in peace" (20:1); sun, moon, and stars roll on in their appointed courses, "in concord, without swerving at all" (20:3); seasons change, giving place to one another "in peace" (20:9); the smallest animals conjoin "in concord and peace" (20:10). So Clement concludes: "All these things did the great creator and master of the universe ordain to be in peace and concord" (20:11). If human beings wish to find their place in the cosmos, as citizens worthy of God, they must accomplish "virtuous deeds before him in concord" (21:1). The great liturgical prayer culminates in an appeal for the peace and concord of the earthly rulers (61:1).

By the end of the 1st century of the Roman empire, "peace and concord" had become a formulaic description of the well-being of the state. One encounters the slogan everywhere, in speeches, in histories, in government documents, on inscriptions and coins. So, for example, in Dio Chrysostom's thirty-ninth oration, *On Concord in Nicaea, Upon the Cessation of Civil Strife:* "But it is fitting that those whose city was founded by the gods should maintain peace and concord toward one another" (39.2; cf. *Or.* 40.26). Plutarch concludes that the plan of Alexander's campaigns demonstrated that he was a true philosopher, because he did not seek to obtain luxury for himself, but to bring "peace and concord to all men" (*De Alex. Fort.* 1.9; cf. Plutarch *De Garr.* 17; Lucian *Hermot.* 22; Dio Cassius *Hist. Rom.* 44.23; 44.25; Dionysius of Halicarnassus *Ant. Rom.* 7.60.2). Diodorus Siculus relates how the inhabitants of Euboea fell into strife, and how their island was devastated; but "at long last the parties came into concord and made peace with one another, having been admonished by their misfortunes" (*Hist.* 16.7.2). The terms "peace and concord" are found together from the 1st century B.C. on, mutually defining a conception of the well-being of the state, in reaction to the bloody civil war (P. Jal 210–31). It is not possible to say whether the combination is typically Roman, and has been taken over into Greek literature (P. Jal 221), or whether *concordia* has been influenced by the Greek concept *homonoia* (Skard 1932). But the origin of the slogan does not lie in Stoic circles exclusively (contra Sanders 1943: 129). For the ideal is found on inscriptions which record the arbitration of disputes (e.g., *SIG* 816) and on coinage celebrating the end of strife between cities. In urging peace and concord, Clement may be seen to follow the advice which Plutarch gave to a young friend who had inquired about the mode of political life appropriate to a citizen of the empire, in which "the affairs of the cities no longer include leadership in wars, or the overthrow of tyrannies, or the conclusion of alliances. . . . There remains, then, for the statesman, of those activities which fall within his province, only this—and it is the equal of the other blessings—always to instill concord and friendship in those who dwell together with him and to remove strifes, discords, and all enmity" (*Praec. ger. rep.* 805A,824C–D).

D. Literary Form

The importance of political context is confirmed by consideration of literary form. The most explicit description of the work is found in 58:2, in the appeal to the readers to "receive our counsel" *(symboulē)*. The letter is conceived, therefore, as a *(symboulē)*, or deliberative discourse, regularly discussed by writers on rhetoric after Aristotle (Arist. *Rh.* 1.3–4.8; *Rh. ad Her.* 1.2.2; Quintilian 3.4.15; 3.8.6; [Aristides] *Ars rh.* in Spengel 1894: 2.503–504; see the studies of the literary category *symboulē* by Klek 1919 and Beck 1970). Epistolary theorists provide definitions of the symbouleutic letter (Ps.-Demetrius *Typoi Epistolikoi* 11 and Ps.-Libanius *Epistolimaioi Xaraktēres* 5 in Weichert 1910). The purpose of such a work is to exhort or dissuade, with reference to some future act; thus, it advocates what is beneficial, as opposed to what is harmful (on the goals of deliberative rhetoric, see Aristotle *Rh.* 1.3.5–4.7; Quint. 3.8.1–3; 3.8.22; 3.8.33; Alexander in Spengel 1894, 3: 1–2 and the more detailed analysis by [Aristides] *Ars rh.* in Spengel 1894, 2: 503–504). Narrative is kept to a minimum, since the deliberative work is concerned with the future and seeks to advise about things to come (Arist. *Rh.* 1.3.4; Quint. 3.8.6). The deliberative orator assigns blame where it is due (Arist. *Rh.* 1.9.28–37; Quint. 3.7.28) and makes use of examples (*Rh.* 1.4.8–9.39; Quint. 3.8.36). A sub-category of the deliberative discourse is the appeal for concord (Isocrates *Paneg.* 3; *Ad Phil.* 16; *Ep.* 3.2; Cicero *De Or.* 1.56; Dio Chrys. *Or.* 38.1–2; Dio Cass. 44.23.3; Aelius Aristides *Or.* 24.825D,826D,827D; Philostr. *VS* 1.9.4; Iamb. *VP* 9.45). A number of examples of this genre have fortunately survived, several in the form of epistles (e.g. Thrasymachus *Peri Politeias* Antiphon *Peri Homonoias;* Isocr. *Or.* 4; *Ep.* 3,8,9; Ps.-Plato *Ep.* 7; Ps.-Demosthenes *Ep.* 1; Socratic Epp. 30–32; Ps.-Sallust *Ep.* 2; Dio Chrys. *Or.* 38–41; Aelius Aristides *Or.* 23–24; [Herodes Atticus] *Peri Politeias;* Ps.-Julian *Or.* 35). Their authors, generally philosophers or rhetoricians, seek to calm the outbreak of faction, within cities or between cities, by dissuading from strife *(stasis)* and exhorting to concord *(homonoia)*.

The *First Epistle of Clement* fully conforms to the definition of a deliberative work (van Unnik 1970: 33–46). The author successfully combines exhortation *(protropē)* with warning *(apotropē)*, e.g., in 30:3; 35:5; 58:1. He uses the recommended topics and arguments, appealing to what is beneficial (19:2–21:2; 35:1–2; 38:6), to what is right and holy, and warning against what causes harm and danger (14:1–2), where the terminology of the *(symboulē)* is especially prominent; on danger as an argument, see also 41:4; 47:7, and the parallel in Dio Chrys. *Or.* 48.14). As Quintilian suggests (3.8.36; 3.8.66), Clement argues for what is right and lawful (63:1–2). Like other works in this genre, *1 Clement* is filled with examples (5; 6; 46; 55; 63:1). The relative absence of narrative, confined to chaps. 1 and 44, is also explained by reference to the genre (Dion. Hal. *Rhet.* 10.14). Even the theme of cosmic harmony in chap. 20 belongs to the topoi of a discourse on concord (cf. Dio Chrys. *Or.* 48.14–16).

In existing speeches and letters on concord, one meets with the same complex of ideas and motifs, adapted by each author to a particular situation. Is it nevertheless possible to discern a structure? When one compares several works from Clement's time, e.g. Dio Chrys. *Or.* 38, [Herodes Atticus] *Peri Politeias,* Ps.-Julian *Or.* 35, Aelius Aristides *Or.* 24.28–37, a schema begins to emerge, in which introduction is followed by proposition, a general appeal for concord, arguments against strife, specific advice, an answer to possible objections, and an epilogue.

E. Occasion and Purpose

1 Clement finds its warrant in the ideology of the empire, and utilizes the popular counsel of concord, ubiquitous in the 2d century (Bowersock 1969: 68). This discovery allows for several conclusions on the occasion and purpose of the work as a whole. First, the fact that Clement draws upon rhetoric and ideology does not mean that the situation is fictitious, or that the letter is a crypto-apology for the faith (Eggenberger 1951). There is no reason to doubt that, as Clement says, "a few rash and self-willed persons have caused strife to blaze up" (1:1), and that several presbyters have been removed from office (44:3–6; 46:9; 47:6), replaced, it seems, by younger men (3:3). That the letter deals sparingly with affairs in Corinth is dictated by the rules of the genre. In the orations of Dio Chrysostom and Aelius Aristides "on concord," the causes of strife are seldom reported. In no case is this a reflection of ignorance; it is simply in keeping with the aims of the genre (Dion. Hal. *Rhet.* 10.14; Quint. 3.8.6–10). In light of these formal and social constraints, one might even say that Clement has told us too much in chap. 44. Thus it is hardly surprising that the background of the conflict is never described, and that the author mentions, as the sources of strife, nothing more concrete than jealousy and envy (4–5). One may conclude that it is impossible to reconstruct the conflict, or the views of those whom Clement combats. It may well be that Lütgert is right in seeing here a conflict between "Spirit and Office" (1911: 50–111), or that W. Bauer was correct in describing the conflict as a special case of the struggle between orthodoxy and heresy (1970: 99–109). But the rules of the genre make it difficult to advance beyond hypotheses.

Whatever the causes of the conflict in Corinth, money seems to have been involved. Contrasting the former humility of the Corinthians with the ambition which has now given rise to strife, the author states that the Corinthians had once been "satisfied with the provision *(ephodios)* of Christ" (2:1). Dionysius of Corinth, in his letter to Soter, observed that it had been the custom of the Roman church from the beginning "to send contributions *(ephodia)* to many churches in every city" (Euseb. *Hist. Eccl.* 4.23.10). From the Roman point of view of Clement, the younger generation of leaders at Corinth are dissatisfied with the provision for their church. What role did this play in the revolt against the presbyters? Were the established presbyters accused of embezzlement? Did the new leaders seek another contribution, to replace the funds their predecessors stole? Polycarp reports that the presbyter Valens was deposed from office for "avarice" (*Ad Phil.* 11). The unrest of the 1st and 2d centuries almost always had economic causes; and the agreements which brought strife to an end usually included concrete provisions which served the interests of all parties.

If one knows less about the situation in Corinth as a result of these insights, one learns more about the purposes of the Roman church. The intervention of Rome into the affairs of Corinth is modelled on the relations of the capital to the provinces. It is thus an expression of the will to power, and not a fraternal correction (Stuiber *RAC* 19: 192) or a kindly (Lietzmann 1832: 202). There is nothing to suggest that Rome's intervention was invited by the Corinthian church, or initiated by the deposed presbyters. The inexact reference to a "report" *(akoē)* in 47:7 seems rather to exclude the possibility of an official communication from Corinth. The Roman church has acted on its own initiative; the division in Corinth only furnished the occasion.

The intervention of the Roman church is modelled on the actions of the Roman senate and the emperor. First, the church decided to dispatch a *symboulē,* in much the same manner that philosophers and orators, with the approval, or on the instruction, of the Roman emperor were sent to troubled cities to counsel concord. Along with its appeal, the church sent three "witnesses" (63:3–4; 65:1) to observe and report on the restoration of peace. The Roman state proceeded in similar fashion in its efforts to quiet faction in the cities. When a class struggle erupted at Rhodes, Aelius Aristides sent a speech on concord in which he described himself as a "witness" (*Or.* 24.833D). In a symbouleutic discourse ascribed to Julian, but dated by Keil (1913) to the 1st century A.D., the author states that a legation *(presbeia)* will be sent to Corinth consisting of two philosopher orators (Ps.-Julian *Or.* 35; Keil 1913: 39). The senate frequently adjudicated disputes between provincial cities, often employing local agents as arbiters (texts and commentary in Sherk [1969]; cf. Tod [1913]; Piccirilli [1973]). Finally, the Roman church recommended exile. *Exsilium* was a Roman practice for escaping trial (frequently mentioned in Cicero, e.g., *Pro Caec.* 100; cf. Suetonius 5.25.4). Clement's solution brings to mind the voluntary exile of Dio under Domitian. Thus the Roman church sought a relation with its sister congregation in Corinth like that which Rome had with the cities of the empire (Cauwelaert 1935), a relationship like that between mother-city and colony (Seibert 1963). In this sense, *1 Clement* belongs in the history of the primacy of Rome (Ziegler 1958: 122).

In adopting the ideology and strategy of the government, Clement endorsed the Roman imperium. The epistle is characterized throughout by a positive attitude toward the Roman state (Wengst 1987). In 37:2–4 the author praises the Roman military, "the soldiers in service of our leader," as a model of obedience, in language which recalls Aelius Aristides' *Eulogy of Rome* (88). In the solemn liturgical prayer with which the work concludes, the author asks that Christians "may be obedient . . . to our rulers and governors on earth," to whom God has given the sovereignty (60:4–61:1). This prayer for princes is more than a show of loyalty; it expresses the conviction that the empire and its rulers have been established by God as the earthly counterpart of the heavenly kingdom.

F. Authorship

1 Clement represents itself as a writing of the Roman church, and gives no hint of the name or person of the author. Yet, it must have been written by a single individual, as the unity of style and content suggest. That his name was Clement, as the manuscripts indicate, was the unanimous opinion of the ancient church. The earliest witnesses are in the letter of Dionysius to Soter (Euseb. *Hist. Eccl.* 4.23.11) and in Hegesippus (Euseb. *Hist. Eccl.* 4.22.1). Irenaeus knows that the Roman community, "during his time in office," sent a letter to Corinth (*Haer.* 3.3.3). Without referring to the epistle, Hermas mentions a Clement who had responsibility for correspondence with the churches without (*Vis.* 2.4.3). One may see in this person the author of *1 Clement.* He must have been a leading personality in the church at Rome, the official correspondent with other churches. More than this, one cannot know.

G. Date

The epistle is customarily dated to the end of the reign of Domitian (95 or 96 C.E.). In the first sentence of the letter, the author explains that the Roman church has been delayed in turning its attention to the dispute at Corinth by "sudden and repeated misfortunes and hindrances which have befallen us" (1:1). This statement is usually interpreted as an allusion to a persecution through which the church at Rome has just been passing. Since chap. 5 speaks of the Neronian persecution as something long past, the sporadic assaults of Domitian must be meant. But the language of 1:1 is so vague that one may doubt whether it refers to persecution at all (Merrill 1924: 160); and the evidence for a persecution under Domitian is tenuous (Merrill 1924: 148–73). In letters and speeches on concord, one often finds an apologetic formula like that which introduces *1 Clement*; it was customary for one who gave advice on concord to excuse his delay by reference to personal or domestic hindrances (e.g. Dio Chrys. *Or.* 40.2; Aelius Aristides *Or.* 24.1; Socratic Ep. 31). The language which Clement uses to describe the causes of the delay, *symphorai* and *periptōseis,* with the adjectives *aiphnidioi* and *epallēloi,* is frequently found in discussions of the circumstances which give rise to discord in literary and epigraphic texts (Diodorus Siculus 16.7.2; *4 Macc.* 3:21; Josephus *JW* 5.32; Euseb. *Hist. Eccl.* 4.2.1; *OGIS* 335.15; 339.17; *SIG* 685.137; 708.7; 730.20; 731.6). The appearance of terms so closely associated with strife in the preface to *1 Clement* suggests that the author has cast the conventional apology in the form of a *captatio benevolentiae*; he wished to include himself and the Roman church in the *nouthetēsis* (admonition), so that they should not appear to be lording it over their brethren. The "misfortunes and hindrances" of which the epistle makes mention may have been internal dissensions like those which troubled the community in Corinth. But it is not necessary to believe that these quarrels had any real existence at all, only that the author found allusion to them, by means of conventional expressions, a convenient way of establishing a sympathetic relationship between himself and his readers. He wished to say: We are faced with the same problems and have need of the same admonition.

Thus one must rely upon more general statements in the epistle and in tradition. The account of the deaths of Peter and Paul in chap. 5 is not that of an eye-witness. The presbyters installed by the apostles have died (44:2), and a second ecclesiastical generation has passed (44:3). The church at Rome is called "ancient" (47:6); and the emissaries from Rome are said to have lived "blamelessly" as Christians "from youth to old age" (63:3). Thus the epistle cannot have been written before the last decades of the 1st century. There are references to the letter by the middle of the next century in the works of Hegesippus and Dionysius of Corinth (*apud* Euseb. *Hist. Eccl.* 3.16; 4.22; 4.23). Thus one may place the composition of *1 Clement* between A.D. 80 and 140.

Bibliography

Text

Bihlmeyer, K. 1970. *Die apostolischen Väter.* Vol. 1. Tübingen.

Fischer, J. A. 1966. *Die apostolischen Väter.* Vol. 1. Darmstadt.

Grant, R. M. 1965. *The Apostolic Fathers.* Vol. 2, *First Clement.* New York.

Jaubert, A. 1971. *Clement de Rome: Epitre aux Corinthiens.* Paris.

Knopf, R. 1920. *Die apostolischen Väter.* Vol. 1, *Zwei Clemensbriefe.* Tübingen.

Lightfoot, J. B. 1890. *The Apostolic Fathers.* Vol. 1, *Clement.* London.

Literature

Bauer, W. 1970. *Orthodoxy and Heresy in Earliest Christianity.* Philadelphia.

Beck, I. 1970. *Untersuchungen zur Theorie des Genos Symnuleutikon.* Hamburg.

Bowersock, G. W. 1969. *Greek Sophists in the Roman Empire.* Oxford.

Cauwelaert, R. 1935. L'intervention de l'église de Rome à Corinthe vers l'an 96. *RHE* 31: 267–306.

Dibelius, M. 1942. Rom und die Christen im ersten Jahrhundert. *SHAW* 1941–42. Heidelberg.

Eggenberger, C. 1951. *Die Quellen der politischen Ethik des I. Klemensbriefs.* Zurich.

Harnack, A. 1929. *Einführung in die alte Kirchengeschichte.* Leipzig.

Jal, P. 1941. "Pax civilis"–"concordia." *Revue des études latines* 34: 210–31.

Keil, B. 1913. Ein *Logos Systatikos. NAWG.* Pp. 1–41.

Klek, J. 1919. *Symbuleutici qui dicitur sermonis historia critica.* Kirchhain.

Lietzmann, H. 1832. *Geschichte der Alten Kirche I.* Tübingen.

Lütgert, W. 1911. *Amt und geist im Kampf.* Gütersloh.

Meinhold, P. 1939. Geschichte und Deutung im ersten Klemensbrief. *ZKG* 58: 87–129.

Merrill, E. T. 1924. *Essays in Early Christian History.* London.

Mikat, P. 1969. *Die Beudeutung der Begriffe Stasis und Aponoia für das Verständnis des I. Clemensbriefes.* Cologne.

Mohrmann, C. 1949. Les origines de la latinité chrétienne à Rome. *VC* 3: 67–106.

Peterson, E. 1950. Das Praescriptum des 1 Clemens. Pp. 351–57 in *Pro Regno Pro Sanctuario.* Nijkerk.

Piccirilli, L. 1973. *Gli Arbitrati Interstali Greci.* Pisa.

Sanders, L. 1943. *L'hellénisme de saint Clement de Rome et le Paulinisme.* Louvain.

Seibert, J. 1963. *Metropolis und Apoikia.* Würzburg.

Sherk, R. K. 1969. *Roman Documents from the Greek East.* Baltimore.

Skard, E. 1932. *Zwei religiös-politische Begriffe.* Oslo.

Spengel, L. von. 1894. *Rhetores graeci.* 3 vols. Bibliotheca Scriptorum Graecorum et Romanorum Teubneriana. Leipzig.

Tod, M. 1913. *International Arbitration Amongst the Greeks.* Oxford.

Unnik, W. C. van. 1950. Is 1 Clement 20 Purely Stoic? *VC* 4: 181–89.

———. 1970. *Studies over de zogenaamde eerste brief van Clemens.* Amsterdam.

Weichert, V., ed. 1910. *Demetrii et Libanii qui feruntur.* Leipzig.

Welborn, L. 1985. On the Date of First Clement. *BR* 29: 35–54.

Wengst, K. 1987. *Pax Romana.* Philadelphia.

Wrede, W. 1891. *Untersuchungen zum Ersten Klemensbriefe.* Göttingen.

Ziegler, A. 1958. *Neue Studien zum Ersten Klemensbrief.* Münich.

LAURENCE L. WELBORN

CLEMENT, SECOND EPISTLE OF. An early Christian epistle transmitted along with *1 Clement* in the biblical Codex Alexandrinus (late 4th century) and the later Jerusalem Codex (1056) which includes the *Didache,* as well as in the Syriac version. It was not written by the author(s) of *1 Clement* and, indeed, is not a letter but a sermon on self-control, repentance, and judgment. The sermon begins abruptly: "Brothers, we must think about Jesus Christ as about God, as about the judge of living and dead; and we must not think little of our salvation." The preacher tells his "brothers and sisters" that he is reading them a "petition" or "plea" (Gk *enteuxis*) to "pay attention to what is written," i.e. to the scriptures which he frequently cites (along with quotations from "the prophetic word," otherwise unknown, and something like the apocryphal Gospel of the Egyptians). He himself refers to "the books (i.e., the OT) and the apostles" as authorities (14.2).

Scholars have noted the "synoptic-type" Jewish piety of the sermon, perhaps surprising around A.D. 140–160 (the epistle's approximate date). The work appears to rely on the Gospel of John as well, however, notably in 9:5–6: "If Christ the Lord who saved us was spirit at first but became flesh [John 1:14] and so called us, so we shall receive the reward in the flesh. Let us then love one another [John 13:34] so that we may all come to the kingdom of God." The kingdom will come when truth and good works are accompanied by ascetic practise (chap. 12). Until then, Christians must preserve the "seal of baptism" (7:6, 8:6) and belong to "the first, spiritual Church, created [like Israel, according to some rabbis] before sun and moon," for Gen 1:27 refers to the male Christ and the female Church, both spiritual; Christ is also the Spirit (chap. 14). The theology is not altogether clear, and the author soon turns to state that he has "given no trivial counsel about self-control," leading into his practical appeal for repentance and going so far as to say that "fasting is better than prayer, but almsgiving is better than both" (16:4).

He urges his hearers "not just to seem to believe and pay attention while being exhorted by the elders" but to remember at home and meet more frequently (17:3). Sinners will be punished in unending fire (17:7, cf. 5:4, 7:6).

Why was it supposed to be from Clement? Three places of origin have been assigned to it because of its connection with *1 Clement:* Corinth, Rome, and (later) Alexandria; but none is fully convincing. It is simply one example of a "garden-variety" 2d century sermon, rhetorically inferior to the work of Melito of Sardis and Hippolytus.

Bibliography

Donfried, K. 1974. *The Setting of Second Clement.* NovTSup 38. Leiden.

Grant, R. M., and Graham, H. H. 1965. *I–II Clement.* New York.

Lake, K., ed. 1912. *The Apostolic Fathers I.* London.

ROBERT M. GRANT

CLEMENTINES, PSEUDO-. "Pseudo-Clementines" is not primarily a generic designation used in all inauthentic writings attached to the name of Clement of Rome. It refers rather to a specific group of pseudonymous compositions that relate a fictitious tale of Clement's conversion to Christianity, of his travels with Peter, and of his recovery of the long-lost and dispersed members of his family. The genre of these writings is the ancient romance of recognitions; the *Pseudo-Clementines* are the first known example of Christian adoption *en bloc* of this literary *Gattung.* The author has thereby used established literary conventions to illustrate his belief that Christian faith leads to the resolution of intellectual difficulties as well as hardships in life.

The main constituents of the *Pseudo-Clementines* are the *Homilies* and the *Recognitions.* The original Greek of the *Hom. Clem.* has survived in two manuscripts from the 11th or 12th and 14th centuries. The Greek of the *Clem. recogn.,* in contrast, has been lost except for small fragments preserved in the church fathers (listed in Rehm 1965: c–cii). Two ancient versions of this work must be employed in lieu of the Greek. A Latin rendering was undertaken by Rufinus of Aquileia in ca. 406 C.E. A Syriac version, containing at least books 1 to 4.1.4, was made somewhat earlier. The surviving Greek and Armenian fragments reveal that these two translations are of approximately equal text-critical value, though the Syriac deserves slight preference. The *Hom. Clem.* and the *Clem. recogn.* originated probably in 4th century Syria, as traces of the Arian debate indicate.

These two main recensions of the *Pseudo-Clementines* have so much material in common that some sort of literary relationship must exist between them. Though simple dependency of the one upon the other was advocated in the 19th century, the view that both are based on an earlier third writing (the basic writing) has gained predominance. It is controversial whether this basic writing was employed independently (Waitz, Strecker) or under the influence of the other recension (Rehm).

There are no undisputed fragments of the basic writing. The most likely candidates are the citations in the *Chron. Pasch.,* Origen *comm. ser. 1–145 in Mt.* at Matt 26:6–13 (series 77, p. 185.18–24), the *Opus imperfectum in Matthaeum* cols. 770–71, and Origen *philoc.,* though Strecker (1981: 260–64, 269) denies that any of these derive from the basic writing. Of decisive importance in this regard is whether Origen himself knew the basic writing. Beyond the passages already mentioned, one should compare also Origen *Cels.* 1.57, 6.11 with *Hom. Clem.* 2.23–24 par. The debate on the genuineness of the citation in Origen *philoc.* (see now Stuiber 1973) has been continued by Junod (1976: 25–33), on the one side, and Rius-Camps (1976: 153–54), on the other; while it is not true that one of the compilers, Basil the Great, did not know the *Pseudo-Clementines* (see Riedinger 1969: 258–59), this citation probably derives from Origen. In contrast, the suggestion by Tetz (1968) regarding a new fragment of the basic writing must be flatly rejected. Other authors who are likely to have used the basic writing are Epiphanius, the *Const. App.* (contra Wehnert 1983: 289–90), and possibly Lactantius. In sum, these witnesses would indicate that the basic writing was composed ca. 220 C.E., and Syria is its probable home.

Great effort has been exerted in attempts to recover the sources of the basic writing. The most important and controversial of these are the so-called *Kerygmata Petrou (Preachings of Peter).* This hypothetical writing, postulated by modern investigators to explain the genesis of the *Pseudo-Clementines*, quite possibly never existed and thus is perhaps only a fiction that has riddled recent scholarship. In any event, the emendations of the text in *Hom. Clem.* 1.20.2 that are used as a main buttress for the theory of this source are not legitimate. Another common source-critical theory assumes that much of the material in *Clem. recogn.* 1 derives from (a recension of) the *Anabathmoi Jakobou (Ascents of James)*, a Jewish Christian writing described by Epiphanius *haer.* 30.16.7–9 as containing a vicious lampoon against Paul. While a source does seem to be reflected in this section of the *Pseudo-Clementines*, the similarities with the *Ascents of James* do not extend beyond widespread Jewish Christian notions, while the differences (e.g., no elements of the lampoon against Paul as reported by Epiphanius) preclude the identification of the *Ascents of James* as the source.

The *Pseudo-Clementines* are significant for biblical studies in a number of ways, but mainly because the author of the basic writing was affected by Syrian Jewish Christianity. He has preserved traditions that evidently extend back to apostolic times and that have survived elsewhere only fragmentarily. Elements of anti-Paulinism in the *Pseudo-Clementines* led F. C. Baur to employ these writings as a cardinal witness to the Jewish Christian wing of earliest Christianity. Early tradition is also reflected in some of the unusual sayings of Jesus that find parallels in a variety of sources, especially Justin Martyr. The thesis that the *Pseudo-Clementines* are directly dependent on a harmony of the Gospels (in particular, one supposedly used by Justin, as assumed by Kline 1975), however, finds insufficient support in the parallels. The history of each saying must be examined independently.

Bibliography

For editions, translations, and a discussion of most of the literature, see:

Jones, F. S. 1982. The Pseudo-Clementines: A History of Research. *Second Cent* 2: 1–33, 63–96.

Supplement

Renoux, C. 1978. Fragments arméniens des Recognitiones du Pseudo-Clément. *OrChr* 62: 103–13.

Strecker, G. 1986–. *Die Pseudoklementinen III: Konkordanz zu den Pseudoklementinen.* GCS. Berlin.

There is also an English translation of the *Recognitions* in:

Whiston, W. 1712. *The Recognitions of Clement: or the Travels of Peter in Ten Books.* Vol. 5 in *Primitive Christianity Reviv'd.* London.

Patristic witnesses are collected in:

Harnack, A. 1958. *Geschichte der altchristlichen Literatur bis Eusebius* 1: 219–29. 2d exp. ed. Leipzig.

They are discussed extensively in:

Hort, F., and Anthony, J. 1901. *Notes Introductory to the Study of the Clementine Recognitions: A Course of Lectures,* pp. 24–78. London.

Bibliography of Older Literature

Richardson, E. C. 1887. Bibliographical Synopsis. Pp. 1–136 in vol. 10 of ANF, ed. A. Cleveland Coxe. Buffalo.

Works Cited Above

Junod, É. 1976. *Origène. Philocalie 21–27: Sur le libre arbitre.* SC 226. Paris.

Kline, L. L. 1975. *The Sayings of Jesus in the Pseudo-Clementine Homilies.* SBLDS 14. Missoula, MT.

Rehm, B. 1965. *Die Pseudoklementinen II: Rekognitionen in Rufins Übersetzung.* GCS 51. Berlin.

Riedinger, R. 1969. Die Parallelen des Pseudo-Kaisarios zu den pseudoklementinischen Rekognitionen, Neue Parallelen aus Basileios *Proseche seautǭ. Byzantinische Zeitschrift* 62: 243–59.

Rius-Camps, J. 1976. Las Pseudoclementinas: Bases filológicas para una nueva interpretación. *Revista Catalana Teologia* 1: 79–158.

Strecker, G. 1981. *Das Judenchristentum in den Pseudoklementinen.* TU 70. 2d, rev. and exp. ed. Berlin.

Stuiber, A. 1973. Ein griechischer Textzeuge für das Opus imperfectum in Matthaeum. *VC* 27: 146–47.

Tetz, M. 1968. Zur Theologie des Markell von Ankyra II: Markells Lehre von der Adamssohnschaft Christi und eine pseudoklementinische Tradition über die wahren Lehrer und Propheten. *ZKG* 79: 342.

Wehnert, J. 1983. Literarkritik und Sprachanalyse: Kritische Anmerkungen zum gegenwärtigen Stand der Pseudoklementinen-Forschung. *ZNW* 74: 268–301.

F. Stanley Jones

CLEODEMUS MALCHUS. A Jewish historian who lived prior to the mid-1st century B.C.E. A brief excerpt of his work is first quoted by the pagan author Alexander Polyhistor, possibly in his now lost book *On Libya.* The fragment is preserved in Josephus *Ant* 1.15.1 §§ 239–41, from which it is later quoted in slightly altered form in Eusebius *Praep. Evang.* 9.20.2–4.

The exact title of his work is not known. Josephus only says that Cleodemus "reported concerning (perhaps, narrated the history of) the Jews." The one surviving fragment expands on Gen 25:1–4, which lists Abraham's descendants through his second wife Keturah. Conflating the biblical account, Cleodemus lists 3 sons of Abraham by Keturah: Iapheras, Sures, and Iaphras (or, as reported by Eusebius, Apher, Assouri, and Aphran), after whom he says the city of Ephra (Afra; otherwise unknown), Assyria, and Africa were named.

Cleodemus displays special interest in traditions relating to Libya (the continent Africa) and Africa (the region around Carthage), in particular the exploits of the Greek hero Heracles in Libya, which were variously reported by ancient authors (cf. *Diod. Sic.* 1.17.3; 21.4; 24.1–8; 4.17.4–5; Plutarch *Sert.* 9.3–5). Especially remarkable is Cleodemus' claim that Abraham's sons joined Heracles in fighting the Libyan giant Antaeus, and that subsequently Heracles married Abraham's granddaughter and fathered a son from whom descended the "barbarian Sophakes" (perhaps a reference to Numidian tribes in N Africa). This willingness to link the biblical account of Abraham's descendants with popular legends current in the Hellenistic-Roman world, thereby providing a distinctly Judaized version of the settling and civilizing of Libya and Africa, is a specific instance of syncretism that typifies certain Gk-speaking Jewish authors of the Hellenistic period, e.g. Artapanus and Pseudo-Eupolemus.

As to the identity of Cleodemus, virtually nothing is

known except that Polyhistor gives his surname as Malchus and calls him "the prophet." Depending on how one interprets each of these biographical data, as well as how one assesses his syncretistic tendencies, scholars have variously identified him as Samaritan (Freudenthal 1875: 131–36), Jewish (Walter 1976: 116), and pagan (Wacholder 1974: 54, 55), either Syrian or Phoenician. The likely Semitic origin of the name Malchus and his demonstrable interest in Abraham argue for his Jewish identity. Generally a Palestinian or Samaritan provenance has been suggested, although the prominence he gives to N African traditions suggests that he was perhaps a member of the Jewish community at Carthage (Walter 1976: 116).

The only firm indicator of his date is that he is quoted by Alexander Polyhistor (ca. 105–30 B.C.E.). How much earlier he flourished is difficult to say. He may have used a Gk translation of Genesis, which would suggest that he lived after the mid-3d century B.C.E. Scholars generally date him between 200–50 B.C.E.

Bibliography

Doran, R. 1985. Cleodemus Malchus. *OTP* 2: 883–87.

Freudenthal, J. 1875. *Alexander Polyhistor und die von him erhaltenen Reste judäischer und samaritanischer Geschichtswerke.* Hellenistische Studien 1–2. Breslau.

Holladay, C. R. 1983. Cleodemus Malchus. Pp. 245–59 in *Fragments from Hellenistic Jewish Authors.* Vol. 1. SBLTT 20. Pseudepigrapha Series 10. Chico, CA.

Schürer, E. 1986. *HJP*² 3/1: 526–28.

Wacholder, B. Z. 1974. *Eupolemus. A Study of Judaeo-Greek Literature.* Monographs of the Hebrew Union College 3. Cincinnati and New York.

Walter, N. 1976. Kleodemos Malchas. Pp. 115–120 in *Jüdische Schriften aus hellenistisch-römischer Zeit* 1/2, ed. W. G. Kümmel. Gütersloh.

CARL R. HOLLADAY

CLEOPAS (PERSON) [Gk *Kleopas*]. One of the 2 disciples whom Jesus joins on their way to Emmaus (Luke 24:18). The name Cleopas has been found on a Gk ostracon from Egypt: it is a shortened form of *Kleopatros* ("illustrious father"), the masculine form of Cleopatra. It is sometimes identified with Clopas (John 19:25), but the latter is of Semitic origin. The evidence for identifying the 2 names is not strong. Probably, Luke is working with a tradition (cf. Mark 16:12–13); otherwise, he would have also named Cleopas' companion (Fitzmyer *Luke x–xxiv* AB, 1554–55, 1563–64). Cleopas was very likely known to Luke's readers. Naturally, there has been some speculation about his unnamed companion; Cleopas' wife or son have been suggested. The former is more reasonable, since if the son was later bishop of Jerusalem, he would have been named (Marshall *Luke* NIGTC, 894). Other suggestions for the identity of Cleopas' companion include: Peter (unlikely in view of vv 33–34), Nathaniel, the deacon Philip, Nicodemus, Simon, Amaon and even Emmaous (Metzger 1980:40–1).

More important is how Cleopas and his companion function in the narrative. They stand for any Christian who was (or is) confused about what happened to Jesus and about where they might now find him (Wanke 1973: 67,122,126). Of course, Jesus' appearance to Cleopas and his companion and the majestic passives express divine initiative and grace (Betz 1969: 34–39,44–46). Cleopas and his companion walk on "the way" (vv 32,35), a name for Christianity (cf. Acts 8:26,36,39;9:2;16:17;19:9,23; 22:4;24:14,22). Their failure to see represents weakness of faith; thus, Jesus describes them as "foolish . . . and slow of heart to believe all that the prophets have spoken!" (Luke 24:25). To be sure, they knew that Jesus of Nazareth was a prophet mighty in work and word and that he had been delivered up, condemned and crucified by the chief priests and rulers. But they failed to realize how well founded was their hope that Jesus was the one to redeem Israel. Now, 3 days had passed, and everything was gloomy, except for the confirmed report of the women that the tomb was empty and their amazing news that they had seen a vision of angels who said that Jesus was alive. Then, before their blind eyes, Jesus opens all the Scriptures. Beginning with Moses and the prophets, he explains everything about himself—that the Christ had to suffer all these things and so enter his glory (cf. Luke 16:31). Some authors (Betz 1969: 37–41; Perry 1986: 59–68) derive from the story a message about the presence of the risen Jesus in every Christian interpretation of scriptures. Koet (1985: 59–73) contends that "discuss" *(synēteō),* "open" *(dianoigō)* and "explain" *(diermēneuō)* are certainly technical terms for scriptural interpretation, and to a lesser extent, "converse" *(homileō).* "Heart" can be associated with such interpretation.

Cleopas and his companion also exemplify hospitality and the recognition of the risen Jesus in the Eucharist. When they reached Emmaus, Jesus appeared to be going further. However, Cleopas and his companion constrained him to remain with them because it was late. At table, Jesus took the bread and blessed it, broke it, and gave it to them. Only then were their eyes opened, and they recognized him (v 31; cf. vv 16,35; Plevnik 1987:94–98), but he vanished. A theme of hospitality (Karris 1987: 58–59; Robinson 1984: 485–94) does not explain the similarity of Jesus' words to those of the Last Supper (Luke 22:19; cf. 9:11–17) nor the parallel with "Philip and the Ethiopian Eunuch" (Acts 8:25–40; Dupont 1953: 361–64). Furthermore, the information that their eyes are opened and their journey ended only at the breaking of bread emphasizes that event even more than the correct understanding of scripture. On the other hand, Luke does associate the breaking of bread with instruction about himself and the mission (Dillon 1978: 105–8).

Cleopas and his companion recalled how on the way their hearts had burned within them when Jesus opened the scriptures. Immediately, they returned to Jerusalem and told the eleven and those with them what happened on the way and how they recognized Jesus in the breaking of bread. Yet their news is subordinated to Jesus' appearance to Peter (Wanke 1974: 186–88), and the return to Jerusalem and the eleven marks the formation of the community (Dillon 1978: 93–103).

Like all Christians, Cleopas and his companion are on the Way. Their inability to see, their lack of faith and hope, calls for a correct understanding of scriptures—that Jesus is the redeemer and, as Christ, had to suffer and thus enter his glory—and of his presence in the Eucharist. Such an understanding brings amazement and joy. Cleopas and his companion also demonstrate the need for grace, hospitality, enthusiasm to share the good news and joining one's proclamation to that of the Church (Borse 1987: 62–66; Wanke 1973:49–53,114–16).

Bibliography

Betz, H. D. 1969. The Origin and Nature of Christian Faith according to the Emmaus Legend. *Int* 23: 32–46.

Borse, U. 1987. Der Evangelist als Verfasser der Emmauserzählung. Pp. 35–67 in SNTU 12, ed. A. Fuchs. Linz.

Dillon, R. J. 1978. *From Eye-Witnesses to Ministers of the Word.* AnBib 82. Rome.

Dupont, J. 1953. Les pèlerins d'Emmaüs (Luc. xxiv, 13–35). Pp. 349–74 in *Miscellanea Biblica B.Bach,* ed. R. M. Diaz. Scripta et Documenta 1. Montisserrati.

Karris, R. J. 1987. Luke 24:13–35. *Int* 41: 57–61.

Koet, B.-J. 1985. Some Traces of a Semantic Field of Interpretation in Luke 24,13–35. *Bij* 46: 59–73.

Metzger, B. M. 1980. *New Testament Studies: Philological, Versional, and Patristic.* NTTS 10. Leiden.

Perry, C. A. 1986. *The Resurrection Promise.* Grand Rapids.

Plevnik, J. 1987. The Eyewitnesses of the Risen Jesus in Luke 24. *CBQ* 49: 90–103.

Robinson, B. P. 1984. The Place of the Emmaus Story in Luke-Acts. *NTS:* 481–497.

Wanke, J. 1973. *Die Emmauserzählung.* ErfThSt 31. Leipzig.

———. 1974. ". . . wie sie ihn beim Brotbrechen erkannten," Zur Auslegung der Emmauserzählung Lk 24,13–35. *BZ* n.s. 18: 180–92.

Robert F. O'Toole

CLEOPATRA (PERSON). Although borne by several minor mythological figures, the name Cleopatra ("born of a famous father") came into prominence during the Hellenistic period mainly as a result of its close association with the royal house of Macedon. The first Cleopatra of historical note was the wife of Perdiccas II of Macedon (ca. 452/35–413 B.C.) and Cleopatra was also the name of the daughter of Philip II at whose wedding celebrations Philip was assassinated in 336 B.C.

It was presumably because of these royal associations that the name later became popular with the Seleucid and Ptolemaic dynasts. Several Ptolemies had wives and daughters called Cleopatra and the best-known bearer of the name—the mistress of Julius Caesar and Mark Antony and last ruler of an independent Egypt before her suicide by asp bite in 30 B.C. and the country's annexation as a Roman province—was actually Cleopatra VII of that line. There are three previous Cleopatras of this dynasty who are of particular biblical interest.

1. *Cleopatra I,* born ca. 215 B.C., was the daughter of Antiochus the Great and Laodice. Married to Ptolemy V in 194/3 B.C. as part of the peace settlement between the two kings in 195 B.C., she brought as her dowry the revenues of Coele-Syria and Palestine (Josephus *Ant* 12.4.1 § 154). Nicknamed Syra ("the Syrian"), she ruled as regent for her young son Ptolemy VI after her husband's death in 180 B.C. She died in 176 B.C., leaving 2 sons, Ptolemy VI and VIII, and a daughter Cleopatra II.

2. *Cleopatra II,* daughter of the foregoing, was married in 175/4 B.C. to her brother Ptolemy VI. Add Esth 11:1 is thought to refer to them. It was to them that Onias IV fled after the installation of the hellenizer Alcimus as high priest (Joseph. *Ant* 12.9.7 §§387–88). In response to his petition citing the prophecy in Isa 29:19, they permitted him to construct at Leontopolis a temple similar to the Temple at Jerusalem (*Ant* 13.3.1–3 §§62–73), as well as favouring the Jews in other ways. In 170–164/3 B.C. Cleopatra was co-regent with Ptolemy VI and her younger brother Ptolemy VIII, with whom she joined in a dynastic marriage with the latter after her husband's death in 145 B.C. Matters deteriorated in 142 B.C. when Ptolemy VIII also married her younger daughter Cleopatra III, adding her to the co-regency. A confused power struggle resulted, with both Cleopatra II and Ptolemy VIII fleeing into exile on occasion. Reconciled in 124 B.C., the three again ruled together until Ptolemy's death in 116 B.C. Cleopatra II herself died soon afterwards, probably in 115 B.C.

3. *Cleopatra Thea,* oldest daughter of the foregoing and Ptolemy VI, was joined in a diplomatic marriage in 150 B.C. to Alexander Balas, who had gained the Seleucid throne with the support of Ptolemy and of Jonathan Maccabaeus (1 Macc 10:57–58; Josephus *Ant* 13.4.1–2 §§80–85). He proved unsatisfactory as king and in 146 B.C. Ptolemy switched his support and Cleopatra's hand to a rival claimant, Demetrius II Nicator (1 Macc 11:9–12; Josephus *Ant.*13.4.7 §§109–110). Demetrius was captured while invading Parthia (139/8 B.C.) but Cleopatra continued as queen by marrying his brother Antiochus VII Sidetas (138–129 B.C.). Later she ruled in her own right for a short period (126 B.C.) and then as regent with her son Antiochus VIII Grypus (125–121 B.C.). Exposed in an attempt to poison him, she was forced to commit suicide by drinking the poison herself (Justin 39.2.7–8).

4. Unrelated is the Cleopatra from Jerusalem, a wife of Herod the Great (Josephus *Ant* 17.1.3 §21) and mother of the tetrarchs Herod and Philip (Luke 3:1). See further in PW 11/1: 738–44, 785–87.

Bibliography

Grant, M. 1972. *Cleopatra.* London.

Lindsey, J. 1971. *Cleopatra.* London.

Otto, W. 1934. *Zur Geschichte der Zeit des 6. Ptolemäers.* ABAW n.s. 11. Munich. Repr. 1976.

Pédech, P. 1973. La Cléopâtre de Corneille devant l'histoire. Pp. 425–33 in *Missions et démarches de la critique. Mélanges offerts au J. A. Vier,* ed. E. Guitton. Paris.

Seibert, J. 1967. *Historische Beiträge zu den dynastischen Verbindungen in hellenistischer Zeit.* Historia Einzelschriften 10. Wiesbaden.

Volkmann, H. 1958. *Cleopatra: A Study in Politics and Propaganda.* Trans. T. J. Cadoux. London.

John Whitehorne

CLERGY. See MINISTRY IN THE EARLY CHURCH.

CLIENT KINGS. Rome's ability to establish friendly contacts and alliances with the powers around her was fundamental to the success of Roman imperial expansion and administration. "Client kings" is a convenient general term employed by modern scholars to denote monarchical rulers who enjoyed such relations with Rome, whether those relations were based upon a formal treaty or not.

A. Terminology and History

The Roman state termed these rulers its *amici* ("friends") and/or *socii* ("allies", a term also applied to provincials). Their kingship was often recognized formally by Roman proclamation *(appellatio),* sometimes, especially under the Republic, with grand ceremony at Rome, as was the case with Herod in 40 B.C. At the same time, individual Romans developed special personal and family relationships with these rulers and might actually describe them as their "clients" *(clientes),* though here, too, the terminology of friendship was the norm. Therefore, the term 'client king' is not a formal title or a common designation so much as a metaphor used to express the *de facto* patronage exercised by Rome and Romans over these rulers. Of course, in practice, the actual nature of that patronage varied greatly from case to case, especially according to the relative strengths of the contracting parties. Thus, for example, the powerful king of Parthia often had a relationship with Rome which, in purely formal terms, was indistinguishable from that of a petty client king (such as Herod), but the vastly greater power of the Parthian king made the realities of his relationship with Rome entirely distinct.

The first client kings were insignificant tribal chieftains of Italy whose names have mostly been lost to history. As Rome expanded into the Hellenistic world, it gained grander "friends and allies." For that reason Hiero II, king of Syracuse (ca. 263 B.C.), is often though erroneously regarded as the first client king of Rome. Client kings remained vital to the Roman empire until the fall of the empire in the West in A.D. 476 (when a client king of sorts, the Germanic Odoacer, seized power). In the East they continued to be vital to the Byzantine state, which could even count kings of Italy among its clients. Yet it is often supposed that Rome conceived of client kingdoms as temporary entities eventually to be replaced by provinces administered directly by Roman governors. The fact is, however, that although kingdoms tended to be annexed over the centuries, there is no evidence that Romans ever thought of such kingdoms as temporary; indeed, such long-term thinking was simply not characteristic of Roman government.

B. Relations with Rome

The frontier of the Roman empire was in practice a broad, ill-defined area, even where fortified lines existed. Within that undefined area, client kings played a crucial role, since most were therefore situated on the margins of the territories directly administered by Rome. Due to their marginality, the Romans themselves disagreed as to whether, strictly speaking, client kings were "inside" or "outside" the *imperium Romanum.* On the frontier, client kings joined Roman military campaigns of attack and defense, providing large forces, necessary resources, information, and strategic positions. Rome seems to have preferred not to tax such kingdoms directly, but rather to leave them as reservoirs upon which she could draw whenever required. Moreover, client kings could use their marginal positions to act as intermediaries for Rome, though they risked accusations of treachery by so doing (see HEROD ANTIPAS).

It must be stressed that client kings enjoyed a great measure of independence and real power by virtue of their powerful friends in Rome and, more generally, because Rome was simply not interested in matters of day-to-day local administration. Rome became genuinely interested in the kings' activities primarily when those activities threatened Roman interests directly or indirectly (e.g., when a king consorted with an enemy of Rome, or if he created or failed to quell unrest within his kingdom). In particular, Rome expected client kings to suppress banditry and piracy within their territories. Should a king fail to satisfy Roman expectations he might be deposed, detained, or even executed. On the other hand, client kings could call upon Roman support and protection against internal and external threats to their kingdoms. Though Rome might refuse to help, usually it was in the interests of its prestige and of future deterrence to be seen rallying to the aid of her friends. In the same way, when a king died he sometimes left a will that called upon Rome to ensure the succession of his chosen heir. Where no such heir existed, kings might bequeath their entire kingdoms to Roman protection and administration.

The relationships between Rome and client kings were structured (and on occasion undermined) by personal and family relationships between kings and leading Romans. These relationships brought great military forces into the hands of the most influential Romans, such as Pompey. In the civil wars which marked the passage from republic to principate at Rome, client kings played important roles. Juba of Numidia and Cleopatra VII of Egypt are the two best-known examples.

After the Battle of Actium in 31 B.C. and the establishment of the principate under Augustus, the patronage exercised over client kings by the Roman state and by individual Romans tended to coalesce, becoming simply the patronage of the emperor and the imperial family. Although other Romans (especially governors in adjoining provinces) continued to form relationships with kings, the emperor took some care to ensure that these did not undermine or contradict his political wishes. Augustus, following precedents set by Caesar and Antony in particular, made client kings a more integral part of the Roman empire than they had been. Most client kings were now granted Roman citizenship and regularly sent their sons to stay with the imperial family at Rome. In their kingdoms, kings founded or re-founded cities which they named Caesarea, cities which often contained edifices named after members of the imperial family. These cities also became centers of the imperial cult, and a few kings, notably in the Crimean Bosporus, actually appointed themselves priests of the imperial cult. Coins were minted depicting the image of the ruling emperor.

Emperors used kings to boost their prestige not only in the empire at large but also within Rome itself, where great ceremonies could be held to celebrate the conclusion of treaties and formal arrangements. The Romans were ambivalent toward these kings, but they nevertheless recognized the exalted status of royalty. It was easy therefore for the emperor to claim honor not only as the "conqueror" of kings but also as their great patron and protector.

In the course of the principate, client kings and leading Romans became increasingly indistinguishable. In the Roman Senate, provincial elites more and more replaced the members of the old aristocracy, which had largely died out. Scions of royal dynasties were very much in the vanguard of this movement into the Senate.

Bibliography

Badian, E. 1958. *Foreign Clientelae, 264–70 B.C.* Oxford.

Braund, D. C. 1984. *Rome and the Friendly King.* New York.

Gruen, E. S. 1984. *The Hellenistic World and the Coming of Rome.* Berkeley.

Luttwak, E. N. 1976. *The Grand Strategy of the Roman Empire.* Baltimore.

Sands, P. C. 1908. *The Client Princes of the Roman Empire under the Republic.* Cambridge.

DAVID C. BRAUND

CLOISONNE. See JEWELRY.

CLOPAS (PERSON) [Gk *Klōpas*]. Husband (or son or father) of a woman who stood near the cross of Jesus during his execution according to John 19:25. The exact relationship cannot be determined from the Gk text, because she is identified only as "the Mary of Clopas." He sometimes has been identified with Cleopas [Gk *Kleopas*], one of the 2 travelers to Emmaus with whom Jesus conversed after the resurrection according to Luke 24:18. While it is possible that the Semitic name Clopas has been transformed into the Gk name Cleopas (abbreviated for *Kleopatros*), or vice versa, there is no reason to assume the identity of the 2 men. No evidence in the Gk texts of Luke and John suggests that the 2 names were interchanged during the course of their transmission. But a tradition found in Origen (*Cels.* 2.62, 68 and elsewhere) suggests that Cleopas and Clopas may have been equated by Christians as early as the 3d century.

Efforts to identify Clopas as a relative of Jesus based on biblical texts are not convincing. John 19:25 appears to depict 4 women near the cross: Jesus' mother "and the sister of his mother, the Mary of Clopas, and Mary Magdalene." Although the phrases "the sister of his mother" and "the Mary of Clopas," seem to refer to separate individuals, the ambiguity of the Gk makes it quite possible that only 3 women are present. Thus if one takes "Mary of Clopas" to stand in apposition to "the sister of his mother," then Clopas could be Jesus' cousin or grandfather or uncle on his mother's side. The last possibility is intriguing because Eusebius knows a tradition from Hegesippus that Clopas was Joseph's brother, hence Jesus' uncle on his father's side (*Hist. Eccl.* 3.11). According to Hegesippus, Clopas was the father of Symeon (Simon) who succeeded Jesus' brother James as bishop of the Jerusalem church (3.32; cf. 3.11; 4.22).

Reading John 19:25 to refer only to 3 women witnesses (as in Mark 15:40 = Matt 27:56; diff. Luke 23:49) has led to further speculation that Mary the wife of Clopas was also Mary the mother of James and Joses named in Mark 15:40. Based on this identification and the conjecture that the James of Mark 15:40 was the son of Alphaeus (Mark 3:18 = Matt 10:3 = Luke 6:15; Acts 1:13), Alphaeus and Clopas would be one and the same person. But the identification of Alphaeus and Clopas depends upon 3 weak presuppositions: (1) the assumption that Mary is Clopas' wife; (2) the inference that Mary of Clopas was the sister of Jesus' mother, which leads to the unlikely result that both sisters had the same name; (3) the arbitrary identification of the James in Mark 15:40 with the James of Mark 3:18. Moreover, there is reason to think that 'Mary the mother of James and Joses' in Mark 15:40 refers not to Clopas' wife but to Jesus' mother, as does a similar description in Mark 6:3. If this is the case, then both Mark and John would agree in portraying the mother of Jesus as present at the crucifixion, but the Mary of Clopas does not readily correspond to any woman in Mark 15:40. (See Platz *IDB* 1:650; *NTApocr* 1: 418–32.)

JON B. DANIELS

CLOTHING. See DRESS AND ORNAMENTATION.

CLOUD, PILLAR OF. See PILLAR OF FIRE AND CLOUD.

CLUB, WAR. See WEAPONS AND IMPLEMENTS OF WARFARE.

CLUBS. See ASSOCIATIONS, CLUBS, THIASOI.

CNIDUS (PLACE) [Gk *Knidos*]. A Greek port on the SW coast of Asia Minor which Paul sailed past on his voyage to Rome (Acts 27:7). Cnidus (pronounced with a silent "c") was situated at the very W tip of a 40-mile peninsula which juts out into the Mediterranean between the islands of Cos and Rhodes, near the modern town of Tekir. This region was called Caria, and in Paul's time was part of the Roman province of Asia. Acts relates that Paul's ship sailed slowly W from Myra to Cnidus, and then was forced by unfavorable autumn winds to turn S and sail to Crete (reference to "the fast" in 27:9 indicates the autumn season). Haenchen detects an error here, claiming that the course was not changed by unfavorable winds but rather was the normal route to Rome (1971: 699). Actually, the text does not say where the normal course for fall sailing was, but simply that "the wind did not allow us to go on." This is not inconsistent with Haenchen's claim that autumn winds typically forced westbound ships to detour S from Cnidus to Crete.

Writing less than a century before Paul's journey, Strabo described Cnidus as a city:

> with two harbours, one of which can be closed, can receive triremes (warships), and is a naval station for twenty ships. Off it lies an island which is approximately seven stadia in circuit, rises high, is theatre-like, is connected by moles with the mainland, and in a way makes

Cnidus a double city, for a large part of its people live on the island, which shelters both harbours. (14.2.15)

The military harbor faces NW while the larger, commercial harbor which Paul's ship approached faces SE. The mountainous island rises W of the city and is connected by a narrow man-made isthmus to the mainland E of the city. Modern excavations have revealed that the city itself may have originally been built on the island and then spread across the isthmus to the mainland. It boasted 2 theaters, the smaller of which seated approximately 4,500 and faced the S commercial harbor. The city also featured numerous temples and a necropolis that is one of the largest ever discovered. A circular temple with 18 Doric columns crowned the westernmost terrace above the city, overlooking both harbors. This almost certainly displayed the famous marble statue of Aphrodite Euploia (the Aphrodite of Fair Sailing) created in the 3d century B.C.E. by Praxiteles. Writing during the 1st century C.E., Pliny the Elder described it as the finest sculpture in the world, a work of art which had made Cnidus a famous city (*HN* 36.20–22).

It was previously hypothesized that ancient Cnidus was founded near modern Burgaz-Datça, about 26 miles E, and was only moved to the present site during the 4th century B.C.E. (*IDB* 1:655). Excavations have disproved this theory by unearthing pottery fragments at the present site dating from the 6th century B.C.E. (Mellink 1978: 324). Anti-Hasmonean Jewish refugees may have fled to Cnidus ca. 142 B.C.E. In that year, at Hasmonean request, the Roman consul Lucius wrote to Cnidus requesting that the city extradite any Jewish refugees to the high priest Simon (1 Macc 15:21–23). Roughly a century later the Romans exempted the city from tribute (Love 1972b: 401). Although Paul sailed past Cnidus, Christian missionaries later came to the area, several churches were constructed, and eventually the city became the seat of a bishop. During the 5th century C.E., a basilica was constructed on the site of the temple of Dionysus (*IDB Sup*, 169).

Bibliography

Haenchen, E. 1971. *The Acts of the Apostles*. Trans. B. Noble et al. Philadelphia.

Love, I. 1972a. A Preliminary Report of the Excavations at Knidos, 1970. *AJA* 76: 61–76.

———. 1972b. A Preliminary Report of the Excavations at Knidos, 1971. *AJA* 76: 393–405.

Mellink, M. J. 1978. Archaeology in Asia Minor. *AJA* 82: 315–38.

MARK J. OLSON

COAT OF MAIL. See WEAPONS AND IMPLEMENTS OF WARFARE.

CODE. See LAW (BIBLICAL AND ANE).

CODEX. The codex (pl. codices), or leaf book, of which the modern book with pages is a direct descendant, came into use as a medium of literature only in the early centuries of the Christian era. Although it was not a Christian invention, the codex was early favored in the Christian circles for the transcription of Christian literature, and its wide use by Christians popularized it and eventually led to its use for the transcription of Greek and Roman literature as well. The replacement of the traditional scroll or roll book (Lat *uolumen,* whence our "volume") by the codex was a development of major importance in the history of book production in general. Within Christianity the codex played an important role in the transmission and collection of Christian writings and contributed to the formation of the Christian Bible.

This entry consists of 10 articles. The first provides a discussion of what exactly a codex is, followed by separate articles on the major codices: Alexandrinus, the Berlin Gnostic codex, Bezae, Brucianus, Claramontanus, Ephraemi Rescriptus, Sinaiticus, Vaticanus, Washingtonianus. A discussion of Codex Askewianus can be found under PISTIS SOPHIA. See also CANON (NT); CHESTER BEATTY PAPYRI; NAG HAMMADI; PAPYRI, EARLY CHRISTIAN.

THE CODEX

The codex made of papyrus or parchment apparently evolved from sets of thin wooden boards, either whitened to receive writing with ink or slightly hollowed and filled with wax to receive writing with a stylus, and then hinged along one edge. Such sets of writing tablets *(tabellae, pugillares)* had long been used as notebooks for jotting memoranda, keeping accounts, doing school exercises, or making rough drafts. The term codex derives from them: *caudex* or *codex* meant originally "a piece of wood." When sheets of papyrus or parchment were substituted for wooden tablets the codex became lighter, easier to handle, and far more capacious. Yet it retained its purely functional status as a notebook and was not immediately regarded as a proper book, that is, a medium of literature.

The papyrus codex was constructed either on a single-quire or a multiple-quire method. A single-quire codex was produced by cutting sheets from a manufactured papyrus roll, stacking them, folding them across at the center, and then fastening them along the crease. Such a codex might contain as many as 50 sheets (yielding 100 leaves or 200 pages). A multiple-quire codex was formed by folding single sheets or small groups of sheets, thus creating a series of gatherings (or quires) which were then stacked and stitched together at their folded edges. On either method, the sheets were usually so arranged that facing pages always exhibited the same side of the papyrus, whether horizontal or vertical fibers. Most early papyrus codices were made as single quires, but the multiple-quire method later prevailed because it permitted the construction of larger codices which did not bulge at the outer edge and tend to spring open. Extant papyrus codices vary in size, but normally are 6–8″ wide and 10–12″ high. Papyrus codices were almost always higher than wide, and thus typically differ from parchment codices, which closely approximate a square shape. Parchment codices could be constructed on the single-quire or the multiple-quire method, but multiple quires are characteristic. Here too the sheets were arranged so that the facing pages showed the same side of the material, in this case either "flesh" or "hair of the skin." Although parchment codices were much outnumbered in the early evidence by papyrus examples, the evidence does not allow a clear determination of what material was originally used for making codices. In the first 3 centuries papyrus seems to have been preferred, for it was plentiful and inexpensive, but by the 4th century parchment predominated, less because of any intrinsic advantage over papyrus than, as some have suggested, because of economic decline in Egypt. Once constructed, the codex was often furnished with a cover of wood or leather which could be fastened with thongs. Few early covers have survived, but the Nag Hammadi codices preserve some fine examples.

The inscribing of a codex posed problems not encountered in a roll. Whereas in a roll all writing was done on the side where the papyrus fibers ran horizontally, in a codex the scribe had to write on both sides of each sheet, and thus also where the papyrus fibers ran vertically. A comparable task was posed by the parchment codex, where the scribe had to write on the hair side as well as on the flesh side. Also, when inscribing a codex it was necessary to calculate carefully in advance how much space would be needed, for the codex, if it was constructed before being inscribed, could not be so easily enlarged as a roll. If, however, the pages were inscribed before the codex was gathered and bound, the sheets had to be carefully maintained in the proper order. Further, whereas rolls were normally inscribed in narrow columns, the relatively narrow pages of codices encouraged the inscription of a rather broader single column per page, and this is the general rule for extant codices. Some, however, have 2 or more columns, but this is more typical of parchment codices with their relatively wider pages.

The first mention of the codex as a medium of literature, and thus as a book proper rather than a notebook, is found in epigrams of the Roman poet Martial in the late 1st century C.E. He refers to the availability of his own poems in a form "which the parchment confines in small pages" (1.2: *quos artat brevibus membrana tabellis*), and mentions the bookseller from whom these could be obtained, so that these were commercial products. He refers also to works of other writers (Homer, Virgil, Cicero) which are *in membranis* or *in pugillaribus membraneis* (14.184–92); at least the latter, but probably all these, were parchment codices. Such inexpensive pocket-editions, which are represented as novelty gifts, must have been produced by a publishing entrepreneur. But the innovation apparently made no headway against the time-honored roll, which continued as the medium of Greek and Latin literature for centuries to come.

It was first of all in Christian circles that the codex gained popularity as a format for literature. The remains of Christian manuscripts from the 2d and 3d centuries are predominately in codex form, and items of Christian "scriptural" literature are almost exclusively in codex form, while the remains of non-Christian manuscripts from this period are by large majority in traditional roll form. The marked departure of Christianity from the established standard in book production cannot be plausibly explained simply by reference to the practical advantages of the codex over the roll, for though there were advantages (economy, portability, ease of reference, comprehensiveness), they would not have been recognized exclusively by Christians. Consequently it has been supposed that the codex was promoted into general Christian usage by the authority of some particular document originally published in a codex, such that the authoritative content of the work carried over to the type of book in which it was known. It has been argued that this document was the gospel of Mark (Roberts 1954), or some early gospel-type document, such as a collection of sayings of Jesus (Roberts and Skeat 1983). A good case might also be made that it was an early collection of Pauline letters. Although such a nonutilitarian stimulus to the Christian adoption of the codex is plausible and probable, the practical advantages of the codex for travelling missionaries (portability, ease of reference, comprehensiveness) ought not be left wholly out of account (McCormick 1985). In any event, the codex early became the standard form of the Christian book, and it was undoubtedly under Christian influence that by the late 3d and early 4th centuries the codex gained parity with the roll as the medium of non-Christian literature, and thereafter almost entirely replaced the roll.

The use of the codex within early Christianity, and most especially for its "scriptural" literature, may be said to imply a functional approach to scripture: this format did not depict its content as cultured literature, but as documentary material for regular uses, such as preaching, teaching, and liturgical reading. Correspondingly, these codices were inscribed in workaday hands rather than calligraphic scripts. And in some ways the codex probably assisted in the conception and formation of a canon of Christian scripture. This type of book provided the technical possibility of compassing a series of documents far more extensive than any single roll could contain, and by the end of the 2d century certain documents were being collectively transcribed on a single codex. Certainly the four Gospels were made available in this way, and so also were the epistles of Paul (cf. the CHESTER BEATTY PAPYRI P^{45} [ca. 250], a codex containing the four Gospels and Acts, and P^{46} [ca. 200], a codex comprising the epistles of Paul). The idea of the exclusive authority of four Gospels, or indeed of a "fourfold Gospel," could find tangible expression only in a codex that contained these and no others, just as the idea that Paul had written to seven churches and no others (and so addressed the church at large) gained concretion by transcribing the letters together in one codex. The form in turn probably helped to promote and to standardize such collections as well as the rationales behind them. Ultimately, when, in the 4th century, all the writings that the Church had come to value as scripture could be transcribed in a single large codex like Codex Sinaiticus or Codex Vaticanus, the codex gave forceful physical representation to the concept of a canon of scripture, connoting its unity, completeness and exclusivity.

Bibliography

Katz, P. 1945. The Early Christians' Use of Codices Instead of Rolls. *JTS* n.s.: 63–65.

McCormick, M. 1985. The Birth of the Codex and the Apostolic Lifestyle. *Scrip* 39: 150–58.

McCown, C. C. 1941. Codex and Roll in the New Testament. *HTR* 34: 219–50.

———. 1943. The Earliest Christian Books. *BA* 6:21–31.
Roberts, C. H. 1949. The Christian Book and the Greek Papyri. *JTS* n.s. 50: 155–68.
———. 1954. The Codex. *Proceedings of the British Academy* 40: 169–204.
Roberts, C. H., and Skeat, T. C. 1983. *The Birth of the Codex.* London.
Robinson, J. M. 1975. The Construction of the Nag Hammadi Codices. Pp. 170–90 in *Essays on the Nag Hammadi Texts in Honor of Pahor Labib.* NHS 6. Leiden.
———. 1975a. On the Codicology of the Nag Hammadi Codices. Pp. 15–31 in *Les Textes de Nag Hammadi,* ed. J.-E. Menard. NHS 7. Leiden.
———. 1984. *The Facsimile Edition of the Nag Hammadi Codices: Introduction.* Leiden.
Schubart, W. 1921. *Das Buch bei den Griechen und Romern.* 2d ed. Berlin and Leipzig.
Skeat, T. C. 1979. 'Especially the Parchments': A Note on 2 Timothy iv. 13. *JTS* n.s. 30: 173–77.
Turner, E. G. 1977. *The Typology of the Early Codex.* Philadelphia.

HARRY Y. GAMBLE

CODEX ALEXANDRINUS

Codex Alexandrinus is a 5th century Gk codex containing both testaments. Because of the early arrival of Alexandrinus to England (only 16 years after the release of the Authorized [King James] Version), this codex was the first early ms of the Gk Bible to be well-known and consulted by scholars. The interest that resulted prompted a search for mss of the Bible, especially of the NT, which has lasted for over 3 centuries.

Codex Alexandrinus was sent as a gift to James I of England by the Greek Patriarch of Constantinople, Cyril Lucar, although the ms did not actually arrive until after the succession of Charles I in 1627. The British Museum became the repository of the codex in 1757 and designated it Royal I.D. V–VIII (Gregory-Aland A). Cyril Lucar had been Patriarch of Alexandria before coming to Constantinople, and it is believed that he brought the ms with him from Egypt (Finegan 1974: 150). A 13th or 14th century note (in Arabic) on the first page of Genesis maintains that the ms belonged to the Patriarchal library in Cairo.

The plain, large, square uncial script on vellum suggests an early date. No original accent or breathing marks occur, but punctuation is provided by the first hand. Ornamentation at the beginning of the books and punctuation or end colophons suggest a date later than Codex Vaticanus and Codex Sinaiticus. Material from Eusebius and Athanasius included before the Psalms requires a later date. It is generally agreed, therefore, that an early 5th century date is correct (see Milne and Skeat 1938:31).

The present codex is bound in 4 volumes with a few missing pages and lucunae defects. Three volumes (629 pages) contain the entire OT with few exceptions. The final volume (144 leaves) contains the NT with the Letters of Clement. Each page measures about 12.6 by 10.4 inches and contains 2 columns with 49–51 lines/column. The codex is composed of quires, usually 8 leaves, with each page numbered with Gk letters in the top center margin.

The OT includes all the books commonly associated with the LXX; in addition are Psalm 151, *3* and *4 Maccabees,* and (after the Psalms) the 14 Odes or liturgical canticles. Therefore, the ms is an important witness to the text of the LXX.

Appended to the entire text of the NT are the two *Epistles of Clement.* According to the table of contents, the *Psalms of Solomon* were originally a part of the codex, but they have been lost.

The type of text of Alexandrinus varies as to section in both testaments. Though opinions vary in the OT, primary text types are pre-Hexaplaric Alexandrian, Hexaplaric, and Lucian (Jellicoe 1968:186 ff.). The NT gospels contain a Byzantine text; Acts and the epistles are Alexandrian with some Western readings. Its greatest textual contributions are in Revelation and some OT books.

Bibliography

Finegan, J. 1974. *Encountering NT Manuscripts.* Grand Rapids.
Jellicoe, S. 1968. *The Septuagint and Modern Study.* Oxford.
Kenyon, F. G. 1909. *The Codex Alexandrinus.* 4 vols. London.
Metzger, B. M. 1981. *Manuscripts of the Greek Bible.* New York.
Milne, H. J. M., and Skeat, T. C. 1938. *Scribes and Correctors of the Codex Sinaiticus.* London.
Spinka, M. 1936. Acquisition of the Codex Alexandrinus by England. *RR* 16: 10–29.
Swete, H. B. 1900. *An Introduction to the OT in Greek.* Cambridge.

JOEL C. SLAYTON

BERLIN GNOSTIC CODEX

The Berlin Gnostic Codex (abbreviation: BG) is also known by the title given it at the Berlin Museum, where it is conserved: Papyrus Berolinensis 8502. It is written in Coptic (Sahidic dialect) and originally contained 142 pages of text, all but the last of which were numbered. Numbered pages 1–6, 11–14 and 133–34 are now missing. It is appropriately called "Gnostic" because 3 of the 4 tractates included in the codex are gnostic: *The Gospel of Mary* ([1.1]–19.5), *The Apocryphon of John* (19.6–77.7), and *The Sophia of Jesus Christ* (77.8–127.12). The 4th tractate, *The Act of Peter* (128.1–141.7), probably comes from Encratite sources (Parrott 1979: 475). The codex is dated, on the basis of paleography, early in the 5th century A.D., which places it in the century after the sequestering of the Nag Hammadi Codices (Till and Schenke 1972: 7). It was discovered in Egypt sometime in the latter part of the 19th century (the date is unknown), and purchased in or near the city of Achmim in 1896 for the Berlin Museum (Schmidt 1896: 839–47). Carl Schmidt proposed to edit it and, in fact, published *Acts Pet.* (Schmidt 1903: 1–25). But the remainder of the codex was unpublished at his death. Walter Till published the 1st edition of the remaining text (1955). Subsequently Hans-Martin Schenke produced a 2d edition of the whole codex (1972).

The cover of BG (presumably leather) is no longer extant. Codicological analysis indicates that the sheets used in the production of the volume were about 13.5 cm. high and 21.6 cm. broad (open position). Three roles of papyrus were used in its manufacture, which resulted in a volume of 146 pages (J. M. Robinson, in Parrott 1979: 36–44). The BG script is bold and square, and is marked by the inconsistent use of superlinear strokes—important elements in Coptic writing that, among other things, help the reader to correctly identify word grouping and the presence of subvocables.

It has recently been proposed that the reason the tractates in BG were collected together is that they all in some way deal with the question of fate or providence. Further, it has been suggested that their arrangement in the codex is determined by that theme, with *Ap. John* serving as the linchpin (Tardieu 1984: 19). This view seems doubtful because (1) the theme of fate or providence is found so generally in gnostic tractates, (2) it is not clear from the extant remains that *Gos. Mary* focused on that theme, and (3) similar codices (i.e., the Nag Hammadi Codices) appear to lack such a theme organization. Therefore, it is likely that the reason for the BG collection could only be discovered if we were to know the special needs and interests of the person or persons for whom the codex was copied.

Bibliography

Parrott, D. M., ed. 1979. *Nag Hammadi Codices V,2–5 and VI with Papyrus Berolinensis 8502, 1 and 4.* NHS 11. Leiden.

Schmidt, C. 1896. Ein vorirenaisches gnostisches Originalwerk in koptischer Sprache. *SPAW* Pp. 839–47.

———. 1903. *Die Alten Petrusakten.* TU 24. Leipzig.

Tardieu, M. 1984. *Écrits Gnostiques: Codex Berlin.* Sources Gnostiques et Manichéennes 1. Paris.

Till, W. C., ed. 1955. *Die gnostischen Schriften des kopischen Papyrus Berolinensis 8502.* TU 60. Berlin.

Till, W. C. and Schenke, H-M., eds. 1972. *Die gnostischen Schriften des koptischen Papyrus Berolinensis 8502.* 2d enl. ed. TU 602. Berlin.

DOUGLAS M. PARROTT

CODEX BEZAE CANTABRIGIENSIS

Codex Bezae, allocated the letter D[ea] and the number 05, originally contained the 4 Gospels (in the order Matthew-John-Luke-Mark), the Catholic Epistles, and Acts. There are a considerable number of lacunae, including all but a leaf of the Epistles, and Acts 22:20 onwards. Out of an original total of 534 leaves, 406 survive. The manuscript has 1 column of 33 lines on each page. The left-hand side of each opening is the Greek text; the right-hand side is an Old Latin version. The lines are of irregular length, with the same content in each column.

The manuscript was written shortly before A.D. 400. The place of writing has long been debated. All the evidence points to an E origin—the style of script has important links with the Roman law school at Berytus (Beirut), the most important Latin center in the E, and an early corrector of the manuscript (B) shows affiliation with a text located in Caesarea. This evidence leads the present writer to favor Berytus as the place where it was written. The character of the manuscript makes it plain that it was written for a church where the Bible was read in Greek and Latin.

The relationship between the 2 columns is complex. It seems that the Latin is derived from a Greek text closely related to D, but not identical with it. It was later revised to bring it into agreement with the Greek column, but with diminishing thoroughness.

A succession of 9 or more hands made corrections, mainly to the Greek, down to about A.D. 700. The manuscript reached Lyons by the 9th century. It stayed there until it passed into the hands of the reformer Theodore Beza, who in 1581 presented it to the University of Cambridge, in whose possession it remains.

In thousands of places the reading of D is unique. A number of factors contribute to its peculiarities.

Firstly, the basic form of the text is much older than the manuscript. It dates from the 2d century, when there was a considerable variety of NT texts.

In the Gospels, there are over 1,500 examples of harmonization (for instance, of the Lord's Prayer in Luke to that of Matthew).

The manuscript is also remarkable for its expansions. One of the more noteworthy is the pericope of the man working on the Sabbath (after Luke 6:4), which is found nowhere else. In particular, the text of Acts contains many significant additions. It has been suggested that theological motives were instrumental in their formation, but there is disagreement as to how distinctive these alleged motives are.

There are readings in the manuscripts that appear to be Semitisms, as well as some Atticisms, and a number of readings that appear actually to introduce Koine idioms into the NT.

The characteristics of the scribe himself are also significant. Many of his errors are due to the influence of the context, where a combination of letters has caught his eye and led him into error. The Gk contains many nonsense readings, and frequently interchanges vowels. But in many ways he carefully reproduced the spellings and practices of his exemplar.

While the distinctive readings of this manuscript have only occasionally laid claim to originality, an understanding of the character of its text is essential to our knowledge of the way in which the early Church handed down the text of the Gospels and Acts.

The editions of Codex Bezae are Scrivener, F. H. 1864. *Bezae Codex Cantabrigiensis, Being an Exact Copy, in Ordinary Type . . . edited with a Critical Introduction, Annotations and Facsimilies.* Cambridge. Repr. 1978. A facsimile edition was produced by Cambridge University Press in 1899: *Codex Bezae Cantabrigiensis. Qvatvor Evangelia et Actus Apostolorum Complectens Graece et Latine.* 2 vols. Cambridge.

Bibliography

Barrett, C. K. 1979. Is There a Theological Tendency in Codex Bezae? Pp. 15–27 in *Text and Interpretation: Studies in the New Testament Presented to Matthew Black,* ed. E. Best and R. McL. Wilson. Cambridge.

Birdsall, J. N. 1986. The Geographical and Cultural Origin of the Codex Bezae Cantabrigiensis. Pp. 102–14 in *Studien zum Text und zur Ethik des Neuen Testaments.* Ed. W. Schrage. Berlin.

Black, M. 1981. The Holy Spirit in the Western Text of Acts. Pp. 159–70 in *New Testament Textual Criticism, Its Significance for Exegesis. Essays in Honour of Bruce M. Metzger,* ed. E. J. Epp and G. D. Fee. Oxford.

Clark, A. C. 1933. *The Acts of the Apostles.* Oxford.

Epp, E. J. 1966. *The Theological Tendency of Codex Bezae in Acts.* SNTSMS 3. Cambridge.

Fischer, B. 1972. Das Neue Testament in lateinischer Sprache, Part 5, Der Codex Bezae und Verwandte Probleme. Pp. 1–92 in *Die alten Ubersetzungen des Neuen Testaments, die Kirchenvaterzitate und Lektionare,* ed. K. Aland. ANTF 5. Berlin. Repr. Pp. 156–274 in *Beitrage zur Geschichte der lateinischen Bibeltexte.* Aus der Geschichte der lateinischen Bibel 12. Freiburg, 1986.

Harris, J. R. 1891. *A Study of Codex Bezae.* TextsS 2/1. Cambridge.

Lowe, E. A. 1972. *Codices Latini Antiquiores* 2. 2d ed. Oxford.

Ropes, J. H. 1926. *The Text of Acts.* Vol. 3 in *The Beginnings of Christianity, Part 1, The Acts of the Apostles.* Ed. F. J. Foakes Jackson and K. Lake. London.

Stone, R. C. 1946. *The Language of the Latin Texts of Codex Bezae.* Urbana, IL.

Vogels, H. J. 1910. *Die Harmonistik im Evangelientext des Codex Cantabrigiensis.* TU 36/1a. Leipzig.

Yoder, J. D. 1961. *Concordance to the Distinctive Greek Text of Codex Bezae.* NTTS 2. Leiden.

D. C. Parker

CODEX BRUCIANUS

Codex Brucianus is the designation for Coptic papyri included among manuscripts purchased in about 1769 in Upper Egypt (perhaps in Medinet Habu) by the Scottish traveler, James Bruce, and eventually acquired by the Bodleian Library in Oxford. The papyri contain the only known manuscripts of 2 ancient Gnostic works: the so-called *First and Second Books of Jeu* and an *Untitled Text.*

The original total of 78 leaves were unbound when acquired, and already in poor physical condition when an early transcription was made, and there has been significant further deterioration. Seven entire leaves and large portions of many others have been lost and are accessible now only in the early copy. Due to the circumstances of their acquisition, the papyri came to be termed collectively the "Bruce Codex," but in reality they seem to be the remains of at least 2 independent codices: 31 leaves containing the *Untitled Text,* inscribed in what is probably a single uncial hand; and the remaining 47 leaves containing the *Books of Jeu.* In this latter group, several scribal hands have been identified, and a more cursive style predominates. The latter fact could indicate that the *Untitled Text* is an older manuscript than the rest of the Bruce Codex, although the dating of these manuscripts is still very uncertain and in need of fresh analysis. Dates ranging from the 3d to the 10th century C.E. have been suggested (Schmidt 1954: xxviii). The Coptic text is probably a translation of works that were composed originally in Gk; the dialect is Sahidic. In the beginning pages of the *Books of Jeu* there are slight dialectical divergences from standard Sahidic. Walter Till (apud Schmidt 1954: xxix) once ascribed these to Subachmimic influence, but they may simply reflect variations deriving from a period before the greater standardization of Sahidic.

Determining the genre of the *Untitled Text* is complicated by the fact that both the beginning and ending have been lost, and there are 5 leaves whose relation to the rest is disputed. The work seems to be a Christian gnostic treatise that describes in systematic fashion the unfolding of the transcendent world and the ordering of material creation. Here and there the author introduces quotations from, or allusions to, both NT and OT writings. The treatise's mythological patterns (e.g., a divine Father-Mother-Son triad), names (e.g., the luminaries Eleleth, Daveide, Oroiael, and [Harmozel]), and terminology are closely related at many points to such texts as the *Apocryphon of John* (NHC II,1; III,1; IV,1; Pap. Berol. 8502,1), *Trimorphic Protennoia* (NHC XIII,1), *Zostrianus* (NHC VIII,1), *Three Steles of Seth* (NHC VII,5), *Allogenes* (NHC XI,3), *Marsanes* (NHC X,1), and a few other "Sethian" gnostic works, as these are often labeled due to the divine Seth who figures prominently in many of them. In the *Untitled Text* a divine entity called "Setheus" does play a central demiurgic role. The precise nature of the relationship among "Sethian" gnostic writings, their respective positions within the history of "Sethian" gnostic doctrines and practices, and the question of how coherent "Sethianism" ever was as a sectarian movement, are issues still in dispute (Layton 1981). The *Untitled Text* is one of several writings important to this discussion.

At one point, the *Untitled Text* appears to allude to works by two Gnostic visionaries, Nicotheus and Marsanes (chap. 7; Schmidt and MacDermot 1978: 235). Epiphanius asserts that a gnostic group whom he labels Archontics spoke of two prophets, Martiades and Marsianos, who were raptured into heaven and returned after 3 days (*Pan.* 40.7.6). This Marsianos could be the same gnostic prophet mentioned by the *Untitled Text* (Schmidt 1892: 602; Puech 1960: 90), and the author of the latter could be alluding to the tractate *Marsanes,* a Platonizing gnostic work of which we now have a fragmentary copy in the Nag Hammadi Library (Pearson 1978: 377; 1981: 229–50). The Neoplatonist Porphyry (*Plot.* 16) mentions an Apocalypse of Nicotheus and an Apocalypse of Zostrianus among other writings already used in Rome in the mid-3d century C.E., by gnostic acquaintances of Plotinus. The Zostrianus apocalypse may be the same as the Nag Hammadi tractate *Zost.,* which in turn shares with the *Untitled Text* certain technical terminology that Plotinus himself mentions as used by his gnostic opponents.

The *Untitled Text* is therefore related to the texts known to this circle of 3d century C.E. Platonist Gnostics in Rome. Schmidt (1892: 664) believed that the treatise dated from around 170–200 C.E., but comparison of its contents with the related writings available since the Nag Hammadi discovery has suggested to some scholars that the *Untitled Text* may represent a later stage of development, in the 3d or 4th century (Sevrin 1986: 208; Turner 1986: 85).

The manuscript containing the *Books of Jeu* consists of 2 principal parts, at the end of the first of which is found the title, "The Book of the Great Mystery-Message" (cf. the reference a few lines earlier in the text to "this great mystery-message of Jeu" [chap. 41]). Though a divine "Jeu" figures prominently in the text, the title *1st and 2d Books of Jeu* does not actually appear in the manuscript. This title was applied to the text by Schmidt, who argued that the contents are to be identified with "the two books of Jeu" mentioned in the closely related *Pistis Sophia* (chaps. 99 and 134) in Codex Askewianus. There Jesus refers his disciples to mysteries that can be found in the 2 books of Jeu that Enoch wrote, when, in an earlier epiphany, Jesus had spoken to Enoch from the trees of Paradise. Early critics of Schmidt's hypothesis noted the absence of any reference to Enoch in Codex Brucianus, and questioned how closely the contents of the manuscript match the description of the teaching that Jesus in *Pistis Sophia* ascribes to the books written by Enoch (Preuschen 1894;

Liechtenhan 1901). Most scholars have nevertheless inclined toward Schmidt's identification.

The manuscript of the *Books of Jeu* has the look of a compilation, the history of which is by no means certain. The surviving leaves seem to preserve only portions of what were originally 2 somewhat longer works, and there are a few extra leaves of uncertain placement, containing fragments of related material in different scribal hands and with some dialectical variations.

The *Books of Jeu* are significant for the history of gnostic ritual. The first book is framed as a revelation dialogue between Jesus and his disciples after his resurrection. Jesus tells them how his Pather brought forth "Jeu, the true God," and then moved Jeu to produce further emanations, themselves called "Jeus" or "fathers of the treasuries." Jesus describes each Jeu in detail, revealing the secret names, numbers, and diagrams corresponding to each one (chaps. 5–32), and then gives instructions about secret numbers, seals, and passwords which will allow the disciples access to each of 60 treasuries of the transcendent world (chaps. 33–40). He takes the disciples into the treasuries and leads them in ritual prayers (chap. 41). In the second book Jesus initiates the disciples into the mysteries of water baptism, baptism of fire, and baptism of the Spirit, each accompanied by elaborate description of the requisite ritual materials and procedures (chaps. 45–48). He then describes the future ascent of their souls through the levels of the transcendent realm, and for each level there is again instruction about cryptic seals, numbers, and passwords to be used in the ascent (chaps. 49–52). Among the most striking features of this manuscript are the numerous cryptograms and seals actually sketched in the text and margins, virtually the only examples of such pictorial elements in a gnostic manuscript (Phinney 1980: 436–37). This fact renders the absence of any facsimile edition of this part of the Bruce Codex all the more regrettable.

Schmidt (1892: 552–98) argued that the *Books of Jeu* and at least the last two books of the *Pistis Sophia* were composed in the 3d century C.E. by members of the same ascetic Severian sect (Epiphanius, *Pan.* 45), and that this sect had come into conflict with libertine Phibionite gnostics who were near relatives as far as sectarian ancestry. Both writings include passages which condemn the ritual consumption of semen and menstrual blood (*Jeu* chap. 43; *Pistis Sophia* chap. 147), and Epiphanius (*Pan.* 26) accuses certain "Phibionites" of a similar practice. A literary connection between *Pistis Sophia* and the *Books of Jeu* remains likely, but a specific link with the Severian gnostics mentioned by Epiphanius is far more tenuous. The shared characteristics upon which Schmidt based his identification (e.g., use of the demiurgic names Ialdabaoth or Sabaoth; ascetic tendencies, etc.) are now found in several texts from Nag Hammadi, and may be too general to allow any narrow identification of the *Books of Jeu* with a gnostic sect that is otherwise so sparsely documented as is the Severian sect.

Bibliography

Abramowski, L. 1983. Nag Hammadi 8,1 "Zostrianus," das Anonymum Brucianum, Plotin Enn. 2,9 (33). Pp. 1–10 in *Platonismus und Christentum: Festschrift für Heinrich Dörrie,* ed. H.-D. Blume and F. Mann. JAC Ergänzungsband 10. Münster.

Amélineau, E. 1891. Notice sur le papyrus gnostique Bruce, Text et traduction. *Notices et extraits des manuscrits de la Bibliothèque Nationale et autres bibliothèques* 29/1: 65–305.

Baynes, C. A. 1933. *A Coptic Gnostic Treatise contained in the Codex Brucianus (Bruce MS. 96. Bod. Lib. Oxford).* Cambridge.

Layton, B. ed. 1981. *The Rediscovery of Gnosticism.* Vol. 2: *Sethian Gnosticism.* SHR 41. Leiden.

Liechtenhan, R. 1901. Untersuchungen zur koptisch-gnostischen Litteratur. *ZWT* 44: 236–53.

Pearson, B., ed. 1978. The Tractate Marsanes (NHC X) and the Platonic Tradition. Pp. 373–84 in *Gnosis: Festschrift für Hans Jonas,* ed. B. Aland. Göttingen.

———. 1981. *Nag Hammadi Codices IX and X.* NHS 15. Leiden: Brill.

Phinney, P. C. 1980. Did Gnostics Make Pictures? Vol. 1, Pp. 434–54 in *The Rediscovery of Gnosticism,* ed. B. Layton. SHR 41. Leiden.

Puech, H.-C. 1960. Plotin et les Gnostiques. Pp. 159–74 in *Les sources de Plotin.* Entretiens sur l'antiquité classique 5. Geneva.

Preuschen, E. 1894. Review of *Gnostische Schriften in koptischer Sprache aus dem Codex Brucianus,* by C. Schmidt. *TLZ* 7: 183–87.

Schmidt, C. 1892. *Gnostische Schriften in koptischer Sprache aus dem Codex Brucianus.* TU 8. Leipzig.

———. 1894. Die in dem koptisch-gnostischen Codex Brucianus enthaltenen "Beiden Bücher Jeû" in ihrem Verhältnis zu der Pistis Sophia untersucht. *ZWT* 37: 555–85.

———. 1901. *Plotinus Stellung nach dem Ursprung des Gnosticismus.* TU 20,4. Leipzig.

———. 1954. *Koptisch-gnostische Schriften.* Vol. 1, *Die Pistis Sophia, Die beiden Bücher des Jeu, Unbekanntes altgnostiches Werk,* ed. W. Till. GCS 45. Berlin.

Schmidt, C., ed., and MacDermot, V. 1978. *The Books of Jeu and the Untitled Text in the Bruce Codex.* NHS 13. Leiden.

Sevrin, J. M. 1986. *Le dossier baptismal séthien.* BCNHE 2. Quebec.

Turner, J. D. 1986. Sethian Gnosticism. Pp. 55–86 in *Nag Hammadi, Gnosticism and Early Christianity,* ed. C. W. Hedrick and R. Hodgson, Jr. Peabody, MA.

MICHAEL A. WILLIAMS

CODEX CLAROMONTANUS

Codex Claromontanus is a 5th- or more likely 6th-century codex containing only the Pauline letters (including Hebrews). It is a bi-lingual Gk and Lat manuscript, consisting of 533 vellum leaves (9⅝″ by 7⅝″), with the Gk text of the letters on the left-hand page, the Lat on the right. Each page bears 1 column of text with 21 lines of irregular length (corresponding to the pauses in the sense).

It is impossible to determine the codex's place of origin. The work of at least 9 different correctors has been identified (the 4th of these added accent and breathing marks in the 9th century). Theodore Beza, the celebrated French scholar who became the successor of Calvin as leader of the Genevan Church, acquired the manuscript between 1565 and 1582. He claimed that it was discovered in a convent at Clermont-en-Beauvais. An edition of the manuscript was published by Tischendorf in 1852.

Codex Claromontanus is an important early witness in the history of the NT text. Like Codex Bezae, which is roughly contemporaneous with this manuscript and contains most of the text of the four Gospels and Acts (with a small fragment of 3 John), the type of text in Codex Claromontanus is distinctly Western. As Metzger (1968) has noted, however, Western readings in the Epistles are not so striking as those in the Gospels and Acts.

Codex Claromontanus is also important for the history of the Christian canon of scripture. After the text of Philemon in this manuscript, and just before the text of Hebrews, there is a stichometric list, in Latin only, of OT and NT books. Whereas the OT books are listed without division, the NT books are subdivided into 2 categories: "The Four Gospels" and "The Epistles of Paul." What is striking is that Paul's letters are not distinguished from the Catholic Epistles and other writings which are also indexed. There is an obvious omission after the listing of Ephesians: Philippians, 1 and 2 Thessalonians are missing. Hebrews is also lacking. The scribe obelizes 4 works at the end of the list: *Barnabas*, the *Shepherd of Hermas*, the *Acts of Paul*, and the *Apocalypse of Peter*. Souter (1954) suggested that these horizontal lines indicate that they are not to be regarded as on the same plane as the others. If that is the case, the canon list included in Codex Claromontanus, granted its careless omissions, would apparently intend to set forth a NT canon of 27 texts.

The presence of such a list in this codex is curious. Jülicher (1931) thought this catalogue belonged to the 4th century and was of W origin. Zahn (1890), however, put forth a compelling argument for a 4th-century date and an E provenance, perhaps Syria-Palestine. As with the MURATORIAN FRAGMENT, how such a list could have come to occupy a place in this codex remains a mystery. Nevertheless, with the exception of Hennecke (*NTApocr* 1) most have followed Zahn in assigning a 4th-century date and an E provenance to the canon list, although the codex in which it appears is W and later.

Bibliography

Jülicher, A. 1931. *Einleitung in das Neue Testament.* 7th edition. Tubingen.

Metzger, B. M. 1968. *The Text of the New Testament.* 2d edition. Oxford.

Souter, A. 1954. *The Text and Canon of the New Testament.* London.

Sundberg, A. C., Jr., 1973. Canon Muratori: A Fourth-Century List. HTR 66: 1–41.

Zahn, T. 1890. *Geschichte des Neutestamentlichen Kanons II.* Erlangen and Leipzig.

Gregory Allen Robbins

CODEX EPHRAIMI RESCRIPTUS

This manuscript (Paris, Bibliothéque Nationale Gr. 9; designated C throughout, and given the number 04 for the NT in the Gregory-Aland catalogue) originally contained the entire Bible. It is a palimpsest, having been broken up and used by a 12th century monk to copy a Gk translation of discourses by Ephraim Syrus. There are 63 OT leaves extant (containing parts of Proverbs, Ecclesiastes, Canticles, Job, Wisdom, and Sirach) and 145 of the NT (in which every canonical book is represented). It may have been written in the 5th century, though Cavallo dates it almost certainly to the 6th. The leaves are 25.6–26.4 × 31.4–32.5 cm; there is a single column, of between 40 and 46 lines on each page. The NT originally contained about 232 (Lyon) or 238 leaves (Kenyon). The OT and NT portions are by separate hands. Arguments that allot the NT to several scribes (Traube, Lyon) are based on differences in forms of the *nomina sacra* and orthography between different books, and have no foundation in the character of the handwriting. The differences are more likely to be due to the use of several separate exemplars in the compilation of the manuscript. This is the appropriate point to note that Oliver has demonstrated that a dislocation of a portion of the text in Revelation is due to the leaves of the exemplar having been bound out of order.

Tischendorf suggested that the manuscript was written in Egypt. This is confirmed by Cavallo, who argues for the Nitrian Desert, associating the script (he is thinking, it appears, of the NT particularly) with those of the Freer manuscript of Deuteronomy and Joshua, the NT uncials 016 (its closest associate) and 027, and two Homer codices (Papyrus Berolinensis 6794 and the Cureton Homer). It belongs to the period of decadence of the biblical uncial script, and was written "without particular care to be calligraphic." The copying, it is alleged, was also careless. These 2 points have led to speculation that the manuscript may have been written for private use.

The text has been reworked by 2 correctors who, it is suggested, are to be placed in 6th-century Caesarea and 9th-century Constantinople. In the early 16th century the codex was brought to Italy, and passed into the possession of Catherine de Medici, with whom it went to Paris, where it has remained ever since.

The great difficulty of deciphering the manuscript has led to its neglect, so that it has been the subject of only a very few studies, and only one edition. The text of the NT is placed by K. and B. Aland in their Category II (of special quality, but contaminated by alien influences). Their analysis of test passages shows that the text of Paul is particularly good. The figures given below show, in order, (a) agreements with the Byzantine text, (b) agreements with the same where it has what the Alands consider to be the original text, (c) agreements with their original text, (d) and readings where it is unique.

	(a)	*(b)*	*(c)*	*(d)*
Gospels	87,	66,	66,	50
Acts	12,	12,	37,	11
Paul	31,	23,	104,	15
Catholic Epistles	15,	3,	41,	12

Bibliography

The manuscript was edited by C. Tischendorf. 1843. *Codex Ephraemi rescriptus sive Fragmenta Novi Testamenti.* Leipzig. For corrections, see R. W. Lyon, below.

Aland, K. and B. 1987. The *Text of the New Testament.* Grand Rapids and Leiden.

Cavallo, G. 1967. *Richerche sulla maiuscola biblica.* 2 vols. *Studi e testi di papirologia* 2. Florence.

Hatch, W. H. P. 1939. *The Principal Uncial Manuscripts of the New Testament.* Chicago.

Jellicoe, S. 1968. *The Septuagint and Modern Study.* Oxford.

Kenyon, F. G. 1912. *Handbook to the Textual Criticism of the New Testament.* 2d ed. London.

Lyon, R. W. 1959. A Re-examination of the Codex Ephraimi Rescriptus. *NTS* 5: 266–72.
Oliver, H. H. 1957. A Textual Transposition in Codex C (Ephraemi Syri Rescriptus). *JBL* 76: 233–36.
Stone, R. B. 1986. The Life and Hard Times of Ephraimi Rescriptus. *TBT* 24: 112–18.
Swete, H. B. 1914. *An Introduction to the Old Testament in Greek.* 2d ed. Cambridge.
Traube, L. 1907. *Nomina Sacra. Versuch einer Geschichte der christlichen Kürzung.* Quellen and Untersuchungen zur lateinischen Philologie des Mittelalters 2. Munich.

D. C. Parker

CODEX SINAITICUS

This codex comes from the Sinai, where it was preserved until the last century in St. Catherine's monastery, which is situated at the foot of Jebel Musa (Mount of Moses) on which, according to ancient traditions, the Ten Commandments were given by God to Israel. This Gk copy of the Bible is now housed in 4 very different places. Most of it, 347 leaves, are proudly displayed on the 1st floor of the British Library (the British Museum). Forty-three leaves are in the University Library at Leipzig. Fragments of 3 leaves are in Leningrad. These collections were removed from St. Catherine's by Constantine Tischendorf: the smaller collection in 1844, the fragments and the major part of the codex in 1859. A fire in St. Catherine's monastery in 1975 revealed around 4,000 manuscripts, including more than a dozen leaves of this precious codex; some of the leaves look as though they came off the table of the copying scribe. These are being prepared for publication by his emminence Archbishop Damianos.

This 4th-century Gk ms, one of the most precious and ancient manuscripts of the Bible, contains most of the OT, the NT, the *Epistle of Barnabas,* and the *Shepherd of Hermas* (up to *Man.* 4.3.6). Scholars estimate that the original manuscript contained at least 730 leaves and would have required approximately 360 goats or sheep to provide the skins. The work was copied by 3 different scribes whose calligraphy is so similar that it is probable that they were trained in the same scriptorium. The manuscript could have been produced in Rome, Caesarea, or Alexandria.

Bibliography

Charlesworth, J. H. 1981. *The New Discoveries in St. Catherine's Monastery: A Preliminary Report on the Manuscripts,* with G. T. Zervos. Foreword by D. N. Freedman. ASORMS 3. Winona Lane, IN.
Lake, H. and K. 1911–1922. *Codex Sinaiticus Petropolitanus.* 2 vols. Oxford.
Metzger, B. M. 1981. Codex Sinaiticus. Pp. 76–79 in *Manuscripts of the Greek Bible.* Oxford and New York.
Milne, H. J. M. and Skeat, T. C. 1951. *The Codex Sinaiticus and the Codex Alexandrinus.* London.
———. 1938. *Scribes and Correctors of the Codex Sinaiticus.* London.
Politis, L. 1980. Nouveau manuscripts grecs découverts au mont sinaï. *Scriptorium* 34: 5–17.

James H. Charlesworth

CODEX VATICANUS

Codex Vaticanus (Vatican Library, Cod. Gr. 1209, given the letter B and, for the NT, the numeral 03) is one of a small number of extant ancient Greek Bibles containing both the OT and NT (though it never contained any of the books of Maccabees). It has been in the Vatican Library since at least 1475, when it was listed in a catalogue (Ropes 1926: xxxi; cf. Kenyon 1912: 77n). During the 15th century, it had certain lacunae filled: Gen 1:1–46:26 (copied from the Vatican Codex Chisianus R VI 38, which is numbered 19 in the catalogue of LXX manuscripts); Ps 105:27–137:6; Heb 9:14 to the end, the Pastoral Epistles, and Revelation (this addition is listed separately amongst NT manuscripts as minuscule 1957). Certain embellishments were added at the same period. In addition to these gaps in the ancient manuscript, part of a leaf (containing 2 Kgdms 2:5–7, 10–13) has been torn away. It has been suggested by Skeat (1984: 463) that B was brought to Rome from Constantinople as a gift by the Greek delegation to the Council of Ferrara-Florence in 1438–39, after a hasty restoration. Attempts to link the manuscript with Cardinal Bessarion and with S Italy are rightly rejected by Skeat (1984: 454–55), following Šagi.

In the 10th or 11th century, the original text was overwritten letter by letter, accents and breathings were newly supplied, and some corrections were made. This activity, apart from destroying the great beauty of the codex, has greatly impeded precise paleographical analysis, so that dating and placing the manuscript's origin is very difficult.

Cavallo suggests the date ca. 350 (after 328 but before 360). It is most likely to have been written in Egypt (Martini 1966: 6; Cavallo 1967: 56). Hatch (1953: xix) suggests Upper Egypt. The attribution to Egypt rests on textual grounds and the order of the books, rather than on a paleographical decision. The theory that the so-called Coptic form of the letter *Mu* indicates an Egyptian origin is not tenable.

It was once a fashionable suggestion that B (with Codex Sinaiticus) was one of 50 copies prepared by Eusebius of Caesarea for the Emperor Constantine in the early 330s. This idea must be abandoned, as must the idea that it was commissioned from Athanasius in Rome by the Emperor Constantine 10 years later.

The ms was written by 2 scribes, "A" and "B," of whom B wrote the NT. The codex is of fine appearance, square (27 × 27cm), composed of 5-sheet quires (quinions), with 3 columns to a page, and 40–44 lines to a column. The text was corrected by a hand contemporary with the scribes, generally identified with the *diorthotes* (official corrector of the scriptorium).

This manuscript is, given its extent, textually the best of any. In the OT it forms the basis of the smaller and larger Cambridge editions. In the NT it was the foundation of Westcott and Hort's text. For the most part, the OT shows a form of LXX text similar to that used by Origen in the 5th column of his Hexapla. It was therefore affected far less than most other manuscripts by the deleterious influence of the Hexapla on the LXX. It is least valuable in Isaiah, Jeremiah, the Minor Prophets, and Job. Its text of Judges is very distinctive, and generally associated with the Hesychian recension.

In the NT, its text is of a high quality throughout (the view that in Paul it shows the influence of the so-called Western text should be treated cautiously). C. M. Martini has demonstrated that the text of B in Luke is substantially that found in the beginning of the 3d century in P. Bodmer XIV–XV. Porter has shown the same to be true for John. In Paul, according to Zuntz, it represents, along with P. Chester Beatty, P. Ann Arbor, and miniscule 1739, the Proto-Alexandrian text of ca. A.D. 200, and preserves the ancient tradition stemming from the creation of the Pauline corpus in ca. 100.

For the story of the early collations, and the first, notoriously inaccurate, full transcription by Mai, see Kenyon (1912: 77–79). A photographic reprint of the whole manuscript was made in 1889–90. A reprint of the NT alone was made in 1968, for presentation to the more distinguished of those attending the Second Vatican Council.

Bibliography

Photographic Reproductions

Novum Testamentum e codice vaticano 1209, nativi textus graeci primo omnium phototypice repraesentatum, auspice Leone XXX, Pont. Max., curante Josepho Cozzaluzi Abate Basiliano. Rome, 1889. The OT was published the following year.

Bibliorum SS. Graecorum Codex Vaticanus 1209 (Cod. B) denuo phototypice expressus jussu et cura praesidum bibliothecae Vaticanae. Testamentum Vetus et Novum. 4 vols. *Codices e Vaticanis selecti phototypice expressi* . . . 4. Milan, 1904–7.

Ta Iera Biblia *Codex Vaticanus graecus 1209. Phototypice expressus iussu Pauli PP VI Pontificis Maximi* He Kaine Diatheke. Vatican, 1965.

Secondary Literature

Aland, B., and K. 1987. *The Text of the New Testament.* Trans. E. F. Rhodes. Leiden.

Cavallo, G. 1967. *Ricerche sulla maiuscola biblica.* Florence.

Hatch, W. H. 1939. *The Principal Uncial Manuscripts of the New Testament.* Chicago.

———. 1953. The Provenance of Codex Vaticanus. *JBL* 72: xviii–xix.

Hoskier, H. C. 1914. *Codex B and Its Allies. A Study and an Indictment.* 2 vols. London.

Jellicoe, S. 1968. *The Septuagint and Modern Study.* Oxford.

Kenyon, F. G. 1912. *Handbook to the Textual Criticism of the New Testament.* 2d ed. London.

Lake, K. 1918. The Sinaitic and Vatican Manuscripts and the Copies sent by Eusebius to Constantine. *HTR* 11: 32–35.

Martini, C. M. 1966. *Il Problema della recensionalita del codice B alla luce del papiro Bodmer XIV.* AnBib 26. Rome.

Payne, J. B. 1949. The Relationship of the Chester Beatty Papyri of Ezekiel to Codex Vaticanus. *JBL* 68: 251–65.

Porter, C. L. 1962. Papyrus Bodmer XV (P75) and the Text of Codex Vaticanus. *JBL* 81: 363–76.

Ropes, J. H. 1926. *The Text of Acts.* Vol. 3, pp. xxxi–xliv, xc–xcviii in *The Beginnings of Christianity.* Pt 1, *The Acts of the Apostles,* ed. F. J. Foakes Jackson and K. Lake. London.

Šagi, J. 1972. Problema historiae codicis B. *DivT* 75: 3–29.

Skeat, T. C. 1984. The Codex Vaticanus in the Fifteenth Century. *JTS* n.s. 35: 454–65.

Zuntz, G. 1953. *The Text of the Apostles. A Disquisition upon the Corpus Paulinum.* London.

D. C. PARKER

CODEX WASHINGTONIANUS

Sometimes referred to as the Freer Manuscript of the Gospels, this ms is designated "W" in the Gregory-Aland list of ms sigla. Housed in the Freer Gallery of Art (Smithsonian, Washington, D.C.), it is an Egyptian-provenance parchment ms of the 4th/5th centuries containing the four Gospels in the "Western" order (Matt, John, Luke, Mark), with 2 lacunae (Mark 15:13–38; John 14:25–16:7, owing to missing pages). Except for the 1st quire of John (1:1–5:11), it is the work of one scribe. There are various indications of formal formatting of the ms for public reading and for study (e.g., punctuation, blank spaces between phrases, paragraph divisions, diacritical marks), and several correctors' hands are evidenced. The pages (averaging 8⅛ × 5⅝″) contain a single column of 30 lines in a clear, sloping hand (ruled lines between 27–35 letters (approx. 3⅞″ long). A major feature of codex W is the mixed nature of its text. Matt and Luke 8:13–24:53 reflect the Byzantine text-type. Luke 1:1–8:12 and John 5:12–21:25 are Alexandrian. Mark 1:1–5:30 (or slightly earlier) is "Western," resembling especially the Old Latin. Mark 5:31–16:20 was long thought a witness to an early stage of the Caesarean text, but has been shown to be insufficiently related to any main text-type, agreeing with P45 most often and showing numerous harmonizations with the other Synoptics as well as deliberate scribal changes, mainly in Markan style. It has been suggested that the varying textual complexion of W derives from an ancestor patchwork manuscript made up after Diocletian's attempt in 303 C.E. to destroy all Christian sacred books.

Probably the most noteworthy reading in W follows Mark 16:14, a reading witnessed to also by Jerome. The undoubtedly apocryphal reading is as follows:

> And they excused themselves, saying, "This age of lawlessness and unbelief is under Satan, who does not allow the truth and power of God to prevail over the unclean things of the spirits. Therefore reveal your righteousness now"—so they spoke to Christ. And Christ replied to them, "The term of years for Satan's authority has been fulfilled, but other terrible things draw near. And for those who have sinned I was delivered over to death, that they may return to the truth and sin no more; that they may inherit the spiritual and incorruptible glory of righteousness which is in heaven."

Bibliography

Gregory, C. R. 1908. *Das Freer-Logion.* Leipzig.

Hurtado, L. W. 1981. *Text-Critical Methodology and the Pre-Caesarean Text: Codex W in the Gospel of Mark.* SD 43. Grand Rapids.

Sanders, H. A. 1912. *Facsimile of the Washington Manuscript of the Four Gospels in the Freer Collection.* Ann Arbor.

———. 1912–18. *The New Testament Manuscripts in the Freer Collection 1: The Washington Manuscript of the Four Gospels.* New York.

L. W. HURTADO

COELE-SYRIA (PLACE) [Gk *Koilē Syria*]. Coele-Syria is a geographical term variously used to describe portions of Syro-Palestine, depending on the historical time period and the author. The term which has been widely interpreted as "hollow Syria" is first attested in its Hellenistic form in the 4th century B.C. While often used by modern writers to describe the N extent of the Great Rift Valley between the Lebanon and Anti-Lebanon Mountains, the name was used by the Hellenistic writers to include a large portion of the E Mediterranean seaboard extending E toward to the Euphrates. Phoenicia however was held to be separate from Coele-Syria. Under Alexander the Great, Coele-Syria was a large administrative unit that included Samaria, which revolted against Andromachus the governor of Coele-Syria whom Alexander had appointed (Curtius Rufus 4.8.9). Under the Ptolemies and Seleucids, the term continued to be used for an administrative region. Under Antiochus III, the Levant was divided into strategia of Coele-Syria and Phoenicia. Coele-Syria in turn was divided into 4 eparchies: Samaria, Idumea, Paralia, and Galaaditis (Diodorus 19.95.2). The names of 6 Seleucid governors of Coele-Syria have been preserved. One of them, Apollonius of Tarsus, the "governor of Coele-Syria and Phoenicia" (2 Macc 3:5–8), fought the Maccabees and was defeated at Jamnia ca. 147 B.C. (1 Macc 10:69ff.). "Coele-Syria" is used to describe S Syria with the exclusion of Phoenicia throughout the Apochrypha (1 Esdr 2:17, 24, 27; 4:48; 1 Macc 10:69; 2 Macc 4:4; etc.). Diodorus of Sicily in describing the Levant prior to the Romans, defined Coele-Syria as being adjacent to Upper Syria, enclosing Phoenicia, and extending as far as Egypt (18.6.3).

The toponym "Coele-Syria" continued to be used after Rome expanded her power into the Levant under Pompey. After Herod gained the enmity of the Jews for his harsh rule over Galilee in 47 B.C., he was made a general over Coele-Syria (Josephus *Ant* 14.9.5 §180). In that position Herod apparently had authority in Damascus, Samaria, and the Transjordan (Josephus *JW* 1.10.8 §213); Josephus, however, uses the term in a variety of ways. At times it is defined as extending from the Euphrates to Egypt (*Ant* 14.4.5 §79).

Among other classical authors, Strabo in his geographical study included all of the arable land E of the Rift Valley in Coele-Syria, with Damascus as its chief city (*Geog* 16.2.2–22), and Ptolemy included the cities of Coele-Syria with those of the Decapolis (*Geog* 5.14).

In the 2d century A.D. the cities of the Decapolis such as Abila, Gadara, Philadelphia, and Scythopolis retained their ancient territorial description by having an abbreviation for Coele-Syria on their coins. The recognition of this region as Coele-Syria was later affirmed by the Roman Emperor Septimius Severus.

The etymology of the word "Coele" is debated. The widely accepted interpretation "hollow Syria" is challenged by E. Schwarz who has postulated that Coele is the hellenized form of the Heb word *kol.* His position is affirmed by A. Shalit, who maintains that Coele-Syria is identical to the usual expression in Gk for "all Syria." B. Mazar buttresses this position by arguing that the Greeks developed the toponym Coele-Syria on the basis of the ancient term "all Aram," which was used by the Aramaic-speaking population, and the word Syria was substituted for Aram (see Mazar 1962: 120 for this discussion).

Bibliography

Bickermann, E. J. 1947. La Coele-Syrie: Notes de Geographie historique. *RB* 54: 256–268.

Mazar, B. 1962. The Aramaean Empire and its Relations with Israel. *BA* 25: 98–120.

ROBERT W. SMITH

COHORT, AUGUSTAN. See AUGUSTAN COHORT.

COHORT, ITALIAN. See ITALIAN COHORT.

COINAGE. Money is a medium of exchange used to acquire goods or services, and therefore serves as a measure of wealth or value. It may also be symbolic of sovereignty or a unit of accounting. Coins are minted metal authorized to function as money; they are culturally accepted media for exchange and designations of value.

A. Money in the Hebrew Bible

When money is mentioned throughout the Hebrew Bible, the text does not refer to coins. The references designate measures of value in goods or in precious metals. The metals are not coined, however, in specific weights. Nor are they generally verified by an official stamp of governmental or religious authorities to meet certain weight standards. The NT, however, has as its background the coined money of the Hellenistic and Roman periods. Coins expressed monetary value more specifically and more easily than bullion, but were still used in tandem with "in kind" transactions, where "money" still existed in the form of sheep, goats, birds, grain, oil, or wine. Indeed, some form of money has existed from earlier times when people bartered with one another or traded commodities. By the time of Jesus and the Apostles of the early Church, coinage was widely accepted and used throughout all lands associated with the Bible. Coinage facilitated exchange of objects, measured value, stored wealth, and provided support and taxation for governments.

In the history of the people of the covenant, the first reference to the use of money is the restitution paid to Abraham by Abimelech for the wrong done to Sarah, Abraham's wife, in Gen 20:14–16. Abimelech pays Abraham "sheep and oxen, and male and female slaves" together with "a thousand pieces of silver" serving as "vindication" for what he had done. In Genesis 23, Abraham purchases a burial place from Ephron the Hittite for 400 shekels of silver. A shekel, on the Babylonian standard, was the equivalent of approx. 8.5 grams of metal. "Abraham weighed out for Ephron the silver which he had named in the hearing of the Hittites, four hundred shekels of silver, according to the weights current among the merchants" (Gen 23:16). The merchants used the Babylonian standard of weights and measures. To "weigh out" this amount was to hand over to Ephron the weight in silver of approx. 8 minas, the equivalent of 26½ gold shekels. The silver would have been in the form of small ingots, pieces of silver foil, rings or silver wire. This was a substantial amount to be sure, although we cannot accurately estimate its value in modern currencies. Ancient measures in grams can be converted to equivalents on the current market value of silver or gold, given market fluctuations. If we can assume that precious metals have always remained fairly stable in their relative value to other goods and services, then we can estimate in late 20th century equivalents what these amounts of money would equal. Clearly, however, this is a haphazard procedure and is best avoided.

The Joseph cycle contains several references to "money," translating the Heb *kesep,* which is also the word for "silver." This "money" included "bundles" which were placed in the traveling bags of Joseph's brothers when they were about to leave Egypt and return to Canaan; the text also mentions the money collected to pay for grain from the Egyptian royal granaries. In Genesis 43, Joseph received money which must have included gold, silver, bronze, and iron, in rings, bars, ingots, or dust (gold only). These were recognized forms of "money," which were weighed in specific amounts and functioned as bullion on the open market. The metals were weighed in specific ratios to one another for terms of standard commerce or taxation. So it is also in Genesis 47, when "Joseph gathered up all the money that was found in the land of Egypt and in the land of Canaan, for the grain which they bought; and Joseph brought the money into Pharaoh's house." When this metallic money was depleted, it was freely interchanged with cattle. "So they brought their cattle to Joseph; and Joseph gave them food in exchange for the horses, the flocks, the herds, and the asses; and he supplied them with food in exchange for all their cattle that year" (Gen 47:17). Specific numbers of animals were considered equally as valuable as their equivalents in metal. Obviously they were harder to handle, but were just as usable in making payments. In Genesis 47, seed and its produce function as money when the Pharoah decreed that harvests will go 80% to him and 20% to the tenant on the land. So it was according to the tradition, while Israel lived in the land of Goshen.

Abraham and the other patriarchs counted their wealth in numbers of sheep, goats, and cattle. The same was true for Job (1:3). Throughout the period of the patriarchs and into the time of the kings of Israel and Judah, the primary means of commerce and trade was barter. Money could be metallic and weighed according to accepted local or international standards, or it could be in kind. When Hiram of Tyre completed construction of Solomon's Temple in Jerusalem, he paid with grain and olive oil, according to 1 Kgs 5:11. Some taxes or forms of tribute were paid in like manner, with grains, oils, wine, sheep/goats, or cattle. On Israelite taxes, see specifically 1 Sam 8:15 and Ezek 45:13–16.

Clearly, transporting herds to administrative or tribal centers to pay tribute or taxes was difficult and most inconvenient for the taxpayer and the taxgatherer. This is probably why equivalent values in metals came to be weighed out and standardized for such transactions. Values could be more easily computed using weights in precious metals as well. For example, if a tax was 10 shekels, or its equivalent of 2 sheep, and the tax was raised by 20% to 12 shekels, the taxation would then equal 2⅖ sheep. Metals became the preferred method of payment when available.

The earliest standards of weights and measures remain unknown. The Bible is mute on the subject, simply referring to numbers of "pieces" or "shekels" of silver (Heb *kesep*). We are not certain what standard this metal was weighed on. The Hebrew renders these expressions only as "silver," implying that an accepted standard or measure was used. The lack of exchange of gold within the Hebrew Bible is strong evidence to suggest that this metal was available in insufficient quantity for use in commerce. For many years, as well, copper was needed for tools, jewelry, or weapons. The copper was mixed with tin and made into bronze. With the coming of the Philistines in the period following 1200 B.C.E., iron began to replace bronze as the metal most used in implements and other hardware. Iron had been smelted in Egypt for many years but had been retained in Egypt; by 1200, its use began to spread.

An early use for precious metals was jewelry, which provided a safe, mobile means for their movement around the country. It is still common for Bedouin women in Palestine to carry all their wealth on their persons in the form of gold, silver, and bronze jewelry. They wear metals in bracelets, anklets, rings, chains, pins, beads, earrings, or settings for precious or semiprecious stones (see Ezekiel 28). Today one is more likely to find strings of coins, pierced and geometrically arranged on necklaces, or coins as earrings or pendants. Some of these forms into which metals were made were probably standardized and accepted on the open market. Even so, as nearly pure forms of the metals, they could be weighed on scales and their value quickly established in commerce if needed, so that they could function as bullion. The Hebrew Bible mentions payment using bars of silver or gold, as well as bracelets, which could have had specific values assigned to them. Abraham's servant gave Rebekah a ring of gold which weighed ½ shekel and 2 bracelets weighing 10 gold shekels (Gen 24:22). In Joshua 7:21, Achan returns from Jericho with 200 shekels of silver and a gold bar (lit. "tongue") weighing 51 shekels. Certainly by the Iron I period, Babylonian weight standards were accepted and current through the lands of the Bible. At Ugarit, in the "Tale of Aqhat," the hero is said to have shed tears like quarter-shekels and fifth-shekels. This is Ugaritic hyperbole to affirm that Aqhat wept bitterly; the glittering metal likened to tears implies a recognizable size and shape, much like money.

Examples of references to weights of silver or money are numerous. In Judges 16:4, Philistine leaders entice Delilah to find the source of Samson's strength by offering her 1,100 pieces of silver (lit. "1000 and 100 *kesep*"). In 1 Sam 9:4, ¼ shekel of silver is the payment to a seer for a prediction on the future success of a journey. When the king of Aramaean Damascus sent a messenger to Israel to seek assistance in healing Naaman of leprosy, the price was considerably higher: 10 talents (lit. "circles" from Heb *kikkār*) of silver and 6,000 shekels of gold. A talent was the equivalent of 60 minas, each of which equalled 50 shekels of silver. One gold shekel was the equivalent of 15 silver shekels. Later during the reign of Azariah in Judah, Menahem reigned for a short time in Samaria doing "what was evil in the sight of the Lord." To confirm his succession as king, he offered the sovereign of Assyria 1,000 talents of silver, exacting it in Israel from wealthy men, asking 50 shekels from each (2 Kgs 15:19–20).

B. Money in the Ancient Near East

1. The shekel. One silver shekel equalled approximately 8.26 g. Fractional shekels were also regularly employed in Palestine and throughout the ANE. A cuneiform text written in Akkadian from the Smith College collection, for example, details an exchange of goods from 2 brothers to their creditors from the time of Samsuiluna of Babylon (18th cent. B.C.E.), in which ⅙ shekel of silver equalled 240 *qa* of barley. Texts show that oxen were normally valued at 1 gold shekel (equal to 15 silver shekels or approx. 2 tons of grain). A ram was worth about 2 shekels according to Lev 5:15. A measure of grain, equal to about 1½ pecks, was valued at a shekel if it was "fine" grain; "common" grain yielded silver double that amount for a shekel. Hoards of precious metals (silver, gold, and electrum) from Shechem, Megiddo, Beth Zur, and Gaza dating from the Late Bronze II through the Iron II periods (*ca.* 1400 B.C.E. to 600 B.C.E.) include pieces of many different weights, including fractions of the standard shekel weight.

2. Egypt. With its military interests encompassing far-off lands, Egypt amassed huge quantities of precious metals during her foreign conquests. Goods were bought and paid for with weights of gold, silver, and copper. Undoubtedly, the treasures of the Pharaoh took up much of the metal in the treasury at any given time in the form of vessels, decorated furniture, jewelry, and other tomb goods. The scenes depicted at Medinet Habu show gold stored in ingots, rings, vases, and dust. The gold was not native to Egypt. Gold usually came into Egyptian hands as booty from wars or as tribute from conquered or vassal countries in Asia and Africa. The Egyptian treasuries processed the gold and cast it into ingots and rings for ease in transportation. Gold dust, however, was apparently left as it was. The Nile Valley, like Mesopotamia and the lower Indus River Valley, was not well endowed in precious metals. In the 18th Dynasty, gold was obtained from Punt at the S end of the Red Sea (probably modern Somalia). The mines of the Sinai were worked from the 12th Dynasty onwards, as were the Red Sea mines. Under Queen Hatshepsut and Seti I, and again under Rameses II, the Sinai mines failed. Mining operations were dependent upon adequate supplies of water, and since there is no evidence that rainfall fluctuated so greatly in these periods, storage systems and cistern networks must have broken down.

The Egyptians, however, appear to have seen the Asiatic provinces under their influence as unlimited sources of gold. Dushratti of Mitanni wrote to his son-in-law, Pharoah Amenhotep IV (Akhenaton) "for was not gold as the dust of the country?" This bit of correspondence from Tell el-Amarna provides some insight into the Egyptian attitude toward gold and its availability. This was a time (the LB Age) when gold was in short supply in Babylon, where metal work prized in Egypt originated. A Babylonian official named Burnaburias wrote to a pharaoh, who hinted that gold would be welcomed in his court. The Babylonian indicated he would be glad to comply if ingots were shipped to Babylon to be worked and returned to Egypt as finished products. The Egyptian demand for gold periodically caused shortages which must have increased the value of silver. Egyptian money was usually gold. Silver was rare, even in tomb treasures, until the 1st millennium when it was more plentiful and popular; but gold in ingots, rings, bags of dust, or lumps remained the most common form of currency. We know from tomb wall reliefs that taxes could be paid in metals or in commodities. Reliefs at Saqqarah also show farmers bringing their payments in kind, with animals, grain, oil, and wine.

3. Mesopotamia. In Babylonia and Assyria weight standards, both "heavy" and "light," were in use by the end of the 3d millennium B.C.E. These systems standardized commercial transactions until the Hellenistic period and the new administrative system initiated by Alexander the Great. Silver was plentiful in Asia Minor and Persia, and earliest smelting of the metal probably occurred in these regions. Mediterranean silver mines were still active when Ezekiel sang the glories of Tyre and Tarshish, "who was her merchant" (Ezekiel 28). Economic texts and receipts for daily commerce are among the most-common clay tablets found at sites in Mesopotamia and Syria. Silver standards were commonly used in local and international trade in the 2d and 1st millennia B.C.E. The Tell el-Amarna letters show evidence for this standard in Syria and Palestine in the 15th century B.C.E. By the 6th century B.C.E., silver was still the metal of account in everyday life; and Babylon was dependent upon Phoenician merchants for its importation. By 550 B.C.E., copper was imported in large quantities from Cyprus and sold at a rate of 3¾ minas to the shekel of silver (by bulk weight). Dealing in bits and pieces of silver or copper in daily commerce became the accepted norm. Bar silver was simply "cut" to furnish fractional amounts.

4. Biblical and Archaeological Evidence. Very little metal money is found at Palestinian sites from *ca.* 1300 to 587 B.C.E. A few hoards from major sites such as Gaza, Shechem, Megiddo, and Beth Shan are the exceptions. Many examples of other types of metal objects are known, including jewelry and weapons. Some of the jewelry undoubtedly functioned as money, since its forms were convenient for transport and commerce.

In the Bible, references to "money" generally fall into 3 categories: (1) prices paid for land; (2) prophetic injunctions against corruption in the market place; and (3) obligations to the temple. Some examples of the first category have already been cited. Temple taxes were usually paid in kind or with money (in metallic form). For example, when a purification rite was required following the birth of a child, an offering was made of a "lamb a year old . . . and a young pigeon or turtledove . . . and the priest [made] atonement for [the woman]" (Lev 12:6–8). Such rites involved charges to worshipers by religious authorities and were common throughout the Near East. The requisite animals could be purchased with grain, oil, wine, or the equivalent in silver. Tariff inscriptions from a number of Canaanite and Punic sources outline elaborate systems of payment for services rendered by cultic officiants (i.e. the Marseille Tariff inscription, Donner and

Röllig 1968: 83–87). Analogous Hebrew customs provided monies for maintenance of the priests and the upkeep of the Temple.

Jehoash, king of Israel in the late 9th century B.C.E., formalized support for the Temple using monies assessed to individuals which were brought to the Temple of the people's own free will for "the house of the Lord." The priests then used his money to repair the Temple (2 Kgs 12:4–5). The uncoined metals were collected in a box, weighed, and then melted down and cast into bars or ingots according to royal standards. The pure metal bars functioned as currency to pay the workmen.

Prophetic injunctions resulted when metals were weighed or examined for purity, because occasional cheating occurred. For example, weights used by merchants were lumps of bronze or iron, or simply stones, supposedly conforming to accepted royal standards. In Deuteronomy 23:13–15, the Israelites were cautioned not to have different sets of stones, i.e., different weights, in their possession. Amos (8:5) preaches against this cheating in the marketplace. Eventually kings verified weight standards with royal seals of legitimacy. Royal identification also occurred on officially sanctioned crops of wine and olive oil. A series of jar handles stamped in paleo-Hebrew script with the phrase *lmlk,* "belonging to the king," dates first from the late 8th century B.C.E. Whether these jar handles simply identified "royal" wine or certified the quality of a crop for international commerce is unclear. See STAMPS, ROYAL JAR HANDLE.

In 1967, excavations at Nush-i Jan, Iran, unearthed a hoard of silver objects in a bronze bowl buried below the floor of a building identified as a "fort." A. D. H. Bivar described these objects as "ingot currency," dating from ca. 600 B.C.E. Hoards like this one are common throughout the Near East in the Persian period, often also containing silver coins from mints in Greece, Anatolia, and Phoenicia. This hoard, for example, included coins, entire or subdivided with chisel cuts; fragments of ancient jewelry; lengths of silver wire; chunks of "cut silver" taken off larger slabs or ingots (usually called by German writers *Hacksilber*); rectangular ingots; and flat, circular ingots of different sizes formed by molten metals solidifying in the bottoms of jars. This particular hoard is important, because it lacks Greek coins and is pre-Achaemenid in date. Any person possessing wealth might have kept a hoard such as this.

Evidence from Nush-i Jan includes ingots in 2 forms, the flat, circular ingot which appears most often in hoards in Egypt, Palestine, and Syria, and the bar ingot, the rectangular form which is more common in Mesopotamia and Persia. The contents of this extensive hoard suggest that standards may have been variable from locality to locality and from time to time. Although there are many pieces in the hoard which closely approximate either the Babylonian standard or the heavier Persic (Achaemenid) standard, there are other bits which fall between the two.

At the same time, there is evidence that Greeks on the Peloponnese were using a currency of iron spits. It is unknown if the spits of iron—which must have originated no earlier than the late 8th or early 7th century B.C.E.—were a new or reformed currency. They may have provided an official standard if made in identical molds. Herodotus (1.68) suggests that iron was not readily available until Greece's colonial expansion in the 8th century B.C.E. (see Koester 1982: 76–77). The iron spits were used into the 6th century, when some Greek and E Greek city states were already striking coins in precious metals. The spits, though still in use, were soon to be obsolete. Coinage may have spread more rapidly among the Greeks since a form of iron-spit currency was already in use and was accepted throughout much of the region. Indeed a "drachma" was literally a "handful" of spits (coming from a root meaning "to grasp"; Grierson 1975: 9–10). The Nush-i Jan hoard, like similar hoards from sites in Palestine, is evidence of a medial development between the use of bullion and coined metals. Small chunks of metal show that pieces of standard weights were in use by the 8th and 7th centuries B.C.E., previewing the denominational systems of true coinage.

C. The Origins of Coinage

Literary evidence contemporaneous with the kings of Judah suggests that coinage began in Anatolia. Passages from cuneiform tablets imply that payments in Mesopotamia were made with coins or coin-like objects called "heads of Ishtar," "heads of Shamash," or "heads of Ashur," all titles suggesting the existence of early stamped currency. Of course, these may be funds belonging to the temples of those deities. Barley, gold, and lead are mentioned in texts as media of exchange; but by far, silver was the most common. Some silver ingots are known from Zingirli inscribed with the name of Bir-Rekeb, son of Panamua, dating to *ca.* 714–710 B.C.E. and weighing one mina.

The places where coinage developed are more certain than the dates of the circumstances, however. In all probability, the first coins were struck in western Asia Minor as small globular pieces of electrum, a natural alloy of silver and gold. The pieces bore a design on one face and a punch mark on the other. These coins, produced either in the late-7th or early-6th centuries B.C.E. were correlated to a weight standard, recognizing the stamp impressed upon the chunks of metal as official recognition that they were legal tender. These early coins bore no inscriptions and did not circulate widely. Their use, however, quickly spread to the Persian empire and the East because of the Persian domination of Asia Minor beginning in the mid-6th century B.C.E. Croesus, according to Greek tradition (Herodotus 1.94), later struck silver and gold coins in the mid-6th century, which probably supplemented and/or expanded the earlier use of electrum.

Some scholars have suggested that the earliest coins were struck by merchants, because the types are diverse and one early inscribed coin reads, "I am the mark of Phanes," presumably a businessman (Grierson 1975: 10; Kraay 1976: 23). However, coinage not only facilitated commerce, it greatly simplified payment and receipt of taxes, temple maintenance, payment of mercenaries and soldiers, and government expenditures on public works. C. M. Kraay has convincingly argued that conversion from bullion to coinage was, therefore, a conscious effort by local communities to simplify monetary transactions. In Kraay's view, coined metals at first remained near the place of origin and were used for governmental purposes. Later, they were traded like any other valuable objects. Neighbors

COI.01. *Coins.*
***a,* PERSIAN DOUBLE DARIC:** *obverse* of gold double daric depicting an archer (probably the Persian king), with spear; ca. 330 B.C.E.

***b,* DOUBLE SHEKEL OF SIDON (PHOENICIA):** *obverse* with Sidonian galley and dating device; *reverse* depicting chariot carrying Great King of Persia, Sidonian king following in obeisance. Struck in silver by ʿAbdʿaštart I, ca. 370–369 B.C.E.

***c,* DOUBLE SHEKEL OF SIDON (PHOENICIA):** *obverse* with Sidonian galley before battlemented walls of city; *reverse* depicting chariot carrying Great King of Persia. Struck in silver by ʿAbdʾešmun, ca. 410–400 B.C.E.

***d,* SILVER SHEKEL OF TYRE (PHOENICIA):** *obverse* with marine deity riding seahorse over waves, with dolphin and murex shell; *reverse* with Tyrian owl and traditional Egyptian symbols of power—the crook and flail in background. Struck ca. 377–357 B.C.E.

***e,* SILVER STATER OF ARADUS (PHOENICIA):** *obverse* depicts head of marine deity in oriental style; *reverse,* Aradian galley, with inscription *mʾ, mamlakt ʾarvad* ("government of Aradus"). Struck ca. 348–338 B.C.E.

***f,* SILVER TETRADRACHMA OF ATHENS (GREECE):** *obverse* with goddess Athena, with olive leaves and helmet; *reverse* depicts Athenian owl, with olive spray and crescent; inscription, *alpha-theta-epsilon.* Struck ca. 460–450 B.C.E. and imitated throughout the E Mediterranean.

***g,* "PHILISTO-ARABIAN" SILVER COIN:** *obverse* depicts man wearing turbanlike headgear; *reverse* with owl and inscription *yhd,* "Yehud." Probably struck near Jerusalem in the 4th century B.C.E.

***h,* "YEHUD DRACHMA":** *obverse* depicts male head in Corinthian helmet; *reverse* depicts male deity(?) seated on throne, with inscription *yhd,* "Yehud." Struck in silver, probably near Jerusalem in the 4th century B.C.E.

***i*, HASMONEAN BRONZE COIN:** *obverse* is a wreath enclosing an inscription which translates "Yeḥohanan, the high priest and the community of Jews"; *reverse* is a double cornucopiae. Struck by John Hyrcanus ca. 135–104 B.C.E. in Jerusalem.

***j*, BRONZE COIN OF HEROD THE GREAT:** *obverse* depicts royal paraphernalia, with abbreviated inscription "Herod the King" in Greek; *reverse* shows tripod between palm branches. Struck in or near Jerusalem, 37–4 B.C.E.

***k*, BRONZE COIN OF ROMAN PROCURATOR:** *obverse* depicts palm branch, with date "year 5 of Caesar"; *reverse* shows an olive branch, with ethnic, "Nero." Struck in Caesarea by the procurator Antonius Felix, ca. 52–60 C.E., under the auspices of the Emperor Nero.

***l*, SILVER SHEKEL OF THE FIRST JEWISH REVOLT:** *obverse* is a chalice, with pellet cover, and inscription, "year 2," "shekel of Israel," in Hebrew; *reverse* shows a stem with three pomegranates and inscription, "Jerusalem the Holy." Struck in Jerusalem, ca. 68–69 C.E. See also Figs. ICO.08 and ICO.09.

***m*, BRONZE COIN OF THE SECOND JEWISH REVOLT:** *obverse* shows a bunch of grapes with leaf and Hebrew inscription, "First year of the Redemption of Israel"; *reverse* depicts a palm tree with two bunches of fruit, and the inscription, "Elazar the Priest." Struck ca. 133–134 C.E. See also Fig. ICO.04.

***n*, ROMAN BRONZE COIN:** *obverse* depicts Emperor Vespasian, with appropriate titles; *reverse* shows Nike standing over body of female, representing JUDEA CAPTA, "captured Judah," following First Jewish Revolt. A dupondius struck in Judea (Ashkelon) and in Rome, ca. 69–79 C.E. Inscription is in Latin; local issues in Palestine often used Greek instead.

***o*, HELLENISTIC SILVER SHEKEL OF TYRE (PHOENICIA):** *obverse* depicts Seleucid ruler in Greek style; *reverse* shows eagle, with inscription identifying Tyre as mint. Struck in Tyre in 2d century B.C.E.; coin commonly accepted as temple tax in Jerusalem. *(Drawings by O. S. Edgerly.)*

of the Greeks were slow to accept coinage until the Persian government decided that a unified monetary system might weld the empire together. *Sigloi* were the standard silver coins struck by Darius the Great and subsequent Persian kings. They copied coins of E Greek manufacture and were used throughout the E Mediterranean. Persian gold *darics* (probably named after Darius I) were struck by the central government and were the standard gold coinage of the realm. The silver *sigloi* were struck by local authorities in the satrapies. By weight, one gold *daric* was equal to 20 silver *sigloi*. Coins with the Great King's likeness were also powerful political tools.

Most classical numismatists argue that coinage was introduced sometime after 650 B.C.E. At first the use of coins spread westward from Lydia. Persian satraps and rulers struck silver and gold coins depicting the Persian king of kings in the guise of a running archer or an archer in the hunt. See Fig. COI.01(a). The scenes are reminiscent of numerous examples of Babylonian, Assyrian, and Persian glyptic art from the 1st millennium B.C.E. Old systems of barter and the use of older forms of money persisted in the E for at least another century; but the use of coinage spread quickly to Greek communities in the Aegean, on mainland Greece, and in the Greek colonial west (Sicily and Italy). Coinage was used in Italy before the end of the 6th century B.C.E. and probably reached Marseilles (a Punic colony) by *ca.* 450 B.C.E. By the second half of the 5th century, coinage was in use and being struck in N Africa and at mints throughout the E Mediterranean, including the important trading centers of the Phoenician league of city states.

The coinage of Sidon, Tyre, Aradus, and Byblos began in the 5th century and became normative for trade in the Near East in the 4th century, supplemented by coins from Greek and E Greek cities (notably Athens whose standard and coinage gained great commercial prominence). Egypt was slow to adopt the use of coinage, using globs of weighed gold with the hieroglyphs *nefer nub,* "fine gold," incised upon them as payment to Greek mercenaries (Grierson 1975: 11). The Greeks probably insisted on being paid in coin, a new concept for the Egyptians.

Sidon was the leading Phoenician city during the Persian period (*ca.* 540–332 B.C.E.). Tyre had been destroyed by Babylonian armies and Sidon, its N neighbor, picked up the commercial slack. Phoenicia provided the navy for the Persian kings and was the critical link in the Persian trading network which connected the spice and silk routes of the E with the Greek and Punic west. By the 5th century, more and more foreign coins appeared in Gaza, the Phoenician cities, and in Jerusalem, so that local authorities sought permission to strike their own coins to make trade simpler and governmental activity more efficient. Merchants no longer weighed out a "shekel" of silver when officially stamped coins were available. The Phoenicians struck coins depicting important symbols of each city-state beginning in *ca.* 450 B.C.E. Sidon, for example, depicted a galley on the obverse types, symbolic of the city's leadership in maritime trade. See Fig. COI.01(b). The reverse types showed the Persian king riding in a chariot followed by the Sidonian king dressed as high priest in the Great King's cult at Sidon. Inscriptions first appeared near the end of the 5th century in the form of abbreviations of the names of the Sidonian kings. Similar inscriptions were tried in Tyre, Aradus, and Byblos. Indeed from Byblos, much fuller inscriptions are known, listing the ruler's name and title—*milk gubl,* "king of Byblos." At Sidon it was common practice to use the 1st initial of the king's name as an abbreviation: i.e. *ʿb* for ʿAbdʿaštart, or *bš* for Baʿlšallim. From an inscription published in the 1960's, the Sidonian king list was greatly expanded so that an accurate, more precise chronology for the Sidonian coinage of the Persian period was made possible. See Fig. COI.01(c)–(e).

These coins were struck on the Phoenician standard, which was directly convertible into the Persic standard of the imperial gold darics. It also exchanged easily with coinage of the Attic standard on which the Athenian and Greek economies were built. By the early 4th century B.C.E., however, Sidon, Tyre, Cyprus, and Egypt revolted against Persia. New coin types developed which depicted the local ruler's likeness, rather than the traditional scenes with the Persian King of Kings. These coins were short-lived because Persia reasserted its control and transferred minting privileges to the Cilician satrap, Mazday, whose name appears on the Sidonian coins in Aram script. One result of this revolt, however, is the adoption of the Attic standard in the Sidonian and Tyrian mints, probably to facilitate trade with Greece.

At the same time, coins were also being struck further S along the Levantine coast in either Gaza or Ashkelon. Most scholars presume that Gaza was the principal regional mint in this period, imitating Attic coins of the 5th century (which depicted Athena on the obverse and the Athenian owl and the Gk letters *alpha-theta-epsilon* ["Athenai" for Athens] on the reverse; see fig. COI.01[f]). The Athenian tetradrachmas, copied in the mint at Gaza, are among the most beautiful coins of this early period. Athenian coins were imitated because they were considered the international monetary standard of their time (late 6th through the early 4th centuries B.C.E.); the owl and head of Athena were symbolic of Athens and conveyed a confidence built up throughout the E Mediterranean in Athenian commerce and statecraft. The Athenians, after all, had been able to withstand the Persian juggernaut at Marathon and Salamis, and they maintained a strong navy. The so-called "Philisto-Arabian" or "Egypto-Arabian" copies are not so well done. See Fig. COI.01(g). They were struck in silver, as were most of the Phoenician coins. Only a few bronze issues are known from Sidon; they supplemented the silver issues which were subdivisions of the more valuable gold darics—the mainstay of the Persian central mint.

The mint at Gaza or Ashkelon struck many different kinds of coins. Besides the Attic imitations, there was a large group which depicted a janiform head—that is, a head of the god Janus which gazes both ways. None of these coins exhibits the quality of craftsmanship known from Greece or Phoenicia. The owls do not measure up to Tyre's owl or that of Athens, and none has the quality of engraving common to the Byblian scenes of a lion attacking a bull.

Suffice it to say, that during the period 450–430 B.C.E., coins were struck along the Levantine coast for the first time. These issues were produced with the permission of the Persian government and under the authority of local rulers loyal to the Great King. Major silver denominations and their fractions facilitated trade and the payment of tribute and taxes to Persepolis and Susa. Each of the coin series depicted local scenes and bore ethnics which had some political or religious significance—a common practice at the time. All of the Phoenician mints used identifiable types peculiar to their own city mints. For the first time, abbreviations of cities' or rulers' names appear on coin flans. The letters, *m*ʾ, for example, were an abbreviation for *mamlakt* ʾ*Arvad,* "the government of Aradus." These coins and numerous examples from Greek and East Greek mints circulated throughout the lands of the Bible as early as the end of the 6th century and beginning of the 5th century B.C.E. This was the period of the great reforms of Ezra and Nehemiah in Jerusalem, when the Temple was rebuilt and the city wall of Jerusalem was restored. Most coins of this time which are known from archaeological contexts, have come from hoards found at sites along major trade routes in the Levant and Mesopotamia. Such hoards have come from excavations or tombs at sites like Abu Shusheh (near Gezer), Acco, Khirbet el-Kerak, Tel Sippor (near modern Qiryat Gat), and Shechem. It was also during this time that coins were first struck under Jewish authority in or near Jerusalem.

D. The Yehud Coins

Investigation and analysis by L. Mildenberg and the author have produced a new chronological picture for the "Yehud" coins. These coins come from the late Persian period, which remains relatively unknown to biblical scholars (the 5th and 4th centuries B.C.E.). Coins bearing the inscription *yhd* have surfaced for many years on antiquities markets and in collections around the world. At first it was thought that they were part of the so-called Philisto-Arabian series already mentioned. The Yehud coins have now been recognized to be a separate series, emanating from a mint in or near Jerusalem. None of the coins bears a mint mark except for the name of the province in paleo-Aramaic or paleo-Hebrew script. When these coins are studied within the context of the larger series from Phoenicia, a clearer picture of the 5th and 4th centuries in Judah emerges.

In the markets of Jerusalem, coined money was first used in the 5th century B.C.E. Evidence of coins in this early period indicates that they were often cut to test the purity of the metal. Indeed at one time in the 4th century in Tyre, inflation was so rapidly devaluing the Tyrian stater, that one enterprising ruler introduced "sandwich" coins, which was a copper core encased in silver. The coins were obviously lighter in weight than pure silver; and following the subsequent public outcry they were withdrawn from circulation (Betlyon 1980: 44–46). Many of the so-called Philisto-Arabian and Egypto-Arabian coins in the collections of the British Museum and the Bibliothèque nationale display punch marks or cuts verifying their purity or weight. Use of officially coined metals, however, made it possible for merchants to transact business without weighing a "shekel" of silver to be certain that the weight in metal matched the accepted weight in stone. While no coins predating the late 6th century have thus far been found in Palestine, the use of metal rings and bars persisted even though the use of coins became more popular. Spreading first from coastal cities along established trade routes, coins were quickly utilized for collection of taxes, both governmental and religious. According to Ezra 2:68–69, the Israelites not only rebuilt Jerusalem, but families made freewill offerings for the rebuilding of the Temple, donating to the treasury "61,000 gold darics *(darkĕmônîm),* 5,000 minas of silver, and other priestly accoutrements."

From comparative analysis, the first coins bearing the ethnic "Yehud," were probably struck soon after 400 B.C.E. They depicted the head of Pallas Athena in typically Attic manner, facing to the right on the obverse. On the reverse was an owl with an olive branch and the legend, in paleo-Aramaic, *Yehud (yhd),* i.e., Judah. The craftsmanship is poor. The die engravers copied Athenian types similar to those presumably copied in Gaza. The legend appears both as it should and on some examples, in retrograde. All of the coins are fractional silver denominations which functioned as small change to complement the larger silver coins of Gaza, Tyre, and Sidon.

By 370 B.C.E., Judah introduced new types including the lily and the falcon with spread wings, again with the legend *Yehud.* Within this group is a coin with the likeness of a local leader, perhaps the high priest, to whom minting authority had devolved. The coin, featuring his bust "in kidaris" (the Persian costume) is very similar to issues from Sidon struck during the first revolt of the 4th century against Persian hegemony. These Sidonian coins from ca. 365/364–362 B.C.E. featured the local king wearing a crown like that of his Persian overlord, identical in style to this example from Judah. The coin stems from the revolt, reflecting Judean participation in the rebellion instigated by the Egyptian leader, Tachos. The Sidonian ʿAbdʿaštart I led the insurrection in the Levant, along with a number of kings from Cyprus. The Judeans, always envious of their own freedom from foreign rulers, participated as well, striking coinage with their own ruler's likeness. It is unusual for a Jew to have agreed to have his face shown on a coin; the use of this type, however, was short-lived, probably due to the public's lack of acceptance. E. Stern has summarized the archaeological evidence for disturbances in the first half of the 4th century at a number of sites in the Shephelah and the Negeb. These destructions were probably due to armed intervention by armies of Artaxerxes II Mnemon, who was doubly anxious when Yohanan, a high priest, killed Yeshua within the Temple. As a result of this act, according to Josephus (*Ant* 11§297–301), a Persian general, Bagoses, entered the Temple, defiled it, and imposed a fee upon each Jewish sacrifice, causing the Jews to suffer for 7 years. This fee may well have been collected in this silver minutiae.

A coin from the British Museum, the so-called Yehud drachma, is probably from this period (ca. 360 B.C.E.) as well. See Fig. COI.01(h). This unique coin depicts a bearded head in Corinthian helmet on the obverse and a bearded figure seated on a winged wheel on the reverse, with a head of the Egyptian god Bes (in incuse) to the side. The legend "Yehud" appears on the reverse. First published by G. F. Hill and E. L. Sukenik many years ago, the coin was thought by some scholars to illustrate a scene from the prophecies of Ezekiel, showing God on the spinning, winged wheel, interpreting Ezekiel 1 and Ezekiel 10 in which God's throne room has whirling wheels, one for each of the cherubim, wheels within wheels. Although the reverse may indeed depict this scene, it is doubtful that it would have been struck by Jewish authorities, given their aversion to depicting God or anything so holy as the cherubim in this early period. This would have been a significant affront to religious authorities in this time of neoorthodoxy following Ezra's reforms. The coin was more likely struck by a satrap like Mazday, on behalf of the Persian government, to maintain commercial activity in Judaea following the Tachos revolt. The coin is not Jewish in character, and represents a foreign, intrusive element. Since only one example is known, this issue must have been intended for limited use.

The next coins struck by Jewish authorities were issued by Yeḥizqiyyah the governor, with a facing head on the obverse and a poorly executed Athenian owl on the reverse. Instead of *Yehud,* the reverse inscription reads *yḥzqh hpḥh, Yeḥizqiyyah happeḥah* ("governor"). The title indicates the rank of the official granted minting privileges by the Persian government. By 346 B.C.E. parts of Judah once again joined in revolt with the Phoenicians and Egyptians against Persia. Yeḥizqiyyah apparently followed the Sidonian lead and put his own head on the coins during this revolt. This time Artaxerxes III Ochus put down the revolt quickly and harshly. Evidence of destruction is found at Hazor, Megiddo, Athlit, Lachish, and Jericho. Diodorus Siculus wrote about this rebellion led by Tennes of Sidon (16.40–46). Scholars have argued that Judah also participated in this revolt. There is some archaeological evidence to indicate that parts of the province revolted, causing more suffering and a deportation of some Jews to the area of the Caspian Sea.

Following the Tennes rebellion there was probably a period when no coinage was struck in Jerusalem; Persian retribution for an indiscretion such as rebellion was swift and sure. Archaeological evidence from the period is scanty, and two destructions cannot be easily reckoned anywhere, especially two destructions only 10 years apart. It is clear, however, that Judah participated at least halfheartedly in these two revolts, so that much of the province had been destroyed at least once by the time that Alexander the Great marched his armies into the E Mediterranean in 332/331 B.C.E.

Following the second revolt (ca. 340 B.C.E.) coins were struck on the same types, but without the inscription Yehud or the name of the fallen Yeḥizqiyyah. A small group of poorly made coins from this period has been recognized by D. Barag to bear the ethnic inscription *yḥnn hkhn, Yoḥanan hakkōhēn,* "Yoḥanan the priest." The listing of high priests in the Chronicler's history does not include the name of a Yoḥanan in the late 4th century. F. M. Cross has argued that the listing in 1–2 Chronicles, Ezra-Nehemiah lacks the names of at least 4 high priests, presumably having been dropped off the list because of scribal errors when the scroll was recopied (specifically by reason of supposed haplography). It may be, however, that the Chronicler's final history of this period was edited by Persian authorities deleting the names of rebellious priests, such as Yoḥanan who took authority on himself to strike coins without an official Persian imprimatur. Nehemiah and Ezra were both highly praised for their loyalty to Persia, and are given special laud for their magnanimity toward the Jews, as Persian officials. The Ezra lists may have been used for propaganda purposes, and only after the histories had passed censorship were they acceptable within the loyalist Jewish community. After all, the Persian period was a time when talk of freedom and revolt was regarded as open rebellion. Zerubbabel, mentioned as a leader in Zechariah 1–8, mysteriously disappeared, probably because he advocated a free, strong Jerusalem once too often.

If this reconstruction of late Persian period history is correct, the high priests apparently had assumed great authority, including the minting of coinage. Some measure, therefore, of civil authority was vested in the high priest as well as his religious function. This scenario corresponds to a time of Persian weakness, ca. 335–332 B.C.E.

These small coins were followed by a series in which old dies were initially reused under Ptolemaic sponsorship following Alexander the Great, with the Aramaic inscription *Yehud* replaced by the Hebrew *Yehudah.* Likenesses of Ptolemy I and his queen eventually appeared upon the types, indicating that secular governmental authorities had taken control of the mint from the high priest. This probably occurred immediately after Alexander's conquest of Judah in 331 B.C.E. Regional mints in Tyre and Alexandria struck the major denominations of silver coinage in this period portraying Alexander's own likeness. Small local mints continued to strike fractional issues such as the Yehud coins found near Jerusalem, Bethlehem, and Hebron.

The Yehud coins are important because they are the first coins struck within the land of Israel and Judah by local authorities. The coins have been found as far S as Beth Zur and Tell Jemmeh, nearly to the border of Egypt. Judah was a province within the Persian satrapy of Abernahara, i.e., the satrapy "across the river," which included Syria, Phoenicia, Palestine, and Cyprus.

E. Coinage in the Apocrypha

After 332/331 B.C.E. no coins were struck in Palestine except in officially sanctioned mints such as the one at Jerusalem where only small minutiae were produced. The major coinage of the period came from Acco and Tyre, where Alexander established large Hellenistic mints. No major monetary changes occurred; the Athenian standard and coins on Greek types predominated until 168 B.C.E. Coinage and the right to produce it were the perquisites of political and military supremacy. As the Ptolemaic and Seleucid Hellenistic kingdoms weakened in the century following Alexander's death, rulers had more and more difficulty dealing with outlying provinces of the kingdoms. Judaea found itself between spheres of Hellenistic influence, which resulted in repressive policies from Syrian Greek rulers early in the 2d century B.C.E. The immediate result was rebellion led by Judas Maccabaeus. The end result was that Jewish authorities were again in control of Jerusalem by 168 B.C.E. Alexander Jannai (ruling from 103–76 B.C.E.) was the first of the Hasmoneans to strike coins in Jerusalem late in the 2d century B.C.E. with a flower (lily?) on the obverse and the ethnic inscription *yhntn hmlk,* "Jonathan the king," referring to himself. These coins were struck mostly in bronze and functioned as supplemental currency with the larger coins circulating from the major mints. Silver and gold were in short supply, so Jonathan later overstruck his own coins altering the title "king" to "high priest and friend of the Jews." The Maccabees were slowly equated not with orthodoxy and revolt against Hellenism, but with Hellenism itself. Their use of an ethnic inference in Greek may have angered more militant Jews in the 2d century, but it was probably a necessary element to insure acceptance of the coins in the marketplaces of the land at the time.

The first Maccabaean coins struck by Alexander Jannai were in bronze. They were fractions of a shekel in weight, including half-, quarter-, and third-shekels. All were minted with similar types and ethnics. These coins probably served as Temple taxes as well as for commerce. The sanguinary family quarreling which marked the early years of Maccabaean/Hasmonean rule, meant that coins were not minted with someone securely in power. In 1 Maccabees 15, Antiochus VII granted to Simon the high priest a letter of privileges. It said among other things, "I give you leave also to coin money for your country with your own stamp." On this basis most scholars have argued that Simon (*Šimᶜon,* d. 134 B.C.E.) struck the first Hasmonean coins. However on a closer reading of 1 Maccabees, it is clear that Antiochus VII went back on his word and revoked Simon's privileges. So who did strike the Hasmonean coins?

The series bears 4 names: Yehoḥanan, Yehudah, Yonatan, and Mittityah. Since the high priestly families commonly practiced papponomy, naming the son after the grandfather, each name could represent more than one person or generation, when the same names recur again and again within a family. The Hasmoneans further complicated this situation, however, because in the 4th generation they stopped using their Hebrew names in favor of Greek ones. The work of B. Kanael, A. Kindler, and Y. Meshorer leads us to the aforementioned conclusion that Alexander Jannai struck the first Hasmonean coins. Seleucid and Ptolemaic coins were circulating at this time throughout Judaea, but by *ca.* 110 B.C.E., the Seleucids had become so weak that subject states and cities often were able to demonstrate autonomy by striking their own types. Tyre was minting autonomous shekels by the mid-2d century B.C.E.; but it was a large, commercial city-state. Smaller states and cities only later began their mints, including renewed coinage from Gaza and Ashkelon, and new coins from Judaea and the Nabataean kingdom. Nabataean coins were struck from *ca.* 80 B.C.E. until about 80 C.E., and regularly circulated in Palestine.

Approximately 20 lead "coins" are known from Alexander Jannai (ruled from 103–76 B.C.E.). The lead flans are usually struck on only one side and appear to be experimental efforts at coin production using soft metal, according to Meshorer (1967: 56–57). Struck between 103 and 76 B.C.E., Alexander Jannai's coins usually depicted a flower on the obverse and an anchor on the reverse. The anchor symbolized his conquest of several maritime cities on the Mediterranean coast. However, it is very similar to other anchors used on the coins of Antiochus VII Sidetes. Some believe that his restriking of coins to delete the royal title "king" and replace it with "high priest and friend of the Jews," was a concession to the Pharisees because the Hasmoneans were not of the house of David and had no legitimate right to the throne.

Alexander Jannai struck other types as well, including reverses depicting double cornucopiae and stars with 8 rays. John Hyrcanus II (high priest from 63–40 B.C.E.) followed Alexander Jannai striking coins on similar types, and repeating the lengthy ethnic—"high priest and friend of the Jews." A crested helmet was used on some smaller bronze issues as a reverse type. Judas Aristobulus II (ruled from 66–63 B.C.E.) and Mattathias Antigonus (ruled from 40–37 B.C.E.) completed the Hasmonean coin series with strikings in 37 B.C.E. No Hasmonean silver is known. Scholars in the last century confused silver from the First Jewish Revolt, *ca.* 67–70 C.E., with Hasmonean coins because of the similar types.

Hasmonean issues weighed a maximum of 14 g. and a minimum of 0.2 g. They were struck on flans which had been cast in open molds. This open mold production method resulted in heavier coins, which were the equivalent of 2 coins pressed together. The only coin struck on the closed mold technique was that of Antigonus depicting a 7-branched menorah. Meshorer argues that this coin was a special issue struck at half the weight of the other issues in 37 B.C.E. when the armies of Herod were laying siege to Jerusalem. Mattathias Antigonus saw his little kingdom slipping into the hands of "strangers"—Rome and Herod. He used this coin with the menorah to proclaim that it was forbidden for the Temple menorah to fall into enemy hands. Meshorer believes that the coin had no economic use, but was intended for "propaganda value only" (1967: 61–62). Mattathias placed his name in Hebrew on the obverse and his Gk name in the genitive, *basileos antigonou,* "belonging to king Antigonus," on the reverse.

F. Coinage of Herod and His Dynasty

In the 1st century B.C.E., coins of Republican Rome began to circulate in the E, especially after the conquests of Pompeii the Great, which established the Roman presence in Egypt and Palestine. With the overthrow of the Hasmoneans, Herod brought some changes to minting operations in Jerusalem: inscriptions (ethnics) would only be in Greek, no Jewish symbols would appear on coins, and a dating system would be attempted for the first time. All of his coins have either a full or abbreviated form of the ethnic, "Herod the King."

Herod's first coins are dated; thereafter they go undated. The symbolism is predominantly pagan, including a tripod, palm branches, crested helmets, shields, winged caduceus, pomegranate, aphlaston (a royal signet), a cross enclosed in a diadem, an anchor, an eagle, and a double cornucopiae. All the coins are in bronze and are meant to support silver from regional mints. See Fig. COI.01(j).

Herod's lands were divided among his 3 sons, Archaelaus, Antipas, and Phillip, after his death in 4 B.C.E. Archaelaus's coins were struck from 4 B.C.E. until 6 C.E. and are maritime in type, perhaps because the principal ports were in his jurisdiction, including Joppa and Caesarea. These coins were struck at Herod's old mint of Jerusalem and continued the same craftsmanship. Herod Antipas, ruling in the Galilee and Peraea (Transjordan) until 39 C.E., began to strike coins in his 24th year, 19/20 C.E. His coins were distinctly Jewish in character, since all the lands he ruled were inhabited primarily by Jews. The designs include the palm tree, palm branches, bunches of dates, and reeds. His coins were struck in a new mint at Tiberias (founded on the W shore of the Sea of Galilee between 17 and 22 C.E.), and were limited to small bronzes which have been found only in N Israel.

Herod Phillip II ruled areas which were predominantly inhabited by pagans, and his coins show foreign influence, including the Roman emperor's bust on the obverse and a Roman temple on the reverse. These coins are extremely rare and were probably struck at Caesarea Philippi (modern Baniyas in the Golan Heights). He even included the name of the Roman emperor, in Greek, on his coins. These examples had a limited, local circulation; only one has surfaced in excavations as far away as Curium, Cyprus.

Agrippa I ruled in the N from 37–44 C.E., and struck coins beginning in his 2d year at Caesarea Philippi. He was a close friend of Claudius who became emperor in 41 C.E. Through his patronage, Agrippa I ruled over almost all the lands which once had been ruled by Herod, uniting the land of the Jews and the first Christians under a single ruler who was the grandson of Herod the Great and his Hasmonean wife Mariamne. Like his contemporaries and his predecessors, his most common issues were *peruṭôt*—small bronze coins—which he struck in Jerusalem or Caesarea. Some of his coins bear types which were intended to circulate in Jewish areas (with types like the canopy); other types, depicting the emperor, Agrippa, a quadriga, and a temple, were intended for areas untouched by Judaism. Agrippa I was the first Jewish ruler since the Persian period to put his own likeness on a coin flan.

The final Herodian ruler was Agrippa II, who sat on the throne until 95 C.E., strongly supporting Roman rule at all times. His coins have been problematic because they were sometimes dated twice, on differing systems; or they bear the names of 2 different emperors. Moreover, the date given by Josephus for his accession is incompatible with the dates on the coins. Josephus argued that Agrippa II came to the throne *ca.* 49/50 C.E.; from inscriptions and his coins, H. Seyrig has more correctly argued that he came to the throne in 56 C.E. (1964: 55–65). Agrippa struck coins on several new types, depicting 4 emperors, including Nero (54–68 C.E.), Vespasian (69–79 C.E.), Titus (79–81 C.E.), and Domitian (81–96 C.E.). He also used divine types such as Pan, Nike, and Tyche with cornucopiae.

During this same period, Roman procurators in Judaea issued coins sporadically between 6 C.E. and 66 C.E. Of the 13 procurators assigned to Judaea, only 5 struck any coins. Under Caesar Augustus (27 B.C.E.–14 C.E.), Coponius struck bronzes in 6 C.E. depicting barley and a palm tree. Ambibulus issued coins on the same types between 9 and 11 C.E. Under Tiberius Caesar (14–37 C.E.), Valerius Gratus issued a series of bronze coins with inscriptions inside a wreath on the obverse and double cornucopiae or lilies on the reverse. He struck them between 15 and 19 C.E. and again in 25 C.E. Pontius Pilate, who replaced him in 26 C.E., struck coins for 3 years, beginning in Caesarea and Jerusalem in 29/30 C.E. New obverse types included the simpulum and the lituus, Roman cult objects which were a source of irritation within the Jewish community of Judaea. Other symbols used by the procurators were not necessarily Jewish, but were less offensive than those chosen by Pilate. The palm tree and a palm branch were most compatible with the Jewish community; but coins depicting spears and shields, symbols of Roman military superiority, appear on some coins of Antonius Felix, issued in 54 and 58 C.E., in the last years of procuratorial minting in Judaea. See Fig. COI.01(k). Felix presided on the Apostle Paul's arrest (Acts 23:26–35). The procuratorial coinage was secondary to imperial and Herodian issues, and was used to fill out the denominational system. Dating mechanisms were used on these coins indicating the year of the procurator's term. Some early scholarly studies described some silver issued of the procurators; these have proven to be forgeries of the modern era.

G. Coins of the New Testament

The coins of the Herodians circulated throughout Palestine during the time when Jesus and the apostles travelled those ancient highways. These coins, with those of the procurators, were the pocket change supplementing silver coins from imperial mints in Rome, Alexandria, and Antiochia. Among these larger silver coins was the *denarius* which was the accepted salary for a day's work by a common laborer. The *denarius* was also the annual Temple tax when Jesus was an adult and is probably the coin mentioned in Matt 22:21. Jesus was questioned concerning the payment of taxes; his response was "render unto Caesar that which is Caesar's," because like so many of the other coins, the emperor's likeness appeared on the obverse. After the revolt of 66–70 C.E., the Temple tax doubled to a half-shekel (two *denarii*).

The coins paid to Judas Iscariot (Matt 26:15) were probably silver shekels of Tyre or Antiochia. Thirty pieces would equal approximately 120 *denarii,* a laborer's salary for up to 4 months. According to Exodus 21:32, however, this sum was considered appropriate "blood money," paid in compensation when someone was killed accidentally. In Mark 12:42 the widow's mite was probably a Greek *lepton,* the smallest coin then in circulation. It was half a Roman *quadrans* or Jewish *peruṭa,* and in diameter would have been smaller than any modern U.S. coin. In 30 C.E., any of these coins may have been seen on the streets of Jerusalem, which was a cosmopolitan city. The coins varied greatly in weight and size from 8 mm or 40 mm in diameter. Because of the variations, simple commercial exchanges often required the services of a moneychanger.

The moneychanger functioned as both a banker and a financier. He sat in the gate of the city or the gate of the Temple and made his services available for a fee. For example, when Antiochian tetradrachmas were exchanged for local shekels, a premium of 4%–8% was exacted. Since coins of different origins were used, the moneychanger's services were often required. The Temple tax of a half-shekel to be paid by adult males was specified in rabbinic instruction to be paid in silver didrachmas (= ½ shekel) of Tyre. According to the Mishna (*Šeqal.* 1:3), the tax was collected in the month preceding Passover and for 20 days immediately before the feast within the Temple precincts. When Jesus "cleansed the Temple" (Matt 21:12–3, Mark 11:15, Luke 19:45–6), moneychangers may have been collecting this tax for the public welfare. Sometimes they cheated when assisting in transactions, especially when converting money or selling animals for Temple sacrifices. Rabbi Simeon reduced the number of obligatory sacrifices (*m. Ker.* 1:7) to eliminate this fraud in the mid-1st century C.E. These same moneychangers also fulfilled the banker's function, paying interest on money held by them, even though there were laws against usury (*m. Šeqal.* 1:6).

H. Coins of the First Jewish Revolt

Mints in Palestine and Phoenicia struck coins for Augustus and his successors, Tiberius, Gaius, Claudius, and Nero. Mints in Judah, Samaria, and neighboring areas included Jerusalem, Caesarea Maritima, Caesarea Samariae (Samaria), Tiberias, Sepphoris, Scythopolis, and Ashkelon. All these mints struck bronze coins which supplemented the silver struck at Tyre.

The monetary situation in the early 1st century C.E. was typical for the Greco-Roman East. Large transactions were conducted in terms of talents; that is, in large masses of coined and uncoined silver by weight, or by barter in commodities, or by gold (Matt 2:11). C. H. V. Sutherland has argued that although there were many mints striking only bronzes, silver remained the principal medium for day-to-day transactions (1974: 129–37). Silver was the metal which fed the Temple treasury, settled moderate debts, furnished the medium for wage-payment, bought lodging and care at an inn for a wounded and exhausted man, covered a mass-purchase of bread for thousands of people, and tempted the traitor. Money was, in short, an essential part of life in Palestine in the 1st century. For a person to hold a purse with coins inside it was not a mark of wealth, but normal behavior for the day.

So there was an established monetary system in place when the Jews revolted against Rome in 66 C.E. Tyrian shekels had been used as payment for the Temple taxes; and for some reason the Romans shut down the Tyrian mint, depriving Jerusalem of this important source of funding for a significant part of its Jewish religious life. When Jewish rebels struck coins in Jerusalem, it was natural for them to be linked to Tyrian coins by weight and other elements—a symbiosis which C. Roth has called "a religious as well as a patriotic necessity." This relationship is clearly seen in a hoard found in Silwan, the modern village of Siloam near Jerusalem, dated from 67–68 C.E. It contained Jewish pieces of "year 2" mixed with Tyrian shekels of the period 13/12 B.C.E. through 64/65 C.E. Another hoard found on Mt. Carmel contained over 4,500 coins, including 3,400 Tyrian shekels, 1,000 Tyrian half-shekels, and 160 Augustan *denarii*—some have suggested that this hoard was Temple tax which had been intercepted by the Romans *en route* to Jerusalem.

The coins struck during the First Jewish Revolt against Rome are among the most studied examples in the world. Struck in silver and bronze, and dated to years 1–5 of the revolt, they emanated from Jerusalem and bore Jewish types. They depicted a chalice, a stem with three fruit (pomegranates?), an amphora with 2 handles, a vine leaf with tendril, the etrog and lulav, two lulavim, a palm tree, and ethnic inscriptions which included "shekel Israel" and denominational designations. See Fig. COI.01(l). Coins were struck in the shekel, half-shekel, and quarter-shekel denominations. Besides the label *šql* and *yšrʾl,* "shekel Israel" or a fraction thereof, several also bear the inscription, "Jerusalem the holy" *(yrwšlym hqdwšh).*

Coins of the revolt have been found all over Judaea, even on Masada. They replaced the Roman coinage of the Herodians which had adapted non-Jewish types. Some Roman coins of the half-peruṭah and peruṭah denominations were struck in Caesarea during the revolt under one of the procurators. These coins were not part of the mass of Jewish coinage coming from Jerusalem. They were an attempt to supply coins to the monetary system of Palestine in this time when more currency was needed since 3 extra legions of soldiers were in the country. The monetary supply must have reached an apex in 67 or 68 C.E. This was especially true in Caesarea, the political capital.

After the revolt was put down in 70 C.E., silver continued to be struck in Antiochia and Tyre, although the old shekel was discontinued in favor of tetradrachmas like those already minted in Antiochia. Bronzes appeared under Vespasian (69–79 C.E.) in Ashkelon, and also under Titus (79–81 C.E.) and Domitian (81–96 C.E.), some coming from Neapolis and Sebaste (Samaria) as well. In the period 71–79 C.E., Vespasian and Titus struck several coins commemorating their victory over the Jews. Probably struck first in Caesarea by Vespasian in 71, these coins depicted the conqueror on the obverse with Nike (Victory) on the reverse with an inscription in Greek, *ioudias ealokuias,* the equivalent of *Judaea capta* in Latin. See Fig. COI.01(n). This latter ethnic was used to continue this massive coin series under Domitian in 92–93 C.E. Titus also struck these coins, which sometimes have on the reverse a trophy with Judaea seated and mourning, her hands tied behind her at its foot.

The coins struck with Gk ethnic inscriptions were intended for the Jewish population of Palestine. The Romans of the Flavian dynasty were very proud of their victory, as the continuing issuance of these coins has shown. Most of the coins, however, are from Titus and Vespasian. The few coins known from the reign of Domitian apparently celebrated the 20th anniversary of the fall of Masada, and probably should not be confused with or grouped together with the issues which immediately followed the war. The Domitian issues came from Rome. Note also that this was an economically and commercially active time: L. Ginzberg has shown that trade from Egypt and Judaea and from Judaea to Rome was extensive, because Palestinian wheat was half the price of wheat in Rome, but double the price of Egyptian wheat (Sperber 1974: 126–7). Ashkelon, Joppa, and Caesarea were points of transshipment (Smallwood 1981: 344–351). Some rabbis, to protect the Palestinian markets, went so far as to declare non-Palestinian goods ritually impure. Rabbi Simeon ben Shetaḥ (in the 1st century B.C.E.) declared imported metalware impure to protect local products (*b. Šabb.* 14b; *j. Pesaḥ* 1,6).

By the end of the revolt, Caesarea had officially become a Roman colony (in 69 C.E.). Roman coins for the province of Arabia were struck at mints in Ashkelon, Caesarea, Gadar, Gaza, Neapolis, and Philadelphia (Amman). Vespasian introduced a new bronze denomination, the *semis* which augmented the *dupondius* already widely in circulation. The *dupondius* was 24–25 mm in diameter and weighed 12.5–16 grams. The *semis* was smaller, ca. 20.5–21 mm, weighing about half as much as the *dupondius.*

I. Coins of the Second Jewish Revolt

By 130 C.E. Jerusalem had also become an official Roman colony: Hadrian (117–138 C.E.) built a new temple to Jupiter and issued coins on the city's new name, Aelia Capitolina. Hadrian officially visited Israel as emperor in 130 C.E., whereupon Simon Bar Kokhba and his followers began their revolt against Rome. This revolt was in reaction to Hadrian's decision to change Jerusalem's character. The Jewish Temple, after all, had been destroyed in 70 C.E. Meshorer argues that the Romanizing of Jerusalem preceded outright rebellion, since a hoard was found on the N edge of the Judaean desert containing 35 *denarii* of Bar Kokhba and a bronze issue of Aelia Capitolina. They were probably salted away together during the war for safekeeping. The contents of the hoard indicate that Jerusalem had been Romanized before Bar Kokhba made his move, not afterward as some have claimed.

The coins of the Second Jewish Revolt were struck under the aegis of Bar Kokhba in an effort to restore the Temple and reinstitute Temple services. See fig. COI.01(m). Coins dated to year 1 of the revolt (132/133 C.E.) depict the facade of the Temple, with a feature (probably the ark of the covenant) in the center and the inscription, "Jerusalem." The reverse depicts the lulav and etrog and the inscription "year one of the redemption of Israel." The coin is a silver tetradrachma weighing over 14 g. and is 27 mm in diameter. A silver *denarius,* 18 mm in diameter and weighing 3.2 g., was also struck, with a jug and palm branch on the obverse and the ethnic, *ʾlʿzr hkhn,* "ʾElʿazar the priest." The reverse depicts a bunch of grapes with the same inscription as the tetradrachma's reverse. Other issues in bronze altered the reverse ethnic to "Shimʿon," "Jerusalem," or "Shimʿon, prince of Israel" *(šmʿn nsʾ yšrʾl).* Palm trees, vines, leaves, and lyres were also shown on the types. Some coins were struck in the 2d year, reusing year 1 dies. New types emerged, including trumpets, and a new ethnic inscription, "year 2 for the freedom of Israel." In year 3, the ethnic was simply "for the freedom of Israel." Bar Kokhba's troops probably occupied Jerusalem in 133–135 C.E. When they finally had to withdraw, their slogan became "for the freedom of Jerusalem," hoping to reverse their fortunes and reestablish the Temple. While most of these coins were undoubtedly struck in Jerusalem, late in the war some coins may have been struck elsewhere (Kindler 1986–87: 46–8).

Some scholars have argued that the "Shimon" mentioned on the coins is not to be connected with any real person. However, the papyri from the Naḥal Ḥever prove that this was really Bar Kokhba himself and no other. For a short-lived revolt, many different coin types were struck. This was in part possible because Bar Kokhba reused coins already circulating throughout Palestine. All of his issues are overstrikes, the silver on Roman *denarii* and Syrian provincial tetradrachmas, and the bronzes on flans from Gaza. At least one bronze was found with the countermark of the Roman 10th Legion on the reverse (from the M. Rosenberger collection in Jerusalem). So Rome freely reused the rebel coins. Bar Kokhba's types include musical instruments used in the Temple (trumpet and lyre) because the Temple was very important to him. It was depicted on the coins, along with many articles of cultic importance, i.e., lulav, etrog, amphora, etc.

With these coins, issues of the Jews from the biblical period came to an end. As M. Avi-Yonah has written, the Roman government in 135 C.E. attempted a radical solution to the "Jewish Question," expelling those Jews who still survived in and around Jerusalem. Religious practices such as circumcision, teaching of the Law, and ordination of rabbis were punishable by death (Avi-Yonah 1976: 13). These historical developments are well documented in the demise of Jewish coinage.

Bibliography

Avi-Yonah, M. 1976. *The Jews under Roman and Byzantine Rule.* New York and Jerusalem.

Babelon, E. 1910. *Traité des monnaies grecques et romaines.* Vol. 2. Paris.

Barag, D. 1985. Some Notes on a Silver Coin of Johanan the High Priest. BA 48: 166–68.

Betylon, J. W. 1980. *The Coinage and Mints of Phoenicia.* HSM 26. Chico, CA.

———. 1986. The Provincial Government of Persian Period Judea and the Yehud Coins. *JBL* 105: 633–642.

Bivar, A. D. H. 1971. A Hoard of Ingot Currency of the Median Period from Nush-i Jan, near Malayir. *Iran* 9: 97–111.

Codrington, K. deB. 1964. The Origins of Coinage. *Bulletin of the Institute of Archaeology of the University of London* 4: 1–24.

Cross, F. M. 1974. The Papyri and their Historical Implications. Pp. 17–29 in *Discoveries in the Wadi ed-Daliyeh,* eds. P. and N. Lapp. AASOR 41. Cambridge, MA.

———. 1975. A Reconstruction of the Judean Restoration. *JBL* 94: 4–18.

Donner, H., and Rollig, W. 1968. *Kanaanaische und Aramaische Inschriften.* Vols. 1–3. Wiesbaden.

Grierson, P. 1975. *Numismatics.* London.

Hill, G. F. 1910. *Catalogue of the Greek Coins of Phoenicia.* London.

———. 1914. *Catalogue of the Greek Coins of Palestine.* London.

Kindler, A. 1986–87. Coins and Remains from a Mobile Mint of Bar Kokhba at Khirbet el-ʿAqd. *INJ* 9: 46–50.

Koester, H. 1982. *Introduction to the New Testament.* Vol. 1. Philadelphia.

Kraay, C. M. 1964. Hoards, Small Change and the Origin of Coinage. *JHS* 84: 76–91.

———. 1976. *Archaic and Classical Greek Coins.* Berkeley.

Meshorer, Y. 1967. *Jewish Coins of the Second Temple Period.* Trans. I. H. Levine. Tel Aviv.

———. 1975. *Nabataean Coins.* Qedem 3. Jerusalem.

———. 1983. *Ancient Jewish Coinage.* Vols. 1–2. Philadelphia.

Mildenberg, L. 1979. Yehud: A Preliminary Study of the Provincial Coinage of Judea. Pp. 183–196. pls. 21–22, in *Greek Numismatics and Archaeology,* ed. O. Morkholm and N. Waggoner. Wetteren, Netherlands.

Robinson, E. S. G. 1950. A "Silversmith's Hoard" from Mesopotamia. *Iraq* 12: 44–51.

Seyrig, M. 1964. Les ères d'Agrippa II. *Revue Numismatique* 6: 55–65.

Smallwood, E. M. 1981. *The Jews Under Roman Rule: From Pompey to Diocletian.* Leiden.

Sperber, D. 1974. *Roman Palestine, 200–400: Money and Prices.* Ramat-Gan.

Sukenik, E. L. 1934. Paralipomena Palaestinensia. *JPOS* 14: 178–82.

Sutherland, C. H. V. 1967. The Pattern of Monetary Development in Phoenicia and Palestine during the early Empire. Pp. 88–

105 in *Proceedings of the International Numismatic Convention, Jerusalem, 1963,* ed. A. Kindler. Jerusalem.
———. 1974. *Roman Coins.* London.
Thompson, M.; Morkholm, O.; and Kraay, C. M. 1973. *An Inventory of Greek Coin Hoards.* New York.

JOHN W. BETLYON

COL-HOZEH (PERSON) [Heb *kol-ḥōzeh*]. A name mentioned in 2 genealogy lists (Neh 3:15 and 11:5). The name means "all seeing" or "everyone's a seer." It is likely that this name was used in the list of names to designate the family profession. There is no apparent relationship between the 2 lists.

GARY C. AUGUSTIN

COLONIES, ROMAN. See ROMAN COLONIES.

COLOSSAE (PLACE) [Gk *Kolossai*]. Best known as the destination of the epistle to the Colossians, this place name occurs in the NT only in the superscription of the letter and in the epistolary greeting (Col 1:2). Colossae was located in the territory of Phrygia in the Roman province of Asia Minor about 120 miles E of Ephesus. Situated near the Lycus river at the foot of Mt. Cadmus (Honaz Dagi; elevation, 8,435 feet), Colossae was only 11 miles SE of Laodicea and 15 miles SSE of Hierapolis. The ancient site was discovered in 1835 by explorer W. J. Hamilton. Surveys of the unexcavated site give evidence of an acropolis and a theater on the S bank of the Lycus river and a necropolis and the remains of other ancient buildings on the N bank.

The city apparently thrived in the 5 centuries before the Christian era as the principal city of the Lycus valley. Herodotus (7.30) refers to Colossae as "a great city of Phrygia" in 480 B.C., and Xenophon (*An.* 1.2.6) describes it as large and prosperous in 400 B.C. (see also Diod. Sic. 14.80.8). In a historical retrospect, Pliny (*HN* 5.145) includes Colossae in a list of famous cities *(oppida celeberrima).*

Colossae was still an important city during the Roman imperial period, as evidenced by inscriptional data and some extant coins showing the usual public officials (Magie 1950: 2.985–86). Based on Strabo's inclusion of Colossae in a list of small towns (*polismata; Geog.* 12.8.13), some scholars have contended that by the 1st-century A.D. Colossae had greatly diminished in size and importance. D. Magie has correctly observed, however, that there is a gap (lacuna) in Strabo's text after *polismata* and it should therefore not be inferred that this description applies to Colossae. Nevertheless, Colossae was increasingly overshadowed by its neighbors, particularly LAODICEA, which became the most prominent city of this valley by the Roman imperial period.

The economic success of the cities of this valley was derived primarily from their textile industries. Colossae was famous for the distinctive purple color of its wool, which was commonly called *colossinus* (Pliny *HN* 21.51; Strab., 12.18.16). The prosperity of these cities was also enhanced by their position on the major trade route leading from the Aegean coast to the hinterland of Asia and on to the E. There was probably a fairly large Jewish population in the cities of the Lycus. Some have estimated that as many as 7,500 Jewish freemen were in the district based upon the amount of Temple tax confiscated by the proconsul Flacus in Laodicea in 62 B.C. (see Cic. *Flac.* 28.68).

The paucity of inscriptions from the unexcavated site make it difficult to reconstruct any detailed history of the city. A number of Colossian coins, however, help to create some impressions about the city, especially concerning the gods worshipped at Colossae. Numismatic evidence points most frequently to the worship of the Ephesian Artemis and the Laodicean Zeus, but also to Artemis (the huntress), Men, Selene, Demeter, Hygieia, Helios, Athena, Tyche, Boule, as well as the Egyptian deities Isis and Sarapis (Head 1906: 154–57).

The fledgling Christian community at Colossae was perceived by Paul (perhaps through the report of Epaphras) as facing the threat of dangerous false teaching resembling aspects both of pagan religion as well as Judaism (see esp. Col 2:6–23). Making an eloquent case for the sole-sufficiency of Christ in his letter, Paul admonishes these believers not to give credence to the claims of the false teachers but to hold firmly to the Lord Jesus Christ alone (see COLOSSIANS).

It is unlikely that Paul had visited the city before he wrote (Col 2:1), although it is not impossible that he did stop off there either on his way to Ephesus (Acts 18:23) or during his lengthy stay at Ephesus. The Colossian church was probably the fruit of the labor of Epaphras, who also ministered in Laodicea and Hierapolis (Col 4:12–13). Paul's expressed desire to visit the city may have been met after his release from prison (Phlm 22; 2 Tim 3:20). Both Philemon and his runaway slave Onesimus were inhabitants of Colossae (Col 4:9; Phlm 10) as were also Archippus and Apphia.

A severe earthquake rocked this region either in A.D. 60 (Tac. *Ann.* 14.27) or in A.D. 64 (Eusebius; see Magie 1950: 2.1421). Laodicea suffered extensive damage and it is probable that Colossae experienced the same devastation. Likely due to the city's susceptibility to damage from recurring earthquakes, the population eventually relocated to the neighboring town of Chonae (Honaz). The comments of Buckler and Calder from a generation ago concerning the unexcavated site of Colossae still apply: "To archaeological research Kolossai offers attractions similar to those of Sardis: historical renown plus an accessible site completely unoccupied" (Buckler and Calder 1939: xi).

Bibliography

Broughton, T. R. S. 1938. Roman Asia Minor. Vol. 4, pp. 499–916 in *An Economic Survey of Ancient Rome,* ed. T. Frank. Paterson, NJ.
Buckler, W. H., and Calder, W. M. 1939. *Monumenta Asiae Minoris Antiqua.* Vol. 6: Monuments and Documents from Phrygia and Caria. Manchester.
Head, B. V., ed. 1906. *Catalogue of the Greek Coins of Phrygia in the British Museum.* London.
Hemer, C. J. 1986. *The Letters to the Seven Churches of Asia in their Local Setting.* JSNTSup 11. Sheffield.
Johnson, S. E. 1950. Laodicea and its Neighbors. *BA* 13: 1–18.

Lightfoot, J. B. 1879. *Saint Paul's Epistles to the Colossians and to Philemon.* Grand Rapids. Repr. 1977.
Magie, D. 1950. *Roman Rule in Asia Minor.* 2 vols. Princeton. NJ.
Mare, W. H. 1976. Archaeological Prospects at Colossae. *Near East Archaeological Society Bulletin* 7: 39–59.
Ramsay, W. M. 1895. *The Cities and Bishoprics of Phrygia.* 2 vols. Oxford.

CLINTON E. ARNOLD

COLOSSIANS, EPISTLE TO THE. Colossians traditionally has been classified as one of the Pauline "imprisonment epistles" since, like Ephesians, Philippians, and Philemon, it appears to have been written while the apostle was in jail (Col 4:3, 10, 18; cf. 1:24). The city of Colossae, in SW Asia Minor, was evidently destroyed by the same earthquake that devastated the neighboring cities of Hierapolis and Laodicea in the 7th year of Nero's reign (60–61 C.E.; see COLOSSAE (PLACE)). It is mentioned nowhere else in the NT, and Paul seems never to have visited the congregation there (see 2:1).

A. Structure, Character, and Contents

The overall structure of Colossians conforms to that of the typical Pauline letter: After the address there is a thanksgiving paragraph; in the body of the letter, affirmations and exhortations are closely related; and the letter is concluded with various personal data, greetings, and a benediction.

Colossians is often described as a polemical writing, since in 2:8–23 false teachings and practices are vigorously opposed. However, this letter does not exhibit the kind of argumentation that one finds in Galatians where Paul seems to be in constant dialogue with his opponents. Colossians is much more admonitory than argumentative, and it is most accurately characterized as a letter of exhortation and encouragement (Bujard 1973: 129, 229). The representation in 1:28 of what Paul does could also be a description of what the letter itself does; it preaches, it admonishes, and it instructs. In the process, various materials from the hymnic (1:15–20), liturgical (2:13–15), and ethical (3:18–4:1) traditions of the church are drawn in. It is striking, however, that no scriptural texts are quoted or discussed, and that even allusions to Scripture are infrequent.

The contents of the letter may be outlined as follows:

I. Letter opening, 1:1–8
  A. Address, 1:1–2
  B. Thanksgiving, 1:3–8
II. Letter body, 1:9–4:6
  A. Affirmations of the apostolic gospel, 1:9–2:7
    1. Introductory prayer for the knowledge of God, 1:9–12
    2. Affirmation of Christ's role in salvation, 1:13–23
      a. Introductory affirmation, 1:13–14
      b. Hymn in praise of Christ, 1:15–20
      c. Appeal to remain faithful to Paul's gospel, 1:21–23
    3. Affirmation of Paul's role, 1:24–2:5
    4. Summary exhortation, 2:6–7
  B. Warnings about false teachers, 2:8–23
    1. General warning about "human tradition," 2:8
    2. Affirmations in support of the warning, 2:9–15
    3. Specific warnings about worthless regulations, 2:16–23
  C. Exhortations to lead a Christian life, 3:1–4:6
    1. Fundamental appeals, 3:1–17
      a. Seek the things that are above, 3:1–4
      b. Put off the old nature, 3:5–11
      c. Put on the new nature, 3:12–17
    2. Counsels about everyday life, 3:18–4:6
      a. The household, 3:18–4:1
      b. Prayer, 4:2–4
      c. Outsiders, 4:5–6
III. Letter closing, 4:7–18
  A. News and greetings of Paul's associates, 4:7–14
  B. Concerning the church in Laodicea, 4:15–16
  C. Concerning Archippus, 4:17
  D. Autograph conclusion and benediction, 4:18

B. Principal Affirmations and Appeals

Although warnings about certain false teachers and their teachings occupy a prominent place in Colossians (2:8–23) the bulk of the letter consists of other kinds of appeals and of the affirmations on which they are based.

1. Affirmations. The principal affirmations of the letter, which are closely related to one another, concerning the truth of the gospel, the supremacy of Christ, and the present reality of the believer's new life.

(a) The gospel is variously described as "the word" (4:3), "the word of the truth" (1:5), "the word of God" (1:25), and "the word of Christ" (3:16). It is said to disclose "the hope laid up for you in heaven" (1:5, 23), and therefore "the grace of God" (1:6). It is identified with "the mystery hidden for ages and generations but now made manifest to his saints," and the content of the mystery is said to be "Christ" (2:2; 4:3), or more specifically, the presence of Christ among the Gentiles (1:27). The awesome scope and generative power of the gospel receive particular emphasis: "In the whole world it is growing and bearing fruit" (1:6) for "it has been preached to every creature under heaven" (1:23). This universal spread of the gospel is to be attributed to Paul himself whose office is to proclaim Christ—"warning every man and teaching every man in all wisdom" (1:28)—and who has been strengthened with a divine power for this purpose (1:29).

(b) The supremacy of Christ is affirmed throughout Colossians, most prominently in a hymn (1:15–20) which portrays Christ as preexistent with God. Echoing descriptions of Wisdom in the literature of Hellenistic Judaism, the hymn praises Christ as "the image of the invisible God" (v 15; 3:10) and "the first-born," both of creation and of those who shall rise from the dead (vv 15, 18b). He is, moreover, the one through whom "all things were created" (vv 15–16), in whom the whole of creation holds together (v 17), in whom "all the fulness [*plērōma*] of God was pleased to dwell" (v 19), and by whom the primal unity of creation is reconstituted (v 20)—"that in everything he might be preeminent" (v 18). He is thus the "head" of the whole cosmic "body" which an interpretive addition to the hymn identifies as "the church" (v 18a; 1:24). The cosmic dimensions of Christ's sovereignty are particularly clear from v 16, where it is declared that "all things," not only earthly but heavenly, including all of the supermundane powers ("thrones," "dominions," "principalities," "authorities"), have been created through him.

This cosmic christology is not confined to the hymn, however. In 2:9 Christ is again identified as the one in whom God's "fulness" dwells and the affirmation in 3:11 that "Christ is all, and in all" harks back to the praise of his role in the creation of all things. The portrayal of him as "head" recurs in 2:10 where he is described as "the head of all rule and authority," and "Head" is actually employed as a christological title in 2:19. The use of a creedal statement in 1:13 further enhances this emphasis on Christ's cosmic supremacy, for it sets the "kingdom" of God's beloved Son over against "the dominion of darkness" from which believers, since their baptism, have been delivered. Thus, in contrast to 1 Cor 15:23–28 where Christ's rule is described as still future and of limited duration, the conception here is of a reign which is already established and enduring. This idea is continued in the reference to Christ's enthronement at God's right hand (3:1) which echoes a creedal formulation based on Ps 110:1 (cf. Heb 1:3–4). In 3:15 Christ's reign is characterized very concretely as the rule of "peace" in the church ("the one body").

(c) Affirmations about the present reality of the believer's new life are also prominent in Colossians. Like those about Christ, these affirmations make frequent use of traditional concepts and terms and tend to be formulated in more or less traditional ways. Believers have not only been "delivered" from the power of darkness, but "transferred" even now into Christ's kingdom (1:13–14); they have not only "died" to the cosmic powers by which they were formerly tyrannized (2:20; 3:3), but "have come to fulness of life" in Christ (2:10); they have not only been "buried" with Christ, but have also been "raised with him" (2:12, 13; 3:1); they have not only "put off the old nature," but have already "put on the new nature" (3:9–10). Their entrance into this new life has been by way of baptism, which is described as "a circumcision made without hands" (2:11–13).

It is through the agency of Christ that believers are able to come into this new life, and his work is designated both as "redemption" (1:14) and as "reconciliation" (1:20, 22). "Redemption" is specifically identified as "the forgiveness of sins" (1:14; 2:13–14; 3:13). "Reconciliation" is also closely associated with forgiveness; through Christ's death believers have been freed from doing the "evil deeds" which had once alienated them from God and are now presented "holy and blameless and irreproachable before him" (1:21–22; 1:28). Although this new life is already fully present, it will not be fully disclosed until Christ's return when believers "will appear with him in glory" (3:3–4; 1:12, 27).

2. Appeals. There are 3 types of appeals in Colossians. Some are of a very fundamental sort, others are best described as instructional, and still others are situational.

(a) Most of the fundamental appeals are quite general: the readers are urged to be "rooted and built up in [Christ] and established in the faith . . ., abounding in thanksgiving (2:6–7), to "seek the things that are above, where Christ is . . ." (3:1–2), and to "do everything in the name of the Lord Jesus, giving thanks to God the Father through him" (3:17). The appeals to let "the peace of Christ" and "the word of Christ" rule their lives, to "admonish one another in all wisdom," and to sing to God with thankfulness in their hearts (3:15–16) are only a little more specific. At several points in the letter there are implicit appeals, some of which are also of this fundamental sort: the readers should "lead a life worthy of the Lord . . ." (1:9–12), "continue in the faith, stable and steadfast . . ." (1:23, 2:5), and be "knit together in love" (2:2). Such appeals have their origin in the view which is implicit in the affirmation of 1:6, that the gospel's worldwide spread is abetted when it bears fruit in the lives of believers (Gnilka *Kolosserbrief* HTKNT, 35).

(b) The appeals in 3:18–4:1 all convey specific instructions about conduct. Ever since Martin Luther's German translation of the Bible (first completed ed., 1534), in which this section and its parallel in Eph 5:22–6:9 appeared under the caption, "Die christliche Haustafel," these and similar passages (1 Pet 2:18–3:7) have been identified as Christian household codes. Whether or not they are only christianized versions of pre-Christian codes, a point on which interpreters are not agreed, it is clear that they belong to the church's fund of catechetical materials. Other appeals involve the listing of practices or attitudes to be avoided (3:5, 8–9) or embraced (3:12–14) and thus provide believers with more general instructions about an appropriate way of life. The admonitions to devote oneself to regular prayer (4:2–4) and to "conduct oneself wisely toward outsiders" (4:5–6) may also be classified as instructional.

(c) The specific requests made of the readers in 4:15–17 (to extend Paul's greetings to the Laodiceans, to exchange letters with the Laodiceans, and to urge Archippus to fulfil his ministry) may be described as situational appeals. The only other such appeals are several warnings about the dangerous beliefs and foolish practices of certain false teachers (2:8, 16, 18).

C. The Errant Teaching

The appeals and warnings in chap. 2 are issued in response to the threat of errant teachings which seem to be getting a hearing in the Christian community to which this letter is addressed. Whether the propagandists are members of that congregation, and how widely their "philosophy" (2:8) may already have been adopted there, are questions that cannot be answered with certainty. However, even though a detailed reconstruction of the philosophy as a whole is not possible, at least a general idea of its principles and practices may be gained from the warnings in 2:8–23 and from certain other passages (1:9–10, 26–28; 2:2–4).

1. Ascetic Practices. The aspect of this philosophy which seems to be of most concern in Colossians is its teaching about the value of rigorous self-denial. It would appear that the technical term for this has been picked up in Col 2:18, 23 where the readers are warned about being led into "self-abasement" (*RSV;* the Greek word is *tapeinophrosynē,* which elsewhere in the NT is used of "humility" in a good sense). Various restrictive rules concerning food and drink (probably including fasting) and perhaps some form(s) of sexual abstinence were intended to check the desires of the flesh (2:16, 20b–23), and one was obligated to the ritual observance of special festivals and days including the sabbath (2:16). Like the asceticism condemned in 1 Tim 4:3–4, this teaching may have involved a rejection of the created order as such, but there is no specific evidence in Colossians that this was the case.

2. Worship of Angels. It is not clear exactly how the reference to "worship of angels" (2:18) should be interpreted since the phrase itself is ambiguous. Are the angels to be understood as the worshippers (Greek: subjective genitive) or as the objects of worship (Greek: objective genitive)? If the latter, as most interpreters believe (Lohse *Colossians* Heremeneia, 117–18; Gnilka, 148–50; Schweizer 1982: 159–60), then one may suppose that a cultic veneration of angels was one further act of self-abnegation required by the errant teachers. This would suggest, in turn, that the difficult word, *ethelothrēskia* in 2:23 (*RSV:* "rigor of devotion") should be interpreted as a reference to that kind of worship (perhaps "self-chosen worship"; Lohse, 126). The alternative interpretation developed by Francis (1973b: 176–81; adopted by O'Brien *Colossians* WBC, xxxvi–xxxviii, 142) regards the angels themselves as the worshippers. According to this reading, the much-debated phrase (*ha heoraken embateuōn*) should be translated, "which he has seen upon entering," and should be understood as a reference to the sort of heavenly journey and participation in the heavenly worship often described in Jewish apocalyptic literature (Francis 1973a, 1973b: 171–76; Rowland, 1983).

3. Cosmic Elements. The ascetic rules, the special calendar, and the veneration of (or worship along with) angels may all be related to teaching about the significance of the "cosmic elements." These are mentioned in 2:8, 20 (*RSV:* "the elemental spirits of the universe") and are probably to be identified with "the principalities and the powers" referred to in 2:15. To judge from what is said here in Colossians, the readers are being encouraged to believe that deliverance from the control of these cosmic forces is not complete without devotion to the specified ascetic, ritual, and cultic practices (2:20–23).

4. Full Knowledge of God. It may be that these practices were also regarded as necessary for gaining access to the full knowledge of God and of God's will. This seems a reasonable inference from the rather polemical way in which Colossians insists on the sufficiency of the knowledge (*epignōsis, gnōsis*), understanding (*synesis*), and wisdom (*sophia*) that are present and disclosed in Christ and the gospel (1:9–10, 26–28; 2:2–3; 3:10). It is possible, but by no means certain, that the false philosophy required some kind of rite akin to that of the Hellenistic mystery cults (Lohse, 117–20; Gnilka, 151; Schweizer, 161–62). At issue is whether the participle *embateuōn* in 2:18 is a technical term for entering into a mystery (Dibelius, 1973) or whether it must be taken here in a more general sense. If the former, the reference would be to having "visions . . . during the mystery rites" (Lohse, 114, 117). If the latter, it could be to the mystical ascent into heaven of an apocalyptic visionary (Francis 1973a, 1973b: 171–76; Rowland 1983).

There are a number of similarities between these beliefs and practices and those of the Jewish sectarians at Qumran, known from the Dead Sea Scrolls; e.g., the strict observance of the sabbath and other special days on the religious calendar (CD iii.13–16; x.14–xi.18; 1QS i.14; x.1–9), the emphasis on distinguishing between clean and unclean foods (CD vi.18), the use of the phrase, "body of flesh" (1QpHab ix.2; Col 1:22), the interest in angels (1QM x.10–11; Col 2:18), and the concern for special religious knowledge (CD ii.3; 1QpHab xi.1; 1QS xi.15–16). Some of these features are also present in gnostic teachings as those are known from the NAG HAMMADI CODICES. The notion of a divine "fullness" (*plērōma*) found in Col 1:9, 19; 2:9, 10 is prominent in gnostic teaching (*Ap. Jas.* 2, 28–3, 11; 3, 34–4, 22; 12, 27–31; Schenke and Fischer 1978: 162).

A few scholars would identify the errant teaching with some form of Judaism (Bruce *Colossians* NICNT, 17–26) or Gnosticism (Schenke and Fischer 1978: 162). With the majority, however, it seems best to regard it as a thoroughly syncretistic philosophy (Bornkamm 1973; Francis 1973a, 1973b; *RGG* 3: 1727; Lohse, 128) which includes elements drawn from several religious movements (including, perhaps, the mystery religions as well as Judaism and Gnosticism), but which may be, in this particular form, unique to the community being addressed (Lindemann *Kolosserbrief* ZBK, 84–85).

D. Authorship

1. Presuming Pauline Authorship. Paul's name occurs as the author of Colossians not only at the beginning and at the end of the letter (1:1; 4:18) but also in 1:23. Various other passages, especially those in which the apostle's friends or associates are named, seem to imply his authorship (1:7, 25; 4:3, 7–17). This is supported as well by the fact that Timothy is named as cosender (1:1; cf. 2 Cor 1:1; Phil 1:1; 1 Thess 1:1; Phlm 1) and by the similarity in overall structure between Colossians and other letters of the Pauline Corpus.

The earliest external attestation to the Pauline authorship of Colossians is provided by the mere existence of Ephesians—written in Paul's name by someone who, because he drew so heavily upon it, must have accepted Colossians as apostolic (see EPHESIANS). This attestation is of course only implicit and indirect. The earliest explicit reference to Colossians as Paul's is by Irenaeus (ca. 180; *Haer.* 3.14.1, quoting Col 4:14); but Marcion, too, must have accepted it as the apostle's, since he seems to have made significant use of it (Tertullian, *Adv. Marc.* 5.19).

There is perhaps an allusion to Col 2:14 in the gnostic *Gos. Truth* (NHC I, 20.25–27), but alleged allusions to Colossians in the Apostolic Fathers (*1 Clem.* 49:2 and Col 3:14; Ign. *Trall.* 5:2 and Col 1:16; Polyc. *Phil.* 12:2 and Col 1:12, 23) and in Justin's *Dial.* (85.2; 138.2) are by no means certain. Because the Church Fathers seem to have preferred Ephesians to Colossians, specific citations of the latter are relatively infrequent in the patristic literature (Frede 1969: 274).

2. Questioning Pauline Authorship. The case against the Pauline authorship of Colossians was first developed by Mayerhoff (1838), who claimed that significant lexical, grammatical, stylistic, and theological differences set it apart from the 6 letters that he regarded as most characteristically Pauline (Romans, 1 and 2 Corinthians, Galatians, Philippians, 1 Thessalonians). He also argued that the author has used Ephesians, which Mayerhoff took to be authentic, and that the kind of teaching which is opposed in this letter did not arise until after Paul's death. The two latter points no longer carry any weight, for there is now general agreement that Colossians must be earlier than Ephesians and that the teaching opposed in Colossians could well have antedated the apostle's death. However, the vocabulary, style, and theological viewpoint of this letter still pose problems. A further difficulty, to which Mayerhoff himself gave no specific attention, is the understanding of Paul's apostolic office that finds expression here. Finally, some interpreters believe that there is good evidence of the literary dependence of Colossians on one or more of the letters which can be safely attributed to Paul.

a. Vocabulary. Most of the lexical differences between Colossians and the letters that are certainly Paul's do not weigh very heavily against Pauline authorship. It is true that Colossians uses a total of 87 words that do not appear in the recognized letters and that 34 of these occur nowhere else in the entire NT (Lohse, 85–86). However, the figures for Philippians, a genuinely Pauline letter of comparable length, are not much different: 76 words are used in no other Pauline letter and 36 of these are present nowhere else in the NT (Percy 1946: 17). Moreover, one must allow for the possibility that the "non-Pauline" words in Colossians were used by the apostle himself to meet a special situation. Nor is it in itself decisive that some important Pauline theological terms are missing from Colossians ("righteousness" and related words: "law," "freedom," "promise," "to save," "salvation" [Lohse, 86–87]). It must also be shown that these are terms Paul would ordinarily use in addressing the topic at hand. It is more important that a number of connective words and inferential articles favored by Paul are missing from Colossians (Lohse, 87); but this verges on the matter of style.

b. Style. Mayerhoff's conclusion that Colossians is written in a style so unlike Paul's that one must assume a different author is not only supported but greatly strengthened in an important study by Bujard (1973). Bujard has shown, for example, that the sentences in Colossians are significantly longer and more complex than Paul's, because conjunctions are used less than half as often while participial constructions and relative clauses are employed much more frequently (1:3–8; 2:6–15; Bujard 1973: 74–75); that the sentences in Colossians are more loosely constructed, with less attention to the logical development of an argument (Bujard 1973: 72–73, 129); and that the use of many synonyms and appositional phrases makes the style of Colossians wordy and tautologous (Bujard 1973: 216–17). These kinds of detailed stylistic differences cannot be explained as merely modifications required by a different subject matter (against Percy 1946: 18–66; see Bujard 1973: 229–30), and they are present throughout the letter, not just where one may suspect the use of traditional materials (against Cannon 1983: 175; see Bujard 1973: 224–29).

c. Theological Viewpoint. Certain ideas that are present in the recognized Pauline letters make an appearance in Colossians as well. For example, Jesus' death (on the cross, 1:20, 2:14) brings reconciliation (1:22); believers have been "buried" with Christ in baptism (2:12); faith involves discarding one's "old" self and becoming a "new" person (3:9–10); the church is "the body" of Christ (1:18; 3:15); in Christ various kinds of worldly barriers that separate people from one another have been broken down (3:11); and all is to be done in love (3:14), with thanksgiving to God (3:17). Although a number of these ideas were already present in the church's traditions on which Paul himself was dependent, it is clear that Colossians stands within the specifically Pauline tradition, even if the apostle himself is not its author.

There are, nevertheless, striking differences between the theological outlook of Colossians and Paul's views as they are known from the undisputed letters. (1) The redemptive work of Christ is identified above all with "the forgiveness of sins" (1:13–14; 2:13; 3:13), whereas the apostle thinks of it mainly as an act of justification (Rom 3:24; 5:6–9, 15–21). (2) In Colossians, Christ is praised as the "head" of the body (1:18; 2:19) which includes the whole cosmos (2:10), but in 1 Cor 12:12–26, 27 and Rom 12:4–5 (where the body in its entirety is identified with Christ), no special status is accorded to the head (v 21), and the body has no special cosmic dimension. (3) While traditional eschatological language and motifs are not entirely missing from Colossians (1:22; 3:4, 6, 24–25), the emphasis falls heavily upon the deliverance that believers have already experienced. Because "hope" is identified as the content of the gospel message, it is understood to be fulfilled in the preaching of Christ (1:5, 23, 27). Hope is not, as in Rom 5:2–5 and elsewhere in Paul's letters, primarily the act of hoping itself. Where Paul speaks of the believer's future resurrection with Christ (Rom 6:5, 8; Phil 3:11, 12), Colossians stresses the present reality of this (2:12–13; 3:1). The apostle's idea of salvation as "already" established but "not yet" fulfilled is missing, and there is no hint of his notion that the Holy Spirit is the down payment on that to which the believer is heir (2 Cor 1:22; 5:5; cf. Rom 5:5; 8:23). (4) It is often observed that one finds nothing in Colossians about such major Pauline topics as God's gift of righteousness, the meaning of justification, faith versus works of the law, the function of the law, or the meaning of freedom in Christ. The example of Galatians, where Paul is opposing teachings similar to those opposed in Colossians, suggests that these are precisely the themes that the apostle himself would have developed in Col 2:8–23. That they are not developed there, or anywhere else in Colossians, adds to the difficulty of accepting this letter as Paul's own.

d. Paul's Apostolic Office. The portrait of Paul that emerges from the pages of Colossians is not easy to reconcile with what the indisputably authentic letters disclose about Paul's own understanding of his apostolic status and role. Two points in particular cause difficulty.

First, Paul is presented here as an apostle without peer in the church. To him alone the preaching of the gospel has been entrusted and the universal spread of the gospel is to be credited (1:23, 24; cf. the emphasis on "every person" in 1:28). Thus, he is not just an apostle to those who have heard and received his gospel, but also to those who, like the Colossians and Laodiceans, have never even seen him (2:1–2; cf. "for you" in 1:25). His apostleship transcends the particularities of time and place and encompasses the world. In the genuinely Pauline letters, however, one meets no such universalist conception of Paul's mission; he regularly refers to other apostles (1 Cor 9:5; 12:28–29; 15:7–9; Gal 1:17, 19), he acknowledges that he is an apostle especially for the churches of his founding (e.g., 1 Cor 9:2), and he does not propose to enter fields into which others have already carried the gospel, or to claim jurisdiction over them (2 Cor 10:13–16; Rom 15:20; Gal 2:9).

A second difficulty is the way Paul's sufferings are interpreted in Colossians. The letter's closing admonition, "Remember my chains" (4:18), leaves no doubt that the readers are to pay special attention to these (Lindemann, 78). The reason for this is apparent in 1:24 where the sufferings that Paul endures as an apostle are interpreted as having a vicarious function. They "complete what is lacking in Christ's afflictions for the sake of his body, that is, the church" which means that they satisfy the quota of sufferings that God's people must endure before the Lord's return (Lohse 69–72). In the acknowledged letters, however, Paul interprets his sufferings as manifesting the sufferings and death of Jesus (2 Cor 4:8–13). He therefore gives them a kerygmatic and not a vicarious interpretation. Moreover, he does not understand them as having universal significance; the beneficiaries are, quite specifically, those to whom he has brought his preaching of the cross (2 Cor 4:15; Phil 2:17).

e. Literary Dependence on Other Letters. Colossians has several things in common with the one to Philemon. In both, Paul writes as a prisoner and Timothy is named as a co-sender; one of the 2 men being sent to the Colossians is Onesimus, on behalf of whom the letter to Philemon is written; 5 of the 6 people to whom greetings are sent in Colossians are also greeted in Philemon; and in Colossians a special appeal is directed to Archippus, one of the 3 individuals addressed in Philemon. Since there is little question about the authenticity of Philemon, it is often argued that these similarities establish the Pauline authorship of Colossians as well (Knox 1938; Cope 1985). However, one can also hold that these connections have been contrived by a later author who, writing in Paul's name, wishes to give an apostolic aura to Colossians (Lohse, 175–77; Schenke and Fischer 1978: 167–68). In this case there would be a literary relationship between the 2 letters but not necessarily a situational one. Evidence has also been adduced for the literary dependence of Colossians on 5 other letters that are certainly Paul's: Romans, 1 and 2 Corinthians, Galatians, and 1 Thessalonians. Using carefully formulated criteria for identifying verbal agreements, E. P. Sanders (1966) has concluded tht materials drawn from 3 or more of these letters have been conflated in Col 1:15–16; 1:20–22a; 1:26–27; 2:12–13; 3:5–11—and in such a way that one can think only of the work of "a secondary imitator" (Sanders 1966: 40).

3. Conclusion. Those who defend the Pauline authorship of Colossians tend to discount the stylistic differences from the authentically Pauline letters, and generally argue that the theological differences amount to no more than changes in emphasis due to the peculiarities of the situation in Colossae (O'Brien *Colossians, Philemon* WBC, 43–44, 49). However, the stylistic differences run very deep, extending even to the manner of argumentation (Bujard); the altered theological outlook that one finds here is no mere change of emphasis; and in addition Paul is accorded a status that he himself had neither claimed nor achieved.

Various scholars have attempted to associate Colossians with Paul despite these non-Pauline features, but none can be judged to have succeeded. (A) The hypothesis that the author of Ephesians is responsible for Colossians in its present form, having greatly expanded an authentically Pauline letter in order to conform it to his own work (Holtzmann 1872; Masson *Colossiens* CNT, 10) overlooks the structural and material integrity of Colossians and reduces it to little more than a patchwork of interpolations. Moreover, on this view one is required to think of Colossians as secondary to Ephesians, whereas a careful comparison of the two letters demonstrates that Ephesians is dependent on Colossians. (B) It is equally speculative to hold that all or most of Colossians was composed at Paul's direction by one of his associates (Klöpper 1882; Schweizer, 21, 23–24; Ollrog 1979: 219–33, 236–42), perhaps because the apostle's circumstances in prison required that. Had someone like Epaphras (Klöpper) or Timothy (Schweizer) written the letter on Paul's behalf, would the first person singular be employed in the biographical notices at 1:23, 24–25, 29; 2:1–5; 4:7–8 (correctly, Lindemann 1981: 116)? And even if one could demonstrate that this was the case, Colossians would still be a "pseudonymous" letter, as Schweizer acknowledges (24).

In sum, the evidence strongly supports the conclusion that Colossians is not only pseudonymous but also post-Pauline (Bornkamm 1971; Lohse, 177–83; Gnilka, 19–26). The style is not Paul's, the theological outlook is in certain respects significantly different from his, and Paul's apostolic status and role are presented in a way that would not have been possible during his own lifetime.

E. The Date and Place of Writing

If this letter was either written or endorsed by Paul himself, it would have to be dated to some period of imprisonment. Since there is circumstantial evidence of an Ephesian imprisonment, one coud date Colossians that early (ca. 55?), as do Suhl (1975: 168), Schweizer (25–26), and Ollrog (1979: 241). On this view, however, it is almost impossible to explain why the theological outlook of Colossians is at points so different from that of Philippians (presumably written about the same time) and Romans (written later). The "theological development" hypothesis has no real force unless Colossians is dated as close to the end of Paul's life as possible, which means either to Caesarea (Acts 23:23–26:32) or to Rome (Acts 28:11–31). One thus arrives at a date somewhere between 57 and 60–61 (when Colossae was destroyed by an earthquake).

If Colossians is post-Pauline, one must allow for the passage of a few years after the apostle's death, which would put the earliest likely date of writing at about 65. A date much later than 90 is ruled out since Ephesians, by whose author Colossians has been used, was probably known to Ignatius, ca. 100. Any closer dating of Colossians seems impossible if the letter is taken as post-Pauline. Moreover, in this case nothing in it suggests a specific place of composition, not even the portrayal of Paul as a prisoner. However, since Colossae and the 2 other cities mentioned, Laodicea (2:1; 4:13, 15, 16) and Hierapolis (4:13), are situated in the Lycus River valley, a location in SW Asia Minor is probable.

F. Occasion and Purpose

This letter has been prompted by the author's concern about a false philosophy which threatens to undermine the readers' faith, luring them into practices which are not in accord with Paul's gospel (2:8–23). The purpose of the letter is stated indirectly in 1:23: The author wants his readers to "continue in the faith, stable and steadfast, not shifting from the hope of the gospel which [they] heard. . . ." The danger posed by the false philosophy is certainly in mind here, just as it is in the summary exhortation of 2:6–7, to be "rooted and built up in [Christ] and established in the faith, just as you were taught. . . ." The errant teaching is more specifically in view in 2:4–5, which may be taken as yet another indirect expression of the purpose of the letter: "I say this in order that no one may delude you with beguiling speech. For though I am absent in body, yet I am with you in spirit, rejoicing to see your good order and the firmness of your faith in Christ." Many of the principal affirmations and appeals in Col 1:9–3:17, and most of the more specific counsels in 3:18–4:6, hark back to the missionary preaching and baptismal instruction with which the readers would have been familiar, because the author wants to remind them of their original commitment "to lead a life worthy of the Lord" (1:10; Meeks 1977: 209–10).

If one regards Colossians as Pauline, then the data that are available concerning its composition and dispatch can be readily summarized. Paul, in prison, has heard about the dangerous situation in Colossae from Epaphras (1:7b–8), who is himself a Colossian and the founder of the congregation (1:5b–7; 4:12–13). This letter is Paul's response and it is probably to be carried to Colossae by Tychicus and Onesimus who are going to tell the Colossians all about Paul's present circumstances and bring them words of encouragement (4:7–9).

If Colossians is actually pseudonymous and post-Pauline, one must doubt whether it was even intended for a congregation in Colossae, since there seems to have been no significant repopulating of the city following the earthquake in 60–61 until the second century (Schweizer, 13–14). Lindemann (1981; *Kolosserbrief* ZB, 12–13) argues that the letter was actually intended for the Laodiceans, whose city (some 10 miles distant) had been devastated by the same earthquake but quickly rebuilt; and the references to Laodicea in 2:1 and 4:15–16 give weight to this hypothesis. Addressing the letter to the Laodiceans themselves, Lindemann suggests, would have required the pseudepigrapher to formulate Paul's words as somewhat oblique prophetic warnings and counsels, provided some years in advance of the situation that the congregation now faces. But composing it as if it had been addressed to the congregation in Colossae allows him to represent the apostle in direct confrontation with doctrines like those now proving attractive to the Laodiceans. The pseudepigrapher must hope that the Laodiceans will recognize this and will hear in "Paul's" warnings to a neighboring congregation an authoritative word for their own (1981: 133; *Kolosserbrief,* 12–13).

The names and personal notices in Colossians (1:7–8; 2:1; 4:7–18) cannot be used as evidence of Pauline authorship, since they can be well enough explained as a pseudepigrapher's attempt to give his letter a believable setting within Paul's ministry. It is noteworthy, however, that Epaphras is singled out for special commendation both at the beginning and at the end of the letter (1:7–8; 4:12–13), perhaps an indication that his standing in the congregation needs bolstering. One could imagine that Epaphras himself is the author of this letter (Suhl 1975: 168, n. 93) but this is unprovable. The important thing is that the author, whoever he is, regards Paul as the church's one great apostle and that he does not hesitate to invoke Paul's authority as he summons the readers to stand firm in their faith, rejecting the teachings and practices of the false philosophy.

Bibliography

Bornkamm, G. 1971. Die Hoffnung im Kolosserbrief. Pp. 206–13 in vol. 2 of *Geschichte und Glaube* (vol. 4 of *Gesammelte Aufsätze).* BEvT 53. München.

———. 1973. The Heresy of Colossians. Pp. 123–45 in Meeks and Francis 1973.

Bujard, W. 1973. *Stilanalytische Untersuchungen zum Kolosserbrief als Beitrag zur Methodik von Sprachvergleichen.* SUNT 11. Göttingen.

Cannon, G. E. 1983. *The Use of Traditional Materials in Colossians.* Macon, GA.

Cope, L. 1985. On Rethinking the Philemon-Colossians Connection. *BR* 30: 45–50.

Dibelius, M. 1973. The Isis Initiation in Apuleius and Related Initiatory Rites. Pp. 61–122 in Meeks and Francis 1973.

Francis, F. O. 1973a. The Background of EMBATEUEIN (Col 2:18) in Legal Papyri and Oracle Inscriptions. Pp. 197–207 in Meeks and Francis 1973.

———. 1973b. Humility and Angelic Worship in Colossae. Pp. 163–95 in Meeks and Francis 1973.

Frede, H. J., ed. 1969. *Epistula ad Colossenses.* Vetus Latina 24/2. Freiburg.

Holtzmann, H. J. 1872. *Kritik der Epheser- und Kolosserbriefe auf Grund eine Analyse ihres Verwandschaftsverhältnisses.* Leipzig.

Klöpper, A. 1882. *Der Brief an die Colosser.* Berlin.

Knox, J. 1938. Philemon and the Authenticity of Colossians. *JR* 18: 144–60.

Lindemann, A. 1981. Die Gemeinde von 'Kolossä': Erwägungen zum 'Sitz im Leben' eines deuteropaulinischen Briefes. *WD* 16: 111–34.

Mayerhoff, E. T. 1838. *Der Brief an die Colosser mit vornehmlicher Berücksichtigung der drei Pastoralbriefe,* ed. J. L. Mayerhoff. Berlin.
Meeks, W. A. 1977. In One Body: The Unity of Humankind in Colossians and Ephesians. Pp. 209–21 in *God's Christ and His People,* ed. J. Jervell and W. Meeks. Oslo.
Meeks, W. A., and Francis, F. O., ed. 1973. *Conflict at Colossae.* SBLSBS 4. Missoula, MT.
Ollrog, W.-H. 1979. *Paulus und seine Mitarbeiter.* WMANT 50. Neukirchen-Vluyn.
Percy, E. 1946. *Die Probleme der Kolosser- und Epheserbriefe.* Acta reg. Societas Humanorum Litterarum Lundensis 39. Lund.
Rowland, C. 1983. Apocalyptic Visions and the Exaltation of Christ in the Letter to the Colossians. *JSNT* 19: 73–83.
Sanders, E. P. 1966. Literary Dependence in Colossians. *JBL* 85: 28–45.
Schenke, H.-M., and Fischer, K. M. 1978. *Die Briefe des Paulus und Schriften des Paulinismus.* Vol. 1 of *Einleitung in die Schriften des Neuen Testaments.* Gütersloh.
Schweizer, E. 1982. *The Letter to the Colossians: A Commentary.* Trans. A. Chester. Minneapolis.
Suhl, A. 1975. *Paulus und seine Briefe. Ein Beitrag zur paulinischen Chronologie.* SNT 11. Gütersloh.

VICTOR PAUL FURNISH

COLUMBARIA. Shelters or coops for pigeons or doves. See ZOOLOGY.

COMMAGENE (PLACE). Ancient Commagene lay just N of the centers of biblical activity, with which it remained involved. The kingdom arose from ancient roots, successfully uniting a Hellenic, Iranian, and Semitic populace, and presenting one of antiquity's most vivid examples of religious syncretism.

It lay W of the Euphrates, between Cappadocia and Syria. Further W ran the formidable barrier of the Taurus Mountains and Cilicia Pedias, which included cities such as Mopsuhestia and Tarsus. Across the Euphrates in Mesopotamia, Commagene fronted Osrhoene and behind it the Parthian Empire.

So placed, it benefited from trade routes running both E–W and N–S; it also controlled one of the most important crossings of the Euphrates. The consequent prosperity made Commagene, by late in the 1st century A.D., richest of the kingdoms allied to Rome, laden with "old wealth" (Tac. *Hist* 2.81.1). This background gave it an international influence disproportionate to its size.

Commagene lay open to influences from its diverse neighbors. At one time, it had been ruled by the Orontids of Armenia, and through a marriage it traced its descent back to Darius the Great of Persia (*OGIS* 388; 391). It had formed part of the Seleucid Empire, but rebelled under Ptolemaios, a local governor, about 163 B.C. as realignments occurred in much of the East (Diodorus 31.19a). Judas Maccabaeus probably made his initial contact with Rome in the preceding year, and events in Bithynia, Cappadocia, Media, and Egypt also reflected the growing tendency to involve Rome. The revolt of Ptolemaios succeeded, signalled by his adoption of the title of king.

A son of Ptolemaios, King Samos, succeeded him about 130 B.C. He probably founded Samosata, and after a reign of indeterminate length passed on the throne to his son, Mithradates I Kallinikos (*OGIS* 402). A state marriage allowed Mithradates to bring into his court a daughter of the Seleucid monarch, Antiochus VIII Grypus. This put Commagene in the top rank of dynastic houses of the East and led to further intermarriage, especially in Judaea and Emesa. A marriage into the Parthian dynasty completed Commagenian credentials in this regard (Dio 49.23.4; now confirmed by Wagner 1983: 208–224).

Perhaps as early as 87 B.C., Commagene fell to the fearsome Tigranes the Great of Armenia, by then "King of Kings" as successor to Mithradates II of Parthia, who was in the process of establishing an empire that stretched from Mesopotamia to Syria. During the 14 or more years that Tigranes ruled Syria, Commagene carried on its native dynasty and national traditions. Mithradates continued the religious cults begun by his 2 predecessors and destined for completion by his son.

Our first glimpse of Antiochus I, son of Mithradates, occurs in a context of 69 B.C., the year in which Tigranes had to leave Syria to defend his homeland against Lucullus.

The restored freedom of Commagene, now allied to Rome, allowed Antiochus leisure for his great religious expression still visible atop Nemrud Dagh. His remarkable fusions of Greek and Iranian gods satisfied the composite population, which could now worship Zeus-Oromasdes (Ahuramazda), Heracles-Artagnes, and the grandly titled Apollo-Mithras-Helios-Hermes!

Antiochus trod a narrow path between Parthia and Rome. He came to blows with Pompey and capitulated; his inscriptions duly bear the title "Friend of Rome" (*Philoromaios: OGIS* 383 ff.). On the other hand, his coinage shows him in an Armenian tiara, which he assumed as a local "successor" to Tigranes. On at least one occasion, he was accused of partiality to the Parthians. Another coin uses Seleucid devices to remind subjects of his lineage on that side.

Both the disaster which befell Crassus in 53 B.C. and the Parthian invasion of Asia Minor in 51 B.C. threatened the stability of Commagene, but it emerged intact. The Roman civil war proved more difficult, and by 38 B.C. Antiochus had incurred the displeasure of Antony, who laid siege to Samosata, assisted by Herod of Judaea. A bribe sent them on their way.

Among the successors of Antiochus, Mithradates II supported Antony down to the battle of Actium in 31 B.C. (Plut. *Ant.* 61). Internal problems suddenly beset the dynasty with a murder and 2 executions. Mithradates III, recognized by Augustus, acceded in 20 B.C. This king married the same Atropatenian princess—Iotape I—whom Antony had sought for marriage to his son Alexander Helios. The progeny of this pair spread into the dynasties of Emesa and Judaea through marriages of the successive Iotapes (Sullivan *ANRW* 2/8: 198–219, 296–354, 732–98). See also IOTAPE (PERSON).

Antiochus III had the melancholy distinction of losing the kingdom in A.D. 18, when Tiberius made it a province (Tac. *Ann* 2.56; Strabo 16.2.3.749). It remained that way for a decade, but in 38 Caligula restored it to the son of Antiochus. The new king, Antiochus IV, had been raised in Rome; with his sister-wife, Iotape VI Philadelphus, he was to enjoy a long and lively reign, from 38 until 72.

A mature man, with at least one child nearly of marriageable age, Antiochus assumed his kingdom by right of inheritance, as son of Antiochus III (Dio 59.8). He celebrated this connection in his inscriptions and sought to strengthen the ties of Commagene to other dynasties. A betrothal of his son, Epiphanes, to a Judaean princess collapsed over the issue of circumcision (*Ant* 19.355; 20.139). His daughter, Iotape VII, did marry into that dynasty; her husband, the later King Alexander of Cilicia, boasted descent from Archelaus of Cappadocia and from Herod the Great of Judaea.

Antiochus began well, thanks to his personal acquaintance with Caligula, who was "raised with" several Eastern princes (Dio 59.24; *IGRR* IV 145). Besides the paternal kingdom in Commagene, he also assumed responsibility for "the coastal portion of Cilicia" in Tracheia (Dio 59.8). Part of this became known as the "Regnum Antiochi," and coins attest his wide rule in Tracheia. Several towns founded by him there (e.g., Iotape; Antioch-on-the-Crag) remain largely unexcavated today.

Antiochus joined a complicated Roman effort to control difficult parts of Asia Minor through native kings. (Strabo 14.5.6.671.) Besides Antiochus, this "circle" involved Archelaus I of Cappadocia and then his son; Polemo II of Pontus and his uncle, Zeno-Artaxias, who ruled in Armenia; Sohaemus of Emesa and Sophene; the Judaeans Aristobulus, Agrippa, and King Alexander.

Antiochus ruled his divided kingdom efficiently despite the Roman vicissitudes which kept Eastern rulers watchful. For some reason, the warmth Caligula once displayed for him turned to anger, and Antiochus found himself deposed. Claudius reversed this, both for Commagene and for some part of Cilicia (Joseph. *Ant.* 19.276; Dio 60.8).

Antiochus joined a meeting of dynasts in 44 hosted by the Judaean Agrippa I at Tiberias (Joseph. *Ant.* 19.338 ff.). This provoked suspicion by the Roman governor of Syria, for they constituted a powerful group: Besides Agrippa, there attended Polemo II of Pontus, Cotys IX of Armenia Minor, Sampsigeramus II of Emesa, Herod of Chalcis, and Antiochus of Commagene.

Random glimpses reveal Commagene active militarily. In A.D. 52, Antiochus fought the wild Cietae in Cilicia. In 54, he joined Nero's mobilization against the Parthians. In 60, he participated in a defensive partition of Armenia (Tac. *Ann* 12.55; 13.7; 13.37; 14.26). He helped install the Judaean Tigranes VI briefly in Armenia.

The Jewish War drew Commagenian contingents, led by sons of Antiochus, to assist Vespasian and Titus. The tumultuous "Year of the Four Emperors" (A.D. 68–69) saw a Commagenian prince wounded while fighting for Otho (Joseph. *JW* 5.460 ff.; Tac. *Hist* 5.1; 2.25).

Despite assistance to Vespasian on his way to the imperial throne, Antiochus could still not relax. Vespasian had been concerned about a Parthian attack "from the rear" while Titus fought in Judaea (Tac. *Hist* 2.82). He therefore worried about "the proximity of the kings" of Commagene and Parthia, realizing that Commagenian control of the Euphrates crossings might afford Parthians "ready passage" should they wish access to Asia Minor; this might "involve the entire Roman Empire in war" out there (Joseph. *JW* 7.222 f.). Euphrates access could also be of importance should Rome wish to try again for control of Armenia, where an Arsacid dynast now ruled, having been recognized in A.D. 66 by Nero.

Accordingly in 72, Antiochus found Romans preparing for war on the charge of intrigue with Parthia. Some fighting did occur, and participants referred to it as the *Bellum Commagenicum* (*ILS* 9198; 9200; *JW* 7.220 ff.). The 2 sons of Antiochus escaped into Parthia, but Antiochus was taken to Rome. There where he had begun his career under the first Julio-Claudians, he ended it in honorable detention under the Flavians. He might have lived in the reigns of all 11 Roman emperors from Augustus to Domitian. He presided over the final decades of a kingdom by now 235 years old.

The 2 sons of Antiochus returned, and with the title of "king" they assumed an honorable place in society. Their sister became the queen of Cilicia for a time, married to King Alexander. Their children, especially Julia Balbilla and C. Iulius Antiochus Philopappus, took notable places in the new absorption of former kings into the Roman aristocracy. Balbilla accompanied Hadrian to Egypt and left extant poetry there. Philopappus became a Roman consul and left a monument on the Mouseion Hill in Athens, where it still faces the Parthenon. Continuation of the intermarriage led eventually to the families of the Emperors Marcus Aurelius and Elagabalus.

The kingdom of Commagene had taken an important role in the long transition from Seleucid to Roman rule, and had stabilized a crucial region between the Hellenic and Iranian societies. The innovations of Antiochus I long influenced religious thought in the vicinity. The old cult-sites remained in use for centuries, as attested by archaeological finds and by literary references. The new cities founded by the dynasty formed the basis for later ecclesiastical organization there.

Commagene greatly influenced the larger society around it even after it was gone.

Bibliography

The archaeological record has been presented especially by Prof. Dr. F. K. Dörner. See F. K. Dörner and T. Göll, *Arsameia am Nymphaios* (Berlin 1963), his forthcoming book on Nemrud Dagh, and his many articles.

Jones, A. H. M. 1971. *Cities of the Eastern Roman Provinces,* 2d ed. Oxford.

Sullivan, R. D. 1989. *Near Eastern Royalty and Rome, 100–30 BC.* Toronto.

Wagner, J. 1983. Dynastie und Herrscherkult in Kommagene. *MDAI(I)* 1/33: 177–224.

———. 1976. *Seleukeia am Euphrat/Zeugma.* Wiesbaden.

RICHARD D. SULLIVAN

COMMANDMENT. The common translation of the Hebrew Bible's *miṣwâ* and the NT *entolē*. All but 8 occurrences of the Bible's *miṣwâ* are translated *entolē* in the LXX. In the Psalms (esp. Psalm 119, LXX), *entolē* is sometimes found as a translation of the Heb *piqqūdîm*. Modern English versions of the Bible sometimes also use "commandment" or "command" to render Heb *mišpaṭ* (Zeph 2:3), *ḥōq* (Amos 2:4), and *piqqūdîm* (Ps 103:18), and Gk *epitagē* (1 Cor 7:25).

Of itself "commandment" denotes that which is commanded by an authority, hence, an authoritative prescription, order, decree, or by extension a directive or instruction. "Commandment" occasionally occurs in the Bible with a secular meaning (2 Chr 35:10, 16; John 11:57; Acts 17:15; etc.), but its biblical usage is predominantly religious: The commandment is a divine ordinance. "Commandment" sometimes appears, somewhat indiscriminately, as one of a series of legal terms (e.g., Gen 26:5), but more often it is used in isolation from other legal terms.

In the Bible, *miṣwâ-entolē* emphasizes the authority of the God who commands rather than the content of the commandment as such. The commandment is the expression of God's will for his people. Rather than suggesting arbitrary demand or constraint, the terminology evokes God's moral authority. Jewish expressions of the significance of the commandments (i.e., their importance and the reasons for them) began to appear during the Hellenistic period (e.g., *Let.Aris.* 142–144; *4 Macc* 5:23–24). From the 2d century onward, largely in response to Christian attacks on the Law, many Jewish replies addressed the issue of the reasons for the commandments. In medieval times, Maimonides held that all commandments had a cause, i.e., a useful purpose.

Deuteronomy and the Deuteronomic literature (including Psalm 119) are the best sources for understanding the biblical notion of commandment. Indeed, the terminology appears but rarely in the prophetic literature (e.g., Isa 48:18; Exod 18:21; Dan 3:29). Commandment, *miṣwâ-entolē,* suggests a "double personal reference" (O'Connell 1960: 361), i.e., the loving God who commands and the one to whom the commandment is addressed. The proper response to a commandment is not merely external compliance, but a total personal response ("from the heart," *leb*). The virtual interchangeability between *miṣwâ-entolē* and *dābār-logos/rhēma,* i.e. "word," (e.g., Deut 5:22; 30:14; Esth 9:32) highlights the personal quality of the commandment. The ultimate significance of the commandments is to relate people to God. Accordingly the commandments are best understood within the covenant context.

The Pentateuch uses *miṣwâ-entolē* in reference to particular laws, and sometimes in the plural (e.g., Deut 15:5). However, in the Deuteronomic paraenesis of Deut 8:1–20, *miṣwâ-entolē* is used comprehensively for the whole law (Deut 8:1; cf. 5:31; 11:22; 19:9; 30:11–14). This is in keeping with the Deuteronomist's holistic view of the relationship between Yahweh and Israel. The commandment, which also has a revelatory function, is intended to make of Israel a holy people. Israel's prosperity is dependent upon its obedience to the commandment. Keeping the commandments indicates a pattern of life, i.e., one of human fidelity to the covenant.

From this perspective, some authors are inclined to identify the Decalog (the covenant prescriptions of Exodus 20 and Deuteronomy 5) as the preeminent referent of "commandment." Jewish tradition, however, going back to tannaitic times and shaped somewhat definitively in the school of R. Akiba, identifies 613 commandments (*taryaq miṣwōt*) in the Bible. Of these, 365 are proscriptions and 248 are prescriptions, as R. Simlai states: "613 commandments were revealed to Moses at Sinai, 365 being prohibitions equal in number to the solar days, and 248 being mandates corresponding in number to the limbs of the human body" (*b. Mak.* 23b). In Jewish writings (e.g., Philo, *Dec.* 29.154; *Num.Rab.* 13:15–16), the biblical commandments are often classified or summarized under the ten headings of the Decalog.

Reference to the developing tradition of the 613 commandments may be part of the background of several pericopes in the synoptic gospels, particularly in their Matthean version (Matt 5:17–20; Matt 19:16–22 = Mark 10:17–22; Luke 18:18–23; Matt 22:34–40 = Mark 12:28–34; Luke 10:25–28). According to Matthew's commandment theory, the entire law and the prophets depend on the two love commandments (Matt 22:37–40 = Mark 12:29–31; Luke 10:27; cf. Matt 19:19b). Matthew affirms that a similarity exists between these two, most probably because of the presence of *agapan* ("to love") in application of the *gezerah shavah* principle of rabbinic hermeneutics. This principle holds that if the same word occurs in two different scriptural passages, one passage may be used to interpret the other. Thus, Matthew stresses the organic unity of the commandments and attributes a summarizing priority to the two-fold love commandment.

Matthew's own catechetical tradition seems also to have underscored the importance of the Decalog among the biblical commandments (Matt 5:21, 27, 33; 15:19 = Mark 7:21–22). As in Deuteronomy, Matthew is aware that the commandments are addressed to the free will of human beings (Matt 19:17; cf. v 21). Matt 15:1–20 has taken over and somewhat modified the Markan controversy story (Mark 7:1–23), in which a precept of the Decalog, "honor your father and your mother," is identified as a commandment of God (Matt 15:3b–4; cf. v 6, "word of God"), distinguished from human precepts (Matt 15:9; cf. v 9 "your tradition"). Matthew's gospel also gives some evidence of intra-Christian debates about the significance of the commandments (Matt 5:17–20).

The Fourth Gospel likewise has a particular understanding of the commandments. In John, the term *entolē,* commandment, is used to characterize the task associated with the mission of the Son (John 10:18; 12:49–50; 15:8). The notion not only implies the Son's obedience to the Father (John 14:31); it also points to the authority with which Jesus fulfills his mission. A specifically Johannine understanding of the commandments is to be found in the idea of Jesus' own commandments ("my commandments," John 14:15, 21; cf. v 24, "my words"). To keep Jesus' commandments is to love him. These commandments are summed up in the love commandment, which is both Jesus' command (John 15:12, 17; cf. 1 John 4:21) and his gift (John 13:34). The love command is called a "new commandment" because of its christological basis (John 13:34; cf. 15:12). Caught up in an inter-Christian contoversy, the author of 1 John reaffirms the christological basis of the new commandment while maintaining that the love commandment is part of the traditional catechesis. As such it is both old and new (1 John 2:7–8).

A unitary understanding of the biblical commandments is also to be found in Paul, where the love commandment (Lev 19:18) summarizes several precepts of the Decalog

(Rom 13:8–10). Keeping this commandment fulfills the law. A particularly significant Pauline notion is that the commandment (*entolē,* in the singular, apparently with reference to the 10th precept of the Decalog), although holy, just, and good, can be exploited by the quasi-demoniac power of sin (*hamartia*). The commandment reveals sin to be sin, leading to death (Rom 7:7–13).

In Pauline usage, with but one exception, *entolē* always refers to the biblical commandments (see Heb 7:5, 16, 18; 9:19). That exception is to be found in 1 Cor 14:37, where the expression "commandment of the Lord" (*Kuriou entole*) is similar to the phrase "commandment of the Lord" (*Kuriou epitage*) found in 1 Cor 7:25. In the NT, the use of commandment-*epitage* is found only in Paul and the Deutero-Pauline literature (Rom 16:26; 1 Cor 7:6, 25; 2 Cor 8:8; 1 Tim 1:1; Tit 1:3; 2:15). Although the term admits of a variety of usages, it appears to enjoy a comprehensive, salvific connotation in Rom 16:26; 1 Tim 1:1, and Tit 1:3. See *TWAT* 4: 1085–95; *EWNT* 1: 1121–25; *TDNT* 2: 545–56; and *EncJud* 5: 760–92.

Bibliography

Braulik, G. 1988. *Studien zur Theologie des Deuteronomiums*. Stuttgarter Biblische Aufsätzbande 2. Stuttgart.

Collins, R. F. 1986. *Christian Morality: Biblical Foundations*. Notre Dame.

Lewittes, M. 1985. Creation and Commandment. *DD* 13: 167–73.

O'Connell, M. J. 1960. The Concept of Commandment in the Old Testament. *TS* 21: 351–403.

Pasinya, L. M. 1973. Pp. 89–93 in *La notion de Nomos dans le Pentateuque grec*. AnBib 52. Rome.

RAYMOND F. COLLINS

COMMANDMENTS, TEN. See TEN COMMANDMENTS.

COMMISSION, GREAT. See GREAT COMMISSION.

COMMUNICATION. See TRAVEL AND COMMUNICATION.

COMMUNION. See LORD'S SUPPER; AGAPE MEAL.

COMMUNITY. This entry consists of two articles, one covering the OT notion of community, the other covering the NT notion.

OLD TESTAMENT

Community in the Bible is a complex subject, amenable to no simple definition. The notion of community not only went through an evolution under the influence of both internal factors and foreign pressures, but frequently competing notions of community coexisted, vying for the allegiance of the people. Another factor complicates the subject. Israel began as a sacral community, that is, as a people organized tribally under the God Yahweh; with the introduction of kingship, however, tribal-theocratic structures gave way to the more secular structures of empire. The Yahwistic community therefore was obliged to assume the more modest status of a voluntary association within the larger society.

As in all other areas of biblical study, the subject of community has been enriched by new discoveries and new methods of analysis. Whereas an earlier age could study community on the basis of divine legislation conferred upon the people at Sinai, scholars today are attentive both to the evidence of social ideals and communal structures attested within the broader ancient Near Eastern environment and to scholarly reconstructions seeking to correlate such evidence with a critical reading of biblical texts. Earlier in the century, Albrecht Alt (1925, 1930) and Martin Noth (1930) rejected as unhistorical the biblical view of a military conquest of Canaan and appealed instead to Nabatean inscriptions of the Roman period and to the structure of the Greek amphictyony. They argued that Israel's origins could be explained as resulting from the infiltration of nomadic elements into the agrarian-urban culture of Canaan. Today social-anthropological studies favor a dimorphic model for understanding the sociology of early Israel; that is to say, the tribes of Israel emerged not through the transplantation of desert nomads onto the soil of sedentary farmers, but within the perennial flux between urban centers and outlying regions. Detribalized elements banded together with disenfranchised city dwellers forming new coalitions and at times merging with older tribal units (Rowton 1976).

As we now examine the shape of Israelite community in its major phases of development, this brief reference to an ever-changing scholarly debate will serve as a reminder of the complexity of the task. Any critical reading of the biblical evidence must factor in archaeological evidence and take seriously methodological insights arising within ancillary disciplines.

A. Tribal Period

Bits and pieces gleaned from extrabiblical epigraphic sources can be combined with central themes found in Israel's epic as preserved in the Pentateuch to produce the following reconstruction of the origins of tribal Israel.

1. El and Kinship. The patriarchal legends reflect in general terms the migration of the Amorites into Mesopotamia and Syro-Palestine during the 2d millennium B.C.E. that is well documented in cuneiform sources. The Amorite personal names first studied by Theo Bauer and more recently by Herbert Huffmon reflect kinship patterns at home in tribal societies. Moreover, they reflect the centrality of the divine kinsman in the life of the tribal groups reflected in the ancestral legends of Genesis that later came to constitute the heart of Israel's concept of covenant. Further light is shed on the background of the divine kinsman of the ancestral stories by the deity El of the Ugaritic texts. El, the tent-dwelling, kindly creator-god and judge, has been plausibly argued to figure prominently in the origins of Israel's god Yahweh on the basis of shared epithets, attributes, and functions (Cross *CMHE,* 44–60). The conclusion to be drawn is this: At the time when

Amorite peoples were establishing themselves as heirs to the earlier civilizations of Mesopotamia, related clans were sojourning in Canaan. The latter encountered a well-established feudal society, living under the hegemony of the royal house of Egypt with local rule exercised by Canaanite lords. Unable to supplant the feudal lords of the land, the Amorites (and whatever other elements merged with them within the dimorphic social structures of Canaan) were obliged to have their patterns of movement and settlement governed by opportunity. What identity they preserved over against the local population was likely derived from their kinship patterns; this included identification with the divine kinsman El (under one of various epithets).

2. ʿApiru. Also germane to the discussion of Israel's origins as a community are references to the *ʿapiru/habiru* found in various MB documents, with the Amarna Letters prominent among them. See also HABIRU/HAPIRU. Though etymologically and sociologically related to the entity referred to in the Bible with the gentilic *ʿibrim,* the groups designated as *ʿapiru* were not ethnically bounded. Instead they were socially defined by their lack of integration into the feudal system of Canaan and, insofar as the local rulers were concerned, by their lawlessness and insubordination. The *ʿapiru* likely included people from different backgrounds, including Amorites, since all that was required to receive this dubious distinction was detribalization or marginalization from village or city. The *ʿapiru* were not confined to Canaan, but wandered freely between countries driven by opportunity and hardship (such as famine). Many of them no doubt eyed the Hyksos interregnum in Egypt as an opportunity (a situation likely reflected by the Joseph legend). With the reestablishment of indigenous rule by the pharaohs of the New Kingdom (cf., Exod 1:8), the *ʿapiru* would have suffered the fate of vast numbers of foreigners, though as inscriptions from the worker-village of Deir el-Medina indicates, the memory of NW Semitic deities was preserved among them. It is a fair assumption, therefore, that the Hebrew slaves of Moses' generation still maintained a sense of separate identity grounded in their ancestral legends and in the sacred stories of their kinsman God.

3. Theocratic Unity. The first mention of Israel outside of the Bible is on the Merneptah Stele of ca. 1210 B.C.E., and it is noteworthy that the preformative designates Israel as a people, not as a nation. This Egyptian encounter with a people identifiable as Israel in 1210 elicits a question: What were the events leading from the rather amorphous tribal backgrounds described above to this more focused community identity?

Earliest Israel appears out of the earliest traditions of the Bible as a loosely confederated group of tribes whose unity centered around a common story featuring the God Yahweh as the central actor. The most likely source of Israel's community structure of tribal organization around the kinsman deity is its ancestral prehistory in Canaan. But the earliest hymnic/epic compositions of the people Israel indicate that the model was infused with a new narrative content and tied to a new divine epithet by subsequent events, namely the story of deliverance from the Egyptian pharaoh effected by the God Yahweh. The reappearance of this story with such regularity in Israel's earliest hymnody offers the following as the most plausible answer to the question of what happened between the shadowy Amorite prehistory and Merneptah's explicit reference to a "people Israel": A group of slaves belonging to the social category of *ʿapiru* managed to escape from their bondage in Egypt under the leadership of Moses, an escape they attributed to the gracious action of their kinsman God, whom they now called Yahweh. The Moses-Jethro story may offer a clue regarding the source from which early Israel derived the divine epithet Yahweh.

Reciting the story of deliverance became the central cult-act of the People Israel. The substitution of an epic in the place of the cult-myth common to most other ANE cultures had a dramatic effect on the community ideals that emerged among the new tribal confederacy. The rules governing the life of the community, though in part drawn from the common traditions of the pervading culture, increasingly included guidelines inferred from the epic of Yahweh's gracious deliverance. An open-ended, historical consciousness challenged the more static values of mythopoeic cultures. Ideals and institutions began to take shape that drew their motivation from "Yahweh who brought you out from the land of Egypt, out of the house of bondage." These ideals and institutions were mixed, to be sure, with those of the environment, as illustrated by the earliest collection of laws in the Bible, the book of the Covenant (Exod 20:21–23:19).

4. Characteristics of the Community. The chief characteristics of Israelite community during the tribal period (i.e., the period of the Judges) can be summarized thus:

First, the basic unit of community was the extended family under the pater familias, with each family in turn fitting into the larger clan and tribe.

Second, within this patriarchal structure, the status of women was defined by male property rights.

Third, ancient kinship patterns made the tribes resistant to urban-based monarchies and their tendency to aggrandize at the expense of small farmers and pastoralists.

Fourth, the autonomy preserved by the individual tribes was qualified by acknowledgement of the sovereignty of the God Yahweh. Therefore, on the level of cult the Israelite tribes were forged into a theocratic unity within 2 contexts: in annual pilgrimage festivals celebrating the common epic of divine deliverance, and in war construed in sacral terms.

Fifth, innovations inspired by the epic tradition coexisted with practices and values drawn from the Canaanite environment, just as the worship of Yahweh was practiced alongside of the rituals of the Baal cult (cf. the Baal names recurring in the book of Judges and the cult background reflected by the Gideon story in Judges 8).

Sixth, the survival and growth of the Yahwistic community in the period of the tribal league seems to be attributable to the religious power inherent in the confession of the God who delivered Hebrew slaves and to the ability of those committed to that confession to extrapolate from this context institutions, practices, and laws that reaffirmed some and challenged other antecedent religious and social structures and values. Among these antecedent structures and values were the ideal of the *naḥălâ,* i.e., the divinely guaranteed right of each family to use of a designated plot of land in perpetuity; protection of vulnerable classes like the alien, the creditor, the widow, and the orphan; the ongoing reform of common law on the basis of the epic, as seen for example in the extension of manumission to women (cf. Exod 21:1–11 with Deut 15:12–18) and the proscription of slavery in Leviticus 25.

Seventh, the most serious structural weakness of the league appeared in the form of centrifugal tendencies, fed by the autonomism of the tribes, that threatened to overwhelm the sense of unity essential for defense against hostile neighbors. Judges 5 mentions simultaneously both the tribes responding to the call to militia duty and those failing to respond to the muster, bearing witness to that weakness. Likewise the ambiguous last verse of the book of Judges: "In those days there was no king in Israel; everyone did what was right in their own eyes." Israel's destiny-ridden response to the structural weakness of tribal-based community was monarchy.

B. Monarchy

The most dramatic example of the impact of foreign influence on community in Israel revolves around the introduction of kingship. The motive given in the elders' request for a king in the narrative of 1 Samuel 8 states this poignantly, "that we may also be like all the nations."

Though variations appear in the different cultures of the ANE, monarchy generally entailed the following common characteristics: (1) ascription of special (and usually to some degree, divine) status to the king, who was regarded as the earthly representative of the chief deity; (2) a hierarchical organization of the society; (3) legitimization of the social system through the cult myth (i.e., the structure of human society reflects the cosmic structure established "in the beginning" by the gods, thereby tying social order inseparably to the natural order); (4) a static ontology, according to which change, and especially revolutionary change, is interpreted as a threat to essential reality; and (5) location of the official cult within the central temple of the capital city with the king as patron.

The open-ended, experimental community ideal that developed over the course of the league period came to be viewed as a source of instability when falling under the intense pressure of rising Philistine power. The response was recourse to the form of governance most closely associated with military and economic might in antiquity: monarchy.

Embedded in the narrative structure of 1 Samuel 8–11 is a conflict between 2 attitudes toward kingship, and although a long and complex history of transmission separates the reader from the events described, the divisions raised within the community from the very onset of kingship seem to be accurately reflected by the text even in its received form. Chapter 8 is particularly interesting in this connection. Written from a critical perspective preserved within prophetic circles, it enumerates the *mišpaṭ hammelek,* that is, the royal ordinance that the king could be expected to impose upon the people. This entailed: (1) Conscription of the youth into military and court service; (2) confiscation of agricultural land belonging to the clans for use as royal grants awarded to servants of the king (e.g., retiring military officers); and (3) taxation to finance an elaborate military and court system.

That final entry in the list, about the military and court, drives home the main point: "and you shall be his slaves." That is, the freedom won by the exodus generation and fiercely defended by the tribes of Yahweh would vanish. As if the point were not yet sufficiently clear, a final phrase—an ironic echo of Exod 3:7–8—is added to indicate that the new generation abdicating its freedom for the security of kingship could not expect a second exodus as the response of the deity: "And in that day you will cry out because of your king, whom you have chosen for yourselves; but the Lord will not answer you in that day." The contrast is clear. Whereas the Hebrews in Egypt had not chosen their royal oppressor, the present generation had. And in so doing they had introduced a deep division into their community, for at important points the ideals developed by the league and royal ideology were incompatible.

Underlying all specific differences was a fundamental dispute over authority stemming from the struggles of the league period. The tribes had acknowledged only one qualification of their autonomy, namely, the claims of the divine suzerain Yahweh that governed Holy War, religious festivals, and the growing tradition of common law defining the moral structure of the community. The delicate balance between unity and freedom upon which the league system was based was safeguarded by the insistence that there could be no king but Yahweh; that is, there could be no human person claiming a privileged position of power and authorized to determine the laws and institutions of the land (Judg 8:23). Because it introduced a human claimant to permanent divine authority, kingship was regarded by many as a direct threat to the central ideals of the community.

In the narratives describing the conflicts that plagued the monarchy, the key issues revolve conspicuously around the question of final authority, as for example: Is the king lord over the fate of his subjects (2 Samuel 11–12)? Is the king authorized to build a temple (2 Samuel 7)? Can the king reorganize the tribes into rational tax districts (2 Samuel 24)?

The result of the introduction of kingship was epoch-making. The community ideal deriving from the epic of divine deliverance and land conferral was removed from the central position that it had enjoyed in the tribal theocracy and became one religious option competing with others. But that ideal did not enter its new phase quiescently. As indicated by a prophetic rumination on the relation between kingship and true Yahwistic faith in 1 Samuel 12, the historical fact of monarchy was not denied in prophetic circles, but it was deprived of all of its mythologically grounded sanctity and ultimacy. Kingship was viewed as a product of human sinfulness, and therefore it possessed no final authority. For the prophets, the viability of the nation continued to be dependent on the archaic Yahwistic principle stemming from the league, obedience to God: "Only fear the Lord, and serve him faithfully with all your heart . . ." (1 Sam 12:25a).

This principle represented a fundamental qualification of royal ideology that few kings were willing to accept. One detects in David an honest attempt to strike a balance, but divisions within the nation were only deepened by the Bathsheba affair, by strife over the census, and above all, by the struggle over the issue of dynastic succession. Solomon emerged from court intrigue as a close replica of the

ANE absolute monarch, and it is not accidental that his reign shaded into civil war. In the conflict between Rehoboam and Ahijah, the lines were drawn between a community ideal predicated on the authority of Yahweh and an imperial ideal resting on royal pretension.

C. Prophecy

1. Concept of Community. Prophecy emerged out of this struggle as a movement committed to preserving the essential values of the older Yahwistic ideal of community within the setting of kingship. Prophecy itself is a complex phenomenon, and the method of carrying out this mission varied from prophet to prophet. In cases like those of Elijah, Hosea, Amos, and Jeremiah, the primary modus operandi was opposition to the king. In the case of Isaiah, we find the attempt to redefine kingship along strictly Yahwistic lines. The underlying principle of divine authority led, nevertheless, to a remarkable consistency within the teachings of the prophets regarding the ideals of community and the relation of the king to them: (1) The king did not stand above the moral standards of the community, but was bound to its laws. (2) All members of the community were equal, and it was the responsibility of the nation's leaders to prevent the exploitation of the weak and the poor by the powerful and the wealthy and to protect the rights especially of vulnerable members of the community. (3) Social order was not identifiable with the natural order established by conflict among the gods, but was to be inferred from the historical example of God's delivery of slaves from their bondage. (4) The cult did not belong to a heavenly order transcending time, but was subservient to the traditional divine mandates of compassion and justice.

2. Reform Movement. The development of the notion of community as the gathering of those responding to God's call to obedience and service thus continued into the monarchial period as a reform movement within the larger society. The degree to which the prophets regarded the dominant society to have strayed from the Yahwistic ideal of community is indicated by the preponderance of indictments and judgments in their recorded words. This negative assessment of society was accompanied by a sober anthropology, epitomized by Jeremiah's words: "The heart is deceitful above all things, and desperately corrupt; who can understand it?" (Jer 17:9). Against this bleak assessment of society, the faithful community came to be viewed increasingly in terms of a remnant, preserved by God as a witness to divine purpose and as agent in the final redemption intended by God.

The reform efforts of the prophets and their followers were not entirely in vain. Asa, Jehoshaphat, Hezekiah, and Josiah paid attention to the traditional Yahwistic ideals, and placed the crown behind efforts to bring the nation into closer conformity with divine law. The tradition of pessimism that seemed to accompany the prophetic movement apparently was vindicated by events, however, for even so godly a king as Josiah failed to secure the land. Jeremiah's bleak outlook (Jer 4:23–26) was supported by that of Ezekiel, who announced that disobedience leading to destruction was written ineluctably on the soul of the nation (Ezekiel 23). The Babylonian destruction of Jerusalem and its temple secured the pessimistic prophetic view against the more self-confident views of kings and prophets like Hananiah, and forced the exilic community that survived the national calamity into a period of reassessment.

D. Exile

Displaced from the familiar setting of temple and land and the traditions associated with them, exilic groups made various efforts to salvage materials for rebuilding their community: (1) Monumental achievements were accomplished by a "priestly" group in collecting traditional laws and placing them in an epic-narrative framework. (2) A prophetic circle associating itself with the name of Isaiah embraced a vision of restoration that broke out of the discredited royal nationalism in the direction of a more universal Yahwism; according to this, the remnant community would act as the servant of divine purpose in a coming age of salvation (Isaiah 40–55). (3) Deuteronomistic tradents adapted their David/Zion centered historiography to the harsh new realities of exile, as indicated by the editorial additions found in 1 and 2 Kings and Jeremiah. (4) Ezekiel and his disciples promulgated a program of restoration based on Zadokite temple theology and conceding a modest role to the royal house (Ezekiel 40–48).

E. Second Temple Period

After the return of a significant number of exiles following Cyrus' Edict of 538 B.C.E., the initiative in rebuilding a sense of Jewish community was taken by a group subscribing to Ezekiel's program. Benefiting from the support of the prophets Haggai and Zechariah, this group emphasized the centrality of a Zadokite-led temple cult as the key to communal vitality. Zechariah sounded a prophetic theme reminiscent of Isaiah that bound cult to faithful observance of the moral commandments. Chapters 56–66 of Isaiah preserve traces of a dissident group highly critical of the Zadokite temple theology and announcing imminent divine judgment on alleged unrighteousness of the majority of the community. The Second Temple Period thus began with competing perspectives on what constituted true community.

Conditions within the Jewish community did not soon improve, judging from the grim pronouncements found in the book of Malachi. Low professional standards within the Zadokite priesthood conspired with even lower standards of morality among the people to undermine community vitality. This bleak picture is confirmed by the books of Ezra and Nehemiah. There we find that the internal weakness of the Jewish community even elicited the attention of the Persian government, concerned as it was with maintaining reasonably stable buffer states between it and its major adversaries. Proponents of strict measures of reform based on the traditional laws collected in the exile by the "priestly" group thus found an unexpected ally in the Persian government. Ezra's being sent by that foreign power as "the scribe of the law of the God of heaven" marked an important turning point in the history of the Jewish community. As a result of his activities, that community received a clear charter that was to become the foundation of its survival through the next 500 years. Torah together with an interpretive process guided by the hermeneutic developed by Ezra and his successors (cf. Nehemiah 10) enabled the community to emerge in a vital new form that adumbrated many of the essential marks of classical Judaism.

This new formulation of community did not give equal emphasis, of course, to all earlier traditions. Conspicuously absent were certain themes favored by earlier visionary circles, such as messianic expectations and announcements of impending divine intervention in judgment and salvation. An orientation favoring careful application of Torah to all aspects of everyday life eclipsed more eschatological themes.

The powerful resurgence of apocalyptic themes in the 2d century B.C.E. indicates that visionary streams were not supplanted, but were merely suppressed by the scribal community. The oppressive measures of the Seleucids forced back to the surface concepts of community emphasizing the fallenness of the majority of the world (including the preponderance of the Jewish population) and the impending intervention of God to cleanse the earth and reestablish the community of the faithful (e.g., Daniel and *1 Enoch*).

In the 2d century B.C.E., therefore, a century well documented by writings from the Bible, the Apocrypha, the Pseudepigrapha, and the Dead Sea Scrolls, we are able to recognize the interplay of several competing notions of community, ranging from the apocalyptic other-worldliness of Qumran to the conservative this-worldliness of the Sadducees, with an increasingly popular proto-Pharisee party in between. It is from this wide range of alternative notions that emergent Judaism and Christianity would begin to forge their own definitions of community during the Roman period.

Bibliography

Alt, A. 1925. *Die Landnahme der Israeliten in Palestina.* Leipzig (ET 1967).

———. 1930. *Die Staatenbildung der Israeliten in Palestina.* Leipzig (ET 1967).

Gottwald, N. K. 1979. *The Tribes of Yahweh: A Sociology of the Religion of Liberated Israel, 1250–150 B.C.E.* Maryknoll, NY.

Hanson, P. D. 1986. *The People Called: The Growth of Community in the Bible.* San Francisco.

Huffman, H. B. 1965. *Amorite Personal Names in the Mari Texts.* Baltimore.

Noth, M. 1930. *Das System der Zwölf Stämme Israel.* BWANT 4/1. Stuttgart.

Rowton, M. B. 1976. Dimorphic Structure and the Problem of the ʿApiru-Ibrim. *JNES* 35: 13–20.

Wilson, R. R. 1977. *Genealogy and History in the Biblical World.* New Haven.

PAUL D. HANSON

NEW TESTAMENT KOINŌNIA

Biblical faith forms a community of those who worship God, who share with one another a common experience of God's salvation and a common call to bear witness to God's salvation-creating power in the world. The diverse descriptions of community found in Scripture reflect the changing religious, social, and political environment in light of which faith and life are constantly being adapted in new and meaningful ways. However, the biblical idea of community is always situated on a theological axis balanced by two convictions: first, that a good God finds forsaken persons who are alienated from all that makes for hope and well-being, and calls them into a covenant people reconciled to all that makes for peace and freedom; and, second, that this redeemed people then responds to God by embodying their experience of God's salvation in their relations with each other.

The development of the idea of community within the biblical tradition is further understood as dynamic and "self-correcting"; indeed, the maintenance of a proper balance between an appreciation of divine grace (orthodoxology) and human responsibility (orthopraxis) is at best tenuous. Throughout the histories of Israel and the Church, specific notions of community were developed to correct certain imbalances in the faith or life of God's people. These different notions of community, enshrined within Scripture, form a whole, greater than the sum of its parts, which provides the current people of God with a normative context for understanding what it means to "be" community and to do as this particular community ought.

A. The OT Idea of Community

The essential features of the NT idea of community are found in the OT. While influenced to some degree by pagan notions, primitive Christianity sought to understand its founding and formative events in light of biblical teaching, and believers assumed a fundamental continuity between their *ekklēsia* and the OT idea of a covenant people, Israel.

From its beginning as a tribal confederacy, Israel understood itself as a community covenanted to God and to each other by virtue of the Exodus event. See COVENANT. Israel experienced God's liberating grace as a people, and as a people who were called together to give adequate response to the God who delivered them from slavery and set them on a course to freedom and *šalôm.* Community was first formed, then, to worship God "as the one who acted in a specific event of history to deliver the oppressed from their oppressor, thereby revealing self as the incomparable God, majestic in holiness" (Hanson 1986: 28).

As Israel sought to live for God in its world of competing deities and nations, its self-understanding as a community rightly related to its redeeming God developed to include an ethical dimension. The compassion of God exacted a demand upon God's people to resist in its own life the very oppression and exploitation from which God had liberated them. In this sense, the worshipping community was also a witnessing community, called forth to reflect in its common life the very character of its transcendent God. Eventually, Torah became the instrument by which the community's life of worship and witness was informed and so formed into a particular people, whose obedience to the Torah of a particular God made clear and concrete God's love and holiness in a pluralistic world.

As the social and political structures of Israel came to be defined by its monarchy, so too was its idea of community. Even as charismatic selection of the confederacy's leadership had given way to dynastic rule, so also were the old convictions about God attached to new, "royalistic" forms. David's covenant with God, and not the Sinaic covenant, became central to how Israel understood itself: God's rule was mediated through Israel's king. The former confederacy, tied together only by its worship of one God and by its muster for holy war on behalf of God, became a *nation* whose future was determined by political alliance and societal syncretism, often at God's expense. The worship of God was institutionalized during the reign of Solomon, who built a temple for God in order to compete with other national religions in the ANE. Under the pressures of international relations, then, the community's witness to God was domesticated. The worshipping community became an established cult, and its official priesthood helped the king as representatives of God on earth. Israel's religion was institutionalized as a critical part of the social order, so that now God's covenant blessing was construed in terms of national peace and prosperity. Accordingly, God, brought from heaven and placed within Solomon's temple, was worshipped as earth's Creator and as the king's God, more than as transcendent Redeemer of a people. God was now worshipped as a God of order, whose creation, like the king's realm, assumed a certain hierarchy into which all persons must fit without fuss.

Besides the deuteronomist's history of the monarchy, the priestly theology of the official cultus, and the advice offered by the prophets tied to the king's court, this community *qua* the king's nation is envisaged by OT Wisdom. According to Israel's sages, the community made wise by its "fear" of God is characterized by those same attributes called for in Torah. However, the deeper logic of Israel's sapiental tradition, especially clear in its preexilic stage (e.g., Proverbs 10–28), moves less from the God whose compassion for a special people is revealed in the events of salvation's history, remembered and interpreted by Israel's sacral institutions, than from human experience and insight into the nature of human relations (von Rad). Attention is now directed toward basic human living—how to cope and how to succeed. The community is informed by the sage's observations of those conventions which maintain the social order and thus enhance the prospects for political *šalôm* and economic prosperity—the very interests of the king.

Further, because David's covenant with God focused upon an individual's (i.e., the king's) relationship with God, so also did the sage's (Brueggemann 1972). Corporate concerns were replaced by individualistic ones, so that the wise individual assumes the primary responsibility to bear witness to God by those virtuous actions which secure his position within the nation. The logic of such "enlightened self-interest," of course, is that the whole Israel *is* the sum of its individual constituents, especially those from its more affluent and influential classes (Gordis 1944). Such an idea of community is more static and secular precisely because it is more hierarchal and institutional; like the monarchy, the concern of Israel's wisdom is for "law and order" and against those evils which promote social chaos, economic exploitation, and political uncertainty.

The prophetic idea of community, also envisaged by the OT, emerged on the fringe of the social order to challenge what Israel's prophets perceived as Israel's "royal consciousness" which was generated by sapiental and sacral impulses alike. According to Brueggemann (1978), Israel, under the aegis of its kings, moved in 3 dangerous directions: (1) a concern for the well-being of the affluent led to the economic exploitation of the rank-and-file; (2) an enforced social hierarchy led to the political oppression of some, especially the social deviant, for the benefit of the state; and (3) the establishment of an official and syncretistic cultus, adopted to serve the king and his political alliances, led to the domestication of God.

The prophetic movement, and the idea of a counter-community it shaped, had two tasks: diagnostic and prognostic. The foundation of both tasks was the covenantal tradition of Moses which forged a community whose life and faith was in marked contrast to the established social order. In order to criticize Israel's social order, the prophet of God appealed to the Torah of Moses for an alternative vision of community whose life and faith are rooted in an economics of equality, a politics of justice, and a religion of divine transcendence. The prophetic call to repent enshrines, then, a reactionary agenda: It recognizes that what bourgeois Israel had become under its kings and their counselors is fundamentally opposed to God's intentions revealed in the Exodus event and the ministry of Moses. As such, the worshipping community bears witness in its particularity, on the margins of the mainstream, to a God who cannot be manipulated by those who manage the social order.

This tensive dialogue between prophet and sage which emerges within the OT can be profitably viewed as self-correcting (Wall 1987b). It is not, however, a conversation between equals. Unlike the shape of Israel's history, the final form of the OT canon is more prophetic than royal, even containing a "prophetic" reformation of the Wisdom tradition (Spina 1983). The OT idea of community is therefore centered through its prophetic voice: In reading its history as narrated by its Bible, Israel is shaped into a prophetic community.

Why then are the canonical voices of the "establishment" retained? Perhaps to prevent prophetic (i.e., normative) Israel from moving in dangerous directions as well. Indeed, the tradition of Israel's wisdom, along with its own canonical correctives, reminds Israel that its worship of an immanent God demands its witness to (and in) specific cultural settings, characterized by particular sociologies and economies. While Israel might continue to live on the margins of the mainstream, its Torah is heard and seen by the outsiders as relevant for their time and space. Further, wisdom reminds Israel that a transcendent God is also present with the necessary resources of human insight and institutions, which, when responsibly used, make it possible for each Israelite to work out one's own salvation with God. The dialectic thus makes clear that the covenant community is formed by a dynamic partnership between a

God who freely redeems a people, the prophet's emphasis, and a redeemed people composed of those who each in turn freely respond by working out one's salvation "in the fear of the Lord," which the sage taught was the beginning of wisdom about life's possibilities and limitations.

B. The NT Gospel and Jesus' Idea of Community

The earliest Christians were not only a biblical people, who sought to live in continuity with their Scriptures; they were also disciples of a person, Jesus from Nazareth. Their worship of and witness to the God of Israel were decisively influenced by their conviction that Jesus was God's Messiah, and that through him God had begun a new Exodus for the restored, eschatological Israel. Because of this, the NT notion of community, which was developed and given ecclesial form after Jesus' death and resurrection, should be viewed as a discrete interpretation of Jewish religious history in the light of Jesus' life and teaching. While Jesus' own notion of community was often at odds with other Jewish communities (i.e., Pharisees, Essenes, Zealots, Sadducees) of his own day, there was no disagreement over those constitutive elements of a covenant people. He was a teacher, perhaps even a revivalist, in and of the Jewish tradition; indeed, many of the themes, especially eschatological, which characterize his ministry place him among the apocalypticists of the Second Temple period.

Although Jesus did not start a new organization, his messianic mission called forth a community of disciples who believed in his teaching as God's word and who followed the pattern of his life as God's will. According to the synoptic evangelists, at the very core of Jesus' proclamation of God's Gospel was the claim that God's kingdom, and the promised salvation with it, had drawn near through him (Mark 1:14–15). In forsaking old, "official" interpretations of God's reign, and in believing that Jesus' interpretation of it was true, the messianic movement formed a people who were called away from worldly concerns (Luke 9:57–62) to a singular worship of God (Matt 6:24; cf. 4:9–10). Jesus "thus began with the heart of classical Yahwism, as it earlier had come to expression in the first commandment, the *šĕmaᶜ*, and Isaiah's call to trust in God" (Hanson 1986: 399).

Luke's portrait of Jesus intensifies two aspects of Jesus' eschatological message which transformed traditional apocalyptical themes. First, Jesus taught that the messianic community could experience God's salvation "today" (4:21; 19:9; 23:43): The day of God's Jubilee, envisioned by the OT prophets and at the center of apocalyptical faith, had already dawned. Rather than awaiting God's future salvation and viewing the surrounding world in a detached way, the disciples were called to a life of engagement in which even enemies were ushered into God's salvation (Luke 10:25–42; cf. 6:36). Second, Jesus taught that anyone could belong to the messianic community. "Official" notions of membership, long tied to a theology of divine election in various Jewish communities, placed social, religious, or ethnic restrictions on those admitted to the covenant community. Jesus extended the membership list to the outsider—the least, last, lame, and lost of Israel (Luke 4:16–30; 7:36–8:21; 14:12–24; 19:1–10; 23:39–43).

According to Matthew's gospel, Jesus calls his disciples to a righteous life in obedience to his interpretation of Torah (Matt 5:17–48; 7:21–24); the Christian *ekklēsia* is a people of a new Torah which gives expression to God's will for the new age of God's salvation. Jesus' teaching about God's Torah, remembered by the ongoing community of his disciples, provides order for its life (18:15–20). The deeper logic of the ethical instruction of Matthew's Jesus follows directly from the Book of the Covenant: The righteousness and mercy of God, disclosed in the (old and new) Exodus events, should now be performed by the covenant people; thus, to love God (18:1–14) is to forgive and restore the neighbor (18:21–35).

This is also true according to the teaching of John's Jesus, although he restricts the scope of the disciple's love to other disciples (13:34; 15:12–17) thus forming a more sectarian idea of community whose essential mission is to nurture itself (21:15–17). Sharply put, then, Jesus taught that the yield of authentic worship is to bear witness in the worshipping community to God's salvation-creating love. In that Jesus' calculus emphasizes the community's love as a *response* to their experience of God's reign rather than as a requirement to enter into it, his teaching holds a tacit challenge to the legalistic (and perhaps antinomistic!) tendencies of other apocalyptic communities in Judaism.

Jesus not only taught by word but by deed. G. Theissen (1978) has called attention to the more charismatic expressions of community in the earliest Christianity as stemming from the radical nature of Jesus' own lifestyle. The pattern, narrated by the canonical gospels—of Jesus wandering on the margins of the social order, forsaking protection and possessions, lacking home and family—make vivid the eschatological claims envisaged by his teaching: The nearness of God's reign made concerns about "this evil age" irrelevant. This pattern of Jesus' itinerancy, and the eschatological hope it envisaged, was embodied in the earliest Christian communities which were profoundly influenced by their memories of him.

However important Theissen's sociological analysis is, it often neglects the relationship between Jesus' own perceptions of God's kingdom and his personal character and ministry as "Son of man." In fact, his understanding of a merciful God is disclosed in his forgiveness of and fellowship with sinners and in his healing of outcasts; his faithfulness to a righteous God is disclosed in his obedient life as God's servant-Son; his economics and politics reflect his commitment to God's vocation, for him more than a self-conscious response to the conditions of his Palestinian world; and in his execution as an innocent man, he makes clear the costs of following God in a world more ordered by ethical casuistry and religious customs than by the norms and values of God's kingdom.

This radical theocentricity, evident in his teaching and life, is at the very core of Jesus' own notion of community. The messianic community is centered by its singular worship of and obedience to the merciful and righteous God, whose reign has been brought near in Messiah's mission. Its life is contretemps, an idealized witness to alternative convictions about the God of the established order. It forgives those whom the society forgets; it welcomes those turned away by the "official" religion; it loves even the nation's enemy; it shares equally in the experience of God's promised *šalôm*; and it obeys the Torah as interpreted and incarnated by Messiah. While accommodating itself to changing social realities and to developing theological understanding, the post-Easter Church retains these same elements at the center of its life: The *ekklēsia* of God is called forth in worship to bear witness to God's liberating grace which is disclosed in the new Exodus of Jesus Christ.

C. The Acts of the Apostles and the NT Idea of Community

The NT book of Acts bridges the canonical gospels to the letters, underscoring the continuity of ministry from Jesus to the apostles and the Church they founded (Wall 1988). In telling the story of the church's formation, Acts not only introduces the more didactic discussion of the Christian *ekklēsia* contained in the letters which follow, but also qualifies it in 3 ways. First, the Church is a missionary community; its essential role is to bear witness, by the Spirit's power, to God's resurrection of faithful Jesus, declaring him both Lord and Christ. Second, the Church is an apostolic community; God has authorized the 12 apostles to rule over the tribes of a new, eschatological Israel. The Church's worship of God and witness to what God has done through Christ and in Christ's Spirit is now guided by apostolic life and teaching. Finally, the Church extends Jesus' messianic mission beyond Jews to include Samaritans, proselyte Jews, and Gentiles: Eschatological Israel is characterized by a diversity of people, called together by God through a diversity of apostolic missions and kerygmata.

Yet, the marks of the messianic community have not changed. Disciples are still called together to worship God and bear witness to the Jubilee of God's salvation which has come through Christ. In Christ's absence, however, his earthly rule is effectively continued by the Spirit through the teaching and life of the apostles; their witness to Christ is now normative. Thus, their writings, which follows Acts in the NT, which re-present their witness, become the Word of God for the ongoing worshipping and witnessing community.

D. The Pauline Idea of the "Body of Christ"

Paul uses his important catchphrase "body of Christ" to relate Christ's death and resurrection to his understanding of the Church as a community of believers. According to Paul, Jesus' physical death is the messianic event in that it testifies to his devotion to God and God's plan of salvation. For him, God's resurrection of Jesus vindicates his scandalous death as truly messianic. The believing community actually participates in the Christ-event by which it enters into the promised New Age of God's salvation (Rom 6:4). This is the great indicative of the Church's redemption: Those who depend upon Christ's dependable work are reconciled with God and each other; it can "now" experience a Christ-like life, characterized by freedom from sin, from death, from legalism, and from all that alienates humanity from God's love (Romans 5–8). Thus, the community's faith in Jesus' faith simply restores a sense of community between God and humanity, and within humanity (2 Cor 5:11–21; cf. Eph 2:11–22). Second, even as the historical Jesus is a single "body," so also the church is "one body" in him. The merging of the two bodies, believer with Christ, underscores the mutuality of the community of believers found "in Christ." Human distinctions are dismantled; an egalitarian community is formed, fulfilling the prophetic vision (Gal 3:14–29). Third, the history of Christ's bodily existence is paradigmatic of the church's own history. Because Jesus is faithful to God, expressed most vividly on the Cross, God's salvation-creating righteousness is disclosed in history (Rom 3:21–26), especially by God's resurrection of Jesus (Phil 2:9–11). The same is promised for the eschatological community whose hope is that through its faith in Christ, God will recognize and exalt the community at the end of time; and whose commitment during the present time is to offer its own body, like the crucified Christ, publicly and concretely in service to God rather than in conformity to the current social order (Rom 12:1–2). Finally, "it is through the church that Christ continues to accomplish the final purpose for which He assumed human nature" (Whiteley 1974: 198). The Church is, in this sense, the ongoing arena for the activity of God on earth. The use of the catchphrase "the body of Christ" intends to underscore the continuity between Jesus' messianic mission and the Church's mission within the history of God's salvation. Is not this the meaning of the "eucharistic body" for Paul (1 Cor 10:14–22; 11:23–26)? Partaking in "communion" as a common act of worship recalls the ongoing foundation of the covenant community: All believers gather around the eucharistic bread and cup to bear witness to God's salvation they continue to experience together since the death of Christ's body.

Paul's use of "body" to characterize the community of believers includes two different tensions. According to 1 Corinthians, tension is felt when individuals seek to understand the relationship of charismatic self to the charismatic community to which self and all the charismata belong. There is no swallowing up of human personality for Paul, but rather those individual believers who are equally baptized into one Lord (1 Cor 12:12–13) by one Spirit are given different gifts of grace (1 Cor 12:4–11; Rom 12:3) in order to effect different ministries for the common goal of edification. The eschatological fitness of the whole body is dependent upon the spiritual fitness of each believer, who uses one's different gifts to prepare the church for the future triumph of God and for its partial realization in the present age.

The second tension arises within the community which seeks to set limits around its newly found freedom in Christ. For example, among the households which comprised the Roman *ekklēsia,* some believers apparently thought that "staying in" the covenant community obligated them to observe a vegetarian diet in strict observance to the holiness code. The Paulinists, on the other hand, thought themselves free from such legalisms since the inauguration of the New Age (Rom 7:6–8:2). Again, in Corinth, where some believers purchased food once offered to pagan idols, other believers, perhaps converts from those very pagan religions, thought this to be a capitulation to an enemy of Christ (1 Cor 8:1–11:1). In both cases, Paul argues for 2 interrelated principles: The actions of both the non-vegetarians in Rome and the meat purchasers in Corinth were acceptable, given the community's newly found freedom in Christ, and should not be condemned by other believers; however, all actions must finally be measured by the growth of the believing community. Actions in accord with God's will edify the insider and evangelize the outsider (1 Cor 10:25–33). Thus, what is acceptable to one's own sensibilities is modified by the sensitivities of others. Paul concludes his advice with a christological creed (1 Cor 11:1; Rom 15:1–13): The community's unity in witness and in life, which is always jeopardized by its own diversity, is held together by a love for one another which imitates Christ's love (1 Cor 8:11; Gal 5:13–15; cf. Eph 5:2). Freedom obligates not a mere acceptance of others, but a participation in their spiritual formation.

By linking his idea of community to the metaphor "body of Christ," Paul concentrates attention on the transformed life *within* the community of faith, rather than on how it impacts the surrounding society. Within the charismatic community, the Spirit of the risen Christ effects a revolution of values, of perceptions, and of relationships. How this internal revolution effects the outsider is not clear in Paul; the oppressive social institutions of the day go unchallenged, even though those institutions have been overturned within the Church. Perhaps Paul's expectation of an imminent parousia led him to encourage his readers to remain neutral toward their societal roles and responsibilities (1 Cor 7:17–31). Surely the hope of an imminent, cosmic transformation causes people to disregard the present for the future! What appears to be a policy of status quo, or even of social apathy, then, is in reality a concrete expression of the belief that God will change society for the good when Christ returns. To engage in God's work might even be presumptuous in light of the parousia's imminency. In any case, Paul's concern was rather with the maintenance of faith and not with changing social or political relationships. The yield of faith in Christ is a new creation which lives in accord with God's will, and which demonstrates its peace with God by living righteously.

Further, Paul's pastoral advice is always informed by his missionary vocation. Indeed, for him the church is a missionary community, whose life and faith is shared to best facilitate a missionary vocation. In understanding that missiological values informed his thinking, the interpreter better understands why Paul is unwilling to challenge the social order of the Greco-Roman world. On the one hand, his interest in the community which does not belong to Christ is primarily evangelistic; he desired the transformation of human souls, not of human society. This perspective is only intensified by his assumption that he lived during the "last days" and that it was his Gentile mission which would usher in the eschaton (Rom 11:25). On the other hand, he was more and more concerned that the Church survive. He was well aware that his apostolic community consisted of small urban households of believers, without much political influence. For them to engage in zealotry would have produced an "official" retaliation against which there would have been little defense, the Gentile mission effectively ended, and the condition for the consummation of the New Age not met.

In this regard, 1 Cor 9:19–27 is quite revealing. Clearly, Paul's missiology informs his ecclesiology. Although in the immediate context he is commenting upon a religious problem that certain Corinthian believers are prone to idolatry, his response to them helps explain his rather conservative posture toward social change. For Paul, the local community takes on particular social structures which best preserve the Gospel within a particular social setting (cf. Luke's portrait of Paul in Acts). The freedom of the believing community in Christ is always limited by their vocation to be a missionary Church. Thus, the Apostle's concern is for "good impressions" (1 Thess 4:11–12; Gal 6:10; Rom 13:3–5; 1 Cor 14:23–5) in order to insure a positive reception of the gospel, and presumably to insure a peaceful environment in which to proclaim it.

Paul commends a sociology of integration, then, as a missionary value. This is not to compromise the community's witness to the Gospel; rather, it is to accommodate outsiders so that they might be won for Christ's sake (1 Cor 10:23–33). This tendency helps explain why, the deutero-Paulinists accommodated the Church to the surrounding culture to an extent well beyond that of Paul. In fact, the distinction between the Church and the other social institutions is collapsed: The church leader is the good citizen rather than gifted believer (1 Tim 3; *contra* 1 Cor 12); the servant does his master's bidding not as a brother nor as unto the Lord but as one deserving honor (1 Tim 6:1–2; *contra* Phil); the woman knows her place (1 Tim 2; *contra* Gal 3:28), and the church supports the civil authority (1 Tim 2; *contra* Rom 13:1–2). While the language of Paul's eschatological message is retained in the Pastorals, his idea of an eschatological community has been severely domesticated for a post-Pauline *Sitz im Leben.*

E. Community as *koinōnia* and the Post-Pauline Situation

As the continuing representative of Christ's body on earth, the Church is viewed by Paul as *koinōnia*—a community of believers who share in equal partnership the spiritual, physical, and material benefits of God's beneficence (Phil 1:5–7; 3:10; 4:14–15; cf. Acts 2:42–47) as mediated by the Spirit (2:1; cf. Acts 2:37–41) in concert with the risen Christ and God's redemptive program disclosed in him (1 Cor 1:9; 9:23; 10:16–20; cf. Acts 2:14–36).

Yet, Paul's perception of believers living together in *koinōnia* is absent in the deutero-Pauline literature of the NT. Mirroring the shift which took place during Israel's transition from charismatic confederacy to nationalistic monarchy, the institutionalizing pressures of a post-Pauline period to which this literature is addressed form a community where pastoral offices (elder, deacon, deaconess) and sociopolitical hierarchies replace the charismata and equality. In fact, the meanings 1 Timothy's author gives to *koinōnei* (5:22) and *koinōnikous* (6:18) intend to insure the authority of the ruling elite in competition with earlier notions of *koinōnia*! According to Dunn, "the Pastorals represent the fruit of a growing reapprochment between the more formal structures which Jewish Christianity took over from the Synagogue and the more dynamic, charismatic structure of the Pauline churches after Paul's death" (1977: 21).

Given its systematic concern for the Church, the absence of *koinōnia* in Ephesians is quite striking as well. Here the author regards the *ekklēsia* not as local, charismatic congregations, but as an invisible, transcendent community of all believers (2:4–7), whose charisms have taken the form of ecclesial offices (4:7–12) rather than particular capacities or ministries given by the Spirit to meet particular needs (1 Cor 12:4–11). No longer is the community "like" Christ's body; it *is* Christ's body (1:23), even elevating the Church's importance to that of Christ's for God's salvation (1:22–23; 4:12–16). Thus, the eschatological perspective of Paul's message, with its keen emphasis on the future of God's salvation, is muted.

Moreover, the rule of the Spirit, dynamically dispensed through *pneumatika* in the charismatic community, is now located in those whose personal qualities also made them "good citizens" (1 Tim 3; Tit 1:6–16) in order that the community might be seen as a respectable institution of the social order. The absence of Paul's charismatic authority and the delay of Christ's return had forced the believing community from society's margins to its mainstream to seek its identity as a worshipping and witnessing people of God.

F. The Community of Pilgrims and the Non-Pauline Letters

The apocalyptic character of Jesus' idea of community is found in the NT collection of non-Pauline letters and the book of Revelation. This is due to a complex of factors, not the least of which is the more sectarian perspective of the Jewish Church and its apostolate with whom these writings are identified. Further, the non-Pauline literature is more concerned with the real threat, even experience, of persecution and the possibility of theological and moral retreat which suffering provokes. These are the very circumstances from which apocalypticism springs as a religious interpretation of suffering and as a motive to prevent disaffection.

For these reasons, the "catholic" letters along with the book of Revelation envisage the church as a *pilgrim* community. The social vision that such a notion forms is characterized by *conflict* rather than integration with social powers. Such an observation may at first appear presumptuous since only Hebrews construes the believing community as on a pilgrimage. However, elements of this motif can be recovered without too much difficulty from each book of the non-Pauline corpus.

In Johnsson's analysis of the pilgrim idea in religious literature (1978), he locates 4 primary themes which comprise the whole: (1) The pilgrim separates him/herself from home; (2) the pilgrim travels to a specific destination; (3) the pilgrim faces hardships along the way; and (4) the pilgrim who completes the pilgrimage receives the promised blessings. These 4 themes organize much of what Hebrews and the General letters articulate about God's people. They also determine the values which shape the relationships within the community of faith as well as set the distance between the community and the surrounding society.

For instance, this material is intensely futuristic; the Church is eschatological Israel (Heb 1:2; Jas 1:2–4; 1 Pet 1:13; 4:7; 5:10). Filtered through the pilgrim motif, God's blessing is posited at the end of the pilgrimage and not before or during it (Heb 11:8–16; 12:1–29; Jas 1:12; cf. 1:4; 5:11a; 1 Pet 5:10; 2 Pet 3:8–13; Rev 2:7, 11, 17, 26–28; 3:5, 12, 21). This perspective only intensifies the Church's sense of its own alienation from the power and prosperity of the present world system (1 Pet 1:1–2; 2:11–12; Revelation 9–11; 16) and encourages noneconomic values for developing human relationships within the community of faith (Jas 1:9–11; 2:5; 4:13–5:6; 1 Pet 1:13-25; cf. Revelation 17–18).

The pilgrim's initial decision is against any ties which are opposed to the pilgrimage's success; the pilgrim is estranged from the very sources of worldly comfort and security. The community of pilgrims lives on society's fringes. They are in conflict with the forces which operate the larger population (Elliott 1981). For the writer of Hebrews, such arrangements are understood religiously; thus, the pilgrim is called to separate self from the competing religious community in which is found the "comforts" of cultic and traditional observance. For James, separation is understood politically: the community stands on the side of the poor rather than on the side of the influential (2:1–13). Perhaps it is public opinion as much as heresy which concerns 2 Peter: to separate from the world means to resist the popular opinion which mocks the Christian hope in the parousia (3:3–7). To separate from the world means to oppose those false teachers whose commitment to worldly values undermines the apostolic witness. In a similar vein, 1 John distinguishes the true community of faith as one which hates the "things of the world" (1 John 2:12–17; cf. Rev 3:14–22) and does not apostatize in capitulation to the popular mocking of the parousia (2:28). When the pilgrim breaks from existing alliances with those outside of the believing community, they view themselves as belonging to a community of aliens, strangers, foreigners—on the margins of the social order in order to gain God's approval through their faith/fullness (Heb 11:37–39; cf. Rev 2:8–11; 16). What is promoted as a community value is the sort of sectarianism one finds in 1 John's demand to "love one another"; that is, the community is committed to the spiritual well-being of other members of the community over and against the outsider. Thus, Hebrews exhorts its readers not to prevent the gathering of the covenant community (10:23–5) or obedience to its leaders (13:17; cf. 13:7–8). James' paraenesis is also a *communal* morality: it intends to secure an apocalyptic community for its end-time salvation. The moral response to the outsider is separation.

The yield of such radical actions is not comfort but hardship; separation from those ties which insure one's personal comforts produce fear and suffering. One might even say that the community's suffering is par for the pilgrim's course. Interpreted in the context of the pilgrim motif, the community's suffering is anticipated and is endured as the by-product of an evil dominion that is passing away (1 John 2:28; cf. Revelation 12–15). The perception of "joy" encouraged by James (1:2; *pasan charan hēgēsasthe*) assumes 2 things: Human trials are inevitable this side of the Lord's parousia (5:7–20), and joy is evoked in knowing that their demise is also inevitable with the coming triumph of God over evil. For 1 Peter, Christian baptism means at once the entering into God's future salvation of souls (1:3–5, 8–9), but not before the distress of human suffering (1:6–7). The history of salvation, then, is dialectical: There is always the hope of future blessing, but this future reality is moderated by the present pain of human suffering. Because this suffering is connected with the outside world, a kind of militant "us-themism" is established. The pilgrim motif only intensifies what is inherently true for the apocalyptic community; that is, believers live in conflict with the surrounding society. A greater solidarity of commitment to those who share in Christ's suffering is then encouraged, while even greater distance between community and culture is effected.

Pilgrimages are not aimless wanderings; there is a destination always in view which gives perspective to human hardships and the risks of breaking old ties. In Hebrews, as with Revelation, that destination is God's city, the heavenly Jerusalem where the blessings of salvation are found (chaps. 11–12; Rev 21:1–22:5). In James, more than eternal life is found (1:12): A jubilary reversal of socioeconomic and political conditions are also promised (1:9–11; 2:5; 4:11–12). For 1 John, it is the completion of eternal life which has already begun, and for 2 Peter it is the new creation, rid of heresy and ambiguity, which constitutes the pilgrim's promised end. In 1 Peter, it is simply the end of alienation and earth's suffering that is in store. This point is important in juxtaposition with the previous one about hardships. The endurance to the end is promoted by the pilgrim's steadfast and focused hope on certain promises which have been revealed to the community of pilgrims. The pilgrim, who stands within the journeying community, believes that God has given each disciple a privileged Word about present suffering and future blessings. Therefore, the pilgrim can look upon the present hardships, even martyrdom, as a test of loyalty and commitment to the coming reign of God. The transcendence of present circumstances depends upon the pilgrim's ability to focus on what lies ahead as the pilgrimage's destiny. Such is the radical nature of the community's witness to the future of God's salvation.

G. The NT Community and the Church Today

The biblical conception of the community is centered by the believers' shared experience of their Exodus from alienation to reconciliation: "Once you were no people but now you are God's people; once you had not received mercy but now you have received mercy" (1 Pet 2:10). Believers gather together to respond in worship and witness to God's antecedent act, so that "you may declare the wonderful deeds of God who called you out of darkness into marvelous light" (1 Pet 2:9b). Such a people, covenanted with God and with each other in celebration of their freedom from evil powers and their newly found *šalôm,* worship God as an eschatological community. That is, their worship of God acknowledges God's continuing and vital presence with them and for them. Further, this people have formed a charismatic community, which bears continuing and vital witness to God's salvation-creating grace in its new life as an alternative to the norms and values of social order.

The NT develops this biblical calculus in the light of the teaching and life of Jesus Christ and in accord with the apostolic traditions about him. For the Pauline tradition, the community of believers, motivated by the urgency of its Gentile mission in light of the imminent inbreaking of God's reign, interacts with the culture in an accommodating way. Such witness runs the risk of becoming so intertwined with the surrounding society that the community loses sense of "conversion" and its force as *contretemps* to life in the world. In fact, the secularizing of the Pauline notion is already indicated in the deutero-Pauline letters, where one finds an institutional mentality, concerned with the survival of the tradition and the institution which secures it for the long haul. The resulting drift from its earlier theological and ethical particularity impoverishes the Church's evangelical witness and a denial of the Spirit's transforming work. When this occurs, the Church ceases being a community.

The egalitarianism of the early charismatic community gave way to an institutional hierarchalism in which women and servants are demoted according to societal norms. It is no doubt the case that such shifts were made necessary by the Church's movement from a household to a social religion in the Greco-Roman world. Yet, such shifts are at odds with the eschatological message of earliest Christianity which stressed the equality of believers who lived at odds with the perceived evils of the outsiders in anticipation of God's coming reign. Their future survival was thought to be insured by living in harmony with God's will and not with social conventions or political powers. Integration with the larger culture was motivated by a theological vision—to bear witness to the new age and to usher people into the eschatological community in time for its full redemption at the parousia. When the church no longer understood the parousia as an imminent reality, that motive was corrupted by institutional self-interest.

Today's Church is a social institution; it no longer views itself as an eschatological community. Like every institution, its *ethos* and *mythoi* are largely shaped by the society's mores and cultural myths; its vision has become secular. Thus, the internal tensions between freedom and responsibility, between unity and diversity are inevitably resolved for the "good of the institution" rather than doxologically. Personal freedom is limited by the institution as well, so that individual charisms and contributions are swallowed up by the institutional demand for conformity.

The intent of this harsh criticism of today's church is to underscore a dangerous appropriation of the Pauline idea of community. Paul's commitment to the Gentile mission and his conviction that the full and final inbreaking of God's reign was imminent leads him to handle Christianity's relationship with the surrounding culture in ambiguous ways: He is more concerned about the changes within the community, which demonstrate the beginning of the age of God's righteousness, than he is about its relationship with the external world.

The NT collection of non-Pauline writings is clearer in this regard and checks those interpretations of Paul which move believers "into *and* of the world" (Wall 1987a). The pilgrim motif, which stresses the themes of separation and suffering, sustains a firmer, clearer distinction between Church and society. This sectarian impulse allows the whole NT canon to forward a view of the Church as witness to a transcendent God: The people of God live and believe in ways which conflict with the idols to Mammon. A pilgrim is an alien and finds reconciliation only from those resources found within the community of faith.

The pilgrim motif, which also stresses the themes of pilgrimage and destination, would have the Gospel and not the world set the Church's agenda. The inner logic of Paul's accommodation principle might lead one to accept the "adversary's" agenda as a tool of evangelism or even as a means of social acceptance. The pilgrim community knows its destination, and sets itself on a course which endures to that particular, "heavenly" end. This transcendent perspective challenges the social order whenever it interferes with the community's forward movement.

Thus, the pilgrim motif is the built-in corrective of Paul's accommodation principle. Yet, the reverse might also be true (Gager 1975). When a community maintains its witness to God's Gospel on society's margins, it tends to drift toward sectarian chaos, toward religious uniformity, toward legalism, and toward a form of witness which is viewed as irrelevant and meaningless by the surrounding society. It becomes a community which worships God without witness. Paul's notion of community, for all its potential dangers, is better able to handle the cultural and personal diversity of the Church catholic. Further, Paul's idea makes clearer the vocation of a missionary church, called to go to all nations and preach the gospel to all persons.

Bibliography

Brueggemann, W. 1972. *In Man We Trust.* Atlanta.

———. 1978. *The Prophetic Imagination.* Philadelphia.

Dunn, J. D. G. 1977. *Unity and Diversity in the New Testament.* Philadelphia.

Elliott, J. H. 1981. *A Home for the Homeless.* Philadelphia.

Gager, J. G. 1975. *Kingdom and Community.* Englewood Cliffs, NJ.

Gordis, R. 1944. Social Background of Wisdom Literature. *HUCA* 19: 77–118.

Hanson, P. D. 1986. *The People Called.* San Francisco.

Johnsson, W. G. 1978. The Pilgrimage Motif in the Book of Hebrews. *JBL* 97: 239–51.

Spina, F. A. 1983. Qoheleth and the Reformation of Wisdom. Pp. 267–79 in *The Quest for the Kingdom of God,* ed. H. B. Huffmon, F. A. Spina, and A. Green. Winona Lake, IN.

Theissen, G. 1978. *Sociology of Early Palestinian Christianity.* Trans. J. Bowden. Philadelphia.

Wall, R. W. 1987a. Ecumenicity and Ecclesiology. *CSR* 16: 336–54.

———. 1987b. Social Justice and Human Liberation. Pp. 109–27 in *The Church in Response to Human Need,* eds. V. Samuel and C. Sugden. Grand Rapids.

———. 1988. Acts of the Apostles in Canonical Context. *BTB* 18: 16–24.

Whiteley, D. E. H. 1974. *The Theology of St. Paul.* Oxford.

Robert W. Wall

COMMUNITY, RULE OF THE (1QS). 1QS was among the first scrolls discovered by the bedouin at the beginning of 1947 in what came to be known as Qumran cave 1. Since the trustworthiness of the intermediaries who spread reports about it around Jerusalem could not be assumed, and their credibility was further compromised by contradictory statements, there was some initial hesitation regarding its authenticity (Trever 1965: 25, 75, 180), but this was quickly overcome. Plates and a transcription of 1QS were published with exemplary speed by Burrows, Trever, and Brownlee in 1951, and in the same year Brownlee furnished an annotated translation.

The script of 1QS dates it to the period 100–75 B.C. (Avigad 1958: 71; Cross 1965: 258 n. 116), making it one of the 3 oldest copies of the *Rule* (Cross 1961: 119). None is an autograph, and so the composition of the *Rule* must be pushed back into the 2d century B.C. (Cross 1961: 120). Ten fragmentary copies of the *Rule* were found in Cave 4. They remain unpublished, but Milik (1960: 411–16) has provided a list of variants (all minor), noting in particular that 3 mss offer a shorter and more intelligible version of col. 5 and that 1QS 8:16–9:11 is missing in one ms. 5Q11 contains part of 1QS 2:4–7, 11–14, and 5Q13 iv 2–3 cites 1QS 3:4–5 (Milik 1962), but since these come from texts that were originally independent of the *Rule,* it is not sure that they represent copies of the *Rule.*

The syntax of 1QS has been studied by Leahy, and the most convenient Heb text is that of Lohse (1964: 4–43), which has a facing German translation. Other important annotated translations are: French (Guilbert), English (Leaney 1966; Wernberg-Møller 1957; Vermes 1983; Knibb 1987: 72–144), Italian (Moraldi 1971: 113–72), and German (Maier 1960, 1:21–45). Reports on the state of research have been published by Bardtke (1973), and in somewhat less detail by Delcor (*DBSup,* 851–57).

Bardtke (1973: 263) perceptively highlighted different literary analyses of 1QS as the most important contributions; they necessarily exercise a decisive influence on all interpretations. The earliest commentators (Dupont-Sommer 1953: 90; Kuhn 1960: 652; Maier 1960, 1:21; Wernberg-Møller 1957: 56, n. 49) recognized the composite character of 1QS, but went no further. An effort by Guilbert (1959) to head off this approach by arguing that 1QS was entirely consistent in style and logical in development won no support. In fact, its effect was just the opposite. Close attention began to be paid to the limits and definition of the various literary units, and this led to a number of important insights and partial hypotheses.

The pioneer in this respect was J. Becker (1963: 39–42), who highlighted significant shifts in style and content, but did not get beyond the level of possibility in explaining their origin. The same is true of Leaney's commentary, and it is regrettable that the new edition of Schürer (*HJP*[2] 3/1: 383) has regressed to this level. Real progress was made by Denis (1964: 40–44) in his analysis of the crucial cols. 8–9, where he discerned 2 interpolations (8:10b–12 and 8:16–9:2). A more detailed examination of the same cols. by Klinzing (1971: 50–66) produced much less satisfactory results (Murphy-O'Connor 1972: 436–38). Although it needed some refinement (Duhaime), von der Osten-Sacken's (1969: 17–27) discovery of 3 levels in the Instruction on the Two Spirits (1QS 3:13–4:26) was a major breakthrough.

The first attempt to find a comprehensive explanation for the composition of the *Rule* was made by Murphy-O'Connor (1969). Rejecting the view that it was a heterogenous compilation, an evolutionary hypothesis involving 4 chronological stages was proposed. The earliest stage was represented by 1QS 8:1–16 plus 9:3–10:8, followed in order by (2) 8:16–9:2; (3) 5:1–7:25; and (4) 1:1–4:26 and 10:9–11:22. This hypothesis was subjected to a book-length critical analysis by J. Pouilly. He found the 4-stage evolution to be correct, but convincingly argued that details needed modification. In consequence he assigned 8:10–12 to stage 2 and 5:13–6:8 to stage 4. His conclusions, which take into account all other contributions to the literary analysis and which have given rise to no serious objections (Davies 1987: 60), must be accorded a very high degree of probability, and can be set forth as follows:

Stage 1: 8:1–10a, 12b–16a; 9:3–10:8.
Stage 2: 8:10b–12a; 8:16b–9:2.
Stage 3: 5:1–13a; 6:8b–7:25.
Stage 4: 1:1–4:26; 5:13b–6:8a; 10:9–11:22.

Stage 1. This is the manifesto that led to the foundation of the Essene community at Qumran. When there have been found 12 men (= the 12 tribes) and 3 priests (= the levitical clans) who live the Law perfectly, "they will be separated from the midst of the habitation of ungodly men in order to go into the desert" (8:13; 9:20). There they will constitute a spiritual temple (8:5) and offer spiritual sacrifices (9:4–5) to expiate the sins of the land (8:6, 10). The hint of a breach with the Jerusalem temple is confirmed by the insistence on the importance of the authentic calendar (10:1–8). In this program the *maskil* has an essential role; he will be responsible for the choice and preparation of candidates (9:12–26). Ultimate authority in the future community will belong to the priestly members (9:7).

Stage 2. The community envisaged in stage 1 has been in existence for some time, and the problems of conventual life have manifested the need for basic penal legislation. The integration of such legislation into the foundation document indicates that the latter retained its value as a definition of the community. The severity of the sanctions is but the other face of the vitality of its idealism.

Stage 3. The life-situation demanded by the material of this stage is that of a large community at some distance from its origins. The redefinition of the community (5:1–6), underscored by the fact that the material of this stage was inserted *before* stages 1–2 in the arrangement of 1QS, clearly manifests the institutionalization and democratization characteristic of a late stage of development. The precise rules for the conduct of a general assembly (6:8–13) and the admission of new members (6:13–23), when taken in conjunction with the casuistry of the penal code (6:24–7:25), confirm this assessment. A significant increase in the numbers at Qumran about 100 B.C. is attested by the extensive building program of period Ib (de Vaux 1973: 5). See also QUMRAN and ESSENES.

Stage 4. This stage is the most complex because a number of elements had an independent existence before being incorporated into the *Rule.* Nonetheless, they are ascribed to the same stage because they all serve a single purpose, viz. revitalization of the fervor of the community. The intention to infuse a new "spirit" into the "letter" of the *Rule* is particularly evident in the way the redactor brackets stages 1–3 with material derived from the liturgy of the renewal of the covenant (1:1–3:12 and 10:9–11:22), whose message is that external observance is meaningless without genuine conversion of the heart. The Instruction on the Two Spirits (3:13–4:23a) had its own literary history (Duhaime 1977) before being adapted to its place in the *Rule* by the addition of 4:23b–26, which emphasizes the responsibility of the individual to choose good rather than evil. The function of the long interpolation 5:13b–6:8a is twofold, to insist on the stringent examination of new members and to highlight the importance of community life with particular stress on the need for continual study of the Law.

Besides attesting to the internal evolution of the Qumran community, the *Rule* is our best witness to its institutions, which are a key element in the identificaiton of its members as Essenes.

Bibliography

Avigad, N. 1958. The Palaeography of the Dead Sea Scrolls and Related Documents. Pp. 56–87 in *Aspects of the Dead Sea Scrolls,* ed. C. Rabin and Y. Yadin. ScrHier 4. Jerusalem.

Bardtke, H. 1973. Literaturbericht über Qumran VII: Die Sektenrolle 1QS. *TRu* 38: 257–91.

Becker, J. 1963. *Das Heil Gottes: Heils- und Sündenbegriffe in den Qumrantexten und im Neuen Testament.* SUNT 3. Göttingen.

Brownlee, W. H. 1951. *The Dead Sea Manual of Discipline.* BASORSup 10–12. New Haven.

Burrows, M., Trever, J. C., and Brownlee, W. H. 1951. *Plates and Transcription of the Manual of Discipline,* Vol 2, fasc 2 of *The Dead Sea Scrolls of St. Mark's Monastery.* New Haven.

Cross, F. M. 1961. *The Ancient Library of Qumran and Modern Biblical Studies.* Rev. ed. Garden City.

———. 1965. The Development of the Jewish Scripts. Pp. 170–264 in *BANE.*

Davies, P. R. 1987. *Behind the Essenes. History and Ideology in the Dead Sea Scrolls.* BJS 94. Atlanta.

Denis, A. M. 1964. Evolution de structures dans le secte de Qumran. Pp. 23–49 in *Aux origines de l'Eglise.* RechBib 7. Brugge.

Duhaime, J. 1977. L'instruction sure les deux esprits et les interpolations dualistes à Qumran. *RB* 84: 566–94.

Dupont-Sommer, A. 1953. *Nouveau aperçus sur les manuscrits de la Mer Morte.* Paris.

Guilbert, P. 1959. Le plan de la Règle de la Communauté. *RevQ* 3: 323–44.

———. 1961. La Règle de la Communauté. Pp. 11–80 in *Les textes de Qumran,* vol. 1. Ed. J. Carmignac and P. Guilbert. Paris.

Klinzing, G. 1971. *Die Umdeutung des Kultus in der Qumran Gemeinde und im Neuen Testament.* SUNT 7. Göttingen.

Knibb, M. 1987. *The Qumran Community.* Cambridge.

Kuhn, K. G. 1960. Der gegenwärtige Stand der Erforschung der in Palästina neu gefundenen hebräischen Handschriften. *TLZ* 85: 649–58.

Leahy, T. 1960. Studies in the Syntax of 1QS. *Bib* 41: 135–57.

Leaney, A. C. R. 1966. *The Rule of Qumran and Its Meaning.* London.

Lohse, E. 1964. *Die Texte aus Qumran. Hebräisch und deutsch mit masoretischer Punktation.* Munich.

Maier, J. 1960. *Die Texte vom Toten Meer.* 2 vols. Munich.

Milik, J. 1960. Review of P. Wernberg-Møller 1957. *RB* 67: 410–16.

———. 1962. Pp. 211–302 in *Les 'petites grottes' de Qumran.* DJD 3. Oxford.

Moraldi, L. 1971. *I Manoscritti di Qumran.* Torino.

Murphy-O'Connor, J. 1969. La genèse littéraire de la Règle de la Communauté. *RB* 76: 528–49.

———. 1972. Review of G. Klinzing 1971. *RB* 79: 435–40.

Osten-Sacken, P. von der. 1969. *Gott und Belial: Traditionsgeschichtliche Untersuchungen zum Dualismus in den Texten aus Qumran.* SUNT 6. Göttingen.

Pouilly, J. 1976. *La Règle de la Communauté de Qumran: Son évolution littéraire.* CahRB 17. Paris.

Trever, J. C. 1965. *The Untold Story of Qumran.* London.

Vaux, R. de. 1973. *Archaeology and the Dead Sea Scrolls.* The Schweich Lectures 1959. Rev. ed. Trans. D. Bourke. London.

Vermes, G. 1983. *The Dead Sea Scrolls in English.* London.

Wernberg-Møller, P. 1957. *The Manual of Discipline translated and annotated.* STDJ 1. Leiden.

J. Murphy-O'Connor

COMPASSION. See LOVE.

COMPUTERS AND BIBLICAL STUDIES.

To achieve a useful level of detail in reasonable scope, this article is focused in two ways. First, it deals with "biblical studies" in the narrow sense of the study of the text, excluding ANE history, archaeology, and geography. Computer science has much to offer these ancillary disciplines, and some impressive applications have been developed, but the common focus of attention of all biblical scholars is the text, and it is there that we direct our attention. Second, this article is methodological, not historical. A history of the application of computers to the Bible would benefit those who study biblical studies (in contrast to the Bible itself), but the field is progressing so rapidly that such a history would immediately be out of date. Furthermore, because of advances in computer science, some of the most important projects historically offer little practical guidance to those planning new research efforts today. Instead, we identify the main stages in the exegetical process and show how computers have been and may be applied to them.

A. Introduction

As does any other science, exegesis involves formulating hypotheses, gathering data, analyzing these data in the light of the hypotheses, and presenting results. This ordering of events is only suggestive, as later stages frequently require repetition of earlier ones. Thus, as one gathers data, an informal analysis often takes place concurrently, leading to a reformulation of the underlying hypotheses and a revision of the plan for gathering data. Still, the division is useful for our purposes. Data collection always presumes some hypothesis about what is interesting or useful to observe and what is not; analysis requires data on which to operate; and effective dissemination of results requires an additional step after analysis is complete.

As we consider each of these steps, we will look both to what has been done and to what can be done. There is not space to describe each of the hundreds of past and present projects, and mention of one or omission of another does not constitute a recommendation or criticism. Surveys of particular projects in computer-assisted biblical (Parunak 1989b; Hughes 1987) and other literary studies (Patton and Holoien 1981), and discussion of technical issues in computer research design for the humanities in general (Hockey 1980), are available elsewhere. These references should be consulted for detailed information about projects and scholars named but not otherwise documented in this article.

B. Formulate Hypotheses

Science never proceeds from a tabula rasa. The scholar always brings to the text some set of ideas to be vindicated or disproven. The better articulated these hypotheses are, the more effective the research process will be, and the less danger there is of implicit hypotheses prejudicing the results.

Computer science, and in particular the specialties of cognitive science and artificial intelligence, have developed rich theoretical frameworks for describing language and thought. By drawing on these models, we can formulate hypotheses about the biblical text with greater precision than was previously possible. In each example in the following (nonexhaustive) list, we discuss how an insight from computer science has been or can be applied to biblical studies.

1. Case Grammar. Case grammar (Fillmore 1968; Cook 1979) is a linguistic model that emerged from the early machine translation work of the 1950s and 1960s. Case grammar focuses attention on the relation between verbs and nouns in sentences. Each verb has associated with it a case frame, which is a set of case slots. These case slots, while suggested by the classical cases marked in the surface structure of languages like German or classical Greek and Latin, differ in important ways from the classical cases. The central difference between the cases in case grammar and classical cases is that between the surface structure of a text and the deep structure of meaning that it represents. The surface level of language contains elements such as verbs, nouns, and (classical) cases. The world of meaning deals with actions, entities, and (case grammar) cases. The relation between these layers is skewed, so that, for example, a noun at the surface level (such as "death") actually represents an action at the deep level. Case grammar cases describe the roles that entities fill with respect to actions at the deep level. For example, commonly used case slots include agent (the one who does the action), experiencer (the one who undergoes the action), and beneficiary (the one who benefits from the action). Case slots are thus characterized semantically, in contrast with surface level (classical) cases (such as nominative, dative, genitive, accusative, vocative), which are syntactic.

Because surface level verbs correspond roughly to deep structure actions, one can associate deep structure case slots with the verbs corresponding to the associated actions. Verbs differ in the case slots they have. For example, "to ache" has an experiencer but no agent; "to hit" has both. At the surface level, a single classical case may correspond on different occasions to different deep structure cases. Thus the experiencer of "to ache" and the agent of "to hit" are both represented by a surface structure nominative, while the experiencer of "to hit" takes a surface structure accusative.

Unlike surface structure cases, case slots are invariant under voice changes or shifts such as those generated through inflection. For example, in both the active sentence "The boy hit the ball" and the passive "The ball was hit by the boy," "boy" is agent and "ball" is experiencer.

Case grammar offers biblical studies a rigorous theoretical framework for lexicography. Once we recognize that case frames do not vary with verbal inflection but do vary with the semantics of the verb, we can use them to classify the vocabulary of a language. It becomes both natural and provocative to classify verbs on the basis of their case frames and the semantic classes of words that can fill them, or to classify nouns on the basis of the case slots that they can fill. Because case slots are a deep structure phenomenon, they offer a theoretical basis for combining the semantic evidence furnished by verbs with that of associated verbal nouns, where the case slots typically appear as surface genitives.

2. Semantic Nets. The term *semantic nets* (Brachman and Levesque 1985) refers to a variety of models of meaning, all characterized by a collection of nodes (representing concepts) and relationships among them. Research in artificial intelligence (AI) has shown that computers need to be able to model large fragments of knowledge about the world in order to perform intelligently. An effective way to store this knowledge is as a network of concepts connected by relations. Two kinds of concepts (*class* and *instance*) and two kinds of relations (*AKO* and *ISA*) are common to the many individual schemes that have been proposed.

An *instance* concept corresponds to a single entity in some world, real or imagined, while a *class* concept is a test that can be applied to any entity and will say "yes" if the entity is a member of the concept, or "no" otherwise. From another perspective, one names instances but describes classes. For example, David, Saul, and Solomon would be instances in a semantic net representing the conceptual world of the Hebrew Bible, while "king of Israel" would be a class. A class may have only one member and still be a class rather than an instance if its function is to describe rather than to name. Thus "creator" is a class whose sole member in orthodox biblical thought is the instance YHWH. One may even have a class with no members (for example, again in orthodox biblical thought, the class "gods other than YHWH").

AKO ("a kind of") relations join related classes, while *ISA* ("is a") relations assign instances to classes. For example, the concept "Prophet" is joined to the concept "Person" with a chain of AKO links, since "Prophet" is a subclass of "Person." (That is, whatever one can describe as "Prophet" can also be described as "Person.") "Person" in turn is AKO "living being." To identify a specific individual (such as Isaiah or Jeremiah) as a prophet, an ISA link connects the instance corresponding to that person with the "Prophet" class.

Semantic nets tend to consist of networks of classes showing the relationships among concepts with a fringe of instances dangling from the bottom. For example, Exhibit 1 (Fig. COM.01) shows a fragment of a semantic net rooted at the concept "Living Being." The nodes printed in light font are all classes, related to one another by AKO links (indicated by bold arrows). At the bottom, in bold font, are specific instances, linked to their most specific classes by ISA links (dashed arrows). In addition to the links actually shown on the diagram, the logic of semantic networks permits us to deduce that "Righteous Person" is AKO "Person" (since any chain of AKO links is equivalent to a single AKO link), and "David" ISA "Living Being" (since an instance of a class is also an instance of any other class of which the first is a subclass).

The AKO and ISA relations are the most common but are not enough for complete semantic modeling. Additional relations among classes (such as *part-of* and *color-of*) are often invented ad hoc to satisfy a particular need but can be derived in a theoretically more satisfying way from the case frames of case grammar.

Semantic nets offer a methodology and framework for describing a semantic space and studying the place of various concepts within it. Together with case grammar, they are an important tool for formalizing lexicography. They also offer a powerful model for studying phenomena such as semantic parallelism in biblical poetry.

One popular theory of parallelism ascribes the repeated pairing of certain lexical items to the existence of a conventional tradition of pairs from which poets drew acceptable matches. If we collect the matched pairs from Ugaritic

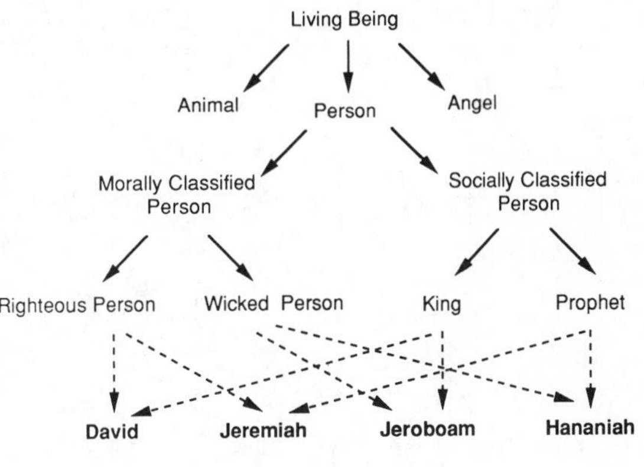

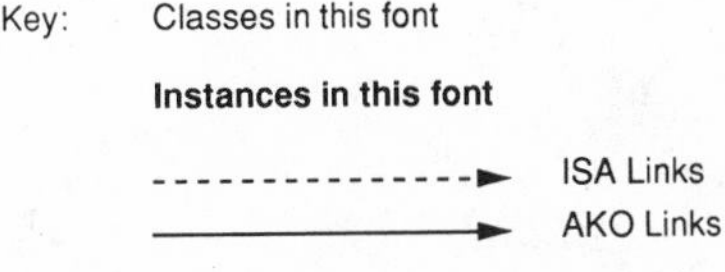

COM.01. Fragment of a semantic network.

poetry or the book of Proverbs and arrange the words on a sheet of paper in such a way that the distance between two words is proportional to the frequency with which those words appear in parallel, the overall pattern falls into clearly delineated regions, each with its own semantic integrity, and the association of individual pairs is seen to be only a detail of the larger picture of regions of associated terms. Such a pattern is easily explained on the hypothesis that humans store their inventory of concepts as a network and tend to associate terms (whether as poetic parallels or in other ways) based on their proximity in the overall network. This overall network is the broader context within which theories about traditional pairs need to be discussed.

For example, Exhibit 2 (Fig. COM.02) distributes 66 nouns in two dimensions in such a way that the closer two words are on the page the more frequently they occur as poetic parallels to one another in Proverbs. Several clear semantic regions are visible. The upper left quadrant, spilling over into the lower left, is dominated by names for body parts. Those toward the right of the cluster are the organs of wisdom and morality, such as "soul," "heart," and "spirit," while those to the left are purely physical, like "foot," "eye," and "hand." Across the top, words like "Sheol," "death," length," "day," "riches," and "honor" reflect the consequences of various styles of life. A vertical region near the center contains nouns descriptive of rational beings (including "Lord," two words for "man," "son," "sinner," and "scorner"). It also contains adjectives that are commonly used as nouns identifying people, such as "wise" and "righteous." Terms at the bottom of the column describe people with regard to their moral condition, while those at the top reflect wisdom and folly. This column bridges two other clusters, one of wisdom terms and the other of morality terms. The rest of the words in the upper right quadrant are the names for wisdom and

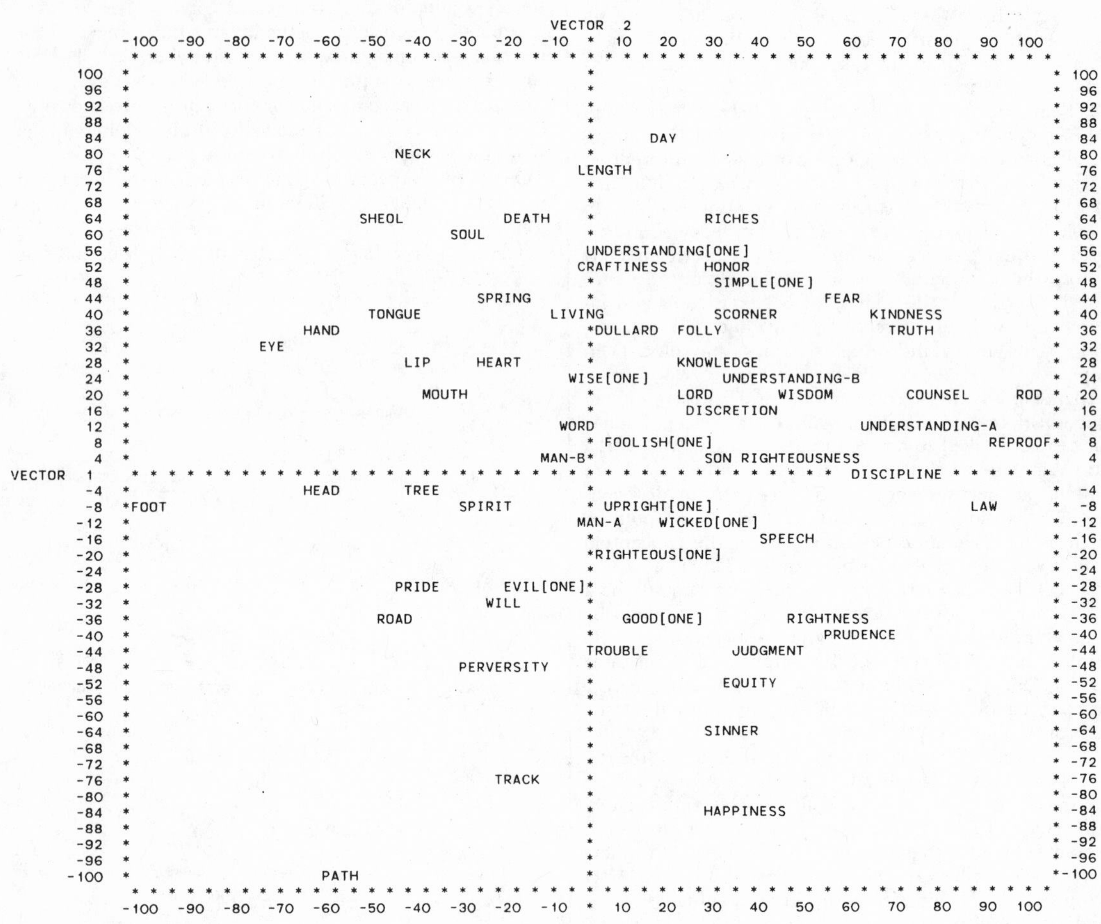

COM.02. 66 words parallel-linked in Proverbs.

understanding, as well as their opposite, "folly." "Fear" is here because of its frequent occurrence in the phrase, "fear of the Lord," which is (as Proverbs often reminds us) the beginning of wisdom. Terms toward the lower right end of this cluster, such as "counsel," "discipline," and "reproof," deal with the communication of wisdom. Across the bottom, merging with the moral words for rational beings, are descriptions of morality and its manifestations, including "pride," "perversity," "rightness," and several metaphors ("road," "track," and "path") that describe the course of a person's life. The existence of such regions is persuasive evidence that parallel pairs are not a stylistic end in themselves but the hem of a whole fabric of semantic interrelations, as suggested by a semantic net model.

The observation that the second member of a poetic pair often intensifies, strengthens, or makes more specific the idea of the first member (Alter 1985) reflects the importance in general of AKO relations in the structure of conceptual spaces.

3. Discourse Analysis. Every exegete has diagrammed sentences to analyze the relations among words within clauses. Recently, interest has mounted in *discourse analysis,* which studies the relations among clauses and larger linguistic units. Much of the impetus for this study has emerged from workers in artificial intelligence, seeking to build formal models for the computational processes underlying human language. One particularly useful methodology, called "rhetorical structure theory," was developed specifically to enable computers to produce text that sounds natural to humans (Mann and Thompson 1987). Important contributions have also been made by the Bible translation community (Beekman and Callow 1974; Longacre 1976; Grimes 1975), but the underlying motivation for this work, as for so much research in modern linguistic theory, is the move toward formal models of human behavior inspired by computer science.

The contribution of discourse analysis highlighted here is the formal definition of a set of relationships that clauses have with one another. Informally, some of these relations (such as Reason or Means) are familiar exegetical categories. The newer contributions offer much more complete sets of these relations than exegetes have been accustomed to using (over fifty in some systems). They provide an underlying theory for these relations (in one case, drawing on propositional calculus to define them precisely). They also show how these relations between clauses can be extended to relations between even larger textual units, thus providing a consistent theory of discourse structure at all levels from the clause to the complete text.

4. Modular Structure. The study of literary architecture, tracing patterns of repetition within texts and studying phenomena such as chiasm, alternation, and formal transitions (Parunak 1979, 1981b, 1983), goes well back before the computer, originating in Lowth's studies of Hebrew verse parallelism. Computer science offers insights that can strengthen and clarify architectural analyses of texts.

As computer programs have grown longer and more complex, new computer languages have provided sophisticated structuring aids to allow the program to be constructed as a series of segments, each with its own identity and function. Without such modularization, people cannot understand long programs, and errors become hard to find and correct. Program structures are an accommodation to human cognitive limitations. Both a structured and an unstructured program may produce the same result, but the structured one is easier for people to understand and manipulate. The development of structure in computer languages is thus a window into human cognitive structure in general and provides a model for analyzing other products of human cognition, such as extended literary texts.

For example, a basic rule in structured programming is the principle of locality of access. Variables used within one module of a program should not be susceptible to change by another module unless the module that owns them explicitly makes them available. This rule reflects the mind's need to package thought into relatively self-contained units and to control the interactions among these units to reduce complexity. Studies of literary architecture have identified a number of techniques for defining textual units, but the resulting analyses are often criticized by observations that a feature (such as a vocabulary item or a grammatical form) appears in several units, outside of the overall pattern of repetition. The principle of locality suggests that such repetition need not invalidate the overall modular structure, since features that are local to individual modules do not interact with one another. Clearly, this approach requires refinement to indicate under what conditions a feature may be considered local and what techniques a module uses to make a feature publicly available to establish relations with other modules. Just as clearly, the whole framework within which the hypothesis is posed, and the directions along which it may be tested and refined, are the results of cognitive tendencies that have been made clear in our attempts to program computers.

5. Transformational Grammar. We have already noted the indirect contribution of early machine translation efforts to linguistic theory in the form of case grammar. Another important contribution of these efforts is *transformational grammar,* developed by Noam Chomsky as a result of studies of the formal structures of mathematical languages. Transformational grammar models how a single semantic representation of an idea inside the mind can emerge as different streams of text. For example, it explains how passive and active forms of a sentence are related to a single underlying meaning.

This particular grammatical theory has been useful in several recent studies of Hebrew poetic parallelism (Collins 1978; O'Connor 1980; Geller 1979), where it has provided a framework for classifying and analyzing parallel poetic structures with much more discrimination than has previously been available. It allows the analyst to identify parallelism not only between words in the surface form of the text but also between elements in the underlying or deep structure, and thus provides a theoretical foundation for extending the application of parallelism to many poetic lines that at the surface level do not exhibit formal parallelism.

C. Gather Data

With a hypothesis in hand, we want to gather data from the text in order to test it. In the days before computers, biblical scholars collected their data by keeping ad hoc notes on various subjects encountered during general reading of the text; by reading the text while looking for a specific phenomenon; or through concordances. The computer was early recognized as a way to accelerate this process. Dozens of programs are available to support the data-gathering phase of exegesis, far too many for us to attempt to review in detail here. Hughes (1987) gives a good survey. We will mention a few that illustrate some of the capabilities we describe.

The two basic components of any computer system for gathering data from the biblical text are the *text base* itself and a *search program* that manipulates this text base. (These correspond respectively to the Bible and the scholar in the pre-computer scenario.) The text base contains at least the text to be studied, which may be in the original languages, translations, or both. (Some programs, like Akiyama's Bible Word program, permit users to consult multiple versions of the same text simultaneously.) It often includes annotations to the text and sometimes provides indices that speed up the search process. The search program is responsible for collecting the user's specifications for a search, applying them to the text base, and returning the results to the user in a useful form.

Data gathering systems differ widely in what is included in the text base, how it is stored, and how the search program manipulates it. Some objectives can be achieved either in the text base or in the search program. For example, if one needs to retrieve verbs according to their parsing, one might code each verb in the text base with its parsing or, alternatively, provide the search program with the capability of parsing verbs as it acquires them. In general (but with many specific exceptions), it is faster to store a linguistic analysis in the text base than to compute it during search, but a stored analysis strategy requires more space for the text base (for instance, a larger hard disk drive) than does one that parses on the run. As computers become faster and high-density storage technologies (such as CD-ROM) become less expensive, both constraints become less important.

1. Text Base. Text bases differ from one another in the detail with which they represent the basic text, the representation of annotations, and the storage strategy.

a. Detail of Representation. The degree of detail that needs to be represented in a coded text varies depending on the purpose for which the text is intended. In many early projects, texts were coded with a specific purpose in mind. For example, scholars interested in lexical and syntactical studies of the OT frequently ignore the cantillation of the text and often do not code it in their text base. Some Hebrew text bases even exclude the vocalization. The GRAMCORD search language (Miller 1984) does not rely on the accentuation of the Greek text, so the text base does not record this accentuation. Some popular computer editions of the KJV do not distinguish the italicized words (those inserted by the translators to smooth the English syntax) from the rest of the text.

Within the context of an individual research project with restricted goals, partial texts can reduce the cost of recording the data and control storage requirements. Also, it is often easier to design search programs if the text base is not cluttered with information (such as cantillation or accentuation) that the search program does not use. All too often, though, a researcher who has coded only some features of a text finds new questions arising in the course of research that require access to the omitted features. As the capacity of storage increases and computers grow faster, and as texts are assembled for general use in repositories such as the Center for Computer Analysis of Texts at the University of Pennsylvania and the Oxford University Computing Service (to name only two) instead of being custom coded for specific projects, text bases will tend to include all of the textual information found in a standard critical edition.

b. Annotations. Many exegetical questions involve the parsed form of words, rather than the form in which they appear in a text. For example, if one is searching a text for "mouse," one often wishes to retrieve at the same time occurrences of the plural form "mice." Though the text contains the string of characters "mice," the analyst may wish to manipulate it as though it had the notation "mouse + plural." This analysis records the "dictionary form" of the word (the entry in a dictionary that one would consult to find information about the word), and its parsing or grammatical code. The dictionary form is also sometimes called the "lemma" (plural "lemmata") and a text that indicates the dictionary form of each word explicitly is thus called a "lemmatized text."

There is less need for lemmatization in English than in Greek and Hebrew. English words change comparatively little in different contexts. Internal plurals (such as "mice") are much rarer than those formed by adding a simple suffix ("houses"), and nouns do not have different forms in subject, object, and indirect object position. Verbs usually retain their basic form, with tense, person, and aspect marked through simple endings and helper verbs. Thus a search program for English can retrieve various inflections of a desired word just by specifying the beginning portion that is common to the various forms of the word.

This strategy is less successful in Greek and Hebrew. The heavy use of prefixes and suffixes in the verbal paradigms, and Hebrew's agglutinative use of prefixed prepositions and articles and postfixed pronouns, together with the less regular spelling characteristic of texts circulated in the centuries before printing, make it difficult to retrieve with a single search pattern all words that the dictionary classes together.

In principle, parsing can be done by the search program. After all, that is how people read texts. The mechanisms that people use, though, are not yet perfectly understood, and what we do know about them shows that they depend on context and even on general background knowledge about the world to resolve parsing ambiguities. Thus, most systems that permit retrieval by lemma or grammatical analysis code the parsing in the text base. Some systems (Morris and James 1975) record only lemmata and grammatical codes and omit the textual form of words entirely. Others record the textual form of each word together with a code indicating its grammatical analysis (Friberg and Friberg 1981), and still others include also lemmata for some (Miller 1984) or all (Radday 1973) words.

Currently available parsed text bases record surface level information. A rudimentary deep structure case scheme has been coded for some OT books and is useful for framing questions of the form, "List all verbs that take God as a patient." If one augments a text base with a semantic network modeling the conceptual world of the community within which the text originally circulated, one can then pose questions of the form, "What does this text have to say about morality?" Even if the word "morality" never appears in the text itself, the semantic network permits identification of subclasses of the concept "morality," and the retrieval can then search for the names of these more specific concepts. For example, a text base augmented with the semantic network of Exhibit 1 could be asked to list all verbs of which righteous people were the agent, and as a result would retrieve passages where "David" and "Jeremiah" occur.

One drawback to extensively parsed text bases is the need for large amounts of storage to record the analysis. Not every researcher requires the same kinds of analysis, and a text base detailed enough to satisfy the needs of all researchers may require so much storage that no researcher can afford to access it. "Adaptive parsing" is a strategy to address this problem. In this strategy, the search engine is able to recover a parsing either from a stored annotation to the text base or (more slowly) by computation from the textual form alone. Specialized parses are obtained by computation but, once found, are added to the text base as annotations. Thus, as one uses the system, it becomes more efficient in retrieving the kinds of information that the user has requested in the past and develops into a highly personalized research assistant.

c. Storage Strategy. In a well-designed retrieval system, the details of how the text is stored in the computer are hidden from the user. To understand how search programs work, though, and to trace the differences among various programs, it is useful to understand three issues concerning textual representation and storage: transcription schemes, indexing, and compression.

The first feature of Greek and Hebrew that strikes the English-speaking novice is that they use alphabets different from that of English. They place characters not only in line with one another but over and under each other, and Hebrew even writes "backward," from right to left instead of from left to right. How are such features represented inside the computer?

Though the average person thinks of interaction with computers as carried out in the Roman alphabet, this alphabet is no more natural to the computer than is any other. Internally, modern computers represent each character as a memory cell (called a "byte") that holds a number from 0 to 255. To store the letter *A* in a byte, the computer places the number 65 there. To store the character *3* (not to be confused with the number 3), the computer uses the number 51. Even the blank space has a number assigned to it (32). This association between numbers and characters is completely arbitrary. To represent Hebrew or Greek, the numbers are assigned to Hebrew or Greek characters instead of Roman ones. Since early programs could only display Roman characters, the assignment schemes for Hebrew and Greek usually assign characters to numbers that also represent Roman letters reminiscent of the Hebrew or Greek letter. For example, Heb *beth* and Gk *beta* are usually represented by the same number that stands for the Roman character *b*. In some cases (such as the Hebrew accents), two bytes together represent a single character. Internally, the computer does not distinguish between "right" and "left," and a suitably programmed terminal can print out Hebrew from right to left just as readily as a conventional one prints English from left to right. Some software, such as the Bible Word, LBase, and GRAMCORD's GRAMGREEK utility, can display and print text in Hebrew and Greek fonts as well as in transliteration.

The Bible is a fairly large text. The KJV, for example, contains about 4,500,000 characters, or nearly 800,000 words, in unlemmatized form. The addition of lemmata or grammatical codes can more than double this figure. Searching such a text by having the computer read it sequentially can be a time-consuming activity, especially if one is seeking a complex pattern.

To speed up a search, some programs follow the example of human readers, who typically search for a passage containing a particular word by looking up the word in a concordance. A concordance is an example of an index. Given the item of interest, it guides one directly to the places in the text that mention that item. In the same way, some biblical retrieval systems use indices to the text to speed up processing. Some systems allow users to build their own indices from sequential searches and use these to speed up future searches. This tactic is a simple version of the adaptive parsing strategy outlined above.

The size of the Bible requires significant external storage resources. Furthermore, one of the slowest operations in a computer is reading information from external storage into memory, so the size of the text slows down processing. To avoid these problems, many systems compress the text. One popular scheme is to replace common sequences of letters in the text with special byte codes that are not used for ordinary characters. For example, if each of the 930 occurrences of "Jesus" in the NT were stored as a single character, 3720 characters could be saved. Compression schemes such as this are one reason that the data files used by many popular retrieval systems must be accessed with their associated search programs and cannot be manipulated with a standard word processor.

2. Search Program. The text base is of relatively little use without a search program to retrieve information from it. Search programs range from general-purpose text manipulation languages (like SNOBOL, Icon, awk, or grep) that can process any ASCII file to programs tailored to the needs of biblical scholars. Their objective is to produce lists, counts, and indices of passages that meet criteria set by the user. Their most important differences are in the flexibility the user has to describe the passages that are to be retrieved, counted, or indexed. These differences concern both the entities out of which a search pattern is constructed and the kinds of constraints among these entities that the user can specify.

a. Search Entities. Every text base contains characters, and general file manipulation languages deal with characters as their basic entity. Character patterns are general and flexible, but most exegetical questions are not posed at the level of characters but in terms of higher-level entities, such as morphemes, phrases, clauses, or literary forms. A search program that manipulates text at the level of characters requires the user to translate search requests from the higher-level objects of exegetical interest into low-level character patterns. A program that explicitly manipulates higher-level groupings is easier to use. If a text base is lemmatized, a search program that understands the differences among text, lemma, and parsing annotations is needed to take full advantage of it. A particularly flexible implementation of such a scheme is Silver Mountain's LBase, which permits the user to define an arbitrary number of nested levels of analysis.

b. Pattern Constraints. A search program provides the user with a language to define relations among the entities that it recognizes. A description phrased in this language is called a *pattern,* and the entities that the pattern matches in the text are its *targets.* Some forms of patterns require that the text be divided into *segments* (typically, lines, sentences, or verses) within which a pattern must be satisfied.

The simplest form of pattern is a fixed list. Thus the character pattern "die" would match all strings of characters that include these characters in this order, including "die" and "died" (which the user probably wants), and also "audience" (which is probably not desired). A fixed list offers no way to retrieve both "of God" and "of our God" with a single pattern. Every character in the pattern must match a character in the target, and in the same order.

A common enhancement to fixed patterns is boolean combinations. This scheme permits the user to build a pattern from two or more simpler patterns (such as fixed lists), and to specify that both of two patterns must appear, or that one or another of two must appear, in an acceptable target. For instance, the pattern "love" and "God" would match every segment containing both the string "love" and the string "God." It would thus retrieve "the love of God" and "thou shalt love the Lord thy God," and also "they loved the praise of men more than the praise of God."

The next level of complexity after boolean combinations allows the user to restrict the order in which the subtargets occur and the material that may occur between them. The most common device for this purpose is some sort of "wild card." For instance, the pattern "." is commonly used to match any character, and * matches any sequence of zero or more occurrences of the preceding character. So the pattern "of.* God" matches all segments containing the string "of," followed by any series of letters, then a space, and finally "God." It thus matches both "of God" and "of our God." A variety of such devices are available in packages like the Bible Word that support the full class of string languages known formally as "regular expression" (Hopcroft and Ullman 1979).

Some pattern languages permit the user to constrain the intervening material in various ways. GRAMCORD, for instance, permits the user to exclude any specific grammatical category from intervening between specified patterns, making it easier for the user to focus in on phrases with a desired structure.

We have been using character patterns to illustrate search. With a search program like LBase that reasons with higher-level entities such as morphemes, words, and sentences, one may encounter fixed patterns, boolean combinations, and wild card possibilities at those levels too. Particularly powerful patterns are possible in a language that allows one to ask (for example) for all verbs that occur within three words of the phrase "in Christ," without intervening verbs. A high proportion of the targets matching such a pattern will be clauses in which the prepositional phrase in fact modifies the verb.

All of the patterns we have discussed up to this point match only on the basis of the collocation of words in the text, not on the basis of their grammatical relations with one another. A true syntactical pattern matcher can retrieve clauses based on words standing in specified relations of modification or dependency to one another. This capability requires either a search program that can effectively diagram the sentences in the text or a text base that is coded for grammatical dependencies. Both approaches are technically feasible, but neither is used in popularly available systems.

D. Analyze Data

In our four-phase model of scholarly activity, data analysis is the third phase, comparing the data gathered in the second phase with the hypotheses formulated in the first phase. From one perspective, analysis is the activity that confirms or disproves a hypothesis. From another perspective, the issue is not confirmation but exploration. The deviations between hypothesis and observation are the most important product of the analysis stage and fuel the formulation of new hypotheses for the next cycle of research. In this second view, a hypothesis summarizes economically the regularities in a set of data and focuses attention on the remaining irregularities.

Analysis can be either qualitative (dealing with categories, themes, and other symbolic, nonnumeric information) or quantitative (focusing on numbers extracted from the text). The computer offers tools to help with both.

1. Qualitative Analysis. Two common computer-based tools for qualitative analysis are the concordance and the data base management system, or DBMS.

a. Concordances. A concordance is a list of extracts from a text, ordered according to some linguistic feature of each. Usually the feature is the occurrence of a word, and the concordance allows us to see in a single place all of the occurrences of that word, together with some context for each one. We have already alluded to the use of a concordance as an index to aid in data gathering. A concordance also presents data in a form that is convenient for many types of analysis. A wide variety of computer-generated concordances is published by Biblical Research Associates in the Computer Bible series.

Concordances were an important tool for scholars for years before the advent of the computer, but the preparation of a concordance for a text the size of the Bible required a lifetime. Now computers collect the data for concordances much more quickly, and in various formats tailored to specific exegetical problems. The popular Key-Word-In-Context or KWIC format lines up the occurrences of the target word down the center of the page (the "gutter"). Within the article for a single word, the entries can be sorted by preceding or following context, permitting the user to note differences in constructions involving the word. Exhibit 3 (Fig. COM.03) shows a portion of a KWIC concordance on the Gk particle *ei,* "if," from 1 Corinthians, from Morton, Michaelson, and Thompson

11:31	και αρρωστοι και κοιμωνται ικανοι·	ει	δε εαυτους διεκρινομεν, ουκ αν εκρινομεθα·
12:19	αυτων, εν τω σωματι καθως ηθελησεν·	ει	δε ην τα παντα εν μελος, που το σωμα; νυν
4:7	διακρινει; τι δε εχεις ο ουκ ελαβες;	ει	δε και ελαβες, τι καυχασαι ως μη λαβων; ηδη
7:15	ακαθαρτα εστιν, νυν δε αγια εστιν·	ει	δε ο απιστος χωριζεται, χωριζεσθω· ου
7:9	καλον αυτοις εαν μεινωσιν ως καγω·	ει	δε ουκ εγκρατευονται γαμησατωσαν, κρειττον
14:35	καθως και ο νομος λεγει·	ει	δε τι μαθειν θελουσιν, εν οικω τους ιδιους
8:3	τι, ουπω εγνω καθως δει γνωναι·	ει	δε τις αγαπα τον θεον, ουτος εγνωσται υπ
14:38	α γραφω υμιν οτι κυριου εστιν εντολη·	ει	δε τις αγνοει, αγνοειται· ωστε, αδελφοι
7:36	και ευπαρεδρον τω κυριω απερισπαστως·	ει	δε τις ασχημονειν επι την παρθενον αυτου
11:16	κομη αντι περιβολαιου δεδοται (αυτη).	ει	δε τις δοκει φιλονεικος ειναι, ημεις
3:12	κειμενον, ος εστιν ιησους χριστος·	ει	δε τις εποικοδομει επι τον θεμελιον χρυσον,
15:12	κηρυσσομεν και ουτως επιστευσατε·	ει	δε χριστος κηρυσσεται οτι εκ νεκρων
15:14	ουκ εστιν, ουδε χριστος εγηγερται·	ει	δε χριστος ουκ εγηγερται, κενον αρα (και) το
15:17	εγειρονται, ουδε χριστος εγηγερται·	ει	δε χριστος ουκ εγηγερται, ματαια η πιστις
10:30	μου κρινεται υπο αλλης συνειδησεως;	ει	εγω χαριτι μετεχω, τι βλασφημουμαι υπερ ου
15:19	οι κοιμηθεντες εν χριστω απωλοντο·	ει	εν τη ζωη ταυτη εν χριστω ηλπικοτες εσμεν
6:2	οτι οι αγιοι τον κοσμον κρινουσιν; και	ει	εν υμιν κρινεται ο κοσμος, αναξιοι εστε
15:44	ψυχικον, εγειρεται σωμα πνευματικον·	ει	εστιν σωμα ψυχικον, εστιν και πνευματικον·

COM.03. Portion of a KWIC concordance on the Greek particle *ei*.

1979. Because the context (in this case, the following context) is sorted, the entry brings together for convenient study such phrases as *ei de, ei de tis,* and *ei de christos.*

Reverse concordances sort words not by their beginnings but by their endings and are useful in identifying manuscript fragments that preserve the end of a word. From a fully analyzed text, concordances can be prepared that organize words by part of speech or conjugation and declension as well as by lemma or textual form. As on-line texts become more widely available and increased computing power becomes less expensive, the notion of a printed concordance will give way to concordance-like displays prepared as they are needed.

b. Data Base Management System. A concordance organizes a set of contexts on the basis of a single feature. A DBMS permits the user to explore the interaction of several features at once. In its simplest form, a DBMS stores information in the form of *records,* each containing a fixed number of *fields.* It is an automated version of the venerable box of index cards. For example, a data base supporting the lexical study of a particular noun might devote a record to each syntactic construction in which the noun occurs. One field of each record might record the biblical reference, another the kind of construction in which the noun occurs, a third the word in the construction to which the noun is bound, a fourth the kind of literature in which the passage occurs, and a fifth a brief definition appropriate to the noun in this context.

Defining the fields for such a data base amounts to constructing a hypothesis about the kinds of information that will prove relevant in determining the meaning of a word in a given context. Once the various constructions are recorded, the DBMS permits the user to sort and retrieve them on the basis of any field or combination of fields in order to explore correlations among fields. Typically, the result of the first day spent perusing such a data base is a redefinition of the fields, reflecting a refinement of the original hypothesis and often requiring a return to the data collection phase to fill out the new categories. The use of a DBMS permits repetition of this process more frequently and easily than is possible with physical index cards.

2. Quantitative Analysis. *Quantitative analysis* has gained in popularity among humanists with the advent of the computer and the development of packages of statistical software. To many people, "computer-assisted biblical studies" is almost synonymous with efforts to assess the authorship of biblical books from counts of stylistic features, such as vocabulary, vocabulary richness, grammatical usages, and idioms (Morton 1978; Radday and Shore 1985).

Modern statistics offers two classes of tools: confirmatory data analysis and exploratory data analysis. While confirmatory analysis has attracted much attention, it is often misapplied. Exploratory data analysis offers tremendous untapped potential for biblical studies.

a. Confirmatory Data Analysis. *Confirmatory data analysis* (CDA) is a mathematical incarnation of the side of analysis that seeks to confirm or disprove a hypothesis. The hypothesis defines a population, from which the data purport to be drawn. CDA assesses this claim, by estimating how likely it is that the data indeed come from that population.

For example, in typical authorship studies, the analyst derives characteristics of an author's style from a sample of text known to be from that author. One hopes that the characteristics chosen remain fairly constant over all works of the author, but vary from one author to another. No one expects an author to produce exactly the same value for such characteristics in every text, but the variation among known texts can be measured and used to estimate how far the author might deviate from the average values. The analyst measures the corresponding characteristics from a text of unknown authorship and computes the probability that a population of texts exhibiting the values and range of variation shown by the known texts could also include texts with the values shown by the unknown texts.

CDA is also a useful set of tools for addressing grammatical and structural questions. For example, the word "spirit" occurs 26 times in Romans, 18 of them in chap. 8. Could such a concentration of vocabulary result from a random distribution of words over the text, or does it reflect the thematic structure of the book? CDA provides quantitative means to assess the significance of such concentrations.

Several challenges must be met by studies applying CDA. We will discuss them in terms of authorship studies, but similar qualifications exist for any application of these methods. For references and further discussion, see Andersen (1976). A model analysis is Mosteller and Wallace (1964).

> The sample used to define the population must indeed be by the author in question. If we have no texts known to be by an author, we can hardly establish parameters for qualifying unknown texts.
>
> If differences between the known and unknown samples are to be attributed to different authors, the samples should not differ in other ways (such as literary genre, subject matter, period of the author's life, later editorial activity, or linguistic register). If samples differ in several ways simultaneously, it becomes very difficult to determine which of the differences is responsible for differing values of the characteristics that the statistician is measuring. Literary studies sometimes seek to circumvent this problem by focusing on function words (like prepositions, conjunctions, relative pronouns, and the copula) rather than content words (like nouns, verbs, and adjectives) on the assumption that an author's usage will show more consistency in function words than in content words. This distinction may be true for subject matter but does not address differences in genre or register. For example, it is well known that some particles occur much less often in Hebrew poetry than in prose, independent of authorship.
>
> In statistical studies in general, more data are better than less. The precision of results often tends to increase as the square root of the number of observations. To get twice as accurate an answer, one needs four times as much data. Landmark authorship studies in nonbiblical literature typically use on the order of 100,000 words of text, well beyond the amount of data available for biblical authorship studies.

Properly applied, CDA is an indispensable tool, but the promise of a "true-false" verdict that it holds out is seductive. It is easy to overlook the extensive methodological pitfalls and assume that, if a procedure yields a number, the answer is certain. Responsible application of these techniques requires close and extended collaboration between exegetes who understand what questions are meaningful in terms of the text and statisticians with a thorough grounding in the capabilities and limitations of their tools. Accessible introductions to CDA include Mosteller, Rourke, and Thomas (1961) and Mosteller and Rourke (1973).

b. Exploratory Data Analysis. Recent years have seen an explosion of statistical interest in *exploratory data analysis* (EDA). Where CDA epitomizes the view of a hypothesis as a claim to be proven or disproven, EDA implements the view that a hypothesis is a partial explanation of the data, whose effects need to be understood and removed so that further patterns may be seen. EDA does not render a verdict on hypotheses but gives one the mathematical equivalent of a magnifying glass, clarifying the data as input to scholarly discretion. Its techniques can reveal structure and order that would otherwise remain hidden in data. The cornerstone of EDA is Tukey (1977), together with Mosteller and Tukey (1977).

These techniques have been used, for example, to explore the distribution of boundary verbs among the tribes in Joshua 14–19. Beginning with a table indicating how many times each tribal boundary list uses each of the verbs, the EDA techniques of median polish and recoding suggest a strong preference for five of the verbs in the boundaries of Benjamin, Judah, Ephraim, and Manasseh, while four other verbs dominate the boundaries of Zebulun, Issachar, Asher, and Naphtali. This observation, which would be difficult to make without these techniques, can be correlated in various ways with the context of the allocation of the land.

The techniques of Tukey (1977) can be applied with paper and pencil, though computer implementations are increasingly common. Other EDA techniques involve massive computations that require computer assistance. Among these are cluster analysis and multidimensional scaling (Parunak 1989a). Both of these techniques give ways to visualize the differences among a number of items (for example, vocabulary words or manuscripts). They begin with an estimate of similarity for each pair of items. Cluster analysis explores how well these similarities can be explained as arising from a set of different categories and seeks to retrieve the underlying categories. Multidimensional scaling (MDS) seeks to build a geometrical model of the set of similarities, thus permitting the scholar to view a spatial arrangement of the items that corresponds to the underlying similarities. Exhibit 2 (Fig. COM.02) is an example of the results of MDS.

A central tenet of EDA is that one picture is worth a thousand digits. Tables of numbers are difficult to understand even if one knows what one is looking for, but an appropriate graph or plot can lead the observer to unanticipated hypotheses. Computers can generate plots easily and thus take advantage of the insight that a picture can give.

For example, Linguistic Density Plots (Parunak 1981a) display the distribution of a linguistic phenomenon (such as a specific word or a grammatical construction) throughout a text, with location in the text on the horizontal axis and concentration on the vertical axis. The result is a series of peaks that show where in the text the phenomenon is concentrated. Such a plot gives the scholar a "feel" for concentrations that is almost impossible to achieve from a concordance list alone. It offers clues to literary structure that would be difficult to find without it.

Exhibits 4–6 show three Density Plots from Paul's Epistle to the Romans. Each dark bullet on the plot represents a separate occurrence of the word being plotted. An integer appears instead of a bullet if two or more occurrences are on top of one another. The horizontal or "REFERENCE" axis shows location in the book, with chapter beginnings labeled and each horizontal position representing four verses. The vertical or "DENSITY" axis is computed in such a way that the higher a point is plotted the closer it is to the adjacent occurrences of the same phenomenon.

Exhibit 4 (Fig. COM.04) shows a dramatic concentration of words beginning with *Israel* (such as "Israel" and "Israelite") in chaps. 9–11. This distribution is not a surprise to

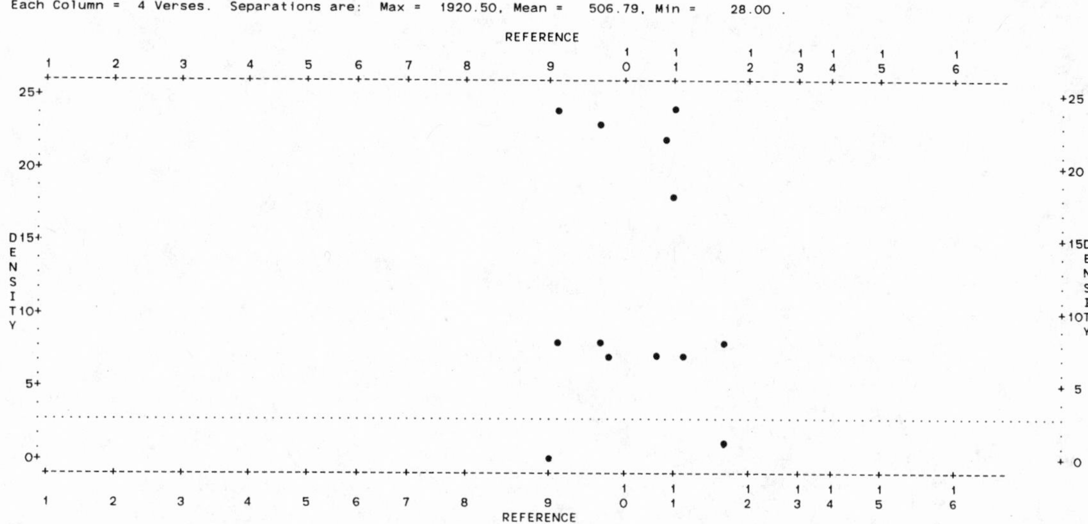

COM.04. Linguistic density plot—Romans 1–16 (13 occurrences of "Israel").

anyone familiar with the overall structure of Romans. Exhibit 5 (Fig. COM.05), though, of the verb *sozo*, "to save," and words beginning *soter* (like "savior" and "salvation"), is arresting. It shows that these words also, which many would suspect to be characteristic of the entire epistle, are concentrated in chaps. 9–11, and suggests that the restoration of Israel contemplated in these chapters is not just an afterthought to the book's preoccupation with salvation but an integral element in the discussion. Exhibit 6 (Fig. COM.06) shows that nouns and verbs describing "mercy" also predominate in these three chapters, this time in concentrations that form an inclusio at the beginning and end of the section.

Not all plots are created equal. Some computer graphics

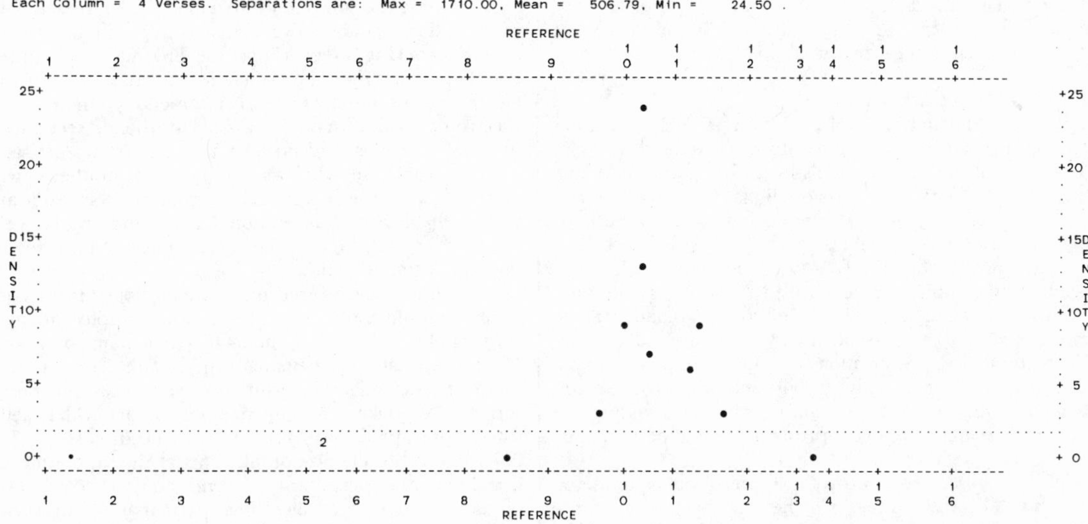

COM.05. Linguistic density plot—Romans 1–16 (13 occurrences of "save" and "savior/salvation").

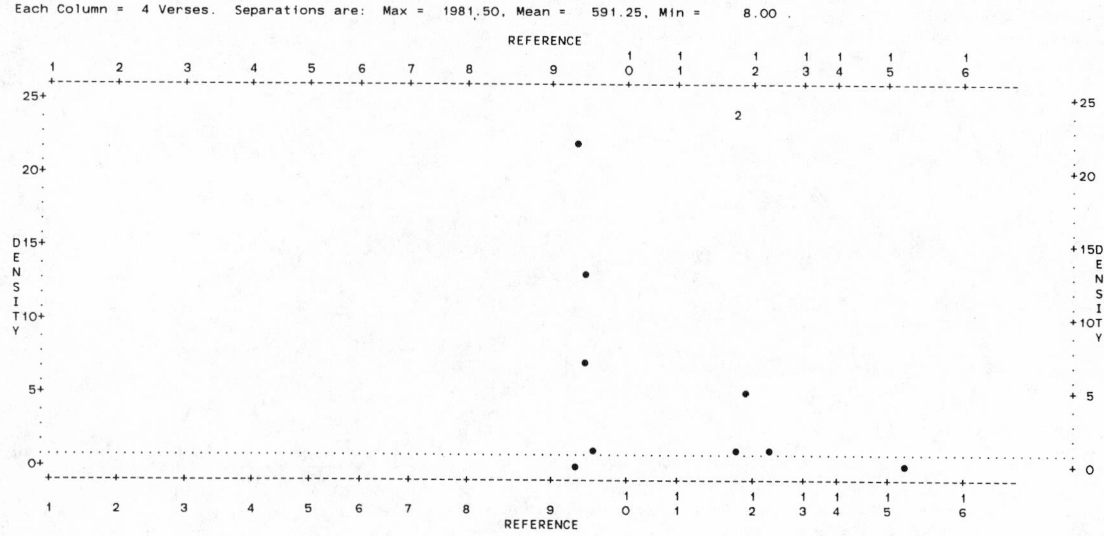

COM.06. Linguistic density plot—Romans 1–16 (11 occurrences of "[have] mercy").

packages create showy graphs that in fact obscure rather than clarify data, and some kinds of displays are better than others at showing specific kinds of data. The ubiquitous pie chart, for example, communicates the preponderance of one category over another, but tests have shown that viewers cannot extract quantitative information from it as reliably as they can from a bar chart or a line graph. As another example, a change in the axes of a line graph or scatterplot (say, from linear to logarithmic or squared) can dramatically change the intuitions suggested by the data. Tufte (1983) and Cleveland (1985) are excellent guides to the graphical presentation of data.

E. Present Results

Biblical scholarship involves an ongoing conversation among the past, present, and future students of the text. The computer offers new tools for assisting and moderating this conversation, both through making more effective use of traditional printed media and as a medium of communication in its own right.

1. Printed Media. The first introduction many humanists have to computers is as word processors. As mundane as this application seems, it has led to a dramatic increase in the ease and speed of moving ideas from mind to page. Corrections and modifications are much simpler to make than formerly, and many publishers can work directly from an author's machine-readable text, thus avoiding the time-consuming and error-prone rekeying of a manuscript for typesetting.

We have discussed concordances and plots as tools for analysis. The ease with which they can be tailored for a specific purpose also makes them attractive as aids to communicate to a reader the evidence that supports an author's arguments, while imposing an added responsibility on the author to ensure that they are clear and not misleading.

2. The Computer as Medium. As well as producing material for printed distribution, computers can themselves be the medium of scholarly activity. Perhaps the earliest example of this tendency is computer-aided instruction. For basic drill of vocabulary and paradigms in language study, computers offer a flexible version of the venerable flash card. More recent technologies that are transforming the computer into a medium of the scholarly conversation include networking and hypermedia.

a. Networking. Networking, the linking of computers together so that they can exchange information, is already a major means of daily scholarly interaction in the sciences. Electronic mail (Email) bypasses letterhead, secretaries, stamps, envelopes, and postal carriers, carrying messages directly from one scholar's computer to another's, with same-day service even across the ocean. Email is faster and more reliable than conventional mail, and (unlike telephone conversation) does not necessitate both parties being free at the same time.

The computer conference or bulletin board is the computer equivalent of a discussion. In its simplest form, it consists of a series of comments by participants on a topic of interest. Later participants can read the comments of earlier participants and offer their responses and observations. Networking permits people who are widely separated geographically to take part in the discussion. The participants usually do not take part at the same time. As with Email, the computer conference holds a record of the discussion so that at any time participants can review comments and add their own.

As more scholars prepare their research in electronic form, it becomes increasingly feasible for publishers to support submissions by networking. In the sciences, research is actively under way to permit the entire process of submission, review, and correction to take place by Email, without the need to circulate paper. The next step is the electronic journal, distributed to the final readers by network rather than on paper.

b. Hypermedia. Hypermedia is the generic term for a collection of information items linked together so that a user may move from one item to any of several associated with it, depending on need and interest. If the information items are restricted to text, one speaks of "hypertext." An encyclopedia is a simple example of hypertext, with the articles constituting the information items and the movement from one item to another guided by cross-references embedded in the articles. The fundamental characteristic of an information repository structured as hypermedia is that it helps the user move through it in many different sequences, rather than in a fixed linear order, as is customary with books and journal articles.

Exhibit 7 (see Fig. COM.07) illustrates SymEdit, one application of hypertext technology. Biblical literature makes extensive use of symmetrical repetitions of words, grammatical constructions, and ideas to define the kinds of structure that paragraph markings and chapter headings provide in modern literature (Parunak 1981b). To discover and analyze such structures, scholars commonly photocopy the passage, cut it into pieces with scissors, and try to arrange the pieces to bring similar sections close to one another for comparison. While the resulting displays are extremely useful, the mechanical manipulations needed to produce them are tedious and clumsy. SymEdit permits an analyst to arrange a text in columns (corresponding to parallel passages) and rows (which contain repeated features). Rows can be labeled to identify the features that they isolate. Individual rows and columns can be collapsed or expanded to bring other material closer together for comparison. The exhibit shows the beginning of four panels in Deuteronomy 12, each of which follows the same structure in legislating worship at a central sanctuary. By expanding the one-dimensional structure of the printed text into two dimensions, SymEdit helps the scholar to identify and analyze repetitive structures. SymEdit is also useful in forming critical comparisons and in studying parallel narrative accounts.

While hypertext has existed for years in the form of encyclopedias, computer technology makes it more compact, easier to use, and more versatile. The volume of information contained in an entire 20-volume encyclopedia can be stored in electronic form on an optical disk less than six inches in diameter and an eighth of an inch thick. A computerized hypertext system can jump quickly from one item to another on such a disk with the touch of a key, without the need for the user to turn pages or change volumes. Because the disk can store sound and graphic images as well as text, such a system can provide full hypermedia.

For example, the CD-Word system currently under development at Dallas Theological Seminary will permit a user who is reading a biblical text in electronic form to call up various translations of a verse, to jump to a lexicon entry for any word in the text, or to access selected commentaries, grammars, and encyclopedias on a passage

12:4 Ye shall not do so unto the LORD your God.	12:8 Ye shall not do after all the things that we do here this day, every man whatsoever is right in his own eyes.	12:13 Take heed to thyself that thou offer not thy burnt offerings in every place that thou seest:	12:17 Thou mayest not eat within thy gates
12:5 But unto the place which the LORD your God shall choose	12:11 Then there shall be a place which the LORD your God shall choose	12:14 But in the place which the LORD shall choose	12:18 (But thou must eat them before the LORD thy God) in the place which the LORD thy God shall choose,
out of all your tribes		in one of thy tribes,	
to put his name there,	to cause his name to dwell there;		
even unto his habitation shall ye seek, and thither thou shalt come:			
12:6 And thither ye shall bring	thither shall ye bring all that I command you;		
your burnt offerings,	your burnt offerings,	there thou shalt offer thy burnt offerings,	
and your sacrifices,	and your sacrifices,		
and your tithes,	your tithes,		the tithe of thy corn, or of thy wine, or of thy oil, or the firstlings of thy herds or of thy flock, nor any of thy vows which thou vowest, nor thy freewill offerings,
and heave offerings of your hand,	and the heave offering of your hand,		or heave offering of thine hand:

COM.07. Illustration of SymEdit on Deuteronomy 12.

under consideration. The objective is to provide in a single computer system an environment comparable to that provided by a shelf of books and a desk in the conventional study. The CELLAR system, a design of the Summer Institute of Linguistics, will enable a linguist to sort field notes, organize lexical studies, and compare multiple translations while preparing a new rendering of a biblical text. Some designs permit users to add their personal annotations to the network of information, just as we now write notes in the margins of paper texts.

At first, such systems will be stand-alone electronic libraries, but the ultimate vision of hypermedia (Nelson 1987) couples the notion of linked information units with computer networking to anticipate a world in which the global resource of human knowledge is accessible from any computer.

Bibliography

Alter, R. 1985. *The Art of Biblical Poetry.* New York.

Andersen, F. I. 1976. Style and Authorship. *The Tyndale Paper* 21:2.

Baird, J. A., and Freedman, D. N., eds. 1971– . The Computer Bible. Wooster, OH.

Beekman, J., and Callow, J. 1974. *Translating the Word of God.* Grand Rapids.

Brachman, R. J., and Levesque, H. J. 1985. *Readings in Knowledge Representation.* Palo Alto.

Cleveland, W. S. 1985. *The Elements of Graphing Data.* Monterey.

Collins, T. 1978. *Line-Forms in Hebrew Poetry.* Studia Pohl: Series Maior 7. Rome.

Cook, W. A. 1979. *Case Grammar: Development of the Matrix Model (1970–1978).* Washington.

Fillmore, C. J. 1968. The Case for Case. In *Universals in Linguistic Theory,* ed. E. Bach and R. Harms. Englewood Cliffs, NJ.

Friberg, T., and Friberg, B. 1981. A Computer-Assisted Analysis of the Greek New Testament Text. In Patton and Holoien 1981.

Geller, S. A. 1979. *Parallelism in Early Biblical Poetry.* HSM 20. Missoula.

Grimes, J. E. 1975. *The Thread of Discourse.* The Hague.

Hockey, S. M. 1980. *A Guide to Computer Applications in the Humanities.* Baltimore.

Hopcroft, J. E., and Ullman, J. D. 1979. *Introduction to Automata Theory, Languages, and Computation.* Reading, PA.

Hughes, J. J. 1987. *Bits, Bytes, and Biblical Studies.* Grand Rapids.

Longacre, R. E. 1976. *An Anatomy of Speech Notions.* Lisse, Netherlands.

Mann, W. C., and Thompson, S. A. 1987. Rhetorical Structure Theory: A Theory of Text Organization. In *The Structure of Discourse,* ed. L. Polanyi. Norwood, NJ.

Miller, P. A. 1984. *GRAMCORD Reference Manual.* Deerfield, MI.

Morris, P. M. K., and James, E. 1975. *A Critical Word Book of Leviticus, Numbers, Deuteronomy.* Computer Bible 8. Wooster, OH.

Morton, A. Q. 1978. *Literary Detection: How to Prove Authorship and Fraud in Literature and Documents.* New York.

Morton, A. Q.; Michaelson, S.; and Thompson, J. D. 1979. *A Critical Concordance to I and II Corinthians.* Computer Bible 19. Wooster, OH.

Mosteller, F., and Rourke, R. E. K. 1973. *Sturdy Statistics.* Reading, PA.

Mosteller, F.; Rourke, R. E. K.; and Thomas, G. B., Jr. 1961. *Probability and Statistics.* Reading, PA.

Mosteller, F., and Tukey, J. W. 1977. *Data Analysis and Regression.* Reading, PA.

Mosteller, F., and Wallace, D. L. 1964. *Inference and Disputed Authorship.* Reading, PA.

Nelson, T. 1987. *Literary Machines.* San Antonio.

O'Connor, M. 1980. *Hebrew Verse Structure.* Winona Lake, IN.

Parunak, H. V. D. 1979. *Structural Studies in Ezekiel.* Ph.D. Diss., U. of Michigan.

———. 1981a. Oral Typesetting: Some Uses of Biblical Structure. *Bib* 62: 2, 153–68.

———. 1981b. Prolegomena to Pictorial Concordances. *Computers and the Humanities* 15: 15–36.

———. 1983. Transitional Techniques in the Bible. *JBL* 102: 525–48.

———. 1989a. Interrogating a Dead Language. In Parunak 1989b.

Parunak, H. V. D., ed. 1989b. *Computer Tools for Ancient Texts.* Winona Lake, IN.

Patton, P. C., and Holoien, R. A. 1981. *Computing in the Humanities.* Lexington, KY.

Radday, Y. T. 1973a. *A Critical Concordance of Haggai, Zechariah, Malachi.* Computer Bible 4. Wooster, OH.

———. 1973b. *The Unity of Isaiah in the Light of Statistical Linguistics.* Hildesheim.

Radday, Y. T., and Shore, H. 1985. *Genesis: An Authorship Study.* Rome.

Tufte, E. R. 1983. *The Visual Display of Quantitative Information.* Cheshire.

Tukey, J. W. 1977. *Exploratory Data Analysis.* Reading, PA.

H. Van Dyke Parunak

CONANIAH (PERSON) [Heb *kônanyāhû*]. Var. JECONIAH. The name of three men mentioned in 2 Chronicles. It means "Yahweh establishes or strengthens."

1. A Levite during the reign of Hezekiah who was given charge over the contributions, tithes, and other gifts given to the newly rededicated temple (2 Chr 31:12–13). His brother, Shimei, was appointed as his immediate deputy along with 10 assistants. One of them was Benaiah, who appears in 2 Chr 35:9 as a LXX variant reading but is absent from the MT. The Masoretic marginal note (the *kĕtîb-qĕrê*) records an orthographic variant spelling omitting a *waw,* which indicates a scribal change from the *polal* ("Yahweh is strengthened") to the *qal* ("Yahweh strengthened") stem of the verbal root *kwn* (*HALAT,* 444). This could be for theological reasons (Yahweh could hardly need to be strengthened or made righteous) or the change could be a dialectical difference in the pronunciation between the two vowels *ā* and *ô* or a historical difference (early vs. a modernized pronunciation).

2. A second person of that name with the same *kĕtîb-qĕrê* mentioned above lived during the time of Josiah, king of Judah (2 Chr 35:9). He was a leader of the Levites, along with his two brothers (or colleagues) and three others mentioned in the text. They contributed 5000 lambs and 500 head of cattle for the Levites' use during the first celebration of the Passover in Josiah's reign. In the parallel account in 1 Esdr 1:9, Jeconiah occurs as an alternate form of this name.

3. An official and judge from the levitical family of Izhar appointed during the time of David (1 Chr 26:29). His administrative duties along with his sons specifically had to do with matters outside of the temple area in the nation at large (*Chronicles* ICC, 288). His name is also spelled with a *šĕwâ* in the first syllable with the LXX and Vg apparently reading an original long *ā* instead.

KIRK E. LOWERY

CONCEPT OF OUR GREAT POWER, THE

(NHC VI,*4*). *The Concept of Our Great Power* (NHC VI,*4*) is the fourth tractate of codex VI (pp. 36–48) of the Nag Hammadi codices. This sole witness to the text is well preserved except for minor lacunae at the tops of most pages (Parrott 1979: 6). A Coptic translation from a Greek original, the text is written in the Sahidic dialect with minor Subachmimic and Achmimic influences (Krause and Labib 1971: 48–52, 63). See also LANGUAGES (COPTIC).

Great Pow. preserves an apocalyptic presentation of salvation history (Wisse and Williams 1979: 291). In this history, ultimate salvation belongs to those who know "our Great Power," the supreme being discussed in the text. Their names will be inscribed in the great light, and they will survive the final purification by fire, which will consume the flesh and everything that burns (matter).

Great Pow. incorporates themes from Genesis, the Jesus traditions, and apocalypticism in a triadic periodization of history. The three periods, which are presented in the text in two versions, include the aeon of the flesh (antediluvian period), the psychic aeon (the postdiluvian period), and the aeon that is to come. The creation of the universe began the aeon of the flesh. This aeon, during which the soul was created, drew to a close with the call of Noah and the flood. The presentation of the psychic aeon, which then ensues, includes the origin of evil, the appearance of the Savior (Jesus), his descent into Hades to humiliate the archons, the rise of an imitator or antichrist, and the final consumption by fire. This consumption will usher in the aeon to come, which is the unchangeable aeon. Matter and flesh will be consumed by the fire and the pure souls (pneumatic) will be joined by the souls that have undergone punishment and become pure (psychic).

The text has been styled as a Christian gnostic apocalypse (Wisse and Williams 1979: 292). While no distinct gnostic cosmogony is outlined, themes and imagery abound which fit into a gnostic world view. The god of Genesis, for example, is called the "father of the flesh" (38,19).

The clarity of the account is clouded by grammatical and logical inconsistencies, the source of which can be traced to the complex literary history of the text (Wisse and Williams 1979: 291–92) and the Coptic translator's failure to fully understand the Gk *Vorlage* (Fischer 1973: 169). The use of the term *anomoean* (40,7; literally meaning "dissimilar things"), if understood as a reference to the Anomoean heresy, offers a *terminus a quo* after the middle of the 4th century. The reference, however, may be a later interpolation (Wisse and Williams 1979: 292, 304). Linguistic analysis has suggested an earlier date for the original text (Cherix 1982: 6, 62).

Great Pow. offers a valuable example of the syncretistic use of Jewish, Greek, and Christian elements in the formation of a periodizing apocalyptic salvation history. It illustrates the far-ranging influence of apocalyptic ideas in the early Christian era and their compatibility with gnostic beliefs in certain circles. The complex literary history of this text, if properly understood, could offer valuable insights into the development of apocalyptic ideas in Jewish, Christian, and gnostic circles.

Bibliography

Cherix, P. 1982. *Le Concept de notre Grande Puissance (CG VI,4)*. OBO 47. Fribourg.

Fischer, K. M. 1973. Der Gedanke unserer grossen Kraft (Noema); Die vierte Schrift aus Nag-Hammadi-Codex VI. *TLZ* 98: 169–76.

Krause, M., and Labib, P. 1971. *Gnostische und hermetische Schriften aus Codex II und Codex VI.* Abhandlungen des Deutschen Archäologischen Instituts Kairo, Koptische Reihe 2. Glückstadt.

Parrott, D. M. 1979. *Nag Hammadi Codices V,2–5 and VI with Papyrus Berolinensis 8502, 1 and 4.* NHS 11. Leiden.

Williams, F. E.; Wisse, F.; and Parrott, D. M. 1977. The Concept of Our Great Power (VI,4). *NHL,* 284–89.

Wisse, F., and Williams, F. E. 1979. The Concept of Our Great Power VI,4: 36,1–48, 15. Pp. 291–323 in *Nag Hammadi Codices V,2–5 and VI with Papyrus Berolinensis 8502, 1 and 4,* ed. D. M. Parrott. NHS 11. Leiden.

JAMES E. GOEHRING

CONEY. See ZOOLOGY.

CONFLATE READINGS IN THE OT.

Conflation is the combination of readings from different texts or parts of a text. More specifically, conflate or double readings in a ms combine two or more variants from two or more mss. These alternative readings can be found in the Hebrew ms tradition (MT, Dead Sea Scrolls, medieval mss), and/or in the ancient versions of the OT, as well as in biblical quotations in Apocrypha, NT, patristic, and rabbinic literature. Conflation by copyists of doubly transmitted texts in related to conflation as a redaction technique, by which two or more variant accounts of the same subject were synthesized by an editor or redactor. There are numerous examples in the Samaritan Pentateuch (e.g., the theophany at Mt. Sinai, Exodus 20), in biblical mss from Qumran (the Sabbath Command, 4QDeut^{n} 5:12–15), in the ancient versions (the two LXX accounts of the rise of Jeroboam in 1 Kgs 11:26–12:24 and 12:24a–z), or in other extrabiblical literature (*Jubilees* and the *Temple Scroll*).

Double readings may have developed early in the composition and transmission process of biblical books. They may witness to different oral or written traditions or to elements introduced in the process of composition or redaction of a biblical book. Conflate readings reflect the textual pluralism that characterizes the history of the biblical text before its standardization around the end of the 1st century A.D. They prove that copyists had great respect for every existing variant reading transmitted in the mss.

This phenomenon is frequent in parallel texts (2 Kgs 18:13–19:37 and Isaiah 36–37, or 2 Kgs 24:18–25:21 and Jeremiah 52), in different versions of a given text (2 Samuel 22 and Psalm 18 contain conflate readings), and it is common in the parallel books of Samuel-Kings and Chronicles. Conflate readings occur mostly in later texts that combine variants of earlier texts or multiple mss: in Isa 37:9, 1QIsa[a] *wyšmʿ wyšwb* and LXX *kai akousas apestrepse* combine MT *wyšmʿ* ("he heard it") and 2 Kgs 19:9 *wyšb* ("again").

Double readings are discovered by comparing two or more witnesses of a same text. They are best observed when each item is preserved independently in different textual witnesses: in 2 Sam 22:43, the MT combines two variants *ʾdqm ʾrqʿm* ("I crushed them, I mashed them"). The LXX[B] text preserves only the first reading and 4QSam[a] the second. Another characteristic is that one of the two items is sometimes ignored in a part of the textual tradition, because it is a secondary development dependent on the older item: in Ezek 1:20 the MT adds *šm hrwḥ llkt . . . šmh hrwḥ llkt,* repeating the phrase "wherever the spirit wanted to go." Some Heb manuscripts, LXX, and Syriac do not contain the second phrase.

A. Classification

Conflate readings can be classified according to different criteria, such as their sources, the extent of the duplication, their location in the sentence, their content, and the particular text-critical phenomenon involved. A comprehensive presentation of these different types of conflate readings follows:

(1) Variant spellings. 1QIsa[a] (1,1) has the Masoretic reading *bymy,* "in the days of," miscorrected toward the Aramaic morphology by superscribing a *waw* above the first *yod* (Talmon 1964: 78). In 1 Sam 10:19 the Targum reading *lw lʾ* ("to him: 'No!' ") combines the MT *lw* and *lʾ*, the equivalent of LXX *ouchi.*

(2) Different vocalizations. Two possible vocalizations of the same Heb consonantal text may generate two readings. In 1 Sam 11:5 and Gk Lucianic *prōi katopisthen tōn boōn* ("early, behind the oxen"), followed by the OL *(mane—post boves),* interprets *hbqr* as both Heb *habbōqer* ("the morning") and Heb *habbāqār* ("the oxen").

(3) Variants in the consonantal text. 1 Sam 10:27 *kmḥryš* ("like someone who keeps silent") is a corruption of *kmw ḥdš* ("about a month"). This reconstruction is attested by 4QSam[a] and suggested by LXX *hōs meta mēna,* which equals Heb *kmḥdš* (see F. M. Cross 1980; McCarter *1 Samuel* AB, 199–200; for a different opinion Barthélemy 1982), however, the Gk Lucianic conflates both readings, *kai egenēthē hos kōpheuon kai egeneto meta mēna hēmerōn,* "and he was like someone who keeps silent and a month later . . ."

(4) Syntactical alternatives. The MT of 1 Sam 23:20 makes a syntactic break after *rd* (*lrdt rd wlnw,* "to come down, come down! And it will be our task . . ."), while the OG agrees with the Heb reading of 4QSam[b] in making no break there (*lrdt yrd ʿlynw,* "to come down, let him come down to us"), and the Syr essays a conflation of both readings. McCarter (*1 Samuel* AB, 377) and Barthélemy (1982) come to opposite conclusions about the "original text" of this verse.

(5) Scribal errors. The OG translation of Judg 1:15, "and Caleb (Heb *klb*) gave her according to her heart (Heb *klbh*)" may have resulted from an accidental dittography in the tradition represented by the OG. The opposite occurrence, haplography, is also possible in the MT. In 2 Sam 19:8, LXX[B] combines MT *wrʿh* ("and will be worse") with the erroneous LXX reading *wdʿh* ("and know").

(6) Juxtaposed synonymous expressions. One expression is sometimes supplemented by another which has the same or a similar meaning and which is probably intended somehow to explain the first. In Isa 51:17 and 22 the *hapax legomenon qbʿt* ("bowl") is followed by *kws* ("cup"), which is omitted in the LXX and the Syriac and is generally agreed to be an explicative gloss (Elliger 1974: 131). Such conflation of synonymous pairs is frequent in the longer text form of the book of Jeremiah transmitted by the MT and is missing in the shorter text form reflected by the LXX. MT of Jer 1:15 adds the first item of the pair *lkl mspḥwt mmlkwt* ("all the clans of the kingdoms"), which is lacking in the LXX *egō sugkalō pasas tas basileias* ("all the kingdoms"); the second item of the pair *qṭr—ʿbd* is added in MT Jer 44:3, *llkt lqṭr lʿbd lʾlhym ʾḥrym* ("to go to burn incense, to serve other gods"), the LXX attesting the shorter reading, *poreuthentes thumiąn theois heterois* (". . . to burn incense to other gods"). Also the conflation of juxtaposed pronominal and nominal variants is frequent in Jeremiah. Personal names are extensively filled out in the MT as in Jer 41:3 *ʾtw ʾt gdlyhw* ("with him with Gedaliah"); OG omits the nominal variant. Occurrences of expressions containing a common and an uncommon word are a particular type of juxtaposition: in Isa 11:6 the older Gk reading *boskethesontai* reflects an uncommon Heb verb, probably *ymrʾw,* "shall grow up" (1QIsa[a] *ymrw*); the alternative reading in the same verse *kai tauros* translates a more common noun *wmryʾ*, "the fatling" (MT 4QIsa[c]).

(7) Attraction of an associated text. In Gen 17:14, "if the flesh of his foreskin has not been cut away," the SamPent and LXX *tę̄ emerą tē ogdoę̄* add *bywm hšmyny,* "on the eighth day," from Lev 12:3 to specify the day of the circumcision.

(8) Assimilation of parallels. In 2 Sam 3:23 the Syr combines MT *hmlk* ("the king") and 4QSam[a] (LXX *dauid*) *dwd,* "David." The reading "David" may be an assimilation to 20:21 (Barthélemy 1982) or, on the contrary, MT may have substituted "the king" in anticipation of v 24 (Ulrich 1978; McCarter *2 Samuel* AB, 109).

(9) Variant locations. Jer 6:13–15 is repeated in 8:10–12, but the OG omits the latter verses.

(10) Exegetical development. The Gk Lucianic in Ezra 6:4 and the A text in 6:24 *kainon enos,* "new one," combine the MT reading *ḥdt* (Aramaic equivalent of *ḥdš*, "new") and the OG *hd* ("one"), which seems to be an exegetical development.

The components of a double reading may be placed side by side, connected with the copulative *w-*, or could form a single syntactical whole. 1QIsa[a], *ʿd ykyn wʿd ykwnn,* "until he establishes and sets up," preserves two variants connected with *w-*, of which MT knows only the first. The MT of 2 Sam 22:38–39, *ʿd klwtm wʾklm,* embraces two readings which grammatically adjust the text: *ʿd klwtm,* "until finishing them," and *ʿd (ʾšr) ʾklm,* "until I finished them." One of the alternative readings may also be placed outside the syntactical context at the end of the sentence. Conflate readings could also enter into the text from marginal or interlinear notations. In Isa 21:17 1QIsa[a] has *gbwry qdr,* "heroes of Kedar," but the word *bny* has been inserted above the line, bringing the shorter reading in line with the conflate MT *gbwry bny qdr,* "the heroes of the sons of Kedar" (Talmon 1964: 119).

The purpose of textual criticism is to establish a critical text by ridding it of all conflation. This is true for the LXX translation and for nonbiblical classical literature. But as far as the Hebrew biblical text is concerned, this is by its very nature a "variant text." Its formative period extended in some books for many centuries and continued even when the textual transmission had already begun. The variant interpretations to which the text was subjected have also left their traces in the text. Therefore the task of editors and critics is not to reduce the plurality and diversity of variants and doublets but to take account of all of them and to try to explain their origin and meaning. Particularly in cases of pairs of synonymous readings, which combine expressions used alternatively in a given context (*ʾdm-ʾys,* "man"; *ntn—śym,* "to give, to put"), neither term can be said to claim textual primacy. Textual and stylistic aspects are here intimately connected (Talmon 1975: 344–57). Conflate readings help the critic in examining phenomena that may have occurred at three different levels in the history of the text. It is not always possible to decide to which of these three levels a given phenomenon is to be assigned.

B. Conflation in the Hebrew Text

Conflation may arise at three different phases in the history of a text. The first is the process of literary formation. At times conflate readings derive from parallel traditions. By inserting the words *wyʿl ʾbytr,* "and Abiathar came up," in 2 Sam 15:24 the redactor blended two traditions which attributed the honor of carrying the ark to different priests, Zadok or Abiathar (Talmon 1960: 189); an editor may also have attempted to remove the reference to Abiathar from the context (Wellhausen 1899: 197).

A second phase at which conflation may arise is the editorial process. The readings of 1 Sam 18:6 *bbwʾm,* "When they came," and *bšwb dwd,* "When David returned," are editorial insertions ignored in the LXX. Their purpose is to connect the following section with two preceding episodes: (1) women came out to meet King Saul on David's return after slaying Goliath the Philistine (17:54); (2) women came out at the approach of Saul and David after their meeting at court (17:55–18:5, omitted in the OG).

The third phase is that of textual transmission. In 2 Sam 13:39, the Targum *npsʾ ddwyd mlkʾ,* "the spirit of David the king," and Gk mss *to pneuma tou basileōs Daueid* combine the OG *to pneuma tou basileōs,* "the king's enthusiasm," which is confirmed by 4QSam[a] *rûaḥ hmlk,* "the spirit of the king," and MT *dwd hmlk,* "David the king." The MT reading is a secondary development, because the verb agrees with *rûaḥ* (feminine), not with the name "David." Different types of textual changes may occur. In 2 Sam 18:3 the Targum *ʾry kʿn ʾt . . . wkʿn,* "for you . . . and now," combines the MT and OG reading *ky ʿth = hoti kai nun* ("for now") and a proto-Masoretic reading *kyʾth* ("but you"), which is reflected by LXX[B] *hoti su* and seems more suitable to the context. Many texts have additions. The Vg of Jer 28:8 reads *et de adflictione et de fame,* which conflates MT *wlrʿh,* "and affliction," and *wlrʿb,* "and famine," supported by many Heb mss. This variant is due to the influence of the following *wldbr,* "and pestilence," which adapts *rʿh* to the usual pair *rʿb* and *dbr;* both words *(wlrʿh wldbr)* were successively added to an older and shorter text reflected by the OG. Enclosed glosses creep into texts, too. The conflate variants in 1 Sam 2:31b *mhywt zqn bbytk* ("so that there will not be an old man in your father's house") and 32b *wlʾ yhyh zqn bbytk* ("and there will not be an old man in your house") form a resumptive repetition that encloses the gloss of v 32a, omitted by LXX.

C. Conflation in the Versions

The conflate readings present in the versions can have arisen in the Hebrew original/s (Vorlage), in the translation process, or along the textual transmission of the version. It is not always possible to establish a clear distinction between these different levels.

Double readings occur in the Hebrew original(s). A translator or a later reviser may have interwoven two renderings drawn from different MT variants. In 2 Chr 23:14, LXX *kai exēlthen . . . kai eneteilato* conflates MT *wywṣʾ,* "brought out," and 2 Kgs 11:15 *wyṣw,* "gave orders to," which is the older reading. One part of the translation may be based on the MT, while another item may translate a divergent non-Masoretic original. For example, in 2 Sam 18:14, OG *dia touto arxomai* (Heb *lākēn ʾaḥălla,* "therefore I shall begin") was supplemented by the proto-Theodotionic reviser with a more literal rendition of the MT *loʾ kēn ʾōḥîlâ = ouch houtōs menō,* "Not thus shall I tarry." A particular type of conflation is that produced because of different interpretations of the Hebrew Vorlage: the LXX of 2 Sam 21:22 *tōn giganton en geth tō rapha oikos,* "of the giants in Gath, to Rapha a house," combines two variants *bgt,* "in Gath," and *byt,* "house," by confusing *g* and *y.*

Double translation is also used as a translation technique. Two alternate renderings or independent equivalents in the target language represent a single parallel item in the parent text. This type of change is to be distinguished from exegetical amplifications or glosses. In Exod 3:8 the verb *lh ʿlwtw mn . . . ʾl,* "to bring them up out . . . into . . . ," is translated in the Greek with two verbs *exagagein* and *eisagagein* in order to express the two aspects provided by the Hebrew verb.

The same Hebrew word may be rendered by two equivalents with the same meaning. These equivalents may be: (1) synonymous readings, as in Exod 22:16 where the verb *mʾn ymʾn,* "he absolutely refuses," is rendered by two equally appropriate verbs *ananeuōn ananeusē kai mē boulētai,* "he absolutely refuses and does not want"; (2) a rendering in good Greek alongside a literal one: In 2 Kings the OG translates the Heb *yhwh ṣbʾwt,* "Lord of the hosts," by *kyrios pantokratōr,* "Lord Almighty" (attested by the Gk Lucianic in 2 Kgs 19:15; 20:16), corrected by the proto-Theodotionic reviser to *kyrios tōn dynameōn,* "Lord of the hosts" (2 Kgs 3:14; 19:31); (3) a regular translation accompanied by a transliteration, 1 Sam 24:23 MT *hmṣwdh,* "the stronghold," is rendered *tēn Messara stenēn;* or (4) it is replaced by a transliteration, 2 Kgs 25:13, 16 *mknwt,* "the trolleys," is rendered by the OG *baseis,* corrected to *mechonoth* in the proto-Theodotionic recension.

This kind of conflation can sometimes be interpreted in different ways, either as preserving an original longer reading or as the result of an inserted gloss. In 1 Sam 16:20, MT *ḥâmôr,* "ass," appears transliterated in LXX as *gomor,* reflecting the vocalization *ḥōmer.* The Gk Lucianic *kai elaben Iessai onon kai apetheken auto gomor artōn,* "Jesse took an ass and ladened it with an omer of bread," and the similar OL *et accepit lesse asinum et imposuit super gomor panis* may preserve here an original longer reading *ḥmwr wyśm ʿlyw ʿmr lḥm* (McCarter, *1 Samuel* AB, 280), or may combine the LXX reading, "took an omer of bread," and a glossed reading attested by the Syr, "took an ass and ladened it with bread" (Barthélemy 1982).

The same Hebrew word is sometimes translated by two equivalents with two different meanings, either for semantic considerations, as in Dan 2:11 *yqyrh* = *barys esti kai epidoxos* ("heavy" and "esteemed"), or because of different etymological derivations, as in Prov 6:3 *rʿk* = *kakōn dia son philon* ("the evil through your fellow"), where *rʿk* is derived from *rʿʿ*, "evil," and *rʿh,* "fellow," or according to two different traditions of translation, as in Isa 41:7 *pʿm* = "hammer" and "at the right time," where the Targum has *bqrnsʾ zmnʾ*, "with the mallet, then," and LXX *sphurē . . . pote,* "hammer . . . then" (Elliger 1974: 134).

A translator who is careful to render his Vorlage as literally as possible is not expected to have recourse to double readings. On the contrary, a free or nonliteral translation like the LXX of Isaiah, which borders on the Midrashic, may be suspected of using such a technique.

Double readings arise in the transmission process of the versions. A copyist or reviser may have interwoven two renderings drawn from different sources. This conflation is characteristic of the Gk recensions, particularly of the Lucianic. In elucidating the priority of one or another of the two renderings, Lagarde's criterion is applied: the free translation is generally older than the literal one. Similarly, the item that translates a divergent Hebrew Vorlage is generally to be preferred to the item based on the MT. This is in accord with a tendency present in the later LXX books to produce a more literal rendition and with a similar tendency of the Gk recensions to bring the original text in line with the increasingly authoritative Hebrew text which served as the base for the Vorlage.

The components of a double translation are usually located next to each other and connected with a copula *(kai).* Sometimes they appear unconnected, as in 1 Kgs 3:25 *hyld,* "the child," = *to paidarion to thēlazon,* "the child the sucking baby." They may also be interwoven with one another, creating a genitive relation between them, as in Josh 9:22, the MT *bqrbnw yšbym* = *egchōrioi (este) tōn katoikountōn en ēmin,* "the inhabitants of the country, who live among us."

Bibliography

Barthélemy, D. 1982. *Josué, Juges, Ruth, Samuel, Rois, Chroniques, Esdras, Néhémie, Esther,* Vol. 1 of *Critique textuelle de l'Ancien Testament,* OBO 50.1. Fribourg.

———. 1986. Isaï, Jérémie, Lamentations, Vol. 2 of *Critique textuelle de l'Ancien Testament,* OBO 50.2. Fribourg.

Boling, R. G. 1966. Some Conflate Readings in Joshua-Judges. VT 16: 293–98.

Cross, F. M. 1980. The Ammonite Oppression of the Tribes of Gad and Reuben: Missing Verses from 1 Samuel 11 Found in 4QSamuel[a]. Pp. 105–19 in *The Hebrew and Greek Texts of Samuel,* ed. E. Tov. Jerusalem.

Elliger, K. 1974. Dubletten im Bibel Text. Pp. 131–39 in *A Light into My Path,* ed. H. N. Bream; R. D. Heim; and C. A. Moore. Gettysburg Theological Studies 4. Pittsburgh, Philadelphia.

Janzen, J. G. 1973. *Studies in the Text of Jeremiah.* HSM 6. Cambridge, MA.

Rahlfs, A. 1911. *Lucians Rezension der Königsbücher.* Vol. 3 of *Septuaginta-Studien.* Göttingen.

Talmon, S. 1960. Double Readings in the Massoretic Text. *Textus* 1: 144–85.

———. 1964. Aspects of Textual Transmission of the Bible in the Light of Qumran Manuscripts. *Textus* 4: 95–132.

———. 1975. The Textual Study of the Bible—A New Outlook. Pp. 321–400 in *Qumran and the History of the Biblical Text,* ed. F. M. Cross, and S. Talmon. Cambridge, MA.

Talshir, Z. 1987. Double Translations in the Septuaginta. Pp. 21–63, *VI Congress of the IOSCS Jerusalem 1986,* ed. C. Cox. Atlanta.

Tigay, J. H. 1985. Conflation as a Redactional Technique. Pp. 53–96 in *Empirical Models for Biblical Criticism,* ed. J. H. Tigay. Philadelphia.

Ulrich, E. 1978. *The Qumran Text of Samuel and Josephus.* HSM 19. Chico, CA.

Wellhausen, J. 1899. *Die Composition des Haxateuchs und der historischen Bücher des Alten Testaments.* Berlin.

Wevers, J. W. 1946. Double Readings in the Books of Kings. *JBL* 65: 307–10.

JULIO TREBOLLE

CONJURING.
See MAGIC (OT).

CONQUEST OF CANAAN.
See ISRAEL, HISTORY OF.

CONSCIENCE. The idea of a human conscience "has existed over since the final verdict of guilt was spoken within man himself, when the true Furies were recognized as the consciousness of guilt" (Dibelius and Conzelmann *Pastoral Epistles* Hermeneia, 19). According to Gooch (1987), the Church has developed three distinct concepts of conscience (Gk *suneidēsis*) as morality's "inner voice": there is (1) a minimal sense by which the term refers to one's self-consciousness (derived from its earlier cognate for "consciousness," *suneidos*) or private knowledge (from the reflexive for knowing one's own knowledge, *sunoida emautō*); (2) a more robust notion where *suneidēsis* refers to "the pain of recognizing that one has done something wrong or bad" (Gooch 1987: 245; also Pierce 1955); and (3) the more recent and common use of *suneidēsis* as an autonomous agent; the repository of moral convictions, which legislates actions in accord with God's will.

A. Background

The first meaning of *suneidēsis* is also earliest and has its origins in popular Hellenistic usage (Maurer *TDNT* 7: 898–907; Davies *IDB* 1: 671–74). Although not prominently used prior to the 1st century B.C.E. (e.g., *suneidēsis* does not appear in Aristotle's *Ethics*), the term was used to describe in a general way a person's moral self-awareness. The conscience was that part of the inner person which continued to judge human actions—usually wrong (a "bad" conscience; Xen. *Ap.* 24). Such a judgment derives from a rational nature and does not have its direct source in a deity (although one's "nature" may be traced to God). Further, conscience bears witness in an immediate sense to a particular act rather than preparing for it to do right or wrong.

From the 1st century on, *suneidēsis* is used more frequently, especially by the Latin rhetoricians, and was taken up into the language of philosophical ethics, most notably by the Stoics (although see Davies *IDB* 1: 671–76). However, its meaning remained essentially the same: an inherent capacity which allows a person to act in accord to what he or she knows is right. Cicero and then Seneca did speak of a "good" conscience *(conscientia)* as directive toward the happy life—a point also made by Epicurus. While not a central notion in Stoicism, Epictetus speaks of conscience as that faculty which helps to override moral timidity and do what one knows is good (cf. *suneidos, Diss.* 3.22.94).

The term also appears in Hellenistic Judaism, especially with Philo, who uses *suneidēsis/suneidos* in common with the Greco-Roman world. However, Judaism's usage carries a religious nuance and is informed by their Scriptures. Thus, the conscience bears witness to biblical truth and produces pain when Torah is not observed. Maurer further argues that Philo's positive use of the notion is in line with the Wisdom tradition in that the truth to which the conscience bears witness directs, even converts, a person onto the path which leads to *šalom* (911–13).

Philo did, however, appropriate the language of conscience from its secular usage, since the OT (LXX) use of the *sunoida* family is quite sparse. That the OT does not have a word for conscience astonishes some but can readily be understood by the Bible's general resistance to an introspective and autonomous anthropology (cf. Stendahl 1976): truth is revealed by God and the individual is encircled (and so limited) by a community covenanted with God and itself. The RSV does translate the Heb *lēb,* "heart," as "conscience" in 1 Sam 25:31, even though the LXX translation is *estai soi touto bdelugmos,* "it (the abomination) will (not) be upon yourself." (The most one can say is that *estai soi* here is perhaps idiomatic for moral self-consciousness.) Wolff (1974) contends that *lēb* "comes to take on the meaning of 'conscience' . . . [in that] what is being described is the reaction of the ethical judgment formed by the conscience" (51). According to OT anthropology, *lēb* is the center of human self-consciousness devoted to making decisions in accord with the word of God. In this sense, the essence of the OT idea of *lēb* is compatible with the general conception of *suneidēsis* in the Greco-Roman world; and it is this conception which provides the background for the NT idea of conscience to which we now turn.

B. Pauline

The connection between the OT notion of *lēb* and the NT *suneidēsis* is nowhere clearer than in Rom 2:15. For Paul, conscience is a universal human capacity which condemns or recommends one's fitness before God against an internalized Torah. As in Hellenistic Judaism, then, Paul ties conscience to the word of God (i.e., Torah) as self-conscious judge of and witness to the community's observance of it.

As with most theological and ethical convictions he inherited from Judaism, Paul further qualifies conscience by linking it to his own apocalyptical gospel, which is focused here on God's eschatological judgment at Christ's Parousia. Thus, human conscience evokes a sense of imminent and inward (*ta krypta tōn anthrōpōn,* Rom 2:16) recognition, whether one stands under God's wrath because of disobedience (which is presumed the case for those outside of Christ, Rom 1:18) or under God's righteousness because of obedience which comes by faith (Rom 2:5–11; cf.1:5). With the exception of 1 Cor 8:1–11:1, other occurrences of *suneidēsis* in Pauline texts (Rom 13:5; 2 Cor 1:12; 4:2; 5:11) reflect this more typical and only modestly refined use of the idea which was current in the Greco-Roman and Jewish worlds.

The most important and innovative text in its use of *suneidēsis* within the Pauline corpus is 1 Cor 8:1–11:1 (Jewett 1971: 421–32). In this passage, Paul seeks to settle a controversy surrounding the permissibility of eating food once offered to idols. His essential point is that under certain circumstances some believers should refrain from eating such food because of negative consequences to the spiritual nurture of other believers. The conscience's pivotal function is twofold: on the one hand, it detects those who are "weak" because they lack and have need of Pauline *gnōsis* (8:7); while, on the other hand, it guides those who are "strong" because they have such *gnōsis* and who now must use it in ways which edify the whole community—to keep the "weak" from returning to idolatry.

The first two meanings of conscience given by Gooch (1987) are discernible in 1 Cor 8:7–13: the scrupulous conscience of the "weak" is pained by the apparently idolatrous acts of the "strong" (vv 7, 12) because it has been informed by previous experiences of idolatry and so bears witness to a non-Christian morality (v 10)). Conscience, then, marks the consistency of a particular act with a particular standard of morality; and when inconsistency to that standard is perceived, pain is produced. Yet the pain produced in the conscience of the "weak" is really the result of competing conceptions of *gnōsis* which have in turn produced competing consciences between those who live either in accord with Pauline *gnōsis* or with pagan *gnōsis*. Thus, the conscience of the "weak" is not itself weak or faulty; rather, it distorts the truth, turning an innocent act (according to Pauline teaching) into an evil one, because of a misguided standard of truth (or *gnōsis* contrary to Pauline teaching).

Paul has, however, already established his working moral principle in 1 Cor 8:1: conscience must bear witness to *love* of others rather than to self-knowledge since the yield of the latter is arrogance (and naturally division) and of the former is edification (and so unity; 8:6). The truth by which any particular act is apprehended by the *suneidēsis* is relational and communal rather than individual and juridical, and is as much a problem for the theologically "strong" as for the "weak"—which seems to be the point of the ironical 8:10 (Jewett 1971: 422–23). Here, then, Paul redefines the current notion of *suneidēsis* by regarding its role as supervising one's relationship with others rather than to a particular *gnōsis*.

Thus, in 1 Cor 9:1–10:22 Paul turns to a discussion of those limits to personal freedom which make this new standard of truth clearer to his readers. Paul contends that even as he and other Christian missionaries adjust their behavior and assessment of personal rights to meet the redemptive needs of others, so also certain Corinthian believers must adjust their behavior, even giving up their rights to certain foods, to keep other believers from going back into idolatry. *The new role of conscience is to regulate this sort of moral accommodation which purposes to edify other people*—to know when and how long to abstain from those "lawful" acts which might, however, "cause a co-believer to stumble."

Paul resumes his discussion of *suneidēsis* at 1 Cor 10:23 and adds yet another meaning to the notion. Especially the use of *krinō* with the individual's *suneidēsis* in 10:29, following the succession of the formulaic *dia tēn suneidēsin* (10:25, 27, 28), suggests an element of autonomy which can help determine obedient acts ahead of time (however, see Gooch 1987: 251–52). The believer's conscience, now armed by the principle of love and delimited by the demand to preserve the commitment of those prone to idolatry, makes "judgments" whether certain behaviors will bring glory to God (10:31) by saving the many (10:33) in agreement with the apostle's gentile mission (11:1). The idea of conscience as an internal and autonomous moral agent, fully developed during the Church's medieval period, has its biblical mooring here.

The early catholicizing tendency of the post-Pauline situation is reflected by the use of *suneidēsis* in the Pastoral Epistles (1 Tim 1:5, 19; 3:9; 4:2; 2 Tim 1:3; Titus 1:15; cf. Acts 23:1; 24:16). The author's concerns are more institutional and less apocalyptical than found in earlier Pauline writings. Thus, the special attributes of the conscience are those found in the "man of God" who is a "good citizen" and best able to rule over the Church of *this* world (1 Tim 1:19; 3:9; cf. Acts 23:1; 24:16; Dibelius and Conzelmann *Pastoral Epistles* Hermeneia, 20). Further, the "good" conscience is shaped by the Church's traditions of the historical Paul (2 Tim 1:3), who is chief exemplar of Christian conduct and teacher of truth; only that conscience which bears witness to apostolic piety and teaching is able to distinguish adequately between orthodoxy and heterodoxy, orthopraxis and heteropraxis (1 Tim 4:2; Titus 1:15). As such, the "good" conscience of the Church's leadership is an element of ecclesiastical *hugiēs* (esp. Titus 1:13–16), "soundness," and is therefore an essential ingredient in maintaining loyalty to "the faith" and its codes and creeds not only in a pluralistic world but also within a Church where the authority of Paul is being challenged. In this context, then, the institutional function of conscience provides for doctrinal as well as moral discernment and stability for the whole Church rather than only for its individual leader.

C. Non-Pauline

The concept of conscience in the Pauline corpus is essentially concerned with human relations. This also seems true of 1 Pet 2:19 and 3:16, where *suneidēsis,* bound to God's will, evaluates behavior toward outsiders. More than Paul, however, the author is concerned with the particular difficulties of living as the Church within an antagonistic (and not simply pluralistic) society; suffering is a real possibility if not already a reality. Conscience, then, is the consciousness of a certain moral particularity which belongs to a divinely elect community of "aliens and strangers" (1 Pet 1:1–2; 2:9–11) and whose common life resists certain sociopolitical standards of behavior; it is an awareness of one's own deviance with the likely result of suffering. Christian baptism inaugurates a manner of life during which the "cleansed conscience" (3:21) seeks to maintain an undivided and difficult loyalty toward God in a world where Christian conduct only marginalizes the people of God. The hope, of course, is that his path of suffering will save the baptized soul (1:3–9; 2:21–25).

The author of Hebrews assumes the essential meaning of *suneidēsis* in the Hellenistic world: the conscience "is the internal faculty within man that causes him to be painfully aware of his sinfulness and, as a result, to experience a sense of guilt" (Selby 1986: 148). However, unlike Paul, who is primarily interested in human relations, the author of Hebrews depicts a guilty conscience as the "one real barrier to an individual's approaching and living in fellowship with *God.* The guilty conscience is thus the impediment to real confidence and stability for the Christian" (ibid).

References to the conscience in Hebrews are gathered together in 9:9, 14 and 10:2, 22, and so at the focal point of the author's exposition on the new covenant. What is "new" in the relationship between God and eschatological Israel is that the work of the priestly Christ has purified Israel's conscience and has made it possible to "draw near" to God (10:22) with inner confidence (10:2; cf.4:16) and to worship God forever (9:11–14). The author's prophetic interest in internal and spiritual transformation (against Judaism's perceived interest in cultic ritual and legal rights) only intensifies the importance of a purified conscience. Judaism's priestly theocracy does not provide a lasting means of ridding Israel's guilt and making easy access to God. Because the priestly Christ offered himself up to God as a "perfect" sacrifice (Heb 7:11–8:13; 10:5–18), the conscience has been cleansed of these legalistic "works which lead to death" (9:1–10; 10:2); indeed, it is the conscience which has now been redeemed in fulfillment of Jeremiah's promise of a new covenant (cf. 8:10).

Bibliography

Gooch, P. W. 1987. "Conscience" in 1 Corinthians 8 and 10. *NTS* 33: 244–54.

Jewett, R. 1971. *Paul's Anthropological Terms.* AGJU 10. Leiden.

Pierce, C. A. 1955. *Conscience in the New Testament.* SBT 15. London.

Selby, G. S. 1986. The Meaning and Function of *Suneidēsis* in Hebrews 9 and 10. *RQ* 28: 145–54.

Stendahl, K. 1976. *Paul Among Jews and Gentiles.* Philadelphia.

Wolff, H. W. 1974. *Anthropology of the Old Testament.* Philadelphia.

Robert W. Wall

CONSTELLATIONS. See ASTROLOGY IN THE ANCIENT NEAR EAST.

CONSTITUTION. See LAW (IN JUDAISM OF THE NT PERIOD).

CONSTITUTIONS AND CANONS, APOSTOLIC.

See APOSTOLIC CONSTITUTIONS AND CANONS.

CONTRIBUTION FOR THE SAINTS.

A project headed by Paul whereby funds from his gentile churches were collected for the poor among the believers in Jerusalem (the recipients are variously named as "the saints," "the poor among the saints," and "the poor").

A. The Contribution in the Letters of Paul

There are references to this project in four of Paul's letters (Romans, 1 and 2 Corinthians, and Galatians). It is generally thought that at least the references in 1 and 2 Corinthians and in Romans refer to different stages of one great project (Hurd 1965: 205, n. 1).

In Rom 15:25–32 Paul speaks about the final stage of the collection as he is on his way to deliver it to Jerusalem (15:26). If the significance of the collection was as a symbol of the unity of the Church (Knox 1950: 54) it may be that Paul's worry over the acceptability of the collection (Rom 15:31) is a concern over whether the Jerusalem church might consider that he had failed to provide such a symbol. The churches of Galatia, who were involved in the project at some stage (1 Cor 16:1), do not appear in Paul's last reference to the collection (Rom 15:26).

In 1 Cor 16:1–4 Paul gives instructions about the contribution. He has previously introduced the collection project to the Corinthian church, perhaps in the previous letter (Hurd 1965: 233), and is now giving more specific instructions about how to proceed, probably in order to encourage a more sizeable contribution (Hurd 1965: 202).

2 Corinthians 8 and 9 are most likely two communications written at separate times (Bornkamm 1965: 77). Betz (*2 Corinthians 8 and 9* Hermeneia, 71) has shown that 2 Corinthians 8 has some of the characteristics of a legal contract in which the mandate given to Titus is set out (2 Cor 8:6) along with a description of his credentials and the task assigned to him (2 Cor 8:16–23). Paul also commends two anonymous brothers (2 Cor 8:18, 19, 22) who, since only Titus is Paul's own partner (2 Cor 8:23b), are under the authority of Titus.

In 2 Corinthians 9, Paul's sending of "the brothers" is explained as necessary in order that the gift will be ready when he arrives with the Macedonians (2 Cor 9:1–5a). 2 Cor 9:5b expresses Paul's concern that the original intention of the contribution not be lost among the Corinthians (Betz, 96).

The three main options for explaining the reference in Gal 2:10 are: (1) that it is an exhortation to continue a standard practice that accompanied Paul's missionary activity (de Burton 1921: 99); (2) that it refers to the collection that Paul subsequently commenced as evidenced in 1 and 2 Corinthians and Romans (Knox 1950: 57); or (3) that it alludes both to the great collection referred to in these letters and to Paul's previous efforts, recorded in Acts 11:17–30, when he and Barnabas brought aid from Antioch to Jerusalem during the famine (Nickle 1966: 59).

B. The Contribution in Acts

There are only two references to the contribution in Acts: in 11:27–30, as referred to above, and in 24:17 where Paul tells Felix that part of the reason he has come to Jerusalem is to bring to the Jews "gifts for the poor."

C. The Significance of the Contribution

That Paul considered the collection project to be highly significant is indicated by the fact that he continued to push for funds even when faced with lethargic and rebellious responses (2 Corinthians 8 and 9) and was willing to risk his life to deliver it (Rom 15:31). It is generally taken that the significance the contribution for the saints had for Paul was as a symbol of the unity of the Church. The collection was meant to represent, primarily to the Jewish Christians in Jerusalem, the unity of both gentile and Jew in Christ, and thereby to be a means of reconciling the Jewish and gentile branches of the Church (Knox 1950: 54). The generosity of the gentile churches was meant to prove the validity of gentile salvation to the church at Jerusalem (Nickle 1966: 127).

Bibliography

Bornkamm, G. 1965. The History of the Origin of the So-Called Second Letter to the Corinthians. Pp. 73–81 in *The Authorship and Integrity of the New Testament.* London.

Buck, C. H. 1950. The Collection for the Saints. *HTR* 43: 1–29.

Burton, E. W. de. 1921. *A Critical and Exegetical Commentary on the Epistle to the Galatians.* Edinbugh.

Hurd, J. C. 1965. *The Origin of I Corinthians.* London.

Knox, J. 1950. *Chapters in a Life of Paul.* Nashville.

Minear, P. S. 1943. The Jerusalem Fund and Pauline Chronology. *ATR* 45: 389–96.

Munck, J. *Paul and the Salvation of Mankind.* Richmond, VA.

Nickle, K. F. 1966. *The Collection. A Study in Paul's Strategy.* London.

L. ANN JERVIS

CONVERSION.

The word "conversion" and the related noun "convert" and verb "to convert" appear infrequently in English translations of the Bible. When they do, they translate the Heb word *šûb* ("to turn") and the Gk *epistrephein.* However, understandings of what conversion involves and what it means are conveyed in diverse ways and cannot be confined to the study of particular terms. To explore the biblical understandings of conversion involves not only a study of particular words but an examination of the varying imagery for conversion.

The unclarity that surrounds the English word "conversion" complicates any discussion of conversion in the Bible. In his classic study of conversion in early Christianity, Arthur Darby Nock defined conversion as "the reorientation of the soul of an individual, his deliberate turning from indifference or from an earlier form of piety to another, a turning which implies a consciousness that a great change is involved, that the old was wrong and the new is right" (Nock 1933: 7). While this definition adequately describes certain uses of the term, it also implicitly eliminates some changes that are customarily described as conversions (e.g., Ruth, whose conversion appears to be a matter of an allegiance to Naomi and her customs; the Ethiopian eunuch and Cornelius, neither of whom appears to undergo a radical change of consciousness). If the term "conversion" is applied more widely than Nock's definition would allow, then there are numerous biblical texts that warrant consideration as examples of conversion.

A. Conversion in the Hebrew Bible

Although the religion of Israel primarily concerned people who were born into Israel, the Bible also speaks of those strangers or sojourners *(gērîm)* among the people. Restrictions governed their participation in Israel's religious life (Exod 12:43–45), but they could offer sacrifices to God and, on condition that males had been circumcised, they could even participate in Passover celebrations (Num 14:13–15; Exod 12:48–49). The best-known example of a sojourner who takes Israel's God for her own is that of Ruth, who apparently acts out of her relationship to her mother-in-law Naomi.

In addition to this motif of the sojourner who converts to Israel's worship is the prominent prophetic motif of the call for Israel's return *(šûb)* to God. Two texts that illustrate this motif are Jer 3:1–4:4 and Isaiah 55. Despite Israel's faithlessness (Jer 3:1–4), she will be allowed to return and will find mercy and pardon (Jer 3:12–13; Isa 55:1–9). What is necessary is that the people sincerely repent and return to God in truth and justice (Jer 4:1–4), a move that itself requires God's strengthening of Israel (Jer 3:22) and that will in turn lead to a renewed relationship with God. This return is not a conversion in the sense of a change of religious affiliation, but the transformation called for here does coincide with part of Nock's definition.

B. Conversion in the New Testament

The Synoptic Gospels portray both John the Baptist and Jesus as preachers of repentance (Gk *metanoia*). While Mark comments merely that John preached "a baptism of repentance for the forgiveness of sins," Luke and Matthew characterize John's preaching as a polemic against those who do not reflect their repentance through good deeds (Matt 3:7–10; Luke 3:7–9). In common with the prophetic motif of repentance and return to God, John's preaching declares God's final judgment on those who do not repent.

While the Synoptic Gospels also present Jesus' preaching as a call for repentance (Mark 1:15; Matt 4:17), it is Jesus' parables that reveal an implicit understanding that repentance involves a converted or transformed understanding of God. For example, several of the parables challenge conventional ways of understanding God (e.g., Luke 15:11–32; Matt 20:1–16) and thereby encourage the reinterpretation of who God is and how God works in the world. The very riddle of the parables presses for new or converted ways of thinking and acting in response to God.

Despite both the vivid accounts in Acts and its well-established place in Christian imagination, Paul's conversion occupies only a fragment of his letters. Indeed, because Paul says so little about this topic, and because he does not speak of changing religions, many students of his letters insist that it is inappropriate to speak of Paul as having experienced a "conversion," and prefer the term "call" in order to capture the motif of the prophetic call that appears in Gal 1:15–16. It has also been suggested that the term "transformation" be used for Paul's particular conversion, since it is not a change of religions but a radical reinterpretation of his understanding of God's actions in and will for the world. This debate itself reflects the previously noted confusion about the English word "conversion."

Whatever term is applied to the change Paul experienced, the evidence about it in his letters is slender. He indicates that he was a faithful Jew whose zeal surpassed that of his peers (Phil 3:5–6; Gal 1:14). Nevertheless, his experience of the risen Jesus (1 Cor 9:1–2; 15:8–10) inaugurated a radical transformation (Phil 3:7); contained within that transformation was Paul's call as apostle to the gentiles (Gal 1:15–16; 1 Cor 9:1–2; 15:8–10). While some interpreters still see in Romans 7 an indication that Paul was driven to his change by guilt over his inability to keep the law, the predominant view is that Romans 7 reflects on some aspect of the human situation and is not an autobiographical reflection. Of the dramatic details included in Acts 9, 22, and 26, Paul says nothing, not even that he was traveling to Damascus (see, however, Gal 1:17).

When referring to the conversions of others, Paul often speaks of God as calling (1 Cor 1:2), purchasing (1 Cor 6:20), liberating (Rom 6:17–18), or giving grace (Rom 3:21–26) to human beings. This is consistent with his conviction that it is God who takes the initiative with the world in a new way in the gospel rather than human beings who act to placate or please God. When he does use the language of converting or turning to God, it is in very traditional contexts that refer to gentiles taking up the worship of the true God, such as in 1 Thess 1:9 (cf. Gal 4:9). More often, he refers to the point at which persons acknowledge God's action in Jesus Christ as "faith" or "belief" (Rom 13:11), which results in radical transformation, a transformation that is still God's gift (Rom 12:1–2).

Because Luke's second volume, the Acts of the Apostles, narrates the formation of the Church and its mission in the gentile world, it is understandable that Acts contains a number of stories of conversion, not only the conversion of Saul or Paul (Acts 9, 22, 26) but also the ETHIOPIAN EUNUCH (8:26–40) and CORNELIUS (10:1–11:18), as well as large numbers of converts who remain unnamed (e.g., 2:41–42; 4:4; 9:35, 42). The first story of the conversion of a group of people comes at the event of Pentecost and appears to present Luke's understanding of conversion, for Peter concludes his sermon with these words: "Repent, and be baptized every one of you in the name of Jesus Christ for the forgiveness of your sins; and you shall receive the gift of the Holy Spirit" (2:38). Later stories do not necessarily conform to this pattern, however. For example, nothing is said about the Ethiopian eunuch repenting or receiving the Holy Spirit (8:26–40). The story of Saul's conversion makes no reference to his repentance (although his behavior might be said to reflect such a change). In the Cornelius episode, there is again no reference to repentance, and here the gift of the Holy Spirit precedes baptism. This inconsistency indicates that Luke is not presenting a systematic interpretation of conversion but is employing the various accounts to weave a story of God's actions in and through the Church. Even the stories of the conversions of individuals are, in Luke's accounting, less about those individuals than they are about God.

In addition to the gospel accounts in which John and Jesus call for repentance, the language of revelation and transformation in the letters of Paul, and the narratives of Acts, some NT texts use imagery of new birth and new life to refer to conversion. This language occurs in both Jewish and pagan literature roughly contemporaneous with the NT, so that its use in the gospel of John and in 1 Peter draws on well-established religious language. The gospel of John includes a story in which Jesus says to Nicodemus: "Truly, truly, I say to you, unless one is born anew *(gennethe anothen)*, he cannot see the kingdom of God" (3:3). This statement turns on a word play, since the Greek word translated "anew" in the RSV also means "from above." While Nicodemus responds to the former meaning of the word, what Jesus intends is clearly the latter. As this birth "from above" stands in its Johannine setting, it refers to life that has its origin in the Spirit, life in radical discontinuity from life in "this world," and life that involves a new relationship with Jesus (e.g., John 15:1–7, 18–19; 17:6–10). In 1 Peter the language of new birth (1:3–5, 14, 23; 2:2) helps to affirm the believer's movement inside the boundaries of a new community. As is the case of John as well, new birth in 1 Peter has ethical as well as social and theological implications, since those who are in the community are enjoined to be holy in their conduct (1:14–15) and to act out of love (1:22–23).

Bibliography

Gaventa, B. R. 1986. *From Darkness to Light: Aspects of Conversion in the New Testament.* Philadelphia.

Holladay, W. L. 1958. *The Root* šûbh *in the Old Testament.* Leiden.

Kim, S. 1982. *The Origin of Paul's Gospel.* Grand Rapids.

MacMullen, R. 1984. *Christianizing the Roman Empire: A.D. 100–400.* New Haven, CT.

Nock, A. D. 1933. *Conversion: The Old and New in Religion from Alexander the Great to Augustine of Hippo.* London.

Stendahl, K. 1976. Call Rather Than Conversion. Pp. 7–23 in *Paul Among Jews and Gentiles.* Philadelphia.

BEVERLY ROBERTS GAVENTA

COOPS, PIGEON. See ZOOLOGY.

COPPER SCROLL (3Q15). In March 1952 a team of archaeologists discovered in Qumran Cave 3 a scroll engraved on two copper sheets which had originally formed one whole 2.40 × 0.30 m in size (de Vaux 1953: 85–86). In 1955/56 H. W. Baker (1956) at Manchester University in England solved the difficult task of opening the brittle and heavily oxidized scroll by sawing it into segments.

Even before the scroll was opened K. G. Kuhn (1954) examined the visible part of the engraving and came to the conclusion that the scroll contained a list of hiding places of the accumulated wealth of the Essenes. Upon further examination the scroll was found to list to twelve columns 64 underground hiding places in various regions of the land of Israel. The deposits include certain amounts of gold, silver, aromatics, scrolls, and also a copy of a more detailed inventory (col. XII, lines 11–13) of the treasures.

J. M. Allegro (1960), who gained access to the newly opened scroll at Manchester, published a transcription and interpretation of it before the official edition was published. His secretive digging around Qumran and elsewhere in search of hidden treasures was severely criticized by the official team. J. T. Milik (1959), a member of the team, published a translation and commentary of the Copper Scroll and maintained that it had no connection with the Qumran Essenes. He declared the scroll a mere compilation of legendary treasures concocted by someone around 100 C.E. (cf. Baillet, Milik, and de Vaux 1962: 199–302). Many scholars were not ready to accept his conclusions. They maintained the reality of the treasures but differed as to their origin. Some ascribed them to the Essenes (Dupont-Sommer 1962: 383–89; Pixner 1983), to the temple of Jerusalem (Kuhn 1956; Rengstrof 1960: 26–28), to the Zealots (Allegro 1964), to other Jewish refugees before 70 C.E. (Golb 1980; 1985), to a collection of money for rebuilding the destroyed sanctuary (Lehmann 1964), or even to the Bar Kokhba revolt (Laperrousaz 1961; Luria 1963). These discussions were summarized by H. Bardtke (1968), Vermes (*HJP*[2], 467–69), and M. Wise (1987: 232).

Despite the intricate difficulties posed by the interior structure of the Copper Scroll, a decisive argument for its dating and origin can be derived from a careful examination of Cave 3Q and its history (Pixner 1983: 334–35). In its original state the cave contained many jars with a variety of documents, which were almost completely destroyed when the outer ceiling collapsed. The few surviving fragments (Baillet, Milik, and de Vaux 1962: 94–104) are universally accepted as genuine Qumran documents. The shape of the cave and the hiding place of the Copper Scroll in it make it inconceivable that this double scroll could have been deposited at a later date while the jars with the other documents were still in place. F. M. Cross dated the scroll on paleographical grounds within the broad limits 25–75 C.E. (Baillet, Milik, and de Vaux 1962: 217–21). Its early Mishnaic Hebrew is not unique among the Qumran documents (Baillet, Milik, and de Vaux 1962: 222). The use of a precious material like copper and the prosaic, factual style of the Copper Scroll argue against a mere folkloristic composition.

Dupont-Sommer (1962: 383–84) points out that even the high sum total of the treasures (ca. 4500 talents) mentioned in the Copper Scroll does not necessarily exclude its reality (contra as J. T. Milik 1959). Since the Essenes had a community of goods and were preparing for the eschatological war (War Scroll) and the rebuilding of the temple (Temple Scroll), the amount of their common wealth is not surprising. The various assets of the community could also be considered a substitute or counterbank to the temple treasure, which the Essenes shunned (Pixner 1983: 339–40).

Since the Copper Scroll was meant to be an aide-mémoire for a secretive team of diggers, it apparently avoids well-known geographical terms. This fact makes it difficult to pinpoint the described hiding places. All scholars believe that some of the hiding places were situated around the monastery of Qumran, named Secacah (cf. Josh 15:62) in the Copper Scroll (IV,*13*–V,*14*; cf. de Vaux 1973: 93). This is another argument for the Qumran relationship of the scroll. Also Jerusalem and its surroundings, e.g., Shiloah (X,*15–16;* cf. John 9:7) and Bethesda (IX,*11–14;* cf. John 5:2), are generally (except Luria: 1963) considered as locations of hidden treasures. While Milik (1959; also in

Baillet et al. 1962) and Allegro (1964) find that the caches were haphazardly distributed all over Palestine, Pixner (1983) professes to see a systematic order in their distribution: nos. 1–17 near the Essene Gate (Jos. *JW* 5.145) on the SW hill of the city, suggesting a special quarter there (Pixner 1983: 342–47; Reisner 1985); nos. 19–34 in and around Qumran; nos. 35–47 in the Yarmuk Valley area ("Land of Damascus"?; cf. CD VII,*15–19*); nos. 48–60 again around the holy city; and nos. 61–64 at diverse locations in the N of the country. The solution to the intricate problems of the topography of Copper Scroll could be of utmost interest, because it might make us understand the general distribution of Essene centers of settlement. The rather poor quality of the original photos has certainly contributed to the divergence of interpretation (Thorion 1985). A new set of pictures of Copper Scroll taken with the help of modern techniques could further advance the research of this very important document.

Bibliography

Allegro, J. M. 1960. *The Treasure of the Copper Scroll.* Garden City, NY. 2d ed. 1964.

Baillet, M.; Milik, J. T.; and Vaux, R. de. 1962. Discoveries in the Judean Desert of Jordan III: *Les "Petites Grottes" de Qumrân.* Oxford.

Baker, H. W. 1956. Notes on the Opening of the "Bronze" Scrolls from Qumran. *Bulletin of the John Rylands Library* 39: 45–56.

Bardtke, H. 1968. Qumran und seine Probleme II/2: Die Kupferrollen. *TR* 33: 185–204.

Dupont-Sommer, A. 1962. *The Essence Writings from Qumran.* Cleveland.

Golb, N. 1980. The Problem of the Origin and Identification of the Dead Sea Scrolls. *Proceedings of the American Philosophical Society* 124: 1–24.

———. 1985. Who Hid the Dead Sea Scrolls? *BA* 48: 68–82.

Kuhn, K. G. 1954. Les Rouleaux de cuivre de Qumrân. *RB* 61: 193–205.

———. 1956. Bericht über neue Qumranfunde und über die öffnung der Kupferrollen. *TLZ* 81: 541–46.

Laperrousaz, E. M. 1961. Remarques sur l'origine des Rouleaux de Cuivre découverts dans la Grotte 3 de Qumrân. *RHR* 159: 157–72.

Lehmann, M. 1964. Identification of the Copper Scroll Based on its Technical Terms. *RevQ* 5: 97–105.

Luria, B. Z. 1963. *Megillat han-Nahoshet mem- Midbar Yehudah.* Jerusalem.

Milik, J. T. 1959. Le Rouleau de cuivre de Qumrân (3Q15). Traduction et commentaire topographique. *RB* 66: 321–57.

Pixner, B. 1983. Unraveling the Copper Scroll Code: A Study on the Topography of 3Q15. *RevQ* 11: 323–66.

Rengstorf, K. H. 1960. *Ḥirbet Qumrân und die Bibliothek vom Toten Meer.* Stuttgart.

Riesner, R. 1985. Essener und urkirche in Jerusalem. *BK* 40: 64–76.

Thorion, Y. 1985. Beiträge zur Erforschung der Sprache der Kupferrolle. *RevQ* 12: 163–76.

Vaux, R. de. 1953. Fouille au Khirbet Qumrân. *RB* 60: 84–85.

———. 1973. *Archaeology and the Dead Sea Scrolls.* Oxford.

Wise, M. 1987. The Dead Sea Scrolls: Part 2, Nonbiblical Manuscripts. *BA* 49: 228–44.

BARGIL (VIRGIL) PIXNER

COPTIC LANGUAGE. See LANGUAGES (COPTIC).

COPTIC VERSIONS. See VERSIONS, ANCIENT (COPTIC).

COR [Heb *kōr; kôr*]. See WEIGHTS AND MEASURES.

CORBAN [Gk *korban*]. The word "corban" appears in Mark 7:11 (cf. Matt 15:5), "As a man should say to his father or mother, That which you should have had from me is *corban,* that is, a gift [to God]. . . ." Matt 15:5 has the same basic text, but without the transliterated Semitic word *cōrbān.* The equivalence *cōrbān* = Gk *doron* [*tou theou*], "gift [to God]," is also attested by Josephus, *Ant* 4.73, where he links it with (a) vows and procedures for gaining release from them, and (b) oaths (cf. also *AgAp* 1.167). This use is now attested in an Aramaic ossuary inscription from Jebel Hellet et-Turi (Fitzmyer 1971), which runs "everything which a man may find to his profit in this ossuary [is] an offering *(qrbn)* to God from the one within it." If it is given to God, then it is banned to men, just as appears in Mark 7:11. The terms *qrbn* and *qwnm* occur in these senses in the Mishnah and Talmud. Thus, in *m. Ned.* 1:4 we read, "If a man said, May what I eat of thine be the Korban, or 'as a Korban' or 'a Korban,' it is forbidden to him." It thus appears in (a) prohibitions of use, and (b) dedication formulas of the 1st century A.D. Further confirmation comes from the finding of a stone jar from the 1st century inscribed with the word *qrbn,* and recalling *m. Maʿaś. Š.* 3:10, "If a man found a vessel and on it was written Korban . . ." (Fitzmyer 1971: 96). In Mark 7:11 the word may thus represent either Hebrew or Aramaic. Matt 27:6 presents the related form, *korbanas,* probably reflecting the Aramaic emphatic state *(qwrbn),* meaning "treasury" and thus equivalent to the Gk *gazophylakion.* The very same use of the term occurs also in Josephus, *JW* 2.175, but so far it does not seem to have been attested in 1st-century Aramaic sources.

Bibliography

Fitzmyer, J. 1971. *Essays on the Semitic Background of the New Testament.* London.

MAX WILCOX

CORINTH (PLACE) [Gk *Korinthos*]. CORINTHIAN. A city on the Peloponnesian coast of Greece (35° 56′N; 22° 56′W) where Paul met Aquila and Priscilla and where he spent eighteen months preaching and teaching (Acts 18:1–18). He later wrote at least two letters to the congregation at Corinth (1 Cor and 2 Cor; but cf. 1 Cor 5:9, 11).

A. Geographic Setting

The 4-km^2 site occupies two broad natural terraces that step up from the coastal plain to the height of Acrocorinth (575 m). This is limited on the E and W by two of the gullies that drain Acrocorinth. The 10-km wall follows the optimum defense line along the edges and is anchored by

Acrocorinth. The built-up area never expanded as far as the walls; in times of danger the extra space could shelter the people and flocks of the agricultural area that fed Corinth. Long walls 2.5 km long and 1.2 km apart linked the city to the port of Lechaeum. See Fig. COR.01. Its artificial double harbor covered 460,000 m^2 and was bordered by 7 km of quays; only a tiny portion of the harbor area has been excavated (Roux 1958: 103). Corinth's second port, CENCHREAE, lay some 9 km to the E on the Saronic Gulf. The artificial harbor enclosed only 30,000 m^2. A large building dominated the N breakwater, and four blocks of warehouses were aligned along the inner part of the S mole (Scranton, Shaw, and Ibrahim 1978: 14, 41).

Control of these two harbors, and its position virtually astride the 6-km-wide isthmus linking the Peloponnese to mainland Greece, made Corinth the great crossroads of the ancient world (Strabo 8.6.20). Set on the edge of a plain whose richness was proverbial, with a tradition of high productivity, and so situated as to be able to levy a percentage on both E–W and N–S trade, the coffers of Corinth were always full. From the time of Homer (*Il.* 2.570) the adjective associated with Corinth was always "wealthy" (Dio Chrysostom, *Or.* 37.36). Today the name Korinthos belongs to a small city on the Peloponnesian coast of the Gulf of Corinth 2.4 km W of the Corinth Canal. Its origins go back only to 1858 when the old city was destroyed by an earthquake. The "light of all Greece" (Cicero, *Leg. Man.* 5) is now represented by the poor village of Archaia (or Palaia) Korinthos, located 5.6 km SW of the modern city.

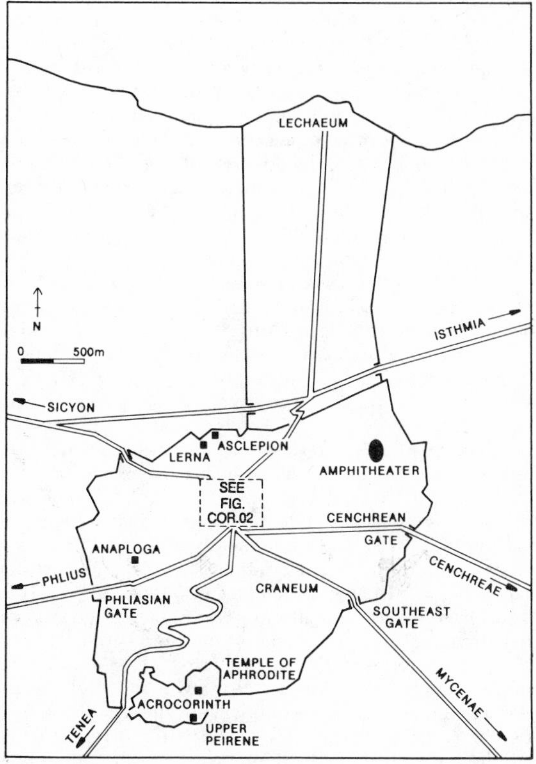

COR.01. City plan of Corinth. *(Redrawn from Murphy-O'Connor 1983a: 20, fig. 4.)*

B. History of Excavations

The first excavations at Corinth were conducted by the German Archaeological Institute (Dörpfeld 1886). In 1896 the American School of Classical Studies at Athens assumed responsibility for the site and has conducted excavations there ever since. Preliminary studies appear in *American Journal of Archaeology* and *Hesperia,* and final reports in the series of volumes entitled *Corinth* (1930–). Remains of all periods from the Early Neolithic have been brought to light. Elsewhere in the Corinthia, major excavations have been carried out at Isthmia (1952–60 and again from 1967 to 1978), and at Cenchreae (1963–68). Final reports on Isthmia have been published by Gebhard (1973) and by Broneer (1971; 1973), and on Cenchreae by Scranton, Shaw, and Ibrahim (1978).

C. History of Corinth

The history of Corinth is long and complex, but the fundamental distinction is between the Greek city, which came to an end in 146 B.C., and the Roman colony founded by Julius Caesar in 44 B.C.

The origins of the city in the 5th millennium and its subsequent development to the 4th century B.C. have been documented by J. B. Salmon (1984). For long centuries Corinth enjoyed unusual social and political stability, partly because of excellent management by the ruling class, who anticipated rather than opposed change, and partly because of an exceptionally diversified and productive economy. In addition to the celebrated Corinthian bronze (Murphy-O'Connor 1983b), the city was renowned for its ceramics, textiles, shipbuilding, and architecture. In order to develop E–W trade a canal joining the Corinthian and Saronic gulfs was mooted as early as the 6th century B.C. (Diog. Laert. 1.99). When the project came to nothing, Periander (ca. 625–585 B.C.) built a paved road (the *diolkos*) across the isthmus, which permitted light ships to be hauled from one sea to the other on a platform running in grooves cut in the pavement. Excavations have revealed a dock and 460 m of the road on the W side of the isthmus. The width varies from 3.4 to 6 m, and the grooves are 1.5 m apart (Wiseman 1978: 45–46). Repaired many times, it remained in use at least until the 9th century A.D., and would also have served for the movement of goods. These facilities permitted merchants to avoid the voyage around Cape Maleae, which was so dangerous as to be proverbial: "When you double Maleae forget your home!" (Strabo 8.6.20).

Such success inevitably provoked the envy of those less fortunate in their location and less industrious in their habits, and so in the 5th–4th centuries B.C., Athenian writers made Corinth the symbol of commercialized love. Aristophanes coined the verb *korinthiazesthai,* "to fornicate" (*Fr.* 354). Philetaerus and Poliochus wrote plays entitled *Korinthiastēs,* "The Whoremonger" (Athenaeus 313c, 559a). Plato used *korinthia korē,* "a Corinthian girl," to mean a prostitute (*Rest.* 404d). These neologisms, however, left no permament mark on the language, because in reality Corinth was neither better nor worse than its contemporaries. It was not dedicated to the goddess of love, Aphrodite (Saffrey 1985), and Strabo's story of 1000 sacred prostitutes (8.6.20) has been shown to be pure fabrication (Conzelmann 1967).

The events leading to the destruction of Corinth in 146 B.C. have been summarized by Wiseman (1979: 450–62). Even though Rome had granted freedom to the cities of Greece after the Second Macedonian War (200–196 B.C.) and permitted them to unite in various leagues, it came to see the latter as a threat. In defiance of a Roman attempt to break up the Achaian League, of which Corinth was a prominent member, the league asserted its independence by going to war to discipline Sparta in 146 B.C. When Metellus reached the isthmus from the N after defeating three Achaian armies, he was joined by the fleet of the consul Lucius Mummius, who assumed command. Corinth, the bastion of Achaia, had only a ragtag army of 14,000 infantry and 600 cavalry recruited from untrained slaves and citizens to face a Roman force of 23,000 infantry and 3500 cavalry plus auxiliaries. The result of the battle on the plain was a foregone conclusion.

The looting of the city is recorded by an eyewitness, Polybius (preserved only in Strabo 8.6.23), but the inference from excavations that the city was neither totally destroyed nor completely depopulated (Wiseman 1979: 494–95) is confirmed by Cicero, who visited Corinth between 79 and 77 B.C. (*Tusc.* 3.53; cf. Feger 1952). Corinth was too natural a market center ever to be abandoned completely, and those citizens who escaped the net cast by Mummius would surely have returned (Dio Cass. 21).

The establishment of the Roman colony is attributed to Julius Caesar by a number of classical authors (all the Greek and Latin references to the colony are conveniently assembled in Murphy-O'Connor 1983a: 1–128), but only Appian gives a precise date, namely 102 years after the sack of Carthage (*Hist.* 8.136), i.e., 44 B.C. Inscriptions show that the new name of the city was Colonia Laus Julia Corinthiensis (Kent 1966: 60, 70). Since the region had been peaceful for over a century and no danger threatened, Caesar's concerns can hardly have been military or political. The economic potential of Corinth was well known in Rome (Cicero, *Leg. Agr.* 1.5; 2.51, 87; cf. E. Salmon 1969: 135), and that this was his motive appears to be demonstrated by the fact that the construction of a canal across the isthmus was part of the project (Suetonius, *Iul.* 44).

Strabo's assertion that the new settlers were for the most part freed slaves (8.136) harmonizes with Appian's view that they were *aporoi* (*Hist.* 8.136), provided that this adjective is understood to apply to those who felt themselves locked into a certain socioeconomic level through lack of opportunity. Thus they were not Romans but had been brought originally from Greece, Syria, Judea, and Egypt (Gordon 1924: 94–95). In a new colony they had everything to gain. Distance would have made their ties to former masters meaningless, and their children would be free. As a group they had the technical, financial, and administrative skills to make the project work. Their enterprise and industry are attested by the fact that, though they had to begin by robbing graves, they quickly found a lucrative market in Rome for the bronze vessels and terracotta reliefs that they discovered (Strabo 8.6.23). The great demand for the former prompted some of the wilier colonists to recommence the production of bronze (Stillwell, Scranton, and Freeman 1941: 273), and other traditional industries were soon reestablished.

Once the colony was securely based, it attracted entrepreneurs from Greece and the major trading countries of the E Mediterranean. Such infusions of new capital in a prime commercial situation inevitably generated more wealth, and within 50 years of its foundation many citizens of Corinth were men of very considerable means. The clearest evidence of this is an inscription commemorating L. Castricius Regulus, who assumed the presidency of the first restored Isthmian Games sometime between 7 B.C. and A.D. 3. He refurbished the facilities, which had not been used for a century, and offered a banquet to all the inhabitants of the colony (Kent 1966: 70). Commercial development demanded banking facilities, and by the mid-1st century A.D. Corinth was an important financial center (Plutarch, *Mor.* 831A).

Urban expansion is also a significant indicator of the city's increasing prosperity (Wiseman 1979: 509–30). The early colonists displaced the center of the old city to the S of the archaic temple, where a racetrack had preserved a large open space. It became the forum (Robinson 1965: 23). A number of ancient elements, e.g., the South Stoa, the Well of Glauce, the Peirene Fountain, were incorporated, but new structures quickly appeared. Ten monumental edifices were erected before the end of the reign of Augustus (31 B.C.–A.D. 14). A further six are ascribed to the long reign of his successor, Tiberius (A.D. 14–37). Thus, the city center at the time of Paul can be reconstructed with a very high degree of accuracy (Murphy-O'Connor 1984). See Fig. COR.02. The ruined walls were still visible but served only as a quarry of cut stone. In an era of great political stability their repair was seen as a completely unprofitable investment.

The Corinth that Paul knew was severely damaged by an earthquake in A.D. 77 (West 1931: 18–19). In gratitude for imperial aid in rebuilding, the city was renamed Colonia Julia Flavia Augusta Corinthiensis (Kent 1966: 42), but the original name returned in the early 2d century A.D. (Edwards 1933: 28–29). The tax-free status accorded the city by Hadrian (Wiseman 1979: 507) stimulated a building boom in the mid-2d century A.D. This was the city depicted (about A.D. 174) by Pausanias in his *Description of Greece* (2.1.1–5.5).

The most attractive residential and recreational area in Corinth was the suburb of Craneum on the lower slopes of Acrocorinth (Plutarch, *Mor.* 601B). According to legend, it was there that Diogenes the Cynic (ca. 400–325 B.C.) lived in his barrel (Dio Chrysostom, *Or.* 8.5) and asked Alexander the Great to move a little to one side because he was blocking the rays of the sun (Plutarch, *Vit. Alex.* 14). In terms of recreational facilities, its only competitor was the Asclepieion and Lerna complex just inside the N wall (Roebuck 1951; Lang 1977). The latter offered a fine swimming pool, while the dining rooms of the latter could have been the setting for 1 Cor 8:10 (Murphy-O'Connor 1983a: 161–67).

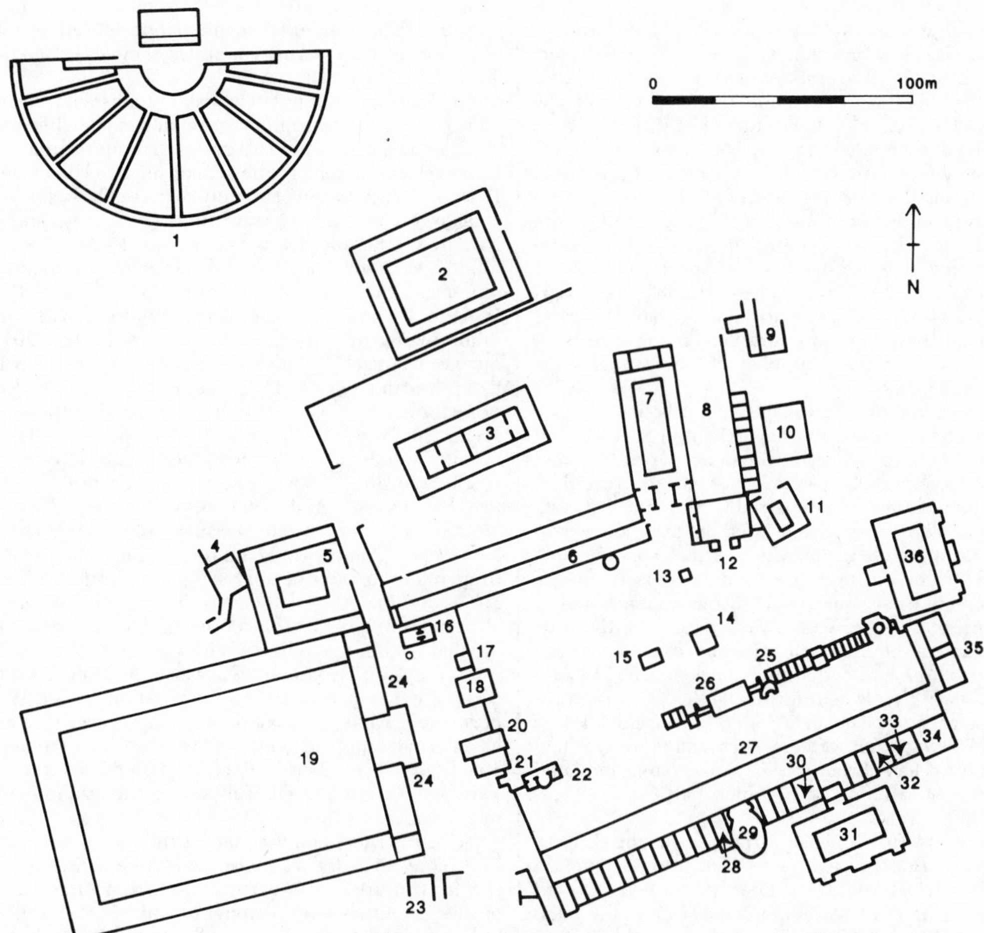

COR.02. Plan of Corinth—central area, ca. 50 c.e. *1,* theater; *2,* N market; *3,* archaic temple, 6th century b.c.e.; *4,* Fountain of Glauke, 6th century b.c.e.; *5,* temple C (unidentified); *6,* NW stoa; *7,* N basilica; *8,* Lechaeum Road; *9,* bath (of Eurycles?); *10,* Peribolos of Apollo; *11,* Fountain of Peirene; *12,* Propylaea; *13,* Tripod; *14,* statue of Athena; *15,* altar (unidentified); *16,* temple D *(Tychē); 17,* Babbius monument; *18,* Fountain of Poseidon (Neptune); *19,* temple of the imperial cult; *20,* temple G (Pantheon?); *21,* temple F (Aphrodite); *22,* unidentified building (temple or civic structure); *23,* "Cellar Building" (public restaurant or tavern); *24,* W shops; *25,* central shops; *26, bēma; 27,* S stoa; *28,* room XX (Sarapis shrine); *29, Bouleutērion; 30,* "Fountain House"; *31,* S basilica; *32,* room C *(Agonotheteion); 33,* room B; *34,* room A; *35,* SE building (Tabularium and library?); *36,* Julian Basilica. *(Redrawn from Furnish,* II Corinthians *AB, 11, fig. 2.)*

When Achaia was set up as a senatorial province in 27 b.c., Corinth presumably was the capital, but this is not confirmed by any direct evidence (Wiseman 1979: 501). In a.d. 15 Tiberius attached Achaia and Macedonia to the imperial province of Moesia (Tacitus, *Ann.* 1.76, 80), but Achaia was restored to the Senate by Claudius in a.d. 44 (Suetonius, *Claud.* 25). Thus, Rome was represented by a proconsul, who served for one year from June 1 to May 30 (Dio Cass. 57.14.5). The most celebrated proconsul is Lucius Iunius Gallio (June 51–May 52), not because of his personal character or achievements but because he is mentioned in Acts 18:12 and so provides the key date in Pauline chronology (Murphy-O'Connor 1983a: 141–52). Since he did not complete his term of office (Seneca, *Ep.* 104.1), Paul must have met him in Corinth in the summer of a.d. 51.

The municipal government was a miniature of that of republican Rome (Kent 1966: 23). Citizen voters, divided into twelve tribes (Wiseman 1979: 497), elected four annual magistrates, who on retirement became eligible for membership of the city council. These offices were open to freedmen (Duff 1928: 66). The senior magistrates were *duoviri iure dicundo,* and to date the names of 58 are known (Kent 1966: 24–26, but the dates there given are subject to revision; Wiseman 1979: 498, n. 224). In addition to juridical duties, they were the chief executive officers of the city. Those elected every fifth year were known as *duoviri quinquennales* and had the additional responsibilities of taking the census and naming new members of the city council.

The *duoviri* were assisted by two *aediles* (11 are listed in Kent 1966: 27). They functioned as city business managers and so presumably were responsible for commercial and financial litigation. An inscription in the paving of the square E of the theater, dated to the mid-1st century A.D., mentions an *aedile* named Erastus. The rarity of the name generally and its absence elsewhere at Corinth (Kent 1966: 99) strengthens the identification of this individual with the Erastus mentioned by Paul as the *oikonomos* of Corinth (Rom 16:23). *Oikonomos,* "steward," however, is not a standard rendering of *aedile,* and Erastus may have occupied a lower office when Paul wrote (Theissen 1982: 79–83). If so, his conversion to Christianity did not block Erastus' advancement. In times of food shortages a *curator annonae* was appointed to ensure supplies at his own expense (Wiseman 1979: 499).

The greatest honor that Corinth could bestow was the presidency of the Isthmian Games, which were celebrated every two years in the spring at the sanctuary of Poseidon at Isthmia. Responsibility for this, the second greatest of the panhellenic festivals, had passed to Sicyon in 146 B.C., but the new colony must have pressed the traditional right of Corinth from the beginning, since great economic benefits flowed from the presence of huge crowds (Strabo 8.6.20). It would have succeeded in this claim, however, only when some of the settlers had become sufficiently wealthy to accept the financially onerous office of *agonothetes.* Paul could have attended the games of A.D. 51 (Kent 1966: 31); it can hardly be coincidental that his first use of athletic imagery appears in a letter to Corinth (1 Cor 9:24–27). The fact that winners at Isthmia were crowned with withered celery (Broneer 1962a) may have stimulated Paul to think of salvation as an imperishable crown (Broneer 1962b).

In addition to furnishing information on the officials and benefactors of the city, inscriptions also document a shift in the official language. Those published by Kent reveal that, of the 104 inscriptions dated prior to the reign of Hadrian (A.D. 117–38), 101 are in Latin and only 3 in Greek, while thereafter there are 39 in Greek and 17 in Latin. There may have been exclusive use of Latin in the early days of the colony, but Greek was the language of trade and commerce, and as the population expanded it would have become the most commonly spoken tongue. Its promotion to an official position, however, was delayed until the 2d century A.D.

The religious and ethnic diversity of the population of Corinth is graphically attested by excavated remains. The imperial cult is attested by a temple just off the forum (Stillwell, Scranton, and Freeman 1941: 168–79), but also by additions to the Isthmian Games. A series of competitions known as the Caesarea and run on a quadrennial basis was added under Augustus, and the imperial contests appear under Tiberius (Kent 1966: 28). Numerous shrines dedicated to Apollo, Athena, Aphrodite, Asclepios, Demeter and Kore, Palaimon, and Sisypus witness to the continuity of Greek cults (detailed references in *2 Corinthians* AB 32A, 15–18). Egyptian influence is documented by the worship of Isis and Sarapis (Smith 1977). The physical evidence for a Jewish community is late (possibly 4th–5th century A.D.) and meager, only a marble impost inscribed with three menorahs separated by lulab and etrog (Scranton 1957: 26, 116) and a cornice stone reused as a lintel and bearing the lettering [*syna*]*gōgē hebr*[*aiōn*] (West 1931: 78–79).

The complete absence of Jewish remains from the early Christian centuries is rather surprising, since Philo's specification of Corinth (and Argos), in counterdistinction to geographical regions in the rest of his description of the Diaspora, would seem to imply a particularly large and vital Jewish community at Corinth (*Leg.* 281). Jews may have fled to Sicyon in 146 B.C. (1 Macc 15:23). If so, they would have returned to join their coreligionists among the settlers of the new colony (*2 Corinthians* AB 32A, 20). Whether Corinth benefited by the expulsion of Jews from Rome by Tiberius in A.D. 19 (Smallwood 1981: 201–10) must remain an open question, and Luke's hint (Acts 18:2) that Jews came to Corinth as a result of the so-called Edict of Claudius in A.D. 41 should be treated with extreme skepticism (Murphy-O'Connor 1983a: 130–40). The community would have increased significantly after A.D. 67 when, according to Josephus, Vespasian sent 6000 Jewish prisoners to work on the canal begun by Nero (*JW* 3.540). Most of them would have become freedmen eventually, because work on the canal did not last long, even though a tremendous amount of work was accomplished (Wiseman 1978: 48–50). Other Jews came from Palestine during and after the revolt of A.D. 132–35 (Justin, *Dial.* 1). On the basis of what is known about conditions elsewhere in the Diaspora, the Jewish community at Corinth would have been recognized as a *politeuma,* a corporation of aliens with permanent right of domicile and empowered to manage its internal affairs through its own officials (Smallwood 1981: 225). Jews, therefore, enjoyed a civic existence but were not citizens in the full sense, though individuals might achieve this status.

Modern writers adopt a view of the moral character of the colony that derives more from Athenian slanders of the 4th century B.C. (see above) and from Athenian envy of the 2d century A.D. (Alciphr. 15 and 24 [3.51, 60]) than from convincing contemporary data. If we exclude the evidence for gladiatorial shows (Apuleius, *Met.* 10.18), which Dio Chrysostom mentions only to indicate that the situation at Athens was worse (*Or.* 31.121), and the mildly erotic tale of a young man in the toils of a vampire (Philostratus, *V.A.* 4.25), all that remains is Apuleius' salacious tale of a woman copulating with a donkey (*Met.* 10.19–23), an act that others considered suitable for the theater (10.34–35). The fact that this episode is set in Corinth (it does not appear in the original Greek novel) owes less to reality than to Apuleius' sojourn in Athens, where he earned the title of the "Platonic philosopher" (Millar 1981). It speaks more of what he learned there than of actual conditions at Corinth. The proverb "Not for everyone is the voyage to Corinth" is used by Strabo in a sexual sense (8.6.20) but, as Horace makes clear (*Epist.* 1.17.36), the original meaning referred not to the danger of losing one's virginity but to the danger of losing one's shirt in the intense cutthroat competition of a boom town.

In choosing as one of his main missionary centers a city in which only the tough were reputed to survive, Paul demonstrated a confidence oddly at variance with his protestations of weakness. Corinth, however, offered advantages that outweighed its dangers. In addition to excellent communications, the extraordinary number of visitors (Dio Chrysostom, *Or.* 37.8; Aelius Aristides, *Or.* 46.24) created the possibility of converts who would carry the gospel back to their homelands. In contrast to the closed complacency of Athens (Geagan 1979: 378–89), Corinth was open and questioning, eager for new ideas but neither docile nor passive, as Paul's relationship with the Christian community there amply documents.

Bibliography

Broneer, O. 1962a. The Isthmian Victory Games. *AJA* 66: 259–63.
———. 1962b. The Apostle Paul and the Isthmian Games. *BA* 25: 1–31.
———. 1971. *Isthmia I. The Temple of Poseidon.* Princeton.
———. 1973. *Isthmia II. Topography and Architecture.* Princeton.
Conzelmann, H. 1967. Korinth und die Mädchen der Aphrodite. Zur Religionsgeschichte der Stadt Korinth. *NAWG* 8: 247–61.
Dörpfeld, W. 1886. Der Tempel von Korinth. *Mitteilungen des deutschen archäologischen Instituts. Athenische Abteilung* 11: 297–308.
Duff, A. M. 1928. *Freedmen in the Early Roman Empire.* Cambridge.
Edwards, K. M. 1933. *Corinth VI. Coins. 1896–1929.* Cambridge, MA.
Feger, R. 1952. Cicero und die Zerstöring Korinths. *Hermes* 80: 436–56.
Geagan, D. 1979. Roman Athens: Some Aspects of Life and Culture. I. 86 B.C.–A.D. 267. *ANRW* 7/1: 371–437.
Gebhard, E. R. 1973. *The Theatre at Isthmia.* Chicago; London.
Gordon, M. L. 1924. The Nationality of Slaves under the Early Roman Empire. *JRS* 14: 93–111.
Kent, J. H. 1966. *Corinth VIII/3. The Inscriptions 1926–1950.* Princeton.
Lang, M. 1977. *Cure and Cult in Ancient Corinth.* Corinth Notes 1. Princeton.
Millar, F. 1981. The World of the *Golden Ass. JRS* 71: 63–75.
Murphy-O'Connor, J. 1983a. *St. Paul's Corinth. Texts and Archaeology.* GNS 6. Wilmington, DE.
———. 1983b. Corinthian Bronze. *RB* 90: 23–26.
———. 1984. The Corinth That Saint Paul Saw. *BA* 47: 147–59.
Robinson, H. S. 1965. *The Urban Development of Ancient Corinth.* Athens.
Roebuck, C. 1951. *Corinth XIV. The Asclepieion and Lerna.* Cambridge, MA.
Roux, G. 1958. *Pausanias en Corinthie (Livre II, 1 à 15). Texte. Traduction Commentaire archéologique et topographique.* Paris.
Saffrey, H.-D. 1985. Aphrodite à Corinthe. Reflexions sur une idée recue. *RB* 92: 359–74.
Salmon, E. T. 1969. *Roman Canonization under the Republic.* Ithaca, NY.
Salmon, J. B. 1984. *Wealthy Corinth. A History of the City to 338 B.C.* Oxford.
Scranton, R. L. 1957. *Corinth XVI. Medieval Architecture in the Central Area of Corinth.* Princeton.
Scranton, R. L.; Shaw, J. W.; and Ibrahim, L. 1978. *Kenchreai. Eastern Port of Corinth I. Topography and Architecture.* Leiden.
Smallwood, E. M. 1981. *The Jews under Roman Rule from Pompey to Diocletian. A Study in Political Relations.* Studies in Judaism in Antiquity 20. Leiden.
Smith, D. E. 1977. The Egyptian Cults at Corinth. *HTR* 70: 201–31.
Stillwell, R.; Scranton, R. L.; and Freeman, S. E. 1941. *Corinth I/2. Architecture.* Cambridge, MA.
Theissen, G. 1982. *The Social Setting of Pauline Christianity, Essays on Corinth.* Ed., trans., intro., J. H. Schütz. Philadelphia.
West, A. B. 1931. *Corinth VIII/2. Latin Inscriptions 1896–1927.* Cambridge, MA.
Wiseman, J. 1978. *The Land of the Ancient Corinthians.* Studies in Mediterranean Archaeology 50. Göteborg.
———. 1979. Corinth and Rome I: 228 B.C.–A.D. 267. *ANRW* 7/1: 438–548.

J. MURPHY-O'CONNOR

CORINTHIANS, FIRST EPISTLE TO THE.

A letter of the apostle Paul to the church at Corinth, found as the seventh book of the NT canon.

A. Introduction

The letter known to us as 1 Corinthians consists of the longest fully extant letter from the correspondence between Paul and the church at Corinth founded by him. The entire correspondence, however, it not extant. A previous letter mentioned in 1 Cor 5:9 has not survived, and from letters subsequent to 1 Corinthians there are one complete and several fragmentary letters now included in 2 Corinthians (whether 2 Cor 6:14–7:1 originally had anything to do with Corinth is not clear). This situation of having substantial parts of an ongoing correspondence is unique as compared with the other letters of the apostle because in all other instances we possess only one letter (Galatians, 1 Thessalonians, Philemon) or some fragments combined in a letter (Philippians, Romans). Methodologically, this requires that all parts of 1 and 2 Corinthians be interpreted not only on their own terms but also within the context of the correspondence as a whole, as far as it is extant. This correspondence consists not only of successive exchanges of letters but also of personal visits, all of it reflecting an important period in the earliest history of the church in Corinth, a period which was decisive for the history of the early Christian mission.

1 Corinthians is characteristically different from the letters included in 2 Corinthians in a number of respects. Being not only the longest of the extant letters sent to Corinth, 1 Corinthians also has its own literary genre and function. The arguments made in this letter have no parallel in 2 Corinthians, although there are many connections between the letters. Issues and events discussed in the later letters (2 Corinthians) can be properly understood only by comparison with the previous letter of 1 Corinthians. To some degree the reverse is also true: 1 Corinthians becomes clearer when one sees from 2 Corinthians what happened to the issues and events later.

1 Corinthians is rich in historical information. The letter reports on the earliest history of the Corinthian church and contains some important clues to Paul's own biography

and career as an apostle. It provides just enough data concerning Paul's opponents to generate a plethora of hypotheses as to the character and theological views of these opponents. On the whole, 1 Corinthians contains the apostle's response to the first phase of the Corinthian crisis which threatened the very existence of that church. Scholarship, especially in the 20th century, has clarified many problems posed by 1 Corinthians, but major challenges still need to be tackled. These pertain to the literary and rhetorical aspects in particular: the problems of literary genre, function, and composition are still being discussed. Also, a consistent interpretation of the letter within the correspondence as a whole is still needed. Considerable progress has been made regarding social history (Hock 1980; Theissen 1982; Malherbe 1983; Meeks 1983); history of religions (Klauck 1982; Willis 1985); and rhetoric (Bünker 1984; Betz 1986; Welborn 1987; Mitchell 1989).

1 Corinthians is comparatively well attested in antiquity (Moffatt 1918: 114–16). *1 Clement* knows it and quotes from it (37:5; 47:1–3; 49:5), as do Ignatius of Antioch (*Eph* 16:1; 18:1; *Rom* 5:1; 9:2; *Phld* 3:3; see Schoedel *Ignatius of Antioch* Hermeneia, 9–10) and Marcion (Harnack 1924: 47–48, *79–*96). In the Muratorian Canon the two Corinthian letters head the list of the Pauline epistles. Early papyri have preserved 1 Corinthians in its entirety (esp. P 46, ca. A.D. 200) or in fragments (Conzelmann *1 Corinthians* Hermeneia, 1–2; Aland 1987: 83–102).

B. Date and Place of Writing

The place of composition of 1 Corinthians is clearly Ephesus, as Paul states in 16:8. The same verse indicates that the letter was composed in or near springtime, as Paul is awaiting Pentecost at Ephesus, yet plans to journey to Corinth and perhaps to winter there (16:6). Beyond the time of year, 1 Corinthians gives us no further specific information about its date of composition.

If we allow evidence from the Acts of the Apostles into the discussion of Pauline chronology, we have two other date markers, not for the composition of 1 Corinthians per se, but for Paul's visit(s) to the city of Corinth (Murphy-O'Connor 1983: 129–52; Lüdemann 1987: 202–12). However, neither of these two date markers is unambiguous.

In Acts 18:1–2 we are told that Paul, upon reaching Corinth, met Aquila and Priscilla, who had just come from Italy because the Roman emperor Claudius (41–54 C.E.) had expelled all the Jews from Rome. The Roman historian Suetonius (*Claud.* 25.4) corroborates the existence of such an event (and adds that these were disturbances at the instigation of a "Chrestus") but gives no date. Parallel accounts supplied by Dio Cassius (*Hist.* 60.6.6) and Augustine's pupil Orosius (*Hist. contra Pag.* 7.6.15–16) provide conflicting testimony in regard to the date and description of such an occurrence involving Claudius and Jews at Rome. Traditionally scholars have supported Orosius' testimony, which dates the Edict of Claudius in 49 C.E., thus roughly compatible with the term of office of Gallio (Conzelmann Hermeneia, 13; Jewett 1979: 38). Challenges to this position have recently been made by Luedemann (1984: 170) and Murphy-O'Connor (1983: 136), who prefer 41 C.E. (with Dio Cassius) for the Edict of Claudius.

In Acts 18:12–17, Paul is said to have made an appearance before the Roman proconsul of Achaia, Gallio, whose name is contained in a fragmentary inscription found at Delphi which is dated to the 26th acclamation of Claudius as emperor. The Gallio inscription permits us to date Gallio's term in office from either 51/52 or 52/53 (Conzelmann, 13). Scholars differ in regard to whether the account in Acts 18 is simply historically unreliable (Murphy-O'Connor 1983: 140) or whether Luke has fused events from more than one Pauline visit to Corinth. G. Luedemann (1984: 162–73) champions the latter position, dating Paul's initial visit to Corinth in 41 C.E. (coinciding with the Edict of Claudius) and places Paul's presentation before Gallio in 51/52 C.E. during Paul's third visit to Corinth. Generally, however, scholars have tended (with Luke) to fuse the two events and date the founding visit to Corinth (which was at least one year and a half in duration according to Acts 18:11) ca. 51 C.E. Proceeding from this date, and allowing enough time for Paul to return to Ephesus from the missionary tour of Acts 18:22–23 results in a date for the composition of 1 Corinthians in the range of 53–55 C.E. (53/54 Barrett *1 Corinthians* HNTC, 5; 54 Bornkamm 1969: 70; 55 Conzelmann, 4, n. 31; 55/56 Jewett 1979: 104).

C. Occasion of the Letter

In 1 Cor 3:6 Paul states that he "planted" the church at Corinth, claiming himself as its founder, while Apollos, he says, "watered" it. This accords with the traditions about the church at Corinth preserved in Acts 18 and 19. According to Acts 18:1–11, Paul arrived in Corinth and, after meeting Aquila and Priscilla, first took his message into the synagogue and persuaded both Jews and Greeks to the gospel. Many Corinthians believed and were baptized (cf. Acts 18:8, 10). Paul encountered Jewish opposition (18:6, 12–17), and we are told that he stayed with Titius Justus, a God-fearer whose house was next door to the synagogue (18:7). Jewish opposition was not unanimous, as two synagogue leaders, Crispus (Acts 18:8; 1 Cor 1:14) and Sosthenes (Acts 18:17; 1 Cor 1:1), became Christians, but it was serious, as Paul was led before the Roman proconsul Gallio (18:12–17).

After remaining in Corinth for more than a year and a half (18:11, 18), Paul set out for Syria and other parts E with Aquila and Priscilla (18:18–22), who stayed at Ephesus when Paul moved on. While Paul was on an extended missionary tour (18:18–23), Apollos, an Alexandrian of rhetorical skill, met Aquila and Priscilla in Ephesus (18:24–26). After they had correctly instructed him in the Christian faith, Apollos, armed with a letter of introduction, journeyed to Achaia and its capital, Corinth (18:27; 19:1). Acts 19:1 explicitly states that Paul and Apollos were not in Corinth at the same time. 1 Corinthians itself demonstrates that it postdates Apollos' appearance at Corinth (1:12; 3:4–6; 4:6; 16:12). Acts 19 recounts a long sojourn by Paul in Ephesus (19:8, 19). This is usually taken to be the time when Paul wrote 1 Corinthians (Barrett, HNTC, 5; Hurd 1983: 14).

1 Cor 5:9 indicates that Paul had written a letter to the Corinthians prior to the letter we know as 1 Corinthians. Most probably this letter is lost (although some scholars identify it with the letter fragment in 2 Cor 6:14–7:1).

Much communication between Paul and the church at Corinth preceded the composition of 1 Corinthians and in fact instigated it. Sosthenes (usually identified with the leader of the synagogue who was persecuted among the Christians in Acts 18:17) is with Paul and is the co-sender of the letter (1:1). "Chloe's people" have come and reported to Paul about the divisions among the community (1:11). A letter has been sent to Paul (7:1) and Paul has also received another delegation of Corinthians including Stephanas, Fortunatus, and Achaicus (16:17). Apollos has left Corinth and is apparently also at Ephesus (16:12). It is impossible to tell which if any of these communiqués belong together (i.e., if one of the delegations brought the letter, if Chloe's people are identical with the group named in 16:17, etc.).

Within 1 Corinthians, Paul explicitly responds to the report by Chloe's people that the community was divided (1:11; cf. 11:18) and to a letter from some members of the church (7:1). The news from Chloe's people (probably confirmed by the other communiqués) is that in Paul's absence the church community has been divided into various groups. The slogans Paul cites in 1:12 show that Corinthian factions claim allegiance to Paul, Apollos, and Cephas, and perhaps Christ. Specific issues are at the heart of this divisive scene: sexual morality, civil litigation, marriage, idol meat consumption, hairstyles, proper behavior in community worship (the Lord's Supper, manifestations of the spirit), and resurrection. This is the situation to which Paul responds in 1 Corinthians.

D. Corinthian Parties and Opposition to Paul

The question of Paul's opponents in Corinth has been under discussion ever since Ferdinand Christian Baur (1845: 259–332; for the history of research, see Räbiger 1847; Hurd 1983: 96–107; Lüdemann 1983: 103–25). The discussion has led to famous theories not only about Corinth but also about developments in early Christianity generally (the so-called Tübingen School). Concerning the opponents in Corinth, however, there is no reliable evidence apart from Paul's polemical and apologetic arguments. This situation raises the methodological problem of how to reconstruct historical facts from strongly biased reports (Berger 1980; Welborn 1987). Basically, these questions must be distinguished: (1) What was the origin and nature of the opposition to Paul? (2) How as the anti-Pauline opposition related to the factions in the church at Corinth? (3) Do 1 and 2 Corinthians presuppose the same opposition, or has the opposition changed after 1 Corinthians?

(1) 1 Corinthians shows that the opposition to Paul originated because of his own claim to be of the same rank as the Jerusalem apostles (1 Cor 9:1–2; 15:3–11). Paul's role as a missionary apostle must not have raised objections, but his claim to higher authority and even independence must have provoked criticism even prior to the writing of 1 Corinthians. See APOSTLE. The apostle's defensive remarks in 9:1–2 and 15:8–9 presuppose such criticism, if not in Corinth, then elsewhere. Paul's self-commendation as the model to imitate (4:16; 11:1) may have intensified the opposition to him. Since there is no reason to doubt that Paul founded the Corinthian church (1:14–17; and many passages in 1/2 Corinthians, Romans, and Acts), this in itself must have looked illegitimate to his opponents. We would know more if more information were available about what actually happened at the founding of the church. It appears that the opposition was in some way related to rivalry between different house churches. In Corinth there seem to have been several house churches (16:15; cf. 11:22) and a full assembly, called *ekklēsia* (1:2; 11:17–34; 14:23, 26).

(2) Since Paul was close to the houses of Stephanas (1:16; 16:15–17) and Gaius (1:14; Rom 16:23), perhaps the opposition arose in other house churches unfriendly to Paul (see Klauck 1981). Such rivalries may stem from their different histories and resulting outlooks. Was the church a union of several house churches? Such a possibility is even suggested by the report in Acts 18:1–17. If this can be assumed, Paul's goal for the church may have been to solidify union among divergent house churches, rather than to prevent an already healthy union from breaking up into factions. Paul's exhortation that the whole church should submit to the leadership of Stephanas (16:16) seems to show that no generally accepted leadership existed at that time.

The four factions named by Paul (1:12; 3:4, 22–23), however, do not seem to have existed at the beginning but emerged later. Because of this development the original founders (1:14, 16; 16:15–17; Acts 18:7–8) were reduced to the Paul party and found themselves competing with other parties named after Apollos, Cephas, and Christ. Little is known about the party of Apollos (1:12; 3:4–6, 22; 4:6; 16:12; Acts 18:24; 19:1); there is no evidence that this party was opposed to Paul (differently, Sellin 1982; cf. Hurd 1983: 97–99). Most likely the Cephas party was the center of the anti-Pauline opposition (1:12; 3:22; cf. 9:5; 15:5). Since Paul tries to dissociate Apollos, Cephas Peter, and even himself from the parties acting in their names, it is difficult to say how much they were involved in the disputes. Although Paul certainly was involved, Apollos does not seem to have been (cf. Paul's commendation in 16:12), while it is not certain whether Cephas ever went to Corinth (Barrett, HNTC 1–12; Hurd 1983: 99–101; Vielhauer 1975: 341–52). No doubt a difficult relationship existed between Paul and Cephas after the conflict at Antioch (Gal 2:11–14). The anti-Pauline opposition in Galatia seems to have been connected with similar opposition in Corinth, Philippi, and Rome. Greatest is the uncertainty with regard to the Christ party mentioned in 1 Cor 1:12 but not in 3:4 and 3:22. In Paul's own view, the Christ party would be the one to which all Christians belong (1:13; 3:23; also 1:2; 2 Cor 10:7). This party would be identical with the "Body of Christ," of which all Christians are "members" (1:4–9, 30; 6:15; 10:16–17; 11:3, 27, 29; 12:12–27). Therefore, did a Christ party exist in Corinth in distinction from the church and in competition with the other parties? Or was the Christ party Paul's invention, intended to show the absurdity of the other parties? Or was the slogan "but I am Christ's" (1:12) a gloss later inserted by a scribe who had well understood Paul's point? Even if Paul invented the Christ party it could also have been invented by somebody else for the same reason. The fact that this party is mentioned only once in 1:12 makes it most likely that it represents an ironic addition by the apostle as he describes the noisy sloganeering (Lüdemann 1983: 118, n. 48).

About Apollos we know almost nothing and even less

about people acting in his name. The Cephas party no doubt subscribed to the Cephas/Peter ideology (3:10–15; cf. Matt 16:17–19; Rom 15: 20). In the history of research much attention has been paid to the elusive Christ party (Baur 1845: 261–322; Hilgenfeld 1865; Räbiger 1847; Lütgert 1908; Rohr 1911; Schlatter 1914; Weiss 1917: 257–58; Hurd 1983: 101–6). More recently Walter Schmithals, building on the work of Lütgert, characterized the opponents of Paul as gnostics who had an already developed gnostic mythology and theology and who identified themselves as "christs" *(christoi)* (Schmithals 1971: 199–208; 374–77). Conzelmann has rightly objected that there is not enough evidence for Schmithals' far-reaching theories. There certainly are "traces of the beginnings of the formation of what later presented itself as 'Gnosticism,' that is, 'Gnosticism *in statu nascendi.* The Corinthians could be described as proto-Gnostics" (Conzelmann, 15). Was this incipient gnosticism represented by one of the parties? Or did it characterize the theology of the whole church? Or if Reitzenstein (1978: 68–89; 426–500) is right, Paul himself may be the gnostic who shared many ideas with the Corinthian enthusiasts, so that the opposition to him may have been anti-gnostic. If the opposition to Paul was connected with the Cephas party, Paul's critique of gnosticizing ideas may not be aimed at his opponents but at wrong conclusions drawn by some from his own earlier preaching. This assumption would explain why Paul, on the one hand, has no fundamental disagreements with the Corinthian "people of the spirit" *(pneumatikoi)* while, on the other hand, he criticizes theological propositions that could have been derived from his own teaching.

(3) While Schmithals still defends his view that the Corinthian gnostics were Paul's opponents in both letters (Schmithals 1983: 107–24), Georgi (1986) has renewed his thesis that, after 1 Corinthians, intruders in Corinth had introduced new opposition. There is no doubt that the letters give the impression that the opponents are different in 1 and 2 Corinthians, a fact insufficiently recognized by Schmithals. On the other hand, Georgi has difficulties in explaining what connections there must have been between the opponents of 2 Corinthians and those of 1 Corinthians. This question, therefore, remains unsolved.

E. Literary Analysis

1. Literary Composition. a. Division Theories. Questions regarding the number of letters Paul wrote to Corinth and their literary integrity began with Johann Salomo Semler (1725–91) and his students (Betz *2 Corinthians 8 and 9* Hermeneia, 3–36). During this debate also the unity of 1 Corinthians was questioned (for surveys and bibliography, see Clemen 1894; Moffatt 1918: 113–14; Kümmel 1975: 276–78; Vielhauer 1975: 140–41; Hurd 1983: 45–58). The theories of Johannes Weiss have been of great influence. In his commentary (1910: xl–xliii) he proposed that 1 Corinthians is the work of a redactor who created the letter out of two letters and who added his own interpolations: Letter A is the epistle mentioned in 1 Cor 5:9, sent from Ephesus and containing 2 Cor 6:14–7:1 and then 1 Cor 10:1–23; 6:12–20; 9:24–27; 11:2–34; 16:7b–9, 15–20. Letter B was sent from Macedonia and contained 1 Cor 1:1–6:11; 7; 8; 13; 10:24–11:1; 9:1–23; 12; 14; 15:1–16:7a; 16:10–14, 21–22. Redactional glosses and interpolations are, according to Weiss: 1:2; 4:17; 7:17; 11:16 (these interpolations giving the letter a "catholic" appeal); and 14:34–35; 10:29–30; 11:11–12. While these theories were meant to be merely suggestive, they became part of the ongoing discussions. By his last work (*Das Urchristentum,* published posthumously in 1917), Weiss had revised his theory, speaking now of four letters: Letter A, a rigorous exhortation to break with paganism, includes 1 Cor 10:1–23; 6:12–20; 11:2–34; 16:7(?), 8–9, 20–21(?); 2 Cor 6:14–7:1. Letter B-1 was written in response to questions from the Corinthians and included 1 Cor 7–9; 10:24–11:1; 12–15; 16:1–6, 7(?), 15–19(?). Another letter, B-2, reacts anxiously to bad news arriving from Corinth (1 Cor 1:1–6:11; 16:10–14, 22–24[?]). Letters C and D are from sections of 2 Corinthians (Weiss 1917: 271–72). While the debate subsided in the thirties, after World War II it was revived by Walter Schmithals in a number of important publications. Schmithals also kept changing his theories. In his dissertation of 1956 he proposed two letters (Schmithals 1971: 87–110, 332–43): Letter A begins with 2 Cor 6:14–7:1 and continues with 1 Cor 9:24–10:22; 6:12–20; 11:2–34; 15; 16:13–24. Letter B contains 1 Cor 1:1–6:11; 7:1–9: 23; 10:23–11:1; 12:1–14: 40 (with chaps. 13 and 14 reversed); 16:1–12. Subsequently Schmithals proposed completely different hypotheses, dividing 1 and 2 Corinthians into 9 (1973: 263–88) and later 13 letters (1984: 19–85). The period between ca. 1950 and 1980 saw the emergence of ever changing division hypotheses by Dinkler (*RGG*³ 3: 17–21); Schenk (1969: 219–43); Suhl (1975: 203–13); Jewett (1978: 389–444); Schenke and Fischer (1978: 92–94; 98–100); and Senft (*Corinthians* CNT, 17–19).

These division hypotheses (also called "partition theories") respond to the following incongruities perceived in 1 Corinthians (for discussion of these arguments, see Weiss 1910: xl–xliii; Schenk 1969; Schmithals 1971: 87–101; 1973; Conzelmann, 2–5; Suhl 1975: 203–13; Jewett 1978; Senft CNT, 17–19; Hurd 1983: 43–47; Merklein 1984):

(1) Contradictions Between 4:17–21 and 16:5–11. In 4:17 Paul announces that Timothy has been sent, but in 16:10 he talks of Timothy's visit conditionally and with a concern for his cordial reception which was absent in 4:17. In 4:19 Paul announces that he will come "quickly" but in 16:8 says that he will remain until Pentecost in Ephesus. The section 4:16–21 with its exhortation and travel plans is characteristic of a letter-closing formula but inappropriate for the middle of a letter (Schenk 1969: 235; Schmithals 1973: 266; Senft, 18). Schmithals has made the same argument in regard to 11:34b (1973: 281). Weiss also argued that the reference in 15:32 to a past persecution in Ephesus is strange if indeed the letter was sent from Ephesus as 16:8 indicates (1910: xli–xlii).

(2) Different Epistolary Occasions. The visit of Chloe's people and their report of divisions in the community seems to provide a different reason for Paul's writing from the Corinthians' letter mentioned in 7:1. In 1:16 Paul refers to the house of Stephanas without further comment, whereas in 16:15–18 he suddenly announces the arrival of a delegation including Stephanas. Most importantly, in 1:11 Paul knows from Chloe's people that divisions exist in the church, but in 11:18 seems ignorant of that fact and of the seriousness of the situation (Weiss

1910: xli, 278; Schmithals 1971: 90–91). 1 Cor 5:9 speaks of a previous Pauline letter to Corinth which is lost if our canonical 1 and 2 Corinthians are unified letters. This "lost letter" has been reconstructed by scholars from 2 Cor 6:14–7:1 and sections of 1 Corinthians (Weiss 1910: xli; Schenk 1969: 221–23; Schmithals 1971: 94–95).

(3) Literary Breaks. It has been argued that all sections of 1 Corinthians beginning *peri de*, "and concerning . . ." (7:1, 25; 8:1, 4; 12:1; 16:1, 12) respond to the Corinthians' letter mentioned in 7:1, and thus must belong to the same letter by Paul, the so-called *Antwortbrief* ("letter of response") (Schmithals 1971: 91; 1973: 268–73; Schenk 1969: 229; Senft, 19). Because "it is to be expected that Paul carries through the answering of the letter without any major digressions" (Schmithals 1971: 91), all sections in chaps. 7–16 not introduced by *peri de* (9:1–11:1; 13:1–15:58; 16:13–24) must belong to a different letter or letters. In general, proponents of division theories have perceived hard transitions throughout 1 Corinthians, which call the unity of the letter into question (5:1; 6:12; 7:1; 9:1; 9:24; 10:1; 10:23; 11:2; 12:1; 13:1; 15:1). In particular, dual treatments of idol meat in chaps. 8 and 10 (one lenient and the other harsh), and spiritual gifts in chaps. 12 and 14, in each case interrupted by the intervening arguments in chaps. 9 and 13, have been of significance for such theories (Weiss 1910: 212; Schmithals 1973: 268–73).

Each division theory resolves these apparent inconsistencies by dividing 1 Corinthians (and often parts of 2 Corinthians) into several distinct letters and constructing a historical scenario to which the letter fragments correspond. Schenk (1969: 242–43), Suhl (1975: 203–13), and Jewett (1978: 398–444) have attempted to reconstruct the redactional work responsible for our canonical 1 Corinthians. The sheer variety of the division theories proposed demonstrates a lack of scholarly consensus as to both proper methodology and specific analysis of the text (Barrett HNTC, 17).

b. Unity Theories. As noted above, the unity of 1 Corinthians went virtually unquestioned until the late nineteenth century (Clemen 1894: 19–57). Since the rise of division theories, the unity of 1 Corinthians has more often been assumed (Marxsen 1968: 76; Bornkamm 1969: 244) or conceded (Barrett, HNTC, 14–17; Conzelmann, 2–4) than argued for. The harsh transitions in the letter have been explained as a result of pauses in dictation (Barrett, 15; Conzelmann, 3, n. 20; Fascher *1 Korinther* THKNT, 44) or of fresh news received by Paul (Barrett, 15).

The first sustained argument in favor of the literary unity of 1 Corinthians was made by J. C. Hurd (1983). Hurd contends that the variety in tone and content within 1 Corinthians is a result of the different kinds of information Paul had received (1983: 47–58). He distinguishes three stages of oral and written communication between Paul and the Corinthians prior to 1 Corinthians: (1) Paul's first preaching in Corinth and the founding of the church; (2) his previous letter to the Corinthians (5:9–10); (3) "Information in reply, partly oral and partly written, brought to Paul from Corinth by Stephanas, Fortunatus and Achaicus and by Chloe's people. Some of this information was in the form of questions addressed to Paul by the Church; some in the form of comments on the situation at Corinth by some or all of the travellers" (Hurd 1983: 58). Hurd also proposes (1983: 213–39) that this Corinthian reply provided the outline for 1 Cor 7–16, where the apostle responds point by point to the Corinthians' questions and objections to his first letter. In sections where Paul responds to oral information (1:11–6:11 except 5:9–13a; 11:17–34), this tone is "aroused, even angry," whereas the sections which reply to the Corinthians' letter (5:9–13a; 7:1–11:16; 12:1–14:40; 16:1–9, 12) are "calm and balanced" (1983: 61–94).

Hurd's theory is significant in its attempt to prove rather than assume the unity of 1 Corinthians, but depends perhaps too much upon historical reconstruction and psychologizing. The assumption behind Hurd's thesis is surprisingly the same as Schmithals' (1971: 91), that by the *peri de* formula Paul responded point by point to the Corinthians' letter. Recent works have argued that, in the arrangement of topics in 1 Corinthians, Paul was governed by his own rhetorical purposes and was not confined to the order of the Corinthians' letter (Lührmann 1986: 305; Mitchell 1989). Similarly, rhetorical rather than historical reasons can account for some of the "inconsistencies" between 4:17–21 and 16:5–11, and between 1:11 and 11:18. An important critique of the bases of partition theories of 1 Corinthians was provided by Merklein (1984: 153–82), who argued for the literary coherence of the letter.

2. Compositional Analysis. The following brief analysis of 1 Corinthians argues for the unity of the letter. 1 Corinthians demonstrates both thematic and rhetorical unity when seen as a deliberative letter convincing the Corinthians to be reconciled and end their factionalism (for a detailed argument, see Mitchell 1989).

1:1–3 Epistolary Prescript.

1:4–9 Epistolary Thanksgiving, forming the *exordium,* which introduces key terms of Corinthian debate and of the epistle (Betz 1986: 26–39). The *exordium* ends appropriately with a call to unity in the *koinōnia* ("partnership") of Jesus Christ.

1:10–17 Statement of Facts, or *narratio,* of the argument in the body of the letter. Verse 1:10 is the *prothesis* or thesis statement of the argument of the entire letter, which calls on the Corinthians to end their factions and be reconciled with one another. In the brief *narratio* Paul rebuts any factionalists' claims resulting from baptism by the leaders (1:13–17).

1:18–15:57 Proof or *probatio,* in 4 subsections.

1:18–4:21 *First Proof Section,* which contains Paul's analysis and interpretation of the terms of the formula in 1:5 ("rich in every form of speech and in every form of knowledge"). The concepts of "speech" *(logos)* and "wisdom" *(sophia)* are discussed in 1:10–2:16, while "knowledge" *(gnōsis)* is examined in 3:1–23 (Betz 1986: 26–39). Corinthian boasting, an obvious expression of p[illegible]y politics, is rejected (1:26–[illegible]

This section lays the groundwork for the rest of the argument in three ways: (1) Paul redefines the goals and standards by which the Christian should make decisions (a common strategy in deliberative rhetoric); (2) he demonstrates their need for his advice for unity by censuring the Corinthians (chaps. 3–4, which contain epideictic elements); (3) Paul argues that he is the best one to advise them by describing his own apostolic office and responsibility in comparison with the Corinthians (esp. 4:14–16). "Therefore, I urge you, brothers, be imitators of me" in 4:16 points both backward (it forms an *inclusio* with 1:10) and forward to Paul's rhetorical strategy throughout 1 Corinthians. He will present himself as the example of the nondivisive behavior he urges the Corinthians to adopt (7:7; 8:13; 9:1–27; 10:33–11:1; 14:18–19).

5:1–11:1 *Second Proof Section* in which Paul treats the specific issues now dividing the community as subordinate arguments in his overall argument to convince the Corinthians to be unified. This section treats relations between Corinthian Christians and outsiders, and among Corinthian Christians within the larger context of the city of Corinth.

Ch. 5–7 *Porneia.* These arguments are grouped around the central issue of *porneia,* "sexual immorality" (mentioned in 5:1, 9, 10, 11; 6:9, 13, 15, 16, 18; 7:2).

5:1–13 *A case of porneia.* Paul begins the second proof section with a discussion of sexual immorality for two reasons: (1) *porneia* stands at the beginning of the list of vices which must have been known to the Corinthians from the beginning (5:10, 11; 6:9–10); (2) before arguing for the unity of the church community Paul must define clearly the boundaries between "insiders" and "outsiders" (5:9–13). Paul executes a legal decision in regard to this man who has married his father's wife. He is to be expelled from the community (5:13) and thus is not included in the unity to which Paul calls the church.

6:1–11 *Court Battles.* In 6:1–11 Paul continues to draw distinctions between "insiders" and "outsiders" (6:1–6). Some persons are taking fellow Christians to civil court. This is another cause and manifestation of the divisions within the community. Paul urges the Corinthians to deal with such issues within the community and not before outsiders.

6:12–20 *Another discussion of porneia,* along with a treatment of the Corinthian definitions of freedom which justify such actions (6:12) to expediency (a part of Paul's argument of redefinition of both freedom and expediency in 1 Corinthians (6:12, 19–20; 8:9; 9:1–27; 10:23–11:1). The "body of Christ" image is introduced (6:15–17) as a corrective to Corinthian individualism and divisiveness; image is fully expanded in chap. 12.

7:1–40 *Marriage and Status.* The section begins "concerning the things you wrote." This *peri de* formula (see above) is used also in 7:25; 8:1, 4; 12:1; 16:1, 12, and introduces a new topic for discussion. The general principle Paul evokes in each of the various cases in chap. 7 is—don't seek to alter your social status (7:8, 17–24, 27, 40) but realize your calling *(klēsis)* (7:15, 17–24; cf. 1:9, 26).

Ch. 8–10 *Idol Worship and Freedom.* Since idol worship *(eidōlolatria)* comes after *porneia* in the vice catalogue (5:10, 11; 6:9), the issues in 8:1–11:1 may be subsumed under this term (see 10:7, 14; cf. 8:1, 4, 7, 10; 10:7, 14, 19). The two complementary treatments of idol meat in chap. 8 and in chap. 10 frame Paul's self-exemplification of the proper use of freedom in chap. 9. The *peri de* formula in 8:1 does not mean that Paul here responds to the Corinthian letter in its order, but is simply a common formula for changing a topic (Mitchell 1989).

8:1–13 *Idolatry, First Treatment.* Paul urges love *(agapē)* over knowledge *(gnōsis)* as the fundamental value. It is true that idols do not exist (8:4–6) but the issue is more complex. 8:9 states a general ethical principle: "lest this your *exousia* ("liberty") might be an offense to this weak." One should sacrifice small freedoms for the sake of the many (8:13).

9:1–27 *Paul the example of proper use of freedom.* Paul establishes that he has the right to support from the gospel (9:3–12a) but has freely renounced that right (9:12b, 17). Such self-renunciation, translated into accommodating social behavior (9:19–23), is what he urges on the Corinthians. 9:24–27 stresses the eschatological goal as the fundamental context of Christian decision making.

10:1–22 *Idolatry, Second Treatment.* A series of rebellious episodes from Israel's wilderness traditions are presented as types (10:6, 11) of Corinthian factionalism and strife. The Corinthians are warned not to destroy themselves as the wilderness generation did—by desiring food, idolatry, and *porneia.* The unifying role of the eucharist in establishing the *koinōnia* of the community is appealed to.

10:23–11:1 This passage provides a conclusion to the second proof section (8:1–11:1). The new ethical principle of *agapē* is stated: "Let no one seek his/her own advantage, but that of the other" (10:24; cf. 13:5). Paul again presents himself as the example of this nonfactionalist behavior (10:33), who is to be imitated, as he imitates Christ (11:1).

11:2–14:40 *Third Proof Section.* Manifestations of Corinthian divisiveness when they come together in worship are discussed, as Paul continues to appeal for unity.

11:2–34 *Corinthians and Tradition.* The two subsections 11:2–16 and 11:17–34 are subsumed under the topic of tradition (11:2, 23; cf. chap. 15).

11:2–16 *Hairstyles in Worship.* A woman should be veiled in prayer but a man should not (11:4–10). Paul rejects the contentiousness which finds expression in the hairstyle controversy (11:16).

11:17–34 *Disorders at the Lord's Supper.* Corinthian factions manifest themselves in changing the celebration of the Lord's Supper. Paul calls the Corinthians to unity in the sacrament by appealing to the original tradition (11:23–26). This important text is our earliest witness to the tradition history of the eucharistic formula in the early Church.

12:1–14:40 *Spiritual Gifts.* Again two treatments of the same topic: spiritual gifts (chaps. 12 and 14) frame an exemplary argument, here on love (chap. 13). Paul urges unity and order in worship as 14:40 forms the conclusion to the third proof section.

12:1–31a *Spiritual Gifts. First Treatment.* Paul applies the political image of the body, theologized into the body of Christ, to the factionalism at Corinth. The goal, as in 1:10, is the end of *schismata,* "divisions" (12:25). Each person has a *charisma,* and all are given, not for individual, but for the communal advantage (12:4–11).

12:31b–13:13 *Love.* This "encomium on love" serves to exemplify the greatest gift—love *(agapē)*—by which the community will be reunified (see esp. 13:4–7). This chapter plays the same rhetorical function as chap. 9, by extrapolating and developing the general unifying principle which Paul embodies.

14:1–40 *Spiritual Gifts. Second Treatment.* Paul tells them to seek those spiritual expressions which promote unity (prophecy and interpretation of tongues, 14:3–5, 13), rather than speaking in tongues, which is divisive (14:2, 6–12). Paul exhorts the Corinthians to build up the church (14:4–5, 26) and stop their partisanship and separation from one another. He urges peace (14:33) and orderliness (14:40) in Corinthian worship.

15:1–57 *Fourth Proof Section.* It is only fitting that chap. 15, dealing with the resurrection from the dead, stands at the end. Divisiveness is caused by the fact that some at Corinth deny the resurrection (15:13), a view here refuted by Paul on the basis of the tradition of Christ's resurrection (15:1–11, 12–28), and an argument on the resurrected body (15:35–57). This eschatological section highlights the final goal in relation to which the Corinthians should make all their decisions. Eschatology plays this role in the *exordium* (1:7–8) and throughout the argument (3:12–15; 4:1–5; 6:3; 9:24–27).

15:58 Conclusion or *peroratio.* Paul sums up his argument in 1:10–15:57 by urging the Corinthians as they stand in expectation of the *eschaton* to follow the course of unity, for it will prove to be to their advantage ("your work is not in vain in the Lord"). This conclusion corresponds to the *exordium* (1:4–9), as it should.

16:1–24 Epistolary Closing, containing travel plans, final admonitions, and greetings.

16:1–12 Information about forthcoming visits of Paul (16:1–9, including instructions on the collection for the saints), Timothy (16:10–11), and Apollos (16:12).

16:13–18 First Paul reiterates the argument in the letter (16:13–14), "Let all things be yours in love" and then supplements this general advice for unity with a concrete political dictum: the Corinthians are to obey the house of Stephanas (16:15–16).

16:19–21 Customary epistolary greetings (16:19–20), to which Paul adds his by his own hand, which serves as an authentication formula (16:21).

16:22–24 Solemn curse (16:22a) and the prayer *maranatha* ("Our Lord, come" [16:22b]). The letter appropriately concludes with a two-part final blessing (16:23–24), for grace *(charis)* and love *(agapē).*

F. Theological Significance

Some scholars have criticized 1 Corinthians for its poverty of theological doctrine (Bauer 1971: 219), while others (Conzelmann, 9) have argued that the letter contains "applied theology." The problem with that view, however, is that all the letters of Paul are applied theology. What is then distinctive about 1 Corinthians? First, there are a number of formal features which make the letter unique: 1 Corinthians as a letter is part of a sequence of exchanges, written and oral, and its theology must be derived from the sequence as a whole as well as its particular expression in this letter. In this dialogue 1 Corinthians represents Paul's answer to a number of questions addressed to him by the Church (7:1, 25; 8:1; 12:1; 16:1, 12). Together with preceding (5:9) and following letters (2 Corinthians), messengers and visitors coming from and going to Corinth, 1 Corinthians is part of an ongoing process of educating the

Church in the belief and practice of the new Christian religion (Betz 1986: 26–27). This educational process does not simply consist of Paul delivering authoritative doctrines and rules for behavior, but the apostle makes his readers partners in a theological debate. His methods of argument show influences from what may be called the Socratic tradition (Betz 1972). Paul not only instructs his readers, he also stimulates their own thinking and elicits their own answers. At any rate he presumed that the matters regarding Christian belief and behavior can be argued in a rational way, especially since rationality was believed to be informed by the Holy Spirit.

In terms of theological doctrines, attention must be given to the situation of the Church in general and of the Corinthian church in particular, to the practical and theological problems at hand, to the presuppositions and conclusions involved on each side of the arguments, and to Paul's own doctrinal stance as he develops his recommendations. The situation of the Corinthian church provided Paul with a novel experience. This church was founded in one of the centers of Hellenistic culture (see the studies on social history by Malherbe 1983; Theissen 1982; Meeks 1983). In Corinth the Pauline mission had succeeded—seemingly for the first time—in winning converts from the better-educated and cultured circles of a prosperous and cosmopolitan city. The congregation had access to material as well as spiritual wealth, both proverbial assets of the city of Corinth. From the scarce evidence available to us we can infer that the church was diverse in its makeup. There were in it sharp distinctions socially, intellectually, and probably ethnically. The considerable number of travelers to the church meant connections with and influences from outsiders, relating to various groups inside. Early on, various members of the church seem to have interpreted Paul's gospel in diverse ways. Some seem to have developed it further in conformity with Hellenistic religiosity. This must have led to changes in the performance and understanding of rituals Paul found disagreeable (1:13–17; 15:29; 11:17–34; Klauck 1982; Willis 1985). The older Jewish-Christian ethos as reflected in the moral catalogs (1 Cor 5:9–11; 6:9–10) gave way to the lifestyle of the big Hellenistic city, where freedom from tradition and convention, experimentation with new ideas, and excitement about spiritual experiences were the standards for achievement. Consequently it is not surprising that the values of Hellenistic city life and religiosity dominate the discussion.

The picture of the Corinthian church which Paul depicts shows a bewildering mixture of positive and negative developments that have taken place since Paul's founding visit. Positively, the church was flourishing; negatively, however, internal dissension threatened to tear it apart. Party slogans (1:12; 3:4; 6:12; 10:23) advocated "political rhetoric" rather than thorough theological thinking. Some church members apparently acted more as an avant-garde, while others expressed a cautious conservatism. One group's expression of freedom must have been a scandal to other groups. Thus, to the apostle the church presented a rather distressing picture: so-called spiritual experiences justifying excesses and abuses of freedom in complete disregard for the life of the community, all signs of a disintegrating community.

As far as we can tell, this situation was without precedent in Paul's missionary experience and thus presented him with a new challenge. In 1 Thessalonians and Galatians the apostle had advocated life in the spirit without reservations. Confronted with the Corinthian problems, however, he was forced to marshal all his available resources in a new way in order to come to grips with the issues. Theologically, Paul begins with the self-understanding of the Corinthians as he sums it up in 1:5: "in everything you have been made rich in him [Christ], in every form of speech and in every form of knowledge." This claim of possessing an abundance of speech and knowledge *(logos kai gnōsis)* becomes the focus of Paul's argumentation throughout the letter and even in 2 Corinthians (Betz 1986: 26–48). Applying to it the christology of the Christ crucified (1:13, 17, 18–25; 8:11) and the doctrine of justification by faith (1:26–31), Paul analyzes critically the notions of speech *(logos),* wisdom *(sophia),* and knowledge *(gnōsis)* in 1:18–3:23. Originally developed in confrontation with the Jewish doctrines of Torah possession and observance, the apostle applies these doctrines to their Greek analog, the claim to possess eloquence and knowledge. This demonstrates Paul's flexibility in applying the principles of his theology to new and different circumstances and problems.

Without denying the Corinthians their claimed abundance of eloquence and knowledge, Paul argues that their spiritual wealth should not simply be taken to coincide with maturity in Christian faith. In fact, he points out, there is an obvious discrepancy between what the Corinthians claim and what they really are. While he concedes that they have plenty of eloquence and knowledge, there are serious shortcomings in the area of practical "deeds" (*erga;* 1:7; 3:13–15; 15:58; 16:10). This discrepancy points to a contradiction between claim and reality and renders their faith "immature" (3:1–4). As long as there is no balance between the claims of eloquence, knowledge, and practice, the goal of "perfection" (cf. 2:'6; 3:1, 18; 4:8) cannot have been reached. Paul's argumentation is designed so as to advise the Corinthians how to bring their praxis *(erga)* up to the same standards as their eloquence and knowledge. This goal is behind the long section of arguments in chaps. 5–15. The key concept in these chapters is that of Christian love (*agapē;* 4:21; 8:1; 13:1–13; 14:1; 16:14, 24), specifically defined as "what which builds up" the community (8:1; 14:4–5; cf. 3:9–15).

Paul, however, does not attempt to talk the Corinthians out of their spiritual wealth. His goal is, on the contrary, to enable them to verify that claim by the practice of the Christian *agapē.* For this purpose Paul develops his lengthy ethical arguments and positions in chaps. 5 and 15. Although several of these arguments show signs of their origin in a Jewish-Christian context, in 1 Corinthians they are clearly applied to the confrontation of new gentile Christians with their Hellenistic pagan background and past. The threat as Paul perceives it is their "Hellenization" in the negative sense of the term. (See HELLENISM). Since no agreed standards yet existed, Paul had to develop rules for behavior anew. How should the new converts conduct their lives with regard to polytheism and its communal and religious practices such as prostitution, the courts of law, the meat markets, invitations to dine in pagan temples, and so forth?

One of the major theological contributions of 1 Corinthians is in the area of ecclesiology. The body of Christ image for the Church runs throughout the epistle (1:13; 6:15–20; 10:16–17; 11:29; 12:4–27; for the extensive literature on this topic, see *sōma* in *TDNT*). Paul confronts the divisiveness of the Corinthian community with a political analogy common in Greek and Roman literature for social cohesion, the body (for references, see Lietzmann *An die Korinther* HNT, 61–63, and Conzelman, 211–14), here radically Christianized. This appropriation provides another example of the apostle's adaptation and transformation of Hellenistic concepts in his theological formulations. The Church is the body of Christ, a unified structure in which each member has a part and function (12:4–27). This ontological reality has ethical implications: the Christian does not own his/her body (6:19), should make decisions on the basis of the entire Church and not merely the self (10:23–11:1; 14:5), and must manifest his/her full solidarity with the other members in both joy and sadness (12:25–26; cf. 13:6). The ecclesiological doctrine of the body of Christ, first introduced by Paul in 1 Corinthians, appears also in Romans (12:3–8) and is later transformed in the deutero-Pauline letters into a spiritual-cosmological doctrine in which Christ appears as the head of the body (Eph 1:22–23; 4:4–16; 5:22, 30; Col 1:18, 24; 2:16–19).

Apart from the specific issues discussed in the letter, 1 Corinthians receives its unique importance because it is only here that Paul develops his theological ideas about Greek cultural and religious values. These values include subjects such as rhetoric, wisdom, and knowledge, that is, the experience of the Christian faith as intellectual enlightenment and inspiration, including forms of ecstasy. In the practical area Corinthian notions of freedom need to be redefined in terms of new forms of Christian communal and individual life (6:12; 8:9; 9:19–23; 10:23–11:1). What Paul is primarily concerned with is the need to safeguard the Christian character of what is advocated as the new life in Christ. The most impressive part of Paul's deliberations is the attempt to spell out rules for Christian behavior vis-à-vis the polytheistic and pluralistic environment within which the Church found itself. Christian theology has never made another such attempt, so that modern Christianity which finds itself again in this situation will become Paul's advice, even if it is conditioned by the situation of the 1st century.

Bibliography

Aland, K. and B. 1987. *The Text of the New Testament.* Trans. Erroll F. Rhodes. Grand Rapids.

Barrett, C. K. 1963. Cephas and Corinth. Pp. 1–12 in *Abraham unser Vater, Festschrift für Otto Michel,* ed. O. Betz; M. Hengel; and P. Schmidt. Leiden.

———. 1982. *Essays on Paul.* Philadelphia.

Bauer, W. 1971. *Orthodoxy and Heresy in Earliest Christianity.* Trans. and ed. by R. A. Kraft and G. Krodel. Philadelphia.

Baur, F. C. 1831. Die Christuspartei in der korinthischen Gemeinde. *Tübinger Zeitschrift für Theologie* 5: 61–206. Repr. *Ausgewählte Werke in Einzelausgaben,* ed. K. Scholder, 1: 1–146. Stuttgart, 1963.

———. 1845. *Paulus, der Apostel Jesu Christi.* Stuttgart.

Berger, K. 1980. Die implizierten Gegner. Pp. 373–400 in *Kirche, Festschrift für Günther Bornkamm,* ed. D. Lührmann and G. Strecker. Tübingen.

Betz, H. D. 1972. *Der Apostel Paulus und die sokratische Tradition.* BHT 45. Tübingen.

———. 1986. The Problem of Rhetoric and Theology according to the Apostle Paul. Pp. 16–48 in *L'Apôtre Paul: Personnalité, style et conception du ministère,* ed. A. Vanhoye. BETL 73. Louvain.

Bornkamm, G. 1969. *Paul.* Trans. D. M. G. Stalker. New York.

Bünker, M. 1984. *Briefformular und rhetorische Disposition im 1. Korintherbrief.* Göttingen.

Clemen, C. 1894. *Die Einheitlichkeit der paulinischen Briefe.* Göttingen.

Dahl, N. A. 1977. *Studies in Paul.* Minneapolis.

Dautzenberg, G. 1975. *Urchristliche Prophetie.* BWANT 104. Stuttgart.

Georgi, D. 1986. *The Opponents of Paul in Second Corinthians.* Philadelphia.

Harnack, A. 1924. *Marcion. Das Evangelium vom fremden Gott.* Leipzig. Repr. Darmstadt, 1960.

Heinrici, G. 1896. *Der erste Brief an die Korinther.* Göttingen.

Hilgenfeld, A. 1865. Die Christus-Leute in Korinth. *ZWT* 3: 241–42.

Hock, R. F. 1980. *The Social Context of Paul's Ministry.* Philadelphia.

Hurd, J. 1983. *The Origin of 1 Corinthians.* 2d ed. Macon, GA.

Jewett, R. 1978. The Redaction of 1 Corinthians and the Trajectory of the Pauline School. *JAARSup 44: 389–444.*

———. 1979. *A Chronology of Paul's Life.* Philadelphia.

Jones, F. S. 1987. *Freiheit bei Paulus.* GTA 34. Göttingen.

Klauck, H.-J. 1981. *Hausgemeinde und Hauskirche im frühen Christentum.* SBS 103. Stuttgart.

———. 1982. *Herrenmahl und hellenistischer Kult.* NTAbh 15. Münster.

———. 1984. *1. Korintherbrief.* Die neue Echter Bibel 7. Würzburg.

Kümmel, W. G. 1975. *Introduction to the New Testament.* Trans. H. C. Kee. 2d ed. Nashville.

Lüdemann, G. 1980–83. *Paulus, der Heidenapostel.* 2 vols. FRLANT 123, 130. Göttingen.

———. 1987. *Das frühe Christentum nach den Traditionen der Apostelgeschichte.* Göttingen.

Luedemann, G. 1984. *Paul, Apostle to the Gentiles.* Trans. F. S. Jones. Philadelphia.

———. 1987. *Antipaulinism in Early Christianity.* Trans. E. Boring. Philadelphia.

Lührmann, D. 1986. Freundschaftsbrief trotz Spannungen. Pp. 298–314 in *Studien zum Text und zur Ethik des Neuen Testaments,* ed. W. Schrage. Berlin.

Lütgert, W. 1908. *Freiheitspredigt und Schwarmgeister in Korinth.* BFCT 12/3. Gütersloh.

Malherbe, A. J. 1983. *Social Aspects of Early Christianity,* 2d ed. Philadelphia.

Marshall, P. 1987. *Enmity in Corinth.* WUNT 2d ser. 23. Tübingen.

Marxsen, W. 1968. *Introduction to the New Testament.* Trans. G. Buswell. Oxford.

Meeks, W. A. 1983. *The First Urban Christians.* New Haven.

Merklein, H. 1984. Die Einheitlichkeit des ersten Korintherbriefes. *ZNW* 75: 153–82.

Mitchell, M. M. 1989. 1 Corinthians: Paul and the Rhetoric of Reconciliation. Ph.D. diss. Chicago.

———. 1991. *Paul and the Rhetoric of Reconciliation.* HUT 27. Tübingen.

Moffatt, J. 1918. *An Introduction to the Literature of the New Testament,* 3d ed. Edinburgh.

Murphy-O'Connor, J. 1983. *St. Paul's Corinth: Texts and Archaeology.* GNS 6. Wilmington.

Räbiger, J. F. 1847. *Kritische Untersuchungen über den Inhalt der beiden Briefs des Apostels Paulus an die korinthische Gemeinde.* Breslau. 2d ed. 1886.

Reitzenstein, R. 1978. *Hellenistic Mystery Religions.* Trans. J. E. Steely. Pittsburgh.

Rohr, I. 1911. Christuspartei und Schwarmgeister in Korinth. *TQ* 93: 165–205.

Schenk, W. 1969. Der erste Korintherbrief als Briefsammlung. *ZNW* 60: 219–43.

Schenke, H. M., and Fischer, K. M. 1978. *Einleitung in die Schriften des Neuen Testaments.* Vol. 1, *Die Briefe des Paulus und Schriften des Paulinismus.* Berlin.

Schlatter, A. 1914. *Die korinthische Theologie.* BFCT 18/2. Gütersloh.

Schmithals, W. 1971. *Gnosticism in Corinth.* Trans. J. E. Steely. Nashville.

———. 1973. Die Korintherbriefe als Briefsammlung. *ZNW* 60: 263–88.

———. 1983. The *Corpus Paulinum* and Gnosis. Pp. 107–24 in *The New Testament and Gnosis,* ed. A. H. B. Logan and A. J. M. Wedderburn. Edinburgh.

———. 1984. *Die Briefe des Paulus in ihrer ursprünglichen Form.* Zurich.

Schreiber, A. 1977. *Die Gemeinde in Korinth.* NTAbh 12. Münster.

Sellin, G. 1982. Das "Geheimnis" der Weisheit und das Rätsel der "Christuspartei" (zu 1 Kor 1–4). *ZNW* 73: 69–96.

———. 1986. *Der Streit um die Auferstehung der Toten.* FRLANT 13. Göttingen.

Suhl, A. 1975. *Paulus und seine Briefe.* SNT 11. Gütersloh.

Theissen, G. 1982. *The Social Setting of Pauline Christianity.* Trans. J. H. Schütz. Philadelphia.

Vanhoye, A., ed. 1986. *L'Apôtre Paul: Personnalité, style et conception du ministère.* BETL 73. Louvain.

Vielhauer, P. 1975. Paulus und die Kephaspartei in Korinth. *NTS* 21: 341–52.

Weiss, J. 1910. *Der erste Korintherbrief.* Göttingen. Repr. 1970.

———. 1917. *Das Urchristentum,* ed. R. Knopf. Göttingen (ET); rep. 1959.

Welborn, L. L. 1987. On the Discord in Corinth. *JBL* 106: 83–111.

Wilckens, U. 1959. *Weisheit und Torheit.* BHT 26. Tübingen.

Willis, W. L. 1985. *Idol Meat in Corinth.* SBLDS 68. Chico, CA.

Wischmeyer, O. 1981. *Der höchste Weg. Das 13. Kapitel des 1. Korintherbriefes.* SNT 13. Gütersloh.

HANS DIETER BETZ
MARGARET M. MITCHELL

CORINTHIANS, SECOND EPISTLE TO THE.

CORINTHIANS, SECOND EPISTLE TO THE. A letter written by the apostle Paul to the church at Corinth, found as the eighth book of the NT canon.

A. Introduction

The letter we call 2 Corinthians abounds with fascinating insights into the activity and mind of the apostle Paul. Some of the passages show how he worked as an administrator, a pastoral adviser, and an ecumenical church leader. The careful reader discovers valuable information about historical developments in the churches of Corinth and elsewhere, finds data concerning the life and personality of Paul, and uncovers aspects of the theologies of Paul and his opponents which do not appear in the apostle's other letters. All these perspectives contribute to an engrossing view of the Pauline mission.

2 Corinthians does not yield its information readily and thus poses problems for its readers and interpreters. Understanding these problems is indispensable not only for 2 Corinthians but also for the interpretation of 1 Corinthians. As with all other correspondence, the letters must be interpreted consecutively and in their entirety, for every section has its place in the context of the entire correspondence. Earlier statements may explain why later events occurred, just as later statements may throw light on what was said earlier. In literary terms, a correspondence contains components of an ongoing conversation, the missing parts of which must be reconstructed to as great a degree as possible. Such reconstruction is a major task for the interpretation of 2 Corinthians.

The publication of 2 Corinthians presents the interpreter with a second difficulty. While there is strong evidence for an early (1st century) attestation of 1 Corinthians, the second letter is not attested before the middle of the 2d century, when its name appears in the canon of Marcion (ca. 140–150; see Harnack 1924: 96*–102*, 128*). It received a second notice a few decades later in the Canon Muratori. Prior to these two lists, however, no external evidence exists for the circulation of the letter. Despite this paucity of attestation, no one in antiquity doubted the letter's authenticity. Thus the circumstances which led to the appearance of 2 Corinthians remain shrouded in mystery.

In light of such interpretative difficulties, we are fortunate to have an extensive history of research on 2 Corinthians. At present, this research is in the midst of a new productive phase. For surveys of the older period, see Moffatt (1918: 116–30) and Windisch (1924: 5–31); for recent developments, see Furnish (*2 Corinthians* AB, 29–54); Betz (*2 Corinthians 8 and 9* Hermeneia, 3–36); Georgi (1986: 333–45), and Welborn (1987).

B. Literary Composition

As most scholars now agree, Paul's second letter to the Corinthians is a collection comprised of fragments from several originally independent letters. The decisive step toward the discovery of these constituent letters was taken by Semler (1776), when he recognized seams in the text between both chaps. 8 and 9 and chaps. 9 and 10. He concluded that 2 Corinthians was composed of pieces of originally separate letters.

Since Semler's discovery, the scholarly debate concerning the division of the letter has not ceased. Questions remain as to whether the letter should be partitioned and, if so, how many sections there are and which passages they comprise (for surveys, see Furnish AB, 30–54; Betz Hermeneia, 3–36). The second of these questions is becoming the more important, as few scholars continue to defend the unity of 2 Corinthians (Hyldahl 1973; Kümmel 1975: 287–93; see Furnish, 33–35, for names and a summary of the arguments).

Important progress in the literary investigation of 2 Corinthians has been made in this century by Bornkamm (1961), who divided 2 Corinthians into fragments from six different letters: (1) an earlier apology (2:14–6:13; 7:2–4); (2) the "letter of tears" (10:1–13:10); (3) the "letter of reconciliation" (1:1–2:13; 7:5–16; 13:11–13); (4) a letter of recommendation for Titus and his companions (chap. 8); (5) a letter to the churches of Achaia (chap. 9); and (6) an interpolated passage (6:14–7:1). Bornkamm assumed that the present letter of 2 Corinthians was the creation of a later editor/redactor. This partition theory, often in somewhat modified form, is now held by a large number of scholars (for a survey, see Betz, 20–25). Furnish (35–41), however, supports the two-letter hypothesis previously held by Windisch, Bruce, and Barrett: 2 Corinthians consists of parts from two originally separate letters: (1) chaps. 1–9 and (2) chaps. 10–13. On the other hand, we have Schmithals' complicated partition theories. Most recently, he has proposed that Paul's Corinthian correspondence consisted of thirteen letters which are now found not only in 1 and 2 Corinthians but in Romans as well (Schmithals 1984: 19–20).

As divisions continue to be discussed, the methodological questions prove to be of primary importance. Since no existing manuscripts of 2 Corinthians show traces of division, evidence for partitioning must come from the internal criteria of philology and comparative literary analysis. Such analyses have been proposed by Betz (Hermeneia) for 2 Corinthians 8 and 9 and by Welborn (1987) for the "letter of reconciliation" (1:1–2:13; 7:5–16; 13:11–13). In addition to careful analyses of the letter fragments, an investigation of the methods and ideas of the redactor who was responsible for the final composition of what we call 2 Corinthians will also be necessary (for interesting suggestions on the redactor's work, see Bornkamm 1961: 24–32).

C. The Letter Fragments in Chronological Sequence

(1) The "first apology" (2:14–6:13; 7:2–4) begins with an expression of thanks to God and a description of the apostle's missionary activity expressed through a field of metaphors which create the image of a triumphal procession (2:14–17). In this procession, Paul functions as the herald (4:5; 5:20–6:2; 6:11–13; 7:2–4). Embedded in the use of this image are arguments in which Paul defends his adequacy for the apostolic office. As an apostle, he describes himself as a "servant of the new covenant" (3:6), which is explained in 3:4–6:10. Although the exact nature of the argumentation is far from clear, Paul additionally uses the occasion to present major christological and soteriological doctrines. The conclusion contains a plea for acceptance and trust (6:11–13; 7:2–3) as well as a confession of confidence and joy (7:4). Since such statements are appropriate to the conclusion of letters, it would seem that only the epistolary pre- and postscripts are omitted.

(2) The "second apology" (10:1–13:10), or "letter of tears" (as it is later characterized in 2:4), was doubtless provoked by Paul's unsuccessful earlier attempts—in particular the earlier apology—to clear himself of suspicion (10:1–2). Yet an escalation must have pushed the matter to a crisis. Facing it, Paul realized that if he were to prevail he must mobilize extraordinary rhetorical armaments (Malherbe 1983: 143–73) and confront the accusers directly (Betz 1986: 40–44). In 10:10, Paul actually quotes from what seems to be a critical report concerning his presence: "His letters," he [or: the report] says, "are weighty and strong, but his physical presence is weak and his speech is contemptible."

The origin of this three-pronged personality profile is unknown. Paul attributes it to a person, but it is not clear whether that person acted as an individual or as the leader of a faction, whether this individual was identical with the unnamed person called "the offender" (7:12), and whether he had any official function. Was an investigator appointed by the church whose report was communicated to Paul (cf. 13:3)? The statement in 10:10 looks like a summary of an investigative report on Paul's performance as a public speaker; it is entirely negative. In order to refute these charges, Paul felt he could only adopt the pose of the fool (11:1; 12:11) and deliver a so-called "fool's speech" (11:1–12:10 [or 12:13]). In this wild and brilliant self-parody, the apostle demolishes the presumptions of his adversaries. He restores his credibility by discrediting theirs through the use of his entire arsenal of irony, sarcasm, and parody. In this fool's speech he demonstrates that, if he wished, he could conform to the standards of his critics but that he had good reason not to do so. In the role of the fool he performs—without actually doing—that which he judges to be inappropriate.

If the critics doubt his skills as a rhetorician, he sheepishly agrees with them: "If I am a layman in speech, I am not in knowledge" (11:6). If they demand the "signs of the apostle," he is ready to deliver them (Betz 1972: 70–100). He presents a testimony about ascending into heaven only to bring back nothing (12:1–4; see Betz 1972: 89–92) and follows with an appeal to a miraculous healing which turns out not to produce the healing (12:7–12; see Betz 1969: 288–305; 1972: 92–100). Paul's own criteria are different (12:11–13). He glorifies God in his weaknesses (12:9, 10; cf. 10:1, 10; 11:21, 23–29; 12:21). He does not accept financial support from the Corinthians (11:7–12; 12:13, 14:18; see Betz 1972: 100–17), and he refuses to be judged in comparison with the other apostles (11:5, 13–15; 12:11–13; see Betz 1972: 118–32). After evaluating his fool's speech, Paul turns to the future, announcing his forthcoming third visit to Corinth (12:14–21; 13:1–4). Typical of a Pauline letter, the last section contains paraenesis and a summary of his concerns (13:5–10). Again, this conclusion suggests that little was omitted by the redactor at the close of the letter.

(3) The "letter of reconciliation" (1:1–2:13; 7:5–16; 13:11–13) is extant in its entirety and provides the frame into which the redactor has inserted the other letter fragments. For an investigation of this "letter of reconciliation," see Welborn 1987.

The letter begins with the epistolary prescript (1:1–2) naming the sender, Paul, with his official title, and the cosender, Timothy, with his rank. There follow the addresses, the church in Corinth and "all the saints living throughout Achaia." The prescript concludes with the usual salutation.

The exordium begins with a praise of God, a *bĕrakâ* or *eulogia* (1:3–4), rather than with the usual prayer of thanksgiving *(eucharistia)*. The main theological concepts of this prayer in praise of God, "affliction" *(thlipsis)* and "consolation" *(paraklēsis)*, are them briefly introduced in preparation for the role they will play in the main body of the letter. Paul's design here is to describe his relationship with the Corinthians, particularly in terms of the crisis just passed, as a partnership in Christian suffering and consolation (1:5–7). In a short narrative (1:8–11), the apostle then demonstrates by his own example—his recent escape from almost certain death in Asia Minor—how God's consolation works in concrete life situations.

From these theological presuppositions the apostle enters into a lengthy discussion of his previous letter (1:12–2:4), the "letter of tears" (10:1–13:10). After giving assurances of his integrity and friendly intentions (1:12–14), he explains apologetically and with some apprehension why he had decided to change his travel plans several times and why these changes should not be construed as evidence of his unreliability and fickleness (1:15–22), the charges by his critics to the contrary. He explains further why he had postponed his third visit to Corinth and why in the meantime he had written the "tearful letter." The intention of that letter had not been to inflict "distress" *(lypē)* on the Corinthians but to make them understand his great love for them (1:23–24; 2:1–4). If the letter had caused severe distress among them, it was not so much due to the letter itself as to the provocations of "the offender" (2:5), an unnamed person in Corinth who fomented the whole crisis. Since this offender had meanwhile been reprimanded by the majority of the church, Paul now generously recommends that they forgive him and, should they do so, he, too, would forgive him (2:5–11). The apostle then describes how in great anguish he went to the Troad and to Macedonia, where he awaited Titus, who was due to come from Corinth to meet him (2:12–13, continued in 7:5). This terrifying "affliction" *(thlipsis)* only ended when Titus appeared with the good news of the accomplishment of a reconciliation (7:6–7).

The report then turns to a theological (and even psychological) analysis of the experience of "distress" *(lypē)*, which Paul admits having caused among the Corinthians with his letter. As he points out, this distress had a positive result in that it turned the Corinthians around and brought them to their senses (*metanoia* [7:9–10]). This change of mind in turn led to Paul's great joy at learning of the reconciliation, which occurrence also confirmed his original confidence in them (7:8–12). In other words, for Paul no less than for the Corinthian church, the whole crisis was another experience of affliction turned into consolation and thus not to be regretted. Paul is now full of joy, pride, and confidence at things having turned out so well (7:13–16), and in these emotions lie the reason for the praise of God at the beginning of the letter (1:3–4). A warm and exuberant postscript concludes the letter (13:11–13).

(4) The "administrative letter" of chap. 8 (see Betz *2 Corinthians 8 and 9* Hermeneia, 37–86, 131–39) was sent to Corinth together with the delegation consisting of Titus and two "brothers." The letter has two parts, an advisory section regarding the collection for the Jerusalem church (8:1–15) and a legal section commending and authorizing the members of the delegation (8:16–23). The letter concludes with a peroration (8:24). Compared with literary and documentary parallels, the fragment is similar to letters of appointment given to political or adminstrative envoys.

(5) The "administrative letter" of chap. 9 (see Betz, 87–128, 139–40) is addressed to the Christians of Achaia and, like chap. 8, is concerned with the collection for the church in Jerusalem. As a literary unit, its purpose is advisory: it seeks to enlist the help of the Achaians in bringing the collection in Corinth to completion. Its two main sections contain information and explanation on the delegation sent to Corinth (9:2–5) and a theological statement about the purpose of the collection (9:6–14) and it concludes with a peroration, an expression of thanksgiving to God (9:15).

(6) The interpolated passage of 6:14–7:1 reflects a situation different from 2 Corinthians' other components: it does not reflect on Paul's relationship with Corinth or on the Jerusalem collection. This difference has resulted in the view held by most scholars today that 2 Corinthians 6:14–7:1 is a non-Pauline interpolation (see Furnish, 360–68, 371–83, with further references), while Betz (1973) has argued that it is even anti-Pauline in its theology, originating perhaps with (some of) Paul's opponents. If this passage did indeed come from Paul's opponents, it might even reflect the party against which Paul had to defend himself elsewhere in his correspondence with the Corinthians. Regardless, the piece is a carefully composed exhortation warning against teaming up with "unbelievers," whoever they may be. Its theology is strongly dualistic and Jewish-Christian. The origin of the piece is as much a puzzle as is the question of how it became mixed up with the Corinthian correspondence.

D. Historical Developments in Corinth

The preceding chronological ordering of the letter fragments provides some clarification of the turbulent events following 1 Corinthians. In 1 Corinthians 16, Paul mentions certain events he expects to take place after the dispatching of that letter. The collection for the church of Jerusalem, begun with Titus during an earlier visit (2 Cor 12:16–18; 8:6), will proceed according to the guidelines set forth in 1 Cor 16:1–2. After the collection, when it is to be taken up to Jerusalem, Paul plans to visit Corinth for the second time. He intends to arrive there from Macedonia, perhaps to spend the winter before going on to Palestine (16:6); however, he is undecided whether he himself will lead the delegation which will deliver the gift to the Jerusalem church (16:3–4). Meanwhile, until his departure for Macedonia, his presence in Ephesus remains crucial (16:8–9). Then he announces the forthcoming visit of Timothy. For reasons we do not know Paul fears that Timothy will not find a friendly reception (16:10–11; cf. 4:17). The letter fragments in 2 Corinthians, however, show that all of these plans could not be carried out as Paul had hoped.

When 2 Corinthians says that Timothy is at Paul's side (1:1), there is no mention of Timothy's visit to Corinth. He probably did go there but upon arrival found the church hostile and in turmoil (see Conzelmann 1973: 104; differently Bornkamm 1961: 9) and returned to Ephesus to inform Paul of the situation. This information, presupposed in 2 Corinthians, included a complete change in the Corinthian situation. While in 1 Corinthians Paul could remain above party factionalism, he now could not avoid facing a full-blown rebellion against him. The problems of his legitimacy, incipient in 1 Corinthians (15:8–10), had worsened, apparently in connection with the collection, which his opponents saw as evidence of a scheme to line his own pockets. Since these charges are already considered in the "first apology" (2 Cor 2:14–6:13; 7:2–4), where Paul responds to accusations of "inadequacy for office" (2:16; 3:5–6) and "peddling the word of God" (2:17; cf. 4:2; 6:3; 7:2; 12:16–17), this letter may be part of his first response and written either before or after Timothy's return to Ephesus. Although Timothy may have taken this letter to Corinth, we have no evidence to substantiate such a hypothesis. At any rate, this "first apology" did not prevent further deterioration in Paul's relationship with Corinth.

At this point, Paul changed his travel plans. The "letter of reconciliation" (2 Cor 1:1–2:13; 7:5–16; 13:11–13), written after the resolution of the conflict, contains lengthy explanations for these changes. His report in 2 Cor 1:15–16, however, indicates that he must twice have altered the plans presented in 1 Cor 16:5–8, for he says that he intended to go from Ephesus to Corinth, passing through Macedonia, and then perhaps to Judea. Upon receiving the bad news about Corinth, he quickly decided to go there directly, and apparently unannounced, to face the opposition head on. This visit, the so-called "sorrowful visit," resulted in a fiasco for the apostle which he says he would not wish to repeat (2:1–3; 12:21; 13:2). Indeed, he postponed his third visit to Corinth (12:14; 13:1) until the conflict had been resolved. At the center of this conflict appears to have been one whom Paul calls "the offender" (7:12) who apparently brought a charge of embezzlement against Paul (12:16–18; 8:20; see Betz *2 Corinthians 8 and 9*, Hermeneia, 76–77). Such suspicion of fraud of course jeopardized Paul's whole credibility. It is possible that the church may even have appointed an investigator, from whose devastating report Paul himself quotes in 2 Cor 10:10 (cf. 11:6; 13:3, 6).

Rejected by his own church as a charlatan and a fraud, Paul made a final desperate attempt to regain his reputation. He wrote the "letter of tears" (10:1–13:10); most likely after he returned to Ephesus, and sent it on to Corinth, probably with Titus and a "brother" (12:18). As we learn from the subsequent "letter of reconciliation" (2 Cor 1:1–2:13; 7:5–16; 13:11–13), both the "letter of tears" and Titus' mission were successful, although Paul was unaware of this fact until much later. In a state of "great tribulation and anguish of heart" (2:4) he left for the Troad in NW Asia Minor; there, anxiously awaiting Titus, he became so restless that he set sail for Macedonia (2:12–13). Titus finally arrived there, bringing with him the good news of the reconciliation (7:5–7). In great joy, the apostle then sent from Macedonia the "letter of reconciliation."

One result of the Corinthian crisis, of course, was the collapse of the collection for the church in Jerusalem from that city. The Macedonian and Achaian churches had finished their part of the collection (8:2–5; 9:2), and at this point the Macedonians proposed to recommence and complete the Corinthian collection (8:4–5) with Titus volunteering to return to Corinth to reorganize the drive (8:17). Paul thus appointed Titus (8:6, 16–17, 23) and two "brothers" (8:18–23; 9:3–5), a carefully chosen delegation representing not only Paul but "all the churches" as well (8:18). Their letter of authorization is extant in chap. 8. In addition, Paul enlisted the aid of the Achaian Christians, who had already completed their part in the endeavor (chap. 9).

From Rom 15:25–31 we learn that the advance team had succeeded in finishing the collection, that Paul had arrived, and that a delegation was ready to take the money to Judea. Paul now decided to lead that delegation, whose members may be listed in Rom 16:21–23; Acts 20:4 (see Betz *2 Corinthians 8 and 9* Hermeneia, 51, 56). His departure from Corinth meant that he would never see Greece again (Acts 19:21; 20:22–25, 36–38).

This reconstruction of events clarifies the otherwise confusing sequence of visits by Paul and his collaborators. Paul made three visits to Corinth, the first being the foundation visit accompanied by Silvanus and Timothy (1 Corinthians *passim;* 2 Cor 1:19; Acts 18:1–18). The second visit, announced in 1 Cor 16:2–9, was made in haste and without advance notice; it became the "sorrowful" visit (2 Cor 2:1). A third visit had been planned but had to be postponed until the crisis had passed (2 Cor 2:1–3; 12:14; 13:1–2). This final visit became a reality when Paul arrived in Corinth to head up the Judean delegation (Rom 15:25–31). Timothy, named as cofounder of the Corinthian church in 2 Cor 1:19 and Acts 18:5, also visited Corinth three times. If his second visit, announced in 1 Cor 16:10–11 (4:17), was carried out, his third visit occurred when he accompanied Paul to Judea (Rom 16:21; Acts 20:4).

Three visits must also be assumed for Titus, whose assignments were closely related to the collection efforts (cf. Gal 2:1–10 for his presence at the Jerusalem conference). His first visit must have occurred prior to the writing of 1 Corinthians because of the subsequent guidelines for the collection as stated in 1 Cor 16:1–4. On this visit he began the fund raising (2 Cor 8:6). His second visit was made in the company of one "brother" (2 Cor 12:18); the main objectives appear to have been the delivery of the "letter of tears" (2 Cor 10:1–13:10) and the attempt to reconcile the church with its apostle. Paul apparently chose Titus rather than Timothy because the Corinthians did not trust the latter (see 1 Cor 16:10–11). Bringing the news of the reconciliation to Paul in Macedonia (2 Cor 7:6–7) quickly led to Titus' third visit to Corinth, accompanied by two "brothers," to restart and finish the collection (2 Cor 8:6, 16–23; 9:3–5). Having completed this task as well, Titus is mentioned no further and his name is not included in the lists of the delegates to Palestine (Rom 16:21–23; Acts 20:4).

E. Dates

Scholars disagree as to whether precise dates can be assigned to the events emerging from the letter fragments of 2 Corinthians. Such variant views depend primarily on the overall view of the chronology of Paul (see CHRONOLOGY [NT]). If Jesus' death is dated early (27 C.E.), Paul's conversion falls in the year 30 C.E.; but if Jesus' death occurred in 30 C.E., Paul's conversion and all other events must be dated later. For Luedemann, who favors earlier dates (see the chronological chart in Luedemann 1984: 262–63), the events involving 2 Corinthians fall in the years 49 (or 52) to 51 (or 54). Jewett (1979; see his appended chart) and Furnish (54–55) date these events in the years 55–56. According to them, Timothy's second visit to Corinth took place in 55 C.E., the year which saw most of the events reported in the letter fragments in 2 Corinthians. Paul spent the winter of 55–56 in Macedonia, went to Corinth in 56, and left for Palestine in the spring of 57. These dates are probable, but good cases can be made as well for two to three years earlier or even for somewhat later (see Schenke and Fischer 1978: 47–63; Vielhauer 1975: 156).

F. Paul's Opponents

Recent decades have seen extensive discussion regarding Paul's opponents in (1 and) 2 Corinthians (for surveys and references, see Barrett 1982: 60–86, 87–107; Barnett 1984: 3–17; Furnish, *2 Corinthians* AB, 48–54; Georgi 1986: 333–450), and notable clarification of the problems and options has been achieved. It is now clear that the issues concerning the factions and Paul's opponents in 1 Corinthians must be distinguished from the factions and Paul's opponents in 2 Corinthians. We can no longer assume that both letters deal with the same kind of opponents. Earlier, Schmithals had advanced the thesis (1971; still defended 1983: 107–24) that there was only one, gnostic, opposition to Paul. Schmithals needs this hypothesis to support his thesis that thirteen letters comprise 1 and 2 Corinthians; most scholars, however, do not accept it (Conzelmann, *1 Corinthians* Hermeneia, 14–16), preferring rather the views of Bornkamm (1971: 169–71) and his student, Georgi (1964), who argue that new opponents moved into Corinth after 1 Corinthians was written.

The discovery of these intruders and their efforts at provocation and agitation sent Timothy back to Ephesus to inform Paul, who then embarked upon his second, unsuccessful, visit to Corinth. The apostle's sarcastic polemics in the subsequent "letter of tears" (2 Cor 10:1–13:10) suggest that these new opponents hold views akin to Hellenistic-Jewish concepts of the "divine man" *(theios anēr)*. As was typical of Jews (1 Cor 1:22), these rival Jewish-Christian missionaries has succeeded in persuading the Corinthians to demand from Paul "the signs of the apostle" (2 Cor 12:1, 7, 12), that is, miracles and revelations which serve as evidence that Christ speaks through the apostle (13:3).

Unfortunately, Paul's polemics do not yield much detail on the views these opponents actually held. To obtain such data, Georgi has therefore interpreted Paul's opponents against the religious background of Diaspora Judaism and that branch of the Church which handed down the miracle stories of the gospels and Acts. Despite the methodological problems of extracting hard data from polemics and counterpolemics, not to mention the slim evidential base generally, Georgi's direction is the right one for future research (see also Betz 1969; 1972; *RAC* 12: Cols. 231–312; Koester 1982, 1: 126–30; Georgi 1986).

If one adopts this line of thought, one immediately sees other questions: Did Paul's opponents in 2 Corinthians have any connection with the factions in 1 Corinthians, and, if so, with which faction(s)? Was there a connection with anti-Pauline forces in Jerusalem (Käsemann 1942; Barrett 1982)? If there was such a connection (2 Cor 11:13–15, 21–23, 24), how do these opponents compare with those against whom Paul defends himself in Galatians? In Galatians, the points of contention surround the Torah and circumcision, not miracles and revelations; thus these opponents must have been different, despite their common goal of discrediting Paul. From the first chapters of the book of Acts it is quite obvious that apostles with different outlooks did mission work under the supervision of the Jerusalem church. Unlike the opponents in 1 Corinthians, those targeted in 2 Corinthians were intruders from outside the city (2 Cor 10:13–16; 11:4, 19–20). Yet the adversary called "the offender" (2 Cor 7:12) was in all probability a resident of Corinth. How was he connected with the parties of 1 Corinthians and the intruders of 2 Corinthians? After the reconciliation, we are told, forgiveness was to be offered to this "offender"; but it is inconceivable that such simple forgiveness was granted to the "pseudo-apostles" and "messengers of Satan" (2 Cor 11:13–14). What happened to these intruders after the reconciliation we do not know. These and other questions may never be answered without the discovery of new sources.

G. Perspectives on the History of the Early Church

The crisis which shattered the relationship between Paul and his church in Corinth had repercussions far beyond Corinth. This particular crisis was just one more piece of evidence that Paul's main mission of bringing the Christian gospel to the gentile world was increasingly threatened from both inside and outside the churches he had founded. Paul's own ambiguous biography had been a source of bewilderment and suspicion from the beginning, and 2 Corinthians shows how well his opponents used this, his Achilles' heel, to undermine his credibility. These doubts about Paul's integrity were compounded by the self-doubts of the Corinthians concerning their salvation. It was not so much that they intended to turn their backs on Christianity altogether as that they had opened themselves up to other Christian missionaries hostile to Paul. These missionaries apparently had better credentials from and connections with the mother church in Palestine. In addition, they offered religious experiences which were more impressive and persuasive in the eyes of people of a Hellenistic religious mentality. Miracles and revelations were easier for the Corinthian Christians to handle than were Paul's complicated theological discourses.

The issue that seemed to have become the focus of the alienation, however, was a monetary one, the collection that Paul had organized in Macedonia and Achaia for the benefit of the church in Jerusalem. Charges, or at least suspicions, of financial irregularities had led the Corinthians to believe that the whole fund drive was a scheme designed to enrich the apostle himself. Their mistrust was justified by the fact that many religious quacks and swindlers with similar schemes operated throughout the Roman Empire. Had one of these con artists duped them? Paul's letter of chap. 9 reveals that the purpose of the collection was to maintain a bond of brotherhood between the Greek churches and the mother church in Jerusalem, thus forestalling their growing alienation from becoming total separation. See also Gal 2:10; GALATIANS.

As the story tells it, Paul's struggle was desperate. Having been driven out of Corinth, he had only a slim chance of regaining his former position. Nevertheless, by the sheer skill of his pen and the diplomatic talents of his envoy Titus, he managed to turn things around, an accomplishment paralleled only in Galatians. Had Paul failed in Corinth, his whole mission work in Greece would have collapsed and passed into other hands. The successful completion of the collection, however, as reported in Rom 15:25–31, meant that he could conclude his mission work in the East and turn his attention to the West, to Rome and Spain (Rom 15:14–24).

H. Theological Significance

The letter fragments assembled in 2 Corinthians give evidence of Paul's methods in dealing with severe crises in his churches. Involving the full repertoire of administrative instruments (visits, envoys, and letters) as well as rhetorical strategies, his major goal was that of theological education. Completing what had been started in the (lost) letter mentioned in 1 Cor 5:9, the letters of 1 and 2 Corinthians have taken the Corinthians through an entire course of theological education. In this course, theological doctrines, rhetorical strategies, and practical experiences went hand in hand (Betz 1986). At the end, Paul could testify that the Corinthians had learned their lessons well. According to 1 Cor 1:5, they could claim an abundance of eloquence and knowledge but lacked mature faith and love. 2 Corinthians can restate this claim in a different form and add another challenge as well: "As you have abundance in everything, in faith and eloquence and knowledge as well as in every kind of zeal and in that kind of love which came from us and dwells in you, you should have abundance in this gift of charity, too" (2 Cor 8:7).

Theological doctrines used in the arguments include here, as elsewhere, those concerned with God, Christ, and Christian salvation, but in the center stands Paul's peculiar doctrine about his apostolic office (see APOSTLE). Much more explicitly than in other letters, Paul devotes two major sections to explanations of his office as an apostle. The "first apology" (2:14–6:13; 7:2–4) contains a self-portrait as the representative of the death and resurrection of Christ. The "letter of tears" (10:1–13:10) goes over this ground again but in a highly sarcastic tone and in the form of an ironic self-parody (the "fool's speech").

While in 1 Corinthians the doctrine of justification by faith (see JUSTIFICATION) is applied to the claim to possess "eloquence and knowledge" (1 Cor 1:18–31), that same doctrine serves in 2 Corinthians (see, especially, in chronological order, 2 Cor 5:17–21; 10:17–18; 12:9–10; 13:3–4; 1:3–7, 18–22) to distinguish between true and false claims of legitimacy. Most important, finally, are the statements and procedures that Paul sets forth concerning the formation of the Church as a theological community of love (see, especially, 2 Cor 5:14; 6:6, 11:13; 11:11; 12:15; 2:4, 8; 13:11, 13; 8:7, 8, 24; 9:6–14).

Bibliography

Barnett, P. W. 1984. Opposition in Corinth. *JSNT* 22: 3–17.

Barrett, C. K. 1982. *Essays on Paul.* Philadelphia.

Betz, H. D. 1967. *Nachfolge und Nachahmung Jesu Christi im Neuen Testament.* BHT 37. Tübingen.

———. 1969. Eine Christus-Aretalogy bei Paulus (2 Kor 12,7–10). *ZTK* 66: 288–305.

———. 1972. *Der Apostel Paulus und die sokratische Tradition.* BHT. 45. Tübingen.

———. 1973. 2 Cor 6:14–7:1: An Anti-Pauline Fragment? *JBL* 92: 88–108.

———. 1986. The Problem of Rhetoric and Theology according to the Apostle Paul. Pp. 16–48 in *L'Apôtre Paul: Personnalité, style et conception du ministère,* ed. A. Vanhoye. BETL 73. Louvain.

Bornkamm, G. 1961. *Die Vorgeschichte des sogenannten zweiten Korintherbriefes.* SHAW 2. Heidelberg. Repr. vol. 2, pp. 162–94 in *Geschichte und Glaube; Gesammelte Auf sätze,* vol. 4. Munich, 1971.

———. 1971. *Paul.* Trans. D. M. G. Stalker. New York.

Bultmann, R. 1967. *Exegetica: Aufsätze zur Erforschung des Neuen Testaments,* ed. E. Dinkler. Tübingen.

———. 1985. *The Second Letter to the Corinthians.* Trans. R. A. Harrisville; ed. E. Dinkler, 1976. Minneapolis.

Carrez, M. 1986. *La deuxième épître de saint Paul aux Corinthiens.* CNT 8. Geneva.

Collange, J.-F. 1972. *Enigmes de la deuxième épître de Paul aux Corinthiens.* SNTSMS 18. Cambridge.

Conzelmann, H. 1973. *History of Primitive Christianity.* Trans. J. E. Steele. Nashville.

Dahl, N. A. 1977. *Studies in Paul.* Minneapolis.

Fallon, F. T. 1980. *2 Corinthians.* NTM 11. Wilmington.

Forbes, C. 1986. Comparison, Self-Praise and Irony: Paul's Boasting and the Conventions of Hellenistic Rhetoric. *NTS* 32: 1–30.

Georgi, D. 1964. *Die Gegner des Paulus im 2. Korintherbrief.* WMANT 11. Neukirchen-Vluyn.

———. 1986. *The Opponents of Paul in Second Corinthians.* Trans. 1964, Philadelphia.

Harnack, A. 1924. *Marcion. Das Evangelium vom fremden Gott.* Leipzig. Repr. 1960.

Hyldahl, N. 1973. Die Frage nach der literarischen Einheit des zweiten Korintherbriefes. *ZNW* 64: 289–306.

Jewett, R. 1979. *A Chronology of Paul's Life.* Philadelphia.

Käsemann, E. 1942. Die Legitimität des Apostels. *ZNW* 41: 33–71. Repr. pp. 475–521 in *Das Paulusbild in der neueren deutschen Forschung,* ed. K. H. Rengsdorf. Darmstadt, 1964.

Koester, H. 1982. *Introduction to the New Testament.* 2 vols. Philadelphia.

Kümmel, W. G. 1975. *Introduction to the New Testament.* Rev. ed. Nashville.

Lüdemann, G. 1982. *Antipaulinismus im frühen Christentum.* Vol. 2 in *Paulus, der Heidenapostel.* FRLANT 130. Göttingen.

Luedemann, G. 1984. *Paul, Apostle to the Gentiles: Studies in Chronology.* Trans. F. S. Jones. Philadelphia.

Malherbe, A. J. 1983. Antisthenes and Odysseus, and Paul at War. *HTR* 76: 143–73.

Moffatt, J. 1918. *An Introduction to the Literature of the New Testament.* 3d ed. Edinburgh.

Schenke, H.-M., and Fischer, K. M. 1978. *Die Briefe des Paulus und*

die Schriften des Paulinismus. Vol. 1 of *Einleitung in die Schriften des Neuen Testaments.* Berlin.
Schmithals, W. 1971. *Gnosticism of Corinth.* Trans. J. E. Steele. Nashville.
———. 1983. The *Corpus Paulinum* and Gnosis. Pp. 107–24 in *The New Testament and Gnosis,* ed. A. H. B. Logan and A. J. M. Wedderburn. Edinburgh.
———. 1984. *Die Briefe des Paulus in ihrer ursprünglichen Form.* Zurich.
Semler, J. S. 1776. *Paraphrasis II. Epistolae ad Corinthios.* Halle.
Suhl, A. 1975. *Paulus und seine Briefe. Ein Beitrag zur paulinischen Chronologie.* SNT 11. Gütersloh.
Vielhauer, P. 1975. *Geschichte der urchristlichen Literatur.* Berlin.
Watson, F. 1984. 2 Cor 10–13 and Paul's Painful Letter to the Corinthians. *JTS* 35: 324–46.
Welborn, L. L. 1987. *Paul's Letter of Reconciliation in 2 Corinthians.* Ph.D. diss. Chicago.
Windisch, H. 1924. *Der zweite Korintherbrief.* Kritisch-exegetischer Kommentar über das Neue Testament 6. Repr. Göttingen, 1970.
Zmijewski, J. 1978. *Der Stil der paulinischen "Narrenrede."* BBB 52. Cologne.

HANS DIETER BETZ

CORINTHIANS, THIRD EPISTLE TO THE.

One of the so-called apocryphal epistles, forming the last part of an apocryphal correspondence between Paul and the Corinthians contained in the *Acts of Paul.* It is preserved in several textual traditions of varying quality: in Armenian through several NT mss; through five rather fragmentary Latin mss; a 6th-century Coptic translation of the *Acts of Paul;* in Greek from the 3d-century Bodmer papyrus (see BODMER PAPYRI); and is attested in Ephrem the Syrian's commentary on the Pauline epistles (*NTApocr* 2: 326–27; Klijn 1963: 2–4). English translations may be found in Schneemelcher and in James.

The Syriac and Armenian churches regarded *3 Corinthians* as authentic and included it with the Pauline letters. Even though it circulated independently and was quite popular among certain groups of early Christians, as early as 1892 Zahn proposed that it was part of the *Acts of Paul* (Zahn; Enslin IDB, 679; *NTApocr* 2: 326; Klijn 1963: 2–5). Discovery of the Coptic Heidelberg papyrus in 1894 showed Zahn to be correct. The Coptic text also indicated that it was written originally in Greek. This was subsequently verified by the discovery of a Greek text which was published in 1959 (Klijn 1963: 5).

While it is now quite apparent that *3 Corinthians* is part of the *Acts of Paul,* opinions vary as to whether the author created the correspondence between Paul and the Corinthians or whether he used already existing writings (Klijn 1963: 10–16; *NTApocr* 2: 340–42).

Establishing the date, place of composition, and the identity of the author of *3 Corinthians* is complicated by its relationship to the *Acts of Paul.* Tertullian says (*De Bapt.* 17; approx. A.D. 200) that the *Acts of Paul* was written by a presbyter in Asia Minor, and the work itself indicates that it was most likely written in Asia Minor. A date between 170 and 195 is usually posited for the composition of the *Acts of Paul* (Klijn 1963: 4; *NTApocr* 2: 351). *3 Corinthians* is at least this early. If *3 Corinthians* was an earlier writing which was used by the author of the *Acts of Paul,* then it is impossible at this time to establish its precise date, place of composition, or the identity of its author.

3 Corinthians is located within the Philippi episode of the *Acts of Paul* and forms part of a correspondence between Paul and the Corinthians. The Corinthians first wrote Paul telling of two men, Simon and Cleobius, who arrived in Corinth and distorted the faith by teaching things they had not heard from Paul or the other apostles. They taught that the Corinthians should not "appeal to the prophets, and that God is not almighty, and that there is no resurrection of the flesh, and that the creation of man is not God's [work], and that the Lord is not come in the flesh, nor was he born of Mary, and that the world is not of God, but of angels" (*NTApocr* 2: 374). This letter was delivered to Paul in prison in Philippi by Threptus and Eutychus. *3 Corinthians* is Paul's response to the Corinthians' request that he either visit or write concerning these teachings.

3 Corinthians begins with a rather typical Pauline greeting, followed by an acknowledgment that his own tribulation is a sign that the teachings of the evil one are gaining ground. Paul then assures the Corinthians that he taught them what he received from the apostles. This is followed by a refutation of the teachings of Simon and Cleobius, which makes up the bulk of the letter. In turn, this is followed by an assurance for those who accept his teachings and condemnation for those who do not. The letter closes with an urge for them to turn away from the false teachings and a blessing of peace, grace, and love.

Bibliography

James, M. R. 1924. *The Apocryphal New Testament.* Oxford.
Klijn, A. F. J. 1963. The Apocryphal Correspondence Between Paul and the Corinthians. *VC* 17: 2–23.
Zahn, T. 1892. *Geschichte des neuentestamentlichen Kanons* 2/2. Leipzig.

DANA ANDREW THOMASON

CORMORANT. See ZOOLOGY.

CORNELIUS (PERSON) [Gk *Kornēlios*].

According to the book of Acts, Cornelius is the first gentile to become a convert to Christianity (Acts 10:1–11:18, cf. 15:6–11). Although the episode occupies a significant place in Luke-Acts, Luke conveys little information about the man himself. Study of the episode has concentrated primarily on the historical development and literary composition of the narrative and its significance in the unfolding story of Luke-Acts.

At the beginning of the Cornelius narrative, Luke notes that Cornelius resides in Caesarea and describes him as "a centurion of what was known as the Italian Cohort, a devout man who feared God with all his household, gave alms liberally to the people, and prayed constantly to God" (10:1–2). This introduction identifies Cornelius in two important ways. First, that he is a gentile may be deduced from the fact that he is a Roman soldier, since being in the military was incompatible with the observance of Jewish law (Joseph. *Ant* 18.84).

Second, with several phrases Luke signals that Cornelius is a religious man. Together with his entire household (cf. 11:14) Cornelius fears God. Whether this statement means that Cornelius belongs to a distinct group of gentiles known as "God-fearers," (i.e., gentiles who worshipped the God of the Jews but did not become proselytes) is a matter of debate. What is not subject to debate is the positive connotation attached to this statement and the ones that follow. Cornelius is charitable toward "the people" (Gk *laos*), a term Luke often employs for the people of Israel; and he prays to God without ceasing. While Cornelius is a gentile, Luke takes care to introduce him as an exceptionally good and pious gentile whose conversion almost becomes a response to his behavior. Indeed, the angel who appears to him and instructs him to send for Peter says that Cornelius' behavior has become a memorial before God (Acts 10:4).

Since Martin Dibelius' essay (1956) on the Cornelius account, interpretation of this episode has revolved around his thesis that the story has its origin in an earlier and simpler story of conversion, such as Dibelius understood had been preserved in the story of the ETHIOPIAN EUNUCH. Dibelius argued that the following elements conflicted with this earlier version of the story and, hence, that they were later additions: (1) Peter's vision (10:9–16) does not appear to be connected with the surrounding narrative, since the vision has to do with food laws but the larger story focuses on the inclusion of gentiles; (2) the description of the arrival of Peter and his colleagues at Cornelius' home (10:27–29), which is literarily awkward; (3) Peter's speech (10:34–43) appears to be a later addition because, according to Dibelius, early conversion stories did not contain speeches and because this particular speech seems to have been modeled on Peter's other speeches; and (4) Peter's defense of his actions in Jerusalem (11:1–18), since it focuses on Peter's social relations with gentiles, which Dibelius finds to be insignificant in the story itself.

Following Dibelius' essay, other interpreters of the Cornelius episode sought to refine his thesis. For example, while Ernst Haenchen (1965) expressed doubts about Dibelius' assumption that the early Church preserved legends about conversions (a criticism more recently revived by Klaus Haacker [1980]), Haenchen's own suggestion was that Luke had received the Cornelius story, in the form Dibelius had suggested, from traditions preserved at Caesarea. Ulrich Wilckens (1958) examined Peter's speech in 10:34–43, contending that this speech is more catechetical than Peter's other speeches in Acts, which are kerygmatic in content. François Bovon (1970) connected Peter's vision (10:9–16) with the Jerusalem discussion in 11:1–18 and argued that together they suggest that within the Cornelius account a second motif pertains to food laws. Karl Löning (1974) has argued that Peter's vision is an integral part of the Cornelius story, even in its earlier forms.

Despite Löning's attempt, the feature of Dibelius' analysis which has been most widely accepted is almost certainly his claim that Peter's vision is extrinsic to the narrative and is, hence, an addition to an earlier and simpler account. However, Dibelius neglected two features of ancient narratives that undermine his argument. First, numerous narratives in the ancient world use the device of double dreams, that is, two characters have separate dreams within one narrative episode (see, for example, Jos. *Ant* 11.321–39). The closest example, of course, occurs in Acts 9, where Saul and Ananias each have a vision concerning the eventual visit of Ananias to Saul. Thus, there is good reason to suspect that the two visions in Acts 10 also belong to the same narrative. The second narrative feature Dibelius neglected is the literary role of dreams or visions. Dibelius found the vision of Peter insufficiently related to the larger narrative, but that is to overlook the fact that dreams or visions often occur at the beginning of an episode, but their significance only unfolds as the story itself unfolds. For example, in Plutarch's treatment of the life of Cicero, he tells of a dream in which Cicero sees Octavius, whom he had actually never met; on the next day, however, Cicero does meet Octavius (*Cic.* 44; cf. *Cim.* 18; *Luc.* 10.23.3–4; *Brut.* 20.8–11). Similarly, in Achilles Tatius' story of *Leucippe and Clitophon,* one of the Hellenistic romances, Clitophon dreams that he has been attached to a wife and then the attachment is severed by someone else. When Clitophon's engagement to Calligone is broken, the dream is fulfilled, and it is fulfilled yet again when Clitophon is separated from Leucippe by a series of misadventures. Numerous such examples suggest that, while Peter's vision does not explicitly address the conversion of gentiles, it may nevertheless be an integral part of the narrative.

The literary structure of the Cornelius account, when read as a unified story, consists of a sequence of parallel scenes: (1a) the vision of Cornelius, in which he receives instructions concerning Peter (10:1–8); (1b) the vision of Peter, in which he receives instructions concerning Cornelius (10:9–16); (2a) Cornelius' agents arrive at Peter's house and are welcomed there (10:17–23a); (2b) Peter and his companions arrive at Cornelius' house and are welcomed there (10:23b–29); (3a) Cornelius speaks to explain the events that have occurred to him (10:30–33); (3b) Peter speaks to explain his insight about God's impartiality and to recount the gospel (10:34–43); (4a) God's impartiality is confirmed by the Holy Spirit and through baptism (10:44–48); (4b) God's impartiality is confirmed by the community gathered in Jerusalem (11:1–18).

Luke narrates this particular story in a careful and even dramatic manner, at least in part because it is a major turning point in his story of the early Church. Beginning in Acts 1:8 (or even Luke 2:32), Luke has laid the groundwork for the inclusion of gentiles within the Christian community. Initially preaching the gospel only within Jerusalem, believers leave Jerusalem when they are forced to do so because of persecution (8:1). With the conversions in Samaria, the conversion of the Ethiopian eunuch, and the conversion of the archenemy Saul, Luke continues to widen the boundaries of the Christian community. The similarities in the stories of the Ethiopian, Saul, and Cornelius suggest that for Luke they are part of one continuous event.

Not only does the Cornelius account bring to a culmination much of Luke's story up to this point, but it paves the way for the Jerusalem council in Acts 15. There, during a debate about the restrictions that ought to be placed upon gentile Christians, Peter refers indirectly to the Cornelius episode (15:6–9). The agreement that then becomes the launching pad for Paul's continued mission among gentiles has as its starting point this conversion of a pious gentile.

By means of this carefully crafted story, Luke conveys several points that are indicative of his theological perspective. Most obvious among these is the understanding that it is God and God alone who determines what the boundaries of the Christian community are to be. In the face of Peter's threefold resistance to the vision (10:9–16) and the Jerusalem community's complaining when Peter joins in table fellowship with gentiles (11:3), God's will has its way. In multiple ways Luke insists that this inclusion is God's will: the vision of Cornelius, the repeated vision of Peter, the gift of the Holy Spirit prior to baptism with water. The conclusion is clear: the inclusion of gentiles was the direct result of God's intervention and was not a merely human act. Despite the reluctance with which Peter becomes the instrument of Cornelius' conversion, his role in this story also conveys an important element in Luke's theological viewpoint. In keeping with the central importance Peter has in the Jerusalem community from the beginning of Acts, he alone is the apostle who has the authority to take this bold step. A third theological issue in this text has to do with the nature of Christian hospitality. Crucial to the Church's inclusion of gentiles is the problem of table fellowship. That is an explicit issue, of course, in Gal 2:12, but it also plays a role in this story with its recurrent motif of hospitality and the sharing of food (10:23, 28, 48; 11:3).

Bibliography

Bovon, F. 1970. Tradition et redaction en Actes 10, 1–11, 18. *TZ* 26: 22–45.

Dibelius, M. 1956. The Conversion of Cornelius. Pp. 109–22 in *Studies in the Acts of the Apostles.* New York.

Gaventa, B. R. 1986. *From Darkness to Light: Aspects of Conversion in the New Testament.* Philadelphia.

Haacker, K. 1980. Dibelius und Cornelius: Ein Beispiel formgeschichtlicher Überlieferungskritik. *BZ* 24: 234–51.

Haenchen, E. 1965. *The Acts of the Apostles.* 14th ed. Philadelphia.

Löning, K. 1974. Die Korneliustradition. *BZ* 18: 1–19.

Wilckens, U. 1958. Kerygma und Evangelium bei Lukas. *ZNW* 49: 223–37.

BEVERLY ROBERTS GAVENTA

CORNER GATE (PLACE) [Heb *šăʿar happinăh; šaʿar happôneh; šaʿar happĕnîm*]. Gate of Jerusalem first mentioned during the reign of Amaziah (2 Kgs 14:13; 2 Chr 25:23) that became increasingly strategic to Uzziah (2 Chr 26:9) and to Hezekiah. After the destruction of Jerusalem in 586 B.C.E., Jeremiah and Zechariah refer to the Corner Gate (Jer 31:37—Eng 38; Zech 14:10) as the westernmost boundary of a future Jerusalem. Where the Corner Gate should be located greatly depends on whether or not there was an Israelite settlement on the Western Hill of Jerusalem and on whether it was included inside the walls of the city (for a full summary, see Simons 1952: 226–81, 447–58). These questions were, for the most part, answered by the archaeological excavations on the Western Hill from 1968 to 1971 with the discovery of pottery, figurines, ostraca, and the more significant "broad wall" and "Israelite tower" dated to the 8th–7th centuries B.C.E. and most likely should be attributed to Hezekiah (Avigad 1980: 23–60). It is at the W end of this 8th-century wall, built along the Transversal Valley to protect the vulnerable NW approach of the city, that the Corner Gate should provisionally be located. The gate most likely began as an avenue of ingress and egress for the settlement on the Western Hill. After Amaziah's defeat at Beth-shemesh, Jehoash, king of Israel, came to Jerusalem and destroyed 400 cubits of a city wall between the Gate of Ephraim and the Corner Gate. Uzziah later strengthened the Corner Gate with defensive towers (2 Chr 26:9) to enhance strategically its vulnerable position for lack of a valley or ravine to protect the gate. The Corner Gate then became the westernmost point of Hezekiah's "broad wall." It ran E–W along the Transversal Valley from the temple enclosure to the Corner Gate where the city wall turned S along the Hinnom Valley (Gibson 1987: 86–87). Nehemiah's lack of reference to the Corner Gate may be attributed to his reinforcing of only the old defensive lines of the smaller City of David and temple area (Avigad 1980: 61–62; Williamson 1984: 85–87).

Bibliography

Avigad, N. 1980. *Discovering Jerusalem.* Nashville.

Geva, H. 1979. The Western Boundary of Jerusalem at the End of the Monarchy. *IEJ* 29: 84–91.

Gibson, S. 1987. The 1961–67 Excavations in the Armenian Garden, Jerusalem. *PEQ* 119: 81–96.

Simons, J. J. 1952. *Jerusalem in the Old Testament.* Leiden.

Williamson, H. G. M. 1984. Nehemiah's Walls Revisited. *PEQ* 116: 81–88.

DALE C. LIID

CORPORATE PERSONALITY. "Corporate personality" is a term used in English law. It refers to the fact that a group or body can be regarded legally as an individual, possessing the rights and duties of an individual. The membership of such a group may change through the death of members or the recruitment of new ones, without affecting the rights and duties of the group as a whole.

Although Wheeler Robinson in 1907 had alluded to the concept in his commentary on Joshua, it wasn't until 1911 that he introduced the term "corporate personality" into biblical interpretation. He believed that it helped to explain features of the OT that were puzzling to modern readers. For example, in Joshua 7, the whole household of Achan was destroyed, even though Achan alone had disobeyed the divine command not to take spoil from Jericho. If Achan's household was a corporate personality, the whole group was culpable, even though only one of its members had offended. Again, in some of the psalms (e.g., 44:5–9—Eng 44:4–8), the language switches abruptly from "I" to "we." If the psalmist belonged to a corporate personality, he could think of himself ("I") as embodying the whole group; yet his sense of solidarity *with* the group allowed him also to employ "we" language.

According to Rogerson (1980), Robinson employed "corporate personality" in at least two different senses: (a) corporate responsibility (e.g., the Achan punishment) and (b) corporate representation (e.g., the corporate "I" of the psalms). Like many scholars of his day, Robinson believed that ancient Hebrew thought was similar to that of "primitive" societies and was impressed by the work of anthropologists on this "primitive" mentality, especially that of Lévy-Bruhl. He believed that the Hebrews analyzed the relation between the individual and the group in ways very different from those of modern man. For example, the Hebrews did not place limits on their individuality but felt themselves to belong to a group in such a way that an individual could be or become the group. Again, a remote ancestor, although dead, could embody the group in such a way that a living member of it could feel the closest identity, even identification, with the ancestor.

Although Robinson took the idea of corporate personality from English law, he applied it to the OT in an imprecise fashion. In English law a corporate personality cannot be punished for the misdemeanor of one of its members. If, however, the offender acted as an authorized representative of the group, then the group as such could be indicted. Furthermore, the idea of a bond of consciousness or identity between individual and group, such as is presupposed in explaining the corporate "I" of the psalms, is foreign to the legal notion adopted by Robinson in order to describe what he believed to be a basic and primitive characteristic of Hebrew thought, one to which modern thought had no parallel.

Since the 1930s many OT scholars believed that Robinson had discovered an important way of avoiding reading modern Western notions of individuality into the OT. Many also believed his work to be confirmed by Pedersen's (1926) mystical account of how Israelites experienced the world. Corporate personality was thus used to explain the individual and collective traits of the servant in the four Servant Songs of Isaiah 42–53 (Robinson 1955; Eissfeldt 1933), the phenomenon of pseudonymity in apocalyptic literature (Russell 1964), the identity between a messenger and the person who sent him (Johnson 1961: 28), and the close affinity between saga characters and Israelite readers of the sagas (Koch 1969). However, the anthropological theories on which Robinson based his notion of Hebrew mentality have since been largely abandoned by anthropologists.

Robinson must be credited, nevertheless, with focusing attention upon an important question: did the Israelites regard a group as a collection of individuals or as a body with various members? In some cases the answer seems to be that a group is regarded primarily as a body whose members are so bound together that they must share a common fate. In Gen 19:22–32, the alternatives are that either Sodom will be destroyed or it will be reprieved should it contain ten righteous persons; that the righteous should be spared and the wicked destroyed is not an option. The city is dealt with as a collective whole.

However, care should be taken not to press this principle into service without careful thought. In the Achan incident there is clear indication of individual responsibility. Achan is identified as the culprit, and, although the people as a whole had been punished by defeat at Ai, it is only Achan's household that is put to death. This punishment need not depend upon corporate personality; it has been explained in terms of the need to execute all those who were defiled by contact with spoil devoted wholly to God (Porter 1965). It has also been seen as an instance of ruler punishment.

The classic instance of ruler punishment (Daube 1947) is 2 Sam 24: 1–17, where David's punishment for holding a census results in the death of 70,000 men. Here again, the idea of individual responsibility is clear: David erred, but his punishment falls upon his property, the 70,000 men.

The above examples should serve as a warning against those who attempt to fit OT texts into simplistic categories. In OT law the principle of individual responsibility was fundamental from the earliest times. Yet some individuals held power over others that might cause them, although innocent, to be punished for the actions of the head. In OT religion the fear of defilement of the whole people by the presence within it of a group or individual that had violated the boundary separating the sacred from the profane was strong enough to require the execution of those responsible. Again, the OT employs the devices of personification and synechdoche: Israel can be described as a virgin girl (Amos 5:2), or a king can represent the whole of his people (Ezek 28:2, 12).

It would be wrong to assume without further investigation that Israelites perceived the relation between the individual and society in exactly the same way as modern scholars. It is equally wrong to suppose that the OT can only be understood by positing a special Hebrew mentality, radically different from that of modern Westerners. Even in modern society, where individualism is a more dominating concept than in the OT, there exist experiences and resources which can be used sensitively to explain features of OT narrative that are at first sight puzzling and alien.

Bibliography

A full bibliography on corporate personality is provided in H. Wheeler Robinson 1964: 61–64, and footnotes to the text. To this bibliography should be added:

Daube, D. 1947. *Studies in Biblical Law.* Cambridge. Repr. New York, 1969.

Eissfeldt, O. 1933. The Ebed-Jahweh in Isaiah xl–lv. *ExpTim* 44: 261–68.

Gordis, R. 1971. *Poets, Prophets and Sagas.* Bloomington, IN.

Johnson, A. R. 1961. *The One and the Many in the Israelite Conception of God.* Cardiff.

———. 1979. *The Cultic Prophet and Israel's Psalmody.* Cardiff.

Joyce, P. 1983. The Individual and the Communities. Pp. 74–89 in *Beginning Old Testament Study,* ed. J. Rogerson. Philadelphia.

Koch, K. 1969. *The Growth of the Biblical Tradition.* London.

Pedersen, J. 1926. *Israel: Its Life and Culture.* 2 vols. London and Copenhagen.

Porter, J. R. 1965. The Legal Aspects of Corporate Personality in the Old Testament. *VT* 15: 361–68.

Robinson, H. W. 1911. *The Christian Doctrine of Man.* Edinburgh.

———. 1955. *The Cross in the Old Testament.* London.

———. 1964. *Corporate Personality in Ancient Israel.* Philadelphia.

Rogerson, J. W. 1980. The Hebrew Conception of Corporate Personality. *JTS* 21: 1–16 = pp. 43–59 in *Anthropological Approaches to the Old Testament,* ed. B. Lang. Philadelphia. 1985.

Russell, D. S. 1964. *The Method and Message of Jewish Apocalyptic.* London.

J. W. Rogerson

CORPUS HELLENISTICUM NOVI TESTAMENTI.

CORPUS HELLENISTICUM NOVI TESTAMENTI. A research project whose purpose is to collect and publish Greco-Roman parallels elucidating the contents of the NT.

A. The History of the Project

Before the 17th century NT exegesis was mainly of a dogmatic nature, both in Protestant and in Roman Catholic circles. The exegete was obligated to "explain" the sacred texts in such a way that the dogmatic interests of the Church were defended. Although as early as 1572 the classical philologist Joachim Camerarius had stated that the NT could only be explained against the background of the linguistic usage of ancient authors (Kümmel 1970: 26–28), it was not until the 17th century that this view became more influential. This period saw the birth and growth of a strictly philological approach to the NT. In the so-called *Observationes* and *Annotationes* literature, the text of the NT books was elucidated on the basis of parallels from one or more classical authors. The most important examples from both the 17th and 18th centuries are works by D. Heinsius, H. Grotius, J. Cappellus, P. Colomesius, J. Dougtaeus, J. B. Carpzovius, C. H. Langius, C. F. Munthe, J. Pricaeus, G. Raphelius, J. T. Krebsius, L. Bos, J. Alberti, C. F. Loesnerus, and J. Elsnerus (for bibliographical details, see Ros 1940: 49–56 and Delling 1963a: 1, n.1). Although *Observationes* and *Annotationes* cannot be strictly distinguished, one may say that, whereas the *Observationes* often merely listed parallels from Greek and Latin authors, the *Annotationes* for the most part have the character of a commentary in which also aspects other than simply elucidating parallels are treated (see the collection of *Annotationes* literature in Pearson 1666).

The practice of collecting classical parallels to the NT reached its zenith in J. J. Wettstein's *Novum Testamentum Graecum* (1751–52). This work, intended to be a new critical edition of the Greek NT, has remained a highly useful tool to the present day (it was reprinted in 1962), not for its edition of the NT, but for its extensive apparatus containing quotations of parallels from Greek, Latin, and rabbinic literature; more than 175 classical authors had been scrutinized by Wettstein over a period of more than forty years in his search for parallels to the NT (see Hulbert-Powell 1938; van Unnik 1964a: 196–99; Mussies fc.). Neither before nor after him has such a comprehensive and systematic collection of materials relevant to the NT been published. Although Wettstein himself declared that much remained to be done (2: 876), after his death this kind of work gradually came to a standstill. In the 19th century historical-critical questions occupied NT scholars much more than philological matters. But by the beginning of the 20th century the climate had again changed. The discovery of papyri in Egypt, excavations in the E Mediterranean area, and the rise of religiohistorical research brought the relationship between the NT and its cultural milieu into focus again. Shortly before World War I, C. F. Georg Heinrici, a Leipzig professor of NT, developed plans for a large-scale project, called by him "a new Wettstein," and later renamed (probably by E. von Dobschütz) *Corpus Hellenisticum Novi Testamenti* (CHNT). Rabbinic writings were excluded from the project when it became known that Paul Billerbeck was working on this material for his monumental *Kommentar zum Neuen Testament aus Talmud und Midrasch* (1926–28). Heinrici enlisted as his collaborators Ernst von Dobschütz, Hans Lietzmann, Hans Windisch, Adolf Deissmann, and Johannes Leipoldt (von Dobschütz 1922: 146–48; van Unnik 1964a: 200–1). During the initial stage of the project, Heinrici died (in 1915) and his responsibility passed to von Dobschütz in Halle. Von Dobschütz organized the project with great enthusiasm and, after World War I, set a great number of assistants (more than fifty, at several universities) to work on it. They checked Wettstein's quotations against modern critical editions, updating and supplementing his material, all of which was recorded on file cards. Soon it was discovered that a team of scholars in England (under F. H. Colson's direction) was also working on a new edition of Wettstein, to be published by SPCK (Hulbert-Powell 1938: 273). Scholars like G. N. L. Hall, G. H. Whitaker, E. R. Bernard, W. O. E. Oesterley, W. Scott, W. K. Lowther Clarke, and others had been collecting materials from Plutarch, Seneca, Josephus, Vettius Valens, Stobaeus, the Corpus Hermeticum, and the Magical papyri. Once von Dobschütz had succeeded in convincing the British that the German project was in a far more advanced stage, they put all their materials at the disposal of the Germans and discontinued the enterprise (von Dobschütz 1922: 147–48).

Between the years 1918 and 1933 much work was done. In 1928 von Dobschütz (1928: 49) wrote that the project could be completed in a few years. However, with the rise of National Socialism the project gradually broke down, the more so after the death of von Dobschütz in 1934. When his successor, Hans Windisch, who hoped to finish the project in the near future (1935: 125), died within a year, the work came to a complete halt (Aland 1955–56: 218). Together with the individual workers, many of the file cards disappeared in the years before and during World War II. In 1941 the Halle NT scholar Erich Klostermann came to an agreement with Anton Fridrichsen in Uppsala that the pagan portion of the materials (the Pagano-Hellenisticum) should be transferred to Uppsala, while the Judeo-Hellenisticum would remain in Halle (Fridrichsen and Klostermann 1941: 255). Fridrichsen had a long-standing interest in the project and had himself written a series of articles with CHNT materials (Bauer 1954: 128). But owing to a long-lasting illness and his early death in 1953, he was not able to advance the project. Only one contribution, a dissertation by one of his pupils (Almqvist 1946), was made in the years between 1941 and 1953. The untimely deaths of J. Schniewind and H. Preisker also considerably slowed progress in the Halle branch.

In 1955 a new start was made. Fridrichsen's successor, Harald Riesenfeld, and the Dutch NT scholar Willem Cornelis van Unnik agreed, after international consultation in the Society of New Testament Studies (van Unnik 1956–57; Aland 1955–56), that the Pagano-Hellenisticum part of the CHNT would be transferred to Utrecht under the direction of van Unnik, while the Judeo-Hellenisticum would remain in Halle, to be directed by Gerhard Delling (Aland 1955–56: 218–19; Delling 1963a: 5). Like von Dobschütz and Windisch, van Unnik, too, expected that the wish to publish a new Wettstein would soon be fulfilled (van Unnik 1964a: 202). In 1956 the file cards arrived in Utrecht and were studied, checked, and reordered by temporary assistants. In the 1960s two full-time researchers began collecting new materials from Hellenistic authors. In 1966 a new branch of the project was begun at the Institute for Antiquity and Christianity in Claremont, California, under Hans Dieter Betz, who had previously published a contribution to the CHNT (Betz 1961).

By this time it had become clear that the ultimate goal, i.e., the publication of an updated and completed Wettstein, could not be reached as easily and quickly as had been wished, both because of the immense amount of ancient literature to be studied and because of the very limited number of researchers who were available to the project. Hence it was decided to aim provisionally at an interim goal, namely, the publication of a series of monographs discussing the relevance of one particular author (or corpus) to the NT. This series, the *Studia ad Corpus Hellenisticum Novi Testamenti* (published by Brill), began in 1970 and continues to the present time (see Petzke 1970; Mussies 1972; Betz 1975 and 1978; Grese 1979; van der Horst 1980). In addition, a series of articles on minor authors (van der Horst 1973, 1974, 1975, 1981, 1983a), and on NT chapters, pericopae, verses, or themes in their relation to Hellenistic literature (van Unnik 1964b, 1970a, 1973a; Betz 1979; van der Horst 1983b, 1985; Mussies 1986) has been and continues to be published in various scholarly journals.

Within these publications, both monographs and articles, three different approaches can be discerned. In the first, the order of the NT text is the point of departure, and the parallels are quoted *seriatim,* from Matthew 1 through Revelation 22, with little or no comment (as in Wettstein). In the second, the order of the writing(s) of the pagan or Jewish author becomes the point of departure, and to it parallels from the NT are quoted, with or without comment. In the third, the material is arranged thematically, with topics from the pagan literature or the NT as the focus; these are elucidated through parallels drawn from the other corpus. Each of the above divergent approaches has its advantages and they are complementary.

Since van Unnik's death in 1978, the work of the Utrecht branch of the CHNT has been continued by his former collaborators Gerard Mussies and Pieter W. van der Horst. Under Delling, and also, since his retirement in 1975, the Judeo-Hellenisticum branch in Halle has been active mainly in bibliographical work (Delling 1975). With Betz's move to Chicago in 1979, the American branch of the Pagano-Hellenisticum moved from Claremont to the Divinity School of the University of Chicago.

In the seventy years of its existence, progress of the project has seriously been hampered by four causes: the First and Second World Wars; the untimely deaths of several of its directors (Heinrici, von Dobschütz, Windisch, Schniewind, Priesker, Fridrichsen, van Unnik); a serious underestimation of the amount of work involved; and in recent times the increasing number of nonresearch duties imposed upon investigators at the universities. The future of the project lies in the steady continuation of the series of books and articles on individual pagan authors or writings and on pericopae, chapters, or themes of the NT.

B. The Purpose of the Project

The primary purpose of the CHNT is to further the understanding of the NT in its cultural context, not only from a religiohistorical, but also from a literary, philosophical, and historical point of view. The work done at this project is necessary in order to learn to hear the words of the NT with the ears of 1st-century people and so to discover the emotional value of these words for the earliest readers or hearers. The aim is to investigate everything that has been preserved from Greek and Roman antiquity in relation to its significance for a proper understanding of the NT (van Unnik 1980: 202, 208). Van Unnik described the project's purpose with the maxim, "Words come to Life" (van Unnik 1971: 199). This does not mean that the project is of a lexicographical nature. In the early *Observationes* literature, as well as in Wettstein, there was a heavy emphasis on lexicographical matters. This was necessary since there were no (or only very inadequate) lexicons in those days. Now with the advent of Walter Bauer (BAGD) and *TDNT,* much of the relevant lexical parallels are easily accessible (Delling 1963a: 8). Moreover, G. H. R. Horsley has undertaken a new collection of lexical material from papyri and inscriptions for a revised Moulton-Milligan (Horsley 1981–87). Of course, there are still several lacunae in NT lexicography, and occasionally CHNT researchers have been able to fill the gaps (see, e.g., van Unnik 1962; Mussies 1978; van der Horst 1976–77, 1978). But more often it is rather the specific combination of words (not indicated by the lexicons) that appears to be relevant. For example, it no longer makes sense to collect occurrences of *gnōmē,* "purpose, mind," and the numeral *heis/mia/hen* in Greek authors; however, it does make sense to collect instances of *mia gnōmē,* "one mind," since only then does it become clear that the author of Revelation is employing a political technical term, which evoked very specific associations (Rev 17:13, 17; van Unnik 1970b).

The main emphasis in CHNT research, however, is on conceptual parallels, which, more often than not, are phrased differently than in the NT so that there is no or only little verbal agreement (the main reason why the computer is of very little use to this project). This is, of course, most obvious when the parallels are found in Latin writings. For example, to the use of spittle in the story of the healing of the blind man by Jesus (Mark 8:23; cf. John 9:6) the closest parallel is Tacitus' story of Vespasian's healing of a blind man by means of the emperor's spittle (*Hist.* 4.81; also Suet. *Ves.* 7.2). Since the languages are different here, there is no verbal agreement, although Greek parallels can be verbally dissimilar as well. As for the story of the ascension in Acts 1:9, there are many pagan parallels, none of which agree verbally (van der Horst 1983b: 20–23). The same applies even to such a motif as the tongues of fire, a manifestation of divine presence or grace in Acts 2:3; here the many parallels in Greek, and especially Latin, sources show little or no verbal similarity (van der Horst 1985: 49–50). Several aspects of Jesus' genealogy in Matt 1:1–17 can be clarified against their Hellenistic and Jewish-Hellenistic background despite the lack of verbal agreement (Mussies 1986). Also Jesus' raising of the widow's son at Nain (Luke 7:11–17) has a striking parallel in a story of Apollonius of Tyana (Philostr. *VA* 4.45), but again there is no verbal agreement (Petzke 1970: 129–30; cf. Betz 1961: 161). In general, there are many pagan parallels to the miracle stories, especially the healing miracles (Betz 1961: 147–60; cf. Weinreich 1909).

Sometimes the agreement between an expression in the NT and its parallels is only partially verbal while conceptually complete. For instance, to the expression *to pneuma mē sbennute,* "Do not quench the Spirit," in 1 Thess 5:19 there are only partial verbal parallels in Plutarch, but nonetheless the background of the concept of extinguishing the spirit can be illuminated from Plutarch, whose writings on inspiration make Paul's meaning clear, i.e., let not rational considerations and the fear to look ridiculous in the eyes of others restrain the activity of God's spirit within you (van Unnik 1968). The formula in Rev 1:19, "what you have seen, what is now, and what will be hereafter" (NEB), has no exact counterpart in Greek and Latin literature, but comparable (as far as meaning is concerned) formulas from Homer through late antiquity make it abundantly clear that this phrase is a formula describing prophecy (van Unnik 1962–63). When in Acts 9:1 it is said that Saul was still "breathing threats and murder" (NEB) against the disciples of the Lord, the use of various verbs for "breathing," with an object in the accusative or genitive to indicate strong emotions at dramatic high points, can again be traced from Homer down to the later imperial period; all such instances are found, significantly enough, in higher literary sources (van der Horst 1970). Acts 22:28 offers an example of a more historical nature. The Roman commander's statement, "It cost me a large sum to acquire this citizenship (NEB), is illustrated in a discourse by Dio Chrysostom (*Or.* 34.23, early 2d century C.E.) where it is stated that one had to pay five hundred drachmas in order to become a Roman citizen of Tarsus (Mussies 1972: 133). The belief of the inhabitants of Jerusalem that Peter's shadow would heal the sick (Acts 5:15) finds its explanation in the whole complex of ideas both in pagan and in Jewish popular belief about the power of an individual's shadow (van der Horst 1976–77, 1979).

A wide variety of parallels have been considered. Sometimes, but not often, they are only lexical. More often they are of a stylistic and literary nature, helping to clarify the linguistic and literary stratum to which the NT writings belong. The most important parallels are the conceptual ones, both in the sphere of the history of religions and in that of ethics and *realia.* "The Corpus Hellenisticum will be a collection of all parallels and antiparallels in expression and contents that exist between the Greek and Roman world and the NT" (van Unnik 1971: 204). All the material collected helps us to see how deeply the earliest Christian writers were rooted in Hellenistic-Roman culture. This is not to deny or doubt the fundamentally Jewish character of the NT writings. The aim of the CHNT is to show what these basically Jewish writings have in common with Greco-Roman and Jewish literary documents. It should also help to measure to what extent 1st-century Jewish (and through it, Christian) thought and diction have been influenced by Hellenistic ideas and modes of expression.

The nature of the work at the CHNT involves the risk that attention is mainly drawn to points where there seems to be a certain agreement or similarity between pagan and early Christian documents, whereas it may rather be the absence of parallels that is significant. Hence it should be stressed that one of the important facets of the project is that, the more work has been done in this field, the better we can identify those passages and concepts in the NT to which no parallels are to be found. Only then will the really distinctive ideas and usages of the NT be brought out in full relief.

Bibliography

Aland, K. 1955. Das Corpus Hellenisticum. *TLZ* 80: 627–28.

———. 1955–56. The Corpus Hellenisticum. *NTS* 2: 217–21.

Almqvist, H. 1946. *Plutarch und das Neue Testament.* ASNU 15. Uppsala.

Bauer, W. 1954. Zur Erinnerung an Anton Fridrichsen. *ZNW* 45: 123–29.

Betz, H. D. 1961. *Lukian von Samosata und das Neue Testament: Religionsgeschichtliche und paränetische Parallelen.* TU 76. Berlin.

———. 1979. Matthew VI 22f and Ancient Greek Theories of Vision. Pp. 43–56 in *Text and Interpretation. Studies in the New Testament Presented to Matthew Black,* ed. E. Best and R. McL. Wilson. Cambridge. Repr. pp. 71–87 in *Essays on the Sermon on the Mount.* Philadelphia.

Betz, H. D., ed. 1975. *Plutarch's Theological Writings and Early Christian Literature.* SCHNT 3. Leiden.

———, ed. 1978. *Plutarch's Ethical Writings and Early Christian Literature.* SCHNT 4. Leiden.

Betz, H. D., and Smith, E. W. 1971. Contributions to the Corpus Hellenisticum. *NovT* 13: 217–35. Repr. in Betz 1975: 85–102.

Bonhöffer, A. 1911. *Epiktet und das Neue Testament.* RVV 10. Giessen. Repr. 1964, Berlin.

Delling, G. 1963a. Zum Corpus Hellenisticum Novi Testamenti. *ZNW* 54: 1–15.

———. 1963b. Bemerkungen zum Corpus Hellenisticum Novi Testamenti. *FuF* 37: 183–85.

———. 1975. *Bibliographie zur jüdisch-hellenistischen und intertestamentarischen Literatur.* 2d ed. TU 106. Berlin.

Dobschütz, E. von 1922. Der Plan eines neuen Wettstein. *ZNW* 21: 146–48.

———. 1925. Zum Corpus Hellenisticum. *ZNW* 24: 43–51.

———. 1928. Ernst von Dobschütz. Pp. 31–62 in vol. 4 of *Die Religionswissenschaft der Gegenwart in Selbstdarstellungen,* ed. E. Stange. Leipzig.

Fridrichsen, A., and Klostermann, E. 1941. Zum Corpus Hellenisticum. *ZNW* 40: 255.

Grese, W. C. 1979. *Corpus Hermeticum XIII and the New Testament.* 5. Leiden.

Horsley, G. H. R. 1981–87. *New Documents Illustrating Early Christianity, 1–4.* 4 vols. North Ryde.

Horst, P. W. van der 1970. Drohung und Mord schnaubend (Acta IX 1). *NovT* 12: 257–69.

———. 1973. Macrobius and the New Testament: A Contribution to the Corpus Hellenisticum. *NovT* 15: 220–32.

———. 1974. Musonius Rufus and the New Testament: A Contribution to the Corpus Hellenisticum. *NovT* 16: 306–15.

———. 1975. Hierocles the Stoic and the New Testament: A Contribution to the Corpus Hellenisticum. *NovT* 17: 156–60.

———. 1976–77. Peter's Shadow: The Religio-Historical Background of Acts 5:15. *NTS* 23: 204–12.

———. 1978. Is Wittiness Unchristian? A note on *eutrapelia* in Eph V 4. Pp. 163–77 in *Miscellanea Neotestamentica* 2, ed. T. Baarda; A. F. J. Klijn; and W. C. van Unnik. Leiden.

———. 1979. Der Schatten im hellenistischen Volksglauben.

Pp. 27–36 in *Studies in Hellenistic Religions,* ed. M. J. Vermaseren. Leiden.

———. 1980. *Aelius Aristides and the New Testament.* SCHNT 6. Leiden.

———. 1981. Cornutus and the New Testament: A Contribution to the Corpus Hellenisticum. *NovT* 23: 165–72.

———. 1983a. Chariton and the New Testament: A Contribution to the Corpus Hellenisticum. *NovT* 25: 348–55.

———. 1983b. Hellenistic Parallels to the Acts of the Apostles (1:1–26). *ZNW* 74: 17–26.

———. 1985. Hellenistic Parallels to the Acts of the Apostles (2:1–47). *JSNT* 25: 49–60.

Hulbert-Powell, C. L. 1938. *John James Wettstein 1693–1754.* London.

Kümmel, W. G. 1970. *Das Neue Testament. Geschichte der Erforschung seiner Probleme.* 2d ed. Orbis Academicus. Freiburg and Munich. (ET: *The New Testament: The History of the Investigation of Its Problems.* Trans. S. MacLean Gilmour and Howard Clark Kee. Nashville, 1972.)

Mussies, G. 1972. *Dio Chrysostom and the New Testament.* SCHNT 2. Leiden.

———. 1978. The Sense of *Syllogidzesthai* at Luke XX:5. Pp. 59–76 in *Miscellanea Neotestamentica* 2, ed. T. Baarda; A. F. J. Klijn; and W. C. van Unnik. Leiden.

———. 1986. Parallels to Matthew's Version of the Pedigree of Jesus. *NovT* 28: 32–47.

———. fc. Johan Jakob Wettstein. *Biografisch Lexicon voor de Geschiedenis van het Nederlandse Protestantisme* 3. Kampen.

Pearson, J., et al. 1666. *Critici Sacri.* London. Repr. 1698.

Petzke, G. 1970. *Die Traditionen über Apollonius von Tyana und das Neue Testament.* SCHNT 1. Leiden.

Ros, J. 1940. *De studie van het Bijbelgrieksch van Hugo Grotius tot Adolf Deissmann.* Nijmegen and Utrecht.

Sevenster, J. N. 1961. *Paul and Seneca.* NovTSup 4. Leiden.

Spiess, E. 1871. *Logos Spermaticós. Parallelstellen zum Neuen Testament aus den Schriften der alten Griechen.* Leipzig. Repr. 1976.

Unnik, W. C. van 1956–57. Second Report on the Corpus Hellenisticum. *NTS* 3: 254–59. Repr. in van Unnik 1980: 175–82.

———. 1962. *Tarsus or Jerusalem? The City of Paul's Youth.* London. Repr. in van Unnik 1973: 259–320.

———. 1962–63. A Formula Describing Prophecy. *NTS* 9: 86–94. Repr. in van Unnik 1980: 183–93.

———. 1964a. Corpus Hellenisticum Novi Testamenti. *JBL* 83: 17–33 Repr. in van Unnik 1980: 194–214.

———. 1964b. Die rechte Bedeutung des Wortes treffen, Lukas 2:19. Pp. 129–47 in *Verbum. Essays on Some Aspects of the Religious Function of Words Dedicated to H. W. Obbink.* Utrecht. Repr. in van Unnik 1973b: 72–91.

———. 1968. Den Geist löschet nicht aus (1 Thess. V 19). *NovT* 10: 255–69.

———. 1970a. "Alles ist dir möglich" (Mk. 14:36). Pp. 27–36 in *Verborum veritas. Festschrift für Gustav Stählin,* ed. O. Böcher and K. Haacker. Wupperthal.

———. 1970b. *Mia gnōmē,* Apocalypse of John XVII: 13, 17. Pp. 209–20 in *Studies in John Presented to J. N. Sevenster.* Leiden.

———. 1971. Words Come to Life. The Work for the "Corpus Hellenisticum Novi Testamenti." *NovT* 13: 199–216.

———. 1973a. Once More St. Luke's Prologue. *Neot* 7: 7–26.

———. 1973b. *Sparsa Collecta* 1. NovTSup 29. Leiden.

———. 1980. *Sparsa Collecta* 2. NovTSup 30. Leiden.

———. 1983. *Sparsa Collecta* 3. NovTSup 31. Leiden.

Weinreich, O. 1909. *Antike Heilungswunder.* RVV 8/1. Giessen. Repr. Berlin, 1969.

Wettstein, J. J. 1751–52. *Hē kainē diathēkē.* Amsterdam. Repr. Graz, 1962.

Windisch, H. 1935. Zum Corpus Hellenisticum. *ZNW* 34: 124–25.

PIETER W. VAN DER HORST

CORRECTIONS OF THE SCRIBES. See SCRIBAL EMENDATIONS; TEXTUAL CRITICISM; MASORAH.

CORRUPTION, MOUNT OF (PLACE) [Heb *har hammašḥît*]. A site mentioned in 2 Kgs 23:13 which tells how King Josiah desecrated "the high places that were east of Jerusalem on the south of the Mount of Corruption." According to 1 Kgs 11:7, this is probably where Solomon had erected shrines to Ashtoreth, Chemosh, and Molech. The specific location of the Mount of Corruption on the hill E of Jerusalem is not exactly clear but seems to have been located on the S end of the hill; in later times it was specifically identified with the S part of the ridge, an area probably to be understood as E of the City of David and up the slope from the modern village of Silwan (Finegan 1969: 89); this area is to the S of the slight depression which separates the N sections of the hill (including the first N summit, Mount Scopus, and the central summit, the Mount of Olives) from the S section of the hill. The same Heb term, used in 2 Kgs 23:13, is also found in Jer 51:25 and translated, "Destroying the Mountain," but in the latter instance refers to Babylon's invasion. The Vg of 2 Kgs 23:13 uses the term Mons Offensionis (Mount of Offense), and this term and a similar one, Mons Scandali (Mountain of Scandal), are often used today to describe the area. Rabbinic tradition identifies the hill by the term, "The Mountain of Anointment," which may have been the earlier name for the hill, because the olives harvested there were used for anointing (Mount of Olives). On this assumption the name of the hill was later changed to "Mount of Corruption" because of Solomon's desecration.

Bibliography

Finegan, J. 1969. *The Archeology of the New Testament.* Princeton.

W. HAROLD MARE

COS (PLACE) [Gk *Kō*]. Small island (approx. 80 stadia in circumference; Strabo 14.2.19) in the Aegean Sea, SW of Asia Minor, with a city by the same name. The Mycenaeans settled on Cos by 1425 B.C.E. and it was heavily populated, according to Homer (*Iliad* 2.184; 14.225; 1 Macc 15:23; Acts 21:1). The island fell to the Dorians sometime after the 12th century B.C.E. and subsequently received settlers from Epidaurus (Str. 14.2.6; Th. 7.57.6). Cos was a major shipping port, exporting excellent wine (Pliny 15.18; 17.30), costly ointments (Athen. 15.688), purple dye, and fabrics of a transparent texture (Hor. *Od* 4.13.7; Tibull. 2.4.6). Cos was celebrated for its Temple of Asclepius (a Greek god associated with healing), as the birthplace of Hippocrates (the so-called father of medicine), and its legendary medical school. In the 3d century B.C.E., Cos developed an outstanding library and several Ptolemaic princes were educated there.

When Judah the Maccabee's emissaries were returning from Rome to Judea in 161 B.C.E., they received a letter of safe-conduct from the Roman consul to the authorities of Cos (*Ant* 14.10.15 §233). The Roman Senate sent a letter to the inhabitants of Cos warning them not to join forces with Tryphon against Judea (1 Macc 15:23). Josephus, quoting Strabo, mentioned that the Jews of Asia Minor deposited their money on Cos during the Mithridatic War (*Ant* 14.7.2). Julius Caesar later issued an edict in favor of the Jews of Cos (*Ant* 14.10.15). Herod the Great conferred many favors on Cos (*JW* 1.21.11) and an inscription also associates Herod Antipas with the island. Another inscription from the island refers to a Jewess or possibly to a "God-fearer" from the island. Cos is mentioned once in the Bible in Acts 21:1. After Paul's third missionary journey, the apostle sailed from Miletus to Cos, where he spent the night before sailing the next day to Rhodes.

SCOTT T. CARROLL

COSAM (PERSON) [Gk *Kōsam*]. The father of Addi and son of Elmadam, according to Luke's genealogy tying Joseph, the "supposed father" of Jesus, to descent from Adam and God (Luke 3:28). D omits Cosam, substituting a genealogy adapted from Matt 1:6–15 for Luke 3:23–31. The name Cosam occurs nowhere else in the biblical documents, including Matthew's genealogy, and falls within a list of eighteen otherwise unknown descendants of David's son Nathan (Fitzmyer *Luke 1–9* AB, 501). Kuhn's (1923: 214–16; endorsed by Schürmann *Luke* HTKNT, 201, n.95) attempt to find a source for Cosam, as part of the group from Neri through Er, in corrupted forms of names in 1 Chr 3:17–18 MT, is particularly unconvincing, especially since there is serious question whether the genealogy at this point is based on 1 Chronicles, which does not have Cosam in 3:18 MT or LXX (Marshall *Luke* NIGTC, 164; cf. Jeremias 1969: 295–96).

Bibliography

Jeremias, J. 1969. *Jerusalem in the Time of Jesus*. Philadelphia.

Kuhn, G. 1923. Die Geschlechtsregister Jesu bei Lukas und Matthäus, nach ihrer Herkunft untersucht. *ZNW* 22: 206–28.

STANLEY E. PORTER

COSMOGONY, COSMOLOGY. The theory and lore concerning the origin and structure of the universe.

A. Definitions
B. Cosmogony and Cosmology in the Hebrew Bible
  1. The Significance of Cosmological Material for Biblical Religion
  2. Varieties of Cosmology in the Hebrew Bible
  3. The Cosmic Battle Pattern
  4. The Creation of the First Humans
  5. The Role of Second Isaiah in Centralizing the Cosmological Argument
  6. The Priestly Account of Creation
  7. The Wisdom Tradition
  8. Cosmogony in Apocalyptic Thought
  9. The Hebrew Bible's Portrait of the Cosmos
C. Cosmology in the NT
  1. Sources of Early Christian Cosmological Thought
  2. Cosmological Assumptions in Pauline Theology
  3. The Johannine Tradition
  4. Later NT Thought
D. The Functions of Religious Cosmogonies/Cosmologies
  1. Older Views
  2. Recent Formulations of the Place of Cosmology in Religion

A. Definitions

Cosmogony and cosmology are both terms whose etymologies remain helpful in defining them for the purposes of discussing their place in biblical thought. The first element in both words is obviously the same Greek word that lies behind the English "cosmos," and thus refers to the entire universe as an organized entity. A cosmogony (*kosmos* + *genia* = "birth") is thus an account, usually in the form of a mythological tale, about the genesis or birth of the structured universe. A cosmology (*kosmos* + *logia* = "report") is a blueprint or map, in the widest sense, of the universe as a comprehensible and meaningful place.

Occasionally, scholars have maintained that it is important to make a firm separation between these two terms—a separation between cosmogony, on the one hand, as a mythical account of the original events that produced an ordered universe, and cosmology, on the other hand, as speculation about meaning and value in the universe in the most general sense and even in the absence of any mention of originating events. Though such a terminological division may be useful in discussing nonbiblical religions, the fact is that the locus of almost all cosmological thought in the Hebrew Bible and in the NT is in cosmogonic texts. Hence, the two terms have traditionally been used almost interchangeably in discussions of early Judaism and Christianity; and they will be so used here.

The present treatment of cosmogony and cosmology in biblical texts is composed of three major sections. The first and much the longest is devoted to the Hebrew Bible, whose lengthy history of composition and transmission has led to a striking variety of quite different cosmological views. A second and shorter section is concerned with cosmological materials in the NT. Finally, the concluding section will concentrate on a series of questions posed by historians of religion but too often neglected in treatments of biblical cosmogonic lore: What is the role of cosmological speculation in religious thought generally? Why is it that almost no religion's scriptures omit some discussion of the origin of the universe?

B. Cosmogony and Cosmology in the Hebrew Bible

1. The Significance of Cosmological Material for Biblical Religion. Initially, one might ask if statements about the origin and meaning of the universe played a significant role in the religion of ancient Israel. Both internal evidence from the Hebrew Bible and the conclusions of a previous stage in biblical scholarship suggest that such a potentially troubling question is not out of place. With regard to the biblical evidence, it has been noted that there is no single word in biblical Hebrew which bears the weight carried by the Greek word *kosmos.* The notion that the universe is a rationally comprehensible totality is one that is met with frequently in Greek thought and that is represented already by the use of this term *kosmos.* The post-biblical usage of the Hebrew word "ancient," "everlasting" *(ʿôlām)* carries similar connotations; but *ʿôlām* is not used in such a cosmic sense within the Hebrew Bible, and other expressions ("earth" [*tēbēl*], "heaven and earth" [*haššāmayim wĕhāʾāreṣ*], or "the all" [*kol*]) are similarly limited. Secondly, only rarely does the Hebrew Bible concentrate at sustained length on cosmogonic narratives. Though hints and allusions abound to what must be assumed to be a popular reservoir of thoughts on the origin and shape of the universe, accounts that extend beyond a few verses are essentially limited to those in Gen 1:1–2:4a and 2:4b–25; and of these, the second is more correctly seen as an account of the origin of humanity (an anthropogony).

On the basis of these observations and others, many scholars, especially those working during the early and mid-20th century, concluded that cosmogonic thought was very much a subsidiary and probably too, a quite late concentration for ancient Israel. Thus, the well-known German form-critic Gerhard von Rad, who placed historiographic concerns at the heart of Israel's theology, urged repeatedly that "Israel's faith is based on history rather than cosmology" (*ROTT* 2: 347). The historian of religion Mircea Eliade concurred: "This God of the Jewish people is no longer an Oriental divinity, creator of archetypal gestures, but a personality who ceaselessly intervenes in history . . . the Hebrews were the first to discover the meaning of history as the epiphany of God, and this conception, as we should expect, was taken up and amplified by Christianity" (1959: 104). Von Rad, Eliade, and others then went on to claim that historiographical, functional, and soteriological concerns dominate in the religion of Israel as speculative, cosmological concerns dominate elsewhere, for example in ancient Egypt, Mesopotamia, or India.

However, the position that cosmological thought plays but a secondary role in the Hebrew Bible is one that has found fewer defenders in the most recent period. The internal evidence most cited for revising the earlier, minimizing assessment of the role of cosmology in biblical religion is, first, that the present shape of the Hebrew Bible does accord primacy to two separate creation accounts. Thus, from a canonical perspective, the ancient Jewish community which based its beliefs and rituals upon the Hebrew Bible clearly saw cosmogony as basic to its religion. Secondly, and especially in the years following the recovery of the ancient, mythological texts from Ugarit (Ras Shamra) on the Syrian coast, the number of allusive references to cosmogonic battles in the Hebrew Bible has been given renewed appreciation.

Beyond this evidence, progress in the study of comparative religion has suggested that no religion entirely omits cosmological reflection. Thus, the French sociologist Emile Durkheim, whose *The Elementary Forms of the Religious Life* has been perhaps the single most influential volume for the study of comparative religion, argued both that "there is no religion that is not a cosmology" (1915: 21) and that "all known religions have been systems of ideas which tend to embrace the universality of things, and to give us a complete representation of the world" (1915: 165). Durkheim's view is that all religions offer their adherents a satisfying explanation of the world, so that cosmology can be sought and found in many texts that are not overt cosmogonies. The analyses of Durkheim and others have begun to persuade biblical scholars that the older view was too limiting and too much in the service of demonstrating the uniqueness of Israel's religion. The position that the Hebrew Bible is essentially concerned solely with history or with soteriology, to the exclusion of cosmology, has had a similar fate. Two recent summaries of Israelite cosmogony can therefore conclude, in opposition to the older view, that creation is not to be seen in the Bible as transformed and historicized, but rather remains fundamentally mythical (McKenzie 1976: 199) and that "at all points in the cosmogonic traditions, even in places where Israel's election or deliverance from enemies is involved, there is a more fundamental level of meaning: the nature of reality itself" (Knight 1985: 134).

Hence, the view commanding increasing assent is that cosmological thought is of greater significance for both ancient Judaism and early Christianity than earlier critics had judged. Still, it remains true and worth accenting that various religious traditions do place a different weight upon such thought, and that on any chart measuring comparative attention granted to cosmology the biblical religions would not rank near the top. Among the neighbors of ancient Israel, both Egypt and Mesopotamia seem to have engaged more fully and at an earlier date in speculations about the origin and the basic blueprint of the cosmos than did Israelites; and early Greek thought shows a similar concentration upon questions of origin and rational organization. Perhaps the most elaborate religious cosmologies are those developed in India, whose chronologies of the ages of the universe are especially noteworthy (*EncRel* 4: 107–13) and contrast greatly with the very brief (cosmically speaking) time spans narrated in the Hebrew Bible and in the NT. Among the reasons for this relative dearth of cosmogonic speculation may be the composite origins of the biblical portrait of Yahweh, the God of Israel. It has been pointed out that elements of both the god Baʿl Haddu and the god 'El from the religion of most ancient Syria-Palestine have gone into the Israelite descriptions of Yahweh *(CMHE);* and the developing polemic against Baʿl Haddu, whose myths are throughout cosmogonic tales, may have militated against the utilization of the full repertoire of cosmogonic myths in portraying Yahweh.

2. Varieties of Cosmology in the Hebrew Bible. A second, prefatory remark about the most general role of cosmology in biblical thought is that this thought displays a notable lack of uniformity and consistency. There is perhaps just sufficient uniformity to allow for the construction of a general world view (see sec. B.9 below); but the contrasts between, for example, the allusions to an original cosmic battle against the forces of chaos, on the one hand, and the portrait of Wisdom's controlling role in the orderly creation of a rational cosmos, on the other hand, remain what is most striking.

The reasons for this lack of uniformity are not difficult to discover. In the first place, the process of the composition and transmission of the materials now in the Hebrew

Bible was one that stretched over something like a full millennium. It should not, therefore, occasion surprise if the cosmogonic accounts which appear to have originated in premonarchical Israel differ dramatically from those now found in Proverbs or the book of Daniel. Secondly, one of the distinctive attributes of the religion of Israel is the allowance for and the preservation of quite different theological positions. Such tolerance of diversity obtains in the area of cosmology as it does elsewhere, so that a recent scholar is on quite firm ground when he concludes of cosmological materials in the Hebrew Bible that "at this point, as in many others, Israel was able to maintain and affirm pluralism as a distinct aspect of her heritage and identity" (Knight 1985: 137).

Of course, both the recent move toward widening the definition of cosmology to include materials previously omitted in discussing cosmology in the Hebrew Bible and the absence of uniformity within this collection of texts create difficulties for any attempt to construct a schematic portrait of cosmology in the Hebrew Bible. In what follows, cosmological materials are treated in rough chronological order, with the frank recognition that the assignment of absolute dates to many strands in the Hebrew Bible must be done with greater hesitancy than was true only a generation ago. Nor is there any attempt, given the constraints of space, to be truly comprehensive. For example, neither the flood story in Genesis 6–9 nor the accounts of the significance of the temple in Jerusalem (e.g., in 1 Kings 8 or Ezekiel 40–48) receives attention below; and yet each could be seen as presenting material of cosmological significance and must be covered in any fuller account.

3. The Cosmic Battle Pattern. Already at the end of the 19th century the great scholar of Israel's preliterary traditions, Hermann Gunkel, noted that a careful reading of the Hebrew Bible revealed allusions to a common ANE cosmogony based upon a primordial combat between the creator and the forces of chaos (Gunkel 1895). Prior to the uncovering and translation of the Ugaritic texts, the source of these traditions was regularly seen to be Mesopotamia, the location of the creation tale *Enuma Eliš* with its account of the battle between the god Marduk and the dragon goddess Tiamat, and perhaps too in Egypt, which knew the tradition of a fundamental combat between the creator god Re and the dragon Apophis. The mythological texts from Ugarit in Syria now demonstrate that there is no need to go so far afield in the search for the literary and theological models which Israelite poets found so useful. These texts, as best the narratives they relate can be reconstructed at present, tell of a primeval battle between the god Baʿl Haddu (familiar as Baʿal in the Hebrew Bible) and the forces of chaotic destruction and death. The latter are called by such titles as Prince Sea *(ym)* and Judge River *(nhr)* in the primary version of this combat tale, while what appear to be alternate versions of the same, basic tale label these forces Lotan (*ltn*, the equivalent of the biblical Leviathan) or the seven-headed serpent (Herdner 1963: CTCA Text 2 or 5).

On the basis of these texts from ancient Syria and of their transformations in the Hebrew Bible, a common Syria-Palestinian pattern for the shape of the cosmogonic battle myth can be reconstructed. This pattern consists of four rounds: (1) a Divine Warrior goes forth to battle the chaotic monsters, variously called Sea, Death, Leviathan, Tannin; (2) the world of nature responds to the wrath of the Divine Warrior and the forces of chaos are defeated; (3) the Divine Warrior assumes his throne on a mountain, surrounded by a retinue of other deities; and (4) the Divine Warrior utters his powerful speech, which leads nature to produce the created world (*CMHE,* 162–63). Though there is no single biblical text which relates this battle in its fullest form, once the pattern is made clear, it seems undeniable that it lies behind and is responsible for a great number of biblical allusions which should be accounted as cosmogonic. For example, the titles Leviathan, Sea, River, Sea Monster (*tannîn* or the like), and Dragon *(rahab)* all are used of opponents of Yahweh the God of Israel in settings describing the earlier days of the cosmos.

The recognition of the existence and the continued power of this cosmic battle pattern has brought to life the cosmogonic significance of a number of biblical texts whose importance for the study of Israelite cosmology had long gone unrecognized. In some cases, the briefest of allusions suggests resonance with a widespread knowledge of this cosmogonic struggle tale. For example, Psalm 29, which was perhaps first composed in honor of Baʿl Haddu and only later transformed into a hymn honoring Yahweh, portrays the victorious God of Israel enthroned upon the "Flood dragon" (*mabbûl;* Ps 29:10). In Ps 68: 22–23 (—Eng 68:21–22) we read of God defeating both the "Serpent" and the "Deep Sea" (see Dahood *Psalms II 51–100* AB, 131, for the text and translation here). Ps 74:13–14, in the midst of a section explicitly devoted to creation, tells of Yahweh's victory over "Sea" *(yam)* and the crushing of the heads of the "Sea Monster" *(tannînîm)* and of Leviathan. Another hymn to God as creator (Psalm 89) refers to Yahweh's reign on the back of "Sea" *(yam)* after defeating the dragon Rahab (Ps 89:10–11—Eng 89: 9–10). Psalm 104, long of special interest because of its similarities with the Egyptian celebration of creation called the Hymn to the Aton, again mentions Leviathan among other watery demons defeated by Yahweh.

It now seems likely that early audiences of all these psalms will have been able to fill out such brief allusions with the larger story so similar to them. Nor are these allusions confined to the Psalter. The hymn in Habakkuk 3, now generally regarded as a very early hymn inserted into a later context, has "River" and "Sea" as the enemies of Yahweh (Hab 3:8). Later prophetic texts display the same awareness of the creator's battle prowess in the struggle against chaotic foes which preceded the present cosmic order. The fire which Yahweh directs, according to one of Amos' visions, devours the "Great Abyss" *(tĕhôm rabbâ),* which appears to be a reference to a sea serpent (Amos 7:4; Wolff *Joel and Amos* Hermeneia, 292–93); and another of this prophet's visions portrays Yahweh commanding the "Serpent" *(nāḥāš)* who dwells in the underworld below (Amos 9:2–3). Leviathan in Isa 27:1 is seen as a "Sea Monster" *(tannîn),* and perhaps too as a fleeing, wriggling snake, if the mythological monsters in this verse are all various epithets for the same cosmic foe. But perhaps the most elaborate series of allusions to this primeval scene made by an Israelite prophet are those contained in the hymn in honor of Yahweh's great strength now to be found in Isa 51:9–11. The setting here is clearly that of the earliest days of the world, the days and generations long past, when Yahweh smote Rahab, pierced the "Sea Monster" *(tannîn),* and dried up the waters of "Sea" *(yam)* and the "Great Abyss" *(tĕhôm rabbâ).* A recent study of this hymn observes that "the allusion is to the cosmogonic myth, the battle of creation, in which the monster of chaos is slain by the God who thereby establishes kingship" (*CMHE,* 108).

Demonstrating both the longevity and the power of this theme in a variety of different Israelite settings, another series of similar allusions are to be found in the poetry of the book of Job (Pope *Job* AB). Job 3:8 refers to Leviathan, 7:12 to the "Sea Monster" *(tannîn)* as cosmic foes of the created order, while 26:12 credits God again with smiting Rahab. At much greater length, the second speech from the whirlwind in Job 40–41 contrasts God's powers over Behemoth and Leviathan with the powerlessness of one such as Job. Leviathan is now well known as Lotan, the enemy of Baʿl and 'Anat from the Ugaritic cosmogonic myths; and, while Behemoth may refer to the hippopotamus in some biblical texts, here the beast is best seen as another power of universal chaos, perhaps even equated with the bull of heaven slain by Gilgamesh and Enkidu in the Epic of Gilgamesh (Pope *Job* AB, 322).

The cumulative effect of all these allusions, tantalizingly brief and vague though each may seem when seen in isolation, is impressive. The texts' very brevity bears witness to the familiarity with the cosmic battle pattern that the author of each could assume on behalf of his listeners. Just as the briefest mention of words and phrases like the Pilgrims, the Founding Fathers, or the Gettysburg Address will resonate widely to an American audience, so too the very spare report of the Sea, the Dragon, or of Yahweh's splitting a sea monster will have called forth for an Israelite audience the entire myth in which these cosmic enemies attempt to play their destructive roles.

Earlier scholars were troubled by the implications of these battle scenes, since they so clearly compromise later Jewish and Christian understandings of the Hebrew Bible as consistently monotheistic. But the Hebrew Bible itself bears clear witness to monotheism as a slowly developing notion within early Israel, and one that for many centuries found no difficulty in portraying Yahweh's creative activity in the terms of the familiar cosmogonic battle pattern.

4. The Creation of the First Humans. The narrative that runs from Gen 2:4b through the remainder of Genesis 2 is, as was observed above, more properly an anthropogony ("human creation account") than a cosmogony. This story is normally credited to the Yahwist or the "J" source of the Tetrateuch. The Yahwist's activity is traditionally placed in the 9th century B.C.E.; but renewed doubt has been expressed of late about our ability to assign a date to this narrative strand with much confidence. The story of the creation of the first man and the first woman in Genesis 2 is surely situated in the remotest past, but as surely this story occurs after the initial cosmogony. About the only clear reference here to events of that earlier, cosmogonic event is that to the underworld reservoir of water which irrigated and hence brought fertility to the otherwise dry and sterile ground (Gen 2:6). The Hebrew word used to designate this reservoir *(ʾd)* is a loan word from Mesopotamia (Sum ID, Akk *edu*), demonstrating again the reliance of many of the details in the primeval history (Genesis 1–11) upon traditions developed in the Tigris-Euphrates Valley.

As is true both of much of the Yahwist's materials in Genesis and of the recently more fully understood Epic of Atrahasis from Mesopotamia, the chief concern in this anthropogony is to describe accurately the status of humanity, and thereby to distinguish humanity from the attributes of the gods (Oden 1981). Another concern of the narrative in Genesis 2, as in so many accounts of the genesis of humanity throughout religious myths, is the origin of the distinction between the sexes (Trible 1978: 72–143). Yahweh here creates humans by forming or shaping them, working as does a potter (Gen 2:7, 19) and using bits of soil as the basic material. As a deity, Yahweh possesses both great wisdom and immortality. Humans initially lack both attributes but hunger ceaselessly for a higher status; and it is this lust for a different position on the cosmic hierarchy that continually causes trouble for humanity. The facts that the tale is set in a garden, so often associated with royalty in the ANE, and that the concern is both the wondrous powers and yet the limitations of humanity have led several scholars to propose the Israelite royal court as the original setting for the narrative's generation and transmission (Coats 1983: 39).

Genesis 2 is not the only account of the creation of primal humanity in the Hebrew Bible, even if it is at once the most familiar and the most sophisticated. Another and related report is to be found in Ezekiel 28, the prophet's lament over the prideful fall of the king of Tyre. Here we encounter again allusion to the creation of early humanity (using the special biblical term for divine creation, *bārāʾ*) in the setting of a garden. And here too read of a human's wickedness and violence requiring his expulsion from the garden. In both stories, the glory of humans as originally created is stressed, but so too is the human propensity to strive pridefully for a status that belongs properly to God.

5. The Role of Second Isaiah in Centralizing the Cosmological Argument. The 6th-century B.C.E. author of the poems now contained in Isaiah 40–55 (and perhaps of material found elsewhere in the book of Isaiah) was hardly the first in ancient Israel to credit Yahweh with creation). But this poet may have been the first to expand upon the series of cosmogonic allusions noted above (B.3) to establish something like a full cosmological argument for the unique and incomparable abilities of the God of Israel. Of the biblical occurrences of the Hebrew word "to create" *(bārāʾ),* used solely of divine creation, over a third occur in this section of the book of Isaiah. Isa 40:12–26 offers a quite complete description of the cosmos shaped by Yahweh, a description of the earth founded upon the seas and of Yahweh enthroned above the vault or disk of the tentlike earth. For this poet, Yahweh is the "Creator of the ends of the earth" (*bôrēʾ qĕṣôt hāʾāreṣ,* Isa 40:28), who created both darkness and light (Isa 45:7).

Many have asked why Second Isaiah first combined the previously scattered allusions to Yahweh as creator into a coherent argument for the superiority of Yahweh over all other so-called deities. An answer ready to hand is provided by the setting in which Second Isaiah's prophetic activity occurred. Isaiah 40–55 are the work of a prophet of the Babylonian Exile, whose Israelite audience will have been bombarded by the cosmogonic claims made on behalf of Mesopotamian deities. These claims are countered and thereby refuted by Second Isaiah's full articulation of the cosmological argument in service of the worship of Yahweh.

6. The Priestly Account of Creation. Both because of its present position opening the Hebrew Bible and because of stylistic features lending to it a tone of high formality and comprehensiveness, the priestly account of creation (Gen 1:1–2:4a) has long been the normative cosmogony for Judaism and Christianity. Like Second Isaiah, those responsible for the composition of this overture have self-consciously utilized the announcement that the God of Israel is creator as a major theological confession. The seven-part, climactic structure helps to indicate that everything in the cosmos is due to the power and generosity of this deity; and the parallelism so noticeable between the various stages in creation adds a tone of purposeful structure (Knight 1985: 144). The rhetorical style of this account, in addition to both a manifest concern for cultic matters and a repetition of blessing formulas, have long pointed to priestly circles for its origin. According to the traditional documentary hypothesis, these indications would assign to Gen 1:1–2:4a a fairly late date, perhaps in the 6th or 5th century B.C.E. However, several scholars have questioned so late a date for any part of the so-called "P Work," and others have observed that even if the seven-day cosmogony here owes its present formulation to activity after the Exile, this cosmogony's remoter origins may lie much earlier in the history of Israel (*ROTT* 1: 140).

Though the creation of humanity is surely accented as the climactic achievement of God's creative activity, the priestly account of creation concentrates less upon anthropogony than does the Yahwistic narrative which follows and does offer something much more in keeping with traditional cosmogonic lore. This almost symphonic overture truly does situate the reader "in the beginning." This remains true whether or not one adheres to the traditional rendering of the first words of Genesis ("In the beginning") or rather adopts the alternative suggestion that the first verses of Genesis 1 are to be read as a dependent clause and hence translated something like "When God set about to create the heaven and earth" (Speiser *Genesis* AB, 3, 12).

The portrait here is of a mighty or divine wind hovering over watery and dark undifferentiated matter. The phrase describing this undifferentiated matter (Heb *tōhû wā-bōhû*), the formless abyss over which the mighty wind of God soars, has prompted two areas of inquiry. The first concerns the origin and meaning of these puzzling words. The phrase is probably best seen as a hendiadys, that is, the use of two words to express but a single notion, in this case that of vast formlessness (Speiser, 5). As such, the matter which existed prior to the formation of a structured cosmos here is much in keeping with other cosmogonies, for example, that of India where again " 'At first there was only darkness wrapped in darkness' " and where everything " 'was only unillumined water' " (Rigveda; *EncRel* 4: 107). Secondly, references in some material which is remotely of Phoenician origin suggest that here too, as in so many areas of the religion of ancient Israel, the ultimate source of the priestly vocabulary and of the resulting portrait is the cosmological speculation of ancient Israel's Canaanite neighbors. The Phoenician cosmology, now found among the works of the church historian Eusebius of Caesarea (3d–4th century C.E.) but attributed to an ancient worthy called Sanchuniathon, mentions both "gas and chaos" as the material existing prior to creation and a certain "Baau" which might well be related to the Heb *bōhû* (Attridge and Oden 1981: 36–39, 75–80). If Phoenician speculation played a role in helping Israel to formulate the priestly account, this is not to say that other influences are not felt as well; for example, the portrait of the cosmos in Psalm 104 is discernibly similar to that in Genesis 1, and the Egyptian nature of this psalm has been noted above.

Out of this mass of undifferentiated and dark primal matter, God creates the cosmos by the power of speech alone. This mode of creation, which is to be encountered elsewhere in the Hebrew Bible (for example, Ps 33:6, where the heavens and their inhabitants are made by Yahweh's "word" and "the breath of his mouth"), is one familiar throughout the ANE. To both the Babylonian deity Marduk, who in *Enuma Eliš* causes a constellation (probably not a "garment," as in older translations) to vanish and then to reappear by speech alone, and to several Egyptian gods is attributed this same awesome power. A question which greatly exercised later theologians is that of whether or not we have to do here with *creatio ex nihilo.* This formulation is surely known elsewhere, for example in Egypt where a creator is called the one who begot himself, in Polynesia where a god is called the parentless (though there is some suggestion that later, Christian influence may be here operative), and also in India. The formulation also does appear in postbiblical Judaism, probably first in 2 Macc 7:28 from the 1st century B.C.E. But the priestly account in Genesis 1 seems not concerned with either affirming or denying *creatio ex nihilo:* it moves very quickly from the simple statement that the world was an undifferentiated waste without limit to a concentration upon the fullness and the surpassing quality of what God created.

The incomparability of the divine creative activity is accented by the priestly account, not just by the formality with which creation's stages progress toward a well-structured fullness, but also by a distinctive vocabulary. Rather than utilizing available terms which suggest that God shaped or formed the cosmos on the model of various human activities, the priestly writers are careful to reserve the term *bārāʾ*, "to create," for God's action alone. Still, if the use of such vocabulary reinforces the theme of the Yahwist's narrative that human status is never divine status, it remains true that the seven-day cosmogony in Gen 1:1–2:4a does grant powerful rank and fearsome responsibility to humanity. Humans are the "image" *(ṣelem)* and "likeness" *(dĕmût)* of divinity itself, and human authority over the earth is overtly portrayed on the analogy of God's own authority over all of creation (Gen 1:26).

7. The Wisdom Tradition. Affirmations of the unique creative power of Israel's God are to be found not only in royal circles and among priests, but also within the wisdom or sapiential tradition. This tradition is that which finds extended expression in genres long designated as works of wisdom, materials such as Proverbs or Job, but additionally in other results of Israel's literary and religious heritage, for example prophetic statements. To Jeremiah is attributed the statements that Yahweh made the world through his "wisdom" *(ḥokmâ)* and "understanding" *(tĕbûnâ)* (Jer 10:12); and Second Isaiah as well portrays Yahweh's creative capacity as part of a comprehensive and comprehendible scheme for the structure of the cosmos (Isaiah 40). If the relatively recent trend in biblical scholarship to attribute a most significant role to the wisdom tradition in shaping the religion of Israel should continue to command assent, then it is quite possible that the major impetus to cosmological thought in ancient Israel resulted from this tradition which attempted most directly to understand and categorize the universe's structuring principles.

The most extended report of creation in this context is that now to be found in Prov 8:22–31 as a part of an entire chapter devoted to extolling the concept of "Wisdom" *(ḥokmâ)*. Wisdom is here portrayed as the oldest of all created things. Wisdom attended upon Yahweh in the formation of the oceans, the mountains, and the earth, and in the stabilizing of various cosmic features. Given the continued interest in Israel and elsewhere in first things and in the order of creation, a long debate has ensued concerning the question of whether Wisdom was "begotten," "acquired," or "created," with the balance of probability now leaning toward the last of these renderings for the Heb verb *qānâ* on the basis of the word's use in the Ugaritic texts (McKane *Proverbs* OTL, 352–54; Dahood 1968: 513). In any case, the emphasis throughout is clearly upon the almost unimaginable intellectual power of Yahweh's attribute of Wisdom in supplying a reasoned blueprint for the cosmos. Toward the conclusion of this cosmogongy from the wisdom tradition, the figure of Wisdom is portrayed both as a child delighting the resulting cosmic order and as perhaps a master craftsman or technician (Prov 8:30–31). The latter description is dependent upon the correct understanding of the noun *ʾāmôn* (Prov 8:30), which may mean "artisan" but might also suggest again "child," or "teacher," or perhaps "faithful companion" (McKane *Proverbs* OTL, 72).

As with the cosmogonies in Genesis 2 and Genesis 1, considerable attention has been granted to the questions of the origin of the role assigned to Wisdom in Proverbs 8 and of the resulting stages in the creation process. Egyptian tradition long established a position of preeminence for the concept of wisdom, often spoken of in terms of a deity called Maat who accompanies the creator's activities, so that here as in the case of Psalm 104 direct Egyptian influence is certainly possible. But the full appreciation of the Ugaritic texts has demonstrated conclusively that Canaanite tradition is the immediate point of impact upon multiple areas of Israel's thinking, whatever may be the more remote origins of any of these thoughts, so that we should probably again look to Canaan for the most direct source of the inspiration for Prov 8:22–31. But the many uncertainties surrounding the origin and translation of these verses should not obscure their chief point, which is to recognize the orderly cosmos as an object of great delight and wonder. As such, Proverbs 8 is very much in keeping with the trajectory of later biblical thought and of Jewish and Christian thinking beyond the biblical period (Philo, for example) with regard to cosmological matters.

8. Cosmogony in Apocalyptic Thought. Eschatology, as teachings about final things, and apocalyptic thought, which reports revelations about these same final matters, might initially seem the least likely locus for cosmogonic materials. However, as soon as one reflects that eschatological speculation is in fact but the future translation of cosmogony, then the bearing of such materials upon cosmology is perhaps clear. Eliade, for example, has noted that the chronological setting of cosmogonies in the remotest period, a period that Eliade labels *in illo tempore,* is in fact repeated in apocalyptic materials: "*in illo tempore* is situated not only at the beginning of time but also at its end. . . . The only difference is that this victory over the forces of darkness and chaos no longer occurs regularly every year but is projected into a future and Messianic *illud tempus*" (1959: 106). Thus, if cosmogonic myths recount the origins of the intelligible universe, apocalyptic myths recount this same universe as created anew in the future.

The initial stages in Israel's development of an apocalyptic tradition are apparent already in the prophets of the exilic period; and it is likely that the apocalyptic tradition is to be traced quite directly to the unfolding of prophetic thought (Hanson 1975). The phrase "in later days," "in following eras" *(ʾaḥărît hayyāmîm),* sometimes refers to a kind of hazy boundary between the near future and the far, clearly eschatological future (as in Jer 23:20), but in later biblical texts has become a technical term for the end of history as previously experienced (*TDOT* 2: 211–12). Perhaps the single and clearest results of this developing apocalyptic tradition are to be seen in Zechariah 14. Those responsible for this chapter extend the thought of Second Isaiah with regard to the revelation of new things and that of Third Isaiah regarding "new heavens and a new earth" (Isa 65:17) to arrive at a portrait of a final cosmogonic battle which will erase the former created order. Zech 14:6–8 shows with particular clarity the announced end of series of paired concepts (day and night, heat and cold, seasons of planting and harvest) which had served to define the originally structured cosmos (Hanson 1975: 376–79). But the very conclusiveness of the former created order's giving way to a new order reveals that such apocalyptic thought should be thought of as additional cosmogonic material within ancient Israel.

9. The Hebrew Bible's Portrait of the Cosmos. The variety in date, origin, and scope of the Hebrew Bible's cosmological materials means that achieving a single, uniform picture of the physical universe is hardly possible. Still, sufficient overlap does obtain between the many accounts of the universe, however these may vary in their details, to allow for a few generalizations. The earth on which humanity dwells is seen as a round, solid object, perhaps a disk, floating upon a limitless expanse of water. Paralleling this lower body of water is a second, similarly limitless, above, from which water descends in the form of rain through holes and channels piercing the heavenly reservoir. The moon, sun, and other luminaries are fixed in a curved structure which arches over the earth. This structure is the familiar "firmament" *(rāqîaʿ)* of the priestly account, perhaps envisioned as a solid but very thin substance on the analogy of beaten and stretched metal.

Though some texts appear to convey a picture of a four-storied universe (Job 11:8–9 or Ps 139:8–9), the great majority of biblical texts assume the three-storied universe so clearly assumed in other, ancient traditions. Thus, the Decalog's prohibition of images specifies "heaven above," "earth below," and "water under the earth" as the possible models for any such forbidden images (Exod 20:4). If we understand the common term "earth" (*ʾereṣ*) as designating at times the "underworld," then the combined references in Ps 77:19 to heaven, the "world" (*tēbēl*), and the "earth" (*ʾereṣ*) are another appeal to the universe as a three-storied structure (for other texts where *ʾereṣ* may refer to the underworld, see Stadelmann 1970: 128, n. 678). Clearer reference still to the same structure is to be found in Ps 115:15–17, where we find grouped together "the heaven of heavens," "the earth," and the realm of "the dead" (cf. Ps 33:6–8 and Prov 8:27–29).

The curving, solid structure which arches over the realm of humanity is sometimes called a "disk" or "vault" (*ḥûg;* Isa 40:22; Prov 8:27). That which allows the heavenly abyss to water the earth are occasional interruptions in this solid structure, openings called variously windows, doors, or channels. In some texts, that which suspends the habitable earth above the underworld's waters (see 1 Sam 2:8 for another reference to these rivers) are pillars or some such foundational structures. These seem envisioned in Job 38:4–6; Pss 24:2; 104:5; Prov 8:29, and elsewhere. Finally, the realm beneath the arena of human activity is not only imagined as one of watery chaos but also given the specific designation "Sheol" (*šĕʾôl*), usually translated "the underworld." In the different elaborations upon just what one should imagine Sheol as including, again there is little consistency. At times, Sheol is personified, with a belly or womb and a mouth (Jonah 2:3—Eng 2:2); Prov 1:23; 30:16; and Ps 141:7), while at others Sheol is rather more architecturally portrayed (Isa 38:10; Job 7:9–10; 14:20–22; 17:13; 18:17–18), as a dark and forgetful land or city (Stadelmann 1970: 166–76).

C. Cosmology in the NT

1. Sources of Early Christian Cosmological Thought. References to the origin of the cosmos and to this cosmos' structure are rather less frequently to be found in the NT than in the Hebrew Bible. This cosmological spareness is to be accounted for partly, and most obviously, because of the smaller size of this collection of texts from early Christianity and partly because the essentials of the portrait painted in the Hebrew Bible are assumed. However, another important reason for the absence of much cosmological lore in the NT is based upon the conclusions of research into the situation in which early Christians felt themselves to lie. Throughout the 20th century, biblical scholarship has confirmed in general the view that the first Christians expected the second coming of the Messiah imminently, and this notable eschatological immediacy does not allow for such speculation as obtains in many religious traditions. One might here contrast Chinese Buddhism, whose expectations of the coming of a future Buddha Maitreya (*EncRel* 4: 116) are certainly messianic; but these expectations still sit quite easily within a vast chronological scheme.

The first and chief source of such NT cosmogonic thought as is to be found is, of course, the material from the Hebrew Bible reviewed above. Especially fruitful ground was found in the cosmological thought of the wisdom tradition, both within the Hebrew Bible and then in later, Hellenistic Judaism. Greek notions of the cosmos' administration through principles of rational organization were also important. To the extent that a fully developed portrait of a cosmic redeemer had been developed within pre-Christian Gnosticism (and the extent of this development remains the subject of scrutiny and disagreement), this portrait too will have exercised its influence upon the first Christian writers, especially in regard to an important departure from Hebrew Bible thought. For gnostic thought, the created world is no longer a divine blessing but is rather evaluated negatively and seen as under the domain of demonic powers. The view of redemption by Christ as redemption from this world obviously shares elements of such thought.

2. Cosmological Assumptions in Pauline Theology. The references to cosmology in letters generally recognized to be of Pauline authorship appear largely, or wholly, to be allusions to pre-Pauline confessional formulas. Thus, the affirmation in 1 Cor 8:6 that there is one God from whom "all things (*ta panta*) come" and also one Lord, Jesus Christ, "through whom all things are" reads like a development of the Jewish confession that Yahweh is one into a twofold formula of one God and one Lord (Conzelmann *1 Corinthians* Hermeneia, 144). God as creator of the cosmos is here affirmed, but the affirmation is assumed rather than developed, and is plainly subsidiary to a confession of Christ's soteriological role. Much the same could be said of the hymn, widely seen as pre-Pauline and often attributed to gnostic influence, in Phil 2:6–11. This hymn insists upon the cosmic and preexistent status of the Christian Lord, whose role in rescuing humanity from domination by earthly powers is again stressed. Indeed, it is perhaps worth accenting that confessions of Christ's cosmic role are at the heart of NT cosmology.

At several places in Paul's letter to the Romans one can again catch glimpses of the cosmological foundations of early Christian thought. In his expansion upon the theme of justification in Romans 4, Paul notes that the God of Abraham is the one who calls into being that which was not (Rom 4:17). As with Gen 1:1–3, this verse has been read as a reference to *creatio ex nihilo,* though in the context of Paul's argument the chief intent is plainly to emphasize the power of God rather than to address this issue at all. Rom 8:19–22 alludes to a position never fully developed, that of creation's pained and groaning longing for release from futility; the background here might equally be gnostic speculation (Bultmann 1951: 174, 230) or the laments about the present world order expressed in Jewish apocalypticism. Finally, quite in keeping with 1 Cor 8:6 is Paul's statement in Rom 11:36 that "everything" (*ta panta*) is from God.

3. The Johannine Tradition. Much as the priestly account of creation in Gen 1:1–2:4a has become determinative for later Jewish and Christian theology, so too the preface to the fourth gospel is the most readily cited piece of cosmogonic teaching in the NT. The literary style of John 1:1–18 once more, as in the case of Phil 2:6–11, has suggested to many scholars an origin in a ritual hymn. In deliberate imitation of Genesis 1 in the LXX version, this preface too opens "In the beginning," here to emphasize the cosmic and remotest origins of the Logos ("Word") figure. Though there is no reflection on the mechanisms of creation at all, that everything was created through the Logos is affirmed by this preface in clear terms (John 1:3). Similarly not reflected upon are a host of questions about this figure which have exercised later theologians and scholars: the Logos is of cosmic status and existed with God from the beginning of all, but how exactly is one to imagine this figure? As a person, or as the personified revealing and creating abilities of God? And how does one deal with the apparent paradox of the Logos as both fully equal with God and yet equally and clearly subordinate to the Father? The question of the origin of the Logos concept in Johannine thought is similarly difficult to answer, with both the wisdom speculation of Jewish thought and the gnostic redeemer scheme possible sources. What is clear throughout John 1:1–18 is just what had been stressed by Paul, the soteriological function of the Logos who became flesh for the salvation of humanity.

The final book in the present NT canon, the book of Revelation, returns in fairly elaborate fashion, to the cosmogonic battle scenes witnessed allusively throughout parts of the Hebrew Bible (Collins 1976). In addition to affirmations of God as the creator of all (Rev 4:11), and as the omnipotent being *(pantokratōr)* who is at once beginning and end (Rev 1:8; 21:6; 22:13), four visions in the book of Revelation are devoted to allegorical rehearsals of the old cosmic battle scenario, as first Gunkel recognized nearly a century ago. In Revelation 12, the chaotic enemy is the serpentine dragon, reminding us of the Sea Monster figure *(tannîn)* in the Hebrew Bible. Revelation 13 introduces two such forces of chaos, perhaps Leviathan and Behemoth in their cosmically destructive modes (Ford *Revelation* AB, 217). The description of the great harlot in Revelation 17 reminds one of many of the Hebrew Bible's allusions to the threat posed by undifferentiated water; and again in Revelation 21 the sea as enemy recalls the opponents of Yahweh's cosmogonic task. In all of these visions, the function of apocalyptic in repeating and renewing the original cosmogony is thus especially clear.

4. Later NT Thought. Even after the initial, creative period of Christian self-expression, little extended discussion of cosmological issues, at least as these are standardly defined, is to be found in the NT. This suggests that the spareness of early Christian cosmology is at least as much the result of a Christian hesitancy to formalize, much less to make of creedal significance, such issues as it is a consequence of the sense that the second coming of the Messiah was imminent. Col 1:15–20 is perhaps the fullest of these brief expressions of what was assumed on behalf of early Christianity about the cosmos. Here, another likely instance of a hymn reutilized in a different context, Christ is affirmed as uniquely preceding all creation, and as the being through whom everything was established. These affirmations recall most centrally the role accorded Wisdom in Proverbs 8 and in postbiblical Jewish thought, though such views, without, of course, the identification of Christ as the medium of creation, can also be found expressed throughout Hellenistic thought. Finally, 2 Peter 3 returns one to the cosmogonic formulations of the Hebrew Bible, in attributing creation to divine speech and in comparing the coming destruction of the known cosmos to that familiar from the biblical flood tale.

D. The Functions of Religious Cosmogonies/ Cosmologies

Most scholarly accounts of the place of cosmogonic lore in the religions of Israel and of early Christianity dwell upon the origin, the initial cultic setting, and the eventual literary context of this lore. Given biblical scholarship's understandable concern for questions of historical origin and transmission (Oden 1987: 1–39), this concentration is hardly surprising. But such concentration requires supplementing with questions of function and meaning. Why is it that few, if any, religious traditions omit some attention to cosmology? Why are the religious communities responsible for collections of sacred texts so concerned, some might say obsessed, with inquiry into the earliest days of the cosmos? Some attention must be paid to these and similar questions here, though the fact that cosmological materials are most frequently to be found in the context of cosmogonic myths means that the following discussion overlaps to some extent issues raised in any account of the origin and role of myths in religion most generally. See MYTH AND MYTHOLOGY.

1. Older Views. Since cosmogonic myths standardly treat data like the shape of the universe, the ultimate sources of meteorological phenomena, and the origin and meaning of the moon and stars, a view long popular was that cosmology is primitive science. This view can be found expressed even in antiquity; but it commanded especially wide assent in the 19th century, during the early days of the systematic study of comparative mythology and of the origin of modern anthropology. However, analyzing cosmologies as strictly analogous to scientific inquiry has never ceased to find a few proponents and has most recently witnessed a revival.

Humans need, this view affirms, satisfying answers to some basic questions about the world of nature; and, this explanation continues, as science answers such questions for moderns, so cosmological narratives answered them for traditional societies. Predictably for the 19th-century heyday of this explanation, cosmogony was thus readily accommodated to an evolutionary scheme. Early humans were seen as adequately served by religious cosmologies; but modern humanity was credited with evolving more demanding standards which could be met only by fully scientific, verifiable explanations. Applying this view to the combat myth in biblical texts, for example, one might say that the origin of such myths was the desire to explain the alternating wet and dry seasons. This desire was long fulfilled by cosmogonies which deified the powers of wetness or aridity; today, however, such early cosmogonies no longer continue to provide satisfactory answers and hence have been replaced by impersonal accounts.

A second explanation, often placed in tandem with the model of cosmogony as primitive science, was the myth-ritual hypothesis. According to this view, all myths originated as rituals. Traditional humans, the proponents of myth-ritualism asserted, acted before they reflected. The myths which have survived are the later attempts to make sense of the primary and generative rituals. These myths are, to use an analogy much favored by myth-ritualists, the libretti to the more fundamental ritual dramas. Assertions about the cultic origins of much biblical material owe a great deal to the base assumptions of the myth-ritual model. For example, we have seen that a setting in the priestly cult is often posited for the seven-day cosmogony in Genesis 1, and a royal cult origin for the anthropogony in Genesis 2.

Attractive as each of these hypotheses is, neither has been able to sustain itself fully in the face of more recent research into the role played by cosmologies in various religious traditions. With regard to the former hypothesis, 20th-century ethnological work has established that so-called "primitive" or "traditional" cultures are fully as capable of scientific, rational, and empirical thinking as are their modern counterparts. If religious cosmologies can exist, as they do, side by side with accounts that must be judged scientific, then it must be that these cosmologies play a role somewhat different from that played by scientific thought. Cosmogonies thus do not necessarily give way in an evolutionary scheme to scientific thought.

With regard to the myth-ritual model, demonstrating that all myths originated as rituals has proved exceptionally difficult. The favored example of the myth-ritualists, the alleged origin of the Babylonian *Enuma Eliš* myth in the setting of the Akitu festival, now turns out to be an example which may rather be that of an earlier myth only later adapted to a ritual setting (Smith 1982: 92). Hence, if some myths originated as rituals, other rituals appear to have begun as myths. Additionally, positing a ritual origin for all cosmogonic myths offered no real explanation of these myths; it only postponed the question of explanation, offering instead a genetic description. That is, even if research should document the general priority of ritual over myth, one would still be left wanting a sustainable account of the meaning and function of ritual.

2. Recent Formulations of the Place of Cosmology in Religion. Given the apparent inadequacy of older hypotheses, many 20th-century scholars have sought alternative explanations for the demonstrable concern on behalf of so many religious traditions to answer cosmological questions. In fairness, it must be said that many or all of these latter explanations have also been found wanting, so that a major agendum for future research remains inquiry into the deepest role played by cosmological materials.

The explanatory model which has continued to play the largest role for contemporary students of cosmology is the so-called "charter" position, in its various formulations. This position, that cosmologies provide a charter for all behavior and for the meaning of all actions to religious communities, is one that received major impetus in the work of Emile Durkheim. According to Durkheim, all of the classification systems to be encountered in religious traditions, including preeminently religious cosmologies, "are modelled upon the social organization" and "have taken the forms of society for their framework" (1915: 169). All such classifications are hierarchical; and, since "hierarchy is exclusively a social affair," these classifications are taken "from society and projected . . . into our conceptions of the world" (1915: 173).

This essential perception that cosmologies owe their origins to human social formations was then greatly extended and worked out in detail by the anthropologist Bronislaw Malinowski. His field work demonstrated to him that "religious faith establishes, fixes, and enhances all valuable mental attitudes, such as reverence for tradition, harmony with environment, courage and confidence in the struggles with difficulties and at the prospect of death" (1954: 89). A cosmological myth "fulfills in primitive culture an indispensable function: it expresses, enhances, and codifies belief; it safeguards and enforces morality; it vouches for the efficiency of ritual and contains practical rules for the guidance of man"; such a myth is thus no "idle tale," nor "an intellectual explanation or an artistic imagery," but rather "a pragmatic charter of primitive faith and wisdom" (1954: 101).

Many subsequent students of religious cosmogony have found further support for the position first defended by Durkheim and Malinowski. C. Long, for example, has very recently argued again that "the cosmogonic myth provides a model that is recapitulated in the creation and founding of all other human modes of existence"; this myth provides "a charter for conduct for other aspects of culture" (*EncRel* 4: 94). So too Bolle's summary of cosmological thought concludes that "views of the cosmos are in harmony with the social order in a tribe or tradition, and as a rule reflect the prevailing mode of production" (*EncRel* 4: 102). Nor is it simply that a cosmology reflects in some fashion the social formation. As charters, cosmologies also carry with them ethical implications: "the behavior required of man is often described and always implied in the account of the world's structure" (*EncRel* 4: 104).

The historian of religion who has devoted the greatest attention to cosmological thought is surely Mircea Eliade. Eliade's position is in many regards a combination of several noted above. Cosmological thought for him often has a ritual origin, satisfies an intellectual need to provide explanations of puzzling phenomena, and is also a comprehensive charter for ethical conduct. Eliade begins by affirming the absolutely central role of cosmogonic lore in traditional societies. Indeed, he repeatedly proposes the presence of cosmogonic lore as the defining characteristic of traditional as opposed to modern, historically based societies: "Whether he abolishes it periodically, whether he devaluates it by perpetually finding transhistorical models and archetypes for it, whether, finally, he gives it a metahistorical meaning (cyclical history, eschatological significations, and so on), the man of the traditional civilizations accorded the historical event no value in itself" (1959: 141). In the alleged absence of a developed historical consciousness, traditional humans, argues Eliade, turn always to accounts of what occurred in the earliest days of the cosmos. Only things that happened "in the beginning, 'in those days,' *in illo tempore, ab origine,*" have full significance for traditional societies (1959: 4).

If this schematic presentation of two worlds of thought offers for Eliade a rationale for the setting of cosmologies in remotest antiquity, their function is then accounted for by utilizing a version of the charter position. Hence, cosmogonic myths "preserve and transmit the paradigms, the exemplary models, for all the responsible activities in which men engage" (Eliade 1959: viii). But, as noted previously, Eliade goes on to combine cosmogonic myths' charter function with the view that these myths also satisfy intellectual needs: "primordial, sacred history . . . is fundamental because it explains, and by the same token justifies, the existence of the world, of man and society. . . . It relates how things came into being, providing the exemplary model and also the justifications of man's activities" (1984: 141).

The many writings of Eliade possess the clear virtue of offering a comprehensive account for the role of cosmological thought, an account evidenced by material drawn from the widest array of religious traditions. Still, the very comprehensiveness of his position means it remains open to some of the same criticisms offered against its component parts. For this reason, others have attempted a fresh approach to the questions of the meaning and function of cosmogony. At once the most novel and the most controversial of these attempts is that provided by the French anthropologist and philosopher Claude Lévi-Strauss. See MYTH AND MYTHOLOGY. Lévi-Strauss begins by stressing the primacy of language. He thus looks to modern linguistics, rather than to sociology or biology, as providing the disciplinary paradigm upon which study of cosmogonic myths should be founded. The unique phenomenon of language means that human beings are caught in a kind of cosmic contradiction: they are at once animals, hence a part of nature, and yet also distinct from the rest of nature since through language they create the mental world in which they live. This contradiction is then found to be mirrored in any number of cultural creations, including kinship structures and religious myths.

Given Lévi-Strauss' prioritizing of linguistics, his analyses of myths always concentrate upon structures of relationship, rather than upon individual items in any mythological repertoire. As meaning in language is always relational rather than essential, so too meaning in myths must be sought structurally. Perhaps the best, brief example of how Lévi-Strauss' structural method works when applied to cosmological myths is his analysis of the British Columbian myth of Asdiwal (1976: 146–97). Although he analyzes this myth in terms of four distinct levels (the geographical, the technoeconomic, the sociological, and the overtly cosmological), he discovers that each level in fact is a redundant expression of the same message. This message is the attempt "to justify the shortcomings of reality" (1976: 173). Similarly, Lévi-Strauss' well known and early analysis of the Oedipus myth concludes that, "although experience contradicts theory, social life validates cosmology by its similarity of structure. Hence cosmology is true" (1963: 216). That is to say, the human situation as one caught in the web of various contradictions has given rise to the repeated articulation of cosmogonic myths whose structures makes these contradictions, not disappear, but in a sense become mentally tolerable.

Though the search for an adequate explanation for the function of cosmologies is hardly completed, many scholars have adopted a version of Lévi-Strauss' analytical model. For example, Jonathan Z. Smith has recently argued that "those myths and rituals which belong to a locative map of the cosmos labor to overcome all incongruity by assuming the interconnectedness of all things, the adequacy of symbolization (usually expressed as a belief in the correspondence between macro- and microcosm) and the power and possibility of repetition" (Smith 1978: 308–9). Finally, Geertz too sees the problematic issues of human religious life, such as the classic theodicy dilemma, giving rise to "the uncomfortable suspicion that perhaps the world, and hence man's life in the world, has no genuine order at all—no empirical regularity, no emotional form, no moral coherence. And the religious response to this suspicion is in each case the same: the formulation, by means of symbols, of an image of such a genuine order of the world which will account for, and even celebrate, the perceived ambiquities, puzzles, and paradoxes in human experience. The effort is not to deny the undeniable—that there are unexplained events, that life hurts, or that rain falls upon the just—but to deny that there are inexplicable events" (Geertz 1973: 108).

Bibliography

Attridge, H., and Oden, R. 1981. *Philo of Byblos: The Phoenician History.* CBQMS 9. Washington.

Bultmann, R. 1951. *Theology of the New Testament.* Vol. 1. New York.

Coats, G. 1983. *Genesis.* FOTL 1. Grand Rapids.

Collins, A. Y. 1976. *The Combat Myth in the Book of Revelation.* Missoula.

Dahood, M. 1968. Proverbs 8,22–31. Translation and Commentary. *CBQ* 30: 512–21.

Durkheim, E. 1915. *The Elementary Forms of the Religious Life.* New York. Repr. 1965.

Eliade, M. 1959. *Cosmos and History: The Myth of the Eternal Return.* New York.

———. 1963. *Myth and Reality.* New York.

———. 1984. Cosmogonic Myth and "Sacred History." Pp. 137–51 in *Sacred Narrative.* ed. A. Dundes. Berkeley.

Geertz, C. 1973. *The Interpretation of Cultures.* New York.

Gunkel, H. 1895. *Schöpfung und Chaos in Urzeit und Endzeit: Eine religionsgeschichtliche Untersuchung über Gen. 1 und Ap. Joh. 12.* Göttingen.

Hanson, P. 1975. *The Dawn of Apocalyptic.* Philadelphia.

Herdner, A. 1963. *Corpus des tablettes en cunéiformes alphabétiques, découvertes à Ras Shamra-Ugarit de 1929 à 1939.* Mission de Ras Shamra, vol. 10. Paris.

Knight, D. 1985. Cosmogony and Order in the Hebrew Tradition. Pp. 133–57 in *Cosmogony and Ethical Order,* ed. R. Lovin and F. Reynolds. Chicago.

Lévi-Strauss, C. 1963. *Structural Anthropology.* New York.

———. 1976. The Story of Asdiwal. Vol. 2, pp. 146–97 in *Structural Anthropology.* New York.

Malinowski, B. 1954. *Magic, Science and Religion, and Other Essays.* Garden City, NY.

McKenzie, J. 1976. *A Theology of the Old Testament.* Garden City, NY.

Oden, R. 1981. Divine Aspirations in Atrahasis and in Genesis 1–11. *ZAW* 93: 197–216.

———. 1987. *The Bible without Theology.* San Francisco.

Smith, J. Z. 1978. *Map Is Not Territory: Studies in the History of Religions.* SJLA 23. Leiden.

———. 1982. *Imagining Religion: From Babylon to Jonestown.* Chicago Studies in the History of Judaism. Chicago.

Stadelmann, L. 1970. *The Hebrew Conception of the World.* AnBib 39. Rome.

Trible, P. 1978. *God and the Rhetoric of Sexuality.* OBT. Philadelphia.

ROBERT A. ODEN, JR.

COTTON. See FLORA; DRESS AND ORNAMENTATION.

COUNCIL. See SANHEDRIN.

COUNCIL OF JAMNIA. See JAMNIA (JABNEH), COUNCIL OF.

COUNCIL OF JERUSALEM. See JERUSALEM, COUNCIL OF.

COUNCIL, HEAVENLY. See DIVINE ASSEMBLY; HOSTS, LORD OF.

COUNSELLORS. See the article on "Postexilic Judean Officials" in PALESTINE, ADMINISTRATION OF.

COUNTING. See NUMBERS AND COUNTING.

COURIER. See TRAVEL AND COMMUNICATION (ANE).

COURT NARRATIVE (2 SAMUEL 9–1 KINGS 2). Traditions about the Davidic court culminating in the accession of Solomon in 2 Samuel 9–20 and 1 Kings 1–2 have been widely regarded as a single narrative unit usually designated the "Court History" or the "Succession Narrative." Within the larger narrative are several more or less distinct smaller narrative units: the story of David and Bathsheba (2 Samuel 10–12); Absalom's revolt, including the account of the rape of Tamar (2 Samuel 13–19); and the accession of Solomon (1 Kings 1–2). 2 Samuel 9 is loosely connected to the larger narrative by David's relations to the house of Saul, and the Sheba rebellion (2 Samuel 20) is part of the aftermath of the Absalom revolt.

A. Content and Structure
   1. David and the House of Saul
   2. The Ammonite War
   3. David and Bathsheba
   4. The Rape of Tamar and Absalom's Revolt
   5. The Accession of Solomon
B. History of Scholarship
   1. Sources, Extent, and Genre of the Court Narrative
   2. L. Rost and the Succession Theme
   3. The Traditio-Historical Approach
   4. History or a Well-Told Story?
   5. Date of Composition
   6. Synthesis

A. Content and Structure

1. David and the House of Saul. The narrative begins with David's expression of concern for the house of Saul (2 Samuel 9). He restored Saul's estate to Mephibosheth, the son of Jonathan, and granted him a permanent right to eat at the king's table. It ends with the accession of Solomon to the throne and the execution of Joab, Shimei, and Adonijah, and a concluding editorial comment in 1 Kgs 2:46: "And the kingdom was established in the hand of Solomon." The account of David's kindness to Mephibosheth is linked to the rebellion of Absalom by Ziba's accusation against Mephibosheth, his master, who, he charges, is expecting the return of his father's kingdom (2 Sam 16:1–4). A further narrative link appears in Mephibosheth's own welcome to David after the death of Absalom (2 Sam 19:24–30).

2. The Ammonite War. A distinct narrative unit appears in the account of the Ammonite war (2 Sam 10:1–11:1; 12:26–31). At the accession of Hanun to the Ammonite throne, David sent condolences to him over the death of his father, Nahash. Hanun rejected David's emissaries, accused them of being spies, and humiliated them by shaving their beards and cutting their garments in half up to their buttocks. David responded by sending Joab into battle against the Ammonites and their allies, the Arameans. This account, which may derive from royal annals contemporary with the events, provides the setting for David's adultery with Bathsheba. Some scholars have noted points of contact with the account of David's exile at Mahanaim in 2 Sam 17:24–29 (Flanagan 1972: 176; McCarter, *2 Samuel* AB, 275–76), which would place the siege of Rabbah, the Ammonite capital, after Absalom's rebellion.

3. David and Bathsheba. The account of David's adultery with Bathsheba (the Chronicler refers to her as Bathshua: 1 Chr 3:5) and its direct consequences is set within the framework of the account of the Ammonite war (2 Sam 11:2–12:25). It is linked to this context by the notice in 2 Sam 11:1: Joab, his servants, and all Israel were sent to battle against Ammon while David remained in Jerusalem. Some have detected a negative connotation in the observation that David remained in Jerusalem. From his roof, David observes Bathsheba, the wife of Uriah the Hittite, cleansing herself from menstrual impurity. He has her brought to his palace, lies with her, and she becomes pregnant. David's sin with Bathsheba is in clear violation of the prohibition of adultery in Deut 22:22 and, according to that law, both should have died.

David's behavior is set in stark contrast to the loyalty of Uriah, her husband, who declined David's deceptive invitation to him to go down to his house and lie with his wife. His refusal was apparently grounded in the rules of holy war which precluded sexual activity in times of battle. The sin of adultery is compounded by murder when David sends Uriah back to the battlefront carrying instructions to Joab which will result in his own death. After Uriah's death Joab sends a messenger to David with a general report on the battle, instructing the messenger to mention Uriah's death should David became angry over the high number of casualties. This report to David concerning Uriah's death contains a narrative link to the account of the death of Abimelech reported in Judg 9:50–57. After Bathsheba's appropriate period of mourning for her husband had passed, David took her to his house and she became his wife, bearing him a son.

In one of the few explicit references to Yahweh's activity in this history, Yahweh sent the prophet Nathan to rebuke David for his adultery and murder. Nathan's condemnation of David took the form of a juridical parable *(māšāl)* eliciting self-judgment, a parable about a rich man who spared his own flock and slaughtered the pet lamb of the poor man to feed a traveler. Whereupon David became enraged and declared that the man doing this deserved to die and must repay fourfold, the restitution specified in Exod 21:37—Eng 22:1. However, many scholars since Wellhausen have preferred the LXX reading "sevenfold" as more in keeping with David's intense anger or with the Deuteronomic use of the number seven (Carlson 1964: 154). Nathan's parable elaborated the relationship between the poor man and his one little ewe lamb. The lamb ate from its owner's food, drank from his cup, and lay in his bosom *(ûbĕḥêqô tiškāb)*. Nathan's rebuke to David contains a reminder of Yahweh's graciousness to David. In addition to rescuing David from the hand of Saul, Yahweh had also given David Saul's wives "to lie in his bosom." This expression occurs again at the end of the Court Narrative in the account of David and Abishag (1 Kgs 1:1–4) which prefaces the account of Solomon's accession, thereby providing a subtle narrative link between the two episodes.

Nathan's parable may not be original to the narrative. Gunkel (1921: 35–36) stressed the lack of fit between the circumstances of the parable and David's actions. On the basis of the namelessness of the characters, the contrast between the rich man and the poor man and the exaggeration of the relationship between the poor man's family and the pet lamb, he characterized the account as a fairy tale *(Märchenstoff)* which is not original to the narrative of David and Bathsheba. Other scholars (Simon 1967; McCarter, *2 Samuel* AB, 299) have, however, stressed the compatibility of the parable and David's actions, identifying the crimes of both David and the rich man as abuses of power.

In an oracle of judgment condemning David for the murder of Uriah and taking his wife for his own, Nathan announces that, because David had slain Uriah with the sword of the Ammonites, the sword will never depart from his house. One of David's own house will arise against him and will lie with his wives in the sight of the sun. In contrast to the secrecy of David's action, this humiliation will be public. Although Yahweh has spared David's life, the son who will be born to David and Bathsheba will die. Some scholars regard this account of Nathan's judgment of David (12:7b–12) as a secondary addition to the larger narrative.

When the child born to Bathsheba became ill, David sought God on behalf of the child, refusing food and lying on the ground, behavior typical of mourning. In a striking reversal of custom, David upon receiving word of the death of the child immediately rose, bathed, anointed himself, and asked for food. At this juncture the narrator records the birth of Solomon, who will ultimately succeed David on the throne, observing that the Lord loved him. Some scholars have suggested that the story of the death of the child is a fiction inserted here to establish the legitimacy of the birth of Solomon (Veijola 1979: 230–50; Würthwein 1974: 32).

This section of the history is rounded off by the report of the conclusion of the Ammonite war. Joab reports success in his siege of Rabbah of the Ammonites and summons David to participate in the conquest so that he will receive the credit for the success of the siege. David's return to Jerusalem concludes a narrative unit which began with David sending his servants to the Ammonite king. There is a concentric and climactic arrangement of 2 Samuel 10–12. The narrative begins with a departure from Jerusalem, the goal of which is Rabbah-Ammon's welfare, and ends with a return to Jerusalem after the destruction of Rabbah-Ammon. Ammon's arrogance stands at the beginning, its fall at the end (Roth 1977). The report of the Ammonite war has thus been skillfully utilized as a framework for the Bathsheba episode.

4. The Rape of Tamar and Absalom's Revolt. Just as the expression "afterward" *(wayhî ʾaḥărê kēn)* marked the beginning of the narrative unit in chaps. 10–12, the same expression in 13:1 marks the beginning of a new literary unity focusing on Absalom (2 Sam 13:1–20:26). This unit begins with a largely self-contained episode, Amnon's rape of Tamar. Absalom's brother Amnon is lovesick with desire for his beautiful half-sister Tamar. He is advised to feign illness and to ask David to send Tamar to prepare food for him in his chamber so that he might eat from her hand. His request is granted. Tamar is sent to him to prepare food for him and Amnon, seizing the opportunity, rapes her. Having assaulted her, he brutally expels her from his presence. The violence of rape is thus compounded by the violence of expulsion. The language of expulsion reduces Tamar to a disposable object since the Hebrew, contrary to many translations, has only the demonstrative pronoun *this* (cf. Trible 1984: 48).

Absalom bides his time for two years after which he invites the king's sons to a sheep shearing at which he arranges the assassination of Amnon. Scholars have devoted considerable attention to this narrative, stressing, in particular, the skill with which the story is told. The kinship element is stressed by the repeated use of the terms *ʾāḥ,* "brother," and *ʾāḥôt,* "sister" (Rideout 1974: 76).

The episode develops in part on the basis of Amnon's deceptions. He first deceives David, then Tamar about his intentions with the ruse of his illness. The denouement also involves deception, Absalom's deceptive invitation to the sheep shearing. The story pivots on the dramatic reversal of Amnon's feelings in v 15: "Then Amnon hated her very greatly; Indeed, the hatred which he had for her was greater than his former love for her." There are striking similarities between the story of this Tamar and Tamar, the daughter-in-law of Judah (Gen 38:1–30). In both narratives there is a foreign woman named Bathshua (the name given Bathsheba in 1 Chr 3:5) and a woman named Tamar who remains unmarried. Both women are eventually vindicated at a sheep-shearing festival and both lose their first child (Blenkinsopp 1966). To this list might also be added the element of deception present in both narratives. On the one hand, Tamar and David are both deceived as to Amnon's intentions and, on the other hand, Judah's daughter-in-law Tamar deceives Judah by disguising herself as a prostitute in order to bear his child.

The rape of Tamar and the consequent elimination of one of the possible successors to the throne (Amnon) sets the stage for the extended narrative of Absalom's revolt beginning in chap. 14. Having murdered his brother, Absalom flees to Geshur to live in exile with Talmai, his maternal grandfather. At the end of three years Joab, in an elaborate ruse, arranges for the return of Absalom to Jerusalem. He enlists the services of a wise woman from

Tekoa who is to pretend that she had two sons, one of whom was slain in a quarrel with the other, and she informs David that the relatives now seek to kill the remaining son as an act of blood vengeance. She will thus be bereaved of all possibility of posterity. David's response to this "self-judgment eliciting story" is to extend protection to the surviving son, thereby trapping himself into the necessity of allowing Absalom to return from exile, although he continues to be banned from the presence of David.

At the end of two more years Absalom enlists Joab's help in lifting that ban, and Absalom is summoned to the king and, in a customary gesture of obeisance, he bows on his face to the ground in what will prove to be a false expression of allegiance. Absalom then acquires a chariot and horses and fifty men running before him. Stationing himself at the gate, he greets those coming to have their cases adjudicated before the king, assuring the petitioners that were he king they would receive satisfaction. Having thus stolen the hearts of the men of Israel, Absalom is ready for action. At the end of four years Absalom comes before the king, asking permission to go to Hebron (where David had himself first become king over Judah) to fulfill a vow he had made while in Geshur. David sends him in peace unaware, apparently, that this is merely a ruse. His supporters are rallied by messengers who instruct the people to proclaim at the sound of the trumpet, "Absalom is king at Hebron."

The rapid growth of Absalom's conspiracy leads to David's withdrawal from Jerusalem. Taking his loyal servants and the Cherethites, Pelethites, and Gittites, he leaves ten concubines behind to administer the house. The narrative then describes a series of events some of which figure in David's eventual success in thwarting Absalom's coup. And all of them portray a generous, humbled, loyal, and noble figure in contrast to the royal arrogance portrayed in the Bathsheba episode. In a touching episode, Ittai the Gittite asks to join with David's beleaguered force, but David encourages him to return home with Yahweh's blessing. Ittai, however, insists and David accepts his aid. Abiathar, Zadok, and the Levites come bearing the ark, setting it down until all the people with David have passed over the Kidron. David then instructs that the ark be returned to Jerusalem, expressing the hope that he may again find favor with Yahweh and eventually be permitted to see the ark in its proper setting. Zadok and Abiathar, the priests, and their two sons, Ahimaaz and Jonathan, are sent back to Jerusalem with the ark to serve as informants to David and his men. In this context, David and his loyal band of followers are portrayed ascending the Mount of Olives weeping and with their heads covered. David is himself barefoot. At the summit he is met by Hushai the Archite, who comes in mourning with his coat torn and dirt on his head. David, rather than accepting Hushai's offer of support, sends him back to Jerusalem "to defeat the counsel of Ahithophel," Absalom's adviser. The introduction of Hushai in the narrative anticipates the eventual reversal of Absalom's success. At this point, Ziba, Mephibosheth's servant, comes with supplies for David and his men, slandering his master by asserting that Mephibosheth has remained in Jerusalem, anticipating the return of the kingdom to the house of Saul. At Bahurim, David and his men are cursed by Shimei, whose life David orders spared.

A pivotal point in the narrative is reached here. David has arrived at the Jordan and Absalom and all the people with him, including Ahithophel, come to Jerusalem. Absalom is on the verge of success in his effort to become king, while David and his loyal band of followers are on the verge of defeat and death. Ahithophel responds to Absalom's request for council by advising him to go in conspicuously to David's concubines, who have been left behind in Jerusalem. This action, to which may be compared Adonijah's request for Abishag (1 Kgs 2:17–25) and Abner's relations with Rizpah, one of Saul's concubines (2 Sam 3:3–11), is usually regarded as a public symbol of the takeover of the royal prerogatives (cf. Tsevat 1958: 241). This action also explicitly fulfills the judgment Nathan uttered against David.

To this advice, Ahithophel, whose counsel is regarded as equivalent to an oracle of God, adds strategic advice. He describes David's desperate situation, of which the reader has already been informed, and he counsels a swift military action of small scale to take David unaware, killing only him and thus avoiding the further alienation which would result from massive bloodshed. The advice is precisely appropriate to the circumstances. However, Absalom also asks Hushai for advice, and he provides him with a strategy which will gain time for David to consolidate his forces. He proposes mustering the troops from Dan to Beersheba, which Absalom will then lead in person to destroy David and his entire force. Absalom's acceptance of this deceptive advice signals the beginning of the end of his rebellion. The rejection of Ahithophel's counsel is attributed to Yahweh, who wanted to bring evil on Absalom (2 Sam 17:14).

David, warned by Jonathan and Ahimaaz, crosses the Jordan to Mahanaim where he is received by a number of local leaders and given provisions for his army. As David and his men prepare for the coming battle, the king says to the men, "I myself will also go out with you." His men, however, refuse this offer, indicating that he is worth ten thousand of them and will better serve the cause by remaining behind to send help from the city if needed. There is irony here in that the entire narrative begins in circumstances in which David does *not* go forth to war against the Ammonites and must ultimately be summoned for the final surrender. In this instance he wants to lead but is refused. In the ensuing conflict, Absalom's forces are routed and Absalom himself is killed, having been caught in an oak while the mule on which he was riding continued on its way. Despite David's order to Joab that the young man Absalom be spared, Joab thrusts three darts into Absalom's heart and his armor bearers strike him and kill him. Although the text does not mention his hair, there is a long tradition of interpretation which links this account to the description of Absalom's beauty and hair (cf. McCarter *2 Samuel* AB, 406). If the narrator indeed intended the reader to make that connection, there is tragic irony in the account. The overriding irony and reversal in the narrative, however, is in the deception of Absalom by Hushai's false counsel. Seen from the perspective of folklore, the entire narrative of Absalom's revolt may be characterized as a story of the deceiver being deceived.

David's reaction to the death of Absalom and the rout of his army evokes another surprise. David does not rejoice in his victory but deeply and publicly grieves for his slain son. This public and excessive grief turns the victory into mourning, the people stealing away as though disgraced (2 Sam 19:1–2). When Joab rebukes David for grieving for his slain enemy, David finally arises and takes his seat in the gate and the people come before him. David's response to the death of Absalom, seen from a personal and family perspective, is appropriate. However, it is behavior, as Joab reminds him, which is not allowable for a king. The narrator, by emphasizing David's grief over his son who is also his enemy, by contrasting David's behavior with that of Uriah, and by noting the ease with which he was dissuaded from going into battle with Absalom (18:4), portrays David as a thoroughly incompetent person in his role as war leader of the kingdom (cf. Ishida 1982: 184).

The strife within David's family is mirrored in the resulting strife over the issue of returning David to the throne (2 Sam 19:1–15). Having won the acceptance of Israel and Judah, David prepares to cross the Jordan and return to Jerusalem. Shimsi and Ziba rush down to meet the king and to assist him across the Jordan. Ahishai, the son of Zeruiah, wants to kill Shimei because he has cursed David, but David orders his life spared. Mephibosheth himself arrives on the scene and expresss loyalty to David, claiming that Ziba has slandered him to the king. Although it appears that Ziba did indeed slander Mephibosheth, David's response is equivocal. Having previously given the estate of Saul to Ziba, David now orders that it be divided between the two of them. Another of the individuals who gave David succor at Mahanaim, Berzillai, comes down to escort David across the Jordan. He refuses David's invitation to come to Jerusalem and to allow David to provide for him. His refusal is based on the infirmities that go with age, and he asks David to take with him in his stead Chimham, who is presumed to be his son. This series of meetings parallels the series of meetings linked to David's flight from Jerusalem (2 Sam 15:13–16:14). The chapter ends with another reference to the strife between Judah and Israel. Thus, within the narrative even the account of David's return to power is surrounded by strife, an implicit reminder of Nathan's prophetic announcement that the sword would never depart from David's house. This strife culminates in a revolt of Israel led by Sheba, the son of Bichri, a Benjaminite. After David returns to Jerusalem he sequesters the ten concubines he had left behind and they live shut up as in widowhood, their plight echoing that of Tamar. The final episode in the revolt of Absalom is the pursuit and elimination of Sheba (2 Sam 20:4–22). The narrative concludes with a list of David's officials which seems to be a variant of the summary list in 8:16–18. (Chaps. 21–24 of 2 Samuel are usually regarded as appendices interrupting the main narrative.)

5. The Accession of Solomon. The resumption of the Court Narrative in 1 Kings 1 presupposes an intervening period. David has become old and cannot get warm even though covered with clothes. The servants offer a solution: a young maiden should be found for the king who will wait upon him and who will lie in his bosom. They search for a beautiful maiden and find Abishag the Shunamite. They bring her to the king and she serves him as a nurse. The narrator, however, informs us that David did not have sexual relations with her (1:4). These details are striking and can best be understood in light of the earlier scene in which David takes Bathsheba. These two scenes form an *inclusio* and they derive their dramatic power in part from their irony. In the opening scene David takes Bathsheba, an illegitimate act from which flows a steady stream of tragic consequences; ironically, in the closing episode, he is incapable of sexual relations with the beautiful virgin Abishag. This kind of ironic reversal seems to be a favorite literary device of the narrator.

The narrative immediately shifts to the account of Adonijah's abortive effort to succeed Solomon. Like Absalom, he prepares for himself chariots and horsemen and fifty men to run before him. The text also notes that, like Absalom, he was a very handsome man and that he was born next after Absalom (1 Kgs 1:6). Adonijah enlists the aid of Joab and Abiathar and invites all his brothers and all the Judean officials to a sacrificial feast at the Serpent's Stone beside En Rogel—with some notable exceptions (1:10). Nathan alerts Bathsheba to Adonijah's actions, advising her to go in to David and to remind him of his promise to her that Solomon will rule after him; while she is speaking, he will come in and confirm her words. There clearly has been no public indication that Solomon is to succeed David. On the contrary, every indication was that Adonijah would be king (1 Kgs 2:15). In terms of the principle of primogeniture, Amnon, Absalom, and Adonijah each would have had a more secure claim to the throne than did Solomon. The strategy of Nathan and Bathsheba works, however, and David orders that Solomon be mounted on the royal she-mule and go down to Gihon where Zadok and Nathan will anoint him king over Israel (1:32–40). This is the third reference to mules in the Court Narrative. The first reference is in the context of the assassination of Amnon. The narrator informs the reader that the other royal sons escaped on their mules (2 Sam 13:29). Again, Absalom met his death when his mule rode out from under him, leaving him hanging helpless before Joab (2 Sam 18:9). These references provide a subtle ironic link between the failed rebellion of Absalom and the accession of Solomon.

When word of Solomon's accession reaches Adonijah, he seizes the horns of the altar and elicits a promise from Solomon that he will be permitted to live if he proves to be an honorable man (1:50–53). Solomon's opportunity to execute his potential rival comes when Adonijah requests (through Bathsheba) that Abishag be given to him. On instructions from David, Joab is executed for his murder of Abner and Amasa; Abiathar is spared because of his role in bearing the ark of the Lord before David, but he is exiled to Anathoth. Shimei violates the order to remain in Jerusalem and he, too, is executed in accordance with the instruction of David. On this note the narrative concludes with the affirmation that the kingdom is securely established in the hand of Solomon. It is in these first two chapters of 1 Kings that the succession motif is most obviously present. Those who see in the Court History a succession document regard the accounts of the murders of Joab and Shimei as efforts to absolve Solomon from full responsibility by shifting some of that responsibility to David. Likewise, Adonijah's request for Abishag is construed as an act of lese majesty necessitating his death.

B. History of Scholarship

1. Sources, Extent, and Genre of the Court Narrative. The traditions which we have called the Court Narrative have by and large been seen as either a distinct narrative unit or a sequence of somewhat independent narrative units. However, some scholars have attempted to trace the sources of the Pentateuch into the books of Samuel. Among these are Karl Budde (*Samuel* KHC) and Otto Eissfeldt, who regarded the court stories of David as a continuation of the J source as well as a masterpiece of Israelite historical writing (1931; 1965: 276–77). Steuernagel was able to trace two sources through 2 Samuel 8, but identified the traditions in 2 Samuel 9–20 (and possibly chap. 24) as a distinct and well-constructed history emanating from Jerusalem, a history which he could describe as one of the most magnificent pieces of Israelite literature (1912: 334–35).

Other scholars saw in the Samuel books a loose compilation of individual narratives. Gressmann, for example, distinguished a series of *Novellen;* the conflict with Ishbaal (2 Samuel 2–5), the story of Amnon and Absalom (2 Sam 13:1–14:33), and the rebellions of Absalom and Sheba (2 Sam 15:1–20:22). At least in the case of the account of Absalom's rebellion. Gressmann defines the narrative as a *Novelle* in the specific sense of a historical account which is deepened by narrative art as opposed to a merely fictional account. This is expressed in part by the psychological depth given to the characters (Gressmann 1921: xiv, 181). Caspari had also singled out the story of Absalom's rebellion in 2 Samuel 15–20 as an independent narrative. This narrative is indeed history, incorporating the transition of the national literature from *Novelle* to history writing (1909: 317–48). Gunkel cited the narrative of Absalom's rebellion (chaps. 13–20) as a parade example of historical writing, *Geschichtserzählung* (1925: 75 [23]), describing it as "the finest gem (*"das köstlichste Kleinod"*) of historical writing in Israel" (1964: 10; *Genesis* HKAT, xii). These scholars, although defining the limits of the narrative units somewhat differently, were in substantial agreement that these traditions collectively and individually be regarded as fine examples of reliable historical writing.

2. L. Rost and the Succession Theme. Modern scholarly discussion of the traditions in the book of 2 Samuel has been shaped primarily by Leonhard Rost's epochal study, *Die Überlieferung von der Thronnachfolge Davids,* which appeared in 1926. Rost isolated the materials of 2 Samuel 6:16 and 20ff.; 7:11b and 16; 9:1–10:5 (10:6–11:1); 11:2–12:7a; 12:13–25 (26–31); 13:1–14:24; 14:28–18:17; 18:19–20:22; 1 Kgs 1:1–2:1; 2:5–10; 2:12–27a; and 2:28–46 as a single literary unit dominated by the thematic problem of the succession to the throne of David (hence the designation "Succession Narrative"). Rost's study has been the touchstone for most subsequent investigation of these traditions and the basis for treating them as a discrete literary unit within the Deuteronomistic History (DH).

Rost's analysis was concerned with both the content and the style of the narrative. It is, however, clear that for Rost content was the decisive criterion for setting these materials apart as a discrete narrative unit. The author made use of the end of the originally independent Ark Narrative with its observation that Michal remained childless until her death (2 Sam 6:23) to introduce the question of who was to succeed David on the throne. The originally independent report on David's war with the Ammonites and the Arameans was used as a framework for the account of David's affair with Bathsheba. The question of David's successor is finally answered with the affirmation of Solomon's sovereignty in 1 Kgs 2:46. In addition to the concern to define the scope and limits of the Succession Narrative, Rost offered a date, provenience, and *Tendenz* for the composition. The author was a member of the royal court writing probably in the early days of the Solomonic era in order to glorify Solomon, "*in majorem gloriam Salomonis.*"

Echoing earlier assessments of the material in 2 Samuel 13–20, Rost characterized the succession narrative as "The finest work of Hebrew narrative art . . ." (1982: 115). Like his predecessors and contemporaries, he accorded "historical trustworthiness" as well as narrative artistry to the Succession Narrative. To be sure, he recognized that the problem of historicity was accentuated by the literary artistry of the narrator, which could be readily interpreted as evidence for regarding it as a fictional account.

Although Rost's analysis was criticized by Eissfeldt and others, his main thesis became the accepted view of the traditions centering on the court of David in 2 Samuel and 1 Kings 1–2, and gave widespread currency to the designation "Succession Narrative" for this body of tradition. This is due in large part to the acceptance of Rost's positions with minor modifications by Albrecht Alt, Martin Noth, and Gerhard von Rad. Alt and von Rad, in particular, emphasized the historicity of the narrative. Von Rad described the narrative as the "oldest specimen of ancient Israelite historical writing," stressing as well its theological contribution, the conception of Yahweh's activity as "concealed in the whole breadth of secular affairs, and pervading every single sphere of human life" (*PHOE,* 176, 204).

It is only within the last two or three decades that extensive criticism and reconsideration of Rost's position have emerged. These criticisms are focused in a variety of ways. Much of the discussion has addressed the question of the *Tendenz* of the narrative. Is the theme of the material really the question of who would rule after David, and is it really a pro-Solomon propaganda piece? This question was raised sharply and effectively by Delekat (1967). He emphasized the negative reports about both David and Solomon. If the theme of the narrative was the succession to the throne of David, Delekat argued, it must be unfavorable to Solomon. If it was correct that Bathsheba was an adulteress, that Adonijah was generally and with David's approbation regarded as the crown prince, and that there was no divine oracle granting the throne to Solomon, the narrative is implicitly critical of Solomon and the process by which he came to the throne. Clearly then, the concern of the narrative is more generally the reign of David until the consolidation of the kingship in the hand of Solomon. The affirmation that the kingdom was secure in Solomon's hands (1 Kgs 2:46) begs the question, How did this come about? The narrator's view is hostile to the arbitrary exercise of royal power evident in both David and Solomon and he is generally an opponent of kingship. His intentions were to shake Israel's loyalty to Solomon, a loyalty which existed despite Solomon's exactions from the people (Delekat 1967).

Delekat's forceful critique of Rost's thesis was not immediately taken up in subsequent analyses of these traditions. Nearly a decade later Würthwein (1974) pursued the issues raised by Delekat, emphasizing the anti-Solomonic tone of 1 Kings 1–2 and the anti-Davidic tone of 2 Samuel 10–12. The account of Bathsheba's entrance into the Davidic court in its original extent clearly shows a critical *Tendenz* against the Davidic kingdom. David is a king who boldly violates the old Israelite commandments against adultery and murder. The narrative portraying David in this light surely is to be regarded as a critique of the form of the monarchy which developed under David. Würthwein's arguments depended in part on the isolation of a number of texts which are to be regarded as later additions and which provide a more favorable portrait of David and those connected with him while placing Solomon's opponents in a less favorable light.

Two other recent analyses of these traditions also delineate an antimonarchical perspective which has subsequently been modified by later additions. Veijola (1975) found evidence of an antimonarchical stance which was subsequently heavily edited within Deuteronomic circles in order to legitimate the Davidic monarchy, while Langlamet (1976) identified a pro-Solomonic redaction in 1 Kings 1–2. On the other hand, McCarter, while acknowledging the tension within the narrative, attributes that tension to the nature of apologetic writing which maintains a tension between apparently unfavorable details and circumstances on the one hand and, on the other, the favorable interpretation of these details by the writer (*2 Samuel* AB, 15–16). Conroy (1978: 102) has noted the omission of any mention of Solomon in the account of Absalom's rebellion (2 Samuel 13–20) and concluded that these chapters deal only with the causes and outcome of Absalom's attempted coup d'état, not with the issue of succession.

3. The Traditio-Historical Approach. Carlson (1964) has applied the traditio-historical methodology of the Uppsala school to 2 Samuel. Following Noth, he sees the traditions of 2 Samuel as a part of the DH, an exilic reflection on the history of Israel. Carlson stressed the importance of the final stage of the process of tradition, its "redactional history" *(Redactionsgeschichte),* the final shape of which is the result of the work of the D-group. The D-group joined units together on the basis of the principle of association by means of catchwords (*Stichworte* or *verba associandi*) used with groups of motifs to link up with earlier traditions, but consistent with the ideological concepts of the prologue, Deuteronomy. The Deuteronomistic approach is to use varied materials to demonstrate that Israel's misfortunes stem from her faithlessness. The D-group used the figure of David as an ideal figure "to give an authoritative demonstration of their faith in a future made possible by turning again to Yahweh and by devotion to him" (Carlson 1964: 26).

Carlson viewed the Samuel traditions in terms of two motifs: David under the blessing *(bĕrākāh),* 2 Samuel 2–5, 6, 7; and David under the curse *(qĕlālāh),* 2 Samuel 9–24. For Carlson, chaps. 9–24 as a whole constitute "a Deuteronomic commentary on the latter half of the Davidic epoch" (1964: 139). He understands 1 Samuel 10–12 as a Deuteronomistic ingress to 2 Sam 13:1–21:14, which is structured in terms of two seven-year periods. The curse introduced by the Bathsheba episode runs in two *šibᶜātayim* phases which constitute the restitution called for in 12:6 (reading with many commentators the LXX's "sevenfold" versus the MT "fourfold"). In addition, 2 Samuel 10–20 as a whole reflects the Deuteronomic laws governing adultery and affinity: Deut 22:22 (2 Samuel 10–12); 22:28–29 (2 Samuel 13–14); and 23:1 (cf. 2 Sam 23:1).

4. History or a Well-Told Story? Rost had himself stressed the importance of the stylistic features of the Court Narrative, although to some recent interpreters Rost's analysis appears idiosyncratic and inadequate. Recent interpretation has to a considerable extent focused on matters of genre and literary artistry. An early example of this recent revival of interest in literary artistry is Jackson's article, which appeared in 1965. For Jackson, the author of the succession story was not simply trying to answer the question of how it came about that Solomon sits upon David's throne. Rather, the author used the techniques of oral narrative along with some of his own to provide a portrait of the varied relations of individuals who contend for temporal power in the secular realm. These techniques include the skillful contrasts of two figures as in the case of David and Joab, the alternation of tension and relaxation, the alternation between terse brevity and wealth of detail, and the heightening of suspense towards a climax and gradual slackening of intensity (1965: 183–95). More recently, Conroy (1978) has focused on the narrative of Absalom's revolt and its aftermarth (2 Samuel 13–20), which he views as a self-contained narrative unity. His detailed analysis of selected pericopes pays close attention to the structural building blocks of the narrative, such as the narrative patterns "command/execution," "desire/fulfillment," and "request and refusal." Conroy also gives careful attention to the movement from complication to resolution within the narrative, as well as to the narrator's point of view and characterization of persons and events. The most elaborate recent literary analysis is that of Fokkelman (1981), whose overarching study finds a series of dominant themes including the dualities of piety-sin, illusion-truth, and unity-duality. Sacon (1982) has applied the insights of the Japanese sentence psychologist, Kanji Hatano, to the Court Narrative. This approach stresses the analysis of paragraphs as the key to clarifying a particular literary work. Sacon, for example, finds a concentric structure in 15:18–19:41 centered around the account of David's reign in exile in 18:1–19:9, which is itself composed of a concentric structure. These studies do not preclude the assessment of the Court Narrative as essentially historical.

However, some of the recent attention to narrative style has to a significant extent called into question the long-standing assessment of the Court Narrative as a fine early example of historical writing. The utilization of motifs and themes characteristic of popular or folk literature, the numerous intimate conversations, the lack of attention to public events, and connections with the Wisdom tradition have led some scholars to conclude that the Court Narrative is not history in intention or in fact. Recognizing that the references to Solomon and his mother in 2 Samuel 11 and 1 Kings 1–2 constitute an *inclusio,* Blenkinsopp distinguished between two separate but connected themes: the legitimation of the Davidic claim to the throne, and the struggle for succession. The *Thronfolgegeschichte* consists of 2 Sam 11:2–27; 12:15b–25; 13–15; 15–20; and 1 Kings 1–2 and is structured by the theme that sin externalized in a sexual form leads to death (1966: 48–49). Blenkinsopp's primary interest, however, was in the affinities with the Yahwist tradition, and he identified several themes common to the David narratives and the Yahwist. These traditional themes included the motifs of the beauty and divine wisdom of the king, brother killing brother, the wise counselor whose advice leads to ruin, and, more prominently, the woman who brings death. Traditional elements in the Court Narrative are also stressed by Gunn. In addition to the themes noted by Blenkinsopp, Gunn notes several traditional motifs: David and the sons of Zeruiah, the judgment-eliciting parable, the woman and the spies, the two messengers, and the letter of death. The author's use of these traditional motifs suggests that the narrative should be seen not as political propaganda but as "first and foremost a fine piece of story-telling" (1978: 37). Whybray (1968) has noted the lack of attention to public events and, *inter alia,* the numerous intimate conversations in the narrative, and on that basis he has characterized the narrative as a work comparable to the modern psychological novel which, in its concerns and perspectives, is linked to the Wisdom tradition. While the author might make use of historical facts, the work itself is not history.

5. Date of Composition. Rost dated the Succession Narrative to the early period of Solomon's kingship. Those scholars who have found evidence of subsequent editing by the Deuteronomist or others may date the finished document later. However, there has been little direct discussion of the widely held assumption that the major part of the traditions contained within the Court Narrative or Succession Document are to be regarded as essentially contemporary with the events which are related. This is the case even though there is little evidence on the basis of which to date the narrative to the 10th century. There are, in fact, some indications of a later date, a number of which have been cited by Gunn. After the death of the child born of the adulterous union with Bathsheba, David goes into the "house" of Yahweh, which would indicate a date after the completion of the temple. There are a number of other references which also suggest temporal distance from the events described. The reference to the attire of the daughters of the king in 2 Sam 13:18 implies a time when this fashion was no longer widely known, and it cannot be easily dismissed as a gloss. There is also apparent confusion about the issue of whether Absalom had sons and about the various parties to Absalom's revolt (Gunn 1978: 32–33).

6. Synthesis. Rost's assessment of the unity and historical worth of 2 Samuel 9–20 and 1 Kings 1–2 as a unified political document stemming from the early days of Solomon's reign no longer reflects a consensus of scholarly opinion. Almost every aspect of Rost's analysis has required reassessment. While literary artistry (including the use of motifs from folklore) does not require rejection of the description of this material as history, it has led to a more critical assessment of its historical worth.

It is also no longer clear that one can talk about a succession document embracing all of 2 Samuel 9–20 and 1 Kings 1–2. The distinction between the themes of the legitimation of David's claims to the throne and the struggle for succession suggests a more complex history for the traditions contained within the document as well. Granted this distinction, the designation "Court Narrative" is beginning to displace Rost's designation of the material as "Succession Narrative." The way in which the references to Solomon, Bathsheba, and Nathan (2 Sam 11:1–12:25; 1 Kgs 1:1–2:46) form an *inclusio* calls into question Rost's definition of the extent of the Court Narrative. There is little reason to try to include 2 Samuel 9 as part of the larger composition, and few scholars have followed Rost in including 2 Sam 6:16, 20ff., and 7:11b, 16. Ironically, Rost's real legacy may be in the growing interest in the literary artistry of the composition, which is characteristic of much of the contemporary writing on the Court Narrative.

Bibliography

Ackroyd, P. R. 1981. The Succession Narrative (so-called). *Int* 35: 383–96.

Bar-Efrat, S. 1978. Literary Modes and Methods in the Biblical Narrative in View of 2 Samuel 10–20 and 1 Kings 1–2. *Immanuel* 8: 19–31.

Blenkinsopp, J. 1966. Theme and Motif in the Succession History (2 Sam. XI 2ff) and the Yahwist Corpus. Pp. 44–57 in *Volume du Congrès. Genève, 1965.* VTSup 15. Leiden.

Carlson, R. A. 1964. *David, the Chosen King.* Stockholm.

Caspari, W. 1909. Literarische Art und historischer Wert von 2 Sam. 15–20. TSK 82: 317–48.

Coats, G. W. 1981. Parable, Fable and Anecdote: Storytelling in the Succession Narrative. *Int* 35: 368–82.

Conroy, C. 1978. *Absalom Absalom! Narrative and Language in 2 Sam 13–20.* AnBib 81. Rome.

Delekat, L. 1967. Tendenz und Theologie der David-Salomo-Erzählung. Pp. 26–36 in *Das Ferne und Nahe Wort,* ed. F. Maas. BZAW 105. Berlin.

Eissfeldt, O. 1931. *Die Komposition der Samuelisbücher.* Leipzig.

———. 1965. *The Old Testament. An Introduction.* Trans. P. R. Ackroyd. New York.

Flanagan, J. W. 1972. Court History or Succession Document? A Study of 2 Samuel 9–20 and 1 Kings 1–2. *JBL* 91: 172–81.

Fokkelman, J. P. 1981. *Narrative Art and Poetry in the Books of Samuel.* Vol. 1. Assen.

Gressmann, H. 1921. *Die alteste Geschichtsschreibung und Prophetie Israels.* SAT 2/1. 2d ed. Göttingen.

Gunkel, H. 1921. *Märchen im alten Testament.* Tübingen.

———. 1925. *Die Israelitische Literatur.* Kultur der Gegenwart 1/7. Leipzig.

———. 1964. *The Legends of Genesis.* New York.

Gunn, D. M. 1978. *The Story of King David.* JSOTSup 6. Sheffield.

Hagan, H. 1979. Deception as Motif and Theme in 2 Sm 9–20; 1 Kgs 1–2. *Bib* 60: 301–26.

Ishida, T. 1982. Solomon's Succession to the Throne of David—A Political Analysis. Pp. 175–87 in *Studies in the Period of David and Solomon and Other Essays,* ed. T. Ishida. Winona Lake, IN.

Jackson, J. J. 1965. David's Throne: Patterns in the Succession Story. *CJT* 11: 183–95.

Knight, D. A. 1985. Moral Values and Literary Traditions: The

Case of the Succession Narrative (2 Samuel 9–20; 1 Kings 1–2). *Semeia* 34: 7–23.

Langlamet, F. 1976. Pour ou contre Salomon? La Rédaction prosalomonienne de I Rois, I–II. *RB* 83: 321–79, 481–529.

McCarter, P. K., Jr. 1981. "Plots, True or False." The Succession Narrative as Court Apologetic. *Int* 35: 355–67.

Rideout, G. 1974. The Rape of Tamar: A Rhetorical Analysis of 2 Sam 13:1–22. Pp. 75–84 in *Rhetorical Criticism: Essays in Honor of James Muilenburg,* ed. J. J. Jackson and M. Kessler. PTMS 1. Pittsburgh.

Rost, L. 1982. *The Succession to the Throne of David.* Trans. M. D. Rutter and D. M. Gunn. Sheffield.

Roth, W. 1977. You Are the Man! Structural Interaction in 2 Samuel 10–12. *Semeia* 8: 1–13.

Sacon, K. K. 1982. A Study of the Literary Structure of "The Succession Narrative," Pp. 27–54 in *Studies in the Period of David and Solomon and Other Essays,* ed. T. Ishida. Winona Lake, IN.

Simon, U. 1967. The Poor Man's Ewe-Lamb. An Example of a Juridical Parable. *Bib* 48: 207–42.

Steuernagel, C. 1912. *Lehrbuch der Einleitung in das Alte Testament.* Tübingen.

Trible, P. 1984. *Texts of Terror.* OBT 13. Philadelphia.

Tsevat, M. 1958. Marriage and Monarchial Legitimacy in Ugarit and Israel. *JSS* 3: 237–43.

Veijola, T. 1975. *Die ewige Dynastie.* AASF 193. Helsinki.

———. 1979. Salomo—der erstgeborene Bathsebas. VTSup 30: 230–50.

Whybray, R. N. 1968. *The Succession Narrative.* SBT 2d series 9. London.

Würthwein, E. 1974. *Die Erzählung von der Thronfolge Davids–theologische oder politische Geschichtsschreibung?* Th Stud 115. Zurich.

HAROLD O. FORSHEY

COURT OF THE GUARD. See GUARD, COURT OF THE.

COURTS. See LAW, BIBLICAL AND ANE.

COVENANT. A "covenant" is an agreement enacted between two parties in which one or both make promises under oath to perform or refrain from certain actions stipulated in advance. As indicated by the designation of the two sections of the Christian Bible—Old Testament (= covenant) and New Testament—"covenant" in the Bible is the major metaphor used to describe the relation between God and Israel (the people of God). As such, covenant is the instrument constituting the rule (or kingdom) of God, and therefore it is a valuable lens through which one can recognize and appreciate the biblical ideal of religious community.

A. Underlying Problems in Approaching the Topic

At the outset it should be noted that two factors often inhibit the ability of many modern Western readers to appreciate fully the biblical portrayal of the covenant between God and Israel. The first is the problem of the so-called "sociology of knowledge" in the modern Western world. On the one hand, the English word "covenant" itself has largely fallen into disuse, and today is limited to certain highly technical legal matters. On the other hand, as a practical form of social organization and behavior, covenant-based relationships in the West have become almost obsolete, the fragile institution of marriage remaining the most noteworthy vestige of such relationships. Thus, one legitimate issue in the study of biblical covenant must be the extent to which modern and Western students of the Bible can conceive and imagine relationships built upon little more than promises reliably made and honorably kept.

The second is generally a problem associated ultimately with the "sociology of knowledge" in ancient Israel. How fully did the ancient Israelite scribes themselves understand what it meant to live in terms of a covenant? As we shall see, in the millennium during which ancient Israelite society and thought developed and changed, and in which the biblical documents were written, the same single term—*bĕrît*—came to be used to refer to many different types of oath-bound promises and relationships. Therefore, any study of covenant in the Bible must be sensitive to the varying social and ideological contexts associated with different types of oath-taking, and it must also be prepared to make careful distinctions between different phenomena underlying the singular use of the Hebrew word *bĕrît.* These phenomena may be roughly classified as "treaties," "loyalty oaths," and "charters." Especially in the later periods of biblical history and in connection with the subsequent utilization of covenant imagery within early Judaism and early Christianity (see H below), it is also necessary to distinguish between covenants as *socially en-*

acted historical realities that were expected to bring about functional changes in patterns of behavior, and covenants as *formal or symbolic dogmatic concepts* that were supposed to be the objects of tradition and belief.

In the past century scholars have rarely been sensitive to such ancient phenomena, and consequently there has been much debate recently as to whether the biblical covenant appeared at the beginning of the history of ancient Israel (the time of Moses) as an adaptation of Late Bronze (LB) Age suzerainty treaty forms, or later during the time of the monarchy (introduced either by the classical prophets or by Josiah) as an adaptation of Iron Age "loyalty oaths" (both McCarthy [1973] and Nicholson [1986] embrace relatively limited perspectives on covenant and opt for its relatively late appearance in Israelite religion).

B. ANE Treaties

1. The Nature of Ancient Covenants. The large number of international treaties preserved in texts from all over the ANE world is dramatic witness to the importance of covenants in ancient social and political life. See also TREATIES. For some periods, especially the Syro-Hittite LB Age, these treaties constitute a major source of our knowledge of the ancient history of the region. As instruments for the creation and regulation of relationships between different social groups, they seem to have been universal in the ancient world. Even the Greek historian Herodotus regarded the forms by which a society established binding covenants as an important element in the description of that culture (e.g. Hdt. 1.74).

By their very nature, covenants are complex *enactments.* As complex acts they combine: (1) historical events that create relationships, usually (though not necessarily) between unequal partners; (2) customary ways of thinking characteristic of both parties, especially common religious ideas associated with deities; (3) descriptions of norms for future behavior (which are often confused with "laws"); (4) literary or oral forms in which the agreement is couched; and (5) almost always some ritual act that is regarded as essential to the ratification of the binding promise. It follows that a covenant cannot be understood merely by regarding it as a rigid literary form, nor can it be understood by reducing it to a literary law code, a ritual act, or a theological or political idea or concept. Thus, most studies of OT covenant in the past quarter century that have been delimited by one or another of such concepts have largely generated a great deal of unnecessary confusion.

Covenants in the form of international treaties appeared almost as soon as writing itself began to be used for literary purposes. From the EB Age at Ebla through the Iron Age a sufficient number of such treaties were recorded and have been preserved so that we can identify changes in the conventional contents and forms of treaties. It is highly probable that these instruments for the regularization of public relationships between sovereigns developed in prehistoric times from customary forms used for making behavior predictable between private persons. One such occasion for private agreements would be marriage contracts, and it is significant that marriage is one of the most pervasive and constant types of covenant throughout history.

Since covenants are typically enacted between parties to create relationships that did not previously exist, both the *substance* and the *form* of covenants must be valid and meaningful to both. Thus, covenants constituted a most important feature of ancient cultures that operated to transcend a narrow parochialism and so to prepare the way for a broader perspective on society and history.

As is the case in so many other features of ancient civilizations, it was the Bronze Age that produced the most highly developed structure of international treaties. Although these treaties are known primarily through Hittite sources, there is no reason to believe that the Hittites originated this treaty form. Since treaties are intrinsically cross-cultural in nature, the basic underlying patterns of thought incorporated in the texts would necessarily have been common property to most ANE cultures of the time. Note, for example, the (parity) treaty between Ḫattusilis and Rameses II (*ANET,* 199–203) which (however temporarily or ephemerally) was meaningful to both an Egyptian audience and a Hittite one. Indeed, the simple fundamental elements of the treaty structure are already found in a text from Byblos dating probably to the end of the EB Age (Mendenhall 1985, chap. 5).

2. The Structure of the LB Age Treaties. The structure of treaties in the LB Age was fully described already in 1931 by V. Korosec, but it was not until 1954 that the extraordinary similarity to certain OT traditions was pointed out (Mendenhall 1954a). Though there has been an enormous amount of discussion since that time, there still seems to be no consensus concerning the historical significance or even the validity of those similarities.

The "ideal structure" of LB Hittite treaties has been abstracted from numerous examples. It is not surprising that not every treaty exhibits all of the individual elements of the structure. The modern idea that all the covenants had to conform to some rigid form defined in advance is characteristic of a "strict law" type of legalistic mentality that not only is quite rare in the history of jurisprudence but also was probably foreign to the ANE historical reality.

a. Identification of the Covenant Giver. This introduction to the treaty text typically begins with the formula "The words of . . . ," followed by the name of the Hittite king, his genealogy, and his various titles, ending with the epithet "the hero." The vast majority of the treaties preserved are suzerainty treaties in which the underlying ideology held that the great and powerful king was bestowing a gracious relationship upon an inferior. It followed, then, that the relationship of the vassal to the overlord had to be an exclusive one: the vassal could not engage in treaty or other relationships with other independent monarchs without being guilty of treason, and therefore becoming subject to the death penalty. (The similarity between this ideology centering upon the Hittite great king and the biblical monotheism seems obvious.)

b. The Historical Prologue. This section, in which the Hittite king recounted his past deeds of benefit to the vassal, is frequently so detailed and extensive as to constitute a major source for our knowledge of ANE history in this period. The motivation for this section was obviously not an academic interest in the past for its own sake, but rather to have that past serve as the foundation for the present obligation of the vassal to be obedient to the stipulations of the covenant. The implications of this element of the covenant structure are far-reaching, but it is difficult if not impossible to prove what those implications might have been. It can at least be suggested that certain concepts were presupposed as present in the minds of both parties to the covenant.

In the first place, the historical prologue is inseparable from the concept of *reciprocity* that is so prevalent in premodern cultures. The narration of the past history emphasized very strongly the benefits that the great king had already bestowed upon the vassal in the past. The implication is, of course, that the common decency of *gratitude* would place the vassal under *obligation* to comply with the wishes of his benefactor. The principles underlying this sort of relationship are illustrated by an old Arabic saying (which actually applies to persons who are equals in an egalitarian society): "If someone does you a favor, you never forget it; if you do someone else a favor, you never mention it." (The latter part of the saying of course does not apply to a king or to a god, who is in the position to specify what he wishes.)

These prologues are not unrelated to the question of the origin of history writing in the ancient world (a subject surrounded by obscurity, mystery, and controversy). This is even more true of the biblical tradition. In view of the fact that the earliest literary materials of the Hebrew Bible (e.g., Exodus 15 and Judges 5) are poetic descriptions of the acts of God, we should consider more seriously the practical purposes associated with the treaty prologues as the *ideological matrix* from which the biblical historiography developed. In short, just as in the LB treaties, so also even in the late repristination of the old covenant traditions of ancient Israel, the past was recounted for the specific purpose of instilling a sense of gratitude as the foundation and ground for future obedience.

c. The Stipulations. This section of the LB treaties, often phrased in the case-law format ("if . . . , then . . ."), described the interests of the great king that the vassal is bound to protect and obey under the covenant relationship. Already in this section there is an implicit distinction between what might be termed public vs. private concerns. The imperial control over vassals involved no interest in the internal affairs of the vassal state other than the obvious one of suppressing or controlling subversive activities and elements that might disrupt the harmonious relationship between the vassal and his overlord.

d. The Provision for Deposit and Periodic Public Reading. This segment of the treaty is again surprisingly sophisticated. Deposit of a copy of the treaty in the temple was an act that now placed that treaty within the interests of the local deity and under its protection. In more modern terminology, the treaty and its contents were to be incorporated into the operating value system of the vassal state, and thus to be internalized as determinants of future behavior. To put it in simplest terms, the treaty was a sacred act and object. (As is often the case, there was undoubtedly a considerable difference between this official doctrine and practical reality.)

The provision for periodic public reading implies that although the treaty was formally established with the vassal king himself, nevertheless it was also binding upon the population over which he ruled. The treaty became a part of the public policy of the king and thus was integrated into the "law" of his kingdom. Interestingly enough, the frequency specified for the periodic public reading varied, but it was usually scheduled from one to four times a year. (It would be interesting to know whether or not these public readings coincided with local festivals, and therefore became part of a public ritual form, but no such information is so far available.)

e. The List of Witnesses to the Treaty. These treaties also typically listed those "third parties" who would witness the enactment of the treaty. It is of especial interest that the witnesses were exclusively deities or deified elements of the natural world. The list of deities was frequently so lengthy as to justify the conclusion that it was intended to be exhaustive: all gods relevant to *both* parties were called upon as witnesses, so that there was no god left that the vassal could appeal to for protection if he wanted to violate his solemn oath. It is especially amusing that often the "*ʿapiru* gods," i.e., even the gods of renegade rebel bands, were included in the list of witnesses.

The witnesses also included the heavens and the earth, and mountains and rivers, a fact of particular significance because the motif continues in the poetic and prophetic traditions of the Bible (Deuteronomy 32; Isa 1:2; Mic 6:1–2), but there is little if any trace of it in any other extra-biblical Iron Age covenant texts and ideologies centuries later. The witnesses were those entities that were called upon to observe the behavior of the party under oath and to carry out the appropriate rewards and punishments (the blessings and curses) connected with the treaty (see below). The fact that these enforcers are all supernatural beings reflects the underlying idea that in this covenant ideology strenuous (if not pretentious) efforts were made to place the entire covenant complex outside the realm of political and military coercive force, and into the realm of a voluntary acceptance of a commonality of interest between suzerain and vassal. In other words, there is expressed here the hope that the vassal's obedience will be "self-policing," i.e., based upon a conscientious regard for higher principles (the gods) than simply upon the fear of superior military force.

f. The Blessings and Curses. This section of the treaty text described in detail the consequences of obedience and disobedience with which the witnesses to the treaty rewarded or punished the vassal. Because the witnesses were the supernatural entities mentioned in the previous section, the blessings and curses were appropriately (in large measure) those experiences that are beyond normal human ability to predict, much less control. Particularly in this prescientific age the most important concerns of humanity were clearly beyond mortal control: health, productivity of fields and flocks and wives, and freedom from external violence. See also BLESSINGS AND CURSES. Thus the treaty made an inseparable connection between ethical adherence to promises made and the consequences of economic prosperity, freedom from disease, and tranquil long life. The text of the treaty typically concluded with this enumeration of the consequences of obedience and disobedience.

It is important to observe that the LB treaty formulas included not only punitive threats to be carried out by supernatural powers but also positive rewards of similar origin. This aspect of international treaties was normal in the LB Age, but later Iron Age treaties typically contained nothing but the curses (see B.3 below).

g. The Ratification Ceremony. It would be extremely naive to think that the mere writing of a treaty text brought into existence the treaty and the relationship it stipulated. Even today a treaty must be signed, ratified, or otherwise formally accepted before it can become binding. In antiquity, the formal ritual by which a covenant came into force had such a variety of forms and procedures that no generalization can be made. These formal rituals are the customs that Herodotus specified for the societies that he described. There is no reason to believe, therefore, that some specified rigid formality was always carried out—indeed, it would be unthinkable in view of the variety of cultures and societies that are involved in the dozens of treaties preserved.

One observation, however, is probably valid: the ratification of the covenant was frequently associated with the sacrifice of an animal. The significance of animal sacrifice in general is a complex and intractable subject, and the problem becomes even more complex when it takes place within the framework of covenant relationships. An Iron Age Assyrian treaty, however (*ANET,* 532–33), makes perfectly clear that at that time and place (N Syria), the sacrificed animal represented, and was identified with, the vassal who was being placed under oath: just as the animal was slaughtered, so would the vassal and his dependents be slaughtered if he violated his oath. The same concept is attested for the earliest Roman covenant traditions (Mendenhall 1954a), so we may safely assume that this sacrificial identification was widespread in both time and space. Once the animal was killed, the vassal could expect the same fate if he violated his oath. Perhaps associated with sacrificial ritual as an enactment ceremony is the well-attested fact that covenants were often officially ratified by a common meal (see G.1 below).

It is characteristic of this period that the treaties do not contain a verbal oath formula. The oath is a conditional self-cursing: i.e., an appeal to the gods to bring certain penalties upon the oath taker if he violates the promise that he is swearing to keep. The sacrifice is thus the *enactment* of the oath; therefore, a verbal formula is unnecessary in the *text* of the treaty itself (though some such verbalization possibly accompanied the slaughter of the animal, as in the early Roman ritual).

h. The Imposition of the Curses. A final element in the entire covenant complex is one which, like the oath formula itself, is not provided in the treaty text but is implied at least by parallels from other cultures of the ancient world. This is the often delicate problem of imprecations and curses. Though there is no certain evidence for a ritual form that effectively imposed the curses for breach of covenant, it seems probable that such a custom did exist. Under what circumstances could a sovereign declare the curses to be in effect, thus depriving the vassal of the protection that the covenant relationship normally would provide? How flagrant must a violation be before the sovereign could legitimately muster his military forces and attack the recalcitrant vassal? Although the treaty texts themselves make no provision for such punitive action *by the suzerain himself* (this would negate the entire ideology of the covenant!), there must have been some means by which the suzerain could proclaim that the covenant no longer existed, and that the vassal therefore could be dealt with by force. In such circumstances, the suzerain could legitimately claim to be the agent of the avenging deities, since the actions of the deities themselves were evidently unreliable (and therefore insufficient). As the ultimate curse for the breach of covenant was the complete destruction of the vassal kingdom, the logical instrument for realizing such a *historical* event (in distinction from the curses of the treaty text that represent *natural* events) would be the suzerain himself.

3. The Structure of Iron Age Loyalty Oaths. The treaties that have become known in recent decades especially from the late Assyrian Empire reveal that structurally and ideologically they belong to a different world from that of the LB Age (Parpola 1987; Grayson 1987). Gone is the historical prologue, except for one example, significantly enough, preserved in extremely rudimentary form in a treaty with an Arab political entity—a culture that we know also preserved Bronze Age linguistic structures. Gone also are most of the other sophisticated and elaborate elements of the treaty forms, such as the gratitude for previous benefits conferred, the blessings, and the provision for deposit and public reading. Instead, these Iron Age treaties give the strong impression that a promise to obey has simply been imposed by superior military force and is now being reinforced by an incredible elaboration of curses. Thus, these treaties have appropriately been termed "loyalty oaths" (Weinfeld 1976).

The structure of the Iron Age loyalty oaths known from Assyrian sources seems to have been very flexible, but usually it included these basic elements:

1. The preamble, giving the name and titles of the Assyrian king, and the name of the vassal who is placed under oath, together with his descendants and the population of his realm.
2. The designation of the Assyrian ruler or successor to whom loyalty is due.
3. The invocation of the deities in whose presence the vassal swears.
4. The definition of the acts of commission and omission that subject the vassal to the curses.
5. The curses, or evils, brought upon the disobedient vassal by each deity, some curses in *mašal* ("parable") form.

Compared with the treaties of the LB Age, these of the Assyrian period are simplistic and one might say almost brutal. Although the text emphasizes the various ills to be brought upon the disloyal by the panoply of gods, the fate of the disobedient vassal is depicted quite tangibly by the Assyrian annals themselves (e.g., *ANET,* 277–301). The ideological matrix of these loyalty oaths suggests that the only motivation for obedience was simply the *self-interested desire* to avoid the fate so graphically illustrated in the Assyrian texts and reliefs, in sharp contrast to the *gratitude* that was supposed to be the foundation of obedience in the LB Hittite treaties. Thus almost all pretense of any transcendent moral or ethical foundations for the suzerain-vassal relationship was abandoned in favor simply of brute military force. Even the power of the supernatural forces to punish violation of oaths was of little importance compared with the vindictive power of the Assyrian king himself to do the punishing (in which some of these Assyrian kings at least seem to have taken a sadistic delight). It is ironic that a major purpose of the 7th-century treaties was to guarantee the succession of the designated heir to the Assyrian throne. The pathetic reliance on subjugated vassals to assure such succession is vivid witness to the *internal* hostilities within the Assyrian court itself.

In conclusion, the LB international treaties exhibit a sophistication and elaboration of concepts that were very largely lost during the Iron Age. In comparison, the treaties of the Iron Age seem to have been based mostly on mere military power reinforced by superstition. It must be observed, however, that the political instruments of the Hittite Empire were precisely that: political instruments. They were devised and adapted from the age-old common property of ancient cultures in the vain hope that they could bring about the voluntary subservience of peoples who in fact had been subjugated by military force. Although the LB covenant ideology certainly represented an admirable attempt to place cross-cultural relationships on a basis of something other than sheer military superiority, the brute facts of the historical evidence lead inevitably to the conclusion that Hittite foreign policy was exclusively military (Goetze 1957). The treaties, in other words, were imposed relationships in which the vassal had freedom to choose either capitulation under the covenant or annihilation; thus, the LB treaties were instruments of propaganda, not of practical reality. Nevertheless, as instruments of propaganda they appealed to a different matrix of ideas than did the (equally propagandistic) loyalty oaths of the Iron Age.

C. The Sinai Covenant

The ongoing scholarly debate concerning the relationship between the LB suzerainty treaties and the biblical traditions depicting a "covenant" in Israel before the monarchy centers on one fundamental point: whether the Sinai covenant was indeed a historical reality known to the Israelite population in the premonarchic period (ca. 1200–1000 B.C.), or whether it was instead nothing more than a pious literary fabrication of the later monarchic period, an attempt to "invent" a (fictitious) past (nevertheless) replete with religious "meaning." If the former applies, then the relationship between the LB treaties and the Sinai covenant traditions are historically significant, and one could justifiably conclude that the Sinai covenant was conceived to be a type of "suzerainty treaty" establishing Yahweh as king and Israel as vassal. If the latter applies, then any similarity between the Sinai covenant traditions and the LB treaties is coincidental, and the real source of inspiration for the biblical idea of covenant must be sought either generally in the monarchic period, specifically at the time of the Assyrian Empire (ca. 750–620 B.C.), or perhaps sometime in the postmonarchic period (after 586 B.C.).

Here it should be stated unequivocally that all of the various elements of the LB suzerainty treaties (presented above) in one way or another are either present or reflected in biblical traditions associated with the premonarchic (Sinai) covenant. But, as will be noted below, these traditions also bear the marks of later "creative writers" who embellished and reworked the traditions from the radically different perspective of the monarchic period. The first task is to delineate the *formal* elements of the premonarchic covenant, and then to establish the *function* that such a covenant could reasonably have been expected to perform in Israel in the century or two before the rise of the monarchy.

1. Formal Elements of the Sinai Covenant. a. Identification and Historical Prologue. The historical investigation of any cultural form must begin with the realization that forms are almost never transferred from one cultural context (such as the international political treaties of the LB Age) to another (such as the hill-country tribes of early Iron Age Palestine) without some modification or adaptation inevitably resulting. This is the "Law of Functional Shift." This principle is aptly illustrated in the first two formal elements of the suzerainty treaty: the identification of the covenant giver and the historical prologue, which have been fused together in the two forms of the Decalogue preserved in Exodus 20 and Deuteronomy 6. Unlike the "great kings" in the Bronze Age political treaties, the one God of Mosaic monotheism was not identified by heaping up divine epithets and attributes so characteristic of ancient polytheism; rather, at the very beginning God was simply identified in terms of what God had done: ". . . who brought you out of the land of Egypt, out of the house of bondage" (Exod 20:2). The identification of the deity thus became synonymous with the historical prologue, and although the entire structure of the Sinai covenant represented a continuity with age-old patterns of thought, both the deity and the historical prologue represented a complete discontinuity from earlier ways of thinking. The historical event that was crucial to the identification of the deity became inseparable from the historical event of the establishment of the covenant itself. As Huffmon (1965) has shown, attempts made by some scholars to separate entirely the Exodus tradition from the Sinai covenant tradition are based upon a rejection of and, at the same time, a failure to understand both the biblical traditions themselves and the ANE patterns of thought that underlie them.

Whether the name of the deity, Yahweh, was a continuation from some earlier tradition is a debated issue to which there is no clear answer (see YAHWEH); it is certain that if there was a god by this name worshipped earlier by some group, it could hardly have been associated with any of the well-known politically organized imperial powers or even city-states of the previous age. The suggestion that it was the name of a Midianite deity simply attempts to explain the obscure by the more obscure.

b. Stipulations. The biblical traditions insist that the text of the covenant established at Sinai (the stipulations) was the Decalogue, the Ten Words (Deut 10:4), and there is no modern evidence that would disprove the ancient information. Virtually all scholars agree that the original Ten Words were the simple prohibitions plus the two positive obligations of sabbath observance and honoring of parents (without all the elaborations that were added at a much later period). According to the Exodus 20 tradition, these were written on two tablets of stone, and contained only the first three of the elements of the suzerainty treaty described above. Some scholars have recently argued that the lack of other LB treaty elements in this text is evidence that the Sinai covenant had nothing to do with the suzerainty treaty. However, this line of reasoning is fatuous because it attempts to draw a historical conclusion from an observation about mere literary forms: even if all the LB elements are not attested in the first 17 verses of Exodus 20 (they are not even all attested in many LB treaties!), virtually all of them are nevertheless reflected in the later elaboration of traditions associated with the Sinai covenant (see below). The most that one can conclude from the literary form of Exod 20:1–17 is that the author (or editor) responsible for its final canonical shape did not believe that he had to pattern the *text* of the Sinai covenant deliberately after LB suzerainty treaties (if he even knew what they were), and felt that it was sufficient simply (1) to identify Yahweh formally (even though contextually this is unnecessary), (2) to restate what Yahweh did on behalf of Israel (again, contextually this is unnecessary), and (3) to list Yahweh's Ten Words. What is surprising is not that the other LB treaty elements are absent in this text but rather that v 2 is present, even though it could just as easily have been omitted. It was included precisely because the *received tradition* already linked item (3) above to items (1) and (2); the only explanation for this linkage is to be found in the LB suzerainty treaties.

The Ten Words are not commands, nor are they couched in command (i.e., imperative) language. They are simple future indicative verbs that indicate the future action that is the expected consequence of the preceding prologue: "I am Yahweh your God who brought you out of the land of Egypt . . . , (and therefore) you will have no other gods before me . . . ," etc. Later biblical tradition itself was utterly confused in its interpretation of the Decalogue, and subsequent postbiblical interpreters have added to the confusion, ranging from the traditional pious view that the phrase "I am Yahweh your God . . ." is the first commandment, to very recent views held by many scholars that the Decalogue is a classical example of an "apodictic" (as opposed to the "casuistic") legal form. See LAW (FORMS OF BIBLICAL LAW).

The confusion continues with the interpretation of the statements themselves, which traditionally have been classified as three (or four) "laws" having to do with obligations to God (Exod 20:2–8), followed by seven (or six) "laws" of obligations to fellow human beings (Exod 20:12–17). Although this classification is admirable in intention, it has nothing to do with ancient religious reality. *All* of the stipulations represent those characteristics of human behavior that constitute the definition of the will of God: they describe the highest value, the "ultimate concern" of the community formed by covenant, for they are the principles upon which the one God directs the historical fate of the community.

c. Deposit and Public Reading, Witnesses, Blessings and Curses. It is true that the Exodus 20 text does not include the provision for deposit and peridic public reading, the list of witnesses, or the curses and blessings. However, it is most inappropriate to conclude that the Sinai covenant therefore had no connection with LB treaty patterns, or that it was a later pious literary invention, or that the Decalogue was completely unrelated to covenant traditions. If these elements were truly absent from the complex of traditions about the very founding of the ancient Israelite community, it is indeed strange that in later times (when most of these elements had been completely forgotten in the process of ANE treaty enactments) some biblical scribes felt it necessary to add them to the complex of the Mosaic tradition.

Since early Israel did not have a temple in which to deposit the text of the covenant written on the tablets of stone, the tablets were deposited in the ark of the covenant (according to numerous variants of the tradition even in Exodus alone). Note also the formal deposit of a text in a "sanctuary" in Josh 24:26. Periodic public reading is not directly attested, but it is certainly implied in ritual customs, such as those described in Exod 23:17 and Deut 27:11–26; and practiced in late OT times and early Judaism ("The recitation of the *Shma*ᶜ is the rabbinic covenantal renewal" [Levenson 1985: 86]). If these traditions did not ultimately derive from the LB/early Iron Age, from whence did the later Israelite scribes derive these motifs, and why would their later audiences find them meaningful?

The list of gods as witnesses was of course incompatible with the monotheistic community, and so the members of the community themselves became the witnesses (cf. Josh 24:22, but also v 27 where the stone is a witness; later tradition evidently did not quite know what to do with this otherwise bizarre *but inherited* element of the treaty structure). Thus the enforcers of the covenant became the members of the community themselves (when Yahweh's enforcement became regarded as not sufficiently predictable, or when it was believed that God was not sufficiently concerned to carry out the duties of reward and punishment [cf. Zeph 1:12]); consequently, the stipulations of covenant became socially enforced law. Again, if this tradition of witnesses was not derived ultimately from the LB/early Iron Age, what would inspire some later scribe to introduce otherwise awkward references to them?

The blessings and curses were enormously elaborated in Deuteronomy 28. In this late elaboration the blessings were enumerated in only 14 verses, while the remaining 68 verses enumerate in vivid detail the curses resulting from breach of covenant. At the later (Assyrian?) period when Deuteronomy 28 was composed, the multiplication of curses is not at all surprising (see MANASSEH); what is surprising in that later milieu is that any blessings were enumerated at all, something that could not have been predicted from the structure and content of the Assyrian loyalty oaths (see B.3 above). It is difficult to imagine how an Israelite scribe of that time could *invent* the covenant idea and include *blessings;* rather that element of the covenant tradition already had to have been preexistent in the earliest biblical tradition, and therefore at the disposal of the Deuteronomic writer (and also of the Priestly writer, who similarly wanted to append a list of blessings and curses to his distinctive version of covenant obligations [Leviticus 26]). On the other hand, the multiplication of *curses* that we find in Deuteronomy 28 (and Leviticus 26) represents later elaboration of a tradition similar to that which is universally found in the ANE (Hillers 1964). Though the text of the Decalogue (Exod 20:1–17) does not refer to either blessings or curses, the latter are implied in the narrative accounts that refer to sacrificed animals ("oxen" according to a later embellishment—inappropriate to a desert environment) and to a common covenant meal with Yahweh (Exod 24:4–8, 11).

d. The Ratification Ceremony. This seems to have two elements, the first a verbal assent to the covenant ("All that the Lord has spoken we will do," Exod 19:8; 24:3; cf. Josh 24:24 for a quite different formula), and the second a ritual act involving the sacrifice of an animal, the blood of which is thrown upon an altar and upon the people (Exod 24:5–8). The latter was a symbolic action in which the people were identified with the sacrificed animal, so that the fate of the latter is presented as the fate to be expected by the people if they violated their sacred promise (i.e., it is a form of self-curse). Thus the ratification ceremony was, in effect, the pledging of their lives as a guarantee of obedience to the divine will. (In time the ratification ceremony simply became a ritual form signaling membership in the ritual society; i.e., circumcision.)

Traces of other ratification ceremonies or covenant enactments have been preserved in later biblical traditions about the premonarchic period, but nevertheless these narratives correspond entirely to what might be expected in the process of the formation of the twelve tribe federation. Most important in this regard is the narrative in Joshua 24 that reproduces much of the content of the LB suzerainty treaty. It contains an elaborate historical prologue (of course in much later language, vv 2–13), an emphasis upon witnesses (the people themselves, v 22; but also the inscribed stone, v 27), and the warning of the curses of divine wrath in case of disobedience (v 20). (Entirely consistent with the late date of this garbled account is the fact that the blessings are entirely absent.) The formal verbal acceptance by the gathered population is accompanied by a brief recapitulation of the historical prologue (vv 16–18), and the stipulations are identified with the "statutes and ordinances" that Joshua wrote in the "book of the law of God" (vv 25–26).

Although the language is much later and the chapter does not reproduce the text of the treaty, Joshua 24 is a narrative description of a covenant enactment. In fact, in its present form the narrative is anachronistically modeled somewhat after the reform of Josiah and the Iron Age "loyalty oath" that was characteristic of that time (see F.1 below). The character of Joshua is a sort of literary prototype of Josiah, and the population is represented as having fallen away from Yahweh, as they had in Josiah's day. But the original event of Joshua's time was that covenant enactment by which various population groups of Canaan proper (who had escaped the collapse of LB Age civilization) formally became members of the Yahwist confederation, and thus the "tribes" of Yahweh. Other features of Josiah's reform that were read back into the time of Joshua include the identification of the covenant stipulations with a written law code (a confusion that is perpetuated to the present day) and the emphasis upon the Abrahamic tradition (vv 2–4, 14–15) that was essential to Josiah's claim to rule over *all* the land of Canaan (after three centuries during which the Jerusalem regime governed only Judah).

The ritual of the recitation of the blessings and curses from Mts. Ebal and Gerizim in Deut 27:11–26 was probably a part of the Shechem covenant enactment recounted in Joshua 24 (cf. Josh 8:30–35, esp. v 34), although the present form of the tradition has completely severed any literary connection between the two, probably because the Deuteronomic tradition had become associated with the commands of Moses. The passage in Deuteronomy plus several others may well contain remote reminiscences of the fact that there had also been a covenant ceremony in Transjordan at the time of Moses, by which population groups of that region had become members of the Yahwist federation. This tradition of a Transjordanian ratification in Moses' latter days is perhaps also reflected in Deut 27:9 "Keep silence and hear, O Israel: this day you have become the people of Yahweh your God" (cf. Deut 32:6, 18).

e. Formal Procedures for Violation of Covenant. Just as later biblical texts such as Joshua 24 preserve certain premonarchic covenant elements discussed above, so they also unwittingly preserve the element pertaining to procedures in case of covenant violations. The narratives of Exodus and Numbers give many illustrations of procedures taken against such violators during the lifetime of Moses himself, but because these are embedded in the late Priestly narratives marked by substantial literary embellishment, it is very difficult to evaluate them historically. Nevertheless, even the very late literary ("envelope"?) structure of the Priestly motif of the "murmuring in the wilderness" illustrates the continuity of this ancient element: the people's complaints about lack of food and water while on the way *to* Sinai (Exod 15:22–17:7) characteristically induce Yahweh to respond favorably, but when they complain about the same things on the way *from* Sinai (Numbers 11; 14; 16) Yahweh characteristically punishes them. Why this reversal?

All historical considerations aside, it is evident even at the literary level that the Priestly writer believed that the status of the people was changed *at* Sinai (i.e., there they became subject to the covenant): consequently, they can no longer be viewed as being in "dire distress" but now rather in outright "rebellion." Therefore the way in which Yahweh (or the narrator) deals with Israel has changed: Yahweh no longer is portrayed as soliciting a relationship by multiplying favors that could potentially be listed in a covenant's historical prologue; he is now depicted taking punitive measures against those who have violated their covenant obligations. Murmuring (grumbling) against an overlord constituted violation of covenant in the Hittite texts, and it is listed (using the same verb, *lūn*) in a syllabic text from Byblos (ca. 2000 B.C.) as the acts against a sovereign that will result in a curse (Mendenhall 1985: 60). Thus, while the Priestly authors of these late biblical texts felt quite comfortable viewing the Sinai event as Yahweh's license now to punish "murmurings," they were probably completely unaware that this religious motif associated with covenant ultimately went back at least to LB notions about formal procedures for dealing with covenant violations.

2. Its Historical and Conceptual Context. The foregoing discussion by no means exhausts the formal similarities between the LB suzerainty treaties and the complex of traditions associated with Israel's premonarchic covenant. Yet in the final analysis the formal links are not the only connections, nor are they necessarily the most important ones (they are simply the ones that modern scholarly method is best equipped to handle). But studies that deal merely at the formal level will inevitably miss an important part of the historical process. Perhaps more important are the substantive links between the ideological matrix of those LB treaties (i.e., their rhetorical appeals to a common interest between suzerain and vassal, and to concepts such as the integrity of promises and the obligations of reciprocity) and the range of biblical concepts associated with the Sinai covenant relationship (such as the "knowledge" of God, the "love" of God, the "fear" of God, righteousness, mercy, justice, repentance, divine wrath, retribution, vengeance, forgiveness, salvation, etc.). Thus, in the absence of any evidence that early Israelite society was defined by any ritual (e.g., "amphictyonic") or political organizations—and excluding outright the later and artificial biblical construct of an Israelite unity mystically based on some primordial blood kinship—the conclusion seems inescapable that early Israel existed largely because such an ideological matrix ceased being mere political rhetoric and became, however imperfectly and temporarily, the functional basis of community life for a vast diversity of villages in Palestine and N Transjordan. Our task here is to delineate that process and ideology, and to trace its subsequent development.

The context of the Sinai covenant was that of an extremely traumatic period in the history of the then civilized world, namely the transition from the LB Age to the early Iron Age (ca. 1250–1150 B.C.). After having been regarded for centuries as divine institutions ruled ultimately by gods or semigods, empires and states were crumbling and eroding, if not being altogether abandoned and destroyed. The attendant economic and demographic chaos is clearly attested or inferable from the historical and archaeological record. The heartland of the ancient Hittite Empire in central Anatolia was almost entirely depopulated (and would remain so for the next three centuries), and much of Syria experienced a significant drop in population that would not be recovered until much later in the Iron Age. But precisely at this time Palestine and Transjordan experienced a very rapid rise in population (this period also reveals the first settlements in the adjacent regions of the NW section of the Arabian Peninsula contiguous to Transjordan). The only conceivable source for this sudden rise of population was the region to the N whence came the Philistines, the "Sea Peoples," and no doubt many Arameans, to name only some identifiable groups. To add to the chaotic conditions of this period, the old power centers of the Canaanite cities were either drastically reduced or destroyed, and considerable segments of their population probably moved into the hill country, establishing new villages. See "Archaeology of the Israelite Settlement" under ISRAEL, HISTORY OF.

Such calamitous events cannot have taken place without an equally traumatic questioning and abandonment of the moral and religious as well as economic systems that undergirded those political institutions, although this is not so well attested outside the biblical record with its bitter condemnation of Baal-worship. This situation furnished an extremely favorable climate for the introduction and initial acceptance of different and "better" ways of envisioning and structuring life in a community that could not possibly be a mere continuation of the old that now lay in ruins.

The only surviving articulation of such a "better" way is that realized in the ancient Israelite covenant, which was initially enacted by a group of fugitive slaves led by Moses, presumably at a place called "Sinai." (Exodus 20–24 of course contains a very complex interweaving of much later, much garbled, and much embellished accounts of what actually transpired there.) The new understanding of the nature of deity and of the course of human experience, both of which were associated with this covenant, also proved attractive to much of the population of Palestine and Transjordan, who in the course of the previous two generations had witnessed the demise of virtually every venerable Bronze Age institution while managing to survive the wholesale destruction of cities and the ravages of war, epidemic disease, famine, and violent death. Thus, for many of these people the ancient Israelite covenant provided a framework within which they could effectively dispose of any lingering attachments to the old order now in ruins, and enact for themselves a new order of community and of self-understanding as the "people" of a transcendent God. Their enactment of the covenant apparently occurred at Shechem (again, Joshua 24 is a much later and distorted account of this event).

Given all that has been said above, and given the probability that there was no place in the ancient civilized world where the political ideology of empire and its mythological legitimation were unknown, the ancient Israelite understanding of a deity who ruled without a human intermediary and his standing contingent of soldiers and tax collectors was very welcome, and it was an understanding that was proclaimed ironically in a formal way similar to that of the old political suzerainty treaties. However, unlike those old and failed political policies, these of the new Sovereign were ones which met the needs of the population of the village farmers and shepherds that he governed: namely, the value and dignity of persons regardless of their social and economic status, the predictability that follows from reciprocity and fairness in their interrelationships, and the reliability of the peace that would result (cf. Isa 32:17). Regardless of how practically these "policies of the new King" could be implemented, they nevertheless furnished an ideological matrix on which a broad and functional unity of hill-country tribes could be based.

For example, it is clear that most of the stipulations of the covenant (the Decalogue) represent the concerns that individuals in community legitimately expect in normal civilized human life (e.g., no lying, killing, stealing, adultery). The first two "commandments" are so specifically relevant to the historical situation of the LB/early Iron Age transition as to present difficulties for religious communities ever since. What was (and is) meant by "other gods" remains a perennial and insoluble problem in the history of religion (and in the modern ecumenical movement). However, the contrast to the one God, Yahweh, was clear and absolute ca. 1200 B.C. The "other gods" could hardly be anything other than the parochial symbols of existent political or tribal entities; Yahweh was the deity who represented concerns beyond the immediate interests of any petty political or tribal group, and who thus opposed the elevation of any political power structure to an object of worship wherein its policies took precedence over all other concerns, especially ethical ones.

Likewise the prohibition of "graven images," etc., represents an ancient iconoclastic movement that was a necessary corollary to the antimonarchic theology of the early Israelite movement. Such images, including those of gold and silver mentioned in Exod 20:23, were largely the product of the urban political establishments that were being destroyed; evidently these "images" were not highly valued anywhere in the E Mediterranean at the time. The graven images were essentially symbols of legitimacy for ancient political regimes in which the differences between gods and kings were always problematic and vague. As such, the images were incompatible with the value system of a community based not upon a monopoly of force but upon an ethical and moral consensus. But perhaps it is the final "commandment" that most powerfully underscores the fact that the *morale* of the early Israelite community (i.e., its ability to act consistently over a period of time and to meet crises effectively) was not dependent upon any political instruments of social control: how can any human control system hope to legislate against covetousness?

Thus arose the celebrated biblical "monotheism," the product not of philosophers and technical theologians but of people who could plainly see that the careful adherence to the stated will of a single God could guarantee community morale only if other competing value systems (represented by "other gods") were rejected as thoroughly as is humanly possible. In turn, this value system could become an operative and tangible reality only so long as a sufficient number of people accepted the suzerainty of Yahweh, so that together they could offer one another some measure of protection and security from those whose value systems were still symbolized by the old state idols of pagan imperialism. The idolatry of the political state and its symbolism of "graven images" of Baals and kings were incompatible with the sovereign rule of Yahweh (i.e., the kingdom of God).

3. History of the Sinai Covenant Tradition. Of course, we should legitimately question the extent to which such a LB/early Iron Age enactment (i.e., such a premonarchic covenant) actually succeeded in exorcising old attachments and in effecting a new self-understanding. For some it no doubt did succeed both deeply and permanently, and at least enough people were sufficiently committed to it so that this "religious experiment" functioned reasonably well for somewhat more than a century. But even later biblical traditions about the ensuing periods of the judges and the kings are quick to point out how many Israelites "fell back" into the old pagan ways. But the crucial point is that at one time *in history,* in the absence of any competing sociopolitical organizations, such a covenant was the practical and functional norm of Israelite self-definition. As such, this covenant would leave a lasting (indeed a permanent) imprint on Israelite traditions and self-understanding, even though at specific times and in particular places (e.g., Jerusalem during the monarchic period) it either failed to have a decisive impact or was grossly distorted.

Nevertheless, even centuries later in Jerusalem the Deuteronomistic Historian, attempting to "reconstruct" a premonarchic period that he little understood, could be found characteristically describing Israelite apostasy in the same sentence that he would mention the past favors of Yahweh (Judg 2:12; 8:33–35). The net effect of this juxtaposition is to characterize the Israelites not simply as sinners but as *ungrateful* sinners. Even though the language of these passages is unquestionably Deuteronomistic and therefore quite late, this motif juxtaposing covenant violation with past favor reflects an ideological matrix quite foreign to the Iron Age loyalty oaths, and quite at home in LB Age treaties. The only conclusion is that this motif was already deeply embedded within traditions about the premonarchic period centuries before it fell into the hands of the Deuteronomistic Historian, and that the latter had little choice but to pass it on. If he considered it important to characterize Israelite covenant trespass in terms of ingratitude (and apparently he did; cf. 2 Kgs 17:7, 35–40; 21:15), he got this idea not from the Assyrian loyalty oaths of his day but because he learned it ultimately from the old Israelite traditions themselves.

Because both the *form* of Assyrian loyalty oaths and the *ideological matrix* to which they appeal is radically different from that of the LB treaties, two major problems would arise if we accepted the recent argument that biblical covenant concepts originated later under the influence of these loyalty oaths. First, how do we account for the presence of certain LB treaty elements in the biblical tradition complex, treaty elements that are not present in the Assyrian loyalty oaths (e.g., the historical prologue and the blessings; see C.1.a and C.1.c above)? Second, how did there arise in Israel a matrix of covenant ideas not reflected in the Assyrian loyalty oaths (e.g., the motif of a relationship based on gratitude and a sense of obligation to values shared by suzerain and vassal alike)? Or if these covenant elements and ideas arose *later than* the Assyrian period, how and from where did they emerge?

On balance, more problems are solved and fewer ones are raised by acknowledging that Hebrew covenant ideas emerged with the formation of the society itself in the premonarchic period and were adaptations of patterns of thought that even then were already centuries old.

This is not to say that this premonarchic covenant tradition was unaffected by the proliferation of Assyrian loyalty oaths of the later Iron Age. The extent to which the state of Judah was thoroughly integrated into ANE culture is indicated by the fact that these Assyrian loyalty oaths *did* have an impact on how some Judeans (particularly in the Jerusalem royal establishment) came to think of their own covenant traditions. In short, over the course of the Iron Age the tradition that God had established a covenant with Israel at Sinai (and at Shechem) was revised and transformed in such a way as to erase gradually (but not completely) the increasingly archaic suzerainty treaty features of that covenant. In the process this Sinaitic tradition was reformulated more along the lines of the prevalent oath-taking procedures of the later period (reflected particularly in the increasing emphasis on curses). In fact, it was precisely this late misunderstanding and reformulation that has led some scholars recently to the mistaken conclusion that the Israelite covenant tradition was actually *created* in this historical context of the Assyrian Empire and derived from its loyalty oaths. It is probably true that the concept of covenant obligations to Yahweh was not taken seriously by the political establishment of either

Israel or Judah until the ephemeral attempt of Josiah to return to the past (see F.1 below), but it is simply wrong to conclude on this basis that earlier traditions of covenant did not exist, particularly outside the royal establishment. Some of those earlier covenant features are still reflected imperfectly in those later texts (see C.1 above and E below), a fact that cannot be explained away by appealing to some Iron Age "inspired creativity." See also MOSAIC COVENANT.

D. The Divine Charter

1. The Nature of the Divine Charter. A charter is, among other definitions, "a written grant of rights by a sovereign." This definition (deriving ultimately from English political history) applies remarkably well to three biblical themes that have traditionally been regarded as "covenants," but which now should rather be reclassified as "charters." (Even in modern American usage, the term "charter" has also come to mean "pact, treaty" among other things.)

The term "charter" is used here to refer to a number of ANE and biblical motifs wherein a deity or group of deities presents some special privilege, power, or status to a human being, almost always a king. There does not seem to be any specific literary form involved; rather the ANE charters are mythological statements about the actions of the gods who characteristically confer the power of kingship upon a successful warrior. The historical background of such concepts is doubtless to be found in military history. The king had succeeded in expanding his economic and political power over realms remote from his home base (which was usually a city-state). In such circumstances, his legitimacy could not possibly rest upon the will of the governed (including the conquered!); now it had to be presented as being based upon the decision of the supernatural powers—especially those identified with his home base.

In the order of their emergence in the developing biblical tradition, these three "charters" are the promise to David (2 Samuel 7), the "covenant" of Abraham (Genesis 15), and the "covenant" of Noah (Gen 9:8–17). Only the latter two narratives specifically designate the divine promise as a "covenant." Although the promise to David is not termed a "covenant" *(bĕrît)* in the narrative of 2 Samuel, it is so designated in the associated traditions (and doubtless royal rituals) recorded in Psalm 89 (see vv 28 and 34; cf. also 2 Sam 23:5). See also DAVIDIC COVENANT. This use of the word *bĕrît* to include now a unilateral divine promise has resulted in enormous confusion in the modern scholarly world, as it probably did in the ancient world as well. (This is another example of the confusion that results from a failure to recognize the fact that verbal classifications often bring together into the same category very diverse historical phenomena simply because they share some important *formal* trait—in this case the fact that a promise is supported by a sworn oath.)

In all three of these biblical traditions—in sharp contrast to the Sinai covenant—it is God, not human beings, who is bound by oath. In all three, some promise is given: first to David and his dynasty (that they would enjoy perpetual rule, 2 Sam 7:12–16), then to Abraham and his offspring (that all Israel would possess the land, Gen 15:18–19), then to Noah and all those on the ark (that all creation need never fear another flood, Gen 9:8–11). The three exhibit an increasing (and very important) transition from covenant as a historical enactment that furnished the foundation of a community to a simple ideological (or theological) assertion. The first two especially presuppose not only an existing *religious community* already ostensibly in a relationship with Yahweh, but also a specific *sociopolitical and economic organization* that is given legitimacy in the context of the existing historical situation. In other words, unlike the ANE treaties and the Sinai covenant, nothing really new is created in any of these "charters"; they are all merely ideological legitimizations of the existing status quo—an expression in traditional theological terms of the value system of the dominant power structure that in the first place created the narratives and in the second place profited by their claims.

The source of this political/religious "charter" tradition is not far to seek (Weinfeld 1970). The old Amorite theory of kingship must certainly have had an elaborate ideology concerning this divine charter. It is specifically stated in the prologue to the Code of Hammurapi (*ANET,* 164–65), and is illustrated on that famous stele as well as elsewhere in ancient Mesopotamian and in Iron Age Syro-Hittite art. Always it is the deity of the king who grants to the king the symbols of sovereignty, for he is the "chosen" one of the committee of gods who in the first place established the kingship as a divine institution.

2. The Davidic Charter. In view of the significant Amorite cultural influence in the city of Jerusalem itself (Ezek 16:3), there is little reason to doubt that the prophet Nathan, in proclaiming the divine promise to David (2 Sam 7:1–17) at the outset of the monarchic period, was simply applying the age-old Amorite political theology of Jebus (now Jerusalem) to its new king (and now in the name of the new king's god, Yahweh). The historical conditions that brought about this fateful ideological development are clearly described, but typically the connections are not delineated—the ancient writer assumed that everyone knew these connections.

David had first become king by two distinct covenants enacted by the two major demographic groups of ancient Israel (each accompanied by the attendant rite of anointing): first with Judah in the S (2 Sam 2:4, though no covenant is specified), and subsequently with the elders of Israel in the N (2 Sam 5:1–3; clearly a suzerainty treaty in form!). Though it is precarious to draw conclusions from the very slight hints of evidence that we have, it is possible to argue that the ritual act of anointing signified the transfer of authority from a superior to his designated agent. For this reason, David's authority over all of the tribes of Israel had been confirmed by covenant.

There were two reasons it was politically necessary subsequently to promote an additional divine covenant that superseded these earlier tribal covenants. First, there had to be some ideological resolution of the latent conflict between the N and S tribes. Both groups in the first place presumably existed because of a prior commitment to Yahweh. Despite this, the narrative goes out of its way to emphasize the fact that the old antagonisms between them continued. Subsequently, however, each group on its own had presumably sworn allegiance to David; although it was an allegiance that could be abrogated for good cause (see 1 Kgs 12:16), both had nevertheless agreed on one fundamental thing: David should rule. Thus, common sense led to the inevitable conclusion that only in the king could the regional, tribal conflict be transcended: this king must therefore represent the will of Yahweh, who would want his people to be one. Nothing would so powerfully affirm this conviction as would Nathan's oracle (2 Samuel 7).

Second, as a result of his military conquests David now ruled over a population comprising far more than the original twelve tribes of Yahwist villagers. His realm now included most, if not all, of the old lowland Canaanite urban power centers that had never been incorporated into the community of Yahweh, and only now were beginning to recover from the ravages of the LB/early Iron Age transition period. These populations (as conditioned as they were to the inevitability and the propriety of ritually reinforced political organizations) could not possibly have had any understanding of the Mosaic tradition, or necessarily any sympathy with its belief that community can proceed directly from the will of God unmediated through ritual or political organizations. Since David and his son-successor Solomon could not afford to alienate further these subjugated peoples, it proved fortunate that in the religious ideology of Jerusalem there existed a type of (Amorite?) sanctification of political authority that David and Solomon could promulgate and that the non-Yahwist populations could comprehend (however grudgingly). This ideology persisted in Jerusalem for centuries after the death of Solomon, and we have every reason to believe that after the schism of 922 B.C. a similar type of ideology was adapted also in the N kingdom to legitimize the various regimes that ruled there over the next two centuries.

Thus the divine charter to David was introduced in an attempt to transcend these two political antipathies. By the proclamation that the king (and his dynasty) was established on the throne in perpetuity by Yahweh himself, it was hoped that the king's vulnerability to the tribal rivalries and conflicts would be greatly reduced. To the conquered Canaanite cities—as well as to the pagan, urban population of Jerusalem—the ideology was normal procedure just as it had been for probably a millennium or more. As far as the Jerusalem regime was concerned, the political doctrine was evidently successful. But although such pious propaganda was normal procedure in antiquity, it was also normal to expect that the behavior of the ruling regime would correspond to the reasonable expectations of the citizenry. Upon the death of Solomon, Rehoboam, his successor, refused to meet those expectations; therefore he was unable to retain the allegiance of the N population (whether Yahwist or urban pagan) and the Israelite kingdom split into two (2 Kgs 12:1–20).

The divine charter theology and literary motif are classified as a "covenant" in the biblical tradition simply because in these three traditions of promises (to David, Abraham, and Noah) it is Yahweh who swears to perform certain acts for the benefit of the recipient *and his descendants* in perpetuity. In all three cases, the recipient is *not* bound by oath, though it is clear that, in the case of the Davidic charter, later tradition attempted lamely to introduce the concept of accompanying conditions, i.e., "obedience to the Torah," that was itself the product of several centuries of development *after* the time of David and Solomon (cf. 2 Sam 7:14b, which is almost unanimously attributed to the Deuteronomistic Historian of the 7th or 6th century B.C.; an even more feeble attachment of obligations to the Davidic charter is evident in 1 Kgs 6:12; see also Ps 89:31–34—Eng vv 30–33; cf. also 1 Kgs 8:25 which is unquestionably [post-]exilic and now sees the Davidic charter as *entirely* conditional).

Despite this, the priority of the Sinaitic covenant structure is still evident in the fact that even this divine charter theology must include some provision for *witnesses* to enforce the stipulations. Just as the people themselves could be witnesses in the Sinai covenant, so also in the divine charter Yahweh is represented as swearing "by himself" as witness (Ps 89:36—Eng v 35), since obviously another deity could not serve in this capacity.

In summary, the Sinai covenant was a historical enactment involving two parties, Yahweh being represented by his agent Moses. In contrast, the divine charter was not something done in a two-party agreement at all, but in the case of David it was simply a prophet's (Nathan's) formal verbal proclamation of a message (privately) received from Yahweh. Similarly, the "covenants" with Abraham and Noah were not functional or historical realities but rather literary ideological motifs undoubtedly superimposed on ancient traditions.

3. The "Covenant" with Abraham. The basic biblical tradition about Abraham stems from the period of the united monarchy, for there is no trace of it in the premonarchic biblical sources (the archaic poetry in Genesis 49; Exodus 15; Numbers 23–24; Deuteronomy 32 and 33), and in those sources it is characteristically Jacob (= Israel), not Abraham, who serves as the common ancestor (cf. also Deut 26:5). On the other hand, recent attempts to see the Abraham traditions as originating late in the monarchy (or even later) have proved unconvincing, if only because they can just as well be explained in terms of a *renewed* interest in those traditions during the later periods (see especially the P materials). As a product of the period of the united monarchy, the covenant with Abraham is a part of that same ideological matrix that brought about the Davidic charter. In fact, it so closely resembles the Davidic charter as to justify the conclusion that they both ultimately come from the same source (see Clements 1967). In its original form, that source was probably the old Canaanite traditions of Jebusite Jerusalem, though certainly the tradition had a long and complex history before it was adapted by biblical writers.

It is probable that the Abrahamic covenant itself went through at least two versions, and more probably three (Mendenhall 1987). The original, Davidic version was not preserved after the demise of David's dynasty, and therefore it must remain hypothetical. In it the divine promise would have been to Abraham and his (Hebronite?) dynasty to which the Davidic dynasty could easily attach itself by the well-known ancient genealogical techniques (note also the association with Hebron and kingship in 2 Sam 2:1–5:5; 15:7–10; and even Josh 12:10).

With the discrediting of the monarchy at the fall of Jerusalem (586 B.C.), this charter had to be revised and depoliticized; now the *population as a whole* became the recipients of the promise as in Genesis 15, where the "seed of Abraham" is now much more than merely David and his descendants. (This transference of motifs from the ruling dynasty to the population as a whole is also illustrated in the development of the idea of the "chosen" of Yahweh. Originally it designated the king or high priest, but in the exilic/postexilic period it became increasingly applied to the community at large ["the chosen people"]). Despite these later revisions, the archaic source of the narrative in Genesis 15 is illustrated by the fact that only here is the divine charter "sealed" by a ritual form: the eerie vision of the smoking fire pot and flaming torch passing between the parts of the sacrificed animals (v 17) represents the manifestation of deity by which the deity identified himself with the slaughtered animals as a guarantee of the reliability of the promise. The similar ritual attested in Jer 34:18 indicates that this was a very archaic ritual form for the ratification of a covenant.

Yahweh's promise of the land (Gen 15:18–21) had nothing to do with the ancient Israelite enjoyment of their allotments under the Sinai covenant, which took place some two hundred years prior to David; rather, it was a religious legitimizing of the Davidic empire that had already been established by military force, and is specifically described in vv 18–21 as extending from the border of Egypt to the Euphrates River, most of it never having been Israelite.

The final adaptation of the Abraham tradition is illustrated in Genesis 17, where the covenant is sealed by the ritual of circumcision—a marker that designates the recipient of the promise. From this time on, into the postbiblical Jewish tradition, "circumcision" and "covenant" became virtually identical (the late Heb term *bĕrît* having both meanings). The historical context of this late reuse of the Abraham tradition seems to have been the continuity of the royal/priestly religious tradition in the postexilic period. This is suggested by the emphasis upon the ritual importance of circumcision, a practice that evidently had no particular religious significance in earlier times, since it is not even mentioned in early law collections (no doubt it was originally a folk custom, since it was very widespread in the ANE from the Chalcolithic of Mesopotamia on). It was especially emphasized in the prophecies of the priest of exile, Ezekiel (44:6–9). In this context, "covenant" is hardly a functional reality that creates community by transcending old parochialisms, but is itself merely a formal, ritual demarcation of a particular preexisting group.

4. The "Covenant" of Noah. The narrative of the covenant established with Noah, his descendants, and all the occupants of the ark (Gen 9:8–17) perhaps illustrates the ultimate demise of the "covenant" tradition. The historical development of the covenant from a constitutive act instrumental in creating a new society and a correspondingly new value system in the time of Moses has, in this late narrative, become little more than a theological motif or literary device by which to confer religious value upon that which already existed, namely, the orderly process of the natural world. Even the oath that upheld a promise is gone, but in its place there is simply the *sign* that serves to remind God of his promise. In place of the rich complexity of the LB suzerainty treaty tradition and its function as a vain attempt to create orderly and peaceful relationships between political entities, the covenant has become a mere word-label giving religious value to an old folkloristic "explanation" of the rainbow.

E. Covenant Traditions in the Prophets

1. Continuity of the Sinai Covenant. On the basis of the politically motivated traditions of "covenants" associated with David and (originally) Abraham (as well as the subsequent politically motivated covenants of Josiah and Nehemiah; see F below), it would be erroneous to conclude that the form, purpose, and ideological matrix of the old premonarchic suzerainty tradition was everywhere forgotten or suppressed. As in any complex society, there was great social and ideological diversity within Israel and Judah, and it would be foolish to assume that the significant transformations of the covenant traditions in the hands of politically ambitious Jerusalem bureaucrats were accepted without question or protest in the rural hinterland where religious values and social processes tended to work differently. Indeed, if any vestiges of the old Sinai covenant tradition should be preserved relatively unadulterated, we would expect to see these emanating from the more conservative villages of the countryside. There the pattern of social life proceeded along lines not much different from that of the early Iron Age, except for the noteworthy intrusions of the kings' tax collectors; and in those villages one might not be too surprised to find an ongoing dissatisfaction with the basic premise of the (Israelite or Judean) state: namely, that meaningful community life must proceed from political bases.

However "theoretical" all this might seem, two points deserve mention. First, the introspective reflections of ancient village agriculturalists and pastoralists are rarely preserved by the "official" religious specialists (priests, scribes, and other functionaries), who tend to dismiss such reflections as unsophisticated and "backward." It is therefore not surprising that most of the biblical narratives dealing with covenant traditions come to us mediated through the minds and pens of various (usually Jerusalem-educated) scribes whom scholars usually identify as J, D, P, DH, "Early Source," "Late Source," etc. Second, what *is* surprising is that the Bible preserves the utterances of certain "prophetic" individuals, a good number of whom came from small rural villages (Tekoa, Moresheth, Anathoth—indeed, Isaiah of Jerusalem is the anomaly!) and who encountered notable opposition from "establishment" officials. Nevertheless, it is within the Iron Age oracles of Amos, Micah, Jeremiah, and even Isaiah that we can find vestiges of the old Sinai suzerainty treaty.

These individuals were neither historiographers intent on recounting the role of covenant in premonarchic Israel (but cf. Jer 7:22–23), nor systematic theologians intent on outlining the various formal elements of premonarchic Israelite covenant theology. However, within their oracles we can discern not only surviving LB covenant forms but, more importantly, a surviving matrix of ideas about covenant that has antecedents in the Bronze Age.

Above, we noted that the LB treaties and some biblical traditions about covenant provide for certain formal procedures by which the suzerain declares the covenant to be broken and the vassal now to be susceptible to the imposition of the curses. In this regard we must examine briefly one recurrent procedural form often used in prophetic utterances: the *rîb*, "indictment, lawsuit." Probably the earliest and most dramatic illustration of such a procedure is preserved in Deuteronomy 32, although the date of this poem is much debated. (Decades ago Albright and Eissfeldt independently argued for an 11th-century date, but some recent studies [*CMHE*, 264, n.193] have unconvincingly opted for a later date.) Regardless of its date, the poem illustrates a theological interpretation of historical processes incorporating virtually every single element of the old suzerainty treaties described above. This literary convention—which begins with an appeal to witnesses (heaven and earth) to hear the case, which recites the previous divine favors conferred upon the "defendant" (i.e., the "vassal"), which describes the defendant's subsequent violation of obligation, and which then announces the punishment—was undoubtedly a well-known form already by the time it was used by both Isaiah (chap. 1) and Micah (6:1–8) toward the end of the 8th century B.C. (see Hillers 1969, chap. 6). The entire structure presupposes that a covenant relationship had existed and was now being abrogated by the behavior of those subject to it. In short, the pattern of ideas represented in the *rîb* had to have existed long before these prophets made use of it, otherwise their contemporaries would not have had the slightest idea what the "message" was within the prophets' words. Simply stated, the prophets of the monarchic period did not invent the *rîb* lawsuit form.

But aside from the formal similarities between the *rîb* and the old suzerainty treaties, the most constant (and specifically biblical) motif shared by the old covenant and the later prophets is the inseparable link between the receipt of past benefits and the consequent obligations binding upon the recipients. The *rîb* form is entirely dependent upon this motif. Insofar as it makes appeal to one's sense of gratitude and obligation as a basis for (re-)establishing a covenant bond, the *rîb* exhibits an ideological matrix similar to that of the LB suzerainty treaties. Theologically, it means that divine "grace" precedes and becomes the foundation for human obedience to the divine will, a will that is revealed most clearly in the experience of "grace" itself and not in some fixed code of social and legal norms. (This lies at the heart of the Christian insistence that "gospel" supersedes "law.") Morally and psychologically, it implies that persons under covenant are capable of recognizing the fact that individually and corporately they have received benefits in their past that they have in no way earned. It furthermore implies that it is the good things in life that they have received in the past (and *not* some politically determined, legally defined, and socially enforced set of formal patterns of behavior) that provide the basis for defining the good they hope to realize in their future choices in community life and in their dealings with other people. It is probably also with regard to this matrix of ideas that we can begin to appreciate the well-known prophetic tendency to think of covenant obligations more broadly in terms of "social justice" than narrowly in terms of "sacred rites" (cf. Deut 24:17–22, esp. vv 18 and 22).

Since the obligations were to the giver of the covenant they were binding upon the individual no matter where and in what context he may find himself: they were not and could not be mere duties to obey culturally or politically prescribed norms and laws. This ethical transcending of political legal systems and ritual cultic systems had as its inevitable correlative the fact that normal social contrasts were also transcended: the community of God cannot be identified merely with the usual "tribal mentality" of political and social organizations that are themselves ephemeral within the broader vision of historical perspective: "Are you not like the Ethiopians to me?" (Amos 9:7).

2. Reappropriation of the Davidic Charter. Despite whatever attachments the Hebrew prophets had to the old Sinai covenant ideology, they were aware of the competing Davidic charter ideology being championed by the official establishment in Jerusalem. In some respects that ideology proclaimed certain "truths" that the prophets could in no way endorse, particularly the assertion that God for eternity had chosen to reconstitute his people as mere subjects of yet another political state. But instead of outright declaring the charter to be a fraud, the prophets instead chose to utilize certain superficial elements of the charter but to reconfigure them against the ideological matrix of the premonarchic covenant tradition. Such a practice of removing something (e.g., the tradition of the promise to David) from its original functional context (e.g., legitimizing a dynasty's political claims) and reapplying it in a new and different functional context is here called "reappropriation."

The dates of the few prophetic allusions to the Davidic dynasty and its privileged position have been the subject of much debate. It is clear, however, that regardless of their dates they have a significantly different point of reference than the two major "Davidic charter" texts of 2 Samuel 7 and Psalm 89. For example, Micah's vision of a David redivivus (5:1–3—Eng 5:2–4) clearly implies at least a major disruption of the political organization of Judah, since the "ruler who will come forth" is not identified with Jerusalem (which will lie in ruins, Mic 3:12) but rather with the village of Bethlehem. It is not clear whether or not the "messianic prophecies" of Isa 9:1–6—Eng 9:2–7 and 11:1–10 originally focused their hopes on a political deliverer (e.g., Hezekiah?). However, the hyperbolic language in these texts heightens expectations for things that no political organization can realistically be expected to provide; the net (and perhaps intended?) effect of the prophecies therefore is ironically to delegitimize any *present-day* Davidic claim to be the fulfillment of God's purpose in the anticipation of some *future* (eschatological?) act of divine favor (note the ubiquitous prophetic phrases such as "in that day," "it will come to pass," and "the days are coming").

The major issue must therefore center on whether the Davidic covenant was so pervasive as to shift the major metaphorical image that Israelites had of their covenant relationship with God. The old Sinai covenant tradition claimed that God himself ruled as king over a religiously constituted body *(thesis)*. The Davidic charter tradition held that God guaranteed that in perpetuity the Davidic dynasty would rule over a politically constituted body *(antithesis)*. Prophetic "messianism" envisioned God eventually reestablishing his rule over his people, but through an ideal Davidite who governs not by any of the well-known "material" means of politics but through "spiritual" means and by the force of moral example (Isa 9:6b—Eng 7b; 11:2–5; Mic 5:3a—Eng 4a; Jer 23:5–6) *(synthesis).* One could argue that indeed the metaphor of covenant did shift decisively during the monarchic period, so much so that from that time on any attempt to envision the relationship between God and his people in some way had to accommodate the new synthesis incorporating some (usually vaguely defined) Davidic figure (cf. Jer 30:8–33; 33:14). But for the prophets this Davidic figure could not be simply another in a line of human politicians; and indeed it is noteworthy that not all prophets in their visions of the future benevolent acts of God felt it necessary to refer to any Davidic figure whatsoever. Indeed, when the Davidic figure is mentioned, often he is so vaguely defined that his identity and that of God merge together (cf. Ezek 34:11–16 with 34:23). The impact that this development had on early Christology and its understanding of Christ's person and role in the covenant between God and [new] Israel is transparent [see H.2 below].) Obviously, early rabbinic Judaism and early Christianity had radically different understandings of the meanings and even the significance of this subsequent prophetic synthesis.

The point is that the original blend of form and substance that made the old Sinai covenant uniquely recognizable and compelling began to dissolve during the monarchic period. Leaving aside the metaphysical forces that would naturally undercut any Israelite's ability to remain faithful to the covenant with God, it is noteworthy that all the significant social forces working against such faithfulness emanated from within official circles in Jerusalem. In the first place, the state-sanctioned Davidic charter forced upon the Israelites a competing way of conceptualizing the nature of their relationship with God. One could challenge its legitimacy only at the risk of his/her own life (Jeremiah 26).

In the second place, the bureaucratic scribes of the monarchy so distorted all Sinai traditions that the ideological matrix associated with the premonarchic covenant began to shift significantly. This is most evident in the Exodus traditions themselves, where originally deliverance from Egypt served ideologically to instill a sense of gratitude among Israelites, leading them to feel obligated to reciprocate accordingly in the future *moral* choices they would make in life (note how memory of the Exodus serves this function in the old "law codes" [Exod 22:21–24; 23:9; cf. also Lev 19:33–36; 25:35–38; Deut 15:12–15; 24:17–22]). Indeed, the prophets preserved this matrix, and a prophetic command to "remember" *(zĕkōr)* the Exodus characteristically envisioned such a *moral* response (Mic 6:4–5, 8). But in the hands of official Priestly historiographers, the memory of God's benevolent deeds during the Exodus became increasingly connected with the establishment of the cult, so much so that a Priestly command to "remember" *(zĕkōr)* the Exodus ideologically envisioned a *ritual* response (Exod 13:3–10). The traditions fared no better in the hands of Deuteronomistic historiographers; there the benevolent deeds of God associated with the Exodus became a literary (and ideological) foil against which to portray (stereotypically) an Israel fundamentally ungovernable by God (and therefore legitimately consigned to human rulers and managers? cf. Judg 2:11–12; 1 Sam 8:8–9). With the ideological matrix of the old historical prologue focusing on the Exodus so effectively dismantled, what remained to instill the requisite sense of gratitude among the people? The prophets' ultimate answer was to envision a new and future act of benevolence by God, but one that must be preceded by the dismantling of the political state (Jer 16:14–15).

3. The "New Covenant." The date and authorship of Jeremiah's remarkable prophecy of a "new covenant" (Jer 31:31–34) are controversial and probably indeterminable, but there is no pressing reason to doubt the traditional attribution to Jeremiah himself. The context and content of the prophecy suggest that it comes from a time shortly after the destruction of Jerusalem in 586 B.C. See also NEW COVENANT.

It should first be noted that in the ancient concepts of covenant the ultimate curse for breach of covenant was the destruction and scattering of the body politic with which the covenant initially was formed. This had happened in 586 B.C. Thus the old covenant was no more—theoretically, there was no longer any body politic to which the covenant would apply. Therefore, if there was to be any continuity in the relationships between Yahweh and the former members of the body politic, it would have to be through the enactment of a new covenant with the people, not with a political organization through its king.

Thus the prophecy of the new covenant actually presupposed conditions much like those at the end of the LB Age, the time of the old Sinai covenant, in which there was likewise no body politic with which the covenant could be established. It was *persons,* not social organizations, who would receive the benefits and accept the obligations involved in the relationship with God. The "house of Judah and the house of Israel" (31:31) are deliberate uses of terminology deriving from family life, not from that of political institutions.

The substance of the prophecy itself emphasizes the discontinuity from the old covenant traditions. There is barely any formal similarity to the old Sinai covenant structure. As always, the covenant is granted by the divine sovereign, but there is no historical prologue—the destruction of Jerusalem and Judah was doubtless too painful a memory. Instead there is a prediction of the *future* acts of God, which consist not of the normal expectations of riches, territory, long life, health, and progeny, but rather of "forgiveness" (i.e., the restoration of a broken relationship; v 34). The restoration of the relationship with God is the only benefit mentioned. There are neither oath, nor curses and blessings, nor witnesses, nor any of the paraphernalia of externally enacted covenants (deposit, public reading, ratification rituals, etc.).

The single element of the Sinai old covenant retained in this "new covenant" is simply the stipulations (which are characteristically absent in divine charters). But no longer are they a set of prohibitions and injunctions, no code of laws or externally enforced and legalistically defined body of "commandments, statutes, and ordinances" such as depicted in the Deuteronomistic History. Instead the *tôrâ* ("teaching") of Yahweh "will be written on their hearts" (not on tablets of stone) and "placed in their inward parts" (v 33). It is a description of the complete internalization of the divine will that makes unnecessary the entire machinery of external enforcement.

Even more astonishing is the abrogation of the entire paraphernalia of religious indoctrination: "they shall no more teach each man his neighbor and each man his brother, saying 'Know Yahweh' " (v 34). Instead of the deposit and periodic reading of the covenant text, the knowledge of the divine will is deposited within the conscience of the members of the community. Special training in theology, doctrine, or *tôrâ* is irrelevant, since "they will all know me, from the least of them to the greatest. . . ." Thus the knowledge of God cannot be identified with the accumulated written corpus of prestigious scribes or theologians: the knowledge of God possessed by the most humble is on a par with that of the elite. The community thus envisioned is not one subject to human social control but one that can only be monitored and maintained by the deity himself. In this regard, the vision and hope associated with this "new covenant" draw deeply from that originally associated with the old.

F. Later Biblical "Covenants"

1. The "Covenant" of Josiah. The narrative of Josiah's reform in 2 Kings 22–23 gives considerable detail concerning not only the events leading up to it but also to the royal acts that ensued; however, it contains virtually nothing concerning the nature of the "covenant" that Josiah made (23:3). Nevertheless, there are sufficient details in the narrative to make it impossible to regard this reform as the basis or origin of the OT covenant tradition. To the contrary, it is presented not as a *novum* (a creative writer could have easily depicted a theophany in 2 Kings 22) but precisely as a *reform,* which by its very nature consists of a return to earlier traditions, or at least what were thought to be earlier traditions.

The chain of events began with the discovery in the Jerusalem temple of a "Book of the Law" (*sēper hattôrâ;* 2 Kgs 22:8–10), which is also called the "Book of the Covenant" (*sēper habbĕrît;* 2 Kgs 23:2–3). The king's distress upon hearing the words of the book indicates in the first place that the contents were previously unknown to him—and presumably unknown also to his whole bureaucracy, since in order to authenticate the document his bureaucrats had to turn to an otherwise obscure wife of a minor functionary resident in the city, who was known to be a "prophetess" (22:13–14).

The second and most important aspect of the king's distress is the fact that the entire procedure was carried out in order to *escape* the curses for violation of covenant that were evidently included in the document that had been found (2 Kgs 22:13). It is this fact that makes it impossible to regard Josiah's action as a mere loyalty oath patterned after Assyrian models. The latter is the procedure by which a vassal initially *becomes* subject to the curses for disobedience. Josiah, however, learned from the "Book of the Covenant" that they were *already* subject to the curses because of past disobedience to a covenant that was currently in effect and binding (even though they had been ignorant of its content). To avoid the curses it is merely necessary to obey the stipulations, which in the case of the Deuteronomic law conveniently enough demanded the extermination of any religiously or ritually based potential rival to his regime (e.g., Deut 12:1–14).

The narrative tells us that Josiah assembled the population to hear all the words of the "Book of the Covenant": at first it was the elders of Judah and Jerusalem (23:1), then it was all the men of Judah and the inhabitants of Jerusalem (v 2). The king then "made a covenant" to obey the commands in the Book of the Law, "and all the people joined in the covenant" (v 3). There is nothing in the narrative to indicate that the procedure was a "covenant" other than the fact that it is labeled as such. There is no reference to an oath, other than that implied in the phrase "to make a covenant." There is no evidence whatever of the old conviction that the ground for obedience was simple gratitude for benefits that had already been received; instead there is simply a concern to escape the curses for disobedience. There is no reference to any ritual or symbolic action that made the covenant binding, which seems to have been a requisite even in the Assyrian treaties of the time. All that is certain is that the king made some public commitment to obey the words of a document found in the temple, and that the people under the king made a similar commitment. In fact, the procedure more properly should be designated as a "vow," since there are not two parties to the process (other than possibly the king and people). The evidence thus seems to justify the conclusion that in Josiah's time "making a covenant" amounted to little more than the repetition of some verbal formula. In more modern terminology, it was simply royal legislation made binding by royal command, but ratified in some way by the assembled population's public promise to obey. It is small wonder that earlier Israelite traditions of covenant suffered under the pens of (Deuteronomistic) scribes who possessed such a limited understanding of what a "covenant" was.

It is quite probable that Josiah's reform was a politically inspired exploitation of an old religious tradition for the purpose of reestablishing old political ambitions (the empire of David) and destroying the religious institutions of any potential political rivals, whether of Israel in the N or of Judah in the S. The wholesale slaughter of the priests of the N shrines (23:20) is reflected in the Deuteronomistic concept that Moses had commanded the utter destruction of the pagan nations of the land (Deut 7:2, 16; 3:12–18). The empire of David was also marked by such wholesale murder of foreigners (1 Kgs 11:15–16, 24).

It should not be surprising that the prophets at that time (and later) barely, if at all, mention this major religio-political event that was carried out by monarchic bureaucrats who evidently had no real understanding of (much less any real commitment to) the religious tradition that derived from the premonarchic period. The reform was superficial and short-lived: after the untimely death of Josiah at the hands of Pharaoh Neco (the direct consequence of Josiah's ambitious dabbling in international politics), the situation in Jerusalem reverted to the normal pluralistic political ideology and policy that had existed previously and that in two short decades would lead inevitably to the destruction of Jerusalem and Judah, just as the prophets had predicted. Even more unfortunate because of its perpetual confusion of religion with politics, however, was the fact that Josiah's hybridized ideas about the religious foundations of ancient Israel—canonized in the Deuteronomistic History—became the "normative" way that much of subsequent Judaism and Christianity (mis)understood the "Old Testament" tradition of Sinai.

2. The "Covenant" of Nehemiah. The latest exemplar of a "covenant" in ancient Israel is narrated in Nehemiah 9–10. Although most, but not all, of the motifs in this narrative have antecedents in earlier OT traditions, the entire description justifies the conclusion that with this episode we have entered an entirely different cultural world in which the underlying concepts and values of the old covenant of Sinai were completely foreign.

As in the covenant of Josiah, here also it is the highest political authority—Nehemiah, the governor appointed by the Persian Empire (10:2—Eng 10:1)—who exercises the initiative in the covenant making. A sort of "historical prologue" still appears, but in this case it is a long prayer by the priest Ezra, who is reminding *God* (!) of all his prior mighty acts (9:6–31). Curiously enough, with this historical narrative (a sort of "canonical version" of the history of Israel beginning now, of course, with Abraham), the prayer combines a repeated litany of covenant violations derived from the old *rîb* structure. The major purpose of the historical prologue/prayer seems to be a theodicy: to show that Yahweh was right in bringing all those curses upon the disobedient society (9:33–35). It certainly has nothing to do with the original purpose of historical prologues: reminding *the people* of past benefits received for the purpose of instilling in them a sense of gratitude as the motivation for future obedience.

Instead it is plainly stated that the reason for entering into the covenant is the fact that the Judeans' economic resources were being tapped by a foreign government in the form of taxes (Neh 9:36–10:1—Eng 9:36–38). This unfortunate situation was seen to be caused by their failure to obey the laws of the Torah; therefore they entered into covenant to remedy this regrettable situation. The motivation for the vow of obedience is thus very similar to that behind Josiah's reform, though in the case of Josiah it was fear of future calamity that prompted the covenant to obey the Deuteronomic law code, while here it is the concern to escape continued subjugation by a foreign empire. In both instances the "covenants" were entirely political undertakings that show concerns only for the political autonomy and ethnic exclusiveness of the society and for the ritual necessities that accompany it (10:33–40—Eng 10:32–39).

Yahweh had nothing to do with the entire procedure except to be the passive recipient of Ezra's long reminder of what he had done in times gone by (the text does not even indicate whether God was moved to respond to this reminder). There are not two parties to this "covenant," unless they be the governor Nehemiah and the rest of the people who are listed in a markedly hierarchical order of decreasing social status. Neh 10:30—Eng 10:29 states that the people were to "enter into a curse and an oath," but no oath formula or ritual enactment is mentioned. The witnesses are completely absent; instead the notables of the time set a seal upon what seems to have been a written document (10:1—Eng 9:38).

By the time of Nehemiah the evolution of the covenant (and of the word *bĕrît*) had run full course from the actual and constitutive foundation of a community to a theological concept to little more now than a ritual form and legal document. In the process the transition was also made from a population seeking through the acts of God a "better" way than that of the economically and ethically bankrupt political empires to a group now ambitious for political power and prestige, for whom deity apparently was (as in the LB Age) a mere symbol for the body politic, legitimizing both its system of enforced legal norms and the social functionaries who presided over it. In some respects this transformation marks the end of "Israelite religion" (in all its complexity) and the rise of a distinctive and new religion called "Judaism" (which understood itself to be a continuation of Israelite Yahwism, and which itself underwent many transformations in the following centuries; see H.1 below).

G. Other Covenant Traditions

1. The Covenant Banquet. Eating and drinking together has been such a universal expression of social solidarities of various sorts that it is not surprising to find common meals appearing very frequently in connection with the creation of covenants, both in the ANE and in the biblical narratives. Their specific association with covenants, however, seems to be a rather archaic cultural trait. In the ANE there are references to such eating and drinking in the Mari documents, interestingly enough, referring specifically to the partaking of bread and (presumably) wine as well as anointing with oil as symbolic acts sealing important legal transactions (ARMT 8: 13). Similarly, in the problematic narrative of Genesis 14, the king of Salem brings forth bread and wine, though there seems to be little or no context for the act—the narrative is evidently only a fragment.

In the LB Age the Amarna Letters include one from the king of Egypt to his vassal king of Amurru, vigorously upbraiding him for having made a covenant with an enemy of the king by eating and drinking with him (EA 162: 22–25). In Gen 26:26–33, Isaac and Abimelech made a nonaggression pact that is represented as a parity treaty, in that both swore oaths, but the oath taking is preceded the evening before by a feast prepared by Isaac. A similar treaty of peace with a related meal is described in Gen 31:43–54 as having been enacted by Jacob and Laban, where mutual nonaggression is combined with a stipulation forbidding Jacob to mistreat Laban's daughters or take additional wives.

One of the several narratives of the Sinai event seems to have been inspired by this kind of covenant. In Exod 24:9–11 seventy of the elders of Israel went up the mountain to eat and drink in the presence of Yahweh, "and Yahweh did not lay a hand on them." The covenant with the Gibeonites narrated in Joshua 9 seems to have been a similar sort of peace covenant that was obtained by fraud and subterfuge; their offer of (moldy) bread and (old) wine was accepted by the Israelites, and the eating and the drinking seem to be related to the ratification of the peace covenant (vv 11–15). It is typical that the oath sworn was regarded as binding even though fraud was involved; instead the pact was downgraded from a parity treaty to a suzerainty treaty in which the Gibeonites became subservient.

2. Marriage as Covenant. The narrative of the covenant between Jacob and Laban mentioned above (Gen 31:43–54) seems to combine two quite distinct acts, one of which involves marriage relationships. Nowhere else in ANE literature is marriage associated with a sworn oath, although it is certainly the most common social institution by which new relationships are created. However, it is interesting to note Malachi's use of the word "covenant" (Heb *bĕrît*) in connection with references to "the wife of (one's) youth" (2:14–15). There, Yahweh is explicitly acknowledged to be a (third-party) "witness" between the two parties of the marriage, and there are clear allusions to (violated) obligations and to resultant curses (2:13). As we have seen, these elements also appear in LB suzerainty treaties.

Although marriage does not correspond formally to the covenant structure as we know it from LB suzerainty treaties, it was an important metaphor for expressing relationships that could also be expressed in political terms. For example, in biblical Hebrew verbs like "love" (*ʾāhab*) and "know" (*yādaʿ*) have nuances of meaning in both conjugal and political contexts (Moran 1963; Huffmon 1966), and biblical prophets often characterized Israelite foreign policy as a series of illicit sexual relations. Therefore it is not surprising that, in addition to the suzerainty treaty analogy, the relationship between God and Israel was also very frequently viewed as analogous to that of husband and wife (Hosea 1–3; Jer 31:32; Ezekiel 16). This metaphor continued in use not only in early rabbinic Judaism but also in NT Christology, where Christ is portrayed as "bridegroom" and the Church as "bride."

In conclusion, these other covenant traditions (banquets and marriage) are noteworthy because they demonstrate how pervasive covenant traditions generally were in the ANE, and how frequently they were utilized in any discussion or presentation of something so fundamental as "community" and "relationships."

H. Postbiblical Developments

In the discussion on Nehemiah (see F.2 above) we noted that by the 5th–4th centuries B.C. the old suzerainty covenant form had been virtually forgotten; even the prophetic *rîb* which was most persistent in preserving (elements of) that form tended to emphasize less the formal components of covenant than the accompanying ideological matrix. Thus, in moving now into a discussion of even later covenant ideas in early Judaism and early Christianity the focus must shift still further away from covenant *forms* and into covenant *ideas;* and in discussing covenant ideas, it must be prepared to distinguish between ideas that were largely *symbolic and rhetorical* and those that were *functional and operational.* In short, the issue now becomes the nature of the early Jewish and early Christian communities themselves: not so much how their traditions formally preserved covenant ideas as how the respective communities themselves were constituted with respect to those ideas.

1. Covenant in Early Judaism. a. Preliminary Remarks. Comparatively little work has been spent on the subject of covenant in early Judaism. Part of the problem is that by the late Hellenistic–early Roman period there was really no such thing as an early "Judaism" in the E Mediterranean world; even within Palestine there were numerous "Judaisms," each claiming to be the legitimate continuation of the people of the God of Israel (perhaps one of the most sharply defined of these being the community revealed in the sectarian documents of Qumran). And yet any discussion of covenant in early Judaism cannot ignore the fact of this marked sectarianism; for if indeed covenant is a device for transcending old parochialisms and factions, then one may reasonably conclude that by the turn of the era it was no longer functioning in this respect. It seems largely to have been symbolic, and there seems to have been simply widespread disagreement as to what specifically it symbolized (i.e., which sect constituted the "true Israel" still in covenant with God?).

Another reason for the comparative lack of study of covenant in early Judaism is that most scholars still seem reluctant to expose one major form of early Judaism—rabbinic Judaism—to any sort of critical "history of religions" investigation. Perhaps there is an underlying fear that, because it is the antecedent of modern Judaism, such critical study will somehow be construed as being "anti-Jewish" (just as the application of this approach to the NT over a century ago was construed as being "anti-Christian"); if so, the reasons for this inhibition are obvious and understandable. Yet if we are to do justice to the history of covenant we cannot avoid subjecting early Judaism to the same level of critical inquiry to which we have subjected ancient Israelite religion. However, we must recognize that such endeavors are still very much in their infancy, and for that reason we offer here in preliminary fashion some of the crucial issues we feel must be addressed critically in any future study not only of covenant in early Judaism but also of the nature of early rabbinic Jewish religion.

First, there is virtually no evidence from the Second Temple period that the notion of "covenant" community was ever effective in transcending existing parochialisms. Indeed, the evidence to the contrary emerges as early as Zerubbabel's unwillingness even to consider searching for "common ground" with the Samaritans, who nonetheless professed devotion to the Judean God (Ezra 4:1–3; note also the tensions with "the people of the land," most of whom were fellow Judeans; see also AM HAʾAREZ). The evidence from the Hellenistic period (books of Maccabees) and the Roman period (especially Josephus) goes even further to document how ineffective *anything* was for transcending the parochialisms that developed *within* Judaism itself. The point to be noted is that in fact the early Judean community (like most of post-Constantinian Christendom) was held together by a socially enforced prestige system, until this degenerated into competing systems within Judaism (as they eventually did within much of Christianity). We shall therefore focus particularly on one system, rabbinic Judaism, that emerged from the debacle of the Jewish War (A.D. 66–70).

b. The Antecedents of Rabbinic Judaism. By tracing itself from Moses and Sinai through the prophets to Ezra and then to subsequent Pharisaic sages *(m. ʾAbot),* rabbinic Judaism formally laid claim to a certain connection with Hebrew covenant thought. Before examining the rabbinic Judaism that is most closely connected with the Mishnah (2d century A.D.) and subsequently with the Talmud, we need to trace this claim backward, examining each "link" in this rabbinic "chain" of tradition.

The Pharisees present a special problem owing to the nature of the historical sources, most of which are either much later (the Mishnah) or demonstrably polemical in tone (the NT). Since the 1960s much research has focused upon the parochial character of the Pharisaic *ḥeber* ("society"), which seems initially to have been based on peculiar class interests of an economic and political sort (Finkelstein 1962: vol. 1, esp. pp. 75–76; Neusner 1973a). It is arguable whether notions of "duty" (a formal equivalent to covenant "obligations"?) were taken more seriously by the Pharisees than by the other sects; however, there can be no doubt that obedience to religious law was paramount in the Pharisaic sect (note the Talmudic reference to "the Pharisee [who says,] 'What is my duty, that I may perform it?' " [*Soṭa* 22a]). It is also noteworthy that some Pharisaic leaders articulated their concept of religious duty more in prophetic than in priestly terms: Rabbi Yohanan ben Zakkai is reported to have said: "We have another atonement as effective as [the temple cult]. And what is it? It is acts of lovingkindness, as it is said, 'For I desire mercy and not sacrifice' " (*ʾAbot R. Nat.* 4; cf. Hos 6:6).

However, Neusner (1973b, esp. pp. 24, 31) notes that for the most part these ideas of obligation were tied in with the Pharisaic sense of "purity," which in fact was morally neutral and unrelated to anything "prophetic." Finkelstein (1962: vol. 1, 31) underscores its parochial character by noting that, when Pharisees were scattered among the various towns and hamlets after the destruction of Jerusalem in A.D. 70, their "rules of purity meant separation from next-door neighbors, [and] refusal to mingle freely with fellow-villagers." If accurate, this suggests that, despite formal, ideological appeals to a "prophetic" sense of ("covenant"?) obligations to an ostensibly transcendent God, in practice the Pharisees were unwilling and therefore unable to transcend existing socioeconomic, political, and ethnic parochialisms (this gap between moral vision and moral practice may in part account for the polemical charges of hypocrisy that the various rival schools within Pharisaism often directed at one another; cf. *b. Ber.* 28a; *Assum. Mos.* 7.4ff.; see also Matt 23:2). The religious obligations *(hălakôt)* were in fact simply a distinctive mark of "in-group" status. As both Finkelstein (1962: vol. 1, 17–20, 266) and Neusner (1973b) point out, and as Josephus' references to the Pharisees seem to confirm (*JW* 1.107–14, 571; 2.162–66; *Ant* 13.171–73, 288–98, 399–418; 17.41–44; 18.11–17), Pharisaic religion in general was a secondary accretion to a group that was primarily constituted by socioeconomic and sociopolitical factors.

Ezra is held to have been the precursor of Pharisaic (and subsequently rabbinic) Judaism, and in that regard he has often been considered a "second Moses" (*b. Sanh.* 21b). If Ezra historically played such a decisive role, then rabbinic Judaism was heir to many of the same sorts of social processes that accompanied the Nehemiah loyalty oath (see F.2 above). In this regard it is noteworthy how in Ezra 9–10 the will of God—i.e., the dynamic equivalent to covenant obligations (intended originally to encourage the transcending of parochialisms)—has for Ezra been reduced to prohibiting intermarriage (reinforcing ethnic parochialisms).

The differences between this understanding of "covenant people" (an endogamous ethnic group) and that reflected earlier in the prophets and still earlier in the Sinai covenant (a unity of diverse tribes/peoples based on shared values) are both obvious and categorical. They perhaps reinforce the conclusion that the reputed links between Ezra and the prophets (and Moses/Sinai) are largely formal and secondary and not substantive or integral; this linkage appears to have been designed at a later time to enhance the prestige (and therefore the authority and power) of rabbinic institutions. (In antiquity the same technique was used by individuals to concoct personal genealogies.)

Early rabbinic Judaism's formal emphasis on the centrality of the Sinai covenant can be adequately understood in light of early rabbinic emphasis on ethnic exclusivity. In the first place, early rabbinic Judaism understandably avoided the prophetic synthesis and reappropriation of the Davidic covenant (see E.2 above) that its chief rival, early Christianity, had embraced and interpreted in light of Jesus. For that reason, it is not surprising that covenant ideas in early rabbinic Judaism characteristically avoided the topics of "messianism" and the Davidic "covenant," and focused instead almost exclusively on the Sinai covenant. In the second place, its understanding of the Sinai covenant (unlike that of the early prophets) was based largely on written Scripture, particularly the canonical Torah, which (as we have seen) depicts the Sinai covenant not as it really was in ancient Israel but as it was later (mis)understood by generations living in a much different (postmonarchic) social context. Chief among these distortions is the canonical sequence itself, which regards the Sinai covenant (Exodus 1–20) as a subsequent event in the history of a community already defined earlier (Genesis 17) in ethnic terms of blood kinship (the covenant of Abraham, understood to refer literally to Abraham's biological offspring; cf. how early Christianity embraced the same canonical sequence but emphasized Abraham's importance in terms of Gen 12:3).

In summarizing the connection between early rabbinic Judaism and earlier biblical covenant ideas, it seems that the chain of transmission in *m. ʾAbot* 1:1 linking rabbinic Judaism to Moses and Mt. Sinai functioned much as the Davidic charter functioned in monarchic Judah: to legitimize an existing social order. The ideological matrix it expresses is actually drawn more from the world of divine charters than from the world of treaties and covenants. This suggests that, if rabbinic authorities realized the historical and *functional* significance of the Sinai covenant (and they probably did not), they chose not to embrace that as a practical means for self-definition and self-understanding. Their covenant ideas did not function practically to articulate a transcendent set of values that could potentially cut across and dissolve old parochialisms as these ideas did in early Israel; indeed they tended to function in just the opposite way—to reinforce and heighten already existing (and increasingly ethnic) parochialisms.

c. Post-Mishnaic Judaism. This is perhaps underscored by rabbinic Judaism's comparative inability to attract converts precisely at a time when the E Mediterranean world was most receptive to monotheism. Instead, in declaring the current inactivity of the Holy Spirit (*Seder ʿOlam Rabbah* 30), early rabbinic Judaism seems to have denied (at least for the time being) the reality of any *religious* forces beyond human control operating to *create* relationships and community where none had previously existed. Instead, early rabbinic Judaism seems to have been content to establish itself in terms of various (parochial) *social* forces operating to *delimit* and *define* an already existing community (note the rabbinic metaphor of "building a fence around the Torah"). These parochial criteria certainly had great "spiritual value" for specific pious Jews, and they received authoritative expression in the Mishnah (although the numerous legal norms contained therein were never regarded as ends unto themselves, nor would early rabbis dare regard them as primarily social or cultural in function). The triumph of parochialism (and the paramount importance of Genesis 17) is perhaps most obvious in the reduction of the term *bĕrît* ("covenant") to mean primarily "circumcision"; the rabbinic need to coin a new word in its place to refer to the Exodus "pact" between God and Israel (Talmudic *dĕyāytîqî,* loan word from Gk *diathēkē*) is evidence that the functional significance of "covenant" had been largely replaced by other concerns. In this context, "covenant" was hardly an operating reality that created community by transcending old parochialisms but was itself merely a formal, ritual demarcation of a particular existing group.

There is little doubt that formal covenant imagery continued to be valued within "orthodox" Jewish circles, and that one's religious obligations continued to be verbalized in prophetic terms as obedience to a transcendent God (cf. especially *b. Mak.* 23b–24a, quoted in Hertzberg 1962: 72–73). However, these obligations were now promulgated within a context that insisted that the orthodox Jewish "circle" be clearly (and ritually) circumscribed. In short, "covenant" was largely symbolic in early Judaism (i.e., a formal part of the tradition), although no doubt for some pious individuals it was a very meaningful symbol insofar as it attempted to inspire Jews to obey an ostensibly transcendent God. In the Talmud (*b. Yebam.* 47a–b) there is an interesting passage about people who convert to Judaism at times when Jews are being persecuted, a passage that implies certain latent covenant forms: the proselyte must first admit that he is not worthy (a statement that perhaps implies he has received some undeserved benefit?), then he is instructed in the lighter and more stringent commandments (obligations), and informed about rewards and punishments that follow from obedience/disobedience (blessings/curses). In lieu of an oath, he is circumcised and later ritually immersed. Despite the apparent survival of old covenant forms, one would have to note that the entire procedure is done in a setting where commandments have a clear social control function, and where circumcision becomes a marker of in-group status. Thus, covenant seems to remain largely symbolic.

The diversity within Judaism, of course, continues to the present; indeed, in the West even most Jews have repudiated as too parochial the rabbinic Judaism manifested in the Mishnah and Talmud. In this regard, a significant issue has been conflicting Jewish understandings about the nature of its covenant with God (Hertzberg 1962: 37–45). Consequently, some Jews have felt it possible to assimilate into a larger pluralistic community without feeling that they have severed their "covenant" bonds to a transcendent God. (This, of course, assumes that such Jews still believe in God; Jewish atheism is another modern Western paradox, perhaps suggesting that the orthodox forms of Judaism were actually counterproductive in their efforts to communicate transcendent values.) Indeed, some Jewish writers (e.g., Feuerlicht 1983) have recently argued that Diaspora and assimilation have been positive experiences (cf. Jer 29:7), enabling Jews to reclaim both the essentially moral character of (Israelite) religious obligations and the (prophetic) vision of a world universally committed to those obligations (cf. Isa 2:2–4).

Perhaps it is no coincidence that, in the West for example, a noteworthy number of Jews have been some of the most outspoken advocates for cultural pluralism. As such they have been in the vanguard of efforts to enact the same sort of "ideological matrix" found in the early Israelite covenant (i.e., a broad human community united by shared commitments to transcendent moral values). Often at some personal risk they have played instrumental roles in such "liberal" causes as the civil rights movement; more recently, a few have even become the most outspoken advocates of justice for the Palestinians (and not surprisingly their efforts have been met with hostile opposition from Zionists for whom the state of Israel has become the ultimate concern). Nevertheless, such Western "liberal" Jewish commitments to pluralism and justice—regardless of how compelling they may or may not be to others in the West—may well be a functioning survival of premonarchic covenant ideas insofar as they embody the same hopes and expectations of the premonarchic Israelite villagers: namely, the value and dignity of persons regardless of their social and economic status or ethnic background, the predictability that follows from reciprocity and fairness in their interrelationships, and the reliability of the peace that would result (cf. Isa 32:17).

2. Covenant in Early Christianity. Just as our treatment of early Jewish covenant ideas focused on the best-known form of early Judaism—"rabbinic Judaism" associated with the Mishnah and Talmud—so our treatment of early Christian covenant ideas will focus only on the best-known form of early Christianity—so called "apostolic Christianity" associated with the canonical OT and NT. The subject of covenant ideas in other early (especially gnostic) forms of Christianity will not be discussed here, although it should be pointed out that their dependence on other "scriptures" and other intellectual wellsprings signals that "covenant" was likely not a significant metaphor by which these early "Christian" groups understood their relationship to God and to Jesus.

a. Covenant and Sacrament. The first and most important context within which we encounter covenant ideas in the NT are the texts recounting the Last Supper Jesus had with his disciples (Matt 26:26–29 and parallels; cf. 1 Cor 11:23–25). In all the NT traditions concerning the Eucharist (except John, of course) it is reported that Jesus gave a cup of wine to his disciples, identifying it as the "covenant" or "new covenant." Here the NT tradition seems to be making some deliberate and conscious connection with older covenant traditions (especially Jer 31:31–34).

The subsequent ritual celebration of the Eucharist (or "Lord's Supper") that arose in conjunction with this Last Supper tradition became a fundamental (and perhaps even a definitive) feature of early Christian gatherings. Around A.D. 112, Pliny the Younger, writing to the Roman emperor Trajan, who was interested in keeping informed of the spread of the Christian movement, reported that the interrogation of a captured Christian yielded the information that Christians gathered *se sacramento obstringere,* "to bind themselves by an oath." The reference is almost certainly to the Eucharist ritual, which perhaps as early as the 1st century was already being identified as a *sacramentum,* "sacrament." Although the English equivalent "sacrament" has subsequently come to mean "having a sacred character or mysterious meaning" (and perhaps it meant such in early Christian mystery sects), the Latin *sacramentum* at the time of the early Church referred to a soldier's oath of loyalty to the Roman emperor.

Thus, a vast number of early Christians seem to have understood the Eucharist in some context associated with oath taking, specifically oath taking with respect to "Christ" (i.e., Jesus), whose interests were understood to transcend those of the Roman Empire (hence Trajan's concern). There was indeed widespread and growing disillusionment with the Roman Empire by the 1st century (not unlike the disillusionment with imperial powers that existed during the LB/early Iron Age transition), and it is in that context that we must note the growing body of diverse peoples throughout the E Mediterranean world who were now participating in this eucharistic rite and identifying themselves as "Christians" (followers of "Christ"). The Roman persecution of Christians indicates that Roman imperial officials took a dim view of their subjects' swearing oaths of loyalty to anyone but the emperor, although it is equally clear from the historical sources that the Christians were categorically different from those power groups seeking politically to unseat the Roman Empire (cf. Rom 13:1–7).

This brings us back to the late developments in ANE thought when covenants had come to be regarded primarily as "loyalty oaths." No doubt this formal similarity between Iron Age Near Eastern, Roman imperial, and early Christian concepts of "covenant" facilitated the communication of early Christianity in the non-Palestinian environment of Mediterranean civilization. However, it would be a grave mistake to conclude (as Roman bureaucrats apparently did) that this formal similarity to political/military loyalty oaths explains the early Christian understanding of covenant.

There is no doubt that, in addition to the formal similarity to Iron Age loyalty oaths, the Christian Eucharist has significant formal connections to other ANE covenant motifs (see Herion 1982). First, its utilization of bread and wine is relevant not just because of general associations with covenant banquet imagery (see G.1 above). Bread and wine appear in ancient Mari in connection with the resolution of enmity and the restoration of personal relationships, and they were associated with the *internalization* of a vassal's obligations in the Assyrian loyalty oaths: "Just as bread and wine enter the intestines, so may the [gods] let this oath enter your intestines" (*ANET,* 539).

Second, some of the Semitic terminology used in the Last Supper narrative (reflected in Gk translation) betrays patterns of thought also attested in early biblical and ANE sources. Specifically, the noteworthy appearance of the word "remembrance" (Gk *anamnēsis*) has a significance in Semitic languages (root *zkr*) that is lacking in Greek (and in English). In the Code of Hammurapi the root *zkr* often means "to swear," and this root seems to convey that meaning in 2 Sam 14:11 (RSV "invoke"); its cognate is still used with this sense in modern village Arabic. The verb "to remember" in the context of (the new) covenant therefore does not mean merely "to call to mind"; it implies recalling some benefit received (in this case the atoning death of Jesus) as a basis for present and future action and decision making. In this we see the revival of the central motif in the ideological matrix of the Sinai covenant (and the earlier LB treaties): the basis for a covenant relationship is the grateful recognition and response to the receipt of an undeserved favor.

Third, the identification of the bread and wine with the body and blood of Christ ("this is my body/blood") in turn made possible the identification of the disciples (who eat and drink it) with the sacrificial victim (cf. Gal 2:20). This has a clear connection with the Iron Age treaties wherein the animal sacrificed is stated specifically to be not a sacrificial animal but the vassal being placed under the loyalty oath (cf. "this is the head/shoulder/etc. of Matʾilu," *ANET,* 532–33). What is certain is that a central metaphor by which the early Church identified itself was "the body of Christ" (Rom 12:4–5; 1 Corinthians 12), and its individual members understood themselves to be the embodiments of the spirit of Christ (1 Cor 6:15ff.; 2 Cor 4:10–11). The "fruit" of this spirit that they were to manifest in their lives was typically those things that make it possible for a diverse body of people to live together in a community that transcends the typical culturally proscribed, parochial bases of social morale (Gal 5:22–25). In this respect, in contrast with the contemporaneous early rabbinic Judaism, there was no codification of culturally bound norms and practices to govern or regulate the behavior of persons in the community (and subsequent attempts to import such norms, whether Jewish or Greco-Roman, were met with strong resistance [Acts 15; Galatians, esp. 3:3]).

In the centuries prior to Constantine, when there was no social reward but often the threat of persecution and possible death for identifying oneself as a Christian, the Eucharist by and large could have been little else but the participants' *sacramentum* ("oath") in which they actually submitted to the lordship of Christ (i.e., to a transcendent, extra-social authority; the "kingdom of God"). This "submission" occurred not merely at the intangible "spiritual" level or simply at the "liturgical" level—both of which Rome would probably have tolerated—but at the tangible level of ethics and values finding expression in the social realm of interpersonal relations. In short, participation in the ritual was an "index" of submission to the transcendent lordship of Christ (on "indexical" rituals whereby participants transmit information about their own current physical, psychic, or sometimes social states, see Rappaport 1979, esp. pp. 179ff.). This would have been a concern to imperial officials, who would understandably want to monitor such a movement closely.

In other words, few Christians in those early centuries could have consumed the bread and wine unless they also really and tangibly became *constituted* as Christ's body in the world (i.e., they were, in fact, subject to something that transcended the interests of the major political powers of their day, or else they would not have taken the risks associated with being recognized as "Christians"). Thus, as in early Israel, the "new covenant" was a socially enacted historical reality that brought into existence a pluralistic community of people from diverse ethnic backgrounds who were united by their commitment to some basic, transcendent values identified with "Christ." (The connection between this development and the OT hopes for the "ingathering of the gentiles" was not lost upon the early Church.)

The situation was, of course, radically reversed when Christianity (especially the church at Rome) became systematically associated with the institutions of political power after the time of Constantine. Under those very different social and historical circumstances, participation in the Christian Eucharist quickly became less constitutive of anything and became much more *symbolic* in nature. In other words, there were now tangible social rewards for participation in the Eucharist, and the distinction between a pledge of loyalty to a transcendent Christ and a pledge of loyalty to the temporal (but now "Christian") emperor in Rome became increasingly fuzzy. At the very least, the ritual was now an "index" of little more than the participants' acceptance of the rule of the new, "Christianized" Roman Empire, which could not be identical to the rule of Christ (on "symbolic" ritual and how it facilitates deception and hypocrisy, see Rappaport 1979).

In the following centuries the original meaning of the eucharistic *sacramentum* was entirely forgotten, and increasingly it came to be viewed either as a mysterious and mystical "communion" with Christ, or (particularly for the laity) as a sacrificial ritual that served to heighten the sanctity (and the authority) of the presiding priestly hierarchy. Despite its claim to transcendence, the bloody history that followed indicates that in practice Christianity by and large had now become the (parochial) handmaid serving the advance of Western culture.

b. OT Covenant Motifs in the NT. The preceding discussion of the covenantal associations of the Eucharist has begged the fundamentally important question: what exactly was this "Christ" with whom the early Christians identified themselves? The creation of the gospel genre seems, in part, designed to answer this question by presenting to the reader the identity and activity of Jesus of Nazareth, who was claimed to be the Messiah (or Christ) of Israel. From these narratives it is fundamentally clear that, while Jesus claimed for himself the title "king," Christians did not regard this as a political claim (John 18:36; supposedly "historical" studies claiming that Jesus *was* a political revolutionary have proven entirely unconvincing). Thus, a *sacramentum* taken with respect to Christ could not legitimately signal any movement of those ambitious for political power and prestige (Matt 5:5).

The complex issue of the historical Jesus need not detain us here, since our main object of study is early Christianity. However, we must point out that the entire NT tradition points to some very important *substantive* connections with the type of suzerainty treaty exhibited in the Sinai covenant. Those connections, however, are not the external, formal continuities that can be easily traced with the standard scholarly methods that compare and classify phenomena in terms of formal features and surface characteristics. For that reason, this tradition must be explicated in terms of its underlying ideological matrix, and not in terms of any formal covenant elements (which were already being atomized at least as early as the writings of the Deuteronomistic Historian). Scholars dependent upon methods of formal classification have sometimes been quick to (mis)understand the formal "new"-ness of Christianity as indicating its fundamental unrelatedness to earlier Hebrew religion. Indeed, comparatively few of the superficial "forms" of Israelite religion are present in early Christianity (as they are in rabbinic Judaism, whose continued reverence for the Hebrew language and onomastics, the rite of circumcision, the levitical dietary laws, and the liturgical calendar insured at least the formal appearance of continuity with [certain aspects of] Israelite religion). But early Christian community and thought each reflect sometimes subtle links with OT covenant traditions, and to appreciate this requires a scholarly sensitivity to something other than formal characteristics. It also probably requires the assumption that the historical Jesus played some role in articulating those old covenant traditions in a new idiom, although it is highly doubtful that even he understood the Sinai covenant in the formal terms of suzerainty treaty elements.

(1) Identification and Historical Prologue. The constant and crucial issue of the identification of the covenant giver is a good case in point. As the Eucharist tradition indicates, the early Church unquestionably understood this to be Jesus himself. The gospel traditions presenting the person and deeds of Jesus of Nazareth assert the same thing, but in a more roundabout way. There, as in the Sinai covenant tradition (Exod 20:2), the identification of the covenant giver is integrally linked to the historical prologue: it is achieved through a narrative of "benevolent deeds" performed, not merely a heaping up of titles and epithets. The importance of this is evident in Matt 11:2–6, where John the Baptist asks Jesus, "Are you he who is to come, or shall we look for another?" The answer indeed identifies Jesus as such by quoting the manifestations of deity envisioned in the book of Isaiah (35:5–6; 61:1; cf. Luke 4:16–21). In other words, Jesus does the things that God does. It is significant that this is a functional rather than a formal identification, and perhaps is based on old concepts that tended to view the Messiah as servant (1 Kgs 12:7) rather than powerful overlord (1 Kgs 12:11; cf. Matt 20:25–28 = Mark 10:42–45; Mendenhall 1986).

Thus, it appears that already during his historical ministry Jesus' identity was being linked to the tangible "benevolent deeds" he was seen to perform (especially the miraculous healings). However, for the early Christians who lived with the knowledge of Jesus' death and resurrection (which for them was a historical reality, not a metaphysical proposition), the most important "benevolent deed" performed by the covenant giver was intangible: the atonement, Jesus' offering of himself for the removal of sin and guilt. This suggests at least a formal connection with the prophecy of the "new covenant" in Jeremiah 31, where the forgiveness of sins is the only act of benevolence mentioned. (It is debatable whether the historical Jesus understood himself to be such an "intangible" [i.e., post-mortem] benefit to his followers.)

In sharp contrast to the use of the historical narrative in the prayer of Ezra, where God is supposed to remember his past deeds performed for the benefit of the corporate body Israel (Nehemiah 9), the historical narrative constituting the gospels emphasizes the direct and immediate benefits that God in Christ bestows on individuals. This understanding of historical events as acts of God that furnish the foundation for a lasting relationship is one of the most striking features of the formative period in early Christianity, and it constitutes a tangible reintroduction of the most fundamental religious feature of the OT tradition; namely, that a covenant relationship with God is based on the receipt of a prior and undeserved act of deliverance (whether physically from the grip of Pharaoh, or metaphysically from the grip of sin and death).

(2) Stipulations. The notion of covenant stipulations was subjected to a most important transformation in the NT traditions, or at least what appears to be a "transformation" with respect to postbiblical and early rabbinic Jewish traditions equating covenant stipulations with written (and oral) "law." But what on first glance appears to be a "transformation" was in fact a way of recovering and returning to early and authentic OT covenant traditions. As in the case of the historical prologue, there was a two-stage development: the first stage associated with the life and teaching of the historical Jesus, and the second associated with the understandings subsequently reflected in early Christian traditions.

Any understanding of Jesus' notion of religious "obligation" (cf. Pharisaic "duty") must begin by recognizing that for several centuries before Jesus there had been no unanimity among Palestinian Jews—indeed, there had been outright hostilities culminating in civil war—over who had the authority to define and enforce the law of God. It is therefore neither unusual nor surprising to find in the teachings of Jesus (and in the gospel narratives) polemical statements directed against most of the prestigious and ambitious *Jewish* power blocs of the time (Sadducees, scribes, and Pharisees). As a growing number of scholars are beginning to concede, this has nothing to do with "anti-Semitism" but rather emphasizes that the early Christian movement was an *inner-Jewish* phenomenon (and as such participated fully in inner-Jewish polemics). The necessary corollary to this hostile polemic is the fact that Jesus of Nazareth and the early Christian movement had no ideology for, and no intention to engage in, the centuries-old power struggle among Palestinian Jewry (Matt 20:25–27). As in the early Iron Age, the rule ("kingdom") of God was a reality that had nothing to do with the usual paraphernalia of social and political organizations that were based on little more than coercive force.

Jesus apparently did have a strong respect for the commandments (Matt 5:17–20). He was no libertarian, and in the Sermon on the Mount—as elsewhere throughout the gospel traditions—Jesus is consistently portrayed as a "commanding" personality speaking in the imperative. It has long been noted that the essence of Jesus' teaching is not to advocate relaxing—much less abolishing—the Law (which subsequently became Paul's position) but rather just the opposite: to advocate a more stringent observation of the Law: "You therefore must be perfect as your Father in heaven is perfect" (Matt 5:48; cf. 5:20!). Of course, since no one can attain such perfection the net rhetorical effect of Jesus' teaching ironically is to condemn in advance anyone who seeks to earn covenant blessings by faithful adherence to the stipulations of the Law (which is a structural premise of the "old covenant" tradition). But while subsequent Christians, particularly Paul, used this as the basis for the classic Law/faith dichotomy (and for proclaiming the end of the "old covenant"), Jesus himself seems to have absolutized the Law for different—but reciprocally interrelated—reasons.

In the first place, he removed religious obligations from the realm of social monitoring and enforcement: thus, his absolutized redefinition of the commandments against killing (Matt 5:21–26) and adultery (5:27–30) effectively removes them from the realm of human monitors and sociopolitical authorities. In short, the concept of religious obligation could no longer be indirectly linked to the perfect *will* of God through a verbal listing of do's and don'ts that can be managed and overseen by imperfect human authorities.

In the second place, in exhorting to absolute moral perfection, Jesus now linked the concept of religious obligation directly to the *character* of God. In short, he advocated a total and complete commonality of interests between suzerain and vassal, and in so doing he (unknowingly) reasserted part of the ideological matrix of the LB treaties. The issue is not just reciprocity ("Do unto others as you would have them do unto you"); rather, it is the recognition that the ultimate character of one's religious obligations proceeds from the character of God as revealed in God's benevolent deeds (his "grace"), not as revealed in God's law (1 John 4:11). To state it covenantally, the ultimate will of the sovereign is manifested more deeply in the character of him whose benevolent deeds are recounted in the historical prologue than in him whose words are recorded in the stipulations. To put it more bluntly, God's actions *(character)* speak truer and deeper than God's words *(will)* (a point Jesus himself seems to make in Matt 19:3–9).

There is here the recognition that in the ongoing quest for a truly "blessed" community, the behavior of individuals ultimately must correspond directly to the "blessings" they have already received (and not to some impersonal codification of laws, statutes, and ordinances). The notion that the Christian's obligations should mirror past benefits is reflected in many NT traditions which define Christian "duty" in terms of what Jesus did: forgive, forsake worldly goods, preach, teach, heal (even raise the dead!), take up a cross, die. If the "new covenant" should require a "new commandment," such is given in John 13:34. What is significant about this is the context, definition, and example given for "love"—". . . even as I have loved you." "Love" (the stipulation of the covenant) is not codified in words but is rather defined by example, more specifically, by the example of a benefit received ("the Word become flesh"). This suggests a return to the same ideological matrix as the prophets, who, like Jesus, understood obligations in absolute moral terms and were likewise considered to be threats to the social authorities, who reserved for themselves the right to define, interpret, and enforce obligations.

(3) Deposit, Witnesses, Curses and Blessings. The provision for deposit and periodic public reading in one respect was almost irrelevant in early Christianity, since there was no material object to deposit. But in another respect, certainly related to the "new covenant" vision of the internalization of the covenant (Jer 31:33), the early

Church seems to have developed notions that the "covenant" was deposited within the believer.

The list of witnesses was also subject to drastic transformation of a most curious and almost inexplicable sort. Originally the witnesses were supposed to enforce the covenant stipulations by bringing to bear the covenant curses, including the death penalty. In the NT from the earliest time the "witness" is the "martyr" (Gk *martus,* "witness") who is put to death as a result of adhering (and thereby testifying) to the truth of the faith.

The formula of blessings and curses also underwent significant transformation. As was true also of pre-Christian Judaism, the rewards and punishments meted out by God were to be realized in the "world to come"; the importance of this is very important to early Christianity as can be seen from the significant role that eschatology plays in early Christian thought. In addition to the eschatological meting out of rewards and punishments in the final judgment, blessings and curses are certainly connected to the "power of the keys" (Matt 16:13–20). The terms translated "binding" and "loosing" have meaning primarily in the ANE context of imposing, and freeing from, a curse. (It is not surprising that after the time of Constantine the Roman church—identifying itself with Peter—claimed for itself this power. In this regard, we see the Matthew 16 text being used as a sort of "divine charter" to legitimize the authority of the Roman priestly hierarchy, an authority that in reality had been conferred on it by imperial concordat.) The several references to the *anathema,* especially in the letters of Paul, probably bear on this same theme, but as in Matt 18:18 and perhaps a parallel in John 20:23 this is not a power given to an authority but is rather a characteristic of the community of the faithful.

c. Summary. At precisely the same time that rabbinic Judaism was "building a fence around the Torah" (and rationalizing such by a general appeal to the OT covenant tradition), apostolic Christianity was expanding. In early rabbinic Judaism, "covenant" was largely a formal or symbolic dogmatic concept that gave meaning mainly to those already within a group whose base of solidarity and cohesion was primarily ethnic. In early apostolic Christianity, on the other hand, "covenant" was largely a socially enacted historical reality that accompanied sufficient functional changes in old patterns of behavior so as to rupture old ethnic and political bases of social solidarity and cohesion and to replace these with a larger vision of the human community. Certainly the tenor here was initially set by Jesus himself, who not only sought relationships with people who were outside the "proper" cultural boundaries (e.g., eating with tax collectors and sinners), but also challenged the religious legitimacy of those boundaries (e.g., sabbath observance). In this we see the reappearance of the same ideological matrix found in the Sinai covenant and prophetic faith: that religious community can cut across old parochialisms and need not be defined in terms of legal norms backed up by coercive power.

The entire covenant complex of NT thought that has been only briefly sketched here illustrates the complete internalization of the ethic of the rule of God, ideally envisioned (but imperfectly realized) in the Sinai suzerainty treaty and so frequently pleaded for (largely in vain) by the OT prophets (Ezek 36:26–27). At the same time, this ethic became freed from the cultural parochialism and political arrogation that inevitably accompanies a defined code of norms and laws. It is clear enough that not all Christians (just as not all early Israelites) succeeded in grasping these points, as illustrated by the reversion to a canon law system in later centuries. In that respect, one could argue that even today the ability of most people to grasp the significance of what it means to be in a "covenant" relationship with a transcendent "God" has advanced little from the LB Age. Nevertheless, the radical transformation that constituted the early Christian Church remains an excellent example of what can happen when new wine is put into old bottles.

I. Conclusion

Because "covenant" is a central biblical metaphor for the relationship between God and his people, it is not surprising that the attempts of biblical theologians to find a thematic "center" *(Mitte)* of the Bible invariably return time and again to the subject of covenant, or to some particular aspect of covenant. But as long as theologians conceive their task as primarily elucidating biblical "ideas," they will continue to miss the fundamental significance of covenant in the biblical tradition. Covenant is not an "idea" to be embraced in the mind, and therefore religious community cannot be defined with respect to "orthodox" appraisals of that idea. Covenant is an "enacted reality" that is either manifested in the concrete choices individuals make, or not. The rule of God is defined with respect to those whose concrete choices arise out of certain positive values that actually transcend culturally bound norms and politically enforced laws.

Similarly, as long as biblical scholars remain content to deal with covenant "ideas" in terms of formal elements and rigidly defined categories, most of the matrix of ideas associated with covenant will remain unnoticed and unappreciated. Covenant form was apparently never that important anywhere in antiquity: even for the LB Hittites it was merely a device for communicating values envisioning human relationships proceeding along some moral plane higher than coercive force.

Bibliography

Baltzer, K. 1964. *Das Bundesformular.* WMANT 4. 2d ed. Neukirchen-Vluyn.

Beyerlin, W. 1965. *Origins and History of the Oldest Sinai Traditions.* Oxford.

Clements, R. 1967. *Abraham and David.* SBT 2/5. London.

Feuerlicht, R. 1983. *The Fate of the Jews.* New York.

Finkelstein, L. 1962. *The Pharisees.* 2 vols. 3d ed. Philadelphia.

Goetze, A. 1957. *Kleinasien.* 2d ed. HAW. Munich.

Grayson, A. 1987. Akkadian Treaties of the Seventh Century B.C. *JCS* 39: 127–60.

Herion, G. 1982. Sacrament as "Covenantal Remembrance." Pp. 97–116 in *Church Divinity 1982,* ed. J. H. Morgan. Notre Dame.

Hertzberg, A., ed. 1962. *Judaism.* Great Religions of Modern Man. New York.

Hillers, D. 1964. *Treaty-Curses and the OT Prophets.* BibOr 16. Rome.

———. 1969. *Covenant: The History of a Biblical Idea.* Baltimore.

Huffmon, H. 1965. The Exodus, Sinai, and the Credo. *CBQ* 27: 101–13.

images, and propositions. Faith is the act of intelligible beings as well as of the human will and affections. Karl Barth has written, "Just because he is *intelligens,* the Christian of all men, has to learn to discern with agonizing clarity what is conceivable by him about God" (1960: 20–21). What cannot be thought clearly and expressed cogently cannot be the basis of life commitment.

Faith itself seeks intelligibility. On the one hand, it seeks the intelligibility of faith itself so that the content of faith can be communicated in intelligible images and in descriptive propositions. On the other hand, faith seeks to understand the world in the light of what it perceives to be the revelation of God.

Creeds are also rooted in and bear the marks of history. Situations in the life of the community of faith have called for creeds, such as heresy, persecution, and worship itself. Controversies within the community have demanded that the community clarify its own judgment as to the content of faith. In addition, great dangers from without which have pressured the church and challenged its deepest commitments have also compelled the church to declare unequivocally its deepest commitments. Creeds therefore bear not only the marks of the believing person, but also the marks of the history in which they have come to be.

Creeds are intentionally catholic. They may bear the marks of their particularity and of a specific perspective and place. The basic intention, however, is to state the faith not of a partisan group but of the one holy catholic church.

The authority of creeds varies. Generally the word "creed" is given to the short and brief statements of the ancient catholic church, such as the Apostles' Creed and the Nicene Creed. The comprehensive Reformed statements of faith are usually labeled confessions. However, there is no established terminology. Protestants in particular have always insisted that creeds are subordinate to Scripture, but at times Protestant churches have used creeds with an equivalent authority. The early Reformed creeds were written with the awareness that a creed ought to be a confession in a particular time and place, and that no one creed should have universal significance. Karl Barth in the 20th century has reiterated the same conviction. Creeds therefore may have normative authority, or they may be the occasional confession of the way the church understands Christian faith in a particular time with no claim to finality. At the other extreme, confessions may be regarded as simply descriptions of Christian belief and practice with no decisive authority.

A. Sources of Creeds

1. Liturgy and Worship. The liturgical life of the church called for creeds of various types. Rules of Faith, varied and without precise language, served the needs of preaching and teaching without stifling creativity. Declarations of faith by the worshiping congregation, in distinction from Rules of Faith, had to be precise, fixed, and economical in the use of words. Rules of Faith may be found in various forms in the writings of such early theologians as Irenaeus, Tertullian, and Origen.

Creedal statements from the beginning have been associated with baptism. Hans Lietzmann argued that the root of all Christian creeds is the formula for belief pronounced by the baptizands or pronounced in their hearing and assented to by them before baptism.

The creedal form that was used in baptismal rites in the 2d and 3d centuries was interrogatory. One of the best examples of the developed form of the interrogatory creed is found in the *Apostolic Traditions of Hippolytus* (ca. 215):

> Do you believe in God the Father all-governing? Do you believe in Christ Jesus, the Son of God, who was begotten by the Holy Spirit from the Virgin Mary, Who was crucified under Pontius Pilate, and died (and was buried) and rose the third day living from the dead, and ascended into the heavens, and sat down on the right hand of the Father, and will come to judge the living and the dead?
>
> Do you believe in the Holy Spirit, in the holy church, and (in the resurrection of the body)?

Creeds also became part of the liturgy of the holy communion in the 5th century. This practice gave the Nicene Creed widespread authority in the life of the church.

2. Education. The teaching ministry of the church also called for creeds. The mother creed of our Apostles' Creed developed in Rome in the 3d century when the interrogatory creed of baptism was turned into a declaratory creed. This became part of catechetical training when the bishop traditioned the creed to the catechumens and when the catechumens rendered it back as their own witness of faith. Creeds were also used as a basis of catechetical lectures, as in the case of the catechetical lectures of Cyril of Jerusalem.

3. Interpretation. Creeds were a useful hermeneutical guide. Biblical studies were carried on and theology was formulated under the guidance of rules of faith and creeds which were the church's best wisdom as to how the Bible should be understood and the faith expressed.

4. Apologetics. Heresy was still another occasion for creedal formulation. Older creedal scholars, such as A. C. McGiffert (1902), argued that the refutation of heresy was a primary factor in the development of the Apostles' Creed. For example, the affirmation that God created the heavens and the earth stood over against the conviction that the created world was evil and the work of a lesser god. Others have argued against McGiffert, that heresy was not a necessity for such Christian affirmations as the goodness of creation.

5. Evangelism. Christian witness made use of creeds as Christians defined themselves over against the pagan society. It also enabled the Christian to render a firm and clear testimony in the face of persecution.

B. Forms of Creeds

1. The Bible. Precise, fixed creeds did not appear until the 3d and 4th centuries of the church's history, but the process that culminated in them had its beginning in the historical credos (Deut 25:5–9 and 6:21–25) and in the declaratory affirmations of the OT (Deut 6:4–5 and 1 Kings 18:39). The NT church in preaching, singing, praying, and witnessing increasingly gave expression to Christian faith in more or less fixed formulas, for example, in 1 Cor 15:3–7; Phil 2:6–11; Matt 28:10; and Rom 10:9. Some creedal statements are simple christological affirmations declaring the lordship of Jesus Christ (Mark 8:9, 1 Tim 3:16, Romans 10:9). Others are two-article formulas confessing both God and Christ (1 Cor 8:6). Three-article statements affirming Father, Son, and Holy Spirit appear in Matt 28:19 and in 2 Cor 13–14, which is a pretrinitarian formulation.

2. Ecumenical Creeds. The creedlike statements of the NT and early Christian writers such as Ignatius, as well as the Rules of Faith, were replaced by precise creedal formulas which served the liturgical and catechetical needs of local churches. In the East, the creeds varied from church to church, but in the West, the creed of Rome exercised a dominating influence over the great churches in the West. One of the daughter creeds of Rome became the established version of the Apostles' Creed. It first appeared in southwest France sometime in the late 6th or 7th century. Its present text is found in the *De singulis libris canonicis scarapsus* of Priminius, which is dated between 710 and 724. This creed, which owed much to Rome, became the common creed of the Frankish empire and was finally adopted in Rome. It became the most universal creed in the West, but it was not known in the East. The first creed to have synodical authority was promulgated by the Council of Nicea (325) in response to the teaching of an Alexandrian presbyter named ARIUS concerning the deity of Jesus Christ. Christians had spoken of Jesus as Lord, Savior, the Word, Son of God, Son of man, prophet, and priest. All these refer to the activity of Jesus Christ and his relation to us.

Arius changed the question. He did not ask how Jesus Christ is related to us or what he means to us. He asks the prior question, "Who is Jesus?" Is he really God? Or is he a creature? Arius declared that he was a creature, but the Council of Nicea took a creed of an Eastern church and added to it four formulas which stated without ambiguity that Jesus Christ was truly God. The key formula was "of the same substance as the Father." The Nicene Creed, which is used in worship today, is dated from the Council of Constantinople in 381. All creeds that use the phrase "of the same substance (reality, being, essence) as the Father" were regarded as Nicene. The Council of Constantinople also eliminated the anathemas from the Creed of 325 and added a statement affirming the deity of the Holy Spirit as well as the one holy catholic church, the forgiveness of sins, and the resurrection of the dead. The Council of Nicea, in affirming that Jesus Christ was truly God, raised the question of the humanity of Christ, and therefore of the doctrine of the person of Christ. The church of the 5th century, in an amazingly catholic theological endeavor, defined its understanding of the person of Jesus Christ at the Council of Chalcedon (431) in which it affirmed that Jesus Christ is truly God and truly man in one person (one acting subject).

The Athanasian Creed was not written by Athanasius but by some Augustinian theologians sometime after the middle of the 5th century. Its use has declined because of its anathemas, but recent studies by J. N. D. Kelly have pointed to its theological excellence. The Definition of the Council of Chalcedon (451) was the definitive statement of the ancient church on the person of Jesus Christ, but it was never used in worship as were the other three creeds.

3. Creeds of the Eastern Church. The Nicene Creed has always been used in the Eastern churches. Later doctrinal statements included the Orthodox Confession of Peter Mogilas (1643), the Answers of Jeremiah (Patriarch of Constantinople) to Lutheran Theologians (1576), the Confession Prepared by Metrophanes Critopolus to Explain Eastern Orthodoxy to Protestants (1625), the Russian Catechisms, especially the Longer Catechism of Philaret (1839), a confession appearing under the name of Cyril Lucar (1629), Patriarch of Constantinople, which was sympathetic to Protestantism and which was repudiated by the majority of Orthodox. The Confession of Dositheus, approved by the Synod of Jerusalem in 1672 in opposition to the Protestant sympathies of the previous document, is more representative of the Eastern church.

4. Roman Catholicism. The Canons and Decrees of the Council of Trent (1545–63) were formulated in the context of the Protestant Reformation. It also narrowed many of the options of the very fluid theology of medieval Catholicism. The creed of the Council of Trent (1564) is a short summary of the lengthy Tridentine document. The Council of Trent fixed the shape of modern Roman Catholicism. There have been other notable pronouncements of doctrine, such as the Dogma of the Assumption of the Virgin Mary (1950), in addition to numerous papal encyclicals of considerable importance. The whole shape of Roman Catholicism received a new interpretation in the work of Vatican Council II (1962–65).

5. Protestantism. Protestants were prolific writers of confessions. These include Martin Luther's Ninety-Five Theses (1517), the Augsburg Confession (1530), the Apology of the Augsburg Confession (1531), the Smalcald Articles (1537), the Treatise on the Power and the Primacy of the Pope (1537), the Small Cathechism of Dr. Martin Luther (1529), and the Large Catechism of Dr. Martin Luther (1529). Calvinists and Reformed Protestants wrote many creeds, the most typical of which are the Ten Theses of Berne (1528), the Gallican Confession (1529), the Scots Confession (1560), and the second Helvetic Confession (1566).

Seventeenth-century Protestantism produced the Westminster Confession (1647) and the Westminster Catechisms, which became the dominant Reformed statement for English-speaking Presbyterians, and also the Canons of Dort (1619). The Thirty-Nine Articles of the Church of England (1563) combined Calvinist and Lutheran influences, as well as an indigenous English tradition with that of the Catholic tradition. At the other extreme of the Protestant Reformation were statements of the radical Reformers such as Schleitheim Articles of 1527.

6. Contemporary Confessions. Numerous confessions have been written in the 20th century. Some of these, such as the Barmen Declaration (1934), were in response to National Socialism. The Confession of 1967 of the United Presbyterian Church (USA) was the attempt of a denomination to formulate its faith in contemporary idiom and in response to contemporary problems. Some of the most interesting of the 20th-century confessions have arisen in younger and non-Western churches, such as the creed of the Batak Church (Great Synod of the Huria Kristen Batak Protestant Church of Indonesia, 1956).

Bibliography

Barth, K. 1960. *Anselm: Fides Quaerens Intellectum.* London.
Kelly, J. N. D. 1972. *Early Christian Creeds.* 3d ed. New York.

Leith, J. H. 1982. *Creeds of the Churches.* 3d ed. Atlanta.
McGiffert, A. C. 1902. *The Apostles' Creed.* New York.
Schaff, P. 1877. *Bibliotheca Symbolica Ecclesiae Universalis: The Creeds of Christendom.* 3 vols. New York. Repr. Grand Rapids, 1966.

JOHN H. LEITH

CRESCENS (PERSON) [Gk *Krēskēs*]. A Christian, apparently a co-worker of Paul, who left him during his Roman imprisonment (assumably in Rome, although Caesarea has been defended) and went to Galatia (2 Tim 4:10). In mentioning Crescens, Paul indicates that he had likewise been left by Titus who went to Dalmatia. While most mss read Galatia as Crescens' destination, a few (e.g., Sinaiticus, C) have Gaul. A later tradition also reports that Paul sent Crescens to Gaul (cf. Eus. *Hist. Eccl.* 3.4.8), where he is thought to have founded the churches in Vienne and Mayence. That Crescens went to Gaul may be supported by the apocryphal *Acts of Paul* where Titus is said to have arrived in Rome from Dalmatia, and Luke (a substitution for Crescens?) is said to have come from Gaul (*Acts Paul* 11:1). Nevertheless, the reading "Galatia" is usually judged as the more strongly favored in the ms witnesses. This does not, however, settle the question of the Gaul tradition since there are instances of some Greeks using the name "Galatia" when they referred to Gaul (Dibelius and Conzelmann *Pastoral Epistles* Hermeneia 122, n. 3). Also to be considered is the context of 2 Timothy. If the imprisonment it portrays was Rome, proximity to Gaul makes it the more probable destination of Crescens; a Caesarean imprisonment, in contrast, would favor reading "Galatia."

FLORENCE MORGAN GILLMAN

CRESCENTS. See JEWELRY.

CRETE (PLACE) [Gk *Krētē; Krētēs*]. CRETANS. The largest and southernmost island in the Aegean Sea. Crete is 156 miles from E to W and 35 miles from N to S (at its broadest point). Mountains, reaching to 7882 feet, run the length of the island. By the 2d century B.C. a formidable Jewish constituency appeared on the island of Crete (Tac. *Hist.* 5. 2) which was centered in the area of Gortyna, lying in Crete's Messara plain. When the Cretans began oppressing the Jews, the latter secured Roman patronage (141 B.C.) and the Romans considered them to be loyal subjects (1 Macc 15:23). From this time through the New Testament era the Cretan Jews continued to flourish. Paul commissioned Titus to oversee the ministry on Crete, and to counteract Judaizing tendencies (Titus 1:5–14). In 67 B.C., Rome finally annexed Crete and Cyrene (Libya); they remained a joint Roman province until Constantine separated them.

Archaeology has revealed a flourishing Minoan civilization on Crete which reached its zenith in the Late Bronze Age (ca. 1700–1450 B.C.). Sir Arthur Evans headed these excavations, focusing on the central city of Knossos, which contains the palace of legendary King Minos. Similar labyrinthine palaces have been found at Mallia, Phaestos, and Zakro. Evans discovered Linear A and B tablets, but only the latter have been deciphered (by Michael Ventris in 1953), proving to be an archaic form of Gk. The Minoan civilization came to an end with a Myceneaen domination, and the cataclysmic eruption of Thera. The subsequent Dorian invasions ushered in Crete's Iron Age (ca. 1200 B.C.). From this time on, Crete was only known for its mercenary soldiers and traders until the Roman annexation.

The Cretan poet Epimenides (ca. 600 B.C.) describes all Cretans as "liars, evil brutes, and lazy gluttons" (quoted both in Titus 1:12 and Acts 17:28). This characterization is found in several ancient sources, e.g., Livy *Epit. Per.* 44:45; Callimachus *Jov.* 8; and Plutarch *Aem* 23. Evidently, after several generations of living in the turbulence of Cretan culture, these characteristics became manifest in the Cretan Jews as well (Titus 3:1).

Bibliography

Cottrell, L. 1953. *The Bull of Minos.* New York.
Willetts, R. F. 1969. *Everyday Life in Ancient Crete.* New York.

JERRY A. PATTENGALE

CRIMES AND PUNISHMENTS. See PUNISHMENTS AND CRIMES.

CRISPUS (PERSON) [Gk *Krispos*]. A Corinthian Jew and ruler of the synagogue who, together with all his household, believed in the Lord because of Paul's preaching (Acts 18:8; 1 Cor 1:14). Crispus is named first, preceding Gaius and the household of Stephanas, as one of the few people baptized by Paul himself (1 Cor 1:14). For that reason, he was probably partial to Paul's position in the disputes among the Corinthians. As a ruler of the synagogue (Gk *ʾarchisynagogos*), Crispus' role was to see that services were conducted in the proper order, to take care of the building, to cover the cost for its upkeep, and possibly to finance the construction of a new synagogue building (see Fee *1 Corinthians* NICNT, 62–63). Hence, he was probably a well-to-do person and highly respected by the Jewish community. His own conversion to Christianity probably led to the conversion not only of his household, but also to that of others from the synagogue. Among the Corinthians he knew, the "worshipper of God" Titius Justus, who lived next door to the synagogue, would have to be included.

Also named as a ruler of presumably the same Corinthian synagogue is Sosthenes (Acts 18:17). While synagogues normally had just one such leader, some had two or more for a time (cf. Acts 13:15). Thus it is not certain whether Crispus was the colleague or predecessor of Sosthenes. A conclusion often drawn—that Sosthenes became ruler because of Crispus' conversion—should be closely examined, for it cannot be assumed that at this early date a synagogue leader who became a Christian had to be replaced. Whatever the case, Paul felt it necessary to withdraw from that particular synagogue because of the opposition he faced (cf. Acts 18:6–7). It is probable that his converts, Crispus among them, followed suit by their own choice because of the animosity experienced.

JOHN GILLMAN

CRITICISM, BIBLICAL. See the BIBLICAL CRITICISM articles.

CROCUS. See FLORA.

CROW. See ZOOLOGY.

CROWN. See JEWELRY.

CRUCIFIXION. The act of nailing or binding a living victim or sometimes a dead person to a cross or stake (*stauros* or *skolops*) or a tree *(xylon)*. Generally Herodotus uses the verb *anaskolopizein* of living persons and *anastauroun* of corpses. After him the verbs become synonyms, "to crucify." Josephus uses only *(ana)stauroun,* Philo only *anaskolopizein.* The verb *stauroun* occurs frequently in the NT, which always employs *stauros* and never *skolops* for the cross of Christ (see *TDNT* 7:572–84).

A. Crucifixion among Non-Romans
B. Crucifixion under the Romans
C. Forms of Crucifixion
D. Jesus' Crucifixion
E. Christian Interpretations of the Crucifixion

A. Crucifixion among Non-Romans

In his *History,* Herodotus notes that the Persians practiced crucifixion as a form of execution (1.128.2; 3.125.3; 3.132.2; 3.159.1). He reports that Darius (512–485 B.C.) had 3000 inhabitants of Babylon crucified. Other ancient sources, which are not necessarily reliable, speak of the use of crucifixion among the people of India (Diod. Sic. 2.18.1), the Assyrians (*ibid.* 2.1.10; Lucian *Iupp. Trag.* 16), the Scythians (Diod. Sic. 2.44.2; Tert. *Adv. Marc.* 1.1.3), the Taurians (Eur. *IT* 1429–30), and the Thracians (Diod. Sic. 33.15.1; 34/35.12.1). Diodorus Siculus says that the Celts crucified criminals as a sacrifice to the gods (5.32.6). According to Tacitus, the Germans (*Ann.* 1.61.4; 4.72.3; *Germ.* 12.1) and the Britons (*Ann.* 14.33.2) practiced crucifixion. Sallust (*Iug.* 14.15) and Julius Caesar (*B Civ.* 66) report that the Numidians used this form of execution. According to many sources (e.g., Polyb. 1.11.5; 24.6; 79.4–5; 86.4; Diod. Sic. 25.5.2; 10.2; 26.23.1; Livy 22.13.9; 28.37.2; 38.48.13), the Carthaginians employed crucifixion. The Romans may have taken over the practice from them.

In the Greek-speaking world, criminals were at times fastened to a flat board *(tympanum)* for public display, torture, or execution. This form of punishment closely resembled crucifixion whenever the victims were nailed to the planks. According to Diodorus Siculus, Dionysius I of Syracuse captured and crucified some Greek mercenaries employed by the Carthaginians (14.53.4). Alexander the Great repeatedly resorted to crucifixion. On one occasion he had 2000 survivors from the siege of Tyre crucified. "Then the anger of the king offered a sad spectacle to the victors. Two thousand persons, for whose killing the general madness had spent itself, hung fixed to crosses over a huge stretch of the shore" (Curtius Rufus *Hist. Alex.* 4.4.17). After Alexander's death Greece itself witnessed mass crucifixions. In 314 B.C. an administrator of Alexander's kingdom quashed a rebellion in the city of Sicyon (near Corinth) and had thirty of its inhabitants crucified (Diod. Sic. 19.67.2). In 303 B.C., after their town fell to Demetrius Poliorcetes, the commander of Orchomenus (in Arcadia) and eighty of his men were crucified (*ibid.* 20.103.6). Under Antiochus IV in 267 B.C. Judea saw the crucifixion of men who remained faithful to the Jewish law (Joseph. *Ant* 12 §256). During the pre-Roman, Hellenistic period in the Greek-speaking East, crucifixion was practiced in the context of war or for acts of high treason. After Roman rule arrived, crucifixion was also used as a punishment for slaves and violent criminals. As Plutarch (ca. A.D. 46–120) remarks, "every criminal condemned to death bears his cross on his back" (*Mor.* 554 A/B).

Among Jews, crucifixion was occasionally practiced during the Hellenistic-Hasmonean period. The Sadducean high priest, Alexander Janneus (in office 103–76 B.C.), had 800 Pharisees crucified and ordered their wives and children to be slaughtered before their eyes as they hung dying (Joseph. *Ant* 13 §380–83; *JW* 1 §97–98). According to Jewish law, the corpses of executed idolaters and blasphemers were hanged on a tree to show that they were accursed by God (Deut 21:22–23). In pre-Christian Palestine this text of Deuteronomy was applied to those who died by crucifixion, as the *pesher* of Nahum from Qumran Cave 4 shows. Another Qumran document (11QTemple 64:6–13) also connects Deuteronomy 21:23 with crucifixion, which was apparently an Essene punishment for some very serious crimes.

B. Crucifixion under the Romans

Cicero calls crucifixion the *summum supplicium* or most extreme form of punishment (*Verr.* 2.5.168). Josephus, who witnessed men dying by crucifixion during Titus' siege of Jerusalem, calls it "the most wretched of deaths" (*JW* 7 §203). In order of increasing severity, the aggravated methods of execution were *decollatio* (decapitation), *crematio* (burning), and crucifixion. At times *damnatio ad bestias* (throwing victims to wild animals) took the place of decapitation, but one needed the animals and an arena to organize such a form of execution. Crucifixion was much easier to carry out and could also serve as a public spectacle. For example, at the time of Caligula (A.D. 37–41) under the prefect Flaccus some Jews were tortured and crucified in the amphitheatre of Alexandria to entertain the people (Philo *Flacc* 72.84–85).

Among the Persians and to some degree in Greece, as we have seen, crucifixion could be a punishment for grave crimes against the state. At times the Carthaginians crucified generals and admirals who had been defeated or had failed in other such ways. Very occasionally Roman citizens were crucified for high treason, desertion during wartime, and similar serious offenses. For instance, just before the outbreak of the Jewish War in A.D. 66, the Roman procurator Gessius Florus had some Jews who were Roman knights flogged and crucified in Jerusalem (Josephus *JW* 2 §308). But normally Roman citizens and, in particular, members of the upper class were safe from the possibility of crucifixion, no matter what their crimes. Death on the cross generally was limited to foreigners and people of the lower class, particularly slaves.

In 63 B.C. Rabirius, a Roman nobleman and senator, was threatened with the penalty of crucifixion. In defending him Cicero argued that the very mention of the "cross" and of the executioner (who tied the criminal's hands, veiled his head, and crucified him) was intolerable for a respectable Roman citizen.

> How grievous a thing it is to be disgraced by a public court; how grievous to suffer a fine, how grievous to suffer banishment; and yet in the midst of any such disaster we retain some degree of liberty. Even if we are threatened with death, we may die free men. But the executioner, the veiling of the head and *the very word "cross"* should be far removed not only from the person of a Roman citizen but his thoughts, his eyes and his ears. For it is not only the actual occurrence of these things but *the very mention of them,* that is unworthy of a Roman citizen and a free man (*Rab. Perd.* 16; italics added).

This speech reflected the horrified disgust which "good" Roman citizens felt for any of their own being subjected to, or even threatened with, crucifixion. For such people, crucifixion was "that most cruel and disgusting penalty," (*crudelissimum taeterrimumque supplicium;* Cic. *Verr.* 2.5.165).

The Romans used crucifixion to bring mutinous troops under control, to break the will of conquered peoples, and to wear down rebellious cities under siege. Dangerous and violent robbers could be crucified—often near or at the scene of their crimes. Quintilian (ca. 35–95 A.D.) approved of crucifixion as a penalty for such criminals, and thought that this form of execution had a better deterrent effect when the crosses were set up along the busiest roads. "Whenever we crucify the guilty, the most crowded roads are chosen, where the most people can see and be moved by this fear. For penalties relate not so much to retribution as to their exemplary effect" (*Decl.* 274). The Romans used crucifixion above all as the *servile supplicium* ("the slaves' punishment"), a terrible form of execution typically inflicted on slaves, (*servitutis extremum summumque supplicium;* Cic. *Verr.* 2.5.169).

Plautus (d. 184 B.C.), who happens to be the first writer to provide evidence about Roman crucifixions, has more to say about the theme than any other Latin author. He writes of the "terrible cross" of slaves (*Poen.* 347; see *Capt.* 469; *Cas.* 611; *Men.* 66, 859; *Pers.* 352; *Rud.* 518; *Trin.* 598), and reflects the grim gallows humor of their subculture. From his time on, the lower classes used "*crux*" as a vulgar taunt. The much-quoted confession of Sceledrus in *Miles Gloriosus* (written about 205 B.C.) suggests that for a long time before Plautus slaves had been frequently crucified: "I know the cross will be my grave: that is where my ancestors are, my father, grandfathers, great-grandfathers, great-great-grandfathers" (372–73).

Livy reports that twenty-five slaves made a conspiracy in Rome (in 217 B.C.) and were crucified (22.33.2). In 196 B.C. the leaders of a slave revolt in Etruria were crucified (Livy 33.36.3). Especially during the 2d century B.C., crucifixion was used to deter rebellions among the masses of slaves who lived in Rome or worked on the great estates elsewhere in Italy. According to Orosius (5.9.4), the first slave war in Sicily (139–132 B.C.) saw the crucifixion of 450 slaves. Appian (*BCiv.* 1.120) states that after the final defeat and death of Spartacus in 71 B.C., Crassus had more than 6000 slaves crucified along the Via Appia between Capua and Rome.

Even under "ordinary" conditions slaves had little legal protection. Juvenal describes the Roman matron who wanted a slave crucified and overrode her husband's objections with the notorious response: *Hoc volo, sic iubeo, sit pro ratione volantas* ("This is my will and my command. If you are looking for a reason, it is simply that I want it" (*Sat.* 6.223). Horace may condemn a master who had his slave crucified for tasting the soup while bringing it from the kitchen (*Sat.* 1.3.80–83), but he can also toss off a cruel remark about slaves "feeding crows on the cross" (*Ep.* 1.16.46–48). At the time of Nero a decree of the Senate revived the custom of executing (often by crucifixion) all the slaves of a household if the master was killed (Tac. *Ann.* 13.32.1). A few years later this was done after the murder of a city prefect (ibid. 14.42–45). A slave called Mithridates was crucified for "having damned the soul" of Caligula (Petron. *Sat.* 53.3). Slaves who questioned astrologers about the future of the emperor, of the state, or even that of their own masters faced crucifixion (Paulus *Sent.* 5.21.3–4). Suetonius says that Caligula (*Calig.* 12.2) and Domitian (*Dom.* 11.1) capriciously crucified imperial slaves and even freedmen. In his *Histories* Tacitus reports the crucifixion of several freedmen (2.72.2; 4.3.2; 4.11.3).

Cicero (see above), Seneca (see below) and other Romans recognized that crucifixion was an atrociously cruel form of execution. Yet Varro (*Sat. Men. Fr.* 24) was practically alone in protesting against the barbarism of crucifixion. Most took it for granted that this frequent form of execution was needed to deter the lower classes from committing serious crimes. Although crucifixion was frequent in Roman times, cultured writers preferred to say little about it. Unlike Josephus, Tacitus does not mention the innumerable crucifixions in Palestine (*Hist.* 5.8–13).

C. Forms of Crucifixion

Generally the victims were crucified alive; at times it was a matter of displaying the corpse of someone already executed in another way. Polycrates of Samos exemplifies the latter case. He was treacherously seized by the Persian satrap Oroites, killed "in an unspeakably cruel way," and his body fastened to a stake (Hdt. 3.125.3). Whether living or already dead, the victims suffered a degrading loss of all dignity by being bound or nailed to a stake. Herodotus offers a few details when reporting the way the satrap Artayctes was crucified by the Athenians at the Hellespont: "They nailed him to planks and hung him there. And they stoned Artayctes' son before his eyes" (9.120). Normally ancient writers were reluctant to describe particular crucifixions in much detail.

Under the Roman Empire, crucifixion normally included a flogging beforehand. At times the cross was only one vertical stake. Frequently, however, there was a crosspiece attached either at the top to give the shape of a "T" *(crux commissa)* or just below the top, as in the form most familiar in Christian symbolism *(crux immissa).* The victims carried the cross or at least a transverse beam *(patibulum)* to the place of execution, where they were stripped and bound or nailed to the beam, raised up, and seated on a *sedile* or small wooden peg in the upright beam. Ropes bound the shoulders or torso to the cross. The feet or heels of the victims were bound or nailed to the upright stake. As crucifixion damaged no vital organs, death could come slowly, sometimes after several days of atrocious pain. See also *IDBSup*, 199–200.

Executioners could vary the form of punishment, as Seneca the Younger indicates: "I see crosses there, not just of one kind but made in many different ways: some have their victims with head down to the ground; some impale their private parts; others stretch out their arms on the gibbet" (*Dial.* 6 [*Cons. Marc.*] 20.3). In his account of what happened to Jewish fugitives from Jerusalem, Josephus also lets us see that there was no fixed pattern for crucifying people. Much depended on the sadistic ingenuity of the moment.

> When they [the fugitives] were going to be taken [by the Romans], they were forced to offer resistance, and when the fighting ended it seemed too late to sue for mercy. Scourged and subjected before death to every torture, they were finally crucified in view of the wall [of Jerusalem]. Titus indeed realized the horror of what was happening, for every day 500—sometimes even more—fell into his hands. However, it was not safe to let men captured by force go free, and to guard such a host of prisoners would tie up a great proportion of his troops. But his chief reason for not stopping the slaughter was the hope that the sight of it would perhaps induce the Jews to surrender in order to avoid the same fate. The soldiers themselves through rage and bitterness nailed up their victims in different postures as a grim joke, till owing to the vast numbers there was no room for the crosses and no crosses for the bodies (*JW* 5 §449–51).

Nero's persecution of the Christians in Rome exemplified a similar capricious cruelty: "Mockery of every sort was added to their deaths. Covered with the skins of wild beasts, they were torn to death by dogs. Or they were fastened on crosses and, when daylight faded, were burned to serve as lamps by night" (Tac. *Ann.* 15.44.4).

In the course of a debate on happiness, Plato's *Gorgias* indicates various kinds of torture that a condemned man might suffer before dying by crucifixion:

> If a man is caught in a criminal plot to make himself tyrant, and when caught is put to the rack and mutilated and has his eyes burnt out and after himself suffering and seeing his wife and children suffer many many other signal outrages of various kinds, is finally crucified or burned on a coat of pitch, will he be happier than if he escaped arrest, established himself as a tyrant and lived the rest of his life a sovereign in his state, doing what he pleased, an object of envy and felicitation among citizens and strangers alike? (473 bc).

Different tortures that could precede crucifixion appear again when Plato describes the fate, not of a would-be tyrant, but of the perfectly just man: "The just man will have to be scourged, racked, fettered, blinded, and finally, after the most extreme suffering, he will be crucified" (*Resp.* 361e–362a).

In Epistle 101 to Lucilius, Seneca argues that it is better to commit suicide than face such extreme and drawn-out suffering as death by crucifixion. To press his argument he describes what such a death was like:

> Can anyone be found who would prefer wasting away in pain dying limb by limb, or letting out his life drop by drop, rather than expiring once for all? Can any man be found willing to be fastened to the accursed tree, long sickly, already deformed, swelling with ugly weals on shoulders and chest, and drawing the breath of life amid long-drawn-out agony? He would have many excuses for dying even before mounting the cross.

D. Jesus' Crucifixion

All four gospels record that Jesus foretold his own death. Matthew specifies that it would be by crucifixion (Matt 20:19; 26:2) and that some of Jesus' followers would suffer the same fate (Matt 23:34).

Jesus' crucifixion is recounted in Matthew 27; Mark 15; Luke 23; and John 19; and is often referred to elsewhere in the NT (e.g., Acts 2:36, 4:10; 1 Cor 2:8; Gal 3:1; Rev 11:8). According to the Synoptics, Simon of Cyrene was forced to carry Jesus' cross. The crucifixion took place at Golgotha or "Place of a skull." It seems that Jesus was nailed to the cross by his hands (Luke 24:39; John 20:25) and feet (Luke 24:39). Two robbers were crucified on either side of Jesus, whose cross carried a sign saying "the King of the Jews," indicating the crime for which he was being executed. Jesus refused the drugged wine offered to deaden his pain. He was taunted by some of the passers-by, used the opening words of Psalm 22 to cry out "My God, my God, why hast thou forsaken me?" and died around three in the afternoon—his death being hastened by the severe scourging he had previously undergone. With Pontius Pilate's permission, Joseph of Arimathea took Jesus' corpse down from the cross and gave it honorable burial.

Beyond doubt, devout reflection on Jesus' death and the desire to find prophetic anticipations of it introduced some details into the passion narratives. Nevertheless, the version just given is a defensible historical account of his crucifixion.

As we saw above, the Romans frequently employed the sadistically cruel and utterly shameful death by crucifixion to uphold civil authority and preserve law and order against troublesome criminals, slaves, and rebels. In Palestine crucifixion was a public reminder of Jewish servitude to a foreign power.

Hence Jesus' cross was a sign of extreme "shame" (Heb 12:2). Paul did not exaggerate when he called the crucified Christ "a stumbling block to Jews and folly to Gentiles" (1 Cor 1:23; see 2:2; Gal 5:11). Nothing in the OT or in other Jewish sources suggests that the Messiah could suffer such a fate. On the contrary, a crucified person—so far from being chosen, anointed, and sent by God—was understood to be cursed by God (see A. above). The nonbelievers it seemed "sheer folly" (1 Cor 1:18) to proclaim the crucified Jesus as God's Son, universal Lord, and coming Judge of the world. The extreme dishonor of his death by crucifixion counted against any such claims. A century after Paul, Justin Martyr (ca. 100–65) noted how utterly offensive it was to acknowledge the divine status of a crucified man: "They say that our madness consists in the fact that we put a crucified man in second place after the unchangeable and eternal God, the Creator of the world" (1 *Apol.* 13.4). In a liturgical rather than an apologetical setting, Melito of Sardis (died ca. 190) also recognized the strange "scandal" of Christian faith in the crucified Jesus.

> He who hung the earth [in its place] hangs there, he who fixed the heavens is fixed there, he who made all things fast is made fast upon the tree, the Master has been insulted, God has been murdered, the King of Israel has been slain by an Israelite hand. O strange murder, strange crime! The Master has been treated in unseemly fashion, his body naked, and not even deemed worthy of a covering that [his nakedness] might not be seen. Therefore the lights [of heaven] turned away, and the day darkened, that it might hide him who was stripped upon the cross (*Pass.* 96–97).

The utter disgrace of crucifixion encouraged Celsus to dismiss derisively the redemptive role of Jesus, who had been "bound in the most ignominious fashion" and "executed in a shameful way" (Origen *Cels.* 6.10). Gnostic docetism eliminated the scandal of the death on the cross by alleging that the living, spiritual Christ remained untouched and laughed when his image was crucified (e.g., *Apoc. Pet.* 82.1–83.15). Against such theorizing Ignatius of Antioch insisted that Christ did not merely appear to suffer but was "truly crucified" (*Trall.* 9.1).

Nothing expresses more forcefully the paradoxical Christian claims about the crucified Jesus than the hymn in Philippians 2:6–11. Whether it existed as a pre-Pauline element or was added by Paul himself, the phrase "even death on a cross" (2:8) presents the extreme contrast between Christ's glory (2:9–11), on the one hand, and the shameful death when he was crucified like a slave *(supplicium servile),* on the other.

E. Christian Interpretations of the Crucifixion

Paul sees in the crucifixion the revelation of Jesus' obedience (Phil 2:8) and love (Gal 2:20). The crucifixion discloses God's power and wisdom (1 Cor 1:24; 2 Cor 13:4). It brings deliverance from sin (Col 2:14) and "the curse of the Law" (Gal 3:13); it effects reconciliation and peace (Col 1:20; Eph 2:16). Becoming Jesus' follower means the crucifixion of one's former, sinful self (Rom 6:6; Gal 2:20; 6:14). The Law has no more claim on those who have died with Christ (Gal 2:19). They renounce sin and leave behind the ungodly world (Gal 6;14). Paul is persecuted because in these terms he accepts and preaches the cross of Christ (Gal 6:12).

To convey what discipleship metaphorically (and sometimes literally) entailed, the Synoptic Gospels spoke of "taking up one's cross" and following Jesus (Mark 8:34; Matt 10:38; 16:24; Luke 9:23; 14:27). "Taking up one's cross" may have been a profane and/or Zealot expression which then was applied to Christian discipleship. For the Synoptics it meant saying no to oneself, accepting suffering, and even surrendering one's life for and with Jesus—in short, being a cross bearer all one's life.

Bibliography

Dinkler, E. 1967. *Signum Crucis.* Tübingen.

Fitzmyer, J. A. 1978. Crucifixion in Ancient Palestine, Qumran Literature, and the New Testament. *CBQ* 40: 493–513.

Hengel, M. 1977. *Crucifixion.* Philadelphia.

Thornton, T. C. G. 1986. The Crucifixion of Haman and the Scandal of the Cross. *JTS* 37: 419–26.

Zias, J., and Sekeles, E. 1985. The Crucified Man from Giv^{c}at ha-Mivtar—A Reappraisal. *BA* 48: 190–91.

GERALD G. O'COLLINS

CRUSE [Heb *ṣappaḥat*]. A translation for a Hebrew word which in several other passages is rendered "jar" (1 Sam 26:11, 12, 16; 2 Kgs 19:6). As "jar," the Hebrew term clearly designates a water container and probably refers to the two-handled lentoid containers known as pilgrim flasks. Such containers are found archaeologically in Late Bronze through Iron II contexts (for illustrations, see Amiran 1969: 166–67, 276; pls. 51, 93–95; Photos 167, 168, 296–98). The biblical passages which use the term for "jar" indicate its portability. The 1 Samuel verses suggest that it functioned as a canteen for soldiers. Travelers too would have carried water in canteens since the mouth of the flask was narrow and convenient for drinking and stoppering (Kelso 1948: 30).

The pilgrim flask makes the most sense as the ceramic vessel meant by *ṣappaḥat,* since the root of that word in other Semitic languages apparently involves flattening or spreading out. The Arabic cognate, e.g., means "to make wide, broad." However, the term *ṣappaḥat* is also used to designate a different vessel, a container used for oil in the story of the oil jar of Elijah and the widow of Zarephath in 1 Kings 17. In that context, it refers to a small container, which contained just a little oil. If this be so, "cruse" designates a small cruet-size ceramic vessel meant for oil as opposed to the larger oil jar (*ʾāsûk;* 2 Kgs 4:2), or to a large storage jar *(nebel)* that could hold oil but also grain or wine. Small juglets used to dip water or to hold oil or another commodity appear in archaeological contexts going back to the Early Bronze Age. Early in the Iron II period, the time of Elijah and the widow's cruse, such small juglets were often black (a black burnished slip) and had rounded bodies, long narrow necks, and handles attached at the middle of the neck (Amiran 1969: 256, 258; pl. 86:12–13; 87:13).

The biblical story of the oil cruse contributes to the characterization of Elijah as a prophetic figure with special powers from God. During a drought, Elijah asks a widow for food and drink. She protests that her supplies are meager (only "a little oil in a cruse," 2 Kgs 17:12). Elijah then assures her that her supplies will not be used up until God ends the drought and her stores can be replenished; and indeed, the cruse of oil [did not] fail" (1 Kgs 17:16).

Bibliography

Amiram, R. 1969. *Ancient Pottery of the Holy Land.* Jerusalem.

Kelso, J. C. 1948. *Ceramic Vocabulary of the Old Testament.* BASORSup 5–6. New Haven.

CAROL MEYERS

CTESIAS. Fifth-century Greek physician in the Persian court who authored a history of Persia *(Persika)* in twenty-three books, a geographical treatise *(Periodos)* in three books, and a book about India (*Indika*).

Scion of a medical family from Cnidus in Asia Minor, Ctesias sojourned for several years in the court of Artaxerxes II. His biography still admits a few obscurities. One of his users, Diodorus of Sicily, thus presents his source in the *Historical Library:* "Ctesias of Cnidus lived during the time of Cyrus' expedition against his brother Artaxerxes; he was taken prisoner, and as he had distinguished himself by his medical knowledge, he was received at the king's court, where he lived seventeen years heaped with honors" (2.32.4). The details here are not clear, however. Diodorus suggests that Ctesias was made a prisoner at the Battle of Cunaxa, possibly in 405, while it is known from other sources that Ctesias' residence in Persia ended in 398. That is why it has been frequently proposed that Diodorus' texts should be corrected to read seven years instead of seventeen. But doubts continue because other sources seem to indicate that Ctesias was part of the royal entourage even before Cunaxa. Photius notes elsewhere that Ctesias attained his *acme* (40 years of age for the Greeks) at the time of Cyrus II (that is, between 408 and 401 B.C.E.); Ctesias thus probably was born around 445.

In the course of his service at the Persian court, he amassed materials for his works that he drafted after his return to Cnidus. Among his known works figures the *Indika,* a sort of ethnographic description of India, of the country and its inhabitants. (A somewhat fantastic ethnography, as notes the epitomizer Photius.) Two other of his works have unfortunately disappeared almost totally; not even the contents would be known if not for the scattered citations made by later authors to whom Athanaeus refers. One of these books gave an account of the stages and relays on the royal road between Ephesus, Bactria, and India. Even the title of the work shows that Ctesias had an administrative and geographical horizon greater than that of Herodotus, who limited the Royal Way to the itinerary between Sardis and Susa. It is not impossible that Ctesias could have used official sources on the subject.

The other book—*Phoroi*—went into particulars of the produce levied by the royal administration to provision the Royal Table. It is an interesting testimony to the ideology of tribute in the Achaemenid empire. Ctesias possibly had access in this case as well to official registers preserved at the court.

His most important work for the historian of ancient Persia was a history of the dynasties that succeeded from Ninos to Semiramis until Artaxerxes II. It is entitled *Persika,* but in reality the first 6 books, extensively cited by Diodorus, concern the history of Assyria. Only books 7 through 23 can be properly considered *Persika* in the strictest sense of the term. Of the 18 books that form this work, 6 of them were dedicated to the activity of the first Persian kings: Cyrus, Cambyses, the magi, Darius, and Xerxes (ca. 550–465). Books 16–17 deal with the reign of Artaxerxes I (465–424). Books 18–20 deal with the reigns of Xerxes II, Sogdianos, and Darius II (424–405/4). Finally the last 3 books (20–23) were devoted to the first seven years (405/4–398) of Artaxerxes II's long reign.

The use of this work poses many problems for historians. Foremost, we don't have access to the text composed by Ctesias' own hand. Outside of a few scattered fragments, we have available only a copious summary compiled by the Byzantine patriarch Photius in the 9th century C.E. It is not always easy to distinguish what belonged to the original work and what has been given prominence by the selection of the abridger. Nonetheless, it appears clear that Photius did not disturb the general structure of the work, which is organized according to a strict annalistic framework, from king to king. The relative importance accorded to each reign seems to derive from Ctesias himself.

Since antiquity, the credibility of Ctesias' information has been doubted. Plutarch, who relied on him heavily in preparing his *Life of Artaxerxes,* criticizes him several times; for, according to him, Ctesias "had introduced in his works incredible and extravagant tales." Photius too stresses Ctesias' tendency toward fabrication, in particular in his work on India. One can point out numerous errors in his accounts of the reigns of earlier kings, in particular in the narrative of the Median Wars; he even inverted the battles of Salamis and Platea! The errors result in part, no doubt, from Ctesias' undisguised desire to polemicize with Herodotus in order to better compete with him. But the comparison is most often to the advantage of the historian of Halicarnassus. For all that, the opposition between the two historians need not be maintained in a systematic fashion. Herodotus resorts to stories and fables too. For example, there is no reason to choose between the respective versions of Herodotus and Ctesias on the origins of Cyrus: both transmit one of the many versions of the legend of the dynast that circulated in their day. In short, to borrow A. Momigliano's expression, there isn't just invention in Ctesias: he is above all marked by the tradition with which he familiarized himself during his days in the Achaemenid court.

It is clear, in fact, that Ctesias did not simply use the works of his precursors. He also did original work. On which documents did he rely? Diodorus tells that Ctesias himself acknowledged using the royal annals; but such a claim seems hardly plausible, least of all for the *Persika;* it had above all the aim of conferring upon the work a pseudoscientific character. Moreover, Photius takes account of nothing but oral testimony: "Ctesias pretends to have seen with his own eyes most of the facts that he records and to have heard them from the Persians themselves when he wasn't a direct witness: it is from these sources that he would have constructed his history." The recourse to oral sources can only cast doubt. Ctesias explicitly indicates as much himself, in making reference to information given by the queen Parysatis, whose health he looked after. Everything also leads one to believe that the long tormented history of Megabyzus was elaborated from information given by representatives of the family: the narrative form given to the story of Megabyzus also contradicts the oral tradition recognizable in numerous passages of *Persika*.

One can only note as well the central importance accorded to the actions and deeds of the kings, queens, and eunuchs. It has less to do with Persian history than with tales of struggles for succession and conflicts of factions within the court. But one should not ask of Ctesias what he never dreamed of offering. In all, his contribution is far from negligible. It can be shown, for example, that the account he gives of the troubled period begun by the assassination of Artaxerxes I and ended by the succession of Ochos-Darius II is in agreement with the conclusions that one can infer from the analysis of Babylonian tablets. In a more general way, he furnishes irreplaceable information on the royal family and on periods of succession.

Historians today have a tendency to accord only little value to Ctesias' information. It is true that comparison with Herodotus and Thucydides devaluates considerably his accounts of the Median Wars or of the struggle between the Athenians and the Persians in Egypt, to give only two examples. But one must remember that the objective of Ctesias was not to write a Persian history in the sense that we understand it. Living at the court, he writes chronologically ordered histories centering around kings and princesses, officers of the court, and nobles. Hence the importance given, for example, to Megabyzus; such a story allows one to show in a quasi-emblematic manner that the power of a noble, as powerful as he might be, depended exclusively on royal favor. It was also a story about a tragic destiny to which Ctesias knew he could attract impassioned readers. In the account of Megabyzus' return from exile, Greek readers could even find a plot close to a model that the return of Ulysses to Ithaca had made familiar to them.

Historiographically, the greatest damage caused by Ctesias comes from the presentation that he give of political life at the Persian court, which he presents as dominated by palace intrigues led by queens and eunuchs who manipulated incapable and irresolute kings. The work is thus dominated by a series of feminine protagonists, in general not very sympathetic; this is particularly true of Parysatis, sister-spouse of Darius II, all of whose actions seem to be inspired by a desire for vengeance against the enemies of his dead son Cyrus and against the representatives of the family of Hydernes, including his own daughter-in-law, the queen Stateira, whose horrible assassination at the hands of Parysatis Ctesias narrates in detail. In doing this, Ctesias conferred on the Persian princesses a political authority that they had never had. In addition, he was one of the creators of the myth of "Persian decadence," which is witnessed in particular by the feminization of the palaces. This myth was obligingly developed after his example by other authors like Plato, Xenophon, and Isocrates, and willingly taken up again in the modern age. This interpretation corresponds to a Hellenocentric vision of the history of the Near East, exacerbated by Greco-Persian conflicts of the 4th century.

Bibliography

Bigwood, J. M. 1976. Ctesias' Account of the Revolt of Inarus. *Phoenix* 30: 1–25.

———. 1978. Ctesias as an Historian of the Persian Wars. *Phoenix* 32: 19–41.

Briant, P. 1982. Sources grecques et histoire achéméide. Pp. 491–506 in *Rois, tributs et paysans.* Paris.

———. 1989. Histoire et idéologie: Les Grecs et la "décadence perse." Vol. 2, pp. 33–47 in *Mélanges Pierre Lévêque.* Paris.

Brown, T. S. 1978. Suggestions for a *Vita* of Ctesias of Cnidus. *Historia* 37: 1–19.

Drews, R. 1973. *The Greek Accounts of Eastern History.* Washington, DC.

König, W. F. 1972. *Die "Persika" des Ktesias von Knidos.* Graz.

Sancisi-Weerdenburg, H. 1987. Decadence in the Empire or Decadence in the Sources: From Source to Synthesis: Ctesias. Vol. 1, pp. 33–45 in *Achaemenid History.* Leiden.

Stolper, M. 1985. *Entrepreneurs and Empire.* Leiden.

PIERRE BRIANT
Trans. Stephen Rosoff

CUB (PLACE). See LIBYA.

CUBIT. See WEIGHTS AND MEASURES.

CUCUMBER. See FLORA.

CUMMIN. See FLORA.

CUN (PLACE) [Heb *kûn*]. Town from which David took much bronze after his defeat of Hadadezer of the kingdom of Zobah in 1 Chr 18:8 (= 2 Sam 8:8). Instead of Cun, 2 Sam 8:8 mentions Berothai. Cun is, according to Albright (1934: 60), the *Ku-nú* found in a catalogue of Ramesses III. The mention in Roman sources of towns named *Conna* and *Cunna* in the N Beqaᶜ Valley of Lebanon at or near Rās Baalbek (34°16′N; 36°28′E) has led many scholars to equate the latter with Cun. Dussaud (1927: 271) accepts that *Conna* may be Rās Baalbek, but he argues that *Cunna* is identical with neither of these. Intense survey of Rās Baalbek in 1972 yielded only a few sherds of the Iron Age or earlier (Müller 1976: 93). Rās Baalbek should not be confused with Baalbek (34°00′N; 36°13′E) about 20 miles to the S. Josephus (*Ant* 7.105) renders the place in 1 Chr 18:8 as *Machōni,* indicating that the *mem,* which the MT regards as a preposition, may be part of the name. Accordingly, one should not overlook the Bronze and Iron Age site of Tell Maqna (34°05′N; 36°13′E), known also as *Mighni* in various sources (cf. Dussaud 1927: 553), as a possible location of the place in 1 Chr 18:8.

Bibliography

Albright, W. F. 1934. *The Vocalization of the Egyptian Syllabic Orthography.* AOS 5. New Haven.

Dussaud, R. 1927. *Topographie historique de la Syrie antique et médiévale.* Paris.

Müller, U. 1976. Die keramnische Befund der alten Siedlungsstätten der nördlichen Biqāᶜ. Pp. 35–100 in *Archäologischer Survey in der nördlichen Biqāᶜ,* ed. A. Kuschke et al. Wiesbaden.

HECTOR AVALOS

CUNEIFORM. From the Lat for "wedge-shaped," the term describes writing systems in which signs were rapidly impressed with a reed stylus on a soft writing surface. The native terms for cuneiform writing, Sum GU-SUM = Akk *miḫiltum/mihiṣtum/mihištum* (Vanstiphout 1988), refer to the stroke of the stylus. The most suitable and ubiquitous writing material was clay; over 99 percent of all cuneiform documents are clay tablets (rarely other shapes, such as cones, prisms, barrels, or vessels) ranging in size from 2×2 cm to 30×30 cm. The only other suitable medium for accepting the stroke of the stylus was wax; wax-covered writing boards are attested from the 2d millennium (one was recently found in a Bronze Age shipwreck off the Turkish coast), and were extensively used in the 1st millennium (Parpola 1983), from which, however, only one, plus some fragments of others, have survived (*RLA* 4: 458–9). For purposes of commemoration or identification, cuneiform signs could be chiseled into stone, engraved in metal, and painted or scratched on wood or ceramic. The cuneiform writing system was used from ca. 3100 B.C. into the first century of this era, originally and finally in Babylonia, but at various times in Iran, Upper Mesopotamia, Anatolia, Armenia, Syria, Palestine, Cyprus, and Egypt.

A. Origin and Development

The widely publicized theories of D. Schmandt-Besserat (1986, 1988), building on the work of P. Amiet, call our attention to small clay tokens found at sites throughout the Near East from the 9th to 2d millennia, which she claims are the earliest form of human record-keeping. Certain tokens are even said to be the direct forerunners of specific cuneiform signs, but these identifications, except for certain numerical signs which may well go back to token shapes, remain highly speculative. However, Schmandt-Besserat has been able to reconstruct a remarkable and convincing sequence that, beginning in the mid-4th millennium, leads from a crude system of numerical notation to the first cuneiform documents.

The sequence begins with hollow clay balls containing clay tokens of various shapes, which have been impressed on the balls before the balls were sealed. The number and shape of the tokens inside the ball matches the impressions on the outside, and one or more seals may have been rolled over the ball. The tokens record a transaction, and have been sealed in the ball to protect the integrity of the record, but have usually also been impressed on the outside for easy consultation. The seal impressions would prevent both tampering with the token impressions and the undetected opening of the clay ball. It was soon recognized that the seal impressions alone could, when necessary, secure the integrity of the impressed numerical data. The tokens were no longer necessary, and the clumsy ball could be flattened into a cushion-shaped tablet. Both tokens and impressions signified quantities, perhaps of specific commodities. Additional information pertaining to the object of the transaction or the individuals and organizations responsible for it were conveyed by the seals (Dittmann 1986). These clay balls and impressed tablets are known best from late 4th millennium Uruk and Susa, but they have also been found at various sites along an arc stretching from the great bend of the Euphrates to southeastern Iran, in assemblages that characterize the Uruk Expansion (Algaze 1989).

The contrast between the clay balls and numerical tablets, and even the earliest inscribed tablets, is striking. They have numerical notation in common, but the inscribed tablets, in addition, have an array of complex signs that is vastly more capable of signifying people, organizations, operations, and commodities than any system of tokens or tokenlike impressions and fixed seal impressions. The elaboration of this writing system was effected by the extension of the substitution of stylus impression for token evidenced in the numerical tablets, to the use of the stylus to produce the kind of pictorial and symbolic representations heretofore best known from seals (Buccellati 1981).

The earliest tablets appear at Uruk around 3100 B.C. (Nissen's Stage IV; see Nissen 1986a–b; Green and Nissen 1987). The bulk of the archaic tablets from Uruk follow immediately on these earliest tablets, and are similar to archaic tablets found outside of Uruk at Jemdet Nasr, Tell ʿUqair, and Tell Asmar (Nissen's Stage III). The presence of the earliest type at Uruk only seems to confirm Uruk as the point of origin for the writing system, which fits well with Uruk's position as the largest urban center, by far, in Babylon at the end of the 4th millennium. The increasing economic and political complexity of urban society was the prime stimulus for the development and implementation of the information storage system represented by the tablets. Curiously, in its archaic stages, cuneiform writing never spread beyond Babylonia to the areas that had been so heavily influenced by Babylonia in previous periods (Algaze 1989), although Elam developed a different archaic writing system of its own, probably through stimulus diffusion from Babylonia (Vallat 1986).

Each sign stood for a Sumerian word of one (the majority) to three syllables. Although most signs were originally pictograms, even if we cannot always determine exactly what a given sign depicts, there were abstract signs as well in the archaic repertoire. For example, in contrast to the cattle signs, which indeed look much like animal heads, the signs for sheep and for goats consist of various combinations of circle, cross, and rectangle, with cross-hatching on the interior or exterior to mark the adult females and female kid, and lozenges to mark the males (Green 1980). See Fig. CUN.01. Pictographs could have an iconic relationship to their signifieds, as GU$_4$ "ox," SAG "head," or TI "arrow", or could point to them in various ways: KA "mouth" seems to be a SAG "head" with added lines about nose level; DU, a foot-shaped sign is used for Sum DU "to go" and GUB "to stand"; AN, a star, stands for Sum AN "heaven" and DINGIR "god." Signs could be combined to form a new sign, whose meaning would be indicated by the sum of its parts: SAG ("head") or KA ("mouth") + NINDA ("food," a pictograph of a ration bowl?) = GU$_7$ "to eat" (fig. 1:5); MINUS (pubic triangle = "woman") + KUR (schematically drawn mountains = "mountains, foreign land") = GEME$_2$ "slave woman" (slaves were frequently foreign captives). As the system evolved, one (or more) of the combined signs might be inscribed within another, as in GU$_7$, or the combined signs might be written side-by-side, as GEME$_2$.

This originally pictographic basis accounts for two characteristic features of cuneiform writing—polyphony and homophony. On the one hand, a given sign may have two or more readings (e.g. /DU/ and /GUB/ for DU). On the other, there may be several signs that have the same read-

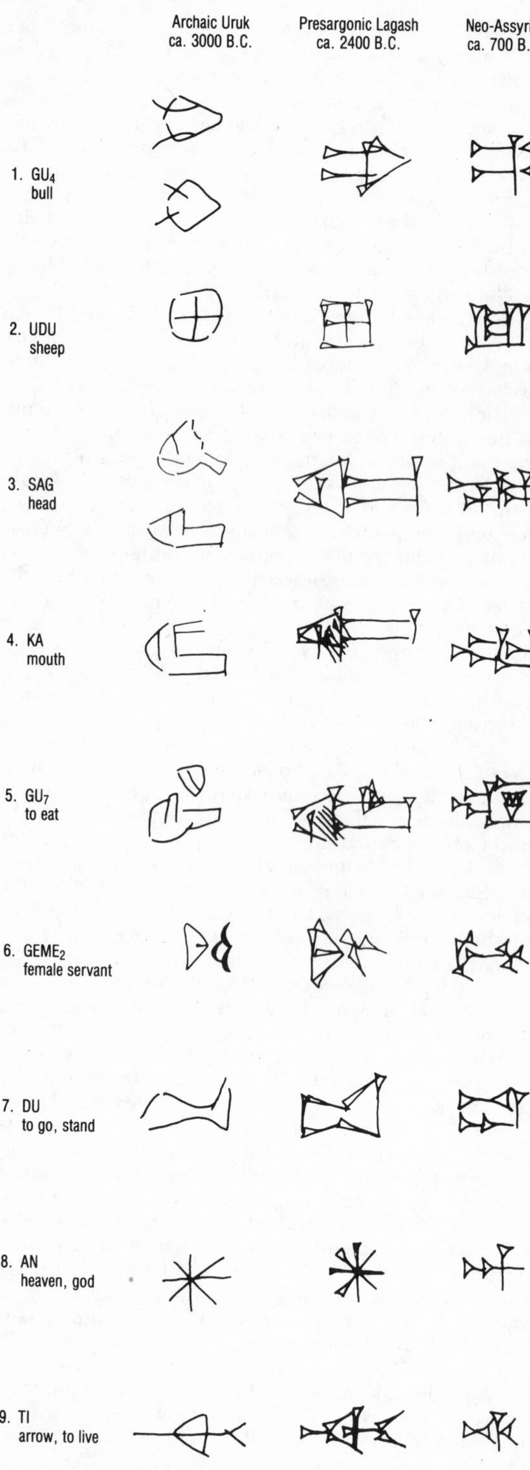

CUN.01. Evolution of cuneiform signs. *(Redrawn from J. Cooper.)*

ing (e.g. GU$_4$ and GU$_7$; the subscripted index number is the scholarly convention for distinguishing homophonic signs in transliteration). The latter phenomenon was exacerbated both because the Sumerian language had a large number of homophones (perhaps distinguished by tone), and because final consonants often drop in Sumerian in word final position (e.g., GU$_4$ is /GUD/ when followed by a vocalic affix).

The signs on the earliest archaic tablets (Stage IV) were *drawn* in the clay, a relatively slow and cumbersome procedure. By archaic Stage III, signs were beginning to be composed out of individually *impressed* strokes. Impression was both rapid and efficient, and imparted the characteristic wedge-shaped head to each stroke in a sign: the wedge was formed by the tip of the stylus, and the trailing line by the stylus's sharpened edge (Green 1981: 351–59). The replacement of drawing by impression quickly led to the signs' loss of pictorialness; within a few centuries of writing's invention, most signs bear little, if any, resemblance to their pictographic antecedents. Other developments obvious from Fig. CUN.01 are the broadening of the wedge at the head of each stroke, the diminution in the number of strokes per sign, the restriction of the possible angles at which a given stroke could be made, and later in Assyria, the resolution of certain groups of angular wedges *(Winkelhacken)* into parallel horizontals (Labat 1988: 1–7). The absolute number of cuneiform signs also declined over time, but not as much as previously thought. A well-educated scribe in 3000 B.C. would know ca. 770 nonnumerical signs; 2300 years later, an Assyrian scholar could be familiar with as many as 600 signs. Although a certain number of signs fell out of use through obsolescence or coalescence with other signs, there was also, over time, a certain amount of differentiation of one sign into two, and the creation of new compounds.

It is immediately apparent from Fig. CUN.01 that the proper orientation of the pictographs is 90 degrees to the right of the normal orientation of the signs in later periods. The motivation and the time of the shift in direction is disputed, but it certainly occurred on tablets by the last centuries of the 3d millennium. Monumental inscription on stone, in keeping with its more solemn and archaizing character, was written to be read in the original orientation well into the 2d millennium (*RLA* 5: 546–67, Powell 1981). In the following discussion, even archaic tablets will be described as if held in the later, "normal" orientation.

Tablet format has an important semiotic as well as organizational role. The use of position, spacing, and horizontal and vertical rulings can convey information not made explicit by the signs alone, and can ease interpretation and help avoid or resolve ambiguities. Although some archaic tablets contain only a few signs deployed on an undifferentiated surface, most already enclose words or phrases in rectangular cases. On larger tablets, these cases can be arranged in vertical rows or columns, read from top to bottom, beginning at obverse left. The tablet was turned on its horizontal axis, and at least by 2500 B.C. but probably earlier, the columns on the reverse were read from right to left. An experiment in very complex columnar subdivisions was abandoned after archaic Stage III (Green 1981).

Within each case, signs originally could be arranged haphazardly, but by ca. 2450 their arrangement, from left to right, corresponded to the order in which they were read. By ca. 2300, the boxlike cases began to evolve into the horizontal lines that are standard by the end of the 3d millennium. The scribes were afflicted with a *horror vacui* at line's end, and spaced the signs on a given line so that the last sign would rest up against the right margin. Words were never broken at the end of a line; if a scribe reached the right margin before finishing a word or a phrase that he wanted to complete on one line, the line would be continued below, indented to the right.

Whereas a pictographic system can adequately represent concrete objects and, as shown above, express certain abstract notions, a writing system in which every word was represented by a different sign would be quite unwieldy. Furthermore, a system with over 700 signs that could give no clue to their reading would be difficult to learn and use. And grammatical features necessary for complete linguistic representation cannot be expressed by a writing system whose individual signs represent lexemes only. The early emergence of rebus phoneticism solved these and other problems, and was essential to the successful development of the cuneiform system. On the lexical level, a sign TI (Fig. CUN.01), originally a picture of an arrow (Sum TI), could be used to write the nearly homonymous abstract verb TIL "to live." As a phonetic indicator, the sign MA (a type of fruit) was combined with an animal head to indicate the final */m/* for the reading as Sum ALIM "bison" (Green and Nissen 1987: 174), or the sign EN is inscribed in GA_2 to create the sign for Sum MEN "crown" (Green and Nissen 1987: 245). This separation of phonetic from semantic content then made it possible to use, say, GA (Sum GA "milk;" pictogram originally a milk jar) to write the Sum verbal prefix GA- "let me," or RA (Sum RA "to strike") to write the dative postposition (possibly incipient at archaic Uruk; see Green and Nissen 1987: 264).

Another aid to distinguishing and reading the signs is the semantic classifier or determinative, a sign set before or after the sign that it classifies to indicate the semantic category to which the sign belongs. Thus GIŠ (Sum "tree, wood") is set before the sign(s) for a tree or wooden object, and KI (Sum "place") follows a toponym. The use of such determinatives is already well attested in the archaic texts from Uruk (Green 1981: 360).

B. Linguistic, Geographic, and Generic Extension

The possibility of using cuneiform signs to express phonetic syllables divorced from any semantic meaning, that is, as syllabograms rather than logograms, created the potential for using the cuneiform writing system to phonetically write languages other than the Sumerian language for which it was originally invented. The first non-Sumerian words to be written, were, no doubt, personal names and toponyms, people and places whose names were not Sumerian but had to be included in the records of the bureaucracies in Babylonia that utilized cuneiform. Some of these names were Semitic; Semitic-speaking peoples were in Babylonia from at least the early 3d millennium, and by 2500 B.C., 50 percent of the scribes known from Abu Salabikh (near Nippur) bore Semitic names, and another thirty Semitic names are known from the Fara tablets (Biggs 1988, Westenholz 1988). A few administrative and literary texts from Abu Salabikh seem to have been meant to be read in Semitic.

The earliest significant corpora of connected texts written in Semitic are arrested from ca. 2400 B.C. at Mari, on the Euphrates near the present Syro-Iraqi border (Charpin 1987), and Ebla in northwestern Syria (see the bibliographies in Cagni 1987, Krebernik 1988). But although personal names and the Semitic words in the bilingual Sumero-Semitic word lists found there are written phonetically, connected Semitic texts rely heavily on Sumerograms, Sumerian logograms meant to be read as Semitic, supplemented by phonetically written Semitic prepositions and pronouns. The language of the Semitic texts and names from Syria and Babylonia ca. 2500–2400 B.C. seems to form "an unbroken linguistic continuum, a cluster of closely related dialects, despite the numerous local peculiarities" (Westenholz 1988: 101). It is closely related to, but not identical with, the Old Akkadian that emerges in Babylonia ca. 2350.

The Semitic Old Akkadian texts known from the time of Sargon of Akkad and his successors in Babylonia (Gelb 1961), in contrast to the Presargonic Semitic texts, write most nouns and nearly all verbs phonetically. A paradigm for writing Akkadian was established that persisted in all subsequent periods: phonetic representation using a restricted corpus of monosyllabic signs, supplemented by a limited number of Sumerograms representing very common terms, such as "king" or "earth," legal and administrative formulas, and technical terms. The major exception is the high frequency of logograms found in certain categories of Akkadian technical literature, especially in the 1st millennium, where the use and spatial deployment of the logograms makes the texts much easier to scan than they would be if written phonetically.

Despite the large number of signs known by academic scribes in any given period or center of cuneiform literacy, the number of signs that a scribe needed to master for everyday purposes was relatively small. There are no studies of how many signs were normally employed by, say, a clerk writing in Sumerian under the 3d Dynasty of Ur (ca. 2100–2000 B.C.), but an OB or OA scribe writing Akkadian could function well with 100–150 signs, and manage to get by with even less (*RLA* 5: 561–62; Larsen 1989: 132–33). Each period and region has its own particular syllabary, or selection of signs, and orthographic practices.

By the middle of the 2d millennium B.C., several of Mesopotamia's neighbors had adapted the Akkadian syllabary together with Sumerian logograms to write their own languages. These include the Elamites in southwestern Iran; the Hurrians, spread in an arc stretching from the Zagros in the east to the Taurus and the Mediterranean in the west; and the Hittites, who controlled a large empire from their capital in central Anatolia. From the early 2d millennium, but especially between 1500–1200 B.C., cuneiform Akkadian was the lingua franca of the Near East and was used regularly in diplomatic communications between capitals and between rulers and their vassals. It was also the language of local law and administration in such non-Akkadian speaking milieux as Mari, Alalakh, Ugarit (alongside Ugaritic), and Emar.

In the first millennium, Sumero-Akkadian cuneiform was used to write other languages only in Elam and Urartu. In Syria and Palestine, cuneiform, stylus, and clay tablets were replaced by the easier-to-learn alphabet, pen, and ink, and papyrus or leather, a process that was occurring in Mesopotamia as well. The change in writing system and medium was accompanied by a change in language, as Aramaic took over the role that Akkadian had played in the preceding millennium.

The earliest cuneiform texts are the records of the bureaucratic organizations whose needs spawned the writing system, and the lexical lists necessary to educate the scribal bureaucrats who used the system. These early records have been aptly characterized as aide-mémoire (Bottéro 1987: 89–112); they listed quantities, commodities, individuals, and sometimes operations, but depended on the user's prior knowledge of context and procedures to ascertain the relationships between those elements. It was only the systematic development of phonetic writing to express the grammatical elements of language that made written literature, letters, and commemorative inscriptions possible. This began ca. 2600, but the earliest literary texts (mainly from Abu Salabikh) are hardly intelligible unless a later version of the same composition exists, and many are written in a peculiar allographic orthography that is only partially deciphered (*RLA* 7: 36–37, Krebernik 1984: 267–86). Full or nearly full expression of grammatical elements, and long, complex narrative texts, begin ca. 2400. Technical and scientific topics (e.g., omens, ritual compendia, astronomy, mathematics, medicine, glassmaking, and grammar) first find written expression in the 2d millennium.

Sumero-Akkadian cuneiform inspired two completely new and radically simplified writing systems utilizing configurations of wedges impressed on clay tablets. From the mid- to late 2d millennium, a cuneiform alphabet, known chiefly from Ugarit, was used to write Ugaritic and other Semitic languages in Syria and Palestine, and presupposes the existence of a linear alphabet (Dietrich and Loretz 1988). In the middle of the 1st millennium, the Achaemenid Persians developed a cuneiform syllabary of 36 signs and 6 logograms for writing Old Persian, which they used for commemorative purposes only; their administrative records are in cuneiform Elamite or alphabetic Aramaic (*RLA* 5: 563–65).

C. Decipherment

Cuneiform first drew the attention of Europeans through artifacts and reports brought back by 17th and 18th century visitors to the Near East, especially Persepolis, the ancient Persian capital. Copies of Achaemenid royal inscriptions on stone were circulated, and it was soon established by formal criteria that some were trilingual. One of the three languages was written in a much simpler writing system, which by the early 19th century was correctly assumed to be the Old Persian language of the Achaemenids. The first steps toward decipherment were taken by the Göttingen scholar Georg Friedrich Grotefend (1775–1853). Substantial progress could be made only when a sufficiently long inscription was found and copied. This was accomplished by the Englishman Henry Rawlinson (1810–1895), who copied the inscription of Darius I on the cliffside at Bisitun. In 1848 he published his decipherment of the Old Persian version, and by the mid-1850s the third language of the inscriptions, Akkadian, had been deciphered through the efforts of Rawlinson, the Irishman Edward Hincks (1792–1866), and the Frenchman Jules Oppert (1825–1905). This was possible only when it was realized that Akkadian was written both syllabically and logographically, and that syllabic Akkadian writing was both polyphonic and homophonic. Because Akkadian was revealed to be a member of the well-known Semitic language family, rapid progress in decipherment followed, in turn facilitating the decipherment of cuneiform texts in a variety of languages during the following decades (Friedrich 1957).

The second language of the Achaemenid inscriptions, Elamite, is without any known relation and is still only imperfectly understood. Sumerian, whose existence was established only after study of the tablets excavated by the British at Nineveh, also has no known cognate languages, but its decipherment was aided by the large corpus of Sumero-Akkadian bilingual literary and lexical texts. Hurrian and Urartian, related to one another, are still far from completely understood, after a century and more of study. Cuneiform Hittite was deciphered in 1915—less than a decade after the first lot of tablets was excavated—by the Czech scholar Bedrich Hrozny (1879–1952). The decipherment of Ugaritic was even more rapid. Soon after the first tablets were discovered by French excavators in 1929, independent decipherments were offered by the French Scholars Charles Virolleaud (1879–1968) and Edouard Dhorme (1881–1966) and the German Theo Bauer (1896–1957). The first Eblaite tablets were published by the Italian scholar Giovanni Pettinato after their discovery in 1974, and work on them has been continued by him and other scholars (Friedrich 1957, Cagni 1987).

D. Myth of Origin and Divine Patrons

The invention of cuneiform is the subject of an episode in the Sumerian epic tale *Enmerkar and the Lord of Aratta* (Cohen 1973). Enmerkar, mythical ruler of the Sumerian city of Uruk, whose historical prototype would have ruled ca. 2700 B.C., demands submission and tribute from the ruler of the distant Iranian city of Aratta, rich in the natural resources that Sumer lacked. Enmerkar's demands are communicated in a series of long messages delivered by a courier. When one message is too long for the courier to remember, Enmerkar invents "writing on clay tablets" to assist him. When the ruler of Aratta was given the tablet he grew angry, because, as H. Vanstiphout has shown (1988: 159), "the words were [just] nails."

This native etiology of writing is implausible, since we know that the earliest use of writing was for information storage, and it was only after many centuries that it was used for long-distance communication (letters). Interesting, however, is that the ancients perceived the wedge shape of the cuneiform signs as moderns do. Before "cuneiform" became a standard term, "nail writing, *Nagelschrift*" were sometimes used, and the equivalent still is in Dutch *(spijkerschrift)* and several other languages (*RLA* 5: 544).

The Sumerian god of wisdom was Enki (Akk Ea), but writing proper was the domain of the goddess Nisaba, tutelary deity of scribes and the scribal academy. By the first millennium, this role had been transferred to the god Nabû, whose emblems were the scribe's stylus and tablet.

E. Cuneiform in Palestine

Although the Hebrew Bible seems not to have recognized cuneiform writing as a phenomenon worthy of particular mention, cuneiform was a fact of life in Palestine from at least the 18th century B.C. to the period of Assyrian domination in the 7th–6th centuries B.C. Biblical authors or redactors might have seen it used by Assyrian officials, such as the two damaged scribes on Sennacherib's relief celebrating the capture of Lachish (Ussishkin 1982: 86–87), or would have surely come across some of the stelas erected by Assyrian kings to celebrate their victories.

It is surprising how little has been found in Palestine: working from Jucquois' list (1966: 32–36), for example, and adding more recent finds, we can estimate that there are between 85 and 100 tablets known to have originated in Palestine in the 2d millennium, but only 32 from that same period have actually been found there. A complete inventory of cuneiform artifacts found in Palestine can be found in Galling (1968: 13–14 and 61). Subsequent finds and bibliography are Rainey 1975, and Owen 1981 (Aphek); Shaffer 1970 and Becking 1982 (Gezer); Hallo and Tadmor 1977 (Hazor); Anbar and Na'aman 1986 (Hebron); Sigrist 1982 (Keisan); Böhl 1974 (Shechem); and Glock 1971 (Ta'anach).

At present, it cannot be determined if Ebla represented the extreme southwestern corner of the cuneiform world in the mid-3d millennium B.C., or if the prolific use of cuneiform known there extended southward as far as Palestine. The earliest cuneiform found in Palestine dates to the 18th to 16th centuries B.C., contemporary with the Mari archives and the later tablets from Alalakh level VII, which correlates well with evidence from Mari showing Hazor to be a participant in a vast network of diplomatic and commercial relations reaching as far east as Babylonia and Elam. Only four or five tablets and an inscribed liver model used for extispicy have been found from this period, at Gezer, Hazor, Hebron, and possibly Shechem, as well as some seals and a jug with a name scratched on its side in cuneiform. But certain of these materials—legal and scholarly texts—never occur as isolated artifacts, and we can safely assume that there were multiple centers in Palestine where cuneiform Akkadian was, as at Alalakh, the language of legal, administrative, and business documents.

The same mix is found in much larger numbers for the first half of the 2d millennium B.C. Twenty-seven tablets of this period have been found, the bulk of which are from Aphek (8) and Ta'anach (13), with others from Gezer, Hesi, Jericho, and Megiddo. To these must be added the letters of Palestinian vassals found in the Egyptian archive at Amarna. Again, we must imagine situations similar to Alalakh, Ugarit, or Emar. We know that at Ugarit the local language, written in a cuneiform alphabet, was used for many of the same purposes as Akkadian. A small number of alphabetic cuneiform tablets have been found in Palestine (Dietrich and Loretz 1988), and one wonders to what extent letters and documents were executed there in local languages, in either cuneiform or linear alphabetic writing.

Cuneiform was not an element of the new cultural paradigm that emerged after the upheavals in the Levant at the end of the 2d millennium B.C. Its reappearance in Palestine coincided with Assyrian domination in the 8th–7th centuries B.C., exemplified by the stela fragments of Sargon II of Assyria found at Ashdod and Samaria. Four legal and administrative tablets were found at Gezer, Keisan, and Samaria, and at the last, an inscribed bulla with the Assyrian royal seal was excavated. Significantly, no school texts were found, suggesting that cuneiform was a device of the conquerors not much propagated on Palestinian soil.

Bibliography

Algaze, G. 1989. The Uruk Expansion: Cross-cultural Exchange as a Factor in Early Mesopotamian Civilization. *Current Anthropology* 30: 571–608.

Anbar, M., and Na'aman, N. 1986. An Account of Sheep from Ancient Hebron. *Tel Aviv* 13: 3–12.

Archi, A. 1988. *Eblaite Personal Names and Semitic Name-giving.* Archivi Reali di Ebla. Studi 1.

Becking, B. 1982. Two Neo-Assyrian Documents from Gezer in Their Historical Context. *JEOL* 27: 76–89.

Biggs, R. 1988. The Semitic Personal Names from Abu Salabikh and the Personal Names from Ebla. Pp. 89–98 in Archi 1988.

Böhl, F. 1974. Der Keilschriftbrief aus Sichem. *Baghdader Mitteilungen* 7: 19–30.

Bottéro, J. 1987. *Mésopotamie. L'écriture, la raison et les dieux.* Paris.

Buccellati, G. 1981. The Origin of Writing and the Beginning of History. Pp. 2–13 in *The Shape of the Past: Studies in Honor of F. D. Murphy,* ed. G. Buccellati and C. Speroni. Los Angeles.

Cagni, L. 1987. *Ebla 1975–1985. Dieci anni di studie linguistici e filologici.* Instituo Universitario Orienatale. Dipartimento di Studi Asiatici. Series Minor 27.

Charpin, D. 1987. Tablettes présargoniques de Mari. *Mari. Annales de Recherches Interdisciplinaires* 5: 65–127.

Cohen, S. 1973. *Enmerkar and the Lord of Aratta.* Diss. U. of Pennsylvania.

Dietrich, M., and Loretz, O. 1988. *Die Keilalphabete: Die phönizisch-kanaanäischen und altarabischen Alphabete in Ugarit.* Abhandlungen zur Literatur Alt-Syrien-Palästinas. Münster.

Dittmann, R. 1986. Seals, Sealings and Tablets. Pp. 332–66 in *Gamdat Nasr. Period or Regional Style?* ed. U. Finkbeiner and W. Röllig. Beihefte zum Tübinger Atlas des Vorderen Orients. Reihe B/62. Wiesbaden.

Friedrich, J. 1957. *Extinct Languages.* New York.

Galling, K. 1968. *Textbuch zur Geschichte Israels.* 2d ed. Tübingen.

Gelb, I. 1961. *Old Akkadian Writing and Grammar.* 2d ed. Materials for the Assyrian Dictionary 2. Chicago.

Glock, A. 1971. A New Ta'annek Tablet. *BASOR* 204: 17–30.

Green, M. 1980. Animal Husbandry at Uruk in the Archaic Period. *JNES* 39: 1–35.

———. 1981. The Construction and Implementation of the Cuneiform Writing System. *Visible Language* 15: 345–72.

———, and Nissen, H. 1987. *Zeichenliste der archaischen Texte aus Uruk.* Ausgrabungen der Deutschen Forschungsgemeinschaft in Uruk-Warka 11. Archaische Texte aus Uruk 2. Berlin.

Hallo, W., and Tadmor, H. 1977. A Lawsuit from Hazor. *IEJ* 27: 1–11 and pl. 1.

Jucquois, G. 1966. *Phonétique comparée des dialectes moyen-babyloniens du nord et de l'ouest.* Bibliothèque du Muséon 53. Louvain.

Krebernik, M. 1984. *Die Beschwörungen aus Fara und Ebla.* Texte und Studien zur Orientalistik 2. Hildesheim.

———. 1988. *Die Personennamen der Ebla-Texte. Eine Zwischenbilanz.* Berliner Beiträge zum Vorderen Orient 7. Berlin.

Labat, R. 1988. *Manuel d'épigraphie akkadienne.* 6th ed. augmented by F. Malbran-Labat. Paris.

Larsen, M. T. 1989. What They Wrote on Clay. Pp. 121–148 in *Literacy and Society,* ed. K. Schousboe and M. T. Larsen. Copenhagen.

Millard, A. 1965. A Letter from the Ruler of Gezer. *PEQ* 97: 140–43.

Nissen, H. 1986a. The Archaic Texts from Uruk. *World Archaeology* 17: 317–34.

———. 1986b. The Development of Writing and of Glyptic Art. Pp. 316–31 in *Ǧamdat Nasr. Period or Regional Style?* ed. U. Finkbeiner and W. Röllig. Beihefte zum Tübinger Atlas des Vorderen Orients. Reihe B/62. Wiesbaden.

Owen, D. 1981. An Akkadian Letter from Ugarit at Tel Aphek. *Tel Aviv:* 1–17.

Parpola, S. 1983. Assyrian Library Records. *JNES* 42: 1–29.

Powell, M. 1981. Three Problems in the History of Cuneiform Writing: Origins, Direction of Script, Literacy. *Visible Language* 15: 419–40.

Rainey, A. 1975. Two Cuneiform Fragments from Tel Aphek. *Tel Aviv* 2: 125–40.

Schmandt-Besserat, D. 1986. An Ancient Token System: The Precursor to Numerals and Writing. *Archaeology* Nov./Dec. 1986: 32–39.

———. 1988. Tokens at Uruk. *Baghdader Mitteilungen* 19: 1–175.

Shaffer, A. 1970. Fragment of an Inscribed Envelope. Pp. 111–13 in W. Dever, et al. *Gezer* I. Jerusalem.

Sigrist, M. 1982. Une tablette cunëiforme de Tell Keisan. *IEJ* 32: 32–35.

Ussishkin, D. 1982. *The Conquest of Lachish by Sennacherib.* Tel Aviv.

Vallat, F. 1986. The Most Ancient Scripts of Iran: The Current Situation. *World Archaeology* 17: 335–47.

Vanstiphout, H. 1988. *Mihiltum,* or the Image of Cuneiform Writing. *The Image in Writing. Visible Religion* 6: 151–68.

Walker, C. 1987. *Cuneiform.* Reading the Past. London.

Westenholz, A. 1988. Personal Names in Ebla and in Pre-Sargonic Babylonia. Pp. 99–118 in Archi 1988.

JERROLD S. COOPER

CURSE. A term associated with a substantial semantic range of concepts and vocabulary in the Bible. The English verb "to curse" renders several Hebrew words (*ʾārar, qālal, ʾālâ, heḥĕrîm, nāqab, qābab, bārak* [a euphemism, lit. "bless"]), and Greek verbs *(kataraomai, anathematizō, katanathematizō, kataraomai, katalaleō).* The English noun "curse" may render any of the Hebrew nouns *ʾalah ḥerem, meʾērāh,* and *taʾalah,* as well as the Greek nouns *katara, epikataratos, anathema,* and *katathema.* We may summarize the predominant usage of the various verbs as follows: to curse is to predict, wish, pray for, or cause trouble or disaster on a person or thing. Correspondingly, the predominant noun usages may be summarized in the following manner: a curse is the expression of such a prediction, wish, prayer, or causation; or the result thereof; or, rarely, the object (person or thing) thereof.

In the Mosaic Law, one means of divine enforcement of the covenant stipulations incumbent on Israel was the curse. Leviticus 26 and Deuteronomy 28–32 contain the sanctions portions of the covenant structure relative to their respective statements of the Law, and in these passages much is made of the many types of curses that will attend the Israelites if they abandon the covenant. Twenty-seven types of curses are found in these contexts, representing virtually all the miseries one could imagine occurring in the ancient world (Stuart *Hosea-Jonah* WBC, xxxi–xlii), but these may be summarized by six terms: defeat, disease, desolation, deprivation, deportation, and death. Such curses are warnings of what God will cause to happen to Israel if they sin. Thus, Jeremiah speaks of the curse that attends the Law (e.g., Jer 11:3) as does Paul (Gal 3:13), with the ultimate curse being that of death, as Rom 6:23 implies. The close relationship between covenant and curse led to a metonymic use of "curse" for "covenant" in Deut 34:12 and Zech 5:3.

As the arbiter of values, God was free to curse those who offended him. Human beings did not have that prerogative. Cursing by people could have serious consequences for themselves depending on who or what it was they had cursed. Cursing one's parents (Exod 21:17; Lev 20:19), the handicapped (Lev 19:14), a king (because he is God's anointed; 2 Samuel 16), or God (Lev 24:11–24) were all crimes or sins punishable by death. In such cases it was the object of the curse that made it wrong rather than the process; pronouncing harm on the innocent was forbidden; pronouncing harm on the evil was appropriate. Thus prophets could utter a curse sinfully (e.g., Balaam against Israel; Num 22:6–17) or righteously (e.g., Joshua on Jericho and Gibeon; Josh 6:26 and 9:23) depending on the object.

It was assumed in ancient times that curses derived their power from the gods (1 Sam 17:43). Merely expressing negative wishes had little force. For the orthodox Israelites, whose God Yahweh was universally sovereign (Gen 12:8, 9; Exod 9:14; Ps 95:3; Amos 1–2), no curse could have effect without Yahweh's superintendence, including that of a foreign or false prophet (Num 23:8). Yahweh could turn a curse against its speaker (Gen 12:3; 27:29) or turn a curse into a blessing (Deut 23:5). In the latter sense he is said by Paul to have made Christ "a curse for us," i.e., a blessing via his taking the penalty of the Law's curse upon himself in his crucifixion (Gal 3:13).

God's word is his deed; it was inconceivable to orthodox believers, whether Christian or Jew, that what God ordered or predicted would not come true either instantly or according to whatever timing he chose. His curses dominate nature (Gen 3:14, 17; Isa 24:6; Mark 11:21) and nations (Gen 9:25; Jer 24:9). They can affect the family (Prov 3:33) or the individual (Matt 25:41; Acts 5:1–11).

When a divine curse has been announced as generally applicable (e.g., Deut 11:26, "I set before you this day blessing and curse . . .") violators of the warning automatically bring upon themselves the miseries implied in the curse (Deut 28:15; Zech 5:1–4; 2 Chr 34:24). Indeed, whenever God so chooses, he may as a punishment bring the intended effect of a curse upon the very individual who uttered it against someone else (Gen 27:12, 13; Ps 109:17).

Curses could accompany any sort of covenant, as part of the oaths made to bind all parties. Individuals who then broke such covenants would be subject to the curses they had agreed to in binding themselves to the covenant (Judg 21:18; Neh 10:29; cf. Matt 26:74; Acts 23:12). A ceremony related to the covenant of marriage could involve the uttering of curses as a part of the process of determining marital infidelity (Num 5:18–27).

Individuals could compose their own curses against other individuals, desiring thereby to hurt them (Job 31:30). They could, as well, give strength to a promise (Gen 34:41) or a legal testimony (1 Kgs 8:31) by an oath.

Words involving the Hebrew root *ḥrm* are sometimes translated "curse" in the sense of a thing banned or made off-limits from society, thus bringing a curse upon the person who breaks the ban and makes contact with it. In so-called Holy War, the enemy and anything belonging to him was *ḥerem,* off-limits, and under penalty of death could not be taken as plunder by victorious Israelite soldiers (Josh 7:1, 12; 1 Sam 15:23). The curse of Mal 4:6 uses the term *ḥerem* in reference to the fate of the land if the future Elijah is not heeded, implying that those who reject the word of God will suffer the same fate as did those who violated the ban in Holy War, i.e., death.

Because cursing was intended to produce negative results, the notion of reversal of cursing in the NT conveys the sense of the dawning of a new age of behavior and expectations. Jesus' teaching, "Bless those who curse you" (Luke 6:28), called for a reversal on the part of his followers of millennia of tradition about personal response to cursing. Revelation 22:3 predicts the cessation of "the curse," i.e., the results of the Genesis fall (sin, disease, death).

Bibliography

Blank, S. H. 1950–51. The Curse, Blasphemy, the Spell, and the Oath. *HUCA* 23: 73–95.

Brichto, H. C. 1963. *The Problem of "Curse" in the Hebrew Bible.* Philadelphia.

Fensham, F. 1962. Malediction and Benediction in Ancient Near Eastern Vassal-Treaties and the OT. *ZAW* 74: 1–9.

Hempel, J. 1925. Die israelitischen Anschauung von Segen und Fluch im Lichte altorientalischer Parallelen *ZDMG* n.s. 4: 20–110.

Herbert, A. G., and Snaith, N. H. 1952. A Study of the Words "Curse" and "Righteousness." *BTrans* 3: 111–14.

Mowinckel, S. 1923. *Segen und Fluch in Israels Kult und Psalmendichtung.* Kristiana.

Pedersen, J. 1914. *Der Eid bei den Semiten.* Strassburg.

Scharbert, J. 1958. "Fluchen" und "Segen" im Alten Testament. *Bib* 34: 1–26.

———. 1958. *Solidaritat in Segen und Flucht im Alten Testament und in seiner Umwelt.* Bonn.

Schottroff, W. 1969. *Der altisraelitische Fluchspruch.* Neukirchen-Vluyn.

DOUGLAS STUART

CUSH (PERSON) [Heb *kûš*]. CUSHITE. Two persons in the OT bear this name.

1. The son of Ham, and father of Seba, Havilah, Sabtah, Raamah, Sabteca, and NIMROD (Gen 10:6–8). This Cush is the eponymous ancestor of the Cushites, but also apparently of a Mesopotamian group, given the relationship to Nimrod in v 8. Thus, in addition to the Ethiopian Cush, Cush has been seen as the ancestor of the Kassites (Gk *Cossaea*), who ruled Babylon until the 12th century B.C. (*Genesis* AB, 66, 72) or of the *Kash,* who conquered Babylon in the 18th century B.C. (*Genesis 1–11* TBC, 119).

2. Benjaminite mentioned in the superscription of Psalm 7 as the person whose activity gave occasion for the composition of the psalm. The LXX reads *chousi* (Heb *kušî*), which may indicate a relationship with 2 Samuel 18:21–32, where the messenger who brought to David word of the defeat and death of Absalom is called *kušî* eight times. This name has been understood as a gentilic, "the Cushite," with no Israelite tribal affiliation. Kyle McCarter, Jr. (*2 Samuel* AB, 402, 408) points out that, in the MT, the second of these eight occurrences of *kušî* does not employ the definite article (thus treating *kušî* as a proper name, Cushi), and that the LXX, Syr, Vg, and Tg. treat *kušî* in all eight occurrences, not as a gentilic, but as a personal name. His conclusion is that it is not impossible to identify the "Cush" of Psalm 7 with "the Cushite" of 2 Samuel 18. Against this view, the "Cush" of Psalm 7 has generally been understood as an enemy of David, e.g., Dalglish (*IDB* 1: 751) describes him as a "calumnious foe of David." This understanding of Cush clearly does not fit the Cushite of 2 Samuel 18, who is no enemy of David, but only a messenger to David from Joab. However, the idea that Cush is David's enemy is based, not on the superscription itself, but rather on the content of the psalm. The superscription reads, "A Shiggaion of David, which he sang to the LORD concerning (Heb *ʿal dibrê*) Cush a Benjaminite." Taken in its plain sense, *ʿal dibrê* means "upon [because of] the words of . . ." So translated, Psalm 7 does not imply an antagonistic relationship of Cush to David, but only states that Cush's words provided the impulse for the composition of the psalm.

SIEGFRIED S. JOHNSON

CUSHAN (PLACE) [Heb *kûšān*]. In the description of a theophany in which Yahweh comes in wrath (Hab 3:3–15), two specific places are pointed out as being distraught, "the tents of Cushan" and "the tent curtains of Midian" (Hab 3:7). The tent dwellings indicate nomads, and such were the Midianites. They are associated with several areas to the S and E of Israel (Gen 37:28, 36; Num 10:29–30; 22; 25). Since this mention of Cushan is unique in the Bible, evidence concerning its location is usually sought elsewhere.

Cush in the OT often is associated with S Egypt and Ethiopia (Gen 10:6; 2 Kgs 19:9), but this appears to be too far S for the context in Habakkuk. Cush is also associated with a more northerly location in its association with the Gihon, one of the four rivers flowing from Eden (Gen 2:13). This seems to place it in the area of Mesopotamia or N Syria. This is also the place of origin of one of Israel's oppressors during the period of the judges, Cushan-rishathaim (Judg 3:8, 10), whose name includes the word under discussion. He comes from Aram-naharaim, "Aram of the two rivers," in the area of the Upper Euphrates and Habur rivers (*MBA*, 4).

Earlier in the 2d millennium B.C., Mesopotamia was controlled by the Kassites (Akk *kaššu;* Gadd *CAH*[3] 2/1:

224–27; Drower *CAH*³ 2/1: 437–44; Gadd *CAH*³ 2/2: 34–44). They are referred to in the Amarna Letters from the 14th century B.C. as *kaša/u*. These people could also be those referred to as the *kwšw* "Cush," in an Egyptian execration text (Cazelles *POTT,* 13). In inscriptions of Ramesses II and Ramesses III, reference is made to *qsn-rm,* "Kusan-rom" in N Syria (Edgerton and Wilson 1936: 110; cf. *ARI,* 205, n. 49). The site is not identified, but it fits in the same area as the other pieces of evidence.

The trouble with these identifications is that the Habakkuk reference to Cushan seems to place it to the S of Israel in the Sinai and Red Sea area based on the allusions to the Exodus events (3:3–15). Cushan could be either an alternative name for the Midianites, or a subgroup of them. They seem to have such names or subgroupings elsewhere as well (Gen 37:27, 28, 36; Judg 8:24; see Baker *Nahum, Habakkuk and Zephaniah* TOTC, 72). If the name is to be understood as indicating an ethnic group rather than a geographical location, it might be expected to occur in association with any number of locations which were within the scope of nomadic travel. Therefore locations in the Sinai and in N Syria are not mutually exclusive.

Bibliography

Edgerton, W. F., and Wilson, J. A. 1936. *Historical Records of Ramses III: The Texts in Medinat Habu.* SAOC 12.

DAVID W. BAKER

CUSHAN-RISHATHAIM (PERSON) [Heb *kûšan riš*ᶜ*ātayim*]. A name which appears in the OT only at Judg 3:7–11, telling how in the Judges period Yahweh sold the Israelites into the hand of Cushan-Rishathaim, king of Mesopotamia (Heb ʾ*ăram nahărāîm*), from whom, after eight years' servitude, they were delivered by Othniel the son of Kenaz, Caleb's younger brother. According to Josh 15:16–19 and Judg 1:12–15, Caleb took Hebron for himself and Othniel captured Debir. Othniel thus belonged to S Judah. In view of this, and because it seems unlikely that this minor figure attacked and defeated a king from N Syria, many scholars have located Cushan (by minor emendation) in Edom, not Aram, excising *nahărāîm* as a gloss (Malamat 1954: 232). The name *riš*ᶜ*ātaîm* was explained in talmudic tradition as meaning "of double wickedness" (Malamat 1954: 232). Marquart (1896: 11), however, explained it as *rôš* ᶜ*ataîm,* "chief of 'Athaim,'" a name he took from the LXX version of the Chronicler's rendering (1 Chr 1:46) of Hadad's city Avith (Gen 36:35). Gray (*Joshua, Judges and Ruth* NCBC, 214–15, 260–61), proposed *rôš hattēmānî,* "chief of the Temanites"; compare the association (Hab 3: 7) of the name "Cushan" with the land of the Midianites. However, while it seems likely that Othniel was involved with some more local opponents than one from N Syria, these suggestions remain speculative, and even if the compiler of the collection of deliverance stories in Judges wrote Edom where Aram(-naharaim) now stands (Judg 3:8, 10), he may not have had any reliable information at hand. Further, the emendation from "Aram" to "Edom" remains doubtful; if the story was composed, as Mayes (*IJH,* 311) suggests, to give an example of God's saving activity by way of introduction to other such stories of deliverance in Judges (and perhaps to provide a suitable deliverer for the tribe of Judah), then the author may have intended to write "Aram," not "Edom," in which case we can draw nothing of any significance for 12th–11th century B.C. Edom from the story. Accepting the reading *Ăram-nahărāîm,* Malamat (1954: 231–42) proposes to identify Cushan-Rishathaim with a certain Arsu or Irsu, a Syrian ruler mentioned in Papyrus Harris 1/75: 1–9 (*ANET,* 260), who, according to Malamat, seized the Egyptian throne in an anarchic period at the end of the 19th Dynasty, about 1200 B.C. The identification of Cushan with Irsu, however, seems highly speculative. E. Taübler (1947: 136–42) argued that the name "Cushan-Rishathaim" derives from a literary attempt to associate the Midianite Cushan with Babylon (the home of wickedness) and so to bring Cushan into contempt. More prosaically, R. Boling (*Judges* AB, 81) suggests that the place name Aram-naharaim results from the mistaken redivision of an original ʾ*rmn hrym,* "fortress of the mountains"; but where was this? The identity of Cushan-Rishathaim and his connection, if any, with Edom remain totally obscure.

Bibliography

Malamat, A. 1954. Cushan Rishathaim and the Decline of the Near East around 1200 B.C. *JNES* 13: 231–42.

Marquart, J. 1896. *Fundamente Israelitischer und Jüdaischer Geschichte.* Göttingen.

Taübler, E. 1947. Cushan-Rishathaim. *HUCA* 20: 137–42.

J. R. BARTLETT

CUSHI (PERSON) [Heb *kûšî*]. The name "Cushi" appears to be cognate with the personal name "Cush," the eponymous son of Ham (Gen 10:6–8; 1 Chr 1:8–10), and the unknown personage mentioned in the title of Psalm 7. It is also conceived to be a geographical or ethnological term in Isa 11:11. The term *kûšî* is used not only as a proper name but also as a *nomen gentilicium* (2 Sam 18:21–23, 31–32). The feminine form "Cushite" (Heb *kûšît*) appears twice in Num 12:1, which the Gk renders *gunè tēs aithiópissēs*.

1. The great-grandfather of the princeling Jehudi. This courtier was dispatched to summon Baruch, the amanuensis of Jeremiah, to appear before the royal cabinet and to read the words of the scroll which Jeremiah had dictated and which Baruch had just read to the people (Jer 36:14). In the enjoinder the ancestry of Jehudi is traced back to the third generation, to Cushi, his great-grandfather, a fact which indicates both the aristocracy of his family lineage and the importance of the assigned mission.

2. The father of Zephaniah, the Judean prophet. The genealogy of the prophet Zephaniah is traced back some four generations to Hezekiah, presumably, the king of Judah. This superscription is unique in the presentation of what appears to be a royal lineage of the prophet. The importance of Cushi can be measured from the above implications suggesting a place in the Judean aristocracy and a deeply committed religious personality. Unfortunately, beyond this, we know no further details of his life.

EDWARD R. DALGLISH

CUTH (PLACE) [Heb *kût*]. Var. CUTHAH. A city in S Mesopotamia (2 Kgs 17:24). Inhabited continuously at least from the 3d to the 1st millennia B.C., this city is best known as the center for the cult associated with the realm of the dead and the chief deity of the Mesopotamian underworld, Nergal. The name "Cuthah" (Heb *kûtâ;* Sum *Gu-du-a,* of unclear etymology) itself may be used in Akkadian as a name for the underworld. The modern Tell Ibrahim, 20 miles NE of Babylon, seems the most likely location for Cuthah, but since extensive excavations have not yet been undertaken, information about Cuthah comes primarily from written sources outside the city. (For further discussion, see Edzard and Gallery *RLA* 6: 384–7.)

When Assyria subdued rebellions in both Israel and Babylonia in the 8th century B.C., the conquered populations of these two lands were resettled elsewhere in accord with Assyrian policy, the Cuthites being relocated 500 miles westward to the territory of subdued Israel and its former capital Samaria (2 Kgs 17:24). Even after being settled in Israel, the former inhabitants of Cuthah continued to venerate their patron deity Nergal (2 Kgs 17:30), presumably maintaining the cult associated with the dead and the underworld with which he was associated. The Assyrian king who was responsible for the deportation of the Cuthites may have been Sargon II if the Babylonian rebellion is to be associated with that of the Merodach-baladan of 2 Kgs 20:12–19. The designation "Cutheans" was later employed by Jews in the first centuries A.D. as an insulting epithet to describe the Samaritans who lived in the region centering on Samaria (Josephus *Ant* 9.14.3; *b. Qidd.* 75–76; *b. Ḥul.* 5b–6a) where the exiles from Cuthah had been settled by the Assyrians.

SAMUEL A. MEIER

CUTHA (PERSON) [Gk *Koutha*]. A temple servant who was the progenitor of a family which returned from Babylon with Zerubbabel (1 Esdr 5:32). Although 1 Esdras is often assumed to have been compiled from Ezra and Nehemiah, this family does not appear among their lists of returning exiles (see Ezra 2:52; Neh 7:54). Omissions such as this also raise questions about 1 Esdras being used as a source by Ezra or Nehemiah. Furthermore, problems associated with dating events and identifying persons described in 1 Esdras have cast doubt on the historicity of the text.

MICHAEL DAVID MCGEHEE

CYAMON (PLACE) [Gk *Kyamōn*]. Site mentioned in the book of Judith whose exact location is unknown (Jdt 7:3). The verse places it in the vicinity of Esdraelon. It has been identified with modern Tell Qeimon (M.R. 160230), which is located near Geba, on the slopes of Mount Carmel, at the N end of the plain of Esdraelon. It is possible that the name "Cyamon" is a corruption of the Hebrew name "Jokmeam" (Heb *yoqmŏʿām*), which appears at 1 Kgs 4:12 as part of the boundary list for one of Solomon's tax districts. Jokmeam is also identified with modern Tell Qeimon, so the hypothesis that Cyamon is a corruption of Jokmeam is plausible. Of course, given the genre of the book of Judith, it is possible that the name is fictitious.

SIDNIE ANN WHITE

CYCLONE. See PALESTINE, CLIMATE OF.

CYMBALS. See the MUSIC AND MUSICAL INSTRUMENTS articles.

CYNICS. Adherents of the Greek school of philosophers who held that virtue is the only good and that its essence lies in self-control and independence.

A. Historical Outline
  1. Early Cynicism
  2. Imperial Cynicism
B. Name
C. Appearance and Manner of Life
D. Cynic Teachings
E. Impact of Cynicism
  1. Cynicism and Greco-Roman Intellectual Life
  2. Cynicism and Early Christianity

A. Historical Outline

1. Early Cynicism. Cynicism began in the 4th century B.C.E. with Socrates' student Antisthenes (ca. 446–366 B.C.E.) and thus is one of the Socratic schools of Greek philosophy. There soon followed Diogenes of Sinope (ca. 404–323 B.C.E.) and his student Crates of Thebes, who flourished during the 113th Olympiad (i.e., 328–324 B.C.E.) (D.L., 6.87) and who died as late as 270 B.C.E. (Susemihl 1891: 1.29–30). No Cynics after them ever eclipsed these three as the school's chief representatives (Lucian, *Fug.* 20; Julian, *Orat.* 6.188B), even though Cynic teachings continued to attract adherents for a thousand years. A brief review of these adherents will draw attention to many of these lesser known Cynics and underscore the long history of this important, if not always appreciated, philosophical movement.

Cynicism's early representatives—from Antisthenes on down to about 200 B.C.E.—are conveniently catalogued by Diogenes Laertius, whose sixth book of *The Lives of the Eminent Philosophers* is our principal source for early Cynicism (Mejer 1978: 1–59). The lives of these early Cynics vary greatly in length, but all tend to include some biographical data; anecdotes of their memorable sayings and actions; summaries, or at least samples, of their teachings; and lists of their writings. Not surprisingly, Diogenes Laertius reserves the most space for Antisthenes (6.1–19), Diogenes (6.20–81), and Crates (6.85–93, 98). He emphasizes Antisthenes' attachment to Socrates (6.2) and his role as founder of Cynicism (2.47), a claim which some scholars doubt (Dudley 1937: 1–16) but without convincing others (Höistad 1948: 8–13; Kusch *RAC* 3: 1063). Diogenes Laertius (6.85–86) illustrates Crates' considerable literary talent with snippets of his poetry, such as the description of a Cynic island utopia called *Pēra* "Begging Bag" (Stenzel *PW* 22: 1625–31, Dudley 1937: 42–53). But he reserves the most space for Diogenes and so clearly announces the importance of this follower of Antisthenes. This longer treatment is justified, as Diogenes became, as it were, the second founder of Cynicism, in that he, more than either Antisthenes or Crates, stamped the movement with his personality and continued to be the point of reference for

Cynics of all kinds down through the centuries (Gerhard 1912; von Fritz 1926; Kusch *RAC* 3: 1063–67).

Diogenes had many students. In addition to Crates (D.L., 6.85), he attracted Monimus of Syracuse (late 4th century B.C.E., von Fritz *PW* 16/1: 126–27) and Onesicritus of Aegina or of Astypalaea (6.84), though more probably the latter (Brown 1949: 2–4). Diogenes Laertius treats both Monimus and Onesicritus very briefly, even though the latter in particular was of some significance. He knows (6.84) that Onesicritus was both a student of Diogenes and an admiral and historian on Alexander's campaigns to India (Brown 1949; cf. Strasburger *PW* 18/1: 460–67), but only Strabo (15.1.63–65) reports Onesicritus' meeting with Indian philosophers, which may have been the source of a radical asceticism in Cynicism (Höistad 1948: 135–38; cf. Brown 1949: 38–53). And other followers of Diogenes are little more than names to Diogenes Laertius: Phocion (6.76), Menander, Hegesias, and Philiscus (6.84), though he seems to make Philiscus the son of Onesicritus (6.75–76) and knows that Satyrus attributed to him some tragedies of Diogenes (6.80; von Fritz *PW* 19/1: 656–63).

Crates likewise had many students, the most famous of which is Zeno of Gitium (333–261 B.C.E.), who eventually left Crates and started the Stoic school (D.L., 7.2–3). Others include: Metrocles of Maroneia (6.94–95; von Fritz *PW* 15/2: 1483–84) and his sister Hipparchia, who later became Crates' celebrated and unconventional wife (6.96–98; von Arnim *PW* 16: 1662); Monimus, who, as already noted, had been a follower of Diogenes (6.82); and perhaps Bion of Borysthenes (ca. 335–245 B.C.E.; 4.51 and Kindstrand 1976: 10–11). At this point, however, Diogenes becomes ambiguous. Scholars usually assign the next Cynics named by Diogenes—Theombrotus (Modrze *PW* 5A/2: 2033–34) and Cleomenes (von Arnim *PW* 11/1: 712)—to the circle of Metrocles, as they are named immediately after the report of Metrocles' death (6.95; Zeller 1922 2/1: 286; Helm *PW* 12: 4). But M.-O. Goulet-Cazé (1986) argues plausibly that the material on Metrocles (6.94–95) is merely a digression in the longer treatment of Crates, so that the reference to "students" here still refers back to Crates. If so, then the dates of Theombrotus and Cleomenes must be pushed back to the late 4th–early 3d century B.C.E. Their students—Demetrius of Alexandria (von Arnim *PW* 4/2: 2842), Timarchus of Alexandria (Nestle *PW* 6A/1: 1238), and Echecles of Ephesus (Natorp *PW* 10: 1909; 6.95)—thus belong to the 3d century, though they are little more than names. More, however, is said about the last two Cynics named by Diogenes Laertius: Menippus of Gadara (6.95, 99–101, Helm *PW* 15/1: 888–93) and Menedemus (6.95, 102, von Fritz *PW* 15/1: 794–95).

Diogenes Laertius has not catalogued all the early Cynics. For example, he omits such 3d-century figures as Teles of Megara, whose diatribes are partially preserved in Stobaeus (O'Neil 1977), and Leonidas of Tarentum, whose epigrams are preserved in the *Greek Anthology* (A.P. 6.293, 298, for fuller lists of early Cynics, see Zeller 1922: 2/1.281–87; Helm *PW* 12: 3–5). And he is often too brief about those Cynics he does include, as was seen above in the case of Onesicritus. Still, despite these shortcomings, the account in Diogenes Laertius is invaluable, and not only in bringing some chronological order to the various early Cynics. For he has also preserved important early materials—fragments of New Comedy which record public perceptions of Cynics (6.83, 93) and summaries of Diogenes' educational and political views (6.70–73; Höistad 1948: 37–47, 138–46).

In fact, the value of a Diogenes Laertius becomes immediately apparent when trying to write the history of Cynicism after 200 B.C.E., the point at which Diogenes' survey ends. The evidence is so sparse that some scholars have claimed that Cynicism died out in the last two centuries B.C.E. (Zeller 1922: 2/1.287). While this claim is not justified (Dudley 1937: 117–24), the little evidence that remains is difficult to pin down. For example, some of the letters attributed to Diogenes belong, according to V. Emeljanow (1967: 4–5), to these centuries (so *epp.* 1–29 [Malherbe 1977: 92–132]), and some Cynic materials on papyrus may belong to this general period too (Dudley 1937: 123). Only Meleager of Gadara (ca. 135–50 B.C.E.) stands out from this period (Garrison 1978: 71–93).

2. Imperial Cynicism. With the beginning of the imperial period, however, the evidence for Cynicism begins to become more plentiful, though again there is no Diogenes Laertius to catalogue them (the fullest lists are in Zeller 1922: 3/1.793–804; Helm *PW* 12: 5–7). The reemergence of evidence has led some scholars to speak of a revival of Cynicism during the early Empire (Billerbeck 1982: 151–58). At the very least, Cynics begin to appear in the 1st century C.E. with some regularity. To be sure, the evidence is often very brief, sometimes little more than a name (so a Plenetiades in Plutarch, *De def. orac,* 413A) and sometimes not even that (so an unnamed Cynic in *AP* 11.158). The evidence is fuller, however, for those Cynics who got caught up in imperial politics—for example, an Isidorus under Nero (Suet. Ner. 39) and a Diogenes and Heras under Vespasian (Dio Cass. 66.15). But the fullest evidence for any 1st-century Cynic is that regarding Demetrius. He, too, played a role in politics which has continued to fascinate scholars (Dudley 1937: 125–42; Moles 1983). He was also a friend of the Stoic philosopher Seneca, whose letters and essays permit a detailed, if also Stoicized, portrait of Demetrius' habits and teachings to emerge (Billerbeck 1979; Kindstrand; cf. Billerbeck 1982: 158–68).

The fullest documentation, however, awaits the scholar of 2d-century Cynicism. To be sure, many of the Cynics are again little more than names: Agathobulus of Alexandria, the teacher of Demonax (Lucian, *Dem.* 3) and of Peregrinus (Lucian, *Peregr.* 17, von Arnim *PW* 1: 745); Honoratus (Lucian, *Dem.* 19, von Arnim *PW* 16: 2276); Pancrates (Philostratus, *VS* 526); and Rhodius (Lucian, *Tox.* 27). Others, however, do emerge more clearly: Demetrius of Sunium (Lucian, *Tox.* 27–34; Jones 1986: 56), Theagenes of Patras (Lucian, *Peregr.* 3 *et passim,* Jones 1986: 131), and especially Oenomaus of Gadara (Dudley 1937: 162–70). Particularly detailed portraits by Lucian of Samosata of the Cynics Demonax of Cyprus and Peregrinus Proteus are useful, even though the former portrait is largely made up of anecdotes (Lucian, *Dem.* 12–67; Jones 1986: 90–98) and the latter, the *De morte Peregrini,* is a vicious attack (von Fritz *PW* 19/1: 656–63; Jones 1986: 117–32). Hence all the more important for a understanding of 2d-century Cynicism is the extensive evidence about Theodorus, nicknamed Cynulcus, in the *Deipnosophistae* of

Athenaeus (1.1d *et passim*); scholars, however, have largely ignored him.

Deserving mention, finally, are many Cynics, who, while not necessarily restricted to the 2d century, seem especially prominent during this period, due in large part to the preservation of many more 2d-century sources. These are the false Cynics whom Lucian in particular attacked; he sometimes lashed out at individuals, such as Alcidamas (*Symp.* 12–14, 16, 19, 35, 44–47), but usually at groups (*Fug.* 12–21; *Pisc.* 44–45; *Vit. auct.* 7–11). And joining Lucian in the condemnation of these Cynics for their abusive, shameless, and greedy behavior which, it was thought, brought reproach on philosophy are Epictetus (*Diss.* 3.22.10–12), Alciphron (*epp.* 2.38; 3.19), and Dio Chrysostom (*Orat.* 32.9) (Malherbe 1970: 204–16; Billerbeck 1978: 1–3, 56–59 *et passim*).

After the 2d century, however, the evidence once again becomes less plentiful, although the emperor Julian is an exception. Writing in the 360s, Julian, like Lucian, is especially bent on attacking Cynics of his day, in particular a Heracleios whose mythmaking Julian found offensive (*Orat.* 7.204A–205A *et passim*). Others who were attacked include an Asclepiades, Serenianus, and Chytron (*Orat.* 7.224D); an Iphicles (*Orat.* 6.198A); and an unnamed Cynic who criticized Diogenes for eating a raw octopus solely for publicity (*Orat.* 6.180D *et passim*).

A century later another Cynic, Maximus of Alexandria, emerges in the record, though in the context of his involvement in ecclesiastical affairs (Dudley 1937: 203–6). And still another century later there is the Cynic Sallustius, who, however, is apparently the last Cynic and who therefore brings an end to the Cynic millennium (Dudley 1937: 206–8).

B. Name

Some people, says Diogenes Laertius (6.13), derive the name "Cynic" (Gk *kynikos*) from Kynosarges, the name of a gymnasium at Athens where Antisthenes lectured. But not only is this derivation linguistically unlikely, it is also historically suspect, in that Antisthenes is the only Cynic associated with this gymnasium and only in traditions claiming this derivation (Antisthenes, *Frag.* 136; see Caizzi 1966: 63). What is more, the derivation seems artificial since it looks like an attempt to establish an architectural locus for the school on the analogy of other philosophical schools—Platonists with another Athenian gymnasium, the Academy; Stoics with the city's colonnade known as the Painted Porch (Gk *stoa poikilē*); and Epicureans with their founder's house in Athens, known as the Garden.

A far more likely explanation—indeed, one that is clearly assumed in other passages of Diogenes Laertius and throughout Greco-Roman literature—derives "Cynic" from *kyōn,* the Greek word for "dog." Hence the term "Cynic" refers to a "doggish philosopher" (Gk *kynikos philosophos*). The specific connotation of the term, however, depends on the characteristics of dogs which were applied to these philosophers. Thus the connotation is positive if the point of the comparison were the desirable characteristics of dogs—their protecting and guarding (Dio, *Orat.* 9.3; Lucian, *Fug.* 16).

But all too often it was the undesirable characteristics of dogs—their constant barking, scavenging, urinating, and mating in public—that lay behind the use of the name "Cynic" (Lucian, *Fug.* 16; Athenaeus, *Deipnos.* 13.611b–d; ps.–Lucian, *Cyn.* 5; Julian, *Orat.* 6.182A). Thus a scholiast on Aristotle's *Categories* explains the term "Cynic" by saying that the prime reason for this designation was these philosophers' *adiaphoria,* their shocking disregard of the conventions of social behavior. Like dogs, the scholiast says, they do such things in public as eat and engage in sex, walk around barefoot, and sleep in large storage jars or at street corners (for the whole text, see Caizzi 1966: 121; cf. von Fritz 1926: 48–49).

And indeed such *adiaphoria* frequently characterizes Cynics in Greco-Roman literature. Lucian refers to Peregrinus' masturbating in public as a demonstration of his *adiaphoria* (*Peregr.* 17; cf. Lucian, *Hermot.* 18). Alciphron illustrates Pancrates' *adiaphoria* by having him urinate and later mate with a flute girl during a symposium (*ep.* 3.19.9). And other examples of such shameless conduct are not hard to find (*AP* 11.153; Quintilian, *Inst.* 4.2.30; Lucian, *Conv.* 46).

Just when the term "Cynic" arose, and precisely with this connotation, however, is difficult to determine. The term, though, is clearly early, as it appears in a fragment of Menander's *Twins* with reference to Crates and in the context of the unconventional marriage to Hipparchia (D.L., 6.93). But the term may well be earlier, originating with Diogenes, if not with Antisthenes (*pace* D.L., 6.13). In any case, the term is especially associated with Diogenes. His practice of sleeping in a large storage jar (D.L., 6.23) is clearly alluded to in the scholiast's remarks discussed above, and many other traditions only confirm this association. Thus he is depicted as eating in public (D.L., 6.58; *Gnom. Vat.* 196; see Sternbach 1887–89: 79), as urinating and doing other bodily functions in public (D.L., 6.46, 56; Dio, *Orat.* 8.36; Julian, *Orat.* 202C), and as engaging in sex acts in public (D.L., 6.69; Dio, *Orat.* 6.17; ps.-Diogenes, *ep.* 44; Malherbe 1977: 174; Julian, *Orat.* 6.200A). Put more generally and also more delicately, Diogenes Laertius says that Diogenes did the works of Demeter and Aphrodite in public (6.69, 76).

In addition, the tradition has Diogenes taunted with the name "dog" (D.L., 6.61; ps.-Diogenes, *ep.* 2; see Malherbe 1977: 92), or has him thrown bones (D.L., 6.46; Dio, *Orat.* 9.9). Diogenes can also turn these taunts around (Aelian, *VH* 14.33; *Gnom. Vat.* 194; see Sternbach 1887–89: 79), and he can even use the term to express his own self-understanding: "Once when Alexander stood over him and said, 'I am Alexander the Great King,' he said, 'And I am Diogenes the Dog' " (D.L., 6.60; Stobaeus, 2.8.21). No wonder then that the Corinthians adorned his grave with a dog carved in stone (D.L., 6.78; *AP* 7.64; Pausanias, 2.2.4).

C. Appearance and Manner of Life

Not only did the name "Cynic" (and its associated shameless behavior) characterize Diogenes and his followers, but appearance and manner of life characterized them just as much. For example, the Cynic typically wore the poor man's threadbare cloak (Gk *tribōn*), carried a begging bag (Gk *pēra*) over his shoulder, and had a staff (Gk *baktēria*) in his hand. These items seem to have characterized Cynics from the beginning—perhaps Antisthenes himself (D.L.,

6.13), probably Diogenes (6.22–23), but certainly his students Monimus and Crates, as the testimony for the last two comes from the near contemporary witness of New Comedy (D.L., 6.83, 93). And from then on this garb is commonplace: Metrocles (Teles, *Frag.* IV^A; see O'Neil 1977: 42), Hipparchia (*AP* 7.413), Bion (D.L., 4.51), Sochares (*AP* 6.298), and Menippus (Lucian, *D. Mort.* 20.2). Likewise for the early empire—for example, Demetrius (Seneca, *ep.* 62.3), Demonax (Lucian, *Dem.* 5), Alcidamas (Lucian, *Conv.* 19), and Peregrinus (Lucian, *Peregr.* 15). To be sure, there was some variation: Honoratus wore a bearskin (Lucian, *Dem.* 19), Cantharus a lionskin (Lucian, *Fug.* 33), and Menedemus dressed like an Erinys (D.L., 6.102). Nevertheless, the *tribōn, pēra,* and *baktēria* were so typical (*AP* 11.158; Lucian, *Peregr.* 37; Epictetus, *Diss.* 3.22.10, 50) that Julian called them the *gnōrismata,* the identifying tokens, as it were, of the Cynic philosopher (*Orat.* 6.200D; cf. ps.-Crates, *ep.* 33.2 [Malherbe 1977: 82], and Kindstrand 1976: 161–64).

Of lesser import for, but still characteristic of, Cynic appearance were long hair (ps.-Crates, *ep.* 23 [Malherbe 1977: 72]; Epictetus, *Diss.* 4.8.34; Julian, *Orat.* 6.201A) and beard (ps.-Socrates, *ep.* 9.3 [Malherbe 1977: 246]; ps.-Lucian, *Cyn.* 1; *AP* 11.154). In addition, Cynics often went barefoot (Dio, *Orat.* 6.15; ps.-Socrates, *ep.* 13.2 [Malherbe 1977: 250]; *AP* 11.153) and frequently presented a rather filthy appearance (Lucian, *Vit. auct.* 7; ps.-Socrates, *ep.* 13.2 [Malherbe 1977: 252]; Epictetus, *Diss.* 3.22.89; *AP* 11.156).

But just as characteristic as the Cynics' appearance was their manner of life, and however put, their life was hard. It meant, as Epictetus says, a life without a house, wife and children, or even a bed, an undershirt, or utensil (*Diss.* 4.8.31). It meant a life at the bare minimum, as illustrated by the anecdote told of Diogenes in which he, on seeing a boy drinking water with his cupped hands, threw away the cup in his *pēra* and said, "A boy has vanquished me in living simply" (D.L., 6.37). It meant, in short, a life of constant hunger and thirst, of being cold, and of sleeping on the ground (ps.-Menippus, *ep.* 1 [Hercher 1876: 400]; cf. Dio, *Orat.* 6.8; Lucian, *Vit. auct.* 9; ps.-Crates, *ep.* 18 [Malherbe 1977: 68]). And this regimen was even recommended for the babies and children of Cynic couples (ps.-Crates, *ep.* 33 [Malherbe 1977: 82]).

What little the Cynic really needed was readily at hand. Temples provided shelter (Plutarch, *An vit. ad inf. suff.* 499A), the furnace of a smith provided some heat (Teles, *Frag.* IV^A; see O'Neil 1977: 42), the quiet of a shoemaker's shop a place to sit and read (Teles, *Frag.* IV^B; see O'Neil 1977: 48). Moreover, drinking water was available at springs or fountains (Athenaeus, *Deipnos.* 10.422c–d; ps.-Socrates, *ep.* 9.2 [Malherbe 1977: 246]), and edible plants grew by the roadside (D.L., 2.68). Usually, though, Cynics got their daily bread from begging—a practice again especially associated with Diogenes (D.L., 6.6, 38, 46, 49, 56, 59, 60, 62, 67) and popular, if not always welcomed, thereafter (D.L., 6.99; Epictetus, *Diss.* 3.22.10; Dio, *Orat.* 32.9; Aulus Gellius, *NA* 9.2.1–11).

To sum up: Half-naked, filthy, exposed to the elements, and living from day to day—no wonder Epictetus cautioned a would-be Cynic from taking up this manner of life (*Diss.* 3.22.1). Indeed, an epigram in the *Greek Anthology* dramatizes the outcome of such a life. The epigram describes the Cynic Sochares' penniless *pēra* and his few other possessions hanging from a bush, the spoils dedicated to the personified deity Hunger (*AP* 6.298).

D. Cynic Teachings

In his apology for Diogenes, the emperor Julian emphasizes the unity of Greek philosophy, in that all the schools can be seen as attempts, say, to carry out the Delphic injunction, "Know thyself" (*Orat.* 6.182D–186A). Still, Julian admits that while Plato did his philosophy with words, Diogenes did his with actions (*Orat.* 6.189A).

Julian's distinction is useful. On the one hand, Cynics often dispensed with many of the intellectual disciplines emphasized in the other schools (ps.-Crates, *ep.* 21 [Malherbe 1977: 70]). Both Antisthenes and Diogenes are claimed to have said that logic and physics, two of the traditional subjects of philosophy, were not necessary, but only the third, ethics (D.L., 6.103). What is more, the study of music, geometry, astronomy, and grammar is ridiculed, and some Cynics had no formal education at all (D.L., 6.27, 73; Lucian, *Fug.* 12; Julian, *Orat.* 6.187D). In this way Cynicism was a shortcut to the happiness which philosophy offered (ps.-Crates, *ep.* 21 [Malherbe 1977: 70]).

On the other hand, the Cynic's manner of life in general and Cynic actions in particular were themselves didactic. Thus the various "doggish" actions discussed above served as illustrations of Diogenes' own Delphic injunction to "alter the currency" (D.L., 6.20–21, 71), to challenge all values and opinions, and to live instead according to nature (Kusch *RAC* 3: 1064). And the simple life also demonstrated, say, the Cynic's claim that he was superior even over Fate (ps.-Diogenes, *ep.* 26 [Malherbe 1977: 118]; Stobaeus, 2.8.21; D.L., 6.93).

And yet, Julian's distinction notwithstanding, Cynicism was more than actions; it, too, had teachings. And, not surprisingly, some of the teachings were as shocking or unconventional as the Cynic's "doggish" actions. Thus Diogenes is held to have advocated having wives and sons in common and to have permitted stealing from temples and even eating human flesh (D.L., 6.72–73; Höistad 1948: 138–49).

Still, Cynic teachings were usually not so shocking as they were sharply critical of misplaced values and human folly. For example: "Diogenes used to say that things of great value were sold for next to nothing and vice versa. At any rate, a statue is sold for three thousand drachmas, but a daily ration of barley for only a couple of copper coins" (D.L., 6.35). Or: "Diogenes observed one of his students associating with scoundrels and said: 'It is absurd that when we wish to sail we select sailors who are our superiors in navigation, but when we decide to live uprightly we choose just anybody to share our life' " (*Gnom. Vat.* 197; see Sternbach 1887–89: 79).

Other Cynic teachings are critical of cooks and feasting (D.L., 6.28, 86), of parasites and courtesans (6.85, 90), of prodigals (6.47), of the rich (6.24), and of tyrants (6.50), and herein lies the principal focus of Cynic teachings: its unrelenting attack on the dominant aristocratic ethos of Greco-Roman society, an ethos that so valued good birth, reputation, and wealth (D.L., 6.72, 104). But it was especially wealth which received censure, as it allowed the satisfaction of every desire and so produced enslavement and immorality (Stobaeus, 3.8.20; ps.-Diogenes, *ep.* 26.5–6 [Malherbe 1977: 122]; cf. Lucian's *Gallus* and *Cataplus,* and Hock 1987: 467–52). Hence the Cynic's wish that his enemies have wealth and a life of pleasure (Lucian, *Gall.* 30; D.L., 6.8), and conversely his praise of toil and poverty which produced a life of virtue—of freedom *(eleutheria),* self-sufficiency *(autarkeia),* and self-control *(sōphrosyne)* (Dio, *Orat.* 7.66; D.L., 6.104; ps.-Socrates, *ep.* 12 [Malherbe 1977: 250]).

E. Impact of Cynicism

1. Cynicism and Greco-Roman Intellectual Life. In the course of a thousand years the Cynics, not surprisingly, had a widespread and, at times, profound impact on those around them. Their impact on other philosophical schools is well known, beginning with Stilpo and the Megarians (Dudley 1937: 95–96). But their influence on Stoicism was especially significant. This influence is natural, as Zeno, the founder of Stoicism, was, as has been said, a student of Crates (D.L., 7.2–3). Cynic features are readily apparent in Zeno's simple life (D.L., 7.16, 27), in his emphasis on living according to nature (6.104), and in his writings (7.4). Thereafter, however, influence varies, in that some Stoics took a Cynicizing direction (so Ariston of Chios according to Diogenes Laertius, 7.37, 160) and others deliberately moved away (so Panaetius of Rhodes according to Cicero, *De fin.* 3.20.68; cf. Dudley 1937: 96–102). In the early empire, though, Cynic influence is once again strong, as is clear in the cases of Attalus, Seneca, Musonius Rufus, and Epictetus (Billerbeck 1982: 156–72).

The impact of Cynicism on Greco-Roman literature is also well known, and particularly influential were the satires of Menippus and the diatribes of Bion (Helm *PW* 12: 15–22). And even if some of the earlier claims of influence of, say, Menippus on Lucian were overstated (Helm 1906), more recent assessments still show clear influence (Hall 1981: 64–150). And the appearance of Cynic anecdotes, usually of Diogenes, in Greco-Roman literature is especially widespread (see the list in Kusch *RAC* 3: 1066). One reason for Cynics being so prevalent in literature is that writers were introduced to Cynics early on, during their school days. Anecdotes of Diogenes have shown up in educational texts preserved on papyri (Collart 1926: 23–24), and the anecdote itself (Gk *chreia*) became a form for exercises in composition called *progymnasmata* and so was learned by all students who went beyond the literary stage of education (Bonner 1977: 250–76). And among the examples of the *chreia* the most popular was this one: "Diogenes the Cynic philosopher, on seeing a boy eating delicacies, struck the paedagogus with his *baktēria*" (Theon, *Progymn* 5 [Walz 1832 1: 205]). In fact, this *chreia* became a favorite topic for a student essay in which Diogenes is presented as a moral "watchdog" (Gk *sōphronistēs*) (Nicolaus, *Progymn.* 3 [Walz 1832 1: 275–76]; cf. Hock and O'Neil 1986: 313–22).

2. Cynicism and Early Christianity. Scholars have long noted similarities between Cynic behavior or teaching and various early Christian texts. Kusch (*RAC* 3: 1067–68) provides a convenient summary of earlier scholarship's identification of such similarities, such as the Diogenes anecdote in which a child teaches the philosopher a lesson in simple living (D.L., 6.37) and the similar function of a child in the gospel tradition (Mark 9:33–37; 10:14–16). Still, many scholars, including Kusch himself (*RAC* 3: 1068), have been, and continue to be, reluctant to posit any direct influence of Cynicism on the NT Gospels (Schottroff and Stegemann 1978: 133–35).

A. J. Malherbe, however, inaugurated a new era in the study of the relationship of Cynicism and early Christianity, although his focus has been on Paul, not on the Gospels. In numerous studies (esp. Malherbe 1968; 1970; 1983) he has provided a careful and sophisticated analysis of Cynicism itself and of such Pauline images as "fighting with beasts" (1 Cor 15:32) and "being gentle as a nurse" (1 Thess 2:7), showing that Paul reflects precise and self-conscious knowledge of important debates going on among Cynics and that such debates are the contexts for understanding Paul's images. And that knowledge extends to other aspects of Paul's teaching and behavior (Hock 1980: 37–42, 52–59).

Scholars have also renewed the study of the gospel tradition from the perspective of Cynic conduct and teaching. Some scholars have focused on specific texts, arguing for Cynic influence on, say, the injunction for disciples to go barefoot in Luke 10:4 (Vaage 1986), or the teaching on wealth and poverty in the Parable of the Rich Man and Lazarus (Luke 16:19–31; see Hock 1987). But of special significance is the thesis of B. Mack (1988: 67–74, 179–92) that the earliest layers of the gospel tradition depict a Jesus whose themes and style of teaching as well as his social role of critic are closest to those of Cynics.

After the NT period the influence of Cynicism becomes explicit, as Church Fathers frequently cite Cynic figures and teachings. Kusch (*RAC* 3: 1069–74) has collected many such references from a variety of Greek and Latin fathers. While Cynic *adiaphoria,* or shamelessness, comes in for frequent censure (*RAC* 3: 1072–73), it must also be stated that many fathers judged Cynics positively, with Clement of Alexandria and Gregory Nazianzus in particular making extensive use of the Diogenes traditions and of the Cynic philosopher as a pagan paradigm of virtue (*RAC* 3: 1069–72).

Bibliography

Billerbeck, M. 1978. *Epiktet, Vom Kynismus.* Philosophia Antiqua 34. Leiden.

———. 1979. *Der Kyniker Demetrius: Ein Beitrag zur Geschichte der frükaiserzeitlichen Popularphilosophie.* Philosophia Antiqua 36. Leiden.

———. 1982. La réception du Cynisme à Rome. *Acta Classica* 51: 151–73.

Bonner, S. 1977. *Education in Ancient Rome from the Elder Cato to the Younger Pliny.* Berkeley.

Brown, T. S. 1949. *Onesicritus: A Study in Hellenistic Historiography.* University of California Publications in History 39. Berkeley.

Caizzi, F. D. 1966. *Antisthenis Fragmenta.* Testi e documenti per lo studio dell' antichita 13. Milan.

Collart, P. 1926. *Les papyrus Bouriant.* Paris.

Dudley, D. R. 1937. *A History of Cynicism from Diogenes to the 6th Century A.D.* London.

Emeljanow, V. 1967. *The Letters of Diogenes.* Ph.D. diss., Stanford University.

Fritz, K. von. 1926. *Quellenuntersuchungen zu Leben und Philosophie des Diogenes von Sinope. Philologus* Supp. vol. 18/2. Leipzig.

Garrison, D. H. 1978. *Mild Frenzy. A Reading of the Hellenistic Love Epigram.* Hermes Einzelschriften 41. Wiesbaden.

Gerhard, G. A. 1912. Zur Legende vom Kyniker Diogenes. *ARW* 15: 388–408.

Goulet-Cazé, M.-O. 1986. Une liste de disciples de Cratès le cynique en Diogène Laërce 6,95. *Hermes* 114: 247–52.

Hall, J. 1981. *Lucian's Satire.* Monographs in Classical Studies. New York.

Helm, R. 1906. *Lucian und Menipp.* Leipzig.

Hercher, R. 1876. *Epistolographi Graeci.* Paris.

Hock, R. F. 1980. *The Social Context of Paul's Ministry.* Philadelphia.

———. 1987. Lazarus and Micyllus: Greco-Roman Backgrounds to Luke 16:19–31. *JBL* 106: 447–63.

Hock, R. F., and O'Neil, E. N. 1986. *The Chreia in Ancient Rhetoric.* Vol. 1 of *The Progymnasmata.* SBLTT 27. Atlanta.

Höistad, R. 1948. *Cynic Hero and Cynic King.* Lund.

Jones, C. P. 1986. *Culture and Society in Lucian.* Cambridge, MA.

Kindstrand, J. F. 1976. *Bion of Borysthenes: A Collection of the Fragments with Introduction and Commentary.* Stockholm.

———. 1979. Demetrius the Cynic. *Philologus* 124: 83–98.

Mack. B. 1988. *A Myth of Innocence: Mark and Christian Origins.* Philadelphia.

Malherbe, A. J. 1968. The Beasts at Ephesus. *JBL* 87: 71–80.

———. 1970. Gentle as a Nurse. The Cynic Background of 1 Thess 2. *NovT* 12: 203–17.

———. 1977. *The Cynic Epistles.* SBLSBS 12. Atlanta.

———. 1983. Antisthenes and Odysseus, and Paul at War. *HTR* 76: 143–73.

Mejer, J. 1978. *Diogenes Laertius and His Hellenistic Background. Hermes.* Einzelschriften 40. Wiesbaden.

Moles, J. 1983. "Honestius quam Ambitiosius"? An Exploration of the Cynic's Attitude to Moral Corruption in His Fellow Men. *JHS* 103: 103–23.

O'Neil, E. N. 1977. *Teles, the Cynic Teacher.* SBLTT 11. Atlanta.

Schottroff, L., and Stegemann, W. 1978. *Jesus von Nazareth: Hoffnung der Armen.* Stuttgart.

Sternbach, L. 1887–89. *Gnomologium Vaticanum e codice vaticano graeco 743.* Berlin.

Susemihl, F. 1891–92. *Geschichte der griechischen Litteratur in der Alexandrinerzeit.* 2 vols. Leipzig.

Vaage, L. 1986. *The Community of Q: The Ethics of an Itinerant Intelligence.* Ph.D. diss., Claremont Graduate School.

Walz, C. 1832. *Rhetores Graeci.* Tübingen.

Zeller, E. 1922. *Die Philosophie der Griechen in ihrer geschichtlichen Entwicklung.* 5th ed. Leipzig.

RONALD F. HOCK

CYPRESS. See FLORA.

CYPRIAN.

Rome had brought with her in her colonization of North Africa a class structure where good education, property, and a say in government tended to remain the privilege of a select few. Cyprian of Carthage was a man of such property and education (Pontius *Vit. Cyp.* 2, 15), and his secular acquaintances included men who belonged to the local governing circles; they came from families of curial, equestrian, and senatorial station (Pontius *Vit. Cyp.* 14). Cyprian's trial and martyr's death followed, accordingly, the course proper for an *honestior,* a man of the upper classes (house arrest, despite the extreme gravity of the charge, and execution by the sword as the method of death); and his style at the very end—twenty-five gold coins *(aurei)* to be presented to his executioner (*Acta procons. Cypriani* 5.4)—continued to be in the manner of handsome public benefaction and patronage traditional in (and expected of) such a level of society. Cyprian was a man with a sense of his position, conscious of his role as a *persona insignis,* a figure of prominence (cf. [Cyp.] *ep.* 8.1.1, written by Roman clergy).

The family of the man is, however, otherwise unknown and his nomenclature (*Caecilius Cyprianus qui et Thascius: ep.* 66 *incipit, ep.* 66.4.1, *Acta procons. Cypriani* 3.3) remains of the obscurest. But the sort of property he possessed in Carthage—it included well-known horti or suburban estates (*ep.* 81.1.1, *Acta procons. Cypriani* 2.1) suggests strongly that he was from a local, established family of some wealth and had inherited the property.

When we meet Cyprian in the 240s, he is living on this estate in Carthage, he has won for himself (according to later, but not uninformed, sources: Hieron. *vir. ill.* 67, 53) reputation and renown as a *rhetor* in a society which prized highly oratorical skills and achievement—and Carthage was *the* center for rhetorically passionate Africa. Late in that decade he is to appear, even though a very recent convert to Christianity, as a man of an authority and stature appropriate for replacing the recently deceased bishop Donatus; the Christian laity urged his candidature with enthusiastic, and successful, acclaim (Pontius *Vit. Cyp.* 5). That suggests a man of some maturity—possibly, to hazard a guess, he was at the time at least into his forties—used to holding a prominent place in his society. Certainly, later as bishop, he gives the appearance of dealing with his laity, his *plebs* as he calls them (clients who had supported his candidacy as bishop) with much greater ease and assurance as their episcopal patron than he does with his more immediate clerical colleagues.

What information of any reliability we have points to Cyprian's secular life as *rhetor* being spent not so much in legal activities in court as an *advocatus* (though some sections in the *Ad Donatum* [on which see below] could suggest this) as in training hopeful devotees in the highly elaborate and stylized art of the public declamation of the time. At all events Cyprian was well equipped for his later episcopal role as preacher and homilist.

Cyprian had not married, and his biographer suggests—no doubt idealistically but perhaps also not without some truth—that there was in him a scholarly dedication to the pursuit of higher learning and accomplishments (Pontius *Vit. Cyp.* 2). Hindsight furthermore suggests that he shared with many of his pagan contemporaries an earnest moral mindedness, espousing exacting and sometimes rigorously unyielding, even puritanical, high principles of behavior and manner. A strong sense of sin, of virtuous living, of moral imperatives, as well as an intense awareness in the reality of a spiritual world, were not notions exclusive to the adherents of Christianity, nor were they confined only to the more thoughtful and philosophic among the pagan members of this society.

By about the middle of the 240s, Cyprian, possessed of such a background, had become attracted to Christianity under the influence and friendship of an aging Carthaginian presbyter Caecilianus (Pontius *Vit. Cyp.* 4; Hieron. *vir.*

ill. 67 [garbled]). Conversion, baptism, renunciation of his worldly estate, and advancement to clerical office, which involved withdrawal from his secular profession (cf. *ep.* 1), followed in swift succession, until by about Easter 249, and probably earlier, he had been installed as bishop of Carthage (see *ep.* 59.6.1 and *ep.* 29.1.2 for the dating). Some older clerics had openly opposed the appointment of this novice Christian and despite a public *refus de pouvoir* and gestures of generosity from the eventual victor toward the defeated, the animosity engendered by this opposition continued to rankle (Pontius *Vit. Cyp.* 5). It sounds as if Cyprian was an unusually well-placed and educated convert for this church; he was too competent and prominent a figure to pass by in filling the vacant *cathedra* of Carthage. Indeed some of the clerical resentment to Cyprian's unusually rapid promotion may well have been roused precisely because of his superior class, education, and manner. To judge from the little evidence we have (e.g., *ep.* 24 [Caldonius]), Cyprian may well have found for company relatively few Christian clerics in Africa who could match his accomplishments. Our closest contemporary social picture is of the Christians in the literary dialogue of Minucius Felix, the *Octavius,* which Cyprian appears to have read; in every probability the protagonists came from African Cirta or thereabouts—but they are of the laity and two of the three are depicted as domiciled in Rome (Min. Fel. *Oct.* 2). In the absence of satisfactorily controlling evidence, it is easy to form an exaggerated perception of the social and cultural isolation which Cyprian may have needed to face in becoming a Christian; but it would be fair to assert that disagreement with his clergy over other issues could readily be sharpened if there were social differences. In an irretrievably class-conscious society it was not possible to overlook such class distinctions.

But on the other side, some of the popular enthusiasm for Cyprian's promotion may have been not just for his eloquent tongue in public oratory and his qualifications for church administration and leadership. This was a man of demonstrable dedication. The gesture of wishing to sell all his worldly goods for the benefit of the Christian poor (so Pontius *Vit. Cyp.* 2, 15) may indeed be in the tradition of the munificent nobility (as of the gospel precepts), but it was nevertheless a personal act of humane charity as well as of total commitment: Cyprian would be selling his secular social status along with his patrimony. For a remarkable feature about Cyprian is how fully a churchman he became in response to his new episcopal role, finding his total career (so far as we know) inside the church, with his talents and energies fully absorbed in the duties of clerical office and ecclesiastical activities. Though others had lived such a life before him, Cyprian's letters allow us to see this new type of churchman clearly delineated for the first time in early church history.

Along with that absorption in church affairs came, it would appear, a corresponding cultural and intellectual absorption; Cyprian was prepared to sell not only his patrimony but much of his cultural birthright as well. All the quotations, allusions, and verbal reminiscences of classical letters, the poets and writers of the past, which richly embellished the compositions of an accomplished rhetorician of the day are astonishingly absent from his churchman's prose, and even the traditional classical *exempla,* the rhetorical stock-in-trade for illustration and elaboration on a theme, are severely limited. This can only be the result of conscious rejection and restriction. Instead, Virgil and Ovid, Cicero and Sallust are replaced by the "sacred letters" to which he devoted study even as a catechumen (Pontius *Vit. Cyp.* 2). Despite the inelegance of quoting verbatim, and often, texts from a Latin version of the Bible which was painfully disharmonious with his own style, Cyprian consistently treats his biblical text with meticulous and exacting reverence; he avoids, by and large, any rewriting of his citation to suit his own paragraph, and even the oblique biblical reference or allusive phrase is relatively rare for one so steeped in the *lectio divina.* In the face of stylistic disadvantages his conscious choice is the direct biblical quotation, normally prefaced by some introductory formula. He has joined a church with a tradition of deep respect for the hallowedness of the sacred word, "the holy and adorable words of the Scriptures," as one of his contemporary African bishops describes his Bible (*Sent. Episc.* LXXXVII. 31). Cyprian has joined a church of *The* Book.

Religious conversion into this church for a man of such dedicated temperament seems to have entailed a kind of linguistic conversion as well. By contrast with other African writers with similar rhetorical backgrounds, say a Minucius Felix a little earlier or an Arnobius or a Lactantius somewhat later, Cyprian is unusually lavish in the range and variety of words with a Christian formation or connotation which he liberally makes his own, not only the almost inevitable technical terms but sometimes ugly Christian neologisms and specialized usages that had been engendered in this close-knit and somewhat beleaguered and separate community. So closely and so wholeheartedly has he identified himself with his new society, and put his literary talents to its service.

Before the year 250 had begun, he had already turned his vigorous pen to the composition of the apologetic essay, the *Ad Donatum,* a rhetorically overblown essay on the marvelous effects of divine grace on his own conversion and regeneration in baptism. Quite probably within the last twelve months he had composed the tractate *De habitu virginum (On the Dress of Virgins),* warning those who have dedicated their virginity to Christ of the perils which beset them from the pagan world with all its vanities and vices. And he had been responsible for the compilation of the three books of biblical *testimonia,* the *Ad Quirinum,* the first book acting as an apology against the Jews, the second as a compendium of christology, and the third (composed later than the first two) as a guide to the Christian duties and virtues.

When in late 249 (or very early 250) the emperor Decius issued orders that all the inhabitants of the empire should make sacrifice to the gods, Cyprian promptly made himself scarce. This action (interpreted by a number as cowardly) was to occasion much, and enduring, criticism (e.g., *ep.* 8, *ep.* 20, *ep.* 66, Pont. *Vit. Cyp.* 7–8), but it was also to occasion Cyprian to correspond from his place of hiding with members of his congregation (clergy, confessors, and laity) as well as with Rome during his sojourn away from Carthage (lasting over twelve months, *ep.* 43.4.1). Hence we have the rich collection of letters numbering from *ep.* 5 to *ep.* 43, nearly half the corpus of correspondence that survives.

In the aftermath of this persecution, his church—as were others—was beset by dispute and schism. Dispute arose everywhere over the treatment appropriate to those who had apostatized during the persecution (perhaps the majority of the Carthaginian flock, *ep.* 14.1.1): the treatise *De lapsis* (*On the Fallen*) expatiates on this penitential dispute and strives hard to find an acceptable pastoral solution to the sin of idolatry, traditionally regarded as irremissible. Schism arose when parties who advocated a more lax discipline, or those who advocated a more severely purist discipline in penitential matters (Novatianists), split off into schismatic churches: by the year 252 Cyprian had two rival bishops of these two different persuasions in Carthage (*ep.* 59.9.1–3). The influential treatise (or to be more accurate the first version of it) *De ecclesiae catholicae unitate (On the Unity of the Catholic Church)* was penned against this background of disunity and disharmony as was probably also the *De dominica oratione (On the Lord's Prayer)*. By this appears the context for three further tractates, *Ad Demetrianum* (defending Christians against the charge of being responsible for natural calamities like plague, famine, and drought), the *De mortalitate (On Mortality)*, and *De opere et eleemosynis (On Good Works and Almsgiving)*.

But the turbulence was to continue. Further, and intense, dissensions over the status of schismatic churches (centered on the validity of Novatianic baptism) were promptly to follow both within the North African communities themselves and then with churches elsewhere (especially with Rome). Cyprian adhered staunchly to an inherited view of the church as an enclosed garden outside of which flowed no source of salvation: the strongly contested issue occasioned a spate of pamphleteering (one sample survives in the anonymous *De rebaptismate* [On Rebaptism]) and in Africa at least a series of conciliar meetings and a flurry of letters (the bulky section of the surviving correspondence from *ep.* 69 to *ep.* 75 is all concerned with this matter). The tracts *De bono patientiae (On the Virtue of Patience)* and most probably *De zelo et livore (On Jealousy and Envy)* as well as a revised version of *De ecclesiae catholicae unitate* (less favorable to the status of Rome) are products of this period. Relations between Rome and many churches elsewhere in the East as well as in Africa had reached the point of breakdown over this issue (*ep.* 75.25.1) when persecution broke out anew under Valerian. Cyprian was relegated to nearby Curubis in August 257 (there perhaps composing the *Ad Fortunatum*, a compendium of scriptural texts on persecution and martyrdom), and when the persecution was intensified in the summer of 258 (*ep.* 80), he was recalled to Carthage, tried, and went to his martyr's death on September 14, 258.

We are fortunate in having not only a dozen pamphlets from Cyprian's own pen, but a body of some 82 letters (including 16 by his correspondents and 6 which are synodal or collective) as well as a short and apologetic biography purportedly written by his deacon Pontius and the *Acta Proconsularia*, which embody transcripts of his trials as confessor and martyr. We thus catch an illuminating glimpse via Cyprian into daily church living of the mid-3d century and witness his struggle (and that of others) to find acceptable pastoral solutions to new challenges as the church found itself more and more required to come to terms with its secular environment.

Bibliography

Bayard, L. 1961–62. *Saint Cyprien. Correspondence.* 2 vols. 2d ed. Paris.

Benson, E. W. 1897. *Cyprian: His Life, His Times, His World.* London.

Bévenot, M. 1961. *The Tradition of Manuscripts: A Study of the Transmission of St. Cyprian's Treatises.* Oxford.

Clarke, G. W. 1984–88. *The Letters of St. Cyprian of Carthage.* 4 vols. ACW. New York.

Hartel, W. 1868–71. *S. Thasci Caecili Cypriani Opera.* 3 vols. CSEL 3. Vienna.

Sage, M. M. 1975. *Cyprian.* Cambridge, MA.

Simonetti, M., and Moreschini, C. 1976. *Sancti Cypriani Episcopi Opera. Pars II.* CCSL 3A. Turnholt, Belgium.

Weber, R., and Bévenot, M. 1972. *Sancti Cypriani Episcopi Opera. Pars I.* CCSL 3. Turnholt, Belgium.

G. W. Clarke

CYPRUS (PLACE) [Heb *kittim;* Gk *Kypros*]. A Mediterranean island located 43 miles S of Asia Minor, 76 miles W of Syria, and 264 miles N of Egypt.

The Hebrew name probably derives from the city of Kition (Roman Citium), which Phoenicians colonized on the SE coast of the island. It may also have been known as Elishah in the OT (Gen 10:4; 1 Chr 1:7; Ezek 27:7). Most, though not all, agree that this is the similar-sounding place often referred to as Alashia or Asy in texts from the ANE. It appears in connection with copper (for which the island was well known in antiquity) on tablets from Alalakh in the 18th century B.C. and Mari in the 17th century B.C. The name occurs frequently in the 14th century B.C., especially in the correspondence between the Egyptian Pharaoh Akhenaten and the king of Alashia, which also refers to a land that produced copper. In the 11th century B.C., an Egyptian priest, Wenamon, sought refuge in Alashia after suffering shipwreck on his return to Egypt from Byblos. This corroborates the location of Alashia to be in Cyprus rather than in Syria. In the *Iliad* (11.21) and the *Odyssey* (4.83; 8.362; 17.442, 443, 448) as well as the NT (i.e., Acts 4:36; 11:19, 20; 13:4; 15:39), the island is known as *kupros* (Cyprus).

Cyprus is the third largest island in the Mediterranean, after Sicily and Sardinia, and only slightly larger than Crete. Its maximum length, E-W, is 138 miles and its maximum width, N-S, is 60 miles, encompassing an area of 3584 square miles. The W half of the island is mountainous, where the Trodos and Kyrenia Mountains reach a height of about 3300 ft and are snow-capped three months out of the year. The E half consists of the Mesaoria Plain and the Karpass Peninsula.

Favorable climate and topography produced a primarily agricultural society on the island throughout its history. However, its most important resources have always been its copper mines and pine forests. These, coupled with a salt industry that undoubtedly flourished in antiquity (from the salt lakes of Limassol and Larnaca), supported the construction of a number of important harbor towns around the island.

The earliest inhabitants of Cyprus, who settled in the SE part of the island and around its central and E coastlines, have been dated by carbon 14 testing to the Pre-Pottery Neolithic period (ca. 7000–6000 B.C.). Circular houses, called *tholoi,* were constructed of mudbrick on stone foundations, and have been found in several settlements around the coastal perimeter of the island (e.g., Khirokitia and Kalavassos-Tenta). They have floors of beaten earth, hearths, platforms built against the walls for sleeping, and posts in the center of the room to support domed ceilings. The inner walls were plastered, and one of them contained a painting of a human figure with uplifted arms. Their dead were interred in the fetal position beneath the floors of their houses or immediately outside. The infant mortality rate was apparently high.

In the Late Neolithic (ca. 4500–3800 B.C.; there are no carbon 14 dates between 6000 and 4500 B.C.), pottery was developed and houses were constructed with greater diversity of forms including wooden structures, stone buildings both circular and rectangular, and partial or total subterranean dwellings like those in Beer-sheba in S Palestine. These people, like those in the PPN, were primarily farmers, but they also hunted wild animals and probably had some domesticated livestock. There was cultural continuity from the Neolithic into the Chalcolithic Period (ca. 3800–2500 B.C.), but settlement patterns shifted to the W side of the island, the central plain, and the Karpass Peninsula.

The EB Age (Early Cypriot, ca. 2500–2000 B.C.) is represented in most of the island except the W half of the Trodos Mountains. Wealthy tomb offerings and beautifully made pottery in a variety of imaginative styles indicate a prosperous culture, supported by an increasing international trade in copper. Tin was imported, probably from Mesopotamia or Asia Minor, evidenced by the production of the many bronze implements which have been found in excavation. Models of sanctuaries show the worship of bulls (after cattle were imported to replace pigs for economic reasons), and testify to a well-developed polytheism.

The MB Age (Middle Cypriot, ca. 2000–1650 B.C.) was brief and continued the basic culture of the earlier period, although the N began to decline when settlement patterns shifted to the SE with the construction of important harbor cities such as Enkomi and Kition. Several forts have been found in the N half of the island, but are completely missing in the S. Apparently hostilities were internal and/or confined to the N, and the S felt no need for such defenses. A clear separation between the E and W is inferred from the differences in pottery produced in each section. The economy of the W was based primarily on copper, while that of the E was based on agriculture.

An abundance of Cypriot pottery from the MB Age has been found in Cilicia, Megiddo, Ras Shamra (Ugarit), and along much of the Syro-Palestinian coast. From this artifactual evidence and later textual evidence (i.e., Tell el-Amarna letters and the library of Boghazkoy), it is clear that trade between Cyprus and countries such as Egypt, Anatolia, and Syria flourished in both the MB and the LB.

A script was developed in Cyprus around 1500 B.C. and was labeled Cypro-Minoan by Sir Arthur Evans. Three forms of the language (Cypro-Minoan 1, 2, and 3) have been found on clay tablets, incised or painted on vases, engraved on votive objects, etc. Whether its roots lie in the west (Crete?) or the east (Ugarit?, etc.) is debatable, but all attempts to decipher the language have been unsuccessful. The fall of Minoan Knossos on Crete to the Mycenaeans, ca. 1380 B.C., brought Mycenaean settlers to Cyprus, (perhaps the "Sea Peoples," some of whom settled in S Palestine) and with them a new type of pottery which is found extensively in Cyprus and the Syro-Palestinian littoral.

Aegean influence continued in Cyprus well into the Iron Age (Cypro-Geometric Age, ca. 1050–750 B.C.), when the Phoenicians arrived around 850 B.C. and established colonies on the island. These colonists from Tyre and Sidon (cf. Isa 23:1, 12; Ezek 27:6) built temples to Astarte and tried to establish close ties between Cyprus and their homelands. One of the largest temples erected to Astarte in the Phoenician world was constructed in Kition around 850–800 B.C. on the ruins of an LB temple.

In the beginning of the Cypro-Archaic Period (ca. 750–475 B.C.), epigraphic evidence records the submission of Cyprus to Sargon II of Assyria. This event, which occurred in 707 B.C., is recorded both on a stele from Kition and in inscriptions from the Assyrian palace at Khorsabad. Ten cities of Cyprus are named on the prism of the Assyrian king Esarhaddon (613 B.C.), among which are Paphos, Idalion, Kourion, and Salamis. Extraordinary tombs made of ashlar blocks (perhaps royal ones) were found at Salamis, and date to the 8th and 7th centuries B.C. Life under the Assyrians seems to have been good, and Mycenaean culture continued to dominate.

Egyptian influence was felt for a brief time when Egypt took advantage of Assyria's decline and invaded the island. In 545 B.C. Cyprus submitted to the rising power of Cyrus, king of Persia, helped him in his war against Babylon, and thereby continued to enjoy considerable autonomy (Hdt. 4.162) until 499 B.C., when the island, identifying with its Greek heritage, joined the unsuccessful Ionic revolt against Persian rule. Two hundred years of slavery followed.

Cyprus suffered often during the early part of the Cypro-Classical Period (475–325 B.C.), when Greeks, who considered Cyprus to be part of the Greek world, attempted repeatedly and unsuccessfully to free the island from Persian control. Greek influence was strong on the W part of the island, while Phoenician and Persian influence continued in the E part. Stasikypros, king of the city of Idalion, repulsed efforts by the Persians and Phoenicians to conquer his city. Archaeologists have recently identified his palace in excavations at Idalion (Stager and Walker 1989). The most influential Cypriot of the period was Euagoras I of Salamis, who introduced the Greek alphabet on the island through his coins. He tried, without success, to unify all Greeks and make Salamis the Athens of the East. He was responsible for spreading the Hellenization at Cyprus into the E Mediterranean world.

Cyprus assisted Alexander the Great in his conquest of Tyre (332 B.C.) and subsequently became a part of his empire, enjoying considerable favor from the conqueror. After Alexander's death and throughout the Hellenistic Period (ca. 325–50 B.C.), Cyprus was controlled by the Ptolemies of Egypt. Hellenistic culture was dominant during this time, manifesting itself especially in the sculpture of Cyprus. Excellent examples found in excavations include a 3d century B.C. limestone head of a woman from Arsos and a 2d century B.C. marble statue of Artemis.

Greek trends are also seen in the production of jewelry, pottery, and terra-cottas.

With the rise of Roman power, Cyprus was made a province after 67 B.C. and, nine years later, was added to the province of Cilicia. After the civil wars ended, Octavian assumed the title of Augustus and controlled most of the area from Britain to Mesopotamia. He combined Cyprus and Cilicia with the province of Syria. After 23 B.C., Cyprus was made a senatorial province and placed under proconsuls. Many of the proconsuls of Cyprus are known for the Roman period (50 B.C.–250 A.D.), although no Cypriot evidence yet exists to attest the proconsulship of Sergius Paulus (Mitford 1979: 1301), who is said to have been one (Acts 13:7) when Paul visited the island in about 47 A.D.

Peace and prosperity existed throughout the early part of the empire, supported by a flourishing trade in wine, copper, shipbuilding, and agriculture. The chief cities of the time were Salamis, Paphos, Lapithos, and Amathus. The Roman way of life is evidenced by the presence of theaters at Paphos, Salamis, Curium, Soli, and Citium, the last attested only epigraphically. Those at Salamis and Soloi are beautifully restored. Further evidence is seen in the presence of gymnasiums preserved at Salamis and Paphos. Others are attested epigraphically for Citium, Curium, Chytri, Lapethus, and Carpasia. There was an amphitheater at Salamis and an odeion at Paphos. A large Roman bath has been found beside the theater and gymnasium at Salamis, and one is also known for Curium.

Roman roads were built around the island, evidenced by numerous milestones and a map drawn up sometime between the 2d and 4th centuries. Inscriptions show that the roads were maintained until the 4th century. Temples of civic gods such as Apollo at Hyle, Aphrodite at Paphos, and Zeus at Salamis, along with floor mosaics such as those in the houses of Paphos testify to the prominence of polytheism. None of these seem to have survived the more immediate appeal of the deified Severan emperors. No evidence exists that any of them outlived the reign of Caracalla (211–17 A.D.). The spiritual vacuum thus created was filled by Christianity, whose presence is seen in the remains of basilical church buildings such as the one at Salamis.

The New Testament mentions two Christians from Cyprus. One was Barnabas, the traveling companion of Paul (Acts 4:36) and the other was Mnason, who lived in Jerusalem and hosted Paul on one occasion (Acts 21:16). Men from Cyprus shared in the evangelizing of the Greek population of Antioch of Syria (Acts 11:19–20). Barnabas and John Mark visited Cyprus following a dispute with Paul (Acts 15:39).

Bibliography

Hunt, D. 1982. *Footprints in Cyprus: An Illustrated History,* ed. D. Hunt. London.

Ieronomachou, I. 1982. Cypriote Bibliography: Archaeology 1979–1981. Pp. 260–69 in *Report of the Department of Antiquities Cyprus.* Nicosia.

Karageorghis, V. 1982. *Cyprus: From the Stone Age to the Romans.* London.

———. 1985. *Archaeology in Cyprus 1960–1985,* ed. V. Karageorghis. Nicosia.

Mitford, T. B. 1979. Roman Cyprus. Pp. 1298–1305 in *Aufstieg und Niedergang der romischen Welt,* II.7.2. Berlin.

Stager, L., and Walker, A. 1989. *American Expedition to Idalion, Cyprus: 1973–80.* Chicago.

Swinney, S. 1985. Recent Developments in Cypriot Prehistoric Archaeology. *AJA* 89: 39–51.

Symons, D. J. 1987. Archaeology in Cyprus, 1981–85. Pp. 62–77 in *Archaeological Reports for 1986–87.* London.

JOHN MCRAY

CYRENE (PLACE) [Gk *Kyrēnē*]. CYRENIANS. The capital of the Roman province of Cyrenaica (Libya) in North Africa. Its name stems from the nature goddess (Kyrana), whose name was given to a perennial spring nearby. The city was founded by Greek colonists from the island of Thera near the end of the 7th century B.C. (Herodotus 4.150–58; *SEG* 9.3). The leader of the expedition, Battus, became its king, and thus instituted a dynasty that lasted nearly two centuries (until ca. 440 B.C.). For the next century it was a republic and subsequently came under the control of Ptolemy I, heir to the North African portion of Alexander the Great's empire, who gave it a constitution (*SEG* 11.1; copy in the museum at Cyrene) establishing a liberal oligarchy, an extensive citizenry, two councils, and a popular court. Under the Ptolemies, the city became an important intellectual center with a celebrated medical school, a classical academy, and a school of philosophers (the "Cyrenaics") who pioneered what came to be known as Epicureanism. Eratosthenes (276–ca. 194 B.C.), a geographer who calculated the circumference of the earth within 50 miles of the presently accepted figure, and Callimachus (ca. 310–240 B.C.), a poet who had a great impact upon the development of Latin poetry, especially that of Catullus and Ovid, were among its famous sons. Both moved to Alexandria, which tended to dominate Cyrene culturally. By the will of Ptolemy Apion (d. 96 B.C.), the city and its territories became Roman; and in 67 B.C. it was united with Crete to form the senatorial province of Cyrenaica. Following a Jewish revolt during the reign of Trajan and its brutal suppression (A.D. 115; see Dio Cassius 68.32), the city embarked on a period of economic and intellectual decline. Its history ended with the Arab conquest in A.D. 642.

Throughout most of its history, Cyrene was very prosperous. Located in the midst of very fertile countryside, it was rich in grain, wool, olive oil, and especially silphium, a spice that was much prized for both culinary and medicinal purposes. According to Herodotus (4.199), the city's climate provided it with three harvest seasons annually. From the time of Ptolemy I, Jews were an important part of its population (Josephus, *AgAp* 2.4; *Ant* 14.114; cf. 1 Macc 15:23; 2 Macc 2:23), which, of course, is why the city is mentioned in the Bible. The noted Jewish writer, Jason (2 Macc 2:19–23), one book of whose five-volume history of the Jewish wars of liberation was abridged in 2 Maccabees, and Ezekiel the Tragedian came from Cyrene.

A citizen of Cyrene by the name of Simon, perhaps a pilgrim to the Passover festival in Jerusalem, is identified in the passion narrative as having been compelled by the Roman soldiers to carry Jesus' cross (Matt. 27:32 = Mark 15:21 = Luke 23:26). Jews from Cyrene are included in the list of those who witnessed the remarkable events resulting from the coming of the Spirit upon the earliest Jerusalem church on the day of Pentecost (Act 2:10). Acts 6:9 suggests that those Jews who "returned home" to Jerusalem from Cyrene and Alexandria were numerous enough to have their own synagogue. Some from this group were active in debate with Stephen and (presumably) the other "Hellenists" and were possibly involved in his lynching; the same group was also numbered among those early Jewish-Christian believers who began to bear witness to gentiles in Syrian Antioch (Acts 11:19–20), the third city of the empire, which was to become so important in the missionary development of the early Christian community. One of the prominent prophets and teachers from the earliest days of the church in Antioch was Lucius of Cyrene (Acts 13:1). With so many Jews moving back and forth between Jerusalem and Cyrene, and between Antioch and Cyrene, it is likely that there was a church established there at a very early date.

The ancient site of Cyrene has been extensively excavated during the present century by Italian, British, and Libyan archaeologists. It has provided a wealth of information concerning ancient Greco-Roman art and architecture, civic and social life, numismatics, and epigraphy. Among the many monuments are a Greek theater; a Roman theater; temples of Zeus, Apollo, and Isis; the agora (marketplace); Roman forum; baths; magnificent houses; a circus (for chariot races); and two early churches (6th century). Two modern museums, one of them devoted primarily to sculpture, house some of the more important artifacts.

Bibliography

Boardman, J. 1964. *The Greeks Overseas.* London.

Graham, A. J. 1964. *Colony and Mother City in Ancient Greece.* New York.

Jones, A. H. M. 1937. *Cities of the Eastern Roman Provinces.* Oxford.

Reynolds, J. 1960. The Christian Inscriptions of Cyrenaica, *JTS* n.s. 11: 284–94.

Romanelli, P. 1943. *La Cirenaica Romana.* Verbania.

Rowe, A. 1948. *A History of Ancient Cyrenaica.* Cairo.

———. ed. 1959. *Cyrenaican Expeditions of the University of Manchester.* Manchester.

W. Ward Gasque

CYRIL OF JERUSALEM, 20TH DISCOURSE OF. See VIRGIN, ASSUMPTION OF THE.

CYRUS (PERSON) [Heb *kōreš*]. A great conqueror and statesman, Cyrus II was the founder of the Achaemenid empire. He was born ca. 590/589 B.C., most probably in Parsa, the modern Iranian province of Fars, but we know nothing historical about his early life (the stories of his childhood related in Herodotus can be dismissed as charming legend).

Much more is known of Cyrus after he came to the throne of Persia in 559 B.C. His career divides into four phases: (1) the triumphant war against Astyages and the Medes in 550 B.C.; (2) his successful campaigns against Lydia in 547 B.C. and the operations against Ionia following the fall of Sardis; (3) campaigns to the NE of the Iranian plateau between 546 and 540 B.C.; and (4) the conquest of Babylon in 539/538 B.C.

Herodotus reports Cyrus as king of Persia was a vassal of Astyages, the last king of the Medes. The basis of his kingdom was several Persian tribes, including his own, the Pasargadae. The extent of his territorial control is unclear, but it certainly included the city of Anshan (modern Malyan). The conflict between Cyrus and Astyages is the first well-documented fact in Achaemenid history. Our two best sources on this event are Herodotus' *Persian Wars* and the Babylonian Chronicle. Herodotus reports that Cyrus successfully rebelled against his master, Astyages. The Babylonian Chronicle suggests that the war with the Medes began with Astyages attempting the conquest of Cyrus, called the King of Anshan. Whatever the cause of the war, the Medes were defeated.

Cyrus spent three years between his defeat of Astyages and war with Lydia (550–547 B.C.) consolidating his control over Medea. His victory had brought under Persian control all of central W and NW Iran, the N and probably the NE parts of the Iranian plateau, some sections of N Mesopotamia and Syria, and large parts of Anatolia, perhaps as far W as the Halys river.

Herodotus tells us the crossing of the Halys by Croesus of Lydia was the cause of the Persian-Lydian war. Cyrus may have been the aggressor. There was an initial and indecisive battle between the two kingdoms in Cappadocia. After the battle Croesus, assuming that it was too late in the autumn to continue campaigning for that year, withdrew his troops to winter quarters in Sardis. Cyrus, on the other hand, continued his advance. A second battle was fought before the walls of Sardis, the Lydians were bested, and withdrew into the citadel in hopes of withstanding a siege. The Persians discovered a way to climb an undefended section of the wall, and a daring assault led to the capture of Croesus and the conquest of Lydia. Cyrus marched on westward from Sardis and, through a combination of war and shrewd diplomacy, conquered most of Ionia.

We know almost nothing in any detail of Cyrus's activities between 547 B.C. and his conquest of Babylon in 539/538 B.C. There are hints in the record that he campaigned extensively to the E and the NE of the Iranian plateau, greatly expanding his new empire in those directions. He almost certainly at this time also undertook the ongoing task of organizing the empire and establishing the administrative controls necessary to command such a vast territory effectively. He may also at this time have begun construction of his imperial capital, Pasargadae, in his home province of Parsa.

Cyrus' defeat of Babylon and the Babylonian empire, along with his previous conquests, brought the whole of the Near East within the Persian empire with the exception of Egypt. Strategically Cyrus's defeat of Babylon began when he conquered Lydia, thus greatly increasing the political and military isolation of Mesopotamia. Tactically the campaign began when Cyrus was fighting in the E and NE, for the Persians mounted a propaganda campaign against Nabonidus, the unpopular king of Babylon, prior to their invasion which proved so successful that the Neo-Babylonian empire ultimately fell almost without a battle.

We have evidence of this propaganda campaign in native Mesopotamian cuneiform sources, but probably our best evidence comes from Second Isaiah. In Isa 45:1–3 the prophet speaks of Cyrus as the anointed of Yahweh who is destined to subdue all nations before him. In return for this favor, of course, the prophet notes (Isa 45:13) that Cyrus will restore the Jewish exiles to their native land. In short, Cyrus has been called by God to capture Babylon, to free the Jews from their bondage, and by inference to permit them to return to Jerusalem. It is suggested that Isaiah could so prophesy because he knew of the discontent with their own government among the Babylonians.

Babylon having been successfully softened up, war actually began early in October of 539 B.C. The decisive battle took place at Opis. The Babylonian army apparently did not stand long before retreating in total chaos. While Cyrus marched to the conquest of the important city of Sippar, another detachment of the Persian army peacefully took Babylon itself on October 12. Cyrus then entered the great city, welcomed by his own troops and (to judge from the Babylonian sources) by the people of the city. Cyrus seized the hands of the statue of the city god, Marduk, and announced that it was his intention to leave local culture and customs undisturbed and to rule the city and the empire as the legitimate successor of the ancient kings of Babylon.

This policy of Cyrus to rule his empire by maintaining respect for local cultures and traditions is, of course, further documented in his famous decree, probably issued in Ecbatana (modern Hamadan), permitting the Jews of Babylon to return to their native land and to rebuild their temple in Jerusalem (Ezra 1:1–4). Such a policy of remarkable tolerance based on a respect for individual people, ethnic groups, other religions, and ancient kingdoms must have seemed amazing to people who had grown accustomed to the governing techniques of the Neo-Assyrian and Neo-Babylonian empires, in which ruthless destruction, the deportation of people, and the forced integration of the conquered into the conqueror's political system had been common practice.

Herodotus reports that Cyrus died in battle in 530 B.C. fighting against the tribe of the Massagetai on Iran's NE frontier. All we really know of the end of his reign is that he was buried in a simple gabled stone tomb at Pasargadae. It is reported that this structure once bore an inscription reading: "Oh man, I am Cyrus the son of Cambyses, who founded the empire of Persia, and was king of Asia. Grudge me not therefore this monument." Standing before the tomb some two centuries later, Alexander the Great is reported to have ordered that it and its supposed treasure be restored, because he was so impressed that Cyrus, founder of the Achaemenid power, creator of the largest empire then known, was the kind of man who would ask so small a favor of posterity.

T. Cuyler Young, Jr.

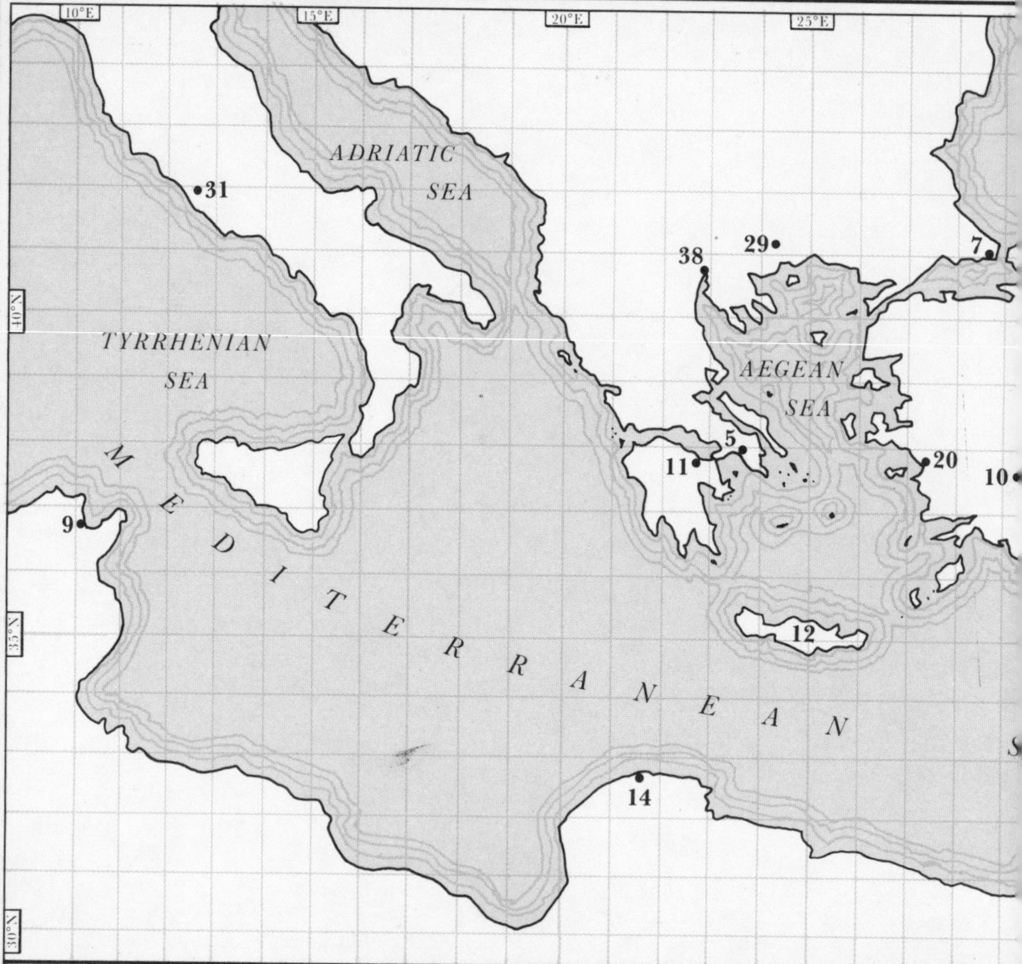

10°E 15°E 20°E 25°E

40°N 35°N 30°N

ADRIATIC SEA

TYRRHENIAN SEA

AEGEAN SEA

MEDITERRANEAN

1 **Alexandria** (31°12′N; 29°53′E)
2 **Amarna, Tell el-** (27°38′N; 30°52′E)
3 **Antioch** (36°12′N; 36°10′E)
4 **Assur** (35°27′N; 43°16′E)
5 **Athens** (37°58′N; 23°43′E)
6 **Babylon** (32°33′N; 44°24′E)
7 **Byzantium/Constantinople** (41°01′N; 28°58′E)
8 **Carchemish** (36°49′N; 38°01′E)
9 **Carthage** (36°54′N; 10°16′E)
10 **Colossae** (37°46′N; 29°15′E)
11 **Corinth** (37°56′N; 22°56′E)
12 **Crete**
13 **Cyprus**
14 **Cyrene** (32°48′N; 21°54′E)
15 **Damascus** (33°30′N; 36°18′E)
16 **Dumah/al-Djawf (Jauf)** (29°48′N; 39°52′E)
17 **Dura-Europus** (34°46′N; 40°46′E)
18 **Ebla/Tell Mardikh** (35°48′N; 36°45′E)
19 **Elephantine** (24°05′N; 32°53′E)
20 **Ephesus** (37°55′N; 27°17′E)
21 **Haran** (36°51′N; 39°00′E)
22 **Hattusas/Boghazköy** (40°02′N; 34°37′E)
23 **Mari** (34°33′N; 40°53′E)
24 **Memphis** (29°51′N; 31°15′E)
25 **Nag Hammadi** (26°04′N; 32°13′E)
26 **Nineveh** (36°25′N; 43°10′E)
27 **Nuzi** (35°22′N; 44°18′E)
28 **Persepolis** (29°57′N; 52°52′E)
29 **Philippi** (41°05′N; 24°19′E)
30 **Qurayya** (28°47′N; 36°00′E)
31 **Rome** (41°53′N; 12°30′E)
32 **Seleucia** (33°05′N; 44°35′E)
33 **Sidon** (33°33′N; 35°22′E)
34 **Susa** (32°11′N; 48°15′E)
35 **Tadmor/Palmyra** (34°36′N; 38°15′E)
36 **Tarsus** (36°52′N; 34°52′E)
37 **Thebes/Luxor** (25°42′N; 32°3
38 **Thessalonica** (40°38′N; 22°58′
39 **Ugarit/Ras Shamra** (35°35′N; 35°45′E)
40 **Ur** (30°56′N; 46°08′E)
41 **Uruk** (31°18′N; 45°40′E)